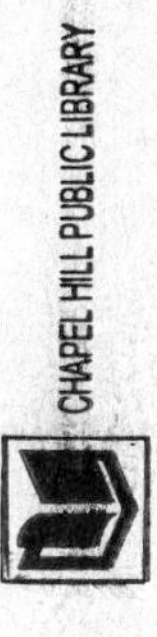

SCOTT®

2010 STANDARD POSTAGE STAMP CATALOGUE

ONE HUNDRED AND SIXTY-SIXTH EDITION IN SIX VOLUMES

VOLUME 4
COUNTRIES OF THE WORLD
J-O

Released July 2009
Includes New Stamp Listings through the July 2009 *Scott Stamp Monthly* Catalogue Update

Scott Publishing Co.

911 Vandemark Road, Sidney, OH 45365-0828
A division of AMOS PRESS, INC., publishers of *Scott Stamp Monthly, Linn's Stamp News, Coin World* and *Coin World's Coin Values.*

Table of Contents

See Volume 1 for United States, United Nations and Countries of the World A-B
See Volume 2, 3, 5, 6 for Countries of the World, C-I, P-Z.

Volume 2: C-F
Volume 3: G-I
Volume 5: P-Sl
Volume 6: So-Z

Scott Publishing Mission Statement

The Scott Publishing Team exists to serve the recreational, educational and commercial hobby needs of stamp collectors and dealers.

We strive to set the industry standard for philatelic information and products by developing and providing goods that help collectors identify, value, organize and present their collections.

Quality customer service is, and will continue to be, our highest priority. We aspire toward achieving total customer satisfaction.

ISBN 0-89487-441-1

Library of Congress Card No. 2-3301

Scott Publishing Co.

SCOTT 911 VANDEMARK ROAD, SIDNEY, OHIO 45365 937-498-0802

Dear Scott Catalogue User:

A time of uncertainty.

We all know that economies worldwide continue to be very weak. As part of that situation, demand for most products is soft. From all information we can gather, it appears that the market for stamps is a bit stronger than most, and for that we can be grateful. However, let's be honest. Unless you have the rarest of the rare or the highest possible grade of a stamp, the market in general is not lively. Most stamps are holding their own, but just barely.

As a result of these circumstances, collectors and dealers will find that somewhat fewer values have changed in this 2010 Volume 4 edition of the *Scott Standard Postage Stamp Catalogue* compared to the near-record number of changes that were seen in last year's edition. Still, there are more than 23,000 value changes in this year's edition, which covers countries of the world from letters J through O.

Where are the value changes in the 2010 Volume 4?

Leading the way in Volume 4, with more than 6,000 value changes, is Korea, which has gone through a thorough review. There are also 1,200 value changes in the Democratic People's Republic of Korea (North Korea). Other countries with large numbers of value changes include Mali (1,635), Niger (1,586), Malagasy Republic (1,132), Mauritania (1,002), Mauritius (983), Jordan (648) and Lithuania (528). Almost every country in Volume 4 shows some value changes, though smaller numbers than the examples cited.

The value changes in Korea begin with the 1946 issues and continue throughout the rest of the listings. Many of the value increases are significant. Collectors and dealers will want to study these changes carefully. In the Democratic People's Republic of Korea, value changes begin with the first issues in 1946 and continue into the 1970s. Value increases of 20 percent are common in the earlier years, with 10 percent advances seen in the later years.

The four African countries with the most value changes are Malagasy Republic, Mali, Mauritania and Niger. Changes in Malagasy Republic are generally small in the years after 1960, but many topical modern issues of the 1980s-1990s show larger increases. The changes in Mali run throughout the country and are mostly small increases, often for both mint never-hinged and used stamps. In Mauritania, many stamps from 1960 to the present show small value increases. And the changes in Niger also are concentrated in the issues after 1960, again with generally small value increases but occasionally larger jumps. Many modern issues from the late 1980s and 1990s that were not valued previously now have values assigned.

The greatest number of value changes in Mauritius are in the issues after 1950, but perhaps the most significant increase is for the used 1859 2p blue on bluish, Scott 15, from the plate re-engraved by Sherwin. From $5,500 in the 2009 Volume 4, this stamp now is valued at $12,000.

What's happening on the editorial side?

More than 70 new minor numbers have been added to the Democratic People's Republic of Korea, representing contemporaneous reprintings of North Korean stamps for domestic sale and use. Typically, these printings were on unsurfaced paper and were made with poorer production qualities. They were issued without gum. The Scott catalogue is the only catalogue that lists these somewhat scarce and very distinctive varieties.

In Latvia, the German occupation stamps handled only by notes after Scott 1N13 in last year's edition have been accorded full recognition as Scott 1N14-1N24. Scott 1N14-1N19 are Russian stamps overprinted "Latvija" and date in three lines, and were used in Latvia under the German occupation in July-September 1941, being replaced by German stamps in October 1941. Scott 1N20-1N24 are the German stamps surcharged "Kurland" plus denomination, and were used in the German-held enclave of Kurland (Courland) from April 20-May 8, 1945, at which time Germany capitulated to Russia.

In Mexico, a number of minor listings have been added, and in the Provisional issues of Guadalajara three new major listings plus minors have been added. The major-number additions are Scott 12A, a 4r black serrate perf stamp on lilac paper; Scott 19A, a 1r black serrate perf stamp on rose paper; and Scott 34A, a 4r black serrate perf stamp on white paper. These stamps were previously unreported on papers of these colors, and all have been competently expertized.

In Montserrat, the $12 and $30 postage and revenue stamps previously mentioned only in a note as being "primarily for revenue purposes" have been accorded major-number status as Scott 501-502. These stamps were available for postal use, and examples used thus are known. Catalogue values are $5 mint never-hinged and $7.50 used for the $12 stamp and $15 mint never-hinged and $20 used for the $30 stamp.

Scott 21C appears for the first time in Orange River Colony. This is the sixth type of "1d." surcharge on Scott 12. This was from a third printing in 1881. Like most of the other surcharges, the new Scott 21C exists with inverted surcharge and double surcharge varieties, Scott 21Ca and 21Cb, respectively.

See the Volume 4 Number Additions, Deletions & Changes listing on page 1626 for these and other changes.

We are close to completing our all-color image project.

Collectors may remember that color images began appearing in the Scott catalogs for the first time in October 2004, when the 2005 *Scott Specialized Catalogue of United States Stamps and Covers* was published for the first time in color. That was followed by the *Scott Classic Specialized Catalogue* of 2005. Then, with the 2006 Standard catalogues, Volumes 1-6, the entire Scott catalogue line appeared in color.

We began scanning stamps from the Scott reference collection in early 2001, and these images (in black and white) started appearing in the 2002 catalogues. Later in 2001, we were blessed by the appearance of a philatelic angel who loaned us, during a period of many months, his entire 400-volume collection of worldwide mint stamps. That angel was Dr. Hsien-ming Meng, an Ohio collector within easy driving distance from our Sidney, Ohio, offices. Between the Scott reference collection and Dr. Meng's collection, we soon approached 90 percent to 100 percent completion in color scans for country after country.

Many other collectors and dealers have helped in the last few years, and we now show close to 100 percent of the stamps in the catalogues in full color. Those who have helped with this project have sent color scans or the actual stamps that were needed. Many thanks to these collectors and dealers. Remember, if you see a Scott image of a stamp in black and white, we probably need a color scan. Any help you can provide will be appreciated. Just call or write us for details concerning what must be done.

We now have begun a new project of replacing images of stamps that are not in an appropriate condition for the catalogues or are in need of color correction. Many hundreds of scans already have been replaced, and many more will be in coming years.

Especially in uncertain economic times such as these, a hobby is a great gift. Happy collecting.

James E Kloetzel

James E. Kloetzel/Catalogue Editor

Acknowledgments

Our appreciation and gratitude go to the following individuals who have assisted us in preparing information included in this year's Scott Catalogues. Some helpers prefer anonymity. These individuals have generously shared their stamp knowledge with others through the medium of the Scott Catalogue.

Those who follow provided information that is in addition to the hundreds of dealer price lists and advertisements and scores of auction catalogues and realizations that were used in producing the catalogue values. It is from those noted here that we have been able to obtain information on items not normally seen in published lists and advertisements. Support from these people goes beyond data leading to catalogue values, for they also are key to editorial changes.

A special acknowledgment to Liane and Sergio Sismondo of The Classic Collector for their extraordinary assistance and knowledge sharing that has aided in the preparation of this year's Standard and Classic Specialized Catalogues.

A. R. Allison (Orange Free State Study Circle)
Roland Austin
Robert Ausubel (Great Britain Collectors Club)
Jack Hagop Barsoumian (International Stamp Co.)
Tim Bartshe
William Batty-Smith
Jules K. Beck (Latin American Philatelic Society)
Vladimir Berrio-Lemm
John Birkinbine II
John D. Bowman (Carriers and Locals Society)
Joshua Buchsbayew (Cherrystone Auctions)
Bernard Bujnak
Timothy Bryan Burgess
Mike Bush (Joseph V. Bush, Inc.)
Tina & John Carlson (JET Stamps)
Carlson Chambliss
Richard A. Champagne (Richard A. Champagne, Inc.)
Henry Chlanda
Richard Clever
Ray Cobb
Leroy P. Collins III (United Postal Stationery Society)
Laurie Conrad
Frank D. Correl
Tony L. Crumbley (Carolina Coin & Stamp, Inc.)
Stephen R. Datz
Tony Davis
Charles Deaton
Bob Dumaine
Sister Theresa Durand
Mark Eastzer (Markest Stamp Co.)
Esi Ebrani (Iran Philatelic Study Circle)
Paul G. Eckman
Marty Farber
George Fedyk
Leon Finik (Loral Stamps)
Henry Fisher
Robert A. Fisher
Jeffrey M. Forster
Ken Fowler
Robert S. Freeman
Ernest E. Fricks (France & Colonies Philatelic Society)
Bob Genisol (Sultan Stamp Center)
Michael A. Goldman (Regency Superior, Ltd.)
Daniel E. Grau
Jan E. Gronwall
Joe Hahn (Associated Collectors of El Salvador)
Bruce Hecht (Bruce L. Hecht Co.)
Clifford O. Herrick (Fidelity Trading Co.)
Peter Hoffman
George W. Holschauer (Colonial Stamp Company)
Armen Hovsepian
Philip J. Hughes (Croatian Philatelic Society)
Doug Iams
Michael Jaffe (Michael Jaffe Stamps, Inc.)
N. M. Janoowalla
Stephen Joe (International Stamp Service)
John Kardos (The Stamp Gallery)
Allan Katz (Ventura Stamp Co.)
Stanford M. Katz
Patricia A. Kaufmann
William V. Kriebel
Dr. Ingert (Ihor) Kuzych-Berlzovsky
Michael Lenard
John R. Lewis (The William Henry Stamp Co.)
William A. Litle
Pedro Llach (Filatelia Llach S.L.)
George Luzitano
Dennis Lynch
Robert L. Markovits (Quality Investors, Ltd.)
Marilyn R. Mattke
William K. McDaniel
Mark S. Miller (India Study Circle)
Allen Mintz (United Postal Stationery Society)
William E. Mooz
Gary M. Morris (Pacific Midwest Co.)
Peter Mosiondz, Jr.
Bruce M. Moyer (Moyer Stamps & Collectibles)
Gregg Nelson
Dr. Marwan Nusair
Robert Odenweller (AIEP)
Albert Olejnik
Dr. Everett L. Parker
Mark Parren
John E. Pearson (Pittwater Philatelic Service)
John Pedneault
Michael O. Perry
Donald J. Peterson (International Philippine Philatelic Society)
Stanley M. Piller (Stanley M. Piller & Associates)
Todor Drumev Popov
Peter W. W. Powell
Stephen Radin (Albany Stamp Co.)
Siddique Mahmudur Rahman
Dr. Reuben A. Ramkissoon
Ghassan D. Riachi
Peter A. Robertson
Omar Rodriquez
Michael Rogers (Michael Rogers, Inc.)
Michael Ruggiero
Mehrdad Sadri (Persiphila)
Richard H. Salz
Alex Schauss (Schauss Philatelics)
Jacques C. Schiff, Jr. (Jacques C. Schiff, Jr., Inc.)
Bernard Seckler (Fine Arts Philatelists)
Guy Shaw
Charles F. Shreve (Spink Shreves Galleries)
Sergio & Liane Sismondo (The Classic Collector)
Jay Smith
Frank J. Stanley, III
Philip & Henry Stevens (postalstationery.com)
Jerry Summers
Scott R. Trepel (Siegel Auction Galleries)
Steve Unkrich
Philip T. Wall
Kristian Wang
Richard A. Washburn
Giana Wayman
William R. Weiss, Jr. (Weiss Philatelics)
Ed Wener (Indigo)
Hans A. Westphal
Don White (Dunedin Stamp Centre)
Kirk Wolford (Kirk's Stamp Company)
Robert F. Yacano (K-Line Philippines)
Ralph Yorio
Val Zabijaka
Michal Zika
John P. Zuckerman (Siegel Auction Galleries)
Alfonsa G. Zulueta, Jr.

Addresses, Telephone Numbers, Web Sites, E-Mail Addresses of General & Specialized Philatelic Societies

Collectors can contact the following groups for information about the philately of the areas within the scope of these societies, or inquire about membership in these groups. Aside from the general societies, we limit this list to groups that specialize in particular fields of philately, particular areas covered by the Scott Standard Postage Stamp Catalogue, and topical groups. Many more specialized philatelic society exist than those listed below. These addresses are updated yearly, and they are, to the best of our knowledge, correct and current. Groups should inform the editors of address changes whenever they occur. The editors also want to hear from other such specialized groups not listed.

Unless otherwise noted all website addresses begin with http://

American Philatelic Society
100 Match Factory Place
Bellefonte PA 16823-1367
Ph: (814) 933-3803
www.stamps.org
E-mail: apsinfo@stamps.org

American Stamp Dealers Association, Inc.
Joe Savarese
3 School St. Suite #205
Glen Cove NY 11542
Ph: (516) 759-7000
www.asdaonline.com
E-mail: asda@erols.com

National Stamp Dealers Association
Dick Keiser, president
2916 NW Bucklin Hill Rd #136
Silverdale WA 98383-8514
Ph: (800) 875-6633
www.nsdainc.org
E-mail: gail@nsdainc.org

International Society of Worldwide Stamp Collectors
Joanne Berkowitz, MD
PO Box 19006
Sacramento CA 95819
www.iswsc.org
E-mail: executivedirector@iswsc.org

Royal Philatelic Society
41 Devonshire Place
London, United Kingdom, W1G 6JY
www.rpsl.org.uk
E-mail: secretary@rpsl.org.uk

Royal Philatelic Society of Canada
PO Box 929, Station Q
Toronto, ON, Canada, M4T 2P1
Ph: (888) 285-4143
www.rpsc.org
E-mail: info@rpsc.org

Young Stamp Collectors of America
Janet Houser
100 Match Factory Place
Bellefonte PA 16823-1367
Ph: (814) 933-3820
www.stamps.org/ysca/intro.htm
E-mail: ysca@stamps.org

Groups focusing on fields or aspects found in worldwide philately (some may cover U.S. area only)

American Air Mail Society
Stephen Reinhard
PO Box 110
Mineola NY 11501
www.americanairmailsociety.org
E-mail: sreinhard1@optonline.net

American First Day Cover Society
Douglas Kelsey
PO Box 16277
Tucson AZ 85732-6277
Ph: (520) 321-0880
www.afdcs.org
E-mail: afdcs@aol.com

American Revenue Association
Eric Jackson
PO Box 728
Leesport PA 19533-0728
Ph: (610) 926-6200
www.revenuer.org
E-mail: eric@revenuer.com

American Topical Association
Ray E. Cartier
PO Box 57
Arlington TX 76004-0057
Ph: (817) 274-1181
americantopicalassn.org
E-mail: americantopical@msn.com

Christmas Seal & Charity Stamp Society
John Denune
234 East Broadway
Granville OH 43023
Ph: (740) 587-0276
http://cscss.home.att.net
E-mail: jdenune@roadrunner.com

Errors, Freaks and Oddities Collectors Club
Stan Raugh
4217 Eighth Ave.
Temple PA 19560
Ph: (717) 445-9420 Nor. Am. Phone No.
www.efocc.org
E-mail: ddprice98@hotmail.com

First Issues Collectors Club
Clark Buchi
P.O. Box 453
Brentwood TN 37024-0453
www.firstissues.org
E-mail: orders@firstissues.org

International Society of Reply Coupon Collectors
Peter Robin
PO Box 353
Bala Cynwyd PA 19004
E-mail: peterrobin@verizon.net

The Joint Stamp Issues Society
Pascal LeBlond
60-600 Rue Cormier
Gatineau, QC, Canada, J9H 6B4
jointissues.ovh.o[illegible]
E-mail: jointiss[illegible]s@yahoo.com

National Duck Stamp Collectors Society
Anthony J. Monico
PO Box 43
Harleysville PA 19438-0043
www.ndscs.org
E-mail: ndscs@hwcn.org

No Value Identified Club
Albert Sauvanet
Le Clos Royal B, Boulevard des Pas Enchantes
St. Sebastien-sur Loire, France, 44230
E-mail: alain.vailly@irin.univ nantes.fr

The Perfins Club
Jerry Hejduk
PO Box 490450.
Leesburg FL 34749-0450
Ph: (352) 326-2117
E-mail: flprepers@comcast.net

Postage Due Mail Study Group
John Rawlins
13, Longacre
Chelmsford
United Kingdom, CM1 3BJ
E-mail: john.rawlins2@ukonline.co.uk.

Post Mark Collectors Club
Beverly Proulx
7629 Homestead Drive
Baldwinsville NY 13027
Ph: (315) 638-0532
www.postmarks.org
E-mail: stampdance@tweny.rr.com

Postal History Society
Kalman V. Illyefalvi
869 Bridgewater Drive
New Oxford PA 17350-8206
Ph: (717) 624-5941
www.stampclubs.com
E-mail: kalphyl@juno.com

Precancel Stamp Society
Jerry Hejduk
PO Box 490450.
Leesburg FL 34749-0450
Ph: (352) 326-2117
www.precancels.com
E-mail: psspromosec@comcast.net

United Postal Stationery Society
Stuart Leven
1445-50 Foxworthy Ave. #187
San Jose, CA 95118-1119
www.upss.org
E-mail: poststat@gmail.com

United States Possessions Philatelic Society
Geoffrey Brewster
6453 E. Stallion Rd.
Paradise Valley AZ 85253
Ph: (480) 607-7184

Groups focusing on U.S. area philately as covered in the Standard Catalogue

Canal Zone Study Group
Richard H. Salz
60 27th Ave.
San Francisco CA 94121-1026

Carriers and Locals Society
John D. Bowman
PO Box 74
Grosse Ile MI 48138
www.pennypost.org
E-mail: jbowman@stx.rr.net

Confederate Stamp Alliance
Gen. Francis J. Crown
PO Box 278
Capshaw AL 35742-0278
Ph. (302) 422-2656
www.csalliance.org
E-mail: csaas@knology.net

Hawaiian Philatelic Society
Kay H. Hoke
PO Box 10115
Honolulu HI 96816-0115
Ph: (808) 521-5721

Plate Number Coil Collectors Club
Ronald E. Maifeld
PO Box 54622
Cincinnati OH 45254-0622
Ph: (513) 231-4208
www.pnc3.org
E-mail: president@pnc3.org

Ryukyu Philatelic Specialist Society
Laura Edmonds, Secy.
PO Box 240177
Charlotte NC 28224-0177
Ph: (704) 519-5157
www.ryukyustamps.org
E-mail: secretary@ryukyustamps.org

United Nations Philatelists
Blanton Clement, Jr.
P.O. Box 146
Morrisville PA 19067-0146
www.unpi.com
E-mail: bclemjr@yahoo.com

United States Stamp Society
Executive Secretary
PO Box 6634
Katy TX 77491-6631
www.usstamps.org
E-mail: webmaster@usstamps.org

U.S. Cancellation Club
Roger Rhoads
6160 Brownstone Ct.
Mentor OH 44060
www.geocities.com/athens/2088/uscchome.htm
E-mail: rrrhoads@aol.com

U.S. Philatelic Classics Society
Rob Lund
2913 Fulton
Everett WA 98201-3733
www.uspcs.org
E-mail: membershipchairman@uspcs.org

Groups focusing on philately of foreign countries or regions

Aden & Somaliland Study Group
Gary Brown
PO Box 106
Briar Hill, Victoria, Australia, 3088
E-mail: garyjohn951@optushome.com.au

American Society of Polar Philatelists (Antarctic areas)
Alan Warren
PO Box 39
Exton PA 19341-0039
Ph: (847) 421-7655
www.polarphilatelists.org
E-mail: cjenner00@yahoo.com

Andorran Philatelic Study Circle
D. Hope
17 Hawthorn Dr.
Stalybridge, Cheshire, United Kingdom, SK15 1UE
http://apsc.free.fr
E-mail: apsc@free.fr

Australian States Study Circle of The Royal Sydney Philatelic Club
Ben Palmer
GPO 1751
Sydney, N.S.W., Australia, 2001

Austria Philatelic Society
Ralph Schneider
PO Box 23049
Belleville IL 62223
Ph: (618) 277-6152
www.austriaphilatelicsociety.com
E-mail: rsstamps@aol.com

American Belgian Philatelic Society
Edward de Bary
11 Wakefield Dr. Apt. 2105
Asheville NC 28803
E-mail: belgam@charter.net

Bechuanalands and Botswana Society
Neville Midwood
69 Porlock Lane
Furzton, Milton Keynes, United Kingdom, MK4 1JY
www.nevsoft.com
E-mail: bbsoc@nevsoft.com

Bermuda Collectors Society
Thomas J. McMahon
PO Box 1949
Stuart FL 34995
www.bermudacollectorssociety.org
E-mail: science29@comcast.net

Brazil Philatelic Association
William V. Kriebel
1923 ManningSt.
Philadelphia PA 19103-5728
Ph: (215) 735-3697
E-mail: kriebewv@drexel.edu

British Caribbean Philatelic Study Group
Dr. Reuben A. Ramkissoon
3011 White Oak Lane
Oak Brook IL 60523-2513
Ph: (630) 963-1439
www.bcpsg.com
E-mail: rramkissoon@juno.com

The King George VI Collectors Society (British Commonwealth)
John Shaw
17 Balcaskie Road, Eltham
London, United Kingdom, SE9 1HQ
www.kg6.info

British North America Philatelic Society (Canada & Provinces)
H. P. Jacobi
6-2168 150A St.
Surrey, B.C., Canada, V4A 9W4
www.bnaps.org
E-mail: pjacobi@shaw.ca

British West Indies Study Circle
W. Clary Holt
PO Drawer 59
Burlington NC 27216
Ph: (336) 227-7461

Burma Philatelic Study Circle
Michael Whittaker
1, Ecton Leys, Hillside
Rugby, Warwickshire, United Kingdom, CV22 5SL
E-mail: whittaker2004@ntlworld.com

Ceylon Study Group
R. W. P. Frost
42 Lonsdale Road, Cannington
Bridgewater, Somerset, United Kingdom, TA5 2JS
E-mail: rodney.frost@tiscali.co.uk

Channel Islands Specialists Society
Moira Edwards
86, Hall Lane, Sandon,
Chelmsford, United Kingdom, CM2 7RQ
www.ciss1950.org.uk
E-mail: am012e5360@blueyonder.co.uk

China Stamp Society
Paul H. Gault
PO Box 20711
Columbus OH 43220
www.chinastampsociety.org
E-mail: secretary@chinastampsociety.org

Colombia/Panama Philatelic Study Group (COPAPHIL)
Thomas P. Myers
7411 Old Post Road #1
Lincoln NE 68506
www.copaphil.org
E-mail: tpmphil@hotmail.com

Association Filatelic de Costa Rica
Giana Wayman
c/o Interlink 102, PO Box 52-6770
Miami, FL 33152
E-mail: scotland@racsa.co.cr

Society for Costa Rica Collectors
Dr. Hector R. Mena
PO Box 14831
Baton Rouge LA 70808
www.socorico.org
E-mail: hrmena@aol.com

Cuban Philatelic Society of America
Ernesto Cuesta
PO Box 34434
Bethesda MD 20827
www.philat.com/cpsa
E-mail: ecuesta@philat.com

Cyprus Study Circle
Colin Dear
10 Marne Close, Wem
Shropshire, United Kingdom, SY4 5YE
www.cyprusstudycircle.org/index.htm
E-mail: colindear@talktalk.net.

Society for Czechoslovak Philately
Phil Rhoade
905 E. Oakside St.
South Bend IN 46614
www.csphilately.org
E-mail: philip.rhoade@mnsu.edu

Danish West Indies Study Unit of the Scandinavian Collectors Club
Arnold Sorensen
7666 Edgedale Drive
Newburgh IN 47630
Ph: (812) 853-2653
dwistudygroup.com
E-mail: valbydwi@hotmail.com

East Africa Study Circle
Jonathan Smalley
1 Lincoln Close
Tweeksbury, United Kingdom, B91 1AE
easc.org.uk
E-mail: jpasmalley@tiscali.co.uk

Egypt Study Circle
Mike Murphy
109 Chadwick Road
London, United Kingdom, SE15 4PY
Dick Wilson: North American Agent
egyptstudycircle.org.uk
E-mail: egyptstudycircle@hotmail.com

Estonian Philatelic Society
Juri Kirsimagi
29 Clifford Ave.
Pelham NY 10803
Ph: (914) 738-3713

Ethiopian Philatelic Society
Ulf Lindahl
21 Westview Place
Riverside CT 06878
Ph: (203) 866-3540
home.comcast.net/~fbheiser/ethiopia5.htm
E-mail: ulindahl@optonline.net

Falkland Islands Philatelic Study Group
Carl J. Faulkner
Williams Inn, On-the-Green
Williamstown MA 01267-2620
www.fipsg.org.uk
Ph: (413) 458-9371

Faroe Islands Study Circle
Norman Hudson
28 Enfield Road
Ellesmere Port, Cheshire, United Kingdom, CH65 8BY
www.faroeislandssc.org.
E-mail: jntropics@hotmail.com

Former French Colonies Specialist Society
BP 628
75367 Paris, Cedex 08, France
www.colfra.com
E-mail: clubcolfra@aol.com

France & Colonies Philatelic Society
Edward Grabowski
111 Prospect St., 4C
Westfield NJ 07090
www.drunkenboat.net/frandcol/
E-mail: edjjg@alum.mit.edu

Germany Philatelic Society
PO Box 6547
Chesterfield MO 63006
www.gps.nu

Gibraltar Study Circle
David R. Stirrups
34 Glamis Drive
Dundee, United Kingdom, DD2 1QP
E-mail: drstirrups@dundee.ac.uk

Great Britain Collectors Club
Timothy Bryan Burgess
3547 Windmill Way
Concord CA 94518
www.gbstamps.com/gbcc
E-mail: Pennyred@earthlink.net

International Society of Guatemala Collectors
Jaime Marckwordt
449 St. Francis Blvd.
Daly City CA 94015-2136
www.guatemalastamps.com

Hellenic Philatelic Society of America (Greece and related areas)
Dr. Nicholas Asimakopulos
541 Cedar Hill Ave.
Wyckoff NJ 07481
Ph: (201) 447-6262
E-mail: nick1821@aol.com

Haiti Philatelic Society
Ubaldo Del Toro
5709 Marble Archway
Alexandria VA 22315
www.haitiphilately.org
E-mail: u007ubi@aol.com

Hong Kong Stamp Society
Dr. An-Min Chung
3300 Darby Rd. Cottage 503
Haverford PA 19041-1064

Society for Hungarian Philately
Robert Morgan
2201 Roscomare Rd.
Los Angeles CA 90077-2222
www.hungarianphilately.org
E-mail: h.alan.hoover@hungarianphilately.org

India Study Circle
John Warren
PO Box 7326
Washington DC 20044
Ph: (202) 564-6876
www.indiastudycircle.org
E-mail: warren.john@epa.gov

Indian Ocean Study Circle
Mrs. S. Hopson
Field Acre, Hoe Benham
Newbury, Berkshire, United Kingdom, RG20 8PD

Society of Indo-China Philatelists
Ron Bentley
2600 North 24th Street
Arlington VA 22207
www.sicp-online.org
E-mail: ron.bentley@verizon.net

Iran Philatelic Study Circle
Mehdi Esmaili
PO Box 750096
Forest Hills NY 11375
www.iranphilatelic.org
E-mail: m.esmaili@earthlink.net

Eire Philatelic Association (Ireland)
David J. Brennan
PO Box 704
Bernardsville NJ 07924
eirephilatelicassoc.org
E-mail: brennan704@aol.com

Society of Israel Philatelists
Paul S. Aufrichtig
300 East 42nd St.
New York NY 10017

Italy and Colonies Study Circle
Andrew DíAnneo
1085 Dunweal Lane
Calistoga CA 94515
www.icsc.pwp.blueyonder.co.uk
E-mail: audanneo@napanet.net

International Society for Japanese Philately
Kenneth Kamholz
PO Box 1283
Haddonfield NJ 08033
www.isjp.org
E-mail: isjp@isjp.org

Korea Stamp Society
John E. Talmage
PO Box 6889
Oak Ridge TN 37831
www.pennfamily.org/KSS-USA
E-mail: jtalmage@usit.net

Latin American Philatelic Society
Jules K. Beck
30 1/2 Street #209
St. Louis Park MN 55426-3551

Liberian Philatelic Society
William Thomas Lockard
PO Box 106
Wellston OH 45692
Ph: (740) 384-2020
E-mail: tlockard@zoomnet.net

Liechtenstudy USA (Liechtenstein)
Paul Tremaine
PO Box 601
Dundee OR 97115-0601
Ph: (503) 538-4500
www.liechtenstudy.org
E-mail: editor@liechtenstudy.org

Lithuania Philatelic Society
John Variakojis
3715 W. 68th St.
Chicago IL 60629
Ph: (773) 585-8649
www.withgusto.org/lps/index.htm
E-mail: variakojis@earthlink.net

Luxembourg Collectors Club
Gary B. Little
7319 Beau Road
Sechelt, BC, Canada, VON 3A8
http://lcc.luxcentral.com
E-mail: gary@luxcentral.com

Malaya Study Group
David Tett
PO Box 34
Wheathampstead, Herts, United Kingdom, AL4 8JY
www.m-s-g/org/uk
E-mail: davidtett@aol.com

Malta Study Circle
Alec Webster
50 Worcester Road
Sutton, Surrey,
United Kingdom, SM2 6QB
E-mail: alecwebster50@hotmail.com

Mexico-Elmhurst Philatelic Society International
David Pietsch
PO Box 50997
Irvine CA 92619-0997
E-mail: mepsi@msn.com

Society for Moroccan and Tunisian Philately
206, bld. Pereire
75017 Paris, France
members.aol.com/Jhaik5814
E-mail: splm206@aol.com

Natal and Zululand Study Circle
Dr. Guy Dillaway
PO Box 181
Weston MA 02493
www.nzsc.demon.co.uk

Nepal & Tibet Philatelic Study Group
Roger D. Skinner
1020 Covington Road
Los Altos CA 94024-5003
Ph: (650) 968-4163
fuchs-online.com/ntpsc/
E-mail: colinhepper@hotmail.co.uk

American Society for Netherlands Philately
Hans Kremer
50 Rockport Ct.
Danville CA 94526
Ph: (925) 820-5841
www.angelfire.com/ca2/asnp
E-mail: hkremer@usa.net

New Zealand Society of Great Britain
Keith C. Collins
13 Briton Crescent
Sanderstead, Surrey, United Kingdom, CR2 0JN
www.cs.stir.ac.uk/~rgc/nzsgb
E-mail: rgc@cs.stir.ac.uk

Nicaragua Study Group
Erick Rodriguez
11817 S.W. 11th St.
Miami FL 33184-2501
clubs.yahoo.com/clubs/nicaraguastudygroup
E-mail: nsgsec@yahoo.com

Society of Australasian Specialists/ Oceania
Henry Bateman
PO Box 4862
Monroe LA 71211-4862
Ph: (800) 571-0293 members.aol.com/stampsho/saso.html
E-mail: hbateman@jam.rr.com

Orange Free State Study Circle
J. R. Stroud
28 Oxford St.
Burnham-on-sea, Somerset, United Kingdom, TA8 1LQ
orangefreestatephilately.org.uk
E-mail: richardstroudph@gofast.co.uk

Pacific Islands Study Circle
John Ray
24 Woodvale Avenue
London, United Kingdom, SE25 4AE
www.pisc.org.uk
E-mail: info@pisc.org.uk

Pakistan Philatelic Study Circle
Jeff Siddiqui
PO Box 7002
Lynnwood WA 98046
E-mail: jeffsiddiqui@msn.com

Centro de Filatelistas Independientes de Panama
Vladimir Berrio-Lemm
Apartado 0823-02748
Plaza Concordia Panama, Panama
E-mail: panahistoria@gmail.com

Papuan Philatelic Society
Steven Zirinsky
PO Box 49, Ansonia Station
New York NY 10023
Ph: (718) 706-0616
www.communigate.co.uk/york/pps
E-mail: szirinsky@cs.com

International Philippine Philatelic Society
Donald J. Peterson
7408 Alaska Ave., NW
Washington DC 20012
Ph: (202) 291-6229
www.theipps.info
E-mail: dpeterson@comcast.net

Pitcairn Islands Study Group
Dr. Everett L. Parker
719 Moosehead Lake Rd.
Greenville ME 04441-3626
Ph: (336) 475-4558
www.pisg.net
E-mail: nalweller@aol.com

Plebiscite-Memel-Saar Study Group of the German Philatelic Society
Clay Wallace
100 Lark Court
Alamo CA 94507
E-mail: clayw1@sbcglobal.net

Polonus Philatelic Society (Poland)
Chris Kulpinski
9350 E. Palm Tree Dr.
Scottsdale AZ 85255
Ph: (480) 585-7114
www.polonus.org
E-mail: ctk@kulpinski.net

International Society for Portuguese Philately
Clyde Homen
1491 Bonnie View Rd.
Hollister CA 95023-5117
www.portugalstamps.com
E-mail: cjh1491@sbcglobal.net

Rhodesian Study Circle
William R. Wallace
PO Box 16381
San Francisco CA 94116
www.rhodesianstudycircle.org.uk
E-mail: bwall8rscr@earthlink.net

Rossica Society of Russian Philately
Edward J. Laveroni
P.O. Box 320997
Los Gatos CA 95032-0116
www.rossica.org
E-mail: ed.laveroni@rossica.org

St. Helena, Ascension & Tristan Da Cunha Philatelic Society
Dr. Everett L. Parker
719 Moosehead Lake Rd.
Greenville ME 04441-3626
Ph: (207) 695-3163
ourworld.compuserve.com/homepages/ ST_HELENA_ASCEN_TDC
E-mail: eparker@hughes.net

St. Pierre & Miquelon Philatelic Society
James R. (Jim) Taylor
2335 Paliswood Rd. SW
Calgary, AB, T2V 3P6, Canada

Associated Collectors of El Salvador
Joseph D. Hahn
1015 Old Boalsburg Rd. Apt G-5
State College PA 16801-6149
www.elsalvadorphilately.org
E-mail: joehahn2@yahoo.com

Fellowship of Samoa Specialists
Donald Mee
23 Leo Street
Christchurch, 8051, New Zealand
www.samoaexpress.org
E-mail: donanm@xtra.co.nz

Sarawak Specialistsí Society
Stu Leven
PO Box 24764
San Jose CA 95154-4764
Ph: (408) 978-0193
www.britborneostamps.org.uk
E-mail: stulev@ix.netcom.com

Scandinavian Collectors Club
Donald B. Brent
PO Box 13196
El Cajon CA 92020
www.scc-online.org
E-mail: dbrent47@sprynet.com

Slovakia Stamp Society
Jack Benchik
PO Box 555
Notre Dame IN 46556

Philatelic Society for Greater Southern Africa
Alan Hanks
34 Seaton Drive
Aurora, ON, L4G 2KI, Canada
Ph: (905) 727-6993
www.psgsa.thestampweb.com
Email: alan.hanks@sympatico.ca

Spanish Philatelic Society
Robert H. Penn
1108 Walnut Drive
Danielsville PA 18038
Ph: (610) 767-6793

Sudan Study Group
c/o North American Agent
Richard S. Wilson
53 Middle Patent Road
Bedford NY 10506
www.sudanphilately.co.uk
E-mail: dadu1@verizon.net

American Helvetia Philatelic Society (Switzerland, Liechtenstein)
Richard T. Hall
PO Box 15053
Asheville NC 28813-0053
www.swiss-stamps.org
E-mail: secretary2@swiss-stamps.org

Tannu Tuva Collectors Society
Ken Simon
513 Sixth Ave. So.
Lake Worth FL 33460-4507
Ph: (561) 588-5954
www.tuva.tk
E-mail: yurttuva@yahoo.com

Society for Thai Philately
H. R. Blakeney
PO Box 25644
Oklahoma City OK 73125
E-mail: HRBlakeney@aol.com

Transvaal Study Circle
J. Woolgar
PO Box 379
Gravesend, DA11 9EW, United Kingdom
www.transvaal.org.uk

Ottoman and Near East Philatelic Society (Turkey and related areas)
Bob Stuchell
193 Valley Stream Lane
Wayne PA 19087
www.oneps.org
E-mail: rstuchell@msn.com

Ukrainian Philatelic & Numismatic Society
George Slusarczuk
PO Box 303
Southfields NY 10975-0303
www.upns.org
E-mail: Yurko@frontiernet.net

Vatican Philatelic Society
Sal Quinonez
1 Aldersgate, Apt. 1002
Riverhead NY 11901-1830
Ph: (516) 727-6426
www.vaticanphilately.org

British Virgin Islands Philatelic Society
Giorgio Migliavacca
PO Box 7007
St. Thomas VI 00801-0007
www.islandsun.com/FEATURES/bviphil9198.html
E-mail: issun@candwbvi.net

West Africa Study Circle
Dr. Peter Newroth
Suite 603
5332 Sayward Hill Crescent
Victoria, BC, Canada, V8Y 3H8
www.wasc.org.uk/

Western Australia Study Group
Brian Pope
PO Box 423
Claremont, Western Australia, Australia, 6910

Yugoslavia Study Group of the Croatian Philatelic Society
Michael Lenard
1514 North 3rd Ave.
Wausau WI 54401
Ph: (715) 675-2833
E-mail: mjlenard@aol.com

Topical Groups

Americana Unit
Dennis Dengel
17 Peckham Rd.
Poughkeepsie NY 12603-2018
www.americanaunit.org
E-mail: info@americanaunit.org

Astronomy Study Unit
John Budd
29203 Coharie Loop
San Antonio FL 33576-4643
Ph: (978) 851-8283
E-mail: jwgbudd@earthlink.net

Bicycle Stamp Club
Norman Batho
358 Iverson Place
East Windsor NJ 08520
Ph: (609) 448-9547
members.tripod.com/~bicyclestamps
E-mail: normbatho@worldnet.att.net

Biology Unit
Alan Hanks
34 Seaton Dr.
Aurora, ON, Canada, L4G 2K1
Ph: (905) 727-6993

Bird Stamp Society
Graham Horsman
23 A East Main Street
Blackburn West Lothian
Scotland, EH47 7QR, United Kingdom
www.bird-stamps.org/bss
E-mail: graham_horsman7@msn.com

Canadiana Study Unit
John Peebles
PO Box 3262, Station ìAî
London, ON, Canada, N6A 4K3
E-mail: john.peebles@sympatico.ca

Captain Cook Study Unit
Brian P. Sandford
173 Minuteman Dr.
Concord MA 01742-1923
www.captaincooksociety.com
E-mail: US@captaincooksociety.com

Casey Jones Railroad Unit
Donald Kesler
709 NW 35th Place
Lawton OK 73505-5121
www.uqp.de/cjr/index.htm
E-mail: normaned@rochester.rr.com

Cats on Stamps Study Unit
Mary Ann Brown
3006 Wade Rd.
Durham NC 27705
www.catsonstamps.org
E-mail: mabrown@nc.rr.com

Chemistry & Physics on Stamps Study Unit
Dr. Roland Hirsch
20458 Water Point Lane
Germantown MD 20874
www.cpossu.org
E-mail: rfhirsch@cpossu.org

Chess on Stamps Study Unit
Anne Kasonic
7625 County Road #153
Interlaken NY 14847
E-mail: akasonic@capital.net

Christmas Philatelic Club
Linda Lawrence
312 Northwood Drive
Lexington KY 40505
www.hwcn.org/link/cpc
E-mail: stamplinda@aol.com

Christopher Columbus Philatelic Society
Donald R. Ager
PO Box 71
Hillsboro NH 03244-0071
http://ccps.maphist.nl/
Ph: (603) 464-5379
E-mail: meganddon@tds.net

Collectors of Religion on Stamps
Verna Shackleton
425 North Linwood Avenue #110
Appleton WI 54914
www://my.vbe.com/~cmfourl/coros1.htm
E-mail: corosec@sbcglobal.net

Dogs on Stamps Study Unit
Morris Raskin
202A Newport Rd.
Monroe Township NJ 08831
Ph: (609) 655-7411
www.dossu.org
E-mail: mraskin@cellurian.com

Earthís Physical Features Study Group
Fred Klein
515 Magdalena Ave.
Los Altos CA 94024
epfsu.jeffhayward.com

Ebony Society of Philatelic Events and Reflections (African-American topicals)
Manuel Gilyard
800 Riverside Drive, Ste 4H
New York NY 10032-7412
www.esperstamps.org
E-mail: gilyardmani@aol.com

Europa Study Unit
Donald W. Smith
PO Box 576
Johnstown PA 15907-0576
www.europanews.emperors.net
E-mail: eunity@aol.com or donsmith65@msn.com

Fine & Performing Arts
Deborah L. Washington
6922 So. Jeffery Boulevard
#7 - North
Chicago IL 60649
E-mail: brasslady@comcast.net

Fire Service in Philately
Brian R. Engler, Sr.
726 1/2 W. Tilghman St.
Allentown PA 18102-2324
Ph: (610) 433-2782
www.firestamps.com

Gay & Lesbian History on Stamps Club
Joe Petronie
PO Box 190842
Dallas TX 75219-0842
www.glhsc.org
E-mail: glhsc@aol.com

Gems, Minerals & Jewelry Study Unit
George Young
PO Box 632
Tewksbury MA 01876-0632
Ph: (978) 851-8283
www.rockhounds.com/rockshop/gmjsuapp.txt
E-mail: george-young@msn.com

Graphics Philately Association
Mark H Winnegrad
PO Box 380
Bronx NY 10462-0380
www.graphics-stamps.org
E-mail: indybruce1@yahoo.com

Journalists, Authors & Poets on Stamps
Ms. Lee Straayer
P.O. Box 6808
Champaign IL 61826
E-mail: lstraayer@dcbnet.com

Lighthouse Stamp Society
Dalene Thomas
8612 West Warren Lane
Lakewood CO 80227-2352
Ph: (303) 986-6620
www.lighthousestampsociety.org
E-mail: dalene@lighthousestampsociety.org

Lions International Stamp Club
John Bargus
108-2777 Barry Rd. RR 2
Mill Bay, BC, Canada, V0R 2P2
Ph: (250) 743-5782

Mahatma Gandhi On Stamps Study Circle
Pramod Shivagunde
Pratik Clinic, Akluj
Solapur, Maharashtra, India, 413101
E-mail: drnanda@bom6.vsnl.net.in

Mask Study Unit
Carolyn Weber
1220 Johnson Drive, Villa 104
Ventura CA 93003-0540
E-mail: cweber@venturalink.net

Masonic Study Unit
Stanley R. Longenecker
930 Wood St.
Mount Joy PA 17552-1926
Ph: (717) 653-1155
E-mail: natsco@usa.net

Mathematical Study Unit
Estelle Buccino
5615 Glenwood Rd.
Bethesda MD 20817-6727
Ph: (301) 718-8898
www.math.ttu.edu/msu/
E-mail: m.strauss@ttu.edu

Medical Subjects Unit
Dr. Frederick C. Skvara
PO Box 6228
Bridgewater NJ 08807
E-mail: fcskvara@optonline.net

Mourning Stamps and Covers Club
John Hotchner
PO Box 1125
Falls Church VA 22041-0125
E-mail: jmhstamp@ix.netcom.com

Napoleonic Age Philatelists
Ken Berry
7513 Clayton Dr.
Oklahoma City OK 73132-5636
Ph: (405) 721-0044
www.nap-stamps.org
E-mail: krb2@earthlink.net

Old World Archeological Study Unit
Caroline Scannel
11 Dawn Drive
Smithtown NY 11787-1761
www.owasu.org
E-mail: editor@owasu.org

Petroleum Philatelic Society International
Dr. Chris Coggins
174 Old Bedford Road
Luton, England, LU2 7HW, United Kingdom
E-mail: WAMTECH@Luton174.fsnet.co.uk

Philatelic Computing Study Group
Robert de Violini
PO Box 5025
Oxnard CA 93031-5025
www.pcsg.org
E-mail: dviolini@adelphia.net

Philatelic Lepidopteristsí Association
Alan Hanks
34 Seaton Dr.
Aurora, ON, Canada, L4G 2K1
Ph: (905) 727-6933
E-mail: alan.hanks@sympatico.ca

Rotary on Stamps Unit
Gerald L. Fitzsimmons
105 Calla Ricardo
Victoria TX 77904
rotaryonstamps.org
E-mail: glfitz@suddenlink.net

Scouts on Stamps Society International
Lawrence Clay
PO Box 6228
Kennewick WA 99336
Ph: (509) 735-3731
www.sossi.org
E-mail: rfrank@sossi.org

Ships on Stamps Unit
Les Smith
302 Conklin Avenue
Penticton, BC, Canada, V2A 2T4
Ph: (250) 493-7486
www.shipsonstamps.org
E-mail: lessmith440@shaw.ca

Space Unit
Carmine Torrisi
PO Box 780241
Maspeth NY 11378
Ph: (718) 386-7882
stargate.1usa.com/stamps/
E-mail: ctorrisi1@nyc.rr.com

Sports Philatelists International
Margaret Jones
5310 Lindenwood Ave.
St. Louis MO 63109-1758
www.sportstamps.org

Stamps on Stamps Collectors Club
Alf Jordan
156 West Elm Street
Yarmouth ME 04096
www.stampsonstamps.org
E-mail: ajordan1@maine.rr.com

Textile Unit
John C. Monson
1062 Bramblewood Dr.
Castle Rock CO 80108-3643
www.caratex.com
E-mail: textilerama@mindspring.com

Windmill Study Unit
Walter J. Hollien
PO Box 346
Long Valley NJ 07853-0346
Ph: (862) 812-0030
E-mail: whollien@earthlink.net

Wine On Stamps Study Unit
Bruce L. Johnson
115 Raintree Drive
Zionsville IN 46077
www.wine-on-stamps.org
E-mail: indybruce@yahoo.com

Women on Stamps Study Unit
Hugh Gottfried
2232 26th St.
Santa Monica CA 90405-1902
E-mail: hgottfried@adelphia.net

Zeppelin Collectors Club
Cheryl Ganz
PO Box 77196
Washington DC 20013
www.americanairmailsociety.org

Expertizing Services

The following organizations will, for a fee, provide expert opinions about stamps submitted to them. Collectors should contact these organizations to find out about their fees andrequirements before submiting philatelic material to them. The listing of these groups here is not intended as an endorsement by Scott Publishing Co.

General Expertizing Services

American Philatelic Expertizing Service (a service of the American Philatelic Society)
100 Match Factory Place
Bellefonte PA 16823-1367
Ph: (814) 237-3803
Fax: (814) 237-6128
www.stamps.org
E-mail: ambristo@stamps.org
Areas of Expertise: Worldwide

B. P. A. Expertising, Ltd.
PO Box 137
Leatherhead, Surrey, United Kingdom KT22 0RG
E-mail: sec.bpa@tcom.co.uk
Areas of Expertise: British Commonwealth, Great Britain, Classics of Europe, South America and the Far East

Philatelic Foundation
70 West 40th St., 15th Floor
New York NY 10018
Ph: (212) 221-6555
Fax: (212) 221-6208
www.philatelicfoundation.org
E-mail:philatelicfoundation@verizon.net
Areas of Expertise: U.S. & Worldwide

Professional Stamp Experts
PO Box 6170
Newport Beach CA 92658
Ph: (877) STAMP-88
Fax: (949) 833-7955
www.collectors.com/pse
E-mail: pseinfo@collectors.com
Areas of Expertise: Stamps and covers of U.S., U.S. Possessions, British Commonwealth

Royal Philatelic Society Expert Committee
41 Devonshire Place
London, United Kingdom W1N 1PE
www.rpsl.org.uk/experts.html
E-mail: experts@rpsl.org.uk
Areas of Expertise: All

Expertizing Services Covering Specific Fields Or Countries

China Stamp Society Expertizing Service
1050 West Blue Ridge Blvd
Kansas City MO 64145
Ph: (816) 942-6300
E-mail: hjmesq@aol.com
Areas of Expertise: China

Confederate Stamp Alliance Authentication Service
Gen. Frank Crown, Jr.
PO Box 278
Capshaw AL 35742-0396
Ph: (302) 422-2656
Fax: (302) 424-1990
www.csalliance.org
E-mail: csaas@knology.net
Areas of Expertise: Confederate stamps and postal history

Errors, Freaks and Oddities Collectors Club Expertizing Service
138 East Lakemont Dr.
Kingsland GA 31548
Ph: (912) 729-1573
Areas of Expertise: U.S. errors, freaks and oddities

Estonian Philatelic Society Expertizing Service
39 Clafford Lane
Melville NY 11747
Ph: (516) 421-2078
E-mail: esto4@aol.com
Areas of Expertise: Estonia

Hawaiian Philatelic Society Expertizing Service
PO Box 10115
Honolulu HI 96816-0115
Areas of Expertise: Hawaii

Hong Kong Stamp Society Expertizing Service
PO Box 206
Glenside PA 19038
Fax: (215) 576-6850
Areas of Expertise: Hong Kong

International Association of Philatelic Experts
United States Associate members:

Paul Buchsbayew
119 W. 57th St.
New York NY 10019
Ph: (212) 977-7734
Fax: (212) 977-8653
Areas of Expertise: Russia, Soviet Union

William T. Crowe
P.O. Box 2090
Danbury CT 06813-2090
E-mail: wtcrowe@aol.com
Areas of Expertise: United States

John Lievsay
(see American Philatelic Expertizing Service and Philatelic Foundation)
Areas of Expertise: France

Robert W. Lyman
P.O. Box 348
Irvington on Hudson NY 10533
Ph and Fax: (914) 591-6937
Areas of Expertise: British North America, New Zealand

Robert Odenweller
P.O. Box 401
Bernardsville, NJ 07924-0401
Ph and Fax: (908) 766-5460
Areas of Expertise: New Zealand, Samoa to 1900

Alex Rendon
P.O. Box 323
Massapequa NY 11762
Ph and Fax: (516) 795-0464
Areas of Expertise: Bolivia, Colombia, Colombian States

Sergio Sismondo
10035 Carousel Center Dr.
Syracuse NY 13290-0001
Ph: (315) 422-2331
Fax: (315) 422-2956
Areas of Expertise: British East Africa, Camerouns, Cape of Good Hope, Canada, British North America

International Society for Japanese Philately Expertizing Committee
32 King James Court
Staten Island NY 10308-2910
Ph: (718) 227-5229
Areas of Expertise: Japan and related areas, except WWII Japanese Occupation issues

International Society for Portuguese Philately Expertizing Service
PO Box 43146
Philadelphia PA 19129-3146
Ph: (215) 843-2106
Fax: (215) 843-2106
E-mail: s.s.washburne@worldnet.att.net
Areas of Expertise: Portugal and Colonies

Mexico-Elmhurst Philatelic Society International Expert Committee
PO Box 1133
West Covina CA 91793
Areas of Expertise: Mexico

Ukrainian Philatelic & Numismatic Society Expertizing Service
30552 Dell Lane
Warren MI 48092-1862
Ph: (810) 751-5754
Areas of Expertise: Ukraine, Western Ukraine

V. G. Greene Philatelic Research Foundation
P.O. Box 204, Station Q
Toronto, ON, Canada M4T 2M1
Ph: (416) 921-2073
Fax: (416) 921-1282
E-mail: vggfoundation@on.aibn.com
www.greenefoundation.ca
Areas of Expertise: British North America

Information on Catalogue Values, Grade and Condition

Catalogue Value

The Scott Catalogue value is a retail value; that is, an amount you could expect to pay for a stamp in the grade of Very Fine with no faults. Any exceptions to the grade valued will be noted in the text. The general introduction on the following pages and the individual section introductions further explain the type of material that is valued. The value listed for any given stamp is a reference that reflects recent actual dealer selling prices for that item.

Dealer retail price lists, public auction results, published prices in advertising and individual solicitation of retail prices from dealers, collectors and specialty organizations have been used in establishing the values found in this catalogue. Scott Publishing Co. values stamps, but Scott is not a company engaged in the business of buying and selling stamps as a dealer.

Use this catalogue as a guide for buying and selling. The actual price you pay for a stamp may be higher or lower than the catalogue value because of many different factors, including the amount of personal service a dealer offers, or increased or decreased interest in the country or topic represented by a stamp or set. An item may occasionally be offered at a lower price as a "loss leader," or as part of a special sale. You also may obtain an item inexpensively at public auction because of little interest at that time or as part of a large lot.

Stamps that are of a lesser grade than Very Fine, or those with condition problems, generally trade at lower prices than those given in this catalogue. Stamps of exceptional quality in both grade and condition often command higher prices than those listed.

Values for pre-1900 unused issues are for stamps with approximately half or more of their original gum. Stamps with most or all of their original gum may be expected to sell for more, and stamps with less than half of their original gum may be expected to sell for somewhat less than the values listed. On rarer stamps, it may be expected that the original gum will be somewhat more disturbed than it will be on more common issues. Post-1900 unused issues are assumed to have full original gum. From breakpoints in most countries' listings, stamps are valued as never hinged, due to the wide availability of stamps in that condition. These notations are prominently placed in the listings and in the country information preceding the listings. Some countries also feature listings with dual values for hinged and never-hinged stamps.

Grade

A stamp's grade and condition are crucial to its value. The accompanying illustrations show examples of Very Fine stamps from different time periods, along with examples of stamps in Fine to Very Fine and Extremely Fine grades as points of reference. When a stamp seller offers a stamp in any grade from fine to superb without further qualifying statements, that stamp should not only have the centering grade as defined, but it also should be free of faults or other condition problems.

FINE stamps (illustrations not shown) have designs that are quite off center, with the perforations on one or two sides very close to the design but not quite touching it. There is white space between the perforations and the design that is minimal but evident to the unaided eye. Imperforate stamps may have small margins, and earlier issues may show the design just touching one edge of the stamp design. Very early perforated issues normally will have the perforations slightly cutting into the design. Used stamps may have heavier than usual cancellations.

FINE-VERY FINE stamps will be somewhat off center on one side, or slightly off center on two sides. Imperforate stamps will have two margins of at least normal size, and the design will not touch any edge. For perforated stamps, the perfs are well clear of the design, but are still noticeably off center. *However, early issues of a country may be printed in such a way that the design naturally is very close to the edges. In these cases, the perforations may cut into the design very slightly.* Used stamps will not have a cancellation that detracts from the design.

VERY FINE stamps will be just slightly off center on one or two sides, but the design will be well clear of the edge. The stamp will present a nice, balanced appearance. Imperforate stamps will be well centered within normal-sized margins. *However, early issues of many countries may be printed in such a way that the perforations may touch the design on one or more sides. Where this is the case, a boxed note will be found defining the centering and margins of the stamps being valued.* Used stamps will have light or otherwise neat cancellations. This is the grade used to establish Scott Catalogue values.

EXTREMELY FINE stamps are close to being perfectly centered. Imperforate stamps will have even margins that are slightly larger than normal. Even the earliest perforated issues will have perforations clear of the design on all sides.

Scott Publishing Co. recognizes that there is no formally enforced grading scheme for postage stamps, and that the final price you pay or obtain for a stamp will be determined by individual agreement at the time of transaction.

Condition

Grade addresses only centering and (for used stamps) cancellation. *Condition* refers to factors other than grade that affect a stamp's desirability.

Factors that can increase the value of a stamp include exceptionally wide margins, particularly fresh color, the presence of selvage, and plate or die varieties. Unusual cancels on used stamps (particularly those of the 19th century) can greatly enhance their value as well.

Factors other than faults that decrease the value of a stamp include loss of original gum, regumming, a hinge remnant or foreign object adhering to the gum, natural inclusions, straight edges, and markings or notations applied by collectors or dealers.

Faults include missing pieces, tears, pin or other holes, surface scuffs, thin spots, creases, toning, short or pulled perforations, clipped perforations, oxidation or other forms of color changelings, soiling, stains, and such man-made changes as reperforations or the chemical removal or lightening of a cancellation.

Grading Illustrations

On the following two pages are illustrations of various stamps from countries appearing in this volume. These stamps are arranged by country, and they represent early or important issues that are often found in widely different grades in the marketplace. The editors believe the illustrations will prove useful in showing the margin size and centering that will be seen on the various issues.

In addition to the matters of margin size and centering, collectors are reminded that the very fine stamps valued in the Scott catalogues also will possess fresh color and intact perforations, and they will be free from defects.

Examples shown are computer-manipulated images made from single digitized master illustrations.

Stamp Illustrations Used in the Catalogue

It is important to note that the stamp images used for identification purposes in this catlaogue may not be indicative of the grade of stamp being valued. Refer to the written discussion of grades on this page and to the grading illustrations on the following two pages for grading information.

Fine-Very Fine
SCOTT CATALOGUES VALUE STAMPS IN THIS GRADE
Very Fine
Extremely Fine
Fine-Very Fine
SCOTT CATALOGUES VALUE STAMPS IN THIS GRADE
Very Fine
Extremely Fine

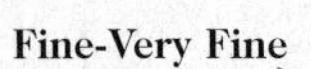

Fine-Very Fine

SCOTT CATALOGUES VALUE STAMPS IN THIS GRADE

Very Fine

Extremely Fine

Fine-Very Fine

SCOTT CATALOGUES VALUE STAMPS IN THIS GRADE

Very Fine

Extremely Fine

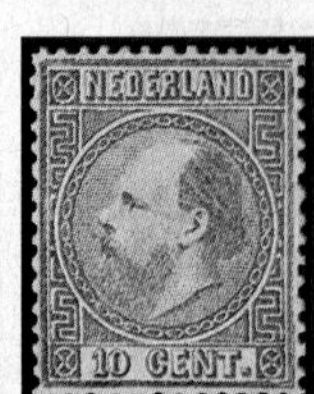

For purposes of helping to determine the gum condition and value of an unused stamp, Scott Publishing Co. presents the following chart which details different gum conditions and indicates how the conditions correlate with the Scott values for unused stamps. Used together, the Illustrated Grading Chart on the previous pages and this Illustrated Gum Chart should allow catalogue users to better understand the grade and gum condition of stamps valued in the Scott catalogues.

Gum Categories:	MINT N.H.	ORIGINAL GUM (O.G.)				NO GUM

	Mint Never Hinged *Free from any disturbance*	**Lightly Hinged** *Faint impression of a removed hinge over a small area*	**Hinge Mark or Remnant** *Prominent hinged spot with part or all of the hinge remaining*	**Large part o.g.** *Approximately half or more of the gum intact*	**Small part o.g.** *Approximately less than half of the gum intact*	**No gum** *Only if issued with gum*
Commonly Used Symbol:	★★	★	★	★	★	(★)
Pre-1900 Issues (Pre-1881 for U.S.)	*Very fine pre-1900 stamps in these categories trade at a premium over Scott value*			Scott Value for "Unused"		Scott "No Gum" listings for selected unused classic stamps
From 1900 to breakpoints for listings of never-hinged stamps	Scott "Never Hinged" listings for selected unused stamps	Scott Value for "Unused" (Actual value will be affected by the degree of hinging of the full o.g.)				
From breakpoints noted for many countries	Scott Value for "Unused"					

Never Hinged (NH; ★★): A never-hinged stamp will have full original gum that will have no hinge mark or disturbance. The presence of an expertizer's mark does not disqualify a stamp from this designation.

Original Gum (OG; ★): Pre-1900 stamps should have approximately half or more of their original gum. On rarer stamps, it may be expected that the original gum will be somewhat more disturbed than it will be on more common issues. Post-1900 stamps should have full original gum. Original gum will show some disturbance caused by a previous hinge(s) which may be present or entirely removed. The actual value of a post-1900 stamp will be affected by the degree of hinging of the full original gum.

Disturbed Original Gum: Gum showing noticeable effects of humidity, climate or hinging over more than half of the gum. The significance of gum disturbance in valuing a stamp in any of the Original Gum categories depends on the degree of disturbance, the rarity and normal gum condition of the issue and other variables affecting quality.

Regummed (RG; (★)): A regummed stamp is a stamp without gum that has had some type of gum privately applied at a time after it was issued. This normally is done to deceive collectors and/or dealers into thinking that the stamp has original gum and therefore has a higher value. A regummed stamp is considered the same as a stamp with none of its original gum for purposes of grading.

Understanding the Listings

On the opposite page is an enlarged "typical" listing from this catalogue. Below are detailed explanations of each of the highlighted parts of the listing.

1 Scott number — Scott catalogue numbers are used to identify specific items when buying, selling or trading stamps. Each listed postage stamp from every country has a unique Scott catalogue number. Therefore, Germany Scott 99, for example, can only refer to a single stamp. Although the Scott catalogue usually lists stamps in chronological order by date of issue, there are exceptions. When a country has issued a set of stamps over a period of time, those stamps within the set are kept together without regard to date of issue. This follows the normal collecting approach of keeping stamps in their natural sets.

When a country issues a set of stamps over a period of time, a group of consecutive catalogue numbers is reserved for the stamps in that set, as issued. If that group of numbers proves to be too few, capital-letter suffixes, such as "A" or "B," may be added to existing numbers to create enough catalogue numbers to cover all items in the set. A capital-letter suffix indicates a major Scott catalogue number listing. Scott uses a suffix letter only once. Therefore, a catalogue number listing with a capital-letter suffix will not also be found with the same letter (lower case) used as a minor-letter listing. If there is a Scott 16A in a set, for example, there will not also be a Scott 16a. However, a minor-letter "a" listing may be added to a major number containing an "A" suffix (Scott 16Aa, for example).

Suffix letters are cumulative. A minor "b" variety of Scott 16A would be Scott 16Ab, not Scott 16b.

There are times when a reserved block of Scott catalogue numbers is too large for a set, leaving some numbers unused. Such gaps in the numbering sequence also occur when the catalogue editors move an item's listing elsewhere or have removed it entirely from the catalogue. Scott does not attempt to account for every possible number, but rather attempts to assure that each stamp is assigned its own number.

Scott numbers designating regular postage normally are only numerals. Scott numbers for other types of stamps, such as air post, semi-postal, postal tax, postage due, occupation and others have a prefix consisting of one or more capital letters or a combination of numerals and capital letters.

2 Illustration number — Illustration or design-type numbers are used to identify each catalogue illustration. For most sets, the lowest face-value stamp is shown. It then serves as an example of the basic design approach for other stamps not illustrated. Where more than one stamp use the same illustration number, but have differences in design, the design paragraph or the description line clearly indicates the design on each stamp not illustrated. Where there are both vertical and horizontal designs in a set, a single illustration may be used, with the exceptions noted in the design paragraph or description line.

When an illustration is followed by a lower-case letter in parentheses, such as "A2(b)," the trailing letter indicates which overprint or surcharge illustration applies.

Illustrations normally are 70 percent of the original size of the stamp. An effort has been made to note all illustrations not illustrated at that percentage. Virtually all souvenir sheet illustrations are reduced even more. Overprints and surcharges are shown at 100 percent of their original size if shown alone, but are 70 percent of original size if shown on stamps. In some cases, the illustration will be placed above the set, between listings or omitted completely. Overprint and surcharge illustrations are not placed in this catalogue for purposes of expertizing stamps.

3 Paper color — The color of a stamp's paper is noted in italic type when the paper used is not white.

4 Listing styles — There are two principal types of catalogue listings: major and minor.

Major listings are in a larger type style than minor listings. The catalogue number is a numeral that can be found with or without a capital-letter suffix, and with or without a prefix.

Minor listings are in a smaller type style and have a small-letter suffix or (if the listing immediately follows that of the major number) may show only the letter. These listings identify a variety of the major item. Examples include perforation, color, watermark or printing method differences, multiples (some souvenir sheets, booklet panes and se-tenant combinations), and singles of multiples.

Examples of major number listings include 16, 28A, B97, C13A, 10N5, and 10N6A. Examples of minor numbers are 16a and C13Ab.

5 Basic information about a stamp or set — Introducing each stamp issue is a small section (usually a line listing) of basic information about a stamp or set. This section normally includes the date of issue, method of printing, perforation, watermark and, sometimes, some additional information of note. *Printing method, perforation and watermark apply to the following sets until a change is noted.* Stamps created by overprinting or surcharging previous issues are assumed to have the same perforation, watermark, printing method and other production characteristics as the original. Dates of issue are as precise as Scott is able to confirm and often reflect the dates on first-day covers, rather than the actual date of release.

6 Denomination — This normally refers to the face value of the stamp; that is, the cost of the unused stamp at the post office at the time of issue. When a denomination is shown in parentheses, it does not appear on the stamp. This includes the non-denominated stamps of the United States, Brazil and Great Britain, for example.

7 Color or other description — This area provides information to solidify identification of a stamp. In many recent cases, a description of the stamp design appears in this space, rather than a listing of colors.

8 Year of issue — In stamp sets that have been released in a period that spans more than a year, the number shown in parentheses is the year that stamp first appeared. Stamps without a date appeared during the first year of the issue. Dates are not always given for minor varieties.

9 Value unused and Value used — The Scott catalogue values are based on stamps that are in a grade of Very Fine unless stated otherwise. Unused values refer to items that have not seen postal, revenue or any other duty for which they were intended. Pre-1900 unused stamps that were issued with gum must have at least most of their original gum. Later issues are assumed to have full original gum. From breakpoints specified in most countries' listings, stamps are valued as never hinged. Stamps issued without gum are noted. Modern issues with PVA or other synthetic adhesives may appear ungummed. Unused self-adhesive stamps are valued as appearing undisturbed on their original backing paper. Values for used self-adhesive stamps are for examples either on piece or off piece. For a more detailed explanation of these values, please see the "Catalogue Value," "Condition" and "Understanding Valuing Notations" sections elsewhere in this introduction.

In some cases, where used stamps are more valuable than unused stamps, the value is for an example with a contemporaneous cancel, rather than a modern cancel or a smudge or other unclear marking. For those stamps that were released for postal and fiscal purposes, the used value represents a postally used stamp. Stamps with revenue cancels generally sell for less.

Stamps separated from a complete se-tenant multiple usually will be worth less than a pro-rated portion of the se-tenant multiple, and stamps lacking the attached labels that are noted in the listings will be worth less than the values shown.

10 Changes in basic set information — Bold type is used to show any changes in the basic data given for a set of stamps. These basic data categories include perforation gauge measurement, paper type, printing method and watermark.

11 Total value of a set — The total value of sets of three or more stamps issued after 1900 are shown. The set line also notes the range of Scott numbers and total number of stamps included in the grouping. The actual value of a set consisting predominantly of stamps having the minimum value of twenty cents may be less than the total value shown. Similary, the actual value or catalogue value of se-tenant pairs or of blocks consisting of stamps having the minimum value of twenty cents may be less than the catalogue values of the component parts.

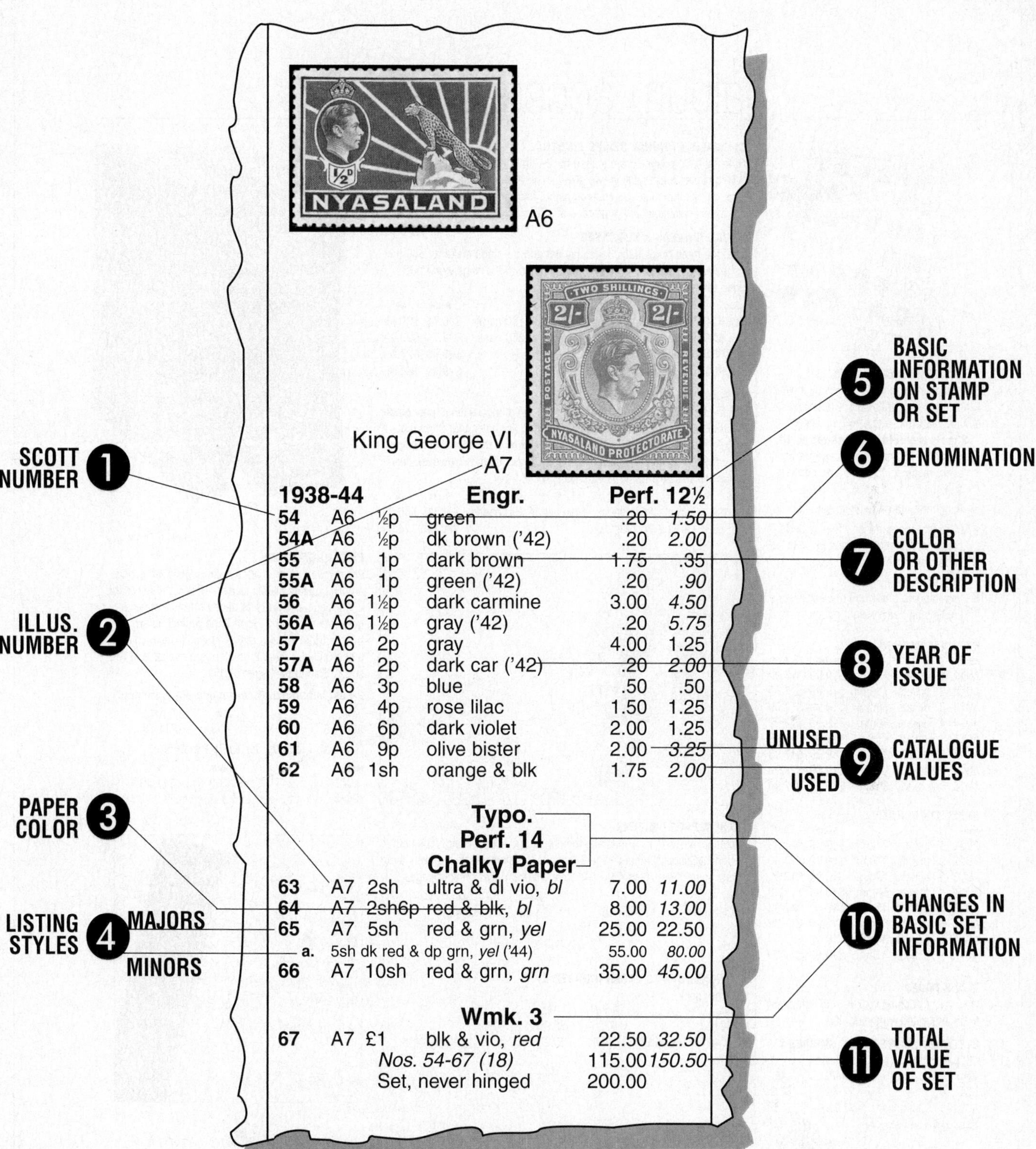

1938-44 **Engr.** **Perf. 12½**

54	A6	½p	green	.20	*1.50*
54A	A6	½p	dk brown ('42)	.20	*2.00*
55	A6	1p	dark brown	1.75	.35
55A	A6	1p	green ('42)	.20	*.90*
56	A6	1½p	dark carmine	3.00	*4.50*
56A	A6	1½p	gray ('42)	.20	*5.75*
57	A6	2p	gray	4.00	1.25
57A	A6	2p	dark car ('42)	.20	*2.00*
58	A6	3p	blue	.50	.50
59	A6	4p	rose lilac	1.50	1.25
60	A6	6p	dark violet	2.00	1.25
61	A6	9p	olive bister	2.00	*3.25*
62	A6	1sh	orange & blk	1.75	*2.00*

Typo.
Perf. 14
Chalky Paper

63	A7	2sh	ultra & dl vio, *bl*	7.00	*11.00*
64	A7	2sh6p	red & blk, *bl*	8.00	*13.00*
65	A7	5sh	red & grn, *yel*	25.00	22.50
a.			5sh dk red & dp grn, *yel* ('44)	55.00	*80.00*
66	A7	10sh	red & grn, *grn*	35.00	*45.00*

Wmk. 3

67	A7	£1	blk & vio, *red*	22.50	*32.50*
			Nos. 54-67 (18)	115.00	*150.50*
			Set, never hinged	200.00	

album accessories

ADVANTAGE STOCK SHEETS

Advantage stock sheets fit directly in your 2-post or 3-ring National or Specialty album. Available with 1 to 8 pockets.

Sheets are sold in packages of 10.

- Stock sheets match album pages in every respect, including size, border, and color.
- Punched to fit perfectly in binder.
- Ideal for storing minor varieties and collateral material. A great place to keep new issues until the next supplement is available.
- Provides the protection of clear acetate pockets on heavyweight pages.

NATIONAL BORDER

Item			*Retail*	*AA**
AD11	1 Pocket	242mm	$19.99	$17.99
AD12	2 Pockets	119mm	$19.99	$17.99
AD13	3 Pockets	79mm	$19.99	$17.99
AD14	4 Pockets	58mm	$19.99	$17.99
AD15	5 Pockets	45mm	$19.99	$17.99
AD16	6 Pockets	37mm	$19.99	$17.99
AD17	7 Pockets	34mm	$19.99	$17.99
AD18	8 Pockets	31mm	$19.99	$17.99

SPECIALTY BORDER

Item			*Retail*	*AA**
AD21	1 Pocket	242mm	$19.99	$17.99
AD22	2 Pockets	119mm	$19.99	$17.99
AD23	3 Pockets	79mm	$19.99	$17.99
AD24	4 Pockets	58mm	$19.99	$17.99
AD25	5 Pockets	45mm	$19.99	$17.99
AD26	6 Pockets	37mm	$19.99	$17.99
AD27	7 Pockets	34mm	$19.99	$17.99
AD28	8 Pockets	31mm	$19.99	$17.99

BLANK PAGES

Ideal for developing your own album pages to be integrated with your album.

SPECIALTY SERIES PAGES (BORDER A)

(20 per pack)

Item		*Retail*	*AA**
ACC110		$7.74	$5.99
ACC111	Quadrille*	$7.74	$5.99

** Graph pattern printed on page.*

SPECIALTY/NATIONAL SERIES BINDERS

National series pages are punched for 3-ring and 2-post binders. The 3-ring binder is available in two sizes. The 2-post binder comes in one size. All Scott binders are covered with a tough green leatherette material that is washable and reinforced at stress points for long wear.

3-RING BINDERS & SLIPCASES

With the three ring binder, pages lay flat and the rings make turning the pages easy. The locking mechanism insure that the rings won't pop open even when the binder is full.

Item			*Retail*	*AA**
ACBR01	Small 3-Ring Binder	Holds up to 100 pages	$36.74	$29.99
ACBR03	Large 3-Ring Binder	Holds up to 250 pages	$36.74	$29.99
ACSR01	Small 3-Ring Slipcase.		$29.99	$24.99
ACSR03	Large 3-Ring Slipcase.		$29.99	$24.99

LARGE 2-POST BINDER & SLIPCASE

For the traditional Scott collector, we offer the standard hinge post binder. Scott album pages are punched with rectangular holes that fit on rectangular posts. The posts and pages are held by a rod that slides down from the top. With the post binder pages do not lie flat. However, filler strips are available for a minimal cost.

Item			*Retail*	*AA**
ACBS03	Large 2-Post Binder	Holds up to 250 pages	$52.99	$45.99
ACSS03	Large 2-Post Slipcase		$29.99	$24.99

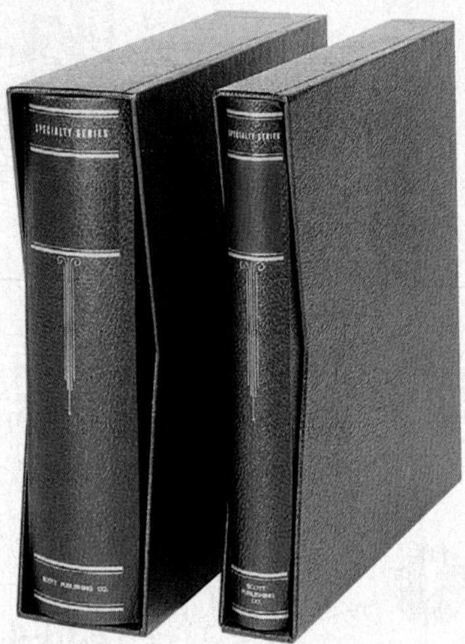

ALBUM PAGE DIVIDERS

Postage, air post, semi-postals; they're all right at your fingertips with National/Specialty Album Page Dividers. The dividers are a great way to keep your albums organized and save wear and tear on your pages.

Item		*Retail*	*AA**
ACC145	Package of 10	$4.49	$3.49

NATIONAL SERIES PAGES (BORDER B)

(20 per pack)

Item		*Retail*	*AA**
ACC120		$7.74	$5.99
ACC121	Quadrille*	$7.74	$5.99

PAGE PROTECTORS

Protect your stamps and album pages with a clear archival quality plastic sleeve. Sleeves fits over the entire page and protects pages from creases, fingerprints and tears. Scott Page protectors are pvc free and thin enough that they won't make your binder bulge. Page Protectors are available in two sizes. Sold in packages of 25.

2-Post Minuteman/International Pg Protectors

Item	*Retail*	*AA**
ACC165	$13.99	$11.75

National/Specialty Series Pg Protectors*

Item	*Retail*	*AA**
ACC166	$13.99	$11.75

*Punched to fit 2-post and 3-ring binder.

To Order Call 1-800-572-6885

www.amosadvantage.com

1. AA* prices apply to paid subscribers of *Scott Stamp Monthly* and *Linn's*.
2. Prices, terms and product availability subject to change.
3. **Shipping & Handling:**
   United States: 10% of order total. Minimum charge $5.99 Maximum charge $40.00.
   Canada: 15% of order total. Minimum charge $14.99 Maximum charge $45.00.
   Foreign orders are shipped via DHL and billed actual freight. Credit cards only.

Catalogue Listing Policy

It is the intent of Scott Publishing Co. to list all postage stamps of the world in the *Scott Standard Postage Stamp Catalogue.* The only strict criteria for listing is that stamps be decreed legal for postage by the issuing country and that the issuing country actually have an operating postal system. Whether the primary intent of issuing a given stamp or set was for sale to postal patrons or to stamp collectors is not part of our listing criteria. Scott's role is to provide basic comprehensive postage stamp information. It is up to each stamp collector to choose which items to include in a collection.

It is Scott's objective to seek reasons why a stamp should be listed, rather than why it should not. Nevertheless, there are certain types of items that will not be listed. These include the following:

1. Unissued items that are not officially distributed or released by the issuing postal authority. If such items are officially issued at a later date by the country, they will be listed. Unissued items consist of those that have been printed and then held from sale for reasons such as change in government, errors found on stamps or something deemed objectionable about a stamp subject or design.

2. Stamps "issued" by non-existent postal entities or fantasy countries, such as Nagaland, Occusi-Ambeno, Staffa, Sedang, Torres Straits and others. Also, stamps "issued" in the names of legitimate, stamp-issuing countries that are not authorized by those countries.

3. Semi-official or unofficial items not required for postage. Examples include items issued by private agencies for their own express services. When such items are required for delivery, or are valid as prepayment of postage, they are listed.

4. Local stamps issued for local use only. Postage stamps issued by governments specifically for "domestic" use, such as Haiti Scott 219-228, or the United States non-denominated stamps, are not considered to be locals, since they are valid for postage throughout the country of origin.

5. Items not valid for postal use. For example, a few countries have issued souvenir sheets that are not valid for postage. This area also includes a number of worldwide charity labels (some denominated) that do not pay postage.

6. Intentional varieties, such as imperforate stamps that look like their perforated counterparts and are usually issued in very small quantities. Also, other egregiously exploitative issues such as stamps sold for far more than face value, stamps purposefully issued in artificially small quantities or only against advance orders, stamps awarded only to a selected audience such as a philatelic bureau's standing order customers, or stamps sold only in conjunction with other products. All of these kinds of items are usually controlled issues and/or are intended for speculation. These items normally will be included in a footnote.

7. Items distributed by the issuing government only to a limited group, club, philatelic exhibition or a single stamp dealer or other private company. These items normally will be included in a footnote.

The fact that a stamp has been used successfully as postage, even on international mail, is not in itself sufficient proof that it was legitimately issued. Numerous examples of so-called stamps from non-existent countries are known to have been used to post letters that have successfully passed through the international mail system.

There are certain items that are subject to interpretation. When a stamp falls outside our specifications, it may be listed along with a cautionary footnote.

A number of factors are considered in our approach to analyzing how a stamp is listed. The following list of factors is presented to share with you, the catalogue user, the complexity of the listing process.

Additional printings — "Additional printings" of a previously issued stamp may range from an item that is totally different to cases where it is impossible to differentiate from the original. At least a minor number (a small-letter suffix) is assigned if there is a distinct change in stamp shade, noticeably redrawn design, or a significantly different perforation measurement. A major number (numeral or numeral and capital-letter combination) is assigned if the editors feel the "additional printing" is sufficiently different from the original that it constitutes a different issue.

Commemoratives — Where practical, commemoratives with the same theme are placed in a set. For example, the U.S. Civil War Centennial set of 1961-65 and the Constitution Bicentennial series of 1989-90 appear as sets. Countries such as Japan and Korea issue such material on a regular basis, with an announced, or at least predictable, number of stamps known in advance. Occasionally, however, stamp sets that were released over a period of years have been separated. Appropriately placed footnotes will guide you to each set's continuation.

Definitive sets — Blocks of numbers generally have been reserved for definitive sets, based on previous experience with any given country. If a few more stamps were issued in a set than originally expected, they often have been inserted into the original set with a capital-letter suffix, such as U.S. Scott 1059A. If it appears that many more stamps than the originally allotted block will be released before the set is completed, a new block of numbers will be reserved, with the original one being closed off. In some cases, such as the U.S. Transportation and Great Americans series, several blocks of numbers exist. Appropriately placed footnotes will guide you to each set's continuation.

New country — Membership in the Universal Postal Union is not a consideration for listing status or order of placement within the catalogue. The index will tell you in what volume or page number the listings begin.

"No release date" items — The amount of information available for any given stamp issue varies greatly from country to country and even from time to time. Extremely comprehensive information about new stamps is available from some countries well before the stamps are released. By contrast some countries do not provide information about stamps or release dates. Most countries, however, fall between these extremes. A country may provide denominations or subjects of stamps from upcoming issues that are not issued as planned. Sometimes, philatelic agencies, those private firms hired to represent countries, add these later-issued items to sets well after the formal release date. This time period can range from weeks to years. If these items were officially released by the country, they will be added to the appropriate spot in the set. In many cases, the specific release date of a stamp or set of stamps may never be known.

Overprints — The color of an overprint is always noted if it is other than black. Where more than one color of ink has been used on overprints of a single set, the color used is noted. Early overprint and surcharge illustrations were altered to prevent their use by forgers.

Se-tenants — Connected stamps of differing features (se-tenants) will be listed in the format most commonly collected. This includes pairs, blocks or larger multiples. Se-tenant units are not always symmetrical. An example is Australia Scott 508, which is a block of seven stamps. If the stamps are primarily collected as a unit, the major number may be assigned to the multiple, with minors going to each component stamp. In cases where continuous-design or other unit se-tenants will receive significant postal use, each stamp is given a major Scott number listing. This includes issues from the United States, Canada, Germany and Great Britain, for example.

Special Notices

Classification of stamps

The *Scott Standard Postage Stamp Catalogue* lists stamps by country of issue. The next level of organization is a listing by section on the basis of the function of the stamps. The principal sections cover regular postage, semi-postal, air post, special delivery, registration, postage due and other categories. Except for regular postage, catalogue numbers for all sections include a prefix letter (or number-letter combination) denoting the class to which a given stamp belongs. When some countries issue sets containing stamps from more than one category, the catalogue will at times list all of the stamps in one category (such as air post stamps listed as part of a postage set).

The following is a listing of the most commonly used catalogue prefixes.

Prefix... Category
C .... Air Post
M....... Military
P .... Newspaper
N .... Occupation - Regular Issues
O .... Official
Q .... Parcel Post
J .... Postage Due
RA ..... Postal Tax
B........ Semi-Postal
E........ Special Delivery
MR .... War Tax

Other prefixes used by more than one country include the following:
H .... Acknowledgment of Receipt
I.......... Late Fee
CO..... Air Post Official
CQ..... Air Post Parcel Post
RAC ... Air Post Postal Tax
CF...... Air Post Registration
CB ..... Air Post Semi-Postal
CBO... Air Post Semi-Postal Official
CE ..... Air Post Special Delivery
EY...... Authorized Delivery
S .... Franchise
G .... Insured Letter
GY ..... Marine Insurance
MC .... Military Air Post
MQ.... Military Parcel Post
NC..... Occupation - Air Post
NO..... Occupation - Official
NJ ...... Occupation - Postage Due
NRA... Occupation - Postal Tax
NB ..... Occupation - Semi-Postal
NE ..... Occupation - Special Delivery
QY ..... Parcel Post Authorized Delivery
AR ..... Postal-fiscal
RAJ .... Postal Tax Due
RAB ... Postal Tax Semi-Postal
F........ Registration
EB...... Semi-Postal Special Delivery
EO ..... Special Delivery Official
QE ..... Special Handling

New issue listings

Updates to this catalogue appear each month in the *Scott Stamp Monthly* magazine. Included in this update are additions to the listings of countries found in the *Scott Standard Postage Stamp Catalogue* and the *Specialized Catalogue of United States Stamps*, as well as corrections and updates to current editions of this catalogue.

From time to time there will be changes in the final listings of stamps from the *Scott Stamp Monthly* to the next edition of the catalogue. This occurs as more information about certain stamps or sets becomes available.

The catalogue update section of the *Scott Stamp Monthly* is the most timely presentation of this material available. Annual subscriptions to the *Scott Stamp Monthly* are available from Scott Publishing Co., Box 828, Sidney, OH 45365-0828.

Number additions, deletions & changes

A listing of catalogue number additions, deletions and changes from the previous edition of the catalogue appears in each volume. See Catalogue Number Additions, Deletions & Changes in the table of contents for the location of this list.

Understanding valuing notations

The *minimum catalogue value* of an individual stamp or set is 20 cents. This represents a portion of the cost incurred by a dealer when he prepares an individual stamp for resale. As a point of philatelic-economic fact, the lower the value shown for an item in this catalogue, the greater the percentage of that value is attributed to dealer mark up and profit margin. In many cases, such as the 20-cent minimum value, that price does not cover the labor or other costs involved with stocking it as an individual stamp. The sum of minimum values in a set does not properly represent the value of a complete set primarily composed of a number of minimum-value stamps, nor does the sum represent the actual value of a packet made up of minimum-value stamps. Thus a packet of 1,000 different common stamps — each of which has a catalogue value of 20-cents — normally sells for considerably less than 200 dollars!

The *absence of a retail value* for a stamp does not necessarily suggest that a stamp is scarce or rare. A dash in the value column means that the stamp is known in a stated form or variety, but information is either lacking or insufficient for purposes of establishing a usable catalogue value.

Stamp values in *italics* generally refer to items that are difficult to value accurately. For expensive items, such as those priced at $1,000 or higher, a value in italics indicates that the affected item trades very seldom. For inexpensive items, a value in italics represents a warning. One example is a "blocked" issue where the issuing postal administration may have controlled one stamp in a set in an attempt to make the whole set more valuable. Another example is an item that sold at an extreme multiple of face value in the marketplace at the time of its issue.

One type of warning to collectors that appears in the catalogue is illustrated by a stamp that is valued considerably higher in used condition than it is as unused. In this case, collectors are cautioned to be certain the used version has a genuine and contemporaneous cancellation. The type of cancellation on a stamp can be an important factor in determining its sale price. Catalogue values do not apply to fiscal, telegraph or non-contemporaneous postal cancels, unless otherwise noted.

Some countries have released back issues of stamps in canceled-to-order form, sometimes covering as much as a 10-year period. The Scott Catalogue values for used stamps reflect canceled-to-order material when such stamps are found to predominate in the marketplace for the issue involved. Notes frequently appear in the stamp listings to specify which items are valued as canceled-to-order, or if there is a premium for postally used examples.

Many countries sell canceled-to-order stamps at a marked reduction of face value. Countries that sell or have sold canceled-to-order stamps at *full* face value include United Nations, Australia, Netherlands, France and Switzerland. It may be almost impossible to identify such stamps if the gum has been removed, because official government canceling devices are used. Postally used copies of these items on cover, however, are usually worth more than the canceled-to-order stamps with original gum.

Abbreviations

Scott Publishing Co. uses a consistent set of abbreviations throughout this catalogue to conserve space, while still providing necessary information.

COLOR ABBREVIATIONS

amb .amber
anil ..aniline
ap ....apple
aqua.aquamarine
az.....azure
bis....bister
bl .....blue
bld ...blood
blk ...black
bril...brilliant
brn...brown
brnshbrownish
brnz .bronze
brt....bright
brnt..burnt
car ...carmine
cer ...cerise
chlky chalky
cham chamois
chnt .chestnut
choc.chocolate
chr ...chrome
cit ....citron
cl .....claret
cob...cobalt
cop...copper
crim .crimson
cr .....cream
dk ....dark
dl .....dull
dp ....deep
db ....drab
emer emerald
gldn .golden
grysh grayish
grn...green
grnsh greenish
hel ...heliotrope
hn....henna
ind ...indigo
int....intense
lav....lavender
lem ..lemon
lil .....lilac
lt......light
mag..magenta
man .manila
mar ..maroon
mv ...mauve
multi multicolored
mlky milky
myr ..myrtle
ol .....olive
olvn .olivine
org ...orange
pck...peacock
pnksh pinkish
Prus .Prussian
pur...purple
redsh reddish
res....reseda
ros ...rosine
ryl ....royal
sal ....salmon
saph .sapphire
scar ..scarlet
sep ...sepia
sien ..sienna
sil.....silver
sl......slate
stl.....steel
turq..turquoise
ultra .ultramarine
Ven ..Venetian
ver ...vermilion
vio ...violet
yel....yellow
yelsh yellowish

When no color is given for an overprint or surcharge, black is the color used. Abbreviations for colors used for overprints and surcharges include: "(B)" or "(Blk)," black; "(Bl)," blue; "(R)," red; and "(G)," green.

Additional abbreviations in this catalogue are shown below:

Adm. ....Administration
AFL.............American Federation of Labor
Anniv. ....Anniversary
APS.............American Philatelic Society
Assoc. ....Association
ASSR............Autonomous Soviet Socialist Republic
b. ....Born
BEP ....Bureau of Engraving and Printing
Bicent. ....Bicentennial
Bklt..............Booklet
Brit. ....British
btwn. ....Between
Bur...............Bureau
c. or ca.........Circa
Cat...............Catalogue
Cent.............Centennial, century, centenary
CIO..............Congress of Industrial Organizations
Conf.............Conference
Cong............Congress
Cpl...............Corporal
CTO.............Canceled to order
d. ....Died
Dbl...............Double
EKU ....Earliest known use
Engr. ....Engraved
Exhib. ....Exhibition
Expo. ....Exposition
Fed. ....Federation
GB ....Great Britain
Gen..............General
GPO.............General post office
Horiz............Horizontal
Imperf..........Imperforate
Impt.............Imprint
Intl..............International
Invtd............Inverted
L..................Left
Lieut., lt. ....Lieutenant
Litho. ....Lithographed
LL ....Lower left
LR................Lower right
mm ....Millimeter
Ms. ....Manuscript
Natl..............National
No. ....Number
NY ....New York
NYC.............New York City
Ovpt. ....Overprint
Ovptd...........Overprinted
P..................Plate number
Perf. ....Perforated, perforation
Phil. ....Philatelic
Photo. ....Photogravure
PO ....Post office
Pr. ....Pair
P.R. ....Puerto Rico
Prec. ....Precancel, precanceled
Pres..............President
PTT..............Post, Telephone and Telegraph
Rio ....Rio de Janeiro
Sgt. ....Sergeant
Soc...............Society
Souv. ....Souvenir
SSR ....Soviet Socialist Republic, see ASSR
St. ....Saint, street
Surch. ....Surcharge
Typo.............Typographed
UL ....Upper left
Unwmkd......Unwatermarked
UPU.............Universal Postal Union
UR ....Upper Right
US................United States
USPOD ....United States Post Office Department
USSR............Union of Soviet Socialist Republics
Vert. ....Vertical
VP................Vice president
Wmk............Watermark
Wmkd..........Watermarked
WWI............World War I
WWII...........World War II

Examination

Scott Publishing Co. will not comment upon the genuineness, grade or condition of stamps, because of the time and responsibility involved. Rather, there are several expertizing groups that undertake this work for both collectors and dealers. Neither will Scott Publishing Co. appraise or identify philatelic material. The company cannot take responsibility for unsolicited stamps or covers sent by individuals.

All letters, E-mails, etc. are read attentively, but they are not always answered due to time considerations.

How to order from your dealer

When ordering stamps from a dealer, it is not necessary to write the full description of a stamp as listed in this catalogue. All you need is the name of the country, the Scott catalogue number and whether the desired item is unused or used. For example, "Japan Scott 422 unused" is sufficient to identify the unused stamp of Japan listed as "422 A206 5y brown."

Basic Stamp Information

A stamp collector's knowledge of the combined elements that make a given stamp issue unique determines his or her ability to identify stamps. These elements include paper, watermark, method of separation, printing, design and gum. On the following pages each of these important areas is briefly described.

Paper

Paper is an organic material composed of a compacted weave of cellulose fibers and generally formed into sheets. Paper used to print stamps may be manufactured in sheets, or it may have been part of a large roll (called a web) before being cut to size. The fibers most often used to create paper on which stamps are printed include bark, wood, straw and certain grasses. In many cases, linen or cotton rags have been added for greater strength and durability. Grinding, bleaching, cooking and rinsing these raw fibers reduces them to a slushy pulp, referred to by paper makers as "stuff." Sizing and, sometimes, coloring matter is added to the pulp to make different types of finished paper.

After the stuff is prepared, it is poured onto sieve-like frames that allow the water to run off, while retaining the matted pulp. As fibers fall onto the screen and are held by gravity, they form a natural weave that will later hold the paper together. If the screen has metal bits that are formed into letters or images attached, it leaves slightly thinned areas on the paper. These are called watermarks.

When the stuff is almost dry, it is passed under pressure through smooth or engraved rollers - dandy rolls - or placed between cloth in a press to be flattened and dried.

Stamp paper falls broadly into two types: wove and laid. The nature of the surface of the frame onto which the pulp is first deposited causes the differences in appearance between the two. If the surface is smooth and even, the paper will be of fairly uniform texture throughout. This is known as *wove paper.* Early papermaking machines poured the pulp onto a continuously circulating web of felt, but modern machines feed the pulp onto a cloth-like screen made of closely interwoven fine wires. This paper, when held to a light, will show little dots or points very close together. The proper name for this is "wire wove," but the type is still considered wove. Any U.S. or British stamp printed after 1880 will serve as an example of wire wove paper.

Closely spaced parallel wires, with cross wires at wider intervals, make up the frames used for what is known as *laid paper.* A greater thickness of the pulp will settle between the wires. The paper, when held to a light, will show alternate light and dark lines. The spacing and the thickness of the lines may vary, but on any one sheet of paper they are all alike. See Russia Scott 31-38 for examples of laid paper.

Batonne, from the French word meaning "a staff," is a term used if the lines in the paper are spaced quite far apart, like the printed ruling on a writing tablet. Batonne paper may be either wove or laid. If laid, fine laid lines can be seen between the batons.

Quadrille is the term used when the lines in the paper form little squares. *Oblong quadrille* is the term used when rectangles, rather than squares, are formed. See Mexico-Guadalajara Scott 35-37 for examples of oblong quadrille paper.

Paper also is classified as thick or thin, hard or soft, and by color if dye is added during manufacture. Such colors may include yellowish, greenish, bluish and reddish.

Brief explanations of other types of paper used for printing stamps, as well as examples, follow.

Pelure — Pelure paper is a very thin, hard and often brittle paper that is sometimes bluish or grayish in appearance. See Serbia Scott 169-170.

Native — This is a term applied to handmade papers used to produce some of the early stamps of the Indian states. Stamps printed on native paper may be expected to display various natural inclusions that are normal and do not negatively affect value. Japanese paper, originally made of mulberry fibers and rice flour, is part of this group. See Japan Scott 1-18.

Manila — This type of paper is often used to make stamped envelopes and wrappers. It is a coarse-textured stock, usually smooth on one side and rough on the other. A variety of colors of manila paper exist, but the most common range is yellowish-brown.

Silk — Introduced by the British in 1847 as a safeguard against counterfeiting, silk paper contains bits of colored silk thread scattered throughout. The density of these fibers varies greatly and can include as few as one fiber per stamp or hundreds. U.S. revenue Scott R152 is a good example of an easy-to-identify silk paper stamp.

Silk-thread paper has uninterrupted threads of colored silk arranged so that one or more threads run through the stamp or postal stationery. See Great Britain Scott 5-6 and Switzerland Scott 14-19.

Granite — Filled with minute cloth or colored paper fibers of various colors and lengths, granite paper should not be confused with either type of silk paper. Austria Scott 172-175 and a number of Swiss stamps are examples of granite paper.

Chalky — A chalk-like substance coats the surface of chalky paper to discourage the cleaning and reuse of canceled stamps, as well as to provide a smoother, more acceptable printing surface. Because the designs of stamps printed on chalky paper are imprinted on what is often a water-soluble coating, any attempt to remove a cancellation will destroy the stamp. *Do not soak these stamps in any fluid.* To remove a stamp printed on chalky paper from an envelope, wet the paper from underneath the stamp until the gum dissolves enough to release the stamp from the paper. See St. Kitts-Nevis Scott 89-90 for examples of stamps printed on this type of chalky paper.

India — Another name for this paper, originally introduced from China about 1750, is "China Paper." It is a thin, opaque paper often used for plate and die proofs by many countries.

Double — In philately, the term double paper has two distinct meanings. The first is a two-ply paper, usually a combination of a thick and a thin sheet, joined during manufacture. This type was used experimentally as a means to discourage the reuse of stamps.

The design is printed on the thin paper. Any attempt to remove a cancellation would destroy the design. U.S. Scott 158 and other Banknote-era stamps exist on this form of double paper.

The second type of double paper occurs on a rotary press, when the end of one paper roll, or web, is affixed to the next roll to save time feeding the paper through the press. Stamp designs are printed over the joined paper and, if overlooked by inspectors, may get into post office stocks.

Goldbeater's Skin — This type of paper was used for the 1866 issue of Prussia, and was a tough, translucent paper. The design was printed in reverse on the back of the stamp, and the gum applied over the printing. It is impossible to remove stamps printed on this type of paper from the paper to which they are affixed without destroying the design.

Ribbed — Ribbed paper has an uneven, corrugated surface made by passing the paper through ridged rollers. This type exists on some copies of U.S. Scott 156-165.

Various other substances, or substrates, have been used for stamp manufacture, including wood, aluminum, copper, silver and gold foil, plastic, and silk and cotton fabrics.

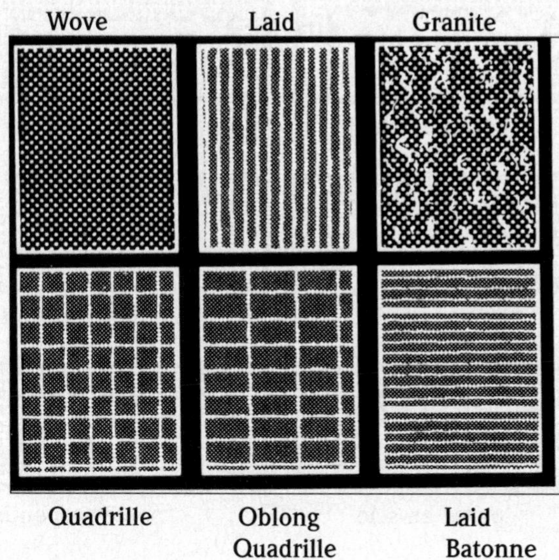

Watermarks

Watermarks are an integral part of some papers. They are formed in the process of paper manufacture. Watermarks consist of small designs, formed of wire or cut from metal and soldered to the surface of the mold or, sometimes, on the dandy roll. The designs may be in the form of crowns, stars, anchors, letters or other characters or symbols. These pieces of metal - known in the paper-making industry as "bits" - impress a design into the paper. The design sometimes may be seen by holding the stamp to the light. Some are more easily seen with a watermark detector. This important tool is a small black tray into which a stamp is placed face down and dampened with a fast-evaporating watermark detection fluid that brings up the watermark image in the form of dark lines against a lighter background. These dark lines are the thinner areas of the paper known as the watermark. Some watermarks are extremely difficult to locate, due to either a faint impression, watermark location or the color of the stamp. There also are electric watermark detectors that come with plastic filter disks of various colors. The disks neutralize the color of the stamp, permitting the watermark to be seen more easily.

Multiple watermarks of Crown Agents and Burma

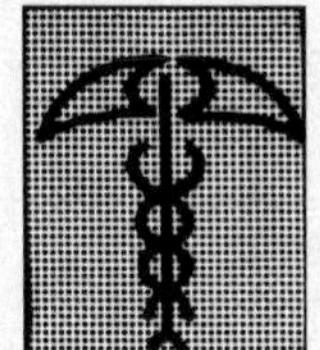
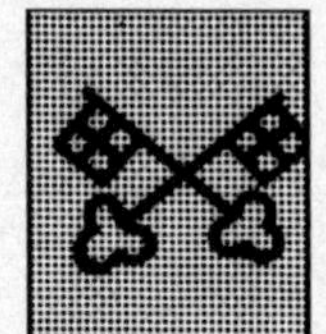

Watermarks of Uruguay, Vatican City and Jamaica

WARNING: Some inks used in the photogravure process dissolve in watermark fluids (Please see the section on Soluble Printing Inks). Also, see "chalky paper."

Watermarks may be found normal, reversed, inverted, reversed and inverted, sideways or diagonal, as seen from the back of the stamp. The relationship of watermark to stamp design depends on the position of the printing plates or how paper is fed through the press. On machine-made paper, watermarks normally are read from right to left. The design is repeated closely throughout the sheet in a "multiple-watermark design." In a "sheet watermark," the design appears only once on the sheet, but extends over many stamps. Individual stamps may carry only a small fraction or none of the watermark.

"Marginal watermarks" occur in the margins of sheets or panes of stamps. They occur on the outside border of paper (ostensibly outside the area where stamps are to be printed). A large row of letters may spell the name of the country or the manufacturer of the paper, or a border of lines may appear. Careless press feeding may cause parts of these letters and/or lines to show on stamps of the outer row of a pane.

Soluble Printing Inks

WARNING: Most stamp colors are permanent; that is, they are not seriously affected by short-term exposure to light or water. Many colors, especially of modern inks, fade from excessive exposure to light. There are stamps printed with inks that dissolve easily in water or in fluids used to detect watermarks. Use of these inks was intentional to prevent the removal of cancellations. Water affects all aniline inks, those on so-called safety paper and some photogravure printings - all such inks are known as *fugitive colors. Removal from paper of such stamps requires care and alternatives to traditional soaking.*

Separation

"Separation" is the general term used to describe methods used to separate stamps. The three standard forms currently in use are perforating, rouletting and die-cutting. These methods are done during the stamp production process, after printing. Sometimes these methods are done on-press or sometimes as a separate step. The earliest issues, such as the 1840 Penny Black of Great Britain (Scott 1), did not have any means provided for separation. It was expected the stamps would be cut apart with scissors or folded and torn. These are examples of imperforate stamps. Many stamps were first issued in imperforate formats and were later issued with perforations. Therefore, care must be observed in buying single imperforate stamps to be certain they were issued imperforate and are not perforated copies that have been altered by having the perforations trimmed away. Stamps issued imperforate usually are valued as singles. However, imperforate varieties of normally perforated stamps should be collected in pairs or larger pieces as indisputable evidence of their imperforate character.

PERFORATION

The chief style of separation of stamps, and the one that is in almost universal use today, is perforating. By this process, paper between the stamps is cut away in a line of holes, usually round, leaving little bridges of paper between the stamps to hold them together. Some types of perforation, such as hyphen-hole perfs, can be confused with roulettes, but a close visual inspection reveals that paper has been removed. The little perforation bridges, which project from the stamp when it is torn from the pane, are called the teeth of the perforation.

As the size of the perforation is sometimes the only way to differentiate between two otherwise identical stamps, it is necessary to be able to accurately measure and describe them. This is done with a perforation gauge, usually a ruler-like device that has dots or graduated lines to show how many perforations may be counted in the space of two centimeters. Two centimeters is the space universally adopted in which to measure perforations.

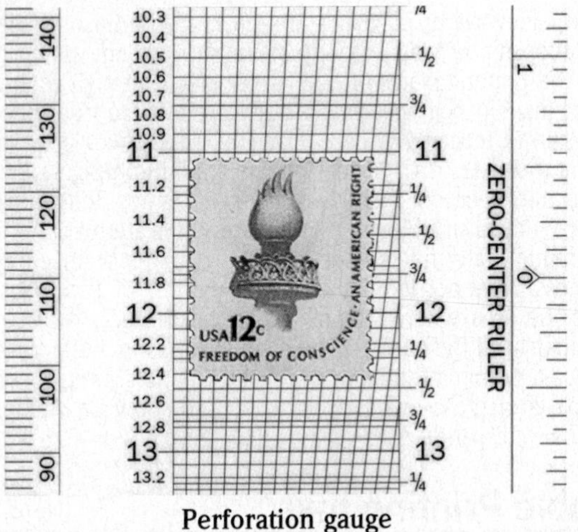

Perforation gauge

To measure a stamp, run it along the gauge until the dots on it fit exactly into the perforations of the stamp. If you are using a graduated-line perforation gauge, simply slide the stamp along the surface until the lines on the gauge perfectly project from the center of the bridges or holes. The number to the side of the line of dots or lines that fit the stamp's perforation is the measurement. For example, an "11" means that 11 perforations fit between two centimeters. The description of the stamp therefore is "perf. 11." If the gauge of the perforations on the top and bottom of a stamp differs from that on the sides, the result is what is known as *compound perforations.* In measuring compound perforations, the gauge at top and bottom is always given first, then the sides. Thus, a stamp that measures 11 at top and bottom and 10 1/2 at the sides is "perf. 11 x 10 1/2." See U.S. Scott 632-642 for examples of compound perforations.

Stamps also are known with perforations different on three or all four sides. Descriptions of such items are clockwise, beginning with the top of the stamp.

A perforation with small holes and teeth close together is a "fine perforation." One with large holes and teeth far apart is a "coarse perforation." Holes that are jagged, rather than clean-cut, are "rough perforations." *Blind perforations* are the slight impressions left by the perforating pins if they fail to puncture the paper. Multiples of stamps showing blind perforations may command a slight premium over normally perforated stamps.

The term *syncopated perfs* describes intentional irregularities in the perforations. The earliest form was used by the Netherlands from 1925-33, where holes were omitted to create distinctive patterns. Beginning in 1992, Great Britain has used an oval perforation to help prevent counterfeiting. Several other countries have started using the oval perfs or other syncopated perf patterns.

A new type of perforation, still primarily used for postal stationery, is known as microperfs. Microperfs are tiny perforations (in some cases hundreds of holes per two centimeters) that allows items to be intentionally separated very easily, while not accidentally breaking apart as easily as standard perforations. These are not currently measured or differentiated by size, as are standard perforations.

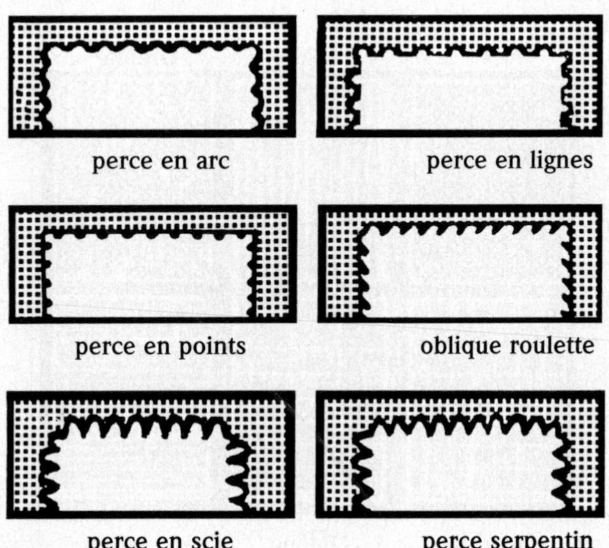

ROULETTING

In rouletting, the stamp paper is cut partly or wholly through, with no paper removed. In perforating, some paper is removed. Rouletting derives its name from the French roulette, a spur-like wheel. As the wheel is rolled over the paper, each point makes a small cut. The number of cuts made in a two-centimeter space determines the gauge of the roulette, just as the number of perforations in two centimeters determines the gauge of the perforation.

The shape and arrangement of the teeth on the wheels varies. Various roulette types generally carry French names:

Perce en lignes - rouletted in lines. The paper receives short, straight cuts in lines. This is the most common type of rouletting. See Mexico Scott 500.

Perce en points - pin-rouletted or pin-perfed. This differs from a small perforation because no paper is removed, although round, equidistant holes are pricked through the paper. See Mexico Scott 242-256.

Perce en arc and *perce en scie* - pierced in an arc or saw-toothed designs, forming half circles or small triangles. See Hanover (German States) Scott 25-29.

Perce en serpentin - serpentine roulettes. The cuts form a serpentine or wavy line. See Brunswick (German States) Scott 13-18.

Once again, no paper is removed by these processes, leaving the stamps easily separated, but closely attached.

DIE-CUTTING

The third major form of stamp separation is die-cutting. This is a method where a die in the pattern of separation is created that later cuts the stamp paper in a stroke motion. Although some standard stamps bear die-cut perforations, this process is primarily used for self-adhesive postage stamps. Die-cutting can appear in straight lines, such as U.S. Scott 2522, shapes, such as U.S. Scott 1551, or imitating the appearance of perforations, such as New Zealand Scott 935A and 935B.

Printing Processes

ENGRAVING (Intaglio, Line-engraving, Etching)

Master die — The initial operation in the process of line engraving is making the master die. The die is a small, flat block of softened steel upon which the stamp design is recess engraved in reverse.

Master die

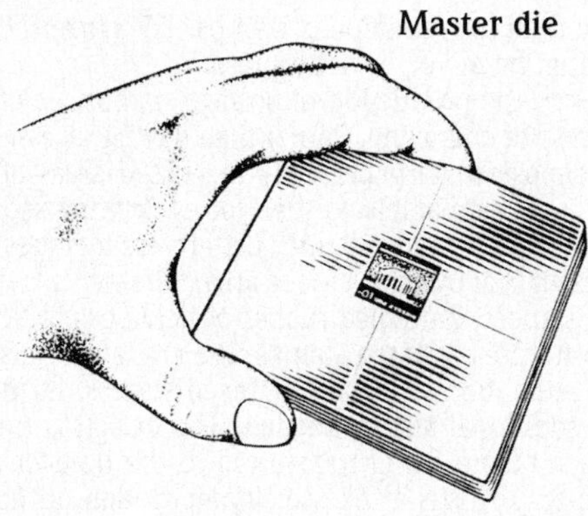

Photographic reduction of the original art is made to the appropriate size. It then serves as a tracing guide for the initial outline of the design. The engraver lightly traces the design on the steel with his graver, then slowly works the design until it is completed. At various points during the engraving process, the engraver hand-inks the die and makes an impression to check his progress. These are known as progressive die proofs. After completion of the engraving, the die is hardened to withstand the stress and pressures of later transfer operations.

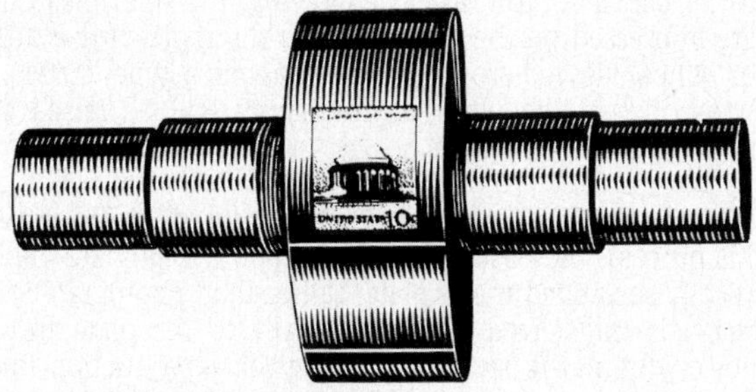

Transfer roll

Transfer roll — Next is production of the transfer roll that, as the name implies, is the medium used to transfer the subject from the master die to the printing plate. A blank roll of soft steel, mounted on a mandrel, is placed under the bearers of the transfer press to allow it to roll freely on its axis. The hardened die is placed on the bed of the press and the face of the transfer roll is applied to the die, under pressure. The bed or the roll is then rocked back and forth under increasing pressure, until the soft steel of the roll is forced into every engraved line of the die. The resulting impression on the roll is known as a "relief" or a "relief transfer." The engraved image is now positive in appearance and stands out from the steel. After the required number of reliefs are "rocked in," the soft steel transfer roll is hardened.

Different flaws may occur during the relief process. A defective relief may occur during the rocking in process because of a minute piece of foreign material lodging on the die, or some other cause. Imperfections in the steel of the transfer roll may result in a breaking away of parts of the design. This is known as a relief break, which will show up on finished stamps as small, unprinted areas. If a damaged relief remains in use, it will transfer a repeating defect to the plate. Deliberate alterations of reliefs sometimes occur. "Altered reliefs" designate these changed conditions.

Plate — The final step in pre-printing production is the making of the printing plate. A flat piece of soft steel replaces the die on the bed of the transfer press. One of the reliefs on the transfer roll is positioned over this soft steel. Position, or layout, dots determine the correct position on the plate. The dots have been lightly marked on the plate in advance. After the correct position of the relief is determined, the design is rocked in by following the same method used in making the transfer roll. The difference is that this time the image is being transferred from the transfer roll, rather than to it. Once the design is entered on the plate, it appears in reverse and is recessed. There are as many transfers entered on the plate as there are subjects printed on the sheet of stamps. It is during this process that double and shifted transfers occur, as well as re-entries. These are the result of improperly entered images that have not been properly burnished out prior to rocking in a new image.

Modern siderography processes, such as those used by the U.S. Bureau of Engraving and Printing, involve an automated form of rocking designs in on preformed cylindrical printing sleeves. The same process also allows for easier removal and re-entry of worn images right on the sleeve.

Transferring the design to the plate

Following the entering of the required transfers on the plate, the position dots, layout dots and lines, scratches and other markings generally are burnished out. Added at this time by the siderographer are any required *guide lines, plate numbers* or other *marginal markings.* The plate is then hand-inked and a proof impression is taken. This is known as a plate proof. If the impression is approved, the plate is machined for fitting onto the press, is hardened and sent to the plate vault ready for use.

On press, the plate is inked and the surface is automatically wiped clean, leaving ink only in the recessed lines. Paper is then forced under pressure into the engraved recessed lines, thereby receiving the ink. Thus, the ink lines on engraved stamps are slightly raised, and slight depressions (debossing) occur on the back of the stamp. Prior to the advent of modern high-speed presses and more advanced ink formulations, paper had to be dampened before receiving the ink. This sometimes led to uneven shrinkage by the time the stamps were perforated, resulting in improperly perforated stamps, or misperfs. Newer presses use drier paper, thus both *wet* and *dry printings* exist on some stamps.

Rotary Press — Until 1914, only flat plates were used to print engraved stamps. Rotary press printing was introduced in 1914, and slowly spread. Some countries still use flat-plate printing.

After approval of the plate proof, older *rotary press plates* require additional machining. They are curved to fit the press cylinder. "Gripper slots" are cut into the back of each plate to receive the "grippers," which hold the plate securely on the press. The plate is then hardened. Stamps printed from these bent rotary press plates are longer or wider than the same stamps printed from flat-plate presses. The stretching of the plate during the curving process is what causes this distortion.

Re-entry — To execute a re-entry on a flat plate, the transfer roll is re-applied to the plate, often at some time after its first use on the press. Worn-out designs can be resharpened by carefully burnishing out the original image and re-entering it from the transfer roll. If the original impression has not been sufficiently removed and the transfer roll is not precisely in line with the remaining impression, the resulting double transfer will make the re-entry obvious. If the registration is true, a re-entry may be difficult or impossible to distinguish. Sometimes a stamp printed from a successful re-entry is identified by having a much sharper and clearer impression than its neighbors. With the advent of rotary presses, post-press re-entries were not possible. After a plate was curved for the rotary press, it was impossible to make a re-entry. This is because the plate had already been bent once (with the design distorted).

However, with the introduction of the previously mentioned modern-style siderography machines, entries are made to the preformed cylindrical printing sleeve. Such sleeves are dechromed and softened. This allows individual images to be burnished out and re-entered on the curved sleeve. The sleeve is then rechromed, resulting in longer press life.

Double Transfer — This is a description of the condition of a transfer on a plate that shows evidence of a duplication of all, or a portion of the design. It usually is the result of the changing of the registration between the transfer roll and the plate during the rocking in of the original entry. Double transfers also occur when only a portion of the design has been rocked in and improper positioning is noted. If the worker elected not to burnish out the partial or completed design, a strong double transfer will occur for part or all of the design.

It sometimes is necessary to remove the original transfer from a plate and repeat the process a second time. If the finished re-worked image shows traces of the original impression, attributable to incomplete burnishing, the result is a partial double transfer.

With the modern automatic machines mentioned previously, double transfers are all but impossible to create. Those partially doubled images on stamps printed from such sleeves are more than likely re-entries, rather than true double transfers.

Re-engraved — Alterations to a stamp design are sometimes necessary after some stamps have been printed. In some cases, either the original die or the actual printing plate may have its "temper" drawn (softened), and the design will be re-cut. The resulting impressions from such a re-engraved die or plate may differ slightly from the original issue, and are known as "re-engraved." If the alteration was made to the master die, all future printings will be consistently different from the original. If alterations were made to the printing plate, each altered stamp on the plate will be slightly different from each other, allowing specialists to reconstruct a complete printing plate.

Dropped Transfers — If an impression from the transfer roll has not been properly placed, a dropped transfer may occur. The final stamp image will appear obviously out of line with its neighbors.

Short Transfer — Sometimes a transfer roll is not rocked its entire length when entering a transfer onto a plate. As a result, the finished transfer on the plate fails to show the complete design, and the finished stamp will have an incomplete design printed. This is known as a "short transfer." U.S. Scott No. 8 is a good example of a short transfer.

TYPOGRAPHY (Letterpress, Surface Printing, Flexography, Dry Offset, High Etch)

Although the word "Typography" is obsolete as a term describing a printing method, it was the accepted term throughout the first century of postage stamps. Therefore, appropriate Scott listings in this catalogue refer to typographed stamps. The current term for this form of printing, however, is "letterpress."

As it relates to the production of postage stamps, letterpress printing is the reverse of engraving. Rather than having recessed areas trap the ink and deposit it on paper, only the raised areas of the design are inked. This is comparable to the type of printing seen by inking and using an ordinary rubber stamp. Letterpress includes all printing where the design is above the surface area, whether it is wood, metal or, in some instances, hardened rubber or polymer plastic.

For most letterpress-printed stamps, the engraved master is made in much the same manner as for engraved stamps. In this instance, however, an additional step is needed. The design is transferred to another surface before being transferred to the transfer roll. In this way, the transfer roll has a recessed stamp design, rather than one done in relief. This makes the printing areas on the final plate raised, or relief areas.

For less-detailed stamps of the 19th century, the area on the die not used as a printing surface was cut away, leaving the surface area raised. The original die was then reproduced by stereotyping or electrotyping. The resulting electrotypes were assembled in the required number and format of the desired sheet of stamps. The plate used in printing the stamps was an electroplate of these assembled electrotypes.

Once the final letterpress plates are created, ink is applied to the raised surface and the pressure of the press transfers the ink impression to the paper. In contrast to engraving, the fine lines of letterpress are impressed on the surface of the stamp, leaving a debossed surface. When viewed from the back (as on a typewritten page), the corresponding line work on the stamp will be raised slightly (embossed) above the surface.

PHOTOGRAVURE (Gravure, Rotogravure, Heliogravure)

In this process, the basic principles of photography are applied to a chemically sensitized metal plate, rather than photographic paper. The design is transferred photographically to the plate through a halftone, or dot-matrix screen, breaking the reproduction into tiny dots. The plate is treated chemically and the dots form depressions, called cells, of varying depths and diameters, depending on the degrees of shade in the design. Then, like engraving, ink is applied to the plate and the surface is wiped clean. This leaves ink in the tiny cells that is lifted out and deposited on the paper when it is pressed against the plate.

Gravure is most often used for multicolored stamps, generally using the three primary colors (red, yellow and blue) and black. By varying the dot matrix pattern and density of these colors, virtually any color can be reproduced. A typical full-color gravure stamp will be created from four printing cylinders (one for each color). The original multicolored image will have been photographically separated into its component colors.

Modern gravure printing may use computer-generated dot-matrix screens, and modern plates may be of various types including metal-coated plastic. The catalogue designation of Photogravure (or "Photo") covers any of these older and more modern gravure methods of printing.

For examples of the first photogravure stamps printed (1914), see Bavaria Scott 94-114.

LITHOGRAPHY (Offset Lithography, Stone Lithography, Dilitho, Planography, Collotype)

The principle that oil and water do not mix is the basis for lithography. The stamp design is drawn by hand or transferred from engraving to the surface of a lithographic stone or metal plate in a greasy (oily) substance. This oily substance holds the ink, which will later be transferred to the paper. The stone (or plate) is wet with an acid fluid, causing it to repel the printing ink in all areas not covered by the greasy substance.

Transfer paper is used to transfer the design from the original stone or plate. A series of duplicate transfers are grouped and, in turn, transferred to the final printing plate.

Photolithography — The application of photographic processes to lithography. This process allows greater flexibility of design, related to use of halftone screens combined with line work. Unlike photogravure or engraving, this process can allow large, solid areas to be printed.

Offset — A refinement of the lithographic process. A rubber-covered blanket cylinder takes the impression from the inked lithographic plate. From the "blanket" the impression is *offset* or transferred to the paper. Greater flexibility and speed are the principal reasons offset printing has largely displaced lithography. The term "lithography" covers both processes, and results are almost identical.

EMBOSSED (Relief) Printing

Embossing, not considered one of the four main printing types, is a method in which the design first is sunk into the metal of the die. Printing is done against a yielding platen, such as leather or linoleum. The platen is forced into the depression of the die, thus forming the design on the paper in relief. This process is often used for metallic inks.

Embossing may be done without color (see Sardinia Scott 4-6); with color printed around the embossed area (see Great Britain Scott 5 and most U.S. envelopes); and with color in exact registration with the embossed subject (see Canada Scott 656-657).

HOLOGRAMS

For objects to appear as holograms on stamps, a model exactly the same size as it is to appear on the hologram must be created. Rather than using photographic film to capture the image, holography records an image on a photoresist material. In processing, chemicals eat away at certain exposed areas, leaving a pattern of constructive and destructive interference. When the phororesist is developed, the result is a pattern of uneven ridges that acts as a mold. This mold is then coated with metal, and the resulting form is used to press copies in much the same way phonograph records are produced.

A typical reflective hologram used for stamps consists of a reproduction of the uneven patterns on a plastic film that is applied to a reflective background, usually a silver or gold foil. Light is reflected off the background through the film, making the pattern present on the film visible. Because of the uneven pattern of the film, the viewer will perceive the objects in their proper three-dimensional relationships with appropriate brightness.

The first hologram on a stamp was produced by Austria in 1988 (Scott 1441).

FOIL APPLICATION

A modern tecnique of applying color to stamps involves the application of metallic foil to the stamp paper. A pattern of foil is applied to the stamp paper by use of a stamping die. The foil usually is flat, but it may be textured. Canada Scott 1735 has three different foil applications in pearl, bronze and gold. The gold foil was textured using a chemical-etch copper embossing die. The printing of this stamp also involved two-color offset lithography plus embossing.

COMBINATION PRINTINGS

Sometimes two or even three printing methods are combined in producing stamps. In these cases, such as Austria Scott 933 or Canada 1735 (described in the preceding paragraph), the multiple-printing technique can be determined by studying the individual characteristics of each printing type. A few stamps, such as Singapore Scott 684-684A, combine as many as three of the four major printing types (lithography, engraving and typography). When this is done it often indicates the incorporation of security devices against counterfeiting.

INK COLORS

Inks or colored papers used in stamp printing often are of mineral origin, although there are numerous examples of organic-based pigments. As a general rule, organic-based pigments are far more subject to varieties and change than those of mineral-based origin.

The appearance of any given color on a stamp may be affected by many aspects, including printing variations, light, color of paper, aging and chemical alterations.

Numerous printing variations may be observed. Heavier pressure or inking will cause a more intense color, while slight interruptions in the ink feed or lighter impressions will cause a lighter appearance. Stamps printed in the same color by water-based and solvent-based inks can differ significantly in appearance. This affects several stamps in the U.S. Prominent Americans series. Hand-mixed ink formulas (primarily from the 19th century) produced under different conditions (humidity and temperature) account for notable color variations in early printings of the same stamp (see U.S. Scott 248-250, 279B, for example). Different sources of pigment can also result in significant differences in color.

Light exposure and aging are closely related in the way they affect stamp color. Both eventually break down the ink and fade colors, so that a carefully kept stamp may differ significantly in color from an identical copy that has been exposed to light. If stamps are exposed to light either intentionally or accidentally, their colors can be faded or completely changed in some cases.

Papers of different quality and consistency used for the same stamp printing may affect color appearance. Most pelure papers, for example, show a richer color when compared with wove or laid papers. See Russia Scott 181a, for an example of this effect.

The very nature of the printing processes can cause a variety of differences in shades or hues of the same stamp. Some of these shades are scarcer than others, and are of particular interest to the advanced collector.

Luminescence

All forms of tagged stamps fall under the general category of luminescence. Within this broad category is fluorescence, dealing with forms of tagging visible under longwave ultraviolet light, and phosphorescence, which deals with tagging visible only under shortwave light. Phosphorescence leaves an afterglow and fluorescence does not. These treated stamps show up in a range of different colors when exposed to UV light. The differing wavelengths of the light activates the tagging material, making it glow in various colors that usually serve different mail processing purposes.

Intentional tagging is a post-World War II phenomenon, brought about by the increased literacy rate and rapidly growing mail volume. It was one of several answers to the problem of the need for more automated mail processes. Early tagged stamps served the purpose of triggering machines to separate different types of mail. A natural outgrowth was to also use the signal to trigger machines that faced all envelopes the same way and canceled them.

Tagged stamps come in many different forms. Some tagged stamps have luminescent shapes or images imprinted on them as a form of security device. Others have blocks (United States), stripes, frames (South Africa and Canada), overall coatings (United States), bars (Great Britain and Canada) and many other types. Some types of tagging are even mixed in with the pigmented printing ink (Australia Scott 366, Netherlands Scott 478 and U.S. Scott 1359 and 2443).

The means of applying taggant to stamps differs as much as the intended purposes for the stamps. The most common form of tagging is a coating applied to the surface of the printed stamp. Since the taggant ink is frequently invisible except under UV light, it does not interfere with the appearance of the stamp. Another common application is the use of phosphored papers. In this case the paper itself either has a coating of taggant applied before the stamp is printed, has taggant applied during the papermaking process (incorporating it into the fibers), or has the taggant mixed into the coating of the paper. The latter method, among others, is currently in use in the United States.

Many countries now use tagging in various forms to either expedite mail handling or to serve as a printing security device against counterfeiting. Following the introduction of tagged stamps for public use in 1959 by Great Britain, other countries have steadily joined the parade. Among those are Germany (1961); Canada and Denmark (1962); United States, Australia, France and Switzerland (1963); Belgium and Japan (1966); Sweden and Norway (1967); Italy (1968); and Russia (1969). Since then, many other countries have begun using forms of tagging, including Brazil, China, Czechoslovakia, Hong Kong, Guatemala, Indonesia, Israel, Lithuania, Luxembourg, Netherlands, Penrhyn Islands, Portugal, St. Vincent, Singapore, South Africa, Spain and Sweden to name a few.

In some cases, including United States, Canada, Great Britain and Switzerland, stamps were released both with and without tagging. Many of these were released during each country's experimental period. Tagged and untagged versions are listed for the aforementioned countries and are noted in some other countries' listings. For at least a few stamps, the experimentally tagged version is worth far more than its untagged counterpart, such as the 1963 experimental tagged version of France Scott 1024.

In some cases, luminescent varieties of stamps were inadvertently created. Several Russian stamps, for example, sport highly fluorescent ink that was not intended as a form of tagging. Older stamps, such as early U.S. postage dues, can be positively identified by the use of UV light, since the organic ink used has become slightly fluorescent over time. Other stamps, such as Austria Scott 70a-82a (varnish bars) and Obock Scott 46-64 (printed quadrille lines), have become fluorescent over time.

Various fluorescent substances have been added to paper to make it appear brighter. These optical brightners, as they are known, greatly affect the appearance of the stamp under UV light. The brightest of these is known as Hi-Brite paper. These paper varieties are beyond the scope of the Scott Catalogue.

Shortwave UV light also is used extensively in expertizing, since each form of paper has its own fluorescent characteristics that are impossible to perfectly match. It is therefore a simple matter to detect filled thins, added perforation teeth and other alterations that involve the addition of paper. UV light also is used to examine stamps that have had cancels chemically removed and for other purposes as well.

Gum

The Illustrated Gum Chart in the first part of this introduction shows and defines various types of gum condition. Because gum condition has an important impact on the value of unused stamps, we recommend studying this chart and the accompanying text carefully.

The gum on the back of a stamp may be shiny, dull, smooth, rough, dark, white, colored or tinted. Most stamp gumming adhesives use gum arabic or dextrine as a base. Certain polymers such as polyvinyl alcohol (PVA) have been used extensively since World War II.

The *Scott Standard Postage Stamp Catalogue* does not list items by types of gum. The *Scott Specialized Catalogue of United States Stamps* does differentiate among some types of gum for certain issues.

Reprints of stamps may have gum differing from the original issues. In addition, some countries have used different gum formulas for different seasons. These adhesives have different properties that may become more apparent over time.

Many stamps have been issued without gum, and the catalogue will note this fact. See, for example, United States Scott 40-47. Sometimes, gum may have been removed to preserve the stamp. Germany Scott B68, for example, has a highly acidic gum that eventually destroys the stamps. This item is valued in the catalogue with gum removed.

Reprints and Reissues

These are impressions of stamps (usually obsolete) made from the original plates or stones. If they are valid for postage and reproduce obsolete issues (such as U.S. Scott 102-111), the stamps are *reissues.* If they are from current issues, they are designated as *second, third,* etc., *printing.* If designated for a particular purpose, they are called *special printings.*

When special printings are not valid for postage, but are made from original dies and plates by authorized persons, they are *official reprints. Private reprints* are made from the original plates and dies by private hands. An example of a private reprint is that of the 1871-1932 reprints made from the original die of the 1845 New Haven, Conn., postmaster's provisional. *Official reproductions* or imitations are made from new dies and plates by government authorization. Scott will list those reissues that are valid for postage if they differ significantly from the original printing.

The U.S. government made special printings of its first postage stamps in 1875. Produced were official imitations of the first two stamps (listed as Scott 3-4), reprints of the demonetized pre-1861 issues (Scott 40-47) and reissues of the 1861 stamps, the 1869 stamps and the then-current 1875 denominations. Even though the official imitations and the reprints were not valid for postage, Scott lists all of these U.S. special printings.

Most reprints or reissues differ slightly from the original stamp in some characteristic, such as gum, paper, perforation, color or watermark. Sometimes the details are followed so meticulously that only a student of that specific stamp is able to distinguish the reprint or reissue from the original.

Remainders and Canceled to Order

Some countries sell their stock of old stamps when a new issue replaces them. To avoid postal use, the *remainders* usually are canceled with a punch hole, a heavy line or bar, or a more-or-less regular-looking cancellation. The most famous merchant of remainders was Nicholas F. Seebeck. In the 1880s and 1890s, he arranged printing contracts between the Hamilton Bank Note Co., of which he was a director, and several Central and South American countries. The contracts provided that the plates and all remainders of the yearly issues became the property of Hamilton. Seebeck saw to it that ample stock remained. The "Seebecks," both remainders and reprints, were standard packet fillers for decades.

Some countries also issue stamps *canceled-to-order (CTO),* either in sheets with original gum or stuck onto pieces of paper or envelopes and canceled. Such CTO items generally are worth less than postally used stamps. In cases where the CTO material is far more prevalent in the marketplace than postally used examples, the catalogue value relates to the CTO examples, with postally used examples noted as premium items. Most CTOs can be detected by the presence of gum. However, as the CTO practice goes back at least to 1885, the gum inevitably has been soaked off some stamps so they could pass as postally used. The normally applied postmarks usually differ slightly from standard postmarks, and specialists are able to tell the difference. When applied individually to envelopes by philatelically minded persons, CTO material is known as *favor canceled* and generally sells at large discounts.

Cinderellas and Facsimiles

Cinderella is a catch-all term used by stamp collectors to describe phantoms, fantasies, bogus items, municipal issues, exhibition seals, local revenues, transportation stamps, labels, poster stamps and many other types of items. Some cinderella collectors include in their collections local postage issues, telegraph stamps, essays and proofs, forgeries and counterfeits.

A *fantasy* is an adhesive created for a nonexistent stamp-issuing authority. Fantasy items range from imaginary countries (Occusi-Ambeno, Kingdom of Sedang, Principality of Trinidad or Torres Straits), to non-existent locals (Winans City Post), or nonexistent transportation lines (McRobish & Co.'s Acapulco-San Francisco Line).

On the other hand, if the entity exists and could have issued stamps (but did not) or was known to have issued other stamps, the items are considered *bogus* stamps. These would include the Mormon postage stamps of Utah, S. Allan Taylor's Guatemala and Paraguay inventions, the propaganda issues for the South Moluccas and the adhesives of the Page & Keyes local post of Boston.

Phantoms is another term for both fantasy and bogus issues.

Facsimiles are copies or imitations made to represent original stamps, but which do not pretend to be originals. A catalogue illustration is such a facsimile. Illustrations from the Moens catalogue of the last century were occasionally colored and passed off as stamps. Since the beginning of stamp collecting, facsimiles have been made for collectors as space fillers or for reference. They often carry the word "facsimile," "falsch" (German), "sanko" or "mozo" (Japanese), or "faux" (French) overprinted on the face or stamped on the back. Unfortunately, over the years a number of these items have had fake cancels applied over the facsimile notation and have been passed off as genuine.

Forgeries and Counterfeits

Forgeries and counterfeits have been with philately virtually from the beginning of stamp production. Over time, the terminology for the two has been used interchangeably. Although both forgeries and counterfeits are reproductions of stamps, the purposes behind their creation differ considerably.

Among specialists there is an increasing movement to more specifically define such items. Although there is no universally accepted terminology, we feel the following definitions most closely mirror the items and their purposes as they are currently defined.

Forgeries (also often referred to as *Counterfeits*) are reproductions of genuine stamps that have been created to defraud collectors. Such spurious items first appeared on the market around 1860, and most old-time collections contain one or more. Many are crude and easily spotted, but some can deceive experts.

An important supplier of these early philatelic forgeries was the Hamburg printer Gebruder Spiro. Many others with reputations in this craft included S. Allan Taylor, George Hussey, James Chute, George Forune, Benjamin & Sarpy, Julius Goldner, E. Oneglia and L.H. Mercier. Among the noted 20th-century forgers were Francois Fournier, Jean Sperati and the prolific Raoul DeThuin.

Forgeries may be complete replications, or they may be genuine stamps altered to resemble a scarcer (and more valuable) type. Most forgeries, particularly those of rare stamps, are worth only a small fraction of the value of a genuine example, but a few types, created by some of the most notable forgers, such as Sperati, can be worth as much or more than the genuine. Fraudulently produced copies are known of most classic rarities and many medium-priced stamps.

In addition to rare stamps, large numbers of common 19th- and early 20th-century stamps were forged to supply stamps to the early packet trade. Many can still be easily found. Few new philatelic forgeries have appeared in recent decades. Successful imitation of well-engraved work is virtually impossible. It has proven far easier to produce a fake by altering a genuine stamp than to duplicate a stamp completely.

Counterfeit (also often referred to as *Postal Counterfeit* or *Postal Forgery*) is the term generally applied to reproductions of stamps that have been created to defraud the government of revenue. Such items usually are created at the time a stamp is current and, in some cases, are hard to detect. Because most counterfeits are seized when the perpetrator is captured, postal counterfeits, particularly used on cover, are usually worth much more than a genuine example to specialists. The first postal counterfeit was of Spain's 4-cuarto carmine of 1854 (the real one is Scott 25). Apparently, the counterfeiters were not satisfied with their first version, which is now very scarce, and they soon created an engraved counterfeit, which is common. Postal counterfeits quickly followed in Austria, Naples, Sardinia and the Roman States. They have since been created in many other countries as well, including the United States.

An infamous counterfeit to defraud the government is the 1-shilling Great Britain "Stock Exchange" forgery of 1872, used on telegraph forms at the exchange that year. The stamp escaped detection until a stamp dealer noticed it in 1898.

Fakes

Fakes are genuine stamps altered in some way to make them more desirable. One student of this part of stamp collecting has estimated that by the 1950s more than 30,000 varieties of fakes were known. That number has grown greatly since then. The widespread existence of fakes makes it important for stamp collectors to study their philatelic holdings and use relevant literature. Likewise, collectors should buy from reputable dealers who guarantee their stamps and make full and prompt refunds should a purchased item be declared faked or altered by some mutually agreed-upon authority. Because fakes always have some genuine characteristics, it is not always possible to obtain unanimous agreement among experts regarding specific items. These students may change their opinions as philatelic knowledge increases. More than 80 percent of all fakes on the philatelic market today are regummed, reperforated (or perforated for the first time), or bear forged overprints, surcharges or cancellations.

Stamps can be chemically treated to alter or eliminate colors. For example, a pale rose stamp can be re-colored to resemble a blue shade of high market value. In other cases, treated stamps can be made to resemble missing color varieties. Designs may be changed by painting, or a stroke or a dot added or bleached out to turn an ordinary variety into a seemingly scarcer stamp. Part of a stamp can be bleached and reprinted in a different version, achieving an inverted center or frame. Margins can be added or repairs done so deceptively that the stamps move from the "repaired" into the "fake" category.

Fakers have not left the backs of the stamps untouched either. They may create false watermarks, add fake grills or press out genuine grills. A thin India paper proof may be glued onto a thicker backing to create the appearance an issued stamp, or a proof printed on cardboard may be shaved down and perforated to resemble a stamp. Silk threads are impressed into paper and stamps have been split so that a rare paper variety is added to an otherwise inexpensive stamp. The most common treatment to the back of a stamp, however, is regumming.

Some in the business of faking stamps have openly advertised foolproof application of "original gum" to stamps that lack it, although most publications now ban such ads from their pages. It is believed that very few early stamps have survived without being hinged. The large number of never-hinged examples of such earlier material offered for sale thus suggests the widespread extent of regumming activity. Regumming also may be used to hide repairs or thin spots. Dipping the stamp into watermark fluid, or examining it under long-wave ultraviolet light often will reveal these flaws.

Fakers also tamper with separations. Ingenious ways to add margins are known. Perforated wide-margin stamps may be falsely represented as imperforate when trimmed. Reperforating is commonly done to create scarce coil or perforation varieties, and to eliminate the naturally occurring straight-edge stamps found in sheet margin positions of many earlier issues. Custom has made straight-edged stamps less desirable. Fakers have obliged by perforating straight-edged stamps so that many are now uncommon, if not rare.

Another fertile field for the faker is that of overprints, surcharges and cancellations. The forging of rare surcharges or overprints began in the 1880s or 1890s. These forgeries are sometimes difficult to detect, but experts have identified almost all. Occasionally, overprints or cancellations are removed to create non-overprinted stamps or seemingly unused items. This is most commonly done by removing a manuscript cancel to make a stamp resemble an unused example. "SPECIMEN" overprints may be removed by scraping and repainting to create non-overprinted varieties. Fakers use inexpensive revenues or pen-canceled stamps to generate unused stamps for further faking by adding other markings. The quartz lamp or UV lamp and a high-powered magnifying glass help to easily detect removed cancellations.

The bigger problem, however, is the addition of overprints, surcharges or cancellations - many with such precision that they are very difficult to ascertain. Plating of the stamps or the overprint can be an important method of detection.

Fake postmarks may range from many spurious fancy cancellations to a host of markings applied to transatlantic covers, to adding normally appearing postmarks to definitives of some countries with stamps that are valued far higher used than unused. With the increased popularity of cover collecting, and the widespread interest in postal history, a fertile new field for fakers has come about. Some have tried to create entire covers. Others specialize in adding stamps, tied by fake cancellations, to genuine stampless covers, or replacing less expensive or damaged stamps with more valuable ones. Detailed study of postal rates in effect at the time a cover in question was mailed, including the analysis of each handstamp used during the period, ink analysis and similar techniques, usually will unmask the fraud.

Restoration and Repairs

Scott Publishing Co. bases its catalogue values on stamps that are free of defects and otherwise meet the standards set forth earlier in this introduction. Most stamp collectors desire to have the finest copy of an item possible. Even within given grading categories there are variances. This leads to a controversial practice that is not defined in any universal manner: stamp *restoration*.

There are broad differences of opinion about what is permissible when it comes to restoration. Carefully applying a soft eraser to a stamp or cover to remove light soiling is one form of restoration, as is washing a stamp in mild soap and water to clean it. These are fairly accepted forms of restoration. More severe forms of restoration include pressing out creases or removing stains caused by tape. To what degree each of these is acceptable is dependent upon the individual situation. Further along the spectrum is the freshening of a stamp's color by removing oxide build-up or the effects of wax paper left next to stamps shipped to the tropics.

At some point in this spectrum the concept of *repair* replaces that of restoration. Repairs include filling thin spots, mending tears by reweaving or adding a missing perforation tooth. Regumming stamps may have been acceptable as a restoration or repair technique many decades ago, but today it is considered a form of fakery.

Restored stamps may or may not sell at a discount, and it is possible that the value of individual restored items may be enhanced over that of their pre-restoration state. Specific situations dictate the resultant value of such an item. Repaired stamps sell at substantial discounts from the value of sound stamps.

Terminology

Booklets — Many countries have issued stamps in small booklets for the convenience of users. This idea continues to become increasingly popular in many countries. Booklets have been issued in many sizes and forms, often with advertising on the covers, the panes of stamps or on the interleaving.

The panes used in booklets may be printed from special plates or made from regular sheets. All panes from booklets issued by the United States and many from those of other countries contain stamps that are straight edged on the sides, but perforated between. Others are distinguished by orientation of watermark or other identifying features. Any stamp-like unit in the pane, either printed or blank, that is not a postage stamp, is considered to be a *label* in the catalogue listings.

Scott lists and values booklet panes. Modern complete booklets also are listed and valued. Individual booklet panes are listed only when they are not fashioned from existing sheet stamps and, therefore, are identifiable from their sheet stamp counterparts.

Panes usually do not have a used value assigned to them because there is little market activity for used booklet panes, even though many exist used and there is some demand for them.

Cancellations — The marks or obliterations put on stamps by postal authorities to show that they have performed service and to prevent their reuse are known as cancellations. If the marking is made with a pen, it is considered a "pen cancel." When the location of the post office appears in the marking, it is a "town cancellation." A "postmark" is technically any postal marking, but in practice the term generally is applied to a town cancellation with a date. When calling attention to a cause or celebration, the marking is known as a "slogan cancellation." Many other types and styles of cancellations exist, such as duplex, numerals, targets, fancy and others. See also "precancels," below.

Coil Stamps — These are stamps that are issued in rolls for use in dispensers, affixing and vending machines. Those coils of the United States, Canada, Sweden and some other countries are perforated horizontally or vertically only, with the outer edges imperforate. Coil stamps of some countries, such as Great Britain and Germany, are perforated on all four sides and may in some cases be distinguished from their sheet stamp counterparts by watermarks, counting numbers on the reverse or other means.

Covers — Entire envelopes, with or without adhesive postage stamps, that have passed through the mail and bear postal or other markings of philatelic interest are known as covers. Before the introduction of envelopes in about 1840, people folded letters and wrote the address on the outside. Some people covered their letters with an extra sheet of paper on the outside for the address, producing the term "cover." Used airletter sheets, stamped envelopes and other items of postal stationery also are considered covers.

Errors — Stamps that have some major, consistent, unintentional deviation from the normal are considered errors. Errors include, but are not limited to, missing or wrong colors, wrong paper, wrong watermarks, inverted centers or frames on multicolor printing, inverted or missing surcharges or overprints, double impressions, missing perforations, unintentionally omitted tagging and others. Factually wrong or misspelled information, if it appears on all examples of a stamp, are not considered errors in the true sense of the word. They are errors of design. Inconsistent or randomly appearing items, such as misperfs or color shifts, are classified as freaks.

Color-Omitted Errors — This term refers to stamps where a missing color is caused by the complete failure of the printing plate to deliver ink to the stamp paper or any other paper. Generally, this is caused by the printing plate not being engaged on the press or the ink station running dry of ink during printing.

Color-Missing Errors — This term refers to stamps where a color or colors were printed somewhere but do not appear on the finished stamp. There are four different classes of color-missing errors, and the catalog indicates with a two-letter code appended to each such listing what caused the color to be missing. These codes are used only for the United States' color-missing error listings.

FO = A *foldover* of the stamp sheet during printing may block ink from appearing on a stamp. Instead, the color will appear on the back of the foldover (where it might fall on the back of the selvage or perhaps on the back of the stamp or another stamp). FO also will be used in the case of foldunders, where the paper may fold underneath the other stamp paper and the color will print on the platen.

EP = A piece of *extraneous paper* falling across the plate or stamp paper will receive the printed ink. When the extraneous paper is removed, an unprinted portion of stamp paper remains and shows partially or totally missing colors.

CM = A misregistration of the printing plates during printing will result in a *color misregistration*, and such a misregistraion may result in a color not appearing on the finished stamp.

PS = A *perforation shift* after printing may remove a color from the finished stamp. Normally, this will occur on a row of stamps at the edge of the stamp pane.

Measurements – When measurements are given in the Scott catalogues for stamp size, grill size or any other reason, the first measurement given is always for the top and bottom dimension, while the second measurement will be for the sides (just as perforation gauges are measured). Thus, a stamp size of 15mm x 21mm will indicate a vertically oriented stamp 15mm wide at top and bottom, and 21mm tall at the sides. The same principle holds for measuring or counting items such as U.S. grills. A grill count of 22x18 points (B grill) indicates that there are 22 grill points across by 18 grill points down.

Overprints and Surcharges — Overprinting involves applying wording or design elements over an already existing stamp. Overprints can be used to alter the place of use (such as "Canal Zone" on U.S. stamps), to adapt them for a special purpose ("Porto" on Denmark's 1913-20 regular issues for use as postage due stamps, Scott J1-J7) or to commemorate a special occasion (United States Scott 647-648).

A *surcharge* is a form of overprint that changes or restates the face value of a stamp or piece of postal stationery.

Surcharges and overprints may be handstamped, typeset or, occasionally, lithographed or engraved. A few hand-written overprints and surcharges are known.

Personalized Stamps — In 1999, Australia issued stamps with se-tenant labels that could be personalized with pictures of the customer's choice. Other countries quickly followed suit, with some offering to print the selected picture on the stamp itself within a frame that was used exclusively for personalized issues. As the picture used on these stamps or labels vary, listings for such stamps are for *any* picture within the common frame (or any picture on a se-tenant label), be it a "generic" image or one produced especially for a customer, almost invariably at a premium price.

Precancels — Stamps that are canceled before they are placed in the mail are known as precancels. Precanceling usually is done to expedite the handling of large mailings and generally allow the affected mail pieces to skip certain phases of mail handling.

In the United States, precancellations generally identified the point of origin; that is, the city and state. This information appeared across the face of the stamp, usually centered between parallel lines. More recently, bureau precancels retained the parallel lines, but the city and state designations were dropped. Recent coils have a service inscription that is present on the original printing plate. These show the mail service paid for by the stamp. Since these stamps are not intended to receive further cancellations when used as intended, they are considered precancels. Such items often do not have parallel lines as part of the precancellation.

In France, the abbreviation *Affranchts* in a semicircle together with the word *Postes* is the general form of precancel in use. Belgian precancellations usually appear in a box in which the name of the city appears. Netherlands precancels have the name of the city enclosed between concentric circles, sometimes called a "lifesaver." Precancellations of other countries usually follow these patterns, but may be any arrangement of bars, boxes and city names.

Precancels are listed in the Scott catalogues only if the precancel changes the denomination (Belgium Scott 477-478); if the precanceled stamp is different from the non-precanceled version (such as untagged U.S. precancels); or if the stamp exists only precanceled (France Scott 1096-1099, U.S. Scott 2265).

Proofs and Essays — Proofs are impressions taken from an approved die, plate or stone in which the design and color are the same as the stamp issued to the public. Trial color proofs are impressions taken from approved dies, plates or stones in colors that vary from the final version. An essay is the impression of a design that differs in some way from the issued stamp. "Progressive die proofs" generally are considered to be essays.

Provisionals — These are stamps that are issued on short notice and intended for temporary use pending the arrival of regular issues. They usually are issued to meet such contingencies as changes in government or currency, shortage of necessary postage values or military occupation.

During the 1840s, postmasters in certain American cities issued stamps that were valid only at specific post offices. In 1861, postmasters of the Confederate States also issued stamps with limited validity. Both of these examples are known as "postmaster's provisionals."

Se-tenant — This term refers to an unsevered pair, strip or block of stamps that differ in design, denomination or overprint.

Unless the se-tenant item has a continuous design (see U.S. Scott 1451a, 1694a) the stamps do not have to be in the same order as shown in the catalogue (see U.S. Scott 2158a).

Specimens — The Universal Postal Union required member nations to send samples of all stamps they released into service to the International Bureau in Switzerland. Member nations of the UPU received these specimens as samples of what stamps were valid for postage. Many are overprinted, handstamped or initial-perforated "Specimen," "Canceled" or "Muestra." Some are marked with bars across the denominations (China-Taiwan), punched holes (Czechoslovakia) or back inscriptions (Mongolia).

Stamps distributed to government officials or for publicity purposes, and stamps submitted by private security printers for official approval, also may receive such defacements.

The previously described defacement markings prevent postal use, and all such items generally are known as "specimens."

Tete Beche — This term describes a pair of stamps in which one is upside down in relation to the other. Some of these are the result of intentional sheet arrangements, such as Morocco Scott B10-B11. Others occurred when one or more electrotypes accidentally were placed upside down on the plate, such as Colombia Scott 57a. Separation of the tete-beche stamps, of course, destroys the tete beche variety.

Currency Conversion

Country	Dollar	Pound	S Franc	Yen	HK $	Euro	Cdn $	Aus $
Australia	1.5615	2.1973	1.3465	0.0159	0.2014	1.9736	1.2136	—
Canada	1.2867	1.8106	1.1095	0.0131	0.1659	1.6263	—	0.8240
European Union	0.7912	1.1134	0.6822	0.0081	0.1020	—	0.6194	0.5067
Hong Kong	7.7550	10.913	6.6871	0.0789	—	9.8016	6.0270	4.9664
Japan	98.270	138.29	84.737	—	12.672	124.20	76.374	62.933
Switzerland	1.1597	1.6319	—	0.0118	0.1495	1.4657	0.9013	0.7427
United Kingdom	0.7106	—	0.6128	0.0072	0.0916	0.8982	0.5523	0.4551
United States	—	1.4072	0.8623	0.0102	0.1289	1.2639	0.7772	0.6404

Country	Currency	U.S. $ Equiv.
Jamaica	dollar	.0114
Japan	yen	.0102
Jordan	dinar	1.410
Kazakhstan	tenge	.0066
Kenya	shilling	.0125
Kiribati	Australian dollar	.6404
Korea (South)	won	.0006
Korea (North)	won	.0070
Kosovo	euro	1.2639
Kuwait	dinar	3.372
Kyrgyzstan	som	.0240
Laos	kip	.0001
Latvia	lat	1.787
Lebanon	pound	.0007
Lesotho	maloti	.0955
Liberia	dollar	.0156
Liechtenstein	Swiss franc	.8623
Lithuania	litas	.3660
Luxembourg	euro	1.2639
Macao	pataca	.1251
Macedonia	denar	.0206
Malagasy Republic	ariary	.0005
Malawi	kwacha	.0071
Malaysia	ringgit (dollar)	.2690
Maldive Islands	rafiyaa	.0782
Mali	Community of French Africa (CFA) franc	.0019
Malta	euro	1.2639
Marshall Islands	U.S. dollar	1.00
Mauritania	ouguiya	.0039
Mauritius	rupee	.0291
Mayotte	euro	1.2639
Mexico	peso	.0658
Micronesia	U.S. dollar	1.00
Moldova	leu	.0929
Monaco	euro	1.2639
Mongolia	tugrik	.0006
Montenegro	euro	1.2639
Montserrat	East Caribbean dollar	.3774
Morocco	dirham	.1145
Mozambique	metical	.0386
Nambia	dollar	.0955
Nauru	Australian dollar	.6404
Nepal	rupee	.0121
Netherlands	euro	1.2639
Netherlands Antilles	guilder	.5602
Nevis	East Caribbean dollar	.3774
New Caledonia	Community of French Pacific (CFP) franc	.0106
New Zealand	dollar	.5024
Nicaragua	cordoba	.0502
Niger	CFA franc	.0019
Nigeria	naira	.0067
Niue	New Zealand dollar	.5024
Norfolk Island	Australian dollar	.6404
Norway	krone	.1415
Oman	rial	2.597

*Source: **Wall Street Journal** Mar. 7, 2009. Figures reflect values as of Mar. 6, 2009.*

COMMON DESIGN TYPES

Pictured in this section are issues where one illustration has been used for a number of countries in the Catalogue. Not included in this section are overprinted stamps or those issues which are illustrated in each country.

EUROPA

Europa, 1956

The design symbolizing the cooperation among the six countries comprising the Coal and Steel Community is illustrated in each country.

Country	Numbers
Belgium	496-497
France	805-806
Germany	748-749
Italy	715-716
Luxembourg	318-320
Netherlands	368-369

Europa, 1958

"E" and Dove — CD1

European Postal Union at the service of European integration.

1958, Sept. 13

Country	Numbers
Belgium	527-528
France	889-890
Germany	790-791
Italy	750-751
Luxembourg	341-343
Netherlands	375-376
Saar	317-318

Europa, 1959

6-Link Enless Chain — CD2

1959, Sept. 19

Country	Numbers
Belgium	536-537
France	929-930
Germany	805-806
Italy	791-792
Luxembourg	354-355
Netherlands	379-380

Europa, 1960

19-Spoke Wheel CD3

First anniversary of the establishment of C.E.P.T. (Conference Europeenne des Administrations des Postes et des Telecommunications.) The spokes symbolize the 19 founding members of the Conference.

1960, Sept.

Country	Numbers
Belgium	553-554
Denmark	379
Finland	376-377
France	970-971
Germany	818-820
Great Britain	377-378
Greece	688
Iceland	327-328
Ireland	175-176
Italy	809-810
Luxembourg	374-375
Netherlands	385-386
Norway	387
Portugal	866-867
Spain	941-942
Sweden	562-563
Switzerland	400-401
Turkey	1493-1494

Europa, 1961

19 Doves Flying as One — CD4

The 19 doves represent the 19 members of the Conference of European Postal and Telecommunications Administrations C.E.P.T.

1961-62

Country	Numbers
Belgium	572-573
Cyprus	201-203
France	1005-1006
Germany	844-845
Great Britain	383-384
Greece	718-719
Iceland	340-341
Italy	845-846
Luxembourg	382-383
Netherlands	387-388
Spain	1010-1011
Switzerland	410-411
Turkey	1518-1520

Europa, 1962

Young Tree with 19 Leaves CD5

The 19 leaves represent the 19 original members of C.E.P.T.

1962-63

Country	Numbers
Belgium	582-583
Cyprus	219-221
France	1045-1046
Germany	852-853
Greece	739-740
Iceland	348-349
Ireland	184-185
Italy	860-861
Luxembourg	386-387
Netherlands	394-395
Norway	414-415
Switzerland	416-417
Turkey	1553-1555

Europa, 1963

Stylized Links, Symbolizing Unity — CD6

1963, Sept.

Country	Numbers
Belgium	598-599
Cyprus	229-231
Finland	419
France	1074-1075
Germany	867-868
Greece	768-769
Iceland	357-358
Ireland	188-189
Italy	880-881
Luxembourg	403-404
Netherlands	416-417
Norway	441-442
Switzerland	429
Turkey	1602-1603

Europa, 1964

Symbolic Daisy — CD7

5th anniversary of the establishment of C.E.P.T. The 22 petals of the flower symbolize the 22 members of the Conference.

1964, Sept.

Country	Numbers
Austria	738
Belgium	614-615
Cyprus	244-246
France	1109-1110
Germany	897-898
Greece	801-802
Iceland	367-368
Ireland	196-197
Italy	894-895
Luxembourg	411-412
Monaco	590-591
Netherlands	428-429
Norway	458
Portugal	931-933
Spain	1262-1263
Switzerland	438-439
Turkey	1628-1629

Europa, 1965

Leaves and "Fruit" CD8

1965

Country	Numbers
Belgium	636-637
Cyprus	262-264
Finland	437
France	1131-1132
Germany	934-935
Greece	833-834
Iceland	375-376
Ireland	204-205
Italy	915-916
Luxembourg	432-433
Monaco	616-617
Netherlands	438-439
Norway	475-476
Portugal	958-960
Switzerland	469
Turkey	1665-1666

Europa, 1966

Symbolic Sailboat — CD9

1966, Sept.

Country	Numbers
Andorra, French	172
Belgium	675-676
Cyprus	275-277
France	1163-1164
Germany	963-964
Greece	862-863
Iceland	384-385
Ireland	216-217
Italy	942-943
Liechtenstein	415
Luxembourg	440-441
Monaco	639-640
Netherlands	441-442
Norway	496-497
Portugal	980-982
Switzerland	477-478
Turkey	1718-1719

Europa, 1967

Cogwheels CD10

1967

Country	Numbers
Andorra, French	174-175
Belgium	688-689
Cyprus	297-299
France	1178-1179
Germany	969-970
Greece	891-892
Iceland	389-390
Ireland	232-233
Italy	951-952
Liechtenstein	420
Luxembourg	449-450
Monaco	669-670
Netherlands	444-447
Norway	504-505
Portugal	994-996
Spain	1465-1466
Switzerland	482
Turkey	B120-B121

Europa, 1968

Golden Key with C.E.P.T. Emblem CD11

1968

Country	Numbers
Andorra, French	182-183
Belgium	705-706
Cyprus	314-316
France	1209-1210
Germany	983-984
Greece	916-917
Iceland	395-396
Ireland	242-243
Italy	979-980
Liechtenstein	442
Luxembourg	466-467
Monaco	689-691
Netherlands	452-453
Portugal	1019-1021
San Marino	687
Spain	1526
Turkey	1775-1776

Europa, 1969

"EUROPA" and "CEPT" CD12

Tenth anniversary of C.E.P.T.

1969

Country	Numbers
Andorra, French	188-189
Austria	837
Belgium	718-719
Cyprus	326-328
Denmark	458
Finland	483
France	1245-1246
Germany	996-997
Great Britain	585
Greece	947-948
Iceland	406-407
Ireland	270-271
Italy	1000-1001
Liechtenstein	453
Luxembourg	474-475
Monaco	722-724
Netherlands	475-476
Norway	533-534
Portugal	1038-1040
San Marino	701-702
Spain	1567
Sweden	814-816

Switzerland 500-501
Turkey 1799-1800
Vatican 470-472
Yugoslavia 1003-1004

Europa, 1970

Interwoven Threads CD13

1970

Andorra, French 196-197
Belgium 741-742
Cyprus 340-342
France 1271-1272
Germany 1018-1019
Greece 985, 987
Iceland 420-421
Ireland 279-281
Italy 1013-1014
Liechtenstein 470
Luxembourg 489-490
Monaco 768-770
Netherlands 483-484
Portugal 1060-1062
San Marino 729-730
Spain 1607
Switzerland 515-516
Turkey 1848-1849
Yugoslavia 1024-1025

Europa, 1971

"Fraternity, Cooperation, Common Effort" CD14

1971

Andorra, French 205-206
Belgium 803-804
Cyprus 365-367
Finland 504
France 1304
Germany 1064-1065
Greece 1029-1030
Iceland 429-430
Ireland 305-306
Italy 1038-1039
Liechtenstein 485
Luxembourg 500-501
Malta 425-427
Monaco 797-799
Netherlands 488-489
Portugal 1094-1096
San Marino 749-750
Spain 1675-1676
Switzerland 531-532
Turkey 1876-1877
Yugoslavia 1052-1053

Europa, 1972

Sparkles, Symbolic of Communications CD15

1972

Andorra, French 210-211
Andorra, Spanish 62
Belgium 825-826
Cyprus 380-382
Finland 512-513
France 1341
Germany 1089-1090
Greece 1049-1050
Iceland 439-440
Ireland 316-317
Italy 1065-1066
Liechtenstein 504
Luxembourg 512-513
Malta 450-453
Monaco 831-832
Netherlands 494-495
Portugal 1141-1143
San Marino 771-772
Spain 1718
Switzerland 544-545
Turkey 1907-1908
Yugoslavia 1100-1101

Europa, 1973

Post Horn and Arrows CD16

1973

Andorra, French 219-220
Andorra, Spanish 76
Belgium 839-840
Cyprus 396-398
Finland 526
France 1367
Germany 1114-1115
Greece 1090-1092
Iceland 447-448
Ireland 329-330
Italy 1108-1109
Liechtenstein 528-529
Luxembourg 523-524
Malta 469-471
Monaco 866-867
Netherlands 504-505
Norway 604-605
Portugal 1170-1172
San Marino 802-803
Spain 1753
Switzerland 580-581
Turkey 1935-1936
Yugoslavia 1138-1139

Europa, 2000

CD17

2000

Albania 2621-2622
Andorra, French 522
Andorra, Spanish 262
Armenia 610-611
Austria 1814
Azerbaijan 698-699
Belarus 350
Belgium 1818
Bosnia & Herzegovina (Moslem) 358
Bosnia & Herzegovina (Serb) 111-112
Croatia 428-429
Cyprus 959
Czech Republic 3120
Denmark 1189
Estonia 394
Faroe Islands 376
Finland 1129
Aland Islands 166
France 2771
Georgia 228-229
Germany 2086-2087
Gibraltar 837-840
Great Britain (Guernsey) 805-809
Great Britain (Jersey) 935-936
Great Britain (Isle of Man) 883
Greece 1959
Greenland 363
Hungary 3699-3700
Iceland 910
Ireland 1230-1231
Italy 2349
Latvia 504
Liechtenstein 1178
Lithuania 668
Luxembourg 1035
Macedonia 187
Malta 1011-1012
Moldova 355
Monaco 2161-2162
Poland 3519
Portugal 2358
Portugal (Azores) 455
Portugal (Madeira) 208
Romania 4370
Russia 6589
San Marino 1480
Slovakia 355
Slovenia 424
Spain 3036
Sweden 2394
Switzerland 1074
Turkey 2762
Turkish Rep. of Northern Cyprus 500
Ukraine 379
Vatican City 1152

The Gibraltar stamps are similar to the stamp illustrated, but none have the design shown above. All other sets listed above include at least one stamp with the design shown, but some include stamps with entirely different designs. Bulgaria Nos. 4131-4132 and Yugoslavia Nos. 2485-2486 are Europa stamps with completely different designs.

PORTUGAL & COLONIES

Vasco da Gama

Fleet Departing CD20

Fleet Arriving at Calicut — CD21

Embarking at Rastello CD22

Muse of History CD23

San Gabriel, da Gama and Camoens CD24

Archangel Gabriel, the Patron Saint CD25

Flagship San Gabriel — CD26

Vasco da Gama — CD27

Fourth centenary of Vasco da Gama's discovery of the route to India.

1898

Azores 93-100
Macao 67-74
Madeira 37-44
Portugal 147-154
Port. Africa 1-8
Port. Congo 75-98
Port. India 189-196
St. Thomas & Prince Islands ... 170-193
Timor 45-52

Pombal
POSTAL TAX
POSTAL TAX DUES

Marquis de Pombal — CD28

Planning Reconstruction of Lisbon, 1755 — CD29

Pombal Monument, Lisbon — CD30

Sebastiao Jose de Carvalho e Mello, Marquis de Pombal (1699-1782), statesman, rebuilt Lisbon after earthquake of 1755. Tax was for the erection of Pombal monument. Obligatory on all mail on certain days throughout the year. Postal Tax Dues are inscribed "Multa."

1925

Angola RA1-RA3, RAJ1-RAJ3
Azores RA9-RA11, RAJ2-RAJ4
Cape Verde RA1-RA3, RAJ1-RAJ3
Macao RA1-RA3, RAJ1-RAJ3
Madeira RA1-RA3, RAJ1-RAJ3
Mozambique RA1-RA3, RAJ1-RAJ3
Nyassa RA1-RA3, RAJ1-RAJ3
Portugal RA11-RA13, RAJ2-RAJ4
Port. Guinea RA1-RA3, RAJ1-RAJ3
Port. India RA1-RA3, RAJ1-RAJ3
St. Thomas & Prince Islands RA1-RA3, RAJ1-RAJ3
Timor RA1-RA3, RAJ1-RAJ3

Vasco da Gama CD34

Mousinho de Albuquerque CD35

Dam CD36

Prince Henry the Navigator CD37

Affonso de Albuquerque CD38

Plane over Globe CD39

1938-39

Angola 274-291, C1-C9
Cape Verde 234-251, C1-C9
Macao 289-305, C7-C15
Mozambique 270-287, C1-C9
Port. Guinea 233-250, C1-C9
Port. India 439-453, C1-C8
St. Thomas & Prince Islands ... 302-319, 323-340, C1-C18
Timor 223-239, C1-C9

Lady of Fatima

Our Lady of the Rosary, Fatima, Portugal — CD40

1948-49

Angola 315-318
Cape Verde 266
Macao 336
Mozambique 325-328
Port. Guinea 271
Port. India 480
St. Thomas & Prince Islands 351
Timor 254

A souvenir sheet of 9 stamps was issued in 1951 to mark the extension of the 1950 Holy Year. The sheet contains: Angola No. 316, Cape Verde No. 266, Macao No. 336, Mozambique No. 325, Portuguese Guinea No. 271, Portuguese India Nos. 480, 485, St. Thomas & Prince Islands No. 351, Timor No. 254. The sheet also contains a portrait of Pope Pius XII and is inscribed "Encerramento do Ano Santo, Fatima 1951." It was sold for 11 escudos.

Holy Year

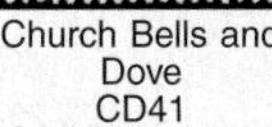

Church Bells and Dove CD41

Angel Holding Candelabra CD42

Holy Year, 1950.

1950-51

Angola 331-332
Cape Verde 268-269
Macao 339-340
Mozambique 330-331
Port. Guinea 273-274
Port. India 490-491, 496-503
St. Thomas & Prince Islands ... 353-354
Timor 258-259

A souvenir sheet of 8 stamps was issued in 1951 to mark the extension of the Holy Year. The sheet contains: Angola No. 331, Cape Verde No. 269, Macao No. 340, Mozambique No. 331, Portuguese Guinea No. 275, Portuguese India No. 490, St. Thomas & Prince Islands No. 354, Timor No. 258, some with colors changed. The sheet contains doves and is inscribed 'Encerramento do Ano Santo, Fatima 1951.' It was sold for 17 escudos.

Holy Year Conclusion

Our Lady of Fatima — CD43

Conclusion of Holy Year. Sheets contain alternate vertical rows of stamps and labels bearing quotation from Pope Pius XII, different for each colony.

1951

Angola 357
Cape Verde 270
Macao 352
Mozambique 356
Port. Guinea 275
Port. India 506
St. Thomas & Prince Islands 355
Timor 270

Medical Congress

CD44

First National Congress of Tropical Medicine, Lisbon, 1952. Each stamp has a different design.

1952

Angola 358
Cape Verde 287
Macao 364
Mozambique 359
Port. Guinea 276
Port. India 516
St. Thomas & Prince Islands 356
Timor 271

Postage Due Stamps

CD45

1952

Angola J37-J42
Cape Verde J31-J36
Macao J53-J58
Mozambique J51-J56
Port. Guinea J40-J45
Port. India J47-J52
St. Thomas & Prince Islands ... J52-J57
Timor J31-J36

Sao Paulo

Father Manuel da Nobrega and View of Sao Paulo — CD46

Founding of Sao Paulo, Brazil, 400th anniv.

1954

Angola 385
Cape Verde 297
Macao 382
Mozambique 395
Port. Guinea 291
Port. India 530
St. Thomas & Prince Islands 369
Timor 279

Tropical Medicine Congress

CD47

Sixth International Congress for Tropical Medicine and Malaria, Lisbon, Sept. 1958. Each stamp shows a different plant.

1958

Angola 409
Cape Verde 303
Macao 392
Mozambique 404
Port. Guinea 295
Port. India 569
St. Thomas & Prince Islands 371
Timor 289

Sports

CD48

Each stamp shows a different sport.

1962

Angola 433-438
Cape Verde 320-325
Macao 394-399
Mozambique 424-429
Port. Guinea 299-304
St. Thomas & Prince Islands ... 374-379
Timor 313-318

Anti-Malaria

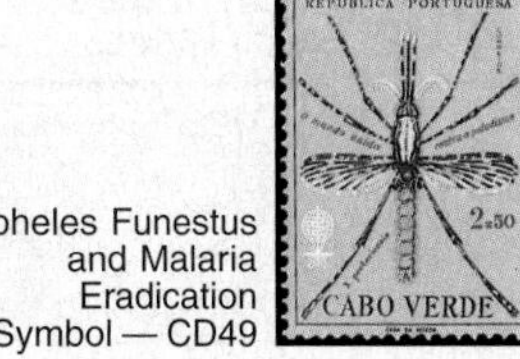

Anopheles Funestus and Malaria Eradication Symbol — CD49

World Health Organization drive to eradicate malaria.

1962

Angola 439
Cape Verde 326
Macao 400
Mozambique 430
Port. Guinea 305
St. Thomas & Prince Islands 380
Timor 319

Airline Anniversary

Map of Africa, Super Constellation and Jet Liner — CD50

Tenth anniversary of Transportes Aereos Portugueses (TAP).

1963

Angola 490
Cape Verde 327
Mozambique 434
Port. Guinea 318
St. Thomas & Prince Islands 381

National Overseas Bank

Antonio Teixeira de Sousa — CD51

Centenary of the National Overseas Bank of Portugal.

1964, May 16

Angola 509
Cape Verde 328
Port. Guinea 319
St. Thomas & Prince Islands 382
Timor 320

ITU

ITU Emblem and the Archangel Gabriel — CD52

International Communications Union, Cent.

1965, May 17

Angola 511
Cape Verde 329
Macao 402
Mozambique 464
Port. Guinea 320
St. Thomas & Prince Islands 383
Timor 321

National Revolution

CD53

40th anniv. of the National Revolution. Different buildings on each stamp.

1966, May 28

Angola 525
Cape Verde 338
Macao 403
Mozambique 465
Port. Guinea 329
St. Thomas & Prince Islands 392
Timor 322

Navy Club

CD54

Centenary of Portugal's Navy Club. Each stamp has a different design.

1967, Jan. 31

Angola 527-528
Cape Verde 339-340
Macao 412-413
Mozambique 478-479
Port. Guinea 330-331
St. Thomas & Prince Islands ... 393-394
Timor 323-324

Admiral Coutinho

CD55

Centenary of the birth of Admiral Carlos Viegas Gago Coutinho (1869-1959), explorer and aviation pioneer. Each stamp has a different design.

1969, Feb. 17

Angola 547
Cape Verde 355
Macao 417
Mozambique 484
Port. Guinea 335
St. Thomas & Prince Islands 397
Timor 335

Administration Reform

Luiz Augusto Rebello da Silva — CD56

Centenary of the administration reforms of the overseas territories.

1969, Sept. 25

Angola	549
Cape Verde	357
Macao	419
Mozambique	491
Port. Guinea	337
St. Thomas & Prince Islands	399
Timor	338

Marshal Carmona

CD57

Birth centenary of Marshal Antonio Oscar Carmona de Fragoso (1869-1951), President of Portugal. Each stamp has a different design.

1970, Nov. 15

Angola	563
Cape Verde	359
Macao	422
Mozambique	493
Port. Guinea	340
St. Thomas & Prince Islands	403
Timor	341

Olympic Games

CD59

20th Olympic Games, Munich, Aug. 26-Sept. 11. Each stamp shows a different sport.

1972, June 20

Angola	569
Cape Verde	361
Macao	426
Mozambique	504
Port. Guinea	342
St. Thomas & Prince Islands	408
Timor	343

Lisbon-Rio de Janeiro Flight

CD60

50th anniversary of the Lisbon to Rio de Janeiro flight by Arturo de Sacadura and Coutinho, March 30-June 5, 1922. Each stamp shows a different stage of the flight.

1972, Sept. 20

Angola	570
Cape Verde	362
Macao	427
Mozambique	505
Port. Guinea	343
St. Thomas & Prince Islands	409
Timor	344

WMO Centenary

WMO Emblem — CD61

Centenary of international meterological cooperation.

1973, Dec. 15

Angola	571
Cape Verde	363
Macao	429
Mozambique	509
Port. Guinea	344
St. Thomas & Prince Islands	410
Timor	345

FRENCH COMMUNITY

Upper Volta can be found under Burkina Faso in Vol. 1

Madagascar can be found under Malagasy in Vol. 3

Colonial Exposition

People of French Empire CD70

Women's Heads CD71

France Showing Way to Civilization CD72

"Colonial Commerce" CD73

International Colonial Exposition, Paris.

1931

Cameroun	213-216
Chad	60-63
Dahomey	97-100
Fr. Guiana	152-155
Fr. Guinea	116-119
Fr. India	100-103
Fr. Polynesia	76-79
Fr. Sudan	102-105
Gabon	120-123
Guadeloupe	138-141
Indo-China	140-142
Ivory Coast	92-95
Madagascar	169-172
Martinique	129-132
Mauritania	65-68
Middle Congo	61-64
New Caledonia	176-179
Niger	73-76
Reunion	122-125
St. Pierre & Miquelon	132-135
Senegal	138-141
Somali Coast	135-138
Togo	254-257
Ubangi-Shari	82-85
Upper Volta	66-69
Wallis & Futuna Isls.	85-88

Paris International Exposition Colonial Arts Exposition

"Colonial Resources" CD74 CD77

Overseas Commerce CD75

Exposition Building and Women CD76

"France and the Empire" CD78

Cultural Treasures of the Colonies CD79

Souvenir sheets contain one imperf. stamp.

1937

Cameroun	217-222A
Dahomey	101-107
Fr. Equatorial Africa	27-32, 73
Fr. Guiana	162-168
Fr. Guinea	120-126
Fr. India	104-110
Fr. Polynesia	117-123
Fr. Sudan	106-112
Guadeloupe	148-154
Indo-China	193-199
Inini	41
Ivory Coast	152-158
Kwangchowan	132
Madagascar	191-197
Martinique	179-185
Mauritania	69-75
New Caledonia	208-214
Niger	72-83
Reunion	167-173
St. Pierre & Miquelon	165-171
Senegal	172-178
Somali Coast	139-145
Togo	258-264
Wallis & Futuna Isls.	89

Curie

Pierre and Marie Curie CD80

40th anniversary of the discovery of radium. The surtax was for the benefit of the Intl. Union for the Control of Cancer.

1938

Cameroun	B1
Cuba	B1-B2
Dahomey	B2
France	B76
Fr. Equatorial Africa	B1
Fr. Guiana	B3
Fr. Guinea	B2
Fr. India	B6
Fr. Polynesia	B5
Fr. Sudan	B1
Guadeloupe	B3
Indo-China	B14
Ivory Coast	B2
Madagascar	B2
Martinique	B2
Mauritania	B3
New Caledonia	B4
Niger	B1
Reunion	B4
St. Pierre & Miquelon	B3
Senegal	B3
Somali Coast	B2
Togo	B1

Caillie

Rene Caillie and Map of Northwestern Africa — CD81

Death centenary of Rene Caillie (1799-1838), French explorer. All three denominations exist with colony name omitted.

1939

Dahomey	108-110
Fr. Guinea	161-163
Fr. Sudan	113-115
Ivory Coast	160-162
Mauritania	109-111
Niger	84-86
Senegal	188-190
Togo	265-267

New York World's Fair

Natives and New York Skyline CD82

1939

Cameroun	223-224
Dahomey	111-112
Fr. Equatorial Africa	78-79
Fr. Guiana	169-170
Fr. Guinea	164-165
Fr. India	111-112
Fr. Polynesia	124-125
Fr. Sudan	116-117
Guadeloupe	155-156
Indo-China	203-204
Inini	42-43
Ivory Coast	163-164
Kwangchowan	121-122
Madagascar	209-210
Martinique	186-187
Mauritania	112-113
New Caledonia	215-216
Niger	87-88
Reunion	174-175
St. Pierre & Miquelon	205-206
Senegal	191-192
Somali Coast	179-180
Togo	268-269
Wallis & Futuna Isls.	90-91

French Revolution

Storming of the Bastille CD83

French Revolution, 150th anniv. The surtax was for the defense of the colonies.

1939

Cameroun	B2-B6
Dahomey	B3-B7
Fr. Equatorial Africa	B4-B8, CB1
Fr. Guiana	B4-B8, CB1
Fr. Guinea	B3-B7
Fr. India	B7-B11
Fr. Polynesia	B6-B10, CB1
Fr. Sudan	B2-B6
Guadeloupe	B4-B8
Indo-China	B15-B19, CB1
Inini	B1-B5
Ivory Coast	B3-B7

Kwangchowan B1-B5
Madagascar...................... B3-B7, CB1
Martinique..................................B3-B7
Mauritania..................................B4-B8
New Caledonia B5-B9, CB1
Niger...B2-B6
Reunion B5-B9, CB1
St. Pierre & Miquelon.................B4-B8
Senegal B4-B8, CB1
Somali Coast..............................B3-B7
Togo..B2-B6
Wallis & Futuna Isls. B1-B5

Plane over Coastal Area CD85

All five denominations exist with colony name omitted.

1940

Dahomey C1-C5
Fr. Guinea C1-C5
Fr. Sudan................................... C1-C5
Ivory Coast C1-C5
Mauritania.................................. C1-C5
Niger.. C1-C5
Senegal C12-C16
Togo... C1-C5

Defense of the Empire

Colonial Infantryman — CD86

1941

Cameroun...................................B13B
Dahomey B13
Fr. Equatorial Africa B8B
Fr. Guiana B10
Fr. Guinea B13
Fr. India B13
Fr. Polynesia.................................B12
Fr. Sudan.......................................B12
Guadeloupe...................................B10
Indo-China...................................B19B
Inini...B7
Ivory Coast B13
Kwangchowan B7
Madagascar.....................................B9
Martinique.......................................B9
Mauritania.....................................B14
New Caledonia B11
Niger...B12
Reunion B11
St. Pierre & Miquelon...................B8B
Senegal B14
Somali Coast...................................B9
Togo...B10B
Wallis & Futuna Isls. B7

Colonial Education Fund

CD86a

1942

Cameroun...................................CB3
Dahomey CB4
Fr. Equatorial Africa CB5
Fr. Guiana CB4
Fr. Guinea CB4
Fr. India CB3
Fr. Polynesia...............................CB4
Fr. Sudan.....................................CB4
Guadeloupe.................................CB3
Indo-China...................................CB5
Inini..CB3
Ivory Coast CB4
Kwangchowan CB4
Malagasy CB5
Martinique....................................CB3
Mauritania....................................CB4
New Caledonia CB4
Niger..CB4
Reunion CB4
St. Pierre & Miquelon...................CB3
Senegal CB5
Somali Coast................................CB3
Togo...CB3
Wallis & Futuna CB3

Cross of Lorraine & Four-motor Plane CD87

1941-5

Cameroun.................................. C1-C7
Fr. Equatorial Africa C17-C23
Fr. Guiana C9-C10
Fr. India C1-C6
Fr. Polynesia............................. C3-C9
Fr. West Africa C1-C3
Guadeloupe C1-C2
Madagascar........................... C37-C43
Martinique................................. C1-C2
New Caledonia C7-C13
Reunion C18-C24
St. Pierre & Miquelon................ C1-C7
Somali Coast............................. C1-C7

Transport Plane CD88

Caravan and Plane CD89

1942

Dahomey C6-C13
Fr. Guinea C6-C13
Fr. Sudan.............................. C6-C13
Ivory Coast C6-C13
Mauritania............................. C6-C13
Niger..................................... C6-C13
Senegal C17-C25
Togo...................................... C6-C13

Red Cross

Marianne CD90

The surtax was for the French Red Cross and national relief.

1944

Cameroun...................................... B28
Fr. Equatorial Africa B38
Fr. Guiana B12
Fr. India B14
Fr. Polynesia.................................. B13
Fr. West Africa B1
Guadeloupe.................................... B12
Madagascar.................................... B15
Martinique...................................... B11
New Caledonia B13
Reunion B15
St. Pierre & Miquelon..................... B13
Somali Coast................................... B13
Wallis & Futuna Isls. B9

Eboue

CD91

Felix Eboue, first French colonial administrator to proclaim resistance to Germany after French surrender in World War II.

1945

Cameroun...............................296-297
Fr. Equatorial Africa 156-157
Fr. Guiana 171-172
Fr. India 210-211
Fr. Polynesia............................150-151
Fr. West Africa 15-16
Guadeloupe 187-188
Madagascar...............................259-260
Martinique.................................196-197
New Caledonia 274-275
Reunion 238-239
St. Pierre & Miquelon...............322-323
Somali Coast.............................238-239

Victory

Victory — CD92

European victory of the Allied Nations in World War II.

1946, May 8

Cameroun..C8
Fr. Equatorial Africa C24
Fr. Guiana C11
Fr. India C7
Fr. Polynesia.....................................C10
Fr. West Africa C4
Guadeloupe C3
Indo-China...C19
Madagascar.......................................C44
Martinique...C3
New Caledonia C14
Reunion C25
St. Pierre & Miquelon.........................C8
Somali Coast.......................................C8
Wallis & Futuna Isls. C1

Chad to Rhine

Leclerc's Departure from Chad — CD93

Battle at Cufra Oasis — CD94

Tanks in Action, Mareth — CD95

Normandy Invasion — CD96

Entering Paris — CD97

Liberation of Strasbourg — CD98

"Chad to the Rhine" march, 1942-44, by Gen. Jacques Leclerc's column, later French 2nd Armored Division.

1946, June 6

Cameroun................................ C9-C14
Fr. Equatorial Africa C25-C30
Fr. Guiana C12-C17
Fr. India C8-C13
Fr. Polynesia......................... C11-C16
Fr. West Africa C5-C10
Guadeloupe C4-C9
Indo-China........................... C20-C25
Madagascar.......................... C45-C50
Martinique............................... C4-C9
New Caledonia C15-C20
Reunion C26-C31
St. Pierre & Miquelon.............. C9-C14
Somali Coast........................... C9-C14
Wallis & Futuna Isls. C2-C7

UPU

French Colonials, Globe and Plane — CD99

Universal Postal Union, 75th anniv.

1949, July 4

Cameroun.......................................C29
Fr. Equatorial Africa C34
Fr. India C17
Fr. Polynesia..................................C20
Fr. West Africa C15
Indo-China.....................................C26
Madagascar...................................C55
New Caledonia C24
St. Pierre & Miquelon....................C18
Somali Coast..................................C18
Togo...C18
Wallis & Futuna Isls. C10

Tropical Medicine

Doctor Treating Infant CD100

The surtax was for charitable work.

1950

Cameroun....................B29
Fr. Equatorial Africa....................B39
Fr. India....................B15
Fr. Polynesia....................B14
Fr. West Africa....................B3
Madagascar....................B17
New Caledonia....................B14
St. Pierre & Miquelon....................B14
Somali Coast....................B14
Togo....................B11

Military Medal

Medal, Early Marine and Colonial Soldier — CD101

Centenary of the creation of the French Military Medal.

1952

Cameroun....................332
Comoro Isls....................39
Fr. Equatorial Africa....................186
Fr. India....................233
Fr. Polynesia....................179
Fr. West Africa....................57
Madagascar....................286
New Caledonia....................295
St. Pierre & Miquelon....................345
Somali Coast....................267
Togo....................327
Wallis & Futuna Isls....................149

Liberation

Allied Landing, Victory Sign and Cross of Lorraine — CD102

Liberation of France, 10th anniv.

1954, June 6

Cameroun....................C32
Comoro Isls....................C4
Fr. Equatorial Africa....................C38
Fr. India....................C18
Fr. Polynesia....................C22
Fr. West Africa....................C17
Madagascar....................C57
New Caledonia....................C25
St. Pierre & Miquelon....................C19
Somali Coast....................C19
Togo....................C19
Wallis & Futuna Isls....................C11

FIDES

Plowmen CD103

Efforts of FIDES, the Economic and Social Development Fund for Overseas Possessions (Fonds d' Investissement pour le Developpement Economique et Social). Each stamp has a different design.

1956

Cameroun....................326-329
Comoro Isls....................43
Fr. Equatorial Africa....................189-192
Fr. Polynesia....................181
Fr. West Africa....................65-72
Madagascar....................292-295
New Caledonia....................303
St. Pierre & Miquelon 350
Somali Coast....................268
Togo....................331

Flower

CD104

Each stamp shows a different flower.

1958-9

Cameroun....................333
Comoro Isls....................45
Fr. Equatorial Africa....................200-201
Fr. Polynesia....................192
Fr. So. & Antarctic Terr....................11
Fr. West Africa....................79-83
Madagascar....................301-302
New Caledonia....................304-305
St. Pierre & Miquelon....................357
Somali Coast....................270
Togo....................348-349
Wallis & Futuna Isls....................152

Human Rights

Sun, Dove and U.N. Emblem CD105

10th anniversary of the signing of the Universal Declaration of Human Rights.

1958

Comoro Isls....................44
Fr. Equatorial Africa....................202
Fr. Polynesia....................191
Fr. West Africa....................85
Madagascar....................300
New Caledonia....................306
St. Pierre & Miquelon....................356
Somali Coast....................274
Wallis & Futuna Isls....................153

C.C.T.A.

CD106

Commission for Technical Cooperation in Africa south of the Sahara, 10th anniv.

1960

Cameroun....................335
Cent. Africa....................3
Chad....................66
Congo, P.R....................90
Dahomey....................138
Gabon....................150
Ivory Coast....................180
Madagascar....................317
Mali....................9
Mauritania....................117
Niger....................104
Upper Volta....................89

Air Afrique, 1961

Modern and Ancient Africa, Map and Planes — CD107

Founding of Air Afrique (African Airlines).

1961-62

Cameroun....................C37
Cent. Africa....................C5
Chad....................C7
Congo, P.R....................C5
Dahomey....................C17
Gabon....................C5
Ivory Coast....................C18
Mauritania....................C17
Niger....................C22
Senegal....................C31
Upper Volta....................C4

Anti-Malaria

CD108

World Health Organization drive to eradicate malaria.

1962, Apr. 7

Cameroun....................B36
Cent. Africa....................B1
Chad....................B1
Comoro Isls....................B1
Congo, P.R....................B3
Dahomey....................B15
Gabon....................B4
Ivory Coast....................B15
Madagascar....................B19
Mali....................B1
Mauritania....................B16
Niger....................B14
Senegal....................B16
Somali Coast....................B15
Upper Volta....................B1

Abidjan Games

CD109

Abidjan Games, Ivory Coast, Dec. 24-31, 1961. Each stamp shows a different sport.

1962

Chad....................83-84
Cent. Africa....................19-20
Congo, P.R....................103-104
Gabon....................163-164, C6
Niger....................109-111
Upper Volta....................103-105

African and Malagasy Union

Flag of Union CD110

First anniversary of the Union.

1962, Sept. 8

Cameroun....................373
Cent. Africa....................21
Chad....................85
Congo, P.R....................105
Dahomey....................155
Gabon....................165
Ivory Coast....................198
Madagascar....................332
Mauritania....................170
Niger....................112
Senegal....................211
Upper Volta....................106

Telstar

Telstar and Globe Showing Andover and Pleumeur-Bodou — CD111

First television connection of the United States and Europe through the Telstar satellite, July 11-12, 1962.

1962-63

Andorra, French....................154
Comoro Isls....................C7
Fr. Polynesia....................C29
Fr. So. & Antarctic Terr....................C5
New Caledonia....................C33
Somali Coast....................C31
St. Pierre & Miquelon....................C26
Wallis & Futuna Isls....................C17

Freedom From Hunger

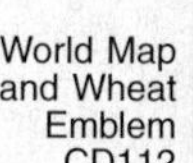
World Map and Wheat Emblem CD112

U.N. Food and Agriculture Organization's "Freedom from Hunger" campaign.

1963, Mar. 21

Cameroun....................B37-B38
Cent. Africa....................B2
Chad....................B2
Congo, P.R....................B4
Dahomey....................B16
Gabon....................B5
Ivory Coast....................B16
Madagascar....................B21
Mauritania....................B17
Niger....................B15
Senegal....................B17
Upper Volta....................B2

Red Cross Centenary

CD113

Centenary of the International Red Cross.

1963, Sept. 2

Comoro Isls....................55
Fr. Polynesia....................205
New Caledonia....................328
St. Pierre & Miquelon....................367
Somali Coast....................297
Wallis & Futuna Isls....................165

African Postal Union, 1963

UAMPT Emblem, Radio Masts, Plane and Mail CD114

Establishment of the African and Malagasy Posts and Telecommunications Union.

1963, Sept. 8

Cameroun.......C47
Cent. Africa.......C10
Chad.......C9
Congo, P.R.......C13
Dahomey.......C19
Gabon.......C13
Ivory Coast.......C25
Madagascar.......C75
Mauritania.......C22
Niger.......C27
Rwanda.......36
Senegal.......C32
Upper Volta.......C9

Air Afrique, 1963

Symbols of Flight — CD115

First anniversary of Air Afrique and inauguration of DC-8 service.

1963, Nov. 19

Cameroun.......C48
Chad.......C10
Congo, P.R.......C14
Gabon.......C18
Ivory Coast.......C26
Mauritania.......C26
Niger.......C35
Senegal.......C33

Europafrica

Europe and Africa Linked — CD116

Signing of an economic agreement between the European Economic Community and the African and Malagasy Union, Yaounde, Cameroun, July 20, 1963.

1963-64

Cameroun.......402
Chad.......C11
Cent. Africa.......C12
Congo, P.R.......C16
Gabon.......C19
Ivory Coast.......217
Niger.......C43
Upper Volta.......C11

Human Rights

Scales of Justice and Globe CD117

15th anniversary of the Universal Declaration of Human Rights.

1963, Dec. 10

Comoro Isls.......58
Fr. Polynesia.......206
New Caledonia.......329
St. Pierre & Miquelon.......368
Somali Coast.......300
Wallis & Futuna Isls.......166

PHILATEC

Stamp Album, Champs Elysees Palace and Horses of Marly CD118

Intl. Philatelic and Postal Techniques Exhibition, Paris, June 5-21, 1964.

1963-64

Comoro Isls.......60
France.......1078
Fr. Polynesia.......207
New Caledonia.......341
St. Pierre & Miquelon.......369
Somali Coast.......301
Wallis & Futuna Isls.......167

Cooperation

CD119

Cooperation between France and the French-speaking countries of Africa and Madagascar.

1964

Cameroun.......409-410
Cent. Africa.......39
Chad.......103
Congo, P.R.......121
Dahomey.......193
France.......1111
Gabon.......175
Ivory Coast.......221
Madagascar.......360
Mauritania.......181
Niger.......143
Senegal.......236
Togo.......495

ITU

Telegraph, Syncom Satellite and ITU Emblem CD120

Intl. Telecommunication Union, Cent.

1965, May 17

Comoro Isls.......C14
Fr. Polynesia.......C33
Fr. So. & Antarctic Terr.......C8
New Caledonia.......C40
New Hebrides.......124-125
St. Pierre & Miquelon.......C29
Somali Coast.......C36
Wallis & Futuna Isls.......C20

French Satellite A-1

Diamant Rocket and Launching Installation — CD121

Launching of France's first satellite, Nov. 26, 1965.

1965-66

Comoro Isls.......C15-C16
France.......1137-1138
Fr. Polynesia.......C40-C41
Fr. So. & Antarctic Terr.......C9-C10
New Caledonia.......C44-C45
St. Pierre & Miquelon.......C30-C31
Somali Coast.......C39-C40
Wallis & Futuna Isls.......C22-C23

French Satellite D-1

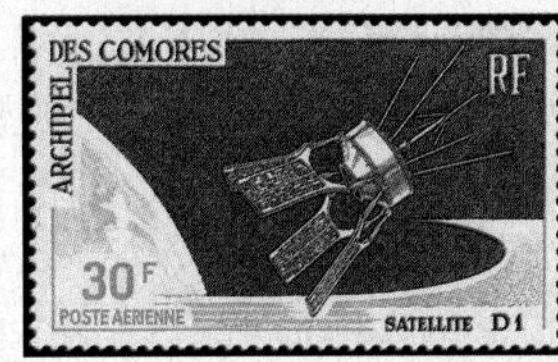

D-1 Satellite in Orbit — CD122

Launching of the D-1 satellite at Hammaguir, Algeria, Feb. 17, 1966.

1966

Comoro Isls.......C17
France.......1148
Fr. Polynesia.......C42
Fr. So. & Antarctic Terr.......C11
New Caledonia.......C46
St. Pierre & Miquelon.......C32
Somali Coast.......C49
Wallis & Futuna Isls.......C24

Air Afrique, 1966

Planes and Air Afrique Emblem — CD123

Introduction of DC-8F planes by Air Afrique.

1966

Cameroun.......C79
Cent. Africa.......C35
Chad.......C26
Congo, P.R.......C42
Dahomey.......C42
Gabon.......C47
Ivory Coast.......C32
Mauritania.......C57
Niger.......C63
Senegal.......C47
Togo.......C54
Upper Volta.......C31

African Postal Union, 1967

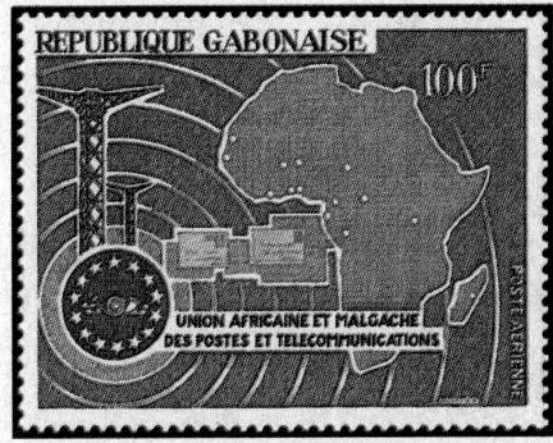

Telecommunications Symbols and Map of Africa — CD124

Fifth anniversary of the establishment of the African and Malagasy Union of Posts and Telecommunications, UAMPT.

1967

Cameroun.......C90
Cent. Africa.......C46
Chad.......C37
Congo, P.R.......C57
Dahomey.......C61
Gabon.......C58
Ivory Coast.......C34
Madagascar.......C85
Mauritania.......C65
Niger.......C75
Rwanda.......C1-C3
Senegal.......C60
Togo.......C81
Upper Volta.......C50

Monetary Union

Gold Token of the Ashantis, 17-18th Centuries — CD125

West African Monetary Union, 5th anniv.

1967, Nov. 4

Dahomey.......244
Ivory Coast.......259
Mauritania.......238
Niger.......204
Senegal.......294
Togo.......623
Upper Volta.......181

WHO Anniversary

Sun, Flowers and WHO Emblem CD126

World Health Organization, 20th anniv.

1968, May 4

Afars & Issas.......317
Comoro Isls.......73
Fr. Polynesia.......241-242
Fr. So. & Antarctic Terr.......31
New Caledonia.......367
St. Pierre & Miquelon.......377
Wallis & Futuna Isls.......169

Human Rights Year

Human Rights Flame — CD127

1968, Aug. 10

Afars & Issas.......322-323

Comoro Isls. 76
Fr. Polynesia...........................243-244
Fr. So. & Antarctic Terr. 32
New Caledonia...............................369
St. Pierre & Miquelon.....................382
Wallis & Futuna Isls. 170

2nd PHILEXAFRIQUE

CD128

Opening of PHILEXAFRIQUE, Abidjan, Feb. 14. Each stamp shows a local scene and stamp.

1969, Feb. 14

Cameroun.................................... C118
Cent. Africa C65
Chad... C48
Congo, P.R.................................... C77
Dahomey C94
Gabon.. C82
Ivory Coast C38-C40
Madagascar.................................. C92
Mali... C65
Mauritania..................................... C80
Niger.. C104
Senegal C68
Togo... C104
Upper Volta................................... C62

Concorde

Concorde in Flight CD129

First flight of the prototype Concorde supersonic plane at Toulouse, Mar. 1, 1969.

1969

Afars & Issas C56
Comoro Isls. C29
France... C42
Fr. Polynesia.................................. C50
Fr. So. & Antarctic Terr. C18
New Caledonia.............................. C63
St. Pierre & Miquelon.................... C40
Wallis & Futuna Isls. C30

Development Bank

Bank Emblem — CD130

African Development Bank, fifth anniv.

1969

Cameroun.......................................499
Chad...217
Congo, P.R.................................181-182
Ivory Coast.....................................281
Mali..127-128
Mauritania......................................267
Niger...220
Senegal 317-318
Upper Volta.....................................201

ILO

ILO Headquarters, Geneva, and Emblem — CD131

Intl. Labor Organization, 50th anniv.

1969-70

Afars & Issas 337
Comoro Isls. 83
Fr. Polynesia............................251-252
Fr. So. & Antarctic Terr. 35
New Caledonia.................................379
St. Pierre & Miquelon.......................396
Wallis & Futuna Isls. 172

ASECNA

Map of Africa, Plane and Airport CD132

10th anniversary of the Agency for the Security of Aerial Navigation in Africa and Madagascar (ASECNA, Agence pour la Securite de la Navigation Aerienne en Afrique et a Madagascar).

1969-70

Cameroun...500
Cent. Africa 119
Chad...222
Congo, P.R.......................................197
Dahomey 269
Gabon...260
Ivory Coast.......................................287
Mali...130
Niger...221
Senegal 321
Upper Volta.......................................204

U.P.U. Headquarters

CD133

New Universal Postal Union headquarters, Bern, Switzerland.

1970

Afars & Issas 342
Algeria 443
Cameroun...................................503-504
Cent. Africa 125
Chad...225
Comoro Isls. 84
Congo, P.R.......................................216
Fr. Polynesia.............................261-262
Fr. So. & Antarctic Terr. 36
Gabon...258
Ivory Coast.......................................295
Madagascar.....................................444
Mali...134-135
Mauritania..283
New Caledonia.................................382
Niger..231-232
St. Pierre & Miquelon.................397-398
Senegal 328-329
Tunisia 535
Wallis & Futuna Isls. 173

De Gaulle

CD134

First anniversary of the death of Charles de Gaulle, (1890-1970), President of France.

1971-72

Afars & Issas 356-357
Comoro Isls. 104-105
France....................................1322-1325
Fr. Polynesia.............................270-271
Fr. So. & Antarctic Terr. 52-53
New Caledonia..........................393-394
Reunion 377, 380
St. Pierre & Miquelon................417-418
Wallis & Futuna Isls. 177-178

African Postal Union, 1971

UAMPT Building, Brazzaville, Congo — CD135

10th anniversary of the establishment of the African and Malagasy Posts and Telecommunications Union, UAMPT. Each stamp has a different native design.

1971, Nov. 13

Cameroun...................................... C177
Cent. Africa C89
Chad.. C94
Congo, P.R.................................... C136
Dahomey C146
Gabon.. C120
Ivory Coast C47
Mauritania...................................... C113
Niger.. C164
Rwanda C8
Senegal C105
Togo.. C166
Upper Volta...................................... C97

West African Monetary Union

African Couple, City, Village and Commemorative Coin — CD136

West African Monetary Union, 10th anniv.

1972, Nov. 2

Dahomey 300
Ivory Coast.......................................331
Mauritania...299
Niger...258
Senegal 374
Togo...825
Upper Volta.......................................280

African Postal Union, 1973

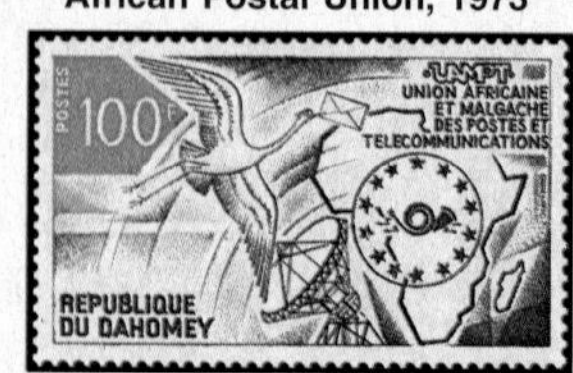

Telecommunications Symbols and Map of Africa — CD137

11th anniversary of the African and Malagasy Posts and Telecommunications Union (UAMPT).

1973, Sept. 12

Cameroun..574
Cent. Africa 194
Chad..294
Congo, P.R..289
Dahomey 311
Gabon..320
Ivory Coast..361
Madagascar......................................500
Mauritania...304
Niger..287
Rwanda 540
Senegal 393
Togo...849
Upper Volta......................................297

Philexafrique II — Essen

CD138

CD139

Designs: Indigenous fauna, local and German stamps. Types CD138-CD139 printed horizontally and vertically se-tenant in sheets of 10 (2x5). Label between horizontal pairs alternately commemoratives Philexafrique II, Libreville, Gabon, June 1978, and 2nd International Stamp Fair, Essen, Germany, Nov. 1-5.

1978-1979

Benin C285-C286
Central Africa C200-C201
Chad C238-C239
Congo Republic................. C245-C246
Djibouti.............................. C121-C122
Gabon................................ C215-C216
Ivory Coast C64-C65
Mali.................................... C356-C357
Mauritania.......................... C185-C186
Niger.................................. C291-C292
Rwanda C12-C13
Senegal C146-C147

BRITISH COMMONWEALTH OF NATIONS

The listings follow established trade practices when these issues are offered as units by dealers. The Peace issue, for example, includes only one stamp from the Indian state of Hyderabad. The U.P.U. issue includes the Egypt set. Pairs are included for those varieties issues with bilingual designs se-tenant.

Silver Jubilee

Windsor Castle and King George V CD301

Reign of King George V, 25th anniv.

1935

Antigua 77-80
Ascension 33-36
Bahamas 92-95
Barbados 186-189
Basutoland....................................11-14
Bechuanaland Protectorate......117-120
Bermuda...................................100-103
British Guiana............................223-226
British Honduras........................108-111
Cayman Islands............................81-84
Ceylon 260-263
Cyprus 136-139
Dominica.......................................90-93
Falkland Islands 77-80
Fiji...110-113
Gambia 125-128
Gibraltar....................................100-103
Gilbert & Ellice Islands..................33-36

Gold Coast 108-111
Grenada 124-127
Hong Kong 147-150
Jamaica 109-112
Kenya, Uganda, Tanganyika 42-45
Leeward Islands 96-99
Malta 184-187
Mauritius 204-207
Montserrat 85-88
Newfoundland 226-229
Nigeria 34-37
Northern Rhodesia 18-21
Nyasaland Protectorate 47-50
St. Helena 111-114
St. Kitts-Nevis 72-75
St. Lucia 91-94
St. Vincent 134-137
Seychelles 118-121
Sierra Leone 166-169
Solomon Islands 60-63
Somaliland Protectorate 77-80
Straits Settlements 213-216
Swaziland 20-23
Trinidad & Tobago 43-46
Turks & Caicos Islands 71-74
Virgin Islands 69-72

The following have different designs but are included in the omnibus set:

Great Britain 226-229
Offices in Morocco 67-70, 226-229, 422-425, 508-510
Australia 152-154
Canada 211-216
Cook Islands 98-100
India 142-148
Nauru 31-34
New Guinea 46-47
New Zealand 199-201
Niue 67-69
Papua 114-117
Samoa 163-165
South Africa 68-71
Southern Rhodesia 33-36
South-West Africa 121-124

249 stamps

Coronation

Queen Elizabeth and King George VI CD302

1937

Aden 13-15
Antigua 81-83
Ascension 37-39
Bahamas 97-99
Barbados 190-192
Basutoland 15-17
Bechuanaland Protectorate 121-123
Bermuda 115-117
British Guiana 227-229
British Honduras 112-114
Cayman Islands 97-99
Ceylon 275-277
Cyprus 140-142
Dominica 94-96
Falkland Islands 81-83
Fiji 114-116
Gambia 129-131
Gibraltar 104-106
Gilbert & Ellice Islands 37-39
Gold Coast 112-114
Grenada 128-130
Hong Kong 151-153
Jamaica 113-115
Kenya, Uganda, Tanganyika 60-62
Leeward Islands 100-102
Malta 188-190
Mauritius 208-210
Montserrat 89-91
Newfoundland 230-232
Nigeria 50-52
Northern Rhodesia 22-24
Nyasaland Protectorate 51-53
St. Helena 115-117
St. Kitts-Nevis 76-78
St. Lucia 107-109
St. Vincent 138-140
Seychelles 122-124
Sierra Leone 170-172
Solomon Islands 64-66
Somaliland Protectorate 81-83
Straits Settlements 235-237
Swaziland 24-26
Trinidad & Tobago 47-49
Turks & Caicos Islands 75-77
Virgin Islands 73-75

The following have different designs but are included in the omnibus set:

Great Britain 234
Offices in Morocco 82, 439, 514
Canada 237
Cook Islands 109-111
Nauru 35-38
Newfoundland 233-243
New Guinea 48-51
New Zealand 223-225
Niue 70-72
Papua 118-121
South Africa 74-78
Southern Rhodesia 38-41
South-West Africa 125-132

202 stamps

Peace

King George VI and Parliament Buildings, London CD303

Return to peace at the close of World War II.

1945-46

Aden 28-29
Antigua 96-97
Ascension 50-51
Bahamas 130-131
Barbados 207-208
Bermuda 131-132
British Guiana 242-243
British Honduras 127-128
Cayman Islands 112-113
Ceylon 293-294
Cyprus 156-157
Dominica 112-113
Falkland Islands 97-98
Falkland Islands Dep. 1L9-1L10
Fiji 137-138
Gambia 144-145
Gibraltar 119-120
Gilbert & Ellice Islands 52-53
Gold Coast 128-129
Grenada 143-144
Jamaica 136-137
Kenya, Uganda, Tanganyika 90-91
Leeward Islands 116-117
Malta 206-207
Mauritius 223-224
Montserrat 104-105
Nigeria 71-72
Northern Rhodesia 46-47
Nyasaland Protectorate 82-83
Pitcairn Island 9-10
St. Helena 128-129
St. Kitts-Nevis 91-92
St. Lucia 127-128
St. Vincent 152-153
Seychelles 149-150
Sierra Leone 186-187
Solomon Islands 80-81
Somaliland Protectorate 108-109
Trinidad & Tobago 62-63
Turks & Caicos Islands 90-91
Virgin Islands 88-89

The following have different designs but are included in the omnibus set:

Great Britain 264-265
  Offices in Morocco 523-524
Aden
  Kathiri State of Seiyun 12-13
  Qu'aiti State of Shihr and Mukalla 12-13
Australia 200-202
Basutoland 29-31
Bechuanaland Protectorate 137-139
Burma 66-69
Cook Islands 127-130
Hong Kong 174-175
India 195-198
  Hyderabad 51
New Zealand 247-257
Niue 90-93
Pakistan-Bahawalpur O16
Samoa 191-194
South Africa 100-102
Southern Rhodesia 67-70
South-West Africa 153-155
Swaziland 38-40
Zanzibar 222-223

164 stamps

Silver Wedding

King George VI and Queen Elizabeth
CD304 CD305

1948-49

Aden 30-31
  Kathiri State of Seiyun 14-15
  Qu'aiti State of Shihr and Mukalla 14-15
Antigua 98-99
Ascension 52-53
Bahamas 148-149
Barbados 210-211
Basutoland 39-40
Bechuanaland Protectorate 147-148
Bermuda 133-134
British Guiana 244-245
British Honduras 129-130
Cayman Islands 116-117
Cyprus 158-159
Dominica 114-115
Falkland Islands 99-100
Falkland Islands Dep. 1L11-1L12
Fiji 139-140
Gambia 146-147
Gibraltar 121-122
Gilbert & Ellice Islands 54-55
Gold Coast 142-143
Grenada 145-146
Hong Kong 178-179
Jamaica 138-139
Kenya, Uganda, Tanganyika 92-93
Leeward Islands 118-119
Malaya
  Johore 128-129
  Kedah 55-56
  Kelantan 44-45
  Malacca 1-2
  Negri Sembilan 36-37
  Pahang 44-45
  Penang 1-2
  Perak 99-100
  Perlis 1-2
  Selangor 74-75
  Trengganu 47-48
Malta 223-224
Mauritius 229-230
Montserrat 106-107
Nigeria 73-74
North Borneo 238-239
Northern Rhodesia 48-49
Nyasaland Protectorate 85-86
Pitcairn Island 11-12
St. Helena 130-131
St. Kitts-Nevis 93-94
St. Lucia 129-130
St. Vincent 154-155
Sarawak 174-175
Seychelles 151-152
Sierra Leone 188-189
Singapore 21-22
Solomon Islands 82-83
Somaliland Protectorate 110-111
Swaziland 48-49
Trinidad & Tobago 64-65
Turks & Caicos Islands 92-93
Virgin Islands 90-91
Zanzibar 224-225

The following have different designs but are included in the omnibus set:

Great Britain 267-268
  Offices in Morocco 93-94, 525-526
Bahrain 62-63
Kuwait 82-83
Oman 25-26
South Africa 106
South-West Africa 159

138 stamps

U.P.U.

Mercury and Symbols of Communications — CD306

Plane, Ship and Hemispheres — CD307

Mercury Scattering Letters over Globe CD308

U.P.U. Monument, Bern CD309

Universal Postal Union, 75th anniversary.

1949

Aden 32-35
  Kathiri State of Seiyun 16-19
  Qu'aiti State of Shihr and Mukalla 16-19
Antigua 100-103
Ascension 57-60
Bahamas 150-153
Barbados 212-215
Basutoland 41-44
Bechuanaland Protectorate 149-152
Bermuda 138-141
British Guiana 246-249
British Honduras 137-140
Brunei 79-82
Cayman Islands 118-121
Cyprus 160-163
Dominica 116-119
Falkland Islands 103-106
Falkland Islands Dep. 1L14-1L17
Fiji 141-144
Gambia 148-151
Gibraltar 123-126
Gilbert & Ellice Islands 56-59
Gold Coast 144-147
Grenada 147-150
Hong Kong 180-183
Jamaica 142-145
Kenya, Uganda, Tanganyika 94-97
Leeward Islands 126-129
Malaya
  Johore 151-154
  Kedah 57-60
  Kelantan 46-49
  Malacca 18-21
  Negri Sembilan 59-62
  Pahang 46-49
  Penang 23-26
  Perak 101-104
  Perlis 3-6
  Selangor 76-79
  Trengganu 49-52
Malta 225-228
Mauritius 231-234
Montserrat 108-111
New Hebrides, British 62-65
New Hebrides, French 79-82
Nigeria 75-78
North Borneo 240-243
Northern Rhodesia 50-53
Nyasaland Protectorate 87-90
Pitcairn Islands 13-16
St. Helena 132-135
St. Kitts-Nevis 95-98
St. Lucia 131-134
St. Vincent 170-173

Sarawak....176-179
Seychelles....153-156
Sierra Leone....190-193
Singapore....23-26
Solomon Islands....84-87
Somaliland Protectorate....112-115
Southern Rhodesia....71-72
Swaziland....50-53
Tonga....87-90
Trinidad & Tobago....66-69
Turks & Caicos Islands....101-104
Virgin Islands....92-95
Zanzibar....226-229

The following have different designs but are included in the omnibus set:

Great Britain....276-279
Offices in Morocco....546-549
Australia....223
Bahrain....68-71
Burma....116-121
Ceylon....304-306
Egypt....281-283
India....223-226
Kuwait....89-92
Oman....31-34
Pakistan-Bahawalpur 26-29, O25-O28
South Africa....109-111
South-West Africa....160-162

319 stamps

University

Arms of University College CD310

Alice, Princess of Athlone CD311

1948 opening of University College of the West Indies at Jamaica.

1951

Antigua....104-105
Barbados....228-229
British Guiana....250-251
British Honduras....141-142
Dominica....120-121
Grenada....164-165
Jamaica....146-147
Leeward Islands....130-131
Montserrat....112-113
St. Kitts-Nevis....105-106
St. Lucia....149-150
St. Vincent....174-175
Trinidad & Tobago....70-71
Virgin Islands....96-97

28 stamps

Coronation

Queen Elizabeth II — CD312

1953

Aden....47
Kathiri State of Seiyun....28
Qu'aiti State of Shihr and Mukalla....28
Antigua....106
Ascension....61
Bahamas....157
Barbados....234
Basutoland....45
Bechuanaland Protectorate....153
Bermuda....142
British Guiana....252
British Honduras....143
Cayman Islands....150
Cyprus....167
Dominica....141
Falkland Islands....121
Falkland Islands Dependencies....1L18
Fiji....145
Gambia....152
Gibraltar....131
Gilbert & Ellice Islands....60
Gold Coast....160
Grenada....170
Hong Kong....184
Jamaica....153
Kenya, Uganda, Tanganyika....101
Leeward Islands....132
Malaya
Johore....155
Kedah....82
Kelantan....71
Malacca....27
Negri Sembilan....63
Pahang....71
Penang....27
Perak....126
Perlis....28
Selangor....101
Trengganu....74
Malta....241
Mauritius....250
Montserrat....127
New Hebrides, British....77
Nigeria....79
North Borneo....260
Northern Rhodesia....60
Nyasaland Protectorate....96
Pitcairn....19
St. Helena....139
St. Kitts-Nevis....119
St. Lucia....156
St. Vincent....185
Sarawak....196
Seychelles....172
Sierra Leone....194
Singapore....27
Solomon Islands....88
Somaliland Protectorate....127
Swaziland....54
Trinidad & Tobago....84
Tristan da Cunha....13
Turks & Caicos Islands....118
Virgin Islands....114

The following have different designs but are included in the omnibus set:

Great Britain....313-316
Offices in Morocco....579-582
Australia....259-261
Bahrain....92-95
Canada....330
Ceylon....317
Cook Islands....145-146
Kuwait....113-116
New Zealand....280-284
Niue....104-105
Oman....52-55
Samoa....214-215
South Africa....192
Southern Rhodesia....80
South-West Africa....244-248
Tokelau Islands....4

106 stamps

Royal Visit 1953

Separate designs for each country for the visit of Queen Elizabeth II and the Duke of Edinburgh.

1953

Aden....62
Australia....267-269
Bermuda....163
Ceylon....318
Fiji....146
Gibraltar....146
Jamaica....154
Kenya, Uganda, Tanganyika....102
Malta....242
New Zealand....286-287

13 stamps

West Indies Federation

Map of the Caribbean CD313

Federation of the West Indies, April 22, 1958.

1958

Antigua....122-124
Barbados....248-250
Dominica....161-163
Grenada....184-186
Jamaica....175-177
Montserrat....143-145
St. Kitts-Nevis....136-138
St. Lucia....170-172
St. Vincent....198-200
Trinidad & Tobago....86-88

30 stamps

Freedom from Hunger

Protein Food CD314

U.N. Food and Agricultural Organization's "Freedom from Hunger" campaign.

1963

Aden....65
Antigua....133
Ascension....89
Bahamas....180
Basutoland....83
Bechuanaland Protectorate....194
Bermuda....192
British Guiana....271
British Honduras....179
Brunei....100
Cayman Islands....168
Dominica....181
Falkland Islands....146
Fiji....198
Gambia....172
Gibraltar....161
Gilbert & Ellice Islands....76
Grenada....190
Hong Kong....218
Malta....291
Mauritius....270
Montserrat....150
New Hebrides, British....93
North Borneo....296
Pitcairn....35
St. Helena....173
St. Lucia....179
St. Vincent....201
Sarawak....212
Seychelles....213
Solomon Islands....109
Swaziland....108
Tonga....127
Tristan da Cunha....68
Turks & Caicos Islands....138
Virgin Islands....140
Zanzibar....280

37 stamps

Red Cross Centenary

Red Cross and Elizabeth II CD315

1963

Antigua....134-135
Ascension....90-91
Bahamas....183-184
Basutoland....84-85
Bechuanaland Protectorate....195-196
Bermuda....193-194
British Guiana....272-273
British Honduras....180-181
Cayman Islands....169-170
Dominica....182-183
Falkland Islands....147-148
Fiji....203-204
Gambia....173-174
Gibraltar....162-163
Gilbert & Ellice Islands....77-78
Grenada....191-192
Hong Kong....219-220
Jamaica....203-204
Malta....292-293
Mauritius....271-272
Montserrat....151-152
New Hebrides, British....94-95
Pitcairn Islands....36-37
St. Helena....174-175
St. Kitts-Nevis....143-144
St. Lucia....180-181
St. Vincent....202-203
Seychelles....214-215
Solomon Islands....110-111
South Arabia....1-2
Swaziland....109-110
Tonga....134-135
Tristan da Cunha....69-70
Turks & Caicos Islands....139-140
Virgin Islands....141-142

70 stamps

Shakespeare

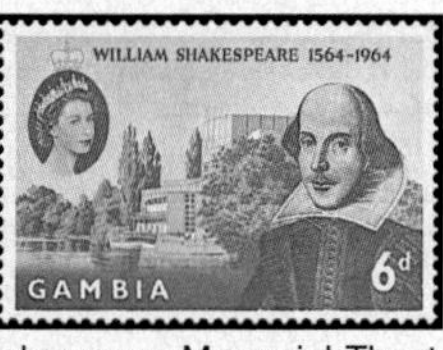

Shakespeare Memorial Theatre, Stratford-on-Avon — CD316

400th anniversary of the birth of William Shakespeare.

1964

Antigua....151
Bahamas....201
Bechuanaland Protectorate....197
Cayman Islands....171
Dominica....184
Falkland Islands....149
Gambia....192
Gibraltar....164
Montserrat....153
St. Lucia....196
Turks & Caicos Islands....141
Virgin Islands....143

12 stamps

ITU

ITU Emblem CD317

Intl. Telecommunication Union, cent.

1965

Antigua....153-154
Ascension....92-93
Bahamas....219-220
Barbados....265-266
Basutoland....101-102
Bechuanaland Protectorate....202-203
Bermuda....196-197
British Guiana....293-294
British Honduras....187-188
Brunei....116-117
Cayman Islands....172-173
Dominica....185-186
Falkland Islands....154-155
Fiji....211-212
Gibraltar....167-168
Gilbert & Ellice Islands....87-88
Grenada....205-206
Hong Kong....221-222
Mauritius....291-292
Montserrat....157-158
New Hebrides, British....108-109
Pitcairn Islands....52-53
St. Helena....180-181
St. Kitts-Nevis....163-164
St. Lucia....197-198
St. Vincent....224-225
Seychelles....218-219
Solomon Islands....126-127
Swaziland....115-116
Tristan da Cunha....85-86
Turks & Caicos Islands....142-143
Virgin Islands....159-160

64 stamps

Intl. Cooperation Year

ICY Emblem CD318

1965

Country	Nos.
Antigua	155-156
Ascension	94-95
Bahamas	222-223
Basutoland	103-104
Bechuanaland Protectorate	204-205
Bermuda	199-200
British Guiana	295-296
British Honduras	189-190
Brunei	118-119
Cayman Islands	174-175
Dominica	187-188
Falkland Islands	156-157
Fiji	213-214
Gibraltar	169-170
Gilbert & Ellice Islands	104-105
Grenada	207-208
Hong Kong	223-224
Mauritius	293-294
Montserrat	176-177
New Hebrides, British	110-111
New Hebrides, French	126-127
Pitcairn Islands	54-55
St. Helena	182-183
St. Kitts-Nevis	165-166
St. Lucia	199-200
Seychelles	220-221
Solomon Islands	143-144
South Arabia	17-18
Swaziland	117-118
Tristan da Cunha	87-88
Turks & Caicos Islands	144-145
Virgin Islands	161-162

64 stamps

Churchill Memorial

Winston Churchill and St. Paul's, London, During Air Attack CD319

1966

Country	Nos.
Antigua	157-160
Ascension	96-99
Bahamas	224-227
Barbados	281-284
Basutoland	105-108
Bechuanaland Protectorate	206-209
Bermuda	201-204
British Antarctic Territory	16-19
British Honduras	191-194
Brunei	120-123
Cayman Islands	176-179
Dominica	189-192
Falkland Islands	158-161
Fiji	215-218
Gibraltar	171-174
Gilbert & Ellice Islands	106-109
Grenada	209-212
Hong Kong	225-228
Mauritius	295-298
Montserrat	178-181
New Hebrides, British	112-115
New Hebrides, French	128-131
Pitcairn Islands	56-59
St. Helena	184-187
St. Kitts-Nevis	167-170
St. Lucia	201-204
St. Vincent	241-244
Seychelles	222-225
Solomon Islands	145-148
South Arabia	19-22
Swaziland	119-122
Tristan da Cunha	89-92
Turks & Caicos Islands	146-149
Virgin Islands	163-166

136 stamps

Royal Visit, 1966

Queen Elizabeth II and Prince Philip CD320

Caribbean visit, Feb. 4 - Mar. 6, 1966.

1966

Country	Nos.
Antigua	161-162
Bahamas	228-229
Barbados	285-286
British Guiana	299-300
Cayman Islands	180-181
Dominica	193-194
Grenada	213-214
Montserrat	182-183
St. Kitts-Nevis	171-172
St. Lucia	205-206
St. Vincent	245-246
Turks & Caicos Islands	150-151
Virgin Islands	167-168

26 stamps

World Cup Soccer

Soccer Player and Jules Rimet Cup CD321

World Cup Soccer Championship, Wembley, England, July 11-30.

1966

Country	Nos.
Antigua	163-164
Ascension	100-101
Bahamas	245-246
Bermuda	205-206
Brunei	124-125
Cayman Islands	182-183
Dominica	195-196
Fiji	219-220
Gibraltar	175-176
Gilbert & Ellice Islands	125-126
Grenada	230-231
New Hebrides, British	116-117
New Hebrides, French	132-133
Pitcairn Islands	60-61
St. Helena	188-189
St. Kitts-Nevis	173-174
St. Lucia	207-208
Seychelles	226-227
Solomon Islands	167-168
South Arabia	23-24
Tristan da Cunha	93-94

42 stamps

WHO Headquarters

World Health Organization Headquarters, Geneva — CD322

1966

Country	Nos.
Antigua	165-166
Ascension	102-103
Bahamas	247-248
Brunei	126-127
Cayman Islands	184-185
Dominica	197-198
Fiji	224-225
Gibraltar	180-181
Gilbert & Ellice Islands	127-128
Grenada	232-233
Hong Kong	229-230
Montserrat	184-185
New Hebrides, British	118-119
New Hebrides, French	134-135
Pitcairn Islands	62-63
St. Helena	190-191
St. Kitts-Nevis	177-178
St. Lucia	209-210
St. Vincent	247-248
Seychelles	228-229
Solomon Islands	169-170
South Arabia	25-26
Tristan da Cunha	99-100

46 stamps

UNESCO Anniversary

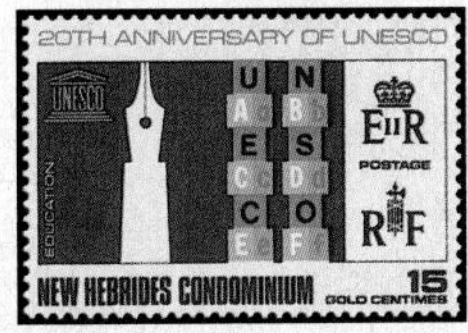

"Education" — CD323

"Science" (Wheat ears & flask enclosing globe). "Culture" (lyre & columns). 20th anniversary of the UNESCO.

1966-67

Country	Nos.
Antigua	183-185
Ascension	108-110
Bahamas	249-251
Barbados	287-289
Bermuda	207-209
Brunei	128-130
Cayman Islands	186-188
Dominica	199-201
Gibraltar	183-185
Gilbert & Ellice Islands	129-131
Grenada	234-236
Hong Kong	231-233
Mauritius	299-301
Montserrat	186-188
New Hebrides, British	120-122
New Hebrides, French	136-138
Pitcairn Islands	64-66
St. Helena	192-194
St. Kitts-Nevis	179-181
St. Lucia	211-213
St. Vincent	249-251
Seychelles	230-232
Solomon Islands	171-173
South Arabia	27-29
Swaziland	123-125
Tristan da Cunha	101-103
Turks & Caicos Islands	155-157
Virgin Islands	176-178

84 stamps

Silver Wedding, 1972

Queen Elizabeth II and Prince Philip — CD324

Designs: borders differ for each country.

1972

Country	Nos.
Anguilla	161-162
Antigua	295-296
Ascension	164-165
Bahamas	344-345
Bermuda	296-297
British Antarctic Territory	43-44
British Honduras	306-307
British Indian Ocean Territory	48-49
Brunei	186-187
Cayman Islands	304-305
Dominica	352-353
Falkland Islands	223-224
Fiji	328-329
Gibraltar	292-293
Gilbert & Ellice Islands	206-207
Grenada	466-467
Hong Kong	271-272
Montserrat	286-287
New Hebrides, British	169-170
Pitcairn Islands	127-128
St. Helena	271-272
St. Kitts-Nevis	257-258
St. Lucia	328-329
St.Vincent	344-345
Seychelles	309-310
Solomon Islands	248-249
South Georgia	35-36
Tristan da Cunha	178-179
Turks & Caicos Islands	257-258
Virgin Islands	241-242

60 stamps

Princess Anne's Wedding

Princess Anne and Mark Phillips — CD325

Wedding of Princess Anne and Mark Phillips, Nov. 14, 1973.

1973

Country	Nos.
Anguilla	179-180
Ascension	177-178
Belize	325-326
Bermuda	302-303
British Antarctic Territory	60-61
Cayman Islands	320-321
Falkland Islands	225-226
Gibraltar	305-306
Gilbert & Ellice Islands	216-217
Hong Kong	289-290
Montserrat	300-301
Pitcairn Island	135-136
St. Helena	277-278
St. Kitts-Nevis	274-275
St. Lucia	349-350
St. Vincent	358-359
St. Vincent Grenadines	1-2
Seychelles	311-312
Solomon Islands	259-260
South Georgia	37-38
Tristan da Cunha	189-190
Turks & Caicos Islands	286-287
Virgin Islands	260-261

44 stamps

Elizabeth II Coronation Anniv.

CD326

CD327

CD328

Designs: Royal and local beasts in heraldic form and simulated stonework. Portrait of Elizabeth II by Peter Grugeon. 25th anniversary of coronation of Queen Elizabeth II.

1978

Country	Nos.
Ascension	229
Barbados	474
Belize	397
British Antarctic Territory	71
Cayman Islands	404
Christmas Island	87
Falkland Islands	275
Fiji	384
Gambia	380
Gilbert Islands	312
Mauritius	464
New Hebrides, British	258
St. Helena	317
St. Kitts-Nevis	354
Samoa	472

Solomon Islands 368
South Georgia 51
Swaziland 302
Tristan da Cunha 238
Virgin Islands 337

20 sheets

Queen Mother Elizabeth's 80th Birthday

CD330

Designs: Photographs of Queen Mother Elizabeth. Falkland Islands issued in sheets of 50; others in sheets of 9.

1980

Ascension 261
Bermuda 401
Cayman Islands 443
Falkland Islands 305
Gambia 412
Gibraltar 393
Hong Kong 364
Pitcairn Islands 193
St. Helena 341
Samoa 532
Solomon Islands 426
Tristan da Cunha 277

12 stamps

Royal Wedding, 1981

Prince Charles and Lady Diana — CD331

CD331a

Wedding of Charles, Prince of Wales, and Lady Diana Spencer, St. Paul's Cathedral, London, July 29, 1981.

1981

Antigua 623-625
Ascension 294-296
Barbados 547-549
Barbuda 497-499
Bermuda 412-414
Brunei 268-270
Cayman Islands 471-473
Dominica 701-703
Falkland Islands 324-326
Falkland Islands Dep. 1L59-1L61
Fiji 442-444
Gambia 426-428
Ghana 759-761
Grenada 1051-1053
Grenada Grenadines 440-443
Hong Kong 373-375
Jamaica 500-503
Lesotho 335-337
Maldive Islands 906-908
Mauritius 520-522
Norfolk Island 280-282
Pitcairn Islands 206-208
St. Helena 353-355
St. Lucia 543-545
Samoa 558-560
Sierra Leone 509-517
Solomon Islands 450-452
Swaziland 382-384
Tristan da Cunha 294-296
Turks & Caicos Islands 486-488
Caicos Island 8-10
Uganda 314-316
Vanuatu 308-310
Virgin Islands 406-408

Princess Diana

CD332

CD333

Designs: Photographs and portrait of Princess Diana, wedding or honeymoon photographs, royal residences, arms of issuing country. Portrait photograph by Clive Friend. Souvenir sheet margins show family tree, various people related to the princess. 21st birthday of Princess Diana of Wales, July 1.

1982

Antigua 663-666
Ascension 313-316
Bahamas 510-513
Barbados 585-588
Barbuda 544-546
British Antarctic Territory 92-95
Cayman Islands 486-489
Dominica 773-776
Falkland Islands 348-351
Falkland Islands Dep. 1L72-1L75
Fiji 470-473
Gambia 447-450
Grenada 1101A-1105
Grenada Grenadines 485-491
Lesotho 372-375
Maldive Islands 952-955
Mauritius 548-551
Pitcairn Islands 213-216
St. Helena 372-375
St. Lucia 591-594
Sierra Leone 531-534
Solomon Islands 471-474
Swaziland 406-409
Tristan da Cunha 310-313
Turks and Caicos Islands 530A-534
Virgin Islands 430-433

250th anniv. of first edition of Lloyd's List (shipping news publication) & of Lloyd's marine insurance.

CD335

Designs: First page of early edition of the list; historical ships, modern transportation or harbor scenes.

1984

Ascension 351-354
Bahamas 555-558
Barbados 627-630
Cayes of Belize 10-13
Cayman Islands 522-525
Falkland Islands 404-407
Fiji 509-512
Gambia 519-522
Mauritius 587-590
Nauru 280-283
St. Helena 412-415
Samoa 624-627
Seychelles 538-541
Solomon Islands 521-524
Vanuatu 368-371
Virgin Islands 466-469

Queen Mother 85th Birthday

CD336

Designs: Photographs tracing the life of the Queen Mother, Elizabeth. The high value in each set pictures the same photograph taken of the Queen Mother holding the infant Prince Henry.

1985

Ascension 372-376
Bahamas 580-584
Barbados 660-664
Bermuda 469-473
Falkland Islands 420-424
Falkland Islands Dep. 1L92-1L96
Fiji 531-535
Hong Kong 447-450
Jamaica 599-603
Mauritius 604-608
Norfolk Island 364-368
Pitcairn Islands 253-257
St. Helena 428-432
Samoa 649-653
Seychelles 567-571
Solomon Islands 543-547
Swaziland 476-480
Tristan da Cunha 372-376
Vanuatu 392-396
Zil Elwannyen Sesel 101-105

Queen Elizabeth II, 60th Birthday

CD337

1986, April 21

Ascension 389-393
Bahamas 592-596
Barbados 675-679
Bermuda 499-503
Cayman Islands 555-559
Falkland Islands 441-445
Fiji 544-548
Hong Kong 465-469
Jamaica 620-624
Kiribati 470-474
Mauritius 629-633
Papua New Guinea 640-644
Pitcairn Islands 270-274
St. Helena 451-455
Samoa 670-674
Seychelles 592-596
Solomon Islands 562-566
South Georgia 101-105
Swaziland 490-494
Tristan da Cunha 388-392
Vanuatu 414-418
Zambia 343-347
Zil Elwannyen Sesel 114-118

Royal Wedding

Marriage of Prince Andrew and Sarah Ferguson CD338

1986, July 23

Ascension 399-400
Bahamas 602-603
Barbados 687-688
Cayman Islands 560-561
Jamaica 629-630
Pitcairn Islands 275-276
St. Helena 460-461
St. Kitts 181-182
Seychelles 602-603
Solomon Islands 567-568
Tristan da Cunha 397-398
Zambia 348-349
Zil Elwannyen Sesel 119-120

Queen Elizabeth II, 60th Birthday

Queen Elizabeth II & Prince Philip, 1947 Wedding Portrait — CD339

Designs: Photographs tracing the life of Queen Elizabeth II.

1986

Anguilla 674-677
Antigua 925-928
Barbuda 783-786
Dominica 950-953
Gambia 611-614
Grenada 1371-1374
Grenada Grenadines 749-752
Lesotho 531-534
Maldive Islands 1172-1175
Sierra Leone 760-763
Uganda 495-498

Royal Wedding, 1986

CD340

Designs: Photographs of Prince Andrew and Sarah Ferguson during courtship, engagement and marriage.

1986

Antigua 939-942
Barbuda 809-812
Dominica 970-973
Gambia 635-638
Grenada 1385-1388
Grenada Grenadines 758-761
Lesotho 545-548
Maldive Islands 1181-1184
Sierra Leone 769-772
Uganda 510-513

Lloyds of London, 300th Anniv.

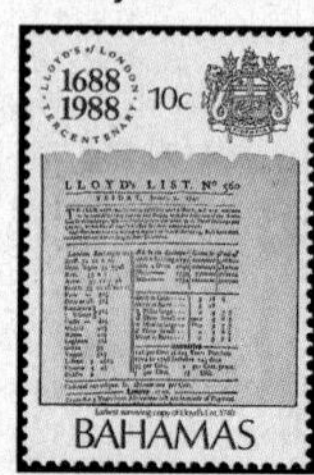

CD341

Designs: 17th century aspects of Lloyds, representations of each country's individual connections with Lloyds and publicized disasters insured by the organization.

1986

Ascension 454-457
Bahamas 655-658
Barbados 731-734
Bermuda 541-544
Falkland Islands 481-484
Liberia 1101-1104
Malawi 534-537
Nevis 571-574
St. Helena 501-504
St. Lucia 923-926
Seychelles 649-652
Solomon Islands 627-630

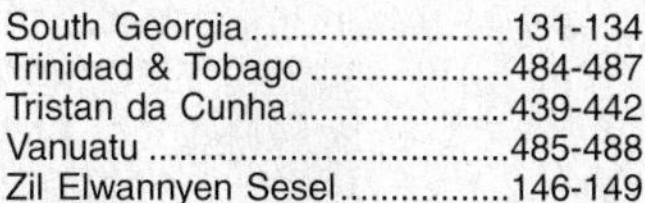

South Georgia 131-134
Trinidad & Tobago 484-487
Tristan da Cunha 439-442
Vanuatu 485-488
Zil Elwannyen Sesel 146-149

Moon Landing, 20th Anniv.

CD342

Designs: Equipment, crew photographs, spacecraft, official emblems and report profiles created for the Apollo Missions. Two stamps in each set are square in format rather than like the stamp shown; see individual country listings for more information.

1989

Ascension Is. 468-472
Bahamas 674-678
Belize 916-920
Kiribati 517-521
Liberia 1125-1129
Nevis 586-590
St. Kitts 248-252
Samoa 760-764
Seychelles 676-680
Solomon Islands 643-647
Vanuatu 507-511
Zil Elwannyen Sesel 154-158

Queen Mother, 90th Birthday

CD343 CD344

Designs: Portraits of Queen Elizabeth, the Queen Mother. See individual country listings for more information.

1990

Ascension Is. 491-492
Bahamas 698-699
Barbados 782-783
British Antarctic Territory 170-171
British Indian Ocean Territory 106-107
Cayman Islands 622-623
Falkland Islands 524-525
Kenya 527-528
Kiribati 555-556
Liberia 1145-1146
Pitcairn Islands 336-337
St. Helena 532-533
St. Lucia 969-970
Seychelles 710-711
Solomon Islands 671-672
South Georgia 143-144
Swaziland 565-566
Tristan da Cunha 480-481
Zil Elwannyen Sesel 171-172

Queen Elizabeth II, 65th Birthday, and Prince Philip, 70th Birthday

CD345

CD346

Designs: Portraits of Queen Elizabeth II and Prince Philip differ for each country. Printed in sheets of 10 + 5 labels (3 different) between. Stamps alternate, producing 5 different triptychs.

1991

Ascension Is. 505-506
Bahamas 730-731
Belize 969-970
Bermuda 617-618
Kiribati 571-572
Mauritius 733-734
Pitcairn Islands 348-349
St. Helena 554-555
St. Kitts 318-319
Samoa 790-791
Seychelles 723-724
Solomon Islands 688-689
South Georgia 149-150
Swaziland 586-587
Vanuatu 540-541
Zil Elwannyen Sesel 177-178

Royal Family Birthday, Anniversary

CD347

Queen Elizabeth II, 65th birthday, Charles and Diana, 10th wedding anniversary: Various photographs of Queen Elizabeth II, Prince Philip, Prince Charles, Princess Diana and their sons William and Henry.

1991

Antigua 1446-1455
Barbuda 1229-1238
Dominica 1328-1337
Gambia 1080-1089
Grenada 2006-2015
Grenada Grenadines 1331-1340
Guyana 2440-2451
Lesotho 871-875
Maldive Islands 1533-1542
Nevis 666-675
St. Vincent 1485-1494
St. Vincent Grenadines 769-778
Sierra Leone 1387-1396
Turks & Caicos Islands 913-922
Uganda 918-927

Queen Elizabeth II's Accession to the Throne, 40th Anniv.

CD348

CD349

Various photographs of Queen Elizabeth II with local Scenes.

1992 - CD348

Antigua 1513-1518
Barbuda 1306-1309
Dominica 1414-1419
Gambia 1172-1177
Grenada 2047-2052
Grenada Grenadines 1368-1373
Lesotho 881-885
Maldive Islands 1637-1642
Nevis 702-707
St. Vincent 1582-1587
St. Vincent Grenadines 829-834
Sierra Leone 1482-1487
Turks and Caicos Islands 978-987
Uganda 990-995
Virgin Islands 742-746

1992 - CD349

Ascension Islands 531-535
Bahamas 744-748
Bermuda 623-627
British Indian Ocean Territory 119-123
Cayman Islands 648-652
Falkland Islands 549-553
Gibraltar 605-609
Hong Kong 619-623
Kenya 563-567
Kiribati 582-586
Pitcairn Islands 362-366
St. Helena 570-574
St. Kitts 332-336
Samoa 805-809
Seychelles 734-738
Solomon Islands 708-712
South Georgia 157-161
Tristan da Cunha 508-512
Vanuatu 555-559
Zambia 561-565
Zil Elwannyen Sesel 183-187

Royal Air Force, 75th Anniversary

CD350

1993

Ascension 557-561
Bahamas 771-775
Barbados 842-846
Belize 1003-1008
Bermuda 648-651
British Indian Ocean Territory 136-140
Falkland Is. 573-577
Fiji 687-691
Montserrat 830-834
St. Kitts 351-355

Royal Air Force, 80th Anniv.

Design CD350 Re-inscribed

1998

Ascension 697-701
Bahamas 907-911
British Indian Ocean Terr 198-202
Cayman Islands 754-758
Fiji 814-818
Gibraltar 755-759
Samoa 957-961
Turks & Caicos Islands 1258-1265
Tuvalu 763-767
Virgin Islands 879-883

End of World War II, 50th Anniv.

CD351

CD352

1995

Ascension 613-617
Bahamas 824-828
Barbados 891-895
Belize 1047-1050
British Indian Ocean Territory 163-167
Cayman Islands 704-708
Falkland Islands 634-638
Fiji 720-724
Kiribati 662-668
Liberia 1175-1179
Mauritius 803-805
St. Helena 646-654
St. Kitts 389-393
St. Lucia 1018-1022
Samoa 890-894
Solomon Islands 799-803
South Georgia & S. Sandwich Is. 198-200
Tristan da Cunha 562-566

UN, 50th Anniv.

CD353

1995

Bahamas 839-842
Barbados 901-904
Belize 1055-1058
Jamaica 847-851
Liberia 1187-1190
Mauritius 813-816
Pitcairn Islands 436-439
St. Kitts 398-401
St. Lucia 1023-1026
Samoa 900-903
Tristan da Cunha 568-571
Virgin Islands 807-810

Queen Elizabeth, 70th Birthday

CD354

1996

Ascension 632-635
British Antarctic Territory 240-243
British Indian Ocean Territory 176-180
Falkland Islands 653-657
Pitcairn Islands 446-449
St. Helena 672-676
Samoa 912-916
Tokelau 223-227
Tristan da Cunha 576-579
Virgin Islands 824-828

Diana, Princess of Wales (1961-97)

CD355

1998

Ascension	696
Bahamas	901A-902
Barbados	950
Belize	1091
Bermuda	753
Botswana	659-663
British Antarctic Territory	258
British Indian Ocean Terr.	197
Cayman Islands	752A-753
Falkland Islands	694
Fiji	819-820
Gibraltar	754
Kiribati	719A-720
Namibia	909
Niue	706
Norfolk Island	644-645
Papua New Guinea	937
Pitcairn Islands	487
St. Helena	711
St. Kitts	437A-438
Samoa	955A-956
Seycelles	802
Solomon Islands	866-867
South Georgia & S. Sandwich Islands	220
Tokelau	252B-253
Tonga	980
Niuafo'ou	201
Tristan da Cunha	618
Tuvalu	762
Vanuatu	719
Virgin Islands	878

Wedding of Prince Edward and Sophie Rhys-Jones

CD356

1999

Ascension	729-730
Cayman Islands	775-776
Falkland Islands	729-730
Pitcairn Islands	505-506
St. Helena	733-734
Samoa	971-972
Tristan da Cunha	636-637
Virgin Islands	908-909

1st Manned Moon Landing, 30th Anniv.

CD357

1999

Ascension	731-735
Bahamas	942-946
Barbados	967-971
Bermuda	778
Cayman Islands	777-781
Fiji	853-857
Jamaica	889-893
Kirbati	746-750
Nauru	465-469
St. Kitts	460-464
Samoa	973-977
Solomon Islands	875-879
Tuvalu	800-804
Virgin Islands	910-914

Queen Mother's Century

CD358

1999

Ascension	736-740
Bahamas	951-955
Cayman Islands	782-786
Falkland Islands	734-738
Fiji	858-862
Norfolk Island	688-692
St. Helena	740-744
Samoa	978-982
Solomon Islands	880-884
South Georgia & South Sandwich Islands	231-235
Tristan da Cunha	638-642
Tuvalu	805-809

Prince William, 18th Birthday

CD359

2000

Ascension	755-759
Cayman Islands	797-801
Falkland Islands	762-766
Fiji	889-893
South Georgia and South Sandwich Islands	257-261
Tristan da Cunha	664-668
Virgin Islands	925-929

Reign of Queen Elizabeth II, 50th Anniv.

CD360

2002

Ascension	790-794
Bahamas	1033-1037
Barbados	1019-1023
Belize	1152-1156
Bermuda	822-826
British Antarctic Territory	307-311
British Indian Ocean Territory	239-243
Cayman Islands	844-848
Falkland Islands	804-808
Gibraltar	896-900
Jamaica	952-956
Nauru	491-495
Norfolk Island	758-762
Papua New Guinea	1019-1023
Pitcairn Islands	552
St. Helena	788-792
St. Lucia	1146-1150
Solomon Islands	931-935
South Georgia & So. Sandwich Is.	274-278
Swaziland	706-710
Tokelau	302-306
Tonga	1059
Niuafo'ou	239
Tristan da Cunha	706-710
Virgin Islands	967-971

Queen Mother Elizabeth (1900-2002)

CD361

2002

Ascension	799-801
Bahamas	1044-1046
Bermuda	834-836
British Antarctic Territory	312-314
British Indian Ocean Territory	245-247
Cayman Islands	857-861
Falkland Islands	812-816
Nauru	499-501
Pitcairn Islands	561-565
St. Helena	808-812
St. Lucia	1155-1159
Seychelles	830
Solomon Islands	945-947
South Georgia & So. Sandwich Isls.	281-285
Tokelau	312-314
Tristan da Cunha	715-717
Virgin Islands	979-983

Head of Queen Elizabeth II

CD362

2003

Ascension	822
Bermuda	865
British Antarctic Territory	322
British Indian Ocean Territory	261
Cayman Islands	878
Falkland Islands	828
St. Helena	820
South Georgia & South Sandwich Islands	294
Tristan da Cunha	731
Virgin Islands	1003

Coronation of Queen Elizabeth II, 50th Anniv.

CD363

2003

Ascension	823-825
Bahamas	1073-1075
Bermuda	866-868
British Antarctic Territory	323-325
British Indian Ocean Territory	262-264
Cayman Islands	879-881
Jamaica	970-972
Kiribati	825-827
Pitcairn Islands	577-581
St. Helena	821-823
St. Lucia	1171-1173
Tokelau	320-322
Tristan da Cunha	732-734
Virgin Islands	1004-1006

Prince William, 21st Birthday

CD364

2003

Ascension	826
British Indian Ocean Territory	265
Cayman Islands	882-884
Falkland Islands	829
South Georgia & South Sandwich Islands	295
Tokelau	323
Tristan da Cunha	735
Virgin Islands	1007-1009

British Commonwealth of Nations

Dominions, Colonies, Territories, Offices and Independent Members

Comprising stamps of the British Commonwealth and associated nations.

A strict observance of technicalities would bar some or all of the stamps listed under Burma, Ireland, Kuwait, Nepal, New Republic, Orange Free State, Samoa, South Africa, South-West Africa, Stellaland, Sudan, Swaziland, the two Transvaal Republics and others but these are included for the convenience of collectors.

1. Great Britain

Great Britain: Including England, Scotland, Wales and Northern Ireland.

2. The Dominions, Present and Past

AUSTRALIA

The Commonwealth of Australia was proclaimed on January 1, 1901. It consists of six former colonies as follows:

New South Wales
Queensland
South Australia
Victoria
Tasmania
Western Australia

The following islands and territories are, or have been, administered by Australia: Australian Antarctic Territory, Christmas Island, Cocos (Keeling) Islands, Nauru, New Guinea, Norfolk Island, Papua.

CANADA

The Dominion of Canada was created by the British North America Act in 1867. The following provinces were former separate colonies and issued postage stamps:

British Columbia and Vancouver Island
New Brunswick
Newfoundland
Nova Scotia
Prince Edward Island

FIJI

The colony of Fiji became an independent nation with dominion status on Oct. 10, 1970.

GHANA

This state came into existence Mar. 6, 1957, with dominion status. It consists of the former colony of the Gold Coast and the Trusteeship Territory of Togoland. Ghana became a republic July 1, 1960.

INDIA

The Republic of India was inaugurated on January 26, 1950. It succeeded the Dominion of India which was proclaimed August 15, 1947, when the former Empire of India was divided into Pakistan and the Union of India. The Republic is composed of about 40 predominantly Hindu states of three classes: governor's provinces, chief commissioner's provinces and princely states. India also has various territories, such as the Andaman and Nicobar Islands.

The old Empire of India was a federation of British India and the native states. The more important princely states were autonomous. Of the more than 700 Indian states, these 43 are familiar names to philatelists because of their postage stamps.

CONVENTION STATES

Chamba
Faridkot
Gwalior
Jhind
Nabha
Patiala

NATIVE FEUDATORY STATES

Alwar
Bahawalpur
Bamra
Barwani
Bhopal
Bhor
Bijawar
Bundi
Bussahir
Charkhari
Cochin
Dhar
Duttia
Faridkot (1879-85)
Hyderabad
Idar
Indore
Jaipur
Jammu
Jammu and Kashmir
Jasdan
Jhalawar
Jhind (1875-76)
Kashmir
Kishangarh
Las Bela
Morvi
Nandgaon
Nowanuggur
Orchha
Poonch
Rajpeepla
Sirmur
Soruth
Travancore
Wadhwan

NEW ZEALAND

Became a dominion on September 26, 1907. The following islands and territories are, or have been, administered by New Zealand:

Aitutaki
Cook Islands (Rarotonga)
Niue
Penrhyn
Ross Dependency
Samoa (Western Samoa)
Tokelau Islands

PAKISTAN

The Republic of Pakistan was proclaimed March 23, 1956. It succeeded the Dominion which was proclaimed August 15, 1947. It is made up of all or part of several Moslem provinces and various districts of the former Empire of India, including Bahawalpur and Las Bela. Pakistan withdrew from the Commonwealth in 1972.

SOUTH AFRICA

Under the terms of the South African Act (1909) the self-governing colonies of Cape of Good Hope, Natal, Orange River Colony and Transvaal united on May 31, 1910, to form the Union of South Africa. It became an independent republic May 3, 1961.

Under the terms of the Treaty of Versailles, South-West Africa, formerly German South-West Africa, was mandated to the Union of South Africa.

SRI LANKA (CEYLON)

The Dominion of Ceylon was proclaimed February 4, 1948. The island had been a Crown Colony from 1802 until then. On May 22, 1972, Ceylon became the Republic of Sri Lanka.

3. Colonies, Past and Present; ControlledTerritory and Independent Members of the Commonwealth

Aden
Aitutaki
Antigua
Ascension
Bahamas
Bahrain
Bangladesh
Barbados
Barbuda
Basutoland
Batum
Bechuanaland
Bechuanaland Prot.
Belize
Bermuda
Botswana
British Antarctic Territory
British Central Africa
British Columbia and Vancouver Island
British East Africa
British Guiana

British Honduras
British Indian Ocean Territory
British New Guinea
British Solomon Islands
British Somaliland
Brunei
Burma
Bushire
Cameroons
Cape of Good Hope
Cayman Islands
Christmas Island
Cocos (Keeling) Islands
Cook Islands
Crete,
British Administration
Cyprus
Dominica
East Africa & Uganda
Protectorates
Egypt
Falkland Islands
Fiji
Gambia
German East Africa
Gibraltar
Gilbert Islands
Gilbert & Ellice Islands
Gold Coast
Grenada
Griqualand West
Guernsey
Guyana
Heligoland
Hong Kong
Indian Native States
(see India)
Ionian Islands
Jamaica
Jersey
Kenya
Kenya, Uganda & Tanzania
Kuwait
Labuan
Lagos
Leeward Islands
Lesotho
Madagascar
Malawi
Malaya
Federated Malay States
Johore
Kedah
Kelantan
Malacca
Negri Sembilan
Pahang
Penang
Perak
Perlis
Selangor
Singapore
Sungei Ujong
Trengganu
Malaysia
Maldive Islands
Malta
Man, Isle of
Mauritius
Mesopotamia
Montserrat
Muscat
Namibia
Natal
Nauru
Nevis
New Britain
New Brunswick
Newfoundland
New Guinea
New Hebrides
New Republic
New South Wales
Niger Coast Protectorate
Nigeria
Niue
Norfolk Island
North Borneo
Northern Nigeria
Northern Rhodesia
North West Pacific Islands
Nova Scotia
Nyasaland Protectorate
Oman
Orange River Colony
Palestine
Papua New Guinea
Penrhyn Island
Pitcairn Islands
Prince Edward Island
Queensland
Rhodesia
Rhodesia & Nyasaland
Ross Dependency
Sabah
St. Christopher
St. Helena
St. Kitts
St. Kitts-Nevis-Anguilla
St. Lucia
St. Vincent
Samoa
Sarawak
Seychelles
Sierra Leone
Solomon Islands
Somaliland Protectorate
South Arabia
South Australia
South Georgia
Southern Nigeria
Southern Rhodesia
South-West Africa
Stellaland
Straits Settlements
Sudan
Swaziland
Tanganyika
Tanzania
Tasmania
Tobago
Togo
Tokelau Islands
Tonga
Transvaal
Trinidad
Trinidad and Tobago
Tristan da Cunha
Trucial States
Turks and Caicos
Turks Islands
Tuvalu
Uganda
United Arab Emirates
Victoria
Virgin Islands
Western Australia
Zambia
Zanzibar
Zululand

POST OFFICES IN FOREIGN COUNTRIES

Africa
East Africa Forces
Middle East Forces
Bangkok
China
Morocco
Turkish Empire

Colonies, Former Colonies, Offices, Territories Controlled by Parent States

Belgium

Belgian Congo
Ruanda-Urundi

Denmark

Danish West Indies
Faroe Islands
Greenland
Iceland

Finland

Aland Islands

France

COLONIES PAST AND PRESENT, CONTROLLED TERRITORIES

Afars & Issas, Territory of
Alaouites
Alexandretta
Algeria
Alsace & Lorraine
Anjouan
Annam & Tonkin
Benin
Cambodia (Khmer)
Cameroun
Castellorizo
Chad
Cilicia
Cochin China
Comoro Islands
Dahomey
Diego Suarez
Djibouti (Somali Coast)
Fezzan
French Congo
French Equatorial Africa
French Guiana
French Guinea
French India
French Morocco
French Polynesia (Oceania)
French Southern & Antarctic Territories
French Sudan
French West Africa
Gabon
Germany
Ghadames
Grand Comoro
Guadeloupe
Indo-China
Inini
Ivory Coast
Laos
Latakia
Lebanon
Madagascar
Martinique
Mauritania
Mayotte
Memel
Middle Congo
Moheli
New Caledonia
New Hebrides
Niger Territory
Nossi-Be
Obock
Reunion
Rouad, Ile
Ste.-Marie de Madagascar
St. Pierre & Miquelon
Senegal
Senegambia & Niger
Somali Coast
Syria
Tahiti
Togo
Tunisia
Ubangi-Shari
Upper Senegal & Niger
Upper Volta
Viet Nam
Wallis & Futuna Islands

POST OFFICES IN FOREIGN COUNTRIES

China
Crete
Egypt
Turkish Empire
Zanzibar

Germany

EARLY STATES

Baden
Bavaria
Bergedorf
Bremen
Brunswick
Hamburg
Hanover
Lubeck
Mecklenburg-Schwerin
Mecklenburg-Strelitz
Oldenburg
Prussia
Saxony
Schleswig-Holstein
Wurttemberg

FORMER COLONIES

Cameroun (Kamerun)
Caroline Islands
German East Africa
German New Guinea
German South-West Africa
Kiauchau
Mariana Islands
Marshall Islands
Samoa
Togo

Italy

EARLY STATES

Modena
Parma
Romagna
Roman States
Sardinia
Tuscany
Two Sicilies
  Naples
  Neapolitan Provinces
  Sicily

FORMER COLONIES, CONTROLLED TERRITORIES, OCCUPATION AREAS

Aegean Islands
  Calimno (Calino)
  Caso
  Cos (Coo)
  Karki (Carchi)
  Leros (Lero)
  Lipso
  Nisiros (Nisiro)
  Patmos (Patmo)
  Piscopi
  Rodi (Rhodes)
  Scarpanto
  Simi
  Stampalia
Castellorizo
Corfu
Cyrenaica
Eritrea
Ethiopia (Abyssinia)
Fiume
Ionian Islands
  Cephalonia
  Ithaca
  Paxos
Italian East Africa
Libya
Oltre Giuba
Saseno
Somalia (Italian Somaliland)
Tripolitania

POST OFFICES IN FOREIGN COUNTRIES

"ESTERO"*
Austria
China
  Peking
  Tientsin
Crete
Tripoli
Turkish Empire
  Constantinople
  Durazzo
  Janina
Jerusalem
Salonika
Scutari
Smyrna
Valona

*Stamps overprinted "ESTERO" were used in various parts of the world.

Netherlands

Aruba
Netherlands Antilles (Curacao)
Netherlands Indies
Netherlands New Guinea
Surinam (Dutch Guiana)

Portugal

COLONIES PAST AND PRESENT, CONTROLLED TERRITORIES

Angola
Angra
Azores
Cape Verde
Funchal
Horta
Inhambane
Kionga
Lourenco Marques
Macao
Madeira
Mozambique
Mozambique Co.
Nyassa
Ponta Delgada
Portuguese Africa
Portuguese Congo
Portuguese Guinea
Portuguese India
Quelimane
St. Thomas & Prince Islands
Tete
Timor
Zambezia

Russia

ALLIED TERRITORIES AND REPUBLICS, OCCUPATION AREAS

Armenia
Aunus (Olonets)
Azerbaijan
Batum
Estonia
Far Eastern Republic
Georgia
Karelia
Latvia
Lithuania
North Ingermanland
Ostland
Russian Turkestan
Siberia
South Russia
Tannu Tuva
Transcaucasian Fed. Republics
Ukraine
Wenden (Livonia)
Western Ukraine

Spain

COLONIES PAST AND PRESENT, CONTROLLED TERRITORIES

Aguera, La
Cape Juby
Cuba
Elobey, Annobon & Corisco
Fernando Po
Ifni
Mariana Islands
Philippines
Puerto Rico
Rio de Oro
Rio Muni
Spanish Guinea
Spanish Morocco
Spanish Sahara
Spanish West Africa

POST OFFICES IN FOREIGN COUNTRIES

Morocco
Tangier
Tetuan

Dies of British Colonial Stamps

DIE A

DIE B

DIE I

DIE II

DIE A:

1. The lines in the groundwork vary in thickness and are not uniformly straight.

2. The seventh and eighth lines from the top, in the groundwork, converge where they meet the head.

3. There is a small dash in the upper part of the second jewel in the band of the crown.

4. The vertical color line in front of the throat stops at the sixth line of shading on the neck.

DIE B:

1. The lines in the groundwork are all thin and straight.

2. All the lines of the background are parallel.

3. There is no dash in the upper part of the second jewel in the band of the crown.

4. The vertical color line in front of the throat stops at the eighth line of shading on the neck.

DIE I:

1. The base of the crown is well below the level of the inner white line around the vignette.

2. The labels inscribed "POSTAGE" and "REVENUE" are cut square at the top.

3. There is a white "bud" on the outer side of the main stem of the curved ornaments in each lower corner.

4. The second (thick) line below the country name has the ends next to the crown cut diagonally.

DIE Ia.
1 as die II.
2 and 3 as die I.

DIE Ib.
1 and 3 as die II.
2 as die I.

DIE II:

1. The base of the crown is aligned with the underside of the white line around the vignette.

2. The labels curve inward at the top inner corners.

3. The "bud" has been removed from the outer curve of the ornaments in each corner.

4. The second line below the country name has the ends next to the crown cut vertically.

Wmk. 1
Crown and C C

Wmk. 2
Crown and C A

Wmk. 3
Multiple Crown and C A

Wmk. 4
Multiple Crown and Script C A

Wmk. 4a

Wmk. 314
St. Edward's Crown and C A Multiple

Wmk. 373

Wmk. 384

Wmk. 406

British Colonial and Crown Agents Watermarks

Watermarks 1 to 4, 314, 373, 384 and 406, common to many British territories, are illustrated here to avoid duplication.

The letters "CC" of Wmk. 1 identify the paper as having been made for the use of the Crown Colonies, while the letters "CA" of the others stand for "Crown Agents." Both Wmks. 1 and 2 were used on stamps printed by De La Rue & Co.

Wmk. 3 was adopted in 1904; Wmk. 4 in 1921; Wmk. 314 in 1957; Wmk. 373 in 1974; Wmk. 384 in 1985; Wmk 406 in 2008.

In Wmk. 4a, a non-matching crown of the general St. Edwards type (bulging on both sides at top) was substituted for one of the Wmk. 4 crowns which fell off the dandy roll. The non-matching crown occurs in 1950-52 printings in a horizontal row of crowns on certain regular stamps of Johore and Seychelles, and on various postage due stamps of Barbados, Basutoland, British Guiana, Gold Coast, Grenada, Northern Rhodesia, St. Lucia, Swaziland and Trinidad and Tobago. A variation of Wmk. 4a, with the non-matching crown in a horizontal row of crown-CA-crown, occurs on regular stamps of Bahamas, St. Kitts-Nevis and Singapore.

Wmk. 314 was intentionally used sideways, starting in 1966. When a stamp was issued with Wmk. 314 both upright and sideways, the sideways varieties usually are listed also – with minor numbers. In many of the later issues, Wmk. 314 is slightly visible.

Wmk. 373 is usually only faintly visible.

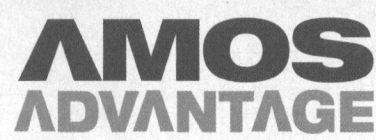

JAMAICA

jə-ˈmā-kə

LOCATION — Caribbean Sea, about 90 miles south of Cuba
GOVT. — Independent state in the British Commonwealth
AREA — 4,411 sq. mi.
POP. — 2,652,443 (1999 est.)
CAPITAL — Kingston

Jamaica became an independent state in the British Commonwealth in August 1962. As a colony, it administered two dependencies: Cayman Islands and Turks and Caicos Islands.

12 Pence = 1 Shilling
20 Shillings = 1 Pound
100 Cents = 1 Dollar (1969)

Catalogue values for unused stamps in this country are for Never Hinged items, beginning with Scott 129 in the regular postage section and Scott B4 in the semi-postal section.

Watermarks

Wmk. 45 — Pineapple

Wmk. 352 — J and Pineapple, Multiple

Values for unused stamps are for examples with original gum as defined in the catalogue introduction. Very fine examples of Nos. 1-12 will have perforations touching the design on at least one side due to the narrow spacing of the stamps on the plates. Stamps with perfs clear on all four sides are scarce and will command higher prices.

Queen Victoria
A1 A2

A3 A4

A5 A6

1860-63 Typo. Wmk. 45 *Perf. 14*

1	A1	1p blue	65.00	15.00
a.		Diagonal half used as ½p on cover		825.00
b.		1p deep blue	140.00	35.00
c.		1p pale blue	77.50	19.00
d.		1p pale greenish blue	100.00	24.00
2	A2	2p rose	160.00	65.00
a.		2p deep rose	240.00	65.00
3	A3	3p green ('63)	160.00	32.50
4	A4	4p brown org	250.00	62.50
a.		4p orange	250.00	27.50
5	A5	6p lilac	225.00	27.50
a.		6p deep lilac	1,050.	65.00
b.		6p gray lilac	350.00	40.00
6	A6	1sh brown	225.00	35.00
a.		1sh lilac brown	700.00	30.00
b.		1sh yellow brown	575.00	32.50

All except No. 3 exist imperforate.

1870-71 Wmk. 1

7	A1	1p blue	75.00	.90
8	A2	2p rose	80.00	.85
a.		2p brownish rose	100.00	1.10
9	A3	3p green	110.00	9.25
10	A4	4p brown org ('72)	210.00	12.00
a.		4p red orange	450.00	6.50
11	A5	6p lilac ('71)	75.00	6.00
12	A6	1sh brown ('73)	27.50	9.50
		Nos. 7-12 (6)	577.50	38.50

The 1p and 4p exist imperf.

See Nos. 17-23, 40, 43, 47-53.

A7 A8

A9 A10

1872, Oct. 29

13	A7	½p claret	16.00	3.75
a.		½p deep claret	19.00	6.00

Exists imperf. See No. 16.

1875, Aug. 27 *Perf. 12½*

14	A8	2sh red brown	45.00	21.00
15	A9	5sh violet	97.50	*150.00*

Exist imperf.

See Nos. 29-30, 44, 54.

1883-90 Wmk. 2 *Perf. 14*

16	A7	½p blue green ('85)	3.75	1.10
a.		½p gray green	1.10	.20
17	A1	1p blue ('84)	350.00	6.00
18	A1	1p carmine ('85)	50.00	.65
a.		1p rose	70.00	1.25
19	A2	2p rose ('84)	215.00	4.50
20	A2	2p slate ('85)	90.00	.65
a.		2p gray	125.00	5.00
21	A3	3p ol green ('86)	2.75	1.40
22	A4	4p red brown	2.25	.40
a.		4p orange brown	440.00	24.00
23	A5	6p orange yel ('90)	6.00	5.00
a.		6p yellow	26.00	8.00
		Nos. 16-23 (8)	719.75	19.70

Nos. 18 and 20 exist imperf. Perf. 12 stamps are considered to be proofs.

For surcharge, see No. 27.

1889-91

24	A10	1p lilac & red vio	5.00	.20
25	A10	2p deep green	12.00	6.50
a.		2p green	22.00	3.75
26	A10	2½p lilac & ultra ('91)	6.25	.75
		Nos. 24-26 (3)	23.25	*7.45*

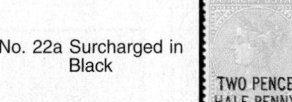

No. 22a Surcharged in Black

1890, June

27	A4	2½p on 4p org brn	37.50	12.00
b.		Double surcharge	350.00	250.00
d.		"PFNNY"	100.00	70.00
f.		As "d," double surcharge	—	

Three settings of surcharge.

1897

28	A6	1sh brown	5.75	*7.00*
29	A8	2sh red brown	32.50	24.00
30	A9	5sh violet	62.50	*92.50*
		Nos. 28-30 (3)	100.75	*123.50*

The 2sh exists imperf.

Llandovery Falls A12 | Arms of Jamaica A13

1900, May 1 Engr. Wmk. 1

31	A12	1p red	4.50	.30

1901, Sept. 25

32	A12	1p red & black	4.00	.25
a.		Pair, imperf. horiz.	10,000.	
b.		Bluish paper	120.00	110.00

1903-04 Typo. Wmk. 2

33	A13	½p green & black	1.75	.40
b.		"SERv ET" for "SERVIET"	45.00	*50.00*
34	A13	1p car & black ('04)	2.25	.20
b.		"SERv ET" for "SERVIET"	35.00	40.00
35	A13	2½p ultra & black	4.25	.45
a.		"SERv ET" for "SERVIET"	70.00	*85.00*
36	A13	5p yel & black ('04)	17.50	*26.00*
a.		"SERv ET" for "SERVIET"	850.00	*1,050.*
		Nos. 33-36 (4)	25.75	*27.05*

1905-11 Chalky Paper Wmk. 3

37	A13	½p green & black	5.00	.20
b.		"SERv ET" for "SERVIET"	32.50	*45.00*
38	A13	1p car & black	20.00	.55
39	A13	2½p ultra & blk ('07)	3.25	4.50
40	A4	4p black, *yel* ('10)	8.00	*45.00*
41	A13	5p yel & black ('07)	65.00	*75.00*
a.		"SERv ET" for "SERVIET"	1,200.	*1,400.*
42	A13	6p red vio & vio ('11)	14.00	13.00
43	A6	1sh black, *green* ('10)	4.75	*9.25*
44	A8	2sh vio, *blue* ('10)	7.00	3.75
45	A13	5sh vio & black	47.50	45.00
		Nos. 37-45 (9)	174.50	196.25

1905-11 Ordinary Paper

46	A13	2½p ultra ('10)	3.00	1.40
47	A3	3p sage green ('07)	6.50	4.00
a.		3p olive green ('07)	5.50	3.25
48	A3	3p pale purple, *yel* ('10)	5.00	3.75
a.		3p vio, *yel* ('10)	2.10	1.60
49	A4	4p red brn ('08)	75.00	80.00
50	A4	4p red, *yel* ('11)	1.60	*8.50*
51	A5	6p dull vio ('09)	30.00	*45.00*
52	A5	6p org yel ('09)	26.50	*55.00*
a.		6p orange ('06)	17.00	*27.50*
53	A6	1sh brown ('06)	20.00	*32.50*
54	A8	2sh red brn ('08)	110.00	*160.00*
		Nos. 46-54 (9)	277.60	*390.15*

Nos. 48 and 51 also come on chalky paper.

A14 A15

1906

58	A14	½p green	4.00	.25
a.		Booklet pane of 6	—	
59	A15	1p carmine	1.60	.20

For overprints see Nos. MR1, MR4, MR7, MR10.

Edward VII A16 | George V A17

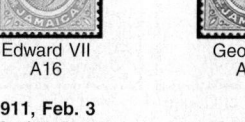

1911, Feb. 3

60	A16	2p gray	4.00	*15.00*

1912-20

61	A17	1p scarlet ('16)	2.50	.80
a.		1p carmine ('12)	1.75	.20
b.		Booklet pane of 6	—	
62	A17	1½p brown org ('16)	1.10	.70
a.		1½p yellow orange	15.00	1.25
63	A17	2p gray	2.25	*2.00*
64	A17	2½p dp br blue	.75	*1.25*
a.		2½p ultra ('13)	1.75	.20

Chalky Paper

65	A17	3p violet, *yel*	.60	.50
66	A17	4p scar & blk, *yel* ('13)	.60	*4.00*
67	A17	6p red vio & dl vio	4.00	2.50
68	A17	1sh black, *green*	2.60	2.25
a.		1sh blk, *bl grn*, olive back ('20)	2.60	*6.25*
69	A17	2sh ultra & vio, *blue* ('19)	15.00	*29.00*
70	A17	5sh scar & green, *yel* ('19)	77.50	*100.00*

Surface-colored Paper

71	A17	3p violet, *yel* ('13)	.65	.45
72	A17	4p scar & black, *yel* ('14)	1.00	*4.50*
73	A17	1sh black, *green* ('15)	2.00	*5.50*
		Nos. 61-73 (13)	110.55	*153.45*

See Nos. 101-102. For overprints see Nos. MR2-MR3, MR5-MR6, MR8-MR9, MR11.

Exhibition Buildings of 1891 — A18 | Arawak Woman Preparing Cassava — A19

World War I Contingent Embarking for Overseas Duty — A20

King's House, Spanish Town — A21 | Return of Overseas Contingent, 1919 — A22

Columbus Landing in Jamaica — A23 | Cathedral in Spanish Town — A24

Statue of Queen Victoria — A26

Memorial to Admiral Rodney — A27

Monument to Sir Charles Metcalfe — A28

Woodland Scene — A29

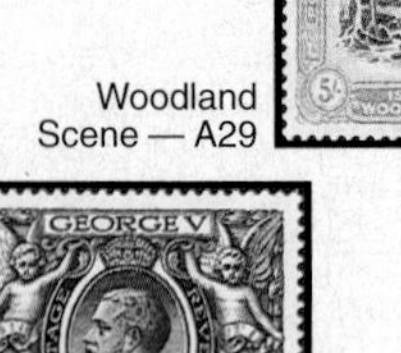
King George V — A30

1919-21 Typo. Wmk. 3 *Perf. 14*

Chalky Paper

No.	Type	Description	Unused	Used
75	A18	½p ol grn & dk grn ('20)	1.10	1.10
76	A19	1p org & car ('21)	2.40	2.00

Engr.

Ordinary Paper

No.	Type	Description	Unused	Used
77	A20	1½p green	.45	*1.10*
78	A21	2p grn & bl ('21)	1.25	*4.50*
79	A22	2½p blue & dk blue ('21)	15.00	3.50
80	A23	3p blue & grn ('21)	1.75	*2.75*
81	A24	4p green & dk brown ('21)	2.75	*10.00*
83	A26	1sh brt org & org ('20)	4.25	*9.00*
a.		Frame inverted	*27,500.*	*20,000.*
		As "a," revenue cancel		*3,000.*
84	A27	2sh brn & bl ('20)	15.00	*30.00*
85	A28	3sh org & violet ('20)	22.50	*92.50*
86	A29	5sh ocher & blue ('21)	62.50	*92.50*
87	A30	10sh dk myrtle grn ('20)	85.00	*175.00*
		Nos. 75-87 (12)	213.95	*423.95*

See note after No. 100.

A 6p stamp depicting the abolition of slavery was sent to the Colony but was not issued. "Specimen" copies exist with wmk. 3 or 4. Value $1,500 each.

Without "Specimen," value $24,000.

Port Royal in 1853 A31

1921-23 Typo. Wmk. 4 *Perf. 14*

Chalky Paper

No.	Type	Description	Unused	Used
88	A18	½p ol grn & dk grn ('22)	.60	.60
a.		Booklet pane of 4		
89	A19	1p orange & car ('22)	1.75	.20
a.		Booklet pane of 6		

Engr.

Ordinary Paper

No.	Type	Description	Unused	Used
90	A20	1½p green	1.50	.55
91	A21	2p grn & blue	7.50	.90
92	A22	2½p bl & dk bl	6.50	2.00
93	A23	3p bl & grn ('22)	2.75	.80
94	A24	4p grn & dk brn	1.10	.35
95	A31	6p bl & blk ('22)	15.00	2.25
96	A26	1sh brn org & dl org	2.00	.90
97	A27	2sh brn & bl ('22)	3.75	.75
98	A28	3sh org & violet	15.50	*11.00*
99	A29	5sh ocher & bl ('23)	35.00	29.00
a.		5sh orange & blue	32.50	26.00
100	A30	10sh dk myrtle green ('22)	60.00	80.00
		Nos. 88-100 (13)	152.95	129.30
		Set, never hinged	350.00	

No. 89 differs from No. 76 in having the words "Postage and Revenue" at the bottom.

On No. 79 the horizontal bar of the flag at the left has a broad white line below the colored line. On No. 92 this has been corrected and the broad white line placed above the colored line.

Watermark is sideways on #76-77, 87, 89-90.

Type of 1912-19 Issue

1921-27 Typo. Wmk. 4

No.	Type	Description	Unused	Used
101	A17	½p green ('27)	2.75	.20
a.		Booklet pane of 6		
102	A17	6p red vio & dl vio	11.50	4.50

No. 102 is on chalky paper.

A32

Type I

Type II

Type II — Cross shading beneath "Jamaica."

1929-32 Engr. *Perf. 13½x14, 14*

No.	Type	Description	Unused	Used
103	A32	1p red, type I	4.50	.20
a.		1p red, type II ('32)	7.00	.20
b.		Booklet pane of 6, type II		
104	A32	1½p brown	3.25	.20
105	A32	9p violet brown	4.50	1.25
		Nos. 103-105 (3)	12.25	1.65
		Set, never hinged	22.00	

The frames on Nos. 103 to 105 differ.

Coco Palms at Columbus Cove — A33

Scene near Castleton, St. Andrew — A34

Priestman's River, Portland Parish — A35

1932 *Perf. 12½*

No.	Type	Description	Unused	Used
106	A33	2p grn & gray blk	22.00	3.25
a.		Vertical pair, imperf. between	*6,500.*	
107	A34	2½p ultra & sl blue	5.25	1.75
a.		Vertical pair, imperf. between	*15,000.*	*15,000.*
108	A35	6p red vio & gray black	22.00	3.00
		Nos. 106-108 (3)	49.25	8.00
		Set, never hinged	70.00	

Common Design Types pictured following the introduction.

Silver Jubilee Issue

Common Design Type

1935, May 6 *Perf. 11x12*

No.	Type	Description	Unused	Used
109	CD301	1p car & blue	.55	.25
a.		Booklet pane of 6	*175.00*	
110	CD301	1½p black & ultra	.75	*1.75*
111	CD301	6p indigo & grn	8.00	*19.50*
112	CD301	1sh brn vio & ind	6.00	*12.00*
		Nos. 109-112 (4)	15.30	*33.50*
		Set, never hinged	25.00	

Coronation Issue

Common Design Type

1937, May 12 *Perf. 13½x14*

No.	Type	Description	Unused	Used
113	CD302	1p carmine	.20	.20
114	CD302	1½p gray black	.30	.30
115	CD302	2½p bright ultra	.45	*.65*
		Nos. 113-115 (3)	.95	1.15
		Set, never hinged	2.25	

King George VI — A36

Coco Palms at Columbus Cove — A37

Scene near Castleton, St. Andrew — A38

Bananas A39

Citrus Grove A40

Priestman's River, Portland Parish — A41

Kingston Harbor A42

Sugar Industry A43

Bamboo Walk — A44

Woodland Scene — A45

King George VI — A46

1938-51 *Perf. 13½x14*

No.	Type	Description	Unused	Used
116	A36	½p dk blue grn	1.40	.20
a.		Booklet pane of 6	9.00	
b.		Wmkd. sideways		
117	A36	1p carmine	1.00	.20
a.		Booklet pane of 6	13.00	
118	A36	1½p brown	1.00	.20

Perf. 12½, 13x13½, 13½x13, 12½x13

No.	Type	Description	Unused	Used
119	A37	2p grn & gray blk, perf. 12½	1.00	1.00
a.		Perf. 13x13½ ('39)	2.25	.60
b.		Perf. 12½x13 ('51)	1.00	.20
120	A38	2½p ultra & sl bl	2.25	*2.25*
121	A39	3p grn & lt ultra	.90	*1.75*
122	A40	4p grn & yel brn	.45	.20
123	A41	6p red vio & gray blk, perf. 13½x13 ('50)	2.00	.20
a.		Perf. 12½	5.50	.35
124	A42	9p rose lake	.55	.55
125	A43	1sh dk brn & brt grn	5.75	.25
126	A44	2sh brn & brt bl	20.00	1.25

Perf. 13, 14

No.	Type	Description	Unused	Used
127	A45	5sh ocher & bl, perf. 13 ('50)	5.50	4.25
a.		Bluish paper, perf. 13 ('49)	5.00	3.50
b.		Perf. 14	11.50	4.00
128	A46	10sh dk myrtle grn, perf. 14	9.00	*10.50*
a.		Perf. 13 ('50)	10.00	*8.00*
		Nos. 116-128 (13)	50.80	22.80
		Set, never hinged	100.00	

See Nos. 140, 148, 149, 152.

Catalogue values for unused stamps in this section, from this point to the end of the section, are for Never Hinged items.

Courthouse, Falmouth A47

Kings Charles II and George VI A48

House of Assembly, 1762-1869 A50

Institute of Jamaica — A49

Allegory of Labor and Learning — A51

Constitution and Flag of Jamaica A52

Perf. 12½

1945, Aug. 20 **Engr.** **Wmk. 4**
129 A47 1½p brown .20 .35
a. Booklet pane of 4 32.50
b. Perf. 12½x13½ ('46) 3.50 .60
130 A48 2p dp grn, perf. 12½x13½ .35 .55
a. Perf. 12½ 7.25 1.10
131 A49 3p bright ultra .20 *.55*
a. Perf. 13 ('46) 1.75 *3.25*
132 A50 4½p slate black .35 .35
a. Perf. 13 ('46) 2.40 *3.50*
133 A51 2sh chocolate .35 .55
134 A52 5sh deep blue 1.75 1.10
135 A49 10sh green 1.75 *2.60*
Nos. 129-135 (7) 4.95 6.05

Granting of a new Constitution in 1944.

Peace Issue
Common Design Type

1946, Oct. 14 **Wmk. 4** ***Perf. 13½***
136 CD303 1½p black brown .20 *1.50*
a. Perf. 13½x14 2.75 .20

Perf. 13½x14
137 CD303 3p deep blue 4.00 1.00
a. Perf. 13½ .60 *4.00*

Silver Wedding Issue
Common Design Types

1948, Dec. 1 **Photo.** ***Perf. 14x14½***
138 CD304 1½p red brown .35 .25

Engr.; Name Typo.
Perf. 11½x11
139 CD305 £1 red 30.00 *60.00*

Type of 1938 and

Tobacco Industry A53

1949, Aug. 15 **Engr.** ***Perf. 12½***
140 A39 3p ultra & slate blue 2.25 1.50
141 A53 £1 purple & brown 42.50 32.50

UPU Issue
Common Design Types
Perf. 13½, 11x11½

1949, Oct. 10 **Wmk. 4**
142 CD306 1½p red brown .20 .20
143 CD307 2p dark green 1.40 1.25
144 CD308 3p indigo .45 *.65*
145 CD309 6p rose violet .55 *1.25*
Nos. 142-145 (4) 2.60 3.35

University Issue
Common Design Types

1951, Feb. 16 ***Perf. 14x14½***
146 CD310 2p brown & gray blk .35 .25
147 CD311 6p rose lilac & gray blk .60 .35

George VI Type of 1938

1951, Oct. 25 ***Perf. 13½x14***
148 A36 ½p orange 1.40 .35
a. Booklet pane of 6 11.00
149 A36 1p blue green 2.25 .20
a. Booklet pane of 6 20.00

Boy Scout Emblem with Map — A54

Map and Emblem A55

Perf. 13½x13, 13x13½

952, Mar. 5 **Typo.** **Wmk. 4**
50 A54 2p blk, yel grn & blue .20 .20
51 A55 6p blk, yel grn & dk red .55 *.60*

1st Caribbean Boy Scout Jamboree, 1952.

Banana Type of 1938

1952, July 1 **Engr.** ***Perf. 12½***
152 A39 3p rose red & green 3.25 .40

Coronation Issue
Common Design Type

1953, June 2 ***Perf. 13½x13***
153 CD312 2p dk green & black .70 .20

Type of 1938 with Portrait of Queen Elizabeth II and Inscription: "ROYAL VISIT 1953"

1953, Nov. 25 ***Perf. 13***
154 A37 2p green & gray black .40 .20

Visit of Queen Elizabeth II and the Duke of Edinburgh, 1953.

Warship off Port Royal A56

Designs: 2½p, Old Montego Bay. 3p, Old Kingston. 6p, Proclaiming abolition of slavery.

1955, May 10 **Engr.** ***Perf. 12x12½***
Center in Black
155 A56 2p olive green .40 .20
156 A56 2½p light ultra .25 .25
157 A56 3p deep plum .25 .20
158 A56 6p rose red .25 .20
Nos. 155-158 (4) 1.15 .85

300th anniv. of Jamaica's establishment as a British territory.

Palm Trees — A57

Blue Mountain Peak — A58

Arms of Jamaica — A59

Arms of Jamaica — A60

1p, Sugar cane. 2p, Pineapple. 2½p, Bananas. 3p, Mahoe flower. 4p, Breadfruit. 5p, Ackee fruit. 6p, Streamer (hummingbird). 1sh, Royal Botanic Gardens, Hope. 1sh6p, Rafting on the Rio Grande. 2sh, Fort Charles.

1956 **Wmk. 4** ***Perf. 12½***
159 A57 ½p org ver & black .20 .20
a. Booklet pane of 6 .30
160 A57 1p emer & blk .20 .20
a. Booklet pane of 6 .50
161 A57 2p rose red & blk .20 .20
a. Booklet pane of 6 .85
162 A57 2½p lt ultra & black .75 .55
a. Booklet pane of 6 4.50
163 A57 3p brown & green .25 .20
164 A57 4p dk blue & ol grn .25 .20
165 A57 5p ol green & car .25 2.75
166 A57 6p car & blk 2.50 .20

Perf. 13½
167 A58 8p red org & brt ultra .40 .20
168 A58 1sh blue & yel grn 1.25 .20
169 A58 1sh6p dp cl & ultra 1.00 .20
170 A58 2sh ol grn & ultra 9.00 2.50

Perf. 11½
171 A59 3sh blue & black 1.75 *2.50*
172 A59 5sh carmine & blk 4.25 *5.50*
173 A60 10sh blue grn & blk 32.50 *20.00*
174 A60 £1 purple & blk 32.50 *20.00*
Nos. 159-174 (16) 87.25 55.60

For overprints see Nos. 185-196. For types overprinted see Nos. 208-216.

West Indies Federation
Common Design Type
Perf. 11½x11

1958, Apr. 22 **Engr.** **Wmk. 314**
175 CD313 2p green .65 .20
176 CD313 5p blue 1.25 *2.50*
177 CD313 6p carmine rose 1.25 .45
Nos. 175-177 (3) 3.15 3.15

Britannia Plane over 1860 Packet Boat A61

1sh Stamps of 1860 and 1956 — A62

6p, Victorian post cart and mail truck.

1960, Jan. 4 ***Perf. 13x13½***
178 A61 2p lilac & blue .55 .20
179 A61 6p ol grn & car rose .55 .40

Perf. 13
180 A62 1sh blue, yel grn & brn .55 .50
Nos. 178-180 (3) 1.65 1.10

Centenary of Jamaican postal service.

Independent State

Zouave Bugler and Map of Jamaica A63

1sh6p, Gordon House (Legislature) & hands of three races holding banner. 5sh, Map & symbols of agriculture & industry.

1962, Aug. 8 **Photo.** ***Perf. 13***
181 A63 2p multicolored 1.00 .20
182 A63 4p multicolored 1.00 .20
a. Yellow omitted
183 A63 1sh6p red, black & brn 3.50 1.00
184 A63 5sh multicolored 4.50 *4.00*
Nos. 181-184 (4) 10.00 5.40

Issue of 1956 Overprinted:

a

b

Perf. 12½

1962, Aug. 8 **Wmk. 4** **Engr.**
185 A57(a) ½p org ver & blk .20 *1.00*
186 A57(a) 1p emer & blk .20 .20
187 A57(a) 2½p lt ultra & blk .20 *1.50*
188 A57(b) 3p brn & grn .20 .20
189 A57(b) 5p ol grn & car .25 *.80*
190 A57(b) 6p car & black 3.00 .20

Perf. 13½
191 A58(b) 8p red org & brt ultra .30 .20
192 A58(b) 1sh bl & yel grn .30 .20
193 A58(b) 2sh ol green & ultra 1.25 *1.75*

Perf. 11½
194 A59(a) 3sh blue & blk 1.40 *1.75*
195 A60(a) 10sh bl grn & blk 4.00 *5.00*
196 A60(a) £1 pur & black 4.00 *6.00*
Nos. 185-196 (12) 15.30 *18.80*

Nos. 181-196 issued to commemorate Jamaica's independence.

"Independence" measures 17½x1½mm on #185-187; 18x1mm on #194-196.
See Nos. 208-216.

Weight Lifting, Soccer, Boxing and Cycling A64

Designs: 6p, Various water sports. 8p, Running and jumping. 2sh, Arms and runner.

Perf. 14½x14

1962, Aug. 11 **Photo.** **Wmk. 314**
197 A64 1p car & dk brown .20 .20
198 A64 6p blue & brown .20 .20
199 A64 8p olive & dk brown .25 .20
200 A64 2sh multicolored .45 *.55*
Nos. 197-200 (4) 1.10 1.15

IX Central American and Caribbean Games, Kingston, Aug. 11-25.

A souvenir sheet containing one each of Nos. 197-200, imperf., was sold exclusively by National Sports, Ltd., at 5sh (face 3sh3p). The Jamaican Post Office sold the entire issue of this sheet to National Sports at face value, plus the printing cost. The stamps are postally valid. The sheet has marginal inscriptions and simulated perforations in ultramarine. Value $14.

Freedom from Hunger Issue

Man Planting Mango Tree and Produce A65

Perf. 12½

1963, June 4 **Unwmk.** **Litho.**
201 A65 1p blue & multi .30 .20
202 A65 8p rose & multi .80 .60

See note after CD314, Common Design section.

Red Cross Centenary Issue
Common Design Type

1963, Sept. 2 **Wmk. 314** ***Perf. 13***
203 CD315 2p black & red .25 .20
204 CD315 1sh6p ultra & red .75 1.00

Carole Joan Crawford — A66

Unwmk.

1964, Feb. 14 **Photo.** ***Perf. 13***
205 A66 3p multicolored .30 .20
206 A66 1sh olive & multi .50 .20
207 A66 1sh6p multicolored .80 .80
a. Souvenir sheet of 3 2.75 2.75
Nos. 205-207 (3) 1.60 1.20

Carole Joan Crawford, Miss World, 1963.
No. 207a contains one each of Nos. 205-207 with simulated perforations. Issued May 25. Sold for 4sh.

Types of 1956 Overprinted like 1962 Independence Issue

Wmk. 314

1963-64 **Engr.** ***Perf. 12½***
208 A57(a) ½p org ver & blk .20 .20
209 A57(a) 1p emer & blk ('64) .20 *1.75*
210 A57(a) 2½p lt ultra & blk ('64) .55 *3.00*
211 A57(b) 3p brn & grn .30 .20
212 A57(b) 5p ol grn & car ('64) .85 *3.00*

Perf. 13½
213 A58(b) 8p red org & brt ultra ('64) .50 *.90*
214 A58(b) 1sh bl & yel grn .75 .75
215 A58(b) 2sh ol grn & ultra ('64) 1.25 *7.50*

Perf. 11½

216 A59(a) 3sh bl & blk ('64) 4.00 *5.25*
Nos. 208-216 (9) 8.60 22.55

Overprint is at bottom on Nos. 214-215, at top on Nos. 192-193.

Lignum Vitae, National Flower, and Map — A67

1½p, Ackee, national fruit, and map. 2p, Blue Mahoe, national tree, and map, vert. 2½p, Land shells (snails). 3p, Flag over map. 4p, Murex antillarum, sea shell. 6p, Papilio homerus. 8p, Streamer (hummingbird). 9p, Gypsum industry. 1sh, Stadium and statue of runner. 1sh6p, Palisadoes International Airport. 2sh, Bauxite mining. 3sh, Blue marlin and boat. 5sh, Port Royal exploration of sunken city, map, ship and artifacts. 10sh, Coat of arms, vert. £1, Flag and Queen Elizabeth II.

Perf. 14½, 14x14½

1964, May 4 Photo. Wmk. 352
Size: 26x22mm, 22x26mm

217 A67 1p bis, vio bl & green .20 .20
a. Booklet pane of 6 .35
218 A67 1½p multicolored .20 .20
219 A67 2p multicolored .20 .20
a. Booklet pane of 6 .85
220 A67 2½p multicolored 1.10 .65
221 A67 3p emer, yel & black .20 .20
a. Booklet pane of 6 3.00
222 A67 4p violet & buff .55 .20
223 A67 6p multicolored 2.50 .20
a. Ultramarine omitted 70.00
224 A67 8p multicolored 2.75 1.75
a. Red omitted 140.00

Perf. 14½x14, 13½x14½, 14x14½

Size: 32x26mm, 26x32mm

225 A67 9p blue & yel 1.75 .35
226 A67 1sh yel brn & blk .25 .20
a. Yellow brown omitted 800.00
b. Black omitted 875.00
227 A67 1sh6p sl, buff & bl 4.50 .20
228 A67 2sh bl, brn red & black 3.00 .35
229 A67 3sh grn, saph & dk bl, perf. 14½x14 .50 .70
a. Perf. 14x14½ 1.75 1.25
230 A67 5sh bl, blk & bis 1.40 1.25
231 A67 10sh multicolored 1.40 1.50
a. Blue ("Jamaica" etc.) omitted 300.00
232 A67 £1 multicolored 2.00 1.25
Nos. 217-232 (16) 22.50 9.40

See Nos. 306-318. For overprints & surcharges see Nos. 248-251, 279-291, 305.

Scout Hat, Globe, Neckerchief — A68

Scout Emblem, American Crocodile — A69

Design: 3p, Scout belt buckle.

Perf. 14½x14, 14

1964, Aug. 27 Wmk. 352

233 A68 3p pink, black & red .20 .20
234 A68 8p ultra, black & olive .20 .20
235 A69 1sh ultra & gold .25 .35
Nos. 233-235 (3) .65 .75

6th Inter-American Scout Conference, Kingston, Aug. 25-29.

Gordon House, Kingston, and Commonwealth Parliamentary Association Emblem — A70

6p, Headquarters House, Kingston. 1sh6p, House of Assembly, Spanish Town.

1964, Nov. 16 Photo. ***Perf. 14½x14***

236 A70 3p yel green & blk .20 .20
237 A70 6p red & black .20 .20
238 A70 1sh6p ultra & black .25 .25
Nos. 236-238 (3) .65 .65

10th Commonwealth Parliamentary Conf.

Eleanor Roosevelt — A71

1964, Dec. 10 Wmk. 352

239 A71 1sh lt green, blk & red .25 .20

Eleanor Roosevelt (1884-1962) on the 16th anniv. of the Universal Declaration of Human Rights.

Map of Jamaica and Girl Guide Emblem — A72

Girl Guide Emblems — A73

Perf. 14x14½, 14

1965, May 17 Photo. Wmk. 352

240 A72 3p lt blue, yel & yel grn .20 .20
241 A73 1sh lt yel grn, blk & bis .25 .30

50th anniv. of the Girl Guides of Jamaica.

Salvation Army Cap — A74

1sh6p, Flag bearer, drummer, globe, vert.

Perf. 14x14½, 14½x14

1965, Aug. 23 Photo. Wmk. 352

242 A74 3p dp blue, yel, mar & blk .25 .20
243 A74 1sh6p emerald & multi .55 .40

Centenary of the Salvation Army.

Paul Bogle, William Gordon and Morant Bay Court House A75

1965, Dec. 29 Unwmk. ***Perf. 14x13***

244 A75 3p vio blue, blk & brn .20 .20
245 A75 1sh6p yel green, blk & brn .25 .20
246 A75 3sh pink & brown .40 *.60*
Nos. 244-246 (3) .85 1.00

Cent. of the Morant Bay rebellion against governor John Eyre.

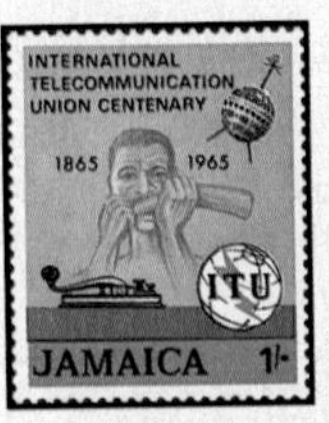

ITU Emblem, Telstar, Telegraph Key and Man Blowing Horn — A76

Perf. 14x14½

1965, Dec. 29 Photo. Wmk. 352

247 A76 1sh gray, black & red .45 .25

Cent. of the ITU.

Nos. 221, 223, 226-227 Overprinted: "ROYAL VISIT / MARCH 1966"

Perf. 14½, 14½x14

1966, Mar. 3 Photo. Wmk. 352
Size: 26x22mm

248 A67 3p emer, yel & black .30 .20
249 A67 6p multicolored 2.75 .35

Size: 32x26mm

250 A67 1sh yel brown & blk .90 .20
251 A67 1sh6p slate, buff & blue 4.00 2.25
Nos. 248-251 (4) 7.95 3.00

See note after Antigua No. 162.

Winston Churchill A77

1966, Apr. 18 ***Perf. 14, 14x14½***

252 A77 6p olive green & gray .60 .35
253 A77 1sh violet & sepia .95 .95

Sir Winston Leonard Spencer Churchill (1874-1965), statesman and WWII leader.

Runner, Flags of Jamaica, Great Britain and Games' Emblem A78

Designs: 6p, Bicyclists and waterfall. 1sh, Stadium. 3sh, Games' Emblem.

Perf. 14½x14

1966, Aug. 4 Photo. Wmk. 352

254 A78 3p multicolored .25 .20
255 A78 6p multicolored .40 .20
256 A78 1sh multicolored .25 .20
257 A78 3sh gold & dk vio blue .40 .45
a. Souvenir sheet of 4 6.50 6.50
Nos. 254-257 (4) 1.30 1.05

8th British Empire and Commonwealth Games, Aug. 4-13, 1966.

No. 257a contains 4 imperf. stamps with simulated perforations similar to Nos. 254-257. Issued Aug. 25, 1966.

Bolivar Statue, Kingston, Flags of Jamaica and Venezuela — A79

1966, Dec. 5 ***Perf. 14x14½***

258 A79 8p multicolored .40 .20

150th anniv. of the "Bolivar Letter," written by Simon Bolivar, while in exile in Jamaica.

Jamaican Pavilion — A80

1967, Apr. 28 ***Perf. 14½x14***

259 A80 6p multicolored .20 .20
260 A80 1sh multicolored .20 .20

EXPO '67 Intl. Exhibition, Montreal, Apr. 28-Oct. 27.

Donald Burns Sangster — A81

Perf. 13x13½

1967, Aug. 28 Unwmk.

261 A81 3p multicolored .20 .20
262 A81 1sh6p multicolored .25 .25

Sir Donald Burns Sangster (1911-1967), Prime Minister.

Traffic Police and Post Office A82

Designs: 1sh, Officers representing various branches of police force in front of Police Headquarters. 1sh6p, Constable, 1867, Old House of Assembly, and 1967 constable with New House of Assembly.

Perf. 13½x14

1967, Nov. 28 Photo. Wmk. 352
Size: 42x25mm

263 A82 3p red brown & multi .50 .20

Size: 56½x20½mm

Perf. 13½x14½

264 A82 1sh yellow & multi .50 .20

Size: 42x25mm

Perf. 13½x14

265 A82 1sh6p gray & multi .80 .90
Nos. 263-265 (3) 1.80 1.30

Centenary of the Constabulary Force.

A Human Rights set of three (3p, 1sh, 3sh) was prepared and announced for release on Jan. 2, 1968. The Crown Agents distributed sample sets, but the stamps were not issued. On Dec. 3, Nos. 271-273 were issued instead. Designs of the unissued set show bowls of food, an abacus and praying hands. Value, $160.

Wicketkeeper, Emblem of West Indies Cricket Team — A82a

Designs: No. 266, Wicketkeeper and emblem of West Indies Cricket Team. No. 267, Batsman and emblem of Marylebone Cricket Club. No. 268, Bowler and emblem of West Indies Cricket Team.

1968, Feb. 8 Photo. *Perf. 14*

266	A82a	6p multicolored	.35	*.40*
267	A82a	6p multicolored	.35	*.40*
268	A82a	6p multicolored	.35	*.40*
a.		Horiz. strip of 3, #266-268	1.75	1.75
		Nos. 266-268 (3)	1.05	1.20

Visit of the Marylebone Cricket Club to the West Indies, Jan.-Feb. 1968.

Sir Alexander and Lady Bustamante — A83

1968, May 23 *Perf. 14½*

269	A83	3p brt rose & black	.25	.20
270	A83	1sh olive green & black	.25	.20

Labor Day, May 23, 1968.

Human Rights Flame and Map of Jamaica A84

Designs: 1sh, Hands shielding Human Rights flame, vert. 3sh, Man kneeling on Map of Jamaica, and Human Rights flame.

1968, Dec. 3 Wmk. 352 *Perf. 14½*

271	A84	3p multicolored	.30	.20
a.		Gold (flame) omitted	110.00	
272	A84	1sh multicolored	.30	.20
273	A84	3sh multicolored	.50	.30
a.		Gold (flame) omitted	130.00	
		Nos. 271-273 (3)	1.10	.70

International Human Rights Year.

ILO Emblem A85

Unwmk.

1969, May 23 Litho. *Perf. 14*

274	A85	6p black & orange yel	.20	.20
275	A85	3sh black & brt green	.30	.30

50th anniv. of the ILO.

WHO Emblem, Children and Nurse — A86

Designs: 1sh, Malaria eradication, horiz. 3sh, Student nurses.

1969, May 30 Photo. *Perf. 14*

276	A86	6p org, black & brown	.20	.20
277	A86	1sh blue grn, blk & brn	.20	.20
278	A86	3sh ultra, black & brn	.25	*.40*
		Nos. 276-278 (3)	.65	.80

WHO, 20th anniv.

Nos. 217-219, 221-223, 225-232 Surcharged with New Value and: "C-DAY 8th SEPTEMBER 1969"

1969, Sept. 8 Wmk. 352 *Perf. 14½*

Size: 26x22mm, 22x26mm

279	A67	1c on 1p multi	.20	.20
280	A67	2c on 2p multi	.20	.20
281	A67	3c on 3p multi	.20	.20
282	A67	4c on 4p multi	1.40	.20
283	A67	5c on 6p multi	1.40	.20
a.		Blue (wing dots) omitted	*70.00*	

Perf. 14½x14, 13½x14½, 14x14½

Size: 32x26mm, 26x32mm

284	A67	8c on 9p multi	.20	.20
285	A67	10c on 1sh multi	.20	.20
286	A67	15c on 1sh6p multi	.55	*1.00*
287	A67	20c on 2sh multi	1.75	*2.00*
288	A67	30c on 3sh multi	2.25	*3.00*
289	A67	50c on 5sh multi	1.40	*3.25*
290	A67	$1 on 10sh multi	1.40	*7.00*
291	A67	$2 on £1 multi	1.40	*7.00*
		Nos. 279-291 (13)	12.55	24.65

Introduction of decimal currency.

The old denomination is obliterated by groups of small rectangles on the 1c and 3c, and with a square on the 2c, 4c and 8c; old denominations not obliterated on others.

Madonna and Child with St. John, by Raphael — A87

Christmas (Paintings): 2c, The Adoration of the Kings, by Vincenzo Foppa. 8c, The Adoration of the Kings, by Dosso Dossi.

1969, Oct. 25 Litho. *Perf. 13*

292	A87	2c vermilion & multi	.20	.30
293	A87	5c multicolored	.25	.30
294	A87	8c orange & multi	.25	.30
		Nos. 292-294 (3)	.70	.90

First Jamaica Penny — A88

Design: 3c, First Jamaica halfpenny.

1969, Oct. 27 *Perf. 12x12½*

295	A88	3c brt pink, blk & silver	.20	.20
296	A88	15c emerald, blk & silver	.20	.20

Centenary of the first Jamaican coinage.

George William Gordon — A89

Crucifixion, by Antonello da Messina — A90

Portraits: 3c, Sir Alexander Bustamante (1884-1977). 5c, Norman W. Manley (1893-1969). 10c, Marcus M. Garvey (1887-1940). 15c, Paul Bogle (1820-1865).

Perf. 12x12½

1970, Mar. 11 Photo. Unwmk.

297	A89	1c lt violet & multi	.20	.20
298	A89	3c lt blue & multi	.20	.20
299	A89	5c lt gray & multi	.20	.20
300	A89	10c pale rose & multi	.20	.20
301	A89	15c pale green & multi	.25	.25
		Nos. 297-301 (5)	1.05	1.05

National heroes connected with Jamaica's independence.

1970, Mar. 23

Easter: 3c, Christ Appearing to St. Peter, by Annibale Carracci. 20c, Easter lily.

302	A90	3c pink & multi	.20	.20
303	A90	10c gray green & multi	.20	.20
304	A90	20c gray & multi	.25	*.50*
		Nos. 302-304 (3)	.65	.90

No. 219 Surcharged

1970, July 16 Wmk. 352 *Perf. 14½*

305	A67	2c on 2p multicolored	.40	.30

Type of Regular Issue, 1964 Values in Cents and Dollars

Designs: 1c, Lignum vitae and map. 2c, Blue mahoe and map, vert. 3c, Flag over map. 4c, Murex antillarum, sea shell. 5c, Papilio homerus. 8c, Gypsum industry. 10c, Stadium and statue of runner. 15c, Palisadoes International Airport. 20c, Bauxite mining. 30c, Blue marlin and boat. 50c, Port Royal exploration of sunken city, map, ship and artifacts. $1, Coat of arms, vert. $2, Flag and Queen Elizabeth II.

1970 Wmk. 352 Photo. *Perf. 14½*

Size: 26x22mm, 22x26mm

306	A67	1c bister & multi	.85	*1.00*
307	A67	2c gray grn & multi	.35	.20
308	A67	3c emer, yel & black	.55	*.80*
309	A67	4c violet & buff	3.00	.35
310	A67	5c green & multi	3.50	.70

Perf. 14½x14, 13½x14½, 14x14½

Size: 32x26mm, 26x32mm

311	A67	8c blue & yellow	2.50	.20
312	A67	10c yel brn & black	.70	.25
313	A67	15c multicolored	3.00	3.00
314	A67	20c multicolored	1.40	*3.00*
315	A67	30c multicolored	4.50	*6.75*
316	A67	50c multicolored	1.40	*4.00*
317	A67	$1 multicolored	1.25	*5.75*
318	A67	$2 multicolored	1.50	*4.25*
		Nos. 306-318 (13)	24.50	30.25

Issued: #306-312, 9/7; #313-318, 11/2.

Bright's Cable Gear on "Dacia" A91

Designs: 3c, Telegraph cable ship "Dacia." 50c, Double current Morse key, 1870, and map of Jamaica.

1970, Oct. 12 Litho. *Perf. 14½*

319	A91	3c red orange & multi	.20	.20
320	A91	10c blue green & multi	.25	.20
321	A91	50c emerald & multi	1.25	1.25
		Nos. 319-321 (3)	1.70	1.65

Centenary of telegraph service.

Bananas, Citrus Fruit, Sugar Cane and Tobacco — A92

1970, Nov. 2 Wmk. 352 *Perf. 14*

322	A92	2c brown & multi	.20	.20
323	A92	10c black & multi	.35	.35

Jamaica Agricultural Society, 75th anniv.

"The Projector," 1845 — A93

Locomotives: 15c, Engine 54, 1944. 50c, Engine 102, 1967.

1970, Nov. 21 Litho. *Perf. 13½*

324	A93	3c green & multi	.20	.20
325	A93	15c org brown & multi	1.00	1.00
326	A93	50c multicolored	3.50	3.50
		Nos. 324-326 (3)	4.70	4.70

125th anniv. of the Jamaican railroad.

Kingston Cathedral — A94

30c, Arms of Jamaica Bishopric. 10c, 20c, like 3c.

1971, Feb. 22 *Perf. 14½*

327	A94	3c lt green & multi	.20	.20
328	A94	10c dull orange & multi	.20	.20
329	A94	20c ultra & multi	.40	.40
330	A94	30c gray & multi	.60	.60
		Nos. 327-330 (4)	1.40	1.40

Centenary of the disestablishment of the Church of England.

Henry Morgan, Ships in Port Royal Harbor A95

Designs: 15c, Mary Read, Anne Bonny and pamphlet on their trial. 30c, 18th century merchantman surrendering to pirate schooner.

1971, May 10 Litho. Wmk. 352

331	A95	3c red brown & multi	1.25	.20
332	A95	15c gray & multi	1.75	.50
333	A95	30c lilac & multi	2.75	1.75
		Nos. 331-333 (3)	5.75	2.45

Pirates and buccaneers.

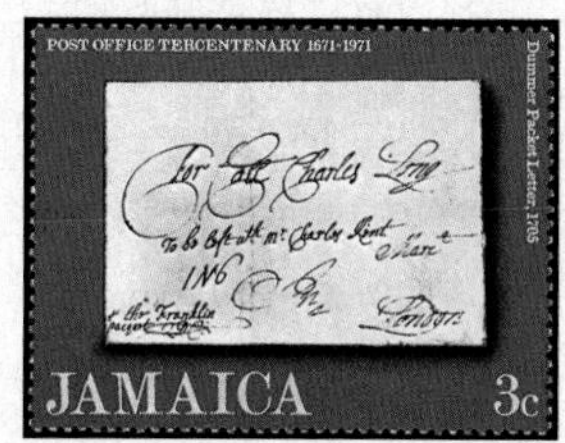

Dummer Packet Letter, 1705 — A96

Designs: 5c, Stampless cover, 1793. 8c, Post office, Kingston, 1820. 10c, Modern date cancellation on No. 312. 20c, Cover with stamps of Great Britain and Jamaica cancellations, 1859. 50c, Jamaica No. 83a, vert.

1971, Oct. 30 *Perf. 13½*

334	A96	3c dk carmine & black	.20	.20
335	A96	5c lt ol grn & black	.20	.20
336	A96	8c purple & black	.20	.20
337	A96	10c slate, black & brn	.25	.25
338	A96	20c multicolored	.50	.50
339	A96	50c dk gray, blk & org	1.25	1.25
		Nos. 334-339 (6)	2.60	2.60

Tercentenary of Jamaica Post Office.

Earth Station and Satellite — A97

1972, Feb. 17 *Perf. 14x13½*

340 A97	3c red & multi		.20	.20
341 A97	15c gray & multi		.40	.40
342 A97	50c multicolored		1.10	1.10
	Nos. 340-342 (3)		1.70	1.70

Jamaica's earth satellite station.

Bauxite Industry — A98

National Stadium A99

Perf. 14½x14, 14x14½

1972-79 **Litho.** **Wmk. 352**

343 A98	1c Pimento, vert.	.20	.20
344 A98	2c Red ginger, vert.	.20	.20
345 A98	3c shown	.20	.20
346 A98	4c Kingston harbor	.20	.20
347 A98	5c Oil refinery	.20	.20
348 A98	6c Senate Building, Univ. of the West Indies	.20	.20

Perf. 13½

349 A99	8c shown	.40	.20
350 A99	9c Devon House, Hope Road	.20	.20
351 A99	10c Stewardess and Air Jamaica plane	.25	.20
352 A99	15c Old Iron Bridge, vert.	2.50	.20
353 A99	20c College of Arts, Science & Technology	.35	.20
354 A99	30c Dunn's River Falls, vert.	.70	.20
355 A99	50c River raft	2.00	.50
356 A99	$1 Jamaica House	1.00	*1.50*
357 A99	$2 Kings House	1.10	*1.50*

Perf. 14½x14

Size: 37x26½mm

358 A99	$5 Map and arms of Jamaica ('79)	1.75	1.75
	Nos. 343-358 (16)	11.45	7.65

For overprints see Nos. 360-362, 451.

Nos. 345, 351, 355 Overprinted: "TENTH ANNIVERSARY INDEPENDENCE 1962-1972"

1972, Aug. 8 *Perf. 14½x14, 13½*

360 A98	3c multicolored	.20	.20
361 A99	10c multicolored	.20	.20
362 A99	50c multicolored	.95	.95
	Nos. 360-362 (3)	1.35	1.35

Arms of Kingston — A100

Design: 5c, 30c, Arms of Kingston, vert.

1972, Dec. 4 *Perf. 13½x14, 14x13½*

363 A100	5c pink & multi	.25	.20
364 A100	30c lemon & multi	.40	.25
365 A100	50c lt blue & multi	.60	*.75*
	Nos. 363-365 (3)	1.25	1.20

Centenary of Kingston as capital.

Mongoose and Map of Jamaica A101

40c, Mongoose & rat. 60c, Mongoose & chicken.

Perf. 14x14½

1973, Apr. 9 **Litho.** **Wmk. 352**

366 A101	8c yel green & blk	.20	.20
367 A101	40c blue & black	.85	.85
368 A101	60c salmon & black	1.60	1.60
a.	Souvenir sheet of 3, #366-368	3.75	3.75
	Nos. 366-368 (3)	2.65	2.65

Centenary of the introduction of the mongoose to Jamaica.

Euphorbia Punicea — A102

Flowers: 6c, Hylocereus triangularis. 9c, Columnea argentea. 15c, Portlandia grandiflora. 30c, Samyda pubescens. 50c, Cordia sebestena.

1973, July 9 *Perf. 14*

369 A102	1c dp green & multi	.25	.20
370 A102	6c vio blue & multi	.35	.20
371 A102	9c orange & multi	.45	.30
372 A102	15c brown & multi	.65	.45
373 A102	30c olive & multi	1.25	1.25
374 A102	50c multicolored	1.90	*2.25*
	Nos. 369-374 (6)	4.85	4.65

Broughtonia Sanguinea — A103

Orchids: 10c, Arpophyllum jamaicense, vert. 20c, Oncidium pulchellum, vert. $1, Brassia maculata.

1973, Oct. 8 *Perf. 14x13½, 13½x14*

375 A103	5c multicolored	.60	.25
376 A103	10c multicolored	.80	.25
377 A103	20c slate & multi	2.00	.50
378 A103	$1 ultra & multi	4.00	*4.50*
a.	Souv. sheet of 4, #375-378, perf 12	8.00	8.00
	Nos. 375-378 (4)	7.40	5.50

Mailboat "Mary" (1808-1815) — A104

Designs: Mailboats.

Perf. 13½ (5c, 50c), 14½ (10c, 15c)

1974, Apr. 8 **Wmk. 352**

379 A104	5c shown	.95	.20
a.	Perf. 14½	2.50	1.25
380 A104	10c "Queensbury" (1814-27)	.95	.35
381 A104	15c "Sheldrake" (1829-34)	1.25	.55
382 A104	50c "Thames" (1842)	2.75	2.75
a.	Souv. sheet of 4, #379-382, perf 13½	6.50	6.50
	Nos. 379-382 (4)	5.90	3.85

Jamaican Dancers — A105

Designs: Dancers.

1974, Aug. 1 **Litho.** *Perf. 13½*

383 A105	5c green & multi	.20	.20
384 A105	10c black & multi	.20	.20
385 A105	30c brown & multi	.50	.40
386 A105	50c lilac & multi	.75	.65
a.	Souvenir sheet of 4, #383-386	3.00	3.00
	Nos. 383-386 (4)	1.65	1.45

National Dance Theatre.

Globe, Letter, UPU Emblem A106

1974, Oct. 9 *Perf. 14*

387 A106	5c plum & multi	.20	.20
388 A106	9c olive & multi	.20	.20
389 A106	50c multicolored	.85	.85
	Nos. 387-389 (3)	1.25	1.25

Centenary of Universal Postal Union.

Senate Building and Sir Hugh Wooding A107

10c, 50c, Chapel & Princess Alice. 30c, like 5c.

1975, Jan. 13 **Wmk. 352**

390 A107	5c yellow & multi	.20	.20
391 A107	10c salmon & multi	.20	.20
392 A107	30c dull orange & multi	.35	.35
393 A107	50c multicolored	.60	.60
	Nos. 390-393 (4)	1.35	1.35

University College of the West Indies, 25th anniversary.

Commonwealth Symbol — A108

Commonwealth Symbol and: 10c, Arms of Jamaica. 30c, Dove of peace. 50c, Jamaican flag.

1975, Apr. 29 **Litho.** *Perf. 13½*

394 A108	5c buff & multi	.20	.20
395 A108	10c rose & multi	.20	.20
396 A108	30c violet blue & multi	.40	.40
397 A108	50c multicolored	.60	.60
	Nos. 394-397 (4)	1.40	1.40

Commonwealth Heads of Government Conference, Jamaica, Apr.-May.

Graphium Marcellinus A109

Koo Koo, "Actor-boy" A110

Butterflies: 20c, Papilio thoas melonius. 25c, Papilio thersites. 30c, Papilio homerus.

1975, Aug. 25 **Litho.** *Perf. 14*

398 A109	10c lt green & multi	1.90	.40
399 A109	20c lt green & multi	1.90	1.40
400 A109	25c lt green & multi	2.60	*2.75*
401 A109	30c lt green & multi	3.00	*3.75*
a.	Souvenir sheet of 4, #398-401	10.00	10.00
	Nos. 398-401 (4)	9.40	*8.30*

See Nos. 423-426, 435-438.

1975, Nov. 3 **Litho.** **Wmk. 352**

Christmas: 10c, Red "set-girls." 20c, French "set-girls." 50c, Jawbone or "House John Canoe." Festival dancers drawn by I. M. Belisario in Kingston, 1837.

402 A110	8c multicolored	.20	.20
403 A110	10c olive & multi	.20	.20
404 A110	20c ultra & multi	.40	.40
405 A110	50c multicolored	1.10	1.40
a.	Souv. sheet of 4, #402-405, perf. 13½	2.75	2.75
	Nos. 402-405 (4)	1.90	2.20

See Nos. 416-418.

Map of Jamaica, by Benedetto Bordone, 1528 — A111

Maps of Jamaica by: 20c, Tommaso Porcacchi, 1576. 30c, Theodor DeBry, 1594. 50c, Barent Langenes, 1598.

1976, Mar. 12 *Perf. 13½x14*

406 A111	10c brown, buff & red	.35	.20
407 A111	20c bister & multi	.65	.40
408 A111	30c lt blue & multi	.90	.90
409 A111	50c multicolored	1.40	*1.75*
	Nos. 406-409 (4)	3.30	3.25

See Nos. 419-422.

Olympic Rings — A112

1976, June 14 **Litho.** *Perf. 13½x14*

410 A112	10c black & multi	.20	.20
411 A112	20c blue & multi	.30	.30
412 A112	25c red & multi	.40	.40
413 A112	50c green & multi	.70	.70
	Nos. 410-413 (4)	1.60	1.60

21st Olympic Games, Montreal, Canada, July 17-Aug. 1.

Map of West Indies, Bats, Wicket and Ball A112a

Prudential Cup — A112b

1976, Aug. 9 Unwmk. *Perf. 14*
414 A112a 10c lt blue & multi .35 .30
415 A112b 25c lilac rose & blk .75 .70

World Cricket Cup, won by West Indies Team, 1975.

Christmas Type of 1975

Belisario Prints, 1837: 10c, Queen of the "set-girls." 20c, Band of Jawbone John Canoe. 50c, Koo Koo, "actor-boy."

1976, Nov. 8 Wmk. 352 *Perf. 13½*
416 A110 10c brick red & multi .20 .20
417 A110 20c bister & multi .35 .30
418 A110 50c tan & multi .90 1.10
a. Souv. sheet of 3, #416-418, perf. 14 1.50 1.75
Nos. 416-418 (3) 1.45 1.60

Christmas.

Map Type of 1976

Maps of Jamaica by: 9c, Edmund Hickeringill, 1661. 10c, John Ogilby, 1671. 25c, House of Visscher, 1680. 40c, John Thornton, 1689.

1977, Feb. 28 Litho. *Perf. 13*
419 A111 9c lt blue & multi .35 .30
420 A111 10c buff & multi .55 .55
421 A111 25c multicolored 1.00 1.00
422 A111 40c multicolored 1.25 *2.50*
Nos. 419-422 (4) 3.15 4.35

Butterfly Type of 1975

10c, Eurema elathea. 20c, Dynamine egaea. 25c, Atlantea pantoni. 40c, Hypolimnas misippus.

1977, May 9 Wmk. 352 *Perf. 13½*
423 A109 10c black & multi .75 .30
424 A109 20c black & multi 1.40 1.00
425 A109 25c black & multi 2.10 2.10
426 A109 40c black & multi 3.25 *4.75*
a. Souv. sheet of 4, #423-426, perf. 14½ 8.00 8.00
Nos. 423-426 (4) 7.50 8.15

Scout Emblem, Doctor Bird, Outline of Jamaica — A113

1977, Aug. 5 Litho. *Perf. 14*
427 A113 10c multicolored .60 .20
428 A113 20c multicolored .90 .35
429 A113 25c multicolored 1.25 .50
430 A113 50c multicolored 1.50 *1.75*
Nos. 427-430 (4) 4.25 2.80

6th Caribbean Jamboree, Hope Gardens, Kingston, Aug. 3-17.

Trumpeter A114

10c, 2 clarinetists and oboist. 20c, kettle drummer and oboist, vert. 25c, Cellist and trumpeter, vert.

1977, Dec. 19 Litho. *Perf. 14*
431 A114 9c multicolored .25 .20
432 A114 10c multicolored .30 .20
433 A114 20c multicolored .70 .50
434 A114 25c multicolored .85 .85
a. Souvenir sheet of 4, #431-434 3.50 3.50
Nos. 431-434 (4) 2.10 1.75

Jamaica Military Band, 50th anniversary.

Butterfly Type of 1975

Butterflies: 10c, Callophrys crethona. 20c, Siproeta stelenes. 25c, Urbanus proteus. 50c, Anaea troglodyta.

1978, Apr. 17 Litho. *Perf. 14½*
435 A109 10c black & multi .70 .25
436 A109 20c black & multi 1.25 .40
437 A109 25c black & multi 1.50 1.00
438 A109 50c black & multi 2.75 *3.25*
a. Souvenir sheet of 4, #435-438 7.00 7.00
Nos. 435-438 (4) 6.20 4.90

Half Figure with Canopy — A115

Norman Manley Statue — A116

Arawak Artifacts, found 1792: 20c, Standing figure. 50c, Birdman.

1978, July 10 Litho. *Perf. 13½x13*
439 A115 10c multicolored .20 .20
440 A115 20c multicolored .30 .25
441 A115 50c multicolored .80 .80
a. Souv. sheet of 3, #439-441, perf. 14 1.25 1.50
Nos. 439-441 (3) 1.30 1.25

1978, Sept. 25 Litho. Wmk. 352

Designs: 20c, Alexander Bustamante statue. 25c, Kingston coat of arms. 40c, Gordon House Chamber, House of Representatives.

442 A116 10c multicolored .20 .20
443 A116 20c multicolored .25 .20
444 A116 25c multicolored .35 .25
445 A116 40c multicolored .40 *.50*
Nos. 442-445 (4) 1.20 1.15

24th Commonwealth Parliamentary Conf.

Salvation Army Band A117

Designs: 20c, Trumpeter. 25c, "S" and Cross entwined on pole of Army flag. 50c, William Booth and Salvation Army shield.

1978, Dec. 4 *Perf. 14*
446 A117 10c multicolored .20 .20
447 A117 20c multicolored .40 .25
448 A117 25c multicolored .40 .30
449 A117 50c multicolored .80 *.90*
Nos. 446-449 (4) 1.80 1.65

Christmas; Salvation Army centenary.

"Negro Aroused," by Edna Manley — A118

Arawak Grinding Stone, c. 400 B.C. — A119

1978, Dec. 11 *Perf. 13*
450 A118 10c multicolored .40 .20

International Anti-Apartheid Year.

No. 351 Overprinted: "TENTH / ANNIVERSARY / AIR JAMAICA / 1st APRIL 1979"

1979, Apr. 2 Litho. *Perf. 13½*
451 A99 10c multicolored .50 .50

1979, Apr. 23 *Perf. 14*

Arawak Artifacts (all A.D.): 10c, Stone implements, c. 500, horiz. 20c, Cooking pot, c. 300, horiz. 25c, Serving boat, c. 300, horiz. 50c, Storage jar fragment, c. 300.

452 A119 5c multicolored .20 .20
453 A119 10c multicolored .20 .20
454 A119 20c multicolored .20 .20
455 A119 25c multicolored .20 .25
456 A119 50c multicolored .20 .50
Nos. 452-456 (5) 1.20 1.35

Jamaica No. 183, Hill Statue A120

Hill Statue and Stamps of Jamaica: 20c, No. 83a. 25c, No. 5. 50c, No. 271.

1979, Aug. 13 Litho. *Perf. 14*
457 A120 10c multicolored .25 .20
458 A120 20c multicolored .25 .20
a. Souvenir sheet of 1 .75 .75
459 A120 25c multicolored .25 .20
460 A120 50c multicolored .45 *.75*
Nos. 457-460 (4) 1.20 1.35

Sir Rowland Hill (1795-1879), originator of penny postage.

Children, IYC Emblem A121

International Year of the Child: 20c, Doll, vert. 25c, "The Family." 25c, "House on the Hill." 25c, 50c are children's drawings.

1979, Oct. 1
461 A121 10c multicolored .20 .20
462 A121 20c multicolored .20 .20
463 A121 25c multicolored .20 .20
464 A121 50c multicolored .30 .35
Nos. 461-464 (4) .90 .95

Tennis, Montego Bay — A122

Jamaican Tody — A123

Designs: 2c, Golfing, Tryall Hanover. 4c, Horseback riding, Negril Beach. 5c, Old Waterwheel, Tryall Hanover. 6c, Fern Gully, Ocho Rios. 7c, Dunn's River Falls, Ocho Rios.

10c, Doctorbird. 12c, Yellow-billed parrot. 15c, Hummingbird. 35c, White-chinned thrush. 50c, Jamaican woodpecker. 65c, Rafting Martha Brae Trelawny. 75c, Blue marlin fishing, Port Antonio. $1, Scuba diving. Ocho Rios. $2, Sail boats, Montego Bay.

Wmk. 352

1979-80 Litho. *Perf. 13½*
465 A122 1c multicolored .80 .80
466 A122 2c multicolored 2.50 2.50
467 A122 4c multicolored .60 *2.50*
468 A122 5c multicolored 1.40 .35
469 A122 6c multicolored 1.75 *2.50*
470 A122 7c multicolored .60 .35
472 A123 8c multicolored 1.25 1.25
473 A123 10c multicolored 1.25 .25
474 A123 12c multicolored 1.25 *2.25*
475 A123 15c multicolored 1.25 .35
476 A123 35c multicolored 1.75 .35
477 A123 50c multicolored 2.00 .35
478 A122 65c multicolored 2.00 *3.25*
479 A122 75c multicolored 2.25 2.25
480 A122 $1 multicolored 2.25 2.25
481 A122 $2 multicolored 2.50 .75
Nos. 465-481 (16) 25.40 22.30

Issued: #465-470, 11/26/79; #472-481, 5/80.
For surcharges see Nos. 581-582, 665-666.

Institute of Jamaica Centenary — A124

1980, Feb. 25 Litho. *Perf. 13½*
484 A124 5c shown .20 .20
485 A124 15c Institute building, 1980 .20 .20
486 A124 35c "The Ascension" on microfilm reader, vert. .35 .30
487 A124 50c Hawksbill and green turtles .60 .60
488 A124 75c Jamaican owl, vert. 2.25 2.25
Nos. 484-488 (5) 3.60 3.55

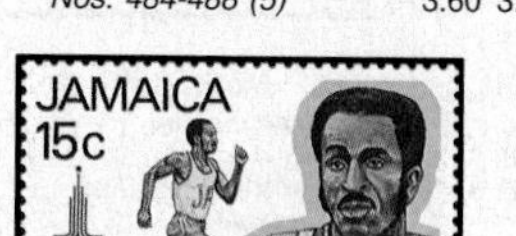

Don Quarrie, 1976 Gold Medalist, 200-Meter Race, Moscow '80 Emblem A125

1952 4x400-meter Relay Team: a, Arthur Wint. b, Leslie Laing. c, Herbert McKenley. d, George Rhoden.

1980, July 21 Litho. *Perf. 13*
489 A125 15c shown .50 .25
490 Strip of 4 3.25 3.25
a.-d. A125 35c any single .75 .75

22nd Summer Olympic Games, Moscow, July 19-Aug. 3.

Parish Church, Kingston A126

1980, Nov. 24 Litho. *Perf. 14*
491 A126 15c shown .20 .20
492 A126 20c Coke Memorial .20 .20
493 A126 25c Church of the Redeemer .20 .20
494 A126 $5 Holy Trinity Cathedral 2.00 2.00
a. Souvenir sheet of 4, #491-494 3.00 3.00
Nos. 491-494 (4) 2.60 2.60

Christmas.

Tube Sponge A127

1981, Feb. 27 Wmk. 352 *Perf. 14*
495 A127 20c Blood cup sponge, vert. .20 .20
496 A127 45c shown .45 .40
497 A127 60c Black coral, vert. .60 .60
498 A127 75c Tire reef .75 .75
Nos. 495-498 (4) 2.00 1.95

See Nos. 523-527.

Indian Coney A128

Designs: b, Facing left. c, Eating. d, Family.

1981, May 25 Wmk. 352 *Perf. 14*
499 Strip of 4 1.10 1.10
a.-d. A128 20c any single .25 .25

Royal Wedding Issue
Common Design Type

1981, July 29 Litho. *Perf. 15*
500 CD331 20c White orchid .20 .20
501 CD331 45c Royal coach .20 .20
502 CD331 60c Couple .30 .25

Perf. 13½
503 CD331 $5 St. James' Palace .75 .50
a. Souvenir sheet of 1 1.75 1.75
b. Bklt. pane of 4, perf 14x14½ 2.00
Nos. 500-503 (4) 1.45 1.15

Also issued in sheets of 5 + label, perf. 13½.

Intl. Year of the Disabled A129

1981, Sept. 14 Wmk. 352 *Perf. 13½*
504 A129 20c Blind weaver .25 .20
505 A129 45c Artist .45 .45
506 A129 60c Learning sign language .60 .60
507 A129 1.50 Basketball players 2.75 2.75
Nos. 504-507 (4) 4.05 4.00

World Food Day — A130

Perf. 13x13½, 13½x13
1981, Oct. 16 Litho. Wmk. 352
508 A130 20c No. 218 .50 .20
509 A130 45c No. 76, vert. .90 .45
510 A130 $2 No. 121 2.50 1.50
511 A130 $4 No. 125 3.75 2.50
Nos. 508-511 (4) 7.65 4.65

Bob Marley (1945-1981), Reggae Musician — A131

Portraits of Bob Marley and song titles.

1981, Oct. 20 Wmk. 373 *Perf. 14½*
512 A131 1c multicolored 1.00 *1.25*
513 A131 2c multicolored 1.00 *1.25*
514 A131 3c multicolored 1.00 *1.25*
515 A131 15c multicolored 3.75 .40
516 A131 20c multicolored 4.00 .40
517 A131 60c multicolored 5.25 4.00
518 A131 $3 multicolored 9.00 *13.00*
Nos. 512-518 (7) 25.00 21.55

Souvenir Sheet
519 A131 $5.25 multicolored 10.00 10.00

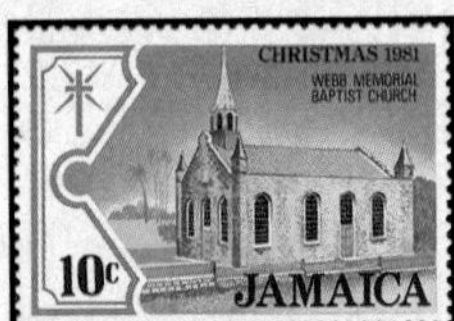

Christmas A132

1981, Dec. 11 Wmk. 352 *Perf. 14*
520 A132 10c Webb Memorial Baptist Church .20 .20
521 A132 45c Church of God .40 .20
522 A132 $5 Bryce United Church 2.75 2.75
a. Souvenir sheet of 3, #520-522, perf. 12½x12 4.50 4.50
Nos. 520-522 (3) 3.35 3.15

See Nos. 547-549.

Marine Life Type of 1981

1982, Feb. 22 Litho. *Perf. 14*
523 A127 20c Gorgonian coral, vert. .60 .20
524 A127 45c Hard sponge .95 .30
525 A127 60c Sea cow 1.25 .55
526 A127 75c Plume worm 1.40 .65
527 A127 $3 Coral-banded shrimp 3.75 2.00
Nos. 523-527 (5) 7.95 3.70

Scouting Year — A133

Princess Diana, 21st Birthday — A134

20c, 45c, 60c, Various scouts. $2, Baden-Powell.

1982, July 12 Litho. *Perf. 13½*
528 A133 20c multicolored .75 .20
529 A133 45c multicolored 1.25 .45
530 A133 60c multicolored 1.60 1.00
531 A133 $2 multicolored 2.50 2.50
a. Souvenir sheet of 4, #528-531 8.50 8.50
Nos. 528-531 (4) 6.10 4.15

1982, Sept. 1 *Perf. 14½*
532 A134 20c Lignum vitae .40 .20
533 A134 45c Couple in coach .60 .45
534 A134 60c Wedding portrait .85 .70
a. Booklet pane of 3, #532-534 2.00
535 A134 75c Saxifraga longifolia 1.50 *3.00*
536 A134 $2 Diana 2.40 3.25
537 A134 $3 Viola gracilis major 2.40 *3.50*
a. Booklet pane of 3, #535-537 7.50
Nos. 532-537 (6) 8.15 11.10

Souvenir Sheet
538 A134 $5 Honeymoon 4.50 4.50

Nos. 535, 537 in sheets of 5.

Nos. 532-538 Overprinted: "ROYAL BABY / 21.6.82"

1982, Sept. 13
539 A134 20c multicolored .35 .20
540 A134 45c multicolored .50 .45
541 A134 60c multicolored .75 .60
a. Booklet pane of 3, #539-541 2.00
542 A134 75c multicolored 1.25 *2.00*
543 A134 $2 multicolored 2.10 2.10
544 A134 $3 multicolored 2.40 *2.50*
a. Booklet pane of 3, #542-544 7.00
Nos. 539-544 (6) 7.35 7.85

Souvenir Sheet
545 A134 $5 multicolored 4.50 4.50

Birth of Prince William of Wales, June 21.

Lizard Cuckoo Capturing Prey — A135

Designs: b, Searching for prey. c, Calling. d, Landing. e, Flying.

1982, Oct. 25
546 Strip of 5 11.00 11.00
a.-e. A135 $1 any single 1.75 1.75

Christmas Type of 1981

Perf. 13x13½
1982, Dec. 8 Wmk. 352
547 A132 20c United Pentecostal Church .80 .25
548 A132 45c Disciples of Christ Church 1.50 .35
549 A132 75c Open Bible Church 2.25 *2.75*
Nos. 547-549 (3) 4.55 3.35

Visit of Queen Elizabeth II — A136

1983, Feb. 14 Litho. *Perf. 14*
550 A136 $2 Queen Elizabeth II 5.00 4.00
551 A136 $3 Arms 6.00 *7.00*

A136a

1983, Mar. 14 Litho. Wmk. 352
552 A136a 20c Dancers .20 .20
553 A136a 45c Bauxite mining .50 .50
554 A136a 75c Map .70 .70
555 A136a $2 Arms, citizens 1.60 *1.75*
Nos. 552-555 (4) 3.00 3.15

Commonwealth Day.

25th Anniv. of Intl. Maritime Org. A137

1983, Mar. 17 Litho. *Perf. 14*
556 A137 15c Cargo ship 1.25 .35
557 A137 20c Cruise liner 1.90 .50
558 A137 45c Container vessel 2.75 .95
559 A137 $1 Intl. Seabed Headquarters 4.25 *5.75*
Nos. 556-559 (4) 10.15 7.55

21st Anniv. of Independence A138

Prime Ministers Alexander Bustamante and Norman Washington Manley.

1983, July 25 Litho. *Perf. 14*
560 A138 15c blue & multi .20 .20
561 A138 20c lt green & multi .20 .20
562 A138 45c yellow & multi .40 .40
Nos. 560-562 (3) .80 .80

World Communications Year — A139

1983, Oct. 18 Wmk. 352 *Perf. 14*
563 A139 20c Ship-to-shore radio 1.00 .20
564 A139 45c Postal services 1.60 .50
565 A139 75c Telephone communication 2.00 *3.50*
566 A139 $1 TV satellite 2.50 *4.00*
Nos. 563-566 (4) 7.10 8.20

Christmas 1983 A140

Paintings: 15c, Racing at Caymanas, by Sidney McLaren. 20c, Seated Figures, by Karl Parboosingh. 75c, The Petitioner, by Henry Daley, vert. $2, Banana Plantation, by John Dunkley, vert.

1983, Dec. 12 Litho. *Perf. 13½*
567 A140 15c multicolored .20 .20
568 A140 20c multicolored .20 .20
569 A140 75c multicolored .75 .50
570 A140 $2 multicolored 1.75 *4.00*
Nos. 567-570 (4) 2.90 4.90

Alexander Bustamante (1884-1977), First Prime Minister — A141

1984, Feb. 24 Litho. *Perf. 14*
571 20c Portrait 1.10 1.10
572 20c Blenheim (birthplace) 1.10 1.10
a. A141 Pair, #571-572 2.50 *3.50*

Sea Planes A142

1984, June 11 Litho. *Perf. 14*
573 A142 25c Gypsy Moth 2.25 .35
574 A142 55c Consolidated Commodore 2.75 1.00
575 A142 $1.50 Sikorsky S-38 5.00 5.00
576 A142 $3 Sikorsky S-40 5.75 5.75
Nos. 573-576 (4) 15.75 12.10

1984 Summer Olympics A143

1984, July 11
577 A143 25c Bicycling 2.50 .60
578 A143 55c Relay race .85 .35
579 A143 $1.50 Running 2.50 *5.50*
580 A143 $3 Women's running 2.25 *4.50*
a. Souvenir sheet of 4, #577-580 8.00 8.00
Nos. 577-580 (4) 8.10 10.95

Nos. 469, 474 Surcharged

1984, Aug. 7 Litho. *Perf. 13½*
581 A122 5c on 6c #469 .55 .45
582 A123 10c on 12c #474 1.60 .60

Early Steam Engines — A144

1984, Nov. 16 Litho. *Perf. 13½*
583 A144 25c Enterprise, 1845 2.10 .35
584 A144 55c Tank Locomotive, 1880 2.75 .85
585 A144 $1.50 Kitson-Meyer Tank, 1904 4.50 4.25

586 A144 $3 Superheater, 1916 5.50 *5.75*
Nos. 583-586 (4) 14.85 11.20

See Nos. 608-611.

Christmas — A145

Local sculptures: 20c, Accompong Madonna, by Namba Roy. 25c, Head, by Alvin Marriott. 55c, Moon, by Edna Manley. $1.50, All Women are Five Women, by Mallica Reynolds.

1984, Dec. 6 Wmk. 352 *Perf. 14*

587 A145 20c multicolored .35 .20
588 A145 25c multicolored .40 .20
589 A145 55c multicolored 1.40 .50
590 A145 $1.50 multicolored 2.50 2.50
Nos. 587-590 (4) 4.65 3.40

Jamaican Boas — A146

1984, Oct. 22 Litho. *Perf. 14½*

591 A146 25c Head of boa *12.50* .75
592 A146 55c Boa over water *15.00* *1.50*
593 A146 70c Boa with young *17.50* *6.50*
594 A146 $1 Boa on branch *25.00* *7.00*
a. Souv. sheet of 4, #591-594 *15.00* *15.00*
Nos. 591-594 (4) *70.00* *15.75*

Stamps in #594a do not have WWF emblem.

Brown Pelicans — A147

1985, Apr. 15 Wmk. 352 *Perf. 13*

595 A147 20c multicolored 1.25 .20
596 A147 55c multicolored 2.25 .45
597 A147 $2 multicolored 3.50 3.50
598 A147 $5 multicolored 5.00 5.00
a. Souvenir sheet of 4, #595-598 12.00 12.00
Nos. 595-598 (4) 12.00 9.15

Birth bicentenary of artist and naturalist John J. Audubon (1785-1851).

Queen Mother 85th Birthday
Common Design Type

1985, June 7 Litho. *Perf. 14½x14*

599 CD336 25c Holding photograph album, 1963 .60 .20
600 CD336 55c With Prince Charles, Windsor Castle, 1983 .80 .25
601 CD336 $1.50 At Belfast University 1.25 1.25
602 CD336 $3 Holding Prince Henry 2.25 *3.25*
Nos. 599-602 (4) 4.90 4.95

Souvenir Sheet

603 CD336 $5 With limousine 4.25 4.25

Maps of Americas and Jamaica, IYY and Jamboree Emblems A148

1985, July 30 Litho. *Perf. 14*

604 A148 25c multicolored 1.50 .20
605 A148 55c multicolored 1.75 .35
606 A148 70c multicolored 2.00 1.60
607 A148 $4 multicolored 4.00 *7.00*
Nos. 604-607 (4) 9.25 9.15

Intl. Youth Year and 5th Pan-American Scouting Jamboree.

Locomotives Type of 1984

1985, Sept. 30 Size: 39x25mm

608 A144 25c Baldwin 1.90 .35
609 A144 55c Rogers 2.60 .40
610 A144 $1.50 Projector 3.75 3.50
611 A144 $4 Diesel 5.00 *6.50*
Nos. 608-611 (4) 13.25 10.75

The Old Settlement, by Ralph Campbell — A149

Christmas (Paintings by local artists): 55c, The Vendor, by Albert Hiue, vert. 75c, Road Menders, by Gaston Tabois. $4, Woman, Must I Not Be About My Father's Business? by Carl Abrahams, vert.

1985, Dec. 9

612 A149 20c multicolored .20 .20
613 A149 55c multicolored .20 .20
614 A149 75c multicolored .25 .25
615 A149 $4 multicolored 1.50 1.50
Nos. 612-615 (4) 2.15 2.15

Birds — A150

A151

1986, Feb. 10 Litho. *Perf. 14*

616 A150 25c Chestnut-bellied cuckoo 1.10 .20
617 A150 55c Jamaican becard 1.40 .25
618 A150 $1.50 White-eyed thrush 1.75 1.40
619 A150 $5 Rufous-tailed flycatcher 3.50 2.75
Nos. 616-619 (4) 7.75 4.60

Queen Elizabeth II 60th Birthday
Common Design Type

Designs: 20c, With Princess Margaret, 1939. 25c, Leaving Liverpool Street Station for Sandringham with Princes Charles and Andrew, 1962. 70c, Visiting the Montego Bay war memorial, Jamaica, 1983. $3, State visit to Luxembourg, 1976. $5, Visiting Crown Agents' offices, 1983.

1986, Apr. 21 *Perf. 14½*

620 CD337 20c scar, blk & sil .20 .20
621 CD337 25c ultra & multi .20 .20
622 CD337 70c green & multi .20 .20
623 CD337 $3 violet & multi 1.00 1.00
624 CD337 $5 rose vio & multi 1.60 1.60
Nos. 620-624 (5) 3.20 3.20

1986, May 19

AMERIPEX '86: 25c, Bustamante Childrens Hospital. 55c, Vacation cities. $3, Norman Manley Law School. $5, Exports.

625 A151 25c multicolored .80 .20
626 A151 55c multicolored 3.00 .45
627 A151 $3 multicolored 1.50 1.50
628 A151 $5 multicolored 8.75 8.75
a. Souvenir sheet of 4, #625-628 13.50 13.50
Nos. 625-628 (4) 14.05 10.90

Royal Wedding Issue, 1986
Common Design Type

Designs: 30c, At the races. $4, Andrew addressing the press.

Perf. 14½x14

1986, July 23 Wmk. 352

629 CD338 20c multicolored .25 .20
630 CD338 $5 multicolored 2.00 2.00

Boxing Champions A152

Champions: 45c, Richard "Shrimpy" Clarke, 1986 Commonwealth flyweight. 70c, Michael McCallum, 1984 WBA junior middleweight. $2, Trevor Berbick, 1986 WBC heavyweight. $4, Clarke, McCallum and Berbick.

1986, Oct. 27 Litho. *Perf. 14*

631 A152 45c multicolored .30 .20
632 A152 70c multicolored .45 .30
633 A152 $2 multicolored 1.00 *1.25*
634 A152 $4 multicolored 2.25 *3.00*
Nos. 631-634 (4) 4.00 4.75

Flowers A153

1986, Dec. 1 *Perf. 14*

635 A153 20c Heliconia wagneriana, vert. .20 .20
636 A153 25c Heliconia psittacorum .20 .20
637 A153 55c Heliconia rostrata, vert. .30 .30
638 A153 $5 Strelitzia reginae 3.00 *3.75*
Nos. 635-638 (4) 3.70 4.45

Christmas. See Nos. 675-678, 706-709.

Shells — A154

1987, Feb. 23 Litho. *Perf. 15*

639 A154 35c Crown cone .70 .20
640 A154 75c Measled cowrie .85 .65
641 A154 $1 Trumpet triton 1.00 *1.10*
642 A154 $5 Rooster-tail conch 2.00 *4.00*
Nos. 639-642 (4) 4.55 5.95

Prime Ministers A155

Natl. Coat of Arms A156

Designs: 1c-9c, 55c, Norman Washington Manley. 10c-50c, 60c-90c, Sir Alexander Bustamante.

1987-94 *Perf. 12½x13*

643	A155	1c dull red	.20	*.55*
644	A155	2c rose pink	.20	*.55*
645	A155	3c light olive	.20	*.55*
646	A155	4c dull green	.20	*.55*
647	A155	5c slate blue	.40	*.50*
648	A155	6c ultramarine	.25	*.55*
649	A155	7c dull magenta	.80	*.55*
650	A155	8c red lilac	.30	.20
651	A155	9c brown olive	.80	.20
652	A155	10c deep rose	.35	*.45*
653	A155	20c bright org	.65	.20
654	A155	30c emerald	.65	.20
655	A155	40c lt blue green	.40	.25
656	A155	50c gray olive	.80	.25
656A	A155	55c olive brown	1.50	.20
657	A155	60c light ultra	.40	.25
658	A155	70c pale violet	.40	.30
659	A155	80c violet	.80	.40
660	A155	90c light brown	1.25	.70
661	A156	$1 dull brn & buff	.80	.45
661A	A156	$1.10 dull brn & buff	2.50	.65
662	A156	$2 orange	.90	.90
663	A156	$5 gray olive & greenish buff	1.25	1.25
664	A156	$10 royal bl & pale bl	2.25	1.75

Perf. 13x13½

664A	A156	$25 vio & pale vio	3.75	1.75
664B	A156	$50 lilac & pale lilac	6.25	3.00
		Nos. 643-664B (26)	28.25	17.15

Issued: $25, $50 (dated "1991"), 10/9/91; 55c, $1.10 (dated "1994"), 10/10/94; others (undated), 5/18/87.

#647, 653 reissued inscribed "1988." #655-656 "1991." #653, 655-656, 660-661 "1992." #652-653, 656, 660-661 "1993." #652-656 "1994." #661-663 "1997."

Nos. 477-478 Surcharged

1986, Nov. 3 *Perf. 13½*

665 A123 5c on 50c multi 2.75 2.75
666 A122 10c on 65c multi 2.00 2.00

A157

Wmk. 352

1987, July 27 Litho. *Perf. 14*

667 A157 55c Flag, sunset 2.00 .75
668 A157 70c Flag, horiz. 2.00 2.00

Natl. Independence, 25th anniv.

A158

1987, Aug. 17

669 25c Portrait 1.90 *2.00*
670 25c Statue 1.90 *2.00*
a. A158 Pair, #669-670 4.25 *4.50*

Marcus Mosiah Garvey (1887-1940), natl. hero. No. 670a has a continuous design.

Salvation Army in Jamaica, Cent. A159

Designs: 25c, School for the Blind. 55c, Col Mary Booth, Bramwell-Booth Memorial H $3, "War Chariot," 1929. $5, Arrival Abram Davey on the S.S. Alene, 1887

1987, Oct. 8 *Perf. 13*
671 A159 25c multicolored 2.25 .40
672 A159 55c multicolored 2.25 .40
673 A159 $3 multicolored 6.00 6.00
674 A159 $5 multicolored 7.25 *8.50*
a. Souvenir sheet of 4, #671-674 19.00 19.00
Nos. 671-674 (4) 17.75 15.30

Flower Type of 1986

1987, Nov. 30 Litho. *Perf. 14½*
675 A153 20c Hibiscus hybrid .25 .20
676 A153 25c Hibiscus elatus .25 .20
677 A153 $4 Hibiscus cannabinus 3.50 3.50
678 A153 $5 Hibiscus rosa sinensis 4.00 4.00
Nos. 675-678 (4) 8.00 7.90

Christmas. Nos. 675-678 vert.

Birds — A160

Designs: No. 679, Chestnut-bellied cuckoo, black-billed parrot, Jamaican euphonia. No. 680, Jamaican white-eyed vireo, rufous-throated solitaire, yellow-crowned elaenia. No. 681, Snowy plover, little blue heron, great white heron. No. 682, Common stilt, snowy egret, black-crowned night heron.

1988, Jan. 22 Litho. *Perf. 14*
679 45c multicolored 2.60 2.60
680 45c multicolored 2.60 2.60
a. A160 Pair, #679-680 6.00 *7.00*
681 $5 multicolored 6.50 *7.00*
682 $5 multicolored 6.50 *7.00*
a. A160 Pair, #681-682 14.00 *15.00*
Nos. 679-682 (4) 18.20 19.20

Nos. 680a, 682a have continuous designs.

Marine Mammals A161

1988, Apr. 14 Litho. *Perf. 14*
683 A161 20c Blue whales 3.50 .85
684 A161 25c Gervais's whales 3.50 .85
685 A161 55c Killer whales 5.25 1.00
686 A161 $5 Common dolphins 8.00 *9.50*
Nos. 683-686 (4) 20.25 12.20

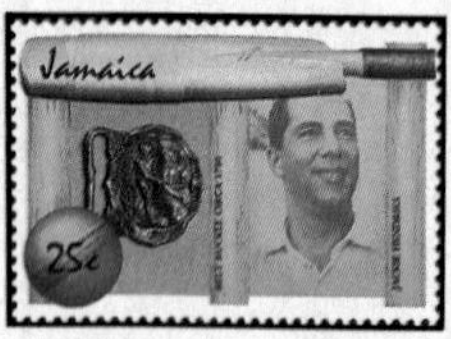

Cricket A162

Bat, wicket posts, ball, 18th cent. belt buckle and batsmen: 25c, Jackie Hendriks. 55c, George Headley. $2, Michael Holding. $3, R.K. Nunes. $4, Allan Rae.

1988, June 6 Litho. *Perf. 14*
687 A162 25c multicolored 2.50 .60
688 A162 55c multicolored 2.50 .60
689 A162 $2 multicolored 4.50 4.00
690 A162 $3 multicolored 5.00 5.00
691 A162 $4 multicolored 5.75 5.75
Nos. 687-691 (5) 20.25 15.95

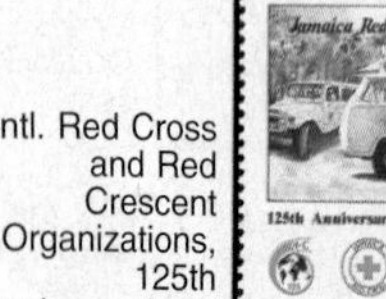
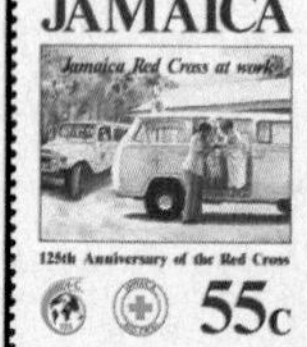

Intl. Red Cross and Red Crescent Organizations, 125th Annivs. — A163

Anniversary emblem, Jamaica Red Cross emblem and: 55c, Ambulances. $5, Jean-Henri Dunant, 1828-1910, treating the wounded after the Battle of Solferino, 1859.

1988, Aug. 8 Litho. *Perf. 14½*
692 A163 55c multicolored .75 .40
693 A163 $5 multicolored 3.75 3.75

1988 Summer Olympics, Seoul A164

1988, Aug. 24 Wmk. 352 *Perf. 14*
694 A164 25c Boxing .50 .20
695 A164 45c Cycling 2.00 .75
696 A164 $4 Women's running 2.50 2.50
697 A164 $5 Hurdling 2.50 2.50
a. Souvenir sheet of 4, #694-697 8.00 8.00
Nos. 694-697 (4) 7.50 5.95

No. 697a sold for $9.90. For surcharges see Nos. B4-B7.

Natl. Olympic Bobsled Team A165

1988, Nov. 4 Litho. *Perf. 14*
698 A165 25c Team members 1.00 1.00
699 A165 25c Two-man bobsled 1.00 1.00
a. Pair, #698-699 2.75 *3.00*
700 A165 $5 Team members, diff. 3.00 3.00
701 A165 $5 Four-man bobsled 3.00 3.00
a. Pair, #700-701 7.00 *8.00*
Nos. 698-701 (4) 8.00 8.00

Nos. 699a, 701a have continuous designs.

Labor Year — A166

Perf. 14½x14

1988, Nov. 24 Wmk. 352
702 A166 25c Medicine, fire fighting 1.00 .50
703 A166 55c Handicrafts 1.00 .50
704 A166 $3 Garment industry 2.00 2.00
705 A166 $5 Fishing 2.50 2.50
Nos. 702-705 (4) 6.50 5.50

Flower Type of 1986

1988, Dec. 15
706 A153 25c Euphorbia pulcherrima, vert. .90 .20
707 A153 55c Spathodea campanulata 1.00 .25
708 A153 $3 Hylocereus triangularis, vert. 2.25 1.75
709 A153 $4 Broughtonia sanguinea 2.75 2.00
Nos. 706-709 (4) 6.90 4.20

Christmas.

Methodist Church in Jamaica, Bicent. — A167

25c, Old York Castle School. 45c, Parade Chapel, Kingston, Rev. Thomas Coke. $5, Fr. Hugh Sherlock, St. John's Church.

1989, Jan. 19 *Perf. 13½*
710 A167 25c multicolored .40 .20
711 A167 45c multicolored .50 .20
712 A167 $5 multicolored 4.00 4.00
Nos. 710-712 (3) 4.90 4.40

Indigenous Moths — A168

Wmk. 352

1989, Aug. 30 Litho. *Perf. 14*
713 A168 25c *Syntomidopsis variegata* 1.00 .20
714 A168 55c *Himantoides undata-perkinsi* 1.75 .30
715 A168 $3 *Hypercompe nigriplaga* 3.00 3.00
716 A168 $5 *Sthenognatha toddi* 4.75 4.75
Nos. 713-716 (4) 10.50 8.25

See #725-728, 752-755. For surcharges & overprints see #729-732, 756-759.

A169

A171

Discovery of America, 500th Anniv. (in 1992): 25c, Arawak spear fisherman. 70c, Smoking tobacco. $5, Ferdinand and Isabella inspecting caravels. $10, Columbus studying chart.

1989, Dec. 22 *Perf. 13½*
717 A169 25c multicolored .30 .20
718 A169 70c multicolored .60 .40
719 A169 $5 multicolored 4.00 4.00
720 A169 $10 multicolored 7.00 *8.50*
a. Souvenir sheet of 4, #717-720, perf. 12½ 25.00 25.00
Nos. 717-720 (4) 11.90 13.10

No. 720a exists imperf.

Wmk. 352

1990, June 28 Litho. *Perf. 14*
721 A171 45c multicolored 2.00 .40
722 A171 55c multi, diff. 2.00 .40
723 A171 $5 multi, diff. 7.25 *9.00*
Nos. 721-723 (3) 11.25 9.80

Girl Guides of Jamaica, 75th anniv.

Indigenous Moths Type of 1989

Wmk. 352

1990, Sept. 12 Litho. *Perf. 14*
725 A168 25c Eunomia rubripunctata 1.50 .50
726 A168 55c Perigonia jamaicensis 2.00 .50
727 A168 $4 Uraga haemorrhoa 4.25 4.25
728 A168 $5 Empyreuma pugione 4.25 4.25
Nos. 725-728 (4) 12.00 9.50

Nos. 725-728 Ovptd. in Black

1990, Sept. 12
729 A168 25c No. 725 1.50 .45
730 A168 55c No. 726 2.25 .45
731 A168 $4 No. 727 4.25 4.25
732 A168 $5 No. 728 4.25 4.25
Nos. 729-732 (4) 12.25 9.40

Expo '90, International Garden and Greenery Exposition, Osaka, Japan.

Intl. Literacy Year A172

Wmk. 352

1990, Oct. 10 Litho. *Perf. 14*
733 A172 55c shown 1.10 .35
734 A172 $5 Mathematics class 6.25 6.25

Christmas — A173

Children's art.

Perf. 13½x14

1990, Dec. 7 Litho. Wmk. 352
735 A173 20c To the market .70 .20
736 A173 25c Untitled (houses) .70 .20
737 A173 55c Jack and Jill .85 .25
738 A173 70c Untitled (market) 1.10 .50
739 A173 $1.50 Lonely (beach) 2.75 2.75
740 A173 $5 Market woman, vert. 4.75 4.75
Nos. 735-740 (6) 10.85 8.65

See Nos. 760-763.

Discovery of America, 500th Anniv. (in 1992) A174

Maps of Columbus' voyages.

1990, Dec. 19 *Perf. 14*
741 A174 25c First, 1492 2.00 .70
742 A174 45c Second, 1493 2.50 .70
743 A174 $5 Third, 1498 7.00 7.00
744 A174 $10 Fourth, 1502 10.00 *11.00*
Nos. 741-744 (4) 21.50 19.40

Souvenir Sheet

745 Sheet of 4 18.00 18.00
a. A174 25c Cuba, Jamaica 1.25 1.25
b. A174 45c Hispaniola, Puerto Rico 1.50 1.50
c. A174 $5 Central America 5.00 5.00
d. A174 $10 Venezuela 9.00 9.00

Souvenir sheet also exists imperf. Value, $25.

See Nos. 764-767.

Natl. Meteorological Service — A175

1991, May 20 Litho. Wmk. 352
746 A175 50c multicolored 1.00 .25
747 A175 $10 multicolored 9.00 9.00

11th World Meteorological Congress.

Intl. Council of Nurses Council of Natl. Representatives, Jamaica — A176

Wmk. 352

1991, June 24 Litho. *Perf. 13½*

748 A176 50c Mary Seacole 1.50 .35
749 A176 $1.10 Mary Seacole House 3.00 3.00

Souvenir Sheet

750 A176 $8 Hospital at Scutari 5.50 5.50

Cyclura Collei (Jamaican Iguana) — A177

Designs: a, Head pointed to UR. b, Facing right. c, Climbing rock. d, Facing left. e, Head pointed to UL.

Wmk. 352

1991, July 29 Litho. *Perf. 13*

751 A177 $1.10 Strip of 5, #a.-e. 6.00 6.00

Natural History Soc. of Jamaica, 50th anniv.

Moths Type of 1989

1991, Aug. 12 *Perf. 14*

752 A168 50c Urania sloanus 1.50 .25
753 A168 $1.10 Phoenicoprocta jamaicensis 1.75 .70
754 A168 $1.40 Horama grotei 2.00 1.00
755 A168 $8 Amplypterus gannascus 5.75 5.75
Nos. 752-755 (4) 11.00 7.70

Nos. 752-755 Overprinted

1991, Sept. 23

756 A168 50c on No. 752 1.50 .25
757 A168 $1.10 on No. 753 2.00 .75
758 A168 $1.40 on No. 754 2.25 1.25
759 A168 $8 on No. 755 7.25 7.25
Nos. 756-759 (4) 13.00 9.50

Children's Christmas Art Type

Children's drawings.

1991, Nov. 27 *Perf. 14x15*

760 A173 50c Doctor bird 1.00 .20
761 A173 $1.10 Road scene 1.75 .30
762 A173 $5 House, people 5.00 4.00
763 A173 $10 Cows grazing 8.25 8.25
Nos. 760-763 (4) 16.00 12.75

Christmas.

Discovery of America Type of 1990

Designs: 50c, Explorers did not land at Santa Gloria because of hostile Indians. $1.10, Fierce dog used to subdue the Indians. $1.40, Indians brought gifts of fruit. $25, Columbus describes Jamaica with crumpled paper.

1991, Dec. 16 *Perf. 13½x14*

764 A174 50c multicolored 1.00 .20
765 A174 $1.10 multicolored 1.25 .50
766 A174 $1.40 multicolored 1.25 .50
767 A174 $25 multicolored 10.00 10.00
a. Souvenir sheet of 4, #764-767 13.00 13.00
Nos. 764-767 (4) 13.50 11.20

Souvenir sheet also exists imperf. Same value as perf.

First Provincial Grand Master of English Freemasonry in Jamaica, 250th Anniv. — A178

Masonic symbols: 50c, Square and compass. $1.10, Stained glass window. $1.40, Square and compass on Bible. $25, Seeing eye.

1992, May 1 *Perf. 13½*

768 A178 50c multicolored 1.25 .40
769 A178 $1.10 multicolored 1.50 .55
770 A178 $1.40 multicolored 1.50 .55
771 A178 $25 multicolored 9.75 9.75
a. Souvenir sheet of 4, #768-771 16.00 16.00
Nos. 768-771 (4) 14.00 11.25

Destruction of Port Royal by Earthquake, 300th Anniv. — A179

Scenes of destruction: 50c, Ship in harbor. $1.10, Homes, church. $1.40, Homes toppling. $5, Port Royal from contemporary broadsheet. $25, Fissure in street.

1992, June 7 *Perf. 14x13½*

772 A179 50c multicolored .80 .45
773 A179 $1.10 multicolored 1.00 .55
774 A179 $1.40 multicolored 1.00 .55
775 A179 $25 multicolored 11.00 11.00
Nos. 772-775 (4) 13.80 12.55

Souvenir Sheet

Perf. 13x12

776 A179 $5 multicolored 8.25 8.25

No. 776 inscribed on reverse.

Independence, 30th Anniv. — A180

1992, Aug. 6 *Perf. 13½*

777 A180 50c black & multi .30 .25
778 A180 $1.10 green & multi .35 .30
779 A180 $25 yellow & multi 4.75 4.75
Nos. 777-779 (3) 5.40 5.30

Credit Union Movement in Jamaica, 50th Anniv. — A181

1992, Aug. 24 *Perf. 14x15*

780 A181 50c Emblem 1.50 .60
781 A181 $1.40 Emblem, O'Hare Hall 2.75 2.75

Pottery — A182

Designs: 50c, "Rainbow" vase, by Cecil Baugh O.D. $1.10, "Yabba Pot," by Louisa Jones (MaLou) O.D. $1.40, "Sculptured Vase," by Gene Pearson. $25, "Lidded Form," by Norma Rodney Harrack.

1993, Apr. 26 *Perf. 13½*

782 A182 50c multicolored .30 .20
783 A182 $1.10 multicolored .50 .25
784 A182 $1.40 multicolored .50 .25
785 A182 $25 multicolored 5.75 5.75
Nos. 782-785 (4) 7.05 6.45

Girls' Brigade, Cent. A183

1993, Aug. 9 *Perf. 14x13½*

786 A183 50c Parade 1.60 .60
787 A183 $1.10 Brigade members 1.75 1.75

Jamaica Combined Cadet Force, 50th Anniv. — A184

Designs: 50c, Tank, cadet, vert. $1.10, Airplane, female cadet. $1.40, Ships, female cadet, vert. $3, Cap badge, cadet.

1993, Nov. 8 *Perf. 14*

788 A184 50c multicolored .60 .25
789 A184 $1.10 multicolored .90 .45
790 A184 $1.40 multicolored .90 .45
791 A184 $3 multicolored 1.25 *1.75*
Nos. 788-791 (4) 3.65 2.90

Golf Courses A185

50c, $1.10, Constant Spring. $1.40, $2, Half Moon. $3, $10, Jamaica Jamaica. $25, Tryall, vert.

1993-94 Litho. Wmk. 352 *Perf. 14*

792 A185 50c yellow & multi .45 .20
793 A185 $1.10 blue & multi .50 .20
794 A185 $1.40 brn org & multi .70 .25
795 A185 $2 lilac & multi .85 .70
796 A185 $3 dark blue & multi 1.10 1.10
797 A185 $10 tan & multi 2.75 2.75
Nos. 792-797 (6) 6.35 5.20

Souvenir Sheets

798 A185 $25 green & multi 8.00 8.00
799 A185 $25 #798 inscribed with Hong Kong '94 emblem 8.00 8.00

Issued: #792-797, Dec. 21, 1993; #798, Dec. 16, 1993; #799, Feb. 18, 1994.

A186

A187

1994, Jan. 12 *Perf. 14x15*

800 A186 $25 Portrait 3.75 *4.00*
801 A186 $50 Portrait, diff. 4.75 *5.00*
a. Pair, #800-801 9.00 *10.00*

Norman Washington Manley, birth cent.

1994, Mar. 1 *Perf. 14*

Royal Visit: $1.10, Jamaican, United Kingdom flags. $1.40, Royal yacht Britannia. $25, Queen Elizabeth II. $50, Prince Philip, Queen.

802 A187 $1.10 multicolored .75 .20
803 A187 $1.40 multicolored 1.60 .40
804 A187 $25 multicolored 3.75 3.75
805 A187 $50 multicolored 7.00 *8.50*
Nos. 802-805 (4) 13.10 12.85

Air Jamaica, 25th Anniv. — A188

Wmk. 352

1994, Apr. 26 Litho. *Perf. 14*

806 A188 50c Douglas DC9 .55 .25
807 A188 $1.10 Douglas DC8 .60 .35
808 A188 $5 Boeing 727 1.10 1.10
809 A188 $50 Airbus A300 5.25 5.25
Nos. 806-809 (4) 7.50 6.95

Giant Swallowtail A189

Various views of the butterfly.

Perf. 14x13½

1994, Aug. 18 Litho. Wmk. 352

810 A189 50c multicolored .60 .30
811 A189 $1.10 multicolored .60 .30
812 A189 $10 multicolored 3.00 3.00
813 A189 $25 multicolored 4.75 4.75
Nos. 810-813 (4) 8.95 8.35

Souvenir Sheet

814 189 $50 multicolored 11.00 11.00

A190

Tourism A191

Designs: 50c, Royal Botanical Gardens, by Sidney McClaren. $1.10, Blue Mountains, coffee beans, leaves. $5, Woman in hammock, waterfalls.

Tourist poster: No. 818a, Flowers, birds (c). b, Diver (d). c, Vegetation, coastline (a, d). d, Guide, tourists on raft.

Wmk. 352

1994, Sept. 7 Litho. *Perf. 14*

815 A190 50c multicolored .75 .25
816 A190 $1.10 multicolored 1.25 .40
817 A190 $5 multicolored 4.00 4.00
Nos. 815-817 (3) 6.00 4.65

Souvenir Sheet

818 A191 $25 Sheet of 4, #a.-d. 10.50 10.50

Caribbean Tourism Conf. (#818).

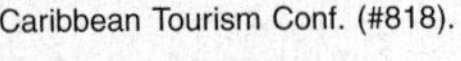

Red Poll Cattle A192

1994, Nov. 16 *Perf. 14x13½*

819 A192 50c Calf .20 .20
820 A192 $1.10 Heifer .20 .20
821 A192 $25 Cow 2.00 2.00
822 A192 $50 Bull 4.50 4.50
Nos. 819-822 (4) 6.90 6.90

Christmas — A193

Paintings by Children: 50c, Clean-up crew. 90c, Hospital Room. $1.10, House. $50, Meadow.

1994, Dec. 1 *Perf. 14x14½*

823 A193 50c multicolored .20 .20
824 A193 90c multicolored .20 .20
825 A193 $1.10 multicolored .20 .20
826 A193 $50 multicolored 4.50 4.50
Nos. 823-826 (4) 5.10 5.10

Birds — A194

Wmk. 384

1995, Apr. 24 Litho. *Perf. 14*

827 A194 50c Ring-tailed pigeon .85 .35
828 A194 90c Yellow-billed parrot 1.10 .35
829 A194 $1.10 Black-billed parrot 1.10 .35
830 A194 $50 Brown owl 7.00 *8.00*
Nos. 827-830 (4) 10.05 9.05

Souvenir Sheet

831 A194 $50 Streamertail 9.00 9.00
a. Ovptd. in sheet margin 7.25 7.25

No. 831 is a continuous design.

No. 831a ovptd. with Singapore '95 emblem. Issued: 9/1/95.

Caribbean Development Bank, 25th Anniv. — A195

Anniversary emblem and: 50c, $1, Jamaican flag, graph, vert. $1.10, Industries, agriculture. $50, Bank notes, coins.

Wmk. 352

1995, May 11 Litho. *Perf. 13½*

832 A195 50c green & multi .20 .20
833 A195 $1 black & multi .20 .20
834 A195 $1.10 multicolored .20 .20
835 A195 $50 multicolored 5.50 5.50
Nos. 832-835 (4) 6.10 6.10

Bob Marley (1945-81), Reggae Musician — A196

Marley performing songs: 50c, Songs of Freedom, by Adrian Boot. $1.10, Fire, by Neville Garrick. $1.40, Time Will Tell, by Peter Murphy. $3, Natural Mystic, by Boot. $10, Live at Lyceum, by Boot.

$100, Legend, by Boot.

Wmk. 352

1995, July 31 Litho. *Perf. 14*

836 A196 50c multicolored .45 .20
837 A196 $1.10 multicolored .65 .25
838 A196 $1.40 multicolored .70 .35
839 A196 $3 multicolored 1.10 .90
840 A196 $10 multicolored 2.00 2.00
Nos. 836-840 (5) 4.90 3.70

Souvenir Sheet

841 A196 $100 multicolored 11.50 11.50

Souvenir Sheet

Queen Mother, 95th Birthday — A197

Illustration reduced.

1995, Aug. 4 *Perf. 14x13½*

842 A197 $75 multicolored 7.00 7.00

Order of the Caribbean Community — A198

Designs: 50c, Michael Manley, former prime minister, Jamaica. $1.10, Sir Alister McIntyre, Vice Chancellor, UWI, Jamaica. $1.40, P. Telford Georges, former Chief Justice, Bahamas. $50, Dame Nita Barrow, Governor General, Barbados.

1995, Aug. 23 *Perf. 14x14½*

843 A198 50c multicolored .25 .25
844 A198 $1.10 multicolored .35 .20
845 A198 $1.40 multicolored .35 .20
846 A198 $50 multicolored 5.50 5.50
Nos. 843-846 (4) 6.45 6.15

UN, 50th Anniv.

Common Design Type

Designs: 50c, Signals Land Rover. $1.10, Antonov AN-32. $3, Bedford Articulated Tanker. $5, Fairchild DC-119 Flying Boxcar. $50, Observation vehicles.

Wmk. 352

1995, Oct. 24 Litho. *Perf. 14*

847 CD353 50c multicolored .35 .25
848 CD353 $1.10 multicolored .65 .30
849 CD353 $3 multicolored .85 .85
850 CD353 $5 multicolored .95 .95
Nos. 847-850 (4) 2.80 2.35

Souvenir Sheet

851 CD353 $50 multicolored 4.00 4.00

No. 851 has continuous design.

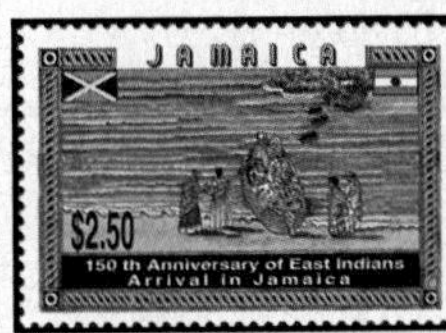

Arrival of East Indians in Jamaica, 150th Anniv. A199

Wmk. 352

1996, May 22 Litho. *Perf. 14*

852 A199 $2.50 Coming ashore .25 .20
853 A199 $10 Musicians, dancers 1.25 1.25

UNICEF, 50th Anniv. — A200

1996, Sept. 2 *Perf. 14½x14*

854 A200 $2.50 multicolored .80 .20
855 A200 $8 multicolored 1.75 1.75
856 A200 $10 multicolored 1.75 1.75
Nos. 854-856 (3) 4.30 3.70

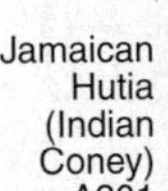

Jamaican Hutia (Indian Coney) A201

$2.50, Two in den. $10, One on ledge. $12.50, Mother, young. $25, One up close.

1996, Sept. 23 *Perf. 13½x14*

857 A201 $2.50 multicolored .25 .20
858 A201 $10 multicolored 1.00 1.00
859 A201 $12.50 multicolored 1.10 1.10
860 A201 $25 multicolored 2.00 *2.75*
Nos. 857-860 (4) 4.35 5.05

World Wildlife Fund.

Kingston Parish Church of St. Thomas the Apostle, 300th Anniv. A202

$2, High altar. $8, Exterior view. $12.50, Carving, "The Angel," by Edna Manley, vert. $60, Exterior view at sunset.

Unwmk.

1997, Feb. 7 Litho. *Perf. 14*

861 A202 $2 multicolored .60 .20
862 A202 $8 multicolored 1.50 .90
863 A202 $12.50 multicolored 2.40 2.40
Nos. 861-863 (3) 4.50 3.50

Souvenir Sheet

864 A202 $60 multicolored 5.00 5.00

No. 864 contains one 42x56mm stamp.

Chernobyl's Children — A203

Perf. 13½x14

1997, Apr. 7 Litho. Unwmk.

865 A203 $55 multicolored 5.50 5.50

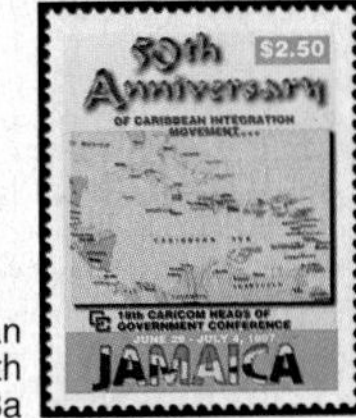

Caribbean Integration, 50th Anniv. — A203a

$2.50, Map of Caribbean. $8, $10, View of coastline.

Wmk. 352

1997, June 30 Litho. *Perf. 14*

865A A203a $2.50 multicolored *6.00 4.00*
865B A203a $8 multicolored *7.00 3.00*
865C A203a $10 multicolored *8.00 3.00*
Nos. 865A-865C (3) *21.00 10.00*

Orchids A204

$1, Coelia triptera. $2, Oncidium pulchellum. $2.50, Oncidium triquetrum. $3, Broughtonia negrilensis. $5, Enclycia frangrans.

Wmk. 352

1997, Oct. 6 Litho. *Perf. 14*

866 A204 $1 multi, vert. .40 .20
867 A204 $2 multi .50 .25
868 A204 $2.50 multi, vert. .55 .25
869 A204 $3 multi, vert. .60 .30
870 A204 $5 multi .60 .45
Nos. 866-870 (5) 2.65 1.45

See Nos. 873-877.

Diana, Princess of Wales (1961-97) — A205

Unwmk.

1998, Feb. 24 Litho. *Perf. 14*

871 A205 $20 Portrait 1.60 1.60

Souvenir Sheet

872 A205 $80 With Mother Teresa 9.00 9.00

No. 871 was issued in sheets of 6. No. 872 contains one 42x56mm stamp.

Orchid Type of 1997

Designs: $4.50, Oncidium gauntlettii. $8, Broughtonia sanguinea. $12, Phaius tankervilleae, vert. $25, Cochleanthes flabelliformis. $50, Broughtonia sanguinea (3 varieties).

Wmk. 352

1997, Dec. 1 Litho. *Perf. 14*

873 A204 $4.50 multicolored .60 .40
874 A204 $8 multicolored .80 .60
875 A204 $12 multicolored 1.10 .85
876 A204 $25 multicolored 1.90 1.75
877 A204 $50 multicolored 3.50 3.50
Nos. 873-877 (5) 7.90 7.10

No. 876 exists inscribed "1999." Value $3.

CARICOM, 25th Anniv. — A206

Perf. 13½

1998, Sept. 17 Litho. Unwmk.

878 A206 $30 multicolored 4.00 4.00

University of the West Indies, Mona, 50th Anniv. A207

$8, Chapel. $10, Philip Sherlock Centre for the Creative Arts. $50, University arms.

1998, July 31 Wmk. 352

879 A207 $8 multi .55 .50
880 A207 $10 multi .65 .60
881 A207 $50 multi, vert. 3.75 3.75
Nos. 879-881 (3) 4.95 4.85

1998 World Cup Soccer Championships, France, Jamaica's Debut in Tournament — A208

Wmk. 373

1998, Sept. 28 Litho. *Perf. 13½*

882 A208 $10 Player, vert. .65 .55
883 A208 $25 Team picture 1.60 1.60
884 A208 $100 Team picture, diff. 5.75 *6.50*
Nos. 882-884 (3) 8.00 8.65

Intl. Year of the Ocean A209

Designs: $10, Underwater scene. $30, Fishermen, Negril. $50, Long spiny black urchin. $100, Design elements from #885-887, vert.

Wmk. 352

1998, Dec. 23 Litho. *Perf. 14*

885 A209 $10 multicolored 1.25 .60
886 A209 $30 multicolored 3.00 1.75
887 A209 $50 multicolored 4.50 4.50

Size: 28x42mm

888 A209 $100 multicolored 8.75 *10.00*
Nos. 885-888 (4) 17.50 16.85

Christmas.

1st Manned Moon Landing, 30th Anniv.

Common Design Type

Designs: $7, Michael Collins. $10, Service module reverses to dock with lunar module. $25, Aldrin walks on lunar surface. $30, Command module back in earth orbit.
$100, Looking at earth from moon.

Perf. 14x13¾

1999, July 20 Litho. Wmk. 352

889 CD357 $7 multicolored .50 .35
890 CD357 $10 multicolored .65 .55
891 CD357 $25 multicolored 1.75 1.75
892 CD357 $30 multicolored 2.00 2.00
Nos. 889-892 (4) 4.90 4.65

Souvenir Sheet

Perf. 14

893 CD357 $100 multicolored 6.75 6.75

#893 contains one 40mm circular stamp.

Athletes A210

Designs: $5, Polo player Lesley Ann Masterton Fong-Yee. $10, Men's cricketers Collie Smith, Lawrence Rowe and Alfred Valentine. $20, Women's cricketer Vivalyn Latty-Scott, vert. $25, Soccer player Lindy Delapenha, vert. $30, Netball player Joy Grant-Charles, vert. $50, Boxers Percy Hayles, Gerald Gray and Bunny Grant.
$100, Delapenha and Grant-Charles.

Perf. 13¼x13¾, 13¾x13¼

1999, Aug. 3 Litho. Wmk. 352

894 A210 $5 multicolored .65 .30
895 A210 $10 multicolored 1.10 .55
896 A210 $20 multicolored 1.60 1.25
897 A210 $25 multicolored 1.75 1.50
898 A210 $30 multicolored 2.00 2.00
899 A210 $50 multicolored 3.25 3.25
Nos. 894-899 (6) 10.35 8.85

Souvenir Sheet

900 A210 $100 multicolored 8.00 8.00

No. 900 contains one 52x38mm stamp.

UPU, 125th Anniv. A211

Designs: $7, Mail ship "Spey." $10, Mail ship "Jamaica Planter." $25, Lockheed Constellation. $30, Airbus A-310.

Wmk. 352

1999, Oct. 8 Litho. *Perf. 14*

901 A211 $7 multicolored 1.50 .40
902 A211 $10 multicolored 1.75 .60
903 A211 $25 multicolored 3.00 3.00
904 A211 $30 multicolored 3.00 3.00
Nos. 901-904 (4) 9.25 7.00

Air Jamaica, 30th Anniv. — A212

Wmk. 352

1999, Nov. 1 Litho. *Perf. 14*

905 A212 $10 A-310 1.00 .45
906 A212 $25 A-320 2.00 2.00
907 A212 $30 A-340 3.00 *3.50*
Nos. 905-907 (3) 6.00 5.95

Dogs — A213

1999, Nov. 25 *Perf. 14¼*

908 A213 $7 Shih tzu 1.50 .60
909 A213 $10 German shepherd 2.00 .80
910 A213 $30 Doberman pinscher 3.50 3.50
Nos. 908-910 (3) 7.00 4.90

Parks A214

Designs: $7, Nelson Mandela Park. $10, St. William Grant Park. $25, Seaview Park. $30, Holruth Park.

1999, Dec. 15 *Perf. 14*

911 A214 $7 multi .40 .35
912 A214 $10 multi .50 .45
913 A214 $25 multi 1.50 1.50
914 A214 $30 multi 1.75 1.75
Nos. 911-914 (4) 4.15 4.05

Edna Manley (1900-87), Sculptor A215

Designs: $10, The Prophet, 1935. $25, Horse of the Morning, 1943. $30, The Angel, 1970. $100, Portrait of Manley.

2000, Mar. 1 Litho. *Perf. 13¾*

915 A215 $10 multi .60 .60
916 A215 $25 multi 1.50 1.50
917 A215 $30 multi 2.00 2.00
918 A215 $100 multi 5.75 5.75
a. Souvenir sheet, #915-918 10.50 10.50
Nos. 915-918 (4) 9.85 9.85

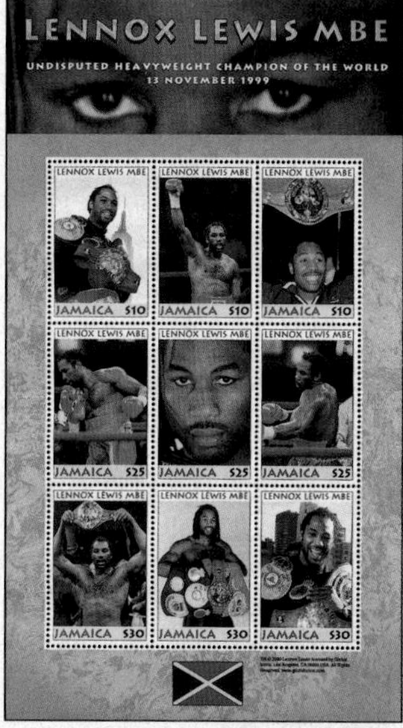

Lennox Lewis, Heavyweight Boxing Champion of the World — A216

a, $10, With belt & Empire State Building. b, $10, Holding up arm. c, $10, Holding up belt. d, $25, In ring with opponent. e, $25, Close-up. f, $25, In ring with referee. g, $30, Holding up belt, diff. h, $30, Holding 4 belts. i, $30, Holding belts in front of buildings.
Illustration reduced.

Wmk. 352

2000, Mar. 24 Litho. *Perf. 14*

919 A216 Sheet of 9, #a.-i. 11.00 11.00

Ferrari Automobiles — A217

Unwmk.

2000, May 26 Litho. *Perf. 14*

920 A217 $10 1947 125S 1.00 1.00
921 A217 $10 1950 375F1 1.00 1.00
922 A217 $10 1966 312F1 1.00 1.00
923 A217 $25 1965 Dino 166P 1.75 1.75
924 A217 $25 1971 312P 1.75 1.75
925 A217 $25 1990 F190 1.75 1.75
Nos. 920-925 (6) 8.25 8.25

Queen Mother, 100th Birthday — A218

Various photos.

2000, Aug. 4 Wmk. 352

926 A218 $10 multi 1.00 .55
927 A218 $25 multi 1.50 1.50
928 A218 $30 multi 2.00 1.75
929 A218 $50 multi 4.25 4.25
Nos. 926-929 (4) 8.75 8.05

2000 Summer Olympics, Sydney — A219

Jamaican flag and various views of sculpture, "The Runner," by Alvin Marriott. Denominations, $10, $25, $30, vert., $50, vert.

Wmk. 352

2000, Sept. 1 Litho. *Perf. 14*

930-933 A219 Set of 4 8.00 8.00

Trees — A220

Designs: $10, Bull thatch palm. $25, Blue mahoe. $30, Silk cotton. $50, Yellow pout.

2000, Oct. 6

934-937 A220 Set of 4 11.00 11.00

Souvenir Sheet

938 A220 $100 Lignum vitae, horiz. 11.00 11.00

Christmas — A221

Designs: $10, Madonna and Child, by Osmond Watson, vert. $20, Boy in the Temple, by Carl Abrahams. $25, Ascension, by Abrahams, vert. $30, Jah Lives, by Watson.

Wmk. 352

2000, Dec. 6 Litho. *Perf. 13¾*
939-942 A221 Set of 4 5.50 5.50

Commonwealth Day, 25th Anniv. — A222

Wmk. 352

2001, Mar. 12 Litho. *Perf. 12½*
943 A222 $30 multi 2.00 2.00

Father Andrew Duffus Mowatt, Founder of Jamaica Burial Scheme Society A223

Wmk. 352

2001, Oct. 12 Litho. *Perf. 13¼*
944 A223 $15 multi 2.00 2.00

Lithographs of Daguerrotypes by Adolphe Duperly (1801-64) — A224

Designs: $15, The Market, Falmouth. $40, Ferry Inn, Spanish Town Road. $45, Coke Chapel. $60, King Street, Kingston.

2001, Nov. 14 *Perf. 13*
945-948 A224 Set of 4 12.00 12.00
a. Souvenir sheet, #945-948 12.00 12.00

Christmas — A225

Poinsettias with background colors of: $15, Light blue. $30, Pink. $40, Pale orange.

2001, Dec. 10 *Perf. 13¼*
949-951 A225 Set of 3 8.00 8.00

Reign Of Queen Elizabeth II, 50th Anniv. Issue

Common Design Type

Designs: Nos. 952, 956a, $15, Princess Elizabeth. Nos. 953, 953b, $40, Wearing striped dress. Nos. 954, 956c, $45, In 1953. Nos. 955, 956d, $60, In 1995. No. 956e, $30, 1955 portrait by Annigoni (38x50mm).

Perf. 14¼x14½, 13¾ (#956e)

2002, Feb. 6 Litho. Wmk. 373

With Gold Frames

952-955 CD360 Set of 4 10.00 10.00

Souvenir Sheet

Without Gold Frames

956 CD360 Sheet of 5, #a-e 11.00 11.00

Visit of Queen Elizabeth II and Prince Philip, Feb. 18-20 A226

Designs: $15, Queen and Prince in 1983, flag of the Royal Standard. $45, Queen in 1983, Jamaican arms.

Perf. 13¼x13¾

2002, Feb. 18 Litho. Wmk. 352
957-958 A226 Set of 2 5.75 5.75

Sir Philip Sherlock (1902-2000), Educator — A227

2002, Mar. 11 *Perf. 13¾*
959 A227 $40 multi 2.25 2.25

Pan-American Health Organization, Cent. — A228

Wmk. 352

2002, Dec. 2 Litho. *Perf. 13¾*
960 A228 $40 multi 3.75 3.75

Christmas — A229

Art: $15, Masquerade, by Osmond Watson, vert. $40, John Canoe in Guanaboa Vale, by Gaston Tabois. $45, Mother and Child, sculpture, by Kapo, vert. $60, Hills of Papine, sculpture by Edna Manley.

2002, Dec. 6
961-964 A229 Set of 4 8.50 8.50

Natl. Dance Theater Company, 40th Anniv. — A230

2002, Dec. 27 *Perf. 14*
965 A230 $15 multi 2.00 2.00

Independence, 40th Anniv. — A231

Flag and: $15, Natl. Dance Theater Company performers. $40, Sir Alexander Bustamante, Michael Manley. $60, Factory workers.

2002, Dec. 27
966-968 A231 Set of 3 9.00 9.00

Kingston, Bicent. — A232

Historical views of Kingston and panel colors of: a, Brown. b, Olive green. c, Indigo.

2002, Dec. 31 *Perf. 13¾*
969 Horiz. strip of 3 4.50 4.50
a.-c. A232 $15 Any single 1.25 1.25

Coronation of Queen Elizabeth II, 50th Anniv.

Common Design Type

Designs: Nos. 970, $15, 972b, $100, Queen in chair awaiting crown. Nos. 971, $45, 972a, $50, Queen and Prince Philip in carriage.

Perf. 14¼x14½

2003, June 2 Litho. Wmk. 352

Vignettes Framed, Red Background

970-971 CD363 Set of 2 5.75 5.75

Souvenir Sheet

Vignettes Without Frame, Purple Panel

972 CD363 Sheet of 2, #a-b 8.00 8.00

Caribbean Community (CARICOM), 30th Anniv. — A233

Wmk. 352

2003, July 4 Litho. *Perf. 14*
973 A233 $40 multi 4.00 4.00

Bird Life International — A234

Designs: $15, Jamaican stripe-headed tanager, vert. $40, Crested quail dove. $45, Jamaican tody. $60, Blue Mountain vireo.

No. 978 — Jamaican blackbird: a, With beak open (35x30mm). b, Chicks in nest (35x30mm). c, In palm fronds, vert. (30x35mm). d, With beak open, vert. (30x35mm) e, With insect in beak (35x30mm).

2003, Sept. 19 *Perf. 14*
974-977 A234 Set of 4 11.00 11.00

Souvenir Sheet

Perf. 14¼x14½, 14½x14¼

978 A234 $30 Sheet of 5, #a-e 11.00 11.00

Maritime Heritage — A235

No. 979: a, Map, sailing ships. b, Sailing ships, ship with passengers. c, The Sugar Refiner and barges.

2003, Sept. 25 *Perf. 14x14¾*
979 Horiz. strip of 3 10.00 10.00
a.-c. A235 $40 Any single 3.00 3.00

Christmas — A236

Flowers and: $15, Adoration of the Magi. $30, Christ child. $60, Holy Family.

2003, Dec. *Perf. 13¼*
980-982 A236 Set of 3 8.00 8.00

Haitian Revolution, Bicent. — A237

Wmk. 352

2004, Jan. 30 Litho. *Perf. 13½*
983 A237 $40 multi 4.00 4.00

Caribbean Bird Festival A238

No. 984: a, Yellow-billed amazon. b, Jamaican oriole. c, Orangequit. d, Yellow-shouldered grassquit. e, Jamaican woodpecker. f, Red-billed streamertail. g, Jamaican mango. h, White-eyed thrush. i, Jamaican lizard cuckoo. j, Arrow-headed warbler.

Wmk. 352

2004, May 17 Litho. *Perf. 13¾*
984 Block of 10 10.00 10.00
a.-j. A238 $10 Any single .85 .85

Miniature Sheet

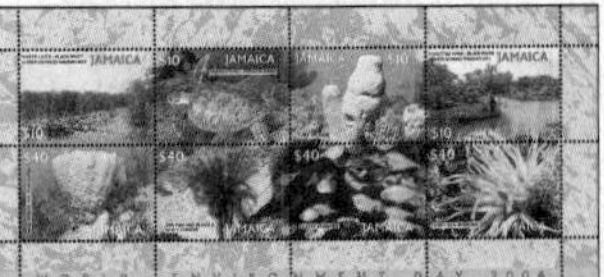

World Environment Day — A239

No. 985: a, $10, Water lilies. b, $10, Hawksbill turtle. c, $10, Tube sponge. d, $10, Boater on Parattee Pond. e, $40, Vase sponge, star coral. f, $40, Sea fan, black and white crinoid. g, $40, Glassy sweepers. h, $40, Giant sea anemone.

Unwmk.

2004, June 4 Litho. *Perf. 14*
985 A239 Sheet of 8, #a-h 9.00 9.00

2004 Summer Olympics, Athens — A240

Jamaican athletes: $30, Women's hurdles. $60, Running. $70, Swimming. $90, Rifle shooting, women's badminton.

Wmk. 352

2004, Aug. 10 Litho. *Perf. 14*
986-989 A240 Set of 4 10.00 10.00

FIFA (Fédération Internationale de Football Association), Cent. — A241

FIFA emblem and various soccer players: $10, $30, $45, $50.

Wmk. 352

2004, Oct. 13 Litho. *Perf. 14*
990-993 A241 Set of 4 8.00 8.00

Jamaica Hotels Law, Cent. A242

Designs: No. 994, Ralph Lauren, Doctors Cave Beach, Montego Bay.

No. 995 — Ambassador John Pringle, Round Hill Hotel and: a, Pink panel. b, Lilac panel.

No. 996 — Tower Isle Hotel and: a, Abe Issa, yellow green panels. b, John Issa, green panels. c, Abe Issa, red panels. d, John Issa, yellow green panels. e, Abe Issa, green panels. f, John Issa, red panels.

2004 Unwmk. *Perf. 13¼x13½*
994 A242 $40 multi 2.50 2.50
995 A242 $40 Pair, #a-b 5.00 5.00
996 A242 $40 Sheet of 6, #a-f 14.00 14.00
Nos. 994-996 (3) 21.50 21.50

Issued: No. 994, 11/19; Nos. 995-996, 11/12. No. 994 printed in sheets of six; No. 995 printed in sheets containing three pairs.

Christmas — A243

White sorrel stalks: $10, $20, $50, $60. $50 and $60 are horiz.

Wmk. 352

2004, Nov. 22 Litho. *Perf. 14¼*
997-1000 A243 Set of 4 7.50 7.50

Founding of Moravian Church in Jamaica, 250th Anniv. A244

Designs: 90c, Mary Morris Knibb, Mizpah Moravian Church. $10, Rev. W. O'Meally, Mizpah Moravian Church. $50, Bishop S. U. Hastings, Redeemer Moravian Church.

2004, Dec. 14
1001-1003 A244 Set of 3 4.00 4.00

Buildings — A245

Designs: 90c, Rose Hall Great House, St. James. $5, Holy Trinity Cathedral. $30, National Commercial Bank, New Kingston. $60, Court House, Falmouth.

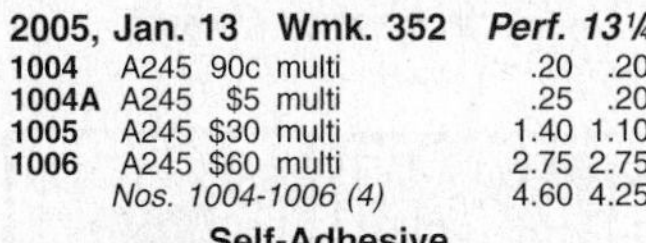

2005, Jan. 13 Wmk. 352 *Perf. 13¼*
1004 A245 90c multi .20 .20
1004A A245 $5 multi .25 .20
1005 A245 $30 multi 1.40 1.10
1006 A245 $60 multi 2.75 2.75
Nos. 1004-1006 (4) 4.60 4.25

Self-Adhesive

Serpentine Die Cut 12¼x12½

Unwmk.

1008 A245 $5 multi .30 .20
1008A A245 $30 multi 1.25 1.10
b. Booklet pane of 10 12.50
Complete booklet, #1008Ab 12.50
1009 A245 $60 multi 2.75 2.75

Nos. 1005 and 1006 exist dated "2008."

Chinese in Jamaica, 150th Anniv. A246

Flags of People's Republic of China and Jamaica and: $30, Food and fruits from China and Jamaica. $60, Chinatown. $90, Chinese Benevolent Association Building.

2005, Feb. 5 Wmk. 352 *Perf. 14¼*
1010-1012 A246 Set of 3 10.00 10.00

European Philatelic Cooperation, 50th Anniv. (in 2006) — A247

Designs: $60, Green square. $70, Yellow diamond. $100 Blue square.

Perf. 13½

2005, June 1 Litho. Unwmk.
1013-1015 A247 Set of 3 10.00 10.00
1015a Souvenir sheet, #1013-1015 10.00 10.00

Europa stamps, 50th anniv. (in 2006).

Battle of Trafalgar, Bicent. — A248

Designs: $20, Gun captain holding powder cartridge. $30, Admiral Horatio Nelson, vert. $50, British 12-pounder cannon. $60, HMS Africa, vert. $70, HMS Leviathan being attacked by the Intrepide, vert. $90, HMS Victory.

$200, HMS Africa at Port Royal, Jamaica.

Wmk. 352, Unwmkd. ($90)

2005, June 23 Litho. *Perf. 13¼*
1016-1021 A248 Set of 6 15.50 15.50

Souvenir Sheet

Perf. 13½

1022 A248 $200 multi 10.00 10.00

No. 1021 has particles of wood from the HMS Victory embedded in areas covered by a thermographic process that produces a raised, shiny effect. No. 1022 contains one 44x44mm stamp.

Rotary International, Cent. — A249

2005, June 30 Wmk. 352 *Perf. 13¾*
1023 A249 $30 multi 2.00 2.00

Pope John Paul II (1920-2005) A250

Unwmk.

2005, Aug. 18 Litho. *Perf. 14*
1024 A250 $30 multi 2.00 2.00

Battle of Trafalgar, Bicent. — A251

Designs: $50, HMS Victory. $90, Ships in battle, horiz. $100, Admiral Horatio Nelson.

Perf. 13¼

2005, Oct. 18 Litho. Unwmk.
1025-1027 A251 Set of 3 11.50 11.50

Mary Seacole (1805-81), Nurse — A252

Seacole and: $30, Herbal remedies and medicines. $50, Seacole Hall, University of the West Indies. $60, Crimean War soldiers. $70, Medals.

Wmk. 352

2005, Nov. 21 Litho. *Perf. 13½*
1028-1031 A252 Set of 4 7.00 7.00

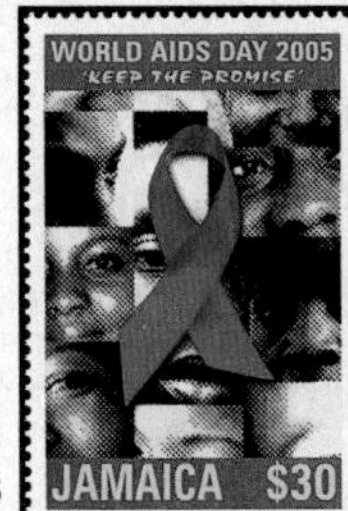

World AIDS Day — A253

2005, Dec. 1 *Perf. 14¾x14*
1032 A253 $30 multi 1.00 1.00

Christmas A254

Star of Bethlehem and poinsettia with various frame designs: $20, $30, $50, $80.

2005, Dec. 1
1033-1036 A254 Set of 4 6.00 6.00

Jessie Ripoll (Sister Mary Peter Claver), Founder of Alpha Schools — A255

2005, Dec. 12 *Perf. 13½*
1037 A255 $30 multi 1.10 1.10

Alpha Schools, 125th anniv.

Buildings Type of 2005

Designs: $10, Court House, Morant Bay. $15, Spanish Town Square, St. Catherine. $20, Mico College. $25, Simms Building, Jamaica College. $50, Devon House, St. Andrew. $70, Ward Theater, Kingston. $90, Vale Royal, St. Andrew. $100, Falmouth Post Office.

Perf. 14x13¼

2006, May 12 Litho. Wmk. 352
1038 A245 $10 multi .30 .30
1039 A245 $15 multi .50 .50
1040 A245 $20 multi .65 .65
1041 A245 $25 multi .80 .80
1042 A245 $50 multi 1.60 1.60
1043 A245 $70 multi 2.25 2.25
1044 A245 $90 multi 3.00 3.00
1045 A245 $100 multi 3.25 3.25
Nos. 1038-1045 (8) 12.35 12.35

Self-Adhesive

Unwmk.

Serpentine Die Cut 13¼x14

1046 A245 $10 multi .30 .30
1047 A245 $15 multi .50 .50
1048 A245 $20 multi .65 .65
1049 A245 $25 multi .80 .80
1050 A245 $50 multi 1.60 1.60
1051 A245 $70 multi 2.25 2.25
1052 A245 $90 multi 3.00 3.00
1053 A245 $100 multi 3.25 3.25
Nos. 1046-1053 (8) 12.35 12.35

Nos. 1038, 1040, 1042, 1043 and 1044 exist dated "2008."

Worldwide Fund for Nature (WWF) A256

Black-billed Amazon parrot: $5, Chicks. $10, Head of adult bird. $30, Bird on branch. $50, Two birds.

Perf. 13¼x13½

2006, Nov. 30 Litho. Wmk. 352
1054-1057 A256 Set of 4 3.50 3.50
1057a Sheet, 4 each #1054-1057 14.00 14.00

Christmas — A257

Flowers: $20, Cup and saucer. $30, Lignum vitae. $50, Neocogniauxia monophylla, vert. $60, Ghost orchid, vert.

Perf. 13¼x13¾, 13¾x13¼

2006, Nov. 30
1058-1061 A257 Set of 4 5.00 5.00

2007 ICC Cricket World Cup, West Indies — A258

Designs: No. 1062, $30, Courtney Walsh. No. 1063, $30, Collie Smith. $40, New Sabrina Park, horiz. $50, Like #1062. $60, Trelawney Multi-purpose Sports Complex, horiz.
$200, ICC Cricket World Cup.

Wmk. 352
2007, Feb. 28 **Litho.** ***Perf. 14***
1062-1066 A258 Set of 5 6.25 6.25

Souvenir Sheet
1067 A258 $200 multi 6.00 6.00

British Abolition of the Slave Trade, Bicent. — A259

Wmk. 352
2007, June 7 **Litho.** ***Perf. 14***
1068 A259 $30 multi .90 .90

Scouting, Cent. A260

Designs: $5, Boy scout, Jamaican flag, Scout salute. $10, Scouts, compass. $30, Scouts, lashed poles. $70, Scouts handling Jamaican flag, Scout making craft.
No. 1073, vert.: a, $50, Scouts on parade. b, $100, Lord Robert Baden-Powell blowing kudu horn.

2007, July 9 ***Perf. 13¾***
1069-1072 A260 Set of 4 3.50 3.50

Souvenir Sheet
1073 A260 Sheet of 2, #a-b 4.50 4.50

Christmas — A261

Flowers: $20, Tolumnia triquetra. $30, Broughtonia negrilensis, horiz. $50, Broughtonia sanguinea, horiz. $60, Spathelia sorbifolia.

Wmk. 352
2007, Nov. 9 **Litho.** ***Perf. 14***
1074-1077 A261 Set of 4 4.50 4.50

2008 Summer Olympics, Beijing A262

Designs: $20, Fish, Asafa Powell. $60, Lanterns, Veronica Campbell-Brown.
No. 1079: a, Bamboo, Aleen Bailey, Veronica Campbell-Brown. b, Sherone Simpson, Tayna Lawrence, dragon.

Wmk. 352
2008, Apr. 30 **Litho.** ***Perf. 13¼***
1078 A262 $20 multi .60 .60
1079 A262 $30 Horiz. pair, #a-b 1.75 1.75
1080 A262 $60 multi 1.75 1.75
Nos. 1078-1080 (3) 4.10 4.10

University of Technology, 50th Anniv. — A263

2008, May 26 **Litho.** ***Perf. 14***
1081 A263 $30 multi .85 .85
a. Souvenir sheet of 1 .85 .85

Associated Board of the Royal Schools of Music in Jamaica, Cent. — A264

Map of Jamaica and: $30, Piano keyboard. $70, Violin.

Wmk. 352
2008, Oct. 30 **Litho.** ***Perf. 14***
1082-1083 A264 Set of 2 2.75 2.75

Christmas A265

Various ferns: $20, $30, $50, $60.

Wmk. 352
2008, Nov. 21 **Litho.** ***Perf. 13¾***
1084-1087 A265 Set of 4 4.25 4.25

SEMI-POSTAL STAMPS

Native Girl — SP1

Native Boy — SP2

Native Boy and Girl — SP3

1923, Nov. 1 **Engr.** ***Perf. 12***
B1 SP1 ½p green & black .70 *6.25*
B2 SP2 1p car & black 2.00 *11.50*
B3 SP3 2½p blue & black 9.75 *20.00*
Nos. B1-B3 (3) 12.45 *37.75*

Each stamp was sold for ½p over face value. The surtax benefited the Child Saving League of Jamaica.

Catalogue values for unused stamps in this section, from this point to the end of the section, are for Never Hinged items.

Nos. 694-697 Surcharged "HURRICANE GILBERT RELIEF FUND" and New Value in Black

Wmk. 352
1988, Nov. 11 **Litho.** ***Perf. 14***
B4 A164 25c +25c multi .20 .20
B5 A164 45c +45c multi .30 .25
B6 A164 $4 +$4 multi 3.00 *3.25*
B7 A164 $5 +$5 multi 3.00 *3.25*
Nos. B4-B7 (4) 6.50 6.95

Red Surcharge
B4a A164 25c + 25c .20 .20
B5a A164 45c + 45c .30 .25
B6a A164 $4 + $4 3.00 *3.25*
B7a A164 $5 + $5 3.00 *3.25*
Nos. B4a-B7a (4) 6.50 6.95

WAR TAX STAMPS

Regular Issues of 1906-19 Overprinted WAR STAMP.

1916 **Wmk. 3** ***Perf. 14***
MR1 A14 ½p green .20 .40
a. Without period 11.00 *27.50*
b. Double overprint 120.00 *140.00*
c. Inverted overprint 100.00 *130.00*
d. As "c," without period 350.00
MR2 A17 3p violet, *yel* 1.10 *20.00*
a. Without period 27.50 *90.00*

Surface-colored Paper
MR3 A17 3p violet, *yel* 17.50 *32.50*
Nos. MR1-MR3 (3) 18.80 *52.90*

Regular Issues of 1906-18 Overprinted

MR4 A14 ½p green .20 .30
a. Without period 12.50 *37.50*
b. Pair, one without ovpt. 4,250. 3,750.
c. "R" inserted by hand 1,500. 1,600.
d. "WAR" only 125.00
MR5 A17 1½p orange .20 .20
a. Without period 5.75 *8.50*
b. "TAMP" 150.00 *160.00*
c. "S" inserted by hand 400.00
d. "R" omitted 2,000. 1,900.
e. "R" inserted by hand 1,100. 900.00
MR6 A17 3p violet, *yel* 3.00 1.10
a. Without period 40.00 *62.50*
b. "TAMP" 600.00 600.00
c. "S" inserted by hand 225.00 225.00
d. Inverted overprint 325.00 175.00
e. As "a," inverted
Nos. MR4-MR6 (3) 3.40 1.60

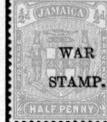

Regular Issues of 1906-19 Overprinted

1917, Mar.
MR7 A14 ½p green .60 .35
a. Without period 10.00 *29.00*
b. Overprinted on back instead of face 210.00
c. Inverted overprint 17.50 45.00
MR8 A17 1½p orange .20 .20
a. Without period 4.00 *20.00*
b. Double overprint 92.50 *100.00*
c. Inverted overprint 92.50 85.00
d. As "a," inverted
MR9 A17 3p violet, *yel* .60 1.60
a. Without period 19.00 *45.00*
b. Vertical overprint 350.00 350.00
c. Inverted overprint 160.00
d. As "a," inverted
Nos. MR7-MR9 (3) 1.40 2.15

There are many minor varieties of Nos. MR1-MR9.

Regular Issues of 1906-19 Overprinted in Red

1919, Oct. 4
MR10 A14 ½p green .20 .20
MR11 A17 3p violet, *yel* 4.25 3.50

OFFICIAL STAMPS

No. 16 Overprinted in Black

Type I — Word 15 to 16mm long.
Type II — Word 17 to 17½mm long.

1890 **Wmk. 2** ***Perf. 14***
O1 A7 ½p green (II) 14.00 2.25
a. Type I 32.50 29.00
b. Inverted overprint (II) 90.00 *95.00*
c. Double overprint (II) 90.00 *95.00*
d. Dbl. ovpt., one invtd. (II) 450.00 450.00
e. Dbl. ovpt., one vert. (II) 1,100.
f. Double overprint (I) 650.00

Missing "O," "L" or one or both "I's" known.

No. 16 and Type of 1889 Overprinted

1890-91
O2 A7 ½p green 11.00 1.75
O3 A10 1p carmine rose 7.25 1.50
O4 A10 2p slate 16.00 1.50
Nos. O2-O4 (3) 34.25 4.75

JAPAN

jə-'pan

LOCATION — North Pacific Ocean, east of China
GOVT. — Constitutional monarchy
AREA — 142,726 sq. mi.
POP. — 126,182,077 (1999 est.)
CAPITAL — Tokyo

1000 Mon = 10 Sen
100 Sen = 1 Yen (or En)
10 Rin = 1 Sen

Catalogue values for unused stamps in this country are for Never Hinged items, beginning with Scott 375 in the regular postage section, Scott B8 in the semi-postal section, and Scott C9 in the airpost section.

Watermarks

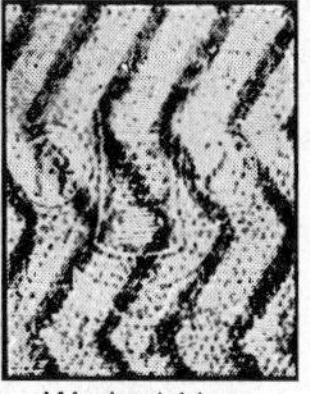

Wmk. 141 — Zigzag Lines

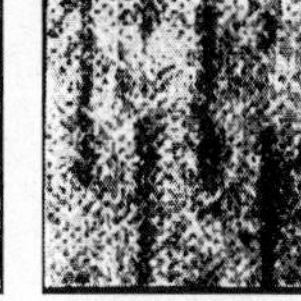

Wmk. 142 — Parallel Lines

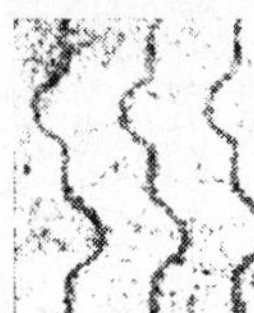

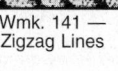

Wmk. 257 — Curved Wavy Lines

After 1945, Wmk. 257 exists also in a narrow spacing on a small number of issues.

Counterfeits of Nos. 1-71 are plentiful. Some are excellent and deceive many collectors.

Nos. 1-54A were printed from plates of 40 with individually engraved subjects. Each stamp in the sheet is slightly different.

Pair of Dragons Facing Characters of Value — A1

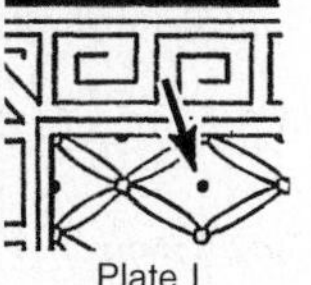

Plate I

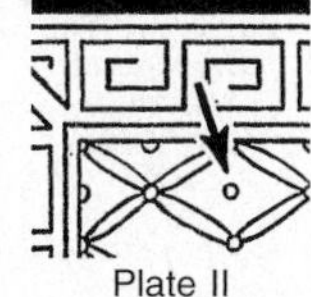

Plate II

48 mon:
Plate I — Solid dots in inner border.
Plate II — Tiny circles replace dots.

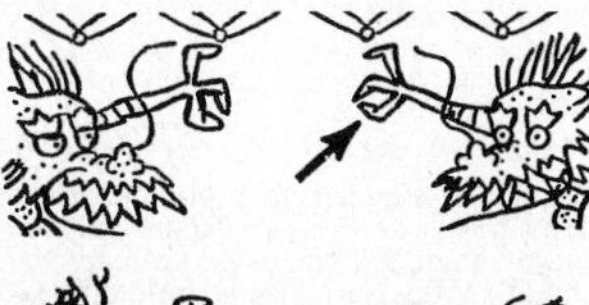

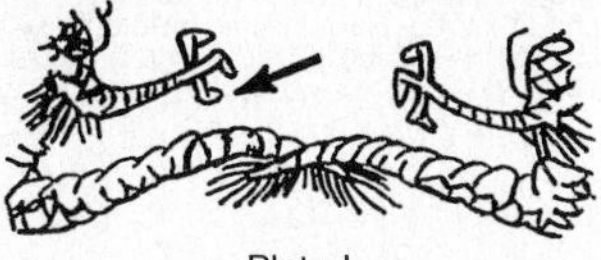

Plate I

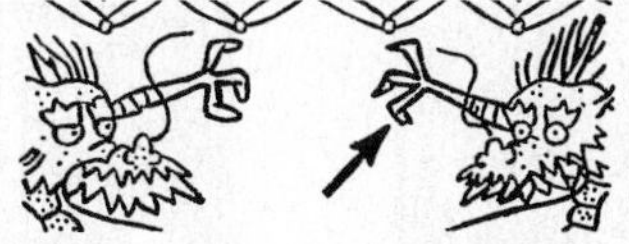

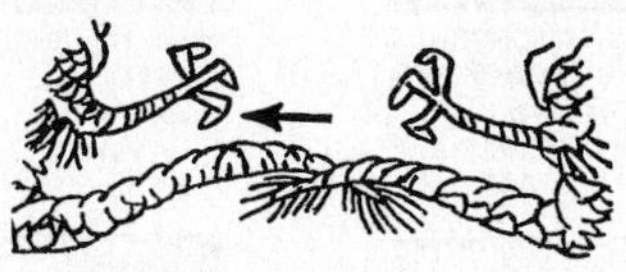

Plate II

100 mon:
Plate I — Lowest dragon claw at upper right and at lower left point upward.
Plate II — Same two claws point downward.

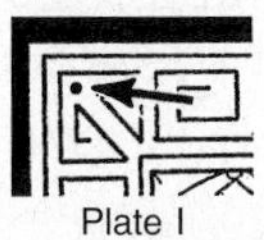

Plate I

Plate II

200 mon:
Plate I — Dot in upper left corner.
Plate II — No dot. (Some Plate I copies show dot faintly; these can be mistaken for Plate II.)

Plate I

Plate II

500 mon:
Plate I — Lower right corner of Greek-type border incomplete
Plate II — Short horizontal line completes corner border pattern.

Unwmk.

1871, Apr. 20 Engr. *Imperf.*

Native Laid Paper Without Gum
Denomination in Black

1	A1	48m brown (I)	250.	275.
a.		48m red brown (I)	325.	325.
b.		Wove paper (I)	275.	275.
c.		48m brown (II)	290.	285.
d.		Wove paper (II)	310.	310.
2	A1	100m blue (I)	225.	225.
a.		Wove paper (I)	300.	300.
b.		Plate II	500.	500.
c.		Wove paper (II)	750.	750.
3	A1	200m vermilion (I)	375.	300.
a.		Wove paper (I)	450.	325.
b.		Plate II	1,750.	1,500.
c.		Wove paper (II)		*3,000.*
4	A1	500m blue green (I)	550.	500.
a.		500m greenish blue (I)	600.	500.
b.		500m green (I)	1,600.	1,000.
c.		500m yellow green (I)	1,750.	1,100.
d.		Wove paper (I)	650.	500.
e.		500m blue green (II)	600.	*3,000.*
f.		500m greenish blue (II)	600.	*3,000.*
g.		Wove paper (II)	1,900.	*4,000.*
h.		Denomination inverted (I)		*175,000.*

Perforations, Nos. 5-8

Perforations on Nos. 5-8 generally are rough and irregular due to the perforating equipment used and the quality of the paper. Values are for stamps with rough perfs that touch the frameline on one or more sides.

Dragons and Denomination — A1a

½ sen:
Plate I — Same as 48m Plate II. Measures not less than 19.8x19.8mm. Some subjects on this plate measure 20.3x20.2mm.
Plate II — Same as 48m Plate II. Measures not more than 19.7x19.3mm. Some subjects measure 19.3x18.7mm.

Plates I & II

Plate III

1 sen:
Plate I — Same as 100m Plate I. Narrow space between frameline and Greek-type border.
Plate II — Same as 100m Plate II. Same narrow space between frameline and border.
Plate III — Space between frameline and border is much wider. Frameline thinner. Shading on dragon heads heavier than on Plates I & II.

Native Laid Paper
With or Without Gum

1872 *Perf. 9-12 & compound*

Denomination in Black

5	A1a	½s brown (II)	100.00	100.00
a.		½s red brown (II)	100.00	100.00
b.		½s gray brown (II)	100.00	100.00
c.		Wove paper (II)	700.00	625.00
d.		½s brown (I)	150.00	150.00
e.		½s red brown (I)	150.00	150.00
f.		½s gray brown (I)	150.00	150.00
g.		Wove paper (I)	200.00	210.00
6	A1a	1s blue (II)	300.00	300.00
a.		Wove paper (II)	600.00	600.00
b.		Plate I	1,000.	*2,250.*
c.		Wove paper (I)	*5,000.*	
d.		Plate III	*7,500.*	1,750.
e.		Wove paper (III)		*5,000.*
7	A1a	2s vermilion	450.00	450.00
a.		Wove paper	450.00	500.00
8	A1a	5s blue green	650.00	550.00
a.		5s yellow green	650.00	550.00
b.		Wove paper	750.00	750.00

In 1896 the government made imperforate imitations of Nos. 6-7 to include in a presentation book.

Expect perforations on Nos. 9-71 to be rough and irregular.

Imperial Crest and Branches of Kiri Tree — A2

Dragons and Chrysanthemum Crest — A3

Imperial Chrysanthemum Crest — A4

Imperial Crest and Branches of Kiri Tree — A5

Perf. 9 to 13 and Compound

1872-73

Native Wove or Laid Paper of Varying Thickness

9	A2	½s brown, *hard wove*	25.00	21.00
a.		Upper character in left label has 2 diagonal top strokes missing	2,100.	1,250.
b.		Laid paper	80.00	—
c.		As "a," laid paper	2,200.	—
d.		½s gray brown, *soft porous native wove*	80.00	—

Nos. 9, 9a are on stiff, brittle wove paper. Nos. 9b, 9c and 9d on a soft, fibrous paper. Nos. 9b, 9c and 9d probably were never put in use, though genuine used examples do exist.

10	A2	1s blue, *wove*	50.00	26.00
a.		Laid paper	52.50	29.00
11	A2	2s ver, *wove*	100.00	50.00
12	A2	2s dull rose, *laid*	75.00	35.00
a.		Wove paper	100.00	50.00
13	A2	2s yel, *laid* ('73)	75.00	21.00
a.		Wove paper ('73)	175.00	26.00
14	A2	4s rose, *laid* ('73)	67.50	26.00
a.		Wove paper ('73)	210.00	32.50
15	A3	10s blue grn, *wove*	260.00	160.00
16	A3	10s yel grn, *laid*	475.00	325.00
a.		Wove paper ('73)	525.00	500.00
17	A4	20s lilac, *wove*	350.00	300.00
a.		20s violet, *wove*	350.00	300.00
b.		20s red violet, *laid*		—
18	A5	30s gray, *wove*	450.00	350.00

See Nos. 24-25, 30-31, 37-39, 51-52.

1874

Foreign Wove Paper

24	A2	4s rose	600.00	200.00
25	A5	30s gray	—	*5,000.*

A6

A7

A8

Design A6 differs from A2 by the addition of a syllabic character in a box covering crossed kiri branches above SEN. Stamps of design A6 differ for each value in border and spandrel designs.

In design A7, the syllabic character appears just below the buckle. In design A8, it appears in an oval frame at bottom center below SE of SEN.

With Syllabic Characters

イ	ロ	ハ	ニ	ホ	ヘ	ト	チ
i	ro	ha	ni	ho	he	to	chi
1	2	3	4	5	6	7	8

リ	ヌ	ル	チ	ワ	カ	ヨ	タ
ri	nu	ru	wo	wa	ka	yo	ta
9	10	11	12	13	14	15	16

レ	ソ	ツ	子	ナ	ラ	ム
re	so	tsu	ne	na	ra	mu
17	18	19	20	21	22	23

Perf. 9½ to 12½ and Compound

1874

Native Laid or Wove Paper

28	A6	2s yellow (syll. 1)	*25,000.*	400.00
		Syllabic 16	400.00	
29	A7	6s vio brn (Syll. 1)	1,500.	450.00
		Syllabic 2	1,750.	475.00
		Syllabic 3	20,000.	1,100.
		Syllabic 4,5	20,000.	600.00
		Syllabic 6	20,000.	700.00
		Syllabic 7	25,000.	550.00
		Syllabic 8	25,000.	550.00
		Syllabic 9	20,000.	700.00
		Syllabic 10		3,500.
		Syllabic 11		3,000.
		Syllabic 12	20,000.	1,900.
30	A4	20s red vio (Syll. 3)	*10,000.*	
		Syllabic 1		*150,000.*
		Syllabic 2	*10,000.*	
31	A5	30s gray (Syll. 1)	2,600.	3,000.
	a.	Very thin laid paper	2,600.	3,000.

No. 30, syll. 1, comes only with specimen dot.

Perf. 11 to 12½ and Compound

1874

Foreign Wove Paper

32	A6	½s brown (Syll. 1)	25.00	25.00
		Syllabic 2	40.00	40.00
33	A6	1s blue (Syll. 4)	160.00	40.00
		Syllabic 1	150.00	35.00
		Syllabic 2	225.00	40.00
		Syllabic 3	200.00	40.00
		Syllabic 5	650.00	150.00
		Syllabic 6, 9	150.00	40.00
		Syllabic 7	350.00	45.00
		Syllabic 8	150.00	40.00
		Syllabic 10	225.00	70.00
		Syllabic 11	215.00	60.00
		Syllabic 12	250.00	65.00
34	A6	2s yel (Syll. 2-4, 15, 17, 20)	200.00	30.00
		Syllabic 1	400.00	35.00
		Syllabic 5	400.00	30.00
		Syllabic 6	2,000.	50.00
		Syllabic 7	2,000.	30.00
		Syllabic 8	200.00	55.00
		Syllabic 9	200.00	35.00
		Syllabic 10	*2,750.*	50.00
		Syllabic 11	200.00	30.00
		Syllabic 12,22	*2,650.*	30.00
		Syllabic 13	*2,500.*	30.00
		Syllabic 14	*2,650.*	45.00
		Syllabic 16	*2,500.*	30.00
		Syllabic 18,19	200.00	30.00
		Syllabic 21	250.00	30.00
		Syllabic 23	265.00	30.00
35	A6	4s rose (Syll. 1)	2,600.	475.00
36	A7	6s vio brn (Syll. 16)	175.00	70.00
		Syllabic 10	500.00	500.00
		Syllabic 11	500.00	
		Syllabic 13	12,500.	*4,500.*
		Syllabic 14	300.00	275.00
		Syllabic 15	20,000.	*2,400.*
		Syllabic 17	215.00	80.00
		Syllabic 18	325.00	115.00
37	A3	10s yel grn (Syll. 2)	300.00	100.00
		Syllabic 1	240.00	75.00
		Syllabic 3	650.00	300.00
38	A4	20s violet (Syll. 5)	300.00	95.00
		Syllabic 4	325.00	100.00
39	A5	30s gray (Syll. 1)	350.00	100.00

1875 *Perf. 9 to 13 and Compound*

40	A6	½s gray (Syll. 2, 3)	22.50	20.00
		Syllabic 4	35.00	1,000.
41	A6	1s brn (Syll. 15)	35.00	22.50
		Syllabic 5	375.00	50.00
		Syllabic 7	2,250.	275.00
		Syllabic 8	*32,500.*	275.00
		Syllabic 12	900.00	225.00
		Syllabic 13	50.00	22.50
		Syllabic 14	50.00	22.50
		Syllabic 16-17	40.00	22.50
42	A6	4s green (Syll. 1)	125.00	27.50
		Syllabic 2	200.00	27.50
		Syllabic 3	125.00	27.50
43	A7	6s orange (Syll. 16,17)	100.00	25.00
		Syllabic 10	175.00	50.00
		Syllabic 11	150.00	40.00
		Syllabic 13	225.00	40.00
		Syllabic 14	160.00	32.50
		Syllabic 15		150,000.
44	A8	6s orange (Syll. 20)	100.00	25.00
		Syllabic 19	100.00	25.00
		Syllabic 21	100.00	25.00
		Syllabic 22	4,250.	1,750.

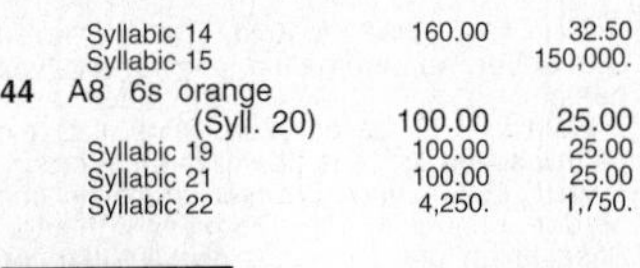

Dragons
A9

Wild Goose
A10

Wagtail — A11

Imperial Crest — A11a

Kiri Branches — A11b

Goshawk — A12

45	A9	10s ultra (Syll. 4)	175.00	27.50
		Syllabic 5	*4,150.*	350.00
46	A10	12s rose (Syll. 1)	350.00	150.00
		Syllabic 2	400.00	175.00
		Syllabic 3	*3,500.*	500.00
47	A11	15s lilac (Syll. 1)	350.00	150.00
		Syllabic 2	400.00	165.00
		Syllabic 3	350.00	175.00
48	A11a	20s rose (Syll. 8)	140.00	20.00
49	A11b	30s vio (Syll. 2-4)	175.00	65.00
50	A12	45s lake (Syll. 1)	450.00	275.00
		Syllabic 2	1,250.	450.00
		Syllabic 3	1,200.	425.00

Issued: #46, syll. 2, 1882; #46, syll. 3, 1883; others, 1875.

The 1s brown on laid paper, type A6, formerly listed as No. 50A, is one of several stamps of the preceding issue which exist on a laid type paper. They are difficult to identify and mainly of interest to specialists.

Without Syllabic Characters

1875

51	A2	1s brown	*6,500.*	675.00
52	A2	4s green	275.00	90.00

Branches of Kiri Tree Tied with Ribbon
A13

Imperial Crest and Kiri Branches
A14

1875-76

53	A13	1s brown	80.00	15.00
54	A13	2s yellow	100.00	16.00
54A	A14	5s green ('76)	200.00	100.00
		Nos. 53-54A (3)	380.00	131.00

A15

A16

Imperial Crest, Star and Kiri Branches
A17

Sun, Kikumon and Kiri Branches
A18

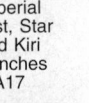

Imperial Crest and Kiri Branches
A19

Kikumon
A20

Perf. 8 to 14 and Compound

1876-77 **Typo.**

55	A15	5r slate	16.00	10.00
56	A16	1s black	37.50	4.25
	a.	Horiz. pair, imperf. btwn.		
57	A16	2s brown ol	52.50	3.00
58	A16	4s blue grn	42.50	4.00
	a.	4s green	42.50	4.00
59	A17	5s brown	65.00	22.50
60	A17	6s orange ('77)	160.00	65.00
61	A17	8s vio brn ('77)	67.50	6.00
62	A17	10s blue ('77)	55.00	2.50
63	A17	12s rose ('77)	210.00	150.00
64	A18	15s yel grn ('77)	150.00	2.50
65	A18	20s dk blue ('77)	160.00	12.00
66	A18	30s violet ('77)	210.00	110.00
	a.	30s red violet	210.00	110.00
67	A18	45s carmine ('77)	625.00	525.00

1879

68	A16	1s maroon	15.00	1.25
69	A16	2s dk violet	40.00	2.00
70	A16	3s orange	60.00	24.00
71	A18	50s carmine	210.00	12.50
		Nos. 68-71 (4)	325.00	39.75

1883

72	A16	1s green	11.50	.60
73	A16	2s car rose	15.00	.25
74	A17	5s ultra	22.50	.50
		Nos. 72-74 (3)	49.00	1.35

1888-92

75	A15	5r gray blk ('89)	5.00	.45
76	A16	3s lilac rose ('92)	15.00	.45
77	A16	4s olive bis	13.00	.45
78	A17	8s blue lilac	19.00	1.60
79	A17	10s brown org	17.00	.45
80	A18	15s purple	57.50	.50
81	A18	20s orange	75.00	1.50
	a.	20s yellow	75.00	1.50
82	A19	25s blue green	150.00	1.50
83	A18	50s brown	100.00	3.25
84	A20	1y carmine	160.00	4.25
		Nos. 75-84 (10)	611.50	14.40

Stamps of types A16-A18 differ for each value, in backgrounds and ornaments.

Nos. 58, 61-62, 64-65, 71-84 are found with telegraph or telephone office cancellations. These sell at considerably lower prices than postally used copies.

Cranes and Imperial Crest — A21

Perf. 11½ to 13 and Compound

1894, Mar. 9

85	A21	2s carmine	24.00	3.00
86	A21	5s ultra	37.50	11.00

25th wedding anniv. of Emperor Meiji (Mutsuhito) and Empress Haru.

Gen. Yoshihisa Kitashirakawa
A22 A23

Field Marshal Akihito Arisugawa
A24 A25

1896, Aug. 1 **Engr.**

87	A22	2s rose	26.00	2.75
88	A23	5s deep ultra	52.50	2.75
89	A24	2s rose	26.00	2.75
90	A25	5s deep ultra	52.50	2.75
		Nos. 87-90 (4)	157.00	11.00

Victory in Chinese-Japanese War (1894-95).

A26

A27

A28

A29

Perf. 11½ to 14 and Compound

1899-1907 **Typo.**

91	A26	5r gray	5.50	1.00
92	A26	½s gray ('01)	3.00	.20
93	A26	1s lt red brn	3.50	.20
94	A26	1½s ultra ('00)	12.00	.85
95	A26	1½s violet ('06)	9.00	.25
96	A26	2s lt green	9.00	.20
97	A26	3s violet brn	8.50	.25
	a.	Double impression		
98	A26	3s rose ('06)	5.00	.25
99	A26	4s rose	6.00	1.25
	a.	4s pink ('06)	7.00	1.75
100	A26	5s orange yel	17.00	.25
101	A27	6s maroon ('07)	29.00	3.50
102	A27	8s olive grn	30.00	5.00
103	A27	10s deep blue	11.00	.20
104	A27	15s purple	40.00	2.00
105	A27	20s red orange	21.00	.25
106	A28	25s blue green	60.00	1.00
107	A28	50s red brown	60.00	2.00
108	A29	1y carmine	70.00	3.00
		Nos. 91-108 (18)	399.50	21.65

For overprints see Nos. M1, Offices in China, 1-18, Offices in Korea, 1-14.

Boxes for Rice Cakes and Marriage Certificates
A30

Symbols of Korea and Japan
A31

Perf. 11½ to 12½ and Compound

1900, May 10

109	A30	3s carmine	28.00	1.00

Wedding of the Crown Prince Yoshihito and Princess Sadako.

For overprints see Offices in China No. 19, Offices in Korea, 15.

1905, July 1

110	A31	3s rose red	80.00	19.00

Issued to commemorate the amalgamation of the postal services of Japan and Korea. Korean stamps were withdrawn from sale June 30, 1905, but remained valid until 1909. No. 110 was used in the Korea and China Offices of Japan, as well as in Japan proper.

Field-piece and Japanese Flag — A32

Empress Jingo — A33

1906, Apr. 29

111 A32 1½s blue 26.00 4.00
112 A32 3s carmine rose 55.00 16.00

Triumphal military review following the Russo-Japanese War.

1908 **Engr.**

113 A33 5y green 750.00 5.00
114 A33 10y dark violet 1,000. 7.50

The frame of No. 114 differs slightly from the illustration.
See Nos. 146-147.
For overprints see Offices in China Nos. 20-21, 48-49.

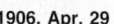

A34

A35

A36

Perf. 12, 12x13, 13x13½

1913 **Typo.** **Unwmk.**

115 A34 ½s brown 6.00 .85
116 A34 1s orange 12.00 .85
117 A34 1½s lt blue 16.00 1.25
a. Booklet pane of 6 175.00
118 A34 2s green 17.00 .85
119 A34 3s rose 24.00 .45
a. Booklet pane of 6 175.00
120 A35 4s red 26.00 10.50
121 A35 5s violet 30.00 1.25
122 A35 10s deep blue 95.00 .60
123 A35 20s claret 95.00 1.25
124 A35 25s olive green 95.00 2.60
125 A36 1y yel grn & mar 650.00 24.00
Nos. 115-125 (11) 1,066. 44.45

1914-25 **Wmk. 141** **Granite Paper**
Size: 19x22½mm ("Old Die")

127 A34 ½s brown 2.10 .20
128 A34 1s orange 2.10 .20
129 A34 1½s blue 2.10 .20
a. Booklet pane of 6 72.50
d. As "a," imperf.
130 A34 2s green 4.25 .20
a. Booklet pane of 6 72.50
131 A34 3s rose 1.60 .20
a. Booklet pane of 6 60.00
132 A35 4s red 14.00 1.00
a. Booklet pane of 6 72.50
133 A35 5s violet 13.00 .45
134 A35 6s brown ('19) 18.00 2.40
136 A35 8s gray ('19) 15.00 9.00
137 A35 10s deep blue 15.00 .20
a. Booklet pane of 6 72.50
138 A35 13s olive brn ('25) 35.00 1.90
139 A35 20s claret 72.50 .60
140 A35 25s olive grn 12.00 .85
141 A36 30s orange brn ('19) 18.00 .50
143 A36 50s dk brown ('19) 26.00 1.00
145 A36 1y yel grn & mar 140.00 1.50
b. Imperf., pair
146 A33 5y green 425.00 4.00
147 A33 10y violet 625.00 6.00
Nos. 127-147 (18) 1,440. 30.40

1924-33
"New Die" Size: 18½x22mm (Flat Plate)
or 18½x22½mm (Rotary)

127a A34 ½s brown 1.75 .95
128a A34 1s orange 1.75 .95
129b A34 1½s blue 2.75 .30
c. Bklt. pane of 6 ('30) 19.00
131b A34 3s rose 1.10 .20
c. Bklt. pane of 6 ('28) 45.00
133a A35 5s violet 15.00 .20
135 A35 7s red org ('30) 7.75 .20
138a A35 13s bister brn ('25) 6.00 .20
140a A35 25s olive green 45.00 .20
142 A36 30s org & grn ('29) 17.00 .30
144 A36 50s yel brn & dk bl ('29) 12.00 .50
145a A36 1y yel grn & mar 67.50 1.00
Nos. 127a-145a (11) 177.60 5.00

See Nos. 212-213, 239-241, 243, 245, 249-252, 255. For overprints see Nos. C1-C2, M2-M5, Offices in China, 22-47.

Ceremonial Cap — A37

Imperial Throne — A38

Enthronement Hall, Kyoto — A39

Perf. 12½

1915, Nov. 10 **Typo.** **Unwmk.**

148 A37 1½s red & blk 2.00 .55
149 A38 3s orange & vio 2.50 .80

Engr.
Perf. 12x12½

150 A39 4s carmine rose 12.00 10.00
151 A39 10s ultra 24.00 16.00
Nos. 148-151 (4) 40.50 27.35

Enthronement of Emperor Yoshihito.

Mandarin Duck — A40

Ceremonial Cap — A41

1916, Nov. 3 **Typo.** ***Perf. 12½***

152 A40 1½s green, red & yel 2.75 1.00
153 A40 3s red & yellow 4.50 1.25
154 A41 10s ultra & dk blue 775.00 225.00

Nomination of the Prince Heir Apparent, later Emperor Hirohito.

A42

Dove and Olive Branch — A43

Perf. 12, 12½, 13½x13

1919, July 1 **Engr.**

155 A42 1½s dark brown 2.00 .60
156 A43 3s gray green 2.50 1.00
157 A42 4s rose 5.50 3.75
158 A43 10s dark blue 23.00 12.00
Nos. 155-158 (4) 33.00 17.35

Restoration of peace after World War I.

Census Officer, A.D. 652 — A44

Meiji Shrine, Tokyo — A45

Perf. 12½

1920, Sept. 25 **Typo.** **Unwmk.**

159 A44 1½s red violet 6.50 2.60
160 A44 3s vermilion 7.00 2.60

Taking of the 1st modern census in Japan. Not available for foreign postage except to China.

1920, Nov. 1 **Engr.**

161 A45 1½s dull violet 2.50 1.10
162 A45 3s rose 2.50 1.10

Dedication of the Meiji Shrine. Not available for foreign postage except to China.

National and Postal Flags — A46

Ministry of Communications Building, Tokyo — A47

Typographed (A46), Engraved (A47)

1921, Apr. 20 ***Perf. 12½, 13x13½***

163 A46 1½s gray grn & red 1.60 .90
164 A47 3s violet brn 2.10 1.00
165 A46 4s rose & red 40.00 17.00
166 A47 10s dark blue 200.00 125.00
Nos. 163-166 (4) 243.70 143.90

50th anniv. of the establishment of postal service and Japanese postage stamps.

Battleships "Katori" and "Kashima" — A48

1921, Sept. 3 **Litho.** ***Perf. 12½***

167 A48 1½s violet 2.00 1.00
168 A48 3s olive green 2.25 1.00
169 A48 4s rose red 30.00 15.00
170 A48 10s deep blue 35.00 18.00
Nos. 167-170 (4) 69.25 35.00

Return of Crown Prince Hirohito from his European visit.

Mount Fuji — A49

Mt. Niitaka, Taiwan — A50

Perf. 13x13½

1930-37 **Typo.** **Wmk. 141**
Granite Paper
Size: 18½x22mm ("New Die")

171 A49 4s green ('37) 2.40 .35
172 A49 4s orange 5.50 .25
174 A49 8s olive green 8.50 .20
175a A49 20s blue ('37) 19.00 26.00
176 A49 20s brown violet 26.00 .20
Nos. 171-176 (5) 61.40 27.00

1922-29
Size: 19x22½mm ("Old Die")

171a A49 4s green 7.50 2.60
172a A49 4s orange ('29) 75.00 7.50
173 A49 8s rose 15.00 5.25
174a A49 8s olive green ('29) 210.00 67.50
175 A49 20s deep blue 17.00 .50
176a A49 20s brown vio ('29) 75.00 1.25
Nos. 171a-176a (6) 399.50 84.60

See Nos. 242, 246, 248.

Perf. 12½

1923, Apr. 16 **Unwmk.** **Engr.**

177 A50 1½s orange 8.50 6.75
178 A50 3s dark violet 13.00 5.75

1st visit of Crown Prince Hirohito to Taiwan. The stamps were sold only in Taiwan, but were valid throughout the empire.

Cherry Blossoms A51

Sun and Dragonflies A52

Empress Jingo — A53

1923 Wmk. 142 Litho. *Imperf.*
Without Gum; Granite Paper

179	A51	½s	gray	4.50	2.25
180	A51	1½s	lt blue	5.00	1.00
181	A51	2s	red brown	4.50	1.00
182	A51	3s	brt rose	3.25	.80
183	A51	4s	gray green	35.00	12.00
184	A51	5s	dull violet	15.00	1.00
185	A51	8s	red orange	55.00	21.00
186	A52	10s	deep brown	27.50	1.00
187	A52	20s	deep blue	30.00	1.25
			Nos. 179-187 (9)	179.75	41.30

#179-187 exist rouletted and with various perforations. These were made privately.

Perf. 12, 13x13½
1924 Engr. Wmk. 141
Granite Paper

188	A53	5y	gray green	240.00	3.00
189	A53	10y	dull violet	350.00	2.00

See Nos. 253-254.

Cranes — A54

Phoenix — A55

Perf. 10½ to 13½ and Compound
1925, May 10 Litho. Unwmk.

190	A54	1½s	gray violet	2.00	1.00
191	A55	3s	silver & brn org	2.60	1.50
a.			Vert. pair, imperf. btwn.	425.00	
192	A54	8s	light red	20.00	11.00
193	A55	20s	silver & gray grn	45.00	35.00
			Nos. 190-193 (4)	69.60	48.50

25th wedding anniv. of the Emperor Yoshihito (Taisho) and Empress Sadako.

Mt. Fuji — A56

Yomei Gate, Nikko — A57

Nagoya Castle — A58

Perf. 13½x13
1926-37 Typo. Wmk. 141
Granite Paper

194	A56	2s	green	1.60	.20
195	A57	6s	carmine	6.00	.20
196	A58	10s	dark blue	7.00	.20
197	A58	10s	carmine ('37)	8.00	7.00
			Nos. 194-197 (4)	22.60	7.60

See Nos. 244, 247. For surcharges see People's Republic of China No. 2L5-2L6.

Baron Hisoka Maejima — A59

Map of World on Mollweide's Projection — A60

Perf. 12½, 13x13½
1927, June 20 Unwmk.

198	A59	1½s	lilac	2.50	1.00
199	A59	3s	olive green	2.50	1.00
200	A60	6s	carmine rose	50.00	45.00
201	A60	10s	blue	62.50	45.00
			Nos. 198-201 (4)	117.50	92.00

50th anniv. of Japan's joining the UPU. Baron Maejima (1835-1919) organized Japan's modern postal system and was postmaster general.

Phoenix — A61

Enthronement Hall, Kyoto — A62

1928, Nov. 10 Engr. *Perf. 12½*
Yellow Paper

202	A61	1½s	deep green	1.00	.50
203	A62	3s	red violet	1.00	.50
204	A61	6s	carmine rose	2.10	1.60
205	A62	10s	deep blue	3.00	2.10
			Nos. 202-205 (4)	7.10	4.70

Enthronement of Emperor Hirohito.

Great Shrines of Ise — A63

Map of Japanese Empire — A64

1929, Oct. 2 *Perf. 12½*

206	A63	1½s	gray violet	1.00	1.00
207	A63	3s	carmine	1.50	1.10

58th rebuilding of the Ise Shrines.

1930, Sept. 25 Unwmk.

208	A64	1½s	deep violet	2.00	1.25
209	A64	3s	deep red	2.25	1.50

2nd census in the Japanese Empire.

Meiji Shrine — A65

1930, Nov. 1 Litho.

210	A65	1½s	green	1.50	.85
211	A65	3s	brown org	2.00	1.00

10th anniv. of dedication of Meiji Shrine.

Coil Stamps
Wmk. Zigzag Lines (141)
1933 Typo. *Perf. 13 Horiz.*

212	A34	1½s	light blue	13.00	17.00
213	A34	3s	rose	14.00	21.00

Japanese Red Cross Badge — A66

Red Cross Building, Tokyo — A67

Perf. 12½
1934, Oct. 1 Engr. Unwmk.

214	A66	1½s	green & red	1.50	1.00
215	A67	3s	dull vio & red	1.75	1.25
216	A66	6s	dk car & red	8.00	5.00
217	A67	10s	blue & red	12.00	8.00
			Nos. 214-217 (4)	23.25	15.25

15th International Red Cross Congress. Sheets of 20 with commemorative marginal inscription. One side of sheet is perf. 13.

White Tower of Liaoyang and Warship "Hiei" — A68

Akasaka Detached Palace, Tokyo — A69

1935, Apr. 2

218	A68	1½s	olive green	1.00	.60
219	A69	3s	red brown	1.50	1.00
220	A68	6s	carmine	6.25	3.00
221	A69	10s	blue	9.00	6.00
			Nos. 218-221 (4)	17.75	10.60

Visit of Emperor Kang Teh of Manchukuo (Henry Pu-yi) to Tokyo, April 6, 1935. Sheets of 20 with commemorative marginal inscription. One side of sheet is perf. 13.

Mt. Fuji — A70

1935 Typo. *Perf. 13x13½*
Granite Paper

222	A70	1½s	rose carmine	10.00	.75
a.			Miniature sheet of 20	700.00	500.00

Issued to pay postage on New Year's cards from Dec. 1-31, 1935. After Jan. 1, 1936, used for ordinary letter postage. No. 222 was issued in sheets of 100.

Mt. Fuji A71

Fuji from Lake Ashi A72

Fuji from Lake Kawaguchi — A73

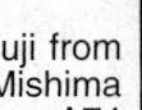

Fuji from Mishima A74

1936, July 10 Photo. Wmk. 141
Granite Paper

223	A71	1½s	red brown	3.00	2.00
224	A72	3s	dark green	4.50	3.00
225	A73	6s	carmine rose	10.00	8.00
226	A74	10s	dark blue	12.00	10.00
			Nos. 223-226 (4)	29.50	23.00

Fuji-Hakone National Park.

Dove, Map of Manchuria and Kwantung — A75

Shinto Shrine, Port Arthur — A76

Headquarters of Kwantung Government A77

1936, Sept. 1 Litho. *Perf. 12½*
Granite Paper

227	A75	1½s	gray violet	18.00	10.00
228	A76	3s	red brown	14.00	12.00
229	A77	10s	dull green	200.00	130.00
			Nos. 227-229 (3)	232.00	152.00

30th anniv. of Japanese administration of Kwangtung Leased Territory and the South Manchuria Railway Zone.

Imperial Diet Building A78

Grand Staircase A79

1936, Nov. 7 Engr. *Perf. 13*

230	A78	1½s	green	2.00	1.00
231	A79	3s	brown vio	3.00	1.50
232	A79	6s	carmine	6.00	4.00
233	A78	10s	blue	10.00	5.75
			Nos. 230-233 (4)	21.00	12.25

Opening of the new Diet Building, Tokyo.

"Wedded Rocks," Futamigaura — A80

1936, Dec. 10 Photo.

234	A80	1½s	rose carmine	3.50	.20

Issued to pay postage on New Year's greeting cards.

Types of 1913-26
Perf. 13½x13, 13x13½
1937 Typo. Wmk. 257

239	A34	½s	brown	1.90	1.00
240	A34	1s	orange yel	2.75	1.25
241	A34	3s	rose	1.00	.20
242	A49	4s	green	3.75	.20
243	A35	5s	violet	5.00	.20
244	A57	6s	crimson	8.00	.95
245	A35	7s	red org	8.00	.25
246	A49	8s	olive bister	8.50	.50

247 A58 10s carmine 6.75 .25
248 A49 20s blue 12.00 .50
249 A35 25s olive grn 35.00 2.00
250 A36 30s org & grn 25.00 .50
251 A36 50s brn org & dk bl 100.00 2.00
252 A36 1y yel grn & mar 55.00 1.50
Nos. 239-252 (14) 272.65 11.30

Engr.

253 A53 5y gray green 275.00 3.25
254 A53 10y dull violet 425.00 3.00

For overprint see People's Republic of China No. 2L6.

Coil Stamp

1938 Typo. *Perf. 13 Horiz.*

255 A34 3s rose 4.00 4.00

New Year's Decoration — A81

1937, Dec. 15 Photo. *Perf. 13*

256 A81 2s scarlet 6.75 .20

Issued to pay postage on New Year's cards, later for ordinary use.

Trading Ship A82

Rice Harvest A83

Gen. Maresuke Nogi — A84

Power Plant — A85

Admiral Heihachiro Togo A86

Mount Hodaka A87

Garambi Lighthouse, Taiwan — A88

Diamond Mountains, Korea — A89

Meiji Shrine, Tokyo — A90

Yomei Gate, Nikko — A91

Plane and Map of Japan — A92

Kasuga Shrine, Nara — A93

Mount Fuji and Cherry Blossoms A94

Horyu Temple, Nara A95

Miyajima Torii, Itsukushima Shrine — A96

Golden Pavilion, Kyoto — A97

Great Buddha, Kamakura A98

Kamatari Fujiwara A99

Plum Blossoms — A100

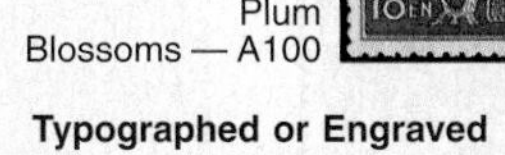

Typographed or Engraved

1937-45 Wmk. 257 *Perf. 13*

257 A82 ½s purple .50 .30
258 A83 1s fawn 1.50 .25
259 A84 2s crimson .35 .20
a. Booklet pane of 20 50.00
b. 2s pink, perf. 12 ('45) 1.25 .85
c. 2s vermilion ('44) 2.10 1.60
260 A85 3s green ('39) .35 .20
261 A86 4s dark green .75 .20
a. Booklet pane of 20 13.00
262 A87 5s dark ultra ('39) .75 .20
263 A88 6s orange ('39) 1.50 .60
264 A89 7s deep green ('39) .50 .20
265 A90 8s dk pur & pale vio ('39) .45 .20
266 A91 10s lake ('38) 2.40 .20
267 A92 12s indigo ('39) .50 .30
268 A93 14s rose lake & pale rose ('38) .50 .25
269 A94 20s ultra ('40) .50 .20
270 A95 25s dk brn & pale brn ('38) .50 .20
271 A96 30s pck blue ('39) 1.10 .20
a. Imperf., pair 400.00
272 A97 50s ol & pale ol ('39) .60 .20
a. Pale olive (forest) omitted
273 A98 1y brn & pale brn ('39) 3.00 1.00
274 A99 5y dp gray grn ('39) 20.00 2.00
275 A100 10y dk brn vio ('39) 14.00 1.50
Nos. 257-275 (19) 49.75 8.40

Nos. 257-261, 265, 268, 270, 272- 273 are typographed; the others are engraved.

Coil Stamps

1938-39 Typo. *Perf. 13 Horiz.*

276 A82 ½s purple ('39) 2.75 *4.00*
277 A84 2s crimson 3.25 *4.25*
278 A86 4s dark green 3.75 *4.25*
279 A93 14s rose lake & pale rose 80.00 70.00
Nos. 276-279 (4) 89.75 82.50

See Nos. 329, 331, 333, 341, 351, 360 and 361. For surcharges see Nos. B4-B5, Burma 2N4-2N27, China-Taiwan, 8-9, People's Republic of China 2L3, 2L7, 2L9-2L10, 2L39, Korea 55-56. For overprints see Ryukyu Islands (US Specialized) Nos. 2X1-2X2, 2X4-2X7, 2X10, 2X13-2X14, 2X17, 2X20, 2X23, 2X27, 2X29, 2X33-2X34, 3X2-3X7, 3X10-3X11, 3X14, 3X17, 3X19, 3X21, 3X23, 3X26-3X30, 5X1-5X3, 5X5-5X8, 5X10.

Mount Nantai — A101

Kegon Falls — A102

Sacred Bridge, Nikko A103

Mount Hiuchi A104

Unwmk.

1938, Dec. 25 Photo. *Perf. 13*

280 A101 2s brown orange 1.00 .50
281 A102 4s olive green 1.00 .50
282 A103 10s deep rose 6.00 3.75
283 A104 20s dark blue 6.00 3.75
a. Souvenir sheet of 4, #280-283 70.00 75.00
Never hinged 100.00
Nos. 280-283 (4) 14.00 8.50
Set, never hinged 35.00

Nikko National Park.
No. 283a sold for 50s.

Many souvenir sheets were sold in folders. Values are for sheets without folders.

Mount Daisen A106

Yashima Plateau, Inland Sea A107

Abuto Kwannon Temple A108

Tomo Bay, Inland Sea A109

1939, Apr. 20

285 A106 2s lt brown 1.00 .50
286 A107 4s yellow grn 1.60 1.00
287 A108 10s dull rose 7.00 4.00
288 A109 20s blue 7.00 4.00
a. Souvenir sheet of 4, #285-288 27.50 40.00
Never hinged 60.00
Nos. 285-288 (4) 16.60 9.50
Set, never hinged 35.00

Daisen and Inland Sea National Parks.
No. 288a sold for 50s.

View from Kuju Village, Kyushu A111

Mount Naka A112

Crater of Mount Naka A113

Volcanic Cones of Mt. Aso A114

1939, Aug. 15

290 A111 2s olive brown	1.00	.50
291 A112 4s yellow green	3.00	2.00
292 A113 10s carmine	17.50	9.00
293 A114 20s sapphire	24.00	10.00
a. Souv. sheet of 4, #290-293	85.00	100.00
Never hinged	140.00	
Nos. 290-293 (4)	45.50	21.50
Set, never hinged	90.00	

Aso National Park. No. 293a sold for 50s.

Globe — A116

Tsunetami Sano — A117

1939, Nov. 15 ***Perf. 12½***

Cross in Carmine

295 A116 2s brown	1.50	.90
296 A117 4s yellow green	1.60	1.00
297 A116 10s crimson	8.00	7.00
298 A117 20s sapphire	8.00	7.00
Nos. 295-298 (4)	19.10	15.90
Set, never hinged	35.00	

Intl. Red Cross Society founding, 75th anniv.

Sacred Golden Kite — A118

Mount Takachiho — A119

Five Ayu Fish and Sake Jar — A120

Kashiwara Shrine — A121

1940 Engr. *Perf. 12*

299 A118 2s brown orange	1.00	1.00
300 A119 4s dark green	.75	.65
301 A120 10s dark carmine	3.75	3.25
302 A121 20s dark ultra	1.00	1.00
Nos. 299-302 (4)	6.50	5.90
Set, never hinged	7.50	

2,600th anniv. of the legendary date of the founding of Japan.

Mt. Hokuchin, Hokkaido A122

Mt. Asahi, Hokkaido A123

Sounkyo Gorge — A124

Tokachi Mountain Range A125

1940, Apr. 20 Photo. *Perf. 13*

303 A122 2s brown	1.00	1.00
304 A123 4s yellow green	3.00	2.00
305 A124 10s carmine	7.00	6.00
306 A125 20s sapphire	7.00	6.25
a. Souv. sheet of 4, #303-306	190.00	200.00
Never hinged	350.00	
Nos. 303-306 (4)	18.00	15.25
Set, never hinged	35.00	

Daisetsuzan National Park. No. 306a sold for 50s.

Mt. Karakuni, Kyushu A127

Mt. Takachiho A128

Torii of Kirishima Shrine A129

Lake of the Six Kwannon A130

1940, Aug. 21

308 A127 2s brown	1.00	.75
309 A128 4s green	2.00	1.50
310 A129 10s carmine	7.00	5.00
311 A130 20s deep ultra	8.00	6.00
a. Souv. sheet of 4, #308-311	190.00	210.00
Never hinged	350.00	
Nos. 308-311 (4)	18.00	13.25
Set, never hinged	40.00	

Kirishima National Park. No. 311a sold for 50s.

Education Minister with Rescript on Education A132

Characters Signifying Loyalty and Filial Piety A133

1940, Oct. 25 Engr. *Perf. 12½*

313 A132 2s purple	1.00	1.00
314 A133 4s green	1.25	1.25
Set, never hinged	2.25	

50th anniv. of the imperial rescript on education, given by Emperor Meiji to clarify Japan's educational policy.

Mt. Daiton, Taiwan A134

Central Peak of Mt. Niitaka A135

Buddhist Temple on Mt. Kwannon A136

View from Mt. Niitaka A137

1941, Mar. 10 Photo. *Perf. 13*

315 A134 2s brown	1.00	.80
316 A135 4s brt green	2.00	1.50
317 A136 10s rose red	6.00	3.75
318 A137 20s brilliant ultra	8.00	5.75
a. Souv. sheet of 4, #315-318	80.00	125.00
Never hinged	175.00	
Nos. 315-318 (4)	17.00	11.80
Set, never hinged	45.00	

Daiton and Niitaka-Arisan National Parks. #318a sold with #323a in same folder for 90s.

Seisui Precipice, East Taiwan Coast — A139

Taroko Gorge — A141

Mt. Tsugitaka A140

Upper River Takkiri District A142

1941, Mar. 10

320 A139 2s brown	1.00	.80
321 A140 4s brt green	2.00	1.00
322 A141 10s rose red	6.00	2.00
323 A142 20s bril ultra	8.00	4.50
a. Souv. sheet of 4, #320-323	80.00	100.00
Never hinged	175.00	
Nos. 320-323 (4)	17.00	8.30
Set, never hinged	30.00	

Tsugitaka-Taroko National Park. See note after No. 318.

War Factory Girl — A144

Building of Wooden Ship — A145

Hyuga Monument and Mt. Fuji A146

War Worker and Planes A147

Palms and Map of "Greater East Asia" A148

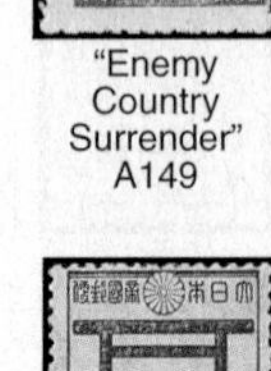

"Enemy Country Surrender" A149

Aviator Saluting and Japanese Flag A150

Torii of Yasukuni Shrine A151

Mt. Fuji and Cherry Blossoms A152

Torii of Miyajima A153

Garambi Lighthouse, Taiwan — A154

Typographed; Engraved

1942-45 Wmk. 257 *Perf. 13*

325 A144 1s orange brn ('43)	.20	.20
328 A145 2s green	.35	.25
329 A84 3s brown ('44)	.45	.20
330 A146 4s emerald	.20	.20
331 A86 5s brown lake	.20	.20
332 A147 6s lt ultra ('44)	.35	.25
a. Imperf., pair		
333 A86 7s org ver ('44)	.20	.20
334 A148 10s crim & dl rose	.35	.20
a. Dull rose (map) omitted	300.00	300.00
335 A149 10s lt gray ('45)	1.90	1.90
336 A150 15s dull blue	1.25	.80
337 A151 17s gray vio ('43)	.45	.35
338 A152 20s blue ('44)	.45	.20
339 A151 27s rose brn ('45)	.45	.35
340 A153 30s bluish grn ('44)	1.25	.50
341 A88 40s dull violet	.35	.20
342 A154 40s dk violet ('44)	.95	.80
Nos. 325,328-342 (16)	9.35	6.80

Nos. 325-335, 337-340 and 342 are typo. Nos. 336 and 341 are engr.

Nos. 329, 331, 333-334, 342 issued with and without gum. No. 335 issued only without gum. These are valued without gum.

#328, 342 exist with watermark sideways. #328 exists printed on gummed side.

Most stamps of the above series exist in numerous shades.

For overprints and surcharges see North Borneo Nos. N34, N37, N41-N42, People's Republic of China 2L4, 2L8, Korea 57-60, Ryukyu Islands (US Specialized) Nos. 2X3, 2X9, 2X12, 2X15-2X16, 2X18-2X19, 2X21-2X22, 2X24-2X26, 2X28, 3X1, 3X8-3X9, 3X12-3X13, 3X15-3X16, 3X18, 3X20, 3X25, 3X31, 4X1-4X2, 5X4.

Kenkoku Shrine, Hsinking — A155

Boys of Japan and Manchukuo A156

Orchid Crest of Manchukuo A157

1942 Unwmk. Engr. *Perf. 12*

No.	Type	Description	Unused	Used
343	A155	2s brown	1.00	1.00
344	A156	5s olive	.65	.65
345	A155	10s red	.75	.75
346	A157	20s dark blue	2.00	2.00
		Nos. 343-346 (4)	4.40	4.40
		Set, never hinged	7.50	

The 2s and 10s were issued Mar. 1 for the 10th anniv. of the creation of Manchukuo; 5s and 20s on Sept. 15 for the 10th anniv. of Japanese diplomatic recognition of Manchukuo.

C-59 Locomotive A158

Yasukuni Shrine, Tokyo A159

1942, Oct. 14 Photo.

No.	Type	Description	Unused	Used
347	A158	5s Prus green	3.50	3.50
		Never hinged	5.00	

70th anniv. of Japan's 1st railway.

1944, June 29 *Perf. 13*

No.	Type	Description	Unused	Used
348	A159	7s Prus green	.55	.55
		Never hinged	.85	

75th anniversary of Yasukuni Shrine.

Kwantung Shrine and Map of Kwantung Peninsula — A160

1944, Oct. 1

No.	Type	Description	Unused	Used
349	A160	3s red brown	4.75	*5.00*
350	A160	7s gray violet	5.25	*5.50*
		Set, never hinged	17.50	

Dedication of Kwantung Shrine, Port Arthur.

Sun and Cherry Blossoms A161

Sunrise at Sea and Plane A162

Coal Miners A163

Yasukuni Shrine A164

Lithographed, Typographed
1945-47 Wmk. 257 *Imperf.*
Without Gum

No.	Type	Description	Unused	Used
351	A84	2s rose red	.30	.30
352	A161	3s rose carmine	.20	.30
353	A162	5s green	.20	.20
a.		5s blue	6.75	6.75
354	A149	10s lt gray	7.50	7.50
354A	A149	10s blue	19.00	
355	A152	10s red orange	.20	.20
356	A152	20s ultra ('46)	.35	.20
357	A153	30s brt blue ('46)	1.25	.75
358	A163	50s dark brown ('46)	.30	.20
a.		Souvenir sheet of 5 ('47)	10.50	12.50
359	A164	1y dp ol grn ('46)	.75	.75
360	A99	5y dp gray grn	4.25	.65
361	A100	10y dk brown vio	30.00	.75
		Nos. 351-361 (12)	64.30	
		Nos. 351-354,355-361 (11)		11.80

Nos. 351 and 354 are typographed. The other stamps in this set are printed by offset lithography.

No. 358a was issued with marginal inscriptions to commemorate the Sapporo (Hokkaido) Philatelic Exhibition, Nov., 1947.

Nos. 351 to 361 are on grayish paper, and Nos. 355 to 361 also exist on white paper.

Most stamps of the above series exist in numerous shades and with private perforation or roulette.

See No. 404. For overprints see Ryukyu Islands (US Specialized) Nos. 2X8, 2X11, 2X30, 3X22, 4X3, 5X9.

Baron Hisoka Maejima A165

Horyu Temple Pagoda A166

"Thunderstorm below Fuji," by Hokusai A167

"First Geese," Print by Hokusai A168

Kintai Bridge, Iwakuni A169

Kiyomizu Temple, Kyoto A170

Goldfish A171

Noh Mask A172

Plum Blossoms — A173

Characters Read Right to Left
1946-47 Wmk. 257 Litho. *Imperf.*
Without Gum

No.	Type	Description	Unused	Used
362	A165	15s dark green	.35	.25
363	A166	30s dull lilac	.45	.20
364	A167	1y ultra	.55	.20
a.		1y deep ultramarine	1.60	.20
b.		1y light blue	.60	.20
365	A168	1.30y olive bister	1.90	.50
366	A169	1.50y dark gray	1.90	.35
367	A170	2y vermilion ('47)	1.60	.20
a.		Souvenir sheet of 5 ('47)	21.00	20.00
368	A171	5y lilac rose	6.00	.45
		Nos. 362-368 (7)	12.75	2.15

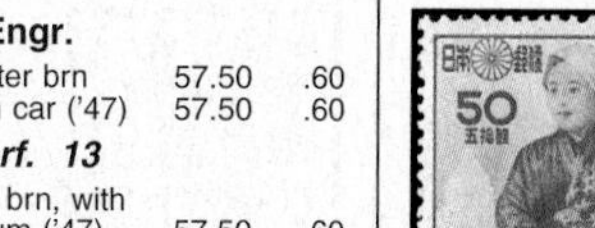

Engr.

No.	Type	Description	Unused	Used
369	A172	50y bister brn	57.50	.60
370	A173	100y brn car ('47)	57.50	.60

Perf. 13

No.	Type	Description	Unused	Used
371	A172	50y bis brn, with gum ('47)	57.50	.60
372	A173	100y brn car, with gum ('47)	57.50	.35

Litho.
Perf. 13x13½, 12, 12x12½

No.	Type	Description	Unused	Used
373	A166	30s dull lilac	3.00	2.75

Rouletted in Colored Lines
Typo. Unwmk.
With Gum

No.	Type	Description	Unused	Used
374	A166	30s deep lilac	.95	1.40

Nos. 363, 368, 373 exist with and without gum, valued without gum, as are Nos. 371-372, 374.

No. 367a for the "Know Your Stamps" exhibition, Kyoto, Aug. 19-24, 1947. Size: 113x71mm

#362, 369 exist with watermark horizontal.

See Nos. 384-387, 512A. For overprints see Ryukyu Islands (US Specialized) Nos. 2X32, 3X24, 4X4.

Catalogue values for unused stamps in this section, from this point to the end of the section, are for Never Hinged items.

Medieval Postman's Bell A175

Baron Hisoka Maejima A176

Design of First Japanese Stamp — A177

Communication Symbols — A178

Perf. 12½, 13½x13
1946, Dec. 12 Engr. Unwmk.

No.	Type	Description	Unused	Used
375	A175	15s orange	5.00	3.00
376	A176	30s deep green	6.00	4.00
377	A177	50s carmine	3.00	2.00
378	A178	1y deep blue	3.00	2.00
a.		Souvenir sheet of 4, #375-378, imperf.	160.00	140.00
		Hinged	75.00	
		Nos. 375-378 (4)	17.00	11.00

Government postal service in Japan, 75th anniv.

No. 378a measures 180-183x125-127mm and is ungummed. There were 2 printings: I — The 4 colors were printed simultaneously. Arched top inscription and other inscriptions in high relief (no more than 2,000 sheets). II — Stamps were printed in one step, sheet inscriptions and 15s orange stamp in another. Lines of top inscription and inscriptions at lower left and lower right (flanking the 1y blue stamp) are much flatter (less raised) than the lines of the green, carmine and blue stamps, almost level with paper's surface (about 49,000 sheets). 1st printing value $950.

Mother and Child, Diet Building — A180

Bouquet of Japanese May Flowers — A181

Wmk. 257
1947, May 3 Litho. *Perf. 12½*
Without Gum

No.	Type	Description	Unused	Used
380	A180	50s rose brown	.25	.30
381	A181	1y brt ultra	.50	.40
a.		Souv. sheet of 2, #380-381, imperf, without gum	9.50	5.00
b.		As "a," 50s stamp omitted	800.00	
c.		As "a," 1y stamp omitted	800.00	

Inauguration of the constitution of May 3, 1947.

A182

1947, Aug. 15 Photo. *Perf. 12½*

No.	Type	Description	Unused	Used
382	A182	1.20y brown	2.10	1.00
383	A182	4y brt ultra	4.25	1.40

Reopening of foreign trade on a private basis.

The ornaments on No. 383 differ from those shown in the illustration.

Types of 1946 Redrawn
Characters Read Left to Right
1947-48 Wmk. 257 Typo. *Perf. 13*

No.	Type	Description	Unused	Used
384	A166	30s deep lilac	1.50	1.25
385	A166	1.20y lt olive grn	1.00	.35
a.		Souvenir sheet of 15	160.00	110.00
386	A170	2y vermilion ('48)	4.00	.20
387	A168	4y lt ultra	2.60	.25
		Nos. 384-387 (4)	9.10	2.05

No. 385a was issued with marginal inscriptions to commemorate the "Know Your Stamps" Exhibition, Tokyo, May, 1947.

On No. 386, the chrysanthemum crest has been eliminated and the top inscription centered.

Plum Blossoms — A183

1947 Typo. *Imperf.*
Without Gum

No.	Type	Description	Unused	Used
388	A183	10y dk brown vio	40.00	.65

This stamp is similar to type A100 but with new inscription "Nippon Yubin" (Japan Post), reading from left to right. The characters for the denomination are likewise transposed.

A184

A185

Baron Hisoka Maejima A186

Whaling A187

National Art, Imperial Treasure House, Nara — A188

1947 Typo. *Perf. 13x13½*

389 A184 35s green .40 .30

Litho.

390 A185 45s lilac rose .55 .50
- *a.* Imperf., pair 700.00
- *b.* Perf. 11x13½ 3.75 3.75

391 A186 1y dull brown 2.40 .35

Typo.

392 A187 5y blue 5.50 .20
- *a.* Imperf., pair 500.00
- *b.* Perf. 11x13½ 19.00 2.40

Engr.

Perf. 13½x13

393 A188 10y lilac 15.00 .20
- *a.* Imperf., pair

Nos. 389-393 (5) 23.85 1.55

No. 389 was produced on both rotary and flat press. Sheets of the rotary press printing have a border. Those of the flat press printing have none.

Lily of the Valley — A188a

1947, Sept. 13 Unwmk. *Perf. 12½*

394 A188a 2y dk Prus green 3.00 1.25

Relief of Ex-convicts Day, Sept. 13, 1947.

Souvenir Sheet

A189

1947 Wmk. 257 Litho. *Imperf.*

Without Gum

395 A189 Sheet of 5, ultra 2.40 2.60

Stamp Hobby Week, Nov. 1-7, 1947. Sheet size: 113½x71½mm, on white or grayish paper.

For overprint, see No. 408.

"Benkei," 1880 Locomotive — A190

1947, Oct. 14 Unwmk. Engr.

Without Gum

396 A190 4y deep ultra 16.50 16.50

75th anniv. of railway service in Japan.

Hurdling — A191

Diving — A192

Discus Throwing A193

Volleyball A194

1947, Oct. 25 Photo. *Perf. 12½*

397 A191 1.20y red violet 9.00 6.00

398 A192 1.20y red violet 9.00 6.00

399 A193 1.20y red violet 9.00 6.00

400 A194 1.20y red violet 9.00 6.00
- *a.* Block of 4, #397-400 52.50 30.00

2nd Natl. Athletic Meet, held in Kanazawa, Oct. 30-Nov. 3.

Souvenir Sheets

A195

1948 Wmk. 257 Litho. *Imperf.*

Without Gum

401 A195 Sheet of 2, As #368, rose carmine 13.50 *15.00*

Same, Inscribed with Three instead of Two Japanese Characters at Bottom Center

402 A195 Sheet of 2, #368 15.00 *17.00*

Philatelic exhibitions at Osaka (No. 401) and Nagoya (No. 402).

For Nos. 401-402 overprinted in green, see Nos. 407, 407b.

Stylized Tree — A196

National Art Treasure, Nara — A197

Perf. 12½

1948, Apr. 1 Unwmk. Photo.

403 A196 1.20y dp yellow grn .90 .90

Forestation movement. Sheets of 30, marginal inscription.

Coal Miners Type of 1946, and Type A197

1948 Wmk. 257 Litho. *Perf. 13*

404 A163 50s dark brown 1.50 .95

Typo.

405 A197 10y rose violet 13.50 .20
- *a.* Imperf., pair

See No. 515A.

School Children — A198

Perf. 12½

1948, May 3 Unwmk. Photo.

406 A198 1.20y dark carmine .90 .80

Reorganization of Japan's educational system. Sheets of 30, marginal inscription.

Souvenir Sheets

No. 402 Overprinted at Top, Bottom and Sides with Japanese Characters and Flowers in Green

1948, Apr. 3

407 A195 Sheet of 2 60.00 37.50
- *a.* Overprint inverted 125.00 125.00
- *b.* Overprint on No. 401 100.00 95.00

Mishima Philatelic Exhibition, Apr. 3-9.

No. 395 Overprinted at Top and Bottom With Japanese Characters in Plum

1948, Apr. 18

408 A189 Sheet of 5, ultra 22.50 19.00

Centenary of the death of Katsushika Hokusai, painter.

Sampans on Inland Sea, Near Suma — A199

Engr. & Litho.

1948, Apr. 22 Unwmk. *Imperf.*

Without Gum

409 A199 Sheet of 2, grn & rose car 12.00 7.50

Communications Exhib., Tokyo, Apr. 27-May 3, 1948. Sheet contains two 2y deep carmine stamps.

Sheet exists with green border omitted.

1948, May 20

Without Gum

410 A199 Sheet of 2, ultra & rose car 14.50 13.50

Aomori Newspaper and Stamp Exhibition. Border design of apples and apple blossoms.

Type A199 With Altered Border and Inscriptions

1948, May 23

Without Gum

411 A199 Sheet of 2, blue & rose car 14.50 13.50

Fukushima Stamp Exhibition. Border design of cherries and crossed lines.

Horse Race — A200

1948, June 6 Photo. *Perf. 12½*

412 A200 5y brown 2.50 .95

25th anniv. of the enforcement of Japan's horse racing laws. Each sheet contains 30 stamps and 2 labels, with marginal inscription.

A201

A202

Wmk. 257

1948, Sept. 10 Litho. *Perf. 13*

413 A201 1.50y blue 2.25 .45

414 A202 3.80y lt brown 6.50 5.25

Souvenir Sheet

Without Gum

Imperf

415 Sheet of 4 32.50 30.00

Kumamoto Stamp Exhibition, Sept. 20. Souvenir sheet, issued Sept. 20, contains two each of 1.50y deep blue (A201) and 3.80y brown (A202).

Rectifying Tower — A203

Perf. 12½

1948, Sept. 14 Photo. Unwmk.

416 A203 5y dark olive bister 2.75 1.50

Government alcohol monopoly.

Swimmer — A204

Runner — A205

Designs: No. 419, High jumper. No. 420, Baseball players. No. 421, Bicycle racers.

1948

417 A204 5y blue 3.50 1.60

418 A205 5y green 8.25 3.50

419 A205 5y green 8.25 3.50

420 A205 5y green 8.25 3.50

421 A205 5y green 8.25 3.50
- *a.* Block of 4, #418-421 42.50 42.50

Nos. 417-421 (5) 36.50 15.60

3rd Natl. Athletic Meet. Swimming matches held at Yawata, Sept. 16-19, field events, Fukuoka, Oct. 29-Nov. 3.

"Beauty Looking Back," Print by Moronobu A206

1948, Nov. 29 *Perf. 13*

422 A206 5y brown 70.00 37.50
- *a.* Sheet of 5 475.00 250.00
- Hinged 300.00

Philatelic Week, Nov. 29-Dec. 5.

See Nos. 2418-2419.

Souvenir Sheet

1948, Dec. 3 *Imperf.*

Without Gum

423 A206 5y brown, sheet of 1 40.00 27.50

Kanazawa and Takaoka stamp exhibitions.

Child Playing Hanetsuki — A207

1948, Dec. 13 Litho. *Perf. 13*

424 A207 2y scarlet 3.75 3.00

Issued to pay postage on New Year's cards, later for ordinary use.

Farm Woman A208

Whaling A209

Miner A210

Tea Picking A211

Girl Printer A212

Factory Girl with Cotton Bobbin A213

Mt. Hodaka A214

Planting A215

Postman A216

Blast Furnace A217

Locomotive Assembly A218

Typographed, Engraved

1948-49 Wmk. 257 *Perf. 13x13½*

No.	Type	Description	Unused	Used
425	A208	2y green	1.50	.20
a.		Overprinted with 4 characters in frame	.55	.75
b.		As "a," overprint inverted	*57.50*	
426	A209	3y lt grnsh bl ('49)	4.25	.20
427	A210	5y olive bis	15.00	.20
a.		Booklet pane of 20	—	110.00
		Hinged	110.00	
428	A211	5y blue grn ('49)	30.00	4.75
429	A212	6y red org ('49)	6.75	.20
430	A210	8y brown org ('49)	6.75	.20
a.		Booklet pane of 20	—	190.00
		Hinged	175.00	
431	A213	15y blue	2.75	.20
432	A214	16y ultra ('49)	6.75	3.50
433	A215	20y dk green ('49)	26.00	.20
434	A216	30y violet bl ('49)	32.50	.20
435	A217	100y car lake ('49)	500.00	1.10
436	A218	500y deep blue ('49)	400.00	1.75
		Nos. 425-436 (12)	1,032.	12.70
		Set, hinged	625.00	

No. 425a has a red control overprint of four characters ("Senkyo Jimu," or "Election Business") arranged vertically in a rectangular frame. Each candidate received 1,000 copies.

Nos. 432, 435-436 are engraved.

See #442, 511-512, 514-515, 518, 520, 521A-521B.

Souvenir Sheets

Typo. and Litho.

1948, Oct. 16 *Imperf.*

437 A213 15y blue, sheet of 1 30.00 30.00

Nagano Stamp Exhibition, Oct. 16.

1948, Nov. 2 *Imperf.*

438 A210 5y ol bis, sheet of 2 35.00 35.00

Shikoku Traveling Stamp Exhib., Nov. 1948.

Sampans on Inland Sea A219

Perf. 13x13½

1949 Wmk. 257 Engr.

No.	Type	Description	Unused	Used
439	A219	10y rose lake	35.00	15.00
440	A219	10y car rose	24.00	14.00
441	A219	10y orange ver	25.00	13.50
442	A214	16y brt blue	10.00	4.50
		Nos. 439-442 (4)	94.00	47.00
		Set, hinged	57.50	

Issued in sheets of 20 stamps with marginal inscription publicizing expositions at Takamatsu (#439), Okayama (#440) and Matsuyama (#441), Nagano Peace Exposition, Apr. 1-May 31, 1949 (#442).

Ice Skater — A221

Ski Jumper — A222

1949 Unwmk. Photo. *Perf. 12*

444 A221 5y violet 2.75 1.25
445 A222 5y ultra 3.00 1.25

Winter events of the 4th Natl. Athletic Meet: skating at Suwa Jan. 27-30, skiing at Sapporo Mar. 3-6. Issued: #444, 1/27; #445, 3/3.

Steamer in Beppu Bay — A223

1949, Mar. 10 Engr. *Perf. 13x13½*

446 A223 2y carmine & ultra 1.00 .65
447 A223 5y green & ultra 3.25 1.00

Scene at Fair — A224

Stylized Trees — A225

1949, Mar. 15 Photo. *Imperf.*

No.	Type	Description	Unused	Used
448	A224	5y brt rose	2.00	1.60
a.		Perf. 13	3.00	1.50
b.		Sheet of 20, imperf.	45.00	45.00

Issued to publicize the Japan Foreign Trade Fair, Yokohama, 1949.

No. 448a was printed in sheets of 50 (10x5); No. 448 in sheets of 20 (4x5) with marginal inscriptions (No. 448b).

1949, Apr. 1 Unwmk. *Perf. 12*

449 A225 5y bright green 8.00 1.50

Issued to publicize the forestation movement.

Lion Rock A226

Daiho-zan (Mt. Ohmine) — A227

Doro Gorge A228

Bridge Pier Rocks A229

1949, Apr. 10 Photo. *Perf. 13*

No.	Type	Description	Unused	Used
450	A226	2y brown	1.10	.75
451	A227	5y yellow grn	3.50	1.10
452	A228	10y scarlet	14.50	8.25
453	A229	16y blue	7.25	3.75
a.		Souv. sheet of 4, #450-453, no gum	27.50	24.00
b.		As "a," 10y stamp omitted		
		Nos. 450-453 (4)	26.35	13.85

Yoshino-Kumano National Park.

No. 453a sold for 40y.

Boy — A230

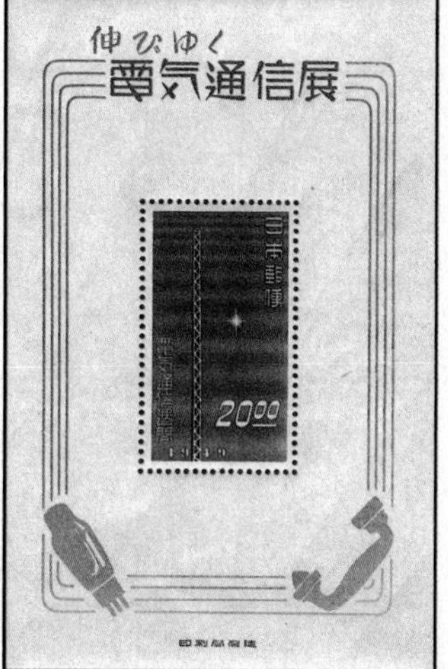

Radio Tower and Star — A231

1949, May 5 *Perf. 12*

455 A230 5y rose brn & org 4.25 1.40
a. Orange omitted 250.00

Children's Day, May 5, 1949.

Souvenir Sheets

1949, May 5 *Imperf.*

456 A230 5y rose brn & org, sheet of 10 350.00 275.00
Hinged 160.00

Children's Exhib., Inuyama, Apr. 1-May 31.

1949, May 11 *Perf. 13*

457 A231 20y dp bl, sheet of 1 120.00 85.00
Hinged 60.00

Electrical Communication Week, May 11-18.

Symbols of Communication A232

Central Meteorological Observatory, Tokyo — A233

Wmk. 257

1949, June 1 Engr. *Perf. 12*

458 A232 8y brt ultra 3.00 1.50

Establishment of the Post Ministry and the Ministry of Electricity and Communication.

1949, June 1 Unwmk. *Perf. 12½*

459 A233 8y deep green 3.00 1.50

75th anniv. of the establishment of the Central Meteorological Observatory.

Mt. Fuji in Autumn A234

Lake Kawaguchi — A235

Fuji from Mt. Shichimen — A236

Shinobuno Village and Mt. Fuji — A237

1949, July 15 Photo. *Perf. 13*

No.	Type	Description	Unused	Used
460	A234	2y yellow brown	3.00	.75
461	A235	8y yellow green	3.50	1.10
462	A236	14y carmine lake	1.50	.45
463	A237	24y blue	5.00	.60
a.		Souv. sheet of 4, #460-463	50.00	35.00
		Nos. 460-463 (4)	13.00	2.90

Fuji-Hakone National Park.

No. 463a sold for 55y.

Allegory of Peace A238

Doves over Nagasaki — A239

Perf. 13x13½, 13½x13

1949 Photo. Unwmk.

465 A238 8y yellow brown 6.50 1.75
466 A239 8y green 4.25 1.75

Establishment of Hiroshima as the City of Eternal Peace and of Nagasaki as the International City of Culture. Issued: #465, Aug. 6; #466, Aug. 9.

Boy Scout — A240

Pen Nib of Newspaper Stereotype Matrix — A241

1949, Sept. 22 *Perf. 13x13½*

467 A240 8y brown 5.75 1.90

Natl. Boy Scout Jamboree.

1949, Oct. 1 *Perf. 13½x13*

468 A241 8y deep blue 4.75 1.90

Natl. Newspaper Week.

Racing Swimmer Poised for Dive — A242

Javelin Thrower — A243

1949 *Perf. 13½*

469 A242 8y dull blue 3.00 1.10

Perf. 12

470 A243 8y shown 5.50 2.10
471 A243 8y Yacht Racing 5.50 2.10
472 A243 8y Relay Race 5.50 2.10
473 A243 8y Tennis 5.50 2.10
a. Block of 4, #470-473 25.00 32.50
Nos. 469-473 (5) 25.00 9.50

4th Natl. Athletic Meet. The swimming matches were held at Yokohama, Sept. 15-18 and the fall events at Tokyo, Oct. 30.

Issued: #469, Sept. 15; #470-473, Oct. 30.

Nos. 470-473 exist perf 12½. Values 50 percent above those of perf 12 copies.

Map and Envelopes Forming "75" — A244

Symbols of UPU — A245

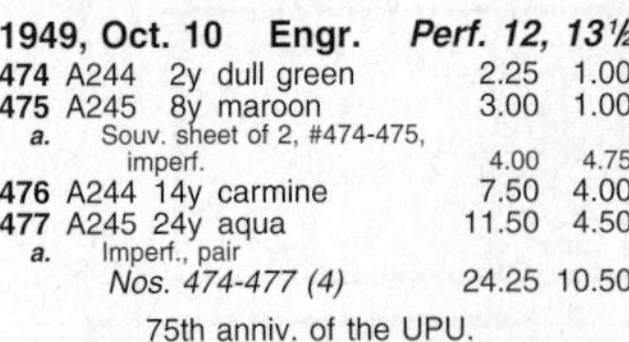

1949, Oct. 10 Engr. *Perf. 12, 13½*

474 A244 2y dull green 2.25 1.00
475 A245 8y maroon 3.00 1.00
a. Souv. sheet of 2, #474-475, imperf. 4.00 4.75
476 A244 14y carmine 7.50 4.00
477 A245 24y aqua 11.50 4.50
a. Imperf., pair
Nos. 474-477 (4) 24.25 10.50

75th anniv. of the UPU.

Floating Zenith Telescope A246

"Moon and Geese," Print by Hiroshige A247

1949, Oct. 30 Photo. *Perf. 12*

478 A246 8y dk blue grn 3.00 1.25

50th anniv. of the Mizusawa Latitudinal Observatory.

1949, Nov. 1 *Perf. 13x13½*

479 A247 8y purple 100.00 40.00
a. Sheet of 5 600.00 350.00
Sheet, hinged 375.00

Postal Week, Nov. 1-7. See #2420-2421.

Dr. Hideyo Noguchi A248

Yukichi Fukuzawa A249

Soseki Natsume A250

Shoyo Tsubouchi A251

Danjuro Ichikawa — A252

Joseph Hardy Niijima — A253

Hogai Kano A254

Kanzo Uchimura A255

Ichiyo Higuchi — A256

Ogai Mori — A257

Shiki Masaoka — A258

Shunso Hishida — A259

Amane Nishi — A260

Kenjiro Ume — A261

Hisashi Kimura — A262

Inazo Nitobe — A263

Torahiko Terada — A264

Tenshin Okakura — A265

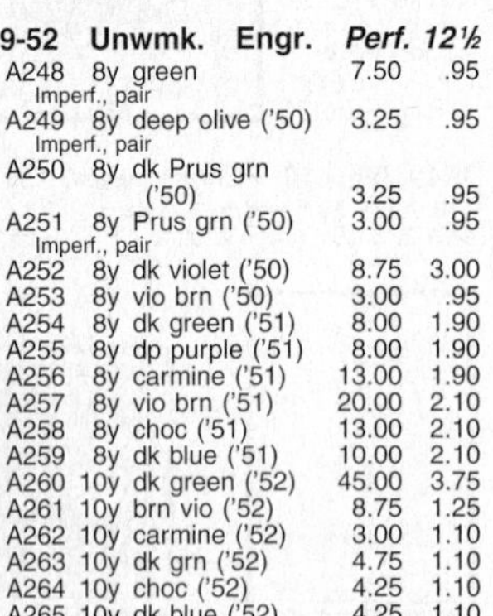

1949-52 Unwmk. Engr. *Perf. 12½*

480 A248 8y green 7.50 .95
a. Imperf., pair
481 A249 8y deep olive ('50) 3.25 .95
a. Imperf., pair
482 A250 8y dk Prus grn ('50) 3.25 .95
483 A251 8y Prus grn ('50) 3.00 .95
a. Imperf., pair
484 A252 8y dk violet ('50) 8.75 3.00
485 A253 8y vio brn ('50) 3.00 .95
486 A254 8y dk green ('51) 8.00 1.90
487 A255 8y dp purple ('51) 8.00 1.90
488 A256 8y carmine ('51) 13.00 1.90
489 A257 8y vio brn ('51) 20.00 2.10
490 A258 8y choc ('51) 13.00 2.10
491 A259 8y dk blue ('51) 10.00 2.10
492 A260 10y dk green ('52) 45.00 3.75
493 A261 10y brn vio ('52) 8.75 1.25
494 A262 10y carmine ('52) 3.00 1.10
495 A263 10y dk grn ('52) 4.75 1.10
496 A264 10y choc ('52) 4.25 1.10
497 A265 10y dk blue ('52) 4.25 1.10
Nos. 480-497 (18) 170.75 29.15
Set, hinged 110.00

Tiger — A266

Microphones of 1925 and 1950 — A267

1950, Feb. 1 Photo. *Perf. 12*

498 A266 2y dark red 5.25 1.50

6th prize (lottery), sheet of 5, value $175.

1950, Mar. 21 *Perf. 13*

499 A267 8y ultra 3.25 1.25

25th anniversary of broadcasting in Japan. Sheets of 20 with marginal inscription.

Dove and Olive Twig on Letter Box — A268

1950, Apr. 20 *Perf. 12*

500 A268 8y dp yellow grn 3.00 1.10

Day of Posts, Apr. 20.

Lake Akan and Mt. Akan A269

Lake Kutcharo, Hokkaido A270

Mt. Akan-Fuji A271

Lake Mashu A272

1950, July 15 Unwmk. *Perf. 13*

501 A269 2y yellow brn 1.50 .75
502 A270 8y dp yellow grn 2.25 1.10
503 A271 14y rose car 10.50 3.75
504 A272 24y brt blue 11.50 4.50
a. Souv. sheet of 4, #501-504 45.00 32.50
Nos. 501-504 (4) 25.75 10.10

Akan National Park.
No. 504a sold for 55y.

Gymnast on Rings — A273

Designs: No. 506, Pole vault. No. 507, Soccer. No. 508, Equestrian.

1950, Oct. 28 *Perf. 13½x13*

505 A273 8y rose brown 26.00 8.25
506 A273 8y rose brown 26.00 8.25
507 A273 8y rose brown 26.00 8.25

508 A273 8y rose brown 26.00 8.25
a. Strip of 4, #505-508 150.00 110.00
b. Block of 4, #505-508 150.00 125.00
As "b," hinged 90.00

5th National Athletic Meet. Sheets of 20 stamps in which each horizontal row contains all four designs.

Types of 1947-49 and

Ishiyama-dera Pagoda A274

Hisoka Maejima A275

Long-tailed Cock of Tosa A276

Goddess Kannon A277

Himeji Castle A278

Nyoirin Kannon of Chuguji A280

Phoenix Hall, Byodoin Temple A279

Perf. 13x13½, 13½x13 (14y)

1950-52 Typo. Unwmk.

509 A274 80s carmine ('51) 1.40 1.25
a. Sheet of 1 7.25 *9.50*

Photo.

510 A275 1y dk brown ('51) 2.75 .55
a. Souvenir sheet of 4 14.00 14.00

Typo.

511 A208 2y green ('51) 1.75 .20
512 A209 3y lt grnsh bl ('51) 37.50 .95
512A A168 4y lt ultra ('52) 30.00 1.10
513 A276 5y dp grn & org brn ('51) 4.75 .20
a. Orange brown omitted 210.00
514 A212 6y red org ('51) 5.50 .45
515 A210 8y dk org brn ('51) 30.00 .55
515A A197 10y rose vio ('51) 57.50 4.75
516 A277 10y red brn & lil ('51) 15.00 .20

Engr.

517 A278 14y brn & car ('51) 50.00 25.00
a. Sheet of 1 65.00 55.00

Typo.

518 A215 20y dk green ('51) 55.00 .95

Engr.

519 A279 24y dp ultra 29.00 12.50
a. Sheet of 1 32.50 35.00

Typo.

520 A216 30y vio bl ('52) 160.00 1.10

Photo.

521 A280 50y dk brown ('51) 115.00 .75
Hinged 95.00
c. Sheet of 1 225.00 210.00
Hinged 150.00

Engr.

521A A217 100y car lake ('52) 400.00 1.00
521B A218 500y dp blue ('52) 375.00 1.25
Nos. 509-521B (17) 1,370. 52.75

No. 510a for the 80th anniv. of Japan's postal service. On No. 512A, characters read from left to right.

Compare designs: A274 with A314c; A275 with A314a, A447, A563a; A277 with A332a; A279 with A385a; A280 with A565f.

Girl and Rabbit — A281

1951, Jan. 1 Photo. *Perf. 12*
522 A281 2y rose pink 5.00 .75

9th prize (lottery), sheet of 5, value $42.50. See No. 2655a.

Scenic Spots Issue

Skiers on Mt. Zao
A282 A283

1951, Feb. 15 *Perf. 13*
523 A282 8y olive 12.50 2.00
524 A283 24y blue 15.00 4.50

Tea Picking — A284

Mt. Fuji Seen from Nihon Plateau A285

Nihon-daira Plateau.

1951, Apr. 2
525 A284 8y olive green 12.50 2.75
526 A285 24y bright blue 75.00 20.00

Hot Springs, Hakone — A286

Lake Ashi, Hakone A287

1951, May 25
527 A286 8y chestnut brown 8.00 2.10
528 A287 24y deep blue 6.50 2.50

Senju Waterfall — A288

Ninai Waterfall A289

Akame 48 Waterfalls.

1951, June 1
529 A288 8y deep green 9.00 2.10
530 A289 24y deep blue 8.75 2.50

Pavilion, Wakanoura Bay — A290

Wakanoura Bay — A291

Wakanoura & Tomogashima.

1951, June 25
531 A290 8y brown 6.00 2.10
532 A291 24y brt blue 5.75 2.50

Uji River — A292

View from Uji Bridge A293

Perf. 13x13½, 13½x13

1951, Aug. 1 Engr.
533 A292 8y brown 6.00 2.10
534 A293 24y deep blue 5.75 2.50

Oura Catholic Church, Nagasaki — A294

Sofuku Temple A295

1951, Sept. 15 Photo. *Perf. 13½*
535 A294 8y carmine rose 8.25 2.10
536 A295 24y dull blue 6.75 2.50

Marunuma — A296

Sugenuma A297

1951, Oct. 1
537 A296 8y rose violet 10.00 2.10
a. Imperf., pair
538 A297 24y dull blue grn 5.25 2.50

Kakuenpo (peak) — A298

Nagatoro Bridge A299

Shosenkyo Gorge.

1951, Oct. 15
539 A298 8y brown red 8.75 2.10
540 A299 24y dp Prus grn 9.00 2.50
Nos. 523-540 (18) 218.75 61.45

Boy's Head and Seedling — A300

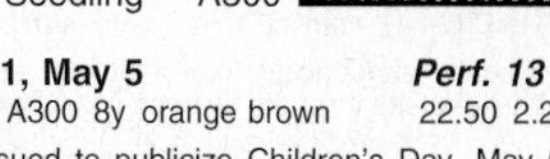

1951, May 5 *Perf. 13½*
541 A300 8y orange brown 22.50 2.25

Issued to publicize Children's Day, May 5, 1951.

Oirase River A301

Lake Towada A302

View from Kankodai A303

Mt. Hakkoda from Mt. Yokodake A304

1951, July 20 Photo. *Perf. 13x13½*
542 A301 2y brown 2.10 .75
543 A302 8y green 7.50 1.10
544 A303 14y dark red 8.25 3.25
545 A304 24y blue 9.50 4.00
a. Souv. sheet of 4, #542-545 45.00 29.00
Nos. 542-545 (4) 27.35 9.10

Towada Natl. Park. No. 545a sold for 55y.

Chrysanthemum A305

National Flag A306

1951, Sept. 9 ***Perf. 13½***

546 A305 2y orange brown 1.90 .95
547 A306 8y slate blue & red 5.75 2.25
548 A305 24y blue green 17.00 6.00
Nos. 546-548 (3) 24.65 9.20

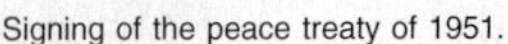

Signing of the peace treaty of 1951.

Putting the Shot — A307

Hockey — A308

1951, Oct. 27

549 A307 2y orange brown 3.25 1.60
550 A308 2y gray blue 3.25 1.60
a. Pair, #549-550 8.75 8.75

6th Natl. Athletic Meet, Hiroshima, 10/27-31.

Okina Mask — A309

1952, Jan. 16 Photo. ***Perf. 13½x13***

551 A309 5y crimson rose 9.50 .75

Sheets reproducing four of these stamps with Japanese inscriptions and floral ornament at left were awarded as sixth prize in the national lottery. Value $100.

Southern Cross from Ship — A310

Earth and Big Dipper — A311

1952, Feb. 19

552 A310 5y purple 5.25 .80
553 A311 10y dark green 13.50 2.00

75th anniv. of Japan's admission to the UPU.

Red Cross and Lilies — A312

Red Cross Nurse — A313

1952, May 1

554 A312 5y rose red & dk red 4.25 .95
555 A313 10y dk green & red 10.00 2.00
a. Red cross omitted
b. Imperf., pair

75th anniv. of the formation of the Japanese Red Cross Society.

Goldfish — A314

A314a

A314b

A314c

Japanese Serow — A315

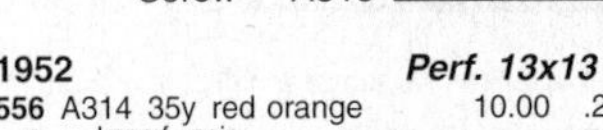

1952 ***Perf. 13x13½***

556 A314 35y red orange 10.00 .20
a. Imperf., pair

Types of 1951
Redrawn; Zeros Omitted
Unwmk.

557 A314a 1y dark brown .40 .20
558 A314b 50y dark brown 4.50 .20

Typo.

559 A314c 4y dp cl & pale rose 1.50 .20
a. Background (pale rose) omitted

Ornamental frame and background added, denomination at upper left, Japanese characters at upper right.

Photo.

560 A315 8y brown .20 .20
Nos. 556-560 (5) 16.60 1.00

Mt. Yari — A316

Kurobe Valley — A317

Mt. Shirouma A318

Mt. Norikura A319

1952, July 5 ***Perf. 13½x13, 13x13½***

561 A316 5y brown 4.50 .50
562 A317 10y blue green 22.50 1.75
563 A318 14y bright red 5.75 3.00
564 A319 24y bright blue 9.50 3.00
a. Souv. sheet of 4, #561-564, imperf. 80.00 60.00
Nos. 561-564 (4) 42.25 8.25

Japan Alps (Chubu-Sangaku) National Park. No. 564a sold for 60y.

Yasuda Hall, Tokyo University A320

Yomei Gate, Nikko A321

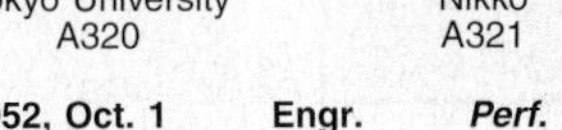

1952, Oct. 1 Engr. ***Perf. 13***

565 A320 10y dull green 14.50 1.75

75th anniversary of the founding of Tokyo University.

1952, Oct. 15 Photo. ***Perf. 13x13½***

566 A321 45y blue 3.50 .20

Mountain Climber — A322

1952, Oct. 18
Dated "1952"

567 A322 5y shown 6.00 1.50
568 A322 5y Wrestlers 6.00 1.50
a. Pair, #567-568 15.00 7.50

7th Nat.l Athletic Meet, Fukushima, 10/18-22.

Mt. Azuma A323

Mt. Asahi A324

Mt. Bandai A325

Mt. Gatsun A326

Unwmk.
1952, Oct. 18 Photo. ***Perf. 13***

569 A323 5y brown 3.75 .60
570 A324 10y olive grn 11.50 1.50
571 A325 14y rose red 4.50 2.25
572 A326 24y blue 10.00 4.00
a. Souv. sheet of 4, #569-572, imperf. 80.00 60.00
Nos. 569-572 (4) 29.75 8.35

Bandai-Asahi National Park. No. 572a sold for 60y.

Kirin — A327

Flag of Crown Prince — A328

Engr. and Photo.
1952, Nov. 10 ***Perf. 13½***

573 A327 5y red org & pur 1.90 .55
574 A327 10y red org & dk grn 2.25 .80
575 A328 24y deep blue 12.00 4.50
a. Souv. sheet of 3, #573-575, imperf. 80.00 175.00
Nos. 573-575 (3) 16.15 5.85

Issued to commemorate the nomination of Crown Prince Akihito as Heir Apparent.

No. 575a measures 130x129mm, and has a background design of phoenix and clouds in violet brown and blue. Sold for 50y.

Sambaso Doll — A329

First Electric Lamp in Japan — A330

Perf. 13½x13
1953, Jan, 1 Photo. Unwmk.

576 A329 5y carmine 6.75 .75

For postage on New Year's cards, later for ordinary use.

Sheets of 4 were awarded as 6th prize in the natl. lottery. Value $67.50.

1953, Mar. 25

577 A330 10y brown 6.25 1.90

75th anniv. of electric lighting in Japan.

"Kintai Bridge," Print by Hiroshige — A331

Kintai Bridge as Rebuilt in 1953 # — A332

1953, May 3 ***Perf. 13***

578 A331 10y chestnut 6.50 2.10
579 A332 24y blue 6.00 3.00

Kannon Type of 1951
Redrawn; Zeros Omitted

A332a

1953-54 **Typo.**

580 A332a 10y red brn & lilac 4.00 .20
a. Booklet pane 10 + 2 labels (souvenir) ('54) 150.00 125.00
b. Bklt. pane 10 + 2 labels ('54) 67.50 60.00

No. 580a was issued in honor of Philatelic Week 1954. The inscriptions on the two labels are arranged in two columns of boldface characters.

On No. 580b, the left-hand label inscriptions are arranged in three columns of mixed heavy and thin characters.

See Nos. 611a-611b and 672.

Lake Shikotsu, Hokkaido A333

Mt. Yotei
A334

1953, July 25 Photo. *Perf. 13*

581 A333 5y ultra 2.10 .55
582 A334 10y green 6.00 1.10
a. Souv. sheet of 2, #581-582, imperf., no gum 37.50 32.50

Shikotsu-Toya National Park.
No. 582a sold for 20 yen.

Akita Dog
A335

Cormorant
Fishing
A336

1953 Unwmk.

583 A335 2y gray .20 .20

Engr.

584 A336 100y dark red 25.00 .20
a. Imperf., pair 525.00

See No. 1622.

Futamigaura Beach — A337

Namikiri
Coast
A338

1953, Oct. 2 Photo.

585 A337 5y red 1.90 .55
586 A338 10y blue 3.75 1.10
a. Souv. sheet of 2, #585-586, imperf., no gum 21.00 17.50

Ise-Shima National Park.

Phoenix — A339

Design: 10y, Japanese crane in flight.

1953, Oct. 12 Engr. *Perf. 12½*

587 A339 5y brown carmine 2.75 1.10

Photo.

588 A339 10y dark blue 5.50 1.90

Nos. 587-588 were issued on the occasion of the return of Crown Prince Akihito from his visit to Europe and America. Issued in sheets of 20 with marginal inscription.

Rugby
Match — A340

Judo — A341

1953, Oct. 22 *Perf. 13½*

589 A340 5y black 5.75 1.25
590 A341 5y blue green 5.75 1.25
a. Pair, #589-590 13.50 7.50

8th Natl. Athletic Meet, Matsuyama, Oct. 22-26.

Sky and Top of
Observatory
A342

1953, Oct. 29

591 A342 10y dk gray blue 9.00 1.50

75th anniversary of the Tokyo Astronomical Observatory.

Mt. Unzen
from Golf
Course
A343

Mt.
Unzen
from
Chijiwa
Beach
A344

1953, Nov. 20 *Perf. 13*

592 A343 5y red 1.75 .55
593 A344 10y blue 4.50 1.10
a. Souv. sheet of 2, #592-593, imperf., no gum 20.00 17.50

Unzen National Park.

Toy
Horse — A345

Racing
Skaters — A346

1953, Dec. 25 *Perf. 13½x13*

594 A345 5y rose 5.25 .55

Issued to pay postage on New Year's cards, later for ordinary use. A sheet reproducing four of these stamps was awarded as sixth prize in the national lottery. Value $37.50.

1954, Jan. 16

595 A346 10y blue 4.50 1.40

World Speed Skating Matches for Men, Sapporo City, Jan. 16-17, 1954.

Golden Hall,
Chusonji
Temple
A347

Thread, Pearls,
Gears, Buttons
and Globe
A348

1954, Jan. 20

596 A347 20y olive green .95 .20

1954, Apr. 10

597 A348 10y dark red 3.25 1.00

International Trade Fair, Osaka, Apr. 10-23.

Little Cuckoo
A349

Wrestlers
A350

1954, May 10 *Perf. 13x13½*

598 A349 3y blue green .20 .20
a. Imperf., pair 300.00

For stamp inscribed "NIPPON," see No. 1067.

1954, May 22 Engr.

599 A350 10y deep green 2.75 1.00

World Free Style Wrestling Championship Matches, Tokyo, 1954.

Mt.
Asama
A351

Mt.
Tanikawa
A352

1954, June 25 *Perf. 13*

600 A351 5y dk gray brn 2.00 .55
601 A352 10y dk blue grn 3.50 1.10
a. Souvenir sheet of 2, #600-601, no gum 19.00 15.00

Jo-Shin-etsu National Park.

Table
Tennis — A353

Archery — A354

1954, Aug. 22 Engr. *Perf. 12*

602 A353 5y dull brown 4.50 1.00
603 A354 5y gray green 4.50 1.00
a. Pair, #602-603 9.50 5.75

9th Natl. Athletic Meet, Sapporo, Aug. 22-26.

Morse Telegraph
Instrument
A355

ITU Monument
A356

1954, Oct. 13 *Perf. 13x13½, 13½x13*

604 A355 5y dark purple brown 1.90 .55
605 A356 10y deep blue 5.00 1.10

75th anniv. of Japanese membership in the ITU.

Daruma
Doll — A357

1954, Dec. 20 Photo. *Perf. 13½x13*

606 A357 5y black & red 5.25 .55

Sheets reproducing four of these stamps with Japanese inscriptions and ornaments were awarded as fifth prize in the national lottery. Value $37.50.

Mountain Stream,
Tama Gorge — A358

Chichibu Mountains — A359

1955, Mar. 1 Engr. *Perf. 13*

607 A358 5y blue 1.50 .55
608 A359 10y red brown 1.90 .75
a. Souv. sheet of 2, #607-608, imperf., no gum 21.00 17.50

Chichibu-Tama National Park.

Bridge and
Iris — A360

1955, Mar. 15 *Perf. 13x13½*

609 A360 500y deep plum 65.00 .40

Paper Carp as Flown
on Boys' Day
A361

Mandarin
Ducks
A362

Unwmk.

1955, May 16 Photo. *Perf. 13*

610 A361 10y multicolored 4.25 1.10

15th congress of the International Chamber of Commerce, Tokyo, May 16-21, 1955.

1955-64

611 A362 5y lt bl & red brn .25 .20
a. Bklt. pane, 4 #611, 8 #580 ('59) 25.00
b. Bklt. pane, 4 #611, 8 #725 ('63) 27.50 17.00
c. Bklt. pane of 4 ('64) 4.25 2.75
d. Imperf., pair 700.00

See Nos. 738, 881d, 914b.

Benten Cape — A363

Jodo Beach A364

1955, Sept. 30
612 A363 5y deep green 1.40 .45
613 A364 10y rose lake 1.90 .75
a. Souv. sheet of 2, #612-613, imperf., no gum 22.50 17.50

Rikuchu-Kaigan National Park. No. 613a sold for 20y.

Gymnastics A365

Runners A366

1955, Oct. 30 **Engr.**
614 A365 5y brown lake 2.00 .75
615 A366 5y bluish black 2.00 .75
a. Pair, #614-615 6.00 5.00

10th National Athletic Meet, Kanagawa Prefecture.
See Nos. 639-640, 657.

"A Girl Blowing Glass Toy," by Utamaro A367

1955, Nov. 1 **Photo.**
616 A367 10y multicolored 10.00 5.75

150th anniv. of the death of Utamaro, wood-cut artist, and to publicize Philatelic Week, Nov. 1955. Issued in sheets of 10.

Kokeshi Dolls — A368

Table Tennis — A369

1955, Dec. 30 **Unwmk.** ***Perf. 13***
617 A368 5y olive grn & red 1.90 .25

Sheets reproducing four of these stamps, were awarded as fifth prize in the New Year's lottery. Value $27.50.

1956, Apr. 2 ***Perf. 13x13½***
618 A369 10y red brown 1.25 .75

Intl. Table Tennis Championship, Tokyo, 4/2-11.

Judo — A370

1956, May 2 ***Perf. 13***
619 A370 10y green & lilac 1.50 .75

Issued to publicize the first World Judo Championship Meet, Tokyo, May 3, 1956.

Boy and Girl with Paper Carp A371

1956, May 5
620 A371 5y lt blue & blk 1.10 .55

Establishment of World Children's Day, 5/5/56.

Water Plants, Lake Akan A372

Big Purple Butterfly A373

1956 **Unwmk.** ***Perf. 13***
621 A372 55y lt blue, grn & blk 12.50 .55
622 A373 75y multicolored 7.00 .55

See Nos. 887A, 917.

Castle Type of 1951
Redrawn; Zeros Omitted

A373a

1956 **Engr.** ***Perf. 13½x13***
623 A373a 14y gray olive 5.00 1.75

Osezaki Promontory — A374

Kujuku Island A375

1956, Oct. 1 **Photo.**
624 A374 5y red brown .95 .45

Engr. & Photo.
625 A375 10y lt blue & indigo 1.40 .75
a. Souv. sheet of 2, #624-625, imperf., no gum 17.00 16.00

Saikai National Park.
No. 625a sold for 20y.

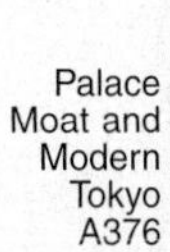

Palace Moat and Modern Tokyo A376

1956, Oct. 1 **Engr.**
626 A376 10y dull purple 1.90 .75

500th anniv. of the founding of Tokyo.

Sakuma Dam — A377

1956, Oct. 15 **Unwmk.** ***Perf. 13***
627 A377 10y dark blue 1.90 .75

Completion of Sakuma Dam.

Long Jump A378

Basketball A379

1956, Oct. 28 ***Perf. 13½x13***
628 A378 5y brown violet 1.10 .55
629 A379 5y steel blue 1.10 .55
a. Pair, #628-629 2.25 2.50

11th Natl. Athletic Meet, Hyogo Prefecture.
See No. 658.

Kabuki Actor Ebizo Ichikawa by Sharaku A380

1956, Nov. 1 **Photo.** ***Perf. 13***
630 A380 10y multicolored 8.50 5.50

Stamp Week. Sheets of 10.

Mount Manaslu A381

1956, Nov. 3
631 A381 10y multicolored 3.00 1.60

Japanese expedition which climbed Mount Manaslu in the Himalayas on May 9 and 11, 1956.

Electric Locomotive and Hiroshige's "Yui Stage" — A382

1956, Nov. 19 **Unwmk.** ***Perf. 13***
632 A382 10y dk ol bis, blk & grn 4.00 1.60

Electrification of Tokaido Line.

Cogwheel, Vacuum Tube and Ship — A383

1956, Dec. 18 **Engr.**
633 A383 10y ultra .90 .75

Japanese Machinery Floating Fair.

Toy Whale — A384

United Nations Emblem A385

1956, Dec. 20 **Photo.**
634 A384 5y multicolored 1.25 .20
a. Imperf., pair

Sheets reproducing four of these stamps, with inscriptions and ornaments, were awarded as sixth prize in the national lottery. Value $13.50.

Photogravure and Engraved

1957, Mar. 8 **Unwmk.** ***Perf. 13½x13***
635 A385 10y lt blue & dk car .70 .55

Japan's admission to the UN, Dec. 18, 1956.

Temple Type of 1950
Redrawn; Zeros Omitted

A385a

1957-59 **Engr.** ***Perf. 13x13½***
636 A385a 24y violet 14.00 2.25
636A A385a 30y rose lilac ('59) 30.00 .40
b. Imperf., pair

IGY Emblem, Penguin and "Soya" — A386

Atomic Reactor — A387

1957, July 1 **Photo.** ***Perf. 13***
637 A386 10y blue, yel & blk .75 .45

International Geophysical Year.

1957, Sept. 18 **Engr.** ***Perf. 13***
638 A387 10y dark purple .45 .25

Completion of Japan's atomic reactor at Tokai-Mura, Ibaraki Prefecture.

Sports Type of 1955

No. 639, Girl on parallel bars. No. 640, Boxers.

1957, Oct. 26 **Unwmk.** ***Perf. 13***
639 A366 5y ultra .35 .20
640 A366 5y dark red .35 .20
a. Pair, #639-640 .90 .75

12th Natl. Athletic Meet, Shizuoka Prefecture.

"Girl Bouncing Ball," by Suzuki Harunobu A388

1957, Nov. 1 **Photo.**
641 A388 10y multicolored 1.50 1.25

1957 Stamp Week. Issued in sheets of 10. See Nos. 646, 671, 728, 757.

Lake Okutama and Ogochi Dam — A389

1957, Nov. 26 **Engr.** ***Perf. 13½***
642 A389 10y ultra .30 .20

Completion of Ogochi Dam, part of the Tokyo water supply system.

Modern and First Japanese Blast Furnaces A390

Toy Dog (Inu-hariko) — A391

1957, Dec. 1 **Photo.** **Unwmk.**
643 A390 10y orange & dk pur .25 .20

Centenary of Japan's iron industry.

1957, Dec. 20 ***Perf. 13½x13***
644 A391 5y multicolored .25 .20

New Year 1958. Sheets reproducing 4 #644, with inscriptions and ornaments, were awarded as 5th prize in the New Year lottery. Value $5.

Shimonoseki-Moji Tunnel — A392

1958, Mar. 9 ***Perf. 13x13½***
645 A392 10y multicolored .25 .20

Completion of the Kan-Mon Underwater Highway connecting Honshu and Kyushu Islands.

Stamp Week Type of 1957

Design: 10y, Woman with Umbrella, woodcut by Kiyonaga.

1958, Apr. 20 **Unwmk.** ***Perf. 13***
646 A388 10y multicolored .50 .20

Stamp Week, 1958. Sheets of 10.

Statue of Ii Naosuke and Harbor A393

Unwmk.
1958, May 10 **Engr.** ***Perf. 13***
647 A393 10y gray blue & car .25 .20

Cent. of the opening of the ports of Yokohama, Nagasaki and Hakodate to foreign powers.

National Stadium — A394

3rd Asian Games, Tokyo: 10y, Torch and emblem. 14y, Runner. 24y, Woman diver.

1958, May 24 **Photo.**
648 A394 5y bl grn, bis & pink .20 .20
649 A394 10y multicolored .25 .30
650 A394 14y multicolored .30 .25
651 A394 24y multicolored .35 .30
Nos. 648-651 (4) 1.10 1.05

Kasato Maru, Map and Brazilian Flag A395

1958, June 18
652 A395 10y multicolored .25 .20

50 years of Japanese emigration to Brazil.

Sado Island and Local Dancer A396

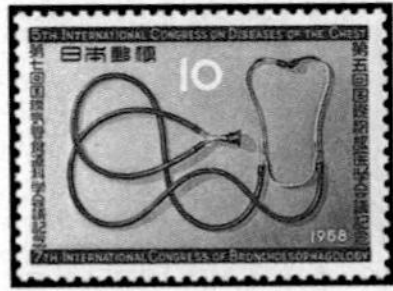
Mt. Yahiko and Echigo Plain — A397

1958, Aug. 20 **Unwmk.** ***Perf. 13***
653 A396 10y multicolored .50 .20
654 A397 10y multicolored .45 .20

Sado-Yahiko Quasi-National Park.

Stethoscope A398

1958, Sept. 7 **Photo.** ***Perf. 13***
655 A398 10y Prussian green .25 .20

5th Intl. Cong. on Diseases of the Chest and the 7th Intl. Cong. of Bronchoesophagology.

"Kyoto" (Sanjo Bridge), Print by Hiroshige A399

1958, Oct. 5
656 A399 24y multicolored 2.00 .70

Issued for International Letter Writing Week, Oct. 5-11. See No. 679.

Sports Types of 1955-56

Designs: No. 657, Weight lifter. No. 658, Girl badminton player.

1958, Oct. 19 **Engr.**
657 A365 5y gray blue .25 .20
658 A379 5y claret .25 .20
a. Pair, #657-658 .75 .75

13th Natl. Athletic Meet, Toyama Prefecture.

Keio University and Yukichi Fukuzawa — A400

1958, Nov. 8 **Engr.** ***Perf. 13½***
659 A400 10y magenta .25 .20

Centenary of Keio University.

Globe and Playing Children A401

1958, Nov. 23 **Photo.** ***Perf. 13***
660 A401 10y deep green .25 .25

9th Intl. Conf. of Social Work and the 2nd Intl. Study Conf. on Child Welfare.

Flame: Symbol of Human Rights — A402

1958, Dec. 10 **Unwmk.** ***Perf. 13***
661 A402 10y multicolored .25 .25

10th anniv. of the signing of the Universal Declaration of Human Rights.

Toy of Takamatsu (Tai-Ebisu) A403

Tractor and Map of Kojima Bay A404

1958, Dec. 20 ***Perf. 13½***
662 A403 5y multicolored .45 .20

New Year 1959. Sheets reproducing 4 #662, with inscriptions and ornaments, were awarded as prizes in the New Year lottery. Size: 103x89mm. Value $5.

1959, Feb. 1 ***Perf. 12½***
663 A404 10y claret & bister brn .25 .25

Completion of the embankment closing Kojima Bay for reclamation.

Karst Plateau A405

Akiyoshi Cave — A406

1959, Mar. 16 **Photo.** ***Perf. 13½***
664 A405 10y green, bl & ocher .80 .20
665 A406 10y multicolored 1.40 .20

Akiyoshidai Quasi-National Park.

Map of Southeast Asia — A407

1959, Mar. 27
666 A407 10y deep carmine .25 .25

Asian Cultural Cong., Tokyo, Mar. 27-31, marking the 2,500th anniv. of the death of Buddha.

Ceremonial Fan — A408

Prince Akihito and Princess Michiko — A409

Photogravure; Portraits Engraved
1959, Apr. 10
667 A408 5y magenta & violet .25 .20
668 A409 10y red brn & dull pur .50 .25
a. Souv. sheet of 2, #667-668, imperf. 4.50 4.50
669 A408 20y org brn & brn .75 .25
670 A409 30y yel grn & dk grn 2.25 .30
Nos. 667-670 (4) 3.75 1.00

Wedding of Crown Prince Akihito and Princess Michiko, Apr. 10, 1959.

Type of 1957

Women Reading Poetry, print by Eishi Fujiwara.

1959, May 20 **Photo.** ***Perf. 13***
671 A388 10y multicolored 2.10 .90

Stamp Week. Issued in sheets of 10.

Redrawn Kannon Type of 1953
Coil Stamp
Perf. 13 Horiz.

1959, Jan. 20 **Typo.** **Unwmk.**
672 A332a 10y red brn & lilac 18.00 *20.00*

Measuring Glass, Tape Measure and Scales — A410

Nurses Carrying Stretcher A411

1959, June 5 Photo. *Perf. 13*
673 A410 10y lt blue & blk .25 .25

Adoption of the metric system.

1959, June 24
674 A411 10y olive grn & red .25 .25

Centenary of the Red Cross idea.

Mt. Fuji and Lake Motosu A412

1959, July 21 Engr. *Perf. 13*
675 A412 10y green, bl & sepia .45 .25

Establishment of Natural Park Day and 1st Natural Park Convention, Yumoto, Nikko, July 21, 1959.

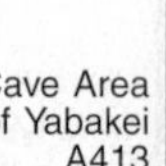

Ao Cave Area of Yabakei A413

Hita, Mt. Hiko and Great Cormorant A414

1959, Sept. 25 Photo. *Perf. 13*
676 A413 10y multicolored .90 .25
677 A414 10y multicolored 1.00 .25

Yaba-Hita-Hiko Quasi National Park.

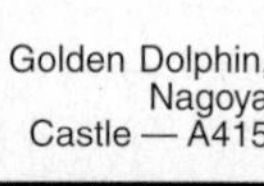

Golden Dolphin, Nagoya Castle — A415

Japanese Crane, IATA Emblem — A416

1959, Oct. 1
678 A415 10y brt bl, gold & blk .50 .25

350th anniversary of Nagoya.

Hiroshige Type of 1958

Design: 30y, "Kuwana," the 7-ri Crossing Point, print by Hiroshige.

1959, Oct. 4 Unwmk.
679 A399 30y multicolored 6.75 1.10

Intl. Letter Writing Week, Oct. 4-10.

1959, Oct. 12 Engr.
680 A416 10y brt grnsh blue .35 .25

15th General Meeting of the International Air Transport Association.

Shoin Yoshida and PTA Symbol — A417

Throwing the Hammer — A418

1959, Oct. 27 Photo. *Perf. 13*
681 A417 10y brown .25 .20

Centenary of the death of Shoin Yoshida, educator, and in connection with the Parent-Teachers Association convention.

1959, Oct. 25 Engr.

Design: No. 683, Woman Fencer.

682 A418 5y gray blue .35 .20
683 A418 5y olive bister .35 .20
a. Pair, #682-683 .75 .75

14th National Athletic Meet, Tokyo.

Globes A419

1959, Nov. 2 Photo.
684 A419 5y brown red .25 .20

15th session of GATT (General Agreement on Tariffs & Trade), Tokyo, Oct. 12-Nov. 21.

Toy Mouse of Kanazawa — A420

1959, Dec. 19 Unwmk. *Perf. 13½*
685 A420 5y gold, red, grn & blk .50 .20

New Year 1960. Sheets reproducing 4 #685, with marginal inscription and ornaments, were awarded as prizes in natl. lottery. Value $5.50.

Yukio Ozaki and Clock Tower, Ozaki Memorial Hall — A421

Nara Period Artwork, Shosoin Treasure House — A422

1960, Feb. 25 Photo. *Perf. 13½*
686 A421 10y red brn & dk brn .25 .20

Completion of Ozaki Memorial Hall, erected in memory of Yukio Ozaki (1858-1954), statesman.

1960, Mar. 10
687 A422 10y olive gray .25 .20

Transfer of the capital to Nara, 1250th anniv.

Scenic Trio Issue

Bay of Matsushima A423

Ama-no-hashidate (Heavenly Bridge) — A424

Miyajima from the Sea — A425

1960 Engr.
688 A423 10y maroon & bl grn 1.25 .45
689 A424 10y green & lt bl 1.60 .45
690 A425 10y vio blk & bl grn 1.60 .45
Nos. 688-690 (3) 4.45 1.35

Issued: #688, 3/15; #689, 7/15; #690, 11/15.

Takeshima, off Gamagori A426

1960, Mar. 20 Photo. *Perf. 13½*
691 A426 10y multicolored .75 .25

Mikawa Bay Quasi-National Park.

Poetess Isé, 13th Century Painting — A427

1960, Apr. 20 Unwmk. *Perf. 13*
692 A427 10y multicolored 1.60 1.60

Stamp Week, 1960.

Kanrin Maru — A428

Design: 30y, Pres. Buchanan receiving first Japanese diplomatic mission.

1960, May 17 Engr.
693 A428 10y bl grn & brn .50 .25
694 A428 30y car & indigo 1.10 .40

Cent. of the Japan-US Treaty of Amity and Commerce. Nos. 694 and 693 form pages of an open book when placed next to each other. Souvenir sheet is No. 703.

Crested Ibis (Toki) — A429

Radio Waves Encircling Globe — A430

1960, May 24 Photo. *Perf. 13½*
695 A429 10y gray, pink & red .45 .30

12th Intl. Congress for Bird Preservation.

1960, June 1 Engr.
696 A430 10y carmine rose .30 .20

25th anniv. of the Intl. Radio Program by the Japanese Broadcasting Corporation.

Flower Garden (Gensei Kaen) — A431

1960, June 15 Photo.
697 A431 10y multicolored .90 .30

Abashiri Quasi-National Park.

Cape Ashizuri A432

1960, Aug. 1 Unwmk.
698 A432 10y multicolored .80 .30

Ashizuri Quasi-National Park.

Rainbow Spanning Pacific, Cherry Blossoms and Pineapples A433

Henri Farman's Biplane and Jet A434

1960, Aug. 20 *Perf. 13½*
699 A433 10y multicolored .55 .25

75th anniversary of Japanese contract emigration to Hawaii.

1960, Sept. 20 *Perf. 13*
700 A434 10y brn & chlky bl .45 .20

50th anniversary of Japanese aviation.

Seat Plan of Diet — A435

"Red Fuji" by Hokusai and Diet Building — A436

1960, Sept. 27
701 A435 5y indigo & org .25 .20
702 A436 10y blue & red brn .60 .25

49th Inter-Parliamentary Conference.

Souvenir Sheet
Type A428

1960, Sept. 27 Engr.
703 Sheet of 2, #693-694 22.50 22.50

Visit of Prince Akihito and Princess Michiko to the US.

"Night Snow at Kambara," by Hiroshige A437

1960, Oct. 9 Photo.
704 A437 30y multicolored 14.00 3.75

Issued for International Letter Writing Week, Oct. 9-15. See Nos. 735, 769.

Japanese Fencing (Kendo) — A438

Okayama Astrophysical Observatory A439

No. 706, Girl gymnast and vaulting horse.

1960, Oct. 23 Engr. *Perf. 13½*
705 A438 5y dull blue .35 .20
706 A438 5y rose violet .35 .20
a. Pair, #705-706 .90 .90

15th National Athletic Meet, Kumamoto.

1960, Oct. 19
707 A439 10y brt violet .50 .20

Opening of the Okayama Astrophysical Observatory.

Lt. Naoshi Shirase and Map of Antarctica — A440

Little Red Calf of Aizu, Gold Calf of Iwate — A441

1960, Nov. 29 Photo.
708 A440 10y fawn & black .45 .20

50th anniv. of the 1st Japanese Antarctic expedition.

1960, Dec. 20 Unwmk. *Perf. 13½*
709 A441 5y multicolored .50 .20

New Year 1961. Sheets reproducing 4 #709 were awarded as prizes in the New Year lottery. Size: 102x89mm. Value $6.

Diet Building at Night — A442

Opening of First Session — A443

1960, Dec. 24 Photo.; Engr. (10y)
710 A442 5y gray & dk bl .35 .20
711 A443 10y carmine .45 .20

70th anniversary of the Japanese Diet.

Narcissus — A444

Nojima Cape Lighthouse and Fisherwomen A445

#713, Plum blossoms. #714, Camellia japonica. #715, Cherry blossoms. #716, Peony. #717, Iris. #718, Lily. #719, Morning glory. #720, Bellflower. #721, Gentian. #722, Chrysanthemum. #723, Camellia sasanqua.

1961 Photo. *Perf. 13½*
712 A444 10y lilac, yel & grn 3.00 .70
713 A444 10y brown, grn & yel 1.40 .70
714 A444 10y lem, grn, pink & yel 1.00 .70
715 A444 10y gray, brn, pink, yel & blk 1.00 .70
716 A444 10y blk, grn, pink & yel .90 .65
717 A444 10y gray, pur, grn & yel .55 .35
718 A444 10y gray grn, yel & brn .40 .30
719 A444 10y lt bl, grn & lil .40 .30
720 A444 10y lt yel grn, vio & grn .40 .30
721 A444 10y org, vio bl & grn .40 .30
722 A444 10y blue, yel & grn .40 .30
723 A444 10y sl, pink, yel & grn .40 .30
Nos. 712-723 (12) 10.25 5.60

1961, Mar. 15
724 A445 10y multicolored .50 .25

South Boso Quasi-National Park.

Cherry Blossoms A446

Hisoka Maejima A447

Unwmk.
1961, Apr. 1 Photo. *Perf. 13*
725 A446 10y lilac rose & gray .30 .20
a. Lilac rose omitted 300.00
b. Imperf., pair 500.00
c. Booklet pane of 4 5.50 2.25
d. Gray omitted 350.00

See No. 611b.

Coil Stamp

1961, Apr. 25 *Perf. 13 Horiz.*
726 A446 10y lil rose & gray 5.00 1.90

1961, Apr. 20 *Perf. 13*
727 A447 10y olive & black 1.10 .20

90th anniv. of Japan's modern postal service from Tokyo to Osaka, inaugurated by Deputy Postmaster General Hisoka Maejima.

Type of 1957

"Dancing Girl" from a "Screen of Dancers."

1961, Apr. 20 *Perf. 13½*
728 A388 10y multicolored .90 .60

Stamp Week, 1961. Sheets of 10 (5x2).

Lake Biwa — A448

1961, Apr. 25
729 A448 10y blk, dk bl & yel grn .50 .25

Lake Biwa Quasi-National Park.

Rotary Emblem and People of Various Races — A449

1961, May 29 Engr. *Perf. 13*
730 A449 10y gray & orange .25 .20

52nd convention of Rotary Intl., Tokyo, May 29-June 1, 1961.

Faucet, Wheat, Insulator & Cogwheel A450

Sun, Earth and Meridian A451

1961, July 7 Photo. *Perf. 13½*
731 A450 10y violet & aqua .30 .20

Aichi irrigation system, Kiso river.

1961, July 12
732 A451 10y yellow, red & blk .30 .20

75th anniv. of Japanese standard time.

Parasol Dance on Dunes of Tottori A452

1961, Aug. 15
733 A452 10y multicolored .55 .25

San'in Kaigan Quasi-National Park.

Onuma Lake and Komagatake Volcano A453

Gymnast on Horizontal Bar — A454

1961, Sept. 15
734 A453 10y grn, red brn & bl .60 .25

Onuma Quasi-National Park.

Hiroshige Type of 1960

1961, Oct. 8 *Perf. 13*

Design: 30y, "Hakone," print by Hiroshige from the 53 Stages of the Tokaido.

735 A437 30y multicolored 5.75 4.50

Intl. Letter Writing Week, Oct. 8-14.

1961, Oct. 8 Engr. *Perf. 13½*

Design: No. 737, Women rowing.

736 A454 5y blue green .30 .20
737 A454 5y ultra .30 .20
a. Pair, #736-737 .75 .75

16th National Athletic Meet, Akita. See Nos. 770-771, 816-817, 852-853.

Duck Type of 1955
Coil Stamp

1961, Oct. 2 Photo. *Perf. 13 Horiz.*
738 A362 5y lt bl & red brn 2.50 2.00

National Diet Library and Book — A455

Papier Maché Tiger — A456

1961, Nov. 1 *Perf. 13½*
739 A455 10y dp ultra & gold .25 .20

Opening of the new Natl. Diet Library, Tokyo.

1961, Dec. 15 *Perf. 13½*
740 A456 5y multicolored .40 .20

New Year 1962. Sheets reproducing 4 #740 were awarded as 5th prize in the New Year lottery. Size: 102x90, Value $6.

Mt. Fuji from Lake Ashi — A457

Minokake-Iwa at Irozaki A458

Mt. Fuji from Mitsu Pass — A459

Mt. Fuji from Cape of Ose — A460

1962, Jan. 16 Unwmk. Photo.
741 A457 5y deep green .40 .20
742 A458 5y dark blue .40 .20
743 A459 10y red brown 1.10 .25
744 A460 10y black 1.10 .30
Nos. 741-744 (4) 3.00 .95

Fuji-Hakone-Izu National Park.

Omishima A461

1962, Feb. 15 *Perf. 13½*
745 A461 10y ultra, red & yel .40 .25

Kitanagato-Kaigan Quasi-National Park.

Perotrochus Hirasei A462

Sacred Bamboo A463

Shari-den of Engakuji
A464

Yomei Gate, Nikko
A465

Noh Mask — A466

Copper Pheasant
A466a

Wind God, Fujin, by Sotatsu
A467

Japanese Crane
A468

Mythical Winged Woman, Chusonji
A469

1962-65 Unwmk. *Perf. 13*

746	A462	4y dk brn & red ('63)	.20	.20
747	A463	6y gray grn & car	.20	.20
748	A464	30y violet black	3.50	.20
749	A465	40y rose red	4.00	.20
750	A466	70y yel brn & blk ('65)	1.75	.20
751	A466a	80y crim & brn ('65)	.95	.20
752	A467	90y brt blue grn	24.00	.25
753	A468	100y pink & blk ('63)	7.50	.20
754	A469	120y purple	7.25	.55
		Nos. 746-754 (9)	49.35	2.20

See Nos. 888, 888A, 1076, 1079, 1257.

Coil Stamp
Perf. 13 Horiz.

755 A464 30y dull violet ('63) 3.50 2.10

Hinamatsuri, Doll Festival — A470

1962, Mar. 3 *Perf. 13½*
756 A470 10y brn, blk, bl & car .85 .40

The Doll Festival is celebrated Mar. 3 in honor of young girls.

Type of 1957

Design: Dancer from "Flower Viewing Party" by Naganobu Kano.

1962, Apr. 20 Photo. *Perf. 13½*
757 A388 10y multicolored .90 .75

Stamp Week, 1962. Sheets of 10.

Sakurajima Volcano and Kagoshima Bay — A471

1962, Apr. 30
758 A471 10y multicolored .30 .25

Kinkowan Quasi-National Park.

Mount Kongo
A472

1962, May 15 *Perf. 13½*
759 A472 10y gray bl, dk grn & sal .30 .25

Kongo-Ikoma Quasi-National Park.

Suigo Park Scene and Iris — A473

1962, June 1 *Perf. 13½*
760 A473 10y multicolored .30 .25

Suigo Quasi-National Park.

Train Emerging from Hokuriku Tunnel — A474

1962, June 10 Photo.
761 A474 10y olive gray .65 .30

Opening of Hokuriku Tunnel between Tsuruga and Imajo, Fukui Prefecture.

Star Festival (Tanabata Matsuri) — A475

Boy Scout Hat on Map of Southeast Asia — A476

1962, July 7 Unwmk. *Perf. 13½*
762 A475 10y multicolored .25 .20

The Tanabata festival is celebrated on the evening of July 7.

1962, Aug. 3
763 A476 10y red org, blk & bis .25 .20

Asian Boy Scout Jamboree, Mt. Fuji, Aug. 3-7.

Ozegahara Swampland and Mt. Shibutsu
A477

Fumes on Mt. Chausu, Nasu — A478

Lake Chuzenji and Mt. Nantai
A479

Senryu-kyo Narrows, Shiobara
A480

1962, Sept. 1

764	A477	5y greenish blue	.25	.20
765	A478	5y maroon	.25	.20
766	A479	10y purple	.35	.20
767	A480	10y olive	.35	.20
		Nos. 764-767 (4)	1.20	.80

Nikko National Park.

Wakato Suspension Bridge — A481

Perf. 13½x13
1962, Sept. 26 Engr. Unwmk.
768 A481 10y rose red .55 .25

Opening of Wakato Bridge over Dokai Bay in North Kyushu.

Hiroshige Type of 1960

Design: 40y, "Nihonbashi," print by Hiroshige from the 53 Stages of the Tokaido.

1962, Oct. 7 Photo. *Perf. 13*
769 A437 40y multicolored 4.50 3.75

Intl. Letter Writing Week, Oct. 7-13.

Sports Type of 1961

Design: No. 770, Woman softball pitcher. No. 771, Rifle shooting.

1962, Oct. 21 Engr. *Perf. 13½*

770	A454	5y bluish black	.25	.20
771	A454	5y brown violet	.25	.20
a.		Pair, #770-771	.50	.50

17th National Athletic Meeting, Okayama.

Shichi-go-san Festival — A482

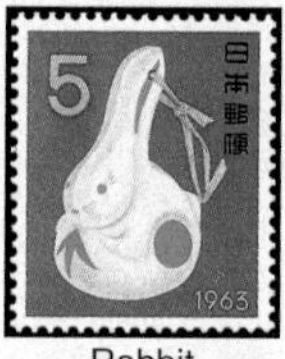
Rabbit Bell — A483

1962, Nov. 15 Photo. *Perf. 13½*
772 A482 10y multicolored .25 .20

This festival for 7 and 3-year-old girls and 5-year-old boys is celebrated on Nov. 15.

1962, Dec. 15
773 A483 5y multicolored .35 .20

New Year 1963. Sheets reproducing 4 #773 were awarded as prizes in the New Year lottery. Value $6.
See No. 2655b.

Mt. Ishizuchi
A484

1963, Jan. 11 Unwmk. *Perf. 13½*
774 A484 10y multicolored .25 .20

Ishizuchi Quasi-National Park.

Setsubun, Spring Festival, Bean Scattering Ceremony
A485

Map of City, Birds, Ship and Factory
A486

1963, Feb. 3 Photo.
775 A485 10y multicolored .25 .20

1963, Feb. 10
776 A486 10y chocolate .25 .20

Consolidation of the communities of Moji, Kokura, Wakamatsu, Yawata and Tobata into Kita-Kyushu City.

"Frost Flowers" on Mt. Fugen
A487

Amakusa Island and Mt. Unzen
A488

1963, Feb. 15

777	A487	5y gray blue	.20	.20
778	A488	10y carmine rose	.25	.20

Unzen-Amakusa National Park.

Green Pond, Midorigaike
A489

Hakusan Range
A490

Perf. 13½
1963, Mar. 1 Unwmk. Photo.

779	A489	5y violet brown	.20	.20
780	A490	10y dark green	.25	.20

Hakusan National Park.

Keya-no-Oto Rock — A491

1963, Mar. 15
781 A491 10y multicolored .25 .20

Genkai Quasi-National Park.

Wheat Emblem and Globe — A492

1963, Mar. 21
782 A492 10y dark green .20 .20

FAO "Freedom from Hunger" campaign.

"Girl Reading Letter," Yedo Screen A493

1963, Apr. 20 *Perf. 13½*

783 A493 10y multicolored .45 .45

Issued to publicize Stamp Week, 1963.

World Map and Centenary Emblem A494

1963, May 8

784 A494 10y multicolored .20 .20

Centenary of the International Red Cross.

Globe and Leaf with Symbolic River System — A495

1963, May 15 **Photo.**

785 A495 10y blue .20 .20

5th Congress of the Intl. Commission on Irrigation and Drainage.

Ito-dake, Asahi Range A496

Lake Hibara and Mt. Bandai A497

1963, May 25 **Unwmk.** *Perf. 13½*

786 A496 5y green .20 .20
787 A497 10y red brown .20 .20

Bandai-Asahi National Park.

Lidth's Jay — A498

#789, Rock ptarmigan. #790, Eastern turtle dove. #791, Japanese white stork. #792, Bush warbler. #792A, Meadow bunting.

1963-64 *Perf. 13½*

Design and Inscription

788	A498	10y	lt green	.60	.40
789	A498	10y	blue	.25	.20
790	A498	10y	pale yellow	.25	.20
791	A498	10y	grnsh blue ('64)	.25	.20
792	A498	10y	green ('64)	.25	.20
792A	A498	10y	lt rose brn ('64)	.25	.20
	Nos. 788-792A (6)			1.85	1.40

Intersection at Ritto, Shiga — A499

Girl Scout and Flag — A500

1963, July 15 **Unwmk.** *Perf. 13½*

793 A499 10y bl grn, blk & org .20 .20

Opening of the Nagoya-Kobe expressway, linking Nagoya with Kyoto, Osaka and Kobe.

1963, Aug. 1 **Photo.**

794 A500 10y multicolored .20 .20

Asian Girl Scout and Girl Guides Camp, Togakushi Heights, Nagano, Aug. 1-7.

View of Nashu A501

Whirlpool at Naruto A502

1963, Aug. 20

795 A501 5y olive bister .20 .20
796 A502 10y dark green .20 .20

Inland Sea National Park.

Lake Shikaribetsu, Hokkaido A503

Mt. Kurodake from Sounkyo Valley — A504

1963, Sept. 1 **Unwmk.** *Perf. 13½*

797 A503 5y deep Prus blue .20 .20
798 A504 10y rose violet .20 .20

Daisetsuzan National Park.

Parabolic Antenna for Space Communications A505

1963, Sept. 9 **Photo.**

799 A505 10y multicolored .20 .20

14th General Assembly of the International Scientific Radio Union, Tokyo.

"Great Wave off Kanagawa," by Hokusai A506

1963, Oct. 10 *Perf. 13*

800 A506 40y gray, dk bl & yel 3.00 1.25

Issued for International Letter Writing Week, Oct. 6-12. Design from Hokusai's "36 Views of Fuji." Printed in sheets of 10 (5x2).

Diver, Pole Vaulter and Relay Runner — A507

Woman Gymnast — A508

1963, Oct. 11 *Perf. 13½*

801 A507 10y bl, ocher, blk & red .20 .20

Tokyo Intl. (Pre-Olympic) Sports Meet, Tokyo, Oct. 11-16.

Perf. 13½

1963, Oct. 27 **Unwmk.** **Engr.**

Design: #803, Japanese wrestling (sumo).

802 A508 5y slate green .20 .20
803 A508 5y brown .20 .20
a. Pair, #802-803 .40 .45

18th National Athletic Meet, Yamaguchi.

Phoenix Tree and Hachijo Island — A509

Toy Dragons of Tottori and Yamanashi — A510

1963, Dec. 10 **Photo.**

804 A509 10y multicolored .20 .20

Izu Islands Quasi-National Park.

1963, Dec. 16

805 A510 5y gold, pink, aqua, ind & red .20 .20
a. Aqua omitted

New Year 1964. Sheets containing 4 #805 were awarded as 5th prize in the New Year lottery. Value $4.25.

Wakasa-Fuji from Takahama A511

1964, Jan 25 *Perf. 13½*

806 A511 10y multicolored .25 .20

Wakasa Bay Quasi-National Park.

Agave and View from Horikiri Pass — A512

1964, Feb. 20 **Unwmk.**

807 A512 10y multicolored .25 .20

Nichinan-Kaigan Quasi-National Park.

Uji Bridge A513

View of Toba — A514

1964, Mar. 15 **Photo.**

808 A513 5y sepia .20 .20
809 A514 10y red lilac .25 .20

Ise-Shima National Park.

Takayama Festival Float and Mt. Norikura — A515

#811, Yamaboko floats & Gion Shrine, Kyoto.

1964 **Photo.** *Perf. 13½*

810 A515 10y lt green & multi .20 .20
811 A515 10y grnsh blue & multi .20 .20

No. 810 issued for the annual Takayama spring and autumn festivals, Takayama City, Gifu Prefecture. No. 811 for the annual Gion festival of Kyoto, July 10-30.

Issue dates: #810, Apr. 15. #811, July 15.

Yadorigi Scene from Genji Monogatari Scroll — A516

1964, Apr. 20

814 A516 10y multicolored .25 .20

Stamp Week, 1964. Sheets of 10 (2x5).

Himeji Castle — A517

1964, June 1 *Perf. 13½*

815 A517 10y dark brown .20 .20

Restoration of Himeji Castle.

Sports Type of 1961

1964, June 6 *Perf. 13½*

816 A454 5y Handball .20 .20
817 A454 5y Woman on beam .20 .20
a. Pair, #816-817 .40 .45

19th National Athletic Meeting, Niigata.

Cable Cross Section, Map of Pacific Ocean A518

Tokyo Expressway Crossing Nihonbashi — A519

1964, June 19

818 A518 10y gray grn, dp mag & yel .20 .20

Opening of the transpacific cable.

1964, Aug. 1 **Photo.**

819 A519 10y green, silver & blk .20 .20

Opening of the Tokyo Expressway.

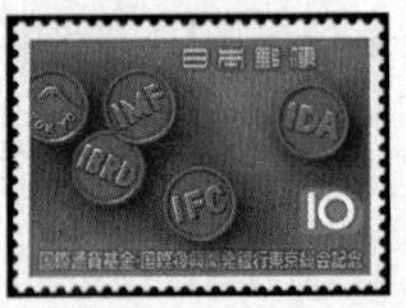

Coin-like Emblems A520

1964, Sept. 7 **Unwmk.** ***Perf. 13½***

820 A520 10y scarlet, gold & blk .20 .20

Annual general meeting of the Intl. Monetary Fund, Intl. Bank for Reconstruction and Development, Intl. Financial Corporation and the Intl. Development Assoc., Tokyo, Sept. 7-11.

Athletes, Olympic Flame and Rings — A521

National Stadium, Tokyo — A522

30y, Nippon Bodokan (fencing hall). 40y, Natl. Gymnasium. 50y, Komazawa Gymnasium.

1964

821 A521 5y multicolored .20 .20
822 A522 10y multicolored .20 .20
823 A522 30y multicolored .35 .20
824 A522 40y multicolored .45 .20
825 A522 50y multicolored .50 .20
a. Souvenir sheet of 5, #821-825 3.25 4.00
Nos. 821-825 (5) 1.70 1.00

18th Olympic Games, Tokyo, Oct. 10-25. Issue dates: 5y, Sept. 9. Others, Oct. 10.

Hand with Grain, Cow and Fruit — A523

Express Train — A524

1964, Sept. 15 ***Perf. 13½***

826 A523 10y violet brn & gold .20 .20

Draining of Hachirogata Lagoon, providing new farmland for the future.

1964, Oct. 1

827 A524 10y blue & black .25 .20

Opening of the new Tokaido railroad line.

Mt. Fuji Seen from Tokaido, by Hokusai A525

1964, Oct. 4 ***Perf. 13***

828 A525 40y multicolored 1.00 .45

Issued for International Letter Writing Week, Oct. 4-10. Issued in sheets of 10 (5x2). See Nos. 850, 896, 932, 971, 1016.

"Straw Snake" Mascot — A526

1964, Dec. 15 **Photo.** ***Perf. 13½***

829 A526 5y crimson, blk & yel .20 .20

New Year 1965. Sheets containing 4 #829 were awarded as prizes in the New Year lottery (issued Jan. 20, 1965). Value $1.75.

Mt. Daisen A527

Paradise Cove, Oki Islands A528

1965, Jan. 20 **Unwmk.** ***Perf. 13½***

830 A527 5y dark blue .20 .20
831 A528 10y brown orange .20 .20

Daisen-Oki National Park.

Niseko-Annupuri — A529

1965, Feb. 15 **Photo.**

832 A529 10y multicolored .20 .20

Niseko-Shakotan-Otarukaigan Quasi-Natl. Park.

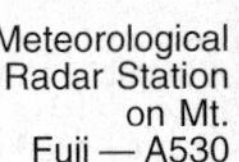

Meteorological Radar Station on Mt. Fuji — A530

1965, Mar. 10 **Photo.** ***Perf. 13½***

833 A530 10y multicolored .20 .20

Completion of the Meteorological Radar Station on Kengamine Heights of Mt. Fuji.

Kiyotsu Gorge — A531

Lake Nojiri and Mt. Myoko A532

1965, Mar. 15

834 A531 5y brown .20 .20
835 A532 10y magenta .20 .20

Jo-Shin-etsu Kogen National Park.

Communications Museum, Tokyo — A533

1965, Mar. 25 **Unwmk.** ***Perf. 13½***

836 A533 10y green .20 .20

Philatelic Exhibition celebrating the completion of the Communications Museum.

"The Prelude" by Shoen Uemura A534

1965, Apr. 20 **Photo.**

837 A534 10y gray & multi .30 .20

Issued for Stamp Week, 1965.

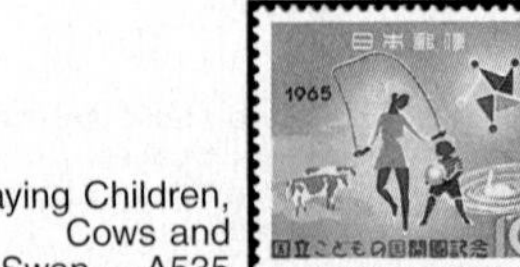

Playing Children, Cows and Swan — A535

Stylized Tree and Sun — A536

1965, May 5 **Unwmk.** ***Perf. 13½***

838 A535 10y pink & multi .20 .20

Opening of the National Garden for Children, Tokyo-Yokohama.

1965, May 9

839 A536 10y multicolored .20 .20

Issued to publicize the forestation movement and the forestation ceremony, Tottori Prefecture.

Globe, Old and New Communication Equipment — A537

1965, May 17

840 A537 10y brt blue, yel & blk .20 .20

Cent. of the ITU.

Crater of Mt. Naka, Kyushu A538

Five Central Peaks of Aso and Mountain Road — A539

1965, June 15 **Photo.** ***Perf. 13½***

841 A538 5y carmine rose .20 .20
842 A539 10y deep green .20 .20

Aso National Park.

ICY Emblem and Doves A540

1965, June 26 **Unwmk.**

843 A540 40y multicolored .45 .20

Intl. Cooperation Year, 1965, and 20th anniv. of the UN.

Horse Chase, Soma A541

Chichibu Festival Scene A542

1965 **Photo.** ***Perf. 13x13½***

844 A541 10y multicolored .20 .20
845 A542 10y multicolored .20 .20

No. 844 issued to publicize the ancient Soma Nomaoi Festival, Fukushima Prefecture; No. 845, to publicize the festival dedicated to the Chichibu Myoken Shrine (built 1584).

Issue dates: #844, July 16; #845, Dec. 3.

Meiji Maru, Black-tailed Gulls — A543

1965, July 20 ***Perf. 13½***

846 A543 10y grn, gray, blk & yel .20 .20

25th Maritime Day, July 20.

Drop of Blood, Girl's Face and Bloodmobile A544

1965, Sept. 1 ***Perf. 13½***

847 A544 10y yel, grn, blk & red .20 .20

Issued to publicize the national campaign for blood donations, Sept. 1-30.

Tokai Atomic Power Station and Structure of Alpha Uranium — A545

1965, Sept. 21 **Photo.**

848 A545 10y multicolored .20 .20

9th General Conf. of the Intl. Atomic Energy Agency, IAEA, Tokyo, Sept. 21-30.

People and Flag — A546

1965, Oct. 1

849 A546 10y multicolored .20 .20

Tenth national census.

Hokusai Type of 1964

Design: No. 850, "Waters at Misaka" by Hokusai (Mt. Fuji seen across Lake Kawaguchi).

1965, Oct. 6 **Unwmk.** ***Perf. 13***

850 A525 40y multicolored .65 .40

Issued for International Letter Writing Week, Oct. 6-12. Issued in sheets of 10 (5x2).

Emblems and Diagram of Seats in National Diet — A547

1965, Oct. 15 ***Perf. 13½***

851 A547 10y multicolored .20 .20

75th anniv. of natl. suffrage, 40th anniv. of universal suffrage and 20th anniv. of women's suffrage.

Sports Type of 1961

Designs: No. 852, Gymnast on vaulting horse. No. 853, Walking race.

1965, Oct. 24 **Engr.** ***Perf. 13½***

852 A454 5y red brown .20 .20
853 A454 5y yellow green .20 .20
a. Pair, #852-853 .35 .45

20th National Athletic Meeting, Gifu.

Profile and Infant A548

1965, Oct. 30 **Photo.** ***Perf. 13***

854 A548 30y car lake, yel & lt bl .30 .20

8th Intl. Conf. of Otorhinolaryngology and the 11th Intl. Conf. of Pediatrics.

Mt. Iwo from Shari Coast, Hokkaido — A549

Rausu Lake and Mt. Rausu A550

1965, Nov. 15 ***Perf. 13½***

855 A549 5y Prus green .20 .20
856 A550 10y bright blue .20 .20

Shiretoko National Park.

Aurora Australis, Map of Antarctica and "Fuji" — A551

1965, Nov. 20

857 A551 10y bl, yel & dk bl .20 .20

Issued to publicize the Antarctic expedition, which left on the observation ship "Fuji," Nov. 20, 1965.

"Secret Horse" Straw Toy, Iwate Prefecture A552

Telephone Dial and 1890 Switchboard A553

1965, Dec. 10

858 A552 5y lt blue & multi .20 .20

Issued for New Year 1966. Sheets containing four of No. 858 were awarded as prizes in the New Year lottery (issued Jan. 20, 1966). Value $1.50.

1965, Dec. 16

859 A553 10y multicolored .20 .20

75th anniversary of telephone service in Japan.

Japanese Spiny Lobster A554

Carp — A555

Bream A555a

Skipjack Tuna A555b

Three Ayu A555c

Eel A555d

Jack Mackerel A555e

Chum Salmon A555f

Yellowtail A555g

Tiger Puffer A555h

Squid A555i

Turbo Cornutus A555j

1966-67 **Photo.** ***Perf. 13***
Multicolored; Background in Colors Indicated

860 A554 10y green & ultra .20 .20
861 A555 10y blue green .20 .20
862 A555a 10y dk blue .20 .20
863 A555b 10y dk ultra .20 .20
864 A555c 10y bis & dk grn .20 .20
865 A555d 15y grnsh bl & yel .30 .20
866 A555e 15y brt grn .30 .20
867 A555f 15y brt grn & bl .30 .20
868 A555g 15y lt bl grn ('67) .30 .20
869 A555h 15y brt grn ('67) .30 .20
870 A555i 15y ultra & grn ('67) .30 .25
871 A555j 15y chlky bl ('67) .55 .25
Nos. 860-871 (12) 3.35 2.50

Famous Gardens Issue

A556

A557

A558

10y, Kobuntei Pavilion and plum blossoms, Kairakuen Garden, Ibaraki. #873, Japanese cranes and Okayama Castle, Korakuen Garden, Okayama. #874, Kenrokuen Garden in the snow.

1966-67 ***Perf. 13½***

872 A556 10y gold, blk & grn .20 .20
873 A557 15y blue, blk & mag .30 .20
874 A558 15y silver, grn & dk brn .30 .20
Nos. 872-874 (3) .80 .60

Issued: 10y, 2/25; #873, 11/3; #874, 1/25/67.

Crater Lake, Zao — A559

1966, Mar. 15

875 A559 10y multicolored .20 .20

Zao Quasi-National Park.

Muroto Cape — A560

Senba Cliffs, Anan Coast — A561

1966, Mar. 22 ***Perf. 13½***

876 A560 10y multicolored .20 .20
877 A561 10y multicolored .20 .20

Muroto-Anan Coast Quasi-National Park.

AIPPI Emblem A562

1966, Apr. 11 *Perf. 13*
878 A562 40y multicolored .75 .20

26th General Assembly of the Intl. Association for the Protection of Industrial Properties, Tokyo, Apr. 11-16.

"Butterflies" by Takeji Fujishima — A563

Photogravure and Engraved

1966, Apr. 20 *Perf. 13½*
879 A563 10y gray & multi .25 .25

Stamp Week, 1966. Sheets of 10 (2x5). See No. 907.

Hisoka Maejima A563a

Goldfish A564

Chrysanthemums — A565

Wisteria A565a

Hydrangea A565b

Golden Hall, Chusonji A565c

Yomei Gate, Nikko A565d

Nyoirin Kannon of Chuguji — A565f

Central Hall, Enryakuji Temple — A566

Ancient Clay Horse (Haniwa) — A567

A567a

A567b

A567c

Katsura Palace Garden — A568

A569

Bodhisattva Playing Flute (from Todaiji Lantern) — A570

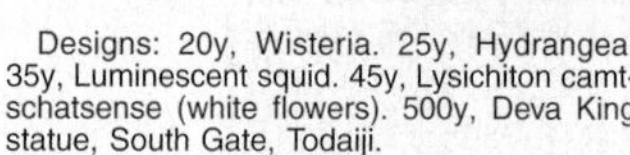

Designs: 20y, Wisteria. 25y, Hydrangea. 35y, Luminescent squid. 45y, Lysichiton camtschatsense (white flowers). 500y, Deva King statue, South Gate, Todaiji.

1966-69 **Photo.** *Perf. 13*

879A A563a 1y olive bis ('68) .20 .20
880 A564 7y ol & dp org 1.10 .20
881 A565 15y bl & yel (bl "15") .95 .20
b. Bklt. pane of 2 + label ('67) 3.25
c. Bklt. pane of 4 ('67) 2.25
d. Bklt. pane of 4 (2 #881 + 2 #611) ('67) 6.00
e. Imperf., pair 300.00
881A A565a 20y vio & multi ('67) 1.90 *2.25*
882 A565b 25y grn & lt ultra .50 .20
882A A565c 30y dp ultra & gold ('68) .55 .20
883 A564 35y blue, gray & blk 1.10 .20
883A A565d 40y bl grn & brn ('68) .75 .20
884 A565 45y blue & multi ('67) .85 .20
885 A565f 50y dk car rose 6.50 .20

Engr.

886 A566 60y slate green 3.25 .20

Photo.

887 A567 65y orange brown 8.50 .20
887A A567a 75y rose, blk, yel & pur 1.40 .20
888 A567b 90y gold & brn 1.75 .20
888A A567c 100y ver & blk ('68) 1.90 .20

Engr.

889 A568 110y brown 2.10 .20
890 A569 120y red 2.25 .20
891 A570 200y Prus grn (22x33mm) 3.75 .20
891A A570 500y dull pur ('69) 9.50 .20
Nos. 879A-891A (19) 48.80 5.85

Nos. 880-881 were also issued with fluorescent frame on July 18, 1966.

See Nos. 913-916, 918, 926, 1072, 1079, 1081, 1244, 1256.

UNESCO Emblem — A571

Map of Pacific Ocean — A572

1966, July 2 **Photo.** *Perf. 13*
892 A571 15y multicolored .30 .20

20th anniv. of UNESCO.

1966, Aug. 22 *Perf. 13*
893 A572 15y bis brn, dl bl & rose .30 .20

11th Pacific Science Congress, Tokyo, Aug. 22-Sept. 10.

Amakusa Bridges, Kyushu — A573

Emblem of Post Office Life Insurance and Family — A574

1966, Sept. 24 **Photo.** *Perf. 13*
894 A573 15y multicolored .30 .20

Completion of five bridges linking Misumi Harbor, Kyushu, with Amakusa islands.

1966, Oct. 1
895 A574 15y yellow grn & multi .30 .20

Post office life insurance service, 50th anniv.

Hokusai Type of 1964

50y, "Sekiya on the Sumida" (horseback riders and Mt. Fuji) from Hokusai's "36 Views of Fuji."

1966, Oct. 6
896 A525 50y multicolored .95 .70

Intl. Letter Writing Week, Oct. 6-12. Printed in sheets of 10 (5x2).

Sharpshooter A575

Design: No. 898, Hop, skip and jump.

1966, Oct. 23 **Engr.** *Perf. 13½*
897 A575 7y ultra .20 .20
898 A575 7y carmine rose .20 .20
a. Pair, #897-898 .45 .40

21st Natl. Athletic Meet, Oita, Oct. 23-28.

National Theater A576

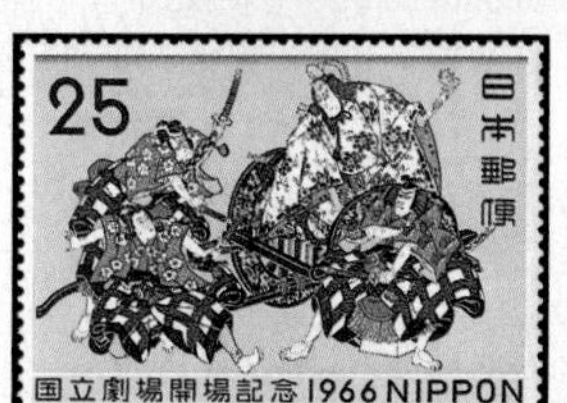

Kabuki Scene — A577

Bunraku Puppet Show — A578

1966, Nov. 1 *Perf. 13, 13½*
899 A576 15y multicolored .20 .20
900 A577 25y multicolored .50 .25
901 A578 50y multicolored .95 .40
Nos. 899-901 (3) 1.65 .85

Inauguration of first National Theater in Japan. Nos. 900-901 issued in sheets of 10.

Rice Year Emblem A579

Ittobori Carved Sheep, Nara Prefecture A580

1966, Nov. 21 *Perf. 13½*
902 A579 15y red, blk & ocher .30 .20

FAO International Rice Year.

1966, Dec. 10 **Photo.** *Perf. 13½*
903 A580 7y bl, gold, blk & pink .20 .20

New Year 1967. Sheets containing 4 #903 were awarded as prizes in the New Year lottery. Value $1.25.

International Communications Satellite, Lani Bird 2 — A581

1967, Jan. 27 *Perf. 13½*
904 A581 15y dk Prus bl & sepia .30 .20

Inauguration in Japan of Intl. commercial communications service via satellite.

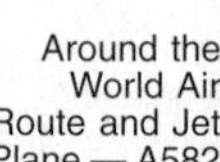

Around the World Air Route and Jet Plane — A582

1967, Mar. 6 **Photo.** *Perf. 13½*
905 A582 15y multicolored .30 .20

Issued to publicize the inauguration of Japan Air Lines Tokyo-London service via New York, which completes the around the world air route.

Library of Modern Japanese Literature A583

1967, Apr. 11
906 A583 15y grnsh bl, lt & dk brn .30 .20

Opening of the Library of Modern Japanese Literature, Komaba Park, Meguro-ku, Tokyo.

Painting Type of 1966

Design: 15y, Lakeside (seated woman), by Seiki (Kiyoteru) Kuroda.

1967, Apr. 20
907 A563 15y multicolored .30 .20

Stamp Week, 1967. Sheets of 10 (2x5).

Kobe Harbor A584

1967, May 8 Photo. *Perf. 13x13½*
908 A584 50y multicolored .95 .20

5th Cong. of the Intl. Association of Ports and Harbors, Tokyo, May 8-13.

Welfare Commissioner's Emblem A585

Traffic Light, Automobile and Children A586

1967, May 12 *Perf. 13½*
909 A585 15y dk brown & gold .30 .20

50th anniversary of the Welfare Commissioner System.

1967, May 22 *Perf. 13x13½*
910 A586 15y emer, red, blk & yel .30 .20

Issued to publicize traffic safety.

Kita and Kai-Koma Mountains A587

Akaishi and Hijiri Mountains A588

1967, July 10
911 A587 7y Prus blue .20 .20
912 A588 15y rose lilac .30 .20

South Japan Alps National Park.

Types of 1966-69 Redrawn and

A588a

Original 20y No. 881A

Redrawn 20y No. 915

1967-69 Photo. *Perf. 13*
913 A564 7y brt yel grn & dp org .20 .20
914 A565 15y bl & yel (white "15") .30 .20
a. Pane of 10 (5x2) ('68) 2.75
b. Bklt. panes of 4 with gutter (6 #914 + 2 #611) ('68) 7.00
c. Imperf., pair 200.00
d. Blue shading omitted
e. Bklt. panes of 2 & 4 with gutter ('68) 45.00 45.00
915 A565a 20y vio & multi ('69) 1.10 .20
916 A565f 50y brt carmine .95 .20
917 A588a 55y lt bl, grn & blk ('69) 1.10 .20
918 A567 65y deep orange 1.25 .20
Nos. 913-918 (6) 4.90 1.20

Issued for use in facer-canceling machines. Issue dates: 7y, Aug. 1; 15y, 50y, July 1; 65y, July 20, 1967; 20y, Apr. 1, 1969; 55y, Sept. 1, 1969.

On No. 913 the background has been lightened and a frame line of shading added at top and right side.

No. 914a is imperf. on four sides.

The two panes of Nos. 914b and 914e are connected by a vertical creased gutter 21mm wide. The left pane of No. 914b consists of 2 No. 914 and 2 No. 611; the right pane, 4 of No. 914. The left pane of 2 of No. 914e includes a 4-line inscription.

On No. 915 the wisteria leaves do not touch frame at left and top. On No. 881A they do.

Coil Stamp

1968, Jan. 9 *Perf. 13 Horiz.*
926 A565 15y bl & yel (white "15") .60 .45

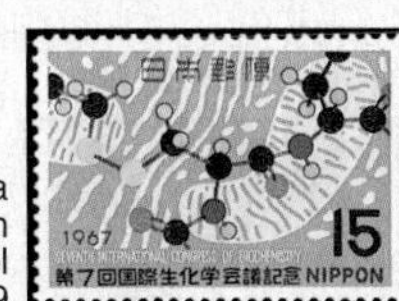

Mitochondria and Protein Model A589

1967, Aug. 19 Photo. *Perf. 13*
927 A589 15y gray & multi .30 .20

7th Intl. Biochemistry Cong., Tokyo, Aug. 19-25.

Gymnast on Horizontal Bar — A590

Universiade Emblem — A591

1967, Aug. 26
928 A590 15y red & multi .30 .20
929 A591 50y yellow & multi .95 .25

World University Games, Universiade 1967, Tokyo, Aug. 26-Sept. 4.

Paper Lantern, ITY Emblem — A592

"Sacred Mt. Fuji" by Taikan Yokoyama — A593

1967, Oct. 2 Photo. *Perf. 13*
930 A592 15y ultra & multi .20 .20
931 A593 50y multicolored 1.25 1.00

International Tourist Year, 1967. No. 931 issued in sheets of 10.

Hokusai Type of 1964

50y, "Kajikazawa, Koshu" (fisherman and waves) from Hokusai's "36 Views of Fuji."

1967, Oct. 6
932 A525 50y multicolored 1.25 .55

Issued for International Letter Writing Week, Oct. 6-12. Sheets of 10 (5x2).

Athlete, Wild Primrose and Chichibu Mountains — A594

1967, Oct. 22 Photo. *Perf. 13*
933 A594 15y gold & multi .30 .20

22nd Natl. Athletic Meet, Saitama, 10/22-27.

Miroku Bosatsu, Koryuji Temple, Kyoto — A595

Kudara Kannon, Horyuji Temple, Nara — A596

Golden Hall and Pagoda, Horyuji Temple, Nara — A597

1967, Nov. 1 Photo.
934 A595 15y multicolored .30 .25

Engr.
935 A596 15y pale grn, blk & red .30 .25

Photo. & Engr.
936 A597 50y multicolored 1.25 .75
Nos. 934-936 (3) 1.85 1.25

National treasures of Asuka Period (6th-7th centuries). No. 936 issued in sheets of 10.

Highway and Congress Emblem A598

1967, Nov. 5 Photo. *Perf. 13*
937 A598 50y multicolored .95 .20

13th World Road Cong., Tokyo, Nov. 5-11.

Mt. Kumotori A599

Lake Chichibu A600

1967, Nov. 27
938 A599 7y olive .20 .20
939 A600 15y red lilac .30 .20

Chichibu-Tama National Park

Climbing Monkey Toy (Noborizaru), Miyazaki Prefecture — A601

1967, Dec. 11 Photo. *Perf. 13*
940 A601 7y multicolored .20 .20

New Year 1968. Sheets containing 4 #940 were awarded as prizes in the New Year lottery. Value $1.25.

Mt. Sobo — A602

Takachiho Gorge — A603

1967, Dec. 20
941 A602 15y multicolored .30 .20
942 A603 15y multicolored .30 .20

Sobo Katamuki Quasi-National Park.

Girl, Boy and Sakura Maru — A604

1968, Jan. 19 Photo. *Perf. 13*
943 A604 15y ultra, ocher & blk .30 .20

Cent. of the Meiji Era, and 1st Japanese Youth Good Will Cruise in celebration of the centenary.

Ashura, Kofukuji Temple, Nara — A605

Gakko Bosatsu, Todaiji Temple, Nara — A606

Kichijo Ten, Yakushiji Temple, Nara — A607

1968, Feb. 1 Engr. *Perf. 13*
944 A605 15y sepia & car .30 .25

Engr. & Photo.

945 A606 15y dk brn, pale grn & org .30 .25

Photo.

946 A607 50y multicolored .95 .95
Nos. 944-946 (3) 1.55 1.45

Issued to show National Treasures of the Nara Period (710-784).

Grazing Cows and Mt. Yatsugatake A608

Mt. Tateshina A609

1968, Mar. 21 Photo. *Perf. 13*
947 A608 15y multicolored .30 .20
948 A609 15y multicolored .30 .20

Yatsugatake-Chushin-Kogen Quasi-Natl. Park.

Young Dancer (Maiko) in Tenjuan Garden, by Bakusen Tsuchida A610

1968, Apr. 20 Photo. *Perf. 13*
949 A610 15y multicolored .30 .20

Stamp Week, 1968. Sheets of 10 (5x2).

Rishiri Isl. Seen from Rebun Isl. — A611

1968, May 10 Photo. *Perf. 13*
950 A611 15y multicolored .30 .20

Rishiri-Rebun Quasi-National Park.

Gold Lacquer and Mother-of-Pearl Box — A612

"The Origin of Shigisan" Painting from Chogo-sonshiji, Nara — A613

Bodhisattva Samantabhadra — A614

1968, June 1 Engr. & Photo.
951 A612 15y lt blue & multi .30 .25

Photo.

952 A613 15y tan & multi .30 .25
953 A614 50y sepia & multi 2.00 1.50
Nos. 951-953 (3) 2.60 2.00

Issued to show national treasures of the Heian Period (8-12th centuries).

Memorial Tower and Badge of Hokkaido — A615

1968, June 14
954 A615 15y grn, vio bl, bis & red .30 .20

Centenary of development of Hokkaido.

Sunrise over Pacific and Fan Palms — A616

1968, June 26 Photo. *Perf. 13*
955 A616 15y blk, org & red org .30 .20

Return of Bonin Islands to Japan by US.

Map of Japan Showing Postal Codes — A617

Two types of inscription:
Type I (enlarged)

"Postal code also on your address"

Type II (enlarged)

"Don't omit postal code on the address"

1968, July 1
956 A617 7y yel grn & red (I) 1.90 .50
957 A617 7y yel grn & red (II) 1.90 .50
a. Pair, #956-957 4.00 4.00
958 A617 15y sky bl & car (I) .75 .50
a. Bklt. panes of 4 with gutter (4 #958 + 2 #959 + 2 #611) 60.00 60.00
959 A617 15y sky bl & car (II) .75 .50
d. Pair, #958-959 3.00 3.00
Nos. 956-959 (4) 5.30 2.00

Introduction of the postal code system.
The double booklet pane, No. 958a, comes in two forms, the positions of the Postal Code types being transposed.

Coil Stamps
Perf. 13 Horiz.

959A A617 15y sky blue & car (I) .90 .75
959B A617 15y sky blue & car (II) .90 .75
c. Pair, #959A-959B 3.75 3.75

Kiso River — A618

Inuyama Castle A619

1968, July 20 *Perf. 13½*
960 A618 15y multicolored .30 .20
961 A619 15y multicolored .30 .20

Hida-Kisogawa Quasi-National Park.

Youth Hostel Emblem, Trees and Sun — A620

1968, Aug. 6 Photo. *Perf. 13*
962 A620 15y citron & multi .30 .20

27th Intl. Youth Hostel Cong., Tokyo, 8/6-20.

Boys Forming Tournament Emblem A621

Pitcher and Tournament Flag — A622

1968, Aug. 9
963 A621 15y yel grn, yel, blk & red .30 .20
964 A622 15y red, yellow & blk .30 .20
a. Pair, #963-964 .65 .60

50th All-Japan High School Baseball Championship Tournament, Koshi-en Baseball Grounds, Aug. 9. Nos. 963-964 printed checkerwise.

Minamoto Yoritomo, Jingoji, Kyoto — A623

Heiji Monogatari Scroll Painting — A624

Red-threaded Armor, Kasuga Shrine, Nara — A625

1968, Sept. 16 Photo. *Perf. 13*
965 A623 15y black & multi .40 .25
966 A624 15y tan & multi .40 .25

Photo. & Engr.

967 A625 50y multicolored 1.25 1.25
Nos. 965-967 (3) 2.05 1.75

National treasures of Kamakura period (1180-1192 to 1333).

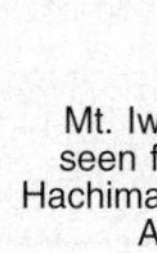

Mt. Iwate, seen from Hachimantai A626

Lake Towada, seen from Mt. Ohanabe A627

1968, Sept. 16 Photo.
968 A626 7y red brown .20 .20
969 A627 15y green .30 .20

Towada-Hachimantai National Park.

Gymnast, Tojimbo Cliff and Narcissus — A628

1968, Oct. 1 Photo. *Perf. 13*
970 A628 15y multicolored .30 .20

23rd National Athletic Meet, Fukui Prefecture, Oct. 1-6.

Hokusai Type of 1964

Design: 50y, "Fujimihara in Owari Province" (cooper working on a barrel) from Hokusai's "36 Views of Fuji."

1968, Oct. 7
971 A525 50y multicolored 1.00 .60

Issued for International Letter Writing Week, Oct. 7-13. Sheets of 10 (5x2).

Centenary Emblem, Sun and First Western Style Warship — A629

Imperial Carriage Arriving in Tokyo (1868), by Tomote Kobori A630

1968, Oct. 23

972 A629 15y vio bl, red, gold & gray .30 .20
973 A630 15y multicolored .30 .20
a. Imperf., pair

Meiji Centenary Festival.

Old and New Lighthouses A631

1968, Nov. 1 Photo. *Perf. 13*

974 A631 15y multicolored .30 .20

Centenary of the first western style lighthouse in Japan.

Ryo'o Court Dance and State Hall, Imperial Palace — A632

1968, Nov. 14

975 A632 15y multicolored .30 .20

Completion of the new Imperial Palace.

Mt. Takachiho A633

Mt. Motobu, Yaku Island A634

1968, Nov. 20

976 A633 7y purple .20 .20
977 A634 15y orange .30 .20

Kirishima-Yaku National Park.

Carved Toy Cock of Yonezawa, Yamagata Prefecture A635

Human Rights Flame, Dancing Children and Globe A636

1968, Dec. 5 Photo. *Perf. 13*

978 A635 7y lt blue & multi .20 .20

New Year 1969. Sheets containing 4 #978 were awarded as prizes in the New Year lottery. Value $1.50.

1968, Dec. 10

979 A636 50y orange & multi .95 .25

International Human Rights Year.

Striped Squirrel A637

Kochomon Cave and Road A638

1968, Dec. 14

980 A637 15y emerald & blk .30 .20

Issued to promote saving.

1969, Jan. 27 Photo.

981 A638 15y multicolored .30 .20

Echizen-Kaga-Kaigan Quasi-National Park.

Silver Pavilion, Jishoji Temple, Kyoto — A639

Pagoda, Anrakuji Temple, Nagano — A640

Winter Landscape by Sesshu A641

1969, Feb. 10 Photo. *Perf. 13*

982 A639 15y multicolored .30 .20

Photo. & Engr.

983 A640 15y lt green & multi .30 .20

Photo.

984 A641 50y tan, blk & ver 1.10 .75
Nos. 982-984 (3) 1.70 1.15

Issued to show national treasures of the Muromachi Period (1333-1572).

Mt. Chokai, seen from Tobishima Island — A642

1969, Feb. 25 Photo.

985 A642 15y brt blue & multi .30 .20

Chokai Quasi-National Park.

Mt. Koya Seen from Jinnogamine A643

Mt. Gomadan and Rhododendron — A644

1969, Mar. 25 Photo. *Perf. 13*

986 A643 15y multicolored .30 .20
987 A644 15y multicolored .30 .20

Koya-Ryujin Quasi-National Park.

Hair (Kami), by Kokei Kobayashi A645

1969, Apr. 20 Photo. *Perf. 13*

988 A645 15y multicolored .30 .20

Issued for Philatelic Week.

Mother, Son Crossing Street A646

Tokyo-Nagoya Expressway and Sakawagawa Bridge A647

1969, May 10 Photo. *Perf. 13*

989 A646 15y lt blue, red & grn .30 .20

National traffic safety campaign.

1969, May 26

990 A647 15y multicolored .30 .20

Completion of Tokyo-Nagoya Expressway.

Nuclear Ship Mutsu and Atom Diagram A648

1969, June 12

991 A648 15y gray, blk, pink & bl .30 .20

Issued to publicize the launching of the first Japanese nuclear ship, Mutsu.

Museum of Modern Art and Palette A649

1969, June 11 Photo. *Perf. 13½*

992 A649 15y lt bl, brn, yel & blk .30 .20

Opening of the new National Museum of Modern Art, Tokyo.

Cable Ship KKD Maru and Map of Japan Sea — A650

1969, June 25

993 A650 15y lt bl, blk & ocher .30 .20

Completion of the Japan sea cable between Naoetsu, Japan, and Nakhodka, Russia.

Postcards, Postal Code Symbol A651

Mailbox, Postal Code Symbol A652

1969, July 1 Photo. *Perf. 13*

997 A651 7y yellow grn & car .20 .20
998 A652 15y sky blue & car .30 .20

1st anniv. of the postal code system and to promote its use.

Lions Emblem and Rose — A653

1969, July 2

999 A653 15y bl, blk, rose & gold .30 .20

52nd Convention of Lions Intl., Tokyo, July 2-5.

Hotoke-ga-ura on Shimokita Peninsula, Northern Honshu A654

1969, July 15

1000 A654 15y multicolored .30 .20

Shimokita Hanto Quasi-National Park.

Himeji Castle, Hyogo Prefecture A655

"Pine Forest" (Detail), by Tohaku Hasegawa A656

"Cypresses," Attributed to Eitoku Kano — A657

1969, July 21 **Photo. & Engr.**

1001 A655 15y lt blue & multi .30 .25

Photo.

1002 A656 15y pale brown & blk .30 .25
1003 A657 50y gold & multi 1.10 .60
Nos. 1001-1003 (3) 1.70 1.10

Issued to show national treasures of the Momoyama period (1573-1614). The 50y is in sheets of 10 (2x5); Nos. 1001-1002 in sheets of 20 (5x4).

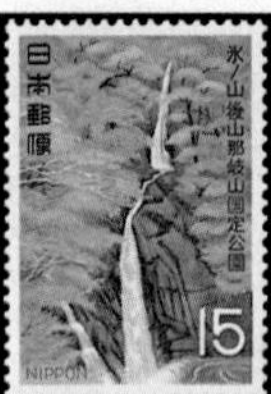

Harano-fudo Waterfall — A658

Mt. Nagisan A659

1969, Aug. 20

1004 A658 15y multicolored .30 .20
1005 A659 15y multicolored .30 .20

Hyobosen-Ushiroyama-Nagisan Quasi-Natl. Park.

Mt. O-akan, Hokkaido — A660

Mt. Iwo — A661

1969, Aug. 25 **Photo.** ***Perf. 13***

1006 A660 7y bright blue .20 .20
1007 A661 15y sepia .30 .20

Akan National Park.

Angling, by Taiga Ikeno — A662

The Red Plum, by Korin Ogata — A663

Pheasant-shaped Incense Burner — A664

No. 1010, The White Plum, by Korin Ogata.

1969, Sept. 25 **Photo.** ***Perf. 13x13½***

1008 A662 15y multicolored .30 .20

Perf. 13

1009 A663 15y gold & multi .30 .20
1010 A663 15y gold & multi .30 .20
a. Pair, #1009-1010 .75 .75

Photo. & Engr.

1011 A664 50y multicolored 1.00 .65
Nos. 1008-1011 (4) 1.90 1.25

Natl. treasures, Edo Period (1615-1867).

Birds Circling Globe and UPU Congress Emblem A665

Woman Reading Letter, by Utamaro A666

Designs (UPU Congress Emblem and): 50y, Two Women Reading a Letter, by Harunobu. 60y, Man Reading a Letter (Miyako Dennai), by Sharaku.

1969, Oct. 1 **Photo.** ***Perf. 13***

1012 A665 15y red & multi .30 .20
1013 A666 30y multicolored .60 .40
1014 A666 50y multicolored .95 .50
1015 A666 60y multicolored 1.10 .65
Nos. 1012-1015 (4) 2.95 1.75

16th UPU Congress, Tokyo, 10/1-11/16. 15y issued in sheets of 20, others in sheets of 10.

Hokusai Type of 1964

Design: 50y, "Passing through Koshu down to Mishima" from Hokusai's 36 Views of Fuji.

1969, Oct. 7 **Photo.** ***Perf. 13***

1016 A525 50y multicolored 1.00 .55

Issued for International Letter Writing Week Oct. 7-13. Sheets of 10 (5x2).

Rugby Player, Camellia and Oura Catholic Church — A667

1969, Oct. 26

1017 A667 15y lt ultra & multi .30 .20

24th Natl. Athletic Meet, Nagasaki, 10/26-31.

Cape Kitayama — A668

Goishi Coast — A669

1969, Nov. 20 **Photo.** ***Perf. 13***

1018 A668 7y gray & dk blue .20 .20
1019 A669 15y salmon & dk red .30 .20

Rikuchu Coast National Park.

Worker in Hard Hat — A670

Dog Amulet, Hokkeji, Nara — A671

1969, Nov. 26

1020 A670 15y ultra, blk yel & brn .30 .20

50th anniv. of the ILO.

1969, Dec. 10

1021 A671 7y orange & multi .20 .20

New Year 1970. Sheets containing 4 #1021 were awarded as prizes in the New Year lottery. Value $1.50.

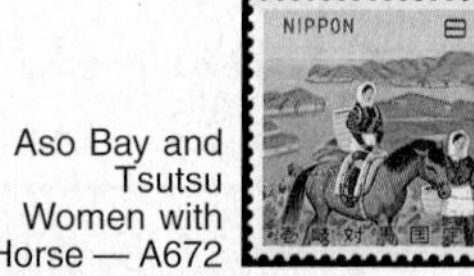

Aso Bay and Tsutsu Women with Horse — A672

1970, Feb. 25 **Photo.** ***Perf. 13***

1022 A672 15y multicolored .30 .20

Iki-Tsushima Quasi-National Park.

Fireworks over EXPO '70 — A673

Cherry Blossoms Around Globe — A674

Irises, by Korin Ogata (1658-1716) — A675

1970, Mar. 14 **Photo.** ***Perf. 13***

1023 A673 7y red & multi .20 .20
1024 A674 15y gold & multi .30 .20
1025 A675 50y gold & multi .95 .65
a. Souv. sheet of 3, #1023-1025 1.75 1.75
b. Bklt. pane of 4 & 3 with gutter 3.00
Nos. 1023-1025 (3) 1.45 1.05

EXPO '70 Intl. Exposition, Senri, Osaka, Mar. 15-Sept. 13.

No. 1025b contains a pane of 4 No. 1023 and a pane with Nos. 1023-1025. A 35mm gutter separates the panes.

Woman with Hand Drum, by Saburosuke Okada A676

1970, Apr. 20 **Photo.** ***Perf. 13***

1026 A676 15y multicolored .45 .20

Issued for Stamp Week, Apr. 20-26.

Mt. Yoshino — A677

Nachi Waterfall A678

1970, Apr. 30 **Photo.** ***Perf. 13***

1027 A677 7y gray & pink .20 .20
1028 A678 15y pale blue & grn .30 .20

Yoshino-Kumano National Park.

Pole Lanterns at EXPO — A679

View of EXPO Within Globe — A680

Grass in Autumn Wind, by Hoitsu Sakai (1761-1828) — A681

1970, June 15 **Photo.** ***Perf. 13***

1029 A679 7y red & multi .20 .20
1030 A680 15y blue & multi .30 .20
1031 A681 50y silver & multi .95 .20
a. Souv. sheet of 3, #1029-1031 1.75
b. Bklt. panes of 4 & 3 with gutter 3.00
Nos. 1029-1031 (3) 1.45 .60

EXPO '70, 2nd issue.

No. 1031b contains a pane of 4 No. 1029 and a pane with Nos. 1029-1031. A 35mm gutter separates the panes.

Buildings and Postal Code Symbol — A682

1970, July 1 **Photo.** ***Perf. 13***

1032 A682 7y emerald & vio .35 .20
1033 A682 15y brt blue & choc .50 .20

Postal code system.

"Maiden at Dojo Temple" A683

Scene from "Sukeroku" A684

"The Subscription List" (Kanjincho) — A685

1970, July 10

1034	A683	15y multicolored	.30	.20
1035	A684	15y multicolored	.30	.20
1036	A685	50y multicolored	.95	.40
		Nos. 1034-1036 (3)	1.55	.80

Issued to publicize the Kabuki Theater.

Girl Scout — A686

1970, July 26

1037	A686	15y multicolored	.30	.20

50th anniversary of Japanese Girl Scouts.

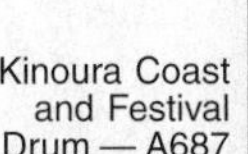

Kinoura Coast and Festival Drum — A687

Tate Mountains Seen from Himi Coast — A688

1970, Aug. 1

1038	A687	15y multicolored	.30	.20
1039	A688	15y multicolored	.30	.20

Noto Hanto Quasi-National Park.

Sunflower and UN Emblem — A689

1970, Aug. 17

1040	A689	15y lt blue & multi	.30	.20

Issued to publicize the 4th United Nations Congress on the Prevention of Crime and the Treatment of Offenders, Kyoto, Aug. 17-26.

Mt. Myogi — A690

Mt. Arafune A691

1970, Sept. 11 Photo. *Perf. 13*

1041	A690	15y multicolored	.30	.20
1042	A691	15y multicolored	.30	.20

Myogi-Arafune-Sakukogen Quasi-Natl. Park.

G.P.O., Tokyo, by Hiroshige III A692

Equestrian, Mt. Iwate and Paulownia A693

1970, Oct. 6

1043	A692	50y multicolored	.95	.30

Intl. Letter Writing Week, Oct. 6-12. Sheets of 10 (5x2). Design from wood block series, "Noted Places in Tokyo."

1970, Oct. 10 Photo. *Perf. 13*

1044	A693	15y silver & multi	.30	.20

25th Natl. Athletic Meet, Morioka, 10/10-16.

Hodogaya Stage, by Hiroshige III — A694

Tree and UN Emblem A695

1970, Oct. 20

1045	A694	15y silver & multi	.30	.20

Centenary of telegraph service in Japan.

1970, Oct. 24

50y, UN emblem and Headquarters with flags.

1046	A695	15y olive, ap grn & gold	.30	.20
1047	A695	50y multicolored	.95	.20

25th anniversary of United Nations.

Vocational Training Competition Emblem — A696

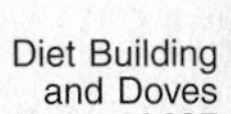

Diet Building and Doves A697

1970, Nov. 10 Photo. *Perf. 13*

1048	A696	15y multicolored	.30	.20

The 19th International Vocational Training Competition, Chiba City, Nov. 10-19.

1970, Nov. 29

1049	A697	15y multicolored	.30	.20

80th anniversary of Japanese Diet.

Wild Boar, Folk Art, Arai City, Niigata Prefecture — A698

1970, Dec. 10

1050	A698	7y multicolored	.20	.20

New Year 1971. Sheets containing 4 #1050 were awarded as prizes in the New Year lottery. Value $1.50.

Gen-jo-raku A699

Ko-cho A700

Tai-hei-raku — A701

1971, Apr. 1 Photo. *Perf. 13*

1051	A699	15y multicolored	.30	.20
1052	A700	15y multicolored	.30	.20
1053	A701	50y multicolored	.95	.20
		Nos. 1051-1053 (3)	1.55	.60

Gagaku, classical Japanese court entertainment.

Woman Voter and Parliament A702

Pines and Maple Leaves A703

1971, Apr. 10 Photo. *Perf. 13*

1054	A702	15y orange & multi	.30	.20

25th anniversary of woman suffrage.

1971, Apr. 18

1055	A703	7y emerald & violet	.20	.20

National forestation campaign.

Woman of Tokyo, by Kiyokata Kaburagi — A704

1971, Apr. 19

1056	A704	15y gray & multi	.35	.20

Philatelic Week, Apr. 19-25.

Mailman A705

Mailbox A706

Railroad Post Office — A707

1971, Apr. 20

1057	A705	15y blk & org brn	.30	.20
1058	A706	15y multicolored	.30	.20
1059	A707	15y multicolored	.30	.20
		Nos. 1057-1059 (3)	.90	.60

Centenary of Japanese postage stamps.

Titmouse A708

Penguins A709

1971, May 10 Photo. *Perf. 13*

1060	A708	15y emer, blk & bis	.30	.20

25th Bird Week.

1971, June 23 Photo. *Perf. 13*

1061	A709	15y dk blue, yel & grn	.30	.20

Antarctic Treaty pledging peaceful uses of and scientific co-operation in Antarctica, 10th anniv.

Goto Wakamatsu Seto Region — A710

Kujukushima ("99 Islands"), Kyushu A711

1971, June 26 Photo. *Perf. 13*

1062	A710	7y dark green	.20	.20
1063	A711	15y deep brown	.30	.20

Saikai National Park.

Arabic Numerals and Postal Code Symbol — A712

1971, July 1

1064 A712 7y emerald & red .20 .20
1065 A712 15y blue & carmine .30 .20

Promotion for postal code system.

Inscribed "NIPPON"
Types of 1962-67 and

Little Cuckoo
A713

Mute Swan
A714

Sika Deer
A715

Beetle
A716

Pine — A717

Noh Mask
A717a

Pheasant
A717b

Golden Eagle — A717c

Bronze Phoenix, Uji — A718

Burial Statue of Warrior, Ota — A718a

Buddha, Sculpture, 685
A718b

Tentoki Sculpture, 11th Century
A718c

Bazara-Taisho, c. 710-794
A718d

Goddess Kissho
A718e

1971-75 Photo. *Perf. 13*

1067 A713 3y emerald .20 .20
a. Bklt. pane of 20 ('72) 2.00
1068 A714 5y bright blue .20 .20
1069 A715 10y yel grn & sep ('72) .20 .20
a. Bklt. pane of 6 (2 #1069, 4 #1071 with gutter btwn.) ('72) 1.40
1070 A716 12y deep brown .20 .20
1071 A717 20y grn & sep ('72) .25 .20
a. Pane of 10 (5x2) ('72) 2.75
1072 A565b 25y emer & lt ultra ('72) .40 .20
1074 A717a 70y dp org & blk 1.00 .20
1075 A717b 80y crimson & brn 1.25 .20
1076 A467 90y org & dk brn 1.50 .20
1077 A717c 90y org & brn ('73) 1.50 .20
1079 A569 120y dk brn & lt grn ('72) 2.00 .20
1080 A718 150y lt & dk green 2.50 .20
1081 A570 200y dp car (18x22mm; '72) 3.50 .20
1082 A718a 200y red brn ('74) 3.50 .30
1083 A718b 300y dk blue ('74) 5.50 .25
1084 A718c 400y car rose ('74) 7.00 .25
1085 A718d 500y green ('74) 9.00 .20
1087 A718e 1000y multi ('75) 17.50 .50
a. Miniature sheet of 1 15.00 15.00
Nos. 1067-1087 (18) 57.20 4.10

No. 1071a is imperf. on four sides.
See #1249-1250, 1254, 1629.

Coil Stamp
Perf. 13 Horiz.

1088 A717 20y green & sep ('72) .45 .30

Boy Scout Bugler — A719

Rose and Rings — A720

1971, Aug. 2

1090 A719 15y lt blue & multi .30 .20

13th World Boy Scout Jamboree, Asagiri Plain, Aug. 2-10.

1971, Oct. 1

1091 A720 15y ultra & multi .30 .20

50th anniv. of Japanese Conciliation System.

Tokyo Horsedrawn Streetcar, by Yoshimura
A721

1971, Oct. 6

1092 A721 50y multicolored .95 .30

Intl. Letter Writing Week. Sheets of 10 (5x2).

Emperor's Flag, Chrysanthemums and Phoenix — A722

"Beyond the Sea," by Empress Nagako
A723

1971, Oct. 14

1093 A722 15y gold, vio, red & bl .30 .20
1094 A723 15y gold, vio, red & bl .30 .20
a. Souv. sheet of 2, #1093-1094, imperf. .85 .85
b. Pair, #1093-1094 .60 .25

European trip of Emperor Hirohito and Empress Nagako, Sept. 28-Oct. 15. No. 1094a has violet map of Asia, Africa and Europe in background.

Tennis, Cape Shiono-misaki, Plum Blossoms — A724

Child's Face and "100" — A725

1971, Oct. 24 Photo. *Perf. 13*

1095 A724 15y orange & multi .30 .20

26th National Athletic Meet, Wakayama Prefecture, Oct. 24-29.

1971, Oct. 27

1096 A725 15y pink, car & blk .30 .20

Centenary of Japanese Family Registration System.

Tiger, by Gaho Hashimoto
A726

Design: No. 1098, Dragon, from "Dragon and Tiger," by Gaho Hashimoto.

1971, Nov. 1 Engr. *Perf. 13*

1097 A726 15y olive & multi .30 .20
1098 A726 15y olive & multi .30 .20
a. Pair, #1097-1098 .75 .30

Centenary of Government Printing Works. Nos. 1097-1098 printed checkerwise.

Mt. Yotei from Lake Toya — A727

Mt. Showa-Shinzan
A728

Treasure Ship
A729

1971, Dec. 6

1099 A727 7y slate grn & yel .20 .20
1100 A728 15y pink & vio bl .30 .20

Shikotsu-Toya National Park.

1971-72

1101 A729 7y emerald, gold & org .20 .20
1102 A729 10y lt blue, org & gold .20 .20

New Year 1972. Sheets containing 3 #1102 were awarded as prizes in the New Year lottery. Value $1.75.
Issued: 7y, Dec. 10; 10y, Jan. 11, 1972.

Downhill Skiing — A730

#1104, Bobsledding. 50y, Figure skating, pairs.

1972, Feb. 3 Photo. *Perf. 13*

Size: 24x34mm

1103 A730 20y ultra & multi .45 .20
1104 A730 20y ultra & multi .45 .20

Size: 49x34mm

1105 A730 50y ultra & multi .95 .25
a. Souv. sheet of 3, #1103-1105 1.75 1.75
Nos. 1103-1105 (3) 1.85 .65

11th Winter Olympic Games, Sapporo, Feb. 3-13. No. 1105a has continuous design extending into margin.

Bunraku, Ningyo Jyoruri Puppet Theater
A731 A732

A733

1972, Mar. 1 Photo. *Perf. 13½*

1106 A731 20y gray & multi .40 .20

Perf. 12½x13

1107 A732 20y multicolored .40 .20

Lithographed and Engraved

Perf. 13½x13

1108 A733 50y multicolored .95 .20
Nos. 1106-1108 (3) 1.75 .60

Japanese classical entertainment.

Express Train on New Sanyo Line — A734

Taishaku-kyo Valley — A735

Hiba Mountains Seen from Mt. Dogo — A736

1972, Mar. 15 **Photo.** ***Perf. 13***

1109 A734 20y multicolored .40 .20

Centenary of first Japanese railroad.

1972, Mar. 24

1110 A735 20y gray & multi .40 .20
1111 A736 20y green & multi .40 .20

Hiba-Dogo-Taishaku Quasi-National Park.

Heart and UN Emblem A737

1972, Apr. 15

1112 A737 20y gray, red & black .40 .20

"Your heart is your health," World Health Day.

"A Balloon Rising," by Gakuryo Nakamura A738

1972, Apr. 20

1113 A738 20y violet bl & multi .40 .20

Philatelic Week, Apr. 20-26.

Shurei Gate, Okinawa A739

Camellia A740

1972, May 15

1114 A739 20y ultra & multi .40 .20

Ratification of the Reversion Agreement with US under which the Ryukyu Islands were returned to Japan.

1972, May 20

1115 A740 20y brt grn, vio bl & yel .40 .20

National forestation campaign and 23rd Arbor Day, May 21.

Mt. Kurikoma and Kijiyama Kokeshi Doll — A741

Naruko-kyo Gorge and Naruko Kokeshi Doll — A742

1972, June 20 **Photo.** ***Perf. 13***

1116 A741 20y blue & multi .40 .20
1117 A742 20y red & multi .40 .20

Kurikoma Quasi-National Park.

Envelope, Postal Code Symbol A743

Mailbox, Postal Code Symbol A744

1972, July 1

1118 A743 10y blue, blk & gray .25 .20
1119 A744 20y emerald & org .40 .20

Publicity for the postal code system.

Mt. Hodaka A745

Mt. Tate — A746

1972, Aug. 10 **Photo.** ***Perf. 13***

1120 A745 10y rose & violet .20 .20
1121 A746 20y blue & buff .40 .20

Chubu Sangaku National Park.

Ghost in "Tamura" A747

Lady Rokujo in "Lady Hollyhock" A748

"Hagoromo" (Feather Robe) — A749

1972, Sept. 20 **Engr.**

1122 A747 20y multicolored .40 .20

Photo.

1123 A748 20y multicolored .40 .20

Perf. 13½x13

1124 A749 50y multicolored .95 .20
Nos. 1122-1124 (3) 1.75 .60

Noh, classical public entertainment.

School Children — A750

Eitai Bridge, Tokyo, by Hiroshige III — A751

1972, Oct. 5 **Photo.** ***Perf. 13***

1125 A750 20y lt ultra, vio bl & car .40 .20

Centenary of modern education system.

1972, Oct. 9

1126 A751 50y multicolored .95 .20

Intl. Letter Writing Week, Oct. 9-15.

Inauguration of Railway Service, by Hiroshige III — A752

Locomotive, Class C62 — A753

1972, Oct. 14

1127 A752 20y multicolored .40 .20
1128 A753 20y multicolored .40 .20

Centenary of Japanese railroad system.

Kendo (Fencing) and Sakurajima Volcano — A754

1972, Oct. 22

1129 A754 10y yellow & multi .20 .20

27th National Athletic Meet, Kagoshima Prefecture, Oct. 22-27.

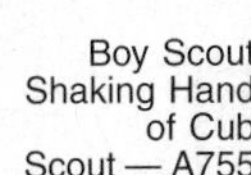

Boy Scout Shaking Hand of Cub Scout — A755

1972, Nov. 4

1130 A755 20y yellow & multi .40 .20

50th anniversary of the Boy Scouts of Japan.

US Ship, Yokohama Harbor A756

"Clay Plate with Plum Blossoms" A757

1972, Nov. 28 **Photo.** ***Perf. 13***

1131 A756 20y multicolored .40 .20

Centenary of Japanese customs. Wood block by Hiroshige III (d. 1896).

1972, Dec. 11

1132 A757 10y blue & multi .20 .20

New Year 1973. Art work by Kenzan Ogata (1663-1743). Sheets containing 3 #1132 were awarded as prizes in the New Year lottery. Value $1.75.

Mt. Tsurugi A758

Oboke Valley — A759

1973, Feb. 20 **Photo.** ***Perf. 13***

1133 A758 20y multicolored .25 .20
1134 A759 20y multicolored .25 .20

Mt. Tsurugi Quasi-National Park.

Mt. Takao — A760

Minoo Falls — A761

1973, Mar. 12 **Photo.** ***Perf. 13***

1135 A760 20y multicolored .25 .20
1136 A761 20y multicolored .25 .20

Meiji Forests Quasi-National Park.

Phoenix Tree — A762

Sumiyoshi Shrine Visitor — A763

1973, Apr. 7 **Photo.** ***Perf. 13***
1137 A762 20y brt grn, yel & dk bl .30 .20

National forestation campaign.

1973, Apr. 20
1138 A763 20y multicolored .30 .20

Philatelic Week, Apr. 20-26. Design from painting by Ryusei Kishida (1891-1929) of his daughter, "A Portrait of Reiko Visiting Sumiyoshi Shrine."

Mt. Kamagatake A764

Mt. Haguro A765

1973, May 25 **Photo.** ***Perf. 13***
1139 A764 20y multicolored .25 .20
1140 A765 20y multicolored .25 .20

Suzuka Quasi-National Park.

Chichijima Beach A766

Coral Reef on Minami Island — A767

1973, June 26
1141 A766 10y grnsh bl & Prus bl .20 .20
1142 A767 20y lilac & dk pur .25 .20

Ogasawara National Park.
5th anniversary of the return of the Bonin (Ogasawara Islands) to Japan.

Tree, Postal Code Symbol A768

Mailman, Postal Code Symbol A769

1973, July 1 **Photo.** ***Perf. 13***
1143 A768 10y brt green & gold .20 .20
1144 A769 20y blue, purple & car .40 .20

Postal code system, 5th anniversary.

Sandan Gorge — A770

Mt. Shinnyu A771

1973, Aug. 28 **Photo.** ***Perf. 13***
1145 A770 20y multicolored .40 .20
1146 A771 20y multicolored .40 .20

Nishi-Chugoku-Sanchi Quasi-National Park.

Tenryu Valley — A772

Mt. Horaiji — A773

1973, Sept. 18 **Photo.** ***Perf. 13***
1147 A772 20y lilac & multi .40 .20
1148 A773 20y vio bl, lt bl & sil .40 .20

Tenryu-Okumikawa Quasi-National Park.

Cock, by Jakuchu Ito (1716-1800) A774

Woman Runner at Start A775

1973, Oct. 6
1149 A774 50y gold & multi .95 .25

International Letter Writing Week, Oct. 7-13. Sheets of 10.

1973, Oct. 14
1150 A775 10y silver & multi .20 .20

28th National Athletic Meet, Chiba Prefecture, Oct. 14-19.

Kan Mon Bridge A776

1973, Nov. 14 **Engr.** ***Perf. 13***
1151 A776 20y black, rose & yel .40 .20

Opening of Kan Mon Bridge connecting Honshu and Kyushu.

Old Man and Dog — A777

Designs: No. 1153, Old man and wife pounding rice mortar, which yields gold. No. 1154, Old man sitting in tree and landlord admiring tree.

1973, Nov. 20 **Photo.**
1152 A777 20y multicolored .40 .20
1153 A777 20y multicolored .40 .20
1154 A777 20y multicolored .40 .20
Nos. 1152-1154 (3) 1.20 .60

Folk tale "Hanasaka-jijii" (The Old Man Who Made Trees Bloom).

Bronze Lantern, Muromachi Period — A778

1973, Dec. 10
1155 A778 10y emerald, blk & org .20 .20

New Year 1974. Sheets containing 3 #1155 were awarded as prizes in the New Year lottery. Value $1.50.

Nijubashi, Tokyo A779

Imperial Palace, Tokyo A780

1974, Jan. 26 **Photo.** ***Perf. 13***
1156 A779 20y gold & multi .40 .20
1157 A780 20y gold & multi .40 .20
a. Souv. sheet of 2, #1156-1157 .90 .40

50th anniversary of the wedding of Emperor Hirohito and Empress Nagako.

Young Wife A781

Crane Weaving A782

Cranes in Flight A783

1974, Feb. 20 **Photo.** ***Perf. 13***
1158 A781 20y multicolored .40 .20
1159 A782 20y multicolored .40 .20
1160 A783 20y multicolored .40 .20
Nos. 1158-1160 (3) 1.20 .60

Folk tale "Tsuru-nyobo" (Crane becomes wife of peasant).

Marudu Falls — A784

Marine Scene — A785

1974, Mar. 15
1161 A784 20y multicolored .40 .20
1162 A785 20y multicolored .40 .20

Iriomote National Park.

"Finger," by Ito Shinsui — A786

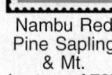

Nambu Red Pine Sapling & Mt. Iwate — A787

1974, Apr. 20 **Photo.** ***Perf. 13***
1163 A786 20y multicolored .40 .20

Philatelic Week, Apr. 20-27.

1974, May 18
1164 A787 20y multicolored .40 .20

National forestation campaign.

Supreme Court Building A788

1974, May 23 **Engr.**
1165 A788 20y redsh brown .40 .20

Completion of Supreme Court Building, Tokyo.

Midget Using Bowl as Boat A789

Designs: No. 1167, Midget fighting demon. No. 1168, Princess and midget changed into prince with magic hammer.

1974, June 10 **Photo.** ***Perf. 13***
1166 A789 20y yellow & multi .40 .20
1167 A789 20y bister & multi .40 .20
1168 A789 20y bister & multi .40 .20
Nos. 1166-1168 (3) 1.20 .60

Folk tale "Issun Hoschi" (The Story of the Mini-mini Boy).

"Police," by Kunimasa Baido — A790

1974, June 17 ***Perf. 13***
1169 A790 20y multicolored .40 .20

Centenary of the Tokyo Metropolitan Police Department.

Japanese Otter A791

Litho. and Engr.; Photo. and Engr. (Nos. 1172-1173)

1974

1170 A791 20y Mayailurus iri-omotensis .40 .20
1171 A791 20y shown .40 .20
1172 A791 20y Pentalagus furnes-si .40 .20
1173 A791 20y Pteropus pse-laphon .40 .20
Nos. 1170-1173 (4) 1.60 .80

Nature conservation.
Issue dates: #1170, Mar. 25; #1171, June 25; #1172, Aug. 30; #1173, Nov. 15.

Transfusion Bottle, Globe, Doves — A794

1974, July 1 **Photo.**
1174 A794 20y brt blue & multi .40 .20

Intl. Red Cross Blood Donations Year.

Discovery of Kaguya Hime in Shining Bamboo A795

Kaguya Hime as Grown-up Beauty A796

Kaguya Hime and Escorts Returning to Moon A797

1974, July 29 **Photo.** ***Perf. 13***
1175 A795 20y multicolored .40 .20
1176 A796 20y multicolored .40 .20
1177 A797 20y multicolored .40 .20
Nos. 1175-1177 (3) 1.20 .60

Folk tale "Kaguya Hime" or "Tale of the Bamboo Cutter."

Rich and Poor Men with Wens A798

Poor Man Dancing With Spirits A798a

Design: No. 1180, Rich man with two wens, poor man without wen, spirits.

1974, Sept. 9 **Photo.** ***Perf. 13***
1178 A798 20y multicolored .40 .20
1179 A798a 20y multicolored .40 .20
1180 A798 20y multicolored .40 .20
Nos. 1178-1180 (3) 1.20 .60

Folk tale "Kobutori Jiisan," or "The Old Man who had his Wen Taken by Spirits."

Goode's Projection and Diet — A799

"Aizen" by Ryushi Kawabata — A800

1974, Oct. 1 **Photo.** ***Perf. 13***
1181 A799 20y multicolored .40 .20
1182 A800 50y multicolored .95 .20

Interparliamentary Union, 61st Meeting, Tokyo, Nov. 2-11.

Pine and Hawk, by Sesson — A801

UPU Emblem — A802

Tending Cow, Fan by Sotatsu Tawaraya — A803

1974, Oct. 7
1183 A801 50y sepia, blk & dk brn .95 .20

Intl. Letter Writing Week, Oct. 6-12.

1974, Oct. 9
1184 A802 20y multicolored .40 .20
1185 A803 50y multicolored .95 .20

Centenary of Universal Postal Union.

Soccer Players and Sailboat A804

Various Mushrooms A805

1974, Oct. 20 **Photo.**
1186 A804 10y multicolored .20 .20

29th National Athletic Meet, Ibaraki Prefecture, Oct. 20-25.

1974, Nov. 2
1187 A805 20y multicolored .40 .20

9th International Congress on the Cultivation of Edible Fungi, Japan, Nov. 4-13.

Steam Locomotive Class D51 — A806

Class C57 — A807

Class 8620 — A808

Class C11 — A809

Designs: Steam locomotives.

1974, Nov. 26 **Photo.** ***Perf. 13***
1188 A806 20y shown .40 .20
1189 A807 20y shown .40 .20
a. Pair, #1188-1189 .80 .20

1975, Feb. 25
1190 A806 20y Class D52 .40 .20
1191 A807 20y Class C58 .40 .20
a. Pair, #1190-1191 .80 .20

1975, Apr. 3
1192 A808 20y shown .40 .20
1193 A809 20y shown .40 .20
a. Pair, #1192-1193 .80 .20

1975, May 15
1194 A806 20y Class 9600 .40 .20
1195 A807 20y Class C51 .40 .20
a. Pair, #1194-1195 .80 .20

1975, June 10 **Photo. & Engr.**
1196 A806 20y Class 7100 .40 .20
1197 A806 20y Class 150 .40 .20
a. Pair, #1196-1197 .80 .20
Nos. 1188-1197 (10) 4.00 2.00

Japanese National Railways.

Ornamental Nail Cover, Katsura Palace — A810

1974, Dec. 10
1198 A810 10y blue & multi .20 .20

New Year 1975. Sheets containing 3 #1198 were awarded as prizes in the New Year Lottery. Value $1.50.

Short-tailed Albatrosses A811

Bonin Island Honey-eater A812

Temminck's Robin A813

Ryukyu-Yamagame Tortoise — A814

Design: No. 1200, Japanese cranes.

1975-76 **Photo. & Engr.** ***Perf. 13***
1199 A811 20y multicolored .40 .20
1200 A811 20y multicolored .40 .20
1201 A812 20y multicolored .40 .20
1202 A813 50y multicolored .95 .20
1203 A814 50y multicolored .95 .20
Nos. 1199-1203 (5) 3.10 1.00

Nature conservation.
Issued: #1199, 1/16; #1200, 2/13; #1201, 8/8; #1202, 2/27/76; #1203, 3/25/76.

Taro Urashima Releasing Turtle A815

Palace of the Sea God and Fish A816

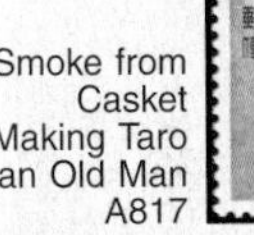

Smoke from Casket Making Taro an Old Man A817

1975, Jan. 28 **Photo.** ***Perf. 13***
1204 A815 20y multicolored .40 .20
1205 A816 20y multicolored .40 .20
1206 A817 20y multicolored .40 .20
Nos. 1204-1206 (3) 1.20 .60

Folk tale "Legend of Taro Urashima."

Kan-mon-sho (Seeing and Hearing), by Shiko Munakata — A818

1975, Mar. 20 **Photo.** ***Perf. 13***
1207 A818 20y brown & multi .40 .20

Japan Broadcasting Corp., 50th anniv.

Old Man Feeding Mouse A819

Man Following Mouse Underground — A820

Mice Entertaining and Bringing Gifts A821

1975, Apr. 15 Photo. *Perf. 13*

1208 A819 20y multicolored .40 .20
1209 A820 20y multicolored .40 .20
1210 A821 20y multicolored .40 .20
Nos. 1208-1210 (3) 1.20 .60

Folk tale "Paradise for the Mice."

Matsuura Screen (detail), 16th Century — A822

1975, Apr. 21

1211 20y denomination at lower left .40 .20
1212 20y denomination at lower right .40 .20
a. A822 Pair, #1211-1212 .80 .20

Philatelic Week, Apr. 21-27.

Oil Derricks, Congress Emblem — A824

1975, May 10 Photo. *Perf. 13*

1213 A824 20y multicolored .40 .20

9th World Petroleum Cong., Tokyo, May 11-16.

Trees and River — A825

IWY Emblem, Sun and Woman — A826

1975, May 24

1214 A825 20y green & multi .40 .20

National forestation campaign.

1975, June 23

1215 A826 20y orange & multi .40 .20

International Women's Year 1975.

Okinawan Dancer, EXPO 75 Emblem A827

Birds in Flight (Bingata) A828

Aquapolis and Globe — A829

1975, July 19 Photo. *Perf. 13*

1216 A827 20y ultra & multi .40 .20
1217 A828 30y blue grn & multi .60 .20
1218 A829 50y ultra & multi .95 .20
a. Souv. sheet of 3, #1216-1218 1.90 1.90
Nos. 1216-1218 (3) 1.95 .60

Oceanexpo 75, 1st Intl. Ocean Exposition, Okinawa, July 20, 1975-Jan. 18, 1976.

Historic Ship Issue

Kentoshi-sen 7th-9th Centuries — A830

Ships: #1220, Kenmin-sen, 7th-9th cent. #1221, Goshuin-sen, merchant ship, 16th-17th cent. #1222, Tenchi-maru, state barge, built 1630. #1223, Sengoku-bune (cargo ship) and fishing vessel. #1224, Shoheimaru, 1852, European-type sailing ship. #1225, Taisei-maru, four-mast bark training ship, 1903. #1226, Tenyomaru, first Japanese passenger liner, 1907. #1227, Asama-maru, passenger liner. #1228, Kinai-maru, transpacific freighter and Statue of Liberty. #1229, Container ship. #1230, Tanker.

1975-76 Engr. *Perf. 13*

1219 A830 20y rose red .40 .20
1220 A830 20y sepia .40 .20
a. Pair, #1219-1220 .80 .20
1221 A830 20y lt olive .40 .20
1222 A830 20y dark blue .40 .20
a. Pair, #1221-1222 .80 .20
1223 A830 50y violet blue .95 .20
1224 A830 50y lilac .95 .20
a. Pair, #1223-1224 1.90 .25
1225 A830 50y gray .95 .20
1226 A830 50y dark brown .95 .20
a. Pair, #1225-1226 1.90 .25
1227 A830 50y olive green .95 .20
1228 A830 50y olive brown .95 .20
a. Pair, #1227-1228 1.90 .25
1229 A830 50y ultra .95 .20
1230 A830 50y violet blue .95 .20
a. Pair, #1229-1230 1.90 .25
Nos. 1219-1230 (12) 9.20 2.40

Printed checkerwise in sheets of 20.
Issued: #1219-1220, 8/30; #1221-1222, 9/25; #1223-1224, 3/11/76; #1225-1226, 4/12/76; #1227-1228, 6/1/76; #1229-1230, 8/18/76.

Apple and Apple Tree — A831

Peacock, by Korin Ogata — A832

1975, Sept. 17 Photo. *Perf. 13*

1231 A831 20y gray, black & red .40 .20

Centenary of apple cultivation in Japan.

1975, Oct. 6 Photo. *Perf. 13*

1232 A832 50y gold & multi .95 .20

Intl. Letter Writing Week, Oct. 6-12.

American Flag and Cherry Blossoms A833

Japanese Flag and Dogwood A834

1975, Oct. 14

1233 A833 20y ultra & multi .40 .20
1234 A834 20y green & multi .40 .20
a. Souv. sheet of 2, #1233-1234 .90 .60

Visit of Emperor Hirohito and Empress Nagako to the United States, Oct. 1-14.

Savings Box and Coins — A835

Weight Lifter — A836

1975, Oct. 24

1235 A835 20y multicolored .40 .20

Japan's Postal Savings System, centenary.

1975, Oct. 25

1236 A836 10y multicolored .20 .20

30th National Athletic Meet, Mie Prefecture, Oct. 26-31.

Papier-mache Dragon, Fukushima Prefecture — A837

1975, Dec. 13 Photo. *Perf. 13*

1237 A837 10y multicolored .20 .20

New Year 1976. Sheets containing 3 #1237 were awarded as prizes in the New Year Lottery. Value $1.50.

Inscribed "NIPPON" Types of 1963-1974 and

Japanese Narcissus A841

Noh Mask, Old Man A843

Guardian Dog, Katori Shrine A845

Sho-Kannon, Yakushiji Temple A846

Designs: 50y, Nyoirin Kannon, Chuguji Temple. 150y, Bronze phoenix, Uji. 200y, Clay burial figure of warrior, Ota.

1976-79 Photo. *Perf. 13*

1244 A565f 50y emerald .95 .20
a. Bklt. panes of 2 & 4 with gutter 6.00
1245 A841 60y multicolored 1.10 .20
1248 A843 140y lil rose & lil 2.50 .20
1249 A718 150y red org & brn 2.75 .20
1250 A718a 200y red orange 3.75 .20
1251 A845 250y blue 4.75 .20
1253 A846 350y dk violet brn 6.50 .20
Nos. 1244-1253 (7) 22.30 1.40

Coil Stamps

Perf. 13 Horiz.

1254 A715 10y yel grn & sep ('79) .20 .20
1256 A565f 50y emerald 1.25 .20
1257 A468 100y ver & blk ('79) 1.90 .30
Nos. 1254-1257 (3) 3.35 .70

See No. 1631.

Hikone Folding Screen (detail), 17th Century — A850

1976, Apr. 20 Photo. *Perf. 13*

1258 50y denomination at lower right .95 .20
1259 50y denomination at upper right .95 .20
a. A850 Pair, #1258-1259 1.90 1.90

Philatelic Week, Apr. 20-26.

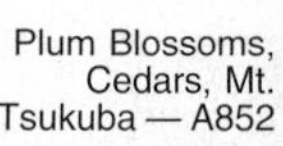

Plum Blossoms, Cedars, Mt. Tsukuba — A852

1976, May 22

1260 A852 50y multicolored .95 .20

National forestation campaign.

Green Tree Frog — A853

Bitterlings
A854

Sticklebacks
A855

1976 Photo. & Engr. *Perf. 13*
1261 A853 50y multicolored .95 .20
1262 A854 50y multicolored .95 .20
1263 A855 50y multicolored .95 .20
Nos. 1261-1263 (3) 2.85 .60

Nature conservation.
Issued: #1261, 7/20; #1262, 8/26; #1263, 9/16.

Crows, by Yosa Buson — A856 Gymnasts and Stadium — A857

1976, Oct. 6 Photo. *Perf. 13*
1264 A856 100y gray, blk & buff 1.90 .20

Intl. Letter Writing Week, Oct. 6-12.

1976, Oct. 23 Photo. *Perf. 13*
1265 A857 20y multicolored .40 .20

31st National Athletic Meet, Saga Prefecture, Oct. 24-29.

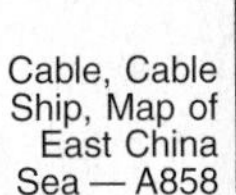

Cable, Cable Ship, Map of East China Sea — A858

1976, Oct. 25
1266 A858 50y blue, blk & silver .95 .20

Opening of Sino-Japanese cable between Shanghai and Reihoku-cho, Kumamoto Prefecture.

Classical Court Dance A859

Imperial Coach A860

1976, Nov. 10 Photo. *Perf. 13*
1267 A859 50y multicolored .95 .20
1268 A860 50y multicolored .95 .20
a. Souv. sheet of 2, #1267-1268 1.90 1.90

Emperor Hirohito's accession to the throne, 50th anniversary.

Kindergarten Class — A861

1976, Nov. 16
1269 A861 50y multicolored .95 .20

Centenary of first kindergarten in Japan.

Healthy Family A862 Bamboo Toy Snake A863

1976, Nov. 24
1270 A862 50y multicolored .95 .20

Natl. Health Insurance, 50th anniv.

1976, Dec. 1 Photo. *Perf. 13*
1271 A863 20y multicolored .40 .20

New Year 1977. Sheets containing 2 #1271 were awarded as prizes in the New Year lottery. Value $1.65.

National Treasures

East Pagoda, Yakushiji Temple, c. 730 — A864

Deva King in Armor Holding Spear, Nara Period A865

1976, Dec. 9 Photo. *Perf. 13*
1272 A864 50y multicolored .95 .20

Engr.

1273 A865 100y green & multi 1.90 .20

Golden Pavilion, Toshodai-ji Temple, 8th Century — A866

Praying Women, from Heike Nokyo Sutra, 12th Century A867

Photogravure and Engraved

1977, Jan. 20 *Perf. 13*
1274 A866 50y multicolored .95 .20

Photo.

1275 A867 100y multicolored 1.90 .20

Comic Picture Scroll, Attributed to Toba Sojo Kakuyu (1053-1140) — A868

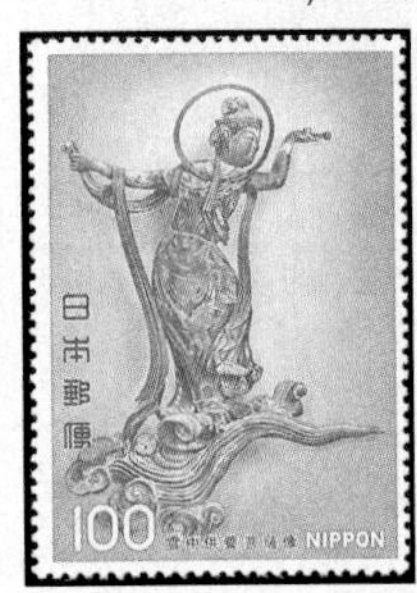

Saint on Cloud, 11th Century Wood Carving, Byodoin Temple A869

1977, Mar. 25 Photo. *Perf. 13*
1276 A868 50y multicolored .95 .20

Engr.

1277 A869 100y multicolored 1.90 .20

Noblemen on Way to Court, from Picture Scroll, Heian Period — A870

Statue of Seitaka-doji, Messenger, Kamakura Period A871

1977, June 27 Photo. *Perf. 13*
1278 A870 50y multicolored .95 .20

Engr.

1279 A871 100y multicolored 1.90 .20

The Recluse Han Shan, 14th Century Painting — A872

Tower, Matsumoto Castle, 16th Century — A873

1977, Aug. 25 Photo. *Perf. 13*
1280 A872 50y multicolored .95 .20

Photogravure and Engraved

1281 A873 100y black & multi 1.90 .20

Pine and Flowers, Chishakuin Temple, Kyoto, 1591 — A874

Main Hall, Kiyomizu Temple, 1633 — A875

1977, Nov. 16 Photo. *Perf. 13*
1282 A874 50y multicolored .95 .20

Engr.

1283 A875 100y multicolored 1.90 .20

Scene from Tale of Genji, by Sotatsu Tawaraya — A876

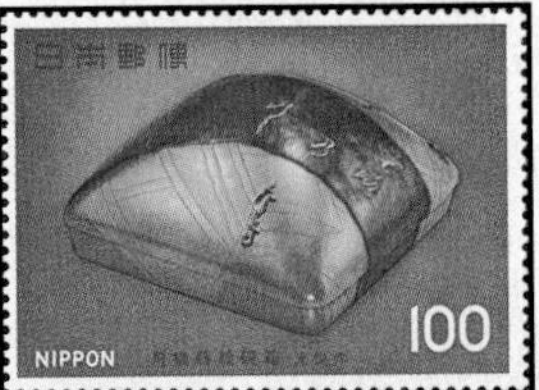

Inkstone Case, by Koetsu Honami — A877

1978, Jan. 26 Photo. *Perf. 13*
1284 A876 50y multicolored .95 .20

Photogravure and Engraved

1285 A877 100y black & multi 1.90 .25

Family Enjoying Cool Evening, by Morikage Kusumi — A878

Yomeimon, Toshogu Shrine, 1636 — A879

1978, Mar. 3 **Photo.** ***Perf. 13***
1286 A878 50y gray & multi .95 .20

Photogravure and Engraved

1287 A879 100y multicolored 1.90 .25

Horseshoe Crabs A884

Graphium Doson Albidum — A885

Firefly A886

Cicada — A887

Dragonfly — A888

1977 **Photo.** ***Perf. 13***
1292 A884 50y multicolored .95 .20

Photogravure and Engraved

1293 A885 50y multicolored .95 .20
1294 A886 50y multicolored .95 .20
1295 A887 50y multicolored .95 .20

Photo.

1296 A888 50y multicolored .95 .20
Nos. 1292-1296 (5) 4.75 1.00

Issued: #1292, 2/18; #1293, 5/18; #1294, 7/22; #1295, 8/15; #1296, 9/14.

Figure Skating — A889

Figure Skating Pair — A890

1977, Mar. 1
1297 A889 50y silver & multi .95 .20
1298 A890 50y silver & multi .95 .20

World Figure Skating Championships, National Yoyogi Stadium, March 1-6.

Sun Shining on Forest — A891

1977, Apr. 16 **Photo.** ***Perf. 13***
1299 A891 50y green & multi .95 .20

National forestation campaign.

Weavers and Dyers (Detail from Folding Screen) — A892

1977, Apr. 20
1300 50y denomination at lower left .95 .20
1301 50y denomination at upper left .95 .20
a. A892 Pair, #1300-1301 1.90 .50

Philatelic Week, Apr. 20-26.

Nurses A894

1977, May 30 **Photo.** ***Perf. 13***
1302 A894 50y multicolored .95 .20

16th Quadrennial Congress of the Intl. Council of Nurses, Tokyo, May 30-June 3.

Fast Breeder Reactor, Central Part — A895

1977, June 6
1303 A895 50y multicolored .95 .20

Experimental fast breeder reactor "Joyo," which began operating Apr. 24, 1977.

Workers and Safety Emblems A896

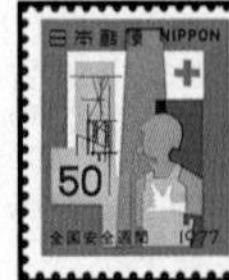

Work on High-rise Buildings A897

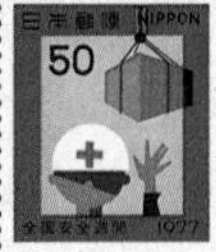

Cargo Unloading A898

Machinery Work A899

1977, July 1
1304 A896 50y multicolored .95 .20
1305 A897 50y multicolored .95 .20
1306 A898 50y multicolored .95 .20
1307 A899 50y multicolored .95 .20
a. Block or strip of 4, #1304-1307 4.00 .75

National Safety Week, July 1-July 7.

Carrier Pigeons, Mail Box, UPU Emblem A900

UPU Emblem, Postal Service Flag of Meiji Era, world Map A900a

1977, June 20 **Photo.** ***Perf. 13***
1308 A900 50y multicolored .95 .20
1309 A900a 100y multicolored 1.90 .20
a. Souv. sheet of 2, #1308-1309 3.00 1.00

Cent. of Japan's admission to the UPU.

Surgeon in Operating Room — A901

1977, Sept. 3 **Photo.** ***Perf. 13***
1310 A901 50y multicolored .95 .20

27th Cong. of the Intl. Surgeon's Society on the 75th anniv. of its founding, Kyoto, 9/3-8.

Child Using Telephone, Map of New Cable Route — A902

1977, Aug. 26
1311 A902 50y multicolored .95 .20

Inauguration of underwater telephone cable linking Okinawa, Luzon and Hong Kong.

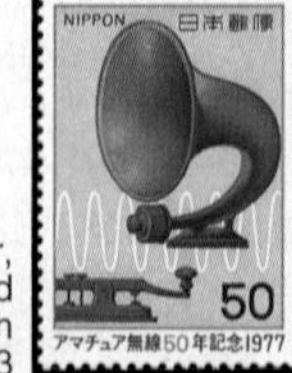

Early Speaker, Waves and Telegraph Key — A903

1977, Sept. 24 **Photo.** ***Perf. 13***
1312 A903 50y multicolored .95 .20

50th anniversary of amateur radio in Japan.

Bicyclist, Mt. Iwaki and Iwaki River — A904

Flowers and Ducks, Attributed to Hasegawa Tohaku — A905

1977, Oct. 1
1313 A904 20y multicolored .40 .20

32nd National Athletic Meet, Aomori Prefecture, Oct. 2-7.

1977, Oct. 6
1314 A905 100y multicolored 1.90 .20

Intl. Letter Writing Week, Oct. 6-12.

Dinosaur, Stars, Museum A906

1977, Nov. 2 **Photo.** ***Perf. 13***
1315 A906 50y multicolored .95 .20

Centenary of National Science Museum.

Decorated Horse, Fushimi Toy — A907

Tokyo Subway, 1927 A908

1977, Dec. 1 **Photo.** ***Perf. 13***
1316 A907 20y multicolored .40 .20

New Year 1978. Sheets containing 2 #1316 were awarded as prizes in the New Year lottery. Value $1.50.

1977, Dec. 6
1317 A908 50y shown .95 .20
1318 A908 50y Subway, 1977 .95 .20
a. Pair, #1317-1318 1.50 .35

Tokyo Subway, 50th anniversary.

Primrose — A909

Pinguicula Ramosa — A910

Dicentra — A911

1978 Photo. & Engr. *Perf. 13*

1319 A909 50y multicolored .95 .20
1320 A910 50y multicolored .95 .20
1321 A911 50y multicolored .95 .20
Nos. 1319-1321 (3) 2.85 .60

Nature protection.

Issued: #1319, 4/12; #1320, 6/8; #1321, 7/25.

Kanbun Bijinzu Folding Screen, Edo Period — A912

1978, Apr. 20 Photo. *Perf. 13*

1322 50y inscribed at left .95 .20
1323 50y inscribed at right .95 .20
a. A912 Pair, #1322-1323 1.90 .35

Philatelic Week, Apr. 16-22.

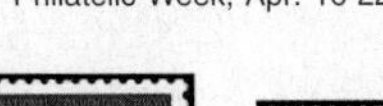

Rotary Emblem, Mt. Fuji A914

Congress Emblem, by Taro Okamoto A915

1978, May 13 Photo. *Perf. 13*

1324 A914 50y multicolored .95 .20

69th Rotary International Convention, Tokyo, May 14-18.

1978, May 15

1325 A915 50y multicolored .95 .20

23rd International Ophthalmological Congress, Kyoto, May 14-20.

Narita International Airport, Tokyo — A916

1978, May 20

1326 A916 50y multicolored .95 .20

Opening of Tokyo International Airport.

Rainbow, Japanese Cedars, Cape Ashizuri A917

Lion, by Sotatsu Tawaraya, Lions Emblem A918

1978, May 20

1327 A917 50y multicolored .95 .20

National forestation campaign.

1978, June 21 Photo. *Perf. 13*

1328 A918 50y multicolored .95 .20

61st Lions Intl. Convention, Tokyo, 6/21-24.

Sumo Print Issues

Grand Champion Hidenoyama with Sword Bearer and Herald, by Kunisada I (Toyokuni III) — A919

Ekoin Drum Tower, Ryogoku, by Hiroshige — A921

Photogravure and Engraved

1978, July 1 *Perf. 13*

1329 50y multicolored .95 .20
1330 50y multicolored .95 .20
a. A919 Pair, #1329-1330 1.90 .30

Photo.

1331 A921 50y multicolored .95 .20
Nos. 1329-1331 (3) 2.85 .60

Champions Tanikaze and Onogawa in Ring-entry Ceremony, 1782, by Shunsho — A922

Jimmaku, Raiden and Referee Shonosuke, 1791 Bout, by Shun'ei — A924

Photogravure and Engraved

1978, Sept. 9 *Perf. 13*

1332 50y multicolored .95 .20
1333 50y multicolored .95 .20
a. A922 Pair, #1332-1333 1.90 .30
1334 A924 50y multicolored .95 .20
Nos. 1332-1334 (3) 2.85 .60

Referee Shonosuke and Champion Onomatsu, by Kunisada I — A925

Children's Sumo Play, by Utamaro — A927

1978, Nov. 11 *Perf. 13*

1335 50y multicolored .95 .20
1336 50y multicolored .95 .20
a. A925 Pair, #1335-1336 1.90 .30
1337 A927 50y multicolored .95 .20
Nos. 1335-1337 (3) 2.85 .60

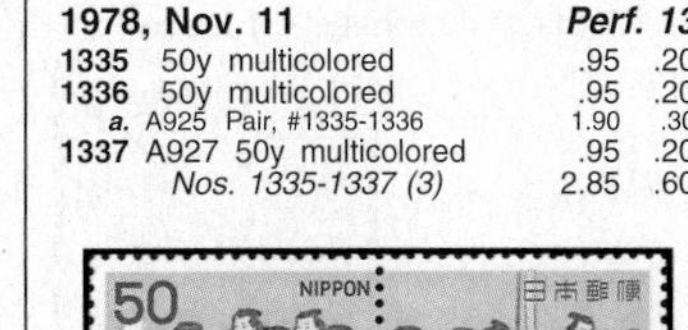

Wrestlers on Ryogoku Bridge, by Kunisada I — A928

Bow-receiving Ceremony at Tournament, by Kunisada II — A930

1979, Jan. 13 *Perf. 13*

1338 50y multicolored .95 .20
1339 50y multicolored .95 .20
a. A928 Pair, #1338-1339 1.90 .30
1340 A930 50y multicolored .95 .20
Nos. 1338-1340 (3) 2.85 .60

Takekuma and Iwamigata (Hidenoyama) Wrestling, by Kuniyoshi — A931

Daidozan (Great Child Mountain) in Ring-entry Ceremony, by Sharaku — A933

1979, Mar. 10 *Perf. 13*

1341 50y multicolored .95 .20
1342 50y multicolored .95 .20
a. A931 Pair, #1341-1342 1.90 .30
1343 A933 50y multicolored .95 .20
Nos. 1341-1343 (3) 2.85 .60

Radio Gymnastics Emblem — A934

1978, Aug. 1 Photo. *Perf. 13*

1344 A934 50y multicolored .95 .20

Radio gymnastics program exercises, 50th anniversary.

Chamber of Commerce and Industry A935

1978, Aug. 28 Photo. *Perf. 13*

1345 A935 50y multicolored .95 .20

Tokyo Chamber of Commerce, centenary.

Symbolic Sculptures, Tokyo Stock Exchange — A936

Flowering Plum with Pheasant, from Screen, Tenkyuin Temple — A937

1978, Sept. 14 Engr. *Perf. 13*

1346 A936 50y lilac, grn & brn .95 .20

Centenary of the Tokyo and Osaka Stock Exchanges.

1978, Oct. 6 Photo. *Perf. 13*

1347 A937 100y multicolored 1.90 .25

Intl. Letter Writing Week, Oct. 6-12.

Softball and Mt. Yarigatake A938

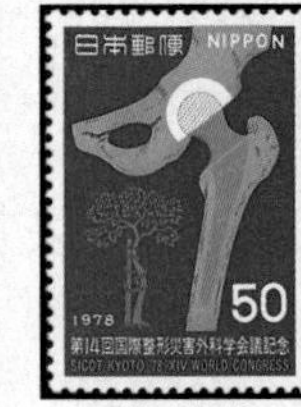

Artificial Hip, Orthopedists' Emblem A939

1978, Oct. 14

1348 A938 20y multicolored .40 .20

33rd National Athletic Meet, Nagano Prefecture, Oct. 15-20.

1978, Oct. 16

1349 A939 50y multicolored .95 .20

14th World Cong. of Intl. Soc. of Orthopedic Surgeons (50th anniv.), Kyoto, Oct. 15-20.

Telescope and Stars — A940

Sheep Bell, Nakayama Toy — A941

1978, Dec. 1 Photo.

1350 A940 50y multicolored .95 .20

Tokyo Astronomical Observatory, cent.

1978, Dec. 4

1351 A941 20y multicolored .40 .20

New Year 1979. Sheets containing 2 #1351 were awarded as prizes in the New Year Lottery. Value $1.50.

Family, Human Rights Emblem — A942

Hands Shielding Children — A943

1978, Dec. 4
1352 A942 50y multicolored .95 .20

Human Rights Week, Dec. 4-10.

1979, Feb. 16 **Photo.** ***Perf. 13***
1353 A943 50y multicolored .95 .20

Education of the handicapped, centenary.

Telephone Dials — A944

Sketch of Man, by Leonardo da Vinci — A945

1979, Mar. 14 **Photo.** ***Perf. 13***
1354 A944 50y multicolored .95 .20

Nation-wide telephone automatization completion.

Photogravure and Engraved

1979, Apr. 7 ***Perf. 13***
1355 A945 50y multicolored .95 .20

Centenary of promulgation of State Medical Act, initiating modern medicine.

Standing Beauties, Middle Edo Period — A946

1979, Apr. 20 **Photo.**
1356 50y multicolored .95 .20
1357 50y multicolored .95 .20
a. A946 Pair, #1356-1357 1.90 .35

Philatelic Week, Apr. 16-22.

Mt. Horaiji and Maple — A948

1979, May 26 **Photo.** ***Perf. 13***
1358 A948 50y multicolored .95 .20

National forestation campaign.

Modern Japanese Art Issue

Merciful Mother Goddess, by Kano Hogai — A949

Sea God's Princess, by Aoki Shigeru — A950

1979, May 30 **Photo.** ***Perf. 13***
1359 A949 50y multicolored .95 .20
1360 A950 50y multicolored .95 .20

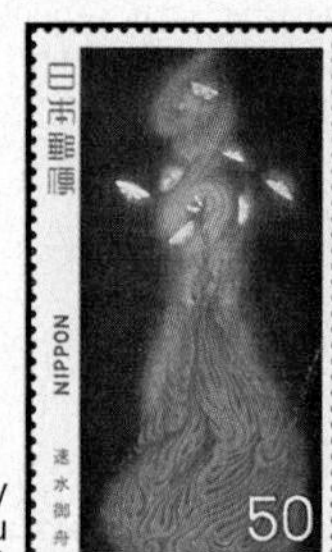
Fire Dance, by Gyoshu Hayami — A951

Leaning Figure, by Tetsugoro Yorozu — A952

1979, June 25 **Photo.** ***Perf. 13***
1361 A951 50y red & multi .95 .20

Photogravure and Engraved

1362 A952 50y red & multi .95 .20

The Black Cat, by Shunso Hishida — A953

Kinyo, by Sotaro Yasui — A954

1979, Sept. 21 **Photo.** ***Perf. 13***
1363 A953 50y multicolored .95 .20
1364 A954 50y multicolored .95 .20

Nude, by Kagaku Murakami A955

Harvest, by Asai Chu — A956

Photogravure and Engraved

1979, Nov. 22 ***Perf. 13***
1365 A955 50y multicolored .65 .20
1366 A956 50y multicolored .65 .20

Salmon, by Yuichi Takahashi A956a

Hall of the Supreme Buddha, by Kokei Kabayashi A956b

Photogravure and Engraved

1980, Feb. 22 ***Perf. 13½***
1367 A956a 50y multicolored .95 .20

Photo.

1368 A956b 50y multicolored .95 .20

Quarantine Officers, Ships, Plane, Microscope A957

1979, July 14 **Photo.**
1369 A957 50y multicolored .95 .20

Centenary of Japanese Quarantine system.

Girl Mailing Letter — A958

Hakata Doll with Letter-paper Roll — A959

1979, July 23
1370 A958 20y multicolored .40 .20
1371 A959 50y multicolored .95 .20

Letter Writing Day.

Pitcher, Baseball with Black Lion Emblem — A960

1979, July 27
1372 A960 50y multicolored .95 .20

50th National Inter-city Amateur Baseball Tournament, Tokyo, August.

Girl Floating in Space A961

Design: No. 1374, Boy floating in space.

1979, Aug. 1
1373 A961 50y magenta & multi .95 .20
1374 A961 50y blue & multi .95 .20
a. Souv. sheet of 2, #1373-1374 1.90 1.90

International Year of the Child.

Japanese Song Issue

Moon over Castle, by Rentaro Taki A962

Evening Glow, by Shin Kusakawa A963

Maple Leaves, by Teiichi Okano A964

The Birthplace, by Teiichi Okano — A965

Winter Landscape A966

Mt. Fuji — A967

Spring Brook A968

Cherry Blossoms A969

1979, Aug. 24 Photo. & Engr.
1375 A962 50y multicolored .95 .20
1376 A963 50y multicolored .95 .20

1979, Nov. 26
1377 A964 50y multicolored .95 .20
1378 A965 50y multicolored .95 .20

1980, Jan. 28 ***Perf. 13***
1379 A966 50y multicolored .95 .20
1380 A967 50y multicolored .95 .20

1980, Mar. 21
1381 A968 50y multicolored .95 .20
1382 A969 50y multicolored .95 .20
Nos. 1375-1382 (8) 7.60 1.60

Great Owl, by Okyo Maruyama — A970

1979, Oct. 8 Photo. ***Perf. 13***
1383 A970 100y multicolored 1.90 .25

Intl. Letter Writing Week, Oct. 8-14.

Runner — A971

"ITU," Globe — A972

1979, Oct. 13
1384 A971 20y multicolored .40 .20

34th National Athletic Meet, Miyazaki, Oct. 4-19.

1979, Oct. 13 Litho. ***Perf. 13½***
1385 A972 50y multicolored .95 .20

Admission to ITU, cent.

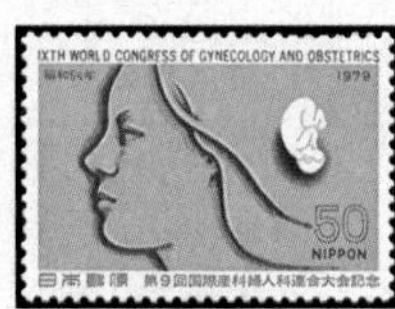
Woman and Fetus — A973

1979, Nov. 12 Photo.
1386 A973 50y multicolored .95 .20

9th World Congress of Gynecology and Obstetrics, Tokyo, Oct. 25-31.

Happy Monkeys, Osaka Toy — A974

Government Auditing Centenary A975

1979, Dec. 1 Photo. ***Perf. 13x13½***
1387 A974 20y multicolored .40 .20

New Year 1980. Sheets of 2 #1387 were New Year Lottery prizes. Value $1.50.

1980, Mar. 5 Photo. ***Perf. 13½***
1388 A975 50y multicolored .95 .20

Scenes of Outdoor Play in Spring, by Sukenobu Nishikawa — A976

1980, Apr. 21 Photo. ***Perf. 13½***
1389 50y multicolored .95 .20
1390 50y multicolored .95 .20
a. A976 Pair, #1389-1390 1.90 .50

Philatelic Week, Apr. 21-27. Sheets of 10.

Japanese Song Issue

The Sea — A978

The Night of the Hazy Moon — A979

Memories of Summer — A981

The Sun Flag — A980

1980 Photo. & Engr. ***Perf. 13***
1391 A978 50y multicolored .95 .20
1392 A979 50y multicolored .95 .20
1393 A980 50y multicolored .95 .20
1394 A981 50y multicolored .95 .20
Nos. 1391-1394 (4) 3.80 .80

Issued: #1391-1392, 4/28; #1393-1394, 6/16.

The Red Dragonfly A982

Song by the Sea — A983

1980, Sept. 18 ***Perf. 13***
1395 A982 50y multicolored .95 .20
1396 A983 50y multicolored .95 .20

Lullaby A984

Coconut, by Toraji Ohnaka — A985

1981, Feb. 9 ***Perf. 13***
1397 A984 60y multicolored 1.10 .20
1398 A985 60y multicolored 1.10 .20

Spring Has Come, by Tatsuyuki Takano — A986

Cherry Blossoms, by Hagoromo Takeshima A987

1981, Mar. 10 ***Perf. 13***
1399 A986 60y multicolored 1.10 .20
1400 A987 60y multicolored 1.10 .20

Modern Japanese Art Issue

Dancers, by Seiki Kuroda — A988

Mother and Child, by Shoen Uemura A989

1980, May 12 Photo. ***Perf. 13½***
1401 A988 50y multicolored .95 .20
1402 A989 50y multicolored .95 .20

The Black Fan, by Takeji Fujishima — A990

Dear Me . . . It's a Shower, by Seiho Takeuchi A991

1980, July 7 Photo. ***Perf. 13½***
1403 A990 50y multicolored .95 .20
1404 A991 50y multicolored .95 .20

Woman, by Morie Ogiwara — A992

Kurofuneya, by Yumeji Takehisa — A993

1980, Oct. 27 Photo. *Perf. 13½*

1405 A992 50y multicolored .95 .20
1406 A993 50y multicolored .95 .20

Nippon Maru, Institute Emblem — A994

1980, May 17

1407 A994 50y multicolored .95 .20

Institute for Nautical Training, training ships Nippon Maru and Kaio Maru, 50th anniversary.

Mt. Gozaisho-dake, Cedars, Flowers — A995

1980, May 24 *Perf. 13x13½*

1408 A995 50y multicolored .95 .20

National forestation campaign.

Yayosu Fire Brigade Review, by Hiroshige III — A996

1980, May 31

1409 A996 50y multicolored .95 .20

Fire fighting centenary.

A997 A997a

Letter Writing Day: 20y, Teddy Bear holding letter. 50y, Folded and tied letter of good wishes, horiz.

1980, July 23 *Perf. 13x13½, 13½x13*

1410 A997 20y multicolored .40 .20
1411 A997a 50y multicolored .95 .20

Lühdorfla Japonica A998

1980, Aug. 2 *Perf. 13½*

1412 A998 50y multicolored .95 .20

16th Intl. Cong. of Entomology, Kyoto, Aug. 3-9.

Three-dimensional World Map — A999

1980, Aug. 25 Photo.

1413 A999 50y multicolored .95 .20

24th Intl. Geographic Cong. and 10th Intl. Cartographic Conf., Tokyo, August.

Integrated Circuit A1000 Camellia A1001

1980, Sept. 29

1414 A1000 50y multicolored .95 .20

Intl. Federation for Information Processing Cong. '80, Tokyo, Oct. 6-9 and World Conf. on Medical Informatics '80, Tokyo, 9/29-10/4.

1980, Oct. 1

1415 A1001 30y shown .60 .20
1416 A1001 40y Rape flower, cabbage butterflies .75 .20
1417 A1001 50y Cherry blossoms .95 .20
Nos. 1415-1417 (3) 2.30 .60

See No. 1437.

Cranes, by Motooki Watanabe A1002

Archery, Mt. Nantai A1003

1980, Oct. 6 *Perf. 13*

1418 A1002 100y multicolored 1.90 .25

24th Intl. Letter Writing Week, Oct. 6-12.

1980, Oct. 11

1419 A1003 20y multicolored .40 .20

35th Natonal Athletic Meet, Tochigi, Oct.

Globe, Jaycee Emblem — A1004

Diet Building and Doves — A1005

1980, Nov. 8 *Perf. 13*

1420 A1004 50y multicolored .95 .25

35th Jaycee (Intl. Junior Chamber of Commerce) World Congress, Osaka, Nov. 9-15.

1980, Nov. 29 *Perf. 13½*

1421 A1005 50y multicolored .95 .20

90th anniversary of Japanese Diet.

Type of 1980 and:

Amur Adonis A1006

White Trumpet Lily A1007

Hanging Bell, Byodoin Temple A1008

Bronze Buddhist Ornament, 7th Century A1009

Writing Box Cover A1010

Mirror with Figures A1011

Heart-shaped Figurine A1012

Silver Crane A1013

Maitreya, Horyuji Temple A1014

Ichiji Kinrin, Chusonji Temple A1015

Komokuten, Todaiji Temple A1016

Lady Maya A1017

Enamel Jar, by Ninsei Nonomura A1018

Miroku Bosatsu, Koryuji Temple A1019

1980-82 Photo. *Perf. 13x13½*

1422 A1006 10y multicolored .25 .20
1423 A1007 20y multicolored .30 .20
1424 A1008 60y multicolored 1.10 .20
a. Bklt. pane (#1424, 4 #1424 with gutter btwn.) ('81) 5.50
1425 A1009 70y multicolored 1.25 .30
1426 A1010 70y multicolored 1.25 .20
1427 A1011 80y multicolored 1.50 .20
1428 A1012 90y multicolored 1.75 .20
1429 A1013 100y multicolored 1.90 .20
1430 A1014 170y multicolored 3.25 .25
1431 A1015 260y multicolored 5.00 .40
1432 A1016 310y multicolored 6.00 .50
1433 A1017 410y multicolored 8.00 .75
1434 A1018 410y multicolored 8.00 .75
1435 A1019 600y multicolored 11.50 1.00
Nos. 1422-1435 (14) 51.05 5.35

Coil Stamps

Perf. 13 Horiz.

1436 A1006 10y multi ('82) .25 .20
1437 A1001 40y as #1416 .75 .30
1438 A1008 60y multi ('82) 1.10 .30
1439 A1013 100y multi ('82) 1.90 .50
Nos. 1436-1439 (4) 4.00 1.30

See Nos. 1627-1628.

Clay Chicken, Folk Toy — A1026

1980, Dec. 1 *Perf. 13 Horiz.*

1442 A1026 20y multicolored .40 .20

New Year 1981.

Sheets of two were New Year Lottery Prizes. Value $1.50.

Modern Japanese Art Issue

Snow-Covered Power Station, by Shikanosuke Oka — A1027

NuKada-no-Ohkimi and Nara in Spring, by Yukihiko Yasuda — A1028

1981, Feb. 26 *Perf. 13½*

1443 A1027 60y multicolored 1.10 .20

Photo.

1444 A1028 60y multicolored 1.10 .20

Artist's Family, by Narashige Koide — A1029

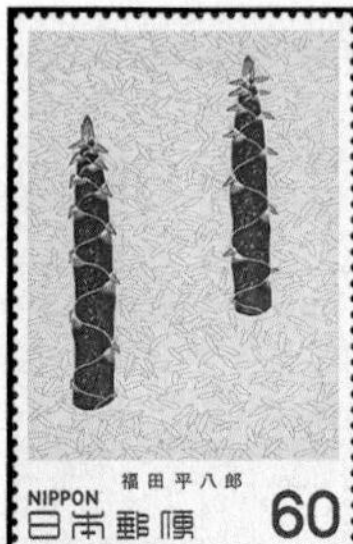

Bamboo Shoots, by Heihachiro Fukuda A1030

Photo. & Engr., Photo.

1981, June 18 *Perf. 13½*

1445 A1029 60y multicolored 1.10 .20
1446 A1030 60y multicolored 1.10 .20

Portrait of Ichiyo, by Kiyokata Kaburagi (1878-1972) A1031

Portrait of Reiko, by Ryusei Kishida (1891-1929) A1032

Photo., Photo. and Engr.

1981, Nov. 27 Engr. *Perf. 13½*

1447 A1031 60y multicolored	1.10	.20
1448 A1032 60y multicolored	1.10	.20

Yoritomo in a Cave, by Seison Maeda — A1033

Advertisement of a Terrace, by Yuzo Saeki — A1034

1982, Feb. 25 Photo. *Perf. 13½*

1449 A1033 60y multicolored	1.10	.20
1450 A1034 60y multicolored	1.10	.20

Emblem, Port Island A1035

1981, Mar. 20 *Perf. 13*

1451 A1035 60y multicolored	1.10	.20

Portopia '81, Kobe Port Island Exhibition, Mar. 20-Sept. 15.

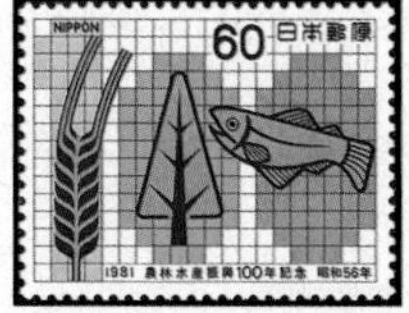
Agriculture, Forestry and Fishery Promotion Centenary A1036

1981, Apr. 7

1452 60y multicolored	1.10	.20

Moonflower, by Harunobu Suzuki — A1037

1981, Apr. 20 Photo. *Perf. 13½*

1453 60y multicolored	1.10	.20
1454 60y multicolored	1.10	.20
a. A1037 Pair, #1453-1454	2.20	.30

Philatelic Week, Apr. 21-27.

Cherry Blossoms — A1039

Cargo Ship and Crane A1040

1981, May 23 Photo. *Perf. 13x13½*

1455 A1039 60y multicolored	1.10	.20

1981, May 25 *Perf. 13*

1456 A1040 60y multicolored	1.10	.20

International Port and Harbor Association, 12th Convention, Nagoya, May 23-30.

Land Erosion Control Cent. — A1041

Stylized Man and Spinal Cord Dose Response Curve A1042

1981, June 27 *Perf. 13½*

1457 A1041 60y multicolored	1.10	.20

1981, July 18 Photo. *Perf. 13*

1458 A1042 60y multicolored	1.10	.20

8th Intl. Pharmacology Cong., Tokyo, July 19-24.

Girl Writing Letter A1043

Japanese Crested Ibis A1044

1981, July 23

1459 A1043 40y shown	.75	.20
1460 A1043 60y Boy, stamp	1.10	.20

Letter Writing Day (23rd of each month).

1981, July 27 Litho.

1461 A1044 60y multicolored	1.10	.20

Plug, faucet A1044a

Plugs A1045

1981, Aug. 1 Photo.

1462 A1044a 40y multicolored	.75	.20
1463 A1045 60y multicolored	1.10	.20

Energy conservation.

Western Architecture Issue

Oura Cathedral — A1046

Hyokei Hall, Tokyo A1047

Photogravure and Engraved

1981, Aug. 22

1464 A1046 60y multicolored	1.10	.20
1465 A1047 60y multicolored	1.10	.20

Old Kaichi School, Nagano A1048

Doshisha University Chapel, Kyoto A1049

1981, Nov. 9 *Perf. 13*

1466 A1048 60y multicolored	1.10	.20
1467 A1049 60y multicolored	1.10	.20

St. John's Church, Meiji-mura A1050

Military Exercise Hall (Former Sapporo Agricultural School), Sapporo A1051

1982, Jan. 29 *Perf. 13*

1468 A1050 60y multicolored	1.10	.20
1469 A1051 60y multicolored	1.10	.20

Former Kyoto Branch of Bank of Japan A1052

Main Building, Former Saiseikan Hospital — A1053

1982, Mar. 10 *Perf. 13*

1470 A1052 60y multicolored	1.10	.20
1471 A1053 60y multicolored	1.10	.20

Oyama Shrine Gate, Kanazawa A1054

Former Iwasaki Family Residence, Tokyo A1055

1982, June 12 *Perf. 13*

1472 A1054 60y multicolored	1.10	.20
1473 A1055 60y multicolored	1.10	.20

Hokkaido Prefectural Govt. Building, Sapporo A1056

Former Residence of Tsugumichi Saigo A1057

1982, Sept. 10 *Perf. 13*

1474 A1056 60y multicolored	1.10	.20
1475 A1057 60y multicolored	1.10	.20

Old Mutsuzawa School — A1058

Sakuranomiya Public Hall — A1059

1983, Feb. 15

1476 A1058 60y multicolored	1.10	.20
1477 A1059 60y multicolored	1.10	.20

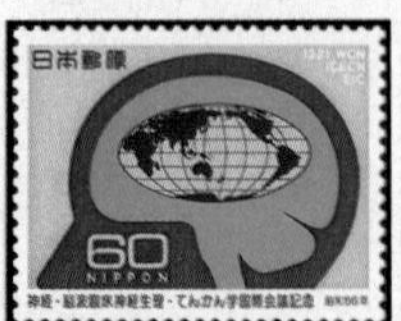
Globe on Brain A1060

1981, Sept. 12 **Photo.**
1478 A1060 60y multicolored 1.10 .20

Intl. medical conferences, Kyoto: 12th Neurology, Sept. 20-25; 10th Brainwaves and Clinical Neurophysiology, Sept. 13-17; 1981 Intl. Epilepsy Conference, Sept. 17-21.

Congress Emblem — A1061

Plum Trees and Fowl, by Sanraku Kano — A1062

1981, Sept. 16
1479 A1061 60y multicolored 1.10 .20

24th World PTTI (Post, Telegraph and Telephone Intl. Labor Federation) Cong., Tokyo, Sept. 16-22.

1981, Oct. 6 **Photo.**
1480 A1062 130y multicolored 2.50 .20

25th Intl. Letter Writing Week, Oct. 6-12.

A1063

A1064

1981, Oct. 9 **Photo. & Engr.**
1481 A1063 60y No. 1 1.10 .20
1482 A1063 60y No. 2 1.10 .20
1483 A1063 60y No. 3 1.10 .20
1484 A1063 60y No. 4 1.10 .20
a. Strip or block of 4, #1481-1484 4.50 4.50

Philatokyo '81 Intl. Stamp Exhibition,Tokyo, Oct. 9-18.

1981, Oct. 13 **Photo.**
1485 A1064 40y multicolored .75 .20

36th Natl. Athletic Meet, Oct. 13-18.

A1065 A1066

1981, Dec. 1 **Photo.** ***Perf. 13x13½***
1486 A1065 40y multicolored .75 .20

New Year of 1982 (Year of the Dog). Sheets of 2 were lottery prizes. Value $1.50.

1982, Mar. 20 **Photo.**

Ueno Zoo Centenary: a, Gorilla, flamingo. b, Penguins, lion. c, Panda, elephants. d, Zebras, giraffe.

1487 Strip of 4 4.50 1.40
a.-d. A1066 60y any single 1.10 .35

Views of the Snow on Matsuchiyama, by Kiyonaga Torii — A1067

1982, Apr. 20 **Photo.** ***Perf. 13½***
1488 60y multicolored 1.10 .30
1489 60y multicolored 1.10 .30
a. A1067 Pair, #1488-1489 2.25 .70

Philatelic Week.

Shisa (Lion-shaped Guard Dog) A1069

Natl. Forestation Campaign A1070

1982, May 15 **Photo.**
1490 A1069 60y multicolored 1.10 .30

10th anniv. of Reversion Agreement returning Ryukyu Islands.

1982, May 22 ***Perf. 13x13½***
1491 A1070 60y multicolored 1.10 .30

16th Intl. Dermatology Conference Tokyo, May 23-28 — A1071

1982, May 24 ***Perf. 13***
1492 A1071 60y Noh mask 1.10 .30

Tohoku-Shinkansen Railroad Line Opening — A1072

1982, June 23
1493 A1072 60y Diesel locomotive 1.10 .30
1494 A1072 60y Steam model 1290 1.10 .30
a. Pair, #1493-1494 2.25 .75

Letter Writing Day — A1073

1982, July 23 ***Perf. 13x13½, 13½x13***
1495 A1073 40y Sea gull, letter .75 .20
1496 A1073 60y Fairy, letter, horiz. 1.10 .30

Modern Japanese Art Issue

Kimono Patterned with Irises, by Saburosuke Okada (1869-1939) A1074

Bodhisattva Kuan-yin on Potalaka Island, by Tessai Tomioka (1837-1924) A1075

1982, Aug. 5 **Photo.** ***Perf. 13½***
1497 A1074 60y multicolored 1.10 .30
1498 A1075 60y multicolored 1.10 .30

The Sarasvati, by Shiko Munakata (1903-1975) A1076

Saltim-banque, by Seiji Togo (1897-1978) A1077

1982, Nov. 24
1499 A1076 60y multicolored 1.10 .30
1500 A1077 60y multicolored 1.10 .30

Snowstorm, by Shinsui Ito — A1078

Spiraeas and Callas with Persian Pot, by Zenzaburo Kojima A1079

1983, Jan. 24 **Photo.**
1501 A1078 60y multicolored 1.10 .30
1502 A1079 60y multicolored 1.10 .30

Innocence, by Taikan Yokoyama (1868-1958) A1080

Roen, by Koun Takamura (1852-1934) A1081

Photo., Photo. and Engr.
1983, Mar. 10 ***Perf. 13½***
1503 A1080 60y multicolored 1.10 .30
1504 A1081 60y multicolored 1.10 .30

A1082

A1083

A1084

1982, Aug. 23 ***Perf. 13x13½***
1505 A1082 60y Wreath 1.10 .35
1506 A1083 60y Crane 1.10 .35
1507 A1084 70y Tortoise 1.25 .35
Nos. 1505-1507 (3) 3.45 1.05

For use on greeting (Nos. 1506-1507) and condolence (No. 1505) cards.

See Nos. 1555-1556, 1836-1839, 2227-2230 and footnotes after Nos. 1708, 1765.

400th Anniv. of Boys' Delegation to Europe, Tensho Era — A1085

1982, Sept. 20 **Photo.** ***Perf. 13***
1508 A1085 60y 16th cent. ship, map 1.10 .30

10th Anniv. of Japanese-Chinese Relations Normalization — A1086

Design: Hall of Prayer for Good Harvests, Temple of Heaven, Peking, by Ryuzaburo Umehara.

1982, Sept. 29
1509 A1086 60y multicolored 1.10 .30

Table Tennis — A1087 "Amusement," Doll by Goyo Hirata — A1088

1982, Oct. 2
1510 A1087 40y multicolored .75 .25

37th Natl. Athletic Meet, Matsue, Oct. 3-8.

1982, Oct. 6
1511 A1088 130y multicolored 2.50 .60

Intl. Letter Writing Week, Oct. 6-12.

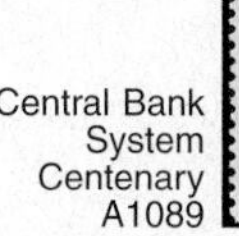

Central Bank System Centenary A1089

Design: The Bank of Japan near Eitaibashi in Snow, by Yasuji Inoue.

Photogravure and Engraved

1982, Oct. 12 ***Perf. 13½***
1512 A1089 60y multicolored 1.10 .30

Opening of Joetsu Shinkansen Railroad Line — A1090

1982, Nov. 15
1513 60y Locomotive, 1982 1.10 .30
1514 60y Locomotive, 1931 1.10 .30
a. A1090 Pair, #1513-1514 2.25 .70

New Year 1983 — A1092

Natl. Museum of History and Folklore Opening A1093

1982, Dec. 1 ***Perf. 13x13½***
1515 A1092 40y Kintaro on Wild Boar .75 .20

Sheets of 2 were lottery prizes. Value, $1.50.

1983, Mar. 16 Photo. ***Perf. 13½x13***
1516 A1093 60y multicolored 1.10 .30

Women Working in the Kitchen, by Utamaro Kitagawa (1753-1806) — A1094

1983, Apr. 20 Photo. ***Perf. 13***
1517 60y multicolored 1.10 .30
1518 60y multicolored 1.10 .30
a. A1094 Pair, #1517-1518 2.25 .70

Philatelic Week.

Natl. Forestation Campaign A1096 50th Nippon Derby A1097

1983, May 21 ***Perf. 13***
1519 A1096 60y Hakusan Mountains, black lily, forest 1.10 .30

1983, May 28
1520 A1097 60y Colt, racing horse 1.10 .30

Islands Cleanup Campaign — A1098

1983, June 13 Photo. ***Perf. 13½***
1521 A1098 60y multicolored 1.10 .30

Western Architecture Series

Hohei Hall Sapporo A1099

Old Glover House, Nagasaki A1100

Gojyuku Bank, Hirosaki A1101

Gakushuin Elementary School, Tokyo A1102

Bank of Japan, Tokyo A1103

Old Hunter House, Kobe A1104

Photogravure and Engraved

1983, June 23 ***Perf. 13***
1522 A1099 60y multicolored 1.10 .30
1523 A1100 60y multicolored 1.10 .30

1983, Aug. 15 ***Perf. 13***
1524 A1101 60y multicolored 1.10 .30
1525 A1102 60y multicolored 1.10 .30

1984, Feb. 16 ***Perf. 13***
1526 A1103 60y multicolored 1.10 .30
1527 A1104 60y multicolored 1.10 .30
Nos. 1522-1527 (6) 6.60 1.80

Official Gazette Centenary A1107 Letter Writing Day A1108

Design: First issue, Drawing of the Government Bulletin Board at Nihonbashi, by Hiroshige Ando III.

1983, July 2 Photo. ***Perf. 13***
1530 A1107 60y multicolored 1.10 .30

1983, July 23 ***Perf. 13x13½, 13½x13***
1531 A1108 40y Boy writing letter .75 .25
1532 A1108 60y Fairy bringing letter, horiz. 1.10 .30

Opening of Natl. Noh Theater, Tokyo A1109

1983, Sept. 14 Photo. ***Perf. 13***
1533 A1109 60y Masked actor, theater 1.10 .30

Endangered Birds Issue

Rallus Okinawae A1110

Ketupa Blakistoni A1111

Photo. and Engr., Photo.

1983, Sept. 22 ***Perf. 13***
1534 A1110 60y multicolored 1.10 .30
1535 A1111 60y multicolored 1.10 .30

Photo., Photo. & Engr.

1983, Nov. 25 ***Perf. 13***
1536 A1110 60y Sapheopipo noguchii 1.10 .30
1537 A1111 60y Branta canadensis leucopareia 1.10 .30

Photo., Photo. and Engr.

1984, Jan. 26 ***Perf. 13***
1538 A1111 60y Megalurus pryeri pryeri 1.10 .30
1539 A1110 60y Spilornis cheela perplexus 1.10 .30

1984, Mar. 15 Photo. ***Perf. 13***
1540 A1110 60y Columba janthina nitens 1.10 .30
1541 A1111 60y Tringa guttifer 1.10 .30

1984, June 22 Photo. ***Perf. 13***
1542 A1110 60y Falco peregrinus frutti 1.10 .30

Photo. and Engr.

1543 A1111 60y Dendrocopus leucutus austoni 1.10 .30
Nos. 1534-1543 (10) 11.00 3.00

Souvenir Sheet

1984, Dec. 10 Photo. & Engr.
1544 Sheet of 3 3.50 3.50
a. A1111 60y Prus grn, engr., #1535 1.10 .30
b. A1110 60y vio brn, engr., #1539 1.10 .30
c. A1110 60y ol blk, engr., #1542 1.10 .30

Intl. Letter Writing Week — A1124 38th Natl. Athletic Meet — A1125

Chikyu Doll by Juzo Kagoshima (1898-1982).

1983, Oct. 6 Photo. ***Perf. 13***
1548 A1124 130y multicolored 2.50 .70

1983, Oct. 15 ***Perf. 13***
1549 A1125 40y Naginata event .75 .25

A1126 World Communications Year — A1127

1983, Oct. 17 Photo. ***Perf. 13***
1550 A1126 60y multicolored 1.10 .30
1551 A1127 60y multicolored 1.10 .30

Showa Memorial National Park Opening
A1128

1983, Oct. 26 **Photo.** ***Perf. 13***
1552 A1128 60y multicolored 1.10 .30

A1129

A1130

1983, Nov. 14 **Photo.**
1553 A1129 60y multicolored 1.10 .30

71st World Dentistry Congress.

1983, Nov. 14 **Photo.** ***Perf. 13***
1554 A1130 60y multicolored 1.10 .30

Shirase, Antarctic observation ship, maiden voyage.

Type of 1982

1983, Nov. 22 **Photo.** ***Perf. 12½***
1555 A1082 40y Wreath .75 .25
1556 A1083 40y Crane .75 .25

For use on condolence and greeting cards.

A1131

A1132

1983, Dec. 1 **Photo.** ***Perf. 13x13½***
1557 A1131 40y Rat riding hammer .75 .25

New Year 1984. Sheets of 2 were lottery prizes. Value, $1.50.

1983, Dec. 5 **Photo.** ***Perf. 13½***
1558 A1132 60y Emblem 1.10 .30

Universal Declaration of Human Rights, 35th anniv.

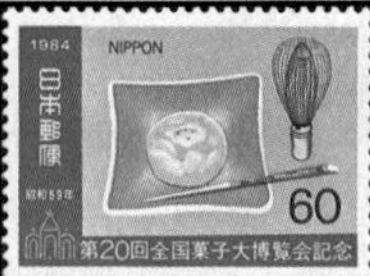

20th Grand Confectionery Fair, Tokyo, Feb. 24-Mar. 12 — A1133

1984, Feb. 24 **Photo.**
1559 A1133 60y Confection, tea whisk 1.10 .30

Natl. Bunraku Theater Opening, Osaka
A1134

1984, Apr. 6 **Photo.** ***Perf. 13***
1560 A1134 60y Bunraku puppet 1.10 .30

A1135

Philatelic Week (Sharaku Prints): No. 1561, Hanshiro Iwai IV (facing right) Playing Shigenoi. No. 1562, Oniji Otani (facing left) Playing Edobe.

Photogravure and Engraved

1984, Apr. 20 ***Perf. 13½***
1561 60y multicolored 1.10 .30
1562 60y multicolored 1.10 .30
a. A1135 Pair, #1561-1562 2.25 .70

Natl. Forestation Campaign
A1137

Weather Forecasting Centenary
A1138

1984, May 19 **Photo.**
1563 A1137 60y Cedar Forest, Sakurajima 1.10 .30

1984, June 1 ***Perf. 13x13½***
1564 A1138 60y Himawari satellite, map 1.10 .30

UNESCO Emblem, Doves — A1139

Letter Writing Day — A1140

1984, July 16 **Photo.**
1565 A1139 60y multicolored 1.10 .30

UNESCO Clubs and Associations World Congress, July 16-24.

1984, July 23 ***Perf. 13x13½, 13½x13***
1566 A1140 40y Birds in tree .75 .20
1567 A1140 60y Bird holding letter, horiz. 1.10 .30

Disaster Relief
A1141

Perf. 13x12½, 12½x13

1984, Aug. 23 **Photo.**
1568 A1141 40y Fire, wind .75 .20
1569 A1141 60y Mother, child, vert. 1.10 .30

Alpine Plant Series

Leontopodium Fauriei — A1142

Lagotis Glauca
A1143

Photogravure and Engraved

Perf. 12½x13, 13x12½

1984, Aug. 27
1570 A1142 60y multicolored 1.10 .30
1571 A1143 60y multicolored 1.10 .30

Trollius Riederianus
A1144

Primula Cuneifolia
A1145

1984, Sept. 21 ***Perf. 13***
1572 A1144 60y multicolored 1.10 .30
1573 A1145 60y multicolored 1.10 .30

Rhododendron Aureum — A1146

Oxytropis Nigrescens Var. Japonica
A1147

1985, Jan. 25 ***Perf. 13***
1574 A1146 60y multicolored 1.10 .30
1575 A1147 60y multicolored 1.10 .30

Draba Japonica — A1148

Dryas Octopetala
A1149

1985, Feb. 28
1576 A1148 60y multicolored 1.10 .30
1577 A1149 60y multicolored 1.10 .30

Callianthemum Insigne Var. Miyabeanum
A1150

Gentiana Nipponica
A1151

1985, July 31 ***Perf. 13***
1578 A1150 60y multicolored 1.10 .30
1579 A1151 60y multicolored 1.10 .30

Campanula Chamissonis
A1152

Viola Crassa
A1153

1985, Sept. 27
1580 A1152 60y multicolored 1.10 .30
1581 A1153 60y multicolored 1.10 .30

Deapensia Lapponica
A1154

Pedicularis Apodochila
A1155

1986, Feb. 13 ***Perf. 13***
1582 A1154 60y multicolored 1.10 .30
1583 A1155 60y multicolored 1.10 .30

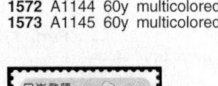

Basho's Street, Sendai — A1156

1984, Sept. 1 **Photo.** ***Perf. 13***
1584 A1156 60y multicolored 1.10 .30

Intl. Microbiological Association's 6th Intl. Congress of Virology, Sendai, Sept. 1-7.

Electronic Mail — A1157

28th Intl. Letter Writing Week, Oct. 6-12 — A1158

1984, Oct. 1 **Photo.**
1585 A1157 500y multicolored 9.50 4.50

1984, Oct. 6
1586 A1158 130y Wooden doll 2.50 .60

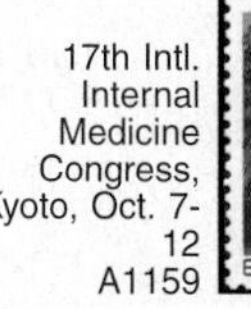

17th Intl. Internal Medicine Congress, Kyoto, Oct. 7-12 A1159

1984, Oct. 8
1587 A1159 60y Ginkakuji Temple 1.10 .30

39th Natl. Athletic Meet, Nara City, Oct. 12-17 — A1160

1984, Oct. 12
1588 A1160 40y Field hockey .75 .25

Traditional Crafts Series

Kutaniyaki Plates — A1161

Nishijinori Weavings — A1163

1984, Nov. 2 **Photo.** ***Perf. 12½x13***
1589 60y Birds 1.10 .30
1590 60y Flowers 1.10 .30
a. A1161 Pair, #1589-1590 2.25 .75
1591 60y Flowers 1.10 .30
1592 60y Leaves 1.10 .30
a. A1163 Pair, #1591-1592 2.25 .75

Edokimekomi Dolls — A1165

Ryukyubingata Cloth — A1167

1985, Feb. 15 **Photo.** ***Perf. 13***
1593 60y Adult figures 1.10 .30
1594 60y Child and pet 1.10 .30
a. A1165 Pair, #1593-1594 2.25 .75
1595 60y Bird and branch 1.10 .30
1596 60y Birds 1.10 .30
a. A1167 Pair, #1595-1596 2.25 .75

Ichii-ittobori Carved Birds — A1169

Imariyaki & Aritayaki Ceramic Ware — A1171

Kamakurabori Wood Carvings — A1173

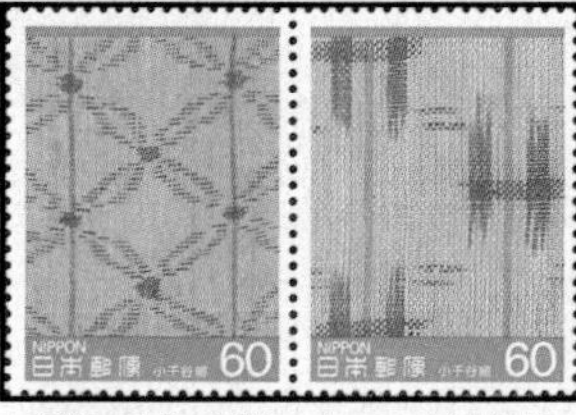
Ojiyachijimi Weavings — A1175

Hakata Ningyo Clay Figures — A1177

Nanbu Tekki Iron Ware — A1179

1985, May 23 **Photo.** ***Perf. 13***
1597 60y Bird 1.10 .30
1598 60y Birds 1.10 .30
a. A1169 Pair, #1597-1598 2.25 .75
1599 60y Bowl 1.10 .30
1600 60y Plate 1.10 .30
a. A1171 Pair, #1599-1600 2.25 .75

1985, June 24 **Photo. & Engr.**
1601 60y Bird and flower panel 1.10 .30
1602 60y Round flower panel 1.10 .30
a. A1173 Pair, #1601-1602 2.25 .75

Litho.
1603 60y Hemp star pattern 1.10 .30
1604 60y Hemp linear pattern 1.10 .30
a. A1175 Pair, #1603-1604 2.25 .75

1985, Aug. 8 **Photo.**
1605 60y Man 1.10 .30
1606 60y Woman and child 1.10 .30
a. A1177 Pair, #1605-1606 2.25 .75

Photogravure and Engraved
1607 60y Silver kettle 1.10 .30
1608 60y Black kettle 1.10 .30
a. A1179 Pair, #1607-1608 2.25 .75

Wajimanuri Lacquerware — A1181

Izumo-ishidoro Sandstone Sculptures — A1183

Photo., Photo. & Engr. (#1611-1612)
1985, Nov. 15
1609 60y Bowl on table 1.10 .30
1610 60y Bowl 1.10 .30
a. A1181 Pair, #1609-1610 2.25 .75
1611 60y Columnar lantern 1.10 .30
1612 60y Lantern on four legs 1.10 .30
a. A1183 Pair, #1611-1612 2.25 .75

Kyo-sensu Silk Fans — A1185

Tobeyaki Porcelain — A1187

1986, Mar. 13 **Photo.** ***Perf. 13***
1613 60y Flower bouquets 1.10 .30
1614 60y Sun and trees 1.10 .30
a. A1185 Pair, #1613-1614 2.25 .75
1615 60y Jug 1.10 .30
1616 60y Jar 1.10 .30
a. A1187 Pair, #1615-1616 2.25 .75
Nos. 1613-1616 (4) 4.40 1.20

Japanese Professional Baseball, 50th Anniv. — A1189

1984, Nov. 15 ***Perf. 13½***
1617 60y Pitcher 1.10 .30
1618 60y Batter 1.10 .30
a. A1189 Pair, #1617-1618 2.25 .80
1619 A1189 60y Matsutaro Shoriki 1.10 .30
Nos. 1617-1619 (3) 3.30 .90

Industrial Education Centenary A1190

New Year 1984 — A1191

1984, Nov. 20 ***Perf. 13x12½***
1620 A1190 60y Workers, symbols 1.10 .30

1984, Dec. 1 **Photo.** ***Perf. 13½x13***
1621 A1191 40y Sakushu Cattle Folk Toy .75 .25

Sheets of 2 were lottery prizes. Value, $1.50.

Ivory Shell
A1200 A1201

A1202 A1203
Hiougi-gai (Bivalve) Rinbo Shell

A1204 A1205

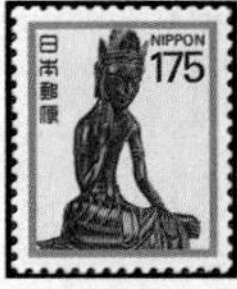

A1206 A1207

A1208 A1209

Photo., Engr. (300y)

1984-89 *Perf. 13x13½*

1622 A1200 2y turq blue ('89) .20 .20
1623 A1201 40y multi ('88) .90 .20
1624 A1202 41y multi ('89) .80 .20
1624B A1202 41y Imperf., self-adhesive .80 .20
1625 A1203 60y multi ('88) 1.10 .20
a. Bklt. pane, 5 each #1623, 1625 9.25
1626 A1204 62y multi ('89) 1.10 .20
a. Bklt. pane, 2 #1624, 4 #1626 6.00
1626B A1204 62y Imperf., self-adhesive 1.10 .20
c. Bklt. pane, 2 #1624B, 4 #1626B ('89) 6.00
1627 A1205 72y dark vio, blk & org yel ('89) 1.40 .20
1628 A1206 175y multi ('89) 3.25 .25
1629 A1207 210y multi ('89) 4.00 .30
1630 A1208 300y dk red brown 5.75 .35
1631 A1209 360y dull pink & brn ('89) 6.75 .35
Nos. 1622-1631 (12) 27.15 2.85

Coil Stamps

Perf. 13 Horiz.

1636 A1202 41y multi ('89) .80 .20
1637 A1204 62y multi ('89) 1.10 .20
Nos. 1636-1637 (2) 1.90 .40

No. 1622 inscribed "Nippon," unlike No. 583.

No. 1626Bc is adhered to the booklet cover, made of peelable paper, folded in half and rouletted down the center fold.

Issued: 40y, 60y, 4/1; 300y, 4/3; 2y, 72y, 4/1; 42y, #1626, 1626a, 41y, #1637, 3/24; 175y, 210y, 360y, 6/1; #1626d, 7/3.

A1210

EXPO '85 — A1211

1985, Mar. 16 **Photo.** *Perf. 13*

1640 A1210 40y multicolored .75 .20
1641 A1211 60y multicolored 1.10 .30
a. Souv. sheet of 2, #1640-1641 1.60

University of the Air — A1212

1985, Apr. 1 **Photo.** *Perf. 13½*

1642 A1212 60y University broadcast tower 1.10 .35

Inauguration of adult education through broadcasting.

Nippon Telegraph & Telephone Co. — A1213

1985, Apr. 1

1643 A1213 60y Satellite receiver 1.10 .30

Inauguration of Japan's new telecommunications system.

World Import Fair, Nagoya A1214

1985, Apr. 5 **Photo.** *Perf. 13*

1644 A1214 60y 16th century map of Japan 1.10 .30

Industrial Proprietary System Cent. — A1215

Design: Portrait of Korekiyo Takashashi, system promulgator, inscriptions in English.

1985, Apr. 18 **Photo.** *Perf. 13½*

1645 A1215 60y multicolored 1.10 .30

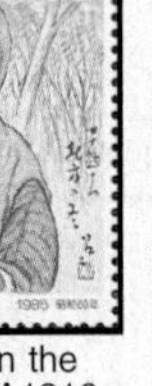

Winter in the North — A1216

To the Morning Light — A1217

Paintings by Yumeji Takehisa (1884-1934).

1985, Apr. 20 *Perf. 13*

1646 A1216 60y multicolored 1.10 .30
1647 A1217 60y multicolored 1.10 .30
a. Pair, #1646-1647 2.25 .75

Philatelic Week. Printed in sheets of 10.

Natl. Land Forestation Project — A1218

Intl. Year of the Forest: Autumn bellflower, camphor tree, cattle and Mt. Aso.

1985, May 10 *Perf. 13½*

1648 A1218 60y multicolored 1.10 .30

Radio Japan, 50th Anniv. — A1219

Painting: Cherry Blossoms at Night, by Taikan Yokoyama.

1985, June 1 **Photo.** *Perf. 13*

1649 60y multi (Left) 1.10 .30
1650 60y multi (Right) 1.10 .30
a. A1219 Pair, #1649-1650 2.25 .70

Hisoka Maejima, 1st Postmaster General — A1220

1985, June 5 **Photo.** *Perf. 13*

1651 A1220 60y Portrait, former P.O. building 1.10 .30

Oonaruto Bridge Opening A1221

1985, June 7 *Perf. 13½*

1652 A1221 60y multicolored 1.10 .30

Intl. Youth Year A1222

Owl Carrying Letter — A1223

1985, July 20 **Photo.** *Perf. 13*

1653 A1222 60y Emblem, silhouette 1.10 .30

Perf. 13½x13, 13x13½

1985, July 23 **Photo.**

1654 A1223 40y shown .75 .25
1655 A1223 60y Girl, cat, bird, letter 1.10 .30

Letter Writing Day (23rd of each month).

Electronic Mail — A1224

Meson Theory, 50th Anniv. A1225

1985, Aug. 1 **Photo.** *Perf. 13x13½*

1656 A1224 500y multicolored 9.50 2.00

1985, Aug. 15 **Photo.** *Perf. 13*

1657 A1225 60y Portrait, nuclear particles 1.10 .30

Dr. Hideki Yukawa was presented the Nobel Prize for Physics for the Meson Theory in 1949, which is the foundation for high-energy physics.

A1226 A1227

1985, Aug. 24 **Photo.** *Perf. 13½*

1658 A1226 60y Gymnast, horse 1.10 .30

Universiade 1985, Kobe.

1985, Sept. 13 **Photo.**

1659 A1227 40y Emblem, competitor .75 .25

28th Intl. Vocational Training Competition, Oct. 21-27.

Normalization of Diplomatic Relations Between Japan and the Republic of Korea, 20th Anniv. — A1228

1985, Sept. 18

1660 A1228 60y Rose of Sharon 1.10 .30

Kan-Etsu Tunnel Opening A1229

1985, Oct. 2 *Perf. 13*

1661 A1229 60y Mountains, diagram, cross sections 1.10 .30

Seisen Doll by Goyo Hirata (1903-1981) A1230

1985, Oct. 7

1662 A1230 130y multicolored 2.50 .75

Intl. Letter Writing Week, Oct. 6-12.

30th Intl. Apicultural Congress, Oct. 10-16, Nagoya A1231

1985, Oct. 9

1663 A1231 60y Honeybee, strawberry plants 1.10 .30

Japanese Overseas Cooperation Volunteers, 20th Anniv. A1232

1985, Oct. 9 **Litho.**

1664 A1232 60y Planting crop 1.10 .30

40th Natl. Athletic Meet, Oct. 20-25, Tottori City Sports Arena — A1233

1985, Oct. 19 **Photo.**

1665 A1233 40y Handball player, Mt. Daisen .75 .25

New Year 1986 — A1234

Natl. Ministerial System of Government, Cent. A1235

1985, Dec. 2 Photo. *Perf. 13x13½*
1666 A1234 40y Shinno papier-mache tiger .75 .25

Sheets of 2 were lottery prizes. Value, $1.40.

1985, Dec. 20 Litho. *Perf. 13½*
1667 A1235 60y Official seal, Cabinet emblem 1.10 .30

Building Institute, Cent. — A1236

Philately Week — A1237

1986, Apr. 9 Photo. *Perf. 13*
1668 A1236 60y multicolored 1.10 .30

1986, Apr. 15

Southern Hateroma (details), by Keigetsu Kikuchi.

1669 A1237 60y Woman standing 1.10 .30
1670 A1237 60y Seated woman 1.10 .30
a. Pair, #1669-1670 2.25 .85

Kyoto Imperial Palace, Phoenix A1238

#1672, Imperial chrysanthemum crest & partridges.

1986, Apr. 28
1671 A1238 60y multicolored 1.10 .30
1672 A1238 60y multicolored 1.10 .30
a. Souv. sheet of 2, #1671-1672 2.25 1.25

Reign of Emperor Hirohito, 60th anniv.

6th Intl. Summit, Tokyo A1239

1986, May 2
1673 A1239 60y Mt. Fuji 1.10 .30

Shrike on Reed, Emperor Nintoku's Mausoleum A1240

1986, May 9 *Perf. 13½*
1674 A1240 60y multicolored 1.10 .30

Natl. Land Afforestation Campaign.

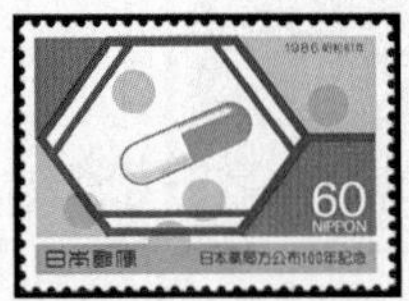
Japanese Pharmaceutical Regulatory Syst., Cent. — A1241

1986, June 25 Photo. *Perf. 13½*
1675 A1241 60y multicolored 1.10 .30

Japanese Standard Time, Cent. — A1242

Letter Writing Day — A1243

1986, July 11 Litho. *Perf. 13*
1676 A1242 60y Meridian, clock 1.10 .30

1986, July 23 Photo. *Perf. 13x13½*
1677 A1243 40y Bird .75 .25
1678 A1243 60y Girl, rabbit, birds 1.10 .35
a. Bklt. pane, 5 each #1677-1678 9.25

Sheets of 2 were lottery prizes. Value, *$60.*

Merchant Marine Education, 110th Anniv. A1244

Training ship Nihonmaru & navigation training institute founders Makoto Kondo, Yataro Iwasaki.

1986, July 26 *Perf. 13*
1679 A1244 60y multicolored 1.10 .35

CTO's exist for Nos. 1680-1681, 1684-1685, 1688-1689, 1694-1695, 1696-1697. They read "Japan" between two arcs in a corner.

Insects

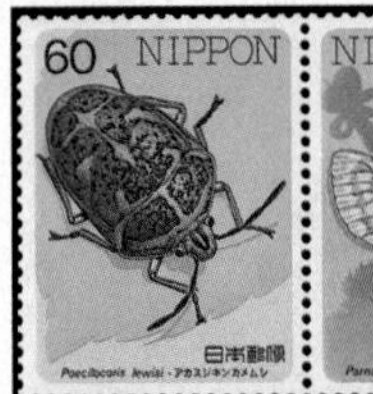

Parnassius Eversmanni — A1245

Photogravure and Engraved

1986, July 30 *Perf. 13*
1680 60y shown 1.10 .35
1681 60y Poecilocoris lewisi 1.10 .35
a. A1245 Pair, #1680-1681 2.25 1.00
1682 60y Rasalia batesi 1.10 .35
1683 60y Epiophlebia superstes 1.10 .35
a. A1245 Pair, #1682-1683 2.25 1.00

1986, Sept. 26 *Perf. 13*
1684 60y Dorcus hopei 1.10 .35
1685 60y Thermo- zephyrus ataxus 1.10 .35
a. A1245 Pair, #1684-1685 2.25 1.00
1686 60y Sympetrum pedemontanum 1.10 .35
1687 60y Damaster blaptoides 1.10 .35
a. A1245 Pair, #1686-1687 2.25 1.00

1986, Nov. 21 *Perf. 13*
1688 60y Elcysma westwoodii 1.10 .35
1689 60y Rhyothemis variegata 1.10 .35
a. A1245 Pair, #1688-1689 2.25 1.00
1690 60y Tibicen japonicus 1.10 .35
1691 60y Chrysochroa holstii 1.10 .35
a. A1245 Pair, #1690-1691 2.25 1.00

1987, Jan. 23 *Perf. 13*
1692 60y Parantica sita 1.10 .35
1693 60y Cheirotonus jambar 1.10 .35
a. A1245 Pair, #1692-1693 2.25 1.00
1694 60y Lucanus maculifemoratus 1.10 .35
1695 60y Anotogaster sieboldii 1.10 .35
a. A1245 Pair, #1694-1695 2.25 1.00

1987, Mar. 12 *Perf. 13*
1696 60y Ascaraphus ramburi 1.10 .35
1697 60y Polyphylla laticollis 1.10 .35
a. A1245 Pair, #1696-1697 2.25 1.00
1698 60y Kallima inachus 1.10 .35
1699 60y Calopteryx cornelia 1.10 .35
f. A1245 Pair, #1698-1699 2.25 1.00
Nos. 1680-1699 (20) 22.00 7.00

Miniature Sheet

1699A Sheet of 4 (#1680, 1692, 1699b-1699c) 3.75 3.75
b. 40y Anthocaris cardamines .75 .35
c. 40y Sasakia charonda .75 .35
d. Bklt. pane, 5 #1680, 5 #1699b 9.25
e. Bklt. pane, 5 #1692, 5 #1699c 9.25
g. A1245 Pair, #1699b, 1680 1.90
h. A1245 Pair, #1699c, 1692 1.90

Booklet panes are perf. 13x13½ on 2 or 3 sides.

Folkways in Twelve Months (Detail), by Shunsho Katsukawa A1265

Electron Microscope A1266

1986, Aug. 23 Photo. *Perf. 13*
1700 A1265 60y multicolored 1.10 .35

52nd conference of the Intl. Federation of Library Associations, Tokyo, Aug. 24-29.

1986, Aug. 30
1701 A1266 60y multicolored 1.10 .35

11th Int. Congress of Electron Microscopy, Kyoto, Aug. 31-Sept. 7.

23rd Intl. Conference on Social Welfare, Tokyo, Aug. 31-Sept. 5 — A1267

1986, Aug. 30 Litho.
1702 A1267 60y multicolored 1.10 .35

Ohmorimiyage Doll, by Juzoh Kagoshima A1268

41st Natl. Athletic Meet, Oct. 12-17, Kofu A1269

1986, Oct. 6 Photo.
1703 A1268 130y multicolored 2.50 .75

Intl. Letter Writing Week.

1986, Oct. 9
1704 A1269 40y multicolored .75 .25

5th World Ikebana Convention A1270

Painting: Flower in Autumn and a Girl in Rakuhoku.

1986, Oct. 17 Photo. *Perf. 13½x13*
1705 A1270 60y multicolored 1.10 .35

A1271

Intl. Peace Year A1272

Lithographed, Photogravure (#1707)
1986, Nov. 28
1706 A1271 40y multicolored .75 .25
1707 A1272 60y multicolored 1.10 .35

New Year 1987 (Year of the Hare) — A1273

Design: A Couple of Rabbits Making Rice Cake, Nagoya clay figurine.

1986, Dec. 1 Photo. *Perf. 13x13½*
1708 A1273 40y multicolored .75 .25

Sheets of two containing Nos. 1506 and 1708 were lottery prizes. Value, $1.75.
See No. 2655c.

Real Estate Registry System, Cent. A1274

1987, Jan. 30 Photo. *Perf. 13½*
1709 A1274 60y multicolored 1.10 .35

Basho Series, Part I

A1275

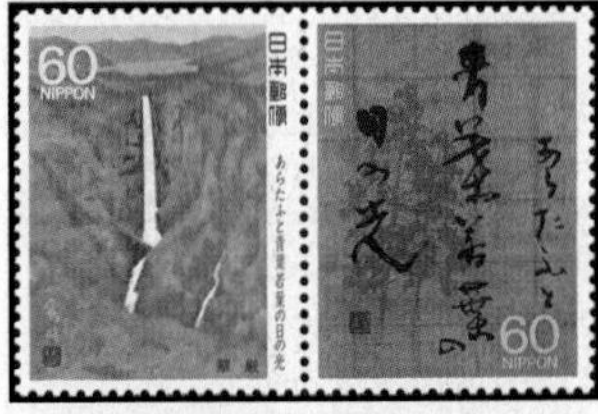
A1277

A1279

A1281

A1283

A1285

A1287

A1289

A1291

A1293

#1710, Basho. #1711, Basho's haiku. #1712, Kegon Falls. #1713, Haiku. #1714, Cuckoo. #1715, Horse and haiku. #1716, Willow Tree. #1717, Rice Paddy and haiku. #1718, Chestnut Tree in Bloom. #1719, Chestnut Leaves and haiku. #1720, Planting Rice Paddy. #1721, Fern Leaves and haiku. #1722, Sweetflags. #1723, Sweetflags and haiku. #1724, Prosperous Man, 17th Cent. #1725, Summer Grass and haiku. #1726, Safflowers in Bloom. #1727, Haiku. #1728, Yamadera (Temple). #1729, Forest and haiku.

1987-89 Photo. *Perf. 13x13½*

1710 60y multicolored 1.10 .35
1711 60y multicolored 1.10 .35
a. Sheet of 2, #1710-1711, imperf. ('89) 2.50
b. A1275 Pair, #1710-1711 2.25 1.00
1712 60y multicolored 1.10 .35
1713 60y multicolored 1.10 .35
a. Sheet of 2, #1712-1713, imperf. ('89) 2.50
b. A1277 Pair, #1712-1713 2.25 1.00
1714 60y multicolored 1.10 .35
1715 60y multicolored 1.10 .35
a. Sheet of 2, #1714-1715, imperf. ('89) 2.50
b. A1279 Pair, #1714-1715 2.25 1.00
1716 60y multicolored 1.10 .35
1717 60y multicolored 1.10 .35
a. Sheet of 2, #1716-1717, imperf. ('89) 2.50
b. A1281 Pair, #1716-1717 2.25 1.00
1718 60y multicolored 1.10 .35
1719 60y multicolored 1.10 .35
a. Sheet of 2, #1718-1719, imperf. ('89) 2.50
b. A1283 Pair, #1718-1719 1.10 1.00
1720 60y multicolored 1.10 .35
1721 60y multicolored 1.10 .35
a. Sheet of 2, #1720-1721, imperf. ('89) 2.50
b. A1285 Pair, #1720-1721 2.25 1.00
1722 60y multi ('88) 1.10 .35
1723 60y multi ('88) 1.10 .35
a. Sheet of 2, #1722-1723, imperf. ('89) 2.50
b. A1287 Pair, #1722-1723 2.25 1.00
1724 60y multi ('88) 1.10 .35
1725 60y multi ('88) 1.10 .35
a. Sheet of 2, #1724-1725, imperf. ('89) 2.50
b. A1289 Pair, #1724-1725 1.10 1.00
1726 60y multi ('88) 1.10 .35
1727 60y multi ('88) 1.10 .35
a. Sheet of 2, #1726-1727, imperf. ('89) 2.50
b. A1291 Pair, #1726-1727 2.25 1.00
1728 60y multi ('88) 1.10 .35
1729 60y multi ('88) 1.00 .35
a. Sheet of 2, #1728-1729, imperf. ('89) 2.50
b. A1293 Pair, #1728-1729 2.25 1.00
Nos. 1710-1729 (20) 21.90 7.00

Issued to commemorate the 300th anniversary of a trip from Edo (now Tokyo) to northern Japan by the famous haiku poet Matsuo Munefusa "Basho" (1644-1694). His prose account of the journey, *Oku no hosomichi* (*Narrow Road to a Far Province*), contains numerous 17-syllable poems (*haiku*), which are shown on the stamps.

In each setenant pair, a complete *haiku* by Basho is inscribed vertically at right on the left stamp and in the center of the right stamp. The same poem appears on both stamps in each pair.

Issued: #1710-1713, 2/26; #1714-1717, 6/23; #1718-1721, 8/25; #1722-1725, 1/3; #1726-1729, 3/26.

See Nos. 1775-1794.

12th World Orchid Congress, Tokyo
A1295 A1296

1987, Mar. 19 Photo. *Perf. 13*

1730 A1295 60y multicolored 1.10 .35
1731 A1296 60y multicolored 1.10 .35

Railway Post Office Termination, Oct. 1, 1986
A1297

1987, Mar. 26 Litho. *Perf. 13½*

1732 A1297 60y Mail car 1.10 .35
1733 A1297 60y Loading mail on car 1.10 .35
a. Pair, #1732-1733 1.60 1.00

Privatization of Japan Railways
A1298

1987, Apr. 1 Photo. *Perf. 13½*

1734 A1298 60y Locomotive No. 137, c. 1900 1.10 .35
1735 A1298 60y Linear induction train, 1987 1.10 .35

Natl. Marine Biology Research, Cent.
A1299

1987, Apr. 2 *Perf. 13*

1736 A1299 60y Sea slugs 1.10 .35

Philately Week — A1300

1987, Apr. 14

1737 60y denomination at upper right 1.10 .35
1738 60y denomination at lower left 1.10 .35
a. A1300 Pair, #1737-1738 1.60 1.00

Map of Asia and Oceania
A1302

1987, Apr. 27 Photo. *Perf. 13½*

1739 A1302 60y multicolored 1.10 .35

20th annual meeting of the Asian Development Bank.

Nat'l. Land Afforestation Campaign
A1303

1987, May 23

1740 A1303 60y Magpie, seashore 1.10 .35

National Treasures Series

A1304

A1305

Golden Turtle Sharito — A1306

Imuyama Castle Donjon, 1469 — A1307

Kongo Sanmai in Tahotoh Temple, Kamakura Era — A1308

Wood Ekoh-Dohji Statue in the Likeness of Kongobuji Fudodo, Kamakura Era, by Unkei — A1309

Itsukushima Shrine, Heian Period
A1310

Kozakura-gawa, Braided Armor Worn by Minamoto-no-Yoshimitsu, Heian Period War Lord, Kai Province — A1311

Statue of *Nakatsu-hime-no-mikoto*, a Hachiman Goddess, Heian Period, Yakushiji Temple — A1312

Murou-ji Temple Pagoda, 9th Cent. — A1313

Designs: No. 1741, Yatsuhashi gold inkstone box, by Kohrin Ogata. No. 1742, Donjon of Hikone Castle, c. 1573-1592.

1987, May 26 Photo. *Perf. 13*
1741 A1304 60y multicolored 1.10 .35

Photo. & Engr.
Perf. 13½
1742 A1305 110y multicolored 2.10 .75

1987, July 17 Photo. *Perf. 13*
1743 A1306 60y multicolored 1.10 .35

Photo. & Engr.
Perf. 13½
1744 A1307 110y multicolored 2.10 .75

1988, Feb. 12 Photo. *Perf. 13*
1745 A1308 60y multicolored 1.10 .35

Photo. & Engr.
Perf. 13½
1746 A1309 110y multicolored 2.10 .75

1988, June 23 Photo. *Perf. 13*
1747 A1310 60y multicolored 1.10 .35

Photo. & Engr.
Perf. 13½
1748 A1311 100y multicolored 1.90 .75

1988, Sept. 26 Photo. *Perf. 13*
1749 A1312 60y multicolored 1.10 .35

Photo. & Engr.
Perf. 13½
1750 A1313 100y multicolored 1.90 .75
Nos. 1741-1750 (10) 15.60 5.50

Letter Writing Day — A1314

1987, July 23 Photo. *Perf. 13x13½*
1751 A1314 40y Flowers, envelope .75 .40
1752 A1314 60y Elephant 1.10 .35
a. Bklt. pane, 5 ea #1751-1752 7.00

Sheets of 2, Nos. 1751-1752, were lottery prizes. Value, *$4.25.*

Kiso Three Rivers Flood Control, Cent. A1315

1987, Aug. 7 Photo. *Perf. 13½*
1753 A1315 60y Kiso, Nagara and Ibi Rivers 1.10 .35

Japan — Thailand Diplomatic Relations, Cent. A1316

Design: Temple of the Emerald Buddha and cherry blossoms.

1987, Sept. 26 *Perf. 13*
1754 A1316 60y multicolored 1.10 .35

Intl. Letter Writing Week — A1317

13th World Congress of Certified Public Accountants, Tokyo, Oct. 11-15 — A1318

Dolls by Goyo Hirata: 130y, Gensho Kanto, by Royojo Hori (1898-1984). 150y, Utage-no-Hana (Fair Woman at the Party).

1987, Oct. 6 Photo. *Perf. 13*
1755 A1317 130y multicolored 2.50 1.00
1756 A1317 150y multicolored 2.75 1.10

1987, Oct. 9 *Perf. 13*

Design: Three Beauties (adaptation), by Toyokuni Utagawa (1769-1825).

1757 A1318 60y multicolored 1.10 .35

Modern Waterworks, Cent. — A1319

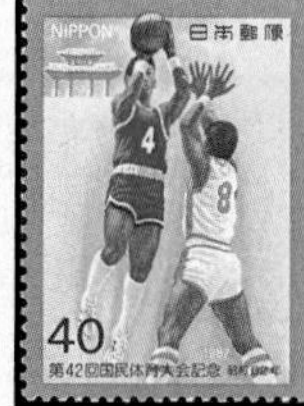

Shurei Gate, Okinawa, Basketball Players — A1320

Design: Lion's head public fountain, 1887, Waterworks Museum, Yokohama.

1987, Oct. 16 Engr.
1758 A1319 60y multicolored 1.10 .35

1987, Oct. 24 Photo.
1759 A1320 40y multicolored .75 .35

42nd Natl. Athletic Meet, Okinawa.

6th World Cong. on Smoking & Health, Nov. 9-12, Tokyo — A1321

World Telecommunications Conf., Nov. 15-18, Tokyo — A1322

1987, Nov. 9
1760 A1321 60y multicolored 1.10 .35

1987, Nov. 13 *Perf. 13½*

Design: Microwave dish antenna at Kashima Station Radio Research Laboratory.

1761 A1322 60y multicolored 1.10 .35

World Conference on Large Historic Cities, Nov. 18-21, Kyoto A1323

Design: Nijo Castle guardhouse roof and Ninomaru Hall, 17th cent.

1987, Nov. 18 *Perf. 13*
1762 A1323 60y multicolored 1.10 .35

Intl. Year of Shelter for the Homeless A1324

Prize-winning illustrations by: 40y, Takahiro Nahahama. 60y, Yoko Sasaki.

1987, Nov. 25
1763 A1324 40y multicolored .75 .35
1764 A1324 60y multicolored 1.10 .35

New Year 1988 (Year of the Dragon) — A1325

Design: Kurashiki papier-mache dragon, 1869, by Tajuro Omizu.

1987, Dec. 1 *Perf. 13x13½*
1765 A1325 40y multicolored .75 .35

Sheets of 2, Nos. 1506, 1765, were lottery prizes. Value, $2.25.

Seikan Tunnel Opening A1326

1988, Mar. 11 Photo. *Perf. 13¼*
1766 A1326 60y ED 79 locomotive, map 1.10 .35
a. Booklet pane of 10 11.00

Opening of Seto-Oohashi Bridge

Kagawa Side
A1327 A1328

Okayama Side
A1329 A1330

1988, Apr. 8 Engr. *Perf. 13½*
1767 A1327 60y multicolored 1.10 .35
1768 A1328 60y multicolored 1.10 .35
1769 A1329 60y multicolored 1.10 .35
1770 A1330 60y multicolored 1.10 .35
a. Strip of 4, #1767-1770 4.50 4.50

Nos. 1767-1768 and 1769-1770 have continuous designs.

Philately Week — A1331

Prints by Kotondo Torii (1900-76): No. 1771, Long Undergarment. No. 1772, Kimono Sash.

1988, Apr. 19 Photo. *Perf. 13*
1771 60y denomination at lower right 1.10 .35
1772 60y denomination at upper left 1.10 .35
a. A1331 Pair, #1771-1772 2.25

Souv. sheet of 2 exists. Value $6.

Silk Road Exposition, Apr. 24-Oct. 23, Nara — A1333

Design: Plectrum guard playing the biwa, detail of Raden-Shitan-no-Gogen-Biwa, a five-panel work of gold lacquer nacre on sandalwood preserved at Shosoin.

1988, Apr. 23 Photo. & Engr.
1773 A1333 60y multicolored 1.10 .35

Natl. Afforestation Campaign A1334

Design: Yahsima, site of the Genji-Heike war, and cuckoo on olive tree branch.

1988, May 20 Photo. *Perf. 13½*
1774 A1334 60y multicolored 1.10 .35

Basho Series, Part II

A1335

A1337

A1339

A1341

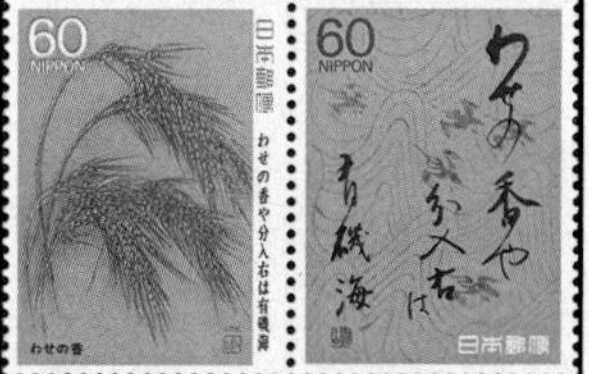

A1343

A1345

A1347

A1349

A1351

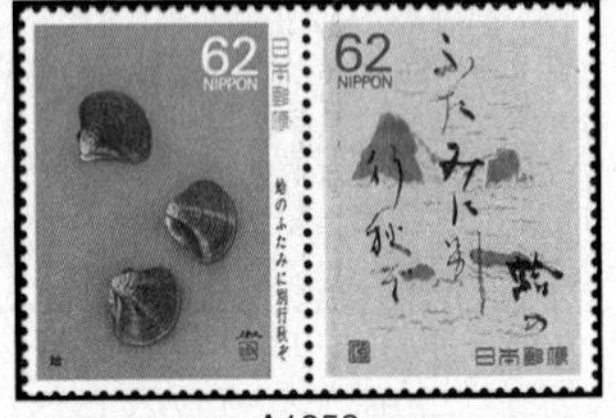

A1353

#1775, Mogami River. #1776, Haiku and flower. #1777, Mt. Gassan. #1778, Haiku and mountain.

1988, May 30 Photo. *Perf. 13x13½*

1775 60y multicolored 1.10 .35
1776 60y multicolored 1.10 .35
a. Souv. sheet of 2, #1775-1776, imperf. ('89) 2.40
b. A1335 Pair, #1775-1776 2.25 1.00
1777 60y multicolored 1.10 .35
1778 60y multicolored 1.10 .35
a. Souv. sheet of 2, #1777-1778, imperf. ('89) 2.40
b. A1337 Pair, #1777-1778 2.25 1.00

1988, Aug. 23

#1779, Mimosa in bloom. #1780, Verse, birds, Kisagata Inlet. #1781, Ocean waves. #1782, Verse and current.

1779 60y multicolored 1.10 .35
1780 60y multicolored 1.10 .35
a. Souv. sheet of 2, #1779-1780, imperf ('89) 2.40
b. A1339 Pair, #1779-1780 2.25 1.00
1781 60y multicolored 1.10 .35
1782 60y multicolored 1.10 .35
a. Souv. sheet of 2, #1781-1782, imperf. ('89) 2.40
b. A1341 Pair, #1781-1782 2.25 1.00

1988, Nov. 11

#1783, Rice. #1784, Birds in flight, haiku. #1785, Sun glow. #1786, Rice, haiku.

1783 60y multicolored 1.10 .35
1784 60y multicolored 1.10 .35
a. Souv. sheet of 2, #1783-1784, imperf. ('89) 2.40
b. A1343 Pair, #1783-1784 2.25 1.00
1785 60y multicolored 1.10 .35
1786 60y multicolored 1.10 .35
a. Souv. sheet of 2, #1785-1786, imperf. ('89) 2.40
b. A1345 Pair, #1785-1786 2.25 1.00

1989, Feb. 13

#1787, Nata-dera Temple. #1788, Haiku, white grass. #1789, Trees. #1790, Haiku, moonlit forest.

1787 60y multicolored 1.10 .35
1788 60y multicolored 1.10 .35
a. Souv. sheet of 2, #1787-1788, imperf. 2.40
b. A1347 Pair, #1787-1788 2.25 1.00
1789 60y multicolored 1.10 .35
1790 60y multicolored 1.10 .35
a. Souv. sheet of 2, #1789-1790, imperf. 2.40
b. A1349 Pair, #1789-1790 2.25 1.00

1989, May 12

#1791, Autumn on the beach. #1792, Haiku. #1793, Clams. #1794, Haiku.

1791 62y multicolored 1.10 .35
1792 62y multicolored 1.10 .35
a. Souv. sheet of 2, #1791-1792, imperf. 2.40
b. A1351 Pair, #1791-1792 2.25 1.00
1793 62y multicolored 1.10 .35
1794 62y multicolored 1.10 .35
a. Souv. sheet of 2, #1793-1794, imperf. 2.40
b. A1353 Pair, #1793-1794 2.25 1.00
Nos. 1791-1794 (4) 4.40 1.40

Haiku from *Oku-no-hosomichi,* "*Narrow Road to a Far Province*," 1694, a travel description written in by Matsuo Munefusa (1644-94), a haiku poet best known by his pen-name Basho.

In each setenant pair, a complete *haiku* by Basho is inscribed vertically at right on the left stamp and in the center of the right stamp. The same poem appears on both stamps in each pair.

Issued: Nos. 1776a-1794a, Aug. 1, 1989.

Intl. Conference on Volcanoes, Kagoshima A1355

1988, July 19 Photo. *Perf. 14*

1795 A1355 60y multicolored 1.10 .35

A1356

A1357

A1358

Letter Writing Day, 10th Anniv. — A1359

Designs and contest-winning children's drawings: No. 1796, Cat and letter. No. 1797, *Crab and Letter,* by Katsuyuki Yamada. No. 1798, Fairy and letter. No. 1799, *Girl and Letter,* by Takashi Ukai.

Photo., Litho. (Nos. 1797, 1799)

1988, July 23 *Perf. 13x13½*

1796 A1356 40y multicolored .75 .50
1796A A1356 40y Imperf., self-adhesive .75 .35
1797 A1357 40y multicolored .75 .35
1798 A1358 60y multicolored 1.10 .70
a. Bklt. pane, 5 each #1796, 1798 9.25

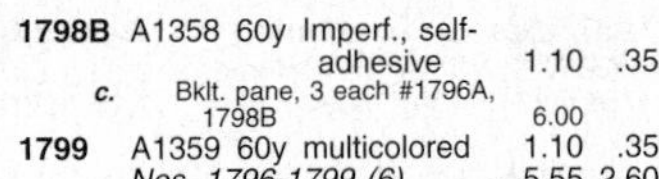

1798B A1358 60y Imperf., self-adhesive 1.10 .35
c. Bklt. pane, 3 each #1796A, 1798B 6.00
1799 A1359 60y multicolored 1.10 .35
Nos. 1796-1799 (6) 5.55 2.60

No. 1798c is adhered to the booklet cover, made of peelable paper, folded in half and rouletted down the center fold, with No. 1796a at left and No. 1798b at right of the roulette.

Sheets of 2 containing Nos. 1796, 1798 were lottery prizes. Value, $5.

15th World Puppetry Festival, July 27-Aug. 11 — A1360

Puppets: No. 1800, *Ohana,* string puppet from the film *Spring and Fall in the Meiji Era,* by Kinosuke Takeda (1923-1979), Japan. No. 1801, Girl, stick puppet from the Natl. Radost Puppet Theater, Brno, Czechoslovakia. No. 1802, Woman, shadow puppet from China. No. 1803, Knight, a marionette from Sicily.

1988, July 27 Photo. *Perf. 13*

1800 60y multicolored 1.10 .35
1801 60y multicolored 1.10 .35
1802 60y multicolored 1.10 .35
1803 60y multicolored 1.10 .35
a. A1360 Block or strip of 4, #1800-1803 3.75 2.50

Japan-China Treaty, 10th Anniv. — A1364

1988, Aug. 12 Photo.

1804 60y Peony 1.10 .35
1805 60y Panda 1.10 .35
a. A1364 Pair, #1804-1805 2.25 1.00

18th World Poultry Congress, Nagoya, Sept. 4-9 — A1366

1988, Sept. 3 *Perf. 13½*

1806 A1366 60y multicolored 1.10 .35

Rehabilitation Intl. 16th World Congress, Tokyo, Sept. 5-9 — A1367

Photo. & Embossed

1988, Sept. 5 *Perf. 13*

1807 A1367 60y multicolored 1.10 .35

A1368 A1369

Prints: 80y, *Kumesaburo Iwai as Chiyo,* by Kunimasa Utagawa (1773-1810), late Edo Period. 120y, *Komazo Ichikawa III as Ganryu Sasaki,* by Toyokuni Utagawa (1769-1825).

1988, Oct. 6 Photo.

1808 A1368 80y multicolored 1.50 .60
1809 A1368 120y multicolored 2.25 1.00

Intl. Letter-Writing Week.

1988, Oct. 14

Design: Gymnast on parallel bars and "Kinkakuji," Temple of the Golden Pavilion.

1810 A1369 40y multicolored .75 .35

43rd Natl. Athletic Meet, Kyoto.

Japan-Mexico Trade Agreement, Cent. A1370

New Year 1989 (Year of the Snake) A1371

1988, Nov. 30 Photo.

1811 A1370 60y multicolored 1.10 .35

1988, Dec. 1

Clay bell snake by Masanobu Ogawa.

1812 A1371 40y multicolored .75 .35

Sheets of two containing Nos. 1506, 1812 were lottery prizes. Value, $2.50.

UN Declaration of Human Rights, 40th Anniv. — A1372

1988, Dec. 5 Litho. *Perf. 13½*

1813 A1372 60y multicolored 1.10 .35

National Treasures Series

Votive Silver Lidded Bowl Used in Todai-ji Temple Ground-Breaking Ceremony, 8th Cent. — A1373

Bronze Yakushi-nyorai Buddha, Asuka Period, 7th Cent. — A1374

Kondo-Sukashibori-Kurakanagu, Bronze Saddle from Ohjin Imperial Mausoleum — A1375

Tamamushi-no-Zushi, Buddhist Altar in Lacquered Cypress from the Asuka Era — A1376

Kin-in, a Gokan Era Gold Seal Given to the King of Na by Emperor Kobutei — A1377

Shinninshaba-gazokyo, a 5th Cent. European Bronze Mirror Back — A1378

Photo., Photo & Engr. (100y)

1989, Jan. 20 *Perf. 13, 13½ (100y)*

1814 A1373 60y multicolored 1.10 .35
1815 A1374 100y multicolored 1.90 .75

1989, June 30

1816 A1375 62y multicolored 1.10 .35
1817 A1376 100y multicolored 1.90 .75

1989, Aug. 15

1818 A1377 62y multicolored 1.10 .35
1819 A1378 100y multicolored 1.90 .75
Nos. 1814-1819 (6) 9.00 3.30

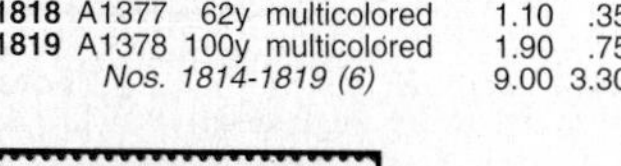

Asian-Pacific Expo, Fukuoka, Mar. 17-Sept. 3 — A1383

1989 **Photo.** *Perf. 13*

1822 A1383 60y multicolored 1.10 .35
1823 A1383 62y multicolored 1.10 .65

Issue dates: 60y, Mar. 16; 62y, Apr. 18.

Yokohama Exposition (Space and Children), Yokohama City, Mar. 25 to Oct. 1 — A1384

Design: Detail of *Russian Lady Sight-seeing at the Port,* by Yoshitora, and entrance to the Yokohama City Art Museum.

1989, Mar. 24 **Litho.**

1824 A1384 60y multicolored 1.10 .35
1825 A1384 62y multicolored 1.10 .35

World Bonsai Convention, Omiya, Apr. 6-9 — A1385

1989, Apr. 6 **Photo.** *Perf. 13*

1826 A1385 62y multicolored 1.10 .35

Awa-odori, by Tsunetomi Kitano (b. 1880) — A1386

1989, Apr. 18 *Perf. 13*

1827 62y multicolored 1.10 .35
1828 62y multicolored 1.10 .35
a. A1386 Pair, #1827-1828 2.25

Philately Week. Sheets of 2 containing #1827-1828 were lottery prizes. Value, $5.

Holland Festival 1989 — A1388

1989, Apr. 19 *Perf. 13½*

1829 A1388 62y Ship 1.10 .35

Fiber-optic Cable, the 3rd Transpacific Line Relay Linking Japan and the US — A1389

1989, May 10 *Perf. 13½x13*

1830 A1389 62y Station tower, map 1.10 .35

Natl. Afforestation Campaign — A1390

1989, May 19 *Perf. 13½*

1831 A1390 62y Bayberry, lime, Mt. Tsurugi 1.10 .35

World Design Exposition, Nagoya, July 15-Nov. 26
A1391 A1392

1989, July 14

1832 A1391 41y multicolored .80 .35
1833 A1392 62y multicolored 1.10 .35

Letter Writing Day
A1393 A1394

1989, July 21 *Perf. 13x13½*

1834 A1393 41y multicolored .80 .35
1835 A1394 62y multicolored 1.10 .35
a. Bklt. pane, 5 each #1834-1835 9.50

Sheets of 2 containing Nos. 1834-1835 were lottery prizes. Value, $3.

Congratulations and Condolences Types of 1982

1989, Aug. 10 **Photo.** *Perf. 13x13½*

1836 A1082 41y Wreath .80 .35
1837 A1083 41y Crane .80 .35
1838 A1083 62y Crane 1.10 .35
1839 A1084 72y Tortoise 1.40 .50
Nos. 1836-1839 (4) 4.10 1.55

6th Interflora World Congress, Tokyo, Aug. 27-30 — A1395

1989, Aug. 25 **Photo.** *Perf. 13½*

1840 A1395 62y multicolored 1.10 .35

Prefecture Issues

Nos. 1841-1990 have been changed to Nos. Z1-Z150. The listings can be found in a new section immediately following the postage section and preceding the semi-postal listings.

Far East and South Pacific Games for the Disabled (FESPIC), Kobe, Sept. 15-20
A1546

1989, Sept. 14 **Photo.** *Perf. 13½*

1991 A1546 62y multicolored 1.10 .35

Okuni Kabuki Screen
A1547 A1548

1989, Sept. 18 *Perf. 13*

1992 A1547 62y multicolored 1.10 .35
1993 A1548 70y multicolored 1.25 .50

EUROPALIA '89, Japan.

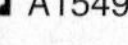

A1549

A1550

Scenes from the Yadorigi and Takekawa Chapters of the Tales of the Genji picture scroll, attributed to Fujiwara-no-Takeyoshi, late Heian Period (897-1185).

1989, Oct. 6 **Photo.** *Perf. 13½*

1994 A1549 80y multicolored 1.50 .60
1995 A1550 120y multicolored 2.25 .75

Intl. Letter Writing Day.

Intl. Conference on Irrigation and Drainage
A1551

100th Tenno Sho Horse Race
A1552

1989, Oct. 13

1996 A1551 62y Rice 1.10 .35

1989, Oct. 27 *Perf. 13*

1997 A1552 62y Jockey riding Shinzan 1.10 .35

9th Hot Air Balloon World Championships, Saga — A1553

1989, Nov. 17 **Photo.** *Perf. 13x13½*

1998 A1553 62y multicolored 1.10 .35

Copyright Control System, 50th Anniv.
A1554

1989, Nov. 17 *Perf. 13*

1999 A1554 62y Conductor 1.10 .35

New Year 1990 (Year of the Horse)
A1555 A1556

1989, Dec. 1 *Perf. 13x13½, 13½*

2000 A1555 41y *Yawata-Uma* festival horse .80 .35
2001 A1556 62y *Kazari-Uma,* Meiji Period 1.10 .35

No. 2001 was sold through Jan. 10, 1990, serving as a lottery ticket.
Sheets of two containing Nos. 1838, 2000 were lottery prizes. Value, $2.

Electric Locomotives

10,000
A1557

Photo. & Engr., Photo.

1990 *Perf. 13*

2002	A1557	62y	shown	1.10	.35
2003	A1557	62y	EF58	1.10	.35
2004	A1557	62y	ED40	1.10	.35
2005	A1557	62y	EH10	1.10	.35
2006	A1557	62y	EF53	1.10	.35
2007	A1557	62y	ED70	1.10	.35
2008	A1557	62y	EF55	1.10	.35
2009	A1557	62y	ED61	1.10	.35
2010	A1557	62y	EF57	1.10	.35
2011	A1557	62y	EF30	1.10	.35
	Nos. 2002-2011 (10)			11.00	3.50

Issued two stamps at a time, the first photo. & engr., the second photo.

Issued: #2002-2003, Jan. 31; #2004-2005, Feb. 28; #2006-2007, Apr. 23; #2008-2009, May 23; #2010-2011, July 18.

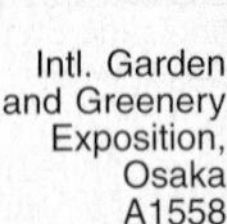

Intl. Garden and Greenery Exposition, Osaka
A1558

1990, Mar. 30 **Photo.** *Perf. 13*
2021 A1558 62y multicolored 1.10 .35

See No. B45.

A1559

A1560

Painting: *Women Gazing at the Stars,* by Chou Ohta.

1990, Apr. 20 **Photo.** *Perf. 13*
2022 A1559 62y multicolored 1.10 .35
a. Souvenir sheet of 1 1.10 .65

Philately Week.

1990, May 18 **Photo.** *Perf. 13½*
2023 A1560 62y Azalea, Mt. Unzen 1.10 .35

Natl. Land Afforestation Campaign.

Flower, Butterfly
A1561

Abstract Art — A1561a

1990, June 1 **Photo.** *Perf. 13*
2024 A1561 62y multicolored 1.10 .35
2025 A1561a 70y multicolored 1.25 .35

Japan-Turkey Relations, Cent. — A1562

1990, June 13
2026 A1562 62y multicolored 1.10 .35

Horses Series

Horse at Stable from Umaya-zu Byobu — A1563

Foals
A1564

Lacquered Saddle, 16th Cent.
A1565

Lacquered Stirrups, 16th Cent.
A1566

Horse by S. Nishiyama
A1567

Kettei
A1568

"Kamo-Kurabeuma-Monyo-Kosode"
A1569

Postal Carriages — A1569a

Inkstone Case "Sano-no-Watashi" — A1570

"Bushu-Senju-zu" by Hokusai — A1571

"Shudan" by Kogetsu Saigo
A1571a

#2027-2031 each show a panel of folding screen with a different horse tied up at a stable.

Perf. 13x13½, 13

1990 **Litho. & Engr.**

Color of Horse

2027	A1563	62y	red brown	1.10	.35
2028	A1563	62y	gray	1.10	.35
2029	A1563	62y	beige	1.10	.35
2030	A1563	62y	tan	1.10	.35
2031	A1563	62y	mottled	1.10	.35
a.	Strip of 5, #2027-2031			5.50	

Photo.

2032 A1564 62y shown 1.10 .35

Photo. & Engr.

2033	A1565	62y	shown	1.10	.35
2034	A1566	62y	shown	1.10	.35
a.	Pair, #2033-2034			2.25	1.00

Photo.

2035	A1567	62y	multicolored	1.10	.35
2036	A1568	62y	multicolored	1.10	.35
2037	A1569	62y	multicolored	1.10	.35

Photo. & Engr., photo. (#2040, 2042)

1991 *Perf. 12½x13*

2038	62y one horse		1.10	.35
2039	62y two horses		1.10	.35
a.	A1569a Pair, #2038-2039		2.25	1.00

Perf. 13½x13

2040	A1570	62y	multicolored	1.10	.35
2041	A1571	62y	multicolored	1.10	.35
2042	A1571a	62y	multicolored	1.10	.35
	Nos. 2027-2042 (16)			17.60	5.60

Issued: #2027-2032, 6/20; #2033-2035, 7/31; #2036-2037, 9/27; #2038-2040, Jan. 31. Nos. 2041-2042, Feb. 28.

38th Intl. Youth Hostel Fed. Conference
A1573

1990, June 25 **Litho.** *Perf. 13*
2057 A1573 62y multicolored 1.10 .35

Letter Writing Day
A1574 A1575

1990, July 23 **Photo.** *Perf. 13½*

2058	A1574	41y	multicolored	.80	.35
2059	A1575	62y	multicolored	1.10	.35
a.	Souv. sheet of 1			1.10	.35
b.	Bklt. pane, 5 ea #2058-2059			9.50	

See No. 2117.

21st Intl. Congress of Mathematicians — A1576

1990, Aug. 17 **Photo.** *Perf. 13*
2060 A1576 62y multicolored 1.10 .35

World Cycling Championships
A1577

1990, Aug. 20 **Litho.** *Perf. 13½*
2061 A1577 62y multicolored 1.10 .35

Ogai Mori, Educator
A1578

1990, Aug. 27 **Photo.**
2062 A1578 62y multicolored 1.10 .35

Intl. Assoc. for Germanic Studies (IVG), 8th Congress.

Character "Ji" in Shape of Rosetta Stone — A1579

1990, Sept. 7 *Perf. 13*
2063 A1579 62y multicolored 1.10 .35

Intl. Literacy Year.

Decade for Natural Disaster Reduction
A1580

1990, Sept. 27 **Photo.**
2064 A1580 62y multicolored 1.10 .35

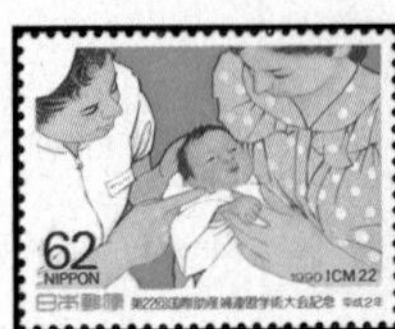
Intl. Confederation of Midwives, 22nd Congress
A1581

1990, Oct. 5 **Photo.**
2065 A1581 62y multicolored 1.10 .35

A1582

"Choju-Jinbutsu-Giga" — A1583

Photo. & Engr.

1990, Oct. 5 *Perf. 13½*

2066 A1582 80y multicolored 1.50 .60
2067 A1583 120y multicolored 2.25 .75

Intl. Letter Writing Week.

"Fumizukai-zu" by Harunobu Suiendo A1584

1990, Oct. 16 **Photo.**

2068 A1584 100y multicolored 1.90 .75
a. Souv. sheet of 1 1.90 1.00

No. 2068a exists with surcharge which paid admission to PHILANIPPON '91. These were not sold by the post office.

Court System, Cent. — A1585

1990, Nov. 1 **Photo.** *Perf. 13x13½*

2069 A1585 62y "Justice" 1.10 .35

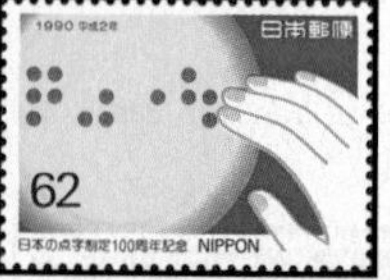

Japanese Braille, Cent. A1586

Photo & Embossed

1990, Nov. 1 *Perf. 13½*

2070 A1586 62y multicolored 1.10 .35

Enthronement of Akihito — A1587

#2071, Chinese phoenix depicted on Emperor's chair. #2072, Diamond pattern for costume worn at banquet ceremony.

1990, Nov. 9 **Photo.** *Perf. 13*

2071 A1587 62y multicolored 1.10 .35
2072 A1587 62y multicolored 1.10 .35
a. Souv. sheet of 2, #2071-2072 2.25 1.10

Japanese Diet, Cent. — A1588

1990, Nov. 29 **Litho.**

2073 A1588 62y multicolored 1.10 .35

New Year 1991 (Year of the Sheep)

A1589 A1590

1990, Dec. 3 **Photo.** *Perf. 13x13½*

2074 A1589 41y multicolored .80 .35

Photo. & Engr.

Perf. 13½

2075 A1590 41y multicolored .80 .45
2076 A1590 62y multi, diff. 1.10 .45
Nos. 2074-2076 (3) 2.70 1.25

Sheets of 2 No. 2074 were lottery prizes. Value, $1.50.

Dr. Yoshio Nishina, Physicist — A1591

Telephone Service, Cent. — A1592

1990, Dec. 6 **Photo.** *Perf. 13*

2077 A1591 62y multicolored 1.10 .35

Use of radio isotopes in Japan, 50th anniv.

1990, Dec. 14

2078 A1592 62y multicolored 1.10 .35

A1593 A1594

1991, Mar. 1 **Photo.** *Perf. 13½*

2079 A1593 41y Figure skating .80 .35

Perf. 13½x13

2080 A1593 62y Speed skating, horiz. 1.10 .35

1991 Winter Universiade.

1991, Apr. 1 **Photo.** *Perf. 13*

2081 A1594 62y multicolored 1.10 .35

Postal Life Insurance System.

Philately Week

A1595 A1596

#2082, Beauty Looking Back by Moronobu. #2083, Opening Dance by Shuho Yamakawa.

1991, Apr. 19

2082 A1595 62y multicolored 1.10 .35
2083 A1596 62y multicolored 1.10 .35
a. Souv. sheet of 2, #2082-2083 1.90 1.10
b. Pair, #2082-2083 1.90 1.10

Postal Service, 120th anniv.

Pairs of Nos. 2082-2083 with label between are available from sheets of 20.

A1597 A1598

1991, Apr. 19 *Perf. 13½*

2084 A1597 62y multicolored 1.10 .35

Ceramic World Shigaraki '91.

1991, May 24 **Photo.** *Perf. 13½*

2085 A1598 41y multicolored .80 .35

Natl. Land Afforestation Campaign.

Standard Datum of Leveling, Cent. — A1599

1991, May 30 **Photo.** *Perf. 13*

2086 A1599m 62y mutlicolored 1.10 .35

Int'l Stamp Design Contest Winning Entries

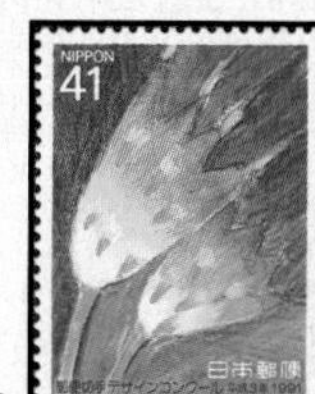

A1600

A1601

A1601a

A1601b

1991, May 31 **Photo.** *Perf. 13*

2087 A1600 41y Flowers .80 .35
2088 A1601 62y Couple in Ethnic Dress 1.10 .35
2089 A1601a 70y World peace 1.25 .50
2090 A1601b 100y Butterfly 1.90 .70
Nos. 2087-2090 (4) 5.05 1.90

Int'l. Stamp Design Contest winning entries.

Kabuki Series

Kagamijishi A1602

Yaegakihime A1603

Koshiro Matsumoto VII A1604

Danjuro Ichikawa XI A1605

Baigyoku Nakamura III A1606

Ganjiro Nakamura II A1607

Kichiemon Nakamura I — A1608

Nizaemon Kataoka XIII — A1609

Enjaku Jitsukawa II A1610

Hakuo Matsumoto I A1611

Fuji-Musume A1612

Kotobuki-Soganotaimen — A1613

Perf. 13 (62y), 13½ (100y)

1991-92 Photo.

2091	A1602	62y	dp bl grn & gold	1.10	.35
2092	A1603	100y	multicolored	1.90	.70
2093	A1604	62y	multicolored	1.10	.35
2094	A1605	100y	multicolored	1.90	.70
2095	A1606	62y	multicolored	1.10	.35
2096	A1607	100y	multicolored	1.90	.70
2097	A1608	62y	multicolored	1.10	.35
2098	A1609	100y	multicolored	1.90	.70
2099	A1610	62y	multicolored	1.10	.35
2100	A1611	100y	multicolored	1.90	.70
2101	A1612	62y	multicolored	1.10	.35
2102	A1613	100y	multicolored	1.90	.70
	Nos. 2091-2102 (12)			18.00	6.30

Issued: #2091-2092, 6/28; #2093-2094, 9/27; #2095-2096, 11/20; #2097-2098, 2/20/92; #2099-2100, 4/10/92; #2101-2102, 6/30/92.

Waterbird Series

Gallinago Hardwickii (Latham's Snipe) A1614

1991-93 Photo. *Perf. 13½*

2103	A1614	62y	shown	1.10	.35
2104	A1614	62y	Sula leucogaster	1.10	.35
2105	A1614	62y	Larus crassirostris	1.10	.35
2106	A1614	62y	Podiceps ruficollis	1.10	.35
2107	A1614	62y	Lunda cirrhata	1.10	.35
2108	A1614	62y	Grus monacha	1.10	.35
2109	A1614	62y	Cygnus cygnus	1.10	.35
2110	A1614	62y	Rostratula benghalensis	1.10	.35
2111	A1614	62y	Calonectris leucomelas	1.10	.35
2112	A1614	62y	Halcyon coromanda	1.10	.35
2113	A1614	62y	Alcedo atthis	1.10	.35
2114	A1614	62y	Bubulcus ibis	1.10	.35
	Nos. 2103-2114 (12)			13.20	4.20

#2103-2104 printed in blocks of 12 with gutter between in sheet of 24.

Issued: #2103-2104, 6/28; #2105-2106, 9/27; #2107-2108, 1/30/92; #2109-2110, 3/25/92; #2111-2112, 8/31/92; #2113-2114, 1/29/93.

See Nos. 2192-2195.

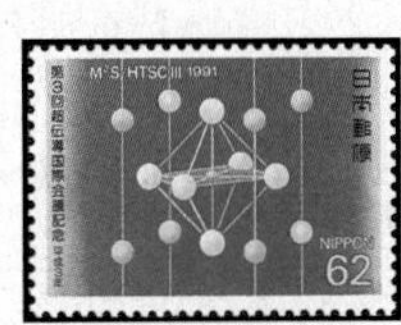

Intl. Conf. on Superconductivity — A1620

1991, July 19 Litho. *Perf. 13½*

2115	A1620	62y	multicolored	1.10	.35

Type of Letter Writing Day of 1990 and

A1621

1991, July 23 Photo. *Perf. 13x13½*

2116	A1621	41y	multicolored	.80	.35
2117	A1575	62y	multicolored	1.10	.35
a.			Souvenir sheet of 1	1.10	.70
b.			Bklt. pane, 5 each #2116-2117	9.50	

Nos. 2117, 2117a have light blue frameline and inscription and violet denomination.

3rd IAAF World Track & Field Championships, Tokyo — A1622

1991, Aug. 23 *Perf. 13*

2118	A1622	41y	High jump	.80	.35
2119	A1622	62y	Shot put	1.10	.35

Intl. Symposium on Environmental Change and Geographical Information Systems — A1623

1991, Aug. 23

2120	A1623	62y	multicolored	1.10	.35

Intl. Letter Writing Week A1624

Bandainagon-emaki picture scroll probably by Mitsunaga Tokiwa: 80y, Crowd of people. 120y, People, house.

Photo. & Engr.

1991, Oct. 7 *Perf. 13½*

2121	A1624	80y	multicolored	1.50	.60
2122	A1624	120y	multicolored	2.25	1.00

A1625

A1627

A1628

62y, Breezy Fine Weather by Hokusai.

1991, Oct. 8 Photo. *Perf. 13*

2123	A1625	62y	multicolored	1.10	.35

Summit Conf. on Earthquake and Natural Disasters Countermeasures.

A1626

1991, Oct. 31 Litho. *Perf. 13*

2124	A1626	62y	multicolored	1.10	.35

Japanese Green Tea, 800th anniv.

Koshaku-Musume by Kunisada Utagawa.

Photo. & Engr.

1991, Nov. 15 *Perf. 13*

2125	A1627	62y	multicolored	1.10	.35
a.			Sheet of 2	2.25	1.60

World Stamp Exhibition, Nippon '91.

1991, Nov. 20 Photo.

2126	A1628	62y	multicolored	1.10	.35

Administrative Counselors System, 30th anniv.

A1629

A1630

New Year 1992 (Year of the Monkey)

A1631 A1632

1991, Dec. 2 Photo. *Perf. 13½*

2127	A1629	41y	multicolored	.80	.45
2128	A1630	62y	multicolored	1.10	.45
2129	A1631	41y	+3y, multi	.85	.55
2130	A1632	62y	+3y, multi	1.25	.55
	Nos. 2127-2130 (4)			4.00	2.00

Sheets of 2 #2127 were lottery prizes.

8th Conference on Intl. Trade in Endangered Species (CITES) A1633

1992, Mar. 2 Photo. *Perf. 13*

2131	A1633	62y	multicolored	1.10	.35

A1634

A1635

Flowers on the Chair, by Hoshun Yamaguchi.

1992, Apr. 20

2132	A1634	62y	multicolored	1.10	.35

Philately Week.

1992, May 15

2133	A1635	62y	multicolored	1.10	.35

Return of Ryukyu Islands to Japan, 20th anniv.

Intl. Space Year — A1636

1992, July 7 Photo. *Perf. 13*

2134		62y	satellite at left	1.10	.35
2135		62y	space station upper right	1.10	.35
a.	A1636		Pair, #2134-2135	2.25	1.56

Letter Writing Day

A1638 A1639

1992, July 23 *Perf. 13x13½*

2136	A1638	41y	multicolored	.80	.35

Perf. 13½

2137 A1639 62y multicolored 1.10 .35
a. Souvenir sheet of 1 1.10 .75
b. Bklt. pane, 5 each #2136-2137 9.50

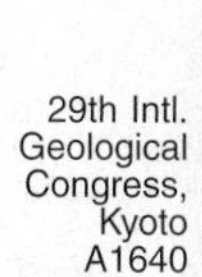

29th Intl. Geological Congress, Kyoto A1640

1992, Aug. 24 Photo. *Perf. 13½x13*
2138 A1640 62y multicolored 1.10 .35

47th Natl. Athletic Meet, Yamagata Prefecture — A1641

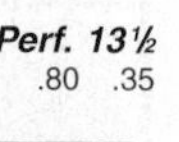

1992, Sept. 4 *Perf. 13½*
2139 A1641 41y multicolored .80 .35

Normalization of Japanese-Chinese Relations, 20th Anniv. — A1642

Photo. & Engr.

1992, Sept. 29 *Perf. 13*
2140 62y jug 1.10 .35
2141 62y long-neck jar 1.10 .35
a. A1642 Pair, #2140-2141 2.25 1.00

Intl. Letter Writing Week — A1644

Heiji picture scroll: 80y, Nobles, servants in carriages by Taikenmon gate. 120y, Fujiwara-no Nobuyori seated before samurai.

Photo. & Engr.

1992, Oct. 6 *Perf. 13½*
2142 A1644 80y multicolored 1.50 .75
2143 A1644 120y multicolored 2.25 1.00

Cat and Birds A1644a

Design: 70y, Santa Claus, snow scene.

Perf. 13½x13, 13x13½

1992, Oct. 9 Photo.
2144 A1644a 62y multicolored 1.10 .35
2145 A1644a 70y multicolored 1.25 .50

Winners of Third Postage Stamp Design contest.

30th Congress of Intl. Cooperative Alliance, Tokyo — A1644b

1992, Oct. 27 *Perf. 13x13½*
2146 A1644b 62y multicolored 1.10 .35

A1645 A1646

Cultural Pioneers: No. 2147, Takakazu Seki (1642?-1708), mathematician. No. 2148, Akiko Yosano (1878-1942), poet.

Photo. & Engr.

1992, Nov. 4 *Perf. 13*
2147 A1645 62y multicolored 1.10 .35
2148 A1645 62y multicolored 1.10 .35

See Nos. 2217-2219, 2642, 2717-2718.

1992, Nov. 9 Photo. *Perf. 13x13½*
2149 A1646 62y multicolored 1.10 .35

Certified Public Tax Accountant System, 50th anniv.

A1647 A1648

New Year 1993 (Year of the Rooster)

A1649 A1650

1992, Nov. 16 *Perf. 13x13½*
2150 A1647 41y multicolored .80 .35
2151 A1648 62y multicolored 1.10 .35
a. Souvenir sheet of 2, #2150-2151 2.00 1.10

Perf. 13½

2152 A1649 41y +3y multi .85 .45
2153 A1650 62y +3y multi 1.25 .45
Nos. 2150-2153 (4) 4.00 1.60

Surtax on Nos. 2152-2153 for lottery.

Flora and Fauna — A1651

1992-94 Photo. *Perf. 13x13½*
2154 A1651 9y Dragonfly .20 .20
2155 A1651 15y Swallowtail .30 .20
2156 A1651 18y Ladybug .35 .20
2157 A1651 41y Mandarin duck .80 .35
2158 A1651 50y Japanese white-eye .95 .45
2159 A1651 62y Rufous turtle dove 1.10 .20
a. Bklt. pane, 5 ea #2157, 2159 9.50
b. Booklet pane of 10 11.00
2160 A1651 72y Varied tit 1.40 .60
2161 A1651 80y Pied kingfisher 1.50 .20
a. Miniature sheet, 5 #2158, 10 #2161 + 3 labels *40.00*
2162 A1651 90y Spotbill duck 1.75 .80
2163 A1651 130y Bullfinch 2.50 1.25
2164 A1651 190y Fringed orchid 3.75 1.90
2165 A1651 270y Wild pink 5.00 2.25
2166 A1651 350y Adder's tongue lily 6.50 3.00
2167 A1651 420y Japanese iris 8.00 3.75
2167A A1651 430y Violet 8.25 4.00
Nos. 2154-2167A (15) 42.35 19.35

Coil Stamps

Perf. 13 Horiz.

2168 A1651 50y like #2156 .95 .45
2169 A1651 80y like #2161 1.50 .70

Booklet Stamps

Self-Adhesive

Die Cut

2170 A1651 41y like #2157 .80 .35
2171 A1651 50y like #2158 .95 .45
2172 A1651 62y like #2159 1.10 .50
a. Bklt. pane, 2 #2170, 4 #2172 5.50
2173 A1651 80y like #2161 1.50 .70
a. Bklt. pane, 4 #2171, 4 #2173 10.00

Issued: 41y, 62y, 72y, 11/30/92; 9y, 18y, #2158, 2161, 90y, 1/13/94; 270y, 350y, 420y, 1/24/94; 15y, 130y, 190y, 430y, 4/25/94.

Nos. 2172a, 2173a are adhered to the booklet cover, made of peelable paper, folded in half and rouletted down the center fold.

See Nos. 2475-2482, 2488B.

World Alpine Skiing Championships, Morioka-Shizukuishi — A1657

1993, Feb. 3 Photo. *Perf. 13*
2174 A1657 41y shown .80 .40
2175 A1657 62y Skier, diff. 1.10 .55

Seasonal Flowers Series

Poppy A1658

Cherry Blossoms A1659

Lily — A1660

Thistle — A1661

Chinese Bellflowers A1662

Chrysanthemums A1663

Plum Blossom A1664

Winter Camellia A1665

Perf. 13½ (41y, 50y), 13 (62y, 80y)

1993-94 Photo.
2176 A1658 41y multicolored .80 .35

Perf. 13

2177 A1659 62y multicolored 1.10 .35
2178 A1660 41y multicolored .80 .35

Perf. 13

2179 A1661 62y multicolored 1.10 .35
2180 A1662 41y multicolored .80 .35
2181 A1663 62y multicolored 1.10 .35
2182 A1664 50y multicolored .95 .35
2183 A1665 80y multicolored 1.50 .70
Nos. 2176-2183 (8) 8.15 3.15

Issued: #2176-2177, 3/12; #2178-2179, 6/18; #2180-2181, 9/16; #2182-2183, 1/28/94.

Waterbird Type

1993 Photo. *Perf. 13½*
2192 A1614 62y Grus vipio 1.10 .35
2193 A1614 62y Ansner albifrons 1.10 .35
2194 A1614 62y Anas formosa 1.25 .35
2195 A1614 62y Haliaeetus albicilla 1.25 .35
Nos. 2192-2195 (4) 4.70 1.40

Issued: #2192-2193, 3/31; #2194-2195, 5/25.

Philately Week A1674

Natl. Land Afforestation Campaign A1675

Painting: In the Studio, by Nampu Katayama.

1993, Apr. 20 Photo. *Perf. 13*
2196 A1674 62y multicolored 1.10 .35

1993, Apr. 23 *Perf. 13½*
2197 A1675 41y multicolored .80 .35

Mandarin Duck in the Nest — A1676

Gardenia in the Nest — A1677

Design: 70y, Mandarin Duck and Gardenia emblems, horiz.

1993, June 8 Photo. *Perf. 13*
2198 A1676 62y multicolored 1.25 .35
2199 A1677 62y multicolored 1.25 .35
a. Pair, #2198-2199 2.50 1.25
2200 A1676 70y multicolored 1.25 .50
Nos. 2198-2200 (3) 3.75 1.20

Royal Wedding of Crown Prince Naruhito and Masako Owada.

5th Meeting of Signatories to Ramsar, Iran Convention on Wetlands and Waterfowl Habitats
A1678

1993, June 10 Photo. *Perf. 13½*

2201 A1678 62y Crane with young 1.25 .35
2202 A1678 62y Crane's head 1.25 .35
a. Pair, #2201-2202 2.50 1.25

Commercial Registration System, Cent. — A1679

1993, July 1 Photo. *Perf. 13x13½*

2203 A1679 62y multicolored 1.25 .35

Letter Writing Day
A1680 A1681

1993, July 23 *Perf. 13x13½*

2204 A1680 41y multicolored .80 .35

Perf. 13½x13

2205 A1681 62y multicolored 1.25 .35
a. Souvenir sheet of 1 1.25 .75
b. Booklet pane, 5 each #2204-2205 10.00

15th Intl. Botanical Congress, Tokyo
A1682

Designs: No. 2206, Glaucidium palmatum. No. 2207, Sciadopitys verticillata.

1993, Aug. 23 Photo. *Perf. 13½x13*

2206 A1682 62y multicolored 1.25 .35
2207 A1682 62y multicolored 1.25 .35
a. Pair, #2206-2207 2.50 1.25

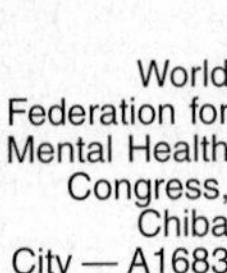

World Federation for Mental Health Congress, Chiba City — A1683

1993, Aug. 23 *Perf. 13½x13*

2208 A1683 62y multicolored 1.25 .35

A1684 A1685

1993, Sept. 3 Photo. *Perf. 13½*

2209 A1684 41y Swimming .80 .35
2210 A1684 41y Karate .80 .35
a. Pair, #2209-2210 1.60 .80

48th natl. athletic meet, Kagawa Prefecture.

1993, Sept. 22 Photo. *Perf. 13*

Japanese-Portuguese Relations, 450th Anniv.: No. 2211, Arrival of Portuguese, folding screen, c. 1560-1630. No. 2212, Mother-of-Pearl Host Box, Jesuit symbols and grape motif.

2211 A1685 62y multicolored 1.25 .35
2212 A1685 62y multicolored 1.25 .35
a. Pair, #2211-2212 2.50 1.25

Intl. Letter Writing Week
A1686

Portraits from Picture Scrolls of the Thirty-Six Immortal Poets: 80y, Ki no Tsurayuki. 120y, Kodai no Kimi.

1993, Oct. 6 *Perf. 13½*

2213 A1686 80y multicolored 1.50 .75
2214 A1686 120y multicolored 2.50 1.00

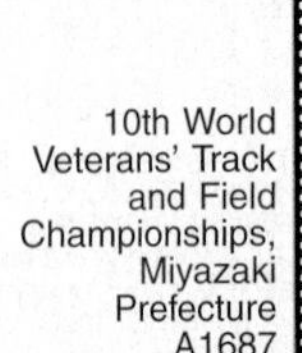

10th World Veterans' Track and Field Championships, Miyazaki Prefecture
A1687

1993, Oct. 7 *Perf. 14*

2215 A1687 62y multicolored 1.25 .35

Souvenir Sheet

Wedding of Crown Prince Naruhito and Princess Masako — A1688

1993, Oct. 13 Photo. *Perf. 13½*

2216 A1688 62y multicolored 1.25 .35

Cultural Pioneers Type of 1992

#2217, Kazan Watanabe (1793-1841), artist. #2218, Umetaro Suzuki (1874-1943), chemist. #2219, Toson Shimazaki (1872-1943), poet.

1993, Nov. 4 Photo. *Perf. 13*

2217 A1645 62y multicolored 1.10 .35

Photo. & Engr.

2218 A1645 62y multicolored 1.10 .35
2219 A1645 62y multicolored 1.10 .35
Nos. 2217-2219 (3) 3.30 1.05

Agricultural Research Center, Cent. — A1689

1993, Nov. 17 *Perf. 13½*

2220 A1689 62y multicolored 1.10 .35

A1690

A1691

New Year 1994 (Year of the Dog)
A1692 A1693

1993, Nov. 17 *Perf. 13x13½*

2221 A1690 41y multicolored .80 .35
2222 A1691 62y multicolored 1.10 .35

Perf. 13½

2223 A1692 41y +3y multi .80 .40
2224 A1693 62y +3y multi 1.25 .40
Nos. 2221-2224 (4) 3.95 1.50

Sheets of 2, Nos. 2221-2222, were lottery prizes. Value, $2.25.

Declaration of Human Rights, 45th Anniv. — A1694

Designs: 62y, Man with bird perched on head. 70y, Globe, dove, person breaking chains, peace symbol.

1993, Dec. 10 Photo. *Perf. 13*

2225 A1694 62y multicolored 1.25 .35
2226 A1694 70y multicolored 1.40 .70

Congratulations and Condolences Types of 1982

1994, Mar. 10 Photo. *Perf. 13x13½*

2227 A1082 50y Wreath .95 .35
2228 A1083 50y Crane .95 .35
2229 A1083 80y Crane 1.50 .40
2230 A1084 90y Tortoise 1.75 .50
Nos. 2227-2230 (4) 5.15 1.60

For use on condolence and greeting cards.

1994 World Figure Skating Championships, Tokyo — A1695

1994, Mar. 17 Photo. *Perf. 13*

2231 A1695 50y Ice dancing .95 .35
2232 A1695 50y Women's singles .95 .35
a. Pair, #2231-2232 2.00 1.00
2233 A1695 80y Men's singles, vert. 1.50 .40
2234 A1695 80y Pairs, vert. 1.50 .40
a. Pair, #2233-2234 3.00 1.50
Nos. 2231-2234 (4) 4.90 1.50

Philately Week — A1696

1994, Apr. 20 Photo. *Perf. 13*

2235 A1696 80y Irises 1.50 .40

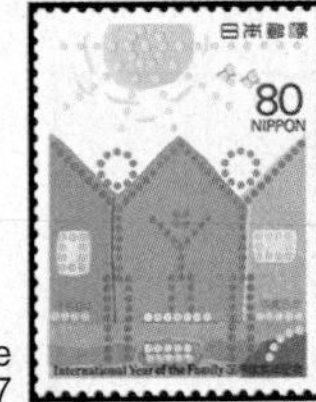

Intl. Year of the Family — A1697

Natl. Land Afforestation Campaign
A1698

Designs: No. 2236, "Love" spelled by people. No. 2237, Faces in flowers. No. 2238, Sun shining on people, homes. No. 2239, Family flying inside bird.

1994, May 13 Photo. *Perf. 13*

2236 A1697 50y multicolored 1.00 .35
2237 A1697 50y multicolored 1.00 .35
2238 A1697 80y multicolored 1.50 .40
a. Pair, #2236, 2238 2.50 1.25
2239 A1697 80y multicolored 1.50 .40
a. Pair, #2237, 2239 2.50 1.25
Nos. 2236-2239 (4) 5.00 1.50

1994, May 20

2240 A1698 50y multicolored 1.00 .35

Intl. Conference on Natural Disaster Reduction
A1699

1994, May 23

2241 A1699 80y multicolored 1.50 .40

No. 2241 printed in sheets of 16 with 4 labels.

A1700 A1701

1994, May 24

2242 A1700 80y multicolored 1.50 .40

Prototype Fast Breeder Reactor, Monju.

1994, June 3 Photo. *Perf. 13*

2243 A1701 80y multicolored 1.50 .40

Environment day.

Letter Writing Day
A1702 A1703

1994, July 22

2244 A1702 50y multicolored 1.00 .35
2245 A1703 80y multicolored 1.50 .40
a. Souvenir sheet of 1 1.50 .75
b. Bklt. pane, 5 each #2244-2245 12.50

Prefecture Issues

Nos. 2246-2400B have been changed to #Z151-Z307. The listings can be found in a new section immediately following the postage section and preceding the semi-postal listings.

10th Intl. Conference on AIDS, Yokohama — A1859

1994, Aug. 5 Photo. *Perf. 13*

2401 A1859 80y multicolored 1.50 .40

Postal History Series

A1860 A1861

A1862

A1863

A1864

First Japanese stamps (Baron Hisoka Maejima and): No. 2402, #1. No. 2403, #2. No. 2404, #3. No. 2405, #4.

CTO's exist for Nos. 2402-2405. They read "Japan" between two arcs in a corner.

Photo. & Engr.

1994, Aug. 10 *Perf. 13*

2402 A1860 80y brown & black 1.50 .40
2403 A1860 80y blue & black 1.50 .40
2404 A1860 80y ver & black 1.50 .40
2405 A1860 80y olive grn & blk 1.50 .40
a. Strip of 4, #2402-2405 6.00 6.00

Photo. & Engr.

1994, Nov. 18 *Perf. 13½*

Early Japanese stamps (Edoardo Chiossone and): No. 2406, #55. No. 2407, Type A16. No. 2408, #63. No. 2409, #65.

2406 A1861 80y buff, slate & blk 1.50 .40
2407 A1861 80y gray & dk brown 1.50 .40
2408 A1861 80y gray lilac & rose 1.50 .40
2409 A1861 80y lt blue & dk blue 1.50 .40
a. Strip of 4, #2406-2409 6.00 6.00

Photo. & Engr.

1995, Jan. 25 *Perf. 13½*

Designs: No. 2410, #85, transporting mail by ricksha. No. 2411, #86, transporting mail by horse-drawn carriage.

2410 A1862 80y multicolored 1.50 .40
2411 A1862 80y multicolored 1.50 .40
Nos. 2402-2411 (10) 15.00 4.00

Photo. & Engr.

1995, May 25 *Perf. 13½*

Designs: No. 2412, #C3, First Osaka-Tokyo airmail flight. No. 2413, #C6, Workers loading freight onto airplane.

2412 A1863 110y multicolored 2.50 .60
2413 A1863 110y multicolored 2.50 .60

Nos. 2412-2413 printed in blocks of 10 with gutter between in sheets of 20.

Photo. & Engr.

1995, Sept. 19 *Perf. 13½*

#2414, Light mail van, #436. #2415, Cherub commemorative mail box, #428. #2416, Mail box, #435. #2417, Van, #433.

2414 A1864 80y multicolored 1.50 .40
2415 A1864 80y multicolored 1.50 .40
2416 A1864 80y multicolored 1.50 .40
2417 A1864 80y multicolored 1.50 .40
a. Block of 4, #2414-2417 6.00 6.00

Postal History Series
Types of 1948-49 With "NIPPON" Inscribed at Bottom

Photo. & Engr.

1996, June 3 *Perf. 13½*

Size: 22x47mm

2418 A206 80y like #422, brown 1.50 .40
2419 A206 80y like #422, multi 1.50 .40
2420 A247 80y like #479, purple 1.50 .40
2421 A247 80y like #479, multi 1.50 .40
a. Strip of 4, #2418-2421 6.00 6.00

Opening of Kansai Intl. Airport — A1877

Designs: No. 2422, Airport, part of plane's vertical stabilizer. No. 2423, Aft section of airplane. No. 2424, Airport, jet.

1994, Sept. 2 Photo. *Perf. 13*

2422 A1877 80y multicolored 1.50 .40
2423 A1877 80y multicolored 1.50 .40
a. Vert. pair, #2422-2423 3.00 3.00
b. Vert. strip of 3, #2422-2424 4.50 4.50
2424 A1877 80y multicolored 1.50 .40
Nos. 2422-2424 (3) 4.50 1.20

A1878 A1879

1994, Sept. 19

2425 A1878 80y multicolored 1.40 .40

ITU Plenipotentiary Conference, Kyoto.

1994, Sept. 30

2426 A1879 50y Kick volleyball 1.00 .35
2427 A1879 80y Steeplechase 1.50 .40
2428 A1879 80y Synchronized swimming 1.50 .40
a. Pair, #2427-2428 3.00 1.75
Nos. 2426-2428 (3) 4.00 1.15

12th Asian Games, Hiroshima.

Intl. Letter Writing Week A1880

Screen paintings of popular indoor games, Momoyama, Edo periods: 90y, Sugoroku. 110y, Japanese chess. 130y, Go.

1994, Oct. 6 Photo. *Perf. 13x13½*

2429 A1880 90y multicolored 1.75 .75
2430 A1880 110y multicolored 2.10 .75
2431 A1880 130y multicolored 2.50 .75
Nos. 2429-2431 (3) 6.35 2.25

49th Natl. Athletic Meet, Aichi Prefecture — A1881

1994, Oct. 28 *Perf. 13½*

2432 A1881 50y multicolored 1.00 .35

A1882

1994, Nov. 4 Photo. *Perf. 13*

2433 A1882 80y multicolored 1.50 .40

Intl. Diabetes Federation, 15th Congress, Kobe.

Cultural Pioneers Type of 1992
Photo. & Engr.

1994, Nov. 4

Cultural pioneers: No. 2434, Michio Miyagi (1894-1956), Musician. No. 2435, Gyoshu Hayami (1894-1935), artist.

2434 A1645 80y multicolored 1.50 .40
2435 A1645 80y multicolored 1.50 .40

Heiankyo (Kyoto), 1200th Anniv.
A1884 A1885

Kanpuzu, by Hideyori Kano, Momoyama period depicts autumn scene on Kiyotakigawa River: No. 2436, People seated, white birds. No. 2437, Bridge, people. No. 2438, Bridge, birds flying. No. 2439, People, Jingoji Temple, Atago-Jinja Shrine. No. 2440, People seated, tree.

No. 2441, Painting of Dry Garden (Sekitei), Ryoanji Temple, by Eizo Kato. No. 2442, Painting of artificial pond, Shugakuin Rikyu, by Kanji Kawai, horiz.

1994, Nov. 8 Photo. *Perf. 13x13½*

2436 A1884 80y multicolored 1.50 .40
2437 A1884 80y multicolored 1.50 .40
2438 A1884 80y multicolored 1.50 .40
2439 A1884 80y multicolored 1.50 .40
2440 A1884 80y multicolored 1.50 .40
a. Strip of 5, #2436-2440 7.50 7.50
2441 A1885 80y multicolored 1.50 .40

Perf. 13½x13

2442 A1885 80y multicolored 1.50 .40
Nos. 2436-2442 (7) 10.50 2.80

A1886 A1887

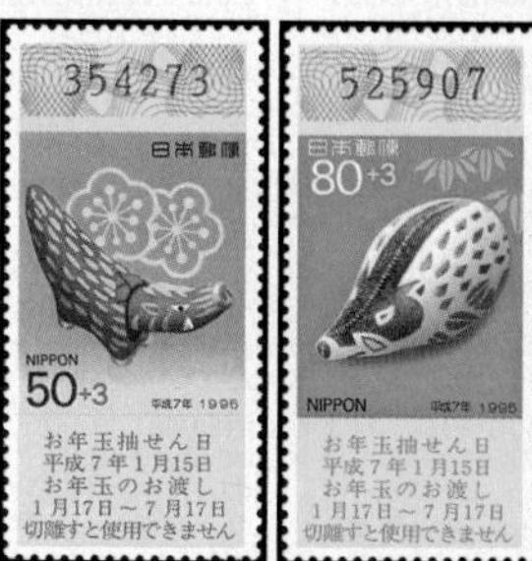

New Year 1995 (Year of the Boar)
A1888 A1889

1994, Nov. 15 *Perf. 13x13½*

2443 A1886 50y multicolored 1.00 .35
2444 A1887 80y multicolored 1.50 .40

Perf. 13½

2445 A1888 50y +3y multi 1.10 .40
2446 A1889 80y +3y multi 1.60 .50
Nos. 2443-2446 (4) 5.20 1.65

World Heritage Series

Himeji Castle
A1890 A1891

A1892

Horyuji Temple
A1893

Cryptomeria Japonica
A1894

Cervus Nippon Yakushimae
A1895

Virgin Beech Forest
A1896

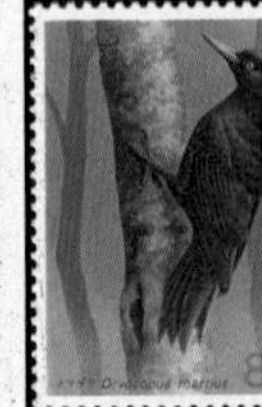
Black Woodpecker
A1897

1994, Dec. 14 Photo. *Perf. 13*

2447 A1890 80y multicolored 1.50 .40
2448 A1891 80y multicolored 1.50 .40

1995, Feb. 22

Designs: 80y, Goddess Kannon from inner temple wall. 110y, Temple exterior.

2449 A1892 80y multicolored 1.50 .40
2450 A1893 110y multicolored 2.25 .75

1995, July 28

2451 A1894 80y multicolored 1.50 .40
2452 A1895 80y multicolored 1.50 .40

1995, Nov. 21 Photo. *Perf. 13*

2453 A1896 80y multicolored 1.50 .40
2454 A1897 80y multicolored 1.50 .40
Nos. 2447-2454 (8) 12.75 3.55

Japan-Brazil Friendship, Cent.
A1898

Designs: No. 2455, Natl. emblems, flowers. No. 2456, Soccer players.

1995, Mar. 3 Photo. *Perf. 13½*

2455 A1898 80y multicolored 1.50 .40
2456 A1898 80y multicolored 1.50 .40

A1899

Fujiwara-Kyo Palace, 1300th Anniv. — A1900

Designs: 50y, Unebiyama, Nijozan Mountains, roofing tile from palace. 80y, Portrait of a Woman, in Asuka and Hakuho era style, by Okada, 1925.

1995, Mar. 28

2457 A1899 50y multicolored 1.00 .35
2458 A1900 80y multicolored 1.50 .40

Modern Anatomical Education
A1901

1995, Mar. 31 *Perf. 13*

2459 A1901 80y multicolored 1.50 .40

A1902

A1903

1995, Apr. 12 Photo. *Perf. 13*

2460 A1902 80y multicolored 1.50 .40

1995 Census.

1995, Apr. 20

2461 A1903 80y multicolored 1.50 .40

Japanese Overseas Cooperation Volunteers, 30th anniv.

A1904

A1905

A1906

A1907

A1908

1995, Apr. 25 *Perf. 13x13½*

2462 A1904 50y multicolored 1.00 .35
2463 A1905 50y multicolored 1.00 .35
2464 A1906 80y multicolored 1.50 .40
2465 A1907 80y multicolored 1.50 .40
2466 A1908 90y multicolored 2.00 .75
Nos. 2462-2466 (5) 7.00 2.25

For use on condolence and greeting cards.

A1909

A1910

1995, May 19 Photo. *Perf. 13½x13*

2467 A1909 50y multicolored 1.00 .35

Natl. land afforestation campaign.

1995, June 1 *Die Cut Perf. 13½*

Greetings: No. 2468, Rainbow, hearts. No. 2469, Girl holding heart-shaped balloon. No. 2470, Flower holding pencil, sign. No. 2471, Star, sun, moon as flowers, fauna. No. 2472, Person, dog with flowers, butterfly in hair.

Self-Adhesive

2468 A1910 80y multicolored 1.50 .40
2469 A1910 80y multicolored 1.50 .40
2470 A1910 80y multicolored 1.50 .40
2471 A1910 80y multicolored 1.50 .40
2472 A1910 80y multicolored 1.50 .40
a. Miniature sheet, #2468-2472 + 5 labels 7.50

Letter Writing Day
A1911 A1912

1995, July 21 Photo. *Perf. 13½*

2473 A1911 50y multicolored 1.00 .35
2474 A1912 80y multicolored 1.50 .40
a. Souvenir sheet of 1 1.50 .75
b. Bklt. pane, 5 ea #2473-2474 12.50
Complete booklet, #2474b 12.50

Flora & Fauna Type of 1992 and

Shikikacho-zu
A1926

Matsutaka-Zu
A1926a

10y, Scarab, dandelions. 20y, Honey bee, flower. 30y, Hairstreak, flowers. 70y, Great tit. 110y, Plover. 120y, Shrike. 140y, Japanese grosbeak. 160y, Jay. 390y, Dayflower.

1995-98 Photo. *Perf. 13½*

2475 A1651 10y multi .20 .20
2476 A1651 20y multi .40 .25
2477 A1651 30y multi .60 .35
2478 A1651 70y multi 1.25 .90
2479 A1651 110y multi 2.10 1.40
2480 A1651 120y multi 2.25 1.40
2481 A1651 140y multi 2.50 1.60
2482 A1651 160y multi 3.00 1.90

Perf. 13x13½

2483 A1651 390y multi 7.50 5.25

Perf. 13½

2484 A1926 700y multi 15.00 11.50

Photo. & Engr.

2485 A1926a 1000y multi 19.00 14.50

Self-Adhesive

Die Cut Perf. 13x13½

2486 A1651 50y Like #2158 .75 .60
2487 A1651 80y Like #2161 1.25 .35

Coil Stamp

Perf. 13 Horiz.

2488 A1651 10y like #2475 .20 .20
Nos. 2475-2488 (14) 56.00 40.40

Issued: 700y, 7/4/95; 390y, 1000y, 3/28/96; 70y, 110y, 7/22/97; #2475, 20y, 30y, 11/28/97; 120y, 140y, 2/16/98 160y, 2/23/98; #2488, 9/11/98. Nos. 2486-2487, 3/25/02.

Nos. 2486 and 2487 were issued in panes of 10.

End of World War II, 50th Anniv.
A1937 A1938

Design: No. 2491, Children holding hands behind stained glass window, peace dove, earth from space.

1995, Aug. 1 Photo. *Perf. 13*

2489 A1937 50y multicolored 1.00 .35
2490 A1938 80y multicolored 1.50 .40
2491 A1938 80y multicolored 1.50 .40
Nos. 2489-2491 (3) 4.00 1.15

A1939

A1940

1995, Aug. 23

2492 A1939 80y multicolored 1.50 .40

18th Universiade, Fukuoka.

1995, Aug. 25

50y, Radio controlled plane, transmitter. 80y, Radio controlled helicopter, competitor, assistant.

2493 A1940 50y multicolored 1.00 .35
2494 A1940 80y multicolored 1.50 .40

1995 Aeromodel World Championships, Okayama Prefecture.

World Veterinary Congress, Yokohama
A1941

World Sports Championships
A1942

1995, Sept. 1 Photo. *Perf. 13*

2495 A1941 80y Dog, cow & horse 1.50 .40

1995, Sept. 28

#2496, 1995 World Judo Championships, Chiba Prefecture. #2497, 1995 World Gymnastics Championships, Sabae, Fuku Prefecture.

1995, Sept. 28

2496 A1942 80y multicolored 1.50 .40
2497 A1942 80y multicolored 1.50 .40

Letter Writing Week A1943

Screen paintings: 90y, Shell-matching game. 110y, Battledore and shuttlecock. 130y, Playing cards.

1995, Oct. 6 *Perf. 13½*

2498 A1943 90y multicolored 1.75 .75
2499 A1943 110y multicolored 2.10 .75
2500 A1943 130y multicolored 2.50 .75
Nos. 2498-2500 (3) 6.35 2.25

A1944 A1945

1995, Oct. 13 *Perf. 13x13½*

2501 A1944 50y multicolored 1.00 .35

50th Natl. athletic meet, Fukushima prefecture.

1995, Oct. 24 *Perf. 13*

2502 A1945 80y UN, hearts 1.50 .40
2503 A1945 80y UNESCO, children 1.50 .40

UN, UNESCO, 50th anniv.

Cultural Pioneers Type of 1992

#2504, Tadataka Ino (1745-1818), cartographer. #2505, Kitaro Nishida (1870-1945), philosopher.

Photo. & Engr.

1995, Nov. 6 *Perf. 13*

2504 A1645 80y multicolored 1.50 .40
2505 A1645 80y multicolored 1.50 .40

A1947 A1948

New Year 1996 (Year of the Rat)
A1949 A1950

1995, Oct. 15 **Photo.** *Perf. 13x13½*

2506 A1947 50y multicolored 1.00 .35
2507 A1948 80y multicolored 1.50 .40

Perf. 13½

2508 A1949 50y +3y multi 1.10 .40
2509 A1950 80y +3y multi 1.60 .45
Nos. 2506-2509 (4) 5.20 1.60

Japanese-Korean Diplomatic Relations, 30th Anniv. — A1951

1995, Dec. 18 *Perf. 13*

2510 A1951 80y multicolored 1.50 .40

Nos. 2511-2512 are unassigned.

A1952 A1953

1996, Feb. 16 **Photo.** *Perf. 13*

2513 A1952 80y multicolored 1.50 .40

Philipp Franz von Siebold (1796-1866), naturalist.

1996, Mar. 1

2514 A1953 80y multicolored 1.50 .40

Labor Relations Commissions, 50th anniv.

Senior Citizens — A1954

1996, Mar. 21 *Perf. 13½*

2515 A1954 80y multicolored 1.50 .40

No. 2515 issued in sheets of 5.

50th Postwar Memorial Year
A1955 A1956

#2516, Crowd, Emperor's limosine approaching Diet. #2517, Prime Minister Yoshida signing Peace Treaty, San Francisco, 9/8/51. #2518, Women performing traditional Okinawan dance.

1996, Apr. 1 **Photo.** *Perf. 13*

2516 A1955 80y multicolored 1.50 .40
2517 A1955 80y multicolored 1.50 .40
a. Pair, Nos. 2516-2517 3.00 1.50
2518 A1956 80y multicolored 1.50 .40
Nos. 2516-2518 (3) 4.50 1.20

Promulgation of the the Constitution, 11/7/46 (#2517a). Return of Okinawa, 5/15/72 (#2518).

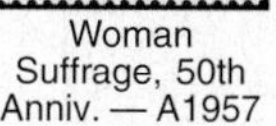

Woman Suffrage, 50th Anniv. — A1957

Philately Week — A1958

1996, Apr. 10 *Perf. 13½*

2519 A1957 80y multicolored 1.50 .40

1996, Apr. 19 *Perf. 13*

2520 A1958 80y multicolored 1.50 .40

UNICEF, 50th Anniv. — A1959

Child Welfare Week, 50th Anniv. — A1960

1996, May 1 **Photo.** *Perf. 13*

2521 A1959 80y multicolored 1.50 .40

1996, May 1

2522 A1960 80y multicolored 1.50 .40

Bird Week, 50th Anniv. — A1961

1996, May 10

2523 80y Birds 1.50 .40
2524 80y Field Glasses 1.50 .40
a. A1961 Pair, #2523-2524 3.00 1.75

Natl. Afforestation Campaign — A1963

1996, May 17

2525 A1963 50y multicolored .95 .35

50th Postwar Memorial Year
A1964 A1965

#2526, 1964 Olympic Games, Tokyo. #2527, Japan Intl. Exposition.

1996, June 24 **Photo.** *Perf. 13*

2526 A1964 80y multicolored 1.50 .40
2527 A1965 80y multicolored 1.50 .40

River Administration System, Cent. — A1966

1996, July 5 **Photo.** *Perf. 13½*

2528 80y denomination lower right 1.50 .40
2529 80y denomination lower left 1.50 .40
a. A1966 Pair, #2528-2529 3.00 1.75

A1968

Marine Day's Establishment A1969

1996, July 19

2530 A1968 50y multicolored .95 .35
2531 A1969 80y multicolored 1.50 .40

Letter Writing Day
A1970 A1971

1996, July 23

2532 A1970 50y multicolored .95 .35
2533 A1971 80y multicolored 1.50 .40
a. Souvenir sheet of 1 1.50 .75
b. Bklt. pane, 5 ea #2532-2533 11.50
Complete booklet 11.50

Cultural Pioneers Type of 1992

No. 2534, Kenji Miyazaw (1896-1933). No. 2535, Hokiichi Hanawa (1746-1821).

Photo. & Engr.

1996, Aug. 27 *Perf. 13*

2534 A1645 80y multicolored 1.50 .40
2535 A1645 80y multicolored 1.50 .40

A1974 A1975

Designs: No. 2536, Advances of women in society, diffusion of home electrical products. No. 2537, Modern highway, railway systems.

1996, Aug. 27 **Photo.** *Perf. 13*

2536 A1974 80y multicolored 1.50 .40
2537 A1975 80y multicolored 1.50 .40

51st Natl. Athletic Meet — A1976

Community Chest, 50th Anniv. — A1977

1996, Sept. 6 Photo. *Perf. 13½*
2538 A1976 50y Archery .95 .35

1996, Sept. 30
2539 A1977 80y multicolored 1.50 .40

Intl. Music Day — A1978

1996, Oct. 1 *Perf. 13*
2540 A1978 80y multicolored 1.50 .40

A1979

Intl. Letter Writing Week A1980

Paintings: #2541, Water wheel, Mt. Fuji. #2542, Flowers. #2543, Mt. Fuji in Clear Weather (Red Fuji), by Hokusai. #2544, Flowers, diff. #2545, Mt. Fuji, lake. #2546, Flowers, diff.

1996, Oct. 7 *Perf. 13½*

2541	A1979	90y multicolored	1.75	.75
2542	A1980	90y multicolored	1.75	.75
a.		Pair, #2541-2542	3.50	1.75
2543	A1979	110y multicolored	2.10	.75
2544	A1980	110y multicolored	2.10	.75
a.		Pair, #2543-2544	4.25	2.00
2545	A1979	130y multicolored	2.50	.75
2546	A1980	130y multicolored	2.50	.75
a.		Pair, #2545-2546	5.00	2.25
		Nos. 2541-2546 (6)	12.70	4.50

18th World Congress of Savings Banks — A1981

1996, Oct. 23 *Perf. 13*
2547 A1981 80y multicolored 1.50 .40

50th Postwar Memorial Year
A1982 A1983

#2548, Earth from space. #2549, Cellular telephone, fiber optic cable, satellite in orbit.

1996, Nov. 8 Photo. *Perf. 13*
2548 A1982 80y multicolored 1.50 .40
2549 A1983 80y multicolored 1.50 .40

A1984 A1985

New Year 1997 (Year of the Ox)
A1986 A1987

1996, Nov. 15 Photo. *Perf. 13x13½*
2550 A1984 50y multicolored .95 .35
2551 A1985 80y multicolored 1.50 .40

Perf. 13½

2552 A1986 50y +3y multi 1.00 .40
2553 A1987 80y +3y multi 1.60 .50
Nos. 2550-2553 (4) 5.05 1.65

Sheets of 2 containing Nos. 2550-2551 were lottery prizes. Value $3.

Yujiro Ishihara, Actor — A1988

Hibari Misora, Entertainer — A1990

Osamu Tezuka, Cartoonist — A1992

1997, Jan. 28 Photo. *Perf. 13*

2554		80y multicolored	1.50	.40
2555		80y multicolored	1.50	.40
a.	A1988	Pair, #2554-2555	3.00	1.75
2556		80y multicolored	1.50	.40
2557		80y multicolored	1.50	.40
a.	A1990	Pair, #2556-2557	3.00	1.75
2558		80y multicolored	1.50	.40
2559		80y multicolored	1.50	.40
a.	A1992	Pair, #2558-2559	3.00	1.75
		Nos. 2554-2559 (6)	9.00	2.40

Sparrow, Rice Plant, Camellia A1994

Sparrow, Maple, Camellia A1995

Perf. 14 Horiz. Syncopated Type A

1997, Apr. 10 Photo.

2560	A1994	50y multi	1.00	.35
2560A	A1994	80y multi	1.50	.40
2560B	A1994	90y multi	1.75	.50
2560C	A1994	120y multi	2.25	.60
2560D	A1994	130y multi	*25.00*	*12.50*
2561	A1995	270y multi	5.00	2.00
		Nos. 2560-2561 (6)	36.50	16.35

Denominations of Nos. 2560-2561 were printed by machine at point of sale, and were limited to the denominations listed.

Daigo, by Okumura Dogyu (1889-1990) A1996

1997, Apr. 18 Litho. *Perf. 13½*
2562 A1996 80y multicolored 1.50 .40

Philately Week.

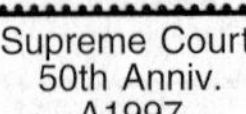

Supreme Court, 50th Anniv. A1997

Doraemon A1998

1997, May 2 Photo. *Perf. 13*
2563 A1997 80y Main court room 1.50 .40

Serpentine Die Cut 13½

1997, May 2

Designs: No. 2564, Shown. No. 2565, With envelope. No. 2566, Standing on hand. No. 2567, With propeller. No. 2568, In love.

Self-Adhesive
Booklet Stamps

2564	A1998	80y multicolored	1.50	.40
2565	A1998	80y multicolored	1.50	.40
2566	A1998	80y multicolored	1.50	.40
2567	A1998	80y multicolored	1.50	.40
2568	A1998	80y multicolored	1.50	.40
a.		Pane of 5, #2564-2568	7.50	

Japanese Migration to Mexico, Cent. — A1999

1997, May 12 *Perf. 13*
2569 A1999 80y multicolored 1.50 .40

See Mexico No. 2035.

A2000

A2001

1997, May 16 *Perf. 13½*
2570 A2000 50y Miyagi bush clover .95 .35

Natl. afforestation campaign.

1997, May 20 *Perf. 13*
2571 A2001 80y Natl. Diet 1.50 .40

Natl. House of Councilors, 50th anniv.

A2002 A2003

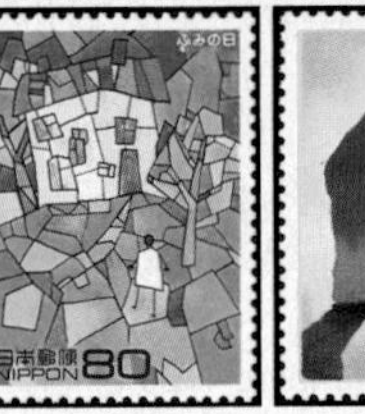

A2004 A2005

Letter Writing Day

1997, July 23 Photo. *Perf. 13*

2572	A2002	50y multicolored	.95	.35
2573	A2003	70y multicolored	1.25	.45
2574	A2004	80y multicolored	1.50	.40
a.		Souvenir sheet of 1	1.50	.40
b.		Bklt. pane, 5 ea #2572, 2574	12.50	
		Complete booklet, #2574b	12.50	
2575	A2005	90y multicolored	1.75	.50
		Nos. 2572-2575 (4)	5.45	1.70

A2006 A2007

1997, Aug. 11 Photo. *Perf. 13*
2576 A2006 50y multicolored .95 .35

Part-time and correspondence education at upper secondary schools, 50th anniv.

1997, Sept. 1
2577 A2007 80y multicolored 1.50 .40

Labor Standards Law, 50th anniv.

Friendship Between Japan and Chile, Cent. A2008

52nd Natl. Sports Festival A2009

1997, Sept. 1 *Perf. 13½*

2578 A2008 80y multicolored 1.50 .40

See Chile No. 1217.

1997, Sept. 12

2579 A2009 50y multicolored .95 .35

Intl. Letter Writing Week A2010

Paintings of Tokaido's 53 Stations by Hiroshige: No. 2580, Hodogaya (bridge over waterway). No. 2582, Kameyama snow-covered mountain slope).

No. 2584, Sumida Riverbank Snowscape (woman in traditional attire beside river), by Hiroshige

From Scrolls of Flowers and Birds of the Four Seasons by Hoitsu Sakai: No. 2581, Bird on tree. No. 2583, Leaves and berries. No. 2585, Bird on tree branch of blossoms.

1997, Oct. 6 **Photo.** *Perf. 13½*

2580	A2010	90y multicolored	1.75	.50
2581	A2010	90y multicolored	1.75	.50
a.		Pair, #2580-2581	3.50	1.75
2582	A2010	110y multicolored	2.10	.60
2583	A2010	110y multicolored	2.10	.60
a.		Pair, #2582-2583	4.25	1.75
2584	A2010	130y multicolored	2.50	.70
2585	A2010	130y multicolored	2.50	.70
a.		Pair, #2584-2585	5.00	1.75
		Nos. 2580-2585 (6)	12.70	3.60

Grand Opening of the Natl. Theater of Tokyo — A2011

1997, Oct. 9 *Perf. 13*

2586 A2011 80y multicolored 1.50 .40

Favorite Songs

A2012 A2013

50y Departure on a Fine Day, by Tanimura Shinji. 80y, Desert Under the Moon, by Kato Masao & Sakasi Suguru.

1997, Oct. 24

2587 A2012 50y multicolored .95 .35

2588 A2013 80y multicolored 1.50 .40

Cultural Pioneers Type of 1992

#2589, Rohan Kouda (1867-1947), writer. #2590, Ando Hiroshige (1797-1858), artist.

1997, Nov. 4

2589 A1645 80y multicolored 1.50 .40

2590 A1645 80y multicolored 1.50 .40

A2016 A2017

New Year 1997 (Year of the Tiger)

A2018 A2019

1997, Nov. 14 *Perf. 13x13½*

2591 A2016 50y multicolored .95 .35

2592 A2017 80y multicolored 1.50 .40

Perf. 13½

2593 A2018 50y +3y multi .95 .40

2594 A2019 80y +3y multi 1.50 .50

Sheets of two containing Nos. 2591-2592 were lottery prizes. Value $2.50.

Return of Okinawa to Japan, 25th Anniv. — A2020

1997, Nov. 21 *Perf. 13*

2595 A2020 80y multicolored 1.50 .40

Shibuya Family's House A2021

Tomizawa Family's House A2022

Photo. & Engr.

1997, Nov. 28 *Perf. 13½*

2596 A2021 80y multicolored 1.50 .40

2597 A2022 80y multicolored 1.50 .40

A2023 A2024

Woodprints: No. 2598, Mother Sea. No. 2599, Mother Earth.

1997, Dec. 1 **Photo.** *Perf. 13*

2598 A2023 80y multicolored 1.50 .40

2599 A2023 80y multicolored 1.50 .40

a. Pair, #2598-2599 3.00 1.90

3rd Conference of the Parties to the UN Framework Convention on Climate Change, Kyoto.

1997, Dec. 2

2600 A2024 80y multicolored 1.50 .40

Agricultural Insurance System, 50th anniv.

Favorite Songs

A2025 A2026

A2027 A2028

1997, Dec. 8

2601 A2025 50y Sunayama .95 .35

2602 A2026 80y Jingle Bells 1.50 .40

1998, Jan. 26 **Photo.** *Perf. 13*

2603 A2027 50y Shabondama .95 .35

2604 A2028 80y Kitaguni no Haru 1.50 .40

1998 Winter Olympic & Paralympic Games, Nagano

A2029 A2030

Paralympic logo and: No. 2605, Glaucidium palmatum. No. 2606, Ice hockey.

Olympic rings and: No. 2607: a, Gentiana nipponica. b, Caltha palustris. c, Fritillaria camtschatcensis. d, Paeonia japonica. e, Erythronium japonicum. f, Snowboarding. g, Curling. h, Speed skating. i, Cross-country skiing. j, Downhill skiing.

1998, Feb. 5

2605	A2029	50y multicolored	.95	.35
2606	A2030	80y multicolored	1.50	.40
a.		Pair, #2605-2606	2.50	1.00
2607		Sheet of 10	12.50	12.50
a.-e.		A2029 50y Any single	.95	.35
f.-j.		A2030 80y Any single	1.50	.40

Historic Houses

A2031

A2032

Photo. & Engr.

1998, Feb. 23 *Perf. 13½*

2608 A2031 80y multicolored 1.50 .40

2609 A2032 80y multicolored 1.50 .40

Japanese Fire Service, 50th Anniv. — A2033

1998, Mar. 6 **Photo.** *Perf. 13*

2610 80y multicolored 1.50 .40

2611 80y multicolored 1.50 .40

a. A2033 Pair, #2610-2611 3.00 1.25

Favorite Songs

A2035 A2036

1998 **Photo.** *Perf. 13*

2612 A2035 50y Medaka-no-Gakko .95 .35

2613 A2036 80y Aoi Sanmyaku 1.50 .40

Issued: 50y, 3/23; 80y, 3/16.

Greetings Stamps — A2037

Designs: a, Puppy. b, Kitten. c, Parakeets. d, Pansies. e, Bunny.

1998, Mar. 13 **Photo.** *Die Cut*

Self-Adhesive

2614 Sheet of 5 7.50

a.-e. A2037 80y any single 1.50 .40

Philately Week — A2038

"Poppies," by Kokei Kobayashi (1883-1957).

1998, Apr. 17 *Perf. 13½*

2615 A2038 80y multicolored 1.50 .40

1998 Year of France in Japan A2039

"Liberty Leading the People," by Delacroix.

1998, Apr. 28 *Perf. 13½*

2616 A2039 110y multicolored 2.10 .75

Natl. Afforestation Campaign — A2040

1998, May 8

2617 A2040 50y Trout, Renge azalea .95 .35

Favorite Songs

A2041 A2042

Designs: 50y, "Wild Roses," by Franz Schubert. 80y, "Hill Abloom with Tangerine Flowers," by Minoru Uminuma and Shogo Kato.

1998, May 25 ***Perf. 13***

2618 A2041 50y multicolored .95 .35
2619 A2042 80y multicolored 1.50 .40

Historic Houses

Kowata Residence A2043

Kamihaga Residence A2044

Photo. & Engr.

1998, June 22 ***Perf. 13½***

2620 A2043 80y multicolored 1.50 .40
2621 A2044 80y multicolored 1.50 .40

Favorite Songs

A2045 A2046

50y, Kono Michi, "This Road." 80y, Ware Wa Umino Ko, "I'm a Boy of the Sea."

1998, July 6 **Photo.** ***Perf. 13***

2622 A2045 50y multicolored .95 .35
2623 A2046 80y multicolored 1.50 .40

Letter Writing Day — A2047

Stylized drawings of children: #2624, Child writing letter. #2625, Child wearing glasses, letter on table. #2626, Child with ink pen, flowers overhead. #2627, Child with ink pen, dove overhead. #2628, Children holding letters, envelopes.

1998, July 23 ***Perf. 13***

2624 A2047 50y multi .95 .35
2625 A2047 50y multi .95 .35
a. Pair, #2624-2625 1.90 .75
2626 A2047 80y multi 1.50 .40
2627 A2047 80y multi 1.50 .40
2628 A2047 80y multi, horiz. 1.50 .40
a. Souvenir sheet of 1 1.50 .40
b. Sheet, 4 each #2626-2627, 2 #2628 15.00 15.00
c. Bklt. pane, 2 ea #2624-2628 13.00 13.00
Complete booklet, #2628c 13.00

See Nos. 2682-2686, 2738-2742, 2779-2783, 2824-2828. See Nos. 2733h-2733j for self-adhesive stamps.

Historic Houses

Kamio Residence A2048

Nakamura Residence A2049

Photo. & Engr.

1998, Aug. 24 ***Perf. 13½***

2629 A2048 80y multicolored 1.50 .40
2630 A2049 80y multicolored 1.50 .40

53rd Natl. Sports Festival, Kanagawa — A2050

1998, Sept. 11 **Photo.** ***Perf. 13½***

2631 A2050 50y multicolored .95 .35

Intl. Letter Writing Week, Greetings — A2051

Details or complete paintings by Jakuchu Ito: #2632, "Birds & Autumn Maple." #2633, "Parakeet in Oak Tree." #2634, "Mandarin Ducks in the Snow." #2635, "Golden Pheasant & Bamboo in Snow." #2636, "Leafy Peonies & Butterflies." #2637, "Parakeet in Rose Bush."

1998, Oct. 6 **Photo.** ***Perf. 13½***

2632 A2051 90y multicolored 1.75 .50
2633 A2051 90y multicolored 1.75 .50
a. Pair, #2632-2633 3.50 1.75
2634 A2051 110y multicolored 2.10 .60
2635 A2051 110y multicolored 2.10 .60
a. Pair, #2634-2635 4.25 1.75
2636 A2051 130y multicolored 2.50 .70
2637 A2051 130y multicolored 2.50 .70
a. Pair, #2636-2637 5.00 1.75
Nos. 2632-2637 (6) 12.70 3.60

Nos. 2632, 2634, 2636 are from "Plants and Animals" and are inscribed for Intl. Letter Writing Week. Nos. 2633, 2635, 2637 are from "Painted Woodcuts of Flowers and Birds."

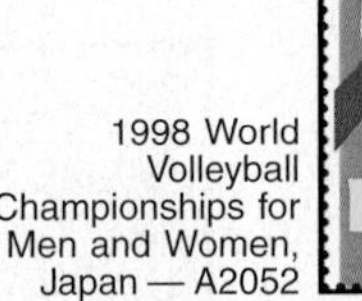

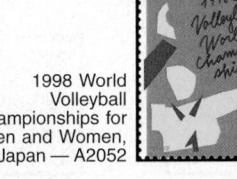

1998 World Volleyball Championships for Men and Women, Japan — A2052

1998, Nov. 2 ***Perf. 13***

2638 A2052 80y Serve 1.50 .40
2639 A2052 80y Receive 1.50 .40
2640 A2052 80y Set & spike 1.50 .40
2641 A2052 80y Block 1.50 .40
a. Strip of 4, #2638-2641 6.00 6.00

Cultural Pioneer Type of 1992 and

Yoshie Fujiwara(1898-1976) — A2053

No. 2642, Bakin Takizawa (1767-1848).

Photo. & Engr.

1998, Nov. 4 ***Perf. 13***

2642 A1645 80y multicolored 1.50 .40
2643 A2053 80y multicolored 1.50 .40

See #2719, 2747-2748, 2839-2840.

A2054 A2055

New Year 1999 (Year of the Rabbit)

A2056 A2057

1998, Nov. 13 **Photo.** ***Perf. 13x13½***

2644 A2054 50y multicolored .95 .35
2645 A2055 80y multicolored 1.50 .40

Perf. 13½x13

2646 A2056 50y +3y multi 1.10 .40
2647 A2057 80y +3y multi 1.60 .50

See No. 2655.

Favorite Songs

A2058 A2059

50y, The Apple Song. 80y, Toys Cha-Cha-Cha at Night.

1998, Nov. 24 ***Perf. 13x13½***

2648 A2058 50y multicolored .95 .35
2649 A2059 80y multicolored 1.50 .40

Japan-Argentina Friendship Treaty, Cent. — A2060

1998, Dec. 2 **Photo.** ***Perf. 13***

2650 A2060 80y multicolored 1.50 .40

A2061 A2062

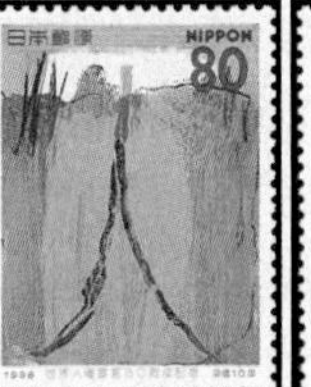

Universal Declaration of Human Rights, 50th Anniv.

A2063 A2064

1998, Dec. 10

2651 A2061 50y multicolored .95 .35
2652 A2062 70y multicolored 1.25 .45
2653 A2063 80y multicolored 1.50 .40
2654 A2064 90y multicolored 1.75 .75
Nos. 2651-2654 (4) 5.45 1.95

Greetings Types of 1951, 1962, 1986 and 1998

1998, Dec. 15 **Photo.** ***Perf. 13x13½***

2655 50y Sheet of 8, 2 each #a.-c., 2644 7.75 7.75
a. A281 rose pink, like #522 .95 .70
b. A483 multi, like #773 .95 .70
c. A1273 multi, like #1708 .95 .70

Favorite Songs

A2065 A2066

50y, Flowing Like a River. 80y, Song of the Four Seasons.

1999, Jan. 26 **Photo.** ***Perf. 13***

2656 A2065 50y multicolored .95 .35
2657 A2066 80y multicolored 1.50 .40

Traditional Houses

Iwase Family House, Gokayama District A2067

Gassho-Zukuri Houses, Shirakawa-mura District — A2068

Gassho-Zukuri House — A2069

Photo. & Engr.

1999, Feb. 16 *Perf. 13½*

2658 A2067 80y multicolored 1.50 .40
2659 A2068 80y multicolored 1.50 .40
2660 A2069 80y multicolored 1.50 .40
a. Pair, #2659-2660 3.00 1.50
Nos. 2658-2660 (3) 4.50 1.20

Rakugo (Comic Storytellers) Stamps

Kokontei Shinshou V — A2070

Katsura Bunraku VIII — A2071

Sanyutei Enshou VI — A2072

Yanagiya Kosan V — A2073

Katsura Beichou III — A2074

1999, Mar. 12 Photo. *Perf. 13*

2661 A2070 80y multicolored 1.50 .40
2662 A2071 80y multicolored 1.50 .40
2663 A2072 80y multicolored 1.50 .40
2664 A2073 80y multicolored 1.50 .40
2665 A2074 80y multicolored 1.50 .40
a. Sheet, 2 each #2661-2665 15.00 15.00

Favorite Songs

Sukiyaki Song A2075

Soushunfu A2076

1999, Mar. 16

2666 A2075 50y multicolored .95 .35
2667 A2076 80y multicolored 1.50 .40

Greetings Stamps — A2077

a, Kitten, daisies. b, Checks, flowers, roses. c, Tartan, puppy. d, Flowers, brown rabbit. e, Gray and white rabbit, moon and stars.

1999, Mar. 23 *Die Cut*

Self-Adhesive

2668 Sheet of 5 7.50
a.-e. A2077 80y Any single 1.50 .40

25th General Assembly of Japan Medical Congress A2078

1999, Apr. 2 *Perf. 13*

2669 A2078 80y multicolored 1.50 .40

Philately Week — A2079

Rabbits Playing in the Field in Spring, by Doumoto Inshou (1891-1975): No. 2670, Three rabbits. No. 2671, Two rabbits.

1999, Apr. 20 *Perf. 13½*

2670 80y three rabbits 1.50 .40
2671 80y Two rabbits 1.50 .40
a. A2079 Pair, #2670-2671 3.00 1.50

No. 2671a is a continuous design.

A2080

A2081

1999, May 18 Photo. *Perf. 13*

2672 A2080 80y multicolored 1.50 .40

Japanese migration to Peru, cent.

1999, May 28 *Perf. 13¼*

2673 A2081 50y multicolored .95 .35

Natl. afforestation campaign.

A2082

A2083

Painting: Ruins of Tholos, by Masayuki Murai.

1999, June 1 Photo. *Perf. 13*

2674 A2082 80y multicolored 1.50 .40

Japanese-Greek Treaty of Commerce & Navigation, cent.

1999, June 3

2675 A2083 80y multicolored 1.50 .40

Japanese emigration to Bolivia, cent.

Land Improvement System, 50th Anniv. — A2084

Family Court, 50th Anniv. — A2085

1999, June 4

2676 A2084 80y multicolored 1.50 .40

1999, June 16

2677 A2085 80y multicolored 1.50 .40

Patent Attorney System in Japan, Cent. — A2086

1999, July 1 Photo. *Perf. 13*

2678 A2086 80y multicolored 1.50 .40

A2087

A2088

1999, July 1

2679 A2087 80y multicolored 1.50 .40

Japanese Community-Based Treatment of Offenders System, 50th anniv.

1999, July 19

Enforcement of Civil and Commercial Codes, Cent.: Masaakira Tomii (1858-1935), Kenjiro Ume (1860-1910) and Nobushige Hozumi (1856-1926), drafters of Civil and Commerical Codes.

2680 A2088 80y multicolored 1.50 .40

Copyright System in Japan, Cent. — A2089

1999, July 22

2681 A2089 80y multicolored 1.50 .40

Letter Writing Day Type of 1998

Stylized drawings of children and toys: No. 2682, Boy and clown, letter. No. 2683, Teddy bear seated on pencil. No. 2684, Girl, ink pen. No. 2685, Clown with yellow hat, jumping up out of envelope.

No. 2686: a, Giraffes. b, Kite, bird, horiz. c, Boy holding kite string. d, Girl with pencil and paper. e, Bunny and bear. f, Boy blowing trumpet. g, Girl playing cello. h, Girl in red. i, Girl in yellow holding envelope. j, Three ducks.

1999, July 23 Photo. *Perf. 13*

2682 A2047 50y multicolored .95 .35
2683 A2047 50y multicolored .95 .35
2684 A2047 50y multicolored .95 .35
2685 A2047 50y multicolored .95 .35
a. Strip of 4, #2682-2685 4.00 1.75
2686 Sheet of 10 15.00 15.00
a.-j. A2047 80y any single 1.50 .40
k. Booklet pane, #2682-2685, 2 each #2686c, 2686g, 2686i 13.00
Complete booklet, #2686k 13.00
l. Sheet of 2, #2682, 2686g 2.50 1.75

Nos. 2686a is 53x27mm. Nos. 2686d, 2685h, 2686j are 30mm in diameter. No. 2686f is 38x39mm. Sheet numbers are in center of rectangles at top of sheets.

The 20th Century — A2090

1900-10 (Sheet 1) — #2687: a, 50y, 1905-06 Serialized novel "Wagahai wa Neko de aru," by Soseki Natsume (stamp 7). b, 50y, 1906 Novel "Bochan," by Natsume (stamp 8). c, 80y, 1901 Collection of poems "Midare-gami," by Akiko Yosano (stamp 1). d, 80y, Opening of Denkikan movie theater in Asakusa, 1903 (stamp 2). e, 80y, Electrification of streetcars, 1903 (stamp 3). f, 80y, Otojirou Kawakami & Sadayakko, actors (stamp 4). g, 80y, Westernization of fashion (stamp 9). h, 80y, Completion of Ryogoku Kokugikan sumo arena, 1909 (stamp 10). i, 80y, Russo-Japanese War soldiers on horseback (stamp 5). j, 80y, Russo-Japanese War soldiers in tent (stamp 6).

A2090a

1910-13 (Sheet 2) — #2688: a, 50y, 1st Japanese-produced airship, tail of 1st Japanese airplane (stamp 3). b, 50y, Front of 1st Japanese airplane (stamp 4). c, 80y, Elementary school song book published by Education ministry, 1910 (stamp 1). d, 80y, Antarctic expedition led by Nobu Shirase, 1910 (stamp 2). e, 80y, Dr. Hideyo Noguchi (stamp 5). f, 80y, Extinction of Japanese wolves (stamp 6). g, 80y, Runner Shizo Kanaguri at 1st participation in Olympic Games, 1912 (stamp 7). h, Takarazuka Musical Review founded, 1913 (stamp 8). i, 80y, "Song of Kachusha," by Sumako Matsui & Hogetsu Shimamura (stamp

9). j, 80y, 1st sale of caramels, 1913 (stamp 10).

A2090b

1914-20 (Sheet 3) — #2689: a, 50y, Painting of couple in boat by Yumeji Takehisa (stamp 9). b, 50y, Takehisa, painting of flowers (stamp 10). c, 80y, 1914 Opening of Tokyo train station (blimp in sky) (stamp 1). d, 80y, Tokyo train station main entrance (stamp 2). e, 80y, Japanese WWI seamen (stamp 3). f, 80y, Western-style women's hair styles (stamp 4). g, 80y, 1915 Poetry book "Rashomon," by Ryunosuke Akutagawa (stamp 5). h, 80y, 1916 Start of postal life insurance (goddess in clouds) (stamp 6). i, 80y, Sakuzo Yoshino, political scientist & democracy advocate, & tree (stamp 7). j, 80y, 1918 Rice riots (painting, photo of crowds) (stamp 8).

A2090c

1920-25 (Sheet 4) — #2690: a, 50y, Silent film star Matsunosuke Onoe (denomination at UR) (stamp 8). b, 50y, Silent film star Tsumasaburo Bandoh (denomination at UL) (stamp 9). c, 80y, 1st Hakone Relay Marathon, 1920 (stamp 1). d, 80y, Popularity of "Gondola Song" recording, spread of phonographs (stamp 2). e, 80y, Ruins from 1923 Kanto earthquake (stamp 3). f, "Nonki na Tosan" comic strip (man with dog) (stamp 4). g, 80y, "Adventures of Sho-chan" comic strip (man with vulture). h, 80y, Japanese crane nears extinction (stamp 6). i, 80y, 1924 Opening of Koshien Stadium (stamp 7). j, 80y, Man, woman in Western-style clothing (stamp 10).

A2090d

1927-28 (Sheet 5) — #2691: a, 50y, 1927 Opening of Tokyo subway (close-up of car) (stamp 2). b, 50y, Subway car approaching station (stamp 3). c, 80y, Movie "Kurama Tengu" (Samurai) (stamp 1). d, 80y, Radio broadcast of "National Health Gymnastics" exercise program (stamp 4). e, 80y, Yoshiyuki Tsuruta, 1928 Olympic swimming champion (stamp 5). f, 80y, Mikio Oda, 1928 Olympic triple jump champion (stamp 6). g, 80y, Olympic Games program (stamp 7). h, 80y, Runner Kinue Hitomi, 1st female Japanese Olympic medalist (stamp 8). i, 80y, Man in Western clothing, cafe (stamp 9). j, 1928 Publishing of "Horoki," by Fumiko Hayashi (stamp 10).

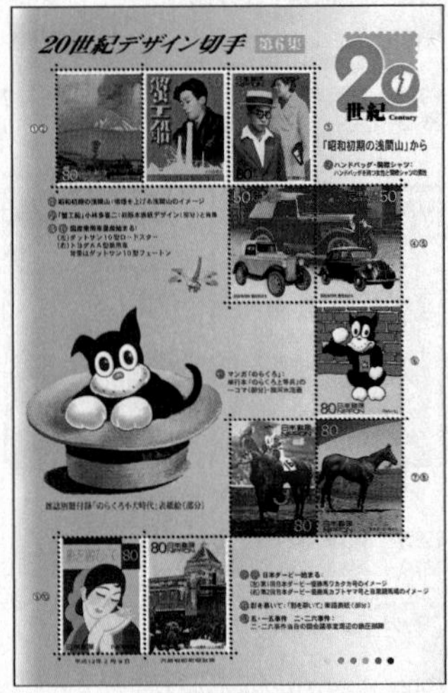

A2090e

1929-32 (Sheet 6) — #2692: a, 50y, Mass production of Japanese automobiles (green 1932 Datsun Model 10) (stamp 4). b, 50y, Black 1936 Toyota Model AA (stamp 5). c, 80y, Volcano, Mt. Asama (stamp 1). d, 80y, Takiji Kobayashi, writer of "Kani-kosen," crane, smokestacks (stamp 2). e, 80y, Man with shirt with open collar, woman with handbag (stamp 3). f, 80y, "Norakuro" comic strip (cat, brick wall) (stamp 6). g, 80y, 1932 Nippon Derby winner Wakataka & jockey (stamp 7). h, 80y, Nippon Derby winner Kabutoyama (stamp 8). i, 80y, Song "Longing for Your Shadow" (woman with closed eyes) (stamp 9). j, 80y, 1932, 1936 Political assassinations (soldiers, truck, building) (stamp 10).

A2090f

1932-36 (Sheet 7) — #2693: a, 50y, Front of D51 steam locomotive (stamp 8). b, 50y, Rear of D51 (stamp 9). c, 80y, Fumihiko Otsuki, lexicographer (Otsuki, geometric design) (stamp 1). d, 80y, Song "Tokyo Ondo" (woman, buildings) (stamp 2). e, 80y, Keinichi Enomoto, comic actor, with feather (stamp 3). f, 80y, Formation of Japanese Baseball League (catcher, umpire) (stamp 4). g, 80y, Batter (stamp 5). h, 80y, Hachiko, dog that waited for dead owner, statue of Hachiko (stamp 6). i, 80y, Eiji Yoshikawa, author of "Miyamoto Musashi." (stamp 7). j, Extinct species Okinawan pigeon (stamp 10).

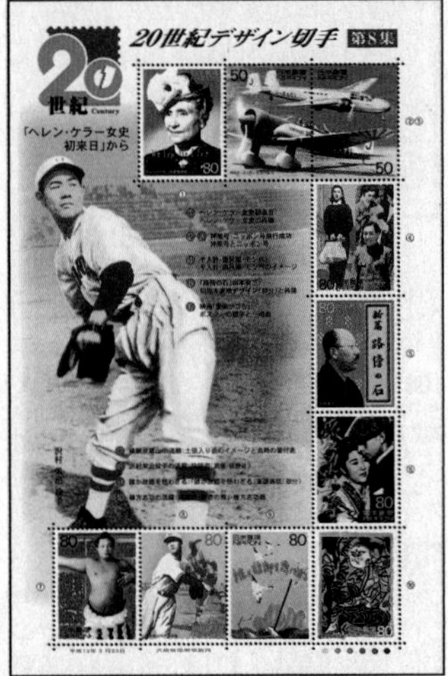

A2090g

1937-40 (Sheet 8) — #2694: a, 50y, Nose of Kamikaze plane, tail of Nippon cargo plane (stamp 2). b, 50y, Nose of Nippon cargo plain, tail of Kamikaze plane (stamp 3). c, 80y, Helen Keller's 1st trip to Japan (stamp 1). d, 80y, Women with senninbari cloths, monpe work pants, man with kokumin-fuku uniform (stamp 4). e, 80y, Yuzo Yamamoto, author of "Robo No Ishi" (stamp 5). f, 80y, Woman & man embracing in movie, "Aizenkatsura" (stamp 6). g, 80y, Sumo wrestler Yokozuna Futabayama, winner of 69 consecutive matches (stamp 7). h, 80y, Baseball pitcher Eiji Sawamura (stamp 8). i, 80y, Song, "Dareka Kokyo" (ducks in flight) (stamp 9). j, 80y, Woodblock art of Shiko Munakata (stamp 10).

A2090h

1940-45 (Sheet 9) — #2695: a, 50y, "Ohgon Bat," cartoon by Ichiro Suzuki (character without hat) (stamp 9). b, 50y, "Ohgon Bat" character wearing hat (stamp 10). c, 80y, Chiune Sugihara, vice-consul in Lithuania who saved Jews from Holocaust (stamp 1). d, 80y, Start of Kokumin Gakko school system (children exercising) (stamp 2). e, 80y, Airplane in attack on Pearl Harbor (stamp 3). f, 80y, Kotaro Takamura, poet, winner of 1st Imperial Art Academy prize, & Japanese characters (stamp 4). g, 80y, Eruption of Mt. Showashinzan (stamp 5). h, 80y, Atomic Bomb Memorial Dome (stamp 6). i, 80y, Statue at Nagasaki Atomic Bomb Museum (stamp 7). j, Signing of World War II surrender documents on USS Missouri (stamp 8).

A2090i

1945-52 (Sheet 10) — #2696: a, 50y, "Captain Atom" cartoon by Osamu Tezuka (stamp 7). b, 50y, "Astro Boy," cartoon by Tezuka (stamp 8). c, 80y, Song, "Ringo No Uta" (Apple Song) (stamp 1). d, 80y, "Sazae San," cartoon by Machiko Hasegawa (stamp 2). e, 80y, Promulgation of Japanese Constitution (woman, child, buildings) (stamp 3). f, 80y, Swimming records by Hironoshin Furuhashi (stamp 4). g, 80y, Dr. Hideki Yukawa, Nobel laurate for Physics (stamp 5). h, 80y, New Year's Eve radio program "Kohaku Uta Gassen" on NHK (stamp 6). i, 80y, Radio soap opera "Kimino Na Wa" (woman and man) (stamp 9). j, 80y, Novel "Nijyu-Yon No Hitomi," by Sakae Tsuboi (stamp 10).

A2090j

1953-58 (Sheet 11) — #2697: a, 50y, Tokyo Tower (olive green panel) (stamp 9). b, 50y, Tokyo Tower from ground (stamp 10). c, 80y, Popularity of radio and television (stamp 1). d, 80y, Director Akira Kurosawa, camera, two Samurai from "Shinchinin No Samurai." (stamp 2). e, 80y, Five Samurai from "Shinchinin No Samurai." (stamp 3). f, 80y, Sumo wrestler Rikidozan and championship belt (stamp 4). g, 80y, Rikidozan in action (stamp 5). h, 80y, Movie "Godzilla" (stamp 6). i, 80y, Taiyozoku fashions (man, woman at seaside) (stamp 7). j, 80y, Portrait of Shotokutaishi from 10,000-yen bank note (stamp 8, 31x42mm oval stamp).

A2090k

1959-64 (Sheet 12) — #2698: a, 50y, Dog Taro, survivor of abandonment in Antarctica, ship's stern (stamp 1). b, 50y, Dog Giro, survivor of abandonment in Antarctic, ship's bow (stamp 2). c, 80y, Commemorative cake box from Wedding of Crown Prince Akihito (stamp 3). d, 80y, Weather map of Isewan Typhoon (stamp 4). e, 80y, "Sukiyaki Song," by Rokusuke Ei (stamp 5). f, 80y, Novelist Ryotaro Shiba and cover from "Ryomaga Yuku," depicting Ryoma Sakamoto (stamp 6). g, 80y, Baby doll, and song "Konnichiwa Akachan," by Ei (stamp 7). h, 80y, Inauguration of Bullet Train (stamp 8). i, 80y, Poster depicting swimmer from Tokyo Olympics (stamp 9). j, 80y, Poster depicting torchbearer from Tokyo Olympics (stamp 10).

A2090l

1964-71 (Sheet 13) — #2699: a, 50y, TV show puppets Don Gabacho and Torahige (stamp 1, 31x30mm semi-oval stamp with straight side at right). b, 50y, TV show puppets Hakase and Lion (stamp 2, 31x30mm semi-oval stamp with straight side at left). c, 80y, Color television, automobile and air conditioner (stamp 3). d, 80y, TV character, Ultraman (stamp 4). e, 80y, Baltan Seijin, character from Ultraman TV series (stamp 5). f, 80y, Electric guitars (stamp 6). g, 80y, Yasunari Kawabata and Kenzaburo Oe, Nobel laureates for Literature (stamp 7). h, 80y, Scene from movie "Otokowa Tsuraiyo" (man holding basket) (stamp 8). i, 80y, Tower from Expo '70, Osaka (stamp 9). j, 80y, Youth fashions and song "Senso O Shiranai Kodomotachi" (stamp 10).

A2090m

1972-74 (Sheet 14) — #2700: a, 50y, Baseball player Sadaharu Oh (leg in air) (stamp 7). b, 50y, Baseball player Shigeo Nagashima (Tokyo uniform) (stamp 8). c, 80y, Two men from Takamatsu Zuka wall paintings, Asuka (stamp 1). d, 80y, Four women from Takamatsu Zuka wall paintings (stamp 2). e, 80y, Pandas Kankan and Ranran, gift from China (stamp 3). f, Shureimon, Return of Okinawa to Japanese control (stamp 4). g, 80y, Oscar, from cartoon "Roses of Versailles," by Riyoko Ikeda (stamp 5). h, 80y, Conductor Seiji Ozawa (stamp 6). i, 80y, Erimo Cape, and song "Erimo Misaki" (stamp 9). j, 80y, Space battleship Yamato from cartoon "Uchu Senkan Yamato," by Reiji Matsumoto (stamp 10).

A2090n

1975-83 (Sheet 15) — #2701: a, 50y, Gundam and Zaku, from TV cartoon series "Kidosenshi Gundam" (blue background) (stamp 7). b, 50y, Amuro and Gundam, from "Kidonsenshi Gundam" (orange background) (stamp 8). c, 80y, Guitar, and song "Jidai" (stamp 1). d, 80y, Fish character Taiyaki Kun, from children's song "Oyoge! Taiyaki Kun" (stamp 2). e, 80y, Musical notes and microphones (popularity of karaoke) (stamp 3). f, 80y, Flower, and song "Cosmos" (stamp 4). g, 80y, UFO, and song "UFO" (stamp 5). h, 80y, Students from TV series, "San Nen B Gumi Kinpachi Sensei" (stamp 6). i, 80y, Musical notes and electronic synthesizer (stamp 9). j, 80y, Oshin, from TV series "Oshin" (stamp 10).

A2090o

1986-93 (Sheet 16) — #2702: a, 50y, Character from cartoon show "Soreike! Anpanman" (stamp 3). b, 50y, Four characters from "Soreike! Anpanman" (stamp 4). c, 80y, Return of Halley's Comet (stamp 1, pentagonal). d, 80y, Opening of Seikan Railroad Tunnel (stamp 2). e, 80y, Watchtower excavated at Yoshinogari Iseki ruins (stamp 5). f, 80y, Singer Hibari Misora, National Medal of Honor recipient (stamp 6). g, 80y, Mascot of J-League Soccer Games (stamp 7, 34x28mm semi-oval stamp with straight side at bottom). h, 80y, Soccer ball (stamp 8, 34x28mm stamp with straight side at top). i, 80y, Selection of Dunjuang as World Heritage Site (Cliffside, stamp 9). j, 80y, Selection of Horyuji Temple as World Heritage Site (Temple and sun, stamp 10).

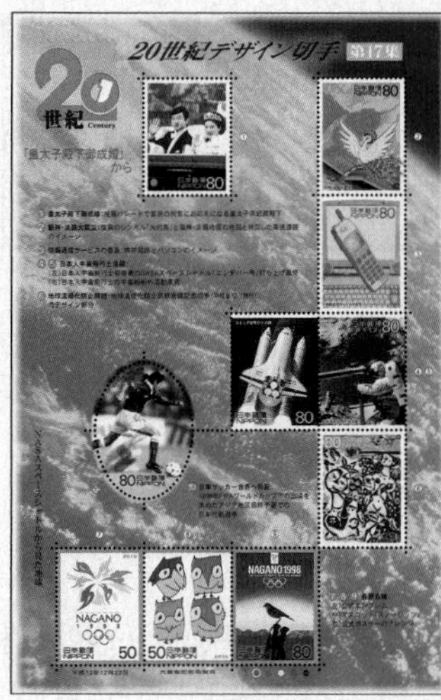

A2090p

1993-98 (Sheet 17) — #2703: a, 50y, Nagano Winter Olympics emblem (stamp 7). b, 50y, Four owl mascots of Nagano Winter Olympics (stamp 8). c, 80y, Wedding of Crown Prince Naruhito and Masako Owada (stamp 1). d, 80y, Phoenix and damage from Hanshin-Awaji earthquake (stamp 2). e, 80y, Cellular phone and computer (stamp 3). f, 80y, Launch of Japanese astronaut aboard Space Shuttle Endeavor (stamp 4). g, 80y, Astronaut Mamoru Mohri in space (stamp 5). h, 80y, Details from Kyoto Climate Change Conf. stamps, #2598-2599 (stamp 6). i, 80y, Poster for Nagano Winter Olympics (stamp 9). j, Soccer player at 1998 World Cup Championships (stamp 10, 42x31mm elliptical stamp).

Illustrations reduced.

1999-2000 Photo. ***Perf. 13x13¼***

Sheets of 10

2687	A2090	#a.-j.	14.00	14.00
a.-b.		50y any single	.95	.35
c.-j.		80y any single	1.50	.40
2688	A2090a	#a.-j.	14.00	14.00
a.-b.		50y any single	.95	.35
c.-j.		80y any single	1.50	.40
2689	A2090b	#a.-j.	14.00	14.00
a.-b.		50y any single	.95	.35
c.-j.		80y any single	1.50	.40
2690	A2090c	#a.-j.	14.00	14.00
a.-b.		50y any single	.95	.35
c.-j.		80y any single	1.50	.40
2691	A2090d	#a.-j.	14.00	14.00
a.-b.		50y any single	.95	.35
c.-j.		80y any single	1.50	.40
2692	A2090e	#a.-j.	14.00	14.00
a.-b.		50y any single	.95	.93
c.-j.		80y any single	1.50	.40
2693	A2090f	#a.-j.	14.00	14.00
a.-b.		50y any single	.95	.35
c.-j.		80y any single	1.50	.40
2694	A2090g	#a-j	14.00	14.00
a.-b.		50y Any single	.95	.35
c.-j.		80y Any single	1.50	.40
2695	A2090h	#a-j	14.00	14.00
a.-b.		50y Any single	.95	.35
c.-j.		80y Any single	1.50	.40
2696	A2090i	#a-j	14.00	14.00
a.-b.		50y Any single	.95	.35
c.-j.		80y Any single	1.50	.40
2697	A2090j	#a-j	14.00	14.00
a.-b.		50y Any single	.95	.35
c.-j.		80y Any single	1.50	.40
2698	A2090k	#a-j	14.00	14.00
a.-b.		50y Any single	.95	.35
c.-j.		80y Any single	1.50	.40
2699	A2090l	#a-j	14.00	14.00
a.-b.		50y Any single	.95	.35
c.-j.		80y Any single	1.50	.40
2700	A2090m	#a-j	14.00	14.00
a.-b.		50y Any single	.95	.35
c.-j.		80y Any single	1.50	.40
2701	A2090n	#a-j	14.00	14.00
a.-b.		50y Any single	.95	.35
c.-j.		80y Any single	1.50	.40
2702	A2090o	#a-j	14.00	14.00
a.-b.		50y Any single	.95	.35
c.-j.		80y Any single	1.50	.40
2703	A2090p	#a-j	14.00	14.00
a.-b.		50y Any single	.95	.35
c.-j.		80y Any single	1.50	.40

Sheet numbers are in UR corner of sheets or in center of rectangles at top of sheet. Stamp numbers are in sheet margin.

Issued: #2687, 8/23; #2688, 9/22; #2689, 10/22; #2690, 12/22; #2691, 1/21/00; #2692, 2/9/00; #2693, 2/23/00; #2694, 3/23/00; #2695, 4/21/00; #2696, 5/23/00; #2697, 6/23/00; #2698, 7/21/00; #2699, 8/23/00; #2700, 9/22/00; #2701, 10/23/00; #2702, 11/22; #2703, 12/22.

Hearts and Doves A2092

Celebration A2093

Red-crowned Crane — A2094

1999, Aug. 16 Photo. *Perf. 13¼*

2704	A2092	50y multi	.95	.35
2705	A2093	80y multi	1.50	.40
2706	A2094	90y multi	1.75	.50
		Nos. 2704-2706 (3)	4.20	1.25

A2095 A2096

1999, Sept. 10

2707	A2095	50y multi	.95	.35

54th Natl. Sports Festival.

1999, Oct. 1 *Perf. 12¾x13*

2708	A2096	80y multi	1.50	.40

Intl. Year of Older Persons.

A2097

A2098

A2099

Intl. Letter Writing Week A2100

Hokusai Paintings: #2709, Sea Route in Kazusa Area. #2710, Roses & a Sparrow. #2711, Rain Beneath the Mountaintop. #2712, Chrysanthemums & a Horsefly. #2713, Under the Fukagawa Bridge. #2714, Peonies & a Butterfly.

1999, Oct. 6 *Perf. 13¼*

2709	A2097	90y multi	1.75	.50
2710	A2098	90y multi	1.75	.50
a.		Pair, #2709-2710	3.50	1.75
2711	A2097	110y multi	2.10	.60
2712	A2099	110y multi	2.10	.60
a.		Pair, #2711-2712	4.25	1.75
2713	A2097	130y multi	2.50	.70
2714	A2100	130y multi	2.50	.70
a.		Pair, #2713-2714	5.00	1.75
		Nos. 2709-2714 (6)	12.70	3.60

Central and Pacific Baseball Leagues, 50th Anniv. — A2101

Mascots wearing uniforms of: a, Yokohama Bay Stars. b, Chunichi Dragons. c, Seibu Lions. d, Nippon Ham Fighters. e, Yomiuri Giants. f, Yakult Swallows g, Orix Blue Wave. h, Fukuoka Daiei Hawks. i, Hiroshima Toyo Carp. j, Hanshin Tigers. k, Kintetsu Buffaloes. l, Chiba Lotte Marines.

1999, Oct. 22 *Die Cut*

Self-Adhesive

2715	A2101	Sheet of 12	18.00	
a.-l.		80y any single	1.50	.40

Natl. Science Council, 50th Anniv. — A2102

1999, Oct. 28 *Perf. 13x13¼*

2716	A2102	80y multi	1.40	.40

Cultural Pioneers Types of 1992-98

#2717, Hokusai (1760-1849), painter. #2718: Yasunari Kawabata (1899-1972), writer. #2719, Shoen Uemura (1875-1949), painter.

1999, Nov. 4 Photo. *Perf. 12¾x13*

2717	A1645	80y multi	1.50	.40

Photo. & Engr.

Perf. 13

2718	A1645	80y multi	1.50	.40
2719	A2053	80y multi	1.50	.40
		Nos. 2717-2719 (3)	4.50	1.20

Reign of Emperor Akihito, 10th Anniv. A2103

Designs: No. 2720, Paulownia and bamboo crest. No. 2721, Phoenix crest.

1999, Nov. 12 Photo. *Perf. 12¼*

2720	A2103	80y red & multi	1.50	.40
2721	A2103	80y yel & multi	1.50	.40
a.		Souvenir sheet, #2720-2721	3.00	3.00

A2104

A2105

New Year 2000 (Year of the Dragon)
A2106 A2107

1999, Nov. 15 *Perf. 13x13¼*

2722	A2104	50y multi	.95	.35
2723	A2105	80y multi	1.50	.40

Perf. 13¼

2724	A2106	50y +3y multi	1.00	.40
2725	A2107	80y +3y multi	1.60	.50

Sheets of 2 containing Nos. 2722-2723 were lottery prizes. Value $2.50.

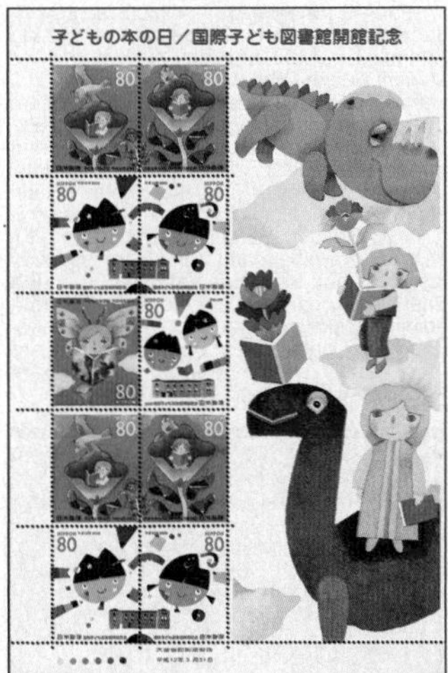

Children's Book Day — A2108

a, Flower with child reading, bird in flight. b, Flower with child reading, bird perched. c, Child, left half of new Intl. Library of Children's Literature. d, Child, right half of library. e, Butterfly with child's head. f, Two children, library.
Illustration reduced.

Perf. 12¾x13¼

2000, Mar. 31 Photo.

2726	A2108	Sheet of 10, #e-f, 2 each #a-d	15.00	15.00
a.-f.		80y any single	1.50	.40

Seishu Hanaoka (1760-1835), Physician, and Flower — A2109

2000, Apr. 11 *Perf. 12¾x13*

2727	A2109	80y multi	1.50	.40

Japan Surgical Society, 100th congress.

Japan-Netherlands Relations, 400th Anniv. — A2110

2000, Apr. 19 *Perf. 13*

2728		80y multi	1.50	.40
2729		80y multi	1.50	.40
a.	A2110	Pair, #2728-2729	3.00	1.50

Dragon and Tiger by Gaho Hashimoto — A2112

Illustration reduced.

2000, Apr. 20 *Perf. 13¼*

2730		80y multi	1.50	.40
2731		80y multi	1.50	.40
a.	A2112	Pair, #2730-2731	3.00	1.50

Philately week.

Natl. Land Afforestation Campaign — A2114

2000, Apr. 21 *Perf. 13¼*

2732	A2114	50y multi	.95	.65

Phila Nippon 2001, Tokyo — A2115

Designs: a, Wild goose (dull green frame background). b, Wagtail (dull violet frame background). c, Goshawk (dull rose frame background). d, A Girl Blowing Glass Toy, by Utamaro. e, Kabuki Actor Ebizo Ichikawa, by Sharaku. f, Flowers. g, Dog and cat. h, Children with pen and envelope (blue background). i, Child with clown. j, Children with pen and envelope (red background).
Illustration reduced.

2000, May 19 Photo. *Die Cut*

Self-Adhesive

2733	A2115	Sheet of 10, #a-j	15.00	
a.-j.		80y any single	1.50	.40

Kyushu-Okinawa Summit — A2116

2000, June 21 Photo. *Perf. 12¾x13*

2734		80y multi	1.50	.40
2735		80y multi	1.50	.40
a.	A2116	Pair, #2734-2735	3.00	1.50

A2117

2000, June 30

2736	80y Three flowers		1.50	.40
2737	80y Two flowers		1.50	.40
a.	A2117 Pair, #2736-2737		3.00	1.50

Crime Prevention Campaign, 50th anniv.

Letter Writing Day Type of 1998

Designs: No. 2738, Girl with bows in hair, pen. No. 2739, Birds, house, letter. No. 2740, Clown with red hat, open envelope. No. 2741, Boy reading letter, puppy.

No. 2742: a, Child, dog, in basket. b, Apple tree, flower (circular stamp). c, Parrots holding envelope (elliptical stamp). d, Bicycle, rabbit, flower (oval stamp). e, Boy, girl, dove. f, Girl, letter, snail, porcupine (oval stamp). g, Child playing harp. h, Child playing recorder. i, Child playing bass (semicircular stamp). j, Girl with blue hat, pen, birds holding envelope.

2000, July 21 *Perf. 12¾x13¼*

2738	A2047 50y multi	.95	.35
2739	A2047 50y multi	.95	.35
2740	A2047 50y multi	.95	.35
2741	A2047 50y multi	.95	.35
a.	Strip of 4, #2738-2741	4.00	4.00
2742	Sheet of 10	15.00	15.00
a.-j.	A2047 80y Any single	1.50	.40
k.	Booklet pane, #2738-2741, 2742g, 2742h, 2 #2742e, 2742j	13.00	
	Booklet, #2742k	13.00	
l.	Souvenir sheet, #2739, 2742e	2.50	2.50

No. 2742b is 30mm in diameter, No. 2742c is 23x34mm, Nos. 2742d, 2742f are 28x40mm, and No. 2742i is 24x40mm.

Women's Private Higher Education, Cent. — A2118

2000, Sept. 22 **Photo.** *Perf. 13*

2743	A2118 80y multi	1.50	.40

Intl. Letter Writing Week A2119

Artwork by Hiroshige: 90y, Okabe. 110y, Maisaka. 130y, Okazaki.

2000, Oct. 6 *Perf. 13¼*

2744	A2119 90y multi	1.75	.75
2745	A2119 110y multi	2.10	.75
2746	A2119 130y multi	2.50	.75
	Nos. 2744-2746 (3)	6.35	2.25

See Nos. 2791-2793, 2835-2837, 2904-2906, 2938-2940, 2999-3001.

Cultural Pioneers Type of 1998 and

Ukichiro Nakaya (1900-62), Snow Crystal Researcher A2120

Designs: No. 2747, Hantaro Nagaoka (1865-1950), physicist. No. 2748, Teijo Nakamura (1900-88), poet.

Photo. & Engr.

2000, Nov. 6 *Perf. 13*

2747	A2053 80y multi	1.50	.40
2748	A2053 80y multi	1.50	.40
2749	A2120 80y multi	1.50	.40
	Nos. 2747-2749 (3)	4.50	1.20

See No. 2841.

A2121

A2122

New Year 2001 (Year of the Snake)

A2123 A2124

2000, Nov. 15 **Photo.** *Perf. 13x13¼*

2750	A2121 50y multi	.95	.35
2751	A2122 80y multi	1.50	.40

Perf. 13¼x13½

2752	A2123 50y +3y multi	1.00	.40
2753	A2124 80y +3y multi	1.60	.50
	Nos. 2750-2753 (4)	5.05	1.65

See No. 2841. Sheets of 2, Nos. 2750-2751, were lottery prizes.

Diet, 110th Anniv. — A2125

2000, Nov. 29 *Perf. 13*

2754	A2125 80y multi	1.50	.40

Internet Expo 2001 — A2126

2001, Jan. 5 *Perf. 13x13¼*

2755	80y Denom. at L	1.50	.40
2756	80y Denom. at R	1.50	.40
a.	A2126 Pair, #2755-2756	3.00	1.50

Intl. Volunteers Year — A2127

2001, Jan. 17 *Perf. 13½x13¼*

2757	A2127 80y multi	1.50	.40

Administrative Scriveners System, 50th Anniv. — A2128

2001, Feb. 22 **Photo.** *Perf. 13¼*

2758	A2128 80y multi	1.50	.40

World Heritage Sites

Sheet 1 — A2129

Sheet 2 — A2130

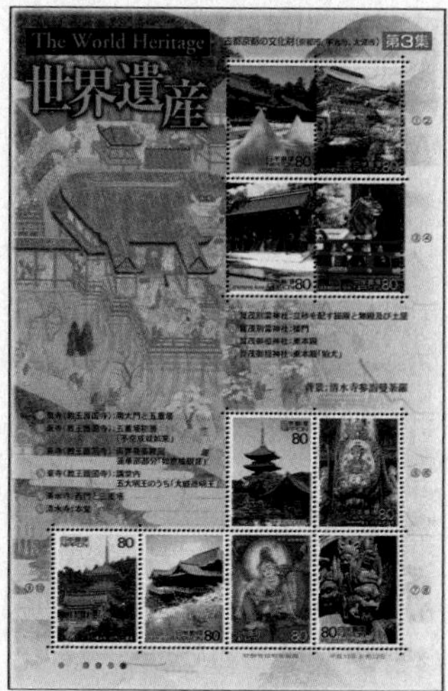

Sheet 3 — A2131

Sheet 4 — A2132

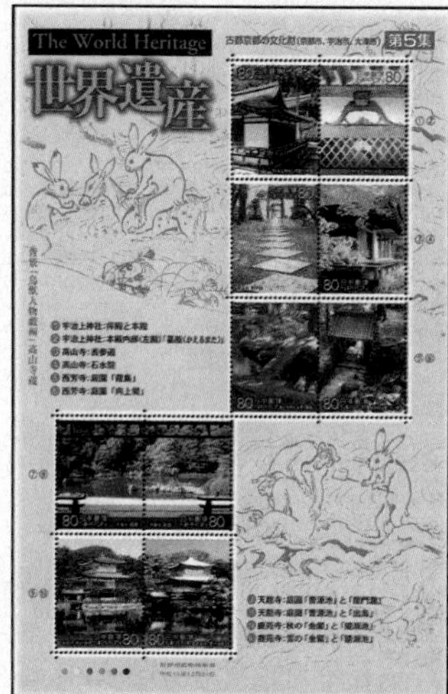

Sheet 5 — A2133

Sheet 6 — A2134

No. 2759 — Nikko: a, Bridge (stamp 1). b, Shrine with pillars in foreground (stamp 2). c, Temple gate (stamp 3). d, Dragon (stamp 4). e, Peacock (stamp 5). f, Cat (stamp 6). g, Statue of blue green figure (stamp 7). h, Statue of red figure (stamp 8). i, Shrine (stamp 9). j, Shrine and walkways (stamp 10).

No. 2760 — Itsukushima: a, Marodo Jinjya and pillar in water (stamp 1). b, Marodo Jinjya (stamp 2). c, Honsha (shrine entrance with steps, stamp 3). d, Koma-inu (lion statue, stamp 4). e, Marodo Jinjya and Gojyuno-tou (stamp 5). f, Bugakumen (sculpture with blue water background, stamp 6). g, Kazari-uma (horse statue, stamp 7). h, Noubutai (building with brown eaves, stamp 8). i, Tahoutou (building with cherry blossoms, stamp 9). j, Oomoto Jinjya (building with red fence, stamp 10).

No. 2761 — Kyoto: a, Hosodono Hall, Maidono Hall and Tsuchinoya Hall, Kamowakeikazuchi Shrine (buildings with cones in foreground, stamp 1). b, Romon Gate, Kamowakeikazuchi Shrine (building with stream, stamp 2). c, East Main Hall, Kamomioya Shrine (building with guardian dog statue on landing, stamp 3). d, Guardian dog statue, Kamomioya Shrine (stamp 4). e, South Great Gate and 5-Story Pagoda (deep blue sky, stamp 5). f, Fukuu Joju Nyorai Statue, Toji Temple (gold statue, stamp 6). g, Nyoirin Kannon, Toji Temple (painting, stamp 7). h, Daiitoku Myoo Statue, Toji Temple (stone statue, stamp 8). i, West Gate, 3-Story Pagoda, Kiyomizudera Temple (red gate and temple, stamp 9). j, Main Hall, Kiyomizudera Temple (building with cherry bloosoms, stamp 10).

No. 2762 — Kyoto: a, Konpon Chudo Hall, Enryakuji Temple (roof, stamp 1). b, Eternal Flame, Enryaluji Temple (stamp 2). c, Ninai-do Hall, Enryakuji Temple (building with large trees in foreground, stamp 3). d, Sanbo-in Temple Garden, Daigoji Temple (building, one end of small bridge, stamp 4). e, Sanbo-in Temple Garden (end of bridge, trees, stamp 5). f, 5-Story Pagoda, Daigoji Temple (white sky, stamp 6). g, Goten, Ninnaji Temple (buildings with walkways, stamp 7). h, 5-Story Pagoda (cherry trees in foreground, stamp 8). i, Phoenix Hall, Byodoin Temple (black sky, stamp 9). j, Wooden carving of Bodhisattvas Floating on Clouds, Byodoin Temple (stamp 10).

No. 2763 — Kyoto: a, Ujikami Shrine (low fence around shrine with denomination at UL, stamp 1). b, Kaeru Mata, Ujikami Shrine (thin, crossing diagonal strips, stamp 2). c, Front approach to Kozanji Temple (walkway of square panels, stamp 3). d, Sekisuiin, Kozanji Temple (yellow tree blossoms in front of temple, stamp 4). e, Kasumijima Garden, Saihoji Temple (moss-covered bridge, stamp 5) f, Kojokan Garden, Saihoji Temple (Stone stairs and rocks, stamp 6). g, View of garden and pond from under roof, Tenryuji Temple (denomination at left, stamp 7). h, View of garden and pond from under roof, Tenryuji Temple (denomination at right, stamp 8). i, Rokuonji Temple in autumn (Building on lake, green leaves on trees, stamp 9). j, Rokuonji Temple in winter (snow covered roofs and trees, stamp 10).

No. 2764 — Kyoto: a, Snow-covered Silver Pavilion, Jishoji Temple (stamp 1). b, Silver Pavilion without snow (stamp 2). c, Moss-covered rock, Hojo Garden, Ryoanji Temple (stamp 3). d, Rock and snow, Hojo Garden (stamp 4). e, Karamon, Honganji Temple (gate with curved roof, stamp 5). f, Hiunkaku, Honganji Temple (building near pond, stamp 6). g, Shoin, Honganji Temple (wall with landscape, stamp 7). h, Ninomaur Palace, Nijo Castle (roof with chrysanthemum crest at peak, stamp 8). i, Detail from "Hawks on Pine," Nijo Castle (hawk looking left, stamp 9). j, Detail from "Hawks on Pine," Nijo Castle (hawk looking down, stamp 10).

2001 Photo. *Perf. 13x13¼*

2759	A2129	Sheet of 10	15.00	15.00
a.-j.		80y Any single	1.50	.40
2760	A2130	Sheet of 10	14.00	15.00
a.-j.		80y Any single	1.50	.40
2761	A2131	Sheet of 10	15.00	15.00
a.-j.		80y Any single	1.50	.40
2762	A2132	Sheet of 10	15.00	15.00
a.-j.		80y Any single	1.50	.40
2763	A2133	Sheet of 10	15.00	15.00
a.-j.		80y Any single	1.50	.40
2764	A2134	Sheet of 10	15.00	15.00
a.-j.		80y Any single	1.50	.40

Issued: No. 2759, 2/23; No. 2760, 3/23; No. 2761, 6/22; No. 2762, 8/23. No. 2763, 12/21. No. 2764, 2/22/02.

Sheet numbers are in center of colored rectangles at top of sheet. Stamp numbers are in sheet margins.

Exhibit of Italian Art at Museum of Western Art, Tokyo — A2135

Designs: 80y, Show emblem. No. 2766, Angel, from The Annunciation, by Botticelli. No. 2767, Virgin Mary, from The Annunciation.

2001, Mar. 19 Photo. *Perf. 13*

2765	A2135	80y multi	1.50	.40

Size: 33x44mm

Perf. 13¼

2766	A2135	110y multi	2.10	.75
2767	A2135	110y multi	2.10	.75
a.		Pair, #2766-2767	4.25	2.00
		Nos. 2765-2767 (3)	5.70	1.90

Japanese Dermatological Association, 100th Annual Meeting — A2136

2001, Apr. 6 *Perf. 13¼*

Color of Triangle Behind "0" in Denomination

2768	A2136	80y pink	1.50	.40
2769	A2136	80y orange	1.50	.40
2770	A2136	80y yellow	1.50	.40
2771	A2136	80y green	1.50	.40
2772	A2136	80y blue	1.50	.40
a.		Vert. strip of 5, #2768-2772	7.50	7.50

Depositing Mail, by Senseki Nakamura A2137

2001, Apr. 20 *Perf. 13x13¼*

2773	A2137	80y multi	1.50	.40

Philately Week, Cent. of red cylindrical mailboxes.

Membership in UNESCO, 50th Anniv. — A2138

2001, July 2 *Perf. 13¼*

2774	A2138	80y multi	1.25	.40

9th FINA World Swimming Championships, Fukuoka A2139

Designs: No. 2775, Swimming race. No. 2776, Synchronized swimming. No. 2777, Diving. No. 2778, Water polo.

2001, July 16 *Perf. 13x13¼*

2775	A2139	80y multi	1.50	.40
2776	A2139	80y multi	1.50	.40
2777	A2139	80y multi	1.50	.40
2778	A2139	80y multi	1.50	.40
a.		Horiz. strip of 4, #2775-2778	6.00	6.00

Letter Writing Day Type of 1998

Designs: No. 2779, Three rabbits, tulip background. No. 2780, Girl with pencil, pencil background. No. 2781, Boy with envelope, bird background. No. 2782, Girl, flower background.

No. 2783: a, Girl with rabbit, bird, flower (oval stamp). b, Bird in tree (circular stamp). c, Boy with pen behind back. d, Girl with envelope and dog. e, Girl on bicycle, flowers (semi-circular stamp). f, Flowers, bird with envelope, insect (circular stamp). g, Bird flying, bird on roof. h, Chicken, chicks, pig (oval stamp). i, Rabbit, flowers (elliptical stamp). j, Boy with hat, rabbit (oval stamp).

2001, July 23 *Perf. 13x13¼*

2779	A2047	50y multi	.95	.35
2780	A2047	50y multi	.95	.35
2781	A2047	50y multi	.95	.35
2782	A2047	50y multi	.95	.35
a.		Horiz. strip of 4, #a-d	4.00	4.00
2783		Sheet of 10	15.00	15.00
a.-j.	A2047	80y Any single	1.50	.40
k.		Booklet pane, #2779-2782, 2 each #2783c, 2783d, 2783g	13.00	
		Booklet, #2783k	13.00	
l.		Souvenir sheet, #2780, 2783g	2.50	2.50

Phila Nippon '01 (Nos. 2783, 2783l). Nos. 2783a and 2783e are 35x29mm; Nos. 2783b and 2783f are 29mm in diameter; No. 2783h is 40x28mm; No. 2783i is 35x23mm; No. 2783j is 34x28mm.

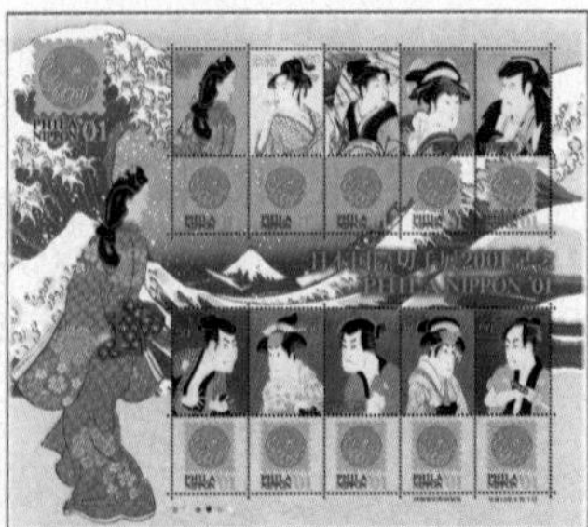

Phila Nippon '01 — A2140

Art: a, Oniji Otani as Edobei (striped kimono), by Sharaku. b, Hanshiro Iwai as Shigenoi (flowered kimono, facing left), by Sharaku. c, Hangoro Sakata as Mizuemon Fujikawa (brown kimono), by Sharaku. d, Kikunojo Segawa as Oshizu, Bunzo Tanabe's Wife (kimono with stars), by Sharaku. e, Omezo Ichikawa as Ippei Yakko (with sword), by Sharaku. f, Beauty Looking Back (flowered kimono), by Moronobu Hishikawa. g, A Girl Whistling a Vidro (checkered kimono), by Utamaro. h, Nishiki Fuzoku Higashino Returning From a Bathhouse in the Rain (with umbrella), by Kiyonaga Torii. i, Kumesaburo Iwai as Chiyo (blue background), by Kunimasa Utagawa. j, Komazo Ichikawa as Ganryu Sasaki (with sword), by Toyokuni Utagawa.

2001, Aug. 1 *Perf. 13*

2784	A2140	Sheet of 10+10 labels	12.50	12.50
a.-e.		50y Any single	.95	.35
f.-j.		80y Any single	1.50	.40

Labels could be personalized by customers at Phila Nippon stamp exhibition.

2001 World Games, Akita — A2141

Designs: No. 2785, Fishing, Frisbee throwing. No. 2786, Aerobics, billiards. No. 2787, Life saving, water skiing. No. 2788, Body building, tug-of-war.

2001, Aug. 16 *Perf. 13*

2785	A2141	50y multi	.95	.35
2786	A2141	50y multi	.95	.35
a.		Pair, #2785-2786	1.90	1.00
2787	A2141	80y multi	1.50	.40
2788	A2141	80y multi	1.50	.40
a.		Pair, #2787-2788	3.00	1.50
		Nos. 2785-2788 (4)	4.90	1.50

Phila Nippon '01 — A2142

Designs: a, Hanshiro Iwai as Shigenoi (figure with stick in hair), by Sharaku. b, Oniji Otani as Edobei (figure with fingers splayed), by Sharaku. c, Mandarin duck in water. d, White-eye on branch. e, Children with letters. f, Kumesaburo Iwai as Chiyo (lilac background), by Kunimasa Utagawa. g, Komazo Ichikawa as Ganryu Sasaki (brown background), by Toyokuni Utagawa. h, Turtledove (blue background). i, Greater pied kingfisher (green background). j, Japan #1.

2001, Aug. 1 Photo. *Die Cut*

Self-Adhesive

2789	A2142	Sheet of 10	12.00	
a.-e.		50y Any single	.95	.35
f.-j.		80y Any single	1.50	.40

San Francisco Peace Treaty, 50th Anniv. — A2143

2001, Sept. 7 *Perf. 13*

2790	A2143	80y multi	1.40	.40

Intl. Letter Writing Week Type of 2000

Hiroshige paintings from 53 Stations of the Tokaido: 90y, Hara. 110y, Oiso. 130y, Sakanoshita.

2001, Oct. 5 *Perf. 13¼*

2791	A2119	90y multi	1.75	.75
2792	A2119	110y multi	2.10	.75
2793	A2119	130y multi	2.50	.75
		Nos. 2791-2793 (3)	6.35	2.25

Town Safety Campaign — A2144

Designs: No. 2794, Boy, duck chicks, owl, frogs, insects. No. 2795, Girl, dogs, cats, birds, insects.

2001, Oct. 11 *Perf. 13x13¼*

2794	80y multi	1.50	.40
2795	80y multi	1.50	.40
a.	A2144 Horiz. pair, #2794-2795	3.00	1.50

1st National Games for the Disabled — A2145

Designs: No. 2796, Disc throwing. No. 2797, Wheelchair race.

2001, Oct. 26 *Perf. 12¾x13*

2796	80y multi	1.50	.40
2797	80y multi	1.50	.40
a.	A2145 Horiz. pair, #2796-2797	3.00	1.50

Norinaga Motoori (1730-1801), Physician, Scholar — A2146

Gidayu Takemoto (1651-1714), Joruri Chanter — A2147

Photo. & Engr.

2001, Nov. 5 *Perf. 12¾x13*

2798	A2146 80y multi	1.50	.40
2799	A2147 80y multi	1.50	.40

Commercial Broadcasting, 50th Anniv. — A2148

2001, Nov. 15 **Photo.**

2800	A2148 80y multi	1.50	.40

A2149 A2150

New Year 2002 (Year of the Horse)

A2151 A2152

2001, Nov. 15 *Perf. 13x13¼*

2801	A2149 50y multi	.95	.35
2802	A2150 80y multi	1.50	.40

Perf. 13¼x13½

2803	A2151 50y +3y multi	1.00	.40
2804	A2152 80y +3y multi	1.60	.50
	Nos. 2801-2804 (4)	5.05	1.65

Sheets of two containing Nos. 2801-2802 were lottery prizes.

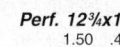

Legal Aid System, 50th Anniv. — A2153

2002, Jan. 24 *Perf. 12¾x13*

2805	A2153 80y multi	1.50	.40

Japan — Mongolia Diplomatic Relations, 30th Anniv. — A2154

2002, Feb. 15

2806	A2154 80y multi	1.50	.40

Lions Clubs in Japan, 50th Anniv. — A2155

2002, Mar. 1 **Photo.** *Perf. 13x13¼*

2807	A2155 80y multi	1.50	.95

2002 World Figure Skating Championships, Nagano — A2156

2002, Mar. 8

2808	80y Men's Singles	1.50	.95
2809	80y Pairs	1.50	.95
a.	A2156 Horiz. pair, #2808-2809	3.00	1.90

Diplomatic Relations Anniversaries A2157

Designs: No. 2810, Taj Mahal, India. No. 2811, Sculpture of "Priest King," Mohenjo Daro excavations, Pakistan. No. 2812, Sigiriya goddess, Lion's Rock, Sri Lanka. No. 2813, Carving from Buddhist Vihara, Paharpur, Bangladesh.

2002, Apr. 12

2810	A2157 80y multi	1.50	.95
2811	A2157 80y multi	1.50	.95
2812	A2157 80y multi	1.50	.95
2813	A2157 80y multi	1.50	.95
	Nos. 2810-2813 (4)	6.00	3.80

Japanese diplomatic relations with India, 50th anniv. (#2810); Pakistan, 50th anniv. (#2811). Sri Lanka, 50th anniv. (#2812), and Bangladesh, 30th anniv. (#2813).

Philately Week — A2158

Folding screen panels depicting horse racing scenes: No. 2814, Denomination at bottom. No. 2815, Denomination at top. Illustration reduced.

2002, Apr. 19 *Perf. 13¼*

2814	80y multi	1.50	.95
2815	80y multi	1.50	.95
a.	A2158 Horiz. pair, #2814-2815	3.00	1.90

Fulbright Exchange Program, 50th Anniv. — A2159

Return of Okinawa, 30th Anniv. — A2160

2002, May 8 *Perf. 12¾x13*

2816	A2159 80y multi	1.50	.95

2002, May 15 *Perf. 13x13¼*

2817	A2160 80y multi	1.50	.95

2002 World Cup Soccer Championships, Japan and Korea — A2161

2002, May 24

2818	80y Soccer field	1.50	.95
2819	80y World Cup	1.50	.95
a.	A2161 Horiz. pair, #2818-2819	3.00	1.90

Nos. 2818-2819 were issued in sheets of 10 stamps, containing five of each. Thirteen different sheet margins exist.

World Heritage Sites

Sheet 7 — A2162

No. 2820 — Todaiji and Koufukuji Temples, Nara: a, Great Buddha Hall, Todaiji Temple (stamp 1). b, Underside of roof of Nandaimon Gate, Todaiji Temple (stamp 2). c, Engraving on lotus petal, Todaiji Temple (stamp 3). d, Head of Koumokuten, Todaiji Temple (stamp 4). e, Hokkedo Hall and steps, Todaiji Temple (stamp 5). f, Five-story pagoda, Koufukuji Temple (stamp 6). g, Hokuendo Hall (with roof ornament), Koufukuji Temple (stamp 7). h, Ashura (statue with four arms), Koufukuji Temple (stamp 8). i, Head of Buddha, Koufukuji Temple (stamp 9). j, Ogre under dragon lantern, Koufukuji Temple (stamp 10).

2002 **Photo.** *Perf. 13x13¼*

2820	A2162 Sheet of 10	15.00	15.00
a.-j.	80y Any single	1.50	1.40

Issued: No. 2820, 6/21.

Numbers have been reserved for additional sheets. Sheet numbers are in center of colored rectangle at top of sheet. Stamp numbers are in sheet margins.

World Heritage Series

Sheet 8 — A2163

Sheet 9 — A2164

Sheet 10 — A2165

No. 2821 — Nara: a, Covered passageway, Kasuga Taisha Shrine (stamp 1). b, Chumon, Kasuga Taisha Shrine (stamp 2). c, Deer in Kasuga-yama Primeval Forest (stamp 3). d, Gokurakubo Zenshitsu and Gokurakubo Hondo, Gango-ji Temple (stamp 4). e, Gokurakubo Five-story Pagoda, Gango-ji Temple (stamp 5). f, East and West Pagodas, Yakushi-ji Temple (stamp 6). g, Yakushi Nyorai (seated Buddha), Yakushi-ji Temple (stamp 7). h, Golden Hall, Toshodai-ji Temple (stamp 8). i, Senju Kannon Ryu-zo (standing image with hands together of Thousand-handed Goddess of Mercy), Toshodai-ji Temple (stamp 9). j, Suzakumon Gate, Heijo Imperial Palace (stamp 10).

No. 2822 — Villages of Shirakawa-go and Gokayama: a, House with large tree at left, Ogimachi (stamp 1). b, Two houses, trees in fall colors Ogimachi (stamp 2). c, House with flowers, Ogimachi (stamp 3). d, Myozen-ji Temple and house, Ogimachi (stamp 4). e, Two houses covered in snow at night, Ogimachi (stamp 5). f, Neighborhood of houses, Ainokura (stamp 6). g, Sonen-ji Temple with stone wall, Ainokura (stamp 7). h, Two houses, Ainokura (stamp 8). i, House with shrub in front, Suganuma (stamp 9). j, House covered in snow, Suganuma (stamp 10).

No. 2823 — Gusuku Sites of the Ryukyu Kingdom: a, Stone lion at royal mausoleum (stamp 1). b, Three steps and stone gate to Sonohyan'utaki Sanctuary (stamp 2). c, Cherry blossoms and ruins of Nakijinjou Castle (stamp 3). d, Steps and stone gate at ruins of Zakimijou Castle (stamp 4). e, Ruins of Katsurenjou Castle walls (stamp 5). f, Ruins of Nakagusukujou Castle citadel (walls with gate, stamp 6). g Kankaimon, main gate of Shurijou Castle (stamp 7). h, Main hall of Shurijou Castle (red building, stamp 8). i, Shikina'en, royal garden (stamp 9). j, Seifautaki Sanctuary (niche in rocks, stamp 10).

2002 Photo. *Perf. 13x13¼*

2821	A2163	Sheet of 10	15.00	15.00
a.-j.		80y Any single	1.50	1.40
2822	A2164	Sheet of 10	15.00	15.00
a.-j.		80y Any single	1.50	1.25
2823	A2165	Sheet of 10	15.00	15.00
a.-j.		80y Any single	1.50	1.40

Issued: No. 2821, 7/23; No. 2822, 9/20; No. 2823, 12/20. Sheet numbers are in center of colored rectangle at top of sheet. Stamp numbers are in sheet margins.

Letter Writing Day Type of 1998

Designs: No. 2824, Girl with bows in hair holding envelope. No. 2825, Monkey in tree holding envelope. No. 2826, House and flowers. No. 2827, Boy with arms raised, fence.

No. 2828: a, Cow and bird (triangular stamp). b, Boy and sheep (elliptical stamp). c, Caterpillar and ladybug under magnifying glass (round stamp). d, Girl with bows in hair, flowers (oval stamp). e, Boy with soccer ball. f, Girl with tennis racquet and ball. g, Man on bicycle. h, Girl with flower in vase (round stamp). i, Truck and automobile. j, Woman holding gift and coat, boy holding envelope

Perf. 13x13¼, 13 (#2828a)

2002, July 23 Photo.

2824	A2047	50y multi	.95	.65
2825	A2047	50y multi	.95	.65
2826	A2047	50y multi	.95	.65
2827	A2047	50y multi	.95	.65
a.		Strip of 4, #2824-2827	4.00	2.60
2828		Sheet of 10	15.00	15.00
a.-j.		A2047 80y Any single	1.50	1.00
k.		Booklet pane, #2824-2827, 3 each #2828g, 2828j	13.00	—
		Booklet, #2828k	13.00	
l.		Souvenir sheet, #2825, 2828j	2.50	2.50

No. 2828a is 34x28mm; No. 2828b is 29x26mm; No. 2828c is 29mm in diameter; No. 2828d is 28x40mm; Nos. 2828e and 2828f are 22x36mm; No. 2828h is 28mm in diameter; No. 2828i is 25x25mm.

12th World Congress of Psychiatry, Yokohama — A2166

2002, Aug. 1 Photo. *Perf. 12¾x13*

2829	A2166	80y multi	1.50	1.00

World Wheelchair Basketball Championships, Kitakyushu A2167

2002, Aug. 9

2830	A2167	80y multi	1.50	1.00

Civil Aviation, 50th Anniv. — A2168

2002, Sept. 6

2831	A2168	80y multi	1.50	1.00

Normalization of Diplomatic Relations Between Japan and People's Republic of China, 30th Anniv. — A2169

Designs: No. 2832, Purple wisteria flowers. No. 2833, Goldfish and cherry blossoms.

2002, Sept. 13 *Perf. 13x13¼*

2832		80y multi	1.50	1.00
2833		80y multi	1.50	1.00
a.		A2169 Horiz. pair, #2832-2833	3.00	2.00

Intl. Fleet Review, Tokyo Bay — A2170

2002, Oct. 1

2834	A2170	80y multi	1.50	1.00

Letter Writing Week Type of 2000

Hiroshige paintings from 53 Stations of the Tokaido Highway: 90y, Yui. 110y, Shono. 130y, Tozuka.

2002, Oct. 7 *Perf. 13¼*

2835	A2119	90y multi	1.75	1.10
2836	A2119	110y multi	2.10	1.25
2837	A2119	130y multi	2.50	1.60
		Nos. 2835-2837 (3)	6.35	3.95

Asian and Pacific Decade of Disabled Persons — A2171

2002, Oct. 10 *Perf. 12¾x13*

2838	A2171	80y multi	1.50	1.00

Cultural Pioneers Types of 1998-2000

Designs: No. 2839, Shiki Masaoka (1867-1902), poet. No. 2840, Ookawabata Yusuzumi-zu, by Kiyonaga Torii (1752-1815), artist. No. 2841, Aikitu Tanakadate (1856-1952), physicist.

Photo. & Engr., Photo. (#2840)

2002, Nov. 5 *Perf. 13*

2839	A2053	80y multi	1.50	1.00
2840	A2053	80y multi	1.50	1.00
2841	A2120	80y multi	1.50	1.00
		Nos. 2839-2841 (3)	4.50	3.00

A2172

A2173

New Year 2003 (Year of the Ram)

A2174 A2175

2002, Nov. 15 Photo. *Perf. 13x13¼*

2842	A2172	50y multi	.95	.60
2843	A2173	80y multi	1.50	1.00

Perf. 13½x13¼

2844	A2174	50y +3y multi	1.00	.65
2845	A2175	80y +3y multi	1.60	1.00
		Nos. 2842-2845 (4)	5.05	3.25

Sheets of two containing Nos. 2842-2843 were lottery prizes.

Kabuki, 400th Anniv. — A2176

Designs: No. 2846, Shibaraku and Tsuchigumo. No. 2847, Okuni Kabuki-zu, detail from painted screen.

2003, Jan. 15 Photo. *Perf. 13x13¼*

2846		80y multi	1.50	1.00
2847		80y multi	1.50	1.00
a.		A2176 Horiz. pair, #2846-2847	3.00	2.00

Japanese Television, 50th Anniv.

A2177 A2178

2003, Jan. 31

2848	A2177	80y multi	1.50	1.00
2849	A2178	80y multi	1.50	1.00

A2179

Greetings — A2180

No. 2850: a, Roses. b, Reindeer. c, Cat and butterfly. d, Rabbits in automobile. e, White flowers.

No. 2851: a, Heart and flower. b, Dog with noisemaker. c, Bird and snowman. d, Bird and strawberries. e, Cranes and turtle.

2003, Feb. 10 *Die Cut Perf. 13½*

Self-Adhesive

2850	A2179	Pane of 5 + 5 labels	7.50	
a.-e.		80y Any single	1.50	1.00
2851	A2180	Pane of 5 + 5 labels	7.50	
a.-e.		80y Any single	1.50	1.00

World Heritage Series

Sheet 11 — A2181

No. 2852 — Hiroshima buildings and stamps on theme of "Peace": a, Atomic Bomb Dome (stamp 1). b, Hiroshima Prefectural Commercial Exhibit Hall (stamp 2). c, Dove over Atomic Bomb Dome, yellow denomination (stamp 3). d, Child's drawing of person with flower (stamp 4). e, Dove over Atomic Bomb Dome, blue denomination (stamp 5). f, Dove over Atomic Bomb Dome, red denomination (stamp 6). g, Doves, stylized person holding child (stamp 7). h, People on hill (stamp 8). i, Bird (stamp 9). j, Rabbit, butterflies and flowers (stamp 10).

2003, Mar. 20 Photo. *Perf. 13x13¼*

2852 A2181 Sheet of 10 14.00 14.00
a.-j. 80y Any single 1.40 1.00

Sheet numbers are in center of colored rectangle at top of sheet. Stamp numbers are in sheet margin.

Inauguration of Japan Post — A2182

No. 2853 — Flowers: a, Adonis (yellow flowers). b, Primrose (pink flowers). c, Violets and Japanese quince (violet and red flowers). d, Field horsetail (flowerless). e, Japanese wisteria (white hanging flowers). f, Weeping cherry tree (pink buds and flowers) and swallow. g, Hydrangea (lilac flowers). h, Japanese magnolia (white and pink flowers). i, Candock (yellow flower) and moorhen. j, Peony (pink flower and bud) and butterfly.

2003, Apr. 1 *Die Cut Perf. 13¼*

Self-Adhesive

2853 A2182 Sheet of 10 14.00
a.-j. 80y Any single 1.40 1.00

Japan Post Mascots — A2183

Designs: a, Aichan (squirrel with pink bow). b, Male Kanchan (with heart on shorts). c, Posuton (with hands extended). d, Yuchan (squirrel with cap). e, Female Kanchan (with flower). f, Posuton (with letter). g, Posuton (with letter). h, Aichan (with pink bow), diff. i, Female Kanchan (with flower), diff. j, Posuton (with hands extended), diff. k, Yuchan (with cap), diff. l, Male Kanchan (waving).

2003, Apr. 1 *Die Cut Perf. 13¼*

Self-Adhesive

2854 A2183 Sheet of 12 13.00
a.-f. 50y Any single .85 .60
g.-l. 80y Any single 1.25 1.00

Ram and Tree Batik Screen Design — A2184

2003, Apr. 18 *Perf. 13¼*

2855 A2184 80y multi 1.40 1.00

Philately Week.

Edo Shogunate, 400th Anniv.

Screen Depicting Edo — A2185

Wall Decoration, Edo Castle — A2186

Armor of Ieyasu Tokugawa A2187

Detail from Writing Box A2188

Noh Mask and Costume — A2189

Sheet 2 — A2190

A2191

No. 2857 — Sheet 2: a, Nihonbashi, from 53 Stations of the Tokaido Road, by Hiroshige (stamp 1). b, Fireman's coat (stamp 2). c, Screen depicting Kabuki theater (stamp 3). d, Hina-matsuri fesitval doll of empress (no number). e, Hina-matsuri festival doll of emperor (stamp 4). f, Danjurou Ichikawa playing role of Goro Takenuki (stamp 5).

No. 2858 — Sheet 3: a, Stern of USS Powhatan (stamp 1). b, Bow of USS Powhatan (no number). c, Screen art depicting return of Commodore Perry's fleet to Japan (stamp 2). d, Ceramic platter for export to Europe (stamp 3). e, Portrait of a European Woman, probably by Gennai Hiraga (stamp 4). f, Perpetual clock (stamp 5).

2003 *Perf. 13x13¼*

2856 Vert. strip of 5 7.00 7.00
a. A2185 80y multi 1.40 1.00
b. A2186 80y multi 1.40 1.00
c. A2187 80y multi 1.40 1.00
d. A2188 80y multi 1.40 1.00
e. A2189 80y multi 1.40 1.00
Sheet, 2 #2856 (Sheet 1) 14.00 14.00
2857 A2190 Sheet of 10, #2857d-2857e, 2 each #2857a-2857c, 2857f 14.00 14.00
a.-f. 80y Any single 1.40 1.00
2858 A2191 Sheet of 10, #2858a-2858b, 2 each #2858c-2858f 14.00 14.00
a.-f. 80y Any single 1.40 1.40

Issued: No. 2856, 5/23; No. 2857, 6/12; No. 2858, 7/1. Sheet numbers are in center of arrows at top of sheet. Stamp numbers are in sheet margins.

ASEAN — Japan Exchange Year — A2192

No. 2859: a, Omar Ali Saifuddien Mosque, Brunei (stamp 1). b, Angkor Wat, Cambodia (stamp 2). c, Borobudur Temple, Indonesia (stamp 3). d, That Luang, Laos (stamp 4). e, Sultan Abdul Samad Building, Malaysia (stamp 5). f, Shwedagon Pagoda, Myanmar (stamp 6). g, Rice terraces, Philippines (stamp 7). h, Merlion Statue, Singapore (stamp 8). i, Wat Phra Kaeo, Thailand (stamp 9). j, Van Mieu, Viet Nam (stamp 10).

2003, June 16 Photo. *Perf. 13x13¼*

2859 A2192 Sheet of 10 14.00 14.00
a.-j. 80y Any single 1.40 1.00

Letter Writing Day — A2193

Designs: No. 2860, Bear with guitar, bird. No. 2861, Monkey with letter. No. 2862, Crocodile with accordion, bird. No. 2863, Cat with camera, letter.

No. 2864: a, Hippopotamus with umbrella, flowers, birds (oval stamp). b, Parakeet with letter. c, Owl (round stamp). d, Bear with letter, bird (oval stamp). e, Elephant with flowers. f, Giraffe with letter (oval stamp). g, Rabbit with letter, flowers (semi-circular stamp). h, Lion with letter, lantern. i, Goat with letter. j, Gorilla with koala, bird and owl.

2003, July 23 Photo. *Perf. 13x13¼*

2860 A2193 50y multi .85 .65
2861 A2193 50y multi .85 .65
2862 A2193 50y multi .85 .65
2863 A2193 50y multi .85 .65
a. Horiz. strip of 4, #2860-2863 3.40 2.60
2864 Sheet of 10 14.00 14.00
a.-j. A2193 80y Any single 1.40 1.00
k. Booklet pane of 10, #2860-2863, 2 each #2864b, 2864h, 2864i 12.00 —
Complete booklet, #2864k 12.00
l. Souvenir sheet, #2860, #2864b 2.25 1.75

Nos. 2864a, 2864d and 2864f are 28x40mm; No. 2864c is 30mm in diameter; No. 2864g is 40x24mm.

Intl. Letter Writing Week Type of 2000

Hiroshige paintings from 53 Stations of the Tokaido Highway: 90y, Kawasaki. 110y, Miya. 130y, Otsu.

2003, Oct. 6 *Perf. 13¼*

2865 A2119 90y multi 1.75 1.25
2866 A2119 110y multi 2.00 1.40
2867 A2119 130y multi 2.40 1.75
Nos. 2865-2867 (3) 6.15 4.40

Cultural Pioneers — A2194

Designs: No. 2868, Mokichi Saito (1882-1953), poet. No. 2869, Shibasaburo Kitasato (1853-1931), bacteriologist.

Photo. & Engr.

2003, Nov. 4 *Perf. 13*

2868 A2194 80y multi 1.50 1.10
2869 A2194 80y multi 1.50 1.10

See Nos. 2907-2909.

Reversion of the Amami Islands to Japanese Control, 50th Anniv. — A2195

2003, Nov. 7 **Photo.**

2870 A2195 80y multi 1.50 1.10

A2196 A2197

New Year 2004 (Year of the Monkey)
A2198 A2199

2003, Nov. 14 *Perf. 13x13¼*

2871 A2196 50y multi .95 .65
2872 A2197 80y multi 1.50 1.10

Photo. & Litho.

Perf. 13½x13¼

2873 A2198 50y +3y multi 1.00 .70
2874 A2199 80y +3y multi 1.60 1.10
Nos. 2871-2874 (4) 5.05 3.55

Sheets of two containing Nos. 2871-2872 were lottery prizes.

Happy Face — A2199a

Sky — A2199b

Serpentine Die Cut 9¼x9

2003, Dec. 1 **Photo.**

Self-Adhesive

2874A A2199a 80y multi + label 1.90 1.90

Serpentine Die Cut 6½x5½

Stamp + Label

Color of Japanese Inscription

2874B A2199b 80y blue 1.90 1.90
2874C A2199b 80y red orange 1.90 1.90
Nos. 2874A-2874C (3) 5.70 5.70

Stamps and labels are separated by a line of rouletting on Nos. 2874B-2874C. Labels could be personalized. No. 2874A was printed in sheets of 4 stamps and 4 labels that sold for 500y, and sheets of 10 stamps and 10 labels that sold for 1000y. Nos. 2874B-2874C were printed in sheets containing five of each stamp and 10 labels that sold for 1000y.

Bubbles — A2199c

Bubbles — A2199d

Rose — A2199e

Serpentine Die Cut 6

2004, Jan. 23 **Photo.**

Self-Adhesive

2874D A2199c 50y multi + label 1.25 1.25
2874E A2199d 50y multi + label 1.25 1.25
2874F A2199e 90y multi + label 1.90 1.90
Nos. 2874D-2874F (3) 4.40 4.40

Stamps and labels are separated by a line of rouletting. Labels could be personalized. Nos. 2874D-2874E were printed in sheets containing ten of each stamp and 20 labels that sold for 1200y. No. 2874F was printed in a sheet of 20 stamps and 20 labels that sold for 2000y.

Science, Technology and Animation

Astro Boy — A2200

Bowman Doll — A2201

Hantaro Nagaoka A2202

H-II Rocket A2203

Morph 3 — A2204

Astro Boy — A2205

Astro Boy — A2206

Astro Boy — A2207

Super Jetter — A2208

Japanese Clock — A2209

Otomo — A2210

KAZ — A2211

Stratospheric Platform Airship — A2212

Super Jetter — A2213

Super Jetter — A2214

Super Jetter — A2215

2003-2004 **Photo.** *Perf. 13x13¼*

2875 Vert. strip of 5 7.50 7.50
a. A2200 80y multi 1.50 1.10
b. A2201 80y multi 1.50 1.10
c. A2202 80y multi 1.50 1.10
d. A2203 80y multi 1.50 1.10
e. A2204 80y multi 1.50 1.10
Sheet, 2 #2875 15.00 15.00
2876 Sheet, #2875b-2875e, 2 each #2876a-2876c 15.00 15.00
a. A2205 80y multi 1.50 1.10
b. A2206 80y multi 1.50 1.10
c. A2207 80y multi 1.50 1.10
2877 Vert. strip of 5 7.50 7.50
a. A2208 80y multi 1.50 1.10
b. A2209 80y multi 1.50 1.10
c. A2210 80y multi 1.50 1.10
d. A2211 80y multi 1.50 1.10
e. A2212 80y multi 1.50 1.10
Sheet, 2 #2875 15.00 15.00
2878 Sheet, #2877b-2877e, 2 each #2878a-2878c 15.00 15.00
a. A2213 80y multi 1.50 1.10
b. A2214 80y multi 1.50 1.10
c. A2215 80y multi 1.50 1.10

Issued: Nos. 2875-2876, 12/16/03; Nos. 2877-2878, 1/23/04.

Science, Technology and Animation

Marvelous Melmo and Baby — A2216

Seishu Hanaoka (1760-1835), Surgeon — A2217

Wooden Microscope A2218

Jokichi Takamine (1854-1922), Chemist A2219

Drug Delivery System — A2220

Marvelous Melmo with Mother — A2221

Marvelous Melmo with Man — A2222

Marvelous Melmo and Others in Bottle — A2223

Science Ninja Team Gatchaman A2224

Proposed Perpetual Motion Machine of Michitaka Kume A2225

OHSUMI Satellite — A2226

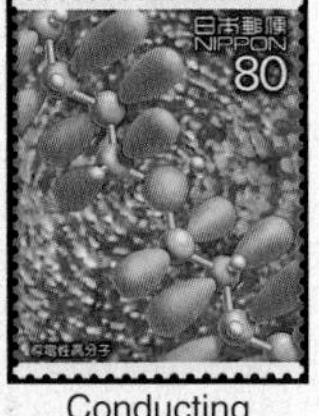

Conducting Polymer — A2227

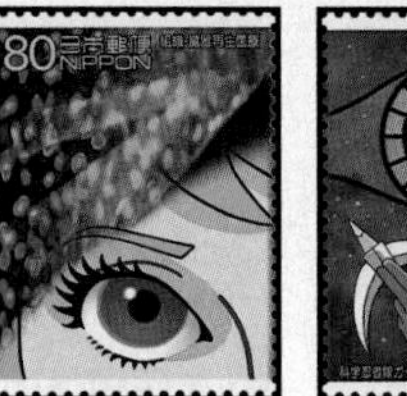

Tissue and Organ Reproduction A2228

Science Ninja Team Gatchaman A2229

Science Ninja Team Gatchaman A2230

Science Ninja Team Gatchaman A2231

2004	**Photo.**	***Perf. 13x13¼***	
2879	Vert. strip of 5	7.25	7.25
a.	A2216 80y multi	1.40	1.00
b.	A2217 80y multi	1.40	1.00
c.	A2218 80y multi	1.40	1.00
d.	A2219 80y multi	1.40	1.00
e.	A2220 80y multi	1.40	1.00
	Sheet, 2 #2879	14.50	14.50
2880	Sheet, #2879b-2879e, 2 each #2880a-2880c	14.50	14.50
a.	A2221 80y multi	1.40	1.00
b.	A2222 80y multi	1.40	1.00
c.	A2223 80y multi	1.40	1.00
2881	Vert. strip of 5	7.75	7.75
a.	A2224 80y multi	1.50	1.10
b.	A2225 80y multi	1.50	1.10
c.	A2226 80y multi	1.50	1.10
d.	A2227 80y multi	1.50	1.10
e.	A2228 80y multi	1.50	1.10
	Sheet, 2 #2881	15.50	15.50
2882	Sheet, #2881b-2881e, 2 each #2882a-2882c	15.50	15.50
a.	A2229 80y multi	1.50	1.10
b.	A2230 80y multi	1.50	1.10
c.	A2231 80y multi	1.50	1.10

Issued: Nos. 2879-2880, 2/23/04. Nos. 2881-2882, 3/23/04.

A2232

Hello Kitty — A2233

No. 2883: a, Red, white and blue flowers under chin. b, Red flower under chin, beige background. c, No flower under chin. d, Blue and red flowers under chin. e, Red flower under chin. f, Two blue flowers under chin. g, White flowers with green leaves under chin. h, Two pink flowers under chin. i, One blue flower under chin. j, Pink, yellow and green flower under chin.

No. 2884 — Head of Kitty with: a, Cherries. b, Bow. c, Strawberries. d, Blue flower. e, Spray of flowers.

Die Cut Perf. 13¼

2004, Feb. 6 Litho.

Self-Adhesive

2883	A2232 Sheet of 10	9.50	
a.-j.	50y Any single	.95	.65
2884	A2233 Sheet of 5	7.75	
a.-e.	80y Any single	1.50	1.10

Uchu-no Sakura Gohiki-no Saru-zu, by Sosen Mori — A2234

Perf. 12½x12¾ Syncopated

2004, Apr. 20		**Photo.**	
2885	A2234 80y multi	1.40	1.00

Philatelic Week.

Japanese Racing Association, 50th Anniv. — A2235

Designs: No. 2886, Ten Point and Tosho Boy, 22nd Armia Memorial Stakes. No. 2887, Narita Brian, 61st Tolyo Yushun.

2004, May 28		***Perf. 13x13¼***	
2886	80y green & multi	1.50	1.10
2887	80y blue & multi	1.50	1.10
a.	A2235 Horiz. pair, #2886-2887	3.00	2.20

Police Law, 50th Anniv. — A2236

2004, June 21		***Perf. 13***	
2888	80y Police car	1.50	1.10
2889	80y Police motorcycle	1.50	1.10
a.	A2236 Horiz. pair, #2888-2889	3.00	2.20

Letter Writing Day — A2237

Designs: No. 2890, Donkichi with pencil. No. 2891, Hime (woman with letter). No. 2892, Shouchan (man with ski cap). No. 2893, Owl with letter.

No. 2894: a, Dove with letter, rainbow. b, Squirrel with wings, rainbow. c, Stork (round stamp). d, Hime with wings (oval stamp). e, Donkichi with wings, letter. f, Kuriko (elf in pink) with wings. g, Megami (woman in white) (oval stamp). h, Shouchan with wings. i, Squirrel with flowers, letter. j, Rabbit (round stamp).

2004, July 23	**Photo.**	***Perf. 13x13¼***	
2890	A2237 50y multi	.90	.65
2891	A2237 50y multi	.90	.65
2892	A2237 50y multi	.90	.65
2893	A2237 50y multi	.90	.65
a.	Horiz. strip of 4, #2890-2893	3.60	2.60
2894	Sheet of 10	14.50	14.50
a.-j.	A2237 80y Any single	1.40	1.00
k.	Booklet pane of 10, #2890-2893, 2 each #2894b, 2894e, 2894f	12.00	—
	Complete booklet, #2894k	12.00	
l.	Souvenir sheet, #2890, #2894f	2.40	1.75

Nos. 2894c, 2894j are 30mm in diameter; No. 2894d is 28x37mm; No. 2894g is 28x40mm; No. 2894i is 28x29mm.

2004 Summer Olympics, Athens — A2238

Olympic rings and: No. 2895, Olympic Flame, Olympia. No. 2896, 2004 Athens Olympics emblem.

2004, Aug. 6		***Perf. 13***	
2895	80y multi	1.50	1.10
2896	80y multi	1.50	1.10
a.	A2238 Horiz. pair, #2895-2896	3.00	2.20

Science, Technology and Animation

Mazinger-Z A2239

Steam Locomotive A2240

New KS Steel A2241

Shinkai 6500 Research Submarine A2242

Fuel Cell A2243

Mazinger-Z A2244

Mazinger-Z A2245

Mazinger-Z A2246

2004, Aug. 23	**Photo.**	***Perf. 13x13¼***	
2897	Vert. strip of 5	7.50	7.50
a.	A2239 80y multi	1.50	1.10
b.	A2240 80y multi	1.50	1.10
c.	A2241 80y multi	1.50	1.10
d.	A2242 80y multi	1.50	1.10

e. A2243 80y multi 1.50 1.10
Sheet, 2 #2897 15.00 15.00
2898 Sheet, #2897b-2897e, 2 each #2898a-2898c 15.00 15.00
a. A2244 80y multi 1.50 1.10
b. A2245 80y multi 1.50 1.10
c. A2246 80y multi 1.50 1.10

Science, Technology and Animation

Doraemon
A2247

Gennai Hiraga
A2248

Mechanical Netsuke
A2249

Television
A2250

Optical Fiber
A2251

Doraemon
A2252

Doraemon
A2253

Doraemon
A2254

2004, Nov. 22 Photo. ***Perf. 13x13¼***
2899 Vert. strip of 5 8.00 8.00
a. A2247 80y multi 1.60 1.10
b. A2248 80y multi 1.60 1.10
c. A2249 80y multi 1.60 1.10
d. A2250 80y multi 1.60 1.10
e. A2251 80y multi 1.60 1.10
Sheet, 2, #2899 16.00 16.00
2900 Sheet, #2899b-2899e, 2 each #2900a-2900c 16.00 16.00
a. A2252 80y multi 1.60 1.10
b. A2253 80y multi 1.60 1.10
c. A2254 80y multi 1.60 1.10

Japan — United States Relationships, 150th Anniv. — A2255

Designs: No. 2901, Mt. Fuji, by Frederick Harris. No. 2902, Cafe, by Yasuo Kuniyoshi.

2004, Sept. 22 ***Perf. 13***
2901 80y multi 1.50 1.10
2902 80y multi 1.50 1.10
a. A2255 Horiz. pair, #2901-2902 3.00 2.20

World Medical Association General Assembly, Tokyo — A2256

2004, Oct. 6 ***Perf. 12¾x13***
2903 A2256 80y multi 1.50 1.10

International Letter Writing Week Type of 2000

Hiroshige paintings from 53 Stations of the Tokaido Highway: 90y, Hiratsuka. 110y, Yokkaichi. 130y, Tsuchiyama.

2004, Oct. 8 ***Perf. 13¼***
2904 A2119 90y multi 1.75 1.25
2905 A2119 110y multi 2.00 1.40
2906 A2119 130y multi 2.40 1.60
Nos. 2904-2906 (3) 6.15 4.25

Cultural Pioneers Type of 2003

Designs: No. 2907, Lafcadio Hearn (1850-1904), writer. No. 2908, Isamu Noguchi (1904-88), sculptor. No. 2909, Masao Koga (1904-78), composer.

Litho. & Engr.

2004, Nov. 4 ***Perf. 12¾x13***
2907 A2194 80y multi 1.50 1.10
2908 A2194 80y multi 1.50 1.10
2909 A2194 80y multi 1.50 1.10
Nos. 2907-2909 (3) 4.50 3.30

A2257

A2258

New Year 2005 (Year of the Cock)
A2259 A2260

2004, Nov. 15 Photo. ***Perf. 13x13¼***
2910 A2257 50y multi 1.00 .65
2911 A2258 80y multi 1.60 1.10

Photo. & Typo.
Perf. 13½x13¼
2912 A2259 50y +3y multi 1.10 .70
2913 A2260 80y +3y multi 1.75 1.10
Nos. 2910-2913 (4) 5.45 3.55

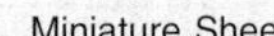

Miniature Sheet

Eto Calligraphy — A2261

Word "tori" in: a, Tensho style. b, Kinbun style (red). c, Kinbun style (black). d, Pictographic tensho style. e, Kana style. f, Sousho style. g, Kobun style (denomination at UR). h, Reisho style. i, Koukotsumoji style. j, Kobun style (denomination at LR).

Photo. & Embossed

2004, Dec. 1 ***Perf. 13***
2914 A2261 Sheet of 10 16.00 16.00
a.-j. 80y Any single 1.60 1.10

"Japan Post" — A2261a

A2261b

A2261c

Rose — A2261d

A2261e

A2261f

Die Cut Perf. 12½
2004, Dec. 15 **Photo.**
Stamp + Label
Denomination Color

2914K A2261a 80y rose 2.00 2.00
2914L A2261a 80y blue 2.00 2.00
2914M A2261b 80y lilac 2.00 2.00
2914N A2261c 80y green 2.00 2.00
2914O A2261d 80y rose 2.00 2.00
2914P A2261e 80y gray 2.00 2.00
2914Q A2261f 80y rose 2.00 2.00
Nos. 2914K-2914Q (7) 14.00 14.00

Stamps and labels are separated by a line of rouletting. Labels could be personalized. Nos. 2914K-2914L were printed in sheets containing five of each stamp and 10 labels that sold for 1000y. Nos. 2914M-2914Q were printed in sheets of two of each stamps and 10 labels that sold for 1000y.

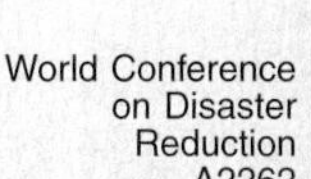
World Conference on Disaster Reduction A2262

2005, Jan. 11 Photo. *Perf. 13*

2915 A2262 80y multi		1.60	1.10

Opening of Chubu Natl. Airport — A2263

2005, Feb. 1

2916 A2263 80y multi		1.60	1.10

Science, Technology and Animation

Time Bokan — A2264

Circular Loom — A2265

Bullet Train — A2266

Micromachines A2267

International Space Station — A2268

Time Bokan — A2269

Time Bokan — A2270

Time Bokan — A2271

2005, Mar. 23 Photo. *Perf. 13x13¼*

2917	Vert. strip of 5	7.50	7.50
a.	A2264 80y multi	1.50	1.10
b.	A2265 80y multi	1.50	1.10
c.	A2266 80y multi	1.50	1.10
d.	A2267 80y multi	1.50	1.10
e.	A2268 80y multi	1.50	1.10
	Sheet, 2 #2917	15.00	15.00
2918	Sheet, #2917b-2917e, 2 each #2918a-2918c	15.00	15.00
a.	A2269 80y multi	1.50	1.10
b.	A2270 80y multi	1.50	1.10
c.	A2271 80y multi	1.50	1.10

Pokémon

Gonbe — A2272

Rayquaza A2273

Mew — A2274

Rizadon — A2275

Pikachu — A2276

2005, June 23 Litho. *Perf. 13x13¼*

2919	Vert. strip of 5	6.25	6.25
a.	A2272 50y multi	.85	.85
b.	A2273 50y multi	.85	.85
c.	A2274 80y multi	1.50	1.50
d.	A2275 80y multi	1.50	1.50
e.	A2276 80y multi	1.50	1.50
	Sheet, 2 #2919	12.50	12.50

Self-Adhesive

Booklet Stamps

2919F	A2272 50y multi	1.40	1.40
i.	Booklet pane of 2	2.80	
2919G	A2276 80y multi	2.25	2.25
2919H	A2274 80y multi	2.25	2.25
j.	Booklet pane, #2919G-2919H	4.50	
	Complete booklet, #2919Fi, 2919Hj + 8 postal cards	18.00	

Complete booklet sold for 1000y.

Mobile Suit Gundam

Freedom Gundam and Kira Yamato — A2277

Justice Gundam and Athrun Zala — A2278

Gundam W — A2279

Hiiro — A2280

Kamille Bidan — A2281

Z Gundam A2282

Zaku — A2283

Char Aznable — A2284

Amuro Ray — A2285

Gundam A2286

2005, Aug. 1

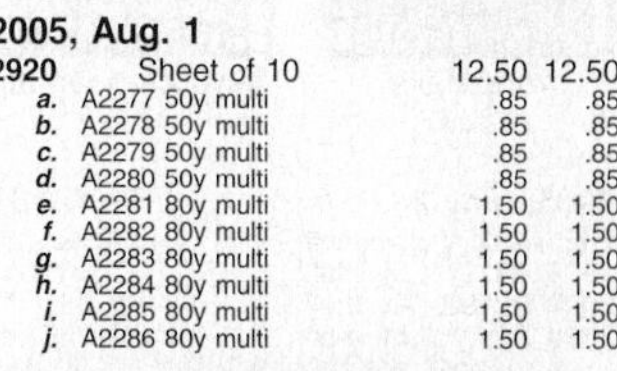

2920	Sheet of 10	12.50	12.50
a.	A2277 50y multi	.85	.85
b.	A2278 50y multi	.85	.85
c.	A2279 50y multi	.85	.85
d.	A2280 50y multi	.85	.85
e.	A2281 80y multi	1.50	1.50
f.	A2282 80y multi	1.50	1.50
g.	A2283 80y multi	1.50	1.50
h.	A2284 80y multi	1.50	1.50
i.	A2285 80y multi	1.50	1.50
j.	A2286 80y multi	1.50	1.50

Expo 2005, Aichi — A2287

Designs: No. 2921, Earth and mammoth skull and tusks. No. 2922, Earth and mammoth.

2005, Mar. 25 Photo. *Perf. 13x13¼*

2921	80y multi	1.50	1.10
2922	80y multi	1.50	1.10
a.	A2287 Horiz. pair, #2921-2922	3.00	2.20

Daikei-shiyu-zu, by Jakuchu Itou — A2288

Perf. 12½x12¾ Syncopated

2005, Apr. 20

2923 A2288 80y multi 1.60 1.10

Philately Week.

Rotary International, Cent. — A2289

2005, Apr. 28 Litho. ***Perf. 12¾x13***

2924 A2289 80y multi 1.60 1.10

Hodakadake A2290

Hakusan-ichige A2291

Yarigatake A2292

Miyama-odamaki A2293

2005, May 2 ***Perf. 13¼***

2925 A2290 50y multi	1.00	.65
2926 A2291 50y multi	1.00	.65
2927 A2292 50y multi	1.00	.65
2928 A2293 50y multi	1.00	.65
a. Horiz. strip of 4, #2925-2928	4.00	2.60

Japanese Alpine Club, cent.

Letter Writing Day — A2294

Designs: No. 2929, Owl on branch with envelope. No. 2930, Kuriko with letter. No. 2931, Squirrel with acorn. No. 2932, Rabbit and flowers.

No. 2933: a, Pigeon with pink letter. b, Donkichi in tree (round stamp). c, Castle and rainbow (oval stamp). d, Shochan with blue ski cap. e, Rabbit with pink letter (round stamp). f, Kuriko with flute on horse. g, Hime with bows in hair. h, Squirrel. i, Fox with letter (round stamp). j, Violets (oval stamp).

2005, July 22 Photo. ***Perf. 13x13¼***

2929 A2294 50y multi	.90	.65
2930 A2294 50y multi	.90	.65
2931 A2294 50y multi	.90	.65
2932 A2294 50y multi	.90	.65
a. Horiz. strip of 4, #2929-2932	3.60	2.60
2933 Sheet of 10	14.50	14.50
a.-j. A2294 80y Any single	1.40	1.00
k. Booklet pane of 10, #2929-2932, 2 each #2933d, 2933f, 2933g	12.00	—
Complete booklet, #2933k	12.00	
l. Souvenir sheet, #2932, #2933d	2.40	1.75

Nos. 2933a, 2933h are 28x29mm, Nos. 2933b, 2933e, 2933i are 30mm in diameter; No. 2933c, 2933j are 28x40mm.

Poetry Collections — A2295

Poets: No. 2934, Ono no Komachi. No. 2935, Fujiwara no Teika.

2005, Sept. 1 Litho. ***Perf. 12¾x13***

2934 80y multi	1.50	1.10
2935 80y multi	1.50	1.10
a. A2295 Horiz. pair, #2934-2935	3.00	2.25

Kokin Wakashu, 1100th anniv. (No. 2934), Shinkokin Wakashu, 800th anniv. (No. 2935).

Intl Astronautics Congress, Fukuoka — A2296

Designs: No. 2936, Himawari-6 satellite. No. 2937, H-IIA rocket launch.

2005, Oct. 3

2936 80y multi	1.40	1.00
2937 80y multi	1.40	1.00
a. A2296 Horiz. pair, #2934-2935	2.80	2.00

Intl. Letter Writing Week Type of 2000

Hiroshige paintings from 53 Stations of the Tokaido Highway: 90y, Mariko. 110y, Minakuchi. 130y, Shinagawa.

2005, Oct. 7 Photo. ***Perf. 13¼***

2938 A2119 90y multi	1.60	1.10
2939 A2119 110y multi	2.00	1.40
2940 A2119 130y multi	2.40	1.60
Nos. 2938-2940 (3)	6.00	4.10

Souvenir Sheets

A2297

Greetings Stamps — A2298

No. 2941: a, Cyclamen. b, Elf and flower. c, Bear and bird. d, Owl, gorilla playing banjo. e, Snowman.

No. 2942: a, Santa Claus. b, Poinsettias and candle. c, Angel with gift. d, Hamster and strawberries. e, Owl, cat playing drums.

Litho. With Foil Application

Serpentine Die Cut 13¼

2005, Oct. 21

Self-Adhesive

2941 A2297 Sheet of 5	4.50	
a.-e. 50y Any single	.90	.65

Serpentine Die Cut 13¼x13½

2942 A2298 Sheet of 5	7.00	
a.-e. 80y Any single	1.40	1.00

A2299

A2300

New Year 2006 (Year of the Dog) A2301 A2302

2005, Nov. 15 Photo. ***Perf. 13x13¼***

2943 A2299 50y multi	.85	.60
2944 A2300 80y multi	1.40	1.00

Photo. & Typo.

Perf. 13¼

2945 A2301 50y +3y multi	.90	.60
2946 A2302 80y +3y multi	1.40	1.00
Nos. 2943-2946 (4)	4.55	3.20

Miniature Sheet

Germany — Japan Exchange Year — A2303

No. 2947: a, Ludwig van Beethoven. b, Benz automobile. c, Meissen porcelain figurine of Japanese man playing drum. d, Meissen porcelain figurine of female musician. e, Meissen porcelain figurine of woman on circus horse. f, Meissen porcelain figurine of a harlequin.

2005, Dec. 1 Photo. ***Perf. 13***

2947 A2303 Sheet of 10, #a-b, 2 each #c-f	14.00	14.00
a.-f. 80y Any single	1.40	1.00

Miniature Sheet

Eto Calligraphy — A2304

Word "inu" in: a, Tensho style (connected lines). b, Kinbun style (on brown red panel). c, Pictograph (denomination at UL). d, Phonetic letters (2 lines unconnected, denomination at LR). e, Tensho style (2 red chops). f, Tensho style (blue half-circle). g, Symbolic characters (red). h, Semi-cursive style (red chop at L, denomination at LL). i, Semi-cursive style (oval chop in red at L). j, Koukotsumoji style (denomination at L, red chop at R).

Photo. & Embossed

2005, Dec. 1 ***Perf. 13x13¼***

2948 A2304 Sheet of 10	14.00	14.00
a.-j. 80y Any single	1.40	1.00

Animation

Galaxy Express 999 — A2305

No. 2949: a, Tetsuro and Galaxy Express 999 in flight. b, Matael and passenger cars. c, Claire holding book. d, The Conductor. e, Freija and Matael. f, Tetsuro and Moriki Yutaka. g, Emeraldas and Count Mecha. h, Herlock. i, Matael and galaxy. j, Galaxy Express 999.

2006, Feb. 1 Litho. ***Perf. 13x13¼***

2949 A2305 Sheet of 10	14.00	14.00
a.-j. 80y Any single	1.40	1.00

Detective Conan — A2306

No. 2950: a, Conan in green jacket. b, Conan wearing glasses, with woman in light blue jacket. c, With Shinichi, scratching chins. d, Ran holding letter. e, Dr. Agasa, Ayumi, front of car. f, Mitushiko, Genta, rear of car. g, Haibara Ai. h, Conan with backpack. i, Mysterious Thief Kid. j, Shinichi and Conan, city in background.

2006, Apr. 3 Litho. *Perf. 13x13¼*

2950	A2306	Sheet of 10	14.00	14.00
a.-j.		80y Any single	1.40	1.00

International Exchanges and Friendships A2307

Designs: No. 2951, Rabbit and flowers. No. 2952, Children kissing. No. 2953, Bears and caught fish. No. 2954, Children's drawing of two animals. No. 2955, Chick, cat, dog, rabbit, squirrel and rocket.

2006, Mar. 1 Photo. *Perf. 13*

2951	A2307	80y multi	1.40	1.00
2952	A2307	80y multi	1.40	1.00
2953	A2307	80y multi	1.40	1.00
2954	A2307	80y multi	1.40	1.00
2955	A2307	80y multi	1.40	1.00
a.		Vert. strip of 5, #2951-2955	7.00	5.00
		Sheet, 2 each #2951-2955	14.00	10.00

Morning Glories and Puppies, Door Painting by Okyu Maruyama — A2308

Designs: No. 2956, Morning glories. No. 2957, Puppies.

Perf. 13½x13 Syncopated

2006, Apr. 20 Photo.

2956		80y multi	1.50	1.10
2957		80y multi	1.50	1.10
a.	A2308	Horiz. pair, #2956-2957	3.00	2.20

Philately Week.

Miniature Sheet

Australia-Japan Year of Exchange — A2309

No. 2958: a, Australian flag, Ayers Rock. b, Kangaroo and Ayers Rock. c, Sydney Opera House. d, Australian flag and Sydney Opera House. e, Fish of Great Barrier Reef. f, Heart Reef. g, Golden wattle flowers. h, Bottlebrush flowers. i, Koalas. j, Kookaburra.

2006, May 23 Photo. *Perf. 13*

2958	A2309	Sheet of 10	15.00	15.00
a.-j.		80y Any single	1.50	1.10

Miniature Sheet

Sacred Sites and Pilgrimage Routes of the Kii Mountains World Heritage Site — A2310

No. 2959: a, Kumano Hongu-Taisha Shrine Building 3 (brown roof, part of stairs seen at bottom). b, Kumano Hongu-Taisha Shrine Building 4 (brown roof, full set of stairs at LR). c, Great Waterfall of Nachi. d, Overhead view of Kumano Nachi-Taisha Shrine (denomination at LL). e, Nachi Fire Festival. f, Seigantoji Temple (dark blue roof). g, Kongobuji Temple (blue green roof). h, Wooden Kongara-Doji-Ryuzo (statue, denomination at UL). i, Kinpusenji Temple (gray roof). j, Wooden Zao-Gongen-Ryuzo (statue, denomination at LL).

2006, June 23 *Perf. 13x13¼*

2959	A2310	Sheet of 10	14.00	14.00
a.-j.		80y Any single	1.40	1.00

Miniature Sheets

A2311

Greetings Stamps — A2312

No. 2960: a, Fairy and flower. b, Church bell. c, Flower bouquet and ribbons. d, Dolphin. e, Hibiscus and hummingbird.

No. 2961: a, Pink cattleya orchid. b, Fairy, flowers and trees. c, Flower and oranges. d, Parrot and flowers. e, Fairy with pail and orange flowers.

Litho. With Foil Application

Serpentine Die Cut 13¼

2006, June 30

Self-Adhesive

2960	A2311	Sheet of 5	5.25	
a.-e.		50y Any single	1.00	.70

Serpentine Die Cut 13½

2961	A2312	Sheet of 5	8.75	
a.-e.		80y Any single	1.75	1.25

No. 2960 sold for 300y; No. 2961 for 500y.

Taifu Iseno, Poet — A2313

Sadaijin Gotokudaijino, Poet — A2314

Mitsune Ooshikochino, Poet — A2315

Akahito Yamabeno, Poet — A2316

Naishi Suono, Poet — A2317

Poets and Poetry — A2318

No. 2963: a, Double Cherry Blossoms, by Yasuko Koyama. b, Iseno and poetry. c, Pale Morning Moon, by Keiso Mitsuoka. d, Gotokudaijino and poetry. e, White Chrysanthemum, by Shiko Miyazaki. f, Ooshikochino and poetry. g, Mt. Fuji, by Eiko Matsumoto. h, Yamabeno and poetry. i, Spring Night, by Soshu Miyake. j, Suono and poetry.

2006, July 21 Photo. *Perf. 13¼*

2962		Vert. strip of 5	4.50	4.50
a.		A2313 50y multi	.90	.65
b.		A2314 50y multi	.90	.65
c.		A2315 50y multi	.90	.65
d.		A2316 50y multi	.90	.65
e.		A2317 50y multi	.90	.65
		Sheet, 2 #2962	9.00	9.00

Perf. 13

2963	A2318	Sheet of 10	14.00	14.00
a.-j.		80y Any single	1.40	1.00

Letter Writing Day.

Horizontal Lines and Colored Circles — A2318a

Die Cut Perf. 13¼

2006, Sept. 1 Litho.

Self-Adhesive

2963K	A2318a	80y multi	2.50	2.50

Printed in sheets of 10 that sold for 1000y. The image portion could be personalized. The image shown is a generic image.

Blue Flowers — A2318b

Pink Flowers — A2318c

Die Cut Perf. 13¼

2006, Sept. 1 Litho.

Self-Adhesive

2963L	A2318b	80y multi	2.50	2.50
2963M	A2318c	80y multi	2.50	2.50

Nos. 2963L-2963M were printed in sheets of 10, containing five of each stamp, that sold for 1000y. The image portions could be personalized. The images shown are generic images.

Accession to the United Nations, 50th Anniv. — A2319

Paintings by Toshiro Sawanuki: 90y, Glorious World To Come. 110y, Eternity.

2006, Sept. 29 Litho. *Perf. 13¾x14*

2964	A2319	90y multi	1.50	1.10
2965	A2319	110y multi	1.90	1.40

Miniature Sheet

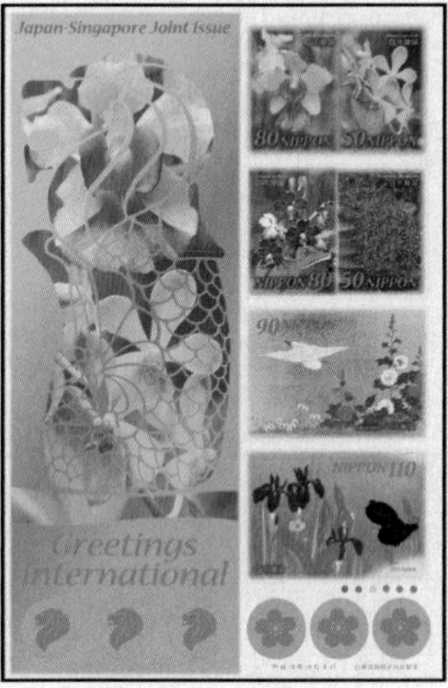

Greetings — A2320

No. 2966: a, Mokara Lion's Gold orchid. b, Renanthera Singaporean orchid. c, Vanda Miss Joaquim orchid. d, Vanda Mimi Palmer orchid. e, Hollyhocks and Egret, by Hoitsu Sakai, horiz. f, Irises and Moorhens, by Sakai, horiz.

Litho. With Foil Application

2006, Oct. 3 *Die Cut Perf. 13½x13¾*

Self-Adhesive

2966	A2320	Sheet of 6	8.50	
a.-b.		50y Either single	.95	.65
c.-d.		80y Either single	1.50	1.10
e.		90y multi	1.60	1.10
f.		110y multi	2.00	1.40

Roulettes separate adjacent 50y and 80y stamps. No. 2966 sold for 500y. See Singapore Nos. 1225-1231.

Miniature Sheets

A2321

Scenes From Japanese Movies — A2322

No. 2967: a, Tange Sazen (scarred samurai, green). b, Carmen Kokyo-Ni-Kaeru (women waving, lilac). c, Ugetsu Monogatari (man and woman, maroon). d, Tokyo Monogatari (man and woman, brown). e, Shichinin-No-Samurai (helmeted samurai, deep green). f, Hawaii-No-Yoru (man and woman, olive green). g, Nemuri Kyoshiro (samurai, blue green). h, Guitar-Wo-Motta-Wataridori (man with guitar, blue). i, Miyamoto Musashi (swordsman, blue gray). j, Cupola-No-Aru-Machi (girl, brown).

No. 2968: a, Sailor-Fuku-To-Kikanju (woman with gun). b, Otoko-Ha-Tsuraiyo (man in light blue kimono). c, Kamata Koshin Kyoku (Three people). d, Yomigaeru Kinro (man in chair). e, Setouchi-Shonen-Yakyu-Dan (woman with baseball glove). f, HANA-BI (man standing). g, Shitsurakuen (Woman hugging man). h, Gamera (monster, denomination at UL). i, Tasogare Seibei (woman grooming man). j, Godzilla (monster, denomination at UR).

2006, Oct. 10 Photo. *Perf. 13*

2967	A2321	Sheet of 10	14.00	14.00
a.-j.		80y Any single	1.40	1.00
2968	A2322	Sheet of 10	14.00	14.00
a.-j.		80y Any single	1.40	1.00

Ikebana International Ninth World Convention — A2323

2006, Oct. 23 Litho. *Perf. 13x13¼*

Background Colors

2969		80y grn & lt grn	1.40	1.00
2970		80y red & yel	1.40	1.00
a.		A2323 Horiz. pair, #2969-2970	2.80	2.00

A2324

A2325

New Year 2007 (Year of the Pig)
A2326 A2327

2006, Nov. 1 Photo. *Perf. 13x13¼*

2971	A2324	50y multi	.85	.60
2972	A2325	80y multi	1.40	1.00

Photo. & Typo.

Perf. 13¼

2973	A2326	50y +3y multi	.90	.65
2974	A2327	80y +3y multi	1.40	1.00
		Nos. 2971-2974 (4)	4.55	3.25

Miniature Sheets

A2328

Greetings Stamps — A2329

No. 2975: a, Squirrel in mug. b, Bell with flowers. c, Clown with flower. d, Skating polar bear. e, Bear in Santa Claus suit, guitar, birds.

No. 2976: a, Cat in Santa Claus suit ringing bell. b, Fairy and cyclamen. c, Snowman with gift. d, Reindeer and star. e, Floral wreath.

Litho. with Foil Application

Die Cut Perf. 13½x13¼

2006, Nov. 24

Self-Adhesive

2975	A2328	Sheet of 5	5.25	
a.-e.		50y Any single	1.00	.70

Die Cut Perf. 13

2976	A2329	Sheet of 5	8.75	
a.-e.		80y Any single	1.75	1.25

No. 2975 sold for 300y; No. 2976 for 500y.

Miniature Sheet

Eto Calligraphy — A2330

No. 2977: a, Semicursive style (white background, red chop at lower left). b, Kinbun style (blue background). c, Reisho style (red background). d, Japanese cursive syllabary (white background, red chop at lower right, character with small arc at top). e, Kinbun style (white background, red chop at lower right, character with funnel-shaped line at top). f, Kinbun style (red character). g, Kinbun style (white background, red chop at lower left, character with flat line at top. h, Kinbun style (white background. red chop at lower right, character with large blotch at top). i, Tensho style (white background, red chop at lower left, character with long curved arc and circle at top) j, Reisho style (white background, red chop at lower right, character with dot and straight line at top).

Litho. & Embossed

2006, Dec. 1 *Perf. 13x13¼*

2977	A2330	Sheet of 10	14.00	14.00
a.-j.		80y Any single	1.40	1.00

Miniature Sheet

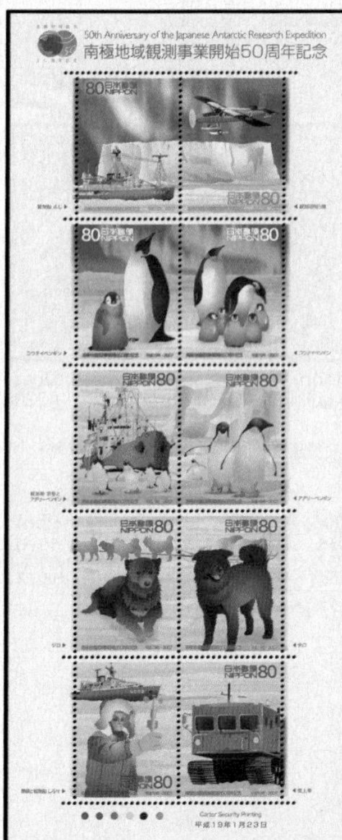

A2331

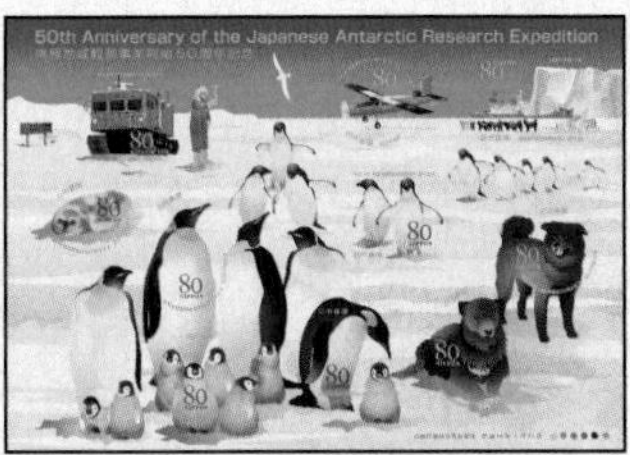

Japanese Antarctic Research Expeditions, 50th Anniv. — A2332

No. 2978: a, Observation ship Fuji. b, Spotter plane. c, Adult emperor penguin and chick. d, Adult emperor penguins and five chicks. e, Observation ship Soya and Adelie penguins. f, Adult Adelie penguins and chick. g, Dog, Jiro, in snow, dog team. h, Dog, Taro, standing, dog sled. i, Scientist, observation ship Shirase. j, Snowmobile with cabin.

No. 2979: a, Snowmobile with cabin (26x28mm). b, Spotter plane (28mm diameter). c, Soya and dog sled (34x26mm). d, Weddell seal (28x23mm ellipse). e, Head of emperor penguin (26x37mm oval). f, Two Adelie penguins (26x28mm). g, Dog, Taro, standing with mouth open (28mm diameter). h, Emperor penguin chicks (28mm diameter). i, Adult emperor penguin and chick (26x28mm). j, Dog, Jiro, in snow (26x37mm oval).

2007, Jan. 23 Litho. *Perf. 13*

2978	A2331	Sheet of 10	14.00	14.00
a.-j.		80y Any single	1.40	1.00

Self-Adhesive

Die Cut Perf. 13¾x13½

2979	A2332	Sheet of 10	14.00	
a.-j.		80y Any single	1.40	1.00

Animation

Miniature Sheet

Neon Genesis Evangelion — A2333

No. 2980: a, Evangelion Unit 01. b, Shinji Ikari. c, Rei Ayanami. d, Evangelion Unit 00. e, Soryu Asuka Langley. f, Evangelion Unit 02. g, Rei Ayanami and Soryu Asuka Langley. h, Misato Katsuragi. i, Kawora Nagisa. j, Sachiel, the third angel.

2007, Feb. 23 *Perf. 13x13¼*

2980	A2333	Sheet of 10	14.00	14.00
a.-j.		80y Any single	1.40	1.00

Animation

Miniature Sheet

Future Boy Conan — A2334

No. 2981: a, Conan (with name). b, Lana (with name). c, Lana (without name). d, Conan (without name). e, Monsley and airplane. f, Lepka. g, Jimsy and Umaso. h, Dyce on running robot. i, Dr. Lao and hovering craft. j, Grandpa.

2007, June 22 Litho. *Perf. 13x13¼*

2981	A2334	Sheet of 10	14.00	14.00
a.-j.		80y Any single	1.40	1.00

World Heritage Sites

Miniature Sheet

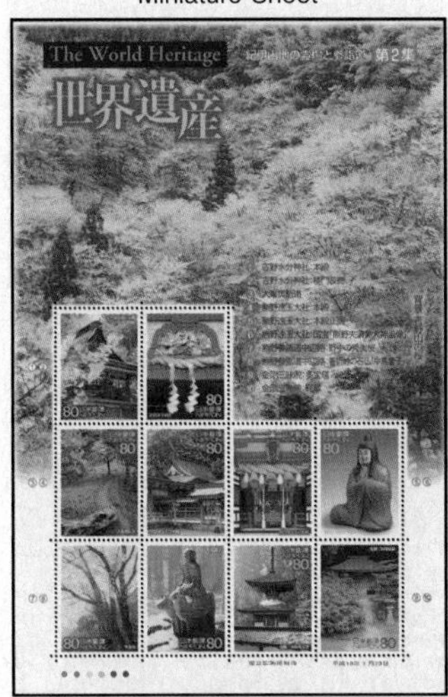

Sacred Sites and Pilgrimage Routes of the Kii Mountains World Heritage Site — A2335

No. 2982: a, Yoshino Mikumari Shrine, cherry blossoms at left. b, Pictoral and rope decoration at Yoshino Mikumari shrine. c, Omine-Okugake-Michi trail. d, Kumano Hayatama-Taisha Shrine (black-roofed building with red trim). e, Kumano Hayatama-Taisha Shrine, diff. f, Wooden icon of Kumano-Fusumino-Okami-Zazo. g, Cherry trees in bloom at Kumano Sankei-Michi Nakahechi. h, Stone sculpture of Emperor Kazan riding ox and horse. i, Kongo-Sanmaiin Temple. j, Steps to Kong-Sanmaiin Temple.

2007, Mar. 23 Photo. *Perf. 13x13¼*

2982	A2335	Sheet of 10	14.00	14.00
a.-j.		80y Any single	1.40	1.00

World Heritage Sites

Miniature Sheet

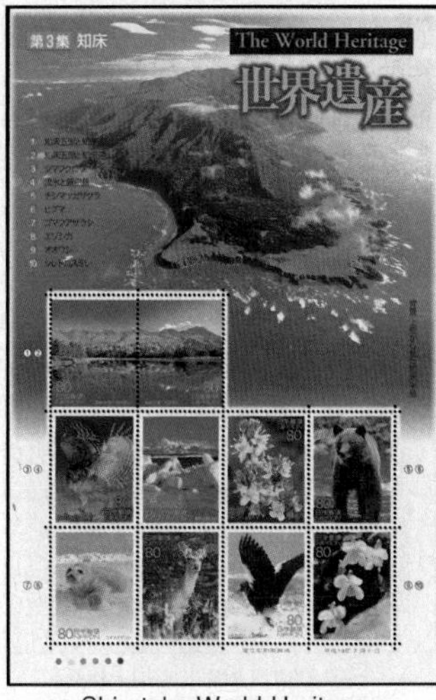

Shiretoko World Heritage Site — A2336

No. 2983: a, Lake and mountain, cloudless sky. b, Lake and mountain, cloud in sky. c, Blakiston's fish owl. d, Sea ice, Mt. Rausu. e, Cherry blossoms. f, Brown bear. g, Harbor seal. h, Ezo deer. i, Sea eagle. j, Shiretoko violets (white and yellow flowers).

2007, July 6 Photo. *Perf. 13x13¼*

2983	A2336	Sheet of 10	14.00	14.00
a.-j.		80y Any single	1.40	1.00

Sleeping Boar, by Ippo Mori — A2337

Boar Loping Across Fields, by Mori — A2338

Sparrow, by Mori — A2339

Cherry Blossoms, by Mori — A2340

Bird Flock, by Mori — A2341

Great Tits Sitting In a Japanese Bush Clover, by Mori — A2342

Perf. 13¼x13 Syncopated

2007, Apr. 20 Photo.

2984	A2337	80y multi	1.40	1.00
2985	A2338	80y multi	1.40	1.00
a.		Horiz. pair, #2984-2985	2.80	2.00
		Sheet, 5 #2985a	14.00	14.00
2986	A2339	80y multi	1.40	1.00
2987	A2340	80y multi	1.40	1.00
2988	A2341	80y multi	1.40	1.00
2989	A2342	80y multi	1.40	1.00
a.		Vert. strip of 4, #2986-2989	5.60	4.00
		Sheet, 2 each #2985-2989	14.00	14.00
		Nos. 2984-2989 (6)	8.40	6.00

Miniature Sheet

Japan - India Friendship Year — A2343

No. 2990: a, Taj Mahal. b, Taj Mahal and camels. c, Bengal tiger. d, Peacock. e, Buddhist monastery, Sanchi, India. f, Statue of goddess, Sanchi. g, Painting of Indian woman facing left. h, Calico print of Indian facing right. i, Indian folk dancer. j, Character from Kathakali, Indian dance drama.

2007, May 23 *Perf. 13*

2990	A2343	Sheet of 10	14.00	14.00
a.-j.		80y Any single	1.40	1.00

Tsurayuki Kino, Poet — A2344

Empress Jito, Poet — A2345

Dayu Sarumaru, Poet — A2346

Kanemasa Minamotono, Poet — A2347

Sanuki Nijoinno, Poet — A2348

Poetry — A2349

No. 2996 — Poetry in Japanese calligraphy and: a, Plum blossoms. b, Tsurayuki Kino. c, Mount Kagu. d, Empress Jito. e, Deer. f, Dayu Sarumaru. g, Plovers. h, Kanemasa Minamotono. i, Stone in sea. j, Sanuki Nijoinno.

2007, July 23 Photo. *Perf. 13½*

2991	A2344 50y multi		.85	.60
2992	A2345 50y multi		.85	.60
2993	A2346 50y multi		.85	.60
2994	A2347 50y multi		.85	.60
2995	A2348 50y multi		.85	.60
a.	Vert. strip of 5, #2991-2995		4.25	3.00

Perf. 13

2996	A2349	Sheet of 10	14.00	14.00
a.-j.	80y Any single		1.40	1.00

Letter Writing Day.

Miniature Sheet

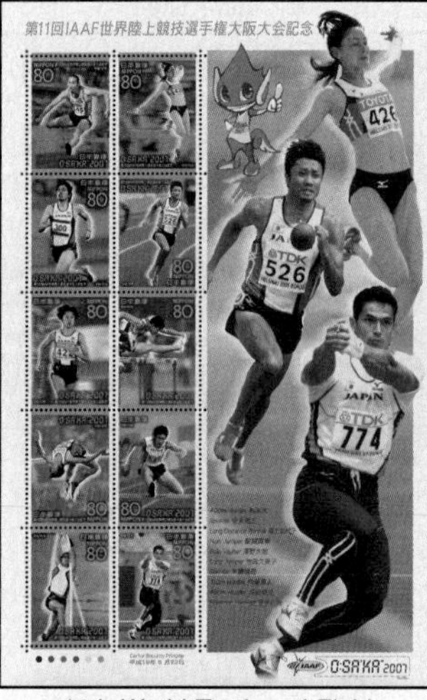

11th World Track and Field Championships, Osaka — A2350

No. 2997: a, Dai Tamesue (athlete 545), hurdler. b, Kumiko Ikeda (athlete 426), sprinter. c, Yuzo Kanemaru (athlete 300), runner. d, Shingo Suetsugu (athlete 526), runner. e, Kayoko Fukushi (athlete 422), runner. f, Masato Naito running over hurdle. g, Naoyuki Daigo high jumping. h, Kenji Narisako (athlete 531), hurdler. i, Daichi Sawano pole vaulting. j, Koji Murofushi (athlete 774), hammer throw.

2007, Aug. 23 Litho. *Perf. 13x13¼*

2997	A2350	Sheet of 10	14.00	14.00
a.-j.	80y Any single		1.40	1.00

Miniature Sheet

Diplomatic Relations Between Japan and Thailand, 120th Anniv. — A2351

No. 2998: a, Maple leaves, bamboo. b, Cherry blossoms. c, Ratchaphruek (yellow flower) blossom. d, Rhynchostylis gigantea (purple and white orchids). e, Mother-of-pearl elephant. f, Mother-of-pearl flower. g, Thai dancer. h, Statue, Wat Phra Keo. i, Elephant with head at left, from Toshogu Shrine, Japan, horiz. j, Elephant with head at right, from Toshogu Shrine, horiz.

Die Cut Perf. and Serpentine Die Cut

2007, Sept. 26 Litho.

Self-Adhesive

2998	A2351	Sheet of 10	14.00	14.00
a.-j.	80y Any single		1.40	1.00

Vertical stamps are die cut perf. 13 at top and bottom, serpentine die cut 10¼ on side adjacent to another stamp, and die cut perf. 12½ on remaining side. Horizontal stamps are die cut perf. 13 at top and bottom, serpentine die cut 10¼ on side adjacent to another stamp, and die cut perf. 12¾ on remaining side.

See Thailand No. 2316.

International Letter Writing Week Type of 2000

Hiroshige paintings from 53 Stations of the Tokaido Highway: 90y, Hodogaya. 110y, Arai. 130y, Kusatsu.

2007, Sept. 28 Litho. *Perf. 14*

2999	A2119 90y multi	1.60	1.10
3000	A2119 110y multi	1.90	1.40
3001	A2119 130y multi	2.25	1.60
	Nos. 2999-3001 (3)	5.75	4.10

Mandarin Duck A2352

Eastern Turtle Dove A2353

2007, Oct. 1 Photo. *Perf. 13x13½*

3002	A2352 50y multi	.85	.60
3003	A2353 80y multi	1.40	1.00

Miniature Sheets

A2354

Establishment of Japan Post Corporation — A2355

No. 3004: a, Baron Hisoka Maejima (red panels). b, Japan #2 (red panels). c, Post office counter (orange panels). d, Postal workers loading mail coach (dark red panels). e, Postal saving counter (green panels). f, People at post office counters (blue panels).

No. 3005 — Paintings of flowers: a, Sunflower, by Hoitsu Sakai. b, Confederate Roses, by Sakai. c, Chrysanthemums, by Sakai. d, Maple Leaves, by Kiitsu Suzuki (showing branch). e, Maple Leaves, by Suzuki (no branch). f, Camellia, by Sakai. g, Cherry Tree, by Sakai (bird in tree). h, Tree Peony, by Sakai. i, Iris, by Sakai, j, Hydrangeas, by Sakai.

2007, Oct. 1 Photo. *Perf. 13¼*

3004	A2354	Sheet of 10, #a-b, 2 each #c-f	14.00	14.00
a.-f.	80y Any single		1.40	1.00
3005	A2355	Sheet of 10	14.00	14.00
a.-j.	80y Any single		1.40	1.00

Miniature Sheet

Intl. Skills Festival For All — A2356

No. 3006: a, Computer operator and robot. b, Computer operator. c, Plasterer and Geisha. d, Plasterer and pillar. e, Pastry chef and cake. f, Pastry chef and bowls. g, Flower arranger and flowers. h, Flower arranger holding scissors. i, Sheet metal worker and automobile. j, Sheet metal worker hammering metal.

2007, Oct. 23 Litho. *Perf. 13*

3006	A2356	Sheet of 10	14.00	14.00
a.-j.	80y Any single		1.40	1.00

A2357

A2358

New Year 2008 (Year of the Rat)

A2359 A2360

2007, Nov. 1 Photo. *Perf. 13x13½*

3007	A2357 50y multi	.90	.60
3008	A2358 80y multi	1.40	1.00

Photo. & Typo.

Perf. 13¼

3009	A2359 50y +3y multi	.95	.65
3010	A2360 80y +3y multi	1.50	1.10
	Nos. 3007-3010 (4)	4.75	3.35

Diamonds — A2360a

Die Cut Perf. 13¼

2007, Nov. 1 Litho.

Self-Adhesive

Green Diamonds

Color of Country Name

3010A	A2360a	50y blue	1.75	1.75
3010B	A2360a	50y green	1.75	1.75
3010C	A2360a	50y red	1.75	1.75
3010D	A2360a	50y purple	1.75	1.75
3010E	A2360a	50y black	1.75	1.75

Blue Diamonds

3010F	A2360a	80y blue	2.50	2.50
3010G	A2360a	80y green	2.50	2.50
3010H	A2360a	80y red	2.50	2.50
3010I	A2360a	80y purple	2.50	2.50
3010J	A2360a	80y black	2.50	2.50

Nos. 3010A-3010E were printed in sheets of 10, containing two of each stamp, that sold for 900y. Nos. 3010F-3010J were printed in sheets of 10, containing two of each stamp, that sold for 1200y. The image portion could be personalized. The image shown is a generic image.

Miniature Sheets

A2361

Greetings Stamps — A2362

No. 3011: a, White buildings. b, Fairies on flying swans. c, Santa Claus. d, Flowers and snow-covered trees. e, Cat and candy cane.

No. 3012: a, Santa Claus and reindeer. b, Fairy and flowers. c, Snowman with green cap. d, Strawberries. e, Snowman and flying reindeer.

2007, Nov. 26 Litho. *Die Cut Perf.*

Self-Adhesive

3011	A2361	Sheet of 5	4.50	
a.-e.		50y Any single	.90	.60

Die Cut Perf. 13

3012	A2362	Sheet of 5	7.50	
a.-e.		80y Any single	1.50	1.10

Miniature Sheet

Edo Calligraphy — A2363

No. 3013 — Charcters for "rat": a, In Kinbun style (red character). b, Black character with three long vertical lines at top, with red chop at LR. c, In Tensho style (gold character on red and brown background). d, In Reisho style (black character resembling a "3" with line through it, with red chop at LR). e, In Shoden style (gold character on blue and pink background). f, In Kana style (black characters resembling "12" with a check mark, with red chop at LR). g, In Reisho style (black characters, with red chop at LL). h, In Sosho style (black character with pink lines, with red chop at LL). i, Black character resembling stick figure with raised arms, with red chop at LR. j, In Kinbun style (black character with five short vertical lines at top, red chop at LL).

Litho. & Embossed

2007, Dec. 3 ***Perf. 13***

3013	A2363	Sheet of 10	15.00	15.00
a.-j.		80y Any single	1.50	1.10

Mt. Fuji A2364

Mt. Fuji A2365

Mt. Fuji A2366

Mt. Fuji A2367

Mt. Fuji A2368

Bamboo — A2369

Someiyoshino Blossoms — A2370

Hydrangea Blossoms — A2371

Maple Leaves A2372

Narcissuses — A2373

2008, Jan. 23 Litho. *Perf. 13¾x14*

3014	Sheet of 10	15.00	15.00
a.	A2364 80y multi	1.50	1.10
b.	A2365 80y multi	1.50	1.10
c.	A2366 80y multi	1.50	1.10
d.	A2367 80y multi	1.50	1.10
e.	A2368 80y multi	1.50	1.10
f.	A2369 80y multi	1.50	1.10
g.	A2370 80y multi	1.50	1.10
h.	A2371 80y multi	1.50	1.10
i.	A2372 80y multi	1.50	1.10
j.	A2373 80y multi	1.50	1.10

Yokoso! Japan Weeks.

Souvenir Sheet

New Year 2008 (Year of the Rat) — A2374

No. 3015: a, Two rats. b, One rat.

2008, Jan. 28 Photo. *Perf. 13*

3015	A2374	Sheet of 2	2.50	2.50
a.		50y multi	1.00	.50
b.		80y multi	1.50	.75

Miniature Sheet

Animated Folktales — A2375

No. 3016: a, Man on horse, cherry trees, pagoda. b, Man in cherry tree. c, Moon Princess in bamboo stump, woodsman with ax. d, Moon Princess, flying horse and wagon, archers. e, Four statues in snow. f, Two statues in snow, man with basket. g, Boy in ship. h, Demons. i, Woman carrying roll of cloth. j, Man, woman, crane.

2008, Feb. 22 Litho. *Perf. 13*

3016	A2375	Sheet of 10	16.00	16.00
a.-j.		80y Any single	1.60	1.25

Folktales "The Old Man Who Made Cherry Trees Blossom" (#3016a-3016b), "The Moon Princess" (#3016c-3016d), "Six Little Statues" (#3016e-3016f), "The Peach Boy" (#3016g-3016h), "The Grateful Crane" (#3016i-3016j).

Miniature Sheet

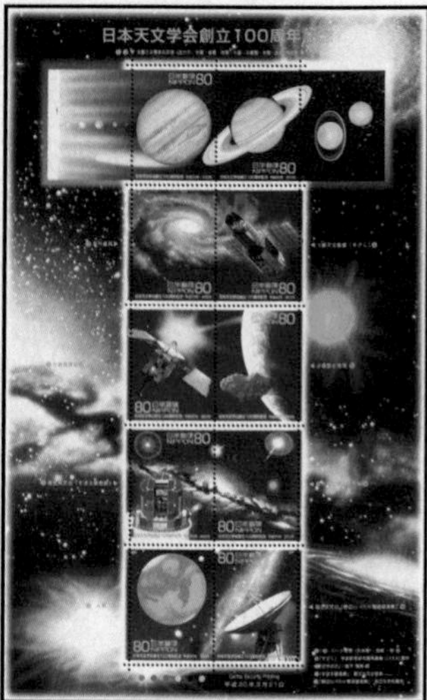

Astronomical Society of Japan, Cent. — A2376

No. 3017: a, Jupiter. b, Saturn. c, Spiral galaxy. d, Suzaku X-ray satellite. e, Hayabusa probe. f, Asteroids and Earth. g, Subaru Telescope. h, Stars. i, Mars. j, Nobeyama Radio Telescope.

2008, Mar. 21

3017	A2376	Sheet of 10	16.00	16.00
a.-j.		80y Any single	1.60	1.25

Miniature Sheet

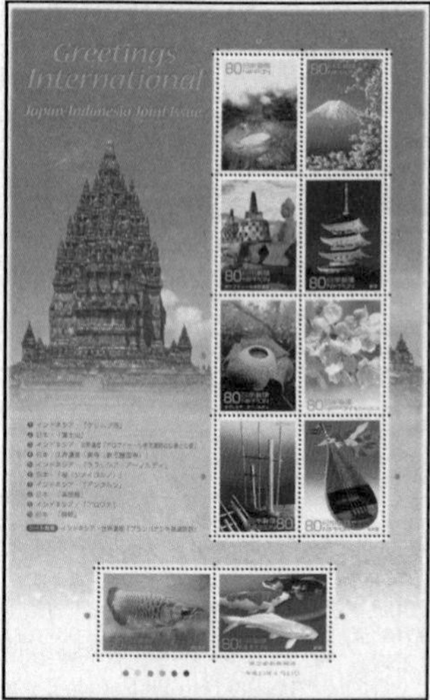

Diplomatic Relations Between Japan and Indonesia, 50th Anniv. — A2377

No. 3018: a, Kelimutu Volcano, Indonesia. b, Mt. Fuji, Japan, and cherry blossoms. c, Borobudur, Indonesia. d, Toji Temple, Kyoto. e, Rafflesia arnoldii. f, Cherry blossoms. g, Angklung (Indonesian musical instrument). h, Gaku biwa (Japanese musical instrument). i, Red arowana fish, horiz. j, Three koi, horiz.

2008, June 23 **Photo.** ***Perf. 13***

3018	A2377	Sheet of 10	15.00	15.00
a.-j.		80y Any single	1.50	1.10

See Indonesia Nos. 2135-2139.

Small Bird in Cherry Blossom, by Seitei Watanabe A2378

Butterfly in Peony Branch, by Watanabe A2379

Egrets in the Rain Beneath Willow Trees, by Watanabe A2380

Grapes, by Watanabe A2381

Sea Birds on a Rocky Crag, by Watanabe A2382

Perf. 13½x13 Syncopated

2008, Apr. 18 **Photo.**

3019	A2378 80y multi		1.60	1.25
3020	A2379 80y multi		1.60	1.25
3021	A2380 80y multi		1.60	1.25
3022	A2381 80y multi		1.60	1.25
3023	A2382 80y multi		1.60	1.25
a.	Vert. strip of 5, #3019-3023		8.00	6.25
	Sheet, 2 #3023a		16.00	16.00

Philately Week.

See note after No. Z827 in the Prefecture Stamp listings.

Miniature Sheet

Home Towns — A2383

No. 3024 — Paintings by Taiji Harada of views of towns: a, Water Shield (Yamamoto District, Akita prefecture). b, Bell of Time (Kawago, Saitama prefecture). c, Enjoying the Evening Cool (Gujo, Gifu prefecture). d, The Little Electric Train (Choshi, Chiba prefecture). e, Sea of the Heart (Shozu District, Kagawa prefecture). f, Lake in the Evening Sun (Gamo District, Shiga prefecture). g, Tanabata Dolls (Matsumoto, Nagano prefecture). h, Town of Outdoor Warehouses (Ise, Mie prefecture). i, The Farm Clock (Aki, Kochi prefecture). j, Late Summer Heat in the Street (Hakusan, Ishikawa prefecture).

2008, May 2 **Photo.** ***Perf. 13***

3024	A2383	Sheet of 10	16.00	16.00
a.-j.		80y Any single	1.60	1.25

Hideyo Noguchi Africa Prize — A2384

2008, May 23 **Litho.** ***Perf. 13***

3025	80y Noguchi		1.60	1.25
3026	80y Map of Africa		1.60	1.25
a.	A2384 Horiz. pair, #3025-3026		3.25	2.50

Miniature Sheet

National Afforestation Campaign — A2385

No. 3027 — Scenes from Akita prefecture: a, Aleutian avens and Mt. Moriyoshi, denomination at UL. b, Aleutian avens and Mt. Moriyoshi, denomination at UR. c, Fringed galax flowers, denomination at LL. d, Fringed galax flowers, denomination at LR. e, Autumn leaves, denomination at LL. f, Autumn leaves, denomination at UR. g, Beech forest in autumn, denomination in UL. h, Beech forest in autumn, denomination in UR. i, Weigela. j, Waterfall.

2008, June 13 **Photo.** ***Perf. 13***

3027	A2385	Sheet of 10	9.25	9.25
a.-j.		50y Any single	.90	.65

Miniature Sheet

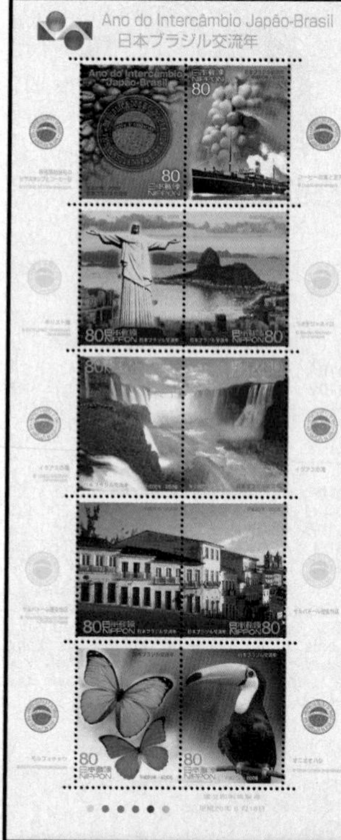

Year of Exchange Between Japan and Brazil — A2386

No. 3028: a, Roasted coffee beans, seal of Brazilian vice-consulate in Kobe. b, Coffee cherries, ship. c, Christ the Redeemer Statue, Rio de Janeiro. d, Sugarloaf Mountain, Rio de Janeiro. e, Iguaçu Falls, denomination at UL. f, Iguaçu Falls, denomination at UR. g, Houses, denomination at LL. h, Houses, denomination at LR. i, Butterflies. j, Toucan.

2008, June 18 **Litho.** ***Perf. 13***

3028	A2386	Sheet of 10	16.00	16.00
a.-j.		80y Any single	1.60	1.25

Miniature Sheet

Publication of *Anne of Green Gables,* by Lucy Maud Montgomery, Cent. — A2387

No. 3029: a, Anne holding buttercups. b, Green Gables House. c, Matthew Cuthbert, wearing hat, vert. d, Marilla Cuthbert, wearing hat, vert. e, Anne, Diana Barry holding hands, vert. f, Diana, vert. g, Anne in black dress, vert. h, Anne and Gilbert Blythe, vert. i, Matthew Cuthbert, without hat, vert. j, Anne, Marilla Cuthbert, vert.

Perf. 13¼x13 (#3026a-3026b), 13x13¼

2008, June 20

3029	A2387	Sheet of 10	16.00	16.00
a.-j.		80y Any single	1.60	1.25

See Canada Nos. 2276-2278.

Lily — A2388

Rugosa Rose — A2389

Rhododendron A2390

Safflower A2391

Gentian — A2392

Lily — A2393

Rugosa Rose A2394

Rhododendron A2395

Safflower A2396

Gentian A2397

2008, July 1 Photo. *Perf. 13¼*

3030	A2388	50y multi	.95	.65
3031	A2389	50y multi	.95	.65
3032	A2390	50y multi	.95	.65
3033	A2391	50y multi	.95	.65
3034	A2392	50y multi	.95	.65
a.		Vert. strip of 5, #3030-3034	4.75	3.25
3035	A2393	80y multi	1.50	1.10
3036	A2394	80y multi	1.50	1.10
3037	A2395	80y multi	1.50	1.10
3038	A2396	80y multi	1.50	1.10
3039	A2397	80y multi	1.50	1.10
a.		Vert. strip of 5, #3035-3039	7.50	5.50
		Nos. 3030-3039 (10)	12.25	8.75

Flowers of Kanagawa, Hokkaido, Fukushima, Yamagata and Nagano prefectures.

Miniature Sheet

Hokkaido Local Autonomy Law, 60th Anniv. — A2398

No. 3040: a, Lake Toya, cranes (32x39mm). b, Goryokaku Fortress (28x33mm). c, Hills around Biei (28x33mm). d, Sea angel (28x33mm). e, Otaru Canal (28x33mm).

2008, July 1 *Perf. 13¼ (#3040a), 13*

3040	A2398	Sheet of 5	7.50	7.50
a.-e.		80y Any single	1.50	1.10

Miniature Sheet

G8 Summit, Toyako — A2399

No. 3041: a, Mt. Yotei (stamp #1). b, Showa Shinzan (stamp #2). c, Mt. Yotei and Lake Toya (stamp #3). d, Mt. Yotei and Fukidashi Park (stamp #4). e, Mt. Eniwa and Lake Shikotsu (stamp #5). f, Pink Japanese wood poppies (stamp #6). g, Squirrel (stamp #7). h, Beardtongue flowers (stamp #8). i, Mountain ash leaves and berries (stamp #9). j, Northern fox (stamp #10).

2008, July 7 Litho. *Perf. 13¾x14*

3041	A2399	Sheet of 10	15.00	15.00
a.-j.		80y Any single	1.50	1.10

Lady Shikibu Murasaki, Poet — A2400

Sanekata Fujiwara, Poet — A2401

Lady Shonagon Sei, Poet — A2402

Kinto Dainagon, Poet — A2403

Lady Shikibu Izumi, Poet — A2404

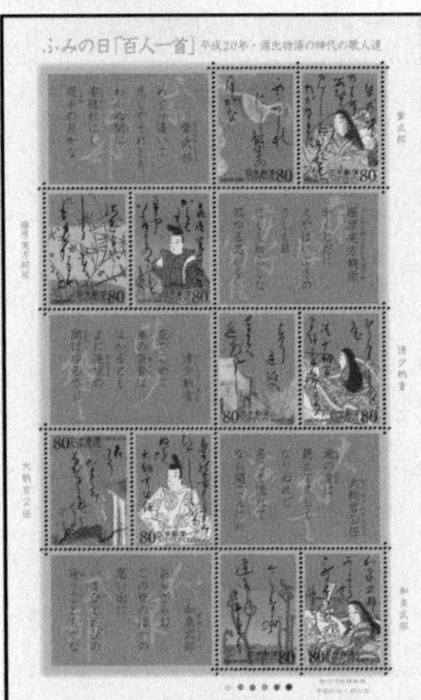
Poetry — A2405

No. 3047 — Poetry in Japanese calligraphy and: a, Moon behind cloud. b, Lady Shikibu Murasaki. c, Mugwort. d, Sanekata Fujiwara. e, Waterfall. f, Lady Shonagon Sei. g, Barrier. h, Kinto Dainagon. i, Bare branches. j, Lady Shikibu Izumi.

2008, July 23 Photo. *Perf. 13¼*

3042	A2400	50y multi	.95	.65
3043	A2401	50y multi	.95	.65
3044	A2402	50y multi	.95	.65
3045	A2403	50y multi	.95	.65
3046	A2404	50y multi	.95	.65
a.		Vert. strip of 5, #3042-3046	4.75	3.25

Perf. 12¾x13

3047	A2405	Sheet of 10	15.00	15.00
a.-j.		80y Any single	1.50	1.10

Letter Writing Day.

Miniature Sheets

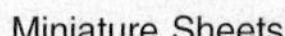

A2406

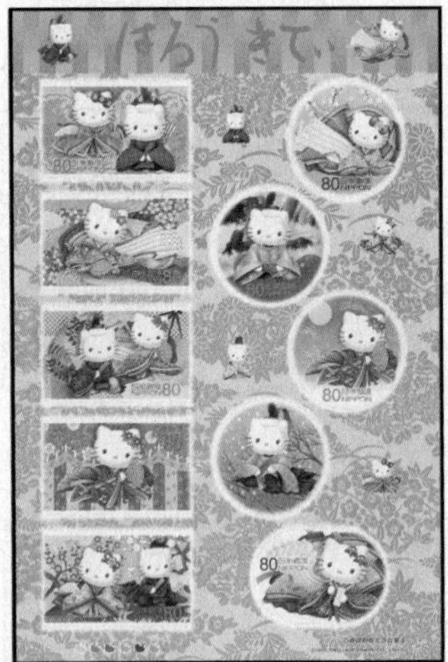
Hello Kitty — A2407

No. 3048 — Hello Kitty characters with: a, Gold denomination at UR. b, Green denomination at UR. c, Yellow denomination at UL, Kitty with pink flowers on head. d, Yellow denomination at UR, Kitty wearing green patterned kimono. e, Green denomination at UL, Kitty wearing black kimono. f, Green denomination at UL, Kitty with pink and blue flowers on head. g, Green denomination at UL, Kitty with bow and flowers on head. h, Yellow denomination at UL, Kitty wearing dark green kimono. i, Green denomination at UL, Kitty wearing brown kimono. j, Green denomination at UL, Kitty with purple and green flowers on head.

No. 3049 — Hello Kitty characters with: a, Green denomination at LL (41x27mm). b, Gold denomination at LR, one Kitty with two pink flowers on head (41x27mm). c, Gold denomination at LR, Kitty at right with purple and green flowers on head (41x27mm). d, Green denomination at UR (41x27mm). e, Gold denomination at LR, Kitty at left with bow and flower on head (41x27mm). f, Blue denomination (34mm diameter). g, Gold denomination, Kitty wearing gray kimono (34mm diameter). h, Gold denomination, Kitty holding fan (34mm diameter). i, Gold denomination, Kitty with snowflakes in background

(34mm diameter). j, Blue denomination (40x28mm oval stamp).

Die Cut Perf. and Serpentine Die Cut (see note)

2008, July 23 Litho.

Self-Adhesive

3048	A2406	Sheet of 10	9.50	
a.-j.		50y Any single	.95	.65

Die Cut Perf. 13x13¼ (#3049a-3049e), Die Cut Perf.

3049	A2407	Sheet of 10	15.00	15.00
a.-j.		80y Any single	1.50	1.10

Stamps on No. 3048 are arranged in five rows of se-tenant pairs. Each pair is die cut perf. 13¾ at top and bottom, die cut perf. 13½ on the outer sides, and serpentine die cut 11¼ between the stamps in the pair.

Love That Meets the Night, by Utamaro A2408

Yatsumi Bridge, by Hiroshige A2409

Mannen Bridge, Fukagawa, by Hiroshige A2410

Koshiro Matsumoto IV as Gorobe Sakanaya of San'ya, by Sharaku A2411

Hanazuma From Hyogoya, by Utamaro A2412

Ayase River at Kanegafuchi, by Hiroshige A2413

Tsukiji Hongan-ji Temple, Teppozu, by Hiroshige A2414

Hikosaburo Bando III as Sanai Sagisaka, by Sharaku A2415

Roko of Tatsumi, by Utamaro A2416

Kameido Plum Gardens, by Hiroshige A2417

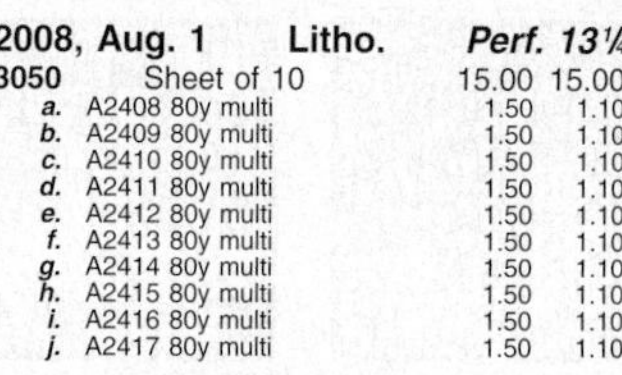

2008, Aug. 1 Litho. *Perf. 13¼*

3050		Sheet of 10	15.00	15.00
a.	A2408 80y multi		1.50	1.10
b.	A2409 80y multi		1.50	1.10
c.	A2410 80y multi		1.50	1.10
d.	A2411 80y multi		1.50	1.10
e.	A2412 80y multi		1.50	1.10
f.	A2413 80y multi		1.50	1.10
g.	A2414 80y multi		1.50	1.10
h.	A2415 80y multi		1.50	1.10
i.	A2416 80y multi		1.50	1.10
j.	A2417 80y multi		1.50	1.10

Life in Edo (Tokyo).

Miniature Sheet

Hometown Festivals — A2418

No. 3051: a, Streamers for Sendai Tanabata Festival, Miyagi prefecture (light green background, denomination at UR). b, Streamers for Sendai Tanabata Festival (light green background, denomination at UL). c, Portable shrine for Kanda Festival, Tokyo prefecture (yellow background, denomination in red at LL). d, Portable shrine for Kanda Festival (yellow background, denomination in blue at UR). e, Dancers from Awa Dance Festival, Tokushima prefecture (pink background, denomination at LR). f, Dancers from Awa Dance Festival (pink background, denomination at UR). g, Participants and lanterns for Hakata Gion Yamakasa Festival, Fukuoka prefecture (light blue background, denomination at UL). h, Participants and float for Hakata Gion Yamakasa Festival (light blue background, denomination at UR). i, Drummers for Eisa Festival, Okinawa prefecture (yellow background, denomination in red at LR). j, Drummers for Eisa Festival (yellow background, denomination in blue at UR).

2008, Aug. 1 Photo. *Perf. 13½x13¼*

3051	A2418	Sheet of 10	9.50	9.50
a.-j.		50y Any single	.95	.65

Miniature Sheet

Treaty of Peace and Friendship Between Japan and People's Republic of China, 30th Anniv. — A2419

No. 3052: a, Temple of Heaven, Beijing. b, Huangshan Mountains, China. c, Mogao Cave Shrines, China. d, Temple of the Flourishing Law, Ikaruga, Japan. e, Female mandarin duck. f, Male mandarin duck. g, Panel from painting by Wang Chuanfeng depicting three stylized fish and red Japanese apricot flower. h, Panel from painting by Wang Chuanfeng depicting two stylized fish and water lily. i, Panel from painting by Wang Chuanfeng depicting one stylized fish and autumn leaves. j, Panel from painting by Wang Chuanfeng depicting two staylized fish and white and red narcissi. Nos. 3052a-3052d, 3052g-3052j are 28x49mm; Nos. 3052e-3052f, 32x49mm.

2008, Aug. 12 Photo. *Perf. 13*

3052	A2419	Sheet of 10	15.00	15.00
a.-j.		80y Any single	1.50	1.10

Animation

Miniature Sheet

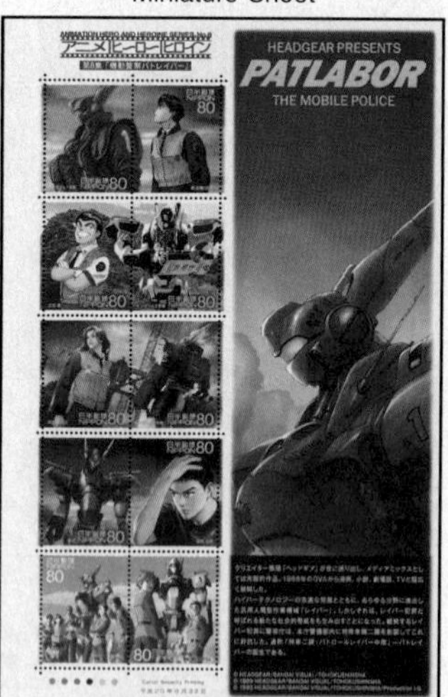

Patlabor — A2420

No. 3053: a, Ingfram Model 1 robot. b, Noa Izumimn, with "2" on sleeve patch. c, Isao Ota, with crossed arms. d, Ingram Model 2 robot. e, Shinobu Nagumo, with long hair. f, Ingram Model 3 robot. g, Robot, diff. h, Asumo Shinohara, with hand on head. i, Ingram Model 1 robot and eight characters. j, Ingram Model 2 robot and three characters.

2008, Aug. 22 Litho. *Perf. 13x13¼*

3053	A2420	Sheet of 10	15.00	15.00
a.-j.		80y Any single	1.50	1.10

Miniature Sheet

Home Towns — A2421

No. 3054 — Paintings by Taiji Harada of views of towns: a, Idyllic Village (Farmhouses, Tonami, Toyama prefecture). b, Blessing (Wedding at Yamate Catholic Church, Yokohama, Kanagawa prefecture). c, Approaching Winter (Lake Nojiri, Kamiminochi District, Nagano prefecture). d, Konjac Field (Farmers planting, Numata, Gunma prefecture). e, Vespers (Family in garden near houses, Nara, Nara prefecture). f, Cosmos (Flowers, boats and boathouses, Mikatakaminaka District, Fukui prefecture). g, Voices of Excited Children (Farmhouse and hill, Haga District, Tochigi prefecture). h, Autumn Colors Everywhere (Farmhouse and train car, Namegata, Ibaraki prefecture). i, Small Market (Family at roadside market, Asakura District, Fukuoka prefecture). j, Lullaby Village (Village and bridge, Kuma District, Kumamoto prefecture).

2008, Sept. 1 Photo. *Perf. 13*

3054	A2421	Sheet of 10	15.00	15.00
a.-j.		80y Any single	1.50	1.10

Miniature Sheet

Kyoto Travel Scenes — A2422

No. 3055: a, Otagi Nebutsu Temple and stone sculptures (stamp #1). b, Toriimoto (stamp #2). c, Adashino Nenbutsu Temple (stamp #3). d, Gio Temple (stamp #4). e, Buddha sculptures, Nison Temple (stamp #5). f, Hut of Fallen Persimmons, persimmons on tree (stamp #6). g, Jojakko Temple (stamp #7). h, Sagano Scenic Railway bridge and trains (stamp #8). i, Rowboats on Hozu River (stamp #9). j, Togetsu Bridge (stamp #10).

2008, Sept. 1 Litho. *Perf. 13x13¼*

3055	A2422	Sheet of 10	15.00	15.00
a.-j.		80y Any single	1.50	1.10

PREFECTURE ISSUES

Japan has 47 prefectures (political subdivisions) and 13 postal regions (12 until 2004). Since 1989, the national postal ministry has issued stamps to publicize each prefecture. These prefectural stamps are valid throughout Japan and were issued not only in the prefecture named on the stamp but in all other prefectures in the postal region, and in one or more post offices in the other 11 or 12 postal regions. Prefectural stamps are distinguishable from other Japanese stamps by the style of the ideographic characters of "Nippon yubin" on each stamp:

日本郵便

Inscr. on National Stamps since 1948

Inscr. on Prefectural Stamps

Monkeys (Nagano) — ZA1

Cherries on Tree (Yamagata) — ZA2

Shurei-mon, Gate of Courtesy (Okinawa) — ZA3

Dogo Hot Spa (Ehime) — ZA4

Blue-eyed Doll (Kanagawa) ZA5

Seto Inland Sea (Hiroshima) — ZA6

Memorial Hall and Mandai Bridge (Niigata) — ZA8

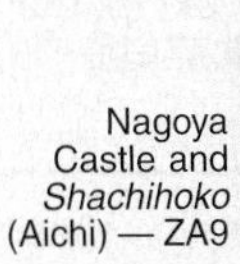

Nagoya Castle and *Shachihoko* (Aichi) — ZA9

Mt. Takasaki Monkey Holding Perilla Leaf, Fruit (Oita) — ZA10

City Hall, 1888 (Hokkaido) ZA11

Runner, Flower (Hokkaido) ZA12

Kumamoto Castle (Kumamoto) ZA13

Stone Lantern, Kenroku-en Park (Ishikawa) — ZA14

Bunraku Puppets and Theater (Osaka) — ZA15

Shigaraki Ware Raccoon Dog and Lake Biwa (Shiga) ZA16

Apples and Blossoms (Aomori) — ZA17

Raccoon Dogs Dancing (Chiba) — ZA18

Blowfish Lanterns (Yamaguchi) ZA19

Tokyo Station (Tokyo) — ZA20

2nd Asian Winter Olympics (Hokkaido) ZA21

Waterfalls (Toyama) ZA22

Perf. 13, 13½ (#Z4, Z11, Z20), 13x13½ (#Z12-Z19)

1989-90 Photo., Litho. (#Z16-Z17)

Z1	ZA1	62y	multicolored	1.10	.65
Z2	ZA2	62y	multicolored	1.10	.65
Z3	ZA3	62y	multicolored	1.10	.65
Z4	ZA4	62y	multicolored	1.10	.65
Z5	ZA5	62y	multicolored	1.10	.65
Z6		62y	sampan, bridge	1.10	.65
Z7		62y	islands, stairs, starbursts	1.10	.65
a.	ZA6		Pair, #Z6-Z7	2.25	1.50
Z8	ZA8	62y	multicolored	1.10	.65
Z9	ZA9	62y	multicolored	1.10	.65
Z10	ZA10	62y	multicolored	1.10	.65
Z11	ZA11	62y	multicolored	1.10	.65
Z12	ZA12	62y	multicolored	1.10	.65
Z13	ZA13	62y	multicolored	1.10	.65
Z14	ZA14	62y	multicolored	1.10	.65
Z15	ZA15	62y	multicolored	1.10	.65
Z16	ZA16	62y	multicolored	1.10	.65
Z17	ZA17	62y	multicolored	1.10	.65
Z18	ZA18	62y	multicolored	1.10	.65
Z19	ZA19	62y	multicolored	1.10	.65
Z20	ZA20	62y	multicolored	1.10	.65
Z21	ZA21	62y	multicolored	1.10	.65
Z22	ZA22	62y	multicolored	1.10	.60
			Nos. Z1-Z22 (22)	24.20	14.25

Sheets containing 4 #Z1, Z2, Z4, Z11 or 3 #Z14 + label, 3 #Z19 + label were lottery prizes.

Issued: #Z1-Z2, 4/1; #Z3, 5/15; #Z4, 6/1; #Z5, 6/2; #Z6-Z7, 7/7; #Z8, 7/14; #Z9, 8/1; #Z10-Z11, 8/15; #Z12, 9/1; #Z13, 9/29; #Z14-Z17, 10/2; #Z18, 10/27; #Z19-Z20, 11/1; #Z21, 3/1/90; #Z22, 4/18/90.

See Nos. Z263, Z285, Z363.

Nos. Z23-Z69 were issued as one set. It is broken into sections for ease of reference. See No. Z69a for sheet containing all 47 stamps.

Hokkaido ZA23

Aomori ZA24

Iwate — ZA25

Miyagi — ZA26

Akita ZA27

Yamagata ZA28

Fukushima ZA29

Ibaraki ZA30

Flowers of the Prefectures.

1990, Apr. 27 Litho. *Perf. 13½*

Z23	ZA23	62y	Sweet briar	3.50	.75
Z24	ZA24	62y	Apple blossom	1.25	.75
Z25	ZA25	62y	Paulowina	1.25	.75
Z26	ZA26	62y	Japanese bush clover	1.25	.75
Z27	ZA27	62y	Butterbur flower	1.25	.75
Z28	ZA28	62y	Safflower	1.25	.75
Z29	ZA29	62y	Alpine rose	1.25	.75
Z30	ZA30	62y	Rose	1.25	.75
			Nos. Z23-Z30 (8)	12.25	6.00

See No. Z190.

Tochigi — ZA31

Gunma — ZA32

Saitama — ZA33

Chiba — ZA34

Tokyo ZA35

Kanagawa ZA36

Yamanashi ZA37

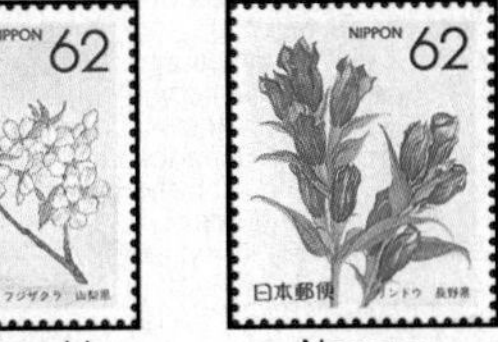

Nagano ZA38

Niigata — ZA39

Toyama — ZA40

Z31	ZA31	62y	Yashio azalea	1.25	.75
Z32	ZA32	62y	Japanese azalea	1.25	.75
Z33	ZA33	62y	Primrose	1.25	.75
Z34	ZA34	62y	Rape blossom	1.25	.75
Z35	ZA35	62y	Cherry blossom	1.25	.75
Z36	ZA36	62y	Gold-banded lily	1.25	.75
Z37	ZA37	62y	Cherry blossom	1.25	.75
Z38	ZA38	62y	Autumn bellflower	3.50	.75
Z39	ZA39	62y	Tulip	1.25	.75
Z40	ZA40	62y	Tulip	1.25	.75
			Nos. Z31-Z40 (10)	14.75	7.50

See No. Z197.

Ishikawa ZA41

Fukui ZA42

Gifu ZA43

Shizuoka ZA44

Aichi — ZA45

Mie — ZA46

Shiga — ZA47

Kyoto — ZA48

Osaka — ZA49

Hyogo — ZA50

Z41	ZA41 62y Black lily	1.25	.75
Z42	ZA42 62y Daffodil	1.25	.75
Z43	ZA43 62y Chinese milk vetch	1.50	.75
Z44	ZA44 62y Azalea	2.00	.75
Z45	ZA45 62y Rabbit-ear iris	1.25	.75
Z46	ZA46 62y Iris	1.25	.75
Z47	ZA47 62y Alpine rose	3.00	.75
Z48	ZA48 62y Drooping cherry blossom	3.00	.75
Z49	ZA49 62y Japanese apricot and primrose	1.25	.75
Z50	ZA50 62y Chrysanthemum	1.25	.75
	Nos. Z41-Z50 (10)	17.00	7.50

Nara ZA51

Wakayama ZA52

Tottori ZA53

Shimane ZA54

Okayama ZA55

Hiroshima ZA56

Yamaguchi ZA57

Tokushima ZA58

Kagawa — ZA59

Ehime — ZA60

Z51	ZA51 62y Double cherry blossom	2.00	.75
Z52	ZA52 62y Japanese apricot	1.50	.75
Z53	ZA53 62y Pear blossom	1.25	.75
Z54	ZA54 62y Peony	1.25	.75
Z55	ZA55 62y Peach blossom	1.25	.75
Z56	ZA56 62y Japanese Maple	1.25	.75
Z57	ZA57 62y Summer orange blossom	1.25	.75
Z58	ZA58 62y Sudachi orange blossom	1.50	.75
Z59	ZA59 62y Olive blossom	5.00	.75
Z60	ZA60 62y Mandarin orange blossom	2.50	.75
	Nos. Z51-Z60 (10)	18.75	7.50

Kochi ZA61

Fukuoka ZA62

Saga ZA63

Nagasaki ZA64

Kumamoto ZA65

Oita ZA66

Miyazaki ZA67

Kagoshima ZA68

Okinawa — ZA69

Z61	ZA61 62y Myrica	2.00	.75
Z62	ZA62 62y Japanese apricot	1.25	.75
Z63	ZA63 62y Laurel	1.25	.75
Z64	ZA64 62y Unzen azalea	1.25	.75
Z65	ZA65 62y Autumn bellflower	1.25	.75
Z66	ZA66 62y Japanese apricot of bungo	1.25	.75
Z67	ZA67 62y Crinum	1.25	.75
Z68	ZA68 62y Rosebay	1.25	.75
Z69	ZA69 62y Coral tree	1.25	.75
a.	Sheet of 47 + 3 labels, #Z23-Z69	110.00	
	Nos. Z61-Z69 (9)	12.00	6.75

Nos. Z23-Z69 were issued in sheets of 20. No. Z69a was released in all prefectures.

Seven Baby Crows (Ibaraki) — ZA70

Inns of Tsumago & Magome (Nagano)

ZA71 ZA72

Mt. Fuji and Tea Picking (Shizuoka) ZA73

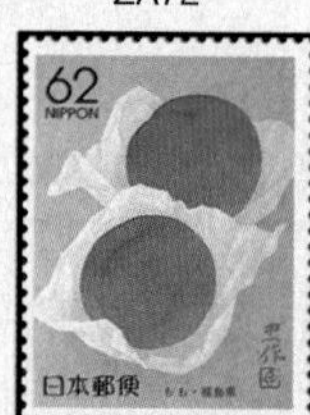

Two Peaches (Fukushima) ZA74

Mt. Sakurajima (Kagoshima) ZA75

Fireworks Festival of Omagari (Akita) ZA76

Travel Expo '90, Nagasaki (Nagasaki) — ZA77

Tokyo Shin Post Office (Tokyo) ZA78

Yasukibushi Folk Song (Shimane) ZA79

Ryukyu Dancer (Okinawa) ZA80

Litho., Litho. & Engr. (#Z70-Z71)

1990 ***Perf. 13***

Z70	ZA70 62y multicolored	1.10	.75
Z71	ZA71 62y blk & buff	1.10	.75
Z72	ZA72 62y blk & pale grn	1.10	.75
a.	Pair, #Z71-Z72	2.25	1.75
Z73	ZA73 62y multicolored	1.10	.70
Z74	ZA74 62y multicolored	1.10	.70
Z75	ZA75 62y multicolored	1.10	.70
Z76	ZA76 62y multicolored	1.10	.70
Z77	ZA77 62y multicolored	1.10	.70
Z78	ZA78 62y multicolored	1.10	.70
Z79	ZA79 62y multicolored	1.10	.70
Z80	ZA80 62y multicolored	1.10	.70
	Nos. Z70-Z80 (11)	12.10	7.85

Issued: #Z70-Z72, 5/1; #Z73, 5/2; #Z74, 6/1; #Z75-Z76, 7/2; #Z77, 8/1; #Z78, 8/6; #Z79-Z80, 8/15.

Sheets of 3 + label of #Z70, Z73, Z80 were lottery prizes. Value, each $3.25.

See Nos. Z332-Z333.

Dancing Girl (Kyoto) ZA81

Old Path of Kumano (Wakayama) ZA82

45th Natl. Athletic Meet (Fukuoka) ZA83

Izu Swamp, Swans (Miyagi) ZA84

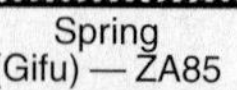

Spring (Gifu) — ZA85

Summer (Gifu) — ZA86

Autumn (Gifu) — ZA87

Winter (Gifu) — ZA88

Nursery Rhyme, Toryanse (Saitama) — ZA89

Japanese Cranes (Hokkaido) ZA90

1990

No.	Design	Description	Unused	Used
Z81	ZA81	62y multicolored	1.10	.75
Z82	ZA82	62y multicolored	1.10	.75
Z83	ZA83	62y multicolored	1.10	.75
Z84	ZA84	62y multicolored	1.10	.75
Z85	ZA85	62y multicolored	1.10	.75
Z86	ZA86	62y multicolored	1.10	.75
Z87	ZA87	62y multicolored	1.10	.75
Z88	ZA88	62y multicolored	1.10	.75
a.		Strip of 4, #Z85-Z88	4.50	4.50
Z89	ZA89	62y multicolored	1.10	.75
Z90	ZA90	62y multicolored	1.10	.75
		Nos. Z81-Z90 (10)	11.00	7.50

Issued: #Z81-Z83, 9/3; #Z84, 10/1; #Z85-Z88, 10/9; #Z89, 10/12; #Z90, 10/30.

Sheets of 3 #Z82 + label were lottery prizes. Value, $3.25.

See Nos. Z171-Z174.

Bizen Ware (Okayama) — ZA92

Battle of Yashima (Kagawa) — ZA91

Yoshinogari Ruins (Saga) — ZA94

Bride Under Cherry Blossoms (Yamanashi) ZA95

Carp (Niigata) ZA96

Lily Bell (Hokkaido) ZA97

Lilac (Hokkaido) ZA98

Day Lily (Hokkaido) ZA99

Rowanberry (Hokkaido) ZA100

Litho., Photo. (#Z94-Z95)

1991 *Perf. 13*

No.	Design	Description	Unused	Used
Z91	ZA91	62y multicolored	1.10	.70
Z92		62y pedestal	1.10	.70
Z93		62y bowl	1.10	.70
a.		ZA92 Pair, #Z92-Z93	2.25	1.50
Z94	ZA94	62y multicolored	1.10	.70
Z95	ZA95	62y multicolored	1.10	.70
Z96	ZA96	62y multicolored	1.10	.70
Z97	ZA97	62y multicolored	1.10	.70
Z98	ZA98	62y multicolored	1.10	.70
Z99	ZA99	62y multicolored	1.10	.70
Z100	ZA100	62y multicolored	1.10	.70
a.		Strip of 4, #Z97-Z100	4.50	4.50
		Nos. Z91-Z100 (10)	11.00	7.00

Issued: #Z91, 2/19; #Z92-Z93, 4/5; #Z94, 4/12; #Z95, 4/18; #Z96, 5/1; #Z97-Z100, 5/31.

See Nos. Z304-Z307.

Nikkou Mountains (Tochigi) — ZA101

Mt. Iwate by Yaoji Hashimoto (Iwate) — ZA102

Wooden Puppet (Tokushima) ZA103

Whales (Kochi) ZA104

Fringed Orchids (Tokyo) ZA105

Cape Toi, Horses (Miyazaki) ZA106

Black Pearls of Kabira Bay (Okinawa) ZA107

Japanese Pears (Tottori) ZA108

Tsujun-kyo Bridge (Kumamoto) ZA109

1991 **Photo.**

No.	Design	Description	Unused	Used
Z101	ZA101	62y multicolored	1.10	.70
Z102	ZA102	62y multicolored	1.10	.70
a.		Booklet pane of 10	11.00	
		Complete booklet, #Z102a	11.00	
Z103	ZA103	62y multicolored	1.10	.70
a.		Pane of 10	11.00	
Z104	ZA104	62y multicolored	1.10	.70
a.		Pane of 10	11.00	
Z105	ZA105	41y multicolored	2.50	1.00
a.		Booklet pane of 10	15.00	
		Complete booklet, #Z105a	15.00	
Z106	ZA106	62y multicolored	1.10	.70
a.		Booklet pane of 10	15.00	
		Complete booklet, #Z106a	15.00	
Z107	ZA107	41y multicolored	.80	.50
Z108	ZA108	62y multicolored	1.10	.70
Z109	ZA109	62y multicolored	1.10	.70
a.		Booklet pane of 10	15.00	
		Complete booklet, #Z108a	15.00	
		Nos. Z101-Z109 (9)	11.00	6.40

Issued: #Z101, 5/29; #Z102, 6/10; #Z103-Z104, 6/26; #Z105-Z106, 7/1; #Z107-Z108, 8/1; #Z109, 8/26.

Sheets of 3 #Z106 + label were lottery prizes. Value, $3.

Ninja, Iga Ueno Castle (Mie) ZA111

46th Natl. Athletic Meet (Ishikawa) ZA110

Eyeglass Industry (Fukui) ZA112

Nursery Rhyme, Tortoise and the Hare — ZA113

Kobe City Weathervane (Hyogo) — ZA114

Spring (Nara) — ZA115

Autumn (Nara, Gunma) — ZA116

Litho., Photo. (#Z110, Z112)

1991 *Perf. 13, 13½ (#Z110)*

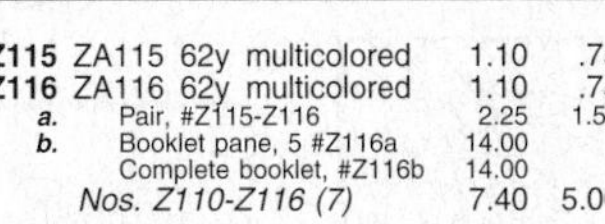

No.	Design	Description	Unused	Used
Z110	ZA110	41y multicolored	.80	.50
a.		Pane of 10	8.00	
Z111	ZA111	62y multicolored	1.10	.75
a.		Booklet pane of 10	14.00	
		Complete booklet, #Z111a	14.00	
Z112	ZA112	62y multicolored	1.10	.75
a.		Booklet pane of 10	14.00	
		Complete booklet, #Z112a	14.00	
Z113	ZA113	62y multicolored	1.10	.75
a.		Booklet pane of 10	14.00	
		Complete booklet, #Z113a	14.00	
Z114	ZA114	62y multicolored	1.10	.75
a.		Booklet pane of 10	14.00	
		Complete booklet, #Z114a	14.00	
Z115	ZA115	62y multicolored	1.10	.75
Z116	ZA116	62y multicolored	1.10	.75
a.		Pair, #Z115-Z116	2.25	1.50
b.		Booklet pane, 5 #Z116a	14.00	
		Complete booklet, #Z116b	14.00	
		Nos. Z110-Z116 (7)	7.40	5.00

Issued: #Z110, 9/2; #Z111, 9/10; #Z112, 10/1; #Z113, 10/23; #Z114-Z116, 10/25.

See Nos. Z177-Z178.

Gogo-An Temple, Sea of Japan (Niigata) ZA117

Natl. Land Afforestation Campaign (Fukuoka) ZA118

Arctic Fox (Hokkaido) ZA119

Tateyama Mountain Range (Toyama) ZA120

Rikuchu Coast (Iwate) — ZA121

Kurushima Strait (Ehime) ZA122

Tsurusaki Dance (Oita) ZA123

Tanabata Lantern Festival (Yamaguchi) ZA124

Shasui-no-taki Waterfall (Kanagawa) ZA125

Kurodabushi Dance (Fukuoka) ZA126

Boat Race (Okinawa)
ZA127

Osaka Castle, Business Park (Osaka)
ZA128

Owl, Mt. Horaiji (Aichi) — ZA129

1992 Litho. *Perf. 13½*

Z117 ZA117 41y multicolored .80 .50
a. Pane of 10 8.00

Photo.

Z118 ZA118 41y multicolored .80 .50
Z119 ZA119 62y multicolored 1.10 .75
a. Souvenir sheet of 3 3.50 3.50

Litho.

Z120 ZA120 62y multicolored 1.10 .75
a. Pane of 10 11.00

Photo.

Z121 ZA121 62y multicolored 1.10 .75
a. Pane of 10 11.00
Z122 ZA122 62y multicolored 1.10 .75
a. Pane of 10 11.00
Z123 ZA123 62y multicolored 1.10 .75
Z124 ZA124 62y multicolored 1.10 .75
Z125 ZA125 62y multicolored 1.10 .75
a. Pane of 10 11.00
b. Souvenir sheet of 3 3.50 3.50

Litho.

Z126 ZA126 62y multicolored 1.10 .90
Z127 ZA127 62y multicolored 1.10 .90
Z128 ZA128 41y multicolored .80 .60

Photo.

Z129 ZA129 62y multicolored 1.10 .75
a. Souvenir sheet of 3 3.50 2.25
b. Pane of 10 11.00
Nos. Z117-Z129 (13) 13.40 9.40

Issued: #Z117, 5/1; #Z118, 5/8; #Z119, 5/29; #Z121-Z122, 6/23; #Z124, 7/7; #Z123, 7/23; #Z125, 7/24; #Z126, 8/3; #Z127, 8/17; #Z129, 10/15.
See also No. Z320.

Oga Peninsula (Akita)
ZA130

Fukuroda Waterfall (Ibaraki)
ZA131

Notojima Bridge, Nanao Bay (Ishikawa)
ZA132

Tama District Mountains (Metropolitan Tokyo)
ZA133

Harbor Seal (Hokkaido) — ZA134

Peace Statue (Kagawa)
ZA135

Hana Ta'ue Rice Planting Festival (Hiroshima)
ZA136

Paradise Flycatcher and Mt. Fuji (Shizuoka)
ZA137

Sailboats on Lake Biwa (Shiga)
ZA138

Matumoto Castle & Japan Alps (Nagano)
ZA139

Ohara Festival (Kagoshima)
ZA140

Oirase Mountain Stream (Aomori)
ZA141

Yourou Valley (Chiba) — ZA142

1993 Litho. *Perf. 13½*

Z130 ZA130 41y multicolored .80 .50
a. Pane of 10 8.00
Z131 ZA131 62y multicolored 1.10 .75
a. Pane of 10 11.00

Photo.

Z132 ZA132 62y multicolored 1.10 .75
a. Pane of 10 11.50
Z133 ZA133 62y multicolored 1.10 .75
a. Booklet pane of 10 11.50
Complete booklet, #Z133a 11.50
Z134 ZA134 62y multicolored 1.10 .75
Z135 ZA135 62y multicolored 1.10 .75
a. Pane of 10 11.00
Z136 ZA136 62y multicolored 1.25 .75
Z137 ZA137 41y multicolored .80 .50
a. Pane of 10 12.00
Z138 ZA138 62y multicolored 1.25 .75
a. Pane of 10 12.00
Z139 ZA139 62y multicolored 1.25 .75
a. Pane of 10 12.00
Z140 ZA140 41y multicolored .80 .50
a. Pane of 10 8.00

Perf. 13x13½

Z141 ZA141 62y multicolored 1.10 .75
a. Pane of 10 11.00

Perf. 13½

Z142 ZA142 41y multicolored .80 .50
a. Pane of 10 8.00
Nos. Z130-Z142 (13) 13.55 8.75

Issued: #Z130, 2/12; #Z131, 3/26; #Z132, 4/2; #Z133, 4/23; #Z134, 5/17; #Z135, 5/21; #Z136, 6/4; #Z137, 6/23; #Z138, 7/1; #Z139, 7/16; #Z140, 9/1; #Z141, 9/22; #Z142, 10/1.
See also No. Z321.

Dream Bridge (Metropolitan Tokyo)
ZA143

Kurobe Canyon & Dam (Toyama)
ZA144

Haiku, Storehouse of Poet Issa (1763-1827) (Nagano)
ZA145

Okuni, Izumo Great Shrine, Taisha (Shimane)
ZA146

Fukiwari Falls (Gunma)
ZA147

Ezoshika (Hokkaido)
ZA148

Watch Tower, Festival in Tajima (Hyogo)
ZA149

Wakura Coast (Wakayama)
ZA150

1994 Photo. *Perf. 13*

Z143 ZA143 50y multicolored .95 .50
a. Pane of 10 9.50
Z144 ZA144 80y multicolored 1.50 .75
a. Pane of 10 15.00
Z145 ZA145 80y multicolored 1.50 .75
a. Pane of 10 15.00
Z146 ZA146 80y multicolored 1.50 .75
a. Pane of 10 15.00

Litho.

Z147 ZA147 80y multicolored 1.50 .75
a. Pane of 10 15.00
Z148 ZA148 50y multicolored 1.00 .75
a. Pane of 10 10.00
Z149 ZA149 50y multicolored 1.00 .65
a. Pane of 10 10.00
Z150 ZA150 80y multicolored 1.50 .75
a. Pane of 10 15.00
Nos. Z143-Z150 (8) 10.45 5.65

Issued: #Z143, 3/23; #Z144, 4/25; #Z145-Z146, 5/2; #Z147, 6/6; #Z148, 6/7; #Z149, 6/23; #Z150, 7/15.

Kentish Plovers (Mie)
ZA151

Awaodori Dance (Tokushima)
ZA152

Tug-of-War (Okinawa)
ZA153

Kehi Pine Wood (Fukui)
ZA154

Matsushima (Miyagi)
ZA155

Kunchi Festival (Nagasaki)
ZA156

1994 Photo. *Perf. 13*

Z151 ZA151 80y multicolored 1.50 .75
a. Pane of 10 15.00
Z152 ZA152 50y multicolored 1.00 .50
a. Pane of 10 10.00
Z153 ZA153 50y multicolored 1.00 .50
Z154 ZA154 50y multicolored 1.00 .50
a. Pane of 10 10.00
Z155 ZA155 80y multicolored 1.60 .75
a. Pane of 10 16.50
Z156 ZA156 80y multicolored 1.60 .75
a. Pane of 10 16.50
Nos. Z151-Z156 (6) 7.70 3.75

Issued: #Z151, 7/22; #Z152-Z153, 8/1; #Z154, 9/1; #Z155, 9/20; #Z156, 10/3.

Hokkaido Chipmunks (Hokkaido) — ZA157

Ushiwakamaru and Benkei (Kyoto) — ZA158

Utopia Flower (Gifu)
ZA159

Jade Bead, Gyofu Soma (1883-1950), Lyricist (Niigata)
ZA160

Cape Ashizuri-Misaki Lighthouse (Kochi) ZA161

Ishikawamon Gate, Kanazawa Castle (Ishikawa) ZA162

Akamon Gate, University of Tokyo (Tokyo) ZA163

Three Waterfalls, Kuroyama (Saitama) ZA164

Lady's Slipper, Rebun Island (Hokkaido) ZA165

Street with Zelkova Trees (Miyagi) ZA166

Eisa Festival (Okinawa) — ZA167

1995 Photo. *Perf. 13*

Z157	ZA157	80y multicolored	1.90	.75
a.		Pane of 10	19.00	

Perf. 13½

Z158	ZA158	80y multicolored	1.90	.75
a.		Pane of 10	19.00	
Z159	ZA159	80y multicolored	1.90	.75
a.		Pane of 10	19.00	
Z160	ZA160	80y multicolored	1.90	.75
a.		Pane of 10	19.00	
Z161	ZA161	80y multicolored	1.90	.75
a.		Pane of 10	19.00	
Z162	ZA162	80y multicolored	1.90	.75
a.		Pane of 10	19.00	
Z163	ZA163	50y multicolored	1.10	.50
a.		Pane of 10	11.00	
Z164	ZA164	80y multicolored	1.75	.75
a.		Pane of 10	17.50	
Z165	ZA165	80y multicolored	1.75	.75
a.		Pane of 10	17.50	
Z166	ZA166	50y multicolored	1.00	.50
a.		Pane of 10	10.00	
Z167	ZA167	80y multicolored	1.60	.75
		Nos. Z157-Z167 (11)	18.60	7.75

Issued: #Z157, 3/3; #Z158, 4/3; #Z159, 4/26; #Z160, 5/1; #Z161-Z162, 6/1; #Z163-Z165, 7/7; #Z166-Z167, 8/1.

Seasons Types of 1990-91 and

Kishiwada Danjiri Festival (Osaka) ZA168

Yamadera Temple (Yamagata) ZA169

Karatsu Kunchi Festival (Saga) ZA170

Niimi-No-Shou Festival (Okayama) ZA171

Kirifuri Waterfall (Tochigi) ZA172

10th All-Japan Holstein Show (Chiba) ZA173

Nos. Z171-Z174: (Gifu).
No. Z177, (Nara). No. Z178, (Nara, Gunma).

1995 Photo. *Perf. 13½*

Z168	ZA168	80y multicolored	1.60	.75
a.		Pane of 10	16.00	
Z169	ZA169	80y multicolored	1.60	.75
a.		Pane of 10	16.00	
Z170	ZA170	80y multicolored	1.60	.75
a.		Pane of 10	16.00	

Perf. 13

Z171	ZA85	80y Spring	1.60	.75
Z172	ZA86	80y Summer	1.60	.75
Z173	ZA87	80y Autumn	1.60	.75
Z174	ZA88	80y Winter	1.60	.75
a.		Strip of 4, #Z171-Z174	6.50	4.50

Perf. 13½

Z175	ZA171	80y multicolored	1.60	.75
Z176	ZA172	50y multicolored	1.00	.50
a.		Pane of 10	10.00	
Z177	ZA115	80y Spring	1.50	.75
Z178	ZA116	80y Autumn	1.50	.75
a.		Pair, #Z177-Z178	3.00	1.75
Z179	ZA173	80y multicolored	1.60	.75
a.		Pane of 10	15.00	
		Nos. Z168-Z179 (12)	18.40	8.75

Issued: #Z168, 9/1; #Z169, 9/15; #Z170-Z174, 10/2; #Z175, 10/13; #Z176, 10/27; #Z177-Z178, 11/6; #Z179, 11/21.

Clione Limancia (Hokkaido) ZA174

Ushibuka Haiya Festival (Kumamoto) ZA175

Peony of Sukagawa (Fukushima) ZA176

Hamayu (Mie) ZA177

Ama Divers (Mie) — ZA178

World Ceramics Expo '96 (Saga) — ZA179

Shosenkyo Gorge (Yamanashi) ZA180

Murasaki Shikibu of Takefu (Fukui) ZA181

1996 Litho. *Perf. 13½x13*

Z180	ZA174	80y multicolored	1.50	.75
a.		Pane of 10	11.50	

Photo.

Z181	ZA175	80y multicolored	1.50	.75
a.		Pane of 10	15.00	
Z182	ZA176	80y multicolored	1.50	.75
a.		Pane of 10	15.00	
Z183	ZA177	80y multicolored	1.50	.75
Z184	ZA178	80y multicolored	1.50	.75
a.		Pair, #Z183-Z184	3.00	1.75
b.		Pane, 5 #Z184a	15.00	
Z185	ZA179	80y multicolored	1.50	.75

Perf. 13½

Z186	ZA180	50y multicolored	.95	.50
a.		Pane of 10	9.50	
Z187	ZA181	80y multicolored	1.50	.75
a.		Pane of 10	15.00	
		Nos. Z180-Z187 (8)	11.45	5.75

Issued: #Z180, 2/6; #Z181, 4/1; #Z182, 4/26; #Z183-Z184, 5/1; #Z185, 5/17; #Z186, 6/3; #Z187, 6/24.

Flower Types of 1990 and

Ancient Trees, Kompon-chudo of Mt. Hiei (Shiga) ZA182

Nishiumi Marine Park (Ehime) ZA183

Nebuta Festival (Aomori) ZA184

Main Palace, Shuri Castle (Okinawa) ZA186

Shimozuru Usudaiko Odori Folk Dance (Miyazaki) ZA185

Asakusa Kaminarimon Gate (Metropolitan Tokyo) ZA187

Tottori Shanshan Festival (Tottori) ZA188

Saito Kinen Festival Matsumoto (Nagano) ZA189

#Z190, (Hokkaido). #Z197, (Nagano).

1996 Photo. *Perf. 13½*

Z188	ZA182	80y multicolored	1.50	.75
a.		Pane of 10	15.00	
Z189	ZA183	80y multicolored	1.50	.75
a.		Pane of 10	15.00	
Z190	ZA23	80y Sweetbriar	1.50	.75
Z191	ZA184	80y multicolored	1.50	.75
a.		Pane of 10	15.00	
Z192	ZA185	80y multicolored	1.50	.75
a.		Pane of 10	15.00	
Z193	ZA186	80y multicolored	1.50	.75
Z194	ZA187	80y multicolored	1.50	.75
a.		Pane of 10	15.00	
Z195	ZA188	80y multicolored	1.50	.75
Z196	ZA189	80y multicolored	1.50	.75
a.		Pane of 10	15.00	
Z197	ZA38	80y Autumn bell-flower	1.50	.75
		Nos. Z188-Z197 (10)	15.00	7.50

Issued: #Z188-Z189, 7/1; #Z190, 7/5; #Z191, 7/23; #Z192-Z193, 8/1; #Z194, 8/8; #Z195, 8/16; #Z196-Z197, 8/22.

Sengokubara Marsh (Kanagawa) ZA190

Nagoya Festival (Aichi) — ZA191

Grass-burning Rite on Mt. Wakakusa (Nara) ZA193

1997 Men's Handball World Championships (Kumamoto) ZA194

Tea Picking (Shizuoka) ZA195

Dahurian Rhododendron (Hokkaido) ZA196

Mt. Fuji (Shizuoka) — ZA197

1996-97 Photo. *Perf. 13½*

Z198	ZA190	80y multicolored	1.50	.75
a.		Pane of 10	15.00	
Z199		80y horse, rider	1.50	.75
Z200		80y two floats	1.50	.75
a.	ZA191	Pair, #Z199-Z200	3.00	1.75
b.		Pane, 5 #Z200a	15.00	
Z201	ZA193	50y multicolored	.95	.50
a.		Pane of 10	9.50	
Z202	ZA194	80y multicolored	1.50	.75
a.		Pane of 10	15.00	
Z203	ZA195	50y multicolored	.95	.50
a.		Pane of 10	9.50	
Z204	ZA196	80y multicolored	1.50	.75
a.		Pane of 10	15.00	
Z205		80y cattle	1.50	.75
Z206		80y orange grasses	1.50	.75
a.	ZA197	Pair, #Z205-Z206	2.50	1.75
b.		Pane, 5 #Z206a	12.50	
		Nos. Z198-Z206 (9)	12.40	6.25

Issued: #Z198, 9/6; #Z199-Z200, 10/1; #Z201, 11/15; #Z202, 4/17/97; #Z203-Z206, 4/25/97.

Marugame Castle (Kagawa) ZA199

Hokkaido Ermine (Hokkaido) ZA200

Okayama Castle (Okayama) ZA201

Okinawan Fruits (Okinawa) ZA202

ZA204 ZA205

ZA206 ZA207

Nagasaki Kaido Highway (Nagasaki, Saga, Fukuoka)

Fukiya Koji's Hanayome Ningyo, Doll of Bride (Niigata) ZA208

The Clock Tower of Kyoto University (Kyoto) ZA209

1997 Photo. *Perf. 13½*

Z207	ZA199	80y multicolored	1.50	.75
a.		Pane of 10	15.00	
Z208	ZA200	50y multicolored	.95	.50
a.		Pane of 10	9.50	
Z209	ZA201	80y multicolored	1.50	.75
a.		Pane of 10	15.00	
Z210		50y pineapple	.95	.60
Z211		50y mango	.95	.60
a.	ZA202	Pair, #Z210-Z211	1.90	1.40
Z212	ZA204	80y multicolored	1.50	.75
Z213	ZA205	80y multicolored	1.50	.75
Z214	ZA206	80y multicolored	1.50	.75
Z215	ZA207	80y multicolored	1.50	.75
a.		Strip of 4, #Z212-Z215	6.00	6.00
Z216	ZA208	50y multicolored	.95	.50
a.		Pane of 10	9.50	
Z217	ZA209	80y multicolored	1.50	.75
a.		Pane of 10	15.00	
		Nos. Z207-Z217 (11)	14.30	7.45

Issued: #Z207, 5/15; #Z208-Z209, 5/30; #Z210-Z211, 6/2; #Z212-Z215, 6/3; #Z216-Z217, 6/18.

Kanto Festival (Akita) ZA210

San-in Yume Minato Exposition (Tottori) ZA211

Waterwheel Plant, Hozoji-numa Pond (Saitama) ZA212

Lake Kasumigaura (Ibaraki) ZA215

Bon Wind Festival, Owara (Toyama) — ZA213

Tokyo Big Site (Tokyo) ZA216

Telecom Center (Tokyo) ZA217

Rainbow Bridge (Tokyo) ZA218

Intl. Forum (Tokyo) ZA219

Tokyo Museum (Tokyo) ZA220

First World Walking Festival (Saitama) ZA221

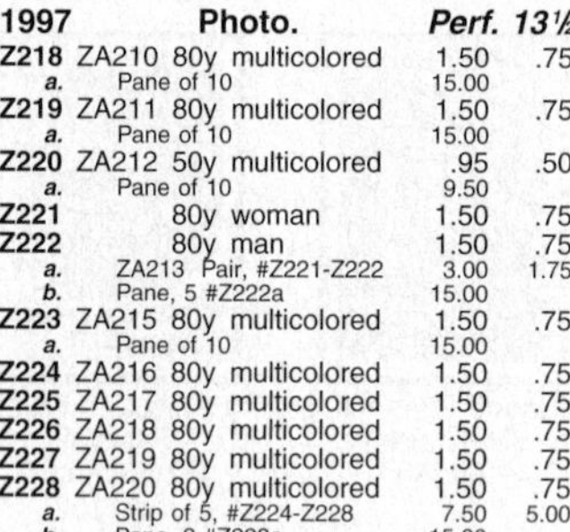

1997 Photo. *Perf. 13½*

Z218	ZA210	80y multicolored	1.50	.75
a.		Pane of 10	15.00	
Z219	ZA211	80y multicolored	1.50	.75
a.		Pane of 10	15.00	
Z220	ZA212	50y multicolored	.95	.50
a.		Pane of 10	9.50	
Z221		80y woman	1.50	.75
Z222		80y man	1.50	.75
a.	ZA213	Pair, #Z221-Z222	3.00	1.75
b.		Pane, 5 #Z222a	15.00	
Z223	ZA215	80y multicolored	1.50	.75
a.		Pane of 10	15.00	
Z224	ZA216	80y multicolored	1.50	.75
Z225	ZA217	80y multicolored	1.50	.75
Z226	ZA218	80y multicolored	1.50	.75
Z227	ZA219	80y multicolored	1.50	.75
Z228	ZA220	80y multicolored	1.50	.75
a.		Strip of 5, #Z224-Z228	7.50	5.00
b.		Pane, 2 #Z228a	15.00	
Z229	ZA221	80y multicolored	1.50	.75
a.		Pane of 10	15.00	
		Nos. Z218-Z229 (12)	17.45	8.75

Issued: #Z218, 7/7; #Z219, 7/11; #Z220, 8/1; #Z221-Z222, 8/20; #Z223, 9/1; #Z224-Z228, 10/1; #Z229, 10/28.

Kanagawa-Chiba Bridge Tunnel (Chiba, Kanagawa) — ZA222

Snow-Covered Tree (Hokkaido) ZA224

Flower in a Dream (Hokkaido) ZA225

Hiyoshi Dam (Kyoto) ZA226

Sanshin (Okinawa) ZA227

Okoshi Daiko (Gifu) ZA228

Kobe-Awaji Expressway (Tokushima, Hyogo) — ZA229

1997-98 Litho. *Perf. 13½*

Z230		80y denomination upper right	1.50	.75
Z231		80y denomination lower left	1.50	.75
a.	ZA222	Pair, #Z230-Z231	3.00	1.75
b.		Pane, 5 #Z231a	15.00	
Z232	ZA224	80y multicolored	1.50	.75
Z233	ZA225	80y multicolored	1.50	.75
a.		Pair, #Z232-Z233	3.00	1.75
b.		Pane, 5 #Z233a	15.00	

Photo.

Perf. 13

Z234	ZA226	80y multicolored	1.50	.75
a.		Pane of 10	15.00	

Perf. 13½

Z235	ZA227	80y multicolored	1.50	.75
a.		Pane of 10	15.00	
Z236	ZA228	80y multicolored	1.50	.75
a.		Pane of 10	15.00	
Z237		80y bridge, whirlpool	1.50	.75
Z238		80y bridge, flowers	1.50	.75
a.	ZA229	Pair, #Z237-Z238	3.00	1.75
b.		Pane, 5 #Z238a	15.00	

Issued: #Z230-Z231, 12/18; #Z232-Z233, 2/5/98; #Z234, 3/2/98; #Z235, 3/4/98; #Z236, 3/19/98; #Z237-Z238, 3/20/98.

Jomon Figurine (Nagano) ZA231

Chaguchagu Umakko, Mt. Iwate (Iwate) ZA232

Tokyo '98 Business Show (Tokyo) ZA233

Mt. Heisei Shinzan (Nagasaki) ZA234

Oze (Gunma) — ZA235

Hanagasa Matsuri (Yamagata) ZA237

9th Women's World Softball Championships (Shizuoka) ZA238

1998	**Photo.**	***Perf. 13½***	
Z239	ZA231 80y multicolored	1.50	.75
a.	Pane of 10	15.00	
Z240	ZA232 80y multicolored	1.50	.75
a.	Pane of 10	15.00	
Z241	ZA233 80y multicolored	1.50	.75
a.	Pane of 10	15.00	
Z242	ZA234 80y multicolored	1.50	.75
a.	Pane of 10	15.00	
Z243	80y blue & multi	1.50	.75
Z244	80y brown & multi	1.50	.75
a.	ZA235 Pair, #Z243-Z244	3.00	1.75
b.	Pane, 5 #Z244a	15.00	
Z245	ZA237 50y multicolored	.95	.50
a.	Pane of 10	9.50	
Z246	ZA238 80y multicolored	1.50	.75
a.	Pane of 10	15.00	
	Nos. Z239-Z246 (8)	11.45	5.75

Issued: #Z239, 4/1; #Z240, 4/24; #Z241, 5/19; #Z242, 5/20/98; #Z243-Z244, 5/21; #Z245, 6/5; #Z246, 6/22.

Mt. Hakusan (Ishikawa) ZA239

Hita Gion (Ohita) ZA240

World Puppetry Festival (Nagano) — ZA241

Views of Seto (Hiroshima) — ZA243

First Postage Stamps of Ryukyu Islands, 50th Anniv. (Ryukyu Islands) — ZA245

1998	**Photo.**	***Perf. 13½***	
Z247	ZA239 50y multicolored	.95	.70
a.	Pane of 10	9.50	
Z248	ZA240 50y multicolored	.95	.50
a.	Pane of 10	9.50	
Z249	50y stage left	.95	.50
Z250	50y stage right	.95	.50
a.	ZA241 Pair, #Z249-Z250	1.90	1.00
b.	Pane, 5 #Z250a	9.50	
Z251	80y harbor	1.50	.75
Z252	80y highway	1.50	.75
a.	ZA243 Pair, #Z251-Z252	3.00	1.75
b.	Pane, 5 #Z252a	15.00	
Z253	80y Ryukyu Islands #1	1.50	.75
Z254	80y Ryukyu Islands #228	1.50	.75
a.	ZA245 Pair, #Z253-Z254	3.00	1.75
	Nos. Z247-Z254 (8)	9.80	5.20

Issued: #Z247-Z248, 7/1; #Z249-Z252, 7/17; #Z253-Z254, 7/23.

Satsuma Pottery, 400th Anniv. (Kogoshima) — ZA247

Seto Ohashi Bridge (Kagawa) ZA249

Kobe Luminaries (Hyogo) ZA250

Apples (Aomori) ZA251

Kumano Path (Wakayama) ZA252

Tama Monorail (Tokyo) — ZA253

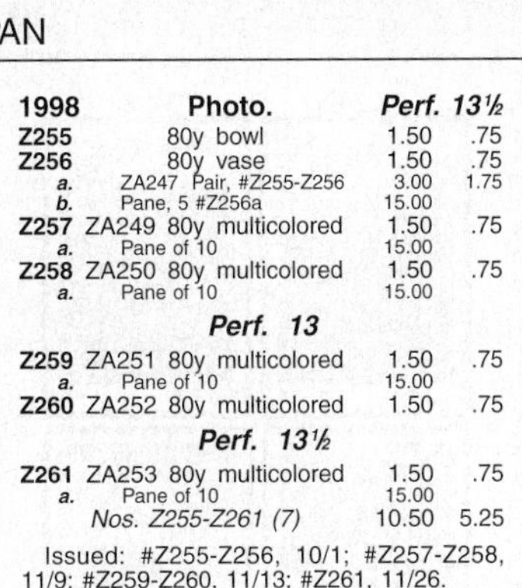

1998	**Photo.**	***Perf. 13½***	
Z255	80y bowl	1.50	.75
Z256	80y vase	1.50	.75
a.	ZA247 Pair, #Z255-Z256	3.00	1.75
b.	Pane, 5 #Z256a	15.00	
Z257	ZA249 80y multicolored	1.50	.75
a.	Pane of 10	15.00	
Z258	ZA250 80y multicolored	1.50	.75
a.	Pane of 10	15.00	
	Perf. 13		
Z259	ZA251 80y multicolored	1.50	.75
a.	Pane of 10	15.00	
Z260	ZA252 80y multicolored	1.50	.75
	Perf. 13½		
Z261	ZA253 80y multicolored	1.50	.75
a.	Pane of 10	15.00	
	Nos. Z255-Z261 (7)	10.50	5.25

Issued: #Z255-Z256, 10/1; #Z257-Z258, 11/9; #Z259-Z260, 11/13; #Z261, 11/26.

Dogo Hot Spa (Ehime) Type of 1989 and

Ibara Line (Okayama, Hiroshima) — ZA254

ZA255

Ao-no-Domon (Oita) — ZA256

ZA257 ZA258

Snow World (Hokkaido) ZA259 ZA260

Tokamachi Snow Festival (Niigata) — ZA261

Orchids (Tokyo) — ZA262

Dinosaurs (Fukui) — ZA264

1999	**Photo.**	***Perf. 13½***	
Z262	ZA254 80y multicolored	1.50	.75
a.	Pane of 10	15.00	
Z263	ZA4 80y multicolored	1.50	.75
Z264	ZA255 80y multicolored	1.50	.75
Z265	ZA256 80y multicolored	1.50	.75
a.	Vert. pair, #Z264-Z265	3.00	1.75
b.	Pane, 5 #Z265a	15.00	
Z266	ZA257 50y multicolored	.95	.50
Z267	ZA258 50y multicolored	.95	.50
Z268	ZA259 80y multicolored	1.50	.75
Z269	ZA260 80y multicolored	1.50	.75
a.	Strip of 4, #Z266-Z269	5.00	3.50
Z270	ZA261 80y multicolored	1.50	.75
a.	Pane of 10	15.00	
Z271	80y white flowers	1.50	.75
Z272	80y purple flowers	1.50	.75
a.	ZA262 Pair, #Z271-Z272	3.00	1.75
b.	Pane, 5 #Z272a	15.00	
Z273	80y denomination upper left	1.50	.75
Z274	80y denomination lower left	1.50	.75
a.	ZA264 Pair, #Z273-Z274	3.00	1.75
b.	Pane, 5 #Z274a	15.00	
	Nos. Z262-Z274 (13)	18.40	9.25

Issued: #Z262, 1/1; #Z263-Z265, 2/1; #Z266-Z269, 2/5; #Z270-Z272, 2/12; #Z273-Z274, 2/22.

Lake Chuzenji (Tochigi) — ZA266

Renowned Cherry Tree (Gifu) ZA268

Kiso Observatory, Mt. Ontake (Nagano) ZA271

Postal Service in Okinawa, 125th Anniv. (Okinawa) — ZA269

ZA272

ZA273

ZA274

The Old Path for Kumano (Mie) — ZA275

1999 Photo. *Perf. 13½*

Z275	80y Spring	1.50	.75
Z276	80y Fall	1.50	.75
a.	ZA266 Pair, #Z275-Z276	3.00	1.75
b.	Pane, 5 #Z276a	15.00	
Z277	ZA268 80y multicolored	1.50	.75
a.	Pane of 10	15.00	
Z278	80y Traditional costume	1.50	.75
Z279	80y Laughing lions	1.50	.75
a.	ZA269 Pair, #Z278-Z279	3.00	1.75
b.	Pane, 5 #Z279a	15.00	
Z280	ZA271 80y multicolored	1.50	.75
a.	Pane of 10	15.00	
Z281	ZA272 80y Tsuzurato Pass	1.50	.75
Z282	ZA273 80y Matsumoto Pass	1.50	.75
Z283	ZA274 80y Umagoshi Pass	1.50	.75
Z284	ZA275 80y Touri Pass	1.50	.75
a.	Strip of 4, #Z281-Z284	6.00	6.00
	Nos. Z275-Z284 (10)	15.00	7.50

Issued: #Z275-Z276, 3/1. #Z277, 3/16. #Z278-Z279, 3/23. #Z280, 4/9. #Z281-Z284, 4/16.

Cherries (Yamagata) Type of 1989 and

Taiko-Mon Gate, Matsumoto Castle (Nagano) ZA276

Firefly Squid (Toyama) ZA277

ZA278

ZA279

Four Seasons, Kenrokuen Garden (Ishikawa)
ZA280 ZA281

No. Z288, Kaisekitou Pagoda, Spring. No. Z289, Fountain, Summer. No. Z290, Kinjoureitaku spring, Autumn. No. Z291, Kotoji stone lantern and yukitsuri, Winter.

1999, Apr. 26 Photo. *Perf. 13*

Z285	ZA2 80y like #Z2	1.50	.75

Perf. 13½

Z286	ZA276 80y multicolored	1.50	.75
a.	Pane of 10	15.00	
Z287	ZA277 80y multicolored	1.50	.75
a.	Pane of 10	15.00	
Z288	ZA278 80y multicolored	1.50	.75
Z289	ZA279 80y multicolored	1.50	.75
Z290	ZA280 80y multicolored	1.50	.75
Z291	ZA281 80y multicolored	1.50	.75
a.	Strip of 4, #Z288-Z291	6.00	6.00
b.	Souvenir sheet, #Z288-Z291	6.00	6.00
	Nos. Z285-Z291 (7)	10.50	5.25

ZA282 ZA283

ZA284 ZA285

ZA286 ZA287

ZA288 ZA289

Opening of Shimanami Seaside Highway (Hiroshima & Ehime)
ZA290 ZA291

Designs: No. Z292, Onomichi-suido Channel. No. Z293, Kurushima-kaikyo Straits. No. Z294, Old, new Onomichi-oohashi Bridges. No. Z295, Kurushima-kaikyo-oohashi Bridge. No. Z296, Innoshima-oohashi Bridge. No. Z297, Kurushima-kaikyo-oohashi Bridge, diff. No. Z298, Ikuchibashi Bridge. No. Z299, Hakatabashi, Ooshima-oohashi Bridges. No. Z300, Tatara-oohashi Bridge. No. Z301, Oomishimabashi Bridge.

1999, Apr. 26 Photo. *Perf. 13½*

Z292	ZA282 80y multicolored	1.50	.75
Z293	ZA283 80y multicolored	1.50	.75
Z294	ZA284 80y multicolored	1.50	.75
Z295	ZA285 80y multicolored	1.50	.75
Z296	ZA286 80y multicolored	1.50	.75
Z297	ZA287 80y multicolored	1.50	.75
Z298	ZA288 80y multicolored	1.50	.75
Z299	ZA289 80y multicolored	1.50	.75
Z300	ZA290 80y multicolored	1.50	.75
Z301	ZA291 80y multicolored	1.50	.75
a.	Block of 10, #Z292-Z301	15.00	15.00
b.	Sheet of 8, # Z294-Z301	12.00	12.00

Flora (Hokkaido) Type of 1991 and

Southern Kii Peninsula (Wakayama) — ZA292

Designs: No. Z302, Nachi-no-taki Falls. No. Z303, Engetsutou Island.

1999, Apr. 28 Photo. *Perf. 13½*

Z302	80y multicolored	1.50	.75
Z303	80y multicolored	1.50	.75
a.	ZA292 Pair, #Z302-Z303	3.00	1.75
b.	Pane, 5 #Z303a	15.00	

Perf. 13

Z304	ZA97 80y Lily bell	1.50	.75
Z305	ZA98 80y Lilac	1.50	.75
Z306	ZA99 80y Daylily	1.50	.75
Z307	ZA100 80y Rowanberry	1.50	.75
a.	Strip of 4, #Z304-Z307	6.00	6.00

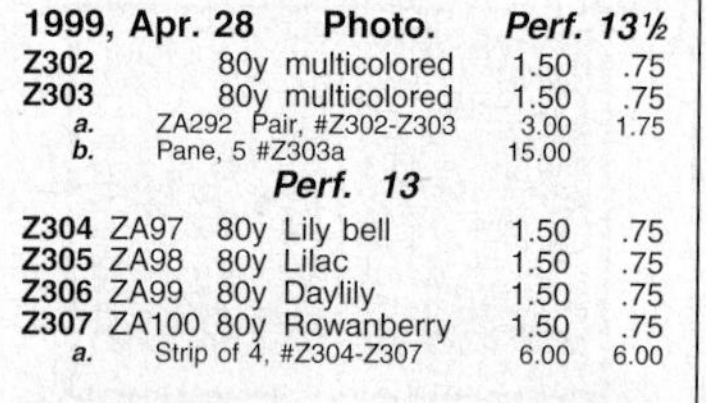

Sendai Tanabata Festival (Miyagi) ZA294

Souma Nomaoi Festival (Fukushima) ZA295

1999, May 14 Photo. *Perf. 13½*

Z310	ZA294 80y multicolored	1.50	.75
Z311	ZA295 80y multicolored	1.50	.75
a.	Pair, #Z310-Z311	3.00	1.75
b.	Pane, 5 #Z311a	15.00	

Ryukyu Dance (Okinawa) — ZA296

1999, May 14

Z312	ZA296 80y multicolored	1.50	.75
a.	Pane of 10	15.00	

ZA297

Northern Paradise (Hokkaido) ZA298

1999, May 25

Z313	ZA297 50y Lavender field	.95	.50
Z314	ZA298 80y Wheat field	1.50	.75

Kurashiki Sightseeing District (Okayama) — ZA299

1999, May 25 Photo. *Perf. 13½*

Z316	ZA299 80y multicolored	1.50	.75
a.	Pane of 10	15.00	

Shirone Big Kite Battle (Niigata)
ZA300 ZA301

1999, June 1 Litho. *Perf. 13½*

Z317	ZA300 80y multicolored	1.50	.75
Z318	ZA301 80y multicolored	1.50	.75
a.	Pair, #Z317-Z318	3.00	1.75
b.	Pane, 5 #Z318a	15.00	

Noto Kiriko Festival (Ishikawa) — ZA302

1999, June 11

Z319	ZA302 80y multicolored	1.50	.75
a.	Pane of 10	15.00	

Hokkaido Types of 1992-93

1999, June 25 Photo. *Perf. 13½*

Z320	ZA119 80y Arctic fox	1.50	.75

Litho.

Z321	ZA134 80y Largha seals	1.50	.75

ZA303

Tokyo: #Z323, morning glories. #Z324, starburst fireworks over Sumida River. #Z325, flower burst fireworks.

1999, July 1 Photo. *Perf. 13½*

Z323	80y multicolored	1.50	.75
Z324	80y multicolored	1.50	.75
Z325	80y multicolored	1.50	.75
a.	ZA303 Block of 3, #Z323-Z325	4.50	4.50
b.	Souv. sheet of 2, #Z324-Z325	3.00	3.00

Hakata Gion Yamagasa Festival (Fukuoka) — ZA306

1999, July 1 Litho.

Z326	ZA306 80y multicolored	1.50	.75
a.	Pane of 10	15.00	

ZA307 ZA308

ZA309 ZA310

Five Fuji Lakes (Yamanashi) ZA311

1999, July 1

Z327	ZA307	80y	Yamanakako	1.50	.75
Z328	ZA308	80y	Kawaguchiko	1.50	.75
Z329	ZA309	80y	Saiko	1.50	.75
Z330	ZA310	80y	Shoujiko	1.50	.75
Z331	ZA311	80y	Motosuko	1.50	.75
a.			Strip of 5, #Z327-Z331	7.70	7.50
b.			Pane, 2 #Z331a	15.00	

Inns of Tsumago, Magome Types of 1990

Photo. & Engr.

1999, July 16 ***Perf. 13***

Z332	ZA71	80y	like #Z71	1.50	.75
Z333	ZA72	80y	like #Z72	1.50	.75
a.			Pair, #Z332-Z333	3.00	2.25

ZA312

Toki (Japanese Crested Ibis) (Niigata) ZA313

1999, July 16 **Litho.** ***Perf. 13½***

Z334	ZA312	80y	Youyou, Yangyang	1.50	.75
Z335	ZA313	80y	Kin	1.50	.75
a.			Pair, #Z334-Z335	3.00	1.75
b.			Pane, 5 #Z335a	15.00	

ZA314

ZA315

Design: Amanohashidate sandbar, Miyatsu Bay (Kyoto).

1999, July 16

Z336	ZA314	80y	multicolored	1.50	.75

1999, July 16

Design: Ooga lotus (Chiba).

Z337	ZA315	80y	multicolored	1.50	.75
a.			Pane of 10	15.00	

ZA316

ZA317

ZA318

ZA319

Designs: Birds (Hokkaido).

1999, July 23 **Photo.** ***Perf. 13½***

Z338	ZA316	50y	Steller's sea-eagle	.95	.50
Z339	ZA317	50y	Tufted puffin	.95	.50
Z340	ZA318	50y	Blakiston's fish owl	.95	.50
Z341	ZA319	50y	Red-crowned crane	.95	.50
a.			Strip of 4, #Z337-Z340	4.00	4.00

Hill on Ie Island, Sabani Boat (Okinawa) — ZA320

1999, July 23 **Litho.** ***Perf. 13¼***

Z343	ZA320	80y	multicolored	1.50	.75
a.			Pane of 10	15.00	

National Treasures (Wakayama) — ZA321

#Z344, Kouyasan, Buddhist monastic complex. #Z345, Natl. treasure, Kongara-douji.

1999, July 26 ***Perf. 13½***

Z344		80y	multicolored	1.50	.75
Z345		80y	multicolored	1.50	.75
a.	ZA321		Pair, #Z344-Z345	3.00	1.75
b.			Pane, 5 #Z345a	15.00	

Autumn Bellflowers (Iwate) — ZA323

1999, July 30

Z346	ZA323	50y	multicolored	.95	.50
a.			Pane of 10	9.50	

Shimizu Port, Cent. (Shizuoka) ZA324

Fishing Boat (Kumamoto) ZA325

1999, Aug. 2 **Litho.** ***Perf. 13¼***

Z347	ZA324	80y	multi	1.50	.75
a.			Pane of 10	15.00	
Z348	ZA325	80y	multi	1.50	.75
a.			Pane of 10	15.00	

Ritsurin Park (Kagawa) ZA326

Artificial Island, Dejima (Nagasaki) ZA327

1999, Aug. 2 ***Perf. 13¼***

Z349	ZA326	80y	multi	1.50	.75
a.			Pane of 10	15.00	

1999, Sept. 1 **Photo.**

Z350	ZA327	80y	multi	1.50	.75
a.			Pane of 10	15.00	

Yoritomo Minamotono (1174-99), Shogun (Kanagawa) ZA328

Shirakami Mountains (Aomori) ZA329

1999, Sept. 2 **Litho.**

Z351	ZA328	80y	multi	1.50	.75
a.			Pane of 10	15.00	

1999, Sept. 6

Z352	ZA329	80y	multi	1.50	.75
a.			Pane of 10	15.00	

Gassho-zukuri Farmhouses and Kokiriko Dance (Toyama) — ZA330

1999, Sept. 14 **Photo.**

Z353	ZA330	80y	multi	1.50	.75
a.			Pane of 10	15.00	

Corn (Hokkaido) ZA331

Potatoes (Hokkaido) ZA332

Asparagus (Hokkaido) ZA333

Muskmelon (Hokkaido) ZA334

1999, Sept. 17 **Litho.**

Z354	ZA331	50y	multi	.95	.50
Z355	ZA332	50y	multi	.95	.50
Z356	ZA333	50y	multi	.95	.50
Z357	ZA334	50y	multi	.95	.50
a.			Strip, #Z354-Z357	4.00	4.00

(Gumma) ZA335

(Osaka) ZA336

1999, Sept. 17 ***Perf. 13¼***

Z358	ZA335	80y	multi	1.50	.75
a.			Pane of 10	15.00	

Iwajuku Paleolithic Site Excavations, 50th anniv.

1999, Sept. 27

Z359	ZA336	80y	multi	1.50	.75

23rd Rhythmic Gymnastics World Championships.

Nihonmatsu Chrysanthemum Exhibition (Fukushima) ZA337

1999, Oct. 1

Z360	ZA337	80y	multi	1.50	.75

Town of Obi (Miyazaki) — ZA338

Designs: No. Z361, Taihei dance, front gate of Obi Castle. No. Z362, Shintokudou School, Komura Jutarou (1855-1911).

1999, Oct. 1 ***Perf. 13¼***

Z361		80y	multi	1.50	.75
Z362		80y	multi	1.50	.75
a.	ZA338		Pair, #Z361-Z362	3.00	1.75
b.			Pane, 5 #Z362a	15.00	

Nagano Monkey Type of 1989

1999, Oct. 13 **Photo.** ***Perf. 12¾x13***

Z363	ZA1	80y	multi	1.50	.75

(Aichi) — ZA340

#Z364, Ichiei Sato. #Z365, "Beautiful Yamato."

1999, Oct. 13 **Photo.** ***Perf. 13¼***

Z364		80y	multi	1.50	.75
Z365		80y	multi	1.50	.75
a.	ZA340		Pair, #Z364-Z365	3.00	1.75
b.			Pane, 5 #Z365a	15.00	

ZA342

#Z366, Hagi (Yamaguchi). #Z367, Tsuwano (Shimane).

1999, Oct. 13

Z366		80y	multi	1.50	.75
Z367		80y	multi	1.50	.75
a.	ZA342		Vert. pair, #Z366-Z367	3.00	1.75
b.			Pane, 5 #Z367a	15.00	

(Nara) — ZA344

#Z368, Yamato Three Mountains. #Z369, Ishibutai Tomb.

1999, Oct. 28 Litho. *Perf. 13¼*

Z368 80y multi 1.50 .75
Z369 80y multi 1.50 .75
a. ZA344 Pair, #Z368-Z369 3.00 1.75
b. Pane, 5 #Z369a 15.00

Shikina-en Garden (Okinawa) — ZA346

1999, Oct. 28

Z370 50y multi .95 .50
Z371 50y multi .95 .50
a. ZA346 Pair, #Z370-Z371 1.90 1.25
b. Pane, 5 #Z371a 9.50

(Fukui) — ZA348

#Z372, Echizen Crab. #Z373, Tojinbou Cliff.

1999, Nov. 4

Z372 80y multi 1.50 .75
Z373 80y multi 1.50 .75
a. ZA348 Pair, #Z372-Z373 3.00 1.75
b. Pane, 5 #Z373a 15.00

Children in Santa's Sleigh (Hokkaido) ZA350

Yoshinogari Dig Site (Saga) ZA351

1999, Nov. 11 *Perf. 13¼*

Z374 ZA350 80y multi 1.50 .75
a. Pane of 10 15.00
Z375 ZA351 80y multi 1.50 .75
a. Pane of 10 15.00

(Kochi) — ZA352

#Z376, Katsura Beach. #Z377, Sakamoto Ryoma.

1999, Nov. 15 Photo.

Z376 80y multi 1.50 .75
Z377 80y multi 1.50 .75
a. ZA352 Pair, #Z376-Z377 3.00 1.75
b. Pane, 5 #Z377a 15.00

Samurai House, Kakunodate (Akita) — ZA354

1999, Dec. 17 Litho. *Perf. 13¼*

Z378 ZA354 80y multi 1.50 .75
a. Pane of 10 15.00

ZA355

ZA356

ZA357

ZA358

Tokyo Scenes (Tokyo) — ZA359

2000, Jan. 12 Litho. *Perf. 13¼*

Z379 ZA355 50y multi .95 .50
Z380 ZA356 50y multi .95 .50
Z381 ZA357 50y multi .95 .50
Z382 ZA358 50y multi .95 .50
Z383 ZA359 50y multi .95 .50
a. Horiz. strip, #Z379-Z383 4.75 4.75
b. Pane, 2 each #Z379-Z383 9.50

ZA360 ZA361

ZA362 ZA363

Snow World (Hokkaido)

2000, Feb. 7 Photo.

Z384 ZA360 80y multi 1.50 .75
Z385 ZA361 80y multi 1.50 .75
Z386 ZA362 80y multi 1.50 .75
Z387 ZA363 80y multi 1.50 .75
a. Strip, #Z384-Z387 6.00 6.00

ZA364

Japan Flora 2000 (Hyogo) — ZA365

2000, Mar. 1 Litho. *Perf. 13¼*

Z388 ZA364 50y multi .95 .50
Z389 ZA365 80y multi 1.50 .75
a. Pane, 5 each #Z388-Z389 12.50

ZA366 ZA367

ZA368 ZA369

Korakuen Gardens, 300th Anniv. (Okayama)

2000, Mar. 2 Photo.

Z390 ZA366 80y multi 1.50 .75
Z391 ZA367 80y multi 1.50 .75
Z392 ZA368 80y multi 1.50 .75
Z393 ZA369 80y multi 1.50 .75
a. Strip, #Z390-Z393 6.00 6.00
b. Souvenir sheet, #Z390-Z393 6.00 6.00

Cherry Blossoms in Takato (Nagano) ZA370

Dyed Fabrics (Okinawa) ZA371

Azumino (Nagano) — ZA372

2000, Mar. 3

Z394 ZA370 80y multi 1.50 .75
a. Pane of 10 15.00

2000, Mar. 17 Litho.

Z395 ZA371 50y multi .95 .50
a. Pane of 10 9.50

2000, Mar. 23 Photo.

Z396 ZA372 80y multi 1.50 .75
a. Pane of 10 15.00

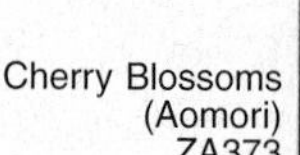

Cherry Blossoms (Aomori) ZA373

Cherry Blossoms (Fukushima) ZA374

Cherry Blossoms (Iwate) — ZA375

Cherry Blossoms (Miyagi) — ZA376

Cherry Blossoms (Akita) — ZA377

Cherry Blossoms (Yamagata) ZA378

2000, Apr. 3 Litho.

Z397 ZA373 80y multi 1.50 .75
a. Pair, #Z397, Z399 3.00 1.75
b. Pair, #Z397, Z400 3.00 1.75
c. Pair, #Z397, Z401 3.00 1.75
d. Pair, #Z397, Z402 3.00 1.75
Z398 ZA374 80y multi 1.50 .75
a. Pair, #Z398, Z399 3.00 1.75
b. Pair, #Z398, Z400 3.00 1.75
c. Pair, #Z398, Z401 3.00 1.75
d. Pair, #Z398, Z402 3.00 1.75
Z399 ZA375 80y multi 1.50 .75
Z400 ZA376 80y multi 1.50 .75
Z401 ZA377 80y multi 1.50 .75
Z402 ZA378 80y multi 1.50 .75
a. Vert. strip, #Z399-Z402 6.00 6.00
Nos. Z397-Z402 (6) 9.00 4.50

Printed in sheets containing one column of four stamps of Nos. Z397 and Z398 at left and right respectively with 3 No. Z402a between.

Tulips (Toyama) — ZA379

2000, Apr. 28 Photo. *Perf. 13¼*

Z403 50y multi .95 .50
Z404 80y multi 1.50 .75
a. ZA379 Pair, #Z403-Z404 2.50 1.50
b. Pane, 5 #Z404a 12.50

Uwajima Castle (Ehime) — ZA381

2000, Apr. 28 *Perf. 13½x13¼*

Z405 ZA381 80y multi 1.50 .75

New Urban Center (Saitama) — ZA382

2000, May 1 *Perf. 13¼*
Z406 50y multi .95 .50
Z407 50y multi .95 .50
a. ZA382 Pair, #Z406-Z407 1.90 1.25
b. Pane, 5 #Z407a 9.50

Flowers of the Chugoku Region

(Tottori) ZA384

(Shimane) ZA385

(Okayama) ZA386

(Hiroshima) ZA387

(Yamaguchi) ZA388

2000, May 1 **Litho.** *Perf. 13¼*
Z408 ZA384 50y multi .95 .50
Z409 ZA385 50y multi .95 .50
Z410 ZA386 50y multi .95 .50
Z411 ZA387 50y multi .95 .50
Z412 ZA388 50y multi .95 .50
a. Vert. strip, #Z408-Z412 4.75 4.75
b. Pane, 2# Z412a 9.50

Cosmos (Tokyo) ZA389

Roses (Tokyo) ZA390

Bird of Paradise Flowers (Tokyo) ZA391

Sasanquas (Tokyo) ZA392

Freesias (Tokyo) — ZA393

2000, June 1 **Photo.** *Perf. 13¼*
Z413 ZA389 50y multi .95 .50
Z414 ZA390 50y multi .95 .50
Z415 ZA391 50y multi .95 .50
Z416 ZA392 50y multi .95 .50
Z417 ZA393 50y multi .95 .50
a. Vert. strip of 5, #Z413-Z417 4.75 4.75
b. Pane, 2 #Z417a 9.50

Shonan Hiratsuka Tanabata Festival (Kanagawa) — ZA394

2000, June 2 **Litho.**
Z418 50y multi .95 .50
Z419 50y multi .95 .50
a. ZA394 Pair, #Z418-Z419 1.90 1.25
b. Pane, 5 #Z419a 9.50

Bankoku Shinryokan (Okinawa) — ZA396

2000, June 21 **Photo.** *Perf. 13¼*
Z420 ZA396 80y multi 1.50 .75
a. Pane of 10 15.00

World Performing Arts Festival (Osaka) — ZA397

Kujuku Islands (Akita) — ZA398

2000, June 28 **Litho.**
Z421 ZA397 80y multi 1.50 .75
a. Pane of 10 15.00

2000, July 7 **Photo.**
Z422 ZA398 80y multi 1.50 .75
a. Pane of 10 15.00

Potato Field (Hokkaido) — ZA399

Hillside and Hay Rolls (Hokkaido) — ZA400

2000, July 19
Z423 50y Flowers, barn .95 .50
Z424 50y Barn, silo .95 .50
a. ZA399 Pair, #Z423-Z424 1.90 1.10
Z425 80y + 20y Hayrolls, houses 1.90 1.00
Z426 80y + 20y Hayrolls, barns 1.90 1.00
a. ZA400 Pair, #Z425-Z426 3.80 2.50
Nos. Z423-Z426 (4) 5.70 3.00

Surtax on Nos. Z425-Z426 for refugees of eruption of Mt. Usu.

Awa-odori (Tokushima) ZA401

Golden Hall of Chusonji Temple (Iwate) ZA402

2000, July 31 **Litho.**
Z427 ZA401 80y multi 1.50 .75
a. Pane of 10 15.00

2000, Aug. 1
Z428 ZA402 80y multi 1.50 .75
a. Pane of 10 15.00

Hakata Doll (Fukuoka) ZA403

55th Natl. Athletic Meet (Toyama) ZA404

2000, Aug. 2
Z429 ZA403 80y multi 1.50 .75
a. Pane of 10 15.00

2000, Sept. 1 **Photo.**
Z430 ZA404 50y multi .95 .50
a. Pane of 10 9.50

25th World Parachuting Championships (Mie) — ZA405

2000, Sept. 13
Z431 80y 2 skydivers 1.50 .75
Z432 80y 3 skydivers 1.50 .75
a. ZA405 Pair, #Z431-Z432 3.00 1.75
b. Pane, 5 #Z432a 15.00

Friendly Tokyo (Tokyo) ZA406

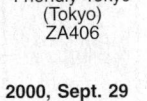

Iwakuni Kintaikyo Bridge (Yamaguchi) ZA407

2000, Sept. 29 **Litho.**
Z433 ZA406 80y multi 1.50 .75
a. Pane of 10 15.00

2000, Oct. 10
Z434 ZA407 80y multi 1.50 .75
a. Pane of 10 15.00

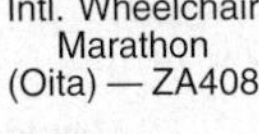
Intl. Wheelchair Marathon (Oita) — ZA408

Willow and Frog (Aichi) — ZA409

2000, Oct. 11
Z435 ZA408 80y multi 1.50 .75
a. Pane of 10 15.00

2000, Oct. 20 **Photo.**
Z436 ZA409 80y multi 1.50 .75
a. Pane of 10 15.00

ZA410 ZA411

ZA412 ZA413
Four Seasons (Kyoto)

2000, Oct. 20 **Litho.**
Z437 ZA410 80y multi 1.50 .75
Z438 ZA411 80y multi 1.50 .75
a. Pane, 5 each #Z437-Z438 15.00
Z439 ZA412 80y multi 1.50 .75
Z440 ZA413 80y multi 1.50 .75
a. Horiz. strip, #Z437-Z440 6.00 3.50
b. Pane, 5 each #Z439-Z440 15.00

Odawarajo Castle (Kanagawa) — ZA414

2000, Oct. 27 *Perf. 13¼*
Z441 50y multi .95 .50
Z442 50y multi .95 .50
a. ZA414 Pair, #Z441-Z442 1.90 1.25
b. Pane, 5 #Z442a 9.50

Intl. Balloon Festival (Saga) — ZA415

2000, Nov. 1 **Litho.** *Perf. 13¼*
Z443 ZA415 80y multi 1.50 .75
a. Pane of 10 15.00

Chichibu Night Festival (Saitama) — ZA416

2000, Nov. 1 **Photo.**

Z444	80y Yatai, fireworks	1.50	.75
Z445	80y Kasahoko	1.50	.75
a.	ZA416 Pair, #Z444-Z445	3.00	1.75
b.	Pane, 5 #Z445a	15.00	

Scenic Izu (Shizuoka) — ZA417

2000, Nov. 29 **Litho.**

Z446	50y Garden	.95	.50
Z447	50y Waterfall	.95	.50
a.	ZA417 Pair, #Z446-Z447	1.90	1.25
b.	Pane, 5 #Z447a	9.50	

Hata Festival, Kohata (Fukushima) ZA418

2000, Dec. 1 **Photo.**

Z448	ZA418 80y multi	1.50	.75
a.	Pane of 10	15.00	

Sekino'o-taki Falls and Kirishima (Miyazaki) — ZA419

2000, Dec. 12 **Photo.**

Z449	80y Waterfall	1.50	.75
Z450	80y Mountain	1.50	.75
a.	ZA419 Pair, #Z449-Z450	3.00	1.75
b.	Pane, 5 #Z450a	15.00	

Megane-bashi Bridge (Gunma) — ZA420

2000, Dec. 15 **Litho.**

Z451	50y Bridge	.95	.50
Z452	50y Transformer substation	.95	.50
a.	ZA420 Pair, #Z451-Z452	1.90	1.25

Song "Shinano-no Kuni" (Nagano) — ZA421

2000, Dec. 15 **Photo.**

Z453	50y Denom. at L	.95	.50
Z454	50y Denom. at R	.95	.50
a.	ZA421 Pair, #Z453-Z454	1.90	1.25

Kobe Earthquake Restoration (Hyogo) — ZA422

2001, Jan. 17 **Photo.** ***Perf. 13¼***

Z455	50y Pandas	.95	.50
Z456	80y Kobe Port	1.50	.75
a.	ZA422 Pair, #Z455-Z456	2.50	1.50
b.	Pane, 5 #Z456a	12.50	

Ooe Kouwaka-mai (Fukuoka) — ZA423

2001, Jan. 19 **Litho.**

Z457	ZA423 80y multi	1.50	.75
a.	Pane of 10	15.00	

Kairakuen Garden (Ibaraki) — ZA424

Designs: No. Z458, Koubuntei Pavilion, tree blossoms. No. Z459, Path, Chumon Gate. No. Z460, Togyokusen Spring, path. No. Z461, Koubuntei Pavilion in winter.

2001, Feb. 1 **Photo.**

Z458	50y multi	.95	.50
Z459	50y multi	.95	.50
Z460	50y multi	.95	.50
Z461	50y multi	.95	.50
a.	ZA424 Horiz. strip, #Z458-Z461	4.00	4.00
b.	Souvenir sheet, #Z461a	4.00	4.00

Ezo Sable (Hokkaido) — ZA425

2001, Feb. 6 **Litho.**

Z462	ZA425 80y multi	1.50	.75
a.	Pane of 10	15.00	

Kochi Castle and Sunday Market (Kochi) — ZA426

2001, Mar. 1 **Photo.** ***Perf. 13¼***

Z463	80y multi	1.50	.75
Z464	80y multi	1.50	.75
a.	ZA426 Pair, #Z463-Z464	3.00	1.75
b.	Pane, 5 #Z464a	15.00	

Takarazuka Revue Dancers (Hyogo) — ZA427

Violets (Hyogo) — ZA428

2001, Mar. 21 **Litho.**

Z465	ZA427 80y multi	1.50	.75
Z466	ZA428 80y multi	1.50	.75
a.	Pane, 5 each #Z465-Z466	15.00	

Matsue Castle and Meimei-an Teahouse (Shimane) — ZA429

2001, Mar. 21

Z467	80y multi	1.50	.75
Z468	80y multi	1.50	.75
a.	ZA429 Pair, #Z467-Z468	3.00	1.75
b.	Pane, 5 #Z468a	15.00	

Grapes, Jewelry and Mt. Fuji (Yamanashi) ZA430

2001, Mar. 30 **Photo.**

Z469	ZA430 80y multi	1.50	.75
a.	Pane of 10	15.00	

Sports Paradise (Osaka) — ZA431

Designs: No. Z470, Thunder god (red) playing table tennis. No. Z471, Wing god (green) playing table tennis. No. Z472, Bowling. No. Z473, Taekwondo.

2001, Apr. 3

Z470	50y multi	.95	.50
Z471	50y multi	.95	.50
Z472	50y multi	.95	.50
Z473	50y multi	.95	.50
a.	ZA431 Horiz. strip, #Z470-Z473	4.00	4.00

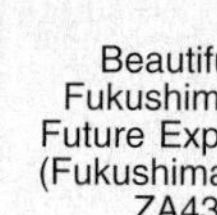

Beautiful Fukushima Future Expo (Fukushima) ZA432

2001, Apr. 10

Z474	ZA432 80y multi	1.50	.75
a.	Pane of 10	15.00	

Cherry Blossoms at Takada Castle (Niigata) — ZA433

2001, Apr. 10 **Litho.**

Z475	ZA433 80y multi	1.50	.75
a.	Pane of 10	15.00	

Hamamatsu Festival (Shizuoka) — ZA434

Designs: No. Z476, Palace Festival. No. Z477, Kite fighting.

2001, May 1

Z476	80y multi	1.50	.75
Z477	80y multi	1.50	.75
a.	ZA434 Pair, #Z476-Z477	3.00	1.75
b.	Pane, 5 #Z477a	15.00	

Ashikaga School Gate (Tochigi) ZA435

Ashikaga School (Tochigi) ZA436

2001, May 11 **Photo.**

Z478	ZA435 80y multi	1.50	.75
Z479	ZA436 50y multi	1.50	.75
a.	Pane, 5 each #Z478-Z479	15.00	

Natl. Afforestation Campaign (Yamanashi) ZA437

2001, May 18

Z480	ZA437 50y multi	.95	.50
a.	Pane of 10	9.50	

Sendai, 400th Anniv. (Miyagi) — ZA438

2001, May 18 **Litho.**

Z481	ZA438 80y multi	1.50	.75
a.	Pane of 10	15.00	

Zenkoji Temple and Mt. Iizunayama (Nagano) — ZA439

2001, May 23

Z482	80y multi	1.50	.75
Z483	80y multi	1.50	.75
a.	ZA439 Pair, #Z482-Z483	3.00	1.75
b.	Pane, 5 #Z483a	15.00	

Ducks (Yamaguchi) ZA440

Kirara Band, Japan Expo Site (Yamaguchi) ZA441

2001, May 25

Z484	ZA440 50y multi	.95	.50
Z485	ZA441 80y multi	1.50	.75
a.	Pane, 5 each #Z484-Z485	12.25	

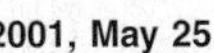

Cherry Blossoms (Tokyo) — ZA442

Hydrangea (Tokyo) — ZA443

Salvia (Tokyo) — ZA444

Chrysanthemums (Tokyo) — ZA445

Camellias (Tokyo) — ZA446

2001, June 1 **Photo.**

Z486	ZA442 50y multi	.95	.50
Z487	ZA443 50y multi	.95	.50
Z488	ZA444 50y multi	.95	.50
Z489	ZA445 50y multi	.95	.50
Z490	ZA446 50y multi	.95	.50
a.	Vert. strip, #Z486-Z490	4.75	4.75
b.	Pane, 2 #Z490a	9.50	

ZA447

Sites (Tottori) — ZA448

Designs: No. Z491, Snow crab, Uradome Coast. No. Z492, Tottori Dunes. No. Z493, Paper Hina dolls in river. No. Z494, Mt. Daisen. No. Z495, Nageiredo Hall. No. Z496, Mukibanda Yayoi Period.
Illustration ZA447 reduced.

2001, June 1

Z491	50y multi	.95	.50
Z492	50y multi	.95	.50
Z493	50y multi	.95	.50
Z494	50y multi	.95	.50
a.	ZA447 Horiz. strip, #Z491-Z494	4.00	4.00
Z495	80y multi	1.50	.75
Z496	80y multi	1.50	.75
a.	ZA448 Horiz. pair, #Z495-Z496	3.00	1.75
	Nos. Z491-Z496 (6)	6.80	3.50

Prosperity in Kaga (Ishikawa) — ZA449

2001, June 4 **Litho.**

Z497	ZA449 80y multi	1.50	.75
a.	Pane of 10	15.00	

Poppies (Hokkaido) ZA450

Calanthe (Hokkaido) ZA451

2001, June 22 **Litho.**

Z498	ZA450 50y multi	.95	.50
a.	Pane of 10	9.50	
Z499	ZA451 50y multi	.95	.50
a.	Pane of 10	9.50	

Cornerstone of Peace (Okinawa) — ZA452

2001, June 22 **Photo.**

Z500	ZA452 80y multi	1.50	.75

Peach Blossoms, Shirane-sanzan Mountains (Yamanashi) ZA453

Irises, Mt. Kitadake (Yamanashi) ZA454

Horses. Mt. Yatsugatake (Yamanashi) ZA455

Oshino-hakkai Pond (Yamanashi) ZA456

Cherry Blossoms, Minobu (Yamanashi) ZA457

2001, July 2

Z501	ZA453 50y multi	.95	.50
Z502	ZA454 50y multi	.95	.50
Z503	ZA455 50y multi	.95	.50
Z504	ZA456 50y multi	.95	.50
Z505	ZA457 50y multi	.95	.50
a.	Vert. strip, #Z501-Z505	4.75	4.75
b.	Pane, 2 #Z505a	9.50	

Automobile City, Toyota (Aichi) — ZA458

Designs: No. Z506, Toyota-oohashi Bridge. No. Z507, Toyota Stadium.

2001, July 2

Z506	50y multi	.95	.50
Z507	50y multi	.95	.50
a.	ZA458 Pair, #Z506-Z507	1.90	1.25
b.	Pane, 5 #Z507a	9.50	

Kitakyushu Expo Festival (Fukuoka) — ZA459

2001, July 4

Z508	ZA459 80y multi	1.50	.75
a.	Pane of 10	15.00	

World Trade Organization, 14th General Assembly (Osaka) — ZA460

Designs: No. Z509, Namdaemun, Seoul, and Doton-bori, Osaka. No. Z510, Bunraku, Nong-ak.

2001, July 6 **Litho.**

Z509	80y multi	1.50	.75
Z510	80y multi	1.50	.75
a.	ZA460 Pair, #Z509-Z510	3.00	1.75

Grand Fireworks of Nagaoka (Niigata) — ZA461

2001, July 23

Z511	50y yel & multi	.95	.50
Z512	50y pink & multi	.95	.50
a.	ZA461 Pair, #Z511-Z512	1.90	1.25
b.	Pane, 5 #Z512a	9.50	

Poplars (Hokkaido) ZA462

Statue, Sheep (Hokkaido) ZA463

2001, Sept. 3 **Litho.** ***Perf. 13¼***

Z513	ZA462 80y multi	1.50	.75
Z514	ZA463 80y multi	1.50	.75
a.	Pane, 5 each #Z513-Z514	15.00	

56th Natl. Athletic Meets (Miyagi) — ZA464

2001, Sept. 7 **Photo.**

Z515	ZA464 50y multi	.95	.50
a.	Pane of 10	9.50	

Matsuyama Castle, Masaoki Shiki (1867-1902), Poet (Ehime) — ZA465

2001, Sept. 12

Z516	50y Castle	.95	.50
Z517	50y Poet	.95	.50
a.	ZA465 Horiz. pair, #Z516-Z517	1.90	1.25

Ibi Traditions (Gifu) — ZA466

Designs: No. Z518, Tanigumi-Odori dance. No. Z519, Train, persimmons.

2001, Sept. 28 **Photo.** ***Perf. 13¼***

Z518	50y multi	.95	.50
Z519	50y multi	.95	.50
a.	ZA466 Horiz. pair, #Z518-Z519	1.90	1.25
b.	Pane, 5 #Z519a	9.50	

Kamakura Igloo (Akita) — ZA467

2001, Oct. 1 **Litho.**

Z520	ZA467 80y multi	1.50	.75
a.	Pane of 10	15.00	

9th Intl. Conference on Lake Conservation & Management (Shiga) — ZA468

2001, Oct. 1

Z521	ZA468 50y multi	.95	.50
a.	Pane of 10	9.50	

World Indoor Cycling Championships (Kagoshima) ZA469

2001, Oct. 1

Z522	ZA469 80y multi	1.50	.75

Okuma Auditorium, Waseda University (Tokyo) — ZA470

2001, Oct. 19

Z523	ZA470 80y multi	1.50	.75
a.	Pane of 10	15.00	

Wild Narcissi (Fukui) ZA471

Echizen Coast and Wild Narcissi (Fukui) ZA472

2001, Nov. 6

Z524	ZA471 50y multi	.95	.50
a.	Pane of 10	9.50	
Z525	ZA472 80y multi	1.50	.75
a.	Pane of 10	15.00	

Tokyo Millenalio (Tokyo) — ZA473

2001, Dec. 3 **Photo.**

Z526	ZA473 80y multi	1.50	.75
a.	Pane of 10	15.00	

Ezo Flying Squirrels (Hokkaido) — ZA474

2002, Feb. 5

Z527	ZA474 80y multi	1.50	.75

Scenes North of Hiroshima (Hiroshima) — ZA475

Designs: No. Z528, Nukui Dam. No. Z529, On-bashi Bridge.

2002, Feb. 22 **Litho.**

Z528	80y multi	1.50	.75
Z529	80y multi	1.50	.75
a.	ZA475 Horiz. pair, #Z528-Z529	3.00	1.75

Azaleas (Wakayama) ZA476

2002, Mar. 1 **Photo.** ***Perf. 13¼***

Z530	ZA476 80y multi	1.50	.95

Glover Garden (Nagasaki) — ZA477

Designs: No. Z531, Houses, fountain, roses. No. Z532, House, tulips.

2002, Mar. 1 **Litho.**

Z531	50y multi	.95	.60
Z532	50y multi	.95	.60
a.	ZA477 Horiz. pair, #Z531-Z532	1.90	1.20

Cherry Blossoms, Hiikawa River (Shimane) ZA478

Cherry Blossoms, Bicchu-Kokubunji Temple (Okayama) ZA479

2002, Mar. 18

Z533	ZA478 50y multi	.95	.60
Z534	ZA479 50y multi	.95	.60
a.	Horiz. pair, #Z533-Z534	1.90	1.20
b.	Pane, 5 #Z534a	9.50	—

Tangerine, Sata Cape (Ehime) ZA480

Citrus Fruit, Mt. Tsurugisan (Tokushima) ZA481

Bayberry, Tengu Highlands (Kochi) ZA482

Olives, Shodo Island (Kagawa) ZA483

2002, Mar. 20 **Photo.**

Z535	ZA480 50y multi	.95	.60
Z536	ZA481 50y multi	.95	.60
Z537	ZA482 50y multi	.95	.60
Z538	ZA483 50y multi	.95	.60
a.	Horiz. strip of 4, #Z535-Z538	4.00	2.40

Flowers (Hokkaido) — ZA484

2002, Apr. 25 **Litho.**

Z539	80y Tulips, windmills	1.50	.95
Z540	80y Sunflowers, field	1.50	.95
a.	ZA484 Horiz. pair, #Z539-Z540	3.00	1.90

54th Intl. Whaling Commission (Yamaguchi) ZA485

2002, Apr. 25

Z541	ZA485 80y multi	1.50	.95

Bonsai Village (Saitama) — ZA486

2002, Apr. 26 **Photo.**

Z542	ZA486 80y multi	1.50	.95

Yokohama (Kanagawa) — ZA487

Designs: No. Z543, Sailing ships. No. Z544, Modern ship, skyline, woman.

2002, May 1

Z543	50y multi	.95	.60
Z544	50y multi	.95	.60
a.	ZA487 Horiz. pair, #Z543-Z544	1.90	1.20
b.	Pane, 5 #Z544a	9.50	

Flowers (Niigata) — ZA488

Designs: No. Z545, Red camellias. No. Z546, Yellow daylilies. No. Z547, Purple and pink irises. No. Z548, Pink iwakagami flowers. Illustration reduced.

2002, May 1 **Litho.**

Z545	50y multi	.95	.60
Z546	50y multi	.95	.60
Z547	50y multi	.95	.60
Z548	50y multi	.95	.60
a.	ZA488 Horiz. strip of 4, #Z545-Z548	4.00	2.40

Natl. Afforestation Campaign (Yamagata) — ZA489

2002, May 31 **Photo.**

Z549	ZA489 50y multi	.95	.60
a.	Pane of 10	9.50	—

Oze (Fukushima) — ZA490

Designs: No. Z550, Flowers, bare trees, walkway. No. Z551, Flowers, evergreens.

2002, June 28 **Litho.**

Z550	50y multi	.95	.60
Z551	50y multi	.95	.60
a.	ZA490 Horiz. pair, #Z550-Z551	1.90	1.20

Mt. Tanigawadake (Gunma) — ZA491

Mountains and: No. Z552, Rhododendrons. No. Z553, Trees in autumn.

2002, June 28

Z552	80y multi	1.50	1.00
Z553	80y multi	1.50	1.00
a.	ZA491 Horiz. pair, #Z552-Z553	3.00	2.00

Tokyo Fair and Market (Tokyo) — ZA492

Designs: No. Z554, Morning Glory Fair. No. Z555, Hozuki Fair.

2002, June 28 **Photo.**

Z554	80y multi	1.50	1.00
Z555	80y multi	1.50	1.00
a.	ZA492 Horiz. pair, #Z554-Z555	3.00	2.00

Alpine Flora (Ishikawa) — ZA493

2002, July 1 **Flower Color**

Z556	50y Purple	.95	.60
Z557	50y Brown	.95	.60
Z558	50y Bright pink	.95	.60
Z559	50y White	.95	.60
a.	ZA493 Horiz. strip of 4, #Z556-Z559	4.00	4.00

Gujou-odori Dance (Gifu) ZA494

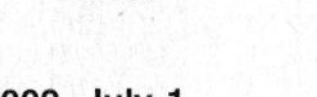

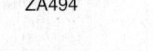

85th Lions Club Intl. Convention (Osaka) ZA495

2002, July 1
Z560 ZA494 50y multi .95 .60

2002, July 1
Z561 ZA495 80y multi 1.50 1.00

23rd Asia-Pacific Scout Jamboree (Osaka) ZA496

Yachiyoza Theater (Kumamoto) ZA497

2002, July 15
Z562 ZA496 50y multi .95 .60

2002, July 15 **Litho.**
Z563 ZA497 80y multi 1.50 1.00

Hikan-zakura, Iejima (Okinawa) ZA498

Hibiscus, Kaichudouro Highway (Okinawa) ZA499

Bougainvillea, House in Tsuboya (Okinawa) ZA500

Lily, Higashihennazaki (Okinawa) ZA501

Seishika Flower, Seishika Bridge (Okinawa) — ZA502

2002, Aug. 23 **Photo.** ***Perf. 13¼***
Z564 ZA498 50y multi .95 .60
Z565 ZA499 50y multi .95 .60
Z566 ZA500 50y multi .95 .60
Z567 ZA501 50y multi .95 .60
Z568 ZA502 50y multi .95 .60
a. Vert. strip of 5, #Z564-Z568 4.75 4.75

Printed in sheets containing two No. Z568a.

Flora (Tokyo) — ZA503

Designs: No. Z569, Azalea (pink flower, blue denomination). No. Z570, Lily. No. Z571, Crape myrtle (pink flower and denomination). No. Z572, Ginkgo leaves.

2002, Sept. 2
Z569 50y multi .95 .60
Z570 50y multi .95 .60
Z571 50y multi .95 .60
Z572 50y multi .95 .60
a. ZA503 Horiz. strip of 4, #Z569-Z572 4.00 2.40

57th Natl. Athletic Meet (Kochi) — ZA504

2002, Sept. 5
Z573 ZA504 50y multi .95 .60

Iga-Ueno (Mie) — ZA505

Designs: No. Z574, Basho Matsuo, Iga-Ueno Castle. No. Z575, Iga-Ueno Castle, Haisei-den Hall.

2002, Sept. 10 **Litho.**
Z574 80y multi 1.50 1.00
Z575 80y multi 1.50 1.00
a. ZA505 Horiz. pair, #Z574-Z575 3.00 2.00

Tohoku's Four Season Story (Aomori) — ZA506

2002, Oct. 23 **Photo.** ***Perf. 13¼***
Z576 ZA506 80y multi 1.50 1.00

Fifth Winter Asian Games (Aomori) — ZA507

2003, Jan. 24 **Photo.** ***Perf. 13¼***
Z577 ZA507 50y multi 1.50 .60

Nobeoka, City of Noh Theater (Miyazaki) — ZA508

Designs: No. Z578, Actor on stage, audience. No. Z579, Actor with red kimono.

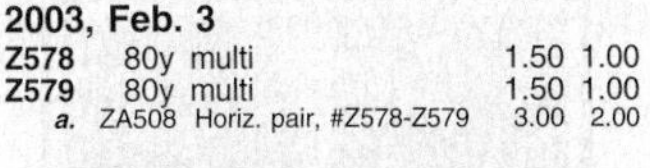

2003, Feb. 3
Z578 80y multi 1.50 1.00
Z579 80y multi 1.50 1.00
a. ZA508 Horiz. pair, #Z578-Z579 3.00 2.00

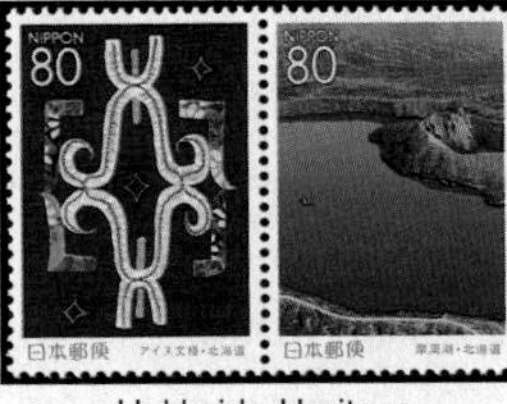

Hokkaido Heritage (Hokkaido) — ZA509

2003, Feb. 5 **Photo.** ***Perf. 13¼***
Z580 80y Ainu design 1.40 1.00
Z581 80y Lake Mashuko 1.40 1.00
a. ZA509 Horiz. pair, #Z580-Z581 2.80 2.00

Flora (Nagano) — ZA510

Designs: No. Z582, Dogtooth Violet (pink flowers) and mountain. No. Z583, Skunk Cabbage (white flower). No. Z584, Nikkoday Lily (yellow flower. No. Z585, Cosmos (white, pink and red flowers).

2003, Mar. 5 **Photo.** ***Perf. 13¼***
Z582 50y multi .85 .60
Z583 50y multi .85 .60
Z584 50y multi .85 .60
Z585 50y multi .85 .60
a. ZA510 Horiz. strip of 4, #Z582-Z585 3.40 2.40

Kibitsu Shrine (Okayama) ZA511

Kompira-Ohshibai Theater (Kagawa) ZA512

2003, Mar. 5
Z586 ZA511 80y multi 1.40 1.00

2003, Mar. 24 **Litho.**
Z587 ZA512 80y multi 1.40 1.00

Imari-Arita Ceramics (Saga) — ZA513

2003, Apr. 10
Z588 ZA513 80y multi 1.40 1.00

Kaneko Misuzu and Poem "Tairyo" (Yamaguchi) — ZA514

2003, Apr. 11 **Photo.**
Z589 80y Misuzu 1.40 1.00
Z590 80y Poem 1.40 1.00
a. ZA514 Horiz. pair, #Z589-Z590 2.80 2.00

Cormorant Fishing and Gifu Castle (Gifu) — ZA515

2003, May 1 ***Perf. 13¼***
Z591 50y Fishermen .85 .60
Z592 50y Castle .85 .60
a. ZA514 Horiz. pair, #Z591-Z592 1.70 1.20

Traditional Events (Kyoto) — ZA516

Designs: No. Z593, Aoi-matsuri (wagon decorated with flowers). No. Z594, Gion-matsuri festival float (tower on wheels). No. Z595, Okuribi (fire on mountain). No. Z596, Jidai-matsuri (parade procession).

2003, May 1 **Litho.**
Z593 50y multi .85 .60
Z594 50y multi .85 .60
Z595 50y multi .85 .60
Z596 50y multi .85 .60
a. ZA516 Horiz. strip of 4, #Z593-Z596 3.40 2.40

Natl. Afforestation Campaign (Chiba) — ZA517

2003, May 16 **Photo.**
Z597 ZA517 50y multi .85 .60

Mt. Tsukuba and Iris (Ibaraki) — ZA518

2003, May 20 **Litho.**
Z598 ZA518 80y multi 1.40 1.00

Tsurugajou Castle, Persimmons (Fukushima) ZA519

2003, July 1 **Photo.** ***Perf. 13¼***
Z599 ZA519 80y multi 1.40 1.00

Kyuya Fukada, Mountineer, Birth Cent. (Ishikawa) — ZA520

2003, July 1 **Litho.**
Z600 ZA520 80y multi 1.40 1.00

Okinawa Urban Monorail (Okinawa) — ZA521

2003, Aug. 8

Z601	50y Shurijo Castle		.85	.65
Z602	50y Naha Airport		.85	.65
a.	ZA521 Horiz. pair, #Z601-Z602		1.70	1.30

58th Natl. Athletics Meets (Shizuoka) — ZA522

2003, Aug. 29 **Photo.**

Z603 ZA520 50y multi .85 .65

Ume (Tokyo) ZA523

Wisterias (Tokyo) ZA524

Irises (Tokyo) ZA525

Tea Blossoms (Tokyo) ZA526

2003, Sept. 1

Z604	ZA523 50y multi	.85	.65
Z605	ZA524 50y multi	.85	.65
Z606	ZA525 50y multi	.85	.65
Z607	ZA526 50y multi	.85	.65
a.	Horiz. strip, #Z604-Z607	3.40	2.60

Chiyojo, Haiku Poet (Ishikawa) — ZA527

2003, Oct. 3 **Litho.**

Z608	80y Haiku text	1.50	1.10
Z609	80y Chiyojo	1.50	1.10
a.	ZA527 Horiz. pair, #Z608-Z609	3.00	2.20

Yasujiro Ozu (1903-63), Film Director (Mie) — ZA528

2003, Oct. 23 **Photo.**

Z610 ZA528 80y multi 1.50 1.10

Kiritappu Wetland and Wakka Primeval Garden (Hokkaido) — ZA529

2004, Feb. 5 **Litho.** ***Perf. 13¼***

Z611	80y Yellow flowers	1.50	1.10
Z612	80y Orange flowers	1.50	1.10
a.	ZA529 Horiz. pair, #Z611-Z612	3.00	2.20

Kyushu Bullet Train (Kagoshima) ZA530

2004, Mar. 12 **Photo.** ***Perf. 13¼***

Z613 ZA530 50y multi .90 .65

Flower Types of 1990

Designs as before.

2004, Mar. 19

Z614	ZA24 50y multi	.95	.65
Z615	ZA25 50y multi	.95	.65
Z616	ZA26 50y multi	.95	.65
Z617	ZA27 50y multi	.95	.65
Z618	ZA28 50y multi	.95	.65
Z619	ZA29 50y multi	.95	.65
	Nos. Z614-Z619 (6)	5.70	3.90

Zuiryuji Temple (Toyama) — ZA531

2004, Mar. 19 **Litho.**

Z620 ZA531 80y multi 1.50 1.10

Hana-Kairou Flower Park (Tottori) — ZA532

2004, Mar. 23

Z621 ZA532 80y multi 1.50 1.10

Gerbera (Shizuoka) ZA533

Carnation (Shizuoka) ZA534

Rose (Shizuoka) ZA535

Lisianthus (Shizuoka) ZA536

2004, Apr. 8

Z622	ZA533 80y multi	1.50	1.10
Z623	ZA534 80y multi	1.50	1.10
Z624	ZA535 80y multi	1.50	1.10
Z625	ZA536 80y multi	1.50	1.10
a.	Horiz. strip of 4, #Z622-Z625	6.00	4.40

Pacific Flora 2004.

National Afforestation Campaign (Miyazaki) — ZA537

2004, Mar. 23 **Photo.**

Z626 ZA537 50y multi .90 .65

Murouji's Five Story Pagoda (Nara) — ZA538

2004, Apr. 26

Z627 ZA538 80y multi 1.40 1.00

Rotary International Convention (Osaka) — ZA539

2004, May 21

Z628 ZA539 80y multi 1.50 1.10

Ice Breaker Garinko-go, Steller's Sea Eagle (Hokkaido) — ZA540

2004, May 28

Z629 ZA540 80y multi 1.50 1.10

Kanto Festival Performer, Namahage (Akita) — ZA541

2004, June 1 **Litho.**

Z630	50y blue & multi	.90	.65
Z631	50y red & multi	.90	.65
a.	ZA541 Horiz. pair, #Z630-Z631	1.80	1.30

Akita City, 400th anniv.

Magnolia (Tokyo) — ZA542

Azalea (Tokyo) — ZA543

Wildflower (Tokyo) — ZA544

Bush Clover (Tokyo) — ZA545

2004, June 1 **Photo.**

Z632	ZA542 50y multi	.90	.65
Z633	ZA543 50y multi	.90	.65
Z634	ZA544 50y multi	.90	.65
Z635	ZA545 50y multi	.90	.65
a.	Horiz. strip of 4, #Z632-Z635	3.60	2.60

Roses and Buildings (Kanagawa) ZA546

Gold-banded Lily and Buildings (Kanagawa) ZA547

Wisteria and Enoshima Island (Kanagawa) ZA548

Hydrangea and Lake Ashinoko (Kanagawa) ZA549

2004, June 1

Z636	ZA546 50y multi	.90	.65
Z637	ZA547 50y multi	.90	.65
Z638	ZA548 50y multi	.90	.65
Z639	ZA549 50y multi	.90	.65
a.	Horiz. strip of 4, #Z636-Z639	3.60	2.60

Daimyo Processions of Lord Takachika Mouri (Yamaguchi) — ZA550

2004, June 21 **Litho.**

Z640	80y red & multi	1.50	1.10
Z641	80y green & multi	1.50	1.10
a.	ZA550 Horiz. pair, #Z640-Z641	3.00	2.20

Rose, Mt. Tsukubasan (Ibaraki) ZA551

Yashio-tsutsuji and Lake Chuzenjiko (Tochigi) ZA552

Renge-tsutsuji and Mt. Akagisan (Gunma) ZA553

Primrose and Tajimagahara Native Primrose Field (Saitama) ZA554

Rape Blossoms and Nojimazaki Lighthouse (Chiba) — ZA555

2004, June 23 **Photo.**

Z642	ZA551	50y multi	.95	.65
Z643	ZA552	50y multi	.95	.65
Z644	ZA553	50y multi	.95	.65
Z645	ZA554	50y multi	.95	.65
Z646	ZA555	50y multi	.95	.65
a.		Vert. strip of 5, #Z642-Z646	4.75	3.25

Owara Dance (Toyama) — ZA556

Designs: No. Z647, Children. No. Z648, Dancers in pink kimonos. No. Z648, Dancers in black clothes. No. Z649, Dancers in blue kimonos.

2004, Aug. 20 **Litho.**

Z647		50y multi	.90	.65
Z648		50y multi	.90	.65
Z649		50y multi	.90	.65
Z650		50y multi	.90	.65
a.	ZA556	Horiz. strip of 4, #Z647-Z650	3.60	2.60

59th National Athletic Meets (Saitama) — ZA557

2004, Sept. 10 **Photo.** ***Perf. 13¼***

Z651	ZA557	50y multi	.95	.65

Miniature Sheet

88 Temples (Shikoku) — ZA558

No. Z652: a, Ryozenji (Temple #1). b, Gokurakuji (Temple #2). c, Konsenji (Temple #3). d, Dainchiji (Temple #4). e, Tatsueji (Temple #19). f, Kakurinji (Temple #20). g, Tairyuji (Temple #21). h, Byoudouji (Temple #22). i, Iwamotoji (Temple #37). j, Kongoufukuji (Temple #38). k, Enkouji (Temple #39). l, Kanjizaiji (Temple #40). m, Nankoubou (Temple #55). n, Taizanji (Temple #56). o, Eifukuji (Temple #57). p, Senyuji (Temple #58). q, Shusshakaji (Temple #73). r, Kouyamaji (Temple #74). s, Zentsuji (Temple #75). t, Kouzouji (Temple #76).

2004, Nov. 5

Z652	ZA558	Sheet of 20	30.00	30.00
a.-t.		80y Any single	1.50	1.10

Temple numbers are found in the first group of small Japanese characters on each stamp. The numbers used are the same as those found under "China" in the Illustrated Identifier at the back of the book. The left and right Japanese characters in this first group of small characters, which ranges from 3 to 5 characters in length, are the same on each stamp. The characters between these two constant characters represent the temple number. As there is no character for zero, the number "20" will show the character for "2" (=) to the left of the character for "10" (+). Numbers 11-19 will have the unit's character to the right of the character for "10." Thus, the numbers "12" and "20" will have the same characters, just in a different order. Two-digit numbers beginning with 21 that are not divisible by 10 will be three characters long. Number 21, as an example, will show the characters for "2," "10," and "1" reading from left to right (= + -).

National Theater (Okinawa) ZA559

2005, Jan. 21 **Litho.** ***Perf. 13¼***

Z653	ZA559	50y multi	1.00	.65

Apple Blossoms (Nagano) ZA560

Renge Azalea (Nagano) ZA561

Lily of the Valley (Nagano) ZA562

Gentian (Nagano) ZA563

2005, Apr. 1 **Litho.** ***Perf. 13¼***

Z654	ZA560	50y multi	.95	.65
Z655	ZA561	50y multi	.95	.65
Z656	ZA562	50y multi	.95	.65
Z657	ZA563	50y multi	.95	.65
a.		Horiz. strip of 4, #Z654-Z657	3.80	2.60

Tulip (Toyama, Ishikawa, Fukui) — ZA564

Hydrangea (Toyama, Ishikawa, Fukui) — ZA565

Rhododendron (Toyama, Ishikawa, Fukui) — ZA566

Lily (Toyama, Ishikawa, Fukui) — ZA567

2005, Apr. 1

Z658	ZA564	50y multi	.95	.65
Z659	ZA565	50y multi	.95	.65
Z660	ZA566	50y multi	.95	.65
Z661	ZA567	50y multi	.95	.65
a.		Horiz. strip of 4, #Z658-Z661	3.80	2.60

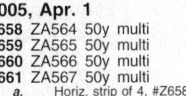

Peace Memorial Park (Hiroshima) — ZA568

Designs: No. Z662, Birds, Cenotaph for Atomic Bomb Victims. No. Z663, Fountains, Hiroshima Peace Memorial Museum.

2005, Apr. 22

Z662		50y multi	.95	.65
Z663		50y multi	.95	.65
a.	ZA568	Horiz. pair, #Z662-Z663	1.90	1.30

Sweetbrier (Hokkaido) ZA569

Lavender (Hokkaido) ZA570

Cowslip (Hokkaido) ZA571

Lily of the Valley (Hokkaido) ZA572

2005, Apr. 26

Z664	ZA569	50y multi	.95	.65
Z665	ZA570	50y multi	.95	.65
Z666	ZA571	50y multi	.95	.65
Z667	ZA572	50y multi	.95	.65
a.		Horiz. strip of 4, #Z664-Z667	3.80	2.60

Momordica Charantia (Okinawa) — ZA573

2005, May 6

Z668	ZA573	50y multi	1.00	.65

Sunflower, Mt. Yatsugatake (Yamanashi) ZA574

Gentian, Mt. Kitadake (Yamanashi) ZA575

Evening Primrose, Mt. Fuji (Yamanashi) ZA576

Lady's Slipper, Mt. Fuji (Yamanashi) ZA577

2005, May 16 **Litho.** ***Perf. 13¼***

Z669	ZA574	80y multi	1.50	1.10
Z670	ZA575	80y multi	1.50	1.10
Z671	ZA576	80y multi	1.50	1.10
Z672	ZA577	80y multi	1.50	1.10
a.		Horiz. strip of 4, #Z669-Z672	6.00	4.40

National Afforestation Campaign (Ibaraki) ZA578

2005, May 27 **Photo.**

Z673	ZA578	50y multi	.95	.65

Orchid (Tokyo) — ZA579

Crinum (Tokyo) — ZA580

Kerria (Tokyo) — ZA581

Azalea (Tokyo) — ZA582

2005, June 1

Z674	ZA579	50y multi	.95	.65
Z675	ZA580	50y multi	.95	.65
Z676	ZA581	50y multi	.95	.65
Z677	ZA582	50y multi	.95	.65
a.		Horiz. strip of 4, #Z674-Z677	3.80	2.60

Une, Dazaifu-Tenmangu (Fukuoka) ZA583

Cherry Blossoms, Kanmon Bridge (Fukuoka) ZA584

Camphor Blossoms, Ariake Sea (Saga) ZA585

Azaleas, Mt. Fugendake (Nagasaki) ZA586

Tulips, Huis Ten Bosch (Nagasaki) ZA587

Gentians, Mt. Aso (Kumamoto) ZA588

Bungo-ume, Mt. Takasaki (Oita) ZA589

Crinums, Nichinan Beach (Miyazaki) ZA590

Azaleas, Kirishima Mountains (Kagoshima) ZA591

Hibiscus, Screw Pine (Kagoshima) ZA592

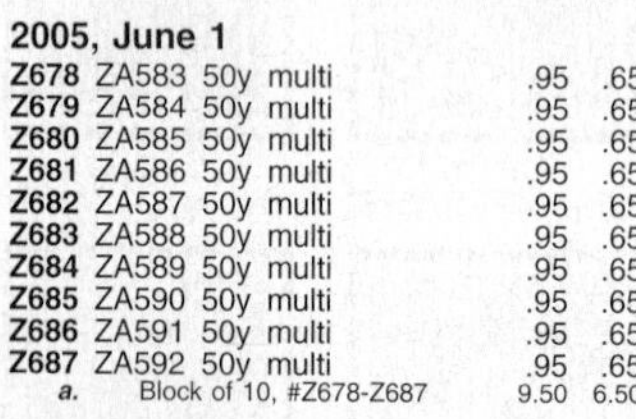

2005, June 1

Z678	ZA583 50y multi		.95	.65
Z679	ZA584 50y multi		.95	.65
Z680	ZA585 50y multi		.95	.65
Z681	ZA586 50y multi		.95	.65
Z682	ZA587 50y multi		.95	.65
Z683	ZA588 50y multi		.95	.65
Z684	ZA589 50y multi		.95	.65
Z685	ZA590 50y multi		.95	.65
Z686	ZA591 50y multi		.95	.65
Z687	ZA592 50y multi		.95	.65
a.	Block of 10, #Z678-Z687		9.50	6.50

Reintroduction of Oriental White Stork (Hyogo) — ZA593

2005, June 6 **Litho.**

Z688	ZA593 80y multi	1.50	1.10

Azaleas, Tsutsujigaoka Park (Gunma) ZA594

Nikko Day Lily, Kirifuri Heights (Tochigi) ZA595

Sunflowers, Hana-hotaru (Chiba) ZA596

Bush Clover, Kairakuen Garden (Ibaraki) ZA597

Allspice, Mt. Bukosan (Saitama) — ZA598

2005, June 23

Z689	ZA594 50y multi	.90	.65
Z690	ZA595 50y multi	.90	.65
Z691	ZA596 50y multi	.90	.65
Z692	ZA597 50y multi	.90	.65
Z693	ZA598 50y multi	.90	.65
a.	Vert. strip of 5, #Z689-Z693	4.50	3.25

Apples (Aomori) ZA599

Apples (Iwate) ZA600

Cherries (Yamagata) ZA601

Peaches (Fukushima) ZA602

2005, June 28 **Litho.**

Z694	ZA599 50y multi	.90	.65
Z695	ZA600 50y multi	.90	.65
Z696	ZA601 50y multi	.90	.65
Z697	ZA602 50y multi	.90	.65
a.	Horiz. strip of 4, #Z694-Z697	3.60	2.60

Miniature Sheet

88 Temples (Shikoku) — ZA603

No. Z698: a, Zizouji (Temple #5). b, Anrakuji (Temple #6). c, Juurakuji (Temple #7). d, Kumadaniji (Temple #8). e, Yakuooji (Temple #23). f, Hotsumisakiji (Temple #24). g, Shinjouji (Temple #25). h, Kongouchouji (Temple #26). i, Ryukouji (Temple #41). j, Butsumokuji (Temple #42). k, Meisekiji (Temple #43). l, Daihouji (Temple #44). m, Kokubunji (Temple #59). n, Yokomineji (Temple #60). o, Kouonji (Temple #61). p, Houjuji (Temple #62). q, Douryuji (Temple #77). r, Goushouji (Temple #78). s, Tennouji (Temple #79). t, Kokubunji (Temple #80).

2005, July 8 **Photo.**

Z698	ZA603 Sheet of 20	30.00	30.00
a.-t.	80y Any single	1.50	1.10

See note under No. Z652 for information on identifying temple numbers.

Swwtbriar, Old Shana Post Office (Hokkaido) ZA604

Sea Otter (Hokkaido) ZA605

Cherry Blossoms (Hokkaido) ZA606

Tufted Puffins (Hokkaido) ZA607

2005, Aug. 22

Z699	ZA604 80y multi	1.50	1.10
Z700	ZA605 80y multi	1.50	1.10
Z701	ZA606 80y multi	1.50	1.10
Z702	ZA607 80y multi	1.50	1.10
a.	Horiz. strip of 4, #Z699-Z702	6.00	4.40

60th Natl. Athletic Meets (Okayama) — ZA608

2005, Sept. 1

Z703	ZA608 50y multi	.95	.65

Kobe Luminarie (Hyogo) — ZA609

2005, Dec. 9 **Litho.**

Z704	50y Yellow denomination	.85	.60
Z705	50y Blue denomination	.85	.60
a.	ZA609 Horiz. pair, #Z704-Z705	1.70	1.20

Kawazu Cherry Blossoms (Shizuoka) — ZA610

2006, Feb. 1 **Photo.** ***Perf. 13¼***

Z706	50y With bird	.85	.60
Z707	50y Without bird	.85	.60
a.	ZA610 Horiz. pair, #Z706-Z707	1.70	1.20

Japanese Characters (Fukui) — ZA611

Maruoka Castle, Hills (Fukui) — ZA612

Maruoka Castle, Clouds (Fukui) — ZA613

Maruoka Castle, Sun (Fukui) — ZA614

Maruoka Castle, Moon (Fukui) — ZA615

2006, Apr. 3 **Litho.**

Z708	ZA611 80y multi	1.40	1.00
Z709	ZA612 80y multi	1.40	1.00
Z710	ZA613 80y multi	1.40	1.00
Z711	ZA614 80y multi	1.40	1.00
Z712	ZA615 80y multi	1.40	1.00
a.	Horiz. strip of 4, #Z709-Z712	5.60	4.00
	Nos. Z708-Z712 (5)	7.00	5.00

Printed in sheets of 20 consisting of 12 #ZA708, and 2 each #Z709-Z712.

Primroses (Osaka) ZA616

Cherry Blossoms (Nara) ZA617

Wild Chrysanthemums (Hyogo) ZA618

Rhododendrons (Shiga) ZA619

Ume Blossoms (Wakayama) ZA620

Weeping Cherry Blossoms (Kyoto) ZA621

2006, Apr. 3

Z713	ZA616 50y multi	.85	.60
Z714	ZA617 50y multi	.85	.60
Z715	ZA618 50y multi	.85	.60
Z716	ZA619 50y multi	.85	.60

Z717 ZA620 50y multi .85 .60
a. Horiz. strip of 4, #Z714-Z717 3.40 2.40
Z718 ZA621 50y multi .85 .60
Nos. Z713-Z718 (6) 5.10 3.60

Printed in sheets containing 4 each #Z713, Z718, 3 each #Z714-Z717.

Pear Blossoms, Yumigahama Beach (Tottori) ZA622

Peonies, Hinomisaki Lighthouse (Shimane) ZA623

Peach Blossoms, Seto-oohashi Bridge (Okayama) ZA624

Scarlet Maple Leaves, Miyajima Shrine (Hiroshima) ZA625

Citron Blossoms, Oomi Island (Yamaguchi) ZA626

2006, May 1 **Photo.**

Z719 ZA622 50y multi .90 .65
Z720 ZA623 50y multi .90 .65
Z721 ZA624 50y multi .90 .65
Z722 ZA625 50y multi .90 .65
Z723 ZA626 50y multi .90 .65
a. Vert. strip of 5, #Z719-Z723 4.50 3.25
Nos. Z719-Z723 (5) 4.50 3.25

National Afforestation Campaign (Gifu) — ZA627

2006, May 19

Z724 ZA627 50y multi .90 .65

Mt. Echigo (Niigata, Nagano) ZA628

Sankayou Flowers (Niigata, Nagano) ZA629

Mt. Asama (Niigata, Nagano) ZA630

Sakurasou Flowers (Niigata, Nagano) ZA631

2006, June 1 **Litho.**

Z725 ZA628 80y multi 1.50 1.10
Z726 ZA629 80y multi 1.50 1.10
Z727 ZA630 80y multi 1.50 1.10
Z728 ZA631 80y multi 1.50 1.10
a. Horiz. strip of 4, #Z725-Z728 6.00 4.40
Nos. Z725-Z728 (4) 6.00 4.40

Daffodils, Nokonoshima Island (Fukuoka) ZA632

Bellflowers, Hirodai (Fukuoka) ZA633

Hydrangeas, Mikaerinotaki Falls (Saga) ZA634

Cosmos, Kujukushima Islands (Nagasaki) ZA635

Camellias, Amakusa Bridges (Kumamoto) ZA636

Flowers, Mt. Aso (Kumamoto) ZA637

Primroses, Mt. Yufudake (Oita) — ZA638

Lavender, Kujurenzan (Oita) — ZA639

Poppies, Mt. Hinamoridake (Miyazaki) ZA640

Nanohana, Mt. Kaimondake (Kagoshima) ZA641

2006, June 1 **Photo.**

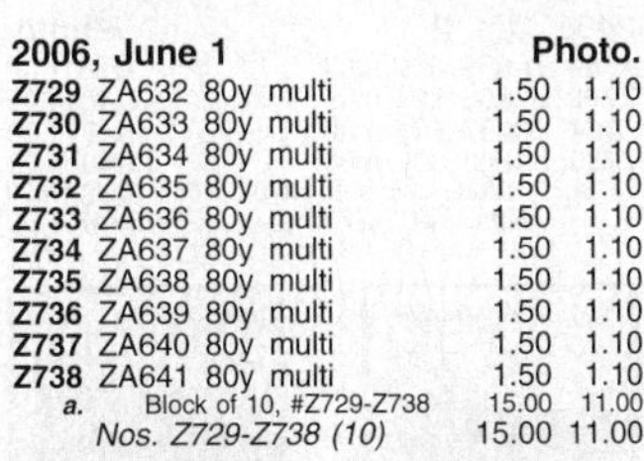

Z729 ZA632 80y multi 1.50 1.10
Z730 ZA633 80y multi 1.50 1.10
Z731 ZA634 80y multi 1.50 1.10
Z732 ZA635 80y multi 1.50 1.10
Z733 ZA636 80y multi 1.50 1.10
Z734 ZA637 80y multi 1.50 1.10
Z735 ZA638 80y multi 1.50 1.10
Z736 ZA639 80y multi 1.50 1.10
Z737 ZA640 80y multi 1.50 1.10
Z738 ZA641 80y multi 1.50 1.10
a. Block of 10, #Z729-Z738 15.00 11.00
Nos. Z729-Z738 (10) 15.00 11.00

Fox (Hokkaido) ZA642

Bears (Hokkaido) ZA643

Squirrel (Hokkaido) ZA644

Owl (Hokkaido) ZA645

2006, June 3

Z739 ZA642 50y multi .90 .65
Z740 ZA643 50y multi .90 .65
Z741 ZA644 50y multi .90 .65
Z742 ZA645 50y multi .90 .65
a. Horiz. strip of 4, #Z739-Z742 3.60 2.60
Nos. Z739-Z742 (4) 3.60 2.60

Aomori Nebuta Festival (Aomori) ZA646

Akita Kanto Festival (Akita) ZA647

Yamagata Hanagasa Festival (Yamagata) ZA648

Sendai Tanabata Festival (Miyagi) ZA649

2006, June 3 **Litho.**

Z743 ZA646 80y multi 1.40 1.00
Z744 ZA647 80y multi 1.40 1.00
Z745 ZA648 80y multi 1.40 1.00
Z746 ZA649 80y multi 1.40 1.00
a. Horiz. strip of 4, #Z743-Z746 5.60 4.00
Nos. Z743-Z746 (4) 5.60 4.00

Azaleas, Eboshi-iwa, Mt. Fuji (Kanagawa) ZA650

Daffodils, Sakawagawa River (Kanagawa) ZA651

Pinks, Tanzawa Mountains (Kanagawa) ZA652

Balloon Flowers, Mt. Fuji (Kanagawa) ZA653

2006, Aug. 1 **Photo.**

Z747 ZA650 80y multi 1.40 1.00
Z748 ZA651 80y multi 1.40 1.00
Z749 ZA652 80y multi 1.40 1.00
Z750 ZA653 80y multi 1.40 1.00
a. Horiz. strip of 4, #Z747-Z750 5.60 4.00
Nos. Z747-Z750 (4) 5.60 4.00

Miniature Sheet

88 Temples (Shikoku) — ZA654

No. Z751: a, Hourinji (Temple #9). b, Kirihata (Temple #10). c, Fujiidera (Temple #11). d, Shouzanji (Temple #12). e, Kounomineji (Temple #27). f, Dainichiji (Temple #28). g, Kokubunji (Temple #29). h, Zenrakuji (Temple #30). i, Iwayaji (Temple #45). j, Joururiji (Temple #46). k, Yasakaji (Temple #47). l, Sairinji (Temple #48). m, Kichijouji (Temple #63). n, Maegamiji (Temple #64). o, Sankakuji (Temple #65). p, Unbenji (Temple #66). q, Shiromineji (Temple #81). r, Negoroji (Temple #82). s, Ichinomiyaji (Temple #83). t, Yashimaji (Temple #84).

2006, Aug. 1

Z751 ZA654 Sheet of 20 28.00 28.00
a.-t. 80y Any single 1.40 1.00

See note under No. Z652 for information on identifying temple numbers.

61st National Athletic Meets (Hyogo) — ZA655

2006, Sept. 1

Z752 ZA655 50y multi .85 .60

Loquats, Byobugaura (Chiba) ZA656

Umes, Fukuroda Waterfall (Ibaraki) ZA657

Apples, Oze (Gunma) ZA658

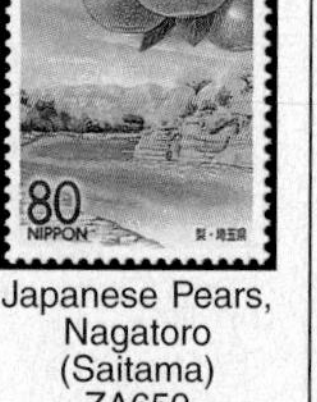

Japanese Pears, Nagatoro (Saitama) ZA659

Strawberries, Kegon Waterfall (Tochigi) — ZA660

2006, Sept. 1

Z753	ZA656	80y	multi	1.40	1.00
Z754	ZA657	80y	multi	1.40	1.00
Z755	ZA658	80y	multi	1.40	1.00
Z756	ZA659	80y	multi	1.40	1.00
Z757	ZA660	80y	multi	1.40	1.00
a.	Vert. strip of 5, #Z753-Z757			7.00	5.00
	Nos. Z753-Z757 (5)			7.00	5.00

Roses (Aichi) — ZA661

Chrysanthemums (Aichi) — ZA662

Orchids (Aichi) — ZA663

Cyclamen (Aichi) — ZA664

2006, Oct. 2 **Litho.**

Z758	ZA661	50y	multi	.85	.60
Z759	ZA662	50y	multi	.85	.60
Z760	ZA663	50y	multi	.85	.60
Z761	ZA664	50y	multi	.85	.60
a.	Horiz. strip of 4, #Z758-Z761			3.40	2.40
	Nos. Z758-Z761 (4)			3.40	2.40

Cherry Blossoms, Chidorigafuchi (Tokyo) — ZA665

Roses, Akasaka Palace (Tokyo) — ZA666

Cosmos, Shouwa Kinen Park (Tokyo) — ZA667

Japanese Apricot Blossoms, Yushima Tenjin Shrine (Tokyo) — ZA668

2006, Oct. 2 **Photo.**

Z762	ZA665	80y	multi	1.40	1.00
Z763	ZA666	80y	multi	1.40	1.00
Z764	ZA667	80y	multi	1.40	1.00
Z765	ZA668	80y	multi	1.40	1.00
a.	Horiz. strip of 4, #Z762-Z765			5.60	4.00
	Nos. Z762-Z765 (4)			5.60	4.00

Iris, Takeshima (Aichi, Mie, Gifu, Shizuoka) ZA669

Chinese Milk Vetch, Shirakawa Village (Aichi, Mie, Gifu, Shizuoka) ZA670

Lily, Nagoya Castle (Aichi, Mie, Gifu, Shizuoka) ZA671

Japanese Iris, Couple Rock (Aichi, Mie, Gifu, Shizuoka) ZA672

Azalea, Jogasaki Coast (Aichi, Mie, Gifu, Shizuoka) — ZA673

2007, Apr. 2 **Photo.** ***Perf. 13¼***

Z766	ZA669	80y	multi	1.40	1.00
Z767	ZA670	80y	multi	1.40	1.00
Z768	ZA671	80y	multi	1.40	1.00
Z769	ZA672	80y	multi	1.40	1.00
Z770	ZA673	80y	multi	1.40	1.00
a.	Vert. strip of 5, #Z766-Z770			7.00	5.00

Cherry Blossom, Yatsugatake (Yamanashi) ZA674

Grapes, Katsunuma Vineyard (Yamanashi) ZA675

Azalea, Syosenkyo (Yamanashi) ZA676

Lavender, Mt. Fuji (Yamanashi) ZA677

Peaches, Southern Japanese Alps (Yamanashi) ZA678

2007, Apr. 2

Z771	ZA674	80y	multi	1.40	1.00
Z772	ZA675	80y	multi	1.40	1.00
Z773	ZA676	80y	multi	1.40	1.00
Z774	ZA677	80y	multi	1.40	1.00
Z775	ZA678	80y	multi	1.40	1.00
a.	Vert. strip of 5, #Z771-Z775			7.00	5.00

Tulips (Niigata) ZA679

Rice (Niigata) ZA680

Pears (Niigata) ZA681

Mealy Primrose (Niigata) ZA682

Iris (Niigata) — ZA683

2007, Apr. 2 **Litho.**

Z776	ZA679	80y	multi	1.40	1.00
Z777	ZA680	80y	multi	1.40	1.00
Z778	ZA681	80y	multi	1.40	1.00
Z779	ZA682	80y	multi	1.40	1.00
Z780	ZA683	80y	multi	1.40	1.00
a.	Vert. strip of 5, #Z776-Z780			7.00	5.00

Cherry Blossom (Saitama) ZA684

Japanese Rose (Ibaraki) ZA685

Skunk Cabbage (Gunma) ZA686

Adder's Tongue Lily (Tochigi) ZA687

Poppies (Chiba) — ZA688

2007, May 1 **Photo.** ***Perf. 13¼***

Z781	ZA684	50y	multi	.85	.60
Z782	ZA685	50y	multi	.85	.60
Z783	ZA686	50y	multi	.85	.60
Z784	ZA687	50y	multi	.85	.60
Z785	ZA688	50y	multi	.85	.60
a.	Vert. strip of 5, #Z781-Z785			4.25	3.00

Mandarin Ducks (Tottori) ZA689

Swans (Shimane) ZA690

Pheasants (Okayama) ZA691

Red-throated Loons (Hiroshima) ZA692

Hooded Cranes (Yamaguchi) ZA693

2007, May 1 **Litho.**

Z786	ZA689	80y	multi	1.40	1.00
Z787	ZA690	80y	multi	1.40	1.00
Z788	ZA691	80y	multi	1.40	1.00
Z789	ZA692	80y	multi	1.40	1.00
Z790	ZA693	80y	multi	1.40	1.00
a.	Vert. strip of 5, #Z786-Z790			7.00	5.00

Japanese Cranes (Hokkaido) ZA694

Hokkaido Mountain Hares (Hokkaido) ZA695

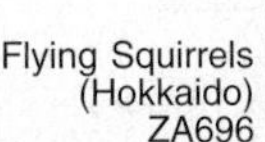

Flying Squirrels (Hokkaido) ZA696

Hokkaido Deer (Hokkaido) ZA697

Spotted Seals (Hokkaido) ZA698

2007, May 1 **Litho.**

Z791	ZA694 80y multi		1.40	1.00
Z792	ZA695 80y multi		1.40	1.00
Z793	ZA696 80y multi		1.40	1.00
Z794	ZA697 80y multi		1.40	1.00
Z795	ZA698 80y multi		1.40	1.00
a.	Horiz. strip of 5, #Z791-Z795		7.00	5.00

Koriyama Castle (Nara) — ZA699

Hikone Castle (Shiga) — ZA700

Himeji Castle (Hyogo) — ZA701

Osaka Castle (Osaka) — ZA702

Wakayama Castle (Wakayama) ZA703

2007, June 1 **Photo.**

Z796	ZA699 50y multi	.85	.60
Z797	ZA700 50y multi	.85	.60
Z798	ZA701 50y multi	.85	.60
Z799	ZA702 50y multi	.85	.60
Z800	ZA703 50y multi	.85	.60
a.	Vert. strip of 5, #Z796-Z800	4.25	3.00

Whale Shark (Okinawa) ZA704

Longfin Bannerfish (Okinawa) ZA705

False Clownfish (Okinawa) ZA706

Blue Damselfish (Okinawa) ZA707

Manta Ray (Okinawa) ZA708

2007, June 1 **Photo.**

Z801	ZA704 80y multi	1.40	1.00
Z802	ZA705 80y multi	1.40	1.00
Z803	ZA706 80y multi	1.40	1.00
Z804	ZA707 80y multi	1.40	1.00
Z805	ZA708 80y multi	1.40	1.00
a.	Horiz. strip of 5, #Z801-Z805	7.00	5.00

National Afforestation Campaign (Hokkaido) ZA709

2007, June 22 ***Perf. 12½x12¾***

Z806	ZA709 50y multi	.85	.60

Dancers, Owara Wind Festival (Toyama) ZA710

Dancers, Owara Wind Festival (Toyama) ZA711

Dancers, Owara Wind Festival (Toyama) ZA712

Dancers, Owara Wind Festival (Toyama) ZA713

Dancers, Owara Wind Festival (Toyama) — ZA714

2007, July 2 **Litho.** ***Perf. 13¼***

Z807	ZA710 80y multi	1.40	1.00
Z808	ZA711 80y multi	1.40	1.00
Z809	ZA712 80y multi	1.40	1.00
Z810	ZA713 80y multi	1.40	1.00
Z811	ZA714 80y multi	1.40	1.00
a.	Vert. strip of 5, #Z807-Z811	7.00	5.00

Tokyo Tower, Japanese Allspice (Tokyo) — ZA715

Double Bridge, Chinese Violet Cress (Tokyo) — ZA716

Meiji shrine Outer Garden, Sweet Olive (Tokyo) — ZA717

Lake Okutama, Gentian (Tokyo) — ZA718

Japan Bridge, Camellia (Tokyo) — ZA719

2007, July 2 **Photo.**

Z812	ZA715 80y multi	1.40	1.00
Z813	ZA716 80y multi	1.40	1.00
Z814	ZA717 80y multi	1.40	1.00
Z815	ZA718 80y multi	1.40	1.00
Z816	ZA719 80y multi	1.40	1.00
a.	Vert. strip of 5, #Z812-Z8161	7.00	5.00

Oirase Mountain Stream (Aomori) ZA720

Hirosaki Castle (Aomori) ZA721

Chuson Temple (Iwate) — ZA722

Jodogahama (Iwate) — ZA723

Matsushima (Miyagi) ZA724

Mt. Zao Crater Lake (Miyagi, Yamagata) ZA725

Oga Peninsula (Akita) ZA726

Mt. Chokai (Akita, Yamagata) ZA727

Oze (Fukushima) ZA728

Gassan Volcano (Yamagata) ZA729

2007, July 2

Z817	Sheet of 10	14.00	14.00
a.	ZA720 80y multi	1.40	1.00
b.	ZA721 80y multi	1.40	1.00
c.	ZA722 80y multi	1.40	1.00
d.	ZA723 80y multi	1.40	1.00
e.	ZA724 80y multi	1.40	1.00
f.	ZA725 80y multi	1.40	1.00
g.	ZA726 80y multi	1.40	1.00
h.	ZA727 80y multi	1.40	1.00
i.	ZA728 80y multi	1.40	1.00
j.	ZA729 80y multi	1.40	1.00

Main Tower, Kumamoto Castle, Cherry Blossoms (Kumamoto) ZA730

Uto Turret, Kumamoto Castle, in Summer (Kumamoto) ZA731

Main Tower, Kumamoto Castle, Gingko Trees (Kumamoto) ZA732

Uto Turret, Kumamoto Castle, in Winter (Kumamoto) ZA733

Three Towers, Kumamoto Castle (Kumamoto) ZA734

2007, Aug. 1 **Litho.**

Z818	ZA730 80y multi	1.40	1.00
Z819	ZA731 80y multi	1.40	1.00
Z820	ZA732 80y multi	1.40	1.00
Z821	ZA733 80y multi	1.40	1.00
Z822	ZA734 80y multi	1.40	1.00
a.	Vert. strip of 5, #Z818-Z822	7.00	5.00

Edo Bridge from Japan Bridge, by Hiroshige (Tokyo) — ZA735

Ohisa Takashima, by Utamaro (Tokyo) — ZA736

Yaozo Ichikawa II as Bunzo Tanabe, by Sharaku (Tokyo) — ZA737

Horikiri Irises, by Hiroshige (Tokyo) — ZA738

Kinryuzan Temple, by Hiroshige (Tokyo) — ZA739

Seven Women Applying Makeup Using a Full Length Mirror, by Utamaro (Tokyo) — ZA740

Ryuzo Arashi II as Kinkichi Ishibe, Moneylender, by Sharaku (Tokyo) — ZA741

Suido Bridge and Surugadai, by Hiroshige (Tokyo) — ZA742

Moon Pine, Ueno Temple, by Hiroshige (Tokyo) — ZA743

Hanaogi from Ogiya, No. 1 District, Edo Town, by Utamaro (Tokyo) — ZA744

2007, Aug. 1

Z823	Sheet of 10	14.00	14.00
a.	ZA735 80y multi	1.40	1.00
b.	ZA736 80y multi	1.40	1.00
c.	ZA737 80y multi	1.40	1.00
d.	ZA738 80y multi	1.40	1.00
e.	ZA739 80y multi	1.40	1.00
f.	ZA740 80y multi	1.40	1.00
g.	ZA741 80y multi	1.40	1.00
h.	ZA742 80y multi	1.40	1.00
i.	ZA743 80y multi	1.40	1.00
j.	ZA744 80y multi	1.40	1.00

ZA745

88 Temples (Shikoku) — ZA746

No. Z824: a, Dainchiji (Temple #13). b, Jorakuji (Temple #14). c, Kokubunji (Temple #15). d, Kanonji (Temple #16). e, Chikurinji (Temple #31). f, Zenjibuji (Temple #32). g, Sekkeiji (Temple #33). h, Tanemaji (Temple #34). i, Jodoji (Temple #49). j, Hantaji (Temple #50). k, Ishiteji (Temple #51). l, Taisanji (Temple #52). m, Daikoji (Temple #67). n, Jinnein (Temple #68). o, Kannonji (Temple #69). p, Motoyamaji (Temple #70). q, Yakuriji (Temple #85). r, Shidoji (Temple #86). s, Nagaoji (Temple #87). t, Okuboji (Temple #88).

No. Z825: a, Idoji (Temple #17). b, Onzanji (Temple #18). c, Kiyotakiji (Temple #35). d, Shoryuji (Temple #36). e, Emmyoji (Temple #53). f, Emmeiji (Temple #54). g, Iyadaniji (Temple #71). h, Mandaraji (Temple #72). i, Deities Cave (no temple number). j, Painting of Daishi Kobo (no temple number).

2007, Aug. 1 Photo. *Perf. 13¼*

Z824	ZA745	Sheet of 20	28.00	28.00
a.-t.		80y Any single	1.40	1.00
Z825	ZA746	Sheet of 10	14.00	14.00
a.-j.		80y Any single	1.40	1.00

See note under No. Z652 for information on identifying temple numbers.

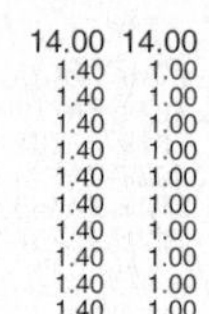
62nd National Athletic Meet (Akita) — ZA747

2007, Sept. 3 Litho.

Z826	ZA747 50y multi	.90	.65

Miniature Sheet

Nagoya Port (Aichi) — ZA748

No. Z827: a, Hibiscus and Antarctic survey. b, Hibiscus and Port Tower. c, Azaleas, killer whale at Nagoya Aquarium. d, Azaleas, dolphins at Nagoya Aquarium. e, Yellow chrysanthemums, Meiko Triton Bridge. f, Orange and yellow chrysanthemums, two bridges. g, Snapdragons and fireworks. h, Sailing ship and snapdragons. i, Azaleas, bridge, Nagoya Aquarium and half of Ferris wheel. j, Azaleas, Port Tower, Nagoya Castle, and half of Ferris wheel.

2007, Nov. 5 Litho. *Perf. 13¼*

Z827	ZA748	Sheet of 10	15.00	15.00
a.-j.		80y Any single	1.50	1.10

Beginning in 2008 the planning and design of prefecture stamps, previously done by regional postal authorities, was taken over by national postal authorities. The national authorities planned issues for 2008 that would be available in more of postal regions, thus making prefectural issues more nationwide and less local in scope. Additionally, the style of the "Nippon yubin" ideographic characters that had been used solely for prefecture stamps reverted to the style used on the national issues for most issues. Because of these changes, prefecture stamps will be listed in the regular postage listings starting with the 2008 issues.

PREFECTURE SEMI-POSTAL STAMPS

Earthquake and Volcano Eruption Refugee Relief (Tokyo) — ZSP1

2000, Nov. 15 Photo.

ZB1	80y +20y Pink ribbon	1.90	1.00
ZB2	80y +20y Blue ribbon	1.90	1.00
a.	ZSP1 Pair, #ZB1-ZB2	4.00	2.50

SEMI-POSTAL STAMPS

Douglas Plane over Japan Alps — SP1

Wmk. Zigzag Lines (141)

1937, June 1 Photo. *Perf. 13*

B1	SP1 2s + 2s rose carmine	1.75	.75
B2	SP1 3s + 2s purple	1.75	1.25
B3	SP1 4s + 2s green	2.50	1.00
	Nos. B1-B3 (3)	6.00	3.00
	Set, never hinged	8.00	

The surtax was for the Patriotic Aviation Fund to build civil airports.

Nos. 259 and 261 Surcharged in Blue or Red

1942, Feb. 16 Wmk. 257 *Perf. 13*

B4	A84 2s + 1s crimson (Bl)	1.00	.90
B5	A86 4s + 2s dk grn (R)	1.25	1.10
	Set, never hinged	3.75	

Fall of Singapore to Japanese forces.

Tank Corps Attack, Bataan — SP2

Pearl Harbor under Japanese Attack — SP3

Unwmk.

1942, Dec. 8 Photo. *Perf. 12*

B6	SP2 2s + 1s rose brown	2.00	1.00
B7	SP3 5s + 2s sapphire	2.25	1.50
	Set, never hinged	6.00	

1st anniv. of the "Greater East Asia War." The surtax was for national defense.

Catalogue values for unused stamps in this section, from this point to the end of the section, are for Never Hinged items.

SP4

1947, Nov. 25 Wmk. 257 *Perf. 12½*

B8	SP4 1.20y + 80s dk rose red	1.00	.85

Japan's 1st Community Chest drive. The surtax was for charitable purposes.

Nurse — SP5

Bird Feeding Young — SP6

1948, Oct. 1 Unwmk. *Perf. 12½*

B9	SP5 5y + 2.50y bright red	12.50	9.00
B10	SP6 5y + 2.50y emerald	12.50	9.00

Souvenir Sheet

Wmk. 257

Imperf

Without Gum

B11	Sheet of 2	55.00	*55.00*

The surtax on Nos. B9-B11 was divided between the Red Cross and Community Chest organizations.

No. B11 contains Nos. B9-B10, imperf.

Javelin Thrower SP8

#B13, Wrestlers. #B14, Diver. #B15, Water polo. #B16, Woman gymnast. #B17, Judo. #B18, Fencing. #B19, Basketball. #B20, Rowing. #B21, Sailing. #B22, Boxing. #B23, Volleyball. #B24, Bicyclist. #B25, Equestrian. #B26, Field hockey. #B27, Pistol shooting. #B28, Modern pentathlon. #B29, Weight lifter. #B30, Women's kayak doubles. #B31, Soccer.

Perf. 13½

1961, Oct. 11 Unwmk. Engr.

B12	SP8 5y + 5y bister	.75	1.00
B13	SP8 5y + 5y dk green	.75	1.00
B14	SP8 5y + 5y carmine	.75	1.00
a.	Souvenir sheet of 3 ('64)	4.25	4.75

1962, June 23

B15	SP8 5y + 5y green	.45	.75
B16	SP8 5y + 5y dk purple	.45	.75
B17	SP8 5y + 5y dk carmine	.45	.75
a.	Souvenir sheet of 3 ('64)	2.75	3.25

1962, Oct. 10

B18	SP8 5y + 5y brick red	.25	.40
B19	SP8 5y + 5y slate grn	.25	.40
B20	SP8 5y + 5y violet	.25	.40
a.	Souvenir sheet of 3 ('64)	2.25	2.50

1963, June 23

B21	SP8 5y + 5y blue	.25	.40
B22	SP8 5y + 5y dk brown	.25	.40
B23	SP8 5y + 5y brown	.25	.40
a.	Souvenir sheet of 3 ('64)	4.75	5.25

1963, Nov. 11

B24	SP8 5y + 5y dk blue	.20	.20
B25	SP8 5y + 5y olive	.20	.20
B26	SP8 5y + 5y black	.20	.20
B27	SP8 5y + 5y claret	.20	.20
a.	Souvenir sheet of 4 ('64)	4.75	5.25

1964, June 23

B28	SP8 5y + 5y bluish vio	.20	.20
B29	SP8 5y + 5y dp olive	.20	.20
B30	SP8 5y + 5y grnsh blue	.20	.20
B31	SP8 5y + 5y rose claret	.20	.20
a.	Souvenir sheet of 4 ('64)	4.75	5.25
	Nos. B12-B31 (20)	6.70	9.25

Issued to raise funds for the 1964 Olympic Games in Tokyo.

The souvenir sheets were issued Aug. 20, 1964. Each contains one each of the stamps in the set it follows. Nos. B14a, B20a, B23a and B27a, exist imperf.

Cobalt Treatment Unit — SP9

Early Cancer Detection with X-rays — SP10

1966, Oct. 21 Photo. *Perf. 13*

B32	SP9 7y + 3y yel org & blk	.20	.20
B33	SP10 15y + 5y multicolored	.40	.20

9th Intl. Anticancer Congress, Tokyo, Oct. 23-29. The surtax was for the fight against cancer and for research.

EXPO '70 Emblem and Globe — SP11

Cherry Blossoms, Screen, Chishakuin Temple — SP12

1969, Mar. 15 Photo. *Perf. 13*

B34	SP11 15y + 5y bl, ocher & ver	.60	.60
B35	SP12 50y + 10y gold, brn & grn	1.25	1.25

Issued to publicize EXPO '70, International Exhibition, Osaka, 1970.

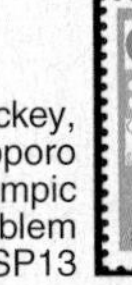

Ice Hockey, Sapporo Olympic Emblem SP13

Design: No. B37, Ski jump and Sapporo Olympic Games emblem, vert.

1971, Feb. 6 Photo. *Perf. 13*

B36	SP13 15y + 5y multi	.40	.20
B37	SP13 15y + 5y multi	.40	.20

To promote the 11th Winter Olympic Games, Sapporo, Japan, 1972.

Blue Dragon, East Wall — SP14

Murals from ancient tomb mound: No. B39, Two men, east wall, vert. 50y+10y, Four women, west wall, vert.

1973, Mar. 26 Photo. *Perf. 13*

Size: 48x27mm, 27x48mm

B38	SP14 20y + 5y multi	.50	.30
B39	SP14 20y + 5y multi	.50	.30

Photogravure and Engraved

Size: 33x48mm

B40	SP14 50y + 10y multi	1.10	.50
	Nos. B38-B40 (3)	2.10	1.10

Surtax was for restoration work on the murals of the Takamatsu-zuka tomb mound, discovered in March, 1972, and excavated in Nara Prefecture.

Reefs, by Hyakusui Hirafuku — SP15

1974, Mar. 2 Photo. *Perf. 13*

B41	SP15 20y + 5y multi	.50	.30

The surtax was for the International Ocean Exposition, Okinawa, 1975.

Intl. Year of the Disabled — SP16

Photogravure and Embossed

1981, Sept. 1 *Perf. 13½*

B42	SP16 60y + 10y multi	1.25	.20

Surtax was for education of the disabled.

TSUKUB'85 Intl. Exposition, Mar. 17-Sept. 16, 1985 — SP17

1984, Feb. 19 Photo. *Perf. 13½*

B43	SP17 60y + 10y multi	1.25	.45

Intl. Garden and Greenery Exposition, Osaka — SP18

1989, June 1 Photo. *Perf. 13*

B44	SP18 62y +10y multi	1.40	.75

Surtax for the preparation and management of the exposition.

Intl. Garden and Greenery Exposition, Osaka SP19

1990, Mar. 30

B45	SP19 41y +4y multi	.85	.45

SP20 SP21

1991, July 5 Photo. *Perf. 13*

B46	SP20 62y +10y multi	1.40	.85

11th World Congress of the World Federation of the Deaf.

1995, Apr. 20 Photo. *Perf. 13*

B47	SP21 80y +20y multi	2.40	1.75

Philately week. Surtax for benefit of victims of Kobe earthquake.

1998 Winter Olympic Games, Nagano — SP22

1997, Feb. 7 Photo. *Perf. 13*

B48	80y +10y emblem	1.75	1.10
B49	80y +10y stylized owls	1.75	1.10
a.	SP22 Pair, #B48-B49	3.50	2.25

2002 Soccer World Cup, Japan and Korea — SP23

Colors of mascots: No. B50, Purple, yellow and blue. No. B51, Purple. No. B52, Blue.

2001, May 31 Photo. *Perf. 13x13¼*

B50	SP23 80y +10y multi	1.75	1.10
B51	SP23 80y +10y multi	1.75	1.10
B52	SP23 80y +10y multi	1.75	1.10
a.	Horiz. pair, #B51-B52	3.50	2.20

Wall Paintings, Kitora Tumulus, Asuka — SP24

Designs: No. B53, White Tiger of the West. No. B54, Red Bird fo the South.

2003, Oct. 15 Photo. *Perf. 13*

B53	80y +10y multi	1.75	1.25
B54	80y +10y multi	1.75	1.25
a.	SP24 Horiz. pair, #B53-B54	3.50	2.50

2005 World Exposition, Aichi — SP25

Exposition mascots and: No. B55, Earth. No. B56, Cherry blossoms.

2004, Mar. 25 Photo. *Perf. 13x13¼*

B55	80y +10y multi	1.75	1.75
B56	80y +10y multi	1.75	1.75
a.	SP25 Horiz. pair, #B55-B56	3.50	3.50

AIR POST STAMPS

Regular Issue of 1914 Overprinted in Red or Blue

Wmk. Zigzag Lines (141)

1919, Oct. 3 *Perf. 13x13½*

Granite Paper

No.	Type	Description	Unused	Used
C1	A34	1½s blue (R)	260.00	72.50
C2	A34	3s rose (Bl)	450.00	210.00

Excellent counterfeits exist.

Passenger Plane over Lake Ashi — AP1

1929-34 **Engr.** *Perf. 13½x13*

Granite Paper

No.	Type	Description	Unused	Used
C3	AP1	8½s orange brn	27.50	14.00
C4	AP1	9½s rose	9.00	3.75
C5	AP1	16½s yellow grn	9.00	4.00
C6	AP1	18s ultra	10.00	3.75
C7	AP1	33s gray	20.00	3.25
		Nos. C3-C7 (5)	75.50	28.75
		Set, never hinged	190.00	

Souvenir Sheet

No.	Type	Description	Unused	Used
C8	AP1	Sheet of 4, #C4-C7	1,400.	1,250.
		Never hinged	2,200.	

Issued: 9½s, 3/1/34; #C8, 4/20/34; others, 10/6/29. #C8 for Communications Commemoration Day (1st observance of establishment of the postal service and issuance of #1-4). Sold only at Phil. Exhib. p.o., Tokyo, 4/20-27. Size: 110x100mm.

Catalogue values for unused stamps in this section, from this point to the end of the section, are for Never Hinged items.

Southern Green Pheasant AP3

Perf. 13x13½

1950, Jan. 10 **Engr.** **Unwmk.**

No.	Type	Description	Unused	Used
C9	AP3	16y gray	30.00	5.75
C10	AP3	34y brown violet	42.50	8.50
C11	AP3	59y carmine	65.00	7.00
C12	AP3	103y orange yellow	47.50	12.00
C13	AP3	144y olive	55.00	12.50
		Nos. C9-C13 (5)	240.00	45.75
		Set, hinged	140.00	

Pagoda and Plane — AP4

Plane and Mt. Tsurugi-dake — AP5

1951-52 **Photo.**

No.	Type	Description	Unused	Used
C14	AP4	15y purple	3.25	2.50
C15	AP4	20y blue	29.00	1.00
C16	AP4	25y yellow grn	26.00	.40
C17	AP4	30y brown red	19.00	.40
C18	AP4	40y gray blk	7.50	.50
C19	AP5	55y brt blue	210.00	35.00
C20	AP5	75y brnsh red	150.00	14.50
C21	AP5	80y magenta	20.00	2.75
C22	AP5	85y black	26.00	6.75
C23	AP5	125y olive bis	13.00	3.00
C24	AP5	160y Prus green	29.00	3.50
		Nos. C14-C24 (11)	532.75	70.30
		Set, hinged	350.00	

Issue dates: 25y, 30y, Dec. 20; 15y, 20y, 40y, Sept. 1; 55y-160y, Feb. 11, 1952.

Redrawn; Underlined Zeros Omitted

1952-62

No.	Type	Description	Unused	Used
C25	AP4	15y purple ('62)	1.60	.50
C26	AP4	20y blue	57.50	.90
C27	AP4	25y yel grn ('53)	1.00	.30
C28	AP4	30y brown red	7.50	.40
C29	AP4	40y gray blk ('53)	5.00	.40
C30	AP5	55y brt blue	72.50	3.75
C32	AP5	75y brnsh red	150.00	8.50
C33	AP5	80y magenta	100.00	2.75
C34	AP5	85y black	6.00	1.25
C36	AP5	125y olive bis	9.00	1.50
C38	AP5	160y Prus green	37.50	1.75
		Nos. C25-C38 (11)	447.60	22.00
		Set, hinged	225.00	

See No. C43.

Great Buddha of Kamakura — AP6

1953, Aug. 15 *Perf. 13½*

No.	Type	Description	Unused	Used
C39	AP6	70y red brown	3.50	.20
C40	AP6	80y blue	5.50	.20
C41	AP6	115y olive green	3.25	.35
C42	AP6	145y Prus green	14.00	1.10
		Nos. C39-C42 (4)	26.25	1.85

Coil Stamp

Redrawn Type of 1952-62

1961, Oct. 2 *Perf. 13 Horiz.*

No.	Type	Description	Unused	Used
C43	AP4	30y brown red	32.50	26.00

MILITARY STAMPS

Nos. 98, 119, 131 Overprinted

1910-14 **Unwmk.** *Perf. 11½ to 13½*

No.	Type	Description	Unused	Used
M1	A26	3s rose	225.00	35.00
M2	A34	3s rose ('13)	350.00	140.00

Wmk. 141

No.	Type	Description	Unused	Used
M3	A34	3s rose ('14)	35.00	16.00
		Nos. M1-M3 (3)	610.00	191.00

Nos. M1-M3 overprint type I has 3.85mm between characters; type II, 4-4.5mm (movable type).

1921 **On Offices in China No. 37**

No.	Type	Description	Unused	Used
M4	A34	3s rose	*5,750.*	*4,750.*

No. M4 is a provisional military stamp issued at the Japanese Post Office, Tsingtao, China. The overprint differs from the illustration, being 12mm high with thicker characters. Counterfeits are plentiful.

Overprint 16mm High

1924 **On No. 131**

No.	Type	Description	Unused	Used
M5	A34	3s rose	100.00	72.50
a.		3s rose (#131b)	100.00	75.00

Excellent forgeries exist of Nos. M1-M5.

JAPANESE OFFICES ABROAD

Offices in China

Regular Issues of Japan Overprinted in Red or Black

Perf. 11½, 12, 12½, 13½, 13x13½

1900-06 **Unwmk.**

No.	Type	Description	Unused	Used
1	A26	5r gray (R)	3.50	2.75
2	A26	½s gray (R) ('01)	2.10	.70
3	A26	1s lt red brn (R)	2.10	.70
4	A26	1½s ultra	9.50	2.10
5	A26	1½s vio ('06)	5.25	.95
6	A26	2s lt grn (R)	5.25	.70
7	A26	3s violet brn	5.75	.70
8	A26	3s rose ('06)	4.25	.50
9	A26	4s rose	4.75	1.25
10	A26	5s org yel (R)	9.50	1.25
11	A27	6s maroon ('06)	18.00	12.00
12	A27	8s ol grn (R)	9.50	6.00
13	A27	10s deep blue	9.50	1.00
14	A27	15s purple	20.00	1.75
15	A27	20s red org	18.00	1.00
16	A28	25s blue grn (R)	37.50	4.00
17	A28	50s red brown	40.00	3.00
18	A29	1y carmine	60.00	3.00
		Nos. 1-18 (18)	264.45	43.35

No. 6 with black overprint is bogus.

Nos. 5, 6, 8, 9 and 13 exist as booklet panes of 6, made from sheet stamps. They are rare.

1900

No.	Type	Description	Unused	Used
19	A30	3s carmine	27.50	15.00

Wedding of Crown Prince Yoshihito and Princess Sadako.

1908

No.	Type	Description	Unused	Used
20	A33	5y green	375.00	47.50
21	A33	10y dark violet	650.00	110.00

On #20-21 the space between characters of the overprint is 6½mm instead of 1½mm.

1913 *Perf. 12, 12x13, 13x13½*

No.	Type	Description	Unused	Used
22	A34	½s brown	15.00	15.00
23	A34	1s orange	16.00	16.00
24	A34	1½s lt blue	42.50	19.00
25	A34	2s green	50.00	21.00
26	A34	3s rose	24.00	8.00
27	A35	4s red	70.00	70.00
28	A35	5s violet	70.00	55.00
29	A35	10s deep blue	70.00	22.50
30	A35	20s claret	275.00	150.00
31	A35	25s olive green	100.00	22.50
32	A36	1y yel grn & mar	825.00	550.00
		Nos. 22-32 (11)	1,557.	949.00

Nos. 24, 25, 26, 27 and 29 exist in booklet panes of 6, made from sheet stamps. The No. 26 pane is very rare.

1914-21 **Wmk. 141**

Granite Paper

No.	Type	Description	Unused	Used
33	A34	½s brown	3.25	.80
34	A34	1s orange	3.75	.80
35	A34	1½s blue	4.25	.80
36	A34	2s green	2.75	.95
37	A34	3s rose	2.40	.80
38	A35	4s red	10.50	4.75
39	A35	5s violet	19.00	1.75
40	A35	6s brown ('20)	32.50	19.00
41	A35	8s gray ('20)	40.00	21.00
42	A35	10s dp blue	13.50	1.25
43	A35	20s claret	45.00	3.25
44	A35	25s olive grn	55.00	3.50
45	A36	30s org brn ('20)	80.00	29.00
46	A36	50s dk brn ('20)	95.00	32.50
47	A36	1y yel grn & mar ('18)	140.00	6.75
48	A33	5y green	1,900.	550.00
49	A33	10y violet ('21)	2,700.	1,700.
		Nos. 33-49 (17)	5,146.	2,376.

On Nos. 48-49 the space between characters of overprint is 4½mm, instead of 6½mm on Nos. 20-21 and 1½mm on all lower values. See No. M4.

No. 42 exists as a booklet pane of 6, made from sheet stamps. It is very rare.

Counterfeit overprints exist of Nos. 1-49.

Offices in Korea

Regular Issue of Japan Overprinted in Red or Black

1900 **Unwmk.** *Perf. 11½, 12, 12½*

No.	Type	Description	Unused	Used
1	A26	5r gray (R)	19.00	8.75
2	A26	1s lt red brn (R)	20.00	5.00
3	A26	1½s ultra	250.00	130.00
4	A26	2s lt green (R)	19.00	10.00
5	A26	3s violet brn	17.00	4.75
6	A26	4s rose	65.00	27.50
7	A26	5s org yel (R)	67.50	27.50
8	A27	8s ol grn (R)	250.00	120.00
9	A27	10s deep blue	35.00	9.00
10	A27	15s purple	62.50	6.00
11	A27	20s red orange	62.50	5.00
12	A28	25s blue grn (R)	220.00	55.00
13	A28	50s red brown	175.00	18.00
14	A29	1y carmine	475.00	14.00
		Nos. 1-14 (14)	1,737.	440.50

1900

No.	Type	Description	Unused	Used
15	A30	3s carmine	100.00	55.00

Wedding of Crown Prince Yoshihito and Princess Sadako.

Counterfeit overprints exist of Nos. 1-15.

Taiwan (Formosa)

Numeral of Value and Imperial Crest — A1

1945 **Unwmk.** **Litho.** ***Imperf.***

Without Gum

No.	Type	Description	Unused	Used
1	A1	3s carmine	30.00	30.00
2	A1	5s blue green	22.50	22.50
3	A1	10s pale blue	35.00	35.00
		Nos. 1-3 (3)	87.50	87.50

Additional values, prepared, but not issued, were: 30s, 40s, 50s, 1y, 5y and 10y. The entire set of nine was overprinted by Chinese authorities after World War II and issued for use in Taiwan.

For overprints see China-Taiwan Nos. 1-7.

JORDAN

'jor-dən

Trans-Jordan

LOCATION — In the Near East, separated from the Mediterranean Sea by Israel
GOVT. — Kingdom
AREA — 38,400 sq. mi.
POP. — 4,561,147 (1999 est.)
CAPITAL — Amman

The former Turkish territory was mandated to Great Britain following World War I. It became an independent state in 1946.

10 Milliemes = 1 Piaster
1000 Mils = 1 Palestine Pound (1930)
1000 Fils = 100 piasters = 1 Jordan Dinar (1951)

Catalogue values for unused stamps in this country are for Never Hinged items, beginning with Scott 221 in the regular postage section, Scott B13 in the semi-postal section, Scott C1 in the air post section, Scott J47 in the postage due section, Scott RA1 in the postal tax section, Scott N1 in the occupation section, Scott NJ1 in the occupation postage due section, and Scott NRA1 in the occupation postal tax section.

Watermarks

Wmk. 305 — Roman and Arabic Initials

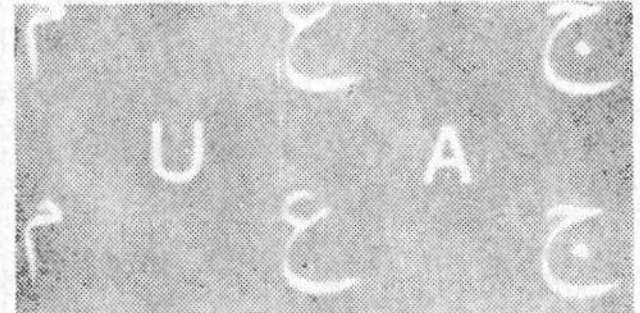

Wmk. 328 — UAR

Wmk. 388 — Multiple "SPM"

British Mandate

Stamps and Type of Palestine 1918 Overprinted in Black or Silver

Perf. 14, 15x14

1920, Nov. Wmk. 33

1 A1 1m dark brown 1.50 *1.50*
a. Inverted overprint 140.00 250.00
b. Perf. 14 1.75 1.60
c. As "b," inverted overprint 160.00
2 A1 2m blue green 1.75 .80
a. Perf. 15x14 9.50 *10.00*
3 A1 3m light brown 2.50 1.25
a. Perf. 14 19.50 17.50
4 A1 4m scarlet 2.25 *1.25*
a. Perf. 14 19.00 *21.00*
5 A1 5m orange 4.00 .90
a. Perf. 15x14 4.00 1.25
6 A1 1pi dark blue (S) 3.25 *1.90*
a. Perf. 15x14 *2,250.*
7 A1 2pi olive green 5.00 3.25
a. Perf. 15x14 5.50 *6.50*
8 A1 5pi plum 4.50 *6.50*
a. Perf. 15x14 29.00 *35.00*
9 A1 9pi bister 6.25 *25.00*
a. Perf. 15x14 1,000. *1,500.*
10 A1 10pi ultramarine 7.25 *25.00*
11 A1 20pi gray 14.00 *40.00*
Nos. 1-11 (11) 52.25 *107.35*

The overprint reads "Sharqi al-ardan" (East of Jordan).
For overprints see Nos. 12-63, 83A.

Stamps of 1920 Issue Handstamp Surcharged "Ashir el qirsh" (tenth of piaster) and numeral in Black, Red or Violet

1922

12 A1 1/10pi on 1m dk brn 32.50 *32.50*
13 A1 1/10pi on 1m dk brn (R) 90.00 67.50
13A A1 1/10pi on 1m dk brn (V) 77.50 70.00
14 A1 2/10pi on 2m bl grn 40.00 29.00
a. 3/10pi on 2m bl grn (error) 125.00 100.00
15 A1 2/10pi on 2m bl grn (R) 100.00 80.00
16 A1 2/10pi on 2m bl grn (V) 135.00 100.00
17 A1 3/10pi on 3m lt brn 15.00 10.00
17A A1 3/10pi on 3m lt brn (V) 175.00 150.00
18 A1 4/10pi on 4m scar 70.00 50.00
19 A1 5/10pi on 5m org 225.00 100.00
c. Perf. 15x14 200.00 100.00
19A A1 5/10pi on 5m dp org (R) 250.00
19B A1 5/10pi on 5m org (V) 325.00

For overprint see No. 83B.

Handstamp Surcharged "El qirsh" (piaster) and numeral in Black, Red or Violet

20 A1 1pi dk bl (R) 210.00 60.00
20A A1 1pi dk bl (V) 425.00
21 A1 2pi ol grn (Bk) 300.00 75.00
22 A1 2pi ol grn (R) 350.00 80.00
22A A1 2pi ol grn (V) 325.00 90.00
23 A1 5pi plum (Bk) 65.00 *70.00*
23A A1 5pi plum (V) *325.00*
24 A1 9pi bister (Bk) 350.00 *350.00*
25 A1 9pi bister (R) 175.00 140.00
a. Perf. 14 600.00 600.00
26 A1 10pi ultra (Bk) 975.00 *1,000.*
27 A1 20pi gray (Bk) 800.00 *850.00*
27A A1 20pi gray (V) 1,000. 950.00

Same Surcharge in Black on Palestine Nos. 13-14

28 A1 10pi on 10pi ultra *2,000.* *2,500.*
29 A1 20pi on 20pi gray *2,600.* *3,000.*

For overprints see Nos. 86, 88, 94, 97, 98.

Stamps of 1920 Handstamped in Violet, Black or Red

1922, Dec. *Perf. 15x14, 14*

30 A1 1m dk brn (V) 30.00 20.00
31 A1 1m dk brn (Bk) 25.00 18.00
32 A1 1m dk brn (R) 15.00 *15.00*
33 A1 2m bl grn (V) 11.00 8.00
34 A1 2m bl grn (Bk) 12.50 10.00
35 A1 2m bl grn (R) 30.00 25.00
36 A1 3m lt brn (V) 10.00 7.00
37 A1 3m lt brn (Bk) 12.00 8.00
38 A1 3m lt brn (R) 50.00 40.00
39 A1 4m scar (V) 60.00 50.00
39A A1 4m scar (Bk) 50.00 50.00
40 A1 4m scar (R) 55.00 50.00
41 A1 5m orange (V) 20.00 10.00
42 A1 5m orange (R) 40.00 *10.00*
a. Perf. 14 325.00 75.00
43 A1 1pi dk blue (V) 20.00 9.00
44 A1 1pi dk blue (R) 30.00 15.00
45 A1 2pi ol grn (V) 27.50 15.00
a. Perf. 14 82.50 80.00
46 A1 2pi ol grn (Bk) 15.00 10.00
47 A1 2pi ol grn (R) 70.00 40.00
48 A1 5pi plum (V) 75.00 *80.00*
a. Perf. 14 110.00 *110.00*
49 A1 5pi plum (R) 100.00 *100.00*
50 A1 9pi bister (V) 250.00 *250.00*
50A A1 9pi bister (Bk) 72.50 *80.00*
50B A1 9pi bister (R) 450.00 *450.00*
51 A1 10pi ultra (V) 1,250. *1,600.*
51A A1 10pi ultra (R) *2,000.* *1,900.*
52 A1 20pi gray (V) 1,250. *1,800.*
52A A1 20pi gray (R) *1,750.* *2,000.*

The overprint reads "Hukumat al Sharqi al Arabia" (Arab Government of the East) and date, 1923. The surcharges or overprints on Nos. 12 to 52A inclusive are handstamped and, as usual, are found inverted and double.
Ink pads of several colors were in use at the same time and the surcharges and overprints frequently show a mixture of two colors.
For overprints see #84, 87, 89, 92-93, 95-96.

Stamps of 1920 Overprinted in Gold

1923, Mar. 1 *Perf. 14, 15x14*

53 A1 1m dark brn (G) 20.00 *24.00*
a. Perf. 15x14 1,600. *1,800.*
54 A1 2m blue grn (G) 18.50 18.00
a. Double overprint 300.00
b. Inverted overprint 375.00 350.00
55 A1 3m lt brn (G) 15.00 *15.00*
a. Black overprint 82.50 *85.00*
56 A1 4m scarlet (Bk) 12.50 *12.00*
57 A1 5m orange (Bk) 15.00 12.00
a. Perf. 15x14 55.00 45.00
58 A1 1pi dk blue (G) 15.00 *14.00*
a. Double overprint 500.00 *475.00*
b. Black overprint *875.00* *850.00*
59 A1 2pi ol grn (G) 19.00 *15.00*
a. Black overprint 275.00 250.00
b. Overprint on back 175.00
60 A1 5pi plum (G) 70.00 *80.00*
a. Inverted overprint 250.00
b. "922" for "921"
61 A1 9pi bister (Bk) 95.00 *100.00*
a. Perf. 15x14 *200.00* *200.00*
62 A1 10pi ultra (G) 82.50 *100.00*
63 A1 20pi gray (G) 85.00 *100.00*
a. Inverted overprint 400.00
b. Double overprint 475.00
c. Double ovpt., one inverted 475.00

The overprint reads "Hukumat al Sharqi al Arabia, Nissan Sanat 921" (Arab Government of the East, April, 1921).
For overprints see Nos. 85, 99, 100, 102.

Stamps of Hejaz, 1922, Overprinted in Black

Coat of Arms (Hejaz A7)

1923, Apr. Unwmk. *Perf. 11½*

64 A7 1/8pi orange brn 3.25 *1.75*
a. Double overprint 225.00
65 A7 1/2pi red 3.25 1.75
a. Inverted overprint 125.00
66 A7 1pi dark blue 1.60 1.00
a. Inverted overprint 140.00 140.00
67 A7 1½pi violet 2.50 *1.75*
a. Double overprint 160.00
68 A7 2pi orange 3.25 *6.00*
a. Inverted overprint
b. Pair, one without overprint
69 A7 3pi olive brn 4.50 *8.50*
a. Inverted overprint 250.00
b. Double overprint 250.00 250.00
c. Pair, one without overprint *400.00*
70 A7 5pi olive green 6.75 *9.50*
Nos. 64-70 (7) 25.10 *30.25*

The overprint is similar to that on the preceding group but is differently arranged. There are numerous varieties in the Arabic letters.
For overprints see Nos. 71-72, 91, J1-J5.

With Additional Surcharge of New Value in Arabic:

a

b

71 A7(a) 1/4pi on 1/8pi 7.00 *8.00*
a. Inverted surcharge 175.00
72 A7(b) 10pi on 5pi 25.00 *26.00*

Independence Issue

Palestine Stamps and Type of 1918 Overprinted Vertically in Black or Gold

1923, May Wmk. 33 *Perf. 15x14*

73 A1 1m dark brn (Bk) 22.50 *17.00*
a. Double ovpt., one reversed 725.00 650.00
73B A1 1m dark brn (G) 175.00 175.00
c. Double ovpt., one reversed 1,000.
74 A1 2m blue grn 35.00 *35.00*
75 A1 3m lt brown 12.50 *12.00*
76 A1 4m scarlet 12.50 *12.00*
77 A1 5m orange 60.00 *60.00*
78 A1 1pi dk blue (G) 60.00 *60.00*
a. Double overprint *650.00* *650.00*
79 A1 2pi olive grn 65.00 *70.00*
80 A1 5pi plum (G) 75.00 *70.00*
a. Double overprint *725.00*
81 A1 9pi bis, perf. 14 65.00 *60.00*
82 A1 10pi ultra, perf. 14 75.00 *80.00*
83 A1 20pi gray 85.00 *90.00*
Nos. 73-83 (12) 742.50 741.00

The overprint reads, "Arab Government of the East (abbreviated), Souvenir of Independence, 25th, May, 1923 ('923')."
There were printed 480 complete sets and a larger number of the 1, 2, 3 and 4m. A large number of these sets were distributed to high officials. The overprint was in a setting of twenty-four and the error "933" instead of "923" occurs once in the setting.
The overprint exists reading downward on all values, as illustrated, and reading upward on all except the 5m and 2pi.
Forged overprints exist.
For overprint see No. 101.

Stamps of Preceding Issues, Handstamp Surcharged

83A A1 2½ 10pi on 5m dp org 175.00 *175.00*
83B A1 5/10pi on 3m (#17) —
84 A1 5/10pi on 3m (#36) 25.00 20.00
85 A1 5/10pi on 3m (#55) 10.00 8.75
86 A1 5/10pi on 5pi (#23) 50.00 42.50
87 A1 5/10pi on 5pi (#48) 5.00 4.00
88 A1 1pi on 5pi (#23) 50.00 42.50
89 A1 1pi on 5pi (#48) *2,100.*

Same Surcharge on Palestine Stamp of 1918

90 A1 5/10pi on 3m lt brn *17,000.*

No. 90 is valued in the grade of fine-very fine. Very fine examples are not known.
As is usual with handstamped surcharges these are found double, inverted, etc.

No. 67 Surcharged by Handstamp

Unwmk. *Perf. 11½*

91 A7 1/2pi on 1½pi vio 4.00 *4.25*
a. Surcharge typographed 30.00 *32.50*

The surcharge reads: "Nusf el qirsh" (half piastre). See note after No. 90.

Stamps of Preceding Issues Surcharged by Handstamp

No. 92

Perf. 14, 15x14

1923, Nov. Wmk. 33

No.	Type	Description	Unused	Used
92	A1	½pi on 2pi (#45)	50.00	45.00
93	A1	½pi on 2pi (#47)	95.00	87.50
94	A1	½pi on 5pi (#23)	30.00	27.50
95	A1	½pi on 5pi (#48)	2,750.	2,000.
96	A1	½pi on 5pi (#49)	1,800.	1,750.
97	A1	½pi on 9pi (#24)	*6,500.*	
98	A1	½pi on 9pi (#25)	95.00	87.50
99	A1	½pi on 9pi (#61)	200.00	160.00

Surcharged by Handstamp 

No. 102

No.	Type	Description	Unused	Used
100	A1	1pi on 10pi (#62)	*2,000.*	*2,000.*
101	A1	1pi on 10pi (#82)	*3,000.*	*3,000.*
102	A1	2pi on 20pi (#63)	30.00	*24.00*

Of the 25 stamps made of No. 100, a few were handstamped in violet.

Stamp of Hejaz, 1922, Overprinted by Handstamp

1923, Dec. Unwmk. *Perf. 11½*

No.	Type	Description	Unused	Used
103	A7	½pi red	4.00	*4.25*

Stamp of Hejaz, 1922, Overprinted 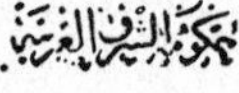

1924

No.	Type	Description	Unused	Used
104	A7	½pi red	4.50	*4.75*

King Hussein Issue

Stamps of Hejaz, 1922, Overprinted

1924

Gold Overprint

No.	Type	Description	Unused	Used
105	A7	½pi red	1.75	1.25
106	A7	1pi dark blue	2.50	1.75
107	A7	1½pi violet	2.25	1.50
108	A7	2pi orange	3.00	2.00

Black Overprint

No.	Type	Description	Unused	Used
109	A7	½pi red	1.00	.65
110	A7	1pi dark blue	1.10	.75
111	A7	1½pi violet	1.25	.90
112	A7	2pi orange	1.50	1.00
		Nos. 105-112 (8)	14.35	9.80

The overprint reads: "Arab Government of the East. In commemoration of the visit of H. M. the King of the Arabs, 11 Jemad el Than i 1342 (17th Jan. 1924)." The overprint was in a setting of thirty-six and the error "432" instead of "342" occurs once in the setting and is found on all values.

Stamps of Hejaz, 1922-24, Overprinted in Black or Red

Coat of Arms (Hejaz A8)

1924

No.	Type	Description	Unused	Used
113	A7	⅛pi red brown	.75	.20
114	A7	¼pi yellow green	.30	.20
a.		Tête bêche pair	2.00	2.00
115	A7	½pi red	.30	.20
116	A7	1pi dark blue	5.00	4.25
117	A7	1½pi violet	4.50	3.75
118	A7	2pi orange	4.00	3.25
119	A7	3pi red brown	3.00	2.40
120	A7	5pi olive green	3.50	*3.75*
121	A8	10pi vio & dk brn (R)	7.75	*7.50*
a.		Pair, one without overprint		
		Nos. 113-121 (9)	29.10	25.50

The overprint reads: "Hukumat al Sharqi al Arabia, 1342." (Arab Government of the East, 1924).

Stamps of Hejaz, 1925, Overprinted in Black or Red

(Hejaz A9)

(Hejaz A10)

(Hejaz A11)

1925, Aug.

No.	Type	Description	Unused	Used
122	A9	⅛pi chocolate	.75	.60
123	A9	¼pi ultramarine	.75	.60
124	A9	½pi carmine rose	.75	.20
125	A10	1pi yellow green	.75	.20
126	A10	1½pi orange	2.00	*2.50*
127	A10	2pi deep blue	2.75	*3.00*
128	A11	3pi dark green (R)	3.25	*4.50*
129	A11	5pi orange brn	5.00	*8.00*
		Nos. 122-129 (8)	16.00	*19.60*

The overprint reads: "Hukumat al Sharqi al Arabi. 1343 Sanat." (Arab Government of the East, 1925). Nos. 122-129 exist imperforate, and with overprint inverted or double.

Type of Palestine, 1918, Overprinted in Black

1925, Nov. 1 Wmk. 4 *Perf. 14*

No.	Type	Description	Unused	Used
130	A1	1m dark brown	.30	.20
131	A1	2m yellow	.30	.20
132	A1	3m Prussian bl	.30	.20
133	A1	4m rose	.30	.20
134	A1	5m orange	.30	.20
135	A1	6m blue green	.30	.20
136	A1	7m yel brown	.30	.20
137	A1	8m red	.30	.20
138	A1	1pi gray	.50	.35
139	A1	13m ultramarine	.60	*.75*
140	A1	2pi olive green	1.00	*1.25*
141	A1	5pi plum	4.50	*4.50*
142	A1	9pi bister	8.50	*9.00*
143	A1	10pi light blue	14.00	*15.00*
144	A1	20pi violet	27.50	*27.50*
		Nos. 130-144 (15)	59.00	*59.95*

This overprint reads: "Sharqi al-ardan" (East of Jordan).

For overprints see Nos. J12-J23.

Perf. 15x14

No.	Type	Description	Unused	Used
142a	A1	9pi	860.	*1,425.*
143a	A1	10pi	100.	*110.*
144a	A1	20pi	1,375.	1,275.
		Nos. 142a-144a (3)	2,335.	*2,810.*

Amir Abdullah ibn Hussein
A1 A2

1927-29 Engr. *Perf. 14*

No.	Type	Description	Unused	Used
145	A1	2(m) Prus blue	.20	*.35*
146	A1	3(m) rose	.55	*1.40*
147	A1	4(m) green	1.10	*2.75*
148	A1	5(m) orange	.55	*.35*
149	A1	10(m) red	1.10	*1.40*
150	A1	15(m) ultra	1.10	.35
151	A1	20(m) olive grn	1.40	1.40
152	A2	50(m) claret	3.75	*5.50*
153	A2	90(m) bister	9.75	*15.00*
154	A2	100(m) lt blue	10.50	16.00
155	A2	200(m) violet	24.50	*35.00*
156	A2	500(m) dp brn ('29)	87.50	*110.00*
157	A2	1000(m) gray ('29)	175.00	*210.00*
		Nos. 145-157 (13)	317.00	*399.50*

For overprints see Nos. 158-168, B1-B12, J24-J29.

Stamps of 1927 Overprinted in Black

1928, Sept. 1

No.	Type	Description	Unused	Used
158	A1	2(m) Prus blue	1.00	*1.90*
159	A1	3(m) rose	1.15	*2.50*
160	A1	4(m) green	1.25	*2.50*
161	A1	5(m) orange	1.25	*1.60*
162	A1	10(m) red	1.90	*4.50*
163	A1	15(m) ultra	1.90	1.90
164	A1	20(m) olive grn	5.00	*10.00*
165	A2	50(m) claret	7.75	*10.00*
166	A2	90(m) bister	17.00	*32.50*
167	A2	100(m) lt blue	32.50	*50.00*
168	A2	200(m) violet	85.00	*125.00*
		Nos. 158-168 (11)	155.70	*242.40*

The overprint is the Arabic word "Dastour," meaning "Constitution." The stamps were in commemoration of the enactment of the law setting forth the Constitution.

A3

"MILS" or "L. P." at lower right and Arabic equivalents at upper left.

1930-36 Engr. *Perf. 14*

Size: 17¾x21mm

No.	Type	Description	Unused	Used
169	A3	1m red brn ('34)	.20	*.95*
170	A3	2m Prus blue	.20	*.55*
171	A3	3m rose	.35	*.80*
172	A3	3m green ('34)	1.40	*1.25*
173	A3	4m green	.90	*2.10*
174	A3	4m rose ('34)	2.25	1.75
175	A3	5m orange	.50	.20
a.		Perf. 13½x14 (coil) ('36)	16.00	10.00
176	A3	10m red	.95	.20
177	A3	15m ultra	.95	.20
a.		Perf. 13½x14 (coil) ('36)	16.00	10.00
178	A3	20m olive grn	1.75	.55

Size: 19¾x23½mm

No.	Type	Description	Unused	Used
179	A3	50m red violet	2.50	2.10
180	A3	90m bister	4.50	*5.75*
181	A3	100m light blue	5.75	*5.75*
182	A3	200m violet	14.00	*17.00*
183	A3	500m deep brown	26.00	*52.50*
184	A3	£1 gray	82.50	*125.00*
		Nos. 169-184 (16)	144.70	*216.65*

See Nos. 199-220, 230-235. For overprint see No. N15a.

1939 *Perf. 13½x13*

Size: 17¾x21mm

No.	Type	Description	Unused	Used
169a	A3	1m red brown	4.00	3.00
170a	A3	2m Prussian blue	10.25	3.00
172a	A3	3m green	17.00	6.25
174a	A3	4m rose	75.00	20.00
175b	A3	5m orange	80.00	4.75
176a	A3	10m red	110.00	6.25
177b	A3	15m ultramarine	42.50	5.50
178a	A3	20m olive green	65.00	19.00
		Nos. 169a-178a (8)	403.75	67.75

For overprint see No. N3a.

Mushetta — A4

Nymphaeum, Jerash — A5

Kasr Kharana — A6

Kerak Castle — A7

Temple of Artemis, Jerash — A8

Aijalon Castle — A9

Khazneh, Rock-hewn Temple, Petra — A10

Allenby Bridge, River Jordan — A11

Amir Abdullah ibn Hussein — A13

Ancient Threshing Floor — A12

1933, Feb. 1 *Perf. 12*

No.	Type	Description	Unused	Used
185	A4	1m dk brn & blk	1.00	*.95*
186	A5	2m claret & blk	1.10	*.75*
187	A6	3m blue green	1.25	*1.25*
188	A7	4m bister & blk	2.00	*1.90*
189	A8	5m orange & blk	2.25	*1.60*
190	A9	10m brown red	2.75	*2.75*
191	A10	15m dull blue	3.75	1.60
192	A11	20m ol grn & blk	5.50	*5.50*
193	A12	50m brn vio & blk	12.00	*12.50*
194	A6	90m yel & black	17.50	*22.50*
195	A8	100m blue & blk	20.00	*22.50*
196	A9	200m dk vio & blk	57.50	*70.00*
197	A10	500m brn & ver	175.00	*225.00*
198	A13	£1 green & blk	600.00	*825.00*
		Nos. 185-198 (14)	901.60	*1,193.*

Nos. 194-197 are larger than the lower values in the same designs.

Amir Abdullah ibn Hussein — A14

Perf. 13x13½

1942, May 18 Litho. Unwmk.

199	A14	1m dull red brn	1.00	*4.00*
200	A14	2m dull green	2.10	1.75
201	A14	3m dp yel green	2.10	*3.00*
202	A14	4m rose pink	2.10	*3.00*
203	A14	5m orange yel	2.40	1.40
204	A14	10m dull ver	2.75	2.75
205	A14	15m deep blue	3.50	3.50
206	A14	20m dull grn	10.50	10.50
		Nos. 199-206 (8)	26.45	29.90

Type A14 differs from A3 in the redrawn inscription above the head and in the form of the "millieme" character at upper left.

For overprint see No. N1.

Abdullah Type of 1930-39

White Paper

1943-44 Engr. Wmk. 4 *Perf. 12*

Size: 17¾x21½mm

207	A3	1m red brown	.20	.60
208	A3	2m Prussian grn	.60	.60
209	A3	3m blue green	1.25	.75
210	A3	4m deep rose	1.25	.75
211	A3	5m orange	1.25	.20
212	A3	10m scarlet	3.00	1.00
213	A3	15m blue	3.00	.20
214	A3	20m olive ('44)	3.00	.90

Size: 20x24mm

215	A3	50m red lil ('44)	3.00	1.10
216	A3	90m ocher	5.50	4.50
217	A3	100m dp bl ('44)	7.50	1.60
218	A3	200m dk vio ('44)	12.00	6.75
219	A3	500m dk brn ('44)	18.00	15.00
220	A3	£1 black ('44)	37.50	30.00
		Nos. 207-220 (14)	97.05	63.95

See Nos. 230-235. For overprints see Nos. 255-256, 259, 264-269, RA23, N2-N4, N7, N12-N17.

Catalogue values for unused stamps in this section, from this point to the end of the section, are for Never Hinged items.

Independent Kingdom

Symbols of Peace and Liberty — A15

Perf. 11½

1946, May 25 Unwmk. Litho.

221	A15	1m sepia	.30	.20
222	A15	2m yel orange	.30	.20
223	A15	3m dl ol grn	.30	.20
224	A15	4m lt violet	.30	.20
225	A15	10m orange brn	.30	.20
226	A15	12m rose red	.30	.20
227	A15	20m dark blue	.35	.20
228	A15	50m ultra	.75	.60
229	A15	200m green	2.25	2.25
		Nos. 221-229 (9)	5.15	4.25

Independence of the Kingdom of Trans-Jordan.

Nos. 221-229 exist imperforate.

Abdullah Type of 1930-39

1947 Wmk. 4 Engr. *Perf. 12*

230	A3	3m rose carmine	.35	.20
231	A3	4m deep yel green	.35	.20
232	A3	10m violet	.40	.20
233	A3	12m deep rose	.95	.65
234	A3	15m dull olive grn	.60	.60
235	A3	20m deep blue	.50	.50
		Nos. 230-235 (6)	3.15	2.35

For overprints see Nos. 257-258, 260-263, RA24-RA25, N5-N6, N8-N11.

Parliament Building, Amman A16

1947, Nov. 1 Engr. Unwmk.

236	A16	1m purple	.30	.20
237	A16	3m red orange	.30	.20
238	A16	4m yel green	.30	.20
239	A16	10m dk vio brn	.30	.20
240	A16	12m carmine	.30	.20
241	A16	20m deep blue	.35	.20
242	A16	50m red vio	.40	.35
243	A16	100m rose	.60	.60
244	A16	200m dark green	1.10	1.00
		Nos. 236-244 (9)	3.95	3.15

Founding of the new Trans-Jordan parliament, 1947.

Nos. 236-244 exist imperforate.

Symbols of the UPU A17

King Abdullah ibn Hussein A18

1949, Aug. 1 Wmk. 4 *Perf. 13*

245	A17	1m brown	.35	.20
246	A17	4m green	.50	.35
247	A17	10m red	.75	.65
248	A17	20m ultramarine	1.15	.90
249	A18	50m dull green	1.25	1.15
		Nos. 245-249 (5)	4.00	3.25

UPU, 75th anniv. For overprints see #N18-N22.

Nos. 207-208, 211, 215-220, 230-235 Surcharged in Carmine, Black or Green

1952 Wmk. 4 *Perf. 12*

Size: 17¾x21½mm

255	A3	1f on 1m red brn (Bk)	.40	.35
256	A3	2f on 2m Prus grn	.40	.35
257	A3	3f on 3m rose car (Bk)	.40	.35
258	A3	4f on 4m dp yel grn	.40	.35
259	A3	5f on 5m org (G)	1.25	.45
260	A3	10f on 10m vio	1.00	.60
261	A3	12f on 12m dp rose (Bk)	1.00	.60
262	A3	15f on 15m dl ol grn	1.00	.40
263	A3	20f on 20m dp bl	1.40	.70

Size: 20x24mm

264	A3	50f on 50m red lil (G)	1.60	1.10
265	A3	90f on 90m ocher (G)	11.00	6.50
266	A3	100f on 100m dp bl	6.75	2.10
267	A3	200f on 200m dk vio	9.50	3.25
268	A3	500f on 500m dk brn	21.00	9.50
269	A3	1d on £1 black	47.50	12.00
		Nos. 255-269 (15)	104.60	38.60

This surcharge also exists on Nos. 199-203, 205, 209-210, 212-214. Numerous inverted, double and wrong color surcharges exist.

Relief Map A19

Amir Abdullah ibn Hussein A20

Perf. 13½x13

1952, Apr. 1 Engr. Wmk. 4

270	A19	1f red brn & yel grn	.35	.20
271	A19	2f dk bl grn & red	.35	.20
272	A19	3f car & gray blk	.35	.30
273	A19	4f green & orange	.45	.30
274	A19	5f choc & rose vio	.45	.30
275	A19	10f violet & brown	.45	.45
276	A19	20f dark bl & blk	.95	.50
277	A19	100f dp blue & brn	3.25	1.90
278	A19	200f purple & orange	6.75	3.25
		Nos. 270-278 (9)	13.35	7.40

Unity of Jordan, Apr. 24, 1950.

For overprints see Nos. 297-305.

1952 Wmk. 4 *Perf. 11½*

279	A20	5f orange	.40	.30
280	A20	10f violet	.40	.30
281	A20	12f carmine	1.25	.95
282	A20	15f olive	.75	.30
283	A20	20f deep blue	.75	.40

Size: 20x24½mm

Perf. 12x12½

284	A20	50f plum	1.60	.75
285	A20	90f brn orange	4.50	2.50
286	A20	100f deep blue	5.00	1.60
		Nos. 279-286 (8)	14.65	7.10

Nos. RA5-RA7 Overprinted in Black or Carmine

Perf. 11½x12½

1953 Unwmk. Engr.

286A	PT1	10m carmine	32.50	25.00
286B	PT1	15m gray (C)	3.00	1.25
286C	PT1	20m dark brown	70.00	47.50

Same Overprint on Nos. NRA4-NRA7

286D	PT1	5m plum	45.00	25.00
286E	PT1	10m carmine	45.00	25.00
286F	PT1	15m gray (C)	45.00	25.00
286G	PT1	20m dk brn (C)	45.00	25.00
		Nos. 286A-286G (7)	285.50	173.75

In addition a few sheets of Nos. RA9, NRA1, NRA3, NRA8-NRA9 and RA37-RA41 have been reported with this overprint. It is doubtful whether they were regularly issued. See Nos. 344-347.

Same Overprint on Nos. RA28-RA31 in Black or Carmine

1953 Wmk. 4 *Perf. 11½x12½*

287	PT1	5f plum	.30	.20
288	PT1	10f carmine	.35	.25
289	PT1	15f gray (C)	.70	.70
290	PT1	20f dark brown (C)	1.25	1.10
		Nos. 287-290 (4)	2.60	2.25

King Hussein A21

Unwmk.

1953, Oct. 1 Engr. *Perf. 12*

Portrait in Black

291	A21	1f dark green	.35	.20
292	A21	4f deep plum	.35	.20
293	A21	15f deep ultra	1.10	.30
294	A21	20f dark purple	2.10	.30
295	A21	50f dark blue grn	4.75	2.25
296	A21	100f dark blue	9.25	6.50
		Nos. 291-296 (6)	17.90	9.75

Accession of King Hussein, May 2, 1953.

Nos. 270-278 Overprinted in Black with Two Bars Through Center Inscription

1953 Wmk. 4 *Perf. 13½x13*

297	A19	1f red brn & yel grn	.40	.20
298	A19	2f dk bl grn & red	.40	.20
299	A19	3f car & gray blk	.40	.20
300	A19	4f green & orange	.40	.25
301	A19	5f choc & rose vio	.40	.25
302	A19	10f violet & brown	1.00	.45
303	A19	20f dark bl & blk	1.00	.60
304	A19	100f dp blue & brn	5.25	1.50
305	A19	200f purple & org	7.00	4.50
		Nos. 297-305 (9)	16.25	8.15

Two main settings of the bars exist on Nos. 297-300 and 304 — the "normal" 1½mm spacing, and the "narrow" ½mm spacing. Values above are for normal spacing. Value of set with narrow spacing, $150.

El Deir Temple, Petra — A22 Dome of the Rock — A23

Designs: 2f, 4f, 500f, 1d, King Hussein. 3f, 5f, Treasury Bldg., Petra. 12f, 50f, 100f, 200f, Al Aqsa Mosque. 20f, as 10f.

1954 Unwmk. Engr. *Perf. 12½*

306	A22	1f dk bl grn & red brn	.35	.20
307	A22	2f red & black	.35	.20
308	A22	3f dp plum & vio bl	.35	.20
309	A22	4f org brn & dk grn	.40	.30
310	A22	5f vio & dk grn	.40	.30
311	A23	10f pur & dk grn	.50	.35
312	A23	12f car rose & sep	1.25	.70
313	A23	20f dp bl & dk grn	1.25	.35
314	A23	50f dk bl & dp rose	3.75	3.50
315	A23	100f dk grn & dp bl	2.75	.75
316	A23	200f dp cl & pck bl	11.00	1.50
317	A22	500f choc & purple	27.50	8.25
318	A22	1d dk ol grn & rose brn	40.00	17.00
		Nos. 306-318 (13)	89.85	33.60

See Nos. 324-337. For overprint see No. 425.

Globe — A23a

Perf. 13½x13

1955, Jan. 1 Photo. Wmk. 195

319	A23a	15f green	.45	.30
320	A23a	20f violet	.45	.30
321	A23a	25f yellow brown	.60	.40
		Nos. 319-321 (3)	1.50	1.00

Founding of the APU, July 1, 1954.

Princess Dina Abdul Hamid and King Hussein — A24

1955, Apr. 19 *Perf. 11x11½*

322	A24	15f ultramarine	1.50	.65
323	A24	100f rose brown	5.75	2.50

Marriage of King Hussein and Princess Dina Abdul Hamid.

Types of 1954

Design: 15f, Dome of the Rock.

Wmk. 305

1955-64 Engr. *Perf. 12½*

324	A22	1f dk bl grn & red brn ('57)	.40	.20
325	A22	2f red & blk ('57)	.40	.20

326 A22 3f dp plum & vio bl ('56) .40 .20
327 A22 4f org brn & dk grn ('56) .40 .20
328 A22 5f vio & dk grn ('56) .40 .20
329 A23 10f pur & grn ('57) .50 .20
330 A23 12f car rose & sep 1.25 .20
331 A23 15f dp brn & rose red .75 .20
332 A23 20f dp bl & dk grn ('57) .60 .20
333 A23 50f dk bl & dp rose 1.50 .35
334 A23 100f dk grn & dp bl ('62) 2.75 .90
335 A23 200f dp cl & pck bl ('65) 7.50 1.75
336 A22 500f choc & pur ('65) 24.00 9.00
337 A22 1d dk ol grn & rose brn ('65) 40.00 15.00
Nos. 324-337 (14) 80.85 28.80

Envelope A25

Wmk. 305

1956, Jan. 15 Engr. *Perf. 14*

"Postmarks" in Black

338 A25 1f light brown .30 .20
339 A25 4f dark car rose .30 .20
340 A25 15f blue .30 .20
341 A25 20f yellow olive .35 .25
342 A25 50f slate blue .55 .25
343 A25 100f vermilion .85 .50
Nos. 338-343 (6) 2.65 1.60

1st Arab Postal Congress in Amman.

Nos. RA1, RA3, RA8 and RA33 Overprinted in Carmine or Black

Perf. 11½x12½

1956, Jan. 5 Unwmk.

344 PT1 1m ultramarine .30 .25
345 PT1 3m emerald .35 .25
346 PT1 50m purple .60 .50

Wmk. 4

347 PT1 100f orange (Bk) 3.25 1.90
Nos. 344-347 (4) 4.50 2.90

Numerous inverted, double and wrong color surcharges exist.

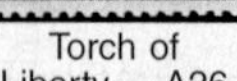

Torch of Liberty — A26

King Hussein — A27

1958 Wmk. 305 Engr. *Perf. 12½*

348 A26 5f blue & red brown .30 .20
349 A26 15f bister brn & blk .30 .25
350 A26 35f blue grn & plum .50 .45
351 A26 45f car & olive grn .60 .55
Nos. 348-351 (4) 1.70 1.45

10th anniv. of the Universal Declaration of Human Rights.

Perf. 12x11½

1959 Wmk. 305 Engr.

Centers in Black

352 A27 1f deep green .35 .20
353 A27 2f violet .35 .20
354 A27 3f deep carmine .35 .20
355 A27 4f brown black .40 .20
356 A27 7f dark green .40 .20
357 A27 12f deep carmine .50 .20
358 A27 15f dark red .50 .20
359 A27 21f green .50 .20
360 A27 25f ocher .70 .20
361 A27 35f dark blue 1.00 .30
362 A27 40f olive green 1.50 .30
363 A27 50f red 2.25 .30
364 A27 100f blue green 3.00 .50

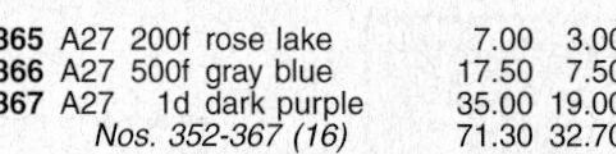

365 A27 200f rose lake 7.00 3.00
366 A27 500f gray blue 17.50 7.50
367 A27 1d dark purple 35.00 19.00
Nos. 352-367 (16) 71.30 32.70

For overprints see Nos. 423-424, 425a, 426-427.

Arab League Center, Cairo, and King Hussein A28

Perf. 13x13½

1960, Mar. 22 Photo. Wmk. 328

368 A28 15f dull green & blk .35 .25

Opening of the Arab League Center and the Arab Postal Museum in Cairo.

World Refugee Year Emblem A29

Wmk. 305

1960, Apr. 7 Litho. *Perf. 13½*

369 A29 15f pale blue & red .35 .25
370 A29 35f bister & blue .50 .45

World Refugee Year, 7/1/59-6/30/60.
For overprints see Nos. 377-378.

Shah of Iran, King Hussein and Flags A30

Perf. 13x13½

1960, May 15 Wmk. 305

Flags in Green, Red & Black

371 A30 15f yellow & black .45 .20
372 A30 35f blue & black .60 .35
373 A30 50f salmon & black .95 .70
Nos. 371-373 (3) 2.00 1.25

Visit of Mohammed Riza Pahlavi, Shah of Iran, to Jordan, Nov. 2, 1959.

Oil Refinery, Zarka A31

1961, May 1 Engr. *Perf. 14x13*

374 A31 15f dull vio & blue .30 .20
375 A31 35f dl vio & brick red .30 .20

Opening of oil refinery at Zarka.

Urban and Nomad Families and Chart A32

Perf. 13x13½

1961, Oct. 15 Photo. Unwmk.

376 A32 15f orange brown .30 .20

First Jordanian census, 1961.

Nos. 369-370 Overprinted in English and Arabic, "In Memorial of Dag Hammarskjoeld 1904-1961," and Laurel Leaf Border

1961 Wmk. 305 Litho. *Perf. 13½*

377 A29 15f pale blue & red 3.75 3.50
378 A29 35f bister & blue 4.25 3.75

Dag Hammarskjold, Secretary General of the UN, 1953-1961.

Malaria Eradication Emblem — A33

Perf. 11x11½

1962, Apr. 15 Unwmk.

379 A33 15f bright pink .35 .20
380 A33 35f blue .45 .30

WHO drive to eradicate malaria. A souvenir sheet exists with one each of #379-380. Value $5.50.

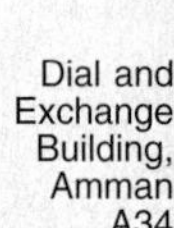

Dial and Exchange Building, Amman A34

1962, Dec. 11 Engr. Wmk. 305

381 A34 15f blue & lilac .30 .20
382 A34 35f lilac & emer .35 .25

Telephone automation in Amman (in 1960).

Opening of the Port of 'Aqaba A35

1962, Dec. 11

383 A35 15f lilac & blk .40 .20
384 A35 35f violet bl & blk .60 .30
a. Souvenir sheet of 2, #383-384 3.75 3.75

No. 384a imperf., same value.

Dag Hammarskjold and UN Headquarters, NY — A36

Perf. 14x14½

1963, Jan. 24 Photo. Unwmk.

385 A36 15f ultra, ol grn & brn red .45 .20
386 A36 35f ol, brn red & ultra .80 .45
387 A36 50f brn red, ol & ultra 1.25 .80
Nos. 385-387 (3) 2.50 1.45

17th anniv. of the UN and in memory of Dag Hammarskjold, Secretary General of the UN, 1953-61. An imperf. souvenir sheet contains one each of #385-387 with simulated perforations. Value $9.

Imperforates

Starting with No. 385, imperforates exist of many Jordanian stamps.

Church of St. Virgin's Tomb, Jerusalem — A37

Arab League Building, Cairo — A38

Designs: No. 389, Basilica of the Agony, Gethsemane. No. 390, Church of the Holy Sepulcher, Jerusalem. No. 391, Church of the Nativity, Bethlehem. No. 392, Haram el-Khalil (tomb of Abraham), Hebron. No. 393, Dome of the Rock, Jerusalem. No. 394, Mosque of Omar el-Khatab, Jerusalem. No. 395, Al Aqsa Mosque, Jerusalem.

1963, Feb. 5 *Perf. 14½x14*

Center Multicolored

388 A37 50f blue .90 .85
389 A37 50f dull red .90 .85
390 A37 50f bright blue .90 .85
391 A37 50f olive green .90 .85
a. Vert. strip of 4, #388-391 9.00
392 A37 50f gray .90 .85
393 A37 50f purple .90 .85
394 A37 50f dull red .90 .85
395 A37 50f light purple .90 .85
a. Vert. strip of 4, #392-395 9.00
Nos. 388-395 (8) 7.20 6.80

1963, July 16 Photo. *Perf. 13½x13*

396 A38 15f slate blue .45 .20
397 A38 35f orange red .65 .20

Arab League.

Wheat and UN Emblem — A39

Perf. 11½x12½

1963, Sept. 15 Litho. Wmk. 305

398 A39 15f lt bl, grn & black .30 .20
399 A39 35f lt grn, grn & blk .30 .20
a. Souvenir sheet of 2, #398-399 1.50 1.50

FAO "Freedom from Hunger" campaign. No. 399a imperf., same value.

East Ghor Canal, Pylon, Gear Wheel and Wheat A40

1963, Sept. 20 *Perf. 14½x14*

400 A40 1f dull yel & black .35 .20
401 A40 4f blue & black .35 .20
402 A40 5f lilac & black .35 .20
403 A40 10f brt yel grn & blk .40 .20
404 A40 35f orange & black 1.25 .50
Nos. 400-404 (5) 2.70 1.30

East Ghor Canal Project.

UNESCO Emblem, Scales and Globe A41

Perf. 13½x13

1963, Dec. 10 Unwmk.

405 A41 50f pale vio bl & red .70 .60
406 A41 50f rose red & blue .70 .60

15th anniv. of the Universal Declaration of Human Rights.

Red Crescent and King Hussein — A42

1963, Dec. 24 Photo. *Perf. 14x14½*

407	A42	1f red & red lilac	.30	.20
408	A42	2f red & bl green	.30	.20
409	A42	3f red & dk blue	.30	.20
410	A42	4f red & dk green	.30	.20
411	A42	5f red & dk brown	.30	.20
412	A42	85f red & dp green	1.10	.95

Design: Red Cross at right, no portrait

413	A42	1f red lilac & red	.30	.20
414	A42	2f blue grn & red	.30	.20
415	A42	3f dk blue & red	.30	.20
416	A42	4f dk green & red	.30	.20
417	A42	5f dk brown & red	.30	.20
418	A42	85f dp green & red	4.00	1.50
		Nos. 407-418 (12)	8.10	4.45

Centenary of the Intl. Red Cross. Two 100f imperf. souvenir sheets, red and red lilac, exist in the Red Crescent and Red Cross designs. Value, pair of sheets $50.

Hussein ibn Ali and King Hussein A43

Perf. 11x11½

1963, Dec. 25 Litho. Unwmk.

419	A43	15f yellow & multi	.50	.20
420	A43	25f multicolored	.75	.35
421	A43	35f brt pink & multi	1.75	.85
422	A43	50f lt blue & multi	2.75	2.00
		Nos. 419-422 (4)	5.75	3.40

Arab Renaissance Day, June 10, 1916. Perf. and imperf. souvenir sheets exist containing one each of Nos. 419-422. Value: perf, $6.50; imperf, $9.

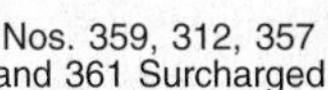

Nos. 359, 312, 357 and 361 Surcharged

Wmk. 305, Unwmk.

Perf. 12x11½, 12½

1963, Dec. 16 Engr.

423	A27	1f on 21f grn & blk	.35	.20
424	A27	2f on 21f grn & blk	.35	.20
425	A23	4f on 12f car rose & sepia	.40	.30
a.		4f on 12f dp car & blk (#357)	16.00	14.50
426	A27	5f on 21f grn & blk	.60	.40
427	A27	25f on 35f dk bl & blk	2.40	.90
		Nos. 423-427 (5)	4.10	*2.00*

Pope Paul VI, King Hussein and Al Aqsa Mosque, Jerusalem — A44

Portraits and: 35f, Dome of the Rock. 50f, Church of the Holy Sepulcher. 80f, Church of the Nativity, Bethlehem.

1964, Jan. 4 Litho. *Perf. 13x13½*

428	A44	15f emerald & blk	.75	.30
429	A44	35f car rose & blk	1.00	.40
430	A44	50f brown & black	1.50	.60
431	A44	80f vio bl & blk	2.25	1.00
		Nos. 428-431 (4)	5.50	2.30

Visit of Pope Paul VI to the Holy Land, Jan. 4-6. An imperf. souvenir sheet contains 4 stamps similar to Nos. 428-431. Value $22.50

A45

Crown Prince Abdullah ben Al-Hussein — A46

Design: 5f, Crown Prince standing, vert.

1964, Mar. 30 Photo. *Perf. 14*

432	A46	5f multicolored	.50	.20
433	A45	10f multicolored	.50	.20
434	A46	35f multicolored	.75	.45
		Nos. 432-434 (3)	1.75	.85

2nd birthday of Crown Prince Abdullah ben Al-Hussein (b. Jan. 30, 1962).

A47

Mercury Astronauts, Spacecraft — A48

Designs: b, M. Scott Carpenter. c, Entering space. d, Alan Shepard. e, At launch pad. f, Virgil Grissom. g, After separation. h, Walter Schirra. i, Lift-off. j, John Glenn. Stamp has point down on b, d, f, h, j.

1964, Mar. 25 Photo. *Perf. 14*

435	A47	20f Block of 10, #a.-j.	9.00	8.25

Imperf

Size: 111x80mm

436	A48	100f multicolored	17.50	15.00

Table Tennis A49

Designs: 1f, 2f, 3f, 5f vertical.

Perf. 14½x14, 14x14½

1964, June 1 Litho. Unwmk.

446	A49	1f Basketball	.50	.20
447	A49	2f Volleyball	.50	.20
448	A49	3f Soccer	.50	.20
449	A49	4f shown	.50	.20
450	A49	5f Running	.50	.20
451	A49	35f Bicycling	1.75	1.10
452	A49	50f Fencing	2.50	1.50
453	A49	100f Pole vault	4.50	2.75
		Nos. 446-453 (8)	11.25	6.35

1964 Olympic Games, Tokyo, Oct. 10-25. An imperf. 200f greenish blue souvenir sheet in design of 100f exists. Value $35.

Mother and Child — A50

1964, June 1 Wmk. 305 *Perf. 14*

454	A50	5f multicolored	.30	.20
455	A50	10f multicolored	.30	.20
456	A50	25f multicolored	.30	.20
		Nos. 454-456 (3)	.90	.60

Social Studies Seminar, fourth session.

Pres. John F. Kennedy — A51

1964, July 15 Unwmk.

457	A51	1f brt violet	.50	.40
458	A51	2f carmine rose	.50	.40
459	A51	3f ultramarine	.50	.40
460	A51	4f orange brown	.50	.40
461	A51	5f bright green	.50	.40
462	A51	85f rose red	18.50	11.00
		Nos. 457-462 (6)	21.00	13.00

President John F. Kennedy (1917-1963). An imperf. 100f brown souvenir sheet exists. Size of stamp: 58x83mm. Value $18.50.

Ramses II A52

Perf. 14½x14

1964, July Litho. Wmk. 305

463	A52	4f lt blue & dark brn	.30	.20
464	A52	15f yellow & violet	.30	.20
465	A52	25f lt yel grn & dk red	.30	.20
		Nos. 463-465 (3)	.90	.60

UNESCO world campaign to save historic monuments in Nubia.

King Hussein and Map of Jordan and Israel — A53

1964, Sept. 5 Unwmk. *Perf. 12*

466	A53	10f multicolored	.40	.20
467	A53	15f multicolored	.40	.20
468	A53	25f multicolored	.40	.20
469	A53	50f multicolored	.70	.25
470	A53	80f multicolored	1.00	.45
		Nos. 466-470 (5)	2.90	1.30

Council of the Heads of State of the Arab League (Arab Summit Conference), Cairo, Jan. 13, 1964. An imperf. souvenir sheet contains Nos. 466-470 with simulated perforations. Value $4.

Pope Paul VI, King Hussein and Patriarch Athenagoras; Church of St. Savior, Church of the Holy Sepulcher and Dome of the Rock — A54

1964, Aug. 17 Litho.

471	A54	10f dk grn, sep & org	.50	.20
472	A54	15f claret, sep & org	.50	.20
473	A54	25f choc, sepia & org	.50	.20
474	A54	50f blue, sepia & org	1.00	.70
475	A54	80f brt grn, sep & org	2.25	.60
		Nos. 471-475 (5)	4.75	1.90

Meeting between Pope Paul VI and Patriarch Athenagoras of the Greek Orthodox Church in Jerusalem, Jan. 5, 1964. An imperf. souvenir sheet contains Nos. 471-475 with simulated perforations. Value $11.

A two-line bilingual overprint, "Papa Paulus VI World Peace Visit to United Nations 1965", was applied to Nos. 471-475 and the souvenir sheet. These overprints were issued Apr. 27, 1966. Value, unused: set, $5; souvenir sheet, $10.

Pagoda, Olympic Torch and Emblem — A55

1964, Nov. 21 Litho. *Perf. 14*

476	A55	1f dark red	.40	.20
477	A55	2f bright violet	.50	.20
478	A55	3f blue green	.60	.20
479	A55	4f brown	.70	.20
480	A55	5f henna brown	.80	.20
481	A55	35f indigo	1.00	.55
482	A55	50f olive	1.75	.75
483	A55	100f violet blue	3.00	1.60
		Nos. 476-483 (8)	8.75	3.90

18th Olympic Games, Tokyo, Oct. 10-25. An imperf. 100f carmine rose souvenir sheet exists. Size of stamp: 82mm at the base. Value $20.

Scouts Crossing Stream on Log Bridge — A56

Designs: 2f, First aid. 3f, Calisthenics. 4f, Instruction in knot tying. 5f, Outdoor cooking. 35f, Sailing. 50f, Campfire.

1964, Dec. 7 Unwmk.

484	A56	1f brown	.70	.20
485	A56	2f bright violet	.70	.20
486	A56	3f ocher	.70	.20
487	A56	4f maroon	.70	.20
488	A56	5f yellow green	.70	.20
489	A56	35f bright blue	2.00	1.25
490	A56	50f dk slate green	3.50	1.75
		Nos. 484-490 (7)	9.00	4.00

Jordanian Boy Scouts. An imperf. 100f dark blue souvenir sheet in campfire design exists. Size of stamp: 104mm at the base. Value $22.50.

Yuri A. Gagarin — A57

Russian Cosmonauts: No. 492, Gherman Titov. No. 493, Andrian G. Nikolayev. No. 494, Pavel R. Popovich. No. 495, Valeri Bykovski. No. 496, Valentina Tereshkova.

1965, Jan. 20 Litho. *Perf. 14*

491	A57 40f sepia & vio bl	1.25	.75
492	A57 40f pink & dk grn	1.25	.75
493	A57 40f lt bl & vio blk	1.25	.75
494	A57 40f olive & dk vio	1.25	.75
495	A57 40f lt grn & red brn	1.25	.75
496	A57 40f chlky bl & blk	1.25	.75
	Nos. 491-496 (6)	7.50	4.50

Russian cosmonauts. A blue 100f souvenir sheet exists showing portraits of the 6 astronauts and space-ship circling globe. This sheet received later an additional overprint honoring the space flight of Komarov, Feoktistov and Yegorov. Value $20, each.

For overprints see Nos. 527-527E.

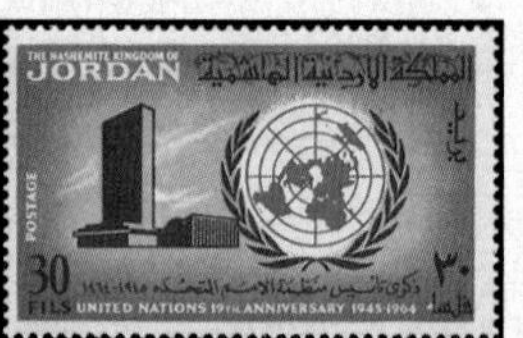

UN Headquarters and Emblem — A58

1965, Feb. 15 *Perf. 14x15*

497	A58 30f yel brn, pur & lt bl	.60	.20
498	A58 70f vio, lt bl & yel brn	1.00	.70

19th anniv. of the UN (in 1964). A souvenir sheet contains Nos. 497-498, imperf. Value $14.

Dagger in Map of Palestine — A59

Volleyball Player and Cup — A60

1965, Apr. 9 Photo. *Perf. 11x11½*

499	A59 25f red & olive	4.50	1.25

Deir Yassin massacre, Apr. 9, 1948.

See Iraq Nos. 372-373 and Kuwait Nos. 281-282.

1965, June Litho. *Perf. 14½x14*

500	A60 15f lemon	1.25	.20
501	A60 35f rose brown	1.50	.20
502	A60 50f greenish blue	2.25	.75
	Nos. 500-502 (3)	5.00	1.15

Arab Volleyball Championships. An imperf. 100f orange brown souvenir sheet exists. Size of stamp: 33x57mm. Value $22.50.

Cavalry Horsemanship A61

Army Day: 10f, Tank. 35f, King Hussein and aides standing in army car.

1965, May 24

503	A61 5f green	.50	.20
504	A61 10f violet blue	.50	.20
505	A61 35f brown red	.75	.40
	Nos. 503-505 (3)	1.75	.80

John F. Kennedy — A62

1965, June 1 Wmk. 305 *Perf. 14*

506	A62 10f black & brt green	.30	.20
507	A62 15f violet & orange	.50	.20
508	A62 25f brown & lt blue	.50	.30
509	A62 50f deep claret & emer	1.50	.60
	Nos. 506-509 (4)	2.80	1.30

John F. Kennedy (1917-63). An imperf. 50f salmon and dark blue souv. sheet exists. Value $17.50.

Pope Paul VI, King Hussein and Dome of the Rock — A63

Perf. 13½x14

1965, June 15 Litho. Wmk. 305

510	A63 5f brown & rose lil	.50	.20
511	A63 10f vio brn & lt yel grn	.90	.40
512	A63 15f ultra & salmon	1.10	.50
513	A63 50f black & rose	3.25	1.60
	Nos. 510-513 (4)	5.75	2.70

1st anniversary of the visit of Pope Paul VI to the Holy Land. An imperf. 50f violet and light blue souvenir sheet exists with simulated perforations. Value $25.

Jordan's Pavilion and Unisphere — A64

Perf. 14x13½

1965, Aug. Unwmk. Photo.

514	A64 15f silver & multi	.45	.20
515	A64 25f bronze & multi	.45	.20
516	A64 50f gold & multi	.85	.40
a.	Souvenir sheet of 1, 100f	3.25	3.00
	Nos. 514-516 (3)	1.75	.80

New York World's Fair, 1964-65.

No. 516a contains a 100f gold and multicolored stamp, type A64, imperf.

Library Aflame and Lamp A64a

1965, Aug. Wmk. 305 *Perf. 11½x11*

517	A64a 25f black, grn & red	.50	.20

Burning of the Library of Algiers, 6/7/62.

ITU Emblem, Old and New Telecommunication Equipment — A65

1965, Aug. Litho. *Perf. 14x13½*

518	A65 25f lt blue & dk bl	.40	.20
519	A65 45f grnsh gray & blk	.60	.35

ITU, centenary. An imperf. 100f salmon and carmine rose souvenir sheet exists with carmine rose border. Size of stamp: 39x32mm. Value $3.

Syncom Satellite over Pagoda — A66

Designs: 10f, 20f, Rocket in space. 15f, Astronauts in cabin.

1965, Sept. *Perf. 14*

521	A66 5f multicolored	.30	.20
521A	A66 10f multicolored	.30	.20
521B	A66 15f multicolored	.50	.25
521C	A66 20f multicolored	.60	.30
521D	A66 50f multicolored	1.50	.75
	Nos. 521-521D (5)	3.20	1.70

Achievements in space research. A 50f multicolored imperf. souvenir sheet shows earth and Syncom satellite. Value $17.50.

Dead Sea A66a

Designs: b, Qumran Caves. c, Dead Sea. d, Dead Sea Scrolls.

1965, Sept. 23 Photo. *Perf. 14*

522	A66a 35f Strip of 4, #a.-d.	5.00	5.00

Visit of King Hussein to France and U.S. — A66b

Wmk. 305

1965, Oct. 5 Litho. *Perf. 14*

523	A66b 5f shown	.30	.20
523A	A66b 10f With Charles DeGaulle	.30	.20
523B	A66b 20f With Lyndon Johnson	.65	.50
523C	A66b 50f like #523	1.50	1.10
	Nos. 523-523C (4)	2.75	2.00

No. 523C exists in a 50f imperf. souvenir sheet. Value $12.

Intl. Cooperation Year — A66c

1965, Oct. 24 *Perf. 14x13½*

524	A66c 5f brt org & dk org	.40	.20
524A	A66c 10f brt bl & dk bl	.75	.35
524B	A66c 45f brt grn & dk violet	2.10	1.40
	Nos. 524-524B (3)	3.25	1.95

Arab Postal Union, 10th Anniv. — A66d

1965, Nov. 5 *Perf. 15x14*

525	A66d 15f violet bl & blk	.30	.20
525A	A66d 25f brt yel grn & blk	.50	.35

Dome of the Rock A66e

1965, Nov. 20 *Perf. 14x15*

526	A66e 15f multicolored	1.10	1.10
526A	A66e 25f multicolored	1.60	1.60

Nos. 491-496 with Spaceship and Bilingual Ovpt. in Blue "Alexei Leonov / Pavel Belyaev / 18-3-65"

1966, Jan. 15 Litho. *Perf. 14*

527	A57 40f on No. 491	3.75	3.50
527A	A57 40f on No. 492	3.75	3.50
527B	A57 40f on No. 493	3.75	3.50
527C	A57 40f on No. 494	3.75	3.50
527D	A57 40f on No. 495	3.75	3.50
527E	A57 40f on No. 496	3.75	3.50
	Nos. 527-527E (6)	22.50	21.00

Both souvenir sheets mentioned after No. 496 exist overprinted in red violet. Value, $50 each.

King Hussein A67

Perf. 14½x14

1966, Jan. 15 Photo. Unwmk.

Portrait in Slate Blue

528	A67 1f orange	.40	.20
528A	A67 2f ultramarine	.40	.20
528B	A67 3f dk purple	.40	.20
528C	A67 4f plum	.40	.20
528D	A67 7f brn orange	.40	.20
528E	A67 12f cerise	.40	.20
528F	A67 15f olive brn	.40	.20

Portrait in Violet Brown

528G A67 21f green .55 .20
528H A67 25f greenish bl .55 .20
528I A67 35f yel bister .80 .35
528J A67 40f orange yel 1.00 .35
528K A67 50f olive grn 1.10 .20
528L A67 100f lt yel grn 2.10 .40
528M A67 150f violet 3.00 1.00
Nos. 528-528M,C43-C45 (17) 44.65 19.35

Anti-tuberculosis Campaign — A67a

1966, May 17 Photo. *Perf. 14x15*

Blue Overprint

529 A67a 15f multicolored .65 .50
529A A67a 35f multicolored 1.10 .95
529B A67a 50f multicolored 1.50 1.25
Nos. 529-529B (3) 3.25 2.70

Unissued Freedom from Hunger stamps overprinted. Two imperf. souvenir sheets exist, one with simulated perforations. Value, each $10.

Nos. 529-529B with Added Surcharge Obliterated with Black Bars

1966, May 17 Photo. *Perf. 14x15*

530 A67a 15f on 15f + 15f .50 .30
530A A67a 35f on 35f + 35f 1.00 .75
530B A67a 50f on 50f + 50f 1.75 1.25
Nos. 530-530B (3) 3.25 2.30

A67b

A67c

Designs: Stations on Jesus' walk to Calvary along Via Dolorosa (Stations of the Cross). Denominations expressed in Roman numerals.

1966, Sept. 14 Photo. *Perf. 15x14*

Design A67b

531 1f Condemned to death .40 .20
531A 2f Takes up cross .40 .20
531B 3f Falls the 1st time .40 .20
531C 4f Meets His mother .50 .25
531D 5f Simon helps carry cross .60 .30
531E 6f Woman wipes Jesus' brow .60 .30
531F 7f Falls 2nd time .80 .40
531G 8f Tells women not to weep .90 .45
531H 9f Falls 3rd time 1.00 .50
531I 10f Stripped of His garment 1.10 .55
531J 11f Nailed to cross 1.25 .60
531K 12f Death on cross 1.40 .65
531L 13f Removal from cross 1.50 .70
531M 14f Burial 1.60 .75
Nos. 531-531M (14) 12.45 6.05

Souvenir Sheet

Imperf

531N 100f like #531 *30.00 27.50*

1966, Nov. 15 Photo. *Perf. 15x14*

Astronauts and spacecraft from Gemini Missions 6-8.

Design A67c

532 1f Walter M. Schirra .35 .20
532A 2f Thomas P. Stafford .35 .20
532B 3f Frank Borman .35 .20
532C 4f James A. Lovell .35 .20
532D 30f Neil Armstrong 1.50 .70
532E 60f David R. Scott 2.10 1.50
Nos. 532-532E (6) 5.00 3.00

Imperf

Size: 119x89mm

532F 100f Gemini 6-8 astronauts *22.50 20.00*

Christmas — A67d

Perf. 14x15, 15x14

1966, Dec. 21 Photo.

533 5f Magi following star .35 .20
533A 10f Adoration of the Magi .35 .20
533B 35f Flight to Egypt, vert. 3.25 1.10
Nos. 533-533B (3) 3.95 1.50

Souvenir Sheet

Imperf

533C 50f like #533A *22.50 20.00*

King Hussein — A67e

Builders of World Peace: No. 534, Dag Hammarskjold. No. 534A, U Thant. No. 534B, Jawaharlal Nehru. No. 534C, Charles DeGaulle. No. 534D, John F. Kennedy. No. 534E, Lyndon B. Johnson. No. 534F, Pope John XXIII. No. 534G, Pope Paul VI. No. 534H, King Abdullah of Jordan.

1967, Jan. 5 Photo. *Perf. 15x14*

Background Color

534 A67e 5f gray .35 .20
534A A67e 5f brt yel grn .35 .20
534B A67e 10f rose lilac .35 .20
534C A67e 10f red brown .35 .20
534D A67e 35f olive green .95 .70
534E A67e 35f orange .95 .70
534F A67e 50f rose claret 1.10 1.00
534G A67e 50f yel bister 1.10 1.00
534H A67e 100f brt blue 2.50 2.10
534I A67e 100f dull blue 2.50 2.10
Nos. 534-534I (10) 10.50 8.40

Imperf

Size: 99x64mm

534J A67e 100f Kennedy, etc. *22.50 22.50*
534K A67e 100f DeGaulle, etc. *22.50 22.50*

King Hussein A67f

Photo. & Embossed

1967, Feb. 7 *Imperf.*

Gold Portrait and Border

Diameter: 50f, 100f, 48mm; 200f, 54mm

Portrait of King Hussein

535 A67f 5f dk bl & salmon .75 .75
535A A67f 10f purple & salmon .75 .75
535B A67f 50f blk brn & vio 4.25 4.25
535C A67f 100f dk ol grn & pink 5.00 5.00
535D A67f 200f dp bl & bl 7.75 7.75

Portrait of Crown Prince Hassan

536 A67f 5f brt yel grn & blk .75 .75
536A A67f 10f vio & blk .75 .75
536B A67f 50f bl & blk 4.25 4.25
536C A67f 100f bister & blk 5.00 5.00
536D A67f 200f brt pink & blk 7.75 7.75

Portrait of John F. Kennedy

537 A67f 5f brt bl & lt grn .75 .75
537A A67f 10f dp grn & pink .75 .75
537B A67f 50f brt rose & org yel 3.25 3.25
537C A67f 100f brn & apple grn 4.25 4.25
537D A67f 200f dk purple & pale grn 5.00 5.00
Nos. 535-537D (15) 51.00 51.00

1968 Summer Olympic Games, Mexico — A67g

Olympic torch and: 1f, Natl. University Library with O'Gormans mosaics, statue, Mexico City. 2f, Fishermen on Lake Patzcuaro. 3f, Natl. University buildings. 4f, Paseo de la Reforma, Mexico City. 30f, Guadalajara Cathedral. 60f, 100f, Palace of Fine Arts, Mexico City.

Perf. 14x15

1967, Mar. Photo. Unwmk.

538 A67g 1f lake, dk bl vio & blk .30 .25
538A A67g 2f blk, lake & dk bl vio .30 .25
538B A67g 3f dark bl vio, blk & lake .30 .25
538C A67g 4f bl, grn & brn .30 .25
538D A67g 30f grn, brn & bl .60 .60
538E A67g 60f brn, bl & grn 1.10 1.10
Nos. 538-538E (6) 2.90 2.70

Souvenir Sheet

Imperf

538F A67g 100f brn, dark bl & grn 22.50 22.50

Symbolic Water Cycle A68

Perf. 14½x14

1967, Mar. 1 Litho. Wmk. 305

539 A68 10f dp org, blk & gray .50 .20
540 A68 15f grnsh bl, blk & gray .50 .35
541 A68 25f brt rose lil, blk & gray .75 .50
Nos. 539-541 (3) 1.75 1.05

Hydrological Decade (UNESCO), 1965-74.

UNESCO Emblem — A69

1967, Mar. 16

542 A69 100f multicolored 1.10 1.10

20th anniv. of UNESCO.

Dromedary — A70

Animals: 2f, Karakul. 3f, Angora goat.

Perf. 14x15

1967, Feb. 11 Photo. Unwmk.

543 A70 1f dark brn & multi 1.10 .20
544 A70 2f yellow & multi 1.10 .20
545 A70 3f lt blue & multi 1.10 .20
Nos. 543-545,C46-C48 (6) 11.30 2.25

A souvenir sheet exists with a 100f in design and colors of No. C47, simulated perforation and marginal animal design. Value $35.

Inauguration of WHO Headquarters, Geneva — A71

1967, Apr. 7 Wmk. 305

546 A71 5f emerald & blk .40 .20
547 A71 45f dl orange & blk .50 .30

Arab League Emblem and Hands Reaching for Knowledge — A72

1968, May 5 Unwmk. *Perf. 11*

548 A72 20f org & slate grn .45 .20
549 A72 20f brt pink & dk bl .45 .20

Issued to publicize the literacy campaign.

"20" and WHO Emblem A73

Perf. 14½x14

1968, Aug. 10 Wmk. 305

550 A73 30f multicolored .60 .20
551 A73 100f multicolored 1.75 1.10

20th anniv. of the WHO.

European Goldfinch — A74

Protected Game: 10f, Rock partridge, vert. 15f, Ostriches, vert. 20f, Sand partridge. 30f, Dorcas gazelle. 40f, Oryxes. 50f, Houbara bustard.

1968, Oct. 5 Unwmk. *Perf. 13½*

552 A74 5f multicolored 3.25 1.25
553 A74 10f multicolored 6.50 1.25
554 A74 15f multicolored 8.50 1.50
555 A74 20f multicolored 8.50 1.75
556 A74 30f multicolored 5.25 1.25
557 A74 40f multicolored 8.00 1.50
558 A74 50f multicolored 12.50 3.00
Nos. 552-558,C49-C50 (9) 77.50 23.00

Human Rights Flame — A75

1968, Dec. 10 Litho. *Perf. 13*

559 A75 20f dp org, lt org & blk .40 .20
560 A75 60f grn, lt blue & blk .75 .45

International Human Rights Year.

Dome of the Rock, Jerusalem A76

5f, 45f, Holy Kaaba, Mecca, & Dome of the Rock.

1969, Oct. 8 Photo. *Perf. 12*

Size: 56x25mm

561 A76 5f dull vio & multi .80 .20

Size: 36x25mm

562 A76 10f vio blue & multi .80 .50
563 A76 20f Prus bl & multi 1.25 .60

Size: 56x25mm

564 A76 45f Prus bl & multi 2.10 .70
Nos. 561-564 (4) 4.95 2.00

ILO Emblem A77

1969, June 10 *Perf. 13½x14*

565 A77 10f blue & black .35 .20
566 A77 20f bister brn & blk .35 .20
567 A77 25f lt olive & black .35 .20
568 A77 45f lil rose & black .50 .30
569 A77 60f orange & black .75 .35
Nos. 565-569 (5) 2.30 1.25

ILO, 50th anniversary.

Horses A78

20f, White stallion. 45f, Mare and foal.

1969, July 6 Unwmk. *Perf. 13½*

570 A78 10f dark bl & multi 1.50 .25
571 A78 20f dl green & multi 3.50 .60
572 A78 45f red & multi 6.50 1.75
Nos. 570-572 (3) 11.50 2.60

Prince Hassan and Princess Tharwat A79

Designs: 60f, 100f, Prince Hassan and bride in western bridal gown.

1969, Dec. 2 Photo. *Perf. 12½*

573 A79 20f gold & multi .50 .20
573A A79 60f gold & multi 1.00 .65
573B A79 100f gold & multi 1.50 1.25
c. Strip of 3, #573-573B 3.25 3.25

Wedding of Crown Prince Hassan, 11/14/68.

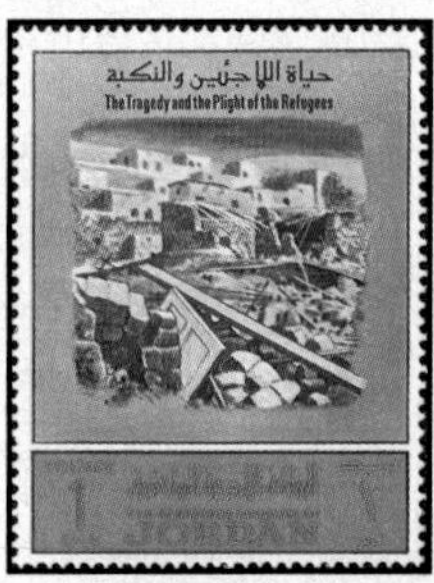

The Tragedy and the Flight of the Refugees A79a

Different design on each stamp. Each strip of 5 has five consecutive denominations.

Perf. 14½x13½

1969, Dec. 10 Photo.

574 A79a 1f-5f Strip of 5 11.00 11.00
f.-j. A79a 1f-5f Any single
574A A79a 6f-10f Strip of 5 11.00 11.00
a.-e. A79a 6f-10f Any single
574B A79a 11f-15f Strip of 5 11.00 11.00
a.-e. A79a 11f-15f Any single
574C A79a 16f-20f Strip of 5 11.00 11.00
a.-e. A79a 16f-20f Any single
574D A79a 21f-25f Strip of 5 11.00 11.00
a.-e. A79a 21f-25f Any single
574E A79a 26f-30f Strip of 5 11.00 11.00
a.-e. A79a 26f-30f Any single

For surcharges see Nos. 870-875.

Inscribed: Tragedy in the Holy Lands

Different design on each stamp. Each strip of 5 has five consecutive denominations.

Perf. 14½x13½

1969, Dec. 10 Photo.

575 A79a 1f-5f Strip of 5 5.00 5.00
f.-j. A79a 1f-5f Any single
575A A79a 6f-10f Strip of 5 5.00 5.00
a.-e. A79a 6f-10f Any single
575B A79a 11f-15f Strip of 5 5.00 5.00
a.-e. A79a 11f-15f Any single
575C A79a 16f-20f Strip of 5 5.00 5.00
a.-e. A79a 16f-20f Any single
575D A79a 21f-25f Strip of 5 5.00 5.00
a.-e. A79a 21f-25f Any single
575E A79a 26f-30f Strip of 5 5.00 5.00
a.-e. A79a 26f-30f Any single

For surcharges see Nos. 876-881.

Pomegranate Flower (inscribed "Desert Scabius") — A80

Oranges — A81

Black Bush Robin — A82

Designs: 15f, Wattle flower ("Caper"). 20f, Melon. 25f, Caper flower ("Pomegranate"). 30f, Lemons. 35f, Morning glory. 40f, Grapes. 45f, Desert scabius ("Wattle"). 50f, Olive-laden branch. 75f, Black iris. 100f, Apples. 180f, Masked shrike. 200f, Palestine sunbird. (Inscriptions incorrect on 5f, 15f, 25f and 45f.)

Perf. 14x13½ (flowers), 12 (fruit), 13½x14 (birds)

1969-70 Photo.

576 A80 5f yel & multi ('70) .40 .20
577 A81 10f blue & multi .40 .20
578 A80 15f tan & multi ('70) .70 .20
579 A81 20f sepia & multi .60 .20
580 A80 25f multi ('70) 1.00 .20
581 A81 30f vio bl & multi 1.00 .20
582 A80 35f multi ('70) 1.50 .20
583 A81 40f dull yel & multi 1.50 .20
584 A80 45f gray & multi ('70) 2.00 .25
585 A81 50f car rose & multi 2.00 .40
586 A80 75f multi ('70) 3.00 1.00
587 A81 100f dk gray & multi 3.25 1.25
588 A82 120f org & multi ('70) 10.00 2.00
589 A82 180f multi ('70) 17.50 4.75
590 A82 200f multi ('70) 20.00 7.00
Nos. 576-590 (15) 64.85 18.25

Issued: Fruits, 11/22; flowers, 3/21; birds, 9/1.

Soccer A83

Designs: 10f, Diver. 15f, Boxers. 50f, Runner. 100f, Bicyclist, vert. 150f, Basketball, vert.

1970, Aug. *Perf. 13½x14, 14x13½*

651 A83 5f green & multi 1.00 .20
652 A83 10f lt bl & multi 1.00 .20
653 A83 15f gray & multi 1.00 .20
654 A83 50f gray & multi 1.50 .65
655 A83 100f yellow & multi 2.25 1.25
656 A83 150f multicolored 3.25 2.25
Nos. 651-656 (6) 10.00 4.75

Refugee Children A84

Emblems and: 10F, Boy Fetching Water, UNICEF and Refugee Emblems. 15f, Girl and tents. 20f, Boy in front of tent.

1970, Aug.

657 A84 5f multicolored .30 .20
658 A84 10f multicolored .40 .20
659 A84 15f multicolored .50 .20
660 A84 20f multicolored .70 .20
Nos. 657-660 (4) 1.90 .80

Issued for Childhood Day.

Nativity Grotto, Bethlehem A85

Church of the Nativity, Bethlehem: 10f, Manger. 20f, Altar. 25f, Interior.

1970, Dec. 25 Photo. *Perf. 13½*

661 A85 5f blue & multi .45 .20
662 A85 10f scarlet & multi .45 .20
663 A85 20f rose lilac & multi .45 .20
664 A85 25f green & multi .60 .20
Nos. 661-664 (4) 1.95 .80

Christmas.

Flag and Map of Arab League Countries A85a

1971, May 10 Photo. *Perf. 11½x11*

665 A85a 10f orange & multi .40 .20
666 A85a 20f lt blue & multi .40 .20
667 A85a 30f olive & multi .40 .20
Nos. 665-667 (3) 1.20 .60

25th anniversary of the Arab League.

Emblem and Doves — A86

Designs: 5f, Emblem and 4 races, vert. 10f, Emblem as flower, vert.

1971, July

668 A86 5f green & multi .30 .20
669 A86 10f brick red & multi .30 .20
670 A86 15f dk blue & multi .30 .20
Nos. 668-670 (3) .90 .60

Intl. Year Against Racial Discrimination.

Dead Sea A87

Views of the Holy Land: 30f, Excavated building, Petra. 45f, Via Dolorosa, Jerusalem, vert. 60f, Jordan River. 100f, Christmas bell, Bethlehem, vert.

1971, Aug. *Perf. 14x13½, 13½x14*

671 A87 5f blue & multi .60 .20
672 A87 30f pink & multi 1.00 .20
673 A87 45f blue & multi 1.50 .70
674 A87 60f gray & multi 2.50 1.25
675 A87 100f gray & multi 3.50 2.25
Nos. 671-675 (5) 9.10 4.60

Tourist publicity.

Opening of UPU Headquarters, Bern in 1970 — A88

1971, Oct. *Perf. 11*

676 A88 10f brn, brn & yel grn .40 .20
677 A88 20f dk vio, grn & yel grn .70 .20

Averroes (1126-1198) A89

Child Learning to Write — A90

Arab Scholars: 5f, Avicenna (980-1037). 20f, ibn-Khaldun (1332-1406). 25f, ibn-Tufail (?-1185). 30f, Alhazen (965?-1039?).

1971, Sept. *Perf. 12*

678 A89 5f gold & multi .35 .20
679 A89 10f gold & multi .35 .20
680 A89 20f gold & multi .65 .20
681 A89 25f gold & multi .65 .20
682 A89 30f gold & multi .85 .35
Nos. 678-682 (5) 2.85 1.15

1972, Feb. 9 Photo. *Perf. 11*

683	A90	5f ultra, brn & grn	.35	.20
684	A90	15f mag, brn & blue	.35	.20
685	A90	20f grn, brn & blue	.35	.20
686	A90	30f org, brn & blue	.75	.30
		Nos. 683-686 (4)	1.80	.90

International Education Year.

Arab Mother and Child — A91

Pope Paul VI and Holy Sepulcher — A92

Mother's Day: 10f, Mothers and children, horiz. 20f, Mother and child.

1972, Mar. *Perf. 14x13½*

687	A91	10f lt grn & multi	.50	.20
688	A91	20f red brown & blk	.50	.20
689	A91	30f blue, brn & blk	.75	.20
		Nos. 687-689 (3)	1.75	.60

1972, Apr. Photo. *Perf. 14x13½*

690	A92	30f black & multi	.40	.20

Easter. See Nos. C51-C52.

UNICEF Emblem, Children A93

UNICEF Emblem and: 20f, Child playing with blocks spelling "UNICEF," vert. 30f, Mother and child.

1972, May *Perf. 11½x11, 11x11½*

691	A93	10f bl, vio bl & blk	.40	.20
692	A93	20f multicolored	.40	.20
693	A93	30f blue & multi	.50	.20
		Nos. 691-693 (3)	1.30	.60

25th anniv. (in 1971) of UNICEF.

UN Emblem, Dove and Grain — A94

1972, July *Perf. 11x11½*

694	A94	5f vio & multi	.50	.20
695	A94	10f multicolored	.50	.20
696	A94	15f black & multi	.50	.20
697	A94	20f green & multi	.50	.20
698	A94	30f multicolored	.85	.50
		Nos. 694-698 (5)	2.85	1.30

25th anniv. (in 1970) of the UN.

Al Aqsa Mosque, Jerusalem — A95

Designs: 60f, Al Aqsa Mosque on fire. 100f, Al Aqsa Mosque, interior.

1972, Aug. 21 Litho. *Perf. 14½*

699	A95	30f green & multi	1.60	.20
700	A95	60f blue & multi	3.50	.85
701	A95	100f ocher & multi	5.50	1.50
		Nos. 699-701 (3)	10.60	2.55

3rd anniversary of the burning of Al Aqsa Mosque, Jerusalem.

House in Desert A96

1972, Nov. *Perf. 14x13½, 13½x14*

702	A96	5f Falconer, vert	.55	.20
703	A96	10f shown	.55	.20
704	A96	15f Man on camel	.55	.20
705	A96	20f Pipe line construction	.95	.20
706	A96	25f Shepherd	.95	.20
707	A96	30f Camels at water trough	1.25	.45
708	A96	35f Chicken farm	1.50	.65
709	A96	45f Irrigation canal	2.00	1.10
		Nos. 702-709 (8)	8.30	3.20

Life in the Arab desert.

Wasfi el Tell and Dome of the Rock A97

Wasfi el Tell, Map of Palestine and Jordan — A98

Perf. 13x13½, 13½x13

1972, Dec. Photo.

710	A97	5f citron & multi	.45	.20
711	A98	10f red & multi	.45	.20
712	A97	20f dl blue & multi	.60	.20
713	A98	30f green & multi	.75	.45
		Nos. 710-713 (4)	2.25	1.05

In memory of Prime Minister Wasfi el Tell, who was assassinated in Cairo by Black September terrorists.

Trapshooting A99

Designs: 75f, Trapshooter facing right, horiz. 120f, Trapshooter facing left, horiz.

1972, Dec. *Perf. 14x13½, 13½x14*

714	A99	25f multicolored	.80	.20
715	A99	75f multicolored	1.10	.80
716	A99	120f multicolored	2.10	1.00
		Nos. 714-716 (3)	4.00	2.00

World Trapshooting Championships.

Aero Club Emblem A100

1973, Jan. Photo. *Perf. 13½x14*

717	A100	5f blue, blk & yel	.50	.20
718	A100	10f blue, blk & yel	.50	.20
		Nos. 717-718,C53-C55 (5)	4.00	1.25

Royal Jordanian Aero Club.

Peace Dove and Jordanian Flag A101

10f, Emblem. 15f, King Hussein. 30f, Map of Jordan.

1973, Mar. *Perf. 11½*

719	A101	5f blue & multi	.45	.20
720	A101	10f pale grn & multi	.45	.20
721	A101	15f olive & multi	.45	.20
722	A101	30f yel grn & multi	.90	.45
		Nos. 719-722 (4)	2.25	1.05

Hashemite Kingdom of Jordan, 50th anniv.

Battle, Flag and Map of Palestine — A102

10f, 2 soldiers in combat, map of Palestine. 15f, Map of Palestine, olive branch, soldier on tank.

1973, Apr. 10 Photo. *Perf. 11*

723	A102	5f crimson & multi	.45	.20
724	A102	10f crimson & multi	.60	.20
725	A102	15f grn, blue & brn	1.10	.50
		Nos. 723-725 (3)	2.15	.90

5th anniversary of Karama Battle.

Father and Child — A103

Father's Day: 20f, Father & infant. 30f, Family.

1973, Apr. 20 *Perf. 13½*

726	A103	10f citron & multi	.50	.20
727	A103	20f lt blue & multi	.50	.20
728	A103	30f multicolored	.75	.50
		Nos. 726-728 (3)	1.75	.90

Phosphate Mine A104

1973, June 25 Litho. *Perf. 13½x14*

729	A104	5f shown	.40	.20
730	A104	10f Cement factory	.40	.20
731	A104	15f Sharmasil Dam	.50	.20
732	A104	20f Kafrein Dam	.70	.25
		Nos. 729-732 (4)	2.00	.85

Development projects.

Camel Racer A105

Designs: Camel racing.

1973, July 21

733	A105	5f multicolored	.80	.20
734	A105	10f multicolored	.80	.20
735	A105	15f multicolored	.80	.20
736	A105	20f multicolored	.80	.20
		Nos. 733-736 (4)	3.20	.80

Book Year Emblem — A106

1973, Aug. 25 Photo. *Perf. 13x13½*

737	A106	30f dk grn & multi	.75	.20
738	A106	60f purple & multi	1.00	.35

Intl. Book Year. For overprints see #781-782.

Family A107

Family Day: 30f, Family around fire. 60f, Large family outdoors.

1973, Sept. 18 Litho. *Perf. 13½*

739	A107	20f multicolored	.50	.20
740	A107	30f multicolored	.50	.20
741	A107	60f multicolored	1.00	.35
		Nos. 739-741 (3)	2.00	.75

Kings of Iran and Jordan, Tomb of Cyrus the Great and Mosque of Omar — A108

1973, Oct. Litho. *Perf. 13*

742	A108	5f ver & multi	.50	.20
743	A108	10f brown & multi	.50	.20
744	A108	15f gray & multi	.75	.20
745	A108	30f blue & multi	1.00	.40
		Nos. 742-745 (4)	2.75	1.00

2500th anniversary of the founding of the Persian Empire by Cyrus the Great.

Palestine Week Emblem A109

Palestine Week: 10f, Torch and laurel. 15f, Refugee family behind barbed wire, vert. 30f, Children, Map of Palestine, globe. Sizes: 5f, 10f, 30f; 38½x22mm. 15f, 25x46mm.

1973, Nov. 17 Photo. *Perf. 11*

746	A109	5f multicolored	.50	.20
747	A109	10f dl bl & multi	.65	.20
748	A109	15f yel grn & multi	.85	.20
749	A109	30f brt grn & multi	1.50	.40
		Nos. 746-749 (4)	3.50	1.00

Traditional Harvest
A110

Traditional and modern agricultural methods.

1973, Dec. 25 *Perf. 13½*

750	A110	5f shown	.65	.20
751	A110	10f Harvesting machine	.65	.20
752	A110	15f Traditional seeding	.65	.20
753	A110	20f Seeding machine	.65	.20
754	A110	30f Ox plow	1.00	.20
755	A110	35f Plowing machine	1.10	.20
756	A110	45f Pest control	1.25	.20
757	A110	60f Horticulture	1.75	1.10
		Nos. 750-757,C56 (9)	9.95	3.50

Red Sea Fish
A111

Designs: Various Red Sea fishes.

1974, Feb. 15 **Photo.** *Perf. 14*

758	A111	5f multicolored	.50	.20
759	A111	10f multicolored	.60	.20
760	A111	15f multicolored	.75	.20
761	A111	20f multicolored	.90	.35
762	A111	25f multicolored	1.25	.40
763	A111	30f multicolored	2.00	.50
764	A111	35f multicolored	2.25	.80
765	A111	40f multicolored	2.75	1.00
766	A111	45f multicolored	3.00	1.10
767	A111	50f multicolored	5.00	1.25
768	A111	60f multicolored	6.25	1.75
		Nos. 758-768 (11)	25.25	7.75

Battle of Muta, 1250
A112

1974, Mar. 15 **Photo.** *Perf. 13½*

769	A112	10f shown	.65	.20
770	A112	20f Yarmouk Battle, 636	1.25	.40
771	A112	30f Hitteen Battle, 1187	1.60	.65
		Nos. 769-771 (3)	3.50	1.25

Clubfooted Boy, by Murillo — A113

Paintings: 10f, Praying Hands, by Dürer. 15f, St. George and the Dragon, by Paolo Uccello. 20f, Mona Lisa, by Da Vinci. 30f, Hope, by Frederic Watts. 40f, Angelus, by Jean F. Millet, horiz. 50f, The Artist and her Daughter, by Angelica Kauffmann. 60f, Portrait of my Mother, by James Whistler, horiz. 100f, Master Hare, by Reynolds.

Perf. 14x13½, 13½x14

1974, Apr. 15 **Litho.**

772	A113	5f black & multi	1.50	.20
773	A113	10f black & gray	1.50	.20
774	A113	15f black & multi	1.50	.20
775	A113	20f black & multi	1.50	.20
776	A113	30f black & multi	1.50	.20
777	A113	40f black & multi	1.75	.20
778	A113	50f black & multi	2.00	.95
779	A113	60f black & multi	2.50	1.00
780	A113	100f black & multi	3.50	1.75
		Nos. 772-780 (9)	17.25	4.90

Nos. 737-738 Overprinted

1974, Apr. 20 **Photo.** *Perf. 13x13½*

781	A106	30f dk grn & multi	.70	.20
782	A106	60f purple & multi	1.00	.50

Intl. Conf. for Damascus History, Apr. 20-25.

UPU Emblem — A114

1974 *Perf. 13x12½*

783	A114	10f yel grn & multi	.40	.20
784	A114	30f blue & multi	.50	.20
785	A114	60f multicolored	.85	.30
		Nos. 783-785 (3)	1.75	.70

Centenary of Universal Postal Union.

Camel Caravan at Sunset
A115

3f, 30f, Palm at shore of Dead Sea. 4f, 40f, Hotel at shore. 5f, 50f, Jars from Qumran Caves. 6f, 60f, Copper scrolls, vert. 10f, 100f, Cracked cistern steps, vert. 20f, like 2f.

1974, June 25 **Photo.** *Perf. 14*

786	A115	2f multicolored	.50	.20
787	A115	3f multicolored	.50	.20
788	A115	4f multicolored	.50	.20
789	A115	5f multicolored	.75	.20
790	A115	6f multicolored	.75	.20
791	A115	10f multicolored	.75	.20
792	A115	20f multicolored	.50	.20
793	A115	30f multicolored	.65	.20
794	A115	40f multicolored	.75	.50
795	A115	50f multicolored	1.75	.40
796	A115	60f multicolored	2.25	.50
797	A115	100f multicolored	3.50	.85
		Nos. 786-797 (12)	13.15	3.85

WPY Emblem — A116

Water Skiing — A117

1974, Aug. 20 **Photo.** *Perf. 11*

798	A116	5f lt green, blk & pur	.30	.20
799	A116	10f lt green, blk & car	.30	.20
800	A116	20f lt green, blk & org	.40	.20
		Nos. 798-800 (3)	1.00	.60

World Population Year.

Perf. 14x13½, 13½x14

1974, Sept. 20

Water Skiing: 10f, 100f, Side view, horiz. 20f, 200f, Turning, horiz. 50f, like 5f.

801	A117	5f multicolored	.50	.20
802	A117	10f multicolored	.50	.20
803	A117	20f multicolored	.50	.20
804	A117	50f multicolored	.65	.20
805	A117	100f multicolored	1.25	.50
806	A117	200f multicolored	2.10	.95
		Nos. 801-806 (6)	5.50	2.25

Holy Kaaba, Mecca, and Pilgrims — A118

1974, Nov. **Photo.** *Perf. 11*

807	A118	10f blue & multi	.50	.20
808	A118	20f yellow & multi	.60	.20

Pilgrimage season.

Amrah Palace
A119

Ruins: 20f, Hisham Palace. 30f, Kharraneh Castle.

1974, Nov. 25 **Photo.** *Perf. 14x13½*

809	A119	10f black & multi	.50	.20
810	A119	20f black & multi	.75	.30
811	A119	30f black & multi	1.25	.50
		Nos. 809-811 (3)	2.50	1.00

Jordanian Woman — A120

Designs: Various women's costumes.

1975, Feb. 1 **Photo.** *Perf. 12*

812	A120	5f lt green & multi	.45	.20
813	A120	10f yellow & multi	.45	.20
814	A120	15f lt blue & multi	.45	.20
815	A120	20f ultra & multi	.60	.20
816	A120	25f green & multi	.90	.45
		Nos. 812-816 (5)	2.85	1.25

Treasury, Petra — A121

Ommayyad Palace, Amman
A122

Designs: 30f, Dome of the Rock, Jerusalem. 40f, Columns, Forum of Jerash.

Perf. 14x13½, 13½x14

1975, Mar. 1 **Photo.**

824	A121	15f lt blue & multi	1.00	.20
825	A122	20f pink & multi	1.00	.20
826	A122	30f yellow & multi	1.25	.20
827	A122	40f lt blue & multi	1.60	.20
		Nos. 824-827,C59-C61 (7)	9.70	3.05

King Hussein — A123

1975, Apr. 8 **Photo.** *Perf. 14*

Size: 19x23mm

831	A123	5f green & ind	.50	.20
832	A123	10f vio & indigo	.50	.20
833	A123	15f car & indigo	.50	.20
834	A123	20f brn ol & ind	.50	.20
835	A123	25f vio bl & ind	.50	.20
836	A123	30f brown & ind	.50	.20
837	A123	35f vio & indigo	.50	.20
838	A123	40f orange & ind	.50	.20
839	A123	45f red lil & ind	.50	.20
840	A123	50f bl green & ind	.65	.20
		Nos. 831-840,C62-C68 (17)	19.15	10.90

Globe, "alia" and Plane — A125

Designs: 30f, Boeing 727 connecting Jordan with world, horiz. 60f, Globe and "alia."

1975, June 15 **Photo.** *Perf. 11*

853	A125	10f multicolored	.70	.20
854	A125	30f multicolored	.75	.20
855	A125	60f multicolored	1.40	.85
		Nos. 853-855 (3)	2.85	1.25

Royal Jordanian Airline, 30th anniversary.

Satellite Transmission System, Map of Mediterranean — A126

1975, Aug. 1 **Photo.** *Perf. 11*

856	A126	20f vio bl & multi	.90	.20
857	A126	30f green & multi	1.10	.75

Opening of satellite earth station.

Chamber of Commerce Emblem — A127

1975, Oct. 15 **Photo.** *Perf. 11*

858	A127	10f yellow & blue	.35	.20
859	A127	15f yel, red & blue	.35	.20
860	A127	20f yel, grn & blue	.35	.20
		Nos. 858-860 (3)	1.05	.60

Amman Chamber of Commerce, 50th anniv.

Hand Holding Wrench, Wall and Emblem — A128

1975, Nov. Photo. Perf. 11½

No.	Type	Description	Mint	Used
861	A128	5f green, car & blk	.35	.20
862	A128	10f car, green & blk	.35	.20
863	A128	20f blk, green & car	.35	.20
		Nos. 861-863 (3)	1.05	.60

Three-year development plan.

Family and IWY Emblem A129

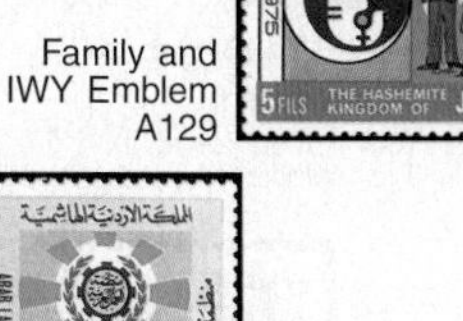

Salt Industry — A130

IWY Emblem and: 25f, Woman scientist with microscope. 60f, Woman graduate.

1976, Apr. 27 Litho. Perf. 14x13½

No.	Type	Description	Mint	Used
864	A129	5f multicolored	.50	.20
865	A129	25f multicolored	.50	.20
866	A129	60f multicolored	1.00	.40
		Nos. 864-866 (3)	2.00	.80

International Women's Year.

1976, June 1 Litho. Perf. 13½x14

Arab Labor Organization Emblem and: 30f, Welders. 60f, Ship at 'Aqaba.

No.	Type	Description	Mint	Used
867	A130	10f gray & multi	.50	.20
868	A130	30f bister & multi	.50	.20
869	A130	60f brown & multi	.75	.40
		Nos. 867-869 (3)	1.75	.80

Arab Labor Organization.

Nos. 574-574E Surcharged

Perf. 14½x13½

1976, July 18 Photo.

Strips of 5

No.	Type	Description	Mint	Used
870	A79a	25f on 1f-5f	32.50	32.50
a.-e.		Any single, 1f-5f		
871	A79a	25f on 6f-10f	32.50	32.50
a.-e.		Any single, 6f-10f		
872	A79a	40f on 11f-15f	32.50	32.50
a.-e.		Any single, 11f-15f		
873	A79a	50f on 16f-20f	32.50	32.50
a.-e.		Any single, 16f-20f		
874	A79a	75f on 21f-25f	32.50	32.50
a.-e.		Any single, 21f-25f		
875	A79a	125f on 26f-30f	32.50	32.50
a.-e.		Any single, 26f-30f		

Nos. 575-575E Surcharged

No.	Type	Description	Mint	Used
876	A79a	25f on 1f-5f	32.50	32.50
a.-e.		Any single, 1f-5f		
877	A79a	25f on 6f-10f	32.50	32.50
a.-e.		Any single, 6f-10f		
878	A79a	40f on 11f-15f	32.50	32.50
a.-e.		Any single, 11f-15f		
879	A79a	50f on 16f-20f	32.50	32.50
a.-e.		Any single, 16f-20f		
880	A79a	75f on 21f-25f	32.50	32.50
a.-e.		Any single, 21f-25f		
881	A79a	125f on 26f-30f	32.50	32.50
a.-e.		Any single, 26f-30f		

Tennis — A132

Designs: 10f, Athlete and wreath. 15f, Soccer. 20f, Equestrian and Jordanian flag. 30f, Weight lifting. 100f, Stadium, Amman.

1976, Nov. 1 Litho. Perf. 14x13½

No.	Type	Description	Mint	Used
990	A132	5f buff & multi	.75	.20
991	A132	10f lt bl & multi	.75	.20
992	A132	15f green & multi	.75	.20
993	A132	20f green & multi	.75	.20
994	A132	30f green & multi	1.00	.20
995	A132	100f multicolored	2.00	1.25
		Nos. 990-995 (6)	6.00	2.25

Sports and youth.

Dam — A133

Telephones, 1876 and 1976 — A134

Designs: Various dams.

1976, Dec. 7 Litho. Perf. 14x13½

No.	Type	Description	Mint	Used
996	A133	30f multicolored	1.00	.20
997	A133	60f multicolored	1.25	.70
998	A133	100f multicolored	2.25	1.10
		Nos. 996-998 (3)	4.50	2.00

1977, Feb. 17 Litho. Perf. 11½x12

125f, 1876 telephone and 1976 receiver.

No.	Type	Description	Mint	Used
999	A134	75f rose & multi	1.50	.95
1000	A134	125f blue & multi	2.00	1.25

Centenary of first telephone call by Alexander Graham Bell, Mar. 10, 1876.

Street Crossing, Traffic Light — A135

Designs: 75f, Traffic circle and light. 125f, Traffic light and signs, motorcycle policeman.

1977, May 4 Litho. Perf. 11x12

No.	Type	Description	Mint	Used
1001	A135	5f rose & multi	.55	.20
1002	A135	75f black & multi	1.50	.85
1003	A135	125f yellow & multi	2.25	1.40
		Nos. 1001-1003 (3)	4.30	2.45

International Traffic Day.

Plane over Ship — A136

Child with Toy Bank — A137

Coat of Arms and: 25f, Factories and power lines. 40f, Fertilizer plant and trucks. 50f, Ground to air missile. 75f, Mosque and worshippers. 125f, Radar station and TV emblem.

1977, Aug. 11 Photo. Perf. 11½x12

No.	Type	Description	Mint	Used
1004	A136	10f sil & multi	.40	.20
1005	A136	25f sil & multi	.40	.20
1006	A136	40f sil & multi	.70	.35
1007	A136	50f sil & multi	.80	.40
1008	A136	75f sil & multi	.95	.60
1009	A136	125f sil & multi	1.75	1.00
		Nos. 1004-1009 (6)	5.00	2.75

Imperf

Size: 100x70mm

No.	Type	Description	Mint	Used
1009A	A136	100f multicolored	8.50	8.50

25th anniv. of the reign of King Hussein.

1977, Sept. 1 Litho. Perf. 11½x12

Postal Savings Bank: 25f, Boy with piggy bank. 50f, Postal Savings Bank emblem. 75f, Boy talking to teller.

No.	Type	Description	Mint	Used
1010	A137	10f multicolored	.40	.20
1011	A137	25f multicolored	.60	.20
1012	A137	50f multicolored	.75	.40
1013	A137	75f multicolored	1.10	.65
		Nos. 1010-1013 (4)	2.85	1.45

King Hussein and Queen Alia — A138

Queen Alia — A139

1977, Nov. 1 Litho. Perf. 11½x12

No.	Type	Description	Mint	Used
1014	A138	10f lt grn & multi	.40	.20
1015	A138	25f rose & multi	.40	.20
1016	A138	40f yellow & multi	.50	.20
1017	A138	50f blue & multi	.70	.20
		Nos. 1014-1017 (4)	2.00	.80

1977, Dec. 1 Litho. Perf. 11½x12

No.	Type	Description	Mint	Used
1018	A139	10f green & multi	.50	.20
1019	A139	25f brown & multi	.50	.20
1020	A139	40f blue & multi	.70	.20
1021	A139	50f yellow & multi	.95	.25
		Nos. 1018-1021 (4)	2.65	.85

Queen Alia, died in 1977 air crash.

Jinnah, Flags of Pakistan and Jordan — A140

APU Emblem, Members' Flags — A141

1977, Dec. 20 Perf. 11½

No.	Type	Description	Mint	Used
1022	A140	25f multicolored	.30	.20
1023	A140	75f multicolored	.70	.40

Mohammed Ali Jinnah (1876-1948), 1st Governor General of Pakistan.

1978, Apr. 12 Litho. Perf. 12x11½

No.	Type	Description	Mint	Used
1024	A141	25f yellow & multi	.75	.50
1025	A141	40f buff & multi	1.25	.75

25th anniv. (in 1977), of Arab Postal Union.

Copper Coffee Set — A142

Roman Amphitheater, Jerash A143

Handicraft: 40f, Porcelain plate and ashtray. 75f, Vase and jewelry. 125f, Pipe holder.

1978, May 30 Photo. Perf. 11½x12

No.	Type	Description	Mint	Used
1026	A142	25f olive & multi	.50	.20
1027	A142	40f lilac & multi	.65	.20
1028	A142	75f ultra & multi	1.10	.65
1029	A142	125f orange & multi	1.75	1.00
		Nos. 1026-1029 (4)	4.00	2.05

1978, July 30 Litho. Perf. 12

Tourist Views: 20f, Roman Columns, Jerash. 40f, Goat, grapes and man, Roman mosaic, Madaba. 75f, Rock formations, Rum, and camel rider.

No.	Type	Description	Mint	Used
1030	A143	5f multicolored	.55	.20
1031	A143	20f multicolored	.55	.20
1032	A143	40f multicolored	1.00	.20
1033	A143	75f multicolored	1.40	.75
		Nos. 1030-1033 (4)	3.50	1.35

King Hussein and Pres. Sadat — A144

Designs: No. 1035, King Hussein and Pres. Assad, Jordanian and Syrian flags, horiz. No. 1036, King Hussein, King Khalid, Jordanian and Saudi Arabian flags, horiz.

1978, Aug. 20 Perf. 11½x12

No.	Type	Description	Mint	Used
1034	A144	40f multicolored	.50	.20
1035	A144	40f multicolored	.50	.20
1036	A144	40f multicolored	.50	.20
		Nos. 1034-1036 (3)	1.50	.60

Visits of Arab leaders to Jordan.

Cement Factory A145

Designs: 10f, Science laboratory. 25f, Printing press. 75f, Artificial fertilizer plant.

1978, Sept. 25 Litho. Perf. 12

No.	Type	Description	Mint	Used
1037	A145	5f multicolored	.60	.20
1038	A145	10f multicolored	.60	.20
1039	A145	25f multicolored	.80	.20
1040	A145	75f multicolored	1.60	.90
		Nos. 1037-1040 (4)	3.60	1.50

Industrial development.

"UNESCO" Scales and Globe — A146

1978, Dec. 5 Litho. Perf. 12x11½

No.	Type	Description	Mint	Used
1041	A146	40f multicolored	.75	.35
1042	A146	75f multicolored	1.25	.70

30th anniversary of UNESCO.

1976-1980 Development Plan — A147

1979, Oct. 25 Litho. Perf. 12½x12

No.	Type	Description	Mint	Used
1043	A147	25f multicolored	.30	.20
1044	A147	40f multicolored	.70	.25
1045	A147	50f multicolored	.95	.25
		Nos. 1043-1045 (3)	1.95	.70

IYC Emblem, Flag of Jordan — A148

1979, Nov. 15 Litho. Perf. 12x12½

No.	Type	Description	Mint	Used
1046	A148	25f multicolored	.50	.20
1047	A148	40f multicolored	.75	.20
1048	A148	50f multicolored	1.25	.35
		Nos. 1046-1048 (3)	2.50	.75

International Year of the Child.

1979 Population and Housing Census
A149

1979, Dec. 25 Litho. *Perf. 12½x12*

1049	A149 25f multicolored	.50	.20
1050	A149 40f multicolored	.70	.25
1051	A149 50f multicolored	.80	.30
	Nos. 1049-1051 (3)	2.00	.75

King Hussein — A150

1980 Litho. *Perf. 13½x13*

1052	A150 5f multicolored	.30	.20
1053	A150 10f multicolored	.30	.20
1055	A150 20f multicolored	.30	.20
1056	A150 25f multicolored	.30	.20
a.	Inscribed 1979	.30	.20
1058	A150 40f multicolored	.60	.20
a.	Inscribed 1979	.50	.20
1059	A150 50f multicolored	.80	.25
1060	A150 75f multicolored	1.00	.30
1061	A150 125f multicolored	1.50	.35
	Nos. 1052-1061 (8)	5.10	1.90

The 5, 10, 20, 25, 40f also come inscribed 1981.

International Nursing Day — A151

El Deir Temple, Petra — A152

1980, May 12 Litho. *Perf. 12x12½*

1062	A151 25f multicolored	.50	.20
1063	A151 40f multicolored	.70	.25
1064	A151 50f multicolored	.85	.25
	Nos. 1062-1064 (3)	2.05	.70

1980 Litho. *Perf. 14½*

1065	A152 25f multicolored	.60	.20
1066	A152 40f multicolored	.90	.50
1067	A152 50f multicolored	1.25	.60
	Nos. 1065-1067 (3)	2.75	1.30

World Tourism Conf., Manila, Sept. 27.

Hegira (Pilgrimage Year) — A153

1980, Nov. 11 Litho. *Perf. 14½*

1068	A153 25f multicolored	.30	.20
1069	A153 40f multicolored	.45	.25
1070	A153 50f multicolored	.75	.30
1071	A153 75f multicolored	1.50	.40
1072	A153 100f multicolored	1.50	.70
	Nos. 1068-1072 (5)	4.50	1.85

Souvenir Sheet

Imperf

1073	A153 290f multicolored	6.50	6.50

#1073 contains designs of #1068-1071.

11th Arab Summit Conference, Amman — A153a

1980, Nov. 25 Litho. *Perf. 14½*

1073A	A153a 25f multi	.40	.20
1073B	A153a 40f multi	.60	.25
1073C	A153a 50f multi	.80	.30
1073D	A153a 75f multi	1.00	.45
1073E	A153a 100f multi	1.10	.65
f.	Souv. sheet of 5, #1073A-1073E, imperf.	6.50	6.50
	Nos. 1073A-1073E (5)	3.90	1.85

A154

A155

1981, May 8 Litho. *Perf. 14½*

1074	A154 25f multicolored	.50	.20
1075	A154 40f multicolored	.80	.60
1076	A154 50f multicolored	.95	.70
	Nos. 1074-1076 (3)	2.25	1.50

Red Crescent Society.

1981, June 17 Litho. *Perf. 14x14½*

1077	A155 25f multicolored	.75	.20
1078	A155 40f multicolored	.90	.90
1079	A155 50f multicolored	1.25	.90
	Nos. 1077-1079 (3)	2.90	2.00

13th World Telecommunications Day.

Nos. 174 and 832 — A156

Perf. 13½x14½, 14½x13½

1981, July 1 Litho.

1080	A156 25f shown	.55	.20
1081	A156 40f Nos. 313, 189, vert.	1.00	.65
1082	A156 50f Nos. 272, 222	1.10	.90
	Nos. 1080-1082 (3)	2.65	1.75

Postal Museum opening.

A157

A158

Arab Women: 25f, Khawla Bint El-Azwar, Ancient Warrior. 40f, El-Khansa (d.645), writer. 50f, Rabia El-Adawiyeh, religious leader.

1981, Aug. 25 Litho. *Perf. 14½x14*

1083	A157 25f multicolored	.20	.20
1084	A157 40f multicolored	2.00	1.25
1085	A157 50f multicolored	3.00	1.50
	Nos. 1083-1085 (3)	5.20	2.95

1981, Oct. 16 Litho. *Perf. 14x14½*

1086	A158 25f multicolored	.20	.20
1087	A158 40f multicolored	.80	.55
1088	A158 50f multicolored	1.00	.65
	Nos. 1086-1088 (3)	2.00	1.40

World Food Day.

Intl. Year of the Disabled A159

Hands Reading Braille — A160

1981, Nov. 14 Litho. *Perf. 14½x14*

1089	A159 25f multicolored	.20	.20
1090	A159 40f multicolored	1.00	.70
1091	A159 50f multicolored	1.40	.90
	Nos. 1089-1091 (3)	2.60	1.80

1981, Nov. 14 *Perf. 14x14½*

1092	A160 25f multicolored	.20	.20
1093	A160 40f multicolored	1.00	.70
1094	A160 50f multicolored	1.40	.90
	Nos. 1092-1094 (3)	2.60	1.80

A161

A162

Design: Hand holding jug and stone tablet.

1982, Mar. 10 Litho. *Perf. 14x14½*

1095	A161 25f multicolored	.50	.20
1096	A161 40f multicolored	1.10	.60
1097	A161 50f multicolored	1.25	.80
	Nos. 1095-1097 (3)	2.85	1.60

Nos. 1095-1097 inscribed 1981.

1982, Apr. 12 Litho. *Perf. 14x14½*

1098	A162 10f multicolored	.20	.20
1099	A162 25f multicolored	.65	.20
1100	A162 40f multicolored	.90	.65
1101	A162 50f multicolored	1.10	.80
1102	A162 100f multicolored	2.40	1.60
	Nos. 1098-1102 (5)	5.25	3.45

30th anniv. of Arab Postal Union.

King Hussein and Rockets A163

1982, May 25 Litho. *Perf. 14½x14*

1103	A163 10f shown	.20	.20
1104	A163 25f Tanks crossing bridge	.65	.20
1105	A163 40f Jet	.90	.65
1106	A163 50f Tanks, diff.	1.25	.75
1107	A163 100f Raising flag	2.25	1.50
	Nos. 1103-1107 (5)	5.25	3.30

Independence and Army Day; 30th anniv. of King Hussein's accession to the throne.

Salt Secondary School A164

1982, Sept. 12 Litho. *Perf. 14½x14*

1108	A164 10f multicolored	.20	.20
1109	A164 25f multicolored	.60	.20
1110	A164 40f multicolored	.85	.60
1111	A164 50f multicolored	1.10	.65
1112	A164 100f multicolored	2.25	1.25
	Nos. 1108-1112 (5)	5.00	2.90

International Heritage of Jerusalem — A165

1982, Nov. 14 Litho. *Perf. 14x14½*

1113	A165 10f Gate to Old City	.20	.20
1114	A165 25f Minaret	1.00	.45
1115	A165 40f Al Aqsa	1.25	.80
1116	A165 50f Dome of the Rock	1.60	.90
1117	A165 100f Dome of the Rock, diff.	3.25	1.75
	Nos. 1113-1117 (5)	7.30	4.10

Yarmouk Forces A166

1982, Nov. 14 *Perf. 14½x14*

1118	A166 10f multicolored	.20	.20
1119	A166 25f multicolored	.45	.20
1120	A166 40f multicolored	.80	.45
1121	A166 50f multicolored	.95	.60
1122	A166 100f multicolored	2.10	1.40
	Nos. 1118-1122 (5)	4.50	2.85

Size: 71x51mm

Imperf

1123	A166 100f Armed Forces emblem	15.00	15.00

2nd UN Conf. on Peaceful Uses of Outer Space, Vienna, Aug. 9-21 — A167

1982, Dec. 1 *Perf. 14½x14*

1124	A167 10f multicolored	.20	.20
1125	A167 25f multicolored	.50	.20
1126	A167 40f multicolored	.75	.50
1127	A167 50f multicolored	.95	.60
1128	A167 100f multicolored	2.00	1.25
	Nos. 1124-1128 (5)	4.40	2.75

Birth Centenary of Amir Abdullah ibn Hussein — A168

1982, Dec. 13 Litho. *Perf. 14½*

1129	A168 10f multicolored	.20	.20
1130	A168 25f multicolored	.40	.20
1131	A168 40f multicolored	.60	.45
1132	A168 50f multicolored	.95	.80
1133	A168 100f multicolored	2.25	1.40
	Nos. 1129-1133 (5)	4.40	3.05

Roman Ruins of Jerash A169

1982, Dec. 29 Litho. *Perf. 15*

1134	A169 10f Temple colonnade	.20	.20
1135	A169 25f Arch	.90	.20
1136	A169 40f Columns	1.40	.90
1137	A169 50f Ampitheater	1.75	1.00
1138	A169 100f Hippodrome	3.25	2.10
	Nos. 1134-1138 (5)	7.50	4.40

King Hussein — A170

1983 Litho. *Perf. 14½x14*

1139	A170 10f multicolored	.20	.20
1140	A170 25f multicolored	.25	.20
1141	A170 40f multicolored	.40	.30
1142	A170 60f multicolored	.60	.40

1143 A170 100f multicolored 1.00 .65
1144 A170 125f multicolored 1.25 .70
Nos. 1139-1144 (6) 3.70 2.45

Issue dates: 10f, 60f, Feb. 1; 40f, Feb. 8; 25f, 100f, 125f, Mar. 3. Inscribed 1982.

Massacre at Shatilla and Sabra Palestinian Refugee Camps A171

10f, 25f, 50f, No. 1149, Various victims. 40f, Children. No. 1150, Wounded child.

1983, Apr. 9 Litho. *Perf. 14½*
1145 A171 10f multicolored *.45 .20*
1146 A171 25f multicolored *.80 .70*
1147 A171 40f multicolored *1.25 .90*
1148 A171 50f multicolored *1.50 1.25*
1149 A171 100f multicolored *2.25 1.75*
Nos. 1145-1149 (5) *6.25 4.80*

Souvenir Sheet

Imperf

1150 A171 100f multicolored *18.00*

Opening of Queen Alia Intl. Airport A172

1983, May 25 Litho. *Perf. 12½*
1151 A172 10f Aerial view .20 .20
1152 A172 25f Terminal buildings .80 .20
1153 A172 40f Hangar 1.10 .80
1154 A172 50f Terminal buildings, diff. 1.40 .90
1155 A172 100f Embarkation Bridge 2.75 1.75
Nos. 1151-1155 (5) 6.25 3.85

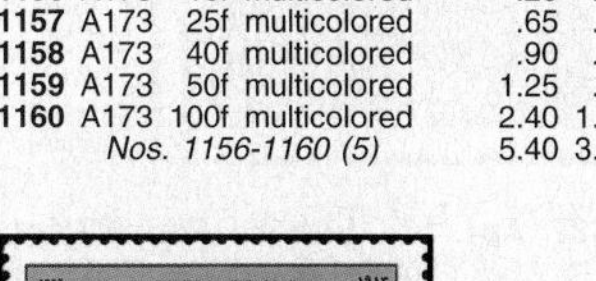

Royal Jordanian Radio Amateurs' Society A173

1983, Aug. 11 Litho. *Perf. 12*
1156 A173 10f multicolored .20 .20
1157 A173 25f multicolored .65 .20
1158 A173 40f multicolored .90 .65
1159 A173 50f multicolored 1.25 .75
1160 A173 100f multicolored 2.40 1.50
Nos. 1156-1160 (5) 5.40 3.30

Royal Academy for Islamic Cultural Research A174

1983, Sept. 16 Litho. *Perf. 12*
1161 A174 10f Academy Bldg. .20 .20
1162 A174 25f Silk carpet .70 .50
1163 A174 40f Mosque, Amman 1.10 .70
1164 A174 50f Dome of the Rock 1.50 .90
1165 A174 100f Islamic city views 2.75 1.75
Nos. 1161-1165 (5) 6.25 4.05

A 100f souvenir sheet shows letter from Mohammed. Value $15.

World Food Day A175

1983, Oct. 16 Litho. *Perf. 12*
1166 A175 10f Irrigation canal .20 .20
1167 A175 25f Greenhouses .60 .20
1168 A175 40f Light-grown crops 1.00 .60
1169 A175 50f Harvest 1.25 .70
1170 A175 100f Sheep farm 2.50 1.40
Nos. 1166-1170 (5) 5.55 3.10

World Communications Year — A176

1983, Nov. 14
1171 A176 10f Radio switchboard operators .20 .20
1172 A176 25f Earth satellite station 1.00 .20
1173 A176 40f Symbols of communication 1.25 1.00
1174 A176 50f Emblems 1.50 1.00
1175 A176 100f Airmail letter 3.25 1.75
Nos. 1171-1175 (5) 7.20 4.15

Intl. Palestinian Solidarity Day A177

Dome of the Rock, Jerusalem.

1983, Nov. 29 *Perf. 12*
1176 A177 5f multicolored .70 .20
1177 A177 10f multicolored .90 .65

35th Anniv. of UN Declaration of Human Rights A178

1983, Dec. 10
1178 A178 10f multicolored .20 .20
1179 A178 25f multicolored .65 .20
1180 A178 40f multicolored .75 .65
1181 A178 50f multicolored 1.25 .75
1182 A178 100f multicolored 2.50 1.50
Nos. 1178-1182 (5) 5.35 3.30

Anti-Paralysis — A179

1984, Apr. 7 *Perf. 13½x11½*
1183 A179 40f multicolored 1.10 .70
1184 A179 60f multicolored 1.60 .95
1185 A179 100f multicolored 2.75 1.60
Nos. 1183-1185 (3) 5.45 3.25

Anti-Polio Campaign.

Israeli Bombing of Iraq Nuclear Reactor — A180

Various designs.

1984, June 7 Litho. *Perf. 13½x11½*
1186 A180 40f multicolored 1.25 .55
1187 A180 60f multicolored 1.75 .70
1188 A180 100f multicolored 2.75 1.25
Nos. 1186-1188 (3) 5.75 2.50

Independence and Army Day — A181

King Hussein and various armed forces.

1984, June 10
1189 A181 10f multicolored .20 .20
1190 A181 25f multicolored .65 .20
1191 A181 40f multicolored 1.00 .65
1192 A181 60f multicolored 1.60 .90
1193 A181 100f multicolored 2.75 1.60
Nos. 1189-1193 (5) 6.20 3.55

1984 Summer Olympics, Los Angeles — A182

1984, July 28
1194 A182 25f shown .30 .20
1195 A182 40f Swimming .50 .30
1196 A182 60f Shooting, archery 1.10 .45
1197 A182 100f Gymnastics 1.60 .75
Nos. 1194-1197 (4) 3.50 1.70

An imperf. 100f souvenir sheet exists picturing pole vaulting. Value $14.

Water and Electricity Year — A183

1984, Aug. 11
1198 A183 25f Power lines, factory .45 .20
1199 A183 40f Amman Power Station .70 .45
1200 A183 60f Irrigation 1.10 .60
1201 A183 100f Hydro-electric dam 1.75 1.10
Nos. 1198-1201 (4) 4.00 2.35

Coins A184

1984, Sept. 26 Photo. *Perf. 13*
1202 A184 40f Omayyad gold dinar 1.10 .60
1203 A184 60f Abbasid gold dinar 1.40 .80
1204 A184 125f Hashemite silver dinar 3.00 1.75
Nos. 1202-1204 (3) 5.50 3.15

Royal Society for the Conservation of Nature — A185

1984, Oct. 18
1205 A185 25f Four antelopes .70 .20
1206 A185 40f Grazing 1.10 .70
1207 A185 60f Three antelopes 1.60 .95
1208 A185 100f King Hussein, Queen Alia, Duke of Edinburgh 2.75 1.60
Nos. 1205-1208 (4) 6.15 3.45

Natl. Universities — A186

Designs: 40f, Mu'ta Military University, Karak. 60f, Yarmouk University, Irbid. 125f, Jordan University, Amman.

1984, Nov. 14 *Perf. 13x13½*
1209 A186 40f multicolored .55 .40
1210 A186 60f multicolored .95 .55
1211 A186 125f multicolored 2.00 1.10
Nos. 1209-1211 (3) 3.50 2.05

Al Sahaba Tombs A187

Designs: 10f, El Harath bin Omier el-Azdi and Derer bin El-Azwar. 25f, Sharhabil bin Hasna and Abu Obaidah Amer bin el-Jarrah. 40f, Muath bin Jabal. 50f, Zaid bin Haretha and Abdullah bin Rawaha. 60f, Amer bin Abi Waqqas. 100f, Jafar bin Abi Taleb.

1984, Dec. 5 Litho. *Perf. 13½x11½*
1212 A187 10f multicolored .20 .20
1213 A187 25f multicolored .50 .20
1214 A187 40f multicolored .75 .50
1215 A187 50f multicolored .95 .55
1216 A187 60f multicolored 1.25 .65
1217 A187 100f multicolored 2.00 1.25
Nos. 1212-1217 (6) 5.65 3.35

Independence and Army Day — A188

Designs: 25f, King Hussein, soldier descending mountain. 40f, Hussein, Arab revolt flag, globe, King Abdullah. 60f, Flag, natl. arms, equestrian. 100f, Natl. flag, arms, King Abdullah.

1985, June 10 *Perf. 13x13½*
1218 A188 25f multicolored .45 .20
1219 A188 40f multicolored .90 .45
1220 A188 60f multicolored 1.40 .75
1221 A188 100f multicolored 2.25 1.40
Nos. 1218-1221 (4) 5.00 2.80

Men in Postal History A189

1985, July 1

1222 A189 40f Sir Rowland Hill .75 .45
1223 A189 60f Heinrich von Stephan 1.10 .65
1224 A189 125f Yacoub al-Sukkar 2.40 1.40
Nos. 1222-1224 (3) 4.25 2.50

1st Convention of Jordanian Expatriates A190

Various designs.

1985, July 20 **Photo.**

1225 A190 40f multicolored .75 .45
1226 A190 60f multicolored 1.10 .65
1227 A190 125f multicolored 2.40 1.40
Nos. 1225-1227 (3) 4.25 2.50

Intl. Youth Year — A191

Various designs.

1985, Aug. 11 Litho. ***Perf. 13½x13***

1228 A191 10f multicolored .20 .20
1229 A191 25f multicolored .50 .20
1230 A191 40f multicolored .80 .50
1231 A191 60f multicolored 1.25 .70
1232 A191 125f multicolored 2.50 1.50
Nos. 1228-1232 (5) 5.25 3.10

World Tourism Organization, 10th Anniv. — A192

1985, Sept. 13 ***Perf. 13½x13***

1233 A192 10f Ruins of the Treasury, Petra .20 .20
1234 A192 25f Jerash Temple .50 .20
1235 A192 40f Roman baths .80 .50
1236 A192 50f Jordanian valley town 1.00 .60
1237 A192 60f Aqaba Bay 1.25 .70
1238 A192 125f Roman amphitheater 2.50 1.40
Nos. 1233-1238 (6) 6.25 3.60

An imperf. 100f souvenir sheet exists picturing flower, 10 and natl. flag. Value $6.50.

UN Child Survival Campaign A193

Various designs.

1985, Oct. 7

1239 A193 25f multicolored .50 .20
1240 A193 40f multicolored .75 .50
1241 A193 60f multicolored 1.25 .70
1242 A193 125f multicolored 2.50 1.50
Nos. 1239-1242 (4) 5.00 2.90

An imperf. 100f souvenir sheet exists picturing campaign emblem and the faces of healthy children. Value $12.

5th Jerash Festival A194

1985, Oct. 21

1243 A194 10f Opening ceremony, 1980 .20 .20
1244 A194 25f Folk dancers .45 .20
1245 A194 40f Dancers .90 .45
1246 A194 60f Choir, Roman theater 1.50 .75
1247 A194 100f King and Queen 2.40 1.50
Nos. 1243-1247 (5) 5.45 3.10

UN, 40th Anniv. A195

1985, Oct. 25 Photo. ***Perf. 13x13½***

1248 A195 60f multicolored 1.25 1.00
1249 A195 125f multicolored 2.50 2.00

King Hussein, 50th Birthday A196

Various photos of King.

1985, Nov. 14 Litho. ***Perf. 14½***

1250 A196 10f multicolored .20 .20
1251 A196 25f multicolored .50 .20
1252 A196 40f multicolored .90 .50
1253 A196 60f multicolored 1.50 .75
1254 A196 100f multicolored 2.40 1.50
Nos. 1250-1254 (5) 5.50 3.15

An imperf. 200f souvenir sheet exists picturing flags, King Hussein and Dome of the Rock. Value $15.

Restoration of Al Aqsa Mosque, Jerusalem A196a

1985, Nov. 25 Litho. ***Perf. 13x13½***

1254A A196a 5f multicolored *1.10 1.10*
1254B A196a 10f multicolored *2.40 2.25*

Police A197

1985, Dec. 18

1255 A197 40f Patrol car 1.10 .20
1256 A197 60f Crossing guard 1.40 1.10
1257 A197 125f Police academy 3.00 2.00
Nos. 1255-1257 (3) 5.50 3.30

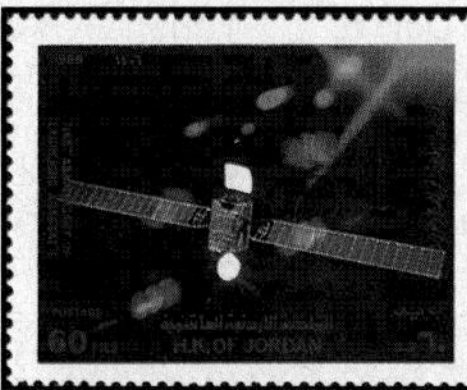

Launch of ARABSAT-1, 1st Anniv. — A198

1986, Feb. 8 Litho. ***Perf. 13½x13***

1258 A198 60f Satellite in orbit .85 .20
1259 A198 100f Over map of Arab countries 1.40 .85

Arabization of the Army, 30th Anniv. A199

40f, King Hussein presenting flag. 60f, Greeting army sergeant. 100f, Hussein addressing army.

1986, Mar. 1 ***Perf. 11½x12½***

1260 A199 40f multicolored .75 .20
1261 A199 60f multicolored .90 .20
1262 A199 100f multicolored 1.60 .90
Nos. 1260-1262 (3) 3.25 1.30

An imperf. souvenir sheet exists with design of 100f. Value $10.

Natl. Independence, 40th Anniv. — A200

Design: King Abdullah decorating soldier.

1986, May 25 ***Perf. 12½x11½***

1263 A200 160f multicolored 2.75 2.10

Arab Revolt against Turkey, 70th Anniv. — A201

Unattributed paintings (details): 40f, The four sons of King Hussein, Prince of Mecca, vert. 60f, Abdullah, retainers and bodyguard. 160f, Abdullah and followers on horseback.

Perf. 12½x11½, 11½x12½

1986, June 10

1264 A201 40f multicolored .65 .20
1265 A201 60f multicolored .85 .20
1266 A201 160f multicolored 2.50 1.25
Nos. 1264-1266 (3) 4.00 1.65

An imperf. 200f souvenir sheet exists picturing the Arab Revolt flag, King Abdullah and text from independence declaration. Value $9.

Intl. Peace Year A202

1986, July 1 Litho. ***Perf. 13½x13***

1267 A202 160f multicolored 2.25 1.25
1268 A202 240f multicolored 3.25 1.90

King Hussein Medical City Cardiac Center A203

1986, Aug. 11

1269 A203 40f Cardiac Center .90 .20
1270 A203 60f Surgery 1.10 .90
1271 A203 100f Surgery, diff. 1.75 .95
Nos. 1269-1271 (3) 3.75 2.05

UN, 40th Anniv. — A204

Excerpts from King Hussein's speech: 40f, In Arabic. 80f, Arabic, diff. 100f, English.

1986, Sept. 27 ***Perf. 12½x11½***

1272 A204 40f multicolored .75 .20
1273 A204 80f multicolored 1.25 .85
1274 A204 100f multicolored 1.60 .85
Nos. 1272-1274 (3) 3.60 1.90

An imperf. 200f stamp 90x70mm exists picturing speech in Arabic and English, King Hussein at podium. Value $8.50.

Arab Postal Union, 35th Anniv. A205

1987, Apr. 12 Litho. ***Perf. 13½x13***

1275 A205 80f Old post office .85 .60
1276 A205 160f New post office 1.90 1.10

Chemical Soc. Emblem and Chemists — A206

Designs: 60f, Jaber ibn Hayyan al-Azdi (720-813). 80f, Abu-al-Qasem al-Majreeti (950-1007). 240f, Abu-Bakr al-Razi (864-932).

1987, Apr. 24

1277 A206 60f multicolored .75 .50
1278 A206 80f multicolored 1.00 .60
1279 A206 240f multicolored 2.75 1.60
Nos. 1277-1279 (3) 4.50 2.70

SOS Children's Village — A207

1987, May 7

1280 A207 80f Village in Amman 1.25 .70
1281 A207 240f Child, bird mural 3.25 1.90

4th Brigade, 40th Anniv. A208

1987, June 10

1282 A208 60f shown 1.40 .95
1283 A208 80f Soldiers in armored vehicle 1.60 1.10

Size: 70x91mm

Imperf

1284 A208 160f Four veterans 8.00 7.50
Nos. 1282-1284 (3) 11.00 9.55

Indigenous Birds — A209

1987, June 24

1285 A209 10f Hoopoe 1.60 .55
1286 A209 40f Palestine sunbird 1.60 .55
1287 A209 50f Black-headed bunting 2.00 .60
1288 A209 60f Spur-winged plover 2.50 .90
1289 A209 80f Greenfinch 3.00 1.25
1290 A209 100f Black-winged stilt 4.00 1.75
Nos. 1285-1290 (6) 14.70 5.60

King Hussein — A210

1987, June 24 Litho. *Perf. 13x13½*

1291 A210 60f multicolored .40 .30
1292 A210 80f multicolored .85 .40
1293 A210 160f multicolored 1.75 1.10
1294 A210 240f multicolored 2.50 1.75
Nos. 1291-1294 (4) 5.50 3.55

Battle of Hittin, 800th Anniv. A211

Dome of the Rock and Saladin (1137-1193), Conqueror of Jerusalem — A212

1987, July 4

1295 A211 60f Battle, Jerusalem .75 .70
1296 A211 80f Horseman, Jerusalem, Dome of the Rock 1.50 .85
1297 A211 100f Saladin 2.25 1.50
Nos. 1295-1297 (3) 4.50 3.05

Souvenir Sheet

Perf. 12x12½

1298 A212 100f shown 8.00 7.75

No. 1298 exists imperf.

Natl. Coat of Arms — A213

Perf. 11½x12½

1987, Aug. 11 Litho.

1299 A213 80f multicolored 1.00 .65
1300 A213 160f multicolored 2.00 1.25

Amman Industrial Park at Sahab — A214

1987, Aug. 11 *Perf. 13½x13*

1301 A214 80f multicolored 1.00 .80

University Crest A215

University Entrance — A216

Perf. 11½x11, 12½x11½

1987, Sept. 2

1302 A215 60f multicolored .80 .50
1303 A216 80f multicolored .95 .65

University of Jordan, 25th anniv.

UN Child Survival Campaign A217

1987, Oct. 5 Litho. *Perf. 13x13½*

1304 A217 60f Oral vaccine .75 .60
1305 A217 80f Natl. flag, child 1.25 .80
1306 A217 160f Growth monitoring 2.50 1.60
Nos. 1304-1306 (3) 4.50 3.00

Parliament, 40th Anniv. — A218

1987, Oct. 20 *Perf. 13½x13*

1307 A218 60f Opening ceremony, 1947 1.00 .60
1308 A218 80f In session, 1987 1.25 .80

A219

Special Arab Summit Conference, Amman — A220

1987, Nov. 8

1309 A219 60f multicolored .55 .50
1310 A219 80f multicolored .90 .55
1311 A219 160f multicolored 2.00 1.25
1312 A219 240f multicolored 2.75 2.00
Nos. 1309-1312 (4) 6.20 4.30

Size: 90x66mm

Imperf

1313 A220 100f multicolored 7.50 7.50

King Hussein, Dag Hammarskjold Peace Prize Winner for 1987 — A221

1988, Feb. 6 Litho. *Perf. 12½*

1314 A221 80f Hussein, woman, vert. .95 .75
1315 A221 160f shown 1.90 1.25

Natl. Victory at the 1987 Arab Military Basketball Championships — A222

1988, Mar. 1 *Perf. 13½x13*

1316 A222 60f Golden Sword Award .80 .50
1317 A222 80f Hussein congratulating team 1.10 .65
1318 A222 160f Jump ball 2.10 1.25
Nos. 1316-1318 (3) 4.00 2.40

WHO, 40th Anniv. — A223

1988, Apr. 7 Photo. *Perf. 13x13½*

1319 A223 60f multicolored 1.00 .70
1320 A223 80f multicolored 1.25 .90

Arab Scouts, 75th Anniv. — A224

1988, July 2 Litho. *Perf. 13x13½*

1321 A224 60f multicolored 1.00 .90
1322 A224 80f multicolored 1.25 1.10

Birds A225

1988, July 21 Litho. *Perf. 11½x12*

1323 A225 10f Crested lark 2.25 .70
1324 A225 20f Stone curlew 2.25 .80
1325 A225 30f Redstart 2.25 .90
1326 A225 40f Blackbird 3.25 1.00
1327 A225 50f Rock dove 4.00 1.10
1328 A225 160f Smyrna kingfisher 11.00 1.75
Nos. 1323-1328 (6) 25.00 6.25

Size: 71x90mm

Imperf

1328A A225 310f Six species 17.50 15.00

Restoration of San'a, Yemen Arab Republic A226

1988, Aug. 11 Litho. *Perf. 12x11½*

1329 A226 80f multicolored .95 .70
1330 A226 160f multicolored 1.90 1.50

Historic Natl. Sites A227

1988, Aug. 11 *Perf. 13½x13*

1331 A227 60f Umm Al-rasas .70 .50
1332 A227 80f Umm Qais .90 .70
1333 A227 160f Iraq Al-amir 1.90 1.50
Nos. 1331-1333 (3) 3.50 2.70

An imperf. souvenir sheet of 3 exists containing one each Nos. 1331-1333. Value $5.

1988 Summer Olympics, Seoul — A228

1988, Sept. 17 Litho. *Perf. 13x13½*

1334 A228 10f Tennis .20 .20
1335 A228 60f Character trademark .90 .70
1336 A228 80f Running, swimming 1.40 .90
1337 A228 120f Basketball 1.75 1.50
1338 A228 160f Soccer 2.50 1.75
Nos. 1334-1338 (5) 6.75 5.05

Size: 70x91mm

Imperf

1339 A228 100f Emblems 17.50 17.50

Royal Jordanian Airlines, 25th Anniv. — A229

1988, Dec. 15 Litho. *Perf. 11½x12*

1340 A229 60f Ruins of Petra 1.00 .75
1341 A229 80f Aircraft, world map 1.25 1.00

UN Declaration of Human Rights, 40th Anniv. — A230

1988, Dec. 10

1342 A230 80f multicolored .75 .60
1343 A230 160f multicolored 1.75 1.10

Arab Cooperation Council, Feb. 16 — A231

1989 Litho. *Perf. 13½x13*

1344 A231 10f shown .20 .20
1345 A231 30f multi, diff. .20 .20
1346 A231 40f multi, diff. .20 .20
1347 A231 60f multi, diff. 1.00 .95
Nos. 1344-1347 (4) 1.60 1.55

Martyrs of Palestine and Their Families — A232

1989 *Perf. 14½*

1348 A232 5f multi .25 .20
1349 A232 10f multi .25 .20

Interparliamentary Union, Cent. — A233

1989 Litho. *Perf. 12*

1350 A233 40f multicolored .35 .20
1351 A233 60f multicolored .55 .35

Arab Housing Day and World Refuge Day A234

Designs: 5f, Housing complex, emblems, vert. 60f, Housing complex, emblem.

1989

1352 A234 5f multicolored .20 .20
1353 A234 40f shown .55 .20
1354 A234 60f multicolored .75 .55
Nos. 1352-1354 (3) 1.50 .95

Ministry of Agriculture, 50th Anniv. — A235

1989 Litho. *Perf. 12*

1355 A235 5f shown .20 .20
1356 A235 40f Tree, anniv. emblem .20 .20
1357 A235 60f Fruit tree, emblem, apiary 2.25 .20
Nos. 1355-1357 (3) 2.65 .60

Arabian Horse Festival A236

1989 *Perf. 12*

1358 A236 5f shown .40 .20
1359 A236 40f Horse, building facade .85 .20
1360 A236 60f Horse's head, vert. 2.40 .20
Nos. 1358-1360 (3) 3.65 .60

Size: 90x70mm

Imperf

1361 A236 100f Mare and foal0 25.00 22.50

Natl. Library Assoc. A237

1989 *Perf. 12*

1362 A237 40f multicolored .20 .20
1363 A237 60f multicolored 1.00 .20

Mosque of the Martyr King Abdullah — A238

1989 *Perf. 12*

1364 A238 40f multicolored .20 .20
1365 A238 60f multicolored 1.00 .20

Size: 90x70mm

Imperf

1366 A238 100f multicolored 6.75 6.75

Mosaics A239

1989, Dec. 23 Litho. *Perf. 12*

1367 A239 5f Man with Basket .60 .30
1368 A239 10f Building .60 .30
1369 A239 40f Deer 1.50 .50
1370 A239 60f Man with stick 2.00 .65
1371 A239 80f Town, horiz. 2.50 .90
Nos. 1367-1371 (5) 7.20 2.65

Size: 90x70mm

Imperf

1372 A239 100f like #1371, horiz. 17.50 17.50

Arab Cooperation Council, 1st Anniv. — A240

1990, Feb. 16 *Perf. 13*

1373 A240 5f multicolored .20 .20
1374 A240 20f multicolored .20 .20
1375 A240 60f multicolored .75 .45
1376 A240 80f multicolored 1.00 .65
Nos. 1373-1376 (4) 2.15 1.50

Nature Conservation — A241

1990, Apr. 22

1377 A241 40f Horses .20 .20
1378 A241 60f Mountain .50 .20
1379 A241 80f Oasis .65 .35
Nos. 1377-1379 (3) 1.35 .75

Prince Abdullah's Arrival in Ma'an, 70th Anniv. — A243

1990 Litho. *Perf. 13½x13*

1382 A243 40f org & multi .20 .20
1383 A243 60f grn & multi .40 .20

Size: 90x70mm

Imperf

1384 A243 200f multicolored 7.00 7.00

UN Development Program, 40th Anniv. — A244

1990 *Perf. 13*

1385 A244 60f multicolored .25 .20
1386 A244 80f multicolored .55 .20

King Hussein — A245

1990-92 Litho. *Perf. 12x13½*

1387 A245 5f yel org & multi .25 .25
1390 A245 20f blue green & multi .25 .25
1391 A245 40f orange & multi .25 .25
1393 A245 60f blue & multi .45 .45
1395 A245 80f pink & multi .70 .70
1397 A245 240f brown & multi 1.25 .90
1398 A245 320f red lilac & multi 1.75 1.25
1399 A245 1d yel green & multi 2.75 2.40
Nos. 1387-1399 (8) 7.65 6.45

#1390 dated 1991.

Issued: 20f, 1992; 5f, 60f, 80f 1990; others 1991.

Nos. 1387, 1395 exist dated "1991," with slightly larger vignette.

Endangered Animals A246

1991, Sept. 1 Litho. *Perf. 13x13½*

1401 A246 5f Nubian ibex .20 .20
1402 A246 40f Onager .50 .25
1403 A246 80f Arabian gazelle 2.25 .40
1404 A246 160f Arabian oryx 1.60 1.10
Nos. 1401-1404 (4) 4.55 1.95

Energy Rationalization Program — A247

Designs: 5f, Light bulbs. 40f, Solar panels, sun, vert. 80f, Electric table lamp, vert.

Perf. 13½x13, 13x13½

1991, Oct. 3 Litho.

1405 A247 5f multicolored .20 .20
1406 A247 40f multicolored .20 .20
1407 A247 80f multicolored .70 .20
Nos. 1405-1407 (3) 1.10 .60

Grain Production for Food Security — A248

1991, Oct. 16 *Perf. 13½x13*

1408 A248 5f Different grains .20 .20
1409 A248 40f shown .20 .20
1410 A248 80f Wheat stalk, kernels .70 .20
Nos. 1408-1410 (3) 1.10 .60

Palestinian Uprising — A249

1991, Nov. 29 Litho. *Perf. 11*

1411 A249 20f multicolored 1.10 .75

Blood Donation Campaign — A250

1991, Nov. 14 Litho. *Perf. 13½x13*

1412 A250 80f multicolored .75 .20
1413 A250 160f multicolored 1.50 .75

Expo '92, Seville A251

1992, Feb. 20

1414 A251 80f multicolored .65 .20
1415 A251 320f multicolored 1.60 .95

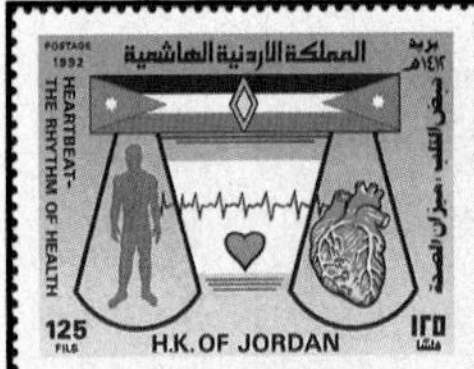

Healthy Hearts A252

80f, Man & woman, heart at center of scale, vert.

Perf. 13x13½, 13½x13

1992, Apr. 7 Litho.

1416 A252 80f multicolored .70 .20
1417 A252 125f multicolored .80 .50

SOS Children's Village, 'Aqaba — A253

1992, Apr. 30 Litho. *Perf. 13½x13*

1418 A253 80f shown .70 .20
1419 A253 125f Village .80 .50

1992 Summer Olympics, Barcelona — A254

Stylized designs with Barcelona Olympic emblem: 5fr, Judo, 40f, Runner, vert. 80f, Diver. 125f, Flag, Cobi, map, vert. 160f, Table tennis.

100f, Incorporates all designs of set.

Perf. 13½x13, 13x13½

1992, July 25 Litho.

1420 A254 5f multicolored .20 .20
1421 A254 40f multicolored .20 .20
1422 A254 80f multicolored .50 .20
1423 A254 125f multicolored .75 .35
1424 A254 160f multicolored 1.10 .50
Nos. 1420-1424 (5) 2.75 1.45

Size: 70x90mm

Imperf

1425 A254 100f multicolored *15.00 12.00*

King Hussein, 40th Anniv. of Accession — A255

Designs: 40f, Flags, King in full dress uniform, vert. 125f, King wearing headdress, flags. 160f, King in business suit, crown. 200f, Portrait.

1992, Aug. 11 *Perf. 13x13½*

1426 A255 40f multicolored .20 .20

Perf. 13½x13

1427 A255 80f shown .45 .20
1428 A255 125f multicolored .75 .35
1429 A255 160f multicolored 1.10 .50
Nos. 1426-1429 (4) 2.50 1.25

Size: 90x70mm

Imperf

1430 A255 200f multicolored *7.25 7.25*

Butterflies — A256

5f, Danaus chrysippus. 40f, Aporia cartaegi. 80f, Papilio machaon. 160f, Pseudochazara telephassa. 200f, Same as #1431-1434.

1992, Dec. 20 Litho. *Perf. 13½x13*

1431 A256 5f multicolored .30 .20
1432 A256 40f multicolored .75 .25
1433 A256 80f multicolored 1.25 .40
1434 A256 160f multicolored 2.75 1.00
Nos. 1431-1434 (4) 5.05 1.85

Imperf

Size: 90x70mm

1435 A256 200f multicolored *16.00 16.00*

See Nos. 1448-1452.

Intl. Customs Day — A257

1993, Jan. 26 Litho. *Perf. 13½x13*

1436 A257 80f green & multi .60 .20
1437 A257 125f pale orange & multi .90 .45

Royal Scientific Society — A258

1993, June 10 Litho. *Perf. 12½x13*

1438 A258 80f multicolored .50 .20

Es Salt Municipality, Cent. — A259

1993, Sept. 1 Litho. *Perf. 12*

1439 A259 80f pink & multi .60 .20
1440 A259 125f green & multi .90 .45
a. Souvenir sheet of 2, #1439-1440, imperf. *6.25 6.25*

No. 1440a sold for 200f.

Great Arab Revolt and Army Day A260

Designs: 5f, Rockets, planes, tank, King Hussein, 40f, King Hussein, military activities. 80f, Amir Abdullah ibn Hussein, Dome of the Rock, map, flags. 125f, Amir Abdullah ibn Hussein, Dome of the Rock, riders. 100f, King Hussein, flags.

1993, June 10

1441 A260 5f multicolored .20 .20
1442 A260 40f multicolored .20 .20
1443 A260 80f multicolored .50 .20
1444 A260 125f multicolored .85 .35
Nos. 1441-1444 (4) 1.75 .95

Size: 90x70mm

Imperf

1445 A260 100f multicolored *6.00 6.00*

White Cane Day A261

Design: 125f, Lighted world, cane, eye, vert.

1993, Oct. 23 Litho. *Perf. 12*

1446 A261 80f shown .60 .20
1447 A261 125f multicolored .90 .45

Butterfly Type of 1992

Designs: 5f, Lampides boeticus. 40f, Melanargria titea. 80f, Allancastria deyrollei. 160f, Gonepteryx cleopatra. 100f, Same designs as Nos. 1448-1451.

1993, Oct. 10 Litho. *Perf. 12*

1448 A256 5f multicolored .40 .20
1449 A256 40f multicolored .75 .30
1450 A256 80f multicolored 1.00 .40
1451 A256 160f multicolored 2.50 1.00
Nos. 1448-1451 (4) 4.65 1.90

Size: 83x65mm

Imperf

1452 A256 100f multicolored *25.00 25.00*

UN Declaration of Human Rights, 45th Anniv. — A262

1993, Dec. 10 *Perf. 12*

1453 A262 40f yellow & multi .20 .20
1454 A262 160f red & multi 1.10 .75

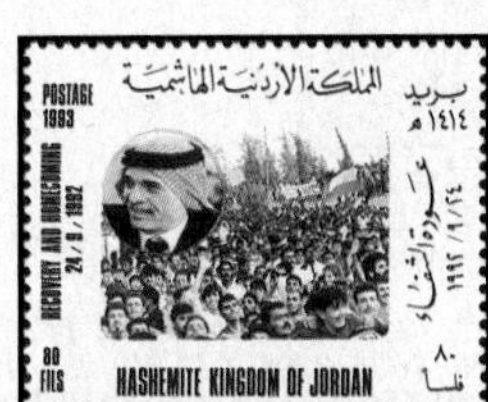

Recovery & Homecoming, 1st Anniv. — A263

King Hussein: 80f, Crowd. 125f, Waving to people. 160f, Embracing woman. 100f, Standing on airplane ramp.

1993, Nov. 25

1455 A263 80f multicolored .50 .20
1456 A263 125f multicolored .85 .40
1457 A263 160f multicolored 1.00 .50
Nos. 1455-1457 (3) 2.35 1.10

Size: 85x65

Imperf

1458 A263 100f multicolored *5.50 3.75*

World AIDS Day — A264

1993, Dec. 1 ***Perf. 12***
1459 A264 80f red & multi .50 .20
1460 A264 125f green & multi .85 .45

Size: 83x70mm

Imperf

1461 A264 200f like #1459-1460 *6.25 4.50*

King Hussein A265

King Hussein wearing: 40f, Military uniform. 80f, Traditional costume. 125f, Business suit. 160f, 100f, Dress uniform in portrait with Queen Noor, horiz.

1993, Nov. 14 ***Perf. 12***
1462 A265 40f multi, horiz. .20 .20
1463 A265 80f multi, horiz. .50 .20
1464 A265 125f multi, horiz. .80 .35
1465 A265 160f multicolored 1.25 .50
Nos. 1462-1465 (4) 2.75 1.25

Size: 82x68mm

Imperf

1466 A265 100f multicolored *8.00 5.75*

Assumption of Constitutional Powers by King Hussein, 40th anniv.

Saladin (1138-1193), Dome of the Rock — A266

1993, Nov. 25 ***Perf. 12***
1467 A266 40f blue & multi .20 .20
1468 A266 80f gray & multi .55 .20
1469 A266 125f yellow & multi .75 .40
Nos. 1467-1469 (3) 1.50 .80

Triumphal Arch, Jerash — A267

Perf. 12x13½ (5f, No. 80f, 1473A, 1475, 160f, 320f, 1d), 12 (25f, 40f, 50f, #1474C, 240f, No. 1478C, No. 1479), 14x13½ (75f, No. 1474, 150f, 200f, 300f, 400f), 13½x14 (#120f), 12¾x13¼ (#1479B)

1993-98 **Litho.**
1470 A267 5f blue & multi .20 .20
1471 A267 25f pale violet & multi .20 .20
1471A A267 40f green & multi .20 .20
1472 A267 50f yellow & multi .25 .25
b. Perf 12¾x13¼ .25 .25
c. Perf 13½x14 .25 .25
1472A A267 75f buff & multi .40 .40
1473 A267 80f green & multi .35 .20
1473A A267 100f red & multi .40 .20
b. Perf. 12 .40 .20
1474 A267 100f apple green & multi .50 .50
a. Perf. 12 .50 .50
1474B A267 120f bl grn & multi .65 .65
1474C A267 125f lt bl & multi .60 .60
1475 A267 125f buff & multi .50 .20
a. Perf. 12 .50 .20
1475B A267 150f salmon pink & multi .90 .90
1476 A267 160f yellow & multi .65 .25
b. Perf. 12 .75 .25
1476A A267 200f gray & multi 1.10 1.10
c. Perf. 12 1.10 1.10
1477 A267 240f pink & multi 1.00 .25
b. Perf. 12x13½ .90 .25
1477A A267 300f pink & multi 1.75 1.75
c. Perf. 12 1.75 1.75
1478 A267 320f brown & multi 1.25 .35
1478A A267 320f sal & multi 1.25 .35
1478C A267 400f bright blue & multi 2.50 2.50
b. Perf. 13x13¼ 2.50 2.50
1479 A267 500f bister & multi 2.00 .85
a. Perf. 12x13½ 2.00 .85
1479B A267 500f yel & multi 2.50 2.50
1480 A267 1d olive & multi 4.00 1.25
a. Perf. 12¾x13¼ 5.00 1.25
Nos. 1470-1480 (22) 23.15 15.65

#Nos. 1472A, 1473, 1473A , 1477b, 1479a are dated 1992; Nos. #1471A, 1473Ab, 1476b, 1993; No. 1474, 1994; No. 1477Ac, 1995; Nos. 1478Ab, 1479B, 1480a, 1997.

Issued: 5f, 320f, 1/13/93 (dated 1992); 25f, 1/18/96 (dated 1995); 40f, 1994; 100f, 200f, 300f, 5/15/96; 1d, 1/13/93; 125f, 160f, 1/13/93; 240f, 3/23/94; 50f, 1995; 150f, 400f, 5/15/96; 500f, 10/25/96; 75f, 5/15/96; #1478Ab, 5/10/98. 80f, Nos. 1473A, 1477b, 1479a, 1/13/93; Nos. 1473Ab, 1476b, 3/23/94; 120f, 5/15/96; No. 1474C, 2/13/95; Nos. 1476Ac, 1477Ac, 1/18/96; No. 1478C, 1993; Nos. 1479B, 1480a, 5/10/98.

No. 1472 exists dated "1996." Nos. 1476b, 1477 exist dated "1994."

No. 1472b exists dated 2003.

No. 1474a exists dated "1995" and "1996."

This is an expanding set. Numbers may change. Numbers have been reserved for additional values in this set.

Hashemite Charity Organization — A268

Designs: 80f, Loading supplies into plane. 125f, People gathering at plane.

1994, Mar. 20 **Litho.** ***Perf. 12***
1481 A268 80f multicolored .55 .20
1482 A268 125f multicolored .80 .50

Third Hashemite Restoration of Al Aqsa Mosque, Dome of the Rock — A269

King Hussein with various scenes of restoration.

1994, Apr. 18 **Litho.** ***Perf. 12x12½***
1483 A269 80f yellow & multi .40 .20
1484 A269 125f lt orange & multi .70 .35
1485 A269 240f lilac & multi 1.25 .60
Nos. 1483-1485 (3) 2.35 1.15

Imperf

Size: 90x70mm

1486 A269 100f green & multi *8.00 5.50*

ILO, 75th Anniv. A270

1994, June 13 **Litho.** ***Perf. 12***
1487 A270 80f yellow & multi .45 .20
1488 A270 125f brt pink & multi .70 .35

Intl. Red Cross and Red Crescent Societies, 75th Anniv. — A271

1994, May 8 ***Perf. 12***
1489 A271 80f shown .45 .20
1490 A271 160f Doves, emblems, vert .80 .45

Size: 61x78mm

Imperf

1491 A271 200f #1489-1490 *11.00 8.25*

Intl. Year of the Family A272

1994, Aug. 11 **Litho.** ***Perf. 12***
1492 A272 80f green & multi .45 .20
1493 A272 125f pink & multi .80 .40
1494 A272 160f yellow & multi 1.00 .45
Nos. 1492-1494 (3) 2.25 1.05

Intl. Olympic Committee, Cent. — A273

Olympic rings and: 80f, Globe, venue symbols, vert. 100f, Jordanian colors. 125f, Venue symbols, diff., vert. 160f, shown. 240f, Torch.

1994, June 23
1495 A273 80f blue & multi .40 .20
1496 A273 125f multicolored .65 .30
1497 A273 160f multicolored 1.10 .40
1498 A273 240f multicolored 1.60 .65
Nos. 1495-1498 (4) 3.75 1.55

Size: 90x70mm

Imperf

1499 A273 100f multicolored *8.50 8.50*

Jordanian Participation in UN Peacekeeping Forces — A274

Designs: 80f, King Hussein greeting troops. 125f, King inspecting troops. 160f, Checkpoint.

1994, Aug. 11 **Litho.** ***Perf. 12***
1500 A274 80f multicolored .45 .20
1501 A274 125f multicolored .70 .35
1502 A274 160f multicolored .85 .45
Nos. 1500-1502 (3) 2.00 1.00

Water Conservation Day — A275

80f, Hands, water droplet. 125f, Water faucet, foods, factory. 160f, Child, rain drops.

1994, Nov. 14 **Litho.** ***Perf. 14***
1503 A275 80f multicolored .60 .20
1504 A275 125f multicolored 1.00 .55
1505 A275 160f multicolored 1.25 .60
Nos. 1503-1505 (3) 2.85 1.35

ICAO, 50th Anniv. A276

1994, Oct. 25 ***Perf. 12***
1506 A276 80f green & multi .45 .20
1507 A276 125f red & multi .70 .35
1508 A276 160f blue & multi .85 .45
Nos. 1506-1508 (3) 2.00 1.00

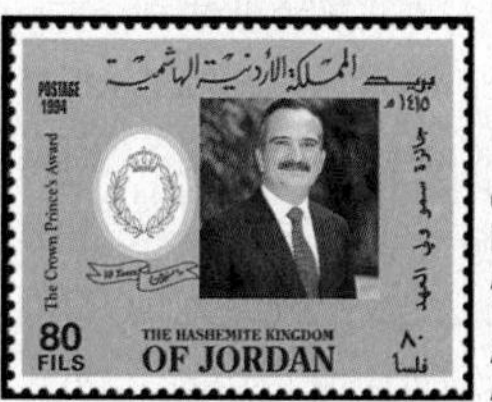

Crown Prince's Award, 10th Anniv. A277

1994, Dec. 11 **Litho.** ***Perf. 12***
1509 A277 80f yel grn & multi .70 .20
1510 A277 125f org brn & multi .90 .55
1511 A277 160f vio bl & multi 1.25 .70
Nos. 1509-1511 (3) 2.85 1.45

UN, 50th Anniv. A278

1995, Apr. 1 **Litho.** ***Perf. 14***
1512 A278 80f green & multi .65 .20
1513 A278 125f pink & multi .95 .55

May Day A279

80f, Emblem, workers, flag. 125f, Emblem, world map, worker. 160f, Hands holding wrench, torch, Jordanian map, emblem.

1995, May 1
1514 A279 80f multicolored .45 .20
1515 A279 125f multicolored .65 .40
1516 A279 160f multicolored .90 .45
Nos. 1514-1516 (3) 2.00 1.05

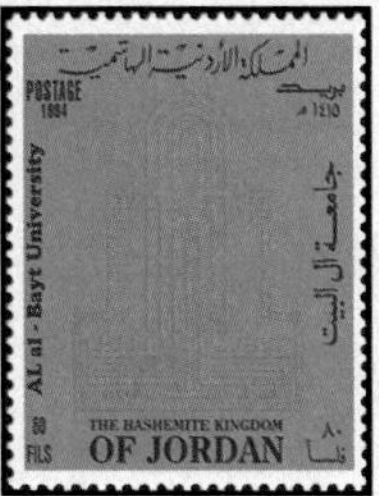

Jordan Week in Japan A280

Globe in two hemishperes with olive branches and: 125f, Japanese, Jordanian flags. 160f, Flags above wall.

1995, May 22 Litho. *Perf. 14*

1517 A280 80f green & multi .45 .20
1518 A280 125f pink & multi .70 .30
1519 A280 160f gray & multi .85 .45
Nos. 1517-1519 (3) 2.00 .95

Opening of Al al-Bayt University A281

1995, Feb. 8 Litho. *Perf. 12*

1520 A281 80f green blue & multi .50 .20
1521 A281 125f olive green & multi .75 .40
a. Souvenir sheet, #1520-1521, imperf. 3.75 3.25

No. 1521a sold for 200f. Nos. 1520-1521 are dated 1994.

Petra, the Rose City A282

Archaeological discoveries: 50f, Amphitheater. 75f, Facial carvings, bowl, pitcher. 80f, Columns of building, vert. 160f, Front of building with columns, vert. 200f, Building in side of mountain.

1995, Aug. 11 Litho. *Perf. 14*

1524 A282 50f multicolored .20 .20
1525 A282 75f multicolored .85 .20
1526 A282 80f multicolored .95 .20
1527 A282 160f multicolored 1.75 .95
Nos. 1524-1527 (4) 3.75 1.55

Size: 90x70mm

Imperf

1528 A282 200f multicolored *20.00 20.00*

Arab League, 50th Anniv. A283

1995, Sept. 20 Litho. *Perf. 14*

1529 A283 80f green & multi .45 .20
1530 A283 125f pink & multi .70 .20
1531 A283 160f gray & multi .85 .45
Nos. 1529-1531 (3) 2.00 .85

FAO, 50th Anniv. A284

Designs: 125f, "50," FAO emblem, shafts of grain. 160f, UN, FAO emblems, "50."

1995, Oct. 16 Litho. *Perf. 14*

1532 A284 80f shown .50 .20
1533 A284 125f multicolored .85 .40
1534 A284 160f multicolored 1.00 .50
Nos. 1532-1534 (3) 2.35 1.10

Middle East and North Africa Economic Summit, Amman — A285

1995, Oct. 29 *Perf. 12*

1535 A285 80f brt pink & multi .50 .20
1536 A285 125f org yel & multi .75 .40

The Deaf A286

1995, Nov. 30 *Perf. 14*

1537 A286 80f shown .50 .20
1538 A286 125f Emblems, hand sign .75 .35

King Hussein, 60th Birthday A287

Designs: 40f, Crown over King's picture in business suit. 80f, Crown, flag, dove, ruins of Petra, King in traditional head wear, military uniform. 100f, King dress uniform, crown, "60." 125f, King in traditional head wear, business suit, crown, flag, olive branch. 160f, Flag, King in business suit. 200f, "60," Dome of the Rock, King in dress uniform, olive branch.

1995, Nov. 14

1539 A287 25f multicolored .20 .20
1540 A287 40f multicolored .20 .20
1541 A287 80f multicolored .45 .20
1542 A287 100f multicolored .50 .20
1543 A287 125f multicolored 1.00 .35
1544 A287 160f multicolored 1.25 .45
Nos. 1539-1544 (6) 3.60 1.60

Size: 83x63mm

Imperf

1545 A287 200f multicolored *6.25 6.25*

Independence, 50th Anniv. — A288

King Hussein and: No. 1547, Outline map of Jordan, crown, dove of peace, Amir Abdullah ibn Hussein. 300f, Jordanian monuments, flag.

No. 1549, Map of Jordan surrounded by wreath, dove, national flags.

1996, May 25 Litho. *Perf. 12*

1546 A288 100f multicolored .55 .20
1547 A288 200f multicolored 1.10 .40
1548 A288 300f multicolored 1.75 .65
Nos. 1546-1548 (3) 3.40 1.25

Size: 86x66mm

1549 A288 200f multicolored *7.50 7.50*

1996 Summer Olympic Games, Atlanta A289

1996 Olympic Games Emblem and: 50f, Natl. flag, Olympic rings, sports pictograms. 100f, Sports pictograms. 200f, Hands. 300f, Torch, Olympic rings, natl. flag.

1996, July 19 Litho. *Perf. 12*

1550 A289 50f multicolored .20 .20
1551 A289 100f multicolored .70 .20
1552 A289 200f multicolored 1.60 .70
1553 A289 300f multicolored 2.50 1.10
Nos. 1550-1553 (4) 5.00 2.20

Protection of the Ozone Layer — A290

1996, Sept. 16

1554 A290 100f multicolored 1.25 .20

UNICEF, 50th Anniv. — A291

1996, Dec. 11 Litho. *Perf. 12*

1555 A291 100f green & multi .60 .20
1556 A291 200f gray lilac & multi 1.00 .60

Crown Prince El-Hassan, 50th Birthday — A292

Designs: 50f, On horseback. 100f, Wearing suit & tie, vert. No. 1559, Natl. flag, wearing traditional attire.

No. 1560, Wearing graduation cap.

1997, Mar. 20 Litho. *Perf. 12*

1557 A292 50f multicolored .20 .20
1558 A292 100f multicolored .70 .20
1559 A292 200f multicolored 1.10 .70
Nos. 1557-1559 (3) 2.00 1.10

Size: 84x64mm

Imperf

1560 A292 200f multicolored *8.25 8.25*

Heinrich von Stephan (1831-97) A293

1997, Apr. 8 Litho. *Perf. 12*

1561 A293 100f multicolored .90 .20
1562 A293 200f multicolored 1.60 .80

Discovery of the Madeba Mosaic Map, Cent. — A294

1997, Apr. 7

1563 A294 100f Karak, vert. .75 .35
1564 A294 200f River Jordan 1.50 .50
1565 A294 300f Jerusalem, vert. 2.50 .90
Nos. 1563-1565 (3) 4.75 1.75

Size: 86x67mm

Imperf

1566 A294 100f Entire map *15.00 15.00*

Jordanian Rosefinch — A295

1997, May 25 Litho. *Perf. 12*

1567 A295 50f multicolored .20 .20
1568 A295 100f multi, diff. .65 .20
1569 A295 150f multi, diff. 1.00 .45
1570 A295 200f multi, diff. 1.50 .65
Nos. 1567-1570 (4) 3.35 1.50

Jerash Festival, 15th Anniv. A296

Designs: 50f, Couples in traditional costumes, ruins. 100f, Symphony orchestra, silhouettes of buildings. 150f, Pillars, parade of dignitaries. 200f, Women in traditional costumes, crowd, ruins.

15d, Queen Noor lighting torch.

1997, July 23 Litho. *Perf. 12*

1571 A296 50f multicolored .20 .20
1572 A296 100f multicolored .60 .20
1573 A296 150f multicolored .95 .45
1574 A296 200f multicolored 1.50 .65
Nos. 1571-1574 (4) 3.25 1.50

Size: 90x70mm

Imperf

1575 A296 15d multicolored 8.50 8.50

Natl. Forum for Women A297

Emblem and: 50f, Women in tradtional and modern dress, vert. 100f, Natl. flag, flame, book. 150fr, Natl. flag, women seated at conference table.

1997, Dec. 20 Litho. *Perf. 12*

1576 A297 50f multicolored .20 .20
1577 A297 100f multicolored .50 .20
1578 A297 150f multicolored .80 .35
Nos. 1576-1578 (3) 1.50 .75

Jordanian Team, 1997 Arab Soccer Champions — A298

Designs: 50f, Team parading in stadium. 75f, Team in red uniforms. 100f, Team in white uniforms, ceremony.
200f, Formal presentation to King Hussein, motorcade.

1997, Dec. 15

1579 A298 50f multicolored .20 .20
1580 A298 75f multicolored .40 .20
1581 A298 100f multicolored .55 .20
Nos. 1579-1581 (3) 1.15 .60

Size: 91x70mm

Imperf

1582 A298 200f multicolored *9.00 7.50*

House of Parliament, 50th Anniv. — A299

100f, Outside view of building, drawing. 200f, Speaker, members assembled in chamber.

1997, Nov. 1 ***Perf. 12½***

1583 A299 100f multicolored .60 .20
1584 A299 200f multicolored .90 .60

53rd General Meeting of Intl. Air Transport Association A300

1997, Nov. 3 Litho. ***Perf. 13x13½***

1585 A300 100f lt blue & multi 1.00 1.00
1586 A300 200f red & multi 1.00 1.00
1587 A300 300f gray & multi 1.00 1.00

Two additional stamps were issued in this set. The editors would like to examine them.

King Hussein II, 62nd Birthday A301

1997, Nov. 14 Litho. ***Perf. 13x13½***

Frame Color

1588 A301 100f red 1.00 1.00
1589 A301 200f gold 1.00 1.00
1590 A301 300f blue 1.00 1.00

Souvenir Sheet

Perf. 12

1590A A301 200f gold 8.50 8.50

No. 1590A contains one 44x60mm stamp.

Earth Day A302

Children's drawings: 50f, Various ways of polluting air and water. 100f, Pollution from factory smoke, automobiles. 150f, Earth chained to various methods of pollution, vert.

1998, Apr. 29 Litho. ***Perf. 14***

1591 A302 50f multicolored .20 .20
1592 A302 100f multicolored .50 .20
1593 A302 150f multicolored .80 .50
Nos. 1591-1593 (3) 1.50 .90

Trans-Jordan Emirate, 75th Anniv. — A303

Designs: 100f, Camel rider holding flag, Amir Abdullah ibn Hussein. 200f, Camel rider holding flag, King Hussein. 300f, King Hussein, arms, #81, Amir Abdullah ibn Hussein.

1998, May 25 ***Perf. 12***

1594 A303 100f multicolored .50 .50
1595 A303 200f multicolored 1.00 1.00
1596 A303 300f multicolored 1.75 1.75
Nos. 1594-1596 (3) 3.25 3.25

Size: 80x70mm

Imperf

1597 A303 300f like #1596 *8.50 8.50*

Mosaics, Um Ar-Rasas A304

1998, July 22 Litho. ***Perf. 14***

1598 A304 100f multicolored .50 .50
1599 A304 200f multi, diff. 1.00 1.00
1600 A304 300f multi, diff. 1.75 1.75
Nos. 1598-1600 (3) 3.25 3.25

Flowers A305

1998, July 7

1601 A305 50f purple & white, thorns .30 .25
1602 A305 100f Poppies .60 .55
1603 A305 150f shown 1.00 .75
Nos. 1601-1603 (3) 1.90 1.55

Size: 60x80mm

Imperf

1604 A305 200f Flower, map of Jordan *8.50 8.50*

2nd Arab Beekeepers Conference — A306

Various pictures of bees, flowers, honeycomb.

1998, Aug. 3 Litho. ***Perf. 14***

1605 A306 50f multicolored .50 .40
1606 A306 100f multi, vert. .85 .50
1607 A306 150f multicolored 1.25 .60
Nos. 1605-1607 (3) 2.60 1.50

Size: 80x60mm

Imperf

1608 A306 200f Bees, flowers, emblem *9.00 9.00*

World Stamp Day A307

1998, Oct. 9 Litho. ***Perf. 14***

1609 A307 50f shown .20 .20
1610 A307 100f World map, emblems .90 .90
1611 A307 150f Globe, stamps 1.75 1.75
Nos. 1609-1611 (3) 2.85 2.85

Universal Declaration of Human Rights, 50th Anniv. — A308

1998, Dec. 10

1612 A308 100f shown .60 .60
1613 A308 200f Emblems, people 1.00 1.00

King Hussein, 63rd Birthday A309

1998, Nov. 14 Litho. ***Perf. 14x14½***

1614 A309 100f green & multi .65 .45
1615 A309 200f violet & multi 1.25 1.00
1616 A309 300f violet blue & multi 2.25 1.50
Nos. 1614-1616 (3) 4.15 2.95

Size: 90x70mm

Imperf

1617 A309 300f gold & multi *8.50 8.50*

Arab Police and Security Chiefs Meeting, 25th Anniv. (in 1997) A310

Map of Arab world and: 100f, King Hussein, emblem. 200f, Flags of Arab countries, emblem, flame, vert. 300f, Beret.

1998, Nov. 18 ***Perf. 14***

1618 A310 100f multicolored .65 .65
1619 A310 200f multicolored 1.10 1.10
1620 A310 300f multicolored 2.00 1.75
Nos. 1618-1620 (3) 3.75 3.50

Mustafa Wahbi (1899-1949), Poet — A311

1999, May 25 Litho. ***Perf. 14¼***

1621 A311 100f multicolored .90 .90

Environmental Protection — A312

Designs: 100f, Children, bandaged Earth. 200f, Earth as fruit in hands.

1999, Oct. 14 Litho. ***Perf. 13¼x13¾***

1622 A312 100f multi .50 .50
1623 A312 200f multi 1.00 1.00

Hijazi Railway Museum A313

Train and: 100f, 200f, Map of Jordan, museum building. 300f, Museum building.

1999, Sept. 7 Litho. ***Perf. 13½x13¾***

1624-1626 A313 Set of 3 6.00 6.00

9th Arab Sports Tournament — A314

Bird mascot, emblem and: 50f, Weight lifting, tennis, wrestling, soccer. 100f, Torch. No. 1629, Shooting, fencing, swimming, track & field, vert. 300f, Flag, map, discus thrower, tennis player.
No. 1631, Basketball, volleyball, boxing, swimming.

Perf. 13¼x13¾, 13¾x13¼

1999, Aug. 15 Litho.

1627 A314 50f multi .20 .20
1628 A314 100f multi .65 .65
1629 A314 200f multi 1.40 1.40
1630 A314 300f multi 2.25 2.25
Nos. 1627-1630 (4) 4.50 4.50

Imperf

Size: 90x70mm

1631 A314 200f multi 3.25 3.25

UPU, 125th Anniv. A315

Designs: 100f, "125," UPU emblems, stripes of airmail envelope. No. 1633, Airmail envelope with UPU emblem.

No. 1634, Like No. 1633, yellow background.

1999, Oct. 9 *Perf. 13¼x13¾*

1632 A315 100f multi .65 .65
1633 A315 200f multi 1.10 1.10

Imperf

Size: 90x70mm

1634 A315 200f multi 2.50 2.50

Gulf of Aqaba Corals A316

Designs: 50f, Pachyseris speciosa. 100f, Acropora digitifera. No. 1637, 200f, Oxypora lacera. 300f, Fungia echinata.

No. 1639, 200f, Gorgonia.

1999, Oct. 2 **Litho.** *Perf. 13½x13¾*

1635-1638 A316 Set of 4 4.00 4.00

Imperf

Size: 90x70mm

1639 A316 200f multi *12.00 12.00*

Cradle of Civilizations — A317

Archaeological sites — Petra: No. 1640, 100f, Al-Deir. No. 1641, 200f, Khazneh. No. 1642, 300f, Obelisk tomb.

Jerash: No. 1643, 100f, Cardo Maximus. No. 1644, 200f, Temple of Artemis. No. 1645, 300f, Nymphaeum.

Amman: No. 1646, 100f, Roman Theater. No. 1647, 200f, Citadel. No. 1648, 300f, Ain Ghazal statues.

Wadi Rum and Aqaba: No. 1649, 100f, Camel riders, Wadi Rum. No. 1650, 200f, House, Aqaba. No. 1651, Ruins, Aqaba.

Madaba: No. 1652, 100f, Mosaic. No. 1653, 200f, Church. No. 1654, 300f, Mosaic map of Jerusalem.

Baptism Site (Bethany): No. 1655, Plant life near water. No. 1656, 200f, Aerial view. No. 1657, 300f, Excavation site.

Aljoun: No. 1658, 100f, Ruins. No. 1659, 200f, Ruins diff. No. 1660, 300f, Ruins, diff.

Pella: No. 1661, 100f, Ruins of Byzantine cathedral. No. 1662, 200f, Three large pillars. No. 1663, 300f, Ruins.

1999-2000 **Litho.** *Perf. 13½x14*

1640-1663 A317 Set of 12 23.00 23.00

Issued: #1640-1645, 10/24; #1646-1651, 10/31; #1652-1654, 12/22; #1655-1657, 12/23; #1658-1663, 3/7/00.

See Nos. 1688-1693.

Museum of Political History — A318

100f, Building interior. 200f, Museum entrance and plaza. 300f, Museum entrance.

1999, Nov. 14 **Litho.** *Perf. 13½x14*

1664-1666 A318 Set of 3 3.75 3.75

Jordan Philatelic Club, 20th Anniv. — A318a

Designs: 100f, #534H and other stamps. 200f, #284 and other stamps.

1999, Nov. 14 *Perf. 14¼*

1666A-1666B A318a Set of 2 1.50 1.50

SOS Children's Village, Irbid — A318b

100f, SOS Children's Village 50th anniv. emblem, Jordanian flag. 200f, Woman, children.

1999, Nov. 23

1666C-1666D A318b Set of 2 1.50 1.50

Coronation of King Abdullah II — A319

1999, Dec. 27 **Litho.** *Perf. 11¾*

Frame Color

1667 A319 100f red .90 .90
1668 A319 200f green .90 .90
1669 A319 300f blue .90 .90

Souvenir Sheet

1670 A319 200f gold 1.00 1.00

King Abdullah II and Queen Rania A319a

1999, Dec. 27 **Litho.** *Perf. 11¾*

1670A A319a 100f red .95 .95
1670B A319a 200f green .95 .95
1670C A319a 300f blue .95 .95

Souvenir Sheet

1670D A319a 200f gold *5.25 5.25*

Issued: 1670D, 12/27/99.

Numbers have been reserved for three additional stamps in this set. The editors would like to examine any examples of them.

King Abdullah II, 38th Birthday A320

King, crown and: 100f, Olive branches. 200f, Nos. #1672 #1674, Flag, "38," horiz. 300f, Flag, "38," eagle, olive branch, horiz.

Perf 12, Imperf (#1674)

2000, Jan. 30 **Litho.**

1671-1673 A320 Set of 3 3.00 3.00

Size: 90x74mm

1674 A320 200f multi *3.50 3.50*

Geneva Convention, 50th Anniv. — A321

Perf. 13½x13¾

2000, Feb. 15 **Litho.**

1675 Horiz. strip of 3 3.50 3.50
a. A321 100f lt bl & multi .50 .50
b. A321 200f ocher & multi 1.00 1.00
c. A321 300f gray & multi 1.50 1.50

Dated 1999.

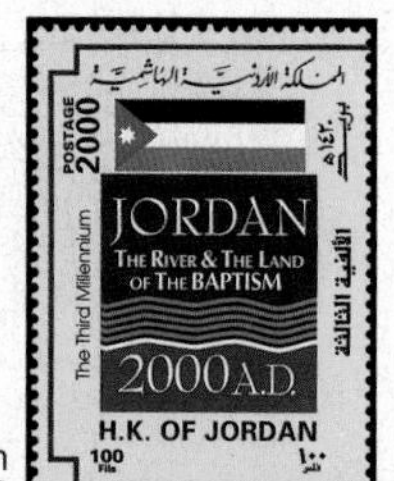

Millennium A322

No. 1678: a, Jordanian flag, "Jordan, The River & The Land of the Baptism" in English. b, Fish in river. c, As "a," with Arabic inscription.

Perf. 13¼x13¾

2000, Feb. 22 **Litho.**

1678 Strip of 3 3.25 3.25
a. A322 100f multi .45 .45
b. A322 200f multi .90 .90
c. A322 300f multi 1.25 1.25

King Abdullah II, Houses of Worship and Pope John Paul II — A323

Color of lower panel: 100f, Dull blue green. 200f, Lilac. 300f, Bright yellow green.

2000, Mar. 20 **Litho.** *Perf. 12*

1679-1681 A323 Set of 3 3.25 3.25

Visit of Pope Paul VI to Jordan, 36th anniv.

Visit of Pope John Paul II to Jordan A324

Pope John Paul II, King Abdullah II and: 100f, "2000." 200f, River. 300f, Vatican and Jordanian flags, map of Jordan. No. 1685, Pope, baptism of Christ, vert.

Perf 12, Imperf (#1685)

2000, Mar. 20

1682-1684 A324 Set of 3 3.25 3.25

Size: 70x90mm

1685 A324 200f multi *17.50 17.50*

World Meteorological Organization, 50th Anniv. — A325

Designs: 100f, Globe, emblem, anniversary emblem. 200f, Globe with arrows, emblem, anniversary emblem.

2000, Mar. 23 **Litho.** *Perf. 12*

1686 A325 100f multi .75 .75
1687 A325 200f multi 1.25 1.25

Cradle of Civilizations Type of 1999

Archaeological sites — Palaces: No. 1688, 100f, Mushatta. No. 1689, 200f, Kharaneh. No. 1690, 300f, Amra.

Um Qais: No. 1691, 100f, Decumanus. No. 1692, 200f, Amphitheater. No. 1693, 300f, Ruins.

2000, Apr. 7 **Litho.** *Perf. 13½x14*

Palaces

1688-1690 A317 Set of 3 4.00 4.00

Um Qais

1691-1693 A317 Set of 3 4.00 4.00
a. Sheet, #1640-1663, 1688-1693 40.00 —

Scouting in Jordan, 90th Anniv. A326

"90" and: 100f, Emblem, Jordanian flag. 200f, Tents. 300f, Tents, Jordanian flag. No. 1697, Like No. 1694.

Perf 12, Imperf (#1697)

2000, May 11 **Litho.**

1694-1696 A326 Set of 3 5.00 5.00

Size: 90x70mm

1697 A326 200f multi *7.50 7.50*

Expo 2000, Hanover — A327

Designs: No. 1698, 200f, Inscribed clay tablet. 300f, Artifact with two heads.

No. 1700, 200f, King, Queen, Jordan pavilion interior.

2000, June 1 **Litho.** *Perf. 11¾*

Granite Paper

1698-1699 A327 Set of 2 3.50 3.50

Imperf
Size: 90x70mm

1700 A327 200f multi 3.00 3.00

Palace of Justice A328

Palace and: 100f, Scales of justice. 200f, Scales, Jordanian flag.

2000, June 25 Unwmk. *Perf. 12*

1701 A328 100f multi .75 .75

Wmk. 388

1702 A328 200f multi 1.25 1.25

A number has been reserved for an additional stamp in this set. The editors would like to examine it.

Al-Amal Cancer Center — A329

Emblem and: 200f, Building. 300f, Family.

Perf. 11¾
2000, July 17 Litho. Unwmk.
Granite Paper

1704-1705 A329 Set of 2 3.75 3.75

Flora and Fauna — A330

Designs: 50f, Dove. 100f, Arabian oryx. 150f, Caracal. 200f, Red fox. 300f, Jal'ad iris. 400f, White broom.

2000, Sept. 28 *Perf. 14¼*
Booklet Stamps

1706 A330 50f multi .35 .30
1707 A330 100f multi .75 .50
a. Booklet pane, 2 each #1706-1707 4.00 —
1708 A330 150f multi 1.25 .60
1709 A330 200f multi 1.50 .80
a. Booklet pane, 2 each #1708-1709 7.00 —
1710 A330 300f multi 2.50 1.75
1711 A330 400f multi 3.00 1.90
a. Booklet pane, 2 each #1710-1711 13.00 —
Booklet, #1707a, 1709a, 1711a 30.00

World Conservation Union — A331

Background color: 200f, Green. 300f, Blue.

2000, Oct. 4 *Perf. 11¾*
Granite Paper

1712-1713 A331 Set of 2 3.50 3.50

Tourist Sites A332

Designs: 50f, Petra. 100f, Jerash. 150f, Mount Nebo. 200f, Dead Sea. 300f, Aqaba. 400f, Wadi Rum.

2000, Oct. 9 *Perf. 14¼*
Booklet Stamps

1714 A332 50f multi .35 .35
1715 A332 100f multi .75 .60
a. Booklet pane, 2 each #1714-1715 2.25 —
1716 A332 150f multi 1.25 .90
1717 A332 200f multi 1.75 1.10
a. Booklet pane, 2 each #1716-1717 6.00 —
1718 A332 300f multi 2.25 1.50
1719 A332 400f multi 2.75 2.25
a. Booklet pane, 2 each #1718-1719 10.00 —
Booklet, #1715a, 1717a, 1719a 22.50

King Hussein (1935-99) A333

Designs: 50f, King, vert. No. 1721, 150f, No. 1723, 200f, King and wreath. No. 1722, 200f, King, symbols of industry and agriculture.

2000, Nov. 14 Litho. *Perf. 11¾*
Granite Paper

1720-1722 A333 Set of 3 *2.75 2.75*

Size: 90x70mm
Imperf

1723 A333 200f multi *4.50 4.50*

UN High Commissioner for Refugees, 50th Anniv. — A334

Designs: 200f, Man, women, child. 300f, Emblem.

2000, Dec. 3 Litho. *Perf. 11¾*
Granite Paper

1724-1725 A334 Set of 2 3.50 3.50

13th Arab Summit Conference A335

Emblem, map of Middle East and: 50f, Jordanian flag. 200f, Jordanian flags. 250f, King Abdullah II.

2001, Aug. 1 *Perf. 14*

1726-1728 A335 Set of 3 3.00 3.00

Palestinian Intifada A336

Dome of the Rock and: 200f, Rock throwers, man carrying flag. 300f, Rock throwers, Israeli troops.

2001, Aug. 5

1729-1730 A336 Set of 2 3.00 3.00

Mohammed Al-Dorra, Boy Killed in Intifada Crossfire A337

Designs: 200f, Al-Dorra and father, Dome of the Rock. 300f, Close-up of Al-Dorra, Al-Dorra dead on father's lap.

2001, Aug. 5

1731-1732 A337 Set of 2 3.00 3.00

Healthy Non-smoking Students — A338

Designs: 200f, Students. 300f, Cartoon character, vert.

2001, Sept. 1

1733-1734 A338 Set of 2 3.00 3.00

Sports For People With Special Needs — A339

Stylized figures and: 200f, Man in wheelchair. 300f, Woman.

2001, Sept. 15

1735-1736 A339 Set of 2 3.00 3.00

Olive Trees A340

Designs: 200f, Olives on branch, tree, map of Jordan. 300f, Woman picking olives, vert.

2001, Oct. 1

1737-1738 A340 Set of 2 3.00 3.00

Year of Dialogue Among Civilizations A341

Emblem and: 200f, Family, handshake, world map. 300f, Other stylized drawings.

2001, Oct. 21

1739-1740 A341 Set of 2 3.00 3.00

Cooperation Between Jordan and Japan — A342

Designs: 200f, Sheikh Hussein Bridge, flags. 300f, King Hussein Bridge, handshake.

2001, Nov. 12 Litho. *Perf. 14¼*

1741-1742 A342 Set of 2 3.00 3.00

Jordan - People's Republic of China Diplomatic Relations, 25th Anniv. A343

Designs: 200f, Dove with envelope. 300f, King Abdullah II and Chinese Pres. Jiang Zemin.

2002 *Perf. 12*

1743-1744 A343 Set of 2 2.25 2.25

Amman, 2002 Arab Cultural Capital A344

Designs: 100f, Arabic script, star. 200f, Pen, torch. 300f, Amphitheater.

2002 *Perf. 14¼*

1745-1747 A344 Set of 3 3.00 3.00

Paintings A345

Paintings by, 100f, Rafiq Laham. 150f, Mahmoud Taha, horiz. 200f, Mohanna Durra. 300f, Wijdan, horiz.

2002, July 2 *Perf. 13¼*

1748-1751 A345 Set of 4 4.50 4.50

Vision 2020 — A346

Designs: 200f, Symbols of business and technology. 300f, Fingers, electronic device.

2002 Litho. *Perf. 13¼*

1752-1753 A346 Set of 2 2.25 2.25

Migratory Birds A347

Designs: 100f, Goldfinch. No. 1755, 200f, Rufous bush robin. 300f, White stork.
No. 1757, 200f, Golden oriole, goshawk, ortolan bunting, hoopoe.

2002 *Perf. 13¼*
1754-1756 A347 Set of 3 4.00 4.00

Imperf
Size: 70x90mm

1757 A347 200f multi *8.50 8.50*

Hashemite Rulers A348

No. 1758: a, Sherif Hussein bin Ali. b, King Abdullah. c, King Talal bin Abdullah. d, King Hussein bin Talal. e, King Abdullah II.

2003, July 2 **Litho.** *Perf. 14*
1758 Miniature sheet of 5 4.50 4.50
a.-e. A348 200f Any single .75 .75

Salt Museum A349

Views of building exterior: 150f, 250f.

2003, July 2
1759-1760 A349 Set of 2 1.75 1.75

Trees A350

Designs: 50f, Cupressus sempervirens. 100f, Pistacia atlantica. 200f, Quercus aegilops.

2003, Aug. 7
1761-1763 A350 Set of 3 2.25 2.25

Flowers A351

Designs: 50f, Cistanche tubulosa. 100f, Ophioglossum polyphyllum, vert. 150f, Narcissus tazetta. 200f, Gynandriris sisyrinchium, vert.

2003, Aug. 7
1764-1767 A351 Set of 4 3.00 3.00

Birds of Prey — A352

Designs: 100f, Ciraetus gallicus. No. 1769, 200f, Falco peregrinus. 300f, Accipiter nisus.
No. 1771, 200f, Ciraetus gallicus, diff.

2003, Dec. 9 **Litho.** *Perf. 14*
1768-1770 A352 Set of 3 3.50 3.50

Size: 70x90mm
Imperf

1771 A352 200f multi 6.00 6.00

Royal Cars Museum A353

Designs: 100f, Red sports car. 150f, Black limousine. 300f, White limousine.
200f, Three automobiles.

2003, Dec. 23 **Litho.** *Perf. 14*
1772-1774 A353 Set of 3 3.50 3.50

Size: 90x70mm
Imperf

1775 A353 200f multi 4.50 4.50

Jordan Post Company A354

Emblem and: 50f, Arch. 100f, Pillars, vert.

2003, Dec. 23 **Litho.** *Perf. 14*
1776-1777 A354 Set of 2 1.00 1.00

Triumphal Arch Type of 1993-98

2003 **Litho.** *Perf. 12¾x13¼*
Granite Paper

1777A A267 25f gray & multi — —

Arabian Horses A355

Various horses: 5pi, 7.50pi, 12.50pi, 15pi, 25pi.
10pi, Two horses, horiz.

2004, Dec. 27 **Litho.** *Perf. 14¼*
Granite Paper

1778-1782 A355 Set of 5 3.25 3.25

Imperf
Size: 90x70mm

1783 A355 10pi multi *8.50 8.50*

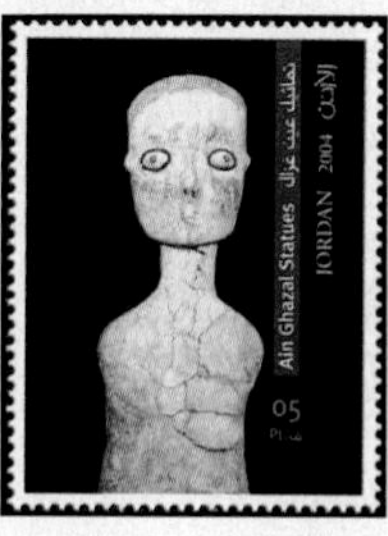

Ain Ghazal Statues A356

Various statues: 5pi, 7.50pi, 12.50pi, 15pi, 25pi.
10pi, Two statues.

2004, Dec. 29
Granite Paper

1784-1788 A356 Set of 5 3.00 3.00

Imperf
Size: 70x90mm

1789 A356 10pi multi *5.00 5.00*

Children's Paintings — A357

Various paintings: 5pi, 7.50pi, 12.50pi, 15pi, 25pi.
10pi, Parts of various paintings.

2004, Dec. 27
Granite Paper

1790-1794 A357 Set of 5 2.75 2.75

Imperf
Size: 90x70mm

1795 A357 10pi multi *5.50 5.50*

Miniature Sheet

Nazareth Iris — A358

No. 1796 — Various photographs of Nazareth Iris: a, 5pi. b, 7.50pi. c, 10pi (70x90mm). d, 12.50pi. e, 15pi. f, 25pi.

2004, Dec. 29 *Perf. 14¼*
Granite Paper

1796 A358 Sheet of 6, #a-f *6.00 6.00*

Miniature Sheet

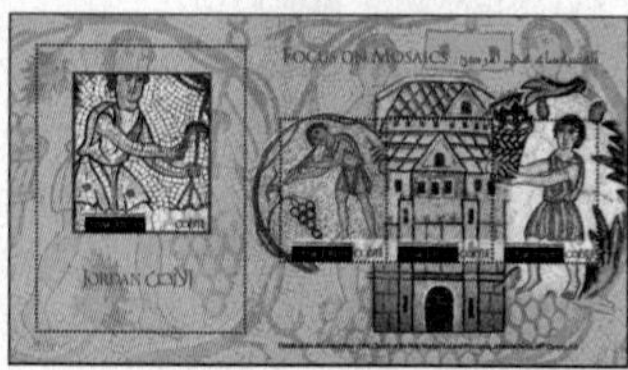

Details From Mosaic Floor of Church of the Holy Martyrs Lot and Procopius, Mount Nebo — A359

No. 1797: a, 10pi, Man with scythe (68x90mm). b, 10pi, Man with flute, grapes. c, 15pi, Building. d, 25pi, Man with Basket.

2004, Dec. 27 **Litho.**
Granite Paper

1797 A359 Sheet of 4, #a-d *6.00 6.00*

Expo 2005, Aichi, Japan A360

No. 1798: a, Dead Sea salt crystal. b, Dead Sea salt crystal, diff. c, Dead Sea salt crystal, diff. d, Dead Sea (70x70mm).

2005, Aug. 7 **Litho.** *Perf. 13¾*
1798 Sheet of 4 3.25 3.25
a. A360 5pi multi .30 .30
b. A360 7.50pi multi .45 .45
c. A360 12.50pi multi .75 .75
d. A360 20pi multi .90 .90

Fish — A361

Various Red Sea fish: 5f, 5pi, 7.50pi, 12.50pi.

Perf. 13½x13¾

2005, Dec. 27 **Litho.**
1799-1802 A361 Set of 4 2.50 2.50

Souvenir Sheet

1803 A361 20pi Lionfish *5.00 5.00*

Intl. Sports Year — A362

Children's drawings of: 1pi, Tennis player. 10pi, Medal winner. 15pi, Soccer game, horiz. No. 1807, 20pi, Swimmer, horiz.
No. 1808, Basketball player.

Perf. 13½x13¾, 13¾x13½

2005, Dec. 27
1804-1807 A362 Set of 4 3.50 3.50

Size: 71x90mm
Imperf

1808 A362 20pi multi *6.00 6.00*

Worldwide Fund for Nature — A363

Arabian oryx: 1.50pi, Grazing. 5pi, Three oryx. 7.50pi, Adults and juvenile. 12.50pi, Two adults.
20pi, Adult, three oryx in background.

2005, Dec. 27 *Perf. 13¾x13½*
1809-1812 A363 Set of 4 *7.25 7.25*

Souvenir Sheet

1813 A363 20pi multi *22.50 22.50*

Child Protection — A364

Designs: 7.50pi, Hands of adult and child. 10pi, Mother holding infant. 12.50pi, Adult hugging child.
20pi, Child.

2005, Dec. 27 ***Perf. 13¾***
1814-1816 A364 Set of 3 3.00 3.00

Size: 70x90mm

Imperf

1817 A364 20pi multi *6.50 6.50*

Friendship of Jordan and Japan — A365

Design: 7.50pi, Gallery of Japanese calligraphy. 12.50pi, Building. 15pi, Building at night.
20pi, Pottery in museum gallery.

2005, Dec. 27 ***Perf. 13¾x13½***
1818-1820 A365 Set of 3 2.75 2.75

Size: 70x90mm

Imperf

1821 A365 20pi multi *5.75 5.75*

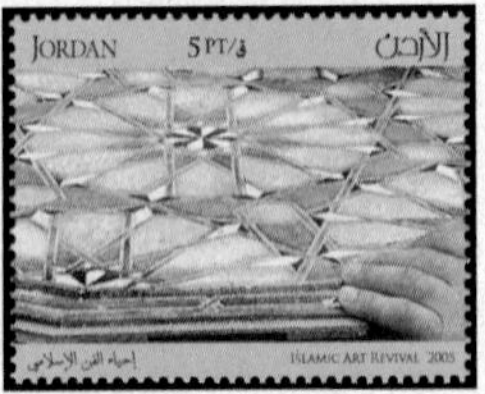

Islamic Art Revival A366

Designs: 5pi, Woodworker. 7.50pi, Engraver. 10pi, Calligrapher. 15pi, Woodworker, diff.
20pi, Calligrapher, diff.

2005, Dec. 27 ***Perf. 13¾x13½***
1822-1825 A366 Set of 4 3.00 3.00

Size: 90x71mm

Imperf

1826 A366 20pi multi *6.00 6.00*

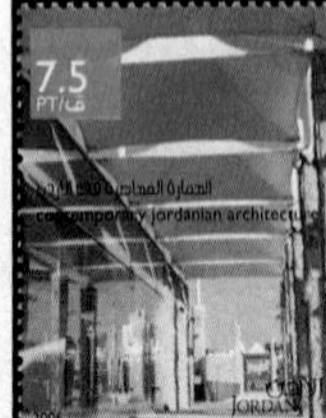

Modern Architecture A367

Various buildings with panel color of: 7.50pi, Green. 10pi, Lemon, horiz. 12.50pi, Red brown.
20pi, Brown, horiz.

2006, Jan. 1 **Litho.** ***Perf. 14***
1827-1829 A367 Set of 3 3.50 3.50

Imperf

Size: 90x70mm

1830 A367 20pi multi *4.50 4.50*

Government Vehicles — A368

Designs: 10pi, Police car. 12.50pi, Fire truck. 17.50pi, Garbage truck. No. 1834, 20pi, Mail vans.
No. 1835, 20pi, Ambulance.

2006, Jan. 1 ***Perf. 14***
1831-1834 A368 Set of 4 3.75 3.75

Imperf

Size: 90x70mm

1835 A368 20pi multi *4.50 4.50*

Ancient Coins — A369

Various coins with background color of: 5pi, Purple. 7.50pi, Yellow brown. 10pi, Gray. 12.50pi, Blue. 15pi, Dark red.
30pi, Dark blue, horiz.

2006, Jan. 1 ***Perf. 13¾***
1836-1840 A369 Set of 5 4.50 4.50

Imperf

Size: 90x70mm

1841 A369 30pi multi *6.50 6.50*

2006 World Cup Soccer Championships, Germany A370

Background color: 5pi, Light blue. 7.50pi, Yellow. 10pi, Tan. 12.50pi, Green. 15pi, Blue.
30pi, Yellow green, horiz.

2006, Jan. 1 ***Perf. 14***
1842-1846 A370 Set of 5 4.50 4.50

Imperf

Size: 90x70mm

1847 A370 30pi multi *5.50 5.50*

Art — A371

Various works of art by unnamed artists: 5pi, 10pi, 15pi. 20pi.
No. 1852, Four works of art, horiz.

2006, Oct. 21 **Litho.** ***Perf. 14¼***

Granite Paper

1848-1851 A371 Set of 4 3.50 3.50

Imperf

Size: 90x70mm

1852 A371 20pi multi *6.00 6.00*

Desert Reptiles A372

Designs: 5pi, Lizard. 7.50pi, Snake. 10pi, Lizards. 12.50pi, Lizard, diff. 15pi, Lizard, horiz. 20pi, Snake, diff.
No. 1859, Lizard, diff., horiz.

2006, Oct. 21 ***Perf. 14¼***

Granite Paper

1853-1858 A372 Set of 6 3.25 3.25

Imperf

Size: 90x70mm

1859 A372 20pi multi *5.25 5.25*

Information and Communications Technology in Education — A373

Design: 7.50pi, Man at computer. 12.50pi, Woman punching keys on keypad. 15pi, Man and computer screen. 20pi, Man using cellular phone.
No. 1864, Circuit board, design of unissued 50f stamp showing finger punching keypad.

2006, Nov. 11 ***Perf. 14¼***

Granite Paper

1860-1863 A373 Set of 4 2.75 2.75

Imperf

Size: 70x90mm

1864 A373 20pi multi *5.50 5.50*

National Symbols A374

Designs: 5pi, King Abdullah II in dress uniform. 7.50pi, King Abdullah II in suit and tie. 10pi, Jordanian soldiers, horiz. 12.50pi, King Abdullah II in camouflage uniform. 15pi, Flag, horiz. 20pi, Men in army uniforms and native garb, horiz. 25pi, Parade of tanks, horiz. 30pi, Flag and rose, horiz.

2006, Nov. 11 ***Perf. 14¼***

Granite Paper

1865-1872 A374 Set of 8 6.25 6.25

Pitchers and Spouted Pots — A375

Designs: 10pi, Spouted pot. 20pi, Spouted pot with legs. 30pi, Pitcher.
25pi, Spouted pot, horiz.

Perf. 13½x13¾

2007, Dec. 31 **Litho.**
1873-1875 A375 Set of 3 1.75 1.75

Imperf

Size: 90x70mm

1876 A375 25pi multi *2.25 2.25*

Culture and Identity A376

Designs: 10pi, Books. No. 1878, 20pi, Lute. 25pi, Bottle. 30pi, Arabic text.
No. 1881, 20pi, Arabic text, paint brushes, bottle, lute, books.

2007, Dec. 31 ***Perf. 13½x13¾***
1877-1880 A376 Set of 4 2.40 2.40

Imperf

Size: 70x90mm

1881 A376 20pi multi *1.50 1.50*

Butterflies A377

Various butterflies with denomination color of: 10pi, Orange. 15pi, Yellow green. 20pi, Gray. 25pi, Olive gray, horiz. 30pi, Orange, horiz.
40pi, Olive green, horiz.

Perf. 13½x13¾, 13¼x13½

2007, Dec. 31
1882-1886 A377 Set of 5 3.00 3.00

Imperf

Size: 90x70mm

1887 A377 40pi multi *4.50 4.50*

Aqaba A378

Designs: 10pi, Arch and beach. 15pi, Scuba diver. 20pi, Motor boats. 30pi, Double-masted ship.

2008, July 16 **Litho.** ***Perf. 14¼***

Granite Paper

1888-1891 A378 Set of 4 2.10 2.10

Traditional Women's Clothing A379

Designs: 10pi, Mafraq. 15pi, Ma'an. 20pi, Amman. 25pi, Jerash. 30pi, Salt.

2008, July 16
Granite Paper

1892-1896 A379 Set of 5 3.00 3.00

Fruit — A380

Designs: 10pi, Oranges. 15pi, Cherries. 20pi, Figs. 25pi, Pomegranates. 30pi, Grapes.

2008, July 16
Granite Paper

1897-1901 A380 Set of 5 3.00 3.00

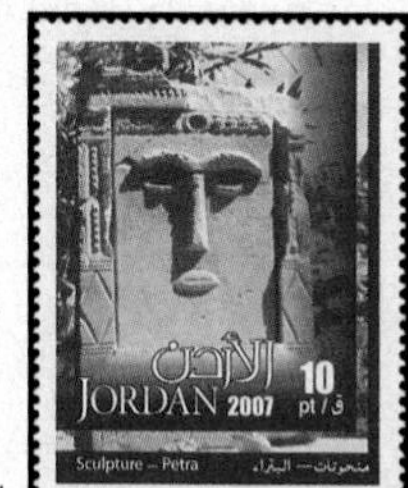
Petra — A381

Designs: 10pi, Sculpture of face. 15pi, Ceramic plate. 20pi, Sculpture of grapevine. 25pi, Siq al Barid fresco. 30pi, Rock formations. 40pi, Treasury.

2008, July 16 Litho. *Perf. 14¼*
Granite Paper

1902-1906 A381 Set of 5 3.00 3.00

Size: 66x86mm

1907 A381 40pi multi 1.25 1.25

Imperf

1908 A381 40pi multi 1.25 1.25

Bridge A382

50th Anniversary Emblem of Engineer's Association A383

2008, Sept. 22 Litho. *Perf. 14¼*
Granite Paper

1909	A382	15pi shown	.45	.45
1910	A383	20pi shown	.60	.60
1911	A382	25pi Power station	.70	.70
		Nos. 1909-1911 (3)	1.75	1.75

2008 Summer Olympics, Beijing A384

Desings: 20pi, Taekwondo. 30pi, Equestrian. 40pi, Table tennis. 50pi, Running.

2008, Sept. 22 Litho.
Granite Paper

1912-1915 A384 Set of 4 4.00 4.00

Musical Instruments A385

Designs: 20pi, Oud. 40pi, Rebab. 60pi, Zither. 80pi, Flutes. 100pi, Tambourine and drum.
50pi, Oud, rebab, zither, flutes, tambourine and drum, horiz.

2008, Sept. 22 *Perf. 14¼*
Granite Paper

1916-1920 A385 Set of 5 8.50 8.50

Imperf
Size: 90x70mm

1921 A385 50pi multi 1.40 1.40

Flowers A386

Designs: 5pi, Egyptian catchfly. 10pi, Lupine. 15pi, Judean viper's bugloss. 20pi, Pimpernel. 30pi, Asiatic crowfoot. 40pi, Grape hyacinth. No. 1928, 50pi, Large flowered sage. 60pi, Star of Bethlehem. 80pi, Pyramidalis. 100pi, Calotropis.
No. 1932, 50pi, Cyclamen, horiz.

2008, Nov. 25 Litho. *Perf. 14¼*
Granite Paper

1922-1931 A386 Set of 10 12.00 12.00

Imperf
Size: 90x70mm

1932 A386 50pi multi 1.40 1.40

Art From Quseir Amra UNESCO World Heritage Site — A387

Designs: 40pi, Woman with arm raised. 60pi, Grapes. 80pi, Hunters on horseback, bath. 100pi, Face of woman.
50pi, Quseir Amra Palace.

2008, Nov. 25 *Perf. 14¼x14*
Granite Paper

1933-1936 A387 Set of 4 8.00 8.00

Imperf
Size: 90x69mm

1937 A387 50pi multi 1.40 1.40

SEMI-POSTAL STAMPS

Locust Campaign Issue

Nos. 145-156 Overprinted

1930, Apr. 1 Wmk. 4 *Perf. 14*

B1	A1	2(m) Prus blue	1.60	*3.50*
	a.	Inverted overprint	200.00	
B2	A1	3(m) rose	1.60	*3.50*
B3	A1	4(m) green	1.75	*4.75*
B4	A1	5(m) orange	18.00	16.75
	a.	Double overprint	300.00	
B5	A1	10(m) red	1.90	*3.50*
B6	A1	15(m) ultra	1.90	*3.50*
	a.	Inverted overprint	200.00	
B7	A1	20(m) olive grn	1.90	*5.00*
B8	A2	50(m) claret	6.75	*11.50*
B9	A2	90(m) bister	15.00	*45.00*
B10	A2	100(m) lt blue	18.00	*47.50*
B11	A2	200(m) violet	42.50	*110.00*
B12	A2	500(m) brown	125.00	*160.00*
	a.	"C" of "Locust" omitted	750.00	650.00
		Nos. B1-B12 (12)	235.90	*414.50*

These stamps were issued to raise funds to help combat a plague of locusts.

Catalogue values for unused stamps in this section, from this point to the end of the section, are for Never Hinged items.

Jerusalem — SP1

1997, Nov. 29 Litho. *Perf. 13½x13*

B13	SP1	100f +10f bl & multi	.75	.75
B14	SP1	200f +20f yel & multi	1.50	1.50
B15	SP1	300f +30f bl grn & multi	2.25	2.25
		Nos. B13-B15 (3)	4.50	4.50

AIR POST STAMPS

Catalogue values for unused stamps in this section are for Never Hinged items.

Plane and Globe — AP1

Temple of Artemis, Jerash — AP2

Perf. 13½x13
1950, Sept. 16 Engr. Wmk. 4

C1	AP1	5f org & red vio	1.25	.20
C2	AP1	10f pur & brown	1.25	.20
C3	AP1	15f ol grn & rose car	1.25	.20
C4	AP1	20f deep blue & blk	1.50	.60
C5	AP1	50f rose pink & dl grn	1.75	.75
C6	AP1	100f blue & brown	3.00	1.50
C7	AP1	150f blk & red org	4.50	2.25
		Nos. C1-C7 (7)	14.50	5.70

1954 Unwmk. *Perf. 12*

C8	AP2	5f blue blk & org	.70	.20
C9	AP2	10f vio brn & ver	.70	.20
C10	AP2	25f bl grn & ultra	.85	.20
C11	AP2	35f dp plum & grnsh bl	1.00	.20
C12	AP2	40f car rose & blk	1.25	.20
C13	AP2	50f dp ultra & org yel	1.40	.40
C14	AP2	100f dk bl & vio brn	1.60	.75
C15	AP2	150f stl bl & red brn	2.50	1.00
		Nos. C8-C15 (8)	10.00	3.15

1958-59 Wmk. 305 *Perf. 12*

C16	AP2	5f blue blk & org	.80	.20
C17	AP2	10f vio brn & ver	.80	.20
C18	AP2	25f bl grn & ultra	.80	.20
C19	AP2	35f dp plum grnsh bl	.80	.20
C20	AP2	40f car rose & blk	1.00	.50
C21	AP2	50f dp ultra & org yel ('59)	1.50	1.00
		Nos. C16-C21 (6)	5.70	2.30

Stadium and Torch AP3

Perf. 11x11½
1964, July 12 Litho. Wmk. 305

C22	AP3	1f yellow & multi	.40	.20
C23	AP3	4f red & multi	.40	.20
C24	AP3	10f blue & multi	.40	.20
C25	AP3	35f yel grn & multi	.75	.40
	a.	Souvenir sheet of 4, #C22-C25	2.00	1.25
		Nos. C22-C25 (4)	1.95	1.00

Opening of Hussein Sports City. No. C25a also exists imperf.

Gorgeous Bush-Shrike — AP4

Birds: 500f, Ornate hawk-eagle, vert. 1d, Gray-headed kingfisher, vert.

Perf. 14x14½
1964, Dec. 18 Photo. Unwmk.
Birds in Natural Colors

C26	AP4	150f lt grn, blk & car	27.50	11.00
C27	AP4	500f brt bl, blk & grn	70.00	30.00
C28	AP4	1d lt ol grn & blk	125.00	50.00
		Nos. C26-C28 (3)	222.50	91.00

Pagoda, Olympic Torch and Emblem — AP5

1965, Mar. 5 Litho. *Perf. 14*

C29	AP5	10f deep rose	.50	.20
C30	AP5	15f violet	.60	.20
C31	AP5	20f blue	.75	.20
C32	AP5	30f green	.90	.20
C33	AP5	40f brown	1.40	.25
C34	AP5	60f carmine rose	2.00	.40
		Nos. C29-C34 (6)	6.15	1.45

18th Olympic Games, Tokyo, Oct. 10-25, 1964. An imperf. 100f violet blue souvenir sheet exists. Size of stamp: 60x60mm. Value $12.50.

For overprints see Nos. C42A-C42F.

Forum, Jerash — AP6

Antiquities of Jerash: No. C36, South Theater. No. C37, Triumphal arch. No. C38, Temple of Artemis. No. C39, Cathedral steps. No. C40, Artemis Temple, gate. No. C41, Columns. No. C42, Columns and niche, South Theater. Nos. C39-C42 are vertical.

1965, June 22 Photo. *Perf. 14x15*
Center Multicolored

C35 AP6 55f bright pink 1.25 .80
C36 AP6 55f light blue 1.25 .80
C37 AP6 55f green 1.25 .80
C38 AP6 55f black 1.25 .80
C39 AP6 55f light green 1.25 .80
C40 AP6 55f carmine rose 1.25 .80
C41 AP6 55f gray 1.25 .80
C42 AP6 55f blue 1.25 .80
Nos. C35-C42 (8) 10.00 6.40

#C35-C38 are printed in horizontal rows of 4; #C39-C42 in vertical rows of 4; sheets of 16.

Nos. C29-C34 with Bilingual Ovpt. "James McDivitt / Edward White / 2-6-1965" and Rocket

1965, Sept. 25 Litho. *Perf. 14*

C42A AP5 10f deep rose 1.50 .95
C42B AP5 15f violet 2.00 1.40
C42C AP5 20f blue 2.50 2.00
C42D AP5 30f green 4.00 3.00
C42E AP5 40f brown 5.00 4.00
C42F AP5 60f carmine rose 6.50 5.75
Nos. C42A-C42F (6) 21.50 17.10

The imperf. 100f blue souvenir sheet exists overprinted. Value $21.50.

King Hussein Type of Regular Issue

1966, Jan. 15 Photo. *Perf. 14½x14*
Portrait in Brown

C43 A67 200f brt blue grn 5.75 1.25
C44 A67 500f light green 10.00 5.00
C45 A67 1d light ultra 17.00 9.00
Nos. C43-C45 (3) 32.75 15.25

Animal Type of Regular Issue, 1967

Animals: 4f, Striped hyena. 30f, Arabian stallion. 60f, Persian gazelle.

1967, Feb. 11 Photo. *Perf. 14x15*

C46 A70 4f dk brn & multi 1.75 .20
C47 A70 30f lt bl & multi 2.25 .45
C48 A70 60f yellow & multi 4.00 1.00
Nos. C46-C48 (3) 8.00 1.65

Game Type of Regular Issue, 1968

Protected Game: 60f, Nubian ibex, vert. 100f, Wild ducks.

1968, Oct. 5 Litho. *Perf. 13½*

C49 A74 60f multicolored 10.00 4.50
C50 A74 100f multicolored 15.00 7.00

Easter Type of Regular Issue

Designs: 60f, Altar, Holy Sepulcher. 100f, Feet Washing, Holy Gate, Jerusalem.

1972, Apr. Photo. *Perf. 14x13½*

C51 A92 60f dk bl & multi 1.40 .70
C52 A92 100f multicolored 1.75 1.10

Aero Club Type of Regular Issue

15f, Two Piper 140s. 20f, R.J.A.C. Beechcraft. 40f, Aero Club emblem with winged horse.

1973, Jan. Photo. *Perf. 13½x14*

C53 A100 15f blue, blk & red .75 .20
C54 A100 20f blue, blk & red .75 .20
C55 A100 40f mag, blk & yel 1.50 .45
Nos. C53-C55 (3) 3.00 .85

Agriculture Type of Regular Issue

Design: 100f, Soil conservation.

1973, Dec. 25 *Perf. 13½*

C56 A110 100f multicolored 2.25 1.00

King Hussein Driving Car — AP7

1974, Dec. 20 *Perf. 12*

C57 AP7 30f multicolored .70 .20
C58 AP7 60f multicolored 1.40 .75

Royal Jordanian Automobile Club.

Building Type of Regular Issue

Designs: 50f, Palms, Aqaba. 60f, Obelisk tomb. 80f, Fort of Wadi Rum.

1975, Mar. 1 Photo. *Perf. 13½x14*

C59 A121 50f pink & multi 1.25 .65
C60 A121 60f lt bl & multi 1.60 .80
C61 A121 80f yellow & multi 2.00 .80
Nos. C59-C61 (3) 4.85 2.25

Hussein Type of Regular Issue

1975, Apr. 8 Photo. *Perf. 14x13½*
Size: 22x27mm

C62 A123 60f dk grn & brn 1.00 .35
C63 A123 100f org brn & brn 1.75 .40
C64 A123 120f dp bl & brn 1.25 .65
C65 A123 180f brt mag & brn 1.60 1.00
C66 A123 200f grnsh bl & brn 1.90 1.25
C67 A123 400f pur & brown 2.75 2.00
C68 A123 500f orange & brn 3.75 3.25
Nos. C62-C68 (7) 14.00 8.90

POSTAGE DUE STAMPS

Stamps of Regular Issue (Nos. 69, 66-68 Surcharged with New Value like No. 91) Overprinted

This overprint reads: "Mustahaq" (Tax or Due)

1923 Unwmk. *Perf. 11½*
Typo. Ovpt. "Mustahaq" 10mm long

J1 A7 ½pi on 3pi ol brn 45.00 55.00
a. Inverted overprint 175.00 175.00
b. Double overprint 175.00 175.00

Handstamped Overprint 12mm long

J2 A7 ½pi on 3pi ol brn 12.50 15.00
J3 A7 1pi dark blue 8.00 9.00
J4 A7 1½pi violet 8.00 9.00
J5 A7 2pi orange 9.00 10.00
Nos. J1-J5 (5) 82.50 98.00

These overprints are found double, inverted, etc. as is usual with handstamps.

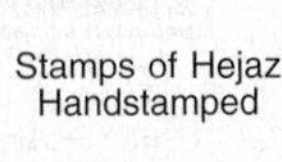

Stamps of Hejaz Handstamped

J6 A7 ½pi red 1.00 1.25
J7 A7 1pi dark blue 1.10 1.75
J8 A7 1½pi violet 1.40 2.25
J9 A7 2pi orange 2.00 3.00
J10 A7 3pi olive brown 3.00 5.50
J11 A7 5pi olive green 5.50 8.00
Nos. J6-J11 (6) 14.00 21.75

Type of Palestine, 1918, Overprinted

1925 Wmk. 4 *Perf. 14*

J12 A1 1m dark brown 1.75 5.00
J13 A1 2m yellow 2.50 3.25
J14 A1 4m rose 4.25 5.00
J15 A1 8m red 5.00 8.50
J16 A1 13m ultramarine 6.75 8.50
J17 A1 5pi plum 7.75 11.50
a. Perf. 15x14 67.50 77.50
Nos. J12-J17 (6) 28.00 41.75

The overprint reads: "Mustahaq. Sharqi al'Ardan." (Tax. Eastern Jordan).

Stamps of Palestine, 1918, Surcharged

1926

J18 A1 1m on 1m dk brn 3.50 5.00
J19 A1 2m on 1m dk brn 3.50 5.00
J20 A1 4m on 3m Prus bl 3.50 6.75
J21 A1 8m on 3m Prus bl 3.75 7.50
J22 A1 13m on 13m ultra 3.75 8.50
J23 A1 5pi on 13m ultra 5.00 10.50
Nos. J18-J23 (6) 23.00 43.25

The surcharge reads "Tax—Eastern Jordan" and New Value.

Stamps of Regular Issue, 1927, Overprinted

1929

J24 A1 2m Prussian bl 1.25 3.75
J25 A1 10m red 2.00 3.75
J26 A2 50m claret 7.75 16.00
Nos. J24-J26 (3) 11.00 23.50

With Additional Surcharge

J27 A1 1(m) on 3(m) rose 1.25 4.25
J28 A1 4(m) on 15(m) ultra 2.00 4.25
a. Inverted surch. and ovpt. 95.00
J29 A2 20(m) on 100(m) lt bl 5.75 13.00
Nos. J27-J29 (3) 9.00 21.50

D1

1929 Engr. *Perf. 14*
Size: 17¼x21mm

J30 D1 1m brown .75 3.25
a. Perf. 13½x13 90.00 45.00
J31 D1 2m orange .75 3.75
J32 D1 4m green .75 4.25
J33 D1 10m carmine 2.00 4.75
J34 D1 20m olive green 7.75 15.00
J35 D1 50m blue 9.50 19.00
Nos. J30-J35 (6) 21.50 50.00

See Nos. J39-J43 design with larger type. For surcharge see No. J52. For overprints see Nos. NJ1a, NJ3, NJ5a, NJ6-NJ7.

D2

1942 Unwmk. Litho. *Perf. 13x13½*

J36 D2 1m dull red brn .20 .20
J37 D2 2m dl orange yel 3.00 3.00
J38 D2 10m dark carmine 4.00 4.00
Nos. J36-J38 (3) 7.20 7.20

For overprints see Nos. NJ8-NJ10.

Type of 1929

1943-44 Engr. Wmk. 4 *Perf. 12*
Size: 17¾x21¼mm

J39 D1 1m orange brn .20 .20
J40 D1 2m yel orange .20 .20
J41 D1 4m yel green .20 .20
J42 D1 10m rose carmine .20 .20
J43 D1 20m olive green 10.00 10.00
Nos. J39-J43 (5) 10.80 10.80

For overprints see Nos. J47-J51, NJ1-NJ2, NJ3a, NJ5, NJ6a.

Catalogue values for unused stamps in this section, from this point to the end of the section, are for Never Hinged items.

Nos. J39-J43, J35 Surcharged "FILS" and its Arabic Equivalent in Black, Green or Carmine

1952 Wmk. 4 *Perf. 12*

J47 D1 1f on 1m org brn (Bk) 2.00 .20
J48 D1 2f on 2m yel org (G) 2.00 .20
J49 D1 4f on 4m yel grn 2.00 .20
J50 D1 10f on 10m rose car (Bk) 2.50 1.75
J51 D1 20f on 20m ol grn 4.50 2.50

Perf. 14

J52 D1 50f on 50m blue 5.00 3.25
Nos. J47-J52 (6) 18.00 8.10

This overprint exists on Nos. J34, J36-J38. Exists inverted, double and in wrong color.

D3

Inscribed: "The Hashemite Kingdom of the Jordan"

1952 Engr. *Perf. 11½*

J53 D3 1f orange brown .65 .45
J54 D3 2f yel orange .65 .45
J55 D3 4f yel green .65 .45
J56 D3 10f rose carmine 1.00 .80
J57 D3 20f yel brown 1.00 .95
J58 D3 50f blue 2.75 2.25
Nos. J53-J58 (6) 6.70 5.35

Type of 1952 Redrawn

Inscribed: "The Hashemite Kingdom of Jordan"

1957 Wmk. 305 *Perf. 11½*

J59 D3 1f orange brown .70 .40
J60 D3 2f yel orange .70 .40
J61 D3 4f yel green .70 .60
J62 D3 10f rose carmine 1.00 .55
J63 D3 20f yel brown 1.40 1.25
Nos. J59-J63 (5) 4.50 3.20

OFFICIAL STAMP

Saudi Arabia No. L34 Overprinted

1924, Jan. Typo. *Perf. 11½*

O1 A7 ½pi red 275.00 100.00

Overprint reads: "(Government) the Arabian East 1342."

POSTAL TAX STAMPS

Catalogue values for unused stamps in this section are for Never Hinged items.

Mosque at Hebron — PT1

Designs: 10m, 15m, 20m, 50m, Dome of the Rock. 100m, 200m, 500m, £1, Acre.

Perf. 11½x12½

1947		Unwmk.		Engr.
RA1	PT1	1m ultra	.35	.20
RA2	PT1	2m carmine	.35	.20
RA3	PT1	3m emerald	.50	.25
RA4	PT1	5m plum	.60	.20
RA5	PT1	10m carmine	.75	.30
RA6	PT1	15m gray	1.00	.30
RA7	PT1	20m dk brown	3.50	1.40
RA8	PT1	50m purple	8.00	3.50
RA9	PT1	100m orange red	15.00	8.00
RA10	PT1	200m dp blue	35.00	24.00
RA11	PT1	500m green	55.00	40.00
RA12	PT1	£1 dk brown	95.00	90.00
		Nos. RA1-RA12 (12)	215.05	168.35

Issued to help the Welfare Fund for Arabs in Palestine. Required on foreign-bound letters to the amount of half the regular postage.

For overprints and surcharges see #286A-286C, 344-346, RA37-RA46, NRA1-NRA12.

Nos. 211, 232 and 234 Overprinted in Black

1950		Wmk. 4	Perf. 12
RA23	A3	5m orange	12.50
RA24	A3	10m violet	20.00
RA25	A3	15m dull olive grn	22.50
		Nos. RA23-RA25 (3)	55.00

Arch and Colonnade, Palmyra, Syria — PT2

Two types of 5m:

Type I — "A" with serifs. Arabic ovpt. 8mm wide.

Type II — "A" without serifs. Arabic ovpt. 5mm wide.

Black or Carmine Overprint

1950-51		Engr.	*Perf. 13½x13*
RA26	PT2	5m orange (I)	20.00
a.		Type II ('51)	27.50
RA27	PT2	10m violet (C)	20.00

The overprint on No. RA27 is similar to that on RA23-RA25 but slightly bolder.

Type of 1947

Designs: 5f, Hebron Mosque. 10f, 15f, 20f, Dome of the Rock. 100f, Acre.

1951		Wmk. 4	*Perf. 11½x12½*	
RA28	PT1	5f plum	.20	.20
RA29	PT1	10f carmine	.20	.20
RA30	PT1	15f gray	.20	.20
RA31	PT1	20f dk brown	.90	.90
RA33	PT1	100f orange	5.75	5.75
		Nos. RA28-RA33 (5)	7.25	7.25

The tax on Nos. RA1-RA33 was for Arab aid in Palestine.

For overprints see Nos. 287-290.

Postal Tax Stamps of 1947 Surcharged "FILS" or "J.D." and Their Arabic Equivalents and Bars in Carmine or Black

1952				Unwmk.
RA37	PT1	1f on 1m ultra	.75	.20
RA38	PT1	3f on 3m emer	.75	.20
RA39	PT1	10f on 10m car	1.25	.75
RA40	PT1	15f on 15m gray	1.60	1.25
RA41	PT1	20f on 20m dk brown	2.40	1.60
RA42	PT1	50f on 50m pur	5.75	3.75
RA43	PT1	100f on 100m org red	15.00	9.50
RA44	PT1	200f on 200m dp blue	40.00	12.00
RA45	PT1	500f on 500m grn	67.50	24.00
RA46	PT1	1d on £1 dk brn	100.00	60.00
		Nos. RA37-RA46 (10)	235.00	113.25

"J.D." stands for Jordanian Dinar.

OCCUPATION STAMPS

Catalogue values for unused stamps in this section are for Never Hinged items.

For Use in Palestine

Stamps of Jordan Overprinted in Red, Black, Dark Green, Green or Orange Red

On No. 200

1948		Unwmk.	*Perf. 13x13½*	
N1	A14	2m dull green (R)	2.00	2.00

On #207-209, 211, 230-235, 215-220

1948		Wmk. 4	*Perf. 12, 13½x13, 14*	
N2	A3	1m red brown	.60	.60
N3	A3	2m Prus green (R)	.60	.60
a.		2m Prussian blue, perf. 13½x13 (R) (#170a)	1.00	*1.25*
N4	A3	3m blue green (R)	.75	.75
N5	A3	3m rose carmine	.40	.35
N6	A3	4m dp yel grn (R)	.40	.35
N7	A3	5m orange (G)	.40	.35
N8	A3	10m violet (OR)	1.00	1.00
N9	A3	12m deep rose	1.00	.80
N10	A3	15m dl ol grn (R)	1.40	1.00
N11	A3	20m dp blue (R)	1.75	1.40
N12	A3	50m red lil (Dk G)	2.10	1.75
N13	A3	90m ocher (Dk G)	9.75	4.75
N14	A3	100m dp blue (R)	11.00	5.50
N15	A3	200m dk vio (R)	7.00	7.00
a.		200m vio, perf. 14 (R) (#182)	35.00	25.00
N16	A3	500m dk brn (R)	42.50	14.00
N17	A3	£1 black (R)	70.00	42.50
		Nos. N2-N17 (16)	150.65	82.70

The first overprinting of these stamps include Nos. N1-N6, N9-N17. The second overprinting includes Nos. N1, N3, N5-N17, in inks differing in shade from the originals.

Many values exist with inverted or double overprint.

Jordan Nos. 245-249 Overprinted in Black or Red

1949, Aug.		Wmk. 4	*Perf. 13*	
N18	A17	1m brown (Bk)	.45	.35
N19	A17	4m green	.45	.35
a.		"PLAESTINE"	25.00	
N20	A17	10m red	.75	.65
N21	A17	20m ultra	.75	.65
N22	A18	50m dull green	1.60	1.60
a.		"PLAESTINE"	25.00	
		Nos. N18-N22 (5)	4.00	3.60

The overprint is in one line on No. N22.

UPU, 75th anniversary.

OCCUPATION POSTAGE DUE STAMPS

Catalogue values for unused stamps in this section are for Never Hinged items.

Jordan Nos. J39, J30a, J40, J32, J41-J43, J34 and J35 Overprinted in Black, Red or Carmine

1948-49		Wmk. 4	*Perf. 12, 14*	
NJ1	D1	1m org brn, perf. 12	1.25	1.25
a.		Perf. 13½x13 (#J30a)	50.00	45.00
NJ2	D1	2m yel orange	1.25	1.25
NJ3	D1	4m grn (R) (#J32)	2.50	2.50
a.		4m yel grn (C) (#J41)	5.00	
NJ5	D1	10m rose car (#J42) ('49)	3.75	3.75
a.		Perf. 14 (#J33)	80.00	
NJ6	D1	20m ol grn (R), perf. 14	2.50	2.50
a.		Perf. 12 (R) (#J43)	62.50	
NJ7	D1	50m blue (R)	3.75	2.50
		Nos. NJ1-NJ3,NJ5-NJ7 (6)	15.00	13.75

The second overprinting of these stamps includes Nos. NJ1-NJ3, NJ3a and NJ5-NJ7, in inks differing in shade from the originals.

Double and inverted overprints exist.

Same Overprint in Black on Jordan Nos. J36-J38

1948-49		Unwmk.	*Perf. 13x13½*	
NJ8	D2	1m dl red brn	*115.00*	*115.00*
NJ9	D2	2m dl org yel ('49)	11.00	11.00
NJ10	D2	10m dark car	9.00	9.00

OCCUPATION POSTAL TAX STAMPS

Catalogue values for unused stamps in this section are for Never Hinged items.

Postal Tax Stamps of 1947 Overprinted in Red or Black

1950				
NRA1	PT1	1m ultra (R)	.30	.35
NRA2	PT1	2m carmine	.35	.35
NRA3	PT1	3m emerald (R)	.50	.35
NRA4	PT1	5m plum	.90	.35
NRA5	PT1	10m carmine	1.50	.50
NRA6	PT1	15m gray (R)	2.40	.90
NRA7	PT1	20m dk brown (R)	3.50	1.10
NRA8	PT1	50m purple (R)	4.25	1.75
NRA9	PT1	100m org red	6.50	2.40
NRA10	PT1	200m dp blue (R)	17.00	6.00
NRA11	PT1	500m green (R)	47.50	18.00
NRA12	PT1	£1 dk brown (R)	95.00	35.00
		Nos. NRA1-NRA12 (12)	179.70	67.05

For overprints see Nos. 286D-286G.

KARELIA

kə-'rē-lə-ə

LOCATION — In northwestern Soviet Russia
GOVT. — An autonomous republic of the Soviet Union
AREA — 55,198 sq. mi. (approx.)
POP. — 270,000 (approx.)
CAPITAL — Petrozavodsk (Kalininsk)

In 1921 the Karelians rebelled and for a short period a form of sovereignty independent of Russia was maintained.

100 Pennia = 1 Markka

Bear — A1

1922 Unwmk. Litho. *Perf. 11½, 12*

1 A1 5p dark gray 12.00 *40.00*
2 A1 10p light blue 12.00 *40.00*
3 A1 20p rose red 12.00 *40.00*
4 A1 25p yellow brown 12.00 *40.00*
5 A1 40p magenta 12.00 *40.00*
6 A1 50p gray green 12.00 *40.00*
7 A1 75p orange yellow 12.00 *40.00*
8 A1 1m pink & gray 20.00 *40.00*
9 A1 2m yel grn & gray 25.00 *90.00*
10 A1 3m lt blue & gray 25.00 *110.00*
11 A1 5m red lil & gray 25.00 *140.00*
12 A1 10m lt brn & gray 25.00 *200.00*
13 A1 15m green & car 25.00 *200.00*
14 A1 20m rose & green 25.00 *200.00*
15 A1 25m yellow & blue 25.00 *200.00*
Nos. 1-15 (15) 279.00 *1,460.*
Set, never hinged 400.00

Nos. 1-15 were valid Jan. 31-Feb. 16, 1922. Use probably ended Feb. 3, although cancellations of the 4th and 5th exist.
Counterfeits abound.

OCCUPATION STAMPS

Issued under Finnish Occupation

Issued in the Russian territory of Eastern Karelia under Finnish military administration.

Types of Finland Stamps, 1930 Overprinted in Black:

On A26

On A27-A28

1941 Unwmk. *Perf. 14*

N1 A26 50p brt yel grn .30 *.60*
N2 A26 1.75m dk gray .70 *1.25*
N3 A26 2m dp org 2.25 *4.00*
N4 A26 2.75m yel org .50 *1.00*
N5 A26 3½m lt ultra 3.00 *5.00*
N6 A27 5m rose vio 3.75 *7.75*
N7 A28 10m pale brn 4.50 *7.75*
Nos. N1-N7 (7) 15.00 *27.35*
Set, never hinged 30.00

Types of Finland Stamps, 1930 Overprinted in Green:

On A26

On A27-A29

N8 A26 50p brt yel grn .30 *.55*
N9 A26 1.75m dk gray .35 *.65*
N10 A26 2m dp org .70 *1.25*
N11 A26 2.75m yel org .50 *.75*
N12 A26 3½m lt ultra .70 *1.25*
N13 A27 5m rose vio 1.60 *4.00*
N14 A28 10m pale brown 3.25 *6.75*
N15 A29 25m green 3.50 *7.25*
Nos. N8-N15 (8) 10.90 *22.45*
Set, never hinged 50.00

Mannerheim Type of Finland Overprinted

1942

N16 A48 50p dk yel grn .65 *1.50*
N17 A48 1.75m slate bl .65 *1.50*
N18 A48 2m red org .65 *1.50*
N19 A48 2.75m brn org .55 *1.50*
N20 A48 3.50m brt ultra .55 *1.50*
N21 A48 5m brn vio .55 *1.50*
Nos. N16-N21 (6) 3.60 *9.00*
Set, never hinged 10.00

Same Overprint on Ryti Type of Finland

N22 A49 50p dk yel grn .55 *1.50*
N23 A49 1.75m slate bl .55 *1.50*
N24 A49 2m red org .55 *1.50*
N25 A49 2.75m brn org .60 *1.50*
N26 A49 3.50m brt ultra .60 *1.50*
N27 A49 5m brn vio .60 *1.50*
Nos. N22-N27 (6) 3.45 *9.00*
Set, never hinged 10.00

The overprint translates, "East Karelia Military Administration."

OCCUPATION SEMI-POSTAL STAMP

Arms of East Karelia — SP1

1943 Unwmk. Engr. *Perf. 14*

NB1 SP1 3.50m + 1.50m dk ol .75 *2.25*
Never hinged 2.25

This surtax aided war victims in East Karelia.

KATANGA

kə-'täŋ-gə

LOCATION — Central Africa
GOVT. — Republic
CAPITAL — Elisabethville

Katanga province seceded from the Congo (ex-Belgian) Republic in July, 1960, but established nations did not recognize it as an independent state. The UN declared the secession ended in Sept, 1961. The last troops surrendered Sept. 1963.

During the secession Katanga stamps were tolerated in the international mails, but the government authorizing them was not recognized.

100 Centimes = 1 Franc

Catalogue values for all unused stamps in this country are for Never Hinged items.

Belgian Congo Nos. 318-322 Overprinted "KATANGA"

Perf. 11½

1960, Sept. 12 Photo. Unwmk.

1 A94 50c golden brn, ocher & red brn
2 A94 1fr dk bl, pur & red brn
3 A94 2fr gray, brt bl & red brn
Nos. 1-3 (3) .75 .75

Inscription in French

4 A95 3fr gray & red 8.00 8.50

Inscription in Flemish

5 A95 3fr gray & red 8.00 8.50

Inverted overprints exist on No. 1-5. Values: 1-3 $4 each; 4-5 $10 each.
For surcharges see Nos. 50-51.

Animal Type of Belgian Congo, Nos. 306-317, Overprinted "KATANGA"

1960, Sept. 19

Granite Paper

6 A92 10c bl & brn
7 A93 20c red org & slate
8 A92 40c brn & bl
9 A93 50c brt ultra, red & sep
10 A92 1fr brn, grn & blk
11 A93 1.50fr blk & org yel
12 A92 2fr crim, blk & brn
13 A93 3fr blk, gray & lil rose
14 A92 5fr brn, dk brn & brt grn
15 A93 6.50fr bl, brn & org yel
16 A92 8fr org brn, ol bis & lil
17 A93 10fr multi
Nos. 6-17 (12) 57.50 27.50

Inverted overprints exist. Value $10 each.

Flower Type of Belgian Congo, Nos. 263-271, 274-281, Overprinted "KATANGA"

1960, Sept. 22

Granite Paper

Flowers in Natural Colors

18 A86 10c dp plum & ocher
19 A86 15c red & yel grn
20 A86 20c grn & gray
21 A86 25c dk grn & dl org
22 A86 40c grn & sal
23 A86 50c dk car & aqua
24 A86 60c bl grn & pink
25 A86 75c dp plum & gray
26 A86 1fr car & yel
27 A86 2fr ol grn & buff
28 A86 3fr ol grn & pink
29 A86 4fr choc & lil
30 A86 5fr dp plum & lt bl grn
31 A86 6.50fr dk car & lil
32 A86 7fr dk grn & fawn
33 A86 8fr grn & lt yel
34 A86 10fr dp plum & pale ol
Nos. 18-34 (17) 65.00 30.00

Inverted overprints exist. Value $12 each.

Carving and Mask Type of Belgian Congo, Nos. 241, 246, 254-256, Surcharged or Overprinted "KATANGA"

1960, Sept. 22 *Perf. 12½*

35 A82 1.50fr on 1.25fr 1.25 .50
36 A82 3.50fr on 2.50fr 1.50 .60
37 A82 20fr red org & vio brn 8.25 4.00
38 A82 50fr dp org & blk 17.50 7.00
39 A82 100fr crim & blk brn 70.00 27.50
Nos. 35-39 (5) 98.50 39.60

Inverted surcharges and overprints exist. Values, No. 37 $42.50, No. 38 $50, No. 39 $80.

Map Type of Congo Democratic Republic, Nos. 356-365, Overprinted "11 / JUILLET / DE / L'ETAT DU KATANGA"

1960, Oct. 26 *Perf. 11½*

Granite Paper

40 A93a 20c brown .20 .20
41 A93a 50c rose red .20 .20
42 A93a 1fr green .20 .20
43 A93a 1.50fr red brn .20 .20
44 A93a 2fr rose car .20 .20
45 A93a 3.50fr lilac .20 .20
46 A93a 5fr brt bl .20 .20
47 A93a 6.50fr gray .20 .20
48 A93a 10fr orange .25 .20
49 A93a 20fr ultra .35 .20
Nos. 40-49 (10) 2.20 2.00

Inverted and double surcharges exist.

Belgian Congo Nos. 321-322 Surcharged

1961, Jan. 16

50 A95 3.50fr on 3fr #321 3.00 3.00
51 A95 3.50fr on 3fr #322 3.00 3.00

Inverted surcharges exist. Value $5.50 each.

A1

A2

Katangan Wood Carvings: 3.50fr-8fr, Preparing meal. 10fr-100fr, Family group.

1961, Mar. 1 *Perf. 11½*

Granite Paper

52 A1 10c grn & lt grn .20 .20
53 A1 20c purple & lil .20 .20
54 A1 50c blue & lt bl .20 .20
55 A1 1.50fr ol grn & lt ol grn .20 .20
56 A1 2fr red brn & lt brn .20 .20
57 A1 3.50fr dk blue & lt bl .20 .20
58 A1 5fr bl grn & lt bl grn .20 .20
59 A1 6fr org brn & tan .20 .20
60 A1 6.50fr bl vio & gray vio .20 .20
61 A1 8fr claret & pink .20 .20
62 A1 10fr dk brn & lt brn .20 .20
63 A1 20fr dk ol & lt grn .30 .25
64 A1 50fr brn & lt brn .70 .40
65 A1 100fr Prus bl & lt bl 1.25 .70
Nos. 52-65 (14) 4.45 3.55

1961, July 8 *Perf. 11½*

1fr, 5fr, Abstract vehicle. 2.50fr, 6.50fr, Gear.

Granite Paper

66 A2 50c blk, grn & red .20 .20
67 A2 1fr blk & blue .20 .20
68 A2 2.50fr blk & yellow .20 .20
69 A2 3.50fr blk, brn & scar .20 .20
70 A2 5fr blk & purple .35 .35
71 A2 6.50fr blk & orange .55 .55
Nos. 66-71 (6) 1.70 1.70

Katanga International Fair.
Imperfs exist. Value, set $45.

Air Katanga A3

Design: 6.50fr, 10fr, Plane on ground.

1961, Aug. 1 *Perf. 11½*

Granite Paper

72 A3 3.50fr multicolored
73 A3 6.50fr multicolored
74 A3 8fr multicolored
75 A3 10fr multicolored
Nos. 72-75 (4) 7.50 7.00

Imperfs exist. Value, set $60.

Katanga Gendarmerie — A4

1962, Oct. 1 *Perf. 11½*

Granite Paper

76 A4 6fr multicolored
77 A4 8fr multicolored
78 A4 10fr multicolored
Nos. 76-78 (3) 5.50 4.50

Imperfs exist.Value, set $40.

SEMI-POSTAL STAMPS

Pres. Moise Tshombe — SP1

1961, July 11 *Perf. 11½*

Granite Paper

B1 SP1 6.50fr + 5fr multi
B2 SP1 8fr + 5fr multi
B3 SP1 10fr + 5fr multi
Nos. B1-B3 (3) 8.00 5.00

Imperf exist. Value, set $65.

POSTAGE DUE STAMPS

Belgian Congo Nos. J8a-J10a, J16-J19 Handstamped "KATANGA" in Blue

1960, Dec. 30 **Unwmk.** *Perf. 12½*

J1 D2 10c olive green
J2 D2 20c dark ultra
J3 D2 50c green

Perf. 11½

J4 D3 1fr light blue
J5 D3 2fr vermilion
J6 D3 4fr purple
J7 D3 6fr violet blue
Nos. J1-J7 (7) 30.00 30.00

This overprint also exists on Belgian Congo Nos. J11a-J12a, J13-J15. Value, set $180.

KAZAKHSTAN

ˌka-ˌzäk-ˈstan

(Kazakstan)

LOCATION — Bounded by southern Russia, Uzbekistan, Kyrgyzstan, and China.
GOVT. — Independent republic, member of the Commonwealth of Independent States.
AREA — 1,049,155 sq. mi.
POP. — 16,824,825 (1999 est.)
CAPITAL — Astana

With the breakup of the Soviet Union on Dec. 26, 1991, Kazakhstan and ten former Soviet republics established the Commonwealth of Independent States.

100 Kopecks = 1 Ruble
100 Tijn = 1 Tenge

Catalogue values for all unused stamps in this country are for Never Hinged items.

Overprinted Stamps

The Philatelic Club of Alma Ata, Kazakhstan, has announced that various overprinted stamps of the USSR were not generally available nor were they in values reflecting actual postal rates.

A1

Perf. 12x12½

1992, Mar. 23 **Litho.** **Unwmk.**

1 A1 50k multicolored .30 .20

Saiga Tatarica A2

1992, Sept. 11 **Litho.** *Perf. 12*

2 A2 75k multicolored .30 .20

Camels and Train, by K. Kasteev — A3

1992, Sept. 11 **Litho.** *Perf. 12½x12*

3 A3 1r multicolored .30 .30

Day of the Republic A3a

1992, Dec. 16 **Litho.** *Perf. 12*

4 A3a 5r multicolored .50 .50

Space Ship and Yurt — A4

Natl. Flag — A5

1993, Jan. 24 **Litho.** *Perf. 13x12½*

22 A4 1r green .20 .20
23 A4 3r red .20 .20
24 A4 10r golden brown .20 .20
25 A4 25r purple .90 .90

Perf. 14

26 A5 50r multicolored 1.75 1.75
Nos. 22-26 (5) 3.25 3.25

See Nos. 64, 69, 108-115.

Space Mail A6

1993, Mar. 5 **Litho.** *Perf. 13½*

35 A6 100r multicolored 2.00 1.40

New Year 1993 (Year of the Rooster) — A7

1993, Mar. 22 **Litho.** *Perf. 13x13½*

36 A7 60r yellow, black & red 1.10 1.10

See Nos. 54, 98, 141, 187A, 220, 268.

Cosmonauts' Day — A8

1993, Apr. 12 *Perf. 13½x13*

37 A8 90r multicolored 1.90 1.40

Pres. Nursultan Nasarbajev — A9

1993, Aug. 2 **Litho.** *Perf. 14*

38 A9 50r multicolored 1.00 .70

Bukar Zhirav Kalkaman (1668-1781), Poet — A10

1993, Aug. 18 *Perf. 13½x13*

39 A10 15r multicolored .35 .20

Map, Pres. Nasarbajev — A11

1993, Sept. 24 **Litho.** *Perf. 13*

40 A11 100r multicolored 1.75 1.10

Wildlife A12

Designs: 5r, Selevinia betpakdalensis. 10r, Hystrix leucura. 15r, Vormela peregusna. 20r, Equis hemionus onager. 25r, Ovis orientalis. 30r, Acinonyx jubatus venaticus.

1993, Nov. 11 *Perf. 12x12½*

41 A12 5r multicolored .30 .20
42 A12 10r multicolored .35 .25
43 A12 15r multicolored .35 .25
44 A12 20r multicolored .40 .30
45 A12 25r multicolored .50 .35
46 A12 30r multicolored .55 .45
Nos. 41-46 (6) 2.45 1.80

Nos. 1-46 were sold after the currency changeover as stamps denominated in one or both of the new currency units. Nos. 47-50, 54, 64 and 69 were sold as stamps denominated in tijn, and later as tenge.

1994 Winter Olympics, Lillehammer A13

1994, Jan. 24 **Litho.** *Perf. 13½x13*

47 A13 15te Ice hockey .30 .30
48 A13 25te Slalom skiing .45 .45
49 A13 90te Ski jumping 1.50 1.50
50 A13 150te Speed skating 2.50 2.50
Nos. 47-50 (4) 4.75 4.75

1994 Winter Olympics, Lillehammer A14

Designs: 2te, Skiers Vladimir Smirnov, Kazakhstan; Bjorn Daehlie, Norway. 6.80te, 12te, Smirnov.

1994, Feb. 19 **Litho.** *Perf. 13x13½*

51 A14 2te multicolored .35 .25
52 A14 6.80te multicolored 1.10 1.10
a. Pair, #51-52 1.60 1.60
53 A14 12te like No. 52 1.25 1.25
Nos. 51-53 (3) 2.70 2.60

No. 53 has an additional two line Cyrillic inscription.

New Year Type of 1993

Size: 26x38mm

1994, Mar. 22 *Perf. 12*

54 A7 30te green, black & blue .70 .25

New Year 1994 (Year of the Dog).

Space Program A15

1994, Apr. 12 *Perf. 13½x13*

55 A15 2te multicolored .50 .50

Souvenir Sheet

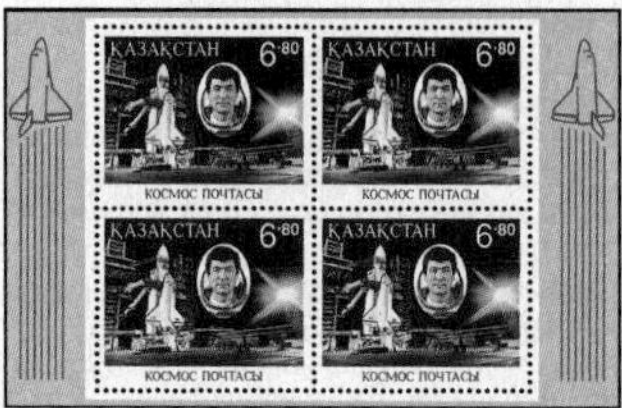

Russian Space Shuttle, Cosmonaut — A16

1994, July 12 *Perf. 13*

56 A16 6.80te Sheet of 4 3.50 3.50

Space Ship and Yurt Type of 1993

1994, July 12 **Litho.** *Perf. 11½*

64 A4 15ti blue .95 .80
69 A4 80ti lake 2.10 1.60

For surcharges see Nos. 70-76, 122.

This is an expanding set. Numbers may change.

Nos. 64, 69 Surcharged in Lake or Purple

1995-2004 **Litho.** *Perf. 11½*

70 A4 1te on 15te #64 .30 .30
71 A4 2te on 15te #64 .30 .30
72 A4 3te on 80te #69 (P) .30 .30
73 A4 4te on 80te #69 (P) .40 .40
74 A4 6te on 80te #69 (P) .45 .45
75 A4 8te on 80ti .75 .75
76 A4 12te on 80te #69 (P) .80 .80
77 A4 20te on 80te #69 (P) .90 .90
78 A4 200te on 80ti #69 (P) 4.50 4.50
Nos. 70-78 (9) 8.70 8.70

Issued: 1te, 2te, 12te, 2/2/95. 3te, 4te, 6te, 20te, 2/10/95. 8te, 9/25/95. 200te, 1/29/04.

Music Competition Festival
A18

Designs: 10te, Snow-covered mountain top. 15te, Aerial view of stadium at night.

1994, Aug. 1 *Perf. 13½*

81	A18	10te multicolored	.75	.75
82	A18	15te multicolored	1.00	1.00

For surcharges see Nos. 119A-119B.

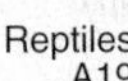

Reptiles
A19

Designs: 1te, Agrionemys horsfieldi. 1.20te, Phrynocephalus mystaceus. 2te, Agkistrodon halys. 3te, Teratoscincus scincus. 5te, Trapelus sanguinolenta. 7te, Ophisaurus apodus. 10te, Varanus griseus.

1994, Oct. 10 *Perf. 12½x12*

83	A19	1te multicolored	.20	.20
84	A19	1.20te multicolored	.25	.25
85	A19	2te multicolored	.30	.30
86	A19	3te multicolored	.35	.35
87	A19	5te multicolored	.45	.45
88	A19	7te multicolored	.50	.50
		Nos. 83-88 (6)	2.05	2.05

Souvenir Sheet

89	A19	10te multicolored	1.50	1.50

Prehistoric Animals
A20

1994, Nov. 24 **Litho.** *Perf. 12½x12*

90	A20	1te Entelodon	.20	.20
91	A20	1.20te Saurolophus	.25	.25
92	A20	2te Plesiosaurus	.30	.30
93	A20	3te Sordes pilosus	.35	.35
94	A20	5te Mosasaurus	.45	.45
95	A20	7te Megaloceros giganteum	.50	.50
		Nos. 90-95 (6)	2.05	2.05

Souvenir Sheet

96	A20	10te Koelodonta antiquitatis	1.50	1.50

Day of the Republic
A21

1994, Oct. 25 *Perf. 11½*

97	A21	2te multicolored	.60	.60

For surcharge see No. 160B.

New Year Type of 1993

1995, Mar. 22 **Litho.** *Perf. 14*

Size: 27x32mm

98	A7	10te blue, black & ultra	.85	.70

New Year 1995 (Year of the Boar).

Abai (Ibraghim) Kynanbaev (1845-1904), Poet — A22

1995, Mar. 31

99	A22	4te Portrait	.30	.30
100	A22	9te Portrait, diff.	.60	.60

Space Day — A23

Designs: 10te, Cosmonauts Malenchenko, Musabaev and Merbold.

1995, Apr. 12 **Litho.** *Perf. 14*

101	A23	2te multicolored	3.75	3.75
102	A23	10te multicolored	16.00	16.00

Mahatma Gandhi (1869-1948) — A24

1995, Oct. 2

103	A24	9te multicolored	2.40	2.40
104	A24	22te multicolored	5.50	5.50

End of World War II, 50th Anniv.
A25

Designs: 1te, Hero, battle scene. 3te, Heroine, tank. 5te, Dove, monument.

1995, May 9 **Litho.** *Perf. 14*

105	A25	1te multicolored	1.00	1.00
106	A25	3te multicolored	3.00	3.00
107	A25	5te multicolored	5.00	5.00
		Nos. 105-107 (3)	9.00	9.00

Spaceship and Yurt Type of 1993

1995, Mar. 24 **Litho.** *Perf. 14x14½*

108	A4	20ti orange	.40	.40
109	A4	25ti yellow brown	.40	.40
110	A4	50ti gray	.40	.40
111	A4	1te green	.60	.60
112	A4	2te blue	.80	.80
113	A4	4te bright pink	1.00	1.00
114	A4	6te gray green	1.25	1.25
115	A4	12te lilac	2.50	2.50
		Nos. 108-115 (8)	7.35	7.35

Nos. 108-115 are inscribed "1995."

Paintings — A26

Designs: 4te, "Springtime," by S. Mambeev. 9te, "Mountains," by Z. Shchardenov. 15te, "Kulash Baiseitova in role of Kyz Zhibek," by G. Ismailova, vert. 28te, "Kokpar," by K. Telzhanov.

1995, June 23 **Litho.** *Perf. 14*

116	A26	4te multicolored	.75	.75
117	A26	9te multicolored	1.60	1.60
118	A26	15te multicolored	2.75	2.75
119	A26	28te multicolored	4.75	4.75
		Nos. 116-119 (4)	9.85	9.85

Nos. 81-82 Ovptd.

1995, July 25 **Litho.** *Perf. 13½*

119A	A18	10te multicolored	1.40	1.40
119B	A18	15te multicolored	1.75	1.75

Dauletkerey (1820-87), Composer — A27

1995, Sept. 1 **Litho.** *Perf. 14*

120	A27	2te yellow & multi	.80	.80
121	A27	28te lake & multi	6.75	6.75

UN, 50th Anniv. — A28

1995, Nov. 24 **Litho.** *Perf. 14*

123	A28	10te multicolored	1.75	1.75
124	A28	36te gold & lt blue	5.25	5.25

Resurrection Cathedral
A29

Circus
A29a

Buildings in Alma-Ata: 2te, Culture Palace. 3te, Opera and Ballet House. 6te, Kazakh Science Academy. 48te, Dramatics Theatre.

Perf. 14, 13x12 (#126, 129)

1995-96 **Litho.**

125	A29	1te green	.30	.30
126	A29a	1te green	.30	.30
127	A29	2te blue	.55	.55
128	A29	3te red	.85	.85
129	A29a	6te olive	1.10	1.10
130	A29	48te brown	8.75	8.75
		Nos. 125-130 (6)	11.85	11.85

Issued: Nos. 125, 127-128, 130, 10/25/95; Nos. 126, 129, 7/5/96.

Raptors
A30

1te, Haliaeetus albicilla. 3te, Pandion haliaetus. 5te, Gypaetus barbatus. 6te, Gyps himalayensis. 30te, Falco cherrug. 50te, Aquila chrysaetus.

1995, Dec. 20 **Litho.** *Perf. 14*

131	A30	1te multicolored	.25	.25
132	A30	3te multicolored	.25	.25
133	A30	5te multicolored	.50	.50
134	A30	6te multicolored	.65	.65
135	A30	30te multicolored	2.75	2.75
136	A30	50te multicolored	4.75	4.75
		Nos. 131-136 (6)	9.15	9.15

New Year Type of 1993

Size: 27x32mm

1996, Mar. 21 **Litho.** *Perf. 14*

141	A7	25te lil, blk & red	1.90	1.90

New Year 1996 (Year of the Rat).

Space Day — A32

1996, Apr. 12

142	A32	6te Earth	2.25	2.25
143	A32	15te Cosmonaut	2.75	2.75
144	A32	20te Space station Mir	5.00	5.00
		Nos. 142-144 (3)	10.00	10.00

Souvenir Sheet

Save the Aral Sea — A33

Designs: a, Felis caracal. b, Salmo trutta aralensis. c, Hyaena hyaena. d, Pseudoscaphirhynchus kaufmanni. e, Aspiolucius esocinus.

1996, Apr. 20 **Litho.** *Perf. 14*

145	A33	20te Sheet of 5, #a.-e.	5.00	5.00

See Kyrgyzstan No. 107, Tadjikistan No. 91, Turkmenistan No. 52, Uzbekistan No. 113.

1996 Summer Olympic Games, Atlanta — A34

1996, June 19 **Litho.** *Perf. 14*

146	A34	4te Cycling	.50	.50
147	A34	6te Wrestling	1.25	1.25
148	A34	30te Boxing	6.25	6.25
		Nos. 146-148 (3)	8.00	8.00

Souvenir Sheet

149	A34	50te Hurdles	4.00	4.00

Issued: #146-148, 6/19/96; #149, 7/19/96.

Architectural Sites — A35

1te, Tomb, 8-9th cent. 3te, Mausoleum, 11-12th cent. 6te, Mausoleum, 13th cent. 30te, Hadji Ahmet Yassauy's Mausoleum, 14th cent.

1996, Sept. 27 **Litho.** *Perf. 14*

150	A35	1te multicolored	.50	.50
151	A35	3te multicolored	1.40	1.40
152	A35	6te multicolored	3.00	3.00
		Nos. 150-152 (3)	4.90	4.90

Souvenir Sheet

153	A35	30te multicolored	3.00	3.00

World Post Day — A37

1996, Oct. 9 Litho. *Perf. 14*

156 A37 9te shown .90 .90
157 A37 40te UPU emblem 3.50 3.50

A38

A39

1996, Aug. 21

158 A38 12te multicolored 1.25 1.25

Schambyl Schabaev (1846-1945).

1996, Oct. 2

159 A39 46te Space station Mir 3.50 3.50
160 A39 46te T. Aubakirov 3.50 3.50
a. Pair, #159-160 8.00 8.00

T. Aubakirov, 1st Kazak cosmonaut.

No. 97 Surcharged

1997, Oct. 25 Litho. *Perf. 11½*

160B A21 21te on 2te multi 1.50 1.50

Surcharge adds numeral 1 to existing value to appear as 21, obliterates original date and adds new date.

Butterflies A40

4te, Saturnia schenki. 6te, Parnassius patricius. 12te, Parnassius ariadne. 46te, Colias draconis.

1996, Nov. 21 Litho. *Perf. 14*

161 A40 4te multicolored .25 .25
162 A40 6te multicolored .25 .25
163 A40 12te multicolored .55 .55
164 A40 46te multicolored 2.25 2.25
Nos. 161-164 (4) 3.30 3.30

Hunting Dogs A41

1996, Nov. 29

165 A41 5te multicolored .50 .50

Souvenir Sheet

166 A41 100te like #165 5.25 5.25

No. 166 is a continuous design.

A42

A43

Traditional Costumes, Furnishings: a, 10te, Woman outside tent. b, 16te, Man outside tent. c, 45te, Interior view of furnishings.

1996, Dec. 5

167 A42 Strip of 3, #a.-c. 6.00 6.00

Nos. 167a-167b have continuous design.

1996, Dec. 24

Archives, Bicent.: 4te, Quill pen, candle, documents. 68te, Scroll, papers, book.

168 A43 4te brown .30 .30
169 A43 68te purple 3.75 3.75

Motion Pictures, Cent. — A44

Film scenes: a, Man in hat holding up fingers. b, Horse, woman, man. c, Two men, from "His Time Arrives." d, Woman holding paper, boy holding hat.

1996, Dec. 25 Litho. *Perf. 14*

170 A44 24te Sheet of 4, #a.-d. 10.00 10.00

Vormela Peregusna — A45

1997, Feb. 12 Litho. *Perf. 14*

171 A45 6te shown .70 .70
172 A45 10te Adult .85 .85
173 A45 32te Two young 1.90 1.90
174 A45 46te Adult, tail up 3.00 3.00
Nos. 171-174 (4) 6.45 6.45

World Wildlife Fund.

Zodiac Constellations A47

1997, Mar. 26 Litho. *Perf. 14*

176 A47 1te Aries .20 .20
177 A47 2te Taurus .20 .20
178 A47 3te Gemini .20 .20
179 A47 4te Cancer .20 .20
180 A47 5te Leo .20 .20
181 A47 6te Virgo .20 .20
182 A47 7te Libra .20 .20
183 A47 8te Scorpio .30 .30
184 A47 9te Sagittarius .35 .35
185 A47 10te Capricorn .35 .35
186 A47 12te Aquarius .50 .50
187 A47 20te Pisces .65 .65
b. Sheet of 12, #176-187 7.50 7.50

New Year Type of 1993 With Kazakhstan Inscribed in Both Cyrillic & Roman Letters

1997, Mar. 22 Litho. *Perf. 14*

187A A7 40te multicolored 1.75 1.75

New Year 1997 (Year of the Ox).

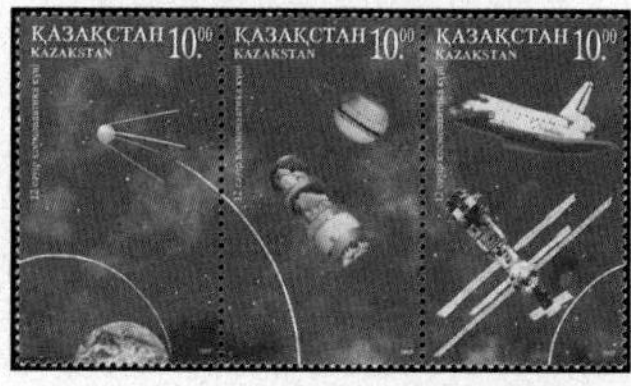

A48

A49

Cosmonauts' Day: a, Earth, Sputnik. b, Space vehicle, Saturn. c, Space shuttle, space station.

1997, Apr. 12

188 A48 10te Strip of 3, #a.-c. 3.00 3.00

No. 188 has continuous design.

1997, Apr. 23

189 A49 15te org yel & grn .60 .60
190 A49 60te org yel & grn 2.00 2.00

UNESCO World Book Day.

Mukhtar Auezov (1897-1961), Writer — A50

1997, May

191 A50 25te House 1.00 1.00
192 A50 40te Auezov at his desk 1.75 1.75

Orders and Medals — A51

Various medals.

1997, June 30 Litho. *Perf. 14*

193 A51 15te grn & yel ribbon .60 .60
194 A51 15te grn, red & pink ribbon .60 .60
195 A51 20te grn bl & multi .85 .85
196 A51 30te grn yel & multi 1.10 1.10
Nos. 193-196 (4) 3.15 3.15

Tulips — A52

15te, Tulipa regelii. No. 198, Tulipa greigii. No. 199, Tulipa alberti.

1997, Aug. 7 Litho. *Perf. 13½*

197 A52 15te multicolored .60 .60
198 A52 35te multicolored 1.40 1.40
199 A52 35te multicolored 1.40 1.40
Nos. 197-199 (3) 3.40 3.40

Paintings — A53

Designs: No. 200, Roping of a Wild Horse, by Moldakhmet S. Kenbaev. No. 201, Shepherd, by Sh. T. Sariev, vert. No. 202, Fantastic Still Life, by Sergei I. Kalmykov, vert.

1997, Sept. 10 Litho. *Perf. 14*

200 A53 25te multicolored 1.10 1.10
201 A53 25te multicolored 1.10 1.10
202 A53 25te multicolored 1.10 1.10
Nos. 200-202 (3) 3.30 3.30

Agate — A54

Azurite — A55

1997, Oct. 15 Litho. *Perf. 14*

203 A54 15te shown .65 .65
204 A54 15te Chalcedony .65 .65
205 A55 20te shown .90 .90
206 A55 20te Malachite .90 .90
a. Souvenir sheet, #203-206 3.00 3.00
Nos. 203-206 (4) 3.10 3.10

Desert Fauna — A56

Designs: No. 207, Gylippus rickmersi. No. 208, Anemelobathus rickmersi. No. 209, Latrodectus pallidus. No. 210, Oculicosa supermirabilis.

1997, Nov. 26 Litho. *Perf. 14*

207 A56 30te multicolored 1.25 1.25
208 A56 30te multicolored 1.25 1.25
209 A56 30te multicolored 1.25 1.25
210 A56 30te multicolored 1.25 1.25
Nos. 207-210 (4) 5.00 5.00

Souvenir Sheet

Nature Park — A57

Designs: a, Mountain goat. b, Trees on side of mountain. c, Rock formations, wildflowers.

1997, Dec. 22

211 A57 30te Sheet of 3, #a.-c. 3.25 3.25

See No. 257A.

A58

Sports A59

Designs: No. 212, Woman, man riding horses. No. 213, Wrestling match. No. 214, Group of men on galloping horses.

1997, Dec. 30 Litho. *Perf. 14*

212 A58 20te multicolored 1.50 1.50
213 A58 20te multicolored 1.50 1.50
214 A58 20te multicolored 1.50 1.50
215 A59 20te multicolored 1.50 1.50
Nos. 212-215 (4) 6.00 6.00

1998 Winter Olympic Games, Nagano — A60

Children's Paintings — A61

1998, Mar. 13 Litho. *Perf. 14*

216 A60 15te Figure skating .70 .70
217 A60 30te Biathlon 1.40 1.40

1998, Mar. 20

218 A61 15te shown .70 .70
219 A61 15te Outdoor scene, horiz. .70 .70

New Year Type of 1993 with "Kazakhstan" inscribed in both Cyrillis and Roman letters

1998, Mar. 22 Litho. *Perf. 14*

220 A7 30te yellow, black & brown 1.50 1.50

New Year 1998 (Year of the Tiger).

Kurmangazy (1823-96), Composer — A62

#222, Ahmet Baitursynov (1873-1937), poet.

1998 Litho. *Perf. 14*

221 A62 30te multicolored 1.25 1.25
222 A62 30te multicolored 1.25 1.25

Issued: No. 221, 4/10/98. No. 222, 4/28/98.

Ancient Gold Folk Art A63

15te, Ram's heads. 30te, Jeweled pendants, vert. 40te, Animal filigree diadem fragment.

1998, Apr. 30

223 A63 15te multicolored .60 .60
224 A63 30te multicolored 1.10 1.10
225 A63 40te multicolored 2.25 2.25
Nos. 223-225 (3) 3.95 3.95

Cosmonaut's Day — A64

#226, Apollo 8, moon, sun. #227, Apollo 8, moon, Earth. 50te, Vostok 6, Earth.

1998, May 4

226 A64 30te multi, vert. 1.25 1.25
227 A64 30te multi, vert. 1.25 1.25
a. Pair, #226-227 2.50 2.50
228 A64 50te multi 2.00 2.00
Nos. 226-228 (3) 4.50 4.50

Astana, New Capital City — A64a

A65

Buildings: 10te, Mosque. 15te, Govt., vert. 20te, Parliament, vert. 25te, Office. 100te, Presidential office.
Illustration A65 reduced.

1998 Litho. *Perf. 13½*

229 A64a 10te brown .80 .80
230 A64a 15te dark blue 1.25 1.25
231 A64a 15te blue 1.25 1.25
232 A64a 20te green blue 1.60 1.60
232A A64a 25te purple 2.00 2.00
Nos. 229-232A (5) 6.90 6.90

Souvenir Sheet

233 A65 100te multicolored 5.00 5.00

Issued: Nos. 229-232, 233, 6/10; 25te, 12/98. No. 230 is inscribed "AKMOLA" in Cyrillic. No. 231 is inscribed "ACTANA."

Souvenir Sheet

Climbing Mt. Everest — A67

1998, July 29 Litho. *Perf. 14*

239 A67 100te multicolored 4.25 4.25

Fauna — A68

Birds: No. 240, Ciconia nigra. No. 241, Phoenicopterus roseus. No. 242, Grus leucogeranus.
Wild cats: No. 243, Lynx lynx isabellinus. No. 244, Felis margarita. No. 245, Uncia uncia.

1998, July 31

240 A68 15te multicolored .70 .70
241 A68 30te multicolored 1.25 1.25
242 A68 50te multicolored 2.10 2.10
Nos. 240-242 (3) 4.05 4.05

1998, Aug. 8

243 A68 15te multicolored .70 .70
244 A68 30te multicolored 1.25 1.25
245 A68 50te multicolored 2.10 2.10
Nos. 243-245 (3) 4.05 4.05

Souvenir Sheet

Admission of Kazakhstan to UPU — A69

Illustration reduced.

1998, Oct. 9 Litho. *Perf. 14*

246 A69 50te multicolored 2.75 2.75

Natl. Arms A70

World Stamp Day A71

Republic, 5th Anniv. — A72

1998 Litho. *Perf. 13½*

247 A70 1te green .20 .20
248 A70 2te blue .20 .20
249 A70 3te red .20 .20
250 A70 4te bright pink .20 .20
251 A70 5te orange yellow .20 .20
252 A70 8te orange .50 .50
253 A71 30te olive 1.60 1.60
254 A72 40te orange 2.25 2.25
Nos. 247-254 (8) 5.35 5.35

Nos. 247, 248, 251 exist dated 1999.
Issued; 1te-5te, 6/29; 8te-40te, 11/12.
See Nos. 296, 299.

Natl. Epic A73

Horseman: 20te, Holding sword. 30te, Shooting bow and arrow. 40te, Charging with spear.

1998, Dec. *Perf. 14*

255 A73 20te multicolored 1.25 1.25
256 A73 30te multicolored 1.90 1.90
257 A73 40te multicolored 2.40 2.40
Nos. 255-257 (3) 5.55 5.55

Souvenir Sheet
Nature Park Type of 1997

Designs: a, Island in middle of lake, mountains. b, Lake, mountain peaks.

1998, Dec. Litho. *Perf. 14*

257A A57 30te Sheet of 2, #a.-b. 3.25 3.25

1999 Census A74

Space Communications A77

K. Satpayev (1899-1964)
A75 A76

1999 Litho. *Perf. 13½*

258 A74 1te green .20 .20
259 A75 15te rose lake .85 .85
260 A76 20te brown 1.10 1.10
261 A77 30te olive 1.60 1.60
Nos. 258-261 (4) 3.75 3.75

Issued: 1te, 2/5/99; 30te, 3/19/99.
See Nos. 270, 272.

Trains — A78

Map showing Orenburg-Tashkent Rail Line, 1890-1906, and: 40te, Steam train. 50te, Diesel locomotive. 60te, Bullet train. 80te, Interurban train.

1999 *Perf. 14*

262 A78 40te yel & multi 1.75 1.75
263 A78 50te pink & multi 2.25 2.25
264 A78 60te grn & multi 3.00 3.00
265 A78 80te blue & multi 4.00 4.00
Nos. 262-265 (4) 11.00 11.00

Space Achievements — A79

1999

266 A79 50te Soviet spacecraft, vert. 6.00 6.00
267 A79 90te Apollo 11 mission 11.50 11.50

Cosmonaut Day (#266), first manned lunar landing, 30th anniv. (#267).

New Year Type of 1993 with "Kazakhstan" inscribed in both Cyrillis and Roman letters

1999, Mar. 19 Litho. *Perf. 14*

268 A7 40te multicolored 2.75 2.75

New Year 1999 (Year of the Rabbit).

Space Communications Type of 1999 and:

A79a

A79b

1999 Litho. *Perf. 13½*

270 A77 3te red .20 .20
271 A79a 4te bright pink .20 .20
272 A77 9te bright green .45 .45
273 A79b 10te purple .50 .50
274 A79a 30te olive green 1.40 1.40
Nos. 270-274 (5) 2.75 2.75

No. 273 is for the UPU, 125th Anniv.

Flowers — A80

Movies — A81

Designs: 20te, Pseudoeremostachys severzowii. 30te, Rhaphidophyton regelii. 90te, Niedzwedkia semiretscenskia.

1999, June 28 Litho. *Perf. 14¼x14*

276	A80 20te multicolored	1.25	1.25
277	A80 30te multicolored	1.75	1.75
278	A80 90te multicolored	5.25	5.25
	Nos. 276-278 (3)	8.25	8.25

1999 Litho. *Perf. 14*

No. 279: a, 15te, Film scene from 1929. b, 20te, Scenes from 1988, 1997, M. Berkovich. c, 30te, Scenes from 1935, 1938, 1957. d, 35te, Scenes from 1989, 1994, 1997. e, 50te, Alfred Hitchcock. f, 60te, Sergei Eisenstein.

279 A81 Sheet of 10, #e.-f., 2 each #a.-d. 12.00 12.00

Foxes A82

Designs: 20te, Vulpes vulpes. 30te, Cuon alpinus. 90te, Vulpes corsac.

1999 Litho. *Perf. 14x 14¼*

280	A82 20te multicolored	1.50	1.50
281	A82 30te multicolored	2.50	2.50
282	A82 90te multicolored	6.50	6.50
	Nos. 280-282 (3)	10.50	10.50

Souvenir Sheet

Environmental Protection — A83

Designs: a, 15te, Cessation of nuclear tests at Semipalatinsk, 10th anniv. b, 45te, Save the ozone layer. c, 60te, Save nature.

1999 Litho. *Perf. 14x13¾*

283 A83 Sheet of 3, #a.-c. 4.50 4.50

Kazakhstan Hockey Team — A84

1999 Litho. *Perf. 14*

284	A84 20te Face-off	.80	.80
285	A84 30te Team photo	1.25	1.25

10th Gusman Kosanov Memorial Track & Field Meet — A85

1999

286 A85 40te multi 1.75 1.75

Cosmonauts — A86

1999 *Perf. 14*

287	A86 40te Talgat Musabayev	1.50	1.50
288	A86 50te Toktar Aubakirov, vert.	1.75	1.75

Souvenir Sheet

UPU, 125th Anniv. — A87

Illustration reduced.

1999, Dec. 20 Litho. *Perf. 14x13¾*

289 A87 20te multi 1.75 1.75

Arms Type of 1998 and

Spireanthus Schrenhianus A88

Echo Satellite A89

Oil Rig A90

Mukhammed Khaidar Dulati (1499-1551), Historian A91

Sabit Mukanov (1900-73), Writer — A92

2000 Litho. *Perf. 13½*

290	A88	1te green	.20	.20
291	A88	2te bright blue	.20	.20
291A	A89	5te orange yellow	.20	.20
292	A90	7te red	.35	.35
293	A91	8te dark blue	.35	.35
294	A92	10te olive green	.35	.35
295	A89	15te violet blue	.45	.45
296	A70	20te orange	.85	.85
297	A89	20te indigo	.60	.60
299	A70	50te blue	1.90	1.90
300	A88	50te blue	1.75	1.75
		Nos. 290-300 (11)	7.20	7.20

Issued: 7te, 20te, 50te, 1/18/00; 1te, 2te, No. 300, 11/24; 5te, 15te, No. 297, 9/28; 8te, 8/25; 10te, 6/30. 20te and 50te are dated 1999.

This is an expanding set. Numbers have been reserved for other values.

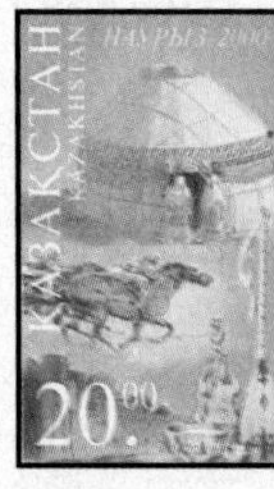

Navruz Bayram — A93

2000, Mar. 21 Litho. *Imperf.*

301 A93 20te multi 1.75 1.75

Millennium — A94

2000, Mar. 24 Litho. *Perf. 13½*

302 A94 30te org & blue green 2.00 2.00

Victory in World War II, 55th Anniv. — A95

2000, May 8 Litho. *Perf. 13½*

303 A95 3te brown & red .25 .25

Souvenir Sheet

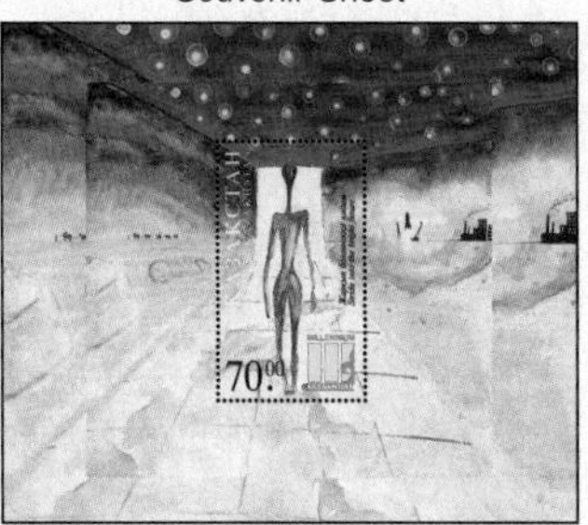

Millennium — A96

2000, June 1 *Perf. 14x13¾*

304 A96 70te multi 3.50 3.50

Containers — A97

No. 305: a, 15te, Leather vessel for koumiss, Kazakhstan. b, 50te, Teapot, China. Illustration reduced.

2000, June 28 *Perf. 12½x12*

305 A97 Horiz. pair, #a-b 5.00 5.00

See China (PRC) Nos. 3042-3043.

2000 Summer Olympics, Sydney — A98

Designs: 35te, Rowing. No. 307, 40te, Taekwondo. No. 308, 40te, Men's gymnastics. 50te, Triathlon.

2000, Sept. 15 *Perf. 12*

306-309 A98 Set of 4 7.00 7.00

Souvenir Sheet

Turkistan, 1500th Anniv. — A99

Mausoleums of: a, 50te, Arystan Bab, 12th-20th cents. b, 50te, Karashash Ana, 12th-18th cents. c, 70te, Hadji Ahmet Yassauy, 14th cent.

2000, Oct. 19 *Perf. 13½*

310 A99 Sheet of 3, #a-c 10.00 10.00
Complete booklet, #310 *24.00*

Bourzhan Momush-Uly (1910-82), Hero of the Soviet Union — A100

2000, Dec. 22 *Perf. 13½*

311 A100 4te black & brown .40 .40

No. B1 Surcharged in Dark Blue

Method and Perf. as Before

2001, Jan. 26

Block of 3, #a-c, + Label

312 SP1 10te on 1te+30ti multi 1.25 1.25

New Year Type of 1993 with "Kazakhstan" Inscribed in Both Cyrillic and Roman Letters

2001, Mar. 2 Litho. *Perf. 13¾x14*

313 A7 40te org, blk & blue 1.25 1.25

Dated 2000. New Year 2000 (Year of the Snail).

Cosmonaut's Day — A101

Designs: 40te, Dogs Belka and Strelka. 70te, Rocket launch, vert.

2001, Mar. 6 *Perf. 14*

314-315 A101 Set of 2 4.25 4.25

Dated 2000. Spaceflight of Belka and Strelka, 40th anniv., Baikonur Cosmodrome, 45th anniv.

New Year Type of 1993 with "Kazakhstan" Inscribed in Both Cyrillic and Roman Letters

2001, Mar. 21 Litho. *Perf. 13¾x14*

316 A7 40te grn, blk & brn 1.40 1.40

New Year 2001 (Year of the Snake).

Souvenir Sheet

Ministry of Communications, 10th Anniv. — A102

2001, Apr. 4 ***Perf. 11½***
317 A102 100te multi 9.00 9.00

Cosmonaut's Day — A103

Designs: 45te, Soyuz 11 and Salyut. 60te, Yuri Gagarin, Earth.

2001, Apr. 12 ***Perf. 14***
318-319 A103 Set of 2 3.50 3.50

Aquilegia Karatavica A104

School, Almaty A105

Phodopus Roborovskii — A106

Perf. 13½, 14 (#321, 326)

2001 **Litho.**

320	A104	3te olive green	.20	.20
321	A105	7te red violet	.20	.20
322	A106	8te orange	.30	.30
323	A104	10te yellow green	.35	.35
324	A106	15te dark blue	.50	.50
325	A106	20te deep blue	.60	.60
326	A105	30te greenish gray	.75	.75
327	A106	50te brown	1.25	1.25
		Nos. 320-327 (8)	4.15	4.15

Issued: 7te, 30te, 10/19/01.

Numbers have been reserved for additional stamps in this set.

Kazakh State Khans — A107

Designs: 50te, Abulkhair Khan (1693-1748). 60te, Abylai Khan (1711-81).

2001, May 24 **Litho.** ***Perf. 13¾x14***
328-329 A107 Set of 2 4.00 4.00

Dated 2000.

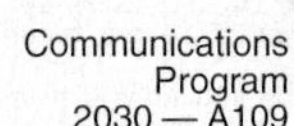

Owls A108

Designs: 30te, Bubo bubo. 40te, Asio otus. 50te, Surnia ulula.

2001, June 7 ***Perf. 14***
330-332 A108 Set of 3 7.00 7.00

Dated 2000.

Communications Program 2030 — A109

2001, June 21 ***Perf. 14x13¾***
333 A109 40te multi 1.50 1.50

Dated 2000.

Souvenir Sheet

Lake Markakol — A110

No. 334: a, Cervus elaphus. b, Ursus arctos. c, Brachymystax lenok.

2001, July 5 ***Perf. 13¾x14***
334 A110 30te Sheet of 3, #a-c 6.00 6.00

Souvenir Sheet

Flora & Fauna — A111

No. 335: a, 9te, Marmota bobac. b, 12te, Otis tarda. c, 25te, Larus relictus. d, 60te, Felis libyca. e, 90te, Nymphaea alba. f, 100te, Pelecanus crispus.

2001, July 19 ***Perf. 14x14¼***
335 A111 Sheet of 6, #a-f 9.00 9.00

Souvenir Sheet

Kazakh Railways, 10th Anniv. — A112

No. 336: a, 15te, Building. b, 20te, Turkestan-Siberia locomotive. c, 50te, Railroad workers.

2001, Aug. 4 ***Perf. 14x13¾***
336 A112 Sheet of 3, #a-c *17.50 17.50*

Medicine — A113

Designs: 1te, WHO emblem, lungs (tuberculosis prevention). 5te, Ribbon, book (AIDS prevention).

2001, Aug. 9 ***Perf. 13½***
337-338 A113 Set of 2 .30 .30

Intl. Year of Mountains (in 2002) — A114

Various mountains: 35te, 60te.

2001, Sept. 26 ***Perf. 14***
339-340 A114 Set of 2 3.25 3.25

Space Achievements — A115

Designs: 50te, Alexei Leonov's walk in space, 1965, vert. 70te, Apollo-Soyuz mission, 1975.

2001, Oct. 2
341-342 A115 Set of 2 7.00 7.00

Dated 2000.

Year of Dialogue Among Civilizations A116

2001, Oct. 9 ***Perf. 13¾x14***
343 A116 45te multi 1.50 1.50

Worldwide Fund for Nature (WWF) — A117

Various views of Equus hemionus kulan: 9te, 12te, 25te, 50te.

2001, Nov. 1 ***Perf. 14***
344-347 A117 Set of 4 4.00 4.00

Commonwealth of Independent States, 10th Anniv. — A118

2001, Dec. 12 **Litho.** ***Perf. 14***
348 A118 40te multi 1.50 1.50

Visit of Pope John Paul II — A119

No. 349: a, 20te, Pres. Nazarbayev, Pope. b, 50te, Pope, Pres. Nazarbayev.
Illustration reduced.

2001, Dec. 14 ***Perf. 11½***
349 A119 Horiz. pair, #a-b 4.00 4.00

A120

Independence, 10th Anniv. — A121

No. 351: a, 9te, Monument of Independence, Almaty. b, 25te, Parliament, Astana. c, 35te, Pres. Nazarbayev.

2001 ***Perf. 13½***
350 A120 40te multi 1.25 1.25

Souvenir Sheet

Perf. 13¾x14

351 A121 Sheet of 3, #a-c 5.50 5.50

Issued: 40te, 12/18; No. 351, 12/16.

Native Attire — A122

No. 352: a, 25te, Male attire. b, 35te, Female attire.
Illustration reduced.

2001, Dec. 25 ***Perf. 14x13¾***
352 A122 Horiz. pair, #a-b 2.00 2.00

2002 Winter Olympics, Salt Lake City A123

Designs: 50te, Women's ice hockey. 150te, Freestyle skiing.

2002, Feb. 14 ***Perf. 14***
353-354 A123 Set of 2 6.50 6.50

New Year Type of 1993 With "Kazakhstan" Inscribed in Both Cyrillic and Roman Letters

2002, Mar. 21 ***Perf. 11½***
355 A7 50te multi 1.60 1.60

New Year 2002 (Year of the Horse).

Horses A124

Horses: 9te, English. 25te, Kustenai. 60te, Akhalteka.

2002, Mar. 28
356-358 A124 Set of 3 5.00 5.00

Pterygostemon Spathulatus A125

Gani Muratbaev (1902-25), Political Leader A126

Salpingotus Pallidus A127

Trade House, Petropavlovsk A128

Monument, Petro-pavlovsk A129

Gabiden Mustafin (1902-85), Writer A130

2002 Litho. *Perf. 13½*

359	A125	1te blue green	.25	.25
360	A125	2te blue	.25	.25
361	A125	3te green	.25	.25
362	A126	3te brown	.25	.25
363	A127	5te rose lilac	.25	.25
364	A128	6te red	.25	.25
365	A128	7te lilac	.25	.25
366	A129	8te orange	.25	.25
367	A125	10te violet	.25	.25
368	A130	10te blue	.25	.25
369	A125	12te pink	.40	.40
370	A127	15te dark blue	.40	.40
371	A129	23te gray blue	.70	.70
372	A125	25te purple	.70	.70
373	A125	35te olive green	.95	.95
374	A127	40te bister brown	1.10	1.10
375	A127	50te brown	1.60	1.60
		Nos. 359-375 (17)	8.35	8.35

Petropavlovsk, 250th anniv. (#364-366, 371). Issued: 1te, 2te, 5/7; Nos. 361, 367, 35te, 4/30; 5te, 15te, 40te, 50te, 4/4; 6te, 7te, 8te, 23te, 7/9; 12te, 25te, 5/14; No. 362, 12/19; No. 368, 12/18.

Cosmonauts Day — A131

Designs: 30te, Cosmonauts Yuri Baturin, Talgat Musabaev and first space tourist Dennis Tito. 70te, Globe, rocket, flags of US, Kazakhstan and Russia.

2002, Apr. 10 Litho. *Perf. 11¾*
376-377 A131 Set of 2 3.75 3.75

2002 World Cup Soccer Championships, Japan and Korea — A132

Two players, one with: No. 378, 10te, Jersey No. 8. No. 379, 10te, Jersey No. 7.

2002, May 31
378-379 A132 Set of 2 1.25 1.25

Transeurasia 2002 Conference — A133

2002, June 6 *Perf. 13½*
380 A133 30te multi .75 .75

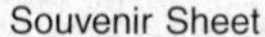

Souvenir Sheet

Flora and Fauna — A134

No. 381: a, Leontopodium fedtschenkoanum. b, Mustela erminea. c, Aport Alexander apples.

2002, June 6 *Perf. 11¾x11½*
381 A134 30te Sheet of 3, #a-c 3.00 3.00

Art — A135

Designs: 8te, Kazakh Folk Epos, by E. Sidorkin, 1961. 9te, Makhambet, by M. Kisamedinov, 1973. 60te, Batyr, by Sidorkin, 1979.

2002, July 19 *Perf. 11¾*
382-384 A135 Set of 3 2.75 2.75

Birds — A136

No. 385: a, 10te, Larus ichthyaetus pallas. b, 15te, Anthropoides virgo.

2002, Aug. 29 *Perf. 12*
385 A136 Horiz. pair, #a-b 1.25 1.25

See Russia No. 6709.

Marine Life — A137

No. 386: a, 20te, Huso huso ponticus. b, 35te, Phoca caspica.
Illustration reduced.

2002, Sept. 6
386 A137 Horiz. pair, #a-b 2.00 2.00

See Ukraine No. 483.

Souvenir Sheet

Taraz, 2000th Anniv. — A138

2002, Sept. 25
387 A138 70te multi 2.25 2.25

Souvenir Sheet

International Year of Mountains — A139

2002, Oct. 4 *Perf. 11½x11¾*
388 A139 50te multi 1.75 1.75

Gabit Musrepov (1902-85) A140

2002, Dec. 30 Litho. *Perf. 11½*
389 A140 20te multi .65 .65

Airplanes A141

Designs: 20te, Ilyushin-86. 40te, Tupolev-144 and map.

Perf. 11½x11¾
2002, Dec. 23 Litho.
390-391 A141 Set of 2 2.00 2.00

First Moscow to Alma Ata flight of Tupolev-144, 25th anniv. (No. 391).

Type of 1999, Types of 2000-01 Redrawn and

Monument to Victims of Political Reprisals A142

Selevinia Betpak-dalensis A143

2003 Litho. *Perf. 13½*

392	A88	1te green	.20	.20
393	A142	1te red violet	.20	.20
394	A88	2te bright blue	.20	.20
394A	A77	3te red	.20	.20
395	A143	4te brown	.20	.20
396	A143	5te bister	.20	.20
397	A143	6te gray green	.20	.20
398	A143	7te dull green	.20	.20
399	A106	8te orange	.20	.20
400	A142	8te red brown	.20	.20
401	A77	9te dark blue	.20	.20
402	A143	10te blue	.20	.20
403	A106	15te deep blue	.45	.45
404	A106	20te gray blue	.55	.55
405	A106	35te dark green	1.00	1.00
406	A143	63te fawn	1.90	1.90
407	A77	84te purple	2.40	2.40
408	A77	100te orange	2.75	2.75
409	A143	150te claret	4.00	4.00
		Nos. 392-409 (19)	15.45	15.45

Issued: No. 392, 2te, 2/24; Nos. 393, 400, 4/17; 4te, 5te, 6te, 7te, 10te, 63te, 150te, 1/31; No. 399, 15te, 20te, 35te, 3/28; 84te, 100te, 5/30; 3te, 9te, 9/12.

Nos. 392 and 394 are dated "2003" and have smaller Cyrillic inscription of country name, and longer Roman inscription of country name than Nos. 290-291.

Nos. 394A is dated "2003" and has a smaller denomination with thinner zeroes than No. 270.

Nos. 399, 403 and 404 are dated "2003" and have taller Cyrillic inscription of country name than Nos. 322, 324-325.

Domestic and Wild Sheep — A144

Various rams, ewes and lambs: 20te, 40te, 50te.

2003, Feb. 26 *Perf. 11½x11¾*
410-412 A144 Set of 3 3.75 3.75

New Year Type of 1993 With "Kazakhstan" Inscribed in Both Cyrillic and Roman Letters

2003, Mar. 21 *Perf. 11½*
413 A7 40te lt bl, blk & dk bl 1.60 1.60

New Year 2003 (Year of the Ram).

Cosmonaut's Day — A145

Designs: 40te, Pioneer 10 and Jupiter. 70te, Mir Space Station, vert.

2003, Apr. 12 *Perf. 11¾*
414-415 A145 Set of 2 3.75 3.75

Intl. Association of Academies of Science, 10th Anniv. — A146

2003, Apr. 23 Litho. *Perf. 11½*
416 A146 50te multi 1.60 1.60

Souvenir Sheet

Ethnic Groups in Kazakhstan — A147

No. 417: a, Kazakhs (woman with red vest). b, Russians (woman with yellow blouse). c, Ukrainians (woman with blue vest).

2003, Apr. 29 Litho. *Perf. 11¾x11½*
417 A147 35te Sheet of 3, #a-c 3.25 3.25

Musical Instruments A148

Designs: 25te, Dombra. 50te, Kobyz.

2003, May 26
418-419 A148 Set of 2 2.25 2.25

Fairy Tales A149

Designs: 30te, Aldar Kose and Alasha Khan. 40te, Aldar Kose and Karynbaj.

2003, June 27 ***Perf. 11½***
420-421 A149 Set of 2 2.50 2.50

Art — A150

Designs: 20te, Chess Match, by Arturo Ricci (1854-1919). 35te, Portrait of the Shepherd, sculpture by H. Nauryzbaev. 45te, Bowls of Koumiss, by Aisha Galimbaeva (1917-).

2003, July 7 ***Perf. 11¾***
422-424 A150 Set of 3 3.50 3.50

Famous Men — A151

Designs: No. 425, 60te, Tole Bey (1663-1756). No. 426, 60te, Kazybek Bey (1667-1763). No. 427, 60te, Aiteke Bey (1689-1766).

2003, Aug. 11 ***Perf. 11¾x11½***
425-427 A151 Set of 3 5.00 5.00

Halyk Bank, 80th Anniv. A152

2003, Aug. 15 ***Perf. 11½x11¾***
428 A152 23te multi .70 .70

International Transit Conference, Almaty — A153

2003, Aug. 28
429 A153 40te multi 1.25 1.25

World Post Day — A154

2003, Oct. 9 ***Perf. 13½***
430 A154 23te pur & blue .70 .70

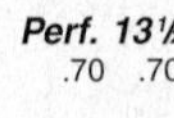

Houses of Worship, Almaty — A155

Designs: No. 431, 50te, Cathedral. No. 432, 50te, Mosque.

2003, Oct. 10 ***Perf. 11¾x11½***
431-432 A155 Set of 2 3.00 3.00

Tenge Currency, 10th Anniv. — A156

2003, Nov. 15 ***Perf. 13½***
433 A156 25te blue & yel org .60 .60

Paintings — A157

No. 434: a, Baxt, by S. Ayitbaev, 1966. b, Tong. Onalik, by R. Ahmedov, 1962.
Illustration reduced.

2003, Nov. 25 ***Perf. 12***
434 A157 100te Horiz. pair, #a-b 6.00 6.00

See Uzbekistan No. 385.

Populus Diversifolia A158

2003, Dec. 10 ***Perf. 11½***
435 A158 100te multi 2.75 2.75

Petroglyphs, Tamgaly — A159

Designs. 25te, Cows. 30te, Man as sun on bull, vert.

Perf. 11½x11¾, 11¾x11½
2003, Dec. 19
436-437 A159 Set of 2 1.50 1.50

Abylkhan Kasteev (1904-73), Artist — A160

2004, Feb. 28 Litho. ***Perf. 11¾***
439 A160 115te multi 2.50 2.50

New Year Type of 1993 With "Kazakhstan" Inscribed in Both Cyrillic and Roman Letters

2004, Mar. 23 ***Perf. 11½***
440 A7 35te lt bl, dk bl & org .90 .90

New Year 2004 (Year of the Monkey).

Cosmonaut's Day — A161

Designs: 40te, Mariner 10, vert. 50te, Luna 3.

Perf. 11¾x11½, 11½x11¾
2004, Apr. 12
441-442 A161 Set of 2 2.25 2.25

Kazakhstan Flag — A162

2004, Apr. 19 ***Perf. 13½***
443 A162 25te yel & brt blue .60 .60

Arms Type of 1998 Redrawn

2004 Litho. ***Perf. 13½***

444	A70	1te	green	.20	.20
445	A70	2te	bright blue	.20	.20
446	A70	4te	bright pink	.20	.20
447	A70	5te	orange yellow	.20	.20
448	A70	10te	olive green	.20	.20
449	A70	16te	brt purple	.40	.40
450	A70	20te	purple	.50	.50
451	A70	35te	bright yellow	.85	.85
452	A70	50te	brt green	1.25	1.25
453	A70	72te	orange	1.75	1.75
454	A70	100te	greenish blue	2.50	2.50
455	A70	200te	vermilion	4.75	4.75
			Nos. 444-455 (12)	13.00	13.00

Issued: 1te, 2te, 4te, 4/19; 20te, 35te, 72te, 100te, 200te, 5/11; 5te, 10te, 16te, 50te, 6/10.

Nos. 444-455 are dated "2004," arms and "Kazakhstan" in Roman letters are larger and denominations are smaller than those features on Nos. 247-254.

No. 447 is dated "2004," arms and "Kazakhstan" in Roman letters are larger and denomination is smaller than those features on No. 251.

Souvenir Sheet

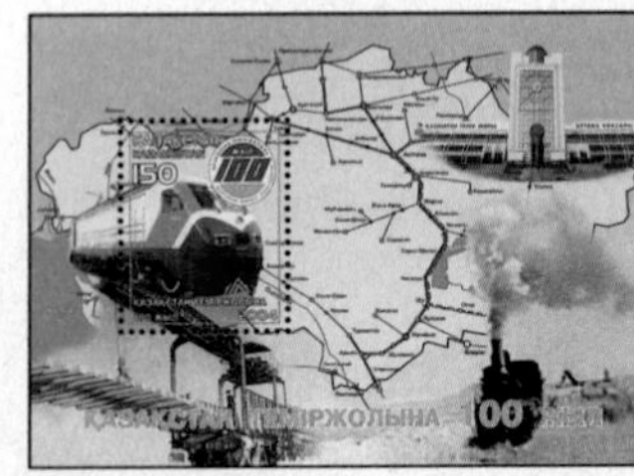

Kazakhstan Railways, Cent. — A163

2004, Apr. 22 Litho. ***Perf. 11¾x11½***
456 A163 150te multi 3.75 3.75

Souvenir Sheet

Ethnic Groups in Kazakhstan — A164

No. 457: a, Uzbeks (denomination at left). b, Germans (denomination at right).

2004, May 12
457 A164 65te Sheet of 2, #a-b 3.00 3.00

FIFA (Fédération Internationale de Football Association), Cent. — A165

FIFA emblem, soccer player and soccer ball at: No. 458, 100te, Left. No. 459, 100te, Center.

2004, May 21 Litho. & Embossed
458-459 A165 Set of 2 4.50 4.50

Children's Art — A166

Designs: No. 460, 45te, Yurts and sheep, by A. Sadykov. No. 461, 45te, Woman, by D. Iskhanova, vert.

2004, June 20 Litho. ***Perf. 11½***
460-461 A166 Set of 2 2.25 2.25

Souvenir Sheet

2004 Summer Olympics, Athens — A167

No. 462: a, 70te, Boxing. b, 115te, Shooting.

Litho., Margin Embossed
2004, June 28
462 A167 Sheet of 2, #a-b 4.00 4.00

Souvenir Sheet

Fauna in Altyn Emel Reserve — A168

No. 463: a, Acgypius monacus. b, Capra sibirica. c, Gazella subgutturosa.

2004, Aug. 11 ***Perf. 11½x11¾***
463 A168 50te Sheet of 3, #a-c 3.75 3.75

Souvenir Sheet

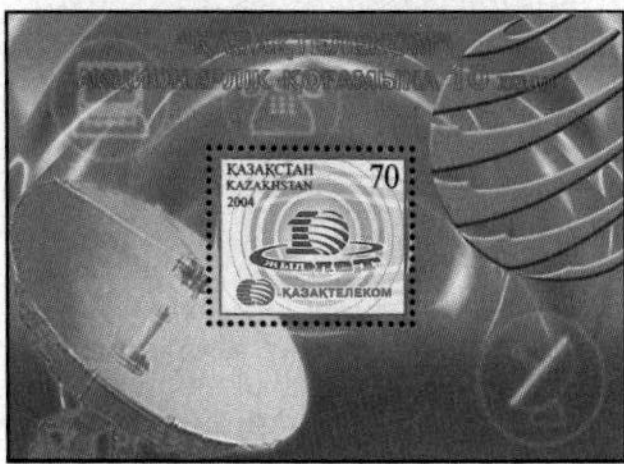

Kazaktelecom, 10th Anniv. — A169

Perf. 11½x11¾
2004, Aug. 18 **Litho.**
464 A169 70te multi 1.75 1.75

Alkei Khakan Margulan (1904-85), Archaeologist A170

2004, Sept. 23
465 A170 115te multi 2.50 2.50

Flowers — A171

2004, Oct. 4 ***Perf. 12¼x11½***
466 A171 25te multi + label .60 .60

Printed in sheets of 12 + 12 labels.

World Post Day Type of 2003

2004, Oct. 9 ***Perf. 13½***
467 A154 3te red vio & blue .20 .20
468 A154 30te yel org & blue .65 .65

New Year 2005 — A172

2004, Nov. 23 ***Perf. 13¼***
469 A172 65te multi 1.50 1.50

Musical Instruments — A173

No. 470: a, Adyma. b, Gizhak and bow. Illustration reduced.

2004, Nov. 29 ***Perf. 11½x11¾***
470 A173 100te Horiz. pair, #a-b 4.75 4.75

See Tajikistan No. 248.

Saken Seifullin (1894-1939), Writer — A174

2004, Dec. 28
471 A174 35te multi .80 .80

Women's Headdresses — A175

No. 472: a, Kazakh headdress, denomination at left. b, Mongol headdress, denomination at right.
Illustration reduced.

2004, Dec. 30
472 A175 72te Horiz. pair, #a-b 3.25 3.25

See Mongolia No. 2590.

Veterinary Research Institute, Cent. — A176

2005, Jan. 14 ***Perf. 13½***
473 A176 7te multi .30 .30

Constitution, 10th Anniv. — A177

2005, Apr. 8 **Litho.** ***Perf. 13½***

474	A177	1te	blue & brn	.20	.20
475	A177	2te	vio & brn	.20	.20
476	A177	3te	brt grn & brn	.20	.20
477	A177	8te	brt bl & brn	.20	.20
478	A177	10te	red & brn	.20	.20
479	A177	A	red vio & brn	.60	.60
480	A177	50te	olive & brn	1.10	1.10
481	A177	65te	bl grn & brn	1.40	1.40
	Nos. 474-481 (8)			4.10	4.10

No. 479 sold for 25te on day of issue.

Europa — A178

2005, Apr. 14 **Litho.** ***Perf. 11½x12¼***
482 A178 90te multi 3.25 3.25

End of World War II, 60th Anniv. — A179

2005, Apr. 28 **Litho.** ***Perf. 13¼x13***
483 A179 72te multi 1.75 1.75

Souvenir Sheet

Baikonur Space Complex, 50th Anniv. — A180

No. 484: a, Rocket. b, Buran space shuttle. c, Capsule and parachute.

2005, June 2 ***Perf. 11½x11¾***
484 A180 72te Sheet of 3, #a-c 5.50 5.50

Peace and Harmony Palace — A181

Litho. & Embossed

2005, July 6 ***Perf. 13¼***
485 A181 65te multi 1.60 1.60

Minerals — A182

Designs: 50te, Azurite. 70te, Agate.

2005, July 12 **Litho.** ***Perf. 11¾x11½***
486-487 A182 Set of 2 3.00 3.00

Fairy Tales Type of 2003

Designs: 35te, Aldar Kose and the Musician. 45te, Aldar Kose and the Raiser of Asses.

2005, Aug. 11
488-489 A149 Set of 2 2.10 2.10

Constitution, 10th Anniv. — A183

2005, Aug. 26
490 A183 72te multi 2.00 2.00

Souvenir Sheet

Olympic Gold Medalists — A184

No. 491: a, Zaksylik Ushkempirov, 1980, 48kg Greco-Roman wrestling. b, Vitaly Savin, 1988, 4x100m relay. c, Vasily Zhirov, 1996, light heavyweight boxing. d, Bekzat Sattarkhanov, 2000, featherweight boxing.

2005, Sept. 22 **Litho.** ***Perf. 11¾***
491 A184 100te Sheet of 4, #a-d 9.50 9.50

Akhmet Baitursynov (1873-1937), Writer — A185

Litho. with Foil Application

2005, Oct. 6 ***Perf. 13¾x14***
492 A185 30te multi .70 .70

No. 492 not issued without gold overprint.

World Post Day — A186

2005, Oct. 8 **Litho.** ***Perf. 13½***
493 A186 35te blue & pur .80 .80
494 A186 40te pur & red .95 .95

Dogs — A187

No. 495: a, Kazakh hound (dog with curled tail). b, Estonian hound (white, black and brown dog).
Illustration reduced.

2005, Oct. 19 ***Perf. 11½x11¾***
495 A187 138te Horiz. pair, #a-b 7.00 7.00

See Estonia No. 523.

United Nations, 60th Anniv. — A188

2005, Oct. 31 ***Perf. 13½***
496 A188 150te multi 3.50 3.50

New Year 2006 — A189

2005, Nov. 10 **Litho.** ***Perf. 13¼***
497 A189 65te multi 1.75 1.75

Evgeny Brusilovsky (1905-81), Composer — A190

2005, Nov. 18 *Perf. 11½x11¾*
498 A190 150te multi 3.50 3.50

Assembly of Peoples of Kazakhstan, 10th Anniv. — A191

2005, Nov. 24 *Perf. 13½*
499 A191 80te multi 2.00 2.00

Souvenir Sheet

National Symbols — A192

No. 500: a, 70te, Flag and eagle. b, 70te, National anthem. c, 300te, Arms.

Litho. & Embossed

2005, Dec. 22 *Perf. 13¼*
500 A192 Sheet of 3, #a-c 10.50 10.50

Turgen Waterfall A193

Mountain Lake A194

2005, Dec. 23 Litho. *Perf. 13½*
501 A193 12te multi .30 .30
502 A194 100te multi 2.40 2.40

Hans Christian Andersen (1805-75), Author — A195

2005, Dec. 30 *Perf. 11¾x11½*
503 A195 200te multi 4.75 4.75

Parliament, 10th Anniv. — A196

2006, Jan. 17 Litho. *Perf. 11½x11¾*
504 A196 50te multi 1.25 1.25

Abylai Khan, by Aubakir Ismailov A197

Litho. With Foil Application

2006, Jan. 27 *Perf. 13x13¼*
505 A197 94te multi 2.25 2.25

2006 Winter Olympics, Turin — A198

Perf. 11½x11¾

2006, Feb. 20 **Litho.**
506 A198 138te multi 3.25 3.25

Cosmonaut's Day — A199

Paintings of cosmonauts by: 100te, P. M. Popov. 120te, A. M. Stepanov.

2006, Apr. 12 *Perf. 11¾x11½*
507-508 A199 Set of 2 5.25 5.25

Traditional Jewelry — A200

No. 509: a, Bracelet, Kazakhstan. b, Brooch, Latvia.
Illustration reduced.

2006, Apr. 19 *Perf. 11½x11¾*
509 A200 110te Horiz. pair, #a-b 5.25 5.25

See Latvia No. 650.

Saksaul Tree — A201

2006, Apr. 27 *Perf. 11¾x11½*
510 A201 25te multi .60 .60

Europa — A202

2006, May 3
511 A202 210te multi 4.25 4.25
a. Tete-beche pair 8.50 8.50

Turkestan-Siberia Railway, 75th Anniv. — A203

2006, May 31 *Perf. 13x13¼*
512 A203 200te multi 4.75 4.75

2006 World Cup Soccer Championships, Germany — A204

2006, June 2 *Perf. 11½x11¾*
513 A204 150te multi 3.50 3.50

Intl. Year of Deserts and Desertification — A205

2006, July 7 *Perf. 13¼*
514 A205 110te multi 2.75 2.75

Mosque, Astana — A206

2006 Litho. *Perf. 13½x13¾*

515	A206	5te	emerald	.20	.20
516	A206	8te	Prus blue	.20	.20
517	A206	10te	olive grn	.25	.25
518	A206	A	purple	.55	.55
518A	A206	100te	dark blue	2.25	2.25
519	A206	110te	brown	2.50	2.50
520	A206	120te	green	2.75	2.75
521	A206	200te	red violet	4.75	4.75
	Nos. 515-521 (8)			13.45	13.45

No. 518 sold for 25te on day of issue.
Issued: 100te, 10/10/06; rest, 7/20/06.

Akzhan Mashani, Geologist, Cent. of Birth — A207

2006, July 21 Litho. *Perf. 11½x11¾*
522 A207 85te multi 2.00 2.00

Houses of Worship in Almaty — A208

Designs: No. 523, 25te, Catholic Church (denomination in orange). No. 524, 25te, Synagogue (denomination in white).

2006, Aug. 17 *Perf. 11¾x11½*
523-524 A208 Set of 2 1.25 1.25

Souvenir Sheet

Famous Men — A209

No. 525: a, Chokan Valikhanov (1835-65), diplomat. b, Saken Sejfullin (1894-1938), poet. c, Nazir Tjurjakulov (1893-1937). d, Kanysh Satpaev (1899-1964), geologist.

2006, Aug. 20 *Perf. 11½*
525 A209 90te Sheet of 4, #a-d 8.25 8.25

Third Meeting of Economic Cooperation Organization Postal Authorities, Turkey — A210

2006, Sept. 15 *Perf. 12*
526 A210 210te multi 4.50 4.50

No. 526 Overprinted in Gold

2006, Sept. 22
527 A210 210te multi 4.50 4.50

Overprint corrects site of meeting from Istanbul to Ankara.

Ahmet Zhubanov (1906-68), Composer A211

2006, Oct. 13 *Perf. 11½*
528 A211 85te multi 1.90 1.90

Coats of Arms — A212

Arms of: 17te, Almaty. 80te, Astana.

2006, Oct. 20 Litho. *Perf. 13½x13¾*
529-530 A212 Set of 2 2.10 2.10

New Year 2007 — A213

2006, Nov. 1 Litho. *Perf. 13¼*
531 A213 25te multi .50 .50

Latif Khamidi (1906-83), Composer A214

2006, Nov. 9 *Perf. 11½x11¾*
532 A214 110te multi 2.25 2.25

Mukagali Makataev (1931-76), Writer — A215

2006, Nov. 29 *Perf. 13½x13¾*
533 A215 1te dark blue .20 .20
534 A215 4te olive grn .20 .20
535 A215 7te rose claret .20 .20
536 A215 15te red brown .30 .30
Nos. 533-536 (4) .90 .90

Manash Kozybaev (1931-2002), Historian — A216

2006, Nov. 29
537 A216 20te brown .45 .45
538 A216 30te brn lake .65 .65

Character From Opera *Silk Girl* — A217

2006, Dec. 15 *Perf. 13¼*
539 A217 80te multi 1.75 1.75

Values are for stamps with surrounding selvage.

18th Century Helmet — A218

2006, Dec. 15 *Perf. 13x12¾*
540 A218 85te multi 1.90 1.90

Nikolai Repinsky (1906-69), Architect — A219

2006, Dec. 20 *Perf. 13½x13¾*
541 A219 2te brown .20 .20
542 A219 3te yel brn .20 .20
543 A219 105te gray grn 2.25 2.25
544 A219 150te blue 3.25 3.25
545 A219 500te rose claret 10.00 10.00
Nos. 541-545 (5) 15.90 15.90

Miniature Sheet

Kurgalzhinsky Nature Reserve — A220

No. 546: a, 25te, Phoenicopterus roseus. b, 100te, Cygnus cygnus. c, 120te, Meles meles.

2006, Dec. 29 *Perf. 11½x11¾*
546 A220 Sheet of 3, #a-c 5.50 5.50

KazTransOil, 10th Anniv. — A221

2007, Apr. 12 Litho. *Perf. 12¾*
547 A221 25te multi .60 .60

Cosmonaut's Day — A222

Designs: 80te, Konstantin E. Tsiolkovsky (1857-1935), rocket pioneer. 110te, Sergei P. Korolev (1906-66), aeronautical engineer.

2007, Apr. 12 *Perf. 12¼x11¾*
548-549 A222 Set of 2 4.25 4.25

Europa — A223

No. 550 — Children's art: a, 25te, Scout bugler and tents. b, 65te, Scouts with backpacks, dog.
Illustration reduced.

2007, May 8 *Perf. 11½x11¾*
550 A223 Pair, #a-b 2.00 2.00
Scouting, cent.

63rd Session of UN Economic and Social Commission for Asia and the Pacific, Almaty — A224

2007, May 17 *Perf. 12¾*
551 A224 25te multi .60 .60

Gali Ormanov (1907-78), Poet — A225

2007, Sept. 28 Litho. *Perf. 11½*
552 A225 25te multi .60 .60

Conference on Interaction and Confidence-Building Measures in Asia, 15th Anniv. — A226

2007, Oct. 17 *Perf. 13½*
553 A226 80te multi 1.75 1.75

Maulen Balakaev (1907-95), Philologist — A227

2007, Oct. 29 Litho. *Perf. 13½*
554 A227 1te red brown .20 .20
555 A227 4te green .20 .20
556 A227 5te dk brown .20 .20
Nos. 554-556 (3) .60 .60

Almaty Zoo Animals — A228

No. 557: a, 25te, Zebras. b, 110te, Elephant.
Illustration reduced.

2007, Oct. 31 Litho. *Perf. 11½*
557 A228 Pair, #a-b 2.40 2.40

Printed in sheets containing 4 each of Nos. 557a and 557b, with a central label.

Hirundo Rustica — A229

2007, Nov. 15 *Perf. 13½*
558 A229 20te multi .35 .35
559 A229 25te multi .45 .45
560 A229 50te multi .90 .90
561 A229 100te multi 1.90 1.90
Nos. 558-561 (4) 3.60 3.60

Saddle A230

2007, Nov. 27 *Perf. 12*
562 A230 80te multi 1.50 1.50

Launch of Sputnik 1, 50th Anniv. — A231

2007, Nov. 27 *Perf. 12½x12¾*
563 A231 500te multi 9.00 9.00

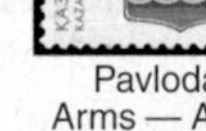

Karagand Arms — A232

Pavlodar Arms — A233

2007, Dec. 10 *Perf. 13½x13¼*
564 A232 10te multi .20 .20
565 A233 10te multi .20 .20

Miniature Sheet

Olympic Gold Medalists — A234

No. 566: a, Vladimir Smirnov, 1994, 50-kilometer skiing. b, Yuri Melinichenko, 1996, Greco-Roman wrestling. c, Olga Shishigina, 2000, 100-meter hurdles. d, Ermahan Ibraimov, 2000, boxing.

2007, Dec. 28 *Perf. 12x11½*
566 A234 150te Sheet of 4, #a-d 10.50 10.50

Souvenir Sheet

Peoples of Kazakhstan — A235

No. 567: a, Uighur man and woman (denomination at left). b, Tatar man and woman (denomination at right).

2007, Dec. 28 *Perf. 11½*
567 A235 105te Sheet of 2, #a-b 3.75 3.75

New Year — A236

2008, Jan. 23 Litho. *Perf. 13¼*
568 A236 25te multi .55 .55

Printed in sheets of 8 + central label.

Miniature Sheet

Women's Day — A237

No. 569 — Various flowers with: a, Denomination at LL. b, Denomination at LR. c, Denomination and country name at UL. d, Denomination and country name at UR, Kazakh text in lower panel justified at right. e, Denomination at L, country name at LL. f, Denomination and country name at UR, Kazakh text in lower panel justified at left.

2008, Mar. 14 ***Perf. 13¼***
569 A237 25te Sheet of 6, #a-f, + 3 labels 3.25 3.25

Navruz Bayram — A238

2008, Mar. 21 ***Perf. 12¾***
570 A238 25te multi .55 .55

2008 Summer Olympics, Beijing — A239

2008, Apr. 2 ***Perf. 14x14¼***
571 A239 25te multi .60 .60

Kazakhstan Postal Service, 15th Anniv. — A240

2008, Apr. 4 ***Perf. 12¾***
572 A240 25te multi .60 .60

Cosmonaut's Day — A241

Designs: 100te, Space Station Mir. 150te, International Space Station.

2008, Apr. 10 ***Perf. 14x14¼***
573-574 A241 Set of 2 5.00 5.00

Europa — A242

No. 575 — Color of dove: a, Blue. b, Red.

2008, May 6 ***Perf. 14x14¼***
575 A242 150te Horiz. pair, #a-b 6.00 6.00

2008 Summer Olympics, Beijing — A243

No. 576: a, Judo. b, Handball.
Illustration reduced.

2008, Aug. 10 Litho. ***Perf. 14x14¼***
576 A243 100te Horiz. pair, #a-b 4.00 4.00

Deer — A244

No. 577: a, Cervus elaphus sibiricus. b, Cervus nippon.
Illustration reduced.

2008, Sept. 18
577 A244 110te Horiz. pair, #a-b 4.50 4.50

See Moldova No. 596.

Ancient Jewelry From Iran and Kazakhstan — A245

No. 578: a, Buckle depicting snow leopard and mountains, 4th-5th cent. B.C., Kazakhstan. b, Gold medal depicting lions, 7th cent. B.C., Iran.

2008, Oct. 3 ***Perf. 14x14¼***
578 Horiz. pair + flanking label 3.50 3.50
a. A245 25te multi .50 .50
b. A245 150te multi 3.00 3.00

See Iran No. 2965.

SEMI-POSTAL STAMP

Cartoons SP1

a, Mother and child. b, Cow, rabbit. c, Horses.

1994, Nov. 3 Litho. ***Perf. 12½x12***
B1 SP1 1te +30ti Block of 3 + label .75 .75

KENYA

'ke-nyə

LOCATION — East Africa, bordering on the Indian Ocean
GOVT. — Republic
AREA — 224,960 sq. mi.
POP. — 28,808,658 (1999 est.)
CAPITAL — Nairobi

Formerly a part of the British colony of Kenya, Uganda, Tanganyika, Kenya gained independence Dec. 12, 1963.

100 Cents = 1 Shilling

Catalogue values for all unused stamps in this country are for Never Hinged items.

Treetop Hotel and Elephants — A1

Designs: 5c, Cattle ranching. 10c, Wood carving. 15c, Riveter. 20c, Timber industry. 30c, Jomo Kenyatta facing Mt. Kenya. 40c, Fishing industry. 50c, Flag and emblem. 65c, Pyrethrum industry (daisies). 1sh, National Assembly bldg. 2sh, Harvesting coffee. 5sh, Harvesting tea. 10sh, Mombasa port. 20sh, Royal College, Nairobi.

Perf. 14x14½
1963, Dec. 12 Photo. Unwmk.
Size: 21x17½mm

1 A1 5c bl, buff & dk brn .20 *.60*
2 A1 10c brown .20 .20
a. Booklet pane of 4 .30
3 A1 15c deep magenta .75 .20
a. Booklet pane of 4 .30
4 A1 20c yel grn & dk brn .20 .20
a. Booklet pane of 4 .40
5 A1 30c yel & black .20 .20
a. Booklet pane of 4 .55
6 A1 40c blue & brown .20 .45
7 A1 50c grn, blk & dp car .25 .20
a. Booklet pane of 4 1.25
8 A1 65c steel blue & yel .50 .90

Perf. 14½
Size: 41½x25½mm

9 A1 1sh multicolored .25 .20
10 A1 1.30sh grn, brn & blk 4.25 .20
11 A1 2sh multicolored 1.25 .45
12 A1 5sh ultra, yel grn & brn 1.25 .90
13 A1 10sh brn & dark brn 8.50 3.25
14 A1 20sh pink & grnsh blk 9.00 *8.50*
Nos. 1-14 (14) 27.00 16.45

President Jomo Kenyatta and Flag of Kenya — A2

Flag and: 15c, Cockerel. 50c, African lion. 1.30sh, Hartlaub's touraco. 2.50sh, Nandi flame flower.

1964, Dec. 12 Photo. ***Perf. 13x12½***
15 A2 15c lt violet & multi .20 .20
16 A2 30c dk blue & multi .25 .20
17 A2 50c dk brown & multi .50 .20
18 A2 1.30sh multicolored 5.50 2.25
19 A2 2.50sh multicolored 1.25 *5.25*
Nos. 15-19 (5) 7.70 *8.10*

Establishment of the Republic of Kenya, Dec. 12, 1964.

Greater Kudu A3

Animals: 5c, Thomson's gazelle. 10c, Sable antelope. 15c, Aardvark. 20c, Senegal bush baby. 30c, Warthog. 40c, Zebra. 50c, Buffalo. 65c, Black rhinoceros. 70c, Ostrich. 1.30sh, Elephant. 1.50sh, Bat-eared fox. 2.50sh, Cheetah. 5sh, Vervet monkey. 10sh, Giant pangolin. 20sh, Lion.

1966-69 Unwmk. ***Perf. 14x14½***
Size: 21x17mm

20 A3 5c gray, black & org .20 .20
21 A3 10c black & yel green .20 .20
22 A3 15c dp orange & black .20 .20
23 A3 20c ultra, lt brn & black .20 .20
24 A3 30c lt ultra & blk .25 .25
25 A3 40c ocher & blk .20 .20
26 A3 50c dp orange & blk .25 .20
27 A3 65c dp yel green & blk 2.00 *2.00*
28 A3 70c rose lake & black 2.00 1.75

Perf. 14½
Size: 41x25mm

29 A3 1sh gray bl, ol & blk .70 .20
30 A3 1.30sh yel grn & blk 2.00 .35
31 A3 1.50sh brn org, brn & black 2.50 *2.50*
32 A3 2.50sh ol bis, yel & blk 3.50 1.75
33 A3 5sh brt grn, ultra & black 3.00 1.00
34 A3 10sh red brn, bis & black 6.25 3.75
35 A3 20sh ocher, bis, gold & black 12.50 *12.50*
Nos. 20-35 (16) 35.95 27.25

Issued: #28, 31, 9/15/69; others, 12/12/66.

Branched Murex — A4

Sea shells: 5c, Morning pink. 10c, Episcopal miter. 15c, Strawberry-top shell. 20c, Humpback cowrie. 30c, variable abalone. 40c, Flame-top shell. 50c, Violet sailor. 60c, Bull's-mouth helmet. 70c, Pearly nautilus. 1.50sh, Neptune's trumpet. 2.50sh, Mediterranean tulip shell. 5sh, Fluctuating turban. 10sh, Textile cone. 20sh, Scorpion shell.

1971 Dec. 13 Photo. ***Perf. 14½x14***
Size: 17x21mm

36 A4 5c bister & multi .20 *.45*
37 A4 10c dull grn & multi .30 .20
a. Booklet pane of 4 .60
38 A4 15c tan & multi .30 .30
a. Booklet pane of 4 .60
39 A4 20c tan & multi .30 .30
a. Booklet pane of 4 .75
40 A4 30c yellow & multi .55 .20
a. Booklet pane of 4 2.25
41 A4 40c gray & multi .55 .20
a. Booklet pane of 4 2.25
42 A4 50c buff & multi *(Janthina globosa)* .85 .30
a. Booklet pane of 4 3.50
43 A4 60c lilac & multi .85 *1.75*
44 A4 70c gray grn & multi *(Nautilus pompileus)* 1.25 *2.10*
a. Booklet pane of 4 5.00

Perf. 14½
Size: 25x41mm

45 A4 1sh ocher & multi .85 .35
46 A4 1.50sh pale grn & multi 2.75 .25
47 A4 2.50sh vio gray & multi 2.75 *.45*
48 A4 5sh lemon & multi 2.75 *.90*
49 A4 10sh multicolored 5.50 *3.50*
50 A4 20sh gray & multi 11.50 *8.00*
Nos. 36-50 (15) 31.25 *19.25*

Used values of Nos. 48-50 are for stamps with printed cancellations.

For surcharges see Nos. 53-55.

Revised Inscription

1974, Jan. 20 ***Perf. 14½x14***
51 A4 50c *(Janthina janthina)* 14.50 2.00
52 A4 70c *(Nautilus pompilius)* 16.50 4.00

Nos. 46-47, 50 Surcharged with New Value and 2 Bars

1975, Nov. 17 Photo. ***Perf. 14½***
53 A4 2sh on 1.50sh multi 5.25 *3.00*
54 A4 3sh on 2.50sh multi 11.50 *20.00*
55 A4 40sh on 20sh multi 13.50 *18.00*
Nos. 53-55 (3) 30.25 *41.00*

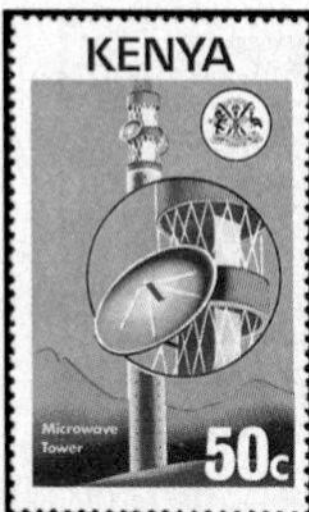

Microwave Tower — A5

Designs: 1sh, Cordless switchboard and operators, horiz. 2sh, Telephones of 1880, 1930 and 1976. 3sh, Message switching center, horiz.

1976, Apr. 15 Litho. *Perf. 14½*

No.	Type	Description	Unused	Used
56	A5	50c blue & multi	.20	.20
57	A5	1sh red & multi	.20	.20
58	A5	2sh yellow & multi	.20	.90
59	A5	3sh multicolored	.60	1.25
a.		Souvenir sheet of 4	3.50	*3.50*
		Nos. 56-59 (4)	1.20	2.55

Telecommunication development in East Africa. No. 59a contains 4 stamps similar to Nos. 56-59 with simulated perforations.

Akii Bua, Ugandan Hurdler — A6

Designs: 1sh, Filbert Bayi, Tanzanian runner. 2sh, Steve Muchoki, Kenyan boxer. 3sh, Olympic torch, flags of Kenya, Tanzania and Uganda.

1976, July 5 Litho. *Perf. 14½*

No.	Type	Description	Unused	Used
60	A6	50c blue & multi	.20	.20
61	A6	1sh red & multi	.25	.20
62	A6	2sh yellow & multi	.60	.50
63	A6	3sh blue & multi	1.10	.75
a.		Souv. sheet of 4, #60-63, perf. 13	9.50	9.50
		Nos. 60-63 (4)	2.15	1.65

21st Olympic Games, Montreal, Canada, July 17-Aug. 1.

Tanzania-Zambia Railway — A7

Designs: 1sh, Nile Bridge, Uganda. 2sh, Nakuru Station, Kenya. 3sh, Class A locomotive, 1896.

1976, Oct. 4 Litho. *Perf. 14½*

No.	Type	Description	Unused	Used
64	A7	50c lilac & multi	.50	.20
65	A7	1sh emerald & multi	1.00	.25
66	A7	2sh brt rose & multi	1.90	1.75
67	A7	3sh yellow & multi	3.00	2.75
a.		Souv. sheet of 4, #64-67, perf. 13	12.00	12.00
		Nos. 64-67 (4)	6.40	4.95

Rail transport in East Africa.

Nile Perch — A8

Game Fish: 1sh, Tilapia. 3sh, Sailfish. 5sh, Black marlin.

1977, Jan. 10 Litho. *Perf. 14½*

No.	Type	Description	Unused	Used
68	A8	50c multicolored	.20	.20
69	A8	1sh multicolored	.55	.20
70	A8	3sh multicolored	2.00	1.50
71	A8	5sh multicolored	2.50	2.00
a.		Souvenir sheet of 4, #68-71	14.50	14.50
		Nos. 68-71 (4)	5.25	3.90

Festival Emblem and Masai Tribesmen Bleeding Cow — A9

Festival Emblem and: 1sh, Dancers from Uganda. 2sh, Makonde sculpture, Tanzania. 3sh, Tribesmen skinning hippopotamus.

1977, Jan. 15 *Perf. 13½x14*

No.	Type	Description	Unused	Used
72	A9	50c multicolored	.20	.20
73	A9	1sh multicolored	.40	.20
74	A9	2sh multicolored	1.60	1.25
75	A9	3sh multicolored	1.90	1.90
a.		Souvenir sheet of 4, #72-75	7.75	7.75
		Nos. 72-75 (4)	4.10	3.55

2nd World Black and African Festival, Lagos, Nigeria, Jan. 15-Feb. 12.

Automobile Passing through Village — A10

Safari Rally Emblem and: 1sh, Winner at finish line. 2sh, Car going through washout. 5sh, Car, elephants and Mt. Kenya.

1977, Apr. 5 Litho. *Perf. 14*

No.	Type	Description	Unused	Used
76	A10	50c multicolored	.25	.20
77	A10	1sh multicolored	.40	.25
78	A10	2sh multicolored	1.25	1.00
79	A10	5sh multicolored	2.75	2.50
a.		Souvenir sheet of 4, #76-79	6.50	6.50
		Nos. 76-79 (4)	4.65	3.95

25th Safari Rally, Apr. 7-11.

Rev. Canon Apolo Kivebulaya — A11

1sh, Uganda Cathedral. 2sh, Early grass-topped Cathedral. 5sh, Early tent congregation, Kigezi.

1977, June 20 Litho. *Perf. 14*

No.	Type	Description	Unused	Used
80	A11	50c multicolored	.20	.20
81	A11	1sh multicolored	.25	.25
82	A11	2sh multicolored	.80	.80
83	A11	5sh multicolored	2.50	2.50
a.		Souvenir sheet of 4, #80-83	4.00	4.00
		Nos. 80-83 (4)	3.75	3.75

Church of Uganda, centenary.

Elizabeth II and Prince Philip at Sagana Lodge — A12

Designs: 5sh, "Treetops" observation hut, Aberdare Forest, and elephants, vert. 10sh, Pres. Jomo Kenyatta, Elizabeth II, crossed spears and shield. 15sh, Elizabeth II and Pres. Kenyatta in open automobile. 50sh, Elizabeth II and Prince Philip at window in Treetops.

1977, July 20 Litho. *Perf. 14*

No.	Type	Description	Unused	Used
84	A12	2sh multicolored	.20	.20
85	A12	5sh multicolored	.75	*.75*
86	A12	10sh multicolored	1.00	*1.00*
87	A12	15sh multicolored	1.50	*1.50*
a.		Souvenir sheet of 1	2.75	2.75
		Nos. 84-87 (4)	3.45	*3.45*

Souvenir Sheet

No.	Type	Description	Unused	Used
88	A12	50sh multicolored	8.50	8.50

Reign of Queen Elizabeth II, 25th anniv.

Pancake Tortoise — A13

Wildlife Fund Emblem and; 1sh, Nile crocodile. 2sh, Hunter's hartebeest. 3sh, Red colobus monkey. 5sh, Dugong.

1977, Sept. 26 Litho. *Perf. 14x13½*

No.	Type	Description	Unused	Used
89	A13	50c multicolored	.55	.25
90	A13	1sh multicolored	.75	.30
91	A13	2sh multicolored	3.00	1.50
92	A13	3sh multicolored	3.50	2.50
93	A13	5sh multicolored	4.50	3.50
a.		Souvenir sheet of 4, #90-93	12.50	12.50
		Nos. 89-93 (5)	12.30	8.05

Endangered species.

Kenya-Ethiopia Border Point — A14

Designs: 1sh, Station wagon at Archer's Post. 2sh, Thika overpass. 5sh, Marsabit Game Lodge and elephant.

1977, Nov. 10 Litho. *Perf. 14*

No.	Type	Description	Unused	Used
94	A14	50c multicolored	.20	.20
95	A14	1sh multicolored	.40	.20
96	A14	2sh multicolored	.95	.95
97	A14	5sh multicolored	2.50	2.50
a.		Souvenir sheet of 4, #94-97	6.25	6.25
		Nos. 94-97 (4)	4.05	3.85

Opening of Nairobi-Addis Ababa highway.

Minerals Found in Kenya — A15

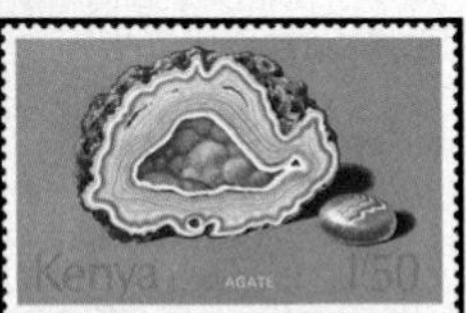

A16

Perf. 14½x14, 14½ (A16)

1977, Dec. 13 Photo.

No.	Type	Denom.	Description	Unused	Used
98	A15	10c	Gypsum	1.60	.20
99	A15	20c	Trona	2.40	.20
100	A15	30c	Kyanite	2.40	.20
101	A15	40c	Amazonite	1.90	.20
102	A15	50c	Galena	1.90	.20
103	A15	70c	Silicified wood	9.00	1.00
104	A15	80c	Fluorite	9.00	1.00
105	A16	1sh	Amethyst	1.90	.20
106	A16	1.50sh	Agate	1.90	.40
107	A16	2sh	Tourmaline	1.90	.45
108	A16	3sh	Aquamarine	2.40	.95
109	A16	5sh	Rhodolite garnet	2.40	1.50
110	A16	10sh	Sapphire	2.40	2.50
111	A16	20sh	Ruby	6.00	5.25
112	A16	40sh	Green grossular garnet	25.00	24.00
			Nos. 98-112 (15)	72.10	38.25

The 10c, 20c, 40c, 50c and 80c were also issued in booklet panes of 4. The 50c was also issued in a booklet pane of 2.

For surcharge see No. 242.

Soccer, Joe Kadenge and World Cup — A17

World Cup and: 1sh, Mohammed Chuma receiving trophy, and his portrait. 2sh, Shot on goal and Omari S. Kidevu. 3sh, Backfield defense and Polly Ouma.

1978, Apr. 10 Litho. *Perf. 14x13½*

No.	Type	Description	Unused	Used
113	A17	50c green & multi	.20	.20
114	A17	1sh lt brown & multi	.20	.20
115	A17	2sh lilac & multi	.50	*.50*
116	A17	3sh dk blue & multi	.90	*.90*
a.		Souvenir sheet of 4, #113-116	5.00	5.00
		Nos. 113-116 (4)	1.80	1.80

World Soccer Cup Championships, Argentina 78, June 1-25.

Boxing and Games' Emblem A18

Games Emblem and: 1sh, Pres. Kenyatta welcoming 1968 Olympic team. 3sh, Javelin. 5sh, Pres. Kenyatta, boxing team and trophy.

1978, July 15 Photo. *Perf. 13x14*

No.	Type	Description	Unused	Used
117	A18	50c multicolored	.20	.20
118	A18	1sh multicolored	.40	.40
119	A18	3sh multicolored	.80	.80
120	A18	5sh multicolored	1.25	1.25
		Nos. 117-120 (4)	2.65	2.65

Commonwealth Games, Edmonton, Canada, Aug. 3-12.

Overloaded Truck — A19

Road Safety: 1sh, Observe speed limit. 1.50sh, Observe traffic lights. 2sh, School crossing. 3sh, Passing. 5sh, Railroad crossing.

1978, Sept. 18 Litho. *Perf. 13½x14*

No.	Type	Description	Unused	Used
121	A19	50c multicolored	.65	.20
122	A19	1sh multicolored	.90	.45
123	A19	1.50sh multicolored	1.10	.90
124	A19	2sh multicolored	1.60	1.00
125	A19	3sh multicolored	1.90	*1.90*
126	A19	5sh multicolored	2.75	*3.00*
		Nos. 121-126 (6)	8.90	7.45

Pres. Kenyatta at Harambee Water Project Opening — A20

Kenyatta Day: 1sh, Prince Philip handing over symbol of independence, 1963. 2sh, Pres. Jomo Kenyatta addressing independence rally. 3sh, Stage at 15th independence anniversary celebration. 5sh, Handcuffed Kenyatta led by soldiers, 1952.

1978, Oct. 16 Litho. *Perf. 14*

No.	Type	Description	Unused	Used
127	A20	50c multicolored	.20	.20
128	A20	1sh multicolored	.40	.40
129	A20	2sh multicolored	.75	.75
130	A20	3sh multicolored	1.40	1.10
131	A20	5sh multicolored	1.50	1.50
		Nos. 127-131 (5)	4.25	3.95

Soldiers and Emblem A21

Anti-Apartheid Emblem and: 1sh, Anti-Apartheid Conference. 2sh, Stephen Biko, South African Anti-Apartheid leader. 3sh, Nelson Mandela, jailed since 1961. 5sh, Bishop Lamont, expelled from Rhodesia in 1977.

1978, Dec. 11 Litho. *Perf. 14x14½*

132 A21 50c multicolored	.20	.20
133 A21 1sh multicolored	.35	.35
134 A21 2sh multicolored	.60	.60
135 A21 3sh multicolored	1.00	1.00
136 A21 5sh multicolored	1.50	1.50
Nos. 132-136 (5)	3.65	3.65

Anti-Apartheid Year and Namibia's struggle for independence.

Children on School Playground — A22

Children's Year Emblem and: 2sh, Boy catching fish. 3sh, Children dancing and singing. 5sh, Children and camel caravan.

1979, Feb. 5 Litho. *Perf. 14*

137 A22 50c multicolored	.35	.35
138 A22 2sh multicolored	.75	.75
139 A22 3sh multicolored	1.00	1.00
140 A22 5sh multicolored	1.90	1.90
Nos. 137-140 (4)	4.00	4.00

International Year of the Child.

"The Lion and the Jewel" A23

National Theater: 1sh, Dancers and drummers. 2sh, Programs of various productions. 3sh, View of National Theater. 5sh, "Genesis," performed by Nairobi City Players.

1979, Apr. 6 Litho. *Perf. 13½x14*

141 A23 50c multicolored	.20	.20
142 A23 1sh multicolored	.40	.40
143 A23 2sh multicolored	.60	.60
144 A23 3sh multicolored	.90	.90
145 A23 5sh multicolored	1.50	1.50
Nos. 141-145 (5)	3.60	3.60

Village Workshop — A24

Salvation Army Emblem and: 50c, Blind telephone operator, vert. 1sh, Care for the aged, vert. 5sh, Vocational training (nurse).

1979, June 4 *Perf. 13½x13, 13x13½*

146 A24 50c multicolored	.20	.20
147 A24 1sh multicolored	.70	.45
148 A24 3sh multicolored	1.90	1.25
149 A24 5sh multicolored	2.75	2.25
Nos. 146-149 (4)	5.55	4.15

Salvation Army Social Services, 50th anniv.

Funeral Procession — A25

British East Africa No. 2, Hill, Signature — A26

Kenyatta: 1sh, Taking oath of office. 3sh, Addressing crowd. 5sh, As young man with wooden trying plane.

1979, Aug. 22 Litho. *Perf. 13½x14*

150 A25 50c multicolored	.20	.20
151 A25 1sh multicolored	.35	.35
152 A25 3sh multicolored	.75	.75
153 A25 5sh multicolored	1.25	1.25
Nos. 150-153 (4)	2.55	2.55

Jomo Kenyatta (1893-1978), first president of Kenya.

1979, Nov. 27 Litho. *Perf. 14*

Hill, Signature and: 1sh, Kenya, Uganda and Tanzania #54. 2sh, Penny Black. 5sh, Kenya #19.

154 A26 50c multicolored	.20	.20
155 A26 1sh multicolored	.35	.35
156 A26 2sh multicolored	.50	.50
157 A26 5sh multicolored	1.00	1.00
Nos. 154-157 (4)	2.05	2.05

Sir Rowland Hill (1795-1879), originator of penny postage.

Highways, Globe, Conference Emblem — A27

Conference Emblem and: 1sh, Truck at Athi River, New Weighbridge. 3sh, New Nyali Bridge, Mombasa. 5sh, Jomo Kenyatta Airport Highway.

1980, Jan. 10 Litho. *Perf. 14*

158 A27 50c multicolored	.20	.20
159 A27 1sh multicolored	.25	.20
160 A27 3sh multicolored	.70	.60
161 A27 5sh multicolored	1.25	1.00
Nos. 158-161 (4)	2.40	2.00

4th IRF African Highway Conference, Nairobi, Jan. 20-25.

Patient Airlift A28

1980, Mar. 20 Litho. *Perf. 14½*

162 A28 50c Outdoor clinic	.20	.20
163 A28 1sh Mule transport of patient, vert.	.40	.35
164 A28 3sh Surgery, vert.	.85	.85
165 A28 5sh shown	1.25	1.25
a. Souvenir sheet of 4, #162-165	3.25	3.25
Nos. 162-165 (4)	2.70	2.65

Flying doctor service.

Hill Statue, Kidderminster and Mt. Kenya — A29

1980, May 6 Litho. *Perf. 14*

166 A29 25sh multicolored	3.50	2.75
a. Souvenir sheet	4.00	3.00

London 1980 International Stamp Exhibition, May 6-14.

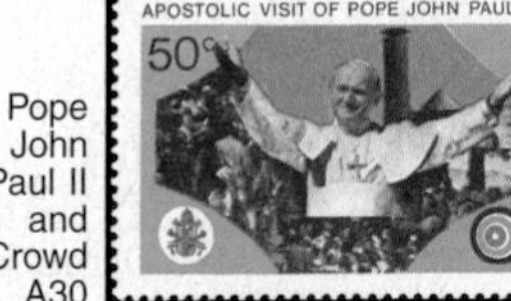

Pope John Paul II and Crowd A30

Visit of Pope John Paul II to Kenya: 1sh, Pope, Nairobi Cathedral, papal flag and arms, vert. 5sh, Pope, papal and Kenya flags, dove, vert. 10sh, Pres. arap Moi of Kenya, Pope, flag of Kenya on map of Africa.

1980, May 8 *Perf. 13½*

167 A30 50c multicolored	.30	.20
168 A30 1sh multicolored	.50	.30
169 A30 5sh multicolored	1.75	1.75
170 A30 10sh multicolored	3.25	3.25
Nos. 167-170 (4)	5.80	5.50

Sting Ray — A31

1980, June 27 Litho. *Perf. 14½*

171 A31 50c shown	.55	.55
172 A31 2sh Alkit snapper	1.40	1.25
173 A31 3sh Sea slug	1.75	1.75
174 A31 5sh Hawksbill turtle	2.75	2.75
Nos. 171-174 (4)	6.45	6.30

National Archives, 1904 A32

1980, Oct. 9 Litho. *Perf. 14*

175 A32 50c shown	.20	.20
176 A32 1sh Commissioner's Office, Nairobi, 1913	.20	.20
177 A32 1.50sh Nairobi House, 1913	.35	.35
178 A32 2sh Norfolk Hotel, 1904	.40	.40
179 A32 3sh McMillan Library, 1929	.65	.65
180 A32 5sh Kipande House, 1913	1.10	1.10
Nos. 175-180 (6)	2.90	2.90

Woman in Wheelchair and Child — A33

1981, Feb. 10 Litho. *Perf. 14x13½*

181 A33 50c shown	.20	.20
182 A33 1sh Pres. arap Moi, team captain	.20	.20
183 A33 3sh Blind mountain climbers, Mt. Kenya, 1965	1.10	1.10
184 A33 5sh Disabled artist	1.60	1.60
Nos. 181-184 (4)	3.10	3.10

International Year of the Disabled.

Longonot Earth Station Complex — A34

1981, Apr. 4 Litho. *Perf. 14x14½*

185 A34 50c shown	.20	.20
186 A34 2sh Intelsat V	.50	.50
187 A34 3sh Longonot I	.90	.80
188 A34 5sh Longonot II	1.25	1.25
Nos. 185-188 (4)	2.85	2.75

Conference Center, OAU Flag — A35

18th Organization for African Unity Conference, Nairobi: 1sh, Map of Africa showing Panaftel earth stations. 3sh, Parliament Building, Nairobi. 5sh, Jomo Kenyatta Intl. Airport. 10sh, OAU flag.

1981, June 24 Wmk. 373 *Perf. 13½*

189 A35 50c multicolored	.20	.20
190 A35 1sh multicolored	.20	.20
191 A35 3sh multicolored	.60	.60
192 A35 5sh multicolored	.90	.90
193 A35 10sh multicolored	2.10	2.10
a. Souvenir sheet of 1, perf. 14½	2.50	2.50
Nos. 189-193 (5)	4.00	4.00

St. Paul's Cathedral — A36

Reticulated Giraffe — A37

1981, July 29 Litho. *Perf. 14, 12*

194 A36 50c Charles, Pres. arap Moi	.20	.20
195 A36 3sh shown	.35	.35
196 A36 5sh Britannia	.55	.55
197 A36 10sh Charles	.90	*1.00*
Nos. 194-197 (4)	2.00	2.10

Souvenir Sheet

198 A36 25sh Couple	3.00	2.75

Royal Wedding.

1981, Aug. 31 Litho. *Perf. 14½*

199 A37 50c shown	.30	.30
200 A37 2sh Bongo	.60	.60
201 A37 5sh Roan antelope	1.40	1.40
202 A37 10sh Mangabey	3.00	3.00
Nos. 199-202 (4)	5.30	5.30

World Food Day — A38

Ceremonial Tribal Costumes A39

1981, Oct. 16 Litho. *Perf. 14*

203 A38 50c Plowing .20 .20
204 A38 1sh Rice field .20 .20
205 A38 2sh Irrigation .50 .50
206 A38 5sh Cattle 1.25 1.25
Nos. 203-206 (4) 2.15 2.15

Perf. 14½x13½

1981, Dec. 18 Litho.

207 A39 50c Kamba .55 .20
208 A39 1sh Turkana .65 .55
209 A39 2sh Giriama 1.50 1.10
210 A39 3sh Masai 2.00 2.00
211 A39 5sh Luo 3.00 *4.00*
Nos. 207-211 (5) 7.70 7.85

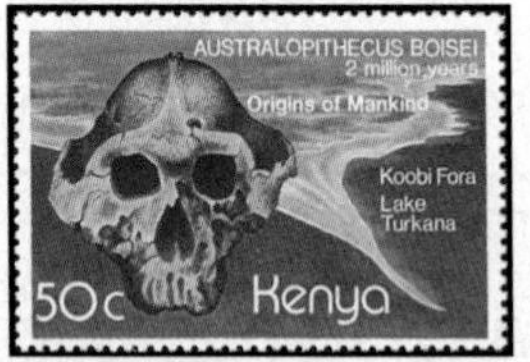

Australopithecus Boisei — A40

1982, Jan. 16 Litho. *Perf. 14*

212 A40 50c shown 2.00 1.00
213 A40 2sh Homo erectus 4.00 2.10
214 A40 3sh Homo habilis 4.00 3.75
215 A40 5sh Proconsul africanus 4.75 4.75
Nos. 212-215 (4) 14.75 11.60

Scouting Year A41

1982, June 2 Litho. *Perf. 14½*

216 A41 70c Tree planting .50 .50
217 A41 70c Paying homage .50 .50
a. Pair, #216-217 1.25 1.25
218 A41 3.50sh Be Prepared 1.25 1.25
219 A41 3.50sh Intl. friendship 1.25 1.25
a. Pair, #218-219 3.00 3.00
220 A41 5sh Helping disabled 2.00 2.00
221 A41 5sh Community service 2.00 2.00
a. Pair, #220-221 4.50 4.50
222 A41 6.50sh Paxtu Cottage 2.75 2.75
223 A41 6.50sh Lady Baden-Powell 2.75 2.75
a. Pair, #222-223 6.25 6.25
Nos. 216-223 (8) 13.00 13.00

Souvenir Sheet

224 Sheet of 4 6.00 6.00
a. A41 70c like #216 .20 .20
b. A41 3.50sh like #218 1.25 .45
c. A41 5sh like #220 1.90 .70
d. A41 6.50sh like #222 2.40 .85

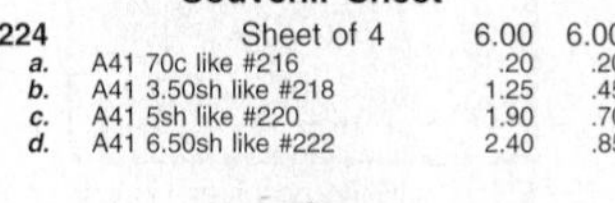

1982 World Cup — A42

Various soccer players on world map.

1982, July 5 Litho. *Perf. 12½*

225 A42 70c multicolored 1.50 .50
226 A42 3.50sh multicolored 3.25 2.50
227 A42 5sh multicolored 4.50 4.25
228 A42 10sh multicolored 6.50 *6.50*
Nos. 225-228 (4) 15.75 13.75

Souvenir Sheet

Perf. 13½x14

229 A42 20sh multicolored 7.75 7.75

A43 A44

1982, Sept. 28 Litho. *Perf. 14½*

230 A43 70c Cattle judging .90 .45
231 A43 2.50sh Farm machinery 1.50 1.25
232 A43 3.50sh Musical ride 2.00 2.00
233 A43 6.50sh Emblem 3.00 3.00
Nos. 230-233 (4) 7.40 6.70

Agricultural Society, 80th anniv.

1982, Oct. 27 Photo. *Perf. 11½*

Granite Paper

234 A44 70c Microwave radio system .20 .20
235 A44 3.50sh Ship-to-shore communication 2.00 1.75
236 A44 5sh Rural telecommunication 2.75 2.50
237 A44 6.50sh Emblem 4.00 3.75
Nos. 234-237 (4) 8.95 8.20

ITU Plenipoteniaries Conf., Nairobi, Sept.

5th Anniv. of Kenya Ports Authority A45

1983, Jan. 20 Litho. *Perf. 14*

238 A45 70c Container cranes 1.00 1.00
239 A45 2sh Cranes, diff. 1.80 1.80
240 A45 3.50sh Cranes, diff. 3.00 3.00
241 A45 5sh Mombasa Harbor map 4.50 4.50
a. Souvenir sheet of 4, #238-241 10.00 10.00
Nos. 238-241 (4) 10.30 10.30

No. 104 Surcharged

1983, Jan. Photo. *Perf. 14½x14*

242 A15 70c on 80c multicolored 1.50 .20

A45a

1983, Mar. 14 Litho. *Perf. 14½*

243 A45a 70c Coffee picking, vert. .20 .20
244 A45a 2sh Pres. arap Moi, vert. .30 .25
245 A45a 5sh Globe .70 .70
246 A45a 10sh Masai dance 1.50 1.50
Nos. 243-246 (4) 2.70 2.65

Commonwealth Day.

Dichrostachys Cinerea A46

Dombeya Burgessiae A47

Perf. 14½x14, 14x14½

1983, Feb. 15 Photo.

247 A46 10c shown .45 .20
248 A46 20c Rhamphicarpa montana .65 .20
249 A46 30c Barleria eranthemoides .65 .20
250 A46 40c Commelina .65 .20
251 A46 50c Canarina abyssinica .65 .20
252 A46 70c Aspilia mossambicensis .70 .20
253 A47 1sh Dombeya burgessiae .75 .20
254 A47 1.50sh Lantana trifolia 2.25 .60
255 A47 2sh Adenium obesum 2.50 .85
256 A47 2.50sh Terminalia orbicularis 3.00 1.00
257 A47 3.50sh Ceropegia ballyana 2.75 1.50
258 A47 5sh Ruttya fruticosa 2.75 1.90
259 A47 10sh Pentanisia ouranogyne 3.00 5.25
260 A47 20sh Brillantaisia nyanzarum 3.50 *6.25*
261 A47 40sh Crotalaria axillaris 5.75 *10.00*
Nos. 247-261 (15) 30.00 *28.75*

See Nos. 350-354.

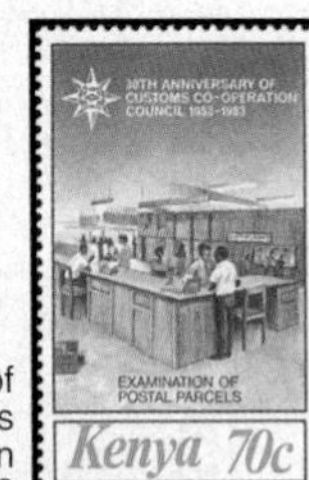

30th Anniv. of Customs Cooperation Council — A48

1983, May 11 Litho. *Perf. 14½*

262 A48 70c Parcel check .30 .20
263 A48 2.50sh Headquarters, Mombasa .70 .55
264 A48 3.50sh Headquarters, Brussels .90 .70
265 A48 10sh Patrol boat 3.00 3.00
Nos. 262-265 (4) 4.90 4.45

World Communications Year — A49

1983, July 4 Litho. *Perf. 14½*

266 A49 70c Satellite, dish antenna, vert. .65 .20
267 A49 2.50sh Mailbox, birthday card, telephone, vert. 1.70 1.25
268 A49 3.50sh Jet, ship 2.25 2.25
269 A49 5sh Railroad bridge, highway 3.50 3.50
Nos. 266-269 (4) 8.10 7.20

Intl. Maritime Organization, 25th Anniv. — A50

1983, Sept. 22 Litho. *Perf. 14½*

270 A50 70c Kilindini Harbor 1.75 1.75
271 A50 2.50sh Life preserver 2.75 2.75
272 A50 3.50sh Mombasa Container Terminal 3.50 3.50
273 A50 10sh Marine Park 5.75 5.75
Nos. 270-273 (4) 13.75 13.75

29th Commonwealth Parliamentary Conference — A51

1983, Oct. 31 Litho. *Perf. 14*

274 A51 70c shown .40 .40
275 A51 2.50sh Parliament Bldg., vert. 1.10 1.10
276 A51 5sh State Opening, vert. 2.75 2.75
a. Souv. sheet of 3, #274-276 + label 5.00 5.00
Nos. 274-276 (3) 4.25 4.25

Royal Visit A52

1983, Nov. 10 Litho. *Perf. 14*

277 A52 70c Flags .85 .55
278 A52 3.50sh Sagana State Lodge 2.40 2.25
279 A52 5sh Tree Tops Hotel 3.25 3.00
280 A52 10sh Elizabeth II and Daniel arap Moi 5.00 5.00
Nos. 277-280 (4) 11.50 10.80

Souvenir Sheet

281 A52 25sh multicolored 6.75 6.75

No. 281 contains Nos. 277-280 without denominations showing simulated perforations.

President Daniel arap Moi, Monument — A53

1983, Dec. 9 Litho. *Perf. 14½*

282 A53 70c shown .20 .20
283 A53 2sh Tree planting .35 .35
284 A53 3.50sh Map, flag, emblem .80 .80
285 A53 5sh School, milk program 1.00 1.00
286 A53 10sh People, flag, banner 2.25 2.25
Nos. 282-286 (5) 4.60 4.60

Souvenir Sheet

Imperf

287 A53 25sh multicolored 4.25 4.25

Independence, 20th Anniv. No. 287 contains Nos. 282, 284-286 without denominations.

Rare Local Birds — A54

1984, Feb. 6 Litho. *Perf. 14½x13½*

288 A54 70c White-backed night heron 2.75 2.75
289 A54 2.50sh Quail plover 4.00 3.50
290 A54 3.50sh Heller's ground thrush 5.00 5.00
291 A54 5sh Papyrus gonolek 5.75 5.75
292 A54 10sh White-winged Apalis 7.25 7.25
Nos. 288-292 (5) 24.75 24.25

Intl. Civil Aviation Org., 40th Anniv. A55

1984, Apr. 2 Litho. *Perf. 14*

293	A55	70c	Radar, vert.	.20	.20
294	A55	2.50sh	Kenya School of Aviation	.65	.65
295	A55	3.50sh	Jet, Moi Intl. Airport	1.00	1.00
296	A55	5sh	Air traffic control center, vert.	1.50	1.50
			Nos. 293-296 (4)	3.35	3.35

1984 Summer Olympics — A56

1984, May 21 *Perf. 14½*

297	A56	70c	Running	.20	.20
298	A56	2.50sh	Hurdles	1.00	1.00
299	A56	5sh	Boxing	2.50	2.40
300	A56	10sh	Field Hockey	4.75	4.75
			Nos. 297-300 (4)	8.45	8.35

Souvenir Sheet

Imperf

301	A56	25sh	Torch bearers	6.00	6.00

No. 301 contains designs of Nos. 297-300.

Bookmobile — A57

1984, Aug. 10 Litho. *Perf. 14½*

302	A57	70c	Emblem	.20	.20
303	A57	3.50sh	shown	.70	.70
304	A57	5sh	Adult library	1.10	1.10
305	A57	10sh	Children's library	2.00	2.00
			Nos. 302-305 (4)	4.00	4.00

Intl. Fed. of Library Associations, 50th Conf.

Kenya Export Year (KEY) A58

1984, Oct. 1 Litho. *Perf. 14*

306	A58	70c	Emblem, vert.	.20	.20
307	A58	3.50sh	Airport	1.90	1.90
308	A58	5sh	Harbor, vert.	3.50	3.50
309	A58	10sh	Exports	5.50	5.50
			Nos. 306-309 (4)	11.10	11.10

A59

Tribal Costumes A60

1984, Aug. 23 Litho. *Perf. 14x14½*

310	A59	70c	Doves, cross	.20	.20
311	A59	2.50sh	Doves, Hinduism symbol	1.50	1.50
312	A59	3.50sh	Doves, Sikhism symbol	2.25	2.25
313	A59	6.50sh	Doves, Islam symbol	4.00	4.00
			Nos. 310-313 (4)	7.95	7.95

World Conference on Religion and Peace, Nairobi, Aug. 23-31, 1984.

1984, Nov. 5 Litho. *Perf. 14½x13½*

314	A60	70c	Luhya	.90	.90
315	A60	2sh	Kikuyu	2.25	2.25
316	A60	3.50sh	Pokomo	3.25	3.25
317	A60	5sh	Nandi	3.50	3.50
318	A60	10sh	Rendile	5.75	5.75
			Nos. 314-318 (5)	15.65	15.65

60th Anniv., World Chess Federation — A61

1984, Dec. 21 Litho. *Perf. 14½*

319	A61	70c	Nyayo Stadium, knight	2.25	.40
320	A61	2.50sh	Fort Jesus, rook	3.25	2.10
321	A61	3.50sh	National Monument, bishop	4.00	4.50
322	A61	5sh	Parliament, queen	4.50	4.50
323	A61	10sh	Nyayo Fountain, king	7.25	7.25
			Nos. 319-323 (5)	21.25	18.75

Energy Conservation — A62

1985, Jan. 22 Litho. *Perf. 13½*

324	A62	70c	Stove, fire pit	.40	.40
325	A62	2sh	Solar panel	.75	.75
326	A62	3.50sh	Biogas tank	1.25	1.25
327	A62	10sh	Plowing field	3.50	3.50
328	A62	20sh	Energy conservation	5.50	2.00
			Nos. 324-328 (5)	11.40	7.90

No. 328 contains Nos. 324-327 without denominations.

Girl Guides, 75th Anniv. A63

1985, Mar. 27 Litho. *Perf. 13½*

329	A63	1sh	Girl Guide, handicrafts	.90	.90
330	A63	3sh	Community service	2.25	2.25
331	A63	5sh	Lady Baden-Powell, Kenyan leader	3.50	3.50
332	A63	7sh	Food project	5.00	5.00
			Nos. 329-332 (4)	11.65	11.65

Intl. Red Cross Day A64

1985, May 8 *Perf. 14½*

333	A64	1sh	Emblem	1.00	.90
334	A64	4sh	First Aid	3.00	3.00
335	A64	5sh	Blood donation	4.00	4.00
336	A64	7sh	Famine relief, cornucopia	6.00	6.00
			Nos. 333-336 (4)	14.00	13.90

A65 A66

Diseases caused by microorganisms carried by insects.

1985, June 25

337	A65	1sh	Malaria	2.25	.75
338	A65	3sh	Leishmaniasis	4.25	2.75
339	A65	5sh	Trypanosomiasis	4.75	4.25
340	A65	7sh	Babesiosis	7.50	*7.50*
			Nos. 337-340 (4)	18.75	15.25

7th Intl. Congress on Protozoology, Nairobi, June 22-29.

1985, July 15

341	A66	1sh	Repairing water pipes	.50	.50
342	A66	3sh	Traditional food processing	1.00	1.00
343	A66	5sh	Basket weaving	1.75	1.75
344	A66	7sh	Dress making	2.25	2.25
			Nos. 341-344 (4)	5.50	5.50

UN Decade for Women.

43rd Intl. Eucharistic Congress, Nairobi, Aug. 11-18 — A67

1985, Aug. 15 *Perf. 13½*

345	A67	1sh	The Last Supper	1.00	1.00
346	A67	3sh	Afro-Christian family	2.10	2.10
347	A67	5sh	Congress altar, Uhuru Park	3.00	3.00
348	A67	7sh	St. Peter Claver's Church	3.75	3.25
			Nos. 345-348 (4)	9.85	9.35

Souvenir Sheet

349	A67	25sh	Pope John Paul II	7.75	7.75

Flower Types of 1983

1985 Photo. *Perf. 14½x14, 14½*

350	A46	80c	like #250	4.50	2.50
351	A46	1sh	Dombeya burgessiae	4.50	1.60
352	A47	3sh	Calotropis procera	8.50	5.00
353	A47	4sh	Momordica foetida	5.25	*6.75*
354	A47	7sh	Oncoba spinosa	7.00	*7.00*
			Nos. 350-354 (5)	29.75	*22.85*

Endangered Wildlife — A68

1985, Dec. 10 Litho. *Perf. 14½*

355	A68	1sh	Diceros bicornis	2.75	1.50
356	A68	3sh	Acinonyx jubatus	3.75	3.25
357	A68	5sh	Cercopithecus neglectus	4.00	4.00
358	A68	10sh	Equus greyvi	7.00	7.00
			Nos. 355-358 (4)	17.50	15.75

Size: 130x122mm

Imperf

359	A68	25sh	Hunter pursuing game	12.00	12.00

Trees A69

1986, Jan. 24 *Perf. 14½*

360	A69	1sh	Borassus aethiopum	1.60	.55
361	A69	3sh	Acacia xanthophloea	3.50	2.75
362	A69	5sh	Ficus natalensis	4.75	3.75
363	A69	7sh	Spathodea nilotica	7.75	6.75
			Nos. 360-363 (4)	17.60	13.80

Size: 117x97mm

Imperf

364	A69	25sh	Glade	7.25	7.25

Intl. Peace Year — A70

1986 World Cup Soccer Championships, Mexico — A71

1986, Apr. 17 *Perf. 14½*

365	A70	1sh	Dove, UN emblem	.55	.55
366	A70	3sh	UN General Assembly, horiz.	1.25	1.25
367	A70	7sh	Mushroom cloud	2.40	2.40
368	A70	10sh	Isaiah 2:4, horiz.	3.75	3.75
			Nos. 365-368 (4)	7.95	7.95

1986, May 9

369	A71	1sh	Dribbling	1.10	.55
370	A71	3sh	Penalty shot	2.25	1.10
371	A71	5sh	Tackling	3.50	2.25
372	A71	7sh	Champions	4.50	4.50
373	A71	10sh	Heading the ball	5.75	5.75
			Nos. 369-373 (5)	17.10	14.15

Size: 110x86mm

Imperf

374	A71	30sh	Harambee Stars	6.50	6.50

EXPO '86, Vancouver — A72

1986, June 11 *Perf. 13½x13*

375	A72	1sh	Rural post office	1.25	.60
376	A72	3sh	Container depot, Embakasi	2.40	1.25
377	A72	5sh	Plane landing	3.75	2.40
378	A72	7sh	Shipping exports	4.75	4.75
379	A72	10sh	Goods transport	6.25	6.25
			Nos. 375-379 (5)	18.40	15.25

TELECOM '86, Nairobi, Sept. 16-23 — A73

1986, Sept. 16 Litho. *Perf. 14½*

380 A73 1sh Telephone-computer links .30 .30
381 A73 3sh Telephones, 1876-1986 1.25 1.25
382 A73 5sh Satellite communications 2.10 2.10
383 A73 7sh Switchboards 3.50 3.50
Nos. 380-383 (4) 7.15 7.15

A74

Dhows (Ships) — A75

1986, Oct. 30 Litho. *Perf. 14½*

384 A74 1sh Mashua 1.00 .45
385 A74 3sh Mtepe 2.00 1.75
386 A74 5sh Dau La Mwao 8.00 2.75
387 A74 10sh Jahazi 5.00 5.00
Nos. 384-387 (4) 16.00 9.95

Souvenir Sheet

388 A75 25sh Lamu, map 8.00 8.00

Christmas A76

1986, Dec. 5 *Perf. 12*

389 A76 1sh Nativity, vert. .40 .40
390 A76 3sh Shepherd boy, vert. 2.00 2.00
391 A76 5sh Angel, map 2.75 2.75
392 A76 7sh Magi 4.50 4.50
Nos. 389-392 (4) 9.65 9.65

UNICEF, 40th Anniv. — A77

Child Survival Campaign: 1sh, Universal immunization by 1990. 3sh, Food and nutrition. 4sh, Oral rehydration. 5sh, Family planning. 10sh, Literacy of women.

1987, Jan. 6 Litho. *Perf. 14½*

393 A77 1sh multicolored .70 .70
394 A77 3sh multicolored 1.40 1.40
395 A77 4sh multicolored 1.90 1.90
396 A77 5sh multicolored 2.40 2.40
397 A77 10sh multicolored 3.75 3.75
Nos. 393-397 (5) 10.15 10.15

A78

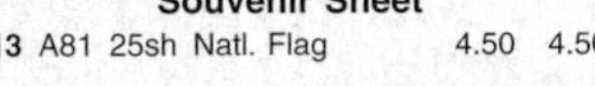

Tourism — A79

1987, Mar. 25 Litho. *Perf. 14½*

398 A78 1sh Akamba carvers 1.25 1.25
399 A78 3sh Beach 3.25 3.25
400 A78 5sh Escarpment 4.75 4.75
401 A78 7sh Pride of lions 7.25 7.25
Nos. 398-401 (4) 16.50 16.50

Souvenir Sheet

402 A79 30sh Kenya geysers 14.00 14.00

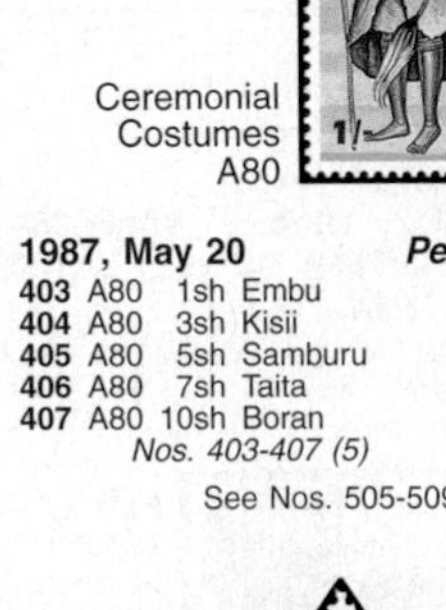

Ceremonial Costumes A80

1987, May 20 *Perf. 14½x13½*

403 A80 1sh Embu 1.25 .60
404 A80 3sh Kisii 2.75 1.40
405 A80 5sh Samburu 4.25 2.40
406 A80 7sh Taita 5.25 4.75
407 A80 10sh Boran 5.50 5.50
Nos. 403-407 (5) 19.00 14.65

See Nos. 505-509.

Posts & Telecommunications Corp., 10th Anniv. — A81

1987, July 1 Litho. *Perf. 13½*

408 A81 1sh Telecommunications satellite 1.25 .60
409 A81 3sh Rural post office, Kajiado 2.00 2.00
410 A81 4sh Athletics 2.40 2.40
411 A81 5sh Rural communication 2.75 2.75
412 A81 7sh Speedpost 4.00 4.00
Nos. 408-412 (5) 12.40 11.75

Souvenir Sheet

413 A81 25sh Natl. Flag 4.50 4.50

A82

A83

1987, Aug. 5 *Perf. 14½x14*

414 A82 1sh Volleyball .20 .20
415 A82 3sh Cycling .55 .55
416 A82 4sh Boxing .75 .75
417 A82 5sh Swimming .90 .90
418 A82 7sh Steeple chase 1.25 1.25
Nos. 414-418 (5) 3.65 3.65

Souvenir Sheet

Perf. 14x14½

419 A82 30sh Kasarani Sports Complex 4.75 4.75

4th All Africa Games, Nairobi, Aug. 1-12. Nos. 414-418, vert.

1987, Oct. 27 Litho. *Perf. 13½x14*

Medicinal herbs.

420 A83 1sh Aloe volkensii 1.10 .65
421 A83 3sh Cassia didymobotrya 2.25 1.50
422 A83 5sh Erythrina abyssinica 3.00 2.40
423 A83 7sh Adenium obesum 4.00 4.00
424 A83 10sh Herbalist's clinic 5.50 5.50
Nos. 420-424 (5) 15.85 14.05

Butterflies — A84

1988-90 Photo. *Perf. 15x14*

424A A84 10c Cyrestis camillus 1.00 1.00
425 A84 20c Iolaus sidus .30 .30
426 A84 40c Vanessa cardui .40 .30
427 A84 50c Colotis euippe omphale .40 .30
428 A84 70c Precis westermanni .40 .30
429 A84 80c Colias electo .40 .30
430 A84 1sh Eronia leda .40 .20
430A A84 1.50sh Papilio dardanus planemoides 5.00 1.00

Size: 25x41mm

Perf. 14½

431 A84 2sh Papilio rex .75 .75
432 A84 2.50sh Colotis phisadia .80 .75
433 A84 3sh Papilio desmondi teita .80 .75
434 A84 3.50sh Papilio demodocus .85 .75
435 A84 4sh Papilio phorcas .90 .80
436 A84 5sh Charaxes druceanus teita 1.00 1.00
437 A84 7sh Cymothoe teita 1.25 1.25
438 A84 10sh Charaxes zoolina 1.75 1.75
439 A84 20sh Papilio dardanus 3.50 3.50
440 A84 40sh Charaxes cithaeron kennethi 7.25 7.25
Nos. 424A-440 (18) 27.15 22.25

Issued: 10c, 9/1/89; 1.50sh, 5/18/90; others, 2/14/88.

Game Lodges A85

1988, May 31 Litho. *Perf. 14½*

441 A85 1sh Samburu .75 .35
442 A85 3sh Naro Moru River 1.10 1.10
443 A85 4sh Mara Serena 1.75 1.75
444 A85 5sh Voi Safari 1.90 1.90
445 A85 7sh Kilimanjaro Buffalo Lodge 2.25 2.25
446 A85 10sh Meru Mulika 2.75 2.75
Nos. 441-446 (6) 10.50 10.10

World Expo '88, Brisbane A86

EXPO '88 and Australia bicentennial emblems plus: 1sh, Stadium, site of the 1982 Commonwealth Games, and runners. 3sh, Flying Doctor Service aircraft. 4sh, HMS Sirius, a 19th cent. immigrant ship. 5sh, Ostrich and emu. 7sh, Pres. Daniel arap Moi, Queen Elizabeth II and Robert Hawke, prime minister of Australia. 30sh, Kenya Pavilion at EXPO '88.

1988, June 10

447 A86 1sh multicolored .70 .60
448 A86 3sh multicolored 2.50 1.75
449 A86 4sh multicolored 3.00 3.00
450 A86 5sh multicolored 4.00 4.00
451 A86 7sh multicolored 5.00 5.00
Nos. 447-451 (5) 15.20 14.35

Souvenir Sheet

452 A86 30sh multicolored 4.25 4.25

World Health Organization, 40th Anniv. — A87

1988, July 1 Litho. *Perf. 14½*

453 A87 1sh shown .35 .35
454 A87 3sh Nutrition 1.40 1.40
455 A87 5sh Immunization 2.50 2.50
456 A87 7sh Water supply 3.75 3.75
Nos. 453-456 (4) 8.00 8.00

1988 Summer Olympics, Seoul — A88

1988, Aug. 1 Litho. *Perf. 14½x14*

457 A88 1sh Handball .50 .20
458 A88 3sh Judo 1.00 .80
459 A88 5sh Weight lifting 1.50 1.50
460 A88 7sh Javelin 2.00 2.00
461 A88 10sh 400-meter relay 3.00 3.00
Nos. 457-461 (5) 8.00 7.50

Souvenir Sheet

462 A88 30sh Tennis 5.00 5.00

Utensils A89

Perf. 14½x14, 14x14½

1988, Sept. 20 Litho.

463 A89 1sh Calabashes, vert. .20 .20
464 A89 3sh Milk gourds, vert. .55 .55
465 A89 5sh Cooking pots .90 .90
466 A89 7sh Winnowing trays 1.25 1.25
467 A89 10sh Reed baskets 1.75 1.75
Nos. 463-467 (5) 4.65 4.65

Souvenir Sheet

468 A89 25sh Gourds, calabash, horn 4.50 4.50

10-Year Presidency of Daniel arap Moi — A90

Designs: 1sh, Swearing-in ceremony, 1978. 3sh, Promoting soil conservation. 3.50sh, Public transportation (bus), Nairobi. 4sh, Jua Kali artisans at market. 5sh, Moi University, Eldoret, established in 1985. 7sh, Hospital ward expansion. 10sh, British Prime Minister Margaret Thatcher and Pres. Moi inaugurating the Kapsabet Telephone Exchange, Jan. 6, 1988.

1988, Oct. 13 Litho. *Perf. 13½x14½*

469 A90 1sh multicolored .70 .70
470 A90 3sh multicolored 1.75 1.75
471 A90 3.50sh multicolored 2.00 2.00

472 A90 4sh multicolored 2.25 2.25
473 A90 5sh multicolored 2.75 2.75
474 A90 7sh multicolored 3.50 3.50
475 A90 10sh multicolored 5.50 5.50
Nos. 469-475 (7) 18.45 18.45

Independence, 25th Anniv. — A91

1988, Dec. 9 Litho. *Perf. 11½*
476 A91 1sh Natl. flag .40 .40
477 A91 3sh Coffee picking 2.10 2.10
478 A91 5sh Model of postal hq. 3.50 3.50
479 A91 7sh Harambee Star Airbus A310-300 5.00 5.00
480 A91 10sh Locomotive 9401 7.00 7.00
Nos. 476-480 (5) 18.00 18.00

Natl. Monuments — A92

1989, Mar. 15 Litho. *Perf. 14½*
481 A92 1.20sh Gedi Ruins, Malindi .40 .40
482 A92 3.40sh Vasco Da Gama Pillar, Malindi, vert. 1.00 1.00
483 A92 4.40sh Ishiakani Monument, Kiunga 2.00 2.00
484 A92 5.50sh Ft. Jesus, Mombasa 2.50 2.50
485 A92 7.70sh She Burnan Omwe, Lamu, vert. 3.50 3.50
Nos. 481-485 (5) 9.40 9.40

Red Cross, 125th Anniv. A93

1989, May 8 Litho. *Perf. 14x13½*
486 A93 1.20sh Anniv. and natl. soc. emblems .35 .35
487 A93 3.40sh First aid 1.25 1.25
488 A93 4.40sh Disaster relief 1.75 1.75
489 A93 5.50sh Jean-Henri Dunant 2.40 2.40
490 A93 7.70sh Blood donation 3.75 3.75
Nos. 486-490 (5) 9.50 9.50

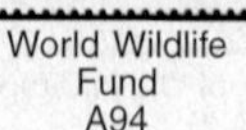

World Wildlife Fund A94

Mushrooms A95

Giraffes, Giraffa Camelopardalis Reticulata.

1989, July 12 Litho. *Perf. 14½*
491 A94 1.20sh multicolored 2.50 2.25
492 A94 3.40sh multicolored 5.25 5.00
493 A94 4.40sh multicolored 6.00 6.00
494 A94 5.50sh multicolored 7.25 *8.00*
Nos. 491-494 (4) 21.00 21.25

Size: 80x110mm
Imperf

495 A94 30sh multicolored 12.00 *12.00*

No. 495 contains four labels like Nos. 491-494, perf. 14½, without denominations or WWF emblem.

1989, Sept. 6 Litho. *Perf. 14½*
496 A95 1.20sh Oyster 2.40 .65
497 A95 3.40sh Chestnut 3.50 2.40
498 A95 4.40sh White button 4.00 3.25
499 A95 5.50sh Termite 4.75 3.75
500 A95 7.70sh Shiitake 6.50 6.50
Nos. 496-500 (5) 21.15 16.55

Jawaharlal Nehru, 1st Prime Minister of Independent India — A96

1989, Nov. 9 Litho. *Perf. 13½x14*
501 A96 1.20sh Independence struggle 2.00 1.50
502 A96 3.40sh Education 2.50 2.00
503 A96 5.50sh Portrait 4.50 4.50
504 A96 7.70sh Industry 7.50 7.50
Nos. 501-504 (4) 16.50 15.50

Costume Type of 1980

1989, Dec. 8 Litho. *Perf. 14½x13½*
505 A80 1.20sh Kipsigis 1.25 .45
506 A80 3.40sh Rabai 2.50 2.50
507 A80 5.50sh Duruma 3.25 2.40
508 A80 7.70sh Kuria 4.50 3.75
509 A80 10sh Bajuni 5.50 5.50
Nos. 505-509 (5) 17.00 14.60

Pan-African Postal Union, 10th Anniv. — A97

Perf. 14x13½, 13½x14
1990, Jan. 31 Litho.
510 A97 1.20sh EMS Speedpost .25 .25
511 A97 3.40sh Mail runner .80 .80
512 A97 5.50sh Mandera P.O. 1.00 1.00
513 A97 7.70sh EMS, diff., vert. 1.25 1.25
514 A97 10sh PAPU emblem, vert. 1.60 1.60
Nos. 510-514 (5) 4.90 4.90

Soccer Trophies — A98

Designs:1.50sh, Moi Golden Cup. 4.50sh, East & Central Africa Challenge Cup. 6.50sh, East & Central Africa Club Championship Cup. 9sh, World Cup.

1990, May 21 Litho. *Perf. 14½*
515 A98 1.50sh multicolored .50 .50
516 A98 4.50sh multicolored 3.25 3.25
517 A98 6.50sh multicolored 4.25 4.25
518 A98 9sh multicolored 6.00 6.00
Nos. 515-518 (4) 14.00 14.00

Penny Black 150th Anniv., Stamp World London '90 — A99

1990, Apr. 27 Litho. *Perf. 11½*
519 A99 1.50sh shown .40 .30
520 A99 4.50sh Great Britain No. 1 1.50 1.50
521 A99 6.50sh Early British cancellations 2.25 2.25
522 A99 9sh Main P.O. 3.25 3.25
a. Souvenir sheet of 4, #519-522 8.50 8.50
Nos. 519-522 (4) 7.40 7.30

No. 522a sold for 30 shillings.

ITU, 125th Anniv. A100

Designs: 4.50sh, Telephone assembly. 6.50sh, ITU Anniv. emblem. 9sh, Telecommunications development.

1990, July 12
523 A100 1.50sh multicolored .45 .20
524 A100 4.50sh multicolored .90 .65
525 A100 6.50sh multicolored 1.25 1.10
526 A100 9sh multicolored 1.60 1.60
Nos. 523-526 (4) 4.20 3.55

Common Design Types pictured following the introduction.

Queen Mother, 90th Birthday
Common Design Types
Perf. 14x15

1990, Aug. 4 Litho. Wmk. 384
527 CD343 10sh Queen Mother 1.50 1.50

Perf. 14½
528 CD344 40sh At garden party, 1947 5.50 5.50

Kenya African National Union (KANU), 50th Anniv. A101

1990, June 11
529 A101 1.50sh KANU flag .35 .20
530 A101 2.50sh Nyayo Monument .40 .35
531 A101 4.50sh KICC Party Headquarters .85 .85
532 A101 5sh Jomo Kenyatta 1.00 1.00
533 A101 6.50sh Daniel T. arap Moi 1.10 1.10
534 A101 9sh KANU mass meeting 1.75 1.75
535 A101 10sh Voters 1.75 1.75
Nos. 529-535 (7) 7.20 7.00

Kenya Postage Stamps, Cent. — A102

Intl. Literacy Year — A103

Designs: 1.50sh, Kenya #431. 4.50sh, East Africa and Uganda Protectorates #2. 6.50sh, British East Africa #1. 9sh, Kenya and Uganda #25. 20sh, Kenya, Uganda, Tanzania #232.

1990, Sept. 5 Litho. *Perf. 14x14½*
536 A102 1.50sh multicolored 1.50 .45
537 A102 4.50sh multicolored 3.00 2.50
538 A102 6.50sh multicolored 4.00 3.75
539 A102 9sh multicolored 5.25 4.75
540 A102 20sh multicolored 8.50 8.50
Nos. 536-540 (5) 22.25 19.95

1990, Nov. 30 Litho. *Perf. 13½x14*
541 A103 1.50sh Adult literacy class .65 .65
542 A103 4.50sh Radio teaching program 1.60 1.60
543 A103 6.50sh Technical training 2.25 2.25
544 A103 9sh Literacy year emblem 3.50 3.50
Nos. 541-544 (4) 8.00 8.00

1992 Summer Olympics, Barcelona — A106

1991, Nov. 29 Litho. *Perf. 14x13½*
554 A106 2sh National flag .45 .45
555 A106 6sh Basketball 1.90 1.90
556 A106 7sh Field hockey 2.50 2.50
557 A106 8.50sh Table tennis 3.00 3.00
558 A106 11sh Boxing 4.50 4.50
Nos. 554-558 (5) 12.35 12.35

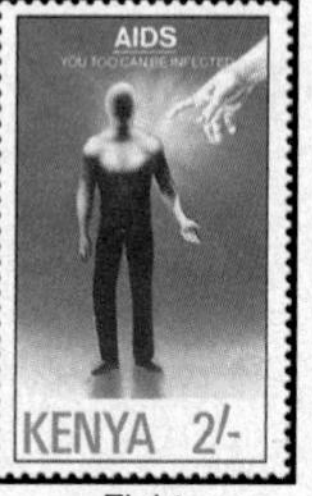

Fight AIDS — A107

Wildlife — A108

1991, Oct. 31 Litho. *Perf. 13½x14*
559 A107 2sh You too can be infected 1.25 .20
560 A107 6sh Has no cure 2.50 2.25
561 A107 8.50sh Casual sex is unsafe 3.50 3.00
562 A107 11sh Sterilize syringe before use 4.75 4.75
Nos. 559-562 (4) 12.00 10.20

Queen Elizabeth II's Accession to the Throne, 40th Anniv.
Common Design Type

1992, Feb. 6 Litho. *Perf. 14x13½*
563 CD349 3sh multicolored .20 .20
564 CD349 8sh multicolored 1.00 1.00
565 CD349 11sh multicolored 1.25 1.25
566 CD349 14sh multicolored 1.50 1.50
567 CD349 40sh multicolored 4.75 4.75
Nos. 563-567 (5) 8.70 8.70

1992, May 8 *Perf. 14½*
568 A108 3sh Leopard 2.25 1.75
569 A108 8sh Lion 4.75 4.75
570 A108 10sh Elephant 6.25 5.75
571 A108 11sh Buffalo 6.25 6.25
572 A108 14sh Rhinoceros 10.50 10.50
Nos. 568-572 (5) 30.00 29.00

Vintage Cars A109

Designs: 3sh, Intl. Harvester S.S. motor truck, 1926. 8sh, Fiat 509, 1924. 10sh, "R" Hupmobile, 1923. 11sh, Chevrolet Box Body, 1928. 14sh, Bentley Parkward, 1934.

1992, June 24 *Perf. 14½*
573 A109 3sh multicolored 2.25 .70
574 A109 8sh multicolored 3.00 1.90
575 A109 10sh multicolored 3.50 2.50
576 A109 11sh multicolored 4.00 3.50
577 A109 14sh multicolored 5.50 5.50
Nos. 573-577 (5) 18.25 14.10

1992 Summer Olympics, Barcelona — A110

1992, July 24 Litho. *Perf. 14½*

No.	Type	Value	Description	Unused	Used
578	A110	3sh	Runners	.55	.55
579	A110	8sh	Judo	2.00	2.00
580	A110	10sh	Women's volleyball	3.25	3.25
581	A110	11sh	4x100-meter relay	3.25	3.25
582	A110	14sh	10,000-meter run	4.25	4.25
			Nos. 578-582 (5)	13.30	13.30

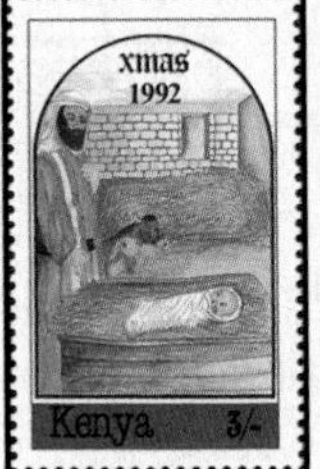

Christmas A111 — Lighthouses A112

Designs: 3sh, Joseph, Jesus & animals in stable. 8sh, Mary holding Jesus in stable. 11sh, Map of Kenya, Christmas tree. 14sh, Adoration of the Magi.

1992, Dec. 14 Litho. *Perf. 13½x14*

No.	Type	Value	Description	Unused	Used
583	A111	3sh	multicolored	.45	.45
584	A111	8sh	multicolored	1.10	1.10
585	A111	11sh	multicolored	1.60	1.60
586	A111	14sh	multicolored	1.75	1.75
			Nos. 583-586 (4)	4.90	4.90

1993, Jan. 25 *Perf. 14½*

Designs: 3sh, Asembo Bay, Lake Victoria. 8sh, Ras Serani, Mombasa. 11sh, Ras Serani, Mombasa, diff. 14sh, Gingira, Lake Victoria.

No.	Type	Value	Description	Unused	Used
587	A112	3sh	multicolored	2.25	.90
588	A112	8sh	multicolored	4.00	2.75
589	A112	11sh	multicolored	5.00	4.50
590	A112	14sh	multicolored	6.75	6.75
			Nos. 587-590 (4)	18.00	14.90

Birds — A113

Designs: 50c, Superb starling. 1sh, Red and yellow barbet. 1.50sh, Ross's turaco. 3sh, Greater honeyguide. 5sh, African fish eagle. 6sh, Vulturine guineafowl. 7sh, Malachite kingfisher. 8sh, Speckled pigeon. 10sh, Cinnamon-chested bee-eater. 11sh, Scarlet-chested sunbird. 14sh, Reichenow's weaver. 50sh, Yellow-billed hornbill. 80sh, Lesser flamingo. 100sh, Hadada ibis.

1993-99 Photo. *Perf. 15x14*

Granite Paper

No.	Type	Value	Description	Unused	Used
594	A113	50c	multi	.20	.20
597	A113	1sh	multi	.20	.20
598	A113	1.50sh	multi	.20	.20
600	A113	3sh	multi	.20	.20
601	A113	5sh	multi	.25	.25
601A	A113	6sh	multi	1.25	.50
602	A113	7sh	multi	.45	.45
603	A113	8sh	multi	.55	.55
604	A113	10sh	multi	.65	.65
605	A113	11sh	multi	.70	.70
606	A113	14sh	multi	.90	.90

Size: 25x42mm

Perf. 14½

No.	Type	Value	Description	Unused	Used
608	A113	50sh	multi	3.25	3.25
609	A113	80sh	multi	5.00	5.00
610	A113	100sh	multi	6.50	6.50
			Nos. 594-610 (14)	20.30	19.55

Issued: 1.50sh, 5sh, 2/14/94; 6sh, 1999; others, 2/22/93.

This is an expanding set. Numbers may change.

17th World Congress of Rehabilatation Intl. — A114

1993, July 1 Litho. *Perf. 14½*

No.	Type	Value	Description	Unused	Used
611	A114	3sh	Health care, vert.	.20	.20
612	A114	8sh	Recreation	1.90	1.90
613	A114	10sh	Vocational training	2.10	2.10
614	A114	11sh	Recreation & sports	2.25	2.25
615	A114	14sh	Emblem, vert.	3.00	3.00
			Nos. 611-615 (5)	9.45	9.45

Maendeleo ya Wanawake Organization, 42th Anniv. — A115

Designs: 3.50sh, Maendeleo House. 9sh, Planting trees. 11sh, Rural family planning services, vert. 12.50sh, Water nearer the people. 15.50sh, Maendeleo improved wood cookstove, vert.

Perf. 14x13½, 13½x14

1994, Mar. 17 Litho.

No.	Type	Value	Description	Unused	Used
616	A115	3.50sh	multicolored	.20	.20
617	A115	9sh	multicolored	1.75	1.75
618	A115	11sh	multicolored	2.00	2.00
619	A115	12.50sh	multicolored	2.50	2.50
620	A115	15.50sh	multicolored	3.00	3.00
			Nos. 616-620 (5)	9.45	9.45

Orchids — A116

Designs: 3.50sh, Ansellia africana. 9sh, Aerangis lutecalba. 12.50sh, Polystachya bella. 15.50sh, Brachycorythis kalbreyeri. 20sh, Eulophia guineensis.

1994, June 27 Litho. *Perf. 13½x14*

No.	Type	Value	Description	Unused	Used
621	A116	3.50sh	multicolored	2.40	.20
622	A116	9sh	multicolored	3.25	2.00
623	A116	12.50sh	multicolored	3.50	3.50
624	A116	15.50sh	multicolored	4.25	4.25
625	A116	20sh	multicolored	5.50	5.50
			Nos. 621-625 (5)	18.90	15.45

African Development Bank, 30th Anniv. — A117

1994, Nov. 21 Litho. *Perf. 14½*

No.	Type	Value	Description	Unused	Used
626	A117	6sh	KICC, Nairobi	1.75	1.75
627	A117	25sh	Isinya, Kajiado	6.25	6.25

Intl. Year of the Family — A118 — Rotary, 50th Anniv. — A119

1994, Dec. 22

No.	Type	Value	Description	Unused	Used
628	A118	6sh	Family planning	1.00	1.00
629	A118	14.50sh	Health	3.25	3.25
630	A118	20sh	Education, horiz.	4.50	4.50
631	A118	25sh	Emblem, horiz.	5.25	5.25
			Nos. 628-631 (4)	14.00	14.00

1994, Dec. 29 *Perf. 13½x14*

Designs: 6sh, Paul P. Harris, founder. 14.50sh, Rotary Club of Mombasa. 17.50sh, Polio plus vaccine. 20sh, Water projects. 25sh, Emblem, motto.

No.	Type	Value	Description	Unused	Used
632	A119	6sh	multicolored	.60	.60
633	A119	14.50sh	multicolored	1.60	1.60
634	A119	17.50sh	multicolored	2.00	2.00
635	A119	20sh	multicolored	2.25	2.25
636	A119	25sh	multicolored	2.75	2.75
			Nos. 632-636 (5)	9.20	9.20

SPCA — A120 — Golf — A121

1995, Jan. 13 Litho. *Perf. 14½*

No.	Type	Value	Description	Unused	Used
637	A120	6sh	Donkey	.50	.50
638	A120	14.50sh	Cattle	1.40	1.40
639	A120	17.50sh	Sheep	1.75	1.75
640	A120	20sh	Dog	1.90	1.90
641	A120	25sh	Cat	2.40	2.40
			Nos. 637-641 (5)	7.95	7.95

Kenya Society for Prevention of Cruelty to Animals.

1995, Feb. 28 Litho. *Perf. 14½*

No.	Type	Value	Description	Unused	Used
642	A121	6sh	Man in vest	1.00	.35
643	A121	17.50sh	Woman	3.25	1.00
644	A121	20sh	Man in red shirt	3.50	1.25
645	A121	25sh	Golf club	4.50	1.50
			Nos. 642-645 (4)	12.25	4.10

Traditional Crafts — A122

1995, Mar. 24 Litho. *Perf. 14x13½*

No.	Type	Value	Description	Unused	Used
646	A122	6sh	Perfume containers	.50	.40
647	A122	14.50sh	Basketry	1.00	.95
648	A122	17.50sh	Preservation pots	1.40	1.40
649	A122	20sh	Gourds	1.75	1.75
650	A122	25sh	Wooden containers	2.40	2.40
			Nos. 646-650 (5)	7.05	6.90

UN, 50th Anniv. A123

Designs: 23sh, UN Headquarters, Nairobi. 26sh, People holding UN emblem. 32sh, UN Peacekeeper's helmet. 40sh, UN emblem.

1995, Oct. 24 Litho. *Perf. 13½*

No.	Type	Value	Description	Unused	Used
651	A123	23sh	multicolored	1.50	1.50
652	A123	26sh	multicolored	1.60	1.60
653	A123	32sh	multicolored	2.25	2.10
654	A123	40sh	multicolored	2.50	2.50
			Nos. 651-654 (4)	7.85	7.70

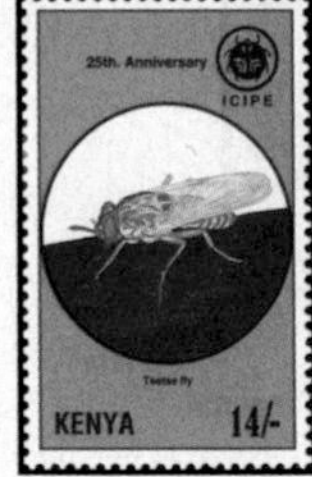

A124 — A125

1995, Sept. 29 Litho. *Perf. 13½*

No.	Type	Value	Description	Unused	Used
655	A124	14sh	Tse-tse fly	.70	.70
656	A124	26sh	Tick	1.25	1.25
657	A124	32sh	Wild silk moth	1.60	1.60
658	A124	33sh	Maize borer	1.75	1.75
659	A124	40sh	Locust	2.10	2.10
			Nos. 655-659 (5)	7.40	7.40

ICIPE, 25th anniv.

1995, Oct. 16

No.	Type	Value	Description	Unused	Used
660	A125	14sh	Maize production	1.00	1.00
661	A125	28sh	Cattle rearing	2.25	2.25
662	A125	32sh	Poultry keeping	2.50	2.50
663	A125	33sh	Fishing	2.50	2.50
664	A125	40sh	Fruits	3.25	3.25
			Nos. 660-664 (5)	11.50	11.50

FAO, 50th anniv.

Miniature Sheets

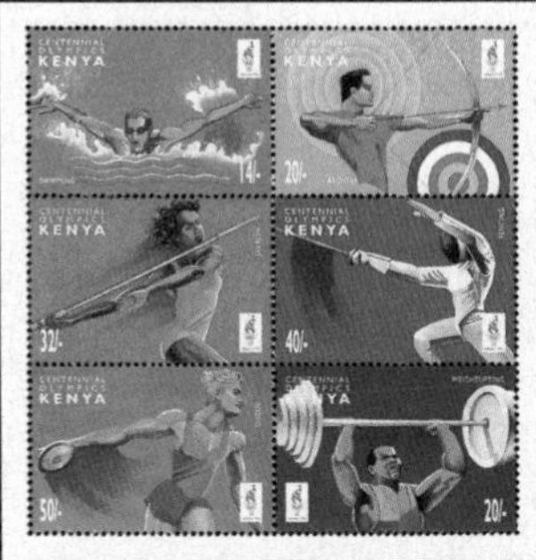

1996 Summer Olympics, Atlanta — A126

No. 665: a, 14sh, Swimming. b, 20sh, Archery. c, 32sh, Javelin. d, 40sh, Fencing. e, 50sh, Discus. f, 20sh, Weight lifting.

No. 666: a, Pole vault. b, Equestrian. c, Diving. d, Track e, Torch bearer. f, Hurdles. g, Kayak. h, Boxing. i, Gymnastics.

No. 667- Medal winners: a, Greg Louganis, diving. b, Muhammed Ali, boxing. c, Nadia Comaneci, gymnastics. d, Daley Thompson, decathlon. e, Kipchoge "Kip" Keino, track and field. f, Kornelia Enders, swimming. g, Jackie Joyner-Kersee, track and field. h, Michael Jordan, basketball. i, Shun Fujimoto, gymnastics.

No. 668, 100sh, Torch bearer. No. 669, 100sh, Gold medalist.

1996, Jan. 5 Litho. *Perf. 14*

No.	Type	Value	Description	Unused	Used
665	A126		Sheet of 6, #a.-f.	12.00	12.00
666	A126	20sh	Sheet of 9, #a.-i.	13.00	13.00
667	A126	25sh	Sheet of 9, #a.-i.	14.00	14.00

Souvenir Sheets

No.	Type	Description	Unused	Used
668-669	A126	Set of 2	12.00	12.00

World Tourism Organization, 20th Anniv. — A127

1996, Jan. 31 Litho. *Perf. 13½*

670 A127 6sh Lions .50 .35
671 A127 14sh Mount Kenya 1.00 1.00
672 A127 20sh Water sports 1.50 1.50
673 A127 25sh Hippopotomus 2.00 2.00
674 A127 40sh Culture 3.00 3.00
Nos. 670-674 (5) 8.00 7.85

Perf. 13x13½

675 A127 50sh Giraffes, vert. 5.00 5.00

Wild Animals A128

1996 *Perf. 13x13½*

Booklet Stamps

676 A128 20sh Water buck 1.25 1.00
677 A128 20sh Rhinoceros 1.25 1.00
678 A128 20sh Cheetah 1.25 1.00
679 A128 20sh Oryx 1.25 1.00
680 A128 20sh Reticulated giraffe 1.25 1.00
681 A128 20sh Bongo 1.25 1.00
a. Booklet pane of 6, #676-681 7.50
Complete booklet, 4 #681a 30.00

Nos. 676-681 appear in No. 681a in two different orders. Complete booklet contains 2 of each type of pane.

1996 Summer Olympic Games, Atlanta — A129

Red Cross — A130

1996, July 18 Litho. *Perf. 13½x14*

682 A129 6sh Woman running .30 .30
683 A129 14sh Steeple chase .60 .60
684 A129 20sh Victory lap .90 .90
685 A129 25sh Boxing 1.10 1.10
686 A129 40sh Man running 1.90 1.90
Nos. 682-686 (5) 4.80 4.80

1996, Aug. 30 Litho. *Perf. 14*

687 A130 6sh Emblem .40 .40
688 A130 14sh Blood donation .80 .80
689 A130 20sh Immunization 1.25 1.25
690 A130 25sh Refugees 1.50 1.50
691 A130 40sh Clean environment 2.50 2.50
Nos. 687-691 (5) 6.45 6.45

A131

A132

1996, Sept. 10 Litho. *Perf. 14½*

693 A131 6sh Impala .40 .40
694 A131 20sh Colobus monkey 1.50 1.50
695 A131 25sh Elephant 1.75 1.75
696 A131 40sh Black rhino 3.25 3.25
Nos. 693-696 (4) 6.90 6.90

East African Wildlife Society.

1996, Oct. 31 Litho. *Perf. 13½*

697 A132 6sh Logo .30 .30
698 A132 14sh Eye camps .95 .95
699 A132 20sh Wheel chair 1.50 1.50
700 A132 25sh Ambulance 1.75 1.75
Nos. 697-700 (4) 4.50 4.50

Lions Club Intl.

COMESA (Common Market for Eastern and Southern Africa — A133

1997, Jan. 15 Litho. *Perf. 13½x14*

701 A133 6sh COMESA logo .20 .20
702 A133 20sh Natl. flag 1.40 1.40

Fish of Lake Victoria A134

Haplochromis: #703, Orange rock hunter. #704, Chilotes. #705, Cinctus. #706, Nigricans.

1997, Jan. 31 *Perf. 14x13½*

703 A134 25sh multicolored *3.50 1.75*
704 A134 25sh multicolored *3.50 1.75*
705 A134 25sh multicolored *3.50 1.75*
706 A134 25sh multicolored *3.50 1.75*
Nos. 703-706 (4) 14.00 7.00

World Wildlife Fund.

Locomotives — A135

1997, Feb. 20 Litho. *Perf. 14x13½*

707 A135 6sh Class 94, 1981 .75 .20
708 A135 14sh Class 87, 1964 1.75 1.10
709 A135 20sh Class 59, 1955 2.10 1.75
710 A135 25sh Class 57, 1939 2.40 1.90
711 A135 30sh Class 23, 1923 2.50 2.40
712 A135 40sh Class 10, 1914 3.50 3.50
Nos. 707-712 (6) 13.00 10.85

Dated 1996.

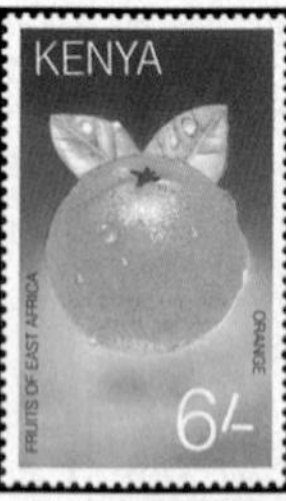

Fruits — A136

A137

1997, Feb. 28 *Perf. 14½*

713 A136 6sh Orange .20 .20
714 A136 14sh Pineapple 2.10 2.10
715 A136 20sh Mango 3.00 3.00
716 A136 25sh Papaya 3.75 3.75
Nos. 713-716 (4) 9.05 9.05

1997, Sept. 1 Litho. *Perf. 14½*

Scouting Organizations: No. 717, Girl Guides, 75th anniv. No. 718, Lord Baden Powell. No. 719, Girl scouts hiking. No. 720, Rangers camping. No. 721, Girl Guides planting trees. No. 722, Boy Scouts first aid. No. 723, Boy Scouts camping. No. 724, Brownies.

717 A137 10sh multicolored .35 .35
718 A137 10sh multicolored .35 .35
a. Pair, #717-718 .75 .75
719 A137 27sh multicolored .90 .90
720 A137 27sh multicolored .90 .90
a. Pair, #719-720 2.25 2.25
721 A137 33sh multicolored 1.25 1.25
722 A137 33sh multicolored 1.25 1.25
a. Pair, #721-722 3.00 3.00
723 A137 42sh multicolored 1.50 1.50
724 A137 42sh multicolored 1.50 1.50
a. Pair, #723-724 3.50 3.50
Nos. 717-724 (8) 8.00 8.00

Tourist Attractions — A138

Designs: 10sh, Crocodile. 27sh, Hot Springs, Lake Bogoria. 30sh, Warthogs. 33sh, Wind surfing. 42sh, Traditional huts.

1997, Oct. 9 *Perf. 13½*

725 A138 10sh multicolored 1.90 .55
726 A138 27sh multicolored 2.50 1.60
727 A138 30sh multicolored 2.75 1.90
728 A138 33sh multicolored 3.25 2.75
729 A138 42sh multicolored 3.50 3.50
Nos. 725-729 (5) 13.90 10.30

Vasco da Gama's Stop in Malindi, 500th Anniv. A139

Designs: 10sh, Residents greeting ships as they arrive. 24sh, Three ships. 33sh, Map of voyage. 42sh, Ships in bay, monument.

1998, Apr. 4 Litho. *Perf. 13*

730 A139 10sh multicolored .60 .60
731 A139 24sh multicolored 1.40 1.40
732 A139 33sh multicolored 2.00 2.00
733 A139 42sh multicolored 2.50 2.50
Nos. 730-733 (4) 6.50 6.50

Pan African Postal Union (PAPU) A140

1998, June 10 Litho. *Perf. 14½*

734 A140 10sh Lion 1.90 .65
735 A140 24sh Buffalo 2.40 1.50
736 A140 33sh Grant's gazelle 3.25 3.25
737 A140 42sh Cheetah 4.25 4.25
Nos. 734-737 (4) 11.80 9.65

Souvenir Sheet

738 A140 50sh Hirola gazelle 3.75 3.75

Pres. Daniel arap Moi Taking Oath of Office, 1998 A141

1998, Dec. 8 Litho. *Perf. 13½*

739 A141 14sh multicolored 2.25 2.25

Turtles A142

Designs: 17sh, Leatherback. 20sh, Green sea. 30sh, Hawksbill. 47sh, Olive Ridley. 59sh, Loggerhead.

2000, Apr. 13 Litho. *Perf. 13½x13¾*

740 A142 17sh multi 1.25 1.25
741 A142 20sh multi 1.50 1.50
742 A142 30sh multi 2.40 2.40
743 A142 47sh multi 3.25 3.25
744 A142 59sh multi 4.50 4.50
Nos. 740-744 (5) 12.90 12.90

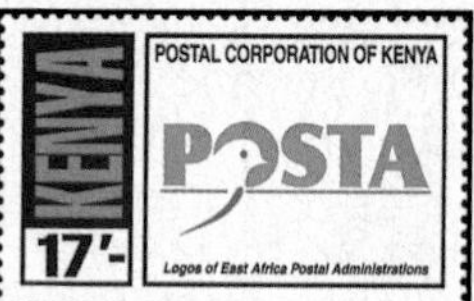

Emblems of East African Postal Administrations — A143

Designs: 17sh, Postal Corporation of Kenya. 35sh, Uganda Posta Limited. 50sh, Tanzania Posts Corporation. 70sh, Postal Corporation of Kenya.

2000, May 31 *Perf. 13¾x13½*

745 A143 17sh multi 1.00 1.00
746 A143 35sh multi 2.10 2.10
747 A143 50sh multi 3.00 3.00
Nos. 745-747 (3) 6.10 6.10

Souvenir Sheet

Perf. 13¼x13

748 A143 70sh multi 5.50 5.50

Crops — A144

2001, Feb. 28 Photo. *Perf. 14½x14*

749 A144 2sh Cotton .20 .20
750 A144 4sh Bananas .25 .25
751 A144 5sh Avocados .30 .30
752 A144 6sh Cassava .45 .45
753 A144 8sh Arrowroot .55 .55
754 A144 10sh Papayas .70 .70
755 A144 19sh Oranges .95 .95
756 A144 20sh Pyrethrum .95 .95
757 A144 30sh Peanuts 1.40 1.40
758 A144 35sh Coconuts 1.75 1.75
759 A144 40sh Sisal 1.90 1.90
760 A144 50sh Cashews 2.40 2.40

Size: 25x42mm

Perf. 14¼

761 A144 60sh Tea 2.75 2.75
762 A144 80sh Corn 4.00 4.00
763 A144 100sh Coffee 5.00 5.00
764 A144 200sh Finger millet 10.00 10.00
765 A144 400sh Sorghum 20.00 20.00
766 A144 500sh Sugar cane 25.00 25.00
Nos. 749-766 (18) 78.55 78.55

2001 Photo. *Perf. 14¾ Horiz.*

Coil Stamps

766A A144 5sh Avocados .30 .30
766B A144 10sh Papayas .70 .70

Historic Sites of East Africa A145

Designs: 19sh, Source of Nile River, Jinja, Uganda. 35sh, Lamu Fort, Kenya (28x28mm). 40sh, Olduvai Gorge, Tanzania. 50sh, Thimlich Ohinga, Kenya (28x28mm).

Perf. 14¼, 13½ (35sh, 50sh)

2002 Litho.

767-770 A145 Set of 4 9.00 9.00

Kenya - People's Republic of China Diplomatic Relations, 40th Anniv. — A146

Flags of Kenya and People's Republic of China and: 21sh, Section of Mombasa Road. 66sh, Kasarani Stadium.

2003, Dec. 14 Litho. *Perf. 12*

771-772 A146 Set of 2 5.50 5.50

Mammals — A147

Designs: 21sh, Lioness and baby oryx. 60sh, Leopard and cub. 66sh, Zebra and calf. 88sh, Bongo and calf.

2004, Nov. 19 Litho. *Perf. 14½*
773-776 A147 Set of 4 6.50 6.50

Easter — A148

Designs: 25sh, Jesus with hand raised. 65sh, Jesus condemned to death. 75sh, Crucifixion. 95sh, Jesus praying.

2005, Apr. 1 Litho. *Perf. 13½*
777-780 A148 Set of 4 7.00 7.00

Rotary International, Cent. — A149

Rotary emblem and: 25sh, Polio vaccination. 65sh, Donation of Jaipur feet. 75sh, Don Bosco Center, Nairobi. 95sh, Donation of sewing machine.

2005, May 26
781-784 A149 Set of 4 12.00 12.00

Native Costumes A150

Designs: 21sh, Gabbra. 60sh, Pokot. 66sh, Meru. 88sh, Digo.

2005, Dec. 6 Litho. *Perf. 14½*
785-788 A150 Set of 4 11.00 11.00

24th Universal Postal Union Congress, Nairobi — A152

2006, Oct. 11 Litho. *Perf. 13½*
793 A152 25sh multi .70 .70

Values are for stamps with surrounding selvage. Due to political unrest in Kenya, the UPU Congress was moved to Geneva, Switzerland.

Hippopotamus and Tortoise — A153

2006, Dec. 15 Litho. *Perf. 12½x13*
794 A153 25sh multi .75 .75

Tourism A155

2006, Dec. 15 *Perf. 13*

Booklet Stamps

795	A155 25sh Roan antelope	*2.60*	*2.60*
796	A155 25sh Weaver bird	*2.60*	*2.60*
797	A155 25sh Monkey	*2.60*	*2.60*
a.	Booklet pane of 3, #795-797	*8.00*	—
798	A155 25sh Turkana hut	*2.60*	*2.60*
799	A155 25sh Sports	*2.60*	*2.60*
800	A155 25sh Golf course	*2.60*	*2.60*
a.	Booklet pane of 3, #798-800	*8.00*	—
801	A155 25sh Abadares Waterfall	*2.60*	*2.60*
802	A155 25sh Balloon safari	*2.60*	*2.60*
803	A155 25sh Bull fighting	*2.60*	*2.60*
a.	Booklet pane of 3, #801-803	*8.00*	—
804	A155 25sh Chimpanzee	*2.60*	*2.60*
805	A155 25sh Maasai	*2.60*	*2.60*
806	A155 25sh Kit Mikaye	*2.60*	*2.60*
a.	Booklet pane of 3, #804-806	*8.00*	—
	Complete booklet, #797a, 800a, 803a, 806a	*32.00*	
	Nos. 795-806 (12)	*31.20*	*31.20*

Mountains — A156

Designs: 25sh, Mt. Kenya, Kenya. 75sh, Mt. Ruwenzori, Uganda. 95sh, Mt. Kilimanjaro, Tanzania.

2007, Feb. 28 Litho. *Perf. 13½*
807-809 A156 Set of 3 5.75 5.75

Breast Cancer Awareness A157

2007, Oct. 28 *Perf. 13¼*
810 A157 25sh multi .75 .75

Ceremonial Costumes — A158

Men's and women's costumes: 25sh, Ogiek. 65sh, Sabaot. 75sh, Ribe. 95sh, Elmolo.

2007, Nov. 21 *Perf. 14½*
811-814 A158 Set f 4 8.25 8.25

National Arboretum, Cent. — A159

Designs: 25sh, Cape chestnut tree and blossom. 65sh, Bhutan cypress tree, Tree Center. 75sh, Nandi flame tree and blossom. 95sh, Calabash nutmeg tree and blossom.

2007, Dec. 13 Litho. *Perf. 13¾*
815-818 A159 Set of 4 8.25 8.25

POSTAGE DUE STAMPS

D1

Perf. 14x13½

1967-85 Litho. Unwmk.

"POSTAGE DUE" 12½mm long

J1	D1	5c dark red	.25	2.75
J2	D1	10c green	.35	2.75
J3	D1	20c dark blue	.70	3.25
J4	D1	30c reddish brown	1.00	4.00
J5	D1	40c brt red lilac	1.25	6.75

Perf. 14

J6	D1	80c brick red	1.00	6.25

Perf. 15x14

J7	D1	1sh orange	3.00	*9.00*

"POSTAGE DUE" 11½mm long

J8	D1	2sh pale violet	.90	.90
		Nos. J1-J8 (8)	8.45	*35.65*

Issued: 80c, 1978. 2sh, 1985; others, 1/3/67.
See Nos. J9-J14.

1969-70 *Perf. 14*

J1a	D1	5c	.20	5.25
J2a	D1	10c	.25	5.25
J3a	D1	20c	.45	5.75
J4a	D1	30c	.70	6.75
J5a	D1	40c	.90	10.50
J7a	D1	1sh	2.00	*13.50*
		Nos. J1a-J7a (6)	4.50	*47.00*

Issued: 1sh, 2/18/70; others, 12/16/69.

1971-73 *Perf. 14x15*

J1b	D1	5c	1.75	5.25
J2b	D1	10c	1.75	5.25
J3b	D1	20c	1.50	5.75
J4b	D1	30c	10.50	13.50
J5b	D1	40c	1.25	9.00
J7b	D1	1sh	2.50	*13.50*
		Nos. J1b-J7b (6)	19.25	52.25

Issued: 30c, 7/13/71; others, 2/20/73. The 10c, 20c, 1sh on chalky paper were issued 7/13/71.

1973, Dec. 12 *Perf. 15*

J1c	D1	5c	.45	4.00
J2c	D1	10c	.45	4.00
J3c	D1	20c	.45	5.00
J4c	D1	30c	.45	5.75
J5c	D1	40c	5.25	10.00
J7c	D1	1sh	1.75	*12.50*
		Nos. J1c-J7c (6)	8.80	41.25

1983 Wmk. 373 *Perf. 14x13½*

J2d	D1	10c
J3d	D1	20c
J5d	D1	40c

Nos. J5, J7-J8 Redrawn

Perf. 15x14

1987-98 Litho. Unwmk.

J8A	D1	30c brown	.20	.20
J9	D1	40c bright red lilac	.20	.20
J10	D1	50c dark green	.20	.20
J10A	D1	80c red brown	.20	.20
J11	D1	1sh light orange	.80	.80
a.		light orange	.20	.20
J12	D1	2sh pale violet	.20	.20
J13	D1	3sh dark blue	.45	.45
J14	D1	5sh red brown	.45	.45
J15	D1	10sh brown	.45	.45
J16	D1	20sh red lilac	.80	.80
		Nos. J8A-J16 (10)	3.95	3.95

"KENYA" is 9mm wide on Nos. J9, J11. "CENTS" is 4½mm wide and "SHILLING" has cross bar on "G"; both are in a new font.

"KENYA" is 8½mm wide on No. J12. "POSTAGE DUE" is 11mm wide on Nos. J10, J11a, J15, J16.

Issued: 40c, 1sh, 1987; 10sh, 20sh, 1998; others, Dec. 6, 1993.

OFFICIAL STAMPS

Nos. 1-5 and 7 Overprinted

Perf. 14x14½

1964, Oct. 1 Photo. Unwmk.

Size: 21x17½mm

O1	A1	5c blue, buff & dk brn	.20	.20
O2	A1	10c brown	.20	.20
O3	A1	15c dp magenta	1.50	.30
O4	A1	20c yel green & dk brn	.30	.45
O5	A1	30c yellow & black	.40	.65
O6	A1	50c green, blk & dp car	2.50	1.10
		Nos. O1-O6 (6)	5.10	2.90

KENYA, UGANDA, TANZANIA

'ke-nyə, ü-'gan-də, ˌtan-zə-'nē-ə

LOCATION — East Africa, bordering on the Indian Ocean
GOVT. — States in British Commonwealth
AREA — 679,802 sq. mi.
POP. — 42,760,000 (est. 1977)
CAPITAL — Nairobi (Kenya), Kampala (Uganda), Dar es Salaam (Tanzania)

Kenya became a crown colony in 1906, including the former East Africa Protectorate leased from the Sultan of Zanzibar and known as the Kenya Protectorate. In 1963 the colony became independent. Its stamps are listed under "Kenya."

The inland Uganda Protectorate, lying west of Kenya Colony, was declared a British Protectorate in 1894. Uganda became independent in 1962.

Tanganyika, a trust territory larger than Kenya or Uganda, was grouped with them postally from 1935 under the East African Posts & Telecommunications Administration. Tanganyika became independent in 1961. When it merged with Zanzibar in 1964, "Zanzibar" was added to the inscriptions on stamps issued under the E.A.P. & T. Administration. In 1965 the multiple inscription was changed to "Kenya, Uganda, Tanzania," variously arranged.

Zanzibar withdrew its own stamps in 1968, and K., U. & T. stamps became valid Jan. 1, 1968.

100 Cents = 1 Rupee
100 Cents = 1 Shilling (1922)
20 Shillings = 1 Pound

Catalogue values for unused stamps in this country are for Never Hinged items, beginning with Scott 90.

East Africa and Uganda Protectorates

King George V
A1 A2

1921 Typo. Wmk. 4 *Perf. 14*

Ordinary Paper

No.	Type	Denom.	Color	Unused	Used
1	A1	1c	black	.90	*1.90*
2	A1	3c	green	6.75	*8.25*
3	A1	6c	rose red	7.75	*12.00*
4	A1	10c	orange	9.75	1.40
5	A1	12c	gray	7.75	*125.00*
6	A1	15c	ultramarine	12.50	*18.50*

Chalky Paper

No.	Type	Denom.	Color	Unused	Used
7	A1	50c	gray lilac & blk	16.50	*120.00*
8	A2	2r	blk & red, *blue*	82.50	*190.00*
9	A2	3r	green & violet	150.00	*260.00*
10	A2	5r	gray lil & ultra	175.00	*275.00*
11	A2	50r	gray grn & red	2,500.	*5,000.*
			Nos. 1-10 (10)	469.40	*1,012.*

The name of the colony was changed to Kenya in August, 1920, but stamps of the East Africa and Uganda types were continued in use. Stamps of types A1 and A2 watermarked Multiple Crown and C A (3) are listed under East Africa and Uganda Protectorates.

For stamps of Kenya and Uganda overprinted "G. E. A." used in parts of former German East Africa occupied by British forces, see Tanganyika Nos. 1-9.

Kenya and Uganda

King George V
A3 A4

1922-27 Wmk. 4

No.	Type	Denom.	Color	Unused	Used
18	A3	1c	brown	1.10	*3.25*
19	A3	5c	violet	4.00	1.00
20	A3	5c	green ('27)	2.40	.55
21	A3	10c	green	1.75	.35
22	A3	10c	black ('27)	4.50	.25
23	A3	12c	black	6.00	*29.00*
24	A3	15c	car rose	1.40	.20
25	A3	20c	orange	3.75	.20
26	A3	30c	ultra	2.75	.60
27	A3	50c	gray	2.75	.20
28	A3	75c	ol bister	6.00	*10.00*
29	A4	1sh	green	4.75	3.00
30	A4	2sh	gray lilac	10.00	*12.00*
31	A4	2sh50c	brown ('25)	24.00	*95.00*
32	A4	3sh	gray black	20.00	7.50
33	A4	4sh	gray ('25)	29.00	*100.00*
34	A4	5sh	carmine	27.50	27.50
35	A4	7sh50c	org ('25)	100.00	*190.00*
36	A4	10sh	ultra	60.00	57.50
37	A4	£1	org & blk	225.00	*275.00*
38	A4	£2	brn vio & grn ('25)	800.00	*1,300.*
39	A4	£3	yel & dl vio ('25)	1,100.	—
40	A4	£4	rose lil & blk ('25)	2,100.	—
41	A4	£5	blue & blk	2,400.	—
			Revenue cancel		55.00
41A	A4	£10	grn & blk	*10,000.*	
41B	A4	£20	grn & red ('25)	*21,000.*	
41C	A4	£25	red & blk	*25,000.*	
41D	A4	£50	red & blk	*32,500.*	
41E	A4	£75	red & blk	*90,000.*	
41F	A4	£100	red & blk	*100,000.*	
			Nos. 18-37 (20)	536.65	*813.10*

High face value stamps are known with revenue cancellations removed and forged postal cancellations added.

Common Design Types pictured following the introduction.

Kenya, Uganda, Tanganyika Silver Jubilee Issue

Common Design Type

1935, May Engr. *Perf. 13½x14*

No.	Type	Denom.	Color	Unused	Used
42	CD301	20c	ol grn & lt bl	1.50	.20
43	CD301	30c	blue & brown	2.50	*3.50*
44	CD301	65c	indigo & green	2.00	*3.25*
45	CD301	1sh	brt vio & indigo	2.25	*3.75*
			Nos. 42-45 (4)	8.25	*10.70*
			Set, never hinged	14.50	

Kavirondo Cranes — A5

Dhow on Lake Victoria — A6

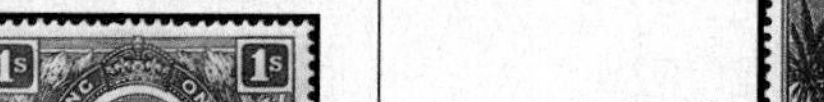

Lion — A7

Mount Kilimanjaro — A8

Jinja Bridge by Ripon Falls — A9

Mount Kenya — A10

Lake Naivasha A11

FIVE CENTS
Type I — Left rope does not touch sail.
Type II — Left rope touches sail.

Perf. 13, 14, 11½x13, 13x11½
Engr.; Typo. (10c, £1)

1935, May 1

No.	Type	Denom.	Color	Unused	Used
46	A5	1c	red brn & blk	1.00	*1.50*
47	A6	5c	grn & blk (I)	2.00	.50
a.			Type II	*22.50*	5.00
b.			Perf. 13x11½ (I)	*3,750.*	*600.00*
c.			Perf. 13x11½ (II)	*675.00*	*200.00*
48	A7	10c	black & yel	4.50	.65
49	A8	15c	red & black	2.75	.20
50	A5	20c	red org & blk	3.50	.20
51	A9	30c	dk ultra & blk	2.50	1.00
52	A6	50c	blk & red vio	3.00	.20
53	A10	65c	yel brn & blk	4.00	*2.00*
54	A11	1sh	grn & black	2.75	.80
a.			Perf. 13x11½ ('36)	*1,350.*	125.00
55	A8	2sh	red vio & rose brn	7.00	4.25
56	A11	3sh	blk & ultra	10.00	*17.50*
a.			Perf. 13x11½	*2,250.*	
57	A9	5sh	car & black	19.00	*35.00*
58	A5	10sh	ultra & red vio	75.00	*100.00*
59	A7	£1	blk & scar	210.00	*250.00*
			Nos. 46-59 (14)	347.00	413.80
			Set, never hinged	725.00	

Coronation Issue

Common Design Type

1937, May 12 Engr. *Perf. 13½x14*

No.	Type	Denom.	Color	Unused	Used
60	CD302	5c	deep green	.20	.20
61	CD302	20c	deep orange	.30	.35
62	CD302	30c	brt ultra	.45	*.65*
			Nos. 60-62 (3)	.95	1.20
			Set, never hinged	2.00	

Kavirondo Cranes — A12

Dhow on Lake Victoria — A13

Lake Naivasha A14

Jinja Bridge, Ripon Falls — A16

Mt. Kilimanjaro — A15

Lion — A17

FIFTY CENTS:
Type I — Left rope does not touch sail.
Type II — Left rope touches sail.

1938-54 Engr. *Perf. 13x13½*

No.	Type	Denom.	Color	Unused	Used
66	A12	1c	vio brn & blk	.25	*.35*
a.			1c red brown & gray black, perf. 13 ('42)	1.50	.45
			Perf. 13x11½		
67	A13	5c	grn & blk	3.00	.25
68	A13	5c	red org & brn ('49)	.40	*2.25*
a.			Perf. 13x12½ ('50)	1.60	*3.00*
69	A14	10c	org & brn	2.00	.20
a.			Perf. 14 ('41)	90.00	7.25
70	A14	10c	grn & blk ('49)	.25	*.75*
a.			Perf. 13x12½ ('50)	1.75	.20
			Perf. 13x12½		
71	A14	10c	gray & red brn ('52)	.80	*.55*
			Perf. 13½x13, 13x13½		
72	A15	15c	car & gray blk ('43)	3.25	*2.75*
a.			Booklet pane of 4	14.00	
b.			Perf. 13	17.00	.50
73	A15	15c	grn & blk ('52)	1.60	*4.00*
74	A12	20c	org & gray blk ('42)	5.75	.20
a.			Booklet pane of 4	24.00	
b.			Imperf., pair		
c.			Perf. 13	*35.00*	.30
d.			Perf. 14 ('41)	*50.00*	12.50
			Perf. 13x12½		
75	A13	25c	car & blk ('52)	1.25	*2.25*
			Perf. 13x13½		
76	A16	30c	dp bl & gray blk ('42)	2.00	.35
a.			Perf. 14 ('41)	*130.00*	12.50
b.			Perf. 13	*40.00*	.40
77	A16	30c	brn & pur ('52)	1.25	.40
78	A12	40c	brt bl & gray blk ('52)	1.50	*3.50*
			Perf. 13x12½		
79	A13	50c	gray blk & red vio (II) ('49)	5.75	.60
a.			Perf. 13x11½ (II)	14.00	1.10
b.			Perf. 13x11½ (I)	175.00	*250.00*
			Perf. 13x11½		
80	A14	1sh	yel brn & gray blk	18.00	.25
a.			Perf. 13x12½ ('49)	10.00	.60
			Perf. 13½x13		
81	A15	2sh	red vio & org brn ('44)	22.50	.30
a.			Perf. 13	*100.00*	2.25
b.			Perf. 14 ('41)	*62.50*	2.25
			Perf. 13x12½		
82	A14	3sh	gray blk & ultra ('50)	27.50	3.00
a.			Perf. 13x11½	35.00	4.00
			Perf. 13x13½		
83	A16	5sh	car rose & gray blk ('44)	27.50	1.40
a.			Perf. 13	*125.00*	17.50
b.			Perf. 14 ('41)	*35.00*	2.50
84	A12	10sh	ultra & red vio ('44)	40.00	4.50
a.			Perf. 13	110.00	21.00
b.			Perf. 14 ('41)	32.50	22.50

Typo.
Perf. 14

85 A17 £1 blk & scar ('41) 22.50 *20.00*
a. Perf. 11½x13 275.00 135.00
b. Perf. 12½ ('54) 12.00 *35.00*
Nos. 66-85 (20) 187.05 *47.85*
Set, never hinged 275.00

See Nos. 98-99.

South Africa Nos. 48, 57, 60 and 62 Surcharged

Basic stamps of Nos. 86-89 are inscribed alternately in English and Afrikaans.

1941-42 Wmk. 201 *Perf. 15x14, 14*

86 A6 5c on 1p car & gray, pair 1.00 *2.00*
a. Single, English .20 .20
b. Single, Afrikaans .20 .20
87 A17 10c on 3p ultra, pair 2.50 *10.00*
a. Single, English .30 .35
b. Single, Afrikaans .30 .35
88 A7 20c on 6p org & grn, pair 2.25 *3.75*
a. Single, English .20 .25
b. Single, Afrikaans .20 .25
89 A11 70c on 1sh lt bl & ol brn, pair 15.00 *7.00*
a. Single, English .50 .45
b. Single, Afrikaans .50 .45
Nos. 86-89 (4) 20.75 22.75
Set, never hinged 30.00

Issued: #86-88, 7/1/41; #89, 4/20/42.

Catalogue values for unused stamps in this section, from this point to the end of the section, are for Never Hinged items.

Peace Issue
Common Design Type
Perf. 13½x14

1946, Nov. 11 Engr. Wmk. 4

90 CD303 20c red orange .20 .20
91 CD303 30c deep blue .40 .30

Silver Wedding Issue
Common Design Types

1948, Dec. 1 Photo. *Perf. 14x14½*

92 CD304 20c orange .20 .20

Engr.; Name Typo.
Perf. 11½x11

93 CD305 £1 red 45.00 *67.50*

UPU Issue
Common Design Types
Engr.; Typo. on Nos. 95 and 96

1949, Oct. 10 *Perf. 13, 11x11½*

94 CD306 20c red orange .20 .20
95 CD307 30c indigo 1.75 *2.25*
96 CD308 50c gray .40 .40
97 CD309 1sh red brown .50 .50
Nos. 94-97 (4) 2.85 3.35

Type of 1949 with Added Inscription: "Royal Visit 1952"

1952, Feb. 1 Engr. *Perf. 13x12½*

98 A14 10c green & black .20 *1.60*
99 A14 1sh yel brn & gray blk 1.25 *2.25*

Visit of Princess Elizabeth, Duchess of Edinburgh, and the Duke of Edinburgh, 1952.

Coronation Issue
Common Design Type

1953, June 2 *Perf. 13½x13*

101 CD312 20c red orange & blk .20 .20

Owen Falls Dam — A18

Giraffe — A19

Elizabeth II — A21

Mt. Kilimanjaro A20

1954, Apr. 28 *Perf. 12½x13*

102 A18 30c dp ultra & black .20 .20

Visit of Queen Elizabeth II and the Duke of Edinburgh, 1954.

1954-59 *Perf. 12½x13, 13x12½*

5c, 30c, Owen Falls Dam (without "Royal Visit 1954"). 20c, 40c, 1sh, Lion. 15c, 1.30sh, 5sh, Elephants. 10sh, Royal Lodge, Sagana.

103 A18 5c choc & blk 1.00 .65
a. Booklet pane of 4 4.00
b. Vignette (dam) inverted *25,000.*
104 A19 10c carmine 1.00 .20
a. Booklet pane of 4 4.00
105 A20 15c lt blue & blk (no period below "c") ('58) .75 1.60
a. Booklet pane of 4 3.50
106 A20 15c lt blue & blk (period below "c") ('59) 1.75 1.60
a. Booklet pane of 4 8.50
107 A19 20c org & black 1.00 .20
a. Booklet pane of 4 4.00
b. Imperf., pair *1,200.*
108 A18 30c ultra & black 1.00 .20
a. Booklet pane of 4 4.00
b. Vignette (dam) inverted *16,000.*
109 A19 40c brown ('58) 2.00 1.00
110 A19 50c dp red lilac 2.00 .20
a. Booklet pane of 4 8.00
111 A20 65c brn car & grn ('55) 3.50 2.00
112 A19 1sh dp mag & blk 2.00 .20
113 A20 1.30sh pur & red org ('55) 11.00 .20
114 A20 2sh dp grn & gray 10.50 1.50
115 A20 5sh black & org 25.00 3.00
116 A20 10sh ultra & black 27.50 4.00
117 A21 £1 black & ver 21.00 16.00
Nos. 103-117 (15) 111.00 32.55

No. 103b is unique.
For "Official" overprints see Tanganyika Nos. O1-O12.

Map Showing Lakes Victoria and Tanganyika A22

Perf. 12½x13

1958, July 30 Engr. Wmk. 314

118 A22 40c green & blue .30 .30
119 A22 1.30sh violet & green .75 .70

Cent. of the discovery of Lakes Victoria and Tanganyika by Sir Richard F. Burton and Capt. J. H. Speke.

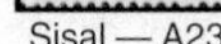

Sisal — A23

A25

Mount Kenya and Giant Plants A24

10c, Cotton. 15c, Coffee. 20c, Gnu. 25c, Ostriches. 30c, Thompson's gazelles. 40c, Manta ray. 50c, Zebras. 65c, Cheetah. 1.30sh, Murchison Falls & hippopotamuses. 2sh, Mt. Kilimanjaro & giraffes. 2.50sh, Candelabra tree & black rhinoceroses. 5sh, Crater Lake & Mountains of the Moon. 10sh, Ngorongoro Crater & buffaloes.

Perf. 14½x14

1960, Oct. 1 Photo. Wmk. 314

120 A23 5c dull blue .20 .20
121 A23 10c lt olive green .20 .20
a. Booklet pane of 4 .60
122 A23 15c dull purple .40 .20
a. Booklet pane of 4 1.75
123 A23 20c brt lilac rose .25 .20
a. Booklet pane of 4 1.20
124 A23 25c olive gray 4.00 1.25
125 A23 30c brt vermilion .20 .20
a. Booklet pane of 4 .90
126 A23 40c bright blue .30 .20
127 A23 50c dull violet .45 .20
a. Booklet pane of 4 1.90
128 A23 65c lemon .65 *1.70*

Engr.
Perf. 14

129 A24 1sh vio & red lilac .90 .20
130 A24 1.30sh choc & dk car 3.75 .20
131 A24 2sh dk bl & dull bl 4.50 .55
132 A24 2.50sh ol grn & dull bl 6.75 2.00
133 A24 5sh rose red & lilac 4.50 4.00
134 A24 10sh sl bl & ol grn 10.00 8.75

Perf. 13½x13

135 A25 20sh lake & bluish violet 20.00 22.50
Nos. 120-135 (16) 57.05 42.55

Booklets issued in 1961.
On Nos. 120-134, positions of "Kenya," "Uganda" and "Tanganyika" are rotated.
For "Official" overprints see Tanganyika Nos. O13-O20.

Agricultural Development — A26

Design: 30c, 1.30sh, Farmer picking corn.

Unwmk.

1963, Mar. 21 Photo. *Perf. 14*

136 A26 15c lt ol grn & ultra .20 .20
137 A26 30c yel & red brown .40 .20
138 A26 50c dp org & ultra .50 .20
139 A26 1.30sh lt blue & red brn .75 .75
Nos. 136-139 (4) 1.85 1.35

FAO "Freedom from Hunger" campaign.

Scholars and Open Book A27

1963, June 28 Unwmk. *Perf. 14*

140 A27 30c multicolored .20 .20
141 A27 1.30sh multicolored .35 .35

Inauguration of University of East Africa.

Red Cross A28

1963, Sept. 2

142 A28 30c blue & red 1.50 .25
143 A28 50c bister brown & red 2.00 1.10

Centenary of International Red Cross.

Kenya, Uganda, Tanganyika and Zanzibar

Issued by the East African Common Services Organization. Not used in Zanzibar.

Japanese Crest and Olympic Rings — A29

Olympic Rings and Banners A30

Unwmk.

1964, Oct. 25 Photo. *Perf. 14*

144 A29 30c org & dk purple .20 .20
145 A29 50c dk purple & org .20 .20
146 A30 1.30sh blue, grn & org .30 .30
147 A30 2.50sh blue, vio & lil rose .60 .60
Nos. 144-147 (4) 1.30 1.30

18th Olympic Games, Tokyo, Oct. 10-25.

Kenya, Uganda, Tanzania

Issued by the East African Common Services Organization.

Safari Rally Emblem and Leopard — A31

1.30sh, 2.50sh, Car on road through national park & emblem of the East African Safari Rally.

1965, Apr. 15 Unwmk. *Perf. 14*

148 A31 30c blue grn, yel & blk .20 .20
149 A31 50c brown, yel & blk .20 .20
150 A31 1.30sh lt ultra, ocher & green .35 .30
151 A31 2.50sh blue, dk grn & dull red .65 .65
Nos. 148-151 (4) 1.40 1.35

13th East African Safari Rally, 4/15-19/65.

ITU Emblem, Old and Modern Communication Equipment — A32

1965, May 17 Photo.

152 A32 30c lilac rose, gold & brn .25 .20
153 A32 50c gray, gold & brown .25 .20
154 A32 1.30sh lt vio bl, gold & brn .65 .30
155 A32 2.50sh brt bl grn, gold & brn 1.50 1.50
Nos. 152-155 (4) 2.65 2.20

Cent. of the ITU.

ICY Emblem — A33

1965, Aug. 4 Unwmk. *Perf. 14*
156 A33 30c green & gold .20 .20
157 A33 50c slate blk & gold .25 .20
158 A33 1.30sh ultra & gold .50 .30
159 A33 2.50sh car & gold 1.25 1.25
Nos. 156-159 (4) 2.20 1.95

International Cooperation Year.

Game Park Lodge A34

Tourist Publicity: 50c, Murchison Falls, Uganda. 1.30sh, Lake Nakuru, Kenya. 2.50sh, Deep-sea fishing, Tanzania.

1966, Apr. 4 Photo. *Perf. 14*
160 A34 30c ocher & multi .20 .20
161 A34 50c green & multi .50 .20
a. Blue omitted
162 A34 1.30sh multicolored 3.25 .35
163 A34 2.50sh gray & multi 2.50 3.50
Nos. 160-163 (4) 6.45 4.25

Javelin Thrower and Games' Emblem A35

1966, Aug. 2 Unwmk. *Perf. 14*
164 A35 30c multicolored .20 .20
165 A35 50c multicolored .20 .20
166 A35 1.30sh multicolored .25 .20
167 A35 2.50sh multicolored .35 .75
Nos. 164-167 (4) 1.00 1.35

8th British Commonwealth and Empire Games, Jamaica, Aug. 4-13, 1966.

UNESCO Emblem — A36

1966, Oct. 3 Photo. *Perf. 14*
168 A36 30c rose red, brt grn & blk .40 .20
169 A36 50c lt brn, brt grn & blk .45 .20
170 A36 1.30sh gray, brt grn & blk 1.25 .25
171 A36 2.50sh yel, brt grn & blk 2.40 4.50
Nos. 168-171 (4) 4.50 5.15

20th anniv. of UNESCO.

Dragon Rapide A37

Planes: 50c, Super VC10. 1.30sh, Comet 4. 2.50sh, F.27 Friendship.

1967, Jan. 23 Unwmk.
172 A37 30c multicolored .35 .20
173 A37 50c multicolored .45 .20
174 A37 1.30sh multicolored .95 .40
175 A37 2.50sh multicolored 2.10 3.50
Nos. 172-175 (4) 3.85 4.30

21st anniversary of East African Airways.

Pillar Tomb, East African Coast — A38

Designs: 50c, Man hunting elephant, petroglyph, Tanzania. 1.30sh, Clay head, Luzira, Uganda. 2.50sh, Proconsul skull, Rusinga Island, Kenya.

1967, May 2 Photo. *Perf. 14*
176 A38 30c rose lake, blk & yel .20 .20
177 A38 50c gray, black & ver .60 .20
178 A38 1.30sh green, yel & blk 1.00 .30
179 A38 2.50sh cop red, yel & blk 2.00 3.50
Nos. 176-179 (4) 3.80 4.20

Archaeological relics of East Africa.

Emblems of Kenya, Tanzania and Tanganyika — A39

Photo.; Gold Impressed
1967, Dec. 1 *Perf. 14½x14*
180 A39 5sh gray, black & gold .60 *1.00*

Establishment of East African Community.

Mount Kenya A40

30c Mountain climber. 1.30sh, Mount Kilimanjaro. 2.50sh, Ruwenzori Mountains.

1968, Mar. 4 Photo. *Perf. 14½*
181 A40 30c multicolored .20 .20
182 A40 50c multicolored .40 .20
183 A40 1.30sh multicolored .70 .35
184 A40 2.50sh multicolored 1.50 *2.75*
Nos. 181-184 (4) 2.80 3.50

Family and Rural Hospital A41

Family and: 50c, Student nurse. 1.30sh, Microscope. 2.50sh, Mosquito and hand holding hypodermic.

1968, May 13 Photo. *Perf. 13½*
185 A41 30c multicolored .20 .20
186 A41 50c rose vio, blk & brt pink .20 .20
187 A41 1.30sh brn org, blk & brt pink .20 .20
188 A41 2.50sh gray, blk & brt pink .30 *.75*
Nos. 185-188 (4) .90 1.35

20th anniv. of the WHO.

Stadium A42

Designs: 50c, Diving tower. 1.30sh, Pylons and tracks. 2.50sh, Boxing ring, vert.

Perf. 14½x14, 14x14½
1968, Oct. 14 Photo.
189 A42 30c dull pur & gray grn .20 .20
190 A42 50c brt grn, blk & gray .20 .20
191 A42 1.30sh gray grn, blk & dk car .30 .30
192 A42 2.50sh buff, brn org & brn blk .50 *.65*
Nos. 189-192 (4) 1.20 1.35

19th Olympic Games, Mexico City, 10/12-27.

Railroad Ferry MV Umoja A43

Water Transport: 50c, Transatlantic liner S.S. Harambee. 1.30sh, Lake motor vessel Victoria. 2.50sh, Ferry St. Michael.

1969, Jan. 20 Photo. *Perf. 14*
193 A43 30c blue, gray & dk bl .40 .20
194 A43 50c blue, gray & scar .45 .20
195 A43 1.30sh bl, dk bl & dk green .90 .60
196 A43 2.50sh bl, dk bl & org 2.00 *4.00*
Nos. 193-196 (4) 3.75 5.00

Farm Workers and ILO Emblem A44

ILO Emblem and: 50c, Construction. 1.30sh, Industry. 2.50sh, Shipping.

1969, Apr. 14 Photo. *Perf. 14*
197 A44 30c green, blk & yel .20 .20
198 A44 50c car rose, blk & car .20 .20
199 A44 1.30sh dp org, blk & org .20 .20
200 A44 2.50sh grnsh bl, blk & ultra .30 .50
Nos. 197-200 (4) .90 1.10

50th anniv. of the ILO.

Pope Paul VI, Mountains of the Moon, Papal Arms, Crested Crane — A45

Euphorbia Tree in Shape of Africa, Development Bank Emblem — A46

1969, July 31 Photo. *Perf. 14*
201 A45 30c dk blue, blk & gold .20 .20
202 A45 70c plum, blk & gold .25 .20
203 A45 1.50sh gray bl, blk & gold .30 .25
204 A45 2.50sh dp vio, blk & gold .35 *.90*
Nos. 201-204 (4) 1.10 1.55

Visit of Pope Paul VI to Uganda, 7/31-8/2.

Perf. 14x13½
1969, Dec. 8 Litho. Unwmk.
205 A46 30c brt grn, dk grn & gold .20 .20
206 A46 70c plum, dk grn & gold .20 .20
207 A46 1.50sh grnsh bl, dk grn & gold .25 .20
208 A46 2.50sh brn org, dk grn & gold .50 .50
Nos. 205-208 (4) 1.15 1.10

African Development Bank, 5th anniv.

Amadinda, Uganda — A47

Musical Instruments: 30c, Marimba, Tanzania. 1.50sh, Nzomari (trumpet), Kenya. 2.50sh, Adeudeu, Kenya.

1970, Feb. 16 Litho. *Perf. 11x12*
209 A47 30c multicolored .20 .20
210 A47 70c multicolored .30 .20
211 A47 1.50sh dk rose brn & org .65 .20
212 A47 2.50sh multicolored 1.25 1.25
Nos. 209-212 (4) 2.40 1.85

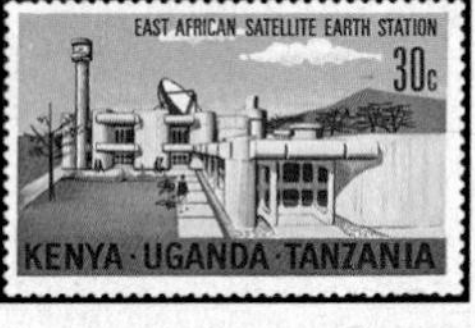

Satellite Earth Station A48

Designs: 70c, Radar station by day. 1.50sh, Radar station by night. 2.50sh, Satellite transmitting communications to and from earth.

1970, May 18 Litho. *Perf. 14½*
213 A48 30c multicolored .20 .20
214 A48 70c multicolored .20 .20
215 A48 1.50sh org, blk & vio .30 .20
216 A48 2.50sh dull bl & multi .60 .80
Nos. 213-216 (4) 1.30 1.40

Opening of the East African Satellite Earth Station, Mt. Margaret, Kenya.

Runner — A49

1970, July 16 Litho. *Perf. 14½*
217 A49 30c org brn, dk brn & blk .20 .20
218 A49 70c grn, dk brn & blk .20 .20
219 A49 1.50sh dull pur, dk brn & blk .20 .20
220 A49 2.50sh grnsh bl, dk brn & blk .30 .50
Nos. 217-220 (4) .90 1.10

9th British Commonwealth Games, Edinburgh, July 16-25.

UN Emblem and People A50

1970, Oct. 19 Photo. *Perf. 14½*
221 A50 30c org brn, gold & black .20 .20
222 A50 70c bl grn, gold & black .20 .20
223 A50 1.50sh dull red brn, gold & blk .20 .20
224 A50 2.50sh olive, gold & blk .30 .80
Nos. 221-224 (4) .90 1.40

25th anniversary of the United Nations.

Conversion from Pounds to Kilograms — A51

Designs: 70c, Conversion from Fahrenheit to centigrade. 1.50sh, Conversion from gallons to liters. 2.50sh, Conversion from miles to kilometers.

1971, Jan. 4 Photo. *Perf. 14½*

225 A51 30c silver & multi .20 .20
226 A51 70c silver & multi .20 .20
227 A51 1.50sh silver & multi .25 .20
228 A51 2.50sh silver & multi .35 .80
Nos. 225-228 (4) 1.00 1.40

Conversion to metric system of weights and measures.

Locomotive — A52

Designs: Various locomotives.

1971, Apr. 19 Photo. *Perf. 14½*

229 A52 30c gold & multi .35 .20
230 A52 70c gold & multi .55 .25
231 A52 1.50sh gold & multi 1.25 1.25
232 A52 2.50sh gold & multi 2.00 3.00
a. Souvenir sheet of 4, #229-232 11.00 11.00
Nos. 229-232 (4) 4.15 4.70

70th anniversary of the completion of the Mombasa to Kisumu line.

Campaign Emblem and Cow — A53

Designs: 1.50sh, Like 30c. 70c, 2.50sh, Bull and Campaign Emblem.

1971, July 5 Photo. *Perf. 14½*

233 A53 30c yel grn, blk & bis .20 .20
234 A53 70c gray bl, blk & bis .20 .20
235 A53 1.50sh mag, blk & bis .20 .20
236 A53 2.50sh red org, blk & bis .30 .50
Nos. 233-236 (4) .90 1.10

Rinderpest campaign by the Organization for African Unity.

Meeting of Stanley and Livingstone — A54

1971, Oct. 28 Litho. *Perf. 14*

237 A54 5sh multicolored .50 .50

Centenary of the meeting at Ujiji of Dr. David Livingstone, missionary, and Henry M. Stanley, journalist, who had been sent to find Livingstone.

Modern Farming Village — A55

Designs: 30c, Pres. Julius K. Nyerere carried in triumph, 1961, vert. 1.50sh, University of Dar es Salaam. 2.50sh, Kilimanjaro International Airport.

1971, Dec. 9 *Perf. 14*

238 A55 30c bister & multi .20 .20
239 A55 70c lt blue & multi .20 .20
240 A55 1.50sh lt green & multi .25 .25
241 A55 2.50sh yel & multi .95 .55
Nos. 238-241 (4) 1.60 1.20

10th anniv. of independence of Tanzania.

Flags of African Nations and Fair Emblem — A56

1972, Feb. 23 *Perf. 13½x14*

242 A56 30c lt bl & multi .20 .20
243 A56 70c gray & multi .20 .20
244 A56 1.50sh yel & multi .25 .25
245 A56 2.50sh multicolored .35 .50
Nos. 242-245 (4) 1.00 1.15

First All-Africa Trade Fair, Nairobi, Kenya, Feb. 23-Mar. 5.

Child Drinking Milk, UNICEF Emblem A57

25th Anniv. (in 1971) of UNICEF: 70c, Children playing ball. 1.50sh, Child writing on blackboard. 2.50sh, Boy playing with tractor.

1972, Apr. 24 Litho. *Perf. 14½x14*

246 A57 30c brn org & multi .20 .20
247 A57 70c lt ultra & multi .20 .20
248 A57 1.50sh yel & multi .20 .20
249 A57 2.50sh green & multi .25 .40
Nos. 246-249 (4) .85 1.00

Hurdles, Olympic and Motion Emblems — A58

1972, Aug. 28

250 A58 40c shown .20 .20
251 A58 70c Running .20 .20
252 A58 1.50sh Boxing .25 .20
253 A58 2.50sh Hockey .60 *2.25*
a. Souvenir sheet of 4, #250-253 8.00 8.00
Nos. 250-253 (4) 1.25 2.85

20th Olympic Games, Munich, 8/26-9/11.

Uganda Kob, Semliki Game Reserve — A59

1972, Oct. 9 Litho. *Perf. 14*

254 A59 40c shown .25 .20
255 A59 70c Intl. Conf. Center .25 .20
256 A59 1.50sh Makerere Univ., Kampala .55 .50
257 A59 2.50sh Uganda arms 1.40 *1.75*
a. Souvenir sheet of 4, #254-257, perf. 13x14 5.50 5.50
Nos. 254-257 (4) 2.45 2.65

Uganda's independence, 10th anniv. #256 also for 50th anniv. of Makerere University, Kampala.

Flag of East Africa — A60

1972, Dec. 1 Litho. *Perf. 14½x14*

258 A60 5sh multicolored 1.25 1.25

5th anniv. of the East African Community.

Anemometer, Lake Victoria Station — A61

WMO Emblem and: 70c, Release of weather balloon, vert. 1.50sh, Hail suppression by meteorological rocket. 2.50sh, Meteorological satellite receiving antenna.

1973, Mar. 5 Litho. *Perf. 14*

259 A61 40c multicolored .20 .20
260 A61 70c ultra & multi .20 .20
261 A61 1.50sh emer & multi .35 .30
262 A61 2.50sh multicolored .65 .65
Nos. 259-262 (4) 1.40 1.35

Cent. of intl. meteorological cooperation.

Scouts Laying Bricks — A62

Designs: 70c, Baden-Powell's gravestone, Nyeri, Kenya. 1.50sh, World Scout emblem. 2.50sh, Lord Baden-Powell.

1973, July 16 Litho. *Perf. 14*

263 A62 40c ocher & multi .20 .20
264 A62 70c multicolored .30 .30
265 A62 1.50sh multicolored .60 .60
266 A62 2.50sh grn & ultra 1.60 1.50
Nos. 263-266 (4) 2.70 2.60

24th Boy Scout World Conference (1st in Africa), Nairobi, Kenya, July 16-21.

International Bank for Reconstruction and Development and Affiliates' Emblems — A63

Designs: 40c, Arrows dividing 4 bank affiliate emblems. 70c, Vert. lines dividing 4 emblems. 1.50sh, Kenyatta Conference Center, Nairobi, vert.

1973, Sept. 24 Litho. *Perf. 14x13½*

267 A63 40c gray, blk & grn .20 .20
268 A63 70c brn, gray & blk .20 .20
269 A63 1.50sh lem, gray & blk .50 .50
270 A63 2.50sh blk, org & gray .95 2.25
a. Souvenir sheet of 4 6.00 6.00
Nos. 267-270 (4) 1.85 3.15

Intl. Bank for Reconstruction and Development and Affiliate Intl. Monetary Fund Meetings, Nairobi.

No. 270a contains stamps similar to Nos. 267-270 with simulated perforations.

INTERPOL Emblem, Policeman and Dog — A64

Designs: 70c, East African policemen and emblem. 1.50sh, INTERPOL emblem. 2.50sh, INTERPOL Headquarters, St. Cloud, France.

1973-74 Litho. *Perf. 14x14½*

271 A64 40c yellow & multi .65 .20
272 A64 70c multicolored 1.25 .20
273 A64 1.50sh violet & multi 2.00 1.25
274 A64 2.50sh lemon & multi *(St. Clans)* 5.00 8.50
275 A64 2.50sh lemon & multi *(St. Cloud)* ('74) 5.00 8.50
Nos. 271-275 (5) 13.90 18.65

50th anniv. of Intl. Criminal Police Org. Issued: Nos. 271-274, Oct. 24, 1973.

Tea Factory, Nandi Hills — A65

1973, Dec. 12 Photo. *Perf. 13x14*

276 A65 40c shown .20 .20
277 A65 70c Kenyatta Hospital .20 .20
278 A65 1.50sh Nairobi Airport .70 .35
279 A65 2.50sh Kindaruma hydroelectric plant 1.25 *2.00*
Nos. 276-279 (4) 2.35 2.75

10th anniversary of independence.

Afro-Shirazi Party Headquarters — A66

Designs: 70c, Michenzani housing development. 1.50sh, Map of East Africa and television screen with flower. 2.50sh, Amaan Stadium.

1974, Jan. 12 Litho. *Perf. 13½x14*

280 A66 40c multicolored .20 .20
281 A66 70c multicolored .20 .20
282 A66 1.50sh black & multi .60 .35
283 A66 2.50sh black & multi 1.25 *3.50*
Nos. 280-283 (4) 2.25 4.25

10th anniversary of Zanzibar revolution.

Symbol of Union A67

Designs: 70c, Map of Tanganyika and Zanzibar, and handshake. 1.50sh, Map of Tanganyika and Zanzibar, and communications symbols. 2.50sh, Flags of Tanu, Tanzania and Afro-Shirazi Party.

1974, Apr. 24 Litho. *Perf. 14½*

284 A67 40c sepia & multi .20 .20
285 A67 70c blue grn & multi .25 .20
286 A67 1.50sh ultra & multi .55 .40
287 A67 2.50sh multicolored 1.50 *2.50*
Nos. 284-287 (4) 2.50 3.30

Union of Tanganyika and Zanzibar, 10th anniv.

Family and Home A68

Designs: 70c, Drummer at dawn. 1.50sh, Family hoeing, and livestock. 2.50sh, Telephonist, train, plane, telegraph lines.

1974, July 15 Litho. *Perf. 14½*

288 A68 40c multicolored .20 .20
289 A68 70c multicolored .20 .20
290 A68 1.50sh multicolored .45 .45
291 A68 2.50sh multicolored 1.00 .80
Nos. 288-291 (4) 1.85 1.65

17th Intl. Conf. on Social Welfare, 7/14-20.

Post and Telegraph Headquarters, Kampala — A69

Cent. of the UPU: 70c, Mail train and truck. 1.50sh, UPU Headquarters, Bern. 2.50sh, Loading mail on East African Airways VC-10.

1974, Oct. 9 Litho. *Perf. 14*

292	A69	40c lt green & multi	.20	.20
293	A69	70c gray & multi	.20	.20
294	A69	1.50sh yel & multi	.25	.25
295	A69	2.50sh lt blue & multi	.75	.80
		Nos. 292-295 (4)	1.40	1.45

Family Planning Clinic A70

World Population Year: 70c, "Tug of War." 1.50sh, Scales and world population figures. 2.50sh, World Population Year emblem.

1974, Dec. 16 Litho. *Perf. 14½*

296	A70	40c multicolored	.20	.20
297	A70	70c purple & multi	.20	.20
298	A70	1.50sh multicolored	.20	.25
299	A70	2.50sh blue blk & multi	.30	.80
		Nos. 296-299 (4)	.90	1.45

Seronera Wild Life Lodge, Tanzania — A71

Game lodges of East Africa: 70c, Mweya Safari Lodge, Uganda. 1.50sh, Ark-Aberdare Forest Lodge, Kenya. 2.50sh, Paraa Safari Lodge, Uganda.

1975, Feb. 24 Litho. *Perf. 14½*

300	A71	40c multicolored	.20	.20
301	A71	70c multicolored	.20	.20
302	A71	1.50sh multicolored	.55	.35
303	A71	2.50sh multicolored	1.10	*3.25*
		Nos. 300-303 (4)	2.05	4.00

Wooden Comb, Bajun, Kenya — A72

African Artifacts: 1sh, Earring, Chaga, Tanzania. 2sh, Armlet, Acholi, Uganda. 3sh, Kamba gourd, Kenya.

1975, May 5 Litho. *Perf. 13½*

304	A72	50c gray & multi	.20	.20
305	A72	1sh gray & multi	.20	.20
306	A72	2sh multicolored	.35	.45
307	A72	3sh multicolored	.65	.75
		Nos. 304-307 (4)	1.40	1.60

Map Showing OAU Members, Ugandan Flag — A73

Elephant, Kenya — A74

OAU Emblem and: 50c, Entebbe Airport, horiz. 2sh, Nile Hotel, Kampala, horiz. 3sh, Ugandan Martyrs' Shrine, Namugongo.

Perf. 11½x11, 11x11½

1975, July 28 Litho.

308	A73	50c multicolored	.35	.20
309	A73	1sh multicolored	.35	.20
310	A73	2sh multicolored	.50	.50
311	A73	3sh multicolored	1.00	*1.25*
		Nos. 308-311 (4)	2.20	2.15

Organization for African Unity (OAU), Summit Conf., Kampala, July 28 - Aug. 1.

1975, Sept. 11 Litho. *Perf. 11x11½*

Protected animals: 1sh, Albino buffalo, Uganda. 2sh, Elephant, exhibit in National Museum, Kenya. 3sh, Abbott's duiker, Tanzania.

312	A74	50c multicolored	.75	.20
313	A74	1sh brown & multi	.90	.20
314	A74	2sh yel green & multi	3.00	2.25
315	A74	3sh blue grn & multi	3.50	*4.25*
		Nos. 312-315 (4)	8.15	6.90

Masai Villagers Bleeding Cow, Masai, Kenya — A75

Festival Emblem and: 1sh, Ugandan dancers. 2sh, Family, Makonde sculpture, Tanzania. 3sh, Skinning hippopotamus, East Africa.

1975, Nov. 3 Litho. *Perf. 13½x14*

316	A75	50c org brown & multi	.25	.20
317	A75	1sh brt green & multi	.25	.20
318	A75	2sh dk blue & multi	.80	.80
319	A75	3sh lilac & multi	1.50	*2.00*
		Nos. 316-319 (4)	2.80	3.20

2nd World Black and African Festival of Arts and Culture, Lagos, Nigeria, Jan. 5 - Feb. 12.

Fokker Friendship, Nairobi Airport — A76

East African Airways, 30th anniv.: 1sh, DC-9 Kilimanjaro Airport. 2sh, Super VC10, Entebbe Airport. 3sh, East African Airways emblem.

1976, Jan. 2 Litho. *Perf. 11½*

320	A76	50c ultra & multi	1.50	.75
321	A76	1sh rose & multi	1.75	.75
322	A76	2sh orange & multi	5.25	4.50
323	A76	3sh black & multi	6.00	6.00
		Nos. 320-323 (4)	14.50	12.00

POSTAGE DUE STAMPS

Kenya and Uganda

D1

D2

Perf. 14½x14

1928-33 Typo. Wmk. 4

J1	D1	5c deep violet	3.00	1.00
J2	D1	10c orange red	3.00	1.00
J3	D1	20c yel green	3.00	4.00
J4	D1	30c ol brn ('31)	22.50	16.00
J5	D1	40c dull blue	8.50	*16.00*
J6	D1	1sh grnsh gray ('33)	77.50	*140.00*
		Nos. J1-J6 (6)	117.50	*178.00*
		Set, never hinged	200.00	

Kenya, Uganda, Tanganyika

1935, May 1 *Perf. 13½x14*

J7	D2	5c violet	3.50	2.25
J8	D2	10c red	.35	.65
J9	D2	20c green	.55	.65
J10	D2	30c brown	1.00	*.90*
J11	D2	40c ultramarine	2.00	*4.00*
J12	D2	1sh gray	25.00	*25.00*
		Nos. J7-J12 (6)	32.40	*33.45*
		Set, never hinged	50.00	

OFFICIAL STAMPS

The 1959-60 "OFFICIAL" overprints on Nos. 103-104, 106-108, 110, 112-117, 120-123, 125, 127, 129, 133 are listed under Tanganyika, as they were used by the Tanganyika government.

KIAUCHAU

(Kiautschou)

LOCATION — A district of China on the south side of the Shantung peninsula.
GOVT. — German colony
AREA — 200 sq. mi.
POP. — 192,000 (approx. 1914).

The area was seized by Germany in 1897 and through negotiations that followed was leased to Germany by China.

100 Pfennig = 1 Mark
100 Cents = 1 Dollar (1905)

Tsingtau Issues

Stamps of Germany, Offices in China 1898, with Additional Surcharge:

a

b

c

On Nos. 1-9, a blue or violet line is drawn through "PF. 10 PF." All exist without this line. All copies of Nos. 1b, 2b and 3b lack the colored line.

The three surcharge types can most easily be distinguished by the differences in the lower loop of the "5."

1900

"China" Overprint at 56 degree Angle

1	A10(a)	5pfg on 10pf car	45.00	*55.00*
c.		Dbl. surch., one inverted	675.00	
2	A10(b)	5pfg on 10pf car	45.00	*55.00*
c.		Dbl. surch., one inverted	675.00	
3	A10(c)	5pfg on 10pf car	45.00	*55.00*
c.		Dbl. surch., one inverted	675.00	
		Nos. 1-3 (3)	135.00	165.00

"China" Overprint at 48 degree Angle

1a	A10(a)	5pfg on 10pf car	140.00	*135.00*
b.		Double surcharge	400.00	*525.00*
2a	A10(b)	5pfg on 10pf car	140.00	*135.00*
b.		Double surcharge	400.00	*525.00*
3a	A10(c)	5pfg on 10pf car	140.00	*135.00*
b.		Double surcharge	400.00	*525.00*
		Nos. 1a-3a (3)	420.00	*405.00*

Surcharged:

d

e

5 Pf.

f

"China" Overprint at 48 degree Angle on Nos. 4-9

4	A10(d)	5pf on 10pf car	*2,250.*	*3,000.*
a.		Double surcharge	*6,750.*	*13,500.*
5	A10(e)	5pf on 10pf car	*2,000.*	*2,750.*
a.		Double surcharge	*6,750.*	*13,500.*
6	A10(f)	5pf on 10pf car	*2,000.*	*2,750.*
a.		Double surcharge	*7,500.*	*16,500.*
b.		5fP		*16,500.*
c.		As "b," double surcharge	—	—

With Additional Handstamp

7	A10(d)	5pf on 10pf car	*37,500.*	*45,000.*
8	A10(f)	5pf on 10pf car	*34,000.*	*40,000.*
a.		On No. 6b	—	—

With Additional Handstamp

9	A10(f)	5pf on 10pf car	*7,500.*	*11,000.*
a.		Double surcharge	32,500.	
b.		On No. 6a		
c.		On No. 6b		
d.		On No. 6c		

Kaiser's Yacht "Hohenzollern"
A1 A2

1901, Jan. Unwmk. Typo. *Perf. 14*

10	A1	3pf brown	2.00	2.00
11	A1	5pf green	2.00	1.75
12	A1	10pf carmine	2.50	2.10
13	A1	20pf ultra	7.50	8.50
14	A1	25pf org & blk, *yel*	13.50	*17.00*
15	A1	30pf org & blk, *sal*	13.50	*16.00*
16	A1	40pf lake & blk	16.00	*21.00*
17	A1	50pf pur & blk, *sal*	16.00	*23.50*
18	A1	80pf lake & blk, *rose*	30.00	*55.00*

Engr. *Perf. 14½x14*

19	A2	1m carmine	50.00	*92.50*
20	A2	2m blue	75.00	*110.00*
21	A2	3m black vio	75.00	*200.00*
22	A2	5m slate & car	210.00	*675.00*
		Nos. 10-22 (13)	513.00	*1,224.*
		Set, never hinged	1,450.	

A3

A4

1905 **Typo.**

23 A3 1c brown 1.25 1.75
24 A3 2c green 1.90 1.25
25 A3 4c carmine 4.25 1.50
26 A3 10c ultra 8.50 5.50
27 A3 20c lake & blk 34.00 20.00
28 A3 40c lake & blk, *rose* 100.00 *100.00*

Engr.

29 A4 $½ carmine 72.50 *85.00*
30a A4 $1 blue 150.00 125.00
31 A4 $1½ black vio 1,200. *1,700.*
32 A4 $2½ slate & car 1,500. *4,400.*
Nos. 23-32 (10) 3,072. *6,440.*
Set, never hinged 7,750.

1905-16 **Wmk. 125** **Typo.**

33 A3 1c brown ('06) 1.25 *1.75*
a. 1c yellow brown ('16) .50 —
34 A3 2c green ('09) 1.10 *1.10*
a. 2c dark green ('14) .50 *2.10*
35 A3 4c carmine ('09) .85 *1.25*
36 A3 10c ultra ('09) 1.10 *3.75*
a. 10c blue 12.00 5.00
37 A3 20c lake & blk ('08) 2.50 *17.50*
38 A3 40c lake & blk, *rose* 3.25 *55.00*

Engr.

39 A4 $½ car ('07) 10.00 *67.50*
40 A4 $1 steel blue ('06) 12.50 *72.50*
41 A4 $1½ blk violet 20.00 *225.00*
42 A4 $2½ slate & car 50.00 *500.00*
Nos. 33-42 (10) 102.55 *945.35*

Four values of the design A3 and A4 stamps in recognizably different shades were printed and released in 1918, but by then Germany had lost control of Kiauchau, and these stamps are not known used. The four stamps and their unused values are: 20c red & black, $1.75; $½ pale rose, $5.50; $1 bright blue, $6.75; $1½ gray violet, $20.

KIONGA

'kyoŋ-gə

LOCATION — Southeast Africa and northeast Mozambique, on Indian Ocean south of Rovuma River
GOVT. — Part of German East Africa
AREA — 400 sq. mi.

This territory, occupied by Portuguese troops during World War I, was allotted to Portugal by the Treaty of Versailles. Later it became part of Mozambique.

100 Centavos = 1 Escudo

Lourenco Marques No. 149 Surcharged in Red

1916, May 29 **Unwmk.** ***Perf. 11½***

1 A2 ½c on 100r bl, *bl* 30.00 20.00
2 A2 1c on 100r bl, *bl* 22.50 17.00
3 A2 2½c on 100r bl, *bl* 22.50 17.00
4 A2 5c on 100r bl, *bl* 22.50 17.00
Nos. 1-4 (4) 97.50 71.00

Most of the stock of Lourenço Marques #149 used for these surcharges lacked gum. Unused examples with original gum are worth approximately 50% more than the values shown.

KIRIBATI

'kir-ə-ˌbas

LOCATION — A group of islands in the Pacific Ocean northeast of Australia
GOVT. — Republic
AREA — 277 sq. mi.
POP. — 85,501 (1999 est.)
CAPITAL — Tarawa

100 Cents = 1 Australian Dollar

Kiribati, former Gilbert Islands, consists of the Gilbert, Phoenix, Ocean and Line Islands.

Catalogue values for all unused stamps in this country are for Never Hinged items.

Watermark

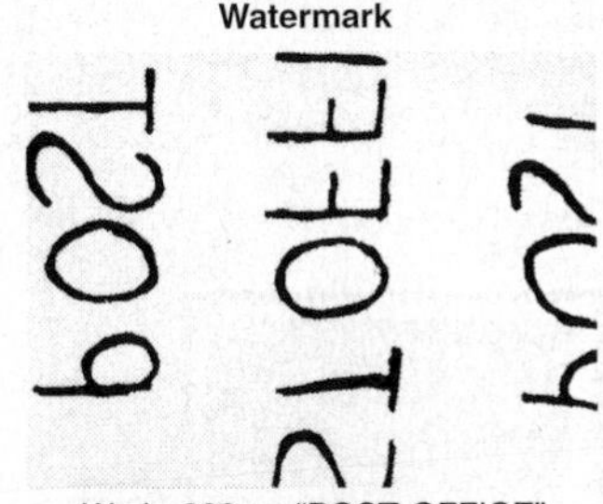

Wmk. 380 — "POST OFFICE"

Kiribati Flag A50

Parliament, London, Assembly, Tarawa — A51

Wmk. 373

1979, July 12 **Litho.** ***Perf. 14***

325 A50 10c multicolored .20 .20
326 A51 45c multicolored .40 .40

Independence.

Training Ship Teraaka A52

Designs: 3c, Passenger launch Tautunu. 5c, Hibiscus. 7c, Cathedral, Tarawa. 10c, House of Assembly, Bikenibeu Island. 12c, Betio harbor. 15c, Reef egret. 20c, Flamboyant tree. 25c, Moorish idol (fish). 30c, Frangipani blossoms. 35c, Chapel, Tangintebu Island. 50c, Hypolimnas bolina elliciana (butterfly). $1, Tarawa Lagoon ferry, Tabakea. $2, Sunset over lagoon. $5, Natl. flag.

1979-80 **Wmk. 373**

327 A52 1c multicolored .20 .60
328 A52 3c multicolored .25 .35
329 A52 5c multicolored .20 .20
330 A52 7c multicolored .20 .20
331 A52 10c multicolored .20 .20
332 A52 12c multicolored .20 *.25*
333 A52 15c multicolored .45 .30
334 A52 20c multicolored .25 *.30*
335 A52 25c multicolored .40 .30
336 A52 30c multicolored .30 .30
337 A52 35c multicolored .30 .30
338 A52 50c multicolored .80 .55
339 A52 $1 multicolored .70 .70
340 A52 $2 multicolored .90 .70
340A A52 $5 multicolored 2.00 *4.00*
Nos. 327-340A (15) 7.35 9.25

Issued: $5, 8/27/80; others, 7/12/79.

1980-81 **Unwmk.**

327a A52 1c multi ('81) .20 .20
328a A52 3c multi ('81) .20 .20
329a A52 5c multi .20 .20
330a A52 7c multi .20 .20
331a A52 10c multi .20 .20
332a A52 12c multi .20 .20
333a A52 15c multi .65 .20
334a A52 20c multi ('81) .20 .20
335a A52 25c multi .35 .20
336a A52 30c multi ('81) .20 .50
337a A52 35c multi ('81) .20 .50
338a A52 50c multi ('81) .90 .75
339a A52 $1 multi .75 .50
340b A52 $2 multi 1.40 .70
340c A52 $5 multi ('80) 2.25 2.50
Nos. 327a-340c (15) 8.10 7.25

For overprints see Nos. O1-O15.

Gilbert and Ellice Islands No. 1 — A53

Simulated Cancel and: 20c, Gilbert and Ellice No. 70. 25c, Great Britain No. 139. 45c, Gilbert and Ellice No. 31.

Wmk. 373

1979, Oct. 4 **Litho.** ***Perf. 14***

341 A53 10c multicolored .20 .20
342 A53 20c multicolored .20 .20
343 A53 25c multicolored .25 .25
344 A53 45c multicolored .25 .25
a. Souvenir sheet of 4, #341-344 1.25 1.25
Nos. 341-344 (4) .90 .90

Sir Rowland Hill (1795-1879), originator of penny postage.

Boy Climbing Coconut Palm, IYC Emblem — A54

IYC Emblem, Coat of Arms and: 10c, Boy and giant clam shell. 45c, Girl reading book. $1, Boy wearing garlands. All vert.

Perf. 14x13½, 13½x14

1979, Nov. 28 **Litho.**

345 A54 10c multicolored .20 .20
346 A54 20c multicolored .20 .20
347 A54 45c multicolored .20 .20
348 A54 $1 multicolored .30 .30
Nos. 345-348 (4) .90 .90

International Year of the Child.

Downrange Station — A55

National Space Development Agency of Japan (NASDA) Satellite Tracking: 45c, Experimental satellite trajectory (map). $1, Rocket launch, Tanegashima, Japan, vert.

1980, Feb. 20 **Litho.** ***Perf. 14½***

349 A55 25c multicolored .20 .20
350 A55 45c multicolored .20 .20
351 A55 $1 multicolored .40 .40
Nos. 349-351 (3) .80 .80

T.S. Teraaka, London 1980 Emblem A56

1980, Apr. 30 **Litho.** **Unwmk.**

352 A56 12c shown .20 .20
353 A56 25c Air Tungaru plane, Bonriki Airport .20 .20
354 A56 30c Radio operator .20 .20
355 A56 $1 Bairiki post office .30 .30
a. Souvenir sheet of 4, #352-355 1.00 1.00
Nos. 352-355 (4) .90 .90

London 1980 Intl. Stamp Exhib., May 6-14.

Achaea Janata A57

1980, Aug. 27 **Litho.** ***Perf. 14***

356 A57 12c shown .25 .25
357 A57 25c Ethmia nigroapicella .30 .30
358 A57 30c Utetheisa pulchelloides .35 .35
359 A57 50c Anua coronata .70 .70
Nos. 356-359 (4) 1.60 1.60

Capt. Cook Hotel A58

1980, Nov. 19 **Wmk. 373** ***Perf. 13½***

360 A58 10c shown .20 .20
361 A58 20c Stadium .20 .20
362 A58 25c Intl. Airport, Bonriki .20 .20
363 A58 35c National Library .20 .20
364 A58 $1 Otintai Hotel .30 .30
Nos. 360-364 (5) 1.10 1.10

Acalypha Godseffiana A59

Perf. 14x13½

1981, Feb. 18 **Litho.** **Wmk. 373**

365 A59 12c shown .20 .20
366 A59 30c Hibiscus schizopetalus .20 .20
367 A59 35c Calotropis gigantea .20 .20
368 A59 50c Euphorbia pulcherrima .30 .30
Nos. 365-368 (4) .90 .90

Abaiang and Marakei Islands, String Figures — A60

Wmk. 380

1981, May 6 **Litho.** ***Perf. 14***

369 A60 12c shown .20 .20
370 A60 30c Butaritari, Little Makin, house .20 .20
371 A60 35c Maiana, Coral Road .25 .25
372 A60 $1 Christmas Isld., Resolution .60 .60
Nos. 369-372 (4) 1.25 1.25

Prince Charles, Lady Diana, Royal Yacht Charlotte A60a

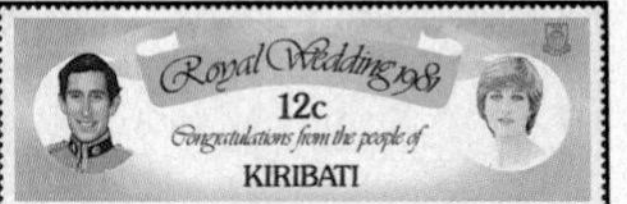

Prince Charles and Lady Diana — A60b

Illustration A60b is greatly reduced.

Wmk. 380

1981, July 29 Litho. *Perf. 14*

373 A60a 12c Couple, The Katherine .20 .20
a. Bklt. pane of 4, perf. 12, unwmkd. .60
374 A60b 12c Couple .30 .20
375 A60a 50c The Osborne .85 .50
376 A60b 50c like #374 .90 .50
a. Bklt. pane of 2, perf. 12, unwmkd. 1.75
377 A60a $2 Britannia 2.50 1.60
378 A60b $2 like #374 2.50 1.60
Nos. 373-378 (6) 7.25 4.60

Souvenir Sheet

Perf. 12

379 A60b $1.20 like #374 3.50 3.50

Royal wedding.

Stamps of the same denomination issued in sheets of 7 (6 type A60a and 1 type A60b).

Bonriki Tuna Fish Bait Breeding Center A61

1981, Nov. 19

380 A61 12c shown .20 .20
381 A61 30c Fishing boat .20 .20
382 A61 35c Cold storage, Betio .25 .25
383 A61 50c Nei Manganibuka .35 .35
a. Souvenir sheet of 4, #380-383 1.25 1.25
Nos. 380-383 (4) 1.00 1.00

Pomarine Jaegers A62

1982-85 Litho. *Perf. 14*

384 A62 1c shown .20 .20
385 A62 2c Mallards .20 .20
386 A62 4c Collared petrels .20 .20
387 A62 5c Blue-faced boobies .25 .20
388 A62 7c Friendly quail dove .30 .20
389 A62 8c Shovelers .30 .20
390 A62 12c Christmas Isld. warblers .35 .25
391 A62 15c Pacific plovers .45 .35
392 A62 20c Reef herons .50 .50
392A A62 25c Brown noddies ('83) 3.50 1.75
393 A62 30c Brown boobies .65 .60
394 A62 35c Audubon's shearwaters .95 .70
395 A62 40c White-throated storm petrels, vert. .85 .80
396 A62 50c Bristle-thighed curlews, vert. .95 .65
396A A62 55c Fairy tern ('85) 15.50 *17.00*
397 A62 $1 Scarlet-breasted lorikeets, vert. 2.00 .85
398 A62 $2 Long-tailed cuckoo, vert. 2.75 1.10
399 A62 $5 Great frigate birds, vert. 5.50 4.00
Nos. 384-399 (18) 35.40 29.75

Issued: 25c, 1/31/83; 55c, 11/19/85; others, 2/18/82.

For overprints see Nos. O16-O20.

Air Tungaru A63

1982, Feb. 18 Wmk. 380

400 A63 12c De Havilland DH114 Heron .20 .20
401 A63 30c Britten-Norman Trislander .25 .25
402 A63 35c Casa 212 Aviocar .25 .25
403 A63 50c Boeing 727 .60 .60
Nos. 400-403 (4) 1.30 1.30

21st Birthday of Princess Diana, July 1 — A64

1982, May 19

404 A64 12c Mary of Teck, 1893 .30 .30
405 A64 50c Teck arms .60 .60
406 A64 $1 Diana .85 .85
Nos. 404-406 (3) 1.75 1.75

Overprinted: "ROYAL BABY"

1982, July 14

407 A64 12c multicolored .30 .30
408 A64 50c multicolored .60 .60
409 A64 $1 multicolored .85 .85
Nos. 407-409 (3) 1.75 1.75

Birth of Prince William of Wales, June 21.

Scouting Year — A65

1982, Aug. 12

410 A65 12c First aid .25 .25
411 A65 25c Repairing boat .25 .25
412 A65 30c Saluting .30 .30
413 A65 50c Gilbert Islds. #304 .50 .50
Nos. 410-413 (4) 1.30 1.30

Visit of Queen Elizabeth II and Prince Philip A66

Wmk. 380

1982, Oct. 23 Litho. *Perf. 14*

414 A66 12c Couple, dancer .20 .20
415 A66 25c Couple, boat .30 .30
416 A66 35c Philatelic Bureau .50 .50
Nos. 414-416 (3) 1.00 1.00

Souvenir Sheet

417 A66 50c Queen Elizabeth II, vert. 1.40 1.40

Nos. 414-416 also issued in sheets of 6.

A67

1983, Mar. 14 Wmk. 380 *Perf. 14*

418 A67 12c Obaia the Feathered legend .20 .20
419 A67 30c Robert Louis Stevenson Hotel, Abemama .20 .20
420 A67 50c Betio Harbor .30 .30
421 A67 $1 Map .70 .70
Nos. 418-421 (4) 1.40 1.40

Commonwealth day.

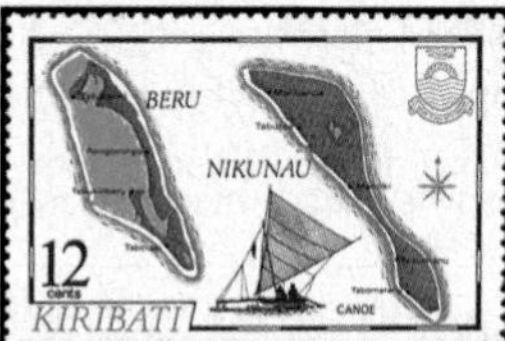

Map of Beru and Nikunau Islds., Canoe — A68

1983, May 19 Litho. *Perf. 14*

422 A68 12c shown .20 .20
423 A68 25c Abemama, Kuria, Aranuka .20 .20
424 A68 35c Nonouti, vert. .30 .30
425 A68 50c Tarawa, vert. .45 .45
Nos. 422-425 (4) 1.15 1.15

See #436-439, 456-459, 475-479, 487-490.

Copra Industry A69

Designs: 12c, Collecting fallen Coconuts. 25c, Selecting Coconuts for Copra. 30c, Removing Husk from Coconuts. 35c, Drying Copra in the Sun. 50c, Loading Copra, Betio Harbor.

1983, Aug. 8 Litho. *Perf. 14*

426 A69 12c multicolored .30 .25
427 A69 25c multicolored .50 .40
428 A69 30c multicolored .65 .60
429 A69 35c multicolored .70 .70
430 A69 50c multicolored .95 .95
Nos. 426-430 (5) 3.10 2.90

Battle of Tarawa, 40th Anniv. A70

1983, Nov. 17 Litho. Wmk. 380

431 A70 12c War memorials .20 .20
432 A70 30c Battle map .20 .20
433 A70 35c Defense gun .20 .20
434 A70 50c Scenes, 1943, 1983 .35 .35
435 A70 $1 Amphibious Assault Ship USS Tarawa .75 .75
Nos. 431-435 (5) 1.70 1.70

Map Type of 1983

1984, Feb. 14 Wmk. 380 *Perf. 14*

436 A68 12c Teraina .20 .20
437 A68 30c Nikumaroro .35 .35
438 A68 35c Kanton .40 .40
439 A68 50c Banaba .60 .60
Nos. 436-439 (4) 1.55 1.55

Local Ships A71

1984, May 9 Litho. Wmk. 380

440 A71 12c Tug boat .55 .20
441 A71 35c Ferry landing craft 1.00 .60
442 A71 50c Ferry 1.25 .85
443 A71 $1 Cargo and passanger boat 2.00 2.00
a. Souvenir sheet of 4, #440-443, perf. 13½ 6.00 6.00
Nos. 440-443 (4) 4.80 3.65

Ausipex '84 — A72

1984, Aug. 21 Litho. *Perf. 14*

444 A72 12c South Tarawa sewer & water system .20 .20
445 A72 30c Fishing boat Nouamake .30 .30
446 A72 35c Overseas communications training .35 .35
447 A72 50c Intl. telecommunications link .50 .50
Nos. 444-447 (4) 1.35 1.35

Legends A73

Designs: 12c, Tabakea supporting Banaba on his back. 30c, Nakaa, Judge of the Dead. 35c, Naareau and Tiku-Tiku-Tamoamoa. 50c, Whistling Ghosts.

1984, Nov. 21 Wmk. 380 *Perf. 14*

448 A73 12c multicolored .20 .20
449 A73 30c multicolored .25 .25
450 A73 35c multicolored .30 .30
451 A73 50c multicolored .45 .45
Nos. 448-451 (4) 1.20 1.20

See Nos. 464-467.

Reef Fish A74

1985, Feb. 19 Litho. *Perf. 14*

452 A74 12c Tang .85 .35
453 A74 25c White-barred triggerfish 1.50 .80
454 A74 35c Surgeon fish 1.75 1.25
455 A74 80c Squirrel fish 3.50 3.50
a. Souvenir sheet of 4, #452-455 8.50 8.50
Nos. 452-455 (4) 7.60 5.90

See Nos. 540-554, 567.

Map Type of 1983

1985, May 9 Litho. *Perf. 13½*

456 A68 12c Tabuaeran, frigate bird 1.50 .45
457 A68 35c Rawaki, coconuts 2.00 .70
458 A68 50c Arorae, xanthid crab 2.25 1.10
459 A68 $1 Tamana, fish hook 2.75 *2.75*
Nos. 456-459 (4) 8.50 5.00

Intl. Youth Year A76

1985, Aug. 5

460 A76 15c Boys playing soccer .85 .50
461 A76 35c Emblems 1.25 1.25
462 A76 40c Girl processing fruit, vert. 1.50 1.50
463 A76 55c Intl. youth exchange 2.00 2.00
Nos. 460-463 (4) 5.60 5.25

Legends Type of 1984

15c, Nang Kineia & the Tickling Ghosts. 35c, Myth of Auriaria & Tituabine. 40c, First Coming of Babai at Arorae. 55c, Riiki & the Milky Way.

1985, Nov. 19 Wmk. 380 *Perf. 14*

464 A73 15c multicolored .70 .70
465 A73 35c multicolored .95 .95
466 A73 40c multicolored 1.10 1.10
467 A73 55c multicolored 1.60 1.60
Nos. 464-467 (4) 4.35 4.35

Transport and Telecommunications Decade 1985-95 — A77

1985, Dec. 9 Litho. *Perf. 14*

468 A77 15c Satellite network 3.25 3.00
469 A77 40c Tarawa-Suva feeder service 4.25 3.75

Common Design Types pictured following the introduction.

Queen Elizabeth II 60th Birthday
Common Design Type

15c, Review of Girl Guides, Windsor Castle, 1938. 35c, Birthday parade, Buckingham Palace, 1980. 40c, With Prince Philip during royal tour, 1982. 55c, Banquet, Austrian embassy in London, 1966. $1, Visiting Crown Agents' offices, 1983.

1986, Apr. 21 *Perf. 14½x14*

470 CD337 15c scar, black & sil .20 .20
471 CD337 35c ultra & multi .30 .30
472 CD337 40c green & multi .35 .35
473 CD337 55c violet & multi .50 .50
474 CD337 $1 rose vio & multi 1.25 1.25
Nos. 470-474 (5) 2.60 2.60

For overprints see Nos. 495-499.

Map Type of 1983

1986, June 17 Wmk. 380 *Perf. 14*

475 A68 15c Manra 3.25 1.50
476 A68 30c Birnie, McKean 4.25 2.00
477 A68 35c Orona 5.00 2.50
478 A68 40c Malden 5.25 3.00
479 A68 55c Vostok, Caroline, Flint 5.50 3.50
Nos. 475-479 (5) 23.25 12.50

Lizards A79

1986, Aug. 26 Unwmk. *Perf. 14*

480 A79 15c Lepidodactylus lugubris 2.25 1.00
481 A79 35c Gehyra mutilata 3.00 1.75
482 A79 40c Hemidactylus frenatus 3.50 2.25
483 A79 55c Gehyra oceanica 5.00 4.50
Nos. 480-483 (4) 13.75 9.50

See Nos. 491-494.

America's Cup — A80

Perf. 14x14½

1986, Dec. 29 Unwmk.

484 Strip of 3 2.50 2.50
a. A80 15c Map of Australia .25 .25
b. A80 55c Course, trophy .60 .60
c. A80 $1.50 Australia II 1.50 1.50

No. 484 has a continuous design.

Transport and Telecommunications Decade (1985-1995) — A81

Designs: 30c, Nei Moamoa, flagship of Kiribati overseas shipping line. 55c, Manual and electronic telephone switching systems.

1987, Mar. 31 Litho. *Perf. 14*

485 A81 30c multicolored 4.00 4.00
486 A81 55c multicolored 5.50 5.50

Map Type of 1983

1987, Sept. 22 Litho. Unwmk.

487 A68 15c Starbuck, red-tailed tropicbird .75 .55
488 A68 30c Enderbury, white tern .80 .55
489 A68 55c Tabiteuea, pandanus 1.10 .65
490 A68 $1 Onotoa, Okai house 1.75 *1.75*
Nos. 487-490 (4) 4.40 3.50

Nos. 487-490 vert.

Lizard Type of 1986

1987, Oct. 27 *Perf. 15*

491 A79 15c Emoia nigra .50 .40
492 A79 35c Cryptoblepharus .70 .60
493 A79 40c Emoia cyanura .70 .75
494 A79 $1 Lipinia noctua 1.50 *1.75*
a. Souvenir sheet of 4, #491-494 3.75 3.75
Nos. 491-494 (4) 3.40 3.50

Nos. 470-474 Overprinted "40TH WEDDING ANNIVERSARY" in Silver

Perf. 14½x14

1987, Nov. 30 Litho. Unwmk.

495 CD337 15c scar, black & sil .20 .35
496 CD337 35c ultra & multi .40 .35
497 CD337 40c green & multi .55 .40
498 CD337 55c violet & multi .75 .50
499 CD337 $1 rose vio & multi 1.50 *1.75*
Nos. 495-499 (5) 3.40 3.35

Intl. Red Cross and Red Crescent Organizations, 125th Annivs. — A83

15c, Jean Henri Dunant (1828-1910), founder. 35c, Red Cross volunteers on parade. 40c, Stretcher bearers. 55c, Gilbert and Ellice Islands #159.

Perf. 14½x14

1988, May 8 Litho. Unwmk.

500 A83 15c multicolored 1.00 .60
501 A83 35c multicolored 1.25 *1.50*
502 A83 40c multicolored 1.50 *1.50*
503 A83 55c multicolored 3.00 *3.50*
Nos. 500-503 (4) 6.75 *7.10*

A84

SYDPEX '88, Australia Bicentennial — A85

Emblem and: 15c, Australia-assisted causeway construction. 35c, Capt. Cook, map of Australia and Kiribati. No. 506, Australia bicentennial banknote obverse. No. 507, Bank note reverse. $2, "Logistic Ace."

1988, July 30 Litho. *Perf. 14½*

504 A84 15c multicolored .35 .35
505 A84 35c multicolored .70 .70
506 A84 $1 multicolored 2.00 2.00
507 A84 $1 multicolored 2.00 2.00
a. Pair, #506-507 4.25 4.25
Nos. 504-507 (4) 5.05 5.05

Souvenir Sheet
Perf. 13½x14

508 A85 $2 multicolored 7.00 7.00

Robert F. Stockton, 1st propeller-driven steamship, 150th anniv.

Transport and Telecommunications Decade (1985-1995) — A86

Wmk. 373

1988, Dec. 28 Litho. *Perf. 14*

509 A86 35c Telephone operator, map 1.25 1.25
510 A86 45c Betio-Bairiki Causeway 1.75 1.75

Ships A87

Wmk. 384

1989, May 26 Litho. *Perf. 14½*

511 A87 15c Brigantine Hound, 1835 1.50 .90
512 A87 30c Brig Phantom, 1854 2.25 1.50
513 A87 40c HMS Alacrity, 1873 2.75 2.75
514 A87 $1 Whaler Charles W. Morgan, 1851 4.25 4.25
Nos. 511-514 (4) 10.75 9.40

See Nos. 557-561, 687-690.

A88

Birds — A89

Perf. 13½x14

1989, July 12 Litho. Wmk. 384

515 A88 15c House of Assembly .50 .50
516 A88 $1 Constitution 3.00 3.00

Natl. Independence, 10th anniv.

Moon Landing, 20th Anniv.
Common Design Type

Apollo 10: 20c, Service and command modules, launch escape system. 50c, Eugene A. Cernan, Thomas P. Stafford and John W. Young. 60c, Mission emblem. 75c, Splashdown, Honolulu. $2.50, Apollo 11 command module in space.

1989, July 20 *Perf. 14*

Size of Nos. 518-519: 29x29mm

517 CD342 20c multicolored .55 .55
518 CD342 50c multicolored 1.00 1.00
519 CD342 60c multicolored 1.25 1.25
520 CD342 75c multicolored 1.50 1.50
Nos. 517-520 (4) 4.30 4.30

Souvenir Sheet

521 CD342 $2.50 multicolored 10.00 10.00

Perf. 14½x14

1989, June 28 Litho. Wmk. 384

522 A89 15c Eastern reef heron 1.75 1.75
523 A89 15c Brood in nest 1.75 1.75
a. Pair, #522-523 4.00 4.00
524 A89 $1 White-tailed tropicbird in flight 3.25 3.25
525 A89 $1 Seated tropicbird 3.25 3.25
a. Pair, #524-525 7.00 7.00
Nos. 522-525 (4) 10.00 10.00

Nos. 523a, 525a have continuous designs. For overprints see Nos. 534-535.

Souvenir Sheets

A90

A91

Perf. 14x13½

1989, Aug. 7 Litho. Wmk. 384

526 A90 $2 Gilbert & Ellice Isls. #58 7.00 7.00

Perf. 14x13½

1989, Sept. 25 Litho. Unwmk.

Workmen renovating the Statue of Liberty: a, Torch. b, Drilling copper sheeting. c, Glancing at a sketch of the statue.

527 Sheet of 3 5.50 5.50
a.-c. A91 35c any single 1.60 1.60

World Stamp Expo '89, Washington, DC, PHILEXFRANCE '89, Paris. No. 526 margin pictures #435, France #634 and US #2224.

Transport and Telecommunications Decade, 1985-95 — A92

1989, Oct. 16 Wmk. 384 *Perf. 14*

528 A92 30c shown 3.00 3.00
529 A92 75c MV *Mataburo* 4.50 4.50

Christmas — A93

Paintings: 10c, *Adoration of the Holy Child* (detail), by Denys Calvert. 15c, *Adoration of the Holy Child* (entire painting). 55c, *The Holy Family and St. Elizabeth,* by Rubens. $1, *Madonna with Child and Mary Magdalene,* School of Corregio.

1989, Dec. 1

530 A93 10c multicolored 1.25 .70
531 A93 15c multicolored 1.60 .85
532 A93 55c multicolored 4.00 2.25
533 A93 $1 multicolored 5.75 *7.50*
Nos. 530-533 (4) 12.60 11.30

Nos. 524-525 Ovptd.

1989, Oct. 21 Litho. *Perf. 14½x14*

534 A89 $1 on No. 524 5.25 5.25
535 A89 $1 on No. 525 5.25 5.25
a. Pair, #534-535 11.00 11.00

STAMPSHOW '89, Melbourne.

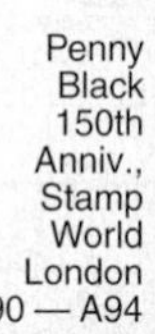

Penny Black 150th Anniv., Stamp World London '90 — A94

Stamps on stamps: 15c, Gilbert & Ellice #15, Great Britain #2. 50c, Gilbert & Ellice #8, Great Britain #1 canceled. 60c, Kiribati #384, Great Britain #58. $1, Gilbert Islands #269, Great Britain #3.

1990, May 1 Litho. *Perf. 14*

536 A94 15c multicolored 1.75 1.75
537 A94 50c multicolored 3.50 3.50
538 A94 60c multicolored 3.50 3.50
539 A94 $1 multicolored 5.50 5.50
Nos. 536-539 (4) 14.25 14.25

Fish Type of 1985

Fish: 1c, Blue-barred orange parrotfish. 5c, Honeycomb rock cod. 10c, Bluefin jack. 15c, Paddle tail snapper. 20c, Variegated emperor. 25c, Rainbow runner. 30c, Black saddled coral trout. 35c, Great barracuda. 40c, Convict surgeonfish. 50c, Violet squirrelfish. 60c, Freckled hawkfish. 75c, Pennant coral fish. $1, Yellow and blue sea perch. $2, Pacific sailfish. $5, Whitetip reef shark.

Wmk. 373

1990, July 12 Litho. *Perf. 14*

540 A74 1c multicolored .40 .40
541 A74 5c multicolored .50 .50
542 A74 10c multicolored .65 .65
543 A74 15c multicolored .75 .75
544 A74 20c multicolored .90 .90
545 A74 25c multicolored 1.00 1.00
546 A74 30c multicolored 1.10 1.10
547 A74 35c multicolored 1.25 1.25
548 A74 40c multicolored 1.50 1.50
549 A74 50c multicolored 2.00 2.00
550 A74 60c multicolored 2.25 2.25
551 A74 75c multicolored 2.50 2.50
552 A74 $1 multicolored 3.50 3.50
553 A74 $2 multicolored 5.00 5.00
554 A74 $5 multicolored 9.50 9.50
Nos. 540-554 (15) 32.80 32.80

Dated 1990. See No. 567. For overprints see Nos. 587-590.

Queen Mother 90th Birthday
Common Design Types

1990, Aug. 4 Wmk. 384 *Perf. 14x15*

555 CD343 75c Queen Mother 1.75 1.75

Perf. 14½

556 CD344 $2 King, Queen & WWII bombing victim, 1940 4.25 4.25

Ships Type of 1989

1990, Nov. 5 Litho. *Perf. 14½*

557 A87 15c Whaling ship Herald, 1851 1.10 .70
558 A87 50c Bark Belle, 1849 2.25 1.75
559 A87 60c Schooner Supply, 1851 2.75 2.75
560 A87 75c Whaling ship Triton, 1848 3.25 3.25
Nos. 557-560 (4) 9.35 8.45

Souvenir Sheet

561 A87 $2 Convict transport Charlotte, 1789 12.00 12.00

Manta Ray A95

1991, Jan. 17 Wmk. 373 *Perf. 14*

562 A95 15c shown 2.00 1.25
563 A95 20c Manta ray, diff. 2.25 1.75
564 A95 30c Whale shark 3.00 2.75
565 A95 35c Whale shark, diff. 3.50 3.25
Nos. 562-565 (4) 10.75 9.00

World Wildlife Fund.

Fish Type of 1985

Design: 23c, Bennett's pufferfish.

1991, Apr. 30 Wmk. 384

567 A74 23c multicolored 2.00 2.00

For overprint see No. 587.

Elizabeth & Philip, Birthdays
Common Design Types

1991, June 17 *Perf. 14½*

571 CD345 65c multicolored 2.00 2.00
572 CD346 70c multicolored 2.00 2.00
a. Pair, #571-572 + label 4.50 4.50

Phila Nippon '91 — A96

Opening of new Tungaru Central Hospital: 23c, Aerial view. 50c, Traditional dancers. 60c, Main entrance. 75c, Foundation stone, plaque. $5, Ambulance, nursing staff.

1991, Nov. 16 *Perf. 13½x14*

573 A96 23c multicolored .65 .65
574 A96 50c multicolored 1.25 1.25
575 A96 60c multicolored 1.75 1.75
576 A96 75c multicolored 2.10 2.10
Nos. 573-576 (4) 5.75 5.75

Souvenir Sheet

577 A96 $5 multicolored 10.50 10.50

Christmas A97

Designs: 23c, Island mother and child. 50c, Family in island hut. 60c, Nativity Scene. 75c, Adoration of the Shepherds.

1991, Dec. 2 Wmk. 373

578 A97 23c multicolored .90 .60
579 A97 50c multicolored 1.50 1.50
580 A97 60c multicolored 2.00 2.00
581 A97 75c multicolored 2.50 2.50
Nos. 578-581 (4) 6.90 6.60

Queen Elizabeth II's Accession to the Throne, 40th Anniv.
Common Design Type

Wmk. 373

1992, Feb. 6 Litho. *Perf. 14*

582 CD349 23c multicolored .40 .40
583 CD349 30c multicolored .60 .60
584 CD349 50c multicolored .90 .90
585 CD349 60c multicolored 1.10 1.10
586 CD349 75c multicolored 1.40 1.40
Nos. 582-586 (5) 4.40 4.40

Nos. 550-551, 553, & 567 Ovptd.

Wmk. 384, 373

1992, June 1 Litho. *Perf. 14*

587 A74 23c on No. 567 1.10 .85
588 A74 60c on No. 550 2.25 2.25
589 A74 75c on No. 551 3.00 3.00
590 A74 $2 on No. 553 3.25 3.50
Nos. 587-590 (4) 9.60 9.60

Marine Training Center, 25th Anniv. A98

1992, Aug. 28 *Perf. 14*

591 A98 23c Entrance .70 .70
592 A98 50c Cadets at morning parade 1.10 1.10
593 A98 60c Fire school 1.40 1.40
594 A98 75c Lifeboat training 1.75 1.75
Nos. 591-594 (4) 4.95 4.95

FAO, WHO A99

Wmk. 373

1992, Dec. 1 Litho. *Perf. 14*

595 A99 23c Children running 1.25 1.25
596 A99 50c Night fishing 1.50 1.50
597 A99 60c Fruit 2.00 2.00
598 A99 75c Ship 3.25 3.25
Nos. 595-598 (4) 8.00 8.00

Water Birds — A100

Wmk. 373

1993, May 28 Litho. *Perf. 14½*

599 A100 23c Phoenix petrel .75 .75
600 A100 23c Cooks petrel .75 .75
a. Pair, #599-600 1.60 1.60
601 A100 60c Northern pintail 1.40 1.40
602 A100 60c Eurasian widgeon 1.40 1.40
a. Pair, #601-602 3.00 3.00
603 A100 75c Spectacled tern 1.75 1.75
604 A100 75c Black naped tern 1.75 1.75
a. Pair, #603-604 3.75 3.75
605 A100 $1 Stilt wader 2.00 2.00
606 A100 $1 Wandering tattler 2.00 2.00
a. Pair, #605-606 4.50 4.50
Nos. 599-606 (8) 11.80 11.80

Insects — A101

Perf. 14½x14

1993, Aug. 23 Litho. Wmk. 373

607 A101 23c Chilocorus nigritus 1.50 1.25
608 A101 60c Rodolia pumila 2.50 2.50
609 A101 75c Rodolia cardinalis 3.00 3.00
610 A101 $1 Cryptolaemus montrouzieri 3.50 *3.75*
Nos. 607-610 (4) 10.50 10.50

Liberation of Kiribati, 50th Anniv. — A102

No. 611: a, Air reconnaissance of Tarawa Atoll. b, USS Nautilus surveys Tarawa. c, USS Indianapolis. d, USS Pursuit leads seaborne assault. e, Kingfisher spotter plane. f, Destroyers USS Ringgold and USS Dashiell. g, Sherman tank on seabed. h, Fighter plane in lagoon. i, Naval gun on seabed. j, First US aircraft to land on Betio Island.

No. 612: a, Transports disembark landing craft. b, Marines assault Betio Island. c, Sea and air assault of Betio. d, Marines pinned down in surf. e, USS Maryland firing broadside. f, Betio from the air. g, Memorial to US Navy dead. h, Memorial to expatriates. i, Memorial to Japanese dead. j, Battle map of Betio.

Wmk. 373

1993, Nov. 1 Litho. *Perf. 14*

Sheets of 10

611 A102 23c #a.-j. + label 8.50 8.50
612 A102 75c #a.-j. + label 22.50 22.50

Christmas — A103

Perf. 13½x14

1993, Dec. 1 Litho. Wmk. 373

613 A103 23c Shepherds .75 .40
614 A103 40c Three kings 1.10 1.00
615 A103 60c Holy Family 1.50 *1.75*
616 A103 75c Mother, children 1.90 *2.10*
Nos. 613-616 (4) 5.25 5.25

Souvenir Sheet

617 A103 $3 Madonna and Child 7.00 7.00

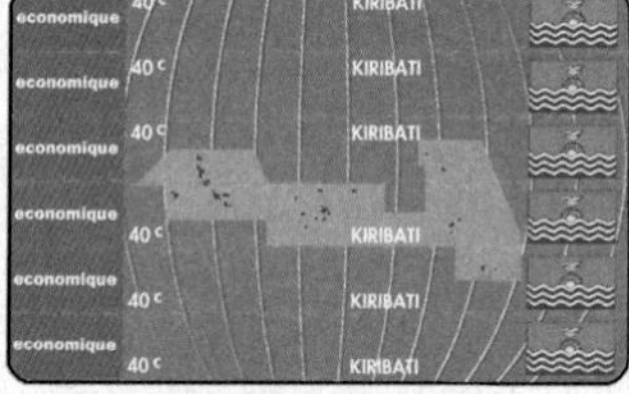

Stampcards — A104

Illustration reduced.

Rouletted 6 on 2 or 3 Sides

1993, Nov. 1 Litho.

Self-Adhesive

Cards of 6 + 6 labels

618 A104 40c #a.-f. *5.00*
619 A104 $1 #a.-f. *12.00*
620 A104 $1.20 #a.-f. *15.00*
621 A104 $1.60 #a.-f. *22.50*
Nos. 618-621 (4) *54.50*

Nos. 619-621 are airmail. Individual stamps measure 70x9mm and have a card backing. Se-tenant labels on No. 618 inscribed "economique." Se-tenant labels on Nos. 619-621 inscribed "prioritaire AIR MAIL."

It has been stated that these stamps were available only from the Philatelic Bureau and were not accepted by local post offices as valid for postage, though this is contradicted by the Controller of Postal Services.

Souvenir Sheet

New Year 1994 (Year of the Dog) — A105

Wmk. 373

1994, Feb. 18 Litho. *Perf. 14*

622 A105 $3 multicolored 7.50 7.50

Hong Kong '94.

Whales
A106

Designs: 23c, Bryde's whale. 40c, Blue whale. 60c, Humpback whale. 75c, Killer whale.

1994, May 2

623 A106 23c multicolored 1.50 1.50
624 A106 23c multicolored 1.50 1.50
a. Pair, #623-624 3.25 3.25
625 A106 40c multicolored 1.75 1.75
626 A106 40c multicolored 1.75 1.75
a. Pair, #625-626 3.75 3.75
627 A106 60c multicolored 2.75 2.75
628 A106 60c multicolored 2.75 2.75
a. Pair, #627-628 6.00 6.00
629 A106 75c multicolored 3.00 3.00
630 A106 75c multicolored 3.00 3.00
a. Pair #629-630 6.50 6.50
Nos. 623-630 (8) 18.00 18.00

Value at UL on Nos. 623, 625, 627, 629; at UR on others.
Nos. 624a-630a have continuous designs.

Environmental Protection — A107

Designs: 40c, Family on beach at sunset. 60c, Fish. 75c, Frigate birds.

1994, July 12

631 A107 40c multicolored 1.10 .90
632 A107 60c multicolored 1.25 1.10
633 A107 75c multicolored 1.75 1.75
Nos. 631-633 (3) 4.10 3.75

Independence, 15th anniv.

Butterflies
A108

Flowers — A109

Designs: 1c, Diaphania indica. 5c, Herpetogamma licarsisalis. 10c, Parotis suralis. 12c, Sufetula sunidesalis. 20c, Aedia sericea. 23c, Anomis vitiensis. 30c, Anticarsia irrorata. 35c, Spodoptera litura. 40c, Mocis frugalis. 45c, Agrius convolvuli. 50c, Cephonodes picus. 55c, Gnathothlibus erotus. 60c, Macroglossum hirundo. 75c, Badamia exclamationis. $1, Precis villida. $2, Danaus plexippus. $3, Hypolimnas bolina (male). $5, Hypolimnas bolina (female).

1994, Aug. 19 *Perf. 14½x14*

634 A108 1c multicolored .20 .20
635 A108 5c multicolored .20 .20
636 A108 10c multicolored .25 .20
637 A108 12c multicolored .30 .25
638 A108 20c multicolored .40 .35
639 A108 23c multicolored .50 .45
640 A108 30c multicolored .65 .55
641 A108 35c multicolored .75 .65
642 A108 40c multicolored .85 .70
643 A108 45c multicolored .90 .80
644 A108 50c multicolored 1.00 .85
645 A108 55c multicolored 1.20 .95
646 A108 60c multicolored 1.25 1.00
647 A108 75c multicolored 1.50 1.25
648 A108 $1 multicolored 2.00 2.00
a. Souvenir sheet of 1 2.75 2.75
649 A108 $2 multicolored 3.75 *4.00*
650 A108 $3 multicolored 5.75 *6.00*
651 A108 $5 multicolored 9.50 *10.00*
Nos. 634-651 (18) 30.95 30.40

No. 648a issued 2/12/97 for Hong Kong '97.
For overprints see #763-767.

1994, Oct. 31

652 A109 23c Nerium oleander .75 .75
653 A109 60c Catharanthus roseus 1.25 1.25
654 A109 75c Ipomea pes-caprae 1.75 1.75
655 A109 $1 Calophyllum mophyllum 2.25 2.25
Nos. 652-655 (4) 6.00 6.00

A110

Constellations.

1995, Jan. 31

656 A110 50c Gemini 1.25 1.25
657 A110 60c Cancer 1.40 1.40
658 A110 75c Cassiopeia 1.75 1.75
659 A110 $1 Southern cross 2.50 2.50
Nos. 656-659 (4) 6.90 6.90

A111

Wmk. 384

1995, Apr. 3 **Litho.** *Perf. 14½*

Scenes of Kiribati: No. 660: a, Architecture. b, Men, canoe, sailboat. c, Gun emplacement, Tarawa. d, Children, shells. e, Outdoor sports.
No. 661: a, Women traditionally attired. b, Windsurfing. c, Filleting fish. d, Snorkeling, scuba diving. e, Weaving.

660 A111 30c Strip of 5, #a.-e. 4.50 4.50
661 A111 40c Strip of 5, #a.-e. 6.50 6.50
f. Booklet pane, #660, #661 + 5 labels 12.00 *12.00*
Complete booklet, #661f 13.00

Visit South Pacific Year.

End of World War II, 50th Anniv.
Common Design Type

Designs: 23c, Grumman TBM-3E Avenger. 40c, Curtiss SOC. 3-1 seagull. 50c, Consolidated B-24J Liberator. 60c, Grumman Goose. 75c, Martin B-26 Marauder. $1, Northrop P-61B Black Widow. $2, Reverse of War Medal 1939-45.

Perf. 14x13½

1995, May 8 **Wmk. 373**

662 CD351 23c multicolored 1.25 1.25
663 CD351 40c multicolored 1.50 1.50
664 CD351 50c multicolored 1.75 1.75
665 CD351 60c multicolored 2.00 2.00
666 CD351 75c multicolored 2.75 2.75
667 CD351 $1 multicolored 3.75 3.75
Nos. 662-667 (6) 13.00 13.00

Souvenir Sheet

Perf. 14

668 CD352 $2 multicolored 5.25 5.25

For overprints see Nos. 691-697.

Souvenir Sheet of 4

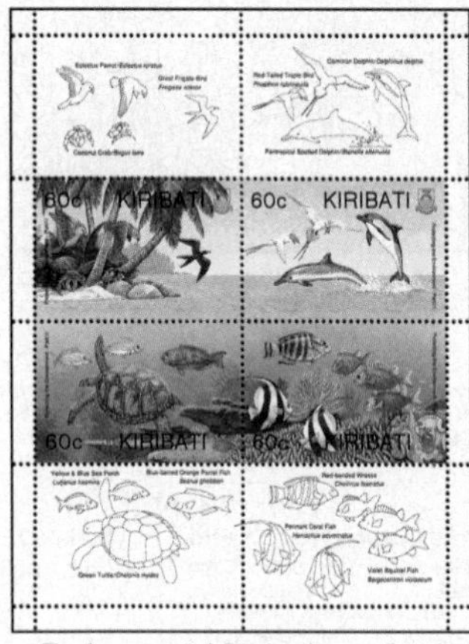

Environmental Protection — A112

Marine life: a, Electus parrot, great frigate bird, coconut crab. b, Red-tailed tropic bird, common dolphin, pantropical spotted dolphin. c, Yellow & blue sea perch, green turtle, blue-barred orange parrot fish. d, Pennant coral fish, red-banded wrasse, violet squirrel fish.

Wmk. 373

1995, July 12 **Litho.** *Perf. 14*

669 A112 60c #a.-d. + 4 labels 5.50 5.50

For overprint see No. 672.

Souvenir Sheet

New Year 1995 (Year of the Boar) — A113

$2, Sow, piglets. Illustration reduced.

1995, Sept. 1 **Litho.** *Perf. 13*

670 A113 $2 multicolored 4.50 4.50

Singapore '95.

Souvenir Sheet

Beijing '95 — A114

Design: $2, like #670, with sheet margin as shown in reduced illustration.

1995, Sept. 14

671 A114 $2 multicolored 4.50 4.50

No. 669 Overprinted for Jakarta '95

Wmk. 373

1995, Aug. 19 **Litho.** *Perf. 14*

672 A112 60c #a.-d. + 4 labels 9.00 9.00

Police Maritime Unit — A115

Patrol boat RKS Teanoai: No. 673, In harbor. No. 674, Under way.

Wmk. 373

1995, Nov. 30 **Litho.** *Perf. 13*

673 75c multicolored 2.50 2.50
674 75c multicolored 2.50 2.50
a. A115 Pair, #673-674 5.25 5.25

Dolphins
A116

Designs: 23c, Pantropical spotted. 60c, Spinner. 75c, Fraser's. $1, Rough-toothed.

Wmk. 384

1996, Jan. 15 **Litho.** *Perf. 14*

675 A116 23c multicolored 1.75 1.00
676 A116 60c multicolored 2.50 1.50
677 A116 75c multicolored 3.25 2.50
678 A116 $1 multicolored 4.00 *4.25*
Nos. 675-678 (4) 11.50 9.25

UNICEF, 50th Anniv. — A117

Portion of UNICEF emblem and: a, Water faucet, clean water. b, Documents, chilren's rights. c, Hypodermic, health care. d, Open book, education.

Wmk. 373

1996, Apr. 22 **Litho.** *Perf. 13*

679 A117 30c Block of 4, #a.-d. 3.00 3.00

No. 679 is a continuous design.

Souvenir Sheet

CHINA '96, 9th Intl. Philatelic Exhibition — A118

Illustration reduced.

1996, Apr. 30 **Wmk. 384** *Perf. 13½*

680 A118 50c multicolored 2.00 2.00

New Year 1996, Year of the Rat.

Souvenir Sheet

No. 5609 Gilbert and Ellice Islands LMS Jubilee Class 4-6-0 Locomotive — A119

Wmk. 373

1996, June 8 Litho. *Perf. 12*

681 A119 $2 multicolored 4.25 4.25

CAPEX '96.

Sea Crabs A120

Wmk. 373

1996, Aug. 6 Litho. *Perf. 14*

682 A120 23c Rathbun red .75 .55
683 A120 60c Red & white painted 1.75 1.25
684 A120 75c Red spotted 2.00 2.00
685 A120 $1 Red spotted white 2.50 *2.75*
Nos. 682-685 (4) 7.00 6.55

Souvenir Sheet

Taipei '96 — A121

Illustration reduced.

Wmk. 384

1996, Oct. 21 Litho. *Perf. 14½*

686 A121 $1.50 Outrigger canoe 4.50 4.50

Ships Type of 1989

23c, Whaling ship, "Potomac," 1843. 50c, Barkentine "Southern Cross IV," 1891. 60c, Bark "John Williams III," 1890. $1, HMS Dolphin, 1765.

Wmk. 384

1996, Dec. 2 Litho. *Perf. 14½*

687 A87 23c multicolored .80 .55
688 A87 50c multicolored 1.25 1.25
689 A87 60c multicolored 1.50 1.50
690 A87 $1 multicolored 2.50 2.50
Nos. 687-690 (4) 6.05 5.80

Nos. 662-668 Ovptd. with PACIFIC 97 Emblem

Perf. 14x13½

1997, May 29 Litho. Wmk. 373

691 CD351 23c multicolored .70 .50
692 CD351 40c multicolored .95 .80
693 CD351 50c multicolored 1.25 1.10
694 CD351 60c multicolored 1.50 1.50
695 CD351 75c multicolored 1.75 1.75
696 CD351 $1 multicolored 2.25 2.25
Nos. 691-696 (6) 8.40 7.90

Souvenir Sheet

697 CD351 $2 multicolored 5.00 5.00

Queen Elizabeth II and Prince Philip, 50th Wedding Anniv. — A122

No. 698, Queen Elizabeth II. No. 699, Horse team going down river bank. No. 700, Queen in open carriage. No. 701, Prince Philip. No. 702, Prince, Queen. No. 703, Riding horse. $2, Queen, Prince in open carriage, horiz.

Perf. 14½x14

1997, July 10 Litho. Wmk. 373

698 50c multicolored 1.50 1.50
699 50c multicolored 1.50 1.50
a. A122 Pair, #698-699 3.25 3.25
700 60c multicolored 1.75 1.75
701 60c multicolored 1.75 1.75
a. A122 Pair, #700-701 3.75 3.75
702 75c multicolored 2.75 2.75
703 75c multicolored 2.75 2.75
a. A122 Pair, #702-703 6.00 6.00
Nos. 698-703 (6) 12.00 12.00

Souvenir Sheet

704 A122 $2 multicolored 7.00 7.00

Birds — A123

#705-706, Rock dove. #707-708, Pacific pigeon. #709-710, Micronesian pigeon.

Wmk. 373

1997, Dec. 1 Litho. *Perf. 14*

705 50c Immature 1.10 1.10
706 50c Adult 1.10 1.10
a. A123 Pair, #705-706 2.40 2.40
707 60c Adult 1.50 1.50
708 60c Immature 1.50 1.50
a. A123 Pair, #707-708 3.25 3.25
709 75c Adult 1.75 1.75
710 75c Immature 1.75 1.75
a. A123 Pair, #709-710 3.75 3.75
Nos. 705-710 (6) 8.70 8.70

Nos. 705-706, 709-710 With Added Inscription

Wmk. 373

1997, Dec. 5 Litho. *Perf. 14*

711 50c on #705 1.25 1.25
712 50c on #706 1.25 1.25
a. A123 Pair, #711-712 2.75 2.75
713 75c on #709 2.00 2.00
714 75c on #710 2.00 2.00
a. A123 Pair, #713-714 4.25 4.25

Asia '97.

Spiny Lobster A124

Wmk. 373

1998, Feb. 2 Litho. *Perf. 14*

715 A124 25c shown .80 .80
716 A124 25c Crawling right .80 .80
717 A124 25c Crawling left .80 .80
718 A124 25c Looking upward .80 .80
a. Strip of 4, #715-718 3.50 3.50

Souvenir Sheet

719 A124 $1.50 Looking straight forward 3.75 3.75

World Wildlife Fund.

Diana, Princess of Wales (1961-97)

Common Design Type

Various portraits — #720: a, 50c. b, 60c. c, 75c.

Perf. 14½x14

1998, Mar. 31 Litho. Wmk. 373

719A CD355 25c multicolored .60 .60

Sheet of 4

720 CD355 #a.-c., 719A 4.75 4.75

No. 720 sold for $2.10 + 50c, with surtax from international sales being donated to the Princess Diana Memorial Fund, and surtax from national sales being donated to designated local charity.

Intl. Year of the Ocean — A125

Whales and dolphins: No. 721, Indo-Pacific humpbacked dolphin. No. 722, Bottlenose dolphin. No. 723, Short-snouted spinner dolphin. No. 724, Risso's dolphin. No. 725, Striped dolphin. No. 726, Sei whale. No. 727, Fin whale. No. 728, Minke whale.

Wmk. 373

1998, Oct. 1 Litho. *Perf. 14*

721 25c multicolored .60 .60
722 25c multicolored .60 .60
a. A125 Pair, #721-722 1.50 1.50
723 60c multicolored 1.25 1.25
724 60c multicolored 1.25 1.25
a. A125 Pair, #723-724 2.75 2.75
725 75c multicolored 1.75 1.75
726 75c multicolored 1.75 1.75
a. A125 Pair, #725-726 3.75 3.75
727 $1 multicolored 2.00 2.00
728 $1 multicolored 2.00 2.00
a. A125 Pair, #727-728 4.50 4.50
Nos. 721-728 (8) 11.20 11.20

Souvenir Sheet

Children of Kiribati — A125a

Illustration reduced.

1998, Sept. 15

729 A125a $1 multicolored 2.25 2.25

Souvenir Sheet

Reuben K. Uatioa Stadium — A126

Illlustration reduced.

Wmk. 373

1998, Oct. 23 Litho. *Perf. 14*

730 A126 $2 multicolored 4.00 4.00

Italia '98 World Philatelic Exhibition.

Greenhouse Effect — A127

Designs: 25c, Contributors to Greenhouse gases. 50c, Explanation of the Greenhouse Effect. 60c, Greenhouse Effect on Tarawa Atoll. 75c, Greenhouse Effect on Kiritimati Island.

$1.50, People in sailboat, "Kiribati way of life."

Wmk. 373

1998, Dec. 1 Litho. *Perf. 13½*

731 A127 25c multicolored .60 .60
732 A127 50c multicolored .90 .90
733 A127 60c multicolored 1.25 1.25
734 A127 75c multicolored 1.75 1.75
Nos. 731-734 (4) 4.50 4.50

Souvenir Sheet

735 A127 $1.50 multicolored 3.75 3.75

Souvenir Sheet

HMS Resolution at Christmas Island — A128

Illustration reduced.

Wmk. 373

1999, Mar. 19 Litho. *Perf. 14*

736 A128 $2 multicolored 4.25 4.25

Australia '99 World Stamp Expo.

IBRA '99, Philatelic Exhibition, Nuremberg — A129

Ducks: 25c, Northern shoveller, male. 50c, Northern shoveller, female. 60c, Green-winged teal, male. 75c, Green-winged teal, female and ducklings.

$3, Green winged teal, male, duckling.

Wmk. 373

1999, Apr. 27 Litho. *Perf. 14*

737 A129 25c multicolored .65 .50
738 A129 50c multicolored 1.25 .80
739 A129 60c multicolored 1.40 1.40
740 A129 75c multicolored 1.75 *2.00*
Nos. 737-740 (4) 5.05 4.70

Souvenir Sheet

741 A129 $3 multicolored 6.00 6.00

Independence, 20th Anniv. — A130

Designs: 25c, Millennium Island. 60c, Map of Kiribati. 75c, Map of Nikumaroro. $1, Amelia Earhart, Lockheed 10E Electra airplane.

Wmk. 373

1999, July 12 Litho. *Perf. 13½*

742 A130 25c multicolored .60 .60
743 A130 60c multicolored 1.10 1.10
744 A130 75c multicolored 1.40 1.40
745 A130 $1 multicolored 3.00 3.00
a. Souvenir sheet, #744-745 4.25 4.25
Nos. 742-745 (4) 6.10 6.10

1st Manned Moon Landing, 30th Anniv.

Common Design Type

Designs: 25c, Edwin Aldrin. 60c, Service module docks with lander. 75c, Apollo 11 on lunar surface. $1, Command module separates from service module.
$2, Earth as seen from moon.

Perf. 14x13¾

1999, July 20 Litho. Wmk. 384

746 CD357 25c multicolored .60 .60
747 CD357 60c multicolored 1.10 1.10
748 CD357 75c multicolored 1.40 1.40
749 CD357 $1 multicolored 1.75 1.75
Nos. 746-749 (4) 4.85 4.85

Souvenir Sheet

Perf. 14

750 CD357 $2 multicolored 4.00 4.00

No. 750 contains one 40mm circular stamp 40mm.

UPU, 125th Anniv., Christmas A131

Wmk. 373

1999, Oct. 9 Litho. *Perf. 13½*

751 A131 25c Santa in canoe .55 .45
752 A131 60c Santa on dock 1.00 .85
753 A131 75c Santa in sleigh 1.25 1.25
754 A131 $1 Santa at computer 1.50 1.50
Nos. 751-754 (4) 4.30 4.05

Millennium A132

Perf. 13¼x13

2000, Jan. 1 Litho. Wmk. 373

755 A132 25c Faith .55 .45
756 A132 40c Harmony .80 .70
757 A132 60c Hope 1.10 1.10
758 A132 75c Enlightenment 1.75 1.75
759 A132 $1 Peace 2.00 2.00
Nos. 755-759 (5) 6.20 6.00

Sesame Street Characters — A133

No. 760: a, Bert. b, Baby Bear. c, Grover. d, Elmo, Cookie Monster. e, Telly Monster. f. Zoe. g, Ernie. h, Big Bird, Rosita. i, Oscar the Grouch.
No. 761, Grover as mailman.
Illustration reduced.

Perf. 14½x14¾

2000, Mar. 22 Litho. Wmk. 373

760 A133 20c Sheet of 9, #a-i 4.00 4.00

Souvenir Sheet

761 A133 $1.50 multi 2.75 2.75

Souvenir Sheet

The Stamp Show 2000, London — A134

Illustration reduced.

2000, May 8 Wmk. 373 *Perf. 13¾*

762 A134 $5 Queen Elizabeth II 8.00 8.00

Nos. 635, 636, 638, 648 and 650 Overprinted " KIRIBATI AT / EXPO 2000 1.06 - 31.10.2000"

Perf. 14½x14

2000, June 1 Wmk. 373

763 A108 5c multi .45 .45
764 A108 10c multi .45 .45
765 A108 20c multi .55 .55
766 A108 $1 multi 1.75 1.75
767 A108 $3 multi 4.50 4.50
Nos. 763-767 (5) 7.70 7.70

Prince William, 18th Birthday A135

Various views of Prince William with Prince Charles.

Wmk. 373

2000, July 24 Litho. *Perf. 12¾*

768 A135 25c multi .40 .40
769 A135 60c multi .90 .90
770 A135 75c multi 1.25 1.25
771 A135 $1 multi 1.50 1.50
Nos. 768-771 (4) 4.05 4.05

Ducks A136

Designs: No. 772, 25c, Blue duck. No. 773, 25c, Green-winged teal. No. 774, 25c, Mallard. No. 775, 25c, Northern shoveler. No. 776, 25c, Pacific black duck. No. 777, 25c, Wandering whistling duck.

Wmk. 373

2001, Jan. 22 Litho. *Perf. 14*

772-777 A136 Set of 6 4.50 4.50

Souvenir Sheet

778 A136 $1 Gray teal 5.00 5.00

Water Conservation A137

Children's art by: 25c, Tiare Hongkai. 50c, Gilbert Z. Tluanga. 60c, Mantokataake Tebaiuea, vert. 75c, Tokaman Karanebo, vert. $2, Taom Simon.

2001, July 12 Litho. *Perf. 13¼*

779-783 A137 Set of 5 6.25 6.25

Phila Nippon '01 A138

Development projects: 75c, Betio Port. $2, New Parliament House.

2001, Aug. 1

784-785 A138 Set of 2 5.00 5.00

Tourism — A139

Designs: 75c, Norwegian Cruise Line ship, map of cruise to Fanning Island. $3, The Betsey, map of Fanning Island.

Perf. 13¼

2001, Nov. 14 Litho. Unwmk.

786-787 A139 Set of 2 5.75 5.75

Fish — A140

Designs: 5c, Paracanthurus hepatus. 10c, Centropyge flavissimus. 15c, Anthias squamipinnis. 20c, Centropyge loriculus. 25c, Acanthurus lineatus. 30c, Oxycirrhites typus. 40c, Dascyllus trimaculatus. 50c, Acanthurus achilles. 60c, Pomacentrus coeruleus. 75c, Acanthurus glaucopareus. 80c, Thalassoma lunare. 90c, Arothron meleagris. $1, Odonus niger. $2, Cephalopholis miniatus. $5, Pomacanthus imperator. $10, Balistoides conspicillum.

2002, Feb. 28 Unwmk. *Perf. 13*

788 A140 5c multi .25 .25
789 A140 10c multi .30 .30
790 A140 15c multi .35 .35
791 A140 20c multi .40 .40
792 A140 25c multi .45 .45
793 A140 30c multi .50 .50
794 A140 40c multi .70 .70
795 A140 50c multi .80 .80
796 A140 60c multi .90 .90
797 A140 75c multi 1.10 1.10
798 A140 80c multi 1.40 1.40
799 A140 90c multi 1.75 1.75
800 A140 $1 multi 2.00 2.00
801 A140 $2 multi 4.00 4.00
802 A140 $5 multi 9.00 9.00
803 A140 $10 multi 16.50 16.50
Nos. 788-803 (16) 40.40 40.40

Pacific Explorers A141

Designs: 25c, Adm. Fabian von Bellingshausen and the Vostok, 1820. 40c, Capt. Charles Wilkes and the Vincennes, 1838-42. 60c, Capt. Edmund Fanning and the Betsey, 1798. 75c, Capt. Coffin and the Transit, 1823. $1, Commodore John Byron and the Dolphin, 1765. $2, Capt. Broughton and HMS Providence, 1795.
$5, Capt. James Cook, 1777, vert.

2002, Mar. 25 Wmk. 373 *Perf. 14*

804-809 A141 Set of 6 8.00 8.00

Souvenir Sheet

810 A141 $5 multi 8.00 8.00

In Remembrance of Sept. 11, 2001 Terrorist Attacks — A142

No. 811: a, 25c. b, $2.

2002, May 3 Wmk. 373 *Perf. 13¾*

811 A142 Vert. pair, #a-b 5.00 5.00

Issued in sheets of 2 pairs.

Reign of Queen Elizabeth II, 50th Anniv. — A143

Various photographs by Dorothy Wilding. Panel colors: 25c, Purple.
No. 812: a, Maroon. b, Purple.

2002, June 3 Wmk. 373 *Perf. 14*

812 A143 25c multi .80 .80

Souvenir Sheet

813 A143 $2 Sheet of 2, #a-b 10.00 10.00

Christmas A144

Ribbons and bow with various basketry weaves: 25c, 60c, 75c, $1, $2.50.

2002, Dec. 2 Litho. *Perf. 13x13¼*

814-818 A144 Set of 5 5.75 5.75

Cowrie Shells — A145

Designs: 25c, Cypraea mappa. 50c, Cypraea eglantina. 60c, Cypraea mauritiana. 75c, Cypraea cribaria. $1, Cypraea talpa. $2.50, Cypraea depressa.

Perf. 14½x14¼

2003, May 12 Litho. Unwmk.

819-824 A145 Set of 6 8.00 8.00
824a Souvenir sheet, #819-824 8.00 8.00

Coronation of Queen Elizabeth II, 50th Anniv.

Common Design Type

Designs: Nos. 825, 25c, 827a, $2, Queen and Prince Philip waving. Nos. 826, $3, 827b, $5, Prince Philip paying homage to Queen at coronation.

Perf. 14¼x14½

2003, June 2 Litho. Wmk. 373

Vignettes Framed, Red Background

825-826 CD363 Set of 2 4.25 4.25

Souvenir Sheet

Vignettes Without Frame, Purple Panel

827 CD363 Sheet of 2, #a-b 9.25 9.25

Powered Flight, Cent. — A146

Designs: 25c, Sopwith Camel. 50c, Northrop Alpha. No. 830, 60c, DeHavilland Comet. 75c, Boeing 727. $1, English Electric Canberra. $2.50, Lockheed Martin F-22.

No. 834: a, 40c, Mitsubishi A6M-5 Zero. b, 60c, Grumman F6F Hellcat.

Illustration reduced.

Wmk. 373

2003, Aug. 29 Litho. *Perf. 14*

Stamp + Label

828-833 A146 Set of 6 10.00 10.00

Souvenir Sheet

834 A146 Sheet of 2, #a-b 3.50 3.50

Christmas — A147

Christmas Island scenes: 25c, Teareba Taomeka, Tabwakea. 40c, Seventh Day Adventist Church, London. 50c, St. Teresa Catholic Church, Tabakea Village. 60c, Betaera Fou, London. 75c, Children, church bells, London. $1.50, Emanuira Church, London. $2.50, Church of Christ (60x24mm).

2003, Dec. 20 Unwmk. *Perf. 13¼*

835-841 A147 Set of 7 12.00 12.00
841a Souvenir sheet, #835-841 12.00 12.00

Road Safety — A148

No. 842: a, Accident. b, Automobile. c, Beverage can, drink, cigarette. d, Children.

2004, Apr. 7 Litho. *Perf. 13x13¼*

842 Horiz. strip of 4 5.00 5.00
a. A148 30c multi .60 .50
b. A148 40c multi .90 .70
c. A148 50c multi 1.00 .90
d. A148 60c multi 1.25 1.10
e. Souvenir sheet, #842 5.25 5.25

World Health Day.

Bird Life International A149

Designs: 25c, Pacific golden plover. 40c, Whimbrel. 50c, Wandering tattler. 60c, Sanderling. 75c, Bar-tailed godwit. $2.50, Ruddy turnstone.

No. 849 — Bristle-thighed curlew: a, One in tree, one at water's edge. b, Head of bird. c, Front of bird, head facing right, vert. d, Back of bird, head facing left, vert. e, Two birds at water's edge.

Perf. 14¼x13¾

2004, Apr. 29 Litho. Unwmk.

843-848 A149 Set of 6 13.00 13.00

Souvenir Sheet

Perf. 14¼x14½

849 A149 $1 Sheet of 5, #a-e 14.00 14.00

2004 Summer Olympics, Athens — A150

Designs: 25c, Runners. 50c, Taekwondo. 60c, Weight lifting. 75c, Women's running.

2004, July 12 Wmk. 373 *Perf. 14*

850-853 A150 Set of 4 4.50 4.50

Souvenir Sheet

Celebration Games — A151

No. 854: a, Runners on track. b, Athletes, dancer, building.

2004, July 12

854 A151 $2.50 Sheet of 2, #a-b 11.00 11.00

Orchids A152

No. 855: a, Dendrobium anosmum. b, Dendrobium chrysotoxum. c, Dendrobium laevifolium. d, Dendrobium mohlianum. e, Dendrobium pseudoglomeratum. f, Dendrobium purpureum. g, Grammatophyllum speciosum. h, Dendrobium williamsianum. i, Spathoglottis plicata. j, Vanda hindsii.

2004, Aug. 28 Unwmk. *Perf. 13½*

855 Block of 10 18.00 18.00
a.-j. A152 $1 Any single 1.60 1.50

Merchant Ships A153

Designs: 50c, MV Montelucia. 75c, MS Pacific Princess. $2.50 MS Prinsendam. $5, MS Norwegian Wind.

2004, Oct. 25 Litho. *Perf. 13¼*

856-859 A153 Set of 4 16.00 16.00

Battle of Trafalgar, Bicent. — A154

Designs: 25c, French 16-pounder cannon. 50c, San Ildefonso in action against HMS Defence. 75c, HMS Victory lashed to the Redoubtable. $1, Emperor Napoleon Bonaparte, vert. $1.50, HMS Victory. No. 865, $2.50, Vice-admiral Sir Horatio Nelson, vert.

No. 866: a, Admiral Federico Gravina. b, Santissima Trinidad.

2005, Mar. 29 Litho. *Perf. 13¼*

860-865 A154 Set of 6 15.00 15.00

Souvenir Sheet

866 A154 $2.50 Sheet of 2, #a-b 10.00 10.00

No. 864 has particles of wood from the HMS Victory embedded in the areas covered by a thermographic process that produces a raised, shiny effect.

End of World War II, 60th Anniv. — A155

No. 867: a, Japanese Type 95 Ha-Go tank invading Gilbert Islands. b, Japanese A6M Zero fighter on Gilbert Islands. c, USS Argonaut and Nautilus land Marines at Butaritari in Carlson Raid. d, Pacific Fleet Admiral Chester W. Nimitz. e, USS Liscome Bay sunk by Japanese submarine. f, US Higgins landing craft approaching Tarawa Red Beach. g, F6F-3 Hellcats provide air cover over Tarawa Red Beach. h, LVTs hit the shore at Tarawa Red Beach. i, Sherman tank at Tarawa Red Beach. j, US Marines take cover on Tarawa Red Beach.

$5, Australian Prime Minister John Curtin, British Prime Minister Winston Churchill.

2005, Apr. 21 *Perf. 13¾*

867 A155 75c Sheet of 10, #a-j 18.00 18.00

Souvenir Sheet

868 A155 $5 multi 11.00 11.00

Pacific Explorer 2005 World Stamp Expo, Sydney (No. 868).

BirdLife International — A156

No. 869, 25c — Birds of Christmas Island: a, Lesser frigatebird. b, Red-tailed tropicbird. c, Blue noddy. d, Christmas shearwater. e, Sooty tern. f, Masked booby.

No. 870, $2 — Birds of Kiribati: a, White-tailed tropicbird. b, Black noddy. c, Red-footed booby. d, Wedge-tailed shearwater. e, White tern. f, Great frigatebird.

2005, Aug. 15 *Perf. 13¼x13*

Sheets of 6, #a-f

869-870 A156 Set of 2 29.00 29.00

Pope John Paul II (1920-2005) A157

2005, Aug. 18 Litho. *Perf. 14*

871 A157 $1 multi 2.25 2.25

Battle of Trafalgar, Bicent. — A158

Designs: 25c, HMS Victory. 50c, Ships, horiz. $5, Admiral Horatio Nelson

2005, Oct. 18 Litho. *Perf. 13½*

872-874 A158 Set of 3 14.00 14.00

Worldwide Fund for Nature (WWF) — A159

Various depictions of harlequin shrimp: 50c, 60c, 75c, $5.

2005, Dec. 1 *Perf. 14*

875-878 A159 Set of 4 12.50 12.50
878a Miniature sheet, 2 each #875-878 24.00 24.00

Queen Elizabeth II, 80th Birthday A160

Queen: 50c, As young woman. 75c, Wearing tiara, sepia photograph. $1, Wearing tiara, color photograph. $2, Wearing pink hat.

No. 883: a, $1.50, Like $1. b, $2.50, Like 75c.

2006, Apr. 21 Litho. *Perf. 14*

Stamps With White Frames

879-882 A160 Set of 4 10.00 10.00

Souvenir Sheet

Stamps Without White Frames

883 A160 Sheet of 2, #a-b 12.00 12.00

Europa Stamps, 50th Anniv. — A161

Flags of European Union and Kiribati with gradiating background colors of: $2, Gray green. $2.50, Purple. $3, Yellowish brown. $5, Blue.

2006, May 4 *Perf. 13¼*

884-887 A161 Set of 4 22.00 22.00
887a Souvenir sheet, #884-887 22.00 22.00

Anniversaries — A162

No. 888, 25c: a, Charles Darwin and marine life. b, Fish and marine life.
No. 889, 50c: a, Isambard Kingdom Brunel. b, Glowing rivet.
No. 890, 75c: a, Christopher Columbus. b, Ship.
No. 891, $1: a, Thomas Alva Edison. b, Tin foil phonograph.
No. 892, $1.25: a, Wolfgang Amadeus Mozart. b, Violin and quill pen.
No. 893, $1.50: a, Concorde. b, Wing of Concorde, Concorde in flight.

2006, May 27 *Perf. 13x12½*
Horiz. Pairs, #a-b

888-893 A162 Set of 6 19.00 19.00

Darwin's voyage on the Beagle, 250th anniv., Birth of Brunel, bicent., Death of Columbus, 500th anniv., Death of Edison, 75th anniv., Birth of Mozart, 250th anniv., Inaugural Concorde flights, 30th anniv.

Dinosaurs A163

Designs: 25c, Ultrasaurus. 50c, Rhamphorhynchus. 60c, Dilophosaurus. 75c, Brachiosaurus. No. 898, $1, Minmi paravertebra. No. 899, $1, Eoraptor. $1.25, Stegosaurus. $1.50, Gigantosaurus.

2006, Sept. 15 *Perf. 13¼x13½*

894-901 A163 Set of 8 12.50 12.50

Miniature Sheet

Victoria Cross, 150th Anniv. — A164

No. 902: a. Troop Sergeant Major John Berryman with Captain Webb at Balaclava. b, Private W. Norman bringing in two Russian prisoners. c, Sergeant Major John Greive saving officer's life at Balaclava. d, Private Thomas Beach rescuing Colonel Carpenter at Inkerman. e, Brevet Major C. H. Lumley engaged with Russian gunners in the Redan. f, Major F. C. Elton working in trenches.

2006, Oct. 20 Litho. *Perf. 13¼x12½*

902 A164 $1.50 Sheet of 6, #a-f, + 6 labels 17.00 17.00

60th Wedding Anniversary of Queen Elizabeth II and Prince Philip — A165

Designs: 50c, Portrait of Elizabeth and Philip. 75c, Wedding procession. $1, Bride and groom waving. $1.50, Queen reading. $5, Wedding portrait.

2007, Jan. 31 Litho. *Perf. 13¾*

903-906 A165 Set of 4 6.00 6.00

Souvenir Sheet
Perf. 14

907 A165 $5 multi 7.75 7.75

No. 907 contains one 42x56mm stamp

Scouting, Cent. A166

Designs: 25c, Scouts with Kiribati flag, hands tying neckerchief. 50c, Scouts learning about AIDS, Scout saluting. 75c, Scout leaders, hand with compass. $2, 1962 Scout shelter, hands lashing rope.
No. 912, vert.: a, $1, Emblem of Kiribati Scouts. b, $1.50, Lord Robert Baden-Powell.

Perf. 13x13¼
2007, Sept. 21 Litho. Wmk. 373

908-911 A166 Set of 4 6.50 6.50

Souvenir Sheet
Perf. 13¼x13

912 A166 Sheet of 2, #a-b 4.50 4.50

Princess Diana (1961-97) A167

Designs: No. 913, 25c, Wearing white dress, facing right. No. 914, 25c, Wearing pink dress, facing left. 50c, Wearing pink dress, diff. No. 916, 75c, Wearing emerald necklace. No. 917, 75c, Wearing black and white dress. $1, Wearing red dress.

Perf. 13¼x12½
2007, Nov. 1 Litho. Unwmk.

913-918 A167 Set of 6 6.50 6.50

Military Uniforms — A168

Uniforms of: 25c, Royal Engineers. 40c, 95th Rifles. 50c, 24th Regiment of Foot. 60c, New Zealand soldiers. 75c, 93rd Sutherland Highlanders. 90c, Irish Guard. $1, Japanese soldiers. $1.50, United States Marine Corps.

2007, Nov. 20 Wmk. 373 *Perf. 14*

919-926 A168 Set of 8 10.50 10.50

Birds — A169

Designs: 5c, Great crested tern. 10c Eurasian teal. 15c, Laughing gull. 20c, Black-tailed godwit. 25c, Pectoral sandpiper. 50c, Band-rumped storm petrel. 60c, Sharp-tailed sandpiper. 75c, Gray-tailed tattler. 90c, Red phalarope. $1, Pink-footed shearwater. $2, Ring-billed gull. $5, Bonin petrel.

Wmk. 373
2008, Feb. 9 Litho. *Perf. 13¾*

927	A169	5c multi	.20	.20
928	A169	10c multi	.20	.20
929	A169	15c multi	.30	.30
930	A169	20c multi	.40	.40
931	A169	25c multi	.45	.45
932	A169	50c multi	.95	.95
933	A169	60c multi	1.10	1.10
934	A169	75c multi	1.40	1.40
935	A169	90c multi	1.75	1.75
936	A169	$1 multi	1.90	1.90
937	A169	$2 multi	3.75	3.75
a.		Souvenir sheet, #929, 933-937	10.50	10.50
938	A169	$5 multi	9.50	9.50
a.		Souvenir sheet, #927-928, 930-932, 938	12.00	12.00
		Nos. 927-938 (12)	21.90	21.90

A170

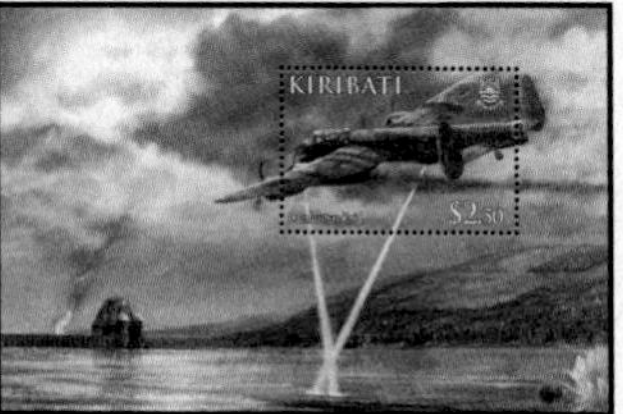
Royal Air Force, 90th Anniv. — A171

Designs: 25c, Avro Shackleton. 50c, Harrier GR3. 75c, Eurofighter Typhoon. $1, Vickers Valiant.
$2.50, Dambusters Raid.

Wmk. 373
2008, Apr. 1 Litho. *Perf. 14*

939-942 A170 Set of 4 4.75 4.75

Souvenir Sheet

943 A171 $2.50 multi 4.75 4.75

Phoenix Island Protected Area A172

Designs: 40c, Huts. 75c, Map of Kanton Island. 80c, Map of various islands. 85c, Phoenix petrel. $1.25, Acropora nobilis and reef fish. $1.75, Blacktip reef shark.

2008, July 12 *Perf. 13¾*

944-949 A172 Set of 6 11.50 11.50
949a Souvenir sheet of 6, #944-949 11.50 11.50

2008 Summer Olympics, Beijing A173

Designs: 25c, Bamboo, weight lifting. 50c, Dragon, running. 60c, Lanterns, cycling. 75c, Fish, javelin.

Wmk. 373
2008, Aug. 8 Litho. *Perf. 13½*

950-953 A173 Set of 4 3.75 3.75

Christmas — A174

No. 954, 25c: a, Lady Sacred Heart Church, Bairiki. b, Kiribati Protestant Church, Bikenibeu.
No. 955, 40c: a, Kaotitaeka Roman Catholic Church, Betio. b, Mormon Church, Iesu Kristo.
No. 956, 50c: a, Moaningaina Church, Eita. b, Sacred Heart Cathedral, Tarawa.
No. 957, 75c: a, St. Paul's Millennium Church, Betio. b, Kainkatikun Kristo Church, Naninimo.
Illustration reduced.

Wmk. 406
2008, Dec. 8 Litho. *Perf. 13*
Pairs, #a-b

954-957 A174 Set of 4 5.00 5.00
957c Souvenir sheet, #954a-954b, 955a-955b, 956a-956b, 957a-957b 5.00 5.00

POSTAGE DUE STAMPS

Natl. Arms — D1

1981, Aug. 27 Litho. *Perf. 14*

J1	D1	1c brt pink & black	.20	.20
J2	D1	2c greenish blue & blk	.20	.20
J3	D1	5c brt yel grn & black	.20	.20
J4	D1	10c lt red brown & blk	.20	.20
J5	D1	20c ultra & black	.20	.20
J6	D1	30c yel bister & black	.20	.25
J7	D1	40c brt pur & black	.30	.35
J8	D1	50c green & black	.40	.50
J9	D1	$1 red orange & blk	.75	.90
		Nos. J1-J9 (9)	2.65	3.00

Imperfs exist from the liquidation of Format International. They are not errors.

OFFICIAL STAMPS

Nos. 327a-340c Overprinted "O.K.G.S."

1981, May Litho. Unwmk. *Perf. 14*

O1	A52	1c multicolored	.20	.20
O2	A52	3c multicolored	.20	.20
O3	A52	5c multicolored	.20	.20
O4	A52	7c multicolored	.20	.20
O5	A52	10c multicolored	.20	.20
O6	A52	12c multicolored	.20	.20
O7	A52	15c multicolored	.20	.20
O8	A52	20c multicolored	.20	.20
O9	A52	25c multicolored	.20	.20
O10	A52	30c multicolored	.25	.25
O11	A52	35c multicolored	.30	.30
O12	A52	50c multicolored	.45	.45
O13	A52	$1 multicolored	.80	.80
O14	A52	$2 multicolored	1.60	1.60
O15	A52	$5 multicolored	4.25	4.25
		Nos. O1-O15 (15)	9.45	9.45

Nos. O1-O15 have thick overprint.

1981 **Wmk. 373**

O1a	A52	1c multi	4.00	4.25
O5a	A52	10c multi	20.00	21.00
O6a	A52	12c multi	6.00	6.00
O7a	A52	15c multi	20.00	20.00
O8a	A52	20c multi	13.00	13.00
O10a	A52	30c multi	8.00	9.00
O12a	A52	50c multi	7.50	7.50
O13a	A52	$1 multi	14.00	14.00
O14a	A52	$2 multi	16.00	17.00
O15a	A52	$5 multi	4.50	4.50
		Nos. O1a-O15a (10)	113.00	116.25

Nos. 390, 393-394, 396, 398 Overprinted "O.K.G.S."

1983, June 28 Litho. *Perf. 14*

O16	A62	12c multicolored	.45	.45
O17	A62	30c multicolored	.80	.80
O18	A62	35c multicolored	.90	.90

O19 A62 50c multicolored 1.25 1.25
O20 A62 $2 multicolored 3.75 3.75
Nos. O16-O20 (5) 7.15 7.15

This overprint has shorter, thinner letters than the one used for Nos. O1-O15. It also exists on Nos. 327, 331-334, 336-340. These have been questioned.

KOREA

kə-ˈrē-ə

(Corea)

(Chosen, Tyosen, Tae Han)

LOCATION — Peninsula extending from Manchuria between the Yellow Sea and the Sea of Japan
GOVT. — Republic
AREA — 38,221 sq. mi.
POP. — 47,904,370 (2001 est.)
CAPITAL — Seoul

Korea (or Corea) an independent monarchy for centuries under Chinese influence, came under Japanese influence in 1876. Chinese and Japanese stamps were used there as early as 1877. Administrative control was assumed by Japan in 1905 and annexation followed in 1910. Postage stamps of Japan were used in Korea from 1905 to early 1946.

At the end of World War II, American forces occupied South Korea and Russian forces occupied North Korea, with the 38th parallel of latitude as the dividing line. A republic was established in 1948 following an election in South Korea. North Korea issues its own stamps.

100 Mon = 1 Poon
5 Poon = 1 Cheun
1000 Re = 100 Cheun = Weun
100 Weun = 1 Hwan (1953)
100 Chun = 1 Won (1962)

Catalogue values for unused stamps in this country are for Never Hinged items, beginning with Scott 283 in the regular postage section, Scott B5 in the semi-postal section, and Scott C23 in the airpost section.

Watermarks

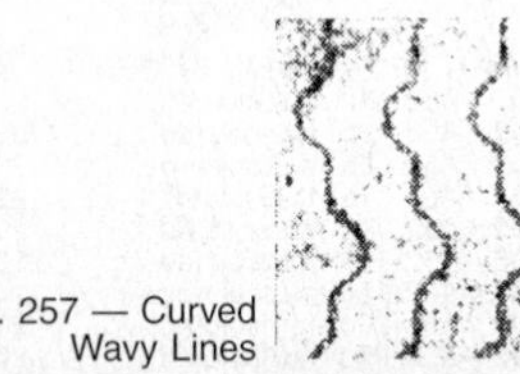

Wmk. 257 — Curved Wavy Lines

Wmk. 312 — Zigzag Lines

Wmk. 317 — Communications Department Emblem

Stylized Yin Yang
A1 A2

Perf. 8½ to 11½

1884 **Typo.** **Unwmk.**
1 A1 5m rose 52.50
2 A2 10m blue 11.00

Reprints and counterfeits of Nos. 1-2 exist.

These stamps were never placed in use. Values: 25 and 50 mon, each $7; 100 mon $10.
Counterfeits exist.

Yin Yang — A6

Two types of 50p:
I — No period after "50."
II — Period after "50."

Perf. 11½, 12, 12½, 13 and Compound

1895 **Litho.**
6 A6 5p green 21.00 15.00
a. 5p pale yellow green 29.00 18.00
b. Vert. pair, imperf horiz. 50.00 50.00
c. Horiz. pair, imperf. vert. 50.00 50.00
d. Vertical pair, imperf. between 55.00 55.00
e. Horiz. pair, imperf. btwn. 55.00 55.00
7 A6 10p deep blue 30.00 16.00
a. Horiz. pair, imperf. between 72.50 72.50
b. Vert. pair, imperf. horiz. 57.50 57.50
8 A6 25p maroon 47.50 27.50
a. Horiz. pair, imperf. between 92.50 92.50
b. Vert. pair, imperf. horiz. 90.00 90.00
9 A6 50p purple (II) 20.00 12.00
a. Horiz. pair, imperf. between 70.00 70.00
b. Vert, pair, imperf. horiz. 40.00 40.00
c. Horiz. pair, imperf. vert. 40.00 40.00
d. Type I 25.00 20.00
Nos. 6-9 (4) 118.50 70.50

For overprints and surcharges see Nos. 10-17C, 35-38.
Counterfeits exist of Nos. 6-9 and all surcharges and overprints.

Overprinted "Tae Han" in Korean and Chinese Characters

1897

Red Overprint

10 A6 5p green 90.00 10.00
a. 5p pale yellow green 200.00 150.00
b. Inverted overprint 150.00 150.00
c. Without ovpt. at bottom 150.00 130.00
d. Without overprint at top 150.00 130.00
f. Double overprint at top 140.00 140.00
g. Overprint at bottom in blk 160.00 160.00
h. Pair, one without overprint 450.00 450.00
i. Double overprint at top, inverted at bottom 550.00
11 A6 10p deep blue 100.00 15.00
a. Without ovpt. at bottom 150.00 150.00
b. Without overprint at top 150.00 150.00
c. Double overprint at top 150.00 150.00
d. Bottom overprint inverted 140.00 140.00
e. Top ovpt. dbl., one in blk 210.00 210.00
f. Top overprint omitted, bottom overprint inverted 450.00
12 A6 25p maroon 110.00 17.00
a. Overprint at bottom invtd. 150.00 150.00
b. Overprint at bottom in blk 210.00 210.00
c. Bottom overprint omitted 150.00 150.00
e. Top ovpt. dbl., one in blk 225.00 225.00
f. Top and bottom overprints double, one of each in blk 250.00 250.00
g. Pair, one without overprint 425.00 425.00
13 A6 50p purple 90.00 12.00
a. Without ovpt. at bottom 110.00 110.00
b. Without overprint at top 110.00 110.00
c. Bottom overprint double 110.00 110.00
e. Pair, one without overprint 275.00 275.00
Nos. 10-13 (4) 390.00 54.00

1897

Black Overprint

13F A6 5p green 300.00 85.00
13G A6 10p deep blue 300.00 100.00
h. Without ovpt. at bottom 350.00
14 A6 25p maroon 300.00 100.00
a. Without ovpt. at bottom 350.00
b. Without overprint at top 325.00
c. Double ovpt at bottom 325.00
15 A6 50p purple 300.00 80.00
a. Without ovpt. at bottom 350.00
Nos. 13F-15 (4) 1,200.

These stamps with black overprint, also No. 16A, are said not to have been officially authorized.

Nos. 6, 6a and 8 Surcharged in Red or Black

1900
15B A6 1p on 5p grn (R) *3,500.* *750.00*
c. Yellow green
16 A6 1p on 25p mar 100.00 60.00

Same Surcharge in Red or Black on Nos. 10, 10a, 12, 12c and 14

16A A6 1p on 5p grn (R) 1,000.
b. 1p on 5p pale yellow green 1,000.
17 A6 1p on 25p (#12) 50.00 22.50
a. Figure "1" omitted 90.00
b. On #12c 80.00 70.00
17C A6 1p on 25p (#14) 775.00 175.00

Counterfeit overprints and surcharges of Nos. 10-17C exist. See note after No. 15.

A8

A9

A10

A11

A12

A13

A14

A15

A16

A17

A18

A19

A20

A21

1900-01 **Typo.** ***Perf. 11***
18 A8 2re gray 5.00 3.50
19 A9 1ch yellow grn 10.50 4.00
20B A11 2ch pale blue 12.00 8.00
21 A12 3ch orange red 12.50 4.50
a. Vert. pair, imperf. horiz. 200.00 200.00
22 A13 4ch carmine 35.00 14.00
23 A14 5ch pink 15.00 8.00
24 A15 6ch dp blue 16.00 6.50
25 A16 10ch purple ('01) 32.50 10.00
26 A17 15ch gray vio 27.50 10.00
27 A18 20ch red brown 37.50 14.00
31 A19 50ch ol grn & pink 300.00 110.00
32 A20 1wn rose, blk & bl 850.00 175.00
33 A21 2wn pur & yel grn 1,400. 275.00
Nos. 18-33 (13) 2,753. 642.50

Nos. 22, 23, 25, 26, 33 exist imperf.
Some examples of Nos. 18-27 exist with forged Tae Han overprints in red. It is believed that Nos. 18 and 21 exist with genuine Tae Han overprints.
Reprints of No. 24 were made in light blue, perf. 12x13, in 1905 for a souvenir booklet. See note after No. 54.
See Nos. 52-54.

Perf. 10

18a A8 2re 8.00 3.50
19a A9 1ch 10.00 4.50
20 A10 2ch blue 35.00 18.00
a. Horiz. pair, imperf. btwn. *725.00*
20Ba A11 2ch pale blue 50.00 45.00
21b A12 3ch 14.00 4.50
22a A13 4ch 45.00 17.50
23a A14 5ch 20.00 9.00
24a A15 6ch 22.50 11.00
26a A17 15ch 160.00 140.00
27a A18 20ch 210.00 190.00
Nos. 18a-27a (10) 574.50 443.00

Emperor's Crown — A22

1902, Oct. 18 ***Perf. 11½***
34 A22 3ch orange 40.00 18.50

40th year of the reign of Emperor Kojong. An imperf. single was part of the 1905 souvenir booklet. See note following No. 54.
Counterfeits exist.

Nos. 8 and 9 Handstamp Surcharged in Black

1ch

2ch

3ch

Perf. 11½, 12, 12½, 13 and Compound

1902

35 A6 1ch on 25p maroon 25.00 6.00
b. Horiz. pair, imperf. btwn. 80.00
c. Imperf. 50.00
d. Vert. pair, imperf. horiz. 50.00
e. On No. 12 90.00 90.00
36 A6 2ch on 25p maroon 29.00 7.00
b. Imperf. 45.00
d. On No. 12 90.00 90.00
36E A6 2ch on 50p purple 160.00 150.00
f. Character "cheun" unabbreviated (in two rows instead of one) 250.00 175.00
37 A6 3ch on 50p purple 25.00 7.00
b. With character "cheun" unabbreviated (in two rows instead of one) 2,100. 800.00
d. Horiz. pair, imperf. btwn. 60.00
e. Vert. pair, imperf. btwn. 75.00
g. On No. 13 75.00 75.00
38 A6 3ch on 25p maroon 65.00 65.00
Nos. 35-38 (5) 304.00 235.00

There are several sizes of these surcharges. Being handstamped, inverted and double surcharges exist.

Counterfeit surcharges exist.

Falcon — A23

1903 *Perf. 13½x14*

39 A23 2re slate 6.50 6.25
40 A23 1ch violet brn 8.00 7.50
41 A23 2ch green 12.50 7.50
42 A23 3ch orange 10.00 7.50
43 A23 4ch rose 19.00 9.50
44 A23 5ch yellow brn 19.00 11.00
45 A23 6ch lilac 25.00 12.50
46 A23 10ch blue 32.50 16.00
47 A23 15ch red, *straw* 45.00 32.50
48 A23 20ch vio brn, *straw* 62.50 32.50
49 A23 50ch red, *grn* 210.00 120.00
50 A23 1wn vio, *lav* 550.00 300.00
51 A23 2wn vio, *org* 550.00 300.00
Nos. 39-51 (13) 1,550. 862.75

Values are for copies with perfs touching the design.

Types of 1901

1903 *Perf. 12½*

Thin, Semi-Transparent Paper

52 A19 50ch pale ol grn & pale pink *300.00 150.00*
53 A20 1wn rose, blk & bl *575.00 190.00*
54 A21 2wn lt vio & lt grn *750.00 250.00*
Nos. 52-54 (3) *1,625.* 590.00

No. 24, perf. 12x13, No. 34 imperf. and most examples of Nos. 52-54 unused are from souvenir booklets made up in 1905 when the Japanese withdrew all Korean stamps from circulation.

WARNING

In 1957 the Ministry of Communications issued 4000 presentation booklets containing Nos. 1-54 reproduced on watermark 312 paper.

Other presentation booklets included full-color reproductions of Nos. 1-54 and Japan No. 110 printed on the pages. Beware of wide-margined imperfs cut from these booklets.

Issued under US Military Rule

Stamps of Japan Nos. 331, 268, 342, 332, 339 and 337 Surcharged in Black

1946, Feb. 1 **Wmk. 257** *Perf. 13*

55 A86 5ch on 5s brn lake 5.50 *12.00*
56 A93 5ch on 14s rose lake & pale rose 1.25 *3.00*
a. 5ch on 40s dark violet (error) 175.00
57 A154 10ch on 40s dk vio 1.25 *3.00*
58 A147 20ch on 6s lt ultra 1.25 *3.00*
a. 20ch on 27s rose brown (error) 175.00
b. Double surcharge 30.00
59 A151 30ch on 27s rose brn 1.25 *3.00*
a. 30ch on 6s light ultra (error) 100.00
b. Double surcharge 25.00
60 A151 5wn on 17s gray vio 6.00 *12.50*
Nos. 55-60 (6) 16.50 *36.50*
Set, never hinged 30.00

Five essays for this provisional issue exist both with and without additional overprint of two Chinese characters ("specimen") in vermilion. The essays are: 20ch on Japan No. 269; 50ch on No. 272; 1wn on No. 336; 1wn on No. 273; 10wn on No. 265. Other denominations have been reported.

Korean Family and Flag — A24

Arms of Korea — A25

Wmk. 257

1946, May 1 **Litho.** *Perf. 10½*

61 A24 3ch orange yellow .60 1.00
62 A24 5ch green .60 1.00
63 A24 10ch carmine .60 1.00
64 A24 20ch dark blue .60 1.00
65 A25 50ch brown violet 1.50 *1.50*
66 A25 1wn lt brown 2.50 *1.75*
Nos. 61-66 (6) 6.40 *7.25*
Set, never hinged 10.00

Liberation from Japan.

Imperfs., Part Perfs.

Imperforate and part-perforate examples of a great many Korean stamps from No. 61 onward exist.

The imperfs. include Nos. 61-90, 93-97, 116-117, 119-126, 132-173, 182-186, 195, 197-199, 202A, 203, 204-205, 217, etc.

The part-perfs. include Nos. 62-65, 69, 72-73, 109, 111-113, 132, etc.

Printers waste includes printed on both sides, etc.

As the field is so extensive, the editors believe that they belong more properly in a specialized catalogue.

Dove — A26

1946, Aug. 15 **Unwmk.**

67 A26 50ch deep violet 4.00 *3.00*
Never hinged 6.00

First anniversary of liberation.

Perforations often are rough on stamps issued between Aug. 1946 and the end of 1954. This is not considered a defect.

Flags of US and Korea A27

1946, Sept. 9 *Perf. 11*

68 A27 10wn carmine 5.00 *3.50*
Never hinged 10.00

Resumption of postal communication with the US.

Astronomical Observatory, Kyongju — A28

Hibiscus with Rice — A29

Map of Korea — A30

Gold Crown of Silla Dynasty — A31

Admiral Li Sun-sin — A32

1946 *Rouletted 12*

69 A28 50ch dark blue .75 *1.50*
70 A29 1wn buff .95 *2.00*
71 A30 2wn indigo 1.10 2.00
72 A31 5wn magenta 9.00 *12.50*
73 A32 10wn emerald 10.00 *12.50*
Nos. 69-73 (5) 21.80 *30.50*
Set, never hinged 40.00

Perf. 11

70a A29 1wn 1.50 *2.00*
71a A30 2wn 75.00 *90.00*
72a A31 5wn 55.00 120.00
Nos. 70a-72a (3) 131.50 212.00
Set, never hinged 160.00

Korean Phonetic Alphabet — A33

1946, Oct. 9 *Perf. 11*

74 A33 50ch deep blue 2.00 1.50
Never hinged 5.00

500th anniv. of the introduction of the Korean phonetic alphabet (Hangul).

Li Jun — A34

Admiral Li Sun-sin — A35

Perf. 11½x11, 11½

1947, Aug. 1 **Litho.** **Wmk. 257**

75 A34 5wn lt blue green 7.00 *7.50*
76 A35 10wn light blue 7.00 *7.50*
Set, never hinged 28.00

Presentation Sheets

Starting in 1947 with No. 75, nearly 100 Korean stamps were printed in miniature or souvenir sheets and given to government officials and others. These sheets were released in quantities of 300 to 4,000. In 1957 the Ministry of Communications began to sell the souvenir sheets at post offices at face value to be used for postage. They are listed from No. 264a onward.

Letter-encircled Globe — A36

1947, Aug. 1 *Perf. 11½x11*

77 A36 10wn light blue 8.00 *9.00*
Never hinged 16.00

Resumption of international mail service between Korea and all countries of the world.

Granite Paper

Starting with No. 77, most Korean stamps through No. 751, except those on Laid Paper, are on Granite Paper. Granite Paper is noted above listing if the issue was printed on both ordinary and Granite Paper, such as Nos. 360a-374A.

Arch of Independence, Seoul — A37

Tortoise Ship, First Ironclad War Vessel — A38

1948, Apr.

78 A37 20wn rose 3.00 *4.00*
79 A38 50wn dull red brown 57.50 40.00
Set, never hinged 120.00

Republic

Flag and Ballot — A39

Woman and Man Casting Ballots — A40

Perf. 11x11½
1948, May 10 Litho. Wmk. 257

80 A39 2wn orange 7.50 7.50
81 A39 5wn lilac rose 12.50 10.00
82 A39 10wn lt violet 19.00 15.00
83 A40 20wn carmine 25.00 25.00
84 A40 50wn blue 19.00 20.00
Nos. 80-84 (5) 83.00 77.50
Set, never hinged 175.00

South Korea election of May 10, 1948.

Korean Flag and Olive Branches — A41

Olympic Torchbearer and Map of Korea — A42

1948, June 1 *Perf. 11x11½, 11½x11*

85 A41 5wn green 55.00 55.00
86 A42 10wn purple 25.00 22.50
Set, never hinged 190.00

Korea's participation in the 1948 Olympic Games.

National Assembly — A43

1948, July 1 Wmk. 257 *Perf. 11½*

87 A43 4wn orange brown 10.00 *12.00*
Never hinged 22.50

Opening of the Assembly July 1, 1948.
Exists without period between "5" and "31."

Korean Family and Capitol — A44

Flag of Korea A45

1948, Aug. 1 Litho.

88 A44 4wn emerald 35.00 35.00
89 A45 10wn orange brown 15.00 *20.00*
Set, never hinged 125.00

Signing of the new constitution, 7/17/48.

Pres. Syngman Rhee — A46

1948, Aug. 5

90 A46 5wn deep blue 150.00 140.00
Never hinged 300.00

Inauguration of Korea's first president, Syngman Rhee.

Dove — A47

Hibiscus — A48

Two types of 5wn:
I — "1948" 3mm wide; top inscription 9mm wide; periods in "8.15." barely visible.
II — "1948" 4mm wide; top inscription 9½mm; periods in "8.15." bold and strong.

1948 *Perf. 11, 11x11½*

91 A47 4wn blue 20.00 *25.00*
92 A48 5wn rose lilac (II) 35.00 32.50
a. Type I 120.00 100.00
Set, never hinged 120.00

Issued to commemorate the establishment of Korea's republican government.

Li Jun — A49

Observatory, Kyongju — A50

1948, Oct. 1 *Perf. 11½x11*

93 A49 4wn rose carmine .75 1.00
94 A50 14wn deep blue .75 1.00
a. 14wn light blue 75.00 45.00
Never Hinged 200.00
Set, never hinged 3.50

For surcharges see Nos. 127, 174, 176.

Doves over UN Emblem — A51

1949, Feb. 12 Wmk. 257 *Perf. 11*

95 A51 10wn blue *20.00 20.00*
Never hinged *40.00*

Arrival of the UN Commission on Korea, Feb. 12, 1949.

Korean Citizen and Census Date — A52

1949, Apr. 25

96 A52 15wn purple 25.00 22.50
Never hinged 52.50

Census of May 1, 1949.

Korean Boy and Girl A53

1949, May 5

97 A53 15wn purple 12.50 12.00
Never hinged 25.00

20th anniv. of Children's Day, May 5, 1949.

Postman — A54

Worker and Factory — A55

Rice Harvesting A56

Japanese Cranes A57

Diamond Mountains A58

Ginseng Plant A59

South Gate, Seoul — A60

Tabo Pagoda, Kyongju — A61

1949 Litho. *Perf. 11*

98 A54 1wn rose 2.50 3.00
99 A55 2wn dk blue gray 2.00 3.00
100 A56 5wn yellow green 8.00 8.00
101 A57 10wn blue green .90 1.20
102 A58 20wn orange brown .60 1.00
103 A59 30wn blue green .60 1.00
104 A60 50wn violet blue .60 1.00
105 A61 100wn dull yellow grn .60 1.00
Nos. 98-105 (8) 15.80 19.20
Set, never hinged 42.50

For surcharges see Nos. 129-131, 175, 177B-179, 181.

Phoenix and Yin Yang — A62

1949, Aug. 25

106 A62 15wn deep blue 17.50 14.00
Never hinged 35.00

1st anniv. of Korea's independence.

Express Train "Sam Chun Li" A63

1949, Sept. 18 *Perf. 11½x12*

107 A63 15wn violet blue 47.50 40.00
Never hinged 120.00

50th anniversary of Korean railroads.

Korean Flag — A64

Perf. 11½x11
1949, Oct. 15 Wmk. 257

108 A64 15wn red org, yel & dk bl 12.00 12.00
Never hinged 27.50

75th anniv. of the UPU.
No. 108 exists unwatermarked. These are counterfeit.

Hibiscus — A65

Magpies and Map of Korea — A66

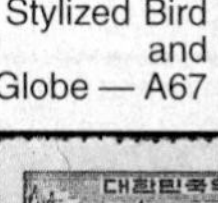
Stylized Bird and Globe — A67

Diamond Mountains A68

Admiral Li Sun-sin A69

1949 Wmk. 257 Litho. *Perf. 11*

109 A65 15wn vermilion .45 *1.20*
110 A66 65wn deep blue 1.00 *2.00*
111 A67 200wn green .45 *1.20*
112 A68 400wn brown .45 *1.20*
113 A69 500wn deep blue .45 *1.20*
Nos. 109-113 (5) 2.80 *6.80*
Set, never hinged 8.00

For surcharges see Nos. 128, 177, 180.

Canceled to Order

More than 100 Korean stamps and souvenir sheets were canceled to order, the cancellation incorporating the date "67.9.20." These include 81 stamps between Nos. 111 and 327, 18 airmail stamps between Nos. C6 and C26, and 5 souvenir sheets between Nos. 313 and 332, etc.

Also exists with later dates and on other stamps.

These c-t-o stamps and souvenir sheets are sold for much less than the values shown below, which are for postally used examples.

A70

A71

Ancient postal medal (Ma-Pae).

1950, Jan. 1

114 A70 15wn yellow green 7.50 *16.00*
115 A70 65wn red brown 5.00 *8.00*
Set, never hinged 50.00

50th anniv. of Korea's entrance into the UPU.

1950, Mar. 10 *Perf. 11½*

Revolutionists.

116 A71 15wn olive 12.00 *15.00*
117 A71 65wn light violet 9.00 6.50
Set, never hinged 65.00

41st anniversary of Korea's declaration of Independence.

Korean Emblem and National Assembly — A72

1950, May 30

118 A72 30wn bl, red, brn & grn 7.50 7.00
Never hinged 17.50

2nd natl. election of the Korean Republic.

Syngman Rhee — A73

Korean Flag and White Mountains — A74

Flags of UN and Korea, Map of Korea A75

1950, Nov. 20 Wmk. 257 *Perf. 11*

119 A73 100wn blue 2.00 *3.00*
120 A74 100wn green 1.75 *3.00*
121 A75 200wn dark green 1.75 *2.00*
Nos. 119-121 (3) 5.50 8.00
Set, never hinged 16.00

Crane — A76

Tiger Mural — A77

Dove and Flag — A78

Postal Medal — A79

Mural from Ancient Tomb — A80

1951 Unwmk. *Perf. 11*
Ordinary Paper

122 A76 5wn orange brown 1.00 *2.25*
123 A77 20wn purple 1.25 *3.00*
124 A78 50wn green 9.00 *17.50*
125 A79 100wn deep blue 15.00 17.50
126 A80 1000wn green 17.50 16.00
Nos. 122-126 (5) 43.75 56.25
Set, never hinged 105.00

Rouletted 12

122a A76 5wn orange brown .80 *2.00*
123a A77 20wn purple .80 *2.00*
124a A78 50wn green 2.00 *5.00*
125a A79 100wn blue 2.00 *5.00*
Nos. 122a-125a (4) 5.60 *14.00*
Set, never hinged 16.00

No. 126 also exists perforated 12½. See Nos. 187-189.

No. 93 Surcharged with New Value and Wavy Lines in Blue

1951 Wmk. 257 *Perf. 11½x11*

127 A49 100wn on 4wn rose car .85 .60
a. Inverted surcharge 24.00 *35.00*
Never hinged 40.00

Nos. 109, 101, 102 and 104 Surcharged in Blue or Brown

Perf. 11

128 A65 200wn on 15wn 2.75 6.00
a. Inverted surcharge 30.00
Never hinged 50.00
129 A57 300wn on 10wn (Br) 5.75 4.50
a. Inverted surcharge 30.00
Never hinged 50.00
130 A58 300wn on 20wn 4.50 4.50
a. Inverted surcharge 35.00
Never hinged 75.00
131 A60 300wn on 50wn (Br) 7.00 3.50
Nos. 127-131 (5) 20.85 19.10
Set, never hinged 100.00

Size and details of surcharge varies. Numeral upright on Nos. 129 and 131; numeral slanted on Nos. 175 and 179. See Nos. 174-181.

On No. 130, the zeros in "300" are octagonal; on No. 177B they are oval.

Flags of US and Korea and Statue of Liberty — A81

Design (blue stamps): Flag of same country as preceding green stamp, UN emblem and doves.

1951-52 Wmk. 257 *Perf. 11*
Flags in Natural Colors, Participating Country at Left

132 A81 500wn green 8.25 4.50
133 A81 500wn blue 8.25 4.50
134 A81 500wn grn *(Australia)* 7.00 4.50
135 A81 500wn blue 8.25 4.50
136 A81 500wn grn *(Belgium)* 7.00 4.00
137 A81 500wn blue 7.00 4.00
138 A81 500wn grn *(Britain)* 7.25 5.00
139 A81 500wn blue 7.25 5.00
140 A81 500wn grn *(Canada)* 7.25 5.00
141 A81 500wn blue 7.00 4.00
142 A81 500wn grn *(Colombia)* 7.00 4.00
143 A81 500wn blue 8.25 5.00
144 A81 500wn grn *(Denmark)* 12.00 *10.00*
145 A81 500wn blue 12.50 *10.00*
146 A81 500wn grn *(Ethiopia)* 7.00 4.00
147 A81 500wn blue 8.25 5.00
148 A81 500wn grn *(France)* 7.00 4.00
149 A81 500wn blue 8.25 5.00
150 A81 500wn grn *(Greece)* 8.25 5.00
151 A81 500wn blue 8.25 5.00
152 A81 500wn grn *(India)* 10.00 5.75
153 A81 500wn blue 11.00 6.50
154 A81 500wn grn *(Italy)* 10.00 5.75
a. Flag without crown ('52) 12.00
155 A81 500wn blue 10.00 5.75
a. Flag without crown ('52) 12.00
156 A81 500wn grn *(Luxembourg)* 10.00 5.75
157 A81 500wn blue 8.25 5.00
158 A81 500wn grn *(Netherlands)* 7.00 4.00
159 A81 500wn blue 7.00 4.00
160 A81 500wn grn *(New Zealand)* 8.25 5.00
161 A81 500wn blue 8.25 5.00
162 A81 500wn grn *(Norway)* 10.00 5.75
163 A81 500wn blue 10.00 5.75
164 A81 500wn grn *(Philippines)* 8.25 5.00
165 A81 500wn blue 8.25 5.00
166 A81 500wn grn *(Sweden)* 7.00 4.00
167 A81 500wn blue 8.25 5.00
168 A81 500wn grn *(Thailand)* 7.00 4.00
169 A81 500wn blue 8.25 5.00
170 A81 500wn grn*(Turkey)* 8.25 5.00
171 A81 500wn blue 8.25 5.00
172 A81 500wn grn *(Union of So. Africa)* 8.25 5.00
173 A81 500wn blue 8.25 5.00
Nos. 132-173 (42) 351.00 214.00
Set, never hinged 600.00

Twenty-two imperf. souvenir sheets of two, containing the green and the blue stamps for each participating country (including both types of Italy) were issued. Size: 140x90mm. Value, set $800.

Nos. 93-94, 101-105, 109-110 Surcharged Like Nos. 128-131 in Blue or Brown

1951 Wmk. 257 *Perf. 11½x11, 11*

174 A49 300wn on 4wn 2.75 *4.00*
a. Inverted surcharge 30.00 —
Never hinged 50.00
175 A57 300wn on 10wn (Br) 1.75 *5.00*
a. Inverted surcharge 30.00 —
Never hinged 50.00
176 A50 300wn on 14wn (Br) 3.25 *4.00*
a. 300wn on 14wn lt bl 3,750. 1,200.
b. Inverted surcharge 30.00 —
Never hinged 50.00
177 A65 300wn on 15wn 2.75 *4.00*
a. Inverted surcharge 30.00 —
Never hinged 50.00
177B A58 300wn on 20wn 7.00 5.00
178 A59 300wn on 30wn (Br) 2.75 *4.00*
a. Inverted surcharge 30.00 —
Never hinged 50.00
179 A60 300wn on 50wn (Br) 2.75 3.50
180 A66 300wn on 65wn (Br) 1.75 *4.00*
a. Inverted monad 90.00 —
181 A61 300wn on 100wn 3.25 3.25
a. Inverted surcharge 45.00 —
Never hinged 75.00
Nos. 174-181 (9) 28.00 36.75
Set, never hinged 75.00

"300" slanted on Nos. 175, 177B and 179; "300" upright on Nos. 129 and 131. The surcharge exists double on several of these stamps.

No. 177B differs from No. 130 in detail noted after No. 131.

Syngman Rhee and "Happiness" — A82

1952, Sept. 10 Litho. *Perf. 12½*

182 A82 1000wn dark green 3.00 *8.00*
Never hinged 8.00

Second inauguration of President Syngman Rhee, Aug. 15, 1952.

Sok Kul Am, Near Kyongju — A83

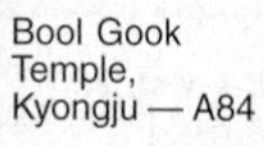

Bool Gook Temple, Kyongju — A84

Tombstone of Mu Yal Wang — A85

Choong Yul Sa Shrine, Tongyung — A86

1952 Wmk. 257 Typo. *Perf. 12½*

183 A83 200wn henna brown .55 *1.25*
184 A84 300wn green 1.00 1.25
185 A85 500wn carmine 1.10 *1.60*
186 A86 2000wn deep blue .85 .85

Rough Perf. 10-11, 11½x11 and Compound

Litho.

186A A83 200wn henna brown .80 *1.60*
186B A84 300wn green .65 *.85*
Nos. 183-186B (6) 4.95 7.40
Set, never hinged 15.00

Types of 1951

(Designs slightly smaller.)

1952-53 *Rough Perf. 10-11*

187 A77 20wn purple 1.00 *3.00*
187A A78 50wn green 14.00 *22.50*
187B A79 100wn deep blue 1.60 1.60
187C A80 1000wn green 82.50 30.00
Nos. 187-187C (4) 99.10 57.10
Set, never hinged 225.00

(Designs slightly larger.)

Perf. 12½

187D A78 50wn green 1.75 2.75
188 A79 100wn deep blue 1.00 *2.00*
189 A80 1000wn green ('53) 3.50 .85
Nos. 187D-189 (3) 6.25 5.60
Set, never hinged 13.00

Type of 1952

1953

189A A85 500wn deep blue 35.00 *160.00*

All examples of No. 189A were affixed to postal cards before sale. Values are for stamps removed from the cards.

See Nos. 191-192, 203B, 248.

Types of 1952 and

Planting Trees — A87

Wmk. 257

1953, Apr. 5 Litho. *Perf. 12½*

190 A87 1h aqua .35 *.65*
191 A85 2h aqua .45 .45
192 A85 5h bright green .55 .45
193 A87 10h bright green 1.60 1.50
194 A86 20h brown 1.90 *1.60*
Nos. 190-194 (5) 4.85 4.65
Set, never hinged 12.00

See Nos. 203A, 247.

Map and YMCA Emblem — A88

1953, Oct. 25 *Perf. 13½*

195 A88 10h dk slate bl & red 2.25 *4.00*
Never hinged 6.50

50th anniv. of the Korean YMCA.

Tombstone of Mu Yal Wang — A88a

A89

Sika Deer — A90

1954, Apr. *Perf. 12½*

196 A88a 5h dark green 1.10 *1.25*
197 A89 100h brown carmine 7.00 3.00
198 A90 500h brown orange 35.00 6.00
199 A90 1000h bister brown 80.00 7.00
Nos. 196-199 (4) 123.10 17.25
Set, never hinged 250.00

See Nos. 203C, 203D, 238-239, 248A, 250-251, 259, 261-262, 269-270, 279, 281-282.

Dok Do (Dok Island) — A91

Design: 10h, Dok Do, lateral view.

1954, Sept. 15

200 A91 2h claret .60 *2.50*
201 A91 5h blue 1.25 *2.50*
202 A91 10h blue green 2.00 *2.50*
Nos. 200-202 (3) 3.85 7.50
Set, never hinged 10.00

A92
Moth and Flag

A92a
Pagoda Park, Seoul

1954, Apr. 16 Wmk. 257 *Perf. 12½*

202A A92 10h brown 2.50 2.00
203 A92a 30h dark blue .55 1.50
Set, never hinged 5.00

See Nos. 203E, 260, 280.

Types of 1952-54

1955-56 Unwmk. *Perf. 12½*

Laid Paper

203A A87 1h aqua ('56) .30 *.50*
203B A85 2h aqua ('56) .30 *.50*
203C A88a 5h brt green ('56) .30 *.40*
203D A89 100h brown carmine 8.00 4.50
203E A92a 200h violet 6.00 2.50
Nos. 203A-203E (5) 14.90 8.40
Set, never hinged 55.00

On No. 203C the right hand character is redrawn as in illustration above No. 212D.

Nos. 203A and 203C are found on horizontally and vertically laid paper.

Erosion Control on Mountainside A93

1954, Dec. 12 Wmk. 257

204 A93 10h dk grn & yel grn 1.50 1.25
205 A93 19h dk grn & yel grn 1.50 *2.00*
Set, never hinged 12.50

Issued to publicize the 1954 forestation campaign.

Presidents Rhee and Eisenhower Shaking Hands — A94

1954, Dec. 25 *Perf. 13½*

206 A94 10h violet blue 1.40 *1.60*
207 A94 19h brown 1.40 *1.60*
208 A94 71h dull green 2.50 2.50
Nos. 206-208 (3) 5.30 5.70
Set, never hinged 15.00

Adoption of the US-Korea mutual defense treaty.

"Reconstruction" A95

Wmk. 257

1955, Feb. 10 Litho. *Perf. 12½*

209 A95 10h brown 1.75 3.00
210 A95 15h violet 1.75 3.00
211 A95 20h blue 500.00 20.00
Never hinged 1,250.
212 A95 50h plum 5.00 1.60
Nos. 209-210,212 (3) 8.50
Set, #209-210, 212, never hinged 20.00
Nos. 209-212 (4) 27.60

Korea's industrial reconstruction.

1955, Oct. 19 Unwmk. *Perf. 12½*

Laid Paper

212A A95 15h violet 1.75 1.00
212B A95 20h blue 1.75 1.00
212C A95 50h plum 3.00 1.40
Nos. 212A-212C (3) 6.50 3.40
Set, never hinged 18.00

No. 212B is found on horizontally and vertically laid paper.

Same with Right Character at Top Redrawn

Original

Redrawn

1956, June 5 Unwmk. *Perf. 12½*

Laid Paper

212D A95 10h brown 2.00 *2.50*
212E A95 15h violet 2.00 *2.50*
212F A95 20h blue 2.00 .85
a. Booklet pane of 6 175.00
Nos. 212D-212F (3) 6.00 5.85
Set, never hinged 16.00

Nos. 212D-212F are found on horizontally and vertically laid paper. See Nos. 248B, 256, 272, 276.

Rotary Emblem — A96

1955, Feb. 23 Wmk. 257 *Perf. 13½*

213 A96 20h violet 4.00 3.00
214 A96 25h dull green 2.00 1.50
215 A96 71h magenta 2.00 1.50
Nos. 213-215 (3) 8.00 6.00
Set, never hinged 15.00

Rotary International, 50th anniversary.

Syngman Rhee, 80th Birthday, Apr. 26 — A98

1955, Mar. 26

217 A98 20h deep blue 8.00 8.00
Never hinged 20.00

Flag and Arch of Independence A99

1955, Aug. 15 Litho. *Perf. 13½*

218 A99 40h Prus green 3.00 2.00
219 A99 100h lake 3.00 3.00
Set, never hinged 18.00

Tenth anniversary of independence.

UN Emblem in Circle of Clasped Hands — A100

1955, Oct. 24

221 A100 20h bluish green 1.75 1.50
222 A100 55h aqua 1.75 1.50
Set, never hinged 9.00

United Nations, 10th anniversary.

Olympic Torch and Runners — A101

1955, Oct. 23

223 A101 20h claret 2.00 2.00
224 A101 55h dark green 2.00 2.00
Set, never hinged 10.00

36th National Athletic Meet.

Adm. Li Sun-sin, Navy Flag and Tortoise Ship A102

Perf. 13x13½

1955, Nov. 11 Unwmk.

Laid Paper

225 A102 20h violet blue 2.00 2.00
Never hinged 9.00

Korean Navy, 10th anniversary.

Rhee Monument near Seoul — A103

1956, Mar. 26 ***Perf. 13½x13***

226 A103 20h dull green 2.50 2.50
Never hinged 7.50

81st birthday of Pres. Syngman Rhee.
No. 226 is found on horizontally and vertically laid paper.

Third Inauguration of Pres. Syngman Rhee — A104

1956, Aug. 15 ***Perf. 13x13½***

227 A104 20h brown 35.00 25.00
228 A104 55h violet blue 15.00 12.00
Set, never hinged 150.00

Olympic Rings and Torch — A105

1956, Nov. 1 **Litho.** ***Perf. 12½***
Laid Paper

229 A105 20h red orange 2.00 *2.50*
230 A105 55h brt green 2.00 *2.50*
Set, never hinged 10.00

16th Olympic Games in Melbourne, 11/22-12/8.

Central Post Office, Seoul A107

Stamp of 1884 — A108

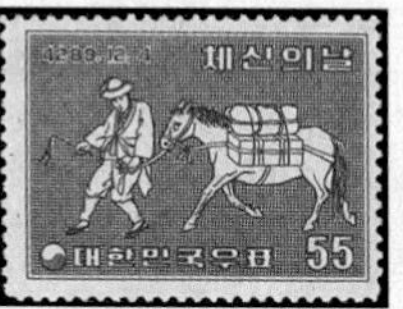

Mail Delivered by Donkey A109

1956, Dec. 4 **Laid Paper** **Unwmk.**

232 A107 20h lt blue green 4.00 3.00
233 A108 50h lt carmine 6.00 5.00
234 A109 55h green 3.00 2.00
Nos. 232-234 (3) 13.00 10.00
Set, never hinged 40.00

Issued to commemorate Postal Day.

Types of 1954 Redrawn and

Hibiscus — A110

King Sejong — A111

Kyongju Observatory A112

No Hwan Symbol; Redrawn Character

1956, Dec. 4 **Unwmk.** ***Perf. 12½***
Laid Paper

235 A110 10h lilac rose .80 .75
236 A111 20h lilac 1.40 .75
237 A112 50h violet 1.75 .75
238 A89 100h brown carmine 10.50 4.50
239 A90 500h brown orange 26.00 5.00
Nos. 235-239 (5) 40.45 11.75
Set, never hinged 100.00

On Nos. 238-239, the character after numeral has been omitted and the last character of the inscription has been redrawn as illustrated above No. 212D.

Nos. 235-236 are found on horizontally and vertically laid paper.

See Nos. 240-242, 253, 255, 258, 273, 275, 278, 291Bd, 291Bf, B3-B4.

Types of 1956

1957, Jan. 21 **Wmk. 312** ***Perf. 12½***

240 A110 10h lilac rose .90 .65
241 A111 20h red lilac 2.10 1.25
242 A112 50h violet 3.00 .65
Nos. 240-242 (3) 6.00 2.55
Set, never hinged 15.00

Telecommunication Symbols — A117

1957, Jan. 31 ***Perf. 13½***

243 A117 40h lt ultra 1.50 1.40
244 A117 55h brt green 1.50 1.40
Set, never hinged 6.00

5th anniv. of Korea's joining the ITU.

Boy Scout and Emblem A118

1957, Feb. 27 **Wmk. 312**

245 A118 40h pale purple 1.00 *1.40*
246 A118 55h lt magenta 1.00 *1.40*
Set, never hinged 5.00

50th anniversary of Boy Scout movement.

Types of 1953-56
Top Right Character Redrawn; Hwan Symbol Retained

1957 **Wmk. 312** ***Perf. 12½***

247 A87 1h aqua .35 *.55*
248 A85 2h aqua .45 *.55*
248A A88a 5h brt green .45 *.55*
248B A95 15h violet 3.50 2.00
Nos. 247-248B (4) 4.75 3.65
Set, never hinged 12.00

Redrawn Types of 1954, 1956 and

Planting Trees — A119

South Gate, Seoul — A120

Tiger A121

Diamond Mountains A122

No Hwan Symbol; Redrawn Character

1957 **Wmk. 312** **Litho.** ***Perf. 12½***

249 A119 2h aqua .30 *.40*
250 A88a 4h aqua .45 .40
251 A88a 5h emerald .45 .40
252 A120 10h green .45 .20
253 A110 20h lilac rose .55 .40
254 A121 30h pale lilac .55 .40
255 A111 40h red lilac .75 .35
a. Booklet pane of 6 80.00
256 A95 50h lake 3.25 .65
257 A122 55h violet brn 1.10 1.00
258 A112 100h violet 1.50 .50
259 A89 200h brown car 1.75 .50
260 A92a 400h brt violet 27.50 5.00
261 A90 500h ocher 27.50 6.50
262 A90 1000h dk ol bis 55.00 12.50
Nos. 249-262 (14) 121.10 29.20
Set, never hinged 300.00

The "redrawn character" is illustrated above No. 212D.

See Nos. 268, 271, 274, 277, 291c, 291e.

Mercury and Flags of Korea and US A123

1957, Nov. 7 **Wmk. 312** ***Perf. 13½***

263 A123 40h dp orange .75 *.90*
264 A123 205h emerald 1.60 *1.90*
a. Souv. sheet of 2, #263-264, imperf. 750.00
Never hinged 1,500.
Set, never hinged 6.00

Treaty of friendship, commerce and navigation between Korea and the US.

Star of Bethlehem and Pine Cone — A124

Designs: 25h, Christmas tree and tassel. 30h, Christmas tree, window and dog.

1957, Dec. 11 **Litho.** ***Perf. 12½***

265 A124 15h org, brn & grn 3.75 *2.00*
a. Souv. sheet of 1, imperf. 600.00
Never hinged 1,000.
266 A124 25h lt grn, yel & red 3.75 *2.00*
a. Souv. sheet of 1, imperf. 600.00
Never hinged 1,000.
267 A124 30h bl, lt grn & yel 7.50 3.00
a. Souv. sheet of 1, imperf. 600.00
Never hinged 1,000.
Nos. 265-267 (3) 15.00 7.00
Set, never hinged 35.00

Issued for Christmas and the New Year.

Redrawn Types of 1954-57
Wmk. 317

1957-59 **Litho.** ***Perf. 12½***

268 A119 2h aqua .30 *.45*
269 A88a 4h aqua .45 .45
270 A88a 5h emerald ('58) .45 .45
271 A120 10h green .55 .45
272 A95 15h violet ('58) 2.25 2.25
273 A110 20h lilac rose .75 .35
274 A121 30h pale lilac ('58) .85 .35
275 A111 40h red lilac .85 .35
276 A95 50h lake ('58) 4.00 .80
277 A122 55h vio brn ('59) 1.25 .85
278 A112 100h violet 1.50 .45
279 A89 200h brn car ('59) 1.75 .45
280 A92a 400h brt vio ('59) 40.00 3.50
281 A90 500h ocher ('58) 35.00 3.50
282 A90 1000h dk ol bis ('58) 60.00 8.50
Nos. 268-282 (15) 149.95 23.15
Set, never hinged 375.00

Nos. 268-282 have no hwan symbol, and final character of inscription is the redrawn one illustrated above No. 212D.

See No. 291B.

Catalogue values for unused stamps in this section, from this point to the end of the section, are for Never Hinged items.

Winged Envelope — A125

1958, May 20 **Wmk. 317**

283 A125 40h dk blue & red 2.00 .75
a. Souv. sheet of 1, imperf. *1,900.*

Issued for the Second Postal Week.

Children Looking at Industrial Growth A126

Design: 40h, Hibiscus forming "10".

1958, Aug. 15 ***Perf. 13½***

284 A126 20h gray 1.60 .65
285 A126 40h dk carmine 2.40 .90
a. Souv. sheet of 2, # 284-285, imperf. 550.00

10th anniversary of Republic of Korea.

UNESCO Building, Paris A127

1958, Nov. 3 **Wmk. 317**

286 A127 40h orange & green 1.25 .60
a. Souv. sheet of 1, imperf. 210.00

Opening of UNESCO. headquarters in Paris, Nov. 3.

Children Flying Kites — A128

Christmas Tree and Fortune Screen — A129

Children in Costume — A130

1958, Dec. 11 Litho. *Perf. 12½*

287 A128 15h yellow green 2.00 .75
 a. Souv. sheet of 1, imperf. 75.00
288 A129 25h blue, red & yel 2.00 .75
 a. Souv. sheet of 1, imperf. 75.00
289 A130 30h yellow, ultra & red 3.50 1.25
 a. Souv. sheet of 1, imperf. 75.00
 Nos. 287-289 (3) 7.50 2.75
 Nos. 287a-289a (3) 225.00

Issued for Christmas and the New Year.

Flag and Pagoda Park A131

1959, Mar. 1 *Perf. 13½*

290 A131 40h rose lilac & brn 1.25 .60
 a. Souv. sheet of 1, imperf. 125.00 125.00

40th anniv. of Independence Movement Day.

Korean Marines Landing A132

1959, Apr. 15

291 A132 40h olive grn 1.25 .60
 a. Souv. sheet of 1, imperf. 12.50 12.50

Korean Marine Corps, 10th anniversary.

Types of 1956-57
Souvenir Sheet
Wmk. 317

1959, May 20 Litho. *Imperf.*

291B Sheet of 4 10.00 *12.00*
 c. A120 10h green 1.40 1.00
 d. A110 20h lilac rose 1.40 1.00
 e. A121 30h pale lilac 1.40 1.00
 f. A111 40h red lilac 1.40 1.00

3rd Postal Week, May 20-26.

WHO Emblem and Family A133

1959, Aug. 17 Wmk. 317 *Perf. 13½*

292 A133 40h pink & rose vio 1.25 .65
 a. Souv. sheet of 1, imperf. 12.50 12.50

10th anniv. of Korea's joining the WHO.

Diesel Train A134

1959, Sept. 18 Litho.

293 A134 40h brown & bister 2.00 1.00
 a. Souv. sheet of 1, imperf. 32.50 32.50

60th anniversary of Korean railroads.

Relay Race and Emblem A135

1959, Oct. 3

294 A135 40h lt bl & red brn 1.50 .70
 a. Souv. sheet of 1, imperf. 15.00 15.00

40th National Athletic Meet.

Red Cross and Korea Map A136

55h, Red Cross superimposed on globe.

1959, Oct. 27 *Perf. 13½*

295 A136 40h red & bl grn 1.00 .50
296 A136 55h pale lilac & red 1.50 .50
 a. Souv. sheet of 2, #295-296, imperf. 35.00 35.00

Centenary of the Red Cross idea.

Old Postal Flag and New Communications Flag — A137

1959, Dec. 4

297 A137 40h blue & red 1.25 .60
 a. Souv. sheet of 1, imperf. 20.00 20.00

75th anniv. of the Korean postal system.

Mice and Chinese Happy New Year Character — A138

Designs: 25h, Children singing Christmas hymns. 30h, Red-crested crane.

1959, Dec. 15 *Perf. 12½*

298 A138 15h gray, vio bl & pink 1.25 .35
 a. Souv. sheet of 1, imperf. 30.00
299 A138 25h blue, red & emer 1.25 .40
 a. Souv. sheet of 1, imperf. 30.00 30.00
300 A138 30h lt lilac, blk & red 2.50 .60
 a. Souv. sheet of 1, imperf. 30.00 30.00
 Nos. 298-300 (3) 5.00 1.35
 Nos. 298a-300a (3) 90.00

Issued for Christmas and the New Year.

UPU Monument and Means of Transportation — A139

Wmk. 317

1960, Jan. 1 Litho. *Perf. 13½*

301 A139 40h grnsh bl & brn 1.50 .75
 a. Souv. sheet of 1, imperf. 25.00 25.00

60th anniv. of Korean membership in the UPU.

Bee, Honeycomb and Clover — A140

Snail and Money Bag — A141

1960, Apr. 1 Wmk. 317 *Perf. 12½*

302 A140 10h emer, brn & org 1.25 .75
303 A141 20h pink, bl & brn 1.50 .75

Issued to encourage systematic saving by children. See No. 313, souvenir sheet. See Nos. 377-380.

Uprooted Oak Emblem and Yin Yang — A142

1960, Apr. 7 Wmk. 312 *Perf. 13½*

304 A142 40h emer, car & ultra 1.25 .60
 a. Souv. sheet of 1, imperf. 50.00 50.00

Issued to publicize World Refugee Year, July 1, 1959-June 30, 1960.

Dwight D. Eisenhower A143

1960, June 19 Litho. Wmk. 317

305 A143 40h bl, red & bluish grn 4.00 2.00
 a. Souv. sheet of 1, imperf. 35.00 35.00

Pres. Eisenhower's visit to Korea, June 19.

Children in School and Ancient Home Teaching A144

1960, Aug. 3 Wmk. 317 *Perf. 13½*

306 A144 40h multicolored 1.25 .50
 a. Souv. sheet of 1, imperf. 7.50 7.50

75th anniv. of the modern educational system.

Hibiscus and House of Councilors A145

1960, Aug. 8

307 A145 40h blue 1.25 .50
 a. Souv. sheet of 1, imperf. 7.50 7.50

Inaugural session, House of Councilors.

Woman Holding Torch and Man with Flag — A146

1960, Aug. 15

308 A146 40h bis, lt bl & brn 1.25 .60
 a. Souv. sheet of 1, imperf. 7.50 7.50

15th anniversary of liberation.

Weight Lifter A147

40h, South Gate, Seoul, & Olympic emblem.

1960, Aug. 25 Litho.

309 A147 20h brn, lt bl & sal 1.50 .75
310 A147 40h brn, lt bl & dk bl 1.50 .75
 a. Souv. sheet of 2, #309-310, imperf. 25.00 25.00

17th Olympic Games, Rome, 8/25-9/11.

Swallow and Telegraph Pole — A148

1960, Sept. 28 *Perf. 13½*

311 A148 40h lt bl, lil & gray 1.50 .75
 a. Souv. sheet of 1, imperf. 7.50 7.50

Establishment of telegraph service, 75th anniv.

Students and Sprout A149

1960, Oct. 1 Wmk. 317

312 A149 40h bl, sal pink & emer 1.25 .50
 a. Souv. sheet of 1, imperf. 6.50 6.50

Rebirth of the Republic.

Savings Types of 1960
Souvenir Sheet

1960, Oct. 7 *Imperf.*

313 Sheet of two 4.50 4.50
 a. A140 10h emer, brn & org 2.00 2.00
 b. A141 20h pink, blue & brown 2.00 2.00

4th Postal Week, Oct. 7-13, and Intl. Letter Writing Week, Oct. 3-9.

Torch — A150

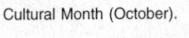

1960, Oct. 15 *Perf. 13½*

314 A150 40h dk bl, lt bl & yel 1.25 .50
 a. Souv. sheet of 1, imperf. 6.50

Cultural Month (October).

UN Flag, Globe and Laurel — A151

1960, Oct. 24 Litho.

315 A151 40h rose lil, bl & grn 1.25 .50
 a. Souv. sheet of 1, imperf. 6.50

15th anniversary of United Nations.

UN Emblem and Grave Markers — A152

1960, Nov. 1 Wmk. 317

316 A152 40h salmon & brn 1.25 .50
 a. Souv. sheet of 1, imperf. 6.50

Establishment of the UN Memorial Cemetery, Tanggok, Pusan, Korea.

"Housing, Agriculture, Population" — A153

1960, Nov. 15 *Perf. 13½*

317 A153 40h multicolored 1.25 .50
 a. Souv. sheet of 1, imperf. 6.50

Issued to publicize the 1960 census.

Boy and Head of Ox — A154

Star of Bethlehem and Korean Sock — A155

Girl Giving New Year's Greeting — A156

1960, Dec. 15 Litho. *Perf. 12½*

318 A154 15h gray, brn & org yel 1.75 .40
 a. Souv. sheet of 1, imperf. 10.00 10.00
319 A155 25h vio bl, red & grn 2.25 .40
 a. Souv. sheet of 1, imperf. 10.00 10.00
320 A156 30h red, vio bl & yel 3.00 .75
 a. Souv. sheet of 1, imperf. 10.00 10.00
 Nos. 318-320 (3) 7.00 1.55
 Nos. 318a-320a (3) 30.00

Issued for Christmas and the New Year.

UN Emblem, Windsock and Ancient Rain Gauge A157

1961, Mar. 23 *Perf. 13½*

321 A157 40h lt blue & ultra 1.25 .50
 a. Souv. sheet of 1, imperf. 4.00 4.00

1st World Meteorological Day.

Children, Globe and UN Emblem A158

1961, Apr. 7 Wmk. 317

322 A158 40h salmon & brown 1.25 .50
 a. Souv. sheet of 1, imperf. 4.00 4.00

10th World Health Day.

Students Demonstrating — A159

1961, Apr. 19 Litho.

323 A159 40h red, grn & ultra 1.50 .60
 a. Souv. sheet of 1, imperf. 10.00 10.00

1st anniv. of the Korean April revolution.

Workers — A160

1961, May 6

324 A160 40h brt green 1.25 .60
 a. Souv. sheet of 1, imperf. 6.00 6.00

International Conference on Community Development, Seoul.

Girl Scout A161

1961, May 10

325 A161 40h brt green 1.25 .60
 a. Souv. sheet of 1, imperf. 12.50 12.50

15th anniversary of Korea's Girl Scouts.

Soldier's Grave — A162

Wmk. 317

1961, June 6 Litho. *Perf. 13½*

326 A162 40h blk & ol gray 2.50 1.25
 a. Souv. sheet of 1, imperf. 10.00 10.00

6th National Mourning Day.

Soldier with Torch — A163

1961, June 16

327 A163 40h brown & yellow 2.50 1.25
 a. Souv. sheet of 1, imperf. 10.00 10.00

Military Revolution of May 16, 1961.

Map of Korea, Torch and Broken Chain — A164

1961, Aug. 15 Wmk. 317 *Perf. 13½*

328 A164 40h dk bl, ver & aqua 2.50 1.25
 a. Souv. sheet of 1, imperf. 5.00 5.00

16th anniv. of liberation.

Flag and Servicemen — A165

1961, Oct. 1 Litho.

329 A165 40h vio bl, red & brn 3.00 1.25
 a. Souv. sheet of 1, imperf. 5.00 5.00

Issued for Armed Forces Day.

Kyongbok Palace Art Museum — A166

1961, Nov. 1 Wmk. 317 *Perf. 13½*

330 A166 40h beige & dk brn 1.50 .60
 a. Souv. sheet of 1, imperf. 4.00 4.00

10th Natl. Exhibition of Fine Arts.

"UNESCO," Candle and Laurel — A167

1961, Nov. 4

331 A167 40h lt grn & dk bl 1.50 .60
 a. Souv. sheet of 1, imperf. 4.00 4.00

15th anniv. of UNESCO.

Mobile X-Ray Unit A168

1961, Nov. 16

332 A168 40h rose beige & red brn 1.25 .60
 a. Souv. sheet of 1, imperf. 4.00 4.00

Tuberculosis Prevention Week.

Ginseng — A169

King Sejong and Hangul Alphabet — A170

Tristram's Woodpecker A171

Rice Farmer A172

Ancient Drums — A173

1961-62 Unwmk. Litho. *Perf. 12½*

338 A169 20h rose brn ('62) 1.90 .60
339 A170 30h pale purple 5.25 .60
340 A171 40h dk blue & red 4.50 .60
341 A172 40h dk green ('62) 7.75 .75
342 A173 100h red brown 10.50 1.50
 Nos. 338-342 (5) 29.90 4.05

See #363-366, 368, 388-392, 517-519, B5-B7.

Globe with Map of Korea and ITU Emblem A175

1962, Jan. 31 Unwmk. *Perf. 13½*

348 A175 40h ver & dk blue 1.75 1.00
 a. Souv. sheet of 1, imperf. 12.00 12.00

10th anniv. of Korea's joining the ITU.

Atomic Reactor and Atom Symbol A176

1962, Mar. 30 Litho. *Perf. 13½*

349 A176 40h lt bl, sl grn & ol gray 1.75 .50

Inauguration of the Triga Mark II atomic reactor.

Malaria Eradication Emblem and Mosquito — A177

1962, Apr. 7 Unwmk.

350 A177 40h green & red org 1.25 .75
 a. Souv. sheet of 1, imperf. 3.50 3.50

WHO drive to eradicate malaria.

YWCA Emblem and Girl A178

1962, Apr. 20 *Perf. 13½*

351 A178 40h pink & dk blue 3.25 .60

40th anniv. of the Korean Young Women's Christian Association.

South Gate and FPA Emblem A179

1962, May 12 **Wmk. 317**

352 A179 40h lt bl, dk vio & red 3.00 .75

Meeting of the Federation of Motion Picture Producers in Asia, May 12-16.

Men Pushing Cogwheel A180

Soldiers on Hang Kang Bridge — A181

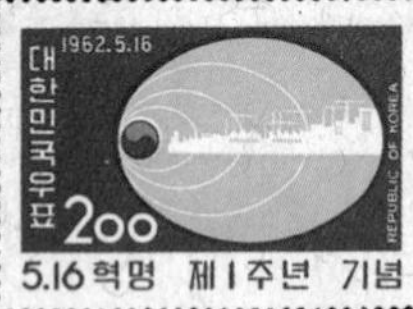
Yin Yang and Factory A182

Wmk. 317

1962, May 16 **Litho.** *Perf. 13½*

353 A180 30h brn & pale olive 3.00 1.00
a. Souv. sheet of 1, Korean text 20.00 20.00
b. Souv. sheet of 1, English text 35.00 35.00
354 A181 40h brn, lt bl & citron 3.00 1.00
a. Souv. sheet of 1, Korean text 20.00 20.00
b. Souv. sheet of 1, English text 35.00 35.00
355 A182 200h ultra, yel & red 22.50 9.00
a. Souv. sheet of 1, Korean text 35.00 35.00
b. Souv. sheet of 1, English text 75.00 75.00
Nos. 353-355 (3) 28.50 11.00

1st anniv. of the May 16th Revolution.
The souvenir sheets are imperf.
The sheets with English text also exist with "E" in "POSTAGE" omitted. The English-text sheets are not watermarked except those with "E" omitted. Value, each $75.

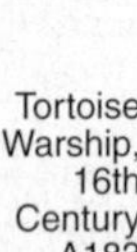

Tortoise Warship, 16th Century A183

Design: 4w, Tortoise ship, heading right.

1962, Aug. 14 **Unwmk.** *Perf. 13½*

356 A183 2w dk bl & pale bl 10.00 1.50
357 A183 4w blk, bluish grn & lil 15.00 2.50

370th anniv. of Korea's victory in the naval battle with the Japanese off Hansan Island.

Flag, Scout Emblem and Tents — A184

Wmk. 312

1962, Oct. 5 **Litho.** *Perf. 13½*

358 A184 4w brown, bl & red 1.90 .75
a. Souv. sheet of 1, imperf., unwmkd. 7.00 7.00

Wmk. 317

359 A184 4w green, bl & red 1.90 .75
a. Souv. sheet of 1, imperf., unwmkd. 7.00 7.00

40th anniv. of Korean Boy Scouts.

Types of 1961-62 and

Hanabusaya Asiatica — A185

Miruk Bosal — A186

Long-horned Beetle — A186a

Symbols of Thrift and Development A186b

Meesun Blossoms and Fruit A186c

Library of Early Buddhist Scriptures A186d

Sika Deer A186e

King Songdok Bell, 8th Cent. — A186f

Bodhisattva in Cavern Temple, Silla Dynasty — A187

Tile of Silla Dynasty — A187a

Designs: 20ch, Jin-Do dog. 1w, Folk dancers. 1.50w, Miruk Bosal. 2w, Ginseng. 3w, King Sejong. 4w, Rice farmer. 5w, Dragon waterpot. 10w, Ancient drums. 500w, Blue dragon fresco, Koguryo dynasty.

1962-63 **Unwmk.** **Litho.** *Perf. 12½*

Ordinary Paper

Size: 22x25mm, 25x22mm

360 A186 20ch gldn brown 1.40 .40
361 A185 40ch blue 1.40 .40
362 A186 50ch claret brn 1.40 .40
363 A169 1w brt blue ('63) 2.75 .40
364 A169 2w red brown 4.25 .40
365 A170 3w violet brown 4.50 .40
366 A172 4w green 5.00 .40
367 A186 5w grnsh blue 5.50 .90
368 A173 10w red brown 85.00 4.00
369 A186c 20w lil rose ('63) 15.00 2.00
370 A186d 40w dl pur ('63) 125.00 5.00
Nos. 360-370 (11) 251.20 14.70

1964-66

Granite Paper

360a A186 20ch org brn .90 .25
361a A185 40ch blue .95 .25
362a A186 50ch claret brn .95 .25
362B A186a 60ch black ('66) .90 .30
363a A169 1w bright blue 3.00 .25
363B A186 1.50w dk sl grn ('66) .70 .30
364a A169 2w red brown 4.50 .40
365a A170 3w vio brown 13.00 .30
366a A172 4w green 5.75 .30
367a A186 5w grnsh blue 30.00 1.50
367B A186b 7w lilac rose ('66) 2.50 .75
368a A173 10w red brown 5.00 .40
369a A186c 20w lilac rose 10.00 1.50
370a A186d 40w vio brown 50.00 2.25
371 A186e 50w red brn 62.50 1.50
372 A186f 100w slate grn 100.00 3.00
373 A187 200w dk & lt grn ('65) 25.00 3.00
374 A187a 300w sl grn & buff ('65) 50.00 4.00
374A A187a 500w dk & lt bl ('65) 25.00 4.00
Nos. 360a-374A (19) 390.65 24.50

The paper of Nos. 360a to 374A contains a few colored fibers; the paper of Nos. 385-396 contains many fibers.
Postal counterfeits exist of Nos. 369a, 370a, 371 and 372.
See Nos. 385-396, 516, 521-522, 582-584, 1076-1079, B8.

Map, Mackerel and Trawler A188

1962, Oct. 10 *Perf. 13½*

375 A188 4w dk bl & grnsh bl 3.50 .75

10th anniv. of the Pacific Fishery Council.

ICAO Emblem and Plane A189

1962, Dec. 11 *Perf. 13½*

376 A189 4w blue & brown 1.75 .75
a. Souv. sheet of 1, imperf. 9.50 9.50

10th anniv. of Korea's joining the ICAO.

Savings Types of 1960

1962-64 **Unwmk.** *Perf. 12½*

377 A140 1w emer, brn & org ('63) 5.50 1.25
a. Granite paper 20.00 9.00
378 A141 2w pink, bl & brn 9.50 1.50
a. Granite paper 12.50 2.50

Wmk. 317

379 A140 1w emer, brn & org ('64) 30.00 10.00
380 A141 2w pink, bl & brn ('64) 12.50 1.75
Nos. 377-380 (4) 57.50 14.50

Wheat Emblem A190

Wmk. 317

1963, Mar. 21 **Litho.** *Perf. 13½*

381 A190 4w emer, dk bl & ocher 1.50 .75
a. Souv. sheet of 1, imperf. 4.25 4.25

FAO "Freedom from Hunger" campaign.

Globe and Letters A191

1963, Apr. 1

382 A191 4w rose lil, ol & dk bl 1.75 .60
a. Souv. sheet of 1, imperf. 4.00 4.00

1st anniv. of the formation of the Asian-Oceanic Postal Union, AOPU.

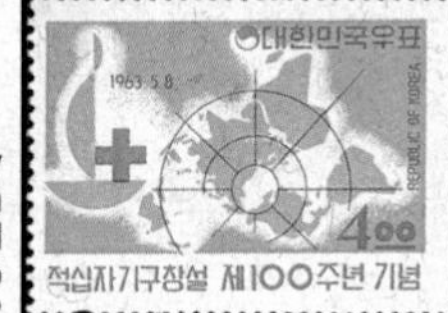
Centenary Emblem and World Map A192

1963, May 8 **Litho.**

383 A192 4w org, red & gray 1.25 .60
384 A192 4w lt bl, red & gray 1.25 .60
a. Souv. sheet of 2, #383-384, imperf. 10.00 10.00

Cent. of the Intl. Red Cross.

Types of 1961-63

Designs as before.

1963-64 **Wmk. 317** *Perf. 12½*

Granite Paper

Size: 22x25mm, 25x22mm

385 A186 20ch gldn brn ('64) .85 .25
386 A185 40ch blue .85 .25
387 A186 50ch cl brn ('64) .85 .25
388 A169 1w brt blue 3.00 .35
389 A169 2w red brown 4.50 .40
390 A170 3w vio brown 13.00 .35
391 A172 4w green 6.00 .60
392 A173 10w red brown 5.00 .60
393 A186c 20w lil rose ('64) 10.00 1.75
394 A186d 40w dull purple 50.00 2.50
395 A186e 50w brown 62.50 2.00
396 A186f 100w slate grn 100.00 4.00
Nos. 385-396 (12) 256.55 13.30

Hibiscus and "15" A193

1963, Aug. 15 **Wmk. 317** *Perf. 13½*

398 A193 4w vio bl, pale bl & red 2.50 1.25

15th anniversary of the Republic.

Army Nurse and Corps Emblem A194

1963, Aug. 26 **Litho.**

399	A194	4w citron, grn & blk	2.00	.85

Army Nurses Corps, 15th anniversary.

First Five-Year Plan Issue

Transformer and Power Transmission Tower A195

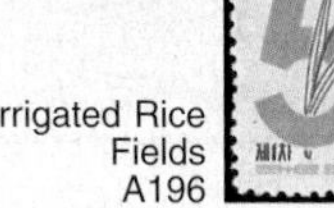
Irrigated Rice Fields A196

#402, Cement factory. #403, Coal Miner. #404, Oil refinery. #405, Fishing industry (ships). #406, Cargo ship and cargo. #407, Fertilizer plant and grain. #408, Radar and telephone. #409, Transportation (plane, train, ship and map).

1962-66 **Unwmk.** ***Perf. 12½***

400	A195	4w org & dk vio	15.00	1.50
401	A196	4w lt bl & vio bl	15.00	1.50
		Wmk. 317		
402	A195	4w dk bl & gray	5.00	1.25
403	A196	4w buff & brn	5.00	1.25
404	A195	4w yel & ultra	2.00	1.00
405	A196	4w lt bl & blk	2.00	1.00
		Unwmk.		
406	A195	4w pale pink & vio bl	2.00	1.00
407	A196	4w bis brn & blk	2.00	1.00
408	A195	7w yel bis & blk	3.75	1.00
409	A196	7w vio bl & lt bl	3.75	1.00
		Nos. 400-409 (10)	55.50	11.50

Economic Development Five-Year Plan.
Issued: #400-401, 12/28/62; #402-403, 9/1/63; #404-405, 6/15/64; #406-407, 6/1/65; #408-409, 6/1/66.

Ramses Temple, Abu Simbel — A197

Wmk. 317

1963, Oct. 1 **Litho.** ***Perf. 13½***

410		3w gray & ol gray	5.00	2.00
411		4w gray & ol gray	5.00	2.00
a.		Souv. sheet of 2, #410-411, imperf.	10.00	10.00
b.		A197 Pair, #410-411	12.00	10.00

UNESCO world campaign to save historic monuments in Nubia.

Rugby and Torch Bearer A199

1963, Oct. 4 **Wmk. 317** ***Perf. 13½***

412	A199	4w pale bl, red brn & dk grn	3.25	1.00

44th National Athletic Games.

Nurse & Mobile X-Ray Unit — A200

1963, Nov. 6 ***Perf. 13½***

413	A200	4w org & bluish blk	2.00	.75

10h anniv. of the Korean Natl. Tuberculosis Association.

Eleanor Roosevelt A201

1963, Dec. 10 **Litho.** **Wmk. 317**

Design: 4w, Hands holding torch and globe.

414	A201	3w lt red brn & dk bl	1.25	.50
415	A201	4w dl org, ol & dk bl	1.75	.75
a.		Souv. sheet of 2, 414-415, imperf.	6.00	6.00

Eleanor Roosevelt; 15th anniv. of the Universary Declaration of Human Rights.

Korean Flag and UN Headquarters A202

1963, Dec. 12 **Wmk. 317** ***Perf. 13½***

416	A202	4w grnsh bl, ol & blk	1.25	.50
a.		Souv. sheet of 1, imperf.	4.50	4.50

15th anniv. of Korea's recognition by the UN.

Tang-piri (Recorder) A203

Musical Instruments: No. 418, Pyen-kyeng (chimes). No. 419, Chang-ko (drums). No. 420, Tai-keum (large flute). No. 421, Taipyeng-so (Chinese oboe). No. 422, Na-bal (brass trumpet). No. 423, Hyang-pipa (Chinese short lute). No. 424, Wul-keum (banjo). No. 425, Kaya-ko (zither), horiz. No. 426, Wa-kong-hu (harp), horiz.

1963, Dec. 17 **Unwmk.**

417	A203	4w pink, blk & car	4.75	.75
418	A203	4w bl, bl grn & blk	4.75	.75
419	A203	4w rose, vio bl & brn	4.75	.75
420	A203	4w tan, dk grn & brn	4.75	.75
421	A203	4w yel, vio bl & brn	4.75	.75
422	A203	4w gray, brn & vio	4.75	.75
423	A203	4w pink, vio bl & red brn	4.75	.75
424	A203	4w grnsh bl, blk & bl	4.75	.75
425	A203	4w rose, red brn & blk	4.75	.75
426	A203	4w lil, blk & bl	4.75	.75
		Nos. 417-426 (10)	47.50	7.50

Pres. Park and Capitol A204

1963, Dec. 17 **Wmk. 317**

427	A204	4w black & brt grn	47.50	12.50

Inauguration of Pres. Park Chung Hee.

Symbols of Metric System A205

1964, Jan. 1 **Litho.**

428	A205	4w multicolored	1.25	.50
a.		Imperf., pair	75.00	

Introduction of the metric system.

UNESCO Emblem and Yin Yang — A206

1964, Jan. 30 **Wmk. 317** ***Perf. 13½***

429	A206	4w red, lt bl & ultra	1.50	.75

Korean Natl. Commission for UNESCO, 10th anniv.

Industrial Census A207

1964, Mar. 23 **Wmk. 317** ***Perf. 13½***

430	A207	4w gray, blk & red brn	1.50	.75

National Mining and Industrial Census.

YMCA Emblem and Head A208

1964, Apr. 12 **Litho.**

431	A208	4w ap grn, dk bl & red	1.25	.50

50th anniv. of the Korean YMCA.

Unisphere, Ginseng and Cargo Ship — A209

Design: 100w, Korean pavilion and globe.

1964, Apr. 22 **Wmk. 317** ***Perf. 13½***

432	A209	40w buff, red brn & grn	6.00	1.00
433	A209	100w bl red brn & ultra	20.00	5.00
a.		Souv. sheet of 2, imperf.	47.50	47.50

New York World's Fair, 1964-65.

Secret Garden, Changdok Palace, Seoul A210

Views: 2w, Whahong Gate, Suwon. 3w, Uisang Pavilion, Yangyang-gun. 4w, Maitreya Buddha, Bopju Temple at Mt. Songni. 5w, Paekma River and Rock of Falling Flowers. 6w, Anab Pond, Kyongju. 7w, Choksok Pavilion, Chinju. 8w, Kwanghan Pavilion. 9w, Whaom Temple, Mt. Chiri. 10w, Chonjeyon Falls, Soguipo.

1964, May 25 **Wmk. 317** ***Perf. 13½***
Light Blue Background

434	A210	1w green	1.10	.50
435	A210	2w gray	1.10	.50
436	A210	3w dk green	1.10	.50
437	A210	4w emerald	2.25	1.00
438	A210	5w violet	4.00	1.50
439	A210	6w vio blue	5.25	2.00
a.		Souv. sheet of 2 (5w, 6w)	17.50	17.50
440	A210	7w dk brown	7.50	2.50
a.		Souv. sheet of 2 (4w, 7w)	17.50	17.50
441	A210	8w brown	8.00	2.50
a.		Souv. sheet of 2 (3w, 8w)	17.50	17.50
442	A210	9w lt violet	8.00	2.50
a.		Souv. sheet of 2 (2w, 9w)	17.50	17.50
443	A210	10w slate grn	11.00	3.00
a.		Souv. sheet of 2 (1w, 10w)	17.50	17.50
		Nos. 434-443 (10)	49.30	16.50
		Nos. 439a-443a (5)	87.50	

The five souvenir sheets are imperf.

Globe and Wheel A211

1964, July 1 **Litho.** ***Perf. 13½***

444	A211	4w lt ol grn, dl brn & ocher	1.25	.60
a.		Souv. sheet of 1, imperf.	4.00	4.00

Colombo Plan for co-operative economic development of south and southeast Asia.

Hands and World Health Organization Emblem — A212

1964, Aug. 17 **Wmk. 317** ***Perf. 13½***

445	A212	4w brt yel grn, yel grn & blk	1.25	.60
a.		Souv. sheet of 1, imperf.	4.00	4.00

15th anniv. of Korea's joining the UN.

Runner A213

1964, Sept. 3

446	A213	4w red lil, grn & pink	3.50	1.25

45th Natl. Athletic Meet, Inchon, Sept. 3-8.

UPU Monument, Bern — A214

1964, Sept. 15

447 A214 4w pink, red brn & bl 1.25 .60
a. Souv. sheet of 1, imperf. 4.00 4.00

1st Intl. Cong. for establishing the UPU, 90th anniv.

Crane Hook and Emblem — A215

1964, Sept. 29 Wmk. 317 *Perf. 13½*

448 A215 4w red brn & dull grn 1.25 .60

5th Convention of the Intl. Federation of Asian and Western Pacific Contractors' Assoc. (IFAWPCA), Seoul, Sept. 29-Oct. 7.

Marathon Runners A216

#453, "V," Olympic rings, laurel & track, vert.

1964, Oct. 10 Litho.

449 A216 4w shown 2.50 .90
450 A216 4w Equestrian 2.50 .90
451 A216 4w Gymnast 2.50 .90
452 A216 4w Rowing 2.50 .90
453 A216 4w multicolored 2.50 .90
Nos. 449-453 (5) 12.50 4.50

18th Olympic Games, Tokyo, Oct. 10-25.

Souvenir Sheets of 1, Imperf., Unwmk.

449a A216 4w 3.50 3.50
450a A216 4w 3.50 3.50
451a A216 4w 3.50 3.50
452a A216 4w 3.50 3.50
453a A216 4w 3.50 3.50
Nos. 449a-453a (5) 17.50 17.50

Stamp of 1885 — A217

Yong Sik Hong — A218

1964, Dec. 4 Unwmk. *Perf. 13½*

454 A217 3w lilac, vio & dl bl grn 3.00 1.00
455 A218 4w gray, vio bl & blk 5.00 1.25

80th anniv. of the Korean postal system. Hong Yong-Sik (1855-84) was Korea's 1st general postmaster.

Pine Branch and Cones — A219

#457, Plum Blossoms. #458, Forsythia. #459, Azalea. #460, Lilac. #461, Sweetbrier. #462, Garden balsam. #463, Hibiscus. #464, Crape myrtle. #465, Chrysanthemum lucidum. #466, Paulownia coreana. #467, Bamboo.

1965 Litho. *Perf. 13½*

456 A219 4w pale grn, dp grn & brn 2.00 .75
457 A219 4w gray, blk, rose & yel 2.00 .75
458 A219 4w lt bl, yel & brn 2.00 .75
459 A219 4w brt grn, lil rose & sal 2.00 .75
460 A219 4w red lil & brt grn 2.00 .75
461 A219 4w yel grn, grn, car & brn 2.00 .75
462 A219 4w bl, grn & red 2.00 .75
463 A219 4w bluish gray, rose red & grn 2.00 .75
464 A219 4w multicolored 2.00 .75
465 A219 4w pale grn, dk brn, grn & car rose 2.00 .75
466 A219 4w buff, ol grn & brn 2.00 .75
467 A219 4w ultra & emer 2.00 .75
Nos. 456-467 (12) 24.00 9.00

Souvenir Sheets of 1, Imperf.

456a A219 4w 3.00 3.00
457a A219 4w 3.00 3.00
458a A219 4w 3.00 3.00
459a A219 4w 3.00 3.00
460a A219 4w 3.00 3.00
461a A219 4w 3.00 3.00
462a A219 4w 3.00 3.00
463a A219 4w 3.00 3.00
464a A219 4w 3.00 3.00
465a A219 4w 3.00 3.00
466a A219 4w 3.00 3.00
467a A219 4w 3.00 3.00
Nos. 456a-467a (12) 36.00

Dancing Women, PATA Emblem and Tabo Tower A220

1965, Mar. 26

468 A220 4w lt bl grn, dk brn & dk vio bl 1.00 .50
a. Souv. sheet of 1, imperf. 3.00 3.00

14th conf. of the Pacific Travel Association, Seoul, Mar. 26-Apr. 2.

Map of Viet Nam and Flag of Korean Assistance Group — A221

1965, Apr. 20 *Perf. 13½*

469 A221 4w blk, lt yel grn & grnsh bl 1.25 .50
a. Souv. sheet of 1, imperf. 3.50 3.50

Issued to honor the Korean military assistance group in Viet Nam.

Symbols of 7-Year Plan — A222

1965, May 1 Litho.

470 A222 4w emer, dk grn & dk brn 1.25 .50

Issued to publicize the 7-year plan for increased food production.

Scales with Families and Homes A223

1965, May 8

471 A223 4w lt & dk grn & gray 1.25 .50
a. Souv. sheet of 1, imperf. 3.00 3.00

May as Month of Family Planning.

ITU Emblem, Old and New Communication Equipment — A224

1965, May 17

472 A224 4w lt bl, car & blk 1.25 .50
a. Souv. sheet of 1, imperf. 3.00 3.00

Cent. of the ITU.

UN Emblem and Flags of Australia, Belgium, Great Britain, Canada and Colombia A225

Gen. Douglas MacArthur and Flags of Korea, UN and US A226

UN Emblem and Flags: No. 474, Denmark, Ethiopia, France, Greece and India. No. 475, Italy, Luxembourg, Netherlands, New Zealand and Norway. No. 476, Philippines, Sweden, Thailand, Turkey and South Africa.

1965, June 25

Flags in Original Colors

473 A225 4w gray & vio bl 1.25 .75
474 A225 4w grnsh bl & vio bl 1.25 .75
475 A225 4w grnsh bl & vio bl 1.25 .75
476 A225 4w grnsh bl & vio bl 1.25 .75
477 A226 10w lt bl, blk, vio bl & red 4.00 1.50
Nos. 473-477 (5) 9.00 4.50

15th anniv. of the participation of UN Forces in the Korean war.

Souvenir Sheets of 1, Imperf.

473a A225 4w 1.75 1.75
474a A225 4w 1.75 1.75
475a A225 4w 1.75 1.75
476a A225 4w 1.75 1.75
477a A226 10w 3.00 3.00
Nos. 473a-477a (5) 10.00 10.00

Flag, Factories and "20" — A227

South Gate, Seoul, Fireworks and Yin Yang — A228

1965, Aug. 15 Litho.

478 A227 4w lt bl, vio bl & red 2.25 .60
479 A228 10w vio bl, lt bl & red 2.75 .80

20th anniv. of liberation from the Japanese.

Factory, Leaf and Ants — A229

1965, Sept. 20 *Perf. 13½*

480 A229 4w brt yel grn, brn & bister 1.25 .50

Issued to publicize the importance of saving.

Parabolic Antenna, Telephone Dial and Punched Tape A230

Telegraph Operator, 1885 A231

1965, Sept. 28

481 A230 3w lt bl, blk & ol 2.00 .50
482 A231 10w citron, Prus bl & blk 4.00 .75

80th anniv. of telegraph service between Seoul and Inchon.

Korean Flag and Capitol, Seoul — A232

1965, Sept. 28

483 A232 3w org, slate grn & bl grn 2.50 1.25

15th anniversary of recapture of Seoul.

Pole Vault A233

1965, Oct. 5

484 A233 3w black, lilac & salmon 2.00 1.00

46th Natl. Athletic Meet, Kwangju, Oct. 5-10.

ICY Emblem A234

UN Flag and Headquarters, NY — A235

1965, Oct. 24 **Litho.**

485 A234 3w lt & dk grn & org brn 1.00 .50
a. Souv. sheet of 1, imperf. 3.50 3.50
486 A235 10w lt bl, vio bl & grn 2.00 .75
a. Souv. sheet of 1, imperf. 3.50 3.50

ICY, 1965, and 20th anniv. of the UN.

Child Posting Letter A236

Design: 10w, Airmail envelope, telephone.

1965, Dec. 4 ***Perf. 13½***

487 A236 3w bl grn, blk, grn & red 2.50 1.00
488 A236 10w ol, dk bl & red 5.00 1.75

Tenth Communications Day.

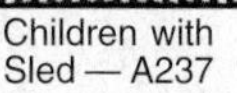

Children with Sled — A237

Children and South Gate — A238

1965, Dec. 11 **Litho.** ***Perf. 12½***

489 A237 3w pale grn, vio bl & red 1.75 .60
490 A238 4w lt bl, grn, vio bl & red 2.75 1.75
a. Souv. sheet of 2, #489-490, imperf. 4.00 4.00

Issued for Christmas and the New Year.

Freedom House A239

1966, Feb. 15 **Unwmk.** ***Perf. 12½***

491 A239 7w brt grn, blk & cit 1.75 .75
492 A239 39w lil, blk & pale grn 10.00 3.00
a. Souv. sheet of 2, #491-492, imperf. 17.50 17.50

Opening of "Freedom House" at Panmunjom.

Wildlife Issue

Mandarin Ducks A240

Alaska Pollack A241

Firefly A242

Badger A243

Birds: 5w, Japanese cranes. 7w, Ring-necked pheasants.

1966, Mar. 15 **Litho.** ***Perf. 12½***

493 A240 3w multicolored 2.00 1.25
494 A240 5w multicolored 2.10 1.25
495 A240 7w multicolored 3.25 1.25

1966, June 15

Fish: 5w, Manchurian trout. 7w, Yellow corvina.

496 A241 3w bl, dk brn & yel 2.50 .90
497 A241 5w grnsh bl, blk & mag 3.00 .90
498 A241 7w brt grnsh bl, blk & yel 4.00 1.00

1966, Sept. 15

Insects: 5w, Grasshopper. 7w, Silk butterfly (sericinus telamon).

499 A242 3w multicolored 2.00 .90
500 A242 5w dp yellow & multi 2.00 .90
501 A242 7w lt blue & multi 2.50 1.00

1966, Dec. 15

Animals: 5w, Asiatic black bear. 7w, Tiger.

502 A243 3w multicolored 2.50 1.00
503 A243 5w multicolored 2.50 1.00
504 A243 7w multicolored 3.25 1.00
Nos. 493-504 (12) 31.60 12.35

Souvenir Sheets of 1, Imperf.

493a	A240	3w	3.00	3.00
494a	A240	5w	3.00	3.00
495a	A240	7w	5.00	5.00
496a	A241	3w	3.00	3.00
497a	A241	5w	3.50	3.50
498a	A241	7w	4.00	4.00
499a	A242	3w	3.00	3.00
500a	A242	5w	3.00	3.00
501a	A242	7w	4.00	4.00
502a	A243	3w	4.00	4.00
503a	A243	5w	4.00	4.00
504a	A243	7w	5.00	5.00
	Nos. 493a-504a (12)		44.50	44.50

Hwansung-gun and Kwangnung Forests — A244

1966, Apr. 5 **Unwmk.** ***Perf. 12½***

505 A244 7w green & brown 1.25 .60

Forestation Movement.

Symbolic Newspaper Printing and Pen — A245

1966, Apr. 7 **Litho.**

506 A245 7w lt bl, vio brn & yel 1.00 .60

Tenth Newspaper Day.

Proper Guidance of Young People — A246

1966, May 1 **Unwmk.** ***Perf. 12½***

507 A246 7w Children & bell 1.00 .60

Opening of WHO Headquarters, Geneva — A247

1966, May 3 **Litho.**

508 A247 7w lt bl, blk & yel 1.25 .60
a. Souv. sheet of 1, imperf. 3.50 3.50
509 A247 39w bluish gray, yel & red 9.75 3.50

Girl Scout and Flag — A248

1966, May 10

510 A248 7w yel, emer & dk bl 2.00 .80

Girl Scouts of Korea, 20th anniversary.

Pres. Park and Flags of Korea, Malaysia, Thailand and Republic of China A249

1966, May 10

511 A249 7w multicolored 7.00 2.50

State visits of President Chung Hee Park.

Women's Ewha University, Seoul, and Student A250

1966, May 31

512 A250 7w lt bl, vio bl & dp org 1.00 .50

80th anniv. of modern education for women.

Types of 1961-66 Inscribed "Republic of Korea," and

Porcelain Incense Burner, 11th-12th Centuries — A253

Celadon Vessel, 12th Century — A254

Unjin Miruk Buddha, Kwanchok Temple — A255

60ch, Long-horned beetle. 1w, Folk dancers. 2w, Ginseng. 3w, King Sejong. 5w, Dragon waterpot. 7w, Symbols of thrift & development.

Perf. 12½

1966, Aug. 20 **Unwmk.** **Litho.**

Size: 22x19mm, 19x22mm

Granite Paper

516 A186a 60ch gray green .40 .20
517 A169 1w green 3.00 4.00
518 A169 2w blue green .50 .20
519 A170 3w dull red brn .50 .20
521 A186 5w gray green 3.50 .70
522 A186b 7w grnsh blue 4.00 .30

Size: 22x25mm

523 A253 13w vio blue 4.00 .75
524 A254 60w green 22.50 1.50
525 A255 80w slate grn 8.50 1.50
Nos. 516-525 (9) 46.90 9.35

Souvenir Sheet

Carrier Pigeons — A258

1966, July 13 **Wmk. 317** ***Imperf.***

Red Brown Surcharge

534 A258 7w on 40h emer & dk grn 3.00 3.00

6th Intl. Letter Writing Week, June 13-19. No. 534 was not issued without surcharge.

Children and World Map Projection A259

1966, July 28 **Unwmk.** ***Perf. 12½***

535 A259 7w lt & dk vio bl & gray 1.25 .50
a. Souv. sheet of 1, imperf. 3.00 3.00

15th annual assembly of WCOTP (World Conf. of Teaching Profession), Seoul, July 28-Aug. 9.

Factory, Money Bag and Honeycomb A260

1966, Sept. 1 **Unwmk.** ***Perf. 12½***

536 A260 7w multicolored 1.00 .50

Issued to publicize systematic saving.

Map of Korea, and People
A261

1966, Sept. 1 **Litho.**
537 A261 7w multicolored 1.00 .50

Ninth national census.

CISM Emblem and Round-Table Conference
A262

1966, Sept. 29 **Unwmk.** ***Perf. 12½***
538 A262 7w multicolored 1.00 .50
a. Souv. sheet of 1, imperf. 3.00 3.00

21st General Assembly of the Intl. Military Sports Council (CISM), Seoul, 9/29-10/9.

Flags of Korea and Viet Nam and Korean Soldiers
A263

1966, Oct. 1
539 A263 7w multicolored 8.00 2.25

1st anniv. of Korean combat troops in Viet Nam.

Wrestlers
A264

1966, Oct. 10
540 A264 7w red brn, buff & blk 2.00 1.00

47th Natl. Athletic Meet, Seoul, Oct. 10-15.

Lions Emblem and Map of Southeast Asia — A265

1966, Oct. 15
541 A265 7w multicolored 1.00 .50
a. Souv. sheet of 1, imperf. 3.00 3.00

5th East and Southeast Asia Lions Convention, Seoul, Oct. 15-17.

Seoul University Emblem
A266

1966, Oct. 15 **Litho.**
542 A266 7w multicolored 1.00 .50

20th anniversary of Seoul University.

Anticommunist League Emblem — A267

1966, Oct. 31 **Unwmk.** ***Perf. 12½***
543 A267 7w multicolored 1.00 .50
a. Souv. sheet of 1, imperf. 3.00 3.00

12th Conf. of the Asian Anticommunist League, Seoul, Oct. 31-Nov. 7.

Presidents Park and Johnson, Flags of US and Korea
A268

1966, Oct. 31 **Litho.** ***Perf. 12½***
544 A268 7w multicolored 2.00 .75
545 A268 83w multicolored 12.00 3.50
a. Souv. sheet of 2, #544-545, imperf. 12.00 12.00

Visit of Pres. Lyndon B. Johnson to Korea.

UNESCO Emblem and Symbols of Learning — A269

1966, Nov. 4
546 A269 7w multicolored 1.00 .40
a. Souvenir sheets 3.00 3.00

20th anniv. of UNESCO.

Good Luck Bag and "Joy"
A270

Ram and "Completion"
A271

1966, Dec. 10 ***Perf. 12½x13, 13x12½***
547 A270 5w multicolored 1.75 .35
a. Souv. sheet of 1, imperf. 3.50 3.50
548 A271 7w multicolored 2.75 .35
a. Souv. sheet of 1, imperf. 3.50 3.50

Issued for Christmas and the New Year.

Syncom Satellite over Globe — A272

1967, Jan. 31 **Litho.** ***Perf. 12½***
549 A272 7w dk blue & multi 1.25 .60
a. Souv. sheet of 1, imperf. 3.50 3.50

15th anniv. of Korea's membership in the ITU.

Presidents Park and Lübke
A273

Perf. 12½

1967, Mar. 2 **Litho.** **Unwmk.**
550 A273 7w multicolored 2.00 1.25
a. Souv. sheet of 1, imperf. 4.00 4.00

Visit of Pres. Heinrich Lübke of Germany, Mar. 2-6.

Hand Holding Coin, Industrial and Private Buildings
A274

1967, Mar. 3
551 A274 7w lt green & blk brn 1.25 .50

1st anniv. of the Natl. Taxation Office.

Folklore Series

Okwangdae Clown — A275

5w, Sandi mask & dance, horiz. 7w, Hafoe mask.

1967, Mar. 15 **Litho.** ***Perf. 12½***
552 A275 4w gray, blk & yel 1.75 .60
553 A275 5w multicolored 1.75 .70
554 A275 7w multicolored 2.50 1.00

Perfect Peace Dance — A276

Designs: 4w, Sword dance, horiz. 7w, Buddhist Monk dance.

1967, June 15
555 A276 4w multicolored 1.75 .60
556 A276 5w multicolored 1.75 .70
557 A276 7w multicolored 2.50 1.00

Girls on Seesaw — A277

Designs: 4w, Girls on swing, horiz. 7w, Girls dancing in the moonlight.

1967, Sept. 15
558 A277 4w multicolored 3.50 .75
559 A277 5w multicolored 3.50 1.00
560 A277 7w multicolored 6.00 1.20

Korean Shuttlecock — A278

Designs: 5w, Girls celebrating full moon, horiz. 7w, Archery.

1967, Dec. 15
561 A278 4w multicolored .75 .20
562 A278 5w multicolored 1.00 .20
563 A278 7w multicolored 1.50 .30
Nos. 552-563 (12) 28.25 8.25

Souvenir Sheets of 1, Imperf.

552a	A275	4w	3.00	3.00
553a	A275	5w	3.00	3.00
554a	A275	7w	4.50	4.50
555a	A276	4w	3.00	3.00
556a	A276	5w	3.00	3.00
557a	A276	7w	4.50	4.50
558a	A277	4w	5.50	5.50
559a	A277	5w	5.50	5.50
560a	A277	7w	7.00	7.00
561a	A278	4w	3.50	3.50
562a	A278	5w	3.50	3.50
563a	A278	7w	4.00	4.00
Nos. 552a-563a (12)			50.00	50.00

JCI Emblem and Kyunghoe Pavilion
A279

1967, Apr. 13 **Litho.** ***Perf. 12½***
564 A279 7w dk brn, brt grn, bl & red 1.25 .40
a. Souv. sheet of 1, imperf. 3.00 3.00

Intl. Junior Chamber of Commerce Conf., Seoul, Apr. 13-16.

Emblem, Map of Far East — A280

1967, Apr. 24 **Unwmk.** ***Perf. 12½***
565 A280 7w vio bl & multi 1.25 .40
a. Souv. sheet of 1, imperf. 3.00 3.00

Issued to publicize the 5th Asian Pacific Dental Congress, Seoul, Apr. 24-28.

EXPO '67 Korean Pavilion
A281

1967, Apr. 28
566 A281 7w yel, blk & red 3.00 .75
567 A281 83w lt bl, blk & red 19.50 5.00
a. Souv. sheet of 2, #566-567, imperf. 16.00 16.00

EXPO '67, Intl. Exhibition, Montreal, Apr. 28-Oct. 27, 1967.

Worker, Soldier, Emblem and Buildings — A282

1967, May 1
568 A282 7w multicolored 1.50 .40

Veterans' Day, May 1.

Second Five-Year Plan Issue

Nut and Arrows
A283

#570, Iron wheel and rail. #571, Express highway. #572, Cloverleaf intersection. #573, Rising income for fishermen and farmers (oysters, silk worm, mushrooms and bull's head). #574, Machine industry (cogwheels, automobile, wrench and motor). #575, Harbor. #576, Housing projects plans. #577, Atomic power plant. #578, Four Great River Valley development.

1967-71 **Litho.** ***Perf. 12½***
569 A283 7w blk, red brn & dl org 6.00 1.00
570 A283 7w dl org, yel & blk 6.00 1.00
571 A283 7w grn, bl & ol 10.00 1.00
572 A283 7w dk brn, yel & grn 7.00 1.00

Perf. 13x12½

573 A283 7w brn, grn, yel & org 1.25 .40
574 A283 7w dk bl, lil rose & buff 1.25 .40
575 A283 10w dk bl, bl, yel & grn 1.25 .40
576 A283 10w lt bl, bl, grn & red 1.25 .40

Photo. Perf. 13

577 A283 10w blk, car & bl 1.25 .40
578 A283 10w blk, grn & brn 1.25 .40
Nos. 569-578 (10) 36.50 6.40

Second Economic Development Five-Year Plan.

Issued: #569-570, 6/1/67; #571-572, 12/5/68; #573-574, 12/5/69; #575-576, 12/5/70; #577-578, 12/5/71.

President Park and Phoenix A284

1967, July 1 Unwmk. Perf. 12½

579 A284 7w multicolored 20.00 3.50
a. Souv. sheet of 1, imperf. 60.00 60.00

Inauguration of President Park Chung Hee for a 2nd term, July 1, 1967.

Korean Boy Scout, Emblem and Tents — A285

20w, Korean Boy Scout emblem, bridge & tents.

1967, Aug. 10 Litho. Perf. 12½

580 A285 7w multicolored 1.00 .60
a. Souv. sheet of 1, imperf. 5.00 5.00
581 A285 20w multicolored 5.00 2.25
a. Souv. sheet of 1, imperf. 5.00 5.00

3rd Korean Boy Scout Jamboree, Hwarangdae, Seoul, Aug. 10-15.

Types of 1962-66 Redrawn (Inscribed "Republic of Korea")

Designs: 20w, Meesun blossoms and fruit. 40w, Library of early Buddhist scriptures. 50w, Deer.

1967, Aug. 25
Granite Paper

582 A186c 20w green & lt bl grn 70.00 1.50
583 A186d 40w dk grn & lt ol 42.50 1.50
584 A186e 50w dk brn & bister 9.00 1.50
Nos. 582-584 (3) 121.50 4.50

The printing of redrawn designs of the regular issue of 1962-66 became necessary upon discovery of large quantities of counterfeits, made to defraud the post. The position of the denominations was changed and elaborate fine background tracings were added.

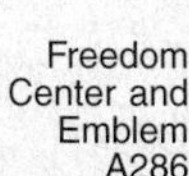

Freedom Center and Emblem A286

Hand Breaking Chain — A287

1967, Sept. 25 Litho. Perf. 12½

586 A286 5w multicolored 1.25 .40
a. Souv. sheet of 1, imperf. 5.00 5.00
587 A287 7w multicolored 1.25 .40
a. Souv. sheet of 1, imperf. 5.00 5.00

1st Conf. of the World Anti-Communist League, WACL, Taipei, China, Sept. 25-29.

Boxing — A288

1967, Oct. 5

Design: 7w, Women's basketball.

588 A288 5w tan & multi 1.75 .75
589 A288 7w pale rose & multi 2.75 .75

48th Natl. Athletic Meet, Seoul, Oct. 5-10.

Students' Memorial, Kwangjoo — A289

1967, Nov. 3 Litho. Perf. 12½

590 A289 7w lt green & multi 1.25 .40

Issued for Student Day commemorating 1929 students' uprising against Japan.

Symbolic Water Cycle — A290

1967, Nov. 20

591 A290 7w multicolored 1.25 .40

Hydrological Decade (UNESCO), 1965-74.

Children Spinning Top — A291

Monkey and Oriental Zodiac — A292

1967, Dec. 10

592 A291 5w sal, org & vio bl 2.50 .35
a. Souv. sheet of 1, imperf. 3.50 3.50
593 A292 7w yel bis, brn & vio bl 3.00 .35
a. Souv. sheet of 1, imperf. 3.50 3.50

Issued for Christmas and New Year.

Parabolic Antenna and Electric Waves — A293

1967, Dec. 21

594 A293 7w lt bl, blk & yel 1.25 .50
a. Souv. sheet of 1, imperf. 3.00 3.00

Opening of the natl. microwave communications network, Dec. 21.

Carving from King Songdok Bell — A294

Earrings, 6th Cent. — A295

Flag — A296

Perf. 13x12½

1968, Feb. 1 Litho. Unwmk.
Granite Paper

595 A294 1w yellow & brown .35 .20
596 A295 5w dk green & yellow 2.75 .40
597 A296 7w dark blue & red 1.25 .25
Nos. 595-597 (3) 4.35 .85

WHO, 20th Anniv. — A297

1968, Apr. 7 Unwmk. Perf. 12½

598 A297 7w multicolored 1.25 .40
a. Souv. sheet of 1, imperf. 3.00 3.00

EATA Emblem and Korean Buildings — A298

1968, Apr. 9 Litho.

599 A298 7w multicolored 1.25 .40
a. Souv. sheet of 1, imperf. 4.00 4.00

2nd General Meeting of the East Asia Travel Association (EATA), Seoul, Apr. 9-13.

Door Knocker, Factories and Emblem A299

1968, May 6 Unwmk. Perf. 12½

600 A299 7w multicolored 1.25 .40
a. Souv. sheet of 1, imperf. 3.50 3.50

2nd Conf. of the Confederation of Asian Chambers of Commerce and Industry, Seoul.

Pres. Park and Emperor Haile Selassie A300

1968, May 18 Litho.

601 A300 7w multicolored 3.50 1.50
a. Souv. sheet of 1, imperf. 7.00 7.00

Visit of Haile Selassie I, May 18-20.

Mailman's Pouch A301

Mailman A302

1968, May 31 Unwmk. Perf. 12½

602 A301 5w multicolored 1.25 .60
603 A302 7w multicolored 1.25 .60

First Postman's Day, May 31, 1968.

Atom Diagram and Symbols of Development A303

1968, June 1 Litho.

604 A303 7w dk bl, citron & ver 1.25 .40

Issued to promote science and technology.

Kyung Hee University and Conference Emblem A304

1968, June 18 Unwmk.

605 A304 7w bl, pink & blk 1.25 .40
a. Souv. sheet of 1, imperf. 5.00 5.00

2nd Conf. of the Intl. Association of University Presidents.

Liberated People A305

1968, July 1 Litho. Perf. 12½

606 A305 7w multicolored 1.25 .40

Issued to publicize the movement to liberate people under communist rule.

Peacock and Industrial Plant — A306

1968, Aug. 15 Unwmk. Perf. 12½

607 A306 7w multicolored 1.50 .40

Republic of Korea, 20th anniversary.

Fair Entrance A307

1968, Sept. 9 Unwmk. Perf. 12½

608 A307 7w lilac & multi 1.50 .40

Issued to publicize the first Korean Trade Fair, Seoul, Sept. 9-Oct. 18.

Assembly Emblem and Pills — A308

1968, Sept. 16 Litho.

609 A308 7w multicolored 1.50 .40

3rd General Assembly of the Federation of Asian Pharmaceutical Associations, Seoul, Sept. 16-21.

Soldier, Insigne and Battle Scene — A309

#611, Sailor, insigne & ship's guns. #612, Servicemen & flags. #613, Aviator, insigne & planes. #614, Marine, insigne & landing group.

1968, Oct. 1

610	A309	7w green & org	6.00	2.00
611	A309	7w lt & dk blue	6.00	2.00
612	A309	7w dk blue & org	6.00	2.00
613	A309	7w dk & lt blue	6.00	2.00
614	A309	7w orange & grn	6.00	2.00
a.		Vert. strip of 5, #610-614	32.50	10.00

20th anniv. of the Korean armed forces.

Colombo Plan Emblem and Globe — A310

1968, Oct. 8 Litho. *Perf. 12½*

615	A310	7w dk brn, pale sal & grn	1.50	.35

19th meeting of the Consultative Committee of the Colombo Plan, Seoul, Oct. 8-28.

Bicycling (Type I) — A311

Type II — (2nd line flush left)

#617, Bicycling, Type II. #618-619, Wrestling. #620-621, Boxing. #622-623, Olympic flame, "68" & symbols of various sports events.

1968, Oct. 12 Unwmk. *Perf. 12½*

616	A311	7w pink & multi (I)	12.50	4.50
617	A311	7w pink & multi (II)	12.50	4.50
a.		Souv. sheet of 2, #616-617, imperf.	10.00	10.00
b.		Pair, #616-617	30.00	10.00
618	A311	7w olive & multi (I)	12.50	4.50
619	A311	7w olive & multi (II)	12.50	4.50
a.		Souv. sheet of 2, #618-619, imperf.	10.00	10.00
b.		Pair, #618-619	30.00	10.00
620	A311	7w orange & multi (I)	12.50	4.50
621	A311	7w orange & multi (II)	12.50	4.50
a.		Souv. sheet of 2, #620-621, imperf.	10.00	10.00
b.		Pair, #620-621	30.00	10.00
622	A311	7w bluish grn & multi (I)	12.50	4.50
623	A311	7w bluish grn & multi (II)	12.50	4.50
a.		Souv. sheet of 2, #622-623, imperf.	10.00	10.00
b.		Pair, #622-623	30.00	10.00
		Nos. 616-623 (8)	100.00	36.00

19th Olympic Games, Mexico City, 10/12-27.
The position of the "7" is reversed on Nos. 619, 621, 623 as are the designs of Nos. 619, 621.

"Search for Knowledge" and School Girls — A312

1968, Oct. 15

624	A312	7w multicolored	1.50	.40

60th anniv. of public secondary education for women.

Coin and Statistics A313

1968, Nov. 1

625	A313	7w multicolored	1.50	.40

National Wealth Survey.

Memorial to Students' Uprising — A314

1968, Nov. 23

626	A314	7w gray & multi	1.50	.40

Issued to commemorate the anti-communist students' uprising, Nov. 23, 1945.

Men With Banners Declaring Human Rights A315

1968, Dec. 10

627	A315	7w multicolored	1.50	.40

Declaration of Human Rights, 20th anniv.

Christmas Decorations A316

Cock and Good Luck Characters A317

1968, Dec. 11

628	A316	5w salmon & multi	9.00	.50
a.		Souv. sheet of 1, imperf.	7.50	7.50
629	A317	7w multicolored	9.00	.50
a.		Souv. sheet of 1, imperf.	7.50	7.50

Issued for Christmas and the New Year.

UN Emblems and Korean House A318

1968, Dec. 12

630	A318	7w lt blue & multi	1.25	.35

20th anniv. of the recognition of the Republic of Korea by the UN.

Regional Boy Scout Conf. — A319

Design: Boy Scout Emblem.

1968, Sept. 30 Litho. *Perf. 12½*

631	A319	7w black & multi	2.00	.75

Sam-il Movement, 50th Anniv. — A320

1969, Mar. 1 Unwmk. *Perf. 12½*

Design: Torch, map and students Demonstrating against Japan, 1919.

632	A320	7w multicolored	1.25	.40

Hyun Choong Sa Shrine and Tortoise Ships A321

1969, Apr. 28 Unwmk. *Perf. 12½*

633	A321	7w deep bl, grn & brn	1.25	.40

Completion of the Hyun Choong Sa Shrine at Onyang, dedicated to the memory of Adm. Li Sun-sin.

Pres. Park and Tuanku Nasiruddin of Malaysia A322

1969, Apr. 29 Litho.

634	A322	7w yellow & multi	1.50	.50
a.		Souv. sheet of 1, imperf.	*25.00*	

Visit of Tuanku Ismail Nasiruddin, ruler of Malaysia, Apr. 29, 1969.

Hanabusaya Asiatica A323

Flag of Korea A324

Ancient Drums A325

Red-crested Cranes A326

Highway and Farm A327

Pitcher (12-13th Centuries) A328

Ceramic Duck (Water Jar) A329

Library of Early Buddhist Scriptures A330

Miruk Bosal — A333

1w, Old man's mask. #637, Stone lamp, 8th cent. #638, Chipmunk. #644, Tiger lily. #649, Bee. #651, Vase, Yi dynasty, 17th-18th centuries. #653, Gold crown, Silla Dynasty.

Zeros Omitted except 7w, No. 639

Perf. 13x12, 12x13 (Litho.); 13½x12½, 12½x13½ (Photo.)

Litho. (40ch, Nos. 641, 650); Photo.

1969-74 Unwmk.

Granite Paper (Lithographed); Ordinary Paper (Photogravure)

635	A323	40ch	green	1.25	.30
636	A326	1w	dk rose brn ('74)	.40	.20
637	A328	5w	brt plum	.95	.25
638	A326	5w	maroon ('74)	.35	.20
639	A324	7w	blue ("7.00")	3.25	.40
640	A324	7w	blue ("7")	1.25	.30
641	A325	10w	ultra	25.00	.70
642	A324	10w	ultra ("10") ('70)	1.25	.25
643	A326	10w	bl & dk bl ('73)	1.25	.40
644	A323	10w	grn & multi ('73)	.95	.20
645	A327	10w	grn, red & gray ('73)	.35	.20
647	A328	20w	green	2.00	.40
648	A329	30w	dull grn ('70)	3.25	.75
649	A326	30w	yel & dk brn ('74)	.75	.20
650	A330	40w	vio bl & pink	40.00	2.25
651	A328	40w	ultra & lilac	2.40	.75
652	A333	100w	dp claret & yel	80.00	2.25
653	A333	100w	brn & yel ('74)	35.00	2.25
			Nos. 635-653 (18)	199.65	12.25

See No. 1090. For surcharge see No. B18.
Counterfeits exist of No. 653.

Red Cross, Faces and Doves A336

1969, May 5 Litho. *Perf. 12½*

654	A336	7w multicolored	1.50	.40
a.		Souv. sheet of 1, imperf.	5.00	5.00

50th anniv. of the League of Red Cross Societies.

Savings Bank, Factories and Highway — A337

1969, May 20 Unwmk. *Perf. 12½*

655	A337	7w yellow grn & multi	1.25	.40

Second Economy Drive.

Pres. Park, Pres. Thieu and Flags of Korea and Viet Nam — A338

1969, May 27 **Litho.**

656 A338 7w pink & multi 2.50 1.00
a. Souv. sheet of 1, imperf. 8.00 8.00

Visit of Pres. Nguyen Van Thieu of Viet Nam, May 27.

"Reforestation and Parched Fields" — A339

Growing and Withering Plants — A340

1969, June 10

657 A339 7w multicolored 1.25 .35
658 A340 7w multicolored 1.25 .35

Issued to publicize the need for prevention of damages from floods and droughts.

Apollo 11, Separation of Second Stage A341

#660, Apollo 11, separation of 3rd Stage. #661, Orbits of command & landing modules around moon. #662, Astronauts gathering rock samples on moon. 40w, Spacecraft splashdown.

1969, Aug. 15 **Unwmk.** ***Perf. 12½***

659 A341 10w indigo, bl & red 3.50 1.00
660 A341 10w indigo, bl & red 3.50 1.00
661 A341 20w indigo, bl, red & lem 3.50 1.00
662 A341 20w indigo, bl, red & lem 3.50 1.00
663 A341 40w indigo, bl & red 3.50 1.00
a. Souv. sheet of 5, #659-663, imperf. 35.00 35.00
b. Strip of 5, #659-663 17.50 9.00

Man's 1st landing on the moon, July 20, 1969. US astronauts Neil A. Armstrong and Col. Edwin E. Aldrin, Jr., with Lieut. Col. Michael Collins piloting Apollo 11.

Fable Issue

Girl and Stepmother A342

Kongji and Patji (Cinderella): 7w, Sparrows help Kongji separate rice. 10w, Ox helps Kongji to weed a field. 20w, Kongji in a sedan chair on the way to the palace.

1969, Sept. 1 **Litho.** ***Perf. 12½***

664 A342 5w apple grn & multi 3.75 .75
665 A342 7w yellow & multi 3.75 .75
666 A342 10w lt violet & multi 5.50 1.25
667 A342 20w lt green & multi 5.50 1.25

The Sick Princess A343

1969, Nov. 1 ***Perf. 13x12½***

"The Hare's Liver": 7w, Hare riding to the palace on back of turtle. 10w, Hare telling a lie to the King to save his life. 20w, Hare mocking the turtle.

668 A343 5w yellow & multi 2.25 .65
669 A343 7w lt vio & multi 2.25 .65
670 A343 10w lt grnsh bl & multi 2.25 .90
671 A343 20w lt yel grn & multi 3.50 .90

Mother Meeting Tiger — A344

1970, Jan. 5

"The Sun and the Moon": 7w, Tiger disguised as mother at children's house. 10w, Tiger, and children on tree. 20w, Children safe on cloud, and tiger falling to his death.

672 A344 5w orange & multi 2.25 .65
673 A344 7w gray grn & multi 2.25 .65
674 A344 10w lt green & multi 2.25 .90
675 A344 20w gray & multi 3.50 .90

Woodcutter Stealing Fairy's Clothes A345

1970, Mar. 5

Designs: No. 677, Woodcutter with wife and children. No. 678, Wife taking children to heaven. No. 679, Husband joining family in heaven.

676 A345 10w dull bl grn & multi 2.50 .90
677 A345 10w buff & multi 2.50 .90
678 A345 10w lt grnsh bl & multi 2.50 .90
679 A345 10w pink & multi 2.50 .90

Heungbu and Wife Release Healed Swallow A346

1970, May 5 ***Perf. 12½***

Designs: No. 681, Heungbu and wife finding gold treasure in gourd. No. 682, Nolbu and wife with large gourd. No. 683, Demon emerging from gourd punishing evil Nolbu and wife.

680 A346 10w lt grnsh bl & multi 5.50 1.00
681 A346 10w orange & multi 5.50 1.00
682 A346 10w apple grn & multi 5.50 1.00
683 A346 10w tan & multi 5.50 1.00
Nos. 664-683 (20) 71.00 17.80

Souvenir Sheets of 1, Imperf.

664a	A342	5w	5.50	5.50
665a	A342	7w	5.50	5.50
666a	A342	10w	5.50	5.50
667a	A342	20w	5.50	5.50
668a	A343	5w	5.00	5.00
669a	A343	7w	5.00	5.00
670a	A343	10w	5.00	5.00
671a	A343	20w	5.00	5.00
672a	A344	5w	5.00	5.00
673a	A344	7w	5.00	5.00
674a	A344	10w	5.00	5.00
675a	A344	20w	5.00	5.00
676a	A345	10w	5.00	5.00
677a	A345	10w	5.00	5.00
678a	A345	10w	5.00	5.00
679a	A345	10w	5.00	5.00
680a	A346	10w	10.00	10.00
681a	A346	10w	10.00	10.00
682a	A346	10w	10.00	10.00
683a	A346	10w	10.00	10.00
Nos. 664a-683a (20)			122.00	122.00

1869 Locomotive and Diesel Train — A347

Design: No. 685, Early locomotive.

Perf. 12½

1969, Sept. 18 **Litho.** **Unwmk.**

684 A347 7w yellow & multi 1.50 .60
685 A347 7w green & multi 1.50 .60

70th anniversary of Korean Railroads.

Formation of F-5A Planes A348

Design: No. 687, F-4D Phantom.

1969, Oct. 1 **Photo.** ***Perf. 13½x13***

686 A348 10w blue, blk & car 5.00 .75

Litho. ***Perf. 13x12½***

687 A348 10w multicolored 6.00 .75

20th anniversary of Korean Air Force.

Cha-jun Game A349

1969, Oct. 3

688 A349 7w ap grn, dk bl & blk 1.00 .35

10th National Festival of Traditional Skills.

Institute of Science and Technology A350

1969, Oct. 23

689 A350 7w bister, grn & choc 1.00 .35

Completion of the Korean Institute of Science and Technology, Hongnung, Seoul.

Pres. Park and Diori Hamani A351

1969, Oct. 27

690 A351 7w yellow grn & multi 2.00 .80
a. Souv. sheet of 1, imperf. 12.50 12.50

Visit of Diori Hamani, Pres. of Niger, Oct. 27.

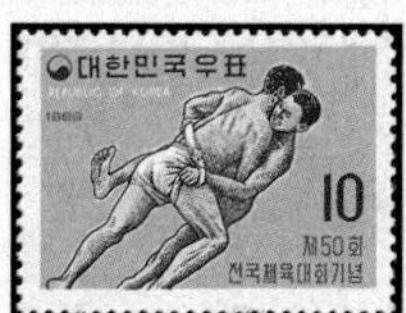

Korean Wrestling A352

#692, Fencing. #693, Korean karate (taekwondo). #694, Volleyball, vert. #695, Soccer, vert.

1969, Oct. 28 ***Perf. 13x12½, 12½x13***

691 A352 10w yellow grn & multi 3.00 .75
692 A352 10w blue & multi 3.00 .75
693 A352 10w green & multi 3.00 .75
694 A352 10w olive & multi 3.00 .75
695 A352 10w ultra & multi 3.00 .75
Nos. 691-695 (5) 15.00 3.75

50th Natl. Athletic Meet, Seoul, Oct. 28-Nov. 2.

Allegory of National Education Charter — A353

1969, Dec. 5 **Litho.** ***Perf. 12½x13***

696 A353 7w dull yel & multi 1.00 .35

1st anniv. of the proclamation of the Natl. Education Charter.

Toy Dogs and Lattice Pattern A354

Candle, Lattice Door and Fence A355

1969, Dec. 11 **Photo.** ***Perf. 13½***

697 A354 5w green & multi 1.25 .40
698 A355 7w blue & multi 1.25 .40

Issued for New Year 1970.

UPU Monument, Bern, and Korean Woman — A356

1970, Jan. 1 **Photo.** ***Perf. 13x13½***

699 A356 10w multicolored 10.00 3.50

70th anniv. of Korea's admission to the UPU.

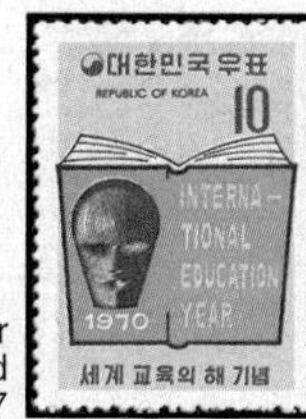

Education Year Emblem and Book — A357

1970, Mar. 10 **Litho.** ***Perf. 12½x13***

700 A357 10w pink & multi 5.50 2.00

International Education Year 1970.

EXPO '70 Emblem, Seated Buddha, Korean Pavilion A358

1970, Mar. 15 ***Perf. 13x12½***

701 A358 10w multicolored 5.50 1.50

Issued to publicize EXPO '70 International Exhibition, Osaka, Japan, March 15-Sept. 13.

Korean Youths and 4-H Club Emblem — A359

1970, Mar. 28 ***Perf. 12½x13***

702 A359 10w yellow & multi 3.50 .75

Issued to publicize the 15th Korean 4-H Club Central Contest, Suwon, March 28.

Money and Bank Emblem A360

1970, Apr. 9 Litho. ***Perf. 13x12½***

703 A360 10w yellow & multi 2.00 .75

3rd annual Board of Governors' meeting of the Asian Development Bank, Seoul, 4/9-11.

Royal Palanquin — A361

1899 Streetcar A362

Historic Means of Transportation: No. 706, Emperor Sunjong's Cadillac, 1903. No. 707, Nieuport biplane, 1922.

Perf. 13x13½, 13½x13

1970, May 20 **Photo.**

704 A361 10w citron & multi 2.50 .90
705 A362 10w yellow & multi 2.50 .90
706 A362 10w ocher & multi 2.50 .90
707 A362 10w aqua & multi 2.50 .90
Nos. 704-707 (4) 10.00 3.60

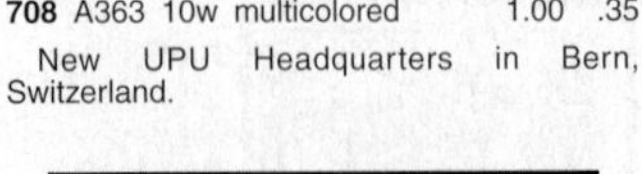

UPU Headquarters A363

1970, May 30 ***Perf. 13½x13***

708 A363 10w multicolored 1.00 .35

New UPU Headquarters in Bern, Switzerland.

Map, Radar and Satellite — A364

1970, June 2 ***Perf. 13x13½***

709 A364 10w sky bl, vio bl & blk 1.50 .75

Issued to commemorate the completion of the Kum San Earth Station of the International Satellite Consortium (INTELSAT).

"PEN" and Manuscript Paper — A365

1970, June 28 Photo. ***Perf. 13x13½***

710 A365 10w bl grn, bl & car 1.00 .35

37th Intl. P.E.N. Cong. (Poets, Playwrights, Editors, Essayists and Novelists), Seoul, June 28-July 4.

Seoul-Pusan Expressway — A366

1970, June 30

711 A366 10w multicolored 1.50 .75

Opening of Seoul-Pusan Expressway.

Postal Code Symbol and Number — A367

Mail Sorting Machine — A368

1970, July 1

712 A367 10w multicolored 1.00 .40

Issued to publicize the introduction of postal zone numbers, July 1, 1970.

1970, July 2

713 A368 10w lt violet & multi 1.00 .40
a. Souv. sheet, 2 each #712-713 90.00 90.00

Mechanization of Korean postal system.

Boy and Children's Hall — A369

1970, July 25

714 A369 10w pink & multi 1.00 .40

Paintings Issue

Jongyangsa Temple and Mt. Kumgang, by Chong Son (1676-1759) — A370

The Fierce Tiger, by Shim Sa-yung (1707-1769) A371

Paintings: No. 716, Mountains and Rivers, by Yi In-moon (1745-1821). No. 717, Mountains and Rivers in Moonlight, by Kim Dooryang (1696-1763).

Perf. 13x13½, 13½x13

1970, Aug. 31 **Photo.**

715 A370 10w blue & multi 2.50 .75
716 A370 10w buff & multi 2.50 .75
717 A371 10w multicolored 2.50 .75

1970, Oct. 30

Paintings: No. 719, Cats and Sparrows, by Pyun Sang-byuk (18th century). No. 720, Dog with puppies, by Yi Am (1499-?).

718 A371 30w multicolored 10.00 2.00
719 A371 30w multicolored 10.00 2.00
720 A371 30w multicolored 10.00 2.00

Nos. 718-720 exist imperf.

1970, Dec. 30

Paintings: No. 721, Cliff and Boat, by Kim Hong-do (1745-?). No. 722, Cock, Hens and Chick, by Pyun Sang-byuk (early 18th century). No. 723, Woman Playing Flute, by Shin Yun-bok (late 18th century).

721 A371 10w yel brn, blk & red 2.50 .75
722 A371 10w pale rose, blk & grn 2.50 .75
723 A371 10w multicolored 2.50 .75
Nos. 715-723 (9) 45.00 10.50

Souvenir Sheets of 2

715a A370 10w 3.50 3.50
716a A370 10w 3.50 3.50
717a A371 10w 3.50 3.50
718a A371 30w Imperf 30.00 30.00
719a A371 30w Imperf 30.00 30.00
720a A371 30w Imperf 30.00 30.00
721a A371 10w 9.00 9.00
722a A371 10w 9.00 9.00
723a A371 10w 9.00 9.00
Nos. 715a-723a (9) 127.50 127.50

Nos. 715a-717a have simulated perforations. Background color of stamps on No. 717a is yellow instead of greenish gray as on No. 717.

Nos. 718a-720a exist perf, twice the imperf values.

Nos. 721a-723a exist imperf. Value, each $3.50.

P.T.T.I. Emblem and Map of Far East — A372

1970, Sept. 6 Litho. ***Perf. 13x12½***

724 A372 10w lt yel grn, bl & dk bl 1.25 .40

Opening of the Councillors' Meeting of the Asian Chapter of the Postal, Telegraph and Telephone Intl. Org., Sept. 6-12.

Korean WAC and Emblem — A373

1970, Sept. 6 Photo. ***Perf. 13x13½***

725 A373 10w blue & multi 1.25 .40

20th anniv. of the founding of the Korean Women's Army Corps.

Pres. Park, Korean Flag and Means of Transportation — A374

Pres. Park, Highways, Factories A375

1970 ***Perf. 13x13½, 13½x13***

726 A374 10w vio bl, blk & car 8.00 3.50
727 A375 10w dk bl, grnsh bl & blk 12.00 3.50

Presidents Park and Hernandez, Flags of Korea, Salvador A376

1970, Sept. 28 Litho. ***Perf. 13x12½***

728 A376 10w dk bl, red & blk 3.00 1.25
a. Souv. sheet of 1, imperf. 100.00 100.00

Visit of Gen. Fidel Sanchez Hernandez, President of El Salvador.

The first printing of 30,000 of No. 728a spelled "Salvadol." Second printing, also 30,000, corrected the error. Value is for first printing. Value, 2nd printing $40, unused or used.

People and Houses A377

1970, Oct. 1 Litho. ***Perf. 13x12½***

729 A377 10w lilac & multi 1.25 .35

Natl. census of population & housing, Oct. 1.

Diver A378

1970, Oct. 6 Photo. ***Perf. 12½x13½***

730 A378 10w shown 4.50 1.00
a. Souv. sheet of 2, imperf. 10.00 10.00
731 A378 10w Field hockey 4.50 1.00
a. Souv. sheet of 2, imperf. 10.00 10.00
732 A378 10w Baseball 4.50 1.00
a. Souv. sheet of 2, imperf. 10.00 10.00
Nos. 730-732 (3) 13.50 3.00
Nos. 730a-732a (3) 30.00

51st Natl. Athletic Games, Seoul, Oct. 6-11.

Police Emblem and Activities A379

1970, Oct. 21 Litho. ***Perf. 12½***

733 A379 10w ultra & multi 1.25 .45

The 25th Policemen's Day.

Freedom Bell, UN Emblem over Globe — A380

1970, Oct. 24 Photo. ***Perf. 13x13½***

734 A380 10w blue & multi 1.25 .45

25th anniversary of United Nations.

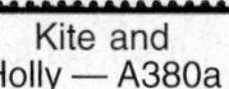
Kite and Holly — A380a

Boar — A381

1970, Dec. 1 Litho. ***Perf. 13***

735 A380a 10w lt blue & multi 1.50 .35
a. Souvenir sheet of 3 7.50 7.50
736 A381 10w green & multi 1.50 .35
a. Souvenir sheet of 3 7.50 7.50

New Year 1971.

Pres. Park Quotation, Globe and Telecommunications Emblems — A382

1970, Dec. 4 **Photo.**

737 A382 10w multicolored 1.25 .45

For the 15th Communications Day.

Power Dam — A383

Coal Mining A384

Highway Intersection — A385

#739, Crate wrapped in world map, & ships. #740, Irrigation project & farm, vert. #742, Cement factory, vert. #743, Fertilizer factory. #744, Increased national income (scales). #745, Increased savings (factories, bee & coins).

1971 ***Perf. 13x13½, 13½x13***

738 A383 10w blue & multi 1.50 .45
739 A383 10w pale lil & multi 1.50 .45
740 A383 10w green & multi 1.50 .45
741 A384 10w bl grn, lt bl & blk 1.25 .35

742 A384 10w lt bl, vio & brt mag 1.25 .35
743 A384 10w vio, grn & bis 1.25 .35
744 A384 10w pink & multi 1.25 .35
745 A384 10w lt bl grn & multi 1.25 .35
746 A385 10w violet & multi 1.25 .35
Nos. 738-746 (9) 12.00 3.45

Economic Development.

Souvenir Sheets of 1, Imperf.

738a A383 10w 6.50 6.50
739a A383 10w 6.50 6.50
740a A383 10w 6.50 6.50

Souvenir Sheets of 2, Imperf.

741a A384 10w 6.50 6.50
742a A384 10w 6.50 6.50
743a A384 10w 6.50 6.50
744a A384 10w 5.00 5.00
745a A384 10w 5.00 5.00
746a A385 10w 5.00 5.00
Nos. 738a-746a (9) 54.00 54.00

No. 739a exists without date. Value $40.

Torch, Globe and Spider — A386

1971, Mar. 1 Litho. ***Perf. 12½x13***

747 A386 10w gray & multi 1.25 .45

March, the month for anti-espionage and victory over communism.

Reservist, Reserve Forces Emblem A387

1971, Apr. 3 Photo. ***Perf. 13½x13***

748 A387 10w lt ultra & multi 1.25 .45

Home Reserve Forces Day, Apr. 3.

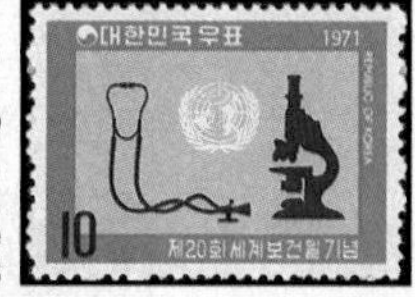

WHO Emblem, Stethoscope, Microscope A388

1971, Apr. 7

749 A388 10w lt bl, pur & yel 1.10 .50

20th World Health Day, Apr. 7.

Subway Tunnel and Train — A389

1971, Apr. 12 Litho. ***Perf. 12½x13***

750 A389 10w multicolored 1.10 .35

Seoul subway construction start.

First Asian Soccer Games, Seoul, May 2-13 — A390

1971, May 2

751 A390 10w grn, dk brn & blk 2.00 .60

Veterans Flag and Veterans — A391

1971, May 8 Photo. ***Perf. 13x13½***

752 A391 10w ultra & multi 1.10 .45

20th Korean Veterans Day.

Girl Scouts and Emblem — A392

1971, May 10

753 A392 10w lilac & multi 1.10 .30

25th anniversary of the Korean Federation of Girl Scouts.

Torch and Development A393

1971, May 16

754 A393 10w lt blue & multi 1.10 .35

10th anniversary of May 16th revolution.

"Telecommunication" — A394

1971, May 17

755 A394 10w blue & multi 1.10 .45

3rd World Telecommunications Day.

UN Organizations A395

Korean Flag — A396

No. 756, ILO. No. 757, FAO. No. 758, General Assembly (UN Headquarters). No. 759, UNESCO. No. 760, WHO. No. 761, World Bank. No. 762, Intl. Development Association (IDA). No. 763, Security Council. No. 764, Intl. Finance Corp. (IFC). No. 765, Intl. Monetary Fund. No. 766, ICAO. No. 767, Economic and Social Council. No. 768, Korean Flag. No. 769, Trusteeship Council. No. 770, UPU. No. 771, ITU. No. 772, World Meteorological Org. (WMO). No. 773, Intl. Court of Justice. No. 774, Intl. Maritime Consultative Org. No. 775, UNICEF. No. 776, Intl. Atomic Energy Agency. No. 777, UN Industrial Development Org. No. 778, UN Commission for the Unification and Rehabilitation of Korea. No. 779, UN Development Program. No. 780, UN Conf. on Trade and Development.

1971, May 30 ***Perf. 13½x13***

756 A395 10w green, blk & pink 3.00 1.20
757 A395 10w pink, blk & bl 3.00 1.20
758 A395 10w bl, blk, grn & pink 3.00 1.20
759 A395 10w pink, blk & bl 3.00 1.20
760 A395 10w green, blk & pink 3.00 1.20
761 A395 10w pink, blk & bl 3.00 1.20
762 A395 10w blue, blk & pink 3.00 1.20
763 A395 10w green, blk & pink 3.00 1.20
764 A395 10w blue, blk & pink 3.00 1.20
765 A395 10w pink, blk & bl 3.00 1.20
766 A395 10w blue, blk & pink 3.00 1.20
767 A395 10w green, blk & pink 3.00 1.20
768 A396 10w blue, blk & pink 3.00 1.20
769 A395 10w green, blk & pink 3.00 1.20
770 A395 10w blue, blk & pink 3.00 1.20
771 A395 10w pink, blk & bl 3.00 1.20
772 A395 10w blue, blk & pink 3.00 1.20
773 A395 10w green, blk & pink 3.00 1.20
774 A395 10w blue, blk & pink 3.00 1.20
775 A395 10w pink, blk & bl 3.00 1.20
776 A395 10w green, blk & pink 3.00 1.20
777 A395 10w pink, blk & bl 3.00 1.20
778 A395 10w blue, blk & pink 3.00 1.20
779 A395 10w pink, blk & bl 3.00 1.20
780 A395 10w green, blk & pink 3.00 1.20
Nos. 756-780 (25) 75.00 30.00

Sheet of 50 incorporates 2 each of #756-780.

Boat Ride, by Shin Yun-bok — A397

Man and Boy under Pine Tree — A398

Paintings by Shin Yun-bok: No. 782, Greeting travelers. No. 783, Sword dance. No. 784, Lady traveling with servants. No. 785, Man and woman on the road.

Perf. 13x13½, 13½x13

1971, June 20 **Photo.**

781 A397 10w multicolored 6.00 1.75
782 A397 10w multicolored 6.00 1.75
783 A397 10w multicolored 6.00 1.75
784 A397 10w multicolored 6.00 1.75
785 A397 10w multicolored 6.00 1.75
b. Vert. strip of 5, #781-785 36.00 36.00
786 A398 10w multicolored 6.00 1.75
Nos. 781-786 (6) 36.00 10.50

Souvenir Sheets of 2

781a A397 10w 12.00 12.00
782a A397 10w 12.00 12.00
783a A397 10w 12.00 12.00
784a A397 10w 12.00 12.00
785a A397 10w 12.00 12.00
786a A398 10w 12.00 12.00
Nos. 781a-786a (6) 72.00 72.00

Types A397-A398 with Inscription at Left

1971, July 20

Paintings: No. 787, Farmyard scene, by Kim Deuk-shin. No. 788, Family living in valley, by

Lee Chae-kwan. No. 789, Man reading book under pine tree, by Lee Chae-kwan.

787 A397 10w pale grn & multi 3.00 1.25
788 A398 10w pale grn & multi 3.00 1.25
789 A398 10w lt yel grn & multi 3.00 1.25
Nos. 787-789 (3) 9.00 3.75

Souvenir Sheets of 2

787a A397 10w 8.00 8.00
788a A398 10w 8.00 8.00
789a A398 10w 8.00 8.00
Nos. 787a-789a (3) 24.00 24.00

Teacher and Students, by Kim Hong-do
A399

Paintings by Kim Hong-do (Yi Dynasty): No. 791, Wrestlers. No. 792, Dancer and musicians. No. 793, Weavers. No. 794, At the Well.

1971, Aug. 20 ***Perf. 13½x13***

790 A399 10w blk, lt grn & rose 5.00 2.50
791 A399 10w blk, lt grn & rose 5.00 2.50
792 A399 10w blk, lt grn & rose 5.00 2.50
793 A399 10w blk, lt grn & rose 5.00 2.50
794 A399 10w blk, lt grn & rose 5.00 2.50
b. Horiz. strip of 5, #790-794 27.50 27.50

Souvenir Sheets of 2

790a A399 10w 12.00 12.00
791a A399 10w 12.00 12.00
792a A399 10w 12.00 12.00
793a A399 10w 12.00 12.00
794a A399 10w 12.00 12.00
Nos. 790a-794a (5) 60.00 60.00

Pres. Park, Highway and Phoenix
A400

1971, July 1 ***Perf. 13½x13***

795 A400 10w grn, blk & org 20.00 2.00
a. Souvenir sheet of 2 70.00 70.00

Inauguration of President Park Chung Hee for a third term, July 1.

Campfire and Tents — A401

1971, Aug. 2 **Photo.** ***Perf. 13x13½***

796 A401 10w blue grn & multi 1.25 .35

13th Boy Scout World Jamboree, Asagiri Plain, Japan, Aug. 2-10.

Symbol of Conference
A402

1971, Sept. 27 ***Perf. 13***

797 A402 10w multicolored 1.25 .45
a. Souvenir sheet of 2 50.00 50.00

Asian Labor Ministers' Conference, Seoul, Sept. 27-30.

Archers — A403

1971, Oct. 8 **Photo.** ***Perf. 13x13½***

798 A403 10w shown 2.00 .75
a. Souvenir sheet of 3 *35.00* 35.00
799 A403 10w Judo 2.00 .75
a. Souvenir sheet of 3 *35.00* 35.00

52nd National Athletic Meet.

Taeguk on Palette
A404

1971, Oct. 11 ***Perf. 13½x13***

800 A404 10w yellow & multi 1.25 .25

20th National Fine Arts Exhibition.

Physician, Globe and Emblem
A405

1971, Oct. 13

801 A405 10w multicolored 1.25 .25

7th Congress of the Confederation of Medical Associations in Asia and Oceania.

Symbols of Contest Events — A406

1971, Oct. 20 **Photo.** ***Perf. 13x13½***

802 A406 10w multicolored 1.25 .25
a. Souvenir sheet of 2 40.00 40.00

2nd National Skill Contest for High School Students.

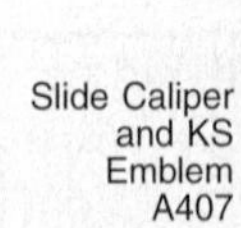

Slide Caliper and KS Emblem
A407

1971, Nov. 11 ***Perf. 13x13½***

803 A407 10w multicolored 1.25 .25

10th anniversary of industrial standardization in Korea.

Rats — A408

Japanese Crane — A409

1971, Dec. 1

804 A408 10w multicolored 1.50 .35
a. Souvenir sheet of 3 25.00 25.00
805 A409 10w multicolored 1.50 .35
a. Souvenir sheet of 3 25.00 25.00

New Year 1972.

Emblem of Hangul Hakhoe and Hangul Letters — A410

1971, Dec. 3 **Photo.**

806 A410 10w dk blue & multi 1.00 .25

50th anniversary of Korean Language Research Society (Hangul Hakhoe).

Red Cross Headquarters and Map of Korea
A411

1971, Dec. 31 ***Perf. 13½x13***

807 A411 10w multicolored 1.25 .60
a. Souvenir sheet of 2 12.50 12.50

First South and North Korean Red Cross Conference, Panmunjom, Aug. 20, 1971.

Globe and Book — A412

1972, Jan. 5 ***Perf. 13x13½***

808 A412 10w multicolored 1.00 .30
a. Souvenir sheet of 2 12.50 12.50

International Book Year 1972.

Intelsat 4 Sending Signals to Korea — A413

1972, Jan. 31 ***Perf. 13½x13***

809 A413 10w dk blue & multi 1.00 .30

Korea's entry into ITU, 20th anniv.

Figure Skating, Sapporo '72 Emblem — A414

Design: No. 811, Speed skating.

1972, Feb. 3 ***Perf. 13x13½***

810 A414 10w lt & dk bl & car 1.25 .60
811 A414 10w lt & dk bl & car 1.25 .60
a. Souvenir sheet of 2, #810-811 12.50 12.50

11th Winter Olympic Games, Sapporo, Japan, Feb. 3-13.

Map of Korea with Forest Sites — A415

1972, Mar. 10 **Photo.** ***Perf. 13x13***

812 A415 10w buff, bl grn & red 1.25 .30

Publicity for forests planted to mark hope for re-unification of Korea.

Junior Chamber of Commerce Emblem and Beetles
A416

1972, Mar. 19 ***Perf. 13½x13***

813 A416 10w pink & multi 1.25 .30

Junior Chamber of Commerce, 20th anniversary.

UN Emblem, Agriculture and Industry — A417

1972, Mar. 28 ***Perf. 13x13½***

814 A417 10w violet, grn & car 1.25 .30

Economic Commission for Asia and the Far East (ECAFE), 25th anniversary.

Flags — A418

1972, Apr. 1 ***Perf. 13½x13***

815 A418 10w blue & multi 1.25 .30

Asian-Oceanic Postal Union, 10th anniv.

Homeland Reserve Forces Flag — A419

1972, Apr. 1 **Photo.** ***Perf. 13x13½***

816 A419 10w yellow & multi 1.50 .40

Homeland Reserve Forces Day, Apr. 1.

YWCA Emblem, Butterflies — A420

1972, Apr. 20

817 A420 10w violet & multi 1.25 .40

50th anniv. of the YWCA of Korea.

Community Projects — A421

1972, May 1 ***Perf. 13x13½***
818 A421 10w pink & multi 1.25 .40

Rural rehabilitation and construction movement.

Korean Flag & Inscription — A422

1972, May 1
819 A422 10w green & multi 1.25 .40

Anti-espionage and victory over communism month.

Children with Balloons A423

1972, May 5 ***Perf. 13½x13***
820 A423 10w yellow & multi 1.25 .40

Children's Day, May 5.

King Munyong's Gold Earrings A424

Design: No. 822, Gold ornament from King's crown, vert.

1972, May 10 ***Perf. 13½x13, 13x13½***
821 A424 10w green & multi 1.25 .40
822 A424 10w green & multi 1.25 .40

National treasures from tomb of King Munyong of Paekche, who reigned 501-523.

Kojo Island — A425

National parks: No. 823, Crater Lake.

1972, May 30 ***Perf. 13½x13***
823 A425 10w blue grn & multi 3.25 .40
824 A425 10w green & multi 3.25 .40

UN Conference on Human Environment, Stockholm, June 5-16 — A426

1972, May 30 Litho. ***Perf. 13x13½***
825 A426 10w Daisy, environment emblem 1.25 .35
a. Souvenir sheet of 2 8.50 8.50

7th Meeting of Asian-Pacific Council (ASPAC) — A427

1972, June 14
826 A427 10w Gwanghwa Gate, flags of participants 1.25 .35

Farm and Fish Hatchery A428

Third Five-Year Plan Issue

1972, July 1 Photo. ***Perf. 13½x13***
827 A428 10w shown 2.00 .50
828 A428 10w Steel industry and products 2.00 .50
829 A428 10w Globe and cargo 2.00 .50
Nos. 827-829 (3) 6.00 1.50

3rd Economic Development Five-Year Plan.

Weight Lifting — A429

1972, Aug. 26 Photo. ***Perf. 13x13½***
830 A429 20w shown 1.25 .50
831 A429 20w Judo 1.25 .50
a. Souvenir sheet of 2, #830-831 6.00 6.00
b. Pair, #830-831 5.00 2.50
832 A429 20w Boxing 1.25 .50
833 A429 20w Wrestling 1.25 .50
a. Souvenir sheet of 2, #832-833 6.00 6.00
b. Pair, #832-833 5.00 2.50
Nos. 830-833 (4) 5.00 2.00

20th Olympic Games, Munich, Aug. 26-Sept. 11. Nos. 831b, 833b each printed checkerwise.

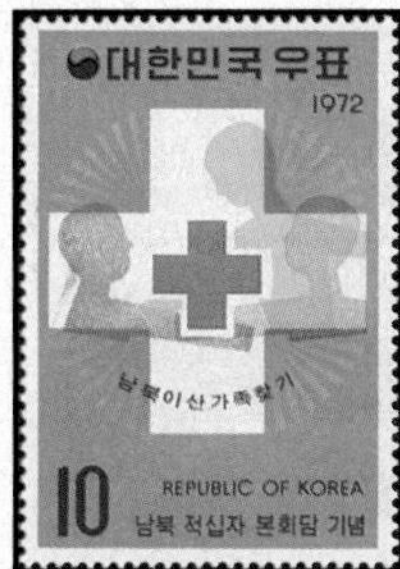

Families Reunited by Red Cross A430

1972, Aug. 30 Photo. ***Perf. 13½x13***
834 A430 10w lt blue & multi 1.75 .60
a. Souvenir sheet of 2 27.50 27.50

Plenary meeting of the South-North Red Cross Conference, Pyongyang, Aug. 30, 1972.

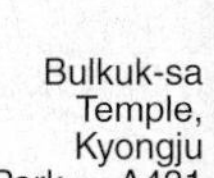

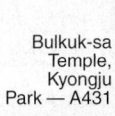

Bulkuk-sa Temple, Kyongju Park — A431

Bopju-sa Temple, Mt. Sokri Park — A432

1972, Sept. 20 Photo. ***Perf. 13½x13***
835 A431 10w brown & multi 1.25 .40
836 A432 10w blue & multi 1.25 .40

National parks.

"5" and Conference Emblem — A433

1972, Sept. 25 ***Perf. 13x13½***
837 A433 10w vio blue & multi 1.20 .35

Fifth Asian Judicial Conf., Seoul, 9/25-29.

Lions Emblem, Taeguk Fan — A434

1972, Sept. 28 ***Perf. 13½x13***
838 A434 10w multicolored 1.20 .35

11th Orient and Southeast Asian Lions Convention, Seoul, Sept. 28-30.

Scout Taking Oath, Korean Flag and Scout Emblem A435

1972, Oct. 5
839 A435 10w yellow & multi 1.50 .45

Boy Scouts of Korea, 50th anniversary.

Children and Ox — A436

Children in Balloon — A437

1972, Dec. 1 Photo. ***Perf. 13x13½***
840 A436 10w green & multi 1.25 .30
a. Souvenir sheet of 2 4.00 4.00
841 A437 10w blue & multi 1.25 .30
a. Souvenir sheet of 2 4.00 4.00

New Year 1973.

Mt. Naejang Park and Temple — A438

Mt. Sorang and Madeungryong Pass — A439

1972, Dec. 10 ***Perf. 13x13½, 13½x13***
842 A438 10w multicolored 1.25 .30
843 A439 10w multicolored 1.25 .30

National parks.

Pres. Park, Korean Flag and Modern Landscape — A440

1972, Dec. 27 ***Perf. 13x13½***
844 A440 10w multicolored 7.50 1.50
a. Souvenir sheet of 2 67.50 67.50

Inauguration of Park Chung Hee for a 4th term as president of Korea.

Tourism Issue

Kyongbok Palace (National Museum) A441

Mt. Sorak and Kejo-am Temple A442

Palmi Island and Beach — A443

Sain-am Rock, Mt. Dokjol — A444

Shrine for Adm. Li Sun-sin — A445

Limestone Cavern, Kusan-ni — A446

Namhae Bridge A447

Hongdo Island — A448

Mt. Mai — A449

Tangerine Orchard, Cheju Island A450

1973, Feb. 20 Photo. *Perf. 13½x13*

845 A441 10w multicolored 1.25 .30
846 A442 10w multicolored 1.25 .30

1973, Apr. 20 *Perf. 13x13½*

847 A443 10w multicolored 1.25 .30
848 A444 10w multicolored 1.25 .30

1973, June 20

849 A445 10w multicolored 1.50 .30
850 A446 10w multicolored 1.50 .30

1973, Aug. 20 *Perf. 13½x13*

851 A447 10w multicolored 1.25 .30
852 A448 10w multicolored 1.25 .30

1973, Oct. 20

853 A449 10w multicolored .85 .25
854 A450 10w multicolored .85 .25
Nos. 845-854 (10) 12.20 2.90

Praying Family — A451

1973, Mar. 1 *Perf. 13x13½*

855 A451 10w yellow & multi 1.00 .30

Prayer for national unification.

Flags of Korea and South Viet Nam, Victory Sign — A452

1973, Mar. 1

856 A452 10w violet & multi 1.00 .30

Return of Korean Expeditionary Force from South Viet Nam.

Workers, Factory, Cogwheel A453

Satellite, WMO Emblem A454

1973, Mar. 10 Unwmk.

857 A453 10w blue & multi .80 .30

10th Labor Day.

1973, Mar. 23

858 A454 10w blue & multi .80 .30
a. Souvenir sheet of 2 5.00 5.00

Cent. of Intl. Meteorological Cooperation.

King's Ceremonial Robe — A455

Traditional Korean Costumes (Yi dynasty): No. 860, Queen's ceremonial dress. No. 861, King's robe. No. 862, Queen's robe. No. 863, Crown Prince. No. 864, Princess. No. 865, Courtier. No. 866, Royal bridal gown. No. 867, Official's wife. No. 868, Military official.

1973 Photo. *Perf. 13½x13*

859 A455 10w ocher & multi 3.50 .70
860 A455 10w salmon & multi 3.50 .70
861 A455 10w rose lilac & multi 3.25 .60
862 A455 10w apple grn & multi 3.25 .60
863 A455 10w lt blue & multi 3.00 .60
864 A455 10w lilac rose & multi 3.00 .60
865 A455 10w yellow & multi 1.50 .50
866 A455 10w lt blue & multi 1.50 .50
867 A455 10w ocher & multi 1.25 .35
868 A455 10w lil rose & multi 1.25 .35
Nos. 859-868 (10) 25.00 5.50

Issued: #859-860, 3/30; #861-862, 5/30; #863-864, 7/30; #865-866, 9/30; #867-868, 11/30.

Souvenir Sheets of 2

859a	A455	10w (#1)		7.50	7.50
860a	A455	10w (#2)		7.50	7.50
861a	A455	10w (#3)		7.50	7.50
862a	A455	10w (#4)		7.50	7.50
863a	A455	10w (#5)		7.50	7.50
864a	A455	10w (#6)		7.50	7.50
865a	A455	10w (#7)		4.00	4.00
866a	A455	10w (#8)		4.00	4.00
867a	A455	10w (#9)		4.00	4.00
868a	A455	10w (#10)		4.00	4.00
		Nos. 859a-868a (10)		61.00	61.00

Parenthetical numbers after souvenir sheet listings appear in top marginal inscriptions.

Nurse Holding Lamp — A456

1973, Apr. 1 *Perf. 13½x13*

869 A456 10w rose & multi 1.00 .20

50th anniv. of Korean Nurses Association.

Homeland Reservists and Flag — A457

1973, Apr. 7 *Perf. 13x13½*

870 A457 10w yellow & multi 1.25 .30

Homeland Reserve Forces Day on 5th anniversary of their establishment.

Table Tennis Player, and Globe — A458

1973, May 23 *Perf. 13x13½*

871 A458 10w pink & multi 1.50 .70

Victory of Korean women's table tennis team, 32nd Intl. Table Tennis Championships, Sarajevo, Yugoslavia, Apr. 5-15.

World Vision Children's Choir — A459

1973, June 25 *Perf. 13x13½*

872 A459 10w multicolored 1.00 .30

20th anniversary of World Vision International, a Christian service organization.

Converter, Pohang Steel Works — A460

1973, July 3 *Perf. 13x13½*

873 A460 10w blue & multi 1.00 .45

Inauguration of Pohang iron and steel plant.

INTERPOL Emblem A461

1973, Sept. 3 *Perf. 13½x13*

874 A461 10w lt violet & multi 1.00 .20

50th anniversary of the International Criminal Police Organization (INTERPOL).

Children with Stamp Albums A462

1973, Oct. 12 *Perf. 13½x13*

875 A462 10w dp green & multi .80 .30
a. Souvenir sheet of 2 15.00 15.00

Philatelic Week, Oct. 12-18.

Woman Hurdler — A463

1973, Oct. 12 *Perf. 12½x13½*

876 A463 10w shown .90 .30
877 A463 10w Tennis player .90 .30

54th Natl. Athletic Meet, Pusan, Oct. 12-17.

Soyang River Dam, Map Showing Location A464

1973, Oct. 15 *Perf. 13½x13*

878 A464 10w blue & multi .50 .20

Inauguration of Soyang River Dam and hydroelectric plant.

Fire from Match and Cigarette — A465

1973, Nov. 1 *Perf. 13x13½*

879 A465 10w multicolored .50 .20

10th Fire Prevention Day.

Tiger and Candles — A466

Toys — A467

1973, Dec. 1 Photo. *Perf. 13x13½*

880 A466 10w emerald & multi 1.00 .30
a. Souvenir sheet of 2 4.50 4.50
881 A467 10w blue & multi 1.00 .30
a. Souvenir sheet of 2 4.50 4.50

New Year 1974.

Human Rights Flame, and Head — A468

1973, Dec. 10 *Perf. 13½x13*

882 A468 10w orange & multi .50 .20

25th anniversary of Universal Declaration of Human Rights.

Musical Instruments Issue

Komunko, Six-stringed Zither — A469

Design: 30w, Nagak, shell trumpet.

1974, Feb. 20 Photo. *Perf. 13x13½*

883 A469 10w lt bl, blk & brn 1.10 .30
884 A469 30w orange & multi 3.00 .60

1974, Apr. 20

Designs: 10w, Tchouk; wooden hammer in slanted box, used to start orchestra. 30w, Eu; crouching tiger, used to stop orchestra.

885 A469 10w brt blue & multi 1.00 .25
886 A469 30w lt green & multi 2.00 .35

1974, June 20

Designs: 10w, A-chaing, 7-stringed instrument. 30w, Kyobang-ko, drum.

887 A469 10w dull yel & multi .90 .25
888 A469 30w salmon pink & multi 1.90 .35

1974, Aug. 20

Designs: 10w, So, 16-pipe ritual instrument. 30w, Kaikeum, 2-stringed fiddle.

889 A469 10w lt blue & multi .90 .30
890 A469 30w brt pink & multi 1.90 .45

1974, Oct. 20

10w, Pak (clappers). 30w, Pyenchong (bell chimes).

891 A469 10w lt lilac & multi .90 .30
892 A469 30w lemon & multi 1.90 .45
Nos. 883-892 (10) 15.50 3.60

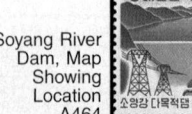

Souvenir Sheets of 2

883a	A469	10w	(#1)	5.00	5.00
884a	A469	30w	(#2)	7.50	7.50
885a	A469	10w	(#3)	3.50	3.50
886a	A469	30w	(#4)	5.50	5.50
887a	A469	10w	(#5)	3.50	3.50
888a	A469	30w	(#6)	5.00	5.00
889a	A469	10w	(#7)	2.75	2.75
890a	A469	30w	(#8)	4.50	4.50
891a	A469	10w	(#9)	2.75	2.75
892a	A469	30w	(#10)	4.50	4.50
	Nos. 883a-892a (10)			44.50	

Fruit Issue

Apricots — A470

1974, Mar. 30 Photo. *Perf. 13x13½*

893 A470 10w shown .75 .30
894 A470 30w Strawberries 2.25 .45

1974, May 30

895 A470 10w Peaches .75 .30
896 A470 30w Grapes 2.25 .45

1974, July 30

897 A470 10w Pears .60 .30
898 A470 30w Apples 2.25 .45

1974, Sept. 30

899 A470 10w Cherries .65 .30
900 A470 30w Persimmons 1.40 .45

1974, Nov. 30

901 A470 10w Tangerines .50 .30
902 A470 30w Chestnuts 1.25 .35
Nos. 893-902 (10) 12.65 3.65

Souvenir Sheets of 2

893a	A470	10w	(#1)	3.50	3.50
894a	A470	30w	(#2)	7.50	7.50
895a	A470	10w	(#3)	3.50	3.50
896a	A470	30w	(#4)	7.00	7.00
897a	A470	10w	(#5)	3.00	3.00
898a	A470	30w	(#6)	7.50	7.50
899a	A470	10w	(#7)	2.00	2.00
900a	A470	30w	(#8)	3.00	3.00
901a	A470	10w	(#9)	2.50	2.50
902a	A470	30w	(#10)	3.00	3.00
	Nos. 893a-902a (10)			42.50	42.50

Reservist and Factory A471

1974, Apr. 6 Photo. *Perf. 13½x13*

903 A471 10w yellow & multi .50 .20

Homeland Reserve Forces Day.

WPY Emblem and Scales — A472

1974, Apr. 10 *Perf. 13x13½*

904 A472 10w salmon & multi .50 .20
a. Souvenir sheet of 2 4.00 4.00

World Population Year 1974.

Train and Communications Emblem — A473

1974, Apr. 22 *Perf. 13½x13*

905 A473 10w multicolored .50 .25

19th Communications Day.

Emblem and Stylized Globe — A474

1974, May 6 Photo. *Perf. 13*

906 A474 10w red lilac & multi .50 .20

22nd Session of Intl. Chamber of Commerce (Eastern Division), Seoul, May 6-8.

New Dock at Inchon A475

1974, May 10

907 A475 10w yellow & multi .50 .20

Dedication of dock, Inchon.

UNESCO Emblem, "20" and Yin Yang — A476

1974, June 14 Photo. *Perf. 13*

908 A476 10w org yel & multi .50 .20

20th anniversary of the Korean National Commission for UNESCO.

EXPLO '74 Emblems — A477

Design: No. 910, EXPLO emblem rising from map of Korea.

1974, Aug. 13 Photo. *Perf. 13*

909 A477 10w orange & multi .45 .20
910 A477 10w blue & multi .45 .20

EXPLO '74, International Christian Congress, Yoido Islet, Seoul, Aug. 13-18.

Subway, Bus and Plane — A478

1974, Aug. 15

911 A478 10w green & multi 1.00 .25

Inauguration of Seoul subway (first in Korea), Aug. 15, 1974.

Target Shooting — A479

1974, Oct. 8 Photo. *Perf. 13x13½*

912 A479 10w shown .40 .20
913 A479 30w Rowing 1.25 .40

55th National Athletic Meet.

UPU Emblem A480

1974, Oct. 9 *Perf. 13*

914 A480 10w yellow & multi .50 .20
a. Souvenir sheet of 2 5.50 5.50

Cent. of UPU. See No. C43.

International Landmarks — A481

1974, Oct. 11

915 A481 10w multicolored .50 .20

Intl. People to People Conf., Seoul, 10/11-14.

Korea Nos. 1-2 — A482

1974, Oct. 17

916 A482 10w lilac & multi .50 .50
a. Souvenir sheet of 2 8.00 8.00

Philatelic Week, Oct. 17-23 and 90th anniversary of first Korean postage stamps.

Taekwondo and Kukkiwon Center A483

1974, Oct. 18

917 A483 10w yellow grn & multi .50 .20

First Asian Taekwondo (self-defense) Games, Seoul, Oct. 18-20.

Presidents Park and Ford, Flags and Globe — A484

1974, Nov. 22 Photo. *Perf. 13*

918 A484 10y multicolored 1.00 .30
a. Souvenir sheet of 2 7.50 7.50

Visit of Pres. Gerald R. Ford to South Korea.

Yook Young Soo — A485

1974, Nov. 29

919 A485 10w green .85 .30
920 A485 10w orange .85 .30
921 A485 10w lilac .85 .30
922 A485 10w blue .85 .30
a. Souvenir sheet of 4, #919-922 35.00 35.00
b. Block of 4, #919-922 3.00 2.00

Yook Young Soo (1925-1974), wife of Pres. Park.

Rabbits — A486

Good-luck Purse — A487

1974, Dec. 1 Litho. *Perf. 12½x13*

923 A486 10w multicolored .60 .20
a. Souvenir sheet of 2 3.75 3.75
924 A487 10w multicolored .60 .20
a. Souvenir sheet of 2 3.75 3.75

New Year 1975.

Good-luck Key and Pigeon A488

1975, Jan. 1 Photo. *Perf. 13*

925 A488 10w lt blue & multi .50 .20

Introduction of Natl. Welfare Insurance System.

UPU Emblem and "75" — A489

UPU Emblem and Paper Plane — A490

1975, Jan. 1

926 A489 10w yellow & multi .50 .20
927 A490 10w lt blue & multi .50 .20

75th anniv. of Korea's membership in UPU.

Dr. Albert Schweitzer, Map of Africa, Hypodermic Needle A491

1975, Jan. 14

928 A491 10w olive .90 .35
929 A491 10w brt rose .90 .35
930 A491 10w orange .90 .35
931 A491 10w brt green .90 .35
a. Block of 4, #928-931 5.00 3.00

Folk Dance Issue

Dancer — A492

Bupo Nori — A492a

#933, Dancer with fan. #934, Woman with butterfly sleeves. #935, Group of Women. #936, Pongsan mask dance. #937, Pusan mask dance. #938, Buddhist drum dance. #939, Bara (cymbals) dance. #940, Sogo dance.

1975, Feb. 20 Photo. *Perf. 13*

932 A492 10w emerald & multi .70 .25
933 A492 10w brt blue & multi .70 .25

1975, Apr. 20

934 A492 10w yel grn & multi .70 .25
935 A492 10w yellow & multi .70 .25

1975, June 20

936 A492 10w pink & multi .70 .25
937 A492 10w blue & multi .70 .25

1975, Aug. 20

938 A492 20w yellow & multi 1.00 .45
939 A492 20w salmon & multi 1.00 .45

1975, Oct. 20

940 A492 20w blue & multi 1.00 .45
941 A492a 20w yellow & multi 1.00 .45
Nos. 932-941 (10) 8.20 3.30

Souvenir Sheets of 2

932a	A492	10w (#1)	2.00	2.00
933a	A492	10w (#2)	2.00	2.00
934a	A492	10w (#3)	1.60	1.60
935a	A492	10w (#4)	1.60	1.60
936a	A492	10w (#5)	1.60	1.60
937a	A492	10w (#6)	1.60	1.60
938a	A492	20w (#7)	2.50	2.50
939a	A492	20w (#8)	2.50	2.50
940a	A492	20w (#9)	2.10	2.10
941a	A492	20w (#10)	2.10	2.10
	Nos. 932a-941a (10)		19.60	19.60

Globe and Rotary Emblem A493

1975, Feb. 23

942 A493 10w multicolored .50 .20

Rotary International, 70th anniversary.

Women and IWY Emblem A494

1975, Mar. 8

943 A494 10w multicolored .50 .20

International Women's Year 1975.

Flower Issue

Violets A495

Anemones A496

Clematis Patens — A496a

Broad-bell Flowers — A496b

Designs: No. 946, Rhododendron. No. 948, Thistle. No. 949, Iris. No. 951, Bush clover. No. 952, Camellia. No. 953, Gentian.

1975, Mar. 15

944 A495 10w orange & multi .60 .25
945 A496 10w yellow & multi .60 .25

1975, May 15

946 A495 10w dk green & multi .75 .25
947 A496a 10w yellow grn & multi .75 .25

1975, July 15

948 A495 10w emerald & multi .75 .25
949 A495 10w blue & multi .75 .25

1975, Sept. 15

950 A496b 20w yellow & multi 1.10 .30
951 A495 20w blue grn & multi 1.10 .30

1975, Nov. 15

952 A495 20w yellow & multi 1.60 .50
953 A496 20w salmon & multi 1.60 .50
Nos. 944-953 (10) 9.60 3.10

Forest and Water Resources — A497

Reduced illustration.

1975, Mar. 20

954 A497 Strip of 4 5.00 3.00
a. 10w Saemaeul forest .75 .30
b. 10w Dam and reservoir .75 .30
c. 10w Green forest .75 .30
d. 10w Timber industry .75 .30

Natl. Tree Planting Month, Mar. 21-Apr. 20.

Map of Korea, HRF Emblem — A498

1975, Apr. 12 Photo. *Perf. 13*

955 A498 10w blue & multi .60 .20

Homeland Reserve Forces Day.

Lily — A499

Ceramic Jar — A500

Ceramic Vase A501

Adm. Li Sun-sin A502

1975 Photo. *Perf. 13½x13*

963 A499 6w green & bl grn .40 .20
964 A500 50w gray grn & brn .75 .25
965 A501 60w brown & yellow .75 .25
966 A502 100w carmine 1.75 .25
Nos. 963-966 (4) 3.65 .95

Issued: Nos. 964-965, 3/15/75; Nos. 963, 966, 10/10/75.

Metric System Symbols A507

1975, May 20 *Perf. 13*

975 A507 10w salmon & multi .50 .20

Centenary of International Meter Convention, Paris, 1875.

Praying Soldier, Incense Burner A508

1975, June 6 Photo. *Perf. 13*

976 A508 10w multicolored .50 .20

20th Memorial Day.

Flags of Korea, UN and US — A509

Designs (Flags of): No. 978, Ethiopia, France, Greece, Canada, South Africa. No. 979, Luxembourg, Australia, Great Britain, Colombia, Turkey. No. 980, Netherlands, Belgium, Philippines, New Zealand, Thailand.

1975, June 25 Photo. *Perf. 13*

977 A509 10w dk blue & multi .75 .30
978 A509 10w dk blue & multi .75 .30
979 A509 10w dk blue & multi .75 .30
980 A509 10w dk blue & multi .75 .30
a. Strip of 4, #977-980 5.00 3.00

25th anniv. of beginning of Korean War.

Presidents Park and Bongo, Flags of Korea and Gabon A510

1975, July 5

981 A510 10w blue & multi .50 .20
a. Souvenir sheet of 2 3.00 3.00

Visit of Pres. Albert Bongo of Gabon, 7/5-8.

Scout Emblem, Tents and Neckerchief — A511

1975, July 29 Photo. *Perf. 13*

982 A511 10w shown .75 .30
983 A511 10w Pick and oath .75 .30
984 A511 10w Tents .75 .30
985 A511 10w Ax, rope and tree .75 .30
986 A511 10w Campfire .75 .30
a. Strip of 5, #982-986 5.00 3.50

Nordjamb 75, 14th Boy Scout Jamboree, Lillehammer, Norway, July 29-Aug. 7.

Flame and Broken Chain A512

Balloons with Symbols of Development over Map — A513

1975, Aug. 15 *Perf. 13½x13*

987 A512 20w gold & multi .70 .25
988 A513 20w silver & multi .70 .25

30th anniversary of liberation.

Taekwondo — A514

1975, Aug. 26 *Perf. 13*

989 A514 20w multicolored .50 .20

2nd World Taekwondo Championships, Seoul, Aug. 25-Sept. 1.

National Assembly and Emblem A515

1975, Sept. 1 Photo. *Perf. 13½x13*

990 A515 20w multicolored .50 .20

Completion of National Assembly Building.

Convention Emblem and Dump Truck — A516

1975, Sept. 7 Photo. *Perf. 13½x13*

991 A516 20w ultra & multi .50 .20

14th Convention of the Intl. Fed. of Asian and Western Pacific Contractors.

Cassegrainian Telescope and Morse Key — A517

1975, Sept. 28

992 A517 20w red lil, org & blk .50 .20

90th anniversary of Korean telecommunications system.

Stalactite Cave, Yeongweol A518

View of Mt. Sorak A519

1975, Sept. 28

993 A518 20w multicolored .50 .20
994 A519 20w multicolored .50 .20

International Tourism Day.

Armed Forces Flag and Missiles — A519a

1975, Oct. 1 Photo. *Perf. 13*

994A A519a 20w multicolored .50 .20

Armed Forces Day.

Gymnastics A520

Handball A521

1975, Oct. 7 Photo. *Perf. 13*

995 A520 20w yellow & multi .50 .20
996 A521 20w multicolored .50 .20

56th Natl. Athletic Meet, Taegu, Oct. 7-12.

Stamp Collecting Kangaroo A522

Hands and UN Emblem A523

1975, Oct. 8

997 A522 20w multicolored .50 .20

Philatelic Week, Oct. 8-14.

1975, Oct. 24

998 A523 20w multicolored .50 .20

United Nations, 30th anniversary.

Red Cross and Activities — A524

Emblem and Dove — A525

1975, Oct. 30

999 A524 20w orange, red & brn .50 .20

Korean Red Cross, 70th anniversary.

1975, Nov. 30 Photo. *Perf. 13*

1000 A525 20w multicolored .50 .20

Asian Parliamentary Union, 10th anniv.

Children Playing — A526

Dragon — A527

1975, Dec. 1

1001 A526 20w multicolored .50 .20
a. Souvenir sheet of 2 2.00 2.00
1002 A527 20w multicolored .50 .20
a. Souvenir sheet of 2 2.00 2.00

New Year 1976.

Inchong-Bukpyong Railroad — A528

1975, Dec. 5 Photo. *Perf. 13*

1003 A528 20w multicolored .75 .20

Opening of electric cross-country railroad.

Butterfly Issue

Dilipa Fenestra A529

Byasa Alcinous Klug — A529a

Graphium Sarpedon A529b

Fabriciana Nerippe A529c

Nymphalis Xanthomelas A529d

Butterflies: No. 1005, Luehdorfia puziloi. No. 1006, Papilio xuthus linne. No. 1007, Parnassius bremeri. No. 1008, Colias erate esper. No. 1010, Hestina assimilis.

1976, Jan. 20 Photo. *Perf. 13*

1004 A529 20w dp rose & multi 1.50 .30
1005 A529 20w dp blue & multi 1.50 .30

1976, Mar. 20

1006 A529 20w yellow & multi 1.50 .30
1007 A529 20w yel grn & multi 1.50 .30

1976, June 20

1008 A529 20w lt violet & multi 1.50 .30
1009 A529a 20w citron & multi 1.50 .30

1976, Aug. 20

1010 A529 20w tan & multi 2.10 .75
1011 A529b 20w lt gray & multi 2.10 .75

1976, Oct. 20

1012 A529c 20w lt green & multi 2.00 .90
1013 A529d 20w lilac & multi 2.00 .90
Nos. 1004-1013 (10) 17.20 5.10

Emblems of Science, Industry and KIST — A530

1976, Feb. 10 Photo. *Perf. 13*

1014 A530 20w multicolored .50 .20

Korean Institute of Science and Technology (KIST), 10th anniversary.

Birds Issue

A531

A532

A532a

A532b

A532c

A532d

A532e

A532f

A532g

A532h

1976, Feb. 20 Photo. *Perf. 13x13½*

1015 A531 20w Siberian Bustard 1.50 .35
1016 A532 20w White-naped Crane 1.50 .35

1976, May 20

1017 A532a 20w Blue-winged pitta 1.50 .35
1018 A532b 20w Tristam's woodpecker 1.50 .35

1976, July 20

1019 A532c 20w Wood pigeon 1.50 .35
1020 A532d 20w Oyster catcher 1.50 .35

1976, Sept. 20

1021 A532e 20w Black-faced spoonbill 1.50 .35
1022 A532f 20w Black stork 1.50 .35

1976, Nov. 20

1023 A532g 20w Whooper swan 3.50 1.40
1024 A532h 20w Black vulture 3.50 1.40
Nos. 1015-1024 (10) 19.00 5.60

1876 and 1976 Telephones, Globe — A533

1976, Mar. 10

1025 A533 20w multicolored .50 .20

Centenary of first telephone call by Alexander Graham Bell, Mar. 10, 1876.

Homeland Reserves A534

1976, Apr. 3 Photo. *Perf. 13½x13*

1026 A534 20w multicolored .50 .20

8th Homeland Reserve Forces Day.

"People and Eye" — A535

1976, Apr. 7 *Perf. 13x13½*

1027 A535 20w multicolored .50 .20

World Health Day; "Foresight prevents blindness."

Pres. Park, Village Movement Flag — A536

Intellectual Pursuits — A537

1976, Apr. 22

1028 A536 20w shown 1.50 .45
1029 A537 20w shown 1.50 .45
1030 A537 20w Village improvement 1.50 .45
1031 A537 20w Agriculture 1.50 .45
1032 A537 20w Income from production 1.50 .45
a. Strip of 5, #1028-1032 10.00 6.00

6th anniv. of Pres. Park's New Village Movement for National Prosperity.

Mohenjo-Daro A538

1976, May 1 *Perf. 13½x13*

1033 A538 20w multicolored .50 .20

UNESCO campaign to save the Mohenjo-Daro excavations in Pakistan.

13-Star and 50-Star Flags — A539

American Bicentennial (Bicentennial Emblem and): No. 1035, Statue of Liberty. No. 1036, Map of US and Mt. Rushmore monument. No. 1037, Liberty Bell. No. 1038, First astronaut on moon.

1976, May 8 *Perf. 13x13½*

1034 A539 100w blk, dp bl & red 3.00 1.00
a. Souvenir sheet of 1 6.00 6.00
1035 A539 100w blk, dp bl & red 3.00 1.00
1036 A539 100w blk, dp bl & red 3.00 1.00
1037 A539 100w blk, dp bl & red 3.00 1.00
1038 A539 100w blk, dp bl & red 3.00 1.00
Nos. 1034-1038 (5) 15.00 5.00

Girl Scouts, Campfire and Emblem — A540

1976, May 10

1039 A540 20w orange & multi .50 .20

Korean Federation of Girl Scouts, 30th anniv.

Stupas, Buddha of Borobudur A541

"Life Insurance" A542

1976, June 10

1040 A541 20w multicolored .50 .20

UNESCO campaign to save the Borobudur Temple, Java.

1976, July 1 **Photo.** *Perf. 13x13½*

1041 A542 20w multicolored .50 .20

National Life Insurance policies: "Over 100 billion-won," Apr. 30, 1976.

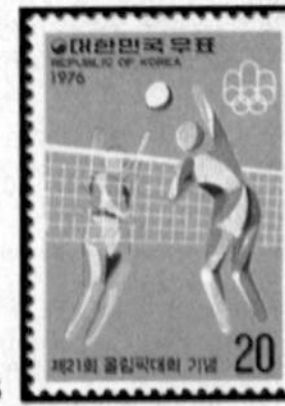
Volleyball — A543

1976, July 17

1042 A543 20w shown .50 .20
1043 A543 20w Boxing .50 .20

21st Olympic Games, Montreal, Canada, July 17-Aug. 1.

Children and Books A544

1976, Aug. 10 *Perf. 13½x13*

1044 A544 20w brown & multi .50 .20

Books for children.

Civil Defense Corps, Flag and Members — A545

1976, Sept. 15 *Perf. 13x13½*

1045 A545 20w multicolored .50 .20

Civil Defense Corps, first anniversary.

Chamsungdan, Mani Mountain — A546

Front Gate, Tongdosa Temple A547

1976, Sept. 28 *Perf. 13½x13*

1046 A546 20w multicolored .75 .25
1047 A547 20w multicolored .75 .25

International Tourism Day.

Cadets and Academy A548

1976, Oct. 1

1048 A548 20w multicolored .50 .20

Korean Military Academy, 30th anniversary.

Leaves and Stones, by Cheong Ju — A549

1976, Oct. 5 *Perf. 13x13½*

1049 A549 20w blk, gray & red .50 .20
a. Souvenir sheet of 2 5.00 5.00

Philatelic Week, Oct. 5-11.

Snake-headed Figure, Bas-relief A550

Door-pull and Cranes A551

1976, Dec. 1 **Photo.** *Perf. 13x13½*

1050 A550 20w multicolored .50 .25
a. Souvenir sheet of 2 2.50 2.50
1051 A551 20w multicolored .50 .25
a. Souvenir sheet of 2 2.50 2.50

New Year 1977.

Arrows, Cogwheels, Worker at Lathe — A552

No. 1053, Arrows, Cogwheels, ship in dock.

1977, Jan. 20 **Photo.** *Perf. 13½x13*

1052 A552 20w multicolored .50 .20
1053 A552 20w multicolored .50 .20

4th Economic Development Five-Year Plan.

Satellite Antenna and Microwaves — A553

1977, Jan. 31 *Perf. 13x13½*

1054 A553 20w multicolored .50 .20

Membership in ITU, 25th anniv.

Korean Broadcasting Center A554

1977, Feb. 16 *Perf. 13½x13*

1055 A554 20w multicolored .50 .20

50th anniversary of broadcasting in Korea.

Parents and Two Children — A555

1977, Apr. 1 **Photo.** *Perf. 13½x13*

1056 A555 20w brt grn & orange 2.00 .25

Family planning.

Reservist on Duty — A556

Head with Symbols — A557

1977, Apr. 2 *Perf. 13x13½*

1057 A556 20w multicolored .50 .20

9th Homeland Reserve Forces Day.

1977, Apr. 21 **Photo.** *Perf. 13x13½*

1058 A557 20w dp lilac & multi .50 .20

10th anniversary of Science Day.

Book, Map, Syringe A558

1977, Apr. 25

1059 A558 20w blue & multi .50 .20

35th Intl. Meeting on Military Medicine.

Boy with Flowers and Dog — A559

Veteran's Emblem and Flag — A560

1977, May 5

1060 A559 20w multicolored .50 .20

Proclamation of Children's Charter, 20th anniversary.

1977, May 8

1061 A560 20w multicolored .50 .20

25th anniversary of Korean Veterans' Day.

Buddha, 8th Century, Sokkulam Grotto — A561

1977, May 25 **Photo.** *Perf. 13x13½*

1062 A561 20w sepia & olive .50 .20
a. Souvenir sheet of 2 5.00 5.00

"2600th" anniversary of birth of Buddha.

Ceramic Issues

Jar with Grape Design, 17th Century — A562

Celadon Vase, Bamboo Design, 12th Century — A563

Celadon Jar with Peonies A564

Vase with Willow Reed Peony Pattern — A565

Celadon Manshaped Wine Jug — A566

Celadon Melon-shaped Vase — A567

Punch'ong Jar — A568

Celadon Cylindrical Vase — A569

1977, Mar. 15 Photo. *Perf. 13x13½*

1063	A562	20w vio brn & multi	2.00	.30
1064	A563	20w gray, grn & bis	2.00	.30

Perf. 13x13½, 13½x13

1977, June 15 Photo.

1065	A564	20w multicolored	.75	.30
1066	A565	20w multicolored	.75	.30

1977, July 15

1067	A566	20w multicolored	.75	.25
1068	A567	20w multicolored	.75	.25

1977, Aug. 15

Designs: No. 1069, White porcelain bowl with inlaid lotus vine design. No. 1070, Black Koryo ware vase with plum blossom vine.

1069	A564	20w multicolored	.75	.25
1070	A565	20w multicolored	.75	.25

1977, Nov. 15

1071	A568	20w multicolored	.75	.25
1072	A569	20w multicolored	.75	.25
		Nos. 1063-1072 (10)	10.00	2.70

Types of 1962-66 Designs as Before

1976-77 Litho. *Perf. 12½*

Granite Paper

1076	A187	200w brown & lt grn	25.00	7.00
1077	A187a	300w sl grn & sal ('76)	50.00	8.00
1078	A187a	300w brown & salmon	50.00	8.00
1079	A187a	500w purple & lt grn	100.00	10.00

Magpie A570

Nature Protection A571

"Family Planning" A572

Children on Swing A573

Ceramic Horseman A574

Muryangsu Hall, Busok Temple A575

Pagoda, Pobjusa Temple A576

Gold Crown, from Chonmachong Mound A577

Monster Mask Tile, 6th or 7th Century — A578

Flying Angels from Bronze Bell from Sangwon-sa, 725 A.D. — A579

Perf. 12½x13½, 13½x12½

1977-79 Photo.

1088	A570	3w lt blue & blk	.75	.25
1090	A326	10w emer & blk	.70	.25
1091	A571	20w multicolored	.50	.20
1092	A572	20w emer & blk ('78)	.50	.20
1093	A573	20w grn & org ('79)	.50	.20
1097	A574	80w lt brn & sep	1.50	.40
1099	A575	200w salmon & brn	2.00	.50
1100	A576	300w brn purple	2.75	.60
1101	A577	500w multicolored	22.50	1.50

Perf. 13½x13

1102	A578	500w brown & pur	11.00	1.00

Perf. 13

1103	A579	1000w slate grn ('78)	10.00	1.50
		Nos. 1088-1103 (11)	52.70	6.60

Ulleung Island — A580

Design: No. 1105, Haeundae Beach.

1977, Sept. 28 Photo. *Perf. 13*

1104	A580	20w multicolored	.50	.20
1105	A580	20w multicolored	.50	.20

World Tourism Day.

Armed Forces Day — A581

1977, Oct. 1 Photo. *Perf. 13*

1106	A581	20w green & multi	.50	.20

Mt. Inwang after the Rain, by Chung Seon (1676-1759) — A582

1977, Oct. 4

1107	20w mountain, clouds	.90	.25
1108	20w mountain, house	.90	.25
a.	Souvenir sheet of 2	8.50	8.50
b.	A582 Pair, #1107-1108	2.25	1.50

Philatelic Week, Oct. 4-10.

Rotary Emblem on Bronze Bell, Koryo Dynasty — A584

1977, Nov. 10 Photo. *Perf. 13*

1109	A584	20w multicolored	.65	.20

Korean Rotary Club, 50th anniversary.

Korean Flag on Mt. Everest A585

1977, Nov. 11

1110	A585	20w multicolored	.65	.20

Korean Mt. Everest Expedition, reached peak, Sept. 15, 1977.

Children and Kites A586

Horse-headed Figure, Bas-relief A587

1977, Dec. 1 Photo. *Perf. 13*

1111	A586	20w multicolored	.45	.25
a.		Souvenir sheet of 2	2.25	2.25
1112	A587	20w multicolored	.45	.25
a.		Souvenir sheet of 2	2.25	2.25

New Year 1978.

Clay Pigeon Shooting A588

Designs: No. 1114, Air pistol shooting. No. 1115, Air rifle shooting and target.

1977, Dec. 3

1113	A588	20w multicolored	.50	.20
a.		Souvenir sheet of 2 ('78)	3.50	3.50
1114	A588	20w multicolored	.50	.20
a.		Souvenir sheet of 2 ('78)	3.50	3.50
1115	A588	20w multicolored	.50	.20
a.		Souvenir sheet of 2 ('78)	3.50	3.50
		Nos. 1113-1115 (3)	1.50	.60
		Nos. 1113a-1115a (3)	10.50	

42nd World Shooting Championships, Seoul, 1978.

Boeing 727 over Globe, ICAO Emblem A589

1977, Dec. 11

1116	A589	20w multicolored	.50	.20

25th anniv. of Korea's membership in the ICAO.

Plane, Cargo, Freighter and Globe A590

1977, Dec. 22 Photo. *Perf. 13*

1117	A590	20w multicolored	.60	.20

Korean exports.

Ships and World Map — A591

1978, Mar. 13 Photo. *Perf. 13*

1118	A591	20w multicolored	.50	.20

Maritime Day.

Stone Pagoda Issue

Four Lions Pagoda, Hwaom-sa A592

Kyongch'on sa Temple A594

Punhwang-sa Temple A593

#1120, Seven-storied pagoda, T'appyongri.

1978, Mar. 20 Photo. *Perf. 13*

1119	A592	20w lt green & multi	1.25	.30
1120	A592	20w ocher & multi	1.25	.30

1978, May 20

Design: No. 1122, Miruk-sa Temple.

1121	A593	20w lt green & blk	1.25	.30
1122	A593	20w grn, brn & yel	1.25	.30

1978, June 20

Designs: #1123, Tabo Pagoda, Pulguk-sa. #1124, Three-storied pagoda, Pulguk-sa.

1123	A592	20w gray, lt grn & blk	.75	.25
1124	A592	20w lilac & black	.75	.25

1978, July 20 *Perf. 13½x12½*

Design: No. 1126, Octagonal Pagoda, Wolchong-sa Temple.

1125	A594	20w gray & brn	1.25	.30
1126	A594	20w lt green & blk	1.25	.30

1978, Nov. 20 *Perf. 13x13½*

Designs: No. 1127, 13-storied pagoda, Jeonghye-sa. No. 1128, Three-storied pagoda, Jinjeon-sa.

1127	A592	20w pale grn & multi	.50	.20
1128	A592	20w lilac & multi	.50	.20
		Nos. 1119-1128 (10)	10.00	2.70

Ants and Coins — A595

Reservist with Flag — A596

1978, Apr. 1

1129 A595 20w multicolored .50 .20

Importance of saving.

1978, Apr. 1

1130 A596 20w multicolored .50 .20

10th Homeland Reserve Forces Day.

Seoul Cultural Center A597

1978, Apr. 1

1131 A597 20w multicolored .50 .20

Opening of Seoul Cultural Center.

National Assembly in Plenary Session A598

1978, May 31

1132 A598 20w multicolored .50 .20

30th anniversary of National Assembly.

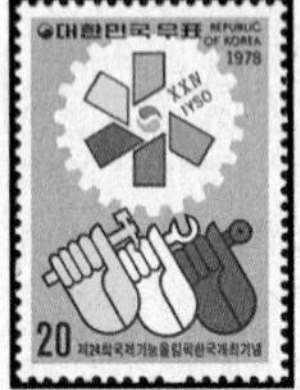

Hands Holding Tools, Competition Emblem — A599

Bell of Joy and Crater Lake, Mt. Baegdu — A600

1978, Aug. 5 Photo. *Perf. 13*

1133 A599 20w multicolored .50 .20

a. Souvenir sheet of 2 3.00 3.00

24th World Youth Skill Olympics, Busan, Aug. 30-Sept. 15.

1978, Aug. 15

1134 A600 20w multicolored .50 .20

Founding of republic, 30th anniversary.

Nurse, Badge and Flowers A601

Sobaeksan Observatory A602

1978, Aug. 26

1135 A601 20w multicolored .50 .20

Army Nurse Corps, 30th anniversary.

1978, Sept. 13 Photo. *Perf. 13*

1136 A602 20w multicolored .50 .20

Opening of Sobaeksan Natl. Observatory.

Kyunghoeru Pavilion, Kyongbok Palace, Seoul A603

Design: No. 1138, Baeg Do (island).

1978, Sept. 28

1137 A603 20w multicolored .40 .20

1138 A603 20w multicolored .40 .20

Tourist publicity.

Customs Flag and Officers A604

1978, Sept. 28

1139 A604 20w multicolored .40 .20

Cent. of 1st Korean Custom House, Busan.

Armed Forces A605

1978, Oct. 1 Photo. *Perf. 13*

1140 A605 20w multicolored .40 .20

Armed Forces, 30th anniversary.

Clay Figurines, Silla Dynasty A606

Portrait of a Lady, by Shin Yoon-bok A607

1978, Oct. 1

1141 A606 20w lt green & blk .40 .20

Culture Month, October 1978.

1978, Oct. 24

1142 A607 20w multicolored .40 .20

a. Souvenir sheet of 2 4.00 4.00

Philatelic Week, Oct. 24-29.

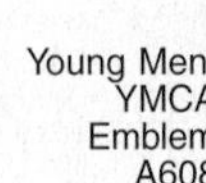

Young Men, YMCA Emblem A608

1978, Oct. 28

1143 A608 20w multicolored .40 .20

75th anniv. of founding of Korean YMCA.

Hand Protecting Against Fire — A609

1978, Nov. 1 Photo. *Perf. 13*

1144 A609 20w multicolored .40 .20

Fire Prevention Day, Nov. 1.

Winter Landscape A610

Ram-headed Figure, Bas-relief A611

1978, Dec. 1 Photo. *Perf. 13x13½*

1145 A610 20w multicolored .45 .20

a. Souvenir sheet of 2 1.75 1.75

1146 A611 20w multicolored .45 .20

a. Souvenir sheet of 2 1.75 1.75

New Year 1979.

Hibiscus, Students, Globe — A612

President Park — A613

1978, Dec. 5

1147 A612 20w multicolored .40 .20

Proclamation of National Education Charter, 10th anniversary.

1978, Dec. 27

1148 A613 20w multicolored .80 .20

a. Souvenir sheet of 2 12.50 12.50

Inauguration of Park Chung Hee for fifth term as president.

Nature Conservation Issue

Golden Mandarinfish A614

Lace-bark Pines A615

Mandarin Ducks — A616

Neofinettia Orchid — A617

Goral — A618

Lilies of the Valley — A619

Rain Frog A620

Asian Polypody A621

Firefly — A622

Meesun Tree — A623

1979, Feb. 20 Photo. *Perf. 13x13½*

1149 A614 20w multicolored 1.50 .20

1150 A615 20w multicolored 1.50 .20

1979, May 20

1151 A616 20w multicolored 1.50 .25

1152 A617 20w multicolored 1.50 .25

1979, June 20

1153 A618 20w multicolored 1.50 .20

1154 A619 20w multicolored 1.50 .20

1979, Nov. 25

1155 A620 20w multicolored 1.50 .20

1156 A621 20w multicolored 1.50 .20

1980, Jan. 20

1157 A622 30w multicolored 1.50 .20

1158 A623 30w multicolored 1.50 .20

Nos. 1149-1158 (10) 15.00 2.10

Samil Monument — A624

1979, Mar. 1 Photo. *Perf. 13x13½*

1159 A624 20w multicolored .40 .20

Samil independence movement, 60th anniv.

Worker and Bulldozer A625

1979, Mar. 10 *Perf. 13½x13*

1160 A625 20w multicolored .40 .20

Labor Day.

Hand Holding Tools, Gun and Grain — A626

1979, Apr. 1 *Perf. 13x13½*

1161 A626 20w multicolored .40 .20

Strengthening national security.

Tabo Pagoda, Pulguk-sa Temple — A627

Women, Silk Screen — A628

Art Treasures: No. 1163, Statue. No. 1164, Crown. No. 1165, Celadon Vase.

1979, Apr. 1

1162	A627	20w gray bl & multi	.45	.20
1163	A627	20w bister & multi	.45	.20
1164	A627	20w violet & multi	.45	.20
1165	A627	20w brt grn & multi	.45	.20
1166	A628	60w multicolored	.90	.30
a.		Souvenir sheet of 2	3.25	3.25
		Nos. 1162-1166 (5)	2.70	1.10

5000 years of Korean art.
See Nos. 1175-1179, 1190.

Pulguk-sa Temple and PATA Emblem A629

1979, Apr. 16 *Perf. 13½x13*
1167 A629 20w multicolored .40 .20

28th Pacific Area Travel Association (PATA) Conf., Seoul, Apr. 16-18, and Gyeongju, Apr. 20-21.

Presidents Park and Senghor A630

1979, Apr. 22 *Perf. 13½x13*
1168 A630 20w multicolored .40 .20
a. Souvenir sheet of 2 1.50 1.50

Visit of Pres. Leopold Sedar Senghor of Senegal.

Basketball — A631

1979, Apr. 29 *Perf. 13x13½*
1169 A631 20w multicolored .50 .20

8th World Women's Basketball Championship, Seoul, Apr. 29-May 13.

Children and IYC Emblem A632

1979, May 5 Photo. *Perf. 13½x13*
1170 A632 20w multicolored .40 .20
a. Souvenir sheet of 2 1.50 1.50

International Year of the Child.

Traffic Pollution — A633

1979, June 5 Photo. *Perf. 13x13½*
1171 A633 20w green & dk brn .75 .25

Pollution control.

Flags, Presidents Park and Carter A634

1979, June 29 *Perf. 13½x13*
1172 A634 20w multicolored .40 .20
a. Souvenir sheet of 2 1.50 1.50

Visit of Pres. Jimmy Carter.

Korean Exhibition Center A635

1979, July 3
1173 A635 20w multicolored .30 .20

Opening of Korean Exhibition Center.

Jet, Globe, South Gate — A636

1979, Aug. 1 Photo. *Perf. 13½x13*
1174 A636 20w multicolored .40 .20

10th anniversary of Korean airlines.

Art Treasure Types

Designs: No. 1175, Porcelain jar, 17th century. No. 1176, Man on horseback, ceremonial pitcher, horiz. No. 1177, Sword Dance, by Shin Yun-bok. No. 1178, Golden Amitabha with halo, 8th century. No. 1179, Hahoe ritual mask.

1979 Photo. *Perf. 13x13½, 13½x13*

1175	A627 20w lilac & multi	.60	.25
1176	A627 20w multicolored	.60	.25
1177	A628 60w multicolored	.85	.30
a.	Souvenir sheet of 2	4.00	4.00
	Nos. 1175-1177 (3)	2.05	.80

Issued: #1177, Sept. 1; #1175-1176, Oct. 15.

1979, Nov. 15
1178 A627 20w dp green & multi .50 .25
1179 A627 20w multicolored .50 .25

Yongdu Rock — A637

1979, Sept. 28
1180 A637 20w shown .40 .20
1181 A637 20w Mt. Mai, vert. .40 .20

World Tourism Day.

People, Blood and Heart — A637a

1979, Oct. 1 *Perf. 13½x13*
1182 A637a 20w multicolored .75 .20

Blood Banks, 4th anniversary.

"My Life in the Year 2000" — A638

1979, Oct. 30 *Perf. 13½x13*
1183 A638 20w multicolored .30 .20
a. Souvenir sheet of 2 1.40 1.40

Philatelic Week, Oct. 30-Nov. 4.

Monkey-headed Figure, Bas-relief A639

Children Playing Yut A640

1979, Dec. 1
1184 A639 20w multicolored .40 .20
a. Souvenir sheet of 2 1.25 1.25
1185 A640 20w multicolored .40 .20
a. Souvenir sheet of 2 1.25 1.25

New Year 1980.

Inauguration of Pres. Choi Kyu-hah A641

1979, Dec. 21
1186 A641 20w multicolored .45 .20
a. Souvenir sheet of 2 5.00 5.00

President Park — A642

1980, Feb. 2 Photo. *Perf. 13x13½*
1187 A642 30w orange brn .45 .20
1188 A642 30w dull purple .45 .20
a. Souvenir sheet of 2 4.00 4.00
b. Pair, #1187-1188 2.25 2.25

President Park Chung Hee (1917-1979) memorial.

Art Treasure Type of 1979 and

Dragon-shaped Kettle — A643

Design: 60w, Landscape, by Kim Hong-do.

Perf. 13½x13, 13x13½
1980, Feb. 20 **Photo.**
1189 A643 30w multicolored .60 .20
1190 A628 60w multicolored 1.00 .30
a. Souvenir sheet of 2 3.50 3.50

Art Treasure Issue

Heavenly Horse, Saddle A644

Dragon Head, Banner Staff A645

Tiger, Granite Sculpture A647

Mounted Nobleman Mural — A646

Human Face, Roof Tile — A648

Deva King Sculpture — A650

White Tiger Mural — A649

Earthenware Ducks — A651

Tiger, Folk Painting — A653

Perf. 13½x13, 13x13½
1980-83 **Photo.**

1191	A644 30w multicolored	.60	.20
1192	A645 30w multicolored	.60	.20
1193	A646 30w multicolored	.60	.20
1194	A647 30w multicolored	.60	.20
1195	A648 30w multicolored	.50	.20
1196	A649 30w multicolored	.50	.20

Engr. *Perf. 12½x13*

1197	A650 30w black	.55	.20
1198	A650 30w red	.55	.20

1983 **Litho.** *Perf. 13*

1199	1000w bis brn & red brn	5.00	.80
1200	1000w bis brn & red brn	5.00	.80
a.	A651 Pair, #1199-1200	10.00	5.00
1201	A653 5000w multicolored	25.00	5.00
a.	Souvenir sheet, perf. 13½x13	30.00	
	Nos. 1191-1201 (11)	39.50	8.20

Issued: #1191-1192, 4/20; #1193-1194, 5/20; #1195-1196, 8/20; #1197-1198, 11/20. #1199-1200, 11/25/83. #1201, 12/1/83.

No. 1201a for PHILAKOREA '84. No. 1201a exists imperf. Value $150.

Lotus Blossoms and Ducks — A656

Tiger and Magpie A657

1980, Mar. 10 ***Perf. 13x13½, 13½x13***

1203	A656 30w multicolored	.55	.20
1204	A657 60w multicolored	1.00	.50

Red Phoenix (in Form of Rooster) — A658

Moon Over Mt. Konryun — A659

No. 1207, Sun over Mt. Konryun. No. 1207a has continuous design.

1980, May 10 ***Perf. 13x13½***

1205	A658 30w multicolored	.50	.20
1206	A659 60w multicolored	1.50	.45
1207	A659 60w multicolored	1.50	.45
a.	Souvenir sheet of 2, #1206-1207	5.00	5.00
b.	Pair, #1206-1207	3.75	3.00
	Nos. 1205-1207 (3)	3.50	1.10

Rabbits Pounding Grain in a Mortar — A660

Dragon in the Clouds — A661

1980, July 10 **Photo.** ***Perf. 13x13½***

1208	A660 30w multicolored	.60	.25
1209	A661 30w multicolored	.60	.25

Pine Tree, Pavilion, Mountain A662

Flowers and Birds, Bridal Room Screen A663

1980, Aug. 9 **Photo.** ***Perf. 13x13½***

1210	A662 30w multicolored	.55	.25
1211	A663 30w multicolored	1.10	.30

Tortoises and Cranes A664

Symbols of longevity: a, cranes, tortoises. b, buck. c, doe. d, waterfall.

1980, Nov. 10 **Photo.** ***Perf. 13½x13***

1212	Strip of 4	6.50	4.50
a.-d.	A664 30w any single	1.40	.20

New Community Movement, 10th Anniv. — A668

Freighters at Sea — A669

1980, Apr. 22 ***Perf. 13x13½***

1216	A668 30w multicolored	.40	.20

1980, Mar. 13

1217	A669 30w multicolored	.40	.20

Increase of Korea's shipping tonnage to 5 million tons.

Soccer — A670

1980, Aug. 23 ***Perf. 13x13½***

1218	A670 30w multicolored	.40	.20

10th President's Cup Soccer Tournament, Aug. 23-Sept. 5.

Mt. Sorak — A671

Paikryung Island — A672

Perf. 12½x13½

1980, Apr. 10 **Photo.**

1219	A671 15w multicolored	.35	.20
1220	A672 90w multicolored	1.00	.20

Flag — A673

1980 ***Perf. 13½x13***

1221	A673 30w multicolored	.45	.20

Coil Stamp

Perf. Vert.

1221A	A673 30w multicolored	1.40	.20

UN Intervention, 30th Anniv. — A674

Election of Miss World in Seoul — A675

1980, June 25 ***Perf. 13x13½***

1222	A674 30w multicolored	.40	.20

1980, July 8

1223	A675 30w multicolored	.40	.20

Women's Army Corps, 30th Anniversary A676

1980, Sept. 6 ***Perf. 13½x13***

1224	A676 30w multicolored	.40	.20

Baegma River — A677

Three Peaks of Dodam A678

1980, Sept. 28

1225	A677 30w multicolored	.40	.20
1226	A678 30w multicolored	.40	.20

Inauguration of Pres. Chun Doo-hwan A679

1980, Sept. 1

1227	A679 30w multicolored	.45	.20
a.	Souvenir sheet of 2	3.00	3.00

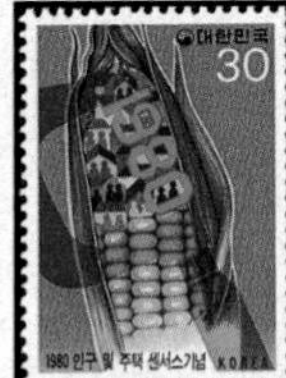
Ear of Corn — A680

Symbolic Tree — A681

1980, Oct. 20 ***Perf. 13x13½***

1228	A680 30w multicolored	.40	.20

12th population and housing census.

1980, Oct. 27

1229	A681 30w multicolored	.40	.20

National Red Cross, 75th anniversary.

"Mail-Delivering Angels" — A682

1980, Nov. 6 ***Perf. 13½x13***

1230	A682 30w multicolored	.40	.20
a.	Souvenir sheet of 2	1.40	1.40

Philatelic Week, Nov. 6-11.

Korea-Japan Submarine Cable System Inauguration A683

1980, Nov. 28 ***Perf. 13x13½***

1231	A683 30w multicolored	.40	.20

Rooster — A684

Cranes — A685

1980, Dec. 1

1232	A684 30w multicolored	.45	.20
a.	Souvenir sheet of 2	1.40	1.40
1233	A685 30w multicolored	.45	.20
a.	Souvenir sheet of 2	1.40	1.40

New Year 1981.

Second Inauguration of Pres. Chun Doo-hwan A686

1981, Mar. 3 **Photo.** ***Perf. 13½x13***

1234	A686 30w multicolored	.40	.20
a.	Souvenir sheet of 2	1.25	1.25

Ship Issue

Oil Tanker A687

Cargo Ship — A688

Oil Tanker A689

Cargo Ship — A690

Tug Boat — A691

Stern Trawler A692

Log Carrier A693

Auto Carrier A694

Chemical Carrier A695

Passenger Boat A696

1981, Mar. 13 ***Perf. 13½x13, 13x13½***

1235 A687 30w multicolored .50 .20
1236 A688 90w multicolored .80 .25

5th Maritime Day.

1981, May 10 **Photo.** ***Perf. 13½x13***

1237 A689 30w multicolored .50 .20
1238 A690 90w multicolored .90 .30

1981, July 10 ***Perf. 13½x13***

1239 A691 40w multicolored .65 .20
1240 A692 100w multicolored 1.10 .30

1981, Aug. 10

1241 A693 40w multicolored .65 .20
1242 A694 100w multicolored 1.10 .30

1981, Nov. 10 **Engr.** ***Perf. 13x12½***

1243 A695 40w black .55 .20
1244 A696 100w dk blue 1.00 .30
Nos. 1235-1244 (10) 7.75 2.45

11th Natl. Assembly Opening Session A697

1981, Apr. 17 **Photo.** ***Perf. 13½x13***

1245 A697 30w gold & dk brn .40 .20

Hand Reading Braille, Helping Hands — A698

1981, Apr. 20 **Photo.** ***Perf. 13x13½***

1246 A698 30w shown .40 .20
1247 A698 90w Man in wheel-chair .75 .20

International Year of the Disabled.

Ribbon and Council Emblem A699

Clena River and Mountains A700

1981, June 5 **Photo.** ***Perf. 13x13½***

1248 A699 40w multicolored .40 .20

Advisory Council on Peaceful Unification Policy (North and South Korea) anniv.

1981, June 5

1249 A700 30w shown .40 .20
1250 A700 90w Seagulls .85 .25

10th World Environment Day.

Pres. Chun and Pres. Suharto of Indonesia A701

Pres. Chun Visit to Asia: b, King of Malaysia. c, Korean, Singapore flags. d, King Bhumibol Adulyadej of Thailand. e, Pres. Marcos of Philippines.

1981, June 25 ***Perf. 13½x13***

1251 Strip of 5 4.50 3.75
a.-e. A701 40w, any single .55 .20
f. Souvenir sheet of 5, imperf. 2.50 2.50

Size: 49x33mm

Perf. 13x13½

1252 A701 40w multicolored .55 .20
a. Souvenir sheet of 2, imperf. 2.25 2.25

36th Anniv. of Liberation — A702

1981, Aug. 15 **Photo.** ***Perf. 13x13½***

1253 A702 40w multicolored .40 .20

Tolharubang, "Stone Grandfather" A704

Rose of Sharon A705

Porcelain Jar, 17th Cent. — A706

Chomsongdae Observatory, 7th Cent. — A707

Mounted Warrior, Earthenware Jug, 5th Cent. A708

Family Planning A709

Walking Stick A710

Ryu Kwan-soon (1904-20), Martyr A711

"Tasan" Chung Yak-yong, Lee Dynasty Scholar A712

Ahn Joong-guen (1879-1910), Martyr A713

Ahn Chang-ho (1878-1938), Independence Fighter A714

Koryo Celadon Incense Burner A715

Kim Ku (1876-1949), Statesman A716

Mountain Landscape Brick Bas-relief A717

Mandarin Duck, Celadon Incense Burner — A718

Perf. 13½x12½ (Nos. 1256, 1257, 1266), 13, 13½x13, 13x13½

1981-89 **Photo., Engr.**

1255 A704 20w multi ('86) .40 .20
1256 A705 40w multi .50 .20
1257 A706 60w multi .50 .20
1258 A707 70w multi .75 .20
1259 A708 80w multi ('83) .85 .20
1260 A709 80w multi ('86) 1.00 .25
1261 A710 80w multi ('89) 2.50 .25
1262 A711 100w lilac 1.00 .20
1263 A712 100w gray blk ('86) 2.50 .20
1264 A713 200w lt ol grn & ol 1.50 .25
1265 A714 300w dl lil ('83) 2.25 .25
1266 A715 400w multi 5.00 .50
1267 A715 400w pale grn & multi ('83) 3.50 .40
1268 A716 450w dk vio brn ('86) 2.75 .40
1269 A717 500w multi 3.50 .75
1270 A718 700w multi ('83) 5.00 .80
Nos. 1255-1270 (16) 33.50 5.25

Inscription and denomination of No. 1266, colorless, No. 1267, dark brown.
See Nos. 1449, 1449C, 1594F.

Coil Stamp

Photo. ***Perf. 13 Horiz.***

1271 A707 70w multicolored 2.00 .50

Girl Flying Model Plane — A721

Air Force Chief of Staff Cup, 3rd Aeronautic Competition: Various model planes.

1981, Sept. 20 ***Perf. 13½x13***

1272 Strip of 5 4.50 3.75
a. A721 10w multi .50 .20
b. A721 20w multi .50 .20
c. A721 40w multi .50 .20
d. A721 50w multi .65 .30
e. A721 80w multi .90 .40

WHO Emblem, Citizens — A722

World Tourism Day — A723

1981, Sept. 22 ***Perf. 13x13½***

1273 A722 40w multicolored .40 .20

WHO, 32nd Western Pacific Regional Committee Meeting, Seoul, Sept. 22-28.

1981, Sept. 28

1274 A723 40w Seoul Tower .40 .20
1275 A723 40w Ulreung Isld. .40 .20

Bicycle Racing A724

1981, Oct. 10 ***Perf. 13½x13***

1276 A724 40w shown .45 .20
1277 A724 40w Swimming .45 .20

62nd Natl. Sports Festival, Seoul, 10/10-15.

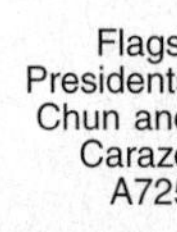

Flags, Presidents Chun and Carazo A725

1981, Oct. 12 ***Perf. 13½x13***

1278 A725 40w multicolored .45 .20

Visit of Pres. Rodrigo Carazo Odio of Costa Rica, Oct. 12-14.

World Food Day — A726

1981, Oct. 16 ***Perf. 13x13½***
1279 A726 40w multicolored .40 .20

First Natl. Aviation Day — A727

1981, Oct. 30 ***Perf. 13½x13***
1280 A727 40w multicolored .45 .20

1988 Olympic Games, Seoul — A728

1981, Oct. 30 ***Perf. 13x13½***
1281 A728 40w multicolored .60 .20

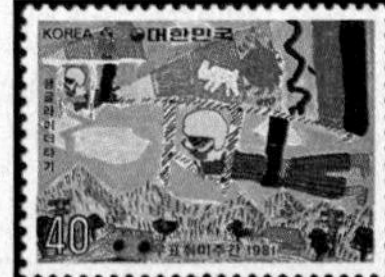

9th Philatelic Week, Nov. 18-24 — A729

1981, Nov. 18 ***Perf. 13½x13***
1282 A729 40w multicolored .40 .20
a. Souvenir sheet of 2 1.60 1.60

Camellia and Dog — A730

Children Flying Kite — A731

1981, Dec. 1 ***Perf. 13x13½***
1283 A730 40w multicolored .40 .20
a. Souvenir sheet of 2 1.60 1.60
1284 A731 40w multicolored .40 .20
a. Souvenir sheet of 2 1.60 1.60

New Year 1982 (Year of the Dog).

Hangul Hakhoe Language Society, 60th Anniv. A732

1981, Dec. 3 ***Perf. 13½x13***
1285 A732 40w multicolored .45 .20

Telecommunications Authority Inauguration A733

1982, Jan. 4 **Photo.** ***Perf. 13x13½***
1286 A733 60w multicolored .50 .20

Scouting Year — A734

1982, Feb. 22
1287 A734 60w multicolored .50 .20

60th Anniv. of YWCA in Korea — A735

1982, Apr. 20 **Photo.** ***Perf. 13x13½***
1288 A735 60w multicolored .45 .20

Intl. Polar Year Centenary A736

1982, Apr. 21 ***Perf. 13½x13***
1289 A736 60w multicolored .50 .20

60th Children's Day — A737

1982, May 5 ***Perf. 13½x13***
1290 A737 60w multicolored .45 .20

Visit of Liberian Pres. Samuel K. Doe, May 9-13 A738

1982, May 9 **Litho.** ***Perf. 13x12½***
1291 A738 60w multicolored .50 .20
a. Souvenir sheet of 2, imperf. 1.60 1.60

Centenary of US-Korea Treaty of Amity — A739

1982, May 18 **Photo.** ***Perf. 13½x13***
1292 A739 60w Statue of Liberty, pagoda .45 .20
1293 A739 60w Emblem .45 .20
a. Souvenir sheet of 2 3.50 3.50
b. Pair, #1292-1293 1.50 1.50

Visit of Zaire Pres. Mobutu Sese Seko, June 7-10 A740

1982, June 7 **Litho.** ***Perf. 13x12½***
1294 A740 60w multicolored .45 .20
a. Souvenir sheet of 2, imperf. 1.60 1.60

Historical Painting Issue

Gen. Kwon Yul's Victory at Haengju, by Oh Seung-woo — A747

Designs: No. 1295, Territorial Expansion by Kwanggaeto the Great, by Lee Chong-sang, 1975. No. 1296, Gen. Euljimunduck's Victory at Salsoo, by Park Kak-soon, 1975. No. 1297, Shilla's Repulse of Tang's Army, by Oh Seung-woo. No. 1298, Gen. Kang Kam-chan's Victory at Kyiju, by Lee Yong-hwan. No. 1299, Admiral Yi Sun-sin's Victory at Hansan, 1592, by Kim Hyung-ku. No. 1300, Gen. Kim Chwa-jin's Battle at Chungsanri, by Sohn Soo-kwang. No. 1302, Kim Chong-suh's Exploitation of Yukjin, 1434, by Kim Tae.

1982 **Photo.** ***Perf. 13x13½***
1295 A747 60w multicolored .75 .40
1296 A747 60w multicolored 1.40 .60
1297 A747 60w multicolored .65 .30
1298 A747 60w multicolored .65 .30
1299 A747 60w multicolored 1.00 .40
1300 A747 60w multicolored 1.00 .40
1301 A747 60w shown 1.10 .40
1302 A747 60w multicolored 1.10 .40
Nos. 1295-1302 (8) 7.65 3.20

Issued: #1295-1296, 6/15; #1297-1298, 7/15; #1299-1300, 10/15; #1301-1302, 12/15.

55th Intl. YMCA Convention, Seoul, July 20-23 — A749

Flags, Presidents Chun and Arap Moi — A750

1982, July 20
1303 A749 60w multicolored .40 .20

1982, Aug. 17 ***Perf. 13½x13***

Pres. Chun's Visit to Africa & Canada: #1304, Kenya (Pres. Daniel T. Arap Moi), Aug. 17-19. #1305, Nigeria (Pres. Alhaji Shehe Shagari), Aug. 19-22. #1306, Gabon (Pres. El Hadj Omar Bongo), Aug. 22-24. #1307, Senegal (Pres. Abdou Diouf), Aug. 24-26. #1308, Canada, Aug. 28-31.

1304 A750 60w multicolored .45 .20
1305 A750 60w multicolored .45 .20
1306 A750 60w multicolored .45 .20
1307 A750 60w multicolored .45 .20
1308 A750 60w multicolored .45 .20
Nos. 1304-1308 (5) 2.25 1.00

Souvenir Sheets of 2

1304a A750 60w 2.25 2.25
1305a A750 60w 2.25 2.25
1306a A750 60w 2.25 2.25
1307a A750 60w 2.25 2.25
1308a A750 60w 2.25 2.25
Nos. 1304a-1308a (5) 11.25

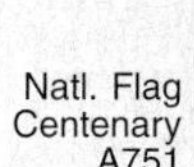

Natl. Flag Centenary A751

1982, Aug. 22
1309 A751 60w multicolored .45 .20
a. Souvenir sheet of 2 2.25 2.25

2nd Seoul Open Intl. Table Tennis Championship, Aug. 25-31 — A752

1982, Aug. 25
1310 A752 60w multicolored .50 .20

27th World Amateur Baseball Championship Series, Seoul, Sept. 4-18 — A753

1982, Sept. 4 **Engr.** ***Perf. 13***
1311 A753 60w red brn .50 .20

Seoul Intl. Trade Fair (SITRA '82), Sept. 24-Oct. 18 — A754

1982, Sept. 17 **Photo.** ***Perf. 13½x13***
1312 A754 60w multicolored .45 .20

Philatelic Week, Oct. 15-21 — A755

Design: Miners reading consolatory letters.

1982, Oct. 15
1313 A755 60w multicolored .45 .20
a. Souvenir sheet of 2 1.50 1.50

Visit of Indonesian Pres. Suharto, Oct. 16-19 — A756

1982, Oct. 16 **Litho.** ***Perf. 13x12½***
1314 A756 60w multicolored .40 .20
a. Souvenir sheet of 2, imperf. 1.40 1.40

37th Jaycee (Intl. Junior Chamber of Commerce) World Congress, Seoul, Nov. 3-18 — A757

1982, Nov. 3 ***Perf. 13½x13***
1315 A757 60w multicolored .40 .20

2nd UN Conference on Peaceful Uses of Outer Space, Vienna, Aug. 9-21 — A758

1982, Nov. 20 *Perf. 13x13½*

1316 A758 60w multicolored .45 .20

New Year 1983 (Year of the Boar) — A759

1982, Dec. 1

1317 A759 60w Magpies, money bag .45 .20
a. Souvenir sheet of 2 2.00 2.00
1318 A759 60w Boar, bas-relief .45 .20
a. Souvenir sheet of 2 2.00 2.00

Flags of Korea and Turkey — A760

1982, Dec. 20 *Perf. 13*

1319 A760 60w multicolored .45 .20
a. Souvenir sheet of 2, imperf. 1.50 1.50

Visit of Pres. Kenan Evren of Turkey, Dec. 20-23.

Letter Writing Campaign — A761

1982, Dec. 31 Photo. *Perf. 13x13½*

1320 A761 60w multicolored .40 .20

First Intl. Customs Day — A762

1983, Jan. 26 *Perf. 13½x13*

1321 A762 60w multicolored .50 .20

Korean-made Vehicle Issue

Hyundai Pony-2 A764

Daewoo Maepsy A765

Super Titan Truck — A768

Flat-bed Truck — A770

1983 Photo. *Perf. 13½x13*

1322 A764 60w Keohwa Jeep .75 .25
1323 A764 60w shown .75 .25
a. Pair, #1322-1323 2.25 2.25
1324 A765 60w shown .75 .25
1325 A764 60w Kia minibus .75 .25
a. Pair, #1324-1325 2.25 2.25
1326 A764 60w Highway bus .75 .25
1327 A768 60w shown .75 .25
1328 A764 70w Dump truck .90 .25
1329 A770 70w shown .90 .25
1330 A764 70w Cement mixer .90 .25
1331 A764 70w Oil truck .90 .25
Nos. 1322-1331 (10) 8.10 2.50

Issued: #1322-1323, Feb. 25; #1324-1325, Mar. 25; #1326-1327, May 25; #1328-1329, July 25; #1330-1331, Aug. 25.

Visit of Malaysian Seri Paduka Baginda, Mar. 22-26 — A773

1983, Mar. 22

1332 A773 60w multicolored .40 .20
a. Souvenir sheet of 2 1.40 1.40

Postal Service Issue

General Bureau of Postal Administration Building A774

Mailman, 1884 — A776

Ancient Mail Carrier A778

Nos. 1-2 — A780

Pre-modern Period Postal Symbol, Mailbox A782

Designs: #1334, Seoul Central PO. #1336, Mailman on motorcycle, 1983. #1338, Modern mail transport. #1340, No. 1201. #1342, Current postal symbol, mailbox.

1983-84 Photo. *Perf. 13½x13*

1333 A774 60w multicolored .60 .25
1334 A774 60w multicolored .60 .25
1335 A776 70w multicolored .70 .25
1336 A776 70w multicolored .70 .25
1337 A778 70w multicolored .90 .25
1338 A778 70w multicolored .90 .25
1339 A780 70w multicolored .60 .20
1340 A780 70w multicolored .60 .20
1341 A782 70w multicolored .60 .20
1342 A782 70w multicolored .60 .20
Nos. 1333-1342 (10) 6.80 2.30

PHILAKOREA '84, Seoul, Oct. 22-31, 1984.
Issued: #1333-1334, Apr. 22; #1335-1336, June 10; #1337-1338, Aug. 10; #1339-1340, Feb. 10, 1984; #1341-1342, Mar. 10, 1984.

Teachers' Day — A784

1983, May 15 Photo. *Perf. 13x13½*

1343 A784 60w Village school-house, score .50 .20
a. Souvenir sheet of 2 2.00 2.00

World Communications Year — A785

1983, June 20

1344 A785 70w multicolored .50 .20
a. Souvenir sheet of 2 1.50 1.50

Communications Life Insurance Inauguration — A786

1983, July 1 Photo. *Perf. 13½x13*

1345 A786 70w multicolored .70 .20

Science and Technology Symposium, Seoul, July 4-8 — A787

1983, July 4

1346 A787 70w multicolored .50 .20

Visit of Jordan's King Hussein, Sept. 10-13 A788

1983, Sept. 10 Litho. *Perf. 13x12½*

1347 A788 70w Pres. Hwan, King Hussein, flags .50 .20
a. Souvenir sheet of 2, imperf. 1.50 1.50

ASTA, 53rd World Travel Congress, Seoul — A789

1983, Sept. 25 Photo. *Perf. 13*

1348 A789 70w multicolored .50 .20

A790 A791

1983, Oct. 4 Photo. *Perf. 13*

1349 A790 70w multicolored .50 .20
a. Souvenir sheet of 2 1.50 1.50

70th Inter-Parliamentary Union Conference.

1983, Oct. 6 Photo. *Perf. 13*

1350 A791 70w Gymnastics .65 .20
1351 A791 70w Soccer .65 .20

64th National Sports Festival.

Pres. Chun and Pres. U San Yu of Burma A791a

Pres. Chun's Curtailed Visit to Southwest Asia: No. 1351B, India. No. 1351C, Pres. Junius R. Jayawardene, Sri Lanka. No. 1351D, Australia, flag. No. 1351E, New Zealand, flag. Withdrawn after one day due to political assassination.

1983, Oct. 8 Photo. *Perf. 13½x13*

1351A A791a 70w multicolored 1.50 .75
1351B A791a 70w multicolored 1.50 .75
1351C A791a 70w multicolored 1.50 .75
1351D A791a 70w multicolored 1.50 .75
1351E A791a 70w multicolored 1.50 .75
Nos. 1351A-1351E (5) 7.50

Souvenir Sheets of 2

1351f A791a 70w 5.00 5.00
1351g A791a 70w 5.00 5.00
1351h A791a 70w 5.00 5.00
1351i A791a 70w 5.00 5.00
1351j A791a 70w 5.00 5.00
Nos. 1351f-1351j (5) 25.00

Water Resource Development A792

1983, Oct. 15 Litho. *Perf. 13*

1352 A792 70w multicolored .50 .20

Newspaper Publication Cent. — A793

1983, Oct. 31 Litho. *Perf. 13*

1353 A793 70w multicolored .50 .20

Natl. Tuberculosis Assoc., 30th Anniv. — A794

1983, Nov. 6 Photo. *Perf. 13*

1354 A794 70w multicolored .50 .20

Presidents Chun and Reagan, Natl. Flags — A795

1983, Nov. 12 Photo. *Perf. 13*

1355 A795 70w multicolored .50 .20
a. Souvenir sheet of 2 3.00 3.00

Visit of Pres. Ronald Reagan, Nov. 12-14.

11th Philatelic Week — A796

1983, Nov. 18 Photo. *Perf. 13*

1356 A796 70w multicolored .50 .20
a. Souvenir sheet of 2 2.75 2.75

New Year 1984
A797 A798

1983, Dec. 1 Photo. *Perf. 13*

1357 A797 70w Mouse, stone wall relief .50 .20
a. Souvenir sheet of 2 2.50 2.50
1358 A798 70w Cranes, pine tree .50 .20
a. Souvenir sheet of 2 2.50 2.50

Bicentenary of Catholic Church in Korea — A799

1984, Jan. 4 Photo. *Perf. 13x13½*

1359 A799 70w Cross .40 .20
a. Souvenir sheet of 2 3.25 3.25

Visit of Brunei's Sultan Bolkiah-Apr. 7-9 — A800

1984, Apr. 7 Litho. *Perf. 13x12½*

1360 A800 70w multicolored .50 .20
a. Souvenir sheet of 2, imperf. 1.50 1.50

Visit of Qatar's Sheik Khalifa, Apr. 20-22 A801

1984, Apr. 20

1361 A801 70w multicolored .50 .20
a. Souvenir sheet of 2, imperf. 1.50 1.50

Girl Mailing Letter — A802

Mailman in City — A803

1984, Apr. 22 Photo. *Perf. 13½x13*

1362 A802 70w multicolored .40 .20
a. Souvenir sheet of 2 1.75 1.75
1363 A803 70w multicolored .40 .20
a. Souvenir sheet of 2 1.75 1.75

Korean postal service.

Visit of Pope John Paul II, May 3-7 — A808

1984, May 3 Engr. *Perf. 12½*

1368 A808 70w dk brn .60 .20

Photogravure & Engraved

1369 A808 70w multicolored .60 .20
a. Souvenir sheet of 2, #1368-1369, perf. 13½ 2.50 2.50

A809 A810

1984, May 11 Photo. *Perf. 13x13½*

1370 A809 70w Tools, brushes, flower .50 .20

Workers' Cultural Festival.

1984, May 21 Photo. *Perf. 13x13½*

1371 A810 70w Jet, ship, Asia map .50 .20

Customs Cooperation Council 63rd-64th Sessions, Seoul, May 21-25.

Visit of Sri Lanka's Pres. Jayewardene, May 27-30 — A811

1984, May 27 *Perf. 13½x13*

1372 A811 70w Asia map, flags, flowers .50 .20
a. Souvenir sheet of 2 1.50 1.50

Advertising Congress Emblem — A812

'88 Olympic Expressway Opening — A813

1984, June 18 Photo. *Perf. 13x13½*

1373 A812 70w ADASIA '84 emblem .50 .20

14th Asian Advertising Cong., Seoul, June 18-21.

1984, June 22

1374 A813 70w multicolored .65 .20

Intl. Olympic Committee, 90th Anniv. — A814

1984, June 23

1375 A814 70w multicolored .50 .20

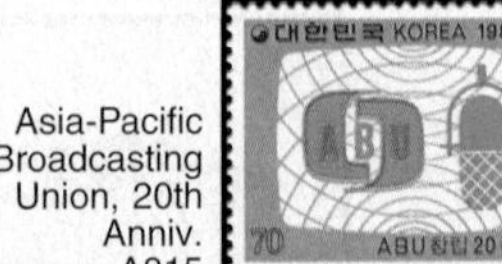

Asia-Pacific Broadcasting Union, 20th Anniv. A815

1984, June 30 *Perf. 13½x13*

1376 A815 70w Emblem, microphone .50 .20

Visit of Senegal's Pres. Diouf, July 9-12 A816

1984, July 9 Litho. *Perf. 13x12½*

1377 A816 70w Flags of Korea & Senegal .50 .20
a. Souvenir sheet of 2, imperf. 2.00 2.00

1984 Summer Olympics A817

Lithographed and Engraved

1984, July 28 *Perf. 12½*

1378 A817 70w Archery .75 .25
1379 A817 440w Fencing 3.00 .75

Korean Protestant Church Cent. A818

Groom on Horseback A819

Stained glass windows.

1984, Aug. 16 *Perf. 13*

1380 A818 70w Crucifixion .75 .20
1381 A818 70w Cross, dove .75 .20
a. Souvenir sheet of 2 6.00 6.00
b. Pair, #1380-1381 2.00 2.00

1984, Sept. 1 Photo. *Perf. 13x13½*

Wedding Procession: a, Lantern carrier. b, Groom. c, Musician. d, Bride in sedan chair (52x33mm).

1382 Strip of 4 3.00 1.50
a.-d. A819 70w any single .70 .25
e. Souvenir sheet 2.50 2.50

No. 1382e contains No. 1382d.

Pres. Chun's Visit to Japan, Sept. 6-8 A820

1984, Sept. 6 Litho. *Perf. 13x12½*

1383 A820 70w Chun, flag, Mt. Fuji .50 .20
a. Souvenir sheet of 2, imperf. 2.00 2.00

Visit of Gambia's Pres. Jawara, Sept. 12-17 A821

1984, Sept. 12

1384 A821 70w Flags of Korea & Gambia .50 .20
a. Souvenir sheet of 2, imperf. 2.00 2.00

Visit of Gabon's Pres. Bongo, Sept. 21-23 — A822

1984, Sept. 21 *Perf. 13*
1385 A822 70w Flags of Korea & Gabon .50 .20
a. Souvenir sheet of 2, imperf. 1.75 1.75

Seoul Intl. Trade Fair — A823

1984, Sept. 18 Photo. *Perf. 13x13½*
1386 A823 70w Products .50 .20

65th Natl. Sports Festival, Taegu, Oct. 11-16 — A824

1984, Oct. 11 Photo. *Perf. 13½x13*
1387 A824 70w Badminton .50 .20
1388 A824 70w Wrestling .50 .20

Philakorea '84 Stamp Show, Seoul, Oct. 22-31 — A825

1984, Oct. 22 *Perf. 13½x13, 13x13½*
1389 A825 70w South Gate, stamps .50 .20
a. Souvenir sheet of 4 3.50 3.50
1390 A825 70w Emblem under magnifier, vert. .50 .20
a. Souvenir sheet of 4 3.50 3.50

Visit of Maldives Pres. Maumoon Abdul Gayoom, Oct. 29-Nov. 1 — A826

1984, Oct. 29 Litho. *Perf. 13x12½*
1392 A826 70w multicolored .50 .20
a. Souvenir sheet of 2, imperf. 2.00 2.00

Chamber of Commerce and Industry Cent. — A827

Children Playing Jaegi-chagi — A828

1984, Oct. 31 Photo. *Perf. 13x13½*
1393 A827 70w "100" .50 .20

1984, Dec. 1 Photo. *Perf. 13x13½*
New Year 1985 (Year of the ox).
1394 A828 70w Ox, bas-relief .50 .20
a. Souvenir sheet of 2 1.75 1.75
1395 A828 70w shown .50 .20
a. Souvenir sheet of 2 1.75 1.75

Intl. Youth Year — A829

1985, Jan. 25 Photo. *Perf. 13½x13*
1396 A829 70w IYY emblem .50 .20

Folkways — A830

1985, Feb. 19 Photo. *Perf. 13x13½*
1397 A830 70w Pounding rice .50 .20
1398 A830 70w Welcoming full moon .50 .20

1985, Aug. 20
1399 A830 70w Wrestling .75 .20
1400 A830 70w Janggi, Korean chess .75 .20

Modern Art Series

Rocky Mountain in the Early Spring, 1915, by Shimjoen, (Ahn Jung-shik) — A831

Still-life with a Doll, 1927, by Suhlcho, (Lee Chong-woo) — A832

Spring Day on a Farm, 1961, by Eijai, (Huh Paik-ryun, 1903-1977) — A833

The Exorcist, 1941, by Chulma, (Kim Chung-hyun, 1901-1953) — A834

Chunhyang-do, by Kim Un-ho — A835

Flowers, by Lee Sang-bum — A836

Image of A Friend, by Ku Bon-wung — A837

Woman in a Ski Suit, by Son Ung-seng — A838

Valley of the Peach Blossoms, 1964, by Pyen Kwan-Sik (1899-1976) — A839

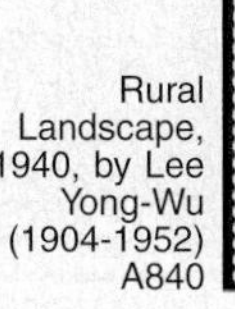

Rural Landscape, 1940, by Lee Yong-Wu (1904-1952) — A840

Male, 1932, by Lee Ma-Dong — A841

Woman with a Water Jar on Her Head, 1944, by Yun Hyo-Chung (1917-1967) — A842

Photo.; Litho. & Engr. (#1411-1412)
1985-87 *Perf. 13½x13, 13x13½*
1401 A831 70w multicolored .75 .25
1402 A832 70w multicolored .75 .25
1403 A833 70w multicolored .75 .25
1404 A834 70w multicolored .75 .25
1405 A835 80w multi ('86) 1.25 .40
1406 A836 80w multi ('86) 1.25 .40
1407 A837 80w multi ('86) 1.25 .40
1408 A838 80w multi ('86) 1.25 .40
1409 A839 80w multi ('87) *3.50* .90
1410 A840 80w multi ('87) *3.50* .90
1411 A841 80w multi ('87) *3.50* .90
1412 A842 80w multi ('87) *3.50* .90
Nos. 1401-1412 (12) 22.00 6.20

Issued: #1401-1402, 4/10; #1403-1404, 7/5; #1405-1408, 12/1; #1409-1412, 6/12.

State Visit of Pres. Chun to the US — A843

Photo. & Engr.
1985, Apr. 24 *Perf. 13*
1413 A843 70w multicolored .50 .20
a. Souvenir sheet of 2 2.00 2.00

Coastal and Inland Fish Series

Gak-si- Bung-eo (silver carp) — A844

Dot-sac-chi (sword fish) — A845

Eoreumchi — A846

Sweetfish A847

Sardine A848

Hammerhead Shark A849

Cham-jung-go-ji — A850

Swi-ri — A851

Oar Fish — A852

Devil-ray A853

1985-87 Photo. *Perf. 13½x13*

1414	A844 70w multicolored	.75	.25
1415	A845 70w multicolored	.75	.25
1416	A846 70w multi ('86)	2.00	.55
1417	A847 70w multi ('86)	2.00	.55
1418	A848 70w multi ('86)	2.00	.55
1419	A849 70w multi ('86)	2.00	.55
1420	A850 80w multi ('87)	2.50	1.00
1421	A851 80w multi ('87)	2.50	1.00
1422	A852 80w multi ('87)	2.50	1.00
1423	A853 80w multi ('87)	2.50	1.00
	Nos. 1414-1423 (10)	19.50	6.70

Issued: #1414-1415, 5/30; #1416-1423, 7/25.

Yonsei University and Medical School, Cent. A854

Photogravure and Engraved

1985, May 6 ***Perf. 13***
1424 A854 70w Underwood Hall .50 .20

State Visit of Pres. Mohammad Zia-Ul-Haq of Pakistan, May 6-10 — A855

1985, May 6 Photo. *Perf. 13x13½*
1425 A855 70w multicolored .50 .20
a. Souvenir sheet of 2 1.50 1.50

State Visit of Pres. Luis Alberto Monge of Costa Rica, May 19-23 — A856

1985, May 18 ***Perf. 13½x13***
1426 A856 70w multicolored .50 .20
a. Souvenir sheet of 2 1.50 1.50

State Visit of Pres. Hussain Muhammad Ershad of Bangladesh, June 15-19 A857

1985, June 15
1427 A857 70w multicolored .50 .20
a. Souvenir sheet of 2, imperf. 1.50 1.50

State Visit of Pres. Joao Bernardo Vieira of Guinea-Bissau, June 25-28 — A858

1985, June 25
1428 A858 70w multicolored .50 .20
a. Souvenir sheet of 2, imperf. 1.50 1.50

Liberation from Japanese Occupation Forces, 40th Anniv. — A859

Heavenly Lake, Mt. Paektu, natl. flower.

1985, Aug. 14 Litho. *Perf. 13x12½*
1429 A859 70w multicolored .50 .20

Folk Music Series

The Spring of My Home, Music by Hong Nan-pa and Lyrics by Lee Won-su A860

A Leaf Boat, Music by Yun Yong-ha and Lyrics by Park Hong-Keun A861

Half Moon, 1924, by Yun Keuk-Young A862

Let's Go and Pick the Moon, by Yun Seok-Jung and Park Tae Hyun A863

Korean Farm Music A864

Barley Field, by Park Wha-mok and Yun Yong-ha — A865

Magnolia, by Cho Young-Shik and Kim Dong-jin — A866

Chusok, Harvest Moon Festival — A867

1985, Sept. 10 Photo. *Perf. 13x13½*
1430 A860 70w multicolored .75 .25
1431 A861 70w multicolored .75 .25

1986, June 25 Photo. *Perf. 13x13½*
1432 A862 70w multicolored 1.00 .30
1433 A863 70w multicolored 1.50 .60

1986, Aug. 26 Photo. *Perf. 13½x13*

Musicians with: a, Flag, hand gong. b, Drum flute. c, Drum, hand gong. d, Taborets, ribbons. e, Taboret, sun, woman, child. Has continuous design.

1434 Strip of 5 7.50 7.50
a.-e. A864 70w, any single 1.25 .25

1987, Mar. 25 Photo. *Perf. 13x13½*
1435 A865 80w multicolored 3.00 1.00
1436 A866 80w multicolored 3.00 1.00

1987, Sept. 10 Photo. *Perf. 13x13½*

Harvest moon dance: No. 1437a, Eight dancers, harvest moon. No. 1437b, Four dancers, festival wheels, balloons. No. 1437c, Three dancers, children on see-saw. No. 1437d, Four dancers, women preparing meal.

1437 A867 Strip of 4 16.00 16.00
a.-d. 80w any single 3.00 1.00

Folklore Series

Tano, Spring Harvest Festival — A868

Sick for Home, by Lee Eun-sang and Kim Kong-jin A869

Pioneer, by Yoon Hae-young and Cho Doo-nam A870

Mask Dance (Talchum) — A871

Designs: a, Woman on shore, riding a swing. b, Sweet flag coiffures. c, Boy picking flowers, girl on swing. d, Boys wrestling.
Illustration reduced.

1988, Aug. 25 Photo. *Perf. 13x13½*
1438 A868 Strip of 4 6.00 6.00
a.-d. 80w multicolored 1.25 .40

1988, Nov. 15
1439 A869 80w multicolored .75 .25
1440 A870 80w multicolored .75 .25

1989, Feb. 25

Designs: a, Two mask dancers with scarves. b, Dancers with fans. c, Dancers with scarf and laurel or fan. d, Three dancers, first as an animal and two more carrying fan and bells or torch.

1441 A871 Strip of 4 5.00 5.00
a.-d. 80w any single 1.25 .40

Korean Telecommunications, Cent. — A872

1985, Sept. 28 ***Perf. 13½x13***
1442 A872 70w Satellite, emblem, dish receiver .50 .20

World Bank Conference, Seoul, Oct. 8-11 — A873

1985, Oct. 8 ***Perf. 13x13½***
1443 A873 70w Emblem .50 .20

Intl. Bank for Reconstruction & Development, 40th Anniv.

UN, 40th Anniv. A874

1985, Oct. 24 ***Perf. 13½x13***
1444 A874 70w Emblem, doves .50 .20

Natl. Red Cross, 80th Anniv. A875

1985, Oct. 26
1445 A875 70w red, blk & bl .50 .20

Segment of Canceled Cover — A876

1985, Nov. 18 Photo. *Perf. 13½x13*
1446 A876 70w multicolored .50 .20

12th Philatelic Week, Nov. 18-23.

New Year 1986 — A877

Lithographed and Engraved

1985, Dec. 2 *Perf. 13x13½*
1447 A877 70w multicolored .50 .20

Mt. Fuji, Korean Airlines Jet — A878

1985, Dec. 18 **Photo.**
1448 A878 70w brt bl, blk & red .75 .30

Normalization of diplomatic relations between Korea and Japan, 20th anniv.
See No. C44.

Statesman Type of 1986 and Types of 1981-86
Engr., Photo. (40w)

1986-87 *Perf. 13*
1449 A716 550w indigo 3.00 .40

Coil Stamps
Perf. 13 Vert.

1449A A704 20w multicolored 1.00 .40
1449B A705 40w multicolored 1.25 .30
1449C A708 80w multicolored 1.75 .60
Nos. 1449A-1449C (3) 4.00 1.30

Issue dates: 550w, Dec. 10; others, 1987.

Intl. Peace Year — A879

1986, Jan. 15 **Photo.** *Perf. 13x13½*
1450 A879 70w multicolored .50 .20

See No. C45.

State Visits of Pres. Chun — A880

Portrait, natl. flags and: No. 1452, Parliament, Brussels. No. 1453, Eiffel Tower, Paris. No. 1454, Cathedral, Cologne. No. 1455, Big Ben, London.

1986, Apr. 4 **Litho.** *Perf. 12½x13*
1452 A880 70w multicolored .75 .30
1453 A880 70w multicolored .75 .30
1454 A880 70w multicolored .75 .30
1455 A880 70w multicolored .75 .30
Nos. 1452-1455 (4) 3.00 1.20

Souvenir Sheets of 2
Perf. 13½

1452a A880 70w 3.50 3.50
1453a A880 70w 3.50 3.50
1454a A880 70w 3.50 3.50
1455a A880 70w 3.50 3.50
Nos. 1452a-1455a (4) 14.00 14.00

Science Series

Observatories — A881

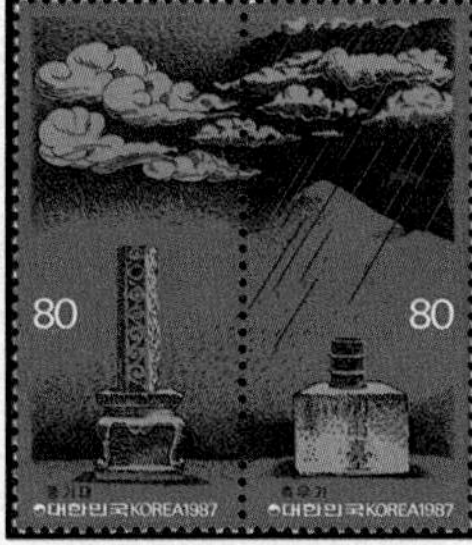

Weather — A883

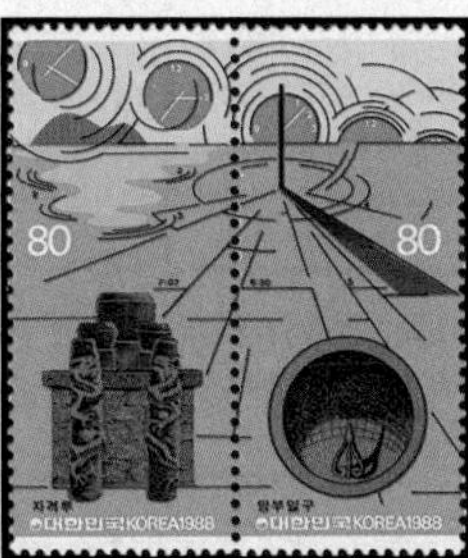

Clocks — A885

Early Printing Methods — A887

A889

Designs: No. 1456, Chomsongdae Observatory, Satellites. No. 1457, Kwanchondae Observatory, Halley's Comet.

1986, Apr. 21 *Perf. 13½x13*
1456 70w multicolored 2.50 .85
1457 70w multicolored 2.50 .85
a. A881 Pair, #1456-1457 7.50 2.75

1987, Apr. 21 **Photo.** *Perf. 13½*

Designs: No. 1458, Wind observatory stone foundation, Chosun Dynasty. No. 1459, Rain gauge, Sejong Period to Chosun Dynasty.

1458 80w multicolored 2.75 1.00
1459 80w multicolored 2.75 1.00
a. A883 Pair, #1458-1459 7.50 4.00

1988, Apr. 21 **Photo.** *Perf. 13½x13*

Designs: No. 1460, *Chagyokru,* water clock invented by Chang Yongshil and Kim Bin in 1434. No. 1461, *Angbuilgu,* sundial completed during King Sejong's reign (1418-1450).

1460 80w multicolored .75 .30
1461 80w multicolored .75 .30
a. A885 Pair, #1460-1461 2.00 2.00

1989, Apr. 21

Designs: No. 1462, Sutra manuscript (detail) printed from wood type, Shila Dynasty, c.704-751. No. 1463, Two characters from a manuscript printed from metal type, Koryo, c.1237.

1462 80w buff & sepia 1.60 .40
1463 80w buff & sepia 1.60 .40
a. A887 Pair, #1462-1463 3.25 3.25

1990, Apr. 21

Designs: No. 1464, 7th century gilt bronze Buddha. No. 1465, Bronze Age dagger, spear molds.

1464 100w multicolored .60 .25
1465 100w multicolored .60 .25
a. A889 Pair, #1464-1465 1.50 1.50
Complete bklt., 2 each #1464-1465 2.50
Nos. 1456-1465 (10) 16.40 5.60

Pairs have continuous designs.

Souvenir Booklets

Booklets containing the stamps listed below have a stamp, pair or strip of stamps, tied to the booklet cover with a first day cancel.

1464-1465, 1523-1524, 1529-1532, 1535-1536, 1539-1540, 1553, 1559-1566, 1572-1576, 1583-1584, 1595-1608, 1613-1621, 1622-1623B, 1624, 1635-1650, 1655-1656, 1657-1668, 1669-1676, 1678-1690, 1693-1699, 1700-1702, 1713-1714, 1745-1748, 1751-1758, 1763-1764, 1767-1768, 1770-1773, 1776-1787, 1797, 1799-1802, 1803-1806, 1810-1811.

Assoc. of Natl. Olympic Committees, 5th General Assembly, Seoul, Apr. 21-25 — A891

1986, Apr. 21 *Perf. 13x13½*
1466 A891 70w multicolored .50 .20

Souvenir Sheet

Butterflies A892

1986, May 22 **Litho.** *Perf. 13½*
1467 Sheet of 6 25.00 25.00
a. A892 70w multicolored 3.00 1.50
b. A892 370w multicolored 3.00 1.50
c. A892 400w multicolored 3.00 1.50
d. A892 440w multicolored 3.00 1.50
e. A892 450w multicolored 3.00 1.50
f. A892 470w multicolored 3.00 1.50

AMERIPEX '86, Chicago, May 22-June 1. No. 1467 contains stamps of different sizes (370w, 42x41mm; 400w, 42x33mm; 440w, 39x45mm; 450w, 32x42mm; 470w, 33x44mm); margin continues the designs.

Women's Education, Cent. A893

1986, May 31 *Perf. 13x12½*
1468 A893 70w multicolored .50 .20

State Visit of Pres. Andre Kolingba, Central Africa A894

1986, June 10 *Perf. 13*
1469 A894 70w multicolored .50 .20
a. Souvenir sheet of 2, imperf. 1.50 1.50

Completion of Han River Development Project — A895

1986, Sept. 10 **Litho.** *Perf. 13*
1470 Strip of 3 4.50 4.50
a. A895 30w Bridge 1.20 .30
b. A895 60w Buildings 1.20 .30
c. A895 80w Seoul Tower, buildings 1.20 .30

Printed in a continuous design.

Fireworks, Seoul Tower — A896

Games Emblem — A897

10th Asian Games, Seoul, Sept. 20-Oct. 5 — A898

Illustration A898 reduced.

1986, Sept. 20 **Photo.** *Perf. 13x13½*
1471 A896 80w multicolored .70 .30
a. Souvenir sheet of 2 7.50 7.50
1472 A897 80w multicolored .70 .30
a. Souvenir sheet of 2 7.50 7.50

Souvenir Sheet

1986, Oct. 31
1473 A898 550w multicolored 21.00 21.00

Juan Antonio Samaranch, Korean IOC Delegation, 1981 — A899

1986, Sept. 30
1474 A899 80w multicolored 1.10 .40

Intl. Olympic Committee decision to hold 24th Olympic Games in Seoul, 5th anniv.

Philatelic Week — A900

1986, Nov. 18 **Photo.** *Perf. 13½x13*
1475 A900 80w Boy fishing for stamp .70 .25

New Year 1987 (Year of the Hare) — A901

Birds — A902

1986, Dec. 1 Photo. *Perf. 13x13½*
1476 A901 80w multicolored .75 .30

1986, Dec. 20 *Perf. 13x14*
1477 A902 80w Waxwing 1.25 .40
1478 A902 80w Oriole 1.25 .40
1479 A902 80w Kingfisher 1.25 .40
1480 A902 80w Hoopoe 1.25 .40
1481 A902 80w Roller 1.25 .40
a. Strip of 5, #1477-1481 7.50 7.50

Coil Stamps
Perf. 14 Horiz.

1481B A902 80w like No. 1479 3.00 .75
1481C A902 80w like No. 1480 3.00 .75
1481D A902 80w like No. 1481 3.00 .75
1481E A902 80w like No. 1477 3.00 .75
1481F A902 80w like No. 1478 3.00 .75
g. Strip of 5, #1481B-1481F 25.00 25.00

Wildlife Conservation A903

Endangered species: No. 1482, Panthera tigris altaica. No. 1483, Felis bengalensis. No. 1484, Vulpes vulpes. No. 1485, Sus scrofa.

1987, Feb. 25 Photo. *Perf. 13½x13*
1482 A903 80w multicolored 2.50 .70
1483 A903 80w multicolored 2.50 .70
1484 A903 80w multicolored 2.50 .70
1485 A903 80w multicolored 2.50 .70
a. Strip of 4, #1482-1485 12.00 12.00

Flowers — A904

1987, Mar. 20 Photo. *Perf. 14x13*
1486 A904 550w Dicentra spectabilis 2.25 .60
1487 A904 550w Hanabusaya asiatica 2.25 .60
1488 A904 550w Erythronium japonicum 2.25 .60
1489 A904 550w Dianthus chinensis 2.25 .60
1490 A904 550w Chrysanthemum zawadskii coreanum 2.25 .60
a. Strip of 5, #1486-1490 12.50 12.50

Coil Stamps
Perf. 13 Vert.

1490B A904 550w like No. 1486 3.00 1.00
1490C A904 550w like No. 1487 3.00 1.00
1490D A904 550w like No. 1488 3.00 1.00
1490E A904 550w like No. 1489 3.00 1.00
1490F A904 550w like No. 1490 3.00 1.00
g. Strip of 5, #1490B-1490F 17.50 17.50

State Visit of Pres. Ahmed Abdallah Abderemane of the Comoro Isls., Apr. 6-9 — A905

1987, Apr. 6 Litho. *Perf. 13½x13*
1491 A905 80w multicolored .50 .20
a. Souvenir sheet of 2 2.00 2.00

Electrification of Korea, Cent. — A906

1987, Apr. 10 Photo.
1492 A906 80w multicolored .50 .20

Int'l. Assoc. of Ports and Harbors, 15th General Session, Seoul — A907

1987, Apr. 25 Photo. *Perf. 13½x13*
1493 A907 80w multicolored .50 .20

State Visit of Pres. U San Yu of Burma A908

1987, June 8 Litho. *Perf. 13½x13*
1494 A908 80w multicolored .50 .20
a. Souvenir sheet of 2 2.00 2.00

Year of The Communications for Information Society — A909

1987, June 30 *Perf. 13x13½*
1495 A909 80w Map, digital telephone .60 .25
1496 A909 80w Emblem .60 .25

Introduction of automatic switching telephone system.

Independence Hall, Monument to the Nation — A910

Statue of Indomitable Koreans, Nat'l. Flag — A911

1987, Aug. 14 Photo. *Perf. 13½x13*
1497 A910 80w multicolored 1.00 .30
a. Souvenir sheet of 2 12.50 12.50
1498 A911 80w multicolored 1.00 .30
a. Souvenir sheet of 2 12.50 12.50

Opening of Independence Hall, Aug. 15.

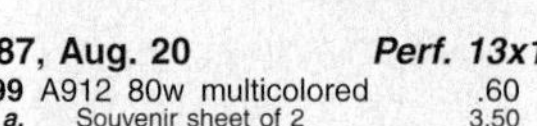

16th Pacific Science Congress, Seoul, Aug. 20-30 — A912

1987, Aug. 20 *Perf. 13x13½*
1499 A912 80w multicolored .60 .20
a. Souvenir sheet of 2 3.50 3.50

State Visit of Pres. Virgilio Barco of Colombia A913

1987, Sept. 8 Litho. *Perf. 13½x13*
1500 A913 80w multicolored .50 .20
a. Souvenir sheet of 2 2.25 2.25

Installation of 10-millionth Telephone A914

1987, Sept. 28 *Perf. 13½x13*
1501 A914 80w multicolored .50 .20

Armed Forces, 39th Anniv. — A915

Armed Forces Day: Servicemen, flags of three military services.

1987, Sept. 30 Litho. *Perf. 13*
1502 A915 80w multicolored .60 .25

14th Philatelic Week, Nov. 18-24 — A916

1987, Nov. 18 Photo. *Perf. 13½*
1503 A916 80w Boy playing the nalrali .60 .25

A917 A918

1987, Nov. 28 Litho.
1504 A917 80w multicolored .75 .40

Signing of the Antarctic Treaty by Korea, 1st anniv.

1987, Dec. 1 Photo.
1505 A918 80w multicolored 1.00 .30

New Year 1988 (Year of the Dragon).

Natl. Social Security Program A919

1988, Jan. 4 Litho. *Perf. 13½x13*
1506 A919 80w multicolored .60 .25

Completion of the Korean Antarctic Base — A919a

1988, Feb. Photo. *Perf. 13x13½*
1506A A919a 80w multicolored 1.00 .30

Inauguration of Roh Tae-Woo, 13th President A920

1988, Feb. 24 Photo. *Perf. 13½x13*
1507 A920 80w multicolored 1.25 .40
a. Souvenir sheet of 2 22.50 22.50

World Wildlife Fund — A921

White-naped crane *(Grus vipio)* displaying various behaviors: a, Calling (1). b, Running (2). c, Spreading wings (3). d, Flying (4).

1988, Apr. 1 *Perf. 13x13½*
1508 Strip of 4 9.00 9.00
a.-d. A921 80w any single 1.40 .80

Intl. Red Cross & Red Crescent Organizations, 125th Annivs. — A922

Telepress Medium, 1st Anniv. — A923

1988, May 7 Photo. *Perf. 13x13½*
1509 A922 80w multicolored .60 .25

1988, June 1 Litho.
1510 A923 80w multicolored .60 .25

Pierre de Coubertin, Olympic Flag — A924

Olympic Temple A925

View of Seoul — A926

Folk Dancers — A927

Litho. & Engr.

1988, Sept. 16 ***Perf. 13½x13***
1511 A924 80w multicolored .75 .30
1512 A925 80w multicolored .75 .30

Photo.
Perf. 13x13½
1513 A926 80w multicolored .75 .30
1514 A927 80w multicolored .75 .30
Nos. 1511-1514 (4) 3.00 1.20

1988 Summer Olympics, Seoul.

Souvenir Sheets of 2
1511a A924 80w 2.25 2.25
1512a A925 80w 2.25 2.25
1513a A926 80w 2.25 2.25
1514a A927 80w 2.25 2.25
Nos. 1511a-1514a (4) 9.00

Margin inscriptions on #1511a-1512a are photo.

OLYMPHILEX '88, Sept. 19-28, Seoul — A928

1988, Sept. 19 Photo. ***Perf. 13x13½***
1515 A928 80w multicolored .50 .20
a. Souvenir sheet of 2 2.00 2.00

22nd Congress of the Intl. Iron and Steel Institute, Seoul A929

1988, Oct. 8 ***Perf. 13½x13***
1516 A929 80w multicolored .50 .20

A930

A931

1988, Oct. 15 ***Perf. 13x13½***
1517 A930 80w shown 1.00 .60
1518 A930 80w Archer seated in wheelchair .75 .30

1988 Natl. Special Olympics (Paralympics), Seoul.

1988, Dec. 1 Photo. ***Perf. 13x13½***
1519 A931 80w multicolored .70 .25

New Year 1989 (Year of the Snake).

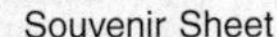
Souvenir Sheet

Successful Completion of the 1988 Summer Olympics, Seoul — A932

1988, Dec. 20 Litho. ***Perf. 13x12½***
1520 A932 550w Opening ceremony 16.00 16.00

Folklore Series

Arirang — A933

Doraji — A934

Pakyon Falls A935

Chonan-Samkori A936

Willowing Bow — A937

Spinning Wheel A938

Treating Threads A939

Weaving Fabric A940

Orchard Avenue — A941

In Flower Garden — A942

A Swing A943

Longing for Mt. Keumkang A944

Natl. ballads.

1989, Mar. 27 Photo. ***Perf. 13x13½***
1521 A933 80w multicolored .75 .25
1522 A934 80w multicolored .75 .25

1990, Feb. 26 **Litho.**
1523 A935 80w multicolored .75 .25
Complete booklet, 4 #1523 6.50
1524 A936 80w multicolored .75 .25
Complete booklet, 4 #1524 6.50

Litho. & Engr.

1990, Sept. 25 ***Perf. 13½x13***
1525 A937 100w multicolored .85 .30
1526 A938 100w multicolored .85 .30
1527 A939 100w multicolored .85 .30
1528 A940 100w multicolored .85 .30
a. Strip of 4, #1525-1528 4.00 4.00

1991, Mar. 27 Litho. ***Perf. 13x13½***
1529 A941 100w multicolored .75 .30
Complete booklet, 4 #1529 6.50
1530 A942 100w multicolored .75 .30
Complete booklet, 4 #1530 6.50

1992, July 13 Litho. ***Perf. 13x13½***
1531 A943 100w multicolored .60 .25
Complete booklet, 4 #1531 6.50
1532 A944 100w multicolored .60 .25
Complete booklet, 4 #1532 6.50
Nos. 1521-1532 (12) 9.10 3.30

14th Asian-Pacific Dental Congress — A945

1989, Apr. 26 Photo. ***Perf. 13x13½***
1533 A945 80w multicolored .50 .20

Rotary Intl. Convention, Seoul, May 21-25 — A946

19th Cong. of the Intl. Council of Nurses, Seoul, May 28-June 2 — A947

1989, May 20 Photo. ***Perf. 13x13½***
1534 A946 80w multicolored .60 .20

1989, May 27
1535 A947 80w multicolored .60 .20
Complete booklet, 4 #1535

Information Industry Month — A948

World Environment Day — A949

1989, June 1
1536 A948 80w multicolored .60 .20
Complete booklet, 4 #1536 2.40

1989, June 5
1537 A949 80w multicolored .50 .20

Asia-Pacific Telecommunity, 10th Anniv. — A950

1989, July 1 Photo. ***Perf. 13x13½***
1538 A950 80w multicolored .50 .20

French Revolution, Bicent. A951

1989, July 14 Litho. ***Perf. 13½x13***
1539 A951 80w multicolored .50 .20
Complete booklet, 4 #1539 2.00

Federation of Asian and Oceanian Biochemists 5th Congress A952

1989, Aug. 12 **Photo.**
1540 A952 80w multicolored .50 .20
Complete booklet, 4 #1540 2.00

Modern Art Series

A White Ox, by Lee Joong-Sub — A953

A Street Stall, by Park Lae-hyun A954

A Little Girl, by Lee Bong-Sang A955

An Autumn Scene, by Oh Ji-ho — A956

Litho. & Engr.; Photo. (#1542, 1544)
1989, Sept. 4 ***Perf. 13x13½, 13½x13***

1541	A953 80w multicolored		.75	.30
1542	A954 80w multicolored		.75	.30
1543	A955 80w multicolored		.75	.30
1544	A956 80w multicolored		.75	.30
	Nos. 1541-1544 (4)		3.00	1.20

Allegory: The Valiant Spirit of Koreans A965

1989, Sept. 12 **Litho.** ***Perf. 13½x13***

1553	A965 80w multicolored	.50	.20
	Complete booklet, 4 #1553	2.00	

1988 Seoul Olympics and the World Korean Sports Festival.

Personification of Justice and Ancient Codex — A966

1989, Sept. 18

1554	A966 80w multicolored	.50	.20

Constitutional Court, 1st anniv.

Fish

A967

A968

A969

A970

A971

A972

A973

A974

A975

A976

A977

A978

1989, Sept. 30 **Photo.** ***Perf. 13½x13***

1555	A967 80w Oplegnathus fasciatus	.75	.30
1556	A968 80w Cobitis multifasciata	.75	.30
1557	A969 80w Liobagrus mediadiposalis	.75	.30
1558	A970 80w Monocentris japonicus	.75	.30

1990, July 2

1559	A971 100w Hapalogenys mucronatus	.75	.30
	Complete booklet, 4 #1559	5.00	
1560	A972 100w Fugu niphobles	.75	.30
	Complete booklet, 4 #1560	5.00	
1561	A973 100w Oncorhynchus masou	.75	.30
	Complete booklet, 4 #1561	5.00	
1562	A974 100w Rhodeus ocellatus	.75	.30
	Complete booklet, 4 #1562	5.00	

1991, June 8

1563	A975 100w Microphysogobio longidorsalis	.75	.25
	Complete booklet, 4 #1563	5.00	
1564	A976 100w Gnathopogon majimae	.75	.25
	Complete booklet, 4 #1564	5.00	
1565	A977 100w Therapon oxyrhnchus	.75	.25
	Complete booklet, 4 #1565	5.00	
1566	A978 100w Psettina ijimae	.75	.25
	Complete booklet, 4 #1566	5.00	
	Nos. 1555-1566 (12)	9.00	3.40

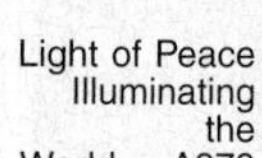

Light of Peace Illuminating the World — A979

1989, Oct. 4

1567	A979 80w multicolored	.50	.20

44th Intl. Eucharistic Cong., Seoul, Oct. 4-8.

29th World Congress of the Intl. Civil Airports Assoc., Seoul, Oct. 17-19 — A980

1989, Oct. 17

1568	A980 80w multicolored	.50	.20

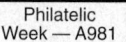

Philatelic Week — A981

Two Cranes — A982

Folk Festival Customs A983

1989, Nov. 18 **Photo.** ***Perf. 13x13½***

1569	A981 80w Lantern	.50	.20
a.	Souvenir sheet of 2	2.00	2.00

1989, Dec. 1 ***Perf. 13x13½, 13½x13***

1570	A982 80w multicolored	.60	.20
a.	Souvenir sheet of 2	1.75	1.75
1571	A983 80w multicolored	.60	.20
a.	Souvenir sheet of 2	1.75	1.75

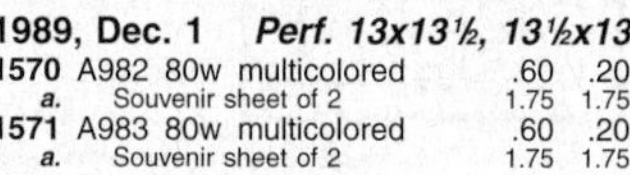

New Year 1990.

World Meteorological Day — A984

1990, Mar. 23 ***Perf. 13½x13***

1572	A984 80w multicolored	.50	.20
	Complete booklet, 4 #1572	5.00	

UNICEF in Korea, 40th Anniv. — A985

1990, Mar. 24 ***Perf. 13x13½***

1573	A985 80w multicolored	.50	.20
	Complete booklet, 4 #1573	5.00	

Cheju-Kohung Fiber Optic Submarine Cable A986

1990, Apr. 21 ***Perf. 13½x13***

1574	A986 80w multicolored	.50	.20
	Complete booklet, 4 #1574	5.00	

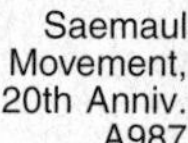

Saemaul Movement, 20th Anniv. A987

1990, Apr. 21

1575	A987 100w multicolored	.50	.20
	Complete booklet, 4 #1575	5.00	

Youth Month A988

1990, May 1

1576	A988 100w multicolored	.45	.20
	Complete booklet, 4 #1576	1.90	

Type of 1981 and

Korean Flag — A989

Korean Stork — A990

White Magnolia A991

Korean White Pine A991a

Cart-shaped Earthenware A992

Fire Safety A993

Environmental Protection A994

Traffic Safety A995

Waiting One's Turn A996

Saving Energy A997

Child Protection A997a

Purification of Language Movement A997b

Rose of Sharon A997c

Give Life to Water A997d

Ginger Jar — A998

Chong-IP'um-Song, Pine Tree Natl. Monument — A999

Drum, Drum Dance A1001

Mask, Wrestlers A1002

Hong Yong-Sik A1003

King Sejong, Korean Alphabet A1004

Dragon Head, Banner Staff — A1005

Gilt-bronze Buddha Triad with Inscription of Keymi — A1006

Photo., Litho. (#1582), Litho. & Engr. (#1594)

1990-96 ***Perf. 13½x13, 13x13½***

1577	A989	10w multi	.30	.20
1578	A990	20w multi	.30	.20
1579	A991	30w multi	.40	.20
1580	A991a	40w multi	.30	.20
1581	A992	50w multi	.40	.20
1582	A993	80w multi	1.75	.30
1583	A994	100w multi	5.00	.40
		Complete booklet, 10 #1583	50.00	
1584	A995	100w multi	1.50	.40
		Complete booklet, 10 #1584	15.00	
1585	A996	100w multi	1.50	.20
1586	A997	100w multi	1.25	.20
1587	A997a	100w multi	1.25	.20
1588	A997b	100w multi	1.25	.20
1589	A997c	110w multi	1.00	.20
1590	A997d	110w multi	1.00	.20
1591	A998	150w multi	1.00	.20
a.		Booklet pane, 20 #1591	20.00	
		Complete booklet, #1591a	20.00	
1592	A999	160w multi	1.50	.25
1593	A1001	370w multi	3.00	.50
1594	A1002	440w multi	4.00	.60
1594A	A1003	600w multi	3.00	.80
1594B	A1004	710w multi	5.00	1.00
1594C	A1005	800w multi	4.00	1.00
1594D	A1006	900w multi	6.00	.85
		Nos. 1577-1594D (22)	44.70	8.50

Issued: #1583, 6/5; 600w, 6/25; 150w, 7/2; 800w, 7/10; #1584, 7/25; 50w, 9/28; 80w, 11/1; #1585, 6/26/91; #1586, 11/1/91; #1587, 4/5/92; #1588, 11/2/92; 370w, 440w, 3/22/93; 10w, #1589, 3/30/93; 160w, 710w, 4/30/93; 20w, 30w, 40w, 5/24/93; #1590, 7/1/93; 900w, 9/20/93; #1591a, 3/20/96.

See #1715-1738, 1846, 1851-1852, 1860, 1862.

Coil Stamps

1990 **Litho.** ***Perf. 13 Horiz.***

1594E	A992	50w multicolored	1.00	.30

Perf. 13 Vert.

1594F	A706	60w multicolored	.75	.25
1594G	A994	100w multicolored	1.75	.75
1594H	A997c	110w multicolored	1.00	.25
		Nos. 1594E-1594H (4)	4.50	1.55

Seoul Mail Center A1007

1990, July 4 **Litho.** ***Perf. 13½x13***

1595 A1007 100w multicolored .50 .20
a. Souvenir sheet of 2 2.00 2.00
Complete booklet, 4 #1595 5.00

8th Korean Boy Scout Jamboree — A1008

1990, Aug. 8 ***Perf. 13x13½***

1596 A1008 100w multicolored .60 .20
Complete booklet, 4 #1596 6.00

Wild Flowers

A1009

A1010

A1011

A1012

A1013

1990, Aug. 25 **Photo.**

1597 A1009 370w Lilium 1.75 .85
Complete booklet, 4 #1597 17.50
1598 A1010 400w Aster 2.25 1.00
Complete booklet, 4 #1598 22.50
1599 A1011 440w Adonis 2.00 .90
Complete booklet, 4 #1599 20.00
1600 A1012 470w Scabiosa 2.40 1.00
Complete booklet, 4 #1600 24.00

1991, July 26

1601 A1013 100w Aerides japonicum .60 .25
Complete booklet, 4 #1601 5.00
1602 A1013 100w Heloniopsis orientalis .60 .25
Complete booklet, 4 #1602 5.00
1603 A1013 370w Aquilegia buergeriana 1.50 .65
Complete booklet, 4 #1603 14.00
1604 A1013 440w Gentiana zollingeri 1.75 .75
Complete booklet, 4 #1604 16.00

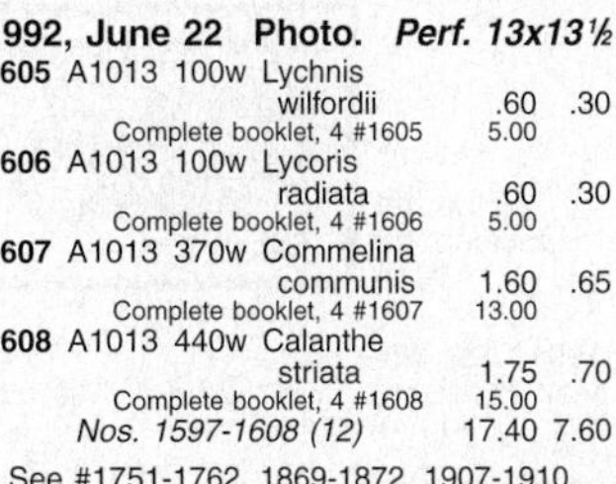

1992, June 22 **Photo.** ***Perf. 13x13½***

1605 A1013 100w Lychnis wilfordii .60 .30
Complete booklet, 4 #1605 5.00
1606 A1013 100w Lycoris radiata .60 .30
Complete booklet, 4 #1606 5.00
1607 A1013 370w Commelina communis 1.60 .65
Complete booklet, 4 #1607 13.00
1608 A1013 440w Calanthe striata 1.75 .70
Complete booklet, 4 #1608 15.00
Nos. 1597-1608 (12) 17.40 7.60

See #1751-1762, 1869-1872, 1907-1910.

A1021

A1022

1990, Sept. 29 **Litho.** ***Perf. 13x13½***

1609 A1021 100w .50 .20

Anglican Church of Korea, cent.

1990, Oct. 15

1610 A1022 100w blk, red & bl .50 .20

Opening of Seoul Tower, 10th anniv.

National Census — A1023

1990, Oct. 20 ***Perf. 13x13½***

1611 A1023 100w multicolored .50 .20

UN Development Program, 40th Anniv. A1024

1990, Oct. 24

1612 A1024 100w multicolored .50 .20

Philatelic Week — A1025

Litho. & Engr.

1990, Nov. 16 ***Perf. 13x13½***

1613 A1025 100w multicolored .50 .20
a. Souvenir sheet of 2 4.50 4.50
Complete booklet, 4 #1613 6.00

New Year 1991 (Year of the Sheep) — A1026

Two Cranes — A1027

1990, Dec. 1 **Litho.** ***Perf. 13x13½***

1614 A1026 100w multicolored .50 .20
Complete booklet, 4 #1614 5.00
1615 A1027 100w multicolored .50 .20
Complete booklet, 4 #1615 5.00
a. Souv. sheet of 2, #1614-1615 6.00 6.00

Taejon Expo '93

A1028

A1029

A1030

A1031

A1032

A1033

Government Pavilion A1034

Intl. Pavilion A1035

Recycling Art Pavilion A1035a

Telcom Pavilion A1035b

1990, Dec. 12

1616 A1028 100w multicolored .85 .30
a. Souvenir sheet of 2 1.75 1.75
Complete booklet, 4 #1616 7.50
1617 A1029 440w multicolored 2.00 .90
a. Souvenir sheet of 2 5.25 5.25
Complete booklet, 4 #1617 17.50

1991, Mar. 23

1618 A1030 100w multicolored .85 .30
a. Souvenir sheet of 2 1.75 1.75
Complete booklet, 4 #1618 7.00
1619 A1031 100w multicolored .85 .30
a. Souvenir sheet of 2 1.75 1.75
Complete booklet, 4 #1619 7.00

1992, Aug. 7 **Photo.** ***Perf. 13½x13***

1620 A1032 100w multicolored .60 .20
a. Souvenir sheet of 2 1.50 1.50
Complete booklet, 4 #1620 4.00
1621 A1033 100w multicolored .60 .20
a. Souvenir sheet of 2 1.50 1.50
Complete booklet, 4 #1621 4.00

1993, July 8

1622 A1034 110w multi .60 .25
a. Souvenir sheet of 2 1.25 1.25
Complete booklet, 4 #1622 5.00
1623 A1035 110w multi .60 .25
c. Souvenir sheet of 2 1.25 1.25
Complete booklet, 4 #1623 5.00
1623A A1035a 110w multi .60 .25
d. Souvenir sheet of 2 1.25 1.25
Complete booklet, 4 #1623A 5.00
1623B A1035b 110w multi .60 .25
e. Souvenir sheet of 2 1.25 1.25
Complete booklet, 4 #1623B 5.00
Nos. 1616-1623B (10) 8.15 3.20

Saemaul Minilibrary, 30th Anniv. A1036

1991, Jan. 2 Litho. *Perf. 13½x13*

1624 A1036 100w multicolored .50 .20
Complete booklet, 4 #1624 4.75

Moth A1037

Beetle A1038

Butterfly A1039

Beetle A1040

Cicada — A1041

1991, Apr. 8 Photo. *Perf. 13½x13*

1625 A1037 100w shown 1.00 .25
1626 A1038 100w shown 1.00 .25
1627 A1039 100w shown 1.00 .25
1628 A1040 100w shown 1.00 .25
1629 A1041 100w shown 1.00 .25
1630 A1040 100w Water beetle 1.00 .25
1631 A1040 100w Bee 1.00 .25
1632 A1040 100w Lady bug 1.00 .25
1633 A1037 100w Dragonfly 1.00 .25
1634 A1037 100w Grasshopper 1.00 .25
a. Strip of 10, #1625-1634 12.00 12.00

Printed in sheets of 100 with each row shifted one design.

Traditional Performing Arts Center, 40th Anniv. — A1042

1991, Apr. 10 *Perf. 13x13½*

1635 A1042 100w multicolored .50 .20
Complete booklet, 4 #1635 5.00

Provisional Government, 72nd Anniv. A1043

1991, Apr. 13 *Perf. 13½x13*

1636 A1043 100w multicolored .50 .20
Complete booklet, 4 #1636 5.00

Hire the Handicapped A1044

1991, Apr. 20

1637 A1044 100w multicolored .50 .20
Complete booklet, 4 #1637 5.00

Teachers' Day, 10th Anniv. A1045

1991, May 15 Litho. *Perf. 13½x13*

1638 A1045 100w multicolored .50 .20
Complete booklet, 4 #1638 5.00

A1046

A1047

1991, Aug. 8 Litho. *Perf. 13x13½*

1639 A1046 100w multicolored .60 .20
a. Souvenir sheet of 2 1.40 1.40
Complete booklet, 4 #1639 9.00

17th World Scouting Jamboree.

1991, Aug. 22 Litho. *Perf. 13x13½*

1640 A1047 100w multicolored .60 .20
Complete booklet, 4 #1640 9.00

YMCA World Assembly.

Natl. Desire for Reunification A1048

1991, Sept. 11 Litho. *Perf. 13x13½*

1641 A1048 100w multicolored .50 .20
Complete booklet, 4 #1641 8.00

Admission to UN — A1049

1991, Sept. 18 *Perf. 13½x13*

1642 A1049 100w multicolored .50 .20
Complete booklet, 4 #1642 6.00

Musical Instruments

Deerskin Drum (Galgo) A1050

Mouth Organ (Saenghwang) A1051

Seated Drum — A1052

Small Gong — A1053

Designs: No. 1645, Brass chimes (Unra). No. 1646, Large gong (Jing). No. 1649, Dragon drum. No. 1650, Single bell chime.

1991-92 Photo. *Perf. 13x13½*

Background color

1643 A1050 100w gray .60 .30
Complete booklet, 4 #1643 5.00
1644 A1051 100w tan .60 .30
Complete booklet, 4 #1644 5.00
1645 A1050 100w lt violet .60 .30
Complete booklet, 4 #1645 5.00
1646 A1050 100w pale green .60 .30
Complete booklet, 4 #1646 5.00
1647 A1052 100w gray .60 .30
Complete booklet, 4 #1647 5.00
1648 A1053 100w tan .60 .30
Complete booklet, 4 #1648 5.00
1649 A1052 100w pale violet .60 .30
Complete booklet, 4 #1649 5.00
1650 A1053 100w pale green .60 .30
Complete booklet, 4 #1650 5.00
Nos. 1643-1650 (8) 4.80 2.40

Issued: #1643-1646, 9/26; others, 2/24/92.

Month of Culture — A1056

Telecom '91 — A1057

1991, Oct. 1 Litho. *Perf. 13x13½*

1655 A1056 100w multicolored .50 .20
Complete booklet, 4 #1655 5.00

1991, Oct. 7 Photo.

1656 A1057 100w multicolored .50 .20
Complete booklet, 4 #1656 6.00

Sixth World Telecommunication Exhibition & Forum, Geneva, Switzerland.

Beauty Series

A1058

A1059

Kottam Architectural Patterns
A1060 A1061

A1062

A1063

Norigae
A1064 A1065

A1066 A1067

Tapestries
A1068 A1069

1991, Oct. 18

1657 A1058 100w multicolored .85 .30
1658 A1059 100w multicolored .85 .30
1659 A1060 100w multicolored .85 .30
1660 A1061 100w multicolored .85 .30
a. Block or strip of 4, #1657-1660 4.50 4.50
Complete booklet, 2 #1660a —

1992, Sept. 21 Photo. & Engr.

1661 A1062 100w multicolored .75 .30
1662 A1063 100w multicolored .75 .30
1663 A1064 100w multicolored .75 .30
1664 A1065 100w multicolored .75 .30
a. Block or strip of 4, #1661-1664 3.50 3.50
Complete booklet, 2 #1664a —

1993, Oct. 11 Photo. *Perf. 13x13½*

1665 A1066 110w multicolored .60 .30
1666 A1067 110w multicolored .60 .30
1667 A1068 110w multicolored .60 .30
1668 A1069 110w multicolored .60 .30
a. Block or strip of 4, #1665-1668 2.75 2.75
Complete booklet, 2 #1668a —

Philatelic Week — A1070

1991, Nov. 16 Photo. *Perf. 13x13½*

1669 A1070 100w multicolored .50 .20
a. Souvenir sheet of 2 1.40 1.40
Complete booklet, 4 #1669 5.00

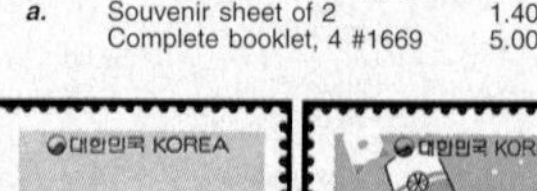

New Year 1992, Year of the Monkey
A1071 A1072

1991, Dec. 2 Photo. & Engr.

1670 A1071 100w multicolored .50 .20
a. Souvenir sheet of 2 1.50 1.50
Complete booklet, 4 #1670 5.00
1671 A1072 100w multicolored .50 .20
a. Souvenir sheet of 2 1.50 1.50
Complete booklet, 4 #1671 5.00

Hibiscus Syriacus, Natl. Flower — A1073

1992, Mar. 9 Photo. *Perf. 13x13½*
Background color

1672 A1073 100w lt green 1.00 .40
1673 A1073 100w lt blue 1.00 .40

Im-Jin War, 400th Anniv. A1074

1992, May 23 Photo. *Perf. 13½x13*

1674 A1074 100w multicolored .50 .20
Complete booklet, 4 #1674 5.00

Science Day, 25th Anniv. A1075

1992, Apr. 21 Photo. *Perf. 13½x13*

1675 A1075 100w multicolored .50 .20
Complete booklet, 4 #1675 6.00

Pong-Gil Yoon, Assassin of Japanese Occupation Leaders, 60th Anniv. of Execution — A1076

Photo. & Engr.
1992, Apr. 29 *Perf. 13x13½*

1676 A1076 100w multicolored .50 .20
Complete booklet, 4 #1676 5.00

A1077 A1078

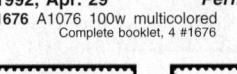

Photo & Engr.
1992, May 25 *Perf. 13x13½*

1678 A1077 100w multicolored .50 .20
Complete booklet, 4 #1678 5.00

60th Intl. Fertilizer Assoc. conf.

1992, July 25 Photo. *Perf. 13x13½*

1679 A1078 100w Pole vault .50 .20
Complete booklet, 4 #1679 5.00
1680 A1078 100w Rhythmic gymnastics .50 .20
Complete booklet, 4 #1680 5.00

1992 Summer Olympics, Barcelona.

21st Universal Postal Congress, Seoul, 1994 A1079

Designs: No. 1681, Korean Exhibition Center, Namdae-mun Gate. No. 1682, Stone statue of Tolharubang, Songsan Ilchulbong Peak.

1992, Aug. 22 Photo. *Perf. 13½x13*

1681 A1079 100w red vio & multi .50 .20
a. Souvenir sheet of 2 1.40 1.40
Complete booklet, 4 #1681 5.00
1682 A1079 100w brown & multi .50 .20
a. Souvenir sheet of 2 1.40 1.40
Complete booklet, 4 #1682 5.00

A1086 A1087

Litho. & Engr.
1992, Oct. 10 *Perf. 13x13½*

1683 A1086 100w salmon & red brn .45 .20
Complete booklet, 4 #1683 5.00

Pong-Chang Yi (1900-1932), would-be assassin of Japanese Emperor Hirohito.

1992, Oct. 10 Litho.

Design: No. 1684, Hwang Young-Jo, 1992 Olympic marathon winner. No. 1685, Shon Kee-Chung, 1936 Olympic Marathon Winner.

1684 A1087 100w multicolored .60 .20
1685 A1087 100w grn & multi .60 .20
a. Pair, #1684-1685 1.50 1.50
b. Souv. sheet of 2, #1684-1685 4.00 4.00
Complete booklet, 2 #1685a 10.00

Discovery of America, 500th Anniv. — A1088

1992, Oct. 12 Photo.

1686 A1088 100w multicolored .60 .20
Complete booklet, 4 #1686 10.00

Philatelic Week A1089

1992, Nov. 14 Photo. *Perf. 13½x13*

1687 A1089 100w multicolored .50 .20
a. Souvenir sheet of 2 1.50 1.50
Complete booklet, 4 #1687 5.00

New Year 1993 (Year of the Rooster)
A1090 A1091

1992, Dec. 1 Photo. *Perf. 13x13½*

1688 A1090 100w multicolored .50 .20
a. Souvenir sheet of 2 1.25 1.25
Complete booklet, 4 #1688 5.00
1689 A1091 100w multicolored .50 .20
a. Souvenir sheet of 2 1.25 1.25
Complete booklet, 4 #1689 5.00

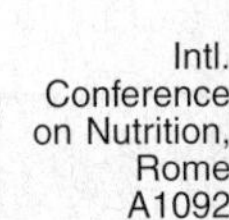

Intl. Conference on Nutrition, Rome A1092

1992, Dec. 5 *Perf. 13½x13*

1690 A1092 100w multicolored .50 .20
Complete booklet, 4 #1690 5.00

Seoul Art Center, Grand Opening A1093

1993, Feb. 15 Photo. *Perf. 13½x13*

1691 A1093 110w multicolored .50 .20

Inauguration of Kim Young Sam, 14th President A1094

1993, Feb. 24

1692 A1094 110w multicolored .75 .30
a. Souvenir sheet of 2 6.00 6.00

A1095 A1096

1993, May 27 Photo. *Perf. 13x13½*

1693 A1095 110w lilac & silver .50 .20
Complete booklet, 4 #1693 6.00

Student Inventions Exhibition.

1993, June 14 Photo. *Perf. 13x13½*

1694 A1096 110w multicolored .50 .20
Complete booklet, 4 #1694 6.00

UN Conference on Human Rights, Vienna.

A1098 A1099

Mushrooms

1993, July 26 Photo. *Perf. 13x13½*

1696 A1098 110w Ganoderma lucidum .50 .25
Complete booklet, 4 #1696 4.00
1697 A1098 110w Pleurotus ostreatus .50 .25
Complete booklet, 4 #1697 4.00
1698 A1098 110w Lentinula edodes .50 .25
Complete booklet, 4 #1698 4.00
1699 A1098 110w Tricholoma matsutake .50 .25
Complete booklet, 4 #1699 4.00
Nos. 1696-1699 (4) 2.00 1.00

See Nos. 1770-1773, 1803-1806, 1883-1886, 1912-1915, 1935.

1993, Aug. 28 Photo. *Perf. 13x13½*

1700 A1099 110w multicolored .50 .20
Complete booklet, 4 #1700 4.00

19th World Congress of Intl. Society of Orthopedic Surgery and Trauma Study.

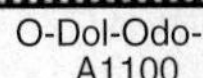

O-Dol-Odo-Gi A1100 Ong-He-Ya A1101

1993, Sept. 13

1701 A1100 110w multicolored .50 .20
Complete booklet, 4 #1701 4.00
1702 A1101 110w multicolored .50 .20
Complete booklet, 4 #1702 4.00

Visit Korea Year '94
A1112 A1113

1993, Sept. 27 Photo. *Perf. 13x13½*

1713 A1112 110w multicolored .50 .20
Complete booklet, 4 #1713 4.00
1714 A1113 110w multicolored .50 .20
Complete booklet, 4 #1714 4.00

Type of 1993 and

Squirrel A1114

Physalis Alkekengi A1115

Scops Owl A1116

Reduce Garbage A1117

Narcissus A1118

Little Tern A1119

Sea Turtle — A1120

Airplane A1122

Passenger Airplane A1123

Porcelain Chicken Water Dropper A1124

Celadon Water Dropper A1125

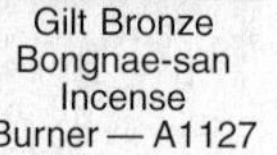

Gilt Bronze Bongnae-san Incense Burner — A1127

Celadon Pitcher — A1128

Designs: 300w, Van. 540w, Train. 1190w, Passenger ship.

Photo., Litho. (#1726), Photo. & Engr. (#1734)

1993-95

Perf. 13½x13, 13x13½ (210w, 1050w, #1728, 1732, 1734), 13½x12½ (60w, 90w), 12½x13½ (180w, 200w)

1715 A1114 60w multi .50 .20
1716 A1115 70w multi .50 .20
1717 A1116 90w multi .65 .25
1718 A1117 110w multi 1.00 .20
1719 A997c 120w multi .80 .20
1720 A1118 130w multi .80 .25
a. Booklet pane of 20 18.00
Complete booklet, #1720a 18.00
1721 A1119 180w multi 1.25 .25
1722 A1120 200w multi 1.25 .30
1723 A1119 210w multi 1.60 .25
1724 A1123 300w multi 2.00 .40
1725 A1122 330w multi 2.00 .20
1726 A1123 390w multi 2.75 .50
a. Booklet pane of 10 30.00
Complete booklet, #1735a 30.00
1727 A1122 400w multi 1.50 .40
a. Booklet pane, 10 #1727 25.00
Complete booklet, #1727a 25.00
1728 A1124 400w multi 1.50 .40
1729 A1125 500w multi 1.75 .65
1730 A1123 540w multi 3.50 .75
1731 A1122 560w multi 3.50 .60
1732 A1127 700w multi 4.00 .95
1733 A1004 910w like #1594B 6.00 1.25
1734 A1128 930w blue & multi 6.00 1.10
1735 A1128 930w tan & multi 6.00 1.25
a. Booklet pane of 10 80.00
Complete booklet, #1735a 80.00
1736 A1128 1050w multi 6.00 1.00
1737 A1123 1190w multi 8.00 1.50
1738 A1122 1300w multi 7.00 1.25
Nos. 1715-1738 (24) 69.85 14.30

Issued: #1718, 11/1/93; 910w, 2/15/94; 90w, 4/22/94; 130w, 8/20/94; 80w, 9/12/94; 390w, #1734, 1190w, 10/1/94; 300w, 540w, 11/1/94; 60w, 200w, 12/19/94; #1720a, 2/28/95; 70w, 3/15/95; #1737, 3/11/95; #1735a, 3/20/95; 700w, 6/15/95; #1728, 8/28/95; #1727, 10/16/95; 1050w, 1300w, 10/5/95; 210w, 560w, 11/1/95; 500w, 11/6/95; 120w, 330w, 11/11/95; #1727a, 3/27/96.

Five versions of booklets with No. 1720a exist with blocks of different colors at the top of the booklet cover. The blocks of color match color bars printed in the selvage of the attached booklet pane.

See Nos. 1847-1848, 1857.

Coil Stamp

1990 Litho. *Perf. 13 Vert.*

1739 A1118 130w multicolored 1.25 .25

Philatelic Week — A1144

21st UPU Congress, Seoul — A1145

1993, Nov. 13 Photo. *Perf. 13x13½*

1745 A1144 110w multicolored .50 .20
a. Souvenir sheet of 2 1.50 1.50
Complete booklet, 4 #1745 10.00

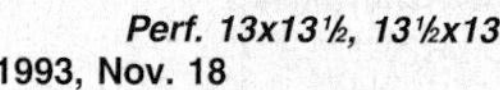

Perf. 13x13½, 13½x13

1993, Nov. 18

1746 A1145 110w Dancer, muscians .50 .20
a. Souvenir sheet of 2 1.50 1.50
Complete booklet, 4 #1746 5.00
1747 A1145 110w Weavers, horiz. .50 .20
a. Souvenir sheet of 2 1.50 1.50
Complete booklet, 4 #1747 5.00

Trade Day, 30th Anniv. A1146

1993, Nov. 30 *Perf. 13½x13*

1748 A1146 110w multicolored .50 .20
Complete booklet, 4 #1748 5.00

New Year 1994 (Year of the Dog) A1147

1993, Dec. 1 *Perf. 13½x13, 13x13½*

1749 A1147 110w shown .50 .20
a. Souvenir sheet of 2 1.40 1.40
1750 A1147 110w Stuffed toy dog, vert. .50 .20
a. Souvenir sheet of 2 1.40 1.40

Flower Type of 1991

1993-95 Photo. *Perf. 13x13½*

1751 A1013 110w Weigela bortensis .50 .25
Complete booklet, 4 #1751 2.50
1752 A1013 110w Caltha palustris .50 .25
Complete booklet, 4 #1752 2.50
1753 A1013 110w Iris ruthenica .50 .25
Complete booklet, 4 #1753 2.50
1754 A1013 110w Aceriphyllum rosii .50 .25
Complete booklet, 4 #1754 2.50
1755 A1013 130w Leontopodium japonicum .50 .25
Complete booklet, 4 #1755 2.50
1756 A1013 130w Geranium eriostemon .50 .25
Complete booklet, 4 #1756 2.50
1757 A1013 130w Lycoris aurea .50 .25
Complete booklet, 4 #1757 2.50
1758 A1013 130w Gentiana jamesii .50 .25
Complete booklet, 4 #1758 1.40
1759 A1013 130w Halenia corniculata .50 .25
Complete booklet, 6 #1759 3.25
1760 A1013 130w Erthyronium japonicum .50 .25
Complete booklet, 6 #1760 3.25
1761 A1013 130w Iris odaesanensis .50 .25
Complete booklet, 6 #1761 3.25
1762 A1013 130w Leontice microrrhyncha .50 .25
Complete booklet, 6 #1762 3.25
Nos. 1755-1762 (8) 4.00 2.00

Issued: #1751-1754, 12/20/93; #1755-1758, 10/4/94; #1759-1762, 7/24/95.

Visit Korea Year
A1148 A1149

1994, Jan. 11 Photo. *Perf. 13x13½*

1763 A1148 110w Masked dancer .50 .20
Complete booklet, 4 #1763 2.50
1764 A1149 110w Piper, clouds .50 .20
Complete booklet, 4 #1764 2.50

21st UPU Congress, Seoul A1150

1994, Jan. 24 *Perf. 13½x13*

1765 A1150 300w multicolored 1.00 .50
a. Souvenir sheet of 2 2.50 2.50
b. Booklet pane of 10 25.00
Complete booklet, #1765b 25.00

Samil Independence Movement, 75th Anniv. — A1151

1994, Feb. 28 Photo. *Perf. 13x13½*

1766 A1151 110w multicolored .50 .20

Wildlife Protection A1152

1994, Mar. 7 Photo. *Perf. 13½x13*

1767 A1152 110w Sasakia charonda .50 .20
a. Souvenir sheet of 2 1.40 1.40
Complete booklet, 4 #1767 2.50
1768 A1152 110w Allomyrina dichotoma .50 .20
a. Souvenir sheet of 2 1.40 1.40
Complete booklet, 4 #1768 2.50

Intl. Year of the Family A1153

1994, May 14 Photo. *Perf. 13*

1769 A1153 110w multicolored .50 .20

Mushroom Type of 1993

#1770, Oudemansiella platyphylla. #1771, Morchella esculenta. #1772, Cortinarius purpurascens. #1773, Gomphus floccosus.

1994, May 30 Photo. *Perf. 13x13½*

1770 A1098 110w multicolored .50 .25
a. Souvenir sheet of 2 1.25 1.25
Complete booklet, 4 #1770 2.50
1771 A1098 110w multicolored .50 .25
a. Souvenir sheet of 2 1.25 1.25
Complete booklet, 4 #1771 2.50
1772 A1098 110w multicolored .50 .25
a. Souvenir sheet of 2 1.25 1.25
Complete booklet, 4 #1772 2.50
1773 A1098 110w multicolored .50 .25
a. Souvenir sheet of 2 1.25 1.25
Complete booklet, 4 #1773 2.50
Nos. 1770-1773 (4) 2.00 1.00
Nos. 1770a-1773a (4) 5.00 5.00

Opening of War Memorial Center A1154

1994, June 10 Photo. *Perf. 13*

1774 A1154 110w multicolored .50 .20

PHILAKOREA '94, Seoul A1155

1994, June 13 *Perf. 13*

1775 A1155 910w multicolored 3.25 1.50
a. Souvenir sheet of 1 3.75 3.75

Beauty Series

Fans — A1156

Gates — A1160

Pouches — A1164

1994, July 18 Photo. *Perf. 13x13½*

1776 110w Taeguk .50 .25
1777 110w Crane .50 .25
1778 110w Pearl .50 .25
1779 110w Wheel .50 .25
a. A1156 Strip of 4, #1776-1779 2.75 2.75
Complete booklet, 2 #1779a 9.50

1995, May 22 Photo. *Perf. 13x13½*

#1780, Lofty Gate, traditional Yungban residence. #1781, Pomosa Temple. #1782, Osumun (Fish Water) Gate, Changdukkung Palace. #1783, Pullomun Gate, Changdukkung Palace.

1780 130w multicolored .50 .25
1781 130w multicolored .50 .25
1782 130w multicolored .50 .25
1783 130w multicolored .50 .25
a. A1160 Strip of 4, #1780-1783 2.75 2.75
Complete booklet, 2 #1783a 10.00

1996, Nov. 1 Photo. *Perf. 13x13½*

1784 150w multicolored .50 .25
1785 150w multicolored .50 .25
1786 150w multicolored .50 .25
1787 150w multicolored .50 .25
a. A1164 Strip of 4, #1784-1787 2.75 2.75
Complete booklet, 2 #1787a 10.00
Nos. 1776-1787 (12) 6.00 3.00

A1168

PHILAKOREA '94 — A1169

1994, Aug. 16 Photo. *Perf. 13*

1788 A1168 130w Winter scene .50 .20
a. Souvenir sheet of 2 1.00 1.00
b. Booklet pane of 10 10.00
Complete booklet, #1788b 10.00
1789 A1168 130w Grape vines .50 .20
a. Souvenir sheet of 2 1.00 1.00
b. Booklet pane of 10 10.00
Complete booklet, #1789b 10.00
1790 A1168 130w Cranes .50 .20
a. Souvenir sheet of 2 1.00 1.00
b. Booklet pane of 10 10.00
Complete booklet, #1790b 10.00
Nos. 1788-1790 (3) 1.50 .60

Souvenir Sheet

Litho. & Engr.

1791 Sheet of 7 8.25 8.25
a. A1169 130w Crane, mountains .35 .20
b. A1169 300w Two cranes, sun .80 .40
c. A1169 370w Two cranes in trees 1.00 .50
d. A1169 400w Two deer 1.10 .55
e. A1169 440w Turtle, rapids 1.25 .60
f. A1169 470w River 1.25 .60
g. A1169 930w Trees 2.50 1.25

A1170

A1171

21st UPU Congress, Seoul: No. 1792, Pens, glasses, stamps. No. 1793, Sword dance. No. 1794, Dove holding envelope. No. 1795, Hong Yong-sik, Heinrich Von Stephan, horiz.

1994, Aug. 22 Photo. *Perf. 13*
1792 A1170 130w multicolored .50 .20
a. Souvenir sheet of 2 1.10 1.10
b. Booklet pane of 10 6.00
Complete booklet, #1792b 6.00
1793 A1170 130w multicolored .50 .20
a. Souvenir sheet of 2 1.10 1.10
b. Booklet pane of 10 6.00
Complete booklet, #1793b 6.00
1794 A1170 130w multicolored .50 .20
a. Souvenir sheet of 2 1.10 1.10
b. Booklet pane of 10 6.00
Complete booklet, #1794b 6.00
1795 A1170 370w multicolored 1.25 .60
a. Souvenir sheet of 2 2.50 2.50
b. Souvenir sheet of 4, #1792-1795 6.25 6.25
c. Booklet pane of 10 42.50
Complete booklet, #1795b 42.50
Nos. 1792-1795 (4) 2.75 1.20

1994, Sept. 27
1796 A1171 130w multicolored .50 .20

Seoul, Capital of Korea, 600th anniv.

A1172

A1173

1994, Nov. 19 Photo. *Perf. 13x13½*
1797 A1172 130w multicolored .50 .25
a. Souvenir sheet of 2 1.25 1.25
Complete booklet, 4 #1797 5.00

Philatelic Week. Complete booklet has one #1797 tied to cover with first day cancel.

1994, Nov. 29
1798 A1173 130w multicolored .50 .20

Seoul becomes Korea's capital, 600th anniv.

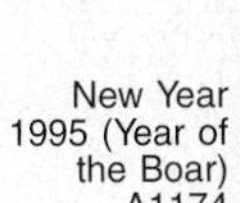

New Year 1995 (Year of the Boar)
A1174

1994, Dec. 1 *Perf. 13½x13*
1799 A1174 130w shown .50 .20
a. Souvenir sheet of 2 1.25 1.25
Complete booklet, 4 #1799 5.00
1800 A1174 130w Family outing .50 .20
a. Souvenir sheet of 2 1.25 1.25
Complete booklet, 4 #1800 5.00

Wildlife Protection
A1175

1995, Jan. 23 Photo. *Perf. 13½x13*
1801 A1175 130w Rana plancyi .65 .30
a. Souv. sheet of 2, imperf. 1.25 1.25
Complete booklet, 4 #1801 5.00
1802 A1175 130w Bufo bufo .65 .30
a. Souv. sheet of 2, imperf. 1.25 1.25
Complete booklet, 4 #1802 5.00

Mushroom Type of 1993

Designs: No. 1803, Russula virescens. No. 1804, Lentinus lepideus. No. 1805, Coprinus comalus. No. 1806, Laetiporus sulphureus.

1995, Mar. 31 Photo. *Perf. 13x13½*
1803 A1098 130w multicolored .60 .30
a. Souvenir sheet of 2 1.50 1.50
Complete booklet, 4 #1803 5.00
1804 A1098 130w multicolored .60 .30
a. Souvenir sheet of 2 1.50 1.50
Complete booklet, 4 #1804 5.00
1805 A1098 130w multicolored .60 .30
a. Souvenir sheet of 2 1.50 1.50
Complete booklet, 4 #1805 5.00
1806 A1098 130w multicolored .60 .30
a. Souvenir sheet of 2 1.50 1.50
Complete booklet, 4 #1806 5.00
Nos. 1803-1806 (4) 2.40 1.20

Completion of HANARO Research Reactor
A1176

1995, Apr. 7 *Perf. 13½x13*
1807 A1176 130w multicolored .65 .35
Complete booklet, 4 #1807 5.00

Modern Judicial System, Cent. — A1177

1995, Apr. 25 Litho. *Perf. 13x13½*
1808 A1177 130w multicolored .40 .20

Modern Legal Education, Cent.
A1178

1995, Apr. 25 *Perf. 13½x13*
1809 A1178 130w multicolored .40 .20

Cartoons
A1179

130w, "Dooly, the Little Dinosaur," baby, porpoise. 440w, "Kochuboo," riding in airplane.

1995, May 4
1810 A1179 130w multicolored .45 .35
a. Souvenir sheet of 1 1.25 1.25
Complete booklet, 4 #1810 5.00
1811 A1179 440w multicolored 1.25 .65
a. Souvenir sheet of 1 2.50 2.50
Complete booklet, 4 #1811 10.00

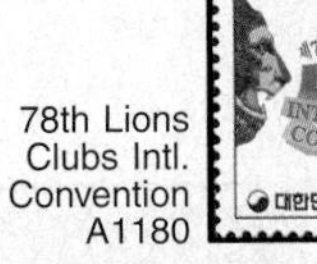
78th Lions Clubs Intl. Convention
A1180

1995, July 4 Photo. *Perf. 13½x13*
1812 A1180 130w multicolored .50 .20

Liberation Day, 50th Anniv.
A1181

Design: 440w, Mountain, yin/yang symbol.

1995, Aug. 14 Photo. *Perf. 13½x13*
1813 A1181 130w multicolored .35 .20
a. Booklet pane of 10 12.00
Complete booklet, #1813a 12.00
b. Souvenir sheet of 2 1.25 1.25

Size: 97x19mm
Perf. 13x13½
1814 A1181 440w multicolored 1.40 .65
a. Souvenir sheet of 1 2.25 2.25

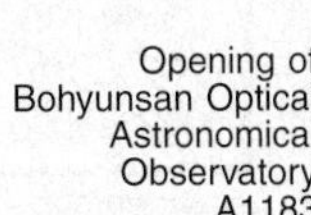
Opening of Bohyunsan Optical Astronomical Observatory
A1183

1995, Sept. 13 Litho. *Perf. 13x13½*
1816 A1183 130w multicolored .50 .20
Complete booklet, 6 #1816 5.00

Literature Series

Kuji-ga Song (The Turtle's Back Song) — A1184

Chongeop-sa Song
A1185

A1186

A1187

Record of Travel to Five Indian Kingdoms — A1188

A Poem to the Sui General Yu Zhong Wen — A1189

A1190

A1191

A1192

A1193

A1194

A1195

Perf. 13x13½, 13½x13
1995-99 Photo.
1817 A1184 130w multicolored .45 .20
a. Souvenir sheet of 2 1.25 1.25
Complete booklet, 6 #1817 5.00
1818 A1185 130w multicolored .45 .20
a. Souvenir sheet of 2 1.25 1.25
Complete booklet, 6 #1818 5.00
1819 A1186 150w multicolored .50 .25
a. Souvenir sheet of 2 1.25 1.25
Complete booklet, 10 #1819 *10.00*
1820 A1187 150w multicolored .50 .25
a. Souvenir sheet of 2 1.25 1.25
Complete booklet, 10 #1820 *10.00*
1821 A1188 170w multicolored .50 .25
a. Souvenir sheet of 2 1.25 1.25
Complete booklet, 10 #1821 7.50
1822 A1189 170w multicolored .50 .25
a. Sheet of 2 1.25 1.25
Complete booklet, 10 #1822 7.50

Photo. & Engr.
1823 A1190 170w multicolored .50 .25
Complete booklet, 10 #1823 7.50
a. Souvenir sheet of 1 .75 .75
1824 A1191 170w multicolored .50 .25
Complete booklet, 10 #1824 7.50
a. Souvenir sheet of 1 .75 .75
1825 A1192 170w multi .50 .30
Complete booklet, 10 #1825 7.50
1826 A1193 170w multi .50 .30
Complete booklet, 10 #1826 7.50
1827 A1194 170w multi .50 .30
Complete booklet, 10 #1827 7.50
1828 A1195 170w multi .50 .30
Complete booklet, 10 #1828 7.50
Nos. 1817-1828 (12) 5.90 3.10

Souvenir Sheets

1828A A1192 340w multi 1.25 .60
1828B A1193 340w multi 1.25 .60
1828C A1194 340w multi 1.25 .60
1828D A1195 340w multi 1.25 .60

Issued: #1817-1818, 9/25/95; #1819-1820, 9/16/96; #1821-1822, 12/12/97; #1823-1824, 9/14/98; #1825-1828D, 10/20/99

FAO, 50th Anniv.
A1196

Litho. & Engr.
1995, Oct. 16 *Perf. 13*
1829 A1196 150w dp vio & blk .50 .25
Complete booklet, 10 #1829 *7.50*

Korean Bible Society, Cent.
A1197

1995, Oct. 18 Litho.
1830 A1197 150w multicolored .50 .25
Complete booklet, 10 #1830 *7.50*

Population and Housing Census — A1198

1995, Oct. 20

1831 A1198 150w multicolored .50 .25
Complete booklet, 10 #1831 *7.50*

UN, 50th Anniv. A1199

1995, Oct. 24 **Photo.**

1832 A1199 150w multicolored .50 .25
Complete booklet, 10 #1832 *7.50*

Wilhelm Röntgen (1845-1923), Discovery of the X-Ray, Cent. A1200

1995, Nov. 8 ***Perf. 13½x13***

1833 A1200 150w multicolored .50 .25
Complete booklet, 10 #1833 7.50

Philatelic Week — A1201

1995, Nov. 18 **Photo.** ***Perf. 13x13½***

1834 A1201 150w multicolored .50 .25
a. Souvenir sheet of 2 1.25 1.25
Complete booklet, 10 #1834 *7.50*

A1202

New Year 1996 (Year of the Rat) — A1203

1995, Dec. 1 ***Perf. 13x13½, 13½x13***

1835 A1202 150w multicolored .50 .25
a. Souvenir sheet of 2 1.25 1.25
Complete booklet, 10 #1835 7.50

1836 A1203 150w multicolored .50 .25
a. Souvenir sheet of 2 1.25 1.25
Complete booklet, 10 #1836 7.50

Normalization of Korea-Japan Relations, 30th Anniv. — A1204

1995, Dec. 18 **Litho.** ***Perf. 13x13½***

1837 A1204 420w multicolored 1.50 .70
Complete booklet, 4 #1837 *7.50*

Types of 1993-97 and

Gallicrex Cinerea A1206

Zosterops Japonica A1208

Luffa Cylindrica A1209

Numenius Madagascariensis A1210

Cambaroides Similis — A1211

747 Airplane A1215

Mare and Colt — A1221

Soksu Stone Carving A1223

Bronze Incense Burner in Shape of Lotus Flowers — A1224

Photo., Photo. & Embossed (#1844)

1996-98 ***Perf. 13x13½, 13½x13***

1839	A1206	50w multi	.30	.20
1840	A1208	80w multi	.30	.20
1841	A1209	100w multi	.45	.20
1842	A1118	140w multi	.45	.25

Perf. 13

1843	A1210	170w multi	.45	.25
1844	A1210	170w like #1843, braille inscription	1.50	.45

Perf. 13x13½, 13½x13

1845	A1211	170w multi	1.00	.30
1846	A997c	190w multi	1.00	.30
1847	A1119	260w multi	1.50	.40

Perf. 13x14

1848	A1119	300w Alauda arvensis	1.00	.40

Perf. 13½x13, 13x13½, 13 (#1855)

1849	A1215	340w green blue & multi	1.60	.45
1850	A1215	380w lt lilac & multi	1.75	.50
1851	A1001	420w like #1593	2.40	.45
1852	A1002	480w like #1594	2.50	.50
1854	A1221	800w multi	2.25	.60
1855	A1223	1000w multi	3.75	1.25
1856	A1224	1170w multi	4.00	2.00
1857	A1128	1190w multicolored	4.00	2.00
1858	A1215	1340w brt green & multi	4.50	1.60
1859	A1215	1380w pink & multi	5.00	1.90
		Nos. 1839-1859 (20)	39.70	14.20

Coil Stamps

Perf. 13 Horiz., 13 Vert. (#1860, 1862)

1996-97 **Photo.**

1860	A998	150w like #1591	1.25	.75
1861	A1211	170w like No. 1845	1.00	.30
1862	A997c	190w like No. 1846	1.00	.30
		Nos. 1860-1862 (3)	3.25	1.35

Issued: 300w, 1/22/96; #1860, 2/1/96; 420w, 480w, 3/20/96; 1000w, 12/16/96; 100w, 3/5/97; 80w, 7/1/97; #1845-1846, 9/1/97; 340w, 380w, 1340w, 1380w, 9/12/97; #1842, 1847, 1856, 1857, 11/1/97; #1861, 1862, 11/18/97; #1843, 12/15/97; 50w, 2/19/98; 800w, 4/4/98; #1844, 10/15/98.

Opening of China-Korea Submarine Fiber Optic Cable System A1229

1996, Feb. 8 **Litho.** ***Perf. 13½x13***

1863 A1229 420w multicolored 1.75 .50
Complete booklet, 4 #1863 *10.00*

See People's Republic of China No. 2647.

Korea Institute of Science and Technology, 30th Anniv. A1230

1996, Feb. 10 **Photo.** ***Perf. 13½x13***

1864 A1230 150w multicolored .50 .25
Complete booklet, 10 #1864 *7.50*

Protection of Nature A1231

1996, Mar. 5 **Photo.** ***Perf. 13½x13***

1865 A1231 150w Geoclemys reevesii .50 .25
a. Souvenir sheet of 2 1.25 1.25
Complete booklet, 10 #1865 *8.50*

1866 A1231 150w Scincella laterale .50 .25
a. Souvenir sheet of 2 1.25 1.25
Complete booklet, 10 #1866 *8.50*

Successful Launches of Mugunghwa Satellites A1232

1996, Mar. 18 **Photo.** ***Perf. 13***

1867 A1232 150w multicolored .50 .25
Complete booklet, 10 #1867 *7.50*

Tongnip Shinmum, First Privately Published Newspaper, Cent. A1233

So Chae-p'il, lead article of first issue.

Litho. & Engr.

1996, Apr. 6 ***Perf. 13***

1868 A1233 150w multicolored .50 .25
Complete booklet, 10 #1868 *8.50*

Wildflower Type of 1992

#1869, Cypripedium macranthum. #1870, Trillium tschonoskii. #1871, Viola variegata. #1872, Hypericum ascyron.

1996, Apr. 22 **Photo.** ***Perf. 13***

1869 A1013 150w multicolored .50 .25
Complete booklet, 10 #1869 *10.00*

1870 A1013 150w multicolored .50 .25
Complete booklet, 10 #1870 *10.00*

1871 A1013 150w multicolored .50 .25
Complete booklet, 10 #1871 *10.00*

1872 A1013 150w multicolored .50 .25
Complete booklet, 10 #1872 *10.00*

Nos. 1869-1872 (4) 2.00 1.00

Korea Military Academy, 50th Anniv. A1234

1996, May 1 **Litho.** ***Perf. 13½x13***

1873 A1234 150w multicolored .50 .25
Complete booklet, 10 #1873 *10.00*

Cartoons A1235

1996, May 4 **Photo.**

1874 A1235 150w Gobau running .50 .25
a. Souvenir sheet of 1 1.25 1.25
Complete booklet, 10 #1874 *10.00*

1875 A1235 150w Kkach'i in swordfight .50 .25
a. Souvenir sheet of 1 1.25 1.25
Complete booklet, 10 #1875 *10.00*

Girl Scouts of Korea, 50th Anniv. A1236

1996, May 10 **Litho.**

1876 A1236 150w multicolored .50 .25
Complete booklet, 10 #1876 *12.00*

35th IAA World Advertising Congress — A1237

1996, June 8 **Litho.** ***Perf. 13***

1877 A1237 150w multicolored .50 .25
Complete booklet, 10 #1877 *9.50*

Campaign Against Illegal Drugs A1238

1996, June 26 **Photo.** ***Perf. 13½x13***

1878 A1238 150w multicolored .60 .25
Complete booklet, 10 #1878 *12.00*

Winter Universiade '97, Muju-Chonju A1239

1996, July 1 ***Perf. 13½x13, 13x13½***

1879 A1239 150w shown .50 .25
Complete booklet, 10 #1879 *10.00*

1880 A1239 150w Emblem, vert. .50 .25
Complete booklet, 10 #1880 *10.00*

1996 Summer Olympic Games, Atlanta
A1240 A1241

1996, July 20 ***Perf. 13x13½***

1881 A1240 150w multicolored .50 .25
Complete booklet, 10 #1881 *10.00*
1882 A1241 150w multicolored .50 .25
Complete booklet, 10 #1882 *10.00*

Mushroom Type of 1993

Designs: No. 1883, Paxillus atrotomentosus. No. 1884, Sarcodon imbricatum. No. 1885, Rhodophyllus crassipes. No. 1886, Amanita inaurata.

1996, Aug. 19 Photo. ***Perf. 13x13½***

1883 A1098 150w multicolored .50 .25
a. Souvenir sheet of 2 1.25 1.25
Complete booklet, 10 #1883 *10.00*
1884 A1098 150w multicolored .50 .25
a. Souvenir sheet of 2 1.25 1.25
Complete booklet, 10 #1884 *10.00*
1885 A1098 150w multicolored .50 .25
a. Souvenir sheet o 2 1.25 1.25
Complete booklet, 10 #1885 *10.00*
1886 A1098 150w multicolored .50 .25
a. Souvenir sheet of 2 1.25 1.25
Complete booklet, 10 #1886 *10.00*
Nos. 1883-1886 (4) 2.00 1.00

Souvenir Sheets

2002 World Cup Soccer Championships, Korea — A1242

#1887, Players, Korean flag. #1888, 2 players.

1996, Aug. 1 Photo. ***Perf. 13½***

1887 A1242 400w Sheet of 4 7.50 7.50
1888 A1242 400w Sheet of 4 7.50 7.50

Korean Alphabet, 550th Anniv. — A1243

Litho. & Engr.

1996, Oct. 9 ***Perf. 13x13½***

1889 A1243 150w multicolored .50 .25
a. Souvenir sheet of 2 1.25 1.25
Complete booklet, 10 #1889 *10.00*

Suwon Castle, Bicent. A1244

Photo. & Engr.

1996, Oct. 10 ***Perf. 13½x13***

1890 A1244 400w multicolored 1.50 .60
Complete booklet, 10 #1890 *20.00*

Seoul Natl. University, 50th Anniv. A1245

1996, Oct. 15 Photo. ***Perf. 13½x13***

1891 A1245 150w multicolored .50 .25
Complete booklet, 10 #1891 *10.00*

Philatelic Week — A1246

Painting: Poppy and a Lizard, by Shin Saimdang.

1996, Nov. 18 Photo. ***Perf. 13x13½***

1892 A1246 150w multicolored .50 .25
a. Souvenir sheet of 2 1.25 1.25
Complete booklet, 10 #1892 *10.00*

A1247

New Year 1997 (Year of the Ox) — A1248

1996, Dec. 2 ***Perf. 13***

1893 A1247 150w multicolored .50 .25
a. Souvenir sheet of 2 1.25 1.25
Complete booklet, 10 #1893 *10.00*
1894 A1248 150w multicolored .50 .25
a. Souvenir sheet of 2 1.25 1.25
Complete booklet, 10 #1894 *10.00*

Winter Universiade '97, Muju-Chonju A1249

1997, Jan. 24 Photo. ***Perf. 13***

1895 A1249 150w Skier .45 .25
Complete booklet, 10 #1895 *10.00*
1896 A1249 150w Ice skater .45 .25
Complete booklet, 10 #1896 *10.00*

Modern Banking System in Korea, Cent. A1250

1997, Feb. 19 Litho. ***Perf. 13½x13***

1897 A1250 150w multicolored .45 .25
Complete booklet, 10 #1897 *9.00*

A1251 A1252

1997, Apr. 10 ***Perf. 13x13½***

1898 A1251 150w multicolored .45 .20
Complete booklet, 10 #1898 *9.00*

97th Inter-Parliamentary Conference, 160th Inter-Parliamentary Council.

1997, Apr. 23 **Litho.**

1899 A1252 150w multicolored .45 .20
Complete booklet, 10 #1899 *9.00*

World Book & Copyright Day.

Cartoons A1253

#1900, Mother holding child from "A Long, Long Journey in Search of Mommy." #1901, Girl in air holding medal from "Run, Run, Hannie."

1997, May 3 Photo. ***Perf. 13½x13***

1900 A1253 150w multicolored .70 .25
a. Souvenir sheet of 1 1.00 1.00
Complete booklet, 10 #1900 *11.00*
1901 A1253 150w multicolored .70 .25
a. Souvenir sheet of 1 1.00 1.00
Complete booklet, 10 #1901 *11.00*

Nos. 1900a, 1901a are continuous designs.

2nd Pusan East Asian Games — A1254

1997, May 10 Litho. ***Perf. 13x13½***

1902 A1254 150w multicolored .50 .25
Complete booklet, 10 #1900 *9.00*

2002 World Cup Soccer, Korea/Japan
A1255 A1256

No. 1903, Jules Rimet, founder of World Cup. No. 1904, Painting of Ch'ukkuk match.

1997, May 31 Photo. ***Perf. 13x13½***

1903 A1255 150w multicolored .60 .25
a. Souvenir sheet of 2 1.50 1.50
Complete booklet, 10 #1903 *10.00*
1904 A1256 150w multicolored .60 .25
a. Souvenir sheet of 3 2.00 2.00
Complete booklet, 10 #1904 *10.00*

Wildlife Protection A1257

Fish: No. 1905, Pungitius sinensis. No. 1906, Coreoperca kawamebari.

1997, June 5 ***Perf. 13***

1905 A1257 150w multicolored .45 .25
a. Souvenir sheet of 2 1.00 1.00
Complete booklet, 10 #1905 *10.00*
1906 A1257 150w multicolored .45 .25
a. Souvenir sheet of 2 1.00 1.00
Complete booklet, 10 #1906 *10.00*

Wildflower Type of 1992

#1907, Belamcanda chinensis. #1908, Hylomecon ernale. #1909, Campanula takesimana. #1910, Magnolia sieboldii.

1997, June 19 Photo. ***Perf. 13***

1907 A1013 150w multicolored .45 .25
Complete booklet, 10 #1907 *12.00*
1908 A1013 150w multicolored .45 .25
Complete booklet, 10 #1908 *12.00*
1909 A1013 150w multicolored .45 .25
Complete booklet, 10 #1909 *12.00*
1910 A1013 150w multicolored .45 .25
Complete booklet, 10 #1910 *12.00*
Nos. 1907-1910 (4) 1.80 1.00

1997 Kwangju Biennale — A1258

1997, July 1

1911 A1258 150w multicolored .45 .25
Complete booklet, 10 #1911 *8.00*

Mushroom Type of 1993

Designs: No. 1912, Inocybe fastigiata. No. 1913, Panaeolus papilionaceus. No. 1914, Ramaria flava. No. 1915, Amanita muscaria.

1997, July 21 Photo. ***Perf. 13x13½***

1912 A1098 150w multicolored .45 .25
a. Souvenir sheet of 2 1.00 1.00
1913 A1098 150w multicolored .45 .25
a. Souvenir sheet of 2 1.00 1.00
1914 A1098 150w multicolored .45 .25
a. Souvenir sheet of 2 1.00 1.00
1915 A1098 150w multicolored .45 .25
a. Souvenir sheet of 2 1.00 1.00
Nos. 1912-1915 (4) 1.80 1.00

85th World Dental Congress, Seoul A1259

1997, Sept. 5 Photo. ***Perf. 13½x13***

1916 A1259 170w multicolored .45 .25

Opening of Port of Mokpo, Cent. A1260

Litho. & Engr.

1997, Oct. 1 ***Perf. 13½x13***

1917 A1260 170w multicolored .45 .25

Soongsil Academy, Cent. A1261

1997, Oct. 10 **Photo. & Engr.**

1918 A1261 170w multicolored .45 .25

Beauty Series

Wrapping Cloths — A1262

1997, Nov. 3 Photo. ***Perf. 13x13½***

1919 170w multicolored .60 .25
1920 170w multicolored .60 .25
1921 170w multicolored .60 .25
1922 170w multicolored .60 .25
a. A1262 Strip of 4, #1919-1922 2.25 2.25

Philatelic Week — A1266

1997, Nov. 18

1923 A1266 170w multicolored .50 .25
a. Souvenir sheet of 2 1.00 1.00

New Year 1998 (Year of the Tiger)
A1267 A1268

1997, Dec. 1 Photo. *Perf. 13x13½*

1924 A1267 170w multicolored .60 .25
a. Souvenir sheet of 2 1.25 1.25

1925 A1268 170w multicolored .60 .25
a. Souvenir sheet of 2 1.25 1.25

Pulguksa Temple — A1269

Litho. & Engr.

1997, Dec. 9 *Perf. 13x13½*

1926 A1269 Sheet of 14 25.00 25.00
a. 170w Buddha, Sokkuram Grotto .85 .85
b. 380w Temple 3.50 3.50

Top part of No. 1926 contains one each #1926a-1926b and is separated from the bottom portion of the sheet by a row of perforations. The lower part of No. 1926 contains 9 #1926a and 3 #1926b.

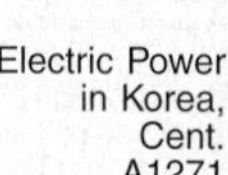

Electric Power in Korea, Cent. A1271

1998, Jan. 26 Photo. *Perf. 13½x13*

1927 A1271 170w multicolored .50 .20

Inauguration of the 15th President, Kim Dae-jung A1272

1998, Feb. 25 Litho. *Perf. 13½x13*

1928 A1272 170w multicolored .80 .40
a. Souvenir sheet of 1 *5.50 5.50*

Protection of Wild Animals and Plants — A1273

Designs: a, Panthera pardus orientalis. b, Selenarctos thibetanus ussuricus. c, Lutra lutra. d, Moschus moschiferus.

1998, Mar. 21 *Perf. 13x13½*

1929 Sheet of 12 20.00 20.00
a.-d. A1273 340w Any single 1.25 .30

Top part of #1929 contains one each #1929a-1929d and is separated from the bottom portion of the sheet by a row of perforations. The lower part of #1929 contains 2 each #1929a-1929d.

Cartoons A1274

Designs: 170w, Boy daydreaming while holding flower, from "Aktong-i," by Lee Hi-jae. 340w, Mother on motorcycle, son making fists from "Challenger," by Park Ki-jong.

1998, May 4 Photo. *Perf. 13½x13*

1930 A1274 170w multicolored .50 .25
a. Souvenir sheet of 1 .75 .75
b. Booklet pane of 10 20.00
Complete booklet, #1930b 20.00

Photo. & Engr.

1931 A1274 340w multicolored 1.10 1.10
a. Souvenir sheet of 1 1.50 1.50
b. Booklet pane of 10 26.00
Complete booklet, #1931b 26.00

Natl. Assembly, 50th Anniv. A1275

1998, May 30 Litho. *Perf. 13½x13*

1932 A1275 170w multicolored .50 .20

2002 World Cup Soccer Championships, Korea/Japan — A1276

Designs: a, Player. b, Two players. c, Player heading ball. d, Player performing bicycle kick.

1998, May 30 *Perf. 13x13½*

1933 Strip of 4, #a.-d. 3.00 3.00
a.-d. A1276 170w any single .60 .25
e. Souvenir sheet, #1933 3.25 3.25

Information Culture Special A1277

Communication through the ages: a, Rock drawings. b, Horseback messenger, beacon fire. c, Telephone, mailbox. d, Computers.

1998, June 1 Litho. *Perf. 13½x13*

1934 Strip of 4 3.50 3.50
a.-c. A1277 170w any single .50 .25
d. A1277 340w multicolored 1.00 .45

No. 1934d is 68x70mm.

Mushroom Type of 1993

Designs: a, Pseudocolus schellenbergiae. b, Cyptotrama asprata. c, Laccaria vinaceoavellanea. d, Phallus rugulosus.

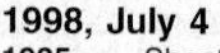

1998, July 4

1935 Sheet of 16 12.00 12.00
a.-d. A1098 170w Any single .75 .30

Left part of #1935 contains 3 each #1935a-1935d, with each strip in a different order. This is separated from the right portion of the sheet by a row of perforations. The right part of #1935 contains 1 each #1935a-1935d.

Republic of Korea, 50th Anniv. A1278

1998, Aug. 14 Photo. *Perf. 13½x13*

1937 A1278 170w multicolored .50 .25

A1279 A1280

1998, Aug. 19 *Perf. 13x13½*

1938 A1279 170w multicolored .50 .25
a. Souvenir sheet of 2 1.10 1.10

Philatelic Week.

1998, Sept. 24 Photo. *Perf. 13x13½*

1939 A1280 170w multicolored .50 .25
Complete booklet, 10 #1939 12.00

1998 Pusan Intl. Film Festival.

Founding of Songkyunkwan, 600th Anniv. — A1281

Photo. & Engr.

1998, Sept. 25 *Perf. 13*

1940 A1281 170w multicolored .50 .25
Complete booklet, 5 #1940 5.00

A1282 A1283

1998, Oct. 1

1941 A1282 170w multicolored .50 .25
Complete booklet, 10 #1941 7.50

Korean Armed Forces, 50th anniv.

1998, Oct. 9

1942 A1283 170w multicolored .50 .25
Complete booklet, 10 #1942 6.50

World Stamp Day.

Beauty Series

Ceramics — A1284

#1944, Box with cranes on lid. #1945, Fish. #1946, Red, white blossom with blue leaf. #1947, Frog. #1948, Dragon. #1949, Monkeys. #1950, Pagoda.

1998, Nov. 20 Photo. *Perf. 13*

1943 A1284 170w multicolored .75 .40
1944 A1284 170w multicolored .75 .40
1945 A1284 170w multicolored .75 .40
1946 A1284 170w multicolored .75 .40
1947 A1284 170w multicolored .75 .40
1948 A1284 170w multicolored .75 .40
1949 A1284 170w multicolored .75 .40
1950 A1284 170w multicolored .75 .40
a. Block of 8, #1243-1250 7.50 7.50

New Year 1999 (Year of the Rabbit) — A1286

1998, Dec. 1 *Perf. 13x13½*

1952 A1286 170w multicolored .50 .25
Complete booklet, 10 #1952 7.50

Woodblock of Buddhist Tripitaka Koreana, Haeinsa Temple A1287

Haeinsa Temple Changgyong P'anjon Complex — A1288

Litho. & Engr.

1998, Dec. 9 *Perf. 13½*

1953 Sheet of 12 20.00 20.00
a. A1287 170w multicolored .75 .50
b. A1288 380w multicolored 2.25 1.50

Top part of #1953 contains one each #1953a-1953b and is separated from the bottom portion of the sheet by a row of perforations. The lower part of #1953 contains 6 #1953a and 4 #1953b.

Opening of Kunsan Port, Cent. A1289

1999, May 1 Litho. *Perf. 13¼*

1954 A1289 170w multicolored .50 .25

Opening of Masan Port, Cent. — A1290

1999, May 1

1955 A1290 170w multicolored .50 .25

Cartoons A1291

No. 1956, Boy and dog, "Tokgo T'ak," by Lee Sang-mu. No. 1957, Choson Dynasty robber, "Im Kkuk-jung," by Lee Du-ho. No. 1958,

Fighter against alien invaders, "Rai-Fi," by Kim San-ho, vert.

1999, May 3 Photo. *Perf. 13½*

1956 A1291 170w multicolored .50 .25
1957 A1291 170w multicolored .50 .25
1958 A1291 170w multicolored .50 .25
Nos. 1956-1958 (3) 1.50 .75

Souvenir Sheets

1959 A1291 340w like #1956 1.40 1.25
1960 A1291 340w like #1957 1.40 1.25
1961 A1291 340w like #1958 1.40 1.25
Nos. 1959-1961 (3) 4.20 3.75

Nos. 1959-1961 are continuous designs.

A1292

A1293

Raptors: a, Falco peregrinus. b, Accipiter soloensis. c, Bubo bubo. d, Haliaeetus pelagicus.

1999, June 5 Litho. *Perf. 13x13¼*

1962 Sheet of 12 24.00 24.00
a.-b. A1292 170w each 1.00 .30
c.-d. A1292 340w each 1.75 .60

Top part of #1962 contains one each #1962a-1962d and is separated from the bottom portion of the sheet by a row of perforations. The lower part of #1962 contains 2 blocks of #1962a-1962d.

1999, June 12 Photo. *Perf. 13x13¼*

1963 A1293 170w multicolored .50 .25
Complete booklet, 10 #1963 12.00

1999 Intl. Olympic Committee Congress, Seoul.

Johann Wolfgang von Goethe, German Poet (1749-1832) A1294

Litho. & Engr.

1999, Aug. 12 *Perf. 13x13½*

1964 A1294 170w multicolored .70 .30

Souvenir Sheet

1965 A1294 480w multicolored 2.00 2.00

Kumgang Mountain by Kyomjae (1676-1759) — A1295

1999, Aug. 13 Litho.

1966 A1295 170w multicolored .50 .30

Souvenir Sheet

1967 A1295 340w multicolored 1.25 1.25

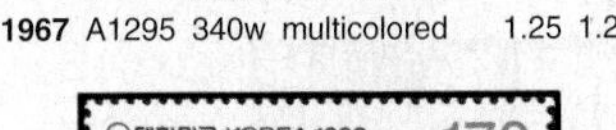

Korean National Railroad, Cent. — A1296

Litho. & Engr.

1999, Sept. 18 *Perf. 13x13¼*

1968 A1296 170w multicolored .70 .30
Complete booklet, 10 #1968 12.00

Millennium — A1297

Prehistoric sites and artifacts — No. 1969: a, Paleolithic ruins, Chungok-ri (black denomination at LL). b, Neolithic sites, Amsa-dong (white denomination at UR). c, Neolithic shell mound ruins, Tongsam-dong (black denomination at LR). d, Dolmen, Pukon-ri (black denomination at UR). e, Bronze Age artifacts and ruins, Songguk-ri. f, Rock carvings, Ulsan.

Three Countries Era artifacts — No. 1970: a, Tiger-shpaed belt buckle from tomb of Sarari, duck-shaped earthenware container, Kyongsang. b, Gold crown, silver cup from Hwangnamdae tomb. c, Wall painting of hunting scene from Tomb of the Dancers, Chibanri. d, Gold diadem ornaments, curved jade pieces from tomb of King Muryong. e, Gold crown from Koryong, armor from Kimhae. f, Decorative tiles, Anapji Pond.

Ancient Choson to Unified Shilla periods — No. 1971: a, Writing, site of Asadal, ancient capital of Choson. b, Korean wrestlers. c, King Kwanggaet'o, stone stele, and circular artifact with writing. d, Archers on horseback. e, Admiral Chang Po-go, ship.

Koryo dynasty — No. 1972: a, Writing and buildings (civil service examinations). b, Monk and Tripitaka Koreana wood blocks. c, Jade and movable metal type. d, Scholar An-hyang, writing and buildings. e, Mun Ik-jom, cotton plants and spinning wheel.

Early Choson dynasty — No. 1973: a, King Sejong and Korean alphabet. b, Korean script and Lady Shin Saimdang, calligrapher and painter. c, Yi Hwang and Yi I and Confucian academy building. d, Admiral Yi Sun-shin and turtle boat. e, Sandae-nori mask dance dramas.

Late Choson Dynasty — No. 1974: a, Tongui Pogam, medical treatises by Huh Joon (anatomic diagram, mortar and pestle) b, Dancer and Musicians, by Kim Hong-do. c, Plum Blossoms and Bird, by Chong Yak-yong and building. d, Map of Korea, by Kim Chong-ho and compass. e, Carved stone monument at Tongchak Peasant Uprsing Memorial Hall.

Historic relics of Koryo and Choson Dynasties — No. 1975: a, Container, pitcher, Kangjin kiln site. b, Fenced-off monument and Nirvana Hall, Pongjungsa Temple (yellow building). c, Hahoe and Pyongsan wooden masks. d, Kunjong Hall, Kyongbok Palace. e, Dream Journey to the Peach Blossom land, by An Kyon. f, Water clock of King Sejong.

Joseon Dynasty — No. 1976: a, Spring Outing, by Sin Yun-bok. b, Chusa-style calligraphy, birthplace of Kim Jeong-hui. c, Beacon Lighthouse, book of technical drawings. d, Myeongdong Cathedral. e, Wongaksa Theater, performers. f, KITSAT-1 satellite.

Vision of the Future — No. 1977: a, Bicycle with wheels represening the two Koreas. b, Rainbow (environmental protection). c, Human genome project. d, IMT 2000 and satellites. e, Children's drawing of space travel. f, Solar-powered vehicle, windmills.

Pre-independence historic events and personalities — No. 1978: a, Kim Ku. b, March 1 Independence Movement, Declaration of Independence. c, Establishment of Korean interim government. d, Ahn Ik-tae, composer of national anthem. e, Yun Dong-ju, poet.

Historic events since independence — No. 1979: a, Liberation after World War II (People with flag). b, Korean War (soldiers, barbed wire). c, Construction of Seoul-Busan Expressway. d, Saemaul Undong movement (workers and flag). e, 1988 Summer Olympics, Seoul.

1999-2001 Litho. *Perf. 13x13½*

1969 Sheet of 6 5.00 5.00
a.-f. A1297 170w any single .60 .30
1970 Sheet of 6 5.00 5.00
a.-f. A1297 170w any single .60 .30

Perf. 13½

1971 Sheet of 5 + label 4.75 4.75
a.-e. A1297 170w any single .60 .30

Photo.

1972 Sheet of 5 + label 4.75 4.75
a.-e. A1297 170w any single .60 .30
1973 Sheet of 5 + label 4.75 4.75
a.-e. A1297 170w any single .60 .30
1974 Sheet of 5 + label 4.75 4.75
a.-e. A1297 170w Any single .60 .30

Perf. 13

1975 Sheet of 6 5.25 5.25
a.-f. A1297 170w Any single .60 .30
1976 Sheet of 6 5.00 5.00
a.-f. A1297 170w Any single .60 .30
1977 Sheet of 6 5.00 5.00
a.-f. A1297 170w Any single .60 .30

Perf. 13½

1978 Sheet of 5 + label 4.50 4.50
a.-e. A1297 170w Any single .60 .30
1979 Sheet of 5 + label 4.50 4.50
a.-e. A1297 170w Any single .60 .30
Nos. 1969-1979 (11) 53.25 53.25

Size of stamps on Nos. 1971-1972, 1974, 1978-1979: 35x36mm.

Issued: #1969, 10/2; #1970, 11/16; #1971, 1/3/00; #1972, 3/2/00; #1973, 5/1/00; #1974, 7/1/00; #1975, 9/1/00; #1976, 11/1/00; #1977, 1/2/01; #1978, 4/2/01; #1979, 7/2/01.

UPU, 125th Anniv. — A1298

1999, Oct. 9 Litho. *Perf. 13x13½*

1980 A1298 170w multi .50 .25

Beauty Series

A1299

a, Purple panel, 4 orange flowers in purple and blue vase, rabbit, duck. b, Blue green panel, red jar, rooster. c, Orange panel, 4 orange flowers in yellow vase. d, Purple panel, fish, purple vase with flower decoration. e, Blue green panel, fish in net. f, Red panel, crab. g, Purple panel, birds, red flowers. h, Orange panel, deer, 3 orange flowers.

1999, Nov. 3 Litho. *Perf. 13x13¼*

1981 A1299 Sheet of 8, #a.-h. 12.00 12.00
a.-h. 340w any single 1.50 .60

New Year 2000 (Year of the Dragon) — A1300

1999, Dec. 1 Photo.

1982 A1300 170w multi .60 .30
a. Souvenir sheet of 2 1.25 1.25

A1301

Registration of Korean Sites on World Heritage List — A1302

Litho. & Engr.

1999, Dec. 9 *Perf. 13x13¼*

1983 Sheet of 10 12.50 12.50
a. A1301 170w multicolored .55 .30
b. A1302 340w multicolored 1.50 .70

Top part of #1983 contains one each #1983a-1983b. The lower part of #1983 contains 4 each #1983a-1983b.

Flag A1303

Nycticorax Nycticorax A1304

Vitis Amurensis A1305

Purpuricenus Lituratus A1306

Eophona Migratoria A1307

Limenitis Populi A1310

Plow A1311

Sseore A1311a

Sowing Basket, Namtae A1311b

Hoes A1311c

Namu-janngun, Jaetbak A1311d

Yongdurei A1311e

Winnower, Thresher A1311f

Meongseok, Wicker Tray A1311g

Mortar, Pestle, Grindstone A1311h

Carrier, Rice Chest A1311i

Hibiscus Syriacus A1312

Chionectes Opilio A1313

Falco Tinnunculus — A1314

Hibiscus Syriacus A1314a

Hibiscus Syriacus A1314b

Ficedula Zanthopygia — A1315

Hibiscus Syriacus A1315a

Celadon Pitcher A1316

Porcelain Container A1316a

Hong Yong-Sik, 1st General Postmaster A1317

Koryo Jade Ornament — A1319

Kylin Roof-End Tile — A1320

Ridge-End Tile — A1321

Porcelain Vase With Bamboo Design — A1322

Crown From Tombs of Shinch'on-ni A1323

Malus Asiatica A1326

Aquilegia Flabeliata — A1327

Perf. 13¼x13 (#2000, 2002, 2004, 2005), 13x13¼ (#2001, 2003, 2006, 2007), 12¾x13¾ (#1984-1990, 1996), 13¾x12¾ (#1986, 1991, 1993, 1994, 1995, 1997, 1998)

1999-2003			**Photo.**	
1984	A1303	10w multi	.20	.20
1985	A1304	20w multi	.30	.30
1986	A1305	30w multi	.50	.35
1987	A1306	40w multi	.30	.30
1988	A1307	60w multi	.55	.35
1989	A1310	160w multi	.55	.30
1990		Horiz. strip of 10	20.00	12.50
a.		A1311 170w multi	1.25	.30
b.		A1311a 170w multi	1.25	.30
c.		A1311b 170w multi	1.25	.30
d.		A1311c 170w multi	1.25	.30
e.		A1311d 170w multi	1.25	.30
f.		A1311e 170w multi	1.25	.30
g.		A1311f 170w multi	1.25	.30
h.		A1311g 170w multi	1.25	.30
i.		A1311h 170w multi	1.25	.30
j.		A1311i 170w multi	1.25	.30
1991	A1312	190w multi	.50	.30
1992	A1313	200w multi	.75	.35
1993	A1314	210w multi	.75	.30
1994	A1314a	220w multi	.75	.30
1995	A1314b	240w multi	.85	.45
1996	A1315	280w multi	1.10	.45
1997	A1315a	310w multi	1.00	.60
1998	A1316	400w multi	1.25	.90
1999	A1316a	500w multi	1.60	1.00
2000	A1317	600w multi	2.50	1.00
2001	A1319	700w multi	3.00	1.00
2002	A1320	1290w multi	4.00	2.50
2003	A1321	1310w multi	4.50	2.50
2004	A1320	1490w buff & multi	5.00	3.50
2005	A1321	1510w brn & multi	5.00	3.50
2006	A1322	1520w multi	5.00	3.50
2007	A1323	2000w multi	6.00	1.50

Booklet Stamps

Self-Adhesive

Serpentine Die Cut 11¼x11½, 11½x11¼

2008	A1326	190w multi	1.00	.35
a.		Booklet pane of 20	20.00	
2008A	A1327	190w multi	1.00	.35
a.		Booklet pane of 20	20.00	
		Nos. 1984-2008A (26)	67.95	38.65

Issued: 600w, 11/15; 2000w, 11/1; 20w, 700w, 1/17/00; 40w, 6/10/00; No. 1992, 1/20/01; 200w, 3/5/01. 160w, 210w, 280w, 1290w, 1310w, 1/15/02; 10w, 3/6/03; 30w, 9/10/01; 60w, 3/15/02; 400w, 4/11/03; 1490w, 1510w, 1/1/03; Nos. 2008-2008A, 7/1/03; 500w, 7/11/03; No. 1991, 220w, 240w, 310w, 1520w, 11/1/04.

2002 World Cup Soccer Championships, Korea & Japan — A1328

Various players in action.

1999, Dec. 31 Photo. *Perf. 13x13½*

Denomination Color

2009	170w orange	.50	.35
2010	170w green	.50	.35
2011	170w red	.50	.35
2012	170w blue	.50	.35
a.	A1328 Strip of 4, #2009-2012	2.75	2.75
b.	Souvenir sheet, #2009-2012	3.50	3.50

Korea's Entry into UPU, Cent. A1329

2000, Jan. 3 Photo. *Perf. 13¼x13*

2013	A1329 170w multi	.50	.30
	Booklet, 10 #2013	12.00	

Steam Locomotives — A1330

Designs: No. 2014, Pashi. No. 2015, Teho. No. 2016, Mika. No. 2017, Hyouki.

2000, Feb. 1 Photo. *Perf. 13¾x12¾*

2014	A1330 170w tan, blk & vio	.60	.30
2015	A1330 170w pink, blk & vio	.60	.30
2016	A1330 170w gray, blk & vio	.60	.30
2017	A1330 170w cit, blk & vio	.60	.30
a.	Block of 4, #2014-2017	2.75	2.75
	Booklet, 2 #2017a	—	

Endangered Flowers — A1331

a, Lilium cernuum. b, Hibiscus hamabo. c, Sedirea japonica. d, Cypripedium japonicum.

2000, Feb. 25 *Perf. 13x13¼*

2018	Sheet of 12	12.00	12.00
a.-d.	A1331 170w any single	.75	.30

Top part of No. 2018 contains one each of Nos. 2018a-2018d and the lower part contains two each. No. 2018 is impregnated with floral scent.

World Water Day — A1332

2000, Mar. 22 Photo. *Perf. 13¼x13*

2019	A1332 170w multi	.50	.30
	Booklet, 10 #2019	10.00	

World Meteorological Organization, 50th Anniv. — A1333

2000, Mar. 23 *Perf. 13x13¼*

2020	A1333 170w multi	.50	.30
	Booklet, 10 #2020	10.00	

Love A1334

2000, Apr. 20 Photo. *Perf. 13¼*

2021	A1334 170w multi	1.00	.30

No. 2021 has floral scent.
Value is for copy with surrounding selvage.

Cyber Korea 21 Technology Plan — A1335

2000, Apr. 22 Litho. *Perf. 13¼x13*

2022	A1335 170w multi	.50	.30
	Booklet, 10 #2022	10.00	

Cartoons — A1336

Designs: No. 2023: Goindol, by Park Soo-dong (cavemen). No. 2024, Youngsim-i, by Bae Gum-taek (girl with lipstick).

2000, May 4 Photo. *Perf. 13x13¼*

2023	A1336 170w multi	.50	.40
a.	Souvenir sheet of 1	.75	.75
	Booklet, 10 #2023	10.00	
2024	A1336 170w multi	.50	.40
a.	Souvenir sheet of 1	.75	.75
	Booklet, 10 #2024	10.00	

Summit Meeting Between North and South Korea A1337

2000, June 12 Photo. *Perf. 13¼x13*

2025	A1337 170w multi	.60	.50

41st Intl. Mathematical Olympiad — A1338

2000, July 13 Photo. *Perf. 13x13¼*

2026	A1338 170w multi	.50	.35
	Booklet, 10 #2026	7.50	

Literature Series

The Nine Cloud Dream, by Kim Man-jung A1339

From the Sea to a Child, by Chun Nam-seon A1340

Tears of Blood, by Yi In-jik A1341

Yolha Diary, by Park Ji-won A1342

The Fisherman's Calendar, by Yun Seon-do A1343

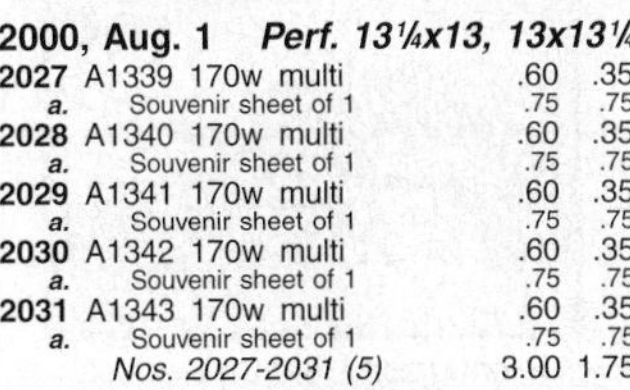
2000, Aug. 1 ***Perf. 13¼x13, 13x13¼***

2027	A1339 170w multi	.60	.35
a.	Souvenir sheet of 1	.75	.75
2028	A1340 170w multi	.60	.35
a.	Souvenir sheet of 1	.75	.75
2029	A1341 170w multi	.60	.35
a.	Souvenir sheet of 1	.75	.75
2030	A1342 170w multi	.60	.35
a.	Souvenir sheet of 1	.75	.75
2031	A1343 170w multi	.60	.35
a.	Souvenir sheet of 1	.75	.75
	Nos. 2027-2031 (5)	3.00	1.75

The Puljongdae Cliff of Mt. Kumgang, by Chong Son — A1344

2000, Aug. 2 **Litho.** ***Perf. 13¼x13***

2032	A1344 340w multi	1.00	.70
a.	Souvenir sheet of 1	1.40	1.40

Philately Week.

2000 Summer Olympics, Sydney — A1345

2000, Sept. 15 **Photo.** ***Perf. 13x13¼***

2033	A1345 170w multi	.60	.45

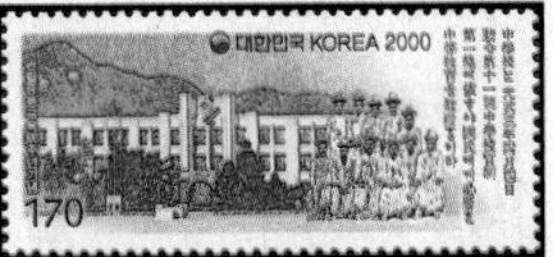
Public Secondary Schools, Cent. — A1346

2000, Oct. 2 **Litho. & Engr.** ***Perf. 13***

2034	A1346 170w multi	.60	.45

Third Asia-Europe Summit Meeting, Seoul A1347

2000, Oct. 20 **Photo.** ***Perf. 13¼x13***

2035	A1347 170w multi	.50	.35

Intl. Council of Graphic Design Associations Millennium Congress — A1348

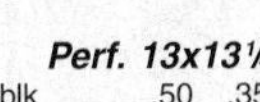
2000, Oct. 25 ***Perf. 13x13¼***

2036	A1348 170w org & blk	.50	.35

Cartoon Character Gobau. 50th Anniv. — A1349

2000, Nov. 1 **Litho.** ***Perf. 13¼***

2037	A1349 170w multi	.60	.35

Beauty Series

Tortoise-shell Comb A1350

Woman's Ceremonial Headdress A1351

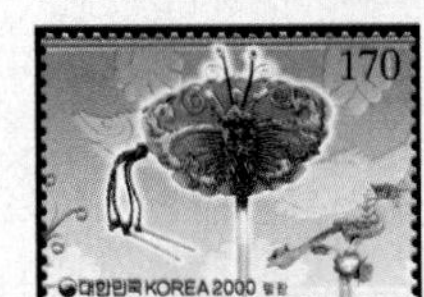
Butterfly-shaped Hair Pin — A1352

Dragon and Phoenix Hair Pins — A1353

2000, Nov. 16 **Photo.** ***Perf. 13¼x13***

2038	Horiz. strip of 4	2.75	2.50
a.	A1350 170w multi	.50	.35
b.	A1351 170w multi	.50	.35
c.	A1352 170w multi	.50	.35
d.	A1353 170w multi	.50	.35

Seoul World Cup Stadium A1354

Busan Sports Complex Main Stadium A1355

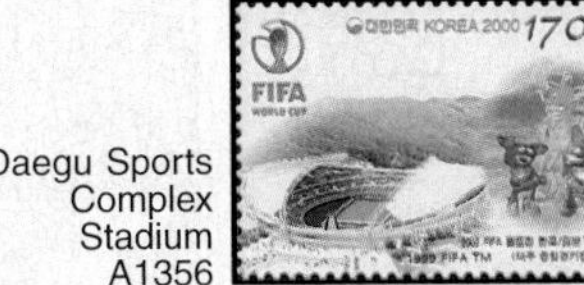
Daegu Sports Complex Stadium A1356

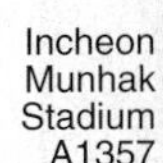

Incheon Munhak Stadium A1357

Gwangju World Cup Stadium A1358

Daejeon World Cup Stadium A1359

Ulsan Munsu Soccer Stadium A1360

Suwon World Cup Stadium A1361

Jeonju World Cup Stadium A1362

Jeju World Cup Stadium A1363

2000, Nov. 24 **Photo.** ***Perf. 13¼x13***

2039	Block of 10	12.00	10.00
a.	A1354 170w multi	1.20	.35
b.	A1355 170w multi	1.20	.35
c.	A1356 170w multi	1.20	.35
d.	A1357 170w multi	1.20	.35
e.	A1358 170w multi	1.20	.35
f.	A1359 170w multi	1.20	.35
g.	A1360 170w multi	1.20	.35
h.	A1361 170w multi	1.20	.35
i.	A1362 170w multi	1.20	.35
j.	A1363 170w multi	1.20	.35
k.	Souvenir sheet, #2039a-2039b	2.50	2.50
l.	Souvenir sheet, #2039c-2039d	2.50	2.50
m.	Souvenir sheet, #2039e-2039f	2.50	2.50
n.	Souvenir sheet, #2039g-2039h	2.50	2.50
o.	Souvenir sheet, #2039i-2039j	2.50	2.50

New Year 2001 (Year of the Snake) A1364

2000, Dec. 1 **Photo.** ***Perf. 13¼***

2040	A1364 170w multi	.60	.35
a.	Souvenir sheet of 2	1.25	1.25

Self-Adhesive

Serpentine Die Cut 10¼

2041	A1364 170w multi	1.00	.35

No. 2041 issued in sheets of 10.

King Sejong and Hunmin Chongun Manuscript — A1365

Annals of the Choson Dynasty and Repository — A1365a

Litho. & Engr.

2000, Dec. 9 ***Perf. 13x13¼***

2042	Sheet of 8	17.00	17.00
a.	A1365 340w multi	1.50	1.10
b.	A1365a 340w multi	1.50	1.10

Addition of Hunmin Chongun manuscript and Annals of the Choson Dynasty to UNESCO Memory of the World Register. Top part of No. 2042 contains one each Nos. 2042a-2042b the lower part contains three each Nos. 2042a-2042b.

Awarding of Nobel Peace Prize to Pres. Kim Dae-jung A1366

2000, Dec. 9 **Photo.**

2043	A1366 170w multi	.60	.35
a.	Souvenir sheet of 1	2.50	2.50

Oksun Peaks, by Kim Hong-do A1367

2001, Jan. 10 **Photo.** ***Perf. 13¼***

2044	A1367 170w multi	.50	.35

Visit Korea Year.

A1368

A1369

A1370

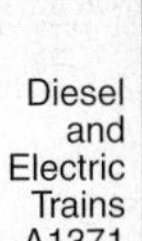
Diesel and Electric Trains A1371

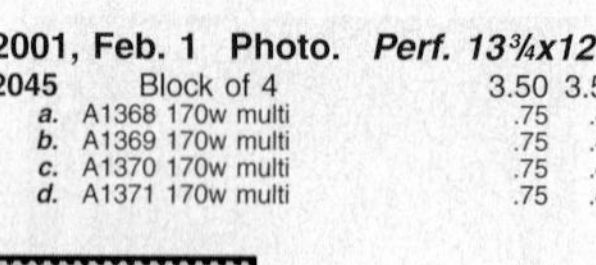

2001, Feb. 1 Photo. ***Perf. 13¾x12¾***

2045	Block of 4	3.50	3.50
a.	A1368 170w multi	.75	.45
b.	A1369 170w multi	.75	.45
c.	A1370 170w multi	.75	.45
d.	A1371 170w multi	.75	.45

Endangered Flowers — A1372

Designs: a, Diapensia lapponica. b, Rhododendron aureum. c, Jeffersonia dubia. d, Sedum orbiculatum.

2001, Feb. 26 ***Perf. 13x13¼***

2046	Sheet of 12	15.00	15.00
a.-d.	A1372 170w Any single	.75	.40

Top part of No. 2046 contains one each Nos. 2046a-2046d, the lower part contains two each Nos. 2046a-2046d.

Opening of Inchon Intl. Airport A1373

2001, Mar. 29

2047	A1373 170w multi	.60	.40

Intl. Olympic Fair, Seoul A1374

2001, Apr. 27 ***Perf. 13¼x13***

2048	A1374 170w multi	.60	.40
a.	Souvenir sheet of 2	1.75	1.75

Personalized Greetings — A1375

Designs: No. 2049, 170w, Hugging bears. No. 2050, 170w, Carnation. No. 2051, 170w, Congratulations. No. 2052, 170w, Birthday cake.

2001 Photo. ***Perf. 13¼***

Stamps + Labels

2049-2052	A1375 Set of 4	6.00	6.00

Issued: Nos. 2049-2050, 4/30; No. 2051, 6/1; No. 2052, 7/2. Each stamp was issued in sheets of 20+20 labels that could be personalized. Each sheet sold for 700w.

Cartoons — A1376

Designs: No. 2053, Iljimae, by Ko Woo-young (shown). No. 2054, Kkeobeongi, by Kil Chang-duk (student at desk).

2001, May 4 Photo. ***Perf. 13x13¼***

2053	A1376 170w multi	.60	.40
a.	Souvenir sheet of 1	1.00	1.00
2054	A1376 170w multi	.60	.40
a.	Souvenir sheet of 1	1.00	1.00

2002 World Cup Soccer Championships, Japan and Korea — A1377

Years of previous championships, soccer players, flags and scenes from host countries: a, 1954, Switzerland, mountains. b, 1986, Mexico, Chichen Itza. c, 1990, Italy, Colosseum. d, 1994, US, World Trade Center and Statue of Liberty. e, 1998, France, Eiffel Tower.

2001, May 31 ***Perf. 13¼x13***

2055	Horiz. strip of 5	5.00	5.00
a.-e.	A1377 170w Any single	.75	.40
f.	Souvenir sheet, 2 #2055a	2.00	2.00
g.	Souvenir sheet, 2 #2055b	2.00	2.00
h.	Souvenir sheet, 2 #2055c	2.00	2.00
i.	Souvenir sheet, 2 #2055d	2.00	2.00
j.	Souvenir sheet, 2 #2055e	2.00	2.00

Kkakdugi A1378

Bossam Kimchi A1379

Dongchimi A1380

Baechu Kimchi A1381

2001, June 15 ***Perf. 13x13¼***

2056	Vert. strip of 4	3.00	3.00
a.	A1378 170w multi	.60	.40
b.	A1379 170w multi	.60	.40
c.	A1380 170w multi	.60	.40
d.	A1381 170w multi	.60	.40

Roses A1382

2001, July 18 Photo. ***Perf. 13¼***

2057	A1382 170w Red Queen	.60	.40
a.	Souvenir sheet of 2	1.50	1.50
2058	A1382 170w Pink Lady	.60	.40
a.	Souvenir sheet of 2	1.50	1.50

Phila Korea 2002, (#2057a, 2058a).

Love — A1383

2001, Aug. 2

2059	A1383 170w multi	.70	.40
a.	Souvenir sheet of 2	1.75	1.75

World Ceramics Exhibition — A1384

2001, Oct. 10 ***Perf. 13x13¼***

2060	A1384 170w multi	.50	.40

53rd Session of the Intl. Statistical Institute A1385

2001, Aug. 22 Litho. ***Perf. 13¼x13***

2061	A1385 170w multi	.50	.40

Korea Minting and Security Printing Corp., 50th Anniv. A1386

Litho. & Engr.

2001, Sept. 28 ***Perf. 13¼***

2062	A1386 170w multi	.50	.40

Intl. Council of Industrial Design Societies Congress, Seoul — A1387

2001, Oct. 8 Photo. ***Perf. 13x13¼***

2063	A1387 170w multi	.50	.40

Year of Dialogue Among Civilizations A1388

2001, Oct. 9 **Litho.**

2064	A1388 170w multi	.50	.40

Intl. Organization of Supreme Audit Institutions, 17th Congress A1389

2001, Oct. 19 ***Perf. 13¼x13***

2065	A1389 170w blue & red	.50	.40

Orchids — A1390

New Year 2002 (Year of the Horse) — A1391

No. 2066: a, Habenaria radiata. b, Orchis cyclochila. c, Dendrobium moniliforme. d, Gymnadenia camschatica.

2001, Nov. 12 Photo. ***Perf. 13¼x13***

2066	Horiz. strip of 4	3.00	3.00
a.-d.	A1390 170w Any single	.60	.40

No. 2066 is impregnated with orchid scent.

2001, Dec. 3 ***Perf. 13x13¼***

2067	A1391 170w multi	.60	.40
a.	Souvenir sheet of 2	1.40	1.40

Seonjeongjeon Hall, Changdeok Palace — A1392

Injeongjeon Hall, Changdeok Palace — A1393

Litho. & Engr.

2001, Dec. 10 ***Perf. 13x13¼***

2068	Sheet of 10	15.00	12.00
a.	A1392 170w multi	.75	.40
b.	A1393 340w multi	1.50	.75

Top part of #2068 contains one each #2068a-2068b. The lower part of #2068 contains 4 each #2068a-2068b.

Priority Mail — A1394

2002, Jan. 15 Photo. ***Perf. 13¼x13***

Background Color

2069	A1394 280w orange	1.10	.40
2070	A1394 310w blue	1.20	.50
2071	A1394 1380w green	3.50	2.40
2072	A1394 1410w red	3.50	2.50
	Nos. 2069-2072 (4)	9.30	5.80

Lily — A1395

Roses — A1395a

Fish — A1396

Chick — A1396a

2002, Jan. 15 Photo. *Perf. 13¼*
Stamp + Label

2073	A1395	190w multi	2.00	1.00
2073A	A1395a	190w multi	2.00	1.00
2074	A1396	190w multi	2.00	1.00
2074A	A1396a	190w multi	2.00	1.00
	Nos. 2073-2074A (4)		8.00	4.00

Nos. 2073, 2073A and 2074 are impregnated with scents of items depicted. Labels could be personalized.

Korea's Entrance in Intl. Telecommunications Union, 50th Anniv. — A1397

2002, Jan. 31 Photo. *Perf. 13x13¼*
2075 A1397 190w multi .60 .40

Trains — A1398

No. 2076: a, Blue and white locomotive. b, Green, yellow and white locomotive. c, Green, yellow and white locomotive pulling cars. d, Red, yellow and white locomotive pulling cars.

2002, Feb. 4 Photo. *Perf. 13¾x12¾*
2076 A1398 190w Block of 4, #a-d 3.00 3.00

Dye Plants — A1399

No. 2077: a, Carthamus tinctorius. b, Lithospermum erythrorhizon. c, Fraxinus rhynchophylla. d, Persicaria tinctoria.

2002, Feb. 25 Photo. *Perf. 13¼x13*
2077 A1399 190w Block of 4, #a-d 3.00 3.00

Intl. Flower Exhibition, Anmyeon Island A1400

2002, Apr. 26 *Perf. 13¼*
2078 A1400 190w multi .40 .40

Cartoons A1401

Designs: No. 2079, Girl from "Wogdoggle Dugdoggle," by Mi-Na Hwang. No. 2080, Schoolmaster and children from "Mengkkong-i Seodang Village School," by Seung-woon Yoon.

2002, May 4 *Perf. 13¼x13*

2079	A1401	190w multi	.60	.40
a.		Souvenir sheet of 1	1.25	1.25
2080	A1401	190w multi	.60	.40
a.		Souvenir sheet of 1	1.25	1.25

64th Rally of Intl. Federation of Camping and Caravanning, Donghae A1402

2002, May 16
2081 A1402 190w multi *10.00* —

2002 World Cup Soccer Championships, Japan and Korea — A1403

No. 2082: a, Player with pink feet, part of map of Europe. b, Player with blue green feet, part of map of North and Central America. c, Player with blue violet feet, part of map of southeast Asia. d, Player with purple feet, part of map of southern Africa. e, Player with brown orange feet, part of map of South America.

2002, May 31 *Perf.*

2082	A1403	190w Sheet, 2 each #a-e, + label	7.50	7.50
f.		Souvenir sheet, 2 #2082a	.70	.40
g.		Souvenir sheet, 2 #2082b	.70	.40
h.		Souvenir sheet, 2 #2082c	.70	.40
i.		Souvenir sheet, 2 #2082d	.70	.40
j.		Souvenir sheet, 2 #2082e	.70	.40

Korean Cuisine — A1404

No. 2083: a, Jeolpyeon (blue background). b, Shirutteok (red background). c, Injeolmi (tan background). d, Songpyeon (green background).

2002, June 15 *Perf. 13x13¼*
2083 A1404 190w Block of 4, #a-d 3.00 3.00

Women's Week — A1405

2002, July 1 Litho. *Perf. 13x13¼*
2084 A1405 190w multi .70 .40

Philakorea 2002 World Stamp Exhibition, Seoul A1406

Designs: No. 2085, Children, globe. No. 2086, Child, stamps showing flags of the world.

2002, July 1 Photo. *Perf. 13¼*

2085	A1406	190w multi	.55	.40
a.		Souvenir sheet of 2	1.50	1.50
2086	A1406	190w multi	.55	.40
a.		Souvenir sheet of 2	1.50	1.50

Regions of Korea

Busan — A1407

Chungbuk — A1408

Chungnam — A1409

Daegu — A1410

Daejeon — A1411

Gangwon — A1412

Gwangju — A1413

Gyeongbuk — A1414

Gyeonggi — A1415

Gyeongnam — A1416

Incheon — A1417

Jeju — A1418

Jeonbuk — A1419

Jeonnam — A1420

Seoul — A1421

Ulsan — A1422

No. 2087: a, Dongnaeyaryu Festival. b, Cliffs.
No. 2088: a, Martial arts. b, Beopju Temple.
No. 2089: a, Weaver. b, Men in sailboat.
No. 2090: a, Forest and river. b, Gwanbong Seokjoyeorae statue.
No. 2091: a, Daeok Science Town, scientist at work. b, Expo Science Park.
No. 2092: a, Gangneung mask drama. b, Ulsanbawi Rock.
No. 2093: a, Men playing tug-of-war game. b, Statues and tower at May 18th Cemetery.
No. 2094: a, Men playing game with tied logs. b, Dokdo Island.
No. 2095: a, Yangjubyeol Sandaenori mask dance. b, Panmunjom Freedom House.
No. 2096: a, Goseong Ogwangdae clowns performing. b, Rock formations in Hallyeo Haesang Natl. Maritime Park.
No. 2097: a, Chamseongdam dancers. b, Cliffs.
No. 2098: a, Traditional house and gate. b, Mt. Halla.
No. 2099: a, Iri folk band. b, Mt. Mai.
No. 2100: a, Ganggang Sullae circle dance. b, Odong Island.
No. 2101: a, Songpa Sandaenori mask dance. b, Heung-injimun Fortress.
No. 2102: a, Cheoyongmu mask dance. b, Cheonjeonnigakseok prehistoric inscriptions.
Illustrations reduced.

2002, Aug. 1 ***Perf. 13x13¼***

2087	A1407	190w Horiz. pair, #a-b	1.40	.75
2088	A1408	190w Horiz. pair, #a-b	1.40	.75
2089	A1409	190w Horiz. pair, #a-b	1.40	.75
2090	A1410	190w Horiz. pair, #a-b	1.40	.75
2091	A1411	190w Horiz. pair, #a-b	1.40	.75
2092	A1412	190w Horiz. pair, #a-b	1.40	.75
2093	A1413	190w Horiz. pair, #a-b	1.40	.75
2094	A1414	190w Horiz. pair, #a-b	1.40	.75
2095	A1415	190w Horiz. pair, #a-b	1.40	.75
2096	A1416	190w Horiz. pair, #a-b	1.40	.75
2097	A1417	190w Horiz. pair, #a-b	1.40	.75
2098	A1418	190w Horiz. pair, #a-b	1.40	.75
2099	A1419	190w Horiz. pair, #a-b	1.40	.75
2100	A1420	190w Horiz. pair, #a-b	1.40	.75
2101	A1421	190w Horiz. pair, #a-b	1.40	.75
2102	A1422	190w Horiz. pair, #a-b	1.40	.75
		Nos. 2087-2102 (16)	22.40	12.00

Philakorea 2002 World Stamp Exhibition, Seoul A1423

2002, Aug. 2 ***Perf. 13¼x13***

2103 A1423 190w multi .60 .40
a. Sheet of 2, imperf. 1.50 1.50

Philately Week A1424

2002, Aug. 2 ***Perf. 13¼***

2104 A1424 190w multi .60 .40
a. Souvenir sheet of 2 1.50 1.50

South Korean Soccer Team's Fourth Place Finish at World Cup Championships — A1425

No. 2105: a, Coach Guus Hiddink. b, Goalie (jersey #1). c, Player with red shirt with white accents. d, Player with red shirt with white accents, with white sock. e, Player with white shirt with red accents, ball near shoulder. f, Player (jersey #5). g, Player (jersey #6). h, Player (jersey #7). i, Player (jersey #8.) j, Player (jersey #9). k, Player (jersey #10). l, Player with ball hiding part of head. m, Goalie with red hair, white gloves with dark trim. n, Player (jersey #13). o, Player (jersey #14). p, Player (jersey #15). q, Player with white shirt with red accents, with white sock. r, Player (jersey #17). s, Player (jersey #18). t, Player (jersey #19). u, Player (jersey #20). v, Player (jersey #21). w, Player (jersey #22). x, Goalie with brown hair, black gloves with red trim.

2002, Aug. 7 ***Perf. 13¼x13***

2105 A1425 190w Sheet of 24, #a-x 15.00 15.00

14th Asian Games, Busan — A1426

2002, Sept. 28 **Litho.** ***Perf. 13***

2106 A1426 190w multi .60 .40
a. Souvenir sheet of 2 1.50 1.50

8th Far East and South Pacific Games for the Disabled, Busan — A1427

2002, Oct. 26 **Photo.** ***Perf. 13x13¼***

2107 A1427 190w multi .60 .40

Orchids — A1428

No. 2108: a, Cymbidium kanran. b, Gastrodia elata. c, Pogonia japonica. d, Cephalanthera falcata.

2002, Nov. 12 ***Perf. 13¼x13***

2108 A1428 190w Block of 4, #a-d 3.00 3.00

No. 2108 is impregnated with orchid scent.

Martial Arts — A1429

No. 2109: a, Taekwondo (white clothes). b, Kung Fu (red clothes).
Illustration reduced.

2002, Nov. 20 ***Perf. 13x13¼***

2109 A1429 190w Horiz. pair, #a-b 1.50 1.50

See People's Republic of China No. 3248.

New Year 2003 (Year of the Ram) — A1430

2002, Dec. 2

2110 A1430 190w multi .60 .40
a. Souvenir sheet of 2 1.40 1.40

Gongsimdon Observation Tower, Hwaseong Fortress — A1431

Banghwasuryu Pavilion, Hwaseong Fortress — A1432

2002, Dec. 9 **Litho. & Engr.**

2111 Sheet of 10 10.00 10.00
a. A1431 190w multi .60 .40
b. A1432 280w multi .90 .55

Top part of No. 2111 contains one each of #2111a-2111b. The lower part contains 4 each #2111a-2111b.

South Korea — Viet Nam Diplomatic Relations, 10th Anniv. — A1433

No. 2112: a, Dabo Pagoda, Gyeongju (denomination at right). b, Mot Cot Pagoda, Hanoi, Viet Nam (denomination at left).

2002, Dec. 21 **Photo.** ***Perf. 13¼x13***

2112 A1433 190w Horiz. pair, #a-b 1.40 1.10

See Viet Nam Nos. 3167-3168.

Priority Mail Type of 2002

2003, Jan. 1 **Photo.** ***Perf. 13¼x13***

Background Color

2113 A1394 1580w lilac 3.75 3.75
2114 A1394 1610w brown 3.75 3.75

Korean Immigration to the US, Cent. — A1434

2003, Jan. 13 **Photo.** ***Perf. 13¼x13***

2115 A1434 190w multi .60 .40

Gondola Car A1435

Box Car A1436

Tanker Car A1437

Hopper Car A1438

2003, Feb. 4 ***Perf. 13¾x13***

2116 Block of 4 3.00 2.25
a. A1435 190w multi .60 .40
b. A1436 190w multi .60 .40
c. A1437 190w multi .60 .40
d. A1438 190w multi .60 .40

Dye Plants Type of 2002

No. 2117: a, Rubia akane. b, Rhus javanica. c, Sophora japonica. d, Isatis tinctoria.

2003, Feb. 22 **Photo.** ***Perf. 13¼x13***

2117 A1399 190w Horiz. strip of 4, #a-d 3.00 2.25

Inauguration of Pres. Roh Moo-hyun A1439

2003, Feb. 25 ***Perf. 13x13¼***

2118 A1439 190w multi .60 .40
a. Souvenir sheet of 1 1.50 1.50

Traditional Culture

Footwear — A1440

Sedan Chairs — A1441

Lighting Implements — A1442

Tables — A1443

No. 2119: a, Unhye (denomination at LL, date at LR). b, Mokhwa (denomination at UR, date at L). c, Jipsin (denomination at UL, date at LR). d, Namaksin (denomination at LR, date at LL).

No. 2120: a, Eoyeon (no handles). b, Choheon (wheeled). c, Saingyo (with handles and roof). d, Nanyeo (with handles only).

No. 2121: a, Jojokdeung (round lantern). b, Deungjan (lamp oil container). c, Juchilmokje Yukgakjedeung (hexagonal lantern). d, Brass candlestick holder with butterfly design.

No. 2122: a, Gujok-ban (round table with legs connected at base. b, Punghyeol-ban (12-sided table, denomination at top). c, Ilju-ban (12-sided table, denomination at top). d, Haeju-ban (octagonal table).

Illustrations reduced.

2003 Engr. *Perf. 12½*

2119	A1440 190w Horiz. strip of 4, #a-d	3.00	2.25
2120	A1441 190w Horiz. strip of 4, #a-d	3.00	2.25
2121	A1442 190w Horiz. strip of 4, #a-d	3.00	2.25
2122	A1443 190w Horiz. strip of 4, #a-d	3.00	2.25
	Nos. 2119-2122 (4)	12.00	9.00

Issued: No. 2119, 3/19; No. 2120, 5/19; No. 2121, 7/25; No. 2122, 9/25.

Cartoons — A1444

Designs: No. 2123, The Goblin's Cap, by Shin Moon-soo (shown). No. 2124, The Sword of Fire, by Kim Hye-rin (woman with sword).

2003, May 2 Photo. *Perf. 13x13¼*

2123 A1444 190w multi	.60	.40
a. Souvenir sheet of 1	1.10	1.10
2124 A1444 190w multi	.60	.40
a. Souvenir sheet of 1	1.10	1.10

Lighthouse Construction in Korea, Cent. — A1445

2003, May 30 *Perf. 13¼x13*

2125 A1445 190w multi .60 .40

Dasik A1446

Yeot Gangjeong A1447

Yakgwa A1448

Yugwa A1449

2003, June 13 *Perf. 13x13¼*

2126 Vert. strip of 4	2.75	2.25
a. A1446 190w multi	.55	.40
b. A1447 190w multi	.55	.40
c. A1448 190w multi	.55	.40
d. A1449 190w multi	.55	.40

Priority Mail Type of 2002

2003, July 1 Photo. *Perf. 13¼x13*

Background Color

2127 A1394 420w blue green 1.25 .90

Philately Week A1450

2003, Aug. 1 *Perf. 13¼*

2128 A1450 190w multi	.60	.40
a. Souvenir sheet of 2, imperf.	1.50	1.50

2003 Summer Universiade, Daegu — A1451

2003, Aug. 21 *Perf. 13x13¼*

2129 A1451 190w multi	.60	.40
a. Souvenir sheet of 2	1.40	1.40

YMCA in Korea, Cent. — A1452

Soong Eui School, Cent. — A1453

2003, Oct. 28 Photo. *Perf. 13¼x13*

2130 A1452 190w multi .60 .40

2003, Oct. 31 *Perf. 13x13¼*

2131 A1453 190w multi .60 .40

Natl. Tuberculosis Association, 50th Anniv. — A1454

2003, Nov. 6 Litho.

2132 A1454 190w black & red .60 .40

Orchids — A1455

No. 2133: a, Cremastra appendiculata. b, Cymbidium lancifolium. c, Orchis graminifolia. d, Bulbophyllum drymoglossum.

2003, Nov. 12 Photo. *Perf. 13¼x13*

2133 A1455 190w Block of 4, #a-d 3.00 2.25

No. 2133 is impregnated with a floral scent.

New Year 2004 (Year of the Monkey) — A1456

2003, Dec. 1 *Perf. 13x13¼*

2134 A1456 190w multi	.60	.40
a. Souvenir sheet of 2	1.40	1.40

A1457

Dolmens — A1458

Litho. & Engr.

2003, Dec. 9 *Perf. 13x13¼*

2135 Sheet of 10	12.00	12.00
a. A1457 190w multi	.70	.40
b. A1458 280w multi	.90	.50

Top part of No. 2135 contains one each of Nos. 2135a-2135b. The lower part contains 4 each Nos. 2135a-2135b.

South Korea — India Diplomatic Relations, 30th Anniv. — A1459

No. 2136: a, Cheomsongdae Astronomical Observatory, Gyeongju, South Korea. b, Jantar Mantar, Jaipur, India.

2003, Dec. 10 Photo. *Perf. 13¼x13*

2136 A1459 190w Horiz. pair, #a-b 1.40 1.10

Dokdo Island Flora and Fauna A1460

No. 2137: a, Calystegia soldanella. b, Aster spathulifolius, butterfly. c, Calonectris laucomelas. d, Larus crassirostris.

2004, Jan. 16 *Perf. 13x13¼*

2137 Horiz. strip of 4	*15.00*	—
a.-d. A1460 190w Any single	*3.50*	*3.50*

Korean National Commission for UNESCO, 50th Anniv. — A1461

2004, Jan. 30

2138 A1461 190w multi .35 .20

Multiple Tie Tamper A1462

Ballast Regulator A1463

Track Inspection Car — A1464

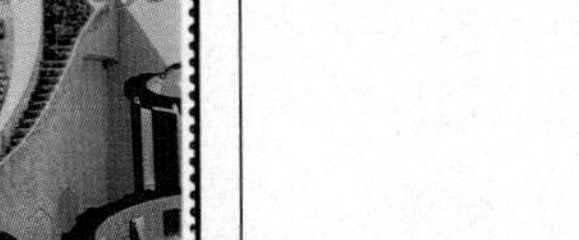

Ballast Cleaner A1465

2004, Feb. 4 *Perf. 13¾x12¾*

2139 Block of 4	2.75	2.75
a. A1462 190w brown & multi	.60	.40
b. A1463 190w lilac & multi	.60	.40
c. A1464 190w blue green & multi	.60	.40
d. A1465 190w blue & multi	.60	.40

Dye Plants Type of 2002

No. 2140: a, Juglans regia. b, Acer ginnala. c, Pinus densiflora. d, Punica granatum.

2004, Feb. 25 *Perf. 13¼x13*

2140 A1399 190w Block of 4, #a-d 2.75 2.75

A1466

A1467

2004, Mar. 22 Litho. *Perf. 13x13¼*
2141 A1466 190w multi .50 .40

12th World Water Day.

2004, Mar. 25 Photo.
2142 A1467 190w multi .50 .40

Korean Meteorological Service, cent.

Inauguration of High Speed Railroads A1468

2004, Apr. 1 *Perf. 13¼x13*
2143 A1468 190w multi .50 .40

A1469

Winners of Future of Science Stamp Design Contest — A1470

Perf. 13¼x13, 13x13¼

2004, Apr. 21 Photo.
2144 A1469 190w multi .50 .40
2145 A1470 190w multi .50 .40

A1471

A1472

Cartoons: No. 2146, Wicked Boy Simsultong, by Lee Jeong-moon (shown). No. 2147, Nation of Winds, by Kim Jin.

2004, May 4 Photo. *Perf. 13x13¼*
2146 A1471 190w multi .50 .40
a. Souvenir sheet of 1 1.00 1.00
2147 A1471 190w multi .50 .40
a. Souvenir sheet of 1 1.00 1.00

2004, May 21
2148 A1472 190w multi .50 .40

FIFA (Fédération Internationale de Football Association), cent.

Korean Cuisine — A1473

No. 2149: a, Sinseollo (blue background). b, Hwayangjeok (green background). c, Bibimbap (pink background). d, Gujeolpan (orange background).
Illustration reduced.

2004, June 15
2149 A1473 190w Block of 4, #a-d 2.50 2.50

Traditional Culture

Needlework Equipment — A1474

Head Coverings — A1475

No. 2150: a, Octagonal storage basket. b, Thimbles with flower decorations. c, Cylindrical bobbin, bobbin and thread. d, Needle cases.
No. 2151: a, Gold crown with tassels. b, Bamboo hat with untied neck band. c, Gauze hat. d, Horsehair hat with tied neck band.
Illustrations reduced.

2004 Engr. *Perf. 12½*
2150 A1474 190w Horiz. strip of 4, #a-d 2.50 2.50
2151 A1475 190w Horiz. strip of 4, #a-d 2.50 2.50

National Academies, 50th Anniv. — A1476

No. 2152: a, National Academy of Science. b, National Academy of Arts.

2004, July 16 Litho. *Perf. 13x13¼*
2152 A1476 190w Horiz. pair, #a-b 1.25 1.25

Congratulations — A1477

2004, July 22 Photo. *Perf. 13¼*
2153 A1477 190w multi .60 .40
a. Souvenir sheet of 2 1.00 1.00

2004 Summer Olympics, Athens — A1478

2004, Aug. 13 *Perf. 13x13¼*
2154 A1478 190w multi .60 .40

Bridges — A1479

No. 2155: a, Geumcheongyo Bridge (two arches). b, Jeongotgyo Bridge (pillars and flat slabs). c, Jincheon Nongdari Bridge (loose rocks). d, Seungseongyo Bridge (single arch).
Illustration reduced.

Perf. 13¼ Syncopated

2004, Sept. 24
2155 A1479 190w Block fo 4, #a-d 2.50 2.50

Intl. Council of Museums, 20th General Conference, Seoul — A1480

2004, Oct. 1 *Perf. 13x13¼*
2156 A1480 190w multi .60 .40

Obaegnahan — A1481

Seonjakjiwat — A1482

Baengnokdam — A1483

Oreum A1484

2004, Oct. 18
2157 Block of 4 2.50 2.50
a. A1481 190w multi .60 .40
b. A1482 190w multi .60 .40
c. A1483 190w multi .60 .40
d. A1484 190w multi .60 .40

Flag — A1485

Flowers — A1486

Flower and Bee — A1487

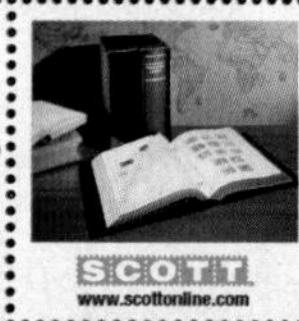
Lamb, Church and Bible — A1488

Children and Lotus Flower — A1489

Stylized Animals — A1490

Teddy Bear — A1491

Dinosaur — A1492

Flower and Envelope — A1493

2004, Nov. 1 Photo. *Perf. 13¼*

2158 A1485 220w multi + label 1.50 1.50
2159 A1486 220w multi + label 1.50 1.50
2160 A1487 220w multi + label 1.50 1.50
2161 A1488 220w multi + label 1.50 1.50
2162 A1489 220w multi + label 1.50 1.50
2163 Strip of 4 + 4 alternating labels 6.00 6.00
a. A1490 220w multi + label 1.50 1.50
b. A1491 220w multi + label 1.50 1.50
c. A1492 220w multi + label 1.50 1.50
d. A1493 220w multi + label 1.50 1.50
Nos. 2158-2163 (6) 13.50 13.50

Labels attached to Nos. 2158-2163 could be personalized.

Orchids — A1494

No. 2164: a, Goodyera maximowicziana. b, Sarcanthus scolopendrifolius. c, Calanthe sieboldii. d, Bletilla striata.

2004, Nov. 12 *Perf. 13¼x13*

2164 A1494 220w Block of 4, #a-d 2.75 2.75

No. 2164 is impregnated with orchid scent.

New Year 2005 (Year of the Chicken) — A1495

2004, Dec. 1 *Perf. 13x13¼*

2165 A1495 220w multi .75 .45
a. Souvenir sheet of 2 1.25 1.25

Daenungwon Tumuli Park, Seosuhyeong Ceramics, Royal Crown of Geumgwanchong — A1496

Anapji Pond, Scissors, Buddha, Lion Incense Burner — A1497

2004, Dec. 9 Litho. & Engr.

2166 Sheet of 10 9.00 9.00
a. A1496 310w multi .75 .45
b. A1497 310w multi .75 .45

Top part of No. 2166 contains one each of Nos. 2166a-2166b. The lower part contains 4 each of Nos. 2166a-2166b.

Fish of Marado Island A1498

No. 2167: a, Girella punctata. b, Epinephelus septemfasciatus. c, Chromis notata. d, Sebastiscus marmoratus.

2005, Jan. 18 Photo.

2167 Horiz. strip of 4 3.50 3.50
a.-d. A1498 220w Any single .60 .45

Cloning of Human Embryonic Stem Cells, 1st Anniv. — A1499

2005, Feb. 12 *Perf. 12¾x13½*

2168 A1499 220w multi .70 .40

Rotary International, Cent. A1500

2005, Feb. 23 *Perf. 13¼x13*

2169 A1500 220w multi .50 .40

Dye Plants Type of 2002

No. 2170: a, Taxus cuspidata. b, Smilax china. c, Clerodendron trichotomum. d, Gardenia jasminoides.

2005, Feb. 25

2170 A1399 220w Block of 4, #a-d 2.50 2.50

Gyeonggi Province Tourism — A1501

2005, Mar. 10 Litho. *Perf. 13x13¼*

2171 A1501 220w multi .50 .40

A1502

Information and Communication of the Future — A1503

2005, Apr. 22 Photo. *Perf. 13¼x13*

2172 A1502 220w multi .50 .40

Perf. 13x13¼

2173 A1503 220w multi .50 .40

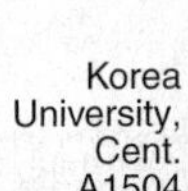

Korea University, Cent. A1504

2005, May 4 Litho. *Perf. 13x13¼*

2174 A1504 220w multi .50 .40

57th Intl. Whaling Commission Meeting, Ulsan A1505

2005, May 27 Photo. *Perf. 13¼x13*

2175 A1505 220w multi .50 .40

Neobani (Broiled Beef) A1506

Bindaetteok (Fried Ground Mung Beans) A1507

Jeongol (Stew) A1508

Hwajeon (Fried Rice Cakes and Flower Petals) A1509

2005, June 15 *Perf. 13x13¼*

2176 Block of 4 3.00 3.00
a. A1506 220w multi .60 .40
b. A1507 220w multi .60 .40
c. A1508 220w multi .60 .40
d. A1509 220w multi .60 .40

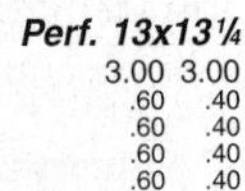

Goguryeo Kingdom — A1510

No. 2177: a, Sword, armored soldier on horse. b, Armored soldiers on horses, Onyeo Fortress, Baek-am Castle.

Perf. 13x13¼ Syncopated

2005, July 1

2177 A1510 310w Vert. pair, #a-b 2.00 2.00

Strix Aluco A1513

Arctous Ruber A1514

Parus Major A1516

Crinum Asiaticum A1517

Planned City — A1521

Brown Hawk Owl — A1522

Rose of Sharon — A1523

Whistling Swans A1525

Buncheong Jar A1529

Euryale Ferox — A1532

2005-07 Photo. *Perf. 13¾x12¾*

2180 A1513 50w multi .75 .25
2181 A1514 70w multi .20 .20

Perf. 12¾x13¾

2183 A1516 90w multi .50 .25

Perf. 13¾x12¾

2184 A1517 100w multi .50 .25

Perf. 13x13¼

2188 A1521 220w multi .50 .25
2189 A1522 250w multi .75 .40

Perf. 13½

2190 A1523 250w multi + label .75 .40

Perf. 13¾x13

2192 A1525 340w multi .75 .40

Perf. 13x13¼

2196 A1529 1720w multi 3.50 1.75

Perf. 13x13½

2197 A1530 1750w multi 3.75 1.90
Nos. 2180-2199 (11) 12.45 6.30

Serpentine Die Cut 11¾x11½

2199 A1532 250w multi .50 .25

Issued: 50w, 9/1; 1720w, 8/1; 90w, 6/5/06; 100w, 3/2/06; 220w, 12/27/05. Nos. 2189, 2190, 2192, 2197, 11/1/06. 70w, 7/10/07. No. 2199, 6/30/08.

No. 2190 was printed in sheets of 20 stamps and 20 labels that could be personalized.

Happy Birthday A1536

2005, Aug. 3 Photo. *Perf. 13¼*

2203 A1536 220w multi .50 .35
a. Souvenir sheet of 2 1.25 1.25

Philately Week. Portions of the design were printed with a thermochromic ink that changes color when warmed.

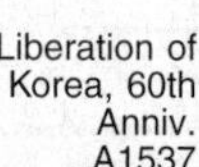

Liberation of Korea, 60th Anniv. A1537

No. 2204: a, Charter and headquarters of provisional government. b, Proclamation of Korean Independence. c, Soldiers taking oath. d, Emblem of 60th anniv. of Korean liberation.

2005, Aug. 12 *Perf. 13¼x13*

2204 Horiz. strip of 4 6.50 6.50
a. A1537 480w multi 1.00 .75
b. A1537 520w multi 1.25 1.00
c. A1537 580w multi 1.40 1.10
d. A1537 600w multi 1.50 1.25

Fusion of Eastern and Western Cultures — A1538

2005, Aug. 18 Litho. *Perf. 13x13¼*

2205 A1538 220w multi .70 .45

Hangang Bridge — A1539

Expogyo — A1540

Banghwa Bridge — A1541

Tongyeong Bridge — A1542

Perf. 13¼ Syncopated

2005, Sept. 23 Photo.

2206 Block of 4 2.50 2.50
a. A1539 220w multi .50 .40
b. A1540 220w multi .50 .40
c. A1541 220w multi .50 .40
d. A1542 220w multi .50 .40

Ikki Falls A1543

Piagol Valley A1544

Cheonwangbong Peak — A1545

Baraebong Peak A1546

2005, Oct. 18 *Perf. 13x13¼*

2207 Horiz. strip of 4 2.50 2.50
a. A1543 220w multi .50 .40
b. A1544 220w multi .50 .40
c. A1545 220w multi .50 .40
d. A1546 220w multi .50 .40

Korean Red Cross, Cent. — A1547

2005, Oct. 27

2208 A1547 220w multi .60 .50

Relocation and Reopening of National Museum A1548

2005, Oct. 28 *Perf. 13¼x13*

2209 A1548 220w multi .75 .50

Orchids — A1549

No. 2210: a, Epipactis thunbergii. b, Cymbidium goeringii. c, Cephalanthera erecta. d, Spiranthes sinensis.

2005, Nov. 11

2210 A1549 220w Block of 4, #a-d 2.50 2.50

2005 Asian-Pacific Economic Cooperation Economic Leaders' Meeting, Busan — A1550

No. 2211: a, The Sun, the Moon and Five Peaks. b, Murimaru APEC House, Dongbaek Island.

2005, Nov. 18 Photo. *Perf. 13x13¼*

2211 A1550 220w Horiz. pair, #a-b 1.00 1.00

New Year 2006 (Year of the Dog) — A1551

2005, Dec. 1

2212 A1551 220w multi .75 .50
a. Souvenir sheet of 2 1.50 1.50

Jikjisimcheyojeol, Book Produced in 1377 by Movable Type — A1552

Seungjeongwon Ilgi, Diaries of the Joseon Dynasty — A1553

2005, Dec. 9 Litho. & Engr.

2213 Sheet of 10 10.00 10.00
a. A1552 310w multi .75 .50
b. A1553 310w multi .75 .50

Top part of No. 2213 contains one each of Nos. 2213a-2213b. The lower part contains 4 each of Nos, 2213a-2213b.

Wildlife of Baengnyeongdo — A1554

Designs: No. 2214, Phoca vitulina largha. No. 2215, Phalacrocorax pelagicus. No. 2216, Orithyia sinica. No. 2217, Ammodytes personatus.

2006, Jan. 18 Photo.

2214 A1554 220w multi .75 .50
2215 A1554 220w multi .75 .50
2216 A1554 220w multi .75 .50
2217 A1554 220w multi .75 .50
Nos. 2214-2217 (4) 3.00 2.00

Nos. 2214-2217 are printed in a checkerboard pattern on the sheet with stamps vertically or horizontally adjacent to labels or the stamp margin, but not being se-tenant to any other stamp.

Designation of Cheju Island as Island of World Peace — A1555

2006, Jan. 27 *Perf. 13¾x12¾*

2218 A1555 220w multi .75 .50

Exports

Automobiles — A1556

Semiconductors — A1557

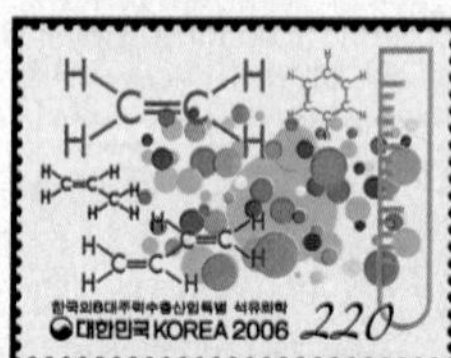

Petrochemicals — A1558

Electronics — A1559

Machinery A1560

Ships A1561

Steel A1562

Textiles A1563

2006, Mar. 15 ***Perf. 13x13¼***

2219	Block of 8	6.50	6.50
a.	A1556 220w multi	.75	.50
b.	A1557 220w multi	.75	.50
c.	A1558 220w multi	.75	.50
d.	A1559 220w multi	.75	.50
e.	A1560 220w multi	.75	.50
f.	A1561 220w multi	.75	.50
g.	A1562 220w black	.75	.50
h.	A1563 220w multi	.75	.50

Gyeongnam Goseong Dinosaur World Expo — A1564

Serpentine Die Cut 11¼x11

2006, Apr. 14

2220	A1564 Horiz. pair	1.50	1.50
a.	220w Iguanodon	.75	.50
b.	220w Megaraptor	.75	.50

A1565

Children's Drawings on Automated World A1566

2006, Apr. 21 ***Perf. 13x13¼, 13¼x13***

2221	A1565 220w multi	.75	.50
2222	A1566 220w multi	.75	.50

Dongguk University, Cent. — A1567

2006, May 8 **Litho.** ***Perf. 13x13¼***

2223 A1567 220w multi .60 .40

Sookmyung Women's University, Cent. — A1568

Perf. 12¾x13¾

2006, May 22 **Photo.**

2224 A1568 220w multi .50 .40

2006 World Cup Soccer Championships, Germany — A1569

2006, June 2 **Photo.** ***Perf. 13¼***

2225 A1569 220w multi + label 1.50 1.50

No. 2225 was printed in sheets of 14 stamps + 14 labels picturing members of South Korean World Cup soccer team + one large label picturing entire team. Sheets sold for 6000w.

A1570

2006 World Cup Soccer Championships, Germany — A1571

Perf. 12¾x13¾

2006, June 9 **Photo.**

2226	Pair	1.50	1.50
a.	A1570 220w multi	.75	.50
b.	A1571 220w multi	.75	.50

Goguryeo Kingdom A1572

No. 2227: a, Janggun Tomb and Sanseongha Tombs. b, Sun and Moon Gods from Ohoebun Tomb No. 4.

Perf. 13x13¼ Syncopated

2006, July 3 **Photo.**

2227 A1572 480w Vert. pair, #a-b 3.00 3.00

No. 2227 was printed in sheets containing seven of each stamp.

Philately Week A1573

No. 2228: a, Denomination below heart. b, Denomination above heart.

2006, Aug. 3 **Photo.** ***Perf. 13¼***

2228	A1573 220w Pair, #a-b	1.00	1.00
c.	Souvenir sheet, #2228a-2228b	1.50	1.50

Skateboarding — A1574

No. 2229: a, Tail stole. b, Drop in. c, Backside spin. d, Backside grab.

Illustration reduced.

Serpentine Die Cut 11¾x11¼

2006, Sept. 5

Self-Adhesive

2229 A1574 220w Block of 4, #a-d 2.00 2.00

World Ginseng Expo, Geumsan — A1575

2006, Sept. 22 ***Perf. 13x13¼***

2230 A1575 220w multi .50 .40

Jindo Bridge — A1576

Changseon-Samcheonpo Bridge — A1577

Olympic Bridge — A1578

Seohae Bridge — A1579

Perf. 13¼ Syncopated

2006, Sept. 26

2231	Block of 4	2.00	2.00
a.	A1576 220w multi	.50	.40
b.	A1577 220w multi	.50	.40
c.	A1578 220w multi	.50	.40
d.	A1579 220w multi	.50	.40

Hangeul Day — A1580

2006, Oct. 9 ***Perf. 13x13¼***

2232 A1580 (220w) multi .60 .40

Use of Hangeul as official Korean writing system, 560th anniv.

Sahmyook University, Cent. — A1581

2006, Oct. 10

2233 A1581 220w multi .60 .40

Lineage — A1582

Maple Story — A1583

Ragnarok
A1584

Gersang
A1585

Legend of Mir
III — A1586

Kartrider
A1587

Mu — A1588

Pangya — A1589

Fortress 2
Forever
Blue — A1590

Mabinogi
A1591

Serpentine Die Cut 11¾

2006, Nov. 9

2234	Block of 10	10.00	10.00
a.	A1582 250w multi	.90	.60
b.	A1583 250w multi	.90	.60
c.	A1584 250w multi	.90	.60
d.	A1585 250w multi	.90	.60
e.	A1586 250w multi	.90	.60
f.	A1587 250w multi	.90	.60
g.	A1588 250w multi	.90	.60
h.	A1589 250w multi	.90	.60
i.	A1590 250w multi	.90	.60
j.	A1591 250w multi	.90	.60

Internet games.

Janggunbong Peak — A1592

Ulsanbawi
Rock
A1593

Daecheongbong Peak — A1594

Sibiseonnyeotang Valley — A1595

2006, Nov. 16 ***Perf. 13x13¼***

2235	Block of 4	3.00	3.00
a.	A1592 250w multi	.75	.60
b.	A1593 250w multi	.75	.60
c.	A1594 250w multi	.75	.60
d.	A1595 250w multi	.75	.60

New Year 2007
(Year of the
Pig) — A1596

2006, Dec. 1 **Photo.** ***Perf. 13x13¼***

2236	A1596 250w multi	.60	.40
a.	Souvenir sheet of 2	1.50	1.50

Text of Heungboga and Pansori
Singer — A1597

Mo Heung-gap, Pansori
Singer — A1598

Litho. & Engr.

2006, Dec. 8 ***Perf. 13x13¼***

2237	Sheet of 10	20.00	20.00
a.	A1597 480w multi	2.00	1.60
b.	A1598 480w multi	2.00	1.60

Top part of No. 2237 contains one each of Nos. 2237a-2237b. The lower part contains 4 each of Nos. 2237a-2237b.

A1599

Sharing and
Caring
A1600

2006, Dec. 14 **Photo.** ***Perf. 13x13¼***

2238	A1599 250w multi	.55	.25

Perf. 13¼x13

2239	A1600 250w multi	.55	.25

No. 2238 is impregnated with a pine scent; No. 2239 with a chocolate scent.

Nakdong River in Autumn — A1601

Nakdong River in Winter — A1602

Nakdong River in Spring — A1603

Nakdong River in Summer — A1604

Perf. 13¼ Syncopated

2007, Jan. 18 **Photo.**

2240	Block of 4	2.25	1.10
a.	A1601 250w multi	.55	.25
b.	A1602 250w multi	.55	.25
c.	A1603 250w multi	.55	.25
d.	A1604 250w multi	.55	.25

Megatron/Matrix — A1605

TV
Buddha
A1606

The More
the Better
A1607

Oh-Mah
(Mother)
A1608

2007, Jan. 29 ***Perf. 13¼***

2241	Sheet of 12, 3 each #a-d	6.75	6.75
a.	A1605 250w multi	.55	.25
b.	A1606 250w multi	.55	.25
c.	A1607 250w multi	.55	.25
d.	A1608 250w multi	.55	.25

Art by Nam June Paik (1932-2006).

National Debt
Repayment
Movement,
Cent. — A1609

2007, Feb. 21 **Photo.** ***Perf. 13x13¼***

2242	A1609 250w multi	.55	.25

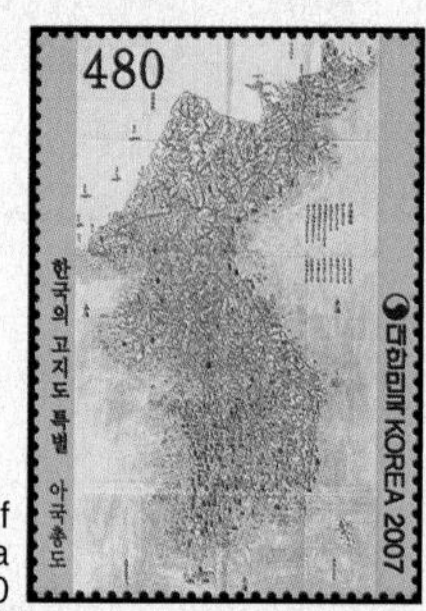

Maps of
Korea
A1610

No. 2243: a, Map from Atlas of Korea, 1780. b, Complete Territorial Map of the Great East, 19th cent. c, Map of the Eight Provinces, 1531. d, Comprehensive Map of the World and Nation's Successive Capitals, 1402.

2007, Feb. 28 **Photo.** ***Perf. 13½x13***

2243	Sheet of 8, 2 each #a-d	9.25	9.25
a.	A1610 480w multi	1.00	.50
b.	A1610 520w multi	1.10	.55
c.	A1610 580w multi	1.25	.60
d.	A1610 600w multi	1.25	.65

Daehan Hospital,
Seoul,
Cent. — A1611

2007, Mar. 15 **Litho.** ***Perf. 13x13¼***

2244	A1611 250w multi	.55	.25

Ninth Asia Pacific
Orchid Conference,
Goyang — A1612

2007, Mar. 16 **Photo.**

2245	A1612 250w multi	.55	.25

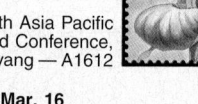

Biology
Year — A1613

2007, Mar. 19 ***Perf. 13¼x13***

2246 A1613 250w multi .55 .25
a. Souvenir sheet of 2 1.10 .50

Sunflower — A1614

2007, Mar. 21 **Litho.** ***Perf. 13¼***

2247 A1614 250w multi + label .80 .40

Printed in sheets of 20 stamps + 20 labels and 14 stamps + 14 labels that sold for 7500w. Labels could be personalized.

Clover — A1615

Pig — A1616

2007, Mar. 21 **Photo.** ***Perf. 13¼***

2248 A1615 250w multi + label 1.00 .50
2249 A1616 250w multi + label 1.00 .50

Nos. 2248-2249 were each printed in sheets of 9 stamps + 9 labels. Each sheet sold for 4300w. Labels could be personalized.

Chinese Bride and Groom — A1617

Indian Bride and Groom — A1618

Malaysian Bride and Groom — A1619

Eurasian Bride and Groom — A1620

No. 2250 — Korean brides and grooms with: e, Mountains in background. f, Flowers on orange background. g, Flowers and foliage in background. h, Ducks in background.

2007, Mar. 30 ***Perf. 13¼x13***

2250 Block of 8 7.00 7.00
a. A1617 250w multi .55 .25
b. A1618 250w multi .55 .25
c. A1619 250w multi .55 .25
d. A1620 250w multi .55 .25
e. A1620 480w multi 1.00 .50
f. A1620 520w multi 1.10 .55
g. A1620 580w multi 1.25 .60
h. A1620 600w multi 1.25 .65

See Singapore No. 1241.

Opening of Fortress Wall in Mt. Bugaksan — A1621

2007, Apr. 5 **Photo.** ***Perf. 13¾x12¾***

2251 A1621 250w multi .55 .25

A1622

Internet Culture A1623

2007, Apr. 20 **Litho.** ***Perf. 13¼x13***

2252 A1622 250w multi .55 .25

Photo.

2253 A1623 250w multi .55 .25

Children's Charter, 50th Anniv. — A1624

Serpentine Die Cut

2007, May 4 **Photo.**

Self-Adhesive

2254 A1624 250w multi .55 .25

No. 2254 is impregnated with a strawberry scent.

Dispatch of Special Envoys to Second Hague Peace Conference, Cent. — A1625

Litho. & Engr.

2007, June 27 ***Perf. 13x13¼***

2255 A1625 250w multi .55 .25

A1626

Goguryeo Kingdom A1627

No. 2256: a, Cooks preparing food. b, Host welcoming guest.

Perf. 13 Syncopated

2007, July 2 **Photo.**

2256 Sheet of 14, 7 each #a-b 14.00 14.00
a. A1626 480w multi 1.00 .50
b. A1627 480w multi 1.00 .50

Philately Week — A1628

No. 2257: a, Korea #1. b, Korea #2. Illustration reduced.

2007, Aug. 2 **Photo.** ***Perf. 13x13¼***

2257 Horiz. pair 1.10 .55
a.-b. A1628 250w Either single .55 .25
c. Souvenir sheet, #2257 1.10 .55

Rollerblading — A1629

No. 2258: a, Drop-in. b, Flip. c, Spin. d, Grind.

Serpentine Die Cut 11¾x11¼

2007, Sept. 5 **Photo.**

Self-Adhesive

2258 A1629 250w Block of 4, #a-d 2.25 1.10

Korean Bar Association, Cent. — A1630

2007, Sept. 21 **Litho.** ***Perf. 13x13¼***

2259 A1630 250w multi .55 .25

Gwangan Bridge — A1631

Seongsu Bridge — A1632

Seongsan Bridge — A1633

Yeongjong Bridge — A1634

Perf. 13¼x13½ Syncopated

2007, Sept. 28 **Photo.**

2260 Block of 4 2.25 1.10
a. A1631 250w multi .55 .25
b. A1632 250w multi .55 .25
c. A1633 250w multi .55 .25
d. A1634 250w multi .55 .25

Inter-Korean Summit, Pyongyang, North Korea — A1635

2007, Oct. 2 ***Perf. 13¼x13***

2261 A1635 250w multi .55 .25

Hyeongje Falls A1636

Rimyeongsu Falls — A1637

Lake Samjiyeon A1638

Lake Chonji A1639

2007, Oct. 18 Photo. ***Perf. 13x13½***

2262	Block of 4	2.25	1.10
a.	A1636 250w multi	.55	.25
b.	A1637 250w multi	.55	.25
c.	A1638 250w multi	.55	.25
d.	A1639 250w multi	.55	.25

A1640

A1641

A1642

Korean Films A1643

No. 2263: a, Arirang, 1926. b, The Ownerless Ferryboat, 1932. c, Looking for Love, 1928. d, Chunhyangjeon, 1935.

2007, Oct. 26 ***Perf. 13x13¼***

2263	Sheet of 16, 4 each #a-d	9.00	9.00
a.	A1640 250w multi	.55	.25
b.	A1641 250w multi	.55	.25
c.	A1642 250w multi	.55	.25
d.	A1643 250w multi	.55	.25

A1644

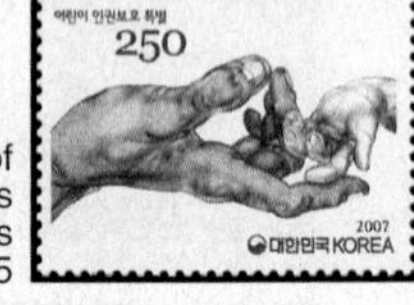

Protection of Children's Rights A1645

2007, Nov. 20 Photo. ***Perf. 13x13¼***

2264 A1644 250w multi .55 .25

Litho.

Perf. 13¼x13

2265 A1645 250w multi .55 .25

Opening of New Central Post Office, Seoul — A1646

No. 2266: a, Hanseong Post Office, 1915, and new building. b, New building.

2007, Nov. 22 Photo. ***Perf. 13x13¼***

2266 A1646 250w Horiz. pair, #a-b 1.10 .55

No. 2266 printed in sheet containing 7 pairs.

New Year 2008 (Year of the Rat) — A1647

2007, Nov. 30

2267	A1647 250w multi	.55	.25
a.	Souvenir sheet of 2	1.10	.50

Tapdeunggut Exorcism, Dano Festival, Gangneung — A1648

Gwanno Mask Drama, Dano Festival — A1649

2007, Dec. 7 **Litho. & Engr.**

2268	Sheet of 10, 5 each #a-b	10.50	10.50
a.	A1648 480w multi	1.00	.50
b.	A1649 480w multi	1.00	.50

Top part of No. 2268 contains one each of Nos. 2268a-2268b. The lower part contains 4 each of Nos. 2268a-2268b.

Seomjin River in Autumn — A1650

Seomjin River in Winter — A1651

Seomjin River in Spring — A1652

Seomjin River in Summer — A1653

Perf. 13½x13¼ Syncopated

2008, Jan. 18 **Photo.**

2269	Block of 4	2.25	1.10
a.	A1650 250w multi	.55	.25
b.	A1651 250w multi	.55	.25
c.	A1652 250w multi	.55	.25
d.	A1653 250w multi	.55	.25

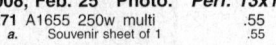

Inauguration of Pres. Lee Myung-Bak — A1655

2008, Feb. 25 Photo. ***Perf. 13x13¼***

2271	A1655 250w multi	.55	.25
a.	Souvenir sheet of 1	.55	.25

African Savanna — A1656

No. 2272: a, African child and mask. b, Leopard. c, Elephant. d, Zebra.
Illustration reduced.

Die Cut Perf. (outer edge) x Serpentine Die Cut 11 (radial sides) x Die Cut (inner edge)

2008, Mar. 26

Self-Adhesive

2272 A1656 250w Block of 4, #a-d, + central label 2.10 1.10

Philakorea 2009 Intl. Stamp Exhibition, Seoul — A1657

No. 2273 — Dancers: a, Buchaechum (orange background). b, Salpurichum (pink background). c, Seungmu (blue background). d, Taepyeongmu (green background).

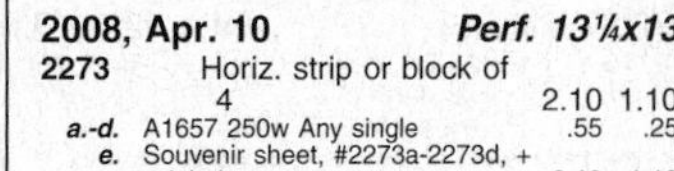

2008, Apr. 10 ***Perf. 13¼x13***

2273	Horiz. strip or block of 4	2.10	1.10
a.-d.	A1657 250w Any single	.55	.25
e.	Souvenir sheet, #2273a-2273d, + label	2.10	1.10

A1658

Winning Designs in "Mailboxes of the Future" Children's Stamp Design Contest — A1659

2008, Apr. 22 Photo. ***Perf. 13¼x13***

2274 A1658 250w multi .50 .25

Litho.

Perf. 13x13¼

2275 A1659 250w multi .50 .25

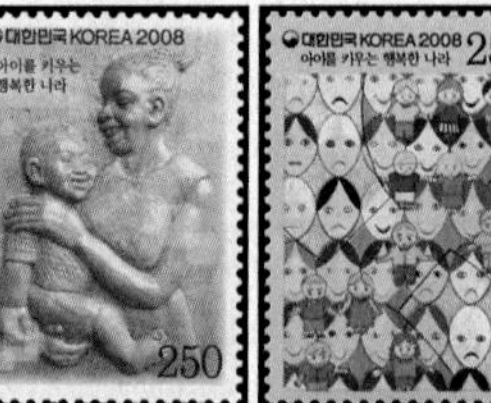

Nurturing of Children
A1660 A1661

Litho., Engr. & Embossed

2008, May 8 ***Perf. 13x13¼***

2276 A1660 250w multi .50 .25

Litho.

2277 A1661 250w multi .50 .25

Sun and Moon — A1662

Hands Making Heart — A1663

Tree-lined Path — A1664

Roses — A1665

2008, May 19 Photo. *Perf. 13¼*

2278 A1662 250w multi + label .50 .25
2279 A1663 250w multi + label .50 .25
2280 A1664 250w multi + label .50 .25
2281 A1665 250w multi + label .50 .25
Nos. 2278-2281 (4) 2.00 1.00

Nos. 2278-2279 each were printed in sheets of 3 stamps + 3 labels, No. 2280 was printed in sheets of 14 stamps + 15 labels, and No. 2281 was printed in sheets of 20 stamps + 20 labels. Labels could be personalized.

Organization for Economic Cooperation and Development Ministerial Meeting, Seoul — A1666

2008, June 17 *Perf. 13¼*

2282 A1666 250w multi .50 .25

Yun Bong-Gil (1908-32), Assassin of Japanese Colonial Generals A1667

2008, June 20

2283 A1667 250w multi .50 .25

Energy Conservation — A1669

No. 2285: a, Open electrical circuit, car, refrigerator, light bulb, fan, meter. b, Hand-straps for public transportation. c, Electrical plugs on flower stems. d, Thermometers.

2008, Aug. 1 Photo. *Perf. 13¼x13*

2285 A1669 250w Block or horiz. strip of 4, #a-d 2.00 1.00

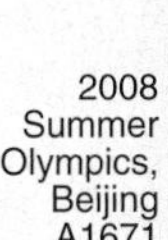

2008 Summer Olympics, Beijing A1671

2008, Aug. 8 Photo. *Perf. 13¼x13*

2287 A1671 250w multi .50 .25

Republic of Korea, 60th Anniv. — A1672

2008, Aug. 14

2288 A1672 250w multi .50 .25

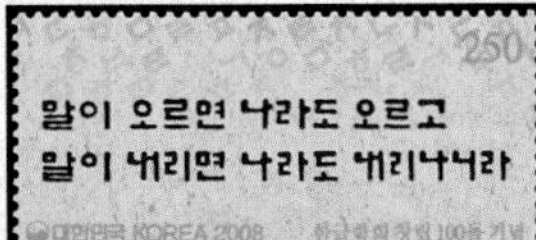

Korean Language Society, Cent. — A1673

2008, Aug. 29 *Perf. 12¾x13½*

2289 A1673 250w multi .50 .25

Seoul Water Works, Cent. — A1674

2008, Sept. 1 Litho. *Perf. 13x13¼*

2290 A1674 250w multi .45 .25

Amateur Radio Direction Finding Championships, Hwaseong A1675

2008, Sept. 2

2291 A1675 250w multi .45 .25

Snowboarding — A1676

No. 2292: a, Carving turn. b, Indy grab. c, Nose grab. d, Air.

Illustration reduced.

Serpentine Die Cut 11¾x11¼

2008, Sept. 5 Photo.

Self-Adhesive

2292 A1676 250w Block of 4, #a-d 1.90 1.00

SEMI-POSTAL STAMPS

Catalogue values for unused stamps in this section are for Never Hinged items.

Field Hospital SP1

Nurses Supporting Patient — SP2

Perf. 13½x14, 14x13½

1953, Aug. 1 Litho. Wmk. 257

Crosses in Red

B1 SP1 10h + 5h bl grn 16.00 4.50
B2 SP2 10h + 5h blue 16.00 4.50

The surtax was for the Red Cross. Nos. B1-B2 exist imperf.

Type of Regular Issue, 1956, with Added inscription at Upper Left

1957, Sept. 1 Wmk. 312 *Perf. 12½*

Granite Paper

B3 A111 40h + 10h lt bl grn 11.00 2.25

Wmk. 317

B4 A111 40h + 10h lt bl grn 11.00 2.25

The surtax was for flood relief.

Rice Farmer Type of Regular Issue, 1961-62

1963, July 10 Wmk. 317 *Perf. 12½*

B5 A172 4w + 1w dk bl 9.00 1.25

The surtax was for flood victims in southern Korea.

1965, Oct. 1 Unwmk. *Perf. 12½*

B6 A172 4w + 2w indigo 4.50 1.25

The surtax was for flood relief.

1965, Oct. 11

B7 A172 4w + 2w magenta 4.50 1.25

The surtax was for a scholarship fund.

Type of Regular Issue 1964-66

1966, Nov. 10 Litho. *Perf. 12½*

Granite Paper

B8 A186b 7w + 2w car rose 6.00 1.75

The surtax was to help the needy.

Soldier with Wife and Child SP3

Reservist SP4

1967, June 20 *Perf. 12½x13*

B9 SP3 7w + 3w rose lil & blk 7.50 1.25

The surtax was for veterans of the war in Viet Nam and their families.

1968, Aug. 1 Litho. *Perf. 13x12½*

B10 SP4 7w + 3w grn & blk 12.50 1.75

Issued for the fund-raising drive to arm reservists.

Flag — SP5

1968, Nov. 1 Litho. Unwmk.

B11 SP5 7w + 3w dk bl & red 40.00 7.50

The surtax was for disaster relief.

1969, Feb. 15

B12 SP5 7w + 3w lt grn, dk bl & red 11.00 1.25

Surtax for military helicopter fund.

Flag Type of 1968 Redrawn Zeros Omitted

1969, Nov. 1 Litho. *Perf. 13x12½*

B13 SP5 7w + 3w dk bl & red 37.50 1.60

The surtax was for the searchlight fund.

"Pin of Love" — SP6

1972, Aug. 1 Photo. *Perf. 13½x12½*

B14 SP6 10w + 5w blue & car 1.90 .75

Disaster relief.

"Pin of Love" — SP7

Paddle and Ball — SP8

1973, July 1 Photo. *Perf. 12½x13½*

B15 SP7 10w + 5w multicolored 1.10 .45

Disaster relief.

1973, Aug. 1 Photo. *Perf. 13½x12½*

B16 SP8 10w + 5w multicolored 1.25 .30

Surtax was for gymnasium to be built to commemorate the victory of the Korean women's table tennis team at the 32nd World Table Tennis Championships.

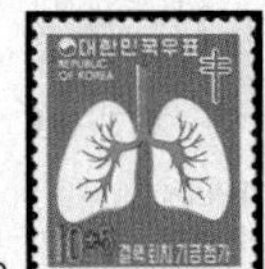

Lungs — SP9

1974, Nov. 1 *Perf. 13½x12½*

B17 SP9 10w + 5w green & red .90 .25

Surtax was for tuberculosis control.

No. 647 Surcharged

Perf. 13½x12½

1977, July 25 Photo.

B18 A328 20w + 10w green *12.00 12.00*

Surtax was for flood relief.

Seoul 1988 Olympic Games Series

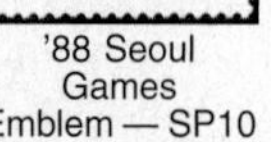

'88 Seoul Games Emblem — SP10

Korean Tiger, Mascot — SP11

Track and Field SP12

Equestrian SP18

1985, Mar. 20 Photo. *Perf. 13x13½*

B19 SP10 70w + 30w blk & multi .50 .30
B20 SP11 70w + 30w blk & multi .50 .30
a. Souvenir sheet of 2, #B19-20 1.75 1.75

1985, June 10

B21 SP12 70w + 30w shown .50 .30
B22 SP12 70w + 30w Rowing .50 .30
a. Souvenir sheet of 2, #B21-B22 1.75 1.75

1985, Sept. 16

B23 SP12 70w + 30w Boxing .50 .30
B24 SP12 70w + 30w Women's basketball .50 .30
a. Souvenir sheet of 2, #B23-B24 1.75 1.75

1985, Nov. 1

B25 SP12 70w + 30w Canoeing .50 .30
B26 SP12 70w + 30w Cycling .50 .30
a. Souvenir sheet of 2, #B25-B26 1.75 1.75

Surtax for the 24th Summer Olympic Games, Sept. 17-Oct. 2, 1988.

1986, Mar. 25 Photo. *Perf. 13x13½*

Designs: No. B28, Fencing. No. B29, Soccer. No. B30, Gymnastic rings.

B27 SP18 70w + 30w multi .50 .30
B28 SP18 70w + 30w multi .50 .30
B29 SP18 70w + 30w multi .50 .30
B30 SP18 70w + 30w multi .50 .30

Souvenir Sheets

B31 Sheet of 4 9.00 9.00
a. SP18 370w + 100w like #B27 2.25 2.25
B32 Sheet of 4 10.00 10.00
a. SP18 400w + 100w like #B28 2.50 2.50
B33 Sheet of 4 12.00 12.00
a. SP18 440w + 100w like #B29 3.00 3.00
B34 Sheet of 4 13.50 13.50
a. SP18 470w + 100w like #B30 3.50 3.50

1986 Photo. *Perf. 13x13½*

B35 SP18 80w +50w Weight lifting 1.50 .75
B36 SP18 80w +50w Team handball 1.50 .75
B37 SP18 80w +50w Judo 1.50 .75
B38 SP18 80w +50w Field hockey 1.50 .75

Souvenir Sheets

B39 Sheet of 4 10.00 10.00
a. SP18 370w + 100w like #B35 2.50 2.50
B40 Sheet of 4 10.00 10.00
a. SP18 400w + 100w like #B36 2.50 2.50
B41 Sheet of 4 12.00 12.00
a. SP18 440w + 100w like #B37 3.00 3.00
B42 Sheet of 4 13.50 13.50
a. SP18 470w + 100w like #B38 3.50 3.50

Issue dates: Nos. B35-B36, B39-B40, Oct. 10; others, Nov. 1.

1987, May 25 Photo. *Perf. 13x13½*

B43 SP18 80w +50w Women's tennis 1.00 .50
B44 SP18 80w +50w Wrestling 1.00 .50
B45 SP18 80w +50w Show jumping 1.00 .50
B46 SP18 80w +50w Diving 1.00 .50

1987, Oct. 10

B47 SP18 80w +50w Table tennis 1.00 .40
B48 SP18 80w +50w Men's shooting 1.00 .40
B49 SP18 80w +50w Women's archery 1.00 .40
B50 SP18 80w +50w Women's volleyball 1.00 .40

1988, Mar. 5 Photo. *Perf. 13x13½*

B51 SP18 80w +20w Sailing .75 .35
B52 SP18 80w +20w Taekwondo .75 .35

1988, May 6 Photo. *Perf. 13½x13*

B53 SP18 80w +20w Torch relay, horiz. .75 .35

Litho. & Engr.

B54 SP18 80w +20w Olympic Stadium, horiz. .75 .35

See Greece No. 1627.

Souvenir Sheets of 2

B43a SP18 80w +50w 2.25 2.25
B44a SP18 80w +50w 2.25 2.25
B45a SP18 80w +50w 2.25 2.25
B46a SP18 80w +50w 2.25 2.25
B47a SP18 80w +50w 2.25 2.25
B48a SP18 80w +50w 2.25 2.25
B49a SP18 80w +50w 2.25 2.25
B50a SP18 80w +50w 2.25 2.25
B51a SP18 80w +20w 3.75 3.75
B52a SP18 80w +20w 3.75 3.75
B53a SP18 80w +20w 2.25 2.25
B54a SP18 80w +20w 2.25 2.25

AIR POST STAMPS

Four-motor Plane and Globe — AP1

Perf. 11½x11

1947-50 Litho. Wmk. 257

C1 AP1 50wn carmine rose 3.00 3.50
a. Horiz. pair, imperf. btwn. *100.00*

Perf. 11

C2 AP1 150wn blue ('49) 1.50 1.50
a. "KORFA" 15.00 *30.00*
C3 AP1 150wn green ('50) 5.00 12.50
Nos. C1-C3 (3) 9.50
Set, never hinged 35.00

#C2-C3 are redrawn and designs differ slightly from type AP1.
Issued: 50wn, 10/1.
For surcharge see No. C5.

Plane and Korea Map — AP2

1950, Jan. 1

C4 AP2 60wn light blue 10.00 7.50
Never hinged 37.50

No. C2 Surcharged with New Value and Wavy Lines in Black

1951, Oct. 10

C5 AP1 500wn on 150wn bl 7.00 3.50
Never hinged 10.50
a. "KORFA" 30.00 *60.00*
b. Surcharge inverted 125.00

Douglas C-47 and Ship — AP3

Perf. 13x12½

1952, Oct. 15 Litho. Wmk. 257

C6 AP3 1200wn red brown 1.50 .75
C7 AP3 1800wn lt blue 1.50 .75
C8 AP3 4200wn purple 5.00 1.50
Nos. C6-C8 (3) 8.00 3.00
Set, never hinged 12.50

Nos. C6-C8 exist imperf.

1953, Apr. 5

C9 AP3 12h dp blue 2.50 .75
C10 AP3 18h purple 3.00 .75
C11 AP3 42h Prus green 4.00 1.50
Nos. C9-C11 (3) 9.50 3.00
Set, never hinged 12.50

Douglas DC-7 over East Gate, Seoul — AP4

1954, June 15 *Perf. 12½*

C12 AP4 25h brown 3.00 1.40
C13 AP4 35h deep pink 3.00 1.60
C14 AP4 38h dark green 3.00 1.60
C15 AP4 58h ultra 3.00 2.00
C16 AP4 71h deep blue 7.50 2.50
Nos. C12-C16 (5) 19.50 9.10
Set, never hinged 37.50

Nos. C12-C16 exist imperf.

Type of 1954 Redrawn

1956, July 20 Unwmk.

Laid Paper

C17 AP4 70h brt bluish grn 4.00 3.50
C18 AP4 110h brown 4.00 3.50
C19 AP4 205h magenta 8.00 3.50
Nos. C17-C19 (3) 16.00 10.50
Set, never hinged 40.00

Nos. C18-C19 are found on horizontally and vertically laid paper.

1957, July Wmk. 312 *Perf. 12½*

Granite Paper

C20 AP4 70h brt bluish grn 6.00 3.50
C21 AP4 110h brown 6.00 3.50
C22 AP4 205h magenta 9.00 3.50
Nos. C20-C22 (3) 21.00 10.50
Set, never hinged 45.00

On the redrawn stamps, Nos. C17-C22, the lines of the entire design are lighter, and the colorless character at right end of bottom row has been redrawn as in illustration above No. 212D.

Catalogue values for unused stamps in this section, from this point to the end of the section, are for Never Hinged items.

Girl on Palace Balcony AP5

Designs: 100h, Suwon Castle. 200h, Songnyu Gate, Tuksu Palace. 400h, Kyunghoeru Pavilion.

Perf. 12½

1961, Dec. 1 Unwmk. Litho.

C23 AP5 50h lt blue & violet 22.50 6.00
C24 AP5 100h pale grn & sepia 30.00 10.00
C25 AP5 200h pale grn & brn 45.00 12.00
C26 AP5 400h grn & pale bl 52.50 12.50
Nos. C23-C26 (4) 150.00 40.50

Values in Won; Same Designs; Underlined Zeros Added

1962-63

C27 AP5 5w lt bl & vio ('63) 90.00 16.00
C28 AP5 10w pale grn & sepia 82.50 16.00
C29 AP5 20w pale grn & brn ('63) 260.00 30.00
C30 AP5 40w grn & pale bl ('63) 90.00 30.00
Nos. C27-C30 (4) 522.50 92.00

1964, May 10 Wmk. 317 *Perf. 12½*

Granite Paper

C32 AP5 10w pale grn & sepia 15.00 4.50
C33 AP5 20w pale grn & brn 52.50 7.50
C34 AP5 40w pale bl & grn 29.00 6.00
Nos. C32-C34 (3) 96.50 18.00

1964, Oct. Unwmk. *Perf. 12½*

Designs: 39w, Girl on palace balcony. 64w, Suwon Castle. 78w, Songnyu Gate, Tuksu Palace. 112w, Kyunghoeru Pavilion.

Granite Paper

C35 AP5 39w vio bl & gray olive 11.00 2.25
C36 AP5 64w bl & grnsh gray 10.00 2.50
C37 AP5 78w grnsh bl & ultra 26.00 4.50
C38 AP5 112w blue & green 12.50 2.50
Nos. C35-C38 (4) 59.50 11.75

World Map and Plane — AP6

Designs: 135w, Plane over eastern hemisphere. 145w, Plane over world map. 180w, Plane over world map.

1973, Dec. 30 Photo. *Perf. 13x12½*

C39 AP6 110w pink & multi 9.00 3.50
C40 AP6 135w yel grn & red 10.00 3.50
C41 AP6 145w lt bl & rose 13.50 4.50
C42 AP6 180w lilac & yellow 32.50 6.50
Nos. C39-C42 (4) 65.00 18.00

UPU Type of 1974

1974, Oct. 9 Photo. *Perf. 13*

C43 A480 110w blue & multi 2.25 1.00
a. Souvenir sheet of 2 20.00 20.00

Mt. Fuji, Korean Airlines Jet Type

1985, Dec. 18 Photo. *Perf. 13x13½*

C44 A878 370w brt bl, blk & red 3.00 1.00

Int'l Year of Peace Type

1986, Jan. 15 Photo. *Perf. 13x13½*

C45 A879 400w multicolored 4.00 1.50

Issued in sheets with two blocks of four.

KOREA, DEMOCRATIC PEOPLE'S REPUBLIC

kə-'rē-ə

LOCATION — Peninsula extending from Manchuria between the Yellow Sea and the Sea of Japan
GOVT. — Republic
AREA — 47,398 sq. mi.
POP. — 22,170,000 (2000 est.)
CAPITAL — Pyongyang

At the end of World War II, American forces occupied South Korea and Russian forces occupied North Korea, with the 38th parallel of latitude as the dividing line. North Korea was administered by a Provisional People's Committee after Feb. 9, 1946. Unoverprinted Japanese stamps continued to be used until the first North Korean issue of March 12, 1946. On Sept. 9, 1948, the Democratic People's Republic of Korea was established, and the last Soviet troops left Korea by the end of the year.

100 Chon = 1 Won (1962)

Catalogue values for unused stamps in this country are for Never Hinged items.

North Korean stamps were issued without gum, unless otherwise noted.
Early issues typically exist in a variety of color shades.
Values for used stamps are for cancelled-to-order copies from 1957-on. Postally used stamps are worth more. Copies on non-philatelic covers are scarce, especially for 1946-1960 issues.

REPRINTS

During 1955-57 the North Korean Postal Administration created "reprints," actually imitations, of most 1946-56 issues for sale to collectors. These reprints were postally valid, and in some cases may have served real postal needs, but most were created for and sold to overseas collectors.
The reprints are more finely printed than the original stamps and are normally printed on a higher quality white wove paper. They often differ from the original printings in both size and design details. Specific distinguishing characteristics are provided below, with the descriptions of each issue.
Value of reprints, $2-$5 each, unused or cto, unless otherwise noted.

SOVIET OCCUPATION

Rose of Sharon — A1

Diamond Mountains (small "50") — A2

Diamond Mountains (large "50") — A3

Perf 11, rouletted 12(#3), 11x Imperf or Imperf x11 (#4,5)

1946, Mar. 12-1955 Litho.

1 A1 20ch red 82.50 *300.00*
2 A2 50ch apple grn ('46) 55.00 *82.50*
 a. 50ch yel green, *buff* 55.00 *82.50*
3 A2 50ch car rose 2,800. *2,300.*
4 A3 50ch rose red 165.00 125.00
 a. Perf 12 ('48) 165.00 125.00
 c. Perf 10 ('55) — —
5 A3 50ch violet 18.00 —
 a. Perf 11 ('50) 300.00 —
 b. Imperf ('50) 55.00 —
 c. Perf 10 ('55) — —
 d. ImperfxPerf 11, soft paper, vert. lines 1,200.
 e. Vert. pair, *tete-beche* 1,250.
 Nos. 1-5 (5) 3,120. 2,807.

No. 4 has lines of colored dots along the horizontal rouletting.
Design sizes: No. 1, 18x21.5-22mm; No. 4, 17.5-18x22-23mm.
Reprints of No. 1 are in yellow green, perf 8½, 8½x9½, 10 or imperf, and measure 18-18.5x23mm. Denomination panel is 4mm high, rather than 3mm. Value $10.
Reprints of No. 4 are perf 10, 10x10½, 11 or imperf, on gummed paper, and measure 17.5-18x22-22.5mm. The double frame lines are clearly separated, and the figures of value are thin and well-formed. Value $6.

Gen. Kim Il Sung (1912-1994) — A4

1946, Aug. 15 Litho. *Pin-Perf*

6 A4 50ch brown 400.00 400.00

First anniversary of liberation from Japan.
No. 6 has lines of colored dots along the horizontal pin perforations.
No. 6 is inscribed in both Korean and Chinese.
No. 6 in chocolate and a 50ch red, similar in design, were printed for presentation to officials and privileged people. Value, $1,500 and $1,800, respectively.

Peasants — A5

Pin-Perf 12, Imperf (#10)

1947, Apr. 22-1955 Litho.

7 A5 1w turquoise 450.00 55.00
8 A5 1w violet ('49) 800.00 175.00
9 A5 1w dark blue, *buff* ('50) 110.00 55.00
10 A5 1w dark blue ('50) 55.00 55.00
 a. Perf 11ximperf ('50) 6.00 *60.00*
 b. Perf 10 ('55) — —

1st anniversary of agrarian reform.
Nos. 7-9 have lines of colored dots along the horizontal pin perforations.
Reprints of type A5 measure 21x24mm, versus the originals' 21-21.5x24-25mm, are finely printed in light blue and are perf 9, 10½, 11 or imperf. Value $10.

Worker and Factory — A6

1948, June 5 Litho. *Perf. 11*

11 A6 50ch dark blue 3,200. 1,000.

Second anniversary of the Labor Law.
Design size: 20-20.5x31mm.
Reprints measure 20x30-30.5mm and are perf 9, 10½, 11 or imperf. Value, $8 perf, $10 imperf.

Workers and Flag — A7

1948, Aug. 15

12 A7 50ch red brown *4,000.* 1,500.

Third anniversary of liberation from Japan.

Flag and Map — A8

1948, Aug. 20

13 A8 50ch indigo & red *2,500.* 450.00

Adoption of the Constitution of the Democratic People's Republic of Korea, July 10, 1948.

DEMOCRATIC PEOPLE'S REPUBLIC

North Korean Flag — A9

1948, Sept. 19 *Rouletted 12*

14 A9 25ch reddish violet 10.00 *100.00*
15 A9 50ch gray blue 20.00 *50.00*
 a. Perf 10½ 40.00 *75.00*

Establishment of the People's Republic, 9/9/48.
Design size: 23x30mm.
Reprints of No. 14 are in blue, on gummed paper, perf 9, 10½ or imperf. Size 20.5x28mm. Value, $6.50.
No. 15a is perforated over rouletting.

North Korean Flag — A10

1949, Feb. 9

16 A10 6w red & blue 4.00 *12.00*
 a. Perf 10¼ 35.00 *35.00*

No. 16 exists on both brownish wove and white wove papers.
Design size: 24x32.5-33mm.
Reprints are perf 10¼, 11 or imperf. Size 19x26.5mm. On the originals, the top and bottom panels are blue, with the center field red. On the reprints, these colors are reversed.

A11

A12

Kim Il Sung University, Pyongyang

1949

17 A11 1w violet 400.00 200.00
18 A12 1w blue 1,200. 125.00

Issue dates: No. 17, 8/9; No. 18, Sept.
Design size: 34x21mm.
Reprints of No. 17 are in slate lilac to reddish lilac, perf 8½, 9, 9x9½, 10 or imperf, on gummed paper. Size 31.5-32x20-20.5mm. Value, $3.50 perf, $10 imperf.

A13

A14

North Korean Flags

Perf 11 or Rouletted 12 (#19)

1949, Aug. 15

With or Without Gum

19 A13 1w red, grn & blue 850.00 175.00
 a. Imperfx11 850.00 175.00
20 A14 1w red, grn & turq 2,000. *1,800.*

4th anniversary of Liberation from Japan.
Design sizes: No. 19, 20.5x31mm; No. 20, 20x29.5mm

Order of the National Flag — A15

#21c Control overprint

Rouletted 12, Imperf (#23)

1950, Apr. 4-1956

Lithographed

21 A15 1w pale sage green 4.50 *12.00*
 a. 1w olive green 4.50 *12.00*
 b. 1w yellow green 4.50 *12.00*
 c. With control overprint ('51) — —
22 A15 1w red orange 20.00 *125.00*

Typographed

23 A15 1w brown orange *3,250.* *1,000.*
24 A15 1w dark green ('51) 60.00 *25.00*
 a. Perf 10¼ ('56) 90.00 —
25 A15 1w light green 150.00 60.00

Design sizes: No. 21, 23-23.5x35mm; No. 22, 20x32mm; No. 23, 22.5-23x36-37mm; No. 24, 22x35.5mm; No. 25, 22.5x36mm.
No. 21c bears the seal of the DPRK MInistry of Posts and Telecommunications, which was applied to validate various stamps during the chaotic months following the landing of United Nations' forces at Inchon in mid-September, 1950, the retreat of North Korean forces to the far north by October, and their renewed advance, after the entry of the Chinese Volunteer Army into the war.
Reprints of type A15 are in dull blue green on white paper, perf 10¼ or imperf, size 22x35mm, or in red orange on white paper, perf 8½, 9, 10½, 10ximperf or imperf, size 20-20.5x32.5mm. Value (orange), $5 perf.

Flags, Liberation Monument A16

Flags, Soldier A17

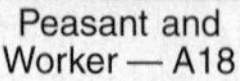

Peasant and Worker — A18

Tractor — A19

1950, June 20-1956

Lithographed, Thin Paper

Roul. 12xImperf, Roul. 12 (#28, 29)

26 A16 1w indigo, lt blue & red 3.50 *17.50*
a. Perf 10¼ ('55) 12.00 *24.50*
27 A16 1w brown orange 9.00 *60.00*
28 A17 2w red, steel blue & black 3.50 *17.50*
a. Perf 10¼ ('55) 12.00 *24.00*
29 A18 6w green 3.50 —
30 A19 10w brown 9.50 —

Typographed, Thin Paper, Roul. 12

31 A18 6w red 3.50 *17.50*
a. Perf 10¼ ('55) 29.00 *24.00*
b. Thick brownish paper, imperf x roul. 12 29.00 *24.00*
32 A19 10w brown 3.50 —
a. Thick brownish paper, imperf x roul. 12 36.00 *32.50*
Nos. 26-32 (7) 36.00 112.50

Fifth anniversary of liberation from Japan.

Design sizes: No. 30, 20x27.5mm; No. 31, 22x33mm; No. 32, 22x30mm.

Reprints of No. 26 are on medium white paper, distinguishable by numerous design differences, among which are: characters in top inscription are 1½mm high, rather than 1mm, with 3 short lines at either side, rather than 2; top corner ornaments have a dark center, rather than white; 4 ray beams at left of monument, rather than 3; no dots on right face of spire, while originals have 3 small dots; value numerals within well-formed circles.

Reprints of Nos. 28 and 29 are on medium white paper, perf 10¼, 11 or imperf. No. 28 reprints are in light green, No. 29 in rose red, dull blue and black.

Reprints of type A19 are 22x31mm in size, on medium white paper and are perf 10¼ or imperf.

Capitol, Seoul — A20

1950, July 10 Litho. *Roul. 12*

33 A20 1w bl grn, red & blue 45.00 —

Capture of Seoul.

Order of Ri Sun Sin — A21

1951, Apr. 5 Typo. *Imperf*

34 A21 6w orange 15.00 15.00
a. Perf 10¼ 30.00 —

No. 34 also exists perf 9x10½.

No. 34 is on brownish laid paper. Design size: 21.5-22x29.5-30mm.

Reprints are on white paper, perf 10¼ or imperf. Size 21.5x30mm. On the reprints, the center of the lower left point of the star is open; on the originals, it is hatched.

Hero Kim Ki Ok — A22

1951, Apr. 17

35 A22 1w blue 19.50 19.50
a. Perf 10¼ *180.00* —

No. 35 was printed on unbleached and off-white wood-pulp laid papers, with wood chips visible. The laid lines are often difficult or impossible to detect.

Design size: 23-23.5x35.5-36mm.

Reprints are on white wove paper, perf 10¼, 10½ or imperf. Size 22.5x33.5mm.

Soviet and North Korean Flags A23

Hero Kim Ki U A24

N. Korean, Chinese & Russian Soldiers — A25

1951, Aug. 15-1955 Litho. *Roul. 12*

36 A23 1w dark blue 105.00 *105.00*
37 A23 1w red 275.00 *275.00*
38 A24 1w dark blue 170.00 *170.00*
39 A24 1w red 170.00 *170.00*
40 A25 2w dark blue 65.00 *65.00*
41 A25 2w red 65.00 *65.00*
Nos. 36-41 (6) 850.00 *850.00*

Perf 10¼ Over Roulette (1955)

36a A23 1w dark blue) 75.00 *75.00*
37a A23 1w red 275.00 *275.00*
38a A24 1w dark blue 275.00 *275.00*
39a A24 1w red 170.00 *170.00*
40a A25 2w dark blue 75.00 *75.00*
41a A25 2w red 40.00 *40.00*
Nos. 36a-41a (6) 910.00 *910.00*

Nos. 36-41 and 36a-41a exist on both coarse buff and white wove papers. Values are the same. Various perfs and roulettes and roulettes exists; not all combinations are known.

Design sizes: Nos. 36 and 37, 17x23.5mm; Nos. 38 and 39, 16x23mm; Nos. 40 and 41, 23x16.5mm.

Reprints of No. 36 are perf 9, 10½x10 or imperf. Size 15.5-16x22.5mm.

Reprints of No. 38 are perf 9, 10 or imperf. They have no lines of shading between the characters in the top inscription.

Reprints of No. 40 are perf 9, 10 or imperf. Size 22-22.5x16.5mm. The Korean "Won" character at lower right is in 4 parts, rather than 3.

Reprints are all light ultramarine.

#16 Surcharged #34 Surcharged

1951, Nov. 1 *Imperf*

42 A10 5w on 6w red & blue (#16) 150.00 60.00
43 A21 5w on 6w orange (#34) 725.00 725.00

Order of Soldier's Honor — A26

1951, Nov. 15-1956

44 A26 40w scarlet (16.5x25mm) 22.50 4.50
a. Perf 10¼ ('56) 22.50 7.75
45 A26 40w scarlet (17x24mm) 12.00 4.50
a. Perf 10¼ ('56) 12.00 7.75

Victory Propaganda — A27

1951, Nov. 15-1956

46 A27 10w dark blue 15.00 7.75
47 A27 10w dark blue 15.00 7.75
a. Perf 10¼ ('56) 22.50 22.50

No. 47 also exists perf 8½.

Design sizes: No. 46, 17x25.5mm; No. 47, 16.5-17x25mm.

Reprints are in light blue, perf 10¼, 11 or imperf. Size 16.5-17x25mm. Value and inscription at bottom are outlined and clear against cross-hatched background.

Ri Su Dok, Guerilla Hero — A28

1952, Jan. 10-1955

48 A28 70w brown 12.00 3.50
a. Perf 10¼ ('55) 24.00 12.00
b. 70w black brown 120.00
c. As "b," perf 10¼ 60.00

Dove, Flag & Globe — A29

1952, Jan. 20-1957

49 A29 20w scarlet, deep blue & lt blue 24.00 6.00
a. Perf 10¼ ('55) 24.00 12.00
b. Perf 9 ('57) — —
c. Perf 9½x8½ ('57) — —

Peace Propaganda.

No. 49 also exists perf 8½, 11 and rouletted 11½.

No. 49 was printed on off-white or buff paper, with broken lines between stamps. Design size: 22x31-31.5mm.

Reprints are perf 10¼ or imperf, in red, slate blue and pale turquoise blue on white paper. Size 22x31mm. They lack the broken lines between stamps. Value, each $20.

Gen. Pang Ho-san — A30

1952, Apr.

50 A30 10w dull purple 60.00 24.00

Honoring Chinese People's Volunteers.

No. 50 is also known with locally-applied rough perforation.

Labor Day — A31

1952, Apr. 20-1955 *Imperf*

51 A31 10w rose red 210.00 *210.00*
a. Perf 10¼ ('55) 210.00 —

Enforcement of the Labor Law, 6th Anniv. — A32

1952, June 1-1955

52 A32 10w light blue 360.00 *325.00*
a. Perf 10¼ ('55) — —

Design size: 18x26mm. Broken lines between stamps.

Reprints are in dull or slate blue, on thick, gummed paper, with no broken lines between stamps. Size 17.5x25.5-26mm.

Day of Anti-U.S. Imperialist Struggle — A33

1952, June 4-1956

53 A33 10w rose red 180.00 150.00
a. Perf 10¼ ('56) 180.00 —

Design size: 17.5x25.5-26mm. Broken lines between stamps.

Reprints are in bright rose red, perf 10, 10¼, 11 or imperf. on thick, gummed paper, with no broken lines between stamps. Size 17.5x26mm.

North Korean-Chinese Friendship — A34

1952, July 25-1956

54 A34 20w deep blue 50.00 24.00
a. Perf 10¼ ('56) 50.00 —

Design size: 18x21.5mm. Printed on thin white wove paper, with clearly discernible mesh pattern.

Reprints are perf 10¼, 11 or imperf, on thick white wove paper, with no pattern visible. Size 18.5-19x21.5-22mm.

Flags & Monument A35 Soldier & Monument A36

1952-55

55 A35 10w carmine 120.00 —
a. Perf 10¼ ('55) — —
56 A36 10w scarlet 240.00 —
a. Perf 10¼ ('55) — —

Seventh Anniversary of Liberation from Japan.

Issue dates: No. 55, 7/25/52; No. 56, 8/1/52.

Design sizes: No. 55, 20.5-21x27.5-28mm; No. 56, 29.5-30x18.5mm.

Reprints of No. 55 are in vermilion, on thick paper, perf 10½, 11 or imperf. Size 20.5x27-27.5mm.

Reprints of No. 56 are in rose red, perf 10, 10¼, 11 or imperf. Size 30.5-31x18.5-19mm.

Note: original are typographed; reprints are lithographed on thin white paper.

International Youth Day — A37

1952, Oct. 20-1955

57 A37 10w deep green 72.50 —
a. Perf 10¼ ('55) 72.50 —

No. 57 is on thick paper, with very thin gum. Design size: 20.5-21x28mm.

Reprints are on thin to medium paper, without gum, perf 10¼, 11 or imperf. Size 20x27mm.

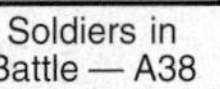
Soldiers in Battle — A38

Soldier and Flag — A39

1953, Jan. 20-1955

58 A38 10w rose carmine 130.00 —
a. Perf 10¼ ('55) 130.00 —
59 A39 40w red brown 60.00 —
a. Perf 10¼ ('55) 75.00 —

Fifth Anniversary of the Founding of the Korean People's Army.

Design sizes: No. 58, 21.5-22x26-26.5mm; No. 59, 21.5x27mm.

Reprints of No. 58 are on thick, gummed paper, perf 10¼, 11 or imperf. Size: 21.5-22x26.5mm.

Reprints of No. 59 are on thick, gummed paper, perf 10, 10½, 11 or imperf. Size: 21.5x26.5mm.

Woman with Flag — A40

Women and Globe — A41

1953, Mar. 1-1955

60 A40 10w carmine 60.00 —
a. Perf 10¼ ('55) 60.00 —
61 A41 40w yellow green 72.50 —
a. Perf 10¼ ('55) 72.50 —

International Women's Day.

Design sizes: No. 60, 20x29.5mm; No. 61, 21x29mm.

Reprints of No. 60 are in rose carmine, on thin paper, perf 10¼, 11 or imperf. Size 20.5x30mm.

Reprints of No. 61 may be distinguished from the originals by design differences: the dove's wing consists of many small feathers (3 large feathers on original), the women's mouths are all open (closed on original), and 3 thin connected lines on center woman's shirt (3 thick separate lines on original).

Worker — A42

Workers Marching — A43

1953, Apr. 15-1955

62 A42 10w yellow green 60.00 —
a. Perf 10¼ ('55) 72.50 —
63 A43 40w orange brown 60.00 —
a. Perf 10¼ ('55) 72.50 —

May Day

Reprints of No. 62 are in green or emerald green, perf 9½x8½, 10¼, 11 or imperf. Among many design differences, they have 4 horizontal lines between flag and frame line at upper left, many short hatching lines between frame line and top inscription, many horizontal lines between flag and flag pole at upper right, and won letter clear. On originals, there are one or no lines at upper left, no lines between frame line and top inscription, no lines between flag and flag pole, and the won character is not clearly defined.

Reprints of No. 63 are perf 10, 10¼ or imperf. On the reprints, the right flag pole touches the frame line, and the left center element of the won character resembles a "T." On the originals, the right flag pole does not touch the frame line, and the center element of the won character resembles an inverted "L."

Soldier — A44

Battle — A45

1953, June 1-1955

64 A44 10w greenish blue 110.00 —
a. Perf 10¼ ('55) 110.00 —
65 A45 40w scarlet 110.00 —
a. Perf 10¼ ('55) 110.00 —

Day of Anti-U.S. Imperialist Struggle.

Nos. 64 and 65 were issued with gum. Design sizes: 10w, 24x33mm; 40w, 24-24.5x33mm.

Reprints of No. 64 and 65 are on thick paper, perf 10¼, 11 or imperf. Design sizes: 10w, 23.5-24x32mm; 40w, 24x32-32.5mm. No. 64 is in turquoise blue, No. 65 in vermilion or orange vermilion.

A46

A47

4th World Festival of Youth & Students

1953, June 10-1955

With Gum

66 A46 10w dp dull blue & pale turq. blue 72.50 —
a. Perf 10¼ ('55) 85.00 —
67 A47 20w gray grn &pink 60.00 36.00
a. Perf 10¼ ('55) 72.50 —

Two types of reprints of No. 66 exist. On the reprints, the forelocks of the center and right heads have detailed hairlines, and the right head shows eye and eyebrow. On the originals, both features are solid.

Victory Issue — A48

1953, June 1-1955

With Gum

68 A48 10w brn & yel 360.00 —
a. Perf 10¼ ('55) 325.00 —

8th Anniversary of Liberation from Japan — A49

1953, Aug. 5-1955

69 A49 10w red orange *3,600.* *3,000.*

Design size: 25x35.5mm.

Reprints are perf 10¼ or imperf. Size: 24.5-25x34.5-35mm. Left side of monument is shaded, and windows are fully drawn and shaded. On the originals, the monument is unshaded, and the windows are only partially drawn and half shaded.

5th Anniv. Founding of D.P.R.K. — A50

1953, Aug. 25-1955

70 A50 10w dp blue & red 72.50 72.50
a. Perf 10¼ ('55) 95.00 —

Design size: 21.5-22x29.5-30mm. Inscribed "1948-1953."

Reprints are in blue and vermilion, perf 9x9½ or imperf and are inscribed "1948-1955." Size: 22.5x30mm. Value, each $30.

Liberation Monument — A51

1953, Dec. 25-1955

With Gum

71 A51 10w deep slate 72.50 47.50
a. Perf 10¼ ('55) 72.50 —

Design size: 20x31mm.

Reprints are in deep gray. Size: 19-19.5x30.5-31mm.

Worker & Crane — A52

1954, Jan. 25-1955

With Gum

72 A52 10w light blue 85.00 55.00
a. Perf 10¼ ('55) 110.00 —

Reconstruction and Economic Development.

Design size: 22x31.5mm.

Reprints are in greenish blue or dull blue, without gum. Size: 21.5x31mm. The horizontal lines defining the sky and clouds are clear and even, and the details of the crane are distinct.

Korean People's Army, 6th Anniv. — A53

1954, Jan. 25-1955

With Gum

73 A53 10w dp car red 725.00 —
a. Perf 10¼ ('55) 725.00 —
b. Rouletted 725.00

Design size: 23.5-24x38mm.

Reprints are in vermilion or orange vermilion. Size: 23-23.5x37.5-38mm. The design is much clearer than in the originals, with thin distinct characters in top inscription and complete unbroken frame line at right.

International Women's Day — A54

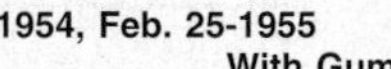

1954, Feb. 25-1955

With Gum

74 A54 10w carmine 220.00 —
a. Perf 10¼ ('55) — —

Design size: 19.5-20x29-29.5mm.

Reprints are in vermilion. Size: 20-20.5x29.5-30mm. The USSR and PRC flags at top right are legible, and the shading under the center and right women's chins is represented by several fine lines (solid on originals).

Labor Day — A55

1954, Apr. 15-1955

With Gum

75 A55 10w vermilion 72.50 —
a. Perf 10¼ ('55) 72.50 —

Design size: 20x27-27.5mm.

Reprints are in orange vermilion, perf 8½x9, 9, 10¼ or imperf. Size: 19-19.5x26-26.5.

#16 overprinted "Fee Collected" in Korean

1954, May (?)

76 A10 6w red & blue 2,500. 2,250.

Day of Anti-U.S. Imperialist Struggle — A56

1954, June 10-1955

With Gum

77 A56 10w red brown 210.00 *210.00*
a. Perf 10¼ ('55) 210.00 *210.00*

National Congress of Young Activists — A57

1954, July 20-1955

With Gum

78 A57 10w blue, red & slate 600.00 300.00
a. Perf 10¼ ('55)

Design size: 20x30mm.

Reprints are in blue, scarlet vermilion & deep slate. Size: 19.5-20x29-29.5mm. On the originals, the worker's hand is beneath the tassel of the flag and is less than 1mm from the frame line. On the reprints, hand is to the right of the tassel and 2mm from frame line.

Liberation from Japan, 9th Anniv. — A58

1954, Aug. 1-1955

With Gum

79 A58 10w chestnut 50.00 50.00
a. Perf 10¼ ('55) 50.00 —

Design size: 20-20.5x30mm.

Reprints of No. 79 are perf 10¼, 11 or imperf. Size: 20x29-29.5mm. Soldier's nose line straight and strong, 3 lines of cooling holes in gun barrel (2 on originals).

North Korean Flag — A59

1954, Aug. 25-1955
With Gum

80 A59 10w blue & dp red 60.00 *60.00*
a. Perf 10¼ ('55) — —

Design size: 24x31.5-32mm.
Reprints are in dull blue and bright rose red. Size: 25-25.5x30.5-31mm.

Taedong Gate, Pyongyang A60

1954, Sept. 1-1956
With Gum

81 A60 5w reddish brown 10.00 3.75
a. Perf 10¼ ('56) 21.00 —
82 A60 5w lilac brown 10.00 3.75
a. Perf 10¼ ('56) 21.00 —

Hwanghae Iron Works — A61

Hwanghae Iron Works & Workers — A61a

#84, Hwanghae Iron Works & workers, horiz.

1954, Nov. 1-1956

83 A61 10w light blue 21.00 3.00
a. Perf 10¼ ('55) 40.00 —
84 A61a 10w chocolate 21.00 3.00
a. Perf 10¼ ('55) 40.00 —
b. Perf 9x8½ ('56) — —

Korean People's Army, 7th Anniversary — A62

1955, Jan. 25
With Gum

85 A62 10w rose red 36.00 36.00
a. Perf 10¼ 36.00 —

International Women's Day — A63

1955, Feb. 25
With Gum

86 A63 10w deep blue 36.00 36.00
a. Perf 10¼ 45.00 —

Reprints are in blue, perf 10¼, imperf and imperf x 10¼. Corners of design are clearly and uniformly indented.

A63A A63B

Labor Day

1955, Apr. 16
With Gum

86A A63A 10w green 60.00 30.00
a. Perf 10¼ — —
86B A63B 10w violet brown 60.00 30.00
a. Perf 10¼ 60.00 —

Design sizes: No. 86A, 19.5-20x30mm. No. 86B, 19x30mm.
Reprints of No. 86A measure 19.5x29mm. Reprints of 86B measure 19x29.5mm and are without gum.

Admiral Ri Sun-Sin — A64

1955, May 14-1956

87 A64 1w blue, *pale green* 15.00 15.00
a. Perf 10¼ ('56) 18.00 —
88 A64 2w rose, *buff* 15.00 1.50
a. Perf 10¼ ('56) 22.00 —
89 A64 2w rose red ('56) 30.00 2.75
a. Perf 10¼ ('56) 30.00 —
Nos. 87-89 (3) 60.00 19.25

No. 89 is redrawn, with a larger "2."
Design sizes: Nos. 87, 88, 20x29-30mm.
Reprints of No. 87 are in dull blue, on pale apple green, perf 10¼, 11½x10½, imperf, or roul. 8½. Size 19x28-28.5mm. Reprints of No. 88 are 19-19.5x28.-28.5mm in size.

Labor Law, 9th Anniv. — A65

1955, May 30

90 A65 10w rose 90.00 90.00
a. Perf 10¼ — —

No. 90 was issued with a very thin yellow gum. Design size: 18.5-19x27.5-28mm.
Reprints exist perf 10¼, 11 or imperf. Size 18-18.5x27-27.5mm. Value unused, $5.

A66 A67

Korea-U.S.S.R. Friendship Month

1955, July ***Perf. 10***

91 A66 10w rose red 30.00 —
a. Imperf 30.00 21.00
92 A66 10w org red & vio blue 30.00 —
a. Imperf 30.00 21.00
93 A67 20w red & lt blue 30.00 —
a. Imperf 30.00 24.00
b. Inscription below flag in two colors — —
c. As "b," imperf — —
94 A67 20w verm & lt blue 24.00 —
a. Imperf 24.00 21.00
Nos. 91-94 (4) 114.00

Issue dates: Nos. 91, 93, 7/16; Nos. 92, 94, 7/20.
Design sizes: No. 91, 22x32.5mm; No. 92, 29.5x43mm; No. 93, 18.5x32mm; No. 94, 24.5-25x42.5x43mm.
Reprints of No. 94 are in light vermilion and light blue, perf 10¼, 11 or imperf, with a very thin gum. Size: 24-24.5x42-43mm. The two blue bands of the flag are solidly colored, with many white spots. On the originals, this area consists of fine lines with few or no white areas.

Liberation from Japan, 10th Anniv. — A68

1955, July 20 ***Perf. 10¼***

95 A68 10w dull green 24.00 —
a. Imperf 24.00 18.00
96 A68 10w ver, dull blue & chestnut 24.00 —
a. Imperf 24.00 18.00

Design sizes: No. 95, 21.5-22x31.5-32mm; No. 96, 29-29.5-42-43mm.
Reprints of No. 95 are in dull blue green, perf 10¼, 11 or imperf, on gummed paper. Size: 21-21.5x31mm. Reprints of No. 96 are in rose red, dull to greenish blue and yellow brown, perf 10¼ or imperf. Size: 28-28.5x42.5-43mm.

Standing Rock in Sea-Kumgang Maritime Park — A69

1956, Jan. 20

97 A69 10w blue, *bluish* 15.00 —
a. Imperf 15.00 8.00

People's Army, 8th Anniv. — A70

1956, Jan. 20

98 A70 10w lt brn, *pale yel grn* 90.00 *90.00*
a. Imperf *72.50 72.50*

Design size: 20x27-27.5mm.
Reprints are in chestnut on pale sage green paper, perf 10¼, 11 or imperf. Size: 19.5-20x27mm. Creases in the soldier's shirt are distinct, and nose and eyes are strongly shaded.

May Day — A71

1956, Apr. 29

99 A71 10w blue *55.00 55.00*
a. Imperf *55.00 55.00*

Design size: 23.5-24x35-35.5mm.
Reprints are perf 10¼, 11 or imperf, on gummed paper. Size: 23.5x35mm. Clear hatching lines at right of top inscription; many feathers in dove's wing.

Ryongwang Pavilion and Taedong Gate, Pyongyang — A72

1956, May 8

100 A72 2w light blue *55.00 55.00*
a. Imperf *55.00 55.00*

Reprints of No. 100 are on thicker, gummed paper. The tail of the central left element in the "won" inscription at lower right extends beyond the left edge of the L-shaped character beneath it.

Moranbong Theater, Pyongyang A73

1956, May 8

101 A73 40w light green 22.50 12.00
a. Imperf 85.00 72.50

Labor Law, 10th Anniv. — A74

1956, June 7

102 A74 10w dark brown 5.00 2.50
a. Perf 9 *80.00 60.00*
b. Imperf 150.00 90.00

Korean Children's Union, 10th Anniv. A75

1956, June 7

103 A75 10w dk brown 12.00 6.50
a. Imperf *135.00 30.00*

Law on Equality of the Sexes, 10th Anniv. A76

1956, July 10

104 A76 10w dark brown 6.50 3.75
a. Perf 9 *25.00 15.00*
b. Imperf 30.00 14.00

Nationalization of Major Industries, 10th Anniv. — A77

1956, July 10

105 A77 10w dark brown 75.00 —
a. Imperf *180.00* —

Liberation from Japan, 11th Anniv. — A78

1956, July 24

106 A78 10w rose red	9.00	3.25
a. Imperf	*130.00*	*25.00*

Machinist A79

1956, July 28

107 A79 1w dark brown	3.75	2.00
a. Perf 9	*12.50*	*8.00*
b. Imperf	27.50	12.00

Kim Il Sung University, 10th Anniv. — A80

1956, Sept. 30

108 A80 10w dark brown	5.75	5.75
a. Imperf	*27.50*	*12.00*

4th Congress, Korean Democratic Youth League — A81

1956, Nov. 3

109 A81 10w dark brown	7.00	3.25
a. Imperf	27.50	15.00

Model Peasant — A82

1956, Nov. 14

110 A82 10w rose	4.00	2.25
a. Imperf	18.00	9.50
b. Rouletted	—	—

220th Anniv. Birth of Pak Ji Won (1737-1805) A83

1957, Mar. 4

111 A83 10w blue	2.50	1.25
a. Imperf	16.00	8.50

Tabo Pagoda in Pulguk Temple A84

Ulmil Pavilion, Pyongyang A85

1957, Mar. 20

112 A84 5w light blue	3.75	2.50
a. Rouletted	—	—
b. Perf 11 (with gum)	—	—
c. Imperf	72.50	18.00
113 A85 40w gray green	4.50	3.25
a. Perf 11	—	—
b. Imperf	19.00	9.50

No. 113b was issued both with and without gum.

Productivity Campaign — A86

1957, July 4
With or Without Gum

114 A86 10w ultramarine	6.75	4.50
a. Perf 11	—	—
b. Imperf	27.50	13.00

Steelworker — A87

Voters Marching — A88

1957, Aug.

115 A87 1w orange	2.25	.75
a. Imperf	8.00	3.50
116 A87 2w brown	2.25	.75
a. Imperf	8.00	3.50
117 A88 10w vermilion	15.00	3.25
a. Imperf	55.00	29.00
Nos. 115-117 (3)	19.50	4.75

Second General Election.

There are two types of the 1w. On type 1, the won character is approx. 2½mm in diameter and is distinct. On type 2, the character is approx. 1½mm in diameter and is virtually illegible.

Issued: 10w, 8/10; 1w, 2w, 8/13.

Founding of Pyongyang, 1530th Anniv. — A89

1957, Sept. 28 ***Perf. 10***

118 A89 10w blue green	2.25	.65
a. Imperf	25.00	7.50

Lenin — A90

Lenin & Flags — A91

Kim Il Sung at Pochonbo A92

Pouring Steel A93

1957

119 A90 10w gray blue	1.90	.95
a. Imperf	25.00	7.50
120 A91 10w blue green	1.90	.95
a. Imperf	25.00	7.50
b. Rouletted 13	—	—
121 A92 10w red	1.90	.95
a. Imperf	25.00	7.50
b. Rouletted 13	—	—
122 A93 10w red orange	4.00	.95
a. Imperf	100.00	11.00
b. Rouletted 13	—	—
Nos. 119-122 (4)	9.70	3.80

40th Anniversary of the Russian October Revolution.

Issued: Nos. 119, 120, 9/30; No. 121, 10/3; 122, 10/16.

No. 120 exists with gum.

4th Congress World Federation of Trade Unions — A94

1957, Oct. 3

123 A94 10w ultra & lt grn	2.50	1.10
a. Imperf	25.00	9.50

No. 123a exists with or without gum.

Russian Friendship Month — A95

1957, Oct. 16

124 A95 10w green	4.50	1.10
a. Imperf	*180.00*	*120.00*

Doctor Weighing Baby — A96

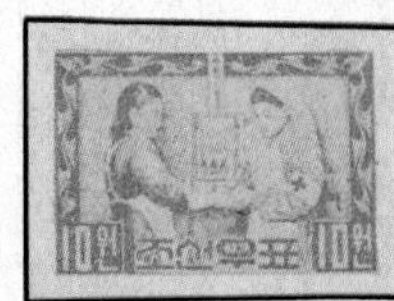

Bandaging Hand — A97

1957, Nov. 1

125 A96 1w red	9.00	1.25
a. Imperf	55.00	11.00
126 A96 2w red	9.00	1.25
a. Imperf	55.00	11.00
b. Rouletted	—	—
127 A97 10w red	35.00	3.75
a. Imperf	110.00	29.00
Nos. 125-127 (3)	53.00	6.25

Red Cross.

No. 126 exists without or without gum. No. 126a was issued with gum.

Flying Dragon Kettle — A98

Flying Dragon Incense Burner — A99

1958, Jan. 14

128 A98 10w blue	12.00	1.60
a. Imperf	72.50	17.00
129 A99 10w gray green	12.00	1.60
a. Imperf	72.50	17.00

Nos. 128a and 129a exist with or without gum.

Woljong Temple Pagoda — A100

1958, Feb. 21 ***10 (#130), 10½ (#131)***

130 A100 5w lt green	1.90	.75
a. Imperf	22.00	11.00
b. Rouletted	—	—
131 A100 10w lt blue	5.50	2.50
a. Imperf	27.50	15.00
b. Rouletted	—	—

No. 130 was issued with gum.

Soldier — A101

Soldier, Flag & Hwanghae Iron Works — A102

Photo (#132), Litho (#133)

1958, Feb. ***Perf. 10***

132 A101 10w blue	8.00	1.10
a. Imperf	44.00	18.00
b. Rouletted	—	—
c. Perf 11	—	—
133 A102 10w rose	11.00	1.25
a. Imperf	44.00	18.00

10th Anniversary of the Korean People's Army.

No. 133 was issued with or without gum.

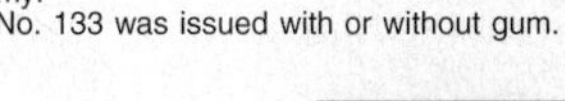

Rocket Launch, Sputnik — A103

Sputnik in Orbit — A104

1958, Mar. 26 **Photo.**

Designs: 40w, Sputnik over observatory.

134 A103 10w dull blue green 8.50 5.00
a. Imperf 55.00 18.00
135 A104 20w dull blue green 8.50 5.00
a. Imperf 55.00 18.00
b. Rouletted — —
136 A104 40w dull blue green 8.50 5.00
a. Imperf 55.00 18.00
137 A103 70w dull blue green 10.00 9.00
a. Imperf 85.00 29.00
Nos. 134-137 (4) 35.50 24.00

International Geophysical Year.
Nos. 134-137 exist with or without gum.

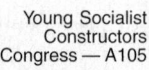

Young Socialist Constructors Congress — A105

1958, May 12 **Litho.**
138 A105 10w blue 4.50 1.25
a. Imperf 25.00 9.50

Opening of Hwanghae Iron Works — A106

1958, May 22
139 A106 10w lt blue 8.50 1.25
a. Imperf 35.00 12.00

Commemorative Badge — A107

1958, May 27
140 A107 10w multicolored 7.00 1.50
a. Imperf 23.00 5.50
b. Perf 11 — —
c. Rouletted — —

Departure of Chinese People's Volunteers. See No. 150.

4th International Democratic Women's Congress — A108

1958, June 5
141 A108 10w blue 1.90 .75
a. Imperf 35.00 9.50

Congress Emblem A109

1958, July 4
142 A109 10w grn & red brn 3.75 2.50
a. Imperf 25.00 5.50
b. Perf 11 12.50 —

First Congress of the Young Workers of the World Federation of Trade Unions.

Apartment House, East Pyongyang A110

1958, July 24
143 A110 10w lt blue 5.00 1.25
a. Imperf 22.00 7.50
b. Perf 11 — —

Workers' Apartment House, Pyongyang A111

1958, Aug. 21
144 A111 10w blue green 5.00 1.25
a. Imperf 22.00 7.50

Hungnam Fertilizer Plant — A112

Pyongyang Railway Station A113

DPRK Arms — A114

Weaver — A115

Dam, Pyongyang A116

1958 **Litho, Photo (#148, 149)**
145 A112 10w blue green 6.00 .95
a. Imperf *110.00* *15.00*
b. Perf 11 —
146 A113 10w dp blue green *22.50* 3.25
a. Imperf *130.00* *36.00*
b. Perf 11 —
147 A114 10w rd brn & yel grn 4.50 .95
a. Imperf *275.00* *90.00*
148 A115 10w sepia 18.00 3.75
a. Imperf *180.00* *47.50*
149 A116 10w sepia 30.00 12.50
a. Imperf *130.00* *30.00*
Nos. 145-149 (5) 81.00 21.40

10th Anniversary Korean People's Republic.
Issued: Nos. 145, 146, 8/21; No. 147, 9/7; Nos. 148, 149, 9/10.

Soldier and Troop Train — A117

1958, Sept. 10 **Photo.** ***Perf. 10***
150 A117 10w sepia 45.00 12.50
a. Imperf *300.00* *65.00*

Departure of Chinese People's Volunteers.

Transplanting Rice Seedlings A118

1958, Sept. 10 **Litho.**
With or Without Gum
151 A118 10w sepia 2.00 .65
a. Imperf 12.50 5.50

Winged Horse of Chollima — A119

1958, Sept. 16
152 A119 10w brick red 3.50 .60
a. Imperf 27.50 3.50

National Congress of the Innovators in Production.

North Korea-China Friendship Month — A120

1958, Oct. 8
With or Without Gum
153 A120 10w multicolored 2.25 .55
a. Imperf 15.00 3.50
b. Rouletted — —

National Congress of Agricultural Cooperatives A121

1959, Jan. 5
With or Without Gum
154 A121 10w dk grnish blue 2.50 .60
a. Imperf 15.00 3.25

Gen. Ulji Mundok — A122

1959, Feb. 11
With Gum
155 A122 10w lilac brn & yel 5.50 1.10
a. Imperf *27.50* *12.00*

See Nos. 157-159 and 209-212.

National Women's Workers Congress — A123

1959, Mar. 29
With or Without Gum
156 A123 10ch brown & red 3.75 1.25
a. Imperf *45.00* —

Jon Pong Jun — A124

Kang Kam Chan — A125

Ulji Mundok — A126

1959, Apr. 1
157 A124 2ch blue, *lt green* 2.50 .45
a. Imperf *90.00* —
158 A125 5ch lilac brn, *buff* 2.90 .50
a. Imperf *130.00* —
159 A126 10ch red brn, *cream* 5.75 .65
a. Imperf *130.00* —
Nos. 157-159 (3) 11.15 1.60

Nos. 157-159 were issued with gum. Nos. 157a-159a were issued with or without gum.

Soviet Luna 1 Moon Rocket Launch A127

1959, May 4 ***Perf. 10, 10½***
160 A127 2ch dk violet, *pale buff* 12.50 6.50
a. Imperf 220.00 47.50
161 A127 10ch blue, *pale green* 25.00 9.50
a. Imperf 220.00 47.50

Issued with gum (perf 10) or without gum (perf 10½). Nos. 160a and 161a were issued with gum.

Land Irrigation Program — A128

1959, May 27 ***Perf. 10***
162 A128 10ch multicolored 10.00 2.75
a. Imperf 36.00 9.50

Slogan-inscribed Tree, Chongbong Bivouac — A129

Statue of Kim Il Sung — A130

Mt. Paektu A131

1959, June 4 ***10, 10¾ (#164)***
163 A129 5ch multicolored 3.25 1.25
a. Imperf *72.50* 15.00
b. Perf 10¾ — —
c. Rouletted — —
164 A130 10ch blue & grnsh bl 3.75 1.25
a. Imperf *55.00* 15.00

165 A131 10ch violet blue	5.00	—
a. Imperf	*55.00*	—
Nos. 163-165 (3)	12.00	2.50

22nd Anniversary of the Battle of Pochondo.
No. 163 also exists perf 10¾.
No. 164 was issued with gum.

Chollima Tractor A132

Jongihwa-58 Electric Locomotive — A133

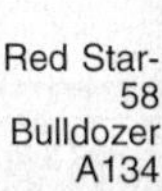

Red Star-58 Bulldozer A134

Chollima Excavator A135

SU-50 Universal Lathe A136

Sungri-58 Truck A137

With or without gum

1959, June 12 ***Perf. 10¾***

166 A132 1ch multicolored	1.50	.50
a. Imperf	*55.00*	*30.00*
b. Rouletted	—	—
167 A133 2ch multicolored	11.00	3.25
a. Imperf	*110.00*	*45.00*
b. Rouletted	—	—
168 A134 2ch multicolored	2.50	.65
a. Imperf	*72.50*	*15.00*
b. Rouletted	—	—
169 A135 5ch multicolored	2.50	1.25
a. Imperf	*180.00*	—
b. Rouletted	—	—
170 A136 10ch multicolored	2.50	.95
a. Imperf	*180.00*	—
b. Rouletted	—	—
171 A137 10ch multicolored	4.50	.65
a. Imperf	*180.00*	—
Nos. 166-171 (6)	24.50	7.25

Machine-building Industry.

Armistice Building, Panmunjom — A138

Anti-U.S. Protester A139

Anti-South Korean Emigration Campaign A140

Peaceful Reunification of Korea — A141

1959, June 25

With Gum

172 A138 10ch dk blue & blue	5.00	.30
a. Imperf	*145.00*	—
b. Perf 10¼	—	—
173 A139 20ch dk blue & lt blue	1.50	.50
174 A140 20ch sepia & brown	7.00	1.90
175 A141 70ch dk brn & lt brn	45.00	12.50
a. Imperf	*145.00*	—
b. Perf 10¼xRoul	—	—
Nos. 172-175 (4)	58.50	15.20

Day of Struggle for the withdrawal of U.S. troops from South Korea.

Metal Type A142

Samil Wolgan Monthly Breaking Chains — A143

Flag with Symbols of Peace and Literature A144

Korean Alphabet of 1443 — A145

1959, Aug. 1

176 A142 5ch sepia	25.00	9.50
177 A143 5ch green & red	7.50	2.90
178 A144 10ch bright blue	7.50	2.90
179 A145 10ch dp bl & pale bl	11.50	4.75
a. Souvenir sheet of 4, #176-179 imperf	110.00	55.00
Nos. 176-179 (4)	51.50	20.05

International Book and Fine Arts Exhibition, Leipzig.
Nos. 176 and 178 were issued with gum. Nos. 177, 179 and 179a were issued without gum.

Milk Cow Farm A146

Pig Farm — A147

1959, Sept. 20

180 A146 2ch multicolored	4.00	.95
181 A147 5ch multicolored	5.50	1.25

No. 180 was issued without gum, No. 181 with gum.

Economic Development

Cement Making A148

Hydroelectrical Dam — A149

Salt Making — A150

Construction A151

Grain A152

Sugar A153

Steel-Making A154

Fishing A155

Iron-Making A156

Coal Mining A157

Textile Production A158

Fruit — A159

Perf. 10½ (#182), 11

1959, Sept. 20-1960

182 A148 1ch multicolored	.75	.55
a. Imperf	*145.00*	—
183 A149 2ch multicolored	1.90	.55
a. Imperf	*145.00*	—
184 A150 5ch multicolored	3.00	.70
a. Imperf	*145.00*	—
185 A151 10ch multicolored	3.50	1.00
a. Imperf	*145.00*	—
186 A152 10ch multicolored	1.50	.55
a. Imperf	*145.00*	—

187	A153 10ch multicolored	2.75	.55
a.	Imperf	*145.00*	—
188	A154 10ch multicolored	2.50	.55
a.	Imperf	*145.00*	—
189	A155 10ch multicolored	2.25	.55
a.	Imperf	*145.00*	—
190	A156 10ch multicolored	1.50	.55
191	A157 10ch multicolored	2.75	.55
192	A158 10ch multicolored	1.50	.55
a.	Imperf	*145.00*	—
193	A159 10ch multicolored ('60)	4.00	.55
	Nos. 182-193 (12)	27.90	7.20

No. 193 issued August 1960.

Nos. 183 and 185 were issued with gum, the other values without gum.

Musk Deer A160

Sable A161

Marten A162

Otter A163

Sika Deer — A164

Pheasant A165

1959-62 ***Perf. 11***

194	A160 5ch multicolored	6.50	.75
195	A161 5ch multicolored	6.50	.75
196	A162 5ch multicolored	6.50	.75
197	A163 5ch multicolored	6.50	.75
198	A164 10ch multicolored	6.50	.75
199	A165 10ch multicolored	30.00	2.50
	Nos. 194-199 (6)	62.50	6.25

Game Preservation.

Issued: No. 198, 10/24/59; No. 199, 3/25/60; No. 194, 11/11/60; Nos. 195-197, 1/24/62.

Nos. 198 and 199 were issued with gum, Nos. 194-197 without gum.

3rd Korean Trade Unions Congress A166

1959, Nov. 4

With Gum

200	A166 5ch multicolored	1.40	.35

Electric Locomotive — A167

Freighter A168

1959, Nov. 5

With Gum

201	A167 5ch brnish purple	20.00	2.90
202	A168 10ch slate green	8.25	2.25

Korean People's Army, 12th Anniv. A169

1960, Feb. 8

With Gum

203	A169 5ch blue	225.00	125.00

Sword Dance — A170

Janggo Dance — A171

Peasant Dance — A172

1960, Feb. 25

204	A170 5ch multicolored	5.00	.45
205	A171 5ch multicolored	5.00	.45
206	A172 10ch multicolored	5.00	.45
	Nos. 204-206 (3)	15.00	1.35

Women of 3 Races, Dove — A173

Woman Worker — A174

1960, Mar. 8

With Gum

207	A173 5ch grnish blue & red vio	2.75	.20
208	A174 10ch grn & org	2.75	.50

50th Anniv. of International Women's Day.

Kim Jong Ho, Geographer A175

Kim Hong Do, Painter A176

Pak Yon, Musician A177

Jong Ta San, Scholar A178

1960

With Gum

209	A175 1ch gray & pale grn	2.75	.20
210	A176 2ch dp blue & yel buff	3.50	.20
211	A177 5ch grnish blue & grnish yel	12.75	.20
212	A178 10ch brn & yel	3.50	.20
	Nos. 209-212 (4)	22.50	.80

Issued: 1ch-5ch, 3/16/60; 10ch 6/60.

Grapes — A179

Wild fruits: No. 214, Fruit of Actinidia arguta planch. No. 215, Pine-cone. No. 216, Hawthorn berries. No. 217, Chestnuts.

1960, Apr. 8

With Gum

213	A179 5ch multicolored	3.25	1.00
214	A179 5ch multicolored	3.25	1.00
215	A179 5ch multicolored	3.25	1.00
216	A179 10ch multicolored	3.75	1.25
217	A179 10ch multicolored	3.75	1.25
	Nos. 213-217 (5)	17.25	5.50

Nos. 214-215 also exist imperf.

Lenin, 90th Birthday — A180

1960, Apr. 22

With Gum

218	A180 10ch violet brown	1.75	.30

Koreans and Caricature of U.S. Soldier — A181

1960, June 20

With Gum

219	A181 10ch dark blue	7.75	.75

Day of Struggle for Withdrawal of U.S. Troops from South Korea.

Mao Tse-Tung Plaza — A182

Taedong River Promenade A183

Youth Street — A184

People's Army Street — A185

Stalin Street — A186

1960, June 29

With Gum

220	A182 10ch gray green	1.25	.20
221	A183 20ch dk bl green	2.50	.30
222	A184 40ch blackish green	4.00	.75
223	A185 70ch emerald	7.25	1.75
224	A186 1w blue	10.00	2.75
	Nos. 220-224 (5)	25.00	5.75

Views of rebuilt Pyongyang.

Luna 3 — A187

Luna 2 — A188

1960, July 15

225 A187 5ch multicolored 7.75 6.00
226 A188 10ch multicolored 11.00 3.00

Soviet space flights.

The 5ch was issued with gum, the 10ch without gum.

Mirror Rock — A189

Devil-faced Rock — A190

Dancing Dragon Bridge A191

Nine Dragon Falls — A192

Mt. Diamond on the Sea A193

1960, July 15-1961

227	A189	5ch multicolored	1.75	.25
228	A190	5ch multicolored	1.75	.25
229	A191	10ch multicolored ('61)	6.25	.35
230	A192	10ch multicolored	5.50	.35
231	A193	10ch multicolored	2.10	.20
		Nos. 227-231 (5)	17.35	1.40

Diamond Mountains scenery.

No. 229 issued 2/8/61.

See Nos. 761-764.

Lily A194

Rhododendron A195

Hibiscus A196

Blue Campanula A197

Mauve Campanula A198

1960, July 15-1961

With Gum

232	A194	5ch multicolored	1.90	.30
233	A195	5ch multicolored	1.90	.30
234	A196	10ch multicolored	2.75	.50
235	A197	10ch multicolored	2.75	.50
236	A198	10ch multicolored ('61)	2.75	.50
		Nos. 232-236 (5)	12.05	2.10

No. 236 issued 6/1/61.

Nos. 232-234 and 236 also exist without gum.

"The Arduous March" A199

Crossing the Amnok River A200

Young Communist League Meeting — A201

Showing the Way at Pochonbo A202

Return to Pyongyang — A203

1960, July 26

237	A199	5ch carmine red	.85	.20
238	A200	10ch deep blue	1.50	.20
239	A201	10ch deep blue	1.50	.20
240	A202	10ch carmine red	1.50	.20
241	A203	10ch carmine red	1.50	.20
		Nos. 237-242 (6)	12.35	1.25

Revolutionary activities of Kim Il Sung.

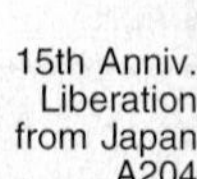

15th Anniv. Liberation from Japan A204

1960, Aug. 6

242 A204 10ch multicolored 5.50 .25

North Korean-Soviet Friendship Month — A205

1960, Aug. 6

243 A205 10ch lake, *cream* 1.40 .25

Okryu Bridge A206

Grand Theater A207

Okryu Restaurant A208

1960, Aug. 11

244	A206	10ch gray blue	4.00	.35
245	A207	10ch dull violet	3.50	.20
246	A208	10ch turquoise	1.40	.20
		Nos. 244-246 (3)	8.90	.75

Pyongyang buildings.

Tokro River Dam — A209

1960, Sept. 9

With Gum

247 A209 5ch slate blue 2.50 .25

Inauguration of Tokro River Hydroelectric Power Station.

World Federation of Trade Unions, 15th Anniv. — A210

1960, Sept. 16

248 A210 10ch blue & lt blue 1.60 .25

Repatriation of Korean Nationals from Japan — A211

1960, Sept. 26

249 A211 10ch brnish violet 5.50 .30

Korean-Soviet Friendship — A212

1960, Oct. 5

With Gum

250 A212 10ch brn & org 1.75 .25

Liberation Day Sports Festival, Pyongyang A213

Designs: 5ch (#251), Runner. 5ch (#252), Weight-lifter. 5ch (#253), Cyclist. 5ch (# 254), Gymnast. 5ch (# 255), Soccer players, horiz. 10ch (#256), Swimmer, horiz. 10ch (#257), Moranbong Stadium, horiz.

1960, Oct. 5

251-257 A213 Set of 7 13.50 2.25

Chinese & North Korean Soldiers A214

Friendship Monument — A215

1960, Oct. 20

With Gum

258 A214 5ch rose 1.40 .20
259 A215 10ch dp blue 1.40 .20

10th Anniversary of Chinese People's Volunteers' Entry into Korean War.

World Federation of Democratic Youth, 15th Anniv. — A216

1960, Nov. 11

260 A216 10ch multicolored 1.40 .25

Woodpecker
A217

Mandarin
Ducks
A218

Scops Owl — A219

Oriole — A220

1960-61

261	A217	2ch	yel grn & multi	7.25	.40
262	A218	5ch	blue & multi	7.75	.50
263	A219	5ch	lt blue & multi	12.50	1.00
264	A220	10ch	lt bl grn & multi	7.75	1.00
			Nos. 261-264 (4)	35.25	2.90

Issued: No. 262, 12/15/60; No. 264, 3/15/61; No. 261, 4/22/61; No. 263, 6/1/61.

Wrestling
A221

Swinging — A222

Archery
A223

Seesaw — A224

1960, Dec. 15-1961

265	A221	5ch	dull grn & multi	1.00	.20
266	A222	5ch	yel & multi ('61)	1.00	.20
267	A223	5ch	yel gold & multi	4.50	.45
268	A224	10ch	lt bl grn & multi	1.00	.20
			Nos. 265-268 (4)	7.50	1.05

No. 266 issued 1/6/61.

Agriculture
A225

Light
Industry
A226

Korean Workers'
Party
Flag — A227

Power
Station
A228

Steel-Making — A229

1960, Dec. 15-1961

269	A225	5ch	multicolored	1.90	.20
270	A226	5ch	multicolored	3.50	.20
271	A227	10ch	multicolored	.95	.20
272	A228	10ch	multicolored	1.90	.20
273	A229	10ch	multicolored	1.40	.20
			Nos. 269-273 (5)	9.65	1.00

Wild Ginseng — A230

Design: 10ch, cultivated ginseng

1961

274	A230	5ch	multicolored	5.00	.25
275	A230	10ch	multicolored	5.00	.25

Issued: 10ch, 1/5; 5ch, 3/15.

A231

A232

A233

A234

Factories

1961, Feb. 8

With Gum

276	A231	5ch	red & pale yel	1.40	.20
277	A232	10ch	bl grn & pale yel	3.00	.25
278	A233	10ch	dp vio blue & pale yel	3.00	.25
279	A234	20ch	vio & pale yel	3.75	.55
			Nos. 276-279 (4)	11.15	1.25

Construction of Vinalon Factory.
See Nos. 350-353.

Pyongyang
Students' and
Children's
Palace
A235

1961, Feb. 8

With Gum

280	A235	2ch	red, *yellow*	1.00	.25

Korean
Revolution
Museum
A236

1961, Feb. 8

With Gum

281	A236	10ch	red	.85	.25

Soviet Venus
Rocket
A237

1961, Feb. 8

282	A237	10ch	turq bl & multi	6.25	.30

Tractor-Plow
A238

Disk-Harrow
A239

Wheat
Harvester
A240

Corn
Harvester
A241

Tractors
A242

1961, Feb. 21

With Gum

283	A238	5ch	violet	.95	.20
284	A239	5ch	blue green	.95	.20
285	A240	5ch	dp gray green	.95	.20
286	A241	10ch	violet blue	1.40	.20
287	A242	10ch	purple	1.40	.20
			Nos. 283-287 (5)	5.65	1.00

Opening of
Industrial
College — A243

1961, Mar. 1

With Gum

288	A243	10ch	red brn, *buff*	3.00	.25

Agrarian
Reform
Law, 15th
Anniv.
A244

1961, Mar. 1

With Gum

289	A244	10ch	dull green, *yel*	2.10	.25

20-Point
Political
Program,
20th Anniv.
A245

1961, Mar. 15

With Gum

290	A245	10ch	dull vio, *pale yel*	1.00	.25

Mackerel
A246

Dolphin
A247

Whale
A248

Tunny — A249

Walleye Pollack A250

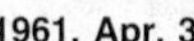

1961, Apr. 3

291	A246	5ch yel grn & multi	5.00	.50
292	A247	5ch lt blue & multi	12.00	1.50
293	A248	10ch lt grnish blue & multi	13.50	.50
294	A249	10ch gray & multi	5.00	.50
295	A250	10ch dk grn & multi	5.00	.50
		Nos. 291-295 (5)	40.50	3.50

Crane-Mounted Tractor — A251

"Sungri-1010" Truck A252

Vertical Milling Machine A253

Victory April-15 Automobile A254

8-Meter Turning Lathe A255

Radial Boring Lathe — A256

Hydraulic Press — A257

750-Kg Air Hammer A258

200mm Boring Lathe A259

3,000-Ton Press A260

3-Ton Air Hammer A261

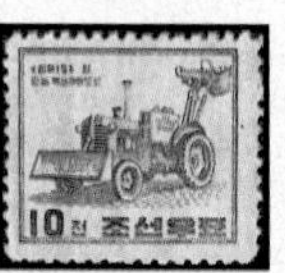
Ssangma-15 Excavator A262

Jangbaek Excavator A263

400-HP Diesel Engine — A264

Honing Lathe — A265

Trolley — A266

8-Meter Planer — A267

Boring Lathe — A268

Hobbing Lathe — A269

Tunnel Drill — A270

1961-65

296	A251	1ch red brown	2.75	.20
297	A252	2ch dk brown	2.75	.20
298	A253	2ch dk green	1.00	.20
299	A253	2ch grayish brn	50.00	12.50
300	A254	4ch dk blue	7.00	.20
301	A255	5ch dk green	4.00	.20
302	A256	5ch dk bl gray	2.10	.20
a.		5ch dark gray green	50.00	12.50
303	A257	5ch bl green	2.10	.20
304	A258	5ch red brown	1.75	.20
305	A259	5ch sl violet	2.50	.20
306	A260	10ch gray violet	3.75	.20
a.		10ch dark blue	50.00	.20
307	A261	10ch blue	3.50	.20
308	A261	10ch brown	*200.00*	*50.00*
309	A262	10ch dk vio gray	1.75	.20
310	A263	10ch dk green	3.75	.20
311	A264	10ch dk sl blue	3.75	.20
312	A265	10ch dk blue	3.25	.20
313	A266	40ch dk blue	13.50	.20
314	A267	90ch dk bl green	6.00	.30
315	A268	1w dk vio brown	17.50	.50
316	A269	5w dk brown	37.50	3.75
317	A270	10w vio brown	50.00	7.50
		Nos. 296-317 (22)	420.20	77.75

Issued: 1ch, 4/22/61; 2ch, 4/27/61; Nos. 301, 306, 5/20/61; Nos. 307, 308, 3/13/62; Nos. 302, 317, 7/30/62; 5w, 9/5/62; No. 302a, 9/15/62; No. 308, 12/26/62; Nos. 297, 298, 2/11/63; No. 303, 4/9/63; 90ch, 5/15/63; 4ch, 6/15/63; 40ch, 9/13/63; 1w, 10/16/63; No. 310, 3/20/64; No. 305, 4/28/64; No. 311, 6/25/64; No. 312, 1/1/65.

Nos. 296, 297, 301, 303, 306 and 316 are perf 10¾. Other values are perf 12½.

Nos. 296-302, 304-307 and 309-315 were issued with gum. Nos. 303, 308, 316 and 317 were issued without gum.

Nos. 296-297, 301, 303, 306-308 and 316 are lithographed. Other values are engraved.

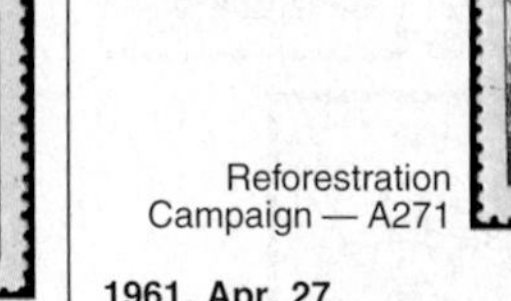

Reforestration Campaign — A271

1961, Apr. 27

With Gum

318	A271	10ch green	2.50	.35

Peaceful Reunification of Korea — A272

1961, May 9

319	A272	10ch multicolored	30.00	2.50

Young Pioneers (Children's Union) of Korea, 15th Anniv. — A273

Designs: 5ch, Pioneers swimming. 10ch (#321), Pioneer bugler. 10ch (#322) Pioneer visiting battlefield.

1961, June 1

320-322	A273	Set of 3	6.50	1.00

Labor Law, 15th Anniv. A274

1961, June 21

With Gum

323	A274	10ch dp blue, *pale yel*	1.75	.30

Plums — A275

Peaches A276

Apples A277

Persimmons A278

Pears — A279

1961, July 11

324	A275	5ch multicolored	1.60	.20
325	A276	5ch multicolored	1.60	.20
326	A277	5ch multicolored	1.60	.20
327	A278	10ch multicolored	1.60	.20
328	A279	10ch multicolored	1.60	.20
		Nos. 324-328 (5)	8.00	1.00

Yuri Gagarin & Vostok I — A280

1961, July 11

329	A280	10ch dp bl & pale bl	2.50	.50
330	A280	10ch red vio & pale bl	2.50	.50

First manned space flight, April 12.

Nationalization of Industry, 15th Anniv. — A281

1961, July 11

With Gum

331	A281	10ch lt red brown	20.00	.90

Sex Equality Law, 15th Anniv. A282

1961, July 27

With Gum

332	A282	10ch brn red & rose	1.25	.25

Children Planting Tree — A283

Children: 5ch (#334), Reading book. 10ch (#335), Playing with ball. 10ch (#336), Building a toy house. 10ch (#337), Waving banner.

1961, Aug. 29

333-337	A283	Set of 5	6.50	.90

Livestock Breeding — A284

Fishing Industry A285

Farming A286

Textile Industry — A287

1961, Aug. 29

338	A284	5ch multicolored	2.25	.20
339	A285	10ch multicolored	1.90	.20
340	A286	10ch multicolored	3.50	.20
341	A287	10ch multicolored	3.25	.30
		Nos. 338-341 (4)	10.90	.90

Improvement of living standards.

Kim Il Sung Writing Under Tree A288

Kim Il Sung at Desk A289

Soldiers Studying A290

1961, Sept. 8

With Gum

342	A288	10ch violet	.85	.35
343	A289	10ch dull violet	.85	.35
344	A290	10ch dp blue & yel	1.60	.35
		Nos. 342-344 (3)	3.30	1.05

15th Anniv. of Kim Il Sung's "Ten-Point Program of the Association for the Restoration of the Fatherland."

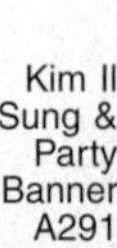

Kim Il Sung & Party Banner A291

Party Emblem, Workers — A292

Chollima Statue — A293

1961, Sept. 8

With Gum

345	A291	10ch brown red	.70	.35
346	A292	10ch green	.70	.35
347	A293	10ch violet	.70	.35
		Nos. 345-347 (3)	2.10	1.05

4th Korean Workers' Party Congress.

Miners' Day — A294

1961, Sept. 12

With Gum

348	A294	10ch brown	13.00	.75

Pak In Ro (1561-1642), Poet — A295

1961, Sept. 12

349	A295	10ch dk blue & gray blue	3.75	.25

Aldehyde Shop A296

Polymerization & Saponification Shops — A297

Glacial Acetic Acid Shops A298

Spinning Shop A299

1961, Oct. 17

With Gum

350	A296	5ch red & pale yel	1.40	.20
351	A297	10ch dp blue & pale yel	2.10	.20
352	A298	10ch dk brn & pale yel	2.10	.20
353	A299	20ch purple & pale yel	3.25	.40
		Nos. 350-353 (4)	8.85	1.00

Completion of Vinalon Factory.

Korean & Soviet Flags — A300

Korean & ChineseFlags A301

1961, Oct. 26

354	A300	10ch multicolored	1.40	.35
355	A301	10ch multicolored	1.40	.35

North Korean Friendship Treaties with the Soviet Union and China.

Day of Sports and Physical Culture — A302

Sports: 2ch, Table tennis. 5ch, Flying model glider. 10ch (#358), Basketball. 10ch (#359), Rowing. 10ch (#360), High jump. 20ch, Emblem.

1961, Nov. 4

With Gum

356-361	A302	Set of 6	10.00	1.75

#209 Surcharged in Violet

1961, Nov. 5

362	5ch on 1ch gray & pale grn	200.00	150.00

Centenary of publication of "Taedongyojido," map.

Janggun Rock — A303

Chonbul Peak A304

Mansa Peak — A305

Kiwajip Rock A306

Mujigae Rock A307

1961, Nov. 29

With Gum

363	A303	5ch slate	1.50	.20
364	A304	5ch brown	1.50	.20
365	A305	10ch br lilac	2.75	.20
366	A306	10ch sl blue	2.75	.20
367	A307	10ch dk blue	2.75	.20
		Nos. 363-367 (5)	11.25	1.00

Mt. Chilbo scenes.

Protection of State Property — A308

1961, Nov. 29

With Gum

368	A308	10ch gray green	1.40	.25

WFTU Emblem — A309

1961, Nov. 29

With Gum

369	A309	10ch multicolored	.85	.25

5th Congress of World Federation of Trade Unions.

"Red Banner" Electric Locomotive A310

1961, Nov. 29

With Gum

370	A310	10ch vio & buff	19.00	1.75

Railway Electrification.

Winter Sports A311

Designs (all 10ch): No. 371, Figure skater. No. 372, Speed skater. No. 373, Ice hockey. No. 374, Skiier.

1961, Dec. 12

With Gum

Figures in Sepia

371-374	A311	Set of 4	11.00	1.00

Six Objectives of Production

Steel — A312

Coal — A313

Grain — A314

Textiles — A315

Sea-Foods — A316

Apartments — A317

1962, Jan. 1

With Gum

375	A312	5ch	multicolored	1.25	.20
376	A313	5ch	multicolored	8.75	.50
377	A314	10ch	multicolored	1.25	.20
378	A315	10ch	multicolored	4.00	.20
379	A316	10ch	multicolored	3.75	.20
380	A317	10ch	multicolored	1.25	.20
			Nos. 375-380 (6)	20.25	1.50

See Nos. 442-447.

Animals

Korean Tiger — A318

Racoon Dog — A319

Badger A320

Bear — A321

1962, Jan. 24

381	A318	2ch	multicolored	5.25	.20
382	A319	2ch	lt grn & brn	3.75	.20
383	A320	5ch	lt bl grn & lt red brn	2.50	.20
384	A321	10ch	grn & brn	3.75	.20
			Nos. 381-384 (4)	15.25	.80

Traditional Musical Instruments

Kayagum — A322

Jotae (Flute) — A323

Wolgum — A324

Haegum — A325

Wagonghu — A326

1962, Feb. 2

385	A322	10ch	multicolored	3.75	.20
386	A323	10ch	multicolored	3.75	.20
387	A324	10ch	multicolored	3.75	.20
388	A325	10ch	multicolored	3.75	.20
389	A326	10ch	multicolored	3.75	.20
			Nos. 385-389 (5)	18.75	1.00

See Nos. 472-476.

Butterflies

Luehdorfia puziloi — A327

Sericinus telamon — A328

Parnassius nomion — A329

Inachusio — A330

1962, Mar. 13

390	A327	5ch	multicolored	4.50	.20
391	A328	10ch	multicolored	4.50	.20
392	A329	10ch	multicolored	4.50	.20
393	A330	10ch	multicolored	4.50	.20
			Nos. 390-393 (4)	18.00	.80

G. Titov & Vostok 2 A331

1962, Mar. 13

394	A331	10ch	multicolored	3.75	.30

Second Soviet Manned Space Flight.

Kim Il Sung Commanding Troops — A332

Kim Il Sung Adressing Workers — A333

Perf. 10¾ (#397), 12½

1962, Apr. 14 **Engr.**

With Gum

395	A332	10ch	blue	1.10	.30
396	A333	10ch	green	1.10	.30
397	A333	10ch	rose red	1.10	.30
			Nos. 395-397 (3)	3.30	.90

Marshall Kim Il Sung's 50th Birthday.

Kim Chaek — A334

Kang Kon — A335

An Kil — A336

Ryu Kyong Su — A337

Kim Jong Suk — A338

Choe Chun Guk — A339

1962, Apr. 23 ***Perf. 12½***

With Gum

398	A334	10ch	dark brown	7.00	.20
399	A335	10ch	dark blue	7.00	.20
400	A336	10ch	rose	7.00	.20
401	A337	10ch	dark brown	7.00	.20
402	A338	10ch	dark blue gray	7.00	.20
403	A338	10ch	dark blue green	7.00	.20
404	A339	10ch	violet brown	7.00	.20
			Nos. 398-404 (7)	49.00	1.40

Anti-Japanese Revolutionary Fighters.

See Nos. 480-484.

National Mothers' Meeting, Pyongyang — A340

1962, May 23 **Litho.** ***Perf. 10¾***

405	A340	10ch	multicolored	.85	.25

Black-faced Spoonbill — A341

Brown Hawk Owl — A342

Eastern Broad-billed Roller — A343

Black Paradise Flycatcher A344

Whistling Swan — A345

1962, May 23 ***Perf. 10¾***

406	A341	5ch multicolored	3.25	.40
407	A342	5ch multicolored	12.00	.50
408	A343	10ch multicolored	7.00	.50
409	A344	10ch multicolored	7.00	.50
410	A345	20ch multicolored	8.75	.55
		Nos. 406-410 (5)	38.00	2.45

Beneficial birds.

Battle of Pochonbo, 25th Anniv. — A346

1962, May 23

411 A346 10ch multicolored 1.90 .25

Croaker A347

Hairtail A348

Japanese Croaker A349

Japanese Sea Bass A350

Gizzard Shad A351

1962, June 28

412	A347	5ch dp grn & multi	1.90	.20
413	A348	5ch dp blue & multi	1.90	.20
414	A349	10ch apple grn & multi	3.25	.20
415	A350	10ch vio blue & multi	3.25	.20
416	A351	10ch grn & multi	3.25	.20
		Nos. 412-416 (5)	13.55	1.00

Sea Fish.

Brush Case — A352

Ink Container — A353

Ink Slab Case A354

Writing Brush Stand A355

Paperweight — A356

Ink Slab A357

Filing Cabinet A358

Kettle — A359

Centers in Black

1962, July 30

417	A352	4ch pale blue	1.40	.20
418	A353	5ch ochre	1.40	.20
419	A354	10ch pale green	1.90	.20
420	A355	10ch salmon	1.90	.25
421	A356	10ch violet	1.90	.25
422	A357	10ch orange brown	1.90	.25
423	A358	10ch pale yellow	1.90	.25
424	A359	40ch gray	4.50	.50
		Nos. 417-424 (8)	16.80	2.10

Antiques of the Koryo and Yi Dynasties.

Nos. 418 and 420 were issued with gum, the other values without gum.

Jong Ta San — A360

1962, July 30 **Engr.** ***Perf. 12½***

425 A360 10ch dp brnish violet 1.60 .25

200th Anniv. birth of Jong Ta San, philosopher.

National Assembly Elections A361 A362

1962, Oct. 3 **Litho.** ***Perf. 10¾***

426	A361	10ch multicolored	1.60	.30
427	A362	10ch multicolored	1.60	.30

Pyongyang, 1535th Anniv. — A363

1962, Oct. 15

With Gum

428 A363 10ch pale blue & blk 1.10 .25

Launch of Soviet Manned Rockets Vostok 3 & 4 — A364

1962, Nov. 12

429 A364 10ch multicolored 3.75 .75

Spiraea — A365

Echinosophoora koreensis — A366

Codonopsis sylvestris — A367

Ginseng — A368

1962, Nov. 30

430	A365	5ch multicolored	1.90	.20
431	A366	10ch multicolored	1.90	.20
432	A367	10ch multicolored	1.90	.20
433	A368	10ch multicolored	1.90	.20
		Nos. 430-433 (4)	7.60	.80

Korean plants.

Uibangryuchui A369

1962, Dec. 26

434 A369 10ch multicolored 5.50 .40

485th anniversary of publication of the medical encyclopedia *Uibangryuchui*, printed with moveable type.

Korean Academy of Sciences, 10th Anniv. A370

1962, Dec. 26

435 A370 10ch dull ultra & pale turq grn 2.25 .25

Fishing — A371

1962, Dec. 30

436 A371 10ch ultra 5.50 .25

European Mink A372

Korean Hare A373

Eurasian Red Squirrel — A374

Goral — A375

Siberian Chipmunk A376

1962, Dec. 30-1963

437 A372 4ch apple green & red brown 1.60 .40
438 A373 5ch lt green & gray ('63) 1.60 .40
439 A374 10ch yellow & gray 2.75 .40
440 A375 10ch pale grn & dk brn 2.75 .40
441 A376 20ch lt gray blue & red brown 5.00 .40
Nos. 437-441 (5) 13.70 2.00

Fur-bearing animals. No. 438 issued 12/30/63.

Coal A377

Grain A378

Textiles A379

Apartment Construction — A380

Steel A381

Sea-Foods — A382

1963, Jan. 1

442 A377 5ch multicolored 1.40 .25
443 A378 10ch multicolored 1.10 .20
444 A379 10ch multicolored 1.40 .20
445 A380 10ch multicolored 1.10 .20
446 A381 10ch multicolored 1.10 .20
447 A382 40ch multicolored 3.25 .45
Nos. 442-447 (6) 9.35 1.50

Consolidation of the Achievement of the 6 Objectives.

A383

Korean People's Army, 15th Anniv.

Designs: 5ch, Airman. 10ch (#449), Soldier. 10ch (#450), Sailor.

1963, Feb. 1 Engr. *Perf. 12½*
With Gum

448-450 A383 Set of 3 6.50 .60

Peony — A384

Rugosa Rose — A385

Rhododendron A386

Campion A387

Orchid — A388

1963, Mar. 21 Litho. *Perf. 10¾*

451 A384 5ch gray & multi 1.10 .20
452 A385 10ch grnsh yel & multi 1.60 .20
453 A386 10ch lemon & multi 1.60 .20
454 A387 10ch br yel & multi 1.60 .20
455 A388 40ch green & multi 5.00 .45
Nos. 451-455 (5) 10.90 1.25

Korean flowers.

Sword Dance — A389

Fan Dance — A390

1963, Apr. 15

456 A389 10ch multicolored 7.75 .30
457 A390 10ch multicolored 7.75 .30

International Music and Dance Competition, Pyongyang, April 16-May 17.

A391

South Korea Uprising of April 19, 3rd Anniv.

1963, Apr. 19

458 A391 10ch multicolored 1.60 .25

A392

Karl Marx, 145th Birth Anniv.

1963, Apr. 23 Engr. *Perf. 12½*
With Gum

459 A392 10ch ultra 2.75 .25

A393

Youth Day

Designs: 2ch, Children in chemistry class. 5ch, Children running. 10ch (#462), Girl chasing butterfly. 10ch (#463), Boy leading chorus.

1963, June 15 Litho. *Perf. 10¾*

460-463 A393 Set of 4 13.00 1.00

Armed Koreans & Caricature of American Soldier — A394

1963, June 25

464 A394 10ch multicolored 1.90 .25

Month of Struggle for the Withdrawal of U.S. Troops from South Korea.

Cyrtoclytus caproides A395

Cicindela chinensis A396

Purpuricenus lituratus A397

Agapanthia pilicornus A398

1963, July 24

465	A395	5ch multicolored	2.50	.20
466	A396	10ch multicolored	3.50	.20
467	A397	10ch multicolored	3.50	.20
468	A398	10ch multicolored	3.50	.20
		Nos. 465-468 (4)	13.00	.80

Korean beetles.

A399

Victory in Korean War, 10th Anniv.

1963, July 27

469	A399	10ch multicolored	1.90	.25

National Emblem — A400

North Korean Flag — A401

1963, Aug. 15

470	A400	10ch multicolored	.65	.30
471	A401	10ch multicolored	.65	.30

No. 471 exists with background in blue. Not issued. Value $750.

Ajaeng (Zither) — A402

Phyongyong (Jade Chimes) — A403

Saenap (Flute) — A404

Rogo (Drums) — A405

Phiri (Pipe) — A406

1963, Sept. 13

472	A402	5ch multicolored	1.60	.20
473	A403	5ch multicolored	1.60	.20
474	A404	10ch multicolored	2.25	.20
475	A405	10ch multicolored	2.25	.20
476	A406	10ch multicolored	2.25	.20
		Nos. 472-476 (5)	9.95	1.00

Korean traditional musical instruments.

Nos. 472 and 475 were issued with gum, the other values without gum.

South Gate, Kaesong A407

Taedong Gate, Pyongyang A408

Pothong Gate, Pyongyang A409

1963, Sept. 13 Engr. *Perf. 12½*
With Gum

477	A407	5ch black	.50	.20
478	A408	10ch brown	1.25	.25
479	A409	10ch black green	1.25	.25
		Nos. 477-479 (3)	3.00	.70

Korean historic buildings.

See Nos. 537-538.

Kwon Yong Byok — A410

Ma Tong Hui — A411

Pak Tal — A412

Ri Je Sun — A413

Kim Yong Bom — A414

1963, Oct. 10
With Gum

480	A410	5ch brown	9.00	—
481	A411	5ch brown purple	9.00	—
482	A412	10ch grnsh slate	9.00	—
483	A413	10ch carmine rose	9.00	—
484	A414	10ch black brown	70.00	50.00

Anti-Japanese revolutionary fighters.

Nurse & Children at Playground A415

Teacher & Children at Fairground A416

1963, Nov. 30 Litho. *Perf. 10¾*

485	A415	10ch multicolored	.85	.25
486	A416	10ch multicolored	.85	.25

Child welfare.

Hwajang Temple — A417

Hyangsan Stream A418

Kwanum Pavilion & Pagoda A419

Sangwon Temple — A420

1963, Nov. 30

487	A417	5ch multicolored	1.10	.20
488	A418	10ch multicolored	5.75	.20
489	A419	10ch multicolored	2.75	.20
490	A420	10ch multicolored	2.75	.20
		Nos. 487-490 (4)	12.35	.80

Mount Myohyang.

Arming the People — A421

Technical Innovation A422

Mining Industry A423

Building Homes — A424

1963, Dec. 5 Engr. *Perf. 12½*
With Gum

491	A421	5ch dp rose red	.55	.20
492	A422	10ch red brown	3.50	.20
493	A423	10ch gray violet	1.90	.30
494	A424	10ch gray black	3.75	.30
		Nos. 491-494 (4)	9.70	1.00

Seven-Year Plan.

Sowing Gourd Seeds A425

Saving a Swallow A426

Swallow Carrying Gourd Seed A427

Sawing Gourd A428

Treasure Pouring from Gourd A429

1963, Dec. 5 Litho. *Perf. 10¾*

495	A425	5ch	multicolored	1.25	.30
496	A426	10ch	multicolored	2.50	.30
497	A427	10ch	multicolored	2.50	.30
498	A428	10ch	multicolored	1.90	.30
499	A429	10ch	multicolored	1.90	.30
			Nos. 495-499 (5)	10.05	1.50

Tale of Hung Bu.

Pistol Shooting A430

Small-Caliber Rifle Shooting — A431

Rifle Shooting A432

1963, Dec. 15

500	A430	5ch	multicolored	.65	.20
501	A431	10ch	multicolored	1.25	.20
502	A432	10ch	multicolored	1.25	.20
			Nos. 500-502 (3)	3.15	.60

Marksmanship Competition.

Chongjin Mill — A433

Sinuiju Mill — A434

1964, Jan. 10 Engr. *Perf. 12½*

With Gum

503	A433	10ch	brn violet	1.25	.20
504	A434	10ch	gray	1.25	.20

Chemical fiber industry.

A435

Wonsan General Strike, 35th Anniv.

1964, Jan. 14

With Gum

505	A435	10ch	brown	1.40	.25

A436

Korean Alphabet, 520th Anniv.

1964, Jan. 15 Litho. *Perf. 10¾*

506	A436	10ch	multicolored	1.40	.25

A437

Lenin's Death, 40th Anniv.

1964, Jan. 22 Engr. *Perf. 12½*

With Gum

507	A437	10ch	rose red	1.10	.25

Whaler A438

Trawler A439

Purse-Seine Boat — A440

Dragnet Boat A441

1964, Feb. 10 Litho. *Perf. 10¾*

508	A438	5ch	multicolored	1.60	.20
509	A439	5ch	multicolored	1.60	.20
510	A440	10ch	multicolored	3.25	.30
511	A441	10ch	multicolored	3.25	.30
			Nos. 508-511 (4)	9.70	1.00

Korean fishing industry.

A442

March 1 Popular Uprising, 45th Anniv.

1964, Feb. 10 Engr. *Perf. 12½*

With Gum

512	A442	10ch	dark violet	1.10	.25

A443

Kabo Peasant War, 70th Anniv.

1964, Feb. 15

With Gum

513	A443	10ch	violet black	1.10	.25

A444

Students' and Children's Palace, Pyongyang

1964, Mar. 3

With Gum

514	A444	10ch	grnsh black	.85	.25

5th Congress, Democratic Youth League of Korea — A445

1964, May 12 Litho. *Perf. 10¾*

515	A445	10ch	multicolored	1.10	.25

A446

Electric Train

1964, May 21

516	A446	10ch	multicolored	10.00	.35

Electrification of Railway between Pyongyang and Sinuiju.

A447

Popular Movement in Chongsan-ri

1964, June 4 Engr. *Perf. 12½*

With Gum

517	A447	5ch	chestnut	275.00	125.00

Drum Dance — A448

Dance of Ecstasy — A449

Small Drum Dance — A450

1964, June 15 Litho. *Perf. 10¾*

518	A448	2ch	multicolored	1.60	.50
519	A449	5ch	multicolored	2.50	.50
520	A450	10ch	multicolored	3.25	.50
			Nos. 518-520 (3)	7.35	1.50

Korean folk dances.

A451

For the Sake of the Fatherland

1964, June 15 Engr. *Perf. 12½*

With Gum

521	A451	5ch	carmine red	1.90	.20

Li Su Bok, soldier.

Nampho Smelter A452

Hwanghae Iron Works A453

1964

With Gum

522	A452	5ch	bronze green	6.50	.20
523	A453	10ch	gray	4.50	.20

Issued: 5ch, 6/15. 10ch, 10/15.

A454

Asian Economic Seminar, Pyongyang

Design: 10ch, Flags, industrial skyline and cogwheel.

1964, June 15 Litho. ***Perf. 10¾***

524 A454 5ch multicolored .90 .20
525 A454 10ch multicolored 1.40 .20

A455

Koreans and Statue of Kang Ho Yong, War Hero

1964, June 25

526 A455 10ch multicolored 1.60 .20

Korean Reunification

Domestic Poultry — A456

Designs: 2ch, Chickens. 4ch, White chickens. 5ch (#529), Black chickens. No. 530, Varicolored chickens. 40ch, Helmet guineafowl.

1964, Aug. 5

527-531 A456 Set of 5 7.75 2.00

9th Winter Olympic Games, Innsbruck A457

Designs: 5ch, Skier. 10ch (#533), Slalom skier. 10ch (#534), Speed skater.

1964, Aug. 5

532-534 A457 Set of 3 4.50 .50

Flags & "Tobolsk," Repatriation Ship — A458

Welcoming Repatriates A459

1964, Aug. 13

535 A458 10ch multicolored 2.50 .20
536 A459 30ch multicolored 2.50 .20

5th anniversary of agreement for the repatriation of Korean nationals in Japan.

Thonggun Pavilion, Uiju — A460

Inphung Pavilion, Kanggye City — A461

1964, Aug. 22 Engr. ***Perf. 12½***
With Gum

537 A460 5ch black violet .75 .20
538 A461 10ch emerald .90 .20

Korean historic sites.

A462

18th Olympic Games, Tokyo

Designs: 2ch, Rifleman. 5ch, Cyclists, vert. 10ch (#541), Runner. 10ch (#542), Wrestlers, vert.. 40ch, Volleyball, vert.

Photo, Centers Litho

1964, Sept. 5 ***Perf. 10¾***

539-543 A462 Set of 5 5.50 1.00

Nos. 539-543 exist imperf. Value, $18 unused, $5 canceled.

A463

Sinking of the *General Sherman,* 1866

1964, Sept. 28 Engr. ***Perf. 12½***
With Gum

544 A463 30ch red brown 6.00 .50

Kim Il Sung & Guerrilla Fighters A464

Kim Il Sung Speaking to Peasants A465

Battle of Xiaowangqing — A466

1964, Sept. 28 Engr. ***Perf. 12½***
With Gum

545 A464 2ch brt violet .65 .20
546 A465 5ch blue 1.00 .20
547 A466 10ch grnsh black 1.10 .20
Nos. 545-547 (3) 2.75 .60

Revolutionary paintings.

A467

Kwangju Students' Uprising, 35th Anniv.

1964, Oct. 15
With Gum

548 A467 10ch blue violet 2.25 .20

Weight Lifter — A468

Runner — A469

Boxers A470

Soccer Goalie A471

GANEFO Emblem A472

1964, Oct. 15 Litho. ***Perf. 10¾***

549 A468 2ch multicolored .65 .20
550 A469 5ch multicolored .65 .20
551 A470 5ch multicolored .65 .20
552 A471 10ch multicolored 1.40 .20
553 A472 10ch multicolored 1.10 .20
Nos. 549-553 (5) 4.45 1.00

1st Games of New Emerging Forces (GANEFO), Djakarta, Indonesia, 1963.

Nos. 549-553 exist imperf. Value, $12 unused, $5 canceled.

Wild Animals A473

Animals: 2ch, Lynx. 5ch, Leopard cat. 10ch (#556), Yellow-throated marten. 10ch (#559), Leopard.

1964, Nov. 20 Engr. ***Perf. 12½***
With Gum

554-557 A473 Set of 4 14.50 1.00

Fighting South Vietnam A474

1964, Dec. 20 Litho. ***Perf. 10¾***

558 A474 10ch multicolored 1.40 .20

Support for North Vietnam.

Prof. Kim Bong Han A475

"Bonghan" Duct — A476

"Bonghan" Corpuscle A477

1964, Dec. 20 Photo. ***Perf. 10¾***

559 A475 2ch olv grn & brown 1.00 .20
560 A476 5ch multicolored 1.40 .20
561 A477 10ch multicolored 2.00 .20
Nos. 559-561 (3) 4.40 .60

Kyongrak Biological System.

Technical Revolution — A478

Ideological Revolution — A479

Cultural Revolution — A480

1964, Dec. 30 Litho.

562 A478 5ch multicolored .30 .20
563 A479 10ch multicolored .55 .20
564 A480 10ch multicolored .55 .20
Nos. 562-564 (3) 1.40 .60

Ideological, Technical and Cultural Revolutions in the Countryside.

"For Arms" A481

1964, Dec. 30 Engr. ***Perf. 12½***
With Gum

565 A481 4ch brown 1.10 .20

Revolutionary painting.

Consumer Goods — A482

Livestock Breeding A483

"All for the Grand Chollima March" — A484

1964, Dec. 30 Litho. *Perf. 10¾*

566 A482 5ch multicolored 1.60 .20
567 A483 10ch multicolored 1.60 .20
568 A484 10ch multicolored 1.10 .20
Nos. 566-568 (3) 4.30 .60

Seven-Year Plan.

No. 566 was issued with gum, Nos. 567 and 568 without gum.

Nos. 566-568 also exist imperf. Value, unused $100.

Battle of Luozigou A485

Battle of Fusong County Seat A486

Battle of Hongqihe A487

1965, Jan. 20 Engr. *Perf. 12½*
With Gum

569 A485 10ch dp slate green 1.10 .20
570 A486 10ch deep violet 1.10 .20
571 A487 10ch slate violet 1.10 .20
Nos. 569-571 (3) 3.30 .60

Guerrilla warfare against Japan 1934-1940.

Tuman River A488

Taedong River — A489

Amnok River A490

1965, Feb. 27 Litho. *Perf. 10¾*

572 A488 2ch multicolored .85 .20
573 A489 5ch multicolored 3.25 .20
574 A490 10ch multicolored 1.40 .20
Nos. 572-574 (3) 5.50 .60

Korean rivers.

A491

1st Congress of the Union of Agricultural Working People of Korea

1965, Mar. 25
With Gum

575 A491 10ch multicolored 1.60 .20

Furnacemen, Workers — A492

1965, Mar. 25
With Gum

576 A492 10ch multicolored 1.10 .20

Ten Major Tasks of Seven-Year Plan.

Sinhung Colliery A493

Tanchou A494

1965, Mar. 31 Engr. *Perf. 12½*
With Gum

577 A493 10ch olive black 1.90 .20
578 A494 40ch violet 1.90 .20

35th anniversary of workers' uprisings.

Sunhwa River Works A495

1965, Mar. 31 Litho. *Perf. 10¾*
With Gum

579 A495 10ch multicolored .85 .20

A496

A497

South Korean Uprising of April 19, 5th Anniv.

1965, Apr. 10
With Gum

580 A496 10ch multicolored .85 .20
581 A497 40ch multicolored 1.40 .20

Nos. 580-581 exist imperf. Value, $5 unused.

A498

Construction of Pyongyang Thermal Power Station

1965, Apr. 10
With Gum

582 A498 5ch dp brn & lt blue 2.10 .20

No. 582 exists imperf. Value, $5 unused.

1st Afro-Asian Conf., Bandung, 10th Anniv. — A499

1965, Apr. 18
With Gum

583 A499 10ch multicolored .95 .20

Crowd Rejoicing — A500

Japanese Koreans Demonstrating for Reunification — A501

1965, Apr. 27 Photo.
With Gum

584 A500 10ch blue & red 1.10 .20
585 A501 40ch multicolored 1.40 .20

10th Anniv. of the General Association of Koreans in Japan.

Nos. 584-585 exist imperf. Value, $25 unused.

Workers Demonstrating — A502

1965, May 10 Engr. *Perf. 12½*
With Gum

586 A502 10ch brown 2.75 .20

35th Anniv. of General Strike at Pyongyang Rubber Goods Factory.

Workers in Battle — A503

Korean & African Soldiers A504

1965, June 20 Photo. *Perf. 10¾*
With Gum

587 A503 10ch multicolored 1.75 .20
588 A504 40ch multicolored 3.25 .30

2nd Asian-African Conference, Algiers (subsequently canceled).

Nos. 587-588 exist imperf. Value, $18 unused.

A505

Victory-64 10-Ton Truck

1965, June 20 Engr. *Perf. 12½*
With Gum

589 A505 10ch grnsh blue 2.50 .20

Kim Chang Gol A506

Jo Kun Sil A507

An Hak Ryong A508

1965, June 20
With Gum

590	A506	10ch slate	.85	.20
591	A507	10ch red brown	.85	.20
592	A508	40ch violet	2.75	.30
		Nos. 590-592 (3)	4.45	.70

War heroes.
See Nos. 775-777 and 827-830.

A509

Postal Ministers' Conference, Peking

1965, June 20 Photo. *Perf. 10¾*
With Gum

593	A509	10ch red, yel & blk	2.25	.30

Lake Samil A510

Jipson Peak A511

Kwanum Waterfalls A512

1965, June 20 Litho.
With Gum

594	A510	2ch multicolored	.95	.20
595	A511	5ch multicolored	1.60	.20
596	A512	10ch multicolored	4.50	.25
		Nos. 594-596 (3)	7.05	.65

Diamond Mountain Scenery.

Nos. 594-596 exist imperf. Value, unused $100.

Kusimuldong — A513

Lake Samji A514

Photo.
1965, June 20
With Gum

597	A513	5ch slate blue	.85	.20
598	A514	10ch grnsh blue	1.10	.20

Revolutionary battle sites.

Soccer Player — A515

Emblem & Stadium — A516

1965, Aug. 1 Litho.
With Gum

599	A515	10ch multicolored	1.60	.20
600	A516	10ch multicolored	1.60	.20

GANEFO Games, Pyongyang.

Nos. 599-600 exist imperf, with gum. Value, $20 unused.

A517

Liberation from Japan, 20th Anniv.

1965, Aug. 15
With Gum

601	A517	10ch multicolored	1.10	.20

Friedrich Engels, 145th Anniv. Birth — A518

1965, Sept. 10 Engr. *Perf. 12½*
With Gum

602	A518	10ch brown	.55	.20

Sports — A519

Designs: 2ch, Pole vault. 4ch, Javelin. 10ch (#605), Discus. 10ch (#606), High jump. 10ch (#607), Shot put.

1965, Sept. 24 Litho. *Perf. 11*
With Gum

603-607	A519	Set of 5	4.50	1.00

Nos. 603-607 exist imperf, without gum. Value. $18 unused.

Korean Workers' Party, 20th Anniv. — A520

Designs: 10ch (#608), Korean fighters. 10ch (#609), Party emblem. 10ch (#610), Lenin & Marx. 10ch (#611), Workers marching. 10ch (#612), Soldiers & armed workers. 40ch, Workers.

Illustration reduced.

1965, Oct. 10 Photo. *Perf. 13X13½*
With Gum

608-613	Set of 6	11.00	5.00
a.	A520 block of 6, #608-613	55.00	25.00
b.	Souvenir sheet of 6, #608-613	600.00	*400.00*

Chongjin Steel Mill A521

Kim Chaek Iron Works A522

1965, Nov. 25 Engr. *Perf. 12½*
With Gum

614	A521	10ch deep violet	5.50	.20
615	A522	10ch sepia	5.50	.20

Rainbow Trout — A523

Dolly Trout — A524

Grass Carp — A525

Carp — A526

Manchurian Trout — A527

Crucian Carp — A528

1965, Dec. 10 Photo. *Perf. 13½*
With Gum

616	A523	2ch multicolored	.85	.20
617	A524	4ch multicolored	1.00	.20
618	A525	10ch multicolored	2.25	.20
619	A526	10ch multicolored	2.25	.20
620	A527	10ch multicolored	2.25	.20
621	A528	40ch multicolored	3.75	.50
		Nos. 616-621 (6)	12.35	1.50

Freshwater fishes.

Nos. 616-621 exist imperf, without gum. Value $20 unused.

House Building — A529

Hemp Weaving — A530

Blacksmith A531

Wrestling A532

School — A533

Dance — A534

1965, Dec. 15 Engr. *Perf. 12½*
With Gum

622	A529	2ch green	.70	.20
623	A530	4ch maroon	1.40	.20
624	A531	10ch violet	1.75	.20
625	A532	10ch carmine red	2.00	.20
626	A533	10ch blue	1.25	.20
627	A534	10ch brown	1.10	.20
		Nos. 622-627 (6)	8.20	1.20

Paintings by Kim Hong Do, 18th century Korean artist.

Students' Extracurricular Activities A535

Designs: 2ch, Children in workshop. 4ch, Boxing. 10ch (#630), Playing violin. 10ch (#631), Chemistry lab.

1965, Dec. 15 Litho. *Perf. 13¼*
With Gum

628-631 A535 Set of 4 3.00 .50

Nos. 628-631 exist imperf. Value, unused $75.

Whaler A536

Service Vessel A537

1965, Dec. 15 Engr. *Perf. 12½*
With Gum

632	A536	10ch deep blue	1.90	.25
633	A537	10ch slate green	1.90	.25

Korean fishing boats.

Black-capped Kingfisher — A538

Korean Great Tit — A539

Blue Magpie A540

White-faced Wagtail A541

Migratory Korean Grosbeak A542

Perf. 11, 13½ (#640)
1965, Dec. 30 Litho.
With Gum

634	A538	4ch pale yel & multi	2.50	.20
635	A539	10ch pale salmon & multi	3.25	.25
636	A540	10ch pale grnsh blue & multi	3.25	.25
637	A541	10ch yel & multi	3.25	.25
638	A542	40ch pale yel grn & multi	9.50	.85
		Nos. 634-638 (5)	21.75	1.80

Korean birds.

Nos. 634-638 exist imperf, without gum. Value $27.50 unused.

Korean sericulture — A543

Designs: 2ch, Silkworm moth & cocoon. No. 640, 10ch, Ailanthus silk moth. No. 641, 10ch, Chinese Oak silk moth.

1965, Dec. 30 Engr. *Perf. 12½*
With Gum

639-641 A543 Set of 3 100.00 3.00

Hooded Crane — A544

Japanese White-necked Crane — A545

Manchurian Crane — A546

Gray Heron — A547

1965, Dec. 30
With Gum

642	A544	2ch olive brown	3.25	.20
643	A545	10ch dp vio blue	3.75	.40
644	A546	10ch slate purple	3.75	.40
645	A547	40ch slate green	6.50	.70
		Nos. 642-645 (4)	17.25	1.70

Wading birds.

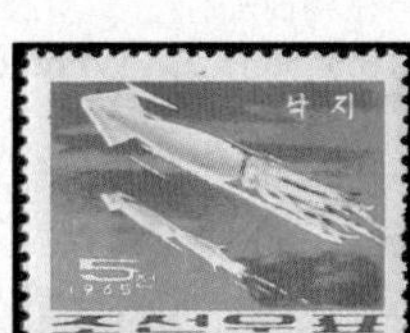
Mollusks A548

Designs: 5ch, Japanese common squid. 10ch, Giant Pacific octopus.

1965, Dec. 31 Litho. *Perf. 11*
With Gum

646-647 A548 Set of 2 5.50 .40

Nos. 646-647 exist imperf, without gum. Value $8 unused.

Korean Ducks — A549

Designs: 2ch, Spotbill. 4ch, Ruddy shelduck. 10ch, Mallard. 40ch, Baikal teal.

1965, Dec. 31 Litho. *Perf. 11*
With Gum

648-651 A549 Set of 4 16.50 2.00

Nos. 648-651 exist imperf. Value $30 unused.

Circus, Pyongyang — A550

Trapeze Performers A551

Balancing Act — A552

Seesawing A553

Tightrope Walker — A554

1965, Dec. 31 Photo.

652	A550	2ch multicolored	.85	.20
653	A551	10ch multicolored	2.25	.20
654	A552	10ch multicolored	2.25	.20
655	A553	10ch multicolored	2.25	.20
656	A554	10ch multicolored	2.25	.20
		Nos. 652-656 (5)	9.85	1.00

Korean acrobatics.

Nos. 652-655 were issued with gum, No. 656 without gum.

Korean Flowers — A555

Designs: No. 657, 4ch, Marvel-of-Peru. No. 658, 10ch, Peony (violet background). No. 659, 10ch, Moss rose (yellow background). No. 660, 10ch, Magnolia (light blue background).

1965, Dec. 31 Litho.

657-660 A555 Set of 4 13.00 1.00

No. 657 was issued without gum, Nos. 658-60 with gum.

Nos. 657-660 exist imperf, without gum. Value $20 unused.

Yachts — A556

Designs: No. 661, 2ch, Finn Class. No. 662, 10ch, Dragon Class (blue background). No. 663, 10ch, 5.5 Class (violet background). No. 664, 40ch, Star Class.

1965, Dec. 31 *Perf. 13½*
With Gum

661-664 A556 Set of 4 6.50 2.00

Nos. 661-664 exist imperf, without gum. Value $10 unused.

10ch depicting Netherlands class yacht, with blue background, not issued. Value $750.

A557

1st Congress of the Org. of Solidarity of Peoples of Asia, Africa and Latin America

1966, Jan. 3 *Perf. 11*
With Gum

665 A557 10ch multicolored .55 .20

Hosta — A558

Dandelion — A559

Lily of the Valley — A560

Pink Convolvulus A561

Catalpa Blossom — A562

1966, Jan. 15
With Gum

666	A558	2ch multicolored	1.40	.25
667	A559	4ch multicolored	1.40	.25
668	A560	10ch multicolored	1.90	.25
669	A561	10ch multicolored	1.90	.25
670	A562	40ch multicolored	6.00	.75
		Nos. 666-670 (5)	12.60	1.75

Korean wildflowers.
Imperfs exist, without gum. Value, $25 unused.

Primrose — A563

Brillian Campion — A564

Amur Pheasant's Eye — A565

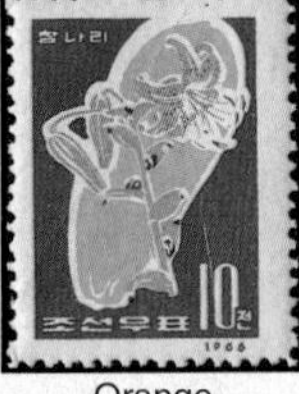
Orange Lily — A566

Rhododendron A567

1966, Feb. 10
With Gum

671	A563	2ch multicolored	1.10	.20
672	A564	4ch multicolored	1.10	.20
673	A565	10ch multicolored	1.60	.20
674	A566	10ch multicolored	1.60	.20
675	A567	90ch multicolored	7.75	1.00
		Nos. 671-675 (5)	13.15	1.80

Korean wildflowers.

A568

Land Reform Law, 20th Anniv.

1966, Mar. 5
With Gum

676	A568	10ch multicolored	1.00	.20

Battle of Jiansanfen A569

Battle of Taehongdan — A570

Battle of Dashahe A571

1966, Mar. 25 Engr. *Perf. 12½*

677	A569	10ch violet brown	.65	.20
678	A570	10ch dp blue green	.65	.20
679	A571	10ch brown carmine	.65	.20
		Nos. 677-679 (3)	1.95	.60

Battles of the anti-Japanese revolution.
No. 678 was issued without gum, the other values with gum.

A572

Art Treasures of the Silla Dynasty

Designs: 2ch, Covered bowl. 5ch, Jar. 10ch, Censer.

1966, Apr. 30
With Gum

680-682	A572	Set of 3	5.00	.60

Labor Day, 80th Anniv. — A573

1966, May 1 Litho. *Perf. 11*
With Gum

683	A573	10ch multicolored	.85	.20

Assoc. for the Restoration of the Fatherland, 30th Anniv. — A574

1966, May 5 Photo.
With Gum

684	A574	10ch brn red & yel	.85	.20

Farmer A575

Worker A576

1966, May 30 Litho.
With Gum

685	A575	5ch multicolored	.55	.20
686	A576	10ch multicolored	.85	.20

A577

Korean Children's Union, 20th Anniv.

1966, June 6
With Gum

687	A577	10ch multicolored	.85	.20

Kangson Steel Works A578

Pongung Chemical Works A579

1966, June 10 Engr. *Perf. 12½*
With Gum

688	A578	10ch gray	5.50	.20
689	A579	10ch deep red	5.50	.20

Korean Factories.

Fish — A580

Designs: 2ch, Saury. 5ch, Pacific cod. No. 692, Chum salmon. No. 693, Mackerel. 40ch, Pink salmon.

1966, June 10 Photo. *Perf. 11*

690-694	A583	Set of 5	16.50	5.00

Nos. 690-692 were issued with gum, Nos. 693-694 without gum.
Nos. 690-694 exist imperf, without gum. Value, $22, either unused or cancelled.

Prof. Kim Bong Han & Kyongrak Biological System — A581

Illustration reduced.

1966, June 30 Photo.
With Gum

695-702	Set of 8	6.50	1.60
a.	A581 Block of 8, #695-702	12.00	9.00
b.	Souvenir sheet of 8, #695-702	125.00	100.00

Voshkod 2 A582

Luna 9 A583

Luna 10 A584

1966, June 30

703	A582	5ch multicolored	.35	.20
704	A583	10ch multicolored	1.10	.30
705	A584	40ch multicolored	1.90	.40
		Nos. 703-705 (3)	3.35	.90

Space Flight Day.
Nos. 703-705 exist imperf. Value, $8 unused.

Jules Rimet Cup A585

Dribbling A586

Goal-keeper A587

1966, July 11 Litho.

706	A585	10ch multicolored	1.90	.25
707	A586	10ch multicolored	1.90	.25
708	A587	10ch multicolored	1.90	.25
		Nos. 706-708 (3)	5.70	.75

World Cup Championship.
Nos. 706-708 exist imperf. Value, $20 unused.

Battle of Naphalsan A588

Battle of Seoul A589

Battle of Height 1211 A590

1966, July 27 Engr. *Perf. 12½*
With Gum

709	A588	10ch red violet	.85	.20
710	A589	10ch deep green	.85	.20
711	A590	10ch violet	.85	.20
		Nos. 709-711 (3)	2.55	.60

Korean War of 1950-53.

A591

Sex Equality Law, 20th Anniv.

1966, July 30 Litho. *Perf. 11*
With Gum

712	A591	10ch multicolored	.85	.20

Nationalization of Industry, 20th Anniv. — A592

1966, Aug. 10
With Gum

713	A592	10ch multicolored	1.10	.20

Water Jar Dance — A593

Bell Dance — A594

Dancer in Mural Painting — A595

Sword Dance — A596

Golden Cymbal Dance — A597

1966, Aug. 10

714	A593	5ch multicolored	1.60	.20
715	A594	10ch multicolored	2.75	.20
716	A595	10ch multicolored	2.75	.20
717	A596	15ch multicolored	2.75	.20
718	A597	40ch multicolored	5.00	.30
		Nos. 714-718 (5)	14.85	1.10

Korean Folk Dances.

5ch and 10ch issued with or without gum. Other values issued without gum.

Nos. 714-718 exist imperf, without gum. Value, $20 unused.

Attacking U.S. Soldier — A598

Worker with Child — A599

Industrialization A600

1966, Aug. 15 Engr. *Perf. 12½*
With Gum

719	A598	10ch deep green	1.40	.20
720	A599	10ch red violet	1.40	.20
721	A600	10ch violet	6.50	.45
		Nos. 719-721 (3)	9.30	.85

Korean Reunification Campaign.

Crop-spraying — A601

Observing Forest Fire — A602

Geological Survey — A603

Fish Shoal Detection A604

1966, Sept. 30 Photo. *Perf. 11*

722	A601	2ch multicolored	.55	.20
723	A602	5ch multicolored	7.75	.20
724	A603	10ch multicolored	1.90	.20
725	A604	40ch multicolored	1.90	.20
		Nos. 722-725 (4)	12.10	.80

Industrial uses of aircraft.

2ch, 5ch issued without gum. 10ch, 40ch issued with gum.

Nos. 722-725 exist imperf, without gum. Value, $20 unused.

A three-value set honoring revolutionary fighters, with designs similar to types A334-A339, was prepared but not issued. Value $3,500.

Kim Il Sung University, 20th Anniv. — A605

1966, Oct. 1 Engr. *Perf. 12½*
With Gum

726	A605	10ch slate violet	.90	.20

Imperforate Stamps

Imperforate varieties are without gum, unless otherwise noted.

A606

1st Asian GANEFO Games

Designs: 5ch, Judo. No. 728, Basketball. No. 729, Table tennis.

1966, Oct. 30 Litho. *Perf. 11*

727-729	A606	Strip of 3	2.25	.60
		Strip of 3, #727-729 imperf	50.00	—

Scarlet Finch — A607

Hoopoe — A608

Korean Crested Lark — A609

Brown Thrush A610

White-bellied Black Woodpecker A611

1966, Oct. 30

730	A607	2ch multicolored	2.50	.20
731	A608	5ch multicolored	2.75	.20
732	A609	10ch multicolored	3.25	.30
733	A610	10ch multicolored	3.25	.30
734	A611	40ch multicolored	6.50	.80
		Nos. 730-734 (5)	18.25	1.80
		Set of 5, imperf	35.00	—

Korean birds.

Construction — A612

Machine-Tool Production — A613

Worker & Graph A614

Miners A615

1966, Nov. 20

735	A612	5ch multicolored	.35	.20
736	A613	10ch multicolored	.60	.20
737	A614	10ch multicolored	.60	.20
738	A615	40ch multicolored	1.90	.40
		Nos. 735-738 (4)	3.45	1.00

Propaganda for increased production.

Nos. 735-737 issued with gum. No. 738 issued without gum.

Parachuting — A616

Show Jumping A617

Motorcycling — A618

Telegraphists' Competition — A619

1966, Nov. 30 Engr. *Perf. 12½*
With Gum

739 A616 2ch dark brown .95 .20
740 A617 5ch org vermilion .70 .20
741 A618 10ch dp violet blue 3.25 .30
742 A619 40ch deep green 2.25 .25
Nos. 739-742 (4) 7.15 .95

National Defense sports.

Samil Wolgan Magazine, 30th Anniv. — A620

1966, Dec. 1 Photo. *Perf. 11*
743 A620 10ch multicolored — —

Korean Deer — A621

Designs: 2ch, Red deer. 5ch, Sika deer. 10ch (#746), Reindeer (grazing). 10ch (#747), Japanese sambar (erect). 70ch, Fallow deer.

1966, Dec. 20 Litho.
744-748 A627 Set of 5 20.00 5.00
Imperf, #744-748 — —

No. 747 was issued with gum. Other values issued without gum.

Wild Fruit — A622

Designs: 2ch, Blueberries. 5ch, Pears. 10ch (#751), Plums. 10ch (#752), Schizandra. 10ch (#753), Raspberries. 40ch, Jujube.

1966, Dec. 30
749-754 A622 Set of 6 6.50 1.00
Imperf, #749-754 14.00 —

Samson Rocks — A623

Ryonju Pond — A624

Jinju Pond — A625

The Ten Thousand Rocks, Manmulsang A626

1966, Dec. 30 Litho. *Perf. 11*
755 A623 2ch multicolored 1.10 .20
756 A624 4ch multicolored 4.50 .20
757 A625 10ch multicolored 1.10 .20
758 A626 10ch multicolored 4.50 .20
Nos. 755-758 (4) 11.20 .80

Diamond Mountains scenery.

Nos. 755-758 are inscribed "1964" but were actually issued in 1966.

2ch and 4ch issued without gum. 10ch values issued with gum.

Onpo A627

Myohyang — A628

Songdowon — A629

Hongwon A630

1966, Dec. 30 Engr. *Perf. 12½*
With Gum

759 A627 2ch blue violet .50 .20
760 A628 4ch turquoise green .55 .20
761 A629 10ch dp blue green .90 .20
762 A630 40ch black 1.60 .35
Nos. 759-762 (4) 3.55 .95

Korean rest homes.

Korean People's Army, 19th Anniv. A631

1967, Feb. 8 Photo. *Perf. 11*
763 A631 10ch multicolored .85 .20

Livestock Farming A632

Designs: 5ch, Sow. 10ch, Goat. 40ch, Bull.

1967, Feb. 28 Litho.
764-766 A632 Set of 3 7.50 1.75
Imperf, #764-766 55.00 —

5ch, 10ch issued without gum. 40ch issued both with and without gum.

Battle of Pochonbo, 30th Anniv. — A633

1967, Feb. 28 Photo.
With Gum

767 A633 10ch multicolored .85 .20

Universal Compulsory Technical Education A634

1967, Apr. 1
768 A634 10ch multicolored .85 .20

29th World Table Tennis Championships, Pyongyang — A635

10ch, 40ch designs similar to 5ch.

1967, Apr. 11 Litho.
769-771 A635 Set of 3 3.50 .60
Imperf, #769-771 100.00 —

5ch issued with or without gum. 10ch, 40ch issued without gum.

People Helping Guerrillas, Wangyugou — A636

Blowing Up Railway Bridge A637

Shooting Down Japanese Plane A638

1967, Apr. 25 Engr.
With Gum

772 A636 10ch deep violet .55 .20
773 A637 10ch dk vio brown 4.50 .25
774 A638 10ch slate .55 .20
Nos. 772-774 (3) 5.60 .65

Paintings of the guerrilla war against Japan.

Ri Tae Hun A639

Choe Jong Un A640

Kim Hwa Ryong A641

1967, Apr. 25
With Gum

775 A639 10ch slate 1.10 .20
776 A640 10ch reddish violet 3.25 .20
777 A641 10ch ultramarine 1.10 .20
Nos. 775-777 (3) 5.45 .60

Heroes of the Republic.

Labor Day A642

1967, May 1 Litho.
778 A642 10ch multicolored .80 .20

Pre-School Education — A643

Designs of children: 5ch, Learning to count. 10ch, Making model tractor. 40ch, Playing with ball.

1967, June 1
779-781 A643 Set of 3 4.00 .60

Victory Monument, Battle of Pochonbo — A644

1967, June 4

782 A644 10ch multicolored 1.10 .20

Military Sculpture A645

Designs: 2ch, Soldier attacking tank. 5ch, Soldiers with musical instruments. 10ch, Soldier in heroic pose. 40ch, Soldier and child.

1967, June 25 **Photo.**

783-786 A645 Set of 4 3.25 .80

2ch issued with or without gum. Other values issued without gum.

Medicinal Plants — A646

Designs: 2ch, Polygonatum japonicum. 5ch, Abelmoschus manihat. 10ch (#789), Scutellaria baicalensis (turquoise blue background). 10ch (#790), Rehmannia glutinosa (olive yellow). 10ch (#791), Pulsatilla koreana (violet blue). 40ch, Tanacetum boreale.

1967, July 20 **Photo.**

787-792 A646 Set of 6 12.50 1.20

Nos. 787-789, 791 issued with or without gum. Nos. 790, 792 issued without gum.

Korean People's Army — A647

Designs: 5ch, Aviator, sailor, soldier. 10ch (#794), Officer decorating soldier. 10ch (#795), Soldier and farmer.

1967, July 25

793-795 A647 Set of 3 1.60 .50

5ch issued with or without gum. 10ch values issued without gum.

Freighter "Chollima" A648

1967, July 30 **Engr.**

With Gum

796 A648 10ch deep green 1.90 .20

Drilling Rock — A649

Felling Trees — A650

Reclaiming Tideland — A651

1967, Aug. 5

797 A649 5ch black brown .65 .20
798 A650 10ch blue green .90 .20
799 A651 10ch slate 1.25 .20
Nos. 797-799 (3) 2.80 .60

Revolutionary paintings.

5ch issued without gum. 10ch values issued with gum.

Crabs A652

Designs: 2ch, Erimaculus isenbeckii. 5ch, Neptunus trituberculatus. 10ch, Paralithodes camtschatica. 40ch, Chionoecetes opilio.

1967, Aug. 10 **Photo.**

800-803 A652 Set of 4 8.75 1.00

Reunification of Korea Propaganda — A653

1967, Aug. 15 **Litho.**

804 A653 10ch Multicolored 4.00 .40

A five-value set, featuring details from famous Korean paintings of the 15th-16th centuries, was prepared for release in August, 1967, but was not issued. Value $2,500.

A 10ch stamp celebrating the 10th anniversary of the launch of the first USSR space satellite was prepared for release on Sept. 10 but was not issued. Value $1,500.

Waterfalls A654

Designs: 2ch, Tongrim waterfalls 10ch, Sanju waterfall, Mt. Myohyang. 40ch, Sambang waterfall, Mt. Chonak.

1967, Oct. 10

805-807 A654 Set of 3 13.00 .80

2ch issued with or without gum. 10ch, 40ch issued without gum.

"For Fresh Great Revolutionary Upsurge" — A655

Designs: 5ch, Ship, train and truck. 10ch (#809), Machine industry. 10ch (#810), Truck, bulldozer, tractor and farmers. 10ch (#811), Construction machinery, buildings. 10ch (#812), Chollima flying horse and banners.

1967, Nov. 1 **Engr.**

808-812 A655 Set of 5 11.00 1.00

Russian Revolution, 50th Anniv. — A656

1967, Nov. 7 **Photo.**

813 A656 10ch Multicolored 1.10 .20

Korean Elections — A657

Designs: 10ch (#814), Voters and flags. 10ch (#815), Woman casting ballot (vert.)

1967, Nov. 23 **Litho.**

814-815 A657 Set of 2 1.40 .40

Raptors A658

Designs: 2ch, Black vulture. 10ch, Rough-legged buzzard. 40ch, White-tailed eagle.

1967, Dec. 1 **Photo.**

816-818 A658 Set of 3 16.00 2.00

2ch issued with or without gum. 10ch, 40ch issued without gum.

Chongjin — A659

Hamhung — A660

Sinuiju A661

1967, Dec. 20 **Engr.**

With Gum

819 A659 5ch bronze green 1.10 .20
820 A660 10ch violet 1.10 .20
821 A661 10ch red violet 1.10 .20
Nos. 819-821 (3) 3.30 .60

Korean cities.

Whaler Firing Harpoon A662

1967, Dec. 30

With or Without Gum

822 A662 10ch ultramarine 2.50 .30

Soldier with Red Book A663

Soldier Mounting Bayonet — A664

Worker and Bayoneted Rifle — A665

Litho or Photo (#829)

1967, Dec. 30

823	A663 10ch multicolored		.55	.20
824	A664 10ch multicolored		.55	.20
825	A665 10ch multicolored		.55	.20
	Nos. 823-825 (3)		1.65	.60

Korean People's Army, 20th Anniv. — A666

Designs: a, Airman, soldier and sailor. b, Soldier, battle in background. c, Soldier & KDPR arms. d, Soldier & flag. e, Soldier with Red Book. f, Three soldiers, North Korean flag. g, Soldier & worker. h, Soldier saluting. i, Soldier attacking. j, Soldier, sailor & airman beneath flag.

Illustration reduced.

1968, Feb. 3 **Litho.**

826	A666 Sheet of 10	80.00	*30.00*
a.-j.	10ch, any single	.45	.20

Ri Su Bok (1934-51) — A667

Han Kye Ryol (1926-51) — A668

1968, Feb. 10 **Engr.**

With Gum

827	A667 10ch dark rose	*550.00*	
828	A667 10ch light violet	.55	.20
829	A668 10ch dark green	550.00	
830	A668 10ch lt blue violet	.55	.20
	Nos. 827-830 (4)	1,101.	.40

War heroes.

Nos. 827 and 829 were prepared but not issued.

Apartment Building, Pyongyang — A669

1968, Mar. 5 **Litho.**

With Gum

831	A669 10ch bright blue	.85	.20

A670

Kim Il Sung, 56th Birthday

1968, Apr. 15

With Gum

832	A670 40ch multicolored	1.10	.40

Printed in sheets of four stamps.

Exists in a miniature sheet of one, which is rare (2 examples reported),

Kim Il Sung's Family Home in Mangyongdae — A671

Leaving Home at Age 13 — A672

Mangyong Hill — A673

Kim Il Sung with Father — A674

Kim Il Sung with Mother — A675

1968, Apr. 15

833	A671 10ch multicolored	.65	.20
834	A672 10ch multicolored	.65	.20
835	A673 10ch multicolored	.65	.20
836	A674 10ch multicolored	.65	.20
837	A675 10ch multicolored	.65	.20
	Nos. 833-837 (5)	3.25	1.00

Childhood of Kim Il Sung.

See Nos. 883-887, 927-930.

Dredger *2 September* A676

1968, June 5

838	A676 5ch green	1.60	.20
839	A676 5ch blue	*850.00*	*600.00*

Matsutake Mushroom A677

Shiitake Mushroom — A678

Meadow Mushroom A679

1968, Aug. 10 **Photo.**

With Gum

840	A677 5ch multicolored	22.50	.60
841	A678 10ch multicolored	45.00	1.00
842	A679 10ch multicolored	45.00	1.00
	Nos. 840-842 (3)	112.50	2.60

Founding of the Korean Democratic People's Republic, 20th Anniv. — A680

Designs: a, Statue of national arms. b, North Korean flag. c, Worker, peasant & flag. d, Soldier & flag. e, Flying Horse of Chollima. f, Soldiers & tanks. g, Battle scene. h, Workers, banner & monument.

Illustration reduced.

1968, Sept. 2 **Litho.**

With Gum

843	A680 Block of 8, #a.-h.	45.00	*40.00*
a.-h.	10ch, any single	1.40	.20

A681

Kaesong Students' and Children's Palace

1968, Oct. 5

With Gum

844	A681 10ch greenish blue	.55	.20

Domestic Goods — A682

Designs: 2ch, Shopper with domestic items. 5ch, Textile manufacturing. 10ch, Cannery.

1968, Nov. 5 **Photo.**

With Gum

845-847	A688 Set of 3	2.75	.60

A683

Kim Il Sung's 10-Point Program

Design: 10ch, Two soldiers, Red Book, horiz.

1968, Dec. 5 **Litho.**

848-849	A683 Set of 2	1.10	.20

Increasing Agricultural Production — A684

Designs: 5ch, Woman carrying eggs. 10ch (#851), Woman harvesting wheat. 10ch (#852), Woman holding basket of fruit.

1968, Dec. 10 **Photo.**

With Gum

850-852	A684 Set of 3	1.40	.50

Shellfish A685

Designs: 5ch (#853), Scallop. 5ch (#854), Clam. 10ch, Mussel.

1968, Dec. 20

With Gum

853-855	A685 Set of 3	6.50	.50

Details of Battle of Pochonbo Victory Monument — A686

Designs (all 10ch): #856, Kim Il Sung at head of columns, vert. #857, shown. #858, Figures marching to right, green sky at right (42.75x28mm). #859, Figures marching to left (55.5x28mm). #860, Figures marching to right

(55.5x28mm). #861, Figures marching to left, sky at right (42.75x28mm). #862, Figures marching to left, sky at left (42.75x28mm).

1968, Dec. 30
856-862 A686 Set of 7 3.75 1.40

Grand Theater, Pyongyang — A687

1968, Dec. 30
863 A687 10ch dark brown 1.10 .20

Revolutionary Museum, Pochonbo — A688

1968, Dec. 30
864 A688 2ch dark green .55 .20

Rural Technical Development — A689

Designs: 2ch, Irrigation. 5ch, Mechanization of agriculture. 10ch, Electrification. 40ch, Mechanical fertilization and spraying.

1969, Feb. 25
865-868 A689 Set of 4 2.50 .80

Rabbits A690

Designs: 2ch, Gray rabbits. 10ch (#870), White rabbits. 10ch (#871), Black rabbits. 10ch (#872), Brown rabbits. 40ch, White rabbits.

1969, Mar. 10
869-873 A690 Set of 5 11.00 1.25

Nos. 869-873 were issued both with and without gum.

Public Health A691

Designs: 2ch, Old man & girl. 10ch, Nurse with syringe. 40ch, Doctor with woman & child.

1969, Apr. 1
874-876 A691 Set of 3 4.50 .60

Farm Machines — A692

Designs: 10ch (#877), Rice sower. 10ch (#878), Rice harvester. 10ch (#879), Herbicide sprayer. 10ch (#880), Wheat & barley thresher.

1969, Apr. 10 **Engr.**
877-880 A692 Set of 4 3.50 .80

Mangyongdae — A693

Ponghwa — A694

1969, Apr. 15 **Litho.**
881 A693 10ch multicolored 1.90 .20
882 A694 10ch multicolored 1.90 .20

Revolutionary historical sites.

Early Revolutionary Years of Kim Il Sung — A695

Designs (all 10ch): #883, Kim crossing into Manchuria 1926, aged 13. #884, Kim talking to four students around table (blue green frame). #885, Kim speaking outdoors to Young Communist League meeting (apple green frame). #886, Kim speaking to Young Communist League meeting indoors (lilac frame). #887, Kim leading demonstration against teachers (peach frame).

1969, Apr. 15
883-887 A695 Set of 5 3.25 1.00

No. 884 was issued with gum. The other values were issued without gum.

Mrs. Kang Pan Sok (1892-1932), Mother of Kim Il Sung — A696

Designs (all 10ch): #888, Birthplace at Chilgol. #889, Resisting Japanese police in home. #890, Meeting with women's revolutionary association.

1969, Apr. 21 **Photo.**
888-890 A696 Set of 3 4.50 .60

A697

Bivouac Sites in War against Japan

Designs: 5ch, Pegaebong. 10ch (#892), Mupho, horiz. 10ch (#893), Chongbong. 40ch, Konchang, horiz.

1969, Apr. 21
891-894 A697 Set of 4 3.00 .80

Chollima Statue — A698

1969, May 1
895 A698 10ch blue .85 .20

Poultry A699

Designs: 10ch (#896), Mangyong chickens. 10ch (#897), Kwangpho ducks.

1969, June 1 **Engr.**
896-897 A699 Set of 2 5.75 .50

Socialist Education System — A700

Designs: 2ch, Kim Il Sung & children. 10ch, Student & worker with books. 40ch, Male & female students, figure "9."

1969, June 1 **Photo.**
898-900 A700 Set of 3 2.25 .60

Pochonbo Battlefield Memorials — A701

Designs: 5ch, Machine gun platform on mountainside. 10ch (#902), Statue of Kim Il Sung, vert. 10ch (#903), Aspen Tree monument (stele & enclosed tree trunk). 10ch (#904), Konjang Hill monument (within forest).

1969, June 4
901-904 A701 Set of 4 2.25 .80

Kim Hyong Jik (1894-1926), Father of Kim Il Sung — A702

Designs: 10ch (#905), Teaching at Myongsin School. 10ch (#906), Outdoor meeting with five other members of Korean National Association.

1969, July 10
905-906 A702 Set of 2 1.90 .40

A 10ch stamp honoring the Juvenile Chess Game of Socialist Countries was prepared for release Aug. 5, 1969, but was not issued. Value $1,000.

Sports Day, 20th Anniv. — A703

1969, Sept. 10
907 A703 10ch multicolored 1.10 .20

Korean Revolution Museum, Pyongyang A704

1969, Sept. 10 **Litho.**
908 A704 10ch dk blue green .85 .20

Pres. Nixon Attacked by Pens — A705

1969, Sept. 18 **Litho.**
909 A705 10ch multi 3.25 .20

Anti-U.S. Imperialism Journalists' Conference, Pyongyang.

Implementation of the 10-Point Program — A706

Designs: 5ch, Soldiers, battle. 10ch (#911), Globe, bayonets attacking dismembered U.S. soldier. 10ch (#912), Workers holding Red Books & slogan, vert.

1969, Oct. 1 **Photo.**
910-912 A706 Set of 3 3.25 .60

Reunification of Korea — A707

Designs: 10ch (#913), Kim Il Sung, marching workers. 10ch (#914), Worker & soldier bayoneting U.S. soldier. 50ch, Armed workers in battle, horiz.

1969, Oct. 1 **Litho.**
913-915 A707 Set of 3 1.60 .60

Refrigerator-Transport Ship "Taesongsan" — A708

1969, Dec. 20 **Engr.**
916 A708 10ch slate purple 1.40 .20

Korean Fishes A709

Designs: 5ch, Yellowtail. 10ch, Dace. 40ch, Mullet.

1969, Dec. 20 **Photo.**
917-919 A709 Set of 3 6.00 .60

Guerrilla Conference Sites A710

Designs: 2ch, Dahuangwai, 1935. 5ch, Yaoyinggou, 1935 (log cabin). 10ch, Xiaohaerbaling, 1940 (tent).

1970, Feb. 10
920-922 A710 Set of 3 1.40 .45

Mt. Paektu, Birthplace of the Revolution — A711

Views of Mt. Paektu (all 10ch): #923, Lake Chon (dull green, tan, black). #924, Janggun Peak (pale peach, dull blue, black). #925, Piryu Peak (dull yellow, blue green, black). #926, Pyongsa Peak (brown orange, blue, red violet).

1970, Mar. 10
923-926 A711 Set of 4 2.75 .60

See Nos. 959-961.

Support for North Vietnam — A712

1970, Mar. 10
927 A712 10ch multicolored .65 .20

Revolutionary Activities of Kim Il Sung — A713

Designs (all 10ch): #928, Receiving his father's pistols from his mother. #929, Receiving smuggled pistols from his mother (other young revolutionaries present). #930, Kim speaking with four farmers in field. #931, Kim speaking at Kalun meeting.

1970, Apr. 15 **Litho.**
928-931 A713 Set of 4 5.50 .90

Lenin Birth Centenary A714

Design: 10ch (#933), Lenin with cap, in three-quarter profile.

1970, Apr. 22 **Photo.**
932-933 A714 Set of 2 1.60 .40

Assoc. of Koreans in Japan, 15th Anniv. — A715

Designs (both 10ch): #934, Red. #935, Maroon.

1970, Apr. 27 **Engr.**
934-935 A715 Set of 2 1.40 .40

Worker-Peasant Red Guard — A716

Design: 10ch (#936), Factory worker in uniform, vert.

1970, May 5 **Photo.**
936-937 A716 Set of 2 1.10 .40

Peasant Education — A717

Designs: 2ch, Students & newspapers. 5ch, Peasant reading book. 10ch, Students in class.

1970, June 25
938-940 A717 Set of 3 1.60 .45

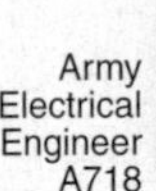

Army Electrical Engineer A718

1970, June 25
941 A718 10ch purple brown .85 .20

Month of the Campaign for Withdrawal of U.S. Troops from South Korea — A719

Design: 10ch, Soldier & partisan.

1970, June 25
942-943 A719 Set of 2 1.50 .20

Anti-U.S., South Korea Propaganda — A720

1970, June 25 **Engr.**
944 A720 10ch deep violet .65 .20

Campaign for Increased Productivity A721

Designs (all 10ch): #945, Quarryman. #946, Steelworker. #947, Machinist. #948, Worker with bag. #949, Construction worker. #950, Railway flagman.

1970, Sept. 10 **Photo.**
945-950 A721 Set of 6 4.50 1.20

Workers' Party Program A722

Designs: 5ch, Peasant, farm scene. 10ch, Steelworker. 40ch, Soldiers.

1970, Oct. 5 **Engr.**
951-953 A722 Set of 3 4.00 .50

Korean Workers' Party, 25th Anniv. — A723

1970, Oct. 10 **Photo.**
954 A723 10ch multicolored .85 .20

5th Korean Workers' Party Congress — A724

Issued in miniature sheet of 10, with one 40ch value (#955a) and nine 10ch values. Designs: a, Kim Il Sung, marchers. b, Family & apartment buildings. c, Soldier with Red Book. d, Soldier with binoculars, various weapons. e, Steelworker. f, Workers killing U.S. soldier. g, Farmers. h, Students. i, Schoolgirl with Red Book, atomic energy symbol. j, Cooperation with South Korean guerillas.

1970, Nov. 2 **Litho.**
955 Sheet of 10, #a.-j. 900.00
a.-i. A724 Any single 1.40 .50
j. A724 10ch 600.00

Soon after release, a design error was discovered on No. 955j, and this stamp was removed from souvenir sheets remaining in stock, usually with the bottom selvage. This is the form in which this set is commonly offered. Value, $25. The full sheet of 10 is scarce.

League of Socialist Working Youth of Korea, 25th Anniv. — A725

1971, Jan. 17 **Photo.**
956 A725 10ch multicolored .55 .20

Nanhutou Conference, 35th Anniv. — A726

1971, Feb. 28
957 A726 10ch multicolored .55 .20

Land Reform Law, 25th Anniv. A727

1971, Mar. 5
958 A727 2ch multicolored .55 .20

Mt. Paektu, Second Issue — A728

Designs: 2ch, Mountainscape. 5ch, Paektu Waterfalls, vert. 10ch, Western Peak.

1971, Mar. 10
959-961 A728 Set of 3 5.00 .60

Revolutionary Museums — A729

Designs (all 10ch): #962, Mangyongdae (red orange & ultramarine). #963, Phophyong (yellow & brown). #964, Junggang (salmon & green).

1971, Apr. 1
962-964 A729 Set of 3 1.60 .60

Coal Production 6-Year Plan — A730

1971, Apr. 1
965 A730 10ch multicolored .85 .20

Revolutionary Activities of Kim Il Sung — A731

Designs (all 10ch): #966, Portrait, vert. #967, Kim addressing crowd at guerrilla base camp. #968, Kim speaking with children on hillside. #969, Kim reviewing Anti-Japanese Guerrilla Army 1932.

1971, Apr. 15 **Litho.**
966-969 A731 Set of 4 3.25 .80

May Day — A732

1971, May 1 **Photo.**
970 A732 1w multicolored 3.75 .40

Association for the Restoration of the Fatherland, 35th Anniv. — A733

1971, May 5
971 A733 10ch multicolored .85 .20

Battles in the Musan Area Command (1939) — A734

Designs: 5ch, Sinsadong Monument. 10ch, Taehongdan Monument, with encased machine guns, horiz. 40ch, Musan headquarters (log cabins in forest), horiz.

1971, May 23
972-974 A734 Set of 3 2.25 .60

Koreans in Japan A735

1971, May 25
975 A735 10ch chocolate .65 .20

A 10ch stamp commemorating the Asia-Africa Invitational Table Tennis Game for Friendship was prepared for release on May 27, 1971, but was not issued. Value $750.

Korean Children's Union, 25th Anniv. — A736

1971, June 6
976 A736 10ch multicolored .55 .20

6th Congress, League of Socialist Working Youth of Korea — A737

Designs: 5ch, Marchers & banners. 10ch, Marchers, banners & globe with map of Korea.

1971, June 21
977-978 A737 Set of 2 1.10 .25

Labor Law, 25th Anniv. A738

1971, June 24
979 A738 5ch multicolored .60 .20

Sex Equality Law, 25th Anniv. A739

1971, July 30
980 A739 5ch multicolored .60 .20

A740

Universal Compulsory Primary Education, 15th Anniv.

1971, Aug. 1
981 A740 10ch multicolored .70 .20

South Korean Revolutionaries — A741

Designs: 5ch, Choe Yong Do (1923-69). 10ch (#983), Kim Jong Thae (1926-69), portrait with rioters killing U.S. soldier. 10ch (#984), Guerrilla fighter with machine gun & Red Book, battle scene.

1971, Aug. 1
982-984 A741 Set of 3 1.40 .45

Nationalization of Industry, 25th Anniv. — A742

1971, Aug. 10
985 A742 5ch multicolored 2.75 .20

Anti-Imperialist, Anti-U.S. Struggle — A743

Designs: 10ch (#986), N. Korean soldier, U.S. prisoners. 10ch (#987), S. Korean guerrilla fighter. 10ch (#988), N. Vietnamese soldiers, map. 10ch (#989), Cuban soldier, map. 10ch (#990), African guerrilla fighters, map. 40ch, six soldiers of various nationalities bayoneting dismembered U.S. soldier.

1971, Aug. 12
986-991 A743 Set of 6 5.00 1.00

Kim Il Sung University, 25th Anniv. A744

1971, Oct. 1
992 A744 10ch multicolored .55 .20

Large Machines — A745

Designs: 2ch, 6,000-ton press. 5ch, Refrigerated cargo ship "Ponghwasan." 10ch (#995), Sungrisan heavy truck. 10ch (#996), Bulldozer.

1971, Nov. 2 **Litho.**
993-996 A745 Set of 4 6.50 .50

Tasks of the 6-Year Plan — A746

Designs (all 10ch): #997, Workers & text on red field. #998, Mining. #999, Consumer goods. #1000, Lathe. #1001, Construction equipment. #1002, Consumer electronic products. #1003, Grains, farming. #1004, Railway track, transportation. #1005, Freighter. #1006, Hand with wrench, manufacturing scenes. #1007, Crate & export goods on dock.

1971, Nov. 2 **Photo.**
997-1007 A746 Set of 11 14.50 1.75

Cultural Revolution — A747

Designs: 2ch, Technical students, university. 5ch, Mechanic. 10ch (#1010), Chemist. 10ch (#1011), Composer at piano. 10ch (#1012), Schoolchildren.

1971, Nov. 2
1008-1012 A747 Set of 5 4.50 .40

Ideological Revolution — A748

Designs (all 10ch): #1013, Workers with Red Books, banners. #1014, Worker with hydraulic drill. #1015, Two workers reading Red Book. #1016, Workers' lecture.

1971, Nov. 2
1013-1016 A748 Set of 4 2.50 .40

Improvement in Living Standards — A749

1971, Nov. 2
1017 A749 10ch multicolored .60 .20

Solidarity with International Revolutionary Forces — A750

Designs (all 10ch): #1018, Revolutionary placards being driven into U.S. soldier. #1019, Japanese militarists being hammered by mallet. #1020, Bayoneted rifles held aloft. #1021, Armed international revolutionaries advancing, horiz.

1971, Nov. 2
1018-1021 A750 Set of 4 3.25 .50

6-Year Plan — A751

1971, Nov. 2
1022 A751 10ch multicolored 1.75 .20

Three sets were prepared for release on Nov. 2, 1971, but were not issued: Butterflies (3 stamps), value $2,500; Korean Reunification (2 10ch stamps), value $750; Cultural Revolution/Improvement of the People's Living Standards (7 10ch stamps), value $5,000.

Samil Wolgan Monthly, 35th Anniv. — A752

1971, Dec. 1
1023 A752 10ch multicolored 1.10 .20

Domestic Printings

Sometime in the early 1970s, the DPRK post office begin to produce separate printings of some issues for domestic use. These stamps were generally printed on poorer quality white or brownish unsurfaced papers and demonstrated poorer overall production values. Serious students of the period are now working to identify just which stamps exist in this form and how to easily distinguish them from the higher-quality printings intended for sale to foreign collectors. At this time, these domestic-use printings are generally sold for $5-$20 per stamp.

Poultry Breeding — A753

Designs: 5ch, Chicks. 10ch, Chickens & automated henhouse. 40ch, Eggs, canned chicken, dead chickens hanging on hooks.

1972, Feb. 1
1024-1026 A753 Set of 3 2.25 .60

War Films A754

Designs (all 10ch): #1027, Man & woman, from *Vintage Shrine.* #1028, Guerrilla bayoneting soldier in back, from *The Fate of a Self-Defense Corps Member.* #1029, Young woman with a pistol, from *Sea of Blood.*

1972, Apr. 1
1027-1029 A754 Set of 3 3.75 .30

A 10ch value picturing *The Flower Girl* was prepared but not issued. Value $2,000.

Kim Il Sung A755

Kim at Military Conference — A756

Kim by Lake Chon — A757

Various portraits of Kim Il Sung: #1030, shown. #1031, In heroic pose. #1032, shown. #1033, In wheatfield. #1034, In factory. #1035, With foundry workers. #1036, Aboard whaling ship. #1037, Visiting hospital. #1038, Visiting fruit farm. #1039, With railroad surveyors. #1040, With women workers. #1041, Sitting with villagers. #1042, Touring chicken plant. #1043, On park bench with children. #1044, Portrait with marchers.

No. 1045, illustration reduced.

1972, Apr. 15 **Litho.**

1030	A755	5ch multicolored	.20	.20
a.		Strip of 3, #1030-1031, 1044	2.25	
1031	A755	5ch multicolored	.20	.20
1032	A756	5ch multicolored	.20	.20
a.		Pair, #1032, 1043	1.10	
1033	A756	10ch multicolored	.50	.20
a.		Block of 10, #1033-1042	10.00	
1034	A756	10ch multicolored	2.25	.40
1035	A756	10ch multicolored	.20	.20
1036	A756	10ch multicolored	.65	.20
1037	A756	10ch multicolored	1.00	.20
1038	A756	10ch multicolored	.20	.20
1039	A756	10ch multicolored	2.25	.20
1040	A756	10ch multicolored	1.40	.20
1041	A756	10ch multicolored	.20	.20
1042	A756	10ch multicolored	.45	.20
1043	A755	40ch multicolored	.60	.20
1044	A756	1wn multicolored	.90	.40
		Nos. 1030-1044 (15)	11.20	3.40

Souvenir Sheet

1045 A757 3wn multicolored 10.00 6.00

60th birthday of Kim Il Sung.

Nos. 1030-1031 and 1044, 1032 and 1043, and 1033-1042, respectively, were printed setenant within their sheets.

A 4-stamp set (2ch, 5ch, 10ch and 15ch values) honoring the 20th Olympic Games were prepared but not issued. Value $3,000.

Guerrilla Army, 40th Anniv. — A758

1972, Apr. 25 **Photo.**
1046 A758 10ch multicolored .95 .20

Revolutionary Sites — A759

Designs: 2ch, Ryongpho. 5ch, Onjong. 10ch, Kosanjin. 40ch, Jonsung.

1972, July 27 **Litho.**
1047-1050 A759 Set of 4 2.25 .50

Olympic Games, Munich A760

Designs: 2ch, Volleyball. 5ch, Boxing, horiz. 10ch (#1053), Judo. 10ch (#1054), Wrestling, horiz. 40ch, Rifle-shooting.

1972, Oct. 1
1051-1055 A760 Set of 5 3.75 1.00

Chollima Street, Pyongyang — A761

Designs (street scenes): 5ch, salmon & black. 10ch (#1057), dull yellow & black. 10ch (#1058), green & black.

1972, Nov. 1
1056-1058 A766 Set of 3 5.50 .85

Resource Management — A762

Designs: 5ch, Dredging river. 10ch, Forest conservation. 40ch, Tideland reclamation.

1972, Nov. 1 **Photo.**
1059-1061 A762 Set of 3 2.75 .35

6-Year Plan - Metallurgical — A763

Designs (all 10ch): #1062, Sheet metal, ingots, smelters. #1063, Pipes, foundry.

1972, Nov. 1
1062-1063 A763 Set of 2 3.75 .35

6-Year Plan — Mining Industry — A764

Designs (all 10ch): #1064, Iron ore. #1065, Coal.

1972, Nov. 1 **Litho.**
1064-1065 A764 Set of 2 4.50 .45

Three Major Goals of the Technical Revolution — A765

Designs (all 10ch): #1066, Agricultural mechanization. #1067, Industrial automation. #1068, Lightening of women's household chores.

1972, Nov. 2 **Photo.**
1066-1068 A765 Set of 3 3.25 .45

6-Year Plan - Machine-Building — A766

Designs (all 10ch): #1069, Machine tools. #1070, Electronics & automation tools. #1071, Single-purpose machines.

1972, Nov. 2 **Photo.**
1069-1071 A766 Set of 3 2.75 .45

6-Year Plan — Chemical Industry — A767

Designs (all 10ch): #1072, Chemical fertilizers, herbicides, insecticides. #1073, Tire, tubing, various chemical products.

1972, Nov. 2
1072-1073 A767 Set of 2 2.25 .35

6-Year Plan — Light Industry — A768

Designs (all 10ch): #1074, Clothing, textiles. #1075, Clothing, kitchenware. #1076, Household Goods.

1972, Nov. 2
1074-1076 A768 Set of 3 2.75 .45

6-Year Plan - Rural Economy — A769

Designs (all 10ch): #1077, Irrigating field. #1078, Bulldozers levelling field. #1079, Applying chemical fertilizer.

1972, Nov. 2 **Litho.**
1077-1079 A769 Set of 3 2.50 .45

6-Year Plan - Transportation — A770

Designs (all 10ch): #1080, Electric train. #1081, New railway construction. #1082, Coastal & river transport.

1972, Nov. 2
1080-1082 A770 Set of 3 6.50 .45

6-Year Plan - Military — A771

Designs (all 10ch): #1083, Soldier with artillery shell. #1084, Navy gunner. #1085, Air Force pilot in cockpit.

1972, Nov. 2
1083-1085 A771 Set of 3 4.50 .45

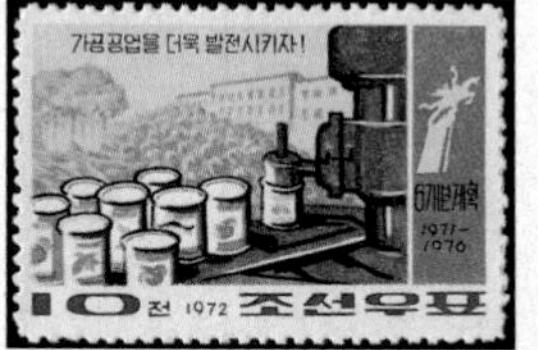

6-Year Plan - Food Storage — A772

Designs (all 10ch): #1086, Food Processing. #1087, Packing foodstuffs. #1088, Food storage (radishes, fruit, fish).

1972, Nov. 2 **Photo.**
1086-1088 A772 Set of 3 8.25 .45

Struggle for Reunification of Korea — A773

Designs (all 10ch): #1089, South Koreans with banners praising Kim Il Sung. #1090, S. Korean guerrillas killing U.S. & S. Korean soldiers. #1091, March of armed S. Korean workers. #1092, S. Koreans rioting, rioters on top of U.S. tank. #1093, N. Koreans demonstrating in support of S. Korean revolutionaries. #1094, International revolutionaries condemning U.S. soldier. #1095, S. Korean marchers carrying banner & Red Book.

1972, Nov. 2
1089-1095 A773 Set of 7 11.00 1.00

A 10ch anti-United States propaganda stamp was prepared for release Nov. 2, 1972, but not issued. Value $750.

Machine Tools A774

Designs: 5ch, Single-axis automatic lathe. 10ch, *Kusong-3* lathe. 40ch, 2,000-ton crank press.

1972, Dec. 1 **Litho.**
1096-1098 A774 Set of 3 2.75 .45

National Elections A775

Designs (both 10ch): #1099, Voter with registration card. #1100, Voter casting ballot.

1972, Dec. 12 **Photo.**
1099-1100 A775 Set of 2 1.90 .30

Korean People's Army, 25th Anniv. — A776

Designs: 5ch, Soldier. 10ch, Sailor. 40ch, Pilot.

1973, Feb. 8
1101-1103 A781 Set of 3 3.75 .75

Mangyongdae Historic Sites — A777

Scenes from Kim Il Sung's childhood: 2ch, Wrestling site. 5ch, "Warship" rock. 10ch (#1106), Swinging tree, vert. 10ch (#1107), Sliding rock. 40ch, Fishing spot on riverside.

1973, Apr. 15
1104-1108 A777 Set of 5 4.50 1.00

Mansu Hill Monument A778

Designs: 10ch (#1109), Anti-Japanese revolutionary monument. 10ch (#1110), Socialist Revolution & Construction monument. 40ch, Statue of Kim Il Sung. 3w, Korean Revolution Museum, hrz.

1973, Apr. 15 **Litho.**
1109-1112 A778 Set of 4 13.00 2.25

Secret Revolutionary Camps in the 1932 Guerrilla War — A780

Designs: 10ch (#1113), Karajibong Camp. 10ch (#1114), Soksaegoi Camp.

1973, Apr. 26
1113-1114 A780 Set of 2 1.40 .20

Anti-Japanese Propaganda — A781

1973, June 1
1115 A781 10ch multicolored .55 .20

Reunification of Korea — A782

Designs: 2ch, Finger pointing down at destroyed U.S. tanks. 5ch, Electric train, crane lifting tractor. 10ch (#1118), Hand holding declaration, map of Korea. 10ch (#1119), Leaflets falling on happy crowd. 40ch, Flag & globe.

1973, June 23
1116-1120 A782 Set of 5 6.50 .75

Trucks & Tractors A783

Designs: 10ch (#1121), Trucks. 10ch (#1122), Bulldozer, tractors.

1973, July 1 **Photo.**
1121-1122 A783 Set of 2 1.60 .30

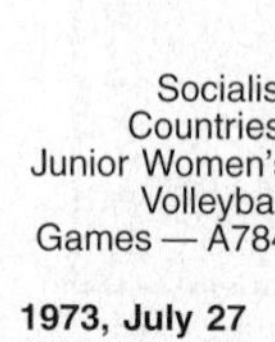

Socialist Countries' Junior Women's Volleyball Games — A784

1973, July 27 **Litho.**
1123 A784 10ch multicolored 1.10 .20

North Korean Victory in the Korean War A785

Designs: 10ch (#1124), Triumphant N. Koreans & battlefield scene. 10ch (#1125), N. Koreans & symbols of military & industrial power.

1973, July 27 **Photo.**
1124-1125 A785 Set of 2 3.25 .30

Mansudae Art Troupe — A786

Dances: 10ch, *Snow Falls*, dancers with red streamers. 25ch, *Bumper Harvest of Apples*. 40ch, *Azalea of the Fatherland*.

1973, Aug. 1 **Litho.**
1126-1128 A786 Set of 3 4.50 .75

Compulsory Secondary Education, 10th Anniv. A787

1973, Sept. 1
1129 A787 10ch multicolored .85 .20

Writings of Kim Il Sung — A788

Designs (all 10ch): #1130, *On Juche in Our Revolution* (claret scene). #1131, *Kim Il Sung Selected Works*, crowd holding glowing book aloft. #1132, *Let Us Further Strengthen Our Socialist System*, four figures holding open book aloft.

1973, Sept. 1
1130-1132 A788 Set of 3 1.90 .30

See Nos. 1180-1181.

DPRK, 25th Anniv. A789

Designs: 5ch, Foundation of the republic ("1948-1973"). 10ch, Korean War ("1950-1953"). 40ch, Farmer, worker & soldier with scenes of economic development in background ("1948-1973").

1973, Sept. 9
1133-1135 A789 Set of 3 2.75 .60

Mt. Myohyang Scenes — A790

Designs: 2ch, Popwang Peak. 5ch, Inhodae Rock. 10ch, Taeha Falls, vert. 40ch, Ryongyon Falls, vert.

1973, Oct. 1 **Photo.**
1136-1139 A790 Set of 4 8.25 .75

Party Founding Museum — A791

1973, Oct. 10
1140 A791 1w multicolored 2.25 .45

People's Athletic Meeting A792

Designs: 2ch, Soccer player, basketball players. 5ch, High jumper, women sprinters. 10ch (#1143), Wrestlers, skier. 10ch (#1144), Speed skaters, skier. 40ch, Parachutist, motorcyclists.

1973, Nov. 1 **Litho.**
1141-1145 A792 Set of 5 6.50 .75

Socialist Countries' Junior Weightlifting Competition A793

1973, Nov. 21
1146 A793 10ch multicolored 1.40 .20

Moran Hill Scenery — A794

Designs: 2ch, Chongryu Cliff. 5ch, Moran Waterfalls. 10ch, Pubyok Pavilion. 40ch, Ulmil Pavilion.

1973, Nov. 1
1147-1150 A794 Set of 4 9.25 1.00

Mt. Kumgang Scenery A795

Designs: 2ch, Mujigae (Rainbow) Bridge. 5ch, Suspension bridge, Okryu Valley, horiz. 10ch (#1153), Chonnyo Peak. 10ch (#1154), Chilchung Rock & Sonji Peak, horiz. 40ch, Sujong & Pari Peaks, horiz.

1973, Nov. 1
1151-1155 A795 Set of 5 8.25 1.00

Magnolia A796

1973, Nov. 1
1156 A796 10ch multicolored 2.25 .40

South Korean Revolutionary Struggle — A797

Designs (both 10ch): #1157, Mob beating U.S. soldier. #1158, Armed demonstrators killing U.S. soldier.

1973, Nov. 2 **Photo.**
1157-1158 A797 Set of 2 5.25 .30

Scenes from *Butterflies and Cock* Fairy Tale — A798

Designs: 2ch, Cock appearing in the village of butterflies. 5ch, Butterflies discussing how to repel cock. 10ch (#1161), Cock chasing butterflies with basket. 10ch (#1162), Butterflies luring cock up cliff. 40ch, Cock chasing butterflies off cliff edge. 90ch, Cock drowning.

1973, Dec. 1 **Litho.**
1159-1164 A798 Set of 6 17.50 1.20

Revolutionary Sites — A799

Designs: 2ch, Buildings, Yonphung. 5ch, Buildings, iron-rail fence, Hyangha. 10ch, Three buildings surrounding courtyard, Changgol. 40ch, Monuments in park-like setting, Paeksong.

1973, Dec. 1
1165-1168 A799 Set of 4 3.25 .60

Modern Buildings in Pyongyang — A800

Designs: 2ch, Science Library, Kim Il Sung University. 5ch, Building No. 2, Kim Il Sung University, vert. 10ch, War Museum. 40ch, People's Palace of Culture. 90ch, Pyongyang Indoor Stadium.

1973, Dec. 1 **Photo.**
1169-1173 A800 Set of 5 4.00 1.00

Socialist Constitution of North Korea — A801

Designs (all 10ch): #1174, Socialist Constitution, national scenes. #1175, Marchers with Red Book & national arms. #1176, Marchers with Red Books, national flag, banners.

1973, Dec. 27 **Litho.**
1174-1176 A801 Set of 3 1.60 .60

Korean Songbirds A802

Designs: 5ch, Great reed warbler. 10ch (#1178), Gray starling (green background). 10ch (#1179), Daurian starling (pink background).

1973, Dec. 28 **Photo.**
1177-1179 A802 Set of 3 14.50 2.00

Writings of Kim Il Sung A803

Designs (both 10ch): #1180, *Let Us Intensify the Anti-Imperialist, Anti-U.S. Struggle*, bayonets threatening U.S. soldier. #1181, *On the Chollima Movement and the Great Upsurge of Socialist Construction*,, Chollima statue.

1974, Jan. 10 **Litho.**
1180-1181 A803 Set of 2 1.60 .30

Opening of Pyongyang Metro — A804

Designs (all 10ch): #1182, Train at platform. #1183, Escalators. #1184, Underground station hall.

1974, Jan. 20
1182-1184 A804 Set of 3 2.75 .45

Socialist Construction — A805

Designs (all 10ch): #1185, Capital construction. #1186, Industry (foundry), vert. #1187, Agriculture. #1188, Transport. #1189, Fishing industry.

1974, Feb. 20
1185-1189 A805 Set of 5 6.50 1.00

Theses on the Socialist Rural Question in Our Country, 10th Anniv. of Publication — A806

Illustration reduced.

1974, Feb. 25
1190-1192 A806 10ch Strip of 3 2.75 .50

Farm Machines A807

Designs: 2ch, Compost sprayer. 5ch, *Jonjin* tractor. 10ch, *Taedoksan* tractor (with flat bed).

1974, Feb. 25 **Photo.**
1193-1195 A807 Set of 3 3.25 .45

N. Korean Victories at 1973 Sports Contests A808

Designs: 2ch, Archery (Grenoble). 5ch, Gymnastics (Varna). 10ch, Boxing (Bucharest). 20ch, Volleyball (Pyongyang). 30ch, Rifle-shooting (Sofia). 40ch, Judo (Tbilisi). 60ch, Model aircraft flying (Vienna), horiz. 1.50w, Table tennis (Beijing), horiz.

Perf. 11, 12 (#1200, 1206)

1974, Mar. 10 **Litho.**
1196-1203 A808 Set of 8 11.00 2.00

D.P.R.K.: World's First Tax-Free Country — A809

1974, Apr. 1 ***Perf. 11***
1204 A809 10ch multicolored 1.10 .20

Revolutionary Activities of Kim Il Sung — A810

Designs (all 10ch): #1205, Kim at Nanhutou Meeting (in log room). #1206, Kim writing the 10-Point Program in forest. #1207, Kim instructing revolutionary (sitting on bench, outdoor winter scene). #1208, Kim at Battle of Laoheishan.

1974, Apr. 15 *Perf. 12*
1205-1208 A810 Set of 4 3.00 .60

Scenes from the Revolutionary Opera *The Flower Girl* — A811

Designs: 2ch, Kkot Pun's blind younger sister. 5ch, Death of Kkot Pun's mother. 10ch, Kkot Pun resists landlord. 40ch, Kkot Pun setting out on the road of revolution.

1974, Apr. 30
1209-1212 A811 Set of 4 12.00 .60

Souvenir Sheet

1213 A811 50ch multicolored 16.50 1.50

No. 1213 contains one larger 50ch value, depicting Kroi Pun (The Flower Girl) and the flowers of Revolution, imperf.

Pyongyang Zoo, 15th Anniv. — A812

A813

Designs: 2ch, Wildcat. 5ch, Lynx. 10ch (#1216), Fox. 10ch (#1217), Wild boar. 20ch, Wolf. 40ch, Bear. 60ch, Leopard. 70ch, Korean tiger. 90ch, Lion.
No. 1223, illustration reduced.

1974, May 10 *Perf. 11*
1214-1222 A812 Set of 9 14.50 2.50

Souvenir Sheet

1223 A813 Sheet of 4, imperf 60.00 —

Wild Roses — A814

Designs: 2ch, Prickly wild rose. 5ch, Yellow sweet briar. 10ch (#1226), Pink aromatic rose. 10ch (#1227), Aronia sweet briar (yellow centers). 40ch, Rosa rugosa.

1974, May 20
1224-1228 A814 Set of 5 8.25 1.00

Kim Il Sung with Children — A815

Illustration reduced.

1974, June 1 *Imperf*
1229 A815 1.20w Souv. Sheet 8.25 7.50

Wild Flowering Plants — A816

Designs: 2ch, Chinese trumpet vine. 5ch, Day lily. 10ch, Shooting star lily. 20ch, Tiger lily. 40ch, Azalea. 60ch, Yellow day lily.

1974, May 20 *Perf. 11*
1230-1235 A816 Set of 6 8.25 1.00

U.P.U. Centenary — A817

Designs, U.P.U. emblem and: 10ch, Postwoman & construction site. 25ch, Chollima statue. 40ch, World map & airplanes.

1974, June 30 *Perf. 12*
1236-1238 A817 Set of 3 6.00 .50

A 60ch souvenir sheet was prepared but not issued. Value $750.

Amphibians — A818

Designs: 2ch, Black spotted frog. 5ch, Oriental fire belly toad. 10ch, North American bull frog. 40ch, Common toad.

1974, July 10 *Perf. 11*
1239-1242 A818 Set of 4 15.50 1.50

Soviet Space Flights — A819

Designs: 10ch, Electron 1 & 2. 20ch, Proton 1. 30ch, Venera 3. 40ch, Venera 5 & 6. 50ch, Launch of Chinese satellite Chicomsat 1. 1w, Space flight of dogs "Bjelka" and "Strjelka."

1974, July 10
1243-1246 A819 Set of 4 3.75 .60

Souvenir Sheets

Imperf

1247 A819 50ch multicolored 8.25 1.00
1248 A819 1w multicolored 18.50 3.00

Nos. 1247-1248 each contain one 47x72mm stamp.

Korean Paintings — A820

Designs: 2ch, *Woman in Namgang Village.* 5ch, *Old Man on the Raktong River.* 10ch, *Inner Kumgang in the Morning.* 20ch, *Mt. Kumgang.* 1.50w, *Evening Glow Over Kangson.*

1974, July 10
1249-1252 A820 Set of 4 5.75 .75

Souvenir Sheet

Imperf

1253 A820 1.50w multicolored 11.00 10.00

Korean Civil Aviation A821

Designs: 2ch, Antonov AN-2. 5ch, Lisunov LI-2. 10ch, Ilyushin IL-14P. 40ch, Antonov AN-24. 60ch, Ilyushin IL-18. 90ch, Antonov AN-24.

1974, Aug. 1
1254-1258 A821 Set of 5 9.25 1.75

Souvenir Sheet

Imperf

1259 A821 90ch multicolored 13.00 6.50

No. 1264 contains one 49x30mm stamp.

Alpine Plants — A822

Designs: 2ch, Rhododendron. 5ch, White mountain-avens. 10ch, Shrubby cinquefoil. 20ch, Poppies. 40ch, Purple mountain heather. 60ch, Oxytropis anertii.

1974, Aug. 10 *Perf. 12*
1260-1265 A822 Set of 6 7.00 1.75

Korean Paintings — A823

Designs: 10ch, *Sobaek Stream in the Morning.* 20ch, *Combatants of Mt. Laohei..* 30ch, *Spring on the Terraced Field.* 40ch, *Night of Tideland.* 60ch, *Daughter.*

1974, Aug. 15 *Perf. 11*
1266-1270 A823 Set of 5 12.00 2.00

Italian Communist Newspaper L'Unita, 50th Anniv. — A824

Illustration reduced.

1974, Sept. 1 *Imperf*
1271 A824 1.50w multicolored 24.50 5.00

Revolutionary Sites — A825

Designs: 5ch, Munmyong. 10ch, Unha (log cabin).

1974, Sept. 9 *Perf. 11*
1272-1273 A825 Set of 2 1.40 .20

Oil-producing Crops — A826

Designs: 2ch, Sesame. 5ch, Perilla-oil plant. 10ch, Sunflower. 40ch, Castor bean.

1974, Sept. 30
1274-1277 A826 Set of 4 5.50 1.00

Revolutionary Activities of Kim Il Sung — A827

Designs (all 10ch): #1278, Portrait in guerrilla uniform, vert. #1279, On horseback.

#1280, Helping a farm family. #1281, Negotiating anti-Japanese united front with Chinese commander.

1974, Oct. 10 ***Perf. 12***
1278-1281 A827 Set of 4 3.25 .60

No. 1278 is 42x65mm. Nos. 1279-1281 are 52x34.5mm.

Grand Monument on Mansu Hill — A828

Designs (all 10ch): #1282, Soldiers marching right, lead figure holding rifle aloft. #1283, Soldiers marching left, lead figure holding rifle aloft. #1284, Workers marching right, lead figure holding torch aloft. #1285, Workers marching left, lead figure holding torch aloft.

1974, Oct. 10 ***Perf. 11***
1282-1285 A828 Set of 4 2.75 .60

Deep-Sea Fishing — A829

Designs: a, 2ch, Factory ship *Chilbosan.* b, 5ch, Factory ship *Paektusan.* c, 10ch, Cargo ship *Moranbong.* d, 20ch, All-purpose ship. e, 30ch, Trawler. f, 40ch, Stern trawler.
Illustration reduced.

1974, Nov. 20
1286 A829 Block of 6 7.75 2.00
a.-f. Any single 1.25 .30

A830

Kim Il Sung's Crossing of the Amnok River, 50th Anniv.

1975, Feb. 3 ***Perf. 12***
1287 A830 10ch multicolored .65 .20

Pak Yong Sun — A831

33rd World Table Tennis Championships — A832

1975, Feb. 16 ***Perf. 11x12***
1288 A831 10ch multicolored 1.90 .20

Souvenir Sheet

Imperf

1289 A832 80ch multicolored 3.25 1.50

Honoring Pak Yong Sun, winner of the 33rd World Table Tennis Championship, Calcutta.

Pyongyang Zoo — A833

Designs: 10ch (#1290), Zebra. 10ch (#1291), African buffalo. 20ch, Giant panda, horiz. 25ch, Bactrian camel. 30ch, Indian elephant, horiz.

Perf. 12¼, 10¾ (#1291, 1294)

1975, Feb. 20
1290-1294 A833 Set of 5 6.25 1.00

Koguryo Period Tomb Paintings, 7th Century — A834

Designs: 10ch, Blue dragon. 15ch, White tiger. 25ch, Red phoenix, vert. 40ch, Turtle and snake.

1975, Mar. 20 ***Perf. 12***
1295-1298 A834 Set of 4 6.50 1.00

The Guerrilla Base in Spring(1968) — A835

Guerrilla Army Landing at Unggi (1969) — A836

The Sewing Team Members (1961) — A837

North Manchuria of China in Spring (1969) — A838

Comrade Kim Jong Suk Giving Guidance to the Children's Corps Members (1970) — A839

Illustrations reduced.

1975, Mar. 30

1299	A835 10ch multicolored	.55	.20
1300	A836 10ch multicolored	.55	.20
1301	A837 15ch multicolored	.85	.20
1302	A838 20ch multicolored	1.75	.20
1303	A839 30ch multicolored	1.40	.20
	Nos. 1299-1303 (5)	5.10	1.00

Korean Paintings, Anti-Japanese Struggle. Compare with Nos. 1325-1329, 1330-1335.

Cosmonauts' Day — A840

Designs: 10ch, Cosmonaut. 30ch, Lunokhod-2 on Moon, horiz. 40ch, Soyuz and Saiyut coupling, horiz.

1975, Apr. 12 ***Perf. 11¾***
1304-1306 A840 Set of 3 3.25 .50

Revolutionary Activities of Kim Il Sung — A841

Multicolor portraits of Kim Il Sung: 10ch (#1307), Speaking with troops in tent (aqua frame). 10ch (#1308), Greeting peasants bringing supplies (tan frame). 10ch (#1309), Speaking to crowd, arm upraised (light blue frame). 10ch (#1310), With soldiers around winter campfire (pale tan frame). 10ch (#1311), Lecturing to troops (pink frame). 15ch, At head of troop column in forest. 25ch, Standing by lake. 30ch, Speaking with peasants, child in lap. 40ch, Presiding over staff meeting, in tent.

1975, Apr. 15 ***Perf. 12***
1307-1315 A841 Set of 9 8.25 2.00

Souvenir Sheet

Victory Monument — A842

1975, Apr. 15 ***Imperf***
1316 A842 1w multicolored 16.50 4.00

Battle of Pochonbo, 38th Anniversary.
Illustration reduced.

Flower Basket & Kim Il Sung's Birthplace A843

Kim Il Sung's Birthplace, Mangyongdae — A844

Illustration of No. 1319 reduced. It is actually slightly larger than No. 1318.

1975, Apr. 15 ***Perf. 12***
1317 A843 10ch multicolored .35 .20
1318 A844 40ch multicolored 1.60 .20

63rd Birthday of Kim Il Sung.

April 19 South Korean Popular Uprising, 15th Anniv. — A845

1975, Apr. 19 *Perf. 11*

1319 A845 10ch multicolored .65 .20

Ri Dynasty Paintings A846

Designs: 5ch, *Kingfisher at Lotus Pond.* 10ch, *Crabs.* 15ch, *Rose of Sharon.* 25ch, *Lotus and Water Bird.* 30ch, *Tree Peony and Cock and Hen.*

1975, May 10

1320-1324 A846 Set of 5 13.00 1.25

On the Road of Advance Southward (1966) A847

The Assigned Post (1968) A848

For the Sake of the Fatherland (1965) — A849

Retaliation (1970) — A850

The Awaited Ranks (1970) — A851

Illustrations of Nos. 1325-1329 reduced.

1975, May 10

1325	A847	5ch multicolored	2.25	.20
1326	A848	10ch multicolored	1.25	.20
1327	A849	15ch multicolored	1.90	.20
1328	A850	25ch multicolored	2.75	.25
1329	A851	30ch multicolored	4.50	.25
		Nos. 1325-1329 (5)	12.65	1.10

Korean Paintings, Anti-Japanese Struggle.

Blue Signal Lamp (1960) A852

Pine Tree (1966) A853

Night with Snowfall (1963) — A854

Smelters (1968) — A855

Reclamation of Tideland (1961) — A856

Mt. Paekgum (1966) — A857

Illustrations of Nos. 1332-1335 reduced.

1975, May 20

1330	A852	10ch multicolored	1.10	.20
1331	A853	10ch multicolored	3.75	.20
1332	A854	15ch multicolored	1.10	.20
1333	A855	20ch multicolored	1.25	.20
1334	A856	25ch multicolored	1.25	.20
1335	A857	30ch multicolored	1.25	.20
		Nos. 1330-1335 (6)	9.70	1.20

Korean Paintings.

Chongryon Assoc. of Koreans in Japan, 20th Anniv. — A858

1975, May 25 *Perf. 11¾*

1336 A858 10ch multicolored 1.10 —

1337 A858 3w multicolored 40.00 —

Marathon Race of Socialist Countries — A859

1975, June 8 *Imperf*

1338 A859 1w multicolored 22.50 4.00

Illustration reduced.

Diving — A860

Divers: 10ch, Man entering water feet-first. 25ch, Man performing somersault pike. 40ch, Woman entering water head-first.

1975, June 20 *Perf. 10¾*

1339-1341 A860 Set of 3 3.25 .75

Month of Anti-U.S. Joint Struggle — A861

1975, June 25 *Perf. 12¼*

1342 A861 10ch multicolored 1.40 .20

Fresh-Water Fish — A862

Fish: 10ch (#1343), Memorial fish, swimming to left. 10ch (#1344), White fish, swimming to right. 15ch, Notch-jowl. 25ch, Amur catfish. 30ch (#1347), Catfish, swimming to right. 30ch (#1348), Snakehead, swimming to left.

1975, June 25 *Perf. 10¾*

1343-1348 A862 Set of 6 9.25 1.25

10th International Socialist Countries' Junior Friendship Soccer Tournament

A863

A864

Soccer players, with diff. stadiums in background: 5ch, Green border. 10ch, Tan border. 15ch, Lilac border. 20ch, Pale violet border. 50ch, Dull gold border.

Perf. 10¾, Imperf (#1354)

1975, July 10

1349-1353 A863 Set of 5 4.50 1.00

Souvenir Sheet

1354 A864 1w multicolored 9.25 3.50

Parrots — A865

Parrots: 10ch, Blue & yellow macaw. 15ch, Sulphur-crested cockatoo. 20ch, Blyth's parakeet. 25ch, Rainbow lory. 30ch, Budgerigar.

1975, July 10 *Perf. 12*

1355-1359 A865 Set of 5 19.50 1.50

Saesallim Street A866

Apartment House — A867

Pothonggang Hotel — A868

1975, July 20 *Perf. 11, 12 (#1360)*

1360	A866	90ch multicolored	20.00	20.00
1361	A867	1w multicolored	25.00	25.00
1362	A868	2w multicolored	35.00	35.00
		Nos. 1360-1362 (3)	80.00	80.00

New street, buildings in Pyongyang.

Blossoms A869

Blossoms of Flowering Trees: 10ch, White peach. 15ch, Red peach. 20ch, Red plum. 25ch, Apricot. 30ch, Cherry.

1975, Aug. 20 *Perf. 10¾*

1363-1367 A869 Set of 5 7.75 1.50

Diamond Mts. Landscapes A870

Designs: 5ch, Sejon Peak. 10ch, Chonson Rock. 15ch, Pisa Gate. 25ch, Manmulsang. 30ch, Chaeha Peak.

1975, Aug. 20 *Perf. 11¾*

1368-1372 A870 Set of 5 7.75 1.00

Flowers A871

Designs: 5ch, Azalea. 10ch, White azalea. 15ch, Mountain rhododendron. 20ch, White rhododendron. 25ch, Rhododendron. 30ch, Yellow rhododendron.

1975, Aug. 30 *Perf. 10¾*

1373-1378 A871 Set of 6 6.50 1.50

Aerial Sports for National Defence

A872

A873

Designs: 5ch (#1379), Gliders. 5ch (#1380), Remote-controlled model airplane. 10ch (#1381), Parachutist in free fall, vert. 10ch (#1382), Parachutists landing, vert. 20ch, Parachutist with bouquet of flowers.

50ch, Formation skydiving.

Perf. 12x11¾, Imperf (#1384)

1975, Sept. 9

1379-1383 A872 Set of 5 5.00 .75

Souvenir Sheet

1384 A873 50ch multicolored 6.00 .50

Flowers — A874

Fruit tree blossoms: 10ch, Wild apple. 15ch, Wild pear. 20ch, Hawthorn. 25ch, Chinese quince. 30ch, Flowering quince.

1975, Sept. 30 *Perf. 12¼x12*

1385-1389 A874 Set of 5 5.00 1.25

Korean Workers' Party, 30th Anniv. A875

Designs: 2ch (#1390), Symbolic creation of the Juche Idea. 2ch (#1391), Korean soldiers above American graves. 5ch (#1392), Hand holding torch with Juche inscription. 5ch (#1393), Monument of Chollima, idealized city. 10ch (#1394), Chollima winged horse and rider with banner. 10ch (#1395), Worker with Red Book. 25ch, South Koreans rioting. 70ch, Map of Korea, Red Book, flowers.

90ch (#1398), Kim Il Sung addressing workers, horiz. stamp, vert. souvenir sheet. 90ch (#1399), Kim with crowd of workers, city skyline in background, horiz. stamp, horiz. souvenir sheet.

Perf. 12, Imperf (#1398-1399)

1975, Oct. 10

1390-1397	A875	Set of 8	4.50	1.00
1398-1399	A875	Set of 2 sheets	8.25	4.00

Return of Kim Il Sung to Pyongyang, 30th Anniv. — A876

1975, Oct. 14 *Perf. 12*

1400 A876 20ch multicolored 1.00 .20

Redong Sinmun, 30th Anniv. — A877

1975, Nov. 1 *Perf. 11*

1401	A877	10ch multicolored	.85	.20
a.		1w, souvenir sheet, imperf	5.50	5.00

Hyonmu Gate A878

Taedong Gate A879

Pothong Gate A880

Jongum Gate A881

Chilsong Gate — A882

Perf. 12x12¼, 12¼x12 (#1406)

1975, Nov. 20

1402	A878	10ch multicolored	1.40	.20
1403	A879	10ch multicolored	1.40	.20
1404	A880	15ch multicolored	1.90	.20
1405	A881	20ch multicolored	3.50	.20
1406	A882	30ch multicolored	5.00	.40
		Nos. 1402-1406 (5)	13.20	1.20

Ancient gates of Pyongyang.

Mt. Chilbo Views — A883

Designs: 10ch (#1407), Mae Rock (pale green border). 10ch (#1408), Jangsu Peak (pale yellow border). 15ch, Suri Peak. 20ch, Jangsu Peak, diff. view. 30ch, Rojok Peak.

1975, Nov. 30 *Perf. 12x11¾*

1407-1411 A883 Set of 5 10.00 1.25

Wangjaesan Monument — A884

Designs: 10ch, Workers marching. 15ch, Soldiers marching. 25ch, Monument beacon tower, vert. 30ch, Base of tower, statues of Kim Il Sung, workers and soldiers.

Perf. 11¾, 10¾ (#1413)

1975, Dec. 20

1412-1415 A884 Set of 4 2.75 .75

Banners, Slogan — A885

Banners, Workers — A886

1976, Jan. 17 *Perf. 12*
1416 A885 2ch multicolored .30 .20
1417 A886 70ch multicolored 1.60 .75

League of Socialist Working Youth, 30th Anniv.

Ducks & Geese A887

Designs: 10ch, Geese. 20ch, Domesticated ducks. 40ch, Kwangpo ducks.

Perf. 12, 12x12¼ (#1418)

1976, Feb. 5
1418-1420 A887 Set of 3 8.25 .50

Korean People's Army, Sculpture A888

Designs: 5ch, *Oath.* 10ch (#1422), *Unity Between Men and Officers,* horiz. 10ch (#1423), *This Flag to the Height.*

Perf. 12, 12¼x12 (#1421)

1976, Feb. 8
1421-1423 A888 Set of 3 2.75 .50

Rural Road at Evening (1965) A889

Passing-on Technique (1970) — A890

Mother (1965) A891

Medical Examination in Kindergarten (1970) — A892

Doctress of the Village (1970) — A893

Illustrations of Nos. 1427-1428 reduced.

1976, Feb. 10 *Perf. 12*
1424 A889 10ch multicolored .65 .20
1425 A890 15ch multicolored .70 .20
1426 A891 25ch multicolored 1.10 .20
1427 A892 30ch multicolored 1.90 .20
1428 A893 40ch multicolored 2.25 .35
Nos. 1424-1428 (5) 6.60 1.15

Modern Korean paintings.

Agrarian Reform Law, 30th Anniv. — A894

1976, Mar. 5 *Perf. 12*
1429 A894 10ch multicolored .65 .20

Telephone Communication Centenary — A895

Designs: 2ch, Telephones and communication satellite. 5ch, Satellite and antenna. 10ch, Satellite and telecommunications systems. 15ch, Telephone and lineman. 25ch, Satellite and map of receiving stations. 40ch, Satellite and cable-laying barge.
50ch, Satellite and antique telephone.

Surface Coated Paper

1976, Mar. 12 *Perf. 13¼*
1430-1435 A895 Set of 6 8.75 1.00
1435a Sheet of 8, as #1430-1436 + label, ordinary paper 10.00 —

Souvenir Sheet

Imperf, Without Gum

1436 A895 50ch multicolored 3.25 .50

Flowers A896

Designs: 5ch, Cosmos. 10ch, Dahlia. 20ch, Zinnia. 40ch, China aster.

1976, Mar. 20 *Perf. 12*
1437-1440 A896 Set of 4 3.00 1.00

Pukchong Conference, 15th Anniv. — A897

Designs: 5ch, Fruit processing industry. 10ch, Fruit and orchards.

1976, Apr. 7 *Perf. 11½x12*
1441-1442 A897 Set of 2 2.25 .25

Locomotives — A898

Designs: 5ch, *Pulgungi* electric train. 10ch, *Jaju* underground electric train. 15ch, *Saeppyol* diesel locomotive.

1976, Apr. 10 *Perf. 11¾*
1443-1445 A898 Set of 3 3.25 .50

Many North Korean issues from 1976-on were also issued imperforate. These imperfs were issued for sale for hard currency, mostly to overseas collectors, and were not valid for postage.

Limited quantities of many sets from Scott No. 1446-on were issued without gum.

Day of Space Flight — A899

Designs: 2ch, Satellite. 5ch, Space station. 10ch, Communications satellite. 15ch, Future space station. 25ch, Satellite. 40ch, Communications satellite.
50ch, Lunar surface vehicle.

1976, Apr. 12 *Perf. 13¼*
1446-1451 A899 Set of 6 3.25 1.00

Souvenir Sheet

Imperf

1452 A899 50ch multicolored 1.60 .50

Kim Il Sung, 64th Birthday

A900

1976, Apr. 15 *Perf. 12*
1453 A900 10ch multicolored .85 .20

Souvenir Sheet

A901

Imperf

1454 A901 40ch multicolored 5.00 .75

Illustrations of Nos. 1453-1454 are reduced.

3rd Asian Table Tennis Championships A902

Designs: 5ch, Paddle and ribbon. 10ch, Three female players with bouquet. 20ch, Female player. 25ch, Male player.

Without Gum

1976, Apr. 25 *Perf. 12*
1455-1458 A902 Set of 4 2.50 1.00

Souvenir Sheet

A903

Illustration reduced.

Imperf

1459 A903 50ch multicolored 2.50 .75

Association for the Restoration of the Fatherland, 40th Anniv. — A904

1976, May 5 *Perf. 12*
1460 A904 10ch multicolored .50 .20

Pheasants — A905

Designs: 2ch, Golden pheasant. 5ch, Lady Amherst's pheasant. 10ch, Silver pheasant. 15ch, Reeves' pheasant. 25ch, Copper pheasant. 40ch, Albino ring-necked pheasant.
50ch, Ring-necked pheasant.

Surface Coated Paper

1976, May 5 *Perf. 11¾*
1461-1466 A905 Set of 6 5.00 1.50
1466a Sheet of 8, as #1461-1467 + label, perf 12, ordinary paper 7.50 7.50

Souvenir Sheet

Imperf

1467 A905 50ch multicolored 3.50 1.50

Potong River Monument A906

1976, May 21 *Perf. 11½*
1468 A906 10ch multicolored 75.00 —

21st Olympic Games, Montreal — A907

Stadium, Olympic rings, and: 2ch, Runners. 5ch, Diver. 10ch, Judo. 15ch, Gymnast. 25ch, Gymnast. 40ch, Fencers.
50ch, Runner with Olympic Torch.

Surface Coated Paper

1976, July 17 *Perf. 13¾*
1469-1474 A907 Set of 6 5.00 1.00
1474a Sheet of 8, as #1469-1475 + label, perf 12, ordinary paper 9.00 —

Souvenir Sheet

Imperf

1475 A907 50ch multicolored 3.50 1.50

For overprints, see Nos. 1632-1638.

Winners, 21st Olympic Games, Montreal A908

Designs: 2ch, Bronze Medal, Hockey — Pakistan. 5ch, Bronze Medal, Free Pistol — Rudolf Dollinger (Austria). 10ch, Silver Medal, Boxing — Li Byong Uk (DPRK). 15ch, Silver Medal, Cycling — Daniel Morelon (France). 25ch, Gold Medal, Marathon — Waldemar Cierpinski (DDR). 40ch, Gold Medal, Boxing — Ku Yong Jo (DPRK).
50ch, Gold, Silver, Bronze Medals.

Multicolored, with Winners' Inscriptions in Silver

Surface Coated Paper

1976, Aug. 2 *Perf. 13¼*
1476-1481 A908 Set of 6 6.00 1.00
1481a Sheet of 8, as #1476-1482 + label, 9.00 —

Souvenir Sheet

Imperf

1482 A908 50ch multicolored 4.00 2.00

Same, with Different Winners' Names

Designs: 2ch, Swimming — David Wilkie (UK). 5ch, Running — Lass Viren (Finland). 10ch, Weight Lifting — Vasili Alexeev (USSR). 15ch Swimming — Kornelia Ender (DDR). 25ch, Platform Diving — Klaus Dibiasi (Italy). 40ch, Boxing — Ku Yong Jo (DPRK). 50ch, Gymnastics — Nadia Comaneci (Romania),

Ordinary Paper

Perf. 13¼

1483-1489 A908 Sheet of 7 + label 10.00 4.00

Souvenir Sheet

Imperf

1490 A908 50ch ovptd. "Kornelia Ender" 4.00 2.00

For overprints, see Nos. 1639-1645.

Winners, 21st Olympic Games, Montreal A909

Designs: 2ch, Boxing — Ku Yong Jo (DPRK). 5ch, Gymnastics — Nadie Comaneci (Romania). 10ch, Pole Vault — Tadeusz Slusarski (Poland). 15ch, Hurdling — Guy Drut (France). 25ch, Cycling — Bernt Johansson (Sweden). 40ch, Soccer (DDR).
50ch, Boxing — Ko Yong Do (DPRK).

Surface Coated Paper

1976, Aug. 2 *Perf. 13¼*
1491-1496 A909 Set of 6 4.50 1.00
1496a Sheet of 12, as #1491-1497 + 5 labels, ordinary paper 8.00 —

Souvenir Sheet

Imperf

1497 A909 50ch multicolored 3.00 .50

International Activities — A910

Designs: 2ch, UPU Headquarters, Bern. 5ch, World Cup. 10ch, Montreal Olympics Stadium. 15ch, Runner with Olympic Torch. 25ch, Satellite, junk. 40ch, Satellites.
50ch, World map.

Surface Coated Paper

1976, Aug. 5 *Perf. 13¼*
1506-1511 A910 Set of 6 5.00 1.50
1511a Sheet of 8, as #1505-1512 + label, ordinary paper 7.00 —

Souvenir Sheet

Imperf

1512 A910 50ch multicolored 2.50 2.50

For overprints, see Nos. 1646-1652.

Embroidery — A911

Designs: 2ch, "Marsh Magpies." 5ch, "Golden Bird." 10ch, "Deer." 15ch, "Golden Bird." 25ch, "Fairy." 40ch, "Tiger."
50ch, "Tiger."

Surface Coated Paper

1976, Aug. 8 *Perf. 12*
1513-1518 A911 Set of 6 7.50 1.50
1518a Sheet of 8, as #1513-1519 + label, perf 13¾, ordinary paper 18.00 —

Souvenir Sheet

Imperf

1519 A911 50ch multicolored 4.00 .50

Model Airplane Championships (1975) — A912

Designs: 5ch, Trophy, certificate and medal. 10ch, Trophy and medals. 20ch, Model airplane and emblem. 40ch, Model glider and medals.

Without Gum

1976, Aug. 15 *Perf. 12*
1520-1523 A912 Set of 4 4.75 1.00

5th Summit Conference of Non-Aligned States — A913

Without Gum

1976, Aug. 16
1524 A913 10ch multicolored .50 .20

Locomotives — A914

Designs: 2ch, "Pulgungi" diesel locomotive. 5ch, "Saeppyol" diesel locomotive. 10ch, "Saeppyol" diesel locomotive (diff.). 15ch, Electric train. 25ch, "Kumsong" diesel locomotive. 40ch, "Pulgungi" electric locomotive.
50ch, "Kumsong" diesel locomotive.

Surface Coated Paper

1976, Sept. 14 *Perf. 12x11¾*
1525-1530 A914 Set of 6 5.50 1.00
1530a Sheet of 8, as #1525-1531 + label, perf 10½ 15.00 —

Souvenir Sheet

Imperf

1531 A914 50ch multicolored 6.00 3.50

House of Culture A915

Without Gum

1976, Oct. 7 *Perf. 12*
1532 A915 10ch black & brown 75.00 —

Revolutionary Activities of Kim Il Sung — A916

Kim Il Sung: 2ch, Visiting the Tosongrang. 5ch, With peasants on hillside. 10ch, With boy and man at seashore. 15ch, Giving house to farm-hand. 25ch, On muddy road at front, with driver and girl. 40ch, Walking in rain with umbrella.
50ch, Watching boy draw picture by roadside.

1976, Oct. 10 *Perf. 13¼*
1533-1538 A916 Set of 6 3.00 .75

Souvenir Sheet

Imperf

1539 A916 50ch multicolored 2.00 1.50

Down-With-Imperialism Union, 50th Anniv. — A917

Without Gum

1976, Oct. 17 *Perf. 12*
1540 A917 20ch black & brown 1.00 .20

21st Olympic Games, Montreal A918

Olympic Rings, stadium and: 5ch, Fencer. 10ch, Weightlifter. 15ch, Horse racer. 20ch, Runner. 25ch, Shot putter. 40ch, Basketball player.
60ch, Yacht race.

Simulated 3-D Printing Using Plastic Overlays

1976, Dec. 21 *Imperf.*
1541-1546 A918 Set of 6 25.00 25.00

Souvenir Sheet

1547 A918 60ch multicolored 45.00 45.00

#1547 Overprinted with Gold Medal Winners' Names, Events

1548 A918 60ch multicolored — —

New Year — A919

Without Gum

1977, Jan. 1 *Perf. 12¼x12*
1549 A919 20ch black & brown .50 .20

21st Olympic Games, Montreal (1976) — A920

Designs: 5ch, Reverse of Bronze Medal, Montreal skyline. 10ch, Obverse of Bronze Medal, diff. Montreal skyline. 15ch, Obverse of Silver Medal, stadium. 20ch, Reverse of Silver Medal, stadium. 25ch, Reverse of Gold Medal, Olympic Flame. 40ch, Obverse of Gold Medal, Olympic Flame.
60ch, Gold, Silver and Bronze Medals.

Simulated 3-D Printing Using Plastic Overlays

1977, Jan. 23 *Imperf.*
1550-1555 A920 Set of 6 25.00 25.00

Souvenir Sheet

1556 A920 60ch multicolored 55.00 55.00

#1556 Overprinted with Gold Medal Winners' Names, Events

1557 A920 60ch multicolored — —

National Costumes of Li Dynasty A921

Seasonal costumes: 10ch, Spring. 15ch, Summer. 20ch, Autumn. 40ch, Winter.

1977, Feb. 10 *Perf. 11¾x12*
1558-1561 A921 Set of 4 3.50 .75
1561a Sheet of 4, #1558-1561 5.00 —

No. 1561 is airmail.

Korean Cultural Relics (5th-12th Centuries) A922

Designs: 2ch, Two Deva kings, Koguryo Dynasty. 5ch, Gold-copper ornament, Koguryo Dynasty. 10ch, Bronze Buddha, Koguryo Dynasty. 15ch, Gold-copper Buddha, Paekje Dynasty. 25ch, Gold crown, Koguryo Dynasty, horiz. 40ch, Gold-copper ornament, Koguryo Dynasty, horiz. 50ch, Gold crown, Silla Dynasty.

1977, Feb. 26 *Perf. 13¼*
1562-1568 A922 Set of 7 5.00 1.50
1568a Sheet of 8, #1562-1568 + label 6.00 —

No. 1568 is airmail.

Five-Point Program for Land Development — A923

Without Gum

1977, Mar. 5 *Perf. 12*
1569 A923 10ch multicolored .50 .20

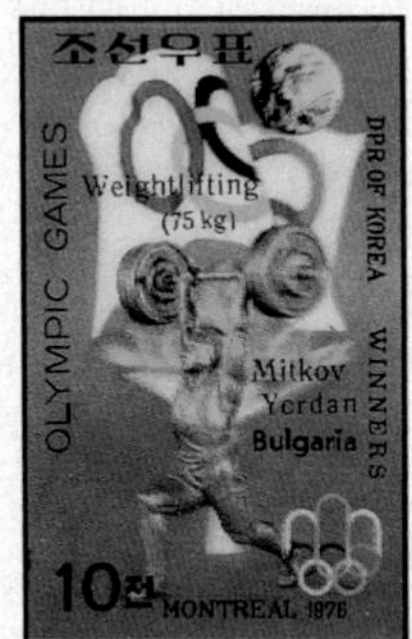

21st Olympic Games, Montreal (1976) A924

Events, winner's name, nationality, and: 5ch, Cycling. 10ch, Weightlifting. 15ch, Judo. 20ch, Wrestling. 25ch, Football (soccer). 40ch, Boxing.
60ch, Boxing.

Simulated 3-D Printing Using Plastic Overlays

1977, Mar.8 *Imperf.*
1570-1575 A924 Set of 6 45.00 45.00

Souvenir Sheet

1576 A924 60ch multicolored — —

Korean National Association, 60th Anniv. — A925

Without Gum

1977, Mar. 23 *Perf. 11¾*
1577 A925 10ch multicolored .65 .20

34th World Table-Tennis Championships — A926

Designs: 10ch, Emblem and trophy. 15ch, Pak Yong Sun. 20ch, Pak Yong Sun with trophy. 40ch, Pak Yong Ok and Yang Ying with trophy.

1977, Apr. 5 *Perf. 12*
1578-1581 A926 Set of 4 3.25 .75

No. 1581 is airmail.

Kim Il Sung, 65th Birthday — A927

Painting of Kim Il Sung: 2ch, Leading Mingyuehkou Meeting. 5ch, Commanding encirclement operation. 10ch, Visiting workers in Kangson. 15ch, Before battle. 25ch, Visiting school. 40ch, Looking over grain fields.

1977, Apr. 15 *Perf. 12*
1582-1587 A927 Set of 6 2.25 .50

Souvenir Sheet

Imperf

1588 A927 50ch multicolored 1.50 .90

Trolley Buses A928

Designs: 5ch, "Chollima 72." 10ch, "Chollima 74."

Without Gum

1977, Apr. 20 *Perf. 12*
1589-1590 A928 Set of 2 3.00 .20

Korean People's Revolutionary Army, 45th Anniv. — A929

Without Gum

1977, Apr. 25 *Perf. 12*
1591 A929 40ch multicolored 1.50 .20

Battle of Pochonbo, 40th Anniv. — A930

Without Gum

1977, June 4 *Perf. 13¼*
1592 A930 10ch multicolored .50 .20

Porcelain A931

Designs: 10ch, White ceramic teapot, Koryo dynasty. 15ch, White ceramic vase, Ri dynasty. 20ch, Celadon vase, Koryo dynasty. 40ch, Celadon vase, Koryo dynasty, diff.

1977, June 10 *Perf. 13¼*
1593-1596 A931 Set of 4 3.50 .75
1596a Sheet of 4, #1593-1596 7.00 .95

No. 1596 is airmail.

Postal Service A932

Designs: 2ch, Railway, ship and trucks. 10ch, Postwoman delivering mail. 30ch, Mil Mi-8 helicopter. 40ch, Airliner and world map.

Without Gum

1977, June 28 *Perf. 13¼*
1597-1600 A932 Set of 4 4.00 1.00

A 3-stamp set and souvenir sheet commemorating the Second Conference of Third World Youth was prepared for release July 1, 1977, but was not issued. Value $3,500.

Butterflies — A933

Designs: 2ch, Rapala arata. 5ch, Colias aurora. 10ch, Limenitis populi. 15ch, Anax parthenope julius. 25ch, Sympetrum pademontanum elatum.
50ch, Papilio maackii.

1977, July 25 *Perf. 12x12¼*

1601-1606 A933 Set of 6 7.00 1.00
1606a Sheet of 6, #1601-1606 15.00 —

No. 1606 is airmail.

Cats and Dogs

A934

A935

Cats: 2ch, Gray cat. 10ch, Black and white cat. 25ch, Ginger cat.
Dogs: 5ch, Brindled dog. 15ch, Chow. 50ch, Pungsang.

1977, Aug. 10 *Perf. 11¾x12*

1607-1609 A934 Set of 3 6.00 .50
1609a Sheet of 3, #1607-1609 8.00 —
1610-1612 A935 Set of 3 4.00 .50
1612a Sheet of 3, #1610-1612 6.00 —

No. 1612 is airmail.

A936

Visit of Pres. Tito of Yugoslavia

1977, Aug. 25 *Perf. 12*

1613-1616 A936 Set of 4 40.00 8.00

11-Year Compulsory Education, 5th Anniv. — A937

Without Gum

1977, Sept. 1 *Perf. 13¼x13½*

1617 A937 10ch multicolored .50 .20

Shell-Fish and Fish — A938

Designs: 2ch, Mactra sulcataria. 5ch, Natica fortunei. 10ch, Arca inflata. 25ch, Rapana thomasiana. 50ch, Sphoeroides porphyreus.

1977, Sept. 5 *Perf. 11¾x12*

1618-1622 A938 Set of 5 5.00 1.00
1622a Sheet of 6, #1618-1622 + label 9.00 —

No. 1622 is airmail.

Publication of Kim Il Sung's *Theses on Socialist Education* A939

Designs: 10ch, Students, banners and *Theses.* 20ch, Students, crowd and *Theses.*

1977, Sept. 5

1623-1624 A939 Set of 2 1.00 .20

Int'l Seminar on the Juche Idea — A940

Designs: 2ch, Juche Torch. 5ch, Interracial crowd holding copies of Kim's Red Book. 10ch, Chollima statue, flags. 15ch, Joined hands of different races, banner and globe. 25ch, Map of Korea. 40ch, Crowd and slogan.
50ch, Seminar emblem.

1977, Sept. 14 *Perf. 11¾x12*

1625-1630 A940 Set of 6 3.50 .60

Souvenir Sheet
Imperf

1631 A940 50ch multicolored 3.00 1.00

Stamps of 1976 Overprinted "Amphilex '77" and Emblem

Methods & Perfs as Before

1977, Nov. 8

On Montreal Olympics, #1469-1474

1632-1637 A907 Set of 6 9.00 —
1637a On #1474a, sheet of 8 10.00 —

Souvenir Sheet
Imperf

1638 A907 50ch multicolored 5.00 —

On Montreal Olympics Medal Winners, #1476-1482

1639-1644 A908 Set of 6 13.00 —
1644a On #1481a, sheet of 8 15.00 —

Souvenir Sheet
Imperf

1645 A908 50ch multicolored 5.00 —

On International Activities, #1506-1512

1646-1651 A910 Set of 6 10.00 —
1651a On #1511a, sheet of 8 15.00 —

Souvenir Sheet
Imperf

1652 A910 50ch multicolored 5.00 —

Amphilex '77 International Stamp Exhibition, Amsterdam.

Election of Deputies, Supreme People's Assembly A941

1977, Nov. 11 *Perf. 12¼x12*

1653 A941 10ch multicolored .50 .20

Argentina '78, World Soccer Championship — A942

Designs: 10ch, Defense. 15ch, Attack. 40ch, Tackle.
50ch, Shot.

1977, Dec. 10 *Perf. 13½*

1654-1656 A942 Set of 3 3.50 .75
1656a Sheet of 4, as #1654-1657 10.00 —

Souvenir Sheet
Imperf

1657 A942 50ch multicolored 2.50 —

Reelection of Kim Il Sung — A943

Illustration reduced.

1977, Dec. 15 *Perf. 12*

1658 A943 10ch multicolored .60 .20

Org. for Communication Cooperation of Socialist Countries, 20th Anniv. — A944

Without Gum

1977, Dec. 16 *Perf. 11¾x12*

1659 A944 10ch multicolored .50 .20

New Year — A945

1978, Jan. 1 *Perf. 13¼*

1660 A945 10ch multicolored .60 .20

Winter Olympic Games, Sapporo-Innsbruck — A946

Designs: 2ch, 19th century skater. 5ch, Skier. 10ch, Ice ballet. 15ch, Hunter on skis. 20ch, 18th century woman skiier. 25ch, Medieval Scandinavian hunter. 40ch, Skiier.
50ch, Landscape. 60ch, Speed skater.

1978, Feb. 18 *Perf. 13¼*

1661-1667 A946 Set of 7 6.00 1.00
1667a Sheet of 10, as #1661-1669 + label 9.00 —

Souvenir Sheets

1668 A946 50ch multicolored 5.00 .50
1669 A946 60ch multicolored 4.00 .50

No. 1667 is airmail.
For overprints, see Nos. 1820-1828.

Postal History A947

Designs: 2ch, Post rider and horse token. 5ch, Postman on motorcycle. 10ch, Electric train and postal van. 15ch, Mail steamer and Mi-8 helicopter. 25ch, Tupolev Tu-154 jetliner and satellite. 40ch, Dove and UPU headquarters.
50ch, Dove and UPU emblem. 60ch, Dove and UPU headquarters.

1978, Mar. 2 *Perf. 13¼*

1670-1675 A947 Set of 6 6.00 1.00
1675a Sheet of 8, as #1670-1677 8.00 —

Souvenir Sheets

1676-1677 A947 Set of 2 6.00 —

No. 1675 is airmail.

Rubens, 400th Anniv. Birth — A948

2ch, 5ch, 40ch, 50ch, Self-portrait, same design.

1978, Mar. 20

1678-1680 A948 Set of 3 2.50 .50
1680a Sheet of 4, as #1678-1681 6.00 —

Souvenir Sheet

1681 A948 50ch multicolored 3.00 1.50

Farm Machines A949

Designs: 10ch (#1682), *Chungsong* tractor. 10ch (#1683), Sprayer.

1978, Apr. 1 ***Perf. 11¾x12***

1682-1683 A949 Set of 2 2.50 .20

Pre-Olympics, Moscow 1980 — A950

Equestrian events: 2ch, Show jumping. 5ch, Jumping bar. 10ch, Cross Country. 15ch, Dressage. 25ch, Water splash. 40ch, Dressage (diff.).
50ch, 3-Step bar jump.

1978, Apr. 1 ***Perf. 13¼***

1684-1689 A950 Set of 6 3.50 1.50
1689a Sheet of 8, as #1684-1690 + label 7.00 —

Souvenir Sheet

1690 A950 50ch multicolored 2.50 —

Korean People's Army Day — A951

Designs: 5ch, Soldier, battle scene. 10ch, Pilot, soldier, sailor saluting.

1978, Apr. 1 ***Perf. 11¾x12***

1691-1692 A951 Set of 2 1.00 .20

Ships — A952

Korean ships: 2ch, Cargo ship *Mangyongbong.* 5ch, Freighter *Hyoksin.* 10ch, Freighter *Chongchongang.* 30ch, Tanker *Sonbang.* 50ch, Freighter *Taedonggang.*

1978, May 5 ***Perf. 13¼***

1693-1697 A952 Set of 5 6.00 1.25
1697a Sheet of 6, as #1693-1697+ label 8.00 —

No. 1697 is airmail.

History of the World Cup — A953

World Cup Winners (all 20ch, except Nos. 1709, 1710): #1698, Uruguay 1930. #1699, Italy 1934. #1700, France 1938. #1701, Brazil 1950. #1702, Switzerland 1954. #1703, Sweden 1958. #1704, Chile 1962. #1705, England 1966. #1706, Mexico 1970. #1707, West Germany 1974. #1708, Argentina 1978. 50ch (#1709), Soccer players and emblem, horiz.
50ch (#1710), World Cup and championship emblem.

1978, June 1

1698-1709 A953 Set of 12 10.00 3.00
1709a Sheet of 12, as #1698-1708, 1710 12.00 —

Souvenir Sheet

1710 A953 50ch multicolored 6.00 .60

No. 1709 is airmail.
For overprints, see Nos. 2051-2062.

World Cup Winners — A954

Designs: 5ch, Uruguay, 1930, 1950. 10ch, Italy, 1934, 1938. 15ch, West Germany, 1954, 1974. 25ch, Brazil, 1958, 1962, 1970. 40ch, England, 1966. 50ch, World Cup, vert.
50ch, World Cup.

1978, June 1

1711-1716 A954 Set of 6 5.00 1.25
1716a Sheet of 6, as #1711-15, 1717 6.00 —

Souvenir Sheet

1717 A954 50ch multicolored 4.00 .75

No. 1716 is airmail.

Art of the Revolution — A955

Designs: 10ch, Opera, *Sea of Love.* 15ch, Embroidered kerchief with floral design in the form of map of Korea. 20ch, *Tansimjul* dance. 40ch, *Song of Korea.*

1978, June 2

1718-1720 A955 Set of 3 2.50 .50

Souvenir Sheet

1721 A955 40ch multicolored 2.50 .50

Domestic Printings

Beginning in the 1970s, a number of North Korean stamps have been reprinted for sale and use within the country. Typically, these printings were on unsurfaced paper, with poorer production qualities, and without gum.

Second Seven-Year Plan — A956

Designs: 5ch, Electricity and Coal. 10ch, Steel and nonferrous metals. 15ch, Machine products and chemical fertilizers. 30ch, Cement and fishing. 50ch, Grain and tideland reclamation.

1978, June 15 ***Perf. 11½x12***

1722-1726 A956 Set of 5 3.25 .90
1722a 5ch, unsurfaced white paper, without gum 8.00 —
1723a 10ch, unsurfaced white paper, without gum 8.00 —
1724a 15ch, unsurfaced white paper, without gum 8.00 —
1725a 30ch, unsurfaced white paper, without gum 5.00 —

History of Olympic Games & Winners — A957

Games emblems / medal winners (all 20ch): #1727, Athens 1896 / Alfred Flatow. #1728, Paris 1900 / Michel Theato. #1729, London 1908 / Wyndham Halswelle. #1730, Stockholm 1912 / William Kinnear. #1731, Antwerp 1920 / Paul Anspach. #1732, Paris 1924 / Ugo Frigerio. #1733, Amsterdam 1928 / Ahmed El Quafi. #1734, Berlin 1936 / Robert Charpentier. #1735, London 1948 / Josef Stalder. #1736, Helsinki 1952 / Laszlo Papp. #1737, Melbourne 1956 / Ronald Delany. #1738, Rome 1960 / Jolanda Balas. #1739, Tokyo 1964 / Valery Brumel. #1740, Mexico 1968 / Vera Caslavska. #1741, Munich 1972 / Li Ho Jun.
50ch, Montreal 1976 / Ku Yong Jo.

1978, June 16 ***Perf. 13¼***

1727-1741 A957 Set of 15 12.00 4.50
1741a Sheet of 16, as #1727-1741 14.00 —

Souvenir Sheet

1742 A957 50ch multicolored 2.00 .75

Passenger Aircraft — A958

Designs: 2ch, Douglas CD-8-63 jetliner and Comte AC-4 Gentleman. 10ch, Ilyushin Il-62M jetliner and Avia BH-25. 15ch, Douglas DC-8-63 jetliner and Savola Marchetti S-71. 20ch, Tupolev Tu-144 jetliner and Kalinin K-5. 25ch, Tupolev Tu-154 jetliner and Antonov An-2 biplane. 30ch, Ilyushin Il-18 airliner and '30s-era airplane. 40ch, Concorde supersonic jetliner and Wibault 283 trimotor.
50ch, Airbus.

1978, July 25

1743-1749 A958 Set of 7 7.00 1.20
1749a Sheet of 8, as #1743-1750 10.00 —

Souvenir Sheet

1750 A958 50ch multicolored 2.50 .50

White-Bellied Black Woodpecker Preservation A959

Designs: 5ch, White-bellied black woodpecker (Tristam's *Dryocopus javensis richardsi*), map of habitat, inset map of Korea. 10ch, Woodpecker and eggs. 15ch, Woodpecker feeding young. 25ch, Woodpecker feeding young (diff.). 50ch, Woodpecker on tree trunk.

1978, Aug. 5 ***Perf. 11¾x12***

1751-1755 A959 Set of 5 7.50 2.00
1755a Sheet of 6, #1751-1755 + label 9.00 —

Democratic People's Republic of Korea, 30th Anniv. A960

Designs (all 10ch): #1756, Building and flag. #1757, Flag with silhouetttes of workers and peasants. #1758, Flag with aviator and two soldiers. #1759, Chollima statue and city. #1760, Workers demonstrating, map of Korea in background. #1761, Asian, European and African clasping hands, with torch and "Solidarity" in background.

Without Gum

1978, Sep. 9 ***Perf. 13½x13¼***

1756-1761 A960 Set of 6 2.75 .50
1758a 10ch, unsurfaced toned paper 10.00 —
1759a 10ch, unsurfaced toned paper 15.00 —
1760a 10ch, unsurfaced toned paper 15.00 —

Paintings by Ri Am (16th Century) A961

Designs: 10ch, *Cat and Pup.* 15ch, *Cat on a Tree.* 40ch, *A Pair of Wild Geese.*

1978, Oct. 16 ***Perf. 13¼***

1762-1764 A961 Set of 3 7.50 1.10
1764a Sheet of 4, #1762-1764 + label 11.00 —

World Cup Winners, Argentina '78 — A962

Soccer players: 10ch, Argentina, Champion. 15ch, Holland, Sub-Champion. 25ch, Brazil, Third Place.
50ch, Argentina, Champion.

1978, Dec. 15
1765-1767 A962 Set of 3 3.00 .50
1767a Sheet of 4, as #1765-1768 12.00 —

Souvenir Sheet

1768 A962 50ch Multicolored 2.50 1.50

New Year — A963

Without Gum

1979, Jan. 1 ***Perf. 12***
1769 A963 10ch Multicolored .50 .20

A964

A965

International Year of the Child

Kim Il Sung and children: 5ch, With Children's Corps members in Maanshan. 10ch, Children's Corps members in classroom. 15ch, "The New Year Gathering." 20ch, by roadside, with snowman, kite. 30ch, Looking at children's school work.

Children: 10ch, Tug of war. 15ch, Ballerinas. 20ch, Children of different races holding hands in circle around globe. 25ch, Singing at piano. 30ch, Playing on toy airplane ride.

50ch (#1780), Kim visiting a kindergarten. 50ch (#1781): As #1776.

1979, Jan. 1 ***Perf. 13¼x13½***
1770-1774 A964 Set of 5 4.00 1.00
1775-1779 A965 Set of 5 3.00 1.00

Souvenir Sheets
Imperf

1780 A964 50ch Multicolored 2.50 1.75
1781 A965 50ch Multicolored 2.50 1.75

Nos. 1770-1779 were issued with setenant labels.

A set of four stamps depicting roses, similar to Type A970, was prepared for release on Jan. 5, 1979, but was not issued.

Story of Two Generals A966

Designs: 5ch, Two warriors on horseback. 10ch (#1783), Man blowing feather. 10ch (#1784), Two generals fighting Japanese invaders. 10ch (#1785), Two generals on horseback.

Without Gum

1979, Jan. 10 ***Perf. 11¾x12***
1782-1785 A966 Set of 4 3.00 .50

Worker-Peasant Red Guards, 20th Anniv. — A967

Without Gum

1979, Jan. 14 ***Perf. 12x11¾***
1786 A967 10ch Multicolored .50 .20

Airships — A968

Designs: 10ch, Clement-Bayard Airship *Fleurus.* 20ch, NI *Norge.*
50ch, *Graf Zeppelin.*

1979, Feb. 27 ***Perf. 13¼***
1787-1788 A968 Set of 2 2.00 .40
1788a Sheet of 3, as #1787-1789 5.00 —

Souvenir Sheet

1789 A968 50ch Multicolored 3.00 1.75

March 1 Popular Uprising, 60th Anniv. A969

Without Gum

1979, Mar. 1 ***Perf. 11¾x12***
1790 A969 10ch Multicolored .60 .20

Roses A970

Designs: 5ch, Rose. 10ch, Red star rose. 15ch, Flamerose. 20ch, Yellow rose. 30ch, White rose. 50ch, Deep pink rose.

1979, Apr. 18 ***Perf. 13¼***
1791-1796 A970 Set of 6 3.50 1.00
1796a Sheet of 6, #1791-1796 4.00 —

No. 1796 is airmail.

35th World Table Tennis Championships, Pyongyang — A971

Designs: 5ch, Championship Cup. 10ch, Female doubles. 15ch, Female singles. 20ch, Male doubles. 30ch, Male singles.
50ch, Chollima statue. "Welcome."

1979, Apr. 25
1797-1801 A971 Set of 5 3.00 .75
1801a Sheet of 6, as #1797-1802 4.00 —

Souvenir Sheet

1802 A971 50ch Multicolored 3.00 .45

"Let Us Step Up Socialist Construction Under the Banner of the Juche Idea" — A972

Designs: 5ch, Marchers, banner. 10ch (#1804), Map of Korea. 10ch (#1805), Hand holding torch.

Without Gum

1979, Apr. 28 ***Perf. 12***
1803-1805 A972 Set of 3 3.00 .25
1803a 5ch, unsurfaced dull white paper 15.00 —
1804a 10ch, unsurfaced dull white paper 15.00 —
1805a 10ch, unsurfaced dull white paper 15.00 —

Order of Honor of the Three Revolutions — A973

Without Gum

1979, May 2
1806 A973 10ch dp blue & lt blue 1.50 .20
a. Unsurfaced dull white paper 15.00 —

World Telecommunications Day — A974

Without Gum

1979, May 17
1807 A974 10ch multicolored 1.00 .20

Battle in Musan Area, 40th Anniv. A975

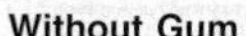
Without Gum

1979, May 23
1808 A975 10ch multicolored .60 .20

Int'l Friendship Exhibition A976

Without Gum

1979, May 29
1809 A976 10ch multicolored .60 .20

Albrecht Dürer, 450th Anniv. Death A977

Details from Dürer paintings: 15ch, "Peonies." 20ch, "Akeley." 25ch, "A Big Tuft of Grass." 30ch, 50ch, "Wing of a Bird."

1979, June 8 ***Perf. 13¼***
1810-1813 A977 Set of 4 5.50 .75
1813a Sheet of 4, as #1810-1813 9.00 —

Souvenir Sheet

1814 A977 50ch Multicolored 3.50 .60

Olympic Games, Moscow 1980 — A978

Olympic Torch, Moscow 1980 emblem and: 5ch, Fencers. 10ch, Gymnast. 20ch, Yacht race. 30ch, Runner. 40ch, Weightlifter.
50ch, Horse jump.

1979, July 1
1815-1819 A978 Set of 5 3.50 1.25
1819a Sheet of 6, as #1815-1820 5.00 —

Souvenir Sheet

1820 A978 50ch Multicolored 3.00 1.50

13th Winter Olympic Games

Nos. 1661-1669 Overprinted

1979, July 17
1821-1827 A946 Set of 7 10.00 3.50
1827a Sheet of 10, as #1821-1829 + label 18.00 —

Souvenir Sheets

1828 A946 50ch Multicolored 4.25 1.50
1829 A946 60ch Multicolored 8.50 —

No. 1827 is airmail.

Koguryo Dynasty Horsemen — A979

Designs: 5ch, Hunting. 10ch, Archery contest. 15ch, Drummer. 20ch, Rider blowing horn. 30ch, Horse and rider in chain mail. 50ch, Hawk hunting.

1979, Aug. 1

1830-1835 A979 Set of 6 6.00 .75
1835a Sheet of 6, as #1830-1835 9.00 —

Olympic Games, Moscow 1980 — A980

Designs: 5ch, Judo. 10ch, Volleyball. 15ch, Cycling. 20ch, Basketball. 25ch, One-oared boat. 30ch, Boxing. 40ch, Shooting. 50ch, Gymnastics.

1979, Aug. 5 ***Perf. 11¾x12***

1836-1842 A980 Set of 7 5.00 1.25
1842a Sheet of 8, as #1836-1843 + label 9.00 —

Souvenir Sheet

1843 A980 50ch Multicolored 3.00 1.00

Ri Dynasty Knights' Costumes A981

Designs: 5ch, Knight in armor. 10ch, Knight in ceremonial dress. 15ch, Knight in armor (diff.) 20ch, Soldier in uniform. 30ch, Knight in armor (diff.) 50ch, Knight in armor (diff.)

1979, Aug. 6 ***Perf. 11¾***

1844-1849 A981 Set of 6 3.75 .75
1849a Sheet of 6, #1844-1849 6.00 —

No. 1849 is airmail.

Olympic Games, Moscow 1980 — A982

Designs: 10ch, Judo. 15ch, Handball. 20ch, Archery. 25ch, Ground hockey. 30ch, Boat race. 40ch, Soccer.
50ch, Horse race.

1979, Sep. 5 ***Perf. 11¾x11½***

1850-1855 A982 Set of 6 5.25 1.25
1855a Sheet of 8, as #1850-1856 + label 8.00 —

Souvenir Sheet

1856 A982 50ch Multicolored 3.00 1.25

Chongbong Monument A983

Without Gum

1979, Sep. 10 ***Perf. 12***

1857 A983 10ch multicolored .60 .20

Sika Deer A984

Designs: 5ch, Breeder feeding fawn from bottle. 10ch, Doe and suckling fawn. 15ch, Deer drinking from stream. 20ch, Buck walking. 30ch, Deer running.
50ch, Antlers.

1979, Oct. 5 ***Perf. 13½***

1858-1863 A984 Set of 6 4.00 1.25
1863a Sheet of 6, #1858-1863 6.00 —

Central Zoo, Pyongyang A985

Designs: 5ch, Moscovy ducks. 10ch, Ostrich. 15ch, Turkey. 20ch, Pelican. 30ch, Guinea fowl. 50ch, Mandarin ducks.

1979, Oct. 9 ***Perf. 12***

1864-1869 A985 Set of 6 5.00 1.50
1869a Sheet of 6, #1864-1869 6.00 —

No. 1869 is airmail.

Int'l Year of the Child — A986

Designs: 20ch (#1870), Girl with toy sail boat. 20ch (#1871), Boy with toy train. 20ch (#1872), Boy with model biplane. 20ch (#1873), Boy with model spaceman. 30ch (#1874), Boy with toy motor boat. 30ch (#1875), Boy sitting on toy train. 30ch (#1876), Boy with model airplane. 30ch (#1877), Boy with model spaceman.
Souvenir Sheets (all 80ch): #1878, Boy and model ocean liner. #1879, Boy and girl with model train. #1880, Boy and Concorde. #1881, Girl and satellite.
Miniature sheets of 4: #1882, Nos. 1870, 1874, 1878 + label. #1883, Nos. 1871, 1875, 1879 + label. #1884, Nos. 1872, 1876, 1880 + label. #1885, Nos. 1873, 1877, 1881 + label.

1979, Oct. 13 ***Perf. 12x11¾***

1870-1877 A986 Set of 8 12.00 2.50

Souvenir Sheets

1878-1881 A986 Set of 4 25.00 2.50

Miniature Sheets

1882-1885 A986 Set of 4 25.00 2.50

Int'l Year of the Child — A987

Children playing soccer: 20ch, Kicking. 30ch, Dribbling.
80ch, Tackling.

1979, Nov. 15 ***Perf. 12x11¾***

1886-1887 A987 Set of 2 5.00 .75
1887a Sheet of 3, as #1886-1888 10.00 —

Souvenir Sheet

1888 A987 80ch Multicolored 5.00 .75

Marine Life — A988

Designs: 20ch, Devil stinger fish (*Inimicas japonicus*). 30ch, Black rockfish (*Sebastes schlegeli*). 50ch, Northern sea lion (*Eumetopias jubatus*).

1889-1891 A988 Set of 3 3.50 .75
1891a Sheet of 3, #1889-1891 5.00 —

Winter Olympics Games, Lake Placid — A989

Designs: 10ch, Figure skating (Irina Rodnina and Aleksandr Zaitsev). 20ch, Ice hockey (Soviet team). 30ch, Ladies' ski relay team. 40ch, Cross-country skiing (Sergei Saveliev, USSR), vert. 50ch, Ladies' speed skating (Tatiana Averina), vert.
60ch, Ice dancing (Ludmila Pakhomova and Aleksandr Gorshkov), stamp vert.

1979, Dec. 9

1892-1896 A989 Set of 5 6.00 1.50
1892a Sheet of 3, #1892-1894 5.00 —
1895a Sheet of 3, as #1895-1897 10.00 —

Souvenir Sheet

1897 A989 60ch Multicolored 5.50 4.50

Honey Bees — A990

Designs: 20ch, Bee gathering nectar. 30ch, Bee and blossoms. 50ch, Bee over flower.

1979, Dec. 22

1898-1900 A990 Set of 3 6.00 .60
1900a Sheet of 3, #1898-1900 7.50 —

Kim Il Sung's Birthplace, Hoeryang A991

Sinpha Revolutionary Museum — A992

1979, Dec. 24

1901 A991 10ch multicolored .75 .20
1902 A992 10ch multicolored .75 .20

Revolutionary historical sites.

New Year A993

1980, Jan. 1

1903 A993 10ch multicolored 1.00 .20

Studying — A994

1980, Jan. 10 ***Perf. 12x11¾***

1904 A994 10ch multicolored .50 .20

Unryul Mine Conveyor Belt — A995

1980, Jan. 20 ***Perf. 11¾x12***

1905 A995 10ch multicolored 1.00 .20

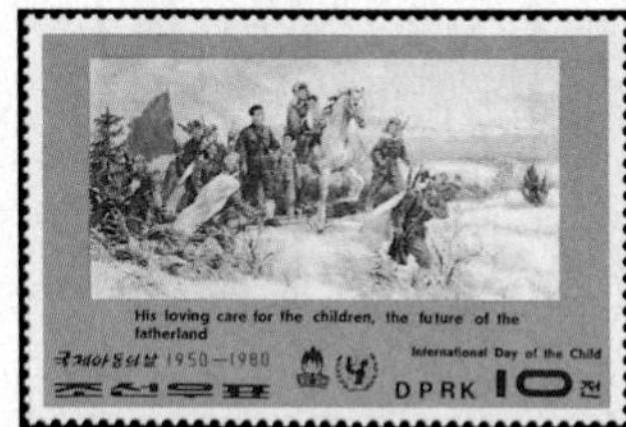
Kim Il Sung, Soldiers and Children — A996

Children Playing — A997

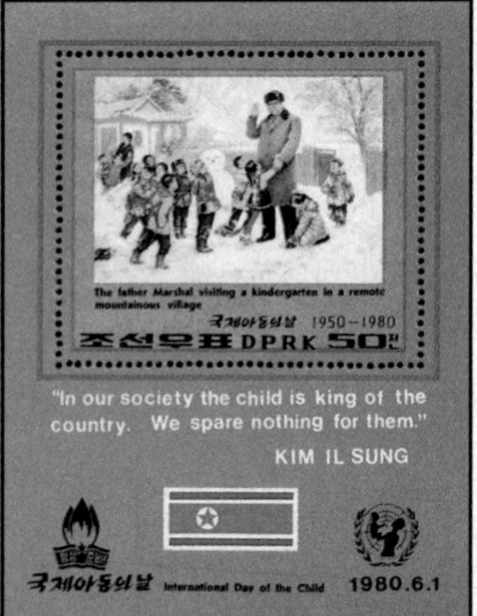

Kim Visiting Kindergarten — A998

International Day of the Child

Type A997 (all 10ch): #1907, Black, Asian and White children with "6" and "1." #1908, Children playing accordion. #1909, Children on airplane ride. #1910, Children on rocket ride. #1911, Children riding tricycles. #1912, Children playing with model train.

Illustrations of types A996 and A998 reduced.

1980, Jan. 28 *Perf. 12x11¾*

1906	A996	10ch multicolored	.35	.20
1907	A997	10ch multicolored	1.50	.35
1908	A997	10ch multicolored	.35	.20
1909	A997	10ch multicolored	.60	.20
1910	A997	10ch multicolored	2.25	.50
1911	A997	10ch multicolored	.50	.20
1912	A997	10ch multicolored	.35	.20
		Nos. 1906-1912 (7)	5.90	1.85

Souvenir Sheet

Perf. 13¼

1913 A998 50ch multicolored 3.00 1.25

Chongsan-ri Monument — A999

Chongsan-ri Party Headquarters — A1000

1980, Feb. 5 *Perf. 11¾x12*

1914 A999 10ch multicolored .50 .20
1915 A1000 10ch multicolored .50 .20

Monument in Honor of Kim Jong Suk's Return A1001

1980, Feb. 16

1916 A1001 10ch multicolored .50 .20

Explorers A1002

Designs: 10ch, Vasco Nunez be Balboa (Spain). 20ch, Francisco de Orellana (Spain). 30ch, Haroun Tazieff (France). 40ch, Sir Edmund Hillary (New Zealand) and Shri Tenzing (Nepal).

70ch, Ibn Battuta (Morocco).

1980, Feb. 18 *Perf. 13¼*

1917-1920 A1002 Set of 4 4.50 1.00
1920a Sheet of 6, as #1917-1921 + label 10.00 —

Souvenir Sheet

1921 A1002 70ch multicolored 4.50 1.50

Ryongpo Revolutionary Museum — A1003

1980, Feb. 23 *Perf. 11¾*

1922 A1003 10ch lt blue & black .50 .20

Rowland Hill (1795-1879), Centenary of Death — A1004

Rowland Hill and stamps of: 30ch, Germany, Great Britain (#1), Russia, Switzerland, DPRK and Wurttemberg. 50ch, Great Britain (#1, pair), France, Roman States, Canada, Two Sicilies and India.

1980, Mar. 1

1923-1924 A1004 Set of 2 7.00 1.00
1924a Sheet of 2, #1923-1924 10.00 —

World Red Cross Day — A1005

Designs (all 10ch): #1925, Emblem of DPRK Red Cross. #1926, J.H. Dunant. #1927, Nurse and infant. #1928, Red Cross ship. #1929, Red Cross helicopter. #1930, Nurse with child and doll. #1931, Map, Red Cross, transports.

50ch, Nurse with syringe.

1980, Apr. 17 *Perf. 11¾x11½*

1925-1931 A1005 Set of 7 8.00 1.50
1931a Sheet of 8, as #1925-1932 15.00 —

Souvenir Sheet

1932 A1005 50ch multicolored 5.50 1.75

For overprints, see Nos. 2043-2050.

Conquerors of the Sea A1006

Designs: 10ch, Fernando Magellan (Portugal). 20ch, Fridtjof Nansen (Norway). 30ch, Auguste and Jacques Piccard (Sweden). 40ch, Jacques Cousteau (France).

70ch, Capt. James Cook (UK).

1980, Apr. 30 *Perf. 13¼*

1933-1936 A1006 Set of 4 8.00 1.50
1936a Sheet of 6, as #1933-1937 + label 15.00 —

Souvenir Sheet

1937 A1006 70ch multicolored 6.50 1.50

London 1980 Int'l Philatelic Exhibition — A1007

Designs: 10ch, Great Britain #1 and Korean stamps. 20ch, British Guiana One-Cent Magenta and Korean cover. 30ch, Korea #1 (in blue) and modern Korean First Day Cover. 40ch, DPRK Nos. 1 (in green) and 1494. 50ch, DPRK Nos. 470-471.

1980, May 6

1938-1942 A1007 Set of 5 10.00 1.50

Souvenir Sheet

1943 A1007 Sheet of 3, #1939, 1941, 1942 15.00 1.50

No. 1941 is airmail.

Conquerors of Sky and Space A1008

Designs: 10ch, Wright Brothers (USA). 20ch, Louis Bleriot (France). 30ch, Anthony Fokker (USA). 40ch, Secondo Campini (Italy) and Sir Frank Whittle (UK).

70ch, Count Ferdinand von Zeppelin (Germany).

1980, May 10

1944-1947 A1008 Set of 4 6.00 1.25
1947a Sheet of 6, as #1944-1948 + label 13.00 —

Souvenir Sheet

1948 A1008 70ch multicolored 5.00 1.25

Conquerors of the Universe A1009

Designs: 10ch, Spaceships. 20ch, Spaceship landing on another planet. 30ch, Spaceships landing on another planet, greeted by dinosaurs. 40ch, Spaceship, dinosaurs.

70ch, Spaceman and dragons.

1980, May 20 *Perf. 11¾x12*

1949-1952 A1009 Set of 4 3.50 1.25
1952a Sheet of 6, as #1949-1953 + label 12.00 —

Souvenir Sheet

1953 A1009 70ch multicolored 3.50 1.25

Chongryon, 25th Anniv. — A1010

1980, May 25 *Perf. 12¼x12*

1954 A1010 10ch multicolored .50 .20

Chongryon is the General Association of Korean Residents in Japan.

Pyongyang Maternity Hospital — A1011

1980, May 30 *Perf. 12*

1955 A1011 10ch multicolored 1.10 .20

Changgwang Health Complex — A1012

1980, June 2 *Perf. 11¾x12*

1956 A1012 2ch black & lt blue .60 .20

Korean Revolutionary Army, 50th Anniv. — A1013

1980, July 6 *Perf. 12*

1957 A1013 10ch multicolored .60 .20

Regular Issue — A1014

Designs (all 10ch): #1958, Workers' hostel, Samjiyon. #1959, *Chongsanri* rice harvester. #1960, *Taedonggang* rice transplanter. #1961, corn harvester. #1962, Samhwa Democratic Propaganda Hall. #1963, Songmun-ri revolutionary historic building (with trees). #1964, Sundial. #1965, Turtle ship. #1966, Phungsan dog. #1967, Quail.

Perf. 11¾, 11½ (#1960, 1965), 12x11¾ (#1964)

1980

1958-1967 A1014 Set of 10 25.00 3.00

Issued: Nos. 1958-1961, 7/25. Nos. 1962-1967, 8/1.

6th Congress, Workers' Party of Korea A1015

"Leading the van in the Arduous March" — A1016

"The great leader inspires and encourages colliers on the spot." — A1017

Designs (all 10ch): #1968, Party emblem, fireworks. #1969, Students, Red Book. #1970, Workers, banner, Red Book. #1971, Young workers, one with accordion. #1972, Worker holding wrench aloft. #1973, Four young workers, one with streamer, building in background. #1974, Map, propaganda slogans. #1975, Workers marching with three banners, smoke stacks in background.

Nos. 1976, 1977 illustrations reduced.

1980, July 30 ***Perf. 12¼x12***

1968-1975 A1015 Set of 8 6.00 1.25

Souvenir Sheets

1976 A1016 50ch multicolored 3.00 .75

1977 A1017 50ch multicolored 2.00 .75

A1018

World Cup Soccer Championship 1978-1982

Designs: 20ch, Two soccer players dribbling ball. 30ch, Tackling.

40ch, Tackling (diff.). 60ch, Moving in to tackle.

1980, Aug. 5 ***Perf. 12***

1978-1979 A1018 Set of 2 7.50 2.00

1979a Sheet of 4, as #1978-1980 — —

Souvenir Sheet

1980 A1018 Sheet of 2 + label 16.00 2.00

a. 40ch multicolored 3.00 1.00

b. 60ch multicolored 4.00 1.00

Winter Olympic Games 1980, Gold Medal Winners — A1019

Designs: 20ch, Irina Rodnina and Aleksandr Zaitsev.

1w, Natalia Linitschnuk and Gennadi Karponosov.

1980, Aug. 10 ***Perf. 13¼***

1981 A1019 20ch multicolored 6.00 1.50

a. Sheet of 2, as #1981-1982 15.00 —

Souvenir Sheet

1982 A1019 1w multicolored 6.50 2.00

A1020

Albrecht Dürer, 450th Anniv. Death

Designs: 20ch, *Soldier with Horse.*

1w, *Horse and Rider.*

1980, Aug. 18 ***Perf. 11¾x12***

1983 A1020 20ch multicolored 6.00 1.50

a. Sheet of 2 as #1983-1984 20.00 —

Souvenir Sheet

1984 A1020 1w multicolored 9.00 2.50

A1021

Johannes Kepler, 350th Anniv. Death

Designs: 20ch, Kepler, astrolabe and satellites.

1w, Kepler, astrolabe and satellites (diff.).

1980, Aug. 25

1985 A1021 20ch multicolored 2.75 1.25

a. Sheet of 2, as #1985-1986 12.00 —

Souvenir Sheet

1986 A1021 1w multicolored 6.00 2.00

3rd Int'l Stamp Fair Essen 1980 — A1022

Designs, Stamps from German and Russian Zeppelin sets, respectively: 10ch, 1m and 30k. 20ch, 2m and 35k. 30ch, 4m and 1r.

50ch, Russian 2r Polar Flight stamp and DPRK No. 1780 stamp.

1980, Sep. 25 ***Perf. 13¼***

1987-1989 A1022 Set of 3 6.50 1.25

1989a Sheet of 4, as #1987-1990 30.00 —

Souvenir Sheet

1990 A1022 50ch multicolored 9.00 2.50

Moscow Olympic Games Winners

A1023

A1024

Designs: 10ch, Free pistol shooting — Aleksandr Melentiev (USSR). 20ch, 4000m Individual pursuit bicycle race — Robert Dill-Bundi (Switzerland). 25ch, Gymnastics — Stoyan Deltchev (Bulgaria). 30ch, Free style wrestling — K). 35ch, Weight-lifting — Ho Bong Choi (DPRK). 40ch, Running — Marita Koch (DDR). 50ch, Modern pentathlon — Anatoly Starostin (USSR).

No. 1997, Boxing — Teofilo Stevenson (Cuba). No. 1998, Ancient Greek rider on horse.

1980, Oct. 20 ***Perf. 12x11¾***

1991-1997 A1023 Set of 7 7.00 2.25

1997a Sheet of 8, as #1991-1998 12.00 —

Souvenir Sheet

1998 A1023 70ch multicolored 2.75 2.00

1999 A1024 70ch multicolored 4.50 2.00

A1025

Josip Broz Tito (1892-1980)

1980, Dec. 4 ***Perf. 12¼x12***

2000 A1025 20ch multicolored 1.00 .20

A1026

First Post-WWII Lufthansa Flight, 25th Anniv.

Designs: 20ch, Convair CV 340 airliner.

1w, Airbus A 300.

1980, Dec. 10 ***Perf. 13¼***

2001 A1026 20ch multicolored 5.50 2.00

a. Sheet of 2, as #2001-2002 15.00 —

Souvenir Sheet

2002 A1026 1w multicolored 7.00 3.00

A1027

Liverpool-Manchester Railway, 150th Anniv.

Designs: 20ch, *The Rocket.*

1w, Locomotive pulling passenger car and horse car.

1980, Dec. 16 ***Perf. 11¾***

2003 A1027 20ch multicolored 6.00 3.00

a. Sheet of 2, as #2003-2004 15.00 —

Souvenir Sheet

2004 A1027 1w multicolored 6.00 2.50

A1028

Electric Train Centenary

Designs: 20ch, First E-type electric and steam locomotives.

1w, Electric locomotive exhibited in Berlin, 1879.

1980, Dec. 24 ***Perf. 13¼***

2005 A1028 20ch multicolored 6.00 2.00

a. Sheet of 2, as #2005-2006 20.00 —

Souvenir Sheet

2006 A1028 1w multicolored 12.00 2.50

A1029

Dag Hammarskjold (1905-61), 75th Anniv. of Birth

Designs: 20ch, Hammarskjold and UN Building.

1w, Hammarskjold (diff.).

1980, Dec. 26 ***Perf. 11¾***

2007 A1029 20ch multicolored 3.25 2.25

a. Sheet of 2, as #2007-2008 10.00 —

Souvenir Sheet

2008 A1029 1w multicolored 4.50 2.75

A1030

World Chess Championship, Merano

Designs: 20ch, Bobby Fischer-Boris Spassky chess match.

1w, Viktor Korchnoi-Anatoly Karpov chess match.

1980, Dec. 28 ***Perf. 13¼***
2009 A1030 20ch multicolored 7.00 2.00
a. Sheet of 2, as #2009-2010 17.00 —

Souvenir Sheet

2010 A1030 1w multicolored 9.00 2.00

A1031

Robert Stolz (1880-1975), Composer, Birth Centen.

Designs: 20ch, Stoltz with music from *At the Flower Bed.*
1w, Stoltz working with stamp collection.

1980, Dec. 30
2011 A1031 20ch multicolored 3.00 1.00
a. Sheet of 2, as #2011-2012 12.00 —

Souvenir Sheet

2012 A1031 1w multicolored 5.00 1.00

New Year — A1032

1981, Jan. 1 ***Perf. 12***
2013 A1032 10ch multicolored .90 .20

Fairy Tales A1033

Designs (all 10ch): #2014 Russian fairy tale. #2015 Icelandic. #2016, Swedish. #2017, Irish. #2018, Italian. #2019, Japanese. #2020, German.
70ch (#2021): Korean fairy tale, *A Gold Nugget and Maize Cake.*

1981, Jan. 30 ***Perf. 13¼***
2014-2020 A1033 Set of 7 10.00 3.50
2020a Sheet of 8, as #2014-2021 15.00 —

Souvenir Sheet

2021 A1033 70ch multicolored 5.75 3.00

International Year of the Child, 1979.

A1034

Changgwang Street, Pyongyang

1981, Feb. 16 ***Perf. 11¾x12***
2022 A1034 10ch multicolored .70 .20

A1035

World Soccer Cup Championship ESPANA '82

Designs: 10ch, Tackling. 20ch, Kicking. 30ch, Feinting.
70ch, Three players.

1981, Feb. 20 ***Perf. 13¼***
2023-2025 A1035 Set of 3 9.00 2.75
2025a Sheet of 4, as #2023-2026 17.00 —

Souvenir Sheet

2026 A1035 70ch multicolored 8.00 3.25

For overprints, see Nos. 2216.

A1036

World Soccer Cup Championship ESPAÑA '82 (2nd issue)

Designs: 10ch, Emblem, map and cup. 20ch, Dribbling. 25ch, Tackling. 30ch, Pass.
70ch, Sliding tackle.

1981, Feb. 28
2027-2031 A1036 Set of 5 9.00 3.75
2031a Sheet of 6, as #2027-2032 18.00 —

Souvenir Sheet

2032 A1036 70ch multicolored 9.00 3.00

A1037

Implementations of Decisions of 6th Korean Workers' Party Congress

Designs: 2ch, Marchers with book, banners. 10ch (#2034), Worker with book. 10ch (#2035), Workers and factory. 10ch (#2036), Electricity generation (horiz.). 10ch (#2037), Factory, construction scene (horiz.). 10ch (#2038), Cement factory, fertilizer (horiz.). 30ch, Fishing, fabrics (horiz.). 40ch, Grain, port facilities (horiz.). 70ch, Clasped hands, map of Korea. 1w, Hand holding torch, "peace" and "solidarity" slogans.

1981, Mar. 15 ***Perf. 12¼***
2033-2042 A1037 Set of 10 6.00 2.50
2033a 2ch, unsurfaced white paper, without gum 10.00 —
2034a 10ch, unsurfaced white paper, without gum 10.00 —
2035a 10ch, unsurfaced white paper, without gum 10.00 —
2039a 30ch, unsurfaced white paper, without gum 10.00 —
2040a 40ch, unsurfaced white paper, without gum 10.00 —
2041a 70ch, unsurfaced white paper, without gum 10.00 —
2042a 1w, unsurfaced white paper, without gum 10.00 —

Nos. 1925-1932 Overprinted **For Nobel Prize Winners in Medicine**

1981, Mar. 20 ***Perf. 11¾x11½***
2043-2049 A1005 Set of 7 9.00 3.00
2049a Sheet of 8, as #2043-2050 12.00 —

Souvenir Sheet

2050 A1005 50ch multicolored 9.00 —

Nos. 1698-1710 Overprinted History of the World Cup

1981, Mar. 20 ***Perf. 13¼***
2051-2062 A953 Set of 12 24.00 —
2062a Sheet of 12, #2051-2062 25.00 —

Souvenir Sheet

2063 A953 50ch multicolored 12.00 —

Copa de Oro Mini-World Cup Championships

A1038

Designs: 20ch, Uruguayan and Brazilian soccer players.
1w, Goalkeeper blocking ball.

1981, Mar. 27
2064 A1038 20ch multicolored 4.00 1.25

Souvenir Sheet

2065 A1038 1w multicolored 8.00 1.00

A1039

Espana '82

Nos. 2066-2068 depict different designs incorporating bleachers and crowds, with images of soccer players and trophy that appear or disappear, depending upon the angle from which the stamps are viewed. This effect is created by printing on multiple layers of thin plastic, with gummed paper backing.

1981, Apr. 10 ***Imperf.***
2066-2067 A1039 Set of 2, 20ch, 30ch 25.00 9.00

Souvenir Sheet

2068 A1039 1w multicolored 25.00 25.00

Nos. 2066-2068 are airmail.

Naposta '81 Int'l Stamp Exhibition, Stuttgart — A1040

Designs: 10ch, Dornier Do-X flying boat. 20ch, Count von Zeppelin and airship LZ-120. 30ch, Goetz von Berlichingen (1480-1562), German knight and subject of poem by Johann von Goethe (1749-1832), also pictured.
70ch, Mercedes-Benz W 196, 1954 automobile.

1981, Apr. 28 ***Perf. 12x11¾***
2069-2071 A1040 Set of 3 8.00 1.60

Souvenir Sheet

Perf. 11½x11¾

2072 A1040 70ch multicolored 5.50 2.75

A1041

World Telecommunications Day

1981, May 17 ***Perf. 11¾x11½***
2073 A1041 10ch multicolored 2.75 .25

Flowers — A1042

Designs: 10ch, Iris pseudodacorus. 20ch, Iris pallasii. 30ch, Gladiolus gandavensis.

1981, May 20 ***Perf. 12x11¾***
2074-2076 A1042 Set of 3 3.50 1.60
2076a Sheet of 3, #2074-2076 3.75 —

WIPA 1981 Stamp Exhibition, Vienna — A1043

Designs: 20ch, Austrian WIPA 1981 and Rudolf Kirchschlager stamps. 30ch, Austrian Maria Theresa and Franz Josef stamps.
50ch, Kim Il Sung and Korean Children's Union choir, vert.

1981, May 22 ***Perf. 13¼***
2077-2078 A1043 Set of 2 6.00 1.60

Souvenir Sheet

Perf. 11½

2079 A1043 50ch multicolored 6.00 2.75

International Gymnastc Federation, Centen. A1044

Gymnastic events: 10ch, Rings. 15ch, Pommel horse. 20ch, Long horse. 25ch, Floor. 30ch, Hoop.
70ch, Ribbon, horiz.

1981, May 25 ***Perf. 11¾x12***
2080-2084 A1044 Set of 5 3.75 1.40
2084a Sheet of 6, as #2080-2085 15.00 —

Souvenir Sheet

Perf. 11½x11¾

2085 A1044 70ch multicolored 3.00 1.00

For surcharges, see Nos. 2270-2275

Mingyuehgou Meeting, 50th Anniv. — A1045

1981, June 15 ***Perf. 12¼x12***
2086 A1045 10ch multicolored .50 .20

A1046

Taen Work System, 20th Anniv.

1981, June 25 ***Perf. 12x12¼***
2087 A1046 10ch multicolored .50 .20

New System of Agricultural Guidance, 20th Anniv. — A1047

1981, June 25
2088 A1047 10ch multicolored .50 .20

A1048

Anti-Japanese Women's Assoc., 55th Anniv.

1981, July 5 ***Perf. 12¼***
2089 A1048 5w multicolored 12.00 1.00

Opera *Sea of Blood*, 10th Anniv. A1049

1981, July 17 ***Perf. 12***
2090 A1049 10w multicolored 30.00 10.00

A1050

Joan of Arc, 550th Anniv. Death

Designs: 10ch (#2091), Joan of Arc. 10ch (#2092a), Archangel Michael. 70ch, Joan of Arc in armor.
No. 2094, as #2093.

1981, July 20
2091 A1050 Set of 3 3.50 .75
2092 Sheet of 2, #2092a-2092b 9.00 —
a. 10ch multicolored — —
b. 70ch multicolored — —

Souvenir Sheet
Perf. 11½
2094 A1050 70ch multicolored 7.00 1.90

A1051

Down-with-Imperialism Union, 55th Anniv.

1981, July 25 ***Perf. 12¼***
2095 A1051 1w multicolored 6.00 2.00

A1052

Rembrandt, 375th Anniv. Birth

Designs: 10ch, *Young Girl by the Window.* 20ch, *Rembrandt's Mother.* 30ch, *Saskia van Uylenburgh.* 40ch, *Pallas Athenae.*
70ch, *Self-portrait.*

1981, July 25 ***Perf. 13¼***
2096-2099 A1052 Set of 4 7.00 2.75

Souvenir Sheet
2100 A1052 70ch multicolored 5.50 3.00

A1053

Symposium of the Non-Aligned Countries on Increasing Agricultural Production

Designs: 10ch, Emblem, banners over Pyongyang. 50ch, Harvesting grain. 90ch, Marchers with banners, tractors, fields, factories.

1981, Aug. 26 ***Perf. 12***
2101-2103 A1053 Set of 3 2.00 1.00

Royal Wedding A1054

Designs: 10ch, St. Paul's Cathedral. 20ch, Prince Charles on Great Britain stamp, Scott #599. 30ch, Princess Diana. 40ch, Prince Charles in military uniform.
70ch, Prince Charles and Princess Diana.

1981, Sept. 18 ***Perf. 13¼***
2104-2107 A1054 Set of 4 10.00 3.00

Souvenir Sheet
2108 A1054 70ch multicolored 15.00 5.00

For overprints, see Nos. 2205-2209.

Reubens Paintings — A1055

Designs: 10ch, *The Four Philosophers.* 15ch, *Portrait of Helena Fourment.* 20ch, *Portrait of Isabella Brandt.* 25ch, *The Education of Maria de Medici.* 30ch, *Helena Fourment and Her Child.* 40ch, *Helena Fourment in Her Wedding Dress.*
70ch, *Portrait of Nikolaas Rubens.*

1981, Sept. 20 ***Perf. 11¾x12***
2109-2114 A1055 Set of 6 9.00 2.75

Souvenir Sheet
Perf 11½
2115 A1055 70ch multicolored 5.50 2.75

Royal Wedding — A1056

Illustration reduced.
Designs: 10ch, Prince Charles and Princess Diana wedding portrait. 20ch, Charles and Diana with Flower Girl. 30ch, Charles and Diana leaving St. Paul's Cathedral. 40ch, Wedding portrait (diff.)
70ch, Charles and Diana with Queen Elizabeth on balcony.

1981, Sept. 29 ***Perf. 13¼***
2116-2119 A1056 Sheet of 4 20.00 4.50

Souvenir Sheet
2120 A1056 70ch multicolored 25.00 6.00

A1057

Philatokyo '81 International Stamp Exhibition, Tokyo

Design: 10ch, Rowland Hill and first stamps of Great Britain, Japan and DPRK. 20ch, DPRK World Fairy Tale stamps. 30ch, Three Japanese stamps.
70ch, Exhibition Hall.

1981, Oct. 9 ***Perf. 11¾x11x½***
2121-2123 A1057 Set of 3 9.00 2.50
2123a Sheet of 4, as #2121-2124, perf 12x11½ 27.50 —

Souvenir Sheet
2124 A1057 70ch multicolored 7.00 2.00

Philatokyo '81 — A1058

Designs (both 10ch): #2125, Two DPRK stamps. #2126, DPRK stamp featuring Juche torch.

1981, Oct. 9 ***Perf. 12x12¼***
2125-2126 A1058 Set of 2 4.00 1.40

League of Socialist Working Youth of Korea, 7th Congress — A1059

1981, Oct. 20 ***Perf. 12x11¾***
2127 A1059 10ch multicolored .20 .20
2128 A1059 80ch multicolored 1.00 .35

A1060

Bulgarian State, 1300th Anniv.

1981, Oct. 20 ***Perf. 12x12¼***
2129 A1060 10ch multicolored .50 .20

A1061

Georgi Dimitrov (1882-1949), Birth Centenary

1981, Nov. 5 ***Perf. 12***
2130 A1061 10ch multicolored .50 .20

Philatelia '81 Int'l Stamp Fair, Frankfurt-am-Main — A1062

1981, Nov. 14 ***Perf. 13¼***
2131 A1062 20ch multicolored 3.00 .45

A1063

A1064

Philexfrance '82 International Stamp Exhibition, Paris

Designs (A1063): 10ch, Count Ferdinand von Zeppelin, *Graf Zeppelin*, Concorde. 20ch, Aircraft — Santos-Dumont 1905, Brequet 1930, Brequet Provence 1950, Concorde 1970. 30ch, Mona Lisa, six French stamps.

No. 2135 (A1064): 10ch, Hotel des Invalides, Paris. 20ch, Pres. Mitterand of France. 30ch, International Friendship Building. 70ch, Kim Il Sung.

No. 2136 (A1063): 60ch, Two French stamps picturing Rembrandt portrait and Picasso painting.

1981, Nov. 14 ***Perf. 13¼***
2132-2134 A1063 Set of 3 10.00 2.00
2135 Sheet of 4, #a.-d. 7.50 2.50
a. A1064 10ch multicolored 1.25 .50
b. A1064 20ch multicolored 1.25 .50
c. A1064 30ch multicolored 1.25 .50
d. A1064 70ch multicolored 1.25 .50

Souvenir Sheet

2136 A1063 60ch multicolored 7.50 2.25

New Year — A1065

1982, Jan. 1 ***Perf. 12***
2137 A1065 10ch multicolored .90 .20

A1066

"Korea Prospering Under the Wise Leadership of the Party"

Party emblem and: 2ch, banners. 10ch (#2139), Iron industry. 10ch (#2140), Produce, city, countryside. 10ch (#2141), Film industry. 10ch (#2142), Mining. 10ch (#2143), Lighthouse, helicopter. 40ch, Idealized cityscape.

1982, Feb. 1
2138-2144 A1066 Set of 7 7.00 1.50

A1067

A1068

Pablo Picasso (1881-1973), Painter, Birth Centenary

Designs (#2145-2148): 10ch, *La Coiffure.* 20ch, *Woman Leaning on Arm.* 25ch, *Child with Pigeon.* 35ch, *Portrait of Gertrude Stein.*

No. 2149: 10ch, *Paulo on a Donkey.* 20ch, *Harlequin.* 25ch, *Reading a Letter.* 35ch, *Harlequin* (diff.) 80ch, *Minotaur.* 90ch, *Mother and Child.*

Nos. 2150-2151: 80ch, *Minotaur.* 90ch, *Mother and Child.*

1982, Mar. 30 ***Perf. 11¾***
2145-2148 A1067 Set of 4 6.00 1.50
2149 Sheet of 6, #a.-f. 14.00 2.75
a. A1067 10ch multicolored 2.25 .45
b. A1067 20ch multicolored 2.25 .45
c. A1067 25ch multicolored 2.25 .45
d. A1067 35ch multicolored 2.25 .45
e. A1067 80ch multicolored 2.25 .45
f. A1067 90ch multicolored 2.25 .45

Souvenir Sheets

2150-2151 A1068 Set of 2 8.00 4.00

A1069

A1070

Kim Il Sung, 70th Birthday

Type A1070 illustration reduced.

Type A1069 (both 10ch): #2152, Kim Il Sung's Birthplace. #2153, Fireworks over Pyongyang.

Type A1070 (10ch), paintings of Kim Il Sung: #2154, "The Day Will Dawn." #2155, Signaling the start of the Pochonbo battle. #2156, Groundbreaking of Potong River Project. #2157, Embracing bereaved children. #2158, Directing operations at front. #2159, "On the Road of Advance." #2160, Speaking with workers at Kangson Steel Plant. #2161, Talking with peasants. #2162, Choosing site for reservoir.

Type A1070 (20ch): #2163, Visiting Komdok Valley. #2164, With Red Flag Company. #2165, With farmers. #2166, Opening metallurgical plant. #2167, Talking with smelters. #2168, At chemical plant. #2169, With fishermen.

Perf. 11¾x12 (#2151-2152), 12x11¾
1982, Apr. 15
2152-2169 Set of 18 8.00 2.25

All type A1070 stamps were issued with setenant labels bearing inscriptions relating to theme of stamp. Values are for stamps with labels attached.

Souvenir Sheets
Perf. 13¼

A1071

Illustration reduced.

Designs: #2170, Kim surrounded by adoring Koreans. #2171, Kim as a boy.

2170-2171 A1071 Set of 2 5.00 1.75

A1072

Korean People's Army, 50th Anniv.

1982, Apr. 25 ***Perf. 12***
2172 A1072 10ch multicolored .50 .20

A1073

ESSEN '82 Int'l Stamp Fair

1982, Apr. 28 ***Perf. 11¾x12***
2173 A1073 30ch multicolored 4.50 .50

A1074

Four Nature-Remaking Tasks

1982, Apr. 30 ***Perf. 12***
2174 A1074 10ch multicolored .60 .20

Issued to publicize the program for nature transformation contained in the Second Seven-Year Plan, which included irrigation, land reclamation, terracing, afforestation and water conservation, and reclamation of tidal lands.

A1075

Princess Diana, 21st Birthday

Princess Diana (#2175-2178): 10ch, As a baby. 20ch, As little girl on swing. 30ch, As little girl wearing red parka.

No. 2179: 50ch, As girl, wearing blue turtleneck sweater. 60ch, With long hair, wearing gray hat. 70ch, Wearing white hat. 80ch, Wearing white blouse and sweater.

Nos. 2180-2181: 40ch, Diana pushing her brother on swing. 80ch, As #2178d.

1982, May 1 ***Perf. 13¼***
2175-2177 A1075 Set of 3 4.00 1.00
2178 Sheet of 4, #a.-d. 18.00 5.50
a. A1075 50ch multicolored 3.50 1.25
b. A1075 60ch multicolored 3.50 1.25
c. A1075 70ch multicolored 3.50 1.25
d. A1075 80ch multicolored 3.50 1.25

Souvenir Sheets

2179-2180 A1075 Set of 2 10.00 5.00

For overprints, see Nos. 2210-2215.

A1076

Tower of the Juche Idea

1982, May 21 *Perf. 12*
2182 A1076 2w multicolored 7.50 2.00

A1077

Arch of Triumph

1982, May 22
2183 A1074 3w multicolored 8.50 2.00

Tigers A1078

(#2184-2185): 20ch, Tiger cubs. 30ch, Tiger cubs (diff.)
No. 2186 (designs horizontal): 30ch, Tiger cub with mother. 40ch, Two cubs playing. 80ch, Two cubs playing, diff.
Nos. 2187: 80ch, Two cubs, horiz.

Perf. 11¾x12 (#2185-2186), 12x11¾
1982, May 30
2184-2185 A1078 Set of 2 7.00 1.00
2186 Sheet of 3, #a.-c. 16.00 3.00
a. A1078 30ch multicolored 3.00 .50
b. A1078 40ch multicolored 3.00 .50
c. A1078 80ch multicolored 3.00 .50

Souvenir Sheet

2187 A1078 80ch Multicolored 6.00 1.50

ESPANA '82 World Cup Championship — A1079

Flags and players of: 10ch, Group 1 countries — Italy, Peru, Poland, Cameroun. 20ch, Group 2 countries — Germany, Chile, Algeria, Austria. 30ch, Group 3 countries — Argentina, Hungary, Belgium, El Salvador. 40ch, Group 4 countries — Great Britain, Czechoslovakia, France, Kuwait. 50ch, Group 5 countries — Spain, Yugoslavia, Honduras, Northern Ireland. 60ch, Group 6 countries — Brazil, Scotland, USSR, New Zealand.
1w, Soccer players, flags, trophy and ESPANA '82 emblem.

1982, June 12 *Perf. 13¼*
2188-2193 A1079 Set of 6 13.00 4.00

Souvenir Sheet

2194 A1079 1w multicolored 11.00 4.00

For overprints, see Nos. 2217-2223.

A1080

Space Exploration

Designs: 10ch, Rocket launch. 20ch, Spaceship over planet. 80ch, Spaceship between planets.
80ch, Spaceship exploring desert area of other planet.

1982, June 20 *Perf. 11¾x11½*
2195-2196 A1080 Set of 2 3.50 1.50
2197 Sheet of 3, #2196-2197 + 2197c + label 6.00 2.50
c. A1080 80ch multicolored 2.00 .75

Souvenir Sheet

2198 A1079 80ch multicolored 3.75 1.50

Nos. 2195, 2196, and 2197c were issued setenant within No. 2197. Nos. 2195 and 2196 were also issued in large sheet format.

A1081

Johann von Goethe (1749-1832), Writer, 150th Anniv. Death

Silhouettes: 10ch, Charlotte von Stein, 20ch, Goethe's sister. 25ch, Charlotte Buff. 35ch, Lili Schönemann.
No. 2203: 10ch, Goethe's mother. 20ch, Angelika Kauffman. 25ch, Anna Amalia. 35ch, Charlotte von Lengefeld. 80ch, Goethe.
No. 2204: 80ch, Goethe.

1982, July 25 *Perf. 11¾x12*
2199-2202 A1081 Set of 4 3.75 1.50
2203 Sheet of 5, #a.-e. + label 9.00 2.00
a. A1081 10ch multicolored 1.75 .50
b. A1081 20ch multicolored 1.75 .50
c. A1081 25ch multicolored 1.75 .50
d. A1081 35ch multicolored 1.75 .50
e. A1081 80ch multicolored 1.75 .50

Souvenir Sheet

2204 A1081 80ch multicolored 4.00 1.75

Princess Diana's 21st Birthday
Nos. 2104-2108 Overprinted in Blue

1982, Aug. 20
2205-2208 A1054 Set of 4 15.00 —

Souvenir Sheet

2209 A1054 70ch multicolored 15.00 —

Birth of Prince William of Wales
Nos. 2175-2179 Overprinted in Blue

1982, Aug. 20
2210-2212 A1075 Set of 3 15.00 —
2213 Sheet of 4 30.00 —

Souvenir Sheet

2214-2215 A1075 Set of 2 25.00 —

Nos. 2025a, 2188-2194 Overprinted in Blue
ESPANA '82 World Soccer Championship Winners

1982, Aug. 25
2216 A1035 Sheet of 4, #a.-d. 14.00 —
a. 10ch multicolored 1.00 —
b. 20ch multicolored 2.00 —
c. 30ch multicolored 3.00 —
d. 70ch multicolored 6.00 —
2217-2222 A1079 Set of 6 15.00 —

Souvenir Sheet

2223 A1079 1w multicolored 12.50 —

A1082

ESPANA '82 World Soccer Cup Winners

Designs: 20ch, Player holding World Cup aloft. 30ch, Three players with World Cup.
No. 2226: 30ch, as No. 2222. 40ch, As No. 2223. 80ch, King Juan Carlos of Spain and two players with World Cup.
No. 2227: 80ch, as No. 2226c.

1982, Aug. 30 *Perf. 13¼*
2224-2225 A1082 Set of 2 4.00 1.00
2226 Sheet of 4, #a.-c. + label 8.00 —
a. A1082 30ch multicolored — —
b. A1082 40ch multicolored — —
c. A1082 80ch multicolored — —

Souvenir Sheet

2227 A1082 80ch multicolored 9.00 2.00

A1083

A1084

1st Wedding Anniv. of Prince and Princess of Wales

No. 2229 illustration reduced.

1982, Sept. 21
2228 A1083 30ch multicolored 10.00 4.00

Souvenir Sheet

2229 A1084 80ch multicolored 15.00 5.00

No. 2228 was issued in sheets of four stamps and two labels.

A1085

Birth of Prince William of Wales

Designs: 10ch, Charles and Diana with Prince William (Charles in suit, Diana in pink hat and dress). 20ch, Couple with William. 30ch, Couple with William (diff.). 40ch, Diana with William. 50ch, Diana with William (diff.).
No. 2235: 10ch, Diana holding bouquet. 20ch, Charles carrying William, with Diana. 30ch, Charles carrying William, with Diana (diff.). 80ch, Couple with William (diff.).
No. 2236 (horiz.): 40ch, Charles and Diana. 50ch, Charles and Diana in evening dress. 80ch, Charles holding William, with Diana.
Nos. 2237-2238 (both 50ch): Diana holding William, with Royal Family; Diana holding William, with godparents.

1982, Sept. 29
2230-2234 A1085 Set of 5 16.00 5.00
2235 Sheet of 4, #a.-d. 15.00 6.00
a. A1085 10ch multicolored 3.25 1.25
b. A1085 20ch multicolored 3.25 1.25
c. A1085 30ch multicolored 3.25 1.25
d. A1085 80ch multicolored 3.25 1.25
2236 Sheet of 3, #a.-c. 15.00 6.00
a. A1085 40ch multicolored 4.00 1.75
b. A1085 50ch multicolored 4.00 1.75
c. A1085 80ch multicolored 4.00 1.75

Souvenir Sheets

2237-2238 A1085 Set of 2 20.00 8.00

A1086

A1087

Birth of Prince William of Wales

Nos. 2239-2244 are composed of layered plastic, on gummed paper, which creates two different images on each stamp, depending on the angle at which it is viewed.

Designs Nos. 2239-2241 (all 30ch): #2239, Charles, Diana and William/Diana holding William. #2240, Charles, Diana and William (diff.)/Couple with William (Charles in suit, Diana in pink hat and dress). #2241, Diana and William/Charles and Diana with William (Charles in suit, Diana in blue dress).

Designs Nos. 2242-2244 (all 80ch): #2242, Diana and William, Portrait of Diana/Charles. #2243, Diana and William, St. Paul's Church/Wedding portrait of Royal Couple. #2244, Charles and Diana with William/Diana holding bouquet.

Type A1087 illustration reduced.

1982, Oct. 1 ***Imperf.***

2239-2241 A1086 Set of 3 35.00 —

Souvenir Sheets

2242-2244 A1087 Set of 3 60.00 —

A1088

Bicentenary of Manned Flight

Designs: 10ch, Baldwin's airship *Nulli Secundus II*, 1908. 20ch, Tissandier Brothers' airship, 1883. 30ch, Parseval *PL VIII*, 1912. 40ch, Count Lennox's balloon *Eagle*, 1834.

No. 2249: 10ch, Pauley and Durs Egg's airship, *The Dolphin*, 1818. 20ch, Guyton de Morveau's balloon, 1784. 30ch, Sir George Cayley's airship, 1837. 40ch, Camille Vert's balloon *Poisson Volant*, 1859. 80ch, Dupuy de Lôme's airship, 1872.

No. 2250: Masse's oar-powered balloon, 1784, vert.

1982, Nov. 21 ***Perf. 13¼***

2245-2248 A1088 Set of 4 7.00 2.00
2249 Sheet of 5, #a.-e. + label 13.00 6.00
a. A1088 10ch multicolored 2.25 1.00
b. A1088 20ch multicolored 2.25 1.00
c. A1088 30ch multicolored 2.25 1.00
d. A1088 40ch multicolored 2.25 1.00
e. A1088 80ch multicolored 2.25 1.00

Souvenir Sheet

2250 A1085 80ch multicolored 4.50 2.00

A1089

Bicentenary of Manned Flight

Designs: 10ch, Balthasar Antoine Dunker's *Utopic Balloon Post*, 1784-90. 20ch, "and they fly into heaven and have no wings." 30ch, Pierre Testu-Brissy's balloon flight with horse, 1796. 40ch, Test flight of Gaston Tissandier's balloon *Zenith*, 1875.

No. 2255: 10ch, Montgolfier balloon at Versailles, 1783. 20ch, Montgolfier Brothers' balloon, 1783. 30ch, Charles' hydrogen balloon landing at Nesle. 40ch, Blanchard and Jeffries' flight over the English Channel, 1785. 80ch, Henri Giffard's balloon *Le Grand Ballon Captif* at World's Fair, 1878.

No. 2256: "Ballons Monte" balloon mail service from besieged Paris, 1870-1871.

1982, Dec. 10

2251-2254 A1089 Set of 4 11.00 4.00
2255 Sheet of 5, #a.-e. + label 25.00 6.50
a. A1089 10ch multicolored 4.50 1.25
b. A1089 20ch multicolored 4.50 1.25
c. A1089 30ch multicolored 4.50 1.25
d. A1089 40ch multicolored 4.50 1.25
e. A1089 80ch multicolored 4.50 1.25

Souvenir Sheet

2256 A1089 80ch multicolored 5.00 2.00

A1090

Tale of the Hare

Designs: 10ch, Turtle searching for hare. 20ch, Turtle and hare going to Dragon King Palace. 30ch, Hare swindling Dragon King, demanding her liver. 40ch, Hare cheating turtle.

1982, Dec. 25 ***Perf. 12***

2257-2260 A1090 Set of 4 8.00 1.25

Socialist Constitution, 10th Anniv. — A1091

1982, Dec. 27

2261 A1091 10ch multicolored .50 .20

New Year — A1092

1983, Jan. 1 ***Perf. 12¼x12***

2262 A1092 10ch multicolored .50 .20

Saenal Newspaper, 55th Anniv. — A1093

1983, Jan. 15 ***Perf. 11½x11¾***

2263 A1093 10ch multicolored .90 .20

Rembrandt Paintings A1094

Designs: 10ch, *Man in Oriental Costume*. 20ch, *The Noble Slav*. 30ch, *Dr. Tulp's Anatomy Lesson* (detail). 40ch, *Two Scholars Disputing*.

No. 2268: 10ch, *Child with Dead Peacocks*. 20ch, *Old Man in Fur Hat*. 30ch, *Portrait of a Fashionable Couple*. 40ch, *Woman with Child*. 80ch, *Woman Holding an Ostrich Feather Fan*.

No. 2269: 80ch, *Self-Portrait*.

1983, Jan. 25 ***Perf. 11¾x11½***

2264-2267 A1094 Set of 4 7.50 1.50
2268 Sheet of 5, #a.-e. + label 15.00 7.50
a. A1094 10ch multicolored 2.00 1.00
b. A1094 20ch multicolored 2.00 1.00
c. A1094 30ch multicolored 2.00 1.00
d. A1094 40ch multicolored 2.00 1.00
e. A1094 80ch multicolored 2.00 1.00

Souvenir Sheet

Perf. 11¾x12

2269 A1094 80ch multicolored 4.00 1.25

Nos. 2080-2085 Overprinted "XXIII Summer Olympic Games 1984" and Olympic Rings

1983, Feb. 10

2270-2274 A1044 Set of 5 20.00 —

Souvenir Sheet

2275 A1044 70ch multicolored 25.00 —

Luposta Int'l Air Mail Exhib., Köln — A1095

1983, Jan. 25 ***Perf. 11¾x11½***

2276 30ch multicolored 3.00 1.00
2277 40ch multicolored 3.00 1.00
a. Pair, #2276-2277 7.00 3.00

Virgin and Child, by Stephan Lochner — A1096

Illustration reduced

Souvenir Sheet

Perf. 13¼

2278 A1096 80ch multicolored 3.50 1.75

A1097

Wangjaesen Meeting, 50th Anniv.

1983, Mar. 11 ***Perf. 11½x11¾***

2279 A1097 10ch multicolored .50 .20

A1098

Karl Marx, Centenary of Death

1983, Mar. 14 ***Perf. 11¾x12***

2280 A1098 10ch multicolored 2.25 .25

Thousand-ri Journey for Learning, 60th Anniv. — A1099

1983, Mar. 16 ***Perf. 12***

2281 A1099 10ch multicolored 1.00 .20

A1100

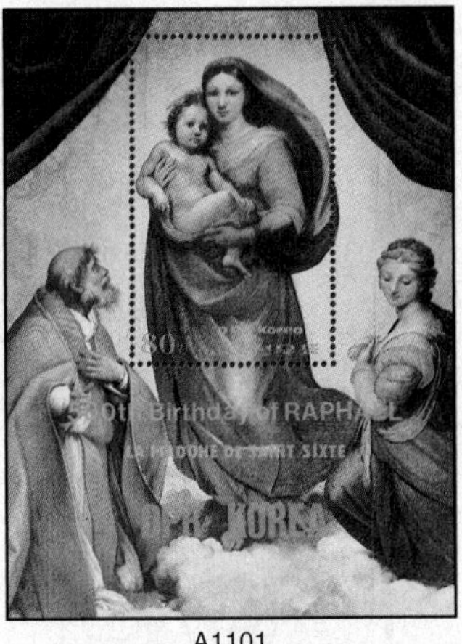

A1101

Designs: 10ch, *Madonna of the Goldfinch.* 30ch, *Madonna of the Grand Duke.* 50ch (#2284), *Madonna of the Chair.*

No. 2285: 20ch, *The School of Athens* (detail). 50ch (#2285b), *Madonna of the Lamb.* 80ch, *The Beautiful Gardener.*

No. 2286: 80ch, *Madonna of St. Sixte,* illustration reduced.

1983, Mar. 20 ***Perf. 13½***

2282-2284 A1100 Set of 3 6.00 1.00

2285 Sheet of 3, #a.-c. + label 15.00 3.50

a. A1100 20ch multicolored 4.00 .75

b. A1100 50ch multicolored 4.00 .75

c. A1100 80ch multicolored 4.00 .75

Souvenir Sheet

2286 A1101 80ch multicolored 4.50 1.25

Pyongyang Buildings — A1102

Designs: 2ch, Chongryu Restaurant. 10ch (#2288), Munsu Street. 10ch (#2289), Ice Rink. 40ch, Department Store No. 1. 70ch, Grand People's Study House.

1983, Apr. 7 ***Perf. 12¼***

2287-2291 A1102 Set of 5 6.00 .75

2287a 2ch, unsurfaced white paper, without gum 10.00 —

2288a 10ch, unsurfaced white paper, without gum 10.00 —

2289a 10ch, unsurfaced white paper, without gum 10.00 —

2290a 40ch, unsurfaced white paper, without gum 10.00 —

2291a 40ch, unsurfaced white paper, without gum 10.00 —

A1103

Int'l Institute of the Juche Idea, 5th Anniv.

1983, Apr. 9 ***Perf. 12¼x12***

2292 A1103 10ch multicolored .50 .20

Pre-Olympic Games, Los Angeles '84 — A1104

Designs (values in gold): 20ch (#2293), Judo. 30ch (#2294), Judo (diff.). 40ch (#2295), Boxing. 50ch (#2296), Weightlifting.

No. 2297 (values in black): 20ch, Wrestling. 30ch, Judo (diff.). 40ch, Shooting. 50ch, Wrestling. (diff.) 80ch, Boxing (diff.).

No. 2298: 80ch, Judo (diff.)

1983, Apr. 20 ***Perf. 11¼***

2293-2296 A1104 Set of 4 13.00 1.50

2297 Sheet of 5, #a.-e. + label 25.00 1.00

a. A1104 20ch multicolored 4.00 .20

b. A1104 30ch multicolored 4.00 .20

c. A1104 40ch multicolored 4.00 .20

d. A1104 50ch multicolored 4.00 .20

e. A1104 80ch multicolored 4.00 .20

Souvenir Sheet

Perf. 13½

2298 A1104 80ch multicolored 10.00 1.00

A1105

World Communications Year

1983, Apr. 30 ***Perf. 11¾x12***

2299 A1105 10ch multicolored 2.00 .20

A1106

TEMBAL '83 Int'l Topical Stamp Exhib., Basel

Designs: 20ch, Emblem, giant panda and stamp. 30ch, Emblem, DPRK flag and "Basel Dove" stamp (Switzerland No. 3L1).

1983, May 21 ***Perf. 12***

2300-2301 A1106 Set of 2 7.50 .75

Old Ships — A1107

Designs: 20ch, *Colourful Cow* (Hamburg, 1402). 35ch, *Great Harry* (England, 1555). 50ch, *Eagle of Lübeck* (Lübeck, 1567).

No. 2305: 20ch, Turtle Boat (Korea, 1592). 35ch, Admiral Li Sun Sin (1545-98), inventor of the Turtle Boat. 50ch, *Merkur* (Prussia, 1847). 80ch, *Duchess Elisabeth* (West Germany).

No. 2306: 80ch, *Christoforo Colombo* (Italy).

1983, May 30 ***Perf. 11x11¼***

2302-2304 A1107 Set of 3 5.00 1.50

2305 Sheet of 4, #a.-d. + 2 labels 12.00 2.50

a. A1107 20ch multicolored 3.00 .50

b. A1107 35ch multicolored 3.00 .50

c. A1107 50ch multicolored 3.00 .50

d. A1107 80ch multicolored 3.00 .50

Souvenir Sheet

Perf. 13½x13¼

2306 A1107 80ch multicolored 6.00 3.00

Steam Locomotives — A1108

Designs: 20ch, *Locomotion* (Great Britain, 1825). 35ch, *De Adler* (Germany, 1835). 50ch, *Austria* (1837).

No. 2310: 20ch, *Drache* (Germany, 1848. 35ch, Korean Train. 50ch, Bristal and Exeter Railway locomotive (Great Britain, 1853). 80ch, Caledonian Railway locomotive (Great Britain, 1859).

No. 2311: 80ch, *Ilmarinen* (Finland, 1860).

1983, June 20 ***Perf. 12x11¾***

2307-2309 A1108 Set of 3 13.00 2.50

2310 Sheet of 4, #a.-d. + 2 labels 40.00 3.50

a. A1108 20ch multicolored 3.00 .75

b. A1108 35ch multicolored 3.00 .75

c. A1108 50ch multicolored 3.00 .75

d. A1108 80ch multicolored 3.00 .75

Souvenir Sheet

Perf. 12

2311 A1108 80ch multicolored 30.00 1.50

A1109

Publication of the Five-Point Policy for Korean Reunification, 10th Anniv.

1983, June 23 ***Perf. 12¼***

2312 A1109 10ch multicolored 1.40 .20

A1110

World Conference of Journalists Against Imperialism and for Friendship and Peace

Designs: 10ch, Emblem, Tower of Juche Idea, fireworks, "Welcome." 40ch, Emblem, clasped hands, rainbow, "Friendship." Emblem, map, hand with raised forefinger, "Korea Is One."

1983, July 2 ***Perf. 12x11¾***

2313-2315 A1110 Set of 3 1.75 .30

A1111

"Let's Create the Speed of the 80s"

1983, July 10 ***Perf. 12x12¼***

2316 A1111 10ch multicolored .50 .20

A1112

Korean War, 30th Anniv.

1983, July 27

2317 A1112 10ch multicolored .50 .20

A1113

Bangkok 1983 Int'l Stamp Exhib.

Designs: 40ch, *Gorch Foch* and 1978 DPRK 2ch stamp depicting the *Mangyongbong* (Scott #1693). 80ch, Bangkok temple, Great Britain Penny Black (Scott #1) and DPRK IYC stamp

1983, Aug. 4 ***Perf. 12x11¾***

2318 A1113 40ch multicolored 3.50 1.00

Souvenir Sheet

Perf. 11½x11¾

2319 A1113 80ch multicolored 7.00 3.50

A1114

A1115

Winter Olympic Games, Sarajevo 1984

Designs: 10ch, Skiier. 30ch, Figure skaters. 50ch, Ski jumper.

No. 2323 (all vert.): 20ch, Woman figure skater. 50ch, Hockey player. 80ch, Speed skater.

No. 2324 (illustration reduced): 80ch, Skier shooting rifle (biathlon).

1983, Aug. 20

2320-2322 A1114 Set of 3 8.00 1.50

2323 Sheet of 3, #a.-c., perf 11¾x12 17.00 2.75

a. A1114 20ch multicolored 4.00 .75

b. A1114 50ch multicolored 4.00 .75

c. A1114 80ch multicolored 4.00 .75

Souvenir Sheet

2324 A1115 80ch multicolored 7.50 1.25

A1116

Democratic People's Republic of Korea, 35th Anniv.

1983, Sept. 9 ***Perf. 13¼x13½***

2325 A1116 10ch multicolored .65 .20

A1117

Folk Games

Designs: 10ch (#2326), Archery. 40ch (#2327), Seesaw. No. 2328: 10ch, Flying kites. 40ch, Swinging.

1983, Sept. 20 ***Perf. 11¾x12***

2326-2327	A1117 Set of 2	5.00	.50
2328	Sheet of 2, #a.-b.	2.50	.40
a.	A1117 10 ch multicolored	.75	.20
b.	A1117 40 ch multicolored	.75	.20

A1118

Korean-Chinese Friendship

1983, Oct. 25 ***Perf. 12***

2329 A1118 10ch multicolored .75 .20

A1119

A1120

World Communications Year

Designs: 30ch (#2330), *Redong Sinmun* and magazine. 40ch (#2331), Letters and forms of postal transport.

No. 2332: 30ch, Communications satellite, satellite dish. 40ch, TV camera and relay tower. 80ch, Telephone and satellite dishes.

No. 2333 (illustration reduced): 80ch, Emblem, communications satellite.

1983, Oct. 30 ***Perf. 13½***

2330-2331	A1119 Set of 2	9.00	1.75
2332	Sheet of 3, #a.-c.	5.50	1.00
a.	A1119 30ch multicolored	1.00	.25
b.	A1119 40ch multicolored	1.00	.25
c.	A1119 80ch multicolored	1.00	.25

Souvenir Sheet

2333 A1120 80ch multicolored 6.00 1.25

A1121

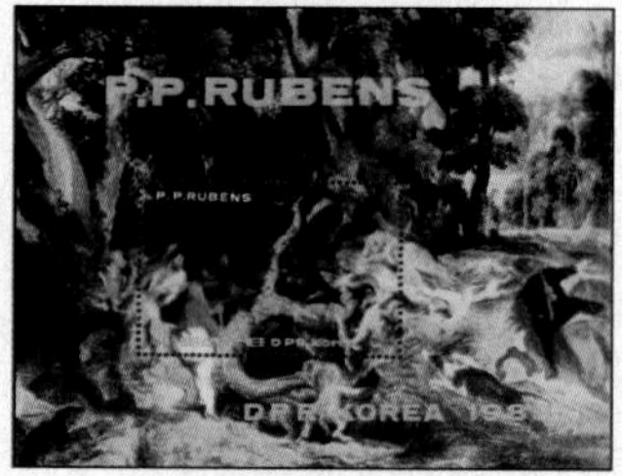

A1122

Rubens Paintings

Designs: 40ch (#2334), *Portrait of Helene Fourmet.*

No. 2335 (both horiz.): 40ch, Detail from *Portrait of a Young Lady.* 80ch, *Diana Returning from Hunt.*

No. 2336 (illustration reduced): 80ch, *The Bear Hunt.*

1983, Nov. 10

2334	A1121 40ch multicolored	1.75	.45
2335	Sheet of 2, #a.-b.	4.50	1.25
a.	A1121 40ch multicolored	1.75	.45
b.	A1121 80ch multicolored	1.75	.45

Souvenir Sheet

2336 A1122 80ch multicolored 3.25 .75

A1123

Olympic Games, Los Angeles 1984

Designs: 10ch, Sprinter. 30ch, Cyclists. 50ch, Volleyball.

No. 2340: 20ch, Show jumping. 50ch, Fencing. 80ch, Gymnastics.

No. 2341: 80ch, Judo.

1983, Nov. 30 ***Perf. 11½***

2337-2339	A1123 Set of 3	10.50	1.25
2340	Sheet of 3, #a.-c.	30.00	2.00
a.	A1123 20ch multicolored	7.00	.50
b.	A1123 50ch multicolored	7.00	.50
c.	A1123 80ch multicolored	7.00	.50

Souvenir Sheet

2341 A1123 80ch multicolored 3.50 1.00

Six deluxe souvenir sheets of one, each denominated 1w, exist. Value, set of 6 sheets, $100.

A1124

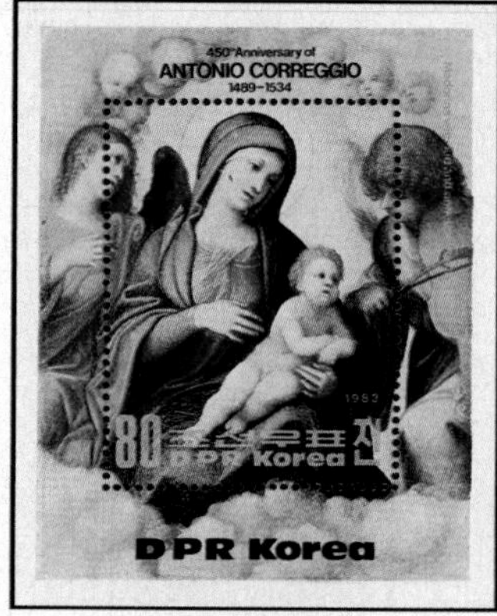

A1125

Antonio Correggio (1489-1534), 450th Anniv. Death

Designs: 20ch, *St. Catherine.* 35ch, *Madonna.* 50ch, *Madonna with St. John.*

No. 2345: 20ch, *Morning* (detail). 35ch, *Morning* (diff. detail). 50ch, *St. Catherine* (diff.). 80ch, *Madonna and Child.*

No. 2346: 80ch, *Madonna and Child with Music-Making Angels.*

1983, Dec. 12 ***Perf. 13¼***

2342-2344	A1124 Set of 3	5.00	1.25
2345	Sheet of 4, #a.-d.	12.00	3.50
a.	A1124 20ch multicolored	2.50	.75
b.	A1124 35ch multicolored	2.50	.75
c.	A1124 50ch multicolored	2.50	.75
d.	A1124 80ch multicolored	2.50	.75

Souvenir Sheet

2346 A1125 80ch multicolored 4.50 1.25

Cats A1126

Domestic cats, each different, denominated 10ch. Frame color: #2347, green. #2348, gray. #2349, gold. #2350, red. #2351, blue.

1983, Dec. 20

2347-2351 A1126 Set of 5 12.00 .50

Six souvenir sheets inscribed Sarajevo '84, each containing one 1w stamp, were issued on Dec. 31, 1983. Value $80.

New Year — A1127

1984, Jan. 1 ***Perf. 12***

2352 A1127 10ch multicolored 1.00 .20

A1128

Korean Workers Party

Designs (both 10ch): No. 2353, Komdok General Mining Enterprise, Ore-dressing Plant No. 3, and Party flag. No. 2354, Worker holding books, and Party flag.

1984, Feb. 16

2353-2354	A1128 Set of 2	1.00	.20
2353a	10ch, unsurfaced white paper, without gum	20.00	—
2354a	10ch, unsurfaced white paper, without gum	20.00	—

Farm Worker, Grain A1129

1984, Feb. 25

2355 A1129 10ch multicolored .60 .20

Publication of the *Theses on the Socialist Rural Question in Our Country*, 20th anniv.

Changdok School, Chilgol A1130

Kim's Birthplace, Rejoicing Crowd A1131

1984, Apr. 15

2356	A1130 5ch multicolored	.50	.20
a.	Unsurfaced white paper, without gum	15.00	—
2357	A1131 10ch multicolored	.50	.20
a.	Unsurfaced white paper, without gum	20.00	—

Kim Il Sung, 72nd birthday.

A1132

A1133

España '84 Int'l Stamp Exhib.

Designs: 10ch, *Spanish Riding School of Vienna*, by Julius von Blaas. 20ch, *Ferdinand of Austria*, by Rubens.
No. 2360: 80ch, *Spanish Riding School*, by von Blaas.

1984, Apr. 27 ***Perf. 13½***
2358-2359 A1132 Set of 2 3.50 .75

Souvenir Sheet

2360 A1133 80ch multicolored 6.50 1.25

A1134

Kiyang Irrigation System, 25th Anniv.

1984, Apr. 30
2361 A1134 10ch multicolored .65 .20

A1135

Raphael, 500th Anniv. of Birth (1983)

Designs: 10ch, *Portrait of Angolo Doni.* 20ch, *Portrait of La Donna Velata.* 30ch, *Portrait of Jeanne d'Aragon.*
80ch, *St. Sebastian.*

1984, Apr. 30 ***Perf. 11¾x12***
2362-2364 A1135 Set of 3 4.00 1.00

Souvenir Sheet
Perf. 11¾x11½

2365 A1135 80ch multicolored 3.50 1.25

A1136

Socialist Construction

1984, May 20 ***Perf. 12***
2366 A1136 10ch multicolored .65 .20

A1137

Winter Olympics Games Medal Winners

Designs: 20ch (#2367), Speed skating (Karin Enke, DDR). 30ch (#2368), Bobsledding (DDR).
No. 2369: 10ch, Ski jumping (Matti Nykaenen, Finland). 20ch (#2369b), Slalom (Max Julen, Switzerland). 30ch (#2369c), Downhill skiing (Maria Walliser, Switzerland).
No. 2370 (both vert.): 40ch, Cross-country skiing (Thomas Wassberg, Sweden). 80ch, Cross-country skiing (Maria Liisa Hamalainen).
No. 2371 (vert.): 80ch, Biathlon (Peter Angerer, West Germany).

1984, May 20 ***Perf. 13½***
2367-2368 A1137 Set of 2 3.00 .75
2369 Sheet of 3, #a.-c. 25.00 1.25
a. A1137 10ch multicolored 6.00 .35
b. A1137 20ch multicolored 6.00 .35
c. A1137 30ch multicolored 6.00 .35
2370 Sheet of 2, #a.-b. 5.00 1.00
a. A1137 40ch multicolored 2.00 .40
b. A1137 80ch multicolored 2.00 .40

Souvenir Sheet

2371 A1137 80ch multicolored 3.50 1.00

A1138

Essen '84 Int'l Stamp Exhib.

Designs: 20ch, Type "202" express locomotive (1939). 30ch, Type "E" freight locomotive (1919).
No. 2375: 80ch, Type "D" locomotive in Germany.

1984, May 26 ***Perf. 12x11¾***
2372-2373 A1138 Set of 2 10.00 1.00

Souvenir Sheet

2374 A1138 80ch multicolored 9.00 1.25

A1139

Edgar Degas, 150th Anniv. Birth

Illustration reduced.
Designs: 10ch, *Mlle. Fiocre in the Ballet 'La Source.'* 20ch, *The Dance Foyer at the Rue le Peletier Opera.* 30ch, *Race Meeting.*
No. 2378: 80ch, *Dancers at the Bars.*

1984, June 10 ***Perf. 12***
2375-2377 A1138 Set of 3 8.00 1.25

Souvenir Sheet
Perf. 11½

2378 A1139 80ch multicolored 4.50 1.25

A1140

Irrigation Experts Meeting

1984, June 16 ***Perf. 11¾x12***
2379 A1140 2ch multicolored .80 .20

A1141

UPU Congress/Hamburg 1984 Stamp Exhib.

No. 2381: 80ch, *Gorch Fock,* DPRK stamp depicting Turtle Boat..

1984, June 19
2380 A1141 20ch multicolored 3.50 .35

Souvenir Sheet
Perf. 11¾x11½

2381 A1141 80ch multicolored 6.00 2.00

A1142

Tripartite Talks Proposal

1984, June 25 ***Perf. 12¼***
2382 A1142 10ch multicolored .65 .20

A1143

Alfred Bernhard Nobel, 150th Anniv. Birth (1983)

Designs: 20ch, Nobel in laboratory. 30ch, Nobel portrait.
No. 2385: 80ch, Nobel portrait, diff.

1984, June 30 ***Perf. 13½***
2383-2384 A1143 Set of 2 8.00 .75

Souvenir Sheet

2385 A1143 80ch multicolored 7.00 2.00

Nos. 2383 and 2384 were issued setenant with labels depicting Nobel's laboratory and home, respectively.

A1144

Improvement of Korean Living Standards

1984, July 10 ***Perf. 11¾x12***
2386 A1144 10ch multicolored .70 .20

A1145

Kuandian Conf., 65th Anniv.

1984, Aug. 17 ***Perf. 12x12¼***
2387 A1145 10ch multicolored 1.25 .20

A1146

Sunhwa School, Mangyongdae

1984, Aug. 17 ***Perf. 12***
2388 A1146 10ch multicolored 1.10 .20

School of Kim Il Sung's father, Kim Hyong Jik.

A1147

Flowers

Designs: 10ch, *Cattleya loddigesii.* 20ch, *Thunia bracteata.* 30ch, *Phalaenopsis amabilis.*
No. 2392: 80ch, *Kimilsungia.*

1984, Aug. 20
2389-2391 A1147 Set of 3 4.00 .60

Souvenir Sheet

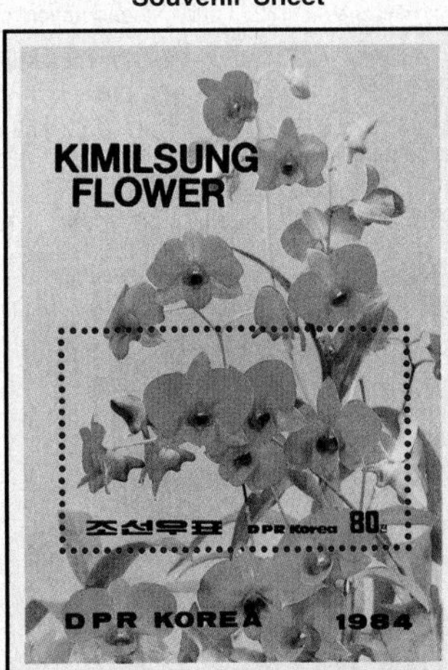

A1148

Illustration reduced.

2392 A1148 80ch multicolored 5.00 1.00

A1149

Fishing Industry

Designs: 5ch, Swordfish and trawler. 10ch, Marlin and trawler. 40ch, *Histiophorus orientalis.*

1984, Aug. 25
2393-2395 A1149 Set of 3 4.50 1.00

A1150

Revolutionary Museum, Chilgol

1984, Aug. 29
2396 A1150 10ch multicolored .90 .20

A1151

"Let's All Become the Kim Hyoks and Cha Gwang Sus of the '80s!"

1984, Aug. 31
2397 A1151 10ch multicolored .90 .20

A1152

Orient Express, 100th Anniv.

Designs: 10ch, Inauguration of a French railway line in 1860. 20ch, Opening of a British railway line in 1821. 30ch, Inauguration of Paris-Rouen line, 1843.
No. 2401: 80ch, Interior views of passenger cars, 1905.

1984, Sept. 7 ***Perf. 13½x13¼***
2398-2400 A1152 Set of 3 8.00 1.25

Souvenir Sheet

2401 A1152 80ch multicolored 7.00 1.75

A1153

Greenwich Meridian Time, Centenary

Designs: 10ch, Clockface, astronomical observatory.
No. 2403: 80ch, Clock face, buildings, Chollima statue.

1984, Sept. 15 ***Perf. 12***
2402 A1153 10ch multicolored 4.00 —

Souvenir Sheet

Perf. 11¾x11½

2403 A1153 80ch multicolored 6.00 1.25

A1154

Hamhung Grand Theater

1984, Sept. 21
2404 A1154 10ch multicolored .90 .20

A1155

Automation of Industry

1984, Sept. 25 ***Perf. 12¼***
2405 A1155 10ch multicolored .90 .25
a. Unsurfaced white paper, without gum 8.00 —

A1156

18th Century Korean Paintings

Designs: 10ch, *Dragon Angler.* 20ch, *Ox Driver*, horiz. 30ch, *Bamboo*, horiz.

1984, Sept. 30 ***Perf. 12 (#2406), 13¼***
2406-2408 A1156 Set of 3 4.00 .60

Souvenir Sheet

A1157

Design: 80ch, *Autumn Night.* Illustration reduced.

Perf. 13¼

2409 A1157 80ch multicolored 3.50 1.25

A1158

K.E. Tsiolkovski (1857-1935), Russian Space Scientist

Designs: 20ch, Portrait. 30ch, Earth, sputnik.
No. 2412: 80ch, Rocket launch.

1984, Oct. 5 ***Perf. 11¾***
2410-2411 A1158 Set of 2 2.00 .45

Souvenir Sheet

Perf. 11¾x11½

2412 A1158 80ch multicolored 4.00 .75

A1159

Container Ships

Designs: 10ch, *Pongdaesan.* 20ch, *Ryongnamsan.* 30ch, *Rungrado.*
No. 2416: 80ch, *Kumgangsan*

1984, Oct. 6 ***Perf. 12x11¾***
2413-2415 A1158 Set of 3 3.50 .75

Souvenir Sheet

Perf. 12

2416 A1159 80ch multicolored 5.00 1.25

A1160

Wild Animals

Designs: 10ch, Spotted hyenas. 20ch, Caracal. 30ch, Black-backed jackals. 40ch, Foxes.

1984, Oct. 13 ***Perf. 13¼***
2417-2420 A1160 Set of 4 4.50 1.00

Souvenir Sheet

A1161

Design: 80ch, Falcon. Illustration reduced.

2421 A1161 80ch multicolored 6.50 1.25

A1162

Marie Curie (1867-1934), Physicist, 50th Anniv. Death

Designs: 10ch, Marie Curie.
No. 2423: 80ch, Portrait of Mme. Curie.

1984, Oct. 21 ***Perf. 12***
2422 A1162 10ch multicolored 4.00 .20

Souvenir Sheet

Perf. 11¾x11½

2423 A1162 80ch multicolored 6.00 1.25

A1163

Birds

Designs: 10ch, Hoopoe. 20ch, South African crowned cranes. 30ch, Saddle-bill stork. 40ch, Chestnut-eared Aracari.
No. 2428: 80ch, Black kite.

1984, Nov. 5 ***Perf. 11½***
2424-2427 A1163 Set of 4 8.50 1.25

Souvenir Sheet

2428 A1163 80ch multicolored 8.50 1.25

A1164

Space Exploration

Designs: 10ch, Cosmonaut. 20ch, Cosmonaut on space-walk. 30ch, Cosmonaut (diff.)
No. 2432: 80ch, Moon vehicle.

1984, Nov. 15 ***Perf. 12***
2429-2431 A1164 Set of 3 2.50 .50

Souvenir Sheet

2432 A1164 80ch multicolored 4.00 1.00

A1165

Russian Icebreakers

Designs: 20ch, *Arktika.* 30ch, *Ermak.*
No. 2435: 80ch, *Lenin.*

1984, Nov. 26 ***Perf. 13¼***
2433-2434 A1165 Set of 2 3.25 .60

Souvenir Sheet

2435 A1165 80ch multicolored 5.00 1.25

A1166

Dmitri Mendeleev (1834-1907), Chemist, 150th Anniv. Birth

1984, Dec. 1 ***Perf. 13¼***
2436 A1166 10ch multicolored 1.75 .20

Souvenir Sheet

A1167

Illustration reduced.

2437 A1167 80ch multicolored 4.00 1.25

A1168

A1169

A1170

Historic European Royalty, Scenes (Type A1168)

No. 2438 (all 10ch): a, Konrad III, 1149 (Germany). b, Henry VIII (England). c, Henry VI (England). d, King John (England). e, Fleet of Elizabeth I (England). f, Philip II Augustus (France). g, Thames and London Bridge, 1616. h, Elizabeth I (England). i, Charles VII, parade (England).

No. 2439 (all 10ch): a, Prince Eugene, 1706 (Savoy). b, Kaiser Wilhelm II (Germany). c, Philip V (Spain). d, Ludwig II (Bavaria). e, Alfonso XIII (Spain). f, Mary Stuart (Scotland). g, Charles Edward Stuart, 1745 (Scotland). h, Marie-Louise (Austria). i, Charles V, 1547 (Spain).

No. 2440 (Horiz., all 10ch): a, Maria Theresa (Austria). b, Francis I, 1814 (Austria). c, Leopold II, 1844 (Austria). d, Louis XVIII (France). e, Versailles, 1688. f, Louis XIV (France). g, Prince Wilhelm (Germany). h, Franz Joseph I (Austria). i, Ludwig II (Bavaria).

No. 2441 (Horiz., all 10ch): a, Napoleon III (France. b, Rudolph of Habsburg, Basel 1273. c, Henry IV (France). d, Louis XII (France). e, Maximilian I (Holy Roman Empire). f, Peter the Great, Amsterdam Harbor (Russia). g, Louis VIII (France). h, Don Juan/Battle of Lepanto, 1571. i, Neuschwaustein Castle.

British Monarchs (Type A1169)

No. 2442 (all 10ch): a, William I. b, Richard II. c, Henry V. d, Henry VI. e, Richard III. f, Edward IV. g, Henry VII. h, Henry VIII, full length portrait. i, Henry VIII, ¾-face portrait, as young man.

No. 2443 (all 10ch): a, Henry VIII, ¾-face portrait, as middle-aged man. b, Mary I. c, Elizabeth I, facing left. d, Edward VI. e, Elizabeth I, facing right. f, Lady Jane Grey. g, Mary, Queen of Scots. h, James I. i, Charles I.

No. 2444 (all 10ch): a, Charles I. b, Henrietta Marie. c, Charles II. d, James II. e, George I, seated. f, William IV. g, Queen Anne, full-length portrait. h, George I, in profile. i. Queen Mary II.

No. 2445 (all 10ch): a, Queen Anne, with her son, William, Duke of Gloucester. b, George II, facing forward. c, George II, in profile. d, George IV. e, George III. f, William III. g, William IV. h, Queen Victoria. i, Prince Albert.

No. 2446 (all 10ch): a, Edward VII. b, Queen Alexandra. c, George V and Royal Family. d, George VI. e, George VI and Royal Family. f, Queen Elizabeth II. g, Prince Charles. h, Prince William of Wales, with Prince Charles and Princess Diana. i, Princess Diana.

No. 2447 (Type A1170): 80ch, Queen Elizabeth II.

Illustrations reduced.

1984, Dec. 20 ***Perf. 12¼x12***
2438-2446 Set, 9 sheets of 9 125.00 —

Souvenir Sheet

Perf. 11½

2447 A1170 80ch multicolored 20.00 12.00

A1171

Kim Il Sung's Visits to Eastern Europe

No. 2448 (all 10ch): a, USSR. b, Poland. c, DDR. d, Czechoslovakia.

No. 2249 (all 10ch): a, Hungary. b, Bulgaria. c, Romania.

No. 2450: 10ch, China.

Illustration reduced.

1984, Dec. 30 ***Perf. 12***
2448 A1171 Sheet of 4, #a.-d. 4.50 1.25
2449 A1171 Sheet of 3, #a.-c. 3.50 1.00

Souvenir Sheet

Perf. 11½

2450 A1171 10ch multicolored 2.75 1.00

A1172

New Year

1985, Jan. 1 ***Perf. 12***
2451 A1172 10ch multicolored 1.90 .20

Kim Il Sung's 1,000-ri Journey, 60th Anniv. — A1173

Illustration reduced.

1985, Jan. 22 ***Perf. 12¼***
2452 A1173 Pair, #a.-b. 2.25 .20
a. 5ch multicolored .75 .20
b. 10ch multicolored .75 .20

A1174

History of the Motorcar

Designs: 10ch, Gugnot's Steam Car, 1769. 15ch, Goldsworthy Steam Omnibus, 1825. 20ch, Gottlieb Daimler diesel car, 1885. 25ch, Benx three-wheeled diesel car, 1886. 30ch, Peugot diesel car, 1891.

1985, Jan. 25 ***Perf. 11½***
2453-2457 A1165 Set of 5 7.00 .85

Souvenir Sheet

A1175

Design: 80ch, Wind-power car, Illustration reduced.

2458 A1175 80ch multicolored 4.50 1.25

Secret Camp, Mt. Paektu — A1176

1985, Feb. 16 ***Perf. 12***
2459 A1176 10ch multicolored .65 .20

Korean Revolution Headquarters

Lighthouses — A1177

10ch, Taechodo. 20ch, Sodo. 30ch, Pido. 40ch, Suundo.

1985, Feb. 23 ***Perf. 12¼x11¾***
2460-2463 A1177 Set of 4 9.00 1.25

A1178

The Hedgehog Defeats the Tiger, Fairy Tale

10ch, Tiger bragging about his strength. 20ch, Tiger going to stamp on rolled-up hedgehog. 30ch, Hedgehog clinging to tiger's nose. 35ch, Fleeing tiger. 40ch, Tiger crawling before hedgehog.

1985, Mar. 6 ***Perf. 11½***
2464-2468 A1178 Set of 5 6.50 1.25

A1179

Mushrooms

10ch, *Pleurotus cornucopiae.* 20ch, *Pleurotus ostreatus.* 30ch, *Catathelasma ventricosum.*

1985, Mar. 16
2469-2471 A1179 Set of 3 6.00 .65

A1180

World Cup Soccer 1954-1966

Designs: 10ch, W. Germany vs. Hungary, 1954. 20ch, Brazil vs. Sweden, 1958. 30ch, Brazil vs. Czechoslovakia, 1962. 40ch, England vs. W. Germany, 1966.

1985, Mar. 20 ***Perf. 13¼***
2472-2475 A1180 Set of 4 4.50 1.00

Souvenir Sheet

A1181

Design: 80ch, DPRK team in quarter final, 1966. Illustration reduced.

2476 A1181 80ch multicolored 4.00 1.25

A1182

World Cup Soccer 1970-1986

Designs: 10ch, Brazil vs. Italy, 1970. 20ch, W. Germany vs. Netherlands, 1974. 30ch, Argentina vs. Netherlands, 1978. 40ch, Italy vs. W. Germany, 1982.

1985, Mar. 20 ***Perf. 13¼***
2477-2480 A1182 Set of 4 4.00 1.00

Souvenir Sheet

A1183

Design: 80ch, Aztec Stadium, Mexico City. Illustration reduced.
2481 A1183 80ch multicolored 4.00 1.25

A1184

Kim Il Sung, 73rd Birthday

1985, April 15 ***Perf. 12***
2482 A1184 10ch multicolored .65 .20

A1185

4th Century Musical Instruments

Designs: 10ch, Horn player. 20ch So (panpipes) player.

1985, May 7 ***Perf. 11½***
2483-2484 A1185 Set of 2 3.50 .25

A1186

Chongryon Hall, Tokyo

1985, May 25
2485 A1186 10ch deep brown .65 .20

30th anniv. of Chongryon, the General Association of Korean Residents in Japan.

A1187

Mammals

Designs: 5ch, Common marmoset (*callithrix jacchus*). 10ch, Ring-tailed lemur (*Lemur catta*).

1985, June 7
2486-2487 A1187 Set of 2 2.50 .20

A1188

National Emblem

1985, June 20
2488 A1188 80ch multicolored 3.00 .70

A1189

Argentina '85 Int'l Stamp Exhib.

Designs: 10ch, Buenos Aires and Argentina stamp. 20ch, Iguaçu Falls and Argentine, DPRK stamps, horiz.

1985, July 5 ***Perf. 11¾***
2489-2490 A1189 Set of 2 3.50 .25

Souvenir Sheet

A1190

Design: 80ch, Gaucho. Illustration reduced.
2491 A1190 80ch multicolored 4.00 4.00

A1191

12th World Youth and Students' Festival, Moscow

Designs: 10ch, Korean dancer with streamer, gymnast. 20ch, Spassky Tower, Festival emblem. 30ch, Youths of different races.

1985, July 27 ***Perf. 12¼***
2492-2494 A1191 Set of 3 3.50 .75

Pyongyang Buildings — A1192

Designs: 2ch, Phyonghwa Pavilion. 40ch, Skyscraper apartments, Chollima Street.

1985, Aug. 1 ***Perf. 12***
2495-2496 A1192 Set of 2 .90 .20
2495a 2ch, thick toned unsurfaced paper, without gum 10.00 —
2496a 40ch, thick toned unsurfaced paper, without gum 5.00 —

A1193

Liberation, 40th Anniv.

Designs: 5ch, Soldiers, battle scene. 10ch (#2498), Korean and Russian soldier with raised arms. 10ch (#2499), Japanese soldiers surrendering. 10ch (#2500), Crowd with banners, Flame of Juche. 10ch (#2501), Student marchers with banners. 10ch (#2502), Liberation monument, vert. 40ch, Students bearing banners.

1985, Aug. 15 ***Perf. 11½***
2497-2503 A1193 Set of 7 2.50 1.00
2497a 5ch, toned unsurfaced paper, without gum 8.00 —
2498a 10ch, toned unsurfaced paper, without gum 8.00 —
2499a 10ch, toned unsurfaced paper, without gum 8.00 —
2500a 10ch, toned unsurfaced paper, without gum 8.00 —
2501a 10ch, toned unsurfaced paper, without gum 8.00 —
2502a 10ch, toned unsurfaced paper, without gum 8.00 —
2503a 40ch, toned unsurfaced paper, without gum 8.00 —

Souvenir Sheet

A1194

Design: 80ch, Monument. Illustration reduced.
2504 A1194 80ch multicolored 2.00 2.00

A1195

Halley's Comet

Designs: 10ch, Halley and Comet. 20ch, Comet, diagram of course, space probe.

1985, Aug. 25 ***Perf. 13½***
2505-2506 A1195 Set of 2 2.00 .25

Souvenir Sheet

A1196

Design: 80ch, Comet's trajectory. Illustration reduced.
2507 A1196 80ch multicolored 4.00 1.25

Flowers — A1197

Designs: 10ch, *Hippeastrum hybridum.* 20ch, *Camellia japonica.* 30ch, *Cyclamen persicum.*

1985, Sept. 10 ***Perf. 12***
2508-2510 A1197 Set of 3 7.00 .65

A1198

Koguryo Culture, 4th-6th Centuries A.D.

Designs: 10ch, Hero. 15ch, Heroine. 20ch, Flying fairy. 25ch, Hunting.

1985, Sep. 30 *Perf. 13¼*
2511-2514 A1198 Set of 4 3.50 .65
2514a Sheet of 4, #2511-2514 4.00 1.00

Nos. 2511-2514 were issued both in separate sheets and in setenant sheetlets of four stamps (#2514a).

Souvenir Sheet

A1199

Perf. 12

Design: 50ch, Pine tree. Illustration reduced.
2515 A1199 50ch multicolored 3.00 .75

A1200

Korean Worker's Party, 40th Anniv.

Designs: 5ch, Party Founding Museum. 10ch (#2517), Soldier, workers. 10ch (#2518), Miner, workers. 40ch, Worker, peasant, professional worker holding up Party emblem.
No. 2520: 90ch, People holding bouquets of flowers.

1985, Oct. 10 *Perf. 11½*
2516-2519 A1200 Set of 4 1.40 .75
2516a 5ch, thick toned unsurfaced paper, without gum 5.00 —
2517a 10ch, thick toned unsurfaced paper, without gum 10.00 —
2518a 10ch, thick toned unsurfaced paper, without gum 5.00 —
2519a 40ch, thick toned unsurfaced paper, without gum 10.00 —

Souvenir Sheet

2520 A1200 90ch multicolored 1.60 .50

A1201

Kim Il Sung's Return, 40th Anniv.

1985, Oct. 14 *Perf. 12*
2521 A1201 10ch red brn & lt grn 1.00 .20
a. Dull white unsurfaced paper, without gum 8.00 —

A1202

Italia '85, Int'l Stamp Exhib., Rome

Designs: 10ch, Colosseum, Rome, and DPRK stamp. 20ch, *The Holy Family*, by Raphael. 30ch. Head of Michelangelo's *David*, vert.
No. 2525: 80ch, Pantheon, Rome.

1985, Oct. 25 *Perf. 11½*
2522-2524 A1200 Set of 3 2.75 .65

Souvenir Sheet

2525 A1202 80ch multicolored 4.00 1.25

A1203

South-West German Stamp Bourse, Sindelfingen

Designs, Mercedes Benz: 10ch, Type 300, 1960. 15ch, Type 770. 20ch, Type W150, 1937. 30ch, Type 600, 1966.
No. 2530: 80ch, Mercedes Benz, Type W31, 1938.

1985, Oct. 25
2526-2529 A1203 Set of 4 6.50 .65

Souvenir Sheet

Perf. 11¾

2530 A1203 80ch multicolored 5.25 .75

A1204

13th World Cup Championship, Mexico City

Designs: 20ch, Dribbling and sliding tackle. 30ch, Jumping kick.

1985, Nov. 1 *Perf. 13¼*
2531-2532 A1204 Set of 2 3.25 .50

Souvenir Sheet

A1205

Design: 80ch, Goalkeeper and Mexican monuments. Illustration reduced.
2533 A1205 80ch multicolored 4.50 1.10

A1206

Int'l Youth Year

Designs: 10ch, Traditional dance. 20ch, Sculpture depicting gymnasts. 30ch, Scientific research.
No. 2537: 80ch, Young people of different races.

1985, Nov. 9 *Perf. 11½*
2534-2536 A1206 Set of 3 3.50 .50

Souvenir Sheet

2537 A1206 80ch multicolored 4.50 1.10

A1207

13th World Cup Championship, Mexico City

Designs: 20ch, Dribbling. 30ch, Tackling. Illustration reduced.

1985, Nov. 20 *Perf. 12*
2538-2539 A1207 Set of 2 3.50 .50

Souvenir Sheet

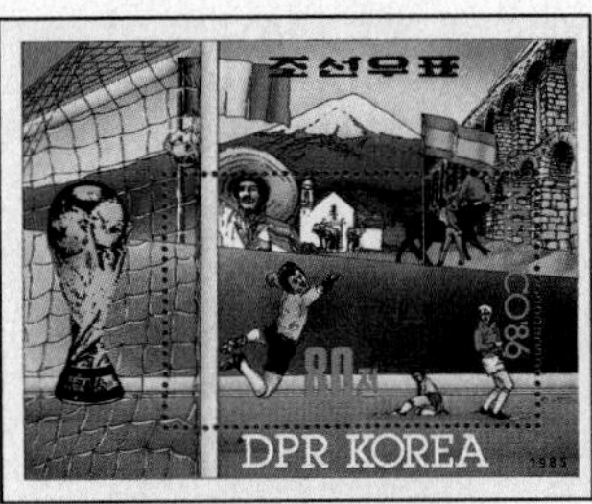
A1208

Design: 80ch, Goalkeeper, bullfighter. Illustration reduced.
2540 A1208 80ch multicolored 5.00 1.10

Juche Torch — A1209

New Year

1986, Jan. 1 *Perf. 12x12¼*
2541 A1209 10ch multicolored 1.25 .20

A1210

History of the Motor Car

Designs: 10ch, Amédée Bollée and Limousine, 1901. 20ch, Stewart Rolls, Henry Royce and Silver Ghost, 1906. 25ch, Giovanni Agnelli and Fiat car, 1912. 30ch, Ettore Bugatti and Royal coupe, 1928. 40ch, Louis Renault and fiacre, 1906.
No. 2547: 80ch, Gottlieb Daimler, Karl Benz and Mercedes S, 1927.

1986, Jan. 20 *Perf. 11½*
2542-2546 A1210 Set of 5 9.50 1.25

Souvenir Sheet

2547 A1210 80ch multicolored 7.50 .75

A1211

World Chess Championship, Moscow

Designs: 20ch, Gary Kasparov.
No. 2549: 80ch, Kasparov-Karpov chess match.

1986, Feb. 5 *Perf. 11¾x12*
2548 A1211 20ch multicolored 2.25 .20

Souvenir Sheet

Perf. 12

2549 A1211 80ch multicolored 5.00 1.25

A1212

Revolutionary Martyrs' Cemetery, Pyongyang

Designs: 5ch, Cemetery Gate. 10ch, Bronze sculpture of draped flag, soldier, workers (detail).

1986, Feb. 10 *Perf. 12*
2550-2551 A1212 Set of 2 1.50 .20

A1213

Songgan Revolutionary Site, 37th Anniv. of Kim Il Sung's Visit

1986, Feb. 16
2552 A1213 10ch multicolored .90 .20

A1214

Mt. Myohyang Historic Buildings

Designs: 10ch, Buddhist Scriptures Museum. 20ch, Taeung Hall of the Pohyon Temple.

1986, Feb. 20 *Perf. 12¼*
2553-2554 A1214 Set of 2 2.00 .20

A1215

Tropical Fish

Designs: 10ch, *Heniochus acuminatus.* 20ch, *Amphiprion frenatus.*

1986, Mar. 12 ***Perf. 11½***
2555-2556 A1215 Set of 2 2.50 .30

A1216

World Cup Championship, Mexico City

Designs, soccer players and flags of: 5ch, Italy, Bulgaria, Argentina. 20ch, Mexico, Belgium, Paraguay, Iraq. 25ch, France, Canada, USSR, Hungary. 30ch, Brazil, Spain, Algeria, Northern Ireland. 35ch, W. Germany, Uruguay, Scotland, Denmark. 40ch, Poland, Portugal, Morocco, England.

No. 2563: 80ch, Soccer players, World Cup, gold soccer ball, boots.

1986, Mar. 21 ***Perf. 12***
2557-2562 A1216 Set of 6 10.00 1.60

Souvenir Sheet

2563 A1216 80ch multicolored 6.50 .65

A1217

4th Spring Friendship Art Festival, Pyongyang

1986, Apr. 5
2564 A1217 1w multicolored 3.00 .65

A1218

Mercedes-Benz, 60th Anniv.

Designs: 10ch (#2565), Dailmer No. 1 ("Motorwagen"), 1886. 10ch (#2566), Benz-Velo, 1894. 20ch (#2567), Mercedes, 1901. 20ch (#2568), Benz limousine, 1909. 30ch (#2569), Mercedes Tourenwagen, 1914. 30ch (#2570), Mercedes Benz 170/6 cylinder, 1931. 40ch (#2571), Mercedes Benz 380, 1933. 40ch (#2572), Mercedes Benz 540K, 1936.

No. 2573: 80ch, Mercedes-Simplex Phaeton, 1904.

1986, Apr. 8 ***Perf. 11½***
2565-2572 A1218 Set of 8 9.00 2.00

Souvenir Sheet

2573 A1218 80ch multicolored 5.00 1.25

A1219

Kim Il Sung, 74th Birthday

1986, Apr. 15 ***Perf. 12***
2574 A1219 10ch multicolored .65 .20

A1220

Association for the Restoration of the Fatherland, 50th Anniv.

1986, May 5 ***Perf. 11¾x12***
2575 A1220 10ch multicolored .65 .20

A1221

Int'l Year of Peace

Designs: 10ch, Dove carrying letter. 20ch, Dove, UN Headquarters. 30ch, Dove, globe, broken missiles.

No. 2579: 80ch, Sculpture of children and dove.

1986, June 18 ***Perf. 11¾x12***
2576-2578 A1221 Set of 3 4.00 1.25

Souvenir Sheet

Perf. 11¾x11½

2579 A1221 80ch multicolored 5.00 .75

A1222

Mona Lisa, by da Vinci

1986, July 9 ***Perf. 13½x13¼***
2580 A1222 20ch multicolored 3.00 .20

A1223

Irises

Designs: 20ch, Pink iris. 30ch, Violet iris.

No. 2583: 80ch, Magenta iris.

1986, July 20 ***Perf. 11½***
2581-2582 A1223 Set of 2 5.00 .50

Souvenir Sheet

2583 A1223 80ch multicolored 6.50 1.10

A1224

Tennis Players

Designs: 10ch, Kim Un Suk. 20ch, Ivan Lendi. 30ch, Steffi Craf. 50ch, Boris Becker. Illustration reduced.

1986, July 30 ***Perf. 13½***
2584 A1224 Block of 4, #a.-d. 7.00 1.00
a. 10ch multicolored 1.50 .20
b. 20ch multicolored 1.50 .20
c. 30ch multicolored 1.50 .20
d. 50ch multicolored 1.50 .20
e. 10ch, on toned unsurfaced paper, without gum 10.00 —

No. 2584 was printed in sheets containing two setenant blocks.

No. 2584d is airmail.

A1225

Stampex '86 Stamp Exhib., Adelaide

Designs: 10ch, Cockatoo; 80ch, Kangaroo, map of Australia, emblems.

1986, Aug. 4 ***Perf. 11½***
2585 A1225 10ch multicolored 5.50 .20

Souvenir Sheet

2586 A1226 80ch multicolored 5.50 1.10

A1227

L'Unita Festival, Milan

Designs: 10ch, First issue of *L'Unita.* 20ch, Milan Cathedral. 30ch, Michelangelo's *Pieta*, vert.

No. 2590: 80ch, Enrico Berlinguer, Italian Communist Party leader.

1986, Aug. 26
2587-2589 A1227 Set of 3 5.50 2.50

Souvenir Sheet

2590 A1227 80ch multicolored 4.50 .75

National Festival of *L'Unita*, the Italian Communist Party newspaper.

A1228

Stockholmia '86 Int'l Stamp Exhib., Stockholm

Design: 10ch, Icebreaker *Express II* and Swedish stamp.

1986, Aug. 28
2591 A1228 10ch multicolored 2.00 .20

Souvenir Sheet

A1229

Design: 80ch, UPU emblem, mail coach and Swedish stamps. Illustration reduced.

2592 A1229 80ch multicolored 7.00 1.50

A1230

DPRK Postage Stamps, 40th Anniv.

Designs: 10ch, Perf green reprint of Scott No. 1. 15ch, Imperf green reprint of Scott No. 1. 50ch, Scott No. 5.

1986, Sep. 12 ***Perf. 12¼x12***
2593-2595 A1230 Set of 3 6.00 1.50

No. 2595 is airmail.

A1231

DPRK Postage Stamps, 40th Anniv.

Designs: 10ch, Postal emblems, DPRK stamps (#387, 2505). 15ch, Postal emblems, General Post Office, Pyongyang, DPRK stamps (#1529, 1749). 50ch, Postal emblems, Kim Il Jung. DPRK stamps (#1, #1 reprint in green), vert.

1986, Oct. 5 ***Perf. 12***
2596-2598 A1231 Set of 3 8.00 1.00

No. 2598 is airmail.

Nos. 2557-2563 Overprinted

World Cup Soccer Championship Results

1986, Oct. 14
2599-2604 A1216 Set of 6 16.00 2.50

Souvenir Sheet

2605 A1216 80ch multicolored 10.00 1.40

A1232

Down-with-Imperialism Union, 60th Anniv.

1986, Oct. 17 *Perf. 11½*
2606 A1232 10ch multicolored .70 .25

A1233

Gift Animals House, 1st Anniv.

1986, Oct. 18 *Perf. 12x11¾*
2607 A1233 2w multicolored 8.50 .90
a. On toned unsurfaced paper, without gum 10.00 —

A1234

United Nations Educational, Scientific and Cultural Organization (UNESCO), 40th anniv.

Designs: 10ch, Schoolchildren. 50ch, UNESCO emblem, Grand People's Study House, televion, communications satellite and dish, horiz.

1986, Nov. 4 *Perf. 12*
2608-2609 A1234 Set of 2 4.50 1.25

A1235

Inter-Sputnik, 15th Anniv.

1986, Nov. 15
2610 A1235 5w multicolored 10.00 2.25
a. On toned unsurfaced paper, without gum 10.00 —

A1236

West Sea Barrage

Designs: 10ch, Oil tanker, lock. 40ch, Aerial view of dam. 1.20w, Aerial view of dam (diff.)

1986, Nov. 20 *Perf. 12x11¾*
2611-2613 A1236 Set of 3 8.50 1.00
2611a 10ch, on toned unsurfaced paper, without gum 5.00 —
2612a 40ch, on toned unsurfaced paper, without gum 8.00 —
2613a 1.20w, on toned unsurfaced paper, without gum 8.00 —

A1237

Mushrooms and Minerals

Designs: a, 10ch Lengenbachite. b, 10ch Clitocybe infundibuliformis. c, 15ch Rhodocrosite. d, 15ch Morchella esculenta. e, 50ch Annabergite. f, 50ch Russula.
Illustration reduced.

1986, Nov. 23 *Perf. 13¼*
2614 A1237 Block of 6, #a.-f. 16.50 1.25
a. 10ch multicolored 2.50 .20
b. 10ch multicolored 2.50 .20
c. 15ch multicolored 2.50 .20
d. 15ch multicolored 2.50 .20
e. 50ch multicolored 2.50 .20
f. 50ch multicolored 2.50 .20

Printed in setenant blocks within the sheet. Nos. 2614e and 2614f are airmail.

A1238

Exhib. of North Korean 3-D Photos and Stamps, Lima

Design: 10ch, Machu Picchu and DPRK Stamp (Scott #1402).

1986, Nov. 25 *Perf. 13¼x13½*
2615 A1238 10ch multicolored 2.00 .20

Souvenir Sheet

A1239

Design: 80ch, Korean and Peruvian children. Illustration reduced.
2616 A1239 80ch multicolored 9.00 2.00

A1240

New Year

Designs: 10ch, Sun, pine tree; 40ch, Hare.

1987, Jan. 1 *Perf. 12*
2617-2618 A1240 Set of 2 3.50 .50

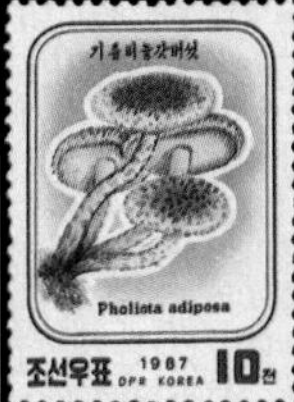

Fungi — A1241

Designs: 10ch, *Pholiota adiposa*; 20ch, *Cantharellus cibarius*; 30ch, *Boletus impolitus*.

1987, Jan. 5 *Perf. 11½*
2619-2621 A1241 Set of 3 5.75 .75

Souvenir Sheet

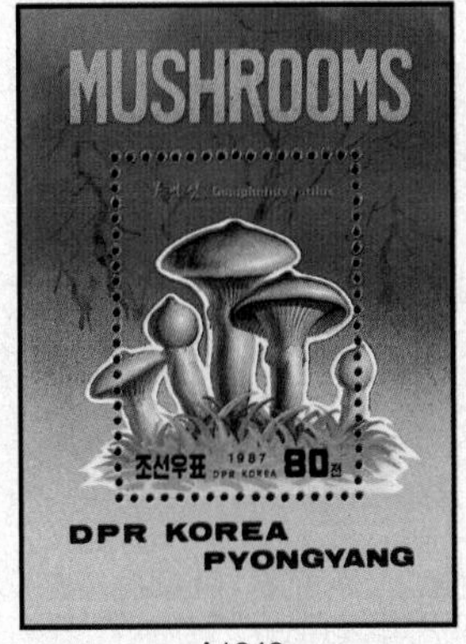

A1242

Design: 80ch, *Gomphidius rutilus*. Illustration reduced.
2622 A1242 80ch multicolored 7.00 1.50

Famous Composers, Death Anniv. — A1243

Designs: 10ch (#2623a), Maurice Ravel (1875-1937); 10ch (#2623b), Kim Ok Song (1916-65); 20ch, Giovanni Lully (1632-67); 30ch, Franz Liszt (1811-86); 40ch (#2623e), Stradivarius violins (Antonio Stradivari, 1644-1737); 40ch (#2623f), Christoph Gluck (1714-87).
Illustration reduced.

1987, Jan. 29 *Perf. 13¼*
2623 A1243 Block of 6, #a.-f. 12.00 1.10
a. 10ch multicolored 1.50 .20
b. 10ch multicolored 1.50 .20
c. 20ch multicolored 1.50 .20
d. 30ch multicolored 1.50 .20
e. 40ch multicolored 1.50 .20
f. 40ch multicolored 1.50 .20

No. 2623 was printed in se-tenant blocks of six within the sheet.

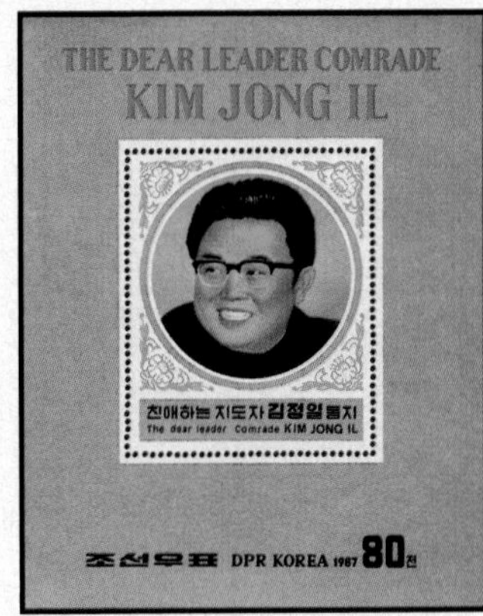

Kim Jong Il, 45th Birthday — A1244

Illustration reduced.

1987, Feb. 16
2624 A1244 80ch multicolored 2.50 .40

Buildings — A1245

Designs: 5ch, East Pyongyang Grand Theater; 10ch, Pyongyang Koryo Hotel (vert.); 3w, Rungnado Stadium.

1987, Feb. 23 *Perf. 12*
2625-2627 A1245 Set of 3 7.50 1.20
2625a 5ch, on stiff paper, without gum 10.00 —
2626a 10ch, on stiff paper, without gum 5.00 —
2627a 3w, on stiff paper, without gum 5.00 —

Sailing Ships — A1246

Designs: 20ch, *Gorch Fock*; 30ch, *Tovarisch* (vert.); 50ch (#2630), *Belle Poule* (vert.); 50ch (#2631), *Sagres II* (vert.); 1w (#2632), Merchantman, Koryo Period (918-1392); 1w (#2633), *Dar Mlodziezy* (vert.).

1987, Feb. 25 *Perf. 13¼*
2628-2633 A1246 Set of 6 11.50 2.75

Nos. 2630-2633 are airmail.

Fire Engines — A1247

Designs: 10ch, German fire engine; 20ch, Benz fire engine; 30ch, Chemical fire engine; 50ch, Soviet fire engine.

1987, Feb. 27 *Perf. 12*
2634-2637 A1247 Set of 4 10.00 1.20

No. 2637 is airmail.

Road Safety — A1248

Designs (multiple traffic signs): 10ch (#2638), Blue sign lower center; 10ch (#2639), Red sign lower center; 20ch, Various signs; 50ch, Various signs (diff.)

1987, Feb. 27

2638-2641	A1248	Set of 4	7.50	.90

Nos. 2641 is airmail.

Butterflies and Flowers — A1249

Designs: 10ch (#2642), *Apatura ilia* and spiraea; 10ch (#2643), *Ypthinia argus* and fuchsia; 20ch (#2644), *Neptis philyra* and aguilegia; 20ch (#2645), *Papilio protenorand* and chrysanthemum; 40ch (#2646), *Parantica sita* and celosia; 40ch (#2847), *Vanessa indica* and hibiscus.

1987, Mar. 12

2642-2647	A1249	Set of 6	11.00	1.50

Korean National Assoc., 70th Anniv. — A1250

Design: 10ch, Association Monument, Pyongyang.

1987, Mar. 23 ***Perf. 11½***

2648	A1250	10ch multicolored	.60	.20

5th Spring Friendship Art Festival — A1251

1987, Apr. 6

2649	A1251	10ch multicolored	.70	.20

A1252

A1253

Kim Il Sung, 75th Birthday

Designs: No. 2650, Mangyong Hill; No. 2651, Kim Il Sung's birthplace, Mangyongdae (horiz.); No 2652, Painting, *Profound Affection for the Working Class*; No. 2653, Painting, *A Bumper Crop of Pumpkins*.

Type A1253 illustration reduced.

1987, Apr. 15 ***Perf. 12***

2650	A1252	10ch multicolored	.50	.20
2651	A1252	10ch multicolored	.50	.20
2652	A1253	10ch multicolored	.50	.20
2653	A1253	10ch multicolored	.50	.20
		Nos. 2650-2653 (4)	2.00	.80

Horses — A1254

Designs: 10ch (#2654a), Bay. 10ch (#2654b), Bay (diff.); 40ch (#2654c), Gray, rearing; 40ch (#2654d), White horse on beach.

Illustration reduced.

1987, Apr. 20 ***Perf. 13¼***

2654	A1254	Block of 4, #a.-d.	7.00	2.10
a.		10ch multicolored	.50	.20
b.		10ch multicolored	.50	.20
c.		40ch multicolored	2.50	.70
d.		40ch multicolored	2.50	.70

No. 2654 was printed in se-tenant blocks of four within the sheet.

Transport — A1255

Designs: 10ch (#2655), Electric train *Juche*; 10ch (#2656), Electric train *Mangyongdae*; 10ch (#2657), *Sputnik I* (vert.); 20ch (#2658), Laika, first animal in space (vert.); 20ch (#2659), Tupolev Tu-144 jetliner; 20ch (#2660), Concorde jetliner; 30ch, Count Ferdinand von Zeppelin and LZ-4; 80ch, Zeppelin and diagrams of airships.

1987, Apr. 30

2655	A1255	10ch multicolored	.60	.20
2656	A1255	10ch multicolored	.60	.20
a.		Pair, #2655-2656	.75	.40
2657	A1255	10ch multicolored	.60	.20
2658	A1255	20ch multicolored	1.10	.20
a.		Pair, #2657-2658	2.00	.40
2659	A1255	20ch multicolored	1.10	.20
2660	A1255	20ch multicolored	1.10	.20
a.		Pair, #2659-2660	2.50	.40
2661	A1255	30ch multicolored	1.50	.25
2662	A1255	80ch multicolored	4.50	1.00
a.		Pair, #2661-2662	7.00	1.25
		Nos. 2655-2662 (8)	11.10	2.45

Nos. 2655/2656, 2657/2658, 2659/2660, 2661/2662 were printed se-tenant within their sheets.

No. 2662 is airmail.

CAPEX '87 Int'l Stamp Exhibition, Toronto — A1256

Designs: 10ch, Musk ox; 40ch, Jacques Cartier, *Grand Hermine* and modern ice-breaker (horiz.); 60ch, Ice hockey, Calgary '88 (horiz.)

1987, May 30 ***Perf. 11***

2663-2665	A1256	Set of 3	6.00	1.25

Int'l Circus Festival, Monaco — A1257

Designs: 10ch (#2666), Trapeze artists; 10ch (#2667), "Brave Sailors" (N. Korean acrobatic troupe) (vert.); 20ch (#2668), Korean performers receiving prize; 20ch (#2669), Clown and elephant (vert.); 40ch, Performing cat, horses; 50ch, Prince Rainier and family applauding.

1987, May 31 ***Perf. 12***

2666-2671	A1257	Set of 6	9.50	1.50

No. 2871 is airmail.

Battle of Pochonbo, 50th Anniv. — A1258

1987, June 4 ***Perf. 11½***

2672	A1258	10ch multicolored	.75	.25

Chongchun Street Sports Complex — A1259

Designs: 5ch, Various sports; 10ch, Indoor swimming pool; 40ch, Weightlifting gymnasium; 70ch, Table-tennis gymnasium; 1w, Angol football stadium; 1.20w, Handball gymnasium.

1987, June 18 ***Perf. 12***

2673-2678 A1259	Set of 6	10.00	2.25
2675a	40ch, on toned unsurfaced paper, without gum	8.00	—
2676a	70ch, on toned unsurfaced paper, without gum	8.00	—
2677a	1w, on toned unsurfaced paper, without gum	8.00	—
2678a	1.20w, on toned unsurfaced paper, without gum	8.00	—

Mandarin Ducks (WWF) — A1260

Designs (ducks): 20ch (#2679), On branch; 20ch (#2680), On shore; 20ch (#2681), In water and on shore; 40ch, In water.

1987, Aug. 4 ***Perf. 13¼***

2679-2682	A1260	Set of 4	11.50	2.00

OLYMPHILEX '87 Stamp Exhibition, Rome — A1261

1987, Aug. 29 ***Perf. 13¼***

2683	A1261	10ch multicolored	1.50	.20

Souvenir Sheet

A1262

Illustration reduced.

2684	A1262	80ch multicolored	7.00	1.25

Railway Uniforms — A1263

Designs: 10ch (#2685), Electric train and Metro dispatcher; 10ch (#2686), Underground station and conductress; 20ch, Train and conductress; 30ch, Train and railway dispatcher; 40ch (#2689), Orient Express and conductor; 40ch (#2690), Express train and ticket inspector.

1987, Sep. 23

2685-2690	A1263	Set of 6	7.50	1.25

HAFNIA '87 Int'l Stamp Exhibition, Copenhagen — A1264

Designs: 40ch, White stork; 60ch, The Little Mermaid and sailing ship *Danmark.*

1987, Sep. 26

2691-2692 A1264 Set of 2 5.25 .70

Winter Olympic Games, Calgary — A1265

Designs (all 40ch): #2693, Figure skating; #2694, Ski jump; #2695, Downhill skiing; #2696, Cross-country skiing.

1987, Oct. 16

2693-2696 A1265 Set of 4 8.00 1.00

Souvenir Sheet

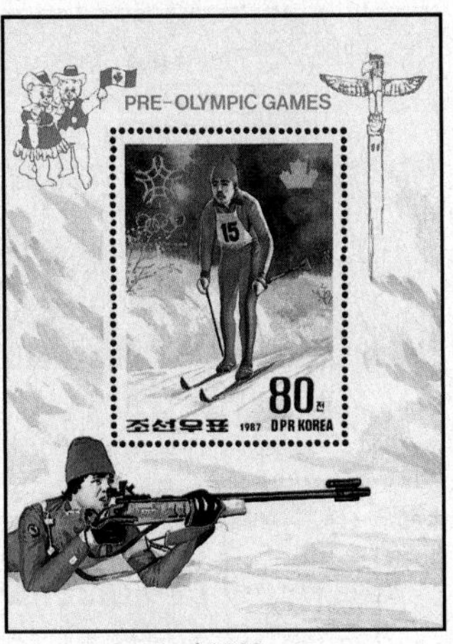

A1266

Illustration reduced.

2697 A1266 80ch multicolored 5.25 1.00

PHILATELIA '87 (Koln) and 750th Anniv. Berlin — A1267

Designs: 10ch, Victory Column; 20ch, Reichstag (horiz.); 30ch, Pfaueninsel Castle; 40ch, Charlottenburg Castle (horiz.).
No. 2706: 80ch, Olympic Stadium.

1987, Nov. 5 ***Perf. 12***

2698-2701 A1267 Set of 4 150.00

Souvenir Sheet

Perf. 11½x12

2702 A1267 80ch multicolored 100.00

Roland Garros Birth Centenary and Tennis as an Olympic Sport — A1268

Designs: 20ch (#2703), Roland Garros (1888-1918), aviator; 20ch (#2704), Ivan Lendl and trophy; 40ch, Steffi Graf.
No. 2706: 80ch, Steffi Graf and trophy.

1987, Nov. 10 ***Perf. 13¼***

2703-2705 A1268 Set of 3 7.50 .75

Souvenir Sheet

Perf. 11½x12

2706 A1268 80ch multicolored 10.00 3.00

Kim Jong Suk — A1269

1987, Dec. 24

2707 A1269 80ch multicolored 2.50 .50

70th anniv. of birth of Kim Jong Suk (1917-49), revolutionary hero.

Pyongyang Buildings — A1270

Dragon — A1271

1988, Jan. 1 ***Perf. 12***

2708 A1270 10ch multicolored .60 .20

2709 A1271 40ch multicolored 1.50 .20

New Year.

Saenal Newspaper, 60th Anniv. — A1272

1988, Jan. 15 ***Perf. 11½***

2710 A1272 10ch multicolored .90 .20

Kim Jong Il's 46th Birthday

A1273

Design: Kim Jong Il's birthplace, Mt. Paektu.

1988, Feb. 16 ***Perf. 12x11¾***

2711 A1273 10ch multicolored .50 .20

Souvenir Sheet

Kim Jong Il — A1274

Illustration reduced.

2712 A1274 80ch multicolored 2.50 .50

Int'l Red Cross, 125th Anniv. — A1275

Designs: 10ch, Henry Dunant; 20ch (#2714), N. Korean Red Cross emblem, map; 20ch (#2715), International Committee Headquarters, Geneva; 40ch, Doctor examining child, Pyongyang Maternity Hospital.
80ch: Red Cross and Red Crescent, flags, globe.
Illustration reduced.

1988, Feb. 17 ***Perf. 12***

2713-2716 Set of 4 6.75 .90

2716a A1275 Sheetlet of 4, #2717-2720 7.00 .90

Souvenir Sheet

2717 A1275 80ch multicolored 4.50 .75

Nos. 2713-2716 were printed in sheetlets of 4 (#2716a).

Columbus' Discovery of America, 500th Anniv.

A1276

Designs: 10ch, *Santa Maria*; 20ch, *Pinta*; 30ch, *Nina*;
Illustration reduced.

1988, Mar. 10 ***Perf. 13¼***

2718 A1276 Strip of 3 5.25 .75

- *a.* 10ch multicolored 1.25 .20
- *b.* 20ch multicolored 1.25 .20
- *c.* 30ch multicolored 1.25 .25

Souvenir Sheet

A1277

Illustration reduced.

2719 A1277 80ch multicolored 5.25 .75

Nos. 2718a-2718c were printed together in the sheet in se-tenant strips of three.

JUVALUX '88 — A1278

Designs: 40ch, Hot air balloons; 60ch, Steam engine, railroad map of Luxembourg 1900.

1988, Mar. 29

2720-2721 A1278 Set of 2 5.25 .75

JUVALUX '88 International Youth Stamp Exhibition, Luxembourg.

6th Spring Friendship Art Festival — A1279

Designs: 10ch, Singer. 1.20w, Dancers.

1988, Apr. 7 ***Perf. 12***

2722-2723 A1279 Set of 2 4.25 1.25

2722a 10ch, on toned unsurfaced paper, without gum 8.00 —

Int'l Institute of the Juche Idea, 10th Anniv. — A1280

1988, Apr. 9
2724 A1280 10ch multicolored .50 .20

Kim Il Sung, 76th Birthday

Kim Il Sung's Birthplace, Mangyongdae — A1281

1988, Apr. 15
2725 A1281 10ch multicolored .50 .20

Souvenir Sheet

A1282

Kim Il Sung and schoolchildren. Illustration reduced.

2726 A1282 80ch multicolored 2.50 .40

FINLANDIA '88 Int'l Stamp Exhibition, Helsinki — A1283

Designs: 40ch, *Urho* ice-breaker; 60ch, Matti Nykänen, Finnish Olympic ski-jumping gold and silver medallist.

1988, May 2 ***Perf. 13¼***
2727-2728 A1283 Set of 2 5.00 .60

ITALIA '90, 14th World Soccer Championships — A1284

Designs: 10ch, Soccer match; 20ch, Postcard for 1934 Championship; 30ch, Player tackling (horiz.)

80ch: Italian team, 1982 winners (horiz.)

1988, May 19
2729-2731 A1284 Set of 3 5.25 .50

Souvenir Sheet

2732 A1284 80ch multicolored 4.50 .60

13th World Festival of Youth and Students — A1285

Designs: 10ch, Festival emblem; 10ch (#2735), Woman dancer; 10ch (#2736), Woman, gymnast, Angol Sports Village; 10ch (#2737), Map of Korea, globe and doves; 10ch (#2738), Finger pointing at broken rockets ("Let's build a new world without nuclear weapons"); 1.20w, Three hands of different races releasing dove.

1988, May 27 ***Perf. 12***
2734-2739 A1285 Set of 6 7.50 1.25
2734a 10ch, on thick toned unsurfaced paper, without gum 8.00 —
2735a 10ch, on thick toned unsurfaced paper, without gum 8.00 —
2736a 10ch, on thick toned unsurfaced paper, without gum 8.00 —
2739a 1.20w, on thick toned unsurfaced paper, without gum 8.00 —

Eight Fairies of Mt. Kumgang, Folk-Tale — A1286

Designs: 10ch, Fairy playing the *haegum*; 15ch, Fairies with rainbow; 20ch, Fairy and herdsman husband; 25ch, Couple with infant; 30ch, Couple with son and daughter; 35ch, Family on rainbow, returning to Mt. Kumgang.

1988, June 20
2740-2745 A1286 Set of 6 5.00 1.10

PRAGA '88 Int'l Stamp Exhibition, Prague — A1287

Designs: 20ch, Mallard ducks; 40ch, Vladimir Remek, Czechoslovak cosmonaut.

1988, June 26 ***Perf. 13¼***
2746-2747 A1287 Set of 2 4.00 .45

Birds — A1288

Designs: 10ch, Red crossbill (*Loxia curvirostra japonica*); 15ch, Stonechat (*Saxicola torquata stejnegeri*); 20ch, European nuthatch (*Sitta eoropaea hondoensis*); 25ch, Great spotted woodpecker (*Dendrocopos major japonicus*); 30ch, Common kingfisher (*Alcedo atthis bengalensis*); 35ch, Bohemian waxwing (*Bombycilla garrula centralasiae*).

1988, July 9 ***Perf. 12***
2748-2753 A1288 Set of 6 10.00 1.75

RICCIONE '88 Int'l Stamp Fair

A1289

1988, July 25
2754 A1289 20ch multicolored .90 .20

Souvenir Sheet

A1290

Illustration reduced.

2755 A1290 80ch multicolored 3.75 .50

Australia Bicentenary

A1291

Designs: 10ch, Emu; 15ch, Statin bower birds; 25ch, Kookaberra (vert.).

1988, July 30 ***Perf. 13¼***
2756-2758 A1291 Set of 3 4.00 .60

Souvenir Sheet

A1292

80ch, H.M.S. *Resolution*. Illustration reduced.

2759 A1292 80ch multicolored 5.00 .65

Ships — A1293

Designs: 10ch, Floating crane *5-28*; 20ch, Cargo ship *Hwanggumsan*; 30ch, Cargo ship *Jangjasan Chongnyon-ho*; 40ch, Passenger ship *Samjiyon*.

1988, Aug. 12 ***Perf. 12***
2760-2763 A1293 Set of 4 5.50 .85

Count Ferdinand von Zeppelin, 150th Birthday

A1294

Designs: 10ch, LZ 13 *Hansa*; 20ch, LZ 10 *Schwaben*; 30ch, LZ 11 *Viktoria Luise*; 40ch, LZ 3.

1988, Aug. 21 ***Perf. 11¼***
2764-2767 A1294 Set of 4 5.50 .85

Souvenir Sheet

A1295

1w, Count von Zeppelin. Illustration reduced.

Perf. 13¼
2768 A1295 1w multicolored 5.00 1.00

Kim Il Sung and Jambyn Batmunkh — A1296

1988, Aug. 30 ***Perf. 12***
2769 A1296 10ch multicolored .75 .20

Kim Il Sung's visit to Mongolia.

National Heroes Congress — A1297

1988, Sep. 1 ***Perf. 11¾***
2770 A1297 10ch multicolored 4.50 .20

Independence, 40th Anniversary

A1298

Designs: 5ch, Tower of Juche Idea. 10ch (#2772), Worker, factory. 10ch (#2773), Soldier and Mt. Paektu. 10ch (#2774), Map, broken U.S. missile. 10ch (#2775), Hand holding sign, peace march, globe, doves.

1988, Sept. 9 ***Perf. 12***
2771-2775 A1298 Set of 5 1.75 .55
2771a 5ch, on toned unsurfaced paper, without gum 20.00 —

Souvenir Sheet

A1299

1.20w, Kim Il Sung presiding over design of DPRK flag and emblem.

Perf. 11½
2776 A1299 1.20w multicolored 2.50 .75

FILACEPT '88 Philatelic Exhib., The Hague

A1300

Designs: 40ch, *Sunflowers*, by Vincent Van Gogh. 60ch, *The Chess Game*, by Lucas van Leyden.

1988, Sept. 18 ***Perf. 13½***
2777-2778 A1300 Set of 2 7.50 1.40

Emblem — A1301

1988, Sep. 23 ***Perf. 11½***
2779 A1301 10ch multicolored .60 .20

16th Conference of the Ministers of Communications of Socialist Countries.

Dump Trucks A1302

Designs: 10ch, *Jaju 82* 10-ton truck. 40ch, *Kumsusan* 40-ton truck.

1988, Sept. 18 ***Perf. 13½***
2780-2781 A1302 Set of 2 2.00 .75

Paintings by O Un Byol — A1303

Designs: 10ch, *Owl*. 15ch, *Dawn*. 20ch, *The Beautiful Rose Received by the Respected Marshall*. 25ch, *The Sun and Bamboo*. 30ch, *Autumn*.

1988, Oct. 5 ***Perf. 11½***
2782-2786 A1303 Set of 5 6.00 .90

Historic Locomotives — A1304

Designs: 10ch, *Junggi No. 35*. 20ch, *Junggi No. 22*. 30ch, *Jongihwa No. 3*. 40ch, *Junggi No. 307*.

1988, Oct. 28 ***Perf. 12***
2787-2790 A1304 Set of 4 5.00 .75

Calgary '88 Winter Olympic Games Winners

A1305

Designs: 10ch, Pirmin Zurbriggen (Switzerland). 20ch, Yvonne Van Gennip (Netherlands). 30ch, Marjo Matikainen (Finland). 40ch, USSR hockey team.

1988, Nov. 1 ***Perf. 13¼***
2791-2794 A1305 Set of 4 3.50 1.25

Souvenir Sheet

A1306

80ch, Katarina Witt (DDR). Illustration reduced.

2795 A1306 80ch multicolored 2.50 .50
a. Overprinted with names of winners in selvage 2.50 .50

First Man and Woman in Space — A1307

Designs: 20ch, Yuri Gagarin. 40ch, Valentina Tereshkova.

1988, Nov. 12 ***Perf. 13¼***
2796 A1307 Pair, #a.-b. 1.75 .60
a. 20ch multicolored .40 .20
b. 40ch multicolored 1.10 .45

INDIA '89 Int'l Philatelic Exhib., New Delhi

A1308

Design: Jawaharlal Nehru (1889-1964), 100th anniversary of birth.

1988, Dec. 15 ***Perf. 11¾x12***
2797 A1308 20ch multicolored 1.20 .20

Souvenir Sheet

A1309

Fan Dance, Korean Folk Dance. Illustration reduced.

Perf. 11¾x11½
2798 A1309 60ch multicolored 3.50 .40

Calgary '88 Winter Olympic Games Winners

New Year — A1310

Designs: 10ch, Chollima Statue. 20ch, Painting, *Dragon Angler*. 40ch, *Tortoise Serpent*, Kangso tomb mural painting (horiz.)

1989, Jan. 1 ***Perf. 13¼***
2799-2801 A1310 Set of 3 3.50 .50

Archery — A1311

Designs: 10ch, Archery. 15ch, Rifle shooting. 20ch, Pistol shooting. 25ch, Parachuting. 30ch, Launching model glider.

1989, Jan. 10 ***Perf. 12***
2802-2806 A1311 Set of 5 4.50 .75

National defense training.

Pets Presented to Kim Il Sung — A1312

Designs: 10ch, Dobermann pinscher. 20ch, Labrador. 25ch, German shepherd. 30ch, Border collies (horiz.). 35ch, Serval (horiz.).

1989, Jan. 23 ***Perf. 13½***
2807-2811 A1312 Set of 5 5.00 .90

Souvenir Sheet

A1313

80ch, *Felix libica*. Illustration reduced.

2812 A1313 80ch multicolored 4.00 .60

Kim Jong Il, 47th Birthday — A1314

Illustration reduced.

1989, Feb. 16 ***Perf. 11¾x12***

2813 A1314 80ch multicolored 2.00 .45

Agriculture — A1315

1989, Feb. 25 ***Perf. 12***

2814 A1315 10ch multicolored .70 .20

a. Toned unsurfaced paper, without gun 5.00 —

25th anniversary of publication of Kim Il Sung's *Theses on the Socialist Rural Question in Our Country.*

Mushrooms and Wild Fruits — A1316

Designs: 10ch, *Rozites caperata* and *Vitisamurensis.* 20ch, *Amanita caesarea* and *Schizandra chinensis.* 25ch, *Lactarius hygrophoides* and *Eleagnus crispa.* 30ch, *Agaricus placomyces* and *Actinidia arguta.* 35ch, *Agaricus arvensis* and *Lycium chinense.* 40ch, *Suillus grevillei* and *Juglans cordiformis.*
1w, *Gomphidius roseus* and *Diospyros lotus.*

1989, Feb. 27 ***Perf. 12***

2815-2820 A1316 Set of 6 8.00 1.25

Souvenir Sheet

Perf. 11½x11¾

2821 A1316 1w multicolored 4.50 .90

13th World Youth and Students' Festival — A1317

Designs: 10ch, Girl. 20ch, Children of different races. 30ch, Fairy, rainbow. 40ch, Young people and Tower of Juche Idea.

1989, Mar. 18 ***Perf. 12¼***

2822-2825 A1317 Set of 4 2.75 1.00

2822a 10ch, on soft toned unsurfaced paper, without gum 15.00 —

2823a 20ch, on soft toned unsurfaced paper, without gum 8.00 —

2824a 30ch, on soft toned unsurfaced paper, without gum 8.00 —

2825a 40ch, on soft toned unsurfaced paper, without gum 8.00 —

2825b 40ch, on stiff dull white unsurfaced paper, without gum 8.00 —

Butterflies and Insects — A1318

Designs: 10ch, *Parnassius eversmanni.* 15ch, *Colias heos.* 20ch, *Dilipa fenestra.* 25ch, *Buthus martensis.* 30ch, *Trichogramma ostriniae.* 40ch, *Damaster constricticollis.*
Illustration reduced.

1989, Mar. 23 ***Perf. 12***

2826 A1318 Shtlet of 6, #a.-f. 6.00 1.00

Souvenir Sheet

Butterflies and Insects — A1319

80ch, *Parnassius nomion.* Illustration reduced.

2827 A1319 80ch multicolored 3.75 .75

Spring Friendship Art Festival — A1320

1989, Apr. 6

2828 A1320 10ch multicolored .80 .20

Kim Il Sung, 77th Birthday — A1321

1989, Apr. 15 ***Perf. 11½***

2829 A1321 10ch multicolored .50 .20

a. Toned unsurfaced paper, without gum 10.00 —

Battle of the Musan Area, 50th Anniv. — A1322

1989, May 19 ***Perf. 12***

2830 A1322 10ch multicolored 1.10 .20

Jamo System of Dance Notation — A1323

Designs: 10ch, Mexican dance. 20ch, Ballet duet in *Don Quixote.* 25ch, Dance of Guinea. 30ch, Cambodian folk dance.
80ch, Korean folk dance.

1989, May 30

2831-2834 A1323 Set of 4 3.75 .65

Souvenir Sheet

2835 A1323 80ch multicolored 3.25 .50

A1324 A1325

13th World Festival of Youth and Students

1989, June 8 ***Perf. 11½***

2836 A1324 5ch Deep blue .25 .20

a. Soft toned unsurfaced paper, without gum 15.00 —

2837 A1325 10ch Red brown .30 .20

Cartoon, *Badger Measures the Height* — A1326

Designs: 10ch, Badger racing cat and bear to flag pole. 40ch, Cat and bear climbing pole, while badger measures shadow. 50ch, Badger winning the prize.

1989, June 21

2838-2840 A1326 Set of 3 4.00 .65

Astronomy A1327

20ch, Chomosongdae Observatory.
80ch, Saturn (horiz.)

1989, June 29 ***Perf. 12***

2841 A1327 20ch multicolored 1.40 .20

Souvenir Sheet

2842 A1327 80ch multicolored 3.00 .50

Eugène Delacroix's *Liberty Guiding the People* — A1328

PHILEXFRANCE '89, Int'l Philatelic Exhib., Paris

Illustration reduced.

1989, July 7 ***Perf. 12x11½***

2843 A1328 70ch multicolored 3.00 2.00

BRASILIANA '89, Int'l Philatelic Exhib., Rio de Janeiro

Pele — A1329

Illustration reduced.

1989, July 28 ***Perf. 12***

2844 A1329 40ch multicolored 1.40 .30

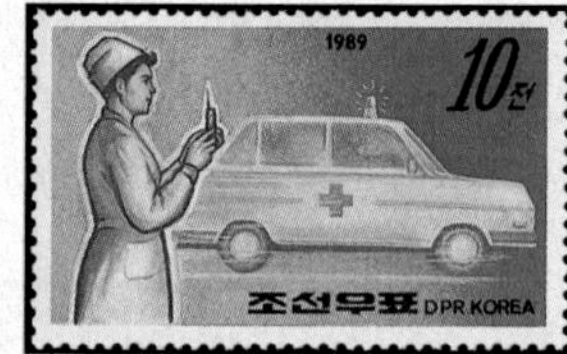

Fire Brigade and Emergency Medical Services — A1330

Designs: 10ch, Nurse and ambulance. 20ch, Surgeon and ambulance. 30ch, Fireman and fire engine. 40ch, Fireman and fire engine (diff.)

1989, Aug. 12

2845-2848 A1330 Set of 4 6.00 .65

Plants Presented as Gifts to Kim Il Sung — A1331

Designs: 10ch, Kafir lily (*Clivia miniata*). 15ch, Tulips (*Tulipa gesneriana*). 20ch, Flamingo lily (*Anthurium andreanum*). 25ch, *Rhododendron obtusum*. 30ch, Daffodils (*Narcissus pseudonarcissus*).
80ch, (*Gerbera hybrida*).

1989, Aug. 19
2849-2853 A1331 Set of 5 5.50 1.00

Souvenir Sheet

2854 A1331 80ch multicolored 4.50 .50

150th Anniv. of Postage Stamps / STAMP WORLD LONDON '90 Int'l Philatelic Exhib. — A1332

Designs: 5ch, Letter, ship, plane, map. 10ch, Letters and mail box. 20ch, Stamps, magnifying glass, tongs. 30ch, Fiirst stamps pf DPRK. 40ch, UPU emblem, headquarters, Berne. 50ch, Sir Rowland Hill and Penny Black.

1989, Aug. 27
2855-2860 A1332 Set of 6 7.50 1.25

Alpine Flowers — A1333

Designs: 10ch, *Iris setosa*. 15ch, *Aquilegia japonica*. 20ch, *Bistorta incana*. 25ch *Rhodiola elongata*. 30ch, *Sanguisorba sitchensis*.

1989, Sept. 8 ***Perf. 11½***
2861-2865 A1333 Set of 5 5.25 1.00

Souvenir Sheet

A1334

80ch, (*Trollius japonicus*). Illustration reduced.

2866 A1334 80ch multicolored 3.50 .55

Trees bearing Anti-Japanese Patriotic Slogans — A1335

Designs: 10ch, "20 million compatriots, an anti-Japanese heroine of Korea rose on Mt. Paektu," inscribed on tree, Mt. Paektu. 3w, "The future of Korea is bright with the Luminous Star of Mt. Paektu," inscribed on tree, Qun-dong, Pyongyang. 5w, "The General Star of Mt. Paektu shines three thousand-ri expanse of land," inscribed on tree, Mt. Kanbaek.

1989, Sept. 21 ***Perf. 12¼***
2867-2869 A1335 Set of 3 18.00 11.00

Compare with No. 2885.

Children's Games — A1336

Designs: 10ch, Girl skipping rope. 20ch, Boy with whirligig. 30ch, Boy flying kite. 40ch, Girl spinning top.

1989, Sept. 30 ***Perf. 12***
2870 A1336 Block of 4, #a.-d. 4.00 .80
a. 10ch multicolored .25 .20
b. 20ch multicolored 1.75 .20
c. 30ch multicolored .50 .20
d. 40ch multicolored .60 .20

Int'l March for Peace and Reunification of Korea — A1337

Illustration reduced.

1989, Oct. 1 ***Perf. 11½x12***
2871 A1337 80ch multicolored 3.00 1.75

Locomotives — A1338

Designs: 10ch, Electric train entering station yard. 20ch, Electric train crossing bridge. 25ch, Diesel locomotive. 30ch, Diesel locomotive (diff.). 40ch, Steam locomotive. 50ch, Steam locomotive (diff.).

1989, Oct. 19 ***Perf. 11¾x12¼***
2872-2877 A1338 Set of 6 6.00 1.25

14th World Soccer Championship, *Italia '90* — A1339

Designs: 10ch, Players and map of Italy. 20ch, Free kick. 30ch, Goal scrimmage. 40ch, Goalkeeper blocking ball.

1989, Oct. 28 ***Perf. 12x11¾***
2878-2881 A1339 Set of 4 4.00 .60

Magellan A1340

1989, Nov. 25 ***Perf. 12***
2882 A1340 30ch multicolored 1.25 .20

Descobrex '89 International Philatelic Exhibition, Portugal.

A1341

A1342

10ch, Mangyong Hill and snow-covered pine branches. 20ch, Koguryo warriors.

Perf. 11½ (#2883), 12 (#2884)

1990, Jan. 1
2883 A1341 10ch multicolored .25 .20
a. Toned unsurfaced paper, without gum 15.00 —
2884 A1342 20ch multicolored 1.20 .20
a. Toned unsurfaced paper, without gum 5.00 —

New Year.

Tree, Mt. Paektu, Bearing Anti-Japanese Patriotic Slogan — A1343

1990, Jan. 12 ***Perf. 11½***
2885 A1343 5ch multicolored .50 .20

Dogs — A1344

Designs: 20ch, Ryukwoli. 30ch, Phalryuki. 40ch, Komdungi. 50ch, Olruki.
Illustration reduced.

1990, Jan. 17
2886 A1344 Block of 4, #a.-d. 5.50 1.50
a. 20ch multicolored .90 .20
b. 30ch multicolored .90 .20
c. 40ch multicolored .90 .20
d. 50ch multicolored .90 .20

Birthplace, Mt. Paektu — A1345

1990, Feb. 16
2887 A1345 10ch deep red brown .50 .20
a. Toned unsurfaced paper, without gum 5.00 —

Kim Jong Il's 48th birthday.

Stone Age Man — A1346

Designs: 10ch, Primitive man, stone tools. 20ch, Paleolithic and Neolithic men, camp scene.

1990, Feb. 21
2888-2889 A1346 Set of 2 3.00 .30

Bridges — A1347

Designs: 10ch, Rungra Bridge, Pyongyang. 20ch, Pothong Bridge, Pyongyang. 30ch, Suspension bridge between Sinuiju-Ryucho Island. 40ch, Chungsongui Bridge, Pyongyang.

1990, Feb. 27 ***Perf. 11½***
2890-2893 A1347 Set of 4 4.50 .60
2890a 10ch, on thin, coarse brownish paper, without gum 5.00 —

Traditional Warriors' Costumes — A1348

Designs: 20ch, Infantryman (3rd century BC-7th century AD). 30ch, Archer. 50ch, Commander in armor (3rd century BC-7th century AD). 70ch, Koguryo Period officer (10th-14th centuries).

1989, Mar. 18

2894-2897 A1348 Set of 4 6.25 2.00
2897a 70ch, on dull white unsurfaced paper, without gum 5.00 —

Crabs — A1349

Designs: 20ch, *Atergatis subdentatus*. 30ch, *Platylambrus validus*. 50ch, *Uca arcuata*.

1990, Mar. 25

2898-2900 A1349 Set of 3 3.00 .60

Dancers — A1350

1990, Apr. 7

2901 A1350 10ch multicolored .50 .20

Spring Friendship Art Festival, Pyongyang.

Kim Il Sung's 78th birthday.

A1351

10ch, 'Fork in the Road' Monument, Mangyongdae Revolutionary Site.

1990, Apr. 15 ***Perf. 11½x11¾***

2902 A1351 10ch multicolored .50 .20

Souvenir Sheet

A1352

80ch, Kim Il Sung.

2903 A1352 80ch multicolored 2.50 .50

Cacti — A1353

Designs: 10ch, *Gynmocalycium sp.* 30ch, *Phyllocactus hybridus.* 50ch, *Epiphyllum truncatum.*

1990, Apr. 21 ***Perf. 12¼***

2904-2906 A1353 Set of 3 4.00 .60

STAMP WORLD LONDON '90 — A1354

20ch, Exhibition emblem.

1990, May 3 ***Perf. 11½***

2907 A1354 20ch multicolored .90 .20

Souvenir Sheet

A1355

70ch, Sir Rowland Hill.

2908 A1355 70ch multicolored 2.75 1.20

Peafowl — A1356

Designs: 10ch, Congo peafowl *Afropavo congensis.* 20ch, Common peafowl *Pavo cristatus.*

1990, May 10 ***Perf. 11¾x12***

2909-2910 A1356 Set of 2 3.00 .60

Souvenir Sheet

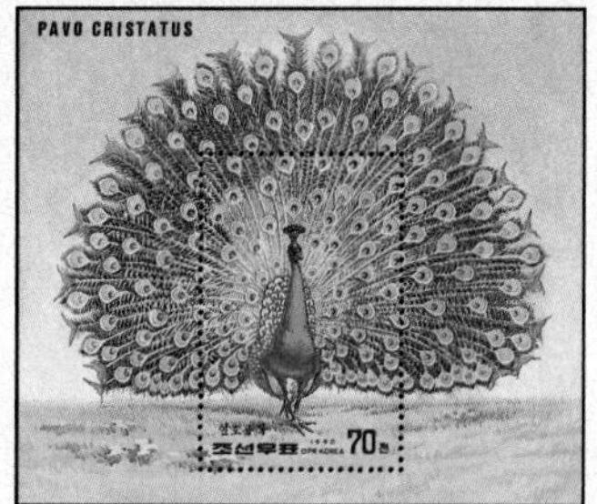

A1357

Design: 70ch, Common peafowl with tail displayed. Illustration reduced.

2911 A1357 70ch multicolored 3.00 .60

Bio-engineering — A1358

Designs: 10ch, Dolphin and submarine. 20ch, Bat and sonar dish, satellite. 30ch, Eagle and airplanes. 40ch, Squid and jets.

1990, May 24

2912 A1358 Sheet of 4, #a.-d. 7.00 1.25
a. 10ch multicolored 1.25 .25
b. 20ch multicolored 1.25 .25
c. 30ch multicolored 1.25 .25
d. 40ch multicolored 1.25 .25

BELGICA '90 Int'l Philatelic Exhib., Brussels — A1359

Designs: 10ch, Rembrandt, *Self Portrait.* 20ch, Raphael, *Self Portrait.* 30ch, Rubens, *Self Portrait.*

1990, June 2 ***Perf. 12¼x12***

2913-2915 A1359 Set of 3 2.25 .40

Düsseldorf '90, 10th Int'l Youth Philatelic Exhib. — A1360

Designs: 20ch, Steffi Graf, tennis player, with bouquet. 30ch, Exhibition emblem. 70ch, K.H. Rummenigge, German soccer player.

1990, June 20

2916-2918 A1360 Set of 3 7.00 .75

A1361

Designs: 10ch, Games mascot, Workers' Stadium, Beijing. 30ch, Chollina Statue and Korean athletes. 40ch, Games emblem, athletes.

1990, July 14

2919-2921 A1361 Set of 3 2.00 .60

11th Asian Games, Beijing (#3021, 3022). Third Asian Winter Games, Samjiyon (#3023).

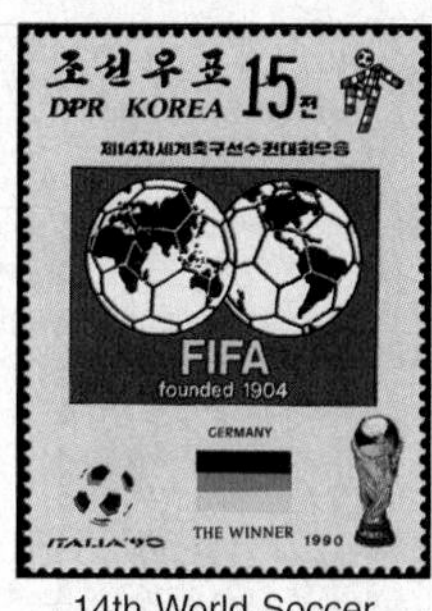

14th World Soccer Championship — A1362

Designs: 15ch, Emblem of F.I.F.A. (Federation of Football Associations). 20ch, Jules Rimet. 25ch, Soccer ball. 30ch, Olympic Stadium, Rome. 35ch, Goalkeeper. 40ch, Emblem of the German Football Association.

80ch, Emblem of German Football Association and trophy.

1990, Aug. 8 ***Perf. 13½***

2922-2927 A1362 Set of 6 6.00 1.00

Souvenir Sheet

2928 A1362 80ch multicolored 3.00 1.50

New Zealand '90 Int'l Philatelic Exhib., Auckland — A1363

1990, Aug. 24 ***Perf. 12***

2929 A1363 30ch multicolored 1.75 .40

Summer at Chipson Peak — A1364

Illustration reduced.

1990, Aug. 24 ***Perf. 11½***

2930 A1364 80ch multicolored 3.00 .50

Europa '90 International Stamp Fair, Riccione.

Koguryo Wedding Procession — A1365

Designs: 10ch, Man on horse blowing bugle. 30ch, Bridegroom on horse. 50ch, Bride in carriage. 1w, Man on horse beating drum.

1990, Sept. 3 *Perf. 12*

2931 Strip of 4, #a.-d. 6.00 .80
a. A1365 10ch multicolored 1.25 .20
b. A1365 30ch multicolored 1.25 .20
c. A1365 50ch multicolored 1.25 .20
d. A1365 1w multicolored 1.25 .20

Printed in setenant strips of four within the sheet.

Pan-National Rally for Peace and Reunification of Korea — A1366

Designs: 10ch, Rally emblem, crowd descending Mt. Paektu.

1990, Sept. 15

2932 A1366 10ch multicolored .50 .20

Souvenir Sheet

A1367

Design: 1w, Crowd watching dancers. Illustration reduced.

2933 A1367 1w multicolored 2.75 .55

Insects — A1368

Designs: 20ch, Praying mantis (*Mantis religiosa*). 30ch, Lady bug (*Coccinella septempunctata*). 40ch, *Pheropsophus jussoensis*. 70ch, *Phyllium siccifolium*.

1990, Sept. 20

2934-2936A A1368 Set of 4 6.00 1.10

Soccer Players — A1369

1990, Oct. 11

2937 A1369 Pair, #a.-b. 2.75 .40
a. 10ch multicolored 1.25 .20
b. 20ch multicolored 1.25 .20

Souvenir Sheet

Design: 1w, North and South Korean players entering May Day Stadium.

2938 A1369 1w multicolored 4.50 .75

North-South Reunification Soccer Games, Pyongyang.

National Reunification Concert — A1370

1990, Oct. 17

2939 A1370 10ch multicolored .50 .20

Farm Animals — A1371

Designs: 10ch, Ox. 20ch, Pig. 30ch, Goat. 40ch, Sheep. 50ch, Horse.

1990, Oct. 18

2940-2944 A1371 Set of 5 5.75 .85
2944a Sheetlet of 10, 2x #2940-2944 13.00 1.75

Nos. 2940-2944 were issued both in separate sheets of 50 stamps and together in sheetlets of 10 stamps.

A1372

A1373

Designs: 10ch, N. Korean and Communist Chinese soldiers. 20ch, Korean civilians welcoming Chinese soldiers. 30ch, Battle scene, victorious soldiers. 40ch, Postwar reconstruction.

1990, Oct. 23

2945 A1372 10ch multicolored .20 .20
2946 A1373 20ch multicolored .75 .20
2947 A1373 30ch multicolored 1.00 .20
2948 A1373 40ch multicolored 1.50 .20
Nos. 2945-2948 (4) 3.45 .80

Souvenir Sheet

A1374

Design: 80ch, Friendship Monument. Illustration reduced.

Perf. 11¾x11½

2949 A1374 80ch multicolored 3.00 .50

40th anniversary of the entry of Chinese troops into the Korean War.

For overprint on No. 2949, see No. 3282.

A1375

1990, Oct. 24 *Perf. 13¼*

2950 A1375 1w multicolored 4.00 1.20

40th anniversary of United Nations Development Program.

Fishes — A1376

Designs: 10ch, Sturgeon (*Acipenser mikadoi*). 20ch, Sea bream (*Sparus macrocephalus*). 40ch, Fat greenling (*Hergrammos otakii*). 50ch, Ray (*Myliobatus tobeijei*).

1990, Nov. 20 *Perf. 12*

2951-2955 A1376 Set of 5 5.75 2.00
2955a Sheetlet of 10, 2x #2951-2955 12.00 4.00

Nos. 2951-2955 were issued both in separate sheets of 50 stamps and together in sheetlets of 10 stamps.

New Year — A1377

1990, Dec. 1

2956 A1377 40ch multicolored 1.75 .20

Birds — A1378

Designs: 10ch, Moorhen (*Gallinula chloropus*). 20ch, Jay (*Garrulus glandarius*). 30ch, Three-toed woodpecker (*Picodes tridactylus*). 40ch, Whimbrel (*Numenius phaeopus*). 50ch, Water rail (*Rallus aquaticus*)

1990, Dec. 18 *Perf. 12*

2957-2961 A1378 Set of 5 6.50 2.00
2961a Sheetlet of 10, 2x #2957-2961 13.00 5.00

Nos. 2957-2961 were issued both in separate sheets of 50 stamps and together in sheetlets of 10 stamps.

Pandas — A1379

Designs: 10ch, Giant panda. 20ch, Two giant pandas feeding. 30ch, Giant panda on limb. 40ch, Giant panda on rock. 50ch, Pair of giant pandas. 60ch, Giant panda in tree.

1991, Jan. 10 *Perf. 11¾x12*

2962-2967 A1379 Set of 6 7.00 1.75
2967a Sheetlet of 6, #2962-2967 7.00 1.75

Souvenir Sheet

A1380

Illustration reduced.

Perf. 11½

2968 A1380 1w multicolored 3.25 .60

Nos. 2962-2967 were issued both in separate sheets and together in sheetlets of 6 stamps.

Revolutionary Sites

Changsan — A1381

Oun A1382

1991, Jan. 10 ***Perf. 12***

2969 A1381 5ch multicolored .25 .20
2970 A1382 10ch multicolored .30 .20

Endangered Birds — A1383

Designs: 10ch, Black-faced spoonbills (*Platalea minor*). 20ch, Gray herons (*Ardea cinerea*). 30ch, Great egrets (*Egretta alba*). 40ch, Manchurian cranes (*Grus japonensis*). 50ch, Japanese white-necked cranes (*Grus vipio*). 70ch, White storks (*Ciconia boyciana*).

1991, Feb. 5

2971-2976 A1383 Set of 6 6.00 1.40
2976a Sheetlet of 6, #2971-2976 7.50 1.75

Nos. 2971-2976 were issued both in separate sheets of 9 and together in sheetlets of 6 stamps.

Alpine Butterflies — A1384

Designs: 10ch, *Clossiana angarensis*. 20ch, *Erebia embla*. 30ch, *Nymphalis antiopa*. 40ch, *Polygonia c-album*). 50ch, *Colias erate*. 60ch, *Thecla betulae*).

1991, Feb. 20 ***Perf. 13¼***

2977-2982 A1384 Set of 6 7.50 2.50
2982a Sheetlet of 6, #2977-2982 7.50 2.50

Nos. 2977-2982 were issued both in separate sheets and together in sheetlets of 6 stamps.

Fungi — A1385

Designs: 10ch, *Hydnum repandum*. 20ch, *Phylloporus rhodoxanthus*. 30ch, *Calvatia craniformis*. 40ch, *Ramaria botrytis*. 50ch, *Russula integra*.

1991, Feb. 26 ***Perf. 12x12¼***

2983-2987 A1385 Set of 5 5.00 1.25
2987a Sheetlet of 10, 2x #2983-2987 10.00 2.50

Nos. 2983-2987 were issued both in separate sheets of 9 stamps and together in sheetlets of 10 stamps.

Revolutionary Sites

Kumchon A1386

Samdung A1387

1991, Mar. 15 ***Perf. 12***

2988 A1386 10ch multicolored .30 .20
2989 A1387 40ch multicolored 1.20 .30

Silkworm Research

Dr. Kye Ung — A1388

Silk Moth — A1389

Designs: 10ch, Dr. Kye Ung (1893-1967), silkworm researcher. 20ch, Chinese oak silk moth, *Antheraea pernyi*. 30ch, *Attacus ricini*. 40ch, *Antheraea yamamai*). 50ch, *Bombyx mori*. 60ch, *Aetias artemis*).

1991, Mar. 27

2990 A1388 10ch multicolored .20 .20
2991 A1389 20ch multicolored .60 .30
2992 A1389 30ch multicolored .80 .40
2993 A1389 40ch multicolored 1.20 .50
2994 A1389 50ch multicolored 1.60 .75
2995 A1389 60ch multicolored 2.00 .80
a. Sheetlet of 6, #2990-2995 6.50 3.50
Nos. 2990-2995 (6) 6.40 2.95

Nos. 2990-2995 were issued both in separate sheets of 21 and together in sheetlets of 6 stamps.

9th Spring Friendship Art Festival, Pyongyang — A1390

1991, Apr. 3

2996 A1390 10ch multicolored .50 .20

Antarctic Exploration — A1391

Designs: 10ch, Penguins. 20ch, Research station. 30ch, Elephant seals. 40ch, Research ship. 50ch, Black-backed gulls.

80ch, DPRK flag and map of Antarctica.

1991, Apr. 20 ***Perf. 11¾x12***

2997-3001 A1391 Set of 5 6.00 1.25

Souvenir Sheet

Perf. 11¾

3002 A1391 80ch multicolored 3.00 .55

85th Interparliamentary Union Conference, Pyongyang — A1392

Designs: 10ch, Peoples Palace of Culture. 1.50w, Conference emblem and azalea.

1991, Apr. 29 ***Perf. 12***

3003-3004 A1392 Set of 2 5.00 1.40

Map and Kim Jong Ho — A1393

1991, May 8 ***Perf. 11¾x12***

3005 A1393 90ch multicolored 2.50 .80

Dinosaurs — A1394

Designs: 10ch, Cynognathus. 20ch, Brontosaurus. 30ch, Stegosaurus and allosaurus. 40ch, Pterosauria. 50ch, Ichthyosaurus.

1991, May 21 ***Perf. 12x11¾***

3006-3010 A1394 Strip of 5 + label 7.50 1.75
3010a Sheetlet of 6 17.00 2.00

Nos. 3006-3010 were issued both in separate sheetlets of 6 (5 stamps + 1 label) and together in sheets of 30 stamps and 6 labels.

Barcelona '92 Olympic Games — A1395

Designs: 10ch (#3011), 100-Meter dash. 10ch (#3012), Hurdle race. 20ch (#3013), Broad jump. 20ch (#3014), Throwing discus. 30ch (#3015), Shot-put. 30ch (#3016), Pole vault. 40ch (#3017), High jump. 40ch (#3018), Javelin throw.

80ch (#3019), 400-meter race. 80ch (#3020), 1500-meter race.

1991, June 18

3011-3018 A1395 Set of 8 4.00 1.40
3018a Sheetlet of 10, #3011-3020 12.50 2.75

Souvenir Sheets

Perf. 11½x11¾

3019-3020 A1395 Set of 2 3.50 1.25

Nos. 3011-3018 were issued both in separate sheetlets of 9 stamps and together in sheets of 10 stamps, with 80ch values from Nos. 3019-3020.

Cats — A1396

Designs: 10ch, Cats and birds. 20ch, Cat and rat. 30ch, Cat and butterfly. 40ch, Cats and ball. 50ch, Cat and frog.

1991, July 21 ***Perf. 13¼***

3021-3025 A1396 Set of 5 5.25 2.25

Riccione '91 Int'l Stamp Fair — A1397

Illustration reduced.

1991, Aug. 27 ***Perf. 11¾x12***

3026 A1397 80ch multicolored 2.75 .60

Horses — A1398

Designs: 10ch, Wild horse (*Equus caballus*). 20ch, Hybrid of wild ass and wild horse (*Equus asinus* and *Equus caballus*). 30ch, Przewalski's horse (*Equus przewalskii*). 40ch, Wild ass (*Equus asinus*). 50ch, Wild horse (*Equus caballus*), diff..

1991, Sept. 2 ***Perf. 13½***

3027-3031 A1398 Set of 5 5.00 1.25
3031a Sheetlet of 5, #3027-3031 5.00 1.40

Nos. 3027-3031 were issued both in separate sheets of 18 stamps and together in sheetlets of 5 stamps.

Fishes

A1399

A1400

Designs: 10ch, Pennant coral fish (*Heniochus acuminatus*). 20ch, Big-spotted trigger fish (*Balistoides conspicillum*). 30ch, Anemone fish (*Amphiprion frenatus*). 40ch, Blue surgeon fish (*Paracanthurus hepatus*). 50ch, Angel fish (*Pterophyllum eimekei*).

80ch, Tetras (*Hyphessobrycon innesi*). Illustration reduced.

1991, Sept. 20 ***Perf. 12x12¼***

3032-3036 A1399 Set of 5 5.00 1.25
3036a Sheetlet of 5, #3032-3036 5.00 1.25

Souvenir Sheet

Perf. 11¾

3037 A1400 80ch multicolored 5.00 .60

Nos. 3032-3036 were issued both in separate sheets of 24 stamps and together in sheetlets of 5 stamps commemorating the Phila Nippon '91 International Stamp Exhibition.

No. 3036 is airmail.

Flowers — A1401

Designs: 10ch, Begonia. 20ch, Gerbera. 30ch, Rhododendrons. 40ch, Phalaenopsis. 50ch, *Impatiens sultani.* 60ch, Streptocarpus.

1991, Oct. 16 ***Perf. 12¼x12***

3038-3043 A1401 Set of 6 6.50 1.75
3043a Sheetlet of 6, #3038-3043 6.50 2.00

Nos. 3041-3043 commemorate Canada '92 International Youth Stamp Exhibition, Montreal, and include the exhibition emblem.

Nos. 3038-3043 were issued both in separate sheets and together in sheetlets of 6 stamps.

Panmunjon — A1402

1991, Oct. 12 ***Perf. 12***

3044 A1402 10ch multicolored .60 .20

Magnolia — A1403

1991, Nov. 1 ***Perf. 11½***

3045 A1403 10ch multicolored .60 .20

DPRK National Flower.

Women's World Soccer Championship, China — A1404

Designs: 10ch, Dribbling. 20ch, Dribbling, diff. 30ch, Heading the ball. 40ch, Overhead kick. 50ch, Tackling. 60ch, Goalkeeper.

1991, Nov. 3 ***Perf. 12***

3046-3051 A1404 Set of 6 6.50 1.75
3051a Sheetlet of 6, #3046-3051 6.50 2.00

Nos. 3046-3051 were issued both in separate sheets and together in sheetlets of 6 stamps.

Monkeys

A1405

A1406

Designs: 10ch, Squirrel monkeys (*Samiri sciureus*). 20ch, Pygmy marmosets (*Cebuella pygmaea*). 30ch, Red-handed tamarins (*Saquinas midas*).

80ch, Monkey leaping. Illustration reduced.

1992, Jan. 1

3052-3054 A1405 Set of 3 2.25 .70
3054a Sheetlet of 3, #3052-3054 2.50 .80

Souvenir Sheet

Perf. 11¾x11½

3055 A1406 80ch multicolored 2.50 1.00

Nos. 3052-3054 were issued both in separate sheets of 21 stamps and together in sheetlets of 3 stamps.

Birds of Prey

A1407

A1408

Designs: 10ch, Great horned owl (*Bubo bubo*). 20ch, Hawk (*Buteo buteo*). 30ch, African fish eagle (*Haliaeetus vocifer*). 40ch, Stellar's sea eagle (*Haliaeetus pelagicus*). 50ch, Golden eagle (*Aquila chrysaetos*).

80ch, Common kestrel (*Falco tinnunculus*). Illustration reduced.

1992, Jan. 5 ***Perf. 13¼***

3056-3060 A1407 Set of 5 4.75 1.75
3060a Sheetlet of 12, 2 #3056-3060 + 2 labels 10.00 3.50

Souvenir Sheet

Perf. 11½

3061 A1408 80ch multicolored 2.50 .60

Nos. 3056-3060 were issued both in separate sheets and together in sheetlets of 12.

No. 3060a commemorates the Granada '92 International Stamp Exhibition.

50th Birthday of Kim Jong Il

A1409

A1410

Designs: 10ch, Birthplace, Mt. Paektu. 20ch, Mt. Paektu. 30ch, Lake Chon on top of Mt. Paektu. 40ch, Lake Samji.

80ch, *Snowstorm in Mt. Paektu.* Illustration reduced.

1992, Feb. 16 ***Perf. 12x11¾***

3062-3065 A1409 Set of 4 3.25 .75

Souvenir Sheet

Perf. 11¾x11½

3066 A1410 80ch multicolored 3.00 .60

Transport

A1411

Designs: 10ch, Bus, "Jipsam 88." 20ch, Bus, "Pyongyang 86." 30ch, Trolley bus, "Chollima 84." 40ch, Bus, "Kwangbok Sonyon." 50ch, Tram. 60ch, July 17 Tram.

1992, Feb. 20 ***Perf. 12¼***

3067-3072 A1411 Set of 6 6.50 1.75
3072a Sheetlet of 6, #3067-3072 6.50 1.90

Nos. 3067-3072 were issued both in separate sheets and together in sheetlets of 6 stamps, with border inscriptions commemorating Essen '92 International Stamp Fair.

Spring Fellowship Art Festival, Pyongyang — A1412

1992, Apr. 7

3073 A1412 10ch multicolored .50 .20

80th Birthday of Kim Il Sung

A1413

Revolutionary Sites: 10ch (#3074), Birthplace, Mangyongdao. 10ch (#3075), Party emblem, Turubong. 10ch (#3076), Map, Ssuksom. 10ch (#3077), Statue of soldier, Tongchang. 40ch (#3078), Chollima Statue, Kangson. 40ch (#3079), Cogwheels, Taean. 1.20w, Monument, West Sea Barrage.

1992, Apr. 15

3074-3080 A1413 Set of 7 7.50 2.25

Souvenir Sheet

A1414

80ch, Kim Il Sung among participants in the April Spring Friendship Art Festival. Illustration reduced.

Perf. 11½

3081 A1414 80ch multicolored 3.00 .60

No. 2080 is airmail.

Kang Ban Sok, Mother of Kim Il Sung, Birth Centenary — A1415

Illustration reduced.

1992, Apr. 21 *Perf. 13¼*

3082 A1415 80ch multicolored 2.25 .60

Korean People's Army, 60th Anniv. — A1416

Designs (all 10ch): #3083, Soldier, troops on parade. #3084, Pilot, soldiers. #3085, Soldier with two civilian women.

1992, Apr. 25 *Perf. 12¼*

3083-3085 A1416 Set of 3 1.10 .25
3085a Sheetlet of 9, 4 #3085, 2 ea. #3083-3084 + label 3.00 1.00

Nos. 3083-3085 were issued both in separate sheets and together in sheetlets of 9 stamps.

25th Olympic Games, Barcelona '92 — A1417

Women's events: 10ch, Hurdle race. 20ch, High jump. 30ch, Shot-put. 40ch, 200-meter race. 50ch, Broad jump. 60ch, Javelin throw. 80ch, 800-meter race.

1992, May 10 *Perf. 12x11¾*

3086-3091 A1417 Set of 6 6.50 1.75
3091a Sheetlet of 8, #3086-3092 + label 9.50 2.50

Souvenir Sheet

3092 A1416 80ch multicolored 2.75 .60

Nos. 3086-3091 were issued both in separate sheets and together in sheetlets of 8 stamps, with type of #3092 and label.

Prehistoric Man — A1418

Designs: 10ch, Planting crops. 20ch, Family in shelter, with cooking pot. 30ch, Plowing. 40ch, Indoor life. 50ch, Laying a dolmen.

1992, June 1 *Perf. 12x11¾*

3093-3097 A1418 Set of 5 5.00 1.25
3097a Sheetlet of 6, #3093-3097 + label 6.00 1.40

Nos. 3093-3097 were issued both in separate sheets and together in sheetlets of 5 stamps and 1 label.

Birds — A1419

Designs: 10ch, White-bellied woodpecker (*Dryocopus javensis*). 20ch, Ring-necked pheasant (*Phasianis colchicus*). 30ch, White stork (*Ciconia boyciana*). 40ch, Blue-winged pitta (*Pitta brachyura*). 50ch, Pallas's sandgrouse (*Syrrhaptes paradoxus*). 60ch, Black grouse (*Lyrurus tetrix*).
80ch, European starling (*Sturnus sturnus*).

1992, June 28 *Perf. 11½*

3098-3103 A1419 Set of 6 7.00 1.75
3103a Sheetlet of 8, #3098-3104 + label 15.00 —

Souvenir Sheet

3104 A1418 80ch multicolored 3.50 1.40

Nos. 3098-3103 were issued both in separate sheets and together in sheetlets of 8 stamps, with the 80ch stamp from No. 3104 and a label.

North-South Joint Statement, 20th Anniv. — A1420

1992, July 4

3105 A1420 1.50w multicolored 4.50 1.40

Souvenir Sheet

3106 A1420 3w multicolored 9.00 2.75

No. 3106 contains two copies of No. 3105 and label.

Flowers — A1421

Designs: 10ch, *Bougainvillea spectabilis*. 20ch, *Ixora chinensis*. 30ch, *Dendrobium taysuwie*. 40ch, *Columnea gloriosa*. 50ch, *Crinum*. 60ch, *Ranunculus asiaticus*.

1992, July 15 *Perf. 12¼*

3107-3112 A1421 Set of 6 6.50 1.75
3112a Sheetlet of 8, #3107-3112 + 2 labels 7.00 2.00

Nos. 3107-3112 were issued both in separate sheets and in sheetlets of 8, with two labels, commemorating Genova '92 International Stamp Exhibition.

The Solar System — A1422

Designs (all 50ch): #3113, Satellite, Venus, Earth, Mars. #3114, Jupiter. #3115, Saturn. #3116, Uranus. #3117, Neptune, Pluto.

1992, Aug. 10 *Perf. 11½*

3113-3117 Strip of 5 8.00 2.50
A1422 50ch Any single
3117a Sheetlet of 10, #3113-3117 + 5 labels 9.00 2.75

Souvenir Sheet

3118 A1422 80ch multicolored 2.50 1.50

Nos. 3113-3117 were issued together in horizontal setenant strips of 5, both within large sheets and in sheetlets of 5 stamps and 5 labels.

Riccione '92 Int'l Stamp Fair — A1423

Designs: 10ch, C-class yacht. 20ch, Sailboard. 30ch, Rager-class yacht. 40ch, Pinclass yacht. 50ch, 470-class yacht. 60ch, Fair emblem.

1992, Aug. 27 *Perf. 12¼*

3119-3124 A1423 Set of 6 6.50 2.25
3119a Sheetlet of 6 stamps, 2 ea. #3119, 3121, 3123 6.50 2.50
3120a Sheetlet of 6 stamps, 2 ea. #3120, 3122, 3124 6.50 2.50

Nos. 3119-3124 were printed both in separate sheets of 24 stamps and in sheetlets of 6, containing two examples each of the 10ch, 30ch and 50ch values, or of the 20ch, 40ch, 60ch values.

U.C. Sampdoria, Italian Soccer Champion 1991

A1424

Designs: 20ch, Moreno Mannini, defender. 30ch, Gianluca Vialli, forward. 40ch, Pietro Vierchowod, back. 50ch, Fausto Pari, centerhalf. 60ch, Roberto Mancini, forward. 1w, club president.
Illustration reduced.

1992, Aug. 31 *Perf. 12*

3125-3130 A1424 Sheet of 6 9.00 3.00

Souvenir Sheet

A1425

1w, Vialli and Riccardo Garrone, president of club sponsor, ERG. Illustration reduced.

Perf. 11½x12

3131 A1425 1w multicolored 3.00 1.50

8th World Taekwondo Championship, Pyongyang

A1426

Designs: 10ch, Team pattern. 30ch, Side kick. 50ch, Flying high kick. 70ch, Flying twisting kick. 90ch, Black-belt breaking tiles with fist.

1992, Sept. 1 *Perf. 12*

3132-3136 A1426 Set of 5 8.00 2.50
3136a Sheetlet of 6, #3132-3136 + label 8.00 2.50

Souvenir Sheet

A1427

1.20w, Flying twin foot side kick; Choe Hong Hin, president of International Taekwon-Do Federation, in margin. Illustration reduced.

3137 A1427 1.20w multicolored 4.00 1.75

Nos. 3132-3136 were issued both in separate sheets and together in sheetlets of 6, with label.
No. 3137 is airmail.

Frogs and Toads — A1428

Designs: 40ch (#3138), *Rana chosenica*. 40ch (#3139), Moor frog (*Rana arvalis*). 40ch (#3140), Common toad (*Bufo bufo*). 70ch (#3141), Common pond frog (*Rana nigromaculata*). 70ch (#3142), Japanese tree toad (*Hyla japonica*). 70ch (#3143), (*Rana coreana*).

1992, Sept. 10 *Perf. 12¼*

3138-3143 A1428 Set of 6 10.00 3.00
3139a Sheet of 8 stamps, 3 #3139, 2 ea. #3138, #3140 + label 15.00 5.00
3142a Sheet of 8 stamps, 3 #3142, 2 ea. #3141, #3143 + label 15.00 5.00

Nos. 3138-3143 were issued both in separate sheets and together in sheetlets of 8.
No. 3143 is airmail.

World Environment Day — A1429

Designs: 10ch, Flower (*Rhododendron mucronulatum*). 30ch, Barn swallow (*Hirundo rustica*). 40ch, Flower (*Stewartia koreana*). 50ch, Beetle (*Dictoptera aurora*). 70ch, Tree (*Metasequoia glyptostroboides*). 90ch, Chinese salamander (*Hynobius leechi*). 1.20w, Tree (*Gingko biloba*). 1.40w, Fish (*Cottus poecilopus*).

1992, Oct. 20 ***Perf. 12***

3144-3151 A1429 Set of 8 19.00 4.75
3151a Sheet of 8 stamps, #3144-3151 20.00 5.25

Nos. 3144-3151 were issued both in separate sheets of 21 and together in sheetlets of 8.

Nos. 3150 and 3151 are airmail.

Whales and Dolphins — A1430

Designs (all 50ch): #3152, Fin whale (*Balaenoptera physalus*). #3153, Common dolphin (*Delphinus delphis*). #3154, Killer whale (*Orcinus orca*). #3155, Hump-backed whale (*Megaptera nodosa*). #3156, Bottle-nosed whale (*Berardius bairdii*). #3157, Sperm whale (*Physeter catadon*).

1992, Oct. 20

3152-3157 A1430 Set of 6 12.00 2.75
3152a Sheet of 3, #3152-3154 5.50 1.25
3155a Sheet of 3, #3155-3157 5.50 1.25

Nos. 3152-3157 were issued both separately in sheets of 25 stamps and together in sheetlets of 3.

No. 3157 is airmail.

New Year (Year of the Rooster) — A1431

Chickens in various cartoon forms: 10ch, Hen and chicks. 20ch, Young hen. 30ch, Strong cock. 40ch, Prince cock. 50ch, Princess hen. 60ch, King cock.
1.20w, Cock.

1992, Dec. 7 ***Perf. 11½***

3158-3163 A1431 Set of 6 6.50 1.75
3163a Sheetlet of 4, #3158-3160, as #3163c 4.00 1.50
3163b Sheetlet of 4, #3161-3163, as #3163c 5.00 2.00
3163c 1.20w Souvenir Sheet 5.00 1.00

Nos. 3158-3163 were issued both separately in large sheets and setenant in two sheetlets of four, one containing Nos. 3158-3160 + the 1.20w value from No. 3163a, the other containing Nos. 3161-3163 + the 1.20w design.

N. Korean Gold Medal Winners at Barcelona Olympics — A1432

Designs: 10ch, Choe Chol Su (boxing). 20ch, Pae Kil Su (gymnastics). 50ch, Ri Hak Son (Wrestling). 60ch, Kim Il (wrestling).

30ch, Archer, flame, gold medal, flags of DPRK and Spain. 40ch, Emblem, game mascot and Church of the Holy Family, Barcelona.

1992, Dec. 20 ***Perf. 12***

3164-3167 A1432 Set of 4 4.50 1.20

Sheet of 6

3168 #3164-3167, 3168a, 3168b 7.00 .60
a. A1432 30ch multicolored .35 .25
b. A1432 40ch multicolored .50 .30

Fungi — A1433

Designs: 10ch, Golden mushroom (*Flammulina velutipes*). 20ch, Shaggy caps (*Coprinus comatus*). 30ch, *Ganoderma lucidum*. 40ch, Brown mushroom (*Lentinus edodes*). 50ch, (*Volvaria bombycina*). 60ch, (*Sarcodon aspratus*).
1w, Scarlet caterpillar (*Cordyceps militaris*).

1993, Jan. 10 ***Perf. 11½***

3169-3174 A1433 Set of 6 7.50 2.50
3169a Sheet of 4, #3169, 3172, 3174, type of 3175 7.00 2.25
3170a Sheet of 4, #3170, 3171, 3173, type of 3175 7.00 2.25

Souvenir Sheet

3175 A1433 1w multicolored 4.50 .80

Nos. 3169-3174 were issued both in separate sheets and together in sheetlets of 4, with the stamp from #3175.

Korean Plants

A1434

Designs: 10ch, (*Keumkangsania asiatica*). 20ch, (*Echinosophora koreensis*). 30ch, (*Abies koreana*). 40ch, (*Benzoin angustifolium*). 50ch, (*Abeliophyllum distichum*). 60ch, (*Abelia mosanensis*).

1993, Jan. 20 ***Perf. 12¼***

3176-3181 A1434 Set of 6 7.00 2.00
3181a Sheet of 6, #3176-3181 7.00 2.25

Souvenir Sheet

A1435

1w, *Pentactina rupicola*. Illustration reduced.

Perf. 11½

3182 A1435 1w multicolored 3.50 2.00

Nos. 3176-3181 were issued both in separate sheets of 16 and together in sheetlets of 4.

8th Congress of the League of Socialist Working Youth of Korea — A1436

Designs: 10ch, Youths, banner. 20ch, Flame, emblem, motto.

1993, Jan. 25 ***Perf. 12¼***

3183-3184 A1436 Set of 2 1.50 .40

Phophyong Revolutionary Site Tower & March Corps Emblem — A1437

1993, Jan. 29 ***Perf. 12x12¼***

3185 A1437 10ch multicolored .50 .20

70th anniv. of the 250-mile Journey for Learning.

Tower of the Juche Idea, Grand Monument, Mt. Wangjae — A1438

1993, Feb. 11

3186 A1438 60ch multicolored .50 .20

60th anniv. of the Wangjaesan Meeting.

51st Birthday of Kim Jong Il

Kimjongilia (Begonia) — A1439

1993, Feb. 16 ***Perf. 12***

3187 A1439 10ch multicolored 1.00 .20

Souvenir Sheet

Kim Il Sung Writing Poem Praising Kim Jong Il — A1440

Illustration of stamp only. The sheet itself is 170mmx95mm, with marginal inscriptions that include reproductions of Kim Il Sung's poem.

Perf. 13¼

3188 A1440 1w multicolored 3.50 .75

Sea Fish — A1441

Designs: 10ch, Pilot fish (*Naucrates ductor*). 20ch, Japanese stingray (*Dasyatis akajei*). 30ch, Moonfish (*Lampris guttatus*). 40ch, Coelacanth (*Latimeria chalumnae*). 50ch, Grouper (*Epinephelus moara*).
1.20w, Mako shark (*Isurus oxyrhynchus*).

1993, Feb. 25 ***Perf. 11½***

3189-3193 A1441 Set of 5 5.00 1.25
3189a Sheetlet of 2, #3189, type of #3194 3.25 .45
3190a Sheetlet of 2, #3190, #3193 3.25 .45
3191a Sheetlet of 2, #3191, #3192 3.25 .45

Souvenir Sheet

3194 A1441 1.20w multicolored 4.50 .80

Nos. 3189-3193 were issued both in separate sheets and in sheetlets of 2.

No. 3194 commemorates Naposta '93, and the exhibition emblem appears as a marginal inscription.

Spring on the Hill, 18th century Korean Painting — A1442

Illustration reduced.

1993, Mar. 20 ***Perf. 12x11½***

3195 A1442 Sheetlet of 5 6.50 1.75
a.-e. 40ch, any single 1.00 .30

Spring Friendship Art Festival — A1443

1993, Apr. 5 ***Perf. 12x12¼***

3196 A1443 10ch multicolored .75 .20

80th Birthday of Kim Il Sung and Publication of *With the Century*

With the Century, Kim Il Sung's Memoir — A1444

1993, Apr. 15

3197 A1444 10ch multicolored .50 .20

Souvenir Sheet

Kim Il Sung Composing *With the Century* — A1445

Illustration reduced.

Perf. 11½

3198 A1445 1w multicolored 3.50 .75

Pyongyang Scenes

A1446

10ch, Kwangbok Street. 20ch, Chollima Street. 30ch, Munsu Street. 40ch, Moranbong Street. 50ch, Thongil Street.

1993, Apr. 20 *Perf. 12x11¾*

3199-3203 A1446 Set of 5 4.50 1.25

Souvenir Sheet

Changgwang Street — A1447

Illustration reduced.

Perf. 11½

3204 A1447 1w multicolored 3.50 .75

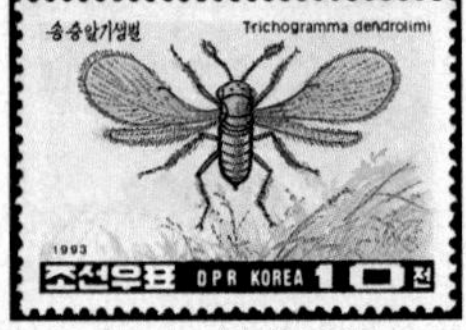

Insects — A1448

Designs: 10ch, Fly (*Trichogramma dendrolimi*). 20ch, Fly (*Brachymeria obscurata*). 30ch, Cricket (*Metrioptera brachyptera*). 50ch, Cricket (*Gryllus campestris*). 70ch, Beetle (*Geocoris pallidipennis*). 90ch, Wasp (*Cyphononyx dorsalis*).

1993, May 10 *Perf. 12x12¼*

3205-3210 A1448 Set of 6 10.00 2.25

3205a Sheetlet of 3, #3205, 3207, 3210 5.00 1.25

3206a Sheetlet of 3, #3206, 3208, 3209 5.00 1.25

Nos. 3205-3210 were issued both in separate sheets and in sheetlets of 3.

A1449

A1450

No. 3212 illustration reduced.

1993, May 19 *Perf. 11½*

3211 A1449 10ch multicolored .50 .20

Souvenir Sheet

Perf. 13¼

3212 A1450 1.20w multicolored 4.00 .80

Release of Ri In Mo, North Korean war correspondent, from South Korean prison.

World Cup Soccer Championship, U.S.A. — A1451

World Cup and soccer players: 10ch, Tackling. 20ch, Kicking. 30ch, Kicking (diff.). 50ch, Tackling (diff.). 70ch, Blocking. 90ch, Feinting.

1993, May 25 *Perf. 11½*

3213-3218 A1451 Set of 6 8.50 2.25

3213a Sheetlet of 3, #3213, 3215, 3218 4.25 1.25

3214a Sheetlet of 3, #3214, 3216, 3217 4.25 1.25

Nos. 3213-3218 were issued both in separate sheets and in sheetlets of 3.

Birds — A1452

Designs: 10ch, Gray-headed green woodpecker (*Picus canus*). 20ch, King of paradise (*Cicinnurus regius*0. 30ch, Lesser bird of paradise (*Paradisea minor*). 40ch, Paradise whydah (*Steganura paradisea*). 50ch, Magnificent bird of paradise (*Diphyllodes magnificus*). 60ch, Greater bird of paradise (*Paradisea apoda*).

1993, May 29 *Perf. 12*

3219-3224 A1452 Set of 6 7.00 1.75

3219a Sheetlet of 4, 2 ea. #3219, 3224 4.00 1.10

3220a Sheetlet of 4, 2 ea. #3220, 3223 4.00 1.10

3221a Sheetlet of 2, #3221, #3222 4.00 1.10

Nos. 3219-3224 were issued both in separate sheets and together in sheetlets of 4 and 2, as described above.

Nos. 3221, 3221a, 3222 commemorate Indopex '93 International Stamp Exhibition, Surabaya, Indonesia.

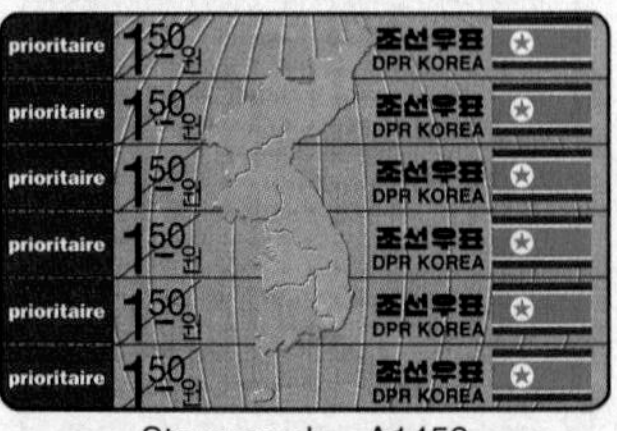

Stampcard — A1453

Map of Korean peninsula. Illustration reduced.

1993, May 29 *Rouletted*

Self-adhesive

3225 A1453 Card of 6 stamps 20.00 20.00

a.-f. 1.50w, any single 3.00 3.00

For surcharges, see No. 3441.

Korean World Champions — A1454

Designs: 10ch, Kim Myong Nam (weight-lifting, 1990). 20ch, Kim Kwang Suk (gymnastics, 1991). 30ch, Pak Yong Sun (table tennis, 1975, 1977). 50ch, Kim Yong Ok (radio direction-finding, 1990). 70ch, Han Yun Ok (taekwondo, 1987, 1988, 1990). 90ch, Kim Yong Sik (free-style wrestling, 1986, 1989).

1993, June 15 *Perf. 12x11¾*

3226-3231 A1454 Set of 6 9.00 2.25

3226a Sheetlet of 6, 2 ea. #3226, 3228, 3231 9.00 2.50

3227a Sheetlet of 6, 2 ea. #3227, 3229, 3230 9.00 2.50

Nos. 3226-3231 were issued both in separate sheets and together in sheetlets of 6, as described above.

Fruits and Vegetables — A1455

Designs: 10ch, Cabbage and chili peppers. 20ch, Squirrel and horse chestnuts. 30ch, Peach and grapes. 40ch, Birds and persimmons. 50ch, Tomatoes, eggplant and cherries. 60ch, Onion, radishes, garlic bulbs.

1993, June 25 *Perf. 11¾x12*

3232-3237 A1455 Set of 6 6.50 1.75

3232a Sheetlet of 3, #3232, 3235, 3237 2.50 .90

3232b As "a.," ovptd. "Polska '93" 5.00 1.25

3233c Sheetlet of 3, #3233, 3234, 3236 2.50 .90

Nos. 3232-3237 were issued both in separate sheets and together in sheetlets of 3, as described above.

National Emblem — A1456

1993, July 5 *Perf. 12*

3238 A1456 10ch vermilion .60 .20

40th Anniv. Korean War

A1457

All 10ch: #3239, Soldiers and civilian women. #3240, Officer and enlisted man. #3241, Anti-aircraft missiles on military trucks. #3242, Guided missiles on carriers. #3243, Self-propelled missile launchers.

1993, July 27

3239-3243 A1457 Set of 5 2.50 .75

Souvenir Sheet

A1458

1w, Kim Il Jong taking salute of paraders. Stamp only illustrated, from 190mmx93mm souvenir sheet, with margins depicting military review in Pyongyang square.

Perf. 13¼

3244 A1458 1w multicolored 4.00 .55

A1459

Designs: 10ch (#3245), Victory statue (soldier with flag). 10ch (#3246), Machine-gunners and refugees. 40ch, Soldiers and flag.

Perf. 11¾x12

3245-3247 A1459 Set of 3 2.25 .50

3247a Sheetlet of 3, #3245-3247 2.50 .60

Nos. 3245-3247 were issued both in separate sheets of 21 and in a setenant sheetlet of 3.

Sheetlets of 2

A1460

Designs: #3248a, 10ch, Kim Il Sung conducting planning meeting; b, 20ch, Kim inspecting artillery unit. #3249a, 10ch, Kim directing battle for Height 1211; b, 20ch, Kim encouraging machine gun crew. #3250a, 10ch, Kim at munitions factory; b, 20ch, Kim directing units of the Second Front. #3251a, 10ch, Kim with tank commanders; b, 20ch, Kim directing airmen. #3252a, 10ch, Kim with victorious soldiers; b, 20ch, Musicians.

Perf. 11½

3248-3252 A1460 Set of 5 5.00 1.40

Souvenir Sheets

Kim Leading Soldiers on the Front — A1461

Kim Surveying Battlefield — A1462

Kim Making 1953 Victory Speech — A1463

Illustrations reduced.

Perf. 13¼

3253 A1461 80ch multicolored 4.50 .60
3254 A1462 80ch multicolored 4.50 .60
3255 A1463 1w multicolored 6.00 .60

National Reunification Prize Winners — A1464

Designs: 10ch, Choe Yong Do (1923-69). 20ch, Kim Gu (1875-1949). 30ch, Hong Myong Hui (1888-1968). 40ch, Ryo Un Hyong (1886-1947). 50ch, Kim Jong Thae (1926-69). 60ch, Kim Chaek (1903-51).

1993, Aug. 1 ***Perf. 12***
3256-3261 A1464 Set of 6 6.50 1.75

Taipei '93 Int'l Philatelic Exhib.

A1465

Designs: 20ch, *Robina sp.* 30ch, *Hippeastrum cv.*

1993, Aug. 14
3262-3263 A1465 Set of 2 1.50 .45

Souvenir Sheet

A1466

1w, Deer. Illustration reduced.

3264 A1466 1w multicolored 3.50 1.50

350th Anniv. Birth of Sir Isaac Newton, Mathematician and Scientist — A1467

Designs: 10ch, Portrait of Newton. 20ch, Apple tree and formula for Law of Gravitation. 30ch, Reflecting telescope invented by Newton. 50ch, Formula of Binomial Theorem. 70ch, Newton's works, statue.

1993, Sept. 1 ***Perf. 12¼x12***
3265-3269 A1467 Set of 5 7.50 1.50
3265a Sheetlet of 3, #3265, 3266, 3269 3.75 3.75
3265b Sheetlet of 3, #3265, 3267, 3268 3.75 3.75

Nos. 3265-3269 were issued both in separate sheets of 21 stamps and together in sheetlets of 3, as described above.

Restoration of the Tomb of King Tongmyong, Founder of Koguryo

A1468

Designs: 10ch, King Tongmyong shooting arrow. 20ch, King Tongmyong. 30ch, Restoration monument. 40ch, Jongrung Temple of the Tomb of King Tongmyong. 50ch, Tomb.

1993, Sept. 10
3270-3274 A1468 Set of 5 4.50 1.25

Souvenir Sheet

A1469

80ch, Kim Il Sung visiting restored tomb. Illustration reduced.

Perf. 11½

3275 A1469 80ch multicolored 2.50 1.50

Bangkok '93 Int'l Philatelic Exhib. — A1470

1.20w, First stamps of North Korea and Thailand. Illustration reduced.

1993, Oct. 1
3276 A1470 1.20w multicolored 5.00 2.00

Orchids — A1471

Designs: 10ch, *Cyrtopodium andresoni.* 20ch, *Cattleya.* 30ch, *Cattleya intermedia* "Oculata." 40ch, *Potinaria* "Maysedo godonsia." 50ch, "Kimilsungia."

1993, Oct. 15 ***Perf. 12***
3277-3281 A1471 Set of 5 6.00 1.25
3281a Strip of 5, #3277-3281 6.00 6.00
3277b-3281b Set of 5 complete booklets, each containing 5 stamps 30.00

Nos. 3277-3281 were issued both in separate sheets of 25 stamps and together in sheets of 25, comprising 5 #3281a.

Nos. 3277b-3281b each contain horizontal strips of 5 of one value, taken from sheets.

Birth Centenary of Mao Zedong, Chinese Leader (1st Issue)

No. 2949 Overprinted

1993, Nov. 16
3282 A1373 80ch vermilion 2.50 1.50

Birth Centenary of Mao Zedong, Chinese Leader (2nd Issue)

A1472

Designs: 10ch, Mao in Yannan (1940). 20ch, Mao in Beijing (1960). 30ch, Mao voting (1953). 40ch, Mao with middle-school students (1959).

1993, Dec. 26 ***Perf. 11½***
3283-3286 A1472 Set of 4 3.25 .90

Souvenir Sheets

A1473

A1474

No. 3287: #3283-3286; 25ch (#3287a), Mao proclaiming People's Republic of China (1949); 25ch (#3287b), Mao and his son, Mao Anying, in Xiangshan, Beijing (1949); 1w (#3287c), Mao and Kim Il Sung (1975).

No. 3288: As No. 3287c.

3287 A1473 Sheet of 7 6.00 6.00
a. 25ch multicolored .50 .30
b. 25ch multicolored .50 .30
c. 1w multicolored 2.00 .90
3288 A1474 1w multicolored 2.00 2.00

Nos. 3283-3286 were printed both in separate sheets of 25 and together within No. 3287.

New Year, Year of the Dog — A1475

Designs: 10ch, Phungsan. 20ch, Yorkshire terriers. 30ch, Gordon setter. 40ch, Pomeranian. 50ch, Spaniel with pups.

1994, Jan. 1 ***Perf. 12***
3289-3293 A1475 Set of 5 5.00 1.00
3289a-3293a Set of 5 complete booklets, each containing 5 stamps 25.00

Nos. 3289a-3293a each contain horizontal strips of 5 of one value, taken from sheets.

Souvenir Sheet

A1476

1w, Pointer. Illustration reduced.

3294 A1476 1w multicolored 4.50 1.25
a. 1w single stamp

Sheetlets of 3

A1477

Nos. 3295-3299 each contain two examples of one design and one exmaple of #3294a.
Illustration reduced.

Perf. 12

3295-3299 A1477 Set of 5 30.00 30.00

52nd Birthday of Kim Jong Il

A1478

Designs: 10ch, Purple hyosong flower (*Prinula polyantha*). 40ch, Yellow hyosong flower (*Prinula polyantha*).

1994, Feb. 16 *Perf. 13¼*

3300-3301 A1478 Set of 2 1.50 .45
a. Pair, #3300-3301 1.75 1.75

Souvenir Sheet

A1479

1w, Kim Il Sung and Kim Jong Il, from embroidery *The Sun of Juche.* Illustration reduced.

3302 A1479 1w multicolored 3.50 1.25

Nos. 3300-3301 were issued both in separate sheets of 25 and in a miniature sheet containing 4 of each value, with central label depicting Jong Il Peak and *Kimjongilia.*

Goldfish — A1480

Designs: 10ch, Red and black dragon-eye. 30ch, Red and white bubble-eye. 50ch, Red and white long-finned wenyu. 70ch, Red and white fringetail.
Illustration reduced.

1994, Feb. 18 *Perf. 12*

3303-3306 A1480 Sheetlet of 4 6.50 1.25

Publication of the *Program of Modeling the Whole Society on the Juche Idea,* 20th Anniv.

A1481

1994, Feb. 19

3307 A1481 20ch multicolored .50 .20

Souvenir Sheet

A1482

Kim Il Sung proclaiming the *Program,* 1974.
Illustration reduced.

Perf. 11½

3308 A1482 1.20w multicolored 4.25 1.25

Publication of Kim Il Sung's *Theses on the Socialist Rural Question in Our Country,* 30th Anniv.

A1483

Designs: 10ch (#3309), Woman propagandist, sound truck. 10ch (#3310), Electrical generator, pylon. 10ch (#3311), Farm, farm equipment, piles of grain. 40ch (#3312), Lab technician with microscope. 40ch (#3313), Dancers celebrating bounty harvest.

1994, Feb. 25 *Perf. 12*

3309-3313 A1483 Set of 5 3.50 .90

Souvenir Sheets

Kim Il Sung in Field — A1484

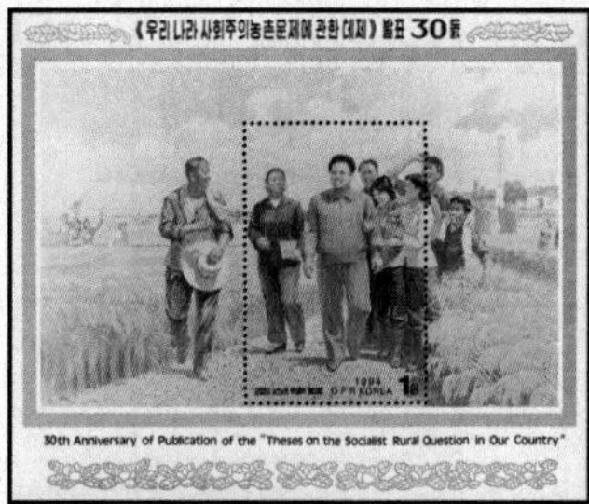
Kim Jong Il Walking Through Field with Peasants — A1485

Illustration reduced.

Perf. 11½

3314 A1484 1w multicolored 2.50 1.25
3315 A1485 1w multicolored 2.50 1.25

Ships — A1486

Designs: 20ch, Passenger ship, *Mangyongbong-92.* 30ch, Cargo ship, *Osandok.* 40ch, Processing stern trawler, *Ryongaksan.* 50ch, Stern trawler.
80ch, Passenger ship, *Maekjon No. 1.*

1994, Mar. 25 *Perf. 12*

3316-3319 A1486 Set of 4 4.50 1.25
3320 Sheetlet of 6, #3316-3319 + 2 #3320a 10.00 2.50
a. A1486 80ch multicolored 2.50 .75

DPRK Flag — A1487

1994, Mar. 30 *Perf. 13¼*

3321 A1487 10ch car & dp blue .50 .20

82nd Birthday of Kim Il Sung

A1488

Designs: 10ch, Magnolia and Kim's home. 40ch, *Kimilsungia* and Kim's home.

1994, Apr. 15 *Perf. 12*

3322-3323 A1488 Set of 2 1.50 .50
a. 10ch Sheetlet of 8 7.00 2.25
b. 40ch Sheetlet of 8 7.00 2.25

Souvenir Sheet

A1489

Five 40ch stamps, together forming design of Lake Chon (crater lake of Mt. Paektu), with *Song of General Kim Il Sung* music within design, lyrics in sheet margin.

3324 A1489 2w sheet of 5 7.00 7.00
a.-e. 40ch, any single 1.25 1.25

Nos. 3322-3323 were issued both in sheets of 25 and in sheetlets of 8.

Alpine Plants of the Mt. Paektu Area

A1490

Designs: 10ch, *Chrysoplenium sphaerospermum.* 20ch, *Campanula cephalotes.* 40ch, *Trollius macropetafus.* 50ch, *Sedum kamtschaticum.*
1w, *Dianthus repens.*

1994, Apr. 25 *Perf. 13¼*

3325-3329 A1490 Set of 5 4.50 1.25
3325a Sheetlet of 3, #3325, 3327, type of #3330 4.25 1.75
3326a Sheetlet of 3, #3326, 3328, 3329 4.25 1.75

Souvenir Sheet

3330 A1490 1w multicolored 3.50 1.50

Nos. 3325-3329 were issued both in sheets of 25 and in sheetlets of 3, as described above.

Int'l Olympic Committee Centenary

A1491

Designs: 10ch, Olympic rings, DPRK flag. 20ch, Pierre de Coubertin, founder. 30ch, Olympic flag, flame. 50ch, IOC Centenary Congress emblem.

1994, May 2 *Perf. 12*

3331-3334 A1491 Set of 4 4.00 1.00

Nos. 3331-3334 were issued in separate sheets of 8.

Souvenir Sheets

A1492

Designs: No. 3335, Runner with Olympic Torch. No. 3336, Juan Antonio Samaranch, IOC President and new IOC headquarters.
Illustration reduced.

Perf. 13¼

3335-3336 A1492 Set of 2 6.50 2.00

A1493

Designs: 10ch, Train, pedestrians crossing on overpass ("Prevention of traffic accident"). 20ch, Medical personnel in Red Cross boat ("Relief on the Sea"). 30ch, Man and girl planting tree ("Protection of the environment"). 40ch, Dam, sailboat on lake ("Protection of drought damage").

1994, May 5
3337-3340 A1493 Strip of 4 3.50 2.50

75th anniv. of founding of the International Federation of Red Cross and Red Crescent societies.
Nos. 3337-3340 were printed in sheetlets of 8, containing two strips of four.

Illustration reduced.

1994, May 29 Self-adhesive ***Imperf***
3341 A1452 1.60w on 1.50w Card of 6 28.00 28.00
a.-f. 1.60w on 1.50w, any single 7.00 7.00

A1494

Designs: 10ch, Northern fur seal (*Callorhinus ursinus*). 40ch, Southern elephant seal (*Mirounga leonina*). 60ch, Southern sea lion (*Otaria byronia*).
No. 3345: 20ch, California sea lion (*Zalophus californianus*). 30ch, Ringed seal (*Phoca hispida*). 50ch, Walrus (*Odobenus rosmarus*).

1994, June 10 ***Perf. 11½***
3342-3344 A1494 Set of 3 4.00 .90
3345 A1494 Sheetlet of 3 4.50 1.00
a. A1493 20ch multicolored .75 .20
b. A1493 30ch multicolored 1.25 .25
c. A1493 50ch multicolored 2.25 .50

Souvenir Sheet

A1495

1w, Harp seal (*Pagophilus groenlandicus*). Illustration reduced.

3346 A1495 1w multicolored 3.50 1.00

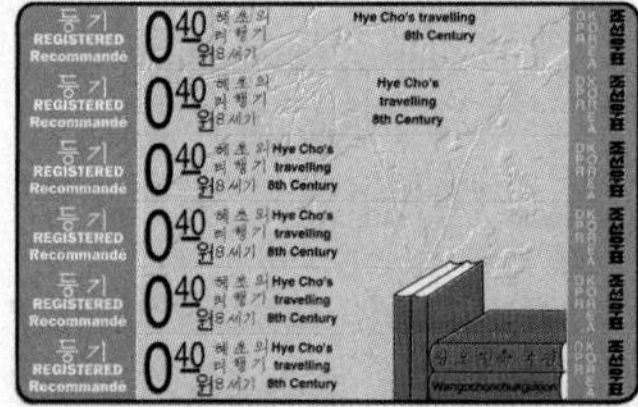
Stampcard — A1496

Map of Asia, books. Illustration reduced.

1994, June 17 ***Rouletted***
Self-adhesive
3347 A1496 Card of 6 stamps 10.00 10.00
a.-f. 40ch, any single 1.65 1.65

Hye Cho's 8th century travels in Central Asia and India.

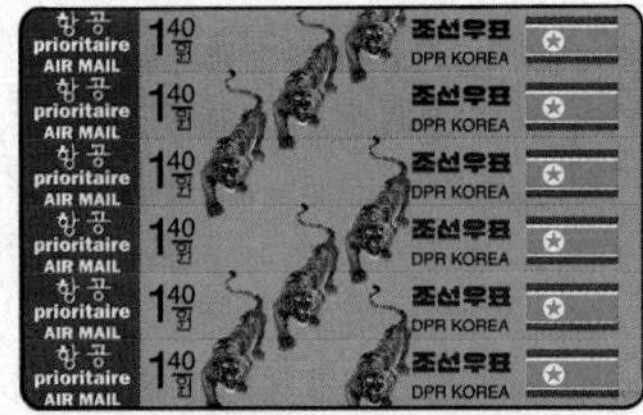
Stampcard — A1497

Korean Tigers. Illustration reduced.

1994, June 18 ***Rouletted***
Self-adhesive
3348 A1497 Card of 6 stamps 30.00 30.00
a.-f. 1.40w, any single 5.00 5.00

Kim Il Sung's Leadership of the Korean Workers' Party, 30th Anniv.

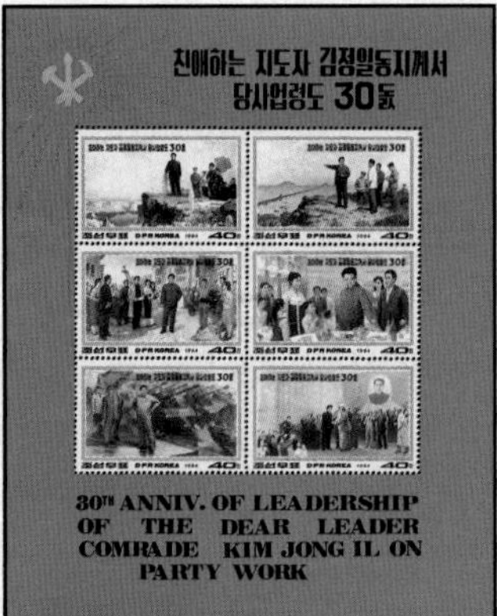

A1498

Designs (all 40ch): #3349, Kim and supporters on cliff ledge, overlooking lake. #3350, Kim on mountain top, pointing across lake to Mt. Paektu. #3351, Kim on film set. #3352, Kim visiting restaurant. #3353, Kim reviewing tank corps. #3354, Kim at conference, shaking hands onstage as audience applauds.
Illustration reduced.

1994, June 19 ***Perf. 12***
3349-3354 A1498 Sheetlet of 6 8.00 2.50
3350a Booklet pane of 6, 3 ea. #3349-3350 8.00 —
Complete booklet, #3350a 8.50
3353a Booklet pane of 6, 3 ea. #3351, 3353 8.00 —
Complete booklet, #3353a 8.50
3354a Booklet pane of 6, 3 ea. #3352, 3354 8.00 —
Complete booklet, #3354a 8.50

Souvenir Sheet

A1499

Illustration reduced.

Perf. 11½
3355 A1499 1w multicolored 3.00 1.00

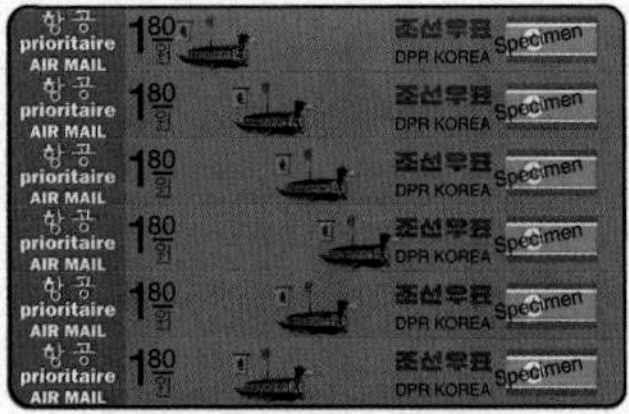
Stampcard — A1500

Turtle ship. Illustration reduced.

1994, June 20 ***Rouletted***
Self-adhesive
3356 A1500 Card of 6 stamps 33.00 33.00
a.-f. 1.80w, any single 5.50 5.50

Mollusks

A1501

Designs: 30ch, Banded bonnet (*Phalium strigatum*). 40ch, Equilateral venus (*Gomphina veneriformis*).

1994, June 25 ***Perf. 12***
3357-3358 A1501 Set of 2 2.50 .60

Sheetlets of 3

A1502

No. 3359: a, 10ch, Cockle (*Cardium muticum*). b, 1.20w, Bladder moon (*Neverita didyma*). c, as No. 3358.
No. 3360: a, 20ch, Whelk (*Buccinum bayani*). b, 30ch, as No. 3357. The 1.20w value, identical to No. 3359b, is included in this sheet.
Illustration reduced.

Perf. 13¼
3359-3360 A1502 Set of 2 14.00 10.00

Souvenir Sheet

A1503

Design: Same as No. 3359b. Illustration reduced.

3361 A1503 1.20w multicolored 5.00 1.40

Circus Acrobats — A1504

Designs: a, 10ch, Flying trapeze. b, 20ch, Rope dance. c, 30ch, Seesaw. d, 40ch, Unicycle show.
Illustration reduced.

1994, July 7 ***Perf. 11½***
3362 A1504 Sheetlet of 4, #a.-d. 4.00 1.25

Centenary of Birth of Kim Hyong Jik (1894-1926), Father of Kim Il Sung

A1505

1994, July 10 ***Perf. 13¼***
3363 A1505 10ch multicolored .50 .20

A1506

Illustrated reduced.

Perf. 11¾x11½
3364 A1506 1w multicolored 3.50 1.25

Jon Pong Pun & Battle Scene — A1507

1994, July 15 *Perf. 12*

3365 A1507 10ch multicolored .60 .20

Centenary of Kabo Peasant War.

Inoue Shuhachi — A1508

Illustration reduced.

1994, July 30 *Perf. 13¼*

3366 A1508 1.20w multicolored 4.00 1.25

Award of the First International Kim Il Sung Prize to Inoue Shuhachi, Director General of the International Institute of the Juche Idea (Japan).

Workers Marching — A1509

1994, Aug. 1 *Perf. 11½*

3367 A1509 10ch multicolored .50 .20

Workers' Party Economic Strategy.

Fossils — A1510

Designs: 40ch (#3368), Onsong fish. 40ch (#3369), Metasequoia. 40ch (#3370), Mammoth teeth. 80ch, Archaeopteryx.

1994, Aug. 10 *Perf. 12*

3368-3371 A1510 Set of 4 13.00 1.75
Complete booklet, 7 #3368 16.00
Complete booklet, 7 #3369 16.00
Complete booklet, 7 #3370 16.00
Complete booklet, 7 #3371 32.00

Souvenir Sheets

No. 3372 contains 2 #3368 and 2 #3371. No. 3373 contains 2 #3369 and 2 #3371. No. 3374 contains 2 #3370 and 2 #3371.

3372-3374 A1510 Set of 3 sheets 26.00 20.00

Medicinal Plants — A1511

Designs: 20ch, *Acorus calamus.* 30ch, *Arctium lappa.*

1994, Aug. 25

3375-3376 A1511 Set of 2 1.75 .50
Complete booklet, 10 #3375 7.00
Complete booklet, 10 #3376 10.50

Souvenir Sheets

No. 3377 (133x86mm): a, 80ch, *Lilium lancifolium.* b, 80ch, *Codonopsis lanceolata.*

No. 3378 (56x83mm): 1w, Ginseng (*Panax schinseng*), vert.

Perf. 13¼

3377-3378 A1511 Set of 2 sheets 8.00 2.00

Calisthenics — A1512

Gymnastic routines: a, 10ch, Ribbon twirling. b, 20ch, Ball. c, 30ch, Hoop. d, 40ch, Ribbon twirling (diff.). e, 50ch, Clubs.

1994, Sept. 7 *Perf. 12*

3379 A1512 Strip of 5 + label 5.50 1.50

No. 3379 was printed in sheets of 18, containing three #3379 in horizontal rows, with a different label in each row.

Zhou Enlai (1898-1976) Birth Centenary

A1513

Portraits of Zhou Enlai: 10ch, As student revolutionary (1919). 20ch, Arrival in Northern Shansi after Long March (1936). 30ch, At Conference of Asian and African Countries, Bandung, Indonesia (1955). 40ch, Speaking with children.

1994, Oct. 1 *Perf. 11½*

3380-3383 A1513 Set of 4, with labels 3.25 1.00

Souvenir Sheets

A1514

A1515

No. 3384: 80ch, Zhou Enlai and Kim Il Sung (1970).

No. 3385: 10ch, as #3380. a, 20ch, Zhou leading Nanchang Uprising (1927). 40ch, as #3383. b, 80ch, as #3384.

No. 3386: 20ch, as #3381. a, 20ch, Zhou and Mao Tzedong at airport, horiz. 30ch, as #3383. 80ch, as #3385b.

Illustrations reduced.

Perf. 13¼

3384 A1514 80ch multicolored 2.75 1.00

Perf 11½ (Vert. stamps), 11¾x12¼ (Horiz. stamps)

3385-3386 A1515 Set of 2 sheets 9.50 4.00

Nos. 3380-3383 were issued in sheets of 30 (6x5), with a label beneath each stamp.

World Environment Day — A1516

Each sheetlet contains two 50ch stamps with designs reflecting environmental issues. Themes: No. 3387, Prevention of air pollution. No. 3388, Preventation of water pollution. No. 3389, Protection of animal resources. No. 3390, Protection of forest resources.

1994, Oct. 5 *Perf. 12*

3387-3390 A1516 Set of 4 sheets 12.50 12.50

Kim Il Sung Memorial, 1st Issue

A1517

A1518

Photos of Kim Il Sung (all 40ch).

No. 3391: a, As young man (1927). b, With Kim Jong Suk, his first wife and mother of Kim Jong Il. c, As captain in Soviet army (1944).

No. 3392: Speaking at lectern upon return to Pyongyang (1945). b, Sitting at desk in office of People's Committee of North Korea. c, Speaking at microphone.

Illustrations reduced.

1994, Oct. 8

3391 A1517 Sheet of 3, #a.-c. 4.00 2.00
3392 A1518 Sheet of 3, #a.-c. 4.00 2.00

Souvenir Sheet

Kim Il Sung — A1519

Illustration reduced.

Perf. 12¼x11¾

3393 A1519 1w multicolored 3.75 1.25

Issued in honor of Kim Il Sung (1912-94), "Great Leader" of North Korea 1948-94.

Compare with Nos. 3401-3403.

"World Cup '94," 15th World Soccer Championship

Soccer Players Dribbling — A1520

Designs: 10ch, Player No. 4. 20ch, Player No. 5. 30ch, Player No. 6. 40ch, Player No. 7. 1w, Player No. 8. 1.50w, Player No. 9.

1994, Oct. 13 *Perf. 13½*

3394-3399 A1520 Set of 6 12.00 6.00
3399a Souvenir Sheet of 6, #3394-3399 18.00 10.00

Souvenir Sheet

A1521

Illustration reduced.

3400 A1521 2.50w multicolored 7.50 4.00

Nos. 3394-3400 were also issued imperf. Value: set, $24; souvenir sheet, $15.

Nos. 3394-3399 exist in sheetlets on one, perf and imperf. Value: perf, $24; imperf, $47.50.

Kim Il Sung Memorial, 2nd Issue

A1522

Photos of Kim Il Sung (all 40ch).

No. 3401: a, Making radio broadcast (1950). b, With soldiers (1951). c, Clapping hands, crowd of soldiers in background (1953).

No. 3402: a, Talking with workers at Chongjin Steel Plant (1959). b, Standing in field, Onchon Plain. c, Talking on telephone.

1994, Oct. 15 ***Perf. 12***

3401-3402 A1522 Set of 2 sheets 8.00 4.00

A1523

1w, Kim Il Sung and Kim Jong Il. Illustration reduced.

Perf. 12¼x11¾

3403 A1523 1w multicolored 3.50 1.50

Issued in honor of Kim Il Sung (1912-94), "Great Leader" of North Korea 1948-94. Compare with Nos. 3391-3393.

North Korean-Chinese Friendship

A1524

1994, Oct. 25 ***Perf. 11½***

3404 A1524 40ch multicolored 1.50 .50

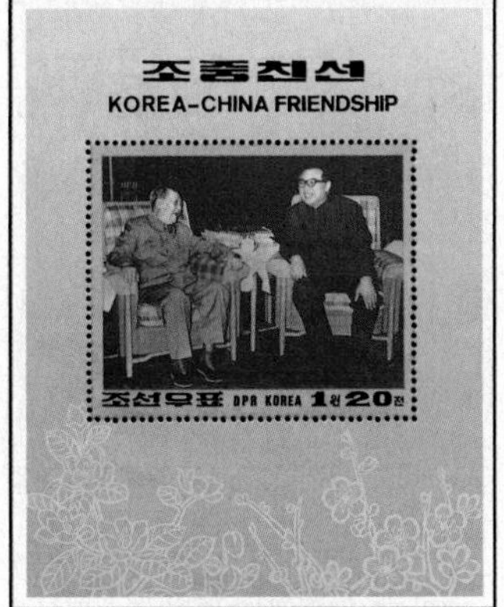

A1525

1w, Kim Il Sung with Mao Zedong. Illustration reduced.

Perf. 13¼

3405 A1525 1.20w multicolored 4.25 2.00

Composers — A1526

All 50ch: #3406, Ri Myon Sang (1908-89), score from *It Snows.* #3407, Pak Han Gyu (1919-92), score from *Nobody Knows.* #3408, Ludwig van Beethoven (1770-1827), score of *Piano Sonata No. 14.* #3409, Wolfgang Mozart (1756-91), score of *Symphony No. 39.*

1994, Nov. 25 ***Perf. 11½***

3406-3409 A1526 Set of 4 6.50 2.25

National Emblem — A1527

1994, Dec. 10 ***Perf. 12***

3410 A1527 1w dp bl green 4.00 1.00

3411 A1527 3w deep brown 8.00 2.50

Gold Medal Winners, Winter Olympic Games, Lillehammer

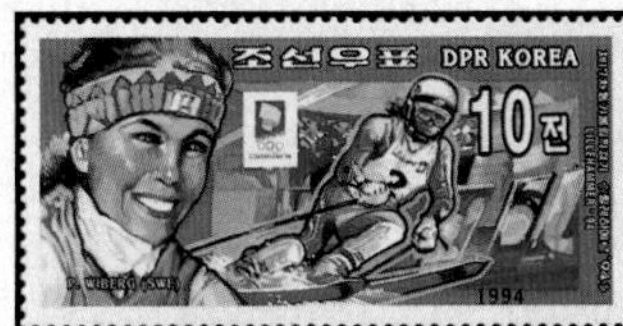

A1528

Designs: 10ch, Pernilla Wiberg (Sweden), Alpine combined skiing. 20ch, Deborah Compagnoni (Italy), Slalom. 30ch, Oksana Baiul (Ukraine), Figure skating. 40ch, Dan Jansen (USA), Speed skating. 1w (#3416), Yubow Jegorowa (Russia), Cross-country skiing. 1w (#3417), Bonnie Blair (USA), Speed skating.

1994, Dec. 20 ***Perf. 13¼***

3412-3417 A1528 Set of 6 11.00 3.00

3417a Sheetlet of 6, #3412-3417 12.00 5.00

Sheetlets of 1

A1529

All 1w: #3418, Bjorn Däehlie and Norwegian skiing team, Alpine combined skiing. #3419, Jekaterina Gordejewa and Serge Grinkow (Russia), Pairs figure skating. #3420, Vreni Schneider (Switzerland), Alpine combined skiing. #3421, Georg Hackl (Germany), Luge. #3422, Jens Weissflog (Germany), Ski jumping. #3423, Masashi Abe, Takanori Kono, Kenji Ogiwara (Japan), Cross-country skiing. Illustration reduced.

3418-3423 A1529 Set of 6 sheets 18.00 6.00

Souvenir Sheet

A1530

2.50w, Tommy Moe (USA), Downhill skiing. Illustration reduced.

3424 A1530 2.50w multicolored 8.00 1.50

Nos. 3412-3417 were issued both in separate sheets of 21 and together in se-tenant sheetlets of 6.

New Year — Year of the Pig — A1531

Designs: 20ch, Pigs relaxing. 40ch, Pigs going to work.

Each 1w: No. 3427, Pigs carrying pumpkin. No. 3428, Piglets bowing to adult pig.

1995, Jan. 1 ***Perf. 11½***

3425-3426 A1531 Set of 2 1.10 .65

Souvenir Sheets

3427-3428 A1531 Set of 2 6.00 5.00

See No. 3478.

World Tourism Org., 20th Anniv. — A1532

Designs, each 30ch: a, Tower of the Juche Idea, Pyongyang. b, Pison Falls on Mt. Myohyang. c, Myogilsang (relief carving of Buddha), Mt. Kumgang.

Illustration reduced.

1995, Jan. 2 ***Perf. 12¼***

3429 A1532 Sheet of 3, #a.-c. 3.50 .90

Mangyondae, Badasgou, Emblem — A1533

1995, Jan. 22 ***Perf. 11½***

3430 A1533 40ch multicolored 1.50 .90

70th anniversary of 250-Mile Journey for the Restoration of the Fatherland.

53rd Birthday of Kim Jong Il

A1534

A1535

A1536

A1537

Designs: 10ch, Jong Il Peak (Mt. Paekdu) and 50th Birthday Ode Monument.

No. 3432 (horiz.): a, 20ch Kim Il Sung and Kim Jong Il; b, 80ch Kim Jong Il inspecting the West Sea Barrage. No. 3433 (vert.): a, 40ch Kim Jong Il in business suit; b, Kim Jong Il in uniform in Taesongsan Martyrs' Cemetary. No. 3434: 1w, Kim Jong Il inspecting the Ryongsong Machine Complex. Illustrations reduced.

1995, Feb. 16 ***Perf. 12¼***

3431 A1534 10ch multicolored .20 .20
3432 A1535 Sheet of 2, #a.-b. 2.00 1.50
3433 A1536 Sheet of 2, #a.-b. 1.75 1.25
3434 A1537 1w Sheet of 1 2.00 2.00

Mausoleum of King Tangun —A1537a

King Tangun and Mausoleum —A1537b

Designs: 10ch, Monument. 30ch, Straight bronze dagger tower. 50ch, Monument inscribed with King Tangun's exploits. 70ch, Gate of mausoleum.

50ch, King Tangun and Mausoleum. Illustration reduced.

1995, Feb. 25 ***Perf. 12¼***

3434A-3434D A1537a Set of 4 3.00 3.00

Souvenir Sheet

Perf. 11½

3434E A1537b 1.40w multi 3.00 3.00

Lighthouses — A1538

Designs: 20ch, Tamaedo Lighthouse. 1.20w, Phido Lighthouse, West Sea Barrage.

1995, Mar. 10 ***Perf. 13½***

3435-3436 A1538 Set of 2 5.00 1.75

Mushrooms — A1539

Designs: 20ch, *Russula virescens.* 30ch, *Russula atropurpurea.*

1w, Caesar's Mushroom (*Amanita caesarea.*

1995, Mar. 25

3437-3438 A1539 Set of 2 2.00 .60
3437a Booklet pane of 10 #3437 3.50 —
Complete booklet, #3437a 4.00
3438a Booklet pane of 10 #3438 17.00 —
Complete booklet, #3438a 17.50

Souvenir Sheet

3439 A1539 1w multicolored 4.50 2.50

Tree Planting Day — A1540

1995, Apr. 6 ***Perf. 11½***

3440 A1540 10ch multicolored .60 .20
a. Sheet of 6 3.50 3.50

No. 3440 was issued both in sheets of 36 and in sheetlets of 6.

Finlandia '95
No. 3225 Surcharged with New Values

1995, Apr. 8 ***Rouletted***

3441 Card of 6 stamps 8.00 8.00
a.-f. 30ch on 1.50w, any single 1.30 1.30

Kim Il Sung, 82nd Birthday

A1541

A1542

A1543

Designs: 10ch, Kim's birthplace, Mangyongdae. 40ch, Tower of the Juche Idea, and *Kimilsungia.*

1w, Kim and children. Illustration reduced.

1995, Apr. 15 ***Perf. 11½***

3442 A1541 10ch multicolored .25 .20
a. Sheet of 6 1.50 1.50
3443 A1542 40ch multicolored 1.25 1.00
a. Sheet of 6 7.50 7.50

Souvenir Sheet

Perf. 13½

3444 A1543 1w multicolored 3.50 3.50

Nos. 3442-3443 were issued both in sheets of 36 and in sheetlets of 6.

Kim Il Sung's Visit to China, 20th Anniv.

A1544

A1545

Designs: 10ch, Deng Xiaoping waving. 20ch, Deng sitting in armchair, vert.

50ch, Kim and Deng sitting in armchairs. Illustration reduced.

1995, Apr. 17 ***Perf. 13½***

3445-3446 A1544 Set of 2 1.25 1.25

Souvenir Sheet

Perf. 11½

3447 A1545 50ch multicolored 2.00 2.00

Asian-African Conf., Bandung, 40th Anniv.

A1546

A1547

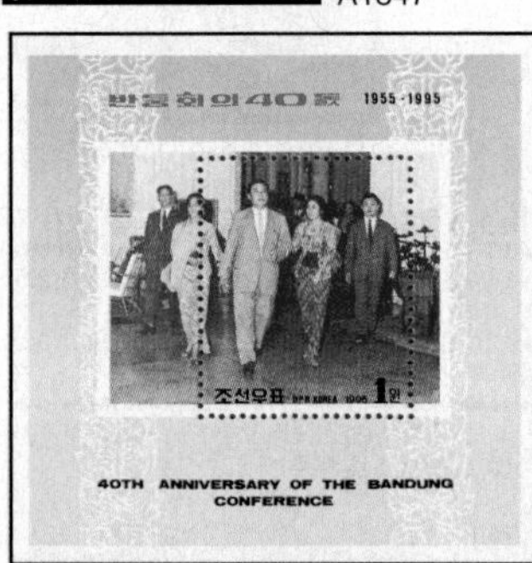

A1548

Designs: 10ch, Site of Bendung Conference. 50ch, Kim Il Sung receiving honorary doctorate from Indonesia University.

1w, Kim Il Sung and Kim Jong Il at Conference 40th Anniversary ceremony. Illustration reduced.

1995, Apr. 18 ***Perf. 11½***

3448 A1546 10ch multicolored .25 .20
3449 A1547 50ch multicolored 1.75 .70

Souvenir Sheet

3450 A1548 1w multicolored 3.50 3.50

Int'l Sports and Cultural Festival for Peace, Pyongyang

A1549

A1550

Designs: 20ch, Emblem. 40ch (#3452), Dancer. 40ch (#3453), Inoki Kanji, leader of Sports Peace Party of Japan.

1w, Nikidozan, wrestling champion. Illustration reduced.

1995, Apr. 28

3451-3453 A1549 Set of 3 3.00 2.00
3451a Sheetlet of 3, 1 #3451 + 2 #3452 3.00 2.00
3453a Sheetlet of 3, 2 #3453 + 1 as #3454 7.00 4.00

Souvenir Sheet

3454 A1550 1w multicolored 3.50 3.50

Nos. 3451-3453 were issued in separate sheets of 36 stamps and in sheetlets of 3 (#3451a and 3453a).

Finlandia '95

Amethyst — A1551

1995, May 2

3455 A1551 20ch multicolored 1.00 .40
a. Sheet of 6 7.50 7.50
b. Booklet pane of 10 10.00 —
Complete booklet, #3455b 11.00

No. 3455 was issued in sheets of 36, miniature sheets of 6, and booklet panes of 10. No. 3455a marginal selvage contains a mountain valley scene and is inscribed "Finlandia 95." No. 3455b has selvage around the block of 10 stamps.

White Animals — A1552

Each 40ch: No. 3456, Tree sparrow (*Passer montanus*). No. 3457, Sea slug (*Stichopus japonicus*).

1995, May 12 ***Perf. 13½***

3456-3457 A1552 Set of 2 2.50 1.50
3457a Sheetlet of 6, 3 #3456 + 3 #3457 9.00

Nos. 3456-3457 were issued both in separate sheets and together in sheetlets of 6.

Fossils — A1553

Designs: a, 50ch, Ostrea. b, 1w, Cladophiebis (fern).

1995, May 15 *Perf. 12*

3458 A1553 Pair, #a.-b. 4.00 1.75

No. 3458 was issued both in sheetlets of 4 stamps, containing two pairs, and in booklets of 7 stamps, containing 4 #3458a and 3 #3458b.

Traditional Games — A1554

Designs: 30ch, Chess. 60ch, Taekwondo. 70ch, Yut.

1995, May 20 *Perf. 11½*

3459-3461 A1554 Set of 3 5.25 2.00
3459a Sheetlet of 2 #3459 + label 1.75 1.75
3460a Sheetlet of 2 #3460 + label 4.00 4.00
3461a Sheetlet of 2 #3461 + label 6.00 6.00
3461b Booklet pane of 6, 2 ea. #3459-3461 10.50 —
Complete booklet, #3461b 11.00

Nos. 3459-3461 were issued in four formats: separately in large sheets; in sheetlets of two stamps of the same denomination, plus label; in booklets of 10 stamps, containing 6 #3459, 2 #3460 and 2 #3461; and in booklet panes of 6, containing 2 se-tenant horizontal strips of Nos. 3459-3461, within inscribed selvage.

General Assoc. of Koreans in Japan, 40th Anniv. — A1555

1995, May 25

3462 A1555 1w multicolored 3.50 .90

Atlanta '96 — A1556

Designs, each 50ch: No. 3463, Weight lifter. No. 3464, Boxing.
1w, Marksman shooting clay pigeon.

1995, June 2

3463-3464 A1556 Set of 2 3.25 1.25
3464a Sheetlet of 2 #3463 + 2 #3464 7.50 7.50

Souvenir Sheet

3465 A1556 1w multicolored 5.00 5.00

Nos. 3464-3465 were issued both in separate large sheets and in se-tenant sheetlets of 4 stamps, containing two of each value.

Fungi — A1557

Designs: 40ch, *Russula citrina.* 60ch, *Craterellus cornucopioides.* 80ch, *Coprinus comatus.*

1995, July 1 *Perf. 13¼*

3466-3468 A1557 Set of 3 6.50 2.00
3466a Booklet pane of 10 #3466 14.00 —
Complete booklet, #3466a 14.50
3467a Booklet pane of 10 #3467 21.00 —
Complete booklet, #3467a 22.00
3468a Booklet pane of 10 #3468 29.00 —
Complete booklet, #3468a 30.00

First Anniv. Death of Kim Il Sung

A1558

A1559

A1560

A1561

No. 3469, 1w, Kim addressing conference for development of agriculture in African countries, 1981.

No. 3470: a, 10ch, Kim greeting Robert Mugabe, President of Zimbabwe. b, 70ch, Kim with King Norodom Sihanouk of Cambodia.

No. 3471: a, 20ch, Kim receiving honorary doctorate, Algeria University, 1975. b, 50ch, Kim with Fidel Castro, 1986.

No. 3472: a, 30ch, Kim talking with Ho Chi Minh, 1958. b, 40ch, Kim greeting Che Guevara, 1960.

Illustrations reduced.

1995, July 8

3469 A1558 1w multicolored 2.75 2.75
3470 A1559 Sheetlet of 2, #a.-b. 2.25 2.25
3471 A1560 Sheetlet of 2, #a.-b. 2.50 2.50
3472 A1561 Sheetlet of 2, #a.-b. 2.00 2.00

Liberation, 50th Anniv. — A1562

Designs: 10ch, Korean army officer. 30ch, Map of Korea, family. 60ch, Hero of the DPRK medal.

No. 3476, Sheet of 4, 2x20ch revolutionary soldier and 2 #3414.

No. 3477, Sheet of 4, 2x40ch demonstrators and 2 #3474.

1995, Aug. 15 *Perf. 11½*

3473-3475 A1562 Set of 3 2.75 1.25
3475a Booklet pane of 5, #3473-3475, 3476a, 3477a 4.50 —
Complete booklet, #3475a 5.00

Souvenir Sheets

3476 Sheetlet of 4 2.50 2.50
a. A1562 20 ch multicolored .50 .20
3477 Sheetlet of 4 4.50 4.50
a. A1562 40 ch multicolored 1.00 .45

No. 3475a contains the five stamps, printed in a se-tenant horizontal strip of four, with inscribed marginal selvage.

Singapore '95 Int'l Stamp Exhib. — A1563

Illustration reduced.

1995, Sept. 1

3478 A1563 Sheet of 4 3.50 3.50

Single stamps from No. 3478 are identical to Nos. 3425-3426.

1st Military World Games — A1564

1995, Sept. 4

3479 A1564 40ch multicolored 1.00 .45

No. 3479 was issued in sheetlets of 4, containing 3 #3479 and one label depicting the Games emblem.

Korea-China Friendship

A1565

A1566

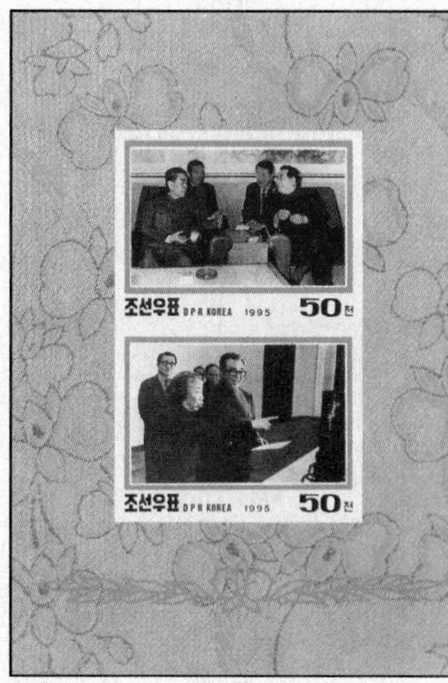

A1567

Designs: No. 3480, 80ch, Kim Il Sung and Mao Zedong. No. 3481, 80ch, Kim and Zhou Enlai.

No. 3482: a, 50ch, Kim and Zhou Enlai. b, 50ch, Kim receiving gift from Deng Ying-Chao, Premier of the State Council of the People's Republic of China.

Illustrations reduced.

1995, Oct. 1 *Perf. 12¼*

3480 A1565 80ch multicolored 1.50 1.50
3481 A1566 80ch multicolored 1.50 1.50
3482 A1567 Sheetlet of 2, #a.-b. 2.25 2.25

Korean Workers' Party, 50th Anniv.

Party Emblem & Banner — A1568

Designs: Designs: 10ch, Korean Workers' Party Emblem and Banner. 20ch, Statue of three workers holding party symbols. 40ch, Monument to founding of Party.

1995, Oct. 10 ***Perf. 11½***
3483-3485 A1568 Set of 3 1.60 .75

Souvenir Sheet

Kim Il Sung — A1569

Illustration reduced.

Perf. 13½
3486 A1569 1w multicolored 2.75 2.75

Kim Il Sung's Return to Korea, 50th Anniv. — A1570

Arch of Triumph, Pyongyang.

1995, Oct. 14 ***Perf. 11½***
3487 A1570 10ch multicolored .60 .20

Great Tunny — A1571

All stamps type A1571, printed in chocolate and black.

1995 ***Perf. 13¼***

Fish

3488 40ch Great tunny 1.25 .35
3489 50ch Pennant coralfish 1.50 .40
3490 50ch Needlefish 1.50 .40
3491 60ch Bullrout 1.75 .45
3492 5w Imperial butterfly fish 15.00 3.50
a. Horiz. strip of 5, #3488-3492 22.50 5.00

Machines

3493 10ch 40-ton truck *Kumsusan* .35 .20
3494 20ch Large bulldozer .75 .20
3495 30ch Hydraulic excavator 1.00 .25
3496 40ch Wheel loader, vert. 1.60 .30
3497 10w Tractor *Chollima-80*, vert. 27.50 7.50
a. Horiz. strip of 5, #3493-3497 32.50 10.00

Animals

3498 30ch Giraffe, vert. .85 .20
3499 40ch Ostrich, vert. 1.10 .35
3500 60ch Bluebuck, vert. 1.60 .50
3501 70ch Bactrian camel 2.00 .55
3502 3w Indian rhinoceros 8.00 2.25
a. Horiz. strip of 5, #3498-3502 16.00 4.00

Sculptures of Children

3503 30ch Boy and pigeon, vert. .85 .20
3504 40ch Boy and goose, vert. 1.10 .35
3505 60ch Girl and geese vert. 1.60 .50
3506 70ch Boy and girl comparing heights, vert. 2.00 .50
3507 2w Boy and girl with soccer ball, vert. 5.75 1.60
a. Vert. strip of 5, #3503-3507 13.00 4.00

Buildings

3508 60ch Pyongyang Circus 1.75 .50
3509 70ch Country apartment bldg. 2.00 .55
3510 80ch Pyongyang Hotel 2.25 .65
3511 90ch Urban apt. towers 2.50 .75
3512 1w Sosan Hotel 2.75 .85
a. Horiz. strip of 5, #3508-3512 13.00 4.00

Issued: Nos. 3488-3492, 10/20; Nos. 3493-3497, 11/2; Nos. 3498-3502, 11/20; Nos. 3503-3507, 12/5; Nos. 3508-3512, 12/15.

Nos. 3488-3492, 3493-3497, 3498-3502, 3503-3507, and 3508-3512 were printed in vertical (#3503-3507) or horizontal se-tenant strips within their sheets.

No. 3512B

No. 3512D

Illustrations reduced.

Self-Adhesive

1995, Oct. 20 ***RoulettedxImperf***
3512B black, *gold*, card of 8 6.00 6.00
a. 20ch, single stamp .75 .75
3512D card of 2 50.00 50.00
e. 20ch, red on gold — —
f. 17.80w on 20ch, red on gold — —

50th anniversary of the first North Korean stamps.

Kim Hyong Gwon — A1572

Illustration reduced.

1995, Nov. 4 ***Perf. 12½x12***
3513 A1572 1w multicolored 2.75 1.50

90th anniv. of birth of Kim Hyong Gwon, Kim Il Sung's uncle.

New Year — A1573

Rodents: 20ch (#3514), Guinea pig. 20ch (#3515), Squirrel. 30ch, White mouse.
Illustration reduced.

1996, Jan. 1 ***Perf. 11½***
3514-3516 A1573 Strip of 3 3.00 .75

Nos. 3514-3516 were issued together in sheetlets of eight stamps, two each #3514 and #3515 and four #3516, plus one center label picturing an idyllic landscape, inscribed "1996."

League of Socialist Working Youth, 50th Anniv. — A1574

1996, Jan. 17
3517 A1574 10ch multicolored .50 .20

Reconstruction of Tomb of King Wanggon of Koryo — A1575

Designs: 30ch, Restoration monument, horiz. 40ch, Entrance gate to royal cemetery. 50ch, King Wanggon's tomb, horiz.

1996, Jan. 30
3518-3520 A1575 Set of 3 3.50 1.00

Teng Li-Chuang (Chinese Singer) — A1576

Illustration reduced.

1996, Feb. 1 ***Perf. 13¼***
3521 A1576 40ch multicolored 1.50 .50

3rd Asian Winter Games, Harbin, China — A1577

Designs, each 30ch: a, Kim Song Sun, Korean speed skater. b, Ye Qiaobo, Chinese sprint skater.
Illustration reduced.

1996, Feb 4 ***Perf. 11½***
3522 A1577 Sheet of 2, #a.-b. 3.50 .50

See No. 3556.

54th Birthday of Kim Jong Il

A1578

A1579

10ch, Jong Il Peak and *Kimjongilia*.
80ch, Kim Jong Il and soldiers. Illustration reduced.

1996, Feb. 16
3523 A1578 10ch multicolored .50 .20

Souvenir Sheet

Perf. 13¼
3524 A1579 80ch multicolored 2.75 .75

A1580

Designs: 10ch, Pairs skating. 20ch, Pairs skating, diff. 30ch, Pairs skating, diff.
50ch, Women's individual skating.

1996, Feb. 17 ***Perf. 11½***
3525-3527 A1580 Set of 3 2.00 .60
3527a Booklet pane of 4, #3525-3527, 3528a 5.50 —
Complete booklet, #3527a 6.00

Souvenir Sheet

3528 Sheet of 4 3.50 1.00
a. A1580 50ch multi 3.25

5th Paektusan Prize International Figure Skating Championship.

No. 3527a contains the four stamps, printed in a se-tenant horizontal strip of four, with unprinted marginal selvage all around.

Folk Tales — A1581

Screen painting by Ryu Suk: 8 stamps in continuous design, within 206mmx84mm skeetlet.

1996, Mar. 2
3529 Sheetlet of 8 5.00 2.25
a.-h. A1581 any single .60 .20

Agrarian Reform Law, 50th Anniv. — A1582

1996, Mar. 5
3530 A1582 10ch multicolored .50 .20

No. 3530 was issued in sheetlets of six, containing 5 #3530 and a label depicting a music score, *Song of Plowing*.

First North Korean Stamps, 50th Anniv. — A1583

1996, Mar. 12

3531 A1583 1w multicolored 3.25 .85

Centenary of Founding of Chinese Imperial Post

Yangzhou, China — A1584

Taihou Lake, China — A1585

Illustrations reduced.

1996, Mar. 20

3532 A1584 50ch multicolored 1.75 .50
3533 A1585 50ch multicolored 1.75 .50

83rd Birthday of Kim Il Sung

A1586

A1587

Designs: 10ch, Birthplace, Mangyondae. 1w, Portrait of Kim Il Sung. Illustration reduced.

1996, Apr. 15

3534 A1586 10ch multicolored .50 .20

Souvenir Sheet

3535 A1587 1w multicolored 3.25 .85

China '96 Int'l Stamp Exhib., Beijing — A1588

Designs, both 10ch: No. 3536, Seacoast gateway. No. 3537, Haiyin Pool. 60ch. Pantuo Stone.

1996, Apr. 22 ***Perf. 13½***

3536-3537 A1588 Set of 2 .50 .25

Souvenir Sheet

Perf. 11½

3538 A1588 60ch multicolored 1.60 .60

Folk Games — A1589

Designs: 20ch, Kicking stone handmill. 40ch, Shuttlecock. 50ch, Sledding.

1996, May 2

3539-3541 A1589 Set of 3 3.50 1.00
3539a-3541a Set of 3 sheetlets 7.00 7.00

Nos. 3539-3541 were each issued both in large sheets and in sheetlets containing two stamps of the same value and a center label.

Assoc. for the Restoration of the Fatherland, 60th Anniv. — A1590

1996, May 5

3542 A1590 10ch multicolored .50 .20
a. Sheetlet of 6, 5 #3542 + label 2.50 1.50

No. 3542 was issued both in large sheets and in sheetlets containing 5 stamps and 1 label.

Ri Po Ik — A1591

Illustration reduced.

1996, May 31 ***Perf. 13½***

3543 A1591 1w multicolored 3.00 .80

120th anniv. of birth of Ri Po Ik, Kim Il Sung's grandmother.

Polar Animals — A1592

Designs, each 50ch: #3544a, Arctic fox. #3544b, Polar bear. #3545a, Emperor penguins. #3546b, Leopard seals.

1996, June 2 ***Perf. 11½***

3544-3545 A1592 Set of 2 sheets 6.50 4.00

Korea Children's Union, 50th Anniv.

A1593

A1594

Designs: 10ch, Boy saluting.
1w, Painting of Kim Il Sung with Children's Union members, *There's Nothing to Envy in the World.* Illustration reduced.

1996, June 6

3546 A1593 10ch multicolored .50 .20

Souvenir Sheet

Perf. 11½x12

3547 A1594 1w multicolored 3.00 .85

Locomotives — A1595

Designs, all 50ch: No. 3548, Steam locomotive, facing left. No. 3549, Electric locomotive, facing right. No. 3550, Steam locomotive, facing right. No. 3551, Electric locomotive, facing left.

1996, June 6 ***Perf. 11½***

3548-3551 A1595 Set of 4 3.50 1.25

Capex '96 World Philatelic Exhibition.
Nos. 3550-3551 were issued in sheetlets of four, containing one of each value plus two labels.

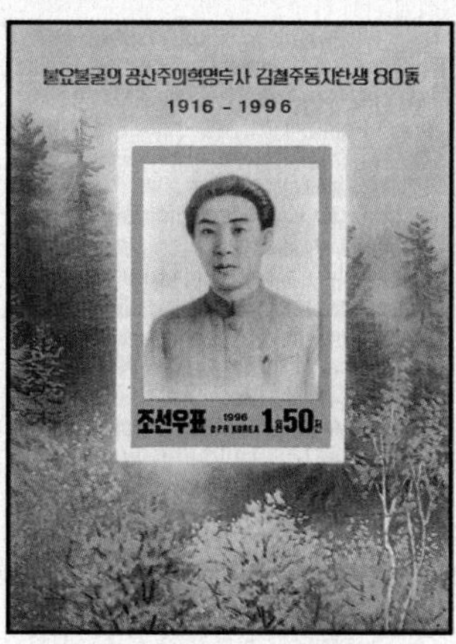

Kim Chol Ju — A1596

Illustration reduced.

1996, June 12 ***Perf. 13¼***

3552 A1596 1.50w multicolored 4.25 2.00

80th anniversary of birth of Kim Chol Ju, Kim Il Sung's brother.

Open Book — A1597

1996, June 15 ***Perf. 13½***

3553 A1597 40ch multicolored 1.10 .50

760th anniversary of publication of the *Complete Collection of Buddhist Scriptures Printed from 80,000 Wooden Blocks.*

Labor Law, 50th Anniv. — A1598

1996, June 24 ***Perf. 11½***

3554 A1598 50ch multicolored .50 .40

Seasonal Birds — A1599

Designs: 10ch, Broad-billed roller. 40ch, Tricolor flycatcher. 50ch, Cuckoo.
Illustration reduced.

1996, July 5

3555 A1599 Sheet of 3, #a.-c. 4.00 2.00

See No. 3569.

3rd Asian Winter Games, Harbin, China (2nd issue) — A1600

Design same as No. 3522, but with a new 30ch value picturing Ye Qiaobo replacing No. 3522b

Illustration reduced.

1996, July 5

3556 A1600 Sheet of 2 1.75 1.00
a. 30ch multi .85 .40

Death of Kim Il Sung, 2nd Anniv.

Kumsusan Memorial Palace — A1601

Outdoor Crowd, Statue of Kim Il Sung — A1602

Hymn, *The Leader will be with us forever* — A1603

Statue of Kim Il Sung in hall of the Kumsusan Memorial Palace — A1604

1996, July 8 *Perf. 12*

3557 A1601 10ch multicolored .25 .20

Souvenir Sheets

Perf. 13¼, 12 (#3558)

3558 A1602 1w multicolored 3.00 1.00
3559 A1603 1w multicolored 3.00 1.00
3560 A1604 1w multicolored 3.00 1.00

A1605

Designs, both 10ch: #3561, Kim Il Sung meeting Mao Zedong of China, 1954. #3562, Kim Il Sung meeting Jiang Zemin of China, 1991.

80ch, Kim shaking hands with Deng Xiaoping of China, horiz.

1996, July 11 *Perf. 11½*

3561-3562 A1605 Set of 2 .50 .25

Souvenir Sheet

3563 A1605 80ch multicolored 2.25 1.00

26th Olympic Games, Atlanta — A1606

Designs, each 50ch: #3564, Soccer. #3565, Tennis. #3566, Hammer throw. #3567, Baseball.

1996, July 19 *Perf. 12¼*

3564-3567 A1606 Set of 4 5.50 2.00

Sexual Equality Law, 50th Anniv. — A1607

1996, July 30 *Perf. 11½*

3568 A1607 10ch multicolored .25 .20

Seasonal Bird Type

Designs: 10ch, Crested shelduck. 40ch, Demoiselle crane. 50ch, White swan.

1996, Aug. 5

3569 A1600 Sheet of 3, #a.-c. 2.75 1.25

Industrial Nationalization, 50th Anniv. — A1608

1996, Aug. 10 *Perf. 11½*

3570 A1608 50ch multicolored .90 .40

UNICEF, 50th Anniv. — A1609

Designs: 10ch, Boy with ball, net. 20ch, Boy playing with building blocks. 50ch, Boy eating meal, holding watermelon slice. 60ch, Girl playing accordion.

1996, Aug. 20

3571-3574 A1609 Set of 4 2.75 1.10

Nos. 3571-3574 were issued in sheetlets of four, one containing 2 #3571, 1 #3574 and a label, the other containing 2 #3572, 1 #3573 and a different label.

1st Asian Gymnastics Championship, Changsha, China — A1610

Designs, each 15ch: #3575, Pae Kil Sun (N. Korea), men's pommel. #3576, Chen Cui Ting (China), rings. #3577, Li Jing (China). #3578, Kim Kwang Suk (N. Korea), asymmetrical bars.

1996, Sept. 24

3575-3578 A1610 Sheet of 4 1.50 .60

Kim Il Sung University, 50th Anniv. — A1611

1996, Oct. 1

3579 A1611 10ch multicolored .50 .20

Tiger — A1612

Designs, each 50ch: #3580, Tiger. #3581, Royal spoonbill.

80ch: Stylized dove/hand nurturing sapling, growing out of planet Earth.

1996, Oct. 13

3580-3581 A1612 Set of 2 3.00 .70

Souvenir Sheet

3582 A1612 80ch multicolored 6.50 1.50

Nos. 3580-3581 were each printed in sheetlets of four, containing three stamps and a label.

Down-with-Imperialism Union, 70th Anniv. — A1613

1996, Oct. 17

3583 A1613 10ch multicolored .25 .20

A1614

Designs: a, 30ch Huang Ji Gwang. b, 10ch, Score of theme song of film *Red Mountain Ridge*. c, 30ch Huang Ji Gwang heroically dying in battle.

1996, Oct. 25

3584 A1614 Sheet of 3, #a.-c. 2.00 1.00

Issued in honor of 44th anniversary of death of Hwang Ji Gwang, Chinese Volunteer, hero of Korean War.

History of the Earth — A1615

Each 50ch: a, Earth 7.5 billion years ago. b, 4.5-5 billion years ago. c, 450 million-4.5 billion years ago. d, 100-450 million years ago. e, 100 million years ago to the present.

Illustration reduced.

1996, Nov. 1 *Perf. 13½*

3585 A1615 Sheet of 5, #a.-e. 8.00 4.00

Freshwater Fishes — A1616

Designs, each 20ch: #3586, Japanese eel. #3587, Menada gray mullet.

80ch, Silver carp.

1996, Nov. 20 *Perf. 11½*

3586-3587 A1616 Set of 2 1.50 .35

Souvenir Sheet

3588 A1616 80ch multicolored 3.00 .75

A1617

1996, Dec. 24 *Perf. 12*

3589 A1617 20ch multicolored .60 .20

5th anniversary of appointment of Kim Jong Il as Supreme Commander of the People's Army.

No. 3589 was issued in sheetlets of 10.

New Year — Year of the Ox — A1618

Designs, each 70ch: #3590, *Ox Driver*, by Kim Tu Ryang. #3591, Bronze ritual plate decorated with a tiger and two bulls. #3592, Cowboy and bull. #3593, Cowboy playing flute, sitting on bull.

80ch, *Kosong People's Support to the Front.*

1997, Jan. 1 ***Perf. 11¾***

3590-3593 A1618 Set of 4 8.00 2.00
3591a, 3593a Set of 2 sheetlets 8.00 2.00

Souvenir Sheet

3594 A1618 80ch multicolored 3.00 .75

No. 3591a contains Nos. 3590 and 3591, with a central label depicting a bull's head surrounded by zodiacal signs. No. 3593a contains Nos. 3592 and 3593, with the same label.

Flowers and Butterflies, by Nam Kye-u (1811-88) — A1619

Designs, each 50ch: a, Three butterflies, flower. b, One small butterfly, flower. c, Large butterfly, leaves.

Illustration reduced.

1997, Jan. 5 ***Perf. 12¼x11¾***

3595 A1618 Sheetlet of 3, #a.-c. 4.50 1.00
b. Complete booklet, pane of 6, 2 ea. #3595a-3595b 9.00

Paintings of Cats and Dogs — A1620

Designs, both 50ch: #3598, Puppy in basket, touching noses with kitten. #3599, Two dogs in basket, kitten.

Both 50ch: #3600a, Cat in basket, with dog and skein of yarn alongside. #3600b, Kitten in basket with fruit and flowers, puppy alongside.

1997, Jan. 25 ***Perf. 11¾x12¼***

3598-3599 A1620 Set of 2 3.25 1.00

Sheetlets of 4

3600-3601 Set of 2 7.00 3.00
3600a A1620 50ch multicolored 1.50
3600b A1620 50ch multicolored 1.50

No. 3600 contains 1 #3598, 2 #3600a and 1 #3600b. No. 3601 contains 1 #3599, 1 #3600a and 2 #3600b.

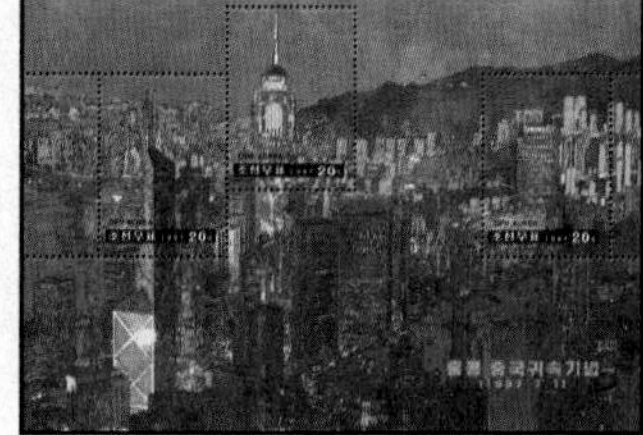

Return of Hong Kong to China — A1621

Hong Kong nightscape, each 20ch: a, Skyscraper with double antennae. b, Skyscraper with single spire. c, Round skyscraper, high-rise apartment buildings.

Illustration reduced.

1997, Feb. 1 ***Perf. 13½***

3602 A1621 Sheetlet of 3, #a.-c. 2.50 .65

55th Birthday of Kim Jong Il

A1622

A1623

10ch, Birthplace, Mt. Paekdu.

Each 1w: #3604, Kim Il Sung and Kim Jong Il with farm machine. #3605, Kim Jong Il inspecting a Korean People's Army unit. Illustration reduced.

1997, Feb. 16 ***Perf. 12***

3603 A1622 10ch multicolored .50 .20

Souvenir Sheets

3604-3605 A1623 Set of 2 5.50 1.75

6th Paektusan Prize Int'l Figure Skating Championships, Pyongyang — A1624

Pairs skating, different routines, each 50ch: #3606, pale reddish brown. #3607, blue. #3608, green.

1997, Feb. 17 ***Perf. 11½***

3606-3608 A1624 Set of 3 4.00 1.00
3608a Booklet pane of 6, 2 ea. #3606-3608 8.00 —
Complete booklet, #3608a 8.50

Sheetlets of 4

3609-3610 A1624 Set of 2 11.00 3.00

Nos. 3606-3608 were each issued in both large separate sheets and in sheetlets of 4: No. 3609 contains 2 #3606 and 2 #3607; No. 3610 contains 2 #3607 and 2 #3608. The booklet pane consists of a se-tenant vertical strip of 6, comprised of two se-tenant strips of #3606-3608.

Kye Sun Hui — A1625

Illustration reduced.

1997, Feb. 20

3611 A1625 80ch multicolored 2.50 .60

Issued to honor Kye Sun Hui, gold medal winner in Women's Judo at 26th Olympic Games, Atlanta.

Choe Un A — A1626

Illustration reduced.

1997, Feb. 25

3612 A1626 80ch multicolored 3.00 .60
a. Booklet pane of 5
Complete booklet, #3612a

Issued to honor Choe Un A, a seven-year-old entrant in the World Go Championships.

Apricots — A1627

Various types of apricots, each 50ch: #3613, *Prunus ansu.* #3614, *Prunus mandshurica.* #3615, *Prunus armeniaca.* #3616, *Prunus sibirica*

1997, Mar. 4 ***Perf. 11¼***

3613-3616 A1627 Set of 4 6.00 1.50
3613a Sheetlet of 8, 2x#3613-3614 12.00 3.00

Nos. 3613-3616 were each issued in both large separate sheets and in a sheetlet of 8, containing two sets in horizontal strips.

Foundation of Korean National Assoc., 80th Anniv. — A1628

1997, Mar. 23 ***Perf. 12¼***

3617 A1628 10ch lt brn & dk grn .50 .20
a. Sheetlet of 8 4.00 1.00

No. 3617 was issued both in large sheets and in a sheetlet of 8, containing two horizontal strips of four separated by inscribed internal selvage.

Reforestation Day, 50th Anniv. — A1629

10ch, Pine sapling.

1997, Apr. 6 ***Perf. 11½***

3618 A1629 10ch multicolored .50 .20
a. Complete booklet, 8 #3618

Souvenir Sheet

A1630

1w, Kim Il Sung planting sapling on Munsu Hill. Illustration reduced.

Perf. 13¼

3619 A1630 1w multicolored 3.00 .90

No. 3618a contains a horizontal strip of eight stamps, apparently taken from the sheet.

Kim Il Sung, 85th Birth Anniv.

A1631

A1632

A1633

Designs: 10ch, Kim's birthplace, Mangyongdae. 20ch, Sliding rock, horiz. 40ch, Warship Rock, horiz.

Each 1w: #3623, Painting of Kim among crowd symbolic of the Korean people. #3624, Kim in business suit, surrounded by flowers.

1997, Apr. 15 ***Perf. 12¼***

3620-3622	A1631	Set of 3	2.00	.55

Souvenir Sheets

Perf. 13¼ (#3623), 11¾x12¼ (#3624)

3623	A1632	1w multicolored	2.75	.90
3624	A1633	1w multicolored	2.75	.90

Korean People's Army, 65th Anniv.

A1634

A1635

10ch, KPA cap badge, rockets and jet fighters.

1w, Kim Il Sung and Kim Jong Il at military review. Illustration reduced.

1997, Apr. 25 ***Perf. 11½***

3625	A1634	10ch multicolored	.50	.20

Souvenir Sheet

Perf. 12¼x11¾

3626	A1635	1w multicolored	3.00	.90

North-South Agreement, 25th Anniv.

A1636

A1637

10ch, Map of Korea.

1w, Monument to Kim Il Sung's Autograph, Phanmunjom. Illustration reduced.

1997, May 4 ***Perf. 11½***

3627	A1636	10ch multicolored	1.00	.20

Souvenir Sheet

Perf. 12x11½

3628	A1637	1w multicolored	4.00	.90

A1638

Each 10ch: #3629, Tower of Juche Idea, flag. #3630, Man with flag. #3631, Soldier, miner, farmer, scientist.

1997, May 25 ***Perf. 12¼x12***

3629-3631	A1638	Set of 3	.90	.40

Int'l Friendship Exhib., Myohyang Mountains — A1639

Each 70ch: #3632, Exhibition Center. #3633, Statue of Kim Il Sung in exhibition entrance hall. #3634, Ivory sculpture *Native House in Mangyongdae* . #3635, Stuffed crocodile holding wooden cups, with ashtray.

1997, May 30 ***Perf. 11¾***

3632-3635	A1639	Set of 4 sheetlets	7.50	5.00

Battle of Poconbo, 60th Anniv. — A1640

1997, June 4 ***Perf. 11½***

3636	A1640	40ch multicolored	1.25	.35
a.		Sheetlet of 6	7.50	7.50
b.		Booklet pane of 6 #3636	7.50	—
		Complete booklet, #3636b	8.00	

No. 3636 was printed in both large sheets and in sheetlets of 6 stamps. No. 3636b contains six stamps in a horizontal strip, within decorative selvage.

Rice Transplantation, Mirin Plain, 50th Anniv. — A1641

Each 1w: #3637, Kim Il Sung transplanting rice. #3638, Kim Il Sung inspecting a rice-transplanting machine.

Illustration reduced.

1997, June 7 ***Perf. 13¼***

3637-3638	A1641	Set of 2 sheetlets	5.75	1.75

Return of Hong Kong to China

A1642

A1643

No. 3639, each 20ch: a, Signing the Nanjing Treaty, 1842. b, Signing the China-Britain Joint Statement, 1984. c, Deng Xiaoping and Margaret Thatcher. d, Jiang Zenin and Tong Jianhua.

97ch, Deng Xiaoping.

Illustrations reduced.

1997, July 1 ***Perf. 11¾***

3639	A1642	Sheetlet of 4, #a.-d.	3.00	.75

Souvenir Sheet

Perf. 13¼

3640	A1643	97ch multicolored	3.00	1.00

Fossils — A1644

Designs: 50ch, *Redlichia chinensis.* 1w, *Ptychoparia coreanica.*

Illustration reduced.

1997, July 5 ***Perf. 11½***

3641-3642	A1644	Pair	5.00	1.25
3641a		Booklet pane, 5 #3641	8.75	—
		Complete booklet #3641a	9.00	
3642a		Booklet pane, 5 #3642	17.50	—
		Complete booklet #3642a	18.00	

Nos. 3641-3642 were printed in sheetlets of four stamps, comprised of two se-tenant pairs. Nos. 3641a-3642a contain horizontal strips of five stamps.

Kim Il Sung, 3rd Anniv. Death — A1645

Each 50ch, Portrait of Kim Il Sung and: #3643, Kim speaking at party conference, 1985. #3644, Kim inspecting Kim Chaek Ironworks, 1985. #3645, Kim at Songsin Cooperative Farm, Sadong District, 1993. #3646, Kim being cheered by performing artists, 1986. #3647, Kim visiting Jonchon Factory, Jagang Province, 1991. #3648, Kim receiving bouquet from soldiers.

1997, July 8 ***Perf. 11¾x12***

3643-3648	A1645	Set of 6	9.00	2.25
3645a		Sheetlet of 3, #3643-3645	4.50	2.00
3648a		Sheetlet of 3, #3646-3648	4.50	2.00

Nos. 3643-3648 were each printed both separately in large sheets and together in two sheetlets of three, one containing #3643-3645 (#3645a) and the other containing #3646-3648 (#3648a).

Folk Games — A1646

Designs: 30ch, Blindman's Bluff. 60ch, Jackstones. 70ch, Arm wrestling.

1997, July 26 ***Perf. 11½***

3649-3651	A1646	Set of 3	4.50	1.25
3649a-3651a		Set of 3 sheetlets	9.00	4.00
3651b		Booklet pane of 6, 2 ea. #3649-3651	9.00	—
		Complete booklet, #3651b	9.50	

Nos. 3649-3651 were each printed both separately in large sheets and in sheetlets containing two stamps and a central label picturing a girl playing jump rope.

No. 3281b contains two each of #3649-3651, printed in a se-tenant block (3x2), with decorative selvage.

Traditional Korean Women's Clothing — A1647

Designs: 10ch, Spring costume. 40ch, Summer. 50ch, Autumn. 60ch, Winter.

1997, Aug. 10

3652-3655 A1647 Set of 4 4.50 2.00
3652a-3654a Set of 3 sheetlets 18.00 12.00

Nos. 3652-3655 were each printed both separately in large sheets and together, in various combinations, in sheetlets of 4. No. 3652a contains 2 #3652 and 2 #3653; No. 3653a contains 2 #3652a contains 2 #3653 and 2 #3654; No. 3654a contains 2 #3654 and 2 #3655.

Chongryu Bridge — A1648

Both 50ch: #3656, Night view of Chongryu Bridge. #3657, Panoramic view.

1997, Aug. 25

3656-3657 A1648 Set of 2 3.00 1.00
3657a Sheetlet of 2 3.50 1.50
3657b Booklet pane of 6, 3 ea. #3656-3657 9.00 —
Complete booklet, #3657b 9.50

Nos. 3656-3657 were each issued both in large sheets and in sheetlets of two, containing one of each value. No. 3657b contains three se-tenant pairs in a vertical strip of six stamps, within inscribed selvage.

Juche Era and Sun Day, 85th Anniv.

A1649

A1650

10ch, Sun, magnolias, banner, balloons. Each 1w: #3659, Kim Il Sung, slogan, doves. #3660, Kim, birthplace Mongyangdae. #3661, Kim, Lake Chon, Mt. Paekdu. #3662, Kim, Kumsusan Memorial Palace. Illustration reduced.

1997, Sept. 3 ***Perf. 13¼***

3658 A1649 10ch multicolored .50 .20

Souvenir Sheets

3659-3662 A1650 Set of 4 sheets 11.00 6.00

Theses on Socialist Education, 20th Anniv. of Publication — A1651

1997, Sept. 5 ***Perf. 11½***

3663 A1651 10ch multicolored .50 .20

No. 3663 was issued in sheetlets of 6.

Air Koryo — A1652

Sheets of 2 stamps and central label: 20ch, TU-134. 30ch, TU-154. 50ch, IL-62. Illustration reduced.

1997, Sept. 14 ***Perf. 13¼***

3664-3666 A1652 Set of 3 sheetlets 5.00 1.50
3665a Complete booklet, pane of 8, 4 ea. #3664, 3666 7.00
3666a Complete booklet, pane of 8, 4 ea. #3665, 3666 8.00

Korean Membership in World Tourism Org., 10th Anniv. — A1653

Views of Mt. Chilbo, each 50ch: #3667, Kim Chol Ung. #3668, Rojok Beach. #3669, Chonbul Peak.

1997, Sept. 22 ***Perf. 12***

3667-3669 A1653 Set of 3 4.50 1.25
3669a Sheetlet, #3667-3669 + label 5.00 1.40

Nos. 3667-3669 were each issued in both large sheets and in sheetlets containing one of each value and a label publicizing Ryohaengsa, the Korean travel company.

Kumgang Mountains — A1654

Each 50ch: #3670, Kumgang Gate. #3671, Podok Hermitage.

1997, Oct. 2

3670-3671 A1654 Set of 2 3.00 .75
3670a Booklet pane of 5 #3670 7.50 —
Complete booklet, #3670a 8.00
3671a Sheetlet of 6, 3 each #3670-3671 10.00 4.00
3671b Booklet pane of 5 #3671 7.50 —
Complete booklet, #3671b 8.00

Nos. 3670-3671 were each issued in large sheets, in sheetlets of 6, containing three of each value in se-tenant pairs, and in booklet panes of 5. Nos. 3670a and 3671b each contain 5 stamps in a horizontal strip, surrounded by decorative selvage.

Mangyongdae Revolutionary School, 50th Anniv. — A1655

Perf. 11½

1997, Oct. 12

3672 A1655 40ch multicolored 1.25 .30
a. Booklet pane of 6 7.50 —
Complete booklet, #3672a 8.00

No. 3672 was issued in sheets of 4. No. 3672a contains six stamps in a vertical strip, with inscribed surrounding selvage.

Gift Animals — A1656

Animals presented to Kim Il Sung as gifts from foreign governments: 20ch, Lion (from Ethiopia, 1987). 30ch, Jaguar (Japan, 1992). 50ch, Barbary sheep (Czechoslovakia, 1992). 80ch, Scarlet macaw (Austria, 1979).

1997, Oct. 15

3673-3676 A1656 Set of 4 5.50 1.25
3673a Sheetlet of 8, 2 each #3673-3676 11.00 5.00
3673b Booklet pane of 8, 2ea. #3673-3676 11.00 —
Complete booklet, #3673b 12.00

Nos. 3673-3676 were each issued separately in large sheets and together in sheetlets of 8, containing two se-tenant horizontal strips of four separated by a large decorative label. No. 3673b contains two se-tenant blocks (or horizontal strips) with decorative selvage.

Qu Shao Yun, Chinese Volunteer Hero — A1657

Designs: a, 30ch, Bust of Qu Shao Yun. b, 10ch, Monument to Qu Shao Yun. c, 30ch, Qu Shao Yun burning to death in battle.

1997, Oct. 18

3677 A1657 Sheetlet of 3, #a.-c. 2.25 .75

Sports — A1658

Each 50ch: #3678, Bowling. #3679, Fencing. #3680, Golf.

1997, Nov. 10 ***Perf. 13¼***

3678-3680 A1658 Set of 3 5.25 1.25
3680a Sheetlet, 2 each #3678-380 + 2 labels 11.00 5.00

Nos. 3678-3680 were each issued separately in large sheets and together in sheetlets of 8, containing two se-tenant vertical strips, each comprised of the three stamps and one label.

Snails — A1659

Each 50ch: #3681, Two snails copulating. #3682, Snail laying eggs. #3683, Snail. Illustration reduced.

1997, Nov. 15 ***Perf. 12¼***

3681-3683 A1659 Strip of 3 4.75 2.00
3683a Sheetlet of 6, 2 each #3681-3683 9.50 4.00
3683b Booklet pane of 6, 2 ea. #3681-3683 9.50 —
Complete booklet, #3683b 10.00

Nos. 3681-3683 were issued both in large sheets, with the three values se-tenant within the sheet, and in sheetlets of 6, containing two se-tenant strips of three.

Shanghai Int'l Stamp & Coin Exhib. — A1660

Illustration reduced.

1997, Nov. 19 ***Perf. 11½***

3684 A1660 Sheetlet of 2, #a.-b. 2.50 1.00
a. 30ch multicolored 1.00 .30
b. 50ch multicolored 1.50 .60

New Year — Year of the Tiger

A1661

A1662

Designs: 10ch, "Juche 87," pine boughs, temple. 50ch (#3686), Tiger in rocket. 50ch (#3687), Tiger in ship. 80ch, Tiger in train.

Perf. 13¼, 11½ (#3686-3687)

1997, Dec. 15

3685 A1661 10ch multicolored .20 .20
3686 A1662 50ch multicolored .90 .25
3687 A1662 50ch multicolored .90 .25
a. Sheetlet of 4, 1 #3686, 1 #3687, 2 as #3688 4.50 2.00
Nos. 3685-3687 (3) 2.00 .70

Souvenir Sheet

3688 A1662 80ch multicolored 2.00 .75

Nos. 3686 and 3687 were printed both separately in large sheets and together with the #3688 value in sheetlets of four.

Kim Jong Suk, 80th Anniv. Birth

Birthplace, Hoeryong — A1663

Kim Jong Suk — A1664

1997, Dec. 24 *Perf. 13¼*
3689 A1663 10ch multicolored .50 .20

Souvenir Sheet

3690 A1664 1w multicolored 3.00 .75

Winter Olympic Games, Nagano, Japan — A1665

Designs: 20ch, Skiing. 40ch, Speed skating.

1998, Feb. 7 *Perf. 11½*
3691-3692 A1665 Set of 2 1.25 .65
3692a Sheetlet of 4, 2 #3691 + 2 #3692 2.50 1.25
3692b Booklet pane of 8, 4 ea. #3691-3692 5.00 —
Complete booklet, #3692b 5.50

Nos. 3691-3692 were issued separately in large sheets, in sheetlets of 4, containing two of each value, and in booklet panes, containing four each, with surrounding inscribed selvage.

56th Birthday of Kim Jong Il

A1666

A1667

Designs: 10ch, Birth date ("2.16").
3w, Birthplace, log cabin on Mt. Paekdu. Illustration reduced.

1998, Feb. 16
3693 A1666 10ch multicolored .50 .20

Souvenir Sheet

3694 A1667 3w multicolored 4.50 2.00

Paintings of Mt. Paekdu Wildlife

A1668

A1669

Designs, each 50ch: #3695, Korean tigers. #3696, White crane.
No. 3697, each 50ch: a, Bears. b, Racoons.

1998, Mar. 6 *Perf. 11¾x12*
3695-3696 A1668 Set of 2 2.00 1.00
3696a Booklet pane of 8, 2 ea. #3695-3696, 3697a-3697b 8.00 —
Complete booklet, #3696a 8.50

Souvenir Sheet

3697 A1669 Sheetlet of 4 4.00 2.00
a. A1668 50ch multicolored 1.00 .50
b. A1668 50ch multicolored 1.00 .50

Nos. 3695-3696 were issued both separately in large sheets, and together with #3697a and #3697b in sheetlets of four.

Kim Il Sung's 1000-ri Journey, 75th Anniv. — A1670

1998, Mar. 16 *Perf. 11½*
3698 A1670 10ch multicolored .50 .20
a. Sheetlet of 10 5.00 1.50

No. 3698 was issued both in large sheets and in sheetlets of 10.

Appt. of Kim Jong Il as Chairman of the Nat'l Defense Commission, 5th Anniv. — A1671

1998, Apr. 9
3699 A1671 10ch multicolored .50 .20

Kim Il Sung, 86th Birth Anniv.

A1672

A1673

10ch, Birthplace, flags, flowers.
Circular stamps, each 80ch, within 84x155mm sheetlets, depicting portraits of Kim Il Sung at different stages in his life: #3701, As child. #3702, As middle school student. #3703, As young revolutionary. #3704, In suit and tie, ca. 1946. #3705, In military uniform during Korean War. #3706, As middle-aged man, in uniform. #3707, As middle-aged man, in suit and tie. #3708, As old man in suit and tie. Illustration reduced.

1998, Apr. 15
3700 A1672 10ch multicolored .50 .20

Souvenir Sheets

3701-3708 A1673 Set of 8 sheets 9.00 4.00

North-South Joint Conference, 50th Anniv. — A1674

1998, Apr. 21 *Perf. 13¼*
3709 A1674 10ch multicolored .50 .20

16th World Cup Soccer Championship, France — A1675

Designs: 30ch, Dribbling. 50ch, Kicking.

1998, May 5 *Perf. 11½*
3710-3711 A1675 Set of 2 1.60 .80
3711a Sheetlet of 6, 2 #3710, 2 #3711 & 2 as #3712 6.00 3.00
3711b Booklet pane of 10, 5 ea. #3710-3711 8.00 —
Complete booklet, #3711b 8.50

Souvenir Sheet

3712 A1675 80ch multicolored 1.60 .80

Nos. 3710-3711 were issued both in large separate sheets and, in combination with the 80ch value from #3712, in sheetlets of 6, containing two se-tenant strips of the three stamps. They were also issued in booklet panes of 10 (5x2), containing #3710-3711 printed se-tenant.

Int'l Friendship Art Exhib., Mt. Myohyang

A1676

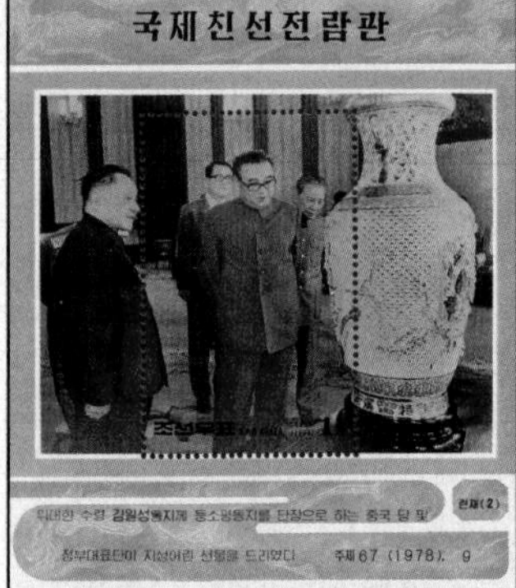
A1677

Designs, each 1w: #3713, *Diagram of Automatic Space Station* (USSR). #3714, Ceramic flower vase (Egypt). #3715, *Crane* (USA).
1w, Kim Il Sung receiving a gift from Deng Xiaoping. Illustration reduced.

1998, May 20 *Perf. 11¾*
3713-3715 A1676 Set of 3 4.50 2.25
3714a Sheetlet of 2, #3712 & #3714 2.75 1.40
3715a Sheetlet of 2, #3712 & #3715 2.75 1.40

Souvenir Sheet

Perf. 13¼

3716 A1677 1w multicolored 2.00 1.00

Nos. 3713-3715 were issued both in large separate sheets and in se-tenant sheetlets of 2 (#3714a, 3715a).

Korean Art Gallery

A1678

A1679

Designs: 60ch, *A Countryside in May.* 1.40w, *Dance.*
3w, *Heart-to-heart Talk with a Peasant.* Illustration reduced.

1998, May 20

3717-3718 A1678 Set of 2 3.00 1.50

Souvenir Sheet

3719 A1679 3w multicolored 4.50 2.25

Vegetables — A1680

Designs: 10ch, Cabbage. 40ch, Radish. 50ch, Green onion. 60ch, Cucumber. 70ch, Pumpkin. 80ch, Carrot. 90ch, Garlic. 1w, Red pepper.

Illustration reduced.

1998, May 20 ***Perf. 13¼***

3720-3727 A1680 Sheet of 8 9.00 4.50

Int'l Year of the Ocean

A1681

A1682

Designs: 10ch, Hydro-Meteorological Headquarters building, ship, oceanographic floating balloons, dolphins, emblem. 80ch, Woman holding child, yachts, emblem.

5w, Vasco da Gama (1460-1524), Portuguese explorer. Illustration reduced.

1998, May 22

3730-3731 A1681 Set of 2 2.00 .90

3731a Sheetlet of 4, 2 ea. #3730-3731 2.00 .90

Souvenir Sheet

3732 A1682 5w multicolored 7.50 3.75

Nos. 3730-3731 were issued both in large separate sheets and in sheetlets containing two se-tenant pairs (#3731a).

Korean Central History Museum, Pyongyang

A1683

A1684

Designs: 10ch, Stone Age tool. 2.50w, Fossil monkey skull.

4w, Kim Il Sung visiting the museum. Illustration reduced.

1998, June 15

3733-3734 A1683 Set of 2 4.00 2.00

Souvenir Sheet

3735 A1684 4w multicolored 6.00 3.00

Dr. Ri Sung Gi (1905-96)

A1685

A1686

Designs: 40ch, Dr. Ri Sung Gi and diagram of vinalon nuclear structure.

80ch, Gi working in laboratory. Illustration reduced.

1998, June 15 ***Perf. 11½***

3736 A1685 40ch multicolored .60 .20

a. Booklet pane of 10
Complete booklet, #3736a

Souvenir Sheet

3737 A1686 80ch multicolored 1.60 1.00

2nd anniv. death of Dr. Ri Sung Gi, inventor of vinalon.

Squirrels and Hedgehogs
Cartoon — A1687

Designs: 20ch, Squirrel and Commander of Hedgehog Unit. 30ch, Commander of Hedgehog Unit receiving invitation to banquet celebrating bumper crop. 60ch, Weasel Commander and mouse. 1.20w, Bear falling dead-drunk. 2w, Weasel Commander and mice invading the flower village. 2.50w, Hedgehog scout saving the squirrel.

1998, June 15

3738-3743 A1687 Set of 6 12.00 6.00

3743a Sheetlet of 6, #3737-3743 12.00 6.00

Nos. 3738-3743 were issued both separately in large sheets and together in se-tenant sheetlets of 6 (#3743a).

Return of Hong Kong to China, 1st Anniv.

A1688

A1689

Designs, each 10w: #3744, Deng Xiaoping (1904-97), Chinese Prime Minister. #3745, Mao Zedong. #3746, Kim Il Sung.

10w, #3747, Deng Xiaoping, Mao Zedong and Kim Il Sung, horiz. Illustration reduced.

1998, July 1

Embossed with gold foil application

3744-3746 A1688 Set of 3 30.00 10.00

Souvenir Sheet

3747 A1689 10w Gold & multi 10.00 10.00

Young Wild Mammals — A1690

Designs: 10ch, Tiger cub. 50ch, Donkey foal. 1.60w, Elephant. 2w, Lion cubs.

1998, July 10 ***Perf. 11½***

3748-3751 A1690 Set of 4 3.00 1.50

Korean War "Victory," 45th Anniv.

A1691

A1692

A1693

45ch, War monument, flag.

Each 2w: #3753, Kim Il Sung inspecting the front. #3754, *Gaz-67* jeep and map of Korea, showing Kim's inspection route.

1998, July 27 ***Perf. 13¼***

3752 A1691 45ch multicolored .25 .20

Souvenir Sheets

3753 A1692 2w multicolored 2.00 1.00

3754 A1693 2w multicolored 2.00 1.00

Embroidery — A1694

Designs: 10ch, *White Herons in Forest.* 40ch, *Carp.* 1.20w, *Hollyhock.* 1.50w, *Cockscomb.*

4w, *Pine and Cranes.*

1998, Aug. 10 ***Perf. 11¾x12***

3755-3758 A1694 Set of 4 2.50 1.25

Sheetlet of 6

Perf. 12x12¼

3759	Sheetlet, #a.-e. + label		5.75	3.00
a.	A1694	10ch multicolored	.20	.20
b.	A1694	40ch multicolored	.40	.20
c.	A1694	1.20w multicolored	1.00	.50
d.	A1694	1.50w multicolored	1.00	.50
e.	A1694	4w multicolored	2.50	1.25

Souvenir Sheet

Perf. 11¾x12

3760 A1694 4w multicolored 3.00 1.50

Traditional Costumes — A1695

Designs: 10ch, Pouch. 50ch, Playthings (dress ornaments). 1.50w, Hairpin. 1.90w, Ornamental silver sword.

1998, Aug. 20 *Perf. 11½*

3761-3764 A1695 Set of 4 3.00 1.50
3763a Sheetlet of 20, 10 se-tenant pairs #3761 and #3763 15.00 7.50
3764a Sheetlet of 20, 10 se-tenant pairs #3762 and #3764 15.00 7.50

Nos. 3761-3764 were printed both separately in large sheets and in combination in two sheetlets of 20 (#3763a, 3764a).

Launch of *Kwangmyongsong I*, DPRK's First Earth Satellite — A1696

Designs: 40ch, Rocket, satellite, world map and flag.
1.50w, Rocket, earth and satellite orbit.

1998, Aug. 31 *Perf. 13¼*

3765 A1696 40ch multicolored .35 .20

Souvenir Sheet

3766 A1696 1.50w multicolored 1.25 .65

Acclamation of Kim Jong Il as Chairman of the DPRK National Defense Commission

Proclamation, *Kimjongilia* — A1697

Kim Jong Il — A1698

1998, Sept. 5 *Perf. 11½*

3767 A1697 10ch multicolored .20 .20

Souvenir Sheet

Perf. 13¼

3768 A1698 1w multicolored .75 .40

Korean DPR, 50th Anniversary

State Arms, Flag, Tower of Juche Idea — A1699

1998, Sept. 9 *Perf. 13¼*

3769 A1699 10ch multicolored .20 .20

Sheetlet of 6

A1700

Designs: Each 1w: #3770, Kim Il Sung saluting crowd from balcony. #3771, Kim raising cap to crowd in street. #3772, Kim in suit and white hat, with fruit, stylized and idealized Korean peninsula in background.
Illustration reduced.

3770-3772 A1700 multicolored 4.50 2.25

Poster: "Let Us Push Ahead with the Forced March for Final Victory" — A1701

1998, Sept. 15 *Perf. 11½*

3773 A1701 10ch multicolored .20 .20

Korean DPR, 50th Anniversary (2nd Issue)

A1702

A1703

Illustrations reduced.

1998, Sept. 20 *Perf. 13¼*

3774 A1702 40ch multicolored .35 .20

Perf. 11½

3775 A1703 1w multicolored 1.00 .50

Summer Olympic Games, Sydney — A1704

Designs: 20ch, Cyclist. 50ch, Soccer. 80ch, Show jumping. 1.50w, Javelin throwing. 2.50w, Basketball.

1998, Sept. 25

3776-3779 A1704 Set of 4 2.50 1.25
3778a Sheetlet of 3, #3777, 3778, as #3780 3.00 1.50
3779a Sheetlet of 3, #3776, 3779, as #3780 3.00 1.50

Souvenir Sheet

3780 A1704 2.50w multi 2.00 1.00

Nos. 3776-3779 were each issued both separately in large sheets and in combination in two sheetlets of 3(#3778a, 3779a).

Plants Presented as Gifts to Kim Jong Il — A1705

Designs: 20ch, *Cyclamen persicum*. 2w, *Dianthus chinensis*.

1998, Sept. 28 *Perf. 11½*

3781-3782 A1705 Set of 2 1.60 .80

Nat'l Vaccination Day — A1706

1998, Oct. 20 *Perf. 13¼*

3783 A1706 40ch multicolored .35 .20
a. Sheetlet of 6 2.10 1.00

No. 3783 was issued both in large sheets and in sheetlets of 6, with the World Health Organization emblem in margins.

Leopard (WWF) — A1707

Designs, each 1w: #3784, Leopard climbing branch. #3785, Leopard walking in snow. #3786, Leopard looking to left. #3787, Lepard's head, full-face.

1998, Oct. 21

3784-3787 A1707 Set of 4 4.00 2.00
3787a Sheetlet of 16, 4 se-tenant blocks of #3784-3787 16.00 8.00

Nos. 3784-3787 were issued both in separate large sheets and together in sheetlets of 16 (#3787a), with "World Wide Fund for Nature," WWF emblems in margin.

Land and Environment Conservation Day

A1708

A1709

Designs: 10ch, Canal, countryside. 40ch, Modern highway exchange, apartment towers.
1w, Kim Il Sung breaking ground for construction of Pothong River project. Illustration reduced.

1998, Oct. 23 *Perf. 11½*

3788-3789 A1708 Set of 2 .45 .25

Souvenir Sheet

Perf. 12x12¼

3790 A1709 1w multicolored .75 .40

Italia '98 Int'l stamp Exhib., Milan — A1710

Illustration reduced.

1998, Oct. 23 *Perf. 12¼x12*

3791 A1710 2w multicolored 1.50 .75

A1711

Designs: 20ch (#3792), Peng Dehuai and Kim Il Sung. 20ch (#3793), Peng Dehuai, Zhou Enlai, Mao Zedong. 30ch (#3794), Marshal Peng Dehuai. 30ch (#3795), Painting, *On the Front*.
Illustration reduced.

1998, Oct. 24 *Perf. 11½*

3792-3795 A1711 Sheetlet of 4 .75 .40

Birth centenary of Peng Dehuai, Commander of the Chinese People's Volunterrs in the Korean War.

Liu Shaoqi — A1712

Designs: 10ch, Liu Shaoqi. 20ch, Liu sitting with Mao Zedong (1965). 30ch, Liu and his daughter, Xiao Xiao (1964). 40ch, Liu sitting with his wife, Wang Guangmei (1961).

1998, Nov 24 ***Perf. 13¼***

3796-3799 A1712 Set of 4 .75 .40

Souvenir Sheet

Perf. 11¾x12¼

3800 A1712 1w multicolored .75 .40

Victory in Korean-Japanese War, 400th Anniv.

Monument — A1713

Sea Battle Off Hansan Islet in 1592 — A1714

Designs: 10ch, Victory monument, Yonsang area, Yonan fortress, banners. 30ch, Naval victory monument, Myongryang area, Gen. Ri Sun Sin, turtleship. 1.60w, Monument to Buddhist priest Hyujong, Sosan-Chonghodang, Hyujong, sword, helmet.

1998, Nov 24 ***Perf. 11½***

3801-3803 A1713 Set of 3 1.50 .75

3803a Sheetlet of 15, containting 5 se-tenant strips of #3801-3803 7.50 3.75

Souvenir Sheet

3804 A1714 10w multicolored 7.50 3.00

Nos. 3801-3803 were issued in both separately in large sheets and together in sheetlets of 15 (#3803a).

DPRK Entry into INTERSPUTNIK, 15th Anniv. — A1715

1998, Nov. 25 ***Perf. 13¼***

3805 A1715 1w dp grn & lt grn .75 .40

Korean Goats — A1716

1998, Nov. 26

3806-3807 A1716 Set of 2 .80 .40

Sculpture, *A Floral Carriage of Happiness* — A1717

Quotation from Kim Il Sung — A1718

Designs: 10ch, Sculpture, panoramic view of Mangyongdae Schoolchildren's Palace.

1w, Kim Il Sung quotation, "Children are the treasure of our country. Korea of the future is theirs." Illustration reduced.

1998, Nov. 26 ***Perf. 11½***

3808 A1717 40ch multicolored .35 .20

a. Sheetlet of 4 2.00 1.00

Souvenir Sheet

3809 A1718 1w multicolored .75 .40

No. 3808 was issued both in large sheets and in sheetlets of 4, with the music and lyrics of song "We are the Happiest in the World" in selvage.

Univeral Declaration of Human Rights, 50th Anniv. — A1719

1998, Dec. 10

3810 A1719 20ch multicolored .20 .20

Reptiles — A1720

Designs: 10ch, Reeves turtle. 40ch, Skink. 60ch, Loggerhead turtle. 1.20w, Leatherback turtle.

Illustration reduced.

1998, Dec. 15 ***Perf. 13¼***

3811-3814 A1720 Block of 4 1.75 .90

3814a Sheetlet of 16, #3811-3814 in 4 se-tenant blocks 17.00 3.50

3814b Complete booklet, 3 ea. #3811-3814 13.00

Nos. 3811-3814 were issued in se-tenant blocks, both in large sheets and in sheetlets of 16. No. 3814b contains three attached se-tenant blocks, apparently made up from sheet stamps.

Mt. Chilbo — A1721

Designs: 30ch, Thajong Rock. 50ch, Peasant Rock. 1.70w, Couple Rock.

1998, Dec. 15 ***Perf. 11½***

3815-3817 A1721 Set of 3 1.75 .90

Tale of Chung Hyang — A1722

Designs: 40ch, Marriage of Ri Mong Ryong and Song Chun Hyang. 1.60w, Pyon Hak Do watching Chun Hyang. 2.50w, Ri Mong Ryong and Chun Hyang.

50ch, Chun Hyang in wedding veil.

1998, Dec. 20

3818-3820 A1722 Set of 3 3.50 1.75

Sheetlet of 4

3821 Sheetlet, #3818-3820, 3821a 5.00 2.50

a. A1722 50ch multicolored 1.00 .50

Nos. 3818-3820 were issued both separately in large sheets and together, in combination with No. 3821a, in sheetlets of 4.

Chollima Statue A1723

Arch of Triumph A1724

Tower of Juche Idea — A1725

Type A1723: 10ch (#3822), 30ch, 70ch (#3829), 1.50w, 5w.

Type A1724: 10ch (#3823), 40ch (#3827), 70ch (#3830), 1.20w, 3w.

Type A1725: 10ch (#3824), 20ch, 40ch (#3828), 2w, 10w.

1998, Dec. 22 ***Perf. 13¼***

3822-3836 Set of 15 25.00 12.50

New Year — Year of the Rabbit — A1726

Designs: 10ch, Rabbit meeting Lion on the road. 1w, Rabbit using mirror to lure lion into pit. 1.50w, Rabbit laughing at Lion in trap.

2.50w, Rabbit.

1999, Jan. 1 ***Perf. 11½***

3837-3839 A1726 Set of 3 2.00 1.00

Sheetlet

3840 Sheetlet of 4, #3837-3839, 3840a 4.00 2.00

a. A1726 2.50w multicolored 2.00 1.00

Worker-Peasant Red Guards, 40th Anniv. — A1727

1999, Jan. 14 ***Perf. 13¼***

3841 A1727 10ch multicolored .20 .20

Kim Jong Il, 57th Birthday — A1728

40ch, Log cabin (birthplace) on Mt. Paekdu.

1999, Feb. 16 ***Perf. 11½***

3842 A1728 40ch multicolored .35 .20

Publication of Kim Il Sung's *Theses on the Socialist Rural Question in Our Country* — A1729

1999, Feb. 25 ***Perf. 13¼***

3843 A1729 10ch multicolored .20 .20

March 1 Popular Uprising, 80th Anniv. — A1730

1999, Feb. 25

3844 A1730 10ch olive brn & black .20 .20

Turtle Ship — A1731

Illustration reduced.

1999, Mar. 19

3845 A1731 2w multicolored 1.60 .80

Australia '99 World Stamp Expo, Melbourne.

Kim Il Sung, 87th Anniv. Birth

Childhood Home, Mangyongdae — A1732

Kim Il Sung — A1733

No. 3847, illustration reduced.

1999, Apr. 15 ***Perf. 11½***
3846 A1732 10ch multicolored .20 .20

Souvenir Sheet

Perf. 11½x12

3847 A1733 2w multicolored 1.60 .80

45th World Table Tennis Championships, Belgrade — A1734

1999, Apr. 26 ***Perf. 11½***
3848 A1734 1.50w multicolored 1.20 .60

Ibra '99 Int'l Stamp Exhib., Nuremberg — A1735

1999, Apr. 27
3849 A1735 1w multicolored .85 .40

Central Zoo, Pyongyang, 40th Anniv. — A1736

Designs: 50ch, Chimpanzee, rhinoceros. 60ch, Manchurian crane, deer. 70ch, Zebra, kangaroo.
2w, Tiger.

1999, Apr. 30 ***Perf. 13¼***
3850-3852 A1736 Set of 3 1.60 .80

Souvenir Sheet

3853 A1736 2w multicolored 1.75 .90

Central Botanical Garden, Pyongyang, 40th Anniv. — A1737

Designs: 10ch, *Benzoin obtusilobum.* 30ch, *Styrax obassia.* 70ch, *Petunia hybrida.* 90ch, *Impatiens hybrida.*
2w, *Kimsungilia* and *Kimjongilia.*

1999, Apr. 30 ***Perf. 11½***
3854-3857 A1737 Set of 4 1.60 .80
3857a Sheetlet of 4, #3854-3857 1.75 .90

Souvenir Sheet

3858 A1737 2w multicolored 1.75 .90

Nos. 3854-3857 were issued both separately in large sheets and together in a se-tenant sheetlet of 4.

Three Revolution Exhibit — A1738

Designs: 60ch, Light Industry Hall. 80ch, Heavy Industry Hall

1999, May 2
3859-3860 A1738 Set of 2 1.20 .60

Three Revolution (ideological, technical, cultural) Exhibition, Ryonmotdong, Sosong District, Pyongyang.

Asia-Pacific Telecommunications Union, 20th Anniv. — A1739

1999, May 8 ***Perf. 13¼***
3861 A1739 1w multicolored .80 .40

Battle of Musan Area, 60th Anniv. — A1740

1999, May 19 ***Perf. 11½***
3862 A1740 10ch multicolored .20 .20

Charles Darwin, 190th Anniv. of Birth — A1741

Designs: 30ch, Seagulls. 50ch, Bats. 1w, Dolphins. 1.20w, Rider on horseback. 1.50w, Korean dancer in traditional dress.

1999, May 20
3863-3867 A1741 Sheetlet of 5 3.00 1.50

Souvenir Sheet

Charles Darwin — A1742

Illustration reduced.

Perf. 13¼x12

3868 A1742 2w multicolored 4.00 2.00

Diego Velazquez (1599-1660), Artist, 400th Anniv. Birth

A1743

Designs, each 50ch: #3869, *Princess Margarita in a White Dress* . #3866, *Men Drawing Water from a Well*
3.50w, *Self-portrait.*

1999, May 30 ***Perf. 11¾***
3869-3870 A1743 Set of 2 1.00 .50
3870a Sheetlet of 3, #3569-3571, 3871a 4.00 2.00

Souvenir Sheet

3871 A1743 3.50w multicolored 3.00 1.50

Medium and Small Hydroelectric Power Stations — A1744

Designs: 50ch, Rimyongsu Power Station. 1w, Janggasan Power Station.

1999, May 30 ***Perf. 11½***
3872-3873 A1744 Set of 2 1.20 .60

3rd Women's World Soccer Championship, USA — A1745

Designs: 1w, Dribbling. 1.50w (#3875), Tackling. 1.50w (#3876), Goal shot. 2w, Knee kick.
Illustration reduced.

1999, June 8 ***Perf. 13¼***
3874-3877 A1745 Sheetlet of 4 5.00 2.50

Mars Exploration — A1746

Designs, each 2w: a, Vostock Rocket. b, Satellite over Martian crater. c, Mars probe landing, Martian moons.
Illustration reduced.

1999, June 10 ***Perf. 11½***
3878 A1746 Sheetlet of 3, #a.-c. 4.75 2.50

Movie, *The Nation and Destiny* — A1747

Scenes from film, each 1w: #3879, Man holding candlestick. #3880, Man in white coat, woman with pistol. #3881, Old man in prison cell. #3882, Man in protective suit, with goggles on hat.
Illustration reduced.

1999, June 10
3879-3882 A1747 Sheetlet of 4 3.20 1.60

Tourism — Mt. Kumgang — A1748

Designs: 20ch, Samil Lagoon. 40ch, Samson Rocks, vert. 60ch, Standing Rock. 80ch, Kuryong Waterfall. 1w, Kwimyon Rock.

1999, June 15 ***Perf. 12***
3883-3887 A1748 Set of 5 2.50 1.25

UPU, 125th Anniv. — A1749

Illustration reduced.

1999, June 20 ***Perf. 11½***
3888 A1749 2w multicolored 1.40 .70

PHILEXFANCE '99 — A1750

2.50w, First stamps of France (1870) and DPRK (1946).
Illustration reduced.

1999, July 2 ***Perf. 12***
3889 A1750 2.50w multicolored 2.00 1.00

Kim Il Sung, 5th Anniv. of Death — A1751

Designs, each 1w: #3890, Kim Il Sung's Mercedes. #3891, Kim's railway car.
Illustration reduced.

1999, July 8 ***Perf. 11½***
3890-3891 A1751 Sheetlet of 2 1.60 .80

Kim Hyong Jik (1894-1926), Revolutionary, 105th Anniv. Birth — A1752

10ch, Chinese characters for "Jiwon" ("Aim High"), Kim Hyong Jik's motto, and Mangyong Hill.

1999, July 10
3892 A1752 10ch multicolored .20 .20

History of Ceramics — A1753

Designs: 70ch, Engraved-patterned vessel (5000 B.C.). 80ch, Wit and beauty jar (3rd-4th Centuries). 1w, Lotus decoration celadon kettle (10th-14th Centuries). 2.50w, White china pot with blue flower (15th Century).

1999, July 15 ***Perf. 13¼***
3893-3897 A1753 Set of 5 5.00 2.50

Fish Breeding — A1754

Designs: 50ch, Silver carp. 1w, Common carp. 1.50w, Spotted silver carp.

1999, July 20
3898-3900 A1754 Set of 3 2.40 1.20

Year of Nat'l Independence and Great Solidarity — A1755

1999, Aug. 5
3901 A1755 40ch multicolored .35 .20

Repatriation of Korean Nationals in Japan, 40th Anniv. — A1756

1999, Aug. 16 ***Perf. 11½***
3902 A1756 1.50w multicolored 1.25 .60

Year For a Turning Point in Building a Powerful Nation — A1757

1999, Aug. 17
3903 A1757 40ch multicolored .35 .20

7th World Athletic Championships, Seville — A1758

Designs: 30ch, 100-Meter Race. 40ch, Hurdles. 80ch, Discus.

1999, Aug. 18
3904-3906 A1758 Set of 3 1.20 .60

Gift Plants — A1759

Designs, all 40ch: #3907, *Acalypha hispida Burm. f.* #3908, *Allamanda neriifolia Hook.* #3909, *Begonia x hiemalis Fotsch.* #3910, *Fatsia japonica Decne.* #3911, *Streptocarpus hydrida hort.* #3912, *Streptocarpus rexii Lindl.*
Illustration reduced.

1999, Aug. 20
3907-3912 A1759 Sheetlet of 6 2.00 1.00

22nd UPU Congress & China '99 World Philatelic Exhib. — A1760

Paintings by Qiu Ying, each 40ch: #3913, *Play a Flute to Call Phoenix.* #3914, *Six Friends in a Pine Forest.* #3915, *Relics Kept in the Bamboo Field.* #3916, *Ladies Morning Dressing.*
Illustration reduced.

1999, Aug. 21
3913-3916 A1760 Sheetlet of 4 1.50 .75

Mushrooms — A1761

Designs: 40ch, *Grifola frondosa.* 60ch *Lactarius volemus.* 1w, *Cariolus versicolor.*

1999, Aug. 25
3917-3919 A1761 Set of 3 2.00 1.00

Cacti — A1762

Designs: 40ch, *Aporocactus flagelliformis.* 60ch *Astrophytum ornatum.* 1w, *Gymnocalycium michanorichii.*

1999, Sept. 1
3920-3922 A1762 Set of 3 1.25 .60

Animals of the Zodiac — A1763

Designs, each 10ch: #3923, Rat. #3924, Ox. #3925, Tiger. #3926, Rabbit. #3927, Dragon. #3928, Snake. #3929, Horse. #3930, Sheep. #3931, Monkey. #3932, Rooster. #3933, Dog. #3934, Pig.
Illustration reduced.

1999, Sept. 10 ***Perf. 12½***
3923-3934 A1763 2 Sheetlets of 6 2.00 1.00

Crustacea — A1764

Designs: 50ch, Shrimp (*Pendalus hypsinotus*). 70ch, Shrimp (*Penaeus orientalis*). 1w, Lobster (*Homarus vulgarus*).

1999, Sept. 10 ***Perf. 11½***
3935-3937 A1764 Set of 3 2.00 1.00

Jong Song Ok, Marathon Runner — A1765

A1766

1999, Sept. 20
3938 A1765 40ch multicolored .35 .20

Souvenir Sheet

3939 A1766 2w multicolored 1.60 .80

Victory of Jong Song Ok, Women's Marathon winner at 7th IAAF World Championships, Seville.
No. 3939 illustration reduced.

DPRK-China Diplomatic Relations, 50th Anniv. — A1767

Designs: 40ch, Mt. Kumgang, Korea. 60ch, Mt. Lushan, China.

1999, Oct. 5 ***Perf. 12¼x11¼***
3940-3941 A1767 Set of 2 1.00 .50
3941a Sheetlet of 4, #3940-3941 + 2 labels 3.00 1.50

Nos. 3940-3941 were printed both in sheetlets of 6, containg three horizontal se-tenant pairs of the two stamps, and in sheetlets of 4, containing a vertical se-tenant pair and two labels.

Return of Macao to China

A1768

A1769

Type A1769, 1w, Pres. Jiang Zemin of China: #3942, Jiang's portrait with gold frame. #3943, Jiang's portrait with green frame.

Type A1769: 20ch (a), Deng Xiaoping sharing toast with Portuguese Prime Minister. 20ch (b), Jiang Zemin shaking hands with He Houhua, newly-appointed mayor of Macao special administrative region. 80ch (c), Mao Zedong at National Day Celebration, Tiananmen Square, 1951. #3944a-c, gold background. #3945a-c, green background.

1999, Nov. 10 ***Perf. 13¼***

3942-3943 A1768 Set of 2 sheetlets 2.00 1.00
3944-3945 A1769 Set of 2 sheetlets 2.50 1.25

New Year — April 19 Uprising, 40th Anniv. — A1770

2000, Jan. 1 ***Perf. 11½***

3946 A1770 10ch multicolored .20 .20

Koguryo Era (2nd Century B.C.-7th Century A.D.)

Yellow Dragon — A1771

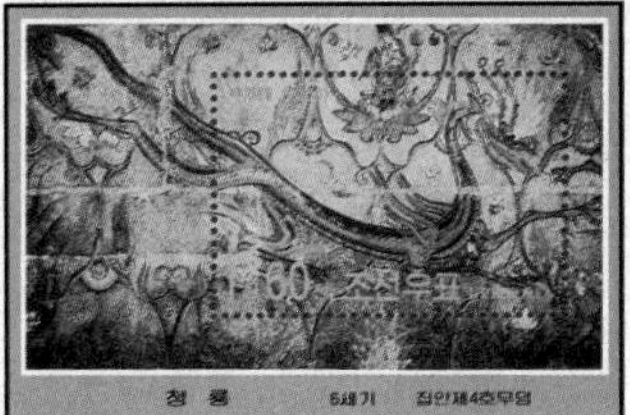

Blue Dragon — A1772

No. 3946, illustration reduced.

2000, Jan. 1

3947 A1771 70ch multicolored .60 .30

Souvenir Sheet

Perf. 11½x11¾

3948 A1772 1.60w multicolored 1.40 .70

Painting, *Rural Life* (18th Century) — A1773

Designs, each 40ch: #3949, Peasants weeding. #3950, Weaving hemp cloth. #3951, Peasants threshing grain. #3952, Riverside market.

Illustration reduced.

2000, Jan. 25 ***Perf. 13¼***

3949-3952 A1773 Sheetlet of 4 1.40 .70

Mt. Paekdu Rock Formations — A1774

Designs, each 20ch: #3953, Dinosaur-shaped rock. #3954, Eagle-shaped rock. #3955, Owl-shaped rock.

2000, Jan. 30

3953-3955 A1774 Set of 3 .60 .30

Pongsan Mask Dance — A1775

Folk dances: 50ch, Chuibari mask dance. 80ch, Ryangban mask dance. 1w, Malttugi mask dance.

Illustration reduced.

2000, Feb. 3 ***Perf. 11½***

3956-3958 A1775 Sheetlet of 3 2.00 1.00

Cats — A1776

Designs, each 50ch: #3959, Cat on window-sill. #3960, Kittens playing. #3961, Mother cat and kittens in basket.

2000, Feb. 3 ***Perf. 13¼***

3959-3961 A1776 Set of 3 1.50 .75

Fauna — A1777

Sheetlets of 4. All values 2w:

No. 3965a, Cats: #3962, Singapura. #3963, Blue Abyssinian. #3964, Oriental. #3965, Scottish fold tabby.

No. 3969a, Dogs: #3966, Shiba inu. #3967, Yorkshire terrier. #3968, Japanese chin. #3969, Afghan hound.

No. 3973a, Horses: #3970, Przewalski's horse. #3971, Gray cob. #3972, White horse. #3973, Donkeys.

No. 3977a, Pandas: #3974, In tree. #3975, Eating. #3976, Leaning against tree. #3977, Mother and cub.

No. 3981a, Bears: #3978, Two polar bears. #3979, Mother and cub. #3980, Bear standing. #3981, Bear reclining.

No. 3985a, Snakes: #3982, Mexican lance-headed rattlesnake (*Crotalus polystictus*). #3983, Scarlet king snake (*Lampropeltis triangulum elapsoides*). #3984, Green tree python (*Chondropython viridis*). #3985, Blood python (*Python curtus*).

No. 3989a, Dinosaurs: #3986, Corythosaurus. #3987, Psittacosaurus. #3988, Megalosaurus. #3989, Muttaburrasaurus.

No. 3993a, Marine Mammals: #3990, Burmeister's porpoise (*Phocoena spinipinnis*). #3991, Finless porpoise (*Neophocaena phocaenoides*). #3992, Bottle-nosed dolphin (*Tursiops truncatus*). #3993, Curvier's beaked whale (*Ziphius cavirostris*.

No. 3997a, Sharks: #3994, Port Jackson shark (*Heterodontus portusjacksoni*). #3995, Great hammerhead shark (*Sphyrna mokarran*). #3996, Zebra shark (*Stegostoma fasciatum*). #3997, Ornate Wobbegong carpet shark (*Orectolobus cavirostris*).

No. 4001a, Ducks: #3998, Ruddy shelduck (*Tadorna ferruginea*). #3999, European widgeon (*Anas penelope*). #4000, Mandarin drake (*Aix galericulata*). #4001, Hottentot teal (*Anas hottentota*).

No. 4005a, Owls: #4002, Little owl (*Athene noctua*). #4003, Ural owl (*Strix uralensis*). #4004, Great horned owl (*Bubo virginianus*). #4005, Snowy owl (*Nyctea scandiaca*).

No. 4009a, Parrots: #4006, Slaty-headed parakeet (*Psittacula himalayana*). #4007, Male eclectus parrot (*Eclectus roratus*). #4008, Major Mitchell's cockatoo (*Cacatua leadbeateri*). #4009, Female eclectus parrot (*Eclectus roratus*).

No. 4013a, Butterflies: #4010, Indian leaf butterfly (*Kallima paralekta*). #4011, Spanish festoon (*Zerynthia rumina*). #4012, Male and female emerald swallowtails (*Papillo palinurus*). #4013, *Bhutanitis lidderdalii*.

No. 4017a, Bees: #4014, Bumble bee. #4015, Bumble bee on flower. #4016, Honey bee (*Apis mellifera*). #4017, Honey bee fighting spider.

No. 4021a, Spiders: #4018, *Micrommata virescens*. #4019, *Araneus quadratus*. #4020, *Dolomedes fimbriatus*. #4021, *Aculepeira ceropegia*.

Illustration reduced.

2000, Feb. 10

3962-4021 A1777 Set of 15 sheetlets 150.00 150.00

58th Birthday of Kim Jong Il — A1778

Design: Birthplace, Mt. Paekdu.

2000, Feb. 16 ***Perf. 11½***

4022 A1778 40ch multicolored .35 .20

Dinosaurs — A1779

Design, each 1w: #4023, Triceratops. #4024, Saltasaurus. #4025, Tyrannosaurus.

Illustration reduced.

2000, Mar. 5 ***Perf. 13¼***

4023-4025 A1779 Sheetlet of 3 3.00 1.50

For overprint, see No. 4080.

Monkeys

A1780

A1781

Design, each 50ch: #4026, Western tarsier (*Tarsius spectrum*). #4027, Patas monkey (*Erythrocebus patas*).

2w, Mona monkey (*Cercopithecus mona*). Illustration reduced.

2000, Mar. 25 ***Perf. 11½***

4026-4027 A1780 Set of 2 .90 .45
4027a Sheetlet of 4, 2 each #4026-4027 2.00 1.00

Souvenir Sheet

4028 A1781 2w multicolored 1.60 .80

Nos. 4026-4027 were issued both separately in panes of 10 and together in sheetlets of 4.

Butterflies — A1782

Designs: 40ch Peacock (*Inachus io*). 60ch, Swallowtail (*Papilio machaon*). 80ch, Mimic (*Hypolimnas misippus Linnaeus*). 1.20w, (*Papilio bianor cramer*).
Illustration reduced.

2000, Mar. 25
4029-4032 A1782 Sheetlet of 4 3.00 1.50

Grand Chollima March — A1783

2000, Mar. 28
4033 A1783 10ch multicolored .20 .20

55th anniversary of the Korean Workers' Party.

April 19 Popular Uprising, 40th Anniv. — A1784

2000, April 1
4034 A1784 10ch multicolored .20 .20

Sun's Day — A1785

2000, April 15
4035 A1785 40ch multicolored .35 .20

88th anniversary of birth of Kim Il Sung.

Mun Ik Hwan — A1786

2000, April 25 ***Perf. 13¼***
4036 A1786 50ch multicolored .50 .25

Issued in honor of Mun Ik Hwan (1918-94), South Korean political activist, winner of 1990 National Reunification Prize.

Millennium, 55th Anniv. Korean Workers' Party — A1787

Designs: 40ch, Chollima statue, flag, symbols of national power. 1.20w, Dove with letter, map, "2000."

2000, May 5
4037-4038 A1787 Set of 2 1.50 .75

Orchids

A1788

A1789

Designs: 20ch, *Cattleya intermedia*. 50ch, *Dendrobium moschatum*. 70ch, *Brassolaeliocattleya*.
2w, *Laeliocattleya*. Illustration reduced.

2000, May 15
4039-4041 A1788 Set of 3 1.40 .70

Souvenir Sheet

4042 A1789 2w multicolored 1.75 .90

Bridges — A1790

Designs: 20ch, Okryn Bridge. 30ch, Ansan Bridge. 1w, Rungna Bridge.

2000, May 21
4043-4045 A1790 Set of 3 2.00 1.00

WIPA 2000 Int'l Stamp Exhib., Vienna — A1791

Traditional Korean musical instruments and folk dances: 1w, Okryugum and Jaenggang dance. 1.50w (#4047), Bungum and Full Moon Viewing dance. 1.50w (#4048), Janggo drum and "Trio" dance.
Illustration reduced.

2000, May 30
4046-4048 A1791 Sheet of 3 3.50 1.75

Nos. 4047-4048 are airmail stamps.

Children's Songs — A1792

Designs: 40ch, Song "Halfmoon," two children in boat. 60ch, Song "Kangram Nostalgia," boy and girl.
1.50w, Song "Spring in Home Village," boy and girl with flowers.

2000, June 1 ***Perf. 11¾x12¼***
4049-4050 A1792 Set of 2 .90 .45

Souvenir Sheet

4051 A1792 1.50w multicolored 1.50 .75

Cephalopods — A1793

Designs: 40ch, Chambered nautilus (*Nautilus pompilius*). 60ch, Octopus (*Octopus vularis*).
1.50w, Squid (*Ommastrephes sloanei pacificus*).

2000, June 15 ***Perf. 11½***
4052-4053 A1793 Set of 2 1.00 .50

Souvenir Sheet

4054 A1793 1.50w multicolored 1.50 .75

Mandarin Ducks — A1794

Designs, each 50ch: #4055, Pair of ducks, couple on bridge. #4056, Pair of ducks, couple in row boat.
1w, Pair of ducks, ducklings.

2000, June 16 ***Perf. 11¾x12¼***
4055-4056 A1794 Set of 2 .90 .45
4056a Sheetlet of 7, 3 #4055 & 4 #4056 3.25 1.60

Souvenir Sheet

4057 A1794 1w multicolored .90 .45

Nos. 4055-4056 were issued both in separate sheets of 9 (3x3) and in sheetlets of 7, containing 3 #4055 and 4 #4056, in an alternating arrangement.
For overprints, see Nos. 4071-4073.

Sports — A1795

Designs: 80ch, Table tennis. 1w (#4059), Basketball. 1.20w (#4060), Baseball.

2000, July 7 ***Perf. 13¼***
4058-4060 A1795 Set of 3 3.00 1.50

Trucks — A1796

Designs: 40ch, *Sungri-61 NA*. 70ch, Flatbed truck. 1.50w, *Konsol* 25-50n dump truck.

2000, July 24 ***Perf. 12***
4061-4063 A1796 Set of 3 2.50 1.25

Korean People's Army — A1797

Portraits of KPA commanders and weapons: 60ch, Ri Tae Hun and 76mm field gun, 80ch, Ko hyon Bink and T-34 tank. 1w, Paek Ki Rah and Yak-9P pursuit plane.

2000, July 27
4064-4066 A1797 Set of 3 2.00 1.00

Minerals — A1798

Designs: 30ch, Fluorite. 60ch, Graphite. 1.60w, Magnesite.

2000, Aug. 15 ***Perf. 13¼***
4067-4069 A1798 Set of 3 1.00 .50

Souvenir Sheet

4070 A1798 1.60w multicolored 1.40 .70

Nos. 4067-4069 were printed together in a pane of 8, comprised of 3 #4067, 3 #4068, and 2 #4070. The 1.60w was also printed separately within a sheetlet of one (#4070).

Nos. 4055-4057 Overprinted

2000, Aug. 15 ***Perf. 13¼***
4071-4072 Set of 2 .90 .45

Souvenir Sheet

4073 1w multicolored .90 .45

International Stamp Exhibition, Jakarta.

Sydney 2000, Summer Olympic Games — A1799

Designs: 80ch, Swimmer. 1.20, Cyclist. 2w, Runner.

Illustration reduced.

2000, Sept. 15 *Perf. 13½*
4074-4076 A1799 Sheet of 3 3.75 2.00

Myohyang Mountain — A1800

Designs: 40ch (#4077), Sanju Falls, wild pig and piglet. 40ch (#4078), Inho Rock, Fallow deer, pair. 1.20w, stag and fawn.

2000, Sept. 27 *Perf. 13¼*
4077-4079 A1800 Set of 3 1.75 .90

Nos. 4023-4025 Sheet Overprinted "Exposicion Mundial de Filatelia 2000.06-14" in Margin

Illustration reduced.

2000, Oct. 6
4080 Sheet of 3 3.00 1.50

Espana 2000 International Stamp Exhibition, Madrid.

Korean Workers' Party, 55th Anniv. (Second Issue)

A1801

A1802

40ch, Party emblem and Party Museum.
No. 4082, each 50ch: a, Kim Il Sung. b, Kim Jong Il. c, Kim Jong Suk. Illustration reduced.

2000, Oct. 10 *Perf. 13¼*
4081 A1801 40ch multicolored .20 .20

Souvenir Sheet

4082 A1802 Sheet of 3, #a-c 1.25 .60

Land Rezoning Project — A1803

10ch, Flags, bulldozer and trucks, urban scene and rice fields.

2000, Oct. 15
4083 A1803 10ch multicolored .20 .20

Taehongdan Potato Farms

A1804

A1805

40ch, Potatoes, pigs, scientist, collective farm.
2w, painting, *The Great Leader President Kim Il Sung Brought a Bumper Crop of Potato in the Paektu Pleateau.*

2000, Oct. 20 *Perf. 11½*
4084 A1804 40ch multicolored .35 .20

Souvenir Sheet

4085 A1805 2w multicolored 1.60 .80

Kim Jong Il & Pres. Jiang Zemin — A1806

Illustration reduced.

2000, Oct. 21 *Perf. 11¾x12¼*
4086 A1806 1.20w multicolored 1.50 .75

Visit of Kim Jong Il to China.

Kim Jong Il & Pres. Kim Dae Jung — A1807

Illustration reduced.

2000, Oct. 23 *Perf. 11½x12*
4087 A1807 2w multicolored 2.50 1.25

North-South Korean Summit Talks, Pyongyang.

Kim Jong Il & Pres. Putin — A1808

Illustration reduced.

2000, Oct. 24 *Perf. 11¾x11½*
4088 A1808 1.50w multicolored 2.00 1.00

Visit of Kim Jong Il to Russia.

50th Anniv. of Chinese People's Volunteers' Entry Into Korean War

Chinese & Korean Soldiers — A1809

2000, Oct. 25 *Perf. 13¼*
4089 A1809 30ch multicolored .55 .30

A1810

Sheet of 5: 10ch (#4090), Soldiers crossing the Amnok River. 10ch (#4091), Battle scene. 50ch (#4092), Kim Il Sung and Chinese officers. 50ch (#4093), Mao Zedong presiding over meeting to decide upon entry into Korean War. 80ch, Chinese soldiers observing battle.

4090-4094 A1810 Sheet of 5 2.00 1.00

Alpine Flowers — A1811

Designs: 30ch, *Aquilegia oxysepala*. 50ch, Brilliant campion (*Lychnis fulgens*). 70ch, Self-heal (*Prunela vulgaris*).

2000, Nov. 5 *Perf. 13½*
4095-4097 A1811 Set of 3 1.25 .60

Nos. 4095-4097 were printed in sheets containing a decorative label.

Repatriation of Long-Term Prisoners of War

A1812

A1813

Designs: 80ch, Returning prisoners receiving bouquets of flowers from women in Pyongyang. 1.20w, Prisoners welcomed by crowd, in front of statue of Kim Il Sung.
Illustrations reduced.

2000, Dec. 20
4098-4099 Set of 2 sheets 2.00 1.00

New Year — A1814

10ch, Flag, trees, factory, missiles, ship, jet planes.

2001, Jan. 1 *Perf. 11½*
4100 A1814 10ch multicolored .20 .20

New Year (2nd Issue) — A1815

Tale of the White Snake: 10ch, White Snake meeting Xu Xian. 40ch, Stealing the Immortal Greass. 50ch, White and Green Snakes and Xu Xian. 80ch, Flooding of Jinshan Hill.
1.20w, White Snake and Green Snake.

2001, Jan. 1 ***Perf. 12½x12***
4101-4104 A1815 Set of 4 3.25 1.60
4104a Sheet of 4, #4101-4104 3.25 1.60

Souvenir Sheet

4105 A1815 1.20w multicolored 2.25 1.00

Nos. 4101-4104 were each issued singly in larger sheets and in combination in sheets of 4 (#4104a).

World Chess Champions

A1816

A1817

Designs: 10ch, E. Lasker (1868-1941) and J.R. Capablanca (1888-1942). 20ch, A. Alekhine (1892-1946) and E. Euwe (1901-80). 30ch, M. Botvinnik (1911-95) and V. Smylov (b. 1921). 40ch, T. Petrosian (1929-84) and M. Tal (1936-93). 50ch, B. Spassky (b. 1937) and R. Fisher (b. 1943). 1w, A. Karpov (b. 1954) and G. Kasparov (b. 1963).
2.50w, Wilhelm Steinmetz (1836-1900). Illustration reduced.

2001, Jan. 5 ***Perf. 13½***
4106-4111 A1816 Set of 6 4.50 2.25
4111a Sheet of 6, #4106-4111 4.50 2.25
4111b Booklet pane of 6, #4116-4111 4.50 —
Complete booklet, #4111a 5.00 —

Souvenir Sheet

4112 A1817 2.50w multicolored 4.50 2.25

No. 4111b contains Nos. 4106-4111 in a se-tenant vertical strip of six, with narrow decorative selvage.
For overprints, see Nos. 4129-4135.

Ri-Dynasty Men's Costumes — A1818

Designs: 10ch, Trousers and jacket. 40ch, Vest. 50ch, Magoja. 70ch, Turumagi
1.50w, Wedding attire.

2001, Jan. 19 ***Perf. 12x12½***
4113-4116 A1818 Set of 4 3.00 1.50
4116a Sheet of 5, #4113-4116, 4117a 6.00 3.00
4116b Booklet pane of 6, #4113-4114, 4116, 4117a, 2 #4115 6.75 —
Complete booklet, #4116b 7.00

Souvenir Sheet

4117 A1818 1.50w multicolored 3.00 1.50
a. 1.50w single stamp 3.00 1.50

Nos. 4113-4116 were each issued both in large sheets and within sheets of 5, in combination with the 1.50w (#4117a) value contained in the souvenir sheet, No. 4117.
No. 4116b contains the six stamps in a se-tenant horizontal strip with narrow distinctive selvage.

Fire Engines — A1819

Fire-fighting vehicles and logos warning against specific fire hazards: 20ch, Small 2-door vehicle (small appliances). 30ch, Large ladder truck (oil can). 40ch, 2-door truck with closed back (match). 60ch, Small truck with ladder and external hose port (gas can).
2w, Old-fashioned fire truck with ladder (cigarette).

2001, Jan. 20 ***Perf. 12½x12***
4118-4121 A1819 Set of 4 3.00 1.50
4121a Booklet pane of 12, 3 ea. #4118-4121 9.00 —
Complete booklet, #4121a 9.00
4121b Sheet of 5, #4118-4121, type of #4122 + label 9.00

Souvenir Sheet

4122 A1819 2w multicolored 4.00 2.00

No. 4121a contains three attached se-tenant blocks of Nos. 4118-4121, arranged horizontally, with inscribed selvage on left and right sides.

Hong Kong 2001 Stamp Exhibition — A1820

1.40w, Black-naped oriole (*Oriolus chinensis*). Illustration reduced.

2001, Feb. 1 ***Perf. 11½***
4123 A1820 1.40w multicolored 2.50 1.25

Kim Jong Il, 59th Birthday — A1821

10ch, Jong Il Peak in Paekdu Range, *Kimjongilia.*

2001, Feb. 10 ***Perf. 13½***
4124 A1821 10ch multicolored .30 .20

New Millenium, Joint Editorial *Rodong Sinmun, Josoninmingun* and *Chongnyonjonwi* Newspapers — A1822

10ch, Flag, symbols of Industry, Agriculture, Transportation

2001, Mar. 5
4125 A1822 10ch multicolored .30 .20

Log Cabin at Revolutionary Headquarters on Mt. Paekdu — A1823

2001, Mar. 7 ***Perf. 11½***
4126 A1823 40ch multicolored .60 .30

Kim Il Sung's Birthplace at Mangyongdae — A1824

Portraits of Kim Il Sung — A1825

No. 1428 (each 80ch): a, As child. b, As Jilin-Yuwen Middle School student. c, As anti-Japanese revolutionary. d, As leader in early DPRK period. e, As supreme commander of the Korean People's Army. f, As leader during post-Korean War period. g, Portrait in middle age. h, Portrait in old age. Illustration reduced.

2001, Apr. 10 ***Perf. 13½***
4127 A1824 10ch multicolored .40 .20

Sheet of 8

4128 A1825 Sheet of 8, #a.-#g 10.00 5.00

Day of the Sun.

Nos. 4106-4112 Overprinted in Gold with Biographical Information

2001, Apr. 20
4129-4134 A1816 Set of 6 5.00 2.50

Souvenir Sheet

4135 A1817 2.50w multicolored 5.00 2.50

Kim Jong Il — A1826

Illustration reduced.

2001, Apr. 25 ***Perf. 12***
4136 A1826 1w multicolored 1.50 .75

Propaganda issue, with the theme "Long Live the Great Victory of Songun Politics!"

Highways — A1827

Designs: 40ch, Pyongyang-Kaesong motorway. 70ch, Pyongyang-Hyangsan tourist expressway. 1.20w, Youth Hero motorway. 1.50w, Pyongyang-Wonsan tourist expressway.

2001, May 7 ***Perf. 12½x12***
4137-4140 A1827 Set of 4 5.50 2.75

Historical Pavilions — A1828

Designs: 40ch, Ryongwang Pavilion in Pyongyang. 80ch, Inphung Pavilion in Kanggye. 1.50w, Paeksang Pavilion in Anju. 2w, Thonggun Pavilion in Uiju.

2001, May 15 ***Perf. 13¼***
4141-4144 A1828 Set of 4 7.00 3.50
4144a Booklet pane of 4, #4141-4144 7.00 —
Complete booklet, #4144a 7.50

No. 4144a contains Nos. 4141-4144 in a se-tenant block of four, within decorative selvage.

Education in Class Consciousness — A1829

2001, June 5
4145 A1829 10ch multicolored .30 .20

Korean Birds — A1830

Designs: 10ch, *Luscinia svecica.* 40ch, *Anser anser.* 80ch, *Diomedea albatrus.* 1w,

Charadrius dubius. 1.20w, *Uria aalge.* 1.50w, *Delichon urbica.*
Illustration reduced.

2001, June 9 ***Perf. 11½***
4146 A1830 Sheet of 6, #a.-f. 9.00 4.50
g. Booklet pane of 8, #4146c-4146f, 2 ea. #4146a-4146b 10.00 —
Complete booklet, #4146g 10.50

BELGICA 2001 Philatelic Exhibition.
No. 4146g contains the eight stamps in a se-tenant horizontal (4x2) block with inscribed selvage on left and right sides.

Chinese Communist Party, 80th Anniv. — A1831

Designs, each 80ch: No. 4147, Mao Zedong. No. 4148, Deng Xiaoping. No. 4149, Jiang Zemin.
Illustration reduced.

2001, June 15
4147-4149 A1831 Set of 3 3.75 1.75

Compare with Nos. 4226-4228.

Mt. Kumol — A1832

Designs: 10ch, Woljong Temple. 40ch, Revolutionary site. 70ch, Potnamu Pavilion. 1.30w, Rock of Tak Peak. 1.50w, Ryongyon Falls.
Illustration reduced.

2001, July 9 ***Perf. 12x12¼***
4150 A1832 Sheet, #a.-e. + label 6.00 3.00
f. Booklet pane of 5, #4150a-4150e + label 6.00 —
Complete booklet, #4150f 6.50

No. 4150f contains the stamps and labels of No. 4150 in the same format, but top and bottom marginal selvage is blank, with side selvage containing maple leaf on left and inscriptions on left and right.

Protected Plants — A1833

Designs: 10ch, *Rheum Coreanum.* 40ch, *Forsythia densiflora.* 1w, *Rhododendron yedoense.* 2w, *Iris setosa.*

2001, July 20 ***Perf. 13½***
4151-4154 A1833 Set of 4 5.50 2.75
4154a Booklet pane of 6, #4152, 4154, 2 ea. #4151, 4153 7.00 —
Complete booklet, #4154a 7.50

No. 4154a contains the six stamps in a se-tenant vertical strip of 6, with inscribed selvage on top and bottom margins.

Orchids — A1834

Designs: 10ch, *Eria pannea.* 40ch, *Cymbidium.* 90ch, *Sophrolaeliocattleya.* 1.60w, *Cattleya trianae.*
No. 4155: 2w, *Cypripedium macranthum.*
Illustration reduced.

2001, Aug. 1
4155-58 A1834 Set of 4 6.00 3.00
4158a Booklet pane of 6, #4155-4156, 4158, #4159a, 2 #4157 11.00 —
Complete booklet, #4158a 11.50

Souvenir Sheet

4159 A1834 2w multicolored 4.00 2.00
a. 2w single stamp 4.00 2.00

No. 4158a contains the six stamps in a se-tenant horizontal strip of 6, with decorative selvage on left and right sides.

Lighthouses — A1835

Designs: 40ch, Pibaldo Lighthouse. 70ch, Soho Lighthouse. 90ch, Komalsan Lighthouse.
No. 4159: 1.50w, Alsom Lighthouse.

2001, Aug. 18
4160-4162 A1835 Set of 3 4.00 2.00
4162a Booklet pane of 6, #4160-4161, 2 #4162, 2 #4163a 12.50 —
Complete booklet, #4162a 13.00
4162b Sheet of 4, #4160-4162, 4163a 7.00 3.50

Souvenir Sheet

4163 A1835 1.50w multicolored 3.00 1.50
a. 1.50w single stamp 3.00 1.50

Nos. 4160-4162 were issued both separately in large sheets and together, with the 1.50w value from No. 4163, in a sheet of 5 (#4162b). No. 4162a contains the six stamps in a horizontal strip of 6, with thin plain selvage.

Kim Po Hyon (1871-1955), Grandfather of Kim Il Sung — A1836

2001, Aug. 19
4164 A1836 1w multicolored 1.50 .75

Protected Animals — A1837

Designs: 10ch, Black stork (*Ciconia nigra*). 40ch, Cinereous vulture (*Aegypius monachus*). 70ch, Chinese water deer (*Hydropotes inermis*). 90ch, Goral (*Nemorhaedus goral*).
No. 4165: 1.30w, Northern eagle owl (*Bubo bubo*).

2001, Sept. 2
4165-4168 A1837 Set of 4 4.00 2.00
4168a Sheet of 5, #4165-4168, 4169a 6.50 —
4168b Booklet pane of 6, #4165-1467, 1469a, 2 x 1468 7.50 —
Complete booklet, #4168b 8.00

Souvenir Sheet

4169 A1837 1.30w multicolored 2.50 1.25
a. 1.30w single stamp 2.50 1.25

Nos. 4165-4168 were issued both separately in large sheets and together, with the 1.30w value from No. #4169, in a sheet of 5 (#4168a).
No. 4168b contains the six stamps in a se-tenant vertical strip, within narrow decorated selvage.

Olympic Games 2008, Beijing — A1838

Designs, each 56ch: a, Deng Ya Ping, Gold medalist ('96), Women's Singles, Table Tennis. b, Jiang Zemin, PRC president. c, Wang Jun Xia, Chinese athlete. d, Li Ning, Chinese gymnast. e, Fu Ming Xia, Chinese diver.
Illustration reduced.

2001, Sept. 10 ***Perf. 12½***
4170 A1838 Sheet of 5, #a.-e. 5.00 2.50

Cycle Sports — A1839

Designs: 10ch, Cycle soccer. 40ch, Road racing. 1.50w, Mountainbike racing. 2w, Indoor race.
Illustration reduced.

2001, Sept. 20 ***Perf. 12***
4171 A1839 Sheet of 4, #a.-d. 7.00 3.50

Space Exploration — A1840

Designs: 10ch, Yuri Gagarin (1934-68), Soviet Cosmonaut. 40ch, Apollo 11 Moon Landing. 1.50w, *Kwangmyongsong,* North Korean satellite (1998). 2w, Edmund Hailey (1656-1742), Halley's Comet and *Giotto* satellite.
Illustration reduced.

2001, Sept. 25
4172 A1840 Sheet of 4, #a.-d. 6.50 3.25
e. Booklet pane of 5, #4172a-4172c, 2 #1472d 10.00 —
Complete booklet, #4172e 11.00

No. 4172e contains five stamps in a se-tenant horizontal strip.

Vladimir Putin and Kim Jong Il — A1841

Illustration reduced.

2001, Oct. 12 ***Perf. 12½x12***

4173 A1841 1.50w multicolored 2.25 1.10

Visit of Kim Jong Il to Russia.

Kim Jong Il and Jiang Zemin — A1842

Illustration reduced.

2001, Oct. 25 ***Perf. 11½x12***

4174 A1842 1.50w multicolored 2.25 1.10

Meeting between Kim Jong Il and Jiang Zemin, president of the People's Republic of China.

Kim Jong Suk in Battle — A1843

Illustration reduced.

2001, Nov. 24 ***Perf. 12½x12***

4175 A1843 1.60w multicolored 3.00 1.50

84th anniv. of birth of Kim Jong Suk, anti-Japanese revolutionary hero.

Kim Jong Il Inspecting Troops — A1844

Illustration reduced.

2001, Dec. 1 ***Perf. 13½***

4176 A1844 1w multicolored 1.50 .75

10th anniv. of appointment of Kim Jong Il as Supreme Commander of the Korean People's Army.

Chollima Statue — A1845

2002, Jan. 1

4177 A1845 10ch multicolored .30 .20

New Year.

A1846

A1847

Horses from painting *Ten Horses*, by Wang Zhi Cheng (1702-68): 10ch, White horse. 40ch, Bay. 60ch, Pinto. 1.30w, Piebald.

1.60w, Black stallion, from painting *Horse Master Jiu Fang Gao*, by Xu Bei Hong (1895-1953). Illustration reduced.

2002, Jan. 1

4178-4181 A1846 Set of 4 3.75 1.75

4181a Sheet of 5, #4178-4181, 4182a 6.25 3.00

Souvenir Sheet

4182 A1847 1.60w multicolored 2.50 1.25

a. 1.60w single stamp 2.50 1.25

Traditional New Year — Year of the Horse.

Nos. 4178-4181 were issued both separately in large sheets and together, with the 1.60w value from No. 4182, in a sheet of 5 (#4181a).

Flower Basket — A1848

Kim Jong Il with Soldiers — A1849

Kim Jong Il — A1850

Kim Il Sung, Kim Jong Il, Kim Jong Suk — A1851

Nos. 4184-4186 illustrations reduced.

2002, Feb. 1

4183 A1848 10ch multicolored .30 .20

Souvenir Sheets

4184 A1849 1.50w multicolored 2.50 1.25

4185 A1850 2w multicolored 3.00 1.50

4186 A1851 Sheet of 3, #a.-c. 6.00 3.00

60th Birthday of Kim Jong Il.

Nos 4183 and 4184 gauge perf 13½, No. 4185 perf 11½x12, and No. 4186 perf 12x12½. No. 4185 bears a golden metallic application.

Centenary of First Zeppelin Flight — A1852

Designs: 40ch, LZ-1. 80ch, LZ-120. 1.20w, Zeppelin NT.

2.40w, Zeppelin NT (different view).

2002, Feb. 5 ***Perf. 12***

4187-4189 A1852 Set of 3 3.75 1.75

4189a Sheet of 4, #4187-4189, 4190a 7.50 3.75

Souvenir Sheet

4190 A1852 2.40w multicolored 3.75 1.75

a. 2.40w single stamp 3.75 1.75

Nos. 4187-4187 were issued both separately in large sheets and together, with the 2.40w value from No. 4190, in a sheet of 4 (#4189a).

Banner, Torch, Soldiers — A1853

2002, Feb. 25 ***Perf. 13½***

4191 A1853 10ch multicolored .30 .20

Annual joint editorial of the three state newspapers, *Rodong Sinmun, Josoninmingum* and *Chongnyonjonwi*

Mushrooms — A1854

Designs: 10ch, *Collybia confluons.* 40ch, *Sparassis laminosa.* 80ch, *Amanita vaginata.* 1.20w, *Russia integra.* 1.50w, *Pholiota squarrosa.*

Illustration reduced.

2002, Feb. 25 ***Perf. 13½***

4192-4196 A1854 Set of 5 6.50 3.25

A1855

A1856

A1857

Designs: 10ch, Kim Il Sung's birthplace, *Kimsungilia.*

Nos. 4198-4200 (each 1.50w): No, 4198, Kim Il Sung with Kim Jong Suk (1941). No. 4199, Kim Il Sung as student, with black cap (1927). No. 4200, Kim Il Sung and Kim Chaek, political commissar. Illustration reduced.

No. 4201: 2w, Portrait of Kim Il Sung. Illustration reduced.

2002, Mar. 15 ***Perf. 13½***

4197 A1855 10ch multicolored .30 .20

Souvenir Sheets

4198-4200 A1856 1.50w Set of 3 6.00 3.00

With Gold Metallic Application

Perf. 11½x12

4201 A1857 2w multicolored 3.00 1.50

90th anniversary of birth of Kim Il Sung (1912-94).

Kang Pan Suk — A1858

Illustration reduced.

2002, Mar. 21 ***Perf. 11½x11¾***

4202 A1858 1w multicolored 1.50 .75

110th anniversary of birth of Kang Pan Sok, mother of Kim Il Sung.

20th April Spring Friendship Art Festival — A1859

2002, Mar. 25 ***Perf. 13¼***

4203 A1859 10ch multicolored .50 .25

Locomotives — A1860

Designs: 10ch, *Kanghaenggun 1.5-01* electric train. 40ch, *Samjiyon 1001* electric train. 1.50w, Steam locomotive. 2w, Steam locomotive (diff.).

No. 4208, 2w, *Pulgungi 5112* diesel locomotive.

2002, Apr. 10 ***Perf. 11½***

4204-4207 A1860 Set of 4 6.00 3.00

Souvenir Sheet

4208 A1860 2w multicolored 3.00 1.50

He Baozhen, 100th Anniv. Birth — A1861

Designs: a, 1w, He Baozhen and Liu Shaoqi in 1923. b, 40ch, He Baozhen's family. c, 30ch, Family home in Dao xian County, Henan Province. d, 10ch, Letter in Chinese, from Liu Ying, a wife of Zhang Wentian, Chinese Communist Party official. e, 20ch, Monument at He Baozhen's birthplace.

Illustration reduced.

2002, Apr. 20 ***Perf. 13¼***

4209 A1861 Sheet of 5, #a.-e. 3.00 1.50

100th anniversary of birth of He Baozhen, first wife of Liu Shaoqi, Chairman of the People's Republic of China 1959-68.

Shellfish — A1862

Designs: 10ch, *Cristaria plicata.* 40ch, *Lanceolaria cospidata kuroda.* 1w, *Schistodesmus lampreyanus.* 1.50w, *Lamprotula coreana.*

2002, Apr. 21

4210-4213 A1862 Set of 4 5.00 2.50

Korean People's Army, 70th Anniv.

A1863

A1864

Designs: 10ch, Soldier, sailor, pilot, symbolizing the three branches of the armed forces.

1.60w, Kim Il Sung and Kim Jong Il walking with army officers and political functionaries.

2002, Apr. 25 ***Perf. 12¼x11¾***

4214 A1863 10ch multicolored .30 .20

Souvenir Sheet

4215 A1864 1.60w multicolored 2.50 1.25

Legend 'Arirang' — A1865

Designs: a, 10ch, Ri Rang and Song Bu as children. b, 40ch, As young adults. c, 50ch, Ri Rang killing the landlord. d, 1.50w, Song Bu

Illustration reduced.

2002, Apr. 28 ***Perf. 13¼***

4216 A1865 Sheet of 4, #a.-d. 3.75 1.75

Mass Gymnastics and Artistic Performance of 'Arirang'

A1866

A1867

Designs: 10ch, Actors. 20ch, Cartoon characters. 30ch, Dancer holding fan. 40ch, Dancer, gymnasts with hoops.

1w, Dancer with tambourine.

2002, Apr. 28 ***Perf. 12¼***

4217-4220 A1866 Set of 4 1.50 .75

Souvenir Sheet

4221 A1867 1w multicolored 1.75 .90

Nos. 4217-4220 were each issued in sheets of 6, with pictorial margins and Arirang logo.

Symbols of Modern Science & Industry — A1868

2002, May 2 ***Perf. 13¼***

4222 A1868 10ch multicolored .30 .20

Science and Technology promotion: "Science and Technology are the Driving Force of Building a Great Prosperous Powerful Nation."

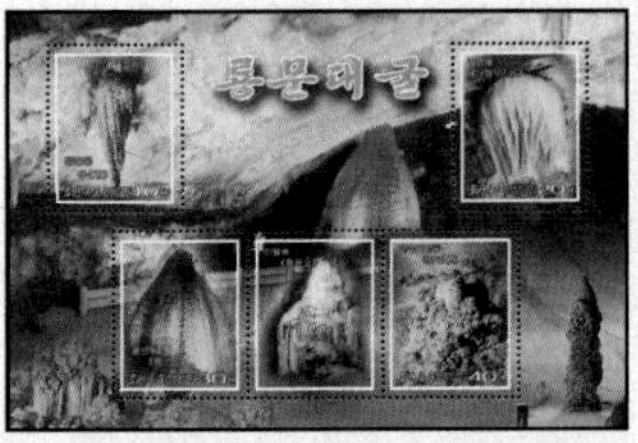

Ryongmun Cavern — A1869

Designs: a, 10ch, Pink stalactite. b, 20ch, Green stalactite. c, 30ch, Golden stalagmite. d, 40ch, Rough-surfaced orange stalagmite.

Illustration reduced.

2002, May 25 ***Perf. 11½***

4223 A1869 Sheet of 4, #a.-d. 2.50 1.25

Monument — A1870

2002, May 2 ***Perf. 13¼***

4224 A1870 10ch multicolored .30 .20

30th Anniv. of the Elucidation of the Three Principles for National Reunification.

Butterflies — A1871

Designs: a, 10ch, *Stauropus fagi.* b, 40ch, *Agrias claudina.* c, 1.50w, *Catocala nupta.* d, 2w, *Morpho rhetenor.*

Illustration reduced.

2002, June 30 ***Perf. 11¾***

4225 A1871 Block of 4, #a.-d. 7.50 3.75

A1872

2002, June 30 *Perf. 11½*
4226-4228 A1872 Set of 3 sheets 4.00 2.00

16th National Congress of the Communist Party of China, Beijing, Nov. 8-14.
Compare with Nos. 4147-4149.

Elderly Man, Child, Hospital — A1873

2002, July 5 *Perf. 12¼*
4229 A1873 10ch multicolored .30 .20

50th Anniv. of Universal Free Medical System.

Kim Jong Suk — A1874

Designs: a, 10ch, As child. b, 40ch, As young woman in Children's Corps. c, 1w, In army uniform. d, 1.50w, With long hair, in civilian clothing.
Illustration reduced.

2002, July 20 *Perf. 13¼*
4230 A1874 Sheet of 4, #a.-d. 2.25 1.10

85th anniv. of birth of Kim Jong Suk (1917-49), first wife of Kim Il Sung and mother of Kim Jong Il.

Soldier, Worker, Farmer — A1875

2002, July 29 *Perf. 11½*
4231 A1875 10ch multicolored .30 .20

30th anniv. of the DPRK Constitution.

World Red Cross & Red Crescent Day

A1876

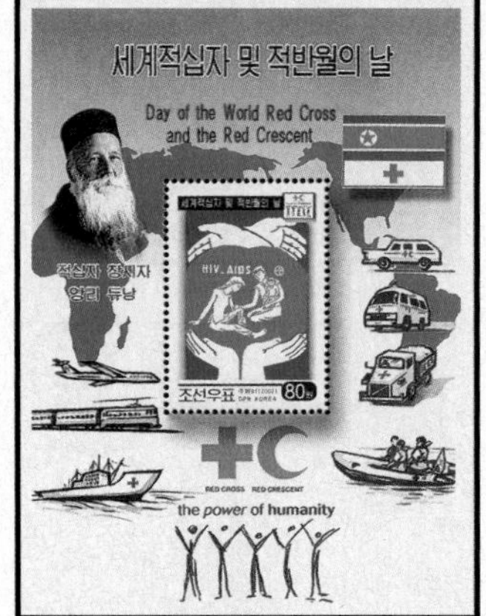

A1877

No. 4232: a, 3w, Korean returnees. b, 12w, Red Cross medics administering first aid. c, 150w, N. Korean truck delivering aid to South Korean flood victims.
No. 4233: 80w, AIDs victim, family.
Illustrations reduced.

2002, Sept. 20 *Perf. 13¼*
Sheet of 6
4232 A1876 Sheet, 2 x #a.-c. 5.00 2.50
Souvenir Sheet
4233 A1877 80w multicolored 1.50 .75

Hong Chang Su, 2000 World Super-Flyweight Boxing Champion — A1878

2002, Sept. 25 *Perf. 11½*
4234 A1878 75w multicolored 1.50 .75

Kim Jong Il's Visit to Russia

Kim Jong Il with Pres. Putin — A1879

Kim Jong Il Shaking Hands with Pres. Putin — A1880

Illustrations reduced. No. 4235 measures 85x70mm, No. 4236 120x100mm.

2002, Oct. 15 *Perf. 13¼*
Souvenir Sheets
4235 A1879 70w multicolored 1.50 .75
4236 A1880 120w multicolored 2.00 1.00

Cats and Dogs

A1881

A1882

Designs: 3w, Siamese cat. 12w, Phungsan dog. 100w, White shorthair cat. 150w, Black and white shorthair cat.
150w, Cavalier King Charles spaniel.

2002, Oct. 20 *Perf. 12*
4237-4240 A1881 Set of 4 5.00 2.50
Souvenir Sheet
4241 A1882 150w multicolored 3.00 1.50
a. Inscr. "World Philatelic Exhibition Bangkok 2003" and emblem in margin 3.00 1.50

No. 4241a issued 10/4/2003.

Minerals — A1883

Designs: 3w, Pyrite. 12w, Magnetite. 130w, Calcite. 150w, Galena.
Illustration reduced.

2002, Oct. 25 *Perf. 13¼*
4242-4245 A1883 Block of 4 5.50 2.75

Japan-Korea Bilateral Declaration

Kim Jong Il and PM Junichiro Signing Declaration — A1884

Kim Jong Il with Japanese Prime Minister Koizumi Junichiro — A1885

Illustrations reduced. No. 4246 measures 90x80mm, No. 4247 75x65mm.

2002, Oct. 25
Souvenir Sheets
4246 A1884 120w multicolored 2.00 1.00
4247 A1885 150w multicolored 3.00 1.50

Kim Il Sung's Birthplace, Mangyongdae — A1886

Kim Jong Il's Birthplace, Mt. Paektu — A1887

Kim Jong Suk's Birthplace, Hoeryong A1888

Kimilsungia A1889

Torch, Tower of Juche Idea A1890

DPRK Flag A1891

Kimjongilia A1892

Magnolia Blossom A1893

DPRK Coat of Arms A1894

Chollima Statue A1895

Victory Monument A1896

Party Founding Monument — A1897

Perf. 11½, 13¼x13½ (#4252-4253, 4256-4259)

2002, Nov. 20

4248 A1886	1w	violet brn	.20	.20
4249 A1887	3w	blue green	.20	.20
4250 A1888	5w	olive brn	.20	.20
4251 A1889	10w	dk lilac rose	.25	.20
4252 A1890	12w	dk reddish brn	.25	.20
4253 A1891	20w	dp blue & red	.35	.20
4254 A1892	30w	brnsh red	.50	.25
4255 A1893	40w	dp grnsh blue	.65	.35
4256 A1894	50w	dk brown	.75	.40
4257 A1895	70w	dk olive grn	1.00	.50
4258 A1896	100w	brown	1.50	.75
4259 A1897	200w	dk lilac rose	3.00	1.50
Nos. 4248-4259 (12)			8.85	4.95

New Year — A1898

2003, Jan. 1 ***Perf. 13¼***

4260 A1898 3w multicolored .30 .20

Animated Film, *Antelopes Defeat Bald Eagles*

A1899

A1900

Designs: 3w, Mother antelope pleading with bald eagle stealing her baby. 50w, Antelopes uniting to defeat bald eagle. 70w, Bald eagle eating fish poisoned by antelopes. 100w, Mother antelope reunited with her child.

150w, Antelopes carrying litter full of fruit.

2003, Jan. 1

4261-4264 A1899 Set of 4 2.50 1.25

Souvenir Sheet

4265 A1900 150w multicolored 1.50 .75

Folk Festivals — A1901

Designs: 3w, Mother and children greeting Full Moon (Lunar New Year, Jan. 15). 12w, Dancers with Full Moon (Lunar New Year). 40w, Two girls on swing (Spring Festival). 70w, Mother and daughter laying flowers on anti-Japanese martyrs' monument (Hangawi - Harvest Moon Festival). 140w, Peasant dance (Hangawi - Harvest Moon Festival).

112w, Wresting (Spring Festival).

2003, Jan. 20 ***Perf. 11¾***

4266-4270 A1901 Set of 5 2.75 1.50

Souvenir Sheet

4271 A1901 112w multicolored 1.50 .75

Soldier — A1902

2003, Feb. 14 ***Perf. 13¼***

4272 A1902 12w multicolored .40 .20

Annual joint editorial of the three state newspapers, *Rodong Sinmun, Josoninmingum* and *Chongnyonjonwi.*

Weapons, Proclamation — A1903

2003, Feb. 15

4273 A1903 30w multicolored .50 .25

North Korean withdrawal from the Nuclear Non-Proliferation Treaty.

Ode Monument — A1904

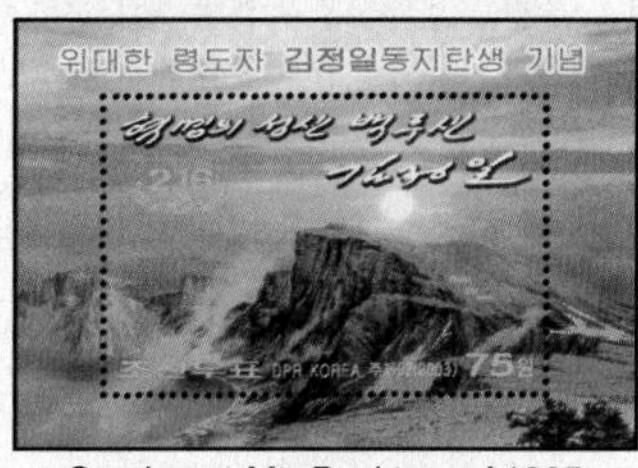
Sunrise at Mt. Paektu — A1905

No. 4275 illustration reduced.

2003, Feb. 16 ***Perf. 12¼x11¼***

4274 A1904 3w multicolored .30 .20

Souvenir Sheet

4275 A1905 75w multicolored 1.00 .50

61st Birthday of Kim Jong Il.

Ships

A1906

A1907

Designs: 15w, Cargo ship *Paekmagang.* 50w, Dredger *Konsol.* 70w, Passenger ship *Undok No. 2.* 112w, Cargo ship *Piryugang.*

150w, Excursion ship *Pyongyang No. 1.* Illustration reduced.

2003, Feb. 18 ***Perf. 11¾***

4276-4279 A1906 Set of 4 3.00 1.50

Souvenir Sheet

4280 A1907 150w multicolored 1.75 .90

Cars Used by Kim Il Sung

A1908

A1909

Designs: 3w, *Zis.* 14w, *Gaz.* 70w, *Pobeda.* 90w, *Mercedes Benz.*

150w, Painting by Kim San Gon *Delaying His Urgent Journey.* Illustration reduced.

2003, Feb. 20

4281-4284 A1908 Set of 4 2.25 1.10

Souvenir Sheet

4285 A1909 150w multicolored 2.00 1.00

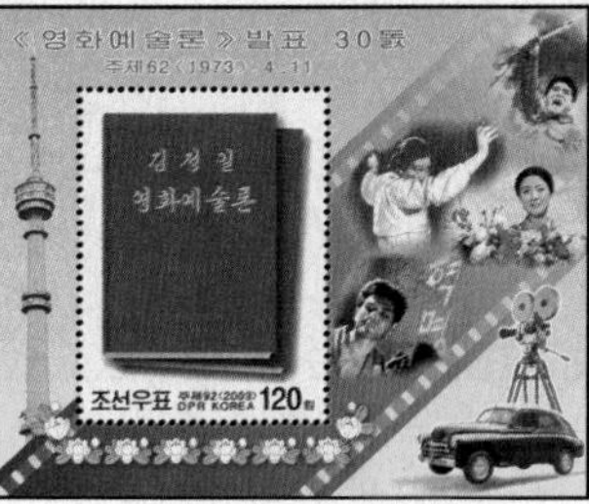
Book — A1910

Illustration reduced.

Souvenir Sheet

2003, Mar. 15

4286 A1910 120w multicolored 1.75 .90

30th anniversary of publication of Kim Jong Il's *On the Art of Cinema.*

Army Trumpeter, Map, Soldiers Marching — A1911

2003, Mar. 16

4287 A1911 15w multicolored .30 .20

80th anniv. of Kim Il Sung's "250-mile Journey for Learning."

Soldier & Workers — A1912

2003, Mar. 29

4288 A1912 3w multicolored .20 .20

Propaganda issue: "Let us meet the requirements of Songun in ideological viewpoint, fighting spirit and way of life!"

A1913

A1914

Designs: 3w, Flags, "10."

No. 4290: a, 12w, Kim Jong Il with computer. b, 70w, Kim with military officers, pointing. c, 112w, Kim, with military officers, hand raised. Illustration reduced.

2003, Apr. 9

4289 A1913 3w multicolored .20 .20

Souvenir Sheet

4290 A1914 Sheet of 3, #a.-c. 3.50 1.75

10th anniv. of election of Kim Jong Il as chairman of the DPRK National Defense Commission.

Kim Il Sung's Birthplace, Mangyongdae, *Kimsungilia* — A1915

2003, Apr. 15

4291 A1915 3w multicolored .20 .20

Day of the Sun — 91st birth anniv. of Kim Il Sung.

Medal — A1916

A1917

Designs: 12w, Order of Suhbaatar (Mongolia, 1953). 35w, National Order of Grand Cross (Madagascar, 1985). 70w, Order of Lenin (USSR, 1987). 140w, Order of Playa Giron (Cuba, 1987).

120w, Kim Il Sung being presented with medal by Fidel Castro (1986). Illustration reduced.

2003, Apr. 15 ***Perf. 13¼***

4292-4295 A1916 Set of 4 3.50 1.75

Souvenir Sheet

Perf. 13¼

4296 A1917 120w multicolored 1.50 .75

Medals and orders presented to Kim Il Sung.

Insects — A1918

Designs: a, 15w, *Pantala flavescens.* b, 70w, *Tibicen japonicus.* c, 220w, Xylotrupes dichotomus. d, 300w, *Lycaena dispar.*

2003, Apr. 20 ***Perf. 13¼***

4297 A1918 Sheet of 4, #a.-d. 9.00 4.50

Korean National Dishes — A1919

Designs: 3w, Glutinous rice cake. 30w, Thongkimchi. 70w, Sinsollo.

120w, Pyongyang cold noodles.

2003, May 1 ***Perf. 11¾***

4298-4300 A1919 Set of 3 1.50 .75

Souvenir Sheet

4301 A1919 120w multicolored 1.50 .75

Victory Monument, Battle in Musan Area — A1920

2003, May 19 ***Perf. 12¾***

4302 A1920 90w multicolored 1.25 .60

Ryangchon Temple — A1921

Designs: 3w, Manse Pavilion. 12w, Buddhist statues. 40w, Painting of Buddha with two saints. 50w, Painting of Buddha with four saints.

120w, Taeung Hall, main shrine of temple.

2003, May 30 ***Perf. 13¼***

4303-4306 A1921 Set of 4 1.75 .90

Souvenir Sheet

4307 A1921 120w multicolored 1.75 .90

Map, Song "We Are One" — A1922

Illustration reduced.

2003, June 1

4308 A1922 60w multicolored 1.00 .50

Wild Animals — A1923

Designs: a, 3w, Tigers. b, 70w, Bears. c, 150w, Wild boars. d, 230w, Roe deer. Illustration reduced.

2003, June 10

4309 A1923 Sheet of 4, #a.-d. 2.25 1.10

Public Bonds of 1950, 2003 — A1924

2003, July 25 ***Perf. 13½***

4310 A1924 140w multicolored 2.25 1.10

Campaign to promote purchase of public bonds.

DPRK "Victory" in Korean War, 50th Anniv.

A1925

A1926

A1927

Designs: 3w, Distinguished Service Medal.

No. 4312: Kim Il Sung in commander's uniform. Illustration reduced.

No. 4313: a, 12w, Kim delivering radio address. 35w, Kim talking to soldiers. c, 70w, Kim ratifying armistace agreement. d, 140w, Kim in uniform. Illustration reduced.

No. 4314: a, 12w, Kim smiling, surrounded by soldiers. 35w, Kim inspecting soldier. c, 70w, Kim Il Sung, Kim Jong Il inspecting army training. d, 140w, Middle-aged Kim Il Sung in suit and tie.

No. 4315: a, 12w, Kim Jong Il receiving bouquet from female soldier. 35w, Kim Jong Il being applauded by soldiers. c, 70w, Kim Jong Il on military inspection. d, 140w, Smiling Kim Jong Il.

2003, July 27 ***Perf. 13¼***

4311 A1925 3w multicolored .20 .20

Souvenir Sheet

4312 A1926 120w multicolored 1.75 .90

Sheets of 4

Perf. 11½

4313-4315 A1927 Set of 3 12.00 6.00

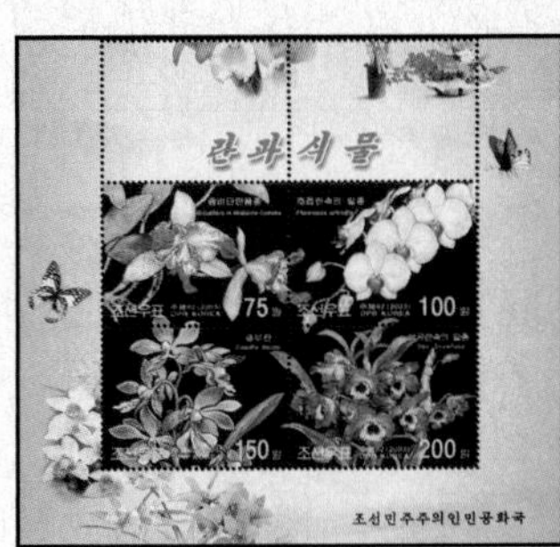

Orchids — A1928

Designs: a, 3w, *Minicattleya coerulea.* b, 100w, *Phalanopsis aphrodite.* c, 150w, *Calanthe discolor.* d, 200w, *Dendrobium snowflake.* Illustration reduced.

2003, July 29 ***Perf. 13¼***

4316 A1928 Sheet of 4, #a.-d. 7.00 3.50

e. Booklet pane of 4, #4316a-4316d 7.00 —

Complete booklet, #4316e 7.50

No. 4316e contains Nos. 4316a-4316d in a horizontal strip of four, with selvage similar to that of No. 4316.

Birds

A1929

A1930

Designs: 12w, *Grus vipio.* 70w, *Nycticorax nycticorax.* 100w, *Columba livia var doestricus.* 120w, *Nymphicus hollandicus.* 150w, *Strix aluco.*

225w, *Pseudogyps africanus.* Illustration reduced.

2003, Aug. 4 ***Perf. 13¼***

4317-4321 A1929 Set of 5 6.00 3.00

Souvenir Sheet

Perf. 11¾

4322 A1930 225w multicolored 3.00 1.50

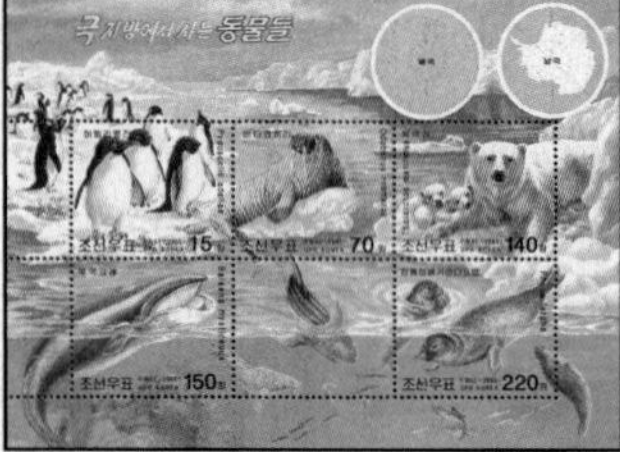

Arctic & Antarctic Animals — A1931

Designs: a, 15w, Adelie penguins *(Pygoscelis adeliae).* b, 70w, Walrus *(Odobenus rosmarus).* c, 140w, Polar bear and cubs *(Thalarctos maritimus).* d, 150w, Bowhead whale *(Balaena mysticetus).* e, 220w, Spotted seals *(Phoca largha).* Illustration reduced.

2003, Aug. 20 ***Perf. 11½***

4323 A1931 Sheet of 5, #a.-e. + label 9.00 4.50

a. Booklet pane of 5 + label —

Complete booklet 13.00

No. 4323a contains one pane, with stamps and label in same arrangement as in No. 4323, surrounded by selvage containing a distinctive arrangement of Polar animals on a primarily yellowish background.

Mushrooms — A1932

Designs: 3w, *Pholiota flammans.* 12w, *Geastrum fimbriatum.* 70w, *Coprinus atramentarius.* 130w, *Pleuotus cornucopiae.* Illustration reduced.

250w, *Elfvingia applanata.*

2003, Sep. 5 ***Perf. 13¼***

4324-4327 A1932 Block of 4 3.50 1.75

Souvenir Sheet

4328 A1932 250w multicolored 4.00 2.00

Korean Stamp Exhibition Hall — A1933

Korean Stamps, Interior of Hall — A1934

2003, Sep. 5

4329 A1933 3w multicolored .20 .20

4330 A1934 60w multicolored 1.00 .50

Korean Stamp Exhibition celebrating the 55th anniversary of the DPRK and the inauguration of the Korean Stamp Exhibition Hall.

55th Anniv. Founding of DPRK

A1935

A1936

A1937

Designs: 3w, DPRK Arms, Flag.

No. 4332: Kim Il Sung. Illustration reduced.

Sheets of 2 with central label: No. 4333: a, 60w, "The Birth of a New Korea" (Kim saluting marchers carrying DPRK flag). b, 60w, "In the Period of Building a New Korea" (Kim Jong Suk and factory workers). No. 4334: a, 60w, "Braving Through a Rain of Bullets Personally" (Kim in jeep in war zone). b, 60w, "Comrade Kim Il Sung, Ever-Victorious Iron-Willed Commander, Personally Commanding the Battle at Height 1211" (Kim on bluff, pointing to battlefield.) No. 4335: a, 60w, "We Trust and Follow Only You, the Leader" (Kim being greeted by villagers). b, 60w, "The Great Leader Kim Il Sung Giving On-the-Spot Guidance to the Pukchang Thermal Power Station" (Kim and factory workers). No. 4336: a, 60w, "The Victory of Korean Revolution Will Be Ensured by the Arms in Our Hand" (Kim speaking to soldiers, Kim Jong Il standing behind). b, 60w, "Keeping Up Songun Politics as All-Powerful Means" (Smiling Kim walking with soldiers symbolizing modern arms). Illustration reduced.

2003, Sep. 9 ***Perf. 11½***

4331 A1935 3w multicolored .20 .20

Souvenir Sheet

Perf. 13¼

4332 A1936 120w multicolored 2.00 1.00

Sheets of 2, #a.-b. + label

Perf. 12¼x12

4333-4336 A1937 Set of 4 6.00 3.00

Birth of Mao Zedong, 110th Anniv.

A1938

Setenant pairs, with label between: No. 4337: a, 20w, Young Mao speaking at political meeting; b, 30w, Mao walking on shore with woman carrying manuscript. No. 4338: a, 30w, Mao addressing Red partisans; b, 30w, Mao (wearing trenchcoat) leading partisans in field. No. 4339: a, 20w, Mao talking with workers, soldiers; b, 30w, Mao in casual setting, leading discussion with soldiers. No. 4340: a, 30w, Mao addressing crowd in Beijing; b, 30w, Mao with people of various races and nationalities.

No. 4341: Sheet containing Nos. 4337-4338, with attached large label depicting 110 stamps picturing Mao and denominated 140w, the price for which the sheet was sold. No. 4342: Same, but containing Nos. 4339-4340. Illustration reduced.

2003, Dec. 26 ***Perf. 13¼***

4337-4340 A1938 Set of 4 pairs 3.50 1.75

Souvenir Sheets

4341-4342 A1938 Set of 2 sheets 4.00 2.00

New Year — A1939

Design: 2w, Soldier, workers, tower.

2004, Jan. 1 ***Perf. 11½***

4343 A1939 3w multicolored .20 .20

Monkeys

A1940

A1941

Designs: 3w, *Cebus apella.* 60w, *Papio doguera.* 70w, *Cercopithecus aethiops.* 100w, *Saguinus oedipus.*

150w, *Macaca mulatta.*

2004, Jan. 1

4344-4347 A1940 Set of 4 4.00 2.00

Souvenir Sheet

4348 A1941 155w multicolored 2.50 2.00

See Nos. 4351-4355.

Lunar New Year's Day — A1942

2004, Jan. 1

4349 A1942 3w multicolored .20 .20

Souvenir Sheet

First Chinese Manned Space Flight — A1943

Designs: a, 91w, Yong Liwei, first Chinese cosmonaut. b, 98w, Landing capsule, parachute, helicopter. Illustration reduced.

2004, Jan. 30 ***Perf. 13¼***
4350 A1943 Sheet of 2, #a.-b. 3.00 1.50

See No. 4356.

Nos. 4344-4348, 4350 with Hong Kong 2004 Emblem.

2004, Jan. 30
4351-4354 A1940 Set of 4 4.00 2.00

Souvenir Sheets

4355 A1941 155w multicolored 2.50 1.25
4356 A1943 Sheet of 2, #a.-b. 3.00 1.50

Joint Editorial *Rodong Sinmun, Josoninmingun* and *Chongnyonjonwi* Newspapers — A1944

2004, Feb. 15 ***Perf. 13¼***
4357 A1944 3w multicolored .20 .20

A1945

A1946

No. 4358: 3w, Kim Jong Il's birthplace, Mt. Paektu.

No. 4359 (each 30w): a, "The Thaw of Sobaek Stream" (Spring). b, "The Thunderclap of Jong Il Peak" (Summer). c, "The Secret Camp in Autumn" (Autumn). d, "Hoarfrost in February" (Winter). Illustration reduced.

2004, Feb. 16 ***Perf. 11½***
4358 A1945 3w multicolored .20 .20

Souvenir Sheet

Perf. 13¼

4359 A1946 Sheet of 4, #a.-d. 2.00 1.00

Kim Jong Il, 62nd birthday.

Kim Jong Il — A1947

Illustration reduced.

2004, Feb. 19 ***Perf. 13¼***
4360 A1947 120w multicolored 2.00 1.00

30th anniv. of publication of the *Program of Modelling the Whole Society on the Juche Idea.*

Rural Village — A1948

Kim Il Sung and Farmers — A1949

2004, Feb. 25 ***Perf. 11½***
4361 A1948 3w multicolored .20 .20

Souvenir Sheet

Perf. 12½ x11¾

4362 A1949 120w multicolored 1.75 1.75

40th anniv. of publication of the "Theses on the Socialist Rural Question in Our Country."

Lighthouses — A1950

Designs: a, 3w, Sokgundo Lighthouse. b, 12w, Yubundo Lighthouse. c, 100w, Jangdokdo Lighthouse. d, 195w, Amryongdan Lighthouse.

2004, Mar. 20 ***Perf. 11¾x12½***
4363 A1950 Sheet of 4, #a.-d. 5.00 2.50
e. Booklet pane of 4, #4363a-4363d 5.00 —
Complete booklet, #4363e 5.50

No. 4363e contains Nos. 4363a-4363d in a horizontal strip of 4, surrounded by a seashore selvage.

Board Games

A1951

A1952

Designs: a, 3w, Korean Chess. b, 12w, Goe. c, 90w, Yut. d, 120w, Kknoni (Chinese Checkers).

98w, Playing Korean Chess.

2004, Mar. 20 ***Perf. 13¼***
4364 A1951 Sheet of 4, #a.-d. 4.00 2.00
e. Booklet pane of 5, #4364a-4364b. 4364d, 2 x 4364c 5.00 —
Complete booklet, #4363e 5.50

Souvenir Sheet

4365 A1952 98w multicolored 2.00 1.00

No. 4364e contains Nos. 4364a-4364d in a horizontal strip of 5, which includes a second copy of the 90w value, with a distinctive printed selvage.

Kim Il Sung's Birthplace, Mangyongdae — A1953

Kim Il Sung — A1954

2004, Apr. 15 ***Perf. 13¼***
4366 A1953 3w multicolored .20 .20

Souvenir Sheet

Perf. 11¾

4367 A1954 120w multicolored 1.75 .90

92nd Anniv. of the birth of Kim Il Sung.

Tok Islands

A1955

A1956

No. 4368: a, 3w, 19th century map of Korea. b, 12w, Western island. c, 106w, Eastern island.

No. 4369: 116w, Both islands, sea gulls. Illustrations reduced.

2004, Apr. 20 ***Perf. 11½***
4368 A1955 Sheet, #a.-c. + label 2.50 1.25

Souvenir Sheet

Perf. 12½

4369 A1956 116w multicolored 2.00 1.00

Fossils — A1957

No. 4370: a, 3w, *Calcinoplax antiqua.* b, 12w, *Podozamites lanceolatus.* c, 70w, *Comptonia naumannii.* d, 140w, *Clinocardium asagaiense.*

No. 4371: 120w, *Tingia carbonica*

Illustration reduced.

2004, May 20 ***Perf. 13¼***
4370 A1957 Sheet of 4, #a.-d. 4.00 2.00
e. Booklet pane of 5, #4370a-4370d, #4371a 5.00 —
Complete booklet, #4370e 5.50 —

Souvenir Sheet

Perf. 12½

4371 A1957 116w multicolored 2.00 1.00
a. A1957 116w Single stamp 2.00 1.00

Cacti — A1958

No. 4372: a, 70w, *Notocactus leninghausii.* b, 90w, *Echinocactus grusonii.* c, 100w, *Gymnocalycium baldianum.* d, 140w, *Mammillaria insularis.*

Illustration reduced.

2004, June 2 ***Perf. 11¾x12¼***
4372 A1958 Sheet of 4, #a.-d. 5.00 2.50
a. Ovptd. "World Stamp Championship 2004" and Singapore 2004 emblem in margin 5.00 2.50

No. 4372a issued Aug. 28.

Unofficial Visit of Kim Jong Il to China

A1959

A1960

No. 4373: a, 74w, Kim Jong Il with Hu Jintao, President of the People's Republic of China.

No. 4374: a, 3w, Kim shaking hands with Hu Jintao. b, 12w, Kim with Jiang Zemin, President of China 1997-2003. c, 40w, Kim with Wu Bangguo, Chinese Communist Party leader. d, 60w, Kim clapping hands at outdoor reception.

No. 4375: a, 3w, Kim with Wen Jiabao, Premier of the State Council of the PRC. b, 12w, Kim with Jia Qinglin, Chinese Communist Party leader. c, 40w, Kim with Zeng Qinghong, Vice-President of the PRC. d, 60w, Kim visiting Tianjin.

Illustrations reduced.

2004, June 18 ***Perf. 13¼***

Souvenir Sheet

4373 A1959 74w multicolored 1.25 .60
a. As No. 4373, diff. (horiz.) selvage 1.25 .60

Sheets of 4

4374-4375 A1960 2 Sheets of 4, #a.-d. 3.50 1.75
4375e Booklet pane of 9, #4373a, 4374a-d, 4375a-d 5.00 —
Complete booklet, #4375e 5.50

No. 4373a is from the booklet No. 4375e.

40th Anniv. of Kim Jong Il's Appointment to the Central Committe of the Workers' Party of Korea

WPK Flag — A1961

A1962

A1963

No. 4377: a, 12w, Kim reading at desk. b, 100w, Kim standing in front of renderings of proposed Samjiyon Battle Site memorial. Illustration reduced.

No. 4378: a, 12w, Kim inspecting power station in Jagang Province. b, 100w, Kim with army officers.

No. 4379: a, 12w, Kim visiting the Komdok mine. b, 100w, Kim, outdoor photo portrait.

No. 4380: 130w, Kim Jong Il and Kim Il Sung. Illustration reduced.

2004, June 19

4376 A1961 3w multicolored .20 .20

Sheets of 4

4377-4379 A1962 3 Sheets, 2 ea. #a.-b. 5.00 2.50

Souvenir Sheet

4380 A1963 130w multicolored 1.25 .60

10th Anniv. Death of Kim Il Sung

A1964

A1965

A1966

No. 4381: 3w, *Kimilsungia*, monument to Kim Il Sung.

No. 4382: a, 12w, Kim Il Sung and Kim Jong Il visiting State Academy of Sciences. b, 116w, Kim Il Sung and Kim Jong Il on Mt. Paektu. Illustration reduced.

No. 4383: a, 12w, Kim iil Sung with workers b, 116w, Kim directing farmers at Chongan co-operative farm.

No. 4384: a, 12w, Kim with soldiers. b, 116w, Kim with children.

No. 4385: a, 12w, Kim embracing Rev. Mun Ik Hwan. 116w, Kim talking on telephone.

No. 4386: 112w, Kim waving. Illustration reduced.

2004, July 8 ***Perf. 11¾***

4381 A1964 3w multicolored .20 .20

Sheets of 4

4382-4385 A1965 4 Sheets of 2 #a.-b. 7.00 3.50

Souvenir Sheet

4386 A1966 112w multicolored 1.50 .75

Monument — A1967

2004, July 10 ***Perf. 11¾***

4387 A1967 112w multicolored 1.50 .75

110th anniv. birth of Kim Hyong Jik, father of Kim Il Sung.

100th Anniv. Birth of Deng Xiaoping

A1968

A1969

A1970

No. 4388: a, 3w, Deng Xiaoping as a student in France. b, 12w, Deng hiking on the Huangshan. c, 35w, Deng saluting at military review. d. 50w, Deng addressing rally celebrating the 35th anniversary of the People's Republic of China.

No. 4389a: Kim Il Sung being greeted by Deng, Chinese crowd during visit to China.

No. 4390: 80w, Deng at seashore.

2004, July 15 ***Perf. 13¼***

4388 A1968 Strip of 4, #4388a-4388d + label 1.50 .75

Sheet of 5

4389 A1969 Sheet, #4388, 4389a, label 2.50 1.25
a. 70w multicolored .75 .40

Souvenir Sheet

4390 A1970 80w multicolored 1.25 .60

Fresh Water Fish — A1971

Designs: a, 3w, *Carassius auratus.* b, 12w, *Tlilapia nilotica.* c, 140w, *Ophiocephalus argus.* d, 165w, *Clarias gariepinus.*

2004, Aug. 10

4391 A1971 Sheet of 4, #a.-d. 4.75 2.40

28th Olympic Games, Athens — A1972

Designs: a, 3w, Boxing. b, 12w, Soccer. c, 85w, Track and field events. d, 140w, Gymnastics.

Illustration reduced.

2004, Aug. 10

4392 A1972 Block or strip of 4, #a.-d. 3.50 1.75
e. Booklet pane of 4, #a.-d. 3.50 —
Complete booklet, #4392e 4.00

No. 4392 was printed in panes of 8 stamps, 2 sets of Nos. 4392a-4392d, with decorative margin depicting athletes, Olympic emblems and Korean inscription. No. 4392e contains Nos. 4392a-4392d in a horizontal strip, with plain marginal selvage.

For overprints, see No. 4409.

Fire Engines — A1973

Designs: a, 3w, Mercedes Benz ladder truck. b, 12w, Fire truck. c, 40w, Jelcz pumper truck. d, 105w, Mercedes Benz fire truck. 97w, ladder truck, diff.

Illustration reduced.

2004, Aug. 15

4393 A1973 Sheet of 4, #a.-d. 2.50 1.25
e. Booklet pane of 4, #a.-d. 2.50 —
Complete booklet, #4393e 3.00
f. A1973 97w Souvenir sheet 1.50 .75

No. 4393e contains Nos. 4393a-4393d in a vertical strip, with marginal selvage similar to that of the sheet.

Airplanes — A1974

Designs: a, 3w, Airbus A340-600. b, 97w, Concorde. c, 104w, Graf Zeppelin DO-X. d, 116w, Junkers JU 52/3m.
Illustration reduced.

2004, Aug. 20 ***Perf. 12***

4394 A1974 Sheet of 4, #a.-d. 5.50 2.75
e. Booklet pane of 4, #a.-d. 5.50 —
Complete booklet, #4394e 6.00

No. 4394e contains Nos. 4394a-4394d in a horizontal strip, with pale yellow marginal selvage, with simple ruled lines and inscription.

Visit of Japanese Prime Minister Koizumi Zunichiro — A1975

Illustration reduced.

2004, Aug. 25 ***Perf. 11¾***

4395 A1975 220w multicolored 3.00 1.50

A1976

Illustration reduced.

2004, Sept. 21

4396 A1976 112w multicolored 1.50 .75

125th anniversary of birth of An Jung Gun (1879-1910), assassin of Japanese Prime Minister Ito Hirdoumi 1909.

A1977

A1978

Designs: 3w, Kim Jong Suk's pistol.
97w, Kim Jong Suk. Illustration reduced.

2004, Sept. 22 ***Perf. 13¼***

4397 A1977 3w multicolored .20 .20

Souvenir Sheet

Perf. 12

4398 A1978 97w multicolored 1.50 .75

Issued in honor of Kim Jong Suk (1917-49), first wife of Kim Il Sung, mother of Kim Jong Il.

World Fund for Wildlife — A1979

Swans: 3w, Swan in profile, looking left. 97w, Swan, ¾ profile, head turned to left. 104w, Two swans, one with outstretched wings. 120w, Two swans in water.

2004, Sept. 30 ***Perf. 11½***

4399-4402 A1979 Set of 4 5.00 2.50
4402a Booklet pane of 4, #4399-4102 5.00 —
Complete booklet, #4402a 5.50

Nos. 4399-4402 were each printed in sheets of 4, with decorative selvage. No. 4402a contains the four stamps in a horizontal se-tenant strip, surrounded by plain selvage.

Simwon Temple

A1980

A1981

Designs: 3w, View of Powkang Hall.
97w, Interior of Powkang Hall, with three golden Buddha statues. Illustration reduced.

2004, Oct. 5 ***Perf. 11¾***

4403 A1980 3w multicolored .20 .20

Souvenir Sheet

Perf. 13¼

4404 A1981 97w multicolored 1.75 .90

Sidelfingen International Stamp Fair

A1982

Electric trains: a, 3w, Red and blue train. b, 40w, Yellow train. c, 75w, Green and white train. d, 150w, Red and green train.
120w, Vintage electric train.

2004, Nov. 5 ***Perf. 11½***

4405 A1982 Sheet of 4, #a.-d. 4.50 2.25

Souvenir Sheet

4406 A1982 120w multicolored 2.00 1.00
a. 120w stamp from souvenir sheet 2.00 1.00
b. Booklet pane of 5, #4405a-4405d, #4606a 6.50 —
Complete booklet, #4406b 7.00

Repatriation of Korean Nationals in Japan, 45th Anniv.

A1983

A1984

Designs: 3w, Repatriation ship *Mangyongbong.*
80w, Kim Il Sung with repatriated Korean children. Illustration reduced.

2004, Dec. 16 ***Perf. 11½***

4407 A1983 3w multicolored .20 .20

Souvenir Sheet

Perf. 11¾

4408 A1984 80w multicolored 1.25 .60

28th Olympic Games Winners No. 4392 Overprinted in Silver

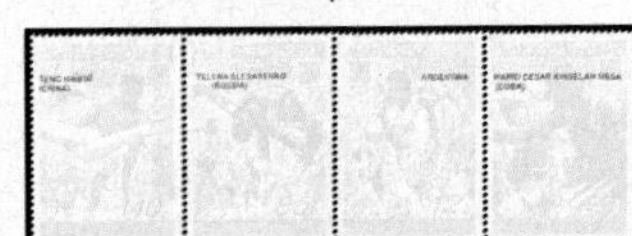

28th Olympic Games, Athens

Overprints: a, 3w, Mario Cesar Kindelan Mesa (Boxing, Cuba). b, 12w, Argentine Soccer Team. c, 85w, Yelena Slesarenko (Women's High Jump, Russia). d, 140w, Teng Haibin (Women's Gymnastics, China).

2004, Dec. 20 ***Perf. 13¼***

4409 A1972 Block or strip of 4, #a.-d. 3.50 1.75

New Year 2005 — A1985

2005, Jan. 1

4410 A1985 3w multicolored .20 .20

New Year 2005 — Year of the Rooster

A1986

A1987

Domestic fowl, millet stalk figures: 3w, Rooster. 12w, Hen.
No. 4413: a, 3w, Chick. b, 70w, Rooster, chick. c, 100w, Rooster. d, 140w, Basket of eggs. Illustration reduced.

2005, Jan. 1

4411 A1986 3w multicolored .20 .20
4412 A1986 12w multicolored .60 .30

Sheet of 4

4413 A1987 Sheet, #a.-d. 4.00 .20
e. Booklet pane of 6, #4411-4412, #4313a-d 4.75 —
Complete booklet, #4413e 5.00

No. 4413e contains all six values of the set, printed in a se-tenant strip of six, within a plain yellow and green border.

Hen, Classic Chinese Painting — A1988

Souvenir Sheet

2005, Jan. 10 ***Perf. 11½***

4414 A1988 97w multicolored 1.50 .75

Kim Il Sung's 250-Mile Journey, 80th Anniv. — A1989

Illustration reduced.

Souvenir Sheet

2005, Jan. 22 *Perf. 11¾*

4415 A1989 120w multicolored 1.50 .75

Statue of Kim Il Sung, Chongsan-ri — A1990

Illustration reduced.

Souvenir Sheet

2005, Feb. 8 *Perf. 13¼*

4416 A1990 120w multicolored 1.50 .75

Creation of the Chongsan-ri Spirit and Chongsan-ri Method.

Songun Scenes — A1991

Designs: a, 3w, Sunrise at Mt. Paektu. b, 12w, Snowscape. c, 40w, Royal azaleas on Chol Pass. d, 50w, Jangja River. e, 60w, Ullim Falls. f, 70w, Handure Plain. g, 70w, Potato blossoms at Taehongdan. h, 100w, Poman-ri. Illustration reduced.

2005, Feb. 10 *Perf. 12¼*

4417 A1991 Sheet of 8, #a.-h. 5.00 2.50

A1992

A1993

A1994

Design: 3w, *Kimjongilia*, mountains.

No. 4419, *216 Peaks Around Lake Chon on Mt. Paektu*, summer scenes, each 50w: a, Mountains, lake on lower right. b, Mountains, lake across foreground. c, Mountains, lake in foreground, shore at lower right.

No. 4420, *216 Peaks Around Lake Chon on Mt. Paektu*, winter scenes, each 50w: a, Mountains, frozen lake in foreground. b, Mountains. lake in foreground, sun showing over peaks. c, Mountains, lake in left foreground.

Nos. 4419-4420 illustrations reduced.

2005, Feb. 16 *Perf. 13¼*

4418 A1992 3w multicolored .20 .20

Sheets of 3, #a.-c.

Perf. 12

4419 A1993 multicolored 2.00 1.00
4420 A1994 multicolored 2.00 1.00

Kim Jong Il, 63rd birthday

Joint Editorial *Rodong Sinmun, Josoninmingun* and *Chongnyonjonwi* Newspapers — A1995

2005, Feb. 16 *Perf. 13¼*

4421 A1995 3w multicolored .20 .20

Naming of the *Kimilsungia*, 40th Anniv.

A1996

A1997

Designs: 3w, *Kimilsungia* and Kimilsungia-Kimjongilia Exhibition Hall.

120w: Kim Il Sung receiving a *Kimilsungia* plant from Pres. Sukarno of Indonesia. Illustration reduced.

2005, Apr. 13

4422 A1996 3w multicolored .20 .20

Souvenir Sheet

4423 A1997 120w multicolored 1.50 .75

Kim Il Sung, 93rd Anniv. of Birth

A1998

A1999

Designs: 3w, *Kimilsungia* and Mangyong Hill.

112w: Kim Il Sung standing in front of straw-thatched house at Mangyongdae.

2005, Apr. 15

4424 A1998 3w multicolored .20 .20

Souvenir Sheet

Perf. 11¾

4425 A1999 112w multicolored 1.50 .75

48th World Table Tennis Championships, Shanghai — A2000

Designs: 3w, Pak Young Sun, Korea. b, 5w, Mao Zedong playing table tennis at the Communist base in Yanan. c, 12w, Wang Liqin, China. d, 20w, J.O. Waldner, Sweden. e, Zhang Yining, China. f, 102w, Werner Schlager, Austria.
Illustration reduced.

2005, Apr. 23 *Perf. 11½*

4426 A2000 Sheet of 6, #a.-f. 3.00 1.50
g. Booklet pane of 6, #4426a-4426f 3.00 —
Complete booklet, #4426g 3.50

No. 4426g contains Nos. 4426a-4426f in a se-tenant horizontal strip of six, surrounded by blue selvage depicting the Shanghai 2005 emblem, stylized athletes and Korean inscription.

Pandas — A2001

Designs: 15w, Panda on tree limb. 45w, Panda walking. 70w, Two pandas. 140w, Panda standing
120w, Panda with cub.

2005, May 3 *Perf. 13¼*

4427-4430 A2001 Set of 4 4.00 .20
4430a Booklet pane of 5, #4427-4430, 4432a 4.00 —
Complete booklet, #4430a 4.50

Sheet of 5

4431 A2001 Sheet, #4427-4430, 4432a 6.00 3.00

Souvenir Sheet

4432 A2001 120w multicolored 3.00 —
a. 120w single stamp

Nos. 4427-4430 were each issued in separate large panes. No. 4430a contains #4427-30, 4432a in a se-tenant horizontal strip of 5, with plain white marginal selvage.

For overprints, see Nos. 4451-4455.

Ecosystem of Tok Island — A2002

Designs: a, 3w, *Dianthus superbus*. b, 3w, *Eumetopia jubata*. c, 12w, Seagull. d, 50w, *Lysimachia mauritania Lam.*
e, 97w: Eastern and Western islands, Tok Island. Illustration reduced.

2005, May 5 *Perf. 11¼*

4433 A2002 Sheet, 2x#4433a-4433d, 1 #4433e, 2 labels 12.00 6.00

A2003

A2004

Designs: 3w, Korean family waving flag.
130w: Kim Il Sung shaking hands with man in suit. Illustration reduced.

2005, May 25 *Perf. 13¼*

4434 A2003 3w multicolored .20 .20

Souvenir Sheet

4435 A2004 130w multicolored 1.50 .75

50th anniversary of the formation on the General Association of Korean Residents in Japan.

Fauna — A2005

Designs, each 40w: No. 4436, Korean Tiger. No. 4437, Sable. Illustration reduced.

2005, June 1

4436	40w multicolored	.75	.40
4437	40w multicolored	.75	.40
a.	A2005 Pair, #4436-4437 with label between	2.00	1.00
b.	Booklet pane, 2 #4437a	2.00	—
	Complete booklet, #4437b	2.50	

See Russia No. 6911.

A2006

A2007

Designs: a, Tomb of a general of Koguryo. b, 70w, Tomb mural depicting hunting scene. c, 100w, Mt. Songsan fortress. d, 130w, Gilded arrowheads.

97w: Monument at Mausoleum of King Kwanggaetho.

2005, June 14

4438	A2006 Sheet of 4, #a.-d.	4.00	2.00
a.	Booklet pane, #4438a-4438d, 4439a	6.00	—
	Complete booklet, #4438a	6.50	

Souvenir Sheet

4439	A2007 97w multicolored	2.00	1.00
a.	97w, single from souvenir sheet	2.00	1.00

Koguryo Historic Site.

No. 4438a contains #4438a-4438d in a horizontal strip of 4, with #4439a placed separately, within a 69mmx279mm sheetlet with selvage depicting hunting scene, artifacts and inscription.

Kim Chol Ju — A2008

Illustration reduced.

Souvenir Sheet

2005, June 14 ***Perf. 11½***

4440	A2008 170w multicolored	1.50	.75

Issued to honor Kim Chol Ju (1919-35), revolutionary hero and younger brother of Kim Il Sung.

A2009

A2010

Designs, all 112w: a, Kim Jong Il and S. Korean President Kim Dae Jung shaking hands. b, Kim Jong Il and Kim Dae Jung standing side-by-side. c, Kim Il Jong and Kim Dae Jung sitting together at table with large flower arrangement. d, Kim Dae Jong and Kim Il Jong at conference table.

167w, Kim Dae Jung and Kim Jong Il smiling, shaking hands, with representatives in background.

Illustrations reduced.

2005, June 15

4441	A2009 Sheet of 4, #a.-d.	6.00	3.00

Souvenir Sheet

4442	A2010 167w multicolored	2.50	1.25

Fifth anniversary of the North-South Joint Declaration.

Amur Tiger

A2011

A2012

Designs: a, 3w, Tiger looking left. b, 12w, Tiger growling. c, 130w, Tiger looking forward. d, 200w, Tiger growling, turned to right.

150w: Tiger with cubs.

Illustrations reduced.

2005, July 10 ***Perf. 11¾***

4443	A2011 Sheet of 4, #a.-d.	4.00	2.00
e.	Booklet pane, #4443a-4443d	4.00	—
	Complete booklet, #4443e	4.50	

Souvenir Sheet

Perf. 11½

4444	A2012 150w multicolored	2.00	1.00

No. 4443e contains #4443a-4443d in a horizontal strip of 4, within selvage depicting forest skyline and inscription "Panthera tigris altaika."

Map of Korea — A2013

Illustration reduced.

Souvenir Sheet

2005, July 25 ***Perf. 11½***

4445	A2013 130w multicolored	1.50	.75

A2014

Design: 3w, Korean soldier, U.S. POWs, military cemetary, military vehicles.

2005, July 27 ***Perf. 12***

4446	A2014 3w multicolored	.20	.20

Propaganda issue, marking "June 25-July 27: Period of Joint Anti-US Struggle."

National Liberation, 60th Anniv.

A2015

A2016

A2017

A2018

Design: 3w, Arch of Triumph, magnolia.

No. 4448: a, 60w, Kim Il Sung receiving his father's pistol from his mother. b, 60w, Kim Il Sung founding the Juche-oriented revolutionary armed force. c, 60w, Kim Il Sung commanding the battle at Taehongdan. 60w, Kim Il Sung addressing staff on eve of final offensive against the Japanese. 102w, Kim Il Sung, WWII-era photo.

No. 4449: a, Kim Il Sung on ship en route to Wonsan Port landing. b, 60w, Kim Il Sung visiting Kangson Steel Works. c, 60w, Kim Il Sung delivering speech. d, 60w, Kim Il Sung

meeting his grandparents, upon his return to Korea. e, 102w, Kim Il Sung with microphone.
No. 4450: 128w, Kim Il Sung.
Nos. 4448-4450 illustrations reduced.

2005, Aug. 15 *Perf. 13¼*
4447 A2015 3w multicolored .20 .20

Sheets of 5

4448 A2016 Sheet, #a.-e. 4.00 2.00
4449 A2017 Sheet, #a.-e. 4.00 2.00

Souvenir Sheet

4450 A2018 128w multicolored 1.50 .75

Nos. 4427-4430, 4432 Overprinted "Taipei 2000" and Emblem in Red and Blue

2005, Aug. 19 *Perf. 13¼*
4451-4454 A2001 Set of 4 4.00 2.00

Souvenir Sheet

4455 A2001 120w multicolored 2.25 1.10

18th Asian International Stamp Exhibition, Taipei.

National Costumes

A2019

A2020

Designs: a, 3w, Woman in red dress. b, 80w, Woman in blue dress. c, 100w, Woman in green dress. d, 120w, Woman in white dress with fur collar.
140w, Children.
Illustrations reduced.

2005, Aug. 30 *Perf. 11½*
4456 A2019 Sheet of 4, #a.-d. 3.50 1.75
4456e Booklet pane of 4, #4456a-d 3.50 —
Complete booklet, #4456e 4.00

Souvenir Sheet
Perf. 11¾

4457 A2020 140w multicolored 1.75 .90

No. 4456e contains Nos. 4456a-d in a horizontal strip of 4, without the small decorative labels that are printed below the stamps in No. 4456. The stamps are surrounded by a narrow selvage similar to that of the sheet of 4.

A2021

Design: 3w, Korean soldier and workers, banners, proclamation of Joint Slogan.

2005, Sept. 8 *Perf. 13¼*
4458 A2021 3w multicolored .20 .20

Propaganda issue, marking the issue of the Joint Slogans by the Workers' Party of Korea and the central military commission of the WPK, celebrating the 60th anniv. of the founding of the party.

Workers' Party of Korea, 60th Anniv.

A2022

A2023

A2024

A2025

A2026

Design: 3w, Monument to founding of Party.
No. 4460: a, 12w, Kim Il Sung organizing Down-with-Imperialism Union. b, 30w, Kim Il Sung forming the first Juche-oriented Party organization. c, 60w, Kim Il Sung discussing a draft resolution to Communist Party leaders. d, 90w, Kim Il Sung addressing Central Committee of the Communist Party.
No. 4461: a, 12w, Kim Il Sung at bank of microphones, addressing 6th Congress of the WPK. b, 30w, Kim Il Sung and Kim Jong Il with military officers. c, 60w, Kim Jong Il inspecting Tabaksol Company, a camouflaged army unit. d, 90w, Kim Jong Il addressing crowd in stadium.
No. 4462: 120w, Kim Il Sung. No. 4463: 120w, Kim Jong Il.
Nos. 4460-4463 illustrations reduced.

2005, Oct. 10 *Perf. 13¼*
4459 A2022 3w multicolored .20 .20

Sheets of 4
Perf. 11¾

4460 A2023 Sheet, #a.-d. 2.00 1.00
4461 A2024 Sheet, #a.-d. 2.00 1.00

Souvenir Sheets
Perf. 13¼

4462 A2025 120w multicolored 1.25 .60
4463 A2026 120w multicolored 1.25 .60

Bees — A2027

Designs: a, 3w, Four bees surrounding queen. 12w, Two bees attending to larva. 128w, Bee filling comb cell with honey. 200w, Bee flying.
Illustration reduced.

2005, Oct. 20 *Perf. 11½*
4464 A2027 Sheet of 4, #a.-d. 4.00 2.00
e. Booklet pane, as #4464a-4464d 4.00 —
Complete booklet, #4443e 4.50

No. 4464e contains four stamps like Nos. 4464a-4464d, but with slightly less yellow in the comb background and a slightly paler blue on the blue design elements. It bears a marginal selvage, with Korean inscription at left and three bees at right.

United Nations, 60th Anniv. — A2028

2005, Oct. 24 *Perf. 13¼*
4465 A2028 15w multicolored .30 .20

Kaesong Historic Site, First Issue

A2029

A2030

No 4466: a, 35w, Pogwang Hall. b, 35w, Monument to Taegakguksa. c, 35w, Pojo Hall. d, 75w, Ryongthong Temple.
No. 4467: a, 35w, Taesong Shrine. b, 35w, Myongryun Hall. c, 35w, Metal type (round). d, 75w, Sam Gate.
Illustrations reduced.

2005, Oct. 31 *Perf. 12*

Sheets of 4, #a.-d.

4466 A2029 multicolored 2.00 1.00
4467 A2030 multicolored 2.00 1.00

Nos. 4466-4467 each contain three non-denominated labels.

Kim Hyong Gwon Monument — A2031

Souvenir Sheet

2005, Nov. 4 *Perf. 11½*
4468 A2031 120w multicolored 1.50 .75

Issued to honor the 100th anniversary of the birth of Kim Hyong Gwon (1905-36), Korean revolutionary, uncle of Kim Il Sung.

A2032

2005, Nov. 17 *Perf. 11¾*
4469 A2032 12w multicolored .30 .20

Centenary of the Ulsa Treaty, under the terms of which Korea became a Japanese protectorate.

Kaesong Historic Site, Second Issue

A2033

A2034

A2035

No 4470: a, 35w, Kaesong Namdaemun. b, 35w, Mausoleum of King Kongmin. c, 35w, Sonjuk Bridge. d, 35w, Sungyang Private School. e, 35w, Anhwa Temple (Five Hundred Rahan). f, 35w, Tomb of Pak Ji Won (Yonam).

No. 4471: a, 35w, King Wanggon, founder of Kingdom of Koryo, 935 A.D., round. b, 35w, Front Gate at Mausoleum of King Wanggon. c, 75w, Mausoleum of King Wanggon.

No. 4472: a, 35w, Fortress on Mt. Taehung (North Gate). b, 35w, Marble statue of Kwanumbosal, Kwanum Temple. c, 75w, Pakyon Falls.

Illustrations reduced.

2005, Nov. 18

Sheet of 6, #a.-f. + 6 labels

Perf. 11½

4470 A2033 multicolored 1.50 .75

Sheet of 3, #a.-c. + 2 labels

Perf. 13¼

4471 A2034 multicolored 1.50 .75

Sheet of 3, #a.-c. + 4 labels

Perf. 12¼ (a, b); 11½ (c)

4472 A2035 multicolored 1.50 .75

A2036

Design: a, 35w, Kim Jong Il meeting with Hu Jintao. b, 35w, Kim Jong Il and Hu Jintao visiting the Taean Friendship Glass Factory. c, 35w, Kim Jong Il and Hu Jintao at state banquet. d, 102w, Kim Jong Il shaking hands with Hu Jintao.

Illustration reduced.

Perf. 11½, 13¼ (#4473d)

2005, Dec. 15

Sheet of 4, #a.-d.

4473 A2036 multicolored 2.50 1.25

Issued in honor of visit to DPRK by Hu Jintao, President of the People's Republic of China.

New Year 2006 — A2037

2006, Jan. 1 **Litho.** ***Perf. 11½***

4474 A2037 3w multi .20 .20

New Year 2006 (Year of the Dog) — A2038

Various dogs: 3w, 70w.

No. 4477 — Various dogs: a, 15w. b, 100w. c, 130w.

2006, Jan. 1 ***Perf. 13¼***

4475-4476 A2038 Set of 2 1.10 .55

4477 A2038 Sheet of 5, #4475-4476, 4477a-4477c 4.50 2.25

d. Souvenir sheet of 1 #4477c 1.90 .95

A2039

League of Socialist Working Youth, 60th Anniv. — A2040

No. 4478: a, 3w, Kim Il Sung and microphone. b, 111w, Kim Il Sung and crowd. c, 150w, Kim Jong Il receiving torch.

2006, Jan. 17 ***Perf. 13¼***

4478 A2039 Sheet of 3, #a-c 3.75 1.90

Souvenir Sheet

Perf. 11½x12

4479 A2040 128w multi 1.90 .95

A2041

New Year 2006 (Year of the Dog) — A2042

Photo. & Engr.

2006, Jan. 29 ***Perf. 11x11¼***

4480 A2041 12w multi .20 .20

Souvenir Sheet

Perf. 11½x11¼

4481 A2042 70w multi 1.00 .50

Down With Imperialism Union, 80th Anniv. — A2043

2006, Feb. 9 **Litho.** ***Perf. 13½***

4482 A2043 3w multi .20 .20

Miniature Sheet

2006 Winter Olymics, Turin — A2044

No. 4483: a, 15w, Ice dancing. b, 85w, Ice hockey. c, 110w, Ski jumping. d, 135w, Speed skating.

2006, Feb. 10 ***Perf. 13¼***

4483 A2044 Sheet of 4, #a-d 5.00 2.50

A2045

Kim Jong Il, 64th Birthday — A2046

No. 4485: a, 12w, Polemonium racemosum. b, 45w, Day lily. c, 100w, Dandelion. d, 140w, Parnassia palustris.

2006, Feb. 16 ***Perf. 13½***

4484 A2045 3w multi .20 .20

Souvenir Sheet

4485 A2046 Sheet of 4, #a-d 4.25 2.10

A2047

Visit of Kim Jong Il to People's Republic of China — A2048

No. 4486 — Kim Jong Il: a, 3w, At Crop Research Institute. b, 12w, At optical fiber factory. c, 35w, At Three Gorges Dam. d, 70w, At Guangzhou Intl. Conference and Exhibition Center. e, 100w, At air conditioner factory. f, 120w, At port of Yandian.

102w, Kim Jong Il and Hu Jintao.

2006, Mar. 4 ***Perf. 12x12¼***

4486 A2047 Sheet of 6, #a-f 4.75 2.40

Souvenir Sheet

Perf. 11¾

4487 A2048 102w multi 1.50 .75

A2049

Agrarian Reform Law, 60th Anniv. — A2050

2006, Mar. 5 ***Perf. 11½***

4488 A2049 12w multi + label .20 .20

Souvenir Sheet

4489 A2050 150w multi 2.10 1.10

Souvenir Sheet

First North Korean Postage Stamps, 60th Anniv. — A2051

2006, Mar. 12 ***Perf. 11¾***

4490 A2051 158w multi 2.25 1.10

Mt. Kumgang Scenery A2052

Designs: 3w, Pibong Falls. 12w, Podok Hermitage. 35w, Sokka Peak. 50w, Jipson Peak. 70w, Chongsok Rocks, horiz. 100w, Sejon Peak, horiz. 120w, Chonhwa Rock, horiz. 140w, Piro Peak, horiz.

2006, Mar. 15 ***Perf. 11¾x12¼***

4491-4498 A2052 Set of 8 7.50 3.75

Belgica 2006 World Youth Philatelic Exhibition, Brussels A2053

Designs: No. 4499, 140w, Jules Verne (1828-1905), writer. No. 4500, 140w, Tyto alba, Volvariella speciosa, Scouting emblem. No. 4501, 140w, Disa grandiflora, Nymphalidae. No. 4502, 140w, Australopithecus afarensis, rocks. No. 4503, 140w, Alaskan malamute, Birman cat, Scouting emblem. No. 4504, 140w, Sunflowers, by Vincent Van Gogh. No. 4505, 140w, Soccer ball, chess knight, table tennis paddle and ball. No. 4506, 140w, Tursiops truncatus, Scouting emblem. No. 4507, 140w, Maglev train, horiz. No. 4508, 140w, 1962 Ernst Grube Type S 4000-1 fire truck, horiz.

2006, Apr. 13 ***Perf. 11¾***

4499-4508 A2053 Set of 10 20.00 10.00

Kim Il Sung, 94th Anniv. of Birth — A2054

2006, Apr. 15 ***Perf. 11½***

4509 A2054 3w multi + label .20 .20

Association for the Restoration of the Fatherland, 70th Anniv. A2055

2006, May 5 ***Perf. 13½***

4510 A2055 3w multi .20 .20

Pothong River Improvement Project, 60th Anniv. — A2056

Illustration reduced.

2006, May 21 ***Perf. 12***

4511 A2056 12w multi .20 .20

Korean Children's Union, 60th Anniv. A2057

2006, June 6 **Litho.** ***Perf. 13½***

4612 A2057 3w multi .20 .20

2006 World Cup Soccer Championships, Germany A2058

Various soccer players in action: 3w, 130w, 160w, 210w.

2006, June 9 ***Perf. 13½***

4613-4616 A2058 Set of 4 7.00 3.50

Souvenir Sheet

Kim Chol Ju (1919-35) — A2059

2006, June 12 ***Perf. 11½x12***

4617 A2059 170w multi 2.40 1.25

Souvenir Sheet

Ri Su Bok (1933-51), War Hero and Poet — A2060

2006, July 27 ***Perf. 11¾***

4618 A2060 120w multi 1.75 .85

Miniature Sheet

Circus Performers — A2061

Designs: a, 3w, Trapeze artists (42x35mm). b, 12w, Aerial acrobatic troupe (42x35mm). c, 130w, Seesaw jumper (42x35mm). d, 200w, Juggler (42x64mm).

Perf. 11½, 11½x12 (200w)

2006, Aug. 10 **Litho.**

4619 A2061 Sheet of 4, #a-d 5.00 2.50

Korean Cuisine A2062

Designs: 3w, Kimchi. 12w, Umegi. 130w, Rice cake dumplings with bean paste. 200w, Sweet rice.

2006, Aug. 12 ***Perf. 13½***

4620-4623 A2062 Set of 4 5.00 2.50

4623a Booklet pane of 4, #4620-4623 5.00 —

Complete booklet, #4623a 5.00

Sea Mammals — A2063

Designs: 3w, Megaptera nodosa. 70w, Balaenoptera musculus. 160w, Physeter catodon. 240w, Inia geoffrensis.

2006, Aug. 20 ***Perf. 11¾***

4624-4627 A2063 Set of 4 6.75 3.25

4627a Booklet pane of 4, #4624-4627 6.75 —

Complete booklet, #4627a 6.75

Motorcycles A2064

Various motorcycles.

2006, Sept. 1 ***Perf. 11½***

4628 Horiz. strip of 4 7.00 3.50

a. A2064 3w multi .20 .20

b. A2064 102w multi 1.40 .70

c. A2064 150w multi 2.10 1.00

d. A2064 240w multi 3.25 1.60

e. Booklet pane of 4, #4628a-4628d 7.00 —

Complete booklet, #4628e 7.00

Sinking of the General Sherman, 140th Anniv. A2065

2006, Sept. 2 **Litho.** ***Perf. 13¼***

4629 A2065 130w multi 1.90 .95

Owls A2066

Designs: 12w, Tyto alba. 111w, Strix uralensis. 130w, Strix aluco. 160w, Nyctea scandiaca.

2006, Sept. 10 ***Perf. 11¾***

4630-4633 A2066 Set of 4 5.75 3.00

4633a Booklet pane of 4, #4630-4633 5.75 —

Complete booklet, #4633a 5.75

For overprints see Nos. 4648-4651.

Souvenir Sheet

Kim Il Sung University, 60th Anniv. — A2067

2006, Oct. 1 ***Perf. 11½x12***
4634 A2067 70w multi 1.00 .50

Famous Koreans A2068

Designs: 3w, Ulgi Mundok, general. 12w, So Hui (942-998), diplomat and general. 35w, Kim Ung So (1564-1624), general. 70w, Kang Kam Chan (948-1031), general. 102w, Yongae Somun, general. 130w, Ri Kyu Bo (1168-1241), poet. 160w, Mun Ik Jom (1329-98), civil official.

2006, Oct. 2 ***Perf. 13½***
4635-4641 A2068 Set of 7 7.25 3.75

Red Cross Society of North Korea, 60th Anniv. — A2071

2006, Oct. 18 **Litho.** ***Perf. 13½***
4644 A2071 30w multi .45 .20

Souvenir Sheet

Secondary Education for Koreans in Japan, 60th Anniv. — A2072

2006, Oct. 21 ***Perf. 13¼***
4645 A2072 110w multi 1.60 .80

Souvenir Sheet

Joson University, 50th Anniv. — A2074

2006, Nov. 4 ***Perf. 11½***
4647 A2074 110w multi + label 1.60 .80

Nos. 4630-4633 Overprinted in Gold

Methods and Perfs As Before

2006, Nov. 16

4648	A2066	12w on #4630		.20	.20
4649	A2066	111w on #4631		1.50	.75
4650	A2066	130w on #4632		1.90	.95
4651	A2066	160w on #4633		2.25	1.10
		Nos. 4648-4651 (4)		5.85	3.00

Belgica 2006 World Youth Stamp Exhibition. Location of the overprint varies.

New Year 2007 A2076

2007, Jan. 1 **Litho.** ***Perf. 13½***
4653 A2076 3w multi .20 .20

New Year 2007 (Year of the Pig) A2077

Various pigs: 3w, 45w.
No. 4656 — Various pigs: a, 70w. b, 130w.

2007, Jan. 1 ***Perf. 11½***

4654-4655	A2077	Set of 2	.70	.35
4656	A2077	Sheet, #4654-4655, 4656a, 4656b	3.50	1.75
c.		Booklet pane, #4654-4655, 4656a, 4656b	3.50	—
		Complete booklet, #4656c	3.50	
d.		Souvenir sheet of 1 #4656a	1.00	.50

A2078

Kim Jong Il, 65th Birthday — A2079

Designs: 3w, Kimiljonghwa begonia and butterfly.
No. 4658 — Mountain, lake and musical score: a, 12w. b, 70w. c, 100w. d, 140w.

2007, Feb. 16 ***Perf. 13¼***
4657 A2078 3w multi .20 .20
4658 A2079 Sheet of 4, #a-d 4.50 2.25

Symbols of Progress A2080

2007, Feb. 28 ***Perf. 13¼***
4659 A2080 3w multi .20 .20

Annual joint editorial of state newspapers.

Butterflies — A2081

Designs: 15w, Callicore selima. 85w, Morpho rhetenor. 110w, Atrophaneura alcinous. 160w, Parnassius bremeri.

2007, Mar. 5

4660-4663	A2081	Set of 4	5.25	2.60
4663a		Booklet pane of 4, #4660-4663	5.25	—
		Complete booklet, #4663a	5.25	

Miniature Sheet

Koguryo Tombs UNESCO World Heritage Site — A2082

No. 4664 — Anak Tomb No. 3 paintings: a, 3w, Stable (60x42mm). b, 70w, Well (60x42mm). c, 130w, Milling area (30x42mm). d, 160w, Man blowing horn (30x42mm).

2007, Mar. 10

4664	A2082	Sheet of 4, #a-d	5.25	2.60
e.		Booklet pane of 4, #4664a-4664d	5.25	—
		Complete booklet, #4664e	5.25	

Korean National Association, 90th Anniv. — A2083

2007, Mar. 23
4665 A2083 12w multi .20 .20

Ludwig van Beethoven (1770-1827), Composer — A2084

2007, Mar. 26
4666 A2084 80w multi 1.10 .55

Mangyongdae, Birthplace of Kim Il Sung — A2085

Paintings of Kim Il Sung — A2086

Kim Il Sung and Family — A2087

No. 4668: a, 45w, The Great Leader Kim Il Sung on the 250-Mile Journey for Learning. b, 70w, The Great Leader Kim Il Sung Who Braved Through the Arduous Road of the Anti-Japanese War. c, 100w, Ever Victorious Road. d, 160w, At the Field Predicting the Rich Harvest.

2007, Apr. 15 ***Perf. 13¼***
4667 A2085 3w multi .20 .20

Perf. 11¾
4668 A2086 Sheet of 4, #a-d 5.25 2.60

Souvenir Sheet

Perf. 11¾x11½

4669 A2087 130w multi 1.90 .95

Kim Il Sung (1912-94).

Miniature Sheet

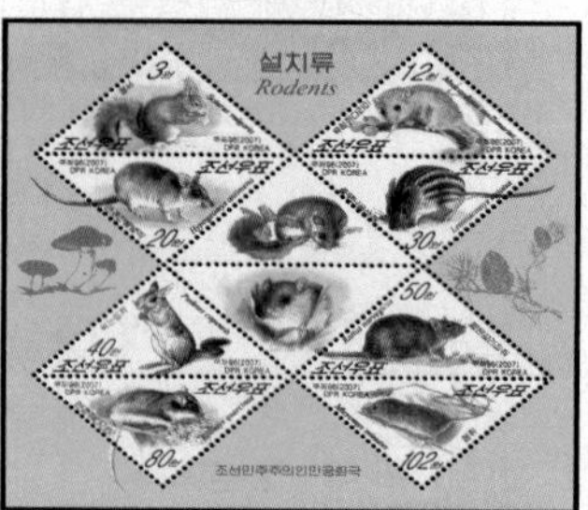

Rodents — A2088

No. 2088: a, 3w, Sciururs vulgaris. b, 12w, Muscardinus avellanarius. c, 20w, Hypogeomys antimena. d, 30w, Lemniscomys striatus. e, 40w, Pedetes capensis. f, 50w, Rattus norvegicus. g, 80w, Eliomys quercinus. h, 102w, Micromys minutus.

2007, Apr. 20 ***Perf. 13x13x12¼***

4670 A2088 Sheet of 8, #a-h, + 2 labels 4.75 2.40

Korean People's Army Soldiers and Mt. Paektu A2089

Leaders Reviewing Troops — A2090

Kim Il Sung and Kim Jong Il Reviewing Troops — A2091

No. 4672: a, 80w, Kim Il Sung and Kim Jong Il reviewing troops. b, 100w, Kim Jong Il and soldiers.

2007, Apr. 25 ***Perf. 13¼***

4671 A2089 12wmulti .20 .20

Perf. 11¾

4672 A2090 Sheet of 2, #a-b 2.50 1.25

Souvenir Sheet

Perf. 12x11½

4673 A2091 120w multi 1.75 .85

Korean People's Army, 75th anniv.

Prevention of Bird Flu — A2092

2007, May 10 ***Perf. 13¼***

4674 A2092 85w multi 1.25 .60

Miniature Sheet

First North Korean Currency, 60th Anniv. — A2093

No. 4675 — Banknotes: a, 3w, 10-won note of 1947. b, 12w, 50-chon note of 1947. c, 35w, 100-won note of 1959. d, 50w, 10-won note of 1959. e, 70w, 10-won note of 1978. f, 110w, 1-won note of 1978. g, 130w, 50-won note of 1992. h, 160w, 100-won note of 1992.

2007, May 20 **Litho.**

4675 A2093 Sheet of 8, #a-h 8.00 4.00

Souvenir Sheet

Battle of Pochonbo, 70th Anniv. — A2094

2007, June 4 ***Perf. 11½x12***

4676 A2094 120w multi 1.75 .85

Fish A2095

Designs: 15w, Naso lituratus. 50w, Carassius auratus. 110w, A. citrinellus. 200w, Symphysodon discus.

2007, July 1 ***Perf. 13¼***

4677-4680 A2095 Set of 4 5.25 2.60

4680a Booklet pane of 4, #4677-4680 5.25 —

Complete booklet, #4680a 5.25

Self-disembowelment of Ri Jun at Hague Intl. Peace Conference, Cent. — A2096

2007, July 14

4681 A2096 110w brn & grn 1.60 .80

Fossils A2097

Designs: 15w, Tetracorallia. 70w, Neuropteridium. 130w, Yoldia. 200w, Rhinoceros mandible.

2007, July 20

4682-4685 A2097 Set of 4 6.00 3.00

4685a Booklet pane of 4, #4682-4685 6.00 —

Complete booklet, #4685a 6.00

Miniature Sheet

Orchids — A2098

No. 4686: a, 3w, Oncidium wyattianum. b, 70w, Cymbidium Red Beauty "Carmen." c, 127w, Dendrobium thyrsifolium. d, 140w, Dendrobium Candy Stripe "Kodama."

2007, Aug. 3 ***Perf. 12¾***

4686 A2098 Sheet of 4, #a-d 4.75 2.40

e. Booklet pane of 4, #4686a-4686d 4.75 —

Complete booklet, #4686e 4.75

Women's Soccer — A2099

No. 4687 — Various women soccer players making plays: a, 12w. b, 40w. c, 70w. d, 110w. e, 140w.

2007, Sept. 10 ***Perf.***

4687 A2099 Sheet of 5, #a-e 5.25 2.60

Souvenir Sheet

4688 A2099 130w shown 1.90 .95

Miniature Sheet

Flowers — A2100

No. 4689: a, Gladiolus gandavensis. b, Iris ensata. c, Rosa hybrida. d, Nelumbo nucifera.

2007, Sept. 26 ***Perf. 13¼***

4689 A2100 30w Sheet of 4, #a-d 1.75 .85

e. Booklet pane of 4, #4689a-4689d 1.75 —

Complete booklet, #4689e 1.75

See Russia No. 7045.

Furniture and Household Furnishings — A2103

Designs: 3w, Seal box. 12w, Ornamental chest. 40w, Collapsible dressing table. 70w, Wardrobe. 110w, Chest of drawers. 130w, Chest of drawers, diff.

2007, Nov. 1 **Litho.** ***Perf. 13¼***

4694-4699 A2103 Set of 6 5.25 2.60

4699a Booklet pane of 6, #4694-4699 5.25 —

Complete booklet, #4699a 5.25

Food A2104

Designs: 12w, Potato and rice cakes. 50w, Yongchae kimchi. 70w, Fermented flatfish. 110w, Potato cakes.

2007, Nov. 5

4700-4703 A2104 Set of 4 3.50 1.75

4703a Booklet pane of 4, #4700-4703 3.50 —

Complete booklet, #4703a 3.50

Souvenir Sheet

Summit Meeting of Pres. Kim Jong Il and South Korean Pres. Roh Moo Hyun — A2105

2007, Nov. 10 ***Perf. 11½x12***

4704 A2105 170w multi 2.40 1.25

Miniature Sheets

Scenes From Arirang Gymnastics Performance — A2106

No. 4705 — Various scenes: a, 12w. b, 50w. No. 4706 — Various scenes: a, 120w. b, 155w.

2007, Nov. 15 ***Perf. 11½***

Sheets of 2, #a-b, + Label

4705-4706 A2106 Set of 2 4.75 2.40

Paintings of Kim Dong Ho — A2107

Designs: 3w, Plowing. 12w, Weaving a Straw Mat. 70w, Thrashing. 130w, Archery.

2007, Nov. 18 ***Perf. 13¼***

4707-4710 A2107 Set of 4 3.00 1.50

4710a Booklet pane of 4, #4707-4710 3.00 —

Complete booklet, #4710a 3.00

Souvenir Sheet

Visit of Viet Nam Communist Party Secretary General Nong Duc Manh — A2108

2007, Dec. 16 ***Perf. 12x11½***
4711 A2108 120w multi 1.75 .85

Home of Kim Jong Suk — A2109

Paintings Depicting Kim Jong Suk — A2110

No. 4713: a, 30w, Kim Jong Suk and Kim Il Sung (54x45mm). b, 70w, Kim Jong Suk (45mm diameter). c, 110w, Kim Jong Suk in battle (54x45mm).
Illustration A2109 reduced.

2007, Dec. 24 ***Perf. 12x11½***
4712 A2109 3w multi .20 .20

Souvenir Sheet

Perf. 13¼, Perf. (#4713b)
4713 A2110 Sheet of 3, #a-c 3.00 1.50

New Year 2008 — A2111

2008, Jan. 1 **Litho.** ***Perf. 13¼***
4714 A2111 3w multi .20 .20

Publication of Saenal Sinmun, 80th Anniv. — A2112

2008, Jan. 15
4715 A2112 85w multi 1.25 .60

Joint Editorials of State Newspapers — A2113

Red flag in upper left corner and: No. 4716, 3w, Arms and flag of North Korea, tower. No. 4717, 3w, Soldiers. No. 4718, 12w, Soldier and flag. No. 4719, 12w, Soldiers, factories and electrical tower, horiz. 30w, Woman and food, horiz. 120w, Musicians, children playing soccer, building. 130w, Men and woman, doves, map of Korea.

2008, Jan. 30 ***Perf. 11¾***
4716-4722 A2113 Set of 7 4.50 2.25

Parrots A2114

Designs: 15w, Melopsittacus undulatus. 85w, Agapornis roseicollis. 155w, Agapornis personata, horiz. 170w, Two Melopsittacus undulatus, horiz.

2008, Feb. 5 ***Perf. 13¼***
4723-4726 A2114 Set of 4 6.00 3.00
4726a Booklet pane of 4, #4723-4726 6.00 —
Complete booklet, #4726a 6.00

Souvenir Sheet

Naming of Kimjongilhwa Begonia, 20th Anniv. — A2115

2008, Feb. 13 ***Perf. 11½x12***
4727 A2115 85w multi 1.25 .60

A2116

Flowers — A2117

Designs: 3w, Pyrethrum hybridum.
No. 4729: a, 12w, Tulipa gesneriana (30x42mm). b, 70w, Adonis amurensis (30x42mm). c, 120w, Mathiola incana (30x42mm). d, 155w, Kimjongilhwa begonia (44mm diameter)

2008, Feb. 16 ***Perf. 13¼***
4728 A2116 3w multi .20 .20
4729 A2117 Sheet of 4, #a-d 5.00 2.50

Kim Jong Il, 66th birthday.

Kim Il Sung Birthplace Type of 2002

2008, Mar. 15 **Litho.** ***Perf. 11½***
4730 A1886 3w red .20 .20

Miniature Sheet

Publication of "On the Art of Cinema," by Kim Jong Il, 35th Anniv. — A2118

No. 4731 — Various actors and actresses: a, 3w, Musician. b, 85w, Man holding gun. c, 135w, Martial artist. d, 170w, Man, woman and children.

2008, Mar. 15 ***Perf. 13¼***
4731 A2118 Sheet of 4, #a-d 5.50 2.75

250-Mile Journey for Learning, 85th Anniv. — A2119

2008, Mar. 16 ***Perf. 12***
4732 A2119 15w multi .20 .20

2008 Summer Olympics, Beijing — A2120

No. 4733: a, 3w, Soccer. b, 12w, Basketball. c, 30w, Tennis. d, 70w, Table tennis.
Illustration reduced.

2008, Mar. 28 ***Perf. 13¼***
4733 A2120 Block or horiz. strip of 4, #a-d 1.60 .80

Famous Men — A2121

Designs: 85w, Choe Yong (1316-88), military leader. 160w, Ho Jun (1546-1615), doctor.

2008, Mar. 29 ***Perf. 12***
4734-4735 A2121 Set of 2 3.50 1.75

Election of Kim Jong Il as Chairman of National Defense Commission, 15th Anniv. — A2122

2008, Apr. 9 ***Perf. 13¼***
4736 A2122 12w multi .20 .20

International Friendship Exhibition A2124

Gifts to Kim Il Sung: 3w, Pitcher and oil lamp. 85w, Painting of rooster. 155w, Throne. 135w, Vase with two handles.

2008, Apr. 15 **Litho.** ***Perf. 11½***
4738-4740 A2124 Set of 3 3.50 1.75

Souvenir Sheet

4741 A2124 135w multi 1.90 .95

North-South Joint Conference, 60th Anniv. — A2125

2008, Apr. 21 ***Perf. 12***
4742 A2125 12w gray green .20 .20

Mushrooms A2126

Designs: 12w, Amanita muscaria. 50w, Armillariella mellea. 135w, Macrolepota procera. 155w, Tricholoma terreum.

2008, May 8 ***Perf. 11½***
4743-4746 A2126 Set of 4 5.00 2.50
4746a Booklet pane of 4, #4743-4746 5.00 —
Complete booklet, #4746a 5.00

Buildings on Mt. Ryongak A2127

Designs: 35w, Two buildings. 155w, Building and wall.

2008, May 25 ***Perf. 13¼***
4747-4748 A2127 Set of 2 2.75 1.40

Musical Instruments — A2128

Designs: 15w, Hyangbipha (stringed instrument). 50w, Phiri (contrabassoon). 120w, Jangsaenap (oboe). 160w, Kayagum (zither), horiz.

2008, June 1 ***Perf. 13¼***
4749-4752 A2128 Set of 4 5.00 2.50
4752a Booklet pane of 4, #4749-4752 5.00 —
Complete booklet, #4752a 5.00

Opera Scenes and Scores — A2129

Designs: 3w, Sea of Blood. 12w, The Flower Girl. 85w, The True Daughter of the Party. 120w, Tell Oh Forest. 155w, The Song of Mt. Kumgang.
Illustration reduced.

2008, June 5 ***Perf. 12x11½***
4753-4757 A2129 Set of 5 5.25 2.60

North Korea No. 1 and Romania No. 1 — A2130

2008, June 20 ***Perf. 12¼x11¾***
4758 A2130 85w multi 1.25 .60

EFIRO 2008 Intl. Stamp Exhibition, Bucharest, Romania.

Capture of the USS Pueblo, 40th Anniv. — A2131

2008, June 25 ***Perf. 12¼x11¾***
4759 A2131 12w multi .20 .20

Souvenir Sheet

Olympic Torch Relay in Pyongyang — A2132

2008, June 26 ***Perf. 11¾x12¼***
4760 A2132 120w multi 1.75 .85

Minerals — A2133

Designs: 12w, Serpentine. 75s, Copper pyrite. 135w, Sphalerite. 155w, Molybdenite.

2008, July 5 ***Perf. 12¼x11¾***
4761-4764 A2133 Set of 4 5.25 2.60
4764a Booklet pane of 4, #4761-4764 5.25 —
Complete booklet, #4764a 5.25

Souvenir Sheets

A2134

A2135

Korean War Ceasefire, 55th Anniv. — A2136

No. 4765: a, 3w, Kim Il Sung leading troop crossing of Han River. b, 120w, Kim Il Sung with troops.
No. 4766: a, 35w, Kim Il Sung and seated troops. b, 155w, Celebration.
85w, Kim Il Sung at battleground.

2008, July 27 ***Perf. 12x11½***
4765 A2134 Sheet of 2, #a-b 1.75 .85
4766 A2135 Sheet of 2, #a-b 2.75 1.40

Perf. 11½
4767 A2136 85w multi 1.25 .60

Souvenir Sheet

Jong Il Peak, 20th Anniv. of Renaming — A2137

2008, Aug. 9 ***Perf. 13¼***
4768 A2137 120w multi 1.75 .85

Food A2138

Designs: 3w, Rice and wormwood cakes. 70w, Rice cakes. 135w, Pancakes. 155w, Garlic in soy sauce.

2008, Aug. 20 **Litho.** ***Perf. 13¼***
4769-4772 A2138 Set of 4 5.25 2.60
4772a Booklet pane of 4, #4769-4772 5.25 —
Complete booklet, #4772a 5.25

A2139

Songun Revolutionary Leadership — A2140

2008, Aug. 25
4773 A2139 12w multi .20 .20

Souvenir Sheet

4774 A2140 135w multi 1.90 .95

Miniature Sheet

Koguryo Tombs UNESCO World Heritage Site — A2141

No. 4775 — Anak Tomb No. 3 paintings: a, 3w, Mask dance (60x42mm). b, 90w, Janghaedok, aide to King Kogukwon (30x42mm). c, 120w, Garage (60x42mm). d, 155w, Stable (60x42mm).

2008, Sept. 2 **Litho.** ***Perf. 13¼***
4775 A2141 Sheet of 4, #a-d, + label 5.25 2.60
e. Booklet pane of 4, #4775a-4775d 5.25 —
Complete booklet, #4775e 5.25

A2142

Flag
A2143

2008, Sept. 9 *Perf. 11½*

4776 A2142 3w multi .20 .20
4777 A2143 155w multi 2.25 1.10

A2144

Creation of North Korea, 60th Anniv. — A2145

Designs: 3w, Chollima Statue, flag of North Korea, city and flowers. 12w, Torch, flag of the Supreme Commander, people. 70w, Soldiers. 120w, People on horses. 160w, Handshake. 155w, Creation of National Flag and Arms.

2008, Sept. 9 *Perf. 13¼*

4778-4782 A2144 Set of 5 5.25 2.60

Souvenir Sheet

4783 A2145 155w multi 2.25 1.10

Transportation — A2146

Designs: No. 4784, 680w, Niña, ship of Christopher Columbus. No. 4785, 680w, 1910 Russian steam engine. No. 4786, 680w, Hindenburg over Lake Constance. No. 4787, 680w, Siberian husky dog sled team. No. 4788, 680w, Ivan Basso, cyclist. No. 4789, 680w, Mercedes-Benz-Mets LF 16 fire truck. No. 4790, 680w, Two Ferrari Enzos. No. 4791, 680w, Eurostar train. No. 4792, 680w, Concorde. No. 4793, 680w, Laika the dog and Sputnik 2.

2008, Sept. 15 *Perf.*

4784-4793 A2146 Set of 10 95.00 47.50

Nos. 4784-4793 each were printed in sheets of 2.

AIR POST STAMPS

Lisunov Li-2 Airliner over Pyongyang
AP1

1958, Feb. 4 **Photo.** *Perf. 10*

C1 AP1 20w blue 11.00 2.00
a. Imperf 22.50 10.00
b. Perf 11 — —
c. Rouletted — —

Korean Civil Aviation.

KUWAIT

ku-'wāt

LOCATION — Northwestern coast of the Persian Gulf
GOVT. — Sheikdom
AREA — 7,000 sq. mi.
POP. — 1,991,115 (1999 est.)
CAPITAL — Kuwait

Kuwait was under British protection until June 19, 1961, when it became a fully independent state.

16 Annas = 1 Rupee
100 Naye Paise = 1 Rupee (1957)
1000 Fils = 1 Kuwaiti Dinar (1961)

Catalogue values for unused stamps in this country are for Never Hinged items, beginning with Scott 72 in the regular postage section, Scott C5 in the air post section, and Scott J1 in the postage due section.

There was a first or trial setting of the overprint with the word "Koweit." Twenty-four sets of regular and official stamps were printed with this spelling. Value for set, $10,000.

Catalogue values for Nos. 1-71 used, are for postally used examples. Stamps with telegraph cancellations are worth less.

Stamps of India, 1911-23, Overprinted

a

b

1923-24 Wmk. 39 *Perf. 14*

1 A47(a) ½a green 4.75 *6.50*
2 A48(a) 1a dk brown 4.50 *3.00*
3 A58(a) 1½a chocolate 3.75 *4.75*
4 A49(a) 2a violet 6.00 *5.00*
5 A57(a) 2a6p ultra 4.50 *10.00*
6 A51(a) 3a brown org 6.75 *22.50*
7 A51(a) 3a ultra ('24) 12.50 *3.00*
8 A52(a) 4a ol green 11.50 *27.50*
9 A53(a) 6a bister 13.00 *16.00*
10 A54(a) 8a red violet 12.00 *38.00*
11 A55(a) 12a claret 22.50 *47.50*
12 A56(b) 1r grn & red brown 30.00 *30.00*
13 A56(b) 2r brn & car rose 55.00 *100.00*
14 A56(b) 5r vio & ultra 125.00 *240.00*
15 A56(b) 10r car & green 175.00 *375.00*
Nos. 1-15 (15) 486.75 *928.75*

Overprint "a" on India No. 102 is generally considered unofficial.

Nos. 1-4, 6-7 exist with inverted overprint. None of these are believed to have been sold at the Kuwait post office.

For overprints see Nos. O1-O13.

Stamps of India, 1926-35, Overprinted type "a"

1929-37 Wmk. 196

17 A47 ½a green 4.00 1.75
18 A71 ½a green ('34) 7.00 1.75
19 A48 1a dark brown 11.00 1.90
20 A72 1a dk brown ('34) 7.00 1.25
21 A60 2a dk violet 5.50 1.25
22 A60 2a vermilion 32.50 *95.00*
23 A49 2a ver ('34) 30.00 6.75
a. Small die 5.00 2.50
24 A51 3a ultramarine 6.00 2.00
25 A51 3a car rose ('34) 9.00 *4.50*
26 A61 4a olive green 35.00 *82.50*
27 A52 4a ol green ('34) 10.00 *14.50*
28 A53 6a bister ('37) 27.50 *65.00*
29 A54 8a red violet 12.00 *17.50*
30 A55 12a claret 32.50 *47.50*

Overprinted

c

31 A56 1r green & brown 20.00 *30.00*
32 A56 2r buff & car rose 21.00 *72.50*
33 A56 5r dk vio & ultra ('37) 115.00 *275.00*
34 A56 10r car & grn ('34) 225.00 *450.00*
35 A56 15r ol grn & ultra ('37) 700.00 *900.00*
Nos. 17-35 (19) 1,310. *2,070.*

For overprints see Nos. O15-O25.

Stamps of India, 1937, Overprinted type "a" (A80, A81) or "c" (A82)

1939 Wmk. 196 *Perf. 13½x14*

45 A80 ½a brown 1.50 *1.60*
46 A80 1a carmine 1.50 *1.60*
47 A81 2a scarlet 2.75 *2.75*
48 A81 3a yel green 3.75 *2.75*
49 A81 4a dark brown 5.50 *16.00*
50 A81 6a peacock blue 5.50 *10.00*
51 A81 8a blue violet 12.00 *37.50*
52 A81 12a car lake 10.00 *55.00*
53 A82 1r brown & slate 3.75 *4.25*
54 A82 2r dk brown & dk violet 13.50 *15.00*
55 A82 5r dp ultra & dk green 17.50 *24.50*
56 A82 10r rose car & dk violet 80.00 100.00
a. Double overprint 350.00 350.00
57 A82 15r dk green & dk brown 105.00 *200.00*
Nos. 45-57 (13) 262.25 *470.95*
Set, never hinged 400.00

Stamps of India 1940-43, Overprinted in Black

1945 Wmk. 196 *Perf. 13½x14*

59 A83 3p slate 2.75 *4.75*
60 A83 ½a rose violet 1.75 *3.50*
61 A83 9p lt green 3.75 *11.50*
62 A83 1a car rose 2.00 *2.50*
63 A84 1½a dark purple 2.75 *11.00*
64 A84 2a scarlet 3.00 *4.50*
65 A84 3a violet 5.00 *6.50*
66 A84 3½a ultramarine 5.50 *11.00*
67 A85 4a chocolate 5.00 *4.75*
68 A85 6a peacock blue 17.50 13.00
69 A85 8a blue violet 9.50 5.00
70 A85 12a car lake 10.00 5.50
71 A81 14a rose violet 17.50 *25.00*
Nos. 59-71 (13) 86.00 *108.50*
Set, never hinged 110.00

Catalogue values for unused stamps in this section, from this point to the end of the section, are for Never Hinged items.

British Postal Administration

See Oman (Muscat) for similar stamps with surcharge of new value only.

Great Britain Nos. 258 to 263, 243 and 248 Surcharged in Black

1948-49 Wmk. 251 *Perf. 14½x14*

72 A101 ½a on ½p grn 2.50 *2.50*
73 A101 1a on 1p ver 2.50 *2.50*
74 A101 1½a on 1½p lt red brown 3.50 2.50
75 A101 2a on 2p lt org 2.75 *2.50*
76 A101 2½a on 2½p ultra 3.75 1.40
77 A101 3a on 3p violet 2.75 1.25
a. Pair, one without surcharge — —
78 A102 6a on 6p rose lil 2.75 1.00
79 A103 1r on 1sh brown 6.00 2.75

Great Britain Nos. 249A, 250 and 251A Surcharged in Black

Wmk. 259 *Perf. 14*

80 A104 2r on 2sh6p yel grn 6.00 *6.25*
81 A104 5r on 5sh dull red 10.00 6.25
81A A105 10r on 10sh ultra 50.00 10.00
Nos. 72-81A (11) 92.50 38.90

Issued: #72-81, Apr., 1948; 10r, July 4, 1949.

Bars of surcharge at bottom on No. 81A.

Silver Wedding Issue

Great Britain Nos. 267 and 268 Surcharged in Black

Perf. 14½x14, 14x14½

1948 Wmk. 251

82 A109 2½a on 2½p brt ultra 3.00 3.00
83 A110 15r on £1 deep chalky blue 42.50 42.50

Three bars obliterate the original denomination on No. 83.

Olympic Games Issue

Great Britain Nos. 271 to 274 Surcharged "KUWAIT" and New Value in Black

1948 *Perf. 14½x14*

84 A113 2½a on 2½p brt ultra 1.50 3.00
85 A114 3a on 3p dp violet 1.50 3.00
86 A115 6a on 6p red violet 1.75 3.50
87 A116 1r on 1sh dk brown 1.75 3.50
Nos. 84-87 (4) 6.50 13.00

A square of dots obliterates the original denomination on No. 87.

UPU Issue

Great Britain Nos. 276 to 279 Surcharged "KUWAIT", New Value and Square of Dots in Black

1949, Oct. 10 Photo.

89 A117 2½a on 2½p brt ultra 1.25 1.00
90 A118 3a on 3p brt vio 1.50 1.25
91 A119 6a on 6p red vio 2.00 *2.50*
92 A120 1r on 1sh brown 2.25 1.50
Nos. 89-92 (4) 7.00 6.25

Great Britain Nos. 280-285 Surcharged Like Nos. 72-79 in Black

1950-51 Wmk. 251 *Perf. 14½x14*

93 A101 ½a on ½p lt org 2.50 1.90
94 A101 1a on 1p ultra 2.50 1.90
95 A101 1½a on 1½p green 2.50 *2.75*
96 A101 2a on 2p lt red brown 2.75 1.90
97 A101 2½a on 2½p ver 2.75 *2.75*
98 A102 4a on 4p ultra ('50) 2.50 1.60

Great Britain Nos. 286-288 Surcharged in Black

Perf. 11x12
Wmk. 259

99 A121 2r on 2sh6p green 17.50 5.50
100 A121 5r on 5sh dl red 27.50 6.50
101 A122 10r on 10sh ultra 35.00 9.25
Nos. 93-101 (9) 95.50 34.05

Longer bars, at lower right, on No. 101.

Issued: 4a, 10/2/50; others, 5/3/51.

Stamps of Great Britain, 1952-54 Surcharged "KUWAIT" and New Value in Black or Dark Blue

1952-54 Wmk. 298 *Perf. 14½x14*

102 A126 ½a on ½p red org ('53) .30 .40
103 A126 1a on 1p ultra ('53) .30 .20
104 A126 1½a on 1½p green .30 .25
105 A126 2a on 2p red brn ('53) .30 .20
106 A127 2½a on 2½p scarlet .30 .25
107 A127 3a on 3p dk pur (Dk Bl) ('54) .75 .20
108 A128 4a on 4p ultra ('53) 2.25 .40
109 A129 6a on 6p lilac rose ('54) 2.25 .20
111 A132 12a on 1sh6p dk green ('53) 7.00 1.25
112 A131 1r on 1sh6p dk blue ('53) 6.00 .50
Nos. 102-112 (10) 19.75 3.85

Coronation Issue

Great Britain Nos. 313-316 Surcharged "KUWAIT" and New Value in Black

1953, June 3

113 A134 2½a on 2½p scarlet 4.00 1.25
114 A135 4a on 4p brt ultra 4.00 1.25
115 A136 12a on 1sh3p dk grn 6.00 2.00
116 A137 1r on 1sh6p dk blue 5.00 1.90
Nos. 113-116 (4) 19.00 6.40

Squares of dots obliterate the original denominations on Nos. 115 and 116.

Great Britain Stamps of 1955-56 Surcharged "KUWAIT" and New Value in Black

1955 Wmk. 308 Engr. *Perf. 11x12*

117 A133 2r on 2sh6p dk brown 9.00 1.50
118 A133 5r on 5sh crimson 10.00 4.25
119 A133 10r on 10sh dp ultra 11.00 4.25
Nos. 117-119 (3) 30.00 10.00

The surcharge on #117-119 exists in two types.

1956 Photo. *Perf. 14½x14*

120 A126 ½a on ½p red org .35 *.40*
121 A126 1a on 1p ultra .75 *.80*
122 A126 1½a on 1½p green .40 *.30*
123 A126 2a on 2p red brown .40 *.30*
124 A127 2½a on 2½p scar .85 *.75*
125 A128 4a on 4p ultra 6.00 2.25
126 A129 6a on 6p lil rose 3.00 .25
127 A132 12a on 1sh3p dk grn 12.50 5.50
128 A131 1r on 1sh6p dk bl 6.25 .20
Nos. 120-128 (9) 30.50 *10.75*

Great Britain Nos. 317-325, 328 and 332 Surcharged "KUWAIT" and New Value in Black

1957-58 Wmk. 308 *Perf. 14½x14*

129 A129 1np on 5p lt brown .35 .35
130 A126 3np on ½p red org 1.00 1.25
131 A126 6np on 1p ultra 1.00 .60
132 A126 9np on 1½p green 1.00 1.00
133 A126 12np on 2p red brn 1.00 1.00
134 A127 15np on 2½p scar, type I 1.00 1.00
a. Type II ('58) 25.00 35.00
135 A127 20np on 3p dk pur 1.00 .20
136 A128 25np on 4p ultra 3.50 2.00
137 A129 40np on 6p lilac rose 1.75 .20
138 A130 50np on 9p dp ol grn 7.75 3.00
139 A132 75np on 1sh3p dk grn 8.00 2.50
Nos. 129-139 (11) 27.35 13.10

The arrangement of the surcharge varies on different values; there are three bars through value on No. 138.

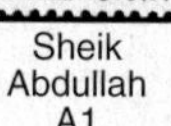

Sheik Abdullah
A1

Dhow
A2

Oil Derrick
A3

Designs: 50np, Pipe lines. 75np, Main square, Kuwait. 2r, Dhow, derrick and Sheik. 5r, Mosque and Sheik. 10r, Oil plant at Burgan and Sheik.

Perf. 12½

1959, Feb. 1 Unwmk. Engr.

140 A1 5np green .60 .20
141 A1 10np rose brown .35 .20
142 A1 15np yellow brown .45 .20
143 A1 20np gray violet .35 .20
144 A1 25np vermilion .50 .20
145 A1 40np rose claret 3.25 .45

Perf. 13½x13

146 A2 40np dark blue .85 .20
147 A2 50np carmine .85 .20
148 A2 75np olive green 1.00 .25

Perf. 14x13½

149 A3 1r claret 1.50 .30
150 A3 2r red brn & dp bl 4.50 .60
151 A3 5r green 6.50 1.25
152 A3 10r purple 20.00 3.75
Nos. 140-152 (13) 40.70 8.00

No. 140-141 and 145 were issued in 1958 for local use. They became valid for international mail on Feb. 1, 1959, but No. 145 was withdrawn after two weeks.

Sheik Abdullah and Flag — A4

1960, Feb. 25 Engr. *Perf. 14*

153 A4 40np olive grn & red .55 .20
154 A4 60np blue & red .80 .30

10th anniv. of the accession of Sheik Sir Abdullah As-Salim As-Sabah.

Types of 1959, Redrawn

Designs: 20f, 3d, Mosque and Sheik. 25f, 100f, Vickers Viscount. 30f, 75f, Dhow, derrick and Sheik. 35f, 90f, Shuwaikh secondary school. 45f, 1d, Wara Hill, Burgan oil field.

1961 *Perf. 12½*

155 A1 1f green .35 .20
156 A1 2f rose brown .35 .20
157 A1 4f yellow brown .35 .20
158 A1 5f gray violet .35 .20
159 A1 8f salmon pink .35 .20
160 A1 15f rose claret .35 .20

Perf. 14x13½, 13½ (40f, 250f)

161 A3 20f green .35 .20
162 A3 25f blue .75 .20
163 A3 30f red brn & dp bl .75 .20
164 A3 35f ver & black .70 .30
165 A2 40f dark blue .55 .20
166 A3 45f violet brown .65 .20
167 A3 75f green & sepia 1.25 .60
168 A3 90f ultra & brown 1.00 .50
169 A3 100f rose red 3.75 .30
170 A2 250f olive green 9.75 1.40
171 A3 1d orange 17.50 4.25
172 A3 3d brick red 45.00 25.00
Nos. 155-172 (18) 84.10 34.55

Nos. 165 and 170 are 32x22mm.
Issued: 75f, 90f, 4/27; 35f, 5/8; others, 4/1.

Symbols of Telecommunications — A5

Perf. 11½

1962, Jan. 11 Unwmk. Photo.

Granite Paper

173 A5 8f blue & black .40 .20
174 A5 20f rose & black .80 .25

4th Arab Telecommunications Union Conference.

Mubarakiya School and Sheiks Abdullah and Mubarak — A6

1962, Apr. 15 Unwmk. *Perf. 11½*

175 A6 8f gldn brn, blk, org & gold .35 .20
176 A6 20f lt blue, blk, org & gold .85 .35

50th anniversary of Mubarakiya School.

Arab League Building, Cairo, and Emblem — A7

1962, Apr. 23 *Perf. 13½x13*

177 A7 20f purple .30 .20
178 A7 45f brown 1.00 .20

Arab Publicity Week, Mar. 22-28.

Flag of Kuwait — A8

Malaria Eradication Emblem — A9

1962, June 19 *Perf. 11½*

Flag in Green, Black & Red

179 A8 8f black & tan .30 .20
180 A8 20f black & yellow .45 .30
181 A8 45f black & lt blue .70 .45
182 A8 90f black & lilac 2.00 .90
Nos. 179-182 (4) 3.45 1.85

Issued for National Day, June 19.

1962, Aug. 1 *Perf. 13½x13*

183 A9 4f slate green & yel grn .30 .20
184 A9 25f green & gray .60 .30

WHO drive to eradicate malaria.
No. 184 has laurel leaves added and inscription rearranged.

Cogwheel, Oil Wells, Camels and Modern Building — A10

Perf. 11x13

1962, Dec. 8 Unwmk. Litho.

185 A10 8f multicolored .50 .20
186 A10 20f multicolored .65 .20
187 A10 45f multicolored 1.00 .35
188 A10 75f multicolored 2.10 .60
Nos. 185-188 (4) 4.25 1.35

Bicentenary of the Sabah dynasty.

Mother and Child — A11

1963, Mar. 21 Photo. *Perf. 14½x14*

189 A11 8f yel, red, blk & green .35 .20
190 A11 20f blue, red, blk & grn .50 .20
191 A11 45f lt ol, red, blk & grn .90 .30
192 A11 75f gray, red, blk & green 1.25 .35
Nos. 189-192 (4) 3.00 1.05

Issued for Mother's Day, Mar. 21, 1963.

Wheat Emblem, Date Palm, Cow and Sheep — A12

1963, Mar. 21 *Perf. 14x14½*

193 A12 4f red brn, lt blue & grn .50 .20
194 A12 8f brown, yel & green .80 .20
195 A12 20f red brn, pale vio & green 1.10 .40
196 A12 45f red brn, rose & green 2.10 .90
Nos. 193-196 (4) 4.50 1.70

FAO "Freedom from Hunger" campaign.

Test Tube, Oil Drops and Ship — A13

1963, Apr. 15 Photo. *Perf. 14½x14*

197 A13 4f brown, yel & blue .30 .20
198 A13 20f green, yel & blue .60 .20
199 A13 45f brt mag, yel & blue 1.25 .30
Nos. 197-199 (3) 2.15 .70

Issued for Education Day.

Sheik Abdullah, Flags and Map of Kuwait A14

1963, June 19 *Perf. 14x13*

Flags in Black, Bright Green & Red; Denominations in Black

200 A14 4f ultramarine 1.40 .35
201 A14 5f ocher 1.60 .65
202 A14 20f bright lilac 5.25 2.75
203 A14 50f olive 9.50 4.50
Nos. 200-203 (4) 17.75 8.25

Second anniversary of National Day.

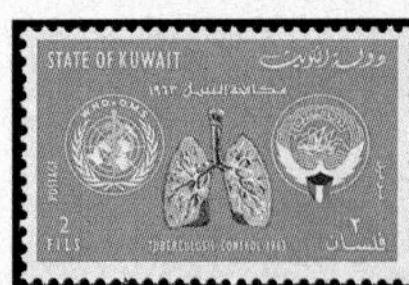

Lungs and Emblems of World Health Organization and Kuwait Tuberculosis Society A15

1963, July 27 *Perf. 13x13½*

Design in Yellow, Black, Emerald & Red

204 A15 2f ocher .35 .20
205 A15 4f dark green .55 .20
206 A15 8f lt violet blue .65 .20
207 A15 20f rose brown 1.10 .30
Nos. 204-207 (4) 2.65 .90

Issued to publicize tuberculosis control.

Sheik Abdullah, Scroll and Scales of Justice — A16

1963, Oct. 29 Photo. *Perf. 11x13*

Center in Gray

208 A16 4f dp red & red brn .40 .20
209 A16 8f dk green & red brn .50 .20
210 A16 20f vio brown & red brn .75 .20
211 A16 45f brown org & red brn 1.25 .20
212 A16 75f purple & red brown 1.75 .50
213 A16 90f ultra & red brown 2.25 .70
Nos. 208-213 (6) 6.90 2.00

Promulgation of the constitution.

Soccer — A17

Sports: 4f, Basketball. 5f, Swimming, horiz. 8f, Track. 15f, Javelin, horiz. 20f, Pole vault, horiz. 35f, Gymnast on rings, horiz. 45f, Gymnast on parallel bars.

1963, Nov. 8 Unwmk. *Perf. 14½x14*

214 A17 1f multicolored .45 .20
215 A17 4f multicolored .45 .20
216 A17 5f multicolored .45 .20
217 A17 8f multicolored .45 .20
218 A17 15f multicolored .60 .20
219 A17 20f multicolored .90 .35
220 A17 35f multicolored 1.75 .45
221 A17 45f multicolored 3.00 .70
Nos. 214-221 (8) 8.05 2.50

Arab School Games of 1963.

UNESCO Emblem, Scales and Globe — A18

1963, Dec. 10 Litho. *Perf. 13x12½*

222 A18 8f violet, blk & pale grn .50 .20
223 A18 20f gray, black & yel .65 .30
224 A18 25f blue, black & tan 1.25 .75
Nos. 222-224 (3) 2.40 1.25

15th anniv. of the Universal Declaration of Human Rights.

Sheik Abdullah — A19

Perf. 12½x13

1964, Feb. 1 Unwmk. Photo.

Portrait in Natural Colors

225 A19 1f gray & silver .30 .20
a. Booklet pane of 6 ('66) 1.90
226 A19 2f brt blue & silver .30 .20
227 A19 4f ocher & silver .30 .20
a. Booklet pane of 6 ('66) 1.90
228 A19 5f fawn & silver .30 .20
229 A19 8f dk brown & sil .30 .20
230 A19 10f citron & sil .30 .20
a. Booklet pane of 6 ('66) 1.90
231 A19 15f brt green & sil 1.00 .45
a. Booklet pane of 6 ('66) 6.00
232 A19 20f blue gray & sil .50 .20
a. Booklet pane of 6 ('66) 3.00
233 A19 25f green & silver .70 .25
234 A19 30f gray grn & sil 1.00 .20
235 A19 40f brt vio & sil 1.10 .20
236 A19 45f violet & silver 1.25 .20
237 A19 50f olive & silver 1.40 .20
238 A19 70f red lilac & sil 1.75 .25
239 A19 75f rose red & sil 2.25 .45
240 A19 90f ultra & silver 3.00 .45
241 A19 100f pale lilac & sil 3.50 .50

Perf. 14x14½

Size: 25x30mm

242 A19 250f brown & sil 8.50 1.50
243 A19 1d brown vio & sil 30.00 6.00
Nos. 225-243 (19) 57.75 12.05

Ramses II Battling the Hittites (from Abu Simbel) — A20

Engr. & Litho.

1964, Mar. 8 *Perf. 13x12½*

244 A20 8f buff, ind & maroon .35 .20
245 A20 20f lt blue, indigo & vio .90 .35
246 A20 30f bluish grn, ind & vio 1.25 .60
Nos. 244-246 (3) 2.50 1.15

UNESCO world campaign to save historic monuments in Nubia.

Mother and Child — A21

1964, Mar. 21 Litho. *Perf. 14x13*

247 A21 8f green, gray & vio blk .35 .20
248 A21 20f green, red & vio blk .45 .20
249 A21 30f green, ol bis & vio blk .60 .20
250 A21 45f green, saph & vio blk 1.10 .45
Nos. 247-250 (4) 2.50 1.05

Issued for Mother's Day, Mar. 21.

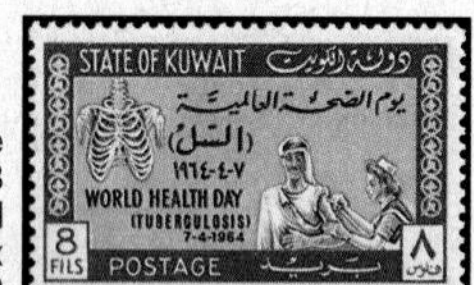

Nurse Giving TB Test, and Thorax A22

Perf. 13x13½

1964, Apr. 7 Photo. Unwmk.

251 A22 8f brown & green .60 .20
252 A22 20f green & rose red 1.60 .35

Issued for World Health Day (fight against tuberculosis), Apr. 7, 1964.

Microscope and Dhow — A23

1964, Apr. 15 *Perf. 12½x13*

253 A23 8f multicolored .30 .20
254 A23 15f multicolored .40 .20
255 A23 20f multicolored .60 .20
256 A23 30f multicolored .90 .45
Nos. 253-256 (4) 2.20 1.05

Issued for Education Day.

Doves and State Seal — A24

1964, June 19 Litho. *Perf. 13½*

Seal in Blue, Brown, Black, Red & Green

257 A24 8f black & bister brn .55 .20
258 A24 20f black & green .65 .20
259 A24 30f black & gray 1.10 .40
260 A24 45f black & blue 1.40 .65
Nos. 257-260 (4) 3.70 1.45

Third anniversary of National Day.

Arab Postal Union Emblem — A25

1964, Nov. 21 Photo. *Perf. 11x11½*

261 A25 8f lt blue & brown .40 .20
262 A25 20f yellow & ultra .90 .20
263 A25 45f olive & brown 1.50 .40
Nos. 261-263 (3) 2.80 .80

Permanent Office of the APU, 10th anniv.

Conference Emblem A26

1965, Feb. 8 Litho. *Perf. 14*

264 A26 8f black, org brn & yel .60 .20
265 A26 20f multicolored 1.10 .20

First Arab Journalists' Conference.

Oil Derrick, Dhow, Sun and Doves — A27

Mother and Children — A28

1965, Feb. 25 *Perf. 13½*

266 A27 10f lt green & multi .45 .20
267 A27 15f pink & multi .75 .20
268 A27 20f gray & multi 1.50 .35
Nos. 266-268 (3) 2.70 .75

Fourth anniversary of National Day.

1965, Mar. 21 Unwmk. *Perf. 13½*

269 A28 8f multicolored .40 .20
270 A28 15f multicolored .55 .20
271 A28 20f multicolored .85 .30
Nos. 269-271 (3) 1.80 .70

Mother's Day, Mar. 21.

Weather Balloon A29

1965, Mar. 23 Photo. *Perf. 11½x11*

272 A29 4f deep ultra & yellow .60 .20
273 A29 5f blue & dp orange 1.00 .20
274 A29 20f dk blue & emerald 1.25 .20
Nos. 272-274 (3) 2.85 .60

Fifth World Meteorological Day.

Census Chart, Map and Family A30

1965, Mar. 28 Litho. *Perf. 13½*

275 A30 8f multicolored .50 .20
276 A30 20f multicolored 1.10 .25
277 A30 50f multicolored 2.25 .55
Nos. 275-277 (3) 3.85 1.00

Issued to publicize the 1965 census.

ICY Emblem A31

1965, Mar. 7 Engr.

278 A31 8f red & black .30 .20
279 A31 20f lt ultra & black .75 .40
280 A31 30f emerald & black 1.50 .65
Nos. 278-280 (3) 2.55 1.25

International Cooperation Year.

Dagger in Map of Palestine — A31a

Perf. 11x11½

1965, Apr. 9 Photo. Unwmk.

281 A31a 4f red & ultra 2.00 .35
282 A31a 45f red & emerald 4.50 .70

Deir Yassin massacre, Apr. 9, 1948. See Iraq Nos. 372-373 and Jordan No. 499.

Tower of Shuwaikh School and Atom Symbol A32

1965, Apr. 15 Litho. *Perf. 14x13*

283 A32 4f multicolored .30 .20
284 A32 20f multicolored .70 .20
285 A32 45f multicolored 1.25 .50
Nos. 283-285 (3) 2.25 .90

Issued for Education Day.

ITU Emblem, Old and New Communication Equipment — A33

1965, May 17 *Perf. 13½x14*

286 A33 8f dk blue, lt bl & red .85 .30
287 A33 20f green, lt grn & red 1.60 .50
288 A33 45f red, pink & blue 2.75 .85
Nos. 286-288 (3) 5.20 1.65

ITU, centenary.

Library Aflame and Lamp A33a

1965, June 7 Photo. *Perf. 11*

289 A33a 8f black, green & red 1.10 .20
290 A33a 15f black, red & green 1.40 .20

Burning of Library of Algiers, June 7, 1962.

Falcon — A34

Book and Wreath Emblem — A35

1965, Dec. 1 Engr. *Perf. 13*

Center in Sepia

291 A34 8f red lilac 2.50 .20
292 A34 15f olive green 2.10 .20
293 A34 20f dark blue 3.00 .30
294 A34 25f orange 3.25 .40
295 A34 30f emerald 3.75 .45
296 A34 45f blue 6.75 .65
297 A34 50f claret 8.50 .80
298 A34 90f carmine 12.50 1.50
Nos. 291-298 (8) 42.35 4.50

1966, Jan. 10 Photo. *Perf. 14x15*

299 A35 8f lt violet & multi .60 .20
300 A35 20f brown red & multi .90 .20
301 A35 30f blue & multi .95 .35
Nos. 299-301 (3) 2.45 .75

Issued for Education Day.

Sheik Sabah as-Salim as-Sabah — A36

1966, Feb. 1 Photo. *Perf. 14x13*

302 A36 4f lt blue & multi .30 .20
303 A36 5f pale rose & multi .30 .20
304 A36 20f multicolored 1.00 .20
305 A36 30f lt violet & multi 1.10 .35
306 A36 40f salmon & multi 1.25 .50
307 A36 45f lt gray & multi 1.50 .60
308 A36 70f yellow & multi 2.75 .85
309 A36 90f pale green & multi 3.75 1.10
Nos. 302-309 (8) 11.95 4.00

Wheat and Fish — A37

1966, Feb. 15 *Perf. 11x11½*

310 A37 20f multicolored 2.50 .90
311 A37 45f multicolored 4.00 1.60

"Freedom from Hunger" campaign.

Eagle, Banner, Scales and Emblems — A38

1966, Feb. 25 Litho. *Perf. 12½x13*
312 A38 20f tan & multi 1.40 .40
313 A38 25f lt green & multi 1.90 .40
314 A38 45f gray & multi 2.75 .75
Nos. 312-314 (3) 6.05 1.55

Fifth anniversary of National Day.

Wheel of Industry and Map of Arab Countries A39

1966, Mar. 1 *Perf. 14x13½*
315 A39 20f brt blue, brt grn & blk .75 .25
316 A39 50f lt red brn, brt grn & black 1.50 .65

Issued to publicize the conference on industrial development in Arab countries.

Mother and Children — A40

1966, Mar. 21 *Perf. 11½x11*
317 A40 20f pink & multi .85 .20
318 A40 45f multicolored 1.90 .45

Mother's Day, Mar. 21.

Medical Conference Emblem — A41

1966, Apr. 1 Photo. *Perf. 14½x14*
319 A41 15f blue & red .75 .20
320 A41 30f red & blue 1.75 .40

Fifth Arab Medical Conference, Kuwait.

Composite View of a City — A42

1966, Apr. 7 Litho. *Perf. 12½x13*
321 A42 8f multicolored .75 .20
322 A42 10f multicolored 1.75 .30

Issued for World Health Day, Apr. 7.

Inauguration of WHO Headquarters, Geneva — A43

1966, May 3 Litho. *Perf. 11x11½*
323 A43 5f dull sal, ol grn & vio bl 1.25 .20
324 A43 10f lt grn, ol grn & vio blue 1.50 .20

Traffic Signal at Night A44

"Blood Transfusion" A45

1966, May 4
325 A44 10f green, red & black 1.50 .20
326 A44 20f green, red & black 2.00 .30

Issued for Traffic Day.

1966, May 5 *Perf. 13½*
327 A45 4f multicolored 1.00 .20
328 A45 8f multicolored 1.25 .20

Blood Bank Day, May 5.

Sheik Ahmad and Ship Carrying First Crude Oil Shipment A46

1966, June 30 *Perf. 13½*
329 A46 20f multicolored 1.25 .25
330 A46 45f multicolored 2.25 .35

20th anniv. of the first crude oil shipment, June 30, 1946.

Ministry of Guidance and Information — A47

1966, July 25 Photo. *Perf. 11½x11*
331 A47 4f rose & brown .35 .20
332 A47 5f yel brown & brt green .40 .20
333 A47 8f brt green & purple .55 .20
334 A47 20f salmon & ultra .65 .20
Nos. 331-334 (4) 1.95 .80

Opening of Ministry of Guidance and Information Building.

Fishing Boat, Lobster, Fish, Crab and FAO Emblem A48

1966, Oct. 10 Litho. *Perf. 13½*
335 A48 4f buff & multi 1.50 .25
336 A48 20f lt lilac & multi 2.00 .40

Fisheries' Conference of Near East Countries under the sponsorship of the FAO, Oct. 1966.

United Nations Flag — A49

UNESCO Emblem — A50

1966, Oct. 24 *Perf. 13x14*
337 A49 20f blue, dk blue & pink 1.75 .30
338 A49 45f blue, dk bl & pale grn 2.50 .65

Issued for United Nations Day.

1966, Nov. 4 Litho. *Perf. 12½x13*
339 A50 20f multicolored 2.00 .80
340 A50 45f multicolored 2.25 1.50

20th anniversary of UNESCO.

Kuwait University Emblem — A51

1966, Nov. 27 Photo. *Perf. 14½*
Emblem in Yellow, Bright Blue, Green and Gold
341 A51 8f lt ultra, vio & gold .50 .20
342 A51 10f red, brown & gold 1.00 .20
343 A51 20f lt yel grn, slate & gold 1.10 .30
344 A51 45f buff, green & gold 2.00 .90
Nos. 341-344 (4) 4.60 1.60

Opening of Kuwait University.

Jabir al-Ahmad al-Jabir and Sheik Sabah A52

1966, Dec. 11 *Perf. 14x13*
345 A52 8f yel green & multi .80 .20
346 A52 20f yellow & multi 1.00 .40
347 A52 45f pink & multi 2.00 1.00
Nos. 345-347 (3) 3.80 1.60

Appointment of the heir apparent, Jabir al-Ahmad al-Jabir.

Scout Badge and Square Knot — A52a

1966, Dec. 21 Litho. *Perf. 14x13*
347A A52a 4f lt ol green & fawn 1.50 .20
347B A52a 20f yel brn & blue grn 4.50 .50

Kuwait Boy Scouts, 30th anniversary.

"Symbols of Science and Peace" — A53

1967, Jan. 15 Litho. *Perf. 13x14*
348 A53 10f multicolored .50 .20
349 A53 45f multicolored 1.50 .40

Issued for Education Day.

Fertilizer Plant — A54

1967, Feb. 19 Unwmk. *Perf. 13*
350 A54 8f lt blue & multi .90 .20
351 A54 20f cream & multi 1.75 .40

Opening of Chemical Fertilizer Plant.

Sun, Dove and Olive Branch — A55

1967, Feb. 25 Litho. *Perf. 13*
352 A55 8f salmon & multi .60 .20
353 A55 20f yellow & multi 1.50 .35

Sixth anniversary of National Day.

Map of Arab States and Municipal Building A56

1967, Mar. 11 *Perf. 14½x13*
354 A56 20f gray & multi 2.00 .40
355 A56 30f lt brown & multi 3.00 .60

1st conf. of the Arab Cities Org., Kuwait.

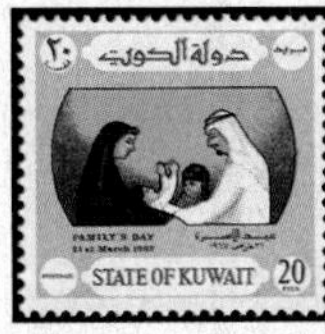

Family — A57

1967, Mar. 21 Litho. *Perf. 13x13½*
356 A57 20f pale rose & multi 1.50 .35
357 A57 45f pale green & multi 3.25 .55

Issued for Family Day, Mar. 21.

Arab League Emblem — A58

1967, Mar. 27 *Perf. 13x14*
358 A58 8f gray & dk blue 1.00 .20
359 A58 10f bister & green 1.25 .20

Issued for Arab Publicity Week.

Sabah Hospital and Physicians at Work — A59

1967, Apr. 7 *Perf. 14x13*
360 A59 8f dull rose & multi 1.50 .20
361 A59 20f gray & multi 1.75 .60

Issued for World Health Day.

Two Heads of Ramses II — A60

1967, Apr. 17 *Perf. 13½*

362 A60 15f citron, green & brn 1.00 .30
363 A60 20f chalky blue, grn & pur 1.75 .35

Arab Week to Save the Nubian Monuments.

Traffic Policeman A61

1967, May 4 **Litho.** *Perf. 14x13*

364 A61 8f lt green & multi 1.75 .35
365 A61 20f rose lilac & multi 2.00 .95

Issued for Traffic Day.

ITY Emblem — A62

1967, June 4 **Photo.** *Perf. 13*

366 A62 20f Prus blue, lt bl & blk 1.25 .65
367 A62 45f rose lilac, lt bl & blk 2.50 1.40

International Tourist Year.

Arab League Emblem and Hands Reaching for Knowledge — A63

Map of Palestine and UN Emblem — A64

1967, Sept. 8 **Litho.** *Perf. 13x14*

368 A63 8f blue & multi 2.00 .20
369 A63 20f dull rose & multi 2.25 .40

Issued to publicize the literacy campaign.

1967, Oct. 24 **Litho.** *Perf. 13*

370 A64 20f blue & pink 2.50 .30
371 A64 45f orange & pink 3.75 .65

Issued for United Nations Day.

Factory and Cogwheels — A65

1967, Nov. 25 **Photo.** *Perf. 13*

372 A65 20f crimson & yellow 1.10 .30
373 A65 45f gray & yellow 2.50 .65

3rd Conf. of Arab Labor Ministers, Kuwait.

Flag and Open Book — A66

Map of Kuwait and Oil Derrick — A67

1968, Jan. 15 **Litho.** *Perf. 14*

374 A66 20f brt blue & multi 1.25 .30
375 A66 45f yel orange & multi 2.25 .70

Issued for Education Day.

1968, Feb. 23 **Litho.** *Perf. 12*

376 A67 10f multicolored 1.25 .50
377 A67 20f multicolored 2.50 .75

30th anniv. of the discovery of oil in the Greater Burgan Field.

Sheik Sabah and Sun — A68

1968, Feb. 25 **Litho.** *Perf. 14x15*

378 A68 8f red lilac & multi .50 .20
379 A68 10f lt blue & multi .60 .20
380 A68 15f violet & multi .75 .25
381 A68 20f vermilion & multi 1.00 .35
Nos. 378-381 (4) 2.85 1.00

Seventh anniversary of National Day.

Open Book and Emblem — A69

1968, Mar. 2 *Perf. 14*

382 A69 8f yellow & multi .85 .20
383 A69 20f lilac rose & multi 1.00 .20
384 A69 45f orange & multi 1.60 .65
Nos. 382-384 (3) 3.45 1.05

Issued for Teachers' Day.

Family Picnic A70

1968, Mar. 21 *Perf. 13½x13*

385 A70 8f blue & multi .50 .20
386 A70 10f red & multi .50 .20
387 A70 15f lilac & multi .75 .20
388 A70 20f dk brown & multi 1.00 .20
Nos. 385-388 (4) 2.75 .80

Issued for Family Day.

Sheik Sabah, Arms of WHO and Kuwait — A71

1968, Apr. 7 **Photo.** *Perf. 12*

389 A71 20f brt lilac & multi 1.00 .80
390 A71 45f multicolored 2.50 1.75

20th anniv. of WHO.

Dagger in Map of Palestine — A72

1968, Apr. 9 **Litho.** *Perf. 14*

391 A72 20f lt blue & vermilion 3.00 .50
392 A72 45f lilac & vermilion 5.00 .75

Deir Yassin massacre, 20th anniv.

Street Crossing A74

1968, May 4 **Photo.** *Perf. 14x14½*

395 A74 10f dk brown & multi 1.60 1.00
396 A74 15f brt violet & multi 1.90 1.25
397 A74 20f green & multi 2.75 1.40
Nos. 395-397 (3) 6.25 3.65

Issued for Traffic Day.

Map of Palestine and Torch — A75

1968, May 15 **Litho.** *Perf. 13½x12½*

398 A75 10f lt ultra & multi .75 .20
399 A75 20f yellow & multi 2.75 .50
400 A75 45f aqua & multi 5.00 .75
Nos. 398-400 (3) 8.50 1.45

Issued for Palestine Day.

Palestinian Refugees — A76

1968, June 5 **Litho.** *Perf. 13x13½*

401 A76 20f pink & multi .85 .20
402 A76 30f ultra & multi 1.00 .20
403 A76 45f green & multi 1.75 .30
404 A76 90f lilac & multi 3.00 .90
Nos. 401-404 (4) 6.60 1.60

International Human Rights Year.

Museum of Kuwait — A77

Perf. 12½

1968, Aug. 25 **Unwmk.** **Engr.**

405 A77 1f dk brown & brt grn .30 .20
406 A77 2f dp claret & grn .30 .20
407 A77 5f black & orange .30 .20
408 A77 8f dk brown & grn .30 .20
409 A77 10f Prus blue & cl .30 .20
410 A77 20f org brown & blue .75 .20
411 A77 25f dk blue & orange .85 .20
412 A77 30f Prus blue & yel grn .90 .25
413 A77 45f plum & vio black 1.50 .30
414 A77 50f green & carmine 1.75 .40
Nos. 405-414 (10) 7.25 2.35

Man Reading Book, Arab League, UN and UNESCO Emblems A78

1968, Sept. 8 **Litho.** *Perf. 12½x13*

415 A78 15f blue gray & multi .80 .20
416 A78 20f pink & multi 1.00 .20

Issued for International Literacy Day.

Map of Palestine on UN Building and Children with Tent — A79

1968, Oct. 25 **Litho.** *Perf. 13*

417 A79 20f multicolored .50 .20
418 A79 30f gray & multi 1.00 .20
419 A79 45f salmon pink & multi 1.10 .30
Nos. 417-419 (3) 2.60 .70

Issued for United Nations Day.

Kuwait Chamber of Commerce A80

1968, Nov. 6 **Litho.** *Perf. 13½x12½*

420 A80 10f dp orange & dk brn .30 .20
421 A80 15f rose claret & vio bl .50 .20
422 A80 20f brown org & dk green .75 .25
Nos. 420-422 (3) 1.55 .65

Opening of the Kuwait Chamber of Commerce Building.

Conference Emblem — A81

1968, Nov. 10 **Litho.** *Perf. 13*

Emblem in Ocher, Blue, Red and Black

423 A81 10f dk brown & blue .50 .20
424 A81 15f dk brown & orange .60 .20
425 A81 20f dk brown & vio blue .75 .25
426 A81 30f dk brown & org brn 1.40 .35
Nos. 423-426 (4) 3.25 1.00

14th Conference of the Arab Chambers of Commerce, Industry and Agriculture.

Shuaiba Refinery — A82

1968, Nov. 18 *Perf. 13½*

Emblem in Red, Black and Blue

427 A82 10f black & lt blue grn .75 .20
428 A82 20f black & gray 1.50 .40
429 A82 30f black & salmon 1.60 .65
430 A82 45f black & emerald 3.00 .85
Nos. 427-430 (4) 6.85 2.10

Opening of Shuaiba Refinery.

Koran, Scales and People A83

1968, Dec. 19 Photo. *Perf. 14x14½*

431	A83	8f multicolored	.60	.20
432	A83	20f multicolored	1.25	.60
433	A83	30f multicolored	1.75	.85
434	A83	45f multicolored	2.50	1.25
		Nos. 431-434 (4)	6.10	2.90

The 1400th anniversary of the Koran.

Boeing 707 — A84

1969, Jan. 1 Litho. *Perf. 13½x14*

435	A84	10f brt yellow & multi	1.00	.20
436	A84	20f green & multi	1.40	.50
437	A84	25f multicolored	1.50	.60
438	A84	45f lilac & multi	2.50	1.10
		Nos. 435-438 (4)	6.40	2.40

Introduction of Boeing 707 service by Kuwait Airways.

Globe, Retort and Triangle — A85

1969, Jan. 15 *Perf. 13*

439	A85	15f gray & multi	.85	.30
440	A85	20f multicolored	1.25	.40

Issued for Education Day.

Kuwait Hilton Hotel — A86

1969, Feb. 15 Litho. *Perf. 14x12½*

441	A86	10f brt blue & multi	.60	.20
442	A86	20f pink & multi	1.25	.20

Opening of the Kuwait Hilton Hotel.

Teachers' Society Emblem, Father and Children — A87

1969, Feb. 15 *Perf. 13*

443	A87	10f violet & multi	.60	.20
444	A87	20f rose & multi	1.25	.45

Issued for Education week.

Wreath, Flags and Dove — A88

1969, Feb. 25 Photo. *Perf. 14½x14*

445	A88	15f lilac & multi	.60	.25
446	A88	20f blue & multi	.90	.30
447	A88	30f ocher & multi	1.25	.55
		Nos. 445-447 (3)	2.75	1.10

Eighth anniversary of National Day.

Emblem, Teacher and Students — A89

1969, Mar. 8 Litho. *Perf. 13x12½*

448	A89	10f multicolored	.50	.20
449	A89	20f deep red & multi	1.00	.20

Issued for Teachers' Day.

Family A90

1969, Mar. 21 *Perf. 13½*

450	A90	10f dark blue & multi	.90	.20
451	A90	20f deep car & multi	1.40	.30

Issued for Family Day.

Avicenna, WHO Emblem, Patient and Microscope — A91

1969, Apr. 7 Litho. *Perf. 13½*

452	A91	15f red brown & multi	1.00	.20
453	A91	20f lt green & multi	2.75	.20

Issued for World Health Day, Apr. 7.

Motorized Traffic Police A92

1969, May 4 Litho. *Perf. 12½x13*

454	A92	10f multicolored	1.00	.25
455	A92	20f multicolored	3.50	.60

Issued for Traffic Day.

ILO Emblem A93

1969, June 1 *Perf. 11½*

456	A93	10f red, black & gold	.50	.20
457	A93	20f lt blue grn, blk & gold	1.00	.20

50th anniv. of the ILO.

S.S. Al Sabahiah A94

1969, June 10 Litho. *Perf. 13½*

458	A94	20f multicolored	1.25	.25
459	A94	45f multicolored	3.00	.80

4th anniversary of Kuwait Shipping Co.

UNESCO Emblem, Woman, Globe and Book — A95

1969, Sept. 8 Litho. *Perf. 13½*

460	A95	10f blue & multi	.35	.20
461	A95	20f rose red & multi	.90	.20

International Literacy Day, Sept. 8.

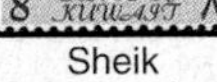

Sheik Sabah — A96

UN Emblem and Scroll — A97

1969-74 Litho. *Perf. 14*

462	A96	8f lt blue & multi	.30	.20
463	A96	10f pink & multi	.30	.20
464	A96	15f gray & multi	.35	.20
465	A96	20f yellow & multi	.50	.20
466	A96	25f violet & multi	.60	.30
467	A96	30f sal & multi	.75	.35
468	A96	45f tan & multi	1.00	.50
469	A96	50f yel grn & multi	1.25	.50
470	A96	70f multicolored	1.50	.75
471	A96	75f ultra & multi	2.10	.90
472	A96	90f pale rose & multi	2.75	1.25
a.		90f brownish rose & multi	2.25	1.00
473	A96	250f lilac & multi	8.25	3.50
473A	A96	500f gray green & multi	15.00	11.00
473B	A96	1d lilac rose & multi	32.50	18.00
		Nos. 462-473B (14)	67.15	37.85

Issued: #473A-473B, 1/12/74; others 10/5/69.

1969, Oct. 24 Litho. *Perf. 13*

474	A97	10f emer & multi	.75	.20
475	A97	20f bister & multi	1.75	.20
476	A97	45f rose red & multi	3.00	.45
		Nos. 474-476 (3)	5.50	.85

Issued for United Nations Day.

Radar, Satellite Earth Station, Kuwait A98

Design: 45f, Globe and radar, vert.

1969, Dec. 15 Photo. *Perf. 14½*

477	A98	20f silver & multi	1.50	.35
478	A98	45f silver & multi	3.00	.70

Inauguration of the Kuwait Earth Station for Satellite Communications.

Globe with Science Symbols, and Education Year Emblem — A99

1970, Jan. 15 Photo. *Perf. 13½x13*

479	A99	20f brt lilac & multi	1.00	.40
480	A99	45f blue & multi	1.50	.85

International Education Year.

Shoue A100

Old Kuwaiti Vessels: 10f, Sambook. 15f, Baghla. 20f, Batteel. 25f, Boom. 45f, Bakkara. 50f, Shipbuilding.

1970, Feb. 1 *Perf. 14½x14*

481	A100	8f multicolored	.60	.20
482	A100	10f multicolored	.80	.20
483	A100	15f multicolored	1.00	.30
484	A100	20f multicolored	1.25	.25
485	A100	25f multicolored	1.75	.30
486	A100	45f multicolored	2.50	.70
487	A100	50f multicolored	3.50	.70
		Nos. 481-487 (7)	11.40	2.65

Refugee Father and Children A101

Kuwait Flag, Emblem and Sheik Sabah A102

1970 Photo. *Perf. 14x12½*

488	A101	20f red brown & multi	2.50	.65
489	A101	45f olive & multi	4.75	1.75

Issued for Universal Palestinian Refugees Week, Dec. 16-22, 1969.

1970, Feb. 25 *Perf. 13½x13*

490	A102	15f silver & multi	.75	.20
491	A102	20f gold & multi	1.00	.20

Ninth anniversary of National Day.

Dome of the Rock, Jerusalem, and Boy Commando — A103

Designs: 20f, Dome and man commando. 45f, Dome and woman commando.

1970, Mar. 4 Litho. *Perf. 13*

492	A103	10f pale violet & multi	1.50	.20
493	A103	20f lt blue & multi	3.00	.65
494	A103	45f multicolored	6.00	1.50
		Nos. 492-494 (3)	10.50	2.35

Honoring Palestinian commandos.

Parents and Children
A104

1970, Mar. 21 ***Perf. 14***

495	A104	20f multicolored	.75	.20
496	A104	30f pink & multi	1.00	.35

Issued for Family Day.

Map of Arab League Countries, Flag and Emblem
A104a

1970, Mar. 22 ***Perf. 11½x11***

497	A104a	20f lt blue, grn & lt brn	.75	.25
498	A104a	45f salmon, grn & dk pur	1.75	.60

25th anniversary of the Arab League.

Census Graph and Kuwait Arms
A105

1970, Apr. 1 **Litho.** ***Perf. 13½x13***

499	A105	15f dull orange & multi	.50	.20
500	A105	20f yellow & multi	.55	.20
501	A105	30f pink & multi	.80	.30
		Nos. 499-501 (3)	1.85	.70

Issued to publicize the 1970 census.

"Fight Cancer," Kuwait Arms, WHO Emblem — A106

1970, Apr. 7 ***Perf. 13½x13***

502	A106	20f blue, vio bl & rose lil	1.25	.30
503	A106	30f dl yel, vio bl & lil rose	1.50	.40

World Health Organization Day, Apr. 7, and to publicize the fight against cancer.

Traffic Signs
A107

1970, May 4 **Photo.** ***Perf. 13½***

504	A107	20f multicolored	1.50	.75
505	A107	30f multicolored	2.50	1.25

Issued for Traffic Day.

Red Crescent
A108

1970, May 8 **Litho.** ***Perf. 12½x13½***

506	A108	10f yellow & multi	.70	.20
507	A108	15f emerald & multi	1.25	.25
508	A108	30f tan & multi	2.25	.70
		Nos. 506-508 (3)	4.20	1.15

Intl. Red Crescent and Red Cross Day.

Opening of UPU Headquarters, Bern — A109

1970, May 25 **Photo.** ***Perf. 12x11½***

509	A109	20f multicolored	1.10	.35
510	A109	30f multicolored	1.40	.55

Sheik Sabah
A110

1970, June 15 **Photo.** ***Perf. 14***

511	A110	20f silver & multi	1.75	.20
512	A110	45f gold & multi	3.25	.50
a.		Miniature sheet of 2	7.50	1.75

Nos. 511-512 have circular perforation around vignette set within a white square of paper, perforated on 4 sides. #512a contains 2 imperf. stamps similar to #511-512.

UN Emblem, Symbols of Peace, Progress, Justice — A111

1970, July 1 **Litho.** ***Perf. 13½x12½***

513	A111	20f lt green & multi	.75	.20
514	A111	45f multicolored	1.25	.40

25th anniversary of the United Nations.

Tanker Loading Crude Oil from Sea Island
A112

1970, Aug. 1 ***Perf. 13½x13***

515	A112	20f multicolored	1.75	.50
516	A112	45f multicolored	4.25	1.10

Issued to publicize the artificial "Sea Island" loading facilities in Kuwait.

"Writing," Kuwait and UN Emblems
A113

1970, Sept. 8 **Photo.** ***Perf. 13½***

517	A113	10f brt blue & multi	1.10	.20
518	A113	15f brt green & multi	1.75	.20

International Literacy Day, Sept. 8.

National Guard and Emblem
A114

1970, Oct. 20 **Photo.** ***Perf. 13x13½***

519	A114	10f gold & multi	1.10	.20
520	A114	20f silver & multi	2.00	.25

First National Guard graduation.

Flag of Kuwait, Symbols of Development
A115

1971, Feb. 25 **Litho.** ***Perf. 12***

521	A115	20f gray & multi	1.50	.40
522	A115	30f multicolored	1.90	.65

Tenth anniversary of National Day.

Charles H. Best, Frederick G. Banting
A116

1971, Apr. 7 **Litho.** ***Perf. 14***

523	A116	20f multicolored	1.75	.20
524	A116	45f multicolored	3.25	.70

World Health Day; discoverers of insulin.

Globe with Map of Palestine
A117

1971, May 3 **Litho.** ***Perf. 12½x13***

525	A117	20f yel green & multi	2.75	1.10
526	A117	45f lilac & multi	4.50	2.25

International Palestine Week.

ITU Emblem and Waves
A118

1971, May 17 **Photo.** ***Perf. 13x13½***

527	A118	20f silver, dk red & blk	1.50	.30
528	A118	45f gold, dk red & blk	3.00	.85

3rd World Telecommunications Day.

Men of 3 Races — A119

1971, June 5 **Litho.** ***Perf. 11½x11***

529	A119	15f red brown & multi	1.00	.30
530	A119	30f ultra & multi	1.50	.70

Intl. Year against Racial Discrimination.

Arab Postal Union Emblem
A120

1971, Aug. 30 ***Perf. 13x12½***

531	A120	20f brown & multi	1.00	.40
532	A120	45f blue & multi	1.75	.55

25th anniv. of the Conf. of Sofar, Lebanon, establishing the Arab Postal Union.

Symbols of Learning, UNESCO and Kuwait Emblems
A121

1971, Sept. 8 ***Perf. 12***

533	A121	25f dull yellow & multi	1.25	.25
534	A121	60f lt blue & multi	2.50	.90

International Literacy Day, Sept. 8.

Soccer
A122

Design: 30f, Soccer, different.

1971, Dec. 10 ***Perf. 13***

535	A122	20f green & multi	2.25	.55
536	A122	30f ultra & multi	2.75	.75

Regional Sports Tournament, Kuwait, Dec.

UNICEF Emblem and Arms of Kuwait — A123

Litho. & Engr.

1971, Dec. 11 ***Perf. 11x11½***

537	A123	25f gold & multi	1.00	.30
538	A123	60f silver & multi	1.75	.70

25th anniv. of UNICEF.

Book Year Emblem
A124

1972, Jan. 2 **Litho.** ***Perf. 14x13***

539	A124	20f black & buff	1.00	.40
540	A124	45f black & lt blue grn	1.75	.90

International Book Year.

Kuwait Emblem with 11 Rays, Olive Branch A125

1972, Feb. 25 Litho. *Perf. 13x13½*

541 A125 20f pink, gold & multi 1.50 .70
542 A125 45f lt blue, gold & multi 2.00 1.25

11th anniversary of National Day.

Telecommunications Center — A126

1972, Feb. 28 *Perf. 13½*

543 A126 20f lt blue & multi 1.75 .60
544 A126 45f multicolored 4.00 1.50

Opening of Kuwait Telecommunications Center.

"Your Heart is your Health" — A127

1972, Apr. 7 Photo. *Perf. 14½x14*

545 A127 20f red & multi 2.25 .60
546 A127 45f red & multi 5.00 1.40

World Health Day.

Nurse and Child — A128

1972, May 8 Litho. *Perf. 12½x13*

547 A128 8f vio blue, red & emer 1.50 .20
548 A128 40f pink & multi 4.00 1.00

Red Cross and Red Crescent Day.

Soccer, Olympic Emblems — A129

1972, Sept. 2 Litho. *Perf. 14½*

549 A129 2f shown .35 .20
550 A129 4f Running .35 .20
551 A129 5f Swimming .35 .20
552 A129 8f Gymnastics .35 .20
553 A129 10f Discus .35 .20
554 A129 15f Equestrian 1.25 .30
555 A129 20f Basketball 1.50 .35
556 A129 25f Volleyball 1.60 .40
Nos. 549-556 (8) 6.10 2.05

20th Olympic Games, Munich, 8/26-9/11.

FAO Emblem, Vegetables, Fish and Ship — A130

1972, Sept. 9 Litho. *Perf. 14x13½*

557 A130 5f blue & multi .60 .40
558 A130 10f emerald & multi 2.00 1.10
559 A130 20f orange & multi 3.50 2.00
Nos. 557-559 (3) 6.10 3.50

11th FAO Regional Conference in the Near East, Kuwait, Sept.

National Bank Emblem A131

1972, Nov. 15 Photo. *Perf. 13x14*

560 A131 10f green & multi .75 .25
561 A131 35f dull red & multi 2.00 1.00

20th anniversary of Kuwait National Bank.

Capitals A132

Relics of Failaka: 5f, View of excavations. 10f, Acanthus leaf capital. 15f, Excavations.

1972, Dec. 4 Litho. *Perf. 12*

562 A132 2f lilac rose & multi .40 .20
563 A132 5f bister & multi .40 .20
564 A132 10f lt blue & multi 1.50 .20
565 A132 15f green & multi 2.00 .40
Nos. 562-565 (4) 4.30 1.00

Flower and Kuwait Emblem — A133

INTERPOL Emblem A134

1973, Feb. 25 Litho. *Perf. 13½x13*

566 A133 10f lt olive & multi .75 .25
567 A133 20f multicolored 1.25 .65
568 A133 30f yellow & multi 1.75 .95
Nos. 566-568 (3) 3.75 1.85

12th anniversary of National Day.

1973, June 3 Litho. *Perf. 12*

569 A134 10f emerald & multi 1.25 .85
570 A134 15f red orange & multi 2.00 1.10
571 A134 20f blue & multi 3.25 1.60
Nos. 569-571 (3) 6.50 3.55

50th anniv. of Intl. Criminal Police Org. (INTERPOL).

I.C.M.S. Emblem and Flag of Kuwait — A135

Kuwait Airways Building — A136

1973, June 24 *Perf. 13*

572 A135 30f gray & multi 1.25 .55
573 A135 40f brown & multi 2.00 .75

Intl. Council of Military Sports, 25th anniv.

1973, July 1 Litho. *Perf. 12½x14*

574 A136 10f lt green & multi 1.00 .20
575 A136 15f lilac & multi 1.10 .30
576 A136 20f lt ultra & multi 1.50 .40
Nos. 574-576 (3) 3.60 .90

Opening of Kuwait Airways Corporation Building.

Weather Map of Suez Canal and Persian Gulf Region — A137

1973, Sept. 4 Photo. *Perf. 14*

577 A137 5f red & multi .75 .20
578 A137 10f green & multi 1.00 .20
579 A137 15f multicolored 1.50 .25
Nos. 577-579 (3) 3.25 .65

Intl. meteorological cooperation, cent.

Sheiks Ahmad and Sabah — A138

1973, Nov. 12 Photo. *Perf. 14*

580 A138 10f lt green & multi 1.00 .20
581 A138 20f yel orange & multi 1.50 .40
582 A138 70f lt blue & multi 4.00 1.40
Nos. 580-582 (3) 6.50 2.00

Stamps overprinted "Kuwait," 50th anniv.

Mourning Dove, Eurasian Hoopoe, Rock Dove, Stone Curlew — A139

Designs: Birds and traps.

1973, Dec. 1 Litho. *Perf. 14*
Size (single stamp): 32x32mm

583 A139 Block of 4 5.50 5.50
a. 5f Mourning dove .70 .25
b. 5f Eurasian hoopoe .70 .25
c. 5f Rock dove .70 .25
d. 5f Stone curlew .70 .25
584 A139 Block of 4 7.25 7.25
a. 8f Great gray shrike .90 .35
b. 8f Red-backed shrike .90 .35
c. 8f Rufous-backed shrike .90 .35
d. 8f Black-naped oriole .90 .35
585 A139 Block of 4 8.00 8.00
a. 10f Willow warbler 1.00 .45
b. 10f Great reed warbler 1.00 .45
c. 10f Blackcap 1.00 .45
d. 10f Common (barn) swallow 1.00 .45
586 A139 Block of 4 12.50 12.50
a. 15f Common rock thrush 1.60 .75
b. 15f European redstart 1.60 .75
c. 15f Wheatear 1.60 .75
d. 15f Bluethroat 1.60 .75
587 A139 Block of 4 14.50 14.50
a. 20f Houbara bustard 1.75 .85
b. 20f Pin-tailed sandgrouse 1.75 .85
c. 20f Ypecaha wood rail 1.75 .85
d. 20f Spotted crake 1.75 .85

Size (single stamp): 35x35mm

588 A139 Block of 4 16.00 16.00
a. 25f American sparrow hawk 2.00 1.00
b. 25f Great black-backed gull 2.00 1.00
c. 25f Purple heron 2.00 1.00
d. 25f Wryneck 2.00 1.00
589 A139 Block of 4 24.00 24.00
a. 30f European bee-eater 3.00 1.40
b. 30f Goshawk 3.00 1.40
c. 30f Gray wagtail 3.00 1.40
d. 30f Pied wagtail 3.00 1.40
590 A139 Block of 4 32.50 32.50
a. 45f Crossbows 4.25 1.90
b. 45f Tent-shaped net 4.25 1.90
c. 45f Hand net 4.25 1.90
d. 45f Rooftop trap 4.25 1.90
Nos. 583-590 (8) 120.25 120.25

Human Rights Flame — A141

1973, Dec. 10 Litho. *Perf. 12*

594 A141 10f red & multi 1.00 .20
595 A141 40f lt green & multi 2.00 .50
596 A141 75f lilac & multi 3.00 .85
Nos. 594-596 (3) 6.00 1.55

25th anniv. of the Universal Declaration of Human Rights.

Promoting Animal Resources A142

Stylized Wheat and Kuwaiti Flag — A143

1974, Feb. 16 Litho. *Perf. 12½*

597 A142 30f violet blue & multi 1.10 .30
598 A142 40f rose & multi 1.50 .40

4th Congress of the Arab Veterinary Union, Kuwait.

1974, Feb. 25 *Perf. 13½x13*

599 A143 20f lemon & multi .50 .20
600 A143 30f bister brn & multi 1.50 .40
601 A143 70f silver & multi 2.25 .90
Nos. 599-601 (3) 4.25 1.50

13th anniversary of National Day.

Conference Emblem and Sheik Sabah — A144

1974, Mar. 8 *Perf. 12½*

602 A144 30f multicolored 2.50 .70
603 A144 40f yellow & multi 3.50 .90

12th Conf. of the Arab Medical Union and 1st Conf. of the Kuwait Medical Soc.

Tournament Emblem — A145

1974, Mar. 15

604 A145 25f multicolored 1.50 .50
605 A145 45f multicolored 2.50 .75

Third Soccer Tournament for the Arabian Gulf Trophy, Kuwait, Mar. 1974.

Scientific Research Institute — A146

1974, Apr. 3 **Photo.** *Perf. 12½*

606 A146 15f magenta & multi 1.50 .25
607 A146 20f green & multi 2.50 .35

Opening of Kuwait Scientific Research Institute.

Arab Postal Union, Kuwait and UPU Emblems A147

1974, May 1 *Perf. 13x14*

608 A147 20f gold & multi .75 .20
609 A147 30f gold & multi 1.00 .30
610 A147 60f gold & multi 1.50 .80
Nos. 608-610 (3) 3.25 1.30

Centenary of Universal Postal Union.

Telephone Dial with Communications Symbols and Globe — A148

1974, May 17 *Perf. 14x13½*

611 A148 10f blue & multi .75 .20
612 A148 30f multicolored 2.00 .60
613 A148 40f black & multi 2.50 .80
Nos. 611-613 (3) 5.25 1.60

World Telecommunications Day, May 17.

Emblem of Unity Council and Flags of Member States — A149

1974, June 25 **Litho.** *Perf. 13½*

614 A149 20f red, black & green 1.10 .40
615 A149 30f green, black & red 1.50 .55

17th anniversary of the signing of the Arab Economic Unity Agreement.

WPY Emblem, Embryo, "Growth" — A150

1974, Aug. 19 **Litho.** *Perf. 14x14½*

616 A150 30f black & multi 1.50 .40
617 A150 70f violet blue & multi 2.50 .90

World Population Year.

Development Building and Emblem — A151

1974, Oct. 30 **Litho.** *Perf. 13x13½*

618 A151 10f pink & multi 1.00 .20
619 A151 20f ultra & multi 1.50 .30

Kuwait Fund for Arab Economic Development.

Emblem of Shuaiba Industrial Area — A152

1974, Dec. 17 **Litho.** *Perf. 12½x12*

620 A152 10f lt blue & multi 1.00 .20
621 A152 20f salmon & multi 2.00 .40
622 A152 30f lt green & multi 2.50 .80
Nos. 620-622 (3) 5.50 1.40

Shuaiba Industrial Area, 10th anniversary.

Arms of Kuwait and "14" — A153

1975, Feb. 25 **Litho.** *Perf. 13x13½*

623 A153 20f multicolored 1.00 .30
624 A153 70f yel green & multi 2.00 .85
625 A153 75f rose & multi 2.75 1.00
Nos. 623-625 (3) 5.75 2.15

14th anniversary of National Day.

Male and Female Symbols — A154

1975, Apr. 14 **Photo.** *Perf. 11½x12*

626 A154 8f lt green & multi .50 .20
627 A154 20f rose & multi .55 .25
628 A154 30f blue & multi .75 .40
629 A154 70f yellow & multi 2.00 .85
630 A154 100f black & multi 3.00 1.40
Nos. 626-630 (5) 6.80 3.10

Kuwaiti census 1975.

IWY and Kuwaiti Women's Union Emblems — A155

1975, June 10 **Litho.** *Perf. 14½*

631 A155 15f brown org & multi 1.00 .25
632 A155 20f olive & multi 1.25 .40
633 A155 30f violet & multi 1.50 .65
Nos. 631-633 (3) 3.75 1.30

International Women's Year.

Classroom and UNESCO Emblem A156

1975, Sept. 8 **Litho.** *Perf. 12½x12*

634 A156 20f green & multi 1.00 .25
635 A156 30f multicolored 1.50 .65

International Literacy Day.

Symbols of Measurements A157

UN Flag, Rifle and Olive Branch — A158

1975, Oct. 14 **Photo.** *Perf. 14x13*

636 A157 10f green & multi .75 .20
637 A157 20f purple & multi 1.10 .40

World Standards Day.

1975, Oct. 24 **Litho.** *Perf. 12x12½*

638 A158 20f multicolored 1.00 .25
639 A158 45f orange & multi 1.75 .70

United Nations, 30th anniversary.

Sheik Sabah — A159

1975, Dec. 22 **Litho.** *Perf. 12½x12*

640 A159 8f yellow & multi .95 .20
641 A159 20f lilac & multi 1.25 .40
642 A159 30f buff & multi 1.60 .50
643 A159 50f salmon & multi 2.50 .90
644 A159 90f lt blue & multi 5.25 1.60
645 A159 100f multicolored 5.75 1.90
Nos. 640-645 (6) 17.30 5.50

"Progress" — A160

1976, Feb. 25 **Litho.** *Perf. 12*

646 A160 10f multicolored .75 .20
647 A160 20f multicolored 1.40 .20

15th anniversary of National Day.

Medical Equipment, Emblem and Surgery — A161

Telephones, 1876 and 1976 — A162

1976, Mar. 1 **Litho.** *Perf. 14½*

648 A161 5f dull green & multi .50 .20
649 A161 10f blue & multi 1.25 .30
650 A161 30f gray & multi 3.50 .80
Nos. 648-650 (3) 5.25 1.30

Kuwait Medical Assoc., 2nd annual conference.

1976, Mar. 10 **Litho.** *Perf. 12*

651 A162 5f orange & black .50 .20
652 A162 15f lt blue & black 1.25 .20

Centenary of first telephone call by Alexander Graham Bell, Mar. 10, 1876.

Human Eye — A163

Photo. & Engr.

1976, Apr. 7 *Perf. 11½*

653 A163 10f multicolored .75 .20
654 A163 20f black & multi 1.25 .30
655 A163 30f multicolored 2.00 .50
Nos. 653-655 (3) 4.00 1.00

World Health Day: "Foresight prevents blindness."

Red Crescent Emblem A164

1976, May 8 Litho. *Perf. 12x11½*

656	A164 20f brt green, blk & red	.85	.30
657	A164 30f vio blue, blk & red	1.40	.35
658	A164 45f yellow, blk & red	2.00	.70
659	A164 75f lilac rose, blk & red	3.25	1.00
	Nos. 656-659 (4)	7.50	2.35

Kuwait Red Crescent Society, 10th anniv.

Modern Suburb of Kuwait A165

1976, June 1 Photo. *Perf. 13x13½*

660	A165 10f light green & multi	.75	.20
661	A165 20f salmon & multi	1.25	.25

Habitat, UN Conference on Human Settlements, Vancouver, Canada, May 31-June 11.

Basketball, Kuwait Olympic Emblem — A166

Various Races, Map of Sri Lanka — A167

Designs: 8f, Running. 10f, Judo. 15f, Fieldball. 20f, Gymnastics. 30f, Water polo. 45f, Soccer. 70f, Swimmers at start.

1976, July 17 Litho. *Perf. 14½*

662	A166 4f black & multi	.40	.20
663	A166 8f red & multi	.40	.20
664	A166 10f green & multi	.40	.20
665	A166 15f lemon & multi	.50	.20
666	A166 20f blue & multi	.75	.20
667	A166 30f lilac & multi	1.00	.40
668	A166 45f multicolored	1.25	.55
669	A166 70f brown & multi	1.75	.85
	Nos. 662-669 (8)	6.45	2.80

21st Olympic Games, Montreal, Canada, July 17-Aug. 1.

1976, Aug. 16 Photo. *Perf. 14*

670	A167 20f dk blue & multi	.60	.20
671	A167 30f purple & multi	.75	.45
672	A167 45f green & multi	1.50	.65
	Nos. 670-672 (3)	2.85	1.30

5th Summit Conf. of Non-aligned Countries, Colombo, Sri Lanka, Aug. 9-19.

"UNESCO," Torch and Kuwait Arms — A168

1976, Nov. 4 Litho. *Perf. 12x11½*

673	A168 20f yel green & multi	1.00	.20
674	A168 45f scarlet & multi	1.75	.70

30th anniversary of UNESCO.

Blindman's Buff A169

Popular games. 5f, 15f, 30f, vertical.

Perf. 14½x14, 14x14½

1977, Jan. 10 Litho.

675	A169 5f Pot throwing	.50	.20
676	A169 5f Kite flying	.50	.20
677	A169 5f Balancing sticks	.50	.20
678	A169 5f Spinning tops	.50	.20
a.	Block of 4, #675-678	2.00	2.00
679	A169 10f shown	.75	.20
680	A169 10f Rowing	.75	.20
681	A169 10f Hoops	.75	.20
682	A169 10f Ropes	.75	.20
a.	Block of 4, #679-682	3.00	3.00
683	A169 15f Rope skipping	1.25	.35
684	A169 15f Marbles	1.25	.35
685	A169 15f Cart steering	1.25	.35
686	A169 15f Teetotum	1.25	.25
a.	Block of 4, #683-686	5.00	5.00
687	A169 20f Halma	1.50	.55
688	A169 20f Model boats	1.50	.55
689	A169 20f Pot and candle	1.50	.55
690	A169 20f Hide and seek	1.50	.55
a.	Block of 4, #687-690	6.00	6.00
691	A169 30f Throwing bones	1.75	.75
692	A169 30f Mystery gifts	1.75	.75
693	A169 30f Hopscotch	1.75	.75
694	A169 30f Catch as catch can	1.75	.75
a.	Block of 4, #691-694	7.00	7.00
695	A169 40f Bowls	3.00	1.00
696	A169 40f Sword fighting	3.00	1.00
697	A169 40f Mother and child	3.00	1.00
698	A169 40f Fivestones	3.00	1.00
a.	Block of 4, #695-698	12.00	12.00
699	A169 60f Hiding a cake	4.00	1.75
700	A169 60f Chess	4.00	1.75
701	A169 60f Dancing	4.00	1.75
702	A169 60f Treasure hunt	4.00	1.75
a.	Block of 4, #699-702	16.00	16.00
703	A169 70f Hobby-horses	4.75	1.90
704	A169 70f Hide and seek	4.75	1.90
705	A169 70f Catch	4.75	1.90
706	A169 70f Storytelling	4.75	1.90
a.	Block of 4, #703-706	19.00	19.00
	Nos. 675-706 (32)	70.00	26.70

Diseased Knee — A170

1977, Feb. 15 *Perf. 13x13½*

707	A170 20f yellow & multi	.75	.25
708	A170 30f multicolored	1.25	.45
709	A170 45f red & multi	1.50	.70
710	A170 75f black & multi	2.50	1.25
	Nos. 707-710 (4)	6.00	2.65

World Rheumatism Year.

Sheik Sabah A171

1977, Feb. 25 Photo. *Perf. 13½x13*

711	A171 10f multicolored	.50	.20
712	A171 15f multicolored	.65	.30
713	A171 30f multicolored	.85	.35
714	A171 80f multicolored	2.25	.95
	Nos. 711-714 (4)	4.25	1.80

16th National Day.

Kuwait Tower — A172

APU Emblem — A173

1977, Feb. 26 *Perf. 14x13½*

715	A172 30f multicolored	1.00	.25
716	A172 80f multicolored	2.50	.80

Inauguration of Kuwait Tower.

1977, Apr. 12 Litho. *Perf. 13½x14*

717	A173 5f yellow & multi	.55	.20
718	A173 15f pink & multi	.60	.20
719	A173 30f lt blue & multi	1.00	.30
720	A173 80f lilac & multi	2.00	.90
	Nos. 717-720 (4)	4.15	1.60

Arab Postal Union, 25th anniversary.

Electronic Tree — A174

1977, May 17 Litho. *Perf. 12x12½*

721	A174 30f brown & red	1.25	.40
722	A174 80f green & red	2.50	1.00

World Telecommunications Day.

Sheik Sabah — A175

Games Emblem — A176

1977, June 1 Photo. *Perf. 11½x12*

723	A175 15f blue & multi	1.40	1.10
724	A175 25f yellow & multi	2.25	1.10
725	A175 30f red & multi	2.75	1.60
726	A175 80f violet & multi	9.00	4.00
727	A175 100f dp org & multi	9.75	4.50
728	A175 150f ultra & multi	13.50	7.25
729	A175 200f olive & multi	18.00	10.00
	Nos. 723-729 (7)	56.65	29.55

1977, Oct. 1 Litho. *Perf. 12*

730	A176 30f multicolored	1.00	.75
731	A176 80f multicolored	2.50	1.50

4th Asian Basketball Youth Championship, Oct. 1-15.

Dome of the Rock, Bishop Capucci, Fatima Bernawi, Sheik Abu Tair — A177

1977, Nov. 1 *Perf. 14*

732	A177 30f multicolored	3.00	1.25
733	A177 80f multicolored	6.50	3.00

Struggle for the liberation of Palestine.

Children and Houses A178

Children's Paintings: No. 735, Women musicians. No. 736, Boats. No. 737, Women preparing food, vert. No. 738, Women and children, vert. No. 739, Seated woman, vert.

1977, Nov. Photo. *Perf. 13½x13*

734	A178 15f lt green & multi	.65	.30
735	A178 15f yellow & multi	.65	.30
736	A178 30f brt yellow & multi	1.10	.60
737	A178 30f lt violet & multi	1.10	.60
738	A178 80f black & multi	2.10	1.60
739	A178 80f rose & multi	2.10	1.60
	Nos. 734-739 (6)	7.70	5.00

Dentist Treating Patient A179

1977, Dec. 3

740	A179 30f green & multi	1.50	1.00
741	A179 80f violet & multi	3.50	1.90

10th Arab Dental Union Congress, Kuwait, Dec. 3-6.

Ships Unloading Water A180

Kuwait water resources. 30f, 80f, 100f, vert.

Perf. 14x13½, 13½x14

1978, Jan. 25 Litho.

742	Block of 4	1.50	1.50
a.	5f shown	.30	.20
b.	5f Home delivery by camel	.30	.20
c.	5f Man with water bags	.30	.20
d.	5f Man with wheelbarrow	.30	.20
743	Block of 4	2.50	2.50
a.	10f Well	.50	.20
b.	10f Trough	.50	.20
c.	10f Water hole	.50	.20
d.	10f Irrigation	.50	.20
744	Block of 4	3.00	3.00
a.	15f Sheep drinking	.60	.20
b.	15f Laundresses	.60	.20
c.	15f Sheep and camels drinking	.60	.20
d.	15f Water stored in skins	.60	.20
745	Block of 4	3.50	3.50
a.	20f Animals at well	.75	.20
b.	20f Water in home	.75	.20
c.	20f Water pot	.75	.20
d.	20f Communal fountain	.75	.20
746	Block of 4	4.25	4.25
a.	25f Distillation plant	.85	.30
b.	25f Motorized delivery	.85	.30
c.	25f Water trucks	.85	.30
d.	25f Water towers	.85	.30
747	Block of 4	6.00	6.00
a.	30f Shower bath	1.25	.30
b.	30f Water tower	1.25	.30
c.	30f Gathering rain water	1.25	.30
d.	30f 2 water towers	1.25	.30
748	Block of 4	13.50	13.50
a.	80f Donkey with water bags	2.75	.90
b.	80f Woman with water can	2.75	.90
c.	80f Woman with water skin	2.75	.90
d.	80f Loading tank car	2.75	.90
749	Block of 4	17.50	17.50
a.	100f Truck delivering water	3.50	1.10
b.	100f Barnyard water supply	3.50	1.10
c.	100f Children at water basin	3.50	1.10
d.	100f Well in courtyard	3.50	1.10
	Nos. 742-749 (8)	51.75	51.75

Radar, Torch, Minarets A181

1978, Feb. 25 Litho. *Perf. 14x14½*

750	A181 30f multicolored	.60	.25
751	A181 80f multicolored	1.50	.75

17th National Day.

Man with Smallpox, Target — A182

1978, Apr. 17 Litho. *Perf. 12½*

752	A182	30f violet & multi	1.25	.50
753	A182	80f green & multi	2.75	1.40

Global eradication of smallpox.

Antenna and ITU Emblem A183

1978, May 17 *Perf. 14*

754	A183	30f silver & multi	.75	.30
755	A183	80f silver & multi	2.00	.75

10th World Telecommunications Day.

Sheik Sabah — A184

1978, June 28 Litho. *Perf. 13x14*

Portrait in Brown

Size: 21½x27mm

756	A184	15f green & gold	.40	.20
757	A184	30f orange & gold	.65	.45
758	A184	80f rose lilac & gold	1.50	1.10
759	A184	100f lt green & gold	1.75	1.25
760	A184	130f lt brown & gold	2.00	1.75
761	A184	180f violet & gold	3.50	2.75

Size: 23½x29mm

762	A184	1d red & gold	15.00	12.50
763	A184	4d blue & gold	62.50	57.50
		Nos. 756-763 (8)	87.30	77.50

Mt. Arafat, Pilgrims, Holy Kaaba A185

1978, Nov. 9 Photo. *Perf. 11½*

764	A185	30f multicolored	1.25	.65
765	A185	80f multicolored	3.00	1.60

Pilgrimage to Mecca.

UN and Anti-Apartheid Emblems — A186

1978, Nov. 27 Litho. *Perf. 12*

766	A186	30f multicolored	.60	.30
767	A186	80f multicolored	1.25	.80
768	A186	180f multicolored	3.25	1.90
		Nos. 766-768 (3)	5.10	3.00

Anti-Apartheid Year.

Refugees, Human Rights Emblems A187

1978, Dec. 10 Photo. *Perf. 13x13½*

769	A187	30f multicolored	.75	.35
770	A187	80f multicolored	1.75	.90
771	A187	100f multicolored	2.50	1.10
		Nos. 769-771 (3)	5.00	2.35

Declaration of Human Rights, 30th anniv.

Information Center — A188

1978, Dec. 26 Photo. *Perf. 13*

772	A188	5f multicolored	.40	.20
773	A188	15f multicolored	.50	.20
774	A188	30f multicolored	.75	.35
775	A188	80f multicolored	1.75	.85
		Nos. 772-775 (4)	3.40	1.60

New Kuwait Information Center.

Kindergarten A189

1979, Jan. 24 Photo. *Perf. 13½x14*

776	A189	30f multicolored	1.25	.50
777	A189	80f multicolored	2.25	1.25

International Year of the Child.

Flag and Peace Doves — A190

1979, Feb. 25 *Perf. 14½x14*

778	A190	30f multicolored	.75	.35
779	A190	80f multicolored	1.50	.85

18th National Day.

Modern Agriculture in Kuwait — A191

1979, Mar. 13 Photo. *Perf. 14*

780	A191	30f multicolored	.85	.45
781	A191	80f multicolored	2.00	1.10

4th Congress of Arab Agriculture Ministers of the Gulf and Arabian Peninsula.

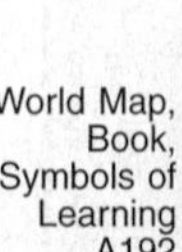

World Map, Book, Symbols of Learning A192

1979, Mar. 22

782	A192	30f multicolored	1.00	.45
783	A192	80f multicolored	2.00	1.10

Cultural achievements of the Arabs.

Children with Balloons — A193

Children's Paintings: No. 785, Boys flying kites. No. 786, Girl and doves. No. 787, Children and houses, horiz. No. 788, Four children, horiz. No. 789, Children sitting in circle, horiz.

1979, Apr. 18 Photo. *Perf. 14*

784	A193	30f yellow & multi	1.00	.45
785	A193	30f buff & multi	1.00	.45
786	A193	30f pale yel & multi	1.00	.45
787	A193	80f lt blue & multi	2.25	1.25
788	A193	80f yel green & multi	2.25	1.25
789	A193	80f lilac & multi	2.25	1.25
		Nos. 784-789 (6)	9.75	5.10

Cables, ITU Emblem, People A194

1979, May 17

790	A194	30f multicolored	1.00	.40
791	A194	80f multicolored	2.00	1.25

World Telecommunications Day.

Military Sports Council Emblem — A195

1979, June 1 Photo. *Perf. 14*

792	A195	30f multicolored	1.00	.40
793	A195	80f multicolored	2.00	1.25

29th Intl. Military Soccer Championship.

Child, Industrial Landscape, Environmental Emblems — A196

1979, June 5 *Perf. 12x11½*

794	A196	30f multicolored	1.25	.60
795	A196	80f multicolored	3.00	1.60

World Environment Day, June 5.

Children Holding Globe, UNESCO Emblem A197

1979, July 25 Litho. *Perf. 11½x12*

796	A197	30f multicolored	1.00	.40
797	A197	80f multicolored	2.00	1.10
798	A197	130f multicolored	2.75	1.75
		Nos. 796-798 (3)	5.75	3.25

Intl. Bureau of Education, Geneva, 50th anniv.

Kuwait Kindergartens, 25th Anniversary A198

Children's Drawings: 80f, Children waving flags.

1979, Sept. 15 Litho. *Perf. 12½*

799	A198	30f multicolored	1.00	.40
800	A198	80f multicolored	2.00	1.10

Pilgrims at Holy Ka'aba, Mecca Mosque A199

1979, Oct. 29 *Perf. 14x14½*

801	A199	30f multicolored	1.25	.50
802	A199	80f multicolored	3.00	1.50

Hegira (Pilgrimage Year).

International Palestinian Solidarity Day — A200

1979, Nov. 29 Photo. *Perf. 11½x12*

803	A200	30f multicolored	3.00	.95
804	A200	80f multicolored	5.75	1.90

Kuwait Airways 25th Anniversary A201

1979, Dec. 24 Photo. *Perf. 13x13½*

805	A201	30f multicolored	1.25	.60
806	A201	80f multicolored	3.00	1.75

19th National Day A202

1980, Feb. 25 Litho. *Perf. 14x14½*

807	A202	30f multicolored	1.00	.40
808	A202	80f multicolored	2.00	1.10

1980 Population Census A203

1980, Mar. 18 *Perf. 13½x14*

809	A203	30f multicolored	1.00	.35
810	A203	80f multicolored	2.00	.85

World Health Day A204

1980, Apr. 7

811 A204 30f multicolored 1.25 .55
812 A204 80f multicolored 3.00 1.60

Kuwait Municipality, 50th Anniversary A205

1980, May 1 Photo. *Perf. 14*

813 A205 15f multicolored .60 .20
814 A205 30f multicolored 1.10 .50
815 A205 80f multicolored 2.50 1.25
Nos. 813-815 (3) 4.20 1.95

Citizens of Kuwait A206

Future Kuwait (Children's Drawings): 80f, Super highway.

1980, May 14 Litho. *Perf. 14x14½*

816 A206 30f multicolored 1.25 .50
817 A206 80f multicolored 3.00 1.60

World Environment Day — A207

1980, June 5 Litho. *Perf. 12x11½*

818 A207 30f multicolored 1.25 .35
819 A207 80f multicolored 2.75 .95

Swimming, Moscow '80 and Kuwait Olympic Committee Emblems — A208

1980, July 19 Litho. *Perf. 12x12½*

820 A208 15f Volleyball .40 .20
821 A208 15f Tennis .40 .20
a. Vert. pair, #820-821 .90 .90
822 A208 30f shown .70 .30
823 A208 30f Weight lifting .70 .30
824 A208 30f Basketball .70 .30
825 A208 30f Judo .70 .30
a. Block of 4, #822-825 3.25 3.25
826 A208 80f Gymnast 1.75 .80
827 A208 80f Badminton 1.75 .80
828 A208 80f Fencing 1.75 .80
829 A208 80f Soccer 1.75 .80
a. Block of 4, #826-829 7.75 7.75
Nos. 820-829 (10) 10.60 4.80

22nd Summer Olympic Games, Moscow, July 19-Aug. 3.

20th Anniversary of OPEC A209

1980, Sept. 16 Litho. *Perf. 14x14½*

830 A209 30f multicolored 1.25 .60
831 A209 80f multicolored 3.00 .90

Hegira (Pilgrimage Year) A210

1980, Nov. 9 Photo. *Perf. 12x11½*

832 A210 15f multicolored .50 .20
833 A210 30f multicolored 1.10 .45
834 A210 80f multicolored 3.00 1.25
Nos. 832-834 (3) 4.60 1.90

Dome of the Rock, Jerusalem — A211

1980, Nov. 29 *Perf. 12x11½*

835 A211 30f multicolored 3.00 .60
836 A211 80f multicolored 5.00 1.60

International Palestinian Solidarity Day.

Avicenna (980-1037), Philosopher and Physician A212

1980, Dec. 7 *Perf. 12x12½*

837 A212 30f multicolored 1.50 .35
838 A212 80f multicolored 2.75 .95

Conference Emblem — A213

1981, Jan. 12 Photo. *Perf. 13½x13*

839 A213 30f multicolored 1.00 .75
840 A213 80f multicolored 3.50 2.10

First Islamic Medical Conference.

Girl in Wheelchair A214

International Year of the Disabled: 30f, Man in wheelchair playing billiards, vert.

Perf. 13½x13, 13x13½

1981, Jan. 26 Photo.

841 A214 30f multicolored 1.00 .55
842 A214 80f multicolored 2.50 1.60

20th National Day A215

1981, Feb. 25 Litho. *Perf. 13x13½*

843 A215 30f multicolored 1.00 .55
844 A215 80f multicolored 2.50 1.60

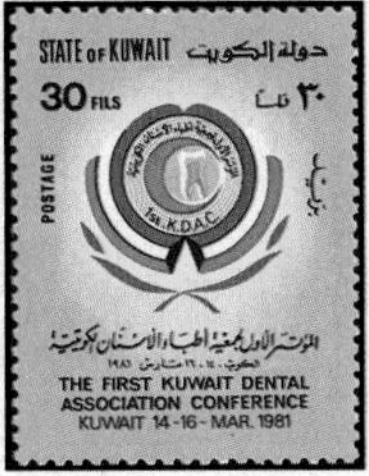

First Kuwait Dental Association Conference A216

1981, Mar. 14 *Perf. 11½x12*

845 A216 30f multicolored 2.00 1.10
846 A216 80f multicolored 6.00 2.75

A217

1981, May 8 Photo. *Perf. 14*

847 A217 30f multicolored 2.00 1.25
848 A217 80f multicolored 6.00 3.50

Intl. Red Cross day.

A218

1981, May 17 Litho. *Perf. 14½x14*

849 A218 30f multicolored 1.75 1.00
850 A218 80f multicolored 4.50 2.40

13th World Telecommunications day.

World Environment Day — A219

1981, June 5 Photo. *Perf. 12*

851 A219 30f multicolored 1.10 .70
852 A219 80f multicolored 3.25 1.90

Sief Palace A220

A221

1981, Sept. 16 Litho. *Perf. 12*

853 A220 5f multicolored .20 .20
854 A220 10f multicolored .20 .20
855 A220 15f multicolored .20 .20
856 A220 25f multicolored .20 .20
857 A220 30f multicolored .25 .20
858 A220 40f multicolored .40 .20
859 A220 60f multicolored .65 .25
860 A220 80f multicolored .85 .45
861 A220 100f multicolored 1.10 .65
862 A220 115f multicolored 1.25 .80
863 A220 130f multicolored 1.40 1.00
864 A220 150f multicolored 1.75 1.00
865 A220 180f multicolored 2.10 1.10
866 A220 250f multicolored 3.00 1.25
867 A220 500f multicolored 5.75 1.60
868 A221 1d multicolored 10.50 2.25
869 A221 2d multicolored 22.50 3.25
870 A221 3d multicolored 32.50 10.00
871 A221 4d multicolored 40.00 12.50
Nos. 853-871 (19) 124.80 37.30

Islamic Pilgrimage A222

1981, Oct. 7 Photo. *Perf. 13x13½*

872 A222 30f multicolored .85 .70
873 A222 80f multicolored 3.00 1.75

World Food Day A223

1981, Oct. 16 Litho. *Perf. 13*

874 A223 30f multicolored .95 .65
875 A223 80f multicolored 3.00 1.75

A224

1981, Dec. 30 Photo. *Perf. 14*

876 A224 30f multicolored 1.00 .65
877 A224 80f multicolored 3.00 1.75

20th anniv. of national television.

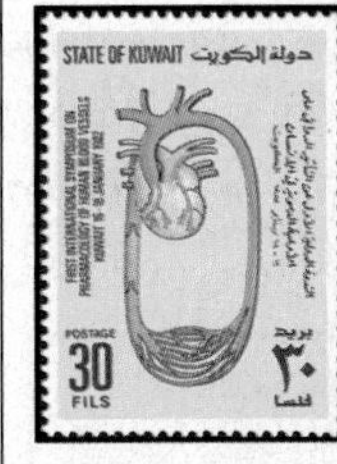

A225

1982, Jan. 16 Photo. *Perf. 14*

878 A225 30f multicolored 1.10 1.10
879 A225 80f multicolored 3.50 1.75

First Intl. Pharmacology of Human Blood Vessels Symposium, Jan. 16-18.

21st Natl. Day — A226

1982, Feb. 25 *Perf. 13½x13*

880 A226 30f multicolored .70 .45
881 A226 80f multicolored 2.00 1.25

Scouting Year A227

1982, Mar. 22 **Photo.** *Perf. 12x11½*

882 A227 30f multicolored .90 .55
883 A227 80f multicolored 2.50 1.50

Arab Pharmacists' Day — A228

1982, Apr. 2 **Litho.** *Perf. 12x11½*

884 A228 30f lt green & multi 1.25 .90
885 A228 80f pink & multi 4.00 2.50

World Health Day — A229

Arab Postal Union, 30th Anniv. — A230

1982, Apr. 7 **Litho.** *Perf. 13½x13*

886 A229 30f multicolored 1.40 .65
887 A229 80f multicolored 4.00 1.75

1982, Apr. 12 **Photo.** *Perf. 13½x13*

888 A230 30f multicolored 1.25 .85
889 A230 80f multicolored 4.00 2.25

TB Bacillus Centenary A231

1982, May 24 **Litho.** *Perf. 11½x12*

890 A231 30f multicolored 2.00 .90
891 A231 80f multicolored 5.75 2.50

1982 World Cup A232

1982, June 17 **Photo.** *Perf. 14*

892 A232 30f multicolored 1.10 .65
893 A232 80f multicolored 3.50 1.75

10th Anniv. of Science and Natural History Museum A233

1982, July 14 *Perf. 14*

894 A233 30f multicolored 3.00 1.50
895 A233 80f multicolored 8.75 4.50

6th Anniv. of United Arab Shipping Co. A234

Designs: Freighters.

1982, Sept. 1 *Perf. 13*

896 A234 30f multicolored 1.25 .40
897 A234 80f multicolored 2.75 1.10

Arab Day of the Palm Tree — A235

1982, Sept. 15 *Perf. 14*

898 A235 30f multicolored .75 .45
899 A235 80f multicolored 2.25 1.25

Islamic Pilgrimage A236

1982, Sept. 26 **Litho.**

900 A236 15f multicolored .50 .30
901 A236 30f multicolored 1.25 .65
902 A236 80f multicolored 3.25 1.75
Nos. 900-902 (3) 5.00 2.70

Desert Flowers & Plants — A237

Frame colors: No. 903a, green. b, violet. c, deep salmon. d, rose red. e, pale brown. f, deep green. g, pale orange. h, brown red. i, tan. j, violet blue.

No. 904: a, yellow green. b, pink. c, pale blue. d, dark blue. e, pale gray green. f, lake. g, pale orange. h, blue. i, red lilac. j, red orange.

No. 905: a, brown. b, pink. c, blue. d, olive green. e, orange red. f, dark blue. g, green. h, rose. i, bister. j, pale orange.

No. 906: a, yellow green. b, dark blue. c, pale orange. d, rose red. e, green. f, gray violet. g, gray blue. h, violet. i, yellow brown. j, orange red.

No. 907: a, lilac. b, blue green. c, pale orange. d, pale brown. e, violet blue. f, yellow. g, green blue. h, purple. i, pale brown. j, pale orange.

1983, Jan. 25 **Litho.** *Perf. 12*

903 Strip of 10 2.50 .90
a.-j. A237 10f any single .25 .20
904 Strip of 10 3.25 1.10
a.-j. A237 15f any single .30 .20
905 Strip of 10 6.25 2.25
a.-j. A237 30f any single .60 .20
906 Strip of 10 7.50 2.75
a.-j. A237 40f any single, horiz. .75 .25
907 Strip of 10 16.00 5.75
a.-j. A237 80f any single, horiz. 1.60 .55
Nos. 903-907 (5) 35.50 12.75

22nd Natl. Day A238

1983, Feb. 25 **Litho.** *Perf. 12½*

908 A238 30f multicolored .80 .50
909 A238 80f multicolored 2.25 1.40

25th Anniv. of Intl. Maritime Org. A239

1983, Mar. 17 **Photo.** *Perf. 14*

910 A239 30f multicolored .50 .30
911 A239 80f multicolored 1.40 .85

Map of Middle East and Africa, Conference Emblem — A240

1983, Mar. 19 *Perf. 13*

912 A240 15f multicolored .40 .20
913 A240 30f multicolored 1.00 .50
914 A240 80f multicolored 3.00 1.40
Nos. 912-914 (3) 4.40 2.10

3rd Intl. Conference on the Impact of Viral Diseases on the Development of the Middle East and Africa, Mar. 19-27.

World Health Day A241

1983, Apr. 7 *Perf. 12x11½*

915 A241 15f multicolored .45 .30
916 A241 30f multicolored .95 .70
917 A241 80f multicolored 2.75 1.90
Nos. 915-917 (3) 4.15 2.90

World Communications Year — A242

1983, May 17 **Photo.** *Perf. 13x13½*

918 A242 15f multicolored .55 .30
919 A242 30f multicolored 1.10 .70
920 A242 80f multicolored 3.25 1.90
Nos. 918-920 (3) 4.90 2.90

World Environment Day — A243

1983, June 5 **Litho.** *Perf. 12½*

921 A243 15f multicolored .65 .30
922 A243 30f multicolored 1.25 .70
923 A243 80f multicolored 3.75 1.90
Nos. 921-923 (3) 5.65 2.90

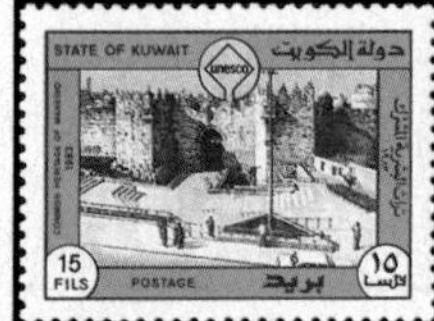

Wall of Old Jerusalem A244

1983, July 25 **Litho.** *Perf. 12*

924 A244 15f multicolored .75 .25
925 A244 30f multicolored 1.75 .55
926 A244 80f multicolored 5.00 1.60
Nos. 924-926 (3) 7.50 2.40

World Heritage Year.

Islamic Pilgrimage A245

1983, Sept. 15 **Photo.** *Perf. 11½*

927 A245 15f multicolored .40 .25
928 A245 30f multicolored 1.00 .55
929 A245 80f multicolored 2.75 1.60
Nos. 927-929 (3) 4.15 2.40

Intl. Palestinian Solidarity Day — A246

1983, Nov. 29 **Photo.** *Perf. 14*

930 A246 15f multicolored .50 .25
931 A246 30f multicolored 1.25 .55
932 A246 80f multicolored 3.50 1.60
Nos. 930-932 (3) 5.25 2.40

21st Pan Arab Medical Congress, Jan. 30-Feb. 2 — A247

1984, Jan. 30 **Litho.** *Perf. 14½x14*

933 A247 15f purple & multi .50 .25
934 A247 30f blue grn & multi 1.25 .55
935 A247 80f pink & multi 3.25 1.60
Nos. 933-935 (3) 5.00 2.40

Key, Natl. Emblem, and Health Establishments Emblem A248

1984, Feb. 20 Photo. ***Perf. 13x13½***

936 A248 15f multicolored .45 .25
937 A248 30f multicolored 1.10 .55
938 A248 80f multicolored 3.00 1.60
Nos. 936-938 (3) 4.55 2.40

Inauguration of Amiri and Al-Razi Hospitals, Allergy Center and Medical Stores Center.

23rd National Day — A249

1984, Feb. 25 Litho. ***Perf. 13½***

939 A249 15f multicolored .40 .25
940 A249 30f multicolored 1.00 .55
941 A249 80f multicolored 2.75 1.60
Nos. 939-941 (3) 4.15 2.40

2nd Kuwait Intl. Medical Science Conf., Mar. 4-8 — A250

1984, Mar. 4 Photo. ***Perf. 12***
Granite Paper

942 A250 15f multicolored .50 .25
943 A250 30f multicolored 1.25 .55
944 A250 80f multicolored 3.25 1.60
Nos. 942-944 (3) 5.00 2.40

30th Anniv. of Kuwait Airways Corp. A251

1984, Mar. 15 ***Perf. 13½***

946 A251 30f multicolored 1.10 .90
947 A251 80f multicolored 2.75 1.60

Al-Arabi Magazine, 25th Anniv. — A252

1984, Mar. 20 ***Perf. 14½x14***

948 A252 15f multicolored .45 .25
949 A252 30f multicolored .95 .50
950 A252 80f multicolored 2.50 1.40
Nos. 948-950 (3) 3.90 2.15

World Health Day — A253

1984, Apr. 7 ***Perf. 12***

951 A253 15f multicolored .40 .25
952 A253 30f multicolored 1.00 .55
953 A253 80f multicolored 2.75 1.60
Nos. 951-953 (3) 4.15 2.40

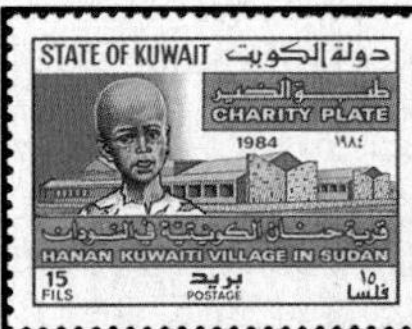

Hanan Kuwaiti Orphan Village, Sudan A254

1984, May 15 Litho. ***Perf. 12***

954 A254 15f multicolored .40 .25
955 A254 30f multicolored 1.00 .55
956 A254 80f multicolored 2.75 1.60
Nos. 954-956 (3) 4.15 2.40

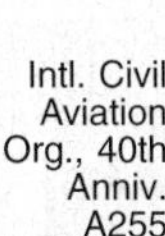

Intl. Civil Aviation Org., 40th Anniv. A255

1984, June 12

957 A255 15f multicolored .40 .25
958 A255 30f multicolored 1.10 .55
959 A255 80f multicolored 3.00 1.60
Nos. 957-959 (3) 4.50 2.40

Arab Youth Day — A256

1984, July 5 ***Perf. 13½***

960 A256 30f multicolored 1.00 .55
961 A256 80f multicolored 2.75 1.60

1984 Summer Olympics A257

1984, July 28 ***Perf. 15x14***

962 A257 30f Swimming .55 .35
963 A257 30f Hurdles .55 .35
a. Pair, #962-963 1.10 1.10
964 A257 80f Judo 1.40 .90
965 A257 80f Equestrian 1.40 .90
a. Pair, #964-965 3.00 3.00
Nos. 962-965 (4) 3.90 2.50

10th Anniv. of the Science Club A258

1984, Aug. 11 Photo. ***Perf. 13½x13***

966 A258 15f multicolored .50 .25
967 A258 30f multicolored 1.25 .55
968 A258 80f multicolored 3.00 1.60
Nos. 966-968 (3) 4.75 2.40

Islamic Pilgrimage — A259

1984, Sept. 4 Photo. ***Perf. 12x11½***

969 A259 30f multicolored 1.25 .55
970 A259 80f multicolored 3.25 1.60

INTELSAT '84, 20th Anniv. A260

1984, Oct. 1 Litho. ***Perf. 13½x14***

971 A260 30f multicolored 1.25 .55
972 A260 80f multicolored 3.00 1.60

G.C.C. Supreme Council, 5th Session A261

1984, Nov. 24 Litho. ***Perf. 15x14***

973 A261 30f multicolored 1.00 .55
974 A261 80f multicolored 2.50 1.60

Map of Israel, Fists, Shattered Star of David — A262

1984, Nov. 29 Photo. ***Perf. 12***

975 A262 30f multicolored 1.40 .55
976 A262 80f multicolored 3.25 1.60

Intl. Palestinian Solidarity Day.

Globe, Emblem A263

1984, Dec. 24 ***Perf. 12x11½***
Granite Paper

977 A263 30f multicolored 1.00 .25
978 A263 80f multicolored 2.75 1.10

Kuwait Oil Co., 50th anniv.

Intl. Youth Year — A264

24th Natl. Day — A265

1985, Jan. 15 ***Perf. 13½***

979 A264 30f multicolored .55 .25
980 A264 80f multicolored 1.60 1.10

1985, Feb. 25 Litho. ***Perf. 14x15***

981 A265 30f multicolored .75 .40
982 A265 80f multicolored 2.75 1.60

Intl. Program for the Development of Communications — A266

1985, Mar. 4 Photo. ***Perf. 11½***
Granite Paper

983 A266 30f multicolored 1.00 .55
984 A266 80f multicolored 2.50 1.60

1st Arab Gulf Week for Social Work — A267

1985, Mar. 13 Photo. ***Perf. 13½x13***

985 A267 30f multicolored 1.00 .55
986 A267 80f multicolored 2.50 1.60

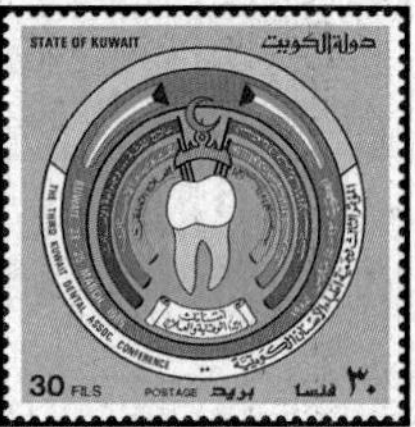

Kuwait Dental Assoc. 3rd Conference A268

1985, Mar. 23 Litho. ***Perf. 13½***

987 A268 30f multicolored 1.00 .55
988 A268 80f multicolored 2.50 1.60

1985 Census — A269

World Health Day — A270

1985, Apr. 1 *Perf. 14x13½*
989 A269 30f multicolored 1.25 .55
990 A269 80f multicolored 2.75 1.60

1985, Apr. 7 Photo. *Perf. 13½x13*
991 A270 30f multicolored 1.25 .55
992 A270 80f multicolored 2.75 1.60

Names of Books, Authors and Poets in Arabic — A271

1985, May 20 *Perf. 12*
Granite Paper
993 A271 Block of 4 5.75 1.75
a.-d. 30f any single 1.40 .40
994 A271 Block of 4 14.50 5.00
a.-d. 80f any single 3.50 1.10

Central Library, 50th anniv.

World Environment Day — A272

1985, June 5 *Perf. 11½*
995 A272 30f multicolored 1.50 .55
996 A272 80f multicolored 3.50 1.60

Org. of Petroleum Exporting Countries, 25th Anniv. A273

1985, Sept. 1 *Perf. 13x13½*
997 A273 30f multicolored 1.25 .55
998 A273 80f multicolored 2.75 1.60

Inauguration of Civil Information System — A274

1985, Oct. 1 Photo. *Perf. 12x11½*
999 A274 30f multicolored 1.10 .55
1000 A274 80f multicolored 2.75 1.60

Intl. Day of Solidarity with Palestinian People A275

1985, Nov. 29 Photo. *Perf. 12*
1001 A275 15f multicolored 1.00 .45
1002 A275 30f multicolored 1.75 .90
1003 A275 80f multicolored 3.75 2.25
Nos. 1001-1003 (3) 6.50 3.60

25th Natl. Day A276

1986, Feb. 25 Litho. *Perf. 15x14*
1004 A276 15f multicolored .25 .20
1005 A276 30f multicolored 1.25 .55
1006 A276 80f multicolored 3.25 1.25
Nos. 1004-1006 (3) 4.75 2.00

Natl. Red Crescent Soc., 20th Anniv. A277

1986, Mar. 26 Photo. *Perf. 13½*
1007 A277 20f multicolored .60 .65
1008 A277 25f multicolored 1.00 1.00
1009 A277 70f multicolored 3.50 2.75
Nos. 1007-1009 (3) 5.10 4.40

World Health Day — A278

1986, Apr. 7 *Perf. 13½x13*
1010 A278 20f multicolored .75 .65
1011 A278 25f multicolored 1.25 1.00
1012 A278 70f multicolored 4.00 2.75
Nos. 1010-1012 (3) 6.00 4.40

Intl. Peace Year A279

1986, June 5 Litho. *Perf. 13½*
1013 A279 20f multicolored .50 .45
1014 A279 25f multicolored 1.25 .70
1015 A279 70f multicolored 3.25 2.00
Nos. 1013-1015 (3) 5.00 3.15

United Arab Shipping Co., 10th Anniv. A280

1986, July 1 Photo. *Perf. 12x11½*
1016 A280 20f Al Mirqab .75 .60
1017 A280 70f Al Mubarakiah 4.00 2.40

Gulf Bank, 25th Anniv. A281

1986, Oct. 1 Photo. *Perf. 12½*
1018 A281 20f multicolored .65 .50
1019 A281 25f multicolored 1.10 .70
1020 A281 70f multicolored 3.25 2.25
Nos. 1018-1020 (3) 5.00 3.45

Sadu Art — A282

Various tapestry weavings.

1986, Nov. 5 Photo. *Perf. 12x11½*
Granite Paper
1021 A282 20f multicolored .65 .35
1022 A282 70f multicolored 2.50 1.40
1023 A282 200f multicolored 6.50 4.00
Nos. 1021-1023 (3) 9.65 5.75

Intl. Day of Solidarity with the Palestinian People — A283

1986, Nov. 29 *Perf. 14*
1024 A283 20f multicolored 1.25 .75
1025 A283 25f multicolored 1.75 1.00
1026 A283 70f multicolored 4.75 3.00
Nos. 1024-1026 (3) 7.75 4.75

5th Islamic Summit Conference — A284

1987, Jan. 26 Litho. *Perf. 14½*
1027 A284 25f multicolored .90 .45
1028 A284 50f multicolored 1.75 1.00
1029 A284 150f multicolored 5.25 3.00
Nos. 1027-1029 (3) 7.90 4.45

26th Natl. Day A285

1987, Feb. 25 *Perf. 13½x14*
1030 A285 50f multicolored 1.50 1.00
1031 A285 150f multicolored 4.50 3.00

Natl. Health Sciences Center A286

1987, Mar. 15 Photo. *Perf. 12x11½*
Granite Paper
1032 A286 25f multicolored .75 .35
1033 A286 150f multicolored 4.25 2.00

3rd Kuwait Intl. Medical Sciences Conference on Infectious Diseases in Developing Countries.

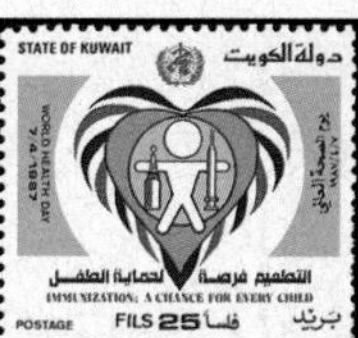

World Health Day — A287

1987, Apr. 7 Photo. *Perf. 13x13½*
1034 A287 25f multicolored .60 .45
1035 A287 50f multicolored 1.50 .90
1036 A287 150f multicolored 4.75 2.50
Nos. 1034-1036 (3) 6.85 3.85

Day of Ghods (Jerusalem) — A288

1987, June 7 Photo. *Perf. 12x11½*
1037 A288 25f multicolored .75 .20
1038 A288 50f multicolored 1.50 .60
1039 A288 150f multicolored 4.50 1.75
Nos. 1037-1039 (3) 6.75 2.55

Islamic Pilgrimage to Miqat Wadi Mihrim — A289

1987, Aug. Photo. *Perf. 13½x14½*
1040 A289 25f multicolored .75 .50
1041 A289 50f multicolored 1.50 .80
1042 A289 150f multicolored 4.75 2.00
Nos. 1040-1042 (3) 7.00 3.30

Arab Telecommunications Day — A290

1987, Sept. 9 Litho. *Perf. 14x13½*
1043 A290 25f multicolored .65 .30
1044 A290 50f multicolored 1.25 .80
1045 A290 150f multicolored 4.00 1.25
Nos. 1043-1045 (3) 5.90 2.35

World Maritime Day A291

1987, Sept. 24 *Perf. 12x11½*
Granite Paper
1046 A291 25f multicolored .85 .30
1047 A291 50f multicolored 1.75 .80
1048 A291 150f multicolored 5.00 2.00
Nos. 1046-1048 (3) 7.60 3.10

Al Qurain Housing Project — A292

1987, Oct. 5 ***Perf. 13x13½***
1049 A292 25f multicolored .50 .30
1050 A292 50f multicolored 1.00 .80
1051 A292 150f multicolored 4.50 2.00
Nos. 1049-1051 (3) 6.00 3.10

Port Authority, 10th Anniv. — A293

1987, Nov. 16 **Litho.** ***Perf. 14½***
1052 A293 25f multicolored .75 .20
1053 A293 50f multicolored 1.50 .50
1054 A293 150f multicolored 5.50 1.75
Nos. 1052-1054 (3) 7.75 2.45

A294

A295

1987, Nov. 29 ***Perf. 14x13½***
1055 A294 25f multicolored .65 .30
1056 A294 50f multicolored 1.25 .60
1057 A294 150f multicolored 4.00 2.00
Nos. 1055-1057 (3) 5.90 2.90

Intl. Day of Solidarity with the Palestinian People

1988, Feb. 3 **Photo.** ***Perf. 14***
1058 A295 25f multicolored .65 .30
1059 A295 50f multicolored 1.00 .50
1060 A295 150f multicolored 3.25 1.25
Nos. 1058-1060 (3) 4.90 2.05

Women's Cultural and Social Soc., 25th anniv.

A296

A297

1988, Feb. 25
1061 A296 25f multicolored .65 .30
1062 A296 50f multicolored 1.00 .50
1063 A296 150f multicolored 3.25 1.25
Nos. 1061-1063 (3) 4.90 2.05

National Day, 27th anniv.

1988, Apr. 7 **Litho.** ***Perf. 14x15***
1064 A297 25f multicolored .85 .20
1065 A297 50f multicolored 1.40 .40
1066 A297 150f multicolored 4.25 1.25
Nos. 1064-1066 (3) 6.50 1.85

World Health Day, WHO 40th anniv.

A298

A299

1988, Apr. 24 **Photo.** ***Perf. 12***
Granite Paper
1067 A298 35f multicolored .90 .35
1068 A298 50f multicolored 1.40 .55
1069 A298 150f multicolored 4.50 1.50
Nos. 1067-1069 (3) 6.80 2.40

Regional Marine Environment Day. Kuwait Regional Convention on the Marine Environment, 10th anniv. See Iraq Nos. 1333-1336.

1988, July 10 **Photo.** ***Perf. 14***
1070 A299 25f multicolored .85 .20
1071 A299 50f multicolored 1.40 .55
1072 A299 150f multicolored 4.75 1.50
Nos. 1070-1072 (3) 7.00 2.25

Kuwait Teachers Soc., 25th anniv.

Pilgrimage to Mecca A300

1988, Sept. 12 **Litho.** ***Perf. 13½x14***
1073 A300 25f multicolored .85 .20
1074 A300 50f multicolored 1.40 .55
1075 A300 150f multicolored 4.75 1.75
Nos. 1073-1075 (3) 7.00 2.50

Palestinian "Children of Stone" Fighting Israelis — A301

1988, Sept. 15 **Photo.** ***Perf. 13x13½***
1076 A301 50f multicolored 2.00 .70
1077 A301 150f multicolored 7.00 2.50

Palestinian Uprising. Dated 1987.

Arab Housing Day — A302

1988, Oct. 3
1078 A302 50f multicolored 1.25 .60
1079 A302 100f multicolored 2.25 1.00
1080 A302 150f multicolored 4.00 1.50
Nos. 1078-1080 (3) 7.50 3.10

Intl. Day for Solidarity with the Palestinian People A303

1988, Nov. 29 **Litho.** ***Perf. 14x13***
1081 A303 50f multicolored 1.10 .60
1082 A303 100f multicolored 2.25 1.00
1083 A303 150f multicolored 4.00 1.75
Nos. 1081-1083 (3) 7.35 3.35

A304

A305

1988, Dec. 5 ***Perf. 13x14***
1084 A304 50f multicolored .90 .50
1085 A304 100f multicolored 2.25 1.00
1086 A304 150f multicolored 3.75 1.25
Nos. 1084-1086 (3) 6.90 2.75

Intl. Volunteers Day.

1989, Feb. 18 **Litho.** ***Perf. 14x13½***
1087 A305 50f multicolored 1.00 .30
1088 A305 100f multicolored 2.00 .55
1089 A305 150f multicolored 3.50 .90
Nos. 1087-1089 (3) 6.50 1.75

18th Arab Engineering Conference.

28th Natl. Day A306

1989, Feb. 25 ***Perf. 13x13½***
1090 A306 50f multicolored 1.00 .30
1091 A306 100f multicolored 2.00 .55
1092 A306 150f multicolored 3.50 .90
Nos. 1090-1092 (3) 6.50 1.75

5th Natl. Dental Assoc. Conference A307

1989, Mar. 30 **Litho.** ***Perf. 13½x13***
1093 A307 50f multicolored 1.25 .40
1094 A307 150f multicolored 2.75 1.00
1095 A307 250f multicolored 4.75 1.60
Nos. 1093-1095 (3) 8.75 3.00

World Health Day A308

1989, Apr. 7 ***Perf. 13x13½***
1096 A308 50f multicolored .90 .40
1097 A308 150f multicolored 2.50 1.00
1098 A308 250f multicolored 4.00 1.60
Nos. 1096-1098 (3) 7.40 3.00

A309

A310

1989, May 10 ***Perf. 13x14***
1099 A309 50f multicolored .90 .25
1100 A309 150f multicolored 2.50 .75
1101 A309 250f multicolored 4.00 1.25
Nos. 1099-1101 (3) 7.40 2.25

Arab Board for Medical Specializations, 10th anniv.

1989, June 10 **Litho.** ***Perf. 14x15***
1102 A310 50f multicolored .90 .40
1103 A310 200f multicolored 3.50 1.50
1104 A310 250f multicolored 4.50 2.00
Nos. 1102-1104 (3) 8.90 3.90

Natl. Journalists Assoc., 25th anniv.

Al-Taneem Mosque — A311

1989, July 9 **Litho.** ***Perf. 13½x14½***
1105 A311 50f multicolored 1.00 .30
1106 A311 150f multicolored 3.00 .50
1107 A311 200f multicolored 4.00 1.40
Nos. 1105-1107 (3) 8.00 2.20

Pilgrimage to Mecca.

Arab Housing Day — A312

1989, Oct. 2 ***Perf. 13½***
1108 A312 25f multicolored .65 .20
1109 A312 50f multicolored 1.60 .25
1110 A312 150f multicolored 5.00 .75
Nos. 1108-1110 (3) 7.25 1.20

Annual Greenery Week Celebration — A313

Dhow — A314

1989, Oct. 15 *Perf. 13½x13*

1111 A313 25f multicolored .65 .20
1112 A313 50f multicolored 1.60 .25
1113 A313 150f multicolored 5.00 .75
Nos. 1111-1113 (3) 7.25 1.20

Numbers in Black, Moon and Dhow in Gold

1989, Nov. 1 *Perf. 14x15*

Coil Stamps

1114 A314 50f brt apple grn *1.75 1.75*
1115 A314 100f brt blue *3.50 3.50*
1116 A314 200f vermilion *7.50 7.50*
Nos. 1114-1116 (3) *12.75 12.75*

Nos. 1114-1116 available only at two post office locations, where they were dispensed from machines. Printed in rolls of 3000 consecutively numbered stamps. Stamps with overprinted asterisks but lacking printed numbers are from the ends of coil rolls.

Gulf Investment Corp., 5th Anniv. — A315

1989, Nov. 4 *Perf. 15x14*

1117 A315 25f multicolored .90 .20
1118 A315 50f multicolored 1.60 .25
1119 A315 150f multicolored 5.00 .75
Nos. 1117-1119 (3) 7.50 1.20

Declaration of Palestinian State, 1st Anniv. — A316

Zakat House, Orphan Sponsorship Program — A317

1989, Nov. 15 Litho. *Perf. 14x15*

1120 A316 50f multicolored 1.00 .25
1121 A316 150f multicolored 3.00 .85
1122 A316 200f multicolored 4.00 1.10
Nos. 1120-1122 (3) 8.00 2.20

1989, Dec. 10 *Perf. 13½x13*

1123 A317 25f multicolored .50 .20
1124 A317 50f multicolored 1.10 .35
1125 A317 150f multicolored 3.25 1.00
Nos. 1123-1125 (3) 4.85 1.55

Kuwait Police, 50th Anniv. — A318

1989, Dec. 30 Litho. *Perf. 15x14*

1126 A318 25f gray & multi .50 .20
1127 A318 50f lt ultra & multi 1.10 .35
1128 A318 150f lt violet & multi 3.25 1.00
Nos. 1126-1128 (3) 4.85 1.55

National Day, 29th Anniv. — A319

1990, Feb. 25 *Perf. 14x13½*

1129 A319 25f multicolored .55 .20
1130 A319 50f multicolored 1.00 .35
1131 A319 150f multicolored 3.25 1.00
Nos. 1129-1131 (3) 4.80 1.55

World Meteorological Day — A320

1990, Mar. 23 Litho. *Perf. 13½x14*

1132 A320 50f multicolored .90 .30
1133 A320 100f multicolored 2.10 .60
1134 A320 150f multicolored 3.00 .90
Nos. 1132-1134 (3) 6.00 1.80

World Health Day — A321

1990, Apr. 7 *Perf. 14x15*

1135 A321 50f multicolored 1.10 .25
1136 A321 100f multicolored 2.25 .60
1137 A321 150f multicolored 3.00 1.00
Nos. 1135-1137 (3) 6.35 1.85

Hawk — A322

Liberation of Kuwait — A323

1990, July 7 Litho. *Perf. 14½*

1138 A322 50f blue & gold 4.00
1139 A322 100f maroon & gold 7.75
1140 A322 150f green & gold 11.50
Nos. 1138-1140 (3) 23.25

1991 Litho. *Perf. 14½*

1141 A323 25f multicolored .60
1142 A323 50f multicolored 1.25
1143 A323 150f multicolored 3.50
Nos. 1141-1143 (3) 5.35

Peace A324

Reconstruction A325

1991, May *Perf. 13½x14*

1144 A324 50f multicolored 1.10
1145 A324 100f multicolored 2.25
1146 A324 150f multicolored 3.50
Nos. 1144-1146 (3) 6.85

1991, May

1147 A325 50f multicolored 1.10
1148 A325 150f multicolored 3.25
1149 A325 200f multicolored 4.25
Nos. 1147-1149 (3) 8.60

Liberation of Kuwait — A326

Flags of forces joining international coalition for liberation of Kuwait: a, Sweden. b, USSR. c, U.S. d, Kuwait. e, Saudi Arabia. f, UN. g, Singapore. h, France. i, Italy. j, Egypt. k, Morocco. l, UK. m, Philippines. n, UAE. o, Syria. p, Poland. q, Australia. r, Japan. s, Hungary. t, Netherlands. u, Denmark. v, New Zealand. w, Czechoslovakia. x, Bahrain. y, Honduras. z, Turkey. aa, Greece. ab, Oman. ac, Qatar. ad, Belgium. ae, Sierra Leone. af, Argentina. ag, Norway. ah, Canada. ai, Germany. aj, South Korea. ak, Bangladesh. al, Bulgaria. am, Senegal. an, Spain. ao, Niger. ap, Pakistan.

No. 1151, Flags of all forces of coalition.

1991, July 25 Litho. *Perf. 14½*

1150 A326 50f Sheet of 42 *50.00*
a.-ap. Any single 1.10

Size: 87x134mm

Imperf

1151 A326 1d multicolored *20.00*

Invasion of Kuwait, 1st Anniv. — A327

1991, Aug. 2 *Perf. 14½*

1152 A327 50f Human terror *1.10*
1153 A327 100f Invasion of Kuwait *2.75*
1154 A327 150f Environmental terrorism, horiz. *4.00*

Size: 90x65mm

Imperf

1155 A327 250f Desert Storm *7.00*
Nos. 1152-1155 (4) *14.85*

12th Gulf Cooperation Council Summit A328

Design: 150f, Tree of flags.

1991, Dec. 23 Litho. *Perf. 14½*

1156 A328 25f multicolored .55
a. see footnote .55
1157 A328 150f multicolored 3.25
a. Sheet, 2 ea #1156-1157 16.00
b. Sheet, 2 ea #1156a, 1157 16.00

No. 1156a has tree with inscriptions (country names in Arabic) in colors of flags shown on No. 1157.

Intl. Literacy Year — A329

OPEC, 30th Anniv. (in 1990) — A330

1992, Feb. 12 Litho. *Perf. 13½x13*

1158 A329 50f dark blue & buff 1.00
1159 A329 100f dark blue & cit 2.00
1160 A329 150f dk blue & pale lil 3.00
Nos. 1158-1160 (3) 6.00

Dated 1990.

1992, Oct. 29 *Perf. 14½x13½*

1161 A330 25f red & multi .55
1162 A330 50f yellow & multi 1.10
1163 A330 150f green & multi 3.25
Nos. 1161-1163 (3) 4.90

31st Natl. Day A331

1992 *Perf. 14½*

1164 A331 50f Flag, doves .60
1165 A331 150f Flags 1.90
a. Min. sheet, 2 ea #1164-1165 5.00

Liberation Day (No. 1165). Issue dates, 50f, Feb. 25; 150f, Feb. 26.

Don't Forget Our P.O.W.'s — A332

1991, Nov. 16

1166 A332 50f Flag, chains 1.10
1167 A332 150f Cell bars, chains 3.25
a. Min. sheet, 2 each #1166-1167 10.00

Dated 1991. Issued: 50f, 2/25; 150f, 2/26.

Camels A333

1991, Nov. 16 *Perf. 12½*

1168 A333 25f pink & multi .40
1169 A333 50f beige & multi .70
1170 A333 150f lt violet & multi 2.25
1171 A333 200f blue & multi 3.00
1172 A333 350f orange & multi 5.25
Nos. 1168-1172 (5) 11.60

Environmental Terrorism, by Jafar Islah — A334

Designs: No. 1174, Snake, flag, map. No. 1175, Skull, dead fish. No. 1176, Dying camel.

1992, June *Perf. 14½*

1173 A334 150f multicolored 2.25
1174 A334 150f multicolored 2.25
1175 A334 150f multicolored 2.25
1176 A334 150f multicolored 2.25
a. Block of 4, #1173-1176 9.00
b. Minature sheet of 4, #1173-1176 11.50

Earth Summit, Rio De Janeiro. No. 1176a printed in continuous design.

EXPO '92, Seville A335

Designs: No. 1177, Kuwaiti Pavilion, La Giralda Tower, Seville. No. 1178, Dhows. No. 1179, Dhow. No. 1180, Pavilion, dhow.

Flags of Spain or Kuwait and: No. 1181, Pavilion. No. 1182, La Giralda Tower. No. 1183, La Giralda Tower, dhow. No. 1184, Pavilion, dhow.

1992, June 19

1177 A335 50f multicolored .50
1178 A335 50f multicolored .50
1179 A335 50f multicolored .50
1180 A335 50f multicolored .50
a. Block of 4, #1177-1180 2.10
1181 A335 150f multicolored 1.60
1182 A335 150f multicolored 1.60
1183 A335 150f multicolored 1.60
1184 A335 150f multicolored 1.60
a. Block of 4, #1181-1184 6.50
b. Miniature sheet of 8, #1177-1184 9.00
Nos. 1177-1184 (8) 8.40

Nos. 1180a, 1184a have continuous designs.

Palace of Justice A336

1992, July 4 *Perf. 12½*

1185 A336 25f lilac & multi .20
1186 A336 50f lilac rose & multi .55
1187 A336 100f yel green & multi 1.75
1188 A336 150f yel orange & multi 1.75
1189 A336 250f blue green & multi 2.75
Nos. 1185-1189 (5) 7.00

1992 Summer Olympics, Barcelona — A337

Olympic flag, Fahed Al Ahmed Al Sabah, member of the Intl. Olympic committee and: 50f, Swimmer, soccer player. 100f, Runner, basketball player. 150f, Judo, equestrian.

1992, July 25 *Perf. 14½*

1190 A337 50f multicolored 1.10
1191 A337 100f multicolored 1.90
1192 A337 150f multicolored 3.00
Nos. 1190-1192 (3) 6.00

Invasion by Iraq, 2nd Anniv. A338

Children's paintings: No. 1193, Tanks, people holding signs, two people being tortured. No. 1194, Truck, Iraqi soldiers looting. No. 1195, Iraqi soldiers killing civilians, tanks. No. 1196, Houses ablaze. No. 1197, Tanks, civilians, soldiers. No. 1198, Planes bombing in attack on fort. No. 1199, Tank, civilians holding flags, signs. No. 1200, Battlefield.

1992, Aug. 2 **Litho.** *Perf. 14x14½*

1193 A338 50f multicolored .50
1194 A338 50f multicolored .50
1195 A338 50f multicolored .50
1196 A338 50f multicolored .50
a. Block of 4, #1193-1196 2.10
1197 A338 150f multicolored 1.60
1198 A338 150f multicolored 1.60
1199 A338 150f multicolored 1.60
1200 A338 150f multicolored 1.60
a. Block of 4, #1197-1200 6.50
b. Min. sheet of 8, #1193-1200 9.00
Nos. 1193-1200 (8) 8.40

Extinguishing of Oil Well Fires, 1st Anniv. — A339

Various scenes showing oil well fire being extinguished.

1992 **Litho.** *Perf. 14½*

1201 A339 25f multi, vert. .20 .20
1202 A339 50f multi, vert. .60 .40
1203 A339 150f multi, vert. 1.60 1.10
1204 A339 250f multicolored 3.00 1.90
Nos. 1201-1204 (4) 5.40 3.60

Kuwait Tower — A340

A341

1993, Jan. 16 **Litho.** *Perf. 14x15*

Background Color

1205 A340 25f lilac .20 .20
1206 A340 100f blue 1.10 .70
1207 A340 150f salmon 1.60 1.10
Nos. 1205-1207 (3) 2.90 2.00

1993, Feb. 25 **Litho.** *Perf. 13½x14*

1208 A341 25f green & multi .20 .20
1209 A341 50f blue & multi .50 .35
1210 A341 150f pink & multi 1.60 1.10
Nos. 1208-1210 (3) 2.30 1.65

National Day, 32nd anniv.

Liberation Day, 2nd Anniv. — A342

1993, Feb. 26 *Perf. 15x14*

1211 A342 25f org yel & multi .25 .25
1212 A342 50f green & multi .55 .55
1213 A342 150f red lilac & multi 1.60 1.60
Nos. 1211-1213 (3) 2.40 2.40

Remembering Prisoners of War — A343

Designs: 50f, Prisoner shackled in cell, vert. 150f, Shackled hand pointing to cell window, bird. 200f, Cell, prisoner's face, vert.

Perf. 13½x14, 14x13½

1993, May 15 **Litho.**

1214 A343 50f multicolored .60 .60
1215 A343 150f multicolored 1.60 1.60
1216 A343 200f multicolored 2.25 2.25
Nos. 1214-1216 (3) 4.45 4.45

A344

A345

1993, Apr. 20 **Litho.** *Perf. 11½x12*

Granite Paper

1217 A344 25f gray & multi .20 .20
1218 A344 50f green & multi .55 .35
1219 A344 150f yellow & multi 1.60 1.10
1220 A344 350f blue & multi 4.00 2.60
Nos. 1217-1220 (4) 6.35 4.25

18th Deaf Child Week.

1993, Aug. 2 **Litho.** *Perf. 13½x14*

1221 A345 50f green & multi .50 .40
1222 A345 150f orange & multi 1.50 1.25

Invasion by Iraq, 3rd anniv.

Kuwait Airforce, 40th Anniv. A346

1993, Dec. 9 **Litho.** *Perf. 13x13½*

1223 A346 50f blue & multi .50 .40
1224 A346 150f green & multi 1.40 1.10

Natl. Day, 33rd Anniv. — A347

Liberation Day, 3rd Anniv. — A348

1994, Feb. 25 **Litho.** *Perf. 13½x14*

1225 A347 25f salmon & multi .20 .20
1226 A347 50f yellow & multi .50 .40
1227 A347 150f green & multi 1.75 1.40
Nos. 1225-1227 (3) 2.45 2.00

1994, Feb. 26

1228 A348 25f yellow & multi .20 .20
1229 A348 50f blue & multi .55 .40
1230 A348 150f gray green & multi 1.50 1.10
Nos. 1228-1230 (3) 2.25 1.70

Central Bank of Kuwait, 25th Anniv. — A349

1994, Apr. 20 **Litho.** *Perf. 13½x13*

1231 A349 25f salmon & multi .20 .20
1232 A349 50f green & multi .60 .40
1233 A349 150f blue violet & multi 1.75 1.25
Nos. 1231-1233 (3) 2.55 1.85

A350

A351

Intl. Year of the Family A352

1994, May 15 **Litho.** *Perf. 13*

1234 A350 50f multicolored .65 .40
1235 A351 150f multicolored 1.75 1.10
1236 A352 200f multicolored 2.40 1.50
Nos. 1234-1236 (3) 4.80 3.00

A353

A354

1994, June 5 Litho. *Perf. 14*

1237	A353	50f yellow & multi	.60	.40
1238	A353	100f blue & multi	1.10	.75
1239	A353	150f green & multi	1.60	1.10
		Nos. 1237-1239 (3)	3.30	2.25

Industrial Bank of Kuwait, 20th anniv.

1994, June 15 Litho. *Perf. 13*

1240	A354	50f Whirlpool	.60	.40
1241	A354	100f Shifting sands	1.10	.75
1242	A354	150f Finger print	1.60	1.10
1243	A354	250f Clouds	2.75	1.90
a.		Min. sheet of 4, #1240-1243	6.50	6.50
		Nos. 1240-1243 (4)	6.05	4.15

Martyr's Day.

A355

A356

1994, June 25 Litho. *Perf. 14*

1244	A355	50f vio & multi	.50	.40
1245	A355	150f pink & multi	1.50	1.00
1246	A355	350f blue & multi	4.00	2.60
		Nos. 1244-1246 (3)	6.00	4.00

ILO, 75th anniv.

1994, Aug. 2 Litho. *Perf. 12½x13½*

1247	A356	50f green blue & multi	.50	.40
1248	A356	150f blue & multi	1.50	1.00
1249	A356	350f lilac & multi	4.00	2.60
		Nos. 1247-1249 (3)	6.00	4.00

Invasion by Iraq, 4th anniv.

Port Authority — A357

Science Club, 20th Anniv. — A358

1994, Aug. 31 Litho. *Perf. 12½x14*

1250	A357	50f pink & multi	.50	.40
1251	A357	150f blue & multi	1.50	1.00
1252	A357	350f green & multi	4.00	2.60
		Nos. 1250-1252 (3)	6.00	4.00

1994, Sept. 11 *Perf. 14*

1253	A358	50f blue & multi	.60	.40
1254	A358	100f green & multi	1.25	.75
1255	A358	150f red & multi	1.60	1.10
		Nos. 1253-1255 (3)	3.45	2.25

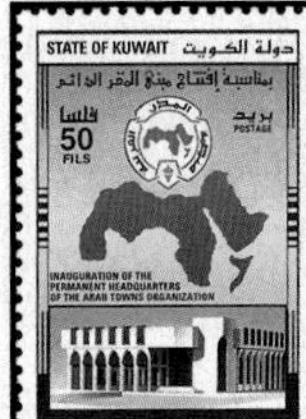

A359

A360

Designs showing emblem and: 50f, Map of Arab countries, building. 100f, Windows, building. 150f, Doors below portico.

1994, Nov. 12 *Perf. 11½*

1256	A359	50f multicolored	.60	.40
1257	A359	100f multicolored	1.25	.75
1258	A359	150f multicolored	1.60	1.10
		Nos. 1256-1258 (3)	3.45	2.25

Arab Towns Organization, opening of headquarters.

1994, Dec. 7 *Perf. 14½*

Designs: 100f, Emblems, sailing ship. 150f, Emblems, co-operation, co-ordination. 350f, Emblem, airplane in flight.

1259	A360	100f silver, gold & multi	1.25	.75
1260	A360	150f silver, gold & multi	1.75	1.10
1261	A360	350f gold & multi	4.50	2.75
		Nos. 1259-1261 (3)	7.50	4.60

ICAO, 50th anniv.

A361

A362

1994, Dec. 20 *Perf. 13x14*

1262	A361	50f lake & multi	.60	.40
1263	A361	100f green & multi	1.25	.75
1264	A361	150f slate & multi	1.60	1.10
		Nos. 1262-1264 (3)	3.45	2.25

Kuwait Airways, 40th anniv.

1995, Feb. 6 Litho. *Perf. 14*

1265	A362	50f yellow & multi	.60	.35
1266	A362	100f green & multi	1.10	.65
1267	A362	150f brown & multi	1.75	1.00
		Nos. 1265-1267 (3)	3.45	2.00

1995 Census.

National Day, 34th Anniv. — A363

Liberation Day, 4th Anniv. — A364

1995, Feb. 25 *Perf. 13*

1268	A363	25f blue & multi	.20	.20
1269	A363	50f yellow & multi	.65	.35
1270	A363	150f lilac & multi	1.90	1.00
		Nos. 1268-1270 (3)	2.75	1.55

1995, Feb. 26

1271	A364	25f blue & multi	.20	.20
1272	A364	50f green & multi	.65	.35
1273	A364	150f rose lilac & multi	1.90	1.00
		Nos. 1271-1273 (3)	2.75	1.55

Medical Research A365

1995, Mar. 20 *Perf. 14*

1274	A365	50f Medical building	.60	.40
1275	A365	100f Classroom instruction	1.25	.75
1276	A365	150f Map of Kuwait	1.60	1.10
		Nos. 1274-1276 (3)	3.45	2.25

Arab League, 50th Anniv. A366

Designs: 50f, Kuwaiti, league flags over emblems, map, vert. 100f, Flags over "50," emblem. 150f, Flags as clasping hands, vert.

1995, Mar. 22 *Perf. 13*

1277	A366	50f multicolored	.60	.40
1278	A366	100f multicolored	1.25	.75
1279	A366	150f multicolored	1.60	1.10
		Nos. 1277-1279 (3)	3.45	2.25

A367

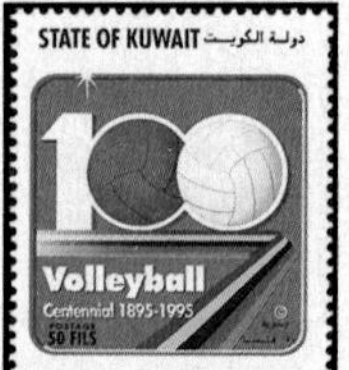

A368

1995, Apr. 7 Litho. *Perf. 13½x13*

1280	A367	50f blue & multi	.65	.40
1281	A367	150f pink & multi	1.75	1.10
1282	A367	200f yellow & multi	2.40	1.50
		Nos. 1280-1282 (3)	4.80	3.00

World Health Day.

1995, June 5 Litho. *Perf. 14*

Designs: 50f, One gold ball. 100f, Gold "1," one gold ball. 150f, "1," both balls in gold.

1283	A368	50f shown	.60	.35
1284	A368	100f multicolored	1.25	.65
1285	A368	150f multicolored	1.75	1.00
		Nos. 1283-1285 (3)	3.60	2.00

Volleyball, cent.

Invasion by Iraq, 5th Anniv. — A369

1995, Aug. 2 Litho. *Perf. 13*

1286	A369	50f purple & multi	.65	.40
1287	A369	100f red & multi	1.25	.75
1288	A369	150f green & multi	1.75	1.10
		Nos. 1286-1288 (3)	3.65	2.25

UN, 50th Anniv. A370

1995, Aug. 12 *Perf. 13x13½*

1289	A370	25f multi	.20	.20
1290	A370	50f orange & multi	.65	.40
1291	A370	150f bl grn & multi	1.75	1.10
		Nos. 1289-1291 (3)	2.60	1.70

FAO, 50th Anniv. — A371

People in traditional dress with: 50f, Cattle, camels, sheep. 100f, Fish, boat. 150f, Poultry, fruits, vegetables.

1995, Sept. 21 *Perf. 13½x13*

1292	A371	50f multicolored	.65	.40
1293	A371	100f multicolored	1.25	.75
1294	A371	150f multicolored	1.75	1.10
a.		Min. sheet of 3, #1292-1294	3.75	3.75
		Nos. 1292-1294 (3)	3.65	2.25

A372

World Standards Day — A373

1995, Oct. 14 *Perf. 13*

1295	A372	50f multicolored	.65	.40
1296	A373	100f green & multi	1.25	.75
1297	A373	150f violet & multi	1.75	1.10
		Nos. 1295-1297 (3)	3.65	2.25

Flowers — A374

Natl. Day, 35th Anniv. — A375

Designs: 5f, Onobrychis ptolemaica. 15f, Convolvulus oxyphyllus. 25f, Papaver rhoeas. 50f, Moltkiopsis ciliata. 150f, Senecio desfontainei.

1995, Nov. 15 Litho. *Perf. 14½*

1298	A374	5f multicolored	.30	.20
1299	A374	15f multicolored	.30	.25
1300	A374	25f multicolored	.55	.40
1301	A374	50f multicolored	.95	.80
1302	A374	150f multicolored	3.00	2.50
		Nos. 1298-1302 (5)	5.10	4.15

1996, Feb. 25 *Perf. 14*

1303	A375	25f lil rose & multi	.20	.20
1304	A375	50f blue green & multi	.55	.40
1305	A375	150f salmon & multi	1.75	1.25
		Nos. 1303-1305 (3)	2.50	1.85

Liberation Day, 5th Anniv. A376

1996, Feb. 26

1306	A376	25f violet & multi	.20	.20
1307	A376	50f brown & multi	.55	.40
1308	A376	150f blue green & multi	1.75	1.25
		Nos. 1306-1308 (3)	2.50	1.85

Arab City Day — A377

A378

1996, Mar. 1 *Perf. 13½*

1309	A377	50f yel grn & multi	.55	.40
1310	A377	100f pink & multi	1.10	.80
1311	A377	150f blue green & multi	1.75	1.25
		Nos. 1309-1311 (3)	3.40	2.45

1996, Jan. 27 *Perf. 14*

1312	A378	50f blue & multi	.55	.40
1313	A378	100f gray & multi	1.10	.80
1314	A378	150f rose lilac & multi	1.75	1.25
		Nos. 1312-1314 (3)	3.40	2.45

Scouting in Kuwait, 60th Anniv. — A379

50f, On top of watchtower. 100f, Drawing water from well. 150f, Planting seedling.

1996, Jan. 14 *Perf. 13½*

1315	A379	50f yellow & multi	.80	.40
1316	A379	100f lilac & multi	1.60	.80
1317	A379	150f blue green & multi	2.50	1.25
		Nos. 1315-1317 (3)	4.90	2.45

Kuwait Money Show — A380

1996, Jan. 2 *Perf. 14*

1318	A380	25f gold & multi	.20	.20
1319	A380	100f blue & multi	1.00	.80
1320	A380	150f dk gray & multi	1.60	1.25
		Nos. 1318-1320 (3)	2.80	2.25

7th Kuwait Dental Assoc. Conference A381

UNESCO, 50th Anniv. A382

1996, Mar. 27 Litho. *Perf. 14x13½*

1321	A381	25f orange & multi	.20	.20
1322	A381	50f violet & multi	.50	.40
1323	A381	150f blue & multi	1.75	1.40
		Nos. 1321-1323 (3)	2.45	2.00

1996, Apr. 10 *Perf. 13½x14*

1324	A382	25f violet & multi	.20	.20
1325	A382	100f green & multi	1.00	.80
1326	A382	150f orange & multi	1.60	1.25
		Nos. 1324-1326 (3)	2.80	2.25

1st Oil Exports, 50th Anniv. — A383

Rule of Al-Sabah Family, Cent. — A384

1996, June 30 Litho. *Perf. 13*

1327	A383	25f multicolored	.25	.25
1328	A383	100f gray & multi	1.25	1.00
1329	A383	150f bister & multi	1.75	1.50
		Nos. 1327-1329 (3)	3.25	2.75

1996, Aug. 12

1330	A384	25f shown	.25	.25
1331	A384	50f Shiek, flags	.60	.50
1332	A384	150f like #1330	1.60	1.50
		Nos. 1330-1332 (3)	2.45	2.25

1996 Summer Olympic Games, Atlanta — A385

1996, Oct. 5 *Perf. 13½*

1333	A385	25f Shooting	.30	.25
1334	A385	50f Running	.60	.50
1335	A385	100f Weight lifting	1.25	1.00
1336	A385	150f Fencing	1.75	1.50
		Nos. 1333-1336 (4)	3.90	3.25

A 750f souvenir sheet exists. Value $75.

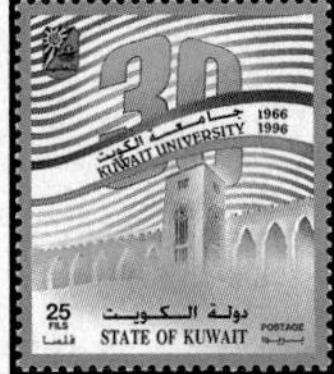

Kuwait University, 30th Anniv. — A386

1st Children's Cultural Festival — A387

1996, Nov. 27 Litho. *Perf. 13½x14*

1337	A386	25f green & multi	.20	.20
1338	A386	100f blue & multi	1.10	.80
1339	A386	150f yellow & multi	1.50	1.10
		Nos. 1337-1339 (3)	2.80	2.10

1996, Nov. 20 *Perf. 14x13½*

1340	A387	25f brn gray & multi	.20	.20
1341	A387	100f multicolored	1.10	.80
1342	A387	150f yel grn & multi	1.50	1.10
		Nos. 1340-1342 (3)	2.80	2.10

3rd Al-Qurain Cultrual Festival — A388

Liberation Tower — A389

1996, Nov. 20 *Perf. 14*

1343	A388	50f orange & multi	.60	.40
1344	A388	100f blue & multi	1.25	.80
1345	A388	150f green & multi	1.60	1.10
		Nos. 1343-1345 (3)	3.45	2.30

1996, Dec. 10 *Perf. 13x13½*

1346	A389	5f red & multi	.20	.20
1347	A389	10f yel bis & multi	.20	.20
1348	A389	15f brt rose & multi	.20	.20
1349	A389	25f pale pink & multi	.25	.20
a.		Booklet pane of 4	—	
		Complete booklet, #1349a	—	
1350	A389	50f violet & multi	.90	.40
a.		Booklet pane of 4	—	
		Complete booklet, #1350a	—	
1351	A389	100f brt yel & multi	1.75	.80
1352	A389	150f blue & multi	2.50	1.10
a.		Booklet pane of 4	—	
		Complete booklet, #1352a	—	
1353	A389	200f pink & multi	3.25	1.50
1354	A389	250f dp blue & multi	4.25	1.90
1355	A389	350f blue & multi	6.50	2.75
		Nos. 1346-1355 (10)	20.00	9.25
		Set of 3 booklets, #1349a-1350a, 1352a	*31.00*	

National Day, 36th Anniv. A390

1997, Feb. 25 Litho. *Perf. 14½*

1356	A390	25f blue & multi	.20	.20
1357	A390	50f lilac & multi	.55	.40
1358	A390	150f orange & multi	1.60	1.10
		Nos. 1356-1358 (3)	2.35	1.70

Liberation Day, 6th Anniv. A391

1997, Feb. 26 *Perf. 13x13½*

1359	A391	25f tan & multi	.20	.20
1360	A391	50f lilac & multi	.55	.40
1361	A391	150f blue & multi	1.60	1.10
		Nos. 1359-1361 (3)	2.35	1.70

Marine Life — A392

No. 1368: Various views of a school of shrimp: a, b, c, d, 25f. e, f, g, h, 50f. i, j, k, l, 100f. m, n, o, p, 150f.

1997, Jan. 15 *Perf. 14½*

1362	A392	25f Maid	.20	.20
1363	A392	50f Sheim	.55	.40
1364	A392	100f Hamoor	1.10	.80
1365	A392	150f Sobaity	1.75	1.25
1366	A392	200f Nagroor	2.25	1.60
1367	A392	350f Zobaidy	3.75	2.75
		Nos. 1362-1367 (6)	9.60	7.00

Sheet of 16

1368	A392	Sheet of 16, #a.-p.	16.00	16.00

Montreal Protocol on Substances that Deplete Ozone Layer, 10th Anniv. — A393

1997, Sept. 16 Litho. *Perf. 13½x13*

1369	A393	25f blue & multi	.20	.20
1370	A393	50f violet & multi	.55	.35
1371	A393	150f bl grn & multi	1.75	1.10
		Nos. 1369-1371 (3)	2.50	1.65

Industries Exhibition A394

1997, Oct. 1

1372	A394	25f brt pink & multi	.20	.20
1373	A394	50f green & multi	.65	.40
1374	A394	150f blue & multi	1.75	1.10
		Nos. 1372-1374 (3)	2.60	1.70

22nd Kuwait Arabic Book Exhibition A395

1997, Nov. 19 Litho. *Perf. 13½x13*

Border Color

1375	A395	25f pink	.20	.20
1376	A395	50f blue	.55	.35
1377	A395	150f blue green	1.75	1.10
		Nos. 1375-1377 (3)	2.50	1.65

Cultural History A396

a, 50f, Qibliya Girls School, 1937. b, 50f, Scissors cutting ribbon, Fine Arts Exhibition, 1959. c, 150f, Folk Theatre Group, 1956. d, 25f, 1st Book Fair, 1975. e, 25f, Kuwait Magazine, 1928. f, 50f, Mubarakiya School, 1912. g, 50f, Kuwait Natl. Museum, 1958. h, 150f, Academy of Music, 1972. i, 25f, A'lam Al-Fikr (periodical), 1970. j, 25f, Al'Bitha Magazine, 1946. k, 50f, Building complex, 1953 (Al-Arabi Magazine). l, 50f, Building, 1959. m, 150f, Al-Sharqiya Cinema, 1955. n, 25f, Al'Lam Al Ma'rifa (periodical), 1978. o, 25f, Dalil Almohtar Fi Alaam al-Bihar (boat), 1923. p, 50f, Alma'had Aldini (arabesques), 1947. q, 50f, Folklore Center, 1956. r, 150f, Theatrical Academy, 1967. s, 25f, Al-Arabi Magazine, 1958. t, 25f, Public Library (book), 1923. u, 50f, Al Ma'Arif Printing Press (Arabic writing), 1947. v, 50f, Literary Club, 1924. w, 150f, Bas Ya Bahar (1st Kuwaitii feature film), 1970. x,

25f, Al Thaqafa Al-Alamiya (periodical), 1981. y, 25f, The World Theatre (periodical), 1969.

1997, Nov. 30

1378	A396	Sheet of 25, #a.-y.	20.00	20.00

Nos. 1378a-1378y each contain year date of event depicted.

Educational Science Museum, 25th Anniv. A397

Designs: 25f, Whale, quadrant, vert. 50f, Space exploration, whale, dinosaur. No. 1381, Astronaut, dinosaur, satellite dish, airplane, globe, skeleton encircling whale, vert. No. 1382, Coelacanth.

Perf. 13½x13, 13x13½

1997, Nov. 1 **Litho.**

1379	A397	25f multicolored	.20	.20
1380	A397	50f multicolored	.70	.40
1381	A397	150f multicolored	1.90	1.10
		Nos. 1379-1381 (3)	2.80	1.70

Souvenir Sheet

1382	A397	150f multicolored	12.00	12.00

No. 1382 is a continuous design and sold for 1d.

18th Summit of Gulf Cooperation Countries — A398

Designs: 25f, Flags of member countries, doves, vert. 50f, Map, birds with flag colors. 150f, Doves perched atop flags, vert.

1997, Dec. 20 *Perf. 13½x14*

1383	A398	25f multicolored	.20	.20
1384	A398	50f multicolored	.80	.40
1385	A398	150f multicolored	2.25	1.10
a.		Bklt. pane of 3, #1383-1385	*12.00*	
		Complete booklet, #1385a	*12.00*	
		Nos. 1383-1385 (3)	3.25	1.70

National Day, 37th Anniv. A399

1998, Feb. 25 **Litho.** *Perf. 13x13½*

1386	A399	25f yellow & multi	.20	.20
1387	A399	50f pink & multi	.75	.35
1388	A399	150f blue & multi	2.25	1.10
		Nos. 1386-1388 (3)	3.20	1.65

Liberation Day, 7th Anniv. A400

1998, Feb. 26

1389	A400	25f yellow & multi	.20	.20
1390	A400	50f orange & multi	.75	.35
1391	A400	150f green & multi	2.25	1.10
		Nos. 1389-1391 (3)	3.20	1.65

A401

A402

1998, Mar. 16 **Litho.** *Perf. 13½x13*

1392	A401	25f tan & multi	.20	.20
1393	A401	50f blue & multi	.75	.35
1394	A401	150f white & multi	2.25	1.10
		Nos. 1392-1394 (3)	3.20	1.65

Say No to Drugs.

1997, May 2 **Litho.** *Perf. 13½x13*

1395	A402	25f orange & multi	.20	.20
1396	A402	50f blue & multi	.75	.35
1397	A402	150f red & multi	2.25	1.10
		Nos. 1395-1397 (3)	3.20	1.65

Chernobyl disaster, 10th anniv.

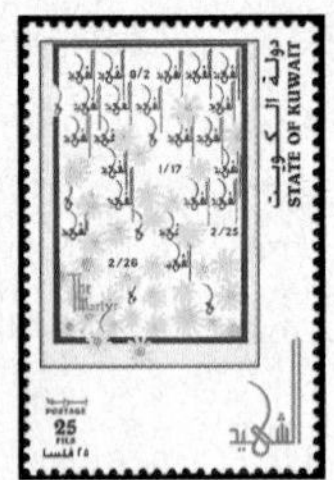

Martyrs — A403

25f, Dates, 1/17, 2/25, 2/26, flowers. 50f, Stylized tree. 150f, Lines, inscriptions. No. 1401: a, Man with hands in dirt. b, Three boys emptying basket of dirt.

1998, Mar. 31 **Litho.** *Perf. 14*

1398	A403	25f multicolored	.20	.20
1399	A403	50f multicolored	.40	.35
1400	A403	150f multicolored	1.25	1.10
a.		Bklt. pane, 2 ea #1398-1400	15.00	
		Complete booklet, #1400a	15.00	

Perf. 14½ Between

Size: 31x54mm

1401	A403	500f Pair, a.-b.	15.00	15.00
		Nos. 1398-1401 (4)	16.85	16.65

Ban Land Mines — A405

Stylized amputees using crutches for support: 25f, Two people. 50f, One person. 150f, Two people, nurse. 500f, Three people, nurse.

1998, Aug. 2 *Perf. 14½*

1402	A405	25f multicolored	.20	.20
1403	A405	50f multicolored	.65	.35
1404	A405	150f multicolored	2.00	1.10

Size: 89x82mm

Imperf

1405	A405	500f multicolored	7.00	7.00
		Nos. 1402-1405 (4)	9.85	8.65

Life in Pre-Oil Kuwait — A406

Designs: 25f, Seated at ceremonial meal. 50f, Building boat. 100f, Weaving. 150f, Loading boat. 250f, Pouring water from water skin into bowl. 350f, Man with pigeons.

1998, Apr. 14 **Litho.** *Perf. 14*

Booklet Stamps

1406	A406	25f multicolored	.45	.20
1407	A406	50d multicolored	.80	.35
1408	A406	100f multicolored	1.60	.70
1409	A406	150f multicolored	2.25	1.00
1410	A406	250f multicolored	4.00	1.75
1411	A406	350f multicolored	5.75	2.50
a.		Booklet pane, #1406-1411	25.00	
		Complete booklet, #1411a	25.00	

1998, Sept. 1 **Litho.** *Perf. 14*

25f, Man shaving another man's head. 50f, Woman using grindstone. 100f, Man pulling thread through cloth. 150f, Man gluing artifacts together. 250f, Potter. 350f, Veiled woman holding rope.

Booklet Stamps

1412	A406	25f multicolored	.40	.20
1413	A406	50f multicolored	.70	.35
1414	A406	100f multicolored	1.40	.70
1415	A406	150f multicolored	2.00	1.00
1416	A406	250f multicolored	3.50	1.75
1417	A406	350f multicolored	5.00	2.50
a.		Booklet pane, #1412-1417	22.50	
		Complete booklet, #1417a	22.50	

Emblem of Kuwait Post A407

1998, Oct. 3 **Litho.** *Perf. 13x13½*

1418	A407	25f green & multi	.20	.20
1419	A407	50f blue & multi	.65	.35
1420	A407	100f brt pink & multi	1.25	.70
1421	A407	150f orange & multi	2.00	1.10
1422	A407	250f brick red & multi	3.25	1.75
		Nos. 1418-1422 (5)	7.35	4.10

Intl. Year of the Ocean — A408

1998, June 1 **Litho.** *Perf. 13½*

1423	A408	25f green & multi	.40	.20
1424	A408	50f blue & multi	.75	.35
1425	A408	150f lilac & multi	2.25	1.10
		Nos. 1423-1425 (3)	3.40	1.65

No. 1424 is 27x37mm.

Union of Consumer Co-operative Societies, 25th Anniv. — A409

1998, July 1 **Litho.** *Perf. 13½x13*

1426	A409	25f buff & multi	.40	.20
1427	A409	50f blue & multi	.65	.35
1428	A409	150f multicolored	2.10	1.10
		Nos. 1426-1428 (3)	3.15	1.65

Children's Cultural House — A410

1998, Nov. 28 **Litho.** *Perf. 13½x13*

1429	A410	25f yellow & multi	.35	.20
1430	A410	50f grn, yel & multi	.65	.35
1431	A410	150f green & multi	2.00	1.10
		Nos. 1429-1431 (3)	3.00	1.65

A411

A412

1998, Dec. 10 *Perf. 14x14½*

1432	A411	25f multicolored	.35	.20
1433	A411	50f multicolored	.65	.35
1434	A411	150f multicolored	2.00	1.10
		Nos. 1432-1434 (3)	3.00	1.65

Universal Declaration of Human Rights, 50th anniv.

1998 **Litho.** *Perf. 14x14½*

1435	A412	25f orange & multi	.20	.20
1436	A412	50f violet & multi	.55	.35
1437	A412	150f green & multi	1.75	1.10
		Nos. 1435-1437 (3)	2.50	1.65

The Public Authority for Applied Education and Training, 25th anniv.

Organ Transplantation in Kuwait, 20th Anniv. — A413

1999 **Litho.** *Perf. 13x13½*

1438	A413	50f Liver	.50	.35
1439	A413	150f Heart	1.50	1.10

Liberation Day, 8th Anniv. A414

1999, Feb. 26

1440	A414	50f Building	2.00	.35
1441	A414	150f Building, diff.	4.00	1.10

Sief Palace Complex — A415

Various buildings in complex. Illustration reduced.

1999 ***Perf. 15x14***

1442 A415 25f multicolored .20 .20
1443 A415 50f multicolored .55 .35
1444 A415 100f multicolored 1.10 .70
1445 A415 150f multicolored 1.75 1.10
1446 A415 250f multicolored 2.75 1.75
1447 A415 350f multicolored 4.00 2.50
a. Booklet pane, #1442-1447 10.00
Complete booklet, #1447a 10.00
Nos. 1442-1447 (6) 10.35 6.60

Al Arabi Magazine A416

1999 ***Perf. 13½x13***

1448 A416 50f violet & multi .50 .35
1449 A416 150f green & multi 1.50 1.10

Natl. Day, 38th Anniv. A417

1999 ***Perf. 13x13½***

1450 A417 50f brown & multi .50 .35
1451 A417 150f blue & multi 1.50 1.10

A418 A419

1999(?)-2003 **Litho.** ***Perf. 14½x14***

1452 A418 25f Hawk .75 .75
1453 A418 50f Camel 1.50 1.50

Coil Stamp

1453A A419 100f multi 1.10 1.10
1454 A419 150f Sailing ship 3.25 3.25
Nos. 1452-1454 (4) 6.60 6.60

Issued: 100f, Jan. 2003.

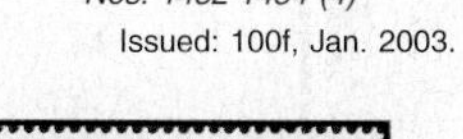

Science Club, 25th Anniv. A420

Background color: 50f, Blue. 150f, Green. 350f, Red.

1999, Oct. 20 **Litho.** ***Perf. 13x13¼***

1455-1457 A420 Set of 3 7.00 3.75

Intl. Civil Aviation Day — A421

1999, Dec. 7 **Litho.** ***Perf. 13x13¼***

1458 A421 50f multi .60 .35
1459 A421 150f multi 1.75 1.00
1460 A421 250f multi 3.00 1.75
Nos. 1458-1460 (3) 5.35 3.10

UPU, 125th Anniv. — A421a

Panel colors: 50f, Orange. 150f, Purple. 350f, Green.
1d, Two hemispheres.

1999 **Litho.** ***Perf. 13¼x13***

1460A-1460C A421a Set of 3 5.00 5.00
1460Ce Booklet pane, #1460A-1460C + label 5.00
Booklet, #1460Ce 5.00

Size: 100x75mm

Imperf

1460D A421a 1d multi 9.00 9.00

Kuwait Intl. Airport — A422

2000, Jan. 2 ***Perf. 13¼x13***

1461 A422 50f multi .60 .35
1462 A422 150f multi 1.75 1.00
1463 A422 250f multi 3.00 1.75
Nos. 1461-1463 (3) 5.35 3.10

National Day, 39th Anniv. — A423

2000

1464 A423 25f multi .40 .20
1465 A423 50f multi .60 .35
1466 A423 150f multi 2.00 1.00
Nos. 1464-1466 (3) 3.00 1.55

Liberation Day, 9th Anniv. — A424

2000

1467 A424 25f multi .40 .20
1468 A424 50f multi .60 .35
1469 A424 150f multi 2.00 1.00
Nos. 1467-1469 (3) 3.00 1.55

Kuwait Conference for Autism and Communication Deficits — A425

Designs: 25f, Puzzle pieces, three children, Kuwait Tower. 50f, Puzzle pieces, children. 150f, Children, Kuwait Tower, flowers.

2000 ***Perf. 13x13¼***

1470 A425 25f multi .40 .20
1471 A425 50f multi .60 .35
1472 A425 150f multi 2.00 1.00
Nos. 1470-1472 (3) 3.00 1.55

Kuwait City — A425a

Background colors: 50f, Blue. 150f, Green. 350f, Red violet.

2000, Apr. 24 **Litho.** ***Perf. 14x14½***

1472A-1472C A425a Set of 3 5.00 5.00

Third Special Education Week — A425b

Background color: 50f, Yellow. 150f, Salmon. 350f, Blue.

2000, May 10 ***Perf. 13¼x13***

1472D-1472F A425b Set of 3 5.00 5.00

2000 Summer Olympics, Sydney A425c

Emblems of 2002 Olympics, Kuwait Olympic Committee and: 25f, Judo. 50f, Shooting. 150f, Swimming. 200f, Weight lifting. 250f, Hurdles. 350f, Soccer.

2000 **Litho.** ***Perf. 13x13¼***

1472G-1472L A425c Set of 6 9.50 —

Souvenir Sheet

Design: 1d, Emblems of 2002 Olympics, Kuwait Olympic Committee and judo, swimming, shooting, weight lifting, hurdles and soccer.

Size: 98x69mm

1472M A425c 1d multi *65.00 65.00*

Sixth Gulf Cooperation Council Countries Joint Stamp Exhibition, Kuwait A425d

Denomination color: 25f, Blue. 50f, Red. 150f, Green.
1d, Emblems of previous exhibitions.

2000 **Litho.** ***Perf. 14¼***

1472N-1472P A425d Set of 3 3.00 3.00

Size: 146x112mm

Imperf

1472Q A425d 1d multi 10.00 10.00

Intl. Investment Forum A426

Background colors: 25f, Gray. 50f, White. 150f, Black.

2000, Mar. 4 **Litho.** ***Perf. 13x13¼***

1473-1475 A426 Set of 3 3.00 3.00

National Committee for Missing and Prisoner of War Affairs A426a

Designs: 25f, Emblem. 50f, Emblem and chains. 150f, Emblem and years.

2000, Aug. 2 **Litho.** ***Perf. 13x13¼***

1475A-1475C A426a Set of 3 — —

Kuwaiti Dental Association, 25th Anniv. — A426b

Frame color: 50f, Pink. 150f, Light blue. 350f, Lilac.

2000, Oct. 15 ***Perf. 13¼x13***

1475D-1475F A426b Set of 3 — —

World Environment Day — A427

Denominations, 50f, 150f, 350f.

2000 **Litho.** ***Perf. 13x13¼***

1476-1478 A427 Set of 3 5.00 5.00

Gulf Investment Corporation, 15th Anniv. — A428

New Gulf Investment Corporation headquarters, emblem, "15" and frame color of: 25f, Green. 50f, Blue. 150f, Red.

2000, Oct. 31 **Litho.** ***Perf. 13x13¼***

1479-1481 A428 Set of 3 — —

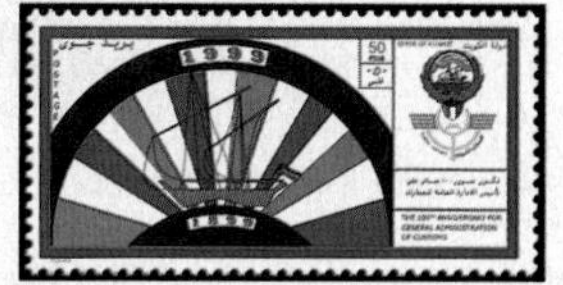

General Administration of Customs, Cent. — A429

Denominations: 50f, 150f, 350f.

2000 **Litho.** ***Perf. 13¼x14***

1482-1484 A429 Set of 3 5.00 5.00

Imperf

Size: 100x75mm

1485 A429 1d multi 9.00 9.00

No. 1485 contains one 47x28mm perf. 13¼x14 non-denominated label.

Hala Fibrayar — A430

Panel colors: 25f, Purple. 50f, Red violet. 150f, Blue.

2001 Litho. ***Perf. 13¼x13***
1486-1488 A430 Set of 3 3.00 3.00

Prisoners of War — A431

Background colors: 25f, White. 50f, Blue & blue green. 150f, Multicolored.

2001 ***Perf. 13x13¼***
1489-1491 A431 Set of 3 3.00 3.00

UN High Commissioner for Refugees, 50th Anniv. — A432

Various depictions of anniversary emblem: 25f, 50f, 150f.

2001
1492-1494 A432 Set of 3 3.00 3.00

Kuwait, 2001 Arab Cultural Capital A433

Background colors: 25f, Yellow. 50f, Green. 150f, Blue.

2001
1495-1497 A433 Set of 3 3.00 3.00

Liberation Day, 10th Anniv. — A434

Frame color: 25f, Lilac. 50f, Blue. 150f, Yellow.

2001 ***Perf. 13¼x13***
1498-1500 A434 Set of 3 3.00 3.00

National Day, 40th Anniv. — A435

Frame color: 25f, Orange. 50f, Yellow. 150f, Blue green.

2001
1501-1503 A435 Set of 3 3.00 3.00

Kuwait Diving Team, 10th Anniv. A436

"10" and: 25f, Fish. 50f, Divers. 150f, Shark, turtle, vert.

2001 ***Perf. 13x13¼, 13¼x13***
1504-1506 A436 Set of 3 3.00 3.00

Radio Kuwait, 50th Anniv. A437

Frame color: 25f, Yellow brown. 50f, Blue, vert. 150f, Red, vert.

2001 ***Perf. 13x13¼, 13¼x13***
1507-1509 A437 Set of 3 3.00 3.00

Intifada A438

Dome of the Rock, Jerusalem: 25f, 50f, 150f.

2001 ***Perf. 13x13¼***
1510-1512 A438 Set of 3 3.00 3.00

Year of Dialogue Among Civilizations A439

Background colors: 25f, Orange & yellow. 50f, Dark & light green. 150f, Rose & pink.

2001 ***Perf. 13¼x13***
1513-1515 A439 Set of 3 3.00 3.00

Human Rights A440

Designs: 25f, Hands covering man's face, vert. 50f, Barbed wire, clock, man's face. 150f, Chains, globe, child, woman.

2001 ***Perf. 13¼x13, 13x13¼***
1516-1518 A440 Set of 3 3.00 3.00

A441

A442

AWQAF Foundation A443

2001 ***Perf. 14x13***
1519 A441 25f multi .40 .20
1520 A442 50f multi .70 .35
1521 A443 150f multi 1.90 .95
Nos. 1519-1521 (3) 3.00 1.50

Kuwait Fund for Arab Economic Development, 40th Anniv. — A444

Background colors: 25f, Yellow. 50f, Green & gray.

2001 ***Perf. 13¼x13***
1522-1523 A444 Set of 2 1.00 1.00

Touristic Enterprises Company, 25th Anniv. — A445

Stylistic flora: 25f, 50f, 100f, 150f. 250f, Combined designs of four stamps.

2001 ***Perf. 13¼x13***
1524-1527 A445 Set of 4 4.50 4.50

Size: 60x80mm

Imperf

1528 A445 250f multi 3.50 3.50

National Bank of Kuwait, 50th Anniv. A447

Emblem and: 25f, Facade of old building. 50f, Modern building. 150f, Camels.

2000, Jan. 16 Litho. ***Perf. 13x13¼***
1532-1534 A447 Set of 3 3.00 3.00

Liberation Day, 11th Anniv. — A448

Background color: 25f, Light blue. 50f, Light yellow. 150f, White.

2002, Feb. 26 ***Perf. 13¼x13***
1535-1537 A448 Set of 3 3.00 3.00

Social Development Office, 10th Anniv. — A449

Background color: 25f, Light yellow. 50f, Light blue.

2002, Apr. 21
1538-1539 A449 Set of 2 1.00 1.00

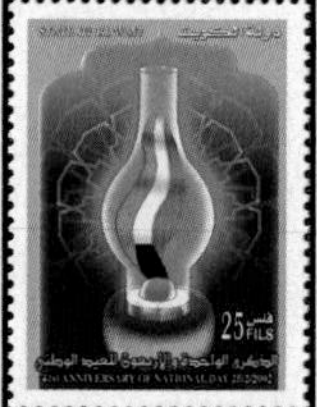

41st National Day — A450

Frame color: 25f, Orange. 50f, Green. 150f, Purple.

2002, Feb. 25 Litho. ***Perf. 13¼x13***
1540-1542 A450 Set of 3 3.00 3.00

Nomadism From the Hejaz to Africa — A451

Top panel color: 25f, Pale orange. 50f, Blue. 150f, Purple.

2002, Mar. 11
1543-1545 A451 Set of 3 3.00 3.00

Rehabilitation of Al-Qurain Landfill Site — A452

Panel color: 25f, Blue. 50f, Purple. 150f, Green.

2002, Apr. 1
1546-1548 A452 Set of 3 3.00 3.00

Kuwait Scientific Center — A453

Designs; Nos. 1549a, 1550e, Lapwing. Nos. 1549b, 1550d, Spur-winged plover. Nos. 1549c, 1550c, Eurasian river otter. Nos. 1549d, 1550b, Saltwater crocodile. Nos. 1549e, 1550i, Fennec fox. Nos. 1549f, 1550h, Caracal. Nos. 1549g, 1550g, Cushion sister starfish. Nos. 1549h, 1550f, Cuttlefish. Nos. 1549i, 1550m, Sand tiger shark. Nos. 1549j, 1550l, Lionfish. Nos. 1549k, 1550k, Kestrel. Nos. 1549l, 1550j, Egyptian fruit bat. Nos. 1549m, 1550a, Science center.

Perf. 13¼x13¾, 14x13¼ (#1550k)

2002, Apr. 17

1549 Sheet of 13 14.00 14.00
a.-l. A453 25f Any single .20 .20
m. A453 50f multi .30 .30
1550 Booklet of 13 panes 40.00
a.-m. A453 50f Any single pane .30 .30

Imperf

Size: 80x60mm

1551 A453 250f shown 7.50 7.50

Stamp sizes: Nos. 1549a-1549l, 30x25mm; No. 1549m, 45x27mm. Nos. 1550a-1550j, 1550l-1550m, 50x36mm; No. 1550k, 32x48mm.

Kuwait Foundation for the Advancement of Sciences, 25th Anniv. (in 2001) — A454

Foundation emblem and: 25f, 25th anniversary emblem. 50f, 25th anniversary emblem and building. 150f, Map of Kuwait, vert.

Perf. 13x13¼, 13¼x13

2002 ? **Litho.**

1552-1554 A454 Set of 3 3.00 3.00

Intl. Volunteers Year (in 2001) — A455

Background colors: 25f, White. 50f, Lilac. 150f, Yellow.

2002 ? *Perf. 13¼x13*

1555-1557 A455 Set of 3 3.00 3.00

National Council for Culture, Arts and Letters, 25th Anniv. — A456

Panel color: 25f, Lilac. 50f, Olive green. 150f, Bright blue.
500f, Lilac.

2002 ? *Perf. 13¼x13*

1558-1560 A456 Set of 3 3.00 3.00

Souvenir Sheet

Imperf

1561 A456 500f multi 5.00 5.00

No. 1561 contains one 42x58mm stamp.

Kuwait Society of Engineers, 40th Anniv. A457

Panel color at LR: 25f, Brown. 50f, Bright green. 150f, Yellow green.

2002 *Perf. 13x13¼*

1562-1564 A457 Set of 3 3.00 3.00

Public Authority for Applied Education and Training, 20th Anniv. — A458

"20," "1982-2002" and: 25f, Men at work. 50f, Surgeon. 100f, Man with machine. 150f, Building and Kuwait flag. 250f, Ironworkers.

2002 *Perf. 13¼x13*

1565-1569 A458 Set of 5 7.50 7.50

42nd National Day — A459

Frame color: 25f, Green. 50f, Red. 150f, Blue.

2003, Feb. 25 **Litho.** *Perf. 13x13¼*

1570-1572 A459 Set of 3 1.50 1.50

Martyr's Bureau A460

Emblem and: 25f, Ship. 50f, Flag on Qarow Island. 150f, Fingerprint. 350f, Map of Kuwait.

2003

1573-1576 A460 Set of 4 4.00 4.00
1576a Booklet pane, #1573-1576 4.00 —
Complete booklet, #1576a 4.00

Intl. Day Against Desertification A461

Designs: 25f, Dead tree. 50f, Log. 150f, Palm trees.

2003 **Litho.** *Perf. 13¼x13*

1577-1579 A461 Set of 3 1.50 1.50

Commercial Bank of Kuwait, 43rd Anniv. — A462

"43" and: 25f, Geometric design. 50f, Old bank building. 150f, New bank building.

2003 *Perf. 13*

1580-1582 A462 Set of 3 1.50 1.50

Kuwait Awqaf Public Foundation, 10th Anniv. A463

Emblem, "10," and: 50f, Building, family. 100f, Fingers. 150f, Man, minaret.

2004, Jan. 19

1583-1585 A463 Set of 3 2.10 2.10

A464

A465

Ministry of Information, 50th Anniv. — A466

2003

1586 A464 25f multi .20 .20
1587 A465 100f multi .65 .65
1588 A466 150f multi 1.00 1.00
Nos. 1586-1588 (3) 1.85 1.85

43rd National Day — A467

Designs: 25f, Palm tree. 50f, Pearl in shell. 150f, Fortress, flags. 350f, Buildings, dhow.

2004, Feb. 25 *Perf. 13¼x13*

1589-1592 A467 Set of 4 4.00 4.00

Kuwait Airways, 50th Anniv. A468

Various airplanes: 25f, 50f, 75f, 100f, 125f, 150f.

2004, Dec. 18 **Litho.** *Perf. 13x13¼*

1593-1598 A468 Set of 6 3.75 3.75

Kuwait Petroleum Corporation, 25th Anniv. — A469

Headquarters: 50f, In daytime. 75f, With sun on horizon. 125f, At night.

2005, Jan. 1 *Perf. 14½*

1599-1601 A469 Set of 3 1.75 1.75

44th National Day — A470

Sheikhs, dhow, eagle and: 75f, Towers. 125f, Truck at port.

2005, Feb. 25 *Perf. 14*

1602-1603 A470 Set of 2 1.40 1.40

Liberation Day, 14th Anniv. — A471

Sheikhs, flag and: 50f, Airplane, satellite dish. 150f, Tower.

2005, Feb. 26

1604-1605 A471 Set of 2 1.40 1.40

Technical Education, 50th Anniv. — A472

Background color: 25f, Purple. 50f, Red. 75f, Orange. 125f, Green.

2005, Mar. 15

1606-1609 A472 Set of 4 1.90 1.90

STATE OF KUWAIT Postage Fils 200 1961

Flags and Emblems A473

Designs: No. 1610, Triangular 1961 ship and harbor flag. No. 1611, 1940 official flag. No. 1612, 1903 special event flag. No. 1613, 1940-50 ruling family flag. No. 1614, Two 1914 right triangle flags. No. 1615, 1921-40, 1956-62 and 1962 emblems.

No. 1616, 1962-56 emblem. No. 1617, 1921-40 emblem.

No. 1618, Right triangle flag of 1914 with Arabic script and emblem in center and script along short side like that on #1613. No. 1619, Right triangle flag of 1914 with Arabic script in center. No. 1620, Right triangle flag of 1914 with Arabic script in center and script along short side.

No. 1621, Triangular 1921 ship and harbor flag. No. 1622, Like #1610. No. 1623, Rectangular 1961 ship and harbor flag. No. 1624, Rectangular 1921 ship and harbor flag.

No. 1625, 1914-61 official flag. No. 1626, 1871-1914 official flag. No. 1627, 1746-1871 official flag. No. 1628, Like #1611. No. 1629, 1921-61 official flag.

No. 1630, 1903 special event flag. No. 1631, 1866 special event flag. No. 1632, 1921 special event flag.

No. 1633, 1921-40 ruling family flag with two white stripes. No. 1634, Like #1613, with colored background. No. 1635, 1921-40 ruling family flag with one white stripe.

2005, Oct. 15 Litho. *Perf. 14x13¾*

1610 A473 200f multi 1.40 1.40
1611 A473 250f multi 1.75 1.75

Perf. 14

Size: 40x30mm

1612 A473 350f multi 2.40 2.40
1613 A473 500f multi 3.50 3.50

Perf. 14x13¾

Size: 60x30mm

1614 A473 1d multi 7.00 7.00
1615 A473 1d multi 7.00 7.00
Nos. 1610-1615 (6) 23.05 23.05

Booklet Stamps

Self-Adhesive

Die Cut Perf. 13

Size:40x34mm

1616 A473 100f multi .70 .70
1617 A473 100f multi .70 .70
a. Booklet pane, #1616-1617 1.40

Die Cut Perf. 13x13¼

Size: 40x30mm

1618 A473 175f multi 1.25 1.25
1619 A473 175f multi 1.25 1.25
1620 A473 175f multi 1.25 1.25
a. Booklet pane, #1618-1620 3.75

Die Cut Perf. 10x10¾

Size: 30x20mm

1621 A473 200f multi 1.40 1.40
1622 A473 200f multi 1.40 1.40
1623 A473 200f multi 1.40 1.40
1624 A473 200f multi 1.40 1.40
a. Booklet pane, #1621-1624 5.75
1625 A473 250f multi 1.75 1.75
1626 A473 250f multi 1.75 1.75
1627 A473 250f multi 1.75 1.75
1628 A473 250f multi 1.75 1.75
1629 A473 250f multi 1.75 1.75
a. Booklet pane #1625-1629 8.75

Die Cut Perf. 13x13¼

Size: 40x30mm

1630 A473 350f multi 2.40 2.40
1631 A473 350f multi 2.40 2.40
1632 A473 350f multi 2.40 2.40
a. Booklet pane, #1630-1632 7.25
1633 A473 500f multi 3.50 3.50
1634 A473 500f multi 3.50 3.50
1635 A473 500f multi 3.50 3.50
a. Booklet pane, #1633-1635 10.50
Complete booklet, #1617a, 1620a, 1624a, 1629a, 1632a, 1635a 37.50
Nos. 1616-1635 (20) 37.20 37.20

Civil Defense A474

Designs: 50f, Civil defense workers and emergency vehicles. 75f, Civil defense workers and children. 125f, Civil defene workers.

2005, Nov. 15 Litho. *Perf. 14½*

1636-1638 A474 Set of 3 1.75 1.75

Al-Arabi Al-Saghir Children's Magazine, 20th Anniv. A475

Background colors: 100f, Blue. 200f, Yellow. 350f, Red.

2006, Feb. 1 Litho. *Perf. 14¼x13¾*

1639-1641 A475 Set of 3 4.50 4.50

45th National Day — A476

Frame color: 75f, Purple. 200f, Green. 250f, Black. 350f, Red.

2006, Feb. 25 *Perf. 13¼*

1642-1645 A476 Set of 4 6.00 6.00

A477

Gulf Cooperation Council, 25th Anniv. — A478

Illustration A478 reduced.

Litho. With Foil Application

2006, May 25 *Perf. 14*

1646 A477 50f multi .35 .35

Imperf

Size: 165x105mm

1647 A478 500f multi 3.50 3.50

See Bahrain Nos. 628-629, Oman Nos. 477-478, Qatar Nos. 1007-1008, Saudi Arabia No. 1378, and United Arab Emirates Nos. 831-832.

Emblem A479

A480

A481

A482

A483

A484

A485

A486

A487

A488

A489

A490

A491

A492

A493

A494

A495

A496

A497

A498

A499

A500

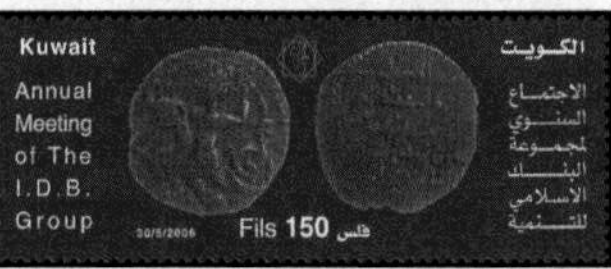

A501

A502

A503

A504

A505

A506

A507

A508

A509

A510

A511

A512

A513

A514

A515

A516

A517

A518

A519

A520

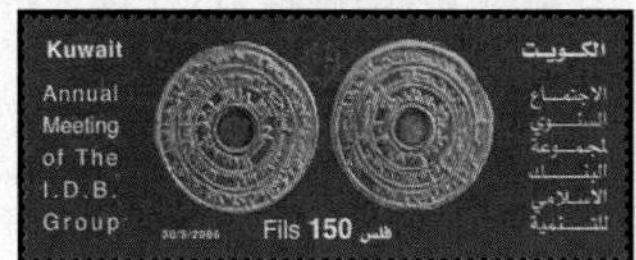

Coins — A521

Illustrations A480-A521 reduced.

2006, May 30 Litho. *Perf. 13¼*

1648	Sheet of 28, #1648b-1648v, 7#1648a	10.00	10.00
a.	A479 50f lt blue & multi	.35	.35
b.	A480 50f multi	.35	.35
c.	A481 50f multi	.35	.35
d.	A482 50f multi	.35	.35
e.	A483 50f multi	.35	.35
f.	A484 50f multi	.35	.35
g.	A485 50f multi	.35	.35
h.	A486 50f multi	.35	.35
i.	A487 50f multi	.35	.35
j.	A488 50f multi	.35	.35
k.	A489 50f multi	.35	.35
l.	A490 50f multi	.35	.35
m.	A491 50f multi	.35	.35
n.	A492 50f multi	.35	.35
o.	A493 50f multi	.35	.35
p.	A494 50f multi	.35	.35
q.	A495 50f multi	.35	.35
r.	A496 50f multi	.35	.35
s.	A497 50f multi	.35	.35
t.	A498 50f multi	.35	.35
u.	A499 50f multi	.35	.35
v.	A500 50f multi	.35	.35
1649	Sheet of 28, #1649b-1649v, 7#1649a	30.00	30.00
a.	A479 150f pink & multi	1.00	1.00
b.	A501 150f multi	1.00	1.00
c.	A502 150f multi	1.00	1.00
d.	A503 150f multi	1.00	1.00
e.	A504 150f multi	1.00	1.00
f.	A505 150f multi	1.00	1.00
g.	A506 150f multi	1.00	1.00
h.	A507 150f multi	1.00	1.00
i.	A508 150f multi	1.00	1.00
j.	A509 150f multi	1.00	1.00
k.	A510 150f multi	1.00	1.00
l.	A511 150f multi	1.00	1.00
m.	A512 150f multi	1.00	1.00
n.	A513 150f multi	1.00	1.00
o.	A514 150f multi	1.00	1.00
p.	A515 150f multi	1.00	1.00
q.	A516 150f multi	1.00	1.00
r.	A517 150f multi	1.00	1.00
s.	A518 150f multi	1.00	1.00
t.	A519 150f multi	1.00	1.00
u.	A520 150f multi	1.00	1.00
v.	A521 150f multi	1.00	1.00

Islamic Development Bank Group annual meeting.

15th Asian Games, Doha, Qatar A522

Designs: 25f, Tennis. 50f, Bowling. 150f, Shooting. 250f, Equestrian. 350f, Fencing.

2006 Litho. *Perf. 14½*
1650-1654 A522 Set of 5 5.75 5.75

Campaign Against Hypertension A523

Frame colors: 50f, Green. 150f, Red. 350f, Brown.

2007, Jan. 15 *Perf. 13¼x13*
1655-1657 A523 Set of 3 4.00 4.00

46th National Day — A524

Sky color: 25f, Dark blue. 50f, Blue. 150f, Orange brown.

2007, Feb. 25
1658-1660 A524 Set of 3 1.60 1.60

Liberation Day, 16th Anniv. A525

Frame color: 25f, Red. 50f, Dark blue. 150f, Purple.

2007, Feb. 26 Litho. *Perf. 13x13¼*
1661-1663 A525 Set of 3 1.60 1.60

Kuwait University, 40th Anniv. (in 2006) A526

Color behind emblem: 25f, Blue. 50f, Yellow. 150f, Green. 350f, Red.

2007, Mar. 20
1664-1667 A526 Set of 4 4.00 4.00

Kuwait Oil Tanker Company, 50th Anniv. A527

Background colors: 25f, Pale blue. 50f, Pale green. 150f, Gray.

Litho. & Embossed With Foil Application

2007, Nov. 25 *Perf. 13*
1668-1670 A527 Set of 3 1.75 1.75

Kuwait Philatelic & Numismatic Society, 1st Anniv. — A528

2007, Dec. 5 Litho. *Perf. 13¼*

1671	Horiz. strip of 3	1.75	1.75
a.	A528 25f Coin	.20	.20
b.	A528 50f Kuwait #146	.40	.40
c.	A528 150f Society emblem	1.10	1.10

No. 1671c is 60x35mm.

47th National Day — A529

Designs: 25f, Women voting. 150f, Stylized people, dhows, fish, towers, horiz.

Perf. 13¼x13, 13x13¼

2008, Feb. 25 Litho.
1672-1673 A529 Set of 2 1.40 1.40

First Gulf Cooperation Council Women's Sports Tournament A531

No. 1676 — Emblem and: a, Gymnastics. b, Running. c, Shooting. d, Basketball. e, Tennis.

No. 1677, horiz. — Emblem, five sports with background color of: a, Orange. b, Red. c, Purple. d, Olive green. e, Red violet.

2008, Mar. 5 Litho. *Perf. 13¼x13*

1676	Vert. strip of 5	.95	.95
a.-e.	A531 25f Any single	.20	.20

Perf. 13x13¼

1677	Horiz strip of 5	5.50	5.50
a.-e.	A531 150f Any single	1.10	1.10

Diplomatic Relations Between Kuwait and Romania, 45th Anniv. — A532

No. 1678: a, Kuwaiti man building ship model. b, Romanian woman weaving.

500f, Flags of Romania and Kuwait, handshake, vert.

2008, June 21 *Perf. 13¼x13*

1678	Horiz. pair + 2 labels	*9.50*	*9.50*
a.-b.	A532 150f Either single + label	*4.75*	*4.75*
c.	Miniature sheet, 4 #1678	*38.00*	—

Souvenir Sheet

Perf. 13x13¼

1679 A532 500f multi *16.00 16.00*

Labels of Nos. 1678a and 1678b are separated from stamps by a partial row of perforations. The labels, which have different designs, are to the left of No. 1678a and to the right of No. 1678b. The labels are adjacent to each other on half of the pairs on No. 1678c. No.

1678 was also printed in sheets containing 6 pairs, two of which have the labels adjacent.
See Romania Nos. 5053-5054.

Old Kuwait A533

Designs: 25f, Drummer and swordsmen. 50f, Drummers and boat painter. 100f, Street with thatched roof. 150f, Fair. 200f, Man and minarets. 250f, Donkey riders at town gate. 350f, Boats in harbor. 500f, People at town gate.

2008, Aug. 1 *Perf. 13*

1680	A533	25f multi	.20	.20
1681	A533	50f multi	.40	.40
1682	A533	100f multi	.75	.75
1683	A533	150f multi	1.10	1.10
1684	A533	200f multi	1.50	1.50
1685	A533	250f multi	1.90	1.90
1686	A533	350f multi	2.75	2.75
1687	A533	500f multi	3.75	3.75
		Nos. 1680-1687 (8)	12.35	12.35

AIR POST STAMPS

Air Post Stamps of India, 1929-30, Overprinted type "c"

1933-34 **Wmk. 196** *Perf. 14*

C1	AP1	2a dull green	12.00	*17.00*
C2	AP1	3a deep blue	2.25	*2.75*
C3	AP1	4a gray olive	110.00	*150.00*
C4	AP1	6a bister ('34)	4.50	*5.00*
		Nos. C1-C4 (4)	128.75	*174.75*

Counterfeits of Nos. C1-C4 exist.

Catalogue values for unused stamps in this section, from this point to the end of the section, are for Never Hinged items.

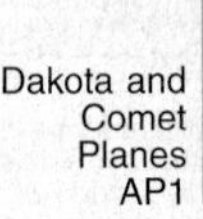

Dakota and Comet Planes AP1

Perf. 11x11½

1964, Nov. 29 **Litho.** **Unwmk.**

C5	AP1	20f multicolored	.90	.30
C6	AP1	25f multicolored	1.00	.40
C7	AP1	30f multicolored	1.25	.40
C8	AP1	45f multicolored	1.50	.60
		Nos. C5-C8 (4)	4.65	1.70

10th anniversary of Kuwait Airways.

POSTAGE DUE STAMPS

Catalogue values for unused stamps in this section are for Never Hinged items.

D1

Perf. 14x15

1963, Oct. 19 **Unwmk.** **Litho.**

Inscriptions in Black

J1	D1	1f ocher	.50	.20
J2	D1	2f lilac	.55	.20
J3	D1	5f blue	.75	.25
J4	D1	8f pale green	1.00	.35
J5	D1	10f yellow	1.25	.60
J6	D1	25f brick red	2.25	1.20
		Nos. J1-J6 (6)	6.30	2.80

D2

1965, Apr. 1 *Perf. 13*

J7	D2	4f rose & yellow	.30	.20
J8	D2	15f dp rose & blue	1.00	.45
J9	D2	40f blue & brt yel grn	1.75	1.00
J10	D2	50f green & pink	2.50	1.25
J11	D2	100f dk blue & yel	4.00	2.50
		Nos. J7-J11 (5)	9.55	5.40

OFFICIAL STAMPS

Stamps of India, 1911-23, Overprinted

Nos. O1-O9

Nos. O10-O14

1923-24 **Wmk. 39** *Perf. 14*

O1	A47	½a green	2.50	*10.00*
O2	A48	1a brown	3.00	*9.00*
O3	A58	1½a chocolate	3.50	*20.00*
O4	A49	2a violet	6.00	*17.50*
O5	A57	2a6p ultra	5.25	*30.00*
O6	A51	3a brown org	5.50	*40.00*
O7	A51	3a ultra ('24)	5.75	*30.00*
O8	A52	4a olive grn	4.75	*45.00*
O9	A54	8a red violet	7.50	*55.00*
O10	A56	1r grn & brn	22.50	*80.00*
O11	A56	2r brn & car rose	25.00	*125.00*
O12	A56	5r vio & ultra	92.50	*325.00*
O13	A56	10r car & grn	175.00	*350.00*
O14	A56	15r ol grn & ultra	240.00	*500.00*
		Nos. O1-O14 (14)	598.75	*1,636.*

Stamps of India, 1926-30, Overprinted

Nos. O15-O20

Nos. O21-O25

1929-33 **Wmk. 196**

O15	A48	1a dk brown	4.50	*20.00*
O16	A60	2a violet	62.50	*150.00*
O17	A51	3a blue	5.00	*30.00*
O18	A61	4a ol green	5.75	*65.00*
O19	A54	8a red violet	6.50	*85.00*
O20	A55	12a claret	32.50	*150.00*
O21	A56	1r green & brn	6.50	*170.00*
O22	A56	2r buff & car rose	10.00	*250.00*
O23	A56	5r dk vio & ultra	34.00	*375.00*
O24	A56	10r car & green	67.50	*500.00*
O25	A56	15r olive grn & ultra	150.00	*1,000.*
		Nos. O15-O25 (11)	384.75	*2,795.*

KYRGYZSTAN

ˌkir-gi-ˈstan

(Kirghizia)

LOCATION — Bounded by Kazakhstan, Uzbekistan, Tadjikistan and China.
GOVT. — Independent republic, member of the Commonwealth of Independent States.
AREA — 77,180 sq. mi.
POP. — 4,546,055 (1999 est.)
CAPITAL — Bishkek

With the breakup of the Soviet Union on Dec. 26, 1991, Kyrgyzstan and ten former Soviet republics established the Commonwealth of Independent States.

100 Kopecks = 1 Ruble
100 Tyiyn = 1 Som

Catalogue values for all unused stamps in this country are for Never Hinged items.

Sary-Chelek Nature Preserve — A1

Unwmk.

1992, Feb. 4 **Litho.** *Perf. 12*

1	A1	15k multicolored	.45	.45

Hawk — A2

1992, Aug. 31 **Litho.** *Perf. 12½x12*

2	A2	50k multicolored	.45	.45

Man with Cattle, by G.A. Aytiev — A3

1992, Aug. 31

3	A3	1r multicolored	.35	.35

Handicrafts A4

1992, Dec. 1 **Litho.** *Perf. 12x11½*

4	A4	1.50r multicolored	.40	.40

Sites and Landmarks A5

Designs: 10k, Petroglyphs. 50k, 11th Cent. tower, vert. 1r + 25k, Mausoleum, vert. 2r + 50k, 12th Cent. mausoleum. 3r, Yurt. 5r + 50k, Statue of epic hero Manas, Pishpek. 9r, Commercial complex, Pishpek. 10r, Native jewelry.

1993, Mar. 21 **Litho.** *Perf. 12*

5	A5	10k multicolored	.20	.20
6	A5	50k multicolored	.20	.20
7	A5	1r +25k multi	.20	.20
8	A5	2r +50k multi	.20	.20
9	A5	3r multicolored	.20	.20
10	A5	5r +50k multi	.30	.30
11	A5	9r multi	.50	.50
		Nos. 5-11 (7)	1.80	1.80

Souvenir Sheet

12	A5	10r multicolored	1.00	1.00

Independence and Admission to UN, 2nd Anniv. — A6

#15a, 120t, like #13. #15b, 130t, like #14.

Perf. 13x12½, 12½x13

1993, Aug. 31 **Litho.**

13	A6	50t Map	.80	.80
14	A6	60t UN emblem, flag, building, vert.	.95	.95

Souvenir Sheet

Imperf

15	A6	Sheet of 2, #a.-b.	5.50	5.50

Nos. 15a-15b have simulated perforations.

Russia Nos. 4598, 5838, 5984 Surcharged in Violet Blue, Prussian Blue or Black

Methods and Perfs as Before

1993, Apr. 6

16	A2765	10r on 1k #5838 (VB)	.25	.20
17	A2765	20r on 2k #5984 (PB)	.30	.25
18	A2139	30r on 3k #4598 (Blk)	.35	.30
		Nos. 16-18 (3)	.90	.75

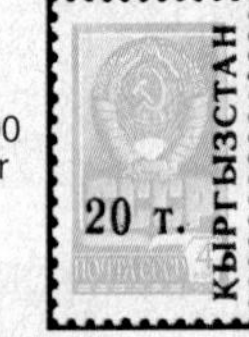
Russia Nos. 4599-4600 Surcharged in Blue or Red

Methods and Perfs as Before

1993, June 29

19	A2138	20t on 4k #4599 (Bl)	.70	.70
20	A2139	30t on 6k #4600 (R)	1.00	1.00

New Year 1994 (Year of the Dog) — A7

1994, Feb. 10 **Litho.** *Perf. 12x12½*

26	A7	60t multicolored	.80	.80

Musical Instrument — A8

1993, Dec. 30 **Litho.** *Perf. 13x12½*

27	A8	30t Komuz	.35	.35

Souvenir Sheet

Perf. 13

28	A8	140t multi	12.00	12.00

No. 28 exists imperf. Value $45.
Issued: #27, 12/30; #28, 4/4/94.

Panthera Uncia A9

1994, Mar. 21 Litho. *Perf. 12½x12*

29	A9	10t shown	.35	.35
30	A9	20t Lying down	.45	.45
31	A9	30t Seated	.65	.65
32	A9	40t Up close	.80	.80
		Nos. 29-32 (4)	2.25	2.25

World Wildlife Fund.

Flowers — A10

Minerals — A11

Perf. 12x12½, 12½x12

1994, Aug. 31 Litho.

Color of Flower

33	A10	1t violet & white	.20	.20
34	A10	3t white & yellow, horiz.	.20	.20
a.		Miniature sheet of 6	1.10	1.10
35	A10	10t red & yellow	.30	.30
36	A10	16t white & yellow	.30	.30
37	A10	20t pink & yellow	.40	.40
38	A10	30t white & yellow	.45	.45
39	A10	40t yellow & brown	.55	.55
a.		Miniature sheet of 6, #33, #35-39	5.25	5.25
b.		Strip of 7, #33-39	4.00	4.00

Souvenir Sheet

40	A10	50t yellow & orange	1.25	1.25

For surcharge see No. 141.

1994, Dec. 1 Litho. *Perf. 13½x13*

41	A11	80t Fluorite-Cinnabar	.60	.60
42	A11	90t Calcite	.65	.65
43	A11	100t Getchellite	.70	.70
44	A11	110t Barite	.80	.80
45	A11	120t Orpiment	.85	.85
46	A11	140t Stibnite	1.25	1.25
		Nos. 41-46 (6)	4.85	4.85

Souvenir Sheet

47	A11	200t Cinnabar	3.75	3.75
a.		Miniature sheet of 6	8.00	8.00

No. 47a contains #42-46 and single from #47.

Fish — A12

Designs: 110t, Glyptosternum reticulatum. 120t, Leuciscus schmidti. 130t, Piptychus dybowskii. 140t, Nemachilus strauchi. 200t, Cyprinus carpio.

1994, Dec. 1 *Perf. 13x13½*

48	A12	110t multicolored	.50	.50
49	A12	120t multicolored	.60	.60
50	A12	130t multicolored	.65	.65
51	A12	140t multicolored	.75	.75
a.		Miniature sheet, #48-51	3.25	3.25
		Nos. 48-51 (4)	2.50	2.50

Souvenir Sheet

52	A12	200t multicolored	2.25	2.25

Wild Animals — A13

#60a, 130t, Raptor, diff. b, 170t, Bighorn sheep.

Perf. 12x12½, 12½x12

1995, Apr. 21 Litho.

53	A13	110t Bear	.40	.40
54	A13	120t Snow leopard, horiz.	.40	.40
55	A13	130t Raptor	.50	.50
56	A13	140t Woodchuck, horiz.	.55	.55
57	A13	150t Raptor, horiz.	.60	.60
58	A13	160t Vulture	.65	.65
59	A13	190t Fox, horiz.	.90	.90
		Nos. 53-59 (7)	4.00	4.00

Souvenir Sheet

60	A13	Sheet of 2, #a.-b.	2.00	2.00

Nos. 53-60 exist imperf. Value $7.

Natl. Costumes — A14

Traffic Safety — A15

1995, Mar. 24 *Perf. 12x12½*

61	A14	50t shown	.30	.30
62	A14	50t Man with mandolin	.30	.30
63	A14	100t Man with falcon	.45	.45
64	A14	100t Woman seated	.45	.45
		Nos. 61-64 (4)	1.50	1.50

Nos. 61-64 exist imperf. Value, set $2.50.

1995, Mar. 24 *Perf. 12*

65	A15	200t multicolored	1.00	1.00

Souvenir Sheet

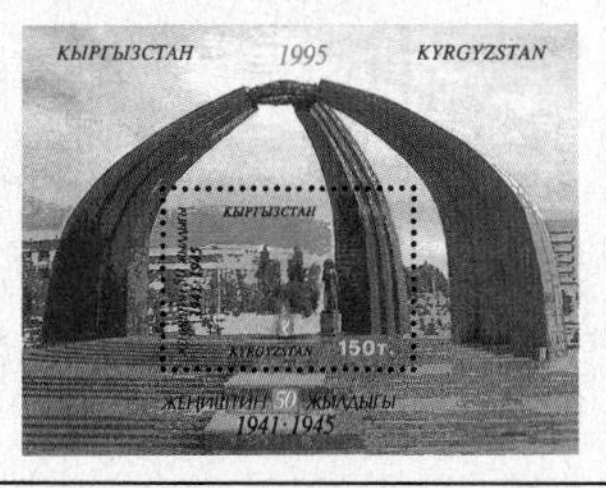
End of World War II, 50th Anniv. — A16

Illustration reduced.

1995, May 4 Litho. *Perf. 12x12½*

66	A16	150t multicolored	1.10	1.10

UPU Intl. Letter Week A17

Natl. Arms — A18

1995, Oct. 3 Litho. *Perf. 12x12½*

67	A17	200t multicolored	1.10	1.10

1995, Oct. 13 *Perf. 12*

68	A18	20t purple	.45	.45
69	A18	50t blue	.45	.45
70	A18	100t brown	.55	.55
71	A18	500t green	1.90	1.90
		Nos. 68-71 (4)	3.35	3.35

Compare with design A37.

Horses A19

Various adult, juvenile horses.

1995, Oct. 16 *Perf. 12½x12, 12x12½*

Background Color

72	A19	10t olive brown	.35	.35
73	A19	50t light brown, vert.	.35	.35
74	A19	100t tan, vert.	.35	.35
75	A19	140t yellow brown, vert.	.40	.40
76	A19	150t lilac	.50	.50
77	A19	200t gray	.60	.60
78	A19	300t yellow green	.85	.85
		Nos. 72-78 (7)	3.40	3.40

Souvenir Sheet

79	A19	600t Herd of horses, vert.	3.00	3.00

Raptors — A20

1995, Sept. 12 *Perf. 12x12½*

80	A20	10t Pandion haliaetus	.30	.30
81	A20	50t Aquila rapax	.35	.35
82	A20	100t Gyps himalayensis	.40	.40
83	A20	140t Falco cherrug	.45	.45
84	A20	150t Circaetus gallicus	.50	.50
85	A20	200t Gypaetus barbatus	.60	.60
86	A20	300t Aquila chrysaetos	.85	.85
		Nos. 80-86 (7)	3.45	3.45

Souvenir Sheet

87	A20	600t Halliaeetus albicilla	3.25	3.25

"Aquila" spelled wrong on #86.

Nos. 80-87 exist imperf. Value: #80-86, $4.25; #87, $2.75.

Souvenir Sheet

UN, 50th Anniv. — A21

Designs: a, UN headquarters, NYC. b, Mountains, rainbow.

1995, Oct. 24 Litho. *Perf. 12½x12*

88	A21	100t Sheet of 2, #a.-b.	1.00	1.00

Natural Wonders of the World — A22

10t, Nile River. 50t, Kilimanjaro. 100t, Sahara Desert. 140t, Amazon River, vert. 150t, Grand Canyon, vert. 200t, Victoria Falls, vert. 350t, Mount Everest. 400t, Niagara Falls.

Issyk-Kul Lake, Kyrgyzstan: No. 97, Raptor, row boat, sail boats. No. 98, Water bird, motor boat, row boat.

1995, Dec. 29 *Perf. 11½*

89	A22	10t multicolored	.30	.30
90	A22	50t multicolored	.35	.35
91	A22	100t multicolored	.45	.45
92	A22	140t multicolored	.50	.50
93	A22	150t multicolored	.55	.55
94	A22	200t multicolored	.70	.70
95	A22	350t multicolored	.90	.90
96	A22	400t multicolored	1.25	1.25
		Nos. 89-96 (8)	5.00	5.00

Souvenir Sheets

97	A22	600t multicolored	1.75	1.75
98	A22	600t multicolored	1.75	1.75

Reptiles A23

Designs: 20t, Psammophis lineolatum. No. 100, Natrix tessellata. No. 101, Eublepharis macularius. 100t, Agkistrodon halys. 150t, Eremias arguta. 200t, Elaphe dione. 250t, Asymblepharus. 500t, Lacerta agilis.

1996, Feb. 2 *Perf. 12½x12*

99	A23	20t multicolored	.25	.25
100	A23	50t multicolored	.25	.25
101	A23	50t multicolored	.25	.25
102	A23	100t multicolored	.30	.30
103	A23	150t multicolored	.40	.40
104	A23	200t multicolored	.50	.50
105	A23	250t multicolored	.65	.65
		Nos. 99-105 (7)	2.60	2.60

Souvenir Sheet

106	A23	500t multicolored	2.25	2.25

Souvenir Sheet

Save the Aral Sea — A24

Designs: a, Felis caracal. b, Salmo trutta aralensis. c, Hyaena hyaena. d, Pseudoscaphirhynchus kaufmanni. e, Aspiolucius esocinus.

1996, Apr. 29 Litho. *Perf. 14*

107	A24	100t Sheet of 5, #a.-e.	4.50	4.50

See Kazakhstan No. 145. Tadjikistan No. 91, Turkmenistan No. 52, Uzbekistan No. 113.

Fauna — A27

a, Aquila chrysaetos. b, Capra falconeri. c, Ovis ammon. d, Gyps himalayensis. e, Equus hemionus. f, Canis lupus. g, Ursus arctor. h, Saiga tatarica.

1997, Aug. 29 Litho. *Perf. 12x12½*
114 A27 600t Sheet of 8, #a.-h. 6.50 6.50

See No. 117.

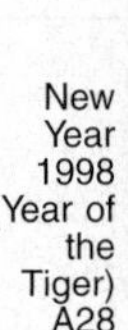

New Year 1998 (Year of the Tiger) A28

1998, June 5 Litho. *Perf. 13½x14*
115 A28 600t multicolored 1.10 1.10

Butterflies — A29

Designs: a, Parnasius actius. b, Colias christophi. c, Papilio machaon. d, Colias thisoa. e, Parnassius delphius. f, Panassius tianschanicus.

1998, June 5
116 A29 600t Sheet of 6, #a.-f. 5.00 5.00

Fauna Type of 1997

a, 600t, Capreolus capreolus. b, 1000t, Oriolus oriolus. c, 600t, Pandion haliaetus. d, 1000t, Uncia uncia. e, 600t, Upupa epops. f, 600t, Ciconia ciconia. g, 1000t, Alcedo atthis. h, 1000t, Falco tinnunculus.

1998, June 5 Litho. *Perf. 12x12½*
117 A27 Sheet of 8, #a-h *10.00 10.00*

Dinosaurs — A31

Designs: a, Saurolophus, vert. b, Euoplocephalus. c, Velociraptor. d, Tyrannosaurus, vert. e, Gallimimus. f, Protoceratops.

Perf. 14x13½, 13½x14
1998, Dec. 4 Litho.
118 A31 10s Sheet of 6, #a.-f. 6.00 6.00

Universal Declaration of Human Rights, 50th Anniv. — A32

a, Andrei Sakharov (1921-89). b, Crowd of people raising their arms. c, Martin Luther King, Jr. d, Mahatma Gandhi. e, Eleanor Roosevelt.

1998, Dec. 4 *Perf. 14x13½*
119 A32 10s Sheet of 5, #a.-e. + label 5.50 5.50

No. 119 exists with 2 different inscriptions on label.

Constitution, 5th Anniv. — A33

1998, Dec. *Perf. 12*
120 A33 1000t multi 1.60 1.60

Imperf

Size: 120x90mm

120A A33 10,000t multi *65.00 65.00*

No. 120A, issued 2/5/99.

Fauna A34

Designs: a, 600t, Fish, denomination UR. b, 1000t, Duck standing beside rocks. c, 1000t, Two birds. d, 1000t, Duck standing beside water. e, 1000t, Duck swimming. f, 1000t, Rodent. g, 1000t, Bird. h, 600t, Fish, denomination UL.

1998, Dec. Litho. *Perf. 12*
121 A34 Sheet of 8, #a.-h. 8.25 8.25

Corsac Fox (Vulpes Corsac) A35

World Wildlife Fund: Nos. 122a, 123a, 10s, Adult sitting. Nos. 122b, 123b, 10s, Adult sleeping. Nos. 122c, 123c, 30s, Two standing. Nos. 122d, 123d, 50s, Adult with young.

1999, Apr. 27 Litho. *Perf. 12½x12*
122 A35 Block of 4, #a.-d. 5.50 5.50

Size: 48x34mm

Perf. 13½

123 A35 Block of 4, #a.-d. 7.00 7.00

Nos. 123a-123d each contain a holographic image. Soaking in water may affect the hologram. IBRA '99, World Philatelic Exhibition, Nuremberg (#123). No. 123 was issued in sheets of 8 stamps.

Aleksandr Pushkin (1799-1837), Poet — A36

No. 124: a, 36t, Knight, giant. b, 6s, Man, woman, fish. c, 10s, Archer, angel. d, 10s, King in carriage.
20s, Portrait of Pushkin.

1999, June Litho. *Perf. 12x12½*
124 A36 Strip of 4, #a.-d. 4.00 4.00

Souvenir Sheet

125 A36 20s multicolored 3.50 3.50

No. 124 printed in sheets of 8 stamps.

Natl. Arms — A37

1999, July Litho. *Perf. 11¼x11½*
126 A37 20t dark blue .80 .80

Souvenir Sheet

China 1999 World Philatelic Exhibition — A38

No. 131: a, 10s, Ailuropoda melanoleuca. b, 15s, Strix leptogrammica.

1999, Aug. 21 Litho. *Perf. 13x12½*
131 A38 Sheet of 2, #a.-b. 2.25 2.25

Exists imperf. Value $3.75.

12th World Kickboxing Championships, Bishkek — A39

Emblem, globe and: No. 132, White background. No. 133, Blue panel. c, No. 134, Green, red, and black panels.
No. 135: a, Black background. b, Yellow and brown panels.

1999, Oct. 7 Litho. *Perf. 13¼*
132 A39 3s multi *.70 .70*
133 A39 3s multi *.70 .70*
134 A39 3s multi *.70 .70*
Nos. 132-134 (3) 2.10 2.10

Souvenir Sheet

Perf. 12½

135 A39 6s Sheet of 2, #a.-b., + label *2.00 2.00*

No. 135 contains 37x26mm stamps.

UPU, 125th Anniv. A40

1999, Oct. *Perf. 14x14¼*
136 A40 3s shown *.50 .50*
137 A40 6s Airplane, man on horse *1.00 1.00*

Dogs — A41

No. 138: a, 3s, Taigan. b, 6s, Tasy. c, 6s, Afghan hound. d, 10s, Saluki. e, 15s, Mid-Asian shepherd. f, 15s, Akbash dog. g, 20s, Chow chow. h, 25s, Akita.
Illustration reduced.

2000, Mar. 18 Litho. *Perf. 12¼x12*
138 A41 Sheet of 8, #a-h 6.75 6.75

Exists imperf. Value $10.

Kyrgyzstan postal officials have declared as "not authentic and not valid" stamps with a face value of 20s depicting the Beatles, Madonna, Pop music stars, Tiger Woods, 2000 French Olympic gold medal winners, Mushrooms, American Political Cartoons concerning the 2000 Presidential election, The Simpsons, Superman, and Warner Brothers cartoon characters.

Bulat Minzhilkiev(1940-98), Opera Singer — A42

2000, Apr. 20 Litho. *Perf. 14x14¼*
139 A42 5s multi *.50 .50*

Victory in World War II, 55th Anniv. A43

Heroes: a, Cholponbay Tuleberdiev (1922-42). b, I. V. Panfilov (1893-1941), vert. c, Duyshenkul Shopokov (1915-41).

Perf. 14x14¼ (#140a, 140c), 14¼x14 (#140b)

2000, May 20 Litho.
140 A43 6s Vert. strip of 3, #a-c *2.50 2.50*

Issued in sheets of 2 each #140a-140c.

No. 33 Surcharged

2000, Sept. 22 Litho. ***Perf. 12x12½***
141 A10 36t on 1t multi *.25 .25*

No. 141 exists with bar obliterators with smaller numerals and with thinner numerals and rosette obliterators in magenta. Value: each, $11.

2000 Summer Olympics, Sydney A44

Designs: 1s, Wrestling. 3s, Hurdles, vert. 6s, Boxing. 10s, Weight lifting, vert.

Perf. 14x14¼, 14¼x14
2000, Sept. 23
142-145 A44 Set of 4 *3.00 3.00*

Kyrgyzstan postal officials have declared as "not authentic and not valid" a sheet of nine 20s stamps depicting the History of Golf.

Atay Ogunbaev, Composer A45

2000, Oct. 28 Litho. ***Perf. 14x14¼***
146 A45 6s multi *.80 .80*

Butterflies — A46

Designs: No. 147, 3s, Aglais urticae. No. 148, 3s, Argynnis aglaja. No. 149, 3s, Colias thisoa. No. 150, 3s, Inachis io. No. 151, 3s, Papilio machaon. No. 152, 3s, Parnassius apollo.

2000, Nov. 18 ***Perf. 13½***
147-152 A46 Set of 6 *3.50 3.50*

Kyrgyzstan postal officials have declared as "not authentic and not valid" stamps with a face value of 20s in sheets of 6 depicting Jennifer Aniston and Tennis, and sheets of 9 depicting Backstreet Boys, Beverly Hills 90210, Minerals, Penguins, Tom and Jerry, Prince William, Babylon 5 and the End of Mir.

Intl. Year of Mountains (in 2002) — A47

Designs: No. 153, 10s, Khan-Tengri Mountain, 7,010 meters. No. 154, 10s, Victory Peak, 7,439 meters. No. 155, 10s, Lenin Peak, 7,134 meters.

2000, Dec. 23 Litho. ***Perf. 13½***
153-155 A47 Set of 3 *3.00 3.00*
a. Souvenir sheet, #153-155 + label *3.00 3.00*

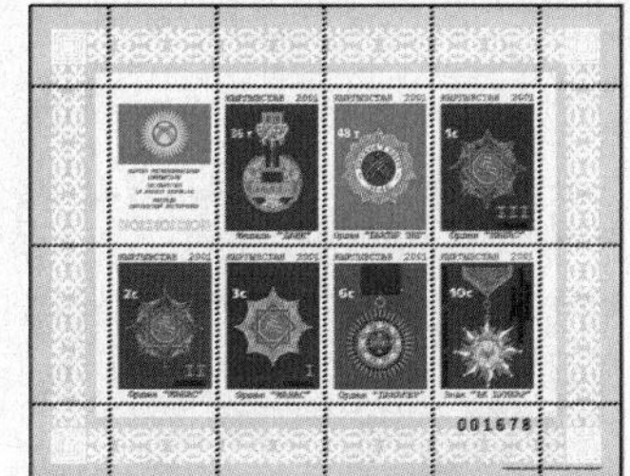

Medals — A48

No. 156: a, 36t, Dank. b, 48t, Baatyr Jene. c, 1s, Manas (third class). d, 2s, Manas (second class). e, 3s, Manas (first class). f, 6s, Danaker. g, 10s, Ak Shumkar.

2001, Jan. 20 Litho. ***Perf. 14¼x14***
156 A48 Sheet of 7, #a-g, + label *2.50 2.50*

UN High Commissioner for Refugees — A49

2001, Mar. 10 Litho. ***Perf. 14x14¼***
157 A49 10s multi *.80 .80*

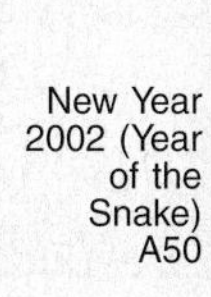

New Year 2002 (Year of the Snake) A50

2001, Mar. 17
158 A50 6s multi *.70 .70*

Exists imperf. Value $2.

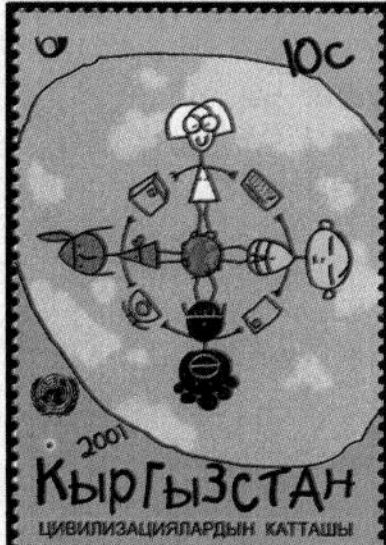

Year of Dialogue Among Civilizations A51

2001, Apr. 14 ***Perf. 13½***
159 A51 10s multi *1.25 1.25*

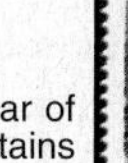

Intl. Year of Mountains A52

Mountains and: Nos. 160, 163a, 10s, Horses crossing stream. Nos. 161, 163b, 10s, Grazing animals, yurt. Nos. 162, 163c, 10s, Valley.

2001, July 7 ***Perf. 14x14¼***
With White Frame
160-162 A52 Set of 3 *2.75 2.75*

Souvenir Sheet
Without White Frame
163 A52 10s Sheet of 3, #a-c, + label *3.25 3.25*

Bishkek Buildings — A53

Designs: 48t, Communications Building. 1s, Town Hall. 3s, Opera House.

2001, July 7 ***Perf. 14x13¼***
164 A53 48t slate gray *.25 .20*
165 A53 1s olive gray *.25 .20*
166 A53 3s violet brown *.30 .25*
a. Horiz. strip, #164-166 *.80 .80*

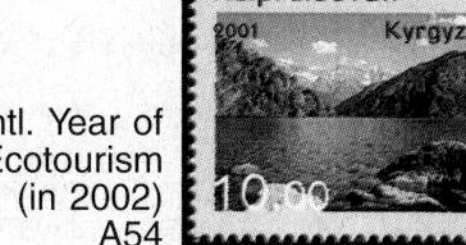

Intl. Year of Ecotourism (in 2002) A54

Designs: No. 167, 10s, Mountains, lake. No. 168, 10s, Mountains, field of flowers. No. 169, 10s, Sailboat on lake.
No. 170, Mosque, vert.

2001, July 21 ***Perf. 14x14¼***
167-169 A54 Set of 3 *3.50 3.50*

Souvenir Sheet
Imperf (Simulated Perfs)
170 A54 10s multi *1.50 1.50*

Independence, 10th Anniv. — A55

Designs: 1.50s, Eagle, mountain. 7s, Pres. Askar Akaev, flag.
11.50s, Governmental building.

2001, Aug. 29 ***Perf. 14x14¼***
171-172 A55 Set of 2 *3.50 3.50*

Souvenir Sheet
173 A55 11.50s Sheet of 1 + 8 labels *4.25 4.25*

Kurmanbek Baatyr, 500th Anniv. of Birth — A56

2001, Sept. 8 ***Perf. 14¼x14***
174 A56 1.50s multi *.70 .70*

Nos. 123a-123b Surcharged

and Nos. 123c-123d Overprinted With Text Only

No. 175: a, 25s on 10s #123a. b, 25s on 10s, #123b. c, 30s #123c. d, 50s #123d.

Litho. With Hologram
2001 ***Perf. 13½***
175 A35 Block of 4, #a-d *8.00 8.00*

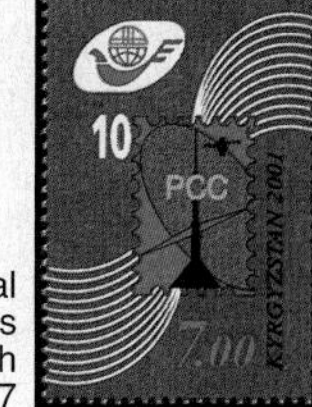

Regional Communications Accord, 10th Anniv. — A57

2001, Oct. 20 Litho. ***Perf. 14¼x14***
176 A57 7s multi *1.00 1.00*

Commonwealth of Independent States, 10th Anniv. — A58

2001, Dec. 8
177 A58 6s Prus bl & yel *1.10 1.10*

Kyrgyzstan postal officials have declared as "illegal:"
Stamps with a face value of 20s in sheets of nine depicting Shrek, Harry Potter, Concorde, Dogs, Tigers, Formula 1 racing, Mother Teresa, and The Beatles;
Stamps with various face values in sheets of nine depicting Defenders of Peace and Freedom, Superman, Green Lantern, Flash, Ironman, Legends of Baseball;
Stamps with various values in sheets of three depicting Princess Diana and Elvis Presley;
Stamps with a face value of 20s in sheets of six depicting Harley Davidson motorcycles;
Souvenir sheets of one 100s stamp depicting Harry Potter and Penguins.

2002 Winter Olympics, Salt Lake City — A59

Designs: 50t, Speed skating. 1.50s, Biathlon. 7s, Ice hockey. 10s, Ski jumping.
50s, Downhill skiing.

2002, Feb. 23 Litho. ***Perf. 14x14¼***
178-181 A59 Set of 4 *2.00 2.00*

Souvenir Sheet
182 A59 50s multi + label *5.00 5.00*

New Year 2002 (Year of the Horse) A60

2002, Mar. 23 ***Perf. 14x14¼***
183 A60 1s multi *1.00 1.00*

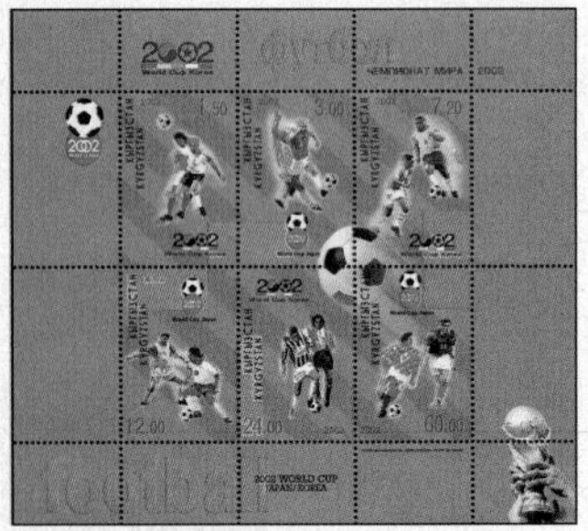

2002 World Cup Soccer Championships, Japan and Korea — A61

No. 184: a, 1.50s. b, 3s. c, 7.20s. d, 12s. e, 24s. f, 60s.

2002, Apr. 13 ***Perf. 14¼x14***
184 A61 Sheet of 6, #a-f *10.00 10.00*

No. 184 exists with an overprint in silver or gold with scores of the final and third place matches of the tournament. Value: each, $25.

Kyrgyzstan/Pakistan Diplomatic Relations, 10th Anniv. — A62

2002, Apr. 18 ***Perf. 14¼x14***
185 A62 12s multi *1.50 1.50*

Kyrgyzstan postal officials have declared as "illegal:"

Stamps with a face value of 20s in sheets of nine depicting Pandas, Dinosaurs, Marine Life, Cats and Scouting Emblem, and the Beatles.

Stamps with various face values in sheets of nine depicting Caricatures of World Cup Soccer Players (3 sheets).

Summer Olympics — A63

No. 186: a, 1s, Discus, Greece #125 (Athens, 1896). b, 2s, Boxing, France #113 (Paris, 1900). c, 3s, Diving, US #324 (St. Louis, 1904). d, 5s, Weight lifting, Great Britain #127 (London, 1908). e, 7s, Rowing, Sweden #97 (Stockholm, 1912). f, 7s, Hurdles, Belgium #B48 (Antwerp, 1920).

No. 187: a, 1s, Rhythmic gymnastics, France #201 (Paris, 1924). b, 2s, Diving, Netherlands #B25 (Amsterdam, 1928). c, 3s, Table tennis, US #718 (Los Angeles, 1932). d, 5s, Running, Germany #B86 (Berlin, 1936). e, 7s, Fencing, Great Britain #274 (London, 1948). f, 7s, Men's gymnastics (pommel horse), Finland #B112 (Helsinki, 1952).

No. 188: a, 1.50s, Volleyball, Australia #277 (Melbourne, 1956). b, 3s, Tennis, Italy #799 (Rome, 1960). c, 5s, Swimming, Japan #B12 (Tokyo, 1964). d, 5s, Judo, Mexico #990 (Mexico City, 1968). e, 7.20s, Kayaking, Germany #B490e (Munich, 1972). f, 12s, Yachting, Canada #B11 (Montreal, 1976).

No. 189: a, 1.50s, Men's gymnastics (rings), Russia #B99 (Moscow, 1980). b, 3s, Synchronized swimming, US #2085a (Los Angeles, 1984). c, 5s, Cycling, South Korea #B54 (Seoul, 1988). d, 5s, High jump, Spain #B197 (Barcelona, 1992). e, 7.20s, Sailboarding, US #3068a (Atlanta, 1996). f, 12s, Women's gymnastics, Australia #1779 (Sydney, 2000).

2002, Aug. 28 Litho. ***Perf. 13x13¼***
Sheets of 6, #a-f, + 3 labels
186-189 A63 Set of 4 *12.00 12.00*

Jalal-Abad A64

Talas A65

Osh — A66

2002, Dec. 7 ***Perf. 13½***

190	A64	20t claret	*.20*	*.20*
191	A65	50t claret	*.20*	*.20*
192	A66	60t claret	*.20*	*.20*
193	A64	1s Prussian bl	*.20*	*.20*
194	A65	1.50s Prussian bl	*.20*	*.20*
195	A66	2s blue gray	*.20*	*.20*
196	A64	3s blue gray	*.35*	*.35*
197	A65	7s blue gray	*.75*	*.75*
198	A66	10s Prussian bl	*1.00*	*1.00*
		Nos. 190-198 (9)	*3.30*	*3.30*

Kyrgyzstan postal officials have declared as "illegal:"

Sheets of 9 with various denominations depicting Looney Tunes Characters (Merry Cristmas! (sic)) (2 different), Harry Potter, 71st Academy Awards, MTV Video Awards.

Sheets of 9 with 20s denominations depicting 20th Century Dreams (5 different), Chess, Teddy bears, MTV Video Awards.

Sheet of 6 with various denominations depicting Dinosaurs.

Sheet of 3 with various denominations depicting Pope John Paul II.

Nos. 33, 35 Surcharged in Red or Black

No. 34 Surcharged

Methods and Perfs As Before
2002, Dec. 28

199	A10	1.50s on 1t multi (R)	*.20*	*.20*
200	A10	3.60s on 3t multi	*.35*	*.35*
201	A10	7s on 10t multi	*.75*	*.75*
		Nos. 199-201 (3)	1.30	1.30

New denomination is at left on No. 201.
Nos. 199-201 exist imperf. Value, set $1.50.

Olmoskhan Atabekova (1922-87) — A67

2003, Jan. 11 Litho. ***Perf. 14¼x14***
202 A67 7.20s multi *.80 .80*

Intl. Association of Academies of Science, 10th Anniv. A68

Emblem and: 1.50s, Atom model. 7.20s, Circles.

2003, Mar. 8 ***Perf. 14x14¼***
203-204 A68 Set of 2 *1.00 1.00*

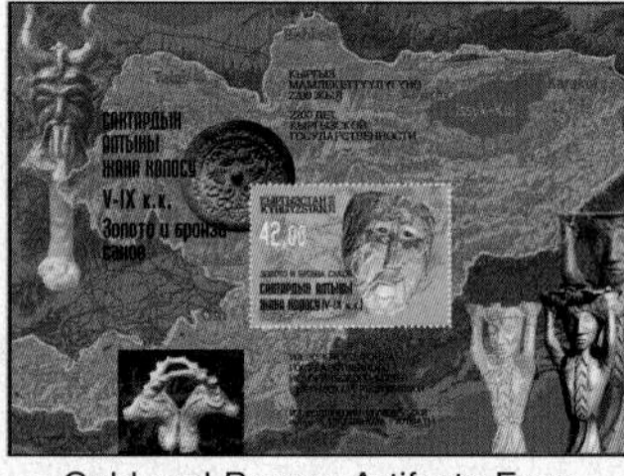

Gold and Bronze Artifacts From Sakov — A69

No. 205: a, 1.50s, Two figurines of people. b, 3s, Coin. c, 3.60s, Lion. d, 5s, Idol with horns. e, 7s, Rooster. f, 10s, Goats. g, 20s, Bird on coin. h, 42s, Animal's head.

No. 206, Mask.

2003, May 10 ***Perf. 14x14¼***
205 A69 Sheet of 8, #a-h *10.00 10.00*

Souvenir Sheet
Imperf. (With Simulated Perforations)
206 A69 42s multi *5.50 5.50*

No. 205 exists imperf. with simulated perforations. Value $12.

Bishkek Post Office, 125th Anniv. A70

Bishkek Post Office, emblem, dove and: 1s, Airplane. 3s, Covered wagon and Jeep. 7s, Covered wagon.

50s, "1878-2003."

2003, May 31 ***Perf. 14x14¼***
207-209 A70 Set of 3 *1.25 1.25*

Souvenir Sheet
Imperf. (With Simulated Perforations)
210 A70 50s multi *4.25 4.25*

Famous Men — A71

Various men: a, 1.50s. b, 3s. c, 3.60s. d, 5s. e, 7.20s. f, 10s. g, 18s. h, 20s. i, 25s. j, 30s.

2003, June 20 ***Perf. 14x14¼***
211 A71 Sheet of 10, #a-j *13.00 13.00*

Issyk Kul — A72

No. 212: a, 1s, Rahat. b, 1.50s, Raduga. c, 2s, Teltoru. d, 3s, Kyrgyzskoe Vzmorije. e, 3.60s, Tamga. f, 5s, Solnyshko. g, 7s, Vityaz. h, 8s, Ak Bermet. i, 12s, Royal Beach. j, 20s, Luchezarnoe Poberejie.

2003, Aug. 15 ***Perf. 13½x13¾***
212 A72 Sheet of 10, #a-j, + 10 labels *6.25 6.25*

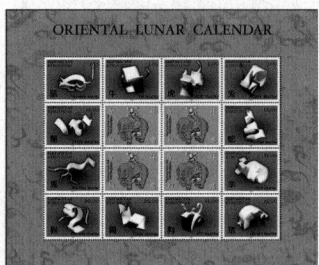

Lunar New Year Animals — A73

No. 213: a, 1.50s, Rat. b, 3s, Ox. c, 5s, Tiger. d, 7s, Hare. e, 12s, Dragon. f, 12s, Snake. g, 15s, Horse. h, 15s, Sheep. i, 20s, Monkey. j, 20s, Cock. k, 25s, Dog. l, 25s, Pig.

2003, Aug. 25 ***Perf. 13x13¼***
213 A73 Sheet of 12, #a-l, +4 labels *13.00 13.00*

National Symbols A74

History of Syma Chan — A75

Designs: No. 214, 3s, Flag. No. 215, 3s, National anthem. 5s, Coat of arms.

2003, Oct. 4 Litho. *Perf. 13½*
214-216 A74 Set of 3 *1.25 1.25*
216a Souvenir sheet, #214-216 *1.25 1.25*

Souvenir Sheet

217 A75 12s multi *1.40 1.40*

New Year 2003 (Year of the Sheep) A76

2003, Dec. 30 Litho. *Perf. 14x14¼*
218 A76 1.50s multi .60 .60

Meerim Fund, 10th Anniv. A77

Designs: 1.50s, Fund emblem, buildings. 7s, Fund emblem, buildings, diff. 20s, Fund emblem.

2004, Feb. 17 Litho. *Perf. 14x14¼*
219-220 A77 Set of 2 *1.10 1.10*

Souvenir Sheet

Perf. 13½

221 A77 20s multi *2.00 2.00*

No. 221 contains one 37x51mm stamp.

New Year 2004 (Year of the Monkey) A78

2004, Apr. 3 Litho. *Perf. 14x14¼*
222 A78 3s multi .50 .50

Automobiles — A79

No. 223: a, 3.60s, 1913 Peugeot. b, 3.60s, 1999 Mercedes-Benz. c, 10s, 1996 Volvo S40. d, 10s, 1908 Ford. e, 15s, 1932 Alfa-Romeo. f, 15s, 1972 VAZ 2101. g, 25s, 1998 Nissan. h, 25s, 1950 ZIS-110.

2004, May 1 Litho. *Perf. 14x13½*
223 A79 Sheet of 8, #a-h *10.00 10.00*

No. 223 exists imperf. Value $15.

Insects — A80

No. 224: a, 3.60s, Insect with red wings. b, 3.60s, Grasshopper. c, 10s, Cricket. d, 10s, Ladybugs. e, 15s, Dragonfly. f, 15s, Praying mantis. g, 25s, Moth with red wings. h, 25s, Bee.

2004, May 15
224 A80 Sheet of 8, #a-h *10.00 10.00*

2004 Singapore World Stamp Championship. No. 224 exists imperf. Value $15.

FIFA (Fédération Internationale de Football Association), Cent. — A81

No. 225: a, 5s, Soccer ball. b, 6s, FIFA emblem, soccer ball, athletic shoes. c, 7s, Soccer player with red shirt. d, 10s, Soccer player with white shirt.
Illustration reduced.

2004, May 21 Litho. *Perf. 14x14¼*
225 A81 Block of 4, #a-d *3.00 3.00*

No. 12 Surcharged

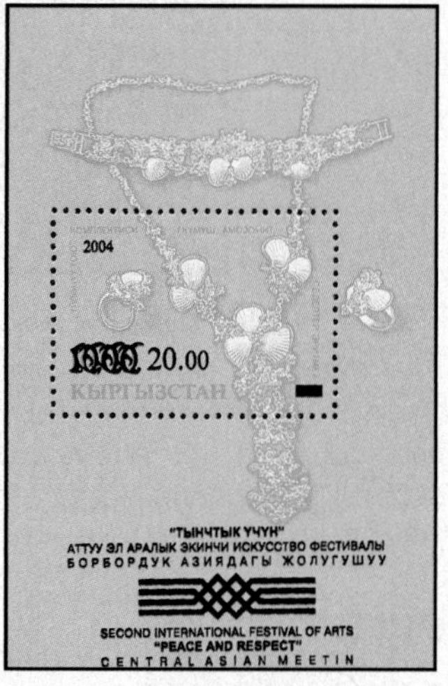

2004, June 19 Litho. *Perf. 12*
226 A5 20s on 10r #12 *2.40 2.40*

Peace and Respect Intl. Festival of Arts.

Karakol Region A82

Naryn Region A83

Tokmok Region — A84

2004, July 6 Litho. *Perf. 13½x13¾*

227	A82	10t indigo	.20	.20
228	A83	20t dark green	.20	.20
229	A84	50t dark brown	.20	.20
230	A82	60t blue	.20	.20
231	A83	1s blue green	.20	.20
232	A84	2s brown	.20	.20
233	A82	3s violet	.40	.40
234	A83	5s green	.60	.60
235	A84	7s light brown	.85	.85
		Nos. 227-235 (9)	3.05	3.05

Chynykei Biy (1788-1874) — A85

2004, Sept. 18 Litho. *Perf. 14x14¼*
236 A85 3s multi .45 .45

National Academy of Sciences, 50th Anniv. A86

Emblem and: 1.50s, Old building. 3.60s, New building.

2004, Nov. 6
237-238 A86 Set of 2 .80 .80

Basketball A87

Basketball player and: 1.50s, Coach Nikolay Zvenchukov. 3.60s, Coach Kubat Karabekov.

2004, Dec. 4
239-240 A87 Set of 2 1.00 1.00

Falcon — A88

2004-05 Litho. *Perf. 13¼x14*

241	A88	10t green	.35	.35
242	A88	50t blue	.35	.35
243	A88	1s brown	.50	.50
		Nos. 241-243 (3)	1.20	1.20

Issued: 1s, 12/28/04. 50t, 2/12/05. 10t, 6/16/05.

New Year 2005 (Year of the Rooster) A89

2005, Mar. 21 Litho. *Perf. 14*
244 A89 3s multi *.90 .90*

Souvenir Sheet

Salizhan Sharipov, Astronaut — A90

2005, Apr. 20 Litho. *Perf. 13¾*
245 A90 100s multi *11.50 11.50*

Folk Art — A91

Various folk art objects.

2005, Apr. 23 *Perf. 14¼x14*

246		Strip of 6	*4.50*	*4.50*
a.	A91	2s orange panel	*.20*	*.20*
b.	A91	3.60s light blue panel	*.25*	*.25*
c.	A91	7s green panel	*.55*	*.55*
d.	A91	12s green panel	*.85*	*.85*
e.	A91	15s bright pink panel	*1.10*	*1.10*
f.	A91	20s orange panel	*1.50*	*1.50*

Souvenir Sheet

247 A91 40s multi *5.50 5.50*

End of World War II, 60th Anniv. A92

2005, May 6 *Perf. 14x14¼*
248 A92 5s multi *.60 .60*

End of World War II, 60th Anniv. — A93

World War II personalities: No. 249, 5s, Gen. Tito. No. 250, 5s, Cervi Brothers. No. 251, 5s, Ferruccio Parri. No. 252, 10s, Air Marshal Sir Hugh Dowding. No. 253, 10s, Gen. George S. Patton. No. 254, 10s, Gen. Konstantin Rokossovsky. No. 255, 10s, Gen. Harold Alexander. No. 256, 10s, Gen. Omar N. Bradley. No. 257, 10s, Gen. Charles de Gaulle. No. 258, 10s, Gen. Jean Leclerc. No. 259, 10s, Field Marshal Bernard Montgomery. No. 260, 10s, Gen. Ivan Konev. No. 261, 10s, Marshal Georgy Zhukov. No. 262, 10s, Gen. Dwight D. Eisenhower. No. 263, 10s, Marshal Semyon Timoshenko. No. 264, 10s, Gen. Vasily Chuikov. No. 265, 15s, Pres. Franklin D. Roosevelt. No. 266, 15s, Prime Minister Winston Churchill. No. 267, 15s, King George VI. No. 268, 15s, Joseph Stalin.

Embossed on Metal

2005, June 18 ***Die Cut Perf 12½***

Self-Adhesive

249-268 A93 Set of 20 *44.00 44.00*

National Games — A94

2005, Aug. 6 Litho. ***Perf. 14¼x14***

269 A94 3s multi *.40 .40*

World Summit on the Information Society, Tunis A95

2005, Sept. 10 ***Perf. 14x14¼***

270 A95 3.60s multi *.45 .45*

Falcon — A96

2005, Sept. 14 Litho. ***Perf. 13¼x14***

271 A96 60t violet .30 .30

No. 271 exists imperf. Value $5.25.

Souvenir Sheet

Lakes — A97

No. 272: a, 7s, Lake Chatyrkul. b, 20s, Lake Sonkul. c, 25s, Lake Sarychelek. d, 30s, Lake Issyk-Kul.

2005, Dec. 10 ***Perf. 14x14¼***

272 A97 Sheet of 4, #a-d 7.25 7.25

Europa Stamps, 50th Anniv. (in 2006) — A98

Designs: 15s, Uzgen Minaret, Kyrgyzstan. 20s, Acropolis, Athens, Greece. 25s, Buran Tower, Kyrgyzstan. 45s, Kolossi Castle, Limassol, Cyprus. 60s, Tash Rabat, Kyrgyzstan. 85s, St. Mark's Basilica, Venice, Italy.

2005, Dec. 29 ***Perf. 13¼x13***

273-278 A98 Set of 6 22.50 22.50

278a Souvenir sheet, #273-278 22.50 22.50

Nos. 273-278 and 278a exist imperf. Values: set, $22.50; sheet, $22.50.

Tugolbai Sydykbekov (1912-97), Writer A99

2006, Jan. 7 ***Perf. 14x14¼***

279 A99 10s multi .85 .85

New Year 2006 (Year of the Dog) A100

2006, Feb. 4

280 A100 3s multi .40 .40

2006 Winter Olympics, Turin A101

2006, Mar. 11

281 A101 5s multi .70 .70

Falcon — A102

2006	**Litho.**	***Perf. 13¼x14***	
282	A102 50t Prus blue	.30	.30
283	A102 1s car lake	.20	.20
284	A102 3s black	.45	.45
	Nos. 282-284 (3)	.95	.95

Issued: 50t, 4/15; 1s, 5/6; 3s, 8/5.

Nos. 282-284 exist imperf. Value, each $5.75.

2006 World Cup Soccer Championships, Germany — A103

2006, June 9 Litho. ***Perf. 14x14¼***

285 A103 15s multi 1.25 1.25

Miniature Sheet

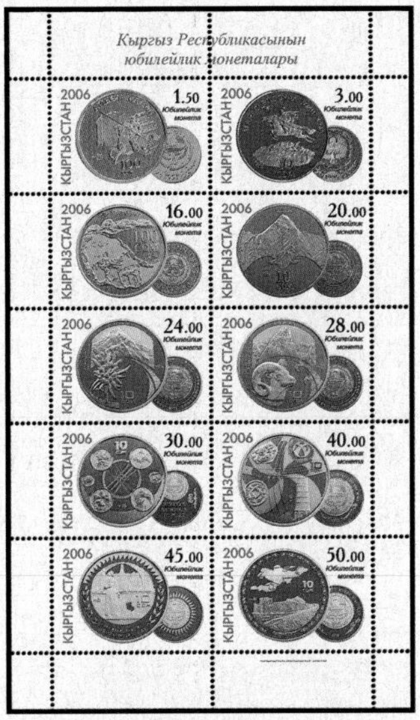

Commemorative Coins — A104

No. 286: a, 1.50s, 1995 100-som gold coin. b, 3s, 1995 10-som silver coin. c, 16s, 2000 100-som gold coin. d, 20s, 2001 10-som silver coin. e, 24s, 2002 10-som silver coin depicting flower. f, 28s, 2002 10-som silver coin depicting ram. g, 30s, 2003 10-som silver and gold coin depicting other coins. h, 40s, 2003 10-som silver and gold coin depicting national symbols. i, 45s, 2005 10-som silver coin. j, 50s, 2005 10-som silver and gold coin.

2006, June 24

286 A104 Sheet of 10, #a-j 19.00 19.00

Regional Communications Commonwealth, 15th Anniv. — A105

2006, Sept. 23 Litho. ***Perf. 14x14¼***

287 A105 12s multi 1.10 1.10

Souvenir Sheet

Public Buildings in Bishkek — A106

No. 288: a, Sports arena (two word inscription, large tree at left). b, Theater (three word inscription). c, Philharmonic hall (one word inscription). d, Museum (two word inscription, no tree).

2006, Sept. 30 ***Perf. 12¾x13¼***

288 A106 12s Sheet of 4, #a-d 4.25 4.25

Intl. Telecommunications Union Plenipotentiary Conference, Antalya, Turkey — A107

2006, Oct. 7 Litho. ***Perf. 13x13½***

289 A107 25s multi 2.10 2.10

Defense of Moscow in World War II, 65th Anniv. A108

2006, Nov. 11 ***Perf. 14x14¼***

290 A108 7s multi .65 .65

Miniature Sheet

Kyrgyz Cinema, 65th Anniv. — A109

No. 291: a, S. Chokmorov (on horse). b, B. Bejshenaliev (man wearing hat). c, T. Tursunbaeva (woman wearing headdress). d, B. Kydykeeva (two women).

2006, Dec. 9

291 A109 12s Sheet of 4, #a-d 4.25 4.25

New Year 2007 (Year of the Pig) A110

2007, Jan. 27 Litho. ***Perf. 14x14¼***

292 A110 3s multi .40 .40

Miniature Sheet

Paintings — A111

No. 293: a, Chingiz Aitmatov (seated man with striped shirt). b, Syimenkul Chokmorov (seated man with clasped hands). c, Kurmangazy Azykbaev (man playing flute). d, Omor Sultanov (seated man wearing light gray suit). e, Zhylkychy Zhakypov (man with dark blue shirt).

2007, Mar. 3 Litho. ***Perf. 14x14¼***

293 A111 12s Sheet of 5, #a-e, + label 4.75 4.75

Kyrgyz National Games A112

2007, May 5 Litho. ***Perf. 14x14¼***

294 A112 7s multi .60 .60

Miniature Sheet

Bishkek-Osh Highway, 50th Anniv. — A113

No. 295: a, Tunnel. b, Road turning to left. c, Road turning to right. d, Straight road.

2007, May 19 *Perf. 13x13¼*
295 A113 25s Sheet of 4, #a-d 7.50 7.50

Aigul — A114

Flower and: 1s, Solid blue background. 100s, Mountains in background.

2007, June 23 *Perf. 13¼x14*
296 A114 1s multi .20 .20

Souvenir Sheet
Perf. 13¼x13

297 A114 100s multi 8.00 8.00

No. 297 contains one 30x40mm stamp.

Miniature Sheet

Seventh Conference of Shanghai Cooperation Organization — A115

No. 298 — Flags of: a, Kazakhstan. b, Kyrgyzstan. c, People's Republic of China. d, Russia. e, Tajikistan. f, Uzbekistan.

2007, Aug. 16 *Perf. 13¾x14½*
298 A115 12s Sheet of 6, #a-f 5.50 5.50

Miniature Sheet

Birds of Prey — A116

No. 299: a, Haliaeetus albicilla. b, Falco rusticolus. c, Aquila chrysaetus. d, Accipiter gentilis. e, Milvus migrans. f, Falco peregrinus.

2007, Nov. 30 **Litho.** *Perf. 14¼*
299 A116 25s Sheet of 6, #a-f 11.00 11.00

Santa Claus — A117

2007, Dec. 1 *Perf. 14x14¼*
300 A117 3s multi .25 .25

New Year 2008 (Year of the Rat) — A118

2008, Jan. 19 *Perf. 14¼x14*
301 A118 7s multi .60 .60

Mammals — A119

Designs: Nos. 302, 310a, 7s, Uncia uncia. Nos. 303, 310b, 7s, Ailuropoda melanoleuca. Nos. 304, 310c, 12s, Panthera tigris. Nos. 305, 310d, 12s, Ailurus fulgens. Nos. 306, 310e, 16s, Hystrix cristata. Nos. 307, 310f, 16s, Pygathrix roxellana. Nos. 308, 310g, 25s, Otocolobus manul. Nos. 309, 310h, 25s, Ovis ammon.

2008, Jan. 19 *Perf. 14x13½*

Stamps With White Frames

302-309 A119 Set of 8 9.75 9.75

Souvenir Sheet

Stamps With Colored Frames

310 A119 Sheet of 8, #a-h 9.75 9.75

Kyrgyz National Games — A120

2008, Mar. 1 *Perf. 14¼x14*
311 A120 5s multi .50 .50

2008 Summer Olympics, Beijing — A121

No. 312: a, Soccer. b, Wrestling. c, Javelin. d, Basketball.
Illustration reduced.

2008, Mar. 1 *Perf. 12½x13*
312 A121 20s Block of 4, #a-d 6.25 6.25

Souvenir Sheet

Mountains — A122

No. 313: a, Khan-Tengri, Kyrgyzstan. b, Sabalan Peak, Iran.

2008, Mar. 8 *Perf. 13x13¼*
313 A122 16s Sheet of 2, #a-b, + central label 3.25 3.25

See Iran No. 2964.

Outlines of Stamps, Mountain, Kyrgyz Post Emblem — A123

2008 **Litho.** *Perf. 14x13¼*
315 A123 1s multi .20 .20
316 A123 3s multi .25 .25

Issued: 1s, 3s, 4/2.

Heroes of the Kyrgyz Republic and Medals A124

Designs: 10s, Sabira Kumushalieva (1917-2007), actress. 15s, Absamat Masaliev (1933-2004), politician.

2008, Apr. 5 **Litho.** *Perf. 14x14¼*
318-319 A124 Set of 2 2.50 2.50

Miniature Sheet

Civil Aircraft — A125

No. 320: a, JAK-12. b, MI-2. c, AN-2. d, TU-154. e, IL-14. f, IL-18. g, AN-24. h, MI-4.
No. 321: a, AN-28. b, JAK-40. c, AN-26. d, TU-134. e, IL-76. f, A-320. g, MI-8.

2008, May 24 *Perf. 14x13¼*
320 A125 20s Sheet of 8, #a-h, + central label 13.50 13.50

Miniature Sheet
Perf. 13x13½

321 A125 20s Sheet of 7, #a-g, + label 12.00 12.00

Hats — A126

Various hats: 6s, 7s, 12s, 50s.

2008, June 28 **Litho.** *Perf. 14¼x14*
323-326 A126 Set of 4 6.75 6.75

Yaks — A127

No. 325: a, Buka yak (denomination on cloud). b, Mamalak yak (denomination on light blue sky and mountain). c, Inek yak facing right (denomination on purple mountain). d, Inek yak facing left (denomination on dark blue sky and mountain).
Illustration reduced.

2008, July 26 *Perf. 13x13¼*
327 A127 25s Block of 4, #a-d 7.25 7.25

Isa Akhunbaev (1908-75), Surgeon — A128

2008, Aug. 30 *Perf. 14¼x14*
328 A128 12s multi 1.10 1.10

SEMI-POSTAL STAMPS

Natl. Epic Poem, Manas, Millennium SP1

SP2

Designs: 10t+5t, Woman with bird in hand. 20t+10t, Bird on man's wrist. No. B3, Women watching as baby held up. No. B4, Woman with spear, leading horse. 40t+15t, Warrior looking at dead dragon. No. B6, Warrior on horse holding axe. No. B7, Man wearing tall hat on horseback. No. B8, Warrior with sword on horseback.

No. B9, Man in red cradling fallen warrior. No. B10, Man in black seated in desert, tornado.

Perf. 12, Imperf

1995, June 16 **Litho.**

B1	SP1	10t +5t blue & bis	.35	.35
B2	SP1	20t +10t blue & bis	.35	.35
B3	SP1	30t +10t blue & bis	.35	.35
B4	SP1	30t +10t blue & bis	.35	.35
B5	SP1	40t +15t blue & bis	.35	.35
B6	SP1	50t +15t blue & bis	.35	.35
B7	SP1	50t +15t blue & bis	.35	.35

B8 SP1 50t +15t blue & bis .35 .35
a. Sheet of 8, #B1-B8 + label 3.75 3.75

Souvenir Sheets

B9 SP2 2s +50t multi 2.00 2.00
B10 SP2 2s +50t multi 2.00 2.00

1996 Summer Olympic Games, Atlanta SP3

Designs: 100t+20t, Equestrian events. 140t+30t, Boxing. 150t+30t, Archery. 300t+50t, Judo, hot air balloon, sailing, water skiing.

1996, July 10 Litho. *Perf. 12½x12*
B11 SP3 100t +20t multi .35 .35
B12 SP3 140t +30t multi .65 .65
B13 SP3 150t +30t multi .90 .90
B14 SP3 300t +50t multi 1.40 1.40
Nos. B11-B14 (4) 3.30 3.30

Town of Osh, 3000th Anniv. — SP4

No. B15: a, Globe, mountains, mosque, "Osh" and "3000." b, Mosque with three arches, mountains (green panel at UR). c, Solomon's Throne (mosque on mountain). d, Mausoleum of Asaf ibn Burkiya (denomination at LL).

Illustration reduced.

2000, Feb. 19 Litho. *Perf. 13½*
B15 SP4 6s +25t Sheet of 4, #a-d *3.50 3.50*

Exists imperf. Value $5.

Kurmanzhan Datka, 190th Anniv. of Birth — SP5

2001, Oct. 13 Litho. *Perf. 14x14¼*
B16 SP5 10s +70t ind & gray *1.50 1.50*

LABUAN

lə-'bü-ən

LOCATION — An island in the East Indies, about six miles off the northwest coast of Borneo
GOVT. — A British possession, administered as a part of the North Borneo Colony
AREA — 35 sq. mi.
POP. — 8,963 (estimated)
CAPITAL — Victoria

The stamps of Labuan were replaced by those of Straits Settlements in 1906.

100 Cents = 1 Dollar

Watermark

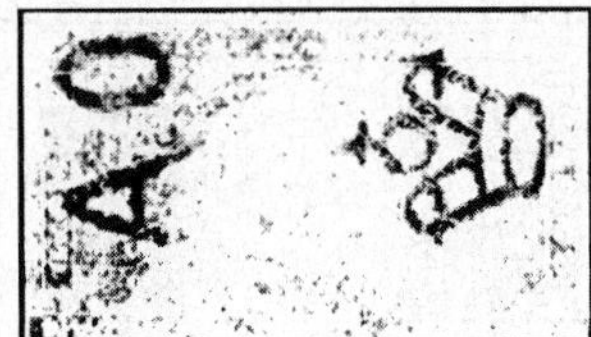

Wmk. 46 — C A over Crown

Queen Victoria — A1

On Nos. 1, 2, 3, 4 and 11 the watermark is 32mm high. It is always placed sideways and extends over two stamps.

1879, May Engr. Wmk. 46 *Perf. 14*
1 A1 2c green 1,325. 975.00
2 A1 6c orange 240.00 210.00
3 A1 12c carmine 1,925. 850.00
4 A1 16c blue 77.50 *160.00*
Nos. 1-4 (4) 3,567. 2,195.

See Nos. 5-10, 16-24, 33-39, 42-48. For surcharges see Nos. 12-15, 25, 31, 40-41.

1880-82 Wmk. 1
5 A1 2c green 27.50 *42.50*
6 A1 6c orange 125.00 *140.00*
7 A1 8c carmine ('82) 125.00 *125.00*
8 A1 10c yel brown 190.00 *100.00*
9 A1 12c carmine 325.00 *375.00*
10 A1 16c blue ('81) 95.00 100.00
Nos. 5-10 (6) 887.50 *882.50*

A2 A3

A3a A4

1880-83 Wmk. 46
11 A2 6c on 16c blue (with additional "6" across original value) (R) 3,000. 1,200.

Wmk. 1

12 A2 8c on 12c carmine 1,700. 1,100.
a. Original value not obliterated 3,300. 2,000.
b. Additional surcharge "8" across original value 2,175. 1,450.
c. "8" inverted 2,100. 1,200.
d. As "a," "8" inverted — —
13 A3 8c on 12c car ('81) 425.00 475.00
14 A3a 8c on 12c car ('81) 140.00 150.00
a. "Eighr" *22,500.*
b. Inverted surcharge 15,000.
c. Double surcharge 2,100. 2,100.
15 A4 $1 on 16c blue (R) ('83) *4,800.*

On No. 12 the original value is obliterated by a pen mark in either black or red.

1883-86 Wmk. 2
16 A1 2c green 25.00 *35.00*
a. Horiz. pair, imperf. btwn. 13,250.
17 A1 2c rose red ('85) 4.00 *14.50*
18 A1 8c carmine 325.00 *115.00*
19 A1 8c dk violet ('85) 30.00 *9.00*
20 A1 10c yellow brn 42.50 *55.00*
21 A1 10c black brn ('86) 16.00 *50.00*
22 A1 16c blue 115.00 *210.00*
23 A1 16c gray blue ('86) 160.00
24 A1 40c ocher 22.50 *115.00*
Nos. 16-24 (9) 740.00 *603.50*

Nos. 1-10, 16-24 are in sheets of 10. For surcharges see Nos. 26-30, 32.

A5 A6

A7 A8

1885 Wmk. 1
25 A5 2c on 16c blue 1,150. *1,100.*

Wmk. 2

26 A5 2c on 8c car 275.00 *500.00*
a. Double surcharge
27 A6 2c on 16c blue 125.00 *190.00*
a. Double surcharge *7,250.*
28 A7 2c on 8c car 80.00 *140.00*

1891

Black or Red Surcharge

29 A8 6c on 8c violet 13.00 11.50
a. 6c on 8c dark violet 160.00 140.00
b. Double surcharge 375.00 —
c. As "a," "Cents" omitted 550.00 550.00
e. Inverted surcharge 90.00 *90.00*
e. Dbl. surch., one inverted 1,100. —
f. Dbl. surch., both inverted 1,100. —
g. "6" omitted 600.00
30 A8 6c on 8c dk vio (R) 1,325. 675.00
a. Inverted surcharge 1,800. 850.00

Wmk. 46

31 A8 6c on 16c blue 2,750. 2,200.
a. Inverted surcharge 11,000. 8,000.

Wmk. 2

32 A8 6c on 40c ocher 12,000. 5,750.
a. Inverted surcharge 11,000. 9,000.

1892 Engr. Unwmk.
33 A1 2c rose 7.25 4.25
34 A1 6c yellow green 10.00 5.75
35 A1 8c violet 7.75 13.00
36 A1 10c brown 17.00 10.00
37 A1 12c deep ultra 9.00 *8.50*
38 A1 16c gray 24.00 *37.50*
39 A1 40c ocher 55.00 *37.50*
Nos. 33-39 (7) 130.00 116.50

The 2c, 8c and 10c are in sheets of 30; others in sheets of 10.

Nos. 39 and 38 Surcharged

1893
40 A1 2c on 40c ocher 210.00 110.00
a. Inverted surcharge 500.00 *675.00*
41 A1 6c on 16c gray 450.00 175.00
a. Inverted surcharge 675.00 350.00
b. Surcharge sideways 675.00 375.00
c. "Six" omitted — —
d. "Cents" omitted — —
e. Handstamped "Six Cents" *2,275.*

Surcharges on Nos. 40-41 each exist in 10 types. Counterfeits exist.

No. 41e was handstamped on examples of No. 41 on which the surcharge failed to print or was printed partially or completely albino.

From Jan. 1, 1890, to Jan. 1, 1906, Labuan was administered by the British North Borneo Co. Late in that period, unused remainders of Nos. 42-83, 53a, 63a, 64a, 65a, 66a, 68a, 85-86, 96-118, 103a, 107a, J1-J9, J3a and J6a were canceled to order by bars forming an oval. Values for these stamps used are for those with this form of cancellation, unless described as postally used, which are for stamps with dated town cancellations. Nos. 63b, 64b, 65b, 104a, J6a, and possibly others, only exist c.t.o.

For detailed listings of Labuan, see the *Scott Classic Specialized Catalogue.*

1894, Apr. Litho.
42 A1 2c bright rose 2.00 .65
43 A1 6c yellow green 16.00 .65
a. Horiz. pair, imperf. btwn. *8,500.*
44 A1 8c bright violet 18.00 .65
45 A1 10c brown 57.50 .65
46 A1 12c light ultra 26.50 .80
47 A1 16c gray 32.50 .65
48 A1 40c orange 60.00 .65
Nos. 42-48 (7) 212.50 4.70

Counterfeits exist.

Dyak Chieftain — A9

Malayan Sambar — A10

Sago Palm A11

Argus Pheasant A12

Arms of North Borneo — A13

Dhow — A14

Saltwater Crocodile — A15

Mt. Kinabalu — A16

Arms of North Borneo — A17

Perf. 12 to 16 and Compound

1894 Engr.
49 A9 1c lilac & black 2.00 .65
a. Vert. pair, imperf. between 1,250. 575.00
50 A10 2c blue & black 3.50 .65
a. Imperf., pair 825.00
51 A11 3c bister & black 5.25 .65
52 A12 5c green & black 42.50 1.10
a. Horiz. pair, imperf. between *1,800.*
53 A13 6c brown red & blk 3.50 .65
a. Imperf., pair 725.00 425.00
54 A14 8c red & black 9.75 .65
55 A15 12c orange & black 37.50 .65
56 A16 18c br bister & blk 29.00 .65
b. Vert. pair, imperf. between *2,000.*
57 A17 24c lilac & blue 18.00 .65
Nos. 49-57 (9) 151.00 6.30

For overprints see Nos. 66-71.

A18

A19

A20

A21

1895, June **Litho.** ***Perf. 14***

No.	Type	Description	Unused	Used
58	A18	4c on $1 red	1.50	.50
59	A18	10c on $1 red	6.00	.50
60	A18	20c on $1 red	35.00	.50
61	A18	30c on $1 red	40.00	.75
62	A18	40c on $1 red	40.00	.75
		Nos. 58-62 (5)	122.50	3.00

1896

No.	Type	Description	Unused	Used
63	A19	25c blue green	32.50	.80
a.		Imperf, pair		72.50
b.		Without overprint	29.00	2.00
c.		As "a," imperf., pair	45.00	
64	A20	50c claret	32.50	.80
a.		Imperf, pair		72.50
b.		Without overprint	26.50	2.00
c.		As "a," imperf., pair	45.00	
65	A21	$1 dark blue	77.50	.80
a.		Imperf, impair		72.50
b.		Without overprint	40.00	2.00
c.		As "a," imperf., pair	47.50	
		Nos. 63-65 (3)	142.50	2.40

For surcharges and overprint see #93-95, 116-118, 120.

Nos. 49-54 Overprinted

1896 ***Perf. 12 to 15 and Compound***

No.	Type	Description	Unused	Used
66	A9	1c lilac & black	22.50	1.00
a.		"JEBILEE"	1,450.	375.00
b.		"JUBILE"	*2,400.*	
c.		Orange overprint	240.00	24.00
e.		Double overprint	450.00	—
67	A10	2c blue & black	47.50	1.25
a.		Vert. pair, imperf. btwn.	1,000.	
b.		"JEBILEE"	1,575.	
c.		"JUBILE"	*2,750.*	
d.		Vert. strip of 3, imperf between	*8,000.*	
68	A11	3c bister & black	45.00	1.00
a.		"JEBILEE"	*2,000.*	925.00
b.		"JUBILE"	—	—
g.		Double overprint	425.00	200.00
h.		Triple overprint	975.00	
69	A12	5c green & black	72.50	1.20
a.		Double overprint	575.00	
70	A13	6c brown red & blk	35.00	1.00
a.		Double overprint	975.00	
b.		"JUBILE"	*3,300.*	
71	A14	8c rose & black	57.50	1.00
a.		Double overprint	—	*3,400.*
		Nos. 66-71 (6)	280.00	6.45

Cession of Labuan to Great Britain, 50th anniv.

Dyak Chieftain A22

Malayan Sambar A23

Sago Palm A24

Argus Pheasant A25

A26

Dhow — A27

Saltwater Crocodile — A28

Mt. Kinabalu "Postal Revenue" — A29

Coat of Arms — A30

Perf. 13½ to 16 and Compound

1897-1900 **Engr.**

No.	Type	Description	Unused	Used
72	A22	1c lilac & black	4.75	.60
72A	A22	1c red brn & black	3.75	.80
73	A23	2c blue & black	30.00	.90
a.		Vert. pair, imperf between		900.00
b.		Horiz. pair, imperf between		950.00
74	A23	2c green & blk ('00)	4.50	.35
a.		Horiz. pair, imperf between	*3,000.*	
75	A24	3c bister & black	10.00	.60
a.		Vert. pair, imperf between	1,100.	675.00
76	A25	5c green & black	60.00	.85
77	A25	5c lt bl & blk ('00)	27.50	.80
78	A26	6c brown red & blk	9.00	.60
a.		Vert. pair, imperf between		850.00
79	A27	8c red & black	21.00	.65
80	A28	12c red & black	40.00	1.20
81	A29	18c ol bister & black	22.50	.65
a.		Vert. pair, imperf between		—
82	A30	24c gray lilac & blue	14.50	.60
		Nos. 72-82 (12)	247.50	8.60

No. 72A used exists only perf 13½x14.
For surcharges see Nos. 87-89, 110-112.

"Postage & Revenue" — A31

"Postage & Revenue" — A32

Perf. 13½ to 16 and Compound

1897

No.	Type	Description	Unused	Used
83	A31	18c bister & black	95.00	2.40
84a	A32	24c ochre & blue	37.50	*2.75*

For surcharges see Nos. 92, 115.

"Postage & Revenue" — A33

"Postage & Revenue" — A34

1898

No.	Type	Description	Unused	Used
85	A33	12c red & black	57.50	4.25
86a	A34	18c bister & black	40.00	3.50

No. 85a cto is always perf 13½x14.
For surcharges see Nos. 90-91, 113-114.

Regular Issue Surcharged in Black

1899

No.	Type	Description	Unused	Used
87	A25	4c on 5c grn & blk	45.00	30.00
88	A26	4c on 6c brn red & blk	27.50	22.00
89	A27	4c on 8c red & blk	70.00	45.00
90	A33	4c on 12c red & blk	47.50	40.00
91	A34	4c on 18c bis & blk	30.00	21.00
a.		Double surcharge	450.00	*525.00*
92a	A32	4c on 24c lil & bl	24.00	*29.00*
93	A19	4c on 25c blue grn	7.00	*8.50*
94	A20	4c on 50c claret	7.50	*8.50*
95	A21	4c on $1 dk blue	7.50	8.50
		Nos. 87-95 (9)	266.00	*212.50*

Orangutan A35

Sun Bear A36

Railroad Train — A37

Crown — A38

Perf. 12 to 16 and Compound

1899-1901

No.	Type	Description	Unused	Used
96	A35	4c yel brown & blk	10.00	.75
a.		Vert. pair, imperf. btwn.	1,350.	
97a	A35	4c car & blk ('00)	6.00	.60
98	A36	10c gray vio & dk brn ('01)	60.00	.75
99	A37	16c org brn & grn (G) ('01)	60.00	3.00
		Nos. 96-99 (4)	136.00	5.10

Perf. 12½ to 16 and Compound

1902-03 **Engr.**

No.	Type	Description	Unused	Used
99A	A38	1c vio & black	5.50	.60
100	A38	2c green & blk	4.75	.35
100A	A38	3c sepia & blk	4.00	.35
101	A38	4c car & black	4.00	.35
102	A38	8c org & black	14.50	.60
103	A38	10c sl blue & brn	4.00	.35
a.		Vert. pair, imperf. between		850.00
104	A38	12c yel & black	10.00	.35
a.		Vert. strip of 3, imperf. horiz.		*4,000.*
105	A38	16c org brn & grn	5.75	.35
106	A38	18c bis brn & blk	4.00	.35
107	A38	25c grnsh bl & grn	9.00	.60
a.		25c greenish blue & black		600.00
108	A38	50c gray lil & vio	12.00	1.50
109	A38	$1 org & red brn	10.00	1.50
		Nos. 99A-109 (12)	87.50	7.25

There are 3 known examples of No. 104a, all cto. A 16c vertical pair, imperf between has been reported. The editors would like to receive evidence of the existence of this item.

Regular Issue of 1896-97 Surcharged in Black

1904

No.	Type	Description	Unused	Used
110	A25	4c on 5c green & blk	55.00	17.00
111	A26	4c on 6c brown red & black	14.50	17.00
112	A27	4c on 8c red & blk	30.00	17.00
113	A33	4c on 12c red & blk	26.50	17.00
114	A34	4c on 18c bis & blk	30.00	17.00
115	A32	4c on 24c brn lil & bl	19.00	17.00
116	A19	4c on 25c blue green	10.00	17.00
117	A20	4c on 50c claret	10.00	17.00
a.		Double surcharge	400.00	
118	A21	4c on $1 dark blue	10.00	17.00
		Nos. 110-118 (9)	205.00	153.00

Stamps of North Borneo, 1893, and Labuan No. 65a Overprinted in Black:

a

b

c

1905

Perf. 14

No.	Type	Description	Unused	Used
119	A30(a)	25c slate blue	1,325.	1,100.
120	A21(c)	$1 blue		1,050.
121	A33(b)	$2 gray green	4,000.	
122	A34(c)	$5 red violet	7,250.	1,700.
123	A35(c)	$10 brown	32,500.	*11,500.*

POSTAGE DUE STAMPS

Regular Issues Overprinted

1901 **Unwmk.** ***Perf. 14***

No.	Type	Description	Unused	Used
J1	A23	2c green & black	21.00	1.10
a.		Double overprint	425.00	
J2	A24	3c bister & black	26.00	.85
J3b	A35	4c car & black	47.50	1.80
a.		Double overprint		850.00
J4	A25	5c lt blue & black	60.00	.90
J5	A26	6c brown red & blk	42.50	.90
J6	A27	8c red & black	85.00	1.80
a.		Center inverted, ovpt. reading down		*11,500.*
J7	A33	12c red & black	120.00	5.00
a.		Overprint reading down		*725.00*

J8	A34	18c ol bister & blk	30.00	1.50
J9	A32	24c brown lil & bl	60.00	6.75
		Nos. J1-J9 (9)	492.00	20.60

See note after No. 41.

The stamps of Labuan were superseded by those of Straits Settlements in 1906.

LAGOS

'lā-,gäs

LOCATION — West Africa, bordering on the former Southern Nigeria Colony
GOVT. — British Crown Colony and Protectorate
AREA — 3,460 sq. mi. (approx.)
POP. — 1,500,000 (1901)
CAPITAL — Lagos

This territory was purchased by the British in 1861 and placed under the Governor of Sierra Leone. In 1874 it was detached and formed part of the Gold Coast Colony until 1886 when the Protectorate of Lagos was established. In 1899 Lagos and the territories of the Royal Niger Company were surrendered to the Crown of Great Britain and formed into the Northern and Southern Nigeria Protectorates. In 1906 Lagos and Southern Nigeria were united to form the Colony and Protectorate of Southern Nigeria.

12 Pence = 1 Shilling

Queen Victoria — A1

1874-75 Typo. Wmk. 1 *Perf. 12½*

1	A1	1p lilac	65.00	37.50
2	A1	2p blue	65.00	32.50
3	A1	3p red brown ('75)	97.50	47.50
4	A1	4p rose	97.50	45.00
5	A1	6p blue green	110.00	15.00
6	A1	1sh orange ('75)	325.00	70.00
a.		Value 15½mm instead of 16½mm long	525.00	160.00
		Nos. 1-6 (6)	760.00	247.50

1876 *Perf. 14*

7	A1	1p lilac	45.00	21.00
8	A1	2p blue	57.50	15.00
9	A1	3p red brown	115.00	21.00
10	A1	4p rose	210.00	12.50
11	A1	6p green	110.00	7.00
12	A1	1sh orange	725.00	95.00
		Nos. 7-12 (6)	1,262.	171.50

The 4p exists with watermark sideways.

1882-1902 Wmk. 2

13	A1	½p green ('86)	2.25	.95
14	A1	1p lilac	22.00	14.50
15	A1	1p car rose	2.25	.95
16	A1	2p blue	175.00	5.75
17	A1	2p gray	80.00	6.75
18	A1	2p lil & bl ('87)	4.75	3.25
19	A1	2½p ultra ('91)	5.00	2.00
a.		2½p blue	90.00	57.50
20	A1	3p orange brn	17.50	5.75
21	A1	3p lilac & brn orange ('91)	3.00	*3.75*
22	A1	4p rose	160.00	14.00
23	A1	4p violet	125.00	9.50
24	A1	4p lil & blk ('87)	2.50	2.00
25	A1	5p lil & grn ('94)	3.00	*12.50*
26	A1	6p olive green	9.00	*47.50*
27	A1	6p lilac & red violet ('87)	5.50	3.50
28	A1	6p lilac & car rose ('02)	5.75	*13.50*
29	A1	7½p lilac & car rose ('94)	2.50	*35.00*
30	A1	10p lil & yel ('94)	3.75	*15.00*
31	A1	1sh orange ('85)	8.00	*22.50*
32	A1	1sh green & blk ('87)	6.50	*27.50*
33	A1	2sh6p ol brn ('86)	375.00	325.00
34	A1	2sh6p green & car rose ('87)	27.50	*92.50*
35	A1	5sh blue ('86)	650.00	500.00
36	A1	5sh green & ultra ('87)	47.50	*175.00*
37	A1	10sh brn vio ('86)	1,700.	1,150.
38	A1	10sh grn & brn ('87)	90.00	*225.00*

Excellent forgeries exist of Nos. 33, 35 and 37 on paper with genuine watermark.

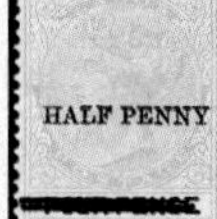

No. 24 Surcharged in Black

1893

39	A1	½p on 4p lilac & blk	5.00	3.00
a.		Double surcharge	62.50	62.50
b.		Triple surcharge	140.00	
c.		½p on 2p lilac & blue (#18)	—	25,000.

Four settings of surcharge.

Double and triple surchages must be clear and complete. Partial doubles caused by loose type exist.

King Edward VII — A3

1904, Jan. 22

40	A3	½p grn & bl grn	1.75	*6.25*
41	A3	1p vio & blk, *red*	1.10	.20
42	A3	2p violet & ultra	6.75	7.00
43	A3	2½p vio & ultra, *bl*	1.25	*1.75*
44	A3	3p vio & org brn	3.25	2.00
45	A3	6p vio & red vio	40.00	11.50
46	A3	1sh green & blk	40.00	*47.50*
47	A3	2sh6p grn & car rose	125.00	*260.00*
48	A3	5sh grn & ultra	150.00	*325.00*
49	A3	10sh green & brn	325.00	*850.00*
		Nos. 40-49 (10)	694.10	*1,511.*

1904-05 Wmk. 3

50	A3	½p grn & bl grn	8.50	3.00
51a	A3	1p vio & blk, *red*	1.75	.20
52	A3	2p violet & ultra	2.50	2.25
53a	A3	2½p vio & ultra, *bl*	2.00	*18.50*
54	A3	3p vio & org brn	4.00	1.50
55a	A3	6p vio & red vio	5.00	1.75
56	A3	1sh green & blk	15.00	21.00
57	A3	2sh6p grn & car rose	18.50	*62.50*
58	A3	5sh grn & ultra	25.00	*110.00*
59	A3	10sh green & brn	67.50	*225.00*
		Nos. 50-59 (10)	149.75	*445.70*

The 2½p is on chalky paper, the other values are on both ordinary and chalky. See *Scott Classic Specialized Catalogue* for detailed listings.

The stamps of Lagos were superseded by those of Southern Nigeria.

LAOS

'laus

LOCATION — In northwestern Indo-China
GOVT. — Republic
AREA — 91,400 sq. mi.
POP. — 5,407,453 (1999 est.)
CAPITAL — Vientiane

Before 1949, Laos was part of the French colony of Indo-China and used its stamps until 1951. The kingdom was replaced by the Lao Peoples Democratic Republic Dec. 2, 1975.

100 Cents = 1 Piaster
100 Cents = 1 Kip (1955)

Imperforates

Most Laos stamps exist imperforate in issued and trial colors, and also in small presentation sheets in issued colors.

Catalogue values for all unused stamps in this country are for Never Hinged items.

Boat on Mekong River — A1

King Sisavang-Vong A2

Laotian Woman A3

Designs: 50c, 60c, 70c, Luang Prabang. 1pi, 2pi, 3pi, 5pi, 10pi, Temple at Vientiane.

1951-52 Unwmk. Engr. *Perf. 13*

1	A1	10c dk grn & emer	.30	.20
2	A1	20c dk car & car	.30	.20
3	A1	30c ind & dp ultra	1.60	.75
4	A3	30c ind & pur ('52)	.70	.25
5	A1	50c dark brown	.35	.45
6	A1	60c red & red org	.35	.45
7	A1	70c ultra & bl grn	.70	.25
8	A3	80c brt grn & dk bl green ('52)	.70	.55
9	A1	1pi dk pur & pur	.70	.45
10	A3	1.10pi dark plum & carmine ('52)	1.10	.70
11	A2	1.50pi blk brn & vio brown	1.25	.65
12	A3	1.90pi indigo & dp blue ('52)	1.25	.50
13	A1	2pi dk grn & gray green	18.00	4.00
14	A1	3pi dk car & red	1.25	.70
15	A3	3pi choc & black brown ('52)	1.50	.65
16	A1	5pi ind & dp ultra	1.60	.75
17	A1	10pi blk brn & vio brown	3.75	1.10
		Nos. 1-17 (17)	35.40	12.60
		Set, hinged	22.50	

A booklet containing 26 souvenir sheets was issued in 1952 on the anniversary of the first issue of Laos stamps. Each sheet contains a single stamp in the center (Nos. 1-17, C2-C4, J1-J6). Value $225.

See No. 223.

UPU Monument and King Sisavang-Vong — A4

1952, Dec. 7

18	A4	80c ind, blue & pur	.55	.55
19	A4	1pi dk car, car & org brown	.55	.55
20	A4	1.20pi dk pur, purple & ultra	.60	.60
21	A4	1.50pi dk grn, bl grn & dk brn	.85	.85
22	A4	1.90pi blk brn, vio brn & dk Prus grn	1.00	1.00
		Nos. 18-22,C5-C6 (7)	12.55	12.55

Laos' admission to the UPU, May 13, 1952.

Court of Love — A5

1953, July 14

23	A5	4.50pi indigo & bl grn	.85	.55
24	A5	6pi gray & dark brn	1.25	.55

Composite of Laotian Temples — A6

1954, Mar. 4

25	A6	2pi indigo & purple	30.00	18.00
26	A6	3pi blk brn & dk red	32.50	19.00
		Nos. 25-26,C13 (3)	237.50	212.00

Accession of King Sisavang-Vong, 50th anniv.

Buddha Statue and Monks — A7

1956, May 24 Engr. *Perf. 13*

27	A7	2k reddish brown	2.50	1.75
28	A7	3k black	3.50	2.25
29	A7	5k chocolate	5.25	3.25
		Nos. 27-29,C20-C21 (5)	69.25	58.25

2500th anniversary of birth of Buddha.

UN Emblem — A8

1956, Dec. 14 *Perf. 13½x13*

30	A8	1k black	.65	.45
31	A8	2k blue	.90	.70
32	A8	4k bright red	1.25	.95
33	A8	6k purple	1.40	1.10
		Nos. 30-33,C22-C23 (6)	15.20	14.20

Admission of Laos to the UN, 1st anniv.

Khouy Player — A9

Khene Player — A10

Musical Instrument: 8k, Ranat.

1957, Mar. 25 Unwmk. *Perf. 13*

34	A9	2k multicolored	1.60	1.00
35	A10	4k multicolored	1.75	1.10
36	A9	8k org, bl & red brn	2.25	1.75
		Nos. 34-36,C24-C26 (6)	14.85	10.85

See No. 224.

Harvesting Rice — A11

Drying Rice — A12

1957, July 22 Engr. *Perf. 13*

37	A11	3k shown	.90	.60
38	A12	5k shown	1.25	.75
39	A12	16k Winnowing rice	2.00	1.50
40	A11	26k Polishing rice	4.00	2.00
		Nos. 37-40 (4)	8.15	4.85

Elephants — A13

Various Elephants: 30c, 5k, 10k, 13k, vert.

1958, Mar. 17

41	A13	10c multi	.70	.45
42	A13	20c multi	.70	.45
43	A13	30c multi	.70	.45
44	A13	2k multi	1.10	.70
45	A13	5k multi	2.25	1.40
46	A13	10k multi	2.50	1.75
47	A13	13k multi	4.25	2.00
		Nos. 41-47 (7)	12.20	7.20

For surcharge see No. B5.

Globe and Goddess — A14

UNESCO Building and Mother with Children — A15

Designs: 70c, UNESCO building, globe and mother with children. 1k, UNESCO building and Eiffel tower.

1958, Nov. 3 Engr. *Perf. 13*

48	A14	50c multicolored	.45	.20
49	A15	60c emer, vio & maroon	.45	.20
50	A15	70c ultra, rose red & brn	.45	.20
51	A14	1k ol bis, cl & grnsh bl	1.00	.60
		Nos. 48-51 (4)	2.35	1.20

UNESCO Headquarters in Paris opening, Nov. 3.

King Sisavang-Vong — A16

1959, Sept. 16 Unwmk.

52	A16	4k rose claret	.35	.35
53	A16	6.50k orange red	.35	.35
54	A16	9k bright pink	.35	.35
55	A16	13k green	.75	.60
		Nos. 52-55 (4)	1.80	1.65

For surcharges see Nos. 112-113, B4.

Dancers A17

Student and Torch of Learning — A18

Portal of Wat Phou, Pakse — A19

Education and Fine Arts: 3k, Globe, key of knowledge and girl student. 5k, Dancers and temple.

1959, Oct. 1 Engr. *Perf. 13*

56	A17	1k vio blk, ol & bl	.40	.20
57	A18	2k maroon & black	.40	.20
58	A17	3k slate grn & vio	.60	.30
59	A18	5k rose vio, yel & brt grn	1.10	.60
		Nos. 56-59 (4)	2.50	1.30

1959, Nov. 2 Unwmk. *Perf. 13*

Historic Monuments: 1.50k, That Inghang, Savannakhet, horiz. 2.50k, Phou Temple, Pakse, horiz. 7k, That Luang, Vientiane. 11k, That Luang, Vientiane, horiz. 12.50k, Phousi, Luang Prabang.

60	A19	50c sepia, grn & org	.20	.20
61	A19	1.50k multi	.35	.20
62	A19	2.50k pur, vio bl & ol	.50	.40
63	A19	7k vio, olive & claret	.75	.50
64	A19	11k brn, car & grn	.90	.75
65	A19	12.50k bl, vio & bister	1.25	.80
		Nos. 60-65 (6)	3.95	2.85

Funeral Urn and Monks — A20

King Sisavang-Vong A21

Designs: 6.50k, Urn under canopy. 9k, Catafalque on 7-headed dragon carriage.

1961, Apr. 29 Engr. *Perf. 13*

66	A20	4k black, bis & org	.70	.50
67	A20	6.50k black & bister	.70	.50
68	A20	9k black & bister	.70	.50
69	A21	25k black	3.00	2.00
		Nos. 66-69 (4)	5.10	3.50

King Sisavang-Vong's (1885-1959) funeral, Apr. 23-29, 1961.

King Savang Vatthana — A22

Boy and Malaria Eradication Emblem — A23

1962, Apr. 16 *Perf. 13*

Portrait in Brown and Carmine

70	A22	1k ultramarine	.25	.20
71	A22	2k lilac rose	.25	.20
72	A22	5k greenish blue	.35	.30
73	A22	10k olive	.90	.40
		Nos. 70-73 (4)	1.75	1.10

1962, July 19 Engr.

9k, Girl. 10k, Malaria eradication emblem.

74	A23	4k bluish grn, blk & buff	.30	.20
75	A23	9k lt bl, blk & lt brn	.70	.40
76	A23	10k ol, bis & rose red	1.25	.45
		Nos. 74-76 (3)	2.25	1.05

WHO drive to eradicate malaria. A souvenir sheet exists. Value, $200.

A24

A25

Designs: 50c, Modern mail service (truck, train, plane). 70c, Globe, stamps, dancer. 1k, Ancient mail service (messenger on elephant). 1.50k, Royal Messenger

1962, Nov. 15 Unwmk. *Perf. 13*

77	A24	50c multicolored	.60	.60
78	A24	70c multicolored	.60	.60
79	A25	1k dp claret, grn & blk	1.25	1.25
80	A25	1.50k multicolored	1.00	1.00
		Nos. 77-80 (4)	3.45	3.45

Souvenir sheets exist. One contains the 50c and 70c; the other, the 1k and 1.50k. The sheets exist both perf and imperf in a souvenir booklet of four sheets. Value intact booklet, $200.

Fishermen with Nets — A26

Threshing Rice — A27

Designs: 5k, Plowing and planting in rice paddy. 9k, Woman with infant harvesting rice.

1963, Mar. 21 *Perf. 13*

81	A26	1k grn, bister & pur	.35	.30
82	A27	4k bister, bl & grn	.45	.35
83	A26	5k grn, bis & indigo	.65	.45
84	A27	9k grn, vio bl & ocher	1.00	.50
a.		Min. sheet of 4, #81-84, imperf.	4.00	4.00
		Nos. 81-84 (4)	2.45	1.60

FAO "Freedom from Hunger" campaign.

Queen Khamphouy Handing out Gifts — A28

1963, Oct. 10 Engr.

85	A28	4k brn, dp car & blue	.40	.40
86	A28	6k grn, red, yel & bl	.55	.50
87	A28	10k bl, dp car & dk brn	.65	.65
a.		Miniature sheet of 3, #85-87	4.00	4.00
		Nos. 85-87 (3)	1.60	1.55

Centenary of the International Red Cross.

Man Holding UN Emblem A29

Perf. 13, Imperf

1963, Dec. 10 Unwmk.

88	A29	4k dk bl, dp org & vio brn	1.50	.80

15th anniv. of the Universal Declaration of Human Rights.

Temple of That Luang, Map of Nubia and Ramses II — A30

1964, Mar. 8 Engr.

89	A30	4k multicolored	.40	.40
90	A30	6k multicolored	.60	.60
91	A30	10k multicolored	.75	.75
a.		Miniature sheet of 3, #89-91	2.50	2.50
		Nos. 89-91 (3)	1.75	1.75

UNESCO world campaign to save historic monuments in Nubia. No. 91a sold for 25k.

Ceremonial Chalice A31

Designs: 15k, Buddha. 20k, Soldier leading people through Mekong River Valley. 40k, Royal Palace, Luang Prabang.

1964, July 30 Unwmk. *Perf. 13*

92	A31	10k multicolored	.40	.30
93	A31	15k multicolored	.60	.40
94	A31	20k multicolored	.80	.60
95	A31	40k multicolored	1.25	.75
a.		Miniature sheet of 4, #92-95	3.50	3.50
		Nos. 92-95 (4)	3.05	2.05

"Neutral and Constitutional Laos." When the stamps are arranged in a block of four with 40k and 15k in first row and 10k and 20k in second row, the map of Laos appears.

Prince Vet and Wife Mathie — A32

Lao Women — A33

Scenes from Buddhist Legend of Phra Vet Sandone: 32k, God of the Skies sending his son to earth. 45k, Phaune's daughter with beggar husband. 55k, Beggar cornered by guard and dogs.

1964, Nov. 17 Photo. *Perf. 13x12½*

96	A32	10k multicolored	.50	.50
97	A32	32k multicolored	.75	.75
98	A32	45k multicolored	1.00	1.00
99	A32	55k multicolored	1.25	1.25
a.		Miniature sheet of 4	5.00	3.75
		Nos. 96-99 (4)	3.50	3.50

#99a contains 4 imperf. stamps similar to #96-99.

1964, Dec. 15 Engr. *Perf. 13*

100	A33	25k blk, org brn & pale ol	.75	.75
		Nos. 100,C43-C45 (4)	3.45	2.35

Butterflies A34

1965, Mar. 13 Unwmk. *Perf. 13*

Size: 36x36mm

101	A34	10k Cethosia biblis	2.00	1.00
102	A34	25k Precis cebrene	3.75	1.25

Size: 48x27mm

103	A34	40k Dysphania militaris	9.00	2.00
		Nos. 101-103,C46 (4)	19.25	6.25

Teacher and School, American Aid — A35

Designs: 25k, Woman at Wattay Airport, French aid, horiz. 45k, Woman bathing child and food basket, Japanese aid. 55k, Musicians broadcasting, British aid, horiz.

1965, Mar. 30 Engr. *Perf. 13*

104	A35	25k bl grn, brn & car rose	.45	.30
105	A35	45k ol grn & brn	.95	.50
106	A35	55k brt bl & bister	1.25	.65
107	A35	75k multicolored	1.75	.80
		Nos. 104-107 (4)	4.40	2.25

Issued to publicize foreign aid to Laos.

Hophabang Temple A36

1965, Apr. 23 Unwmk. *Perf. 13*

108	A36	10k multicolored	.65	.25

Telewriter, Map of Laos and Globe A37

30k, Communication by satellite & map of Laos. 50k, Globe, map of Laos & radio.

1965, June 15 Engr. *Perf. 13*

109	A37	5k vio bl, brn & red lil	.20	.20
110	A37	30k bl, org brn & sl grn	.65	.50
111	A37	50k crim, lt bl & bis	1.25	.90
a.		Miniature sheet of 3, #109-111	4.25	4.25
		Nos. 109-111 (3)	2.10	1.60

ITU, centenary.

Nos. 52-53 Surcharged in Dark Blue with New Value and Bars

1965, July 5 Unwmk. *Perf. 13*

112	A16	1k on 4k rose claret	.50	.30
113	A16	5k on 6.50k org red	.55	.35

Mother and Child, UNICEF and WHO Emblems — A38

Map of Laos and UN Emblem — A39

1965, Sept. 1 Engr. *Perf. 13*

114	A38	35k lt ultra & dk red	.85	.70
a.		Miniature sheet	4.50	4.50

Mother and Child Protection movement, 6th anniv.

1965, Nov. 3 *Perf. 12½x13*

115	A39	5k emer, gray & vio bl	.30	.25
116	A39	25k lil rose, gray & vio bl	.45	.35
117	A39	40k bl, gray & vio bl	.70	.50
		Nos. 115-117 (3)	1.45	1.10

UN, 20th anniv. Although first day covers were canceled "Oct. 24," the actual day of issue is reported to have been Nov. 3.

Tikhy (Hockey) A40

Pastimes: 10k, Two bulls fighting. 25k, Canoe race. 50k, Rocket festival.

1965, Dec. 23 *Perf. 13*

118	A40	10k org, brn & gray	.30	.25
119	A40	20k grn, ver & dk bl	.40	.30
120	A40	25k brt blue & multi	.40	.35
121	A40	50k orange & multi	.80	.50
		Nos. 118-121 (4)	1.90	1.40

Slaty-headed Parakeet — A41

Birds: 15k, White-crested laughing thrush. 20k, Osprey. 45k, Bengal roller.

1966, Feb. 10 Engr. *Perf. 13*

122	A41	5k car rose, ol & brn	.85	.50
123	A41	15k bluish grn, brn & blk	1.10	.60
124	A41	20k dl bl, sep & bister	1.60	1.00
125	A41	45k vio, Prus bl & sepia	4.50	2.40
		Nos. 122-125 (4)	8.05	4.50

WHO Headquarters, Geneva — A42

1966, May 3 Engr. *Perf. 13*

126	A42	10k bl grn & indigo	.25	.20
127	A42	25k car & dk green	.40	.30
128	A42	50k ultra & black	.75	.70
a.		Miniature sheet of 3, #126-128	17.50	17.50
		Nos. 126-128 (3)	1.40	1.20

Inauguration of the WHO Headquarters, Geneva. No. 128a sold for 150k.

Ordination of Buddhist Monk — A43

Folklore: 25k, Women building ceremonial sand hills. 30k, Procession of the Wax Pagoda, vert. 40k, Wrist-tying ceremony (3 men, 3 women), vert.

1966, May 20 *Perf. 13*

129	A43	10k multicolored	.30	.25
130	A43	25k multicolored	.45	.30
131	A43	30k multicolored	.75	.50
132	A43	40k multicolored	1.00	.70
		Nos. 129-132 (4)	2.50	1.75

UNESCO Emblem A44

1966, July 7 Engr. *Perf. 13*

133	A44	20k ocher & gray	.20	.20
134	A44	30k brt blue & gray	.40	.30
135	A44	40k brt green & gray	.55	.30
136	A44	60k crimson & gray	.75	.35
a.		Miniature sheet, #133-136	6.00	6.00
		Nos. 133-136 (4)	1.90	1.15

UNESCO, 20th anniv. No. 136a sold for 250k.

Addressed Envelope Carrier Pigeon, Globe and Hand with Quill Pen — A45

1966, Sept. 7 Engr. *Perf. 13*

137	A45	5k red, brn & bl	.25	.20
138	A45	20k bl grn, blk & lil	.45	.30
139	A45	40k bl, red brn & dk ol bister	.55	.35
140	A45	45k brt rose lil, bl grn & black	.75	.50
a.		Min. sheet of 4, #137-140	6.00	6.00
		Nos. 137-140 (4)	2.00	1.35

Intl. Letter Writing Week, Oct. 6-12. No. 140a sold for 250k.

Sculpture from Siprapouthbat Temple — A46

Sculptures: 20k, from Visoun Temple. 50k, from Xiengthong Temple. 70k, from Visoun Temple.

1967, Feb. 21 Engr. *Perf. 12½x13*

No.	Type	Description	Unused	Used
141	A46	5k olive grn & grn	.30	.25
142	A46	20k brn ol & gray bl	.70	.40
143	A46	50k dk brn & dp claret	1.25	.50
144	A46	70k dk brn & dk magenta	1.50	.80
		Nos. 141-144 (4)	3.75	1.95

General Post Office A47

1967, Apr. 6 Engr. *Perf. 13*

No.	Type	Description	Unused	Used
145	A47	25k brn, grn & vio brn	.35	.25
146	A47	50k ind, brt blue & grn	.55	.40
147	A47	70k dk red, grn & brn	1.25	.75
		Nos. 145-147 (3)	2.15	1.40

Inauguration of the new Post and Telegraph Headquarters.

Snakehead A48

Fish: 35k, Giant catfish. 45k, Spiny eel. 60k, Knifefish.

1967, June 8 Engr. *Perf. 13x12½*

No.	Type	Description	Unused	Used
148	A48	20k dl bl, bis & blk	1.25	.50
149	A48	35k aqua, bis & gray	1.50	.60
150	A48	45k pale grn, bis & ol brn	2.50	.70
151	A48	60k sl grn, bis & blk	3.75	.80
		Nos. 148-151 (4)	9.00	2.60

Drumstick Tree Flower — A49

Blossoms: 55k, Turmeric. 75k, Peacock flower. 80k, Pagoda tree.

1967, Aug. 10 Engr. *Perf. 12½x13*

No.	Type	Description	Unused	Used
152	A49	30k red lil, yel & grn	.60	.35
153	A49	55k org, mag & lt grn	.90	.45
154	A49	75k bl, red & lt grn	1.25	.65
155	A49	80k brt grn, mag & yel	1.50	.75
		Nos. 152-155 (4)	4.25	2.20

Banded Krait — A50

Reptiles: 40k, Marsh crocodile. 100k, Malayan moccasin. 200k, Water monitor.

1967, Dec. 7 Engr. *Perf. 13*

No.	Type	Description	Unused	Used
156	A50	5k emer, ind & yel	.60	.40
157	A50	40k sep, lt grn & yel	1.60	.80
158	A50	100k lt grn, brn & ocher	3.50	1.75
159	A50	200k grn, blk & bister	6.25	3.25
		Nos. 156-159 (4)	11.95	6.20

Human Rights Flame — A51

1968, Feb. 8 Engr. *Perf. 13*

No.	Type	Description	Unused	Used
160	A51	20k brt grn, red & grn	.30	.25
161	A51	30k brn, red & grn	.40	.30
162	A51	50k brt bl, red & grn	.80	.60
a.		Souv. sheet of 3, #160-162	5.00	5.00
		Nos. 160-162 (3)	1.50	1.15

Intl. Human Rights Year. #162a sold for 250k.

WHO Emblem — A52

1968, July 5 Engr. *Perf. 12½x13*

No.	Type	Description	Unused	Used
163	A52	15k rose vio, ver & ocher	.25	.20
164	A52	30k brt bl, brt grn & ocher	.25	.20
165	A52	70k ver, plum & ocher	.55	.40
166	A52	110k brn, brt rose lil & ocher	.90	.55
167	A52	250k brt grn, brt bl & ocher	2.40	1.50
a.		Souv. sheet of 5, #163-167	6.50	6.50
		Nos. 163-167 (5)	4.35	2.85

WHO, 20th anniv. No. 167a sold for 500k.

Parade and Memorial Arch — A53

Designs: 20k, Armored Corps with tanks. 60k, Three soldiers with Laotian flag.

1968, July 15 *Perf. 13*

No.	Type	Description	Unused	Used
168	A53	15k multicolored	.35	.25
169	A53	20k multicolored	.45	.35
170	A53	60k multicolored	.90	.45
		Nos. 168-170,C52-C53 (5)	5.80	3.15

Laotian Army. For souvenir sheet see No. C53a.

Chrysochroa Mnizechi — A54

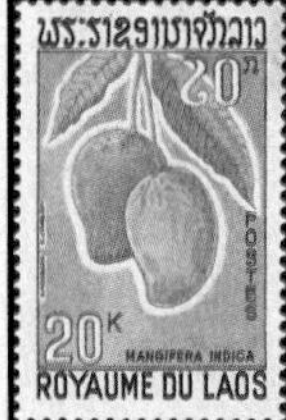

Mangoes — A55

Insects: 50k, Aristobia approximator. 90k, Eutaenia corbetti.

1968, Aug. 28 Engr. *Perf. 13*

No.	Type	Description	Unused	Used
171	A54	30k vio bl, grn & yel	.90	.35
172	A54	50k lil, blk & ocher	1.50	.50
173	A54	90k bis, blk & org	2.25	1.25
		Nos. 171-173,C54-C55 (5)	8.40	4.20

1968, Oct. 3 Engr. *Perf. 13*

Fruits: 50k, Tamarind. 180k, Jackfruit, horiz. 250k, Watermelon, horiz.

No.	Type	Description	Unused	Used
174	A55	20k ind, lt bl & emer	.40	.25
175	A55	50k lt bl, emer & brn	.70	.40
176	A55	180k sep, org & yel grn	2.00	1.10
177	A55	250k sep, bis & emer	2.75	1.60
		Nos. 174-177 (4)	5.85	3.35

Hurdling — A56

1968, Nov. 15 Engr. *Perf. 13*

No.	Type	Description	Unused	Used
178	A56	15k shown	.50	.50
179	A56	80k Tennis	1.00	.50
180	A56	100k Soccer	1.00	.50
181	A56	110k High jump	1.50	1.00
		Nos. 178-181 (4)	4.00	2.50

19th Olympic Games, Mexico City, 10/12-27.

Wedding of Kathanam and Nang Sida A57

Design: 200k, Thao Khathanam battling the serpent Ngou Xouang and the giant bird Phanga Houng. Design from panels of the central gate of Ongtu Temple, Vientiane. Design of 150k is from east gate.

1969, Feb. 28 Photo. *Perf. 12x13*

No.	Type	Description	Unused	Used
182	A57	150k blk, gold & red	2.00	1.25
183	A57	200k blk, gold & red	2.75	1.75

Soukhib Ordered to Attack — A58

Scenes from Royal Ballet: 15k, Pharak pleading for Nang Sita. 20k, Thotsakan reviewing his troops. 30k, Nang Sita awaiting punishment. 40k, Pharam inspecting troops. 60k, Hanuman preparing to rescue Nang Sita.

1969 Photo. *Perf. 14*

No.	Type	Description	Unused	Used
184	A58	10k multicolored	.40	.25
185	A58	15k blue & multi	.55	.40
186	A58	20k lt bl & multi	.65	.50
187	A58	30k salmon & multi	1.00	.55
188	A58	40k salmon & multi	1.40	.70
189	A58	60k pink & multi	2.00	1.10
		Nos. 184-189,C56-C57 (8)	14.25	8.50

For surcharges see #B12-B17, CB1-CB2.

ILO Emblem and Basket Weavers at Vientiane Vocational Center A59

1969, May 7 Engr. *Perf. 13*

No.	Type	Description	Unused	Used
190	A59	30k claret & violet	.45	.40
191	A59	60k slate grn & vio brn	1.00	.75
		Nos. 190-191,C58 (3)	6.20	4.40

ILO, 50th anniv.

Chinese Pangolin — A60

1969, Nov. 6 Photo. *Perf. 13x12*

No.	Type	Description	Unused	Used
192	A60	15k multicolored	.60	.25
193	A60	30k multicolored	1.00	.50
		Nos. 192-193,C59-C61 (5)	7.45	3.85

That Luang, Luang Prabang A61

King Sisavang-Vong — A62

1969, Nov. 19 Engr. *Perf. 13*

No.	Type	Description	Unused	Used
194	A61	50k dk brn, bl & bister	.80	.60
195	A62	70k maroon & buff	1.40	1.00
a.		Pair, #194-195 + label	3.00	3.00

Death of King Sisavang-Vong, 10th anniv.

Carved Capital from Wat Xiengthong A63

1970, Jan. 10 Photo. *Perf. 12x13*

No.	Type	Description	Unused	Used
196	A63	70k multicolored	1.75	1.25
		Nos. 196,C65-C66 (3)	5.15	2.90

Kongphene (Midday) Drum — A64

Designs: 55k, Kongthong (bronze) drum.

1970, Mar. 30 **Engr.** ***Perf. 13***
197 A64 30k bl gray, ol & org 1.00 .60
198 A64 55k ocher, blk & yel grn 1.75 1.35
Nos. 197-198,C67 (3) 5.75 3.45

Lenin Explaining Electrification Plan, by L. Shmatko — A65

1970, Apr. 22 **Litho.** ***Perf. 12½x12***
199 A65 30k blue & multi 1.10 .55
200 A65 70k rose red & multi 1.40 .75

Lenin (1870-1924), Russian communist leader.

Silk Weaver and EXPO Emblem A66

1970, July 7 **Engr.** ***Perf. 13***
201 A66 30k shown .50 .30
202 A66 70k Woman winding thread .90 .80
Nos. 201-202,C69 (3) 2.80 2.35

Laotian silk industry; EXPO '70 Intl. Exposition, Osaka, Japan, Mar. 15-Sept. 13.

Wild Boar A67

1970, Sept. 7 **Engr.** ***Perf. 13***
203 A67 20k green & dp brn .45 .25
204 A67 60k dp brn & ol bis .90 .45
Nos. 203-204,C70-C71 (4) 7.35 4.45

Buddha, UN Headquarters and Emblem — A68

1970, Oct. 24
Size: 22x36mm
205 A68 30k ultra, brn & rose red .60 .40
206 A68 70k brt grn, sep & vio .90 .60
Nos. 205-206,C75 (3) 3.25 2.10

UN, 25th anniv.

Nakhanet, Symbol of Arts and Culture — A69

1971, Feb. 5
207 A69 70k shown .90 .60
208 A69 85k Rahu swallowing the moon 1.10 .85
Nos. 207-208,C76 (3) 4.25 2.45

Silversmithing — A70

1971, Apr. 12 **Engr.** ***Perf. 13***
Size: 36x36mm
209 A70 30k shown .35 .25
210 A70 50k Pottery .55 .35
Size: 47x36mm
211 A70 70k Boat building 1.10 .40
Nos. 209-211 (3) 2.00 1.00

Laotian and African Children, UN Emblem — A71

60k, Women musicians, elephants, UN emblem.

1971, May 1 **Engr.** ***Perf. 13***
212 A71 30k lt grn, brn & blk .50 .30
213 A71 60k yel, pur & dull red 1.10 .50

Intl. year against racial discrimination.

Miss Rotary, Wat Ho Phrakeo — A72

Dendrobium Aggregatum A73

Design: 30k, Monk on roof of That Luang and Rotary emblem, horiz.

1971, June 28 **Engr.** ***Perf. 13***
214 A72 30k purple & ocher .60 .40
215 A72 70k gray ol, dk bl & rose 1.25 .55

Rotary International, 50th anniversary.

Perf. 12½x13, 13x12½
1971, July 7 **Photo.**
Size: 26x36, 36x26mm
216 A73 30k shown .75 .40
217 A73 50k Asocentrum ampullaceum, horiz. 1.30 .95
218 A73 70k Trichoglottis fasciata, horiz. 2.00 1.25
Nos. 216-218,C79 (4) 7.55 4.10

See Nos. 230-232, C89.

Palm Civet A74

Animals: 40k, like 25k. 50k, Lesser Malay chevrotain. 85k, Sika deer.

1971, Sept. 16 **Engr.** ***Perf. 13***
219 A74 25k pur, dk bl & blk .80 .45
220 A74 40k grn, ol bis & blk 1.00 .60
221 A74 50k brt grn & ocher 1.50 .70
222 A74 85k sl grn, grn & brn orange 2.50 1.25
Nos. 219-222,C83 (5) 10.05 5.75

Types of 1952-57 with Ornamental Panels and Inscriptions

Designs: 30k, Laotian woman. 40k, So player (like #C25). 50k, Rama (like #C19).

1971, Nov. 2
223 A3 30k brn vio & brn .45 .30
a. Souvenir sheet of 3 5.00 5.00
224 A10 40k sepia, blk & ver .55 .50
225 AP7 50k ultra, blk & salmon 1.00 .70
Nos. 223-225,C84 (4) 3.40 2.90

20th anniv. of Laotian independent postal service. All stamps inscribed: "Vingtième Anniversaire de la Philatélie Lao," "Postes" and "1971." No. 223a contains No. 223 and 60k and 85k in design of 30k, sold for 250k.

Children Learning to Read A75

1972, Jan. 30 **Engr.** ***Perf. 13***
Size: 36x22mm
226 A75 30k shown .25 .25
227 A75 70k Scribe writing on palm leaves .50 .50
Nos. 226-227,C87 (3) 1.75 1.75

Intl. Book Year.

Nam Ngum Hydroelectric Dam, Monument and ECAFE Emblem — A76

1972, Mar. 28 **Engr.** ***Perf. 13***
228 A76 40k grn, ultra & lt brn .30 .25
229 A76 80k grn, brn ol & dk bl .50 .40
Nos. 228-229,C88 (3) 1.60 1.45

25th anniv. of the Economic Commission for Asia and the Far East (ECAFE), which helped build the Nam Ngum Hydroelectric Dam.

Orchid Type of 1971

Orchids: 40k, Rynchostylis giganterum. 60k, Paphiopedilum exul. 80k, Cattleya, horiz.

1972, May 1 **Photo.** ***Perf. 13***
Size: 26x36mm, 36x26mm
230 A73 40k lt bl & multi .80 .35
231 A73 60k multicolored 1.40 .45
232 A73 80k lt bl & multi 1.75 .50
Nos. 230-232,C89 (4) 7.95 2.80

Woman Carrying Water, UNICEF Emblem — A77

Children's drawings: 80k, Child learning bamboo-weaving, UNICEF emblem.

1972, July 20 **Engr.** ***Perf. 13***
233 A77 50k blue & multi .60 .45
234 A77 80k brown & multi .80 .65
Nos. 233-234,C90 (3) 2.40 2.10

25th anniv. (in 1971) of UNICEF.

Attopeu Costume, Religious Ceremony — A78

Lion from Wat That Luang and Lions Emblem — A79

Design: 90k, Phongsaly festival costume.

1973, Feb. 16 **Engr.** ***Perf. 13***
235 A78 40k maroon & multi .45 .25
236 A78 90k multicolored 1.00 .50
Nos. 235-236,C101-C102 (4) 3.25 2.55

1973, Mar. 30 **Engr.** ***Perf. 13***
237 A79 40k vio bl, rose cl & lil .50 .25
238 A79 80k pur, org brn & yel .80 .40
Nos. 237-238,C103 (3) 2.55 1.40

Lions International of Laos.

Dr. Hansen, Map of Laos, "Dok Hak" Flowers — A80

1973, June 28 **Engr.** ***Perf. 13***
239 A80 40k multicolored .55 .30
240 A80 80k multicolored 1.00 .45

Centenary of the discovery by Dr. Armauer G. Hansen of the Hansen bacillus, the cause of leprosy.

Wat Vixun, Monk Blessing Girl Scouts — A81

1973, Sept. 1 **Engr.** ***Perf. 13***
241 A81 70k ocher & brown .60 .40
Nos. 241,C106-C107 (3) 2.15 1.10

25th anniv. of Laotian Scout Movement.

INTERPOL Headquarters — A82

1973, Dec. 22 Engr. *Perf. 13x12½*

242	A82	40k greenish bl	.25	.25
243	A82	80k brown	.65	.60
		Nos. 242-243,C110 (3)	2.00	1.45

Intl. Criminal Police Org., 50th anniv.

Boy Mailing Letter — A83

Eranthemum Nervosum — A84

1974, Apr. 30 Engr. *Perf. 13*

244	A83	70k bl, lt grn & ocher	.50	.25
245	A83	80k lt grn, bl & ocher	.60	.35
		Nos. 244-245,C114-C115 (4)	6.10	3.60

UPU, cent.

1974, May 31

Size: 26x36mm, 36x26mm

246	A84	30k grn & vio	.55	.40
247	A84	50k Water lilies, horiz.	.80	.50
248	A84	80k Scheffler's kapokier, horiz.	1.25	.75
		Nos. 246-248,C116 (4)	7.60	4.65

Mekong River Ferry — A85

90k, Samlo (passenger tricycle), vert.

1974, July 31 Engr. *Perf. 13*

249	A85	25k red brn & choc	.40	.40
250	A85	90k brown ol & lt ol	1.25	1.25
		Nos. 249-250,C117 (3)	4.15	3.15

Marconi, Indigenous Transmission Methods, Transistor Radio — A86

1974, Aug. 28 Engr. *Perf. 13*

251	A86	60k multicolored	.50	.50
252	A86	90k multicolored	.75	.75
		Nos. 251-252,C118 (3)	3.50	2.35

Guglielmo Marconi (1874-1937), Italian electrical engineer and inventor.

Diastocera Wallichi Tonkinensis A87

1974, Oct. 23 Engr. *Perf. 13*

253	A87	50k shown	.90	.60
254	A87	90k Macrochenus isabellunus	1.40	.85
255	A87	100k Purpuricenus malaccensis	1.75	.90
		Nos. 253-255,C119 (4)	5.80	3.35

Temple, Houeisai, and Sapphire A88

1975, Feb. 12 Engr. *Perf. 13x12½*

256	A88	100k bl, brn & grn	.80	.50
257	A88	110k Sapphire panning at Attopeu	1.25	.75

King Sisavang-Vong, Princes Souvanna Phouma and Souphanou-Vong — A89

1975, Feb. 21 Engr. *Perf. 13*

258	A89	80k olive & multi	.60	.40
259	A89	300k multicolored	1.25	.90
260	A89	420k multicolored	1.40	1.25
		Nos. 258-260 (3)	3.25	2.55

1st anniv. of Peace Treaty of Vientiane.

A souvenir sheet exists, embossed on paper with a foil application. Value, $10.

Fortuneteller Working on Forecast for New Year (Size of pair: 100x27mm) — A90

New Year Riding Rabbit, and Tiger (Old Year) — A92

Designs: 40k, Chart of New Year symbols. 200k, Fortune teller. 350k, As shown.

1975, Apr. 14 Engr. *Perf. 13*

261		40k bister & red brn	.50	.20
262		200k bis, red brn & sl	1.40	.80
a.		A90 Pair, #261-262	2.25	1.75
263	A92	350k blue & multi	2.50	1.60
		Nos. 261-263 (3)	4.40	2.60

New Year 1975, Year of the Rabbit.

UN Emblem, "Equality" — A93

200k, IWY emblem, man and woman.

1975, June 19 Engr.

264	A93	100k dl bl & vio bl	.40	.40
265	A93	200k multi	.85	.85
a.		Miniature sheet of 2, #264-265	4.50	4.50

International Women's Year.

UPU, Cent. — A93a

Designs: 15k, Runner, rocket reaching orbit, vert. 30k, Docked Soyuz capsules, chariot, vert. 40k, Biplane, Concorde. 1000k, Apollo spacecraft in orbit. 1500k, Apollo spacecraft, astronaut, vert. No. 266G, Mail truck, Concorde. No. 266H, Wagon train, Lunar Rover. No. 266I, Zeppelin, locomotive.

Perf. 13x14, 14x13

1975, July 7 Litho.

266	A93a	10k multicolored	.20	.20
266A	A93a	15k multicolored	.40	.20
266B	A93a	30k multicolored	.50	.20
266C	A93a	40k multicolored	.80	.25
266D	A93a	1000k multicolored	2.50	1.00
266E	A93a	1500k multicolored	4.00	1.50
		Nos. 266-266E (6)	8.40	3.35

Litho. & Embossed

Perf. 13½

266G	A93a	3000k gold & multi	—	

Souvenir Sheets

266H	A93a	2500k gold & multi	8.00	2.50
266I	A93a	3000k gold & multi	8.00	2.50

Nos. 266D-266E, 266G-266I are airmail.
Nos. 266-266I also exist imperf.

Apollo-Soyuz Mission — A93b

Designs: 125k, Astronauts, Thomas Stafford, Vance D. Brand, Donald Slayton. 150k, Cosmonauts Alexei Leonov, Valery Koubasov. 200k, Apollo-Soyuz link-up. 300k, Handshake in space. 450k, Preparation for re-entry. 700k, Apollo splashdown.

1975, July 7 Litho. *Perf. 14x13*

267	A93b	125k multicolored	.40	.20
267A	A93b	150k multicolored	.60	.20
267B	A93b	200k multicolored	1.00	.30
267C	A93b	300k multicolored	2.00	.75
267D	A93b	450k multicolored	2.75	.60
267E	A93b	700k multicolored	3.75	1.50
		Nos. 267-267E (6)	10.50	3.55

Nos. 267D-267E are airmail.
Nos. 267-267E also exist imperf.

Scene from Vet Sandone Legend — A94

Designs: Scenes from Buddhist legend of Prince Vet Sandone.

1975, July 22 Photo. *Perf. 13*

268	A94	80k multicolored	.65	.30
268A	A94	110k multicolored	.70	.40
268B	A94	120k multicolored	.90	.50
268C	A94	130k multicolored	1.50	.60
		Nos. 268-268C (4)	3.75	1.80

American Revolution, Bicent. — A94a

Presidents: 10k, Washington, J. Adams, Jefferson, Madison. 15k, Monroe, J.Q. Adams, Jackson, Van Buren. 40k, Harrison, Tyler, Polk, Taylor. 1000k, Truman, Eisenhower, Kennedy. 1500k, L. Johnson, Nixon, Ford.

1975, July 30 Litho. *Perf. 13½*

269	A94a	10k multicolored	—
269A	A94a	15k multicolored	—
269B	A94a	40k multicolored	—
269C	A94a	1000k multicolored	—
269D	A94a	1500k multicolored	—

Nos. 269C-269D are airmail. Stamps of similar design in denominations of 50k, 100k, 125k, 150k, and 200k exist but were not available in Laotian post offices. Value for set of 10, $60.

Buddha, Stupas of Borobudur — A95

Design: 200k, Borobudur sculptures and UNESCO emblem.

1975, Aug. 20 Engr. *Perf. 13*

270	A95	100k indigo & multi	.75	.40
271	A95	200k multicolored	1.40	.85
a.		Miniature sheet of 2, #270-271	2.50	2.50

UNESCO campaign to save Borobudur Temple, Java.

Coat of Arms of Republic — A96

Thathiang Pagoda, Vientiane — A97

1976, Dec. 2 Litho. *Perf. 14*

272	A96	1k blue & multi	.20	.20
273	A96	2k rose & multi	.20	.20
274	A96	5k brt grn & multi	.25	.20
275	A96	10k lilac & multi	.45	.40

276 A96 200k orange & multi 3.00 2.25
a. Min. sheet of 5, #272-276 7.50 7.50
Nos. 272-276 (5) 4.10 3.25

Miniature sheets of 1 exist. Value $50.
For overprints, see Nos. 426A, 426V, 508C, 676H.

1976, Dec. 18 ***Perf. 13½***

Designs: 2k, 80k, 100k, Phonsi Pagoda, Luang Prabang. 30k, 300k, like 1k.

277 A97 1k multicolored .20 .20
278 A97 2k multicolored .25 .20
279 A97 30k multicolored .75 .50
280 A97 80k multicolored 1.50 1.00
281 A97 100k multicolored 2.25 1.40
282 A97 300k multicolored 3.75 2.50
Nos. 277-282 (6) 8.70 5.80

Silversmith — A98

Perf. 13x12½, 12½x13
1977, Apr. 1 **Litho.**

283 A98 1k shown .20 .20
284 A98 2k Weaver .20 .20
285 A98 20k Potter .65 .25
286 A98 50k Basket weaver, vert. 1.25 .40
Nos. 283-286 (4) 2.30 1.05

Miniature sheets of 2 exist, perf. and imperf. Value $7.50, perf or imperf.
For overprints, see Nos. 426B, 426C, 426D, 426R, 676B.

Cosmonauts A.A. Gubarev, G.M. Grechko A99

Government Palace, Vientiane, Kremlin, Moscow — A100

20k, 50k, Lenin speaking on Red Square.

Perf. 12x12½, 12½x12
1977, Oct. 25 **Litho.**

287 A99 5k multicolored .20 .20
288 A99 20k multicolored .20 .20
289 A99 50k multicolored .50 .25
290 A99 60k multicolored .55 .40
291 A100 100k multicolored 1.00 .65
a. Souv. sheet of 3, #288, 290-291 4.50 4.50
292 A100 250k multicolored 2.25 1.50
a. Souv. sheet of 3, #287, 289, 292 5.00 5.00
Nos. 287-292 (6) 4.70 3.20

60th anniv. of Russian October Revolution.
For overprints, see Nos. 426F, 426N, 676C, 676F, 676I.

Natl. Arms — A101

A102

1978, May 26 **Litho.** ***Perf. 12½***

293 A101 5k dull org & blk .20 .20
294 A101 10k tan & black .20 .20
295 A101 50k brt pink & blk .50 .20
296 A101 100k yel grn & blk 1.00 .45
297 A101 250k violet & blk 2.00 .85
Nos. 293-297 (5) 3.90 1.90

For overprints, see Nos. 426G, 676J.

Perf. 12½x12¼, 12½x12¾
1978, Sept. 15 **Litho.**

Army Day: 20k, Soldiers with flag. 40k, Fighters and burning house, horiz. 300k, Anti-aircraft battery.

298 A102 20k multicolored .20 .20
299 A102 40k multicolored .25 .20
300 A102 300k multicolored 1.75 1.00
Nos. 298-300 (3) 2.20 1.40

For overprints see No. 426O, 426Q, 676A, 676L.

Marchers with Banner A103

1978, Dec. 2 **Litho.** ***Perf. 11½***

301 A103 20k shown .30 .20
302 A103 50k Women with flag .30 .20
303 A103 400k Dancer 2.25 1.40
a. Sheet of 3, #301-303, imperf. 4.25
Nos. 301-303 (3) 2.85 1.80

National Day. A second printing in slightly different colors and with rough perforation exists; values the same. Stamps in souvenir sheet are in reverse order.

Electronic Tree, Map of Laos, ITU Emblem — A104

Design: 250k, Electronic tree, map of Laos and broadcast tower.

1979, Jan. 18 **Litho.** ***Perf. 12½***

304 A104 30k multicolored .20 .20
305 A104 250k multicolored 1.50 .75

World Telecommunications Day, 1978.
For overprints, see Nos. 426P, 426W, 676K.

Woman Mailing Letter A105

10k, 80k, Processing mail. 100k, like 5k.

1979, Jan. 18

306 A105 5k multicolored .20 .20
307 A105 10k multicolored .20 .20
308 A105 80k multicolored .75 .30
309 A105 100k multicolored 1.00 .40
Nos. 306-309 (4) 2.15 1.10

Asian-Oceanic Postal Union, 15th anniv.
For overprints, see Nos. 426H, 426J, 426K, 426T, 426U, 676E, 676G.

Intl. Year of the Child A106

1979 **Litho.** ***Perf. 11***
Without Gum

310 A106 20k Playing with ball, vert. .25 .20
311 A106 50k Studying .40 .20
312 A106 100k Playing musical instruments .50 .35
313 A106 200k Breast-feeding, vert. 2.00 .65
314 A106 200k Map, globe, vert. 1.00 .65
315 A106 500k Immunization, vert. 5.25 1.50
316 A106 600k Girl dancing, vert. 3.00 1.50
Nos. 310-316 (7) 12.40 5.05

Issued: #310-311, 313, 315, 8/1; others, 12/25.
Imperf sheets of 4 containing #310-311, 313, 315 and of 3 containing #312, 314, 316 exist. Value for both sheets $25.

Traditional Modes of Transportation — A107

1979, Oct. 9 ***Perf. 12½x13***

317 A107 5k Elephants, buffalo, pirogues .20
318 A107 10k Buffalo, carts .20
319 A107 70k like 10k .60
320 A107 500k like 5k 2.50
Nos. 317-320 (4) 3.50

For overprints, see Nos. 426I, 426L, 426S, 676D.

5th Anniv. of the Republic — A108

1980, May 30 ***Perf. 11***

321 A108 30c Agriculture, vert. .20
322 A108 50c Education, health services .20
323 A108 1k Three women, vert. .60
324 A108 2k Hydroelectric energy 1.25
Nos. 321-324 (4) 2.25

Imperf. souvenir sheet of 4 exists. Value $10.

Lenin, 110th Birth Anniv. A109

1980, July 5 ***Perf. 12x12½, 12½x12***

325 A109 1k Lenin reading .25
326 A109 2k Writing .45
327 A109 3k Lenin, red flag, vert. .65
328 A109 4k Orating, vert. 1.10
Nos. 325-328 (4) 2.45

Imperf. souvenir sheet of 4 exists. Value $5.

From this point forward, all issues exist CTO and, unless otherwise noted, are worth 20% of the mint value.

5th Anniv. of the Republic — A110

1980, Dec. 2 ***Perf. 11***
Without Gum

329 A110 50c Threshing rice .20
330 A110 1.60k Logging .35
331 A110 4.60k Veterinary medicine .75
332 A110 5.40k Rice paddy 1.10
Nos. 329-332 (4) 2.40

Imperf. souvenir sheet of 4 exists. Value $10.

26th Communist Party (PCUS) Congress A111

1981, June 26 ***Perf. 12x12½***
Without Gum

333 A111 60c shown .20
334 A111 4.60k Globe, broken chains 1.50
335 A111 5.40k Grain, cracked bomb 2.00
a. Souv. sheet of 3, #333-335, imperf. 6.00
Nos. 333-335 (3) 3.70

No. 335a sold for 15k.

Souvenir Sheet

PHILATOKYO '81 — A112

1981, Sept. 20 ***Perf. 13***
Without Gum

336 A112 10k Pandas 5.50

1982 World Cup Soccer Championships, Spain — A113

Intl. Year of the Disabled A114

1981, Oct. 15 *Perf. 12½*

Without Gum

337 A113 1k Heading ball .20
338 A113 2k Dribble .40
339 A113 3k Kick .55
340 A113 4k Goal, horiz. .75
341 A113 5k Dribble, diff. 1.00
342 A113 6k Kick, diff. 1.40
Nos. 337-342 (6) 4.30

1981 *Perf. 13*

Without Gum

343 A114 3k Office worker 1.25
344 A114 5k Teacher 1.40
345 A114 12k Weaver, fishing net 3.50
Nos. 343-345 (3) 6.15

Wildcats — A115

1981 *Perf. 12½*

Without Gum

346 A115 10c Felis silvestris ornata .20
347 A115 20c Felis viverrinus .20
348 A115 30c Felis caracal .20
349 A115 40c Neofelis nebulosa .20
350 A115 50c Felis planiceps .20
351 A115 9k Felis chaus 3.50
Nos. 346-351 (6) 4.50

6th Anniv. of the Republic A116

1981, Dec. *Perf. 13*

Without Gum

352 A116 3k Satellite dish, flag .60
353 A116 4k Soldier, flag .75
354 A116 5k Map, flag, women, soldier 1.00
Nos. 352-354 (3) 2.35

Indian Elephants A117

1982, Jan. 23 *Perf. 12½x13*

Without Gum

355 A117 1k Head .20
356 A117 2k Carrying log in trunk .50
357 A117 3k Transporting people .65
358 A117 4k In trap .90
359 A117 5k Adult and young 1.25
360 A117 5.50k Herd 1.60
Nos. 355-360 (6) 5.10

Laotian Wrestling A118

Various moves.

1982, Jan. 30 *Perf. 13*

Without Gum

361 A118 50c multicolored .20
362 A118 1.20k multi, diff. .20
363 A118 2k multi, diff. .30
364 A118 2.50k multi, diff. .35
365 A118 4k multi, diff. .60
366 A118 5k multi, diff. 1.00
Nos. 361-366 (6) 2.65

Water Lilies A119

1982, Feb. 10 *Perf. 12½x13*

Without Gum

367 A119 30c Nymphaea zanzibariensis .20
368 A119 40c Nelumbo nucifera gaertn rose .20
369 A119 60c Nymphaea rosea .20
370 A119 3k Nymphaea nouchali .65
371 A119 4k Nymphaea white 1.00
372 A119 7k Nelumbo nucifera gaertn white 1.75
Nos. 367-372 (6) 4.00

Birds A120

1982, Mar. 9 *Perf. 13*

Without Gum

373 A120 50c Hirundo rustica, vert. .20
374 A120 1k Upupa epops, vert. .20
375 A120 2k Alcedo atthis, vert. .50
376 A120 3k Hypothymis azurea .65
377 A120 4k Motacilla cinerea 1.25
378 A120 10k Orthotomus sutorius 2.75
Nos. 373-378 (6) 5.55

A121

1982 World Cup Soccer Championships, Spain — A122

Various match scenes.

1982, Apr. 7

Without Gum

379 A121 1k multicolored .25
380 A121 2k multicolored .40
381 A121 3k multicolored .55
382 A121 4k multicolored .70
383 A121 5k multicolored 1.00
384 A121 6k multicolored 1.25
Nos. 379-384 (6) 4.15

Souvenir Sheet

385 A122 15k multicolored 4.00

Butterflies A123

1982, May 5 *Perf. 12½x13*

Without Gum

386 A123 1k Herona marathus .25
387 A123 2k Neptis paraka .60
388 A123 3k Euripus halitherses .75
389 A123 4k Lebadea martha 1.25

Size: 42x26mm

Perf. 12½

390 A123 5k Iton semamora 1.75

Size: 54x36½mm

Perf. 13x12½

391 A123 6k Elymnias hypermnestra 2.25
Nos. 386-391 (6) 6.85

Souvenir Sheet

PHILEXFRANCE '82 — A124

1982, June 9 *Perf. 13*

Without Gum

392 A124 10k Temple, Vientiane 2.75

River Vessels A125

1982, June 24

Without Gum

393 A125 50c Raft .20
394 A125 60c River punt .20
395 A125 1k Houseboat .20
396 A125 2k Passenger steamer .35
397 A125 3k Ferry .55
398 A125 8k Self-propelled barge 1.50
Nos. 393-398 (6) 3.00

Pagodas A126

1982, Aug. 2

Without Gum

399 A126 50c Chanh .20
400 A126 60c Inpeng .20
401 A126 1k Dong Mieng .20
402 A126 2k Ho Tay .35
403 A126 3k Ho Pha Keo .60
404 A126 8k Sisaket 1.60
Nos. 399-404 (6) 3.15

Dogs A127

1982, Oct. 13

Without Gum

405 A127 50c Poodle .20
406 A127 60c Samoyed .20
407 A127 1k Boston terrier .25
408 A127 2k Cairn terrier .40
409 A127 3k Chihuahua .75
410 A127 8k Bulldog 2.50
Nos. 405-410 (6) 4.30

World Food Day — A128

1982, Oct. 16

Without Gum

411 A128 7k Watering seedlings 1.75
412 A128 8k Planting rice 2.00

Classic Automobiles — A129

1982, Nov. 7

Without Gum

413 A129 50c 1925 Fiat .20
414 A129 60c 1925 Peugeot .20
415 A129 1k 1925 Berliet .20
416 A129 2k 1925 Ballot .40
417 A129 3k 1926 Renault .75
418 A129 8k 1925 Ford 2.00
Nos. 413-418 (6) 3.75

7th Anniv. of the Republic A130

1982, Dec. 2

Without Gum

419 A130 50c Kaysone Phomvihan, vert. .20
420 A130 1k Tractors, field, industry .20
421 A130 2k Cows, farm .45

422 A130 3k Truck, microwave dish .65
423 A130 4k Nurse, child, vert. .90
424 A130 5k Education 1.10
425 A130 6k Folk dancer, vert. 1.40
Nos. 419-425 (7) 4.90

Bulgarian Flag, Coat of Arms and George Dimitrov (1882-1949), Bulgarian Statesman — A131

1982, Dec. 15 ***Perf. 12½***

Without Gum

426 A131 10k multicolored 1.90

Nos. 272, 276, 283, 284, 286-288, 293, 298, 299, 304-309, 317-319 Overprinted in Red or Black

Methods and Perfs as before

1982

426A A96 1k multi 30.00
426B A98 1k multi (Bk) 10.00
a. "I" instead of "1" in overprint —
b. "à" instead of "2" in overprint —
c. Inverted "8n overprint —
426C A98 1k multi — —
a. "I" instead of "1" in overprint —
b. "9" in overprint omitted —
c. Inverted "8n overprint —
426D A98 2k multi — —
426F A99 5k multi 10.00
a. Double overprint —
426G A101 5k dull org & blk 10.00
426H A105 5k multi 10.00
a. Inverted "8" in overprint — —
b. Inverted "1" in overprint —
426I A107 5k multi 10.00
426J A105 10k multi (Bk) — —
a. Inverted "8" in overprint — —
b. Double overprint, one inverted —
426K A105 10k multi 10.00
426L A107 10k multi (Bk) 10.00
a. Inverted "8" in overprint — —
426N A99 20k multi 20.00
426O A102 20k multi 20.00
a. Small "2" in overprint — —
426P A104 30k multi 25.00
a. Small "2" in overprint —
426Q A102 40k multi 30.00
a. Inverted "8" in overprint — —
426R A98 50k multi 40.00
a. Inverted "8" in overprint — —
426S A107 70k multi 50.00
a. Inverted "8" in overprint — —
426T A105 80k multi (Bk) 60.00
a. Inverted "8" in overprint — —
426U A105 100k multi 75.00
a. Inverted "8" in overprint — —
426V A96 200k org & multi (Bk) 125.00
426W A104 250k multi (Bk) 150.00
a. Inverted "8n overprint —
b. Double overprint, one inverted —
Nos. 426A-426W (18) 695.00

Five additional stamps were issued in this set. The editors would like to examine any examples.

Constitution of the USSR, 60th Anniv. — A132

1982, Dec. 30

Without Gum

427 A132 3k Kremlin .65
428 A132 4k Maps .90

Souvenir Sheet

Perf. 13½x13

428A Sheet of 2 3.75
b. A132 5k like 3k 1.25
c. A132 10k like 4k 2.50

Nos. 428Ab-428Ac not inscribed in Laotian at top; buff and gold decorative margin contains the inscription.

1984 Summer Olympics, Los Angeles A133

1983, Jan. 25 ***Perf. 13***

Without Gum

429 A133 50c Hurdling .20
430 A133 1k Women's javelin .20
431 A133 2k Basketball .35
432 A133 3k Diving .55
433 A133 4k Gymnastics .75
434 A133 10k Weight lifting 2.10
Nos. 429-434 (6) 4.15

Souvenir Sheet

435 A133 15k Soccer 3.25

No. 435 contains one stamp 32x40mm.

Horses A134

Various breeds.

1983, Feb. 1

Without Gum

436 A134 50c multicolored .20
437 A134 1k multi, diff. .25
438 A134 2k multi, diff. .40
439 A134 3k multi, diff. .65
440 A134 4k multi, diff. .80
441 A134 10k multi, diff. 2.75
Nos. 436-441 (6) 5.05

A135

Raphael, 500th Birth Anniv. — A136

Paintings (details) by Raphael: 50c, St. Catherine of Alexandra, Natl. Gallery, London. 1k, Adoration of the Kings (spectators), Vatican. 2k, Granduca Madonna, Pitti Gallery, Florence. 3k, St. George and the Dragon, The Louvre, Paris. 4k, Vision of Ezekiel, Pitti Gallery. 10k, Adoration of the Kings (Holy Family), Vatican. No. 448, Coronation of the Virgin, Vatican.

1983, Mar. 9 ***Perf. 12½x13***

Without Gum

442 A135 50c multicolored .20
443 A135 1k multicolored .20
444 A135 2k multicolored .35
445 A135 3k multicolored .60
446 A135 4k multicolored .75
447 A135 10k multicolored 2.50
Nos. 442-447 (6) 4.60

Souvenir Sheet

Perf. 13x13½

448 A136 10k multicolored 2.50

INTERCOSMOS Space Cooperation Program — A137

Cosmonaut and flags of USSR and participating nations.

1983, Apr. 12 ***Perf. 12½***

449 A137 50c Czechoslovakia .20
450 A137 50c Poland .20
451 A137 1k East Germany .25
452 A137 1k Bulgaria .25
453 A137 2k Hungary .40
454 A137 3k Mongolia .65
455 A137 4k Romania .80
456 A137 6k Cuba 1.25
457 A137 10k France 2.25
Nos. 449-457 (9) 6.25

Souvenir Sheet

Perf. 13½x13

458 A137 10k Vietnam 2.75

No. 458 contains one stamp 32x40mm.

A138

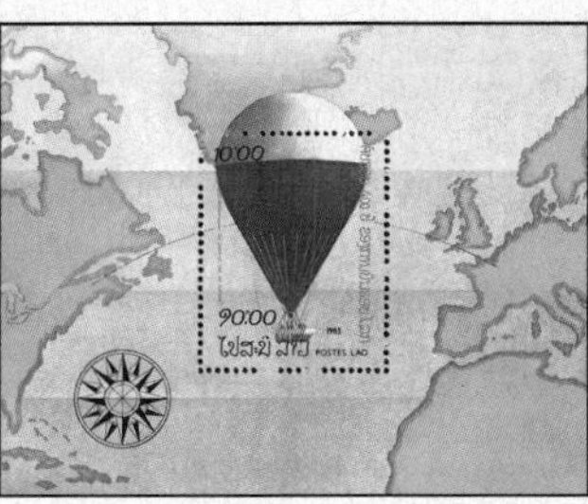

First Manned Balloon Flight, Bicent. — A139

Various balloons.

1983, May 4 ***Perf. 12½x13***

459 A138 50c shown .20
460 A138 1k multi, diff. .20
461 A138 2k multi, diff. .35
462 A138 3k multi, diff. .50
463 A138 4k multi, diff. .65
464 A138 10k multi, diff. 2.25
Nos. 459-464 (6) 4.15

Souvenir Sheet

Perf. 13½x13

465 A139 10k shown 2.40

Souvenir Sheet

TEMBAL '83, Basel — A140

1983, May 21 ***Perf. 13x13½***

Without Gum

466 A140 10k German Maybach 3.00

Flora A141

1983, June 10 ***Perf. 13***

Without Gum

467 A141 1k Dendrobium sp. .25
468 A141 2k Aerides odoratum .40
469 A141 3k Dendrobium aggregatum .60
470 A141 4k Dendrobium .75
471 A141 5k Moschatum 1.10
472 A141 6k Dendrobium sp., diff. 1.40
Nos. 467-472 (6) 4.50

1984 Winter Olympics, Sarajevo — A142

1983, July 2

Without Gum

473 A142 50c Downhill skiing .20
474 A142 1k Slalom .25
475 A142 2k Ice hockey .40
476 A142 3k Speed skating .70
477 A142 4k Ski jumping .85
478 A142 10k Luge 2.25
Nos. 473-478 (6) 4.65

Souvenir Sheet

Perf. 13x13½

479 A142 15k 2-Man bobsled 3.50

No. 479 contains one 40x32mm stamp.

Souvenir Sheet

BANGKOK '83 — A143

1983, Aug. 4 *Perf. 13½x13*

480 A143 10k Boats on river 2.25

Mekong River Fish — A144

1983, Sept. 5 *Perf. 12½*

Without Gum

481 A144 1k Notopterus chitala .25
482 A144 2k Cyprinus carpio .40
483 A144 3k Pangasius sp. .65
484 A144 4k Catlocarpio siamensis .75
485 A144 5k Morulius sp. 1.10
486 A144 6k Tilapia nilotica 1.50
Nos. 481-486 (6) 4.65

Explorers and Their Ships — A145

1983, Oct. 8 *Perf. 13x12½*

Without Gum

487 A145 1k Victoria, Magellan .25
488 A145 2k Grand Hermine, Cartier .40
489 A145 3k Santa Maria, Columbus .65
490 A145 4k Cabral and caravel .75
491 A145 5k Endeavor, Capt. Cook 1.10
492 A145 6k Pourquoi-Pas, Charcot 1.50
Nos. 487-492 (6) 4.65

No. 492 incorrectly inscribed "CABOT."

Domestic Cats A146

1983, Nov. 9 *Perf. 12½x13*

Without Gum

493 A146 1k Tabby .25
494 A146 2k Long-haired Persian .60
495 A146 3k Siamese .75
496 A146 4k Burmese .85
497 A146 5k Persian 1.25
498 A146 6k Tortoiseshell 1.75
Nos. 493-498 (6) 5.45

Karl Marx (1818-1883) — A147

1983, Nov. 30 *Perf. 13*

Without Gum

499 A147 1k shown .25
500 A147 4k Marx, 3 flags, diff., vert. 1.00
501 A147 6k Marx, flag of Laos 1.60
Nos. 499-501 (3) 2.85

8th Anniv. of the Republic — A148

1983, Dec. 2 *Perf. 12½x13, 13x12½*

Without Gum

502 A148 1k Elephant dragging log, vert. .25
503 A148 4k Oxen, pig 1.00
504 A148 6k Produce, vert. 1.60
Nos. 502-504 (3) 2.85

World Communications Year — A149

1983, Dec. 15 *Perf. 13*

505 A149 50c Teletype .20
506 A149 1k Telephone .20
507 A149 4k Television .65
508 A149 6k Satellite, dish receiver 1.00
Nos. 505-508 (4) 2.05

Nos. 275, 306 Overprinted in Red

1983 **Method and Perf. As Before**

508B A105 5k multi — —
508C A96 10k lilac & multi

Additional stamps were issued in this set. The editors would like to examine any examples.

1984 Winter Olympics, Sarajevo — A150

1984, Jan. 16

509 A150 50c Women's figure skating .20
510 A150 1k Speed skating .25
511 A150 2k Biathlon .40
512 A150 4k Luge .80
513 A150 5k Downhill skiing 1.00
514 A150 6k Ski jumping 1.25
515 A150 7k Slalom 1.50
Nos. 509-515 (7) 5.40

Souvenir Sheet

Perf. 13½x13

516 A150 10k Ice hockey 2.25

Nos. 509-511, 514-515 vert. No. 516 contains one stamp 32x40mm.

World Wildlife Fund A151

Panthera tigris.

1984, Feb. 1 *Perf. 13*

517 A151 25c Adult, vert. *.50*
518 A151 25c shown *.50*
519 A151 3k Nursing cubs *5.00*
520 A151 4k Two cubs, vert. *8.00*
Nos. 517-520 (4) *14.00*

1984 Summer Olympics, Los Angeles A152

Gold medals awarded during previous games, and athletes. 50c, Athens 1896, women's diving. 1k, Paris 1900, women's volleyball. 2k, St. Louis 1904, running. 4k, London 1908, basketball. 5k, Stockholm 1912, judo. 6k, Antwerp 1920, soccer. 7k, Paris 1924, gymnastics. 10k, Moscow 1980, wrestling.

1984, Mar 26

521 A152 50c multicolored .20
522 A152 1k multicolored .25
523 A152 2k multicolored .60
524 A152 4k multicolored 1.10
525 A152 5k multicolored 1.25
526 A152 6k multicolored 1.60
527 A152 7k multicolored 1.90
Nos. 521-527 (7) 6.90

Souvenir Sheet

Perf. 12½

528 A152 10k multicolored 2.75

No. 528 contains one stamp 32x40mm.

Musical Instruments — A153

1984, Mar. 27 *Perf. 13*

529 A153 1k Tuned drums .25
530 A153 2k Xylophone .40
531 A153 3k Pair of drums .65
532 A153 4k Hand drum .90
533 A153 5k Barrel drum 1.10
534 A153 6k Pipes, string instrument 1.25
Nos. 529-534 (6) 4.55

Natl. Day — A154

Chess A155

1984, Mar. 30 *Perf. 12½*

535 A154 60c Natl. flag .25
536 A154 1k Natl. arms .40
537 A154 2k like 1k .60
Nos. 535-537 (3) 1.25

1984, Apr. 14 *Perf. 12½x13*

Illustrations of various medieval and Renaissance chess games.

538 A155 50c multi .20
539 A155 1k multi, diff. .25
540 A155 2k multi, red brn board, diff. .50
541 A155 2k multi, blk board, diff. .50
542 A155 3k multi, diff. .70
543 A155 4k multi, diff. 1.25
544 A155 8k multi, diff. 2.25
a. Souv. sheet of 6, #538-540, 542-544, with gutter between 6.00
Nos. 538-544 (7) 5.65

Souvenir Sheet

Perf. 13½x13

545 A155 10k Royal game, human chessmen 2.75

World Chess Federation, 60th anniv. No. 545 contains one stamp 32x40mm.

ESPANA '84, Madrid — A156

Woodland Flowers — A157

Paintings: 50c, Cardinal Nino de Guevara, by El Greco. 1k, Gaspar de Guzman, Duke of Olivares, on Horseback, byVelazquez. No. 548, The Annunciation, by Murillo. No. 549, Portrait of a Lady, by Francisco de Zurburan (1598-1664). 3k, The Family of Charles IV, by Goya. 4k, Two Harlequins, by Picasso. 8k, Abstract, by Miro. 10k, Burial of the Count of Orgaz, by El Greco.

1984, Apr. 27 *Perf. 12½*

546 A156 50c multicolored .20
547 A156 1k multicolored .25
548 A156 2k multicolored .45
549 A156 2k multicolored .45
550 A156 3k multicolored .65
551 A156 4k multicolored .90
552 A156 8k multicolored 1.75
Nos. 546-552 (7) 4.65

Souvenir Sheet

Perf. 13½x13

553 A156 10k multicolored 2.75

No. 553 contains one stamp 32x40mm.

1984, May 11 *Perf. 13*

554 A157 50c Adonis aestivalis .20
555 A157 1k Alpinia speciosa .25
556 A157 2k Aeschynanthus speciosus .45
557 A157 2k Cassia lechenaultiana .45
558 A157 3k Datura meteloides .65
559 A157 4k Quamoclit pennata .90

560 A157 8k Commelina benghalensis 1.75
Nos. 554-560 (7) 4.65

A158

19th UPU Congress, Hamburg — A159

Classic sport and race cars.

1984, June 19
561 A158 50c Nazzaro .20
562 A158 1k Daimler .20
563 A158 2k Delage .35
564 A158 2k Fiat S 57/14B .35
565 A158 3k Bugatti .50
566 A158 4k Itala .65
567 A158 8k Blitzen Benz 1.40
Nos. 561-567 (7) 3.65

Souvenir Sheet
Perf. 12½
568 A159 10k Winton Bullet 1.90

Paintings by Correggio (1494-1534) A160

Designs: 50c, Madonna and Child (Holy Family). 1k, Madonna and Child (spectators). No. 571, Madonna and Child (Holy Family, diff.). No. 572, Mystical Marriage of St. Catherine (Catherine, child, two women). 3k, The Four Saints. 4k, Noli Me Tangere. 8k, Christ Bids Farewell to the Virgin Mary. 10k, Madonna and Child, diff.

1984, June 26 ***Perf. 13***
569 A160 50c multicolored .20
570 A160 1k multicolored .25
571 A160 2k multicolored .45
572 A160 2k multicolored .45
573 A160 3k multicolored .65
574 A160 4k multicolored .75
575 A160 8k multicolored 1.40
Nos. 569-575 (7) 4.15

Souvenir Sheet
Perf. 13½x13
576 A160 10k multicolored 3.25

No. 576 contains one stamp 32x40mm.

Space Exploration A161

1984, July 12 ***Perf. 13***
577 A161 50c Luna 1 .20
578 A161 1k Luna 2 .20
579 A161 2k Luna 3 .30
580 A161 2k Sputnik 2, Kepler, horiz. .30
581 A161 3k Lunokhod 2, Newton, horiz. .45
582 A161 4k Luna 13, Jules Verne, horiz. .65
583 A161 8k Space station, Copernicus, horiz. 1.10
Nos. 577-583 (7) 3.20

Reptiles A162

1984, Aug. 20
584 A162 50c Malaclemys terrapin .20
585 A162 1k Bungarus fasciatus .25
586 A162 2k Python reticulatus .40
587 A162 2k Python molurus, vert. .40
588 A162 3k Gekko gecko .75
589 A162 4k Natrix subminiata 1.00
590 A162 8k Eublepharis macularius 1.90
Nos. 584-590 (7) 4.90

Marsupials — A163

1984, Sept. 21
591 A163 50c Schoinobates volans .20
592 A163 1k Ornithorhynchus anatinus .25
593 A163 2k Sarcophilus harrisii .40
594 A163 2k Lasiorhinus latifrons .40
595 A163 3k Thylacinus cynocephalus .75
596 A163 4k Dasyurops maculatus 1.00
597 A163 8k Wallabia isabelinus 1.90
Nos. 591-597 (7) 4.90

Souvenir Sheet
Perf. 12½
598 A163 10k Macropus rufus 2.75

AUSIPEX '84, Melbourne. No. 598 contains one stamp 32x40mm.

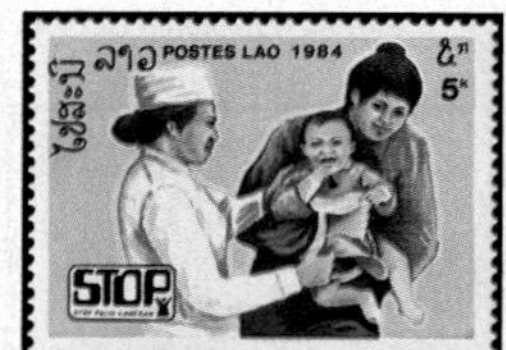
Stop Polio Campaign — A164

1984, Sept. 29 ***Perf. 13***
599 A164 5k shown .85
600 A164 6k Vaccinating child 1.00

Art A165

1984, Oct. 26
601 A165 50c Dragon (hand rail) .20
602 A165 1k Capital .20
603 A165 2k Oval panel .35
604 A165 2k Deity .35
605 A165 3k Leaves .55
606 A165 4k Floral pattern .65
607 A165 8k Lotus flower (round panel) 1.40
Nos. 601-607 (7) 3.70

Nos. 601-604 and 607 vert.

9th Anniv. of the Republic — A166

1984, Dec. 17
608 A166 1k River boats .20
609 A166 2k Aircraft .45
610 A166 4k Bridge building .90
611 A166 10k Surveying, construction 2.25
Nos. 608-611 (4) 3.80

1986 World Cup Soccer Championships, Mexico — A167

Various match scenes and flag of Mexico.

1985, Jan. 18
612 A167 50c multicolored .20
613 A167 1k multi, diff. .25
614 A167 2k multi, diff. .50
615 A167 3k multi, diff. .65
616 A167 4k multi, diff. .85
617 A167 5k multi, diff. 1.10
618 A167 6k multi, diff. 1.40
Nos. 612-618 (7) 4.95

Souvenir Sheet
Perf. 12½
619 A167 10k multi, diff. 2.25

No. 619 contains one stamp 32x40mm.

Motorcycle, Cent. — A168

1985, Feb. 25 ***Perf. 12½***
620 A168 50c shown .20
621 A168 1k 1920 Gnome Rhone .20
622 A168 2k 1928 F.N. M67C .35
623 A168 3k 1930 Indian Chief .50
624 A168 4k 1914 Rudge Multi .65
625 A168 5k 1953 Honda Benly J .85
626 A168 6k 1938 CZ 1.00
Nos. 620-626 (7) 3.75

Mushrooms — A169

Lenin, 115th Birth Anniv. — A170

1985, Apr. 8 ***Perf. 13***
627 A169 50c Amanita muscaria .20
628 A169 1k Boletus edulis .25
629 A169 2k Coprinus comatus .50
630 A169 2k Amanita rubescens .50
631 A169 3k Xerocomus subtomentosus .75
632 A169 4k Lepiota procera 1.00
633 A169 8k Paxillus involutus 2.00
Nos. 627-633 (7) 5.20

End of World War II, 40th Anniv. A169a

1k, Battle of Kursk. 2k, Red Army parade, Moscow. 4k, Battle of Stalingrad. 5k, Battle for Berlin. 6k, Victory parade through Brandenburg Gate.

1985, May **Litho.** ***Perf. 12½x12***
633A A169a 1k multicolored .30
633B A169a 2k multicolored .65
633C A169a 4k multicolored 1.10
633D A169a 5k multicolored 1.50
633E A169a 6k multicolored 2.00
Nos. 633A-633E (5) 5.55

1985, June 28 ***Perf. 12½***
634 A170 1k Reading Pravda, horiz. .25
635 A170 2k shown .55
636 A170 10k Addressing revolutionaries 1.75
Nos. 634-636 (3) 2.55

Orchids — A171

Fauna — A172

1985, July 5 ***Perf. 13***
637 A171 50c Cattleya percivaliana .20
638 A171 1k Odontoglossum luteo-purpureum .25
639 A171 2k Cattleya luedemanniana .45
640 A171 2k Maxillaria sanderiana .45
641 A171 3k Miltonia vexillaria .70
642 A171 4k Oncidium varicosum 1.00
643 A171 8k Cattleya dowiana aurea 2.25
Nos. 637-643 (7) 5.30

Souvenir Sheet
Perf. 13½x13
644 A171 10k Catasetum fimbriatum 2.75

ARGENTINA '85, Buenos Aires. No. 644 contains one stamp 32x40mm.

1985, Aug. 15 ***Perf. 13***
645 A172 2k Macaca mulatta .35
646 A172 3k Bos sauveli .55
647 A172 4k Hystrix leucura, horiz. .80
648 A172 5k Selenarctos thibotanus, horiz. 1.00
649 A172 10k Manis pentadactyla 2.00
Nos. 645-649 (5) 4.70

Apollo-Soyuz Flight, 10th Anniv. — A173

1985, Sept. 6

650 A173 50c Apollo launch pad, vert. .20
651 A173 1k Soyuz launch pad, vert. .20
652 A173 2k Apollo approaching Soyuz .40
653 A173 2k Soyuz approaching Apollo .65
654 A173 3k Apollo, astronauts .80
655 A173 4k Soyuz, cosmonauts 1.00
656 A173 8k Docked spacecrafts 1.60
Nos. 650-656 (7) 4.85

Aircraft A174

1985, Oct. 25

657 A174 50c Fiat .20
658 A174 1k Cant z.501 .20
659 A174 2k MF-5 .40
660 A174 3k Macchi Castoldi .65
661 A174 4k Anzani .80
662 A174 5k Ambrosini 1.00
663 A174 6k Piaggio 1.10
Nos. 657-663 (7) 4.35

Souvenir Sheet

Perf. 13x13½

664 A174 10k MF-4 4.50

ITALIA '85, Rome. No. 664 contains one stamp 40x32mm.

Miniature Sheet

Columbus's Fleet — A175

1985, Oct. 25 ***Perf. 13***

665 Sheet of 5 + 4 labels 2.75
a. A175 1k Pinta .20
b. A175 2k Nina .30
c. A175 3k Santa Maria .50
d. A175 4k Columbus .65
e. A175 5k Map of 1st voyage .80

ITALIA '85.

UN, 40th Anniv. — A176

Health — A177

1985, Oct.

666 A176 2k UN and natl. flag .55
667 A176 3k Coats of arms .80
668 A176 10k Map, globe 2.50
Nos. 666-668 (3) 3.85

1985, Nov. 15

669 A177 1k Mother feeding child .20
670 A177 3k Immunization, horiz. .50
671 A177 4k Hospital care, horiz. .65
672 A177 10k Breast-feeding 1.75
Nos. 669-672 (4) 3.10

10th Anniv. of the Republic A178

1985, Dec. 2

673 A178 3k shown .65
674 A178 10k multi, diff. 2.00

People's Revolutionary Party, 30th Anniv. — A179

1985, Dec. 30

675 A179 2k shown .55
676 A179 8k multi, diff. 1.90

Nos. 276, 286, 289, 291-292, 297, 299-300, 305, 308-309, 319 Overprinted in Red

Methods and Perfs As Before

1985

676A A102 40k multi 10.00
m. Inverted "8n overprint —
676B A98 50k multi 10.00
n. Inverted overprint —
o. "1895" instead of "1985" —
676C A99 50k multi 10.00
676D A107 70k multi 10.00
676E A105 80k multi 20.00
676F A100 100k multi 20.00
676G A105 100k multi 20.00
676H A96 200k org & multi 40.00
676I A100 250k multi 50.00
676J A101 250k vio & blk
676K A104 250k multi 100.00
p. Inverted overprint —
676L A102 300k multi 100.00
Nos. 676A-676L (11) 390.00

1986 World Cup Soccer Championships, Mexico — A180

Flowering Plants — A181

Various match scenes.

1986, Jan. 20

677 A180 50c multicolored .20
678 A180 1k multi, diff. .25
679 A180 2k multi, diff. .40
680 A180 3k multi, diff. .50
681 A180 4k multi, diff. .70
682 A180 5k multi, diff. .80
683 A180 6k multi, diff. 1.10
Nos. 677-683 (7) 3.95

Souvenir Sheet

Perf. 13x13½

684 A180 10k multi, diff. 2.00

No. 684 contains one stamp 40x32mm.

27th Congress of the Communist Party of the Soviet Union A180a

1986, Jan. **Litho.** ***Perf. 12x12½***

684A A180a 4k Cosmonaut, spacecraft 1.00
684B A180a 20k Lenin 4.25

1986, Feb. 28 ***Perf. 13***

685 A181 50c Pelargonium grandiflorum .20
686 A181 1k Aquilegia vulgaris .25
687 A181 2k Fuchsia globosa .45
688 A181 3k Crocus aureus .65
689 A181 4k Althaea rosea .80
690 A181 5k Gladiolus purpureo 1.00
691 A181 6k Hyacinthus orientalis 1.25
Nos. 685-691 (7) 4.60

Butterflies A182

1986, Mar. 30

692 A182 50c Aporia hippia .20
693 A182 1k Euthalia irrubescens .25
694 A182 2k Japonica lutea .45
695 A182 3k Pratapa ctesia .65
696 A182 4k Kallina inachus .80
697 A182 5k Ixias pyrene 1.00
698 A182 6k Parantica sita 1.25
Nos. 692-698 (7) 4.60

A183

First Man in Space, 25th Anniv. — A184

Designs: 50c, Launch, Baikonur Space Center, vert. 1k, Interkosmos communications satellite, vert. 2k, Salyut space station. 3k, Yuri Gagarin, Sputnik 1 disengaging stage. 4k, Luna 3, the Moon, vert. 5k, Komarov on first space walk, vert. 6k, Luna 16 lifting off Moon, vert. 10k, Spacecrafts docking.

1986, Apr. 12

699 A183 50c multicolored .20
700 A183 1k multicolored .25
701 A183 2k multicolored .40
702 A183 3k multicolored .65
703 A183 4k multicolored .80
704 A183 5k multicolored 1.00
705 A183 6k multicolored 1.10
Nos. 699-705 (7) 4.40

Souvenir Sheet

Perf. 13x13½

706 A184 10k multicolored 2.50

Fauna — A185

1986, May 22 ***Perf. 12½x13, 13x12½***

707 A185 50c Giraffa camelopardalis .20
708 A185 1k Panthera leo .25
709 A185 2k Loxodonta africana africana .40
710 A185 3k Macropus rufus .70
711 A185 4k Gymnobelideus leadbeateri 1.00
712 A185 5k Phoenicopterus ruber 1.25
713 A185 6k Ailuropoda melanoleucus 1.50
Nos. 707-713 (7) 5.30

Souvenir Sheet

Perf. 13½x13

714 A185 10k Bison, vert. 3.00

Nos. 707-712 vert.

No. 714 has the Ameripex '86 stamp exhibition logo in the margin.

Pheasants — A187

1986, June 29 ***Perf. 12½x13***

715 A187 50c Argusianus argus .20
716 A187 1k Cennaeus nycthemerus .25
717 A187 2k Phasianus colchicus .45
718 A187 3k Chrysolophus amherstiae .60
719 A187 4k Symaticus reevesii .80
720 A187 5k Chrysolophus pictus 1.00
721 A187 6k Syrmaticus soemmerringii 1.25
Nos. 715-721 (7) 4.55

Snakes — A188

1986, July 21 ***Perf. 12½x13, 13x12½***

722 A188 50c Elaphe guttata .20
723 A188 1k Thalerophis richardi .30
724 A188 1k Lampropeltis doliata annulata .35
725 A188 2k Diadophis amabilis .40
726 A188 4k Boiga dendrophila .70
727 A188 5k Python molurus 1.00
728 A188 8k Naja naja 1.25
Nos. 722-728 (7) 4.20

Nos. 722-723 and 728 vert.

Halley's Comet — A189

50c, Acropolis, Athens. #730a, 1k, Bayeux Tapestry. #730b, 2k, Edmond Halley. #731a, 3k, Vega space probe. #731b, 4k, Galileo. #732a, 5k, Comet. #732b, 6k, Giotto probe.

1986, Aug. 22 ***Perf. 12½x13***

729 A189 50c multi .20
730 A189 Pair, #a.-b. .75
731 A189 Pair, #a.-b. 1.25
732 A189 Pair, #a.-b. 2.25
Nos. 729-732 (4) 4.45

Souvenir Sheet

Perf. 13x13½

733 A189 10k Comet, diff. 2.50

#730-732 printed in continuous designs. Sizes of #730a, 731a, 732a: 46x25mm; #730b, 731b, 732b; 23x25mm. #733 contains one 40x32mm stamp.

Dogs — A190

Cacti — A191

1986, Aug. 28 ***Perf. 13***

737 A190 50c Keeshond .20
738 A190 1k Elkhound .25
739 A190 2k Bernese .45
740 A190 3k Pointing griffon .65
741 A190 4k Sheep dog (border collie) .85
742 A190 5k Irish water spaniel 1.00
743 A190 6k Briard 1.25
Nos. 737-743 (7) 4.65

Souvenir Sheet

Perf. 13x13½

744 A190 10k Brittany spaniels 2.10

STOCKHOLMIA '86. Nos. 738-743 horiz. No. 744 contains one 40x32mm stamp.

1986, Sept. 28 ***Perf. 13***

Designs: 50c, Mammillaria matudae. 1k, Mammillaria theresae. 2k, Ariocarpus trigonus. 3k, Notocactus crassigibbus. 4k, Astrophytum asterias hybridum. 5k, Melocactus manzanus. 6k, Astrophytum ornatum hybridum.

745 A191 50c multicolored .20
746 A191 1k multicolored .25
747 A191 2k multicolored .40
748 A191 3k multicolored .65
749 A191 4k multicolored .80
750 A191 5k multicolored 1.00
751 A191 6k multicolored 1.10
Nos. 745-751 (7) 4.40

Intl. Peace Year — A192

UNESCO Programs in Laos — A193

1986, Oct. 24

752 A192 3k Natl. arms, dove, globe .75
753 A192 5k Dove, shattered bomb 1.10
754 A192 10k Emblem held aloft 2.25
Nos. 752-754 (3) 4.10

1986, Nov. 4

755 A193 3k Vat Phu Champasak ruins .60
756 A193 4k Satellite dish, map, globe .85
757 A193 9k Laotians learning to read, horiz. 1.60
Nos. 755-757 (3) 3.05

1988 Winter Olympics, Calgary — A194

1987, Jan. 14

758 A194 50c Speed skating .20
759 A194 1k Biathlon .25
760 A194 2k Pairs figure skating .40
761 A194 3k Luge .60
762 A194 4k 4-Man bobsled .75
763 A194 5k Ice hockey 1.00
764 A194 6k Ski jumping 1.10
Nos. 758-764 (7) 4.30

Souvenir Sheet

Perf. 13½x13

765 A194 10k Slalom 2.25

Nos. 758-760 vert. No. 765 contains one stamp 32x40mm.

1988 Summer Olympics, Seoul — A195

1987, Feb. 2 ***Perf. 12½x13, 13x13½***

766 A195 50c Women's gymnastics .20
767 A195 1k Women's discus .25
768 A195 2k Running .40
769 A195 3k Equestrian .65
770 A195 4k Women's javelin .75
771 A195 5k High jump 1.00
772 A195 6k Wrestling 1.10
Nos. 766-772 (7) 4.35

Souvenir Sheet

Perf. 12½

773 A195 10k Runners leaving start 2.00

Nos. 766, 768, 770 and 772 vert. No. 773 contains one 40x32mm stamp.

Dogs A196

1987, Mar. 5 ***Perf. 12½x13***

774 A196 50c Great Dane .20
775 A196 1k Labrador retriever .25
776 A196 2k St. Bernard .40
777 A196 3k Schippercke .65
778 A196 4k Alsatian (German shepherd) .75
779 A196 5k Beagle 1.00
780 A196 6k Spaniel 1.25
Nos. 774-780 (7) 4.50

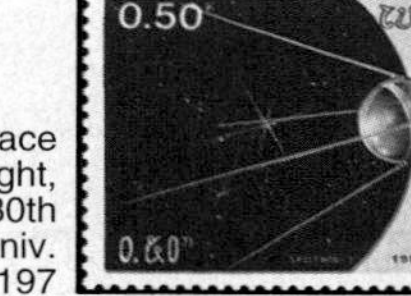

Space Flight, 30th Anniv. A197

1987, Apr. 12 ***Perf. 13***

781 A197 50c Sputnik 1 .20
782 A197 1k Sputnik 2 .25
783 A197 2k Cosmos 87 .40
784 A197 3k Cosmos .50
785 A197 4k Mars .65
786 A197 5k Luna 1 .80
787 A197 9k Luna 3, vert. 1.25
Nos. 781-787 (7) 4.05

Packet Ships and Stampless Packet Letters — A198

Canada No. 282 — A199

1987, May 12

788 A198 50c "Montreal" .20
789 A198 1k "Paid Montreal" .25
790 A198 2k "Paid" and "Montreal Nov 24" .35
791 A198 3k "Williamsbvrg" and "Forwarded" .55
792 A198 4k "Montreal Fe 18 1844" .75
793 A198 5k "Paid" and "Montreal Jy 10 1848" .85
794 A198 6k "Paid" and "Montreal Paid Ap 16 1861 Canada" 1.10
Nos. 788-794 (7) 4.05

Souvenir Sheet

Perf. 12½

795 A199 10k multicolored 2.50

CAPEX '87.

Orchids — A200

1987, Aug. 10 **Litho.** ***Perf. 13***

796 A200 3k *Vanda teres* .20
796A A200 7k *Laeliocattleya* .25
796B A200 10k *Paphiopedilum hibrido* .40
796C A200 39k *Sobralia* .75
796D A200 44k *Paphiopedilum hibrido*, diff. .80
796E A200 47k *Paphiopedilum hibrido*, diff. 1.00
796F A200 50k *Cattleya trianaei* 1.10
Nos. 796-796F (7) 4.50

Souvenir Sheet

Perf. 12½

796G A200 95k *Vanda tricolor* 2.25

No. 796G contains one 32x40mm stamp.

Automobiles — A201

1987, July 2 **Litho.** ***Perf. 12½***

797 A201 50c Toyota 480 .20
798 A201 1k Alfa 33 .25
799 A201 2k Ford Fiesta .40
800 A201 3k Datsun .65
801 A201 4k Vauxhall Cavalier .80
802 A201 5k Renault 5 1.00
803 A201 6k Rover-800 1.25
Nos. 797-803 (7) 4.55

Miniature Sheet

Perf. 13

804 A201 10k Talbot 2.10

HAFNIA '87, Denmark A202

Various Indian elephants.

1987, Sept. 2 ***Perf. 13***

805 A202 50c Adult, calf .20
806 A202 1k Two adults, calf .25
807 A202 2k Adult eating grass .40
808 A202 3k Adult, diff. .60
809 A202 4k Adult, calf drinking .75
810 A202 5k Adult, diff. .90
811 A202 6k Adult, vert. 1.10
Nos. 805-811 (7) 4.20

Souvenir Sheet

812 A202 10k Herd, diff. 2.25

No. 812 contains one stamp 40x32mm.

Horses — A203

Perf. 13x12½, 12½x13

1987, June 3 **Litho.**

813 A203 50c multicolored .20
814 A203 1k multi, diff. .25
815 A203 2k multi, diff. .40
816 A203 3k multi, diff. .60
817 A203 4k multi, diff. .75
818 A203 5k multi, diff. 1.00
819 A203 6k multi, diff. 1.10
Nos. 813-819 (7) 4.30

Nos. 814-819 vert.

Fish A204

Designs: 3k, Botia macracantha. 7k, Oxymocanthus longirostris. 10k, Adioryx caudimaculatus. 39k, Synchiropus splendidus. 44k, Cephalopolis miniatus. 47k, Dendrochirus zebra. 50k, Pomacantus semicirculatus.

1987, Oct. 14 **Litho.** *Perf. 13x12½*

820 A204 3k multicolored .20
821 A204 7k multicolored .25
822 A204 10k multicolored .40
823 A204 39k multicolored .70
824 A204 44k multicolored .80
825 A204 47k multicolored 1.00
826 A204 50k multicolored 1.10
Nos. 820-826 (7) 4.45

World Food Day A205

1987, Oct. 16 *Perf. 13*

827 A205 1k Tending crops .20
828 A205 3k Harvesting corn, vert. .25
829 A205 5k Harvesting wheat .30
830 A205 63k Youths, fish, vert. 1.25
831 A205 142k Tending pigs, chickens 2.40
Nos. 827-831 (5) 4.40

Cultivation of Rice in Mountainous Regions — A206

1987, Nov. 9 *Perf. 13*

832 A206 64k Tilling soil 1.25
833 A206 100k Rice paddy 1.90

October Revolution, Russia, 70th Anniv. A207

Paintings: 1k, Wounded soldier on battlefield. 2k, Mother and child. 4k, Storming the Winter Palace. 8k, Lenin and revolutionaries. 10k, Rebuilding Red Square.

1987, Nov. *Perf. 12x12½*

834 A207 1k multicolored .20
835 A207 2k multicolored .40
836 A207 4k multicolored .70
837 A207 8k multicolored 1.25
838 A207 10k multicolored 1.75
Nos. 834-838 (5) 4.30

Women Wearing Regional Costumes A208

1987, Dec. 2

839 A208 7k Mountain .20
840 A208 38k Urban .80
841 A208 144k Mountain, diff. 2.75
Nos. 839-841 (3) 3.75

A209

1988 Winter Olympics, Calgary — A210

1988, Jan.10 *Perf. 13x12½*

842 A209 1k Bobsled .20
843 A209 4k Biathlon .25
844 A209 20k Skiing .45
845 A209 42k Ice hockey .75
846 A209 63k Speed skating 1.10
847 A209 70k Slalom 1.25
Nos. 842-847 (6) 4.00

Souvenir Sheet

Perf. 13

848 A210 95k Slalom, diff. 2.25

No. 848 contains one stamp 40x32mm.

ESSEN '88 — A211

Locomotives: 6k, Nonpareil, vert. 15k, Rocket, vert. 20k, Royal George. 25k, Trevithick. 30k, Novelty. 100k, Tom Thumb. 95k, Locomotion.

1988 *Perf. 12½x13, 13x12½*

849 A211 6k multicolored .20
850 A211 15k multicolored .25
851 A211 20k multicolored .45
852 A211 25k multicolored .55
853 A211 30k multicolored .65
854 A211 100k multicolored 1.90
Nos. 849-854 (6) 4.00

Souvenir Sheet

Perf. 13

855 A211 95k multicolored 2.25

No. 855 contains one stamp 40x32mm.

Intl. Year of Shelter for the Homeless — A212

1988 **Litho.** *Perf. 13*

856 A212 1k Building frame of house .20
857 A212 27k Cutting lumber .55
858 A212 46k Completed house 1.00
859 A212 70k Community 1.60
Nos. 856-859 (4) 3.35

Dinosaurs — A213

Perf. 13x12½, 12½x13

1988, Mar. 3 **Litho.**

860 A213 3k Tyrannosaurus .20
861 A213 7k Ceratosaurus nasicornis .25
862 A213 39k Iguanodon bernissartensis .75
863 A213 44k Scolosaurus .80
864 A213 47k Phororhacus 1.00
865 A213 50k Trachodon 1.10
Nos. 860-865 (6) 4.10

Souvenir Sheet

Perf. 12½

866 A213 95k Pteranodon 2.25

JUVALUX '88. Nos. 861-864 vert.
Identifications on Nos. 860 and No. 865 are switched.
No. 866 contains one 40x32mm stamp.

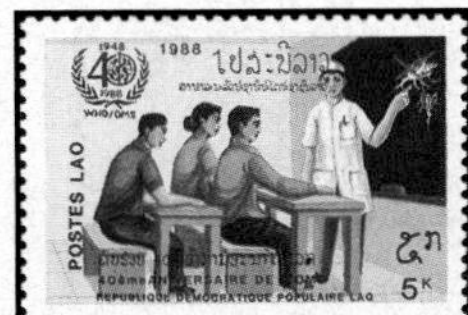

WHO, 40th Anniv. A214

1988, Apr. 8 *Perf. 12½*

867 A214 5k Students, teacher .20
868 A214 27k Pest control .50
869 A214 164k Public water supply, vert. 3.00
Nos. 867-869 (3) 3.70

Flowers — A215

Birds — A216

1988 *Perf. 13x12½*

870 A215 8k *Plumieria rubra* .20
871 A215 9k *Althaea rosea* .25
872 A215 15k *Ixora coccinea* .40
873 A215 33k *Cassia fistula* .75
874 A215 64k *Dahlia coccinea* (pink) 1.25
875 A215 69k *Dahlia coccinea* (yellow) 1.50
Nos. 870-875 (6) 4.35

Souvenir Sheet

Perf. 13

876 A215 95k Plumieria, Althaea, Ixora 2.50

FINLANDIA '88. No. 876 contains one 32x40mm stamp.

1988 *Perf. 13*

877 A216 6k *Pelargopsis capensis* .20
878 A216 10k *Coturnix japonica* .25
879 A216 13k *Psittacula roseata* .40
880 A216 44k *Treron bicincta* .85
881 A216 63k *Pycnonotus melanicterus* 1.10
882 A216 64k *Ducula badia* 1.10
Nos. 877-882 (6) 3.90

1988 Summer Olympics, Seoul — A217

1988 *Perf. 12½x12*

883 A217 2k Javelin .20
884 A217 5k Long jump .25
885 A217 10k Horizontal bar .40
886 A217 12k Canoeing .50
887 A217 38k Balance beam .80
888 A217 46k Fencing 1.00
889 A217 100k Wrestling 2.00
Nos. 883-889 (7) 5.15

Souvenir Sheet

Perf. 13

889A A217 95k Horizontal bar, diff. 2.10

No. 889A contains one 40x32mm stamp.

Decorative Stencils — A218

1988 *Perf. 13*

890 A218 1k Scarf .20
891 A218 2k Pagoda entrance, vert. .25
892 A218 3k Pagoda wall, vert. .35
893 A218 25k Pagoda pillar .50
894 A218 163k Skirt 3.00
Nos. 890-894 (5) 4.30

Completion of the 5-Year Plan (1981-85) — A219

1988 **Litho.** *Perf. 13*

895 A219 20k Health care .40
896 A219 40k Literacy .80
897 A219 50k Irrigation 1.00
898 A219 100k Communication, transport 1.75
Nos. 895-898 (4) 3.95

Intl. Red Cross and Red Crescent Organizations, 125th Annivs. — A220

Designs: 4k, Dove, 3 stylized figures representing mankind, vert. 52k, Giving aid to the handicapped, vert. 144k, Child immunization.

1988

899 A220 4k multi .20
900 A220 52k multi 1.10
901 A220 144k multi 2.75
Nos. 899-901 (3) 4.05

Chess Champions — A220a

1988 **Litho.** *Perf. 13*

901A A220a 1k R. Segura .20
901B A220a 2k Adolph Anderssen .20
901C A220a 3k P. Morphy .20
901D A220a 6k W. Steinitz .25
901E A220a 7k E. Lasker .30
901F A220a 12k J.R. Capablanca .40
901G A220a 172k A. Alekhine 3.00
Nos. 901A-901G (7) 4.55

Nos. 901C is incorrectly inscribed "Murphy."

1990 World Cup Soccer Championships, Italy — A221

Various plays.

1989 *Perf. 13x12½*

902 A221 10k multi .20
903 A221 15k multi, diff. .25
904 A221 20k multi, diff. .40
905 A221 25k multi, diff. .55
906 A221 45k multi, diff. .80
907 A221 105k multi, diff. 2.00
Nos. 902-907 (6) 4.20

Souvenir Sheet
Perf. 13

907A A221 95k multi, diff. 2.10

No. 907A contains one 40x32mm stamp.

INDIA '89 A222

Cats.

1989, Jan. 7 *Perf. 12½*

908 A222 5k multi .20
909 A222 6k multi, diff. .25
910 A222 10k multi, diff. .40
911 A222 20k multi, diff. .60
912 A222 50k multi, diff. 1.10
913 A222 172k multi, diff. 3.25
Nos. 908-913 (6) 5.80

Souvenir Sheet
Perf. 13

914 A222 95k multi, diff. 2.10

No. 914 contains one 32x40mm stamp.

1992 Winter Olympics, Albertville — A223

Various figure skaters.

1989, May 1 *Perf. 13*

915 A223 9k multi, vert. .20
916 A223 10k shown .25
917 A223 15k multi, diff., vert. .35
918 A223 24k multi, diff., vert. .50
919 A223 29k multi, diff., vert. .65
920 A223 114k multi, diff., vert. 2.00
Nos. 915-920 (6) 3.95

Souvenir Sheet
Perf. 12½

921 A223 95k Pairs figure skating 2.10

No. 921 contains one 32x40mm stamp.

People's Army, 40th Anniv. A224

1989, Jan. 20 *Perf. 13*

922 A224 1k shown .20
923 A224 2k Military school, vert. .20
924 A224 3k Health care .20
925 A224 250k Ready for combat 6.00
Nos. 922-925 (4) 6.60

1992 Summer Olympics, Barcelona — A225

Perf. 12x12½, 12½x12

1989, June 1 **Litho.**

926 A225 5k Pole vault, vert. .20
927 A225 15k Gymnastic rings, vert. .20
928 A225 20k Cycling .30
929 A225 25k Boxing .40
930 A225 70k Archery, vert. 1.10
931 A225 120k Swimming, vert. 1.75
Nos. 926-932 (7) 6.05

Souvenir Sheet
Perf. 13

932 A225 95k Baseball 2.10

No. 932 contains one 32x40mm stamp.

PHILEXFRANCE '89 — A226

Paintings by Picasso: 5k, *Beggars by the Edge of the Sea.* 7k, *Maternity.* 8k, *Portrait of Jaime S. Le Bock.* 9k, *Harlequins.*95k, *Spanish Woman from Majorca.* 105k, *Dog with Boy.* 114k, *Girl Balancing on Ball.*
95k *Woman in Hat.*

1989, July 17 *Perf. 12½x13*

933 A226 5k multi .20
934 A226 7k multi .25
935 A226 8k multi .25
936 A226 9k multi .35
937 A226 105k multi 1.75
938 A226 114k multi 2.00
Nos. 933-938 (6) 4.80

Souvenir Sheet
Perf. 12½

939 A226 95k shown 2.10

No. 939 contains one 32x40mm stamp.

Cuban Revolution, 30th Anniv. — A227

1989, Apr. 20 **Litho.** *Perf. 13*

940 A227 45k shown 1.10
941 A227 50k Flags 1.25

Fight the Destruction of Forests — A228

1989, Mar. 30 **Litho.** *Perf. 13*

942 A228 4k Planting saplings .20
943 A228 10k Fight forest fires .25
944 A228 12k Do not chop down trees .25
945 A228 200k Map of woodland 3.25
Nos. 942-945 (4) 3.95

Nos. 944-945 are vert.

Jawaharlal Nehru (1889-1964), Indian Statesman A229

1989, Nov. 9 **Litho.** *Perf. 12½*

946 A229 1k multicolored .20
947 A229 60k multi, horiz. 1.10
948 A229 200k multi, diff. 3.50
Nos. 946-948 (3) 4.80

Mani Ikara Zapota — A230

A231

1989, Sept. 18 *Perf. 12½x13*

949 A230 5k shown .20
950 A230 20k Psidium guajava .40
951 A230 20k Annona sguamosa .40
952 A230 30k Durio zibethinus .55
953 A230 50k Punica granatum .90
954 A230 172k Moridica charautia 3.00
Nos. 949-954 (6) 5.45

1989, Oct. 19 **Litho.** *Perf. 12½*

Historic Monuments: No. 955, That Sikhotabong, Khammouane. No. 956, That Dam, Vientiane. No. 957, That Ing Hang, Savannakhet. No. 958, Ho Vay Phra Thatluang, Vientiane.

955 A231 5k multicolored .20
956 A231 15k multicolored .30
957 A231 61k multicolored 1.10
958 A231 161k multicolored 2.75
Nos. 955-958 (4) 4.35

1992 Summer Olympics, Barcelona A232

1990, Mar. 5 **Litho.** *Perf. 12½x13*

959 A232 10k Basketball .20
960 A232 30k Hurdles .45
961 A232 45k High jump .65
962 A232 50k Cycling .75
963 A232 60k Javelin .90
964 A232 90k Tennis 1.40
Nos. 959-964 (6) 4.35

Souvenir Sheet

965 A232 95k Rhythmic gymnastics 2.00

1992 Winter Olympics, Albertville — A233

1990, June 20 *Perf. 13*

966	A233	10k	Speed skating	.20
967	A233	25k	Cross country skiing, vert.	.40
968	A233	30k	Slalom skiing	.45
969	A233	35k	Luge	.55
970	A233	80k	Ice dancing, vert.	1.25
971	A233	90k	Biathlon	1.40
			Nos. 966-971 (6)	4.25

Souvenir Sheet

972	A233	95k	Hockey, vert.	2.00

New Zealand Birds A234

Designs: 10k, Prosthemadera novaeseelandie. 15k, Alauda arvensis. 20k, Haemotopus unicolor. 50k, Phalacrocorax carbo. 60k, Demigretta sacra. 100k Apteryx australis mantelli. 95k, Phalacrocorax corunculatus.

1990, Aug. 24 *Perf. 12½*

973	A234	10k	multicolored	.20
974	A234	15k	multicolored	.35
975	A234	20k	multicolored	.45
976	A234	50k	multicolored	.90
977	A234	60k	multicolored	1.10
978	A234	100k	multicolored	1.90
			Nos. 973-978 (6)	4.90

Souvenir Sheet

979	A234	95k	multicolored	2.25

World Stamp Expo, New Zealand '90. No. 979 contains one 32x40mm stamp.

That Luang Temple, 430th Anniv. A235

1990, July 25 *Perf. 13x12½, 12½x13*

980	A235	60k	1867	1.10
981	A235	70k	1930	1.25
982	A235	130k	1990, vert.	2.40
			Nos. 980-982 (3)	4.75

Ho Chi Minh (1890-1969), Vietnamese Leader — A236

1990, May 11 *Perf. 13*

983	A236	40k	Addressing people	.60
984	A236	60k	With Laotian President	.90
985	A236	160k	Waving, vert.	2.50
			Nos. 983-985 (3)	4.00

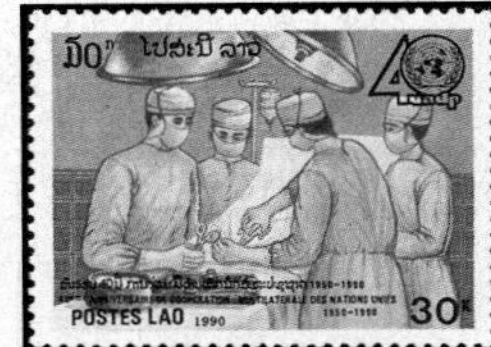

UN Development Program, 40th Anniv. — A237

1990, Oct. 24 **Litho.** *Perf. 13*

986	A237	30k	Surgeons	.50
987	A237	45k	Fishermen	.70
988	A237	80k	Flight controller, vert.	1.40
989	A237	90k	Power plant	1.50
			Nos. 986-989 (4)	4.10

15th Anniv. of the Republic A238

Designs: 15k, Placing flowers at monument. 20k, Celebratory parade. 80k, Visiting sick. 120k, Women marching with banner.

1990, Dec. 2 **Litho.** *Perf. 13*

990	A238	15k	multicolored	.30
991	A238	20k	multicolored	.40
992	A238	80k	multicolored	1.60
993	A238	120k	multicolored	2.50
			Nos. 990-993 (4)	4.80

New Year's Day A239

1990, Nov. 20

994	A239	5k	shown	.20
995	A239	10k	Parade	.30
996	A239	50k	Ceremony	.90

Size: 40x29mm

997	A239	150k	Ceremony, diff.	2.50
			Nos. 994-997 (4)	3.90

World Cup Soccer Championships, Italy — A240

Designs: Various soccer players in action.

1990 **Litho.** *Perf. 13*

998	A240	10k	multicolored	.25
999	A240	15k	multicolored	.30
1000	A240	20k	multicolored	.45
1001	A240	25k	multicolored	.55
1002	A240	45k	multicolored	.85
1003	A240	105k	multicolored	1.90
			Nos. 998-1003 (6)	4.30

Souvenir Sheets

Perf. 12½

1004	A240	95k	multi, horiz.	2.00

Perf. 13

1004A	A240	95k	multi	2.00

No. 1004 contains one 39x31mm stamp; No. 1004A one 32x40mm stamp.

Intl. Literacy Year A241

1990, Feb. 27 **Litho.** *Perf. 12½*

1005	A241	10k	shown	.35
1006	A241	50k	Woman with child, vert.	1.60
1007	A241	60k	Monk teaching class	2.00
1008	A241	150k	Two women, man reading	4.75
			Nos. 1005-1008 (4)	8.70

Stamp World London '90 — A242

Stamps, modes of mail transport: 15k, Great Britain #1, stagecoach. 20k, US #1, train. 40k, France #3, balloons. 50k, Sardinia #1, post rider. 60k, Indo-China #3, elephant. 95k, Laos #272, jet. 100k, Spain #1, sailing ship.

1990, Apr. 26 **Litho.** *Perf. 13x12½*

1009	A242	15k	multicolored	.25
1010	A242	20k	multicolroed	.40
1011	A242	40k	multicolored	.70
1012	A242	50k	multicolored	1.00
1013	A242	60k	multicolored	1.10
1014	A242	100k	multicolored	1.90
			Nos. 1009-1014 (6)	5.35

Souvenir Sheet

Perf. 13

1015	A242	95k	multicolored	2.00

No. 1015 contains one 40x32mm stamp.

Endangered Animals — A242a

1990, Sept. 15 **Litho.** *Perf. 12½*

1015A	A242a	10k	Brow-antlered deer	.25
1015B	A242a	20k	Gaur	.40
1015C	A242a	40k	Wild water buffalo	.70
1015D	A242a	45k	Kouprey	.75
1015E	A242a	120k	Javan rhinoceros	1.75
			Nos. 1015A-1015E (5)	3.85

A243

1992 Olympics, Barcelona and Albertville — A244

Perf. 12½x12, 12x12½, 13 (A244)

1991, Jan. 25

1016	A243	22k	2-man canoe	.20
1017	A243	32k	1-man kayak	.20
1018	A244	32k	Bobsled, vert.	.20
1019	A244	135k	Cross country skiing	.25
1020	A244	250k	Ski jumping	.55
1021	A244	275k	Biathlon	.60
1022	A243	285k	Diving, vert.	.65
1023	A243	330k	Sailing, vert.	.70
1024	A244	900k	Speed skating	1.90
1025	A243	1000k	Swimming	2.00
			Nos. 1016-1025 (10)	7.25

Souvenir Sheets

Perf. 12½, 13½x13

1026	A243	700k	2-man kayak	2.00
1027	A244	700k	Slalom skiing, vert.	2.00

No. 1026 contains one 40x32mm stamp. No. 1027 contains one 32x40mm stamp.

Tourism — A245

Designs: 155k, Rapids, Champassak. 220k, Vangvieng. 235k, Waterfalls, Saravane, vert. 1000k Plain of Jars, Xieng Khouang, vert.

1991 *Perf. 13x12½, 12½x13*

1028	A245	155k	multicolored	.45
1029	A245	220k	multicolored	.60
1030	A245	235k	multicolored	.70
1031	A245	1000k	multicolored	2.25
			Nos. 1028-1031 (4)	4.00

1994 World Cup Soccer Championships — A246

Designs: Various players in action.

1991 **Litho.** *Perf. 13*

1032	A246	32k	multicolored	.20
1033	A246	330k	multicolored	.75
1034	A246	340k	multi, vert.	.85
1035	A246	400k	multicolored	1.00
1036	A246	500k	multicolored	1.25
			Nos. 1032-1036 (5)	4.05

Souvenir Sheet

Perf. 13½x13

1037	A246	700k	multi, vert.	2.00

No. 1037 contains one 32x40mm stamp.

Espamer '91, Buenos Aires — A247

Espamer '91 Type

1991, June 30 **Litho.** *Perf. 12½x12*

1038	A247	25k	Mallard 4-4-2	.20
1039	A247	32k	Pacific 231 4-6-2	.25
1040	A247	285k	American style 4-8-4	.90
1041	A247	650k	Canadian Pacific 4-6-2	2.00
1042	A247	750k	Beyer-Garrant 4-8-2 2-8-4	2.25
			Nos. 1038-1042 (5)	5.60

Souvenir Sheet

Perf. 12½

1043	A247	700k	Inter-city diesel	2.00

Espamer '91, Buenos Aires. No. 1039 does not show denomination or country in Latin characters. Size of Nos. 1038, 1040-1042: 44x28mm.

Musical Celebrations — A248

Designs: 220k, Man playing mong, vert. 275k, Man, woman singing Siphandone, vert. 545k, Man, woman singing Khapngum. 690k, People dancing.

1991, July 10 Litho. *Perf. 13*

1044 A248 20k multicolored .20
1045 A248 220k multicolored .55
1046 A248 275k multicolored .75
1047 A248 545k multicolored 1.25
1048 A248 690k multicolored 1.75
Nos. 1044-1048 (5) 4.50

Butterflies — A248a

1991, Oct. 15 Litho. *Perf. 12½x12*

1048A A248a 55k Sasakia charonda .25
1048B A248a 90k Luendorfia puziloi .30
1048C A248a 255k Papilio bianor .90
1048D A248a 285k Papilio machaon 1.00
1048E A248a 900k Graphium doson 2.50
Nos. 1048A-1048E (5) 4.95

Souvenir Sheet

Perf. 13

1048F A248a 700k Cyrestis thyodamas 3.25

No. 1048F contains one 40x32mm stamp. Phila Nippon '91.

Arbor Day A249

700k, 6 people planting trees. 800k, Nursery.

1991, June 1 *Perf. 12½*

1049 A249 250k multicolored .70
1050 A249 700k multicolored 1.60
1051 A249 800k multicolored 2.00
Nos. 1049-1051 (3) 4.30

1992 Winter Olympics, Albertville A250

Perf. 12½x12, 12x12½

1992, Jan. 12 Litho.

1052 A250 200k Bobsled .50
1053 A250 220k Skiing .60
1054 A250 250k Skiing, horiz. .70
1055 A250 500k Luge 1.25
1056 A250 600k Figure skater 1.50
Nos. 1052-1056 (5) 4.55

Souvenir Sheet

Perf. 12½

1057 A250 700k Speed skater 2.00

No. 1057 contains one 32x40mm stamp.

1992 Summer Olympics, Barcelona A251

1992, Feb. 21 Litho. *Perf. 12½*

1058 A251 32k Women's running .20
1059 A251 245k Baseball .70
1060 A251 275k Tennis .80
1061 A251 285k Basketball .90
1062 A251 900k Boxing, horiz. 2.25
Nos. 1058-1062 (5) 4.85

Souvenir Sheet

1062A A251 700k Diving 2.00

No. 1062A contains one 40x32mm stamp.

World Health Day A252

Designs: 200k, Spraying for mosquitoes. 255k, Campaign against smoking. 330k, Receiving blood donation. 1000k, Immunizing child, vert.

1992, Apr. 7

1063 A252 200k multicolored .50
1064 A252 255k multicolored .70
1065 A252 330k multicolored .90
1066 A252 1000k multicolored 2.25
Nos. 1063-1066 (4) 4.35

A253

A254

Flags, ball and players: 260k, Argentina, Italy. 305k, Germany, Great Britain. 310k, US, World Cup trophy (no players). 350k, Italy, Great Britain. 800k, Germany, Argentina.

1992, May 1 Litho. *Perf. 13*

1067 A253 260k multicolored .60
1068 A253 305k multicolored .65
1069 A253 310k multicolored .70
1070 A253 350k multicolored .80
1071 A253 800k multicolored 1.90
Nos. 1067-1071 (5) 4.65

Souvenir Sheet

Perf. 12½

1072 A253 700k Goalie 3.25

1994 World Cup Soccer Championships, US.

1992, Nov. 8 Litho. *Perf. 13*

Children playing.

1073 A254 220k Playing drum .85
1074 A254 285k Jumping rope, horiz. 1.10
1075 A254 330k Walking on stilts 1.25
1076 A254 400k Escape from line, horiz. 1.60
Nos. 1073-1076 (4) 4.80

Poisonous Snakes — A255

Perf. 12½x13, 13x12½

1992, July 10 Litho.

1078 A255 280k Naja naja kaouthia .85
1079 A255 295k Naja naja atra .85
1080 A255 420k Trimeresurus wagleri 1.25
1081 A255 700k Ophiophagus hannah, vert. 2.25
Nos. 1078-1081 (4) 5.20

Restoration of Wat Phou — A256

Different views of Wat Phou.

Perf. 13x12½, 12½x13

1992, Aug. 22 Litho.

1082 A256 185k multicolored .50
1083 A256 220k multicolored .60
1084 A256 1200k multi, horiz. 2.75
Nos. 1082-1084 (3) 3.85

Genoa '92 — A257

Sailing ships and maps by: 100k, Juan Martinez. 300k, Piri Reis, vert. 350k, Paolo del Pozo Toscanelli. 400k, Gabriel de Vallseca. 455k, Juan Martinez, diff. 700k, Juan de la Cosa.

Perf. 13x12½, 12½x13

1992, Sept. 12

1085 A257 100k multicolored .25
1086 A257 300k multicolored .75
1087 A257 350k multicolored .90
1088 A257 400k multicolored 1.00
1089 A257 455k multicolored 1.25
Nos. 1085-1089 (5) 4.15

Souvenir Sheet

Perf. 13

1090 A257 700k multicolored 2.00

Traditional Costumes of the Montagnards A258

Various costumes.

1992, Oct. 2 Litho. *Perf. 13*

1091 A258 25k multicolored .20
1092 A258 55k multicolored .25
1093 A258 400k multicolored 1.00
1094 A258 1200k multicolored 2.75
Nos. 1091-1094 (4) 4.20

A259

A260

UN, UNESCO emblems, stylized faces and: 330k, Drum. 1000k, Traditional flute.

1991, Nov. 1 Litho. *Perf. 13*

1095 A259 285k shown .80
1096 A259 330k multicolored 1.00
1097 A259 1000k multicolored 2.75
Nos. 1095-1097 (3) 4.55

Cultural Development Decade, 1988-1997.

1992, Dec. 22

Designs: Apes.

1098 A260 10k Black gibbon .20
1099 A260 100k Douc langur .25
1100 A260 250k Pileated gibbon .75
1101 A260 430k Francois langur 1.10
1102 A260 800k Pygmy loris 2.00
Nos. 1098-1102 (5) 4.30

Natl. Customs A261

Designs: 100k, Woman praying before Buddha, vert. 160k, Procession. 1500k, People giving food to monks.

1992, Dec. 2 *Perf. 12½*

1103 A261 100k multicolored .30
1104 A261 140k multicolored .40
1105 A261 160k multicolored .45
1106 A261 1500k multicolored 4.50
Nos. 1103-1106 (4) 5.65

First Subway System, 130th Anniv. A262

1993, Jan. 9 Litho. *Perf. 13*

1107 A262 15k New York .20
1108 A262 50k Berlin .25
1109 A262 100k Paris .30
1110 A262 200k London .75
1111 A262 900k Moscow 2.75
Nos. 1107-1111 (5) 4.25

Souvenir Sheet

Perf. 13x13½

1112 A262 700k Antique engine, vert. 2.50

No. 1112 contains one 32x40mm stamp.

Frogs
A263

1993, Feb. 1 Litho. *Perf. 12½*

1113 A263 55k Kaloula pulchra .25
1114 A263 90k Xenopus muelleri .30
1115 A263 100k Centrolenella vireovittata, vert. .35
1116 A263 185k Bufo marinus .70
1117 A263 1200k Hyla arborea, vert. 3.50
Nos. 1113-1117 (5) 5.10

Animals
A264

1993, Mar. 13 Litho. *Perf. 13*

1118 A264 45k Tupaia glis .25
1119 A264 60k Cynocephalus volans .25
1120 A264 120k Loris grasilis .45
1121 A264 500k Tarsium spectrum 1.60
1122 A264 600k Symphalangus syndactylus 1.90
Nos. 1118-1122 (5) 4.45

Native Houses
A265

Various houses.

1993, July 12 Litho. *Perf. 13*

1123 A265 32k multi, vert. .20
1124 A265 200k multicolored .75
1125 A265 650k multicolored 2.50
1126 A265 750k multicolored 2.75
Nos. 1123-1126 (4) 6.20

Campaign Against Illegal Drugs — A266

Designs: 200k, Drugs, skull smoking cigarette. 430k, Burning confiscated drugs. 900k, Instructor showing danger of drugs to audience.

1993, June 26 *Perf. 12½*

1127 A266 200k multicolored .65
1128 A266 430k multicolored 1.50
1129 A266 900k multicolored 3.25
Nos. 1127-1129 (3) 5.40

A267

A268

Shells: 20k, Chlamys senatorius nobilis. 30k, Epitonium prestiosum. 70k, Lambis rugosa. 500k, Conus aulicus. 1000k, Lambis millepeda.

1993, May 29 Litho. *Perf. 12x12½*

1130 A267 20k multicolored .20
1131 A267 30k multicolored .20
1132 A267 70k multicolored .30
1133 A267 500k multicolored 1.60
1134 A267 1000k multicolored 3.00
Nos. 1130-1134 (5) 5.30

1993, Aug. 10 Litho. *Perf. 13*

Birds of prey.

1135 A268 10k Aquila clanga .20
1136 A268 100k Athene brama .50
1137 A268 330k Circus melanoleucos 1.50
1138 A268 1000k Circaetus gallicus 4.00
Nos. 1135-1138 (4) 6.20

No. 1137 is horiz.

Environmental Protection — A269

Designs: 32k, Fighting forest fire. 40k, Animals around clean river. 260k, Rice paddies. 1100k, Water buffalo, people in water.

1993, Sept. 25 Litho. *Perf. 13*

1139 A269 32k multicolored .20
1140 A269 40k multicolored .20
1141 A269 260k multicolored 1.00
1142 A269 1100k multicolored 4.25
Nos. 1139-1142 (4) 5.65

Bangkok '93
A270

Butterflies: 35k, Narathura atosia. 80k, Parides philoxenus. 150k, Euploea harrisi. 220k, Ixias pyrene. 500k, Elymnias hypermnestra. 700k, Stichopthalma louisa.

1993, Oct. 1 Litho. *Perf. 13*

1143 A270 35k multicolored .20
1144 A270 80k multicolored .25
1145 A270 150k multicolored .45
1146 A270 220k multicolored .75
1147 A270 500k multicolored 2.00
Nos. 1143-1147 (5) 3.65

Souvenir Sheet

1148 A270 700k multicolored 3.00

No. 1148 contains one 40x32mm stamp.

1994 World Cup Soccer Championships, US — A271

Various soccer players.

1993, Nov. 3 *Perf. 13*

1149 A271 10k multicolored .20
1150 A271 20k multicolored .20
1151 A271 285k multicolored 1.10
1152 A271 400k multicolored 1.60
1153 A271 800k multicolored 3.25
Nos. 1149-1153 (5) 6.35

Souvenir Sheet

Perf. 12½

1154 A271 700k multicolored 2.75

Nos. 1154 contains one 32x40mm stamp.

Prehistoric Birds — A272

1994, Jan. 20 Litho. *Perf. 13*

1155 A272 10k Hesperornis .20
1156 A272 20k Dronte .20
1157 A272 150k Archaeopterix .60
1158 A272 600k Phororhachos 2.00
1159 A272 700k Dinornis maximus 2.25
Nos. 1155-1159 (5) 5.25

Souvenir Sheet

1160 A272 700k Teratornis, horiz. 2.50

Intl. Olympic Committee, Cent. — A273

100k, Flag, flame. 250k, Ancient Olympians. 1000k, Baron de Coubertin, Olympic runner.

Perf. 12x12½, 12½x12

1994, Mar. 15 Litho.

1161 A273 100k multi, vert. .25
1162 A273 250k multi .75
1163 A273 1000k multi, vert. 3.25
Nos. 1161-1163 (3) 4.25

1994 World Cup Soccer Championships, U.S. — A274

Various soccer plays.

1994, June 15 Litho. *Perf. 12½*

1164 A274 40k multicolored .20
1165 A274 50k multicolored .25
1166 A274 60k multicolored .30
1167 A274 320k multicolored 1.75
1168 A274 900k multicolored 5.00
Nos. 1164-1168 (5) 7.50

Souvenir Sheet

Perf. 13

1169 A274 700k multicolored 3.75

No. 1169 contains one 32x40mm stamp.

Pagodas
A275

Various ornate gables.

1994, July 1 Litho. *Perf. 12½*

1170 A275 30k multicolored .20
1171 A275 150k multicolored .65
1172 A275 380k multicolored 1.60
1173 A275 1100k multicolored 4.50
Nos. 1170-1173 (4) 6.95

Ursus Malayanus — A276

1994, July 23

1174 A276 50k shown .75 .20
1175 A276 90k Adult 1.00 .40
1176 A276 200k Cub, adult 2.25 1.00
1177 A276 220k Adult standing 3.25 1.25
Nos. 1174-1177 (4) 7.25 2.85

World Wildlife Fund.

Reptiles — A277

Intl. Year of the Family — A278

70k, Natrix natrix. 80k, Natrix tessellata. 90k, Salamandra salamandra. 600k, Triturus alpestris. 700k, Triturus cristatus. 800k, Lacerta viridis.

1994, Aug. 1 Litho. *Perf. 12½*

1178 A277 70k multi, horiz. .30
1179 A277 80k multi, horiz. .35
1180 A277 90k multi, horiz. .40
1181 A277 600k multi, horiz. 2.50
1182 A277 800k multicolored 3.25
Nos. 1178-1182 (5) 6.80

Souvenir Sheet

1183 A277 700k multi, horiz. 3.25

No. 1183 contains one 40x32mm stamp.

1994, Sept. 24

Designs: 500k, Mother taking child to school, horiz. No. 1186, Mother walking with children. No. 1187, Family.

1184 A278 200k multicolored .85
1185 A278 500k multicolored 2.10
1186 A278 700k multicolored 3.25
Nos. 1184-1186 (3) 6.20

Souvenir Sheet

1187 A278 700k multicolored 3.25

No. 1187 contains one 32x40mm stamp.

Drums
A279

Designs: 440k, Two people with hanging drum. 450k, Barrel shaped drum. 600k, Hanging drum.

Perf. 12½, 13x12½ (#1189)

1994, Oct. 20 **Litho.**

1188 A279 370k multicolored 1.60
1189 A279 440k multicolored 1.75
1190 A279 450k multicolored 1.75
1191 A279 600k multicolored 2.40
Nos. 1188-1191 (4) 7.50

No. 1189 is 40x29mm.

Elephants — A280

1994, Nov. 25

1192 A280 140k shown .55
1193 A280 400k Beside railing 1.60
1194 A280 890k Being ridden, vert. 3.25
Nos. 1192-1194 (3) 5.40

Peace Bridge Between Laos and Thailand — A281

1994, Apr. 8 **Litho.** ***Perf. 14x14½***

1195 A281 500k multicolored 1.75

Buddha — A282

Dinosaurs
A283

15k, Phra Xayavoraman 7. 280k, Phra Thong Souk. 390k, Phra Monolom. 800k, Phra Ongtu.

1994, Aug. 25 **Litho.** ***Perf. 13***

1196 A282 15k multicolored .20
1197 A282 280k multicolored 1.25
1198 A282 390k multicolored 1.60
1199 A282 800k multicolored 3.50
Nos. 1196-1199 (4) 6.55

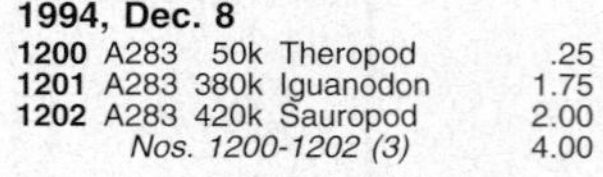

1994, Dec. 8

1200 A283 50k Theropod .25
1201 A283 380k Iguanodon 1.75
1202 A283 420k Sauropod 2.00
Nos. 1200-1202 (3) 4.00

World Tourism Organization, 20th Anniv. — A284

1995, Jan. 2 **Litho.** ***Perf. 12½***

1203 A284 60k Traditional music .25
1204 A284 250k Traditional dance 1.00
1205 A284 400k Traditional food 1.75
1206 A284 650k Waterfalls, vert. 2.75
Nos. 1203-1206 (4) 5.75

Souvenir Sheet

Perf. 13

1207 A284 700k like #1206, vert. 4.00

No. 1207 contains one 32x44mm stamp.

Dinosaurs
A285

1995, Feb. 20 ***Perf. 12½***

1208 A285 50k Tracodont .20
1209 A285 70k Protoceratops .30
1210 A285 300k Brontosaurus 1.25
1211 A285 400k Stegosaurus 1.75
1212 A285 600k Tyranosaurus 2.50
Nos. 1208-1212 (5) 6.00

Birds
A286

1995, Mar. 10

1213 A286 50k Acridotheres javanicus .20
1214 A286 150k Starnus burmannicus .65
1215 A286 300k Acridotheres tristis 1.25
1216 A286 700k Gracula religiosa 3.00
Nos. 1213-1216 (4) 5.10

Francophonie, 25th Anniv. — 1216A

Designs: 50k, People with arms linked. 380k, Temple. 420k, Map of Laos.

1995, Mar. 20 **Litho.** ***Perf. 13***

1216A A286a 50k multi .20
1216B A286a 380k multi 1.50
1216C A286a 420k multi 1.75
Nos. 1216A-1216C (3) 3.45

Antique Containers
A287

1995, May 1 **Litho.** ***Perf. 12½***

1217 A287 70k "Hanche" cup, vert. .30
1218 A287 200k Resin bowl .85
1219 A287 450k Button design bowl 1.90
1220 A287 600k Loving cup 2.50
Nos. 1217-1220 (4) 5.55

1996 Atlanta Pre-Olympics
A288

1995, Apr. 5

1221 A288 60k Pole vault .25
1222 A288 80k Javelin .35
1223 A288 200k Hammer throw .85
1224 A288 350k Long jump 1.60
1225 A288 700k High jump 3.25
Nos. 1221-1225 (5) 6.30

Souvenir Sheet

1226 A288 700k Baseball 3.25

No. 1226 contains one 40x32mm stamp.

Rocket Festival
A289

Designs: 80k, Launching rocket from scaffolding, vert. 160k, Carrying rocket in procession led by monk. 500k, Man carrying rocket on shoulder. 700k, People looking at rockets on tripods.

1995, June 1 **Litho.** ***Perf. 13***

1227 A289 80k multicolored .30
1228 A289 160k multicolored .65
1229 A289 500k multicolored 1.90
1230 A289 700k multicolored 2.50
Nos. 1227-1230 (4) 5.35

Domestic Cats
A290

Designs: 40k, Red tabby longhair. 50k, Siamese seal point. 250k, Red tabby longhair. 400k, Tortoise-shell shorthair. 650k, Tortoise-shell shorthair, vert. 700k, Tortoise-shell shorthair.

1995, July 25 **Litho.** ***Perf. 12½***

1231 A290 40k multicolored .20
1232 A290 50k multicolored .20
1233 A290 250k multicolored 1.00
1234 A290 400k multicolored 1.75
1235 A290 650k multicolored 3.00
Nos. 1231-1235 (5) 6.15

Souvenir Sheet

1236 A290 700k multicolored 3.25

No. 1236 contains one 40x32mm stamp.

Insect-Eating Plants — A291

Designs: 90k, Nepenthes villosa. 100k, Dionaea muscipula. 350k, Sarracenia flava. 450k, Sarracenia purpurea. 500k, Nepenthes ampullaria.
1000k, Nepenthes gracilis.

1995, Aug. 24

1237 A291 90k multicolored .20
1238 A291 100k multicolored .20
1239 A291 350k multicolored .65
1240 A291 450k multicolored .85
1241 A291 500k multicolored .90
Nos. 1237-1241 (5) 2.80

Souvenir Sheet

1242 A291 1000k multicolored 5.75

No. 1242 contains one 40x32mm stamp.

Insects
A292

Designs: 40k, Lucanus cervus. 50k, Melolontha melolontha. 500k, Xylocopa violacea. 800k, Tettigonia viridissima.

1995, Sept. 20

1243 A292 40k multicolored .20
1244 A292 50k multicolored .20
1245 A292 500k multicolored 2.00
1246 A292 800k multicolored 3.25
Nos. 1243-1246 (4) 5.65

FAO, 50th Anniv.
A293

Designs: 80k, Cattle grazing. 300k, Farmer tilling rice paddy. 1000k, Planting, irrigating rice paddies, stocking pond with fish.

1995, Oct. 16 **Litho.** ***Perf. 12½***

1247 A293 80k multicolored .25
1248 A293 300k multicolored 1.00
1249 A293 1000k multicolored 3.50
Nos. 1247-1249 (3) 4.75

Traditional Culture — A294

Designs: 50k, Man with musical instrument, two women. 280k, Dance. 380k, Playing game with bamboo poles. 420k, Woman, man with musical instruments.

1996, Jan. 10

1250 A294 50k multicolored .25
1251 A294 280k multicolored 1.40
1252 A294 380k multicolored 2.00
1253 A294 420k multicolored 2.25
Nos. 1250-1253 (4) 5.90

1996 Summer Olympics, Atlanta — A295

1996, Feb. 20

1254 A295 30k Cycling .20
1255 A295 150k Soccer .75
1256 A295 200k Basketball, vert. 1.00
1257 A295 300k Running, vert. 1.50
1258 A295 500k Shooting 2.50
Nos. 1254-1258 (5) 5.95

Souvenir Sheet

1259 A295 1000k Pole vault 3.50

No. 1259 contains one 38x30mm stamp.

Fauna — A296

Designs: 40k, Helarctos malayanus. 60k, Pelecanus philippensis. 200k, Panthera pardus. 250k, Papilio machaon. 700k, Python molurus.

1996, Feb. 26 **Litho.** ***Perf. 13***

1260 A296 40k multicolored .25
1261 A296 60k multicolored .35
1262 A296 200k multicolored 1.10
1263 A296 250k multicolored 1.25
1264 A296 700k multicolored 3.00
Nos. 1260-1264 (5) 5.95

Intl. Women's Day A297

20k, Weaving textile. 290k, Instructing calisthenics. 1000k, Feeding infant, vert.

1996, Mar. 8

1265 A297 20k multicolored .20
1266 A297 290k multicolored 1.10
1267 A297 1000k multicolored 3.50
Nos. 1265-1267 (3) 4.80

A298

A299

Various soccer plays.

1996, May 3 **Litho.** ***Perf. 13***

1268 A298 20k multicolored .20
1269 A298 50k multicolored .25
1270 A298 300k multicolored 1.25
1271 A298 400k multicolored 1.50
1272 A298 500k multicolored 2.00
Nos. 1268-1272 (5) 5.20

Souvenir Sheet

1273 A298 1000k multicolored 3.50

1998 World Soccer Cup Championships, France.

No. 1273 contains one 32x40mm stamp.

1996, Apr. 15 **Litho.** ***Perf. 13½x13***

Various rats.

1274 A299 50k purple & multi .25
1275 A299 340k blue & multi 1.25
1276 A299 350k green & multi 1.25
1277 A299 370k red & multi 1.25
Nos. 1274-1277 (4) 4.00

New Year 1996 (Year of the Rat).

Laos Rural Development Program, 20th Anniv. — A300

50k, Instruction for giving medical care. 280k, Irrigation system. 600k, Bridge over waterway.

1995, Dec. 2 ***Perf. 13***

1278 A300 50k multicolored .20
1279 A300 280k multicolored 1.00
1280 A300 600k multicolored 2.10
Nos. 1278-1280 (3) 3.30

UN, 50th Anniv. A301

Designs: 290k, Men seated at round table. 310k, Men playing game, checkers. 440k, Boys in swing, playing ball.

1995, Oct. 24

1281 A301 290k multicolored 1.00
1282 A301 310k multicolored 1.10
1283 A301 440k multicolored 1.50
Nos. 1281-1283 (3) 3.60

Antique Aircraft A302

1996, July 5 **Litho.** ***Perf. 13***

1284 A302 25k Morane .20
1285 A302 60k Sopwith Camel .25
1286 A302 150k De Haviland DH-4 .65
1287 A302 250k Albatros 1.10
1288 A302 800k Caudron 2.50
Nos. 1284-1288 (5) 4.70

Capex '96.

Carts A303

1996, Aug. 21

1289 A303 50k shown .25
1290 A303 100k Cart, diff. .40
1291 A303 440k Pulled by oxen 1.50
Nos. 1289-1291 (3) 2.15

Flowers — A304

Designs: 50k, Dendrobium secundum. 200k, Ascocentrum miniatum. 500k, Aerides multiflorum. 520k, Dendrobium aggregatum.

1996, Oct. 25 **Litho.** ***Perf. 13***

1292 A304 50k multicolored .20
1293 A304 200k multicolored .75
1294 A304 500k multicolored 1.90
1295 A304 520k multicolored 2.00
Nos. 1292-1295 (4) 4.85

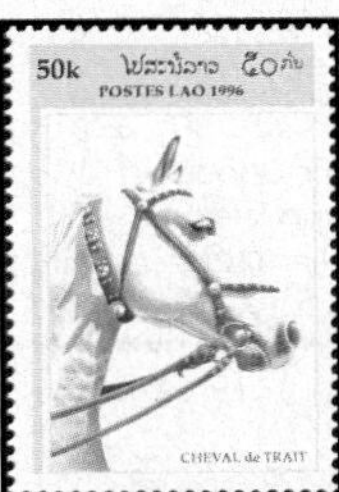

Draft Horses — A305

Various breeds.

1996, Nov. 5 **Litho.** ***Perf. 13***

1296 A305 50k yellow & multi .20
1297 A305 80k green & multi .25
1298 A305 200k pink & multi .55
1299 A305 400k blue & multi 1.25
1300 A305 600k yellow & multi 1.75
Nos. 1296-1300 (5) 4.00

Souvenir Sheet

1301 A305 1000k pink & multi 3.00

No. 1301 contains one 32x40mm stamp.

UNICEF, 50th Anniv. A306

1996, Dec. 11 **Litho.**

1302 A306 200k Children in school .80
1303 A306 500k Child breastfeeding, vert. 2.00
1304 A306 600k Woman pumping water 2.40
Nos. 1302-1304 (3) 5.20

Greenpeace, 25th Anniv. — A306a

Turtles: 150k, Dermochelys coriacea on sand. 250k, Dermochelys coriacea in surf. 400k, Erethochelys imbricata. 450k, Chelonia agassizi.

1996, Dec. 27 **Litho.** ***Perf. 13***

1304A A306a 150k multicolored .80
1304B A306a 250k multicolored 1.25
1304C A306a 400k multicolored 2.00
1304D A306a 450k multicolored 2.25
e. Souvenir sheet, #1304A-1304D 6.50
Nos. 1304A-1304D (4) 6.30

Steam Locomotives — A307

Designs: 100k, Kinnaird, 1846. 200k, Pioneer, 1836, portrait of George Stephenson. 300k, Portrait of Robert Stephenson, Long Boiler Express, 1848. 400k, Adler, 1835. 500k, Lord of the Isles, 1851-84. 600k, The Columbine, 1845.

2000k, Best friend of Charleston, 1830.

Perf. 12½x12, 12x13 (#1306-1309)

1997 **Litho.**

1305 A307 100k multicolored .30
1306 A307 200k multicolored .60
1307 A307 300k multicolored .95
1308 A307 400k multicolored 1.25
1309 A307 500k multicolored 1.50
1310 A307 600k multicolored 1.75
Nos. 1305-1310 (6) 6.35

Souvenir Sheet

Perf. 12½

1311 A307 2000k multicolored 5.75

Nos. 1306-1309 are 42x21mm.

No. 1311 contains one 40x32mm stamp.

Parrots — A308

Designs: 50k, Agapornis personata. 150k, Agapornis cana. 200k, Agapornis lilianae. 400k, Agapornis fischeri. 500k, Agapornis nigregenis. 800k, Agapornis roseicollis.

2000k, Agapornis taranta.

1997 ***Perf. 12½***

1312 A308 50k multicolored .20
1313 A308 150k multicolored .45
1314 A308 200k multicolored .60
1315 A308 400k multicolored 1.25
1316 A308 500k multicolored 1.50
1317 A308 800k multicolored 2.40
Nos. 1312-1317 (6) 6.40

Souvenir Sheet

1318 A308 2000k multicolored 6.50

No. 1318 contains one 32x40mm stamp.

Year of the Ox — A308a

Designs: 300k, Ox, rider with flag, vert. 440k, Ox, rider with umbrella.

1997 **Litho.** ***Perf. 13x13½, 13½x13***

1318A A308a 50k multi .20
1318B A308a 300k multi 1.60
1318C A308a 440k multi 2.25
Nos. 1318A-1318C (3) 4.05

Cooking Utensils A309

50k, Cooking over open fire, vert. 340k, Traditional food containers. 370k, Traditional meal setting.

1997

1319	A309	50k	multicolored	.20
1320	A309	340k	multicolored	1.00
1321	A309	370k	multicolored	1.00
			Nos. 1319-1321 (3)	2.20

Orchids A310

Designs: 50k, Roeblingiana. 100k, Findlayanum. 150k, Crepidatum. 250k, Sarcanthus birmanicus. 400k, Cymbidium lowianum. 1000k, Dendrobium gratiosissimum. 2000k, Chamberlainianum.

1997 Litho. *Perf. 12½*

1322	A310	50k	multicolored	.20
1323	A310	100k	multicolored	.30
1324	A310	150k	multicolored	.45
1325	A310	250k	multicolored	.80
1326	A310	400k	multicolored	1.25
1327	A310	1000k	multicolored	3.00
			Nos. 1322-1327 (6)	6.00

Souvenir Sheet

1328 A310 2000k multicolored 6.00

No. 1328 contains one 32x40mm stamp.

Elephants — A311

Elephas maximus: 100k, Adult, vert. 250k, Adult holding log. 300k, Adult, calf.

Loxodonta africana: 350k, Adult. 450k, Adult in water. 550k, Adult, vert. 2000k, Head of adult.

1997 Litho. *Perf. 12½*

1329	A311	100k	multicolored	.30
1330	A311	250k	multicolored	.75
1331	A311	300k	multicolored	.85
1332	A311	350k	multicolored	1.10
1333	A311	450k	multicolored	1.25
1334	A311	550k	multicolored	1.60
			Nos. 1329-1334 (6)	5.85

Souvenir Sheet

1335 A311 2000k multicolored 5.75

No. 1335 contains one 32x40mm stamp.

Head Pieces and Masks A312

Various designs.

1997 Litho. *Perf. 12½*

1336	A312	50k	multi, vert.	.20
1337	A312	100k	multi, vert	.25
1338	A312	150k	multi	.40
1339	A312	200k	multi, vert.	.55
1340	A312	350k	multi, vert.	1.25
			Nos. 1336-1340 (5)	2.65

1998 World Cup Soccer Championships, France — A313

Various soccer plays.

1997 Litho. *Perf. 12½*

1341	A313	100k	multicolored	.25
1342	A313	200k	multicolored	.50
1343	A313	250k	multicolored	.65
1344	A313	300k	multicolored	.75
1345	A313	350k	multicolored	.90
1346	A313	700k	multicolored	1.75
			Nos. 1341-1346 (6)	4.80

Souvenir Sheet

1347 A313 2000k multicolored 5.00

Sailing Ships A314

50k, Phoenician. 100k, 13th cent. ship. 150k, 15th cent. vessel. 200k, Portuguese caravel, 16th cent. 400k, Dutch, 17th cent. 900k, HMS Victory.

2000k, Grand Henry, 1514.

1997 *Perf. 13*

1348	A314	50k	multicolored	.20
1349	A314	100k	multicolored	.25
1350	A314	150k	multicolored	.40
1351	A314	200k	multicolored	.55
1352	A314	400k	multicolored	1.10
1353	A314	900k	multicolored	2.50
			Nos. 1348-1353 (6)	5.00

Souvenir Sheet

1354 A314 2000k multicolored 5.00

No. 1354 contains one 40x28mm stamp.

Canoe Races A315

Designs: 50k, Team in red shirts, team in yellow shirts rowing upward. 100k, Crowd cheering on teams. 300k, Teams rowing left. 500k, People standing in canoe cheering on teams.

1997 Litho. *Perf. 12½*

1355	A315	50k	multicolored	.20
1356	A315	100k	multicolored	.25
1357	A315	300k	multicolored	.75
1358	A315	500k	multicolored	1.25
			Nos. 1355-1358 (4)	2.45

Admission of Laos to ASEAN — A316

Central flag: a, Brunei. b, Indonesia. c, Laos. d, Malaysia. e, Taiwan. f, Philippines. g, Singapore. h, Thailand. i, Viet Nam.

1997, July 23 Litho. *Perf. 14x14½*

1359 A316 550k Strip of 9, #a.-i. 9.50 9.50
j. Sheet of 9, #1359a-1359i + label 9.50 9.50

Nos. 1359a-1359i also exist in souvenir sheets of 1. No. 1359 was not available in the philatelic market until 8/98.

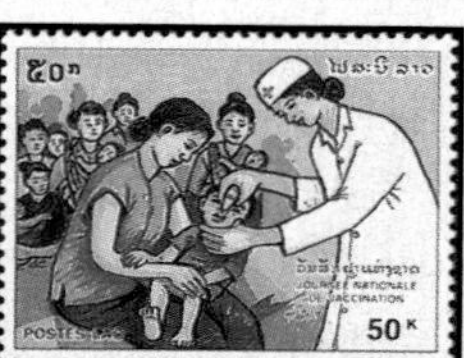

Vaccination Day — A317

Design: 50k, Child receiving oral vaccination. 340k, Child receiving shot. 370k, Child in wheelchair.

1997, Jan. 3 Litho. *Perf. 13x13¼*

1363	A317	50k	multi	*.20*
1364	A317	340k	multi	*1.50*
1365	A317	370k	multi	*1.60*
			Nos. 1363-1365 (3)	*3.30*

Pseudoryx Saola — A319

Various views of Pseudoryx saola.

1997, Feb. 10 *Perf. 13x13¼, 13¼x13*

1366	A319	350k	multi	*1.60*	*1.60*
1367	A319	380k	multi, vert.	*1.75*	*1.75*
1368	A319	420k	multi	*2.00*	*2.00*
			Nos. 1366-1368 (3)	*5.35*	*5.35*

ASEAN (Assoc. of South East Asian Nations), 30th Anniv. — A321

1997, Aug. 8 Litho. *Perf. 13*

1373	A321	150k	Headquarters	.90
1374	A321	600k	Map of Laos	3.50

Fishing A322

Designs: 50k, Holding large net with a pole, vert. 100k, Casting net. 450k, Woman using small net, vert. 600k, Placing fish traps in water.

1997

1375	A322	50k	multicolored	.30
1376	A322	100k	multicolored	.60
1377	A322	450k	multicolored	2.00
1378	A322	600k	multicolored	2.75
			Nos. 1375-1378 (4)	5.65

New Year 1998 (Year of the Tiger) A323

1998

1379	A323	150k	green & multi	.90
1380	A323	350k	gray & multi	1.75
1381	A323	400k	pale lilac & multi	1.90
			Nos. 1379-1381 (3)	4.55

Canoes — A325

Designs: 1100k, Barque. 1200k, Covered pirogue. 2500k, Motorized pirogue.

1998 Litho. *Perf. 14½x14*

1387	A325	1100k	multicolored	2.50	2.50
1388	A325	1200k	multicolored	2.75	2.75
1389	A325	2500k	multicolored	6.25	6.25
			Nos. 1387-1389 (3)	11.50	11.50

A326

A327

Various wind musical instruments.

1998 *Perf. 14x14½*

1390	A326	900k	multicolored	2.25	2.25
1391	A326	1200k	multicolored	3.25	3.25
1392	A326	1500k	multicolored	4.00	4.00
			Nos. 1390-1392 (3)	9.50	9.50

1998

Buddha Luang, Phabang.

1393 A327 3000k multicolored 7.50 7.50

Orchids — A328

Designs: 900k, Paphiopedilum callosum. 950k, Paphiopedilum concolor. 1000k, Dendrobium thyrsiflorum, vert. 1050k, Dendrobium lindleyi, vert.

1998 *Perf. 14½x14, 14x14½*

1394	A328	900k	multicolored	2.75	2.75
1395	A328	950k	multicolored	3.00	3.00
1396	A328	1000k	multicolored	3.00	3.00
1397	A328	1050k	multicolored	3.25	3.25
			Nos. 1394-1397 (4)	12.00	12.00

Universal Declaration of Human Rights, 50th Anniv. — A329

Designs: 170k, Women voting. 300k, Children in classroom.

1998 *Perf. 14½x14*

1398	A329	170k	multicolored	2.25	2.25
1399	A329	300k	multicolored	3.75	3.75

Historic Sites — A330

Designs: 10,000k, Hotay Vat Sisaket, vert. 25,000k, Vat Phou. 45,000k, That Luong.

1998 Litho. *Perf. 14x14¼, 14¼x14*

1400-1402	A330	Set of 3	*35.00*	*35.00*

People's Army, 50th Anniv. — A331

Designs: 1300k, Soldiers, flag, flowers. 1500k, Soldiers, cave, jungle, vert.

1999 Litho. *Perf. 13¼*

1403	A331	1300k multi	*1.40*	*1.40*
1404	A331	1500k multi	*1.50*	*1.50*

Souvenir Sheet

Visit Laos Year (in 2000) — A331a

Various temples: b, 2500k. c, 4000k, d, 5500k, e, 8000k.

1999 ? Typo. *Perf. 13¼*
Gold Stamps

1404A	A331a	Sheet of 4, #b-e	5.25	5.25
f.		As 1404A, with larger margins with Thaipex 99 and China Stamp Exhibition 99 emblems	5.25	5.25
g.		As 1404A, with larger margins with China 1999 Philatelic Exhibition emblem	5.25	5.25

Luang Prabang World Heritage Site — A332

Designs: 400k, Commemorative marker, vert. 1150k, Building. 1250k, Vat Xiengthong (building with curved roof).

1999

1405	A332	400k multi	*.40*	*.40*
1406	A332	1150k multi	*1.10*	*1.10*
1407	A332	1250k multi	*1.25*	*1.25*
		Nos. 1405-1407 (3)	*2.75*	*2.75*

Tourism — A333

Designs: 200k, Yaos, Muong Sing. 500k, Phadeang, Vangvieng District. 1050k, That Makmo, Luang Prabang. 1300k, Patuxay, Vientiane, vert.

1999 Litho. *Perf. 14¾x14, 14x14¾*

1408	A333	200k multi	*.30*
1409	A333	500k multi	*.60*
1410	A333	1050k multi	*1.10*
1411	A333	1300k multi	*1.50*
		Nos. 1408-1411 (4)	*3.50*

Nocturnal Creatures A334

Designs: 900k, Glaucidium brodiei. 1600k, Otus lempiji. 2100k, Tyto alba. 2800k, Chironax melanocephalus.

1999 Litho. *Perf. 14x14½*

1412	A334	900k multi	*.70*	*.70*
1413	A334	1600k multi	*1.50*	*1.50*
1414	A334	2100k multi	*2.00*	*2.00*
1415	A334	2800k multi	*2.75*	*2.75*
		Nos. 1412-1415 (4)	*6.95*	*6.95*

New Year 1999 (Year of the Rabbit) — A335

1500k, Rabbit, other animals of calendar cycle. 1600k, Rabbit.

1999 Litho. *Perf. 14x14¼*

1416	A335	1500k multi, vert.	*4.00*	*5.00*

Perf. 14¾x14

1417	A335	1600k multi, horiz.	*5.00*	*6.00*

Farming Implements — A336

1999 Litho. *Perf. 14¾x14*

1418	A336	1500k Plow	*1.00*	*1.00*
1419	A336	2000k Yoke	*1.50*	*1.50*
1420	A336	3200k Plow, diff.	*2.25*	*2.25*
		Nos. 1418-1420 (3)	*4.75*	*4.75*

UPU, 125th Anniv. A337

1999

1421	A337	2600k shown	*2.00*	*2.00*
1422	A337	3400k Postman	*2.50*	*2.50*

Wildlife — A338

700k, Rhinoceros sondaicus. 900k, Bubalus bubalis. 1700k, Prionodon pardicolor. 1800k, Cervus unicolor. 1900k, Panthera leo.

1999 *Perf. 14¾x14, 14x14¾*

1423	A338	700k multi	*.60*	*.60*
1424	A338	900k multi, vert.	*.80*	*.80*
1425	A338	1700k multi	*1.50*	*1.50*
1426	A338	1800k multi	*1.75*	*1.75*
1427	A338	1900k multi, vert.	*1.90*	*1.90*
		Nos. 1423-1427 (5)	*6.55*	*6.55*

Expo '99, Kunming, China — A339

Designs: 300k, Carved tree stump. 900k, China Hall. 2300k, Science and Technology Hall. 2500k, Laos traditional wooden house.

1999 *Perf. 14¾x14*

1428	A339	300k multi	*.25*	*.25*
1429	A339	900k multi	*.75*	*.75*
1430	A339	2300k multi	*1.90*	*1.90*
1431	A339	2500k multi	*2.00*	*2.00*
		Nos. 1428-1431 (4)	*4.90*	*4.90*

Millennium — A340

No. 1432, 2000k: a, Airport, bus, hospital. b, Temple, tractor, elephant. c, Building, truck. d, River, waterfalls.
Illustration reduced.

2000, Jan. 1 Litho. *Perf. 13½*

1432	A340	Block of 4, #a-d	*5.50*	*5.50*
e.		Souvenir sheet, #1432	*6.75*	*6.75*

No. 1432e sold for 10,000k.

New Year 2000 (Year of the Dragon) — A341

Dragons: 1800k, And other zodiac animals. 2300k, In water.

2000, Apr. 1 *Perf. 14½x14*

1433-1434	A341	Set of 2	1.25	1.25

Wedding Costumes A342

Designs: 800k, Lao Theung. 2300k, Lao Lum. 3400k, Lao Sung.

2000, Oct. 30 *Perf. 14x14½*

1435-1437	A342	Set of 3	2.60	2.60

Children's Drawings — A343

Designs: 300k, Waterfall. 400k, Forest fire. 2300k, Animals at river. 3200k, Animals at river, vert.

2000, June 1 *Perf. 14½x14, 14x14½*

1438-1441	A343	Set of 4	3.00	3.00

Bangkok 2000 Stamp Exhibition — A344

Orchids: 500k, Dendrobium draconis. 900k, Paphiopedilum hirsutissimum. 3000k, Dendrobium sulcatum. 3400k, Rhynchostylis gigantea.

2000, Mar. 25 *Perf. 14x14½*

1442-1445	A344	Set of 4	3.00	3.00
1445a		Souv. sheet, #1442-1445, perf. 13½	4.00	4.00

No. 1445a sold for 10,000k.

Peacocks A345

700k, Male with feathers down, vert., 1000k, Male with feathers up, vert., 1800k, Female. 3500k, Male and female.
10,000k, Male with feathers up, vert.

2000, July 10 *Perf. 14x14½, 14½x14*

1446-1449	A345	Set of 4	2.50	2.50

Souvenir Sheet
Perf. 13½
Litho. With Foil Application

1450	A345	10,000k multi	4.00	4.00

2000 Summer Olympics, Sydney — A346

Designs: 500k, Cycling. 900k, Boxing. 2600k, Judo. 3600k, Kayaking.

2000, Sept. 15 Litho. *Perf. 14½x14*

1451-1454	A346	Set of 4	3.00	3.00
1454a		Souvenir sheet, #1451-1454, perf. 13½	3.75	3.75

No. 1454a sold for 10,000k.

Laotian postal officials have declared as "illegal" a sheet of stamps for Great People of the 20th Century (Elvis Presley, Roberto Clemente, Marilyn Monroe, Dr. Martin Luther King, Jr., Pope John Paul II, Frank Sinatra, Albert Einstein, Princess Diana and Walt Disney) and stamps depicting Tiger Woods, Payne Stewart, Arnold Palmer, Elvis Presley, Marilyn Monroe, John Lennon and the Beatles.

Women's Costumes — A347

2000, Mar. 8 Litho. *Perf. 14¼x14½*

1455	A347	100k Kor Loma	.20	.20
1456	A347	200k Kor Pchor	.20	.20
1457	A347	500k Nhuan Krom	.20	.20

1458	A347	900k Taidam	.40	.40
1459	A347	2300k Yao	1.00	1.00
1460	A347	2500k Meuy	1.10	1.10
1461	A347	2600k Sila	1.10	1.10
1462	A347	2700k Hmong	1.25	1.25
1463	A347	2800k Yao, diff.	1.25	1.25
1464	A347	3100k Kor Nukkuy	1.40	1.40
1465	A347	3200k Kor Pouxang	1.40	1.40
1466	A347	3300k Yao Lanten	1.40	1.40
1467	A347	3400k Khir	1.50	1.50
1468	A347	3500k Kor	1.50	1.50
1469	A347	3900k Hmong, diff.	1.75	1.75
	Nos. 1455-1469 (15)		15.65	15.65

Laotian-Japanese Bridge Project — A348

Flags, various views of bridge: 900k, 2700k, 3200k.

2000, Aug. 2 ***Perf. 14½x14***
1470-1472 A348 Set of 3 2.75 2.75

Souvenir Sheet

No. 1472A: b, 4000k, Similar to #1470. c, 7500k, Similar to #1471. d, 8500k, Similar to #1472.

2000 **Typo.** ***Perf. 13¼x13½***
1472A A348 Sheet of 3, #b-d 7.00 7.00

No. 1472A contains three 48x33mm stamps in gold.

Tourism — A349

Designs: 300k, Phousy Stupa, Luang Prabang. 600k, Than Chang Cave. 2800k, Inhang Stupa. 3300k, Buddha, Phiawat Temple.

2000, Nov. 20 ***Perf. 14x14½***
1473-1476 A349 Set of 4 3.00 3.00

Lao People's Democratic Republic, 25th Anniv. — A350

2000, Dec. 2 ***Perf. 13¼***
1477 A350 4000k multi 1.50 1.50

Mekong River at Twilight A351

Various views: 900k, 2700k, 3400k.

2000, June 20 ***Perf. 14½x14***
1478-1480 A351 Set of 3 2.50 2.50

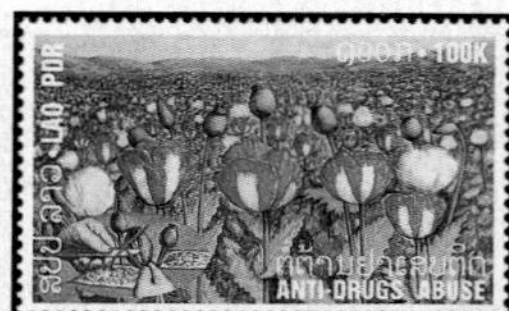

Anti-Drug Campaign — A352

Designs: 100k, Poppy field. 4000k, Burning of seized drugs.

2000, June 26 **Litho.**
1481-1482 A352 Set of 2 1.50 1.50

Souvenir Sheet

Route 13 Bridge Reconstruction Project — A353

Bridge in: a, Savannakhet. b, Saravane. c, Pakse.

2000, Feb. 14 ***Perf. 13¼***
1483 A353 4000k Sheet of 3, #a-c 4.00 4.00

Souvenir Sheet

Anti-Polio Campaign — A354

No. 1484: a, 900k, People receiving vaccine. b, 2500k, Family, map of Laos.

2000, June 1
1484 A354 Sheet of 2, #a-b 1.25 1.25

Millennium A355

Designs: 3200k, Satellite, telecommunication dishes, map of Laos, student. 4000k, High tension lines, dam.

2001, Jan. 1 ***Perf. 14x14½***
1485-1486 A355 Set of 2 2.25 2.25

New Year 2001 (Year of the Snake) A356

Designs: 900k, Snake coiled around branch. 3500k, Snake, other zodiac animals.

2001, Apr. 15 ***Perf. 14½x14***
1487-1488 A356 Set of 2 1.50 1.50

Cockfighting — A357

Pair of cocks fighting: 500k, 900k, 3300k, 3500k.
10,000k, Single cock, vert.

2001, Mar. 10 ***Perf. 14½x14***
1489-1492 A357 Set of 4 3.25 3.25

Souvenir Sheet

Perf. 13¼

1493 A357 10,000k multi 4.00 4.00

No. 1493 contains one 36x50mm stamp.

Laos-People's Republic of China Diplomatic Relations, 40th Anniv. — A358

Illustration reduced.

2001, Apr. 25 ***Perf. 14¼x14½***
1494 A358 1000k multi .40 .40

Phila Nippon '01 A359

Birds: Nos. 1495, 1499a, 700k, Egretta intermedia. Nos. 1496, 1499b, 800k, Bubulcus ibis (36x50mm). Nos. 1497, 1499c, 3100k, Ardea cinera (36x50mm). Nos. 1498, 1499d, 3400k, Egretta alba.

Perf. 14½x14, 13¼ (#1496-1497)
2001, Aug. 1

With White Frames

1495-1498 A359 Set of 4 2.75 2.75

Souvenir Sheet

Without White Frames

Perf. 13¼

1499 A359 Sheet of 4, #a-d 2.75 2.75

No. 1499 sold for 10,000k.

Mortars and Pestles — A360

Designs: 900k, Two women using large hand-held pestle, vert. 2600k, Water-driven mortar and pestle. 3500k, Woman operating mechanical mortar and pestle, vert.

Perf. 14x14½, 14½x14
2001, Nov. 15
1500-1502 A360 Set of 3 2.25 2.25

Ceremonies — A361

Designs: 300k, Pou Nyer and Nya Nyer, vert. 600k, Hae Nang Sangkhan, vert. 1000k, Sand Stupa. 2300k, Hae Prabang, vert. 4000k, Takbat, vert.

2001, Apr. 13 ***Perf. 14x14½, 14½x14***
1503-1507 A361 Set of 5 3.50 3.50

Buddhist Art — A362

Designs: 200k, Himavanta. 900k, Vanapavesa. 3200k, Kumarakanda. 3600k, Sakkapabba.

2001, Dec. 5 ***Perf. 13¼***
1508-1511 A362 Set of 4 3.25 3.25
1511a Souvenir sheet, #1508-1511 3.25 3.25

Men's Costumes — A363

Designs: 100k, Yao Mane. 200k, Gnaheun. 500k, Katou. 2300k, Hmong Dam. 2500k, Harlak. 2600k, Kui. 2700k, Krieng. 3100k, Khmu Nhuan. 3200k, Ta Oy. 3300k, Tai Theng. 3400k, Hmong Khao. 3500k, Gnor. 3600k, Phouthai Na Gnom. 4000k, Yao. 5000k, Hmong.

2001, Feb. 20 ***Perf. 14¼x14½***

1512	A363	100k multi	.20	.20
1513	A363	200k multi	.20	.20
1514	A363	500k multi	.20	.20
1515	A363	2300k multi	.80	.80
1516	A363	2500k multi	.85	.85
1517	A363	2600k multi	.85	.85
1518	A363	2700k multi	.90	.90
1519	A363	3100k multi	1.00	1.00
1520	A363	3200k multi	1.10	1.10
1521	A363	3300k multi	1.10	1.10
1522	A363	3400k multi	1.25	1.25
1523	A363	3500k multi	1.25	1.25
1524	A363	3600k multi	1.25	1.25
1525	A363	4000k multi	1.50	1.50
1526	A363	5000k multi	1.90	1.90
	Nos. 1512-1526 (15)		14.35	14.35

Buddhist Temple Doors — A364

Various doors: 600k, 2300k, 2500k, 2600k.

2001, Sept. 17 **Litho.** ***Perf. 14x14½***
1527-1530 A364 Set of 4 2.50 2.50

Frangipani Flowers — A365

Designs: 1000k, White flowers. 2500k, Pink flowers, vert. 3500k, Red flowers.

2001, Oct. 2 ***Perf. 14½x14, 14x14½***
1531-1533 A365 Set of 3 2.25 2.25
a. Souvenir sheet, #1531-1533, perf. 13¼ 2.25 2.25

Intl. Volunteers Year — A366

Illustration reduced.

2001, Dec. 29 ***Perf. 13¼***
1534 A366 1000k multi .40 .40

Women's Costumes — A367

Designs: 200k, Meuy. 300k, Leu. 500k, Tai Kouane. 700k, Tai Dam. 1000k, Tai Men. 1500k, Lanten. 2500k, Hmong. 3000k, Phouxang. 3500k, Taitheng. 4000k, Tai O. 5000k, Tai Dam, diff.

2002, Jan. 10 ***Perf. 14x14½***
1535 A367 200k multi .20 .20
1536 A367 300k multi .20 .20
1537 A367 500k multi .20 .20
1538 A367 700k multi .25 .25
1539 A367 1000k multi .30 .30
1540 A367 1500k multi .45 .45
1541 A367 2500k multi .75 .75
1542 A367 3000k multi .95 .95
1543 A367 3500k multi 1.10 1.10
1544 A367 4000k multi 1.25 1.25
1545 A367 5000k multi 1.60 1.60
Nos. 1535-1545 (11) 7.25 7.25

Intl. Year of Mountains — A368

Designs: No. 1546, 1500k, Pha Tang. No. 1547, 1500k, Phou Phamane.

2002, Mar. 30 ***Perf. 14½x14***
1546-1547 A368 Set of 2 1.10 1.10

New Year 2002 (Year of the Horse) A369

Designs: 1500k, Horse, zodiac animals. 3500k, Galloping horse.

2002, Apr. 14
1548-1549 A369 Set of 2 1.60 1.60

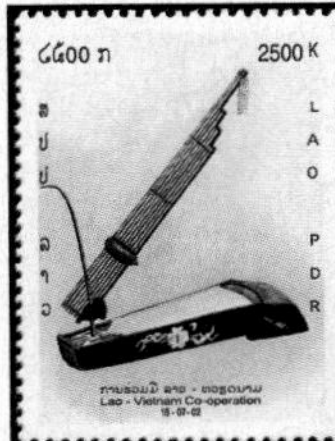

Laos - Viet Nam Cooperation A370

Designs: 2500k, Musical instruments. 3500k, Laotian leader with Ho Chi Minh, horiz.

2002, July 18 ***Perf. 13***
1550-1551 A370 Set of 2 1.90 1.90

Phila Korea 2002 World Stamp Exhibition, Seoul — A371

Insects: Nos. 1552a, 1553a, Sagra femorata. Nos. 1552b, 1552c, Cerambycidae. Nos. 1552c, 1552c, Chrysochroa mniszechii. Nos. 1552d, 1553d, Anoplophora sp. Nos. 1552e, 1553e, Chrysochroa sandersi. Nos. 1552f, 1553f, Mouhotia batesi. Nos. 1552g, 1553g, Megaloxantha assamensis. Nos. 1552h, 1553h, Eupatorus gracillicornis.

2002, Aug. 1 ***Perf. 14½x14***
Insects and Colored Backgrounds
1552 Vert. strip of 8 2.50 2.50
a.-h. A371 1000k Any single .30 .30

Souvenir Sheet
Insects On Vegetation
1553 A371 1000k Sheet of 8, #a-h 2.75 2.75

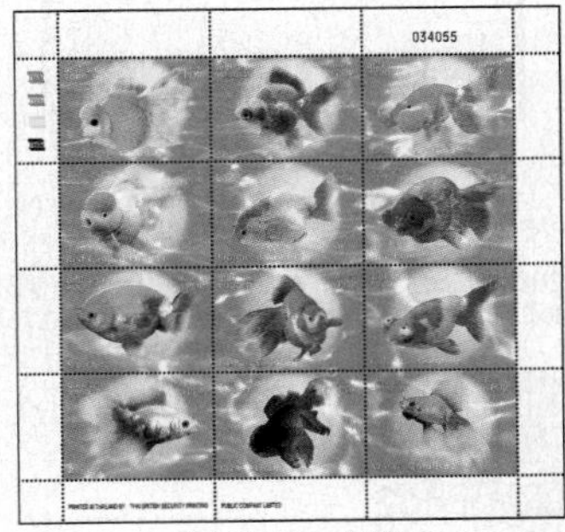

Admission to UPU, 50th Anniv. A372

2002, May 20 **Litho.** ***Perf. 13x13¼***
1554 A372 3000k black .95 .95

Goldfish — A373

No. 1555: a, Pearlscale goldfish. b, Moor. c, Bubble eyes goldfish. d, Red-capped oranda. e, Lionhead goldfish. f, Pom pom. g, Ranchu. h, Fantail goldfish. i, Celestial goldfish. j, Ryukin. k, Brown oranda. l, Veiltail goldfish.

2002, Oct. 2 ***Perf. 13¼***
1555 A373 1000k Sheet of 12, #a-l 4.00 4.00

Buffalo Fighting A374

Various buffalo: 200k, 300k, 3000k, 4000k.

2002, Dec. 15 ***Perf. 13x13¼***
1556-1559 A374 Set of 4 2.50 2.50

Souvenir Sheet

National Route 9 Improvement Project — A375

No. 1560: a, Curve. b, Interchange. c, Curve and building.

2002, Dec. 18 **Litho.** ***Perf. 13¼***
1560 A375 1500k Sheet of 3, #a-c 1.60 1.60

Vat Phou World Heritage Site — A376

Designs: 1500k, Temple, vert. 3000k, Temple, diff. 4000k, Statue of Buddha, vert. 10,000k, Stone carving.

2003, Feb. 14 ***Perf. 14x14½, 14½x14***
1561-1563 A376 Set of 3 2.60 2.60

Souvenir Sheet
Perf. 13¼
1564 A376 10,000k multi 3.50 3.50

No. 1564 contains one 93x27mm stamp.

Butterflies — A377

No. 1565: a, Hasora schoenherr. b, Spindasis lohita. c, Graphium sarpedon. d, Polyura schreiber. e, Castalius rosimon. f, Dalias pasithoe. g, Pachliopta aristolochiae. h, Papilio memnon.
10,000k, Danaus genutia.

2003, Mar. 8 ***Perf. 14½x14***
1565 Block of 8 3.50 3.50
a.-h. A377 1000k Any single .40 .35

Souvenir Sheet
Perf. 13¼
1566 A377 10,000k multi 4.25 4.25

No. 1566 exists imperf.

New Year 2003 (Year of the Goat) A378

Designs: 2500k, Two goats. 5000k, Goat, zodiac animals.

2003, Apr. 15 ***Perf. 14½x14***
1567-1568 A378 Set of 2 2.25 2.25

Orchids — A379

Designs: 200k, Phalaenopsis Paifang's Golden Lion. 300k, Coelogyne lentiginosa. 500k, Phalaenopsis sumatrana. 1000k, Phalaenopsis bellina. 1500k, Paphiopedilum appletonianum. 2000k, Vanda bensonii. 2500k, Dendrobium harveyanum. 3000k, Paphiopedilum glaucophyllum. 3500k, Paphiopedilum gratrixianum. 4000k, Vanda roeblingiana. 5000k, Phalaenopsis Lady Sakhara.

2003, Apr. 25 ***Perf. 14½x14¼***
1569 A379 200k multi .20 .20
1570 A379 300k multi .20 .20
1571 A379 500k multi .20 .20
1572 A379 1000k multi .30 .30
1573 A379 1500k multi .45 .45
1574 A379 2000k multi .60 .60
1575 A379 2500k multi .75 .75
1576 A379 3000k multi .90 .90
1577 A379 3500k multi 1.00 1.00
1578 A379 4000k multi 1.25 1.25
1579 A379 5000k multi 1.50 1.50
Nos. 1569-1579 (11) 7.35 7.35

Wood Handicrafts — A380

Designs: 500k, Bowl. 1500k, Pitcher and goblets. 2500k, Fluted bowl. 3500k, Bowl, vert.

2003, May 10 ***Perf. 13***
1580-1583 A380 Set of 4 2.40 2.40

Traditional Games A381

Designs: 1000k, Walking on stringed coconut shells. 3000k, Top spinning. 4000k, Field hockey.

2003, June 1
1584-1586 A381 Set of 3 2.40 2.40

Stop Hunting Campaign A382

Designs: 1500k, Deer. 2000k, Gun. 4500k, Wild animals.

2003, July 25 **Litho.** ***Perf. 13***
1587-1589 A382 Set of 3 2.50 2.50

Fruit A383

Designs: 500k, Mango. 1500k, Watermelon. 2500k, Custard apple. 4000k, Pineapple.

2003, Aug. 8 ***Perf. 14½x14***
1590-1593 A383 Set of 4 2.60 2.60

Palm Leaf Manuscripts A384

Designs: 500k, Monk writing palm leaf manuscript. 1500k, Palm leaf manuscript. 2500k, Manuscript casket. 3000k, Ho Tai.

2003, Sept. 12 *Perf. 14x14½*
1594-1597 A384 Set of 4 3.00 3.00

Bangkok 2003 Intl. Philatelic Exhibition — A385

Buddhas of Luang Prabang: 500k, Pha Sene Souk. 1500k, Pha Gnai. 3000k, Pha Ong Luang. 3500k, Pha Ong Sene.
10,000k, Pha Attharatsa.

2003, Oct. 4 *Perf. 14x14½*
1598-1601 A385 Set of 4 3.25 3.25

Souvenir Sheet

Perf. 13½

1602 A385 10,000k multi 3.75 3.75

No. 1602 contains one 30x95mm stamp and exists imperf.

Textiles — A386

Various textiles with panel colors of: 500k, Blue. 1000k, Red brown. 3000k, Green. 4000k, Yellow brown.

2003, Dec. 1 *Perf. 14x14½*
1603-1606 A386 Set of 4 3.00 3.00

Installed Emerald Buddha — A387

2004, Feb. 5 **Litho.** *Perf. 14½x14*
1607 A387 5500k multi 1.90 1.90

Birds — A388

Designs: 2000k, Buceros bicornis. 2500k, Pycnonotus jocosus. 3000k, Ploceus hypoxanthus. 3500k, Alcedo atthis. 4000k, Magalaima incognita. 4500k, Serilophus lunatus. 5000k, Lacedo pulchella. 5500k, Eurylaimus ochromalus.

2004, Feb. 20 *Perf. 14¼x14½*
1608-1615 A388 Set of 8 11.00 11.00

Dolphins — A389

Two dolphins: 1500k With heads above water. 2500k, Leaping out of water. 3500k, Underwater.

2004, Mar. 29 *Perf. 14½x14*
1616-1618 A389 Set of 3 2.50 2.50

New Year 2004 (Year of the Monkey) — A390

Designs: 500k, Two monkeys. 4500k, Monkey, zodiac animals.

2004, Apr. 15
1619-1620 A390 Set of 2 1.75 1.75

FIFA (Fédération Internationale de Football Association), Cent. — A391

No. 1621 — FIFA emblem and: a, Flags of various countries. b, Soccer players.
Illustration reduced.

2004, May 21 *Perf. 13½*
1621 A391 12,000k Pair, #a-b 8.00 8.00

Values are for stamps with surrounding selvage,

Children's Day — A392

Designs: 3500k, Four children. 4500k, Children, globe, school.

2004, June 1 *Perf. 14½x14*
1622-1623 A392 Set of 2 2.60 2.60

11th ASEAN Postal Business Meeting — A393

2004, July 5 **Litho.** *Perf. 14x14½*
1624 A393 5000k multi 1.75 1.75

Worldwide Fund for Nature (WWF) — A394

No. 1625 — Cuora amboinensis: a, 5000k, In water. b, 5500k, On rock near water. c, 6000k, Pair. d, 7000k, Head, feet and shell.

Illustration reduced.

2004, Aug. 16 **Litho.** *Perf. 13½x14*
1625 A394 Block of 4, #a-d 5.00 5.00

Dances — A395

Designs: 1000k, Tangwai. 1500k, Khabthoume Luangprabang. 2000k, Lao Lamvong. 2500k, Salavan.

2004, Aug. 23 *Perf. 14x14¾*
1626-1629 A395 Set of 4 2.10 2.10
1629a Souvenir sheet, #1626-1629, perf. 13¼ 3.00 3.00

No. 1629a sold for 10,000k and exists imperf.

Marigolds A396

Designs: 3500k, Yellow, orange marigolds. 5000k, Red and orange marigolds. 5500k, Decorations made with marigolds.

2004, Sept. 28 *Perf. 13¼x13*
1630-1632 A396 Set of 3 4.75 4.75

Scenes From Ramakian — A397

Various scenes: 3500k, 4500k, 5500k, 6500k.

2004, Oct. 10 *Perf. 13¼*
1633-1636 A397 Set of 4 6.75 6.75

Naga Fireball — A398

Designs: 2000k, Figure above river, serpent in river. 3000k, Buildings, serpent, horiz. 3500k, Fireball in serpent's mouth, horiz. 4000k, Fireballs above serpent.

2004, Oct. 28 *Perf. 13 Syncopated*
1637-1640 A398 Set of 4 4.25 4.25

Betel Tray A399

Designs: 2000k, Betel nuts, bowls and containers. 4000k, Betel nut and leaf. 6000k, Betel tray.

2004, Nov. 11 **Litho.** *Perf. 13*
1641-1643 A399 Set of 3 4.00 4.00

Laos — Sweden Diplomatic Relations, 40th Anniv. — A400

Illustration reduced.

2004, Dec. 12 **Litho.** *Perf. 13x13½*
1644 A400 8500k multi 2.75 2.75

Handicrafts — A401

Designs: 1000k, Short, round basket. 2000k, Paddle. 2500k, Basket with handle, vert. 5500k, Basket with handle and lid, vert.

Perf. 14½x14, 14x14½

2005, Mar. 10 **Litho.**
1645-1648 A401 Set of 4 3.25 3.25

New Year 2005 (Year of the Rooster) — A402

Rooster and: 2000k, Hen. 7500k, Zodiac animals.

2005, Apr. 13 *Perf. 14½x14*
1649-1650 A402 Set of 2 3.50 3.50

Daily Buddhas — A403

Buddha for: 500k, Sunday. 1000k, Monday. 1500k, Tuesday, horiz. 2000k, Wednesday. 2500k, Thursday. 3000k, Friday. 3500k, Saturday.

Perf. 14x14½, 14½x14

2005, May 15 **Litho.**
1651-1657 A403 Set of 7 4.50 4.50

Rice — A404

Designs: 1500k, Rice plants. 3000k, Cooked rice on plate, horiz. 6500k, Bundles of rice plants, horiz.

Perf. 13 Syncopated

2005, June 1 **Litho.**
1658-1660 A404 Set of 3 3.25 3.25

Mekong River Giant Catfish — A405

Designs: 3500k, Shown. 6500k, Catfish, diff.

2005, July 13 Litho. *Perf. 14½x14*
1661-1662 A405 Set of 2 3.25 3.25

Gold Panning — A406

Designs: 2000k, Pan. 7500k, Woman panning for gold, vert.

Perf. 13 Syncopated

2005, Aug. 1 Litho.
1663-1664 A406 Set of 2 3.00 3.00

Folk Songs — A407

Designs: 1000k, Two musicians standing. 3500k, Two musicians seated. 5500k, Four musicians, horiz.

2005, Sept. 2
1665-1667 A407 Set of 3 3.00 3.00

Europa Stamps, 50th Anniv. (in 2006) A408

Designs: 6000k, Stonehenge, England, and Plain of Jars, Laos. No. 1669, 7000k, Knossos Palace, Greece, and Patuxay, Laos. No. 1670, 7000k, Colosseum, Rome, and Wat Phu, Laos. No. 1671, 7500k, Stave Church, Lom, Norway, and Wat Xieng Thong, Laos. No. 1672, 7500k, Notre Dame Cathedral, Paris, and That Luang, Laos. 8000k, Trier Cathedral, Germany, and Wat Phra Keo, Laos.

2005, Oct. 24 Litho. *Perf. 14¾x14*
1668-1673 A408 Set of 6 12.50 12.50
1673a Souvenir sheet, #1668-1673 12.50 12.50

No. 1673a exists imperf.

People's Democratic Republic, 30th Anniv. — A409

Designs: 500k, Flag and building. 1000k, Flag and people. 2000k, Flag and coat of arms. 5000k, People and coat of arms.

2005, Dec. 2 *Perf. 13*
1674-1677 A409 Set of 4 2.50 2.50

Diplomatic Relations with Thailand, 55th Anniv. — A410

2005, Dec. 19
1678 A410 7500k multi 2.25 2.25

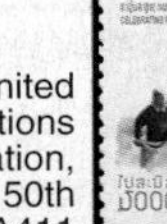

Laos-United Nations Cooperation, 50th Anniv. — A411

Designs: No. 1679, 3000k, Rice harvesters. No. 1679A, 3000k, Children at school gate. No. 1679B, 3000k, Infant health care.

2005, Oct. 24 Litho. *Perf. 13x13¼*
1679-1679B A411 Set of 3 3.50 3.50
1679Bc Souvenir sheet, #1679-1679B 5.25 5.25

No. 1679Bc sold for 15,000k.

Lao People's Democratic Republic, 30th Anniv. — A411a

Designs: 500k, Buildings and flag. 1000k, Map, people and flag. 2000k, Flag, coat of arms. 5000k, Arms, people.

2005, Dec. 2 Litho. *Perf. 13*
1679D-1679G A411a Set of 4 4.50 4.50

Lao People's Democratic Republic, 30th Anniv. — A411b

2005, Dec. 16 Litho. *Perf. 13¼x13*
1679H A411b 15,500k multi 5.50 5.50

Souvenir Sheet

1679I A411b 20,000k multi 7.00 7.00

Diplomatic Relations Between Laos and Japan, 50th Anniv. — A411c

Designs: 7000k, Flowers. 20,000k, Temples.

2005, Dec. 30 *Perf. 13*
1679J A411c 7000k multi 2.60 2.60

Size: 170x130mm

Imperf

1679K A411c 20,000k multi 7.00 7.00

Statue of King Phangum Lenglathorany A412

2006, Mar. 9 Litho. *Perf. 14x14½*
1680 A412 8500k multi 2.60 2.60

A souvenir sheet containing one perf. 13½ example of No. 1680 sold for 20,000k.

New Year 2006 (Year of the Dog) A413

Designs: 2000k, Dog. 6500k, Dog, zodiac animals.

2006, Apr. 14 *Perf. 14½x14*
1681-1682 A413 Set of 2 3.50 3.50

AGL Insurance in Laos, 15th Anniv. — A414

AGL Insurance emblem and: 8000k, Car, minivan and motorcycle. 8500k, Map of Laos. 9500k, Family.

2006, May 1 *Perf. 13*
1683-1685 A414 Set of 3 7.75 7.75

Friendship Between Vientiane and Moscow — A415

Laotian and Russian: 7500k, Women. 8500k, Sculptures and houses of worship.

2006, May 1
1686-1687 A415 Set of 2 4.75 4.75
1687a Souvenir sheet, #1686-1687 6.00 6.00

No. 1687a sold for 20,000k.

Diplomatic Relations Between Laos and People's Republic of China, 45th Anniv. — A416

Illustration reduced.

2006, May 24 *Perf. 13x12¾*
1688 A416 8500k multi 2.60 2.60

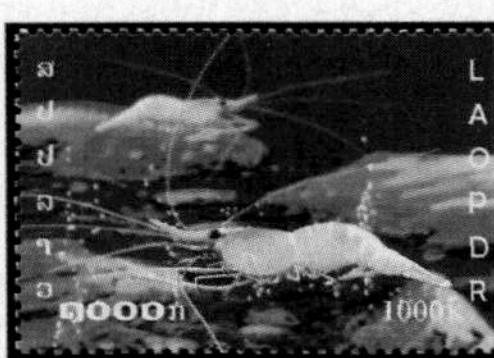

Shrimp A417

Various depictions of shrimp: 1000k, 2000k, 4000k, 6000k.

2006, July 10 *Perf. 13*
1689-1692 A417 Set of 4 4.00 4.00
1692a Souvenir sheet, #1689-1692 4.50 4.50

No. 1692a sold for 15,000k.

Léopold Sédar Senghor (1906-2001), First President of Senegal — A418

2006, Sept. 4
1693 A418 8500k multi 2.60 2.60

Bronze Drums A419

Various drums with background colors of: 2000k, Red brown. 3500k, Blue. 7500k, Olive green.

2006, Oct. 9
1694-1696 A419 Set of 3 4.00 4.00
1696a Souvenir sheet, #1694-1696 5.50 5.50

No. 1696a sold for 15,000k.

Xieng Khouane Temple — A420

Various views of temple and sculptures: 1000k, 2500k, 3000k, 5000k.

2006, June 10 Litho. *Perf. 13*
1697-1700 A420 Set of 4 4.00 4.00

Bananas A421

Designs: 1000k, Pisang Masak Hijau. 2000k, Pisang Mas. 4000k, Pisang Ambon. 8000k, Pisang Awak.

2006, Nov. 1
1701-1704 A421 Set of 4 5.00 5.00

Opening of Second Thai-Lao Friendship Bridge — A422

Designs: No. 1705, 7500k, Bridge in daylight. No. 1706, 7500k, Bridge at night.

2006, Dec. 20

1705-1706 A422 Set of 2 5.00 5.00

Jewelry — A423

Designs: 2000k, Pins. 5000k, Bracelet. 7000k, Earrings. 7500k, Necklace and pendant.

2007, Jan. 15 Litho. *Perf. 13¼x13*

1707-1710 A423 Set of 4 8.00 8.00
1710a Souvenir sheet, #1707-1710 9.50 9.50

No. 1710a sold for 25,000k.

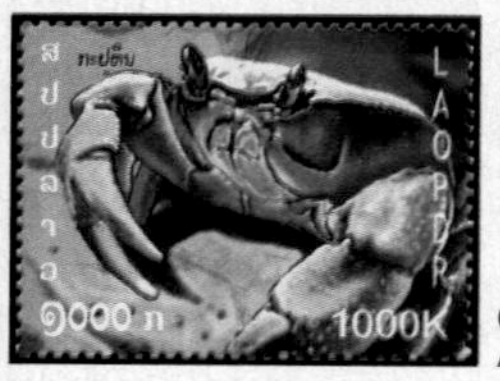

Crabs A424

Various crabs: 1000k, 2000k, 7000k, 7500k.

2007, Feb. 20 *Perf. 13x13¼*

1711-1714 A424 Set of 4 6.50 6.50
1714a Souvenir sheet, #1711-1714, perf. 13½x13¾ 7.50 7.50

No. 1714a sold for 20,000k.

New Year 2007 (Year of the Pig) A425

Designs: No. 1715, 7500k, Pig and piglets. No. 1716, 7500k, Pig, zodiac animals.

2007, Apr. 15 *Perf. 13x13¼*

1715-1716 A425 Set of 2 5.75 5.75

Worldwide Fund for Nature (WWF) A427

Hylobates lar: 6000k, Head. 7000k, Adult and juvenile. 8000k, With open mouth. 9000k, Two adults.

2008 Litho. *Perf. 13½x14*

1719-1722 A427 Set of 4 7.25 7.25
1722a Miniature sheet, 4 each #1719-1722 29.00 29.00

Nos. 1719-1722, 1722a exist imperf.

2008 Summer Olympics, Beijing A428

Designs: No. 1723, 5000k, Taekwondo. No. 1724, 5000k, High jump. No. 1725, 5000k, Cycling. No. 1726, 5000k, Soccer.

2008 *Perf. 12½x13*

1723-1726 A428 Set of 4 4.75 4.75

SEMI-POSTAL STAMPS

Laotian Children — SP1

Unwmk.

1953, July 14 Engr. *Perf. 13*

B1 SP1 1.50pi + 1pi multi 2.25 1.75
B2 SP1 3pi + 1.50pi multi 2.25 1.75
B3 SP1 3.90pi + 2.50pi multi 2.25 1.75
Nos. B1-B3 (3) 6.75 5.25

The surtax was for the Red Cross.

Nos. 52 and 46 Surcharged: "1k ANNEE MONDIALE DU REFUGIE 1959-1960"

1960, Apr. 7

B4 A16 4k + 1k rose claret 1.25 1.25
B5 A13 10k + 1k multicolored 1.25 1.25

World Refugee Year, July 1, 1959-June 30, 1960. The surcharge was for aid to refugees.

Flooded Village SP2

40k+10k, Flooded market place and truck. 60k+15k, Flooded airport and plane.

1967, Jan. 18 Engr. *Perf. 13*

B6 SP2 20k + 5k multi .50 .25
B7 SP2 40k + 10k multi .50 .25
B8 SP2 60k + 15k multi 1.25 1.00
a. Miniature sheet of 3 3.00 3.00
Nos. B6-B8 (3) 2.25 1.50

The surtax was for victims of the Mekong Delta flood. No. B8a contains one each of Nos. B6-B8. Size: 148x99mm. Sold for 250k.

Women Working in Tobacco Field — SP3

1967, Oct. 5 Engr. *Perf. 13*

B9 SP3 20k + 5k multi .50 .50
B10 SP3 50k + 10k multi .75 .75
B11 SP3 60k + 15k multi 1.00 1.00
a. Souv. sheet of 3, #B9-B11 3.00 3.00
Nos. B9-B11 (3) 2.25 2.25

Laotian Red Cross, 10th anniv. No. B11a sold for 250k+30k.

Nos. 184-189 Surcharged: "Soutien aux Victimes / de la Guerre / + 5k"

1970, May 1 Photo. *Perf. 14*

B12 A58 10k + 5k multi .50 .25
B13 A58 15k + 5k multi .50 .25
B14 A58 20k + 5k multi .50 .25
B15 A58 30k + 5k multi .50 .25
B16 A58 40k + 5k multi .75 .50
B17 A58 60k + 5k multi 1.00 .50
Nos. B12-B17,CB1-CB2 (8) 9.75 6.50

AIR POST STAMPS

Weaving — AP1

Design: 3.30pi, Wat Pra Keo.

Unwmk.

1952, Apr. 13 Engr. *Perf. 13*

C1 AP1 3.30pi dk pur & pur 1.00 .75
C2 AP1 10pi ultra & bl grn 2.00 1.50
C3 AP1 20pi deep cl & red 3.75 2.75
C4 AP1 30pi blk brn & dk brn violet 4.25 3.75
Nos. C1-C4 (4) 11.00 8.75

See note following No. 17.

UPU Monument and King Sisavang-Vong — AP2

1952, Dec. 7

C5 AP2 25pi vio bl & indigo 4.00 4.00
C6 AP2 50pi dk brn & vio brn 5.00 5.00

Laos' admission to the UPU, May 13, 1952.

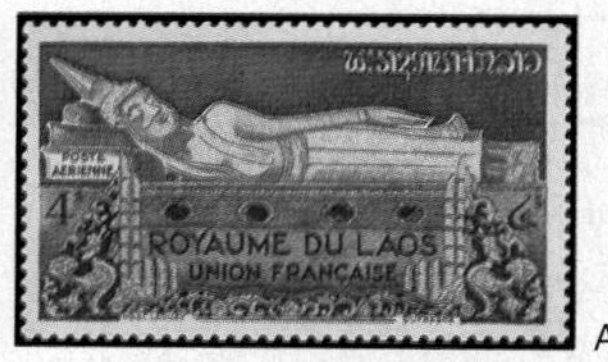

AP3

AP4

Designs: Various Buddha statues.

1953, Nov. 18

C7 AP3 4pi dark green 1.00 .50
C8 AP4 6.50pi dk bl green 1.00 .50
C9 AP4 9pi blue green 1.50 .75
C10 AP3 11.50pi red, yel & dk vio brn 2.50 1.00
C11 AP4 40pi purple 4.00 1.50
C12 AP4 100pi olive 7.50 4.00
Nos. C7-C12 (6) 17.50 8.25

Great Oath of Laos ceremony.

Accession Type of Regular Issue

1954, Mar. 4 Unwmk.

C13 A6 50pi indigo & bl grn 175.00 175.00
Hinged 100.00

Ravana — AP6

Sita and Rama — AP7

Scenes from the Ramayana: 4k, Hanuman, the white monkey. 5k, Ninh Laphath, the black monkey. 20k, Lucy with a friend of Ravana. 30k, Rama.

1955, Oct. 28 Engr. *Perf. 13*

C14 AP6 2k bl grn, emer & ind 1.00 .50
C15 AP6 4k red brn, dk red brn & ver 1.50 1.00
C16 AP6 5k scar, sep & olive 2.50 1.50
C17 AP7 10k blk, org & brn 5.00 1.75
C18 AP7 20k vio, dk grn & olive 6.00 2.50
C19 AP7 30k ultra, blk & salmon 8.00 4.00
Nos. C14-C19 (6) 24.00 11.25

See No. 225.

Buddha Type of Regular Issue, 1956

1956, May 24

C20 A7 20k carmine rose 29.00 23.50
C21 A7 30k olive & olive bister 29.00 27.50

2500th anniversary of birth of Buddha.

UN Emblem AP8

1956, Dec. 14

C22 AP8 15k light blue 4.50 4.50
C23 AP8 30k deep claret 6.50 6.50

Admission of Laos to the UN, 1st anniv.

Types of Regular Issue, 1957

Musical Instruments: 12k, Khong vong. 14k, So. 20k, Kong.

1957, Mar. 25 Unwmk. *Perf. 13*

C24 A9 12k multicolored 2.75 1.75
C25 A10 14k multicolored 3.00 2.25
C26 A10 20k bl grn, yel grn & pur 3.50 3.00
Nos. C24-C26 (3) 9.25 7.00

Monk Receiving Alms — AP9

Monks Meditating in Boat — AP10

18k, Smiling Buddha. 24k, Ancient temple painting (horse and mythological figures.)

1957, Nov. 5

C27 AP9 10k dk pur, pale brn & dk grn 1.00 1.00
C28 AP10 15k dk vio brn, brn org & yel 1.00 1.00
C29 AP9 18k slate grn & ol 1.25 1.25
C30 AP10 24k claret, org yel & blk 3.00 3.00
Nos. C27-C30 (4) 6.25 6.25

No. C28 measures 48x27mm. No. C30, 48x36mm. See No. C84.

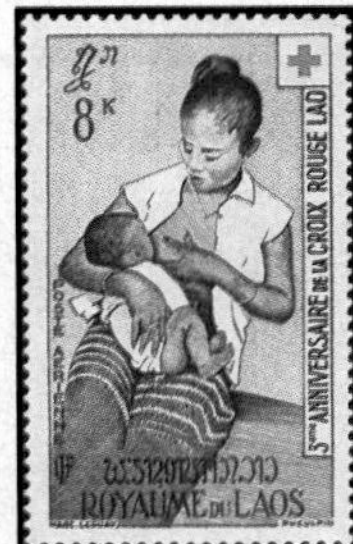

Mother Nursing Infant — AP11

1958, May 2

Cross in Red

C31 AP11 8k lil gray & dk gray 1.50 .75
C32 AP11 12k red brn & brn 1.75 1.00
C33 AP11 15k sl grn & bluish green 2.00 1.00
C34 AP11 20k bister & vio 2.50 1.50
Nos. C31-C34 (4) 7.75 4.25

3rd anniversary of Laotian Red Cross.

Plain of Stones, Xieng Khouang AP12

Papheng Falls, Champassak — AP13

Natl. Tourism Industry: 15k, Buffalo cart. 19k, Buddhist monk and village.

1960, July 1 Engr. *Perf. 13*

C35 AP12 9.50k bl, ol & claret .50 .50
C36 AP13 12k vio bl, red brn & gray .50 .50
C37 AP13 15k yel grn, ol gray & cl .75 .75
C38 AP12 19k multicolored 1.00 1.00
Nos. C35-C38 (4) 2.75 2.75

Pou Gneu Nha Gneu Legend — AP14

Garuda — AP15

Hanuman, the White Monkey — AP16

Nang Teng One Legend AP17

1962, Feb. 19 Unwmk. *Perf. 13*

C39 AP14 11k grn, car & ocher .60 .60
C40 AP15 14k ultra & org .60 .60
C41 AP16 20k multicolored .80 .80
C42 AP17 25k multicolored .90 .90
Nos. C39-C42 (4) 2.90 2.90

Makha Bousa festival.

Yao Hunter — AP18

Phayre's Flying Squirrel — AP19

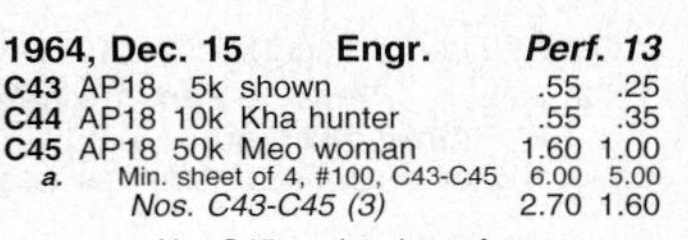

1964, Dec. 15 Engr. *Perf. 13*

C43 AP18 5k shown .55 .25
C44 AP18 10k Kha hunter .55 .35
C45 AP18 50k Meo woman 1.60 1.00
a. Min. sheet of 4, #100, C43-C45 6.00 5.00
Nos. C43-C45 (3) 2.70 1.60

No. C45a exists imperf.

Butterfly Type of 1965

1965, Mar. 13

Size: 48x27mm

C46 A34 20k Atlas moth 4.50 2.00

1965, Oct. 7 Engr. *Perf. 13*

Designs: 25k, Leopard cat. 75k, Javan mongoose. 100k, Crestless porcupine. 200k, Binturong.

C47 AP19 25k dk brn, yel grn & ocher .40 .20
C48 AP19 55k brown & blue .65 .30
C49 AP19 75k brt grn & brn .85 .45
C50 AP19 100k ocher, brn & blk 1.50 1.00
C51 AP19 200k red & black 3.25 2.25
Nos. C47-C51 (5) 6.65 4.20

Army Type of Regular Issue

Design: 200k, 300k, Parading service flags before National Assembly Hall.

1968, July 15 Engr. *Perf. 13*

C52 A53 200k multicolored 1.60 .85
C53 A53 300k multicolored 2.50 1.25
a. Souv. sheet of 5, #168-170, C52-C53 5.00 5.00

No. C53a sold for 600k.

Insect Type of Regular Issue

Insects: 120k, Dorysthenes walkeri, horiz. 160k, Megaloxantha bicolor, horiz.

1968, Aug. 28 Engr. *Perf. 13*

C54 A54 120k brn, org & blk 1.50 .85
C55 A54 160k rose car, Prus bl & yel 2.25 1.25

Ballet Type of Regular Issue

Designs: 110k, Sudagnu battling Thotsakan. 300k, Pharam dancing with Thotsakan.

1969 Photo. *Perf. 14*

C56 A58 110k multicolored 2.75 1.75
a. Souv. sheet of 4, #187-189, C56, imperf. 17.50 17.50
C57 A58 300k multicolored 5.50 3.25
a. Souv. sheet of 4, #184-186, C57, imperf. 17.50 17.50

No. C56a sold for 480k; No. C57a for 650k. For surcharges see Nos. CB1-CB2.

Timber Industry, Paksane AP20

1969, May 7 Engr. *Perf. 13*

C58 AP20 300k olive bister & blk 4.75 3.25

ILO, 50th anniversary.

Animal Type of Regular Issue

Animals: 70k, Asiatic black bear. 120k, White-handed gibbon, vert. 150k, Tiger.

1969, Nov. 6 Photo. *Perf. 12x13*

C59 A60 70k multicolored 1.10 .60
C60 A60 120k multicolored 2.00 1.10
C61 A60 150k multicolored 2.75 1.40
Nos. C59-C61 (3) 5.85 3.10

Hairdressing, by Marc Leguay — AP21

Paintings: No. C63, Village Market, by Marc Leguay, horiz. No. C64, Tree on the Bank of the Mekong, by Marc Leguay, horiz.

1969-70 Photo. *Perf. 12x13, 13x12*

C62 AP21 120k multicolored 1.00 .40
C63 AP21 150k multicolored 2.00 .65
C64 AP21 150k multi ('70) 2.00 .65
Nos. C62-C64 (3) 5.00 1.70

See Nos. C72-C74.

Wat Xiengthong, Luang Prabang — AP22

1970, Jan. 10 *Perf. 12x13, 13x12*

C65 AP22 100k Library, Wat Sisaket, vert. 1.40 .65
C66 AP22 120k shown 2.00 1.00

Drum Type of 1970

1970, Mar. 30 Engr. *Perf. 13*

C67 A64 125k Pong wooden drum, vert. 3.00 1.50

Franklin D. Roosevelt (1882-1945) — AP23

1970, Apr. 12

C68 AP23 120k olive & slate 1.60 1.10

EXPO '70 Type of Regular Issue

Design: 125k, Woman boiling cocoons in kettle, and spinning silk thread.

1970, July 7 Engr. *Perf. 13*

C69 A66 125k olive & multi 1.40 1.25

See note after No. 202.

Animal Type of Regular Issue

1970, Sept. 7 Engr. *Perf. 13*

C70 A67 210k Leopard 2.00 1.25
C71 A67 500k Gaur 4.00 2.50

Painting Type of 1969-70

Paintings by Marc Leguay: 100k, Village Foot Path. 120k, Rice Field in Rainy Season, horiz. 150k, Village Elder.

Perf. 11½x13, 13x11½

1970, Dec. 21 Photo.

C72 AP21 100k multicolored 1.10 1.10
C73 AP21 120k multicolored 1.40 1.40
C74 AP21 150k multicolored 1.60 1.60
Nos. C72-C74 (3) 4.10 4.10

UN Type of Regular Issue

125k, Earth Goddess Nang Thorani wringing her hair; UN Headquarters and emblem.

1970, Oct. 24

Size: 26x36mm

C75 A68 125k brt bl, pink & dk grn 1.75 1.10

Hanuman and Nang Matsa — AP24

1971, Feb. 5
C76 AP24 125k multicolored 2.25 1.00

Orchid Type of Regular Issue

Design: 125k, Brasilian cattleya.

1971, July Photo. *Perf. 13x12½*
Size: 48x27mm
C79 A73 125k Brasilian cattleya 3.50 1.50

Laotian and French Women, That Luang Pagoda and Arms AP25

1971, Aug. 6 Engr. *Perf. 13*
C80 AP25 30k brn & dull red .25 .20
C81 AP25 70k vio & lilac .50 .40
C82 AP25 100k slate grn & grn .70 .55
Nos. C80-C82 (3) 1.45 1.15

Kinship between the cities Keng Kok, Laos, and Saint Astier, France.

Animal Type of Regular Issue

1971, Sept. 16
C83 A74 300k Javan rhinoceros 4.25 2.75

Type of 1957 with Ornamental Panel and Inscription

Design: Monk receiving alms (like No. C27).

1971, Nov. 2 Engr. *Perf. 13*
C84 AP9 125k dk pur, pale brn & dk grn 1.40 1.40

20th anniv. of Laotian independent postal service. No. C84 inscribed: "Vingtième Anniversaire de la Philatélie Lao," "Poste Aerienne" and "1971."

Sunset Over the Mekong, by Chamnane Prisayane — AP26

Design: 150k, "Quiet Morning" (village scene), by Chamnane Prisayane.

1971, Dec. 20 Photo. *Perf. 13x12*
C85 AP26 125k black & multi 1.00 1.00
C86 AP26 150k black & multi 1.25 1.25

Book Year Type of Regular Issue

Design: 125k, Father teaching children to read palm leaf book.

1972, Jan. 30 Engr. *Perf. 13*
Size: 48x27mm
C87 A75 125k bright purple 1.00 1.00

Dam Type of Regular Issue

Design: 145k, Nam Ngum Hydroelectric Dam and ECAFE emblem.

1972, Mar. 28 Engr. *Perf. 13*
C88 A76 145k brown, bl & grn .80 .80

Orchid Type of Regular Issue 1971

1972, May 1 Photo. *Perf. 13x12½*
Size: 48x27mm
C89 A73 150k Vanda teres, horiz. 4.00 1.50

UNICEF Type of Regular Issue

Design: 120k, Boy riding buffalo to water hole (child's drawing).

1972, July Engr. *Perf. 13*
C90 A77 120k multicolored 1.00 1.00

Nakharath, Daughter of the Dragon King AP27

Wood carvings from Wat Sikhounvieng Dongmieng, Vientiane: 120k, Nang Kinnali, Goddess from Mt. Kailath. 150k, Norasing, Lion King from Himalayas.

1972, Sept. 15 Engr. *Perf. 13*
C91 AP27 100k blue green .70 .70
C92 AP27 120k violet .80 .80
C93 AP27 150k brn orange 1.10 1.10
Nos. C91-C93 (3) 2.60 2.60

That Luang Religious Festival — AP28

1972, Nov. 18 Engr. *Perf. 13*
C94 AP28 110k Presentation of wax castles .90 .90
C95 AP28 125k Procession 1.10 1.10

Workers in Rice Field, by Leguay AP29

Paintings by Mark Leguay: No. C97, Women and water buffalo in rice field. Nos. C98, Rainy Season in Village (Water buffalo in water). No. C99, Rainy Season in Village (Water buffalo on land). 120k, Mother and Child.

1972, Dec. 23 Photo. *Perf. 13*
C96 AP29 50k multicolored .45 .45
C97 AP29 50k multicolored .45 .45
C98 AP29 70k multicolored .65 .65
C99 AP29 70k multicolored .65 .65
C100 AP29 120k yel & multi 1.25 1.25
Nos. C96-C100 (5) 3.45 3.45

Nos. C97, C99 have denomination and frame at right.

Costume Type of Regular Issue

Women's Costumes: 120k, Luang Prabang marriage costume. 150k, Vientiane evening costume.

1973, Feb. 16 Engr. *Perf. 13*
C101 A78 120k multicolored .80 .80
C102 A78 150k brown & multi 1.00 1.00

Lions Club Emblems, King Sayasettha-Thirath — AP30

1973, Mar. 30 Engr. *Perf. 13*
C103 AP30 150k rose & multi 1.25 .75

Lions Club of Vientiane.

Rahu with Rockets and Sputnik — AP31

Space achievements: 150k, Laotian festival rocket and US lunar excursion module.

1973, May 11 Engr. *Perf. 13*
C104 AP31 80k ultra & multi .55 .35
C105 AP31 150k buff & ultra 1.00 .45

Dancing Around Campfire — AP32

Design: 125k, Boy Scouts helping during Vientiane Flood, 1966.

1973, Sept. 1 Engr. *Perf. 13*
C106 AP32 110k vio & orange .65 .30
C107 AP32 125k Prus grn & bis .90 .40

Laotian Scout Movement, 25th anniv.

Sun Chariot and WMO Emblem — AP33

Design: 90k, Nang Mékhala, the weather goddess, and WMO emblem, vert.

1973, Oct. 24 Engr. *Perf. 13*
C108 AP33 90k vio, red & ocher .75 .35
C109 AP33 150k ocher, red & brn ol .85 .50

Intl. meteorological cooperation, cent.

Woman in Poppy Field, INTERPOL Emblem — AP34

1973, Dec. 22 Engr. *Perf. 13*
C110 AP34 150k vio, yel grn & red 1.10 .60

Intl. Criminal Police Org., 50th anniv.

Phra Sratsvady, Wife of Phra Phrom AP35

Designs: 110k, Phra Indra on 3-headed elephant Erawan. 150k, Phra Phrom, the Creator, on phoenix. Designs show giant sculptures in park at Thadeua.

1974, Mar. 23 Engr. *Perf. 13*
C111 AP35 100k lilac, red & blk .80 .40
C112 AP35 110k car, vio & brn 1.00 .50
C113 AP35 150k ocher, vio & sepia 1.25 .70
Nos. C111-C113 (3) 3.05 1.60

UPU Emblem, Women Reading Letter — AP36

1974 Engr. *Perf. 13*
C114 AP36 200k lt brn & car 1.25 1.00
C115 AP36 500k lilac & red 3.75 2.00
a. Souvenir sheet 5.50 5.50

Centenary of Universal Postal Union. Issue dates: 200k, Apr. 30; 500k, Oct. 9.

Flower Type of 1974

1974, May 31
Size: 36x36mm
C116 A84 500k Pitcher plant 5.00 3.00

Transportation Type of Regular Issue

1974, July 31 Engr. *Perf. 13*
C117 A85 250k Sampan 2.50 1.50

Marconi Type of 1974

Old & new means of communications.

1974, Aug. 28 Engr. *Perf. 13*
C118 A86 200k vio bl & brn 2.25 1.10

Insect Type of 1974

1974, Oct. 23 Engr. *Perf. 13*
C119 A87 110k Sternocera multipunctata 1.75 1.00

Boeing 747 — AP37

1986, June 2 Litho. *Perf. 12½*
C120 AP37 20k shown 3.50
C121 AP37 50k IL86 8.00

AIR POST SEMI-POSTAL STAMPS

Nos. C56-C57 Surcharged: "Soutien aux Victimes / de la Guerre / + 5k"

1970, May 1 Photo. *Perf. 13*
CB1 A58 110k + 5k multi 2.00 1.50
CB2 A58 300k + 5k multi 4.00 3.00

The surtax was for war victims.

POSTAGE DUE STAMPS

Vat-Sisaket Monument D1

Boat and Raft D2

Perf. 13½x13

1952-53 Unwmk. Engr.

J1	D1	10c	dark brown	.25	.25
J2	D1	20c	purple	.25	.25
J3	D1	50c	carmine	.25	.25
J4	D1	1pi	dark green	.25	.25
J5	D1	2pi	deep ultra	.25	.25
J6	D1	5pi	rose violet	1.00	1.00
J7	D2	10pi	indigo ('53)	1.25	1.25
			Nos. J1-J7 (7)	3.50	3.50

Serpent — D3

1973, Oct. 31 Photo. *Perf. 13*

J8	D3	10k	yellow & multi	.25	.25
J9	D3	15k	emerald & multi	.25	.25
J10	D3	20k	blue & multi	.25	.25
J11	D3	50k	scarlet & multi	.50	.50
			Nos. J8-J11 (4)	1.25	1.25

PARCEL POST STAMPS

Wat Ong Theu PP1

2000, June 7 Litho. *Die Cut*

Self-Adhesive

Serial Number in Black

Q1	PP1	5000k	orange	*5.00*	*5.00*
Q2	PP1	40,000k	milky blue	*25.00*	*25.00*
Q3	PP1	60,000k	gray blue	*32.50*	*32.50*
Q4	PP1	80,000k	cerise	*50.00*	*50.00*
Q5	PP1	100,000k	carmine	*60.00*	*60.00*
Q6	PP1	250,000k	ultra	*150.00*	*150.00*
			Nos. Q1-Q6 (6)	322.50	322.50

Phra That Luang — PP2

2003, Aug. 14 *Die Cut*

Self-Adhesive

Serial Number in Black

Q7	PP2	5000k	vio bl & bl	3.00	3.00
Q8	PP2	40,000k	claret & red	15.00	15.00
Q9	PP2	60,000k	grn & claret	25.00	25.00
Q10	PP2	90,000k	red & blue	35.00	35.00
			Nos. Q7-Q10 (4)	78.00	78.00

LATAKIA

ˌla-tə-ˈkē-ə

LOCATION — A division of Syria in Western Asia
GOVT. — French Mandate
AREA — 2,500 sq. mi.
POP. — 278,000 (approx. 1930)
CAPITAL — Latakia

This territory, included in the Syrian Mandate to France under the Versailles Treaty, was formerly known as Alaouites. The name Latakia was adopted in 1930. See Alaouites and Syria.

100 Centimes = 1 Piaster

Stamps of Syria Overprinted in Black or Red

Perf. 12x12½, 13½

1931-33 Unwmk.

1	A6	10c	red violet	1.25	1.25
2	A6	10c	vio brn ('33)	1.60	1.60
3	A7	20c	dk blue (R)	1.25	1.25
4	A7	20c	brown org ('33)	1.60	1.60
5	A8	25c	gray grn (R)	1.25	1.25
6	A8	25c	dk bl gray (R) ('33)	1.60	1.60
7	A9	50c	violet	2.00	2.00
8	A15	75c	org red ('32)	3.25	3.25
9	A10	1p	green (R)	2.40	2.40
10	A11	1.50p	bis brn (R)	3.25	3.25
11	A11	1.50p	dp grn ('33)	4.00	4.00
12	A12	2p	dk vio (R)	3.25	3.25
13	A13	3p	yel grn (R)	5.25	5.25
14	A14	4p	orange	5.25	5.25
15	A15	4.50p	rose car	5.50	5.50
16	A16	6p	grnsh blk (R)	5.50	5.50
17	A17	7.50p	dl blue (R)	4.50	4.50
18	A18	10p	dp brown (R)	9.50	9.50
19	A19	15p	dp green (R)	10.00	10.00
20	A20	25p	violet brn	20.00	20.00
21	A21	50p	dk brown (R)	20.00	20.00
22	A22	100p	red orange	47.50	47.50
			Nos. 1-22 (22)	159.70	159.70

AIR POST STAMPS

Air Post Stamps of Syria, 1931, Overprinted in Black or Red

1931-33 Unwmk. *Perf. 13½*

C1	AP2	50c	ocher	1.25	1.25
a.			Inverted overprint	1,200.	1,200.
C2	AP2	50c	blk brn (R) ('33)	2.40	2.40
C3	AP2	1p	chestnut brn	2.40	2.40
C4	AP2	2p	Prus blue (R)	3.50	3.50
C5	AP2	3p	blue grn (R)	4.75	4.75
C6	AP2	5p	red violet	6.50	6.50
C7	AP2	10p	slate grn (R)	8.00	8.00
C8	AP2	15p	orange red	11.00	11.00
C9	AP2	25p	orange brn	22.50	22.50
C10	AP2	50p	black (R)	36.00	36.00
C11	AP2	100p	magenta	40.00	40.00
			Nos. C1-C11 (11)	138.30	138.30

POSTAGE DUE STAMPS

Postage Due Stamps of Syria, 1931, Overprinted like Regular Issue

1931 Unwmk. *Perf. 13½*

J1	D7	8p	blk, *gray bl* (R)	24.00	24.00
J2	D8	15p	blk, *dl rose* (R)	24.00	24.00

Stamps of Latakia were superseded in 1937 by those of Syria.

LATVIA

ˈlat-vē-ə

(Lettonia, Lettland)

LOCATION — Northern Europe, bordering on the Baltic Sea and the Gulf of Riga
GOVT. — Independent Republic
AREA — 25,395 sq. mi.
POP. — 2,353,874 (1999 est.)
CAPITAL — Riga

Latvia was created a sovereign state following World War I and was admitted to the League of Nations in 1922. In 1940 it became a republic in the Union of Soviet Socialist Republics. Latvian independence was recognized by the Soviet Union on Sept. 6, 1991.

100 Kapeikas = 1 Rublis
100 Santims = 1 Lat (1923, 1993)
100 Kopecks = 1 Ruble (1991)

Catalogue values for unused stamps in this country are for Never Hinged items, beginning with Scott 1 in the regular postage section, Scott B1 in the semi-postal section, Scott C1 in the air post section, Scott CB1 in the air post semi-postal section, and Scott 2N45 in the Russian Occupation section.

Catalogue values for unused stamps in this section are for Never Hinged items.

Watermarks

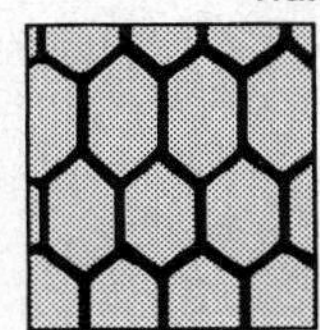
Wmk. 108 Honeycomb

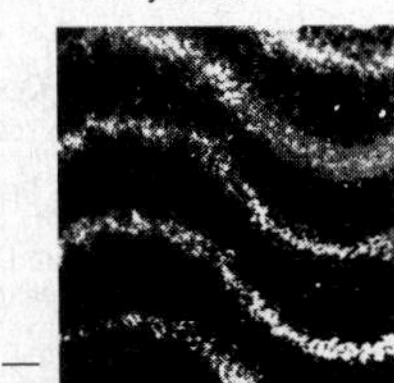
Wmk. 145 — Wavy Lines

Wmk. 181 Wavy Lines

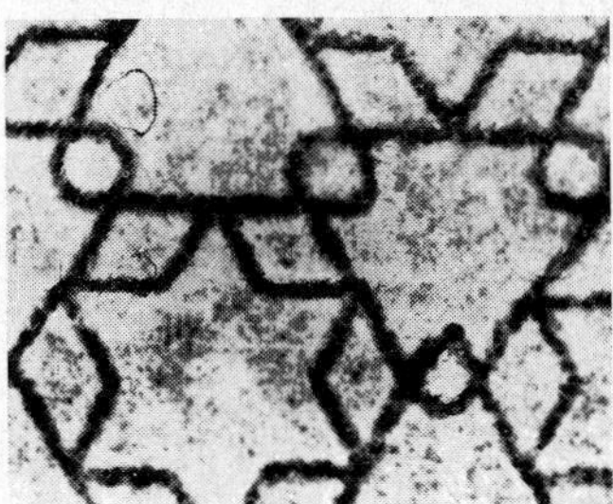
Wmk. 197 — Star and Triangles

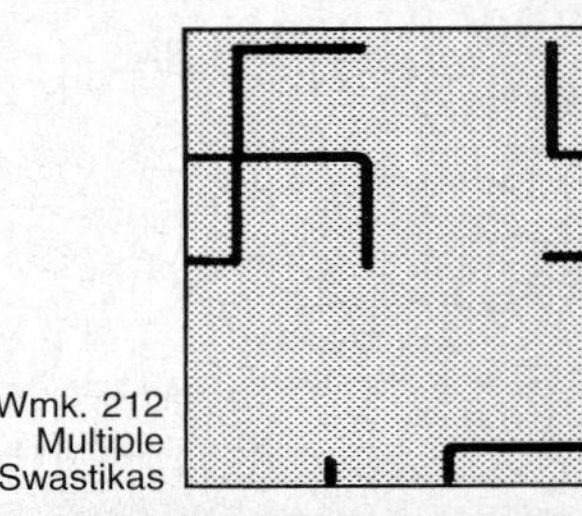
Wmk. 212 Multiple Swastikas

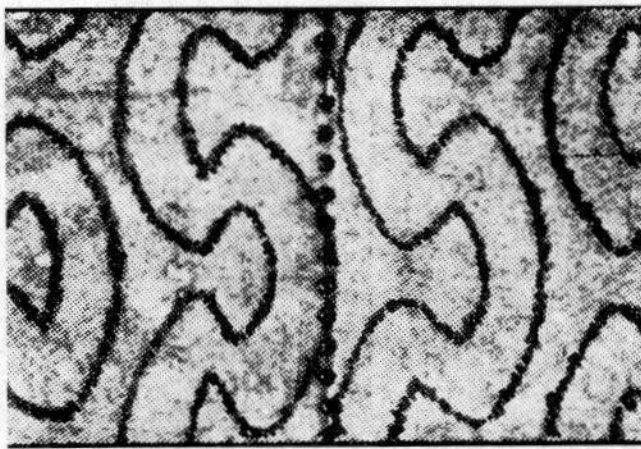
Wmk. 265 — Multiple Waves

Wmk. 387 — Squares and Rectangles

Arms — A1

Printed on the Backs of German Military Maps

Unwmk.

1918, Dec. 18 Litho. *Imperf.*

1	A1	5k	carmine	1.25	1.25

Perf. 11½

2	A1	5k	carmine	1.25	1.25

Values given are for stamps where the map on the back is printed in brown and black. Maps printed only in black are valued at $3.50 each mint or used. Stamps with no map at all sell for more. Stamps with no printing on the back are from the outer rows of some sheets.

Redrawn

Paper with Ruled Lines

1919 *Imperf.*

3	A1	5k	carmine	.50	.25
4	A1	10k	dark blue	.50	.25
5	A1	15k	green	.50	.25

Perf. 11½

6	A1	5k	carmine	2.75	2.75
7	A1	10k	dark blue	2.75	2.75
8	A1	15k	deep green	7.75	7.75
			Nos. 3-8 (6)	14.75	14.00

In the redrawn design the wheat heads are thicker, the ornament at lower left has five points instead of four, and there are minor changes in other parts of the design.

The sheets of this and subsequent issues were usually divided in half by a single line of perforation gauging 10. Thus stamps are found with this perforation on one side.

1919 Pelure Paper *Imperf.*

9	A1	3k	lilac	7.00	6.00
10	A1	5k	carmine	.20	.20
11	A1	10k	deep blue	.20	.20
12	A1	15k	dark green	.20	.20
13	A1	20k	orange	.20	.20
13A	A1	25k	gray	45.00	40.00
14	A1	35k	dark brown	.25	.25
15	A1	50k	purple	.25	.25
16	A1	75k	emerald	5.00	5.00
			Nos. 9-16 (9)	58.30	52.30

Perf. 11½, 9½

No.	Type	Value	Color	Unused	Used
17	A1	3k	lilac	35.00	25.00
18	A1	5k	carmine	1.00	.80
19	A1	10k	deep blue	4.00	3.00
20	A1	15k	dark green	3.00	3.00
21	A1	20k	orange	3.75	3.75
22	A1	35k	dark brown	4.50	4.50
23	A1	50k	purple	6.00	6.00
24	A1	75k	emerald	15.00	15.00
			Nos. 17-24 (8)	72.25	61.05

Values are for perf 11½. Examples Perf 9½ sell for more.

Nos. 17-24 are said to be unofficially perforated varieties of Nos. 9-16.

1919 Wmk. 108 *Imperf.*

No.	Type	Value	Color	Unused	Used
25	A1	3k	lilac	.30	.20
26	A1	5k	carmine	.30	.20
27	A1	10k	deep blue	.30	.20
28	A1	15k	deep green	.35	.20
29	A1	20k	orange	.40	.25
30	A1	25k	gray	.85	.50
31	A1	35k	dark brown	.45	.25
32	A1	50k	purple	.45	.25
33	A1	75k	emerald	.55	.25
			Nos. 25-33 (9)	3.95	2.30

The variety "printed on both sides" exists for 3k, 10k, 15k, 20k and 35k. Value, $20 each.

See #57-58, 76-82. For surcharges and overprints see #86, 132-133, 2N1-2N8, 2N12-2N19.

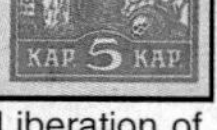

Liberation of Riga — A2

Rising Sun — A4

1919 Wmk. 108

No.	Type	Value	Color	Unused	Used
43	A2	5k	carmine	.50	.25
44	A2	15k	deep green	.50	.25
45	A2	35k	brown	.70	.45
			Nos. 43-45 (3)	1.70	.95

Unwmk.
Pelure Paper

No.	Type	Value	Color	Unused	Used
49	A2	5k	carmine	15.00	9.50
50	A2	15k	deep green	15.00	9.50
51	A2	35k	brown	30.00	9.50
			Nos. 49-51 (3)	60.00	28.50

For surcharge and overprints see Nos. 87, 2N9-2N11, 2N20-2N22.

1919 *Imperf.*

No.	Type	Value	Color	Unused	Used
55	A4	10k	gray blue	.85	.60

Perf. 11½

No.	Type	Value	Color	Unused	Used
56	A4	10k	gray blue	1.50	1.50

Type of 1918

1919 Laid Paper *Perf. 11½*

No.	Type	Value	Color	Unused	Used
57	A1	3r	slate & org	1.60	1.00
58	A1	5r	gray brn & org	2.50	1.00

Independence Issue

Allegory of One Year of Independence A5

1919, Nov. 18 Unwmk.
Wove Paper
Size: 33x45mm

No.	Type	Value	Color	Unused	Used
59	A5	10k	brown & rose	1.25	1.00

Laid Paper

No.	Type	Value	Color	Unused	Used
60	A5	10k	brown & rose	1.25	1.00

Size: 28x38mm

No.	Type	Value	Color	Unused	Used
61	A5	10k	brown & rose	.30	.25
a.			Imperf.	50.00	
62	A5	35k	indigo & grn	.30	.20
a.			Vert. pair, imperf. btwn.	45.00	40.00

Wmk. 197
Thick Wove Paper
Blue Design on Back

No.	Type	Value	Color	Unused	Used
63	A5	1r	green & red	.90	.75
			Nos. 59-63 (5)	4.00	3.20

There are two types of Nos. 59 and 60. In type I the trunk of the tree is not outlined. In type II it has a distinct white outline.

No. 63 was printed on the backs of unfinished 5r bank notes of the Workers and Soldiers Council, Riga.

For surcharges see Nos. 83-85, 88, 94.

Warrior Slaying Dragon — A6

1919-20 Unwmk. *Perf. 11½*
Wove Paper

No.	Type	Value	Color	Unused	Used
64	A6	10k	brown & car	.50	.25
a.			Horiz. pair, imperf. btwn.	55.00	45.00
65	A6	25k	ind & yel grn	.60	.35
a.			Pair, imperf. btwn.	55.00	45.00
66	A6	35k	black & bl ('20)	.75	.35
a.			Horiz. pair, imperf. btwn.	55.00	45.00
67	A6	1r	dk grn & brn ('20)	1.50	.70
a.			Horiz. pair, imperf. vert.	50.00	40.00
b.			Horiz. pair, imperf. btwn.	50.00	40.00
			Nos. 64-67 (4)	3.35	1.65

Issued in honor of the liberation of Kurzeme (Kurland). The paper sometimes shows impressed quadrille lines.

For surcharges see Nos. 91-93.

Latgale Relief Issue

Latvia Welcoming Home Latgale Province — A7

1920, Mar.
Brown and Green Design on Back

No.	Type	Value	Color	Unused	Used
68	A7	50k	dk green & rose	1.00	.40
a.			Horiz. pair, imperf. vert.	50.00	
69	A7	1r	slate grn & brn	1.10	.45
a.			Horiz. pair, imperf. vert.	50.00	

No. 68-69 were printed on the backs of unfinished bank notes of the government of Colonel Bermondt-Avalov and on the so-called German "Ober-Ost" money.

For surcharges see Nos. 95-99.

First National Assembly Issue

Latvia Hears Call to Assemble — A8

1920

No.	Type	Value	Color	Unused	Used
70	A8	50k	rose	.85	.30
a.			Imperf., pair	10.00	6.00
71	A8	1r	blue	.85	.20
a.			Vert. pair, imperf. btwn.	45.00	45.00
b.			Imperf., pair	20.00	15.00
72	A8	3r	dk brn & grn	.85	.75
73	A8	5r	slate & vio brn	2.25	.80
			Nos. 70-73 (4)	4.80	2.05

For surcharges see Nos. 90, 134.

Type of 1918 Issue
Wove Paper

1920-21 Unwmk. *Perf. 11½*

No.	Type	Value	Color	Unused	Used
76	A1	5k	carmine	.20	.20
78	A1	20k	orange	.20	.20
79	A1	40k	lilac ('21)	.60	.20
80	A1	50k	violet	.60	.20
81	A1	75k	emerald	.60	.20
82	A1	5r	gray brn & org ('21)	3.75	.20
			Nos. 76-82 (6)	5.95	1.20

No. 63 Surcharged in Black, Brown or Blue

1920, Sept. 1

No.	Type	Description	Unused	Used
83	A5	10r on 1r grn & red (Bk)	2.50	1.50
84	A5	20r on 1r grn & red (Br)	4.75	3.00
85	A5	30r on 1r grn & red (Bl)	7.50	5.00
		Nos. 83-85 (3)	14.75	9.50

Types of 1919 Surcharged

1920-21 Wmk. 108 *Perf. 11½*

No.	Type	Description	Unused	Used
86	A1	2r on 10k dp blue	3.00	*4.00*
87	A2	2r on 35k brown	.95	*3.75*

No. 62 Surcharged in Red

Unwmk.

No.	Type	Description	Unused	Used
88	A5	2r on 35k ind & grn	.70	.50

No. 70 Surcharged in Blue

1921

No.	Type	Description	Unused	Used
90	A8	2r on 50k rose	.90	.60

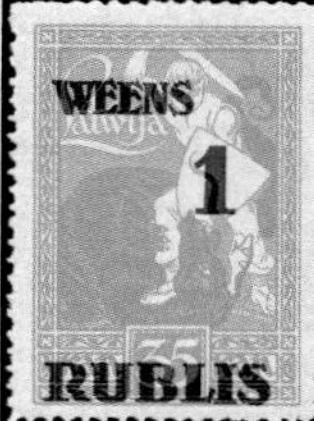

Nos. 64-66 Surcharged in Red or Blue

1920-21

No.	Type	Description	Unused	Used
91	A6	1r on 35k blk & bl (R)	.55	.35
92	A6	2r on 10k brn & rose (Bl)	1.00	.75
93	A6	2r on 25k ind & grn (R)	.65	.40
a.		Imperf.	—	
		Nos. 91-93 (3)	2.20	1.50

On Nos. 92 and 93 the surcharge reads "DIVI 2 RUBLI."

No. 83 with Added Surcharge

1921 Wmk. 197

No.	Type	Description	Unused	Used
94	A5	10r on 10r on 1r	2.50	1.00

Latgale Relief Issue of 1920 Surcharged in Black or Blue

1921, May 31 Unwmk.

No.	Type	Description	Unused	Used
95	A7	10r on 50k	2.25	1.25
a.		Imperf.	—	
96	A7	20r on 50k	7.50	3.50
97	A7	30r on 50k	9.50	2.75
98	A7	50r on 50k	17.50	5.50
99	A7	100r on 50k (Bl)	35.00	13.00
		Nos. 95-99 (5)	71.75	26.00

Excellent counterfeits exist.

Arms and Stars for Vidzeme, Kurzeme & Latgale — A10

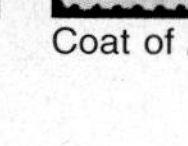

Coat of Arms — A11

Type I, slanting cipher in value.
Type II, upright cipher in value.

Perf. 10, 11½ and Compound
Wmk. Similar to 181

1921-22 Typo.

No.	Type	Value	Color	Unused	Used
101	A10	50k	violet (II)	1.00	.30
102	A10	1r	orange yel	.60	.30
103	A10	2r	deep green	.40	.20
104	A10	3r	brt green	1.25	.45
105	A10	5r	rose	1.40	.20
106	A10	6r	dp claret	2.10	.75
107	A10	9r	orange	1.50	.40
108	A10	10r	blue (I)	1.50	.20
109	A10	15r	ultra	3.50	.60
a.			Printed on both sides	*50.00*	
110	A10	20r	dull lilac (II)	22.50	4.00

1922, Aug. 21 *Perf. 11½*

No.	Type	Value	Color	Unused	Used
111	A11	50r	dk brn & pale brn (I)	35.00	4.50
112	A11	100r	dk bl & pale bl (I)	40.00	6.00
			Nos. 101-112 (12)	110.75	17.90

#101-131 sometimes show letters of a paper maker's watermark "PACTIEN LIGAT MILLS."

See Nos. 126-131, 152-154.

A12

2 SANTIMS
Type A, tail of "2" ends in an upstroke.
Type B, tail of "2" is nearly horizontal.

1923-25 *Perf. 10, 11, 11½*

No.	Type	Value	Color	Unused	Used
113	A12	1s	violet	1.00	.20
114	A12	2s	org yel (A)	1.75	.25
115	A12	4s	dark green	1.50	.20
a.			Horiz. pair, imperf. btwn.	55.00	50.00
116	A12	5s	lt green ('25)	4.50	.40
117	A12	6s	grn, *yel* ('25)	6.00	.20

118 A12 10s rose red (I) 3.00 .20
a. Horiz. pair, imperf. btwn. 55.00 50.00
119 A12 12s claret .45 .25
120 A12 15s brn, *sal* 6.00 .20
a. Horiz. pair, imperf. btwn. 55.00 50.00
121 A12 20s dp blue (II) 3.50 .20
122 A12 25s ultra ('25) .85 .20
123 A12 30s pink (I) ('25) 9.00 .25
124 A12 40s lilac (I) 3.50 .20
125 A12 50s lil gray (II) 6.50 .25
126 A11 1 l dk brn & pale brn 21.00 .60
127 A11 2 l dk blue & blue 34.00 1.00
130 A11 5 l dp grn & pale grn 100.00 5.00
131 A11 10 l car rose & pale rose (I) 6.00 6.00
Nos. 113-131 (17) 208.55 15.60

Value in "Santims" (1s); "Santimi" (2s-6s) or "Santimu" (others).

See note after No. 110.

See Nos. 135-151, 155-157. For overprints and surcharges see Nos. 164-167, B21-B23.

Nos. 79-80 Surcharged — No. 72 Surcharged

1927 Unwmk. *Perf. 11½*

132 A1 15s on 40k lilac .90 .30
133 A1 15s on 50k violet 2.50 1.00
134 A8 1 l on 3r brn & grn 21.00 6.50
Nos. 132-134 (3) 24.40 7.80

Types of 1923-25 Issue

1927-33 Wmk. 212 *Perf. 10, 11½*

135 A12 1s dull violet .25 .20
136 A12 2s org yel (A) 1.50 .20
137 A12 2s org yel (B) ('33) 1.00 .20
138 A12 3s org red ('31) .25 .20
139 A12 4s dk green ('29) 6.50 1.40
140 A12 5s lt green ('31) .85 .20
141 A12 6s grn, *yel* .20 .20
142 A12 7s dk green ('31) 1.25 .20
143 A12 10s red (I) 4.25 .40
144 A12 10s grn, *yel* (I) ('32) 20.00 .20
145 A12 15s brn, *sal* 7.50 .20
146 A12 20s pink (I) 9.00 .20
147 A12 20s pink (II) 8.00 .20
148 A12 30s lt blue (I) 3.50 .20
149 A12 35s dk blue ('31) 2.50 .20
150 A12 40s dl lil (I) ('29) 3.75 .20
151 A12 50s gray (II) 5.00 .25
152 A11 1 l dk brn & pale brn 14.00 .30
153 A11 2 l dk bl & bl ('31) 50.00 1.25
154 A11 5 l grn & pale grn ('33) 225.00 30.00
Nos. 135-154 (20) 364.30 36.40

The paper of Nos. 141, 144 and 145 is colored on the surface only.

See note above No. 113 for types A and B, and note above No. 101 for types I and II.

Type of 1927-33 Issue
Paper Colored Through

1931-33 *Perf. 10*

155 A12 6s grn, *yel* .20 .20
156 A12 10s grn, *yel* (I) ('33) 30.00 .20
157 A12 15s brn, *salmon* 8.00 .20
Nos. 155-157 (3) 38.20 .60

View of Rezekne — A13

Designs (Views of Cities): 15s, Jelgava. 20s, Cesis (Wenden). 30s, Liepaja (Libau). 50s, Riga. 1 l, Riga Theater.

1928, Nov. 18 Litho. *Perf. 10, 11½*

158 A13 6s dp grn & vio 1.75 .40
159 A13 15s dk brn & ol grn 1.75 .40
160 A13 20s cerise & bl grn 2.10 .45
161 A13 30s ultra & vio brn 2.50 .40
162 A13 50s dk gray & plum 2.50 1.00
163 A13 1 l blk brn & brn 6.50 1.75
Nos. 158-163 (6) 17.10 4.40

10th anniv. of Latvian Independence.

Riga Exhibition Issue

Stamps of 1927-33 Overprinted

1932, Aug. 30 *Perf. 10, 11*

164 A12 3s orange 1.75 1.10
165 A12 10s green, *yel* 3.25 .35
166 A12 20s pink (I) 3.75 1.00
167 A12 35s dark blue 5.00 2.25
Nos. 164-167 (4) 13.75 4.70

Riga Castle — A19

Arms and Shield — A20

Allegory of Latvia — A21

Ministry of Foreign Affairs — A22

1934, Dec. 15 Litho. *Perf. 10½, 10*

174 A19 3s red orange .25 .20
175 A20 5s yellow grn .25 .20
176 A20 10s gray grn 2.00 .20
177 A21 20s deep rose 2.00 .20
178 A22 35s dark blue .60 .20
179 A19 40s brown .60 .20
Nos. 174-179 (6) 5.70 1.20

Atis Kronvalds A23

A. Pumpurs A24

Juris Maters A25

Mikus Krogzemis (Auseklis) A26

1936, Jan. 4 Wmk. 212 *Perf. 11½*

180 A23 3s vermilion 2.75 *3.75*
181 A24 10s green 2.75 *3.75*
182 A25 20s rose pink 2.75 *3.75*
183 A26 35s dark blue 2.75 *3.75*
Nos. 180-183 (4) 11.00 15.00

President Karlis Ulmanis — A27

1937, Sept. 4 Litho. *Perf. 10, 11½*

184 A27 3s org red & brn org .50 .90
185 A27 5s yellow grn .50 .90
186 A27 10s dk sl grn .75 .90
187 A27 20s rose lake & brn lake 1.25 .60
188 A27 25s black vio 1.75 .90
189 A27 30s dark blue 1.90 1.00
190 A27 35s indigo 1.90 2.50
191 A27 40s lt brown 1.75 2.00
192 A27 50s olive blk 1.90 2.50
Nos. 184-192 (9) 12.20 12.20

60th birthday of President Ulmanis.

Independence Monument, Rauna (Ronneburg) A28

Independence Monument, Jelgava — A30

Monument Entrance to Cemetery at Riga A29

War Memorial, Valka — A31

Independence Monument, Iecava — A32

Independence Monument, Riga — A33

Tomb of Col. Kalpaks — A34

Unwmk.

1937, July 12 Litho. *Perf. 10*

Thick Paper

193 A28 3s vermilion .75 *.90*
194 A29 5s yellow grn .75 *.90*
195 A30 10s deep grn .75 *.90*
196 A31 20s carmine 1.75 1.10
197 A32 30s lt blue 2.25 2.25

Wmk. 212

Engr. *Perf. 11½*

Thin Paper

198 A33 35s dark blue 2.25 2.25
199 A34 40s brown 3.50 3.25
Nos. 193-199 (7) 12.00 *11.55*

View of Vidzeme — A35

General J. Balodis A37

President Karlis Ulmanis A38

Views: 5s, Latgale. 30s, Riga waterfront. 35s, Kurzeme. 40s, Zemgale.

1938, Nov. 17 *Perf. 10, 10½x10*

200 A35 3s brown org .40 .20
a. Booklet pane of 4 40.00
201 A35 5s yellow grn .50 .20
a. Booklet pane of 4 40.00
202 A37 10s dk green .60 .20
a. Booklet pane of 2 40.00
203 A38 20s red lilac .40 .20
a. Booklet pane of 2 40.00
204 A35 30s deep blue 1.50 .20
205 A35 35s indigo 1.50 .20
a. Booklet pane of 2 40.00
206 A35 40s rose violet 2.50 .25
Nos. 200-206 (7) 7.40 1.45

The 20th anniversary of the Republic.

School, Riga — A42

Independence Monument, Riga — A45

President Karlis Ulmanis A49

Designs: 5s, Castle of Jelgava. 10s, Riga Castle. 30s, Symbol of Freedom. 35s, Community House Daugavpils. 40s, Powder Tower and War Museum, Riga.

1939, May 13 Photo. *Perf. 10*

207 A42 3s brown orange .60 .75
208 A42 5s deep green .90 .75
209 A42 10s dk slate grn 1.25 .75
210 A45 20s dk car rose 2.75 1.25
211 A42 30s brt ultra 1.75 .75
212 A42 35s dark blue 2.50 1.75

213 A45 40s brown violet 3.50 1.50
214 A49 50s grnsh black 6.00 1.50
Nos. 207-214 (8) 19.25 9.00

5th anniv. of National Unity Day.

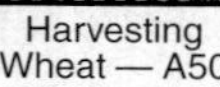
Harvesting Wheat — A50

Apple — A51

1939, Oct. 8
215 A50 10s slate green 1.25 .60
216 A51 20s rose lake 1.75 .65

8th Agricultural Exposition held near Riga.

Arms and Stars for Vidzeme, Kurzeme and Latgale — A52

1940
217 A52 1s dk vio brn .45 .40
218 A52 2s ocher .75 .60
219 A52 3s red orange .20 .20
220 A52 5s dk olive brn .20 .20
221 A52 7s dk green .45 .40
222 A52 10s dk blue grn 1.25 .25
224 A52 20s rose brown 1.25 .25
225 A52 30s dp red brn 1.75 .40
226 A52 35s brt ultra .20 .50
228 A52 50s dk slate grn 2.50 .75
229 A52 1 l olive green 6.00 2.25
Nos. 217-229 (11) 15.00 6.20

Natl. Arms — A70

1991, Oct. 19 Litho. *Perf. 13x12½*
300 A70 5k multicolored *5.00* *5.00*
301 A70 10k multicolored .35 .35
302 A70 15k multicolored .45 .45
303 A70 20k multicolored .60 .60
304 A70 40k multicolored 1.25 1.25
305 A70 50k multicolored 1.75 1.75

Size: 28x32mm

Perf. 13½x14
306 A70 100k silver & multi 2.75 2.75
307 A70 200k gold & multi 5.00 5.00
Nos. 300-307 (8) 17.15 17.15

Most issues, Nos. 300-342, have one blocked value that was not freely available at Latvian post offices.

Russia Nos. 5984, 5985a Ovptd. "LATVIJA" and Surcharged in Red Lilac, Orange, Green, Violet

1991, Dec. 23 Photo. *Perf. 12x11½*
308 A2765 100k on 7k (RL) *.50* .50
a. Vert. pair, one without ovpt. 9.50
b. Litho., perf. 12x12½ *.50* .50

Perf. 12x12½

Litho.
309 A2765 300k on 2k (O) *.85* .85
a. Vert. pair, one without ovpt. 9.50
310 A2765 500k on 2k (G) *1.25* 1.25
a. Vert. pair, one without ovpt. 9.50
311 A2765 1000k on 2k (V) *2.40* 2.40
a. Vert. pair, one without ovpt. 9.50
Nos. 308-311 (4) *5.00* 5.00

On Nos. 308-311 the sixth row of the sheet was not surcharged.
Forgeries exist.

Liberty Monument, Riga — A71

1991, Dec. 28 *Perf. 12½x13*
312 A71 10k ol brn & multi .40 .40
313 A71 15k violet & multi *.75* *.75*
314 A71 20k bl grn & multi .70 .70
315 A71 30k ol grn & multi .85 .85
316 A71 50k choc & multi 1.40 1.40
317 A71 100k dp blue & multi 2.00 1.10
Nos. 312-317 (6) 6.10 5.20

A72 A73

Monuments — A74

1992, Feb. 29 *Perf. 14*
318 A72 10k black .20 .20
319 A73 20k violet black .45 .20
320 A73 30k brown .60 .20
321 A72 30k purple .60 .20
322 A74 40k violet blue .80 .20
323 A74 50k green .90 .20
324 A73 50k olive green .90 .20
325 A74 100k red brown 1.90 .50
326 A72 200k blue 3.00 1.00
Nos. 318-326 (9) 9.35 2.90

Russia Nos. 4599, 5984, 5985a Ovptd. "LATVIJA" and Surcharged in Red, Brown, Emerald and Violet

1992, Apr. 4 Photo. *Perf. 12x11½*
327 A2765 1r on 7k (R) .20 .20

Perf. 12x12½

Litho.
328 A2765 3r on 2k (Br) .40 .25
329 A2765 5r on 2k (E) .65 .35
330 A2765 10r on 2k (V) 1.10 .75
331 A2138 25r on 4k 2.25 1.75
Nos. 327-331 (5) 4.60 3.30

Surcharged denominations expressed in rubles (large numerals) and kopecks (small zeros).

Birds of the Baltic Shores — A75

Litho. & Engr.

1992, Oct. 3 *Perf. 12½x13*

Booklet Stamps
332 A75 5r Pandion haliaetus .30 .30
333 A75 5r Limosa limosa .30 .30
334 A75 5r Mergus merganser .30 .30
335 A75 5r Tadorna tadorna .30 .30
a. Booklet pane of 4, #332-335 2.25

See Estonia Nos. 231-234a, Lithuania Nos. 427-430a, and Sweden Nos. 1975-1978a.

Christmas A76

2r, 10r Angels with children around Christmas tree. 3r, Angels with musical instruments, Christmas tree. 15r, Nativity scene.

1992, Nov. 21 Litho. *Perf. 13½x13*
336 A76 2r silver & multi *1.00* *1.00*
337 A76 3r multicolored *.30* *.20*
338 A76 10r gold & multi *.85* *.60*
339 A76 15r multicolored *1.10* *1.00*
Nos. 336-339 (4) *3.25* *2.80*

Russia Nos. 4728, 5107, 5109 Surcharged in Brown or Blue

Perfs. & Printing Methods as Before

1993, Feb. 26
340 A2229 50r on 6k #4728 (Br) *1.10* *.55*
341 A2435 100r on 6k #5109 *2.25* *1.00*
342 A2435 300r on 6k #5107 *6.00* *3.00*
Nos. 340-342 (3) *9.35* *4.55*

Traditional Costumes — A77

1993, Apr. 29 Litho. *Perf. 13x13½*
343 A77 5s Kuldiga *.20* *.20*
344 A77 10s Alsunga *.30* *.20*
345 A77 20s Lielvarde *.55* *.30*
346 A77 50s Rucava *1.50* *.80*
347 A77 100s Zemgale *3.00* *1.50*
348 A77 500s Ziemellatgale *15.00* *12.00*
a. Miniature sheet of 6, #343-348 *25.00* *25.00*
Nos. 343-348 (6) *20.55* *15.00*

See #400-401, 415-416, 440-441, 466-467.

21st Natl. Song Festival
A78 A79

1993, July 3 Litho. *Perf. 12½x13*
349 A78 3s rose brn, gold & black *1.40* *.50*
350 A78 5s purple, gold & black *2.60* *.80*
351 A79 15s multicolored *3.50* *1.25*
Nos. 349-351 (3) *7.50* *2.55*

A80

A81

1993, Aug. 28 Litho. *Perf. 14*
352 A80 15s Pope John Paul II *1.25* *1.00*

1993, Nov. 11 Litho. *Perf. 12½x13*
353 A81 5s silver, black & red *.90* *.30*
354 A81 15s gold, black & red *1.60* *.45*

Independence, 75th anniv.

A82

A83

1994, Apr. 2 Litho. *Perf. 14*
355 A82 15s multicolored *1.40* *.35*

Evalds Valters, actor, 100th birthday.

1994, Apr. 20 Litho. *Perf. 12½x13*
356 A83 5s Biathlon *.40* *.40*
357 A83 10s 2-man bobsled *.85* *.40*
358 A83 15s Luge *1.25* *.65*
359 A83 100s Men's figure skating *7.50* *3.75*
Nos. 356-359 (4) *10.00* *5.20*

Souvenir Sheet
360 A83 200s like #357 *11.00* *9.50*

1994 Winter Olympics, Lillehammer.

Ethnographical Open Air Museum — A84

1994, Apr. 30 Litho. *Perf. 13x12½*
361 A84 5s multicolored *1.50* *.35*

1994 Basketball Festival, Riga — A85

1994, June 4 Litho. *Perf. 12½x13*
362 A85 15s multicolored *1.75* *.45*

Provincial Municipal Arms — A86

1994-2006 *Perf. 13x12½, 14 (#373)*
363 A86 1s Kurzeme *.30* *.20*
b. Perf. 13¼x13¾ ('06) .30 .20
364 A86 2s Auce *.30* *.20*
b. Perf 13¼x13¾ ('05) .30 .20
365 A86 3s Zemgale *.30* *.20*
b. Perf 13¼x13¾ ('05) .30 .20
366 A86 5s Vidzeme *.30* *.20*
b. Perf. 13¼x13¾ ('06) .30 .20
367 A86 8s Livani *.40* *.20*
368 A86 10s Latgale *.50* *.20*
369 A86 13s Preili *.55* *.30*
370 A86 16s Ainazi *.70* *.35*
371 A86 20s Grobina *.85* *.45*
372 A86 24s Tukums *1.00* *.50*
373 A86 28s Madona *1.25* *.55*
374 A86 30s Riga *1.40* *.60*
375 A86 36s Priekule *1.50* *.70*
376 A86 50s Natl. arms *2.10* *1.00*

Size: 29x24mm

Perf. 14
377 A86 100s Riga *4.25* *2.50*
377A A86 200s Natl. arms *8.75* *4.75*
Nos. 363-377A (16) *24.45* *12.90*

The 1s, 5s, 8s, 16s, 20s, 24s exist dated "1996"; 1s, 2s, 10s "1997"; 1s, 2s, 10s "1998." Nos. 364b and 365b exist dated "2006."

Issued: 1s, #365, 5s, 10s, 6/21/94; 30s, 50s, 100s, 200s, 12/21/94; 8s, 16s, 20s, 24s, 4/8/95; #364, 13s, 4/12/96; 28s, 36s, 11/5/96. #364a, 365a, 9/10/05.

See Nos. 450-451, 472-473, 482-483, 506-507, 525-526. Nos. 363b, 366b, 9/9/06. Nos. 364b and 365b exist dated "2006." Nos. 363b, 364b and 365b exist dated "2007."

Perf. 14

363a	A86	1s	*1.75*	*.75*
364a	A86	2s	*1.75*	*.75*
365a	A86	3s	*1.75*	*.75*
366a	A86	5s	*1.75*	*.75*

Dated "1999." Issued: #363a, 364a, 366a, 1/20/99; #365a, 3/3/99. Nos. 364a, 365a and 366a exist dated "2000." Nos. 363a, 364a, 365a exist dated "2002."

A87

A88

1994, Sept. 24 Litho. *Perf. 14*

378 A87 5s multicolored *.75 .30*

University of Latvia, 75th anniv.

1994, Oct. 29 Litho. *Perf. 14x13½*

Items balanced on scales (Europa): 10s, Latvian coins. 50s, Locked chest, money card.

379	A88 10s multicolored		*.65*	*.25*
a.	Tete-beche pair		*1.40*	*.50*
380	A88 50s multicolored		*3.50*	*1.50*
a.	Tete-beche pair		*7.00*	*3.00*

Doormouse A89

1994, Nov. 19 Litho. *Perf. 13½x13*

381	A89 5s shown	*.55*	*.35*
382	A89 10s Among leaves	*.85*	*.35*
383	A89 10s Eating berries	*.85*	*.35*
384	A89 15s Berry, large mouse	*1.75*	*.50*
	Nos. 381-384 (4)	*4.00*	*1.55*

World Wildlife Fund.

A90

LATVIJA 5 1994

A91

Christmas: 3s, Angel. 8s, Angels playing flute & violin. 13c, Angels singing. 100s, Candles.

1994, Dec. 3 *Perf. 14*

385	A90 3s multicolored	*.30*	*.20*
386	A90 8s multicolored	*.55*	*.20*
387	A90 13s multicolored	*1.25*	*.30*
388	A90 100s multicolored	*5.50*	*2.10*
	Nos. 385-388 (4)	*7.60*	*2.80*

Perf. 13x12½ on 3 Sides

1994, Dec. 17

Children's Fairy Tales, by Margarita Staraste: 5s, Elf with candle. No. 390, Small bear in snow. No. 391, Boy on sled.

Booklet Stamps

389	A91 5s multicolored	*.25*	*.20*
390	A91 10s multicolored	*.50*	*.20*
391	A91 10s multicolored	*.50*	*.20*
a.	Booklet pane, 2 each #389-391	*2.75*	
	Complete booklet, #391a + label	*3.50*	
	Nos. 389-391 (3)	*1.25*	*.60*

A92

LATVIJA 15 ANO-50 1995

A93

1995, Feb. 18 *Perf. 14*

392 A92 10s multicolored *.70 .30*

European safe driving week.

1995, Mar. 4 Litho. *Perf. 14*

393 A93 15s silver, blue & red *1.00 .50*

UN, 50th anniv.

A94

A95

Via Baltica Highway Project: 8s, No. 395b, Castle, Bauska, Latvia. No. 395a, Beach Hotel, Parnu, Estonia. c, Kaunas, Lithuania.

1995, Apr. 20 Litho. *Perf. 14*

394 A94 8s multicolored *.40 .20*

Souvenir Sheet

395 A94 18s Sheet of 3, #a.-c. *3.25 2.00*

See Estonia #288-289, Lithuania #508-509.

1995, July 8 Litho. *Perf. 12½*

396	A95 8s Dendrocopos leucotos	*.35*	*.20*
397	A95 20s Crex crex	*.85*	*.40*
398	A95 24s Chlidonias leucopterus	*1.10*	*.50*
	Nos. 396-398 (3)	*2.30*	*1.10*

European nature conservation year.

Julian Cardinal Vaivods, Birth Cent. — A96

1995, Aug. 18 Litho. *Perf. 14*

399 A96 8s multicolored *.60 .25*

Traditional Costume Type of 1993

1995, Sept. 8 Litho. *Perf. 13x13½*

400 A77 8s Nica *.45 .20*

Souvenir Sheet

401 A77 100s Like #400 *4.50 4.50*

Friendly Appeal, by Karlis Ulmanis, 60th Anniv. — A97

1995, Sept. 8 *Perf. 14*

402 A97 8s multicolored *.60 .25*

Riga, 800th Anniv. — A98

1995, Sept. 23 *Perf. 13½*

403	A98 8s Natl. Opera	*.35*	*.20*
404	A98 16s Natl. Theatre	*.70*	*.35*

Size: 45x27mm

405	A98 24s Academy of Arts	*1.00*	*.55*
406	A98 36s State Art Museum	*1.50*	*.80*
	Nos. 403-406 (4)	*3.55*	*1.90*

See Nos. 508-511.

Peace and Freedom — A99

Heroes from national epic, Lacplesis, dates of independence: 16s, Spidola with sword and shield, 1918. 50s, Lacplesis with leaves and banner, 1991.

1995, Nov. 15 Litho. *Perf. 13½*

407	A99 16s multicolored	*.75*	*.30*
408	A99 50s multicolored	*2.25*	*.95*

Europa.

Christmas A100

Designs: No. 409, Characters surrounding Christmas tree at night. No. 410, Santa gliding through sky holding candle. 15s, Characters outside snow-covered house. 24s, Santa standing between dog and cat.

1995, Dec. 2

409	A100 6s multicolored	*.45*	*.20*
410	A100 6s multicolored	*.45*	*.20*
411	A100 15s multicolored	*.25*	*.55*
412	A100 24s multicolored	*2.10*	*.90*
	Nos. 409-412 (4)	*3.25*	*1.85*

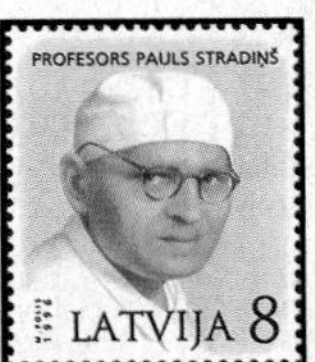

Pauls Stradins (1896-1958), Physician — A101

1996, Jan. 17 Litho. *Perf. 14*

413 A101 8s multicolored *.50 .25*

Zenta Maurina (1897-1978) A102

1996, May 10 Litho. *Perf. 13½x14*

414 A102 36s multicolored *1.60 .95*

Europa.

Traditional Costume Type of 1993

1996, May 18 Litho. *Perf. 13x13½*

415 A77 8s Barta *.50 .25*

Souvenir Sheet

416 A77 100s like No. 415 *4.50 3.00*

Souvenir Sheet

Children's Games — A103

1996, June 8 Litho. *Perf. 14x13½*

417 A103 48s Sheet of 1 *2.10 1.50*

1996 Summer Olympic Games, Atlanta A104

Perf. 14x13½, 13½x14

1996, June 19

418	A104 8s Cycling,vert.	*.40*	*.20*
419	A104 16s Basketball, vert	*.85*	*.40*
420	A104 24s Walking, vert.	*1.00*	*.50*
421	A104 36s Canoeing	*1.60*	*.80*
	Nos. 418-421 (4)	*3.85*	*1.90*

Souvenir Sheet

422 A104 100s Javelin *4.00 2.25*

Nature Museum, 150th Anniv. A105

Butterflies: 8s, Papilio machaon. 24s, Catocala fraxini. 80s, Pericallia matronula.

1996, Aug. 30 *Perf. 13*

423	A105 8s multicolored	*.35*	*.20*
424	A105 24s multicolored	*.90*	*.45*
425	A105 80s multicolored	*3.75*	*1.90*
	Nos. 423-425 (3)	*5.00*	*2.55*

Car Production in Latvia — A106

Designs: 8s, 1912 Russo-Balt fire truck. 24s, 1899 Leutner-Russia. 36s, 1939 Ford-Vairogs.

1996, Oct. 25 Litho. *Perf. 13x12½*

426	A106 8s multicolored	*.35*	*.20*
427	A106 24s multicolored	*1.25*	*.55*
428	A106 36s multicolored	*1.75*	*.85*
	Nos. 426-428 (3)	*3.35*	*1.60*

City of Riga, 800th Anniv. — A107

1996, Dec. 5 Litho. *Perf. 13½*

429 A107 8s Building front *.40 .20*

Size: 30x26mm

430 A107 16s Stained glass window *.75 .40*

Size: 37x26mm

431	A107 24s Buildings	*1.25*	*.55*
432	A107 30s Art figures	*1.40*	*.70*
	Nos. 429-432 (4)	*3.80*	*1.85*

Christmas A108

Designs: 6s, Santa's elves, presents. 14s, Santa on skis, dog, children in animal costumes. 20s, Child in front of Christmas tree, santa in chair, pets.

1996, Dec. 7 *Perf. 14*
433 A108 6s multicolored .30 .20
434 A108 14s multicolored .70 .35
435 A108 20s multicolored 1.00 .50
Nos. 433-435 (3) 2.00 1.05

See Nos. 458-460.

Birds — A109

Designs: 10s, Caprimulgus eurpaeus. 20s, Aquila clanga. 30s, Acrocephalus paludicola.

1997, Feb. 8 *Perf. 13x12½*
436 A109 10s multicolored .50 .25
437 A109 20s multicolored .90 .45
438 A109 30s multicolored 1.40 .70
Nos. 436-438 (3) 2.80 1.40

Turn of the Epochs — A110

Legend of Rozi Turaidas — A111

1997, Mar. 25 **Litho.** *Perf. 14*
439 A110 10s multicolored .70 .35

Traditional Costume Type of 1993

1997, Apr. 3 *Perf. 13x13½*
440 A77 10s Rietumvidzeme 1.75 .80

Souvenir Sheet

441 A77 100s like #440 4.00 2.25

Stamp Day.

1997, Apr. 26 **Litho.** *Perf. 12½x13*
442 A111 32s multicolored 1.25 .60

Europa.

Old Baltic Ships — A112

Designs: 10s, Linijkugis, 17th cent.
No. 444: a, Linijkugis, 17th cent., diff. b, Kurenas 16th cent. c, Maasilinn ship, 16th cent.

1997, May 10 *Perf. 14x14½*
443 A112 10s multicolored .85 .40

Souvenir Sheet

444 A112 20s Sheet of 3, #a.-c. 3.50 2.75

See Estonia #322-323, Lithuania #571-572.

Port of Ventspils, Cent. — A113

1997, May 21 **Litho.** *Perf. 13½x14*
445 A113 20s Hermes, Poseidon 1.00 .50

Children's Activities A114

Designs: 10s, Stamp collecting. 12s, Riding dirt bike, vert. 20s, Boy in hockey uniform, girl in skiwear, vert. 30s, Tennis, soccer, basketball.

1997, June 7 *Perf. 13½x13*
446 A114 10s multicolored .45 .20
447 A114 12s multicolored .60 .30
448 A114 20s multicolored .95 .45
449 A114 30s multicolored 1.50 .75
Nos. 446-449 (4) 3.50 1.70

Municipal Arms Type of 1994

1997, Sept. 6 **Litho.** *Perf. 13x12½*
450 A86 10s Valmiera .85 .40
a. Perf 14 .85 .40
b. Perf. 13¼x14 .85 .40
451 A86 20s Rezekne 1.75 .85

No. 450 exists dated "1998." No. 450a exists dated "2000." No. 450b exists dated "2005." Issued: No. 450b, 9/12/01.

Nature Preserves A115

1997, Oct. 18 **Litho.** *Perf. 13x12½*
452 A115 10s Moricsala, 1912 .45 .20
453 A115 30s Slitere, 1921 1.40 .70

See Nos. 464-465.

City of Riga, 800th Anniv. A116

10s, Woman, house, 12th cent. 20s, Monument to Bishop Albert, seal of the bishop, rosary, writing tool, 13th-16th cent. 30s, Riga castle, weapons used during Middle Ages. 32s, Houses, arms of Riga, statue of St. John.

1997, Nov. 27 **Litho.** *Perf. 13x14*
454 A116 10s multicolored .45 .20
455 A116 20s multicolored .80 .40
456 A116 30s multicolored 1.25 .60

Size: 27x26mm

457 A116 32s multicolored 1.40 .70
Nos. 454-457 (4) 3.90 1.90

See Nos. 468-471, 488-491.

Christmas Type of 1996

People dressed in masks, costumes for mummery: 8s, Santa, bear. 18s, Two goats. 28s, Horse.

1997, Nov. 29 *Perf. 14*
458 A108 8s multicolored .40 .20
459 A108 18s multicolored .80 .40
460 A108 28s multicolored 1.25 .60
Nos. 458-460 (3) 2.45 1.20

A117

A118

1998, Jan. 31 **Litho.** *Perf. 14x13½*
461 A117 20s multicolored 1.00 .50

1998 Winter Olympic Games, Nagano.

1998, Feb. 21 **Litho.** *Perf. 13½*

Statue at Spridisi, museum home of Anna Brigadere(1861-1933), writer.

462 A118 10s multicolored .50 .25

National Song Festival — A119

1998, Mar. 28 **Litho.** *Perf. 13x14*
463 A119 30s multicolored 2.00 1.00

Europa.

Nature Preserves Type of 1997

1998, Apr. 30 *Perf. 13x12½*
464 A115 10s Grini, 1936 .45 .20
465 A115 30s Teici, 1982 1.50 .75

Traditional Costume Type of 1993

#467, Krustpils, man wearing crown of leaves.

1998, May 9 *Perf. 13x13½*
466 A77 10s Krustpils region .50 .25

Souvenir Sheet

467 A77 100s multicolored 4.75 3.25

City of Riga, 800th Anniv., Type of 1997

10s, Dannenstern House, 16th and 17th cent. coins issued by kings of Poland and Sweden, 17th cent. wooden sculpture. 20s, City Library, monument to G. Herder, poet, philosopher, teacher. 30s, 18th cent. arsenal, column celebrating defeat of Napoleon's troops, octant, compass. 40s, Sculpture of Mother Latvia at Warriors' Cemetery, entrance to Cemetery, obv. & rev. of 5 lat coin, 1930.

1998, May 29 **Litho.** *Perf. 13x14*
468 A116 10s multicolored .35 .20
469 A116 20s multicolored .70 .35
470 A116 30s multicolored 1.00 .50
471 A116 40s multicolored 1.40 .70
Nos. 468-471 (4) 3.45 1.75

No. 468 is 30x26mm.

Municipal Arms Type of 1994

Perf. 13¼x13¾

1998, Sept. 26 **Litho.**
472 A86 15s Bauska .75 .35
473 A86 30s Liepaja 1.50 .75

No. 473 exists dated 2004.

World Stamp Day — A120

1998, Oct. 20 **Litho.** *Perf. 14*
474 A120 30s #2, various stamps 1.25 .60

Dome Church, Riga, 1211 A121

Pres. Janis Cakste (1859-1927) A122

1998, Oct. 23
475 A121 10s multicolored .60 .30

1998, Nov. 11 *Perf. 14x13½*
476 A122 10s multicolored .60 .30

See No. 497, 515.

Independence, 80th Anniv. — A123

1998, Nov. 14 *Perf. 13x12½*
477 A123 10s shown .45 .20
478 A123 30s Arms, flags 1.50 .75

Christmas A124

Christmas elves: 10s, Rolling snow balls. 20s, Decorating tree, preparing presents. 30s, Pulling sled over snow.

1998, Nov. 28 *Perf. 13½x14*
479 A124 10s multicolored .50 .25
480 A124 20s multicolored 1.10 .55
481 A124 30s multicolored 1.50 .75
Nos. 479-481 (3) 3.10 1.55

Municipal Arms Type of 1994

1999 **Litho.** *Perf. 13¼x13¾*
482 A86 15s Ogre .80 .40
483 A86 40s Jelgava 2.00 1.00

Issued: 15s, 2/12; 40s, 4/10. No. 482 exists dated "2000."
No. 483 exists dated 2004.

Nature Parks and Reserves A125

Europa: 30s, Krustkalnu Nature Reserve. 60s, Gauja Natl. Nature Park.

1999, Mar. 20 *Perf. 13x12½*
484 A125 30s multicolored 1.50 .75
485 A125 60s multicolored 3.00 1.50

Council of Europe, 50th Anniv. — A126

1999, Apr. 24
486 A126 30s multicolored 1.40 .70

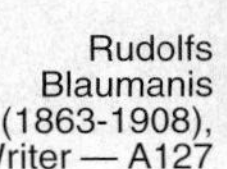

Rudolfs Blaumanis (1863-1908), Writer — A127

1999, Apr. 24 *Perf. 14x13*
487 A127 110s multicolored 4.25 2.10

City of Riga, 800th Anniv. Type

10s, Streetcar. 30s, Schooner "Widwud." 40s, Airplane. 70s, TK-type locomotive.

Perf. 13¼x13¾

1999, June 26 **Litho.**
488 A116 10s multicolored .45 .20
489 A116 30s multicolored 1.40 .70
490 A116 40s multicolored 1.90 .95
491 A116 70s multicolored 3.25 1.60
Nos. 488-491 (4) 7.00 3.45

No. 488 is 30x27mm.

Aglona Basilica — A129

"Baltic Chain," 10th Anniv. — A130

1999, July 10 **Litho.** *Perf. 14x14½*
492 A129 15s multicolored .65 .30
Complete booklet, 6 #492 12.00

1999, Aug. 23 **Litho.** *Perf. 12½x13*

Families and flags: 15s, No. 494a, Latvian. No. 494: b, Lithuanian. c, Estonian.

493 A130 15s multicolored .80 .40

Souvenir Sheet

494 A130 30s Sheet of 3, #a.-c. 4.50 4.00

See Estonia Nos. 366-367, Lithuania Nos. 639-640.

Rundâle Palace — A131

1999, Sept. 25 **Litho.** *Perf. 14*
495 A131 20s multicolored 1.00 .50

See No. 512.

Landscape, by Julijs Feders (1838-1909) — A132

1999, Oct. 13 **Litho.** *Perf. 13½*
496 A132 15s multi .80 .40

Presidents Type of 1998

1999, Nov. 16 **Litho.** *Perf. 14x13½*
497 A122 15s Pres. Gustavs Zemgals (1871-1939) .80 .40

A134

A135

1999, Nov. 25 *Perf. 14x14½*
498 A134 40s multi 1.75 .85

UPU, 125th anniv.

1999, Nov. 27 *Perf. 14¼*

Christmas and Millennium: 12s, Santa, tree, candle. 15s, Santa, tree, children. 40s, Santa, tree with ornaments.

499 A135 12s multi .55 .25
500 A135 15s multi .70 .35
501 A135 40s multi 1.75 .85
Nos. 499-501 (3) 3.00 1.45

Nude, by J. Rozentals A136

Perf. 14½x14¼

2000, Feb. 26 **Litho.**
502 A136 40s multi 2.00 1.00

Aleksandrs Caks (1901-50), Poet — A137

2000, Apr. 8 **Litho.** *Perf. 14x13½*
503 A137 40s multi 1.75 .85
Booklet, 6 #503 10.00

Europa, 2000
Common Design Type

2000, May 9
504 CD17 60s multi 4.25 2.10

Ice Hockey — A138

Illustration reduced.

Wmk. 387

2000, June 21 **Litho.** *Perf. 14*
505 A138 70s multi + label 3.00 1.25

Issued in sheets of 8 + 8 labels. Vertical columns of four labels, which depict players Helmut Balderis, Vitalijs Samoilovs, Sandis Ozolinsh and Arturs Irbe, flank a central block of eight stamps. Color photos of the players appear at left or right of the labels.

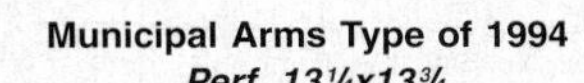

Municipal Arms Type of 1994

Perf. 13¼x13¾

2000, July 6 **Unwmk.**
506 A86 15s Daugavpils .85 .40
507 A86 15s Jūrmala .85 .40

No. 506 exists dated "2005." No. 507 exists dated 2001, 2002 and 2005.

City of Riga, 800th Anniv. Type of 1995

20s, Central Market. #509, Riga Zoo. #510, Riga Dome Organ. 70s, Powder Tower.

2000, July 22 *Perf. 13¼x14*

Size: 40x28mm

508 A98 20s multi 1.00 .50

Size: 47x28mm

509 A98 40s multi 2.00 1.00

Perf. 14x13¼

Size: 28x32mm

510 A98 40s multi 2.00 1.00
511 A98 70s multi 3.50 1.25
Nos. 508-511 (4) 8.50 3.75

Palace Type of 1999

2000, Aug. 12 *Perf. 13¼x14*
512 A131 40s Jelgava Palace 2.00 1.00
Booklet, 6 #512 15.00

2000 Summer Olympics, Sydney — A139

2000, Sept. 15 *Perf. 14¼x14*
513 A139 70s multi + label 2.75 1.75

See No. 518.

Millennium — A140

No. 514: a, 15s, Freedom Monument, Riga. b, House of Blackheads, Riga.
Illustration reduced.

Perf. 14x13¼

2000, Sept. 28 **Litho.** **Wmk. 387**
514 A140 Pair + label 2.50 1.25
a. 15s multi .75 .35
b. 50s multi 1.75 .90

President Type of 1998

Perf. 13¾x13¼

2000, Nov. 11 **Unwmk.**
515 A122 15s Alberts Kveisis (1881-1936) .80 .40

Orthodox Cathedral — A141

2000, Nov. 17 *Perf. 14*
516 A141 40s multi 2.00 1.00

Red Cross — A142

2000, Nov. 22
517 A142 15s multi .80 .40

Olympics Type of 2000

2000, Nov. 22
518 A139 40s multi 1.75 .85

Issued in sheets of 4 + 2 different labels depicting gold medal winner Igors Vihrovs.

Christmas — A143

Designs: 12s, Watch. No. 520, 15s, Angels. No. 521, 15s, Madonna and child.

2000, Nov. 25
519-521 A143 Set of 3 2.00 1.00

International Recognition of Latvia, 80th Anniv. — A144

2001, Jan. 13 **Litho.** *Perf. 14*
522 A144 40s multi 2.00 1.00

Kad Silavas Mostas, by Vilhelmis Purvitis A145

Perf. 14¼x14½

2001, Feb. 1 **Litho.** **Unwmk.**
523 A145 40s multi 2.00 1.00
Booklet, 6 #523 12.00

President Type of 1998

2001, Feb. 17 *Perf. 13¾x13¼*
524 A122 15s Karlis Ulmanis (1877-1942) .75 .35

Municipal Arms Type of 1994

2001, Mar. 5 *Perf. 13¼x13¾*
525 A86 5s Smiltene .50 .25
526 A86 15s Kuldiga .60 .30

Nos. 525-526 exist dated 2002. No. 525 exists dated "2005."

Narrow Gauge Locomotive A146

2001, Mar. 24 *Perf. 14*
527 A146 40s multi 2.10 1.00

Europa — A147

2001, Apr. 14
528 A147 60s multi 2.25 1.10

Riga, 800th Anniv. Type of 1995

Riga in: No. 529a, 20th cent. No. 529b, 21st cent. 60s, 16th cent. 70s, 17th cent.

2001, May 24 **Litho.** *Perf. 13¾x13½*

Size: 29x33mm (each stamp)

529 A98 15s Horiz. pair, #a-b 1.50 .75

Size: 47x28mm
Perf. 13½x13¾

530 A98 60s multi 2.50 1.25
531 A98 70s multi 2.75 1.40
Nos. 529-531 (3) 6.75 3.40

Kakisa Dzirnavas, by Karlis Skalbe — A148

2001, June 9 ***Perf. 13¾***
532 A148 40s multi 2.00 1.00
Booklet, 6 #532 12.00

Souvenir Sheet

Mikhail Tal (1936-92), Chess Champion — A149

2001, Aug. 18 Litho. ***Perf. 14***
533 A149 100s multi 4.00 2.00

Baltic Coast Landscapes A150

Designs: 15s, No. 535a, Vidzeme. No. 535b, Palanga. No. 535c, Lahemaa.

2001, Sept. 15 ***Perf. 13½***
534 A150 15s multi 1.50 .75
Booklet, 6 #534 10.00

Souvenir Sheet

535 Sheet of 3 5.00 2.50
a.-c. A150 30s Any single 1.60 .80

See Estonia Nos. 423-424, Lithuania Nos. 698-699.

Palace Type of 1999

2001, Oct. 24 ***Perf. 14½x14***
536 A131 40s Cesvaines Palace 2.00 1.00
a. Perf. 13¼x14 2.00 1.00
b. Booklet pane, 6 #536a 10.00 —
Booklet, #536b 10.00

House of Worship Type of 2000

2001, Nov. 3 ***Perf. 13¾x14***
537 A141 70s Riga Synagogue 3.00 1.50
Booklet, 6 #537 24.00

Latvian Seamen — A151

Designs: 15s, Krisjanis Valdemars (1825-91), founder of Naval College. 70s, Duke Jekabs Ketlers (1610-82), shipbuilder.

2001, Nov. 14 ***Perf. 13¼x14***
538-539 A151 Set of 2 3.00 1.50

Christmas A152

Designs: 12s, Rabbits. No. 541, 15s, Dog, rabbit. No. 542, 15s, Lambs.

2001, Nov. 22 ***Perf. 13¼***
540-542 A152 Set of 3 2.00 1.00

Town Arms — A153

2002, Jan. 29 Litho. ***Perf. 13¼x13¾***
543 A153 5s Ludza .35 .35
544 A153 10s Dobele .50 .35
545 A153 15s Sigulda .75 .40
Nos. 543-545 (3) 1.60 1.10

2002 Winter Olympics, Salt Lake City — A154

2002, Feb. 8 ***Perf. 13¼x13¾***
546 A154 40s multi 1.75 .85
a. Booklet pane of 6, perf. 13¼x13¾ on 3 sides 15.00 —
Booklet, #546a 15.00

2002 Winter Paralympics, Salt Lake City — A155

2002, Mar. 5 ***Perf. 14¼x13¾***
547 A155 15s multi .60 .30

Refugees, by Jekabs Kazaks — A156

2002, Apr. 20 Litho. ***Perf. 14½x14¼***
548 A156 40s multi 1.75 .85

Europa — A157

2002, May 4 ***Perf. 14***
549 A157 60s multi 2.50 1.25
a. Tete-beche pair 5.00 2.50

Endangered Plants — A158

Designs: 15s, Cypripedium calceolus. 40s, Trapa natans.

2002, May 25 ***Perf. 13¾***
550-551 A158 Set of 2 2.75 1.40

Latvian Armed Forces — A159

2002, June 15 ***Perf. 13¾x13¼***
552 A159 40s multi 1.60 .80

Janis Jaunsudrabins (1877-1962), Writer — A160

2002, July 6 ***Perf. 13¾x13½***
553 A160 40s multi 2.00 1.00
a. Booklet pane of 6, perf. 13¾x13½ on 3 sides 12.00
Booklet, #553a 12.00

Kristians Johans Dals (1839-1904) and Ship — A161

2002, July 20 ***Perf. 13¼x13¾***
554 A161 70s multi 2.75 1.40

Fish — A162

Designs: 15s, Gadus morhua callarias. 40s, Siluris glanis.

2002, Aug. 10 Litho. ***Perf. 14***
555-556 A162 Set of 2 2.50 1.25
a. Booklet pane, perf. 14 on 3 sides 11.00
Booklet, #556a 11.00

Souvenir Sheet

Venta River Bridge — A163

2002, Aug. 24 ***Perf. 12¾x12½***
557 A163 100s multi 4.50 2.25

Jaunmoku Palace — A164

2002, Sept. 14 ***Perf. 14¼x13¾***
558 A164 40s multi 1.60 .80

House of Worship Type of 2000

2002, Oct. 12 ***Perf. 13¾x14***
559 A141 70s Grebenschikov Old Belief Praying House 2.75 1.40
a. Booklet pane of 6, perf. 13¾x14 on 3 sides 17.00
Booklet, #559a 17.00

Mittens A165

2002, Nov. 2 ***Perf. 13¼x13¾***
560 A165 15s multi .65 .30

Christmas — A166

Designs: 12s, Elf on sack, Christmas tree. No. 562, 15s, Angel, Christmas tree. No. 563, 15s, Elves on gift.

2002, Nov. 23 ***Perf. 13¾x13¼***
561-563 A166 Set of 3 2.00 1.00

A Man Entering a Room, by Niklavs Strunke (1894-1966) A167

2003, Jan. 25 Litho. ***Perf. 13¼x14***
564 A167 40s multi 2.00 1.00

Town Arms Type of 2002

2003, Feb. 15 ***Perf. 13¼x13¾***
565 A153 10s Balvi .50 .25
566 A153 15s Gulbene .75 .35
567 A153 20s Ventspils 1.00 .50
Nos. 565-567 (3) 2.25 1.10

Protected Plants Type of 2002

Designs: 15s, Ophrys insectifera. 30s, Taxus baccata.

2003, Mar. 21 ***Perf. 13¾***
568 A158 15s multi .60 .30
569 A158 30s multi 1.40 .70
a. Perf. 14½x14¼ on 3 sides 1.40 .70
b. Booklet pane, 6 #569a 8.50 —
Complete booklet, #569b 8.50

Straumeni, by Edvarts Virza (1883-1940) A168

2003, Apr. 12 ***Perf. 13¾x13¼***
570 A168 40s multi 1.50 .75

Europa — A169

2003, May 3 Litho. ***Perf. 13¼x13¾***
571 A169 60s multi 2.50 1.25

Kolka Lighthouse — A170

2003, May 17 *Perf. 13¾x13¼*
572 A170 60s multi 2.25 1.10

House of Worship Type of 2000

2003, June 6 *Perf. 13¼x13¾*
573 A141 70s Salvation Temple, horiz. 2.75 1.40

Souvenir Sheet

Gauja River Bridge, Sigulda — A171

2003, July 19
574 A171 100s multi 4.50 2.25

Fish — A172

Designs: 15s, Thymallus thymallus. 30s, Salmo salar.

2003, Aug. 2 *Perf. 14x13¾*
575 A172 15s multi .60 .30
576 A172 30s multi 1.40 .70
a. Booklet pane of 6, perf. 14x13¾ on 3 sides 8.50 —
Complete booklet, #576a 8.50

Motacilla Alba — A173

2003, Aug. 30 *Perf. 14¾x14*
577 A173 15s multi .70 .35

Palace Type of 1999

2003, Sept. 27 *Perf. 14¼x13¾*
578 A131 40s Birini Palace 1.75 .85
a. Booklet pane of 6 11.00
Complete booklet, #578a 11.00

Mittens Type of 2002

2003, Oct. 11 *Perf. 14x13¾*
579 A165 15s Libiesi mittens .75 .35

Motorcycle Racing A174

2003, Oct. 31 *Perf. 13¼x13¾*
580 A174 70s multi 2.75 1.40
a. Booklet pane of 6 17.00 —
Complete booklet, #580a 17.00

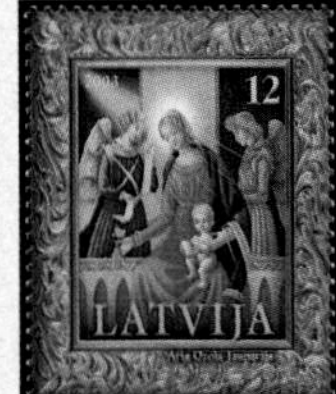
Christmas — A175

Designs: 12s, Madonna and Child with two angels. No. 582, 15s, The Annunciation (golden brown frame). No. 583, 15s, Nativity (gray frame).

2003, Nov. 22 *Perf. 13¾x14¼*
581-583 A175 Set of 3 1.75 .85

Still Life with Triangle, by Romans Suta — A176

2004, Jan. 25 Litho. *Perf. 13¼x14*
584 A176 40s multi 1.75 .85

Arms Type of 2002

2004, Feb. 14 *Perf. 13¼x13¾*
585 A153 5s Valka .25 .20
586 A153 15s Cesis .65 .35
587 A153 20s Saldus .85 .45
Nos. 585-587 (3) 1.75 1.00

Reinis (1839-1920) and Matiss (1848-1926) Kaudzites, Writers — A177

2004, Mar. 20 *Perf. 13¾*
588 A177 40s multi 1.60 .80

Endangered Plants Type of 2002

Designs: 15s, Gentiana cruciata. 30s, Onobrychis arenaria.

2004, Apr. 3
589-590 A158 Set of 2 1.90 .95

2006 World Ice Hockey Championships, Riga — A178

2004, Apr. 17 Litho. *Perf. 13¼x13¾*
591 A178 30s multi 1.25 .60
a. Booklet pane of 4, perf. 13¼x13¾ on 3 sides 5.00 —
Complete booklet, #591a 5.00

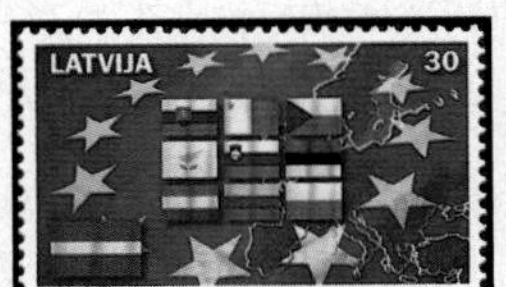
Admission to European Union — A179

Designs: No. 592, 30s, Stars, map of Europe, flags of newly-added countries. No. 593, 30s, Seven stars.

2004, May 1 *Perf. 13x13¼*
592-593 A179 Set of 2 2.50 1.25

Europa — A180

2004, May 8 Litho. *Perf. 13¼x13¾*
594 A180 60s multi 2.50 1.25

European Soccer Championships, Portugal — A181

2004, June 3 *Perf. 14x13½*
595 A181 30s multi 1.25 .60

Fish — A182

Designs: 15s, Oncorhynchus mykiss. 30s, Psetta maxima.

2004, June 26 *Perf. 13¼x14*
596 A182 15s multi .60 .30
597 A182 30s multi 1.40 .70
a. Booklet pane of 6, perf. 13¼x14 on 3 sides 8.50 —
Complete booklet, #597a 8.50

Visit of Pres. Bill Clinton to Latvia, 10th Anniv. — A183

2004, July 6 *Perf. 13¾x13¼*
598 A183 40s multi 1.50 .75

Souvenir Sheet

Dzelzcela Bridge, Riga — A184

2004, July 24 *Perf. 13¼x13¾*
599 A184 100s multi 4.50 4.50

2004 Summer Olympics, Athens A185

2004, Aug. 14 Litho. *Perf. 14*
600 A185 30s multi 1.10 .55

St. Jacob's Cathedral — A186

Perf. 13¾x13¼

2004, Aug. 28 Litho.
601 A186 40s multi 1.50 .75

Lighthouse Type of 2003

2004, Sept. 18
602 A170 60s Mikelbaka 2.50 1.25
a. Booklet pane of 4, perf. 13¾x13¼ on 3 sides 10.00 —
Complete booklet, #602a 10.00

Jaunpils Palace — A187

2004, Oct. 15 *Perf. 14¼x13¾*
603 A187 40s multi 1.50 .75
a. Booklet pane of 6, perf. 14¼x13¾ on 3 sides 9.00 —
Complete booklet, #603a 9.00

Mittens Type of 2002

2004, Nov. 6 *Perf. 13¼x13¾*
604 A165 15s Piebalga mittens .70 .35

Christmas — A188

Designs: 12s, Children, rabbit, bird, heart. No. 606, 15s, Snowman, birds. No. 607, 15s, Angel.

2004, Dec. 4 *Perf. 13¾x13¼*
605-607 A188 Set of 3 1.75 .85

1905 Revolution, Cent. A189

2005, Jan. 13 Litho. *Perf. 13¾x13¼*
608 A189 15s multi .85 .45

Arms Type of 2002

2005, Feb. 11 *Perf. 13¼x13¾*
609 A153 15s Aluksne .55 .30
610 A153 15s Talsi .55 .30
611 A153 40s Jekabpils 1.50 .75
Nos. 609-611 (3) 2.60 1.35

Endangered Plants Type of 2002

Designs: 20s, Pulsatilla patens. 30s, Allium ursinum.

2005, Mar. 5 *Perf. 13¼*
612-613 A158 Set of 2 2.00 1.00
613a Booklet pane of 6 #613, perf. 13¼ on 3 sides 7.25 —
Complete booklet, #613a 7.25

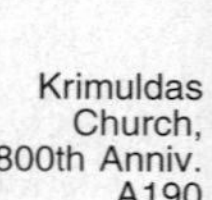

Krimuldas Church, 800th Anniv. A190

2005, Mar. 19 ***Perf. 13¼x13¾***

614 A190 40s multi 1.50 .75

The Adventures of Baron Munchausen, by Rudolph Erich Raspe A191

2005, Apr. 1 Litho. ***Perf. 13¼x13¾***

615 A191 30s multi 1.10 .55

Europa — A192

2005, Apr. 23

616 A192 60s multi 2.25 1.10

a. Tete beche pair 4.50 2.25

Mother and Child, by Janis Rozentals A193

2005, May 8 ***Perf. 14x13¼***

617 A193 40s multi 1.40 .70

a. Booklet pane of 4, perf. 14x13¼ on 3 sides 5.75 —

Complete booklet, #617a 5.75

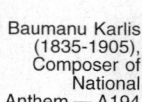

Baumanu Karlis (1835-1905), Composer of National Anthem — A194

2005, May 21 ***Perf. 13¾x13¼***

618 A194 20s multi .70 .35

Kaive Oak — A195

Serpentine Die Cut 14

2005, June 11

Self-Adhesive

619 A195 15s multi 1.10 .55

Printed in sheets of 8.

Fish Type of 2004

Designs: 15s, Lampetra fluviatilis. 40s, Clupea harengus membras.

2005, Aug. 13 Litho. ***Perf. 13¼x14***

620-621 A182 Set of 2 2.00 1.00

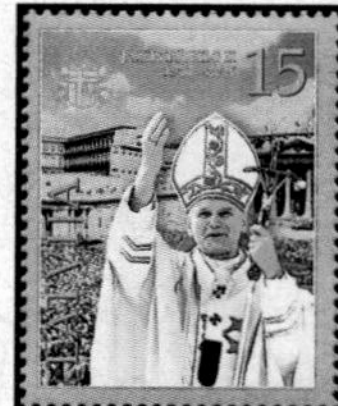

Pope John Paul II (1920-2005) A196

2005, Aug. 14 ***Perf. 14¼x13½***

622 A196 15s multi .70 .35

Souvenir Sheet

Latvian National Library — A197

2005, Aug. 27 ***Perf. 13¼x12¾***

623 A197 100s multi 4.25 2.10

Janis Plieksans (Rainis), (1865-1929), Writer — A198

2005, Sept. 10 ***Perf. 14¼***

624 A198 40s multi 1.50 .75

a. Booklet pane of 6, perf. 14¼ on 3 sides 9.00 —

Complete booklet, #624a 9.00

Souvenir Sheet

Bridge Over Railroad Tracks, Riga — A199

2005, Sept. 24 ***Perf. 13¼x13¾***

625 A199 100s multi 5.00 2.50

Lighthouse Type of 2003

2005, Oct. 8 Litho. ***Perf. 14x13¼***

626 A170 40s Daugavgrivas 1.50 .75

a. Booklet pane of 4, perf. 14x13¼ on 3 sides 6.25 —

Complete booklet, #626a 6.25

Gunars Astra (1931-88), Human Rights Activist in Soviet Union — A200

2005, Oct. 22 ***Perf. 13½x14¼***

627 A200 15s multi .60 .30

Palace Type of 2004

2005, Nov. 5 ***Perf. 13¼x14***

628 A187 40s Durbes Palace, horiz. 1.50 .75

Mittens Type of 2002

2005, Nov. 26 ***Perf. 13¼x13¾***

629 A165 20s Dienvidlatgale mittens .80 .40

Christmas A201

Designs: 12s, Goat riding on wolf's back. No. 631, 15s, Woman, dog near tree, vert. No. 632, 15s, Cat, woman carrying rooster, vert.

2005, Dec. 3 ***Serpentine Die Cut 15***

Self-Adhesive

630-632 A201 Set of 3 1.50 .75

Europa Stamps, 50th Anniv. A202

Latvian Europa stamps: Nos. 633, 637a, 10s, #414. Nos. 634, 637b, 15s, #463. Nos. 635, 637c, 15s, #442. Nos. 636, 637d, 20s, #484-485.

2006, Jan. 7 Litho. ***Perf. 13¾x13¼***

633-636 A202 Set of 4 2.10 1.10

Souvenir Sheet

Perf. 13½ Syncopated

637 A202 Sheet of 4, #a-d 2.10 1.10

No. 637 contains four 45x28mm stamps.

Town Arms Type of 2002

2006, Jan. 11 ***Perf. 13¼x13¾***

638 A153 7s Aizkraukle .25 .20

639 A153 22s Kraslava .75 .40

640 A153 31s Limbazi 1.10 .55

Nos. 638-640 (3) 2.10 1.15

2006 Winter Olympics, Turin — A203

2006, Feb. 4 ***Perf. 14***

641 A203 45s multi 1.60 .80

Stamerienas Palace — A204

2006, Feb. 25 ***Perf. 14¼x13¾***

642 A204 95s multi 3.50 1.75

Zvartes Iezis — A205

Serpentine Die Cut 14

2006, Mar. 11

Self-Adhesive

643 A205 22s multi .80 .40

Printed in sheets of 8.

Souvenir Sheet

Raunu Railroad Bridge — A206

2006, Mar. 25 ***Perf. 13½x14***

644 A206 100s multi 3.75 1.90

2006 World Ice Hockey Championships, Riga — A207

Illustration reduced.

Perf. 13½x14¼

2006, Mar. 31 **Litho.**

645 A207 55s multi + label 2.00 1.00

a. Booklet pane of 4, perf. 13½x14¼ on 3 sides, without labels 8.00 —

Complete booklet, #645a 8.00

Cesis, 800th Anniv. — A208

Various sites in Cesis: 22s, 31s, 45s, 55s. 45s and 55s are horiz.

Perf. 13¼x13¾, 13¾x13¼

2006, Apr. 7

646-649 A208 Set of 4 5.50 2.75

Traditional Jewelry — A209

No. 650: a, Brooch, Latvia. b, Bracelet, Kazakhstan.

Illustration reduced.

2006, Apr. 19 ***Perf. 14x13¾***

650 A209 22s Horiz. pair, #a-b 1.60 .80

See Kazakhstan No. 509.

Europa — A210

2006, May 3 ***Perf. 13½x14¼***

651 A210 85s multi 3.25 1.60

a. Tete beche pair 6.50 3.25

Ciganiete ar Tamburinu, by Karlis Huns — A211

2006, May 13 ***Perf. 13¼x14***

652 A211 40s multi 1.50 .75
a. Booklet pane of 4, perf. 13¼x14 on 3 sides 6.00 —
Complete booklet, #652a 6.00

A212

Personalizable Stamps A213

2006, June 9 ***Perf. 13¾***

653 A212 31s yel bister 1.25 .60
654 A213 31s yel bister 1.25 .60

Stamp vignettes could be personalized by customers, presumably for an extra fee.

"Big Christopher" Statue — A214

2006, June 16 ***Perf. 14x13½***

655 A214 36s multi 1.40 .70

Art by Anna Koshkina — A215

Die Cut Perf. 14½x13 on 3 Sides

2006, Aug. 11

Booklet Stamp

Self-Adhesive

656 A215 22s multi .80 .40
a. Booklet pane of 8 6.50

Volunteer Army, 15th Anniv. — A216

2006, Aug. 23 ***Perf. 13½x14***

657 A216 22s multi .80 .40

Staburags — A217

2006, Sept. 9 Litho. ***Perf. 14¼x13¾***

658 A217 58s multi 2.10 1.10
a. Tete beche pair 4.25 2.25

Wild Animals and Their Tracks — A218

Designs: 45s, Lynx lynx. 55s, Cervus elaphus.

2006, Sept. 23 ***Perf. 14¼x13½***

659-660 A218 Set of 2 3.75 1.90
659a Booklet pane of 4 #659, perf. 14¼x13½ on 3 sides 6.50 —
Complete booklet, #659a 6.50
659b Tete beche pair 3.50 3.50
660a Tete beche pair 4.00 4.00

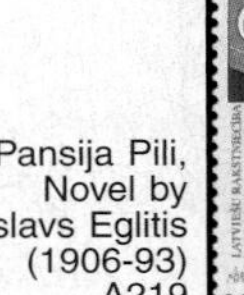

Pansija Pili, Novel by Anslavs Eglitis (1906-93) A219

2006, Oct. 14 Litho. ***Perf. 13¼x13½***

661 A219 67s multi 2.50 1.25

Lighthouse Type of 2003

2006, Oct. 27 ***Perf. 14¼x13½***

662 A170 40s Mersraga Lighthouse 1.50 .75
a. Booklet pane of 4, perf. 14¼x13½ on 3 sides 6.00 —
Complete booklet, #662a 6.00

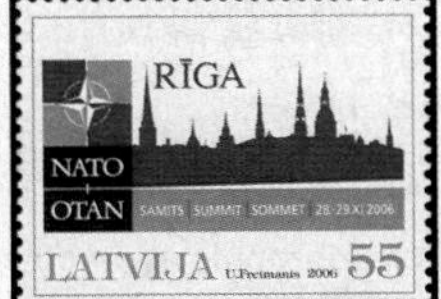

NATO Summit, Riga A220

2006, Nov. 17 ***Perf. 13¾x13¼***

663 A220 55s multi 2.10 1.10

Christmas A221

Cookies in shape of: 18s, Christmas tree. 22s, Star. 31s, Crescent moon. 45s, Bell.

Serpentine Die Cut 14

2006, Nov. 17

Self-Adhesive

664-667 A221 Set of 4 4.50 2.25

Oskars Kalpaks (1882-1919), First Commander-in-chief of Latvian Army — A222

2007, Jan. 6 ***Perf. 14¼x14***

668 A222 22s multi .85 .40

Mobile Telecommunications in Latvia, 15th Anniv. — A223

2007, Jan. 19

669 A223 22s multi .85 .40
a. Tete beche pair 1.75 .80

Town Arms Type of 2002

2007, Feb. 3 ***Perf. 13¼x13¾***

670 A153 5s Staicele .20 .20
671 A153 10s Sabile .40 .20
672 A153 22s Vecumnieki .85 .40
Nos. 670-672 (3) 1.45 .80

Tilts Tornkalna, Painting by Ludolfs Liberts (1895-1959) A224

2007, Feb. 17 ***Perf. 14¼x14***

673 A224 58s multi 2.25 1.10

Pauls Stradins Museum of the History of Medicine, Riga, 50th Anniv. A225

2007, Mar. 9 ***Perf. 14x14¼***

674 A225 22s multi .85 .40

Baltic Coast — A226

Serpentine Die Cut 14

2007, Mar. 24

Self-Adhesive

675 A226 22s multi .85 .40

Lighthouse Type of 2003

2007, Apr. 14 ***Perf. 13¾x13½***

676 A170 67s Papes Lighthouse 2.75 1.40
a. Booklet pane of 4, perf. 13¾x13½ on 3 sides 10.50 —
Complete booklet, #676a 10.50

Europa — A227

2007, Apr. 28 Litho. ***Perf. 13½x14¼***

677 A227 85s multi 3.50 1.75
a. Tete beche pair 7.00 3.50

Scouting, cent.

Palace Type of 2004

2007, June 8 Litho. ***Perf. 13½x14¼***

678 A187 22s Krustpils, horiz. .85 .40

UNESCO World Heritage Sites — A228

Designs: 36s, Historic Center of Riga. 45s, Historic Centers of Straslund and Wismar, Germany.

2007, July 12 Litho. ***Perf. 14x13¾***

679-680 A228 Set of 2 3.25 1.60

See Germany Nos. 2449-2450.

Sigulda, 800th Anniv. — A229

Designs: 22s, New Sigulda Castle. 31s, Bobsled course. 40s, Sigulda Castle ruins.

Serpentine Die Cut 15¼

2007, Aug. 10

Self-Adhesive

681-683 A229 Set of 3 4.00 2.00

Berries and Mushrooms A230

Designs: 22s, Vaccinium vitis-idaea. 58s, Cantharellus cibarius.

2007, Aug. 25 ***Perf. 14x13½***

684-685 A230 Set of 2 3.50 1.60
685a Booklet pane of 4, perf. 14x13½ on 3 sides 10.00 —
Complete booklet, #685a 10.00

Organized Soccer in Latvia, Cent. — A231

2007, Sept. 8 ***Perf. 13¾***

686 A231 45s multi 2.00 1.00

Values are for stamps with surrounding selvage.

Souvenir Sheet

Aiviekstí Railroad Bridge — A232

2007, Oct. 13 *Perf. 14*
687 A232 100s multi 4.25 2.10

Latvia Post, 375th Anniv. A233

Designs: 22s, Postrider. 31s, Postal worker and van.

Serpentine Die Cut 15

2007, Oct. 20 **Litho.**

Self-Adhesive

688-689 A233 Set of 2 2.25 1.10

13th Century Decorations A234

2007, Nov. 3 *Perf. 13¼x14*
690 A234 60s multi 2.50 1.25

Wild Animals and Their Tracks Type of 2006

Designs: 45s, Vulpes vulpes. 55s, Alces alces.

2007, Nov. 16 *Perf. 14¼x13½*
691-692 A218 Set of 2 4.25 2.10

Christmas A235

Christmas tree and children with: 22s, Musical instruments. 31s, Cookies. 45s, Skis and sled.

Serpentine Die Cut 15

2007, Nov. 24

Self-Adhesive

693-695 A235 Set of 3 4.25 2.10

Town Arms Type of 2002 With Country Name at Top

2008, Feb. 9 *Perf. 13¼x13¾*
696 A153 22s Salaspils .95 .50
697 A153 28s Plavinas 1.25 .60
698 A153 45s Saulkrasti 2.00 1.00
Nos. 696-698 (3) 4.20 2.10

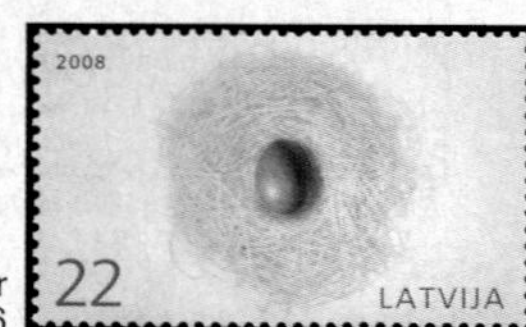

Easter A236

2008, Feb. 23 *Perf. 13¼x13*
699 A236 22s multi 1.00 .50

Augli, by Leo Svemps A237

2008, Mar. 8 **Litho.** *Perf. 13x13¼*
700 A237 63s multi 3.00 3.00

State Awards of the Baltic Countries — A238

Designs: Nos. 701, 702a, Order of Three Stars, Latvia. No. 702b, Order of Vytautas the Great, Lithuania. No. 702c, Order of the National Coat of Arms, Estonia.

2008, Mar. 15 *Perf. 13½x13¾*
701 A238 31s multi 1.40 1.40

Souvenir Sheet

702 A238 31s Sheet of 3, #a-c 4.25 4.25

On No. 701, the second line of type above the medal is 18mm wide, while it is 15mm wide on No. 702a.

See Estonia Nos. 592-593, Lithuania Nos. 862-863.

Worldwide Fund for Nature (WWF) — A239

Bats: 22s, Barbastella barbastellus. 31s, Myotis dasycneme. 45s, Barbastella barbastellus, vert. 55s, Myotis dasycneme, vert.

Perf. 13½x14¼, 14¼x13½

2008, Apr. 12
703-706 A239 Set of 4 6.75 6.75

Europa A240

Designs: 45s, Letters and postcards. 85s, Person writing letter.

2008, Apr. 22 *Perf. 13½*
707-708 A240 Set of 2 5.75 5.75

Lighthouse Type of 2003

2008, May 5 *Perf. 14¼x13½*
709 A170 63s Akmenraga 3.00 3.00

European Orienteering Championships, Ventspils — A241

2008, May 23 **Litho.** *Perf. 13x13¼*
710 A241 45s multi 2.10 2.10

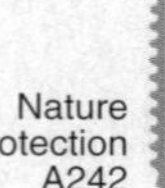

Nature Protection A242

Serpentine Die Cut 12½

2008, June 7

Self-Adhesive

711 A242 22s multi .95 .95

Riga Museum Foundations — A243

2008, June 26 *Perf. 13x13½*
712 A243 22s multi 1.00 1.00

2008 Summer Olympics, Beijing — A244

2008, Aug. 8 *Perf. 13½x13*
713 A244 63s multi 2.75 2.75

Sudraba Fairy Tale — A245

Perf. 14¼x13½

2008, Aug. 23 **Litho.**
714 A245 22s multi .95 .95

Berries and Mushrooms Type of 2007

Designs: 22s, Vaccinium myrtillus. 58s, Lecinum aurantiacum.

2008, Sept. 6 *Perf. 14x13½*
715 A230 22s multi .90 .90
716 A230 58s multi 2.25 2.25
a. Perf. 13½x14 on 3 sides 2.25 2.25
b. Booklet pane of 4 #716a 9.00 —
Complete booklet, #716b 9.00

Souvenir Sheet

Kandavas Bridge — A246

2008, Sept. 27 *Perf. 14*
717 A246 100s multi 4.00 4.00

Tautas Fronte Newspaper, 20th Anniv. — A247

2008, Oct. 8 *Perf. 13½*
718 A247 22s multi .85 .85

Wild Animals and Their Tracks Type of 2006

Designs: 45s, Martes martes. 55s, Castor fiber.

2008, Oct. 10 *Perf. 14¼x13½*
719-720 A218 Set of 2 3.75 3.75

Maris Strombergs, 2008 BMX Cycling Olympic Gold Medalist — A248

2008, Oct. 24 *Perf. 13½*
721 A248 22s multi .80 .80

Plate, Bow and Tablecloth A249

2008, Oct. 25 *Perf. 13½x13¾*
722 A249 28s multi 1.00 1.00

Latvian Republic, 90th Anniv. — A250

2008, Nov. 7 *Perf. 13¼x13*
723 A250 31s multi 1.10 1.10

Mezotnes Palace A251

2008, Nov. 8 *Perf. 13½x14¼*
724 A251 63s multi 2.25 2.25

Christmas — A252

2008, Nov. 28 *Perf. 14¼x13¾*
725 A252 25s multi .90 .90

Town Arms Type of 2002 With Country Name at Top

2009, Jan. 10 Litho. *Perf. 14x14¼*
726 A153 33s Dagda 1.25 1.25
727 A153 35s Balozi 1.40 1.40
728 A153 60s Stende 2.25 2.25
Nos. 726-728 (3) 4.90 4.90

Brooch, 8th Cent. A. D. — A253

2009, Jan. 24 *Perf. 14*
729 A253 98s multi 3.75 3.75

Dancing Boy and Animals Folktale A254

2009, Feb. 21 *Perf. 13¼*
730 A254 40s multi 1.50 1.50

SEMI-POSTAL STAMPS

Catalogue values for unused stamps in this section are for Never Hinged items.

"Mercy" Assisting Wounded Soldier — SP1

1920 Unwmk. Typo. *Perf. 11½*
Brown and Green Design on Back
B1 SP1 20(30)k dk brn & red 1.25 *1.25*
B2 SP1 40(55)k dk bl & red 1.25 *1.25*
B3 SP1 50(70)k dk grn & red 1.25 *1.50*
B4 SP1 1(1.30)r dl sl & red 1.50 *2.50*

Wmk. Star and Triangles (197)
Blue Design on Back
B5 SP1 20(30)k dk brn & red 1.25 *1.25*
B6 SP1 40(55)k dk bl & red 1.25 *1.25*
a. Vert. pair, imperf. btwn. 40.00
B7 SP1 50(70)k dk grn & red 1.25 *1.50*
B8 SP1 1(1.30)r dk sl & red 2.00 *2.50*

Wmk. Similar to 145
Pink Paper *Imperf.*
Brown, Green and Red Design on Back
B9 SP1 20(30)k dk brn & red 1.75 *2.50*
B10 SP1 40(55)k dk bl & red 1.75 *2.50*
B11 SP1 50(70)k dk grn & red 1.75 *2.50*
B12 SP1 1(1.30)r dk sl & red 3.50 *4.25*
Nos. B1-B12 (12) 19.75 *24.75*

These semi-postal stamps were printed on the backs of unfinished bank notes of the Workers and Soldiers Council, Riga, and the Bermondt-Avalov Army. Blocks of stamps showing complete banknotes on reverse are worth approximately three times the catalogue value of the stamps.

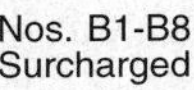
Nos. B1-B8 Surcharged

1921 Unwmk. *Perf. 11½*
Brown and Green Design on Back
B13 SP1 20k + 2r dk brn & red 3.00 *4.00*
B14 SP1 40k + 2r dk bl & red 3.00 *4.00*
B15 SP1 50k + 2r dk grn & red 3.00 *4.00*
B16 SP1 1r + 2r dk sl & red 3.00 *4.00*

Wmk. Star and Triangles (197)
Blue Design on Back
B17 SP1 20k + 2r dk brn & red 30.00 *30.00*
B18 SP1 40k + 2r dk bl & red 30.00 *30.00*
B19 SP1 50k + 2r dk grn & red 30.00 *30.00*
B20 SP1 1r + 2r dk sl & red 30.00 *30.00*
Nos. B13-B20 (8) 132.00 *136.00*

Regular Issue of 1923-25 Surcharged in Blue

1923 Wmk. Similar to 181 *Perf. 10*
B21 A12 1s + 10s violet 1.00 1.00
B22 A12 2s + 10s yellow 1.00 1.00
B23 A12 4s + 10s dk green 1.00 1.00
Nos. B21-B23 (3) 3.00 3.00

The surtax benefited the Latvian War Invalids Society.

Lighthouse and Harbor, Liepaja (Libau) SP2

Church at Liepaja — SP5

Coat of Arms of Liepaja — SP6

Designs: 15s (25s), City Hall, Liepaja. 25s (35s), Public Bathing Pavilion, Liepaja.

1925, July 23 *Perf. 11½*
B24 SP2 6s (12s) red brown & deep blue 4.25 3.50
B25 SP2 15s (25s) dk bl & brn 2.50 *2.75*
B26 SP2 25s (35s) violet & dark green 4.00 2.00
B27 SP5 30s (40s) dark blue & lake 7.50 *8.50*
B28 SP6 50s (60s) dark grn & violet 11.00 *11.00*
Nos. B24-B28 (5) 29.25 *27.75*

Tercentenary of Liepaja (Libau). The surtax benefited that city. Exist imperf. Value, unused set $450.

President Janis Cakste — SP7

1928, Apr. 18 Engr.
B29 SP7 2s (12s) red orange 4.00 3.00
B30 SP7 6s (16s) deep green 4.00 3.00
B31 SP7 15s (25s) red brown 4.00 3.00
B32 SP7 25s (35s) deep blue 4.25 3.50
B33 SP7 30s (40s) claret 4.25 3.50
Nos. B29-B33 (5) 20.50 16.00

The surtax helped erect a monument to Janis Cakste, 1st pres. of the Latvian Republic.

Venta River — SP8

Allegory, "Latvia" — SP9

View of Jelgava SP10

National Theater, Riga — SP11

View of Cesis (Wenden) SP12

Riga Bridge and Trenches SP13

Perf. 11½, Imperf.
1928, Nov. 18 Wmk. 212 Litho.
B34 SP8 6s (16s) green 4.00 2.75
B35 SP9 10s (20s) scarlet 4.00 2.75
B36 SP10 15s (25s) maroon 4.00 2.75
B37 SP11 30s (40s) ultra 4.25 2.75
B38 SP12 50s (60s) dk gray 4.50 3.00
B39 SP13 1 l (1.10 l) choc 4.75 3.50
Nos. B34-B39 (6) 25.50 17.50

The surtax was given to a committee for the erection of a Liberty Memorial.

Z. A. Meierovics SP14

1929, Aug. 22 *Perf. 11½, Imperf.*
B46 SP14 2s (4s) orange 5.75 3.75
B47 SP14 6s (12s) dp grn 5.75 3.75
B48 SP14 15s (25s) red brown 5.75 3.75
B49 SP14 25s (35s) deep blue 6.00 3.75
B50 SP14 30s (40s) ultra 6.50 3.75
Nos. B46-B50 (5) 29.75 18.75

The surtax was used to erect a monument to Z. A. Meierovics, Latvian statesman.

Tuberculosis Cross — SP15

Allegory of Hope for the Sick — SP16

Gustavs Zemgals — SP17

Riga Castle — SP18

Daisies and Double-barred Cross — SP20

Tuberculosis Sanatorium, near Riga — SP22

Cakste, Kviesis and Zemgals SP23

Designs: No. B61, Janis Cakste, 1st pres. of Latvia. No. B63, Pres. Alberts Kviesis.

1930, Dec. 4 Typo. *Perf. 10, 11½*
B56 SP15 1s (2s) dk vio & red orange 1.40 1.40
B57 SP15 2s (4s) org & red orange 1.40 1.40
a. Cliché of 1s (2s) in plate of 2s (4s) *700.00 700.00*
B58 SP16 4s (8s) dk grn & red 1.75 1.75
B59 SP17 5s (10s) brt grn & dk brown 1.75 1.75
B60 SP18 6s (12s) ol grn & bister 1.75 1.75
B61 SP17 10s (20s) dp red & black 2.25 2.25
B62 SP20 15s (30s) mar & dl green 1.90 2.25
B63 SP17 20s (40s) rose lake & ind 2.75 2.25
B64 SP22 25s (50s) multi 6.00 6.00
B65 SP23 30s (60s) multi 6.00 6.00
Nos. B56-B65 (10) 26.95 26.80

Surtax for the Latvian Anti-Tuberculosis Soc.
For surcharges see Nos. B72-B81.

J. Rainis and New Buildings, Riga SP24

Character from Play and Rainis SP25

Characters from Plays — SP26

Rainis and Lyre SP27

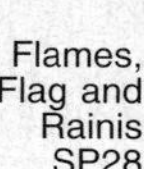

Flames, Flag and Rainis SP28

1930, May 23 Wmk. 212 *Perf. 11½*

No.	Type	Value	Unused	Used
B66	SP24	1s (2s) dull violet	1.25	1.00
B67	SP25	2s (4s) yellow org	1.25	1.00
B68	SP26	4s (8s) dp green	1.25	1.00
B69	SP27	6s (12s) yel grn & red brown	1.25	1.00
B70	SP28	10s (20s) dark red	32.50	*35.00*
B71	SP27	15s (30s) red brn & yellow green	35.00	*40.00*
		Nos. B66-B71 (6)	72.50	*79.00*

Sold at double face value, surtax going to memorial fund for J. Rainis (Jan Plieksans, 1865-1929), writer and politician.
Exist imperf. Value twice that of perf. stamps.

Nos. B56 to B65 Surcharged in Black

1931, Aug. 19 *Perf. 10, 11½*

No.	Type	Value	Unused	Used
B72	SP18	9s on 6s (12s)	1.75	1.10
B73	SP15	16s on 1s (2s)	21.00	15.00
B74	SP15	17s on 2s (4s)	2.10	1.40
B75	SP16	19s on 4s (8s)	6.50	6.00
B76	SP17	20s on 5s (10s)	4.25	*6.00*
B77	SP20	23s on 15s (30s)	2.00	2.00
B78	SP17	25s on 10s (20s)	4.25	3.00
B79	SP17	35s on 20s (40s)	6.50	3.75
B80	SP22	45s on 25s (50s)	22.50	*25.00*
B81	SP23	55s on 30s (60s)	27.50	*30.00*
		Nos. B72-B81 (10)	98.35	93.25

The surcharge replaces the original total price, including surtax.
Nos. B73-B81 have no bars in the surcharge. The surtax aided the Latvian Anti-Tuberculosis Society.

Lacplesis, the Deliverer SP29

Designs: 1s, Kriva telling stories under Holy Oak. 2s, Enslaved Latvians building Riga under knight's supervision. 4s, Death of Black Knight. 5s, Spirit of Lacplesis over freed Riga.

Inscribed: "AIZSARGI" (Army Reserve)

1932, Feb. 10 *Perf. 10½, Imperf.*

No.	Type	Value	Unused	Used
B82	SP29	1s (11s) vio brn & bluish	3.25	3.25
B83	SP29	2s (17s) ocher & ol green	3.25	3.25
B84	SP29	3s (23s) red brn & org brown	3.25	3.25
B85	SP29	4s (34s) dk green & green	3.50	3.50
B86	SP29	5s (45s) green & emerald	4.00	4.00
		Nos. B82-B86 (5)	17.25	17.25

Surtax aided the Militia Maintenance Fund.

Marching Troops SP30

Infantry in Action SP31

Nurse Binding Soldier's Wound — SP32

Army Soup Kitchen — SP33

Gen. J. Balodis — SP34

1932, May *Perf. 10½, Imperf.*

No.	Type	Value	Unused	Used
B87	SP30	6s (25s) ol brn & red violet	7.00	6.00
B88	SP31	7s (35s) dk bl grn & dark blue	7.00	6.00
B89	SP32	10s (45s) ol green & black brown	7.00	6.00
B90	SP33	12s (55s) lake & ol green	7.50	6.50
B91	SP34	15s (75s) red org & brown violet	8.50	7.50
		Nos. B87-B91 (5)	37.00	32.00

The surtax aided the Latvian Home Guards.

Symbolical of Unified Latvia — SP35

Aid to the Sick — SP37

Symbolical of the Strength of the Latvian Union SP36

"Charity" SP38

Wmk. Multiple Swastikas (212)

1936, Dec. 28 Litho. *Perf. 11½*

No.	Type	Value	Unused	Used
B92	SP35	3s orange red	2.50	*4.00*
B93	SP36	10s green	2.50	*4.00*
B94	SP37	20s rose pink	2.50	*4.50*
B95	SP38	35s blue	2.50	*4.50*
		Nos. B92-B95 (4)	10.00	*17.00*

Souvenir Sheets

SP39

1938, May 12 Wmk. 212 *Perf. 11*

No.	Type	Value	Unused	Used
B96	SP39	Sheet of 2	15.00	*20.00*
a.		35s Justice Palace, Riga	4.50	*5.00*
b.		40s Power Station, Kegums	4.50	*5.00*

Sold for 2 l. The surtax of 1.25 l was for the National Reconstruction Fund.
No. B96 exists imperf.

Overprinted in Blue with Dates 1934 1939 and "15" over "V"

1939

No.	Type	Value	Unused	Used
B97	SP39	Sheet of 2	30.00	*40.00*

5th anniv. of Natl. Unity Day. Sold for 2 lats. Surtax for the Natl. Reconstruction Fund.

Natl. Olympic Committee SP50

1992, Feb. 8 Litho. *Perf. 13½x13*

Background Color

No.	Type	Value	Unused	Used
B150	SP50	50k +25k gray	.85	.85
B151	SP50	50k +25k buff	1.75	1.75
B152	SP50	100k +50k bister	1.25	1.25
		Nos. B150-B152 (3)	3.85	3.85

No. B150 inscribed "Berlin 18.09.91."

AIR POST STAMPS

Catalogue values for unused stamps in this section are for Never Hinged items.

Blériot XI — AP1

Wmk. Wavy Lines Similar to 181

1921, July 30 Litho. *Perf. 11½*

No.	Type	Value	Unused	Used
C1	AP1	10r emerald	5.00	4.00
a.		Imperf.	13.00	*13.00*
C2	AP1	20r dark blue	5.00	4.00
a.		Imperf.	12.00	*13.00*

1928, May 1

No.	Type	Value	Unused	Used
C3	AP1	10s deep green	5.00	1.50
C4	AP1	15s red	3.00	1.50
C5	AP1	25s ultra	6.00	3.50
a.		Pair, imperf. btwn.	35.00	
		Nos. C3-C5 (3)	14.00	6.50

Nos. C1-C5 sometimes show letters of a paper maker's watermark "PACTIEN LIGAT MILLS."

1931-32 Wmk. 212 *Perf. 11, 11½*

No.	Type	Value	Unused	Used
C6	AP1	10s deep green	1.75	.90
C7	AP1	15s red	2.50	1.40
C8	AP1	25s deep blue ('32)	14.00	1.60
		Nos. C6-C8 (3)	18.25	3.90

Type of 1921 Overprinted or Surcharged in Black

1933, May 26 Wmk. 212 *Imperf.*

No.	Type	Value	Unused	Used
C9	AP1	10s deep green	55.00	*75.00*
C10	AP1	15s red	55.00	*75.00*
C11	AP1	25s deep blue	55.00	*75.00*
C12	AP1	50s on 15s red	275.00	*500.00*
C13	AP1	100s on 25s dp blue	275.00	*500.00*
		Nos. C9-C13 (5)	715.00	*1,225.*

Honoring and financing a flight from Riga to Bathurst, Gambia. The plane crashed at Neustettin, Germany.
Counterfeits exist of Nos. C1-C13.

AIR POST SEMI-POSTAL STAMPS

Catalogue values for unused stamps in this section are for Never Hinged items.

Durbes Castle, Rainis Birthplace — SPAP1

Wmk. 212

1930, May 26 Litho. *Perf. 11½*

No.	Type	Value	Unused	Used
CB1	SPAP1	10s (20s) red & olive green	10.00	*12.00*
CB2	SPAP1	15s (30s) dk yel green & copper red	10.00	*12.00*

Surtax for the Rainis Memorial Fund.

Imperf.

No.	Type	Value	Unused	Used
CB1a	SPAP1	10s (20s)	20.00	*17.50*
CB2a	SPAP1	15s (30s)	20.00	*17.50*

Nos. C6-C8 Surcharged in Magenta, Blue or Red

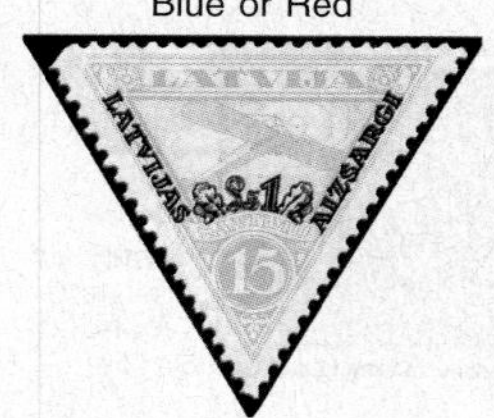

1931, Dec. 5

No.	Type	Value	Unused	Used
CB3	AP1	10s + 50s deep green (M)	13.00	*14.00*
CB4	AP1	15s + 1 l red (Bl)	13.00	*14.00*
CB5	AP1	25s + 1.50 l deep blue	13.00	*14.00*
		Nos. CB3-CB5 (3)	39.00	*42.00*

Surtax for the Latvian Home Guards.

Imperf.

No.	Type	Value	Unused	Used
CB3a	AP1	10s + 50s	13.50	*14.50*
CB4a	AP1	15s + 1 l	13.50	*14.50*
CB5a	AP1	25s + 1.50 l	13.50	*14.50*
		Nos. CB3a-CB5a (3)	40.50	*43.50*

SPAP2

1932, June 17 *Perf. 10½*

No.	Type	Value	Unused	Used
CB6	SPAP2	10s (20s) dk sl grn & green	22.50	*22.50*
CB7	SPAP2	15s (30s) brt red & buff	22.50	*22.50*
CB8	SPAP2	25s (50s) dp bl & gray	22.50	*22.50*
		Nos. CB6-CB8 (3)	67.50	*67.50*

Surtax for the Latvian Home Guards.

Imperf.

No.	Type	Value	Unused	Used
CB6a	SPAP2	10s (20s)	22.50	22.50
CB7a	SPAP2	15s (30s)	22.50	22.50
CB8a	SPAP2	25s (50s)	22.50	22.50
		Nos. CB6a-CB8a (3)	67.50	*67.50*

Icarus — SPAP3

Leonardo da Vinci — SPAP4

Charles Balloon — SPAP5

Wright Brothers Biplane SPAP6

Bleriot Monoplane SPAP7

1932, Dec. ***Perf. 10, 11½***

CB9	SPAP3	5s (25s) ol bister & green	25.00	25.00
CB10	SPAP4	10s (50s) ol brn & gray grn	25.00	25.00
CB11	SPAP5	15s (75s) red brown & gray grn	25.00	25.00
CB12	SPAP6	20s (1 l) gray grn & lil rose	25.00	25.00
CB13	SPAP7	25s (1.25 l) brn & bl	25.00	25.00
		Nos. CB9-CB13 (5)	125.00	125.00

Issued to honor pioneers of aviation. The surtax of four times the face value was for wounded Latvian aviators.

Imperf.

CB9a	SPAP3	5s (25s)	22.00	*24.00*
CB10a	SPAP4	10s (50s)	22.00	*24.00*
CB11a	SPAP5	15s (75s)	22.00	*24.00*
CB12a	SPAP6	20s (1 l)	22.00	*24.00*
CB13a	SPAP7	25s (1.25 l)	22.00	*24.00*
		Nos. CB9a-CB13a (5)	110.00	120.00

Icarus Falling SPAP8

Monument to Aviators SPAP9

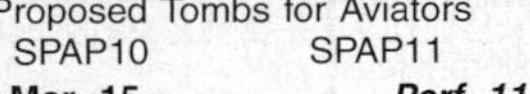

Proposed Tombs for Aviators
SPAP10 SPAP11

1933, Mar. 15 ***Perf. 11½***

CB14	SPAP8	2s (52s) blk & ocher	20.00	*20.00*
CB15	SPAP9	3s (53s) blk & red org	20.00	*20.00*
CB16	SPAP10	10s (60s) blk & dk yel green	20.00	*20.00*
CB17	SPAP11	20s (70s) blk & cerise	20.00	*20.00*
		Nos. CB14-CB17 (4)	80.00	*80.00*

50s surtax for wounded Latvian aviators.

Imperf.

CB14a	SPAP8	2s (52s)	21.00	21.00
CB15a	SPAP9	3s (53s)	21.00	21.00
CB16a	SPAP10	10s (60s)	21.00	21.00
CB17a	SPAP11	20s (70s)	21.00	21.00
		Nos. CB14a-CB17a (4)	84.00	84.00

Monoplane Taking Off SPAP12

Designs: 7s (57s), Biplane under fire at Riga. 35s (1.35 l), Map and planes.

1933, June 15 **Wmk. 212** ***Perf. 11½***

CB18	SPAP12	3s (53s) org & sl blue	40.00	*40.00*
CB19	SPAP12	7s (57s) sl bl & dk brn	40.00	*40.00*
CB20	SPAP12	35s (1.35 l) dp ultra & ol black	40.00	*40.00*
		Nos. CB18-CB20 (3)	120.00	*120.00*

Surtax for wounded Latvian aviators. Counterfeits exist.

Imperf.

CB18a	SPAP12	3s (53s)	40.00	*42.50*
CB19a	SPAP12	7s (57s)	40.00	*42.50*
CB20a	SPAP12	35s (1.35 l)	40.00	*42.50*
		Nos. CB18a-CB20a (3)	120.00	*127.50*

American Gee-Bee SPAP13

English Seaplane S6B SPAP14

Graf Zeppelin over Riga SPAP15

DO-X SPAP16

1933, Sept. 5 ***Perf. 11½***

CB21	SPAP13	8s (68s) brn & gray black	80.00	*85.00*
CB22	SPAP14	12s (1.12 l) brn car & ol green	80.00	*85.00*
CB23	SPAP15	30s (1.30 l) blue & gray black	90.00	*90.00*
CB24	SPAP16	40s (1.90 l) brn vio & indigo	85.00	*85.00*
		Nos. CB21-CB24 (4)	335.00	345.00

Surtax for wounded Latvian aviators.

Imperf.

CB21a	SPAP13	8s (68s)	85.00	85.00
CB22a	SPAP14	12s (1.12 l)	85.00	85.00
CB23a	SPAP15	30s (1.30 l)	95.00	95.00
CB24a	SPAP16	40s (1.90 l)	90.00	90.00
		Nos. CB21a-CB24a (4)	355.00	*355.00*

OCCUPATION STAMPS

Issued under German Occupation

German Stamps of 1905-18 Handstamped

1919 **Wmk. 125** ***Perf. 14, 14½***

Red Overprint

1N1	A22	2½pf gray	225.00	225.00
1N2	A16	5pf green	175.00	90.00
1N3	A22	15pf dk violet	275.00	90.00
1N4	A16	20pf blue vio	110.00	40.00
1N5	A16	25pf org & blk, *yel*	375.00	275.00
1N6	A16	50pf pur & blk, *buff*	375.00	275.00

Blue Overprint

1N7	A22	2½pf gray	225.00	225.00
1N8	A16	5pf green	110.00	60.00
1N9	A16	10pf carmine	92.50	35.00
1N10	A22	15pf dk violet	275.00	150.00
1N11	A16	20pf blue vio	110.00	35.00
1N12	A16	25pf org & blk, *yel*	375.00	275.00
1N13	A16	50pf pur & blk, *buff*	375.00	275.00
		Nos. 1N1-1N13 (13)	3,097.	2,050.

Inverted and double overprints exist, as well as counterfeit overprints.

Some experts believe that Nos. 1N1-1N7 were not officially issued. All used stamps are canceled to order.

Russian Stamps Overprinted

1941, July

1N14	A331	5k red (#734)	.80	*4.25*
1N15	A109	10k blue (#616)	.80	*4.25*
1N16	A332	15k dark green (#735)	27.50	*67.50*
1N17	A97	20k dull green (#617)	.80	*4.25*
1N18	A333	30k deep blue (#736)	.80	*4.25*
1N19	A111	50k dp brn (#619A)	3.25	*10.00*
		Nos. 1N14-1N19 (6)	33.95	*94.50*
		Set, never hinged	50.00	

Issued: 20k, 30k, 7/17; 5k, 10k, 7/18; 15k, 7/19; 50k, 7/23.

Nos. 1N14-1N19 were replaced by German stamps in mid-October. On Nov. 4, 1941, German stamps overprinted "Ostland" (Russia Nos. N9-N28) were placed into use.

The overprint exists on imperf examples of the 10k and 50k stamps. Value, each $800.

Counterfeit overprints exist.

KURLAND

German Stamps Overprinted

1945, Apr. 20

1N20	A115	6pf on 5pf dp yellow grn (#509)	37.50	*62.50*
		Never hinged	65.00	
1N21	A115	6 pf 10pf dk brown (#511A)	15.00	*30.00*
		Never hinged	25.00	
a.		Inverted surcharge	100.00	*175.00*
		Never hinged	175.00	
b.		Double surcharge	85.00	*150.00*
		Never hinged	150.00	
1N22	A115	6 pf on 20pf blue	8.50	*13.50*
		Never hinged	15.00	
a.		Inverted surcharge	100.00	*175.00*
		Never hinged	175.00	
b.		Double surcharge	85.00	*150.00*
		Never hinged	150.00	

Perf 13½

1N23	MPP1	12pf on (-) red brown, (#MQ1)	42.50	*72.50*
		Never hinged	82.50	
a.		Inverted surcharge	150.00	*275.00*
		Never hinged	275.00	
b.		Double surcharge	150.00	*275.00*
		Never hinged	275.00	

Rouletted

1N24	MPP1	12pf on (-) red brown, (#MQ1a)	6.50	*10.00*
		Never hinged	12.50	
a.		Inverted surcharge	75.00	*135.00*
		Never hinged	135.00	
b.		Double surcharge	67.50	*120.00*
		Never hinged	120.00	
		Nos. 1N20-1N24 (5)	110.00	*188.50*
		Set, never hinged	200.00	

Nos. 1N20-1N24 were used in the German-held enclave of Kurland (Courland) from April 20-May 8, 1945.

Counterfeit surcharges are plentiful.

ISSUED UNDER RUSSIAN OCCUPATION

Fake overprints/surcharges exist on Nos. 2N1-2N36.

The following stamps were issued at Mitau during the occupation of Kurland by the West Russian Army under Colonel Bermondt-Avalov.

Stamps of Latvia Handstamped

1919 **Wmk. 108** ***Imperf.***

On Stamps of 1919

2N1	A1	3k lilac	12.50	*17.50*
2N2	A1	5k carmine	12.50	*17.50*
2N3	A1	10k dp blue	67.50	*92.50*
2N4	A1	20k orange	12.50	*17.50*
2N5	A1	25k gray	12.50	*17.50*
2N6	A1	35k dk brown	12.50	*17.50*
2N7	A1	50k purple	12.50	*17.50*
2N8	A1	75k emerald	15.00	*22.50*

On Riga Liberation Stamps

2N9	A2	5k carmine	7.50	*12.50*
2N10	A2	15k dp green	7.50	*12.50*
2N11	A2	35k brown	7.50	*12.50*

Stamps of Latvia Overprinted

On Stamps of 1919

2N12	A1	3k lilac	5.00	*7.50*
2N13	A1	5k carmine	5.00	*7.50*
2N14	A1	10k dp blue	60.00	*92.50*
2N15	A1	20k orange	10.00	*15.00*
2N16	A1	25k gray	17.50	*35.00*
2N17	A1	35k dk brown	12.50	*17.50*
2N18	A1	50k purple	12.50	*17.50*
2N19	A1	75k emerald	12.50	*17.50*

On Riga Liberation Stamps

2N20	A2	5k carmine	4.00	*6.00*
2N21	A2	15k dp green	4.00	*6.00*
2N22	A2	35k brown	4.00	*6.00*
a.		Inverted overprint	*110.00*	
		Nos. 2N1-2N22 (22)	327.00	*485.50*

The letters "Z. A." are the initials of "Zapadnaya Armiya"-i.e. Western Army.

Russian Stamps of 1909-17 Surcharged

Perf. 14, 14½x15

Unwmk.

On Stamps of 1909-12

2N23	A14	10k on 2k grn	4.00	*5.00*
a.		Inverted surcharge	*30.00*	
2N24	A15	30k on 4k car	3.50	*4.50*
2N25	A14	40k on 5k cl	3.50	*4.50*
2N26	A15	50k pn 10k dk bl	3.50	*4.50*
2N27	A11	70k on 15k red brn & bl	3.50	*4.50*
a.		Inverted surcharge	*50.00*	
2N28	A8	90k on 20k bl & car	3.50	*4.50*
2N29	A11	1r on 25k grn & vio	3.50	4.50
2N30	A11	1½r on 35k red brn & grn	22.50	37.50
2N31	A8	2r on 50k vio & grn	4.50	6.50
a.		Inverted surcharge	*35.00*	
2N32	A11	4r on 70k brn & org	12.50	15.00

Perf. 13½

2N33	A9	6r on 1r pale brn, brn & org	12.50	15.00

On Stamps of 1917

Imperf

2N34	A14	20k on 3k red	4.50	*5.00*
2N35	A14	40k on 5k claret	32.50	*42.50*
2N36	A12	10r on 3.50r mar & lt grn	32.50	*42.50*
a.		Inverted surcharge	*100.00*	
		Nos. 2N23-2N36 (14)	146.50	*196.00*

Eight typographed stamps of this design were prepared in 1919, but never placed in use. They exist both perforated and imperforate. Value, set, imperf. $1, perf. $2.

Reprints and counterfeits exist.

Catalogue values for unused stamps in this section, from this poit to the end of the section, are for Never Hinged items.

Arms of Soviet Latvia — OS1

1940 Typo. Wmk. 265 *Perf. 10*

2N45	OS1	1s dk violet	.20	.20
2N46	OS1	2s orange yel	.20	.20
2N47	OS1	3s orange ver	.20	.20
2N48	OS1	5s dk olive grn	.20	.20
2N49	OS1	7s turq green	.20	.20
2N50	OS1	10s slate green	1.40	.20
2N51	OS1	20s brown lake	.85	.20
2N52	OS1	30s light blue	2.10	.25
2N53	OS1	35s brt ultra	.20	.20
2N54	OS1	40s chocolate	1.40	.20
2N55	OS1	50s lt gray	2.00	.20
2N56	OS1	1 l lt brown	2.75	.25
2N57	OS1	5 l brt green	20.00	7.50
		Nos. 2N45-2N57 (13)	31.70	10.00

Used values of #2N45-2N57 are for CTOs. Commercially use are worth three times as much.

LEBANON

'le-bə-nən

(Grand Liban)

LOCATION — Asia Minor, bordering on the Mediterranean Sea
GOVT. — Republic
AREA — 4,036 sq. mi.
POP. — 3,562,699 (1999 est.)
CAPITAL — Beirut

Formerly a part of the Syrian province of Turkey, Lebanon was occupied by French forces after World War I. It was mandated to France after it had been declared a separate state. Limited autonomy was granted in 1927 and full independence achieved in 1941. The French issued two sets of occupation stamps (with T.E.O. overprint) for Lebanon in late 1919. The use of these and later occupation issues (of 1920-24, with overprints "O.M.F." and "Syrie-Grand Liban") was extended to Syria, Cilicia, Alaouites and Alexandretta. By custom, these are all listed under Syria.

100 Centimes = 1 Piaster
100 Piasters = 1 Pound

Watermark

Wmk. 400

Catalogue values for unused stamps in this country are for Never Hinged items, beginning with Scott 177 in the regular postage section, Scott B13 in the semi-postal section, Scott C97 in the airpost section, Scott CB5 in the airpost semi-postal section, Scott J37 in the postage due section, and Scott RA11 in the postal tax section.

Issued under French Mandate

Stamps of France 1900-21 Surcharged

1924 Unwmk. *Perf. 14x13½*

1	A16	10c on 2c vio brn	2.00	1.00
a.		Inverted surcharge	30.00	27.50
2	A22	25c on 5c orange	2.00	.90
3	A22	50c on 10c green	2.00	.90
4	A20	75c on 15c sl grn	3.00	1.90
5	A22	1p on 20c red brn	2.25	.75
a.		Double surcharge	32.50	27.50
b.		Inverted surcharge	35.00	32.50
6	A22	1.25p on 25c blue	5.00	2.40
7	A22	1.50p on 30c org	3.00	2.25
8	A22	1.50p on 30c red	3.00	2.25
9	A20	2.50p on 50c dl bl	2.50	1.00
a.		Inverted surcharge	27.50	27.50

Surcharged

10	A18	2p on 40c red & pale bl	5.50	3.75
a.		Inverted surcharge	27.50	27.50
11	A18	3p on 60c violet & ultra	8.00	6.75
12	A18	5p on 1fr cl & ol green	10.00	7.50
13	A18	10p on 2fr org & pale bl	15.00	12.00
a.		Inverted surcharge	50.00	50.00
14	A18	25p on 5fr dk bl & buff	22.50	19.00
a.		Inverted surcharge	85.00	85.00
		Nos. 1-14 (14)	85.75	62.35

Broken and missing letters and varieties of spacing are numerous in these surcharges.

For overprints see Nos. C1-C4.

Stamps of France, 1923, (Pasteur) Surcharged "GRAND LIBAN" and New Values

15	A23	50c on 10c green	3.50	1.10
a.		Inverted surcharge	35.00	25.00
16	A23	1.50p on 30c red	4.50	2.25
17	A23	2.50p on 50c blue	3.75	1.10
a.		Inverted surcharge	30.00	27.50
		Nos. 15-17 (3)	11.75	4.45

Commemorative Stamps of France, 1924, (Olympic Games) Surcharged "GRAND LIBAN" and New Values

18	A24	50c on 10c gray grn & yel grn	32.50	*32.50*
a.		Inverted surcharge	350.00	
19	A25	1.25p on 25c rose & dk rose	32.50	*32.50*
a.		Inverted surcharge	350.00	
20	A26	1.50p on 30c brn red & blk	32.50	*32.50*
a.		Inverted surcharge	350.00	
21	A27	2.50p on 50c ultra & dk bl	32.50	*32.50*
a.		Inverted surcharge	350.00	
		Nos. 18-21 (4)	130.00	130.00

Stamps of France, 1900-24, Surcharged

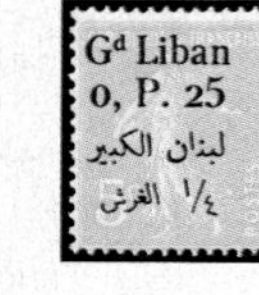

1924-25

22	A16	10c on 2c vio brn	1.00	.50
23	A22	25c on 5c orange	1.25	.75
24	A22	50c on 10c green	2.00	1.40
25	A20	75c on 15c gray grn	1.75	1.10
26	A22	1p on 20c red brn	1.50	.95
27	A22	1.25p on 25c blue	2.25	1.60
28	A22	1.50p on 30c red	2.00	1.25
29	A22	1.50p on 30c orange	62.50	57.50
30	A22	2p on 35c vio ('25)	2.25	1.60
31	A20	3p on 60c lt vio ('25)	3.00	2.10
32	A20	4p on 85c ver	3.50	2.50

Surcharged

33	A18	2p on 40c red & pale bl	2.25	1.60
a.		2nd line of Arabic reads "2 Piastre" (singular)	2.50	.50
34	A18	2p on 45c green & blue ('25)	27.50	22.50
35	A18	3p on 60c violet & ultra	3.50	2.50
36	A18	5p on 1fr cl & ol green	4.25	3.25
37	A18	10p on 2fr org & pale bl	9.75	8.50
38	A18	25p on 5fr dk bl & buff	15.00	13.50
		Nos. 22-38 (17)	145.25	123.10

Last line of surcharge on No. 33 has four characters, with a 9-like character between the third and fourth in illustration. Last line on No. 33a is as illustrated.

The surcharge may be found inverted on most of Nos. 22-38, and double on some values.

For overprints see Nos. C5-C8.

Stamps of France 1923-24 (Pasteur) Surcharged as Nos. 22-32

39	A23	50c on 10c green	2.00	.85
a.		Inverted surcharge	35.00	25.00
b.		Double surcharge	40.00	21.00
40	A23	75c on 15c green	2.25	1.40
41	A23	1.50p on 30c red	2.75	1.40
a.		Inverted surcharge	35.00	25.00
42	A23	2p on 45c red	5.00	3.50
a.		Inverted surcharge	35.00	21.00
43	A23	2.50p on 50c blue	2.00	.95
a.		Inverted surcharge	35.00	21.00
b.		Double surcharge	40.00	21.00
44	A23	4p on 75c blue	5.00	3.50
		Nos. 39-44 (6)	19.00	11.60

France Nos. 198 to 201 (Olympics) Surcharged as Nos. 22-32

45	A24	50c on 10c	32.50	*32.50*
46	A25	1.25p on 25c	32.50	*32.50*
47	A26	1.50p on 30c	32.50	*32.50*
48	A27	2.50p on 50c	32.50	*32.50*
		Nos. 45-48 (4)	130.00	130.00

France No. 219 (Ronsard) Surcharged as Nos. 22-32

49	A28	4p on 75c bl, *bluish*	3.50	3.50
a.		Inverted surcharge	65.00	50.00

Cedar of Lebanon — A1

Crusader Castle, Tripoli — A3

View of Beirut A2

Designs: 50c, Crusader Castle, Tripoli. 75c, Beit-ed-Din Palace. 1p, Temple of Jupiter, Baalbek. 1.25p, Mouktara Palace. 1.50p, Harbor of Tyre. 2p, View of Zahle. 2.50p, Ruins at Baalbek. 3p, Square at Deir-el-Kamar. 5p, Castle at Sidon. 25p, Square at Beirut.

1925 Litho. *Perf. 12½, 13½*

50	A1	10c dark violet	.50	.20

Photo.

51	A2	25c olive black	.95	.20
52	A2	50c yellow grn	.75	.20
53	A2	75c brn orange	.75	.20
54	A2	1p magenta	2.00	.80
55	A2	1.25p deep green	2.25	1.40
56	A2	1.50p rose red	1.00	.20
57	A2	2p dark brown	1.25	.20
58	A2	2.50p peacock bl	2.00	.80
59	A2	3p orange brn	2.75	1.10
60	A2	5p violet	3.00	1.40
61	A3	10p violet brn	7.50	2.10
62	A2	25p ultramarine	20.00	12.00
		Nos. 50-62 (13)	44.70	20.80

For surcharges and overprints see Nos. 63-107, B1-B12, C9-C38, CB1-CB4.

Stamps of 1925 with Bars and Surcharged

1926

63	A2	3.50p on 75c brn org	1.50	1.50
64	A2	4p on 25c ol blk	2.50	2.50
65	A2	6p on 2.50p pck bl	2.00	2.00
66	A2	12p on 1.25p dp grn	1.40	1.40
67	A2	20p on 1.25p dp grn	6.75	6.75

Stamps of 1925 with Bars and Surcharged

68	A2	4.50p on 75c brn org	2.75	2.75
69	A2	7.50p on 2.50p pck bl	2.75	2.75
70	A2	15p on 25p ultra	2.75	2.75
		Nos. 63-70 (8)	22.40	22.40

No. 51 with Bars and Surcharged

1927

71	A2	4p on 25c ol blk	2.50	2.50

Issues of Republic under French Mandate

Stamps of 1925 Issue Overprinted in Black or Red

1927

72	A1	10c dark vio (R)	.55	.20
a.		Black overprint	35.00	

73 A2 50c yellow grn .55 .20
74 A2 1p magenta .55 .20
75 A2 1.50p rose red .80 .60
76 A2 2p dark brown 1.10 .90
77 A2 3p orange brn .90 .20
78 A2 5p violet 1.75 1.00
79 A3 10p violet brn 2.25 1.10
80 A2 25p ultramarine 19.00 8.00
Nos. 72-80 (9) 27.45 12.40

On Nos. 72 and 79 the overprint is set in two lines. On all stamps the double bar obliterates GRAND LIBAN.

Same Overprint on Provisional Issues of 1926-27

15 PIASTERS ON 25 PIASTERS
TYPE I — "République Libanaise" at foot of stamp.
TYPE II — "République Libanaise" near top of stamp.

81 A2 4p on 25c ol blk .75 .20
82 A2 4.50p on 75c brn org .85 .20
83 A2 7.50p on 2.50p pck bl 1.10 .20
84 A2 15p on 25p ultra (I) 7.50 5.25
a. Type II 11.50 8.00
Nos. 81-84 (4) 10.20 5.85

Most of Nos. 72-84 are known with overprint double, inverted or on back as well as face.

Stamps of 1927 Overprinted in Black or Red

1928
86 A1 10c dark vio (R) .80 .60
a. French overprint omitted, on #50
87 A2 50c yel grn (Bk) 2.00 1.50
a. Arabic overprint inverted 35.00 25.00
88 A2 1p magenta (Bk) 1.00 .70
a. Inverted overprint 35.00 25.00
89 A2 1.50p rose red (Bk) 2.00 1.50
90 A2 2p dark brown (R) 2.75 2.10
90A A2 2p dk brn (Bk+R) 110.00 110.00
91 A2 3p org brown (Bk) 1.90 1.40
92 A2 5p violet (Bk+R) 3.50 2.75
93 A2 5p violet (R) 3.00 2.40
a. French ovpt. below Arabic 30.00 14.00
94 A3 10p vio brn (Bk) 5.00 4.25
a. Double overprint 100.00 90.00
b. Double overprint inverted
c. Inverted overprint 100.00 70.00
95 A2 25p ultra (Bk+R) 11.50 10.50
95A A2 25p ultra (R) 13.00 13.00
Nos. 86-95A (12) 156.45 150.70

On all stamps the double bar with Arabic overprint obliterates Arabic inscription.

Same Overprint on Nos. 81-84

96 A2 4p on 25c (Bk+R) 2.00 1.50
97 A2 4.50p on 75c (Bk) 2.00 1.50
98 A2 7.50p on 2.50p (Bk+R) 4.50 3.50
99 A2 7.50p on 2.50p (R) 7.00 6.00
100 A2 15p on 25p (II) (Bk+R) 11.00 9.50
a. Arabic overprint inverted
101 A2 15p on 25p (I) (R) 14.00 12.00
Nos. 96-101 (6) 40.50 34.00

The new values are surcharged in black. The initials in ( ) refer to the colors of the overprints.

Stamps of 1925 Surcharged in Red or Black

1928-29 *Perf. 13½*
102 A2 50c on 75c brn org (Bk) ('29) 1.50 1.90
103 A2 2p on 1.25p dp grn 1.50 1.90
104 A2 4p on 25c ol blk 1.50 1.90
a. Double surcharge 35.00 25.00
105 A2 7.50p on 2.50p pck bl 2.50 2.75
a. Double surcharge 40.00 25.00
b. Inverted surcharge 55.00 25.00
106 A2 15p on 25p ultra 22.50 10.00
Nos. 102-106 (5) 29.50 18.45

On Nos. 103, 104 and 105 the surcharged numerals are 3¼mm high, and have thick strokes.

No. 86 Surcharged in Red

1928
107 A1 5c on 10c dk vio 1.75 .30

Silkworm, Cocoon and Moth — A4

1930, Feb. 11 **Typo.** *Perf. 11*
108 A4 4p black brown 15.00 15.00
109 A4 4½p vermilion 15.00 15.00
110 A4 7½p dark blue 15.00 15.00
111 A4 10p dk violet 15.00 15.00
112 A4 15p dark green 15.00 15.00
113 A4 25p claret 15.00 15.00
Nos. 108-113 (6) 90.00 90.00

Sericultural Congress, Beirut. Presentation imperfs exist.

Pigeon Rocks, Ras Beirut — A5

View of Bickfaya A8

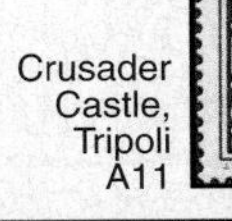

Beit-ed-Din Palace A10

Crusader Castle, Tripoli A11

Ruins of Venus Temple, Baalbek A12

Ancient Bridge, Dog River A13

Belfort Castle A14

Afka Falls — A19

20c, Cedars of Lebanon. 25c, Ruins of Bacchus Temple, Baalbek. 1p, Crusader Castle, Sidon Harbor. 5p, Arcade of Beit-ed-Din Palace. 6p, Tyre Harbor. 7.50p, Ruins of Sun Temple, Baalbek. 10p, View of Hasbeya. 25p, Government House, Beirut. 50p, View of Deir-el-Kamar. 75c, 100p, Ruins at Baalbek.

1930-35 **Litho.** *Perf. 12½, 13½*
114 A5 10c brown orange .60 .20
115 A5 20c yellow brn .60 .20
116 A5 25c deep blue .75 .45

Photo.
117 A8 50c orange brn 3.00 1.50
118 A11 75c ol brn ('32) 1.50 1.00
119 A8 1p deep green 1.75 1.25
120 A8 1p brn vio ('35) 3.00 1.00
121 A10 1.50p violet brn 3.25 1.90
122 A10 1.50p dp grn ('32) 3.50 1.50
123 A11 2p Prussian bl 4.50 1.60
124 A12 3p black brown 4.50 1.60
125 A13 4p orange brn 4.75 1.60
126 A14 4.50p carmine 5.00 1.60
127 A14 5p greenish blk 3.00 1.50
128 A13 6p brn violet 5.25 2.75
129 A10 7.50p deep blue 5.00 1.60
130 A10 10p dk ol grn 9.00 1.60
131 A19 15p blk violet 11.50 3.50
132 A19 25p blue green 20.00 6.00
133 A8 50p apple grn 60.00 15.00
134 A11 100p black 65.00 19.00
Nos. 114-134 (21) 215.45 66.35

See Nos. 135, 144, 152-155. For surcharges see Nos. 147-149, 161, 173-174.

Pigeon Rocks Type of 1930-35 Redrawn

1934 **Litho.** *Perf. 12½x12*
135 A5 10c dull orange 6.75 4.00

Lines in rocks and water more distinct. Printer's name "Hélio Vaugirard, Paris," in larger letters.

Cedar of Lebanon A23

President Emile Eddé A24

Dog River Panorama A25

1937-40 **Typo.** *Perf. 14x13½*
137 A23 10c rose car .50 .20
137A A23 20c aqua ('40) .50 .20
137B A23 25c pale rose lilac ('40) .50 .20
138 A23 50c magenta .50 .20
138A A23 75c brown ('40) .50 .20

Engr.
Perf. 13
139 A24 3p dk violet 4.00 .75
140 A24 4p black brown .75 .20
141 A24 4.50p carmine 1.00 .20
142 A25 10p brn carmine 2.25 .20
142A A25 12½p dp ultra ('40) 1.00 .20
143 A25 15p dk grn ('38) 4.00 .75
143A A25 20p chestnut ('40) 1.00 .20
143B A25 25p crimson ('40) 1.50 .60
143C A25 50p dk vio ('40) 5.00 1.60
143D A25 100p sepia ('40) 3.50 2.25
Nos. 137-143D (15) 26.50 7.95

Nos. 137A, 137B, 138A, 142A, 143A, 143B, 143C, and 143D exist imperforate.
For surcharges see Nos. 145-146A, 150-151, 160, 162, 175-176.

View of Bickfaya A26

Type A8 Redrawn

1935 (?) **Photo.** *Perf. 13½*
144 A26 50c orange brown 17.50 9.75

Arabic inscriptions more condensed.

Stamps of 1930-37 Surcharged in Black or Red

1937-42 *Perf. 13, 13½*
145 A24 2p on 3p dk vio 1.50 1.50
146 A24 2½p on 4p blk brn 1.50 1.50
146A A24 2½p on 4p black brown (R) ('42) 1.50 1.50
147 A10 6p on 7.50p dp bl (R) 4.00 4.00

Stamps of 1930-35 and Type of 1937-40 Surcharged in Black or Red

Perf. 13½, 13
148 A8 7.50p on 50p ap grn 2.50 2.50
149 A11 7.50p on 100p blk (R) 2.50 2.50
150 A25 12.50p on 7.50p dk bl (R) 5.00 5.00

Type of 1937-40 Surcharged in Red with Bars and

1939 **Engr.** *Perf. 13*
151 A25 12½p on 7.50p dk bl 2.00 2.00
Nos. 145-151 (8) 20.50 20.50

Type of 1930-35 Redrawn
Imprint: "Beiteddine-Imp.-Catholique-Beyrouth-Liban."

1939 **Litho.** *Perf. 11½*
152 A10 1p dk slate grn 2.25 .20
153 A10 1.50p brn violet 2.25 .75
154 A10 7.50p carmine lake 2.25 1.10
Nos. 152-154 (3) 6.75 2.05

Bridge Type of 1930-35
Imprint: "Degorce" instead of "Hélio Vaugirard"

1940 **Engr.** *Perf. 13*
155 A13 5p grnsh blue 1.50 .20

Exists imperforate.

Independent Republic

Amir Beshir Shehab — A27

1942, Sept. 18 **Litho.** *Perf. 11½*
156 A27 50c emerald 3.75 3.75
157 A27 1.50p sepia 3.75 3.75
158 A27 6p rose pink 3.75 3.75
159 A27 15p dull blue 3.75 3.75
Nos. 156-159 (4) 15.00 15.00

1st anniv. of the Proclamation of Independence, Nov. 26, 1941.
Nos. 156-159 exist imperforate.

Nos. 140, 154 and 142A Surcharged in Blue, Green or Black

1943 *Perf. 13, 11½*

No.	Type	Description	Unused	Used
160	A24	2p on 4p (Bl)	6.75	7.25
161	A10	6p on 7.50p (G)	3.00	1.00
162	A25	10p on 12½p (Bk)	3.00	1.00
		Nos. 160-162 (3)	12.75	9.25

The surcharge is arranged differently on each value.

Parliament Building A28

Government House, Beirut — A29

1943 **Litho.** *Perf. 11½*

No.	Type	Description	Unused	Used
163	A28	25p salmon rose	15.00	6.00
164	A29	50p bluish green	15.00	6.00
165	A28	150p light ultra	15.00	6.00
166	A29	200p dull vio brn	15.00	6.00
		Nos. 163-166 (4)	60.00	24.00
		Nos. 163-166,C82-C87 (10)	134.25	83.50

2nd anniv. of Proclamation of Independence. Nos. 163-166 exist imperforate. For overprints see Nos. 169-172.

Quarantine Station, Beirut A30

1943, July 8 **Photo.**

Black Overprint

No.	Type	Description	Unused	Used
167	A30	10p cerise	7.00	4.00
168	A30	20p light blue	7.00	4.00
		Nos. 167-168,C88-C90 (5)	28.00	16.25

Arab Medical Congress, Beirut.

Nos. 163 to 166 Overprinted in Blue, Violet, Red or Black

1944

No.	Type	Description	Unused	Used
169	A28	25p sal rose (Bl)	16.00	13.50
170	A29	50p bluish green (V)	16.00	13.50
171	A28	150p lt ultra (R)	16.00	13.50
172	A29	200p dull vio brn (Bk)	22.50	19.00
		Nos. 169-172,C91-C96 (10)	226.25	207.75

Return to office of the president and his ministers, Nov. 22, 1943.

Type of 1930 and No. 142A Surcharged in Violet, Black or Carmine

1945 **Unwmk.** **Engr.** *Perf. 13*

No.	Type	Description	Unused	Used
173	A13	2p on 5p dk bl grn (V)	1.50	.20
174	A13	3p on 5p dk bl grn (Bk)	1.50	.20
175	A25	6p on 12½p deep ultra (Bk)	2.00	.35
176	A25	7½p on 12½p deep ultra (C)	3.00	.95
		Nos. 173-176 (4)	8.00	1.70

Trees at bottom on Nos. 175 and 176.

Catalogue values for unused stamps in this section, from this point to the end of the section, are for Never Hinged items.

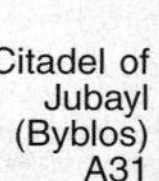

Citadel of Jubayl (Byblos) A31

Crusader Castle, Tripoli A32

1945 **Litho.** *Perf. 11½*

No.	Type	Description	Unused	Used
177	A31	15p violet brown	5.50	4.00
178	A31	20p deep green	5.50	4.00
179	A32	25p deep blue	5.50	4.00
180	A32	50p dp carmine	9.50	4.50
		Nos. 177-180,C97-C100 (8)	77.00	37.10

See Nos. 229-233.

Soldiers and Flag of Lebanon A33

1946 **Litho.**

Stripes of Flag in Red Orange

No.	Type	Description	Unused	Used
181	A33	7.50p red & pale lil	1.75	.20
182	A33	10p lil & pale lilac	3.00	.20
183	A33	12.50p choc & yel grn	4.00	.20
184	A33	15p sepia & pink	5.00	.25
185	A33	20p ultra & pink	4.25	.30
186	A33	25p dk grn & yel green	7.00	.35
187	A33	50p dk bl & pale bl	15.00	1.50
188	A33	100p gray blk & pale bl	20.00	3.00
		Nos. 181-188 (8)	60.00	6.00

Type of 1946 Overprinted in Red

1946, May 8

Stripes of Flag in Red

No.	Type	Description	Unused	Used
189	A33	7.50p choc & pink	1.50	.20
190	A33	10p dk vio & pink	1.75	.20
191	A33	12.50p brn red & pale lilac	2.00	.45
192	A33	15p lt grn & yel green	3.25	.65
193	A33	20p sl grn & yel green	3.00	.70
194	A33	25p sl bl & pale bl	5.00	.95
195	A33	50p ultra & gray	7.50	.90
196	A33	100p blk & pale bl	11.00	2.25
		Nos. 189-196 (8)	35.00	6.30

See Nos. C101-C106, note after No. C106.

Cedar of Lebanon — A34

Night Herons over Mt. Sanin A35

1946-47 **Unwmk.** *Perf. 10½*

No.	Type	Description	Unused	Used
197	A34	50c red brn ('47)	1.50	.20
198	A34	1p purple ('47)	1.50	.20
199	A34	2.50p violet	2.75	.20
200	A34	5p red	4.00	.20
201	A34	6p gray ('47)	4.00	.20

Perf. 11½

No.	Type	Description	Unused	Used
202	A35	12.50p deep car	30.00	.20
		Nos. 197-202,C107-C110 (10)	121.25	10.50

For surcharge see No. 246.

A36

Crusader Castle, Tripoli A37

1947 **Litho.** *Perf. 14x13½*

No.	Type	Description	Unused	Used
203	A36	50c dark brown	2.00	.20
204	A36	2.50p bright green	3.25	.20
205	A36	5p car rose	4.00	.20

Perf. 11½

No.	Type	Description	Unused	Used
206	A37	12.50p rose pink	10.50	.50
207	A37	25p ultramarine	12.50	.55
208	A37	50p turq green	32.50	1.10
209	A37	100p violet	45.00	5.75
		Nos. 203-209 (7)	109.75	8.50

A38 Zubaida Aqueduct — A39

1948 *Perf. 14x13½*

No.	Type	Description	Unused	Used
210	A38	50c blue	.75	.20
211	A38	1p yel brown	.90	.20
212	A38	2.50p rose violet	1.10	.20
213	A38	3p emerald	2.75	.20
214	A38	5p crimson	3.25	.20

Perf. 11½

No.	Type	Description	Unused	Used
215	A39	7.50p rose red	7.00	.20
216	A39	10p dl violet	5.00	.20
217	A39	12.50p blue	10.50	.40
218	A39	25p blue vio	18.00	.90
219	A39	50p green	32.50	4.75
		Nos. 210-219 (10)	81.75	7.45

See Nos. 227A-228A, 234-237. For surcharge see No. 245.

Europa A40

Avicenna — A41

1948 **Litho.**

No.	Type	Description	Unused	Used
220	A40	10p dk red & org red	6.00	1.40
221	A40	12.50p pur & rose	7.00	1.90
222	A40	25p ol grn & pale green	8.00	1.50
223	A41	30p org brn & buff	9.00	1.50
224	A41	40p Prus grn & buff	13.00	1.50
		Nos. 220-224 (5)	43.00	7.80

UNESCO. Nos. 220 to 224 exist imperforate (see note after No. C145).

Camel Post Rider A42

1949, Aug. 16 **Unwmk.** *Perf. 11½*

No.	Type	Description	Unused	Used
225	A42	5p violet	2.00	.40
226	A42	7.50p red	3.00	.60
227	A42	12.50p blue	4.00	1.00
		Nos. 225-227,C148-C149 (5)	29.00	10.50

UPU, 75th anniv. See note after No. C149.

Cedar Type of 1948 Redrawn and Jubayl Type of 1945

1949 **Litho.** *Perf. 14x13½*

No.	Type	Description	Unused	Used
227A	A38	50c blue	2.75	.20
228	A38	1p red orange	2.75	.20
228A	A38	2.50p rose lilac	13.00	.35

Perf. 11½

No.	Type	Description	Unused	Used
229	A31	7.50p rose red	4.00	.20
230	A31	10p violet brn	7.00	.20
231	A31	12.50p deep blue	14.00	.20
232	A31	25p violet	25.00	.40
233	A31	50p green	47.50	1.90
		Nos. 227A-233 (8)	116.00	3.65

On No. 227A in left numeral tablet, top of "P" stands higher than flag of the 1¼mm high "5." On No. 210, tops of "P" and the 2mm "5" are on same line.

On No. 228, "1 P." is smaller than on No. 211, and has no line below "P."

On No. 228A, the "O" does not touch tablet frame; on No. 212, it does. No. 228A exists on gray paper.

Cedar Type of 1948 Redrawn and

Ancient Bridge across Dog River — A43

1950 **Litho.** *Perf. 14x13½*

No.	Type	Description	Unused	Used
234	A38	50c rose red	1.00	.20
235	A38	1p salmon	1.50	.20
236	A38	2.50p violet	2.00	.20
237	A38	5p claret	3.50	.20

Cedar slightly altered and mountains eliminated.

Perf. 11½

No.	Type	Description	Unused	Used
238	A43	7.50p rose red	5.00	.20
239	A43	10p rose vio	5.50	.20
240	A43	12.50p light blue	8.00	.20
241	A43	25p deep blue	1.75	1.00
242	A43	50p emerald	32.50	4.00
		Nos. 234-242 (9)	60.75	6.40

See Nos. 251-255, 310-312.

Flags and Building A44

Cedar — A45

1950, Aug. 8 *Perf. 11½*

No.	Type	Description	Unused	Used
243	A44	7.50p gray	2.50	.20
244	A44	12.50p lilac rose	2.50	.20
		Nos. 243-244,C150-C153 (6)	20.50	4.10

Conf. of Emigrants, 1950. See note after #C153.

Nos. 213 and 201 Surcharged with New Value and Bars in Carmine

1950 Unwmk. ***Perf. 14x13½, 10½***

No.	Type	Description	Unused	Used
245	A38	1p on 3p emerald	1.25	.20
246	A34	2.50p on 6p gray	2.00	.20

1951 Litho. ***Perf. 14x13½***

No.	Type	Description	Unused	Used
247	A45	50c rose red	1.50	.20
248	A45	1p light brown	2.25	.20
249	A45	2.50p slate gray	5.00	.20
250	A45	5p rose lake	5.00	.20

Bridge Type of 1950, Redrawn

Typo. ***Perf. 11½***

No.	Type	Description	Unused	Used
251	A43	7.50p red	6.00	.20
252	A43	10p dl rose vio	8.50	.20
253	A43	12.50p blue	14.00	.20
254	A43	25p dull blue	17.50	.50
255	A43	50p green	37.50	3.50
		Nos. 247-255 (9)	97.25	5.40

Nos. 238-242 are lithographed from a fine-screen halftone; "P" in the denomination has serifs. Nos. 251-255 are typographed and much coarser; "P" without serifs.

Cedar — A46

Ruins at Baalbek A47

Design: 50p, 100p, Beaufort Castle.

1952 Litho. ***Perf. 14x13½***

No.	Type	Description	Unused	Used
256	A46	50c emerald	1.25	.20
257	A46	1p orange brn	1.25	.20
258	A46	2.50p grnsh blue	2.50	.20
259	A46	5p car rose	3.25	.20
		Perf. 11½		
260	A47	7.50p red	4.50	.20
261	A47	10p brt violet	6.50	.70
262	A47	12.50p blue	7.25	.70
263	A47	25p violet bl	8.00	1.25
264	A47	50p dk blue grn	22.50	2.50
265	A47	100p chocolate	45.00	7.00
		Nos. 256-265 (10)	102.00	13.15

Cedar of Lebanon A48

Postal Administration Building A49

1953 ***Perf. 14x13½***

No.	Type	Description	Unused	Used
266	A48	50c blue	2.00	.20
267	A48	1p rose lake	2.00	.20
268	A48	2.50p lilac	2.25	.20
269	A48	5p emerald	3.25	.20
		Perf. 11½		
270	A49	7.50p car rose	4.50	.20
271	A49	10p dp yel grn	5.00	.65
272	A49	12.50p aquamarine	6.00	.75
273	A49	25p ultra	9.00	1.25
274	A49	50p violet brn	14.00	2.75
		Nos. 266-274 (9)	48.00	6.40

See No. 306.

A50

Gallery, Beit-ed-Din Palace — A51

1954 ***Perf. 14x13½***

No.	Type	Description	Unused	Used
275	A50	50c blue	1.50	.20
276	A50	1p dp orange	1.75	.20
277	A50	2.50p purple	2.00	.20
278	A50	5p blue green	3.50	.20
		Perf. 11½		
279	A51	7.50p dp carmine	5.00	.20
280	A51	10p dl ol grn	6.00	.20
281	A51	12.50p blue	8.00	.80
282	A51	25p vio blue	11.00	2.50
283	A51	50p aqua	19.00	4.50
284	A51	100p black brn	37.50	8.00
		Nos. 275-284 (10)	95.25	17.00

Arab Postal Union Issue

Globe — A52

1955, Jan. 1 Litho. ***Perf. 13½x13***

No.	Type	Description	Unused	Used
285	A52	12.50p blue green	1.25	.20
286	A52	25p violet	1.50	.25
		Nos. 285-286,C197 (3)	4.25	.65

Founding of the APU, July 1, 1954.

Cedar A53

Jeita Cave A54

1955 ***Perf. 14x13½***

No.	Type	Description	Unused	Used
287	A53	50c violet blue	1.75	.20
288	A53	1p vermilion	1.75	.20
289	A53	2.50p purple	1.75	.20
290	A53	5p emerald	2.00	.20
		Perf. 11½		
291	A54	7.50p deep orange	2.50	.20
292	A54	10p yellow grn	2.75	.20
293	A54	12.50p blue	3.00	.20
294	A54	25p dp vio blue	4.25	.20
295	A54	50p dk gray grn	5.75	.30
		Nos. 287-295 (9)	25.50	1.90

See Nos. 308-309, 315-318, 341-343A. For overprint see No. 351.

Cedar of Lebanon A55

Globe and Columns A56

1955 Unwmk. ***Perf. 13x13½***

No.	Type	Description	Unused	Used
296	A55	50c dark blue	1.50	.20
297	A55	1p deep orange	1.50	.20
298	A55	2.50p deep violet	1.75	.20
299	A55	5p green	2.00	.20
300	A56	7.50p yel org & cop red	2.25	.20
301	A56	10p emer & sal	2.00	.20
302	A56	12.50p ultra & bl grn	2.50	.20
303	A56	25p dp ultra & brt pink	4.00	.20
304	A56	50p dk grn & lt bl	4.50	.20
305	A56	100p dk brn & sal	7.00	.40
		Nos. 296-305 (10)	29.00	2.20

For surcharge see No. 333.

Cedar Type of 1953 Redrawn

1956 Litho. ***Perf. 13x13½***

No.	Type	Description	Unused	Used
306	A48	2.50p violet	9.00	1.50

No. 306 measures 17x20½mm. The "2p.50" is in Roman (upright) type face.

Cedar Type of 1955 Redrawn and Bridge Type of 1950, Second Redrawing

1957 Litho. ***Perf. 13x13½***

No.	Type	Description	Unused	Used
308	A53	50c light ultra	1.25	.20
309	A53	2.50p claret	1.75	.20
		Perf. 11½		
310	A43	7.50p vermilion	2.00	.35
311	A43	10p brn orange	2.75	.40
312	A43	12.50p blue	3.75	.50
		Nos. 308-312 (5)	11.50	1.65

On Nos. 308 and 309 numerals are slanted and clouds slightly changed.

Nos. 310-312 inscribed "Liban" instead of "Republique Libanaise," and different Arabic characters.

Runners — A57

1957, Sept. 12 Litho. ***Perf. 13***

No.	Type	Description	Unused	Used
313	A57	2.50p shown	1.50	.20
314	A57	12.50p Soccer players	2.00	.35
		Nos. 313-314,C243-C244 (4)	10.75	4.30

Second Pan-Arab Games, Beirut.

A souvenir sheet of 4 contains Nos. 313-314, C243-C244.

Cedar Type of 1955 Redrawn and

Workers — A58

Ancient Potter — A59

1957 Unwmk. ***Perf. 13x13½***

No.	Type	Description	Unused	Used
315	A53	50c light blue	1.50	.20
316	A53	1p light brown	1.50	.20
317	A53	2.50p bright vio	1.75	.20
318	A53	5p light green	2.25	.20
		Perf. 11½, 13½x13 (A59)		
319	A58	7.50p crim rose	2.25	.20
320	A58	10p dull red brn	2.25	.20
321	A58	12.50p bright blue	2.50	.20
322	A59	25p dull blue	2.50	.20
323	A59	50p yellow grn	4.00	.20
324	A59	100p sepia	5.00	.60
		Nos. 315-324 (10)	25.50	2.40

The word "piaster" is omitted on No. 315; on Nos. 316 and 318 there is a line below "P"; on No. 317 there is a period between "2" and "50."

Nos. 315-318 are 16mm wide and have three shading lines above tip of cedar. See No. 343A and footnote.

For surcharges see Nos. 334-335, 339.

Cedar of Lebanon A60

Soldier and Flag A61

1958 Litho. ***Perf. 13***

No.	Type	Description	Unused	Used
325	A60	50c blue	1.50	.20
326	A60	1p dull orange	1.50	.20
327	A60	2.50p violet	1.50	.20
328	A60	5p yellow grn	1.75	.20
329	A61	12.50p bright blue	2.00	.20
330	A61	25p dark blue	2.25	.20
331	A61	50p orange brn	2.50	.20
332	A61	100p black brn	3.75	.25
		Nos. 325-332 (8)	16.75	1.65

For surcharges see Nos. 336-338.

No. 304 Surcharged

1959, Sept. 1

No.	Type	Description	Unused	Used
333	A56	30p on 50p dk grn & lt bl	2.25	.25

Arab Lawyers Congress. See No. C265.

No. 323 Surcharged

1959 ***Perf. 13½x13***

No.	Type	Description	Unused	Used
334	A59	30p on 50p yel grn	2.00	.20
335	A59	40p on 50p yel grn	2.25	.35

Convention of the Assoc. of Arab Emigrants in the United States.

Nos. 329-330 and 323 Surcharged with New Value and Bars

1959 ***Perf. 13, 13½x13***

No.	Type	Description	Unused	Used
336	A61	7.50p on 12.50p brt bl	1.00	.20
337	A61	10p on 12.50p brt bl	1.10	.20
338	A61	15p on 25p dark blue	1.25	.20
339	A59	40p on 50p yel grn	2.00	.20
		Nos. 336-339,C271 (5)	8.35	1.10

Arab League Center, Cairo A62

Perf. 13x13½

1960, May 23 Unwmk. Litho.

No.	Type	Description	Unused	Used
340	A62	15p lt blue green	1.75	.20

Opening of the Arab League Center and the Arab Postal Museum in Cairo.

For overprint see No. 352.

Cedar Type of 1955, Second Redrawing

1960 Litho. ***Perf. 13x13½***

No.	Type	Description	Unused	Used
341	A53	50c light violet	1.25	.20
342	A53	1p rose claret	1.25	.20
343	A53	2.50p ultramarine	1.50	.20
343A	A53	5p light green	1.75	.20
		Nos. 341-343A (4)	5.75	.80

Nos. 341-343A are 16½-17mm wide and have two shading lines above cedar. In other details they resemble the redrawn A53 type of 1957 (Nos. 315-318).

President Fuad Chehab
A63 A64

1960 Photo. *Perf. 13½*
344 A63 50c deep green 1.25 .20
345 A63 2.50p olive 1.25 .20
346 A63 5p green 1.25 .20
347 A63 7.50p rose brown 1.50 .20
348 A63 15p bright blue 1.75 .20
349 A63 50p lilac 2.00 .20
350 A63 100p brown 2.50 .20
Nos. 344-350 (7) 11.50 1.40

Nos. 343A and 340 Overprinted in Red

1960, Nov. Litho. *Perf. 13x13½*
351 A53 5p light green 1.25 .20
352 A62 15p lt blue green 1.75 .20

Arabian Oil Conference, Beirut.

1961, Feb. Litho. *Perf. 13½x13*
353 A64 2.50p blue & light bl 1.25 .20
354 A64 7.50p dark vio & pink 1.25 .20
355 A64 10p red brn & yel 1.25 .20
Nos. 353-355 (3) 3.75 .60

Cedar — A65

Post Office, Beirut
A66

1961 Unwmk. Litho. *Perf. 13*
356 A65 2.50p green 2.50 .20

Redrawn

357 A65 2.50p orange 2.50 .25
358 A65 5p maroon 1.25 .20
359 A65 10p black 1.75 .20

Nos. 357-359 have no clouds.

Perf. 11½

361 A66 2.50p rose carmine 1.25 .20
362 A66 5p bright green 2.00 .20
363 A66 15p dark blue 3.25 .20
Nos. 356-363 (7) 14.00 1.45

Cedars — A67

10p, 15p, 50p, 100p, View of Zahle.

1961 Litho. *Perf. 13*
365 A67 50c yellow green 1.50 .20
366 A67 1p brown 1.50 .20
367 A67 2.50p ultramarine 1.50 .20
368 A67 5p carmine 1.75 .20
369 A67 7.50p violet 2.00 .20
370 A67 10p dark brown 2.25 .20
371 A67 15p dark blue 2.50 .20
372 A67 50p dark green 2.75 .25
373 A67 100p black 3.25 .35
Nos. 365-373 (9) 19.00 2.00

See Nos. 381-384.

Unknown Soldier Monument — A68

1961, Dec. 30 Unwmk. *Perf. 12*
374 A68 10p shown 3.00 .20
375 A68 15p Soldier & flag 3.75 .20

Anniv. of Lebanon's independence; evacuation of foreign troops, Dec. 31, 1946.
See Nos. C329-C330.

Bugler — A69

Scout Carrying Flag and Scout Emblem
A70

Designs: 2.50p, First aid. 6p, Lord Baden-Powell. 10p, Scouts building campfire.

1962, Mar. 1 Litho. *Perf. 12*
376 A69 50c yel grn, blk & yel 1.50 .20
377 A70 1p multicolored 1.50 .20
378 A70 2.50p dk red, blk & grn 1.50 .20
379 A69 6p multicolored 1.50 .20
380 A70 10p dp bl, blk & yel 1.50 .20
Nos. 376-380,C331-C333 (8) 10.75 1.80

50th anniversary of Lebanese Boy Scouts.

Type of 1961 Redrawn

Designs as before.

1962 Unwmk. *Perf. 13*
381 A67 50c yellow green 1.50 .20
382 A67 1p brown 1.50 .20
383 A67 2.50p ultramarine 1.60 .20
384 A67 15p dark blue 4.00 .20
Nos. 381-384,C341-C342 (6) 15.95 1.40

Temple of Nefertari, Abu Simbel — A71

Cherries — A72

1962, Aug. 1 Unwmk. *Perf. 13*
390 A71 5p light ultra 1.25 .20
391 A71 15p brn lake & mar 1.75 .20

Campaign to save the historic monuments in Nubia. See Nos. C351-C352.

1962 Litho.

Designs: 50c, 2.50p, 7.50p, Cherries. 1p, 5p, Figs. 10p, 17.50p, 30p, Grapes. 50p, Oranges. 100p, Pomegranates.

Vignette Multicolored

392 A72 50c violet blue 1.50 .20
393 A72 1p gray blue 1.50 .20
394 A72 2.50p brown 1.50 .20
395 A72 5p bright blue 1.50 .20
396 A72 7.50p lilac rose 1.50 .20
397 A72 10p chocolate 1.75 .20
398 A72 17.50p slate 2.50 .20
399 A72 30p slate grn 2.75 .20
400 A72 50p green 3.00 .20
401 A72 100p brown blk 5.00 .50
Nos. 392-401,C359-C366 (18) 31.65 4.30

Elementary Schoolboy — A73

1962, Oct. 1 Litho. *Perf. 12*
404 A73 30p multicolored 1.50 .20

Students' Day, Oct. 1. See No. C355.

Cedar of Lebanon
A74 A75

1963-64 Unwmk. *Perf. 13x13½*
405 A74 50c green 7.00 .20
406 A75 50c gray grn ('64) 1.50 .20
407 A75 2.50p ultra ('64) 1.50 .20
408 A75 5p brt pink ('64) 1.60 .20
409 A75 7.50p orange ('64) 1.75 .20
410 A75 17.50p rose lil ('64) 2.25 .20
Nos. 405-410 (6) 15.60 1.20

Bicyclist — A76

Hyacinth — A77

1964, Feb. 11 Litho. *Perf. 13*
415 A76 2.50p shown 1.50 .20
416 A76 5p Basketball 1.50 .20
417 A76 10p Track 1.50 .20
Nos. 415-417,C385-C387 (6) 6.70 1.20

4th Mediterranean Games, Naples, Sept. 21-29, 1963.

1964 Unwmk. *Perf. 13x13½*
Size: 26x27mm
418 A77 50c shown 1.50 .20
419 A77 1p Hyacinth 1.50 .20
420 A77 2.50p Hyacinth 1.50 .20
421 A77 5p Cyclamen 1.50 .20
422 A77 7.50p Cyclamen 1.50 .20

Perf. 13
Size: 26x37mm
423 A77 10p Poinsettia 1.50 .20
424 A77 17.50p Anemone 2.50 .20
425 A77 30p Iris 3.50 .20
426 A77 50p Poppy 7.00 .45
Nos. 418-426,C391-C397 (16) 29.20 3.55

See Nos. C391-C397.

Temple of the Sun, Baalbek
A78

1965, Jan. 11 Litho. *Perf. 13x13½*
429 A78 2.50p blk & red org 2.00 .20
430 A78 7.50p black & blue 2.75 .20
Nos. 429-430,C420-C423 (6) 9.10 1.65

International Festival at Baalbek.

Swimmer
A79

1965, Jan. 23 Engr. *Perf. 13*
431 A79 2.50p shown 2.50 .20
432 A79 7.50p Fencer 2.75 .20
433 A79 10p Basketball, vert. 4.00 .20
Nos. 431-433,C424-C426 (6) 11.10 1.20

18th Olympic Games, Tokyo, Oct. 10-25, 1964.

Golden Oriole
A80

1965 Engr. *Perf. 13*
434 A80 5p Bullfinch 8.00 .20
435 A80 10p European goldfinch 13.00 .20
436 A80 15p Hoopoe 10.00 .20
437 A80 17.50p Rock partridge 12.00 .20
438 A80 20p shown 15.00 .20
439 A80 32.50p European bee-eater 20.00 .20
Nos. 434-439 (6) 78.00 1.20

For surcharge see No. 459.

Cow and Calf — A81

1965 Photo. *Perf. 11x12*
440 A81 50c shown 2.00 .20
441 A81 1p Rabbit 2.25 .20
442 A81 2.50p Ewe & lamb 2.50 .20
Nos. 440-442 (3) 6.75 .60

Hippodrome, Beirut — A82

1p, Pigeon Rocks. 2.50p, Tabarja. 5p, Ruins, Beit-Méry. 7.50p, Statue and ruins, Anjar.

1966 Unwmk. *Perf. 12x11½*
443 A82 50c gold & multi 1.75 .20
444 A82 1p gold & multi 2.00 .20
445 A82 2.50p gold & multi 2.25 .20
446 A82 5p gold & multi 2.50 .20
447 A82 7.50p gold & multi 2.75 .20
Nos. 443-447 (5) 11.25 1.00

See #C486-C492. For surcharge see #460.

ITY Emblem and Cedars A83

1967 Photo. *Perf. 11x12*
448 A83 50c lem, blk & brt bl 4.00 .20
449 A83 1p sal, blk & brt bl 4.00 .20
450 A83 2.50p gray, blk & brt bl 4.00 .20
451 A83 5p lt rose lil, blk & brt bl 4.00 .20
452 A83 7.50p yel, blk & brt bl 4.00 .20
Nos. 448-452 (5) 20.00 1.00

Intl. Tourist Year; used as a regular issue. See #C515-C522. For surcharge see #461.

Goat and Kid A84

1968, Feb. Photo. *Perf. 12x11½*
453 A84 50c shown 3.00 .20
454 A84 1p Cattle 4.00 .20
455 A84 2.50p Sheep 5.00 .20
456 A84 5p Camels 6.00 .20
457 A84 10p Donkey 7.00 .20
458 A84 15p Horses 9.00 .20
Nos. 453-458 (6) 34.00 1.20

See Nos. C534-C539.

No. 439 Surcharged

1972, Apr. Engr. *Perf. 13*
459 A80 25p on 32.50p multi 22.50 .20

Nos. 447 and 452 Surcharged with New Value and Bars
Perf. 12x11½, 11x12
1972, May Photo.
460 A82 5p on 7.50p multi *4.50* .20
461 A83 5p on 7.50p multi *4.50* .20

Cedar — A85

Army Badge — A86

1974 Litho. *Perf. 11*
462 A85 50c orange & olive *.25* .25

1980, Dec. 28 Litho. *Perf. 11½*
463 A86 25p multicolored 2.50 .20

Army Day. See Nos. C792-C793.

Pres. Elias Sarkis — A87

World Communications Year — A89

World Food Day, Oct. 16, 1981 A88

1981, Sept. 23 Photo. *Perf. 14x13½*
464 A87 125p multicolored 2.75 .80
465 A87 300p multicolored 2.75 1.60
466 A87 500p multicolored 7.50 2.40
Nos. 464-466 (3) 13.00 4.80

1982, Nov. 23 Photo. *Perf. 12x11½*
467 A88 50p Stork carrying food packages 1.75 .30
468 A88 75p Wheat, globe 2.00 .50
469 A88 100p Produce 2.25 .65
Nos. 467-469 (3) 6.00 1.45

1983, Dec. 19 Photo. *Perf. 14*
470 A89 300p multicolored 6.00 1.75

Illustrations from Khalil Gibran's The Prophet A90

1983, Dec. 19 *Perf. 13½x14*
471 A90 200p The Soul Is Back 2.75 1.00
472 A90 300p The Family 4.25 1.75
473 A90 500p Self-portrait 7.50 2.40
474 A90 1000p The Prophet 15.00 4.75
a. Souvenir sheet, #471-474 37.50 37.50
Nos. 471-474 (4) 29.50 9.90

No. 474a sold for £25.

Scouting Year — A91

Cedar of Lebanon — A93

1983, Dec. 19 *Perf. 14*
475 A91 200p Rowing 3.50 .65
476 A91 300p Signaling 4.00 .80
477 A91 500p Camp 7.25 1.25
Nos. 475-477 (3) 14.75 2.70

1984, Dec. Photo. *Perf. 14½x13½*
481 A93 5p multicolored 2.00 .25

Flowers — A94

Defense — A95

1984, Dec. Photo. *Perf. 14½x13½*
482 A94 10p Iris of Sofar 2.00 .20
483 A94 25p Periwinkle 3.00 .30
484 A94 50p Flowering thorn 4.00 .40
Nos. 482-484 (3) 9.00 .90

For surcharges see Nos. 531-532.

1984, Dec. Photo. *Perf. 14½x13½*
485 A95 75p Dove over city 3.50 .90
486 A95 150p Soldier, cedar 4.75 1.90
487 A95 300p Olive wreath, cedar 6.25 3.50
Nos. 485-487 (3) 14.50 6.30

Temple Ruins A96

1985 Photo. *Perf. 13½x14½*
488 A96 100p Fakra 3.00 .55
489 A96 200p Bziza 3.50 1.10
490 A96 500p Tyre 6.50 2.75
Nos. 488-490 (3) 13.00 4.40

Pres. Gemayel, Map of Lebanon, Dove, Text — A97

Pres. Gemayel, Military Academy Graduate — A98

1988, Feb. 1 Litho. *Perf. 14*
491 A97 £50 multicolored 5.00 2.00

1988, Mar. 9
492 A98 £25 multicolored 5.50 1.50

Arab Scouts, 75th Anniv. A99

1988, Mar. 9 *Perf. 13½x14½*
493 A99 £20 multicolored 5.50 1.25

UN Child Survival Campaign A100

1988, Mar. 9 *Perf. 14½x13½*
494 A100 £15 multicolored 3.50 .75

Prime Minister Rashid Karame (1921-1987), Satellite, Flags, Earth A101

1988, Mar. 9 *Perf. 13½x14½*
495 A101 £10 multicolored 2.50 .60

1st World Festival for Youths of Lebanese Descent in Uruguay A102

1988, Mar. 9
496 A102 £5 multicolored 3.25 .50

Cedar — A103

1989 Photo. *Perf. 13x13½*
497 A103 £50 dk grn & vio 3.00 .35
498 A103 £70 dk grn & brn 3.50 .50
499 A103 £100 dk grn & brt yel 4.00 .50
500 A103 £200 dk grn & bluish grn 6.00 1.25
501 A103 £500 dk grn & brt yel grn 11.00 3.00
Nos. 497-501 (5) 27.50 5.60

Independence, 50th Anniv. — A104

Designs: £200, Al Muntazah Restaurant, Zahle, 1883. £300, Sea Castle, Sidon, vert. £500, Presidential Palace, Baabda. £1000, Army graduation ceremony, vert. £3000, Beirut 2000, architectural plan. £5000, Pres. Elias Harawi, Lebanese flag, vert.

1993 Litho. *Perf. 14*
502 A104 £200 multi 1.75 .20
503 A104 £300 multi 2.25 .55
504 A104 £500 multi 3.50 .85
505 A104 £1000 multi 5.00 1.75
506 A104 £3000 multi 9.25 3.00
507 A104 £5000 multi 17.50 8.25
Nos. 502-507 (6) 39.25 14.60

For overprints, see Nos. 533B, 533C, 533G.

Size: 126x150mm
Imperf
508 A104 £10,000 multi 57.50 57.50

A105

A106

Environmental Protection: £100, Stop polluting atmosphere. £200, Stop fires. £500, Trees, building. £1000, Birds, trees in city. £2000, Mosaic of trees. £5000, Green tree in middle of polluted city.

1994, May 7 Litho. ***Perf. 13½x13***

509 A105 £100 multicolored 1.75 .20
510 A105 £200 multicolored 2.00 .45
511 A105 £500 multicolored 3.25 .95
512 A105 £1000 multicolored 5.25 1.60
513 A105 £2000 multicolored 8.75 2.75
514 A105 £5000 multicolored 20.00 6.50
Nos. 509-514 (6) 41.00 12.45

For overprints see Nos. 533D, 533H, 537.

1995, May 6 Litho. ***Perf. 13½x13***

515 A106 £1500 Martyr's Day 7.00 3.00

For overprint see No. 534.

Anniversaries and Events — A107

Anniversaries and Events of 1995 — A108

£500, UNICEF, 50th anniv., horiz. £1000, Intl. Year of the Family (1994), horiz. £2000, ILO, 75th anniv. (in 1994), horiz. £3000, Bar Association (Berytus Nutrix Legum), 75th anniv.

1996, Feb. 21 Litho. ***Perf. 14***

516 A107 £500 multi, horiz. 4.25 1.10
517 A107 £1000 multi, horiz. 6.75 2.25
518 A107 £2000 multi, horiz. 12.00 4.25
519 A107 £3000 multicolored 17.50 6.75
Nos. 516-519 (4) 40.50 14.35

For overprints, see Nos. 533E, 534A, 535A.

1996, Feb. 21 ***Perf. 13½x13***

£100, Opening of Museum of Arab Postage Stamps. £500, FAO, 50th anniv. £1000, UN, 50th anniv. £2000, Arab League, 50th anniv. £3000, Former Pres. René Moawad (1925-89).

520 A108 £100 multicolored 2.75 .20
521 A108 £500 multicolored 4.25 1.10
522 A108 £1000 multicolored 7.00 2.10
523 A108 £2000 multicolored 11.50 4.00
524 A108 £3000 multicolored 17.50 6.50
Nos. 520-524 (5) 43.00 13.90

For overprints see Nos. 533A, 533F, 533I, 535-536.

Massacre at Cana A109

1997, Oct. 13 Litho. ***Perf. 14***

525 A109 £1100 multicolored 11.00 2.75

For overprint, see No. 533J.

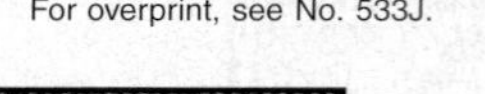

1997 Visit of Pope John Paul II to Lebanon A110

1997 Litho. ***Perf. 13½x13***

526 A110 £10,000 multi 100.00 32.50

For overprint see Nos. 533O, 538.

Fakhr al-Din Palace, Deir-el-Kamar — A111

1999 Litho. ***Perf. 12***

527 A111 £100 Chehab Palace, Hasbaya, vert. 1.50 .20
528 A111 £300 ESCWA Building, Beirut, vert. 2.50 .45
529 A111 £500 shown 3.00 .80
530 A111 £1100 Grand Seraglio, Beirut 6.00 1.75
Nos. 527-530 (4) 13.00 3.20

Nos. 484, 485 and C775 Surcharged in Silver and Black

Methods and Perfs. as before

1999

531 A94 £100 on 50p (#484) 1.75 .20
532 A95 £300 on 75p (#485) 2.50 .45
533 AP154 £1100 on 70p (#C775) 6.00 1.75
Nos. 531-533 (3) 10.25 2.40

Nos. 502, 504-505, 511-512, 516, 518-522, 525 Overprinted in Gold

Similar to Nos. 534-538 but with Symbol Oriented as a Cross

Methods and Perfs As Before

1999 (?)

533A A108 £100 multi 15.00
533B A104 £200 multi 15.00
533C A104 £500 multi 25.00
533D A105 £500 multi 25.00
533E A107 £500 multi 25.00
533F A108 £500 multi 25.00
533G A104 £1000 multi 50.00
533H A105 £1000 multi 47.50
533I A108 £1000 multi 30.00
533J A109 £1100 multi 300.00
533K A106 £1500 multi 40.00
533L A107 £2000 multi 75.00
533M A107 £3000 multi 115.00
533N A105 £5000 multi 225.00
533O A110 £10,000 multi 425.00
Nos. 533A-533O (15) 1,437.

Nos. 514, 515, 523, 524 and 526 Overprinted in Gold or Silver

Methods and Perfs As Before

2000 (?)

534 A106 £1500 multi 6.00 2.50
535 A108 £2000 multi 8.50 3.25
536 A108 £3000 multi (S) 13.00 5.25
537 A105 £5000 multi 19.00 8.50
538 A110 £10,000 multi 37.50 17.00
Nos. 534-538 (5) 84.00 36.50

Cedar of Lebanon — A112

Wmk. 400 (£500, 1000, 1100, 1500), Unwmk.

Perf. 13x13¼, 11x11¼ (£500, 1000, 1100)

2000 ? Litho.

539 A112 £100 dark red .50 .20
540 A112 £300 Prus blue 1.00 .35
541 A112 £500 green 1.50 .65
a. Perf. 13x13¼ 1.50 .65
b. Booklet pane, 10 #541a 15.00
Booklet, #541b 15.00
542 A112 £1000 blue 3.50 1.25
543 A112 £1100 olive brn 3.75 1.40
a. Perf. 13x13¼ 3.75 1.40
b. Booklet pane, 10 #543a 37.50
Booklet, #543b 37.50
544 A112 £1500 vio blue 4.50 1.90
a. Booklet pane, 10 #544 45.00
Booklet, #544a 45.00
b. Perf. 11x11¼ 4.50 1.90
Nos. 539-544 (6) 14.75 5.75

No. 544 and minors have watermark 400.

A113

2001 ? Litho. ***Perf. 11¼x11***

545 A113 £1100 multi 4.00 1.50

Geneva Conventions, 50th Anniv. (in 1999) — A114

Red Cross/Red Crescent A115

2001 Litho. ***Perf. 11x11½***

546 A114 £500 shown 2.00 .70
547 A114 £1100 "50," fist 4.00 1.50
548 A115 £1500 shown 5.00 2.10
Nos. 546-548 (3) 11.00 4.30

SOS Children's Villages A116

2001

549 A116 £300 multi 1.25 .40

Prisoners in Israel A117

2001

550 A117 £500 multi 2.00 .70

Ibrahim Abd el Al (1908-59), Hydrologist A118

2001

551 A118 £1000 multi 3.50 1.40

Abdallah Zakher (1680-1748), Printer — A119

2001

552 A119 £1000 multi 3.50 1.40

Elias Abu Chabke (1904-49), Poet — A120

2001 ***Perf. 11½x11***

553 A120 £1500 multi 5.00 2.10

Saint Joseph University, 125th Anniv. (in 2000) A121

2001 ***Perf. 11x11½***

554 A121 £5000 multi 15.00 7.00

Economic & Social Commission for Western Asia, 25th Anniv. (in 1999) — A122

2001 *Perf. 11½x11*

555 A122 £10,000 multi 32.50 20.00

Arab Woman's Day — A123

2002, Feb. 1 Litho. *Perf. 13¼x13½*

556 A123 £1000 multi 3.25 2.60

Arab League Summit Conference, Beirut — A124

Arab League member flags and: £2000, Emblem. £3000, Cedar tree, Lebanese Pres. Emile Lahoud.

2002, Mar. 27

557-558 A124 Set of 2 11.00 9.25

Souvenir Sheet

Israeli Withdrawal From Southern Lebanon, 2nd Anniv. — A125

No. 559: a, Pres. Emile Lahoud, flag. b, Pres. Lahoud holding book. c, Pres. Lahoud and map. d, Pres. Lahoud receiving sword.

2002, Mar. 27 *Perf. 13¼*

559 A125 £1100 Sheet of 4, #a-d 10.50 9.50

Souvenir Sheet

Martyrs of Justice — A126

2002, June 14 *Perf. 13¼x13½*

560 A126 £3000 multi 7.00 5.75

UPU, 125th Anniv. (in 1999) A127

2002, Oct. 11 Litho. *Perf. 13½x13¼*

561 A127 £2000 multi 7.00 5.75

City Views — A128

Ruins — A129

Paleontonlogy — A130

Designs: £100 Old souk, Zouk Mikael. £300, Old souk, Sidon. £500, Byblos. £1000, Souk, Tripoli. £1100, Bziza. £1500, Arqa. £2000, Niha. £3000, Mousailaha Citadel. £5000, Libanobythus milkii in amber. £10,000, Nematonotus longispinus fossil.

Perf. 13¼x13½, 13½x13¼

2002-03 **Litho.**

562	A128	£100 multi	.50	.20
563	A128	£300 multi	.90	.50
564	A128	£500 multi	1.75	.90
565	A128	£1000 multi	2.50	1.75
566	A129	£1100 multi	3.00	2.00
567	A129	£1500 multi	3.50	2.75
568	A129	£2000 multi	4.50	3.75
569	A129	£3000 multi	7.25	5.75
570	A130	£5000 multi	10.50	9.25
571	A130	£10,000 multi	21.00	18.00
		Nos. 562-571 (10)	55.40	44.85

Issued: £100, £300, 10/11; £1000, £1500, £2000, £3000, £10,000, 11/20; £500, £1100, 12/20; £5000, 1/8/03.

Ninth Francophone Summit, Beirut — A131

Summit emblem and: No. 572, £1500, Mountains. No. 573, £1500, Pres. Emile Lahoud.

2002, Oct. 23 *Perf. 13¼x13½*

572-573 A131 Set of 2 7.00 5.50

Beirut, 1999 Arab Cultural Capital — A132

2002, Nov. 13

574 A132 £2000 multi 5.00 4.00

Independence, 60th Anniv. (in 2001) — A133

Stylized flag and: No. 575, £1250, Crowd viewing horse and rider. No. 576, £1250, Men and flag on staff. No. 577, £1750, Arabic text. No. 578, £1750, Soldier saluting group of men. £6000, Vignettes of Nos. 575-578.

2003, Dec. 5 Litho. *Perf. 12¾x13*

575-578 A133 Set of 4 14.00 14.00

Imperf

Size: 160x110mm

579 A133 £6000 multi 14.00 14.00

Faqra Ski Resort A134

2004 Litho. *Perf. 11x11¼*

580 A134 £500 multi 1.25 1.25

General Post Office, Beirut — A135

Post office in: £100, 1953. £300, 2002.

2004 *Perf. 11¼x11*

581-582 A135 Set of 2 1.00 1.00

Al Bustan Festival A136

2004 Litho. *Perf. 11x11¼*

583 A136 £1000 multi 2.50 2.50

St. George's Hospital, Beirut, 125th Anniv. (in 2003) — A137

2004, Oct. 28 Litho. *Perf. 11x11¼*

584 A137 £3000 multi 4.00 4.00

Ski Resorts A138

2004 Litho. *Perf. 11x11¼, 11¼x11*

586	A138	£100	Aayoun Siman	.20	.20
587	A138	£250	Laklouk, vert.	.35	.35
589	A138	£300	Kanat Bakish	.40	.40
590	A138	£1000	Cedres	1.40	1.40
			Nos. 586-590 (4)	2.35	2.35

Issued: £250, 11/26; Nos. 586, 589, £1000, 12/10. Numbers have been reserved for two additional stamps in this set.

Baalbeck Intl. Festival A139

Tyre Festival — A140

Beiteddine Festival — A141

Byblos Intl. Festival — A142

Perf. 11x11¼, 11¼x11

2004, Nov. 26 **Litho.**

591	A139	£500 multi	.70	.70
592	A140	£1250 multi	1.75	1.75
593	A141	£1400 multi	1.90	1.90
594	A142	£1750 multi	2.40	2.40
		Nos. 591-594 (4)	6.75	6.75

Rotary International, Cent. — A143

2005, Feb. 23 ***Perf. 11¼x11***
595 A143 £3000 multi 4.00 4.00

Beirut Buildings A144

Designs: £100, Rafiq Hariri Intl. Airport. £250, Parliament. £300, Camille Chamoun Sports Center. £500, National Museum. £1000, Governmental Palace. £1250, Bank of Lebanon. £1400, St. Paul's Cathedral. £1750, Bahaeddine Hariri Mosque. £2000, Presidential Palace.

2005 **Litho.** ***Perf. 13x13½***
596-604 A144 Set of 9 15.00 15.00

Issued: £100, £300, £500, £1000, 10/11; others, 11/11.

Pres. Rafiq Hariri (1944-2005) — A145

Designs: No. 605, £1250, Pres. Hariri, flag. No. 606, £1250, Pres. Hariri, mosque, church and statues. No. 607, £1750, Pres. Hariri, mosque. No. 608, £1750, Child kissing picture of Pres. Hariri.

2006, Feb. 13 ***Perf. 13¼x13***
605-608 A145 Set of 4 10.50 10.50
608a Souvenir sheet, #605-608, imperf. 10.50 10.50

No. 608a has embossed margin and simulated perforations between stamps.

Arabic Book Exhibition A146

2007, Apr. 18 **Litho.** ***Perf. 13x13¼***
609 A146 £1000 multi 1.40 1.40

Basil Fuleihan (1963-2005), Economy Minister — A147

Fuleihan: £500, Wearing cap and gown, suit and tie. £1500, With flags of Lebanon and European Union. £2000, With flag of Lebanon.
£4000, Vignettes of Nos. 610-612, map and flag of Lebanon.

2007, Apr. 18 ***Perf. 13¼x13***
610-612 A147 Set of 3 5.75 5.75

Size: 160x100mm

Imperf

613 A147 £4000 multi 5.75 5.75

Pres. Fouad Chehab (1902-73) — A148

2007, June 4 ***Perf. 13¼x13***
614 A148 £1400 multi 1.90 1.90

World Summit on the Information Society, Tunis (in 2005) A149

2007, July 2 ***Perf. 13x13¼***
615 A149 £100 multi .20 .20

Léopold Sédar Senghor (1906-2001), First President of Senegal — A150

2007, July 2 ***Perf. 13¼x13***
616 A150 £300 multi .45 .45

Intl. Year of Sports and Physical Education (in 2005) A151

2007, July 2 ***Perf. 13x13¼***
617 A151 £500 multi .70 .70

OPEC Development Fund, 30th Anniv. — A152

2007, July 2
618 A152 £1400 multi 1.90 1.90

Baalbeck Intl. Festival, 50th Anniv. — A153

50th anniv. emblem and: £1000, Names of performers. £5000, Female performers.

2007, July 2 ***Perf. 13¼x13***
619-620 A153 Set of 2 7.50 7.50

Islamic Makassed Association of Sidon, 125th Anniv. (in 2004) — A154

Emblem and: £1400, Pres. Rafiq Hariri. £1750, Prime Minister Riad El Solh.

2007, July 2
621-622 A154 Set of 2 4.00 4.00

Islamic Makassed Association of Beirut, 125th Anniv. (in 2003) — A155

Emblem and: £250, "125" in Arabian script. £500, Prime Minister Saeb Salam. £1400, Pres. Rafiq Hariri. £1750, Omar El Daouk.

2007, July 2
623-626 A155 Set of 4 5.00 5.00

Souvenir Sheet

2006 Ascent of Mt. Everest by Maxime Chaya — A156

2007, July 2
627 A156 £3000 multi 3.75 3.75

2004 Return of Freed Prisoners — A157

Illustration reduced.

2007, July 2 ***Imperf.***
628 A157 £5000 multi 6.25 6.25

Souvenir Sheet

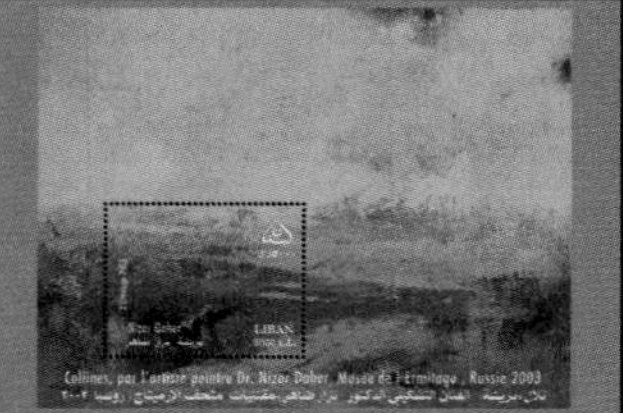

Hills, by Nizar Daher — A158

2007, July 2 **Litho.** ***Perf. 13¼x13***
629 A158 £5000 multi 6.25 6.25

Rotary International District 2450 Conference, Beirut — A159

2008, Apr. 30 **Litho.** ***Perf. 13¼x13***
630 A159 £2000 multi 3.00 3.00

Kahlil Gibran (1883-1931), Writer and Artist — A160

Designs: £100, Mother and Her Child. £500, Sultana. £1400, Gibran Museum, Bsharri. £2000, Gibran.
£4000, Gibran and vignettes of Nos. 631-634, horiz.

2008, Apr. 30 *Perf. 13x13¼*
631-634 A160 Set of 4 5.75 5.75

Imperf

Size: 160x110mm

635 A160 £4000 multi 5.75 5.75

Army Day A161

Emblem and: £500, Soldier and flag of Lebanon. £1000, Stylized flag of Lebanon. £1250, Soldier holding wheat stalks. £1750, Eye.
£4500, Soldiers and vignettes of Nos. 636-639.

2008 **Litho.** *Perf. 13¼x13*
636-639 A161 Set of 4 6.00 6.00

Size: 160x110mm

Imperf

640 A161 £4500 multi 6.00 6.00

Souvenir Sheet

Arab Postal Day — A162

No. 641 — Emblem and: a, World map and pigeon. b, Camel caravan.

Perf. 13¼ Vert. Through Center

2008
641 A162 £5000 Sheet of 2, #a-b 13.50 13.50

Stamps have simulated perforations on three sides.

Lebanon Post, 10th Anniv. — A163

Simulated postmarks, Lebanon Post emblem, streamers, airplane and: £1250, "10" in Arabian script. £1750, Open envelope and "10th anniversary."
£3000, Simulated postmarks, Lebanon Post emblem, streamers, airplane and vignettes of Nos. 642-643.

2008 *Perf. 13¼x13*
642-643 A163 Set of 2 4.00 4.00

Size: 160x110mm

Imperf

644 A163 £3000 multi 4.00 4.00

Trees and Map of Mediterranean Area — A164

2008, Nov. 20 *Perf. 13*
645 A164 £1750 multi 2.40 2.40

See France No. 3569.

Gen. François El Hajj (1953-2007) — A165

2009, Jan. 8 *Perf. 13x13¼*
646 A165 £1750 multi 2.60 2.60

Universal Declaration of Human Rights, 60th Anniv. — A166

2009, Jan. 8 *Perf. 13¼x13*
647 A166 £2000 multi 3.00 3.00

Dated 2008.

SEMI-POSTAL STAMPS

Regular Issue of 1925 Surcharged in Red or Black

1926 **Unwmk.** *Perf. 14x13½*
B1 A2 25c + 25c ol blk 4.25 4.25
B2 A2 50c + 25c yellow green (B) 4.25 4.25
B3 A2 75c + 25c brown orange (B) 4.25 4.25
B4 A2 1p + 50c mag 4.25 4.25
B5 A2 1.25p + 50c dp grn 4.75 4.75
B6 A2 1.50p + 50c rose red (B) 4.75 4.75
a. Double surcharge 40.00 30.00
B7 A2 2p + 75c dk brn 4.25 4.25
B8 A2 2.50p + 75c pck bl 4.75 4.75
B9 A2 3p + 1p org brn 4.75 4.75
B10 A2 5p + 1p vio (B) 4.75 4.75
B11 A3 10p + 2p violet brown (B) 4.75 4.75
B12 A2 25p + 5p ultra 4.75 4.75
Nos. B1-B12 (12) 54.50 54.50

On No. B11 the surcharge is set in six lines to fit the shape of the stamp. All values of this series exist with inverted surcharge. Value each, $14.
See Nos. CB1-CB4.

Catalogue values for unused stamps in this section, from this point to the end of the section, are for Never Hinged items.

Boxing — SP1

1961, Jan. 12 **Litho.** *Perf. 13*
B13 SP1 2.50p + 2.50p shown .50 .20
B14 SP1 5p + 5p Wrestling .50 .20
B15 SP1 7.50p + 7.50p Shot put .50 .20
Nos. B13-B15,CB12-CB14 (6) 10.50 5.40

17th Olympic Games, Rome, Aug. 25-Sept. 11, 1960.

Nos. B13-B15 with Arabic and French Overprint in Black, Blue or Green and two Bars through Olympic Inscription: "CHAMPIONNAT D'EUROPE DE TIR, 2 JUIN 1962"

1962, June 2
B16 SP1 2.50p + 2.50p blue & brn (Bk) .50 .20
B17 SP1 5p + 5p org & brn (G) .90 .20
B18 SP1 7.50p + 7.50p vio & brn (Bl) 1.00 .40
Nos. B16-B18,CB15-CB17 (6) 8.65 4.25

European Marksmanship Championships held in Lebanon.

Red Cross SP2

1988, June 8 **Litho.** *Perf. 14*
B19 SP2 £10 + £1 shown 1.75
B20 SP2 £20 + £2 Stylized profile 2.75
B21 SP2 £30 + £3 Globe, emblems, dove 3.75
Nos. B19-B21 (3) 8.25

AIR POST STAMPS

#10-13 with Additional Overprint

1924 **Unwmk.** *Perf. 14x13½*
C1 A18 2p on 40c 12.50 *12.50*
a. Double surcharge
C2 A18 3p on 60c 12.50 *12.50*
C3 A18 5p on 1fr 12.50 *12.50*
a. Dbl. surch. and ovpt.
C4 A18 10p on 2fr 12.50 *12.50*
a. Invtd. surch. and ovpt. 95.00
Nos. C1-C4 (4) 50.00 *50.00*

Nos. 33, 35-37 Overprinted

C5 A18 2p on 40c 12.50 7.00
C6 A18 3p on 60c 12.50 7.00
C7 A18 5p on 1fr 12.50 7.00
a. Overprint reversed 40.00
C8 A18 10p on 2fr 12.50 7.00
a. Overprint reversed 40.00
b. Double surcharge 40.00
Nos. C5-C8 (4) 50.00 28.00

Nos. 57, 59-61 Overprinted in Green

1925
C9 A2 2p dark brown 4.50 4.50
C10 A2 3p orange brown 4.50 4.50
C11 A2 5p violet 4.50 4.50
a. Inverted overprint
C12 A3 10p violet brown 4.50 4.50
Nos. C9-C12 (4) 18.00 18.00

Nos. 57, 59-61 Overprinted in Red

c

1926
C13 A2 2p dark brown 4.50 4.50
C14 A2 3p orange brown 4.50 4.50
C15 A2 5p violet 4.50 4.50
C16 A3 10p violet brown 4.50 4.50
Nos. C13-C16 (4) 18.00 18.00

Airplane poited down on No. C16.
Exist with inverted overprint. Value, each $15.

Issues of Republic under French Mandate

Nos. C13-C16 Overprinted

d

1927
C17 A2 2p dark brown 5.50 5.50
C18 A2 3p orange brown 5.50 5.50
C19 A2 5p violet 5.50 5.50
C20 A3 10p violet brown 5.50 5.50
Nos. C17-C20 (4) 22.00 22.00

On No. C19 "Republique Libanaise" is above the bars. Overprint set in two lines on No. C20.

Nos. C17-C20 with Additional Overprint

e

1928

Black Overprint

C21 A2 2p brown 12.50 5.50
a. Double overprint 25.00
b. Inverted overprint 25.00
C22 A2 3p orange brown 12.50 5.50
a. Double overprint 25.00
C23 A2 5p violet 12.50 5.50
a. Double overprint 15.00
C24 A3 10p violet brown 12.50 5.50
a. Double overprint 15.00
Nos. C21-C24 (4) 50.00 22.00

On Nos. C21-C24 the airplane is always in red.

Nos. 52, 54, 57, 59-62 Overprinted in Red or Black (No. C34)

f

1928
C25 A2 2p dark brown 3.00 .85
C26 A2 3p orange brown 3.00 .85
C27 A2 5p violet 3.00 .85
C28 A3 10p violet brown 3.50 .85

1929
C33 A2 50c yellow green .75 .40
a. Inverted overprint 35.00 15.00

C34 A2 1p magenta (Bk) 1.00 .50
  a. Inverted overprint 35.00 15.00
C35 A2 25p ultra 190.00 100.00
  a. Inverted overprint 350.00 250.00
  Nos. C25-C34 (6) 14.25 4.30
  Nos. C25-C35 (7) 204.25 104.30

On Nos. C25-C28 the airplane is always in red.

On No. C28 the overprinted orientation is horizontal. The bars covering the old country names are at the left.

The red overprint of a silhouetted plane and "Republique Libanaise," as on Nos. C25-C27, was also applied to Nos. C9-C12. These are believed to have been essays, and were not regularly issued.

No. 62 with Surcharge Added in Red

Two types of surcharge:

I — The "5" of "15 P." is italic. The "15" is 4mm high. Arabic characters for "Lebanese Republic" and for "15 P." are on same line in that order.

II — The "5" is in Roman type (upright) and smaller; "15" is 3½mm high. Arabic for "Lebanese Republic" is centered on line by itself, with Arabic for "15 P." below right end of line.

C36 A2 15p on 25p ultra (I) 225.00 175.00
  a. Type II (#106) *600.00* *600.00*

Nos. 102 Overprinted Type "c" in Blue

C37 A2 50c on 75c .75 .30
  a. Airplane inverted 45.00
  b. French and Arabic surch. invtd.
  c. "P" omitted
  d. Airplane double 50.00

No. 55 Surcharged in Red

1930
C38 A2 2p on 1.25p dp green 1.75 1.00
  a. Inverted surcharge 30.00 15.00

Airplane over Rachaya AP2

Designs: 1p, Plane over Broumana. 2p, Baalbek. 3p, Hasroun. 5p, Byblos. 10p, Kadicha River. 15p, Beirut. 25p, Tripoli. 50p, Kabeljas. 100p, Zahle.

1930-31 **Photo.** ***Perf. 13½***
C39 AP2 50c dk violet ('31) .50 .20
C40 AP2 1p yellow grn ('31) .50 .20
C41 AP2 2p dp orange ('31) 2.75 1.50
C42 AP2 3p magenta ('31) 2.75 1.50
C43 AP2 5p indigo 2.75 1.50
C44 AP2 10p orange red 5.75 2.50
C45 AP2 15p orange brn 3.75 2.25
C46 AP2 25p gray vio ('31) 5.25 3.75
C47 AP2 50p dp claret 17.50 12.00
C48 AP2 100p olive brown 21.00 15.00
  Nos. C39-C48 (10) 62.50 40.40

Nos. C39 to C48 exist imperforate.

Tourist Publicity Issue

Skiing in Lebanon AP12

Bay of Jounie AP13

1936, Oct. 12
C49 AP12 50c slate grn 3.00 3.00
C50 AP13 1p red orange 3.75 3.75
C51 AP12 2p black violet 3.75 3.75
C52 AP13 3p yellow grn 4.00 4.00
C53 AP12 5p brown car 4.00 4.00
C54 AP13 10p orange brn 4.00 4.00
C55 AP13 15p dk carmine 37.50 37.50
C56 AP12 25p green 125.00 125.00
  Nos. C49-C56 (8) 185.00 185.00

Nos. C49 to C56 exist imperforate.

Lebanese Pavilion at Exposition AP14

1937, July 1 ***Perf. 13½***
C57 AP14 50c olive black 1.50 1.50
C58 AP14 1p yellow green 1.50 1.50
C59 AP14 2p dk red orange 1.50 1.50
C60 AP14 3p dk olive grn 1.50 1.50
C61 AP14 5p deep green 2.00 2.00
C62 AP14 10p carmine lake 9.00 9.00
C63 AP14 15p rose lake 10.00 10.00
C64 AP14 25p orange brn 17.50 17.50
  Nos. C57-C64 (8) 44.50 44.50

Paris International Exposition.

Arcade of Beit-ed-Din Palace AP15

Ruins of Baalbek AP16

1937-40 **Engr.** ***Perf. 13***
C65 AP15 50c ultra ('38) .35 .20
C66 AP15 1p henna brn ('40) .35 .20
C67 AP15 2p sepia ('40) .35 .20
C68 AP15 3p rose ('40) 3.25 1.25
C69 AP15 5p lt green ('40) .35 .20
C70 AP16 10p dull violet .35 .20
C71 AP16 15p turq bl ('40) 2.75 1.75
C72 AP16 25p violet ('40) 6.00 5.00
C73 AP16 50p yellow grn ('40) 11.00 7.00
C74 AP16 100p brown ('40) 6.00 3.50
  Nos. C65-C74 (10) 30.75 19.50

Nos. C65-C74 exist imperforate.

Medical College of Beirut AP17

1938, May 9 **Photo.** ***Perf. 13***
C75 AP17 2p green 3.00 *3.50*
C76 AP17 3p orange 3.00 *3.50*
C77 AP17 5p lilac gray 5.50 *6.50*
C78 AP17 10p lake 10.50 *12.00*
  Nos. C75-C78 (4) 22.00 *25.50*

Medical Congress.

Maurice Noguès and View of Beirut — AP18

1938, July 15 ***Perf. 11***
C79 AP18 10p brown carmine 4.00 1.50
  a. Souv. sheet of 4, perf. 13½ 35.00 20.00
  b. Perf. 13½ 7.50 4.00

10th anniversary of first Marseille-Beirut flight, by Maurice Noguès.

No. C79a has marginal inscriptions in French and Arabic. Exists imperf.; value $250.

Independent Republic

Plane Over Mt. Lebanon AP19

1942, Sept. 18 **Litho.** ***Perf. 11½***
C80 AP19 10p dk brown vio 7.00 *8.00*
C81 AP19 50p dk gray grn 7.00 *8.00*

1st anniv. of the Proclamation of Independence, Nov. 26, 1941.

Nos. C80 and C81 exist imperforate.

Bechamoun AP20

Rachaya Citadel AP21

Air View of Beirut AP22

1943, May 1 ***Perf. 11½***
C82 AP20 25p yellow grn 4.00 2.50
C83 AP20 50p orange 5.50 3.25
C84 AP21 100p buff 5.50 2.75
C85 AP21 200p blue vio 6.75 5.00
C86 AP22 300p sage green 20.00 16.00
C87 AP22 500p sepia 32.50 30.00
  Nos. C82-C87 (6) 74.25 59.50

2nd anniv. of the Proclamation of Independence. Nos. C82-C87 exist imperforate.

See #163-166. For overprints see #C91-C96.

Bhannes Sanatorium AP23

1943, July 8 **Photo.**

Black Overprint

C88 AP23 20p orange 3.75 2.25
C89 AP23 50p steel blue 4.25 2.25
C90 AP23 100p rose violet 6.00 3.75
  Nos. C88-C90 (3) 14.00 8.25

Arab Medical Congress, Beirut.

Nos. C82 to C87 Overprinted in Red, Blue or Violet

1944, Nov. 23
C91 AP20 25p yel grn (R) 7.25 7.25
C92 AP20 50p orange (Bl) 12.00 12.00
C93 AP21 100p buff (V) 14.00 14.00
C94 AP21 200p blue vio (R) 25.00 25.00
C95 AP22 300p sage grn (R) 32.50 30.00
C96 AP22 500p sepia (Bl) 65.00 60.00
  Nos. C91-C96 (6) 155.75 148.25

Return to office of the President and his ministers, Nov. 22, 1943.

Catalogue values for unused stamps in this section, from this point to the end of the section, are for Never Hinged items.

Falls of Litani — AP24

The Cedars AP25

1945, July **Unwmk.** **Litho.**
C97 AP24 25p gray brown 3.50 2.10
C98 AP24 50p rose violet 5.00 2.75
C99 AP25 200p violet 15.00 5.25
C100 AP25 300p brown black 27.50 10.50
  Nos. C97-C100 (4) 51.00 20.60

Lebanese Soldiers at Bir Hacheim AP26

1946, May 8
C101 AP26 15p bl blk, org & red org 1.00 .25
C102 AP26 20p red, lil & bl 1.00 .60
C103 AP26 25p brt bl, org & red 1.25 .20
C104 AP26 50p gray blk, bl & red 1.75 .50
C105 AP26 100p pur, pink & red 5.00 1.25
C106 AP26 150p brn, pink & red 6.00 3.75
  Nos. C101-C106 (6) 16.00 6.55

Victory of the Allied Nations in WWII, 1st anniv.

Three imperf. souvenir sheets of 14 exist. They contain one each of Nos. C101-C106 and 189-196 in changed colors. One has sepia inscriptions, and one on thin white card has blue inscriptions. Value $30 each. The third, with blue inscriptions, is on thick honeycombed chamois card. Value $110.

Night Herons Type

1946, Sept. 11
C107 A35 10p orange 7.00 1.00
C108 A35 25p ultra 8.00 .20
C109 A35 50p blue green 25.00 1.60
C110 A35 100p dk vio brn 37.50 6.50
  Nos. C107-C110 (4) 77.50 9.30

Symbols of Communications — AP28

1946, Nov. 22
C111 AP28 25p deep blue 1.75 .70
C112 AP28 50p green 2.50 .80
C113 AP28 75p orange red 4.25 1.75
C114 AP28 150p brown black 6.00 2.75
  Nos. C111-C114 (4) 14.50 6.00

Arab Postal Congress, Sofar, 1946.

Stone Tablet, Dog River and Pres. Bechara el-Khoury AP29

1947, Feb. 11
C115 AP29 25p ultra 7.00 .35
C116 AP29 50p dull rose 9.00 .60
C117 AP29 75p gray black 11.00 .65
C118 AP29 150p blue green 17.50 1.40
  Nos. C115-C118 (4) 44.50 3.00

Evacuation of foreign troops from Lebanon, Dec. 31, 1946.

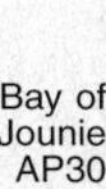

Bay of Jounie AP30

Government House, Beirut — AP31

1947, Feb. 11

Grayish Paper

C119	AP30	5p	dp blue grn	.60	.20
C120	AP30	10p	rose vio	.90	.20
C121	AP30	15p	vermilion	2.25	.20
C122	AP30	20p	orange	2.50	.20
a.			20p red orange, white paper	2.25	.20
C123	AP30	25p	deep blue	3.00	.20
C124	AP30	50p	henna brn	5.00	.20
C125	AP30	100p	chocolate	10.50	.30
C126	AP31	150p	dk vio brn	18.00	.50
C127	AP31	200p	slate	27.50	2.40
C128	AP31	300p	black	45.00	6.00
			Nos. C119-C128 (10)	115.25	10.40

See Nos. C145A-C147B.

Post Horn and Letter — AP32

Phoenician Galley AP33

1947, June 17 **Litho.**

C129	AP32	10p	brt ultra	1.75	.50
C130	AP32	15p	rose car	2.00	.50
C131	AP32	25p	bright blue	2.50	.80
C132	AP33	50p	dk slate grn	5.75	.90
C133	AP33	75p	purple	7.00	1.90
C134	AP33	100p	dark brown	9.00	2.50
			Nos. C129-C134 (6)	28.00	7.10

Lebanon's participation in the 12th UPU congress, Paris.

Lebanese Village AP34

1948, Sept. 1 ***Perf. 11½***

C135	AP34	5p	dp orange	.75	.20
C136	AP34	10p	rose lilac	1.75	.20
C137	AP34	15p	orange brn	3.50	.20
C138	AP34	20p	slate	4.50	.20
C139	AP34	25p	Prus blue	10.50	1.00
C140	AP34	50p	gray black	17.50	1.40
			Nos. C135-C140 (6)	38.50	3.20

Apollo — AP35

Minerva AP36

1948, Nov. 23 **Unwmk.**

C141	AP35	7.50p	blue & lt blue	4.00	1.00
C142	AP35	15p	black & gray	5.00	1.25
C143	AP35	20p	rose brn & rose	5.25	1.90
C144	AP36	35p	car rose & rose	8.00	2.50
C145	AP36	75p	bl grn & lt green	15.00	5.00
			Nos. C141-C145 (5)	37.25	11.65

UNESCO. Nos. C141-C145 exist imperforate, and combined with Nos. 220-224 in an imperforate souvenir sheet on thin buff cardboard, with black inscriptions in top margin in Arabic and at bottom in French. Value $275.

Bay Type of 1947 Redrawn

1949

White Paper

C145A	AP30	10p	rose lilac	9.00	1.00
C146	AP30	15p	dark green	11.00	1.25
C147	AP30	20p	orange	25.00	9.00
C147A	AP30	25p	dark blue	65.00	3.25
C147B	AP30	50p	brick red	275.00	35.00
			Nos. C145A-C147B (5)	385.00	49.50

In the redrawn designs, Nos. C145A, C147 and C147B have zeros with broader centers than in the 1947 issue (Nos. C120, C122 and C124).

Helicopter Mail Delivery — AP37

1949, Aug. 16 **Unwmk.** ***Perf. 11½***

C148	AP37	25p	deep blue	8.00	4.00
C149	AP37	50p	green	12.00	4.50
a.			Souvenir sheet of 5, #225-227, C148-C149	75.00	35.00

UPU, 75th anniv. No. 149a exists on thin cardboard. Value $250.

Homing Birds AP38

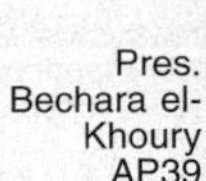

Pres. Bechara el-Khoury AP39

1950, Aug. 8 **Litho.**

C150	AP38	5p	violet blue	3.75	.65
C151	AP38	15p	rose vio	4.25	.70
C152	AP39	25p	chocolate	3.00	.95
C153	AP39	35p	gray green	4.50	1.40
a.			Souvenir sheet of 6, #243-244, C150-C153, chamois paper	70.00	55.00
			Nos. C150-C153 (4)	15.50	3.70

Conference of Emigrants, 1950.

Crusader Castle, Sidon Harbor AP40

1950, Sept. 7

C154	AP40	10p	chocolate	1.00	.20
C155	AP40	15p	dark green	2.00	.20
C156	AP40	20p	crimson	4.00	.20
C157	AP40	25p	ultra	7.00	.80
C158	AP40	50p	gray black	10.00	2.25
			Nos. C154-C158 (5)	24.00	3.65

1951, June 9 **Redrawn** **Typo.**

C159	AP40	10p	grnsh black	2.00	.20
C160	AP40	15p	black brown	3.00	.20
C161	AP40	20p	vermilion	3.00	.20
C162	AP40	25p	deep blue	4.00	.20
C163	AP40	35p	lilac rose	8.00	2.40
C164	AP40	50p	indigo	11.00	2.40
			Nos. C159-C164 (6)	31.00	5.60

Nos. C154-C158 are lithographed from a fine-screen halftone; Nos. C159-C164 are typographed and much coarser, with larger plane and many other differences.

Khaldé International Airport, Beirut — AP41

Design: 50p to 300p, Amphitheater, Byblos.

1952 **Litho.** ***Perf. 11½***

C165	AP41	5p	crimson	1.50	.20
C166	AP41	10p	dark gray	1.50	.20
C167	AP41	15p	rose lilac	1.75	.20
C168	AP41	20p	brown org	2.00	.20
C169	AP41	25p	grnsh blue	2.00	.20
C170	AP41	35p	violet bl	2.75	.20
C171	AP41	50p	blue green	14.00	.60
C172	AP41	100p	deep blue	55.00	2.40
C173	AP41	200p	dk blue grn	35.00	3.50
C174	AP41	300p	black brn	52.50	7.50
			Nos. C165-C174 (10)	168.00	15.20

Lockheed Constellation — AP42

1953, Oct. 1

C175	AP42	5p	yellow green	.90	.20
C176	AP42	10p	deep plum	1.25	.20
C177	AP42	15p	scarlet	1.75	.20
C178	AP42	20p	aqua	2.25	.20
C179	AP42	25p	blue	4.00	.20
C180	AP42	35p	orange brn	5.75	.20
C181	AP42	50p	violet blue	11.00	.30
C182	AP42	100p	black brown	16.00	2.40
			Nos. C175-C182 (8)	42.90	3.90

Ruins at Baalbek AP43

Irrigation Canal, Litani AP44

1954, Mar.

C183	AP43	5p	yel green	.75	.20
C184	AP43	10p	dull purple	.90	.20
C185	AP43	15p	carmine	1.50	.20
C186	AP43	20p	brown	2.00	.20
C187	AP43	25p	dull blue	2.50	.20
C188	AP43	35p	black brn	3.00	.20
C189	AP44	50p	dk olive grn	10.00	.25
C190	AP44	100p	deep carmine	19.00	.35
C191	AP44	200p	dark brown	27.50	.70
C192	AP44	300p	dk gray blue	50.00	1.50
			Nos. C183-C192 (10)	117.15	4.00

Khaldé International Airport, Beirut — AP45

1954, Apr. 23 ***Perf. 11½***

C193	AP45	10p	pink & rose red	1.25	.20
C194	AP45	25p	dp bl & gray bl	2.75	.50
C195	AP45	35p	dl brn & yel brn	4.25	.90
C196	AP45	65p	dp grn & grn	6.25	1.60
			Nos. C193-C196 (4)	14.50	3.20

Opening of Beirut's Intl. Airport. Exist imperf.

Arab Postal Union Type of Regular Issue, 1955

1955, Jan. 1 ***Perf. 13½x13***

C197	A52	2.50p	yellow brn	1.50	.20

Rotary Emblem AP47

1955, Feb. 23 ***Perf. 11½***

C198	AP47	35p	dull green	1.50	.40
C199	AP47	65p	dull blue	2.50	.55

Rotary International, 50th anniversary.

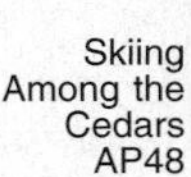

Skiing Among the Cedars AP48

1955, Feb. 24 **Litho.**

C200	AP48	5p	blue green	2.00	.20
C201	AP48	15p	crimson	2.25	.20
C202	AP48	20p	lilac	2.75	.20
C203	AP48	25p	blue	5.00	.20
C204	AP48	35p	olive brn	6.50	.20
C205	AP48	50p	chocolate	11.00	.70
C206	AP48	65p	deep blue	17.50	2.10
			Nos. C200-C206 (7)	47.00	3.80

See #C233-C235. For surcharge see #C271.

Tourist — AP49

1955, Sept. 10 **Unwmk.** ***Perf. 13***

C207	AP49	2.50p	brn vio & lt bl	.50	.20
C208	AP49	12.50p	ultra & lt bl	.65	.20
C209	AP49	25p	indigo & lt bl	1.50	.20
C210	AP49	35p	ol grn & lt bl	1.75	.20
a.			Sheet of 4, #C207-C210, imperf.	22.50	7.75
			Nos. C207-C210 (4)	4.40	.80

Tourist Year. No. C210a is printed on cardboard.

Oranges AP50

Designs: 25p, 35p, 50p, Grapes, vert. 65p, 100p, 200p, Apples.

1955, Oct. 15

C211	AP50	5p	yel grn & yel	1.10	.20
C212	AP50	10p	dk grn & dp orange	1.25	.20
C213	AP50	15p	yel grn & red orange	1.40	.20
C214	AP50	20p	olive & yel org	2.00	.20
C215	AP50	25p	blue & vio bl	2.75	.20
C216	AP50	35p	green & cl	3.25	.20
C217	AP50	50p	blk brn & dl yellow	3.25	.20
C218	AP50	65p	green & lemon	6.50	.20
C219	AP50	100p	yel grn & dp orange	8.50	.85
C220	AP50	200p	green & car	15.00	4.25
			Nos. C211-C220 (10)	45.00	6.70

For surcharge see No. C265.

United Nations Emblem AP52

1956, Jan. 23 ***Perf. 11½***

C221	AP52	35p	violet blue	5.25	1.90
C222	AP52	65p	green	6.50	2.25

UN, 10th anniv. (in 1955).

An imperf. souvenir sheet contains one each of Nos. C221 and C222. Value $90.

Temple of the Sun Colonnade, Masks and Lion's Head — AP53

Temple of Bacchus, Baalbek AP54

Design: 35p, 65p, Temple of the Sun colonnade, masks and violincello.

1956, Dec. 10 **Litho.** ***Perf. 13***

C223	AP53	2.50p	dark brown	.85	.20
C224	AP53	10p	green	1.10	.20
C225	AP54	12.50p	light blue	1.10	.20
C226	AP54	25p	brt vio bl	1.60	.35
C227	AP53	35p	red lilac	3.00	.45
C228	AP53	65p	slate blue	4.25	.90
	Nos. C223-C228 (6)			11.90	2.30

International Festival at Baalbek.

Skiing Type of 1955 Redrawn and

Irrigation Canal, Litani AP55

1957 **Litho.** ***Perf. 11½***

C229	AP55	10p	brt violet	.65	.20
C230	AP55	15p	orange	.90	.20
C231	AP55	20p	yel green	1.00	.20
C232	AP55	25p	slate blue	1.10	.20
C233	AP48	35p	gray green	2.50	.20
C234	AP48	65p	dp claret	4.00	.20
C235	AP48	100p	brown	6.00	.65
	Nos. C229-C235 (7)			16.15	1.85

Different Arabic characters used for the country name; letters in "Liban" larger.

For surcharge see No. C271.

Pres. Camille Chamoun and King Saud AP56

King Saud, Pres. Chamoun, King Hussein, Pres. Kouatly, King Faisal, Pres. Nasser — AP57

Pres. Chamoun and: No. C237, King Hussein. No. C238, Pres. Kouatly. No. C239, King Faisal. No. C240, Pres. Nasser. 25p, Map of Lebanon.

1957, July 15 **Litho.** ***Perf. 13***

C236	AP56	15p	green	.75	.20
C237	AP56	15p	blue	.75	.20
C238	AP56	15p	red lilac	.75	.20
C239	AP56	15p	red orange	.75	.20
C240	AP56	15p	claret	.75	.20
C241	AP56	25p	blue	.75	.20
C242	AP57	100p	dl red brn	6.00	1.50
	Nos. C236-C242 (7)			10.50	2.70

Congr. of Arab Leaders, Beirut, 11/12-15/56.

Fencing AP58

50p, Pres. Chamoun and stadium with flags.

1957, Sept. 12 **Unwmk.** ***Perf. 13***

C243	AP58	35p	claret	3.25	1.50
C244	AP58	50p	lt green	4.00	2.25

2nd Pan-Arab Games, Beirut. See note on souvenir sheet below No. 314.

Symbols of Communications — AP59

Power Plant, Chamoun AP60

1957 ***Perf. 13x13½, 11½ (AP60)***

C245	AP59	5p	brt green	.55	.20
C246	AP59	10p	yel orange	.60	.20
C247	AP59	15p	brown	.60	.20
C248	AP59	20p	maroon	.80	.20
C249	AP59	25p	violet blue	1.10	.20
C250	AP60	35p	violet brn	1.40	.20
C251	AP60	50p	green	1.60	.20
C252	AP60	65p	sepia	2.25	.20
C253	AP60	100p	dark gray	3.00	.55
	Nos. C245-C253 (9)			11.90	2.15

Plane at Airport AP61

Cogwheel AP62

1958-59 **Unwmk.** ***Perf. 13***

C254	AP61	5p	green	.55	.20
C255	AP61	10p	magenta	.75	.20
C256	AP61	15p	dull violet	.90	.20
C257	AP61	20p	orange ver	1.10	.20
C258	AP61	25p	dk vio bl	1.40	.20
C259	AP62	35p	grnsh gray	1.60	.20
C260	AP62	50p	aquamarine	2.25	.20
C261	AP62	65p	pale brown	3.75	.30
C262	AP62	100p	brt ultra	4.25	.20
	Nos. C254-C262 (9)			16.55	1.90

Nos. C259 and C261 Surcharged in Black or Dark Blue

1959 **Unwmk.** **Litho.** ***Perf. 13***

C263	AP62	30p	on 35p grnsh gray	1.00	.20
C264	AP62	40p	on 65p pale brn (Bl)	1.40	.45

Arab Engineers Congress.

No. C217 Surcharged

1959, Sept. 1

C265	AP50	40p	on 50p blk brn & dull yel	1.50	.50

Arab Lawyers Congress.

Myron's Discobolus — AP63

Wreath and Hand Holding Torch AP64

1959, Oct. 11 **Litho.** ***Perf. 11½***

C266	AP63	15p	shown	1.00	.20
C267	AP63	30p	Weight lifter	1.25	.30
C268	AP64	40p	shown	1.90	.40
	Nos. C266-C268 (3)			4.15	.90

3rd Mediterranean Games, Beirut.

A souvenir sheet on white cardboard contains one each of Nos. C266-C268, imperf. Sold for 100p. Value *$67.50*

Soldiers and Flag — AP65

Hands Planting Tree — AP66

1959, Nov. 25 ***Perf. 13½x13***

C269	AP65	40p	sep, brick red & sl	1.50	.30
C270	AP65	60p	sep, dk grn & brick red	2.00	.35

Lebanon's independence, 1941-1959.

No. C234 Surcharged with New Value and Bars

1959, Dec. 15 ***Perf. 11½***

C271	AP48	40p	on 65p dp claret	3.00	.30

1960, Jan. 18 **Litho.** ***Perf. 11½***

C272	AP66	20p	rose vio & grn	1.00	.20
C273	AP66	40p	dk brn & green	1.25	.40

Friends of the Tree Society, 25th anniv.

Postal Administration Building — AP67

1960, Feb. **Unwmk.** ***Perf. 13***

C274	AP67	20p	green	.90	.20

President Fuad Chehab AP68

Uprooted Oak Emblem AP69

1960, Mar. 12 **Photo.** ***Perf. 13½***

C275	AP68	5p	green	.50	.20
C276	AP68	10p	Prus blue	.50	.20
C277	AP68	15p	orange brn	.50	.20
C278	AP68	20p	brown	.55	.20
C279	AP68	30p	olive	.80	.20
C280	AP68	40p	dull red	.90	.20
C281	AP68	50p	blue	1.00	.20
C282	AP68	70p	red lilac	1.10	.20
C283	AP68	100p	dark green	2.00	.40
	Nos. C275-C283 (9)			7.85	2.00

1960, Apr. 7 **Litho.** ***Perf. 13½x13***

Size: 20½x36½mm

C284	AP69	25p	yellow brn	1.00	.20
C285	AP69	40p	green	1.25	.30
a.	Souv. sheet of 2, #C284-C285, imperf.			45.00	19.00

Size: 20x36mm

C284b	AP69	25p	yellow brown	1.00	.40
C285b	AP69	40p	green	1.75	.65

World Refugee Year, 7/1/59-6/30/60.

No. C285a sold for 150p.

Nos. C284b-C285b appear fuzzy and pale when compared to the bolder, clear-cut printing of Nos. C284-C285. Issue date: July 18.

Nos. C284b-C285b exist with carmine surcharges of "30P.+15P." (on C284b) and "20P.+10P." (on C285b), repeated in Arabic, with ornaments covering original denominations.

Martyrs' Monument — AP70

Martyrs of May 6th: 70p, Statues from Martyrs' monument, vert.

1960, May 6 ***Perf. 13x13½, 13½x13***

C286	AP70	20p	rose lilac & grn	.80	.20
C287	AP70	40p	Prus grn & dk grn	1.00	.30
C288	AP70	70p	gray olive & blk	2.00	.50
	Nos. C286-C288 (3)			3.80	1.00

Pres. Chehab and King of Morocco AP71

1960, June 1 ***Perf. 13x13½***

C289	AP71	30p	choc & dk brn	1.00	.30
C290	AP71	70p	blk, dk brn & buff	2.00	.35

Visit of King Mohammed V of Morocco.

A souvenir sheet of 2 on white cardboard contains Nos. C289-C290, imperf. Value $72.

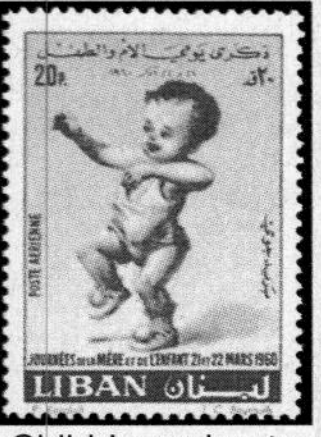

Child Learning to Walk — AP72

Bird, Ribbon of Flags and Map of Beirut — AP73

1960, Aug. 16 Litho. *Perf. 13½x13*

C291 AP72 20p shown 1.00 .20
C292 AP72 60p Mother & child 2.00 .40
Nos. C291-C292,CB10-CB11 (4) 5.90 1.40

Day of Mother and Child, Mar. 21-22.

Perf. 13½x13, 13x13½

1960, Sept. 20 Unwmk.

40p, Cedar & birds. 70p, Globes & cedar, horiz.

C293 AP73 20p multicolored .50 .20
C294 AP73 40p vio, bl & grn .75 .20
C295 AP73 70p multicolored 1.00 .20
Nos. C293-C295 (3) 2.25 .60

Union of Lebanese Emigrants in the World. A souvenir sheet of 3 contains Nos. C293-C295, imperf., printed on cardboard. Sold for 150p. Value $22.50.

Pres. Chehab and Map of Lebanon — AP74

Casino, Maameltein Lebanon AP75

1961, Feb. Litho. *Perf. 13½x13*

C296 AP74 5p bl grn & yel grn .50 .20
C297 AP74 10p brown & bister .50 .20
C298 AP74 70p vio & rose lilac 1.25 .35

1961 *Perf. 13x13½*

C299 AP75 15p rose claret .60 .20
C300 AP75 30p greenish blue 1.00 .20
C301 AP75 40p brown 1.25 .20
C302 AP75 200p bis brn & dl bl 5.25 1.40
Nos. C296-C302 (7) 10.35 2.75

On Nos. C299-C301, the denomination, inscription and trees differ from type AP75.

UN Headquarters, New York — AP76

20p, UN Emblem & map of Lebanon. 30p, UN Emblem & symbolic building. 20p, 30p are vert.

1961, May 5 *Perf. 13½x13, 13x13½*

C306 AP76 20p lake & lt blue .70 .20
C307 AP76 30p green & beige .85 .20
C308 AP76 50p vio bl & grnsh bl 1.40 .20
a. Souvenir sheet of 3 9.00 9.00
Nos. C306-C308 (3) 2.95 .60

UN, 15th anniv. (in 1960).

No. C308a contains one each of Nos. C306-C308, imperf., against a light blue background showing UN emblem. Sold for 125p.

Pottery Workers AP77

1961, July 11 Litho. *Perf. 13x13½*

C309 AP77 30p shown 2.75 .20
C310 AP77 70p Weaver 1.60 .20

Issued for Labor Day, 1961.

Fireworks AP78

Water Skiing AP79

70p, Tourists on boat ride through cave.

1961, Aug. 8 *Perf. 13½x13, 13x13½*

C311 AP78 15p lt pur & dk bl 1.50 1.00
C312 AP79 40p blue & pink 2.10 1.25
C313 AP79 70p dull brn & pink .90 .50
Nos. C311-C313 (3) 4.50 2.75

Issued to publicize tourist month.

Highway Circle at Dora, Beirut Suburb AP80

1961, Aug. *Perf. 11½*

C314 AP80 35p yellow green 1.00 .30
C315 AP80 50p orange brown 1.25 .45
C316 AP80 100p gray 1.25 .55
Nos. C314-C316 (3) 3.50 1.30

Beach at Tyre — AP81

Afka Falls — AP82

1961, Sept. Litho. *Perf. 13*

C317 AP81 5p carmine rose .50 .20
C318 AP81 10p brt violet .75 .20
C319 AP81 15p bright blue .80 .20
C320 AP81 20p orange 1.00 .20
C321 AP81 30p brt green 1.25 .20
C322 AP82 40p dp claret 1.00 .20
C323 AP82 50p ultramarine 1.10 .20
C324 AP82 70p yellow green 1.50 .25
C325 AP82 100p dark brown 2.00 .35
Nos. C317-C325 (9) 9.90 2.00

See Nos. C341-C342.

Entrance to UNESCO Building AP83

"UNESCO" and Cedar — AP84

Design: 50p, UNESCO headquarters, Paris.

1961, Nov. 20 Unwmk. *Perf. 12*

C326 AP83 20p bl, buff & blk .65 .20
C327 AP84 30p lt grn, blk & mag .80 .20
C328 AP83 50p multicolored 1.25 .20
Nos. C326-C328 (3) 2.70 .60

UNESCO, 15th anniv.

Emir Bechir and Fakhr-el-Din El Maani — AP85

Design: 25p, Cedar emblem.

1961, Dec. 30 Litho.

C329 AP85 25p Cedar emblem .65 .20
C330 AP85 50p shown 1.00 .30

See note after No. 375.

Scout Types of Regular Issue, 1962

15p, Trefoil & cedar emblem. 20p, Hand making Scout sign. 25p, Lebanese Scout emblem.

1962, Mar. 1 Unwmk. *Perf. 12*

C331 A70 15p grn, blk & red .80 .20
C332 A69 20p lil, blk & yel .95 .20
C333 A70 25p multicolored 1.50 .40
Nos. C331-C333 (3) 3.25 .80

Arab League Building, Cairo — AP86

1962, Mar. 20 *Perf. 13*

C334 AP86 20p ultra & lt bl .60 .20
C335 AP86 30p red brn & pink .75 .20
C336 AP86 50p grn & grnsh bl 1.00 .30
Nos. C334-C336 (3) 2.35 .70

Arab League Week, Mar. 22-28. See Nos. C372-C375.

Blacksmith AP87

Farm Tractor AP88

Perf. 13½x13, 13x13½

1962, May 1 Litho.

C337 AP87 5p green & lt blue .50 .20
C338 AP87 10p blue & pink .50 .20
C339 AP88 25p brt vio & pink .75 .20
C340 AP88 35p car rose & blue 1.00 .20
Nos. C337-C340 (4) 2.75 .80

Issued for Labor Day.

Types of 1961 Redrawn with Large Numerals Similar to Redrawn Regular Issue of 1962

1962 *Perf. 13*

C341 AP81 5p carmine rose 1.10 .20
C342 AP82 40p deep claret 6.25 .40

Hand Reaching for Malaria Eradication Emblem — AP89

Bas-relief of Isis, Kalabsha Temple, Nubia — AP90

Design: 70p, Malaria eradication emblem.

1962, July 2 Litho. *Perf. 13½x13*

C349 AP89 30p tan & brown 1.00 .20
C350 AP89 70p bluish lil & vio 1.25 .50

WHO drive to eradicate malaria.

1962, Aug. 1 Unwmk. *Perf. 13*

C351 AP90 30p yellow green 2.00 .25
C352 AP90 50p slate 4.00 .60

Campaign to save historic monuments in Nubia.

Spade, Heart, Diamond, Club — AP91

College Student — AP92

1962, Sept.

C353 AP91 25p car rose, blk & red 3.25 1.25
C354 AP91 40p multicolored 4.50 1.25

European Bridge Championship Tournament.

1962, Oct. 1 *Perf. 12*

C355 AP92 45p multicolored .90 .20

Issued for Students' Day, Oct. 1.

Sword Severing Chain — AP93

Harvest — AP94

1962, Nov. 22 **Litho.** ***Perf. 13***
C356 AP93 25p vio, lt bl & red 1.00 .25
C357 AP93 25p bl, lt bl & red 1.00 .25
C358 AP93 25p grn, lt bl & red 1.00 .25
Nos. C356-C358 (3) 3.00 .75

19th anniversary of independence.

Fruit Type of Regular Issue, 1962

5p, Apricots. 10p, 30p, Plums. 20p, 40p, Apples. 50p, Pears. 70p, Medlar. 100p, Lemons.

1962

Vignette Multicolored
C359 A72 5p orange brown .50 .20
C360 A72 10p black .55 .20
C361 A72 20p brown .60 .20
C362 A72 30p gray .75 .20
C363 A72 40p dark gray 1.00 .20
C364 A72 50p light brown 1.25 .20
C365 A72 70p gray olive 1.50 .30
C366 A72 100p blue 3.00 .50
Nos. C359-C366 (8) 9.15 2.00

1963, Mar. 21 **Litho.** ***Perf. 13***

Design: 15p, 20p, UN Emblem and hand holding Wheat Emblem, horiz.

C367 AP94 2.50p ultra & yel .50 .20
C368 AP94 5p gray grn & yel .50 .20
C369 AP94 7.50p rose lil & yel .50 .20
C370 AP94 15p rose brn & pale grn .80 .20
C371 AP94 20p rose & pale grn 1.00 .20
Nos. C367-C371 (5) 3.30 1.00

FAO "Freedom from Hunger" campaign.

Redrawn Type of 1962, Dated "1963"

Design: Arab League Building, Cairo.

1963, Mar. **Unwmk.** ***Perf. 12***
C372 AP86 5p violet & lt blue .50 .20
C373 AP86 10p green & lt blue .50 .20
C374 AP86 15p claret & lt blue .55 .20
C375 AP86 20p gray & lt blue .70 .25
Nos. C372-C375 (4) 2.25 .85

Issued for Arab League Week.

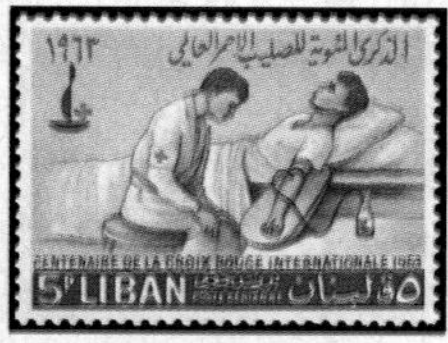

Blood Transfusion AP95

Design: 35p, 40p, Nurse and infant, vert.

1963, Oct. 5 **Unwmk.** ***Perf. 13***
C376 AP95 5p green & red .50 .20
C377 AP95 20p grnsh bl & red .55 .20
C378 AP95 35p org, red & blk .70 .20
C379 AP95 40p purple & red 1.00 .20
Nos. C376-C379 (4) 2.75 .80

Centenary of International Red Cross.

Lyre Player and Columns — AP96

Lebanon Flag, Rising Sun — AP97

1963, Nov. 7 **Unwmk.** ***Perf. 13***
C380 AP96 35p lt bl, org & blk 1.50 .30

International Festival at Baalbek.

1964, Jan. 8 **Litho.**
C381 AP97 5p bluish grn, ver & yel .50 .20
C382 AP97 10p yel grn, ver & yel .55 .20
C383 AP97 25p ultra, ver & yel .75 .25
C384 AP97 40p gray, ver & yel 1.10 .35
Nos. C381-C384 (4) 2.90 1.00

20th anniversary of Independence.

Sports Type of Regular Issue, 1964

1964, Feb. 11 **Unwmk.** ***Perf. 13***
C385 A76 15p Tennis .55 .20
C386 A76 17.50p Swimming, horiz. .65 .20
C387 A76 30p Skiing, horiz. 1.00 .20
a. Souvenir sheet of 3 13.50 10.50
Nos. C385-C387 (3) 2.20 .60

No. C387a contains three imperf. stamps similar to Nos. C385-C387 with simulated orange brown perforations and green marginal inscription. Sold for 100p.

Anemone AP98

Flame and UN Emblem — AP100

Girls Jumping Rope AP99

1964, June 9 **Unwmk.** ***Perf. 13***
C391 AP98 5p Lily .50 .20
C392 AP98 10p Ranunculus .60 .20
C393 AP98 20p shown .75 .20
C394 AP98 40p Tuberose 1.00 .20
C395 AP98 45p Rhododendron 1.10 .20
C396 AP98 50p Jasmine 1.25 .20
C397 AP98 70p Yellow broom 2.00 .30
Nos. C391-C397 (7) 7.20 1.50

1964, Apr. 8

Children's Day: 20p, 40p, Boy on hobby-horse, vert.

C398 AP99 5p emer, org & red .50 .20
C399 AP99 10p yel brn, org & red .55 .20
C400 AP99 20p dp ultra, lt bl & org .60 .20
C401 AP99 40p lil, lt bl & yel 1.00 .30
Nos. C398-C401 (4) 2.65 .90

1964, May 15 **Litho.** **Unwmk.**

40p, Flame, UN emblem and broken chain.

C402 AP100 20p salmon, org & brn .50 .20
C403 AP100 40p lt bl, gray bl & org .75 .20

15th anniv. (in 1963) of the Universal Declaration of Human Rights.

Arab League Conference — AP101

1964, Apr. 20 ***Perf. 13x13½***
C404 AP101 5p blk & pale sal 1.00 .20
C405 AP101 10p black 1.25 .35
C406 AP101 15p green 1.75 .50
C407 AP101 20p dk brn & pink 2.25 .65
Nos. C404-C407 (4) 6.25 1.70

Arab League meeting.

Child in Crib — AP102

Beit-ed-Din Palace and Children — AP103

1964, July 20 ***Perf. 13½x13, 13½***
C408 AP102 2.50p multicolored .50 .20
C409 AP102 5p multicolored .50 .20
C410 AP102 15p multicolored .60 .20
C411 AP103 17.50p multicolored .80 .20
C412 AP103 20p multicolored .90 .20
C413 AP103 40p multicolored 1.00 .20
Nos. C408-C413 (6) 4.30 1.20

Ball of the Little White Beds, Beirut, for the benefit of children's hospital beds.

Clasped Hands and Map of Lebanon AP104

1964, Oct. 16 **Litho.** ***Perf. 13½x13***
C414 AP104 20p yel grn, yel & gray .65 .20
C415 AP104 40p slate, yel & gray 1.10 .40

Congress of the Intl. Lebanese Union.

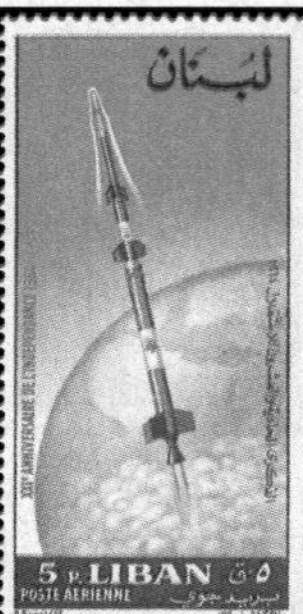

Rocket Leaving Earth — AP105

Woman in Costume AP107

Battle Scene — AP106

1964, Nov. 24 **Unwmk.** ***Perf. 13½***
C416 AP105 5p multicolored .50 .20
C417 AP105 10p multicolored .50 .20
C418 AP106 40p sl blue & blk 1.00 .30
C419 AP106 70p dp claret & blk 2.00 .50
Nos. C416-C419 (4) 4.00 1.20

21st anniversary of independence.

1965, Jan. 11 **Litho.** ***Perf. 13½***

Design: 10p, 15p, Man in costume.

C420 AP107 10p multicolored .70 .20
C421 AP107 15p multicolored .90 .20
C422 AP107 25p green & multi 1.25 .35
C423 AP107 40p brown & multi 1.50 .50
Nos. C420-C423 (4) 4.35 1.25

International Festival at Baalbek.

Equestrian AP108

1965, Jan. 23 **Engr.** ***Perf. 13***
C424 AP108 15p shown .50 .20
C425 AP108 25p Target shooting, vert. .60 .20
C426 AP108 40p Gymnast on rings .75 .20
a. Souvenir sheet of 3, #C424-C426, imperf. 18.00 9.25
Nos. C424-C426 (3) 1.85 .60

18th Olympic Games, Tokyo, Oct. 10-25, 1964. No. 426a sold for 100p.

Heliconius Cybria AP109

30p, Pericallia matronula. 40p, Red admiral. 45p, Satyrus semele. 70p, Machaon. 85p, Aurore. 100p, Morpho cypris. 200p, Erasmia sanguiflua. 300p, Papilio crassus. 500p, Charaxes ameliae.

1965 Unwmk. *Perf. 13*
Size: 36x22mm

C427 AP109 30p multicolored 2.10 .20
C428 AP109 35p multicolored 2.40 .20
C429 AP109 40p multicolored 2.75 .20
C430 AP109 45p multicolored 3.50 .20
C431 AP109 70p multicolored 4.75 .35
C432 AP109 85p multicolored 6.25 .35
C433 AP109 100p multicolored 7.50 .35
C434 AP109 200p multicolored 12.50 .60
C435 AP109 300p multicolored 17.50 1.10

Engr. and Litho.
Perf. 12
Size: 35x25mm

C436 AP109 500p lt ultra & blk 45.00 2.75
Nos. C427-C436 (10) 104.25 6.30

For surcharges see Nos. C654-C656.

Pope Paul VI and Pres. Chehab — AP110

1965, June 28 Photo. *Perf. 12*
C437 AP110 45p gold & brt vio 5.25 1.00
a. Souv. sheet of 1, imperf. 52.50 32.50

Visit of Pope Paul VI to Lebanon. No. C437a sold for 50p.

Cedars of Friendship AP111

1965, Oct. 16 Photo. *Perf. 13x12½*
C438 AP111 40p multicolored 1.50 .20

Cocoon, Spindle and Silk — AP112

15p, 30p, 40p, 50p, Silk weaver at loom.

1965, Oct. 16 *Perf. 12½x13*
Design in Buff and Bright Green

C439 AP112 2.50p brown 1.25 .20
C440 AP112 5p dk olive grn 1.25 .20
C441 AP112 7.50p Prus blue 1.25 .20
C442 AP112 15p deep ultra 1.25 .20
C443 AP112 30p deep claret 1.50 .20
C444 AP112 40p brown 2.40 .20
C445 AP112 50p rose brown 3.50 .60
Nos. C439-C445 (7) 12.40 1.80

Parliament Building AP113

1965, Oct. 26 *Perf. 13x12½*
C446 AP113 35p red, buff & brn .80 .20
C447 AP113 40p emer, buff & brn 1.00 .20

Centenary of the Lebanese parliament.

UN Headquarters, NYC, UN Emblem and Lebanese Flags — AP114

1965, Nov. 10 Engr. *Perf. 12*
C448 AP114 2.50p dull blue .50 .20
C449 AP114 10p magenta .50 .20
C450 AP114 17.50p dull violet .50 .20
C451 AP114 30p green .60 .20
C452 AP114 40p brown .85 .20
Nos. C448-C452 (5) 2.95 1.00

UN, 20th anniv. A souvenir sheet contains one 40p imperf. stamp in bright rose lilac. Sold for 50p. Value $15.

Playing Card King, Laurel and Cedar AP115

Dagger in Map of Palestine AP116

1965, Nov. 15 Photo. *Perf. 12½x13*
C453 AP115 2.50p multicolored .70 .20
C454 AP115 15p multicolored 1.10 .20
C455 AP115 17.50p multicolored 1.25 .20
C456 AP115 40p multicolored 1.40 .20
Nos. C453-C456 (4) 4.45 .80

Intl. Bridge Championships. A souvenir sheet contains two imperf. stamps similar to Nos. C454 and C456. Sold for 75p. Value $22.50.

1965, Dec. 12 *Perf. 12½x11*
C457 AP116 50p multicolored 4.50 .55

Deir Yassin massacre, Apr. 9, 1948.

ITU Emblem, Old and New Communication Equipment and Syncom Satellite — AP117

1966, Apr. 13 *Perf. 13x12½*
C458 AP117 2.50p multi .50 .20
C459 AP117 15p multi .55 .20
C460 AP117 17.50p multi .60 .20
C461 AP117 25p multi 1.00 .20
C462 AP117 40p multi 1.25 .20
Nos. C458-C462 (5) 3.90 1.00

ITU, centenary (in 1965).

Folk Dancers Before Temple of Bacchus — AP118

Designs: 7.50p, 15p, Dancers before Temple of Jupiter, vert. 30p, 40p, Orchestra before Temple of Bacchus.

1966, July 20 Unwmk. *Perf. 12*
Gold Frame

C463 AP118 2.50p brn vio, bl & orange .50 .20
C464 AP118 5p mag, bl & org .50 .20
C465 AP118 7.50p vio bl, bl & pink .50 .20
C466 AP118 15p pur, bl & pink .60 .20
C467 AP118 30p dk grn, org & blue .65 .20
C468 AP118 40p vio, org & bl 1.10 .20
Nos. C463-C468 (6) 3.85 1.20

11th International Festival at Baalbek.

Opening of WHO Headquarters, Geneva — AP119

1966, Aug. 25 Engr. *Perf. 12*
C469 AP119 7.50p dp yel grn .50 .20
C470 AP119 17.50p car rose .60 .20
C471 AP119 25p blue 1.00 .20
Nos. C469-C471 (3) 2.10 .60

Skier AP120

Designs: 5p, Children on toboggan. 17.50p, Cedar in snow. 25p, Ski lift.

1966, Sept. 15 Photo. *Perf. 12x11½*
C472 AP120 2.50p multi .50 .20
C473 AP120 5p multi .50 .20
C474 AP120 17.50p multi .75 .20
C475 AP120 25p multi 1.00 .20
Nos. C472-C475 (4) 2.75 .80

International Festival of Cedars.

Sarcophagus of King Ahiram with Early Alphabet — AP121

15p, Phoenician ship. 20p, Map of the Mediterranean Sea showing Phoenician travel routes, and ship. 30p, Phoenician with alphabet tablet.

Litho. & Engr.
1966, Sept. 25 *Perf. 12*
C476 AP121 10p dl grn, blk & lt brn .50 .20
C477 AP121 15p rose lil, brn & ocher .50 .20
C478 AP121 20p tan, dk brn & bl .60 .20
C479 AP121 30p org, dk brn & yel 1.00 .20
Nos. C476-C479 (4) 2.60 .80

Invention of alphabet by Phoenicians.

Child in Bathtub and UNICEF Emblem AP122

5p, Boy in rowboat. 7.50p, Girl skier. 12p, Girl feeding bird. 20p, Boy doing homework. 50p, Children of various races, horiz.

1966, Oct. 10 Photo. *Perf. 11½x12*
C480 AP122 2.50p multi .50 .20
C481 AP122 5p multi .50 .20
C482 AP122 7.50p multi .60 .20
C483 AP122 15p multi .75 .20
C484 AP122 20p multi 1.00 .20
Nos. C480-C484 (5) 3.35 1.00

Miniature Sheet
Imperf

C485 AP122 50p dl yellow & multi 7.50 3.50

UNICEF; World Children's Day. No. C485 contains one horizontal stamp 43x33mm.

Scenic Type of Regular Issue, 1966

Designs: 10p, Waterfall, Djezzine. 15p, Castle of the Sea, Saida. 20p, Amphitheater, Jubayl (Byblos). 30p, Temple of the Sun, Baalbek. 50p, Beit-ed-Din Palace. 60p, Church of Christ the King, Nahr-el-Kalb. 75p, Abu Bakr Mosque, Tripoli.

1966, Oct. 12 *Perf. 12x11½*
C486 A82 10p gold & multi .50 .20
C487 A82 15p gold & multi .60 .20
C488 A82 20p gold & multi .75 .20
C489 A82 30p gold & multi 1.00 .20
C490 A82 50p gold & multi 1.75 .20
C491 A82 60p gold & multi 2.00 .20
C492 A82 75p gold & multi 3.00 .20
Nos. C486-C492 (7) 9.60 1.40

Symbolic Water Cycle — AP123

Daniel Bliss — AP124

15p, 20p, Different wave pattern without sun.

1966, Nov. 15 Photo. *Perf. 12½*
C493 AP123 5p red, bl & vio bl .50 .20
C494 AP123 10p org, bl & brn .50 .20
C495 AP123 15p org, emer & dk brn .60 .20
C496 AP123 20p org, emer & grnsh blue .75 .20
Nos. C493-C496 (4) 2.35 .80

Hydrological Decade (UNESCO), 1965-74.

1966, Dec. 3

Designs: 30p, Chapel, American University, Beirut. 50p, Daniel Bliss, D.D., and American University, horiz.

C497 AP124 20p grn, yel & brn .50 .20
C498 AP124 30p red brn, grn & blue .60 .20

Souvenir Sheet
Imperf

C499 AP124 50p grn, brn & org brown 2.50 1.00

Cent. of American University, Beirut, founded by the Rev. Daniel Bliss (1823-1916). Nos. C497-C498 are printed each with alternating labels showing University emblem.
No. C499 contains one stamp 59x37mm.

Flags of Arab League Members, Hand Signing Scroll — AP125

1967, Aug. 2 Photo. *Perf. 12x11½*

C500 AP125	5p brown & multi	.50	.20
C501 AP125	10p multicolored	.50	.20
C502 AP125	15p black & multi	.55	.20
C503 AP125	20p multicolored	.65	.20
Nos. C500-C503 (4)		2.20	.80

Signing of Arab League Pact in 1945.

Veteran's War Memorial Building, San Francisco — AP126

10p, 20p, 30p, Scroll, flags of Lebanon & UN.

1967, Sept. 1 Photo. *Perf. 12x11½*

C504 AP126	2.50p blue & multi	.50	.20
C505 AP126	5p multicolored	.50	.20
C506 AP126	7.50p multicolored	.50	.20
C507 AP126	10p blue & multi	.50	.20
C508 AP126	20p multicolored	.60	.20
C509 AP126	30p multicolored	.75	.20
Nos. C504-C509 (6)		3.35	1.20

San Francisco Pact (UN Charter), 22nd anniv.

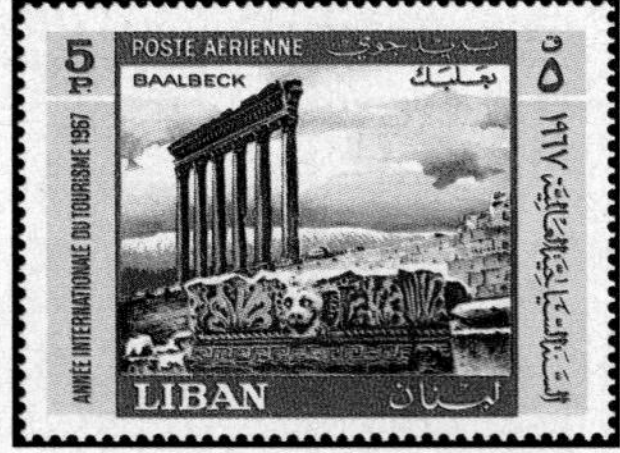

Ruins at Baalbek — AP127

Intl. Tourist Year: 10p, Ruins at Anjar. 15p, Bridge over Ibrahim River and ruins. 20p, Boat on underground lake, Jaita cave. 50p, St. George's Bay, Beirut.

1967, Sept. 25 *Perf. 12½*

C510 AP127	5p multicolored	.50	.20
C511 AP127	10p multicolored	.60	.20
C512 AP127	15p violet & multi	.80	.20
C513 AP127	20p brown & multi	.95	.20
Nos. C510-C513 (4)		2.85	.80

Souvenir Sheet

Imperf

C514 AP127 50p multicolored *27.50* *20.00*

View of Tabarja AP128

Views: 15p, Pigeon Rock and shore, Beirut. 17.50p, Beit-ed-Din Palace. 20p, Ship at Sidon. 25p, Tripoli. 30p, Beach at Byblos. 35p, Ruins, Tyre. 40p, Temple of Bacchus, Baalbek.

1967, Oct. *Perf. 12x11½*

C515 AP128	10p multi	*.50*	.20
C516 AP128	15p multi	*1.00*	.20
C517 AP128	17.50p multi	*1.50*	.20
C518 AP128	20p multi	*1.50*	.20
C519 AP128	25p multi	*1.50*	.20
C520 AP128	30p multi	*2.00*	.20
C521 AP128	35p multi	*2.50*	.20
C522 AP128	40p multi	*3.50*	.20
Nos. C515-C522 (8)		*14.00*	1.60

Intl. Tourist Year; used as a regular airmail issue.

India Day — AP129

1967, Oct. 30 Engr. *Perf. 12*

C523 AP129	2.50p orange	.50	.20
C524 AP129	5p magenta	.50	.20
C525 AP129	7.50p brown	.50	.20
C526 AP129	10p blue	.55	.20
C527 AP129	15p green	.60	.20
Nos. C523-C527 (5)		2.65	1.00

Globe and Arabic Inscription — AP130

Design: 10p, 20p, 30p, UN emblem.

1967, Nov. 25 Engr. *Perf. 12*

C528 AP130	2.50p rose	.50	.20
C529 AP130	5p gray blue	.50	.20
C530 AP130	7.50p green	.50	.20
C531 AP130	10p brt carmine	.50	.20
C532 AP130	20p violet blue	.60	.20
C533 AP130	30p dark green	.80	.20
Nos. C528-C533 (6)		3.40	1.20

Lebanon's admission to the UN. A 100p rose red souvenir sheet in the globe design exists. Value $6.25.

Basking Shark AP131

Fish: 30p, Needlefish. 40p, Pollack. 50p, Cuckoo wrasse. 70p, Red mullet. 100p, Rainbow trout.

1968, Feb. Photo. *Perf. 12x11½*

C534 AP131	20p multi	1.90	.20
C535 AP131	30p multi	1.90	.20
C536 AP131	40p multi	2.75	.20
C537 AP131	50p multi	4.00	.20
C538 AP131	70p multi	7.00	.20
C539 AP131	100p multi	9.00	.20
Nos. C534-C539 (6)		26.55	1.20

Ski Jump — AP132

5p, 7.50p, 10p, Downhill skiers (various). 25p, Congress emblem (skis and cedar).

1968 *Perf. 12½x11½*

C540 AP132	2.50p multicolored	.50	.20
C541 AP132	5p multicolored	.50	.20
C542 AP132	7.50p multicolored	.50	.20
C543 AP132	10p multicolored	.50	.20
C544 AP132	25p multicolored	.75	.20
Nos. C540-C544 (5)		2.75	1.00

26th Intl. Ski Congress, Beirut. A 50p imperf. souvenir sheet exists in design of the 25p. Value $7.25.

Emir Fakhr al-Din II — AP133

2.50p, Emira Khaskiah. 10p, Citadel of Sidon, horiz. 15p, Citadel of Chekif & grazing sheep, horiz. 17.50p, Citadel of Beirut & harbor, horiz.

Perf. 11½x12, 12x11½

1968, Feb. 20 Litho.

C546 AP133	2.50p multicolored	.50	.20
C547 AP133	5p multicolored	.50	.20
C548 AP133	10p multicolored	.50	.20
C549 AP133	15p multicolored	.75	.20
C550 AP133	17.50p multicolored	.75	.20
Nos. C546-C550 (5)		3.00	1.00

In memory of the Emir Fakhr al-Din II. A 50p imperf. souvenir sheet exists showing the Battle of Anjar. Value $11.50.

Roman Bust AP134

Ruins of Tyre: 5p, Colonnade, horiz. 7.50p, Arch, horiz. 10p, Banquet, bas-relief.

Litho. & Engr.

1968, Mar. 20 *Perf. 12*

C552 AP134	2.50p pink, brn & buff	.50	.20
C553 AP134	5p yel, brn & lt bl	.60	.20
C554 AP134	7.50p lt grnsh bl, brn & yel	.80	.20
C555 AP134	10p sal, brn & lt bl	.95	.20
a.	Souvenir sheet	22.50	17.50
Nos. C552-C555 (4)		2.85	.80

No. C555a contains one dark brown and light blue stamp, perf. 10½x11½. Sold for 50p. Exists imperf. Value $22.50.

For surcharge see No. C657.

Emperor Justinian AP135

Design: 15p, 20p, Justinian and map of the Mediterranean, horiz.

Perf. 11½x12, 12x11½

1968, May 10 Photo.

C556 AP135	5p blue & multi	.50	.20
C557 AP135	10p blue & multi	.50	.20
C558 AP135	15p red & multi	.55	.20
C559 AP135	20p blue & multi	.60	.20
Nos. C556-C559 (4)		2.15	.80

Beirut, site of one of the greatest law schools in antiquity; Emperor Justinian (483-565), who compiled and preserved the Roman law.

Arab League Emblem AP136

1968, June 6 Photo. *Perf. 12x11½*

C560 AP136	5p orange & multi	.50	.20
C561 AP136	10p multicolored	.50	.20
C562 AP136	15p pink & multi	.60	.20
C563 AP136	20p multicolored	.75	.20
Nos. C560-C563 (4)		2.35	.80

Issued for Arab League Week.

Cedar and Globe Emblem — AP137

1968, July 10

C564 AP137	2.50p sal pink, brn & green	.50	.20
C565 AP137	5p gray, brn & grn	.55	.20
C566 AP137	7.50p brt bl, brn & grn	.60	.20
C567 AP137	10p yel grn, brn & green	.75	.20
Nos. C564-C567 (4)		2.40	.80

3rd Congress of Lebanese World Union.

Temple of Jupiter, Baalbek AP138

Designs: 10p, Fluted pilasters, cella of Bacchus Temple. 15p, Corniche, south peristyle of Jupiter Temple, horiz. 20p, Gate, Bacchus Temple. 25p, Ceiling detail, south peristyle of Bacchus Temple.

1968, Sept. 25 Photo. *Perf. 12½*

C568 AP138	5p gold & multi	.50	.20
C569 AP138	10p gold & multi	.50	.20
C570 AP138	15p gold & multi	.60	.20
C571 AP138	20p gold & multi	.75	.20
C572 AP138	25p gold & multi	1.00	.20
Nos. C568-C572 (5)		3.35	1.00

13th Baalbek International Festival.

Broad Jump and Phoenician Statue — AP139

Designs: 10p, High jump and votive stele, Phoenician, 6th century B.C. 15p, Fencing and Olmec jade head, 500-400 B.C. 20p, Weight lifting and axe in shape of human head, Vera Cruz region. 25p, Aztec stone calendar and Phoenician ship.

1968, Oct. 19 Photo. *Perf. 12x11½*

C573 AP139 5p lt ultra, yel & gray .50 .20
C574 AP139 10p mag, lt ultra & blk .50 .20
C575 AP139 15p cit, ocher & brn .50 .20
C576 AP139 20p dp org, brn & ocher .60 .20
C577 AP139 25p light brown 1.00 .20
Nos. C573-C577 (5) 3.10 1.00

19th Olympic Games, Mexico City, 10/12-27.

Human Rights Flame and Tractor AP140

Human Rights Flame and: 15p, People. 25p, Boys of 3 races placing hands on globe.

1968, Dec. 10 Litho. *Perf. 11½*

C578 AP140 10p multicolored .50 .20
C579 AP140 15p yellow & multi .60 .20
C580 AP140 25p lilac & multi 1.00 .20
Nos. C578-C580 (3) 2.10 .60

International Human Rights Year.

Minshiya Stairs, Deir El-Kamar AP141

Views in Deir El-Kamar: 15p, The Seraglio Kiosk. 25p, Old paved city road.

1968, Dec. 26

C581 AP141 10p multicolored .50 .20
C582 AP141 15p multicolored .60 .20
C583 AP141 25p multicolored .80 .20
Nos. C581-C583 (3) 1.90 .60

1st Municipal Council in Lebanon, established in Deir El-Kamar by Daoud Pasha, cent.

Nurse Treating Child, and UN Emblem — AP142

Designs: 10p, Grain, fish, grapes and jug. 15p, Mother and children. 20p, Reading girl and Phoenician alphabet. 25p, Playing children.

1969, Jan. 20 Litho. *Perf. 12*

C584 AP142 5p blk, lt bl & sepia .50 .20
C585 AP142 10p blk, brt yel & grn .50 .20
C586 AP142 15p blk, red lil & ver .50 .20
C587 AP142 20p blk, citron & bl .50 .20
C588 AP142 25p blk, pink & bis brn .70 .20
Nos. C584-C588 (5) 2.70 1.00

UNICEF, 22nd anniversary.

Silver Coin from Byblos, 5th Century B.C. — AP143

National Museum, Beirut: 5p, Gold dagger, Byblos, 18th cent. B.C. 7.50p, King Dining in the Land of the Dead, sarcophagus of Ahiram, 13-12th cent. B.C. 30p, Breastplate with cartouche of Amenemhat III (1849-1801 B.C.). 40p, Phoenician bird vase from Khalde, 8th cent. B.C.

Photogravure; Gold Impressed

1969, Feb. 20 *Perf. 12*

C589 AP143 2.50p grn, yel & lt bl .50 .20
C590 AP143 5p vio, brn & yel .60 .20
C591 AP143 7.50p dl yel, brn & pink .80 .20
C592 AP143 30p blue & multi 1.00 .20
C593 AP143 40p multicolored 1.10 .20
Nos. C589-C593 (5) 4.00 1.00

Intl. Congress of Museum Councils; 20th anniv. of the Intl. Council of Museums.

Water Skier AP144

Designs: 5p, Water ballet. 7.50p, Parachutist, vert. 30p, Yachting, vert. 40p, Regatta.

1969, Mar. 3 Litho. *Perf. 11½*

C594 AP144 2.50p multicolored .50 .20
C595 AP144 5p multicolored .50 .20
C596 AP144 7.50p multicolored .50 .20
C597 AP144 30p multicolored 1.00 .20
C598 AP144 40p multicolored 1.25 .25
Nos. C594-C598 (5) 3.75 1.05

Tomb of Unknown Soldier at Military School — AP145

2.50p, Frontier guard. 7.50p, Soldiers doing forestry work. 15p, Army engineers building road. 30p, Ambulance and helicopter. 40p, Ski patrol.

1969, Aug. 1 Litho. *Perf. 12x11½*

C599 AP145 2.50p multicolored .50 .20
C600 AP145 5p multicolored .50 .20
C601 AP145 7.50p multicolored .50 .20
C602 AP145 15p multicolored .50 .20
C603 AP145 30p multicolored .60 .20
C604 AP145 40p multicolored .75 .20
Nos. C599-C604 (6) 3.35 1.20

25th anniversary of independence.

Crosses and Circles AP146

1971, Jan. 6 Photo. *Perf. 11½x12*

C605 AP146 15p shown .50 .20
C606 AP146 85p Crosses, cedar 1.75 .45

Lebanese Red Cross, 25th anniversary.

Foil Fencing AP147

10p, Flags of participating Arab countries. 15p, Flags of participating non-Arab countries. 40p, Sword fencing. 50p, Saber fencing.

1971, Jan. 15 Litho. *Perf. 12*

C607 AP147 10p yellow & multi .50 .20
C608 AP147 15p yellow & multi .50 .20
C609 AP147 35p yellow & multi .60 .20
C610 AP147 40p yellow & multi .80 .20
C611 AP147 50p yellow & multi .95 .20
Nos. C607-C611 (5) 3.35 1.00

10th World Fencing Championships, held in Lebanon.

Agricultural Workers, Arab Painting, 12th Century — AP148

1971, Feb. 1

C612 AP148 10p silver & multi 1.00 .20
C613 AP148 40p gold & multi 1.75 .20

International Labor Organization.

UPU Building and Monument, Bern — AP149

1971, Feb. 15 Litho. *Perf. 12*

C614 AP149 15p yel, blk & dp org 1.00 .20
C615 AP149 35p dp org, yel & blk 1.75 .35

Opening of new UPU Headquarters in Bern, Switzerland.

Ravens Burning Owls — AP150

Children's Day: 85p, Jackal and lion. Designs of the 15p and 85p are after 13th-14th century paintings, illustrations for the "Kalila wa Dumna."

1971, Mar. 1 Photo. *Perf. 11*

Size: 30x30mm

C616 AP150 15p gold & multi .20 .20

Perf. 12x11½

Size: 38½x29mm

C617 AP150 85p gold & multi 2.75 .70

Map and Flag of Arab League AP151

1971, Mar. 20 *Perf. 12x11½*

C618 AP151 30p orange & multi .55 .20
C619 AP151 70p yellow & multi 1.25 .35

Arab League, 25th anniv.

Bechara el Khoury AP152

Famous Lebanese Men: No. C620, Symbolic design for Imam al Ouzai. No. C622, Hassan Kamel al Sabbah. No. C623, Kahlil Gibran.

1971, Apr. 10

C620 AP152 25p lt grn, gold & brn .25 .20
C621 AP152 25p yel, gold & brn .40 .20
C622 AP152 25p yel, gold & brn .40 .20
C623 AP152 25p lt grn, gold & brn .40 .20
Nos. C620-C623 (4) 1.45 .80

Education Year Emblem, Computer Card — AP153

1971, Apr. 30 Photo. *Perf. 11½x12*

C624 AP153 10p blk, vio & bl .35 .20
C625 AP153 40p blk, org & yel .70 .20

Intl. Education Year.

Maameltein Bridge — AP154

5p, Jamhour Substation. 15p, Hotel Management School. 20p, Litani Dam. 25p, Television set wiring. 35p, Temple of Bziza. 40p, Jounieh Port. 45p, Airport radar. 50p, Flower. 70p, New School of Sciences. 85p, Oranges. 100p, Arbanieh earth satellite station.

1971, May Litho. *Perf. 12*

C626 AP154 5p multicolored *.20* .20
C627 AP154 10p multicolored *.20* .20
C628 AP154 15p multicolored *.45* .20
C629 AP154 20p multicolored *.85* .20
C630 AP154 25p multicolored *1.25* .20
C631 AP154 35p multicolored *1.60* .20
C632 AP154 40p multicolored *1.60* .20
C633 AP154 45p multicolored *1.75* .20
C634 AP154 50p multicolored *2.75* .20
C635 AP154 70p multicolored *4.00* .20
C636 AP154 85p multicolored *5.50* .20
C637 AP154 100p multicolored *7.00* .40
Nos. C626-C637 (12) *27.15* 2.60

For overprints and surcharges see Nos. C771, C775, C779, 533.

Dahr-el-Bacheq Sanatorium AP155

1971, June 1
C638 AP155 50p shown 1.25 .20
C639 AP155 100p multi, diff. 1.75 .60

Campaign against tuberculosis.

Solar Wheel (Festival Emblem) AP156

1971, July 1 Photo. *Perf. 11*
C640 AP156 15p ultra & org .20 .20
C641 AP156 85p Corinthian capital 1.25 .35

16th Baalbek International Festival.

Mirage fighters flying over Baalbek ruins AP157

Army Day: 15p, 155mm Cannon. 40p, Army Headquarters. 70p, Naval patrol boat.

1971, Aug. 1 *Perf. 12x11½*
C642 AP157 15p gold & multi *3.25* .20
C643 AP157 25p gold & multi *5.75* .20
C644 AP157 40p gold & multi *7.75* .20
C645 AP157 70p gold & multi *13.00* .25
Nos. C642-C645 (4) *29.75* .85

Wooden Console, Al Aqsa Mosque AP158

1971, Aug. 21 *Perf. 12*
C646 AP158 15p dk brn & ocher .75 .20
C647 AP158 35p dk brn & ocher 1.25 .20

2nd anniversary of the burning of Al Aqsa Mosque in Jerusalem.

Lenin (1870-1924) — AP159

1971, Oct. 1 *Perf. 12x11½*
C648 AP159 30p gold & multi .60 .20
C649 AP159 70p multicolored 1.40 .30

UN Emblem, World Map AP160

1971, Oct. 24 *Perf. 13x12½*
C650 AP160 15p multicolored .35 .20
C651 AP160 85p multicolored 1.25 .35

UN, 25th anniv. (in 1970).

The Rape of Europa, Mosaic from Byblos AP161

1971, Nov 20 Litho. *Perf. 12*
C652 AP161 10p slate & multi *.50* .20
C653 AP161 40p gold & multi *2.50* .20

Publicity for World Lebanese Union (ULM).

Nos. C435-C436 Surcharged

Engr.; Engr. & Litho.
1972, May *Perf. 13, 12*
C654 AP109 100p on 300p *20.00* .40
C655 AP109 100p on 500p *20.00* .40
C656 AP109 200p on 300p *35.00* .80
Nos. C654-C656 (3) *75.00* 1.60

The numerals on No. C655 are taller (5mm) and bars spaced 1½mm apart.

No. C554 Surcharged

(Reduced)

1972, June Litho. & Engr. *Perf. 12*
C657 AP134 5p on 7.50p multi *3.00* .20

Hibiscus — AP162

Lebanese House AP163

1973 Litho. *Perf. 12*
C658 AP162 2.50p shown *.20* .20
C659 AP162 5p Roses *.20* .20
C660 AP162 15p Tulips *.35* .20
C661 AP162 25p Lilies *1.00* .20
C662 AP162 40p Carnations *1.10* .20
C663 AP162 50p Iris *1.60* .20
C664 AP162 70p Apples *1.25* .20
C665 AP162 75p Grapes *1.40* .20
C666 AP162 100p Peaches *1.90* .35
C667 AP162 200p Pears *6.75* .25
C668 AP162 300p Cherries *7.25* .55
C669 AP162 500p Oranges *12.00* .90
Nos. C658-C669 (12) *35.00* 3.65

For overprints see #C758-C759, C763, C766, C769, C772, C776, C778, C782, C785-C787.

1973 *Perf. 14*

Designs: Old Lebanese houses.

C670 AP163 35p yel & multi *2.50* .20
C671 AP163 50p lt bl & multi *3.50* .20
C672 AP163 85p buff & multi *5.75* .30
C673 AP163 100p multicolored *7.75* .40
Nos. C670-C673 (4) *19.50* 1.10

For overprints see #C768, C773, C780, C783.

Woman with Rose — AP164

Lebanese Costumes: 10p, Man. 20p, Man on horseback. 25p, Woman playing mandolin.

1973, Sept. 1 Litho. *Perf. 14*
C674 AP164 5p yellow & multi *1.25* .20
C675 AP164 10p yellow & multi *3.75* .20
C676 AP164 20p yellow & multi *5.75* .20
C677 AP164 25p yellow & multi *8.25* .20
Nos. C674-C677 (4) *19.00* .80

For overprints see Nos. C760-C761, C764, C767.

Swimming, Temple at Baalbek — AP165

Designs: 10p, Running and portal. 15p, Woman athlete and castle. 20p, Women's volleyball and columns. 25p, Basketball and aqueduct. 50p, Women's table tennis and buildings. 75p, Handball and building. 100p, Soccer and cedar.

1973, Sept. 25 Photo. *Perf. 11½x12*
C678 AP165 5p multicolored .20 .20
C679 AP165 10p multicolored .20 .20
C680 AP165 15p grn & multi .35 .20
C681 AP165 20p multicolored .35 .20
C682 AP165 25p ultra & multi .50 .20
C683 AP165 50p org & multi 1.25 .30
C684 AP165 75p vio & multi 1.50 .40
C685 AP165 100p multicolored 2.75 .80
a. Souvenir sheet 3.75 1.75
Nos. C678-C685 (8) 7.10 2.50

5th Pan-Arabic Scholastic Games, Beirut. No. C685a contains one stamp with simulated perforations similar to No. C685; gold inscription and denomination.

View of Brasilia — AP166

20p, Old Salvador (Bahia). 25p, Lebanese sailing ship enroute from the Old World to South America. 50p, Dom Pedro I & Emir Fakhr al-Din II.

1973, Nov. 15 Litho. *Perf. 12*
C686 AP166 5p gold & multi .40 .20
C687 AP166 20p gold & multi 2.25 .35
C688 AP166 25p gold & multi 2.25 .35
C689 AP166 50p gold & multi 4.75 .65
Nos. C686-C689 (4) 9.65 1.55

Sesquicentennial of Brazil's independence.

Inlay Worker AP167

1973, Dec. 1
C690 AP167 10p shown *.80* .20
C691 AP167 20p Weaver *1.25* .25
C692 AP167 35p Glass blower *2.00* .35
C693 AP167 40p Potter *2.75* .50
C694 AP167 50p Metal worker *3.00* .50
C695 AP167 70p Cutlery maker *5.00* .65
C696 AP167 85p Lace maker *7.00* 1.00
C697 AP167 100p Handicraft Museum *8.00* 1.40
Nos. C690-C697 (8) *29.80* 4.85

Lebanese handicrafts.

For overprints see Nos. C762, C765, C770, C774, C777, C781, C784.

Camp Site, Log Fire and Scout Emblem — AP168

Designs: 5p, Lebanese Scout emblem and map. 7½p, Lebanese Scout emblem and map of Middle East. 10p, Lord Baden-Powell, ruins of Baalbek. 15p, Girl Guide, camp and emblem. 20p, Lebanese Girl Guide and Scout emblems. 25p, Scouts around camp fire. 30p, Symbolic globe with Lebanese flag and Scout emblem. 35p, Flags of participating nations. 50p, Old man, and Scout chopping wood.

1974, Aug. 24 Litho. *Perf. 12*
C698 AP168 2.50p multi *.75* .25
C699 AP168 5p multi *.75* .25
C700 AP168 7.50p multi *1.40* .25
C701 AP168 10p multi *1.40* .25
C702 AP168 15p multi *1.75* .55
a. Vert. strip of 5, #C698-C702 *7.00*
C703 AP168 20p multi *2.50* .65
C704 AP168 25p multi *3.50* .65
C705 AP168 30p multi *4.75* .65
C706 AP168 35p multi *5.75* .90
C707 AP168 50p multi *7.00* 1.40
a. Vert. strip of 5, #C703-C707 *25.00*
Nos. C698-C707 (10) *29.55* 5.80

11th Arab Boy Scout Jamboree, Smar-Jubeil, Aug. 1974. Nos. C702-C703 are for the 5th Girl Guide Jamboree, Deir-el-Kamar.

Mail Train and Postman Loading Mail, UPU Emblem — AP169

UPU Emblem and: 20p, Postal container hoisted onto ship. 25p, Postal Union Congress Building, Lausanne, and UPU Headquarters, Bern. 50p, Fork-lift truck loading mail on plane.

1974, Nov. 4 Photo. *Perf. 11½x12*
C708 AP169 5p multicolored *.45* .20
C709 AP169 20p multicolored *2.00* .25
C710 AP169 25p multicolored *3.00* .25
C711 AP169 50p ultra & multi *6.25* .70
Nos. C708-C711 (4) *11.70* 1.40

Centenary of Universal Postal Union.

Congress Building, Sofar — AP170

Arab Postal Union Emblem and: 20p, View of Sofar. 25p, APU Headquarters, Cairo. 50p, Ministry of Post, Beirut.

1974, Dec. 4 Litho. *Perf. 13x12½*
C712 AP170 5p orange & multi *.35* .20
C713 AP170 20p yellow & multi *.60* .20
C714 AP170 25p blue & multi *.90* .25
C715 AP170 50p multicolored *4.25* 1.00
Nos. C712-C715 (4) *6.10* 1.65

Arab Postal Union, 25th anniversary.

Mountain Road, by Omar Onsi — AP171

Paintings by Lebanese artists: No. C717, Clouds, by Moustapha Farroukh. No. C718, Woman, by Gebran Kahlil Gebran. No. C719, Embrace, by Cesar Gemayel. No. C720, Self-portrait, by Habib Serour. No. C721, Portrait of a Man, by Daoud Corm.

1974, Dec. 6 Litho. *Perf. 13x12½*

C716 AP171 50p lilac & multi *2.00* .50
C717 AP171 50p blue & multi *2.00* .50
C718 AP171 50p green & multi *2.00* .50
C719 AP171 50p lt vio & multi *2.00* .50
C720 AP171 50p brown & multi *2.00* .50
C721 AP171 50p gray brn & multi 2.00 .50
Nos. C716-C721 (6) 12.00 3.00

Hunter Spearing Lion — AP172

Excavations at Hermel: 10p, Statue of Astarte. 25p, Dogs hunting boar, tiled panel. 35p, Greco-Roman tomb.

1974, Dec. 13

C722 AP172 5p blue & multi *.40* .20
C723 AP172 10p lilac & multi *.90* .20
C724 AP172 25p multicolored *2.25* .20
C725 AP172 35p multicolored *2.75* .40
Nos. C722-C725 (4) *6.30* 1.00

UNESCO Emblems and Globe AP173

1974, Dec. 16 *Perf. 12½x13*

C726 AP173 5p violet & multi .40 .20
C727 AP173 10p bister & multi .85 .20
C728 AP173 25p blue & multi 2.00 .30
C729 AP173 35p multicolored 2.50 .40
Nos. C726-C729 (4) 5.75 1.10

International Book Year.

Symbolic Stamp under Magnifying Glass — AP174

Designs (Symbolic): 10p, Post horns. 15p, Stamp printing. 20p, Mounted stamp.

1974, Dec. 20 *Perf. 13x12½*

C730 AP174 5p blue & multi .20 .20
C731 AP174 10p olive & multi .40 .20
C732 AP174 15p brown & multi .80 .20
C733 AP174 20p lilac & multi 1.00 .20
Nos. C730-C733 (4) 2.40 .80

Georgina Rizk — AP175

5p, 25p, Georgina Rizk in Lebanese costume.

1974, Dec. 21

C734 AP175 5p multicolored .20 .20
C735 AP175 20p violet & multi .55 .20
C736 AP175 25p yellow & multi .75 .20
C737 AP175 50p blue & multi 1.50 .20
a. Souvenir sheet of 4 8.00 4.25
Nos. C734-C737 (4) 3.00 .80

Georgina Rizk, Miss Universe 1971. No. C737a contains 4 stamps similar to Nos. C734-C737 with simulated perforations.

UNICEF Emblem, Helicopter, Camel, Supplies — AP176

UNICEF Emblem and: 25p, Child welfare clinic. 35p, Kindergarten class. 70p, Girls in chemistry laboratory.

1974, Dec. 28 Litho. *Perf. 12½x13*

C738 AP176 20p multicolored .20 .20
C739 AP176 25p multicolored .20 .20
C740 AP176 35p blue & multi .75 .20
C741 AP176 70p blue & multi 1.75 .20
a. Souvenir sheet of 4 5.75 3.00
Nos. C738-C741 (4) 2.90 .80

UNICEF, 25th anniv. No. C741a contains 4 stamps similar to Nos. C738-C741 with simulated perforations. Sold for 200p.

Discus and Olympic Rings — AP177

1974, Dec. 30 *Perf. 13x12½*

C742 AP177 5p shown .20 .20
C743 AP177 10p Shot put .30 .20
C744 AP177 15p Weight lifting .40 .20
C745 AP177 35p Running .85 .25
C746 AP177 50p Wrestling 1.25 .25
C747 AP177 85p Javelin 2.00 .35
a. Souvenir sheet of 6 8.00 5.25
Nos. C742-C747 (6) 5.00 1.45

20th Olympic Games, Munich, Aug. 26-Sept. 11, 1972. No. C747a contains 6 stamps similar to Nos. C742-C747 with simulated perforations.

Clouds and Environment Emblem AP178

1975

C748 AP178 5p shown .20 .20
C749 AP178 25p Landscape .55 .20
C750 AP178 30p Flowers and tree .55 .20
C751 AP178 40p Waves .85 .20
a. Souvenir sheet of 4 7.00 4.75
Nos. C748-C751 (4) 2.15 .80

UN Conf. on Human Environment, Stockholm, June 5-16, 1972. No. C751a contains four stamps similar to Nos. C748-C751 with simulated perforations. Sold for 150p.

Archaeology — AP179

Symbols of: 25p, Science & medicine. 35p, Justice & commerce. 70p, Industry & commerce.

1975, Aug. Litho. *Perf. 12½x13*

C752 AP179 20p multicolored *.90* .20
C753 AP179 25p multicolored *1.25* .25
C754 AP179 35p blue & multi *1.75* .40
C755 AP179 70p buff & multi *4.00* .70
Nos. C752-C755 (4) *7.90* 1.55

Beirut, University City.

Stamps of 1971-73 Overprinted with Various Overall Patterns Including Cedars in Blue, Red, Orange, Lilac, Brown or Green

1978 Litho. *Perf. 12, 14*

C758 AP162 2.50p (#C658;B) .20 .20
C759 AP162 5p (#C659;R) .20 .20
C760 AP164 5p (#C674;B) .20 .20
C761 AP164 10p (#C675;B) .20 .20
C762 AP167 10p (#C690;O) .20 .20
C763 AP162 15p (#C660;R) 1.00 .20
C764 AP164 20p (#C676;B) .70 .20
C765 AP167 20p (#C691;B) .70 .20
C766 AP162 25p (#C661;L) .70 .20
C767 AP164 25p (#C677;B) 1.40 .20
C768 AP163 35p (#C670;Br) 1.60 .20
C769 AP162 40p (#C662;L) 1.60 .20
C770 AP167 40p (#C693;G) 1.60 .20
C771 AP154 45p (#C633;L) 1.60 .20
C772 AP162 50p (#C663;L) 2.50 .20
C773 AP163 50p (#C671;L) 2.50 .20
C774 AP167 50p (#C694;Br) 2.50 .20
C775 AP154 70p (#C635;L) 2.75 .55
C776 AP162 70p (#C664;L) 2.75 .55
C777 AP167 70p (#C695;B) 2.75 .55
C778 AP162 75p (#C665;B) 4.50 .55
C779 AP154 85p (#C636;R) 3.25 .60
C780 AP163 85p (#C672;B) 3.25 .60
C781 AP167 85p (#C696;G) 3.25 .60
C782 AP162 100p (#C666;O) 5.00 .80
C783 AP163 100p (#C673;B) 5.00 .80
C784 AP167 100p (#C697;L) 5.00 .80
C785 AP162 200p (#C667;O) 10.00 2.75
C786 AP162 300p (#C668;O) 14.50 5.25
C787 AP162 500p (#C669;O) 21.00 7.50
Nos. C758-C787 (30) 102.40 25.30

Heart and Arrow — AP180

1978, Apr. 7 Litho. *Perf. 12*

C788 AP180 50p blue, blk & red 1.00 .80

World Health Day; drive against hypertension.

Poet Mikhail Naimy and Sannine Mountains — AP181

Designs: 50p, Naimy and view of Al Chakhroub Baskinta. 75p, Naimy portrait in sunburst, vert.

1978, May 17

C789 AP181 25p gold & multi *.90* .25
C790 AP181 50p gold & multi *1.60* .55
C791 AP181 75p gold & multi *2.50* .80
Nos. C789-C791 (3) *5.00* 1.60

Mikhail Naimy Festival.

Army Day Type of 1980

Designs: 50p, Emir Fakhr al-Din statue, vert. 75p, Soldiers and flag.

1980, Dec. 28 Litho. *Perf. 11½*

C792 A86 50p multicolored *1.50* .25
C793 A86 75p multicolored *2.00* .40

28th UPU Congress, Rio de Janeiro, 1979 — AP182

1981, Feb. 17 Photo. *Perf. 12x11½*

C794 AP182 25p multicolored 1.10 .20
C795 AP182 50p multicolored 2.40 .70
C796 AP182 75p multicolored 3.50 1.00
Nos. C794-C796 (3) 7.00 1.90

Intl. Year of the Child (1979) AP183

1981, Mar. 25 Litho. *Perf. 12x11½*

C797 AP183 100p multicolored 4.50 1.40

1974 Chess Championships — AP184

Various chess pieces. #C799-C802 vert.

Perf. 12x11½, 11½x12

1980-81 Photo.

C798 AP184 50p multicolored 1.90 .65
C799 AP184 75p multicolored 2.25 .85
C800 AP184 100p multicolored 2.75 1.25
C801 AP184 150p multicolored 4.50 2.40
C802 AP184 200p multicolored 5.75 3.25
Nos. C798-C802 (5) 17.15 8.40

Makassed Islamic Institute Centenary (1978) AP185

1981 Photo. *Perf. 13½x14*

C803 AP185 50p Children 1.00 .20
C804 AP185 75p Institute 1.50 .20
C805 AP185 100p Makassed 1.75 .40
Nos. C803-C805 (3) 4.25 .80

AIR POST SEMI-POSTAL STAMPS

#C13-C16 Surcharged Like #B1-B12

1926 *Perf. 13½*

CB1 A2 2pi + 1pi dark brown 12.00 8.00
CB2 A2 3pi + 2pi orabge brown 12.00 8.00
CB3 A2 5pi + 3pi violet 12.00 8.00
CB4 A3 10pi + 5pi violet brown 12.00 8.00
Nos. CB1-CB4 (4) 48.00 32.00

These stamps were sold for their combined values, original and surcharged. The latter represented their postal franking value and the former was a contribution to the relief of refugees from the Djebel Druze War.

Catalogue values for unused stamps in this section, from this point to the end of the section, are for Never Hinged items.

Independent Republic

Natural Bridge, Faraya SPAP1

Bay of Jounie SPAP2

Perf. 11½

1947, June 27 Unwmk. Litho.

Cross in Carmine

CB5 SPAP1 12.50 + 25pi brt bl grn 11.00 3.75
CB6 SPAP1 25 + 50pi blue 13.00 4.50
CB7 SPAP2 50 + 100pi choc 15.00 5.25
CB8 SPAP2 75 + 150pi brt pur 30.00 10.00
CB9 SPAP2 100 + 200pi sl 50.00 14.00
Nos. CB5-CB9 (5) 119.00 37.50

The surtax was for the Red Cross.

Mother & Child Type of Air Post Stamps, 1960

1960, Aug. 16 ***Perf. 13½x13***

CB10 AP72 20p + 10p dk red & buff .80 .20
CB11 AP72 60p + 15p bl & lt bl 2.10 .60

Olympic Games Type of Semi-Postal Issue, 1961

1961, Jan. 12 Unwmk. ***Perf. 13***

CB12 SP1 15p + 15p Fencing 3.00 1.60
CB13 SP1 25p + 25p Bicycling 3.00 1.60
CB14 SP1 35p + 35p Swimming 3.00 1.60
Nos. CB12-CB14 (3) 9.00 4.80

An imperf. souvenir sheet exists, containing one each of Nos. CB12-CB14. Value $32.50.

Nos. CB12-CB14 with Arabic and French Overprint in Green, Red or Maroon and two Bars through Olympic Inscription: "CHAMPIONNAT D'EUROPE DE TIR, 2 JUIN 1962"

1962, June 2

CB15 SP1 15p + 15p (G) 1.25 .60
CB16 SP1 25p + 25p (M) 2.25 1.25
CB17 SP1 35p + 35p (R) 2.75 1.60
Nos. CB15-CB17 (3) 6.25 3.45

European Marksmanship Championships held in Lebanon.

POSTAGE DUE STAMPS

Postage Due Stamps of France, 1893-1920, Surcharged like Regular Issue

1924 Unwmk. ***Perf. 14x13½***

J1 D2 50c on 10c choc 6.50 4.00
J2 D2 1p on 20c ol grn 6.50 4.00
J3 D2 2p on 30c red 6.50 4.00
J4 D2 3p on 50c vio brn 6.50 4.00
J5 D2 5p on 1fr red brn, *straw* 7.50 3.00
Nos. J1-J5 (5) 33.50 19.00

Postage Due Stamps of France, 1893-1920, Surcharged

1924

J6 D2 50c on 10c choc 7.00 3.25
J7 D2 1p on 20c ol grn 7.00 3.25
J8 D2 2p on 30c red 7.00 3.25
J9 D2 3p on 50c vio brn 7.00 3.25
J10 D2 5p on 1fr red brn, *straw* 7.00 3.25
Nos. J6-J10 (5) 35.00 16.25

Ancient Bridge across Dog River — D3

Designs: 1p, Village scene. 2p, Pigeon Rocks, near Beirut. 3p, Belfort Castle. 5p, Venus Temple at Baalbek.

1925 Photo. ***Perf. 13½***

J11 D3 50c brown, *yellow* .90 .20
J12 D3 1p violet, *rose* 1.25 .35
J13 D3 2p black, *blue* 2.00 .60
J14 D3 3p black, *red org* 3.25 1.10
J15 D3 5p black, *bl grn* 5.50 2.10
Nos. J11-J15 (5) 12.90 4.35
Set, never hinged 42.50

Nos. J11 to J15 Overprinted

1927

J16 D3 50c brown, *yellow* 1.50 .20
J17 D3 1p violet, *rose* 2.50 .55
J18 D3 2p black, *blue* 3.25 .85
J19 D3 3p black, *red org* 7.00 2.50
J20 D3 5p black, *bl grn* 9.00 3.00
Nos. J16-J20 (5) 23.25 7.10
Set, never hinged 35.00

Nos. J16 to J20 with Additional Overprint

1928

J21 D3 50c brn, *yel* (Bk+R) 1.40 .70
J22 D3 1p vio, *rose* (Bk) 1.40 .70
J23 D3 2p blk, *bl* (Bk+R) 2.75 1.40
J24 D3 3p blk, *red org* (Bk) 5.50 2.75
J25 D3 5p blk, *bl grn* (Bk+R) 6.25 3.00
Nos. J21-J25 (5) 17.30 8.55
Set, never hinged 65.00

No. J23 has not the short bars in the upper corners.

Postage Due Stamps of 1925 Overprinted in Red like Nos. J21-J25

1928

J26 D3 50c brn, *yel* (R) .75 .20
J27 D3 2p blk, *bl* (R) 3.75 2.25
J28 D3 5p blk, *bl grn* (R) 10.50 6.00
Nos. J26-J28 (3) 15.00 8.45
Set, never hinged 32.50

No. J28 has not the short bars in the upper corners.

D4

Bas-relief of a Ship — D5

D6

D7

D8

Bas-relief from Sarcophagus of King Ahiram — D9

D10

1930-40 Photo.; Engr. (No. J35)

J29 D4 50c black, *rose* .55 .45
J30 D5 1p blk, *gray bl* 1.00 .70
J31 D6 2p blk, *yellow* 1.40 1.00
J32 D7 3p blk, *bl grn* 1.40 1.00
J33 D8 5p blk, *orange* 6.75 4.50
J34 D9 8p blk, *lt rose* 4.50 3.00
J35 D8 10p dk green ('40) 7.00 4.00
J36 D10 15p black 5.75 2.50
Nos. J29-J36 (8) 28.35 17.15
Set, never hinged 60.00

Nos. J29-J36 exist imperf.

Catalogue values for unused stamps in this section, from this point to the end of the section, are for Never Hinged items.

Independent Republic

National Museum, Beirut D11

1945 Unwmk. Litho. ***Perf. 11½***

J37 D11 2p brn black, *yel* 8.00 1.40
J38 D11 5p ultra, *rose* 8.75 1.60
J39 D11 25p blue, *bl green* 13.50 2.50
J40 D11 50p dark bl, *blue* 17.50 2.50
Nos. J37-J40 (4) 47.75 8.00

D12

1947

J41 D12 5p black, *green* 5.50 .75
J42 D12 25p blk, *yellow* 55.00 2.10
J43 D12 50p black, *blue* 27.50 4.50
Nos. J41-J43 (3) 88.00 7.35

Hermel Monument D13

1948

J44 D13 2p blk, *yellow* 4.25 3.75
J45 D13 3p black, *pink* 7.75 1.25
J46 D13 10p black, *blue* 20.00 2.40
Nos. J44-J46 (3) 32.00 7.40

D14

1950

J47 D14 1p carmine rose 3.25 .20
J48 D14 5p violet blue 12.00 .35
J49 D14 10p gray green 25.00 .65
Nos. J47-J49 (3) 40.25 1.20

D15

1952

J50 D15 1p dp rose lilac .60 .20
J51 D15 2p bright violet .60 .20
J52 D15 3p dk blue green 1.25 .20
J53 D15 5p blue 1.60 .20
J54 D15 10p chocolate 2.25 .20
J55 D15 25p black 18.00 .65
Nos. J50-J55 (6) 24.30 1.65

D16

D17

1953

J56 D16 1p carmine rose .20 .20
J57 D16 2p blue green .20 .20
J58 D16 3p orange .20 .20
J59 D16 5p lilac rose .40 .20
J60 D16 10p brown .75 .20
J61 D16 15p deep blue 1.40 .50
Nos. J56-J61 (6) 3.15 1.50

1955 Unwmk. ***Perf. 13***

J62 D17 1p orange brown .20 .20
J63 D17 2p yellow green .20 .20
J64 D17 3p blue green .20 .20
J65 D17 5p carmine lake .20 .20
J66 D17 10p gray green .40 .20
J67 D17 15p ultramarine .50 .20
J68 D17 25p red lilac 1.10 .30
Nos. J62-J68 (7) 2.80 1.50

Cedar of Lebanon D18

Emir Fakhr al-Din II D19

1966 Photo. ***Perf. 11½***

J69 D18 1p bright green .40 .20
J70 D18 5p rose lilac .40 .20
J71 D18 15p ultramarine .50 .20
Nos. J69-J71 (3) 1.30 .60

1968 Litho. ***Perf. 11***

J72 D19 1p dk & lt gray .50 .20
J73 D19 2p dk & lt blue grn .50 .20
J74 D19 3p deep org & yel .50 .20
J75 D19 5p brt rose lil & pink .50 .20
J76 D19 10p olive & lemon .50 .20
J77 D19 15p vio & pale violet .75 .20
J78 D19 25p brt & lt blue 1.00 .20
Nos. J72-J78 (7) 4.25 1.40

POSTAL TAX STAMPS

Fiscal Stamp Surcharged in Violet

Wmk. A T 39 Multiple

1945 ***Perf. 13½***

RA1 R1 5pi on 30c red brn 325.00 1.50

The tax was for the Lebanese Army.

No. RA1 Overprinted in Black

1948

RA2 R1 5pi on 30c red brn 16.50 1.40

Fiscal Stamps Surcharged in Various Colors

RA3 R1 5pi on 15pi dk vio bl (R) 14.00 1.60
 a. Brown surcharge 18.00 2.25
RA4 R1 5pi on 25c dk blue green (R) 14.00 1.60
RA5 R1 5pi on 30c red brn (Bl) 16.00 1.60
RA6 R1 5pi on 60c lt ultra (Br) 22.50 1.60
RA7 R1 5pi on 3pi salmon rose (Ult) 14.00 1.60

No RA4 exists with watermarks "AT37" or "AT38."

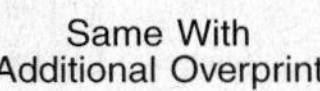

Same With Additional Overprint

RA8 R1 5pi on 10pi red *65.00* 5.00

Fiscal Stamp Surcharged Like Nos. RA3-RA7 with Top Arabic Characters Replaced by

RA9 R1 5pi on 3pi rose (Bk+V) 16.50 1.40

Fiscal Stamp Surcharged in Black and Violet

RA10 R1 5pi on 3pi sal rose *190.00* 15.00

The tax was to aid the war in Palestine.

Catalogue values for unused stamps in this section, from this point to the end of the section, are for Never Hinged items.

Family among Ruins — R2

Building a House — R3

1956 **Unwmk.** **Litho.** ***Perf. 13***

RA11 R2 2.50pi brown 4.00 .20

The tax was for earthquake victims. These stamps were obligatory on all inland mail and all mail going to Arab countries.

1957-58 ***Perf. 13½x13***

RA12 R3 2.50p brown 4.00 .20
RA13 R3 2.50p dk blue grn ('58) 2.25 .20

Type of 1957 Redrawn

1959

RA14 R3 2.50p light brown 2.50 .20

On No. RA14 the denomination is on top and the Arabic lines are at the bottom of design.

R4

Building a House — R5

1961 **Unwmk.** ***Perf. 13½x13***

RA15 R4 2.50p yellow brown 2.25 .20

1962 ***Perf. 13½x14***

RA16 R5 2.50p blue green 3.75 .20

The tax was for the relief of earthquake victims.

LEEWARD ISLANDS

'lē-wərd 'ī-ləndz

LOCATION — A group of islands in the West Indies, southeast of Puerto Rico
GOVT. — British Colony
AREA — 423 sq. mi.
POP. — 108,847 (1946)
CAPITAL — St. John

While stamps inscribed "Leeward Islands" were in use, 1890-1956, the colony consisted of the presidencies (now colonies) of Antigua, Montserrat, St. Christopher (St. Kitts) with Nevis and Anguilla, the British Virgin Islands and Dominica (which became a separate colony in 1940).

Each presidency issued its own stamps, using them along with the Leeward Islands general issues. The Leeward Islands federation was abolished in 1956.

12 Pence = 1 Shilling
20 Shillings = 1 Pound
100 Cents = 1 Dollar

Catalogue values for unused stamps in this country are for Never Hinged items, beginning with Scott 116.

Queen Victoria — A1

1890 **Typo.** **Wmk. 2** ***Perf. 14***

1 A1 ½p lilac & green 3.75 1.40
2 A1 1p lilac & car 5.00 .20
3 A1 2½p lilac & ultra 7.00 .30
4 A1 4p lilac & org 6.50 *9.50*
5 A1 6p lilac & brown 12.50 14.00
6 A1 7p lilac & slate 7.00 *13.00*
7 A1 1sh green & car 24.00 *52.50*
8 A1 5sh green & ultra 135.00 *275.00*
 Nos. 1-8 (8) 200.75 *365.90*

Denomination of Nos. 7-8 are in color on plain tablet: "ONE SHILLING" or "FIVE SHILLINGS."

For overprints and surcharges see Nos. 9-19.

Jubilee Issue

Regular Issue of 1890 Handstamp Overprinted

1897, July 22

9 A1 ½p lilac & green 5.50 *17.50*
10 A1 1p lilac & car 6.50 *17.50*
11 A1 2½p lilac & ultra 7.00 *17.50*
12 A1 4p lilac & org 47.50 *80.00*
13 A1 6p lilac & brown 55.00 *110.00*
14 A1 7p lilac & slate 55.00 *105.00*
15 A1 1sh green & car 130.00 *220.00*
16 A1 5sh green & ultra 525.00 *850.00*
 Nos. 9-16 (8) 831.50 *1,417.*

Double Overprints

9a A1 ½p *1,350.*
 b. Triple overprint *12,000.*
10a A1 1p *1,150.*
 b. Triple overprint *3,750.*
11a A1 2½p *1,350.*
12a A1 4p *1,350.*
13a A1 6p *1,600.*
14a A1 7p *1,600.*
15a A1 1sh *2,100.*
16a A1 5sh *5,750.*

60th year of Queen Victoria's reign.
Excellent counterfeits of Nos. 9-16 exist.

Stamps of 1890 Surcharged in Black or Red:

b

c

1902, Aug.

17 A1(b) 1p on 4p lilac & org 4.50 *6.50*
 a. Tall narrow "O" in "One" 40.00 *80.00*
18 A1(b) 1p on 6p lilac & brn 5.50 *12.50*
 a. Tall narrow "O" in "One" 60.00 *125.00*
19 A1(c) 1p on 7p lilac & sl 5.00 *9.25*
 Nos. 17-19 (3) 15.00 28.25

King Edward VII — A4

Numerals of ¼p, 2p, 3p and 2sh6p of type A4 are in color on plain tablet. The 1sh and 5sh denominations are expressed as "ONE SHILLING" and "FIVE SHILLINGS" on plain tablet.

1902

20 A4 ½p violet & green 6.00 1.10
21 A4 1p vio & car rose 7.50 .20
22 A4 2p violet & bister 3.00 *4.50*
23 A4 2½p violet & ultra 6.00 2.50
24 A4 3p violet & black 5.00 *8.00*
25 A4 6p violet & brown 2.75 *8.50*
26 A4 1sh grn & car rose 3.75 *20.00*
27 A4 2sh6p green & blk 29.00 *75.00*
28 A4 5sh green & ultra 50.00 *80.00*
 Nos. 20-28 (9) 113.00 *199.80*

1905-11 **Wmk. 3**

Chalky Paper (Ordinary Paper #29, 33)

29 A4 ½p vio & grn ('06) 3.75 2.25
 a. Chalky paper ('08) 22.00 13.50
30 A4 1p vio & car rose 9.00 .90
31 A4 2p vio & bis ('08) 5.25 *15.00*
32 A4 2½p vio & ultra 65.00 35.00
33 A4 3p violet & black 17.50 *52.50*
 a. Chalky paper ('08) 55.00 95.00
34 A4 3p violet, *yel* ('10) 3.75 *8.00*
35 A4 6p vio & brn ('08) 42.50 *75.00*
36 A4 6p violet & red violet ('11) 9.00 7.50
37 A4 1sh grn & car rose ('08) 45.00 *110.00*
38 A4 1sh blk, *grn* ('11) 6.00 *22.50*
39 A4 2sh6p blk & red, *blue* ('11) 42.50 *50.00*
40 A4 5sh grn & red, *yel* ('11) 45.00 *70.00*
 Nos. 29-40 (12) 294.25 *448.65*

Nos. 29 and 33 are valued on ordinary paper. Values on chalky paper; No. 29, $20 unused, $12 used; No. 33, $42.50 unused, *$75* used.

1907-11

Ordinary Paper

41 A4 ¼p brown ('09) 3.00 1.90
42 A4 ½p green 3.75 1.40
43 A4 1p red 11.00 .85
 a. 1p rose carmine 40.00 3.75
44 A4 2p gray ('11) 3.75 *8.00*
45 A4 2½p ultramarine 7.50 4.50
 Nos. 41-45 (5) 29.00 *16.65*

King George V
A5 A6

For description of dies I and II, see "Dies of British Colonial Stamps" in Table of Contents.

The ½p, 1p, 2½p and 6p denominations of type A5 show the numeral on horizontally-lined tablet. The 1sh and 5sh denominations are expressed as "ONE SHILLING" and "FIVE SHILLINGS" on plain tablet.

Die I

1912

Ordinary Paper

46 A5 ¼p brown 1.90 1.10
47 A5 ½p green 5.25 1.75
48 A5 1p carmine 5.25 1.10
 a. 1p scarlet 6.75 1.10
49 A5 2p gray 4.25 *5.75*
50 A5 2½p ultramarine 3.50 *7.25*
 Nos. 46-50 (5) 20.15 *16.95*

1912-22

Chalky Paper

51 A5 3p violet, *yel* 1.90 *11.00*
52 A5 4p blk & red, *yel* (Die II) ('22) 4.00 *22.50*
53 A5 6p vio & red vio 3.25 *8.50*
54 A5 1sh blk, *bl grn, ol* back 9.50 *8.50*
 a. 1sh black, *green* 3.25 *8.50*
55 A5 2sh vio & ultra, *bl* (Die II) ('22) 9.00 *57.50*
56 A5 2sh6p black & red, *blue* ('14) 13.00 *40.00*
57 A5 5sh green & red, *yellow* ('14) 55.00 *100.00*
 Nos. 46-57 (12) 115.80 *264.95*

1913, Nov.

Surface-colored Paper

58 A5 3p violet, *yel* 67.50 *125.00*
59 A5 1sh black, *green* 55.00 40.00
60 A5 5sh green & red, *yel* 45.00 *85.00*
 Nos. 58-60 (3) 167.50 250.00

Die II

1921-32 **Wmk. 4**

Ordinary Paper

61 A5 ¼p dk brown ('22) 2.50 1.10
a. ¼p dark brown (I) ('32) 6.25 *17.00*
62 A5 ½p green 1.10 .80
a. ½p green (I) ('32) 27.50 *35.00*
63 A5 1p carmine 2.50 .60
a. 1p rose red (I) ('32) 32.50 .90
b. 1p bright scarlet (II) ('29) 12.50 2.50
64 A5 1p dp violet ('22) 2.50 1.10
65 A5 1½p rose red ('26) 3.50 2.10
66 A5 1½p red brn ('29) 1.40 .20
a. 1½p red brown (I) ('32) 4.50 *3.00*
68 A5 2p gray ('22) 2.10 .85
69 A5 2½p orange ('23) 6.75 *52.50*
70 A5 2½p ultra ('27) 3.75 1.40
a. Die I ('32) 7.50 3.75
71 A5 3p ultra ('23) 5.00 *27.50*
a. 3p deep ultramarine ('25) 65.00 65.00

Chalky Paper

72 A5 3p violet, *yel* *1.60* *6.75*
73 A5 4p black & red, *yel* ('23) 3.25 *22.50*
74 A5 5p vio & olive grn ('22) 2.75 *4.50*
75 A5 6p vio & red vio ('23) 16.00 *42.50*
a. Die I ('32) 22.50 *85.00*
76 A5 1sh blk, *emerald* ('23) 7.25 *8.50*
a. 1sh black, *green* (I) ('32) 52.50 *80.00*
77 A5 2sh vio & ultra, *bl* ('22) 17.50 *42.50*
a. 2sh red purple & blue, *blue* ('26) 8.50 *52.50*
78 A5 2sh6p blk & red, *bl* ('23) 6.75 *24.00*
79 A5 3sh green & vio 12.50 *26.00*
80 A5 4sh black & scar 12.50 *42.50*
81 A5 5sh grn & red, *yel* 40.00 *75.00*
82 A6 10sh red & grn, *emer* ('28) 62.50 *100.00*

Wmk. 3

83 A6 £1 black & vio, *red* ('28) 240.00 275.00
Nos. 61-66,68-83 (22) 453.70 *757.90*

Common Design Types pictured following the introduction.

Silver Jubilee Issue
Common Design Type
Perf. 11x12

1935, May 6 **Engr.** **Wmk. 4**
96 CD301 1p car & dk blue 1.25 3.25
97 CD301 1½p blk & ultra 2.50 1.60
98 CD301 2½p ultra & brn 4.00 4.75
99 CD301 1sh brn vio & ind 9.75 17.50
Nos. 96-99 (4) 17.50 27.10
Set, never hinged 30.00

Coronation Issue
Common Design Type

1937, May 12 ***Perf. 13½x14***
100 CD302 1p carmine .50 .70
101 CD302 1½p brown .50 1.25
102 CD302 2½p bright ultra .55 1.25
Nos. 100-102 (3) 1.55 3.20
Set, never hinged 2.25

A7

King George VI — A8

1938-51 **Typo.** ***Perf. 14***
103 A7 ¼p brown .30 1.25
a. ¼p deep brown, chalky paper ('49) .20 *1.60*
104 A7 ½p green .40 .65
105 A7 1p carmine .75 7.25
a. 1p scarlet ('42) 1.10 1.60
b. 1p red ('48) 3.00 *3.75*
106 A7 1½p red brown .80 .45
107 A7 2p gray 1.60 1.25
a. 2p slate gray ('42) 3.00 2.75
108 A7 2½p ultramarine .40 *1.10*
a. 2½p bright blue 10.00 2.25
109 A7 3p dl org ('42) 2.50 *.90*
a. 3p brown orange 22.50 2.50
110 A7 6p vio & red vio 4.00 2.50
a. 6p deep dull purple * bright purple 13.00 5.00
b. 6p purple & deep magenta ('47) 5.00 3.50
111 A7 1sh blk, *emerald* ('42) 4.50 1.50
a. 1sh black, *emerald*, chalky paper 10.00 2.25
112 A7 2sh vio & ultra, *bl* 6.50 1.75
a. 2sh reddish purple & blue, *blue*, chalky paper 12.50 3.00

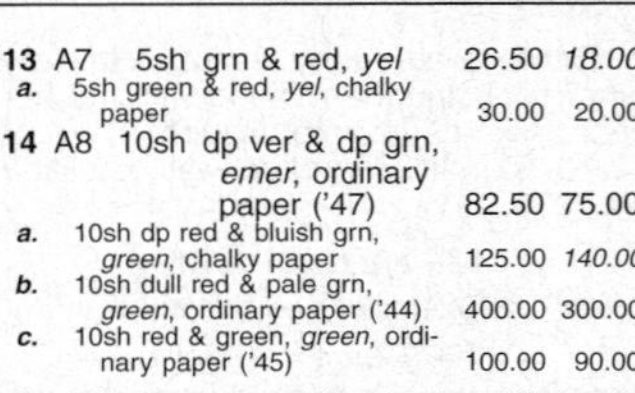

113 A7 5sh grn & red, *yel* 26.50 *18.00*
a. 5sh green & red, *yel*, chalky paper 30.00 20.00
114 A8 10sh dp ver & dp grn, *emer*, ordinary paper ('47) 82.50 75.00
a. 10sh dp red & bluish grn, *green*, chalky paper 125.00 *140.00*
b. 10sh dull red & pale grn, *green*, ordinary paper ('44) 400.00 300.00
c. 10sh red & green, *green*, ordinary paper ('45) 100.00 90.00

Two dies were used for the 1p, differing in thickness of shading line at base of "1."

Wmk. 3 ***Perf. 13***

115 A8 £1 blk & vio, *scar* ('51) 37.50 *47.50*
a. £1 black & brown purple, *red*, perf. 14 225.00 175.00
Never hinged 350.00
b. £1 black & purple, *carmine*, perf. 14 ('41) 55.00 45.00
Never hinged 80.00
c. £1 black & brown purple, *salmon*, perf. 14 ('43) 32.50 32.50
Never hinged 45.00
d. Wmkd. sideways (as #115, perf. 13) *3,000.*
Never hinged 4,000.
Nos. 103-115 (13) 168.25 159.10
Set, never hinged 300.00

The 3p-£1 were issued on chalky paper in 1938 and on ordinary paper in 1942. Values are for the most common varieties.

Issued: #115, 12/13/51; others, 11/25/38.

See Nos. 120-125.

Catalogue values for unused stamps in this section, from this point to the end of the section, are for Never Hinged items.

Peace Issue
Common Design Type
Perf. 13½x14

1946, Nov. 1 **Wmk. 4** **Engr.**
116 CD303 1½p brown .20 .25
117 CD303 3p deep orange .20 .25

Silver Wedding Issue
Common Design Types

1949, Jan. 2 **Photo.** ***Perf. 14x14½***
118 CD304 2½p bright ultra .20 .20

Perf. 11½x11
Engr.; Name Typographed
119 CD305 5sh green 5.75 5.75

George VI Type of 1938

1949, July 1 **Typo.** ***Perf. 13½x14***
120 A7 ½p gray .25 .65
121 A7 1p green .55 .20
122 A7 1½p orange & black .55 .20
123 A7 2p crimson rose 1.40 .65
124 A7 2½p black & plum .55 .20
125 A7 3p ultramarine .65 .20
Nos. 120-125 (6) 3.95 2.10

UPU Issue
Common Design Types
Engr.; Name Typo. on 3p and 6p

1949, Oct. 10 ***Perf. 13½, 11x11½***
126 CD306 2½p slate .20 .65
127 CD307 3p indigo 1.60 .90
128 CD308 6p red lilac .65 .90
129 CD309 1sh blue green .75 .90
Nos. 126-129 (4) 3.20 3.35

University Issue
Common Design Types
Perf. 14x14½

1951, Feb. 16 **Engr.** **Wmk. 4**
130 CD310 3c gray black & org .35 .45
131 CD311 12c lilac & rose car 1.00 .90

Coronation Issue
Common Design Type

1953, June 2 ***Perf. 13½x13***
132 CD312 3c dk green & black .60 *2.25*

A9

Queen Elizabeth II — A10

1954, Feb. 22 **Typo.** ***Perf. 14***
133 A9 ½c brown .20 .60
134 A9 1c gray .90 1.50
135 A9 2c green .70 .20
136 A9 3c orange & blk 2.25 1.50
137 A9 4c rose red 1.60 .20
138 A9 5c blk & claret 2.25 1.50
139 A9 6c orange 2.25 .65
140 A9 8c deep ultra 2.75 .20
141 A9 12c rose vio & mag 2.00 .20
142 A9 24c black & green 2.00 .30
143 A9 48c rose vio & ultra 7.00 4.00
144 A9 60c brown & green 7.00 3.25
145 A9 $1.20 yel grn & rose red 5.75 4.50

Perf. 13
146 A10 $2.40 red & blue grn 7.50 7.75
147 A10 $4.80 black & claret 7.50 10.25
Nos. 133-147 (15) 51.65 *36.60*

LESOTHO

lə-'sō-ₒₒtō

LOCATION — An enclave within the Republic of South Africa
GOVT. — Independent state in British Commonwealth
AREA — 11,720 sq. mi.
POP. — 2,128,950 (1999 est.)
CAPITAL — Maseru

Basutoland, the British Crown Colony, became independent, October 4, 1966, taking the name Lesotho.

100 Cents = 1 Rand
100 Lisente (s) = 1 Maloti (1979)

Catalogue values for all unused stamps in this country are for Never Hinged items.

Watermark

Wmk. 362 — Basotho Hat Multiple

Moshoeshoe I and II — A1

Perf. 12½x13

1966, Oct. 4 Photo. Unwmk.

1 A1 2½c red brn, blk & red .20 .20
2 A1 5c red brn, blk & brt bl .20 .20
3 A1 10c red brn, blk & brt green .30 .25
4 A1 20c red brn, blk & red lilac .50 .45
Nos. 1-4 (4) 1.20 1.10

Lesotho's independence, Oct. 4, 1966.

Basutoland Nos. 72-74, 76-82 Overprinted

Perf. 13½

1966, Nov. 1 Wmk. 4 Engr.

5 A7 ½c dk brown & gray .20 .20
6 A7 1c dp grn & gray blk .20 .20
7 A7 2c orange & dp blue .70 .20
8 A7 3½c dp blue & indigo .35 .20
9 A7 5c dk grn & org brn .20 .20
10 A7 10c rose vio & dk ol .30 .20
11 A7 12½c aqua & brown 5.75 .35
12 A7 25c lil rose & dp ultra .50 .20
13 A7 50c dp car & black 1.00 .65

Perf. 11½

14 A8 1r dp claret & blk 1.00 *2.50*
a. "Lseotho" 100.00
Nos. 5-14 (10) 10.20 4.90

Same Overprint on Nos. 87-91 and Type of 1954

Wmk. 314 *Perf. 13½*

15 A7 1c green & gray blk .20 .20
16 A7 2½c car & ol green 1.00 .20
17 A7 5c dk grn & org brn .40 .20
18 A7 12½c aqua & brown .60 .40
19 A7 50c dp car & black 1.25 .75

Perf. 11½

20 A8 1r dp claret & blk 1.50 1.50
a. "Lseotho" 55.00
Nos. 15-20 (6) 4.95 3.25

UNESCO Emblem, Microscope, Book, Violin and Retort — A2

Unwmk.

1966, Dec. 1 Litho. *Perf. 14*

21 A2 2½c green & ocher .20 .20
22 A2 5c olive & brt green .20 .20
23 A2 12½c ver & lt blue .40 .20
24 A2 25c dull blue & orange .75 .50
Nos. 21-24 (4) 1.55 1.10

20th anniv. of UNESCO.

King Moshoeshoe II and Corn — A3

King Moshoeshoe II — A4

Designs: 1c, Bull. 2c, Aloes. 2½c, Basotho hat. 3½c, Merino sheep. 5c, Basotho pony. 10c, Wheat. 12½c, Angora goat. 25c, Maletsunyane Falls. 50c, Diamonds. 1r, Coat of Arms.

Perf. 13½x14½

1967, Apr. 1 Photo. Unwmk.

25 A3 ½c violet & green .20 .20
26 A3 1c dk red & brown .20 .20
27 A3 2c green & yellow .20 .20
28 A3 2½c yel bister & blk .20 .20
29 A3 3½c yellow & black .20 .20
30 A3 5c brt blue & yel bis .30 .20
31 A3 10c gray & ocher .40 .20
32 A3 12½c orange & blk .50 .45
33 A3 25c ultra & blk .95 .85
34 A3 50c Prus green & blk 6.75 2.00
35 A3 1r gray & multi 1.25 1.50

Perf. 14½x13½

36 A4 2r mag, blk & gold 1.75 3.00
Nos. 25-36 (12) 12.90 9.20

See Nos. 47-59.

University Buildings and Graduates — A4a

1967, Apr. 7 *Perf. 14x14½*

37 A4a 1c yel, sep & dp blue .20 .20
38 A4a 2½c blue, sep & dp bl .20 .20
39 A4a 12½c dl rose, sep & dp bl .20 .20
40 A4a 25c lt vio, sep & dp bl .30 .20
Nos. 37-40 (4) .90 .80

1st conferment of degrees by the Univ. of Botswana, Lesotho and Swaziland at Roma, Lesotho.

Statue of Moshoeshoe I — A5

1st Anniv. of Independence: 12½c, Flag of Lesotho. 25c, Crocodile.

1967, Oct. 4 Photo. *Perf. 14*

41 A5 2½c apple green & black .20 .20
42 A5 12½c multicolored .55 .55
43 A5 25c tan, blk & dp green 1.00 1.00
Nos. 41-43 (3) 1.75 1.75

Boy Scout and Lord Baden-Powell — A6

1967, Nov. 1 Unwmk. *Perf. 14x14½*

44 A6 15c lt ol grn, dk grn & brn .40 .25

60th anniversary of the Boy Scouts.

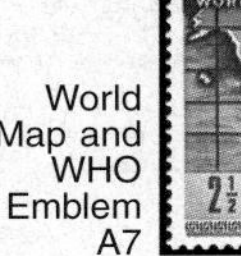

World Map and WHO Emblem A7

20th anniv. of WHO: 25c, Nurse and child, arms of Lesotho and WHO emblem.

1968, Apr. 8 Photo. *Perf. 14x14½*

45 A7 2½c dp bl, car rose & gold .20 .20
46 A7 25c gold, gray grn & redsh brown .50 .40

Types of 1967

Design: 3c, Sorghum. Others as before.

Perf. 13½x14½

1968-69 Photo. Wmk. 362

47 A3 ½c violet & green .20 .20
48 A3 1c dk red & brown .20 .20
49 A3 2c green & yellow .20 .20
50 A3 2½c yel bister & blk .20 .20
51 A3 3c lt brn, dk brn & green .20 .20
52 A3 3½c yellow & black .20 .20
53 A3 5c brt bl & yel bis .35 .20
54 A3 10c gray & ocher .70 .60
55 A3 12½c org & blk ('69) 1.10 1.00
56 A3 25c ultra & blk ('69) 2.10 1.60
57 A3 50c Prussian grn & black ('69) 14.00 3.50
58 A3 1r gray & multi 4.00 4.00

Perf. 14½x13½

59 A4 2r magenta, blk & gold ('69) 11.50 15.00
Nos. 47-59 (13) 34.95 27.10

Hunters, Rock Painting A8

Rock Paintings: 3½c, Baboons. 5c, Javelin thrower, vert. 10c, Archers. 15c, Cranes, vert. 20c, Eland. 25c, Hunting scene.

Perf. 14½x14, 14x14½

1968, Nov. 1 Photo. Wmk. 362

60 A8 3c dk & lt green & brn .35 .20
61 A8 3½c dk brown & yel .45 .20
62 A8 5c sepia, yel & red brn .50 .20
63 A8 10c black, brt rose & org .65 .30
64 A8 15c olive brn & buff 1.00 .50
65 A8 20c black, yel & lt grn 1.25 .70
66 A8 25c dk brown, yel & org 1.40 1.10
Nos. 60-66 (7) 5.60 3.20

Protection for Lesotho's rock paintings.

Queen Elizabeth II Hospital A9

Designs: 10c, Radio Lesotho. 12½c, Leabua Jonathan Airport. 25c, Royal Palace.

1969, Mar. 11 Litho. *Perf. 14x13½*

67 A9 2½c multicolored .20 .20
68 A9 10c multicolored .20 .20
69 A9 12½c multicolored .40 .20
70 A9 25c multicolored .25 .20
Nos. 67-70 (4) 1.05 .80

Centenary of Maseru, capital of Lesotho.

Mosotho Horseman and Car — A10

Designs: 12½c, Car on mountain pass. 15c, View from Sani Pass and signal flags. 20c, Map of Lesotho and Independence Trophy.

1969, Sept. 26 Photo. *Perf. 14½x14*

71 A10 2½c brown & multi .20 .20
72 A10 12½c multicolored .25 .25
73 A10 15c multicolored .30 .30
74 A10 20c yellow & multi .35 .35
Nos. 71-74 (4) 1.10 1.10

Roof of Africa Auto Rally, Sept. 19-20.

Gryponyx A11

Prehistoric Reptile Footprints, Moyeni: 3c, Dinosaur. 10c, Plateosauravus and Footprints. 15c, Tritylodon. 25c, Massospondylus.

Perf. 14½x14

1970, Jan. 5 Wmk. 362

Size: 60x23mm

75 A11 3c brown, yel & black 1.00 .75

Perf. 15x14

Size: 40x23mm

76 A11 5c maroon, blk & pink 1.40 .40
77 A11 10c sepia, blk & yel 1.75 .45
78 A11 15c slate grn, blk & yel 2.75 3.00
79 A11 25c gray blue, blk & bl 3.75 3.00
Nos. 75-79 (5) 10.65 7.60

Moshoeshoe I A12

Design: 25c, Moshoeshoe I with top hat.

Perf. 14x13½

1970, Mar. 11 Litho. Wmk. 362

80 A12 2½c brt grn & car rose .20 .20
81 A12 25c lt blue & org brn .25 .25

Cent. of the death of Moshoeshoe I, chief of the Bakoena clan of the Basothos.

UN Headquarters, New York — A13

2½c, UN emblem. 12½c, UN emblem, people. 25c, UN emblem, peace dove.

1970, June 26 Litho. *Perf. 14½x14*

82 A13 2½c pink, red brn & bl .20 .20
83 A13 10c blue & multi .20 .20
84 A13 12½c olive, ver & lt blue .20 .20
85 A13 25c tan & multi .20 .20
Nos. 82-85 (4) .80 .80

25th anniversary of the United Nations.

Basotho Hat Gift Shop, Maseru A14

Tourism: 5c, Trout fishing. 10c, Horseback riding. 12½c, Skiing, Maluti Mountains. 20c, Holiday Inn, Maseru.

1970, Oct. 27 *Perf. 14x14½*

86 A14 2½c multicolored .20 .20
87 A14 5c multicolored .20 .20
88 A14 10c multicolored .40 .30
89 A14 12½c multicolored .40 .30
90 A14 20c multicolored .50 .40
Nos. 86-90 (5) 1.70 1.40

Corn — A15

Designs: 1c, Bull. 2c, Aloes. 2½c, Basotho hat. 3c, Sorghum. 3½c, Merino sheep. 4c, National flag. 5c, Basotho pony. 10c, Wheat. 12½c, Angora goat. 25c, Maletsunyane Falls. 50c, Diamonds. 1r, Coat of Arms. 2r, Statue of King Moshoeshoe I in Maseru, vert.

1971 Litho. Wmk. 362 *Perf. 14*

91 A15 ½c lilac & green .20 .20
92 A15 1c brn red & brn .20 .20
93 A15 2c yel brn & yel .20 .20
94 A15 2½c dull yel & blk .20 .20
95 A15 3c bis, brn & grn .20 .20
96 A15 3½c yellow & black .20 .20
97 A15 4c ver & multi .20 .20
98 A15 5c blue & brown .20 .20
99 A15 10c gray & ocher .35 .30
100 A15 12½c orange & brn .40 .35
101 A15 25c ultra & black .70 .60
102 A15 50c lt bl grn & blk 6.50 3.25
103 A15 1r gray & multi 2.40 2.10
104 A15 2r ultra & brown 2.40 *4.50*
a. Unwmkd. ('80) 1.75 *2.00*
Nos. 91-104 (14) 14.35 12.70

Issue dates: 4c, Apr. 1; others, Jan. 4.
For overprints and surcharges see #132-135, 245, 312.

Lammergeier A16

Birds: 5c, Bald ibis. 10c, Rufous rock jumper. 12½c, Blue korhaan (bustard). 15c, Painted snipe. 20c, Golden-breasted bunting. 25c, Ground woodpecker.

1971, Mar. 1 *Perf. 14*

105 A16 2½c multicolored 3.00 .25
106 A16 5c multicolored 4.00 1.90
107 A16 10c multicolored 4.00 1.40
108 A16 12½c multicolored 4.50 3.00
109 A16 15c multicolored 5.25 4.00
110 A16 20c multicolored 5.25 4.00
111 A16 25c multicolored 6.25 4.00
Nos. 105-111 (7) 32.25 18.55

Lionel Collett Dam A17

Designs: 10c, Contour farming. 15c, Earth dams. 25c, Beaver dams.

1971, July 15 Litho. Wmk. 362

112 A17 4c multicolored .20 .20
113 A17 10c multicolored .20 .20
114 A17 15c multicolored .30 .30
115 A17 25c multicolored .40 .40
Nos. 112-115 (4) 1.10 1.10

Soil conservation and erosion control.

Diamond Mining A18

10c, Potter. 15c, Woman weaver at loom. 20c, Construction worker and new buildings.

1971, Oct. 4

116 A18 4c olive & multi .95 .40
117 A18 10c ocher & multi .40 .20
118 A18 15c red & multi .60 .60
119 A18 20c dk brown & multi .80 1.25
Nos. 116-119 (4) 2.75 2.45

Mail Cart, 19th Century A19

Designs: 10c, Postal bus. 15c, Cape of Good Hope No. 17, vert. 20c, Maseru Post Office.

1972, Jan. 3

120 A19 5c pink & black .20 .20
121 A19 10c lt blue & multi .25 .20
122 A19 15c gray, black & blue .40 .20
123 A19 20c yellow & multi .50 .50
Nos. 120-123 (4) 1.35 1.10

Centenary of mail service between Maseru and Aliwal North in Cape Colony.

Runner and Olympic Rings — A20

1972, Sept. 1

124 A20 4c shown .20 .20
125 A20 10c Shot put .25 .25
126 A20 15c Hurdles .40 .35
127 A20 25c Broad jump .60 .60
Nos. 124-127 (4) 1.45 1.40

20th Olympic Games, Munich, 8/26-9/11.

Adoration of the Shepherds, by Matthias Stomer — A21

1972, Dec. 1 Litho. *Perf. 14*

128 A21 4c blue & multi .20 .20
129 A21 10c red & multi .25 .25
130 A21 25c emerald & multi .35 .35
Nos. 128-130 (3) .80 .80

Christmas.

WHO Emblem — A22

1973, Apr. 7 Litho. *Perf. 13½*

131 A22 20c blue & yellow .50 .50

WHO, 25th anniversary.

Nos. 94, 97-99 overprinted: "O.A.U. / 10th Anniversary / Freedom in Unity"

1973, May 25 Wmk. 362 *Perf. 14*

132 A15 2½c dull yellow & black .20 .20
133 A15 4c vermilion & multi .20 .20
134 A15 5c blue & brown .20 .20
135 A15 10c gray & ocher .30 .30
Nos. 132-135 (4) .90 .90

Basotho Hat, WFP/FAO Emblem — A23

Designs: 15c, School lunch. 20c, Child drinking milk and cow. 25c, Map of mountain roads and farm workers.

1973, June 1 *Perf. 13½*

136 A23 4c ultra & multi .20 .20
137 A23 15c buff & multi .20 .20
138 A23 20c yellow & multi .20 .20
139 A23 25c violet & multi .40 .40
Nos. 136-139 (4) 1.00 1.00

World Food Program, 10th anniversary.

Christmas Butterfly A24

Designs: Butterflies of Lesotho.

1973, Sept. 3 *Perf. 14x14½*

140 A24 4c Mountain Beauty 1.40 .20
141 A24 5c shown 1.60 .60
142 A24 10c Painted lady 2.40 .60
143 A24 15c Yellow pansy 4.00 2.25
144 A24 20c Blue pansy 4.00 2.40
145 A24 25c African monarch 4.75 3.25
146 A24 30c Orange tip 4.75 4.50
Nos. 140-146 (7) 22.90 13.80

Map of Northern Lesotho and Location of Diamond Mines — A25

Designs: 15c, Kimberlite (diamond-bearing) rocks. 20c, Diagram of Kimberlite volcano, vert. 30c, Diamond prospector, vert.

Perf. 13½x14, 14x13½

1973, Oct. 1 Litho. Wmk. 362

147 A25 10c gray & multi 2.50 .40
148 A25 15c multicolored 2.75 2.10
149 A25 20c multicolored 2.75 2.25
150 A25 30c multicolored 4.50 6.25
Nos. 147-150 (4) 12.50 11.00

International Kimberlite Conference.

Nurses' Training and Medical Care — A26

Designs: 10c, Classroom, student with microscope. 20c, Farmers with tractor and bullock team and crop instruction. 25c, Potter and engineers with lathe. 30c, Boy scouts and young bricklayers.

1974, Feb. 18 Litho. *Perf. 13½x14*

151 A26 4c lt blue & multi .20 .20
152 A26 10c ocher & multi .20 .20
153 A26 20c multicolored .30 .20
154 A26 25c bister & multi .35 .25
155 A26 30c yellow & multi .35 .30
Nos. 151-155 (5) 1.40 1.15

Youth and development.

Open Book and Wreath — A27

Designs: 15c, Flags of Botswana, Lesotho and Swaziland; cap and diploma. 20c, Map of Africa and location of Botswana, Lesotho and Swaziland. 25c, King Moshoeshoe II, Chancellor of UBLS, capping graduate.

1974, Apr. 7 Litho. *Perf. 14*

156 A27 10c multicolored .20 .20
157 A27 15c multicolored .25 .20
158 A27 20c multicolored .30 .25
159 A27 25c multicolored .35 .35
Nos. 156-159 (4) 1.10 1.00

10th anniversary of the University of Botswana, Lesotho and Swaziland.

Senqunyane River Bridge, Marakabei — A28

5c, Tsoelike River Bridge. 10c, Makhaleng River Bridge. 15c, Seaka Bridge, Orange/Senqu River. 20c, Masianokeng Bridge, Phuthiatsana River. 25c, Mahobong Bridge, Hlotse River.

1974, June 26 Wmk. 362 *Perf. 14*

160 A28 4c multicolored .20 .20
161 A28 5c multicolored .20 .20
162 A28 10c multicolored .30 .30
163 A28 15c multicolored .60 .45
164 A28 20c multicolored .75 .60
165 A28 25c multicolored .95 .70
Nos. 160-165 (6) 3.00 2.45

Bridges and rivers of Lesotho.

UPU Emblem A29

1974, Sept. 6 Litho. *Perf. 14x13*

166 A29 4c shown .20 .20
167 A29 10c Map of Lesotho .20 .20
168 A29 15c GPO, Maseru .20 .40
169 A29 20c Rural mail delivery .80 1.00
Nos. 166-169 (4) 1.40 1.80

Centenary of Universal Postal Union.

Siege of Thaba-Bosiu — A30

King Moshoeshoe I A31

5c, King Moshoeshoe II laying wreath at grave of Moshoeshoe I. 20c, Makoanyane, warrior hero.

Perf. 12½x12, 12x12½

1974, Nov. 25

No.	Type	Description	Unused	Used
170	A30	4c multicolored	.20	.20
171	A30	5c multicolored	.20	.20
172	A31	10c multicolored	.25	.20
173	A31	20c multicolored	.60	.40
		Nos. 170-173 (4)	1.25	1.00

Sesquicentennial of Thaba-Bosiu becoming the capital of Basutoland and Lesotho.

Mamokhorong — A32

Musical Instruments of the Basotho: 10c, Lesiba. 15c, Setolotolo. 20c, Meropa (drums).

Perf. 14x14½

1975, Jan. 25 **Wmk. 362**

No.	Type	Description	Unused	Used
174	A32	4c multicolored	.20	.20
175	A32	10c multicolored	.20	.20
176	A32	15c multicolored	.30	.30
177	A32	20c multicolored	.50	.50
a.		Souvenir sheet of 4, #174-177	2.00	2.00
		Nos. 174-177 (4)	1.20	1.20

View, Sehlabathebe National Park — A33

5c, Natural arch. 15c, Mountain stream. 20c, Lake and mountains. 25c, Waterfall.

1975, Apr. 8 **Litho.** ***Perf. 14***

No.	Type	Description	Unused	Used
178	A33	4c multicolored	.35	.20
179	A33	5c multicolored	.35	.20
180	A33	15c multicolored	.70	.70
181	A33	20c multicolored	.70	.70
182	A33	25c multicolored	.90	.90
		Nos. 178-182 (5)	3.00	2.70

Sehlabathebe National Park.

Moshoeshoe I (1824-1870) A34

Mofumahali Mantsebo Seeiso (1940-1960) A35

Leaders of Lesotho: 4c, Moshoeshoe II. 5c, Letsie I (1870-1891). 6c, Lerotholi (1891-1905). 10c, Letsie II (1905-1913). 15c, Griffith (1913-1939). 20c, Seeiso Griffith Lerotholi (1939-1940).

1975, Sept. 10 **Litho.** **Wmk. 362**

No.	Type	Description	Unused	Used
183	A34	3c dull blue & black	.20	.20
184	A34	4c lilac rose & black	.20	.20
185	A34	5c pink & black	.20	.20
186	A34	6c brown & black	.20	.20
187	A34	10c rose car & black	.20	.20
188	A34	15c orange & black	.25	.25
189	A34	20c olive & black	.30	.30
190	A35	25c lt blue & black	.35	.35
		Nos. 183-190 (8)	1.90	1.90

No. 190 issued for Intl. Women's Year.

Mokhibo, Women's Dance A36

Traditional Dances: 10c, Ndlamo, men's dance. 15c, Raleseli, men and women. 20c, Mohobelo, men's dance.

1975, Dec. 17 ***Perf. 14x14½***

No.	Type	Description	Unused	Used
191	A36	4c blue & multi	.20	.20
192	A36	10c black & multi	.25	.25
193	A36	15c black & multi	.30	.30
194	A36	20c blue & multi	.40	.40
a.		Souvenir sheet of 4, #191-194	5.50	5.50
		Nos. 191-194 (4)	1.15	1.15

Enrollment in Junior Red Cross — A37

Designs: 10c, First aid team and truck. 15c, Red Cross nurse on horseback in rural area. 25c, Supplies arriving by plane.

1976, Feb. 20 **Litho.** ***Perf. 14***

No.	Type	Description	Unused	Used
195	A37	4c red & multi	.60	.40
196	A37	10c red & multi	.85	.60
197	A37	15c red & multi	1.10	.75
198	A37	25c red & multi	1.75	1.25
		Nos. 195-198 (4)	4.30	3.00

Lesotho Red Cross, 25th anniversary.

Mosotho Horseman — A38

King Moshoeshoe II A39

2c, Tapestry (weavers and citation). 4c, Map of Lesotho. 5c, Hand holding Lesotho brown diamond. 10c, Lesotho Bank. 15c, Flags of Lesotho and Organization of African Unity. 25c, Sehlabathebe National Park. 40c, Pottery. 50c, Pre-historic rock painting.

1976, June 2 ***Perf. 14***

No.	Type	Description	Unused	Used
199	A38	2c multicolored	.20	.20
200	A38	3c multicolored	.20	.20
201	A38	4c multicolored	1.10	.20
202	A38	5c multicolored	.40	.20
203	A38	10c multicolored	.30	.30
204	A38	15c multicolored	1.10	.60
205	A38	25c multicolored	.80	.95
206	A38	40c multicolored	1.25	1.90
207	A38	50c multicolored	2.25	1.90
208	A39	1r multicolored	1.40	*2.50*
		Nos. 199-208 (10)	9.00	8.95

For surcharges see Nos. 302-311.

Soccer A40

Rising Sun of Independence A41

Olympic Rings and: 10c, Weight lifting. 15c, Boxing. 25c, Discus.

1976, Aug. 9 **Litho.** **Wmk. 362**

No.	Type	Description	Unused	Used
209	A40	4c citron & multi	.20	.20
210	A40	10c lilac & multi	.25	.20
211	A40	15c salmon & multi	.30	.25
212	A40	25c blue & multi	.65	.50
		Nos. 209-212 (4)	1.40	1.15

21st Olympic Games, Montreal, Canada, July 17-Aug. 1.

1976, Oct. 4 ***Perf. 14***

Designs: 10c, Opening gates. 15c, Broken chain. 25c, Plane over Molimo Restaurant.

No.	Type	Description	Unused	Used
213	A41	4c yellow & multi	.20	.20
214	A41	10c pink & multi	.20	.20
215	A41	15c blue & multi	.60	.20
216	A41	25c dull blue & multi	.70	.50
		Nos. 213-216 (4)	1.70	1.10

Lesotho's independence, 10th anniversary.

Telephones, 1876 and 1976 — A42

Designs: 10c, Woman using telephone, and 1895 telephone. 15c, Telephone operators and wall telephone. 25c, A.G. Bell and 1905 telephone.

Perf. 13x13½

1976, Dec. 6 **Wmk. 362**

No.	Type	Description	Unused	Used
217	A42	4c multicolored	.20	.20
218	A42	10c multicolored	.30	.30
219	A42	15c multicolored	.40	.40
220	A42	25c multicolored	.60	.60
		Nos. 217-220 (4)	1.50	1.50

Centenary of first telephone call by Alexander Graham Bell, Mar. 10, 1876.

Aloe Striatula — A43

Aloes and Succulents: 4c, Aloe aristata. 5c, Kniphofia caulescens. 10c, Euphorbia pulvinata. 15c, Aloe saponaria. 20c, Caralluma lutea. 25c, Aloe polyphylla.

1977, Feb. 14 **Litho.** ***Perf. 14***

No.	Type	Description	Unused	Used
221	A43	3c multicolored	.35	.20
222	A43	4c multicolored	.40	.20
223	A43	5c multicolored	.50	.20
224	A43	10c multicolored	.65	.20
225	A43	15c multicolored	2.10	.40
226	A43	20c multicolored	2.10	.60
227	A43	25c multicolored	2.25	.80
		Nos. 221-227 (7)	8.35	2.60

Rock Rabbits A44

Perf. 14x14½

1977, Apr. 25 **Wmk. 362**

No.	Type	Description	Unused	Used
228	A44	4c shown	*8.25*	.55
229	A44	5c Porcupine	*8.25*	.75
230	A44	10c Polecat	*8.25*	.90
231	A44	15c Klipspringers	*24.50*	3.75
232	A44	25c Baboons	*30.00*	5.00
		Nos. 228-232 (5)	*79.25*	10.95

Man with Cane, Concentric Circles — A45

Man with Cane: 10c, Surrounded by flames of pain. 15c, Surrounded by chain. 25c, Man and globe.

1977, July 4 **Litho.** ***Perf. 14***

No.	Type	Description	Unused	Used
233	A45	4c red & yellow	.20	.20
234	A45	10c dk blue & lt blue	.20	.20
235	A45	15c blue green & yellow	.60	.20
236	A45	25c black & orange	.70	.70
		Nos. 233-236 (4)	1.70	1.30

World Rheumatism Year.

Small-mouthed Yellow-fish — A46

Fresh-water Fish: 10c, Orange River mud fish. 15c, Rainbow trout. 25c, Oreodaimon quathlambae.

1977, Sept. 28 **Wmk. 362** ***Perf. 14***

No.	Type	Description	Unused	Used
237	A46	4c multicolored	.45	.20
238	A46	10c multicolored	.85	.25
239	A46	15c multicolored	1.60	.60
240	A46	25c multicolored	1.75	1.25
		Nos. 237-240 (4)	4.65	2.30

White and Black Equal — A47

Designs: 10c, Black and white jigsaw puzzle. 15c, White and black cogwheels. 25c, Black and white handshake.

1977, Dec. 12 **Litho.** ***Perf. 14***

No.	Type	Description	Unused	Used
241	A47	4c lilac rose & black	.20	.20
242	A47	10c brt blue & black	.20	.20
243	A47	15c orange & black	.20	.20
244	A47	25c lt green & black	.40	.30
		Nos. 241-244 (4)	1.00	.90

Action to Combat Racism Decade.

No. 99 Surcharged

1977, Dec. 7

No.	Type	Description	Unused	Used
245	A15	3c on 10c gray & ocher	1.50	1.25

Poppies — A48

Edward Jenner Vaccinating Child — A49

Flowers of Lesotho: 3c, Diascia integerrima. 4c, Helichrysum trilineatum. 5c, Zaluzianskya maritima. 10c, Gladioli. 15c, Chironia krebsii. 25c, Wahlenbergia undulata. 40c, Brunsvigia radulosa.

1978, Feb. 13 Litho. Wmk. 362

246 A48 2c multicolored .20 .30
247 A48 3c multicolored .20 .30
248 A48 4c multicolored .20 .20
249 A48 5c multicolored .20 .20
250 A48 10c multicolored .40 .30
251 A48 15c multicolored .65 .45
252 A48 25c multicolored 1.00 .95
253 A48 40c multicolored 1.75 1.90
Nos. 246-253 (8) 4.60 4.60

1978, May 8 Litho. *Perf. 13½x13*

Global Eradication of Smallpox: 25c, Child's head and WHO emblem.

254 A49 5c multicolored .40 .20
255 A49 25c multicolored 1.40 1.50

Tsoloane Falls — A50

Lesotho Waterfalls: 10c, Qiloane Falls. 15c, Tsoelikana Falls. 25c, Maletsunyane Falls.

1978, July 28 Litho. *Perf. 14*

256 A50 4c multicolored .20 .20
257 A50 10c multicolored .40 .40
258 A50 15c multicolored .65 .65
259 A50 25c multicolored 1.00 1.00
Nos. 256-259 (4) 2.25 2.25

Flyer 1 A51

25c, Orville and Wilbur Wright, Flyer 1.

1978, Oct. 9 Wmk. 362 *Perf. 14½*

260 A51 5c multicolored .20 .20
261 A51 25c multicolored 1.00 1.00

75th anniversary of 1st powered flight.

Dragonflies A52

Trees A53

Insects: 10c, Winged grasshopper. 15c, Wasps. 25c, Praying mantis.

1978, Dec. 18 Litho. *Perf. 14*

262 A52 4c multicolored .20 .20
263 A52 10c multicolored .30 .30
264 A52 15c multicolored .45 .45
265 A52 25c multicolored .75 .75
Nos. 262-265 (4) 1.70 1.70

1979, Mar. 26 Litho. *Perf. 14*

266 A53 4c Leucosidea Sericea .20 .20
267 A53 10c Wild olive .25 .25
268 A53 15c Blinkblaar .40 .40
269 A53 25c Cape holly .65 .65
Nos. 266-269 (4) 1.50 1.50

Reptiles A54

1979, June 4 Wmk. 362 *Perf. 14*

270 A54 4s Agama Lizard .20 .20
271 A54 10s Berg adder .35 .30
272 A54 15s Rock lizard .50 .45
273 A54 25s Spitting snake .85 .75
Nos. 270-273 (4) 1.90 1.70

A55

A56

1979, Oct. 22 Litho. *Perf. 14½*

274 A55 4s Basutoland No. 2 .20 .20
275 A55 15s Basutoland No. 72 .40 .40
276 A55 25s Penny Black .60 .60
Nos. 274-276 (3) 1.20 1.20

Souvenir Sheet

277 A55 50s Lesotho No. 122 1.25 1.25

Sir Rowland Hill (1795-1879), originator of penny postage.

1979, Dec. 10 Wmk. 362 *Perf. 14½*

Children's Games, by Brueghel the Elder, and IYC emblem: 4s, Children Climbing Tree. 10s, Follow the leader. 15s, Three cup montie. 25s, Entire painting.

278 A56 4s multicolored .20 .20
279 A56 10s multicolored .20 .20
280 A56 15s multicolored .35 .35
Nos. 278-280 (3) .75 .75

Souvenir Sheet

281 A56 25s multicolored .80 .80

International Year of the Child.

Beer Strainer, Brooms and Mat A57

1980, Feb. 18 Litho. *Perf. 14½*

282 A57 4s shown .20 .20
283 A57 10s Winnowing basket .20 .20
284 A57 15s Basotho hat .30 .30
285 A57 25s Grain storage pots .50 .50
Nos. 282-285 (4) 1.20 1.20

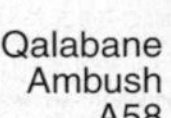

Qalabane Ambush A58

Gun War Centenary: 4s, Praise poet, text. 5s, Basotho army commander Lerotholi. 15s, Snider and Martini-Henry rifles. 25s, Map of Basutoland showing battle sites.

1980, May 6 Litho. *Perf. 14*

286 A58 4s multicolored .20 .20
287 A58 5s multicolored .20 .20
288 A58 10s multicolored .30 .30
289 A58 15s multicolored .70 .40
290 A58 25s multicolored .90 .65
Nos. 286-290 (5) 2.30 1.75

St. Basil's, Moscow, Olympic Torch A59

1980, Sept. 20 Litho. *Perf. 14½*

291 A59 25s shown .35 .35
292 A59 25s Torch and flags .35 .35
293 A59 25s Soccer .35 .35
294 A59 25s Running .35 .35
295 A59 25s Misha and stadium .35 .35
a. Strip of 5, #291-295 2.25 2.25

Souvenir Sheet

296 A59 1.40m Classic and modern torch bearers 2.25 2.25

22nd Summer Olympic Games, Moscow, July 19-Aug. 3.

Beer Mug and Man Drinking A60

Prince Philip — A61

Wmk. 362

1980, Oct. 1 Litho. *Perf. 14*

297 A60 4s shown .20 .20
298 A60 10s Beer brewing pot .20 .20
299 A60 15s Water pot .20 .20
300 A60 25s Pots and jugs .30 .20
Nos. 297-300 (4) .90 .80

Souvenir Sheet

Perf. 14x14½

301 Sheet of 4 1.80 1.80
a. A61 40s shown .40 .40
b. A61 40s Queen Elizabeth .40 .40
c. A61 40s Prince Charles .40 .40
d. A61 40s Princess Anne .40 .40

Traditional pottery; 250th birth anniversary of Josiah Wedgewood, potter.

Nos. 104, 199-208 Surcharged

Wmk. 362

1980, Oct. 20 Litho. *Perf. 14*

302 A38 2s on 2c multi .20 .20
303 A38 3s on 3c multi .20 .20
304 A38 5s on 5c multi .20 .20
a. 5s on 6s on 5c multi .20 .20
305 A38 6s on 4c multi .20 .20
306 A38 10s on 10c multi .20 .20
307 A38 25s on 25s multi .35 .35
308 A38 40s on 40c multi .55 .55
309 A38 50s on 50c multi .80 .80
310 A38 75s on 15c multi 2.00 2.00
311 A39 1m on 1r multi 2.40 2.40
312 A15 2m on 2r multi 4.50 4.50
Nos. 302-312 (11) 11.60 11.60

Numerous surcharge errors exist (double triple, inverted, etc.).

Souvenir Sheet

Queen Mother Elizabeth and Prince Charles — A62

Basutoland No. 36, Flags of Lesotho and Britain — A63

1980, Dec. 1 Unwmk. *Perf. 14½*

313 Sheet of 9 3.25 3.25
a. A62 5s shown .20 .20
b. A62 10s Portrait .20 .20
c. A63 1m shown .90 .90

Queen Mother Elizabeth, 80th birthday. No. 313 contains 3 each Nos. 313a-313c.

St. Agnes' Anglican Church, Teyateyaneng — A63a

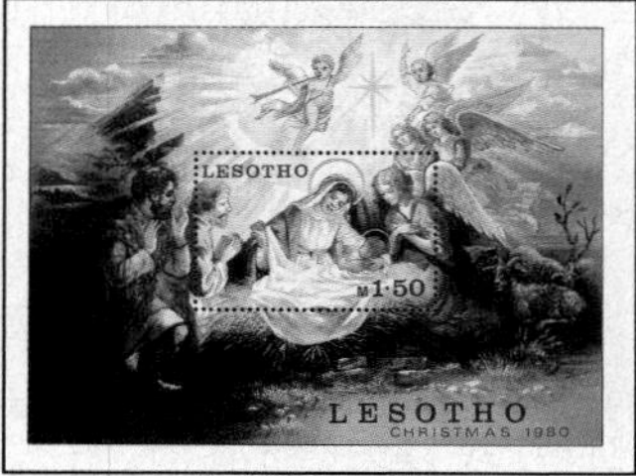

Nativity — A64

1980, Dec. 8 *Perf. 14x14½*

314 A63a 4s Lesotho Evangelical Church, Morija .20 .20
315 A63a 15s shown .20 .20
316 A63a 25s Our Lady's Victory Cathedral, Maseru .20 .20
317 A63a 75s University Chapel, Roma .40 .40
Nos. 314-317 (4) 1.00 1.00

Souvenir Sheet

318 A64 1.50m shown 1.00 1.00

Christmas.

Voyager Satellite and Saturn — A65

1981, Mar. 15 Litho. *Perf. 14*

319 Strip of 5 2.75 2.75
a. A65 25s Voyager, planet .45 .40
b. A65 25s shown .45 .40
c. A65 25s Voyager, Saturn's rings .45 .40
d. A65 25s Columbia space shuttle .45 .40

e. A65 25s Columbia, diff. .45 .40

Souvenir Sheet

320 A65 1.40m Saturn 2.75 2.75

Voyager expedition to Saturn and flight of Columbia space shuttle.

Rock Pigeons — A66

1981, Apr. 20 Unwmk. *Perf. 14½*

321 A66 1s Greater kestrel, vert. .20 .20
322 A66 2s shown .20 .20
323 A66 3s Crowned cranes, vert. .25 .20
324 A66 5s Bokmakierie, vert. .25 .20
325 A66 6s Cape robins, vert. .40 .20
326 A66 7s Yellow canary, vert. .40 .20
327 A66 10s Red-billed teal .40 .25
328 A66 25s Malachite kingfisher, vert. 1.00 .60
329 A66 40s Malachite sunbirds 1.25 1.00
330 A66 60s Orange-throated longclaw 1.60 1.50
331 A66 75s African hoopoe 2.00 1.75
332 A66 1m Red bishops 2.50 2.50
333 A66 2m Egyptian goose 4.75 4.75
334 A66 5m Lilac-breasted rollers 10.00 10.00
Nos. 321-334 (14) 25.20 23.55

For surcharges see Nos. 558A, 561-563, 598A, 599, 600B, 600C.

1981 *Perf. 13*

321a A66 1s 1.40 .70
322a A66 2s 1.60 .70
324a A66 5s 2.00 .70
327a A66 10s 2.00 .70
Nos. 321a-327a (4) 7.00 2.80

1982, June 14 Wmk. 373 *Perf. 14½*

321b A66 1s .20 .40
322b A66 2s .20 .40
323a A66 3s .35 .40
324b A66 5s .35 .45
325a A66 6s .35 .20
326a A66 7s .35 .20
327b A66 10s .35 .20
328a A66 25s 1.00 .45
329a A66 40s 1.10 .50
330a A66 60s 1.50 .90
331a A66 75s 2.00 .90
332a A66 1m 2.40 *2.75*
333a A66 2m 3.00 *4.00*
334a A66 5m 6.00 *10.00*
Nos. 321b-334a (14) 19.15 21.75

Common Design Types pictured following the introduction.

Royal Wedding Issue

Common Design Type and

Royal Wedding — A66a

Illustration reduced.

Unwmk.

1981, July 22 Litho. *Perf. 14*

335 CD331 25s Bouquet .20 .20
a. Booklet pane of 3 + label .80
336 CD331 50s Charles .40 .40
a. Booklet pane of 3 + label 1.60
337 CD331 75s Couple .60 .60
b. Booklet pane of 3 + label 2.00
c. Bklt. pane of 3, #335-337 + label 1.50
Nos. 335-337 (3) 1.20 1.20

1981 Litho. *Perf. 14½*

337A A66a 1.50m Couple 1.75 1.75

Nos. 335-337A exist imperf.

Tree Planting A67

1981, Oct. 30 Litho. *Perf. 14½*

338 A67 6s Duke of Edinburgh .20 .20
339 A67 7s shown .20 .20
340 A67 25s Digging .35 .35
341 A67 40s Mountain climbing .55 .55
342 A67 75s Emblem 1.00 1.00
Nos. 338-342 (5) 2.30 2.30

Souvenir Sheet

343 A67 1.40m Duke of Edinburgh, diff. 2.10 2.10

Duke of Edinburgh's Awards, 25th anniv. #343 contains 1 45x29mm stamp, perf. 13½.

Santa Claus at Globe, by Norman Rockwell A68

The Mystic Nativity, by Botticelli — A69

Christmas: Saturday Evening Post covers by Norman Rockwell.

1981, Oct. 5 *Perf. 13½x14*

344 A68 6s multicolored .20 .20
345 A68 10s multicolored .20 .20
346 A68 15s multicolored .25 .25
347 A68 20s multicolored .35 .35
348 A68 25s multicolored .40 .40
349 A68 60s multicolored 1.00 1.00
Nos. 344-349 (6) 2.40 2.40

Souvenir Sheet

350 A69 1.25m multicolored 2.25 2.25

Chacma Baboons A70

Perf. 14x13½, 14½ (20s, 40s, 50s)

1982, Jan. 15 Litho.

351 A70 6s African wild cat *3.00* .45
352 A70 20s shown *4.00* 1.10
353 A70 25s Cape eland *5.00* 1.60
354 A70 40s Porcupine *6.00* 2.10
355 A70 50s Oribi *6.25* 2.75
Nos. 351-355 (5) *24.25* 8.00

Souvenir Sheet

Perf. 14

356 A70 1.50m Black-backed jackal 13.50 11.00

6s, 25s; 50x37mm. No. 356 contains one stamp 48x31mm.

Scouting Year — A71

1982, Mar. 5 Litho. *Perf. 14x13½*

357 A71 6s Bugle call .20 .20
358 A71 30s Hiking .60 .60
359 A71 40s Drawing .80 .80
360 A71 50s Holding flag 1.00 1.00
361 A71 75s Salute 1.50 1.50
a. Booklet pane of 10 + sheet 12.50
Nos. 357-361 (5) 4.10 4.10

Souvenir Sheet

362 A71 1.50m Baden-Powell 2.75 2.75

No. 361a contains 2 each Nos. 357-361 with gutter and No. 362.

#357-361 issued in sheets of 8 with gutter.

1982 World Cup Soccer A72

Championships, 1930-1978: a, Uruguay, 1930. b, Italy, 1934. c, France, 1938. d, Brazil, 1950. e, Switzerland, 1954. f, Sweden, 1958. g, Chile, 1962. h, England, 1966. i, Mexico, 1970. j, Germany, 1974. k, Argentina, 1978. l, World Cup.

1982, Apr. 14 *Perf. 14½*

363 Sheet of 12 4.25 4.25
a.-l. A72 15s any single .25 .25

Souvenir Sheet

364 A72 1.25m Stadium 2.50 2.50

Nos. 363b, 363c, 363f, 363g, 363j, 363k exist se-tenant in sheets of 72.

George Washington's Birth Bicentenary — A73

Designs: Paintings.

1982, June 7

365 A73 6s Portrait .20 .20
366 A73 7s With children .20 .20
367 A73 10s Indian Chief's Prophecy .20 .20
368 A73 25s With troops .40 .40
369 A73 40s Arriving at New York .60 .60
370 A73 1m Entry into New York 1.25 1.25
Nos. 365-370 (6) 2.85 2.85

Souvenir Sheet

371 A73 1.25m Crossing Delaware 2.00 2.00

Princess Diana Issue

Common Design Type

Wmk. 373

1982, July 1 Litho. *Perf. 14*

372 CD333 30s Arms .90 .90
373 CD333 50s Diana .90 .90
374 CD333 75s Wedding 1.25 1.25
375 CD333 1m Portrait 1.90 1.90
Nos. 372-375 (4) 4.95 4.95

Sesotho Bible Centenary A74

Birth of Prince William of Wales, June 21 — A75

1982, Aug. 20 Litho. *Perf. 14½*

376 A74 6s Man reading bible .20 .20
377 A74 15s Angels, bible .20 .20

Size: 59½x40½mm

378 A74 1m Bible, Maseru Cathedral .50 .50
Nos. 376-378 (3) .90 .90

Issued in sheets of 9 (3 each Nos. 376-378).

1982, Sept. 30

379 A75 6s Congratulation 4.00 4.00
380 A75 60s Diana, William 2.00 2.00

Issued in sheets of 6 (No. 379, 5 No. 380).

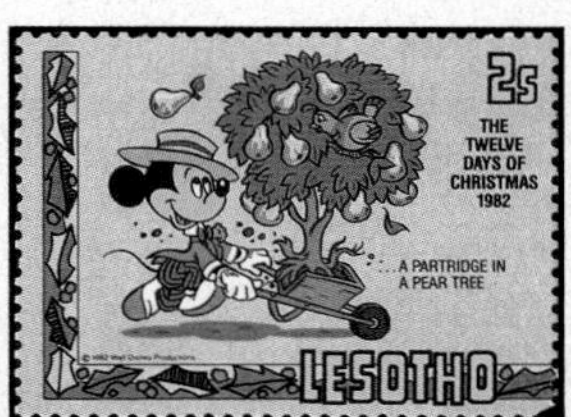

Christmas — A76

Designs: Scenes from Walt Disney's The Twelve Days of Christmas. Stamps of same denomination se-tenant.

1982, Dec. 1 Litho. *Perf. 11*

381 A76 2s multicolored .20 .20
382 A76 2s multicolored .20 .20
383 A76 3s multicolored .20 .20
384 A76 3s multicolored .20 .20
385 A76 4s multicolored .20 .20
386 A76 4s multicolored .20 .20
387 A76 75s multicolored 2.25 2.25
388 A76 75s multicolored 2.25 2.25
Nos. 381-388 (8) 5.70 5.70

Souvenir Sheet

Perf. 14x13½

389 A76 1.50m multicolored 5.00 5.00

Local Mushrooms — A77

1983, Jan. 11 *Perf. 14½*

390 A77 10s Lepista caffrorum .20 .20
391 A77 30s Broomexia congregate .50 .40
a. Booklet pane of 2, #390, 391 .75
392 A77 50s Afroboletus luteolus .90 .80
393 A77 75s Lentinus tuberregium 1.25 1.10
a. Booklet pane of 4, #390-393 2.75
Nos. 390-393 (4) 2.85 2.50

Commonwealth Day — A78

1983, Mar. 14 Litho. *Perf. 14½*

394 A78 5s Ba-Leseli dance .20 .20
395 A78 30s Tapestry weaving .20 .20
396 A78 60s Elizabeth II .35 .35
397 A78 75s Moshoeshoe II .40 .40
Nos. 394-397 (4) 1.15 1.15

Trance Dancers A79

Hunters — A79a

Rock Paintings: 25s, Baboons, Sehonghong Thaba Tseka. 60s, Hunter attacking mountain reedbuck, Makhetha Berera. 75s, Eland, Leribe.

1983, May 20 Litho. *Perf. 14½*

398 A79 6s multicolored .45 .40
399 A79 25s multicolored .85 .85
400 A79 60s multicolored .95 .90
401 A79 75s multicolored 1.00 1.00
Nos. 398-401 (4) 3.25 3.15

Souvenir Sheet

402 Sheet of 5, #398-401, 402a 3.75 3.75
a. A79a 10s multicolored .35 .20

Manned Flight Bicentenary — A80

1983, July 11 Litho. *Perf. 14½*

403 A80 7s Montgolfier, 1783 .20 .20
404 A80 30s Wright brothers .45 .35
405 A80 60s 1st airmail plane .85 .75
406 A80 1m Concorde 3.00 3.00
Nos. 403-406 (4) 4.50 4.30

Souvenir Sheet

407 Sheet of 5 4.00 4.00
a. A80 6s Dornier 228 .40 .40

#407 contains #403-406, 407a (60x60mm).

Sesquicentennial of French Missionaries' Arrival — A81

1983, Sept. 5 Litho. *Perf. 13½x14*

408 A81 6s Rev. Eugene Casalis, flags .40 .40
409 A81 25s Morija, 1833 .40 .40
410 A81 40s Baptism of Libe .40 .40
411 A81 75s Map of Basutoland, 1834 .80 .80
Nos. 408-411 (4) 2.00 2.00

Christmas — A82

Scenes from Disney's Old Christmas, from Washington Irving's Sketch Book.

1983, Dec. Litho. *Perf. 14*

412 A82 1s shown .20 .20
413 A82 2s Christmas Eve, diff. .20 .20
414 A82 3s Christmas Day .20 .20
415 A82 4s Christmas Day, diff. .20 .20
416 A82 5s Christmas dinner .20 .20
417 A82 6s Christmas dinner, diff. .20 .20
418 A82 75s Christmas games 2.75 2.75
419 A82 1m Christmas dancers 3.25 3.25
Nos. 412-419 (8) 7.20 7.20

Souvenir Sheet

420 A82 1.75m Christmas Eve 6.00 6.00

African Monarch A83

Butterflies.

1984, Jan. 20 Litho.

421 A83 1s shown .45 .35
422 A83 2s Mountain Beauty .45 .35
423 A83 3s Orange Tip .50 .40
424 A83 4s Blue Pansy .50 .40
425 A83 5s Yellow Pansy .50 .40
426 A83 6s African Migrant .50 .40
427 A83 7s African Leopard .50 .40
428 A83 10s Suffused Acraea .60 .50
429 A83 15s Painted Lady 1.00 1.10
430 A83 20s Lemon Traveller 1.25 1.25
431 A83 30s Foxy Charaxes 1.50 1.75
432 A83 50s Broad-Bordered Grass Yellow 1.50 1.75
433 A83 60s Meadow White 1.50 1.75
434 A83 75s Queen Purple Tip 1.60 2.00
435 A83 1m Diadem 1.60 2.00
436 A83 5m Christmas Butterfly 2.50 3.25
Nos. 421-436 (16) 16.45 18.05

For surcharges see Nos. 559-560, 561A, 564-566, 600, 600A, 600D, 617A-617B.

Easter A84

Designs: Nos. 437a-437j, The Ten Commandments. 1.50m, Moses holding tablets.

1984, Mar. 30 Litho. *Perf. 14*

437 Sheet of 10 + 2 labels 7.00 7.00
a.-j. A84 20s any single .35 .35

Souvenir Sheet

438 A84 1.50m multicolored 2.50 2.50

No. 438 contains one stamp 45x29mm.

1984 Summer Olympics — A85

1984, May 5 Litho. *Perf. 13½*

439 A85 10s Torch bearer .20 .20
440 A85 30s Equestrian .20 .20
441 A85 50s Swimming .35 .35
442 A85 75s Basketball .45 .45
443 A85 1m Running .55 .55
Nos. 439-443 (5) 1.75 1.75

Souvenir Sheet

444 A85 1.50m Flags, flame, stadium 2.00 2.00

Prehistoric Footprints — A86

1984, July 2 Litho. *Perf. 13½*

445 A86 10s Sauropodomorph .35 .35
446 A86 30s Lesothosaurus 1.00 1.00
447 A86 50s Carnivorous dinosaur 1.75 1.75
Nos. 445-447 (3) 3.10 3.10

Mail Coach Bicentenary and Ausipex '84 — A87

6s, Wells Fargo, 1852. 7s, Basotho mail cart, 1900. 10s, Bath mail coach, 1784. 30s, Cobb coach, 1853. 50s, Exhibition buildings. 1.75m, Penny Black, Basutoland #O4, Western Australia #3.

1984, Sept. 5 Litho. *Perf. 14*

448 A87 6s multicolored .20 .20
449 A87 7s multicolored .20 .20
450 A87 10s multicolored .20 .20
451 A87 30s multicolored .20 .20

Size: 82x26mm

451A A87 50s multicolored .45 .45
Nos. 448-451A (5) 1.25 1.25

Souvenir Sheet

452 A87 1.75m multicolored 3.75 3.75

No. 452 contains one stamp 82x26mm.

Trains — A88

1984, Nov. 5 Litho. *Perf. 13½*

453 A88 6s Orient Express, 1900 .20 .20
454 A88 15s 05.001, Class 5, 1935 .30 .30
455 A88 30s Cardean, Caledonian, 1906 .55 .55
456 A88 60s Santa Fe, Super Chief, 1940 1.10 1.10
457 A88 1m Flying Scotsman, 1934 2.00 2.00
Nos. 453-457 (5) 4.15 4.15

Souvenir Sheet

Perf. 14x13½

458 A88 2m The Blue Train, 1972 2.50 2.50

Indigenous Young Animals — A89

1984, Dec. 20 *Perf. 14½*

459 A89 15s Cape Eland calf .25 .25
460 A89 20s Chacma baboons .30 .30
461 A89 30s Oribo calf .45 .45
462 A89 75s Red rock hares 1.10 1.10

Size: 47x28mm

Perf. 13½

463 A89 1m Black-backed jackals 1.60 1.60
Nos. 459-463 (5) 3.70 3.70

King Moshoeshoe II — A90

1985, Jan. 30 Litho. *Perf. 15*

464 A90 6s Royal crown, 1974 .20 .20
465 A90 30s Moshoeshoe II, 1966 .20 .20
466 A90 75s In Basotho dress .50 .50
467 A90 1m In military uniform .70 .70
Nos. 464-467 (4) 1.60 1.60

25th anniversary of reign.

Miniature Sheet

Easter A91

Stations of the Cross: a, Condemned to death. b, Bearing cross. c, Falls the first time. d, Meets his mother. e, Cyrenean helps carry cross. f, Veronica wipes His face. g, Second fall. h, Consoles women of Jerusalem. i, Third fall. j, Stripped. k, Nailed to cross. l, Dies on cross. m, Taken down from cross. n, Laid in sepulchre. No. 469, The Crucifixion, detail, by Mathias Grunewald (c. 1460-1528).

1985, Mar. 8 *Perf. 11*

468 Sheet of 14 + label 7.00
a.-n. A91 20s any single .20 .20

Souvenir Sheet

Perf. 14

469 A91 2m multicolored 3.00 3.00

Queen Mother, 85th Birthday — A92

Photographs: 10s, Queen Mother, Princess Elizabeth, 1931. 30s, 75th birthday portrait. 60s With Queen Elizabeth II and Princess Margaret, 80th birthday. No. 473, With Queen Elizabeth II, Princess Diana, Princes Henry and Charles, christening of Prince Henry. No. 474, like No. 473, with Prince William.

1985, May 30 *Perf. 13½x14*

470 A92 10s multicolored .20 .20
471 A92 30s multicolored 1.10 1.10
472 A92 60s multicolored 1.25 1.25
473 A92 2m multicolored 2.25 2.25
Nos. 470-473 (4) 4.80 4.80

Souvenir Sheet

474 A92 2m multicolored 2.25 2.25

No. 474 contains one stamp 38x51mm.

Automobile Centenary — A93

Luxury cars.

1985, June 10 *Perf. 14*

475 A93 6s BMW 732i .40 .20
476 A93 10s Ford LTD Crown Victoria .60 .20
477 A93 30s Mercedes-Benz 500SE .90 .60
478 A93 90s Cadillac Eldorado Biarritz 1.75 1.50
479 A93 2m Rolls Royce Silver Spirit 3.50 3.50
Nos. 475-479 (5) 7.15 6.00

Souvenir Sheet

480 A93 2m 1907 Rolls Royce Silver Ghost Tourer, vert. 6.00 6.00

No. 480 contains one stamp 38x51mm.

Audubon Birth Bicentenary — A94

Illustrations of North American bird species by artist and naturalist John J. Audubon.

1985, Aug. 5 *Perf. 14½*

481 A94 5s Cliff swallow, vert. .55 .45
482 A94 6s Great crested grebe .70 .45
483 A94 10s Vesper sparrow 1.25 .60
484 A94 30s Greenshank 1.75 1.75
485 A94 60s Stilt sandpiper 2.25 2.25
486 A94 2m Glossy ibis 3.50 3.50
Nos. 481-486 (6) 10.00 9.00

Nos. 481-486 printed in sheets of 5 with labels picturing various birds.

Intl. Youth Year, Girl Guides 75th Anniv. — A95

1985, Sept. 26 *Perf. 15*

487 A95 10s Mountain climbing .20 .20
488 A95 30s Medical research .65 .60
489 A95 75s Guides on parade 1.40 1.25
490 A95 2m Guide saluting 2.75 2.25
Nos. 487-490 (4) 5.00 4.30

Souvenir Sheet

491 A95 2m Lady Baden-Powell, World Chief Guide 4.00 4.00

UN, 40th Anniv. — A96

Wildflowers — A97

Designs: 10s, UN No. 1, flag, horiz. 30s, Dish satellite, Ha Sofonia Earth Satellite Station, ITU emblem. 50s, Aircraft, Maseru Airport, ICAO emblem, horiz. 2m, Maimonides (1135-1204), medieval Jewish scholar, WHO emblem.

1985, Oct. 15 **Litho.** *Perf. 15*

492 A96 10s multicolored .35 .35
493 A96 30s multicolored .65 .65
494 A96 50s multicolored 1.25 1.25
495 A96 2m multicolored 6.00 5.00
Nos. 492-495 (4) 8.25 7.25

1985, Nov. 11 *Perf. 11*

496 A97 6s Cosmos .55 .20
497 A97 10s Small agapanthus .70 .20
498 A97 30s Pink witchweed 1.25 .75
499 A97 60s Small iris 2.00 2.00
500 A97 90s Wild geranium 2.50 2.50
501 A97 1m Large spotted orchid 3.50 3.50
Nos. 496-501 (6) 10.50 9.15

Mark Twain, Author, Jacob and Wilhelm Grimm, Fabulists A98

Disney characters acting out Mark Twain quotes or portraying characters from The Wishing Table, by the Grimm Brothers.

1985, Dec. 2 *Perf. 11*

502 A98 6s multicolored .20 .20
503 A98 10s multicolored .20 .20
504 A98 50s multicolored 1.50 1.50
505 A98 60s multicolored 2.10 2.10
506 A98 75s multicolored 2.50 2.50
507 A98 90s multicolored 3.00 3.00
508 A98 1m multicolored 3.25 3.25
509 A98 1.50m multicolored 5.50 5.50
Nos. 502-509 (8) 18.25 18.25

Souvenir Sheets

Perf. 14

510 A98 1.25m multicolored 7.00 7.00
511 A98 1.50m multicolored 7.00 7.00

Christmas. #505, 507 printed in sheets of 8.

World Wildlife Fund — A99

Flora and Fauna — A100

Lammergeier vulture.

1986, Jan. 20 *Perf. 15*

512 A99 7s Male *2.00 .75*
513 A99 15s Male, female *4.00 1.00*
514 A99 50s Male in flight *6.00 2.40*
515 A99 1m Adult, young *8.00 4.25*
Nos. 512-515 (4) 20.00 8.40

1986, Jan. 20

516 A100 9s Prickly pear .50 .20
517 A100 12s Stapelia .50 .20
518 A100 35s Pig's ears .75 .50
519 A100 2m Columnar cereus 2.75 2.50
Nos. 516-519 (4) 4.50 3.40

Souvenir Sheet

520 A100 2m Black eagle 11.00 8.25

1986 World Cup Soccer Championships, Mexico — A101

Various soccer plays.

1986, Mar. 17 *Perf. 14*

521 A101 35s multicolored 1.25 1.25
522 A101 50s multicolored 1.75 1.75
523 A101 1m multicolored 3.50 3.50
524 A101 2m multicolored 7.00 7.00
Nos. 521-524 (4) 13.50 13.50

Souvenir Sheet

525 A101 3m multicolored 11.00 11.00

New Currency, 1st Anniv. (in 1980) A101a

No. 525A — Both sides of: b, 1979 Intl. Year of the Child gold coin. c, Five-maloti banknote. d, 1979 50-lisente coin. e, Ten-maloti banknote. f, 1979 1-sente coin.

1986, Apr. 1 **Litho.** *Perf. 13¾x14*

525A Horiz. strip of 5 *37.50 37.50*
b.-f. A101a 30s Any single *7.50 7.50*

A102

Halley's Comet — A103

Designs: 9s, Hale Telescope, Mt. Palomar, Galileo. 15s, Pioneer Venus 2 probe, 1985 sighting. 70s, 684 sighting illustration, Nuremberg Chronicles. 3m, 1066 sighting, Norman conquest of England. 4m, Comet over Lesotho.

1986, Apr. 5

526 A102 9s multicolored .75 .20
527 A102 15s multicolored 1.00 .20
528 A102 70s multicolored 2.25 .75
529 A102 3m multicolored 6.00 6.00
Nos. 526-529 (4) 10.00 7.15

Souvenir Sheet

530 A103 4m multicolored 10.00 10.00

Queen Elizabeth II, 60th Birthday

Common Design Type

Designs: 90s, In pantomime during youth. 1m, At Windsor Horse Show, 1971. 2m, At Royal Festival Hall, 1971. 4m, Age 8.

1986, Apr. 21

531 CD339 90s lt yel bis & black .60 .60
532 CD339 1m pale grn & multi .70 .70
533 CD339 2m dull vio & multi 1.40 1.40
Nos. 531-533 (3) 2.70 2.70

Souvenir Sheet

534 CD339 4m tan & black 3.00 3.00

For overprints see Nos. 636-639.

Statue of Liberty, Cent. A104

Statue and famous emigrants: 15s, Bela Bartok (1881-1945), composer. 35s, Felix Adler (1857-1933), philosopher. 1m, Victor Herbert (1859-1924), composer. No. 538, David Niven (1910-1983), actor. No. 539, Statue, vert.

1986, May 1

535 A104 15s multicolored 1.00 .20
536 A104 35s multicolored 1.00 .35
537 A104 1m multicolored 3.50 1.75
538 A104 3m multicolored 5.50 3.00
Nos. 535-538 (4) 11.00 5.30

Souvenir Sheet

539 A104 3m multicolored 7.00 7.00

AMERIPEX '86 — A105

Walt Disney characters.

1986, May 22 *Perf. 11*

540 A105 15s Goofy, Mickey 1.10 .20
541 A105 35s Mickey, Pluto 1.40 .45
542 A105 1m Goofy 3.00 1.90
543 A105 2m Donald, Pete 3.50 2.50
Nos. 540-543 (4) 9.00 5.05

Souvenir Sheet

Perf. 14

544 A105 4m Goofy, Chip'n'Dale 12.00 12.00

Royal Wedding Issue, 1986

Common Design Type

Designs: 50s, Prince Andrew and Sarah Ferguson. 1m, Andrew. 3m, Andrew at helicopter controls. 4m, Couple, diff.

1986, July 23 *Perf. 14*

545 CD340 50s multicolored .50 .50
546 CD340 1m multicolored .95 .95
547 CD340 3m multicolored 2.50 2.50
Nos. 545-547 (3) 3.95 3.95

Souvenir Sheet

548 CD340 4m multicolored 4.00 4.00

Natl. Independence, 20th Anniv. — A106

1986, Oct. 20 **Litho.** *Perf. 15*

549 A106 9s Basotho pony, rider .20 .20
550 A106 15s Mohair spinning .20 .20
551 A106 35s River crossing .35 .35
552 A106 3m Thaba Tseka P.O. 3.00 3.00
Nos. 549-552 (4) 3.75 3.75

Souvenir Sheet

553 A106 4m Moshoeshoe I 8.00 8.00

Christmas A107

Walt Disney characters.

1986, Nov. 4 **Litho.** ***Perf. 11***

554 A107 15s Chip'n'Dale .95 .20
555 A107 35s Mickey, Minnie 1.40 .40
556 A107 1m Pluto 1.90 1.60
557 A107 2m Aunt Matilda 2.75 2.75
Nos. 554-557 (4) 7.00 4.95

Souvenir Sheet

Perf. 14

558 A107 5m Huey and Dewey 11.00 11.00

Butterfly and Bird Type of 1981-84 Surcharged

1986 **Litho.** ***Perf. 14, 14½***

558A A66 9s on 10s #327b
b. 9s on 10s #327
559 A83 9s on 30s No. 431 .20 .20
a. 9s on 30s #431 (surcharge smaller & sans serif)
560 A83 9s on 60s No. 433 .20 .20
561 A66 15s on 1s No. 321 .20 .20
b. 15s on 1s #321a
c. 15s on 1s #321b
561A A83 15s on 1s No. 421 2.00 2.00
562 A66 15s on 2s No. 322 .20 .20
563 A66 15s on 60s No. 330 .20 .20
a. 15s on 60s #330a
564 A83 15s on 2s No. 422 .20 .20
565 A83 15s on 3s No. 423 .20 .20
566 A83 35s on 75s No. 434 .35 .35
a. 35s on 75s #434, small "s"

Issued: Nos. 559-560, July 1. Nos. 561-563, Aug. 22. Nos. 561A, 564-566, June 25.

See Nos. 617A-617B.

Roof of Africa Rally — A108

1988 Summer Olympics, Seoul — A109

1987, Apr. 28 **Litho.** ***Perf. 14***

567 A108 9s White car .45 .20
568 A108 15s Motorcycle #26 .55 .20
569 A108 35s Motorcycle #25 .75 .35
570 A108 4m Red car 4.00 4.00
Nos. 567-570 (4) 5.75 4.75

1987, May 29 ***Perf. 14***

571 A109 9s Tennis .90 .20
572 A109 15s Judo .90 .20
573 A109 20s Running 1.00 .20
574 A109 35s Boxing 1.10 .45
575 A109 1m Diving 1.40 1.10
576 A109 3m Bowling 3.25 3.25
Nos. 571-576 (6) 8.55 5.40

Souvenir Sheet

577 A109 2m Tennis, diff. 2.75 2.75
577A A109 4m Soccer 5.25 5.25

See Nos. 606-611.

No. 577A shows green at lower left diagonal half of the flag.

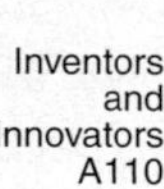

Inventors and Innovators A110

Designs: 5s, Sir Isaac Newton, reflecting telescope. 9s, Alexander Graham Bell, telephone. 75s, Robert H. Goddard, liquid fuel rocket. 4m, Chuck Yeager (b. 1923), test pilot. No. 582, Mariner 10 spacecraft.

1987, June 30 ***Perf. 15***

578 A110 5s multicolored .45 .20
579 A110 9s multicolored .45 .20
580 A110 75s multicolored 1.00 .75
581 A110 4m multicolored 4.00 4.00
Nos. 578-581 (4) 5.90 5.15

Souvenir Sheet

582 A110 4m multicolored 5.00 5.00

Fauna and Flora A111

1987, Aug. 14

583 A111 5s Gray rhebuck .50 .20
584 A111 9s Cape clawless otter .50 .20
585 A111 15s Cape gray mongoose .70 .20
586 A111 20s Free state daisy .80 .20
587 A111 35s River bells .90 .35
588 A111 1m Turkey flower 2.00 1.00
589 A111 2m Sweet briar 2.50 2.00
590 A111 3m Mountain reedbuck 3.00 3.00
Nos. 583-590 (8) 10.90 7.15

Souvenir Sheet

591 A111 2m Pig-lily 3.25 3.25
592 A111 4m Cape wildebeest 5.75 5.75

Nos. 586-589 and 591 vert.

16th World Scout Jamboree, Australia, 1987-88 — A112

1987, Sept. 10 **Litho.** ***Perf. 14***

593 A112 9s Orienteering .20 .20
594 A112 15s Playing soccer .20 .20
595 A112 35s Kangaroos .65 .65
596 A112 75s Salute, flag 1.25 1.25
597 A112 4m Windsurfing 7.25 7.25
Nos. 593-597 (5) 9.55 9.55

Souvenir Sheet

598 A112 4m Map, flag of Australia 6.00 6.00

Nos. 324, 425, 424, 328 and 427 Surcharged

1987 **Litho.** ***Perf. 14½, 14***

598A A66 9s on 5s No. 324 .20 .20
599 A66 15s on 5s No. 324 .20 .20
600 A83 15s on 5s No. 425 .20 .20
600A A83 20s on 4s No. 424 .20 .20
600B A66 35s on 25s No. 328 .35 .35
e. 35s on 25s #328, small "s"
f. 35s on 25s #328a
g. 35s on 25s #328a, small "s"
600C A66 35s on 75s #331
h. 35s on 75s #331, small "s"
600D A83 40s on 7s No. 427 .40 .40

Issued: #599-600, Nov. 16; #600B, Dec. 15; #598A, 600A, 600D, Dec. 30.

A113

A114

Religious paintings (details) by Raphael: 9s, Madonna and Child. 15s, Marriage of the Virgin. 35s, Coronation of the Virgin. 90s, Madonna of the Chair. 3m, Madonna and Child Enthroned with Five Saints.

1987, Dec. 21 ***Perf. 14***

601 A113 9s multicolored .20 .20
602 A113 15s multicolored .20 .20
603 A113 35s multicolored 1.25 1.25
604 A113 90s multicolored 3.25 3.25
Nos. 601-604 (4) 4.90 4.90

Souvenir Sheet

605 A114 3m multicolored 5.00 5.00

Christmas.

Summer Olympics Type of 1987

1987, Nov. 30 **Litho.** ***Perf. 14***

606 A109 5s like 9s .20 .20
607 A109 10s like 15s .20 .20
608 A109 25s like 20s .25 .25
609 A109 40s like 35s .35 .35
610 A109 50s like 1m .50 .50
611 A109 3.50m like 3m 3.50 3.50
Nos. 606-611 (6) 5.00 5.00

Souvenir Sheet

612 A109 4m Soccer 4.00 4.00

No. 612 shows green at lower right diagonal half of the flag.

Discovery of America, 500th Anniv. (in 1992) A115

Columbus's fleet and marine life: 9s, Spotted trunkfish. 15s, Green sea turtle. 35s, Common dolphin. 5m, White-tailed tropicbird. 4m, Ship.

1987, Dec. 14 **Litho.** ***Perf. 14***

613 A115 9s multicolored .20 .20
614 A115 15s multicolored .20 .20
615 A115 35s multicolored .60 .60
616 A115 5m multicolored 8.50 8.50
Nos. 613-616 (4) 9.50 9.50

Souvenir Sheet

617 A115 4m multicolored 7.00 7.00

Nos. 328, 559 Surcharged

Methods and Perfs as Before

1988

617A A83 3s on 9s on 30s
617B A83 7s on 9s on 30s

Birds A116

1988, Apr. 5 **Litho.** ***Perf. 15***

618 A116 2s Pied kingfisher .20 .20
619 A116 3s Three-banded plover .20 .20
620 A116 5s Spurwing goose .20 .20
621 A116 10s Clapper lark .20 .20
622 A116 12s Red-eyed bulbul .20 .20
623 A116 16s Cape weaver .20 .20
624 A116 20s Red-headed finch .20 .20
625 A116 30s Mountain chat .30 .30
626 A116 40s Stone chat .40 .40
627 A116 55s Pied barbet .55 .55
628 A116 60s Cape glossy starling .60 .60
629 A116 75s Cape sparrow .75 .75
630 A116 1m Cattle egret 1.00 1.00
631 A116 3m Giant kingfisher 3.00 3.00
632 A116 10m Crowned guinea fowl 10.00 10.00
Nos. 618-632 (15) 18.00 18.00

For surcharges see Nos. 755, 805-806.

1989, Sept. 18 ***Perf. 14***

620a A116 5s multicolored .20 .20
622a A116 12s multicolored .20 .20
623a A116 16s multicolored .20 .20
624a A116 20s multicolored .20 .20
630a A116 1m multicolored .80 .80
631a A116 3m multicolored 2.40 2.40
632a A116 10m multicolored 8.00 8.00
Nos. 620a-632a (7) 12.00 12.00

Dated 1989.

1990 ***Perf. 12½x12***

620b A116 5s multicolored .20 .20
622b A116 12s multicolored .20 .20
623b A116 16s multicolored .20 .20
624b A116 20s multicolored .20 .20
630b A116 1m multicolored .80 .80
631b A116 3m multicolored 2.40 2.40
632b A116 10m multicolored 8.00 8.00
Nos. 620b-632b (7) 12.00 12.00

Dated 1989.

1991 (?) ***Perf. 11½x13***

620c A116 5s multicolored .20 .20
622c A116 12s multicolored .20 .20
623c A116 16s multicolored .20 .20
624c A116 20s multicolored .20 .20
630c A116 1m multicolored .80 .80
631c A116 3m multicolored 2.40 2.40
632c A116 10m multicolored 8.00 8.00
Nos. 620c-632c (7) 12.00 12.00

Dated 1989.

Nos. 531-534 Overprinted "40th WEDDING ANNIVERSARY / H.M. QUEEN ELIZABETH II / H.R.H. THE DUKE OF EDINBURGH" in Silver

1988, May 3 ***Perf. 14***

636 CD339 90s lt yel bis & blk 1.00 1.00
637 CD339 1m pale grn & multi 1.10 1.10
638 CD339 2m dull vio & multi 2.25 2.25
Nos. 636-638 (3) 4.35 4.35

Souvenir Sheet

639 CD339 4m tan & black 4.50 4.50

FINLANDIA '88, Helsinki, June 1-12 — A117

Disney animated characters and Helsinki sights.

1988, June 2 **Litho.** ***Perf. 14x13½***

640 A117 1s Touring President's Palace .20 .20
641 A117 2s Sauna .20 .20
642 A117 3s Lake Country fishing .20 .20
643 A117 4s Finlandia Hall .20 .20
644 A117 5s Photographing Sibelius Monument .20 .20
645 A117 10s Pony trek, youth hostel .30 .30
646 A117 3m Olympic Stadium 4.75 3.50
647 A117 5m Santa Claus, Arctic Circle 6.00 4.75
Nos. 640-647 (8) 12.05 9.55

Souvenir Sheets

Perf. 14x13½, 13½x14

648 A117 4m Market Square 4.75 4.75
649 A117 4m Lapp encampment, vert. 4.75 4.75

Mickey Mouse, 60th anniv.

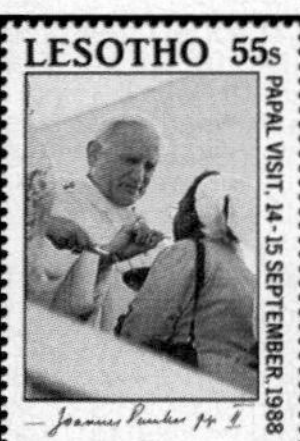

A118

A119

1988, Sept. 1 Litho. *Perf. 14*

650 A118 55s Pope giving communion .55 .55
651 A118 2m Leading procession 2.00 2.00
652 A118 3m Walking in garden 3.00 3.00
653 A118 4m Wearing scullcap 4.00 4.00
Nos. 650-653 (4) 9.55 9.55

Souvenir Sheet

654 A118 5m Pope, Archbishop Morapeli of Lesotho, horiz. 8.50 8.50

Visit of Pope John Paul II, Sept. 14-16.

1988, Oct. 13 Litho. *Perf. 14*

Small indigenous mammals.

655 A119 16s Rock hyrax .20 .20
656 A119 40s Honey badger .85 .85
657 A119 75s Genet 1.50 1.50
658 A119 3m Yellow mongoose 6.25 6.25
Nos. 655-658 (4) 8.80 8.80

Souvenir Sheet

659 A119 4m Meerkat 6.00 6.00

Birth of Venus, 1480, by Botticelli A120

Paintings: 25s, View of Toledo, 1608, by El Greco. 40s, Maids of Honor, 1656, by Diego Velazquez. 50s, The Fifer, 1866, by Manet. 55s, The Starry Night, 1889, by Van Gogh. 75s, Prima Ballerina, 1876, by Degas. 2m, Bridge over Water Lilies, 1899, by Monet. 3m, Guernica, 1937, by Picasso. No. 668, The Presentation of the Virgin in the Temple, c. 1534, by Titian. No. 669, The Miracle of the Newborn Infant, 1511, by Titian.

1988, Oct. 17 Litho. *Perf. 13½x14*

660 A120 15s multicolored .40 .20
661 A120 25s multicolored .55 .25
662 A120 40s multicolored .65 .40
663 A120 50s multicolored .75 .50
664 A120 55s multicolored .80 .55
665 A120 75s multicolored .90 .90
666 A120 2m multicolored 2.00 2.00
667 A120 3m multicolored 3.00 3.00
Nos. 660-667 (8) 9.05 7.80

Souvenir Sheets

668 A120 4m multicolored 4.00 4.00
669 A120 4m multicolored 4.00 4.00

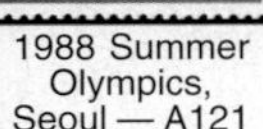

1988 Summer Olympics, Seoul — A121

Intl. Tennis Federation, 75th Anniv. — A122

1988, Nov. 11 Litho. *Perf. 14*

670 A121 12s Wrestling, horiz. .20 .20
671 A121 16s Equestrian .20 .20
672 A121 55s Shooting, horiz. .40 .40
673 A121 3.50m like 16s 2.75 2.75
Nos. 670-673 (4) 3.55 3.55

Souvenir Sheet

674 A121 4m Olympic flame 5.25 5.25

1988, Nov. 18

Tennis champions, views of cities or landmarks: 12s, Yannick Noah, Eiffel Tower, horiz. 20s, Rod Laver, Sydney Opera House and Harbor Bridge, horiz. 30s, Ivan Lendl, Prague, horiz. 65s, Jimmy Connors, Tokyo. 1m, Arthur Ashe, Barcelona. 1.55m, Althea Gibson, NYC. 2m, Chris Evert, Vienna. 2.40m, Boris Becker, London. 3m, Martina Navratilova, Golden Gate Bridge, horiz. 4m, Steffi Graf, Berlin, West Germany.

675 A122 12s multi .70 .20
676 A122 20s multi .90 .20
677 A122 30s multi .80 .35
678 A122 65s multi .95 .80
679 A122 1m multi 1.25 1.25
680 A122 1.55m multi 1.75 1.75
681 A122 2m multi 2.40 2.40
682 A122 2.40m multi 2.75 2.75
683 A122 3m multi 3.50 3.50
Nos. 675-683 (9) 15.00 13.20

Souvenir Sheet

684 A122 4m multi 5.00 5.00

No. 676 has "Sidney" instead of "Sydney." No. 679 has "Ash" instead of "Ashe."

Paintings by Titian A123

Designs: 12s, The Averoldi Polyptych. 20s, Christ and the Adulteress (Christ). 35s, Christ and the Adulteress (adultress). 45s, Angel of the Annunciation. 65s, Saint Dominic. 1m, The Vendramin Family. 2m, Mary Magdalen. 3m, The Tribute Money. No. 693, Christ and the Woman Taken in Adultery. No. 694, The Mater Dolorosa.

1988, Dec. 1 *Perf. 14x13½*

685 A123 12s multicolored .40 .20
686 A123 20s multicolored .50 .20
687 A123 35s multicolored .60 .35
688 A123 45s multicolored .70 .45
689 A123 65s multicolored .70 .65
690 A123 1m multicolored 1.00 1.00
691 A123 2m multicolored 2.00 2.00
692 A123 3m multicolored 3.00 3.00
Nos. 685-692 (8) 8.90 7.85

Souvenir Sheets

693 A123 5m multicolored 5.00 5.00
694 A123 5m multicolored 5.00 5.00

Birth of Titian, 500th anniv. Nos. 685-693 inscribed "Christmas 1988."

Intl. Red Cross, 125th Anniv. A124

Anniv. emblem, supply and ambulance planes: 12s, Pilatus PC-6 Turbo Porter. 20s, Cessna Caravan. 55s, De Havilland DHC-6 Otter. 3m, Douglas DC-3 in thunderstorm. 4m, Douglas DC-3, diff.

1989, Jan. 30 Litho. *Perf. 14*

695 A124 12s multicolored .20 .20
696 A124 20s multicolored .20 .20
697 A124 55s multicolored 1.25 1.25
698 A124 3m multicolored 6.00 6.00
Nos. 695-698 (4) 7.65 7.65

Souvenir Sheet

699 A124 4m multi, vert. 10.00 10.00

Landscapes by Hiroshige — A125

Designs: 12s, Dawn Mist at Mishima. 16s, Night Snow at Kambara. 20s, Wayside Inn at Mariko Station. 35s, Shower at Shono. 55s, Snowfall on the Kisokaido Near Oi. 1m, Autumn Moon at Seba. 3.20m, Evening Moon at Ryogaku Bridge. 5m, Cherry Blossoms, Arashiyama. No. 708, Listening to the Singing Insects at Dokanyama. No. 709, Moonlight, Nagakubo.

1989, June 19 Litho. *Perf. 14x13½*

700 A125 12s multi .40 .20
701 A125 16s multi .45 .20
702 A125 20s multi .45 .20
703 A125 35s multi .45 .30
704 A125 55s multi .70 .45
705 A125 1m multi 1.00 .80
706 A125 3.20m multi 2.75 2.75
707 A125 5m multi 4.50 4.50
Nos. 700-707 (8) 10.70 9.40

Souvenir Sheets

708 A125 4m multi 4.50 4.50
709 A125 4m multi 4.50 4.50

Hirohito (1901-1989) and enthronement of Akihito as emperor of Japan.

PHILEXFRANCE '89, French Revolution Bicent. — A126

Disney characters wearing insurgent uniforms.

1989, July 10 *Perf. 13½x14, 14x13½*

710 A126 1s General .20 .20
711 A126 2s Infantry .20 .20
712 A126 3s Grenadier .20 .20
713 A126 4s Cavalry .20 .20
714 A126 5s Hussar .20 .20
715 A126 10s Marine .20 .20
716 A126 3m Natl. guard 3.50 3.50
717 A126 5m Admiral 5.75 5.75
Nos. 710-717 (8) 10.45 10.45

Souvenir Sheets

718 A126 4m Natl. guard, royal family, horiz. 5.50 5.50
719 A126 4m La Marseillaise 5.50 5.50

Maloti Mountains A127

Mushrooms A128

No. 720: a, Sotho thatched dwellings. b, Two trees, cliff edge. c, Waterfall. d, Tribesman.

1989, Sept. Litho. *Perf. 14*

720 Strip of 4 4.25 4.25
a.-d. A127 1m any single .80 .80

Souvenir Sheet

721 A127 4m Flora 4.50 4.50

1989, Sept. 8 Litho. *Perf. 14*

722 A128 12s *Paxillus involutus* .35 .20
723 A128 16s *Ganoderma applanatum* .35 .20
723A A128 55s *Suillus granulatus* .65 .55
724 A128 5m *Stereum hirsutum* 5.00 4.75
Nos. 722-724 (4) 6.35 5.70

Souvenir Sheet

725 A128 4m *Scleroderma flavidum* 6.75 6.75

Birds A129

1989, Oct. 23 Litho. *Perf. 14*

726 A129 12s Marsh sandpipers .20 .20
727 A129 65s Little stints 1.10 1.10
728 A129 1m Ringed plovers 1.75 1.75
729 A129 4m Curlew sandpipers 7.00 7.00
Nos. 726-729 (4) 10.05 10.05

Souvenir Sheet

730 A129 5m Ruff, vert. 12.00 12.00

1st Moon Landing, 20th Anniv. A130

Highlights of the Apollo 11 mission.

1989, Nov. 6 *Perf. 14*

731 A130 12s Liftoff .20 .20
732 A130 16s Eagle landing .20 .20
733 A130 40s Astronaut on ladder .40 .40
734 A130 55s Buzz Aldrin .60 .60
735 A130 1m Solar wind experiment 1.10 1.10
736 A130 2m Eagle lifting off 2.25 2.25
737 A130 3m Columbia in orbit 3.25 3.25
738 A130 4m Splashdown 4.50 4.50
Nos. 731-738 (8) 12.50 12.50

Souvenir Sheet

739 A130 5m Astronaut, Eagle 7.50 7.50

Nos. 731, 733, 738-739 vert.

World Stamp Expo '89 A131

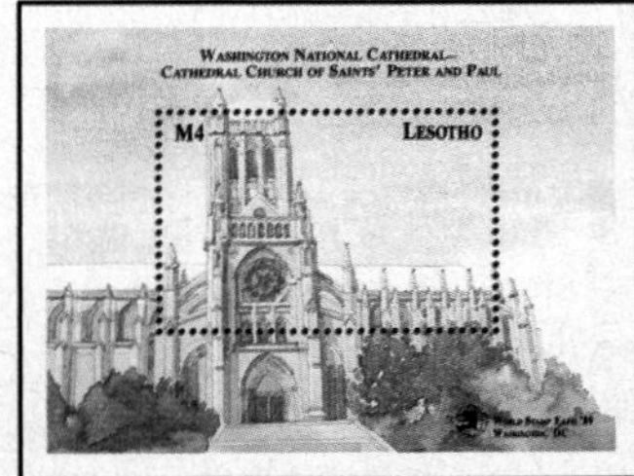

Cathedral Church of Sts. Peter and Paul, Washington, DC — A132

No. 740: a, Postal marking, England, 1680. b, Wax seal and feather, Germany, 1807. c, Crete #1. d, Perot postmaster's provisional, Bermuda, 1848. e, Pony Express handstamp, US, 1860. f, Finland #1. g, Fiji #1. h, Swedish newspaper handstamp, 1823. i, Bhor #1.

1989, Nov. 17 Litho. *Perf. 14*

740 Sheet of 9 9.00 9.00
a.-i. A131 75s any single .40 .40

Souvenir Sheet

741 A132 4m shown 4.50 4.50

Christmas — A133

Religious paintings by Velazquez: 12s, The Immaculate Conception. 20s, St. Anthony Abbot and St. Paul the Hermit. 35s, St. Thomas the Apostle. 55s, Christ in the House of Martha and Mary. 1m, St. John Writing the Apocalypse on Patmos. 3m, The Virgin Presenting the Chasuble to St. Ildephonsus. 4m, The Adoration of the Magi. 5m, The Coronation of the Virgin.

1989, Dec. 18

742 A133 12s multicolored .20 .20
743 A133 20s multicolored .20 .20
744 A133 35s multicolored .35 .35
745 A133 55s multicolored .55 .55
746 A133 1m multicolored .90 .90
747 A133 3m multicolored 2.75 2.75
748 A133 4m multicolored 3.50 3.50
Nos. 742-748 (7) 8.45 8.45

Souvenir Sheet

749 A133 5m multicolored 11.00 11.00

1990 World Cup Soccer Championships, Italy — A134

Various athletes, emblem and name of previous championship host nations.

1989, Dec. 27

750 A134 12s England, 1966 .20 .20
751 A134 16s Mexico, 1970 .20 .20
752 A134 55s West Germany, 1974 1.00 1.00
753 A134 5m Spain, 1982 7.50 7.50
Nos. 750-753 (4) 8.90 8.90

Souvenir Sheet

754 A134 4m Diego Maradona, Argentina 8.00 8.00

No. 622a Surcharged

1990 Litho. *Perf. 14*

755 A116 16s on 12s multi .20 .20

Orchids A135

1990, Mar. 12 Litho. *Perf. 14*

756 A135 12s Satyrium princeps .20 .20
757 A135 16s Huttonaea pulchra .20 .20
758 A135 55s Herschelia graminifolia .90 .90
759 A135 1m Ansellia gigantea 1.60 1.60
760 A135 1.55m Polystachya pubescens 2.50 2.50
761 A135 2.40m Penthea filicornis 3.75 3.75
762 A135 3m Disperis capensis 4.75 4.75
763 A135 4m Disa uniflora 6.50 6.50
Nos. 756-763 (8) 20.40 20.40

Souvenir Sheet

764 A135 5m Stenoglottis longifolia 11.00 11.00

Expo '90.

Butterflies — A136

1990, Feb. 26 Litho. *Perf. 14*

765 A136 12s Pseudo ergolid .95 .20
766 A136 16s Painted lady 1.10 .20
767 A136 55s Ringed pansy 1.60 .55
768 A136 65s False acraea 1.75 .65
769 A136 1m Eyed pansy 2.40 1.10
770 A136 2m Golden pansy 3.75 2.25
771 A136 3m African monarch 5.25 3.25
772 A136 4m African giant swallowtail 6.50 5.50
Nos. 765-772 (8) 23.30 13.70

Souvenir Sheet

773 A136 5m Citrus swallowtail 12.00 12.00

Queen Mother, 90th Birthday — A137

1990, July 5 Litho. *Perf. 14*

774 1.50m In hat 1.25 1.25
775 1.50m Two children 1.25 1.25
776 1.50m Young woman 1.25 1.25
a. A137 Strip of 3, #774-776 4.50 4.50
Nos. 774-776 (3) 3.75 3.75

Souvenir Sheet

777 A137 5m Child 6.00 6.00

A139 A140

Designs: 12s, King Moshoeshoe II, Prince Mohato wearing blankets. 16s, Prince Mohato in Seana-Marena blanket. 1m, Pope John Paul II in Seana-Marena blanket. 3m, Basotho men on horses. 5m, Pope with blanket and hat.

1990, Aug. 17 Litho. *Perf. 14*

778 A139 12s multicolored .20 .20
779 A139 16s multicolored .20 .20
780 A139 1m multicolored 1.40 1.40
781 A139 3m multicolored 4.00 4.00
Nos. 778-781 (4) 5.80 5.80

Souvenir Sheet

782 A139 5m multi, horiz. 8.25 8.25

1990, Aug. 24

Highland Water Project: 16s, Moving gravel. 20s, Fuel truck. 55s, Piers for bridge construction. 2m, Road construction. 5m, Drilling blasting holes.

783 A140 16s multicolored .20 .20
784 A140 20s multicolored .20 .20
785 A140 55s multicolored .90 .90
786 A140 2m multicolored 2.75 2.75
Nos. 783-786 (4) 4.05 4.05

Souvenir Sheet

787 A140 5m multicolored 8.25 8.25

A141 A142

1990, Sept. 26 Litho. *Perf. 14*

788 A141 12s Breastfeeding .20 .20
789 A141 55s Oral rehydration 1.75 1.75
790 A141 1m Baby being weighed 2.50 2.50
Nos. 788-790 (3) 4.45 4.45

UNICEF Save the Children campaign.

1990, Oct. 5

791 A142 16s Triple jump .20 .20
792 A142 55s 200-meter race 1.00 1.00
793 A142 1m 5000-meter race 1.50 1.50
794 A142 4m Equestrian show jumping 6.00 6.00
Nos. 791-794 (4) 8.70 8.70

Souvenir Sheet

795 A142 5m Lighting Olympic flame 9.00 9.00

1992 Summer Olympics, Barcelona.

Christmas A143

Different details from paintings by Rubens: 12s, 1m, 3m, Virgin and Child. 16s, 80s, 2m, 4m, Adoration of the Magi. 55s, Head of One of the Three Kings, diff. 5m, Assumption of the Virgin.

1990, Dec. 5 Litho. *Perf. 13½x14*

796 A143 12s multicolored .20 .20
797 A143 16s multicolored .20 .20
798 A143 55s multicolored .55 .55
799 A143 80s multicolored .85 .85
800 A143 1m multicolored 1.00 1.00
801 A143 2m multicolored 2.10 2.10
802 A143 3m multicolored 3.00 3.00
803 A143 4m multicolored 4.25 4.25
Nos. 796-803 (8) 12.15 12.15

Souvenir Sheet

804 A143 5m multicolored 7.50 7.50

Nos. 625-626 Surcharged

1991, Jan. 18 Litho. *Perf. 15*

805 A116 16s on 30s #625 .20 .20
806 A116 16s on 40s #626 .20 .20

Phila Nippon '91 — A144

Walt Disney characters visit Japan: 20s, Mickey at Nagasaki Peace Park. 30s, Mickey at Kamakura Beach. 40s, Mickey, Donald entertain at Bunraku Puppet Theater. 50s, Mickey, Donald eat soba at noodle shop. 75s, Minnie, Mickey at tea house. 1m, Mickey, Bullet Train. 3m, Mickey, deer at Todaiji Temple. 4m, Mickey, Minnie before Imperial Palace. No. 815, Mickey skiing at Happo-One, Nagano. No. 816, Mickey, Minnie at Suizenji Park.

1991, June 10 Litho. *Perf. 14x13½*

807 A144 20s multicolored .20 .20
808 A144 30s multicolored .25 .25
809 A144 40s multicolored .50 .50
810 A144 50s multicolored .70 .70
811 A144 75s multicolored 1.40 1.40
812 A144 1m multicolored 1.40 1.40
813 A144 3m multicolored 4.00 4.00
814 A144 4m multicolored 5.50 5.50
Nos. 807-814 (8) 13.95 13.95

Souvenir Sheets

815 A144 6m multicolored 6.25 6.25
816 A144 6m multicolored 6.25 6.25

Entertainers in Films About Africa — A145

Designs: 12s, Stewart Granger, King Solomon's Mines. 16s, Johnny Weissmuller, Tarzan, the Ape Man. 30s, Clark Gable, Grace Kelly, Mogambo. 55s, Sigourney Weaver, Gorillas in the Mist. 70s, Humphrey Bogart, Katharine Hepburn, The African Queen. 1m, John Wayne, Hatari. 2m, Meryl Streep, Out of Africa. 4m, Eddie Murphy, Arsenio Hall, Coming to America. 5m, Elsa, Born Free.

1991, June 20 Litho. *Perf. 14*

817 A145 12s multicolored .65 .20
818 A145 16s multicolored .65 .20
819 A145 30s multicolored .80 .25
820 A145 55s multicolored .95 .70
821 A145 70s multicolored 1.25 .90
822 A145 1m multicolored 1.60 1.25
823 A145 2m multicolored 2.50 2.50
824 A145 4m multicolored 5.25 5.25
Nos. 817-824 (8) 13.65 11.25

Souvenir Sheet

825 A145 5m multicolored 7.25 7.25

Butterflies A146

1991, Aug. 1 Litho. *Perf. 13½*

827 A146 2s Satyrus aello .20 .20
828 A146 3s Erebia medusa .20 .20
829 A146 5s Melanargia galathea .20 .20
830 A146 10s Erebia aethiops .20 .20
831 A146 20s Coenonympha pamphilus .30 .20
832 A146 25s Pyrameis atalanta .30 .20
833 A146 30s Charaxes jasius .45 .30
834 A146 40s Colias palaeno .45 .35
835 A146 50s Colias cliopatra .50 .45
836 A146 60s Colias philodice .60 .55
837 A146 70s Rhumni gonepterix .60 .60
838 A146 1m Colias caesonia .90 .90
839 A146 2m Pyrameis cardui 1.75 1.75
840 A146 3m Danaus chrysippus 2.50 2.50
840A A146 10m Apatura iris 8.75 8.75
Nos. 827-840A (15) 17.90 17.35

Exist dated 1992. Value, set $21.
For surcharge see No. 1062.

SADCC, 10th Anniv. A147

Tourism: 12s, Wattled cranes. 16s, Butterfly, flowers in national parks. 25s, Tourist bus and Mukurub, the Finger of God. 3m, People in traditional dress.

1991, Oct. 10 Litho. *Perf. 14x13½*

841 A147 12s multicolored 2.00 2.00
842 A147 16s multicolored 2.00 2.00
843 A147 25s multicolored 2.00 2.00
Nos. 841-843 (3) 6.00 6.00

Souvenir Sheet

844 A147 3m multicolored 6.00 6.00

Say No to Drugs A148

1991, Oct. 10

845 A148 16s multicolored 2.40 2.40

Charles de Gaulle, Birth Cent. — A149

DeGaulle: 40s, Wearing brigadier general's kepi. 50s, Facing left. 60s, Facing right. 4m, In later years.

1991, Dec. 6 Litho. *Perf. 14*

846 A149 20s black & brown .20 .20
847 A149 40s black & violet .65 .65
848 A149 50s black & olilve .85 .85
849 A149 60s black & dk blue 1.00 1.00
850 A149 4m black & brn org 6.75 6.75
Nos. 846-850 (5) 9.45 9.45

Christmas A150

Engravings by Albrecht Durer: 20s, St. Anne with Mary and the Child Jesus. 30s, Mary on the Grass Bench. 50s, Mary with the Crown of Stars. 60s, Mary with Child beside a Tree. 70s, Mary with Child beside the Wall. 1m, Mary in a Halo on the Crescent Moon. 2m, Mary Breastfeeding Her Child. 4m, Mary with the Infant in Swaddling Clothes. No. 859, Holy Family with the Dragonfly. No. 860, The Birth of Christ.

1991, Dec. 13 Litho. *Perf. 12*

851 A150 20s rose & black .20 .20
852 A150 30s blue & black .50 .50
853 A150 50s green & black .80 .80
854 A150 60s red & black 1.00 1.00
855 A150 70s yellow & black 1.10 1.10
856 A150 1m yel org & black 1.60 1.60
857 A150 2m violet & black 3.00 3.00
858 A150 4m dk blue & black 6.50 6.50
Nos. 851-858 (8) 14.70 14.70

Souvenir Sheets

Perf. 14½

859 A150 5m blue & black 6.00 6.00
860 A150 5m pink & black 6.00 6.00

Games A151

Walt Disney characters playing games: 20s, Mickey, Pluto playing pin the tail on the donkey. 30s, Mickey enjoying board game, Mancala. 40s, Mickey hoop rolling. 50s, Minnie with hula hoops. 70s, Mickey throwing Frisbee to Pluto. 1m, Donald trying to play Diabolo. 2m, Huey, Dewey and Louie playing marbles. 3m, Donald frustrated by Rubik's cube. No. 869, Donald and Mickey's nephews in tug-of-war. No. 870, Mickey, Donald stick fighting.

1991, Dec. 16 *Perf. 13½x14*

861 A151 20s multicolored .20 .20
862 A151 30s multicolored .55 .55
863 A151 40s multicolored .65 .65
864 A151 50s multicolored .90 .90
865 A151 70s multicolored 1.25 1.25
866 A151 1m multicolored 1.75 1.75
867 A151 2m multicolored 3.50 3.50
868 A151 3m multicolored 5.75 5.75
Nos. 861-868 (8) 14.55 14.55

Souvenir Sheets

869 A151 5m multicolored 6.50 6.50
870 A151 5m multicolored 6.50 6.50

Royal Family Birthday, Anniversary

Common Design Type

1991, Dec. 9 Litho. *Perf. 14*

871 CD347 50s multicolored .70 .70
872 CD347 70s multicolored .95 .95
873 CD347 1m multicolored 1.40 1.40
874 CD347 3m multicolored 4.25 4.25
Nos. 871-874 (4) 7.30 7.30

Souvenir Sheet

875 CD347 4m Charles, Diana, sons 7.00 7.00

Charles and Diana, 10th wedding anniversary. Numbers have been reserved for additional values in this set.

Queen Elizabeth II's Accession to the Throne, 40th Anniv.

Common Design Type

1992, Feb. 6 Litho. *Perf. 14*

881 CD348 20s multicolored .20 .20
882 CD348 30s multicolored .40 .40
883 CD348 1m multicolored 1.25 1.25
884 CD348 4m multicolored 4.75 4.75
Nos. 881-884 (4) 6.60 6.60

Souvenir Sheet

885 CD348 5m multicolored 6.75 6.75

Birds — A152

Designs: a, Lanner falcon. b, Bataleur. c, Red-headed finch. d, Lesser-striped swallow. e, Alpine swift. f, Diederik cuckoo. g, Malachite sunbird. h, Crimson-breasted shrike. i, Pin-tailed whydah. j, Lilac-breasted roller. k, Black korhaan. l, Black-collared barbet. m, Secretary bird. n, Red-billed quelea. o, Red bishop. p, Ring-necked dove. q, Yellow canary. r, Orange-throated longclaw. s, Blue waxbill. t, Golden bishop.

1992, Feb. 10 *Perf. 14½*

886 A152 30s Sheet of 20, #a.-t. 16.00 16.00

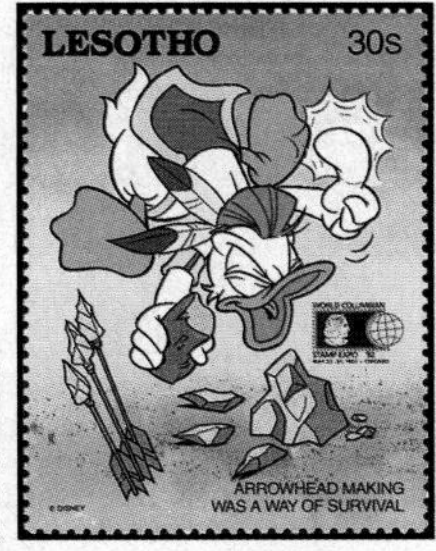

World Columbian Stamp Expo '92, Chicago A153

Walt Disney characters depicting native Americans: 30s, Donald Duck making arrowheads. 40s, Goofy playing lacrosse. 1m, Mickey, Donald planting corn. 3m, Minnie Mouse mastering art of beading. No. 891, Mickey as "Blackhawk" hunting for moose.

1992, Apr. Litho. *Perf. 13½x14*

887 A153 30s multicolored .55 .55
888 A153 40s multicolored .65 .65
889 A153 1m multicolored 1.75 1.75
890 A153 3m multicolored 5.25 5.25
Nos. 887-890 (4) 8.20 8.20

Souvenir Sheet

891 A153 5m multicolored 8.50 8.50

Granada '92 — A154

Walt Disney characters in Spanish costumes: 20s, Minnie Mouse as Lady of Rank, 1540-1660. 50s, Mickey as conqueror of Lepanto, 1571. 70s, Donald Duck from Galicia, 1880. 2m, Daisy Duck from Aragon, 1880. No. 901, Goofy as bullfighter.

1992, Apr. 13 Litho. *Perf. 13½x14*

897 A154 20s multicolored .20 .20
898 A154 50s multicolored 1.25 1.25
899 A154 70s multicolored 1.60 1.60
900 A154 2m multicolored 4.75 4.75
Nos. 897-900 (4) 7.80 7.80

Souvenir Sheet

901 A154 5m multicolored 8.50 8.50

Dinosaurs A155

1992, June 9 *Perf. 14*

907 A155 20s Stegosaurus .20 .20
908 A155 30s Ceratosaurus .65 .65
909 A155 40s Procompsognathus .75 .75
910 A155 50s Lesothosaurus 1.00 1.00
911 A155 70s Plateosaurus 1.40 1.40
912 A155 1m Gasosaurus 2.00 2.00
913 A155 2m Massospondylus 4.00 4.00
914 A155 3m Archaeopteryx 6.00 6.00
Nos. 907-914 (8) 16.00 16.00

Souvenir Sheet

915 A155 5m Archaeopteryx, diff. 8.50 8.50
916 A155 5m Lesothosaurus, diff. 8.50 8.50

No. 915 printed in continuous design.

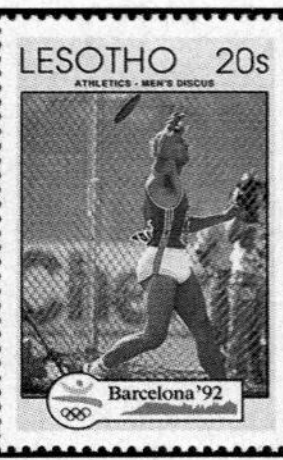

1992 Olympics, Barcelona and Albertville — A156

Designs: 20s, Discus. 30s, Long jump. 40s, Women's 4x100-meter relay. 70s, Women's 100-meter dash. 1m, Parallel bars. 2m, Two-man luge, horiz. 3m, Women's cross-country skiing, horiz. 4m, Biathlon. No. 925, Ice hockey, horiz. No. 926, Women's figure skating.

1992, Aug. 5 Litho. *Perf. 14*

917 A156 20s multicolored .20 .20
918 A156 30s multicolored .25 .25
919 A156 40s multicolored .30 .30
920 A156 70s multicolored .65 .65
921 A156 1m multicolored .95 .95
922 A156 2m multicolored 1.90 1.90
923 A156 3m multicolored 2.75 2.75
924 A156 4m multicolored 4.00 4.00
Nos. 917-924 (8) 11.00 11.00

Souvenir Sheet

925 A156 5m multicolored 6.00 6.00
926 A156 5m multicolored 6.00 6.00

Christmas A158

Details or entire paintings: 20s, Virgin and Child, by Sassetta. 30s, Coronation of the Virgin, by Master of Bonastre. 40s, Virgin and Child, by Master of Saints Cosmas and Damian. 70s, The Virgin of Great Panagia, by Russian School, 12th cent. 1m, Madonna and Child, by Vincenzo Foppa. 2m, Madonna and Child, by School of Lippo Memmi. 3m, Virgin and Child, by Barnaba da Modena. 4m, Virgin and Child, by Simone Dei Crocifissi. No. 935, Virgin & Child Enthroned & Surrounded by Angels, by Cimabue. No. 936, Virgin and Child with Saints (entire triptych), by Dei Crocifissi.

1992, Nov. 2 Litho. *Perf. 13½x14*

927 A158 20s multicolored .20 .20
928 A158 30s multicolored .45 .45
929 A158 40s multicolored .55 .55
930 A158 70s multicolored 1.10 1.10
931 A158 1m multicolored 1.50 1.50
932 A158 2m multicolored 2.75 2.75
933 A158 3m multicolored 4.25 4.25
934 A158 4m multicolored 5.75 5.75
Nos. 927-934 (8) 16.55 16.55

Souvenir Sheets

935 A158 5m multicolored 7.00 7.00
936 A158 5m multicolored 7.00 7.00

Souvenir Sheet

World Trade Center, New York City — A159

1992, Oct. 28 Litho. *Perf. 14*

937 A159 5m multicolored 8.50 8.50

Postage Stamp Mega Event '92, NYC.

Anniversaries and Events — A160

Designs: 20s, Baby harp seal. 30s, Giant panda. 40s, Graf Zeppelin, globe. 70s, Woman grinding corn. 4m, Zeppelin shot down over Cuffley, UK by Lt. Leefe Robinson flying BE 2c, WWI. No. 943, Valentina Tereshkova, first woman in space. No. 944, West African crowned cranes. No. 945, Dr. Ronald McNair.

1993, Jan. Litho. *Perf. 14*

938 A160 20s multicolored .20 .20
939 A160 30s multicolored .40 .40
940 A160 40s multicolored .50 .50
941 A160 70s multicolored .90 .90
942 A160 4m multicolored 5.25 5.25
943 A160 5m multicolored 6.25 6.25
Nos. 938-943 (6) 13.50 13.50

Souvenir Sheets

944 A160 5m multicolored 7.25 7.25
945 A160 5m multicolored 7.25 7.25

Earth Summit, Rio de Janeiro (#938-939, 944). Count Zeppelin, 75th death anniv. (#940, 942). Intl. Conference on Nutrition, Rome (#941). Intl. Space Year (#943, 945).

A number has been reserved for an additional value in this set.

Louvre Museum, Bicent. A161

No. 947 — Details or entire paintings, by Nicolas Poussin: a, Orpheus and Eurydice. b-c, Rape of the Sabine Women (left, right). d-e, The Death of Sapphira (left, right). f-g, Echo and Narcissus (left, right). h, Self-portrait.

No. 948, The Moneychanger and His Wife, by Quentin Metsys.

1993, Mar. 19 Litho. *Perf. 12*

947 A161 70s Sheet of 8, #a.-h. + label 9.50 9.50

Souvenir Sheet

Perf. 14½

948 A161 5m multicolored 8.00 8.00

No. 948 contains one 55x88mm stamp.

Flowers — A162

1993, June Litho. *Perf. 14*

949 A162 20s Healing plant .20 .20
950 A162 30s Calla lily .25 .25
951 A162 40s Bird of Paradise .30 .30
952 A162 70s Belladonna .75 .75
953 A162 1m African lily 1.00 1.00
954 A162 2m Veldt lily 2.00 2.00
955 A162 4m Watsonia 4.25 4.25
956 A162 5m Gazania 5.25 5.25
Nos. 949-956 (8) 14.00 14.00

Souvenir Sheets

957 A162 7m Leadwort 6.25 6.25
958 A162 7m Desert rose 6.25 6.25

Miniature Sheet

Coronation of Queen Elizabeth II, 40th Anniv. — A163

No. 959: a, 20s, Official coronation photograph. b, 40s, St. Edward's Crown, Scepter with the Cross. c, 1m, Queen Mother. d, 5m, Queen, family.

7m, Conversation Piece at Royal Lodge, Windsor, by Sir James Gunn, 1950.

1993, June 2 Litho. *Perf. 13½x14*

959 A163 Sheet, 2 each, #a.-d. 16.00 16.00

Souvenir Sheet

Perf. 14

960 A163 7m multicolored 7.50 7.50

Butterflies A164

1993, June 30 Litho. *Perf. 14*

961 A164 20s Bi-colored pansy .20 .20
962 A164 40s Golden pansy .35 .35
963 A164 70s Yellow pansy .55 .55
964 A164 1m Pseudo ergolid .90 .90
965 A164 2m African giant swallowtail 1.75 1.75
966 A164 5m False acraea 4.50 4.50
Nos. 961-966 (6) 8.25 8.25

Souvenir Sheets

967 A164 7m Seasonal pansy 5.75 5.75
968 A164 7m Ringed pansy 5.75 5.75

African Trains A165

Designs: 20s, East African Railways Vulcan 2-8-2, 1929. 30s, Zimbabwe Railways Class 15A, 1952. 40s, South African Railways Class 25 4-8-4, 1953. 70s, East African Railways A58 Class Garratt. 1m, South Africa Class 9E Electric. 2m, East African Railways Class 87, 1971. 3m, East African Railways Class 92, 1971. 5m, South Africa Class 26 2-D-2, 1982. #977, Algeria 231-132BT Class, 1937. #978, South African Railway Class 6E Bo-Bo, 1969.

1993, Sept. 24 Litho. *Perf. 14*

969 A165 20s multicolored .20 .20
970 A165 30s multicolored .40 .40
971 A165 40s multicolored .45 .45
972 A165 70s multicolored .90 .90
973 A165 1m multicolored 1.25 1.25
974 A165 2m multicolored 2.40 2.40
975 A165 3m multicolored 3.75 3.75
976 A165 5m multicolored 6.00 6.00
Nos. 969-976 (8) 15.35 15.35

Souvenir Sheets

977 A165 7m multicolored 7.50 7.50
978 A165 7m multicolored 7.50 7.50

Taipei '93 — A166

Disney characters in Taiwan: 20s, Chung Cheng Park, Keelung. 30s, Chiao-Tienkung Temple Festival. 40s, Procession. 70s, Temple Festival. 1m, Queen's Head Rock Formation, Yehliu, vert. 1.20m, Natl. Concert Hall, Taiwan, vert. 2m, C.K.S. Memorial Hall, Taiwan, vert. 2.50m, Grand Hotel, Taipei.

No. 987, 5m, Natl. Palace Museum, Taipei. No. 988, 6m, Presidential Palace Museum, Taipei, vert.

1993 Litho. *Perf. 14x13½, 13½x14*

979-986 A166 Set of 8 14.00 14.00

Souvenir Sheets

987-988 A166 Set of 2 12.00 12.00

Domestic Cats — A167

Various cats: 20s, 30s, 70s, 5m.

No. 992A, Brown cat eating mouse, vert.

1993, Oct. 29 Litho. *Perf. 14*

989-992 A167 Set of 4 7.00 7.00

Souvenir Sheet

992A A167 5m multicolored 6.00 6.00

Traditional Houses A168

Designs: 20s, Khoaling, Khotla. 30s, Lelapa le seotloana morao ho, 1833. 70s, Thakaneng, Baroetsana. 4m, Mohlongoafatse pele ho, 1833.

No. 996A, Lelapa litema le mekhabiso.

1993, Sept. 24

993-996 A168 Set of 4 8.00 8.00

Souvenir Sheet

996A A168 4m multicolored 6.00 6.00

A169

A170

Players, country: 20s, Khomari, Lesotho. 30s, Mohale, Lesotho. 40s, Davor, Yugoslavia; Rincon, Colombia. 50s, Lekhotla, Lesotho. 70s, Khali, Lesotho. 1m, Milla, Cameroun. 1.20m, Platt, England. 2m, Rummenigge, Germany; Lerby, Denmark.

No. 1005, Stejskal & Hasek, Czechoslovakia; Baresi, Italy, horiz. No. 1006, Lindenberger, Czechoslovakia; Schillaci, Italy.

1993 Litho. *Perf. 13½x14*

997-1004 A169 Set of 8 10.50 10.50

Souvenir Sheets

Perf. 13

1005-1006 A169 6m Set of 2 12.00 12.00

1994 World Cup Soccer Championships, US.

1994, Apr. 2 Litho. *Perf. 14*

New Democratic Government: 20s, King Letsie III signs oath of office under new constitution. 30s, Parliament building. 50s, Dr. Ntsu Mokhehle sworn in as prime minister. 70s, Transfer of power from Major Gen. P. Ramaema to Dr. Mokhehle.

30s, 50s, 70s are horizontal.

1007 A170 20s multicolored .20 .20
1008 A170 30s multicolored .45 .45
1009 A170 50s multicolored .70 .70
1010 A170 70s multicolored 1.00 1.00
Nos. 1007-1010 (4) 2.35 2.35

A171

PHILAKOREA '94 — A172

Frogs: 35s, Aquatic river. 50s, Bubbling kassina. 1m, Guttural toad. 1.50m, Common river.

No. 1015, 5m, Green frog statue. No. 1016, 5m, Black spotted frog, oriental white-eye bird, vert.

1994, Aug. 16 Litho. *Perf. 14*

1011-1014 A171 Set of 4 3.25 3.25

Souvenir Sheets

1015-1016 A172 Set of 2 12.00 12.00

ICAO, 50th Anniv. A173

Designs: 35s, Airplane, passengers on ground. 50s, Airplane, control tower. 1m, Airplane banking, terminal, control tower. 1.50m, Airplane ascending.

1994 Litho. *Perf. 14*

1017 A173 35s multicolored .20 .20
1018 A173 50s multicolored .65 .65
1019 A173 1m multicolored 1.25 1.25
1020 A173 1.50m multicolored 2.00 2.00
Nos. 1017-1020 (4) 4.10 4.10

Medicinal Plants — A174

Designs: 35s, Tagetes minuta. 50s, Plantago lanceolata. 1m, Amaranthus spinosus. 1.50m, Taraxacum officinale. 5m, Datura stramonium.

1995, May 22 Litho. *Perf. 14*

1021-1024 A174 Set of 4 2.25 2.25

Souvenir Sheet

1025 A174 5m multicolored 3.00 3.00

Pius XII Natl. University, 50th Anniv. A175

Designs: 35s, Pius XII College, 1962. 50s, Univ. of Basutoland, Bechuanaland Protectorate & Swaziland, 1965. 70s, Univ. of Botswana, Lesotho & Swaziland, 1970. 1m, Univ. of Bostswana, Lesotho & Swaziland, 1975. 1.50m, Natl. Univ. of Lesotho, 1988. 2m, Natl. Univ. of Lesotho, procession of vice-chancellors at celebration.

1995, July 26 Litho. *Perf. 14*

1026-1031 A175 Set of 6 4.50 4.50

A176 A177

Designs: 35s, Qiloane Pinnacle, Thaba-Bosiu, horiz. 50s, Rock Formation, Ha Mohalenyane, horiz. 1m, Botsoela Falls, Malealea. 1.50m, Backpacking, Makhaleng River Gorge, horiz.
4m, Red hot pokers.

1995, Aug. 28 Litho. *Perf. 14*
1032-1035 A176 Set of 4 3.00 3.00

Souvenir Sheet

1036 A176 4m multicolored 2.50 2.50

No. 1036 contains one 38x58mm stamp.
World Tourism Organization, 20th anniv.
No. 1036 withdrawn 9/15 because "Pokers" was misspelled "Porkers."

1995, Sept. 26

UN emblem and: 35s, Peace dove. 50s, Scales of justice. 1.50m, Handshake of reconciliation, horiz.

1037-1039 A177 Set of 3 2.50 2.50

UN, 50th anniv.

Christmas A178

Roses: 35s, Sutter's Gold. 50s, Michele Meilland. 1m, J. Otto Thilow. 2m, Papa Meilland.

1995, Nov. 1 Litho. *Perf. 14*
1040-1043 A178 Set of 4 3.00 3.00

A179 A180

UNICEF, 50th Anniv.: 35s, Using iodized salt. 50s, Taking care of livestock, horiz. 70s, Children in classroom. horiz. 1.50m, Children learning traditional dance, singing, horiz.

1996, July 30 Litho. *Perf. 14*
1044-1047 A179 Set of 4 2.50 2.50

1996, Aug. 1

1996 Summer Olympic Games, Atlanta: 1m, US Basketball team, 1936, horiz. 1.50m, Olympic Stadium, Brandenburg Gate, Berlin, horiz. 2m, Jesse Owens, 1936. 3m, Motor boating, horiz.

Past Olympic medalists: No. 1052a, Glen Morris, long jump, decathlon, 1936. b, Said Aouita, 5000-meters, 1984. c, Arnie Robinson, long jump, 1976. d, Hans Woellke, shot put, 1936. e, Renate Stecher, 100-meters, 1972. f, Evelyn Ashford, 100-meters, 1984. g, Willie Davenport, 110-meter hurdles, 1968. h, Bob Beamon, long jump, 1968. i, Heidi Rosendhal, long jump, 1972.

No. 1053, 8m, Michael Gross, swimming, 1984. No. 1054, 8m, Kornelia Ender, swimming, 1976.

1048-1051 A180 Set of 4 4.50 4.50
1052 A180 1.50m Sheet of 9, #a.-i. 11.50 11.50

Souvenir Sheets

1053-1054 A180 Set of 2 12.50 12.50

Maps of Lesotho — A181

No. 1055 — 1911 map: a, Lephaqlioa. b, Maqaleng. c, Molapo. d, Nkeu. e, No area specified. f, Rafanyane. g, No area specified (7800). h, Madibomatso River. i, Konyani. j, Semena River.

No. 1056 — 1978 map: a, No area specified. b, Lepaqoa. c, Mamoha (name). d, Ha Nkisi. e, Ha Rafanyan, Ha Thoora. f, Ha Mikia, Ha Ntseli. g, Ha Kosetabole, Ha Mpeli. h, Ha Selebeli, Ha Theko. i, Ha Rapooane, Ha Ramabotsa. j, Ha Ramani, Khohlontso (Kolberg).

No. 1057 — Locations on 1994 Map: a, Mafika-Lisiu Pass. b, Rampai's Pass, Ha Lesaoana. c, Ha Masaballa. d, Ha Nkisi, Ha Molotanyan. e, Ha Rafanyane, Kobong. f, Laitsoka Pass. g, Katse Reservoir. h, Seshote. i, Ha Rapoeea, Ha Kennan. j, Katse (i, name), Ha Mense.

1996

Sheets of 10, #a-j

1055-1057 A181 35s Set of 3 15.00 15.00

Trains A182

No. 1058, 1.50m: a, ETR 450, Italy. b, TGV, France. c, XPT, Australia. d, Blue Train, South Africa. e, IC 255, Great Britain. f, Bullet Train, Japan.

No. 1059, 1.50m: a, WP Streamlined 4-6-2, India. b, Canadian Pacific 2471, Canada. c, The Caledonian 4-2-2, Scotland. d, William Mason 4-4-0, US. e, Trans-Siberian Express, Russia. f, Swiss Federal 4-6-0, Switzerland.

No. 1060, 8m, 52 Class, Germany. No. 1061, 8m, ICE, Germany.

1996, Sept. 1 Litho. *Perf. 14*

Sheets of 6, #a-f

1058-1059 A182 Set of 2 12.50 12.50

Souvenir Sheets

1060-1061 A182 Set of 2 12.00 12.00

Nos. 1060-1061 each contain one 56x42mm stamp.

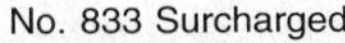

No. 833 Surcharged

1996 Litho. *Perf. 13½*
1062 A146 20s on 30s multi .20 .20

Christmas — A183

Women from Mother's Unions: 35s, Methodist Church. 50s, Roman Catholic Church. 1m, Lesotho Evangelical Church. 1.50m, Anglican Church.

1996, Dec. 10 Litho. *Perf. 14*
1063-1066 A183 Set of 4 2.75 2.75

Highlands Water Project A184

Designs: 35s, "Cooperation for Development." 50s, "Nature and Heritage." 1m, "An Engineering Feat." 1.50m, "LHDA 10th Anniv., 1986-1996."

1997, Apr. 21 Litho. *Perf. 14*
1067-1070 A184 Set of 4 3.25 3.25

No. 1070 is 72x25mm.

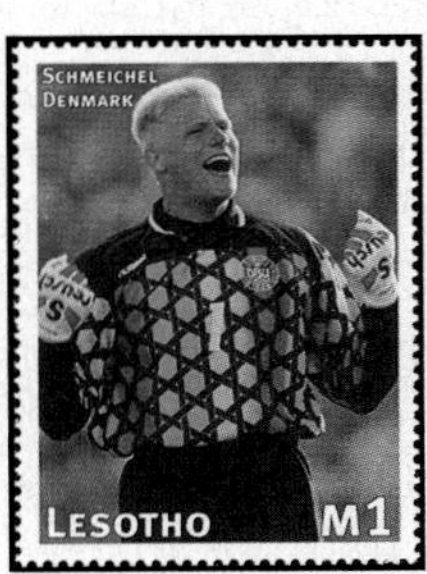

1998 World Cup Soccer Championships, France — A185

Players: 1m, Schmeichel, Denmark. 1.50m, Bergkamp, Holland. 2m, Southgate, England. 2.50m, Asprilla, Colombia. 3m, Gascoigne, England. 4m, Giggs, Wales.

No. 1077: Various action scenes of Argentina vs. Holland, 1978.

No. 1078, 8m, Littbarski, W. Germany, horiz. No. 1079, 8m, Shearer, England.

1997, Oct. 31 Litho. *Perf. 13½*
1071-1076 A185 Set of 6 7.00 7.00
1077 A185 1.50m Sheet of 6, #a.-f. 11.50 11.50

Souvenir Sheets

1078-1079 A185 Set of 2 9.50 9.50

Butterflies A186

No. 1080: a, Spialia spio. b, Cyclyrius pirithous. c, Acraea satis. d, Belenois aurota. e, Spindasis natalensis. f, Torynesis orangica. g, Lepidochrysops variabilis. h, Pinacopteryx eriphea. i, Anthene butleri.

No. 1081, 8m, Bematistes aganice. No. 1082, 8m, Papilio demodocus.

1997, Nov. 28 *Perf. 14*
1080 A186 1.50m Sheet of 9, #a.-i. 7.00 7.00

Souvenir Sheets

1081-1082 A186 Set of 2 12.00 12.00

Morija Museum and Archives, 40th Anniv. A187

Designs: 35s, Rock paintings, child, vert. 45s, Lower jaw of hippopotamus, hippo walking in water. 50s, Traditional attire, vert. 1m, Traditional musical instruments, vert. 1.50m, Award, Man with ceremonial garb, vert. 2m Boy riding bull.

Perf. 14½ Syncopated Type A

1998, Jan. 30 Litho.
1083-1088 A187 Set of 6 3.50 3.50

Diana, Princess of Wales (1961-97) — A188

Designs: No. 1089, Various portaits. No. 1090, Taking flowers from child.

1998, Mar. 16 Litho. *Perf. 13½*
1089 A188 3m Sheet of 6, #a.-f. 9.00 9.00

Souvenir Sheet

1090 A188 9m multicolored 9.50 9.50

A189

A190

Wildlife — A191

No. 1091 — Cape vulture: a, Head. b, Perched on rock with head down. c, Looking left. d, Looking right.

No. 1092: a, Atitlan grebe. b, Cabot's tragopan. c, Spider monkey. d, Dibatag. e, Right whale. f, Imperial parrot. g, Cheetah. h, Brown-eared pheasant. i, Leatherback turtle. j, Imperial woodpecker. k, Andean condor. l, Barbary deer. m, Grey gentle lemur. n, Cuban parrot. o, Numbat. p, Short-tailed albatross. q, Green turtle. r, White rhinoceros. s, Diademed sifaka. t, Galapagos penguin.

No. 1093: a, Impala. b, Black bear. c, Buffalo. d, Elephant. e, Kangaroo. f, Lion. g, Panda. h, Tiger. i, Zebra.

No. 1094, 8m, Nectarinia talatala. No. 1095, 8m, Psephotus chrysopterygius. No. 1096, 8m, Percina tanasi.

No. 1097, 8m, Monkey.

1998, Apr. 27 Litho. *Perf. 14*
1091 A189 1m Strip of 4, #a.-d. *5.00 5.00*
1092 A190 1m Sheet of 20, #a.-t. 12.00 12.00
1093 A191 1.50m Sheet of 9, #a.-i. 7.50 7.50

Souvenir Sheets

1094-1096 A190 Set of 3 12.00 12.00
1097 A191 8m multicolored 4.00 4.00

No. 1091 was issued in sheets of 12 stamps. World Wildlife Fund (#1091).

Cats A192

Designs: 70s, Siamese. 1m, Chartreux. 2m, Korat. 3m, Egyptian mau. 4m, Bombay. 5m, Burmese.

No. 1104, 2m: a, Japanese bobtail. b, British white. c, Bengal. d, Abyssinian. e, Snowshoe. f, Scottish fold.

No. 1105, 2m: a, Maine coon. b, Balinese. c, Persian. d, Javanese. e, Turkish angora. f, Tiffany.

No. 1106, 8m, Singapura. No. 1107, 8m, Tonkinese.

1998, May 18

1098-1103 A192 Set of 6 7.75 7.75

Sheets of 6, #a-f

1104-1105 A192 Set of 2 16.00 16.00

Souvenir Sheets

1106-1107 A192 Set of 2 10.00 10.00

Mushrooms — A193

Designs: 70s, Laccaria laccata. 1m, Mutinus caninus. 1.50m, Tricholoma lascivum. 2m, Clitocybe geotrapa. 3m, Amanita excelsa. 4m, Red-capped bolete.

No. 1114: a, Parrot wax cap. b, Cortinarius obtusus. c, Volvariella bombycina. d, Continarius caerylescens. e, Laccaria amethystea. f, Tricholoma aurantium. g, Amanita excelsa. h, Clavaria helvola. i, Cortinarius caerylescens. j, Russula queletii. k, Amanita phalloides. l, Lactarius delicious.

No. 1115, 8m, Amanita pantherina. No. 1116, 8m, Boletus satanus.

1998, June 15 Litho. *Perf. 14*

1108-1113 A193 Set of 6 7.00 7.00

1114 A193 1m Sheet of 12, #a.-l. 7.00 7.00

Souvenir Sheets

1115-1116 A193 Set of 2 10.00 10.00

Japanese Film Stars A194

No. 1117: a, Takamine Hideko. b, James Shigeta. c, Miyoshi Umeki. d, May Ishimara. e, Sessue Hayakawa. f, Miiko Taka. g, Mori Masayuki. h, Hara Setsuko. i, Kyo Machiko.

10m, Toshiro Mifune.

1998, July 14 Litho. *Perf. 14*

1117 A194 2m Sheet of 9, #a.-i. 8.00 8.00

Souvenir Sheet

1118 A194 10m multicolored 4.00 4.00

Prehistoric Animals — A195

No. 1119, 2m: a, Nyctosaurus (b). b, Volcanoes, wings of nyctosaurus, eudimorphadon. c, Eudimorphodon (b). d, Apatosaurus (g). e, Peteinosaurus (d, f, i). f, Tropeognathus. g, Pteranodon ingens (d). h, Ornithodesmus (g, i). i, Wuerhosaurus.

No. 1120, 2m: a, Ceresiosaurus (b, c, d). b, Rhomaleosaurus (d, e, f). c, Anomalocaris (b, f). d, Mixosaurus (e, g, h). e, Stethacanthus. f, Dunklosteus (c, e, i). g, Tommotia. h, Sanctacaris. i, Ammonites (a, f, h).

No. 1121, 2m: a, Rhamphorhynchus (b, d). b, Brachiosaurus (c, f). c, Mamenchisaurus hochuanensis (a, d, e, f). d, Ceratosaurus nasicornis (e, g, h). e, Archaeopteryx (b). f, Leaellynasaura amicargraphica (e, h, i). g, Chasmosaurus belli (h). h, Deinonychus, Pachyrhinosaurus (g). i, Deinonychus (h).

No. 1122, 10m, Woolly rhinoceros. No. 1123, 10m, Tyrannosaurus. No. 1124, 10m, Coelophysis.

1998, Aug. 10

Sheets of 9, #a-i

1119-1121 A195 Set of 3 27.00 27.00

Souvenir Sheets

1122-1124 A195 Set of 3 18.00 18.00

Intl. Year of the Ocean A196

Fish: No. 1125, 1m, Treefish. No. 1126, 1m, Tiger barb. No. 1127, 1m, Bandtail puffer. No. 1128, 1m, Cod. No. 1129, 1.50m, Filefish. No. 1130, 1.50m, Clown loach. No. 1131, 1.50m, Sicklefin killie. No. 1132, 1.50m, Christy's lyretail. No. 1133, 2m, Brook trout. No. 1134, 2m, Pacific electric ray. No. 1135, 2m, Bighead searobin. No. 1136, 2m, Emerald betta. 3m, Harlequin tuskfish. 4m, Half-moon angelfish. 5m, Spotted trunkfish. 6m, Wolf-eel. 7m, Cherubfish.

No. 1142, 2m: a, Platy variatus. b, Archerfish. c, Clown knifefish. d, Angelicus. e, Black arowana. f, Spotted scat. g, Kribensis. h, Golden pheasant.

No. 1143, 2m: a, Bluegill. b, Grayling. c, Walleye. d, Brown trout. e, Atlantic salmon. f, Northern pike. g, Large mouth bass. h, Rainbow trout.

No. 1144, 2m: a, Purple firefish. b, Halequin sweetlips. c, Clown wrasse. d, Bicolor angelfish. e, False cleanerfish. f, Mandarinfish. g, Regal tang. h, Clownfish.

No. 1145, 2m: a, Weakfish. b, Red drum. c, Blue marlin. d, Yellowfin tuna. e, Barracuda. f, Striped bass. g, White shark. h, Permit.

No. 1146, 12m, Cyprinus carpio. No. 1147, 12m,Oncorhychus. No. 1148, 12m,Pseudopleuronectes americanus. No. 1149, 12m, Heterodontus francisci.

1998, Oct. 15 Litho. *Perf. 14*

1125-1141 A196 Set of 17 17.25 17.25

Sheets of 8, #a-h

1142-1145 A196 Set of 4 26.00 26.00

Souvenir Sheets

1146-1149 A196 Set of 4 19.00 19.00

Africa in Films A197

No. 1150: a, "Simba." b, "Call to Freedom." c, "Cry the Beloved Country." d, "King Solomon's Mines." e, "Flame and the Fire." f, "Cry Freedom." g, "Bopha!" h, "Zulu."

10m "Born Free," horiz.

1998, July 14 Litho. *Perf. 14*

1150 A197 2m Sheet of 8, #a.-h. 8.00 8.00

Souvenir Sheet

1151 A197 10m multicolored 4.00 4.00

Flowers — A198

Designs: 10s, Pelargonium sidoides. 15s, Aponogeton ranunculiflorus. 20s, Sebaea leiostyla. 40s, Sebaea grandis. 50s, Satyrium neglectum. 60s, Massonia jasminiflora. 70s, Ajuga ophrydis. 80s, Nemesia fruticans. 1m, Aloe broomii. 2m, Wahlenbergia androsacea. 2.50m, Phygelius capensis. 3m, Dianthus basuticus. 4.50m, Rhodohypoxis baurii. 5m, Turbina oblongata. 6m, Hibiscus microcarpus. 10m, Lobelia erinus, moraea stricta.

1998 Litho. *Perf. 14*

1152	A198	10s	multicolored	.20	.20
1153	A198	15s	multicolored	.20	.20
1154	A198	20s	multicolored	.20	.20
1155	A198	40s	multicolored	.20	.20
1156	A198	50s	multicolored	.20	.20
1157	A198	60s	multicolored	.20	.20
1158	A198	70s	multicolored	.25	.25
1159	A198	80s	multicolored	.40	.40
1160	A198	1m	multicolored	.50	.50
1161	A198	2m	multicolored	1.00	1.00
1162	A198	2.50m	multicolored	1.25	1.25
1163	A198	3m	multicolored	1.50	1.50
1164	A198	4.50m	multicolored	2.25	2.25
1165	A198	5m	multicolored	2.40	2.40
1166	A198	6m	multicolored	3.00	3.00
1167	A198	10m	multicolored	5.25	5.25
	Nos. 1152-1167 (16)			19.00	19.00

Nos. 1152-1167 are dated 1997.

Coronation of King Letsie III, 1st Anniv. — A199

No. 1168: a, Receiving crown. b, Waving. c, Facing left.

1998, Oct. 31

1168 A199 1m Strip of 3, #a.-c. 2.40 2.40

Dogs A200

Designs: 70s, Akita. 1m, Canaan. 2m, Eskimo. 4.50m, Norwegian elkhound.

No. 1173, 2m: a, Cirneco dell'etna. b, Afghan hound. c, Finnish spitz. d, Dalmatian. e, Basset hound. f, Shar-pei.

No. 1174, 2m: a, Boxer. b, Catalan sheepdog. c, English toy spaniel. d, Greyhound. e, Keeshond. f, Bearded collie.

No. 1175, 8m, Rough collie. No. 1176, 8m, Borzoi.

1999, May 18 Litho. *Perf. 14*

1169-1172 A200 Set of 4 4.00 4.00

Sheets of 6, #a-f

1173-1174 A200 Set of 2 11.00 11.00

Souvenir Sheets

1175-1176 A200 Set of 2 11.00 11.00

Birds A201

Designs: 70s, Belted kingfisher. 1.50m, Palm cockatoo, vert. 2m, Red-tailed hawk. 3m, Tufted puffin. 4m, Reddish egret. 5m, Hoatzin, vert.

No. 1183, 2m: a, Evening grosbeak. b, Lesser blue-winged pitta. c, Altamira oriole. d, Rose-breasted grosbeak. e, Yellow warbler. f, Akiapolaau. g, American goldfinch. h, Northern flicker. i, Western tanager.

No. 1184, 2m, vert: a, Blue jay. b, Northern cardinal. c, Yellow-headed blackbird. d, Red. crossbill. e, Cedar waxwing. f, Vermilion flycatcher. g, Pileated woodpecker. h, Western meadowlark. i, Kingfisher.

No. 1185, 8m, Great egret. No. 1186, 8m, Zosterops erythropleura.

1999, June 28 Litho. *Perf. 14*

1177-1182 A201 Set of 6 8.00 8.00

Sheets of 9, #a-i

1183-1184 A201 Set of 2 19.00 19.00

Souvenir Sheets

1185-1186 A201 Set of 2 11.00 11.00

No. 1183c is incorrectly inscribed "Atlamira."

Orchids — A202

Chinese Art — A203

Designs: 1.50m, Cattleya dowiana. 3m, Diurus behri. 4m, Ancistrochilus rothchildianus. 5m, Aerangis curnowiana. 7m, Arachnis flos-aeris. 8m, Aspasia principissa.

No. 1193, 2m: a, Dendrobium bellaudum. b, Dendrobium trigonopus. c, Dimerandra emarginata. d, Dressleria eburnea. e, Dracula tubeana. f, Disa kirstenbosch. g, Encyclia alata. h, Epidendrum pseudepidendrum. i, Eriopsis biloba.

No. 1194, 2m: a, Apasia epidendroides. b, Barkaria lindleyana. c, Bifrenaria terragona. d, Bulbophyllum graveolens. e, Brassavola flagellaris. f, Bollea lawrenceana. g, Caladenia carnea. h, Catasetum macrocarpum. i, Cattleya aurantiaca.

No. 1195, 2m: a, Cochleanthes discolor. b, Cischweinfia dasyandra. c, Ceratostylis retisquama. d, Comparettia speciosa. e, Cryptostylis subulata. f, Cycnoches ventricsum. g, Dactylorhiza maculata. h, Cypripedium calceolus. i, Cymbidium finlaysonianum.

No. 1196, 10m, Paphiopedilum tonsum. No. 1197, 10m, Laelia rubescens. No. 1198, 10m, Ansellium africana. No. 1199, 10m, Ophrys apifera.

1999, July 30 Litho. *Perf. 14*

1187-1192 A202 Set of 6 13.00 13.00

Sheets of 9, #a-i

1193-1195 A202 Set of 3 22.50 22.50

Souvenir Sheets

1196-1199 A202 Set of 4 16.00 16.00

1999, Aug. 16 *Perf. 13x13¼*

No. 1200 — Paintings by Pan Tianshou (1897-1971): a, Water Lily at Night. b, Hen and Chicks. c, Plum Blossom and Orchid. d, Plum Blossom and Banana Tree. e, Crane and Pine. f, Swallows. g, Eagle on the Pine (black eagle). h, Palm Tree. i, Eagle on the Pine (gray eagle). j, Orchids.

No. 1201: a, Sponge Gourd. b, Dragonfly.

1200 A203 1.50m Sheet of 10, #a.-j. 9.00 9.00

Souvenir Sheet

1201 A203 6m Sheet of 2, #a.-b. 7.00 7.00

China 1999 World Philatelic Exhibition. No. 1201 contains two 51x40mm stamps.

Souvenir Sheet

UN Rights of the Child Convention, 10th Anniv. — A204

No. 1202: a, Black boy. b, Asian girl. c, Caucasian boy.

1999, Aug. 16 *Perf. 14*

1202 A204 2m Sheet of 3, #a.-c. 4.00 4.00

Paintings by Hokusai (1760-1849) — A205

No. 1203, 3m: a, Nakamaro Watching the Moon from a Hill. b, Peonies and Butterfly. c, The Blind (bald man, both eyes open). d, The Blind (bald man, one eye shut). e, People Crossing an Arched Bridge (two at crest). f, People Crossing an Arched Bridge (river).

No. 1204, 3m: a, A View of Sumida River in Snow. b, Two Carp. c, The Blind (man with hair, both eyes shut). d, The Blind (man with hair, one eye open). e, Fishing by Torchlight. f, Whaling off the Goto Islands.

No. 1205, 10m, The Moon Above Yodo River and Osaka Castle, vert. No. 1206, 10m, Bellflower and Dragonfly, vert.

1999, Aug. 16 ***Perf. 13¾***

Sheet of 6, #a-f

1203-1204 A205 Set of 2 14.00 14.00

Souvenir Sheets

1205-1206 A205 Set of 2 8.00 8.00

Queen Mother (b. 1900) — A206

No. 1207: a, Wearing hat, 1938. b, With King George VI, 1948. c, Wearing tiara, 1963. d, Wearing hat, 1989.

15m, Waving at Clarence House.

1999, Aug. 16 ***Perf. 14***

1207 A206 5m Sheet of 4, #a.-d., + label 9.00 9.00

Souvenir Sheet

Perf. 13¾

1208 A206 15m multicolored 7.00 7.00

No. 1208 contains one 38x51mm stamp.

Johann Wolfgang von Goethe (1749-1832) — A207

No. 1209: a, Mephistopheles appears as a dog in Faust's study. b, Portraits of Goethe and Friedrich von Schiller. c, Mephistopheles disguised as dog scorching the earth.

12m, Mephistopheles.

1999, Aug. 16 ***Perf. 14***

1209 A207 6m Sheet of 3, #a.-c. 7.00 7.00

Souvenir Sheet

1210 A207 12m multicolored 5.00 5.00

IBRA '99, Nuremberg, Germany — A208

Designs: 7m, Austerity 2-10-10 locomotive, building in Frankfurt am Main. 8m, Adler locomotive, Brandenburg Gate.

1999, Aug. 16 ***Perf. 14x14½***

1211 A208 7m multicolored 3.00 3.00

1212 A208 8m multicolored 3.50 3.50

Ships A209

No. 1213, 4m: a, James Watt. b, Savannah. c, Amistad. d, Brick. e, Great Briain. f, Sirius.

No. 1214, 4m: a, France. b, Queen Elizabeth II. c, United States. d, Queen Elizabeth I. e, Michelangelo. f, Mauretania.

No. 1215, 4m: a, New Jersey. b, Aquila. c, De Zeven Provincien. d, Formidable. e, Vittorio Veneto. f, Hampshire.

No. 1216, 4m: a, Shearwater. b, British submarine. c, Hovercraft SRN 130. d, Italian submarine. e, Sr. N/3. f, Soucoupe Plongeante.

No. 1217, 15m, E. W. Morrison. No. 1218, 15m, Titanic. No. 1219, 15m, German U-boat. No. 1220, 15m, Enterprise.

1999, Dec. 31 **Litho.** ***Perf. 14***

Sheets of 6, #a.-f.

1213-1216 A209 Set of 4 32.00 32.00

Souvenir Sheets

1217-1220 A209 Set of 4 22.50 22.50

Names of ships are only found on sheet margins.

Millennium A210

No. 1221 — Highlights of the 12th century: a, Chinese make first rocket. b, Burmese temple guardian. c, Troubador. d, Abbé Suger. e, Pope Adrian IV. f, King Henry II of England. g, Holy Roman Emperor Barbarossa. h, Yoritomo establishes shogunate in Japan. i, Crusader monument. j, Ibn Rushd translates Aristotle. k, Archbishop Thomas Becket. l, Leaning Tower of Pisa. m, Pivot windmill. n, Saladin. o, Richard the Lion-Hearted. p, Easter Island statues (60x40mm) q, Third Crusade begins.

1999, Dec. 31 ***Perf. 12¾x12½***

1221 A210 1.50m Sheet of 17, #a.-q. 11.00 11.00

Wedding of King Letsie III to Karabo Anne Motsoeneng A211

No. 1222: a, King, bride in Western attire. b, Bride. c, King. d, King, bride in native attire.

2000, Feb. 18 **Litho.** ***Perf. 14***

1222 A211 1m Sheet of 4, #a.-d., + label 4.00 4.00

Prince William, 18th Birthday — A212

No. 1223: a, Wearing bow tie. b, Wearing scarf. c, Wearing striped shirt. d, Wearing sweater, holding car door.

15m, Wearing sweater, diff.

2000, June 21 **Litho.** ***Perf. 14***

1223 A212 4m Sheet of 4, #a-d 7.00 7.00

Souvenir Sheet

Perf. 13¾

1224 A212 15m multi 7.00 7.00

No. 1223 contains four 28x42mm stamps.

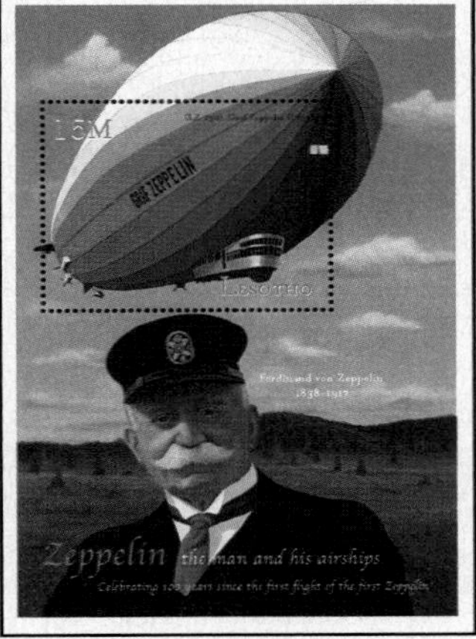

First Zeppelin Flight, Cent. — A213

No. 1225 — Ferdinand von Zeppelin and: a, LZ- 127. b, LZ-130. c, LZ-10.

15m, LZ-130, diff.

2000, July 6 ***Perf. 14***

1225 A213 8m Sheet of 3, #a-c 9.00 9.00

Souvenir Sheet

1226 A213 15m multi 7.00 7.00

No. 1225 contains three 42x28mm stamps.

Berlin Film Festival, 50th Anniv. — A214

No. 1227: a, Gena Rowlands. b, Vlastimil Brodsky. c, Carlos Saura. d, La Collectioneuse. e, Le Depart. f, Le Diable Probablement.

15m, Stammheim.

2000, July 6

1227 A214 6m Sheet of 6, #a-f 13.00 13.00

Souvenir Sheet

1228 A214 15m multi 7.00 7.00

Souvenir Sheets

2000 Summer Olympics, Sydney — A215

No. 1229: a, Nedo Nadi. b, Swimming. c, Aztec Stadium, Mexico City and Mexican flag. d, Ancient Greek boxers.

2000, July 6

1229 A215 6m Sheet of 4, #a-d 9.00 9.00

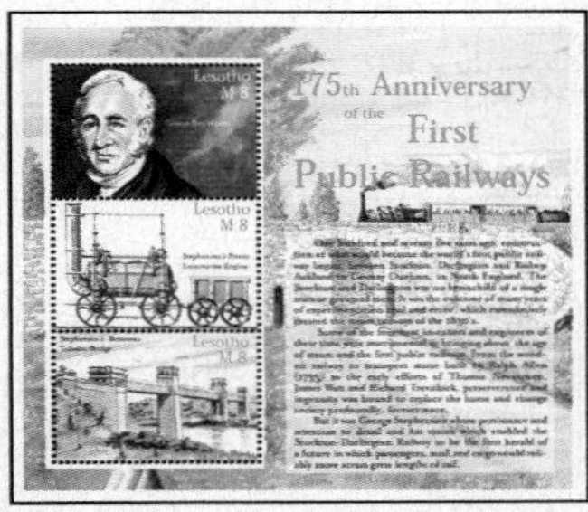

Public Railways, 175th Anniv. — A216

No. 1230: a, George Stephenson. b, Stephenson's patent locomotive engine. c, Stephenson's Britannia Tubular Bridge.

2000, July 6

1230 A216 8m Sheet of 3, #a-c 9.00 9.00

Johann Sebastian Bach (1685-1750) — A217

Illustration reduced.

2000, July 6

1231 A217 15m multi 7.00 7.00

Flowers — A218

Designs: 4m, Moore's crinum. 5m, Flame lily. 6m, Cape clivia. 8m, True sugarbush.

No. 1236, 3m: a, Spotted leaved arum. b, Christmas bells. c, Lady Monson. d, Wild pomegranate. e, Blushing bride. f, Bot River protea.

No. 1237, 3m: a, Starry gardenia. b, Pink hibiscus. c, Dwarf poker. d, Coast kaffirboom. e, Rose cockade. f, Pride of Table Mountain.
No. 1238, 3m: a, Drooping agpanthus. b, Yellow marsh afrikander. c, Weak stemmed painted lady. d, Impala lily. e, Beatrice watsonia. f, Pink arum.
No. 1239, 15m, Green arum. No. 1240, 15m, Red hairy erica, horiz.

2000, July 12
1232-1235 A218 Set of 4 9.00 9.00

Sheets of 6, #a-f
1236-1238 A218 Set of 3 21.00 21.00

Souvenir Sheets
1239-1240 A218 Set of 2 16.00 16.00

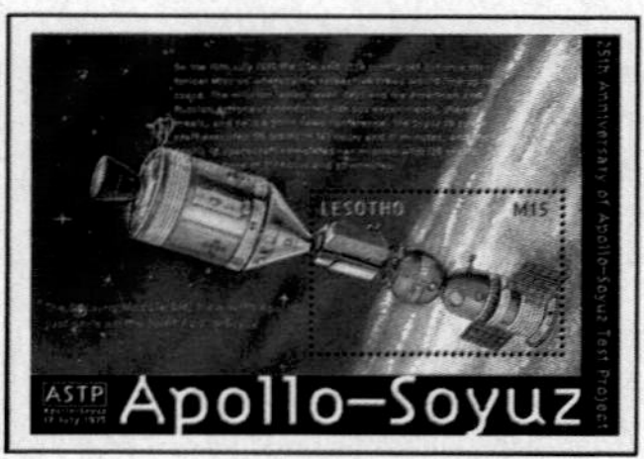

Apollo-Soyuz Mission, 25th Anniv. — A219

No. 1241: a, Apollo 18 and Soyuz 19 docked. b, Apollo 18. c, Soyuz 19.

2000, July 6 Litho. *Perf. 14*
1241 A219 8m Sheet of 3, #a-c 10.00 10.00

Souvenir Sheet
1242 A219 15m shown 7.00 7.00

Souvenir Sheet

Albert Einstein (1879-1955) — A220

2000, July 6 *Perf. 14¼*
1243 A220 15m multi 7.00 7.00

Endangered Wildlife — A221

No. 1244, 4m, horiz.: a, Alethe. b, Temminck's pangolin. c, Cheetah. d, African elephant. e, Chimpanzee. f, Northern white rhinoceros.
No. 1245, 4m, horiz.: a, African black rhinoceros. b, Leopard. c, Roseate tern. d, Mountain gorilla. e, Mountain zebra. f, Zanzibar red colobus monkey.
No. 1246, horiz: a, Wildebeest. b, Tree hyrax. c, Red lechwe. d, Eland.
No. 1247, 15m, Dugong. No. 1248, 15m, West African manatee.

2000, Aug. 10 Litho. *Perf. 14*

Sheets of 6, #a-f
1244-1245 A221 Set of 2 18.00 18.00
1246 A221 5m Sheet of 4, #a-d 7.75 7.75

Souvenir Sheets
1247-1248 A221 Set of 2 16.00 16.00

The Stamp Show 2000, London.

Automobiles — A222

No. 1249, 3m: a, 1960 Cadillac El Dorado Seville. b, 1955-75 Citroen DS. c, 1961 Ford Zephyr Zodiac Mk II. d, 1945-55 MG TF. e, 1949-65 Porsche 356. f, 1955 Ford Thunderbird.
No. 1250, 3m: a, 1948-52 Cisitalia 202 Coupe. b, 1990s Dodge Viper. c, 1968-69, TVR Vixen SI. d, 1957-70 Lotus 7. e, 1964-68 Ferrari 275 GTB/4. f, 1951 Pegasus Touring Spider.
No. 1251, 4m: a, 1913 Fiat Type O. b, 1914 Stutz Bearcat. c, 1924 French Levat. d, 1888 Benz Motorwagen. e, 1925 Isota Fraschini Type 8A. f, 1887 Markus Motor Carriage.
No. 1252, 4m: a, 1951 Morris Minor. b, 1935 Hispano-Suiza Type 68. c, 1949 MG TC. d, 1955 Morgan 4/4. e, 1950 Jaguar XK120. f, 1946-49 Triumph 1800/2000 Roadster.
No. 1253, 15m, 1896 Bersey Electric Car. No. 1254, 15m, 1948-71 Morris Minor 1000. No. 1255, 15m, 1953-63 AC Ace. No. 1256, 15m, Ferrari F40, vert.
Illustration reduced.

2000, Sept. 1

Sheets of 6, #a-f
1249-1252 A222 Set of 4 32.50 32.50

Souvenir Sheets
1253-1256 A222 Set of 4 26.50 26.50

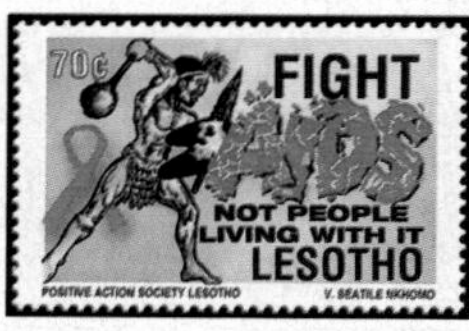

Fight Against AIDS A223

Designs: 70s, "Fight AIDS, not people living with it." 1m, "Speed kills, so does AIDS. Go Slow!" 1.50m, "People with AIDS need friends, not rejection," vert. 2.10m, "Even when you're off duty, protect the nation."

2001, Jan. 22 Litho. *Perf. 14*
1257-1260 A223 Set of 4 4.25 4.25

Butterflies A224

Designs: 70s, Great orange tip. 1m, Red-banded pereute. 1.50m, Sword grass brown. No. 1264, 2m, Striped blue crow. No. 1265, 3m, Alfalfa. 4m, Doris.
No. 1267, 2m: a, African migrant. b, Large oak blue. c, Wanderer. d, Tiger swallowtail. e, Union jack. f, Saturn. g, Broad-bordered grass yellow. h, Hewitson's uraneis.
No. 1268, 2m: a, Orange-banded sulfur. b, Large wood nymph. c, Postman. d, Palmfly. e, Gulf fritillary. f, Cairns birdwing. g, Common morpho. h, Common dotted border.
No. 1269, 3m: a, Bertoni's antwren (bird). b, Clorinde. c, Iolas blue. d, Mocker swallowtail. e, Common Indian crow. f, Grecian shoemaker. g, Small flambeau. h, Orchid swallowtail.
No. 1270, 15m, Crimson tip. No. 1271, 15m, Forest queen.

2001, Mar. 1 Litho. *Perf. 13¼x13¾*
1261-1266 A224 Set of 6 5.00 5.00

Sheets of 8, #a-h
1267-1269 A224 Set of 3 21.00 21.00

Souvenir Sheets
1270-1271 A224 Set of 2 13.50 13.50

Phila Nippon '01, Japan A225

Designs: 1.50m, Man in carriage from The Battle of Lepanto and the Map of the World, by unknown artist. 2m, Battle scene from The Battle of Lepanto and the Map of the World. 3m, Crane from Birds and Flowers of the Four Seasons, by Eitoku Kano. 4m, The Four Elegant Pastimes. 7m, Maple Viewing at Mount Takao, by unknown artist. 8m, The Four Accomplishments, by Yusho Kaiho.
No. 1278, 5m: a, Portrait of a Lady, by unknown artist. b, Portrait of Tadakatsu Honda, by unknown artist. c, Portrait of the Wife of Tokujo Goto, by unknown artist. d, Portrait of Emperor Go-yosei, by Takanobu Kano. e, Portrait of Tenzuiin, Hideyoshi's Mother, by Sochin Hoshuku.
No. 1279, 6m: a, Portrait of Yusai Hosokawa, by Suden Ishin. b, Portrait of Sen No Rikyu, attributed to Tohaku Hasegawa. c, Portrait of Oichi No Kata, by unknown artist. d, Portrait of Ittetsu Inaba, attributed to Hasegawa. e, Portrait of Nobunaga Oda, by Sochin Kokei.
No. 1280, 15m, Portrait of Ieyasu Tokugawa, by unknown artist. No. 1281, 15m, Portrait of Hideyoshi Toyotomi, by unknown artist.

Perf. 13¾, 14 (#1278-1279)
2001, May 31 Litho.
1272-1277 A225 Set of 6 6.00 6.00

Sheets of 5, #a-e
1278-1279 A225 Set of 2 30.00 30.00

Souvenir Sheets
1280-1281 A225 Set of 2 14.00 14.00

Size of stamps on Nos. 1278-1279: 85x28mm.
Nos. 1274-1275 are incorrectly inscribed. No. 1274 actually depicts "Landscape with Flowers and Birds." No. 1275 shows a detail from"The Four Elegant Pastimes," by Eitoku Kano.

Mushrooms A226

Designs: No. 1282, 5m, Bell-shaped panaeolus. No. 1283, 5m, Golden false pholiota. No. 1284, 5m, Shiny cap. No. 1285, 5m, Sooty brown waxy cap.
No. 1286, 3m: a, Violet cortinarius. b, Angel's wings. c, Collybia velutibes. d, Lentinellus. e, Anthurus aseroiformis. f, Caesar's mushroom.
No. 1287, 4m: a, Pungent cortinarius. b, Peziza sarcosphaera. c, Emetic russula. d, Questionable stropharia. e, Apricot jelly mushroom. f, Anise-scented clitocybe.
No. 1288, 15m, Cone-shaped waxy cap, horiz. No. 1289, 15m, Boletus, horiz.

2001, June 29 *Perf. 14*
1282-1285 A226 Set of 4 9.00 9.00

Sheets of 6, #a-f
1286-1287 A226 Set of 2 19.00 19.00

Souvenir Sheets
1288-1289 A226 Set of 2 14.00 14.00

Belgica 2001 Intl. Stamp Exhibition, Brussels (Nos. 1286-1289).

UN High Commissioner for Refugees, 50th Anniv. — A227

Designs: 70s, Silhouette of woman and child. 1m, Child and animal. 1.50m, Woman, vert. 2.10m, Information technology, vert.

2001, Aug. 20 *Perf. 14*
1290-1293 A227 Set of 4 3.00 3.00

Birds of Prey — A228

Designs: 70s, Black kite. 1m, Martial eagle. 1.50m, Bateleur. 2.10m, African goshawk. 2.50m, Bearded vulture. 3m, Jackal buzzard.

2001, Oct. 1 Litho. *Perf. 14*
1294-1299 A228 Set of 6 5.00 5.00

Southern African Wildlife A229

Designs: 1m, Grass owl. 2.10m, Klipspringer. 3m, Saddlebacked jackal. 5m, Black wildebeest.
No. 1304, 4m: a, Damara zebra. b, Bontebok. c, Eland. d, Lion. e, Saddlebacked jackal, diff. f, Yellow-billed kite.
No. 1305, 4m: a, Aardvark. b, Rock kestrel. c, Black-footed cat. d, Springhare. e, Aardwolf. f, Rock hyrax.
No. 1306, 15m, black-shouldered kite. No. 1307, 15m, Caracal, vert.

2001, Oct. 15 Litho. *Perf. 14*
1300-1303 A229 Set of 4 4.25 4.25

Sheets of 6, #a-f
1304-1305 A229 Set of 2 18.00 18.00

Souvenir Sheets
1306-1307 A229 Set of 2 14.00 14.00

Reign of Queen Elizabeth II, 50th Anniv. — A230

No. 1308: a, Queen seated. b, Queen with Prince Philip and British flag. c, Queen with man. c, Prince Philip.
20m, Queen wearing black suit.

2002, Feb. 6 **Litho.** ***Perf. 14¼***
1308 A230 8m Sheet of 4, #a-d 10.00 10.00

Souvenir Sheet

1309 A230 20m multi 8.00 8.00

United We Stand — A231

2002, Aug. 13 ***Perf. 14***
1310 A231 7m multi 4.25 4.25

Printed in sheets of 4.

SOS Children's Village, Lithabaneng — A232

2002, Aug. 13
1311 A232 10m multi 5.00 5.00

Rotary International in Lesotho, 25th Anniv. — A233

Designs: 8m, Horner Wood. 10m, Paul Harris.
No. 1314, 25m, Stylized globe and clasped hands. No. 1315, 25m, Golden Gate Bridge, horiz.

2002, Aug. 13
1312-1313 A233 Set of 2 7.00 7.00

Souvenir Sheets

1314-1315 A233 Set of 2 16.00 16.00

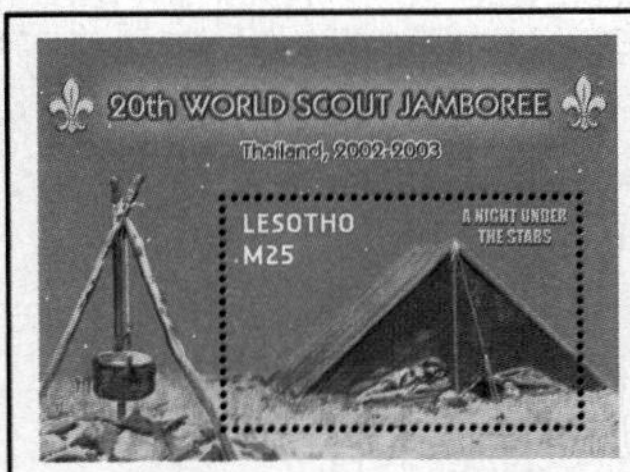

20th World Scout Jamboree, Thailand — A234

No. 1316: a, Sheet bend knots. b, Pup and forester tents. c, Canoeing. d, Water rescue.
25m, A night under the stars.

2002, Aug. 13
1316 A234 9m Sheet of 4, #a-d 9.50 9.50

Souvenir Sheet

1317 A234 25m multi 9.00 9.00

Intl. Year of Mountains — A235

No. 1318, horiz.: a, Mt. Machache. b, Mt. Thabana Li-Mèle. c, Mt. Qiloane. d, Mt. Thaba Bosiu.
25m, Mt. Rainier, US.

2002, Aug. 13
1318 A235 8m Sheet of 4, #a-d 6.00 6.00

Souvenir Sheet

1319 A235 25m multi 4.75 4.75

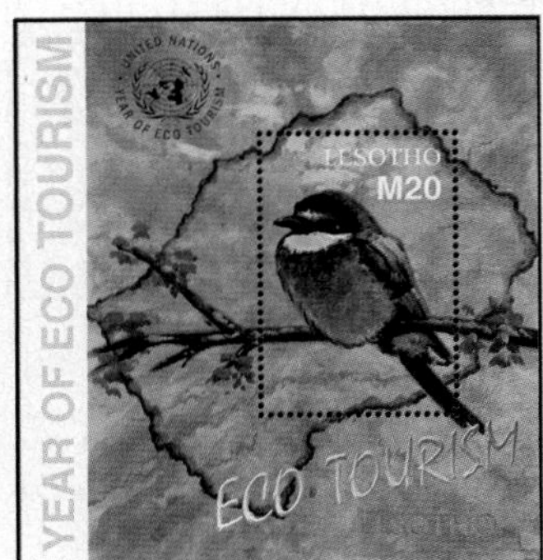

Intl. Year of Ecotourism — A236

No. 1320, horiz.: a, Plant. b, Flowers. c, Man and horses. d, Lion. e, Frog. f, House.
20m, Bird.

2002, Aug. 13
1320 A236 6m Sheet of 6, #a-f 6.75 6.75

Souvenir Sheet

1321 A236 20m multi 3.75 3.75

Flowers, Insects and Spiders — A237

No. 1322, 6m — Flowers: a, Angel's fishing rod. b, Marigold. c, Joan's blood. d, Mule pink. e, Tiger lily. f, Comtesse de Bouchaud.
No. 1323, 6m — Orchids: a, Phragmipedium besseae. b, Cypripedium calceolus. c, Cattleya Louise Georgiana. d, Brassocattleya binosa. e, Laelia gouldiana. f, Paphiopedilum maudiae.
No. 1324, 6m, horiz. — Insects: a, Leaf grasshopper. b, Golden-ringed dragonfly. c, Weevil-hunting wasp. d, European grasshopper. e, Thread-waisted wasp. f, Mantid.
No. 1325, 20m, Bleeding heart. No. 1326, 20m, Brassavola tuberculata. No. 1327, 20m, Orb web spider.

2002, Aug. 30 ***Perf. 14***

Sheets of 6, #a-f

1322-1324 A237 Set of 3 21.00 21.00

Souvenir Sheets

1325-1327 A237 Set of 3 11.50 11.50

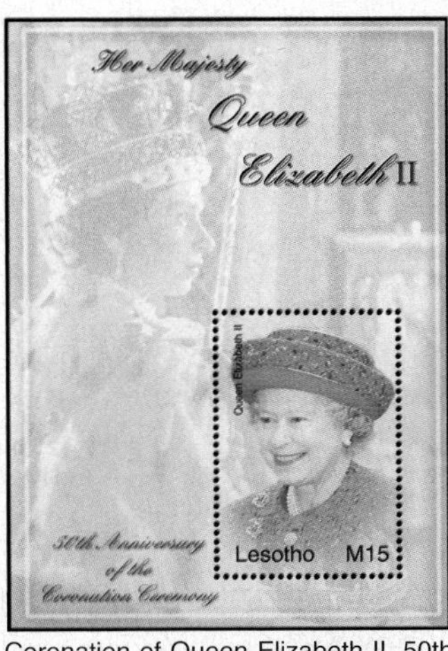

Coronation of Queen Elizabeth II, 50th Anniv. (in 2003) — A238

No. 1328: a, Wearing blue hat. b, Wearing white hat. c, Wearing black hat.
15m, Wearing red hat.

2004, May 17 **Litho.** ***Perf. 14***
1328 A238 8m Sheet of 3, #a-c 7.50 7.50

Souvenir Sheet

1329 A238 15m multi 4.75 4.75

Prince William, 21st Birthday (in 2003) — A239

No. 1330: a, Wearing sunglasses. b, Wearing suit and tie c, Wearing sports shirt.
15m, As young boy.

2004, May 17
1330 A239 8m Sheet of 3, #a-c 7.50 7.50

Souvenir Sheet

1331 A239 15m multi 4.75 4.75

Intl. Year of Fresh Water (in 2003) — A240

No. 1332: a, Top of Qiloane Falls (gray water at top). b, Middle portion of Qiloane Falls (narrow at top). c, Bottom portion of Qiloane Falls.
15m, Orange River.

2004, May 17 ***Perf. 14¼***
1332 A240 8m Sheet of 3, #a-c 7.50 7.50

Souvenir Sheet

1333 A240 15m multi 4.75 4.75

Powered Flight, Cent. (in 2003) — A241

No. 1334: a, Louis Blériot's Canard at Bagatelle, 1906. b, Blériot's Double-winged Libellule, 1907. c, Cross-country flight of Blériot VIII, Toury to Artenay, 1908. d, Blériot XII test flight, 1909.
15m, Blériot XI.

2004, May 17
1334 A241 6m Sheet of 4, #a-d 7.50 7.50

Souvenir Sheet

1335 A241 15m multi 4.75 4.75

Worldwide Fund for Nature (WWF) — A242

No. 1336 — Southern bald ibis: a, On nest, country name in white at LR. b, Flying to right, black denomination. c, Standing on rock, black denomination. d, Facing left.
No. 1337 — Southern bald ibis: a, Standing on rock, red denomination. b, Flying to left, red denomination. c, On nest, country name in black at UR.

2004, May 17 ***Perf. 14***
1336 Horiz. strip of 4 3.75 3.75
a.-d. A242 3m Any single .90 .90
1337 Horiz. strip of 4, #1336d, 1337a-1337c 3.75 3.75
a.-c. A242 3m Any single .90 .90

No. 1336 printed in sheets of 4 strips. No. 1337 printed in sheets of 2 strips.

Mammals A243

Designs: 1m, Cape porcupine. 1.50m, Brown rat. 2.10m, Springhare, vert. No. 1341, 5m, South African galago, vert.
No. 1342, 5m: a, Striped grass mouse. b, Greater galago. c, Ground pangolin. d, Banded mongoose.
15m, Egyptian rousette, vert.

2004, May 17
1338-1341 A243 Set of 4 3.00 3.00
1342 A243 5m Sheet of 4, #a-d 6.25 6.25

Souvenir Sheet

1343 A243 15m multi 4.75 4.75

Birds — A244

Designs: 1.50m, Secretary bird. 2.10m, Gray-crowned crane. 3m, Pied avocet. 5m, Common kestrel.
No. 1348: a, European roller. b, Common cuckoo. c, Great spotted cuckoo. d, Pel's fishing owl.
15m, Kori bustard.

2004, May 17
1344-1347 A244 Set of 4 3.50 3.50
1348 A244 6m Sheet of 4, #a-d 7.50 7.50

Souvenir Sheet

1349 A244 15m multi 4.75 4.75

Butterflies A245

Designs: 1.50m, Acraea rabbaiae. 2.10m, Alaena margaritacea. 4m, Bematistes aganice. No. 1353, 6m, Acraea quirina.
No. 1354, 6m: a, Bematistes excisa male. b, Bematistes excisa female. c, Bematistes epiprotea. d, Bematistes poggei.
15m, Acraea satis.

2004, May 17
1350-1353 A245 Set of 4 4.25 4.25
1354 A245 6m Sheet of 4, #a-d 7.50 7.50

Souvenir Sheet

1355 A245 15m multi 4.75 4.75

Flowers — A246

Designs: 1.50m, Sparaxis grandiflora. 2.10m, Agapanthus africanus. 3m, Protea linearis. No. 1359, 5m, Nerine cultivars.
No. 1360, 5m: a, Kniphofia uvaria. b, Amaryllis belladonna. c, Cazania splendens. d, Erica coronata.
15m, Saintpaulia cultivars.

2004, May 17
1356-1359 A246 Set of 4 3.50 3.50
1360 A246 5m Sheet of 4, #a-d 6.25 6.25

Souvenir Sheet

1361 A246 15m multi 4.75 4.75

Houses A247

Designs: 70s, Mokhoro. 1m, Heisi. 1.50m, Lesotho. 2.10m, Mohlongoa-Fat'se.

2005, Feb. 21 Litho. *Perf. 14*
1362-1365 A247 Set of 4 1.90 1.90

Girl Guides A248

Girl Guides: 70s, Dancing. 1m, Marching in parade. 1.50m, Collecting cans, vert. 2.10m, Standing near building.
10m, Leader holding microphone, vert.

2005, May 20 Litho. *Perf. 14*
1366-1369 A248 Set of 4 1.60 1.60

Souvenir Sheet

1370 A248 10m multi 3.00 3.00

Pope John Paul II (1920-2005) A249

2005, Aug. 22 *Perf. 12¾*
1371 A249 10m multi 3.25 3.25

Printed in sheets of 4.

Souvenir Sheet

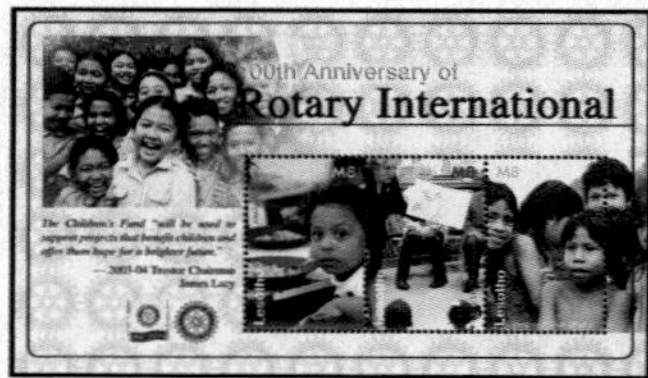

Rotary International, Cent. — A250

No. 1372: a, Alleviating poverty. b, Advancement of literacy. c, Helping at-risk children.

2005, Aug. 22
1372 A250 8m Sheet of 3, #a-c 7.75 7.75

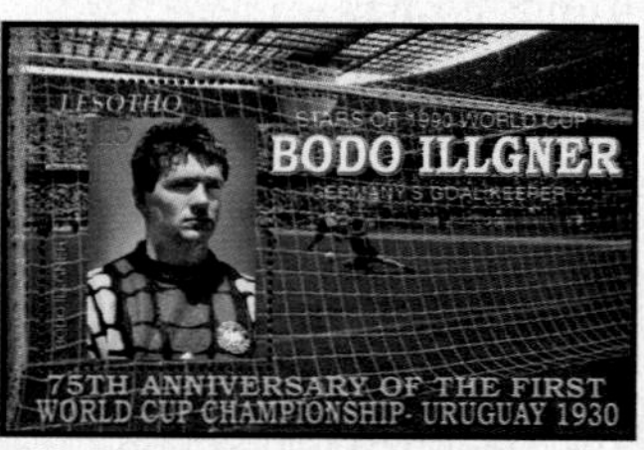

World Cup Soccer Championships, 75th Anniv. — A251

No. 1373, horiz. — Players from final match from: a, 1930. b, 1938. c, 1990.
15m, Bodo Illgner, 1990 goalie for Germany.

2005, Aug. 22 *Perf. 12*
1373 A251 8m Sheet of 3, #a-c 7.75 7.75

Souvenir Sheet

1374 A251 15m multi 4.75 4.75

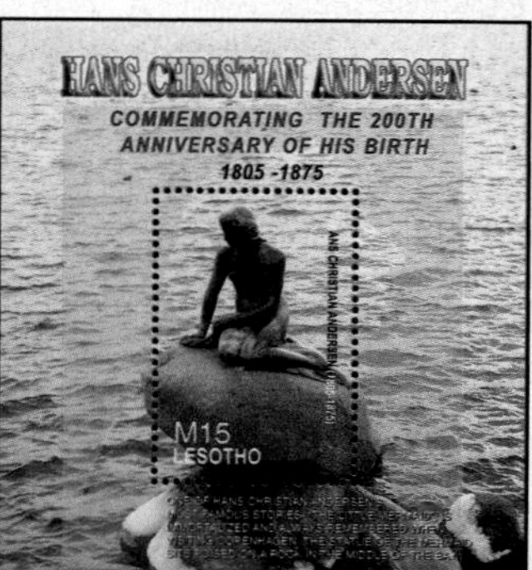

Hans Christian Andersen (1805-75), Author — A252

No. 1375: a, Statue of Andersen, Copenhagen. b, Childhood home of Andersen, Odense, Denmark. c, Scene from "The Steadfast Tin Soldier".
15m, Little Mermaid statue, Copenhagen.

2005, Aug. 22 *Perf. 12¾*
1375 A252 8m Sheet of 3, #a-c 7.75 7.75

Souvenir Sheet

1376 A252 15m multi 4.75 4.75

Jules Verne (1828-1905), Writer — A253

No. 1377, horiz.: a, Journey to the Center of the Earth. b, Verne, without hat. c, 20,000 Leagues Under the Sea.
15m, Verne wearing hat.

2005, Aug. 22
1377 A253 8m Sheet of 3, #a-c 7.75 7.75

Souvenir Sheet

1378 A253 15m multi 4.75 4.75

Albert Einstein (1879-1955), Physicist — A254

No. 1379, horiz. — Einstein and: a, Country name in black. b, Nikola Tesla, Charles Steinmetz. c, Country name in red violet.
15m, Time Magazine "Person of the Century" cover.

2005, Aug. 22
1379 A254 8m Sheet of 3, #a-c 7.75 7.75

Souvenir Sheet

1380 A254 15m multi 4.75 4.75

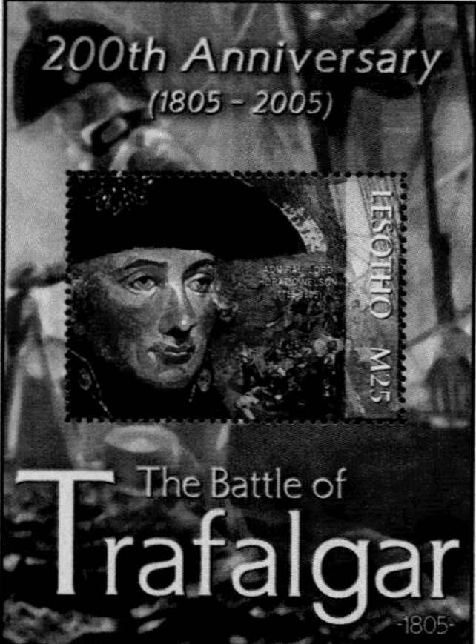

Battle of Trafalgar, Bicent. — A255

No. 1381: a, HMS Victory. b, Admiral Horatio Nelson facing left. c, Nelson wounded in battle. d, Ships in battle.
25m, Nelson facing right.

2005, Aug. 22 *Perf. 12¾*
1381 A255 8m Sheet of 4, #a-d 10.50 10.50

Souvenir Sheet
Perf. 12

1382 A255 25m multi 8.00 8.00

No. 1381 contains four 42x28mm stamps.

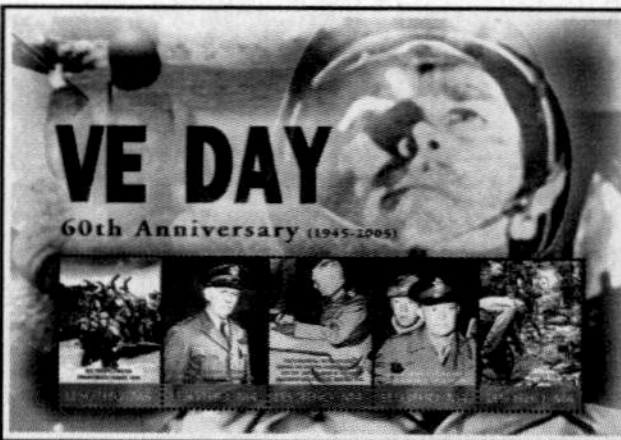

End of World War II, 60th Anniv. — A256

No. 1383, 4m — V-E Day: a, U.S. troops land on Omaha Beach, 1944. b, Gen. George C. Marshall. c, German Field Marshal Wilhelm Keitel signing surrender. d, Generals Dwight D. Eisenhower and George S. Patton. e, Soldiers sifting through war damage.
No. 1384, 4m — V-J Day: a, USS Arizona. b, Bunker, Chula Beach, Tinian Island. c, Bockscar flight crew. d, Newspaper announcing Japanese surrender. e, Historic marker commemorating loading of second atomic bomb on Tinian Island.

2005, Aug. 22 *Perf. 12¾*
Sheets of 5, #a-e
1383-1384 A256 Set of 2 13.00 13.00

A257

People and Livestock — A258

Designs: 70 l, Boy riding calf. 1m, Man feeding cattle. 1.50m, Cattle tenders playing game. 2.10m, Shepherd carrying lamb.
10m, Dancers.

2006, Mar. 13 Litho. *Perf. 14*
1385-1388 A257 Set of 4 1.75 1.75

Souvenir Sheet

1389 A258 10m multi 3.25 3.25

A259

Women Balancing Items on Heads — A260

Women carrying: 70 l, Sticks. 1m, Cooking pot. 1.50m, Water jar. 2.10m, Bowl of fruit.
10m, Bowl of grain.

2006, June 19

1390-1393 A259 Set of 4 1.50 1.50

Souvenir Sheet

1394 A260 10m multi 3.00 3.00

A261

Handicrafts — A262

Designs: 70 l, Baskets. 1m, Artist and drawing, vert. 1.50m, Painted pottery. 2.10m, Figurines of stork and fish, decorated bull's horn.

10m, Boy, native costume.

2006, Oct. 9 Litho. *Perf. 14¼*

1395-1398 A261 Set of 4 1.40 1.40

Souvenir Sheet

1399 A262 10m multi 2.75 2.75

Birds — A263

Designs: 1m, Crested caracara. 1.50m, Wood storks. 2.10m, Tawny-shouldered blackbird. No. 1403, 15m, Jabiru.

No. 1404: a, Great blue heron. b, Anna's hummingbird. c, Gray silky flycatcher. d, Limpkin.

No. 1405, 15m, Western reef heron. No. 1406, 15m, Monk parakeet.

2007, Aug. 20 Litho. *Perf. 14*

1400-1403 A263 Set of 4 5.50 5.50

1404 A263 6m Sheet of 4, #a-d 6.75 6.75

Souvenir Sheets

1405-1406 A263 Set of 2 8.50 8.50

Butterflies — A264

Designs: 1m, Mylothris erlangeri. 1.50m, Papilio nireus. 2.10m, Acraea terpiscore. 10m, Salamis temora.

No. 1411: a, Danaus chrysippus. b, Myrina silenus. c, Chrysiridia madagascariensis. d, Hypolimnas dexithea.

No. 1412, 15m, P. demodocus. No. 1413, 15m, Amphicallia tigris.

2007, Aug. 20

1407-1410 A264 Set of 4 4.25 4.25

1411 A264 6m Sheet of 4, #a-d 6.75 6.75

Souvenir Sheets

1412-1413 A264 Set of 2 8.50 8.50

Orchids — A265

Designs: 1.50m, Spiranthes laciniata. 2.10m, Triphora craigheadii. 3m, Arethusa bulbosa. 10m, Calypso bulbosa.

No. 1418: a, Encyclia tampensis. b, Prosthechea cochleata. c, Vanilla pompona. d, Cypripedium acaule.

No. 1419, 15m, Vanilla barbellata. No. 1420, 15m, Epidendrum radicans.

2007, Aug. 20

1414-1417 A265 Set of 4 4.75 4.75

1418 A265 6m Sheet of 4, #a-d 6.75 6.75

Souvenir Sheets

1419-1420 A265 Set of 2 8.50 8.50

A266

A267

Mushrooms — A268

Designs: 1m, Amanita pantherina. 1.50m, Agaricus xanthodermus. 2.10m, Amanita rubescens. No. 1424, 15m, Amanita phalloides.

No. 1425: a, Amanita phalloides, diff. b, Amanita pantherina, diff. c, Panaeolus papilionaceus. d, Amanita rubescens, diff.

No. 1426, 15m, Amanite panther. No. 1427, 15m, Podaxis pistillaris.

2007, Aug. 20

1421-1424 A266 Set of 4 5.50 5.50

1425 A267 6m Sheet of 4, #a-d 6.75 6.75

Souvenir Sheets

1426 A267 15m multi 4.25 4.25

1427 A268 15m multi 4.25 4.25

Miniature Sheet

2008 Summer Olympics, Beijing — A269

No. 1428: a, Rowing. b, Softball. c, Wrestling. d, Volleyball.

2008, Aug. 18 Litho. *Perf. 12*

1428 A269 3.50m Sheet of 4, #a-d 3.75 3.75

POSTAGE DUE STAMPS

Basutoland Nos. J9-J10 Overprinted: "LESOTHO"

Wmk. 314

1966, Nov. 1 Typo. *Perf. 14*

J1 D2 1c carmine .20 .25
a. "Lseotho" *50.00*

J2 D2 5c dark purple .75 .60
a. "Lseotho" *85.00*

D1

D2

Perf. 13½

1967, Apr. 1 Unwmk. Litho.

J3 D1 1c dark blue .20 .20

J4 D1 2c dull rose .25 .30

J5 D1 5c emerald .55 .70

Nos. J3-J5 (3) 1.00 1.20

1976, Nov. 30 Wmk. 362

J7 D1 2c dull rose 3.00 3.00

J8 D1 5c emerald 3.00 3.00

1986 Litho. *Perf. 13x13½*

J9 D2 2s green .50 .50

J10 D2 5s blue .50 .50

J11 D2 25s purple .50 .50

Nos. J9-J11 (3) 1.50 1.50

This is an expanding set. Numbers will change if necessary.

LIBERIA

lī-'bir-ē-ə

LOCATION — West coast of Africa, between Ivory Coast and Sierra Leone

GOVT. — Republic

AREA — 43,000 sq. mi.

POP. — 2,602,100 (1997 est.)

CAPITAL — Monrovia

100 Cents = 1 Dollar

Catalogue values for unused stamps in this country are for Never Hinged items, beginning with Scott 330 in the regular postage section, Scott B19 in the semi-postal section, Scott C67 in the airpost section, and Scott CB4 in the airpost semi-postal section.

Values for unused stamps are for examples with original gum as defined in the catalogue introduction. Any exceptions will be noted. Very fine examples of Nos. 1-3, 13-21 and 157-159 will have perforations just clear of the design due to the narrow spacing of the stamps on the plates and/or imperfect perforating methods.

Watermarks

Wmk. 116 — Crosses and Circles

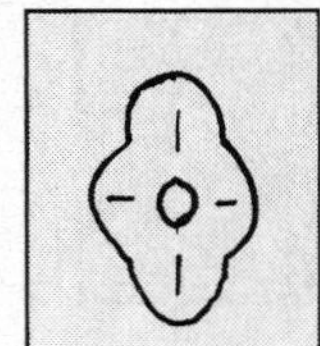
Wmk. 143

For watermarks 373 and 384 see British Watermark page.

"Liberia" — A1

1860 Unwmk. Litho. *Perf. 12*

Thick Paper

1 A1 6c red 400.00 *300.00*
a. Imperf, pair 500.00

2 A1 12c deep blue 22.50 *50.00*
a. Imperf, pair 250.00

3 A1 24c green 50.00 *50.00*
a. Imperf, pair 300.00

Nos. 1-3 (3) 472.50 *400.00*

Stamps set very close together. Copies of the 12c occasionally show traces of a frame line around the design.

Medium to Thin Paper

With a single-line frame around each stamp, about 1mm from the border

1864 *Perf. 11, 12*

7 A1 6c red 62.50 *77.50*
a. Imperf, pair 200.00

8 A1 12c blue 72.50 *87.50*
a. Imperf, pair 200.00

9 A1 24c lt green 82.50 *95.00*
a. Imperf, pair 200.00

Nos. 7-9 (3) 217.50 *260.00*

Stamps set about 5mm apart. Margins large and perforation usually outside the frame line.

Without Frame Line

1866-69

13 A1 6c lt red 25.00 *30.00*

14 A1 12c lt blue 25.00 *30.00*

15 A1 24c lt yellow grn 25.00 *30.00*

Nos. 13-15 (3) 75.00 *90.00*

Stamps set 2-2½mm apart with small margins. Stamps are usually without frame line but those from one transfer show broken and irregular parts of a frame.

With Frame Line

1880 *Perf. 10½*

16 A1 1c ultra 5.00 7.50

17 A1 2c rose 5.00 *5.25*
a. Imperf, pair 175.00

18 A1 6c violet 5.00 5.25

19 A1 12c yellow 5.00 *5.25*

20 A1 24c rose red 5.00 5.25

Nos. 16-20 (5) 25.00 28.50

Unused values for Nos. 16-20 are for copies without gum.

For surcharges see Nos. 157-159.

Counterfeits

Counterfeits exist of Nos. 1-28, 32 and 64.

From Arms of Liberia — A2

1881

21 A2 3c black 15.00 10.00

Unused value is for copies without gum.

A3

A4

1882 ***Perf. 11½, 12, 14***

No.	Type	Description	Unused	Used
22	A3	8c blue	50.00	10.00
23	A4	16c red	8.00	5.00

On No. 22 the openings in the figure "8" enclose a pattern of slanting lines. Compare with No. 32.

Canceled to Order

Beginning with the issue of 1885, values in the used column are for "canceled to order" stamps. Postally used copies sell for much more.

A5

A6

From Arms of Liberia — A7

A8

Perf. 10½, 11, 12, 11½x10½, 14, 14½

1885

No.	Type	Description	Unused	Used
24	A5	1c carmine	2.00	2.00
a.		1c rose	2.00	2.00
25	A5	2c green	2.00	2.00
26	A5	3c violet	2.00	2.00
27	A5	4c brown	2.00	2.00
28	A5	6c olive gray	2.00	2.00
29	A6	8c bluish gray	4.00	4.00
a.		8c lilac	7.00	7.00
30	A6	16c yellow	12.00	12.00
31	A7	32c deep blue	29.00	29.00
		Nos. 24-31 (8)	55.00	55.00

In the 1885 printing, the stamps are spaced 2mm apart and the paper is medium. In the 1892 printing, the stamps are 4½mm apart.

For surcharges see Nos. J1-J2.

Imperf., Pair

No.	Type	Description	Unused	Used
24b	A5	1c	3.00	
25a	A5	2c	4.25	
26a	A5	3c	5.00	
27a	A5	4c	5.00	
28a	A5	6c	4.25	4.25
29b	A6	8c	12.50	
30a	A6	16c	15.00	
31a	A7	32c	30.00	

Imperf. pairs with 2mm spacing sell for higher prices.

1889 ***Perf. 12, 14***

No.	Type	Description	Unused	Used
32	A8	8c blue	4.25	4.25
a.		Imperf., pair	20.00	

The openings in the figure "8" are filled with network. See No. 22.

A9

Elephant — A10

Oil Palm — A11

Pres. Hilary R. W. Johnson — A12

Vai Woman in Full Dress — A13

Coat of Arms — A14

Liberian Star — A15

Coat of Arms — A16

Hippopotamus A17

Liberian Star — A18

President Johnson — A19

1892-96 Wmk. 143 Engr. *Perf. 15*

No.	Type	Description	Unused	Used
33	A9	1c vermilion	.50	.40
a.		1c blue (error)	40.00	
34	A9	2c blue	.50	.40
a.		2c vermilion (error)	240.00	
35	A10	4c green & blk	1.75	1.00
a.		Center inverted	175.00	
36	A11	6c blue green	.70	.50
37	A12	8c brown & blk	.95	.95
a.		Center inverted	600.00	600.00
b.		Center sideways	750.00	
38	A12	10c chrome yel & indigo ('96)	.95	.65
39	A13	12c rose red	.95	.65
40	A13	15c slate ('96)	.95	.65
41	A14	16c lilac	3.50	1.75
a.		16c deep greenish blue (error)	110.00	
42	A14	20c vermilion ('96)	3.50	1.75
43	A15	24c ol grn, *yel*	2.00	1.10
44	A15	25c yel grn ('96)	2.00	1.40
45	A16	30c steel bl ('96)	6.25	4.50
46	A16	32c grnsh blue	3.50	2.75
a.		32c lilac (error)	*110.00*	
47	A17	$1 ultra & blk	10.00	9.00
a.		$1 blue & black	11.00	11.00
48	A18	$2 brown, *yel*	9.00	8.00
49	A19	$5 carmine & blk	10.00	10.00
a.		Center inverted	500.00	500.00
		Nos. 33-49 (17)	57.00	45.45

Many imperforates, part-perforated and misperforated varieties exist.

The 1c, 2c and 4c were issued in sheets of 60; 6c, sheet of 40; 8c, 10c, sheets of 30; 12c, 15c, 24c, 25c, sheets of 20; 16c, 20c, 30c, sheets of 15; $1, $2, $5, sheets of 10.

For overprints & surcharges see #50, 64B-64F, 66, 71-77, 79-81, 85-93, 95-100, 160, O1-O13, O15-O25, O37-O41, O44-O45.

No. 36 Surcharged:

a

5 5 Five Cents
b

1893

No.	Type	Description	Unused	Used
50	A11 (a)	5c on 6c blue grn	1.75	1.10
a.		"5" with short flag	6.00	6.00
b.		Both 5's with short flags	5.00	5.00
c.		"i" dot omitted	19.00	19.00
d.		Surcharge "b"	30.00	30.00

"Commerce," Globe and Krumen — A22

1894 Unwmk. Engr. *Imperf.*

No.	Type	Description	Unused	Used
52	A22	5c carmine & blk	5.00	5.00

Rouletted

No.	Type	Description	Unused	Used
53	A22	5c carmine & blk	10.00	7.50

For overprints see Nos. 69, O26-O27.

Oil Palm A23

Hippopotamus A24

Elephant — A25

Liberty — A26

1897-1905 Wmk. 143 *Perf. 14 to 16*

No.	Type	Description	Unused	Used
54	A23	1c lilac rose	1.00	.65
a.		1c violet	1.00	.65
55	A23	1c deep green ('00)	1.25	.95
56	A23	1c lt green ('05)	3.00	1.60
57	A24	2c bister & blk	2.50	1.60
58	A24	2c org red & blk ('00)	5.00	2.10
59	A24	2c rose & blk ('05)	2.50	1.60
60	A25	5c lake & black	2.50	1.60
a.		5c lilac rose & black	2.50	1.60
61	A25	5c gray bl & blk ('00)	5.00	5.00
62	A25	5c ultra & blk ('05)	3.50	2.75
a.		Center inverted	1,250.	
63	A26	50c red brn & blk	3.25	3.50
		Nos. 54-63 (10)	29.50	21.35

For overprints & surcharges see #65, 66A-68, 70, 78, 82-84, M1, O28-O36, O42, O92.

A27

Two types:
I — 13 pearls above "Republic Liberia."
II — 10 pearls.

1897 Unwmk. Litho. *Perf. 14*

No.	Type	Description	Unused	Used
64	A27	3c red & green (I)	.25	.60
a.		Type II	*10.00*	.20

No. 64a is considered a reprint, unissued. "Used" copies are CTO.

For surcharge see No. 128.

Official Stamps Handstamped in Black **ORDINARY**

1901-02 Wmk. 143

On Nos. O7-O8, O10-O12

No.	Type	Description	Unused	Used
64B	A14	16c lilac	*525.00*	*500.00*
64C	A15	24c ol grn, *yel*	*575.00*	*400.00*
64D	A17	$1 blue & blk	*3,000.*	*2,000.*
64E	A18	$2 brown, *yel*		
64F	A19	$5 carmine & blk		

On Stamps with "O S" Printed

No.	Type	Description	Unused	Used
65	A23	1c green	*37.50*	*40.00*
66	A9	2c blue	*100.00*	*100.00*
66A	A24	2c bister & blk	—	*150.00*
67	A24	2c org red & blk	*45.00*	*40.00*
68	A25	5c gray bl & blk	*37.50*	*35.00*
69	A22	5c vio & grn (No. O26)	*300.00*	*300.00*
70	A25	5c lake & blk	*275.00*	*225.00*
71	A12	10c yel & blue blk	*37.50*	*60.00*
a.		"O S" omitted		
72	A13	15c slate	*200.00*	*60.00*
73	A14	16c lilac	*475.00*	*300.00*
74	A14	20c vermilion	*42.50*	*50.00*
75	A15	24c ol grn,*yel*	*52.50*	*50.00*
76	A15	25c yellow grn	*42.50*	*50.00*
a.		"O S" omitted	*750.00*	
77	A16	30c steel blue	*42.50*	*40.00*
78	A26	50c red brn & blk	*100.00*	*52.50*
79	A17	$1 ultra & blk	*325.00*	*275.00*
a.		"O S" omitted		
80	A18	$2 brn, *yel*	*2,000.*	*1,800.*
81	A19	$5 car & blk	*2,250.*	*2,000.*
a.		"O S" omitted	*3,000.*	*2,750.*

On Stamps with "O S" Handstamped

No.	Type	Description	Unused	Used
82	A23	1c deep green	62.50	
83	A24	2c org red & blk	75.00	
84	A25	5c lake & blk	200.00	
85	A12	10c yel & bl blk	125.00	
86	A14	20c vermilion	140.00	
87	A15	24c ol grn, *yel*	140.00	
88	A15	25c yel grn	160.00	
89	A16	30c steel blue	525.00	
90	A16	32c grnsh blue	210.00	

Varieties of Nos. 65-90 include double and inverted overprints.

Nos. 47, O10, O23a Surcharged in Carmine

1902

No.	Type	Description	Unused	Used
91	A17	75c on $1 #47	15.00	13.00
a.		Thin "C" and comma	19.00	19.00
b.		Inverted surcharge	62.50	62.50
c.		As "a," inverted		
92	A17	75c on $1 #O10	*2,500.*	
a.		Thin "C" and comma	*3,500.*	
93	A17	75c on $1 #O23a	*3,500.*	
a.		Thin "C" and comma	*4,250.*	

Liberty — A29

1903 Unwmk. Engr. *Perf. 14*

No.	Type	Description	Unused	Used
94	A29	3c black	.30	.20
a.		Printed on both sides	45.00	
b.		Perf. 12	20.00	6.00

For overprint see No. O43.

Stamps of 1892 Surcharged in Blue

a

b

1903 Wmk. 143

No.	Type	Description	Unused	Used
95	A14 (a)	10c on 16c lilac	3.00	4.00
96	A15 (b)	15c on 24c ol grn, *yel*	4.50	5.50

97 A16 (b) 20c on 32c grnsh bl 6.25 7.75
Nos. 95-97 (3) 13.75 17.25

Nos. 50, O3 and 45 Surcharged in Black or Red

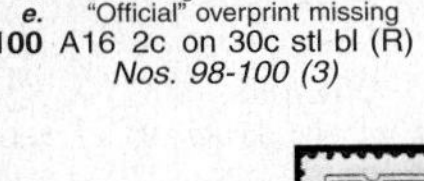

1904

98 A11 1c on 5c on 6c bl grn .60 .55
- *a.* "5" with short flag 4.25 4.25
- *b.* Both 5's with short flags 8.75 8.75
- *c.* "i" dot omitted 10.00 10.00
- *d.* Surcharge on #50d 12.50 12.50
- *e.* Inverted surcharge 6.75 6.75

99 A10 2c on 4c grn & blk 1.50 2.75
- *a.* Pair, one without surcharge 35.00
- *b.* Double surcharge
- *c.* Double surcharge, red and blk 62.50
- *d.* Surcharged on back also 19.00
- *e.* "Official" overprint missing 30.00

100 A16 2c on 30c stl bl (R) 8.75 14.00
Nos. 98-100 (3) 10.85 17.30

African Elephant — A33

Mercury — A34

Chimpanzee A35

Great Blue Touraco — A36

Agama — A37

Egret — A38

Head of Liberty From Coin — A39

A40

Liberian Flag — A41

Pygmy Hippopotamus A42

Liberty with Star of Liberia on Cap — A43

Mandingos — A44

Executive Mansion and Pres. Arthur Barclay — A45

1906 Unwmk. Engr. *Perf. 14*

101 A33 1c green & blk 1.50 .50
102 A34 2c carmine & blk .30 .20
103 A35 5c ultra & blk 2.75 .65
104 A36 10c red brn & blk 4.00 .65
105 A37 15c pur & dp grn 14.50 3.00
106 A38 20c orange & blk 8.50 2.00
107 A39 25c dull blue & gray .85 .20
108 A40 30c deep violet 1.00 .20
109 A41 50c dp green & blk 1.00 .20
110 A42 75c brown & blk 12.00 2.00
111 A43 $1 rose & gray 3.00 .20
112 A44 $2 dp green & blk 4.50 .35
113 A45 $5 red brown & blk 9.25 .50
Nos. 101-113 (13) 63.15 10.65

For surcharges see Nos. 114, 129, 130, 141, 145-149, 161, M2, M5, O72-O73, O82-O85, O96. For overprints see Nos. O46-O58.

Center Inverted

101a A33 1c 110.00 55.00
102a A34 2c 120.00 35.00
103a A35 5c 175.00 175.00
104a A36 10c 80.00 80.00
105a A37 15c 175.00 175.00
106b A38 20c 175.00 175.00
107a A39 25c 75.00 75.00
109b A41 50c 75.00 75.00
110b A42 75c 125.00 125.00
111a A43 $1 100.00 100.00
112a A44 $2 95.00 95.00

Imperf., Pairs

101b A33 1c 11.00
102b A34 2c 4.50
106a A38 20c 17.00
107b A39 25c 45.00 45.00
109a A41 50c 17.00
110a A42 75c 17.00
113a A45 $5 22.50

No. 104 Surcharged in Black

1909

114 A36 3c on 10c red brn & blk 6.00 6.00

Coffee Plantation — A46

Pres. Barclay — A47

S. S. Pres. Daniel E. Howard, former Gunboat Lark — A48

Commerce with Caduceus — A49

Vai Woman Spinning Cotton — A50

Blossom and Fruit of Pepper Plants — A51

Circular House — A52

President Barclay — A53

Men in Canoe — A54

Liberian Village — A55

1909-12 *Perf. 14*

115 A46 1c yel grn & blk .70 .55
116 A47 2c lake & blk .70 .55
117 A48 5c ultra & blk .70 .55
118 A49 10c plum & blk, perf. 12½ ('12) .70 .55
- *a.* Imperf, pair 19.00
- *b.* Perf 14 ('12) 2.25 2.25
- *c.* As "b," pair, imperf between 27.50
- *d.* Perf 12½x14 2.75 2.25

119 A50 15c indigo & blk 3.50 .60
120 A51 20c rose & grn 4.50 .60
- *b.* Imperf.

121 A52 25c dk brn & blk 1.40 .60
- *a.* Imperf.

122 A53 30c dark brown 4.50 .60
123 A54 50c green & blk 4.50 .60
124 A55 75c red brn & blk 4.50 .60
Nos. 115-124 (10) 25.70 5.80

Rouletted

125 A49 10c plum & blk .75 .45

For surcharges see Nos. 126-127E, 131-133, 136-140, 142-144, 151-156, 162, B1-B2, M3-M4, M6-M7, O70-O1, O74-O81, O86-O91, O97.

For overprints see Nos. O59-O69.

Center Inverted

116a A47 2c 70.00 60.00
117a A48 5c 62.50 55.00
119a A50 15c 100.00 60.00
120a A51 20c 70.00 55.00
121b A52 25c 47.50 42.50
123a A54 50c 95.00 80.00

Stamps and Types of 1909-12 Surcharged in Blue or Red

1910-12 *Rouletted*

126 A49 3c on 10c plum & blk (Bl) .40 .25
- *a.* "3" inverted

126B A49 3c on 10c blk & ultra (R) 30.00 5.00

#126B is roulette 7. It also exists in roulette 13.

Perf. 12½, 14, 12½x14

127 A49 3c on 10c plum & blk (Bl) ('12) .40 .25
- *a.* Imperf., pair 22.50
- *b.* Double surcharge, one invtd. 22.50
- *c.* Double vertical surcharge

127E A49 3c on 10c blk & ultra (R) ('12) 17.00 .55
Nos. 126-127E (4) 47.80 6.05

Nos. 64, 64a Surcharged in Dark Green

1913

128 A27 8c on 3c red & grn (I) .30 .20
- *a.* Surcharge on No. 64a 3.00 .20
- *b.* Double surcharge 6.25
- *c.* Imperf., pair 20.00
- *d.* Inverted surcharge 25.00

Stamps of Preceding Issues Surcharged

a

b

1914

On Issue of 1906

129 A39 (a) 2c on 25c dl bl & gray 11.50 3.25
130 A40 (b) 5c on 30c dp violet 11.50 3.25

On Issue of 1909

131 A52 (a) 2c on 25c brn & blk 11.50 3.25
132 A53 (b) 5c on 30c dk brown 11.50 3.25
133 A54 (a) 10c on 50c grn & blk 11.50 3.25
Nos. 129-133 (5) 57.50 16.25

Liberian House A57

Providence Island, Monrovia Harbor A58

1915 Engr. Wmk. 116 *Perf. 14*

134 A57 2c red	.20	.20
135 A58 3c dull violet	.20	.20

For overprints see Nos. 196-197, O113-O114, O128-O129.

Nos. 109, 111-113, 119-124 Surcharged with New Values in Dark Blue, Black or Red:

c

d

e

f

g

1915-16 Unwmk.

136 A50 (c) 2c on 15c (R)	.90	.90
137 A52 (d) 2c on 25c (R)	8.00	8.00
138 A51 (e) 5c on 20c (Bk)	1.10	5.75
139 A53 (f) 5c on 30c (R)	4.50	4.50
a. Double surcharge	14.00	14.00
140 A53 (g) 5c on 30c (R)	40.00	40.00

h

i

141 A41 (h) 10c on 50c (R)	8.00	8.00
a. Double surch., one invtd.		
142 A54 (i) 10c on 50c (R)	14.00	14.00
a. Double surcharge red & blk	35.00	35.00
b. Blue surcharge	35.00	35.00
143 A54 (i) 10c on 50c (Bk)	20.00	15.00

j

k

144 A55 (j) 20c on 75c (Bk)	3.50	5.75
145 A43 (k) 25c on $1 (Bk)	42.50	42.50

l

50
Cents
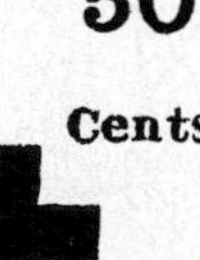
m

146 A44 (l) 50c on $2 (R)	11.00	11.00
a. "Ceuts"	22.50	22.50
147 A44 (m) 50c on $2 (R)	800.00	800.00

n

148 A45 $1 on $5 (Bk)	65.00	65.00
a. Double surcharge	90.00	90.00

o

149 A45 $1 on $5 (R)	52.50	52.50

The color of the red surcharge varies from light dull red to almost brown.

Handstamped Surcharge, Type "i"

150 A54 10c on 50c (Dk Bl)	14.00	14.00

No. 119 Surcharged in Black

2

151 A50 2c on 15c	700.00	500.00

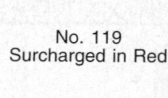

No. 119 Surcharged in Red

152 A50 2c on 15c	45.00	40.00
a. Double surcharge	92.50	

Nos. 116-117 Surcharged in Black or Red

1 — a1

1c — b1

one cemt — c1

1ct — d1

one one — e1

1c (inverted) — f1

1cent * * * * * * — g1

h1 — 1 c 1

i1 — one c one

j1 — 1cts

k2 — Two cemts

l2 — Two cents

m2 — 2cents

n2 — Two cts (inverted)

o2 — 2c

p2 — 2. 2.

q2 — two c two

r2 — 2 2

s2 — two

t2 — 2cent

153 A47 1c on 2c lake & blk	2.50	2.50
a. Strip of 10 types	35.00	
154 A48 2c on 5c ultra & blk (R)	3.50	2.50
a. Black surcharge	14.00	14.00
b. Strip of 10 types (R)	35.00	
c. Strip of 10 types (Bk)	165.00	

The 10 types of surcharge are repeated in illustrated sequence on 1c on 2c in each horiz. row and on 2c on 5c in each vert. row of sheets of 100 (10x10).

No. 116 and Type of 1909 Surcharged:

one ct.

155 A47 1c on 2c lake & blk	190.00	190.00

2ct

156 A48 2c on 5c turq & blk	140.00	140.00

Nos. 18-20 Surcharged

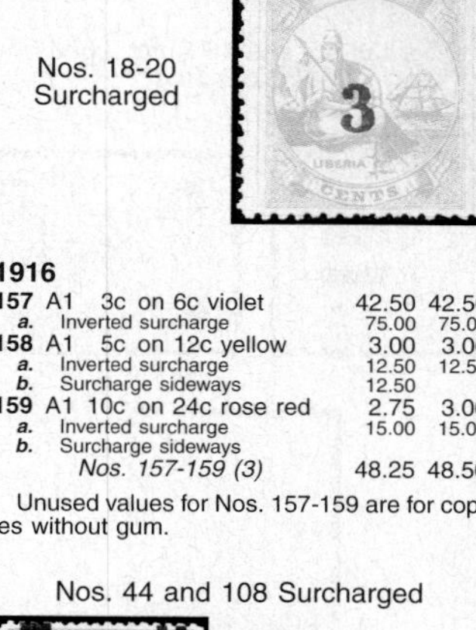

1916

157 A1 3c on 6c violet	42.50	42.50
a. Inverted surcharge	75.00	75.00
158 A1 5c on 12c yellow	3.00	3.00
a. Inverted surcharge	12.50	12.50
b. Surcharge sideways	12.50	
159 A1 10c on 24c rose red	2.75	3.00
a. Inverted surcharge	15.00	15.00
b. Surcharge sideways		
Nos. 157-159 (3)	48.25	48.50

Unused values for Nos. 157-159 are for copies without gum.

Nos. 44 and 108 Surcharged

p

r

1917 Wmk. 143

160 A15 (p) 4c on 25c yel grn	11.00	11.00
a. "OUR"	25.00	25.00
b. "FCUR"	25.00	25.00

Unwmk.

161 A40 (r) 5c on 30c dp vio	90.00	90.00

No. 118 Surcharged in Red

1918

162 A49 3c on 10c plum & blk	2.25	2.25
a. "3" inverted	9.25	9.25

Bongo Antelope — A59

Symbols of Liberia — A61

Two-spot Palm Civet A60

A62

Palm-nut Vulture — A66

Oil Palm — A63

Mercury — A64

Traveler's Tree — A65

"Mudskipper" or Bommi Fish — A67

Mandingos A68

"Liberia" A71

Coast Scene A69

Liberia College A70

1918 **Engr.** ***Perf. 12½, 14***

163	A59	1c	dp grn & blk	.65	.20
164	A60	2c	rose & blk	.80	.20
165	A61	5c	gray bl & blk	.20	.20
166	A62	10c	dark green	.20	.20
167	A63	15c	blk & dk grn	3.00	.20
168	A64	20c	claret & blk	.35	.20
169	A65	25c	dk grn & grn	3.25	.20
170	A66	30c	red vio & blk	15.00	.80
171	A67	50c	ultra & blk	26.50	3.50
172	A68	75c	ol bis & blk	.90	.20
173	A69	$1	yel brn & bl	7.25	.20
174	A70	$2	lt vio & blk	6.50	.20
175	A71	$5	dark brown	7.00	.40
			Nos. 163-175 (13)	71.60	6.70

For surcharges see Nos. 176-177, 228-229, 248-270, B3-B15, O111-O112, O155-O157.

For overprints see Nos. O98-O110.

Nos. 163-164, F10-F14 Surcharged

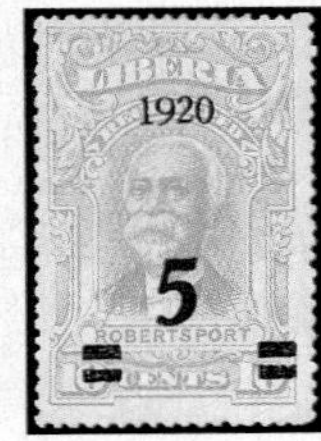

1920

176	A59	3c on 1c grn & blk	1.00	1.00
a.		"CEETS"	17.00	17.00
b.		Double surcharge	10.00	10.00
c.		Triple surcharge	15.00	15.00
177	A60	4c on 2c rose & blk	1.00	1.00
a.		Inverted surcharge	20.00	20.00
b.		Double surcharge	10.00	10.00
c.		Double surcharge, one invtd.	18.00	
d.		Triple surcharge, one inverted	25.00	25.00
e.		Quadruple surcharge	30.00	30.00
f.		Typewritten surcharge		
g.		Same as "f" but inverted		
h.		Printed and typewritten surcharges, both inverted		
178	R6	5c on 10c bl & blk	2.50	2.50
a.		Inverted surcharge	10.00	10.00
b.		Double surcharge	10.00	10.00
c.		Double surcharge, one invtd.	15.00	15.00
d.		Typewritten surcharge ("five")		100.00
e.		Printed and typewritten surcharges	100.00	
179	R6	5c on 10c org red & blk	2.50	2.50
a.		5c on 10c orange & black	4.00	2.75
b.		Inverted surcharge	15.00	
c.		Double surcharge	15.00	
d.		Double surcharge, one invtd.	18.00	15.00
e.		Typewritten surch. in violet	100.00	100.00
f.		Typewritten surch. in black		
g.		Printed and typewritten surcharges	100.00	
180	R6	5c on 10c grn & blk	2.50	2.50
a.		Double surcharge	10.00	10.00
b.		Double surcharge, one invtd.	18.00	18.00
c.		Inverted surcharge		18.00
d.		Quadruple surcharge	25.00	25.00
e.		Typewritten surcharge		100.00
f.		Printed and typewritten surcharges		
181	R6	5c on 10c vio & blk (Monrovia)	4.00	4.00
a.		Double surcharge, one invtd.	25.00	25.00
182	R6	5c on 10c mag & blk (Robertsport)	2.00	2.00
a.		Double surcharge	15.00	15.00
b.		Double surcharge, one invtd.	15.00	15.00
c.		Double surcharge, both invtd.	25.00	
		Nos. 176-182 (7)	15.50	15.50

Cape Mesurado A75

Pres. Daniel E. Howard — A76

Arms of Liberia — A77

Crocodile A78

Pepper Plant A79

Leopard A80

Village Scene A81

Kru men in Dugout A82

Rapids in St. Paul's River A83

Bongo Antelope A84

Hornbill A85

Elephant A86

1921 **Wmk. 116** ***Perf. 14***

183	A75	1c	green	.20	.20
184	A76	5c	dp bl & blk	.20	.20
185	A77	10c	red & dl bl	.20	.20
186	A78	15c	dl vio & grn	6.50	.30
187	A79	20c	rose red & grn	2.75	.20
188	A80	25c	org & blk	7.50	.30
189	A81	30c	grn & dl vio	.40	.20
190	A82	50c	org & ultra	.45	.20
191	A83	75c	red & blk brn	.80	.20
a.			Center inverted		70.00
192	A84	$1	red & blk	32.50	1.75
193	A85	$2	yel & ultra	10.50	.70
194	A86	$5	car rose & vio	32.50	.95
			Nos. 183-194 (12)	94.50	5.40

For overprints see Nos. 195, 198-208, O115-O127, O130-O140.

Nos. 134-135, 183-194 Overprinted "1921"

195	A75	1c	green	22.50	.40
196	A57	2c	red	22.50	.40
197	A58	3c	dull violet	32.50	.40
198	A76	5c	dp bl & blk	3.50	.30
199	A77	10c	red & dull bl	50.00	.40
200	A78	15c	dull vio & grn	22.50	1.40
201	A79	20c	rose red & grn, ovpt. invtd.	7.25	.75
202	A80	25c	orange & blk	22.50	1.40
203	A81	30c	grn & dull vio	2.50	.30
204	A82	50c	orange & ultra	3.50	.30
205	A83	75c	red & blk brn	4.75	.30
206	A84	$1	red & blk	62.50	2.10
207	A85	$2	yellow & ultra	22.50	2.10
208	A86	$5	car rose & vio	60.00	2.75
			Nos. 195-208 (14)	339.00	13.30

Overprint exists inverted in Nos. 195-208 and normal on No. 201.

First Settlers Landing at Cape Mesurado from U. S. S. Alligator A87

1923 **Litho.**

209	A87	1c	lt blue & blk	18.00	.30
210	A87	2c	claret & ol gray	26.00	.30
211	A87	5c	ol grn & ind	26.00	.30
212	A87	10c	bl grn & vio	1.00	.30
213	A87	$1	rose & brn	3.25	.30
			Nos. 209-213 (5)	74.25	1.50

Centenary of founding of Liberia.

Memorial to J. J. Roberts, 1st Pres. — A88

Hall of Representatives, Monrovia — A89

Liberian Star — A90

A91

Pres. Charles Dunbar Burgess King — A92

Hippopotamus — A93

Antelope
A94

West
African
Buffalo
A95

Grebos
Making
Dumboy
A96

Pineapple
A97

Carrying
Ivory Tusk
A98

Rubber Planter's House — A99

Stockton Lagoon — A100

Grebo Houses — A101

1923 *Perf. 13½x14½, 14½x13½*

214 A88 1c yel grn & dp grn 7.50 1.25
215 A89 2c claret & brn 7.50 .20
216 A90 3c lilac & blk .35 .20
217 A91 5c bl vio & blk 115.00 .20
218 A92 10c slate & brn .35 .20
219 A93 15c bister & bl 35.00 .50
220 A94 20c bl grn & vio 2.50 .35
221 A95 25c org red & brn 160.00 .60
222 A96 30c dk brn & vio .60 .20
223a A97 50c dull vio & org 1.00 .20
224 A98 75c gray & bl 1.90 .40
225a A99 $1 dp red & dk vio 4.50 .60
226 A100 $2 orange & blue 7.50 .80
227a A101 $5 dp grn & brn 8.50 .90
Nos. 214-227a (14) 352.20 6.60

Nos. 222-227 exist on white, buff or brownish paper. Values are for the most common variety. See the Scott Classic Specialized Catalogue for detailed listings.

For overprints see Nos. O141-O154.

No. 163 Surcharged

1926 **Unwmk.** ***Perf. 14***

228 A59 2c on 1c dp grn & blk 3.50 3.50
a. Surcharge with ornamental design as on #O155 17.00

No. 163 Surcharged in Red

1927

229 A59 2c on 1c dp grn & blk 9.50 9.50
a. "Ceuts" 14.00
b. "Vwo" 14.00
c. "Twc" 14.00
d. Double surcharge 27.50
e. Wavy lines omitted 17.50

Palms
A102

Map of
Africa — A103

President
King — A104

1928 **Engr.** ***Perf. 12***

230 A102 1c green .75 .50
231 A102 2c dark violet .50 .35
232 A102 3c bister brn .50 .35
233 A103 5c ultra 1.00 .55
234 A104 10c olive gray 1.40 .55
235 A103 15c dull violet 6.25 2.25
236 A103 $1 red brown 77.50 26.50
Nos. 230-236 (7) 87.90 31.05

For surcharges & overprints see Nos. 288A, 289A, 290A-291, 292A, C1-C3, O158-O165.

Nos. 164-168, 170-175 Surcharged in Various Colors and Styles, "1936" and New Values

1936 ***Perf. 12½, 14***

248 A60 1c on 2c (Bl) .55 *3.50*
249 A61 3c on 5c (Bl) .20 *2.00*
250 A62 4c on 10c (Br) .20 *2.00*
251 A63 6c on 15c (Bl) .55 *3.50*
252 A64 8c on 20c (V) .20 *2.00*
253 A66 12c on 30c (V) 1.00 *9.75*
254 A67 14c on 50c (Bl) 1.10 *11.00*
255 A68 16c on 75c (Br) .55 *5.50*
256 A69 18c on $1 (Bk) .55 *5.50*
a. 22c on $1 yellow brown & blue 7.25
257 A70 22c on $2 (V) .75 7.75
258 A71 24c on $5 (Bk) 1.00 9.75
Nos. 248-258 (11) 6.65 62.25

Official Stamps, Nos. O99-O110, Surcharged or Overprinted in various colors and styles with 6 pointed star and "1936"

1936

259 A60 1c on 2c (Bl) .40 *4.00*
260 A61 3c on 5c (Bl) .40 *4.00*
261 A62 4c on 10c (Bl) .40 *4.00*
262 A63 6c on 15c (Bl) .40 *4.00*
263 A64 8c on 20c (V) .40 *4.00*
264 A66 12c on 30c (V) 1.50 *20.00*
a. "193" instead of "1936" 19.00
265 A67 14c on 50c (Bl) 2.00 *21.00*
266 A68 16c on 75c (Bk) 1.00 *12.00*
267 A69 18c on $1 (Bk) 1.00 *12.00*
268 A70 22c on $2 (Bl) 1.25 *15.00*
269 A71 24c on $5 (Bk) 1.50 *17.00*
270 A65 25c (Bk) 2.00 *21.00*
Nos. 259-270 (12) 12.25 138.00

Hornbill — A106

Designs: 2c, Bushbuck. 3c, West African dwarf buffalo. 4c, Pygmy hippopotamus. 5c, Lesser egret. 6c, Pres. E. J. Barclay.

Perf. Compound of 11½, 12, 12½, 14
1937, Apr. 10 **Engr.** **Unwmk.**

271 A106 1c green & blk 1.50 .80
272 A106 2c carmine & blk 1.50 .20
273 A106 3c violet & blk 1.50 .80
274 A106 4c orange & blk 2.25 1.25
275 A106 5c blue & blk 2.25 .95
276 A106 6c green & blk .80 .20
Nos. 271-276 (6) 9.80 4.20

Coast Line of Liberia, 1839 — A107

Seal of Liberia, Map and Farming Scenes — A108

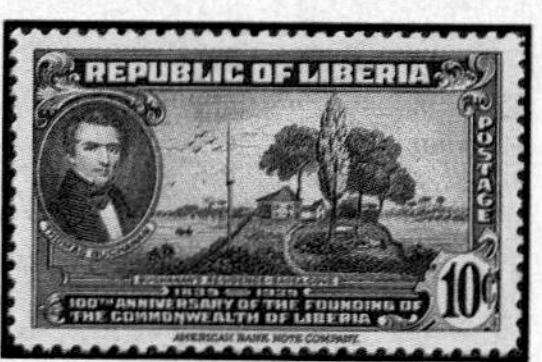

Thomas Buchanan and Residence at Bassa Cove — A109

1940, July 29 **Engr.** ***Perf. 12***

277 A107 3c dark blue .35 .35
278 A108 5c dull red brn .35 .35
279 A109 10c dark green .35 .35
Nos. 277-279 (3) 1.05 1.05

100th anniv. of the founding of the Commonwealth of Liberia.

For overprints & surcharges see Nos. 280-282, B16-B18, C14-C16, CB1-CB3, CE1, CF1, E1, F35.

Nos. 277-279 Overprinted in Red or Blue

1941, Feb. 21

280 A107 3c dk blue (R) 2.50 2.50
281 A108 5c dull red brn (Bl) 2.50 2.50
282 A109 10c dark green (R) 2.50 2.50
Nos. 280-282,C14-C16 (6) 15.75 15.75

Royal
Antelope
A110

Bay-thighed Diana
Monkey — A115

2c, Water chevrotain. 3c, White-shouldered duiker. 4c, Bushbuck. 5c, Zebra antelope.

1942 **Engr.**

283 A110 1c violet & fawn 1.10 .20
284 A110 2c brt ultra & yel brn 1.40 .20
285 A110 3c brt grn & yel brn 1.90 .90
286 A110 4c blk & red org 2.40 1.90
287 A110 5c olive & fawn 3.00 1.90
288 A115 10c red & black 5.25 2.40
Nos. 283-288 (6) 15.05 7.50

Nos. 231, 233-234, 271-276 Surcharged with New Values and Bars or X's in Violet, Black, Red Brown or Blue

Perf. 12, 12x12½, 14
1944-46 **Unwmk.**

288A A102 1c on 2c (Bk) 9.25 6.50
289 A106 1c on 4c (Bk) 50.00 47.50
289A A104 1c on 10c (R Br) 12.50 9.50
290 A106 2c on 3c 62.50 50.00
290A A103 2c on 5c (Bk) 2.75 2.75
290B A103 2c on 5c (Bl) 21.00 9.25
291 A102 3c on 2c 30.00 30.00
292 A106 4c on 5c 11.00 7.25
292A A104 4c on 10c (Bk) 3.25 3.25
b. Double surch., one inverted
293 A106 5c on 1c (Bk) 85.00 50.00
294 A106 6c on 2c (Bk) 11.00 9.50
295 A106 10c on 6c 11.00 9.50
Nos. 288A-295 (12) 309.25 235.00

Surcharges on Nos. 289, 290, 293, 294 are found inverted. Values same as normal.

Pres. Franklin D. Roosevelt Reviewing Troops — A116

1945, Nov. 26 **Engr.** ***Perf. 12½***
Grayish Paper

296 A116 3c brt violet & blk .20 .20
297 A116 5c dk blue & blk .45 .45
Nos. 296-297,C51 (3) 1.90 2.05

In memory of Pres. Franklin D. Roosevelt (1882-1945).

Monrovia Harbor — A117

1947, Jan. 2

298 A117 5c deep blue .20 .20

Opening of the Monrovia Harbor Project, Feb. 16, 1946. See No. C52.

Without Inscription at Top

1947, May 16

299 A117 5c violet .20 .20

See No. C53.

1st US Postage Stamps and Arms of Liberia — A118

1947, June 6

300 A118 5c carmine rose .20 .20

Nos. 300,C54-C56 (4) .80 .80

Cent. of US postage stamps and the 87th anniv. of Liberian postal issues.

Matilda Newport Firing Cannon — A119

1947, Dec. 1 Engr. & Photo.

Center in Gray Black

301 A119 1c brt blue green .20 .20
302 A119 3c brt red violet .20 .20
303 A119 5c brt ultra .60 .20
304 A119 10c yellow 3.25 .80
Nos. 301-304,C57 (5) 5.50 1.70

125th anniv. of Matilda Newport's defense of Monrovia, Dec. 1, 1822.

Liberian Star — A120

Cent. of Independence: 2c, Liberty. 3c, Liberian Arms. 5c, Map of Liberia.

1947, Dec. 22 Engr.

305 A120 1c dark green .55 .20
306 A120 2c brt red vio .55 .20
307 A120 3c brt purple .55 .20
308 A120 5c dark blue .55 .20
Nos. 305-308,C58-C60 (7) 3.80 1.65

Centenary of independence.

Natives Approaching Village — A124

Rubber Tapping and Planting A125

Landing of First Colonists — A126

Jehudi Ashmun and Defenders — A127

1949, Apr. 4 Litho. *Perf. 11½*

309 A124 1c multicolored .45 .75
310 A125 2c multicolored .45 .75
311 A126 3c multicolored .45 .75
312 A127 5c multicolored .45 .75
Nos. 309-312,C63-C64 (6) 2.50 4.30

Nos. 309-312 exist perf. 12½ and sell at a much lower price. The status of the perf. 12½ set is indefinite.

Stephen Benson — A128

Liberian Presidents: 1c, Pres. Joseph J. Roberts. 3c, Daniel B. Warner. 4c, James S. Payne. 5c, Executive mansion. 6c, Edward J. Roye. 7c, A. W. Gardner and A. F. Russell. 8c, Hilary R. W. Johnson. 9c, Joseph J. Cheeseman. 10c, William D. Coleman. 15c, Garretson W. Gibson. 20c, Arthur Barclay. 25c, Daniel E. Howard. 50c, Charles D. B. King. $1, Edwin J. Barclay.

1948-50 Unwmk. Engr. *Perf. 12½*

Caption and Portrait in Black

313 A128 1c green ('48) 2.75 *7.00*
314 A128 2c salmon pink .40 *.65*
315 A128 3c rose violet .40 *.65*
a. "1876-1878" added 16.00 *40.00*
316 A128 4c lt olive grn .90 .90
317 A128 5c ultra .50 *.90*
318 A128 6c red orange .90 *1.75*
319 A128 7c lt blue ('50) 1.10 *2.10*
320 A128 8c carmine 1.10 *2.40*
321 A128 9c red violet 1.25 *2.10*
322 A128 10c yellow ('50) .85 .55
323 A128 15c yellow orange 1.00 .70
324 A128 20c blue gray 1.40 1.40
325 A128 25c cerise 2.00 2.10
326 A128 50c aqua 3.75 1.40
327 A128 $1 rose lilac 6.25 1.40
Nos. 313-327,C65 (16) 25.15 *26.65*

Issued: 1c, 11/18; 7c, 10c, 1950; others, 7/21/49.

See Nos. 328, 371-378, C118.

Pres. Joseph J. Roberts — A129

1950

328 A129 1c green & blk .25 .25

Hand Holding Book — A130

1950, Feb. 14

329 A130 5c deep blue .45 .20

National Literacy Campaign. See No. C66.

Catalogue values for unused stamps in this section, from this point to the end of the section, are for Never Hinged items.

UPU Monument — A131

First UPU Building, Bern — A132

1950, Apr. 21 Engr. Unwmk.

330 A131 5c green & blk .25 .25
331 A132 10c red vio & blk .25 .25
Nos. 330-331,C67 (3) 3.25 3.25

UPU, 75th anniv. (in 1949). Exist imperf., same value.

Jehudi Ashmun and Seal of Liberia — A133

John Marshall, Ashmun and Map of Town of Marshall — A134

Designs (Map or View and Two Portraits): 2c, Careysburg, Gov. Lott Carey (1780-1828), freed American slave, and Jehudi Ashmun (1794-1828), American missionary credited as founder of Liberia. 3c, Town of Harper, Robert Goodloe Harper (1765-1825), American statesman, and Ashmun. 5c, Upper Buchanan, Gov. Thomas Buchanan and Ashmun. 10c, Robertsport, Pres. Joseph J. Roberts and Ashmun.

1952, Apr. 10 *Perf. 10½*

332 A133 1c deep green .25 .25
333 A133 2c scarlet & ind .25 .25
334 A133 3c purple & grn .25 .25
335 A134 4c brown & grn .25 .25
336 A133 5c ultra & org red .25 .25
337 A134 10c org red & dk bl .25 .25
Nos. 332-337,C68-C69 (8) 2.40 2.40

Nos. 332-337 exist imperf. Value about two and one-half times that of the perf. set.

No. 334 exists with center inverted. Value $50.

See No. C69a.

UN Headquarters Building A135

Scroll and Flags A136

10c, Liberia arms, letters "UN" and emblem.

1952, Dec. 20 Unwmk. *Perf. 12½*

338 A135 1c ultra .30 .30
339 A136 4c car & ultra .30 .30
340 A136 10c red brn & yel .30 .30
a. Souvenir sheet of 3, #338-340 2.00 2.00
Nos. 338-340,C70 (4) 1.80 1.55

Nos. 338-340 and 340a exist imperforate.

Pepper Bird — A137

Roller A138

1953, Nov. 18 *Perf. 10½*

341 A137 1c shown 1.00 .20
342 A138 3c shown 1.00 .20
343 A137 4c Hornbill 1.60 .20
344 A137 5c Kingfisher 1.75 .20
345 A138 10c Jacana 1.90 .20
346 A138 12c Weaver 2.50 .20
Nos. 341-346 (6) 9.75 1.20

Exist imperf. Value, set unused $20.

Tennis A139

Callichilia Stenosepala A140

1955, Jan. 26 Litho. *Perf. 12½*

347 A139 3c shown .25 .25
348 A139 5c Soccer .25 .25
349 A139 25c Boxing .25 .25
Nos. 347-349,C88-C90 (6) 1.65 1.65

1955, Sept. 28 Unwmk.

Various Native Flowers: 7c, Gomphia subcordata. 8c, Listrostachys caudata. 9c, Musaenda isertiana.

350 A140 6c yel grn, org & yel .30 .30
351 A140 7c emer, yel & car .30 .30
352 A140 8c yel grn, buff & bl .30 .30
353 A140 9c orange & green .30 .30
Nos. 350-353,C91-C92 (6) 1.80 1.80

Rubber Tapping A141

1955, Dec. 5 *Perf. 12½*

354 A141 5c emerald & yellow .25 .25
Nos. 354,C97-C98 (3) 1.15 .65

50th anniv. of Rotary Intl. No. 354 exists printed entirely in emerald.

Statue of Liberty A142

Coliseum, New York City — A143

Design: 6c, Globe inscribed FIPEX.

1956, Apr. 28 *Perf. 12*

355 A142 3c brt grn & dk red brn .20 .20
356 A143 4c Prus grn & bis brn .20 .20
357 A143 6c gray & red lilac .20 .20
Nos. 355-357,C100-C102 (6) 1.90 1.20

Fifth International Philatelic Exhibition (FIPEX), NYC, Apr. 28-May 6, 1956.

Kangaroo and Emu — A144

Discus Thrower A145

Designs: 8c, Goddess of Victory and Olympic symbols. 10c, Classic chariot race.

1956, Nov. 15 Litho. Unwmk.

358 A144 4c lt ol grn & gldn brn .20 .20
359 A145 6c emerald & gray .20 .20
360 A144 8c lt ultra & redsh brn .20 .20
361 A144 10c rose red & blk .20 .20
Nos. 358-361,C104-C105 (6) 1.80 1.80

16th Olympic Games at Melbourne, Nov. 22-Dec. 8, 1956.

Idlewild Airport, New York A146

5c, Roberts Field, Liberia, plane & Pres. Tubman.

Lithographed and Engraved

1957, May 4 *Perf. 12*

362 A146 3c orange & dk blue .20 .20
363 A146 5c red lilac & blk .20 .20
Nos. 362-363,C107-C110 (6) 2.95 1.20

1st anniv. of direct air service between Roberts Field, Liberia, and Idlewild (Kennedy), NY.

Orphanage Playground — A147

Orphanage and: 5c, Teacher and pupil. 6c, Singing boys and natl. anthem. 10c, Children and flag.

1957, Nov. 25 Litho. *Perf. 12*

364 A147 4c green & red .20 .20
365 A147 5c bl grn & red brn .20 .20
366 A147 6c brt vio & bis .20 .20
367 A147 10c ultra & rose car .20 .20
Nos. 364-367,C111-C112 (6) 2.00 1.20

Founding of the Antoinette Tubman Child Welfare Foundation.

Windmill and Dutch Flag — A148

Designs: No. 369, German flag and Brandenburg Gate. No. 370, Swedish flag, palace and crowns.

Engraved and Lithographed

1958, Jan. 10 Unwmk. *Perf. 10½*

Flags in Original Colors

368 A148 5c reddish brn .20 .20
369 A148 5c blue .20 .20
370 A148 5c lilac rose .20 .20
Nos. 368-370,C114-C117 (7) 2.40 2.40

European tour of Pres. Tubman in 1956.

Presidential Types of 1948-50

Designs as before.

1958-60 Engr. *Perf. 12*

Caption and Portrait in Black

371 A129 1c salmon pink .45 .20
372 A128 2c brt yellow .45 .20
373 A128 10c blue gray .55 .55
374 A128 15c brt bl & blk ('59) .20 .20
375 A128 20c dark red .65 .65
376 A128 25c blue .65 .65
377 A128 50c red lil & blk ('59) .75 .65
378 A128 $1 bister brn ('60) 5.75 .75
Nos. 371-378,C118 (9) 10.70 4.75

Many shades of 1c.

Open Globe Projection — A149

Designs: 5c, UN Emblem and building. 10c, UN Emblem. 12c, UN Emblem and initials of agencies.

1958, Dec. 10 Litho. *Perf. 12*

379 A149 3c gray, bl & blk .20 .20
380 A149 5c blue & choc .20 .20
381 A149 10c black & org .20 .20
382 A149 12c black & car 1.10 1.10
Nos. 379-382 (4) 1.70 1.70

10th anniv. of the Universal Declaration of Human Rights. See No. C119.

People of Africa on the March — A150

Symbols of UNESCO A151

1959, Apr. 15

383 A150 20c orange & brown .45 .45

African Freedom Day, Apr. 15. See No. C120.

1959, May 11 Unwmk.

384 A151 25c dp plum & emer .55 .55

Opening of UNESCO Headquarters in Paris, Nov. 3, 1958.
See Nos. C121, C121a.

Abraham Lincoln — A152

1959, Nov. 20 Engr. *Perf. 12*

385 A152 10c ultra & blk .40 .40
386 A152 15c orange & blk .40 .40
a. Souv. sheet of 3, Nos. 385-386, C122, imperf. 2.50 4.00
Nos. 385-386,C122 (3) 1.70 1.70

150th anniv. of the birth of Abraham Lincoln.

Touré, Tubman and Nkrumah A153

1960, Jan. 27 Litho. Unwmk.

387 A153 25c crimson & blk .55 .55

1959 "Big Three" conference of Pres. Sékou Touré of Guinea, Pres. William V. S. Tubman of Liberia and Prime Minister Kwame Nkrumah of Ghana at Saniquellie, Liberia. See No. C123.

World Refugee Year Emblem — A154

Map of Africa — A155

1960, Apr. 7 *Perf. 11½*

388 A154 25c emerald & blk .70 1.00

World Refuge Year, July 1, 1959-June 30, 1960. See No. C124, C124a.

1960, May 11 Litho. *Perf. 11½*

389 A155 25c green & black .60 .60

10th anniv. of the Commission for Technical Cooperation in Africa South of the Sahara (C.C.T.A.). See No. C125.

Weight Lifter and Porter — A156

Liberian Stamps of 1860 — A157

Designs: 10c, Rower and canoeists, horiz. 15c, Walker and porter.

1960, Sept. 6 Unwmk.

390 A156 5c dk brn & emer .20 .20
391 A156 10c brown & red lil .20 .20
392 A156 15c brown & org .70 .75
Nos. 390-392,C126 (4) 2.00 1.85

17th Olympic Games, Rome, 8/25-9/11.

1960, Dec. 1 Litho. *Perf. 11½*

393 A157 5c multicolored .20 .20
394 A157 20c multicolored .70 .70
Nos. 393-394,C128 (3) 1.90 1.90

Liberian postage stamps, cent.

Laurel Wreath — A158

1961, May 19 Unwmk. *Perf. 11½*
395 A158 25c red & dk blue .60 .60

Liberia's membership in the UN Security Council. Exists imperf. See Nos. C130-C131 and note after No. C131.

Anatomy Class A159

1961, Sept. 8 *Perf. 11½*
396 A159 25c green & brown .60 .60

15th anniv. of UNESCO. See #C132-C133.

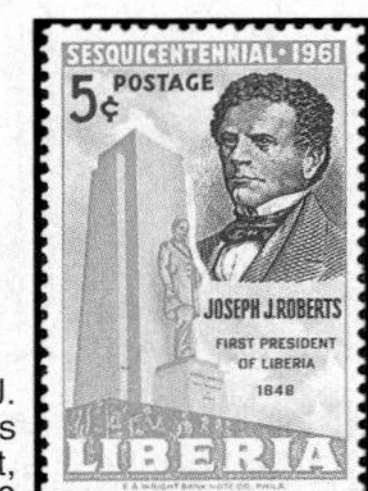

Joseph J. Roberts Monument, Monrovia — A160

Design: 10c, Pres. Roberts and old and new presidential mansions, horiz.

1961, Oct. 25 Litho.
397 A160 5c orange & sepia .40 .40
398 A160 10c ultra & sepia .40 .40
Nos. 397-398,C134 (3) 1.50 1.50

150th anniv. of the birth of Joseph J. Roberts, 1st pres. of Liberia.

Boy Scout A161

Design: Insignia and Scouts camping.

1961, Dec. 4 Unwmk. *Perf. 11½*
399 A161 5c lilac & sepia .20 .20
400 A161 10c ultra & bister .50 .50
Nos. 399-400,C135 (3) 2.10 2.10

Boy Scouts of Liberia. Exist imperf.

Dag Hammarskjold and UN Emblem — A162

1962, Feb. 1 *Perf. 12*
401 A162 20c black & ultra .45 .45

Dag Hammarskjold, Secretary General of the UN, 1953-61. See Nos. C137-C138.

Malaria Eradication Emblem — A163

1962, Apr. 7 Litho. *Perf. 12½*
402 A163 25c dk green & red .55 .45

WHO drive to eradicate malaria. See Nos. C139-C140.

United Nations Emblem A164

1962, Oct. 22 *Perf. 12x12½*
403 A164 20c green & yel bister .35 .35

Issued to mark the observance of United Nations Day, Oct. 24, as a national holiday. See Nos. C144-C145.

Executive Mansion, Monrovia A165

1c, 80c, Executive Mansion, Monrovia. 5c, Treasury Department Building, Monrovia. 10c, Information Service. 15c, Capitol.

1962-64
403A A165 1c vio bl & dp org ('64) .20 .20
404 A165 5c lt blue & pur .20 .20
405 A165 10c bister & brn .20 .20
406 A165 15c salmon & dk bl .20 .20
406A A165 80c brn & yel ('64) 1.75 .85
Nos. 403A-406A,C146-C148 (9) 9.10 8.20

"FAO" Emblem and Food Bowl — A166

1963, Mar. 21 *Perf. 12½*
407 A166 5c aqua & dk car .25 .25

FAO "Freedom from Hunger" campaign. See Nos. C149-C150.

Rocket in Space A167

Design: 15c, Space capsule and globe.

1963, May 27 Litho. *Perf. 12½*
408 A167 10c dp vio bl & yel .20 .20
409 A167 15c blue & red brn .60 .60
Nos. 408-409,C151 (3) 1.50 1.50

Achievements in space exploration for peaceful purposes.

Red Cross A168

10c, Centenary emblem and torch, vert.

1963, Aug. 26 Unwmk. *Perf. 11½*
410 A168 5c blue grn & red .20 .20
411 A168 10c gray & red .20 .20
Nos. 410-411,C153-C154 (4) 1.50 1.50

Intl. Red Cross, cent.

Palm Tree and Scroll — A169

Ski Jump — A170

1963, Oct. 28 *Perf. 12½*
412 A169 20c brown & green .45 .45

Conference of African heads of state for African Unity, Addis Ababa, May, 1963. See No. C156.

1963, Dec. 11 Unwmk. *Perf. 12½*
413 A170 5c rose red & dk vio bl .25 .25
Nos. 413,C157-C158 (3) 1.25 1.25

9th Winter Olympic Games, Innsbruck, Austria, Jan. 29-Feb. 9, 1964.

John F. Kennedy A171

1964, Apr. 6 Litho.
414 A171 20c blk & brt blue .35 .35

John F. Kennedy (1917-63). See #C160-C161.

Syncom Satellite A172

Satellites: 15c, Relay I, vert. 25c, Mariner II.

1964, June 22 Unwmk. *Perf. 12½*
415 A172 10c orange & emer .20 .20
416 A172 15c brt car rose & vio .20 .20
417 A172 25c blue, org & blk .70 .70
Nos. 415-417 (3) 1.10 1.10

Progress in space communications and the peaceful uses of outer space. See No. C162.

Mt. Fuji A173

Designs: 15c, Torii and Olympic flame. 25c, Cherry blossoms and stadium.

1964, Sept. 15 Litho.
418 A173 10c orange yel & emer .20 .20
419 A173 15c lt red & purple .20 .20
420 A173 25c ocher & red .95 .95
Nos. 418-420 (3) 1.35 1.35

Issued for the 18th Olympic Games, Tokyo, Oct. 10-25, 1964. See No. C163.

Boy Scout Emblem and Scout Sign — A174

"Emancipation" by Thomas Ball — A175

10c, Bugle and Liberian Scout emblem, horiz.

1965, Mar. 8 Litho. *Perf. 12½*
421 A174 5c lt blue & brown .25 .25
422 A174 10c dk green & ocher .25 .25
Nos. 421-422,C164 (3) 1.30 1.30

Liberian Boy Scouts.

1965, May 3 Unwmk. *Perf. 12½*

Designs: 20c, Abraham Lincoln and John F. Kennedy, horiz. 25c, Lincoln by Augustus St. Gaudens, Lincoln Park, Chicago.

423 A175 5c dk gray & brn org .20 .20
424 A175 20c emer & lt gray .50 .50
425 A175 25c maroon & blue .65 .65
Nos. 423-425 (3) 1.35 1.35

Centenary of the death of Abraham Lincoln. See No. C166.

ICY Emblem A176

1965, June 21 Litho. *Perf. 12½*
426 A176 12c orange & brn .20 .20
427 A176 25c vio blue & brn .40 .40
428 A176 50c emerald & brn .85 .85
Nos. 426-428 (3) 1.45 1.45

Intl. Cooperation Year. See No. C167.

ITU Emblem, Old and New Communication Equipment — A177

1965, Sept. 21 Unwmk. ***Perf. 12½***

429 A177 25c brt grn & red brn .40 .40
430 A177 35c black & car rose .50 .50
Nos. 429-430,C168 (3) 1.70 1.60

Cent. of the ITU.

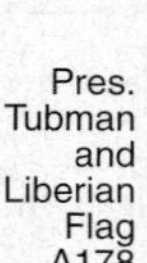

Pres. Tubman and Liberian Flag A178

1965, Nov. 29 Litho.

431 A178 25c red, ultra & brn .60 .60

Pres. William V. S. Tubman's 70th birthday. See No. C169, C169a.

Churchill in Admiral's Uniform A179

Pres. Joseph J. Roberts — A180

Designs: 15c, Churchill giving "V" sign, vert.

1966, Jan. 18 Litho. ***Perf. 12½***

432 A179 15c orange & blk .20 .20
433 A179 20c black & brt grn .90 .90
Nos. 432-433,C170 (3) 1.80 1.65

Issued in memory of Sir Winston Spencer Churchill (1874-1965), statesman and World War II leader.

1966-69 Litho. ***Perf. 12½***

Presidents: 2c, Stephen Benson. 3c, Daniel Bashiel Warner. 4c, James S. Payne. 5c, Edward James Roye. 10c, William D. Coleman. 25c, Daniel Edward Howard. 50c, Charles Dunbar Burgess King. 80c, Hilary R. W. Johnson. $1, Edwin J. Barclay. $2, Joseph James Cheeseman ("Cheesman" on stamp).

434 A180 1c black & brick red .20 .20
435 A180 2c black & yellow .20 .20
436 A180 3c black & lilac .20 .20
437 A180 4c ap grn & blk ('67) .20 .20
438 A180 5c black & dull org .20 .20
439 A180 10c pale grn & blk ('67) .20 .20
440 A180 25c black & lt blue .60 .20
441 A180 50c blk & brt lil rose 1.25 .90
442 A180 80c dp rose & blk ('67) 1.90 1.10
443 A180 $1 black & ocher 2.25 .20

Perf. 11½x11

443A A180 $2 blk & dp red lil ('69) 4.50 3.00
Nos. 434-443A,C182 (12) 12.30 6.90

Soccer Players and Globe A181

Designs: 25c, World Championships Cup, ball and shoes, vert. 35c, Soccer player dribbling, vert.

1966, May 3 Litho. ***Perf. 12½***

444 A181 10c brt green & dk brn .20 .20
445 A181 25c brt pink & brn .60 .20
446 A181 35c brown & orange .80 .45
Nos. 444-446 (3) 1.60 .85

World Cup Soccer Championships, Wembley, England, July 11-30. See No. C172.

Pres. Kennedy Taking Oath of Office A182

20c, 1964 Kennedy stamps, #414, C160.

1966, Aug. 16 Litho. ***Perf. 12½***

447 A182 15c red & blk .35 .35
448 A182 20c brt bl & red lil .35 .35
Nos. 447-448,C173-C174 (4) 1.80 1.10

3rd anniv. of Pres. Kennedy's death (Nov. 22).

Children on Seesaw and UNICEF Emblem A183

Design: 80c, Boy playing doctor.

1966, Oct. 25 Unwmk. ***Perf. 12½***

449 A183 5c brt blue & red .20 .20
450 A183 80c org brn & yel grn 1.10 1.10

20th anniv. of UNICEF.

Giraffe — A184

Jamboree Badge — A185

Designs: 3c, Lion. 5c, Slender-nosed crocodile, horiz. 10c, Baby chimpanzees. 15c, Leopard, horiz. 20c, Black rhinoceros, horiz. 25c, Elephant.

1966, Dec. 20

451 A184 2c multicolored 1.25 1.25
452 A184 3c multicolored 1.25 1.25
453 A184 5c multicolored 1.25 1.25
a. Black omitted ("5c LIBERIA" and imprint) 50.00
454 A184 10c multicolored 1.25 1.25
455 A184 15c multicolored 1.60 1.25
456 A184 20c multicolored 2.25 1.25
457 A184 25c multicolored 3.25 1.25
Nos. 451-457 (7) 12.10 8.75

1967, Mar. 23 Litho. ***Perf. 12½***

Designs: 25c, Boy Scout emblem and various sports, horiz. 40c, Scout at campfire and vision of moon landing, horiz.

458 A185 10c brt lil rose & grn .20 .20
459 A185 25c brt red & blue .65 .55
460 A185 40c brt grn & brn org 1.10 .85
Nos. 458-460 (3) 1.95 1.60

12th Boy Scout World Jamboree, Farragut State Park, Idaho, Aug. 1-9. See No. C176.

A186

A187

Pre-Hispanic Sculpture of Mexico: 25c, Aztec Calendar and Olympic rings. 40c, Mexican pottery, sombrero and guitar, horiz.

1967, June 20 Litho. ***Perf. 12½***

461 A186 10c ocher & violet .20 .20
462 A186 25c lt bl, org & blk .35 .25
463 A186 40c yel grn & car .55 .40
Nos. 461-463 (3) 1.10 .85

Issued to publicize the 19th Olympic Games, Mexico City. See No. C177.

1967, Aug. 28 Litho. ***Perf. 12½***

Designs: 5c, WHO Office for Africa, horiz. 80c, WHO Office for Africa.

464 A187 5c blue & yellow .20 .20
465 A187 80c brt grn & yel 2.10 2.10

Inauguration of the WHO Regional Office for Africa in Brazzaville, Congo.

Boy Playing African Rattle A188

Africans Playing Native Instruments: 3c, Tom-tom and soko violin, horiz. 5c, Mang harp, horiz. 10c, Alimilim. 15c, Xylophone drums. 25c, Large tom-toms. 35c, Large harp.

1967, Oct. 16 Litho. ***Perf. 14***

466 A188 2c violet & multi .20 .20
467 A188 3c blue & multi .20 .20
468 A188 5c lilac rose & multi .20 .20
469 A188 10c yel grn & multi .20 .20
470 A188 15c violet & multi .40 .20
471 A188 25c ocher & multi .90 .40
472 A188 35c dp rose & multi 1.40 .65
Nos. 466-472 (7) 3.50 2.05

Ice Hockey — A189

Pres. William Tubman — A190

Designs: 25c, Ski jump. 40c, Bobsledding.

1967, Nov. 20 Litho. ***Perf. 12½***

473 A189 10c emer & vio bl .20 .20
474 A189 25c grnsh bl & dp plum .40 .20
475 A189 40c ocher & org brn .70 .50
Nos. 473-475 (3) 1.30 .90

10th Winter Olympic Games, Grenoble, France, Feb. 6-18, 1968. See No. C178.

1967, Dec. 22 Litho. ***Perf. 12½***

476 A190 25c ultra & brown 1.00 .50

Souvenir Sheet

Imperf

477 A190 50c ultra & brown 2.50 2.50

Inauguration of President Tubman, Jan. 1, 1968. No. 477 contains one stamp with simulated perforations and picture frame.

Human Rights Flame — A191

Martin Luther King, Jr. — A192

1968, Apr. 26 Litho. ***Perf. 12½***

478 A191 3c ver & dp bl .20 .20
479 A191 80c brown & emer 1.40 1.40

Intl. Human Rights Year. See No. C179.

1968, July 11 Unwmk. ***Perf. 12½***

Designs: 15c, Mule-drawn hearse and Dr. King. 35c, Dr. King and Lincoln monument by Daniel Chester French, horiz.

480 A192 15c brt bl & brn .20 .20
481 A192 25c indigo & brn .40 .20
482 A192 35c olive & blk .65 .40
Nos. 480-482 (3) 1.25 .80

Rev. Dr. Martin Luther King, Jr. (1929-1968), American civil rights leader. See No. C180.

Javelin and Diana Statue, Mexico City A193

Designs: 25c, Discus, pyramid and serpent god Quetzalcoatl. 35c, Woman diver and Xochicalco from ruins near Cuernavaca.

1968, Aug. 22 Litho. ***Perf. 12½***

483 A193 15c dp vio & org brn .40 .20
484 A193 25c red & brt blue .70 .20
485 A193 35c brown & emer 1.00 .45
Nos. 483-485 (3) 2.10 .85

19th Olympic Games, Mexico City, Oct. 12-27. See No. C181.

Pres. Wm. V. S. Tubman A194

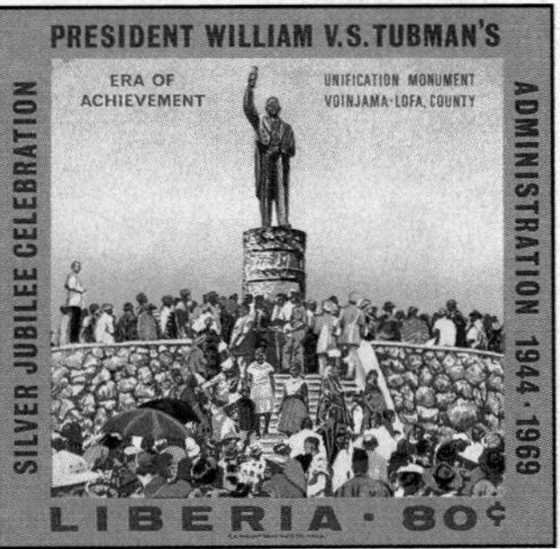

Unification Monument, Voinjama-Lofa County — A195

1968, Dec. 30 Unwmk. *Perf. 12½*

486 A194 25c silver, blk & brn 1.60 1.00

Souvenir Sheet

Imperf

487 A195 80c silver, ultra & red 3.25 3.25

25th anniv. of Pres. Tubman's administration.

"ILO" with Cogwheel and Wreath A196

1969, Apr. 16 Litho. *Perf. 12½*

488 A196 25c lt blue & gold .70 .40

50th anniv. of the ILO. See No. C183.

Red Roofs, by Camille Pissarro — A197

Paintings: 3c, Prince Balthasar Carlos on Horseback, by Velazquez, vert. 10c, David and Goliath, by Caravaggio. 12c, Still Life, by Jean Baptiste Chardin. 15c, The Last Supper, by Leonardo da Vinci. 20c, Regatta at Argenteuil, by Claude Monet. 25c, Judgment of Solomon, by Giorgione. 35c, Sistine Madonna, by Raphael.

1969, June 26 Litho. *Perf. 11*

489 A197 3c gray & multi .20 .20
490 A197 5c gray & multi .20 .20
491 A197 10c lt blue & multi .20 .20
492 A197 12c gray & multi .50 .20
493 A197 15c gray & multi .50 .20
494 A197 20c gray & multi .80 .20
495 A197 25c gray & multi .95 .20
496 A197 35c gray & multi 1.25 .40
Nos. 489-496 (8) 4.60 1.80

See Nos. 502-509.

African Development Bank Emblem — A198

1969, Aug. 12 Litho. *Perf. 12½*

497 A198 25c blue & brown .60 .50
498 A198 80c yel grn & red 1.90 1.00

5th anniversary of the African Development Bank.

Moon Landing and Liberia No. C174 A199

15c, Memorial tablet left on moon, rocket, earth & moon, horiz. 35c, Take-off from moon.

1969, Oct. 15 Litho. *Perf. 12½*

499 A199 15c blue & bister .65 .20
500 A199 25c dk vio bl & org 1.00 .20
501 A199 35c gray & red 1.50 .40
Nos. 499-501 (3) 3.15 .80

Man's 1st landing on the moon, July 20, 1969. US astronauts Neil A. Armstrong and Col. Edwin E. Aldrin, Jr., with Lieut. Col. Michael Collins piloting Apollo 11. See No. C184.

Painting Type of 1969

1969, Nov. 18 Litho. *Perf. 11*

Paintings: 3c, The Gleaners, by Francois Millet. 5c, View of Toledo, by El Greco, vert. 10c, Heads of Negroes, by Rubens. 12c, The Last Supper, by El Greco. 15c, Dancing Peasants, by Brueghel. 20c, Hunters in the Snow, by Brueghel. 25c, Detail from Descent from the Cross, by Rogier van der Weyden, vert. 35c, The Ascension, by Murillo (inscribed "The Conception"), vert.

502 A197 3c lt blue & multi .20 .20
503 A197 5c lt blue & multi .20 .20
504 A197 10c lt blue & multi .20 .20
505 A197 12c gray & multi .40 .20
506 A197 15c gray & multi .55 .20
507 A197 20c lt blue & multi .70 .20
508 A197 25c gray & multi .95 .40
509 A197 35c lt blue & multi 1.25 .40
Nos. 502-509 (8) 4.45 2.00

Peace Dove, UN Emblem and Atom — A200

1970, Apr. 16 Litho. *Perf. 12½*

510 A200 5c green & silver .30 .30

25th anniv. of the UN. See No. C185.

Official Emblem — A201

Designs: 10c, Statue of rain god Tlaloc, vert. 25c, Jules Rimet cup and sculptured wall, vert. 35c, Sombrero and soccer ball. 55c, Two soccer players.

1970, June 10 Litho. *Perf. 12½*

511 A201 5c pale blue & brn .20 .20
512 A201 10c emerald & ocher .20 .20
513 A201 25c dp rose lil & gold .70 .20
514 A201 35c ver & ultra 1.00 .35
Nos. 511-514 (4) 2.10 .95

Souvenir Sheet

Perf. 11½

515 A201 55c brt bl, yel & grn 1.75 1.60

9th World Soccer Championships for the Jules Rimet Cup, Mexico City, May 30-June 21, 1970.

EXPO '70 Emblem, Japanese Singer and Festival Plaza — A202

Designs (EXPO '70 Emblem and): 3c, Male Japanese singer, EXPO Hall and floating stage. 5c, Tower of the Sun and view of exhibition. 7c, Tanabata Festival. 8c, Awa Dance Festival. 25c, Sado-Okesa Dance Festival. 50c, Ricoh Pavilion with "eye," and Mt. Fuji, vert.

1970, July Litho. *Perf. 11*

516 A202 2c multicolored .20 .20
517 A202 3c multicolored .20 .20
518 A202 5c multicolored .45 .20
519 A202 7c multicolored .60 .20
520 A202 8c multicolored .75 .20
521 A202 25c multicolored 1.75 .65
Nos. 516-521 (6) 3.95 1.65

Souvenir Sheet

522 A202 50c multicolored 3.25 1.00

Issued to publicize EXPO '70 International Exhibition, Osaka, Japan, Mar. 15-Sept. 13.

UPU Headquarters and Monument, Bern — A203

Design: 80c, Like 25c, vert.

1970, Aug. 25 *Perf. 12½*

523 A203 25c blue & multi 1.25 1.10
524 A203 80c multicolored 3.00 2.50

Inauguration of the new UPU Headquarters in Bern.

Napoleon as Consul, by Joseph Marie Vien, Sr. A204

Paintings of Napoleon: 5c, Visit to a School, by unknown painter. 10c, Napoleon Bonaparte, by François Pascal Gerard. 12c, The French Campaign, by Ernest Meissonier. 20c, Napoleon Signing Abdication at Fontainebleau, by François Bouchot. 25c, Napoleon Meets Pope Pius VII, by Jean-Louis Demarne. 50c, Napoleon's Coronation, by Jacques Louis David.

1970, Oct. 20 Litho. *Perf. 11*

525 A204 3c blue & multi .20 .20
526 A204 5c blue & multi .20 .20
527 A204 10c blue & multi .55 .20
528 A204 12c blue & multi .75 .20
529 A204 20c blue & multi 1.10 .20
530 A204 25c blue & multi 2.10 .20
Nos. 525-530 (6) 4.90 1.20

Souvenir Sheet

Imperf

531 A204 50c blue & multi 3.25 .80

200th anniv. of the birth of Napoleon Bonaparte (1769-1821). No. 531 contains one stamp with simulated perforations.

Pres. Tubman A205

1970, Nov. 20 Litho. *Perf. 13½*

532 A205 25c multicolored 1.10 .55

Souvenir Sheet

Imperf

533 A205 50c multicolored 2.00 1.10

Pres. Tubman's 75th birthday. No. 533 contains one imperf. stamp with simulated perforations.

Adoration of the Kings, by Rogier van der Weyden — A206

Paintings (Adoration of the Kings, by): 5c, Hans Memling. 10c, Stefan Lochner. 12c, Albrecht Altdorfer, vert. 20c, Hugo van der Goes, Adoration of the Shepherds. 25c, Hieronymus Bosch, vert. 50c, Andrea Mantegna (triptych).

Perf. 13½x14, 14x13½

1970, Dec. 21 Litho.

534 A206 3c multicolored .20 .20
535 A206 5c multicolored .20 .20
536 A206 10c multicolored .20 .20
537 A206 12c multicolored .35 .20
538 A206 20c multicolored .50 .20
539 A206 25c multicolored .75 .20
Nos. 534-539 (6) 2.20 1.20

Souvenir Sheet

Imperf

540 A206 50c multicolored 3.00 .85

Christmas 1970.
No. 540 contains one 60x40mm stamp.

Dogon Tribal Mask A207

African Tribal Ceremonial Masks: 2c, Bapendé. 5c, Baoulé. 6c, Dédougou. 9c, Dan. 15c, Bamiléké. 20c, Bapendé mask and costume. 25c, Bamiléké mask and costume.

1971, Feb. 24 **Litho.** ***Perf. 11***

541	A207	2c lt green & multi	.20	.20
542	A207	3c pink & multi	.20	.20
543	A207	5c lt blue & multi	.20	.20
544	A207	6c lt green & multi	.20	.20
545	A207	9c lt blue & multi	.20	.20
546	A207	15c pink & multi	.45	.20
547	A207	20c lt green & multi	.85	.55
548	A207	25c pink & multi	.45	.20
		Nos. 541-548 (8)	2.75	1.95

Astronauts on Moon — A208

Designs: 5c, Astronaut and lunar transport vehicle. 10c, Astronaut with US flag on moon. 12c, Space capsule in Pacific Ocean. 20c, Astronaut leaving capsule. 25c, Astronauts Alan B. Shepard, Stuart A. Roosa and Edgar D. Mitchell.

1971, May 20 **Litho.** ***Perf. 13½***

549	A208	3c vio blue & multi	.20	.20
550	A208	5c vio blue & multi	.20	.20
551	A208	10c vio blue & multi	.45	.20
552	A208	12c vio blue & multi	.60	.20
553	A208	20c vio blue & multi	.85	.20
554	A208	25c vio blue & multi	1.00	.35
		Nos. 549-554 (6)	3.30	1.35

Apollo 14 moon landing, Jan. 31-Feb. 9. See No. C186.

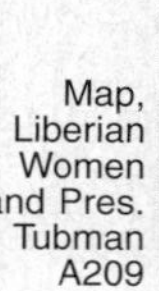

Map, Liberian Women and Pres. Tubman A209

3c, Pres. Tubman & women at ballot box, vert.

1971, May 27 ***Perf. 12½***

555	A209	3c ultra & brn	.20	.20
556	A209	80c green & brn	2.10	2.10

25th anniversary of women's suffrage.

Hall of Honor, Munich, and Olympic Flag — A210

Munich Views and Olympic Flag: 5c, General view. 10c, National Museum. 12c, Max Joseph's Square. 20c, Propylaeum on King's Square. 25c, Liesel-Karlstadt Fountain.

1971, June 28 **Litho.** ***Perf. 11***

557	A210	3c multicolored	.20	.20
558	A210	5c multicolored	.20	.20
559	A210	10c multicolored	.20	.20
560	A210	12c multicolored	.25	.20
561	A210	20c multicolored	1.10	.20
562	A210	25c multicolored	1.90	.90
		Nos. 557-562 (6)	3.85	1.90

Publicity for the 20th Summer Olympic Games, Munich, Germany, 1972. See No. C187.

Boy Scout, Emblem and US Flag A211

Boy Scout, Natl. Flag & Boy Scout Emblem of: 5c, German Federal Republic. 10c, Australia. 12c, Great Britain. 20c, Japan. 25c, Liberia.

1971, Aug. 6 **Litho.** ***Perf. 13½***

563	A211	3c multicolored	.20	.20
564	A211	5c multicolored	.20	.20
565	A211	10c multicolored	.20	.20
566	A211	12c multicolored	.35	.20
567	A211	20c multicolored	.60	.20
568	A211	25c multicolored	.75	.20
		Nos. 563-568 (6)	2.30	1.20

13th Boy Scout World Jamboree, Asagiri Plain, Japan, Aug. 2-10. See No. C188.

Pres. Tubman (1895-1971) A212

1971, Aug. 23 ***Perf. 12½***

569	A212	3c black, ultra & brn	.20	.20
570	A212	25c blk, brt rose lil & brn	1.10	1.10

Zebra and UNICEF Emblem — A213

Animals (UNICEF Emblem and Animals with their Young): 7c, Koala. 8c, Llama. 10c, Red fox. 20c, Monkey. 25c, Brown bear.

1971, Oct. 1 ***Perf. 11***

571	A213	5c multicolored	.20	.20
572	A213	7c multicolored	.50	.20
573	A213	8c multicolored	.50	.20
574	A213	10c multicolored	.65	.20
575	A213	20c multicolored	1.25	.50
576	A213	25c multicolored	1.60	.65
		Nos. 571-576 (6)	4.70	1.95

25th anniv. of UNICEF. See No. C189.

Sapporo 72 Emblem, Long-distance Skiing, Sika Deer — A214

3c, Sledding & black woodpecker. 5c, Ski Jump & brown bear. 10c, Bobsledding & murres. 15c, Figure skating & pikas. 25c, Downhill skiing & Japanese cranes.

1971, Nov. 4 ***Perf. 13x13½***

577	A214	2c multicolored	.20	.20
578	A214	3c multicolored	.20	.20
579	A214	5c multicolored	.20	.20
580	A214	10c multicolored	.30	.20
581	A214	15c multicolored	1.75	.20
582	A214	25c multicolored	3.75	.20
		Nos. 577-582 (6)	6.40	1.20

11th Winter Olympic Games, Sapporo, Japan, Feb. 3-13, 1972. See No. C190.

Dove Carrying Letter, APU Emblem A215

1971, Dec. 9 ***Perf. 12½***

583	A215	25c ultra & dp org	.60	.55
584	A215	80c gray & dp brn	2.00	1.60

10th anniversary of African Postal Union.

Pioneer Fathers' Monument, Monrovia A216

Pres. William R. Tolbert, Jr. — A217

Designs: 3c, 25c, Sailing ship "Elizabeth," Providence Island, horiz. 35c, as 20c.

1972, Jan. 1

585	A216	3c blue & brt grn	.20	.20
586	A216	20c orange & blue	.95	.70
587	A216	25c orange & purple	1.00	.85
588	A216	35c lil rose & brt grn	1.75	1.25
		Nos. 585-588 (4)	3.90	3.00

Founding of Liberia, sesqui. See No. C191.

1972, Jan. 1

25c, Pres. Tolbert and map of Liberia, horiz.

589	A217	25c emerald & brown	.65	.40
590	A217	80c blue & brown	2.25	.70

Inauguration of William R. Tolbert, Jr. as 19th president of Liberia.

Soccer and Swedish Flag — A218

Olympic Rings, "Motion" Symbol and: 5c, Swimmers at start, Italian flag. 10c, Equestrian, British flag. 12c, Bicycling, French flag. 20c, Long jump, US flag. 25c, Running and Liberian flag.

1972, May 19 **Litho.** ***Perf. 11***

591	A218	3c lemon & multi	.20	.20
592	A218	5c lt lilac & multi	.20	.20
593	A218	10c multicolored	.75	.20
594	A218	12c gray & multi	1.00	.20
595	A218	20c lt blue & multi	1.40	.60
596	A218	25c pink & multi	1.90	.75
		Nos. 591-596 (6)	5.45	2.15

20th Olympic Games, Munich, Aug. 26-Sept. 10. See No. C192.

Y's Men's Club Emblem, Map A219

Design: 90c, Y's Men's Club emblem and globe; inscribed "fifty and forward."

1972, June 12 ***Perf. 13½***

597	A219	15c purple & gold	.50	.20
598	A219	90c vio bl & emer	2.40	2.00

Intl. Y's Men's Club, 50th anniv.

Astronaut and Lunar Rover — A220

5c, Moon scene reflected in astronaut's helmet. 10c, Astronauts with cameras. 12c, Astronauts placing scientific equipment on moon. 20c, Apollo 16 badge. 25c, Astronauts riding lunar rover.

1972, June 26

599	A220	3c lt blue & multi	.20	.20
600	A220	5c red org & multi	.20	.20
601	A220	10c pink & multi	.50	.20
602	A220	12c yellow & multi	.80	.20
603	A220	20c lt vio & multi	1.00	.20
604	A220	25c emerald & multi	1.40	.20
		Nos. 599-604 (6)	4.10	1.20

Apollo 16 US moon mission, Apr. 15-27, 1972. See No. C193.

Emperor Haile Selassie — A221

1972, July 21 ***Perf. 14x14½***

605	A221	20c olive grn & yel	.70	.70
606	A221	25c maroon & yel	.85	.85
607	A221	35c brown & yel	1.25	1.25
		Nos. 605-607 (3)	2.80	2.80

80th birthday of Emperor Haile Selassie of Ethiopia.

Ajax, 1809, and Figurehead — A222

1972, Sept. 6 ***Perf. 11***

608	A222	3c *shown*	.20	.20
609	A222	5c *Hogue, 1811*	.20	.20
610	A222	7c *Ariadne, 1816*	.55	.20
611	A222	15c *Royal Adelaide, 1828*	1.00	.20
612	A222	20c *Rinaldo, 1860*	1.25	.20
613	A222	25c *Nymphe, 1888*	1.45	.45
		Nos. 608-613 (6)	4.65	1.45

Famous sailing ships and their figureheads. See No. C194.

Pres. Tolbert Taking Oath, Richard A. Henries — A223

1972, Oct. 23 Litho. *Perf. 13½*

614 A223 15c green & multi 1.10 .95
615 A223 25c vio blue & multi 1.50 1.45

Pres. William R. Tolbert, Jr. sworn in as 19th President of Liberia, July 23, 1971. See No. C195.

Klaus Dibiasi, Italy, Diving — A224

8c, Valery Borzov, USSR, running. 10c, Hideaki Yanagida, Japan, wrestling. 12c, Mark Spitz, US, swimming. 15c, Kipchoge Keino, Kenya, 3000-meter steeplechase. 25c, Richard Meade, Great Britain, equestrian. 55c, Hans Winkler, Germany, grand prix jumping.

1973, Jan. 5 Litho. *Perf. 11*

616 A224 5c lt blue & multi .20 .20
617 A224 8c violet & multi .20 .20
618 A224 10c multicolored .20 .20
619 A224 12c green & multi .55 .20
620 A224 15c orange & multi .80 .20
621 A224 25c pale salmon & multi 1.10 .55
Nos. 616-621 (6) 3.05 1.55

Souvenir Sheet

622 A224 55c multicolored 4.50 2.25

Gold medal winners in 20th Olympic Games.

Astronaut on Moon and Apollo 17 Badge — A225

Designs (Apollo 17 Badge and): 3c, Astronauts on earth in lunar rover. 10c, Astronauts collecting yellow lunar dust. 15c, Astronauts in lunar rover exploring moon crater. 20c, Capt. Eugene A. Cernan, Dr. Harrison H. Schmitt and Comdr. Ronald E. Evans on launching pad. 25c, Astronauts on moon with scientific equipment.

1973, Mar. 28 Litho. *Perf. 11*

623 A225 2c blue & multi .20 .20
624 A225 3c blue & multi .20 .20
625 A225 10c blue & multi .20 .20
626 A225 15c blue & multi .70 .20
627 A225 20c blue & multi 1.00 .50
628 A225 25c blue & multi 1.25 .60
Nos. 623-628 (6) 3.55 1.90

Apollo 17 US moon mission, Dec. 7-19, 1972. See No. C196.

Locomotive, England — A226

Designs: Locomotives, 1895-1905.

1973, May 4

629 A226 2c shown .20 .20
630 A226 3c Netherlands .20 .20
631 A226 10c France .90 .20
632 A226 15c United States 1.25 .20
633 A226 20c Japan 2.25 .20
634 A226 25c Germany 3.25 .75
Nos. 629-634 (6) 8.05 1.75

See No. C197.

OAU Emblem and Flags — A227

1973, May 24 Litho. *Perf. 13½*

635 A227 3c multicolored .20 .20
636 A227 5c multicolored .20 .20
637 A227 10c multicolored .20 .20
638 A227 15c multicolored .45 .20
639 A227 25c multicolored .55 .45
640 A227 50c multicolored 1.25 .95
Nos. 635-640 (6) 2.85 2.20

10th anniv. of the Organization for African Unity.

WHO Emblem, Edward Jenner and Roses — A228

Designs (WHO Emblem and): 4c, Sigmund Freud and pansies. 10c, Jonas E. Salk and chrysanthemums. 15c, Louis Pasteur and scabiosa caucasia. 20c, Emil von Behring and rhododendron. 25c, Alexander Fleming and tree mallows.

1973, June 26 Litho. *Perf. 11*

641 A228 1c gray & multi .20 .20
642 A228 4c orange & multi .20 .20
643 A228 10c lt blue & multi .20 .20
644 A228 15c rose & multi .40 .20
645 A228 20c blue & multi .50 .20
646 A228 25c yel grn & multi .75 .40
Nos. 641-646 (6) 2.25 1.40

25th anniv. of WHO. See No. C198.

Stanley Steamer, 1910 — A229

Designs: Classic automobiles.

1973, Sept. 11 Litho. *Perf. 11*

647 A229 2c shown .20 .20
648 A229 3c Cadillac, 1903 .20 .20
649 A229 10c Clement-Bayard, 1904 .40 .20
650 A229 15c Rolls Royce, 1907 .55 .20
651 A229 20c Maxwell, 1905 .80 .20
652 A229 25c Chadwick, 1907 1.00 .50
Nos. 647-652 (6) 3.15 1.50

See No. C199.

Copernicus, Armillary Sphere, Satellite Communication — A230

Portraits of Copernicus and: 4c, Eudoxus solar system. 10c, Aristotle, Ptolemy, Copernicus and satellites. 15c, Saturn and Apollo spacecraft. 20c, Orbiting astronomical observatory. 25c, Satellite tracking station.

1973, Dec. 14 Litho. *Perf. 13½*

653 A230 1c yellow & multi .20 .20
654 A230 4c lt violet & multi .20 .20
655 A230 10c lt blue & multi .20 .20
656 A230 15c yel grn & multi .50 .20
657 A230 20c bister & multi .65 .20
658 A230 25c pink & multi .80 .40
Nos. 653-658 (6) 2.55 1.40

Nicolaus Copernicus (1473-1543), Polish astronomer. See No. C200.

Radio Tower, Map of Africa A231

15c, 25c, Map of Liberia, Radio tower and man listening to broadcast. 17c, like 13c.

1974, Jan. 16 Litho. *Perf. 13½*

659 A231 13c multicolored .60 .60
660 A231 15c yellow & multi .60 .50
661 A231 17c lt gray & multi .75 .60
662 A231 25c brt green & multi 1.00 .65
Nos. 659-662 (4) 2.95 2.35

20th anniv. of Radio ELWA, Monrovia.

Thomas Coutts, 1817; Aureal, 1974; UPU Emblem — A232

Designs (UPU Emblem and): 3c, Jet, satellite, Post Office, Monrovia, ship. 10c, US and USSR telecommunication satellites. 15c, Mail runner and jet. 20c, Futuristic mail train and mail truck. 25c, American Pony Express rider.

1974, Mar. 4 Litho. *Perf. 13½*

663 A232 2c ocher & multi .20 .20
664 A232 3c lt green & multi .20 .20
665 A232 10c lt blue & multi .20 .20
666 A232 15c pink & multi .50 .20
667 A232 20c gray & multi .65 .20
668 A232 25c lt lilac & multi .85 .40
Nos. 663-668 (6) 2.60 1.40

Cent. of UPU. See No. C201.

Fox Terrier — A233

1974, Apr. 16 Litho. *Perf. 13½*

669 A233 5c shown .20 .20
670 A233 10c Boxer .20 .20
671 A233 16c Chihuahua .65 .20
672 A233 19c Beagle .70 .20
673 A233 25c Golden retriever .80 .20
674 A233 50c Collie 1.75 .40
Nos. 669-674 (6) 4.30 1.40

See No. C202.

Soccer Game, West Germany and Chile — A234

Designs: Games between semi-finalists, and flags of competing nations.

1974, June 4 Litho. *Perf. 11*

675 A234 1c shown .20 .20
676 A234 2c Australia and East Germany .20 .20
677 A234 5c Brazil and Yugoslavia .20 .20
678 A234 10c Zaire and Scotland .20 .20
679 A234 12c Netherlands and Uruguay .20 .20
680 A234 15c Sweden and Bulgaria .45 .20
681 A234 20c Italy and Haiti .65 .20
682 A234 25c Poland and Argentina .75 .45
Nos. 675-682 (8) 2.85 1.85

World Cup Soccer Championship, Munich, June 13-July 7. See No. C203.

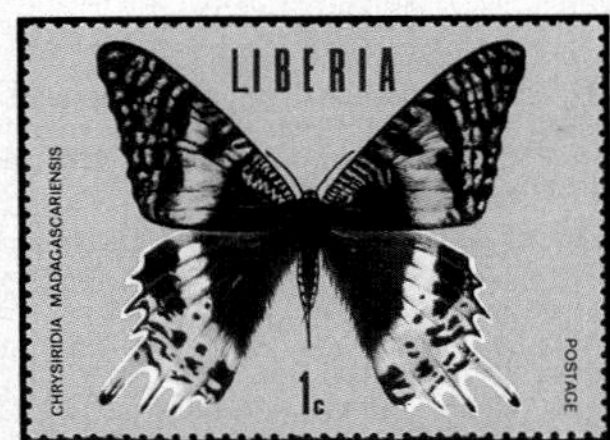

Chrysiridia Madagascariensis — A235

Tropical Butterflies: 2c, Catagramma sorana. 5c, Erasmia pulchella. 17c, Morpho cypris. 25c, Agrias amydon. 40c, Vanessa cardui.

1974, Sept. 11 Litho. *Perf. 13½*

683 A235 1c gray & multi .20 .20
684 A235 2c gray & multi .20 .20
685 A235 5c gray & multi .20 .20
686 A235 17c gray & multi .95 .20
687 A235 25c gray & multi 1.25 .40
688 A235 40c gray & multi 2.40 .65
Nos. 683-688 (6) 5.20 1.85

See No. C204.

Pres. Tolbert and Medal — A236

$1, Pres. Tolbert, medal & Liberian flag.

1974, Dec. 10 Litho. *Perf. 13½*

689 A236 3c multi .20 .20
690 A236 $1 multi, vert. 2.75 2.75

Pres. William R. Tolbert, Jr., recipient of 1974 Family of Man Award.

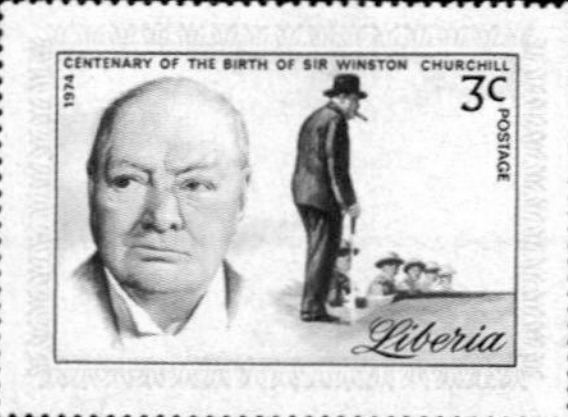

Winston Churchill, 1940 — A237

Churchill and: 10c, RAF planes in dog fight. 15c, In naval launch on way to Normandy. 17c, In staff car reviewing troops in desert. 20c, Aboard landing craft crossing Rhine. 25c, In conference with Pres. Roosevelt.

1975, Jan. 17 Litho. *Perf. 13½*

691	A237	3c multicolored	.20	.20
692	A237	10c multicolored	.20	.20
693	A237	15c multicolored	.20	.20
694	A237	17c multicolored	.45	.20
695	A237	20c multicolored	.55	.20
696	A237	25c multicolored	.90	.45
		Nos. 691-696 (6)	2.50	1.45

Sir Winston Churchill (1874-1965), birth centenary. See No. C205.

Women's Year Emblem and Marie Curie — A238

3c, Mahalia Jackson with microphone. 5c, Joan of Arc. 10c, Eleanor Roosevelt and children. 25c, Matilda Newport firing cannon. 50c, Valentina Tereshkova in space suit.

1975, Mar. 14 Litho. *Perf. 14½*

697	A238	2c citron & multi	.20	.20
698	A238	3c dull orange & multi	.20	.20
699	A238	5c lilac rose & multi	.20	.20
700	A238	10c yellow & multi	.20	.20
701	A238	25c yellow grn & multi	.55	.20
702	A238	50c lilac & multi	1.00	.65
		Nos. 697-702 (6)	2.35	1.65

Intl. Women's Year 1975. See No. C206.

Old State House, Boston, US No. 627 — A239

10c, George Washington, US #645. 15c, Town Hall & Court House, Philadelphia, US #798. 20c, Benjamin Franklin, US #835. 25c, Paul Revere's Ride, US #618. 50c, Santa Maria, US #231.

1975, Apr. 25 Litho. *Perf. 13½*

703	A239	5c multicolored	.20	.20
704	A239	10c multicolored	.50	.20
705	A239	15c multicolored	.60	.20
706	A239	20c multicolored	.80	.20
707	A239	25c multicolored	1.25	.20
708	A239	50c multicolored	2.50	.50
		Nos. 703-708 (6)	5.85	1.50

American Revolution Bicentennial. See No. C207.

Dr. Schweitzer, Hospital and Baboon Mother — A240

Designs (Dr. Schweitzer and): 3c, Elephant, and tribesmen poling boat. 5c, Water buffalo, egret, man and woman paddling canoe. 6c, Antelope and dancer. 25c, Lioness, woman cooking outdoors. 50c, Zebra and colt, doctor's examination at clinic.

1975, June 26 Litho. *Perf. 13½*

709	A240	1c multicolored	.20	.20
710	A240	3c multicolored	.20	.20
711	A240	5c multicolored	.20	.20
712	A240	6c multicolored	.20	.20
713	A240	25c multicolored	.55	.20
714	A240	50c multicolored	1.25	.65
		Nos. 709-714 (6)	2.60	1.65

Dr. Albert Schweitzer (1875-1965), medical missionary, birth centenary. See No. C208.

American-Russian Handshake in Space — A241

Designs (Apollo-Soyuz Emblem and): 5c, Apollo. 10c, Soyuz. 20c, Flags and maps of US and USSR. 25c, A. A. Leonov, and V. N. Kubasov. 50c, D. K. Slayton, V. D. Brand, T. P. Stafford.

1975, Sept. 18 Litho. *Perf. 13½*

715	A241	5c multicolored	.20	.20
716	A241	10c multicolored	.20	.20
717	A241	15c multicolored	.40	.20
718	A241	20c multicolored	.55	.20
719	A241	25c multicolored	.75	.20
720	A241	50c multicolored	1.40	.45
		Nos. 715-720 (6)	3.50	1.45

Apollo Soyuz space test project (Russo-American cooperation), launching July 15; link-up, July 17. See No. C209.

Presidents Tolbert, Siaka Stevens; Treaty Signing; Liberia and Sierra Leone Maps — A242

1975, Oct. 3 Litho. *Perf. 13½*

721	A242	2c gray & multi	.20	.20
722	A242	3c gray & multi	.20	.20
723	A242	5c gray & multi	.20	.20
724	A242	10c gray & multi	.20	.20
725	A242	25c gray & multi	.65	.40
726	A242	50c gray & multi	1.25	.80
		Nos. 721-726 (6)	2.70	2.00

Mano River Union Agreement between Liberia and Sierra Leone, signed Oct. 3, 1973.

Figure Skating — A243

Designs (Winter Olympic Games Emblem and): 4c, Ski jump. 10c, Slalom. 25c, Ice hockey. 35c, Speed skating. 50c, Two-man bobsled.

1976, Jan. 23 Litho. *Perf. 13½*

727	A243	1c lt blue & multi	.20	.20
728	A243	4c lt blue & multi	.20	.20
729	A243	10c lt blue & multi	.20	.20
730	A243	25c lt blue & multi	.90	.20
731	A243	35c lt blue & multi	1.25	.20
732	A243	50c lt blue & multi	1.75	.90
		Nos. 727-732 (6)	4.50	1.90

12th Winter Olympic Games, Innsbruck, Austria, Feb. 4-15. See No. C210.

Pres. Tolbert Taking Oath of Office — A244

25c, Pres. Tolbert at his desk, vert. $1, Seal & flag of Liberia, $400 commemorative gold coin.

1976, Apr. 5 Litho. *Perf. 13½*

733	A244	3c multicolored	.20	.20
734	A244	25c multicolored	.50	.50
735	A244	$1 multicolored	2.50	2.50
		Nos. 733-735 (3)	3.20	3.20

Inauguration of President William R. Tolbert, Jr., Jan. 5, 1976.

Weight Lifting and Olympic Rings — A245

Designs (Olympic Rings and): 3c, Pole vault. 10c, Hammer and shot put. 25c, Yachting. 35c, Women's gymnastics. 50c, Hurdles.

1976, May 4 Litho. *Perf. 13½*

736	A245	2c gray & multi	.20	.20
737	A245	3c orange & multi	.20	.20
738	A245	10c lt violet & multi	.20	.20
739	A245	25c lt green & multi	.90	.20
740	A245	35c yellow & multi	1.25	.70
741	A245	50c pink & multi	1.75	.70
		Nos. 736-741 (6)	4.50	2.20

21st Olympic Games, Montreal, Canada, July 17-Aug. 1. See No. C211.

A. G. Bell, Telephone and Receiver, 1876, UPU Emblem — A246

UPU Emblem and: 4c, Horsedrawn mail coach and ITU emblem. 5c, Intelsat IV satellite, radar and ITU emblem. 25c, A. G. Bell, ship laying underwater cable, 1976 telephone. 40c, A. G. Bell, futuristic train, telegraph and telephone wires. 50c, Wright brothers' plane, Zeppelin and Concorde.

1976, June 4 Litho. *Perf. 13½*

742	A246	1c green & multi	.20	.20
743	A246	4c ocher & multi	.20	.20
744	A246	5c orange & multi	.20	.20
745	A246	25c green & multi	.90	.20
746	A246	40c lilac & multi	1.25	.20
747	A246	50c blue & multi	1.50	.70
		Nos. 742-747 (6)	4.25	1.70

Cent. of 1st telephone call by Alexander Graham Bell, Mar. 10, 1876. See No. C212.

Gold Nugget on Chain, Gold Panner — A247

1976-81 Litho. *Perf. 14½*

749	A247	1c Mano River Bridge	.20	.20
750	A247	3c shown	.20	.20
751	A247	5c "V" ring	.20	.20
752	A247	7c like 5c ('81)	.20	.20
753	A247	10c Rubber tire, tree	.45	.20
754	A247	15c Harvesting	.75	.60
755	A247	17c like 55c ('81)	.80	.60
756	A247	20c Hydroelectric plant	1.00	.80
757	A247	25c Mesurado shrimp	1.25	.20
758	A247	27c Woman tie-dying cloth	1.40	1.00
759	A247	55c Lake Piso, barracuda	2.75	.75
760	A247	$1 Train hauling iron ore	5.00	3.50
		Nos. 749-760 (12)	14.20	8.45

See Nos. 945-953.

Rhinoceros — A249

African Animals: 3c, Zebra antelope. 5c, Chimpanzee, vert. 15c, Pigmy hippopotamus. 25c, Leopard. $1, Gorilla, vert.

1976, Sept. 1 Litho. *Perf. 13½*

763	A249	2c orange & multi	.60	.60
764	A249	3c gray & multi	.60	.60
765	A249	5c blue & multi	.60	.60
766	A249	15c brt blue & multi	.60	.60
767	A249	25c ultra & multi	1.00	.75
768	A249	$1 multicolored	3.50	2.25
		Nos. 763-768 (6)	6.90	5.40

See No. C213.

Maps of US and Liberia; Statue of Liberty, Unification Monument, Voinjama and Liberty Bell — A250

$1, George Washington, Gerald R. Ford, Joseph J. Roberts (1st Pres. of Liberia), William R. Tolbert, Jr., Bicentennial emblem, US & Liberian flags.

1976, Sept. 21 Litho. *Perf. 13½*

769	A250	25c multicolored	.55	.40
770	A250	$1 multicolored	1.75	.95

American Bicentennial and visit of Pres. William R. Tolbert, Jr. to the US, Sept. 21-30. See No. C214.

Baluba Masks and Festival Emblem A251

Tribal Masks: 10c, Bateke. 15c, Basshilele. 20c, Igungun. 25c, Masai. 50c, Kifwebe.

1977, Jan. 20 Litho. *Perf. 13½*

771	A251	5c	yellow & multi	.20	.20
772	A251	10c	green & multi	.20	.20
773	A251	15c	salmon & multi	.20	.20
774	A251	20c	lt blue & multi	.65	.20
775	A251	25c	violet & multi	.80	.20
776	A251	50c	lemon & multi	1.50	.65
			Nos. 771-776 (6)	3.55	1.65

FESTAC '77, 2nd World Black and African Festival, Lagos, Nigeria, Jan. 15-Feb. 12. See No. C215.

Latham's Francolin — A252

Birds of Liberia: 10c, Narina trogon. 15c, Rufous-crowned roller. 20c, Brown-cheeked hornbill. 25c, Common bulbul. 50c, Fish eagle. 80c, Gold Coast touraco.

1977, Feb. 18 Litho. *Perf. 14*

777	A252	5c	multicolored	.20	.20
778	A252	10c	multicolored	.55	.20
779	A252	15c	multicolored	.75	.20
780	A252	20c	multicolored	1.10	.20
781	A252	25c	multicolored	1.40	.20
782	A252	50c	multicolored	3.50	.65
			Nos. 777-782 (6)	7.50	1.65

Souvenir Sheet

783	A252	80c	multicolored	4.50	3.00

Edmund Coffin, Combined Training, US — A253

Designs: 15c, Alwin Schockemohle, single jump. Germany, vert. 20c, Christine Stuckelberger, Switzerland, individual dressage. 25c, Prix de Nations (team), France.

1977, Apr. 22 Litho. *Perf. 13½*

784	A253	5c	ocher & multi	.20	.20
785	A253	15c	ocher & multi	.95	.20
786	A253	20c	ocher & multi	1.10	.20
787	A253	25c	ocher & multi	1.40	.80
			Nos. 784-787,C216 (5)	6.90	3.00

Equestrian gold medal winners in Montreal Olympic Games. See No. C217.

Elizabeth II Wearing Crown — A254

Designs: 25c, Elizabeth II Prince Philip, Pres. and Mrs. Tubman. 80c, Elizabeth II, Prince Philip, royal coat of arms.

1977, May 23 Litho. *Perf. 13½*

788	A254	15c	silver & multi	.45	.20
789	A254	25c	silver & multi	.85	.20
790	A254	80c	silver & multi	2.50	.70
			Nos. 788-790 (3)	3.80	1.10

25th anniversary of the reign of Queen Elizabeth II. See No. C218.

Jesus Blessing Children A255

Christmas: 25c, The Good Shepherd. $1, Jesus and the Samaritan Woman. Designs after stained-glass windows, Providence Baptist Church, Monrovia.

1977, Nov. 3 Litho. *Perf. 13½*

791	A255	20c	lt blue & multi	.45	.20
792	A255	25c	lt blue & multi	.60	.45
793	A255	$1	lt blue & multi	1.90	1.10
			Nos. 791-793 (3)	2.95	1.75

Dornier DOX, 1928 — A256

Progress of Aviation: 3c, Piggyback space shuttle, 1977. 5c, Eddie Rickenbacker and Douglas DC 3. 25c, Charles A. Lindbergh and Spirit of St. Louis. 35c, Louis Bleriot and Bleriot XI. 50c, Orville and Wilbur Wright and flying machine, 1903. 80c, Concorde landing at night at Dulles Airport, Washington, DC.

1978, Jan. 6 Litho. *Perf. 13½*

794	A256	2c	multicolored	.20	.20
795	A256	3c	multicolored	.20	.20
796	A256	5c	multicolored	.20	.20
797	A256	25c	multicolored	.65	.20
798	A256	35c	multicolored	.90	.55
799	A256	50c	multicolored	1.60	.75
			Nos. 794-799 (6)	3.75	2.10

Souvenir Sheet

800	A256	80c	multicolored	3.50	2.50

Baladeuse by Santos-Dumont, 1903 — A257

Airships: 3c, Baldwin's, 1908, and US flag. 5c, Tissandier brothers', 1883. 25c, Parseval PL VII, 1912. 40c, Nulli Secundus II, 1908. 50c, R34 rigid airship, 1919.

1978, Mar. 9 Litho. *Perf. 13½*

801	A257	2c	multicolored	.20	.20
802	A257	3c	multicolored	.20	.20
803	A257	5c	multicolored	.20	.20
804	A257	25c	multicolored	.55	.20
805	A257	40c	multicolored	.85	.20
806	A257	50c	multicolored	1.10	.20
			Nos. 801-806 (6)	3.10	1.20

75th anniv. of the Zeppelin. See No. C219.

Soccer, East Germany and Brazil — A258

Soccer Games: 2c, Poland and Argentina, vert. 10c, West Germany and Netherlands. 25c, Yugoslavia and Brazil. 35c, Poland and Italy, vert. 50c, Netherlands and Uruguay.

1978, May 16 Litho. *Perf. 13½*

807	A258	2c	multicolored	.20	.20
808	A258	3c	multicolored	.20	.20
809	A258	10c	multicolored	.20	.20
810	A258	25c	multicolored	.75	.20
811	A258	35c	multicolored	1.00	.50
812	A258	50c	multicolored	1.50	.75
			Nos. 807-812 (6)	3.85	2.05

11th World Cup Soccer Championships, Argentina, June 1-25. See No. C220.

Coronation Chair — A259

Designs: 25c, Imperial state crown. $1, Buckingham Palace, horiz.

1978, June 12

813	A259	5c	multicolored	.20	.20
814	A259	25c	multicolored	.75	.20
815	A259	$1	multicolored	2.75	1.00
			Nos. 813-815 (3)	3.70	1.40

25th anniversary of coronation of Queen Elizabeth II. See No. C221.

Jinnah, Liberian and Pakistani Flags — A260

1978, June Litho. *Perf. 13*

816	A260	30c	multicolored	*37.50*	8.25

Mohammed Ali Jinnah (1876-1948), first Governor General of Pakistan.

Carter and Tolbert Families — A261

Designs: 25c, Pres. Tolbert, Rosalynn Carter and Pres. Carter at microphone, Robertsfield Airport. $1, Jimmy Carter and William R. Tolbert, Jr. in motorcade from airport.

1978, Oct. 26 Litho. *Perf. 13½*

817	A261	5c	multicolored	.20	.20
818	A261	25c	multicolored	.85	.85
819	A261	$1	multicolored	3.50	3.50
			Nos. 817-819 (3)	4.55	4.55

Pres. Carter's visit to Liberia, Apr. 1978.

Soccer Game: Italy-France — A262

Soccer Games: 1c, Brazil-Spain, horiz. 10c, Poland-West Germany, horiz. 27c, Peru-Scotland. 35c, Austria-West Germany. 50c, Argentina the victor.

1978, Dec. 8 Litho. *Perf. 13½*

820	A262	1c	multicolored	.20	.20
821	A262	2c	multicolored	.20	.20
822	A262	10c	multicolored	.40	.20
823	A262	27c	multicolored	.95	.65
824	A262	35c	multicolored	1.25	.80
825	A262	50c	multicolored	1.75	1.25
			Nos. 820-825 (6)	4.75	3.30

1978 World Cup Soccer winners. See No. C222.

Liberian Lumbermen — A263

Designs: 10c, Hauling timber by truck, vert. 25c, Felling trees with chain saw. 50c, Moving logs.

1978, Dec. 15 Litho. *Perf. 13½x14*

826	A263	5c	multicolored	.20	.20
827	A263	10c	multicolored	.20	.20
828	A263	25c	multicolored	.85	.25
829	A263	50c	multicolored	1.75	1.25
			Nos. 826-829 (4)	3.00	1.90

8th World Forestry Congress, Djakarta, Indonesia.

"25" and Waves — A264

Design: $1, Radio tower and waves.

1979, Apr. 6 Litho. *Perf. 14x13½*

830 A264 35c multicolored .70 .70
831 A264 $1 multicolored 1.90 1.90

25th anniversary of Radio ELWA.

Emblems of IYC, African Child's Decade and SOS Village — A265

Designs: 25c, $1, like 5c, with UNICEF emblem replacing SOS emblem. 35c, like 5c.

1979, Apr. 6 *Perf. 13½x14*

832 A265 5c multicolored .20 .20
833 A265 25c multicolored .20 .20
834 A265 35c multicolored .60 .60
835 A265 $1 multicolored 1.40 1.40
Nos. 832-835 (4) 2.40 2.40

IYC and Decade of the African Child.

Presidents Gardner and Tolbert, and Post Office, Monrovia — A266

Design: 35c, Anthony W. Gardner, William R. Tolbert, Jr. and UPU emblem.

1979, Apr. 2 Litho. *Perf. 13½x14*

836 A266 5c multicolored .20 .20
837 A266 35c multicolored 1.10 1.10

Cent. of Liberia's joining UPU.

Unity Problem, Map of Africa, Torches — A267

Designs: 27c, Masks. 35c, Elephant, giraffe, lion, antelope, cheetah and map of Africa. 50c, Huts, pepper birds and map of Africa.

1979, July 6 Litho. *Perf. 14x13½*

838 A267 5c multicolored .20 .20
839 A267 27c multicolored .75 .75
840 A267 35c multicolored 1.00 1.00
841 A267 50c multicolored 1.50 1.50
Nos. 838-841 (4) 3.45 3.45

Organization for African Unity, 16th anniversary, and OAU Summit Conference.

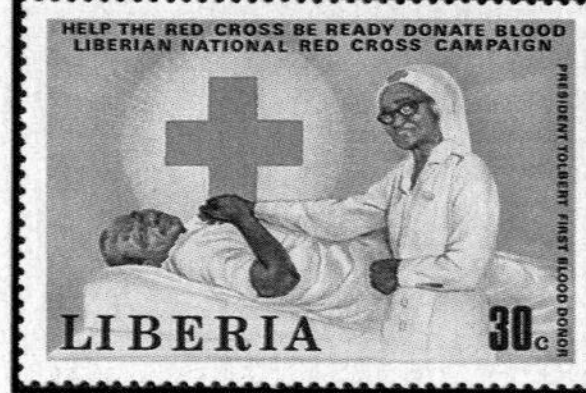

Liberia No. 666, Rowland Hill — A268

10c, Pony Express rider, 1860. 15c, British mail coach, 1800. 25c, Mail steamship John Penn, 1860. 27c, Stanier Pacific train, 1939. 50c, Concorde. $1, Curtiss Jenny, 1916.

1979, July 20

842 A268 3c multicolored .20 .20
843 A268 10c multicolored .20 .20
844 A268 15c multicolored .45 .45
845 A268 25c multicolored .85 .65
846 A268 27c multicolored 1.00 .75
847 A268 50c multicolored 1.75 1.40
Nos. 842-847 (6) 4.45 3.65

Souvenir Sheet

848 A268 $1 multicolored 3.50 2.50

Sir Rowland Hill (1795-1879), originator of penny postage.

Red Cross, Pres. Tolbert Donating Blood — A269

Design: 50c, Red Cross, Pres. Tolbert.

1979, Aug. 15 Litho. *Perf. 13½*

849 A269 30c multicolored .65 .65
850 A269 50c multicolored 1.25 1.25

National Red Cross, 30th anniversary and blood donation campaign.

M.S. World Peace — A270

Design: $1, M.S. World Peace, diff.

1979, Aug. 15

851 A270 5c multicolored .20 .20
852 A270 $1 multicolored 3.25 3.25

2nd World Maritime Day, March 16; Liberia Maritime Program, 30th anniversary.

A Good Turn, by Norman Rockwell A271

Paintings — Scouting through the eyes of Norman Rockwell (1925-76): #853: a, Stories. b, 3 branches of Scouts. c, camping. d, Church. e, Animal care. f, advancements. g, Scout, Lincoln. h, First aid on puppy. i, Reading with elderly and dog. j, Scout teaching cubs..

#854: a, "1910." b, Feeding dog. c, Man, dog, Scout on top of rock. d, Merit badges. e, Hiking in mountains. f, With explorer and eagle. g, Wearing new uniform. h, Indian lore. i, First camping. j, Group saluting.

#855: a, Eagle ceremony. b, Hiking with compass. c, The Scouting Trail. d, Phyical fitness. e, Prayer. f, Tales of the sea. g, Foreign and US scouts dancing. h, Building a birdhouse. i, In front of flag. j, Rescueing girl and kitten.

#856: a, Painting outdoors. b, Scout saluting in front of flag. c, Scout, Lincoln, Washington, eagle. d, Starting on hike. e, Knot tying. f, Reading instructions. g, Scouts of 6 nations. h, Boy, Girl Scouts and leaders. i, "On my honor..." j, Cooking outdoors.

#857: a, Portaging. b, "Spirit of '76." c, Saluting flag with astronaut. d, 5 branches of scouting. e, Planting trees. f, Washington praying. g, First aid on dog. h, Saying grace in mess tent. i, First time in Scout uniform. j, Rock climbing.

1979, Sept. 1 Litho. *Perf. 11*

853 A271 5c #a.-j, any single .50 .30
854 A271 10c #a.-j, any single .50 .30
855 A271 15c #a.-j, any single .80 .40
856 A271 25c #a.-j, any single 1.40 .45
857 A271 35c #a.-j, any single 2.00 .85
Nos. 853-857, Set of 50 in 5 strips of 10 85.00 85.00

Mrs. Tolbert, Children, Children's Village Emblem — A272

40c, Mrs. Tolbert, children, emblem, vert.

1979, Nov. 14 Litho. *Perf. 14*

858 A272 25c multicolored .60 .60
859 A272 40c multicolored 1.40 1.40

SOS Children's Village in Monrovia, Liberia.

Rotary International Headquarters, Evanston, Ill., Emblem — A273

Rotary Emblem and: 5c, Vocational services. 17c, Man in wheelchair, nurse, vert. 27c, Flags of several nations. 35c, People of various races holding hands around globe. 50c, Pres. Tolbert, map of Africa, vert. $1, "Gift of Life."

1979, Dec. 28 *Perf. 11*

860 A273 1c multicolored .20 .20
861 A273 5c multicolored .20 .20
862 A273 17c multicolored .40 .40
863 A273 27c multicolored .85 .85
864 A273 35c multicolored 1.00 1.00
865 A273 50c multicolored 1.75 1.75
Nos. 860-865 (6) 4.40 4.40

Souvenir Sheet

866 A273 $1 multicolored 3.25 3.25

Rotary International, 75th anniversary.

Ski Jump, Lake Placid '80 Emblem — A274

Lake Placid '80 Emblem and: 5c, Figure skating. 17c, Bobsledding. 27c, Cross-country skiing. 35c, Women's speed skating. 50c, Ice hockey. $1, Slalom.

1980, Jan. 21

867 A274 1c multicolored .20 .20
868 A274 5c multicolored .20 .20
869 A274 17c multicolored .95 .95
870 A274 27c multicolored 1.90 1.90
871 A274 35c multicolored 1.90 1.90
872 A274 50c multicolored 2.75 2.75
Nos. 867-872 (6) 7.90 7.90

Souvenir Sheet

873 A274 $1 multicolored 3.50 3.50

13th Winter Olympic Games, Lake Placid, NY, Feb. 12-24.

Pres. Tolbert, Pres. Stevens, Maps of Liberia and Sierra Leone, Mano River — A275

1980, Mar. 6 Litho. *Perf. 14x13½*

874 A275 8c multicolored .20 .20
875 A275 27c multicolored .80 .80
876 A275 35c multicolored 1.10 1.10
877 A275 80c multicolored 2.40 2.40
Nos. 874-877 (4) 4.50 4.50

Mano River Agreement, 5th anniversary; Mano River Postal Union, 1st anniversary.

Sgt. Doe and Soldiers, Clenched Hands Angel — A276

1981 Litho. *Perf. 14*

878 A276 1c Redemption horn, vert. .20 .20
879 A276 6c like 1c .20 .20
880 A276 10c shown .20 .20
881 A276 14c Citizens, map, Flag .20 .20
882 A276 23c like 10c .30 .30
883 A276 31c like 14c .45 .45
884 A276 41c like $2 .60 .60
885 A276 $2 Sgt. Samuel Doe, vert. 3.00 3.00
Nos. 878-885 (8) 5.15 5.15

Establishment of new government under the People's Redemption Council, Apr. 12, 1980.

Soccer Players, World Cup, Flags of 1930 and 1934 Finalists — A277

Soccer Players, Cup, Flags of Finalists from: 5c, 1938, 1950. 20c, 1954, 1958. 27c, 1962, 1966. 40c, 1970, 1974. 55c. 1978. $1, Spanish team.

1981, Mar. 4 Litho. *Perf. 14*

886 A277 3c multicolored .20 .20
887 A277 5c multicolored .20 .20
888 A277 20c multicolored .55 .55
889 A277 27c multicolored .80 .80
890 A277 40c multicolored 1.25 1.25
891 A277 55c multicolored 1.75 1.75
Nos. 886-891 (6) 4.75 4.75

Souvenir Sheet

892 A277 $1 multicolored 3.50 3.50

ESPANA '82 World Cup Soccer Championship.

Sgt. Samuel Doe and Citizens — A278

1981, Apr. 7 Litho. *Perf. 14*

893 A278 22c shown .70 .70
894 A278 27c Doe, Liberian flag .90 .90
895 A278 30c Clasped arms 1.40 1.40
896 A278 $1 Doe, soldiers, Justice 3.50 3.50
Nos. 893-896 (4) 6.50 6.50

People's Redemption Council government, first anniversary.

Royal Wedding A279

1981, Aug. 12 Litho. *Perf. 14x13½*

897 A279 31c Couple .85 .85
898 A279 41c Initials, roses 1.10 1.10
899 A279 62c St. Paul's Cathedral 2.10 2.10
Nos. 897-899 (3) 4.05 4.05

Souvenir Sheet

900 A279 $1 Couple 3.50 3.50

John Adams, US President, 1797-1801 A280

Washington Crossing the Delaware — A281

1981, July 4 *Perf. 11*

901 A280 4c shown *.20 .20*
902 A280 5c Wm. H. Harrison *.20 .20*
903 A280 10c Martin Van Buren *.20 .20*
904 A280 17c James Monroe *.50 .40*
905 A280 20c John Q. Adams *.60 .50*
906 A280 22c James Madison *.70 .55*
907 A280 27c Thomas Jefferson *.75 .65*
908 A280 30c Andrew Jackson *.85 .70*
909 A280 40c John Tyler *1.25 .95*
910 A280 80c George Washington *2.40 1.50*
Nos. 901-910 (10) *7.65 5.85*

Souvenir Sheet

911 A281 $1 multi *3.50 3.50*

1981, Nov. 26 Litho. *Perf. 11*

912 A280 6c Rutherford B. Hayes *.20 .20*
913 A280 12c Ulysses S. Grant *.20 .20*
914 A280 14c Millard Fillmore *.20 .20*
915 A280 15c Zachary Taylor *.20 .20*
916 A280 20c Abraham Lincoln *.60 .20*
917 A280 27c Andrew Johnson *.70 .60*
918 A280 31c James Buchanan *.80 .60*
919 A280 41c James A. Garfield *1.00 .80*
920 A280 50c James K. Polk *1.25 .95*
921 A280 55c Franklin Pierce *1.40 1.00*
Nos. 912-921 (10) *6.55 4.95*

Souvenir Sheet

922 A281 $1 Washington at Valley Forge *5.50 5.50*

1982, Apr. 7 Litho. *Perf. 11*

923 A280 4c William H. Taft *.20 .20*
924 A280 5c Calvin Coolidge *.20 .20*
925 A280 6c Benjamin Harrison *.20 .20*
926 A280 10c Warren G. Harding *.20 .20*
927 A280 22c Grover Cleveland *.65 .50*
928 A280 27c Chester Arthur *.75 .55*
929 A280 31c Woodrow Wilson *.80 .65*
930 A280 41c William McKinley *1.25 .95*
931 A280 80c Theodore Roosevelt *2.25 1.75*
Nos. 923-931 (9) *6.50 5.20*

Souvenir Sheet

932 A281 $1 Signing Constitution, horiz. *3.50 3.50*

1982, July 15 Litho. *Perf. 11*

933 A280 4c Jimmy Carter *.20 .20*
934 A280 6c Gerald Ford *.20 .20*
935 A280 14c Harry Truman *.20 .20*
936 A280 17c F. D. Roosevelt *.20 .20*
937 A280 23c L. B. Johnson *.55 .20*
938 A280 27c Richard Nixon *.65 .20*
939 A280 31c John F. Kennedy *.75 .55*
940 A280 35c Ronald Reagan *.90 .65*
941 A280 50c Herbert Hoover *1.25 .90*
942 A280 55c Dwight D. Eisenhower *1.40 1.00*
Nos. 933-942 (10) *6.30 4.30*

Souvenir Sheet
Perf. 14x13½

943 A281 $1 Battle of Yorktown *3.50 3.50*

See No. 1113.

Type of 1976

1981-83 Litho. *Perf. 14½x13½*
Size: 34x20mm

945 A247 1c like #749 .20 .20
946 A247 3c like #750 .20 .20
947 A247 6c like #753 .20 .20
948 A247 15c like #754 .60 .60
949 A247 25c like #757 1.00 1.00
950 A247 31c like #756 1.25 1.25
951 A247 41c like #758 1.75 1.75
952 A247 80c like #759 3.50 3.50
953 A247 $1 like #760 5.00 5.00
Nos. 945-953 (9) 13.70 13.70

Issued: #946-947, 949, 950, 11/27/81; #945, 953, 10/12/82; #948, 951, 12/10/82; #952, 11/3/83.

Intl. Year of the Disabled (1981) — A282

Designs: Various disabled people.

1982, Mar. 24 Litho. *Perf. 14*

954 A282 23c multi, vert. .55 .55
955 A282 62c multicolored 1.25 1.25

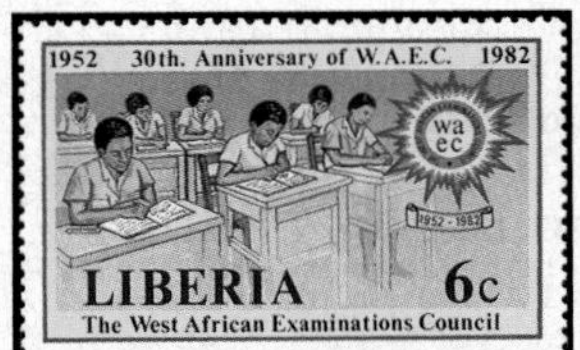

30th Anniv. of West African Examinations Council — A283

1982, Mar. 24

956 A283 6c multicolored .20 .20
957 A283 31c multicolored 1.25 1.25

21st Birthday of Princess Diana — A284

31c, 41c, 62c, Diana portraits. $1, Wedding.

1982, July 1 *Perf. 14x13½*

958 A284 31c multicolored .85 .85
959 A284 41c multicolored 1.25 1.25
960 A284 62c multicolored 2.25 2.25
Nos. 958-960 (3) 4.35 4.35

Souvenir Sheet

961 A284 $1 multicolored 3.50 3.50

Nos. 958-961 Overprinted in Silver: "ROYAL BABY / 21-6-82 / PRINCE WILLIAM"

1982, Aug. 30 Litho. *Perf. 14x13½*

962 A284 31c multicolored .85 .85
963 A284 41c multicolored 1.25 1.25
964 A284 62c multicolored 2.25 2.25
Nos. 962-964 (3) 4.35 4.35

Souvenir Sheet

965 A284 $1 multicolored 3.50 3.50

Birth of Prince William of Wales, June 21.

3rd Natl. Redemption Day — A285

1983, Apr. 5 Litho. *Perf. 13½*

966 A285 3c Fallah Varney .20 .20
967 A285 6c Samuel Doe .20 .20
968 A285 10c Jlatoh N. Podier, Jr. .20 .20
969 A285 15c Jeffry S. Gbatu .40 .40
970 A285 31c Thomas G. Quiwonkpa .95 .95
971 A285 41c Abraham D. Kollie 1.75 1.75
Nos. 966-971 (6) 3.70 3.70

Souvenir Sheet

972 A285 $1 like 6c 3.50 3.50

Natl. Archives Opening — A286

Building views.

1983, Apr. 5

973 A286 6c multicolored *1.60 1.60*
974 A286 31c multicolored *2.75 2.75*

Christmas 1983 A287

Raphael Paintings: 6c, Circumcision of Christ. 15c, Adoration of the Magi. 25c, Announcement to Mary. 31c, Madonna with Baldachin. 41c, Holy Family. 62c, Detail of Madonna with Child Surrounded by Five Saints. $1.25 Madonna of Foligno.

1983, Dec. 14 Litho. *Perf. 13½*

975 A287 6c multicolored .20 .20
976 A287 15c multicolored .20 .20
977 A287 25c multicolored .50 .50
978 A287 31c multicolored .70 .70
979 A287 41c multicolored .85 .85
980 A287 62c multicolored 1.10 1.10
Nos. 975-980 (6) 3.55 3.55

Souvenir Sheet

981 A287 $1.25 multicolored 2.50 2.50

Sheets of 1 showing entire painting exist.

Mano River Union, 10th Anniv. (1983) — A288

1984, Apr. 6 Litho. *Perf. 14x13½*

982 A288 6c Training school graduates .20 .20
983 A288 25c Emblem .85 .85
984 A288 31c Maps, leaders 1.10 1.10
985 A288 41c Guinea's accession 1.75 1.75
Nos. 982-985 (4) 3.90 3.90

Souvenir Sheet

986 A288 75c Guinea's accession, diff. 3.50 3.50

4th Natl. Redemption Day — A289

1984, Apr. 12 *Perf. 14½*

987 A289 3c Hospital, New Kru Town .20 .20
988 A289 10c Ganta-Harper Highway construction .20 .20
989 A289 20c Constitution Assembly opening .60 .60
990 A289 31c Doe at highway construction 1.10 1.10
991 A289 41c Draft Constitution presentation 1.75 1.75
Nos. 987-991 (5) 3.85 3.85

Adoration of the Wise Men, by Rubens (1577-1640) — A290

1984, June 1 Litho. Perf. 13½

992 A290 6c shown .20 .20
993 A290 15c Crowning of Katharina .20 .20
994 A290 25c Mother and Child Adored by Wise Men .55 .55
995 A290 31c Madonna and Child with Halo .75 .75
996 A290 41c Adoration of the Shepherds .95 .95
997 A290 62c Madonna and Child with Saints 1.50 1.50
Nos. 992-997 (6) 4.15 4.15

Souvenir Sheet

998 A290 $1.25 Madonna Adored by Saints *5.50 5.50*

Sheets of 1 showing entire painting exist.

1984 Summer Olympics A291

1984, July 2 Perf. 13½x14

999 A291 3c Jesse Owens, 1936 .20 .20
1000 A291 4c Rafer Johnson, 1960 .20 .20
1001 A291 25c Miruts Yifter, 1980 1.00 1.00
1002 A291 41c Kipchoge Keino, 1968, 1972 1.60 1.60
1003 A291 62c Muhammad Ali, 1960 2.25 2.25
Nos. 999-1003 (5) 5.25 5.25

Souvenir Sheet
Perf. 14x13½

1004 A291 $1.25 Wilma Rudolph, 1960, horiz. 5.50 5.50

1984 Louisiana Expo — A292

1984, July 24 Perf. 14½

1005 A292 6c Water birds .20 .20
1006 A292 31c Ship, Buchanan Harbor 1.25 1.25
1007 A292 41c Fish 1.50 1.50
1008 A292 62c Train carrying iron ore 2.50 2.50
Nos. 1005-1008 (4) 5.45 5.45

Pygmy Hippopotamus, World Wildlife Fund Emblem — A293

Various pygmy hippopotomi.

1984, Nov. 22 Litho. Perf. 14½

1009 A293 6c multicolored .75 .75
1010 A293 10c multicolored 1.00 1.00
1011 A293 20c multicolored 2.75 2.75
1012 A293 31c multicolored 4.00 4.00
Nos. 1009-1012 (4) 8.50 8.50

Indigent Children Home, Bensonville — A294

First Lady Mrs. Nancy Doe and various children.

1984, Dec. 14

1013 A294 6c multicolored .20 .20
1014 A294 31c multicolored 1.25 1.25

Natl. Redemption Day, Apr. 12 — A295

1985, Apr. 5 Litho. Perf. 14½

1015 A295 6c Army barracks, Monrovia .20 .20
1016 A295 31c Pan-African Plaza, Monrovia 1.25 1.25

Liberian Revolution, fifth anniv.

Audubon Birth Bicentenary — A296

Illustrations by artist/naturalist J. J. Audubon.

1985, Apr. 5

1017 A296 1c Bohemian waxwing .20 .20
1018 A296 3c Bay-breasted warbler .20 .20
1019 A296 6c White-winged crossbill .20 .20
1020 A296 31c Red phalarope 1.10 1.10
1021 A296 41c Eastern bluebird 1.60 1.60
1022 A296 62c Northern cardinal 2.40 2.40
Nos. 1017-1022 (6) 5.70 5.70

Venus and Mirror A297

Paintings (details) by Rubens: 15c, Adam & Eve in Paradise. 25c, Andromeda. 31c, The Three Graces. 41c, Venus & Adonis. 62c, The Daughters of Leucippus. $1.25, The Judgement of Paris.

1985, Nov. 14 Litho. Perf. 14

1023 A297 6c multicolored .20 .20
1024 A297 15c multicolored .70 .70
1025 A297 25c multicolored 1.00 1.00
1026 A297 31c multicolored 1.25 1.25
1027 A297 41c multicolored 1.75 1.75
1028 A297 62c multicolored 3.00 3.00
Nos. 1023-1028 (6) 7.90 7.90

Souvenir Sheet

1029 A297 $1.25 multicolored 4.50 4.50

Sheets of 1 showing entire painting exist.

1986 World Cup Soccer Championships, Mexico — A298

1985, Nov. 14

1030 A298 6c Germany-Morocco, 1970 .20 .20
1031 A298 15c Zaire-Brazil, 1974 .50 .50
1032 A298 25c Tunisia-Germany, 1978 .85 .85
1033 A298 31c Cameroun-Peru, 1982, vert. 1.00 1.00
1034 A298 41c Algeria-Germany, 1982 1.25 1.25
1035 A298 62c 1986 Senegal team 2.10 2.10
Nos. 1030-1035 (6) 5.90 5.90

Souvenir Sheet

1036 A298 $1.25 Liberia-Nigeria 4.50 4.50

Queen Mother, 85th Birthday — A299

World Food Day — A300

1985, Dec. 12 Litho. Perf. 14½

1037 A299 31c Elizabeth in garter robes .80 .80
1038 A299 41c At the races 1.00 1.00
1039 A299 62c In garden, waving 1.60 1.60
Nos. 1037-1039 (3) 3.40 3.40

Souvenir Sheet

1040 A299 $1.25 Wearing diadem 3.00 3.00

1985, Dec. 12

1041 A300 25c multicolored .50 .50
1042 A300 31c multicolored .75 .75

AMERIPEX '86 — A301

Statue of Liberty, Cent. — A302

1986, June 10 Litho. Perf. 14½

1043 A301 25c The Alamo 1.25 1.25
1044 A301 31c Liberty Bell 1.40 1.40
1045 A301 80c #344, 802, C102 3.75 3.75
Nos. 1043-1045 (3) 6.40 6.40

1986, June 10

1046 A302 20c Unveiling, 1886 .40 .40
1047 A302 31c Frederic A. Bartholdi .62 .62
1048 A302 $1 Statue close-up 2.00 2.00
Nos. 1046-1048 (3) 3.02 3.02

1988 Winter Olympics, Calgary — A303

1984 Gold medalists: 3c, Max Julen, Switzerland, men's giant slalom. 6c, Debbie Armstrong, U.S., women's giant slalom. 31c, Peter Angerer, West Germany, biathlon. 60c, Bill Johnson, U.S., men's downhill. 80c, East Germany, 4-man bobsled. $1.25, H. Stangassinger, F. Wembacher, West Germany, 2-man luge.

1987, Aug. 21 Litho. Perf. 14

1049 A303 3c multicolored .20 .20
1050 A303 6c multicolored .20 .20
1051 A303 31c multicolored .75 .75
1052 A303 60c multicolored 1.75 1.75
1053 A303 80c multicolored 2.25 2.25
Nos. 1049-1053 (5) 5.15 5.15

Souvenir Sheet

1054 A303 $1.25 multicolored 2.50 2.50

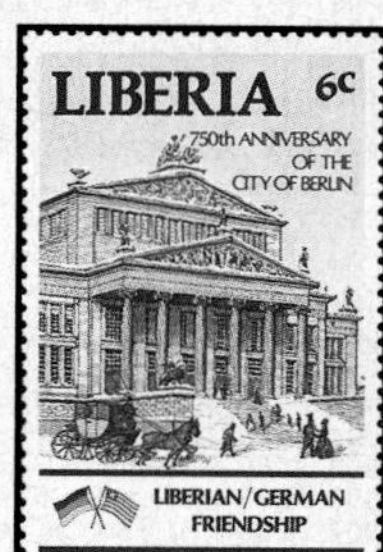

City of Berlin, 750th Anniv. — A304

6c, State (Royal) Theater in the Gendarmenmarkt, c. 1820, architect Schinkel. 31c, Kaiser Friedrich Museum, Museum Is. on River Spree. 60c, Charlottenburg Castle, 17th cent. 80c, Modern church bell tower & Kaiser Wilhelm Gedachtniskirche. $1.50, MIRAK rocket development, Spaceship Society Airfield, Reinickendorf, 1930.

1987, Sept. 4

1055 A304 6c multicolored .20 .20
1056 A304 31c multicolored .85 .85
1057 A304 60c multicolored 1.60 1.60
1058 A304 80c multicolored 2.00 2.00
Nos. 1055-1058 (4) 4.65 4.65

Souvenir sheet

Perf. 11½

1059 A304 $1.50 buff & dk brown 4.50 4.50

No. 1059 contains one 25x61mm stamp.

Shakespearean Plays — A305

1987, Nov. 6 **Litho.** ***Perf. 14***

1060 Sheet of 8 8.50 8.50
a. A305 3c Othello .35 .35
b. A305 6c Romeo & Juliet .35 .35
c. A305 10c The Merry Wives of Windsor .35 .35
d. A305 15c Henry IV .35 .35
e. A305 31c Hamlet .60 .60
f. A305 60c Macbeth .60 .60
g. A305 80c King Lear 1.50 1.50
h. A305 $2 Shakespeare and the Globe Theater, 1598 3.50 3.50

Amateur Radio Association, 25th Anniv. — A306

1987, Nov. 23 **Litho.** ***Perf. 14***

1061 A306 10c Emblem .45 .45
1062 A306 10c Village .45 .45
1063 A306 35c On-the-Air certificate 1.50 1.50
1064 A306 35c Globe, flags 1.50 1.50
Nos. 1061-1064 (4) 3.90 3.90

Miniature Sheets

Statue of Liberty, Cent. (in 1986) — A307

#1065: a, Torch, southern view of NYC. b, Overhead view of crown and scaffold. c, 4 workmen repairing crown. d, 5 workmen, crown. e, Statue's right foot.
#1066: a, Tall ship, statue. b, Bay Queen ferry. c, Statue on poster at a construction site, NYC. d, Tug boat, tall ship. e, Building frieze.
#1067: a, Statue flanked by fireworks. b, Lighting of the statue. c, Crown observatory illuminated. d, Statue surrounded by fireworks. e, Crown and torch observatories illuminated.
#1068: a, Liberty "Happy Birthday" poster at a construction site. b, Ships in NY Harbor. c, Woman renovating statue nose. d, Man & woman renovating nose. e, Man, nose.
#1068a-1068e vert.

1987, Dec. 10 ***Perf. 13½***

1065 Sheet of 5 + label .95
a.-e. A307 6c any single .20 .20
1066 Sheet of 5 + label 3.00
a.-e. A307 15c any single .50 .50
1067 Sheet of 5 + label 5.75
a.-e. A307 31c any single .95 .95
1068 Sheet of 5 + label 10.00
a.-e. A307 60c any single 1.75 1.75
Nos. 1065-1068 (4) 19.70

Nos. 1065-1068 contain label inscribed "CENTENARY OF THE STATUE OF LIBERTY" in two or five lines.

Second Republic, 2nd Anniv. A308

Design: Natl. flag, coat of arms, hand grip, Pres. Doe and Vice Pres. Moniba.

1988, Jan. 6 ***Perf. 14½***

1069 A308 10c multicolored .60 .60
1070 A308 35c multicolored 1.90 1.90

UN Child Survival Campaign — A309

1988, Jan. 15 ***Perf. 13x13½, 13½x13***

1071 A309 3c Breast-feeding .20 .20
1072 A309 6c Oral rehydration therapy, vert. .20 .20
1073 A309 31c Immunization 2.00 2.00
1074 A309 $1 Growth monitoring, vert. 5.75 5.75
Nos. 1071-1074 (4) 8.15 8.15

Inauguration of the Second Republic — A310

Design: Pres. Doe greeting Chief Justice Emmanuel N. Gbalazeh.

1988, Jan. 15 ***Perf. 13x13½***

1075 A310 6c multicolored 1.50 1.50

Samuel Kanyon Doe Sports Complex, Opened Apr. 12, 1986 A311

1988, Jan. 15

1076 A311 31c multicolored .65 .65

Green (Agricultural) Revolution — A312

1988, Apr. 4 ***Perf. 15***

1077 A312 10c multicolored .40 .40
1078 A312 35c multicolored 1.50 1.50

US Peace Corps in Liberia, 25th Anniv. A313

1988, Apr. 4

1079 A313 10c multicolored .40 .40
1080 A313 35c multicolored 1.50 1.50

Souvenir Sheet

1988 Summer Olympics, Seoul — A314

1988, Apr. 14 ***Perf. 14***

1081 A314 $3 multicolored 10.00 10.00

Organization of African Unity, 25th Anniv. — A315

1988, May 25

1082 A315 10c multicolored .45 .45
1083 A315 35c multicolored 1.50 1.50
1084 A315 $1 multicolored 4.50 4.50
Nos. 1082-1084 (3) 6.45 6.45

Rail Transport A316

1988, July 30 **Litho.** ***Perf. 14½***

1085 A316 10c GP10 at Nimba .30 .30
1086 A316 35c Triple-headed iron ore train .90 .90

Souvenir Sheets

Perf. 11

1087 A316 $2 King Edward II, 1930 *5.50 5.50*
1088 A316 $2 GWR 57 No. 3697, 1941 *5.50 5.50*
1089 A316 $2 GWR 0-4-2T No. 1408, 1932 *5.50 5.50*
1090 A316 $2 GWR No. 7034 Ince Castle, 1950 *5.50 5.50*

#1087-1090 contain one 64x44mm stamp each.

Nos. 1087-1090 with Added Text

1993, Aug. 3

Souvenir Sheets

1087a With added text in margin 7.50 7.50
1088a With added text in margin 7.50 7.50
1089a With added text in margin 7.50 7.50
1090a With added text in margin 7.50 7.50

Added text on Nos. 1087a-1090a reads: "25th ANNIVERSARY OF THE LAST STEAM TRAIN TO / RUN ON BRITISH RAIL 1968-1993."

1988 Summer Olympics, Seoul — A317

1988, Sept. 13 **Litho.**

1091 A317 10c Baseball .20 .20
1092 A317 35c Hurdles .85 .85
1093 A317 45c Fencing 1.00 1.00
1094 A317 80c Synchronized swimming 1.90 1.90
1095 A317 $1 Yachting 2.25 2.25
Nos. 1091-1095 (5) 6.20 6.20

Souvenir Sheet

1096 A317 $1.50 Tennis 3.00 3.00

Intl. Tennis Federation, 75th anniv. ($1.50).

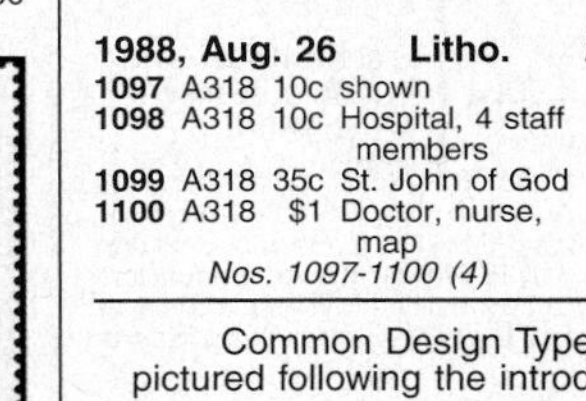

St. Joseph's Catholic Hospital, 25th Anniv. A318

1988, Aug. 26 **Litho.** ***Perf. 14½***

1097 A318 10c shown .20 .20
1098 A318 10c Hospital, 4 staff members .20 .20
1099 A318 35c St. John of God .80 .80
1100 A318 $1 Doctor, nurse, map 2.25 2.25
Nos. 1097-1100 (4) 3.45 3.45

Common Design Types pictured following the introduction.

Lloyds of London, 300th Anniv.

Common Design Type

CD341

Designs: 10c, Royal Exchange destroyed by fire, 1838, vert. 35c, Air Liberia BN2A aircraft. 45c, Supertanker Chevron Antwerp. $1, Lakonia on fire off Madeira, 1963, vert.

1988, Oct. 31 **Litho.** ***Perf. 14***

1101 CD341 10c multicolored .20 .20
1102 CD341 35c multicolored 1.00 1.00
1103 CD341 45c multicolored 1.25 1.25
1104 CD341 $1 multicolored 2.75 2.75
Nos. 1101-1104 (4) 5.20 5.20

Sasa Players A319

Perf. 14x14½, 14½x14

1988, Sept. 30 **Litho.**

1105 A319 10c Monkey bridge, vert. .50 .50
1106 A319 35c shown 1.40 1.40
1107 A319 45c Snake dancers, vert. 1.90 1.90
Nos. 1105-1107 (3) 3.80 3.80

Intl. Fund for Agricultural Development, 10th Anniv. — A320

1988, Oct. 7 **Litho.** ***Perf. 14x14½***

1108 A320 10c Crops .50 .50
1109 A320 35c Spraying crops, livestock 1.90 1.90

3rd Anniv. of the 2nd Republic — A321

1989, Jan. 6 Litho. *Perf. 14*

1110 A321 10c Pres. Doe, officials .50 .50
1111 A321 35c like 10c 1.90 1.90
1112 A321 50c Pres. Doe, doctor 2.40 2.40
Nos. 1110-1112 (3) 4.80 4.80

US Presidents Type of 1981-82

1989, Jan. 20 *Perf. 13½x14*

1113 A280 $1 George Bush 4.75 4.75

Rissho Kosei-Kai Buddhist Assoc., Tokyo, 50th Anniv. — A322

Natl. flags and: No. 1114, "Harmony" in Japanese. No. 1115, Organization headquarters, Tokyo. No. 1116, Nikkyo Niwano, founder. 50c, Statue of Buddha in the Great Sacred Hall.

1989, Feb. 28 Litho. *Perf. 14x14½*

1114 A322 10c multicolored .60 .60
1115 A322 10c multicolored .60 .60
1116 A322 10c multicolored .60 .60
1117 A322 50c multicolored 2.50 2.50
Nos. 1114-1117 (4) 4.30 4.30

Liberian-Japanese friendship.

Souvenir Sheet

Emperor Hirohito of Japan (1901-1989) — A323

Commemorative coins: a, Silver. b, Gold.

1989, Feb. 28 Unwmk. *Perf. 14½*

1118 A323 Sheet of 2 8.00 8.00
a.-b. 75c any single 3.25 3.25

For overprint see No. 1147.

Mano River Union, 15th Anniv. A324

Natl. flag, crest and: 10c, Union Glass Factory, Gardnersville, Monrovia. 35c, Pres. Doe, Momoh of Sierra Leone and Conte of Guinea. 45c, Monrovia-Freetown Highway. 50c, Sierra Leone-Guinea land postal services. $1, Communique, 1988 summit.

Unwmk.

1989, May 8 Litho. *Perf. 14*

1119 A324 10c multicolored .20 .20
1120 A324 35c multicolored 1.25 1.25
1121 A324 45c multicolored 1.75 1.75
1122 A324 50c multicolored 1.90 1.90
1123 A324 $1 multicolored 3.75 3.75
Nos. 1119-1123 (5) 8.85 8.85

World Telecommunications Day — A325

1989, May 17 Litho. *Perf. 12½*

1124 A325 50c multicolored 1.40 1.40

Moon Landing, 20th Anniv.

Common Design Type

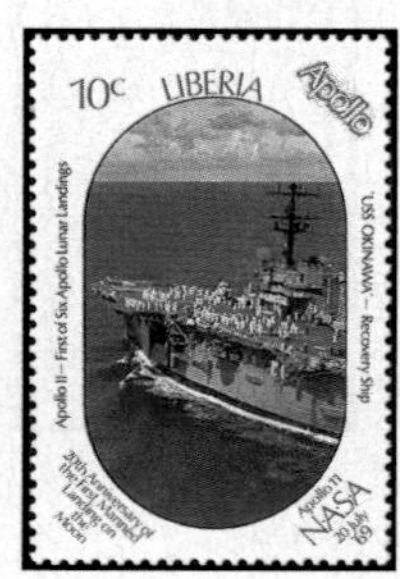

CD342

Apollo 11: 10c, Recovery ship USS Okinawa. 35c, Buzz Aldrin, Neil Armstrong and Michael Collins. 45c, Mission emblem. $1, Aldrin steps on the Moon. $2, Aldrin preparing to conduct experiments on the Moon's surface.

Perf. 14x13½, 14 (35c, 45c)

1989, July 20 Litho. Wmk. 384

Size of Nos. 1126-1127: 29x29mm

1125 CD342 10c multicolored .20 .20
1126 CD342 35c multicolored .90 .90
1127 CD342 45c multicolored 1.25 1.25
1128 CD342 $1 multicolored 2.75 2.75
Nos. 1125-1128 (4) 5.10 5.10

Souvenir Sheet

1129 CD342 $2 multicolored 5.50 5.50

Souvenir Sheet

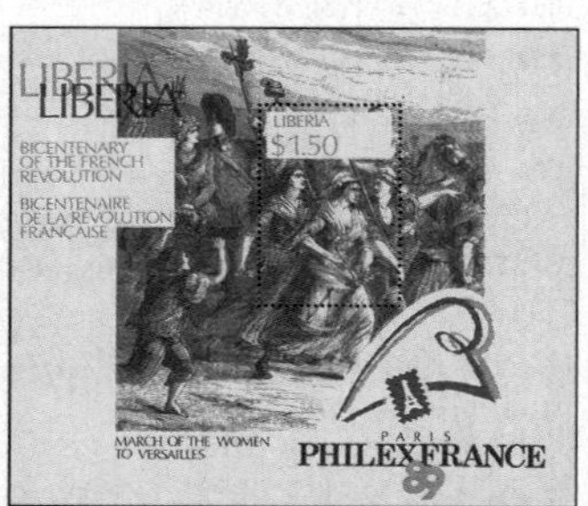

The Women's March on Versailles — A326

1989, July 7 Wmk. 384 *Perf. 14*

1130 A326 $1.50 multicolored 4.00 4.00

French revolution, bicent., PHILEXFRANCE '89.

Souvenir Sheet

Renovation and Re-dedication of the Statue of Liberty, 1986 — A327

Photographs: a, Workman. b, French dignitary, US flag. c, Dignitaries at ceremony, statue.

Perf. 14x13½

1989, Oct. 2 Litho. Wmk. 373

1131 Sheet of 3 2.25 2.25
a.-c. A327 25c any single .75 .75

World Stamp Expo '89 and PHILEXFRANCE '89.

Souvenir Sheet

A328

1989, Nov. 17 Unwmk. *Perf. 14½*

1132 A328 $2 black 5.50 5.50

World Stamp Expo '89, Washington, DC.

Jawaharlal Nehru, 1st Prime Minister of Independent India — A329

1989, Dec. 22 Unwmk. *Perf. 14*

1133 A329 45c Nehru, signature, flag 1.50 1.50
1134 A329 50c Nehru, signature 3.25 3.25

New Standard-A Earth Satellite Station — A330

1990, Jan. 5

1135 A330 10c shown .20 .20
1136 A330 35c multi, diff. 1.25 1.25

US Educational & Cultural Foundation in Liberia, 25th Anniv. (in 1989) — A331

1990, Jan. 5

1137 A331 10c multicolored .20 .20
1138 A331 45c multicolored 1.40 1.40

Pan-African Postal Union, 10th Anniv. — A332

1990, Jan. 18 *Perf. 13x12½*

1139 A332 35c multicolored 1.00 1.00

Flags of Liberian Counties — A333

Designs: a, Bomi. b, Bong. c, Grand Bassa. d, Grand Cape Mount. e, Grand Gedeh. f, Grand Kru. g, Lofa. h, Margibi. i, Maryland. j, Montserrado. k, Nimba. l, Rivercess. m, Sinoe.

Perf. 14x13½

1990, Mar. 2 Litho. Unwmk.

1140 Strip of 13 5.00 5.00
a.-m. A333 10c any single .30 .30
1141 Strip of 13 17.00 17.00
a.-m. A333 35c any single 1.00 1.00
1142 Strip of 13 22.50 22.50
a.-m. A333 45c any single 1.50 1.50
1143 Strip of 13 25.00 25.00
a.-m. A333 50c any single 1.60 1.60
1144 Strip of 13 50.00 50.00
a.-m. A333 $1 any single 3.00 3.00
Nos. 1140-1144 (5) 119.50 119.50

Queen Mother, 90th Birthday

Common Design Types

At Age 6 — CD343

At Age 22 — CD344

Perf. 14x15

1991, Oct. 28 Wmk. 384

1145 CD343 10c multicolored .20 .20

Perf. 14½

1146 CD344 $2 brn & blk 4.00 4.00

For overprints see Nos. 1162-1163.

Souvenir Sheet

No. 1118 Overprinted

Perf. 14½

1991, Nov. 16 Litho. Unwmk.

1147 A323 Sheet of 2 4.50 4.50
a.-b. 75c any single 2.25 2.25

National Unity — A334

Designs: 35c, Hands clasp over map of Liberia. 45c, Liberian flag, hands, African map. 50c, All Liberia conference, March 1991, conferees, flag, map.

1991, Dec. 30 *Perf. 13½*
1148 A334 35c multicolored 1.10 1.10
1149 A334 45c multicolored 1.60 1.60
1150 A334 50c multicolored 1.75 1.75
Nos. 1148-1150 (3) 4.45 4.45

1992 Summer Olympics, Barcelona — A335

1992, Aug. 7 **Litho.** *Perf. 14*
1151 A335 45c Boxing 2.00 2.00
1152 A335 50c Soccer 2.25 2.25
1153 A335 $1 Weight lifting 4.50 4.50
1154 A335 $2 Water polo 8.25 8.25
Nos. 1151-1154 (4) 17.00 17.00

Souvenir Sheet

1155 A335 $1.50 Running 6.00 6.00

Disarmament — A336

Designs: 50c, Disarm today. $1, Join your parents & build Liberia. $2, Peace must prevail in Liberia.

1993, Feb. 10 **Litho.** *Perf. 13½x14*
1156 A336 50c multicolored 1.90 1.90
1157 A336 $1 multicolored 3.75 3.75
1158 A336 $2 multicolored 7.25 7.25
Nos. 1156-1158 (3) 12.90 12.90

See Nos. 1237-1239.

Miniature Sheets

Flora and Fauna — A337

No. 1159 — Flora: a, Papaya. b, Sausage tree. c, Angraecum eichlerianum. d, Arachnis flos-aeris. e, Screw pine. f, African tulip tree. g, Coffee tree. h, Bolusiella talbotii. i, Bulbophyllum lepidum. j, Oeceoclades maculata. k, Plectrelminthus caudatus. l, Diaphananthe rutila.

No. 1160 — Fauna: a, Diana monkey. b, Flying squirrel. c, Egyptian rousette. d, Serval. e, Potto. f, Chimpanzee. g, African horned chameleon. h, Royal python. i, Golden cat. j, Banded duiker. k, Pygmy hippopotamus. l, Water chevrotain.

No. 1161 — Birds: a, Grey heron. b, Bat hawk. c, Martial eagle. d, Little sparrow hawk. e, Hoopoe. f, Red bishop. g, Purple-throated sunbird. h, African fish eagle. i, African grey parrot. j, Black-crowned night heron. k, Swallow. l, Great white egret.

1993-94 **Litho.** *Perf. 14*
1159 A337 70c Sheet of 12, #a.-l. 35.00 35.00
1160 A337 90c Sheet of 12, #a.-l. 37.50 37.50
1161 A337 $1 Sheet of 12, #a.-l. 37.50 37.50
Nos. 1159-1161 (3) 110.00 110.00

Issued: 70c, 10/14; 90c, 11/18; $1, 1/14/94.

Nos. 1145-1146 Ovptd. with Hong Kong '94 Emblem

Perf. 14x15

1994, Feb. 18 **Litho.** **Wmk. 384**
1162 CD343 10c multicolored .20 .20

Perf. 14½

1163 CD344 $2 multicolored 7.75 7.75

Miniature Sheet

Roberts Field, Monrovia, 50th Anniv. A338

No. 1164: a, Vickers Supermarine Spitfire Mk IX. b, Boeing B-17G. c, Douglas A-20 Boston. d, North American B-25J Mitchell. e, Beech C-45 Expeditor. f, Douglas C-54. g, Piper L4 Cub. h, Martin PBM-3C.

1994, July 11 **Litho.** *Perf. 13½x13*
1164 A338 35c Sheet of 8, #a.-h. + label 11.00 11.00

Souvenir Sheets

Locomotives — A339

Designs: No. 1165, $1, Class A3 #60044 Melton, Class A4 #60017 Silver Fox. No. 1166, $1, GWR 2-6-2 Prairie Tank #4561. No. 1167, $1, GWR 2-6-2 Small Prairie. No. 1168, $1, GWR Castle Class 4-6-0 No. Kinswear Castle. No. 1169, $1, GWR 0-6-0 Pannier Tank. No. 1170, $1, Bong Mining Company diesel hauling iron ore. Illustration reduced.

1994, Aug. 16 **Litho.** *Perf. 14*
1165-1170 A339 Set of 6 18.00 18.00

See Nos. 1194-1199, 1205.

Liberian Natl. Red Cross, 75th Anniv. — A340

Designs: 70c, No. 1172, Globe. No. 1173, $2, Jean-Henri Dunant.

1994, Oct. 3 **Litho.** *Perf. 14½x14*
1171 A340 70c multicolored 2.50 2.50
1172 A340 $1 multicolored 3.50 3.50
1173 A340 $1 multicolored 3.50 3.50
1174 A340 $2 multicolored 7.25 7.25
Nos. 1171-1174 (4) 16.75 16.75

End of World War II, 50th Anniv.

Common Design Types

Designs: 70c, Sunderland on U-boat patrol. 90c, US Army Engineer Task Force. $1, MV Abosso sunk off Liberia, 1942. #1178, MV Adda sunk off Liberia, 1941.

#1179, Obverse of U.S. Victory Medal depicting Liberty.

1995, May 8 **Litho.** *Perf. 13½*
1175 CD351 70c multicolored 2.10 2.10
1176 CD351 90c multicolored 2.75 2.75
1177 CD351 $1 multicolored 3.00 3.00
1178 CD351 $2 multicolored 5.75 5.75
Nos. 1175-1178 (4) 13.60 13.60

Souvenir Sheet

Perf. 14

1179 CD352 $2 multicolored 6.00 6.00

Wild Animals A341

1995, June 1 *Perf. 14*
1180 A341 70c Cheetah 2.50 2.50
1181 A341 70c Giraffe 2.50 2.50
1182 A341 90c Rhinoceros 3.25 3.25
1183 A341 $1 Elephant 3.75 3.75
1184 A341 $2 Lion 7.50 7.50
Nos. 1180-1184 (5) 19.50 19.50

Souvenir Sheet

1995 IAAF World Track & Field Championships, Gothenburg — A342

No. 1185: a, Merlene Ottey. b, Heike Drechsler. Illustration reduced.

1995, Aug. 4 **Litho.** *Perf. 14*
1185 A342 $1 Sheet of 2, #a.-b. 8.50 8.50

Miniature Sheet

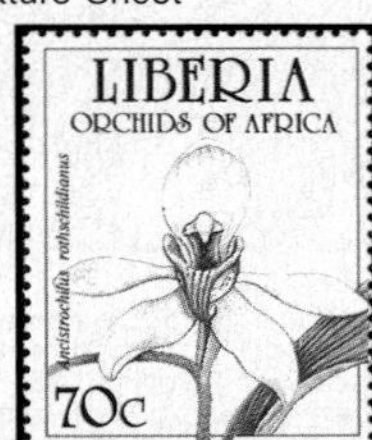

Orchids — A343

No. 1186: a, Ancistrochilus rothschildianus. b, Disa uniflora. c, Polystachya ottoniana. d, Aerangis brachycarpa. e, Plectrelminthus caudatus. f, Polystachya bella. g, Ansellia africana. h, Bulbophyllum cochleatum.

1995, Sept. 1 *Perf. 13*
1186 A343 70c Sheet of 8, #a.-h. + label 24.00 24.00

Singapore '95.

UN, 50th Anniv.

Common Design Type

Designs: 25c, UN Land Rovers. 50c, Delivering food supplies. $1, Ilyushin IL-76 freighter airlifting supplies. $2, MIL MI-8 helicopter.

1995, Oct. 24 **Litho.** *Perf. 14*
1187 CD353 25c multicolored 1.00 1.00
1188 CD353 50c multicolored 2.00 2.00
1189 CD353 $1 multicolored 4.00 4.00
1190 CD353 $2 multicolored 8.00 8.00
Nos. 1187-1190 (4) 15.00 15.00

Economic Community of West African States, 20th Anniv. — A344

Designs: 25c, Map, Liberian flag, soldiers, civilians. 50c, Soldier carrying child, vert. $1, Logo, vert.

Perf. 13½x13, 13½x13

1995, Nov. 10 **Litho.**
1191 A344 25c multicolored 1.00 1.00
1192 A344 50c multicolored 2.00 2.00
1193 A344 $1 multicolored 4.00 4.00
Nos. 1191-1193 (3) 7.00 7.00

Train Type of 1994

Souvenir Sheets

Designs: No. 1194, $1, 4-4-0 locomotive 11 "The Reno," galloping horses. No. 1195, $1, Halwill station, Southern Region T9 class locomotive #30719. No. 1196, $1, GWR 0-4-2T "1400" class locomotive #1408, cricket match. No. 1197, $1, LMS Jubilee class 4-6-0, #45684 "Jutland," Kettering station. No. 1198, $1, GWR 2-6-2 "Prairie" locomotive #4547, Lustleigh station. No. 1199, $1, Wainwright "H" class 0-4-4T locomotive, winter countryside.

1996, Feb. 29 **Litho.** *Perf. 14x15*
1194-1199 A339 Set of 6 18.00 18.00

Modern Olympic Games, Cent. — A345

1996, Apr. 22 **Litho.** *Perf. 13*
1200 A345 20c Runners .70 .70
1201 A345 35c Boxing 1.25 1.25
1202 A345 50c Javelin 1.75 1.75
1203 A345 $1 Hurdles 3.50 3.50
Nos. 1200-1203 (4) 7.20 7.20

Butterflies A346

No. 1204: a, Papilio zalmoxis. b, Papilio dardanus. c, Charaxes varanes. d, Acraea natalica. e, Euphaedra neophron. f, Craphium antheus. g, Salamis anacardii. h, Kallima cymodoce. i, Precis hierta.

1996, May 22 **Litho.** *Perf. 13½*
1204 A346 70c Sheet of 9, #a.-i. 18.00 18.00

Train Type of 1994

Souvenir Sheet

Design: G4a Class Pacific locomotive, Canadian Pacific Railroad.

1996, June 8 **Litho.** *Perf. 14x15*
1205 A339 $1 multi 3.00 3.00

CAPEX '96.

Fish A347

No. 1206: a, Atlantic Sailfish. b, Guinean flyingfish. c, Blue marlin. d, Little tunny (e). e, Common dolphinfish (f). f, Guachanche barracuda. g, Guinean parrotfish. h, Cadenat's chromis (g). i, Dusky grouper (h). j, Hoefler's butterflyfish (k). k, African hind (l). l, West African Angelfish.

1996, July 15 Litho. *Perf. 14*
1206 A347 90c Sheet of 12, #a.-l. 32.50 32.50

The government of Liberia has been in chaos, and the country has been in a state of anarchy for some time. New issue stamps continue to be released into the philatelic market by agents. Stamps canceled-to-order and on first day covers probably exist.

Butterflies — A348

No. 1207: a, Euphaedra judith. b, Euphaedra eleus. c, Acraea encedon. d, Euphaedra neophron. e, Liptena praestans. f, Neptis exalenca. g, Palla decius. h, Salamis cytora. i, Pseudacraea dolomena. j, Anaphaeis eriphia. k, Euphaedra themis. l, Hadrodontes varanes.

No. 1208: a, Papilio mnestheus. b, Papilio nobilis. c, Graphium antheus. d, Asterope benguelae. e, Graphium illyris. f, Emphaedra eupalus. g, Charaxes protoclea. h, Cymothoe beckeri. i, Euphaedra cyparissa. j, Coliades chalybe. k, Mimacraea neokoton. l, Charaxes ethalion.

$2, Charaxes pelias.

1996 Litho. *Perf. 14*
1207 A348 20c Sheet of 12, #a.-l. 7.00
1208 A348 25c Sheet of 12, #a.-l. 9.00

Souvenir Sheet

1209 A348 $2 multicolored 6.00

Birds — A349

Designs, horiz: 35c, African jacana. 50c, Pel's fishing owl. $1, Paradise whydah.

No. 1213: a, Turtle dove. b, Bee-eater. c, Golden oriole. d, Pied flycatcher. e, Sardinian warbler. f, Goliath heron. g, Rock thrush. h, Kestrel. i, Cattle egret. j, Woodchat shrike. k, Hoopoe. l, Great egret.

No. 1214, horiz: a, Red faced crimsonwing. b, Egyptian goose. c, African pitta. d, Paradise flycatcher. e, Garganey. f, Southern carmine bee-eater. g, Fulvous whistling duck. h, Village weaver. i, Martial eagle.

$2, Pintail duck, horiz.

1996
1210-1212 A349 Set of 3 5.50
1213 A349 25c Sheet of 12, #a.-l. 9.50
1214 A349 35c Sheet of 9, #a.-i. 9.50

Souvenir Sheet

1215 A349 $2 multicolored 6.00

Marilyn Monroe (1926-62) A350

1996
1216 A350 20c multicolored .70

No. 1216 was issued in sheets of 16.

UNICEF, 50th Anniv. — A351

Designs: 35c, Education for all. 70c, Health care. $1, Children first.

1996, Sept. 16 *Perf. 13½x13*
1217-1219 A351 35c Set of 3 7.00

1996 Summer Olympic Games, Atlanta A352

Designs: No. 1220, 20c, Cricket (discontinued sport), vert. No. 1221, 20c, Babe Didrikson, vert. No. 1222, 35c, Vitaly Scherbo, winner of 6 gold medals, 1992, vert. No. 1223, 35c, Betty Robinson, vert. No. 1224, 50c, Cuban baseball team, gold medal, 1992. No. 1225, 50c, Ancient Greek wall painting of boxers, vert. No. 1226, $1, Stadium, Barcelona, 1992. No. 1227, $1, Stadium, Amsterdam, 1928, vert.

No. 1228, 35c, vert. — Olympic events: a, Men's athletics. b, Men's gymnastics. c, Weight lifting. d, Women's volleyball. e, Women's diving. f, Women's gymnastics. g, Women's track. h, Women's tennis. i, Discus.

No. 1229, 35c, vert. — Boxing gold medalists, boxing: a, Tyrell Biggs, U.S. b, Isan Gura, Tanzania (no medal). c, Mark Breland, U.S. d, Teofilo Stevenson, Cuba. e, Ray Leonard, U.S. f, Michael Spinks, U.S. g, Joe Frazier, U.S. h, Floyd Patterson, US. i, George Foreman, US.

$2, Evelyn Ashford.

1996 Litho. *Perf. 14*
1220-1227 A352 Set of 8 14.00

Sheets of 9, #a-i

1228-1229 A352 Set of 2 22.50

Souvenir Sheet

1230 A352 $2 multicolored 7.00

Flowers and Flowering Trees — A353

No. 1231: a, Olive tree. b, Olive flower. c, Fig tree. d, Almond tree. e, Almug tree. f, Cedar. g, Pomegranate (b). h, Citron. i, Date palm (d, e, j). j, Date palm (fruit). k, Cedar of Lebanon. l, Rock rose. m, Narcissus. n, Oleander (i). o, Date palm (flower). p, Shittah tree. q, Hyacinth. r, Barley, flax (s). s, Grape vine. t, Lily of the field. u, Mandrake. v, Caper desire. w, Madonna lily. x, Aloe (s). y, Date palm tree.

1996
1231 A353 25c Sheet of 25, #a.-y. 30.00

History of Rock and Roll A354

No. 1232: a, Wilson Pickett. b, Bill Haley. c, Otis Redding. d, Fats Domino. e, Buddy Holly. f, Chubby Checker. g, Marvin Gaye. h, Jimi Hendrix.

1996 *Perf. 13½x14*
1232 A354 35c Sheet of 8, #a.-h. + label 10.00

Kingfisher A355

No. 1233 — Kingfishers: a, Striped. b, Grey-headed. c, Pied. d, Giant. e, Shining-blue.

1996, Oct. 7 Litho. *Perf. 13½*
1233 A355 75c Strip of 5, #a.-e. 11.00

See No. 1236.

Mao Zedong, 20th Anniv. of Death — A356

1996, Nov. 1 Litho. *Perf. 14½x14*
1234 A356 $1 shown 3.25
1235 A356 $1 As older man 3.25

Kingfisher Type of 1996
Souvenir Sheet

1997, Feb. 3 Litho. *Perf. 14*
1236 A355 $1 Like #1233b 3.00

Hong Kong '97. No. 1236 contains one 29x43mm stamp.

Disarmament Type of 1993
Inscribed "PEACE TODAY"

1997 Litho. 13½x14
1237 A336 $1 Like #1157 *4.00*
1238 A336 $2 Like #1158 *8.25*
1239 A336 $3 Like #1156 *12.50*
Nos. 1237-1239 (3) 24.75

Nos. 1237-1239 are dated 1996.

Wildlife — A357

No. 1240: a, Olive baboon. b, Leopard. c, African tree pangolin. d, Vervet. e, Aardvark. f, Spotted hyena. g, Hunting dog. h, Thomson's gazelle. i, Warthog. j, African civet. k, Nile crocodile. l, African polecat.

1997, Apr. 2 Litho. *Perf. 14*
1240 A357 50c Sheet of 12, #a.-l. 18.00

Deng Xiaoping (1904-97), British Transfer of Hong Kong — A358

Different portraits of Deng Xiaoping, "July 1, 1997," Hong Kong: 70c, In daylight, vert. $1, At night.

No. 1243: a, 50c. b, 70c. c, $1.20. Illustration reduced.

1997 Litho. *Perf. 14*
1241 A358 70c multicolored 2.00
1242 A358 $1 multicolored 3.25
1243 A358 Sheet of 3, #a.-c. 7.75

No. 1241 is 28x44mm, and was issued in sheets of 4. No. 1242 was issued in sheets of 3.

UNESCO, 50th Anniv. — A359

No. 1244, 50c, vert.: a, Canals, Venice, Italy. b, Mosque of Badshahi, Gardens of Shalamar, Lahore, Pakistan. c, Palace of Orando, Spain. d, Grounds of Temple of Hera, Greece. e, Church and Monastery of Daphni, Greece. f, Fraser Island, Australia. g, Canadian Rocky Mountains Park, Canada. h, Church of Santo Domingo Puebla, Mexico.

No. 1245, 50c, vert.: a, City of Ohrid and lake, Macedonia. b, Thracian Tomb of Sveshtari, Bulgaria. c, Monastery of Hossios Luckas, Greece. d, Church of Santa Cristina of Lena, Spain. e, Church of Santa Maria Della Salute, Venice, Italy. f, Center of Puebla, Mexico. g, Bagrati Cathedral, Georgia. h, Quebec City, Canada.

No. 1246: a, Ngorongoro Conservation Area, Tanzania. b, Garamba Natl. Park, Zaire. c, Canaima Natl. Park, Venezuela. d, Simien Natl. Park, Ethiopia. e, Mana Pools Natl. Park, Zimbabwe.

No. 1247, $2, Palace of Diocletian, Split, Croatia. No., 1248, $2, Monument of Nubia at Abu Simbel, Egypt. No. 1249, $2, Quedlinberg, Germany.

Perf. 13½x14, 14x13½
1997, June 17 Litho.

Sheets of 8, #a-h + Label

1244-1245 A359 Set of 2 27.50
1246 A359 70c Sheet of 5, #a-e, + label 12.50

Souvenir Sheets

1247-1249 A359 Set of 3 21.00

Queen Elizabeth II, Prince Philip, 50th Wedding Anniv. — A360

No. 1250: a, Queen holding umbrella. b, Royal arms. c, Prince in white uniform, Queen. d, Queen waving, Prince. e, Windsor Castle. f, Prince Philip.

No. 1251, $2, Queen seated on sofa. No. 1252, $2, Queen, Prince wearnig robes of Order of the Garter.

1997, June 17 *Perf. 14*
1250 A360 50c Sheet of 6, #a.-f. 11.00

Souvenir Sheet

1251-1252 A360 $2 Set of 2 14.00

Grimm's Fairy Tales A361

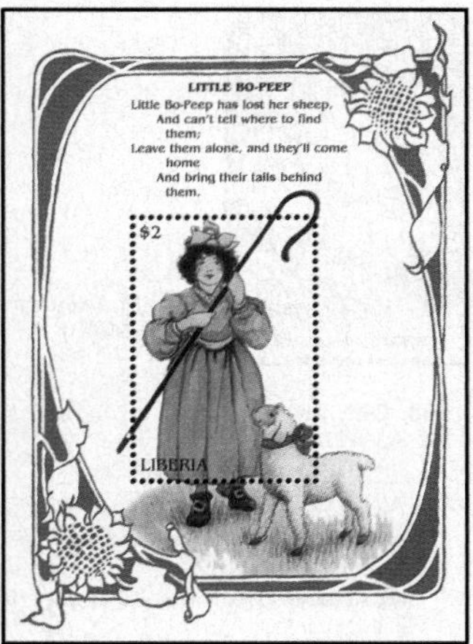

Mother Goose — A362

No. 1253 — Scenes from Rapunzel: a, Girl. b, Wicked person, raven. c, Prince.

No. 1254, Prince rescuing girl.

No. 1255, Little Bo Peep, sheep.

1997, June 17 *Perf. 13½x14*

1253 A361 $1 Sheet of 3, #a.-c. 10.00

Souvenir Sheets

1254 A361 $2 multicolored 7.00

Perf. 14

1255 A362 $2 multicolored 7.00

1998 Winter Olympics, Nagano — A363

Designs: 50c, Olympic Stadium, Lillehammer, 1994. 70c, Johann Koss, speed skating. $1, Katarina Witt, figure skating. $1.50, Sonia Henie, figure skating.

No. 1260: a, K. Seizinger, Alpine downhill skiing. b, J. Weissflog, 120-m ski jump. c, T. Kono, Nordic combined. d, G. Hackl, luge.

No. 1261: a, E. Bredesen, 90-m ski jump. b, L. Kjus, downhill skiing. c, B. Daehlie, cross-country skiing. d, P. Wiberg, combined Alpine skiing. e, S.L. Hattestad, freestyle skiing. f, G. Weder, D. Acklin, 2-man bobsled. g, Swedish hockey player. h, T. Alsgaard, cross-country skiing.

No. 1262, $2, German biathlete, 1994. No. 1263, $2, M. Wasmeier, giant slalom. No. 1264, $2, J. Koss, speed skating, diff. No. 1265, $2, V. Schneider, slalom.

1997, June 23 *Perf. 14*

1256-1259 A363 Set of 4 13.00

1260 A363 50c Strip or block of 4, #a.-d. 7.00

1261 A363 50c Sheet of 8, #a.-h. 14.00

Souvenir Sheets

1262-1265 A363 Set of 4 27.50

No. 1260 was issued in sheets of 8 stamps.

Flowers — A364

No. 1266, 50c: a, Sugar cane dahlia. b, Windsor tall phlox. c, Creative art daylily. d, Columbine. e, Infinite Grace bearded iris. f, Fairy lilies mini amaryllis.

No. 1267, 50c: a, White coneflower. b, Peggy Lee hybrid tea rose. c, Daffodil. d, Bowl of Beauty peony. e, Hardy lily. f, Windflower.

No. 1268, $2, Lily-flowered tulip. No. 1269, $2, Chrysanthemum Potomac.

1997, July 1 **Litho.** *Perf. 14*

Sheets of 6, #a-f

1266-1267 A364 Set of 2 20.00 20.00

Souvenir Sheets

1268-1269 A364 Set of 2 16.00 16.00

Flora and Fauna A365

No. 1270: a, Lovebirds. b, Genet. c, Leopard, crowned night heron. d, Gorilla. e, Giant wild boar. f, Elephant. g, Sterculia flower, skink. h, Ladybugs, bush baby. i, Cape primroses, ground hornbill.

No. 1271, $2, Rufus-crowned roller. No. 1272, $2, Gray heron.

1997, July 1

1270 A365 50c Sheet of 9, #a.-i. 13.00 13.00

Souvenir Sheets

1271-1272 A365 Set of 2 12.00 12.00

Chernobyl Disaster, 10th Anniv. A366

1997, June 17 **Litho.** *Perf. 13½x14*

1273 A366 $1 UNESCO 3.25 3.25

Marcello Mastroianni (1923-96), Actor — A367

No. 1274 — Scenes from motion pictures: a, Casanova, 1970. b, Divorce Italian Style. c, 8½. d, La Dolce Vita.

1997, Sept. 3

1274 A367 75c Sheet of 4, #a.-d. 10.00 10.00

Contemporary Artists and Paintings — A368

No. 1275, 50c: a, Andy Warhol (1927-87). b, "Multicolored Retrospective," by Warhol, 1979. c, "The Three Musicians," by Picasso, 1921. d, Pablo Picasso (1881-1973). e, Henri Matisse (1869-1954). f, "The Dance," by Matisse, 1910. g, "Lavender Mist," by Pollock, 1950. h, Jackson Pollock (1912-56).

No. 1276, 50c: a, Piet Mondrian (1872-1944). b, "Broadway Boogie Woogie," by Mondrian, 1942-43. c, "Persistence of Memory," by Dali, 1931. d, Salvador Dali (1904-89). e, Roy Lichtenstein (1923-97). f, "Artist's Studio: The Dance," by Lichtenstein, 1974. g, "Europe After the Rain," by Ernst, 1940-42. h, Max Ernst (1891-1976).

1997, Sept. 3 *Perf. 14*

Sheets of 8, #a-h

1275-1276 A368 Set of 2 27.50 27.50

Nos. 1275b-1275c, 1275f-1275g, 1276b-1276c, 1276f-1276g are 53x38mm.

Owls — A369

No. 1277: a, Akun eagle owl. b, Shelley's eagle owl. c, African wood owl. d, Rufous fishing owl. e, Maned owl. f, Sandy scops owl.

1997

1277 A369 50c Sheet of 6, #a.-f. 9.00 9.00

Birds — A370

Designs: 1c, Black bee-eater. 2c, Yellow-billed barbet. 3c, Carmine bee-eater. 4c, Malachite kingfisher. 5c, Emerald cuckoo. 10c, Blue-throated roller. 15c, Blue-headed bee-eater. 20c, Black-collared lovebird. 25c, Broad-billed roller. 50c, Blue-breasted kingfisher. 70c, Little bee-eater. 75c, Yellow spotted barbet. 90c, White-throated bee-eater. $1, Double-toothed barbet. $2, Blue-cheeked bee-eater. $3, Narina's trogon.

1997

1278	A370	1c multicolored	.20	.20
1279	A370	2c multicolored	.20	.20
1280	A370	3c multicolored	.20	.20
1281	A370	4c multicolored	.20	.20
1282	A370	5c multicolored	.20	.20
1283	A370	10c multicolored	.20	.20
1284	A370	15c multicolored	.40	.40
1285	A370	20c multicolored	.50	.50
1286	A370	25c multicolored	.65	.65
1287	A370	50c multicolored	1.25	1.25
1288	A370	70c multicolored	1.90	1.90
1289	A370	75c multicolored	2.00	2.00
1290	A370	90c multicolored	2.40	2.40
1291	A370	$1 multicolored	2.75	2.75
1292	A370	$2 multicolored	5.25	5.25
1293	A370	$3 multicolored	7.75	7.75
		Nos. 1278-1293 (16)	26.05	26.05

1998 World Cup Soccer — A371

Players, country, vert: 50c, Salenko, Russia. 70c, Schillaci, Italy. $1, Lineker, England. $1.50, Pele, Brazil. $2, Fontaine, France. $2, Rahn, W. Germany.

No. 1300, 50c, vert: a, Ardiles, Argentina. b, Romario, Brazil. c, Rummenigge, Germany. d, Charlton, England. e, Villa, Argentina. f, Matthäus, Germany. g, Maradona, Argentina. h, Lineker, England.

No. 1301, 50c: a, Paulo Rossi, Italy. b, Ademir, Brazil. c, Grzegorz Lato, Poland. d, Gary Lineker, England. e, Gerd Muller, W. Germany. f, Johan Cruyff, Holland. g, Karl-Heinz Rummenigge, Germany. h, Mario Kempes, Argentina.

No. 1302, $6, Beckenbauer, W. Germany, vert. No. 1303, $6, Maier, W. Germany, vert.

Perf. 13½x14, 14x13½

1997, Oct. 1 **Litho.**

1294-1299 A371 Set of 6 18.00 18.00

Sheets of 8, #a-h, + Label

1300-1301 A371 Set of 2 27.50 27.50

Souvenir Sheets

1302-1303 A371 Set of 2 40.00 40.00

Marine Life A372

No. 1304: a, Flamingoes (beach, palm trees). b, Six flamingoes. c, Sailfish (d). d, Egret. e, Yellow-tail snapper. f, Manatee. g, Clown coris. h, White-collar butterflyfish. i, Royal angelfish. j, Titan triggerfish. k, Three-striped wrasse. l, Pacific blue-eye. m, Wobbegono. n, Jellyfish. o, Sea urchin, red sea triggerfish. p, Harlequin fish.

No. 1305, $2, Seahorses, vert. No. 1306, $2, Anemone fish.

1998, Mar. 9 **Litho.** *Perf. 14*

1304 A372 20c Sheet of 16, #a.-p. 9.50 9.50

Souvenir Sheets

Perf. 13½x14, 14x13½

1305-1306 A372 Set of 2 12.00 12.00

No. 1305 contains one 38x51mm stamp, No. 1306 contains one 51x38mm stamp.

Butterflies — A373

Designs: No. 1307, 50c, Orange tip. No. 1308, 50c, Saturn. No. 1309, 50c, Queen of Spain fritillary. No. 1310, 50c, Plain tiger. No. 1311, 50c, Doris. No. 1312, 50c, Forest queen. No. 1313, 50c, Figure-of-eight. No. 1314, 50c, Orange-barred sulphur.

No. 1315, 50c: a, Alfalfa. b, Orange-barred sulphur, diff. c, Union jack. d, Mocker swallowtail. e, Large green-banded blue. f, Common dotted border.

No. 1316, 50c: a, Cairns birdwing. b, Leafwing. c, Banded kin shoemaker. d, Tiger swallowtail. e, Adonis blue. f, Palmfly.

No. 1317, $2, Great orange tip. No. 1318, $2, Japanese emperor.

1998, Apr. 6 **Litho.** *Perf. 14*

1307-1314 A373 Set of 8 12.00 12.00

Sheets of 6, #a-f

1315-1316 A373 Set of 2 18.00 18.00

Souvenir Sheets

1317-1318 A373 Set of 2 12.00 12.00

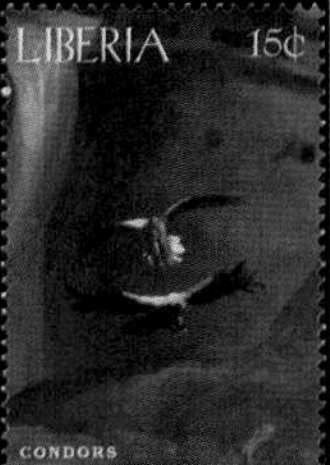

Noah's Ark — A374

No. 1319: a, Condors. b, Giraffes, skunks. c, Mallard ducks. d, Snowy owl. e, Snowy owl (face forward). f, Noah. g, Noah's wife. h, Polar bears. i, Elephants. j, Zebras. k, Rhinoceros. l, Sheep. m. Ruby-throated hummingbird. n, Wives of Noah's sons. o, Bats. p, Ring-necked pheasant. q, Tiger. r, Deer. s, Kangaroos. t, Camels. u, Red-eyed frogs. v, Raccoons. w, Rooster, hen. x, Marmosets. y, Lions.

$2, Black-legged kittiwake gull, ark on top of mountain, horiz.

1998, May 4 Litho. *Perf. 14*

1319 A374 15c Sheet of 25, #a.-y. 11.00 11.00

Souvenir Sheet

1320 A374 $2 multicolored 6.00 6.00

World Wildlife Fund A375

No. 1321 — Liberian Mongoose: a, Looking straight ahead. b, Holding object between front paws. c, With front legs on branch. d, With mouth wide open.

1998, June 16 Litho. *Perf. 14*

1321 A375 32c Block or strip of 4, #a.-d. 5.50 5.50

Issued in sheets of 12 stamps.

Mushrooms A376

Designs: 10c, Lepiota cristata. 15c, Russula emetica. 20c, Coprinus comatus. 30c, Russula cyanoxantha. 50c, Cortinarius violaceus. 75c, Amanita cothurnata. $1, Stropharia cyanea. $1.20, Panaeolus semiovatus.

No. 1330, 40c: a, Collybia butryacea. b, Asterophora parasitica. c, Tricholomopsis rutilans. d, Marasmius alliaceus. e, Mycena crocata. f, Mycena polygramma. g, Oudemansiella mucida. h, Entoloma conferendum. i, Entoloma serrulatum.

No. 1331, 40c: a, Cordyceps militaris. b, Xylaria hypoxlon. c, Sarcoscypha austriaca. d, Auriscalpium. e, Fomitopsis pinicola. f, Pleurotus ostreatus. g, Lepista flaccida. h, Clitocybe metachroa. i, Hygrocybe conica.

No. 1332, $2, Gomphidus roseus. No. 1333, $2, Paxillus atrotomentosus. No. 1334, $2, Russula occidentalis. No. 1335, $2, Cantharellus cibarius.

1998, July 1

1322-1329 A376 Set of 8 14.00 14.00

Sheets of 9, #a-i

1330-1331 A376 Set of 2 24.00 24.00

Souvenir Sheets

1332-1335 A376 Set of 4 27.50 27.50

Monarchs A377

No. 1336, 50c: a, Kaiser Wilhelm II, Germany. b, Qabus Bin Said, Oman. c, King Albert, Belgium. d, Haile Selassie, Ethiopia. e, King Hussein, Jordan. f, Sheik Jaber Al-Ahmad Al-Sabah, Kuwait.

No. 1337, 50c: a, Alexander the Great, Greece. b, Charlemagne, France. c, Cleopatra, Egypt. d, Henry VIII, England. e, Peter the Great, Russia. f, Frederick the Great, Prussia.

No. 1338, 50c: a, Queen Beatrix, Netherlands. b, King Juan Carlos, Spain. c, Queen Elizabeth II, England. d, Franz Joseph I, Austria-Hungary. e, Princess Grace, Monaco. f, King Carl XVI Gustaf, Sweden.

No. 1339, $2, Empress Michiko, Japan. No. 1340, $2, Emperor Akihito, Japan. No. 1341, $2, Kublai Khan, China.

1998, July 27 Litho. *Perf. 14*

Sheets of 6, #a-f

1336-1338 A377 Set of 3 24.00 24.00

Souvenir Sheets

1339-1341 A377 Set of 3 21.00 21.00

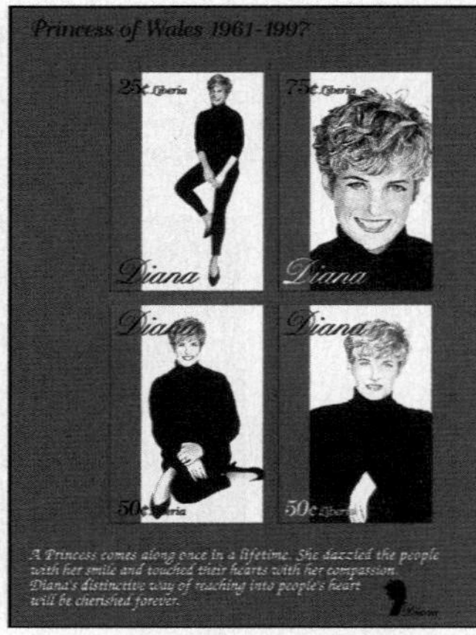

Diana, Princess of Wales (1961-97) — A378

Various portraits of Diana in black outfit.

1998 *Imperf.*

1342 A378 50c Sheet of 4, #a.-d. 4.00 4.00

Birds A379

No. 1343, 32c, Great green macaw. No. 1344, 32c, Crowned pigeon, vert. No. 1345, 32c, Blue-gray tanager. No. 1346, 32c, Roseate spoonbill, vert. No. 1347, 32c, Red-capped manakin. No. 1348, 32c, Groove-billed ani. No. 1349, 32c, South African crowned crane, vert.

No. 1350, vert: a, African sunbird. b, Seven-colored tanager. c, Red-throated bee-eater. d, Blue-crowned motmot. e, Duvaucel's trogon. f, Green bulbul. g, Grass-green tanager. h, Turaco. i, Hammer-head. j, Sarus crane. k, Limpkin. l, Ground hornbill.

No. 1351, $2, Red-crested touraco. No. 1352, $2, Flamingo, vert.

1998, Aug. 31 Litho. *Perf. 14*

1343-1349 A379 Set of 7 7.00 7.00

1350 A379 32c Sheet of 12, #a.-l. 12.00 12.00

Souvenir Sheets

1351-1352 A379 Set of 2 12.00 12.00

Children's Stories A380

No. 1354: a, Tom Sawyer, by Mark Twain. b, Peter Rabbit, by Beatrix Potter. c, The Nutcracker, by E.T.A. Hoffman. d, Hansel & Gretel, by The Brothers Grimm. e, The Princess and the Pea, by Hans Christian Andersen. f, Oliver Twist, by Charles Dickens. g, Little Red Riding Hood, by The Brothers Grimm. h, Rumpelstiltskin, by The Brothers Grimm. i, The Wind & the Willows, by Kenneth Grahame.

$2, Rapunzel, by Brothers Grimm.

1998, Sept. 16 Litho. *Perf. 14½*

1354 A380 40c Sheet of 9, #a.-i. 12.00 12.00

Souvenir Sheet

Perf. 13½

1355 A380 $2 multicolored 7.00 7.00

No. 1355 contains one 38x51mm stamp.

Island, Marine Life A381

No. 1356: a, Litoria peronii. b, Volcano, denomination UL. c, Volcano, denomination UR. d, Egretta alba. e, Graphium antiphates itamputi. f, Rhododendron zoelleri. g, Boat. h, Lava flow. i, Cormorants. j, Vaccinium. k, Caranx latus. l, Dugongs. m, Underwater lava flow. n, Cetocarus bicolor. o, Chilomycterus spilostylus. p, Lienardella fasliatus. q, Aerobatus. r, Gray reef shark. s, Acanthurus leucosternon, denomination UR. t, Hippocampus kuda. u, Coral, denomination UR. v, Chelonia. w, Myripristis hexogona. x, Coral, denomination, UL. y, Acanthurus leucosternon, denonination UL.

No. 1357: a, Sperm whale (b, c). b, Lollipop tang. c, Bottlenose dolphin (b, f). d, Jackass penguin (h). e, Harlequin tuskfish. f, Manta ray (a, b, e, j). g, Sealion. h, Grouper (g, l). i, Hammerhead shark (m). j, Butterfly fish. k, Garibaldi (g). l, Marine iguana (p). m, Loggerhead turtle (n). n, Seahorse. o, Horseshow crab (n, p). p, Moray eel.

No. 1358, 32c: a, Walrus. b, Pockfish-harlequin. c, Striped marlin. d, Whale shark. e, Spiny boxfish. f, Porcupine fish. g, Octopus. h, Dragonfish. i, Sea krait.

No. 1359, 32c: a, Snapping turtle. b, Atlantic spadefish. c, Bottlenose dolphin. d, Humpback whale. e, Whitetip shark. f, Twilight and deep seafish. g, Moorish idol. h, American lobster. i, Stingrays.

No. 1360, $2, Great white shark. No. 1361, $2, Banner fish. No. 1362, $2, Killer whale. No. 1363, $2, Surgeon fish.

1998, Oct. 15 *Perf. 14*

1356 A381 15c Sheet of 25, #a.-y. 12.00 12.00

1357 A381 20c Sheet of 16, #a.-p. 10.00 10.00

Sheets of 9, #a-i

1358-1359 A381 Set of 2 18.00 18.00

Souvenir Sheets

1360-1363 A381 Set of 2 22.50 22.50

International Year of the Ocean.

Diana, Princess of Wales (1961-97) A382

Design: a, 50c, Inscription panel on left. b, 50c, panel on right.

1998, Oct. 26 Litho. *Perf. 14½x14*

1364 A382 50c Pair, a.-b. 3.25 3.25

No. 1364 was issued in sheets of 6.

Pablo Picasso (1881-1973) — A383

Entire paintings or details: 50c, Woman Throwing a Stone, 1931. 70c, Man with Sword and Flower, 1969, vert. $1, Large Bather with a Book, 1937, vert.

$2, French Cancan, 1901.

1998, Oct. 26 *Perf. 14½*

1365-1367 A383 Set of 3 7.50 7.50

Souvenir Sheet

1368 A383 $2 multicolored 7.00 7.00

Mahatma Gandhi (1869-1948) A384

1998, Oct. 26 *Perf. 14*

1369 A384 50c shown 1.75 1.75

Souvenir Sheet

1370 A384 $2 Portrait, diff. 7.00 7.00

No. 1369 was issued in sheets of 4.

1998 World Scout Jamboree, Chile — A385

No. 1371: a, Daniel Carter Beard, Ernest Thompson Seton, award scouts, 1912. b, Robert Baden-Powell in Matabeleland, 1896. c, Scout repairing small girl's wagon.

1998, Oct. 26

1371 A385 $1 Sheet of 3, #a.-c. 10.00 10.00

Enzo Ferrari (1898-1988), Automobile Manufacturer — A386

No. 1372: a, King Leopold Cabriolet. b, 195 S. c, 250 GTO 64.

$2, 250MM Cabriolet.

1998, Oct. 26 Litho. *Perf. 14*

1372 A386 $1 Sheet of 3, #a.-c. 9.00 9.00

Souvenir Sheet

1373 A386 $2 multicolored 8.50 8.50

No. 1373 contains one 91x35mm stamp.

Royal Air Force, 80th Anniv. A387

No. 1374: a, Hawker Hurricane XII. b, Avro Lancaster in flight. c, Avro Lancaster B2. d, Supermarine Spitfire HG Mk 1XB.

No. 1375, $2, Bristol F2B fighter, Eurofighter. No. 1376, $2, Hawk, biplane.

1998, Oct. 26

1374 A387 70c Sheet of 4, #a.-d. 9.50 9.50

Souvenir Sheet

1375-1376 A387 Set of 2 14.00 14.00

Famous People and Events of the Twentieth Cent. — A388

No. 1380, 40c: a, Mao Tse-tung. b, Cultural Revolution begins. c, Promoting Third World unity. d, Zhou Enlai. e, Deng Xiaoping. f, Hong Kong returns to China, 1997. g, Shanghai, an Asian metropolis. h, Jiang Zemin.

No. 1381, 40c: a, Robert E. Peary. b, Expedition to the North Pole. c, Climbing Mt. Everest. d, Sir Edmund Hillary. e, Neil Armstrong. f, Walking on the moon. g, Expedition to the South Pole. h, Roald Amundsen.

$2, Matthew Henson.

1998, Dec. 1 Litho. *Perf. 14*

Sheets of 8, #a-h

1380-1381 A388 Set of 2 22.50 22.50

Souvenir Sheet

1382 A388 $2 multicolored 6.50 6.50

Nos. 1380b-1380c, 1380f-1380g, 1381b-1381c, 1380f-1381g are each 53x38mm.

Classic Cars A389

Designs: No. 1383, 32c, 1966-72 Lamborghini Miura. No. 1384, 32c, 1966-93 Alfa Romeo Spider. No. 1385, 32c, 1948-61 Jaguar XK140. No. 1386, 32c, 1959-63 Lotus Elite.

No. 1387, 50c: a, 1949-53 Bristol 401. b, 1952-55 Bentley Continental R. c, 1973-75 Lancia stratos. d, 1963-67 Chevrolet Corvette Stingray. e, 1948-52 Austin A90 Atlantic. f, 1969-90 Aston Martin V8.

No. 1388, 50c: a, 1961-75 Jaguar E-Type. b, 1955-57 Ford Thunderbird. c, 1964-73, Ford Mustang GT350. d, 1957-77 Fiat 500. e, 1955-59 BMW 507. f, 1963-65 Buick Riviera.

No. 1389, $2, 1945-55 MG TD. No. 1390, $2, 1959-65 Rolls Royce Silver Cloud.

1998, Dec. 24

1383-1386 A389 Set of 4 4.00 4.00

Sheets of 6, #a-f

1387-1388 A389 Set of 2 20.00 20.00

Souvenir Sheets

1389-1390 A389 Set of 2 13.00 13.00

New Year 1999 (Year of the Rabbit) — A390

Paintings, by Liu Jiyou (1918-83): No. 1391, Two rabbits. No. 1392, Three rabbits.

No. 1393, Two rabbits, flowers, vert.

1999, Jan. 5

1391 A390 50c multicolored 1.75 1.75
1392 A390 50c multicolored 1.75 1.75

Souvenir Sheet

1393 A390 $2 multicolored 6.50 6.50

Nos. 1391-1392 were issued in sheets of 2 each. No. 1393 contains one 43x52mm stamp.

US Presidents A391

No. 1394, 75c, Various portraits of Abraham Lincoln. No. 1395, 75c, Various portraits of Bill Clinton.

1998, Dec. 1 Litho. *Perf. 14*

Sheets of 4, #a-d

1394-1395 A391 Set of 2 20.00 20.00

Zhou Enlai (1898-1976), Chinese Premier — A392

Various portraits.

1999 Litho. *Perf. 14*

1396 A392 50c Sheet of 6, #a.-f. 10.00 10.00

Souvenir Sheet

1397 A392 $2 multicolored 7.00 7.00

Raptors — A393

Designs: 50c, Snowy owl. 70c, Barn owl. $1, American kestrel $1.50, Golden eagle.

No. 1402, 50c: a, Eurasian eagle owl. b, Osprey. c, Egyptian vulture. d, Lizard buzzard. e, Pale chanting goshawk. f, Bald eagle.

No. 1403, 50c: a, Goshawk. b, Laughing falcon. c, Oriental bay-owl. d, Swallow-tailed kite. e, Secretary bird. f, Brown falcon.

No. 1404, $2, Northern harrier. No. 1405, $2, Peregrine falcon.

1999, Jan. 4

1398-1401 A393 Set of 4 11.00 11.00

Sheets of 6, #a-f

1402-1403 A393 Set of 2 20.00 20.00

Souvenir Sheets

1404-1405 A393 Set of 2 13.00 13.00

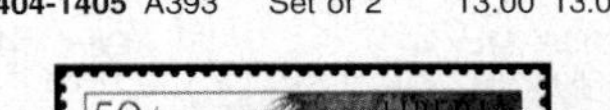

Dinosaurs — A395

No. 1406, 50c, Pachyrinosaur. No. 1407, 50c, Centrosaurus, vert. No. 1408, 70c, Pentaceratops, vert. No. 1409, 70c, Oviraptor, vert. $1, Corythosaur. $1.50, Stegosaurus, vert.

No. 1412, 40c: a, Baryonyx (e). b, Pachycephalosaur (a, c). c, Homalocephale. d, Pterodustro (c, g). e, Pycnosteroides. f, Giant nautiloid. g, Kronosaur (e, f). h, Giant cephalopod (g).

No. 1413, 40c: a, Camarasaur. b, Albertosaur (c, f, g). c, Eudimorhodon (b, d). d, Dimorphodon (c). e, Compsognathus. f, Torosaurus. g, Nodosaurid (h). h, Probactrosaurus.

No. 1414, $2, Tarbosaurus, vert. No. 1415, $2, Shunosaurus, vert.

1999, Jan. 18

1406-1411 A395 Set of 6 12.00 12.00

Sheets of 8, #a-h

1412-1413 A395 Set of 2 22.50 22.50

Souvenir Sheets

1414-1415 A395 Set of 2 13.00 13.00

Dinosaurs — A396

Designs: 50c, Brachiosaurus, vert. 70c, Tyrannosaurus, vert. $1, Mosasaurus. $1.50, Triceratops.

No. 1420: a, Albertosaurus. b, Parasaurolophus. c, Styracosaurus. d, Struthiomimus. e, Ankylosaurus. f, Chasmosaurus.

No. 1421, $2, Deinonychus. No. 1422, $2, Stegosaurus.

1999

1416-1419 A396 Set of 4 9.00 9.00
1420 A396 50c Sheet of 6, #a.-f. 10.00 10.00

Souvenir Sheets

1421-1422 A396 Set of 2 13.00 13.00

Flowers — A397

Designs: No. 1423, 50c, Tecophilaea cyanocrocus. 70c, Nymphoides peltata. $1, Angraecum scottianum. $1.50, Grevillea dielsiana.

No. 1427, 50c: a, Cyrtopodium parvilforum. b, Catharanthus roseus. c, Acacia acuminata. d, Herbertia lahue. e, Protea venusta. f, Clianthus formosus.

No. 1428, 50c: a, Dendrobium rarum. b, Cyrtorchis arcuata. c, Zygopetalum intermedium. d, Cassia fistula. e, Saintpaulia ionantha. f, Heliconia collinsiana.

No. 1429, $2, Hibiscus tilliaceus. No. 1430, $2, Rhododendron thomsonii.

1999, Feb. 8

1423-1426 A397 Set of 4 11.00 11.00

Sheets of 6, #a-f

1427-1428 A397 Set of 2 20.00 20.00

Souvenir Sheets

1429-1430 A397 Set of 2 13.00 13.00

Orchids — A398

Designs: No. 1431, 50c, Tridactyle bicaudata. No. 1432, 50c, Angraecum infundibulare. No. 1433, 70c, Oeceoclades maculata. No. 1434, 70c, Ophyrs fusca. No. 1435, $1, Sobennikoffia robusta. No. 1436, $1, Stenoglottis fimbriata. No. 1437, $1.50, Plectrelminthus caudatus. No. 1438, $1.50, Satyrium erectum.

No. 1439, 50c: a, Angraecrum eichlerianum. b, Ansellia africana. c, Cymbidiella pardalina. d, Angraecum eburnium. e, Ancistrochilus rothchildianus. f, Aerangis luteoalba.

No. 1440, 50c: a, Dis cardinalis. b, Cytorchus arcuata. c, Cynorkis compacta. d, Disa kewensis. e, Eulophia guineensis. f, Eulophia speciosa.

No. 1441, Angraecum compactum. No. 1442, Calanthe vestita.

1999, Mar. 13

1431-1438 A398 Set of 8 22.50 22.50

Sheets of 6, #a-f

1439-1440 A398 Set of 2 19.00 19.00

Souvenir Sheets

1441-1442 A398 Set of 2 13.00 13.00

Orchids — A399

Designs: No. 1443, 50c, Calypso bulbosa. No. #1444, 50c, Maclellanara pagan lovesong. No. 1445, 70c, Masdevallia chimaera. No. 1446, 70c, Yamadara midnight. $1, Cleistes divaricata. $1.50, Oncidium golden sunset.

No. 1449: a, Trichopilia tortilis. b, Stenoglottis longifolia. c, Telipogon pulcher. d, Esmeralda clarkei. e, Papilionanthe teres. f, Mormodes rolfeanum. g, Cypripedium acaule. h, Serapias lingua.

1999, Mar. 13

1443-1448 A399 Set of 6 15.00 15.00
1449 A399 30c Sheet of 8, #a.-h. 9.00 9.00

Wildlife — A400

No. 1450: a, Mink. b, Arctic fox. c, Lynx. d, Snowy owl. e, Polar bear. f, Golden eagle.

$2, Big horn sheep.

1999, Feb. 24 Litho. *Perf. 14*

1450 A400 50c Sheet of 6, #a.-f. 7.00 7.00

Souvenir Sheet

1451 A400 $2 multicolored 5.00 5.00

Flora and Fauna A401

No. 1452: a, Madgascan red fody. b, Indri (e). c, Coral-billed nuthatch. d, Safaka (g, j). e, Golden piper. f, Aye aye (i). g, Croad-bordered grass yellowy. h, Ring-tailed lemur (g, j, k). i, Parson's chameleon. j, Madagascar day gecko. k, Leaf-tailed gecko. l, Orchid.

No. 1453, $2, Wattled false sunbird. No. 1454, $2, Parson's chameleon. No. 1455, $2, Ring-tailed lemur.

1999, Apr. 1

1452 A401 20c Sheet of 12, #a.-l. 7.00 7.00

Souvenir Sheets

1453-1455 A401 Set of 3 15.00 15.00

Seabirds — A402

Designs: No. 1456, 50c, Harlequin duck. No. 1457, 50c, Eleonor's falcon, vert. No. 1458, 70c, Wilson's plover. No. 1459, 70c, Common eider. No. 1460, $1, Little tern. No. 1461, $1, American oystercatcher. No. 1462, $1.50, Herring gull, vert. No. 1463, $1.50, Brown pelican, vert.

No. 1464, 30c, vert: a, Great cormorant. b, Crested cormorant. c, Red faced cormorant. d, Whimbrel. e, Tufted puffin. f, Ivory gull. g, Common murre. h, Shelduck. i, Razorbill.

No. 1465, 30c: a, Common tern. b, Black-legged kittiwake. c, Bernacle goose. d, Black-headed gull. e, Semipalmated plover. f, Northern gannet. g, King eider. h, Iceland gull. i, Ring-billed gull.

No. 1466, $2, Arctic loon. No. 1467, $2, Atlantic puffin. No. 1468, $2, California gull, vert.

1999, Apr. 1 Litho. *Perf. 14*
1456-1463 A402 Set of 8 17.00 17.00

Sheets of 9, #a-i
1464-1465 A402 Set of 2 13.00 13.00

Souvenir Sheets
1466-1468 A402 Set of 3 15.00 15.00

Queen Mother (b. 1900) — A404

No. 1475: a, With King George VI at wedding, 1923. b, In Nairobi, 1959. c, Wearing tiara, 1953. d, Wearing hat, 1990.
$2, Wearing hat, 1990, diff.

1999, Aug. 4 *Perf. 14*
1475 A404 $1 Sheet of 4, #a.-d., + label 9.00 9.00

Souvenir Sheet
Perf. 13¾
1476 A404 $2 multicolored 5.00 5.00

No. 1476 contains one 38x51mm stamp.

Trains A405

Designs: 32c, Nozomi Train, Japan. 40c, 401 Intercity Express, Germany. 50c, C53, Japan Railways. 70c, Beuth 2-2-2, Germany.
No. 1481, 40c: a, "Adler," Germany. b, Suburban EMU, Japan. c, Class 01, 4-6-2, Germany. d, Class 120 Bo-Bo, Germany. e, Class P8, 4-6-0, Germany. f, Fujikawa Express, Japan. g, Class 081, Germany. h, Kodama 8-car train, Japan. i, Class C62, 4-6-4, Japan.
No. 1482, 40c: a, KF Type, 4-8-4, China. b, Minobu Line train, Japan. c, Class S34-40, Germany. d, Class EF81, Bo-Bo, Japan. e, V200, B-B, Germany. f, SVT 877 "Flying Hamburger," Japan. g, C51, 4-6-2 Japan Railways. h, AEO Single rail car, Germany. i, Class D51, Japan.
No. 1483, $2, Yamonote Line train, Japan. No. 1484, $2, Class B8, Germany.

1999, Aug. 25 Litho. *Perf. 14*
1477-1480 A405 Set of 4 4.50 4.50

Sheets of 9, #a-i
1481-1482 A405 Set of 2 17.00 17.00

Souvenir Sheets
1483-1484 A405 Set of 2 10.00 10.00

Dogs A406

No. 1485, Lhasa apso. 70c, Samoyed.
No. 1487, vert.: a, Dalmatian. b, Pyrennean Mountain dog. c, Golden retriever. d, Bearded collie. e, Basset hound. f, Bernese Mountain dog.
No. 1488, Beagle, vert.

1999, Aug. 30 *Perf. 14*
1485 A406 50c multicolored 1.25 1.25
1486 A406 70c multicolored 1.75 1.75
1487 A406 50c Sheet of 6, #a.-f. 7.50 7.50

Souvenir Sheet
1488 A406 $2 multicolored 5.00 5.00

During 1999-2004 Liberia was torn by a brutal and chaotic civil war that reduced the nation to a state of anarchy. Government services, including postal operations, functioned erratically, if at all, for months at a time. During this period, overseas stamp agents continued to produce stamps under pre-war contracts, and a large number of issues appeared that were marketed to overseas collectors. It appears that some of these stamps have been released in Liberia since the end of hostilities. These will be listed when their sale and postal use has been confirmed.

Paintings by Norman Rockwell A580

Paintings: $15, Playing Party Games. $30, Saturday Night Out. $35, The Portrait. No, 2328, $50, Grandpa's Little Ballerina.
No. 2329, $50: a, The Cave of the Winds. b, Redhead Loves Hatty. c, The Rivals. d, Three's Company.
No. 2330, $50: a, Distortion. b, Summer Vacation. c, Runaway Pants. d, Tumble.
No. 2331, $50: a, Daydreams. b, A Patient Friend. c, Lands of Enchantment. d, The Little Spooners.
No. 2332, $50: a, The Skating Lesson. b, The Fortune Teller. c, God Bless You. d, Knowledge is Power.

2005, Jan. 10 Litho. *Perf. 14¼*
2325-2328 A580 Set of 4 7.00 7.00

Sheets of 4, #a-d
2329-2332 A580 Set of 4 40.00 40.00

Jules Verne (1828-1905), Writer — A581

No. 2333, $30: a, The Adventures of Captain Hatteras. b, The Mysterious Island (deflated balloon). c, The Mysterious Island (Men looking at ape). d, 20,000 Leagues Under the Sea (spotlights on ship).
No. 2334, $30: a, Around the World in Eighty Days. b, From the Earth to the Moon (people watching man on space capsule ladder). c, Paris in the Twentieth Century. d, Master of the World (ship captain at wheel).
No. 2335, $30: a, The Chase of the Golden Meteor. b, Master of the World (flying machine, country name in white). c, Five Weeks in a Balloon. d, From the Earth to the Moon (rocket in space).
No. 2336, $30: a, The Mysterious Island (People in balloon basket). b, Robur the Conqueror. c, Round the Moon. d, Master of the World (flying machine, country name in black).
No. 2337, $30 — Scenes from 20,000 Leagues Under the Sea: a, Ships on water. b, Shark and octopus attacking ship. c, Shark attacking diver. d, Squid attacking ship.
No. 2338, $100, Deep sea divers. No. 2339, $100, Admiral Richard E. Byrd. No. 2340, $100, Radio satellite communication. No. 2341, $100, Long range ballistic missile. No. 2342, $100, Extravehicular satellite repair.

2005, Jan. 11 *Perf. 13¼x13½*
Sheets of 4, #a-d
2333-2337 A581 Set of 5 32.50 32.50

Souvenir Sheets
2338-2342 A581 Set of 5 27.50 27.50

Marilyn Monroe (1926-62), Actress — A582

2005, Jan. 26 *Perf. 14*
2343 A582 $12 multi .70 .70

Prehistoric Animals — A583

No. 2344, $50: a, Torosaurus. b, Tyrannosaurus. c, Polacanthus. d, Stegosaurus.
No. 2345, $50: a, Smilodon. b, Brontothere. c, Doedicurus. d, Moeritherium.
No. 2346, $50: a, Cymbospondylus. b, Archelon. c, Xiphactinus. d, Dunkleosteus.
No. 2347, $120, Stegosaurus, diff. No. 2348, $120, Woolly rhinoceros. No. 2349, $120, Odobenocetops.

2005, Jan. 26 *Perf. 13¼x13½*
Sheets of 4, #a-d
2344-2346 A583 Set of 3 32.50 32.50

Souvenir Sheet
2347-2349 A583 Set of 3 18.00 18.00

Battle of Trafalgar, Bicent. — A584

Various ships: $10, $20, $40, $50.
$100, Death of Admiral Horatio Nelson.

2005, May 4 *Perf. 14¼*
2350-2353 A584 Set of 4 6.00 6.00

Souvenir Sheet
2354 A584 $100 multi 5.50 5.50

Hans Christian Andersen (1805-75), Author — A585

No. 2355: a, Medal. b, Open book. c, Andersen.
$100, Sketch of Little Mermaid.

2005, May 4 *Perf. 14¼*
2355 A585 $50 Sheet of 3, #a-c 7.50 7.50

Souvenir Sheet
2356 A585 $100 multi 5.50 5.50

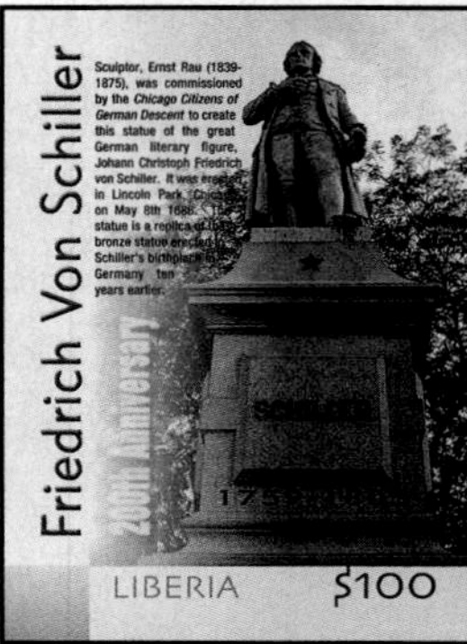

Friedrich von Schiller (1759-1805), Writer — A586

No. 2357: a, Bust of Schiller on round pedestal. b, Bust and foliage. c, Bust on monument.
$100, Statue of Schiller, Chicago.

2005, May 4 *Perf. 14¼*
2357 A586 $50 Sheet of 3, #a-c 7.50 7.50

Size: 48x67mm
Imperf
2358 A586 $100 multi 5.50 7.50

No. 2357 contains three 28x42mm stamps.

Miniature Sheets

Elvis Presley (1935-77) — A587

No. 2359, $35 — Presley in: a, 1956. b, 1969. c, 1969 (country name in yellow). d, 1969 (country name in pink). e, 1970.
No. 2360, $35 — Presley wearing: a, Red suit and white shirt. b, Yellow sweater. c, Red shirt. d, Brown suit. e, Gray suit.

2005, May 19 *Perf. 13½x13¼*
Sheets of 5, #a-e
2359-2360 A587 Set of 2 19.00 19.00

Pope John Paul II (1920-2005) A588

2005, Aug. 22 *Perf. 12¾*
2361 A588 $50 multi 2.50 2.50

Printed in sheets of 4.

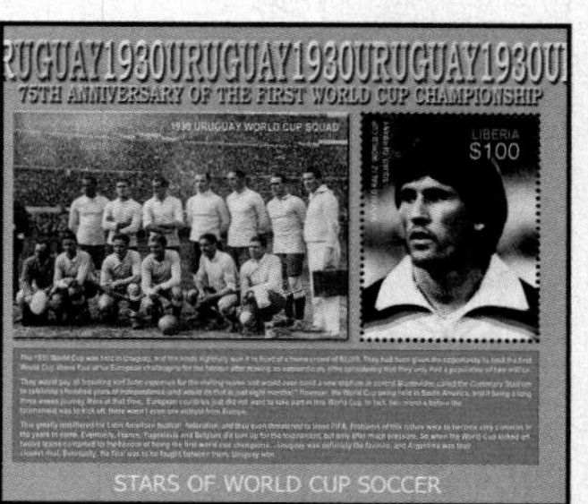

World Cup Soccer Championships, 75th Anniv. — A589

No. 2362: a, Norbert Eder. b, Paul Breitner. c, Thomas Helmer.
$100, Manfred Kaltz.

2005, Aug. 22 ***Perf. 13¼***
2362 A589 $60 Sheet of 3, #a-c 10.00 10.00

Souvenir Sheet
Perf. 12
2363 A589 $100 multi 5.50 5.50

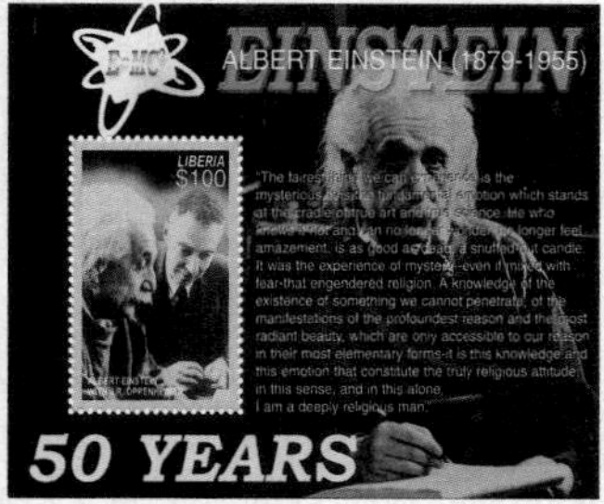

Albert Einstein (1879-1955), Physicist — A590

No. 2364 — Einstein and: a, Charlie Chaplin. b, Max Planck. c, William Allen White.
$100, J. Robert Oppenheimer

2005, Aug. 22 ***Perf. 12¾***
2364 A590 $60 Sheet of 3, #a-c 7.50 7.50

Souvenir Sheet
2365 A590 $100 multi 4.25 4.25

End of World War II, 60th Anniv. — A591

No. 2366, $40 — V-E Day: a, Gen. Dwight D. Eisenhower. b, Prime Minister Winston Churchill. c, Gen. George Patton. d, Field Marshal Bernard Montgomery.
No. 2367, $40 — V-E Day: a, Air Marshal Sir Arthur "Bomber" Harris. b, Gen. Douglas MacArthur. c, Field Marshal Alan Brooke. d, Pres. Franklin D. Roosevelt.
No. 2368, $40 — V-J Day: a, RAF Wellington bomber. b, Mitsubishi A6M Zero. c, RAF Hudson bomber. d, B-17 bomber.
No. 2369, $40 — V-J Day: a, P-51 Mustang. b, RAF Hamilcar glider. c, P-38 Lightning. d, RAF Supermarine Spitfire.

2005, Aug. 22 ***Perf. 13¼x13½***
Sheets of 4, #a-d
2366-2369 A591 Set of 4 26.00 26.00

Worldwide Fund for Nature (WWF) — A592

No. 2370: a, Jentink's duiker. b, Head of Ogilby's duiker. c, Ogilby's duiker. d, Head of Jentink's duiker.

2005, Aug. 31 ***Perf. 14***
2370 A592 $20 Block or vert. strip of 4, #a-d 3.25 3.25
e. Miniature sheet, 2 each #2370a-2370d 6.50 6.50

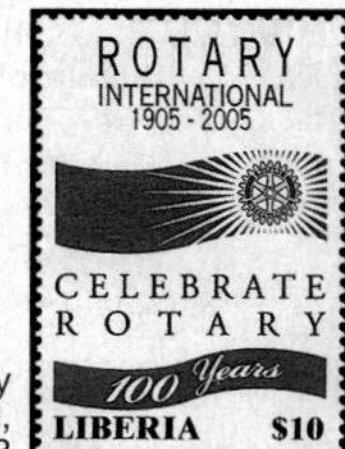

Rotary International, Cent. — A593

Emblem: $10, $25, $35, $50.
$100, Mother Teresa.

2005, Sept. 22 ***Perf. 14***
2371-2374 A593 Set of 4 5.00 5.00

Souvenir Sheet
2375 A593 $100 multi 4.25 4.25

Christmas — A594

Paintings: $20, Glory to God, by Kim Ki-chang. $25, Flight Into Egypt, by Fra Angelico. $30, Christmas Mom, by Will Hickock Low. $50, The Nativity, by Bernadino Luini.
$100, Adoration of the Magi, by Nicolas Poussin.

2005, Dec. 1
2376-2379 A594 Set of 4 5.25 5.25

Souvenir Sheet
2380 A594 $100 multi 4.25 4.25

Elvis Presley (1935-77) — A595

Illustration reduced.

Variable Serpentine Die Cut
2006, Jan. 17 Litho. & Embossed
Without Gum
2381 A595 $350 gold & multi 14.50 14.50

African Antelopes — A596

No. 2382: a, Gemsbok. b, Kudu. c, Sable antelope. d, Impala.
$100, Springbok.

2006, Jan. 17 Litho. ***Perf. 13½***
2382 A596 $45 Sheet of 4, #a-d 7.50 7.50

Souvenir Sheet
2383 A596 $100 multi 4.25 4.25

Mammals — A597

No. 2384: a, Jackal. b, Fox. c, Wolf. d, Coyote.
$100, Hyena.

2006, Jan. 17
2384 A597 $45 Sheet of 4, #a-d 7.50 7.50

Souvenir Sheet
2385 A597 $100 multi 4.25 4.25

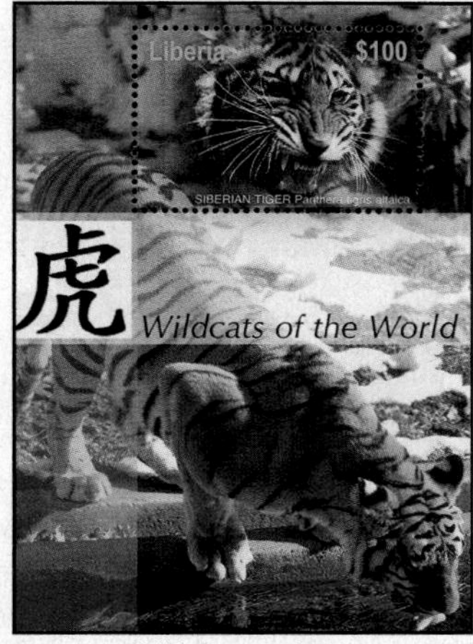

Wild Cats — A598

No. 2386: a, Jaguar. b, Lion. c, Puma. d, Cheetah.
$100, Siberian tiger.

2006, Jan. 17
2386 A598 $45 Sheet of 4, #a-d 7.50 7.50

Souvenir Sheet
2387 A598 $100 multi 4.25 4.25

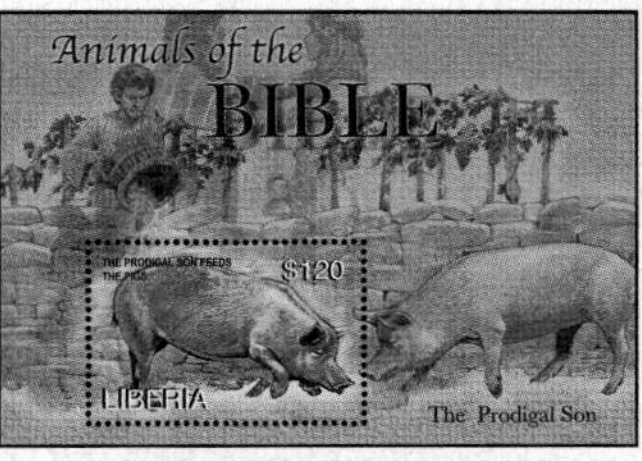

Animals of the Bible — A599

No. 2388, $45: a, Lions. b, Camels. c, Doves. d, Donkey.
No. 2389, $45: a, Foxes. b, Vultures. c, Turtles. d, Ducks.
No. 2390, $45: a, Goat. b, Bear. c, Ravens. d, Sheep.
No. 2391, $120, Pig. No. 2392, $120, Whale. No. 2393, $120, Snake.

2006, Jan. 17
Sheets of 4, #a-d
2388-2390 A599 Set of 3 22.50 22.50

Souvenir Sheets
2391-2393 A599 Set of 3 15.00 15.00

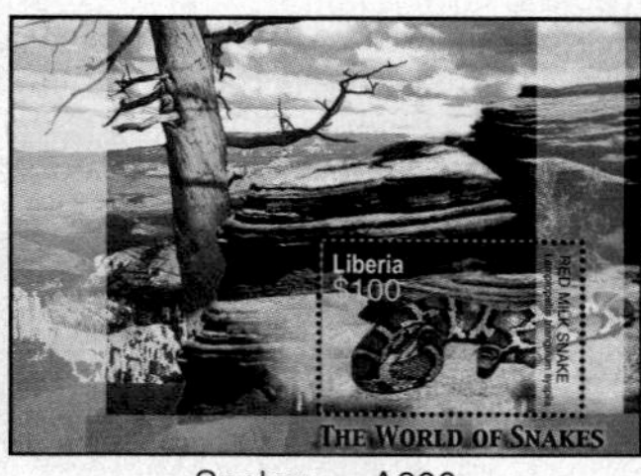

Snakes — A600

No. 2394: a, Rough green snake. b, Speckled king snake. c, Garter snake. d, Brown snake.
$100, Red milk snake.

2006, Jan. 27
2394 A600 $45 Sheet of 4, #a-d 7.50 7.50

Souvenir Sheet
2395 A600 $100 multi 4.25 4.25

2006 Winter Olympics, Turin — A601

Designs: $20, Austria #B337. $25, Poster for 1976 Innsbruck Winter Olympics, vert. $35, Austria #B338. $50, Austria #B335. $70, US #3555. $100, Poster for 2002 Salt Lake City Winter Olympics, vert.

2006, Apr. 6 ***Perf. 13½***
2396-2399 A601 Set of 4 5.50 5.50
2399A A601 $70 multi 3.00 3.00
2399B A601 $100 multi 4.25 4.25

Nos. 2399A-2399B were not made available until 2007.

Souvenir Sheet

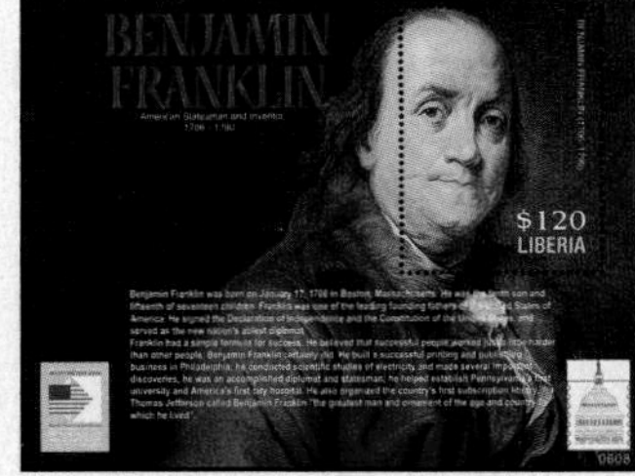

Benjamin Franklin (1706-90), Statesman — A602

2006, May 27 ***Perf. 13½***
2400 A602 $120 multi 5.00 5.00

Washington 2006 World Philatelic Exhibition.

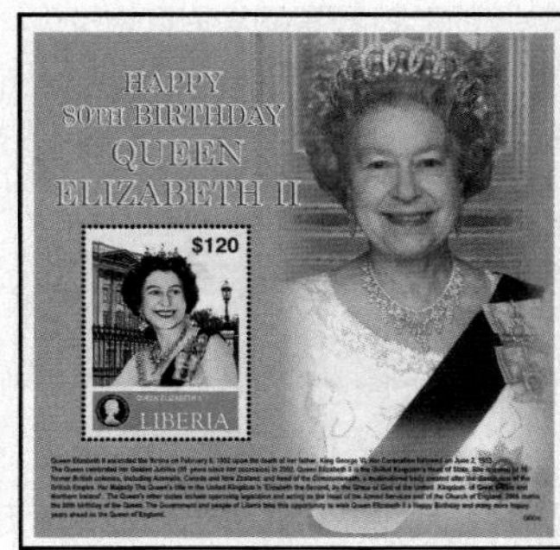

Queen Elizabeth II, 80th Birthday — A603

No. 2401 — Hat color: a, Green. b, Blue. c, Beige. d, Black.
$120, Queen wearing tiara.

2006, June 13 ***Perf. 14¼***
2401 A603 $40 Sheet of 4, #a-d 6.50 6.50

Souvenir Sheet

2402 A603 $120 multi 5.00 5.00

Rembrandt (1606-69), Painter A604

Artwork: $15, Young Man in a Turban. $30, Man Leaning on a Windowsill. $40, Officer with a Gold Chain. $45, The Art Dealer Clement de Jonghe.

No. 2407, $60: a, Self-portrait, 1633. b, Self-portrait, 1634. c, Self-portrait, 1639. d, Self-portrait, 1640.

No. 2408, $60: a, Christ and the Canaanite Woman. b, The Mocking of Christ. c, Head of an Old Man (Three-quarters view). d, Head of an Old Man (profile).

No. 2409, $60: a, David and Jonathan. b, Nude Woman with a Snake. c, The Abduction of Europa. d, Daniel and Cyrus Before the Idol Bel.

No. 2410, $60: a, Shah Jahan and Dara Shikoh. b, Farm Building Surrounded by Trees. c, Two Thatched Cottages with Figures at Window. d, A Sailing Boat on Wide Expanse of Water.

No. 2411, $120, Bearded Old Man with a Gold Chain. No. 2412, $120, A Scholar in His Study. No. 2413, $120, Rembrandt's Mother. No. 2414, $120, Portrait of Jan Six.

2006, June 13 **Litho.**
2403-2406 A604 Set of 4 5.50 5.50

Sheets of 4, #a-d

2407-2410 A604 Set of 4 40.00 40.00

Imperf

Size: 76x103mm

2411-2414 A604 Set of 4 20.00 20.00

Souvenir Sheet

Wolfgang Amadeus Mozart (1756-91), Composer — A605

2006, July 25 ***Perf. 12¾***
2415 A605 $120 multi 5.00 5.00

Miniature Sheet

Chinese Ceramics — A606

No. 2416: a, Bowl with red, black and white exterior, brown interior. b, Bowl with blue and white exterior, blue, red and white interior. c, Bowl with green on white exterior, square opening. d, Bowl with red, white and blue exterior, brown interior. e, Bowl with green on white exterior, circular opening. f, Bowl with red, white and green exterior, square opening.

2006, Aug. 16 ***Perf. 12x12¼***
2416 A606 $35 Sheet of 6, #a-f 8.75 8.75

Inauguration of Pres. Ellen Johnson-Sirleaf — A607

Designs: $10, Pres. Johnson-Sirleaf and flag. $25, Certification by National Election Commission, horiz. $30, Casting of ballots. $40, Pres. Johnson-Sirleaf holding child, horiz.

$100, Pres. Johnson-Sirleaf at microphone.

2006, Aug. 22 ***Perf. 13¼***
2417-2420 A607 Set of 4 4.25 4.25

Souvenir Sheet

2421 A607 $100 multi 4.25 4.25

Millennium Development Goals — A608

Goals: No. 2422, $10, Achieve universal primary education (graduates). No. 2423, $10, Promote gender equality and empower women. No. 2424, $25, Eradicate extreme hunger and poverty. No. 2425, $25, Reduce child mortality. No. 2426, $30, Develop a global partnership for development (map). No. 2427, $30, Develop a global partnership for development (ships and airplane). $40, Improve maternal health. $50, Achieve universal primary education (classroom). No. 2430, $100, Ensure environmental sustainability. No. 2431, $100, Combat HIV/AIDS, malaria and other diseases.

No. 2432, Achieve universal primary education (classroom), vert.

2006, Sept. 22
2422-2431 A608 Set of 10 17.50 17.50

Souvenir Sheet

2432 A608 $100 multi 4.25 4.25

Space Achievements — A609

No. 2433, $40 — Intl. Space Station: a, Country name and denomination in black, at top. b, Country name in black, denomination in white. c, Country name and denomination in white, at top. d, Country name and denomination in black, at bottom. e, Space shuttle (country name and denomination in white, at bottom). f, Astronaut (country name and denomination in white, at bottom.

No. 2434, $40, vert. — Apollo 11: a, Lunar module. b, Rocket on launch pad. c, Nose cone of rocket. d, Astronaut on moon. e, Command module. f, Astronauts and rocket.

No. 2435, $55, vert. — First Flight of Space Shuttle Columbia: a, Astronaut Bob Crippen. b, Front of space shuttle. c, Astronaut John Young. d, Tail of space shuttle.

No. 2436, $55 — Space Shuttle returns to space: a, Wing. b, Fuselage, reflection of sunlight. c, Wing inscribed "Discovery." d, Fuselage and Earth.

No. 2437, $120, Apollo-Soyuz. No. 2438, $120, Mars Reconnaissance Orbiter. No. 2439, $120, Venus Express. No. 2440, $120, Deep Impact Probe.

2006, Oct. 3 **Litho.** ***Perf. 12¾***

Sheets of 6, #a-f

2433-2434 A609 Set of 2 20.00 20.00

Sheets of 4, #a-d

2435-2436 A609 Set of 2 18.00 18.00

Souvenir Sheets

2437-2440 A609 Set of 4 20.00 20.00

Christopher Columbus (1451-1506), Explorer — A610

Designs: $25, Columbus, drawings of ships. $50, Columbus, ships, horiz. $70, Columbus and Santa Maria, horiz. $100, Ship, crew encountering natives, horiz.

$120, Men on shore.

2006, Nov. 15
2441-2444 A610 Set of 4 10.00 10.00

Souvenir Sheet

2445 A610 $120 multi 5.00 5.00

Souvenir Sheet

Christmas — A611

No. 2446 — Details from The Adoration of the Magi, by Peter Paul Rubens: a, Man and boy. b, Mary. c, Man with headcovering. d, Infant Jesus.

2006, Dec. 21 **Litho.** ***Perf. 14***
2446 A611 $40 Sheet of 4, #a-d 6.75 6.75

A612

Concorde — A613

No. 2447, $30 — Concorde: a, G-BOAF. b, G-BOAB.

No. 2448, $35 — Concorde: a, F-BVFA on runway. b, G-BOAA taking off.

Illustrations reduced.

2007, Mar. 1 **Litho.** ***Perf. 13½***

Horiz. Pairs, #a-b

2447-2448 A612 Set of 2 5.50 5.50

Litho. & Embossed

Without Gum

Irregular Serpentine Die Cut

2449 A613 $350 gold & multi 14.50 14.50

Souvenir Sheet

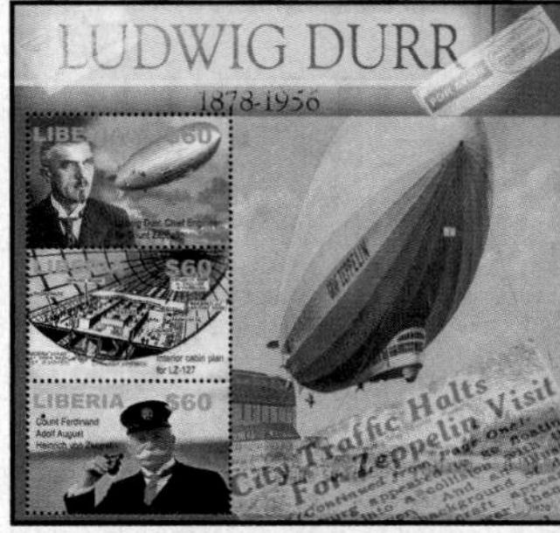
Ludwig Durr (1878-1956), Engineer — A614

No. 2450: a, Durr and Zeppelin. b, Interior cabin plan for LZ-127. c, Count Ferdinand von Zeppelin.

2007, Mar. 1 **Litho.** ***Perf. 13¼***
2450 A614 $60 Sheet of 3, #a-c 7.50 7.50

Souvenir Sheet

Marilyn Monroe (1926-62), Actress — A615

Various portraits.

2007, Mar. 1
2451 A615 $50 Sheet of 4, #a-d 8.25 8.25

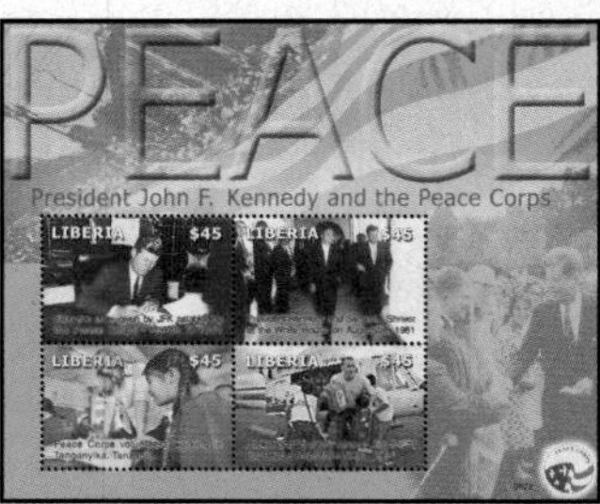
Pres. John F. Kennedy (1917-62) — A616

No. 2452, $45: a, Signing executive order establishing the Peace Corps. b, With Sargent Shriver. c, Peace Corps volunteers in Tanganyika. d, Jack Hood Vaughn, second director of Peace Corps.

No. 2453, $45 — Kennedy: a, And Eleanor Roosevelt. b, Delivering Alliance for Progress speech. c, With Mrs. Kennedy in Venezuela. d, And Secretary of State Dean Rusk.

2007, Mar. 1 **Litho.**

Sheets of 4, #a-d

2452-2453 A616 Set of 2 15.00 15.00

Mushrooms A617

Designs: $25, Boletus edulis. $35, Begriipt russula. No. 2456, $45, Lactarius helvus. $50, Amanita pantherina.

No. 2458, $45: a, Russula cyanoxantha. b, Cantharellus subalbidus. c, Leccinum oxydalile. d, Boletus badius.

No. 2459, $45: a, Amanita bingensis. b, Chlorophyllum molybdites. c, Calvatia utriformis. d, Amanita loosii.

No. 2460, $100, Amanita muscaria. No. 2461, $100, Chlorophyllum molybdites, diff. No. 2462, $100, Agaricus silvaticus.

2007, Mar. 1
2454-2457 A617 Set of 4 6.50 6.50

Sheets of 4, #a-d

2458-2459 A617 Set of 2 15.00 15.00

Souvenir Sheets

2460-2462 A617 Set of 3 12.50 12.50

Scouting, Cent. A618

Designs: $50, Scouts and 2006 World Jamboree emblem. $150, Scouts, horiz.

2007, Mar. 15
2463 A618 $50 multi 1.75 1.75

Souvenir Sheet

2464 A618 $150 multi 5.00 5.00

No. 2463 was printed in sheets of 4.

Pope Benedict XVI — A619

2007, Nov. 30 Litho. ***Perf. 13¼***
2465 A619 $30 multi 1.00 1.00

Miniature Sheet

New Year 2007 (Year of the Boar) — A620

No. 2466 — Wild Boar, by Liu Jiyou with text "Year of the Boar" in: a, Red. b, Green. c, Brown. d, Blue.

2007, Nov. 30
2466 A620 $30 Sheet of 4, #a-d 4.00 4.00

Miniature Sheet

Wedding of Queen Elizabeth II and Prince Philip, 60th Anniv. — A621

No. 2467: a, Couple, denomination in white. b, Queen, denomination in yellow. c, Couple, denomination in lilac. d, Queen, denomination in white. e, Couple, denomination in yellow. f, Queen, denomination in lilac.

2007, Nov. 30
2467 A621 $35 Sheet of 6, #a-f 7.00 7.00

Princess Diana (1961-97) — A622

No. 2468 — Various depictions of Diana with denomination in: a, Red violet. b, Blue. c, Green. d, Red.
$125, Red denomination.

2007, Nov. 30
2468 A622 $45 Sheet of 4, #a-d 6.00 6.00

Souvenir Sheet

2469 A622 $125 multi 4.25 4.25

Souvenir Sheets

Pres. Ellen Johnson-Sirleaf and Foreign Dignitaries — A623

Pres. Johnson-Sirleaf meeting with: No. 2470, $100, Chinese Pres. Hu Jintao. No. 2471, $100, U.S. Pres. George W. Bush.

2007, Nov. 30
2470-2471 A623 Set of 2 6.50 6.50

Miniature Sheet

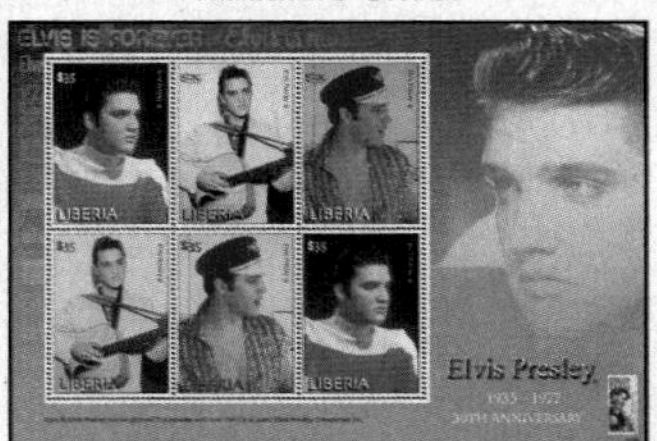

Elvis Presley (1935-77) — A624

No. 2472 — Presley: a, Wearing red and white sweater, country name in white. b, Holding guitar, country name in blue. c, Wearing cap, country name in white. d, Holding guitar, country name in purple. e, Wearing cap, country name in red violet. f, Wearing red and white sweater, country name in yellow.

2007, Nov. 30
2472 A624 $35 Sheet of 6, #a-f 7.00 7.00

Souvenir Sheet

Japanese Prime Minister Junchiro Koizumi, U.S. Pres. George W. Bush and Wife at Graceland — A625

2007, Nov. 30
2473 A625 $100 multi 3.25 3.25

New Year 2008 (Year of the Rat) A626

2007, Dec. 26 Litho. ***Perf. 11½x12***
2474 A626 $25 multi .85 .85

Printed in sheets of 4.

Birds — A627

Designs: $20, Pin-tailed whydahs. $30, Lesser honeyguides. $40, African jacanas. $50, Malachite sunbirds.

No. 2479, $45, horiz.: a, White-brown sparrow weavers. b, Parasitic weavers. c, Black-winged orioles. d, Crested guineafowl.

No. 2480, $45, horiz.: a, Red-billed francolins. b, Rufous-crowned rollers. c, African golden orioles. d, Black-crowned tchagras.

No. 2481, $100, Kori bustard. No. 2482, $100, Ostrich. No. 2483, $100, Great white pelican, horiz.

2007, Dec. 26 ***Perf. 14***
2475-2478 A627 Set of 4 4.75 4.75

Sheets of 4, #a-d

2479-2480 A627 Set of 2 12.00 12.00

Souvenir Sheets

2481-2483 A627 Set of 3 10.00 10.00

Butterflies — A628

Designs: $20, Appias epaphia. $30, Papilio bromius. $40, Charaxes jasius. $50, Mimacraea marshalli dohertyi.

No. 2488, $45: a, Belenois thysa. b, Papilio pelodorus. c, Cymothoe sangaris. d, Colotis aurigineus.

No. 2489, $45: a, Junonia hierta. b, Myrina silenus. c, Byblia ilithyia. d, Argyrogrammana attsonii.

No. 2490, $100, Iolaus menas. No. 2491, $100, Leptomyrina hirundo. No. 2492, $100, Pinacopteryx eriphia.

2007, Dec. 26
2484-2487 A628 Set of 4 4.75 4.75

Sheets of 4, #a-d

2488-2489 A628 Set of 2 12.00 12.00

Souvenir Sheets

2490-2492 A628 Set of 3 10.00 10.00

Orchids — A629

Designs: $20, Neobenthamia gracilis. $30, Eulophia guineensis. $40, Aerangis curnowiana. $50, Cymbidiella pardalina.

No. 2497, $45: a, Ophrys lutea. b, Ophrys holoserica. c, Ophrys fusca. d, Ophrys scolopax.

No. 2498, $45: a, Disa veitchii. b, Disa racemosa. c, Disa kewensis. d, Disa diores.

No. 2499, $100, Disa crassicornis. No. 2500, $100, Aerangis citrata. No. 2501, $100, Angraecum sororium.

2007, Dec. 26
2493-2496 A629 Set of 4 4.75 4.75

Sheets of 4, #a-d

2497-2498 A629 Set of 2 12.00 12.00

Souvenir Sheets

2499-2501 A629 Set of 3 10.00 10.00

Christmas A630

Designs: $30, Madonna and Child. $40, Holy Family. $45, Flight into Egypt. $50, The Three Magi, horiz.

2007, Dec. 26 ***Perf. 14x14¾, 14¾x14***
2502-2505 A630 Set of 4 5.50 5.50

Miniature Sheet

2008 Summer Olympics, Beijing — A631

No. 2506: a, Babe Didrikson. b, 1932 Summer Olympics poster. c, Helene Madison. d, Chuhei Nambu.

2008, Apr. 8 ***Perf. 12¾***
2506 A631 $30 Sheet of 4, #a-d 4.00 4.00

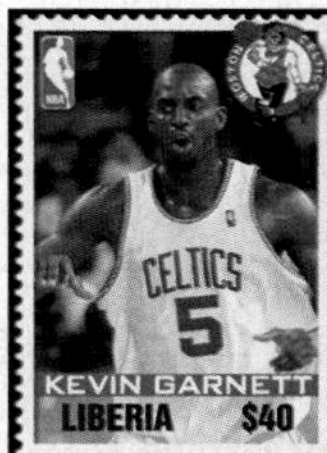

National Basketball Association Players — A632

No. 2507 — NBA and Boston Celtics emblems and Kevin Garnett: a, Wearing white uniform, not holding basketball. b, Wearing green uniform. c, Wearing white uniform, holding basketball.

No. 2508 — NBA and Boston Celtics emblems and Paul Pierce: a, Wearing white uniform, hands at side. b, Wearing green uniform. c, Wearing white uniform, pointing.

No. 2509 — NBA and Washington Wizards emblems and Gilbert Arenas: a, Wearing white uniform, hands on hips. b, Wearing blue uniform. c, Wearing white uniform, with basketball.

No. 2510 — NBA and Milwaukee Bucks emblems and Yi Jianlian: a, Wearing white uniform, basketball at left. b, Wearing blue green uniform. c, Wearing white uniform, basketball at right.

2008, Apr. 30 *Perf. 13½x13¼*

2507	Vert. strip of 3	4.00	4.00
a.-c.	A632 $40 Any single	1.25	1.25
2508	Vert. strip of 3	4.00	4.00
a.-c.	A632 $40 Any single	1.25	1.25
2509	Vert. strip of 3	4.00	4.00
a.-c.	A632 $40 Any single	1.25	1.25
2510	Vert. strip of 3	4.00	4.00
a.-c.	A632 $40 Any single	1.25	1.25
	Nos. 2507-2510 (4)	16.00	16.00

Nos. 2507-2510 each printed in sheets of 6 containing 2 of each stamp in strip.

Souvenir Sheet

Meeting of Liberian Pres. Ellen Johnson-Sirleaf and US Pres. George W. Bush. — A633

No. 2511: a, Pres. Bush. b, Pres. Johnson-Sirleaf.

2008, June 12 *Perf. 13¼*

2511 A633 $125 Sheet of 2, #a-b 8.00 8.00

Elvis Presley (1935-77) — A634

No. 2512 — Presley: a, Holding microphone, red background. b, Holding microphone, "Elvis" in lights. c, Holding microphone, blue background. d, Wearing glasses.

2008, June 12 *Perf. 13¼*

2512 A634 $60 Sheet of 4, #a-d 7.75 7.75

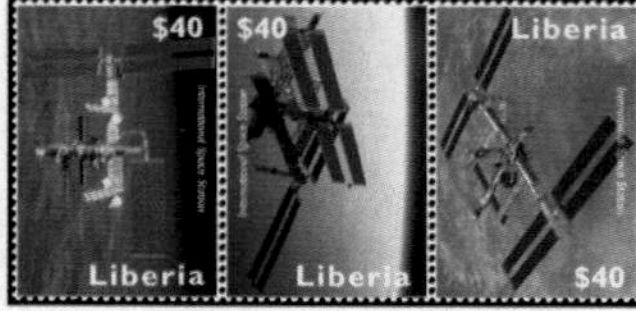

Space Achievements — A635

No. 2513, $40 — International Space Station with denomination at: a, UR. b, UL. c, LR.

No. 2514, $40 — Chandra X-ray Observatory: a, Observatory below nebula. b, Interior of Observatory. c, Observatory above nebula.

No. 2515: a, Calisto, Europa, Voyager I, Jupiter and Io. b, Lift-off of Voyager I. c, Voyager I record cover. d, Voyager I, Titan and Saturn.

No. 2516, $150, International Space Station, horiz. No. 2517, $150, Chandra X-ray Observatory, horiz. No. 2518, $150, Voyager I and rings of Saturn, horiz.

Illustration reduced.

2008, June 12 *Perf. 13¼*

Horiz. Strips of 3, #a-c

2513-2514 A635 Set of 2 7.75 7.75

Miniature Sheet

2515 A635 $60 Sheet of 4, #a-d 7.75 7.75

Souvenir Sheets

2516-2518 A635 Set of 3 14.50 14.50

Nos. 2513-2514 were each printed in sheets of 6 containing 2 of each stamp in strip.

Pope Benedict XVI — A636

2008, June 30 **Litho.**

2519 A636 $45 multi 1.50 1.50

Printed in sheets of 4.

County Flags A637

Flag of: No. 2520, $10, Maryland County. No. 2521, $10, Montserrado County. No. 2522, $25, Gbarpolu County. No. 2523, $25, Grand Bassa County. No. 2524, $30, Grand Cape Mount County. No. 2525, $30, Nimba County. No. 2526, $40, Lofa County. No. 2527, $40, Sinoe County. No. 2528, $50, Bong County. No. 2529, $50, Margibi County. No. 2530, $100, Bomi County. No. 2531, $100, Grand Gedeh County. No. 2532, $100, Grand Kru County. No. 2533, $100, River Cess County. No. 2534, $100, River Gee County.

2008, June 30

2520-2534 A637 Set of 15 26.00 26.00

Miniature Sheet

Ferrari F2008 — A638

No. 2535: a, "F" under "E" of "Liberia." b, "F" under "B" of Liberia. c, Side view of car. d, Car straddling yellow line on track.

2008, Sept. 5 **Litho.** *Perf. 13½*

2535 A638 $60 Sheet of 4, #a-d 7.75 7.75

A639

Election of Barack Obama as US President — A640

Inscriptions: No. 2537, Joseph Biden. No. 2539a, Joseph Robinette Biden, Jr.

Perf. 14¼x14¾, 12¼x11¾ (#2538)

2008, Nov. 5

2536	A639 $45 shown	1.50	1.50
2537	A639 $45 multi	1.50	1.50
2538	A640 $65 shown	2.10	2.10
	Nos. 2536-2538 (3)	5.10	5.10

Souvenir Sheet

2539	Sheet of 2, #2536, 2539a	3.00	3.00
a.	A639 $45 multi	1.50	1.50

No. 2536 was printed in sheets of 9 and in No. 2539. No. 2537 was printed in sheets of 9. No. 2538 was printed in sheets of 4.

A641

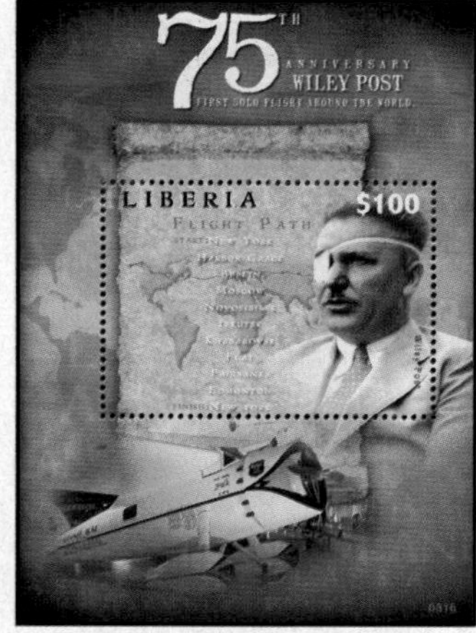

Solo Aerial Circumnavigation of the World by Wiley Post, 75th Anniv. — A642

No. 2540: a, Post arriving in Cleveland. b, Harold Gatty, navigator. c, Post wearing pressure suit. d, Post atop plane. e, Post and wife Mae. f, The Winnie Mae.

$100, Post and map of flight.

2008, Nov. 24 *Perf. 13¼*

2540 A641 $40 Sheet of 6, #a-f 7.75 7.75

Souvenir Sheet

2541 A642 $100 multi 3.25 3.25

SEMI-POSTAL STAMPS

No. 127 Surcharged in Red

1915 **Unwmk.** *Perf. 14*

B1	A49 2c + 3c on 10c	1.00	*3.50*
a.	Double red surcharge		
b.	Double blue surcharge		
c.	Both surcharges double		
d.	Pair, one without "2c"		

Same Surcharge On Official Stamp of 1912

B2	A49 2c + 3c on 10c blk & ultra	1.00	*3.50*
a.	Double surcharge		

Regular Issue of 1918 Surcharged in Black and Red

1918 *Perf. 12½, 14*

B3	A59 1c + 2c dp grn & blk	1.40	*10.50*
B4	A60 2c + 2c rose & blk	1.40	*10.50*
a.	Double surch., one inverted		
b.	Invtd. surch., cross double		
c.	Invtd. surch., cross omitted	17.00	
B5	A61 5c + 2c gray bl & blk	.65	*3.00*
a.	Imperf., pair	19.00	
B6	A62 10c + 2c dk green	1.25	*3.00*
a.	Inverted surcharge	5.75	27.50
B7	A63 15c + 2c blk & dk grn	5.25	10.50
B8	A64 20c + 2c claret & blk	2.10	*8.50*
B9	A65 25c + 2c dk grn & grn	4.25	*15.00*
B10	A66 30c + 2c red vio & blk	10.00	*10.50*
B11	A67 50c + 2c ultra & blk	8.50	*16.00*
B12	A68 75c + 2c ol bis & blk	3.75	*30.00*
B13	A69 $1 + 2c yel brn & bl	6.25	*57.50*
B14	A70 $2 + 2c lt vio & blk	8.50	*80.00*
B15	A71 $5 + 2c dk brown	20.00	*200.00*
	Nos. B3-B15 (13)	73.30	*455.00*

Used values are for postally canceled stamps.

Nos. 277-279 Surcharged in Red or Blue

1941 **Unwmk.** *Perf. 12*

B16	A107 3c + 2c dk blue (R)	2.25	2.25
B17	A108 5c + 2c dull red brn	2.25	2.25
B18	A109 10c + 2c dk grn (R)	2.25	2.25
	Nos. B16-B18 (3)	6.75	6.75

Catalogue values for unused stamps in this section, from this point to the end of the section, are for Never Hinged items.

Research — SP1

Lithographed and Engraved

1954 **Unwmk.** *Perf. 12½*

B19	SP1 5c + 5c rose lilac & blk	.20	.20
	Nos. B19,CB4-CB6 (4)	.80	.80

The surtax was for the Liberian Government Hospital. No. B19 exists imperforate.

Remember the African Child SP2

Designs: 25c + 10c, Village life. 70c + 20c, Mr. Sean feeding children. 75c + 15c, Fleeing conflict. 80c + 20c, Nuns teaching children. No. B24, Nuns killed in Oct. 1992, vert. No. B25, Sean Devereux (1964-93), vert.

Perf. 13½x14

1994, Jan. 6 Unwmk. Litho.

B20	SP2	25c +10c multi	1.00	1.00
B21	SP2	70c +20c multi	3.25	3.25
B22	SP2	75c +15c multi	3.25	3.25
B23	SP2	80c +20c multi	3.50	3.50
		Nos. B20-B23 (4)	11.00	11.00

Souvenir Sheets

B24	SP2	$1.50 +50c multi	7.50	7.50
B25	SP2	$1.50 +50c multi	7.50	7.50

Surtax for Sean Devereux Liberian Children's Fund.

Charities — SP3

Designs: 25c+10c, No. B30, Natl. map in flag colors, blind man with cane. No. B27, Logo depicting children. No. B28, Blind man crossing street. No. B29, Dr. Herman Gmeiner, children.

1995 Litho. *Perf. 14*

B26	SP3	25c +10c multi	1.25	1.25
B27	SP3	80c +20c multi	3.50	3.50
B28	SP3	80c +20c multi	3.50	3.50
B29	SP3	$1.50 +50c multi	6.75	6.75
B30	SP3	$1.50 +50c multi	6.75	6.75
		Nos. B26-B30 (5)	21.75	21.75

Christian Assoc. of the Blind, 10th anniv. (#B26, B28, B30). SOS Children's Village (#B27, B29).

Issued: #B27, B29, 4/26; others, 4/28.

George Weah, Soccer Player — SP4

Designs: 50c+20c, In AC Milan strip. 75c+25c, In Liberia Natl. strip. 80c+20c, With 1989 Golden Ball Award. $1.50+50c, Two-time Golden Ball Winner.

1995, Oct. 6 Litho. *Perf. 13x13½*

B31	SP4	50c +20c multi	2.50	2.50
B32	SP4	75c +25c multi	3.50	3.50
B33	SP4	80c +20c multi	3.50	3.50
B34	SP4	$1.50 +50c multi	7.25	7.25
a.		Souvenir sheet of 1, perf. 13	7.25	7.25
		Nos. B31-B34 (4)	16.75	16.75

Issued: No. B34a, 6/24/96. Surcharge for Liberian charities supported by George Weah.

AIR POST STAMPS

Regular Issue of 1928 Surcharged in Black "AIR MAIL" and New Values

1936, Feb. 28 Unwmk. *Perf. 12*

C1	A102	6c on 2c violet	250.00	*275.00*
C2	A102	6c on 3c bis brn	250.00	*275.00*

Same Surcharge on Official Stamp of 1928

C3	A102	6c on 1c green	250.00	*275.00*
m.		On No. 230 (error)	*750.00*	
		Nos. C1-C3 (3)	750.00	825.00

Values are for stamps with disturbed gum. Many counterfeits exist.

Waco Plane — AP1

1936, Sept. 30 Engr. *Perf. 14*

C3A	AP1	1c yellow grn & blk	.20	.20
C3B	AP1	2c carmine & blk	.20	.20
C3C	AP1	3c purple & blk	.20	.20
C3D	AP1	4c orange & blk	.20	.20
C3E	AP1	5c blue & blk	.20	.20
C3F	AP1	6c green & blk	.20	.20
		Nos. C3A-C3F (6)	1.20	1.20

Liberia's 1st air mail service of Feb. 28, 1936.

Nos. C3A-C3F exist in pairs imperf. between (value, $50 each) and in pairs imperf. (value $15 each).

Eagle in Flight — AP2

Sikorsky Amphibian — AP5

Trimotor Plane AP3

Egrets — AP4

Designs: 3c, 30c, Albatross.

1938, Sept. 12 Photo. *Perf. 12½*

C4	AP2	1c green	.20	.20
C5	AP3	2c red orange	.40	.20
C6	AP3	3c olive green	.50	.20
C7	AP4	4c orange	.60	.20
C8	AP4	5c brt blue grn	1.00	.20
C9	AP3	10c violet	1.00	.20
C10	AP5	20c magenta	1.25	.20
C11	AP3	30c gray black	2.25	.20
C12	AP2	50c brown	3.00	.20
C13	AP5	$1 blue	5.25	.20
		Nos. C4-C13 (10)	15.45	2.00

For surcharges see Nos. C17-C36, C45-C46, C47-C48, C49-C50.

Nos. 280-282 Overprinted in Red or Dark Blue

1941, Feb. 25 *Perf. 12*

C14	A107	3c dark blue (R)	2.75	2.75
C15	A108	5c dull red brn (DB)	2.75	2.75
C16	A109	10c dark green (R)	2.75	2.75
		Nos. C14-C16 (3)	8.25	8.25

Nos. C4-C13 Surcharged in Black

1941 *Perf. 12½*

C17	AP2	50c on 1c green	*3,000.*	325.00
C18	AP3	50c on 2c red org	175.00	105.00
C19	AP3	50c on 3c ol grn	175.00	105.00
C20	AP4	50c on 4c orange	70.00	42.50
C21	AP4	50c on 5c brt bl grn	70.00	42.50
C22	AP3	50c on 10c violet	70.00	42.50
C23	AP5	50c on 20c magenta	*2,500.*	70.00
C24	AP3	50c on 30c gray blk	55.00	30.00
C25	AP2	50c brown	55.00	30.00
C26	AP5	$1 blue	70.00	30.00

Nos. C17 to C26 with Additional Overprint of Two Bars, Obliterating "1941"

1942

C27	AP2	50c on 1c green	6.75	6.75
C28	AP3	50c on 2c red org	6.75	5.75
C29	AP3	50c on 3c ol grn	6.00	5.75
C30	AP4	50c on 4c orange	4.75	6.00
C31	AP4	50c on 5c brt bl grn	3.00	3.00
C32	AP3	50c on 10c violet	4.25	4.25
C33	AP5	50c on 20c magenta	4.25	4.25
C34	AP3	50c on 30c gray blk	4.75	4.75
C35	AP2	50c brown	4.75	4.75
C36	AP5	$1 blue	4.25	4.25
		Nos. C27-C36 (10)	49.50	49.50

Plane and Air Route from United States to South America and Africa AP6

Plane over House AP7

1942-44 Engr. *Perf. 12*

C37	AP6	10c rose	.20	.20
C38	AP7	12c brt ultra ('44)	.20	.20
C39	AP7	24c turq grn ('44)	.20	.20
C40	AP6	30c brt green	.20	.20
C41	AP6	35c red lilac ('44)	.20	.20
C42	AP6	50c violet	.20	.20
C43	AP6	70c olive gray ('44)	.60	.20
C44	AP6	$1.40 scarlet ('44)	1.50	.60
		Nos. C37-C44 (8)	3.30	2.00

No. C3A-C3C, C5-C8, C12 Surcharged with New Values and Large Dot, Bar or Diagonal Line in Violet, Blue, Black or Violet and Black

1944-45 *Perf. 12½*

C45	AP3	10c on 2c (V+Bk)	35.00	25.00
C46	AP4	10c on 5c (V+Bk) ('45)	12.00	12.00
C46A	AP1	30c on 1c (Bk)	140.00	70.00
C47	AP3	30c on 3c (V)	150.00	65.00
C48	AP4	30c on 4c (V+Bk)	12.00	12.00
C48A	AP1	50c on 3c (Bk)	32.50	32.50
C48B	AP1	70c on 2c (Bk)	60.00	60.00
C49	AP3	$1 on 3c (Bl)	22.50	22.50
C50	AP2	$1 on 50c (V)	35.00	26.50
		Nos. C45-C50 (9)	499.00	325.50

These surcharges were handstamped with the possible exception of the large "10 CTS." of No. C46 and the "30 CTS." of No. C48. On No. C47, the new value was created by handstamping a small, violet, broken "O" beside the large "3" of the basic stamp.

Surcharges on Nos. C46A, C48A, C48B are found inverted. Values same as normal.

Roosevelt Type of Regular Issue

1945, Nov. 26 Engr.

C51	A116	70c brn & blk, *grysh*	1.25	1.40

Copies on thick white paper appeared later on the stamp market at reduced prices.

Monrovia Harbor Type

1947, Jan. 2

C52	A117	24c brt bluish grn	1.00	1.25
		Never hinged	2.50	

Without Inscription at Top

1947, May 16

C53	A117	25c dark carmine	.40	.45
		Never hinged	1.50	

1st US Postage Stamps Type

1947, June 6

C54	A118	12c green	.20	.20
C55	A118	25c brt red violet	.20	.20
C56	A118	50c brt blue	.20	.20
a.		Souv. sheet of 4, #300, C54-C56	42.50	
		Never hinged	100.00	
		Nos. C54-C56 (3)	.60	.60
		Set, never hinged	2.10	

No. C56a exists imperf. Values: hinged $65; never hinged $160.

Matilda Newport Firing Cannon — AP11

1947, Dec. 1 Engr. & Photo.

C57	AP11	25c scar & gray blk	1.25	.30
		Never hinged	3.50	

See note after No. 304.

Monument to Joseph J. Roberts — AP12

Centenary Monument AP14

Design: 25c, Flag of Liberia.

1947, Dec. 22 **Engr.**

C58 AP12 12c brick red .30 .20
C59 AP12 25c carmine .50 .20
C60 AP14 50c red brown .80 .45
Nos. C58-C60 (3) 1.60 .85
Set, never hinged 5.50

Centenary of independence.

L. I. A. Plane in Flight AP15

1948, Aug. 17 ***Perf. 11½***

C61 AP15 25c red 1.50 1.50
C62 AP15 50c deep blue 1.00 1.00
Set, never hinged 5.00

1st flight of Liberian Intl. Airways, Aug. 17, 1948.

Map and Citizens — AP16

Farm Couple, Arms and Agricultural Products — AP17

1949, Apr. 12 **Litho.** ***Perf. 11½***

C63 AP16 25c multicolored .35 .65
C64 AP17 50c multicolored .35 .65
Set, never hinged 2.00

Nos. C63-C64 exist perf. 12½. Definite information concerning the status of the perf. 12½ set has not reached the editors. The set also exists imperf.

Type of Regular Issue of 1948-50

Design: William V. S. Tubman.

1949, July 21 **Engr.** ***Perf. 12½***

C65 A128 25c blue & black .60 .65
Set, never hinged 1.60

See No. C118.

Sun and Open Book — AP18

UPU Monument AP19

1950, Feb. 14 **Engr.** ***Perf. 12½***

C66 AP18 25c rose carmine 1.00 .50
Set, never hinged 2.75
a. Souv. sheet of 2, #329, C66, imperf. 1.75 1.75
Set, never hinged 4.75

Campaign for National Literacy.

Catalogue values for unused stamps in this section, from this point to the end of the section, are for Never Hinged items.

1950, Apr. 21

C67 AP19 25c orange & vio 2.75 2.75
a. Souv. sheet of 3, #330-331, C67, imperf. 24.00 24.00

UPU, 75th anniv. (in 1949).
No. C67 exists imperf.

Map of Monrovia, James Monroe and Ashmun — AP20

50c, Jehudi Ashmun, President Tubman & map.

1952, Apr. 1 ***Perf. 10½***

C68 AP20 25c lilac rose & blk .20 .20
C69 AP20 50c dk blue & car .70 .70
a. Souvenir sheet of 8 24.00

Nos. C68-C69 exist imperf. Value about two and one half times that of the perf. set.

Nos. C68-C69 exist with center inverted. Value $50 each.

No. C69a contains one each of Nos. 332 and C68, and types of Nos. 333-337 and C69 with centers in black; imperf.

The 25c exists in colors of the 50c and vice versa. Value, each $8.

Flags of Five Nations — AP21

1952, Dec. 10 ***Perf. 12½***

C70 AP21 25c ultra & carmine .90 .65
a. Souvenir sheet 2.25 2.25

Nos. C70 and C70a exist imperforate.

Road Building — AP22

Designs: 25c, Ships in Monrovia harbor. 35c, Diesel locomotive. 50c, Free port, Monrovia. 70c, Roberts Field. $1, Wm. V. S. Tubman bridge.

1953, Aug. 3 **Litho.**

C71 AP22 12c orange brown .20 .20
C72 AP22 25c lilac rose .20 .20
C73 AP22 35c purple 1.00 .20
C74 AP22 50c orange 1.00 .20
C75 AP22 70c dull green 1.75 .20
C76 AP22 $1 blue 2.25 1.00
Nos. C71-C76 (6) 6.40 2.00

See Nos. C82-C87.

Flags, Emblem and Children — AP23

1954, Sept. 27

Size: 51x39mm

C77 AP23 $5 bl, red, vio bl & blk 40.00 40.00

A reproduction of No. C77, size 63x49mm, was prepared for presentation purposes. Value $35.

Half the proceeds from the sale of No. C77 was given to the UNICEF.

UN Technical Assistance Agencies — AP24

Designs: 15c, Printing instruction. 20c, Sawmill maintenance. 25c, Geography class.

1954, Oct. 25

C78 AP24 12c black & blue .20 .20
C79 AP24 15c dk brown & yel .20 .20
C80 AP24 20c black & yel grn .20 .20
C81 AP24 25c vio blue & red .80 .20
Nos. C78-C81 (4) 1.40 .80

UN Technical Assistance program.

Type of 1953 Inscribed: "Commemorating Presidential Visit U. S. A.-1954"

Designs as before.

1954, Nov. 19

C82 AP22 12c vermilion .20 .20
C83 AP22 25c blue .20 .20
C84 AP22 35c carmine rose .30 .20
C85 AP22 50c rose violet .40 .20
C86 AP22 70c orange brown .55 .25
C87 AP22 $1 dull green .80 .30
Nos. C82-C87 (6) 2.45 1.35

Visit of Pres. William V.S. Tubman to the US. Exist imperforate.

Baseball AP25

1955, Jan. 26 **Litho.** ***Perf. 12½***

C88 AP25 10c shown .30 .30
C89 AP25 12c Swimming .30 .30
C90 AP25 25c Running .30 .30
a. Souvenir sheet 18.00 18.00
Nos. C88-C90 (3) .90 .90

#C90a contains 1 each of #349, C90 with colors transposed. Exists imperf.; same value.

Costus AP26

Design: 25c, Barteria nigritiana.

1955, Sept. 28 **Unwmk.** ***Perf. 12½***

C91 AP26 20c violet, grn & yel .30 .30
C92 AP26 25c green, red & yel .30 .30

UN Emblem — AP27

UN Charter AP28

15c, General Assembly. 25c, Gabriel L. Dennis signing UN Charter for Liberia.

1955, Oct. 24 **Unwmk.** ***Perf. 12***

C93 AP27 10c ultra & red .20 .20
C94 AP27 15c violet & blk .20 .20
C95 AP27 25c green & red brn .60 .20
C96 AP28 50c brick red & grn 1.50 .20
Nos. C93-C96 (4) 2.50 .80

10th anniv. of the UN, Oct. 24, 1955.

Rotary International Headquarters, Evanston, Ill. — AP29

Design: 15c, View of Monrovia.

1955, Dec. 5 **Litho.** ***Perf. 12½***

C97 AP29 10c deep ultra & red .20 .20
C98 AP29 15c redsh brn, red & bis .70 .20

Souvenir Sheet

C99 AP29 50c deep ultra & red 1.75 1.75
Nos. C97-C99 (3) 2.65 2.15

No. C99 design as No. C97, but redrawn and with leaves omitted.

50th anniversary of Rotary International.

Nos. C97-C99 exist without Rotary emblem; No. C97 printed entirely in deep ultramarine; No. C98 with bister impression omitted.

FIPEX Type of Regular Issue

10c, New York Coliseum. 12c, Globe inscribed FIPEX. 15c, 50c, Statue of Liberty.

1956, Apr. 28 **Unwmk.** ***Perf. 12***

C100 A143 10c rose red & ultra .20 .20
C101 A143 12c orange & purple .20 .20
C102 A142 15c aqua & red lilac .90 .20
Nos. C100-C102 (3) 1.30 .60

Souvenir Sheet

C103 A142 50c lt green & brn 1.75 1.75

Olympic Park, Melbourne — AP32

20c, 40c, Map of Australia & Olympic torch.

1956, Nov. 15 **Unwmk.** ***Perf. 12***

C104 AP32 12c emerald & vio .50 .50
C105 AP32 20c multicolored .50 .50

Souvenir Sheet

C106 AP32 40c multicolored 7.50 7.50
Nos. C104-C106 (3) 8.50 8.50

16th Olympic Games, Melbourne, 11/22-12/8.

Type of Regular Issue, 1957.

12c, 25c, Idlewild airport, NYC. 15c, 50c, Roberts Field, Liberia, plane & Pres. Tubman.

Lithographed and Engraved

1957, May 4 ***Perf. 12***

C107 A146 12c brt grn & dk bl .20 .20
C108 A146 15c red brn & blk .20 .20
C109 A146 25c carmine & dk bl .75 .20
C110 A146 50c lt ultra & blk 1.40 .20
Nos. C107-C110 (4) 2.55 .80

Type of Regular Issue, 1957

Orphanage and: 15c, Nurse inoculating boy. 35c, The Kamara triplets. 70c, Children and flag.

1957, Nov. 25 **Litho.** ***Perf. 12***

C111 A147 15c lt blue & brn .20 .20
C112 A147 35c maroon & lt gray 1.00 .20

Souvenir Sheet

C113 A147 70c ultra & rose car 1.50 1.25
Nos. C111-C113 (3) 2.70 1.65

Type of Regular Issue, 1958

10c, Italian flag & Colosseum. #C115, French flag & Arc de Triomphe. #C116, Swiss flag & chalet. #C117, Vatican flag & St. Peter's.

Engr. and Litho.

1958, Jan. 10 ***Perf. 10½***

Flags in Original Colors

C114 A148 10c dark gray .45 .45
C115 A148 15c dp yellow grn .45 .45
C116 A148 15c ultra .45 .45
C117 A148 15c purple .45 .45
Nos. C114-C117 (4) 1.80 1.80

Type of Regular Issue, 1948-50

Design: William V. S. Tubman.

1958 **Engr.** ***Perf. 12***

C118 A128 25c lt green & blk 1.25 .90

Souvenir Sheet

Preamble to Declaration of Human Rights — AP33

1958, Dec. 17 **Litho.** ***Perf. 12***

C119 AP33 20c blue & red 2.75 2.75

10th anniv. of the signing of the Universal Declaration of Human Rights.

Liberians Reading Proclamation AP34

1959, Apr. 15 **Unwmk.**

C120 AP34 25c blue & brown .60 .60

African Freedom Day, Apr. 15.

UNESCO Building, Paris AP35

1959, May 1

C121 AP35 25c ultra & red .60 .50
a. Souvenir sheet 1.75 1.75

Opening of UNESCO Headquarters in Paris, Nov. 3, 1958.

Lincoln Type of Regular Issue

1959, Nov. 20 **Engr.** ***Perf. 12***

C122 A152 25c emerald & black .90 .90

For souvenir sheet see No. 386a.

Touré, Tubman and Nkrumah AP36

1960, Jan. 27 **Litho.** **Unwmk.**

C123 AP36 25c beige, vio bl & blk .60 .80

See note after No. 387.

WRY Type of Regular Issue, 1960

1960, Apr. 7 ***Perf. 11½***

C124 A154 25c ultra & black .80 .70
a. Souv. sheet of 2, #388, C124, imperf. 2.75 2.75

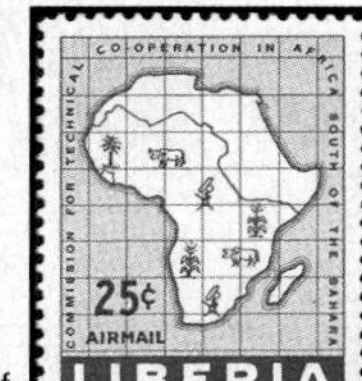

Map of Africa — AP37

1960, May 11 ***Perf. 11½***

C125 AP37 25c ultra & brown .80 .80

See note after No. 389.

Olympic Games Type of 1960

Designs: 25c, Javelin thrower and hunter, horiz. 50c, Runner and stadium, horiz.

1960, Sept. 6 ***Perf. 11½***

C126 A156 25c brown & brt ultra .90 .70

Souvenir Sheet

Imperf

C127 A156 50c lilac & brown 3.50 3.50

Stamp Centenary Type of 1960

1960, Dec. 1 **Litho.** ***Perf. 11½***

C128 A157 25c multicolored 1.00 1.00

Souvenir Sheet

C129 A157 50c multicolored 1.75 1.75

Globe, Dove and UN Emblem AP38

Design: 50c, Globe and dove.

1961, May 19 **Unwmk.** ***Perf. 11½***

C130 AP38 25c indigo & red .50 .50

Souvenir Sheet

C131 AP38 50c red brn & emerald 2.25 2.25

Liberia's membership in the UN Security Council.

A second souvenir sheet contains one each of Nos. 395, C130 and the 50c from No. C131, imperf. Size: 133x83mm.

No. C130 exists imperf.

Science Class AP39

Design: 50c, Science class, different design.

1961, Sept. 8 **Litho.**

C132 AP39 25c purple & brown .50 .20

Souvenir Sheet

C133 AP39 50c blue & brown 1.75 1.75

15th anniv. of UNESCO.

Joseph J. Roberts and Providence Island — AP40

1961, Oct. 25 **Litho.** ***Perf. 11½***

C134 AP40 25c emerald & sepia .70 .70
a. Souvenir sheet of 3 1.75 1.75

150th anniv. of the birth of Joseph J. Roberts, 1st pres. of Liberia.

No. C134a contains three imperf. stamps similar to Nos. 397-398 and C134, but printed in different colors; 5c, emerald & sepia. 10c, orange & sepia. 25c, ultramarine & sepia.

Scout Type of Regular Issue and

Boy Scout — AP41

1961, Dec. 4 **Unwmk.** ***Perf. 11½***

C135 AP41 25c emerald & sepia 1.40 1.40

Souvenir Sheet

Design: Like No. 399.

C136 A161 35c dull blue & sepia 5.00 5.00

Dag Hammarskjold Type of 1962

1962, Feb. 1 **Unwmk.** ***Perf. 12***

C137 A162 25c black & red lilac .60 .60

Souvenir Sheet

Imperf

C138 A162 50c black & ultra 1.75 1.75

Malaria Eradication Emblem AP42

1962, Apr. 7 ***Perf. 12½***

C139 AP42 25c purple & orange .60 .50

Souvenir Sheet

Imperf

C140 AP42 50c dark red & ultra 1.50 1.50

Pres. Tubman, Statue of Liberty, New York Skyline and Flags of US and Liberia AP43

1962, Sept. 17 **Litho.** ***Perf. 11½x12***

C141 AP43 12c multicolored .20 .20
C142 AP43 25c multicolored .60 .50
C143 AP43 50c multicolored 1.25 .85
Nos. C141-C143 (3) 2.05 1.55

Pres. Tubman's visit to the US in 1961.

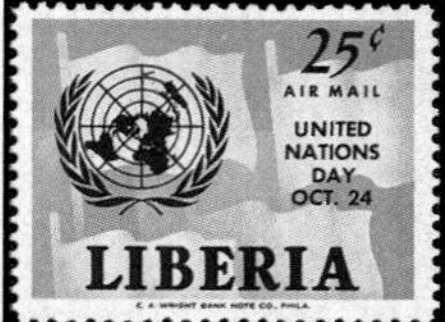

United Nations Emblem and Flags AP44

Design: 50c, UN emblem.

1962, Oct. 22 ***Perf. 12x12½***

C144 AP44 25c lt ultra & dk bl .50 .50

Souvenir Sheet

Imperf

C145 AP44 50c brt grnsh bl & blk 1.25 1.25

Observance of UN Day, Oct. 24, as a national holiday.

Building Type of Regular Issue

12c, 70c, Capitol. 50c, Information Service. $1, Treasury Department Building, Monrovia.

1962-63 ***Perf. 12x12½, 12 (70c)***

C146 A165 12c brt yel grn & mar .20 .20
C147 A165 50c orange & ultra 1.50 1.50
C147A A165 70c brt pink & dk bl ('63) 2.10 2.10
C148 A165 $1 salmon & blk ('63) 2.75 2.75
Nos. C146-C148 (4) 6.55 6.55

"FAO" Emblem and Globe — AP45

Design: 50c, "FAO" and UN Emblems.

1963, Mar. 21 **Unwmk.** ***Perf. 12½***

C149 AP45 25c dk green & yel .70 .70

Souvenir Sheet

Perf. 12

C150 AP45 50c emerald & ultra 1.75 1.75

FAO "Freedom from Hunger" campaign.

Type of Regular Issue, 1963

Designs: 25c, Telstar satellite, vert. 50c, Telstar and rocket, vert.

1963, May 27 **Litho.** ***Perf. 12½***

C151 A167 25c Prus blue & org .70 .70

Souvenir Sheet

Perf. 12

C152 A167 50c dp violet & yel 3.00 1.60

Red Cross Type of Regular Issue

Design: 25c, Red Cross and globe. 50c, Centenary emblem and globe.

1963, Aug. 26 **Unwmk.** ***Perf. 12***

C153 A168 25c purple & red .40 .40
C154 A168 50c deep ultra & red .70 .70

Map of Africa — AP46

1963, Oct. 28 ***Perf. 12½***

C156 AP46 25c red orange & grn .40 .40

See note after No. 412.

Olympic Type of Regular Issue

10c, Torch and mountains. 25c, Mountains, horiz. 50c, Torch, background like No. 413.

1963, Dec. 11 **Litho.** ***Perf. 12½***

C157 A170 10c vio blue & red .20 .20
C158 A170 25c green & orange .80 .80

Souvenir Sheet

Perf. 12

C159 A170 50c gray & red 1.75 1.75

Kennedy Type of Regular Issue, 1964

Designs: 25c, John F. Kennedy, vert. 50c, John F. Kennedy (like No. 414).

1964, Apr. 6 Unwmk. *Perf. 12½*
C160 A171 25c blk & red lil .60 .50

Souvenir Sheet

Perf. 12

C161 A171 50c blk & red lil 1.75 1.40

An imperf. miniature sheet containing one of No. C160 exists. No marginal inscription.

Satellite Type of Regular Issue
Souvenir Sheet

Design: Launching rocket separating from booster in space, vert.

1964, June 22 Litho.
C162 A172 50c vio bl & red 3.00 3.00

Olympic Type of Regular Issue
Souvenir Sheet

Design: 50c, Runner and Olympic rings.

1964, Sept. 15 Unwmk. *Perf. 12*
C163 A173 50c grnsh bl & red 3.00 1.25

Scout Type of Regular Issue, 1965

Designs: 25c, Liberian flag and fleur-delis. 50c, Globe and Scout emblem.

1965, Mar. 8 Litho. *Perf. 12½*
C164 A174 25c crimson & ultra .80 .80

Souvenir Sheet

Perf. 12

C165 A174 50c yellow & lilac 4.00 4.00

Lincoln Type of Regular Issue
Souvenir Sheet

50c, Lincoln and John F. Kennedy, horiz.

1965, May 3 Unwmk. *Perf. 12*
C166 A175 50c dp plum & lt gray 1.75 1.75

ICY Type of Regular Issue, 1965
Souvenir Sheet

1965, June 21 Litho.
C167 A176 50c car rose & brn 1.75 1.75

ITU Type of Regular Issue, 1965

1965, Sept. 21 Unwmk. *Perf. 12½*
C168 A177 50c red org & vio bl .80 .70

Tubman Type of Regular Issue

25c, Pres. Tubman and coat of arms.

1965, Nov. 29 Litho. *Perf. 12½*
C169 A178 25c ultra, red & brn .70 .70
a. Souv. sheet of 2, #431, C169, imperf. 1.75 1.75

Churchill Type of Regular Issue

25c, "Angry Lion" portrait by Karsh & Parliament, London. 50c, "Williamsburg Award Dinner" portrait by Karsh & map of Europe.

1966, Jan. 18 Litho. *Perf. 12½*
C170 A179 25c blk & vio bl .70 .55

Souvenir Sheet

Perf. 12

C171 A179 50c blk & red lil 1.75 1.75

Soccer Type of Regular Issue
Souvenir Sheet

Design: 50c, Soccer match in stadium.

1966, May 3 Litho. *Perf. 11½*
C172 A181 50c ultra & red brn 2.50 2.50

Kennedy Type of Regular Issue

25c, UN General Assembly & Pres. Kennedy. 35c, Pres. Kennedy & rocket on launching pad, Cape Kennedy. 40c, Flame on grave at Arlington.

1966, Aug. 16 Litho. *Perf. 12½*
C173 A182 25c ultra, blk & ocher .50 .20
C174 A182 35c dk vio bl & pink .60 .20

Souvenir Sheet

Perf. 11½

C175 A182 40c dk vio bl & multi 2.50 2.50

Boy Scout Type of Regular Issue
Souvenir Sheet

50c, Scout at campfire & vision of moon landing.

1967, Mar. 23 Litho. *Perf. 12½*
C176 A185 50c brt red lil & scar 5.00 5.00

Olympic Type of Regular Issue
Souvenir Sheet

Design: 50c, Pre-Hispanic sculpture, serape and Olympic rings, horiz.

1967, June 20 Litho. *Perf. 12½*
C177 A186 50c vio & car 3.75 1.60

Winter Olympic Games Type of Regular Issue
Souvenir Sheet

Design: 50c, Woman skater.

1967, Nov. 20 Litho. *Perf. 11½*
C178 A189 50c ver & blk 2.25 .70

Human Rights Type of Regular Issue
Souvenir Sheet

1968, Apr. 26 Litho. *Perf. 11½*
C179 A191 80c bl & red 3.00 1.10

M. L. King Type of Regular Issue
Souvenir Sheet

55c, Pres. Kennedy congratulating Dr. King.

1968, July 11 Litho. *Perf. 11½*
C180 A192 55c brn & blk 3.75 1.00

Olympic Type of Regular Issue
Souvenir Sheet

Design: 50c, Steeplechase and ancient sculpture.

1968, Aug. 22 Litho. *Perf. 11½*
C181 A193 50c brt bl & org brn 2.25 1.10

President Type of Regular Issue 1966-69

Design: 25c, Pres. William V. S. Tubman.

1969, Feb. 18 Litho. *Perf. 11½x11*
C182 A180 25c blk & emer .60 .30

ILO Type of Regular Issue

Design: 80c, "ILO" surrounded by cogwheel and wreath, vert.

1969, Apr. 16 Litho. *Perf. 12½*
C183 A196 80c emer & gold 2.50 1.10

Apollo 11 Type of Regular Issue
Souvenir Sheet

65c, Astronauts Neil A. Armstrong, Col. Edwin E. Aldrin, Jr., & Lieut. Col. Michael Collins, horiz.

1969, Oct. 15 Litho. *Perf. 11½*
C184 A199 65c dk vio bl & brt red 2.50 1.10

UN Type of 1970

Design: $1, UN emblem, olive branch and plane as symbols of peace and progress, vert.

1970, Apr. 16 Litho. *Perf. 12½*
C185 A200 $1 ultra & sil 2.40 1.40

Apollo 14 Type of Regular Issue
Souvenir Sheet

Design: 50c, Moon, earth and star.

1971, May 20 Litho. *Imperf.*
C186 A208 50c multi 3.50 3.50

Souvenir Sheet

Olympic Yachting Village, Kiel, and Yachting — AP47

Illustration reduced.

1971, June 28 Litho. *Perf. 14½x14*
C187 AP47 Sheet of 2 3.50 3.50
a. 25c multi .50 .50
b. 30c multi .60 .60

Publicity for the 20th Summer Olympic Games, and the yachting races in Kiel, Germany, 1972.

Boy Scout Type of Regular Issue
Souvenir Sheet

Boy Scouts of various nations cooking, horiz.

1971, Aug. 6 Litho. *Perf. 15*
C188 A211 50c multi 4.25 4.25

UNICEF Type of Regular Issue
Souvenir Sheet

UNICEF emblem & Bengal tigress with cubs.

1971, Oct. 1 *Imperf.*
C189 A213 50c multi 3.00 3.00

Souvenir Sheet

Japanese Royal Family — AP48

1971, Nov. 4 *Perf. 15*
C190 AP48 50c multi 4.25 4.25

11th Winter Olympic Games, Sapporo, Japan, Feb. 3-13, 1972.

Sesquicentennial Type of Regular Issue
Souvenir Sheet

Design: 50c, Sailing ship "Elizabeth" between maps of America and Africa, horiz.

1972, Jan. 1 Litho. *Imperf.*
C191 A216 50c car & vio bl 3.00 3.00

Olympic Type of Regular Issue
Souvenir Sheet

Design: 55c, View of Olympic Stadium and symbol of "Motion."

1971, May 19 Litho. *Perf. 15*
C192 A218 55c multi 5.50 5.50

Apollo 16 Type of Regular Issue
Souvenir Sheet

Lt. Comdr. Thomas K. Mattingly, 2nd, Capt. John W. Young & Lt. Col. Charles M. Duke, Jr.

1972, June 26 Litho. *Perf. 15*
C193 A220 55c pink & multi 2.50 2.50

Ship Type of 1972
Souvenir Sheet

Design: Lord Nelson's flagship Victory, and her figurehead (1765).

1972, Sept. 6 Litho. *Perf. 15*
C194 A222 50c multi 3.00 3.00

Pres. Tolbert Type of 1972.
Souvenir Sheet

1972, Oct. 23 Litho. *Perf. 15*
C195 A223 55c multi 2.00 2.00

Apollo 17 Type of Regular Issue
Souvenir Sheet

55c, Apollo 17 badge, moon and earth.

1973, Mar. 28 Litho. *Perf. 11*
C196 A225 55c bl & multi 2.50 2.50

Locomotive Type of Regular Issue
Souvenir Sheet

Design: 55c, Swiss locomotive.

1973, May 4 Litho. *Perf. 11*
C197 A226 55c multi 4.00 4.00

WHO Type of Regular Issue 1973
Souvenir Sheet

Design: 55c, WHO emblem, Paul Ehrlich and poppy anemones.

1973, June 26 Litho. *Perf. 11*
C198 A228 55c lt vio & multi 2.50 2.50

Automobile Type of Regular Issue
Souvenir Sheet

Franklin 10 HP cross-engined 1904-05 models.

1973, Sept. 11 Litho. *Perf. 11*
C199 A229 55c multi 2.50 2.50

Copernicus Type of Regular Issue
Souvenir Sheet

Design: 55c, Copernicus and concept of orbiting station around Mars.

1973, Dec. 14 Litho. *Perf. 13½*
C200 A230 55c gray & multi 2.25 2.25

UPU Type of Regular Issue
Souvenir Sheet

55c, UPU emblem and English coach, 1784.

1974, Mar. 4 Litho. *Perf. 13½*
C201 A232 55c multi 3.00 3.00

Dog Type of Regular Issue
Souvenir Sheet

Design: Hungarian sheepdog (kuvasz).

1974, Apr. 16 Litho. *Perf. 13½*
C202 A233 75c multi 4.50 4.50

Soccer Type of Regular Issue
Souvenir Sheet

Design: 60c, World Soccer Championship Cup and Munich Stadium.

1974, June 4 Litho. *Perf. 11*
C203 A234 60c multi 2.50 2.50

Butterfly Type of Regular Issue
Souvenir Sheet

Tropical butterfly: 60c, Pierella nereis.

1974, Sept. 11 Litho. *Perf. 13½*
C204 A235 60c gray & multi *4.50 4.50*

Churchill Type of 1974
Souvenir Sheet

60c, Churchill at easel painting landscape.

1975, Jan. 17 Litho. *Perf. 13½*
C205 A237 60c multi 2.00 2.00

Women's Year Type of 1975
Souvenir Sheet

Design: 75c, Vijaya Lakshmi Pandit, Women's Year emblem and dais of UN General Assembly.

1975, Mar. 14 Litho. *Perf. 13*
C206 A238 75c gray & multi 1.50 1.50

American Bicentennial Type
Souvenir Sheet

Design: 75c, Mayflower and US No. 548.

1975, Apr. 25 Litho. *Perf. 13½*
C207 A239 75c multi 3.50 3.50

Dr. Schweitzer Type, 1975
Souvenir Sheet

Schweitzer as surgeon in Lambarene Hospital.

1975, June 26 Litho. *Perf. 13½*
C208 A240 60c multi 3.00 3.00

Apollo-Soyuz Type, 1975
Souvenir Sheet

75c, Apollo-Soyuz link-up and emblem.

1975, Sept. 18 Litho. *Perf. 13½*
C209 A241 75c multi 2.50 2.50

Winter Olympic Games Type, 1976
Souvenir Sheet

Downhill skiing & Olympic Games emblem.

1976, Jan. 23 Litho. *Perf. 13½*
C210 A243 75c multi 2.00 2.00

Olympic Games Type, 1976
Souvenir Sheet

Design: 75c, Dressage and jumping.

1976, May 4 Litho. ***Perf. 13½***
C211 A245 75c multi 2.50 2.50

Bell Type
Souvenir Sheet

Design: 75c, A. G. Bell making telephone call, UPU and ITU emblems.

1976, June 4 Litho. ***Perf. 13½***
C212 A246 75c ocher & multi 3.00 3.00

Animal Type of 1976
Souvenir Sheet

Design: 50c, Elephant, vert.

1976, Sept. 1 Litho. ***Perf. 13½***
C213 A249 50c org & multi 4.00 4.00

Bicentennial Type of 1976
Souvenir Sheet

Design: 75c, Like No. 770.

1976, Sept. 21 Litho. ***Perf. 13½***
C214 A250 75c multi 3.00 3.00

Mask Type of 1977
Souvenir Sheet

75c, Ibo mask and Festival emblem.

1977, Jan. 20 Litho. ***Perf. 13½***
C215 A251 75c lil & multi 2.25 2.25

Equestrian Type of 1977

Designs: 55c, Military dressage (team), US. 80c, Winners receiving medals, vert.

1977, Apr. 22 Litho. ***Perf. 13½***
C216 A253 55c ocher & multi 3.25 1.60

Souvenir Sheet

C217 A253 80c ocher & multi 3.00 3.00

Elizabeth II Type of 1977
Souvenir Sheet

75c, Elizabeth II, laurel and crowns.

1977, May 23 Litho. ***Perf. 13½***
C218 A254 75c sil & multi 1.75 1.25

Zeppelin Type of 1978
Souvenir Sheet

75c, Futuristic Goodyear aerospace airship.

1978, Mar. 9 Litho. ***Perf. 13½***
C219 A257 75c multi 2.50 2.50

Soccer Type of 1978
Souvenir Sheet

Soccer game Netherlands & Uruguay, vert.

1978, May 16 Litho. ***Perf. 13½***
C220 A258 75c multi 2.50

Coronation Type of 1978
Souvenir Sheet

Design: 75c, Coronation coach, horiz.

1978, June 12
C221 A259 75c multi 3.25

Soccer Winners' Type of 1978
Souvenir Sheet

Design: 75c, Argentine team, horiz.

1978, Dec. 8 Litho. ***Perf. 13½***
C222 A262 75c multi 3.25

AIR POST SEMI-POSTAL STAMPS

Nos. C14-C16 Overprinted in Red or Blue Like Nos. B16-B18

1941 Unwmk. ***Perf. 12***
CB1 A107 3c +2c dk bl (R) 4.00 4.00
CB2 A108 5c +2c dl red brn (Bl) 4.00 4.00
CB3 A109 10c +2c dk grn (R) 4.00 4.00
Nos. CB1-CB3 (3) 12.00 12.00

Catalogue values for unused stamps in this section, from this point to the end of the section, are for Never Hinged items.

Nurses Taking Oath — SPAP1

Designs: 20c+5c, Liberian Government Hospital. 25c+5c, Medical examination.

1954, June 21 Litho. & Engr.
Size: 39½x28½mm
CB4 SPAP1 10c +5c car & blk .20 .20
CB5 SPAP1 20c +5c emer & blk .20 .20
Size: 45x34mm
CB6 SPAP1 25c +5c ultra, car & blk .20 .20
Nos. CB4-CB6 (3) .60 .60

Surtax for the Liberian Government Hospital. Nos. CB4-CB6 exist imperf. No. CB6 exists with carmine omitted.

AIR POST SPECIAL DELIVERY STAMP

No. C15 Overprinted in Dark Blue Like No. E1

1941 Unwmk. ***Perf. 12***
CE1 A108 10c on 5c dl red brn 2.00 2.00

AIR POST REGISTRATION STAMP

No. C15 Overprinted in Dark Blue Like No. F35

1941 Unwmk. ***Perf. 12***
CF1 A108 10c on 5c dl red brn 2.00 2.00

SPECIAL DELIVERY STAMP

No. 278 Surcharged in Dark Blue

1941 Unwmk. ***Perf. 12***
E1 A108 10c on 5c dl red brn 2.00 2.00

REGISTRATION STAMPS

R1

1893 Unwmk. Litho. ***Perf. 14, 15***
Without Value Surcharged
F1 R1 (10c) blk (Buchanan) 250.00 250.00
F2 R1 (10c) blk (Greenville) *2,250. 2,250.*
F3 R1 (10c) blk (Harper) *2,250. 2,250.*
F4 R1 (10c) blk (Monrovia) 30.00 30.00
F5 R1 (10c) blk (Robertsport) 1,000. 1,000.

Types of 1893 Surcharged in Black

1894 ***Perf. 14***
F6 R1 10c bl, *pink* (Buchanan) 5.00 5.25
F7 R1 10c grn, *buff* (Harper) 5.00 5.25
F8 R1 10c red, *yel* (Monrovia) 5.00 5.25
F9 R1 10c rose, *bl* (Robertsport) 5.00 5.25
Nos. F6-F9 (4) 20.00 21.00

Exist imperf or missing one 10. Value, each $10.

President Garretson W. Gibson — R6

1903 Engr. ***Perf. 14***
F10 R6 10c bl & blk (Buchanan) 1.10 .20
a. Center inverted 100.00
F11 R6 10c org red & blk ("Grenville") 1.10
a. Center inverted 100.00
b. 10c orange & black 1.90 .20
F12 R6 10c grn & blk (Harper) 1.10 .20
a. Center inverted 100.00
F13 R6 10c vio & blk (Monrovia) 1.10 .20
a. Center inverted 100.00
b. 10c lilac & black 1.90
F14 R6 10c mag & blk (Robertsport) 1.10 .20
a. Center inverted 100.00
Nos. F10-F14 (5) 5.50
Nos. F10, F11b, F12-F14 .75

For surcharges see Nos. 178-182.

S.S. Quail on Patrol — R7

1919 Litho. ***Serrate Roulette 12***
F15 R7 10c blk & bl (Buchanan) 1.40 2.75

Serrate Roulette 12, Perf. 14
F16 R7 10c ocher & blk ("Grenville") 1.40 2.75
F17 R7 10c grn & blk (Harper) 1.40 2.75
F18 R7 10c vio & bl (Monrovia) 1.40 2.75
F19 R7 10c rose & blk (Robertsport) 1.40 2.75
Nos. F15-F19 (5) 7.00 13.75

Gabon Viper — R8

Wmk. Crosses and Circles (116)
1921 Engr. ***Perf. 13x14***
F20 R8 10c cl & blk (Buchanan) 90.00 3.50
F21 R8 10c red & blk (Greenville) 22.50 3.50
F22 R8 10c ultra & blk (Harper) 22.50 3.50
F23 R8 10c org & blk (Monrovia) 22.50 3.50
a. Imperf., pair 225.00
F24 R8 10c grn & blk (Robertsport) 22.50 3.50
a. Imperf., pair 225.00
Nos. F20-F24 (5) 180.00 17.50

Preceding Issue Overprinted "1921"
F25 R8 10c (Buchanan) 20.00 6.25
F26 R8 10c (Greenville) 20.00 6.25
F27 R8 10c (Harper) 70.00 6.25
F28 R8 10c (Monrovia) 20.00 6.25
F29 R8 10c (Robertsport) 20.00 6.25
Nos. F25-F29 (5) 150.00 31.25

Nos. F20-F24 are printed tete-beche. Thus, the "1921" overprint appears upright on half the stamps in a sheet and inverted on the other half. Values are the same for either variety.

Passengers Going Ashore from Ship — R9

Designs: No. F31, Transporting merchandise, shore to ship (Greenville). No. F32, Sailing ship (Harper). No. F33, Ocean liner (Monrovia). No. F34, Canoe in surf (Robertsport).

1924 Litho. ***Perf. 14***
F30 R9 10c gray & carmine 7.00 .60
F31 R9 10c gray & blue grn 7.00 .60
F32 R9 10c gray & orange 7.00 .60
F33 R9 10c gray & blue 7.00 .60
F34 R9 10c gray & violet 7.00 .60
Nos. F30-F34 (5) 35.00 3.00

No. 278 Surcharged in Dark Blue

1941 Unwmk. ***Perf. 12***
F35 A108 10c on 5c dull red brn 2.00 2.00

POSTAGE DUE STAMPS

Nos. 26, 28 Surcharged

1892 Unwmk. ***Perf. 11***
J1 A5 3c on 3c violet 6.50 4.25
a. Imperf., pair 22.50
b. Inverted surcharge 45.00 45.00
c. As "a," inverted surcharge 110.00

Perf. 12
J2 A5 6c on 6c olive gray 15.00 13.50
a. Imperf., pair 32.50
b. Inverted surcharge 52.50 35.00

D2

Engr.; Figures of Value Typographed in Black
1893 Wmk. 143 ***Perf. 14, 15***
J3 D2 2c org, *yel* 2.00 1.00
J4 D2 4c rose, *rose* 2.00 1.00
J5 D2 6c brown, *buff* 2.00 1.25
J6 D2 8c blue, *blue* 2.00 1.25
J7 D2 10c grn, *lil rose* 2.25 1.50
J8 D2 20c vio, *gray* 2.25 1.50
a. Center inverted 110.00 110.00
J9 D2 40c ol brn, *grnsh* 4.50 3.00
Nos. J3-J9 (7) 17.00 10.50

All values of the above set exist imperforate.

MILITARY STAMPS

"LFF" are the initials of "Liberian Frontier Force." Nos. M1-M7 were issued for the use of troops sent to guard the frontier.

Issues of 1905, 1906 and 1909 Surcharged

1916 **Wmk. 143**

M1 A23 1c on 1c lt grn 175.00 175.00
a. 2nd "F" inverted 250.00 250.00
b. "FLF" 250.00 250.00
c. Inverted surcharge 250.00 250.00

Unwmk.

M2 A33 1c on 1c grn & blk 500.00 500.00
a. 2nd "F" inverted 550.00 550.00
b. "FLF" 550.00 550.00
M3 A46 1c on 1c yel grn & blk 3.75 4.50
a. 2nd "F" inverted 7.50 7.50
b. "FLF" 7.50 7.50
M4 A47 1c on 2c lake & blk 3.75 4.50
a. 2nd "F" inverted 7.50 7.50
b. "FLF" 7.50 7.50

Surcharge exists sideways on Nos. M2, M5; double on Nos. M1-M4; inverted on Nos. M2-M4.

Nos. O46, O59-O60 Surcharged

M5 A33 1c on 1c 400.00 400.00
a. 2nd "F" inverted 550.00 550.00
b. "FLF" 550.00 550.00
M6 A46 1c on 1c 3.75 4.50
a. 2nd "F" inverted 7.50 7.50
b. "FLF" 7.50 7.50
c. "LFF 1c" inverted 10.00 10.00
d. As "a" and "1c" inverted 14.00
e. "FLF 1c" inverted 14.00
M7 A47 1c on 2c 2.75 3.25
a. 2nd "F" inverted 5.75 5.75
b. "FLF" 5.75 5.75
c. Pair, one without "LFF 1c"

OFFICIAL STAMPS

Types of Regular Issues Overprinted "OFFICIAL" in Various Colors

Perf. 12½ to 15 and Compound

1892 **Wmk. 143**

O1 A9 1c vermilion .80 .80
O2 A9 2c blue .80 .80
O3 A10 4c grn & blk .80 .80
O4 A11 6c bl grn .80 .80
O5 A12 8c brn & blk .80 .80
O6 A13 12c rose red 2.00 2.00
O7 A14 16c red lilac 2.00 2.00
O8 A15 24c ol grn, *yel* 2.00 2.00
O9 A16 32c grnsh bl 2.00 2.00
O10 A17 $1 bl & blk 40.00 16.00
O11 A18 $2 brn, *yel* 16.00 11.50
O12 A19 $5 car & blk 24.00 9.00
Nos. O1-O12 (12) 92.00 48.50

1893

O13 A11 (a) 5c on 6c bl grn (No. 50) .95 .95
a. "5" with short flag 5.00 5.00
b. Both 5's with short flags 5.00 5.00
c. "i" dot omitted 19.00 19.00
d. Overprinted on #50d 45.00 45.00

1894

Overprinted "O S" in Various Colors

O15 A9 1c vermilion .70 .35
O16 A9 2c blue .85 .40
a. Imperf.
O17 A10 4c grn & blk 1.00 .55
O18 A12 8c brn & blk 1.00 .55
O19 A13 12c rose red 1.40 .60
O20 A14 16c red lilac 1.40 .60
O21 A15 24c ol grn, *yel* 1.40 .70
O22 A16 32c grnsh bl 2.75 .80
O23 A17 $1 bl & blk 27.50 21.00
a. $1 ultra & black 27.50 21.00
O24 A18 $2 brn, *yel* 27.50 21.00
O25 A19 $5 car & blk 125.00 87.50
Nos. O15-O25 (11) 190.50 134.05

Unwmk.

Imperf

O26 A22 5c vio & grn 3.00 1.90

Rouletted

O27 A22 5c vio & grn 3.00 1.90

Regular Issue of 1896-1905 Overprinted "O S" in Black or Red

1898-1905 **Wmk. 143** ***Perf. 14, 15***

O28 A23 1c lil rose .90 .90
O29 A23 1c dp grn ('00) .90 .90
O30 A23 1c lt grn (R) ('05) .90 .90
O31 A24 2c bis & blk 1.75 .60
a. Pair, one without overprint 87.50
O32 A24 2c org red & blk ('00) 2.75 1.50
O33 A24 2c rose & blk ('05) 4.50 2.75
O34 A25 5c lake & blk 3.00 1.50
O35 A25 5c gray bl & blk ('00) 3.50 1.50
O36 A25 5c ultra & blk (R) ('05) 6.00 3.75
O37 A12 10c chr yel & ind 1.75 1.75
O38 A13 15c slate 1.75 1.75
O39 A14 20c vermilion 3.00 2.10
O40 A15 25c yel grn 1.75 1.75
O41 A16 30c steel blue 4.50 2.75
O42 A26 50c red brn & blk 4.50 2.75
Nos. O28-O42 (15) 41.45 27.15

For surcharge see No. O92.

Official stamps overprinted "ORDINARY" or with a bar with an additional surcharge are listed as Nos. 64B-90, 92-93, 99.

Red Overprint

1903 **Unwmk.** ***Perf. 14***

O43 A29 3c green .20 .20
a. Overprint omitted 5.00
b. Inverted overprint

Two overprint types: I — Thin, sharp, dark red. II — Thick, heavier, orange red. Same value.

On No. 50

O3

1904 **Black Surcharge** **Wmk. 143**

O44 A11 1c on 5c on 6c bl grn 1.25 1.50
a. "5" with short flag 4.25
b. Both "5s" with straight flag 8.00 8.00

Red Surcharge

O45 O3 2c on 30c steel blue 8.00 8.00
a. Double surcharge, red and black
b. Surcharge also on back

Types of Regular Issue Overprinted in Various Colors (a)

1906 **Unwmk.**

O46 A33 1c grn & blk (R) .65 .40
O47 A34 2c car & blk (Bl) .20 .20
a. Center and overprint inverted 30.00 3.00
b. Inverted overprint 6.00
O48 A35 5c ultra & blk (Bk) .65 .40
a. Inverted overprint 15.00 15.00
b. Center and overprint invtd. 50.00
O49 A36 10c dl vio & blk (R) .75 .55
a. Inverted overprint 10.00 10.00
b. Center and overprint invtd. 50.00
O50 A37 15c brn & blk (Bk) 3.00 .55
a. Inverted overprint 4.50
b. Overprint omitted 12.00 6.00
c. Center and overprint invtd. 60.00
O51 A38 20c dp grn & blk (R) .75 .55
a. Overprint omitted 15.00
O52 A39 25c plum & gray (Bl) .50 .20
a. With 2nd ovpt. in blue, invtd. 15.00
O53 A40 30c dk brn (Bk) .55 .20
O54 A41 50c org brn & dp grn (G) .75 .20
a. Inverted overprint 5.00 4.00
O55 A42 75c ultra & blk (Bk) 1.40 .95
a. Inverted overprint 9.50 5.75
b. Overprint omitted 22.50
O56 A43 $1 dp grn & gray (R) .90 .20
a. Inverted overprint
O57 A44 $2 plum & blk (Bl) 2.75 .20
a. Overprint omitted 22.50 15.00
O58 A45 $5 org & blk (Bk) 5.50 .20
a. Overprint omitted 11.00
b. Inverted overprint 12.00 8.00
Nos. O46-O58 (13) 18.35 4.80

Nos. O52, O54, O55, O56 and O58 are known with center inverted.

For surcharges see Nos. O72, O82-O85, O96.

(b)

1909-12

O59 A46 1c emer & blk (R) .40 .20
O60 A47 2c car rose & brn (Bl) .40 .20
a. Overprint omitted
O61 A48 5c turq & blk (Bk) .45 .20
a. Double overprint, one inverted 7.50
O62 A49 10c blk & ultra (R) ('12) .60 .20
O63 A50 15c cl & blk (Bl) .60 .45
O64 A51 20c bis & grn (Bk) 1.10 .55
O65 A52 25c ultra & grn (Bk) 1.10 .55
a. Double overprint 4.75 4.75
O66 A53 30c dk bl (R) .85 .20
O67 A54 50c brn & grn (Bk) 1.40 .40
a. Center inverted 27.50
b. Inverted overprint 4.00 2.75
O68 A55 75c pur & blk (R) 1.50 .20
Nos. O59-O68 (10) 8.40 3.15

Nos. O63, O64, O67 and O68 are known without overprint and with center inverted.

For surcharges see Nos. O74-O81, O86-O90, O97.

Rouletted

O69 A49 10c blk & ultra (R) .70 .70

Nos. 126B and 127E Overprinted type "a" ("OS") in Red

1910-12 ***Rouletted***

O70 A49 3c on 10c blk & ultra .60 1.00

Perf. 12½, 14, 12½x14

O71 A49 3c on 10c blk & ultra ('12) .60 .30
a. Pair, one without surch., the other with dbl. surch., one invtd.
b. Double surcharge, one inverted 3.75

Stamps of Preceding Issues Surcharged with New Values like Regular Issue and

(c)

1914

On Nos. O52 and 110

O72 A39 (a) 2c on 25c plum & gray 25.00 10.50
O73 A42 (c) 20c on 75c brn & blk 8.75 5.25

On Nos. O66 and O68

O74 A53 (b) 5c on 30c dk bl 8.75 5.25
O75 A55 (c) 20c on 75c pur & blk (R) 13.00 5.25
Nos. O72-O75 (4) 55.50 26.25

Official Stamps of 1906-09 Surcharged Like Regular Issues of Same Date

1915-16

O76 A50 (c) 2c on 15c (Bk) .75 .50
O77 A52 (d) 2c on 25c (Bk) 4.25 4.25
O78 A51 (e) 5c on 20c (Bk) .75 .50
O79 A53 (g) 5c on 30c (R) 7.00 7.00
O80 A54 (i) 10c on 50c (Bk) 4.50 2.75
O81 A55 (j) 20c on 75c (R) 2.25 2.25
O82 A43 (k) 25c on $1 (R) 16.00 16.00
a. "25" double 22.50
b. "OS" inverted 22.50
O83 A44 (l) 50c on $2 (Bk) 50.00 50.00
a. "Ceuts" 70.00 70.00
O84 A44 (m) 50c on $2 (Br) 18.00 18.00
O85 A45 (n) $1 on $5 (Bk) 17.00 17.00

Handstamped Surcharge

O86 A54 (i) 10c on 50c (Bk) 8.50 8.50

Nos. O60-O61 Surcharged like Nos. 153-154 in Black or Red

a1, b1

c1, d1

e1, f1

g1, h1

i1, j1

O87 A47 1c on 2c 2.25 2.25
Strip of 10 types 25.00

O88 A48 2c on 5c (R) 2.25 2.25
  Strip of 10 types (R) 25.00
  a. Black surcharge 8.50 8.50
  Strip of 10 types (Bk) 125.00

See note following Nos. 153-154.

#O60-O61 Surcharged like #155-156

O90 A47 1c on 2c 125.00 125.00
O91 A48 2c on 5c 100.00 100.00

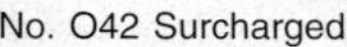
No. O42 Surcharged

O92 A26 10c on 50c (Bk) 11.00 11.00

No. O53 Surcharged like No. 161

1917

O96 A40 5c on 30c dk brn 17.00 17.00
  a. "FIV" 27.50 27.50

The editors consider the 1915-17 issues unnecessary and speculative.

#O62 Surcharged in Red like #162

1918

O97 A49 3c on 10c blk & ultra 1.90 1.90

Types of Regular Issue of 1918 Overprinted Type "a" ("OS") in Black, Blue or Red

1918 **Unwmk.** ***Perf. 12½, 14***

O98 A59 1c dp grn & red brn (Bk) .60 .20
O99 A60 2c red & blk (Bl) .60 .20
O100 A61 5c ultra & blk (R) 1.10 .20
O101 A62 10c ultra (R) .60 .20
O102 A63 15c choc & dk grn (Bl) 2.75 .60
O103 A64 20c gray lil & blk (R) .85 .20
O104 A65 25c choc & grn (Bk) 5.25 .65
O105 A66 30c brt vio & blk (R) 6.50 .65
O106 A67 50c mar & blk (Bl) 7.75 .65
  a. Overprint omitted 11.00
O107 A68 75c car brn & blk (Bl) 3.00 .20
O108 A69 $1 ol bis & turq bl (Bk) 6.00 .20
O109 A70 $2 ol bis & blk (R) 9.25 .20
O110 A71 $5 yel grn (Bk) 12.00 .40
  Nos. O98-O110 (13) 56.25 4.55

For surcharges see Nos. 259-269, O111-O112, O155-O157. For overprint see No. 270.

Official Stamps of 1918 Surcharged like Regular Issue

1920

O111 A59 3c on 1c grn & red brn .90 .55
  a. "CEETS" 15.00 15.00
  b. Double surcharge 8.00 8.00
  c. Double surch., one invtd. 15.00 15.00
  d. Triple surcharge 20.00 20.00
O112 A60 4c on 2c red & blk .55 .55
  a. Inverted surcharge 12.00 12.00
  b. Double surcharge 12.00 12.00
  c. Double surch., one invtd. 10.00 10.00
  d. Triple surcharge 15.00 15.00

Types of Regular Issues of 1915-21 Overprinted

1921 **Wmk. 116** ***Perf. 14***

O113 A57 2c rose red 8.25 .20
O114 A58 3c brown 1.75 .20
O115 A79 20c brn & ultra 2.25 .40

Same, Overprinted "O S"

O116 A75 1c dp grn 1.75 .20
O117 A76 5c dp bl & brn 1.75 .20
O118 A77 10c red vio & blk .85 .20
O119 A78 15c blk & grn 4.75 .60
  a. Double overprint
O120 A80 25c org & grn 6.50 .60
O121 A81 30c brn & red 1.75 .20
O122 A82 50c grn & blk 1.75 .20
  a. Overprinted "S" only
O123 A83 75c bl & vio 3.25 .20
O124 A84 $1 bl & blk 22.50 .65
O125 A85 $2 grn & org 12.00 .95
O126 A86 $5 grn & bl 13.50 2.10
  Nos. O113-O126 (14) 82.60 6.90

Preceding Issues Overprinted "1921"

1921

O127 A75 1c dp grn 7.50 .20
O128 A57 2c rose red 7.50 .20
O129 A58 3c brown 7.50 .20
O130 A76 5c dp bl & brn 4.50 .20
O131 A77 10c red vio & blk 7.50 .20
O132 A78 15c blk & grn 8.50 .20
O133 A79 20c brn & ultra 8.50 .40
O134 A80 25c org & grn 8.25 .80
O135 A81 30c brn & red 7.50 .20
O136 A82 50c grn & blk 8.75 .20
O137 A83 75c bl & vio 5.50 .20
O138 A84 $1 bl & blk 15.00 2.00
O139 A85 $2 org & grn 19.00 2.25
O140 A86 $5 grn & bl 15.00 3.25
  Nos. O127-O140 (14) 130.50 10.50

Types of Regular Issue of 1923 Overprinted "O S"

1923 ***Perf. 13½x14½, 14½x13½***

White Paper

O141 A88 1c bl grn & blk 8.75 .20
O142 A89 2c dl red & yel brn 8.75 .20
O143 A90 3c gray bl & blk 8.75 .20
O144 A91 5c org & dk grn 8.75 .20
O145 A92 10c ol bis & dk vio 8.75 .20
O146 A93 15c yel grn & bl 1.10 .40
O147 A94 20c vio & ind 1.10 .40
O148 A95 25c brn & red brn 32.50 .40

White, Buff or Brownish Paper

O149a A96 30c dp ultra & brn 1.10 .20
  b. Overprint omitted
O150a A97 50c dl bis & red brn 2.25 .45
O151 A98 75c gray & grn 2.25 .20
O152a A99 $1 red org & grn 2.25 .65
  b. Overprint omitted 11.00
O153 A100 $2 red lil & ver 6.00 .20
O154a A101 $5 bl & brn vio 4.50 2.25
  Nos. O141-O154a (14) 96.80 6.15

Nos. O149-154 exist on white, buff or brownish paper. Values are for the most common varieties. For detailed listings, see the Scott Classic Specialized Catalogue.

No. O98 Surcharged in Red Brown

1926 **Unwmk.** ***Perf. 14***

O155 A59 2c on 1c 2.25 2.25
  a. "Gents" 7.25
  b. Surcharged in black 5.75
  c. As "b," "Gents" 9.50

No. O98 Surcharged in Black

1926

O156 A59 2c on 1c .85 .85
  a. Inverted surcharge 20.00
  b. "Gents" 10.00

No. O98 Surcharged in Red

1927

O157 A59 2c on 1c 35.00 35.00
  a. "Ceuts" 55.00
  b. "Vwo" 55.00
  c. "Twc" 55.00

Regular Issue of 1928 Overprinted in Red or Black

1928 ***Perf. 12***

O158 A102 1c grn (R) 1.10 .55
O159 A102 2c gray vio (R) 3.50 2.10
O160 A102 3c bis brn (Bk) 3.75 4.25
O161 A103 5c ultra (R) 1.10 .55
O162 A104 10c ol gray (R) 3.50 1.75
O163 A103 15c dl vio (R) 3.50 1.00
O164 A103 $1 red brn (Bk) 77.50 25.50
  Nos. O158-O164 (7) 93.95 35.70

For surcharges see Nos. C3, O165.

No. O162 Surcharged with New Value and Bar in Black

1945 **Unwmk.** ***Perf. 12***

O165 A104 4c on 10c (Bk) 12.00 12.00

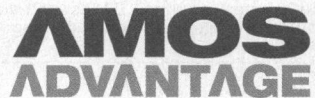

LIBYA

'li-bē-ə

(Libia)

LOCATION — North Africa, bordering on the Mediterranean Sea
GOVT. — Republic
AREA — 679,358 sq. mi.
POP. — 4,992,838 (1999 est.)
CAPITAL — Tripoli

In 1939, the four northern provinces of Libya, a former Italian colony, were incorporated in the Italian national territory. Included in the territory is the former Turkish Vilayet of Tripoli, annexed in 1912. Libya became a kingdom on Dec. 24, 1951. The Libyan Arab Republic was established Sept. 1, 1969. "People's Socialist . . ." was added to its name in 1977. See Cyrenaica and Tripolitania.

100 Centesimi = 1 Lira
Military Authority Lira (1951)
Franc (1951)
1,000 Milliemes = 1 Pound (1952)
1,000 Dirhams = 1 Dinar (1972)

Watermarks

Wmk. 140 — Crown

Wmk. 195 — Multiple Crown and Arabic F

Wmk. 310 — Multiple Crescent and Star

Catalogue values for unused stamps in this country are for Never Hinged items, beginning with Scott 102 in the regular postage section, Scott C51 in the airpost section, Scott E13 in the special delivery section, Scott J25 in the postage due section, Scott O1 in the official section, Scott N1 in the Fezzan-Ghadames section, Scott 2N1 in the Fezzan section, Scott 2NB1 in the Fezzan semi-postal section, Scott 2NC1 in the Fezzan airpost section, Scott 2NJ1 in the Fezzan postage due section, Scott 3N1 in the Ghadames section, and Scott 3NC1 in the Ghadames airpost section.

Used values in italics are for postally used stamps. CTO's sell for about the same as unused, hinged stamps.

Stamps of Italy Overprinted in Black

1912-22 **Wmk. 140** ***Perf. 14***

No.	Type	Description	Unused	Used
1	A42	1c brown ('15)	1.75	1.00
a.		Double overprint	250.00	250.00
2	A43	2c orange brn	1.75	.65
3	A48	5c green	1.75	.40
a.		Double overprint	160.00	160.00
b.		Imperf., pair	400.00	
c.		Inverted overprint		—
d.		Pair, one without overprint	425.00	425.00
4	A48	10c claret	17.00	.40
a.		Pair, one without overprint	425.00	425.00
b.		Double overprint	190.00	190.00
5	A48	15c slate ('22)	4.25	*6.75*
6	A45	20c orange ('15)	4.25	.40
a.		Double overprint	210.00	210.00
b.		Pair, one without overprint	750.00	750.00
7	A50	20c brn org ('18)	4.25	*6.00*
8	A49	25c blue	4.25	.40
a.		Double overprint	175.00	175.00
9	A49	40c brown	12.50	1.25
10	A45	45c ol grn ('17)	30.00	27.50
a.		Inverted overprint	550.00	
11	A49	50c violet	34.00	1.75
12	A49	60c brn car ('18)	17.00	*23.00*
13	A46	1 l brown & green ('15)	85.00	2.10
14	A46	5 l bl & rose ('15)	425.00	350.00
15	A51	10 l gray green & red ('15)	47.50	*175.00*
		Nos. 1-15 (15)	690.25	*596.60*

Two types of overprint were applied to this issue. Type I has bold letters, with dots close within "i"; type II has thinner letters, with dots further away within "i." All values, along with Nos. E1 and E2, received the type I overprint, and values shown are for this type. Nos. 1, 3-4, 6, 8, 11, 13-15 and E1-E2 also received the type II overprint. For detailed listings, see the *Scott Specialized Catalogue of Stamps and Covers.*

For surcharges see Nos. 37-38.

Overprinted in Violet

1912 **Unwmk.**

No.	Type	Description	Unused	Used
16	A58	15c slate	240.00	2.10
a.		Blue black overprint	*19,000.*	37.50

No. 16 Surcharged

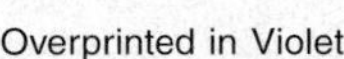

1916, Mar. **Unwmk.**

No.	Type	Description	Unused	Used
19	A58	20c on 15c slate	37.50	10.00

Roman Legionary — A1

Diana of Ephesus — A2

Ancient Galley Leaving Tripoli — A3

"Victory" — A4

1921 **Engr.** **Wmk. 140** ***Perf. 14***

No.	Type	Description	Unused	Used
20	A1	1c blk & gray brn	3.25	6.75
21	A1	2c blk & red brn	3.25	6.75
22	A1	5c black & green	4.25	.85
a.		5c black & red brown (error)	1,700.	
b.		Center inverted	65.00	92.50
c.		Imperf., pair	600.00	600.00
23	A2	10c blk & rose	4.25	.85
a.		Center inverted	65.00	92.50
24	A2	15c blk brn & brn org	110.00	3.25
a.		Center inverted	140.00	*275.00*
25	A2	25c dk bl & bl	4.25	.20
a.		Center inverted	21.00	30.00
b.		Imperf., pair	850.00	850.00
26	A3	30c blk & blk brn	30.00	.85
a.		Center inverted	2,400.	2,400.
27	A3	50c blk & ol grn	12.50	.20
a.		50c black & brown (error)	525.00	
b.		Center inverted		*3,400.*
28	A3	55c black & vio	12.50	25.00
29	A4	1 l dk brn & brn	45.00	.20
30	A4	5 l blk & dk blue	25.00	25.00
31	A4	10 l dk bl & ol grn	290.00	170.00
		Nos. 20-31 (12)	544.25	239.90

Nos. 20-31 also exist perf. 14x13. Values substantially higher.

See #47-61. For surcharges see #102-121.

Italy Nos. 136-139 Overprinted

1921, Apr.

No.	Type	Description	Unused	Used
33	A64	5c olive green	2.10	*7.50*
a.		Double overprint	340.00	340.00
34	A64	10c red	2.10	*7.50*
a.		Double overprint	340.00	340.00
b.		Inverted overprint	550.00	550.00
35	A64	15c slate green	2.10	*12.00*
36	A64	25c ultramarine	2.10	*12.00*
		Nos. 33-36 (4)	8.40	*39.00*

3rd anniv. of the victory of the Piave.

Nos. 11, 8 Surcharged

1922, June 1

No.	Type	Description	Unused	Used
37	A49	40c on 50c violet	2.50	2.50
38	A49	80c on 25c blue	2.50	*7.50*

Libyan Sibyl — A6

1924-31 **Unwmk.** ***Perf. 14½x14***

No.	Type	Description	Unused	Used
39	A6	20c deep green	.85	.20
c.		Vert. pair, imperf between and top	1,325.	
d.		Horiz. pair, imperf between and at right	1,325.	
e.		Horiz. pair, imperf between and at left	1,325.	
40	A6	40c brown	1.75	.85
b.		Imperf single	325.00	*425.00*
41	A6	60c deep blue	.85	.20
b.		Imperf single	290.00	
42	A6	1.75 l orange ('31)	.35	.20
43	A6	2 l carmine	3.00	1.10
b.		Imperf single	240.00	*275.00*
44	A6	2.55 l violet ('31)	6.00	12.50
		Nos. 39-44 (6)	12.80	15.05

1926-29 ***Perf. 11***

No.	Type	Description	Unused	Used
39a	A6	20c	35.00	.35
40a	A6	40c	27.50	3.00
41a	A6	60c	27.50	.55
43a	A6	2 l ('29)	13.00	6.25
		Nos. 39a-43a (4)	103.00	10.15

Type of 1921

1924-40 **Unwmk.** ***Perf. 13½ to 14***

No.	Type	Description	Unused	Used
47	A1	1c blk & gray brown	3.25	6.50
48	A1	2c blk & red brn	3.25	6.50
49	A1	5c blk & green	4.25	.85
50	A1	7½c blk & brown ('31)	.45	85.00
51	A2	10c blk & dl red	3.50	.35
b.		10c black & carmine	3.50	.35
c.		As "b," center inverted	210.00	
52	A2	15c blk brn & org	6.75	1.25
b.		Center inverted, perf. 11	3,000.	5,200.
53	A2	25c dk bl & bl	50.00	.65
a.		Center inverted	300.00	340.00
54	A3	30c blk & blk brn	3.40	.65
55	A3	50c blk & ol grn	3.40	.35
b.		Center inverted	3,000.	
56	A3	55c black & vio	500.00	750.00
57	A4	75c violet & red ('31)	3.40	.20
58	A4	1 l dk brn & brn	8.50	.45
59	A3	1.25 l indigo & ultra ('31)	.35	.20
60	A4	5 l blk & dark blue ('40)	140.00	140.00
		Nos. 47-60 (14)	730.50	992.95

Perf. 11

No.	Type	Description	Unused	Used
47a	A1	1c	300.00	
48a	A1	2c	300.00	
49a	A1	5c	75.00	12.50
51a	A2	10c	50.00	6.75
52a	A2	15c	375.00	42.50
54a	A3	30c	150.00	2.50
55a	A3	50c	850.00	.20
58a	A4	1 l	340.00	.45
60a	A4	5 l ('37)	*2,750.*	400.00
61	A4	10 l dk bl & olive grn ('37)	550.00	475.00

Italy #197 and 88 Overprinted Like #1-15

1929 **Wmk. 140** ***Perf. 14***

No.	Type	Description	Unused	Used
62	A86	7½c light brown	6.75	*42.50*
a.		Double overprint	—	—
63	A46	1.25 l blue & ultra	47.50	24.00
a.		Inverted overprint	2,500.	

Italy #193 Overprinted Like #33-36

1929 **Unwmk.** ***Perf. 11***

No.	Type	Description	Unused	Used
64	A85	1.75 l deep brown	60.00	2.50
h.		Perf 13¾		8,500.

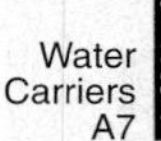

Water Carriers A7

Man of Tripoli — A8

Designs: 25c, Minaret. 30c, 1.25 l, Tomb of Holy Man near Tagiura. 50c, Statue of Emperor Claudius at Leptis. 75c, Ruins of gardens.

1934, Feb. 17 **Photo.** ***Perf. 14***

No.	Type	Description	Unused	Used
64A	A7	10c brown	5.00	*17.00*
64B	A8	20c carmine rose	5.00	*15.00*
64C	A8	25c green	5.00	*15.00*
64D	A7	30c dark brown	5.00	*15.00*
64E	A8	50c purple	5.00	*12.50*
64F	A7	75c rose	5.00	*25.00*
64G	A7	1.25 l blue	50.00	*75.00*
		Nos. 64A-64G (7)	80.00	*174.50*
		Nos. 64A-64G,C14-C18 (12)	432.00	*801.50*

8th Sample Fair, Tripoli.

Bedouin Woman — A15

Highway Memorial Arch — A16

1936, May 11 **Wmk. 140** ***Perf. 14***

No.	Type	Description	Unused	Used
65	A15	50c purple	1.70	*3.25*
66	A15	1.25 l deep blue	1.70	*9.25*

10th Sample Fair, Tripoli.

1937, Mar. 15

No.	Type	Description	Unused	Used
67	A16	50c copper red	2.50	*5.00*
68	A16	1.25 l sapphire	2.50	*12.00*
		Nos. 67-68,C28-C29 (4)	10.00	*33.75*

Coastal road to the Egyptian frontier, opening.

Nos. 67-68 Overprinted in Black

1937, Apr. 24

69 A16 50c copper red 15.00 *37.50*
70 A16 1.25 l sapphire 15.00 *37.50*
Nos. 69-70,C30-C31 (4) 60.00 *150.00*

11th Sample Fair, Tripoli.

Roman Wolf and Lion of St. Mark A17

View of Fair Buildings A18

1938, Mar. 12

71 A17 5c brown .25 1.25
72 A18 10c olive brown .25 .85
73 A17 25c green .60 1.50
74 A18 50c purple .70 .65
75 A17 75c rose red 1.25 *2.50*
76 A18 1.25 l dark blue 1.40 *6.00*
Nos. 71-76,C32-C33 (8) 6.95 *21.25*

12th Sample Fair, Tripoli.

Augustus Caesar (Octavianus) A19

Goddess Abundantia A20

1938, Apr. 25

77 A19 5c olive brown .25 1.70
78 A20 10c brown red .25 1.70
79 A19 25c dk yel green .60 .75
80 A20 50c dk violet .60 .55
81 A19 75c orange red 1.70 *2.10*
82 A20 1.25 l dull blue 1.70 *3.40*
Nos. 77-82,C34-C35 (8) 6.75 *16.80*

Birth bimillenary of Augustus Caesar (Octavianus), first Roman emperor.

Desert City — A21

View of Ghadames A22

1939, Apr. 12 **Photo.**

83 A21 5c olive brown .40 1.25
84 A22 20c red brown .85 1.25
85 A21 50c rose violet .85 1.25
86 A22 75c scarlet .85 *2.50*
87 A21 1.25 l gray blue .85 *3.75*
Nos. 83-87,C36-C38 (8) 5.70 *16.70*

13th Sample Fair, Tripoli.

Modern City — A23

Oxen and Plow A24

Mosque — A25

1940, June 3 **Wmk. 140** ***Perf. 14***

88 A23 5c brown .35 1.25
89 A24 10c red orange .35 .85
90 A25 25c dull green .75 *1.25*
91 A23 50c dark violet .75 *.85*
92 A24 75c crimson .85 *3.40*
93 A25 1.25 l ultramarine 1.25 *5.00*
94 A24 2 l + 75c rose lake 1.25 *17.00*
Nos. 88-94,C39-C42 (11) 9.25 *50.95*

Triennial Overseas Exposition, Naples.

"Two Peoples, One War," Hitler and Mussolini A26

1941, May 16

95 A26 5c orange 1.75 *6.75*
96 A26 10c brown 1.75 *6.75*
97 A26 20c dull violet 2.50 *6.75*
98 A26 25c green 2.50 *6.75*
99 A26 50c purple 2.50 *6.75*
100 A26 75c scarlet 2.50 *19.00*
101 A26 1.25 l sapphire 2.50 *19.00*
Nos. 95-101,C43 (8) 18.50 *106.75*
Set, never hinged 12.50

The Rome-Berlin Axis.

Catalogue values for unused stamps in this section, from this point to the end of the section, are for Never Hinged items.

United Kingdom of Libya

Stamps of Cyrenaica 1950 Surcharged in Black

For Use in Tripolitania

1951, Dec. 24 **Unwmk.** ***Perf. 12½***

102 A2 1mal on 2m rose car .25 .25
103 A2 2mal on 4m dk grn .25 .25
104 A2 4mal on 8m red org .25 .25
105 A2 5mal on 10m pur .45 .45
106 A2 6mal on 12m red .45 .45
a. Inverted surcharge 30.00 30.00
107 A2 10mal on 20m dp bl .85 .85
a. Arabic "20" for "10" 25.00 25.00
108 A3 24mal on 50m choc & ultra 3.00 3.00
109 A3 48mal on 100m bl blk & car rose 12.50 12.50
110 A3 96mal on 200m vio & pur 27.50 27.50
111 A3 240mal on 500m dk grn & org 72.50 72.50
Nos. 102-111 (10) 118.00 *118.00*

The surcharge is larger on Nos. 108 to 111.

Same Surcharge in Francs

For Use in Fezzan

112 A2 2fr on 2m rose car .25 .50
113 A2 4fr on 4m dk grn .25 .50
114 A2 8fr on 8m red org .35 .70
115 A2 10fr on 10m pur .50 1.00
116 A2 12fr on 12m red .90 1.75
117 A2 20fr on 20m dp bl 2.00 *4.25*
118 A3 48fr on 50m choc & ultra 40.00 *225.00*
119 A3 96fr on 100m bl blk & car rose 40.00 *225.00*
120 A3 192fr on 200m vio & pur 110.00 *225.00*
121 A3 480fr on 500m dk grn & org 210.00 *240.00*
Nos. 112-121 (10) 404.25 *923.70*

The surcharge is larger on Nos. 118-121.

A second printing of Nos. 118-121 has an elongated first character in second line of Arabic surcharge.

Cyrenaica Nos. 65-77 Overprinted in Black

For Use in Cyrenaica

122 A2 1m dark brown .20 .35
123 A2 2m rose carmine .25 .35
124 A2 3m orange .25 .50
125 A2 4m dark green 30.00 47.50
126 A2 5m gray .25 *.50*
127 A2 8m red orange .60 *1.20*
128 A2 10m purple .85 *1.75*
129 A2 12m red 1.10 *2.10*
130 A2 20m deep blue 1.75 *3.50*
131 A3 50m choc & ultra 9.00 *18.00*
132 A3 100m bl blk & car rose 15.00 *21.00*
133 A3 200m violet & pur 50.00 *65.00*
134 A3 500m dk grn & org 150.00 *175.00*
Nos. 122-134 (13) 259.25 *336.75*

Wider spacing between the two lines on Nos. 131-134.

King Idris

A27 A28

1952, Apr. 15 **Engr.** ***Perf. 11½***

135 A27 2m yellow brown .20 .20
136 A27 4m gray .20 .20
137 A27 5m blue green 19.00 .65
138 A27 8m vermilion .75 .55
139 A27 10m purple 19.00 .35
140 A27 12m lilac rose 1.60 .35
141 A27 20m deep blue 22.50 .90
142 A27 25m chocolate 22.50 .90
143 A28 50m brown & blue 2.75 1.25
144 A28 100m gray blk & car rose 5.00 2.75
145 A28 200m dk blue & pur 10.00 5.50
146 A28 500m dk grn & brn orange 32.50 20.00
Nos. 135-146 (12) 136.00 33.60

For surcharge and overprints see #168, O1-O8.

Globe — A29

Perf. 13½x13

1955, Jan. 1 **Photo.** **Wmk. 195**

147 A29 5m yellow brown 1.90 1.30
148 A29 10m green 2.75 2.00
149 A29 30m violet 5.00 3.25
Nos. 147-149 (3) 9.65 6.55

Arab Postal Union founding, July 1, 1954.

Nos. 147-149 Overprinted

1955, Aug. 1

150 A29 5m yellow brn .90 .65
151 A29 10m green 1.60 1.10
152 A29 30m violet 3.25 1.90
Nos. 150-152 (3) 5.75 3.65

Arab Postal Congress, Cairo, Mar. 15.

Emblems of Tripolitania, Cyrenaica and Fezzan with Royal Crown — A30

1955 **Engr.** **Wmk. 310** ***Perf. 11½***

153 A30 2m lemon 2.00 .70
154 A30 3m slate blue .20 .20
155 A30 4m gray green 2.60 1.20
156 A30 5m light blue grn .85 .20
157 A30 10m violet 1.40 .20
158 A30 18m crimson .25 .20
159 A30 20m orange .50 .20
160 A30 30m blue .85 .20
161 A30 35m brown 1.20 .25
162 A30 40m rose carmine 1.80 .60
163 A30 50m olive 1.20 .60

Size: 27½x32½mm

164 A30 100m dk green & pur 2.60 1.20
165 A30 200m ultra & rose car 12.00 2.50
166 A30 500m grn & orange 20.00 12.00

Size: 26½x32mm

167 A30 £1 ocher, brn & grn, *yel* 30.00 18.00
Nos. 153-167 (15) 77.45 38.30

See Nos. 177-179, 192-206A.

No. 136 Surcharged

1955, Aug. 25 **Unwmk.**

168 A27 5m on 4m gray 2.00 .90

Tomb of El Senussi, Jagbub A31

Perf. 13x13½

1956, Sept. 14 **Photo.** **Wmk. 195**

169 A31 5m green .50 .50
170 A31 10m bright violet .50 .50
171 A31 15m rose carmine 1.25 1.25
172 A31 30m sapphire 2.00 1.40
Nos. 169-172 (4) 4.25 3.65

Death centenary of the Imam Seyyid Mohammed Aly El Senussi (in 1859).

Map, Flags and UN Headquarters A32

Globe and Postal Emblems A33

1956, Dec. 14 Litho. *Perf. 13½x13*

173 A32 15m bl, ocher & ol bis .75 .35
174 A32 35m bl, ocher & vio brn 1.60 .75

Libya's admission to the UN, 1st anniv.

1957 Wmk. 195 *Perf. 13½x13*

175 A33 15m blue 1.50 1.50
176 A33 500m yellow brown 21.00 11.00

Arab Postal Congress, Tripoli, Feb. 9.

Emblems Type of 1955

1957 Wmk. 310 Engr. *Perf. 11½*

177 A30 1m black, *yellow* .20 .20
178 A30 2m bister brown .20 .20
179 A30 4m brown carmine .35 .35
Nos. 177-179 (3) .75 .75

UN Emblem and Broken Chain — A34

Unwmk.

1958, Dec. 10 Photo. *Perf. 14*

180 A34 10m bluish violet .35 .25
181 A34 15m green .60 .35
182 A34 30m ultramarine 1.50 .85
Nos. 180-182 (3) 2.45 1.45

Universal Declaration of Human Rights, 10th anniv.

Date Palms and FAO Emblem A35

1959, Dec. 5 Unwmk. *Perf. 14*

183 A35 10m pale vio & black .40 .25
184 A35 15m bluish grn & blk .60 .45
185 A35 45m light blue & blk 1.50 1.20
Nos. 183-185 (3) 2.50 1.90

1st Intl. Dates Conf., Tripoli, Dec. 5-11.

Arab League Center, Cairo, and Arms of Libya A36

Perf. 13x13½

1960, Mar. 22 Wmk. 328

186 A36 10m dull grn & blk .60 .35

Opening of the Arab League Center and the Arab Postal Museum in Cairo.

Emblems of WRY and UN, Arms of Libya — A37

Palm Tree and Radio Mast — A38

1960, Apr. 7 Unwmk. *Perf. 14*

187 A37 10m violet & black .60 .35
188 A37 45m blue & black 1.75 1.25

World Refugee Year, 7/1/59-6/30/60.

1960, Aug. 4 Engr. *Perf. 13x13½*

189 A38 10m violet .35 .25
190 A38 15m blue green .50 .25
191 A38 45m dk carmine rose 1.80 1.25
Nos. 189-191 (3) 2.65 1.75

3rd Arab Telecommunications Conf., Tripoli, Aug. 4.

Emblems Type of 1955

1960 Wmk. 310 Engr. *Perf. 11½*

Size: 18x21½mm

192	A30	1m black, *gray*	.20	.20
193	A30	2m bis brn, *buff*	.20	.20
194	A30	3m blue, *bluish*	.20	.20
195	A30	4m brn car, *rose*	.20	.20
196	A30	5m grn, *greenish*	.20	.20
197	A30	10m vio, *pale vio*	.25	.20
198	A30	15m brown, *buff*	.25	.20
199	A30	20m orange, *buff*	.50	.20
200	A30	30m red, *pink*	.50	.20
201	A30	40m rose car, *rose*	.75	.25
202	A30	45m blue, *bluish*	.85	.25
203	A30	50m olive, *buff*	.85	.25

Size: 27½x32½mm

204	A30	100m dk grn & pur, *gray*	1.50	.70
205	A30	200m bl & rose car, *bluish*	4.25	1.40
206	A30	500m green & org, *greenish*	30.00	9.00

Size: 26½x32mm

206A	A30	£1 ocher, brn & grn, *brn*	35.00	18.00
		Nos. 192-206A (16)	75.70	31.65

Watchtower and Broken Chain — A39

1961, Aug. 9 Photo. Unwmk.

207 A39 5m lt yel grn & brn .50 .25
208 A39 15m light blue & brn .85 .35

Issued for Army Day, Aug. 9, 1961.

Map of Zelten Oil Field and Tanker at Marsa Brega — A40

1961, Oct. 25 *Perf. 11½*

209 A40 15m ol grn & buff .50 .25
210 A40 50m red brn & pale vio 1.50 1.00
211 A40 100m ultra & blue 3.25 1.25
Nos. 209-211 (3) 5.25 2.50

Opening of first oil pipe line in Libya.

Hands Breaking Chain, Tractor and Cows — A41

Designs: 50m, Modern highways and buildings. 100m, Machinery.

1961, Dec. 24 *Perf. 11½*

Granite Paper

212 A41 15m pale grn, grn & brown .25 .25
213 A41 50m buff & brown .90 .60
214 A41 100m sal, vio & brn 3.25 1.25
Nos. 212-214 (3) 4.40 2.10

10th anniversary of independence.

Camel Riders — A42

15m, Well. 50m, Oil installations in desert.

1962, Feb. 20 Photo. *Perf. 12*

215 A42 10m choc & org brn .85 .25
216 A42 15m plum & yel grn 1.00 .60
217 A42 50m emer & ultra 2.75 2.10
a. Souv. sheet of 3, #215-217, imperf. 65.00 30.00
Nos. 215-217 (3) 4.60 2.95

Intl. Fair, Tripoli, Feb. 20-Mar. 20.

Nos. 215-217 exist imperf. Value about twice that of perf.

Malaria Eradication Emblem and Palm — A43

Ahmed Rafik El Mehdawi (1898-1961), Poet — A44

1962, Apr. 7 Unwmk. *Perf. 11½*

218 A43 15m multicolored .60 .50
219 A43 50m grn, yel & brn 1.50 1.20

WHO drive to eradicate malaria.

Exist imperf. Value $10.

Two imperf. souvenir sheets exist, one containing the 15m, the other the 50m. Sold for 20m and 70m respectively. Value for both, $30.

1962, July 6 Engr. *Perf. 13x14*

220 A44 15m green .40 .20
221 A44 20m brown .85 .50

El Mehdawi, 1st death anniv.

Clasped Hands and Scout Emblem — A45

Drop of Oil with New City, Desert, Oil Wells and Map of Coast Line — A46

Designs: 10m, 30m, Boy Scouts. 15m, 50m, Scout emblem and tents.

1962, July 13 Photo. *Perf. 12*

222 A45 5m yel, blk & red .25 .20
223 A45 10m bl, blk & yel .50 .25
224 A45 15m multicolored .60 .50
Nos. 222-224 (3) 1.35 .95

Souvenir Sheet

Imperf

225 Sheet of 3 18.00 18.00
a. A45 20m yellow, black & red 5.00 5.00
b. A45 30m blue, black & yellow 5.00 5.00
c. A45 50m blue gray, yel, blk & grn 5.00 5.00

Third Libyan Scout meeting (Philia).

Nos. 222-224 exist imperf. Value for set, $3.

1962, Nov. 25 *Perf. 11x11½*

226 A46 15m grn & vio blk .50 .25
227 A46 50m brn org & ol 1.40 .75

Opening of the Essider Terminal Sidrah pipeline system.

Centenary Emblem — A47

Litho. & Photo.

1963, Jan. 1 *Perf. 11½*

228 A47 10m rose, blk, red & bl .75 .40
229 A47 15m citron, blk, red & bl .85 .60
230 A47 20m gray, blk, red & bl 1.60 .85
Nos. 228-230 (3) 3.20 1.85

Centenary of the International Red Cross.

Rainbow and Arches over Map of Africa and Libya — A48

1963, Feb. 28 Litho. *Perf. 13½*

231 A48 15m multicolored .50 .35
232 A48 30m multicolored .85 .35
233 A48 50m multicolored 1.80 1.00
Nos. 231-233 (3) 3.15 1.70

Tripoli Intl. Fair "Gateway of Africa," Feb. 28-Mar. 28. Every other horizontal row inverted in sheet of 50 (25 tête bêche pairs). Value, set of tête bêche pairs, $6.

Date Palm and Well — A49

Designs: 15m, Camel and flock of sheep. 45m, Sower and tractor.

1963, Mar. 21 Photo. *Perf. 11½*

234 A49 10m green, lt bl & bis .50 .25
235 A49 15m pur, lt grn & bis .60 .50
236 A49 45m dk bl, sal & sep 1.60 1.00
Nos. 234-236 (3) 2.70 1.75

FAO "Freedom from Hunger" campaign.

Man with Whip and Slave Reaching for UN Emblem A50

1963, Dec. 10 Unwmk. *Perf. 11½*

237 A50 5m red brown & bl .25 .20
238 A50 15m deep claret & bl .50 .25
239 A50 50m green & blue 1.25 .75
Nos. 237-239 (3) 2.00 1.20

Universal Declaration of Human Rights, 15th anniv.

Exhibition Hall and Finger Pointing to Libya — A51

1964, Feb. 28 Photo. *Perf. 11½*

240 A51 10m red brn, gray grn & brn 1.00 .25
241 A51 15m pur, gray grn & brn 1.40 .60

242 A51 30m dk bl, gray grn & brn 2.00 1.40
Nos. 240-242 (3) 4.40 2.25

3rd Intl. Fair, Tripoli, Feb. 28-Mar. 20.

Child Playing with Blocks — A52

Design: 15m, Child in bird's nest.

1964, Mar. 22 ***Perf. 11½***
243 A52 5m multicolored .25 .25
244 A52 15m multicolored .60 .25
245 A52 45m multicolored 1.75 .85
a. Souvenir sheet of 3, #243-245, imperf. 4.50 4.50
Nos. 243-245 (3) 2.60 1.35

Children's Day. Exist imperf. Value about 1½ times that of perf.
No. 245a sold for 100m.

Lungs and Stethoscope — A53

1964, Apr. 7 **Photo.** ***Perf. 13½x14***
246 A53 20m deep purple 1.25 .60

Campaign against tuberculosis.

Map of Libya A54

1964, Apr. 27 **Unwmk.** ***Perf. 11½***
247 A54 5m emerald & org .25 .20
248 A54 50m blue & yellow 1.50 .60

First anniversary of Libyan union.

Moth Emerging from Cocoon, Veiled and Modern Women — A55

Hand Giving Scout Sign, Scout and Libyan Flags — A56

1964, June 15 **Litho. & Engraved**
249 A55 10m vio bl & lt grn .35 .25
250 A55 20m vio blue & yel .75 .60
251 A55 35m vio bl & pink 1.25 1.10
a. Souv. sheet of 3, #249-251 4.50 4.50
Nos. 249-251 (3) 2.35 1.95

To honor Libyan women in a new epoch. No. 251a sold for 100m.

1964, July 24 **Photo.** ***Perf. 12x11½***

Design: 20m, Libyan Scout emblem and hands.

252 A56 10m lt bl & multi .85 .35
253 A56 20m multicolored 1.75 .85
a. Souvenir sheet of 2, #252-253, imperf. 11.00 11.00

Opening of new Boy Scout headquarters; installation of Crown Prince Hassan al-Rida el Senussi as Chief Scout. No. 253a sold for 50m.
Nos. 252-253 exist imperf. Value about 1½ times that of perf.

Bayonet, Wreath and Map A57

Ahmed Bahloul el-Sharef A58

1964, Aug. 9 **Litho.** ***Perf. 14x13½***
254 A57 10m yel grn & brn .25 .20
255 A57 20m org & blk .75 .35

Founding of the Senussi Army.

1964, Aug. 11 **Engr.** ***Perf. 11½***
256 A58 15m lilac .50 .20
257 A58 20m greenish blue .85 .50

Poet Ahmed Bahloul el-Sharef, died 1953.

Soccer A59

1964, Oct. 1 **Litho.** ***Perf. 14***
Black Inscriptions and Gold Olympic Rings
258 A59 5m shown .75 .50
259 A59 10m Bicycling .75 .50
260 A59 20m Boxing .75 .50
261 A59 30m Sprinter .75 .60
262 A59 35m Woman diver .75 .60
263 A59 50m Hurdling .75 .60
a. Block of 6, #258-263 5.00 5.00

18th Olympic Games, Tokyo, Oct. 10-25. No. 263a printed in sheet of 48. The two blocks in each double row are inverted in relation to the two blocks in the next row, providing various tete beche and se-tenant arrangements.
#258-263 exist imperf. Value for set, $27.50.
Perf. and imperf. souvenir sheets exist containing six 15m stamps in the designs and colors of Nos. 258-263. Sheets sold for 100m. Value for both, $32.50.

Arab Postal Union Emblem — A59a

1964, Dec. 1 **Photo.** ***Perf. 11x11½***
264 A59a 10m yellow & blue .25 .20
265 A59a 15m pale vio & org brn .50 .25
266 A59a 30m lt yel grn & brn 1.40 .85
Nos. 264-266 (3) 2.15 1.30

Permanent Office of the APU, 10th anniv.

International Cooperation Year Emblem — A60

1965, Jan. 1 **Litho.** ***Perf. 14½x14***
267 A60 5m vio bl & gold .50 .25
268 A60 15m rose car & gold 1.50 .70

Imperfs. exist. Value about twice that of perfs.
See Nos. C51-C51a.

European Bee Eater — A61

Birds: 5m, Long-legged buzzard, vert. 15m, Chestnut-bellied sandgrouse. 20m, Houbara bustard. 30m, Spotted sandgrouse. 40m, Libyan Barbary partridge, vert..

1965, Feb. 10 **Photo.** ***Perf. 11½***
Granite Paper
Birds in Natural Colors
269 A61 5m gray & black 1.10 .45
270 A61 10m lt bl & org brn 1.75 .45
271 A61 15m lt green & blk 2.00 .55
272 A61 20m pale lil & blk 3.50 .80
273 A61 30m tan & dark brn 4.50 1.40
274 A61 40m dull yel & blk 5.25 1.75
Nos. 269-274 (6) 18.10 5.40

Map of Africa with Libya A62

1965, Feb. 28 **Photo.** ***Perf. 11½***
Granite Paper
275 A62 50m multicolored 1.00 .55

4th Intl. Tripoli Fair, Feb. 28-Mar. 20.

Compass Rose, Rockets, Balloons and Stars — A63

1965, Mar. 23 **Litho.**
276 A63 10m multicolored .25 .20
277 A63 15m multicolored .50 .35
278 A63 50m multicolored 1.50 1.00
Nos. 276-278 (3) 2.25 1.55

Fifth World Meteorological Day.

ITU Emblem, Old and New Communication Equipment — A64

1965, May 17 **Unwmk.**
279 A64 10m sepia .25 .20
280 A64 20m red lilac .35 .20
281 A64 50m lilac rose 1.25 .90
Nos. 279-281 (3) 1.85 1.30

ITU, centenary.

Library Aflame and Lamp — A65

1965, June **Litho.** ***Perf. 11½***
282 A65 15m multicolored .50 .25
283 A65 50m multicolored 1.25 .55

Burning of the Library of Algiers, June 7, 1962.

Rose — A66

Jet Plane and Globe — A67

1965, Aug. **Litho.** ***Perf. 14***
284 A66 1m shown .25 .20
285 A66 2m Iris .25 .20
286 A66 3m Opuntia .35 .20
287 A66 4m Sunflower .75 .20
Nos. 284-287 (4) 1.60 .80

1965, Oct. **Photo.** ***Perf. 11½***
288 A67 5m multicolored .25 .20
289 A67 10m multicolored .50 .20
290 A67 15m multicolored 1.00 .20
Nos. 288-290 (3) 1.75 .60

Issued to publicize Libyan Airlines.

Forum, Cyrene — A68

Mausoleum at Germa — A69

Designs: 100m, Arch of Trajan. 200m, Temple of Apollo, Cyrene. 500m, Antonine Temple of Jupiter, Sabratha, horiz. £1, Theater, Sabratha.

Perf. 12x11½, 11½x12
1965, Dec. 24 **Engr.** **Wmk. 310**
291 A68 50m vio blue & olive 1.75 .55
292 A68 100m Prus bl & dp org 2.50 .80
293 A68 200m pur & Prus bl 6.25 1.40
294 A68 500m car rose & grn 14.00 3.75
295 A68 £1 grn & dp org 30.00 9.50
Nos. 291-295 (5) 54.50 16.00

Nos. 293-295 with "Kingdom of Libia" in both Arabic and English blocked out with a blue felt-tipped pen were issued June 21, 1970, by the Republic.

Perf. 11½
1966, Feb. 10 **Unwmk.** **Litho.**
296 A69 70m purple & salmon 3.00 1.00

"POLIGRAFICA & CARTEVALORI-NAPLES" and Libyan Coat of Arms printed on back in yellow green. See No. E13.
Booklet pane containing 4 No. 296 and 4 No. E13 exists. Value $30.

Globe in Space, Satellites — A70

1966, Feb. 28 ***Perf. 12***
297 A70 15m multicolored .50 .20
298 A70 45m multicolored 1.00 .45
299 A70 55m multicolored 1.25 .65
Nos. 297-299 (3) 2.75 1.30

5th Intl. Fair at Tripoli, Feb. 28-Mar. 20.

Arab League Center, Cairo, and Emblem — A71

Litho. & Photo.

1966, Mar. 22 *Perf. 11*

300 A71 20m car, emer & blk .35 .35
301 A71 55m brt bl, ver & blk 1.50 .65

Issued to publicize the Arab League.

Souvenir Sheet

WHO Headquarters, Geneva, and Emblem — A72

1966, May 3 **Litho.** *Imperf.*

302 A72 50m multicolored 9.00 15.00

Inauguration of the WHO headquarters. See Nos. C55-C57.

Tuareg and Camel — A73

A74

Three Tuareg Riders — A75

Design: 20m, like 10m, facing left.

1966, June 20 **Unwmk.** *Perf. 10*

303 A73 10m bright red 1.25 .80
304 A73 20m ultramarine 2.75 1.50
305 A74 50m multicolored 6.00 4.00
a. Strip of 3, Nos. 303-305 10.00 6.00

Imperf

306 A75 100m multicolored 15.00 15.00

Gazelle — A76

Emblem — A77

Perf. 13x11, 11x13

1966, Aug. 12 **Litho.**

307 A76 5m lt grn, blk & red .50 .25
308 A77 25m multicolored .90 .35
309 A77 65m multicolored 2.50 .65
Nos. 307-309 (3) 3.90 1.25

1st Arab Girl Scout Camp (5m); 7th Arab Boy Scout Camp, Good Daim, Libya, Aug. 12 (25m, 60m).

UNESCO Emblem A78

1967, Jan. **Litho.** *Perf. 10x10½*

310 A78 15m multicolored .50 .25
311 A78 25m multicolored 1.10 .45

UNESCO, 20th anniv. (in 1966).

Castle of Columns, Tolemaide A79

Fair Emblem A80

Design: 55m, Sebha Fort, horiz.

Perf. 13x13½, 13½x13

1966, Dec. 24 **Engr.**

312 A79 25m lil, red brn & blk .65 .35
313 A79 55m blk, lil & red brn 1.25 .65

1967, Feb. 28 **Photo.** *Perf. 11½*

314 A80 15m multicolored .65 .20
315 A80 55m multicolored 1.00 .55

6th Intl. Fair, Tripoli, Feb. 28-Mar. 20.

Oil Tanker, Marsa Al Hariga Terminal — A81

1967, Feb. 14 **Litho.** *Perf. 10*

316 A81 60m multicolored 2.25 .75

Opening of Marsa Al Hariga oil terminal.

Tourist Year Emblem — A82

1967, May 1 **Litho.** *Perf. 10½x10*

317 A82 5m gray, blk & brt bl .20 .20
318 A82 10m lt bl, blk & brt bl .25 .25
319 A82 45m pink, blk & brt bl .75 .35
Nos. 317-319 (3) 1.20 .80

International Tourist Year.

Map of Mediterranean and Runners — A83

1967, Sept. 8 **Litho.** *Perf. 10½*

320 A83 5m shown .20 .20
321 A83 10m Javelin .20 .20
322 A83 15m Bicyling .25 .20
323 A83 45m Soccer .75 .55
324 A83 75m Boxing 1.10 .75
Nos. 320-324 (5) 2.50 1.90

5th Mediterranean Games, Tunis, Sept. 8-17.

A84

A85

Arab League emblem and hands reaching for knowledge.

1967, Oct. 1 **Litho.** *Perf. 12½x13*

325 A84 5m orange & dk pur .25 .20
326 A84 10m brt grn & dk pur .25 .20
327 A84 15m lilac & dk pur .25 .25
328 A84 25m blue & dk pur .50 .25
Nos. 325-328 (4) 1.25 .90

Literacy campaign.

1968, Jan. 15 **Litho.** *Perf. 13½x14*

Human rights flame.

329 A85 15m grn & vermilion .35 .20
330 A85 60m org & vio bl .90 .55

International Human Rights Year.

Map, Derrick, Plane and Camel Riders — A86

1968, Feb. 28 **Photo.** *Perf. 11½*

331 A86 55m car rose, brn & yel 1.25 .75

7th Intl. Fair, Tripoli, Feb. 28-Mar. 20.

Arab League Emblem A87

1968, Mar. 22 **Engr.** *Perf. 13½*

332 A87 10m blue gray & car .25 .20
333 A87 45m fawn & green .90 .65

Issued for Arab League Week.

Children, Statuary Group A88

Children's Day: 55m, Mother and children.

1968, Mar. 21 **Litho.** *Perf. 11*

334 A88 25m gray, blk & mag .65 .35
335 A88 55m gray & multi 1.25 .65

Hands Reaching for WHO Emblem — A89

1968, Apr. 7 **Photo.** *Perf. 13½x14½*

336 A89 25m rose cl, dk bl & gray bl .60 .25
337 A89 55m bl, blk & gray .90 .55

WHO, 20th anniversary.

From Oil Field to Tanker A90

1968, Apr. 23 **Litho.** *Perf. 11*

338 A90 10m multicolored .50 .20
339 A90 60m multicolored 1.50 .80

Opening of the Zueitina oil terminal.

Teacher and Crowd A91

1968, Sept. 8 **Litho.** *Perf. 13½*

340 A91 5m bright pink .25 .20
341 A91 10m orange .25 .20
342 A91 15m blue .25 .25
343 A91 20m emerald .50 .50
Nos. 340-343 (4) 1.25 1.15

Literacy campaign.

Arab Labor Emblem A92

1968, Nov. 3 **Photo.** *Perf. 14x13½*

344 A92 10m multicolored .25 .20
345 A92 15m multicolored .50 .20

4th session of the Arab Labor Ministers' Conf., Tripoli, Nov. 3-10.

Wadi el Kuf Bridge and Road Sign — A93

1968, Dec. 25 Litho. *Perf. 11x11½*

346 A93 25m ultra & multi .40 .35
347 A93 60m emer & multi 1.00 .90

Opening of the Wadi el Kuf Bridge.

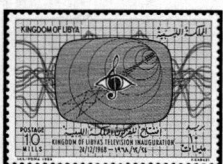

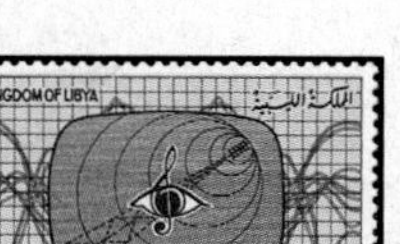

Television Screen and Chart A94

1968, Dec. 25 Photo. *Perf. 14x13½*

348 A94 10m yellow & multi .25 .20
349 A94 30m lilac & multi .90 .45

Inauguration of television service, Dec. 24.

Melons — A95

1969, Jan. Photo. *Perf. 11½*
Granite Paper

350 A95 5m shown .25 .20
351 A95 10m Peanuts .25 .20
352 A95 15m Lemons .25 .20
353 A95 20m Oranges .40 .20
354 A95 25m Peaches .65 .35
355 A95 35m Pears 1.25 .55
Nos. 350-355 (6) 3.05 1.70

Nos. 350-355 with "Kingdom of Libya" in both English and Arabic blocked out with a blue felt-tipped pen were issued in December, 1971, by the Republic.

Tripoli Fair Emblem A96

1969, Apr. 8
Granite Paper

356 A96 25m silver & multi .40 .20
357 A96 35m bronze & multi .65 .35
358 A96 40m gold & multi .75 .45
Nos. 356-358 (3) 1.80 1.00

8th Intl. Fair, Tripoli, Mar. 6-26.

Weather Balloon and Observer A97

1969, Mar. 21 Photo. *Perf. 14x13*

359 A97 60m gray & multi 1.50 .80

World Meteorological Day, Mar. 23.

Cogwheel and Workers A98

1969, Mar. 29 Litho. *Perf. 13½*

360 A98 15m blue & multi .25 .20
361 A98 55m salmon & multi .75 .55

10th anniversary of Social Insurance.

ILO Emblem — A99

1969, June 1 Photo. *Perf. 14*

362 A99 10m bl grn, blk & lt ol .25 .20
363 A99 60m car rose, blk & lt ol .90 .65

ILO, 50th anniversary.

African Tourist Year Emblem — A100

1969, July *Perf. 11½*
Emblem in Emerald, Light Blue & Red

364 A100 15m emer & silver .45 .20
365 A100 30m blk & gold .90 .65

Issued to publicize African Tourist Year.

Libyan Arab Republic

Soldiers, Tanks and Planes — A101

Radar, Flags and Carrier Pigeon — A102

1969, Dec. 7 Photo. *Perf. 12x12½*

366 A101 5m org & multi .40 .20
367 A101 10m ultra & multi .65 .35
368 A101 15m multicolored .90 .45
369 A101 25m multicolored 1.40 .65
370 A101 45m brt bl & multi 1.60 1.00
371 A101 60m multicolored 2.75 1.25
Nos. 366-371 (6) 7.70 3.90

Establishment of the Libyan Arab Republic, Sept. 1, 1969. See Nos. 379-384.

1970, Mar. 1 Photo. *Perf. 11½*
Granite Paper

372 A102 15m multicolored .65 .20
373 A102 20m multicolored 1.00 .35
374 A102 25m multicolored 1.40 .45
375 A102 40m multicolored 2.00 1.00
Nos. 372-375 (4) 5.05 2.00

Map of Arab League Countries, Flag and Emblem A102a

1970, Mar. 22

376 A102a 10m lt bl, brn & grn .35 .20
377 A102a 15m org, brn & grn .60 .20
378 A102a 20m ol, brn & grn 1.00 .45
Nos. 376-378 (3) 1.95 .85

25th anniversary of the Arab League.

Type A101 Redrawn — A103

1970, May 2 Photo. *Perf. 12x12½*

379 A103 5m org & multi .35 .20
380 A103 10m ultra & multi .60 .55
381 A103 15m multicolored .90 .45
382 A103 25m multicolored 1.40 1.25
383 A103 45m brt bl & multi 1.60 1.00
384 A103 60m multicolored 2.75 1.25
Nos. 379-384 (6) 7.60 4.70

On Nos. 379-384 the numerals are in black, the bottom inscription is in 2 lines and several other changes.

Inauguration of UPU Headquarters, Bern — A104

1970, May 20 Photo. *Perf. 11½x11*

385 A104 10m multicolored .25 .20
386 A104 25m multicolored .60 .20
387 A104 60m multicolored 1.25 .65
Nos. 385-387 (3) 2.10 1.05

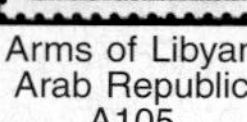

Arms of Libyan Arab Republic A105

Flags, Soldiers and Tank A106

1970, June 20 Photo. *Perf. 11*

388 A105 15m black & brt rose .25 .20
389 A105 25m vio bl, yel & brt rose .50 .20
390 A105 45m emer, yel & brt rose 1.75 .45
Nos. 388-390 (3) 2.50 .85

Evacuation of US military base in Libya.

1970, Sept. 1 Photo. *Perf. 11x11½*

391 A106 20m multicolored .75 .20
392 A106 25m multicolored 1.00 .55
393 A106 30m blue & multi 1.60 .75
Nos. 391-393 (3) 3.35 1.50

Libyan Arab Republic, 1st anniv.

UN Emblem, Dove and Scales — A107

1970, Oct. 24 Photo. *Perf. 11x11½*

394 A107 5m org & multi .60 .35
395 A107 10m olive & multi .90 .45
396 A107 60m multicolored 2.50 .90
Nos. 394-396 (3) 4.00 1.70

25th anniversary of the United Nations.

Map and Flags of UAR, Libya, Sudan A107a

1970, Dec. 27 Photo. *Perf. 11½*

397 A107a 15m lt grn, car & blk 7.00 2.25

Signing of the Charter of Tripoli affirming the unity of UAR, Libya and the Sudan, Dec. 27, 1970.

UN Emblem, Dove and Globe — A108

1971, Jan. 10 Litho. *Perf. 12x11½*

398 A108 15m multicolored .60 .20
399 A108 20m multicolored .90 .45
400 A108 60m lt vio & multi 2.50 .90
Nos. 398-400 (3) 4.00 1.55

UN declaration on granting of independence to colonial countries and peoples, 10th anniv.

Education Year Emblem — A109

Al Fatah Fighter — A110

1971, Jan. 16

401 A109 5m red, blk & ocher .25 .20
402 A109 10m red, blk & emer .60 .55
403 A109 20m red, blk & vio bl 1.60 .80
Nos. 401-403 (3) 2.45 1.55

International Education Year.

1971, Mar. 14 Photo. *Perf. 11*

404 A110 5m ol & multi .50 .20
405 A110 10m yel & multi .80 .20
406 A110 100m multicolored 1.90 .20
Nos. 404-406 (3) 3.20 .60

Fight for the liberation of Palestine.

Tripoli Fair Emblem — A111

10th Anniv. of OPEC — A112

1971, Mar. 18 Litho. *Perf. 14*

407 A111 15m multicolored .35 .20
408 A111 30m org & multi .90 .45

9th International Fair at Tripoli.

1971, May 29 Litho. *Perf. 12*

409 A112 10m yellow & brown .25 .20
410 A112 70m pink & vio bl 1.60 .65

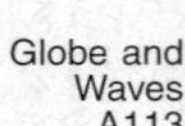

Globe and Waves A113

1971, June 10 *Perf. 14½x13½*
411 A113 25m brt grn, blk & vio bl .50 .20
412 A113 35m gray & multi 1.25 1.00

3rd World Telecommunications Day, May 17, 1971.

Map of Africa and Telecommunications Network — A114

1971, June 10
413 A114 5m yel, blk & grn .20 .20
414 A114 15m dl bl, blk & grn .40 .20

Pan-African telecommunications system.

Torchbearer and Banner — A115

Ramadan Suehli — A116

1971, June 15 Photo. *Perf. 11½x12*
415 A115 5m yel & multi .25 .20
416 A115 10m org & multi .35 .35
417 A115 15m multicolored .50 .45
Nos. 415-417 (3) 1.10 1.00

Evacuation of US military base, 1st anniv.

1971, Aug. 24 *Perf. 14x14½*
418 A116 15m multicolored .20 .20
419 A116 55m bl & multi 1.00 .55

Ramadan Suehli (1879-1920), freedom fighter.
See #422-423, 426-427, 439-440, 479-480.

Date Palm — A117

Gamal Abdel Nasser (1918-1970), President of Egypt — A118

1971, Sept. 1
420 A117 5m multicolored .20 .20
421 A117 15m multicolored 1.25 1.25

Sept. 1, 1969 Revolution, 2nd anniv.

Portrait Type of 1971

Portrait: Omar el Mukhtar (1858-1931), leader of the Martyrs.

1971, Sept. 16 *Perf. 14x14½*
422 A116 5m lt grn & multi .20 .20
423 A116 100m multicolored 2.50 1.50

1971, Sept. 28 Photo. *Perf. 11x11½*
424 A118 5m lil, grn & blk .35 .20
425 A118 15m grn, lil & blk 1.25 .20

Portrait Type of 1971

Ibrahim Usta Omar (1908-50), patriotic poet.

1971, Oct. 8 Litho. *Perf. 14x14½*
426 A116 25m vio bl & multi .60 .60
427 A116 30m multicolored 1.10 .45

Racial Equality Emblem A119

Arab Postal Union Emblem — A120

1971, Oct. 24 *Perf. 13½x14½*
428 A119 25m multicolored .60 .20
429 A119 35m multicolored 1.10 .45

Intl. Year Against Racial Discrimination.

1971, Nov. 6 Litho. *Perf. 14½*
Emblem in Black, Yellow and Blue
430 A120 5m red .25 .20
431 A120 10m violet .40 .20
432 A120 15m bright rose lilac .40 .20
Nos. 430-432 (3) 1.05 .60

Conference of Sofar, Lebanon, establishing Arab Postal Union, 25th anniv.

Postal Union Emblem and Letter A121

25m, 55m, APU emblem, letter and dove.

1971, Dec. Photo. *Perf. 11½x11*
433 A121 10m org brn, bl & blk .35 .20
434 A121 15m org, lt bl & blk .50 .35
435 A121 25m lt grn, org & blk .75 .55
436 A121 55m lt brn, yel & blk 1.60 .70
Nos. 433-436 (4) 3.20 1.80

10th anniversary of African Postal Union. Issued: 25m, 55m, 12/2; 10m, 15m, 12/12.

Despite the change from milliemes to dirhams in 1972, both currencies appear on stamps until August.

Book Year Emblem A122

Coat of Arms A123

1972, Jan. 1 Litho. *Perf. 12½x13*
437 A122 15m ultra, brn, gold & blk .35 .35
438 A122 20m gold, brn, ultra & blk .60 .60

International Book Year.

Portrait Type of 1971

Ahmed Gnaba (1898-1968), poet of unity.

1972, Jan. 12 *Perf. 14x14½*
439 A116 20m red & multi .60 .20
440 A116 35m olive & multi .85 .45

1972, Feb. 10 Photo. *Perf. 14½*
Size: 19x23mm
441 A123 5m gray & multi .20 .20
442 A123 10m lt ol & multi .20 .20
443 A123 15d lilac & multi .20 .20
445 A123 25m lt bl & multi .25 .20
446 A123 30m rose & multi .35 .20
447 A123 35m lt ol & multi .45 .20
448 A123 40m dl yel & multi .60 .20
449 A123 45m lt grn & multi .75 .35
451 A123 55m multicolored 1.00 .50
452 A123 60m bister & multi 1.90 .65
453 A123 65d multicolored .75 .55
454 A123 70d lt vio & multi 1.00 .65
455 A123 80d ocher & multi 1.50 .80
456 A123 90m bl & multi 1.90 .90

Size: 27x32mm
Perf. 14x14½
457 A123 100d multicolored 2.25 1.20
458 A123 200d multicolored 3.75 2.25
459 A123 500d multicolored 9.50 6.50
460 A123 £1 multicolored 17.50 11.00
Nos. 441-460 (18) 44.05 26.75

During the transition from millimemes and pounds to dirhams and dinars, stamps were issued in both currencies.

A124

A124a

A124b

Coil Stamps

1972, July 27 Photo. *Perf. 14½x14*
461 A124 5m sl bl, ocher & black 2.50 2.00
462 A124a 20m bl, lil & blk 11.00 2.00
463 A124b 50m bl, ol & blk 26.00 5.00
Nos. 461-463 (3) 39.50 9.00

See Nos. 496-498, 575-577.

Tombs at Ghirza — A125

Fair Emblem A126

Designs: 10m, Kufic inscription, Agedabia, horiz. 15m, Marcus Aurelius Arch, Tripoli. 25m, Exchange of weapons, mural from Wan Amil Cave. 55m, Garamanthian (Berber) chariot, petroglyph, Wadi Zigza. 70m, Nymph Cyrene strangling a lion, bas-relief, Cyrene.

1972, Feb. 15 Litho. *Perf. 14*
464 A125 5m lilac & multi .50 .50
465 A125 10m multicolored .50 .50
466 A125 15m dp org & multi 1.00 .35
467 A125 25m emer & multi 1.50 .90
468 A125 55m scar & multi 3.50 .90
469 A125 70m ultra & multi 7.00 1.25
Nos. 464-469 (6) 14.00 4.40

1972, Mar. 1
470 A126 25d gray & multi .60 .20
471 A126 35d multicolored .65 .20
472 A126 50d multicolored 1.40 .35
473 A126 70d multicolored 1.60 .60
Nos. 470-473 (4) 4.25 1.35

10th International Fair at Tripoli.

Dissected Arm, and Heart — A127

"Arab Unity" — A128

1972, Apr. 7 *Perf. 14½*
474 A127 15d multicolored 1.50 .45
475 A127 25d multicolored 3.25 1.00

"Your heart is your health," World Health Day.

Litho. & Engr.
1972, Apr. 17 *Perf. 13½x13*
476 A128 15d bl, yel & blk .25 .20
477 A128 20d lt grn, yel & blk .60 .20
478 A128 25d lt ver, yel & blk 1.25 .80
Nos. 476-478 (3) 2.10 1.20

Fed. of Arab Republics Foundation, 1st anniv.

Portrait Type of 1971

Suleiman el Baruni (1870-1940), patriotic writer.

1972, May 1 Litho. *Perf. 14x14½*
479 A116 10m yellow & multi 1.25 .80
480 A116 70m dp org & multi 2.00 1.00

Environment Emblem A129

Olympic Emblems A130

1972, Aug. 15 Litho. *Perf. 14½*
481 A129 15m red & multi .60 .20
482 A129 55m green & multi 1.40 .40

UN Conference on Human Environment, Stockholm, June 5-16.

1972, Aug. 26
483 A130 25d brt bl & multi 2.00 .60
484 A130 35d red & multi 3.00 1.25

20th Olympic Games, Munich, 8/26-9/11.

Emblem and Broken Chain A131

Dome of the Rock, Jerusalem A132

1972, Oct. 1 Litho. *Perf. 14x13½*
485 A131 15d blue & multi .40 .20
486 A131 25d yellow & multi .90 .35

Libyan Arab Republic, 3rd anniv.

1972 *Perf. 12½x13*
487 A132 10d multicolored .40 .20
488 A132 25d multicolored .60 .20

Nicolaus Copernicus (1473-1543), Polish Astronomer
A133

Blind Person, Books, Loom and Basket
A135

Eagle and Fair Buildings
A134

Design: 25d, Copernicus in Observatory, by Jan Matejko, horiz.

Perf. 14½x13½, 13½x14½

1973, Feb. 26

489 A133 15d yellow & multi .40 .20
490 A133 25d blue & multi .60 .35

1973, Mar. 1 ***Perf. 13½x14½***

491 A134 5d dull red & multi .40 .20
492 A134 10d blue grn & multi .60 .20
493 A134 15d vio blue & multi 1.25 .20
Nos. 491-493 (3) 2.25 .60

11th International Fair at Tripoli.

1973, Apr. 18 Photo. ***Perf. 12x11½***

494 A135 20d gray & multi 8.00 1.50
495 A135 25d dull yel & multi 11.00 5.00

Role of the blind in society.

Coil Stamps
Numeral Type of 1972 Denominations in Dirhams

1973, Apr. 26 Photo. ***Perf. 14½x14***

496 A124 5d sl bl, ocher & blk 1.00 1.00
497 A124 20d blue, lilac & blk 1.50 1.50
498 A124 50d blue, olive & blk 5.50 5.50
Nos. 496-498 (3) 8.00 8.00

Map of Africa — A136

1973, May 25 Photo. ***Perf. 11x11½***

499 A136 15d yel, green & brown .50 .20
500 A136 25d lt yel grn, grn & blk 1.00 .50

"Freedom in Unity" (Org. for African Unity).

INTERPOL Emblem and General Secretariat, Paris — A138

Perf. 13½x14½

1973, June 30 **Litho.**

501 A138 10d lilac & multi .25 .20
502 A138 15d ocher & multi .50 .20
503 A138 25d lt grn & multi .75 .20
Nos. 501-503 (3) 1.50 .60

50th anniv. of Intl. Criminal Police Org.

Map of Libya, Houses, People, Factories, Tractor
A139

1973, July 15 Photo. ***Perf. 11½***

504 A139 10d rose red, black & ultra 4.00 .80
505 A139 25d ultra, blk & grn 5.75 1.75
506 A139 35d grn, blk & org 11.00 3.50
Nos. 504-506 (3) 20.75 6.05

General census.

UN Emblem — A140

1973, Aug. 1 ***Perf. 12½x11***

507 A140 5d ver, blk & bl .25 .20
508 A140 10d yel grn, blk & bl .50 .50

Intl. meteorological cooperation, cent.

Soccer — A141

1973, Aug. 10 Photo. ***Perf. 11½***

509 A141 5d yel grn & dk brn .50 .20
510 A141 25d orange & dk brn 1.10 .70

2nd Palestinian Cup Soccer Tournament.

Torch and Grain — A142

Writing Hand, Lamp and Globe — A143

1973, Sept. 1 Litho. ***Perf. 14***

511 A142 15d brown & multi .50 .20
512 A142 25d emer & multi 1.40 .20

4th anniv. of Sept. 1 Revolution.

1973, Sept. 8

513 A143 25d multicolored .60 .60

Literacy campaign.

Gate of First City Hall
A144

Militia, Flag and Factories
A145

1973, Sept. 18 ***Perf. 13***

514 A144 10d shown .50 .50
515 A144 25d Khondok fountain .60 .60
516 A144 35d Clock tower .90 .35
Nos. 514-516 (3) 2.00 1.45

Centenary of Tripoli as a municipality.

1973, Oct. 7 Photo. ***Perf. 11½x11***

517 A145 15d yel, blk & red .50 .20
518 A145 25d green & multi .75 .35

Libyan Militia.

Revolutionary Proclamation by Khadafy — A146

70d, as 25d, with English inscription.

1973, Oct. 15 Litho. ***Perf. 12½***

519 A146 25d orange & multi .50 .50
520 A146 70d green & multi 1.50 .75

Proclamation of People's Revolution by Pres. Muammar Khadafy.

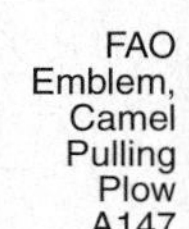

FAO Emblem, Camel Pulling Plow
A147

1973, Nov. 1 Photo. ***Perf. 11***

521 A147 10d ocher & multi .20 .20
522 A147 25d dk brn & multi .50 .50
523 A147 35d black & multi .75 .35
Nos. 521-523 (3) 1.45 1.05

World Food Org., 10th anniv.

Human Rights Flame — A148

1973, Dec. 20 Photo. ***Perf. 11x11½***

524 A148 25d pur, car & dk bl .35 .35
525 A148 70d lt grn, car & dk bl 1.50 .65

Universal Declaration of Human Rights, 25th anniv.

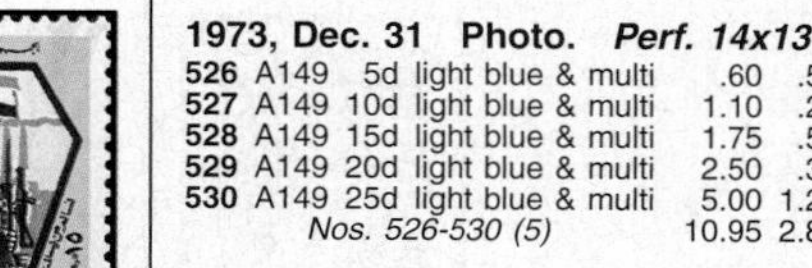

Fish
A149

Designs: Various fish from Libyan waters.

1973, Dec. 31 Photo. ***Perf. 14x13½***

526 A149 5d light blue & multi .60 .50
527 A149 10d light blue & multi 1.10 .25
528 A149 15d light blue & multi 1.75 .50
529 A149 20d light blue & multi 2.50 .35
530 A149 25d light blue & multi 5.00 1.25
Nos. 526-530 (5) 10.95 2.85

1975, Jan. 5

526a A149 5d greenish blue & multi 2.10 1.25
527a A149 10d greenish blue & multi 4.25 1.25
528a A149 15d greenish blue & multi 4.25 1.25
529a A149 20d greenish blue & multi 6.25 .60
530a A149 25d greenish blue & multi 8.00 2.50
Nos. 526a-530a (5) 24.85 6.85

Scout, Sun and Scout Signs
A150

Fair Emblem, Flags of Participants
A151

1974, Feb. 1 Litho. ***Perf. 11½***

531 A150 5d blue & multi 1.10 .35
532 A150 20d light lilac & multi 3.25 .60
533 A150 25d light green & multi 5.50 2.50
Nos. 531-533 (3) 9.85 3.45

Libyan Boy Scouts.

1974, Mar. 1 Litho. ***Perf. 12x11½***

534 A151 10d lt ultra & multi .60 .35
535 A151 25d tan & multi .90 .60
536 A151 35d lt green & multi 1.75 .20
Nos. 534-536 (3) 3.25 1.15

12th Tripoli International Fair.

Protected Family, WHO Emblem — A152

Minaret and Star — A153

1974, Apr. 7 Litho. ***Perf. 12½***

537 A152 5d lt green & multi .35 .20
538 A152 25d red & multi .60 .60

World Health Day.

1974, Apr. 16 ***Perf. 11½x11***

539 A153 10d pink & multi .50 .50
540 A153 25d yellow & multi 1.00 .60
541 A153 35d orange & multi 1.40 .50
Nos. 539-541 (3) 2.90 1.60

City University of Bengazi, inauguration.

UPU Emblem and Star — A154

Traffic Signs — A156

1974, May 22 Litho. ***Perf. 13½x14½***
542 A154 25d multicolored 7.50 1.10
543 A154 70d multicolored 14.00 2.25

Centenary of Universal Postal Union.

1974, June 8 Photo. ***Perf. 11***
547 A156 5d gold & multi .20 .20
548 A156 10d gold & multi .40 .20
549 A156 25d gold & multi .50 .20
Nos. 547-549 (3) 1.10 .60

Automobile and Touring Club of Libya.

Tank, Oil Refinery, Book — A157

Symbolic "5" — A158

1974, Sept. 1 Litho. ***Perf. 14***
550 A157 5d red & multi .20 .20
551 A157 20d violet & multi .40 .40
552 A157 25d vio bl & multi .40 .40
553 A157 35d green & multi .50 .50
Nos. 550-553 (4) 1.50 1.50

Souvenir Sheet

Perf. 13

554 A158 55d yel & maroon 9.00 9.00

Revolution of Sept. 1, 5th anniv. English inscription on No. 553.

WPY Emblem and Crowd — A159

Libyan Woman — A160

1974, Oct. 19 ***Perf. 14***
555 A159 25d multicolored .35 .20
556 A159 35d lt brn & multi .75 .60

World Population Year.

1975, Mar. 1 Litho. ***Perf. 13x12½***

Libyan Costumes: 10d, 15d, Women. 20d, Old man. 25d, Man riding camel. 50d, Man on horseback.

557 A160 5d org yel & multi .20 .20
558 A160 10d org yel & multi .20 .20
559 A160 15d org yel & multi .50 .20
560 A160 20d org yel & multi .75 .20
561 A160 25d org yel & multi 1.50 .75
562 A160 50d org yel & multi 2.75 .75
Nos. 557-562 (6) 5.90 2.30

Congress Emblem — A161

1975, Mar. 4 Litho. ***Perf. 12x12½***
563 A161 10d brown & multi .20 .20
564 A161 25d vio & multi .40 .40
565 A161 35d gray & multi .75 .20
Nos. 563-565 (3) 1.35 .80

Arab Labor Congress.

Teacher Pointing to Blackboard A162

1975, Mar. 10 ***Perf. 11½***
566 A162 10d gold & multi .20 .20
567 A162 25d gold & multi .50 .20

Teacher's Day.

Bodies, Globe, Proclamation A163

Woman and Man in Library — A164

1975, Apr. 7 Litho. ***Perf. 12½***
568 A163 20d lilac & multi .40 .40
569 A163 25d emer & multi .50 .20

World Health Day.

1975, May 25 Litho. ***Perf. 12½***
570 A164 10d bl grn & multi .20 .20
571 A164 25d olive & multi .50 .50
572 A164 35d lt vio & multi .60 .60
Nos. 570-572 (3) 1.30 1.30

Libyan Arab Book Exhibition.

Festival Emblem — A165

Games Emblem and Arms — A166

1975, July 5 Litho. ***Perf. 13x12½***
573 A165 20d lt bl & multi .40 .40
574 A165 25d orange & multi .50 .50

2nd Arab Youth Festival.

Coil Stamps

Redrawn Type of 1973 Without "LAR"

1975, Aug. 15 Photo. ***Perf. 14½x14***
575 A124 5d blue, org & blk .50 .50
576 A124 20d blue, yel & blk 1.00 1.00
577 A124 50d blue, grn & blk 2.00 2.00
Nos. 575-577 (3) 3.50 3.50

1975, Aug. 23 ***Perf. 13x12½***
578 A166 10d salmon & multi .20 .20
579 A166 25d lilac & multi .50 .50
580 A166 50d yellow & multi 1.40 .40
Nos. 578-580 (3) 2.10 1.10

7th Mediterranean Games, Algiers, 8/23-9/6.

Peace Dove, Symbols of Agriculture and Industry — A167

Khadafy's Head Over Desert — A168

Design: 70d, Peace dove, diff.

1975, Sept. Litho. ***Perf. 13x12½***
581 A167 25d multicolored .40 .20
582 A167 70d multicolored 1.40 .50

Souvenir Sheet

Imperf

Litho. & Embossed

583 A168 100d multicolored 6.00 6.00

6th anniversary of Sept. 1 revolution. No. 583 contains one stamp with simulated perforations.

Khalil Basha Mosque — A169

Al Kharruba Mosque — A170

Mosques: 10d, Sidi Abdulla El Shaab. 15d, Sidi Ali El Fergani. 25d, Katikhtha. 30d, Murad Agha. 35d, Maulai Mohammed.

1975, Dec. 13 Litho. ***Perf. 12½***
584 A169 5d gray & multi .20 .20
585 A169 10d purple & multi .20 .20
586 A169 15d green & multi .20 .20
587 A170 20d ocher & multi .40 .20
588 A170 25d multicolored .40 .20
589 A170 30d multicolored .50 .20
590 A170 35d lilac & multi .75 .60
Nos. 584-590 (7) 2.65 1.80

Mohammed's 1405th birthday.

Arms of Libya and People — A171

Islamic- Christian Dialogue Emblem — A172

1976, Jan. 15 Photo. ***Perf. 13***
591 A171 35d blue & multi .50 .20
592 A171 40d multicolored .60 .20

General National (People's) Congress.

1976, Feb. 5 Litho. ***Perf. 13x12½***
593 A172 40d gold & multi .60 .20
594 A172 115d gold & multi 1.90 .90

Seminar of Islamic-Christian Dialogue, Tripoli, Feb. 1-5.

Woman Blowing Horn — A173

National Costumes: 20d, Lancer. 30d, Drummer. 40d, Bagpiper. 100d, Woman carrying jug on head.

1976, Mar. 1 Litho. ***Perf. 13x12½***
595 A173 10d multicolored .20 .20
596 A173 20d multicolored .50 .40
597 A173 30d pink & multi 1.00 .20
598 A173 40d multicolored 1.25 .20
599 A173 100d yel & multi 3.00 .50
Nos. 595-599 (5) 5.95 1.50

14th Tripoli International Fair.

Telephones, 1876 and 1976, ITU and UPU Emblems — A174

70d, Alexander Graham Bell, telephone, satellites, radar, ITU & UPU emblems.

1976, Mar. 10 Photo. ***Perf. 13***
600 A174 40d multicolored 2.25 .75
a. Souvenir sheet of 4 9.00 9.00
601 A174 70d multicolored 3.75 .75
a. Souvenir sheet of 4 15.00 15.00

Centenary of first telephone call by Alexander Graham Bell, Mar. 10, 1876.

Nos. 600a and 601a exist imperf. Value, both sheets $90.

Mother and Child — A175

Hands, Eye and Head — A176

1976, Mar. 21 *Perf. 12*
602 A175 85d gray & multi 1.50 1.25
603 A175 110d pink & multi 1.60 1.50

International Children's Day.

1976, Apr. 7 Photo. *Perf. 13½x13*
604 A176 30d multicolored .35 .35
605 A176 35d multicolored .50 .50
606 A176 40d multicolored .60 .60
Nos. 604-606 (3) 1.45 1.45

"Foresight prevents blindness;" World Health Day.

Little Bittern A177

Birds of Libya: 10d, Great gray shrike. 15d, Songbird. 20d, European bee-eater, vert. 25d, Hoopoe.

Perf. 13x13½, 13½x13
1976, May 1 **Litho.**
607 A177 5d orange & multi .60 .45
608 A177 10d ultra & multi 1.25 1.00
609 A177 15d rose & multi 2.50 1.25
610 A177 20d yellow & multi 4.50 1.25
611 A177 25d blue & multi 9.00 2.50
Nos. 607-611 (5) 17.85 6.45

Al Barambekh A178

Bicycling — A179

Designs: 15d, Whale, horiz. 30d, Lizard (alwaral), horiz. 40d, Mastodon skull, horiz. 70d, Hawk. 115d, Wild mountain sheep.

1976, June 20 Litho. *Perf. 12½*
612 A178 10d multicolored 1.25 1.00
613 A178 15d multicolored 2.25 1.75
614 A178 30d multicolored 2.75 2.25
615 A178 40d multicolored 4.75 4.00
616 A178 70d multicolored 8.50 7.00
617 A178 115d multicolored 14.00 12.00
Nos. 612-617 (6) 33.50 28.00

Museum of Natural History.

1976, July 17 Litho. *Perf. 12x11½*
Granite Paper
618 A179 15d shown .20 .20
619 A179 25d Boxing .50 .50
620 A179 70d Soccer 1.50 1.50
Nos. 618-620 (3) 2.20 2.20

Souvenir Sheet
621 A179 150d Symbolic of various sports 15.00 15.00

21st Olympic Games, Montreal, Canada, July 17-Aug. 1.

Tree Growing from Globe — A180

Symbols of Agriculture and Industry — A181

Drummer and Pipeline — A182

1976, Aug. 9 *Perf. 13*
622 A180 115d multicolored 1.25 .90

5th Conference of Non-Aligned Countries, Colombo, Sri Lanka, Aug. 9-19.

Beginning with No. 622 numerous issues are printed with multiple coats of arms in pale green on back of stamps.

1976, Sept. 1 *Perf. 14½x14*
623 A181 30d yel & multi .40 .20
624 A181 40d multicolored .50 .20
625 A181 100d multicolored 1.25 .90
Nos. 623-625 (3) 2.15 1.30

Souvenir Sheet
Perf. 13
626 A182 200d multicolored 6.00 6.00

Sept. 1 Revolution, 7th anniv.

Sports, Torch and Emblems A183

Chess Board, Rook, Knight, Emblem — A184

145d, Symbolic wrestlers and various emblems.

1976, Oct. 6 Litho. *Perf. 13*
627 A183 15d multicolored .20 .20
628 A183 30d multicolored .35 .35
629 A183 100d multicolored 1.60 .90
Nos. 627-629 (3) 2.15 1.45

Souvenir Sheet
630 A183 145d multi, horiz. 4.50 4.50

5th Arab Games, Damascus, Syria.

1976, Oct. 24 Photo. *Perf. 11½*
631 A184 15d pink & multi 2.00 .40
632 A184 30d buff & multi 3.25 .90
633 A184 100d multicolored 10.00 1.90
Nos. 631-633 (3) 15.25 3.20

The "Against" (protest) Chess Olympiad, Tripoli, Oct. 24-Nov. 15.

A185

Designs: Various local flowers.

1976, Nov. 1 Photo. *Perf. 11½*
Granite Paper
634 A185 15d lilac & multi .35 .35
635 A185 20d multicolored .35 .35
636 A185 35d yellow & multi .80 .20
637 A185 40d salmon & multi 1.25 .35
638 A185 70d multicolored 3.00 .50
Nos. 634-638 (5) 5.75 1.75

International Archives Council Emblem and Document — A186

1976, Nov. 10 Litho. *Perf. 13x13½*
639 A186 15d brown, org & buff .20 .20
640 A186 35d brn, brt grn & buff .35 .35
641 A186 70d brown, blue & buff .75 .75
Nos. 639-641 (3) 1.30 1.30

Arab Regional Branch of International Council on Archives, Baghdad.

Holy Ka'aba and Pilgrims A187

Numeral A188

1976, Dec. 12 Litho. *Perf. 14*
642 A187 15d multicolored .20 .20
643 A187 30d multicolored .20 .20
644 A187 70d multicolored .80 .80
645 A187 100d multicolored 1.00 1.00
Nos. 642-645 (4) 2.20 2.20

Pilgrimage to Mecca.

Coil Stamps
1977, Jan. 15 Photo. *Perf. 14½x14*
646 A188 5d multicolored .20 .20
647 A188 20d multicolored .35 .35
648 A188 50d multicolored .90 .90
Nos. 646-648 (3) 1.45 1.45

Covered Basket — A189

Designs: 20d, Leather bag. 30d, Vase. 40d, Embroidered slippers. 50d, Ornate saddle. 100d, Horse with saddle and harness.

1977, Mar. 1 Litho. *Perf. 12½x12*
649 A189 10d multicolored .20 .20
650 A189 20d multicolored .20 .20
651 A189 30d multicolored .35 .20
652 A189 40d multicolored .60 .35
653 A189 50d multicolored 1.00 .35
Nos. 649-653 (5) 2.35 1.30

Souvenir Sheet
Imperf
654 A189 100d multicolored 4.50 4.50

15th Tripoli International Fair. No. 654 contains one stamp 49x53mm with simulated perforations.

Girl and Flowers, UNICEF Emblem A190

Children's drawings, UNICEF Emblem and: 30d, Clothing store. 40d, Farm yard.

1977, Mar. 28 Litho. *Perf. 13x13½*
655 A190 10d multicolored .35 .20
656 A190 30d multicolored .60 .35
657 A190 40d multicolored .75 .50
Nos. 655-657 (3) 1.70 1.05

Children's Day.

Gun, Fighters, UN Headquarters A191

1977, Mar. 13 *Perf. 13½*
658 A191 15d multicolored *.25* .20
659 A191 25d multicolored *.25* .20
660 A191 70d multicolored *1.25* 1.25
Nos. 658-660 (3) *1.75* 1.65

Battle of Al-Karamah, 9th anniversary.

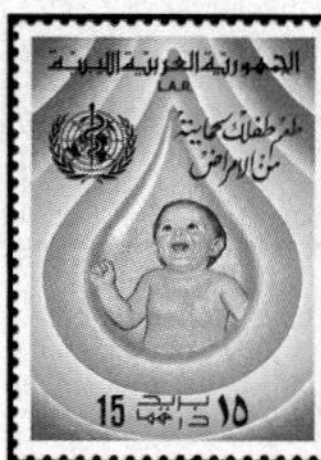
Child, Raindrop, WHO Emblem — A192

Maps of Africa and Libya A194

Arab Postal Union, 25th Anniv. — A193

1977, Apr. 7 Litho. *Perf. 13x12½*
661 A192 15d multicolored .20 .20
662 A192 30d multicolored .50 .50

World Health Day.

1977, Apr. 12 *Perf. 13½*
663 A193 15d multicolored .20 .20
664 A193 30d multicolored .35 .35
665 A193 40d multicolored .50 .50
Nos. 663-665 (3) 1.05 1.05

1977, May 8 Litho. *Perf. 14x13½*
666 A194 40d multicolored 1.50 1.25
667 A194 70d multicolored 2.25 1.90

African Labor Day.

Map of Libya and Heart — A195

1977, May 10		*Perf. 14½x14*	
668 A195 5d multicolored		.35	.20
669 A195 10d multicolored		.50	.35
670 A195 30d multicolored		1.40	.60
Nos. 668-670 (3)		2.25	1.15

Libyan Red Crescent Society.

Electronic Tree, ITU Emblem, Satellite and Radar A196

Electronic Tree, ITU Emblem and: 115d, Communications satellite, Montreal Olympics emblem, boxer on TV screen. 200d, Spacecraft over earth. 300d, Solar system.

1977, May 17	**Litho.**	*Perf. 13½x13*	
671 A196 60d multicolored		.30	.20
672 A196 115d multicolored		.60	.40
673 A196 200d multicolored		3.00	2.50
Nos. 671-673 (3)		3.90	3.10

Souvenir Sheet

674 A196 300d multicolored		*3.00*	*3.00*

9th World Telecommunications Day. No. 674 contains one stamp 52x35mm.

Nos. 671-673 exist imperf. Value, set $40. They also exist in miniature sheets of 4, perf and imperf. Values: set perf, $100; set imperf, $125.

Plane over Tripoli, Messenger A197

UPU Emblem and: 25d, Concorde, messenger on horseback. 150d, Loading transport plane and messenger riding camel. 300d, Graf Zeppelin LZ127 over Tripoli.

1977, May 17	**Litho.**	*Perf. 13½*	
675 A197 20d multicolored		.75	.75
676 A197 25d multicolored		1.60	1.60
677 A197 150d multicolored		3.25	3.25
Nos. 675-677 (3)		5.60	5.60

Souvenir Sheet

678 A197 300d multicolored		*7.00*	*5.00*

UPU centenary (in 1974). No. 678 contains one stamp 52x35mm.

Nos. 675-678 exist imperf. Values: set $55; souvenir sheet, $50. Nos. 675-677 also exist in miniature sheets of 4, perf and imperf. Values: set perf, $75; set imperf, $150.

Mosque A198

Various Mosques. 50d, 100d, vertical.

1977, June 1	**Photo.**	*Perf. 14*	
679 A198 40d multicolored		.50	.50
680 A198 50d multicolored		.75	.75
681 A198 70d multicolored		1.00	1.00
682 A198 90d multicolored		1.25	1.25
683 A198 100d multicolored		1.50	1.50
684 A198 115d multicolored		2.00	2.00
Nos. 679-684 (6)		7.00	7.00

Palestinian Archbishop Hilarion Capucci, Jailed by Israel in 1974, Map of Palestine — A199

1977, Aug. 18	**Litho.**	*Perf. 13½*	
687 A199 30d multicolored		.35	.35
688 A199 40d multicolored		.50	.50
689 A199 115d multicolored		2.00	.90
Nos. 687-689 (3)		2.85	1.75

Raised Hands, Pylons, Wheel, Buildings — A200

Star and Ornament — A201

1977, Sept. 1	**Litho.**	*Perf. 13½x12½*	
690 A200 15d multicolored		.20	.20
691 A200 30d multicolored		.35	.35
692 A200 85d multicolored		1.25	.60
Nos. 690-692 (3)		1.80	1.15

Souvenir Sheet

Perf. 12½

693 A201 100d gold & multi		4.50	2.75

8th anniversary of Sept. 1 Revolution.

Team Handball — A202

1977, Oct. 8		*Perf. 13½*	
694 A202 5d Swimmers, vert.		.20	.20
695 A202 10d shown		.20	.20
696 A202 15d Soccer, vert.		.20	.20
697 A202 25d Table tennis		.75	.75
698 A202 40d Basketball, vert.		1.60	.90
Nos. 694-698 (5)		2.95	2.25

7th Arab School Games.

Steeplechase — A203

Show Emblem and: 10d, Bedouin on horseback. 15d, Show emblem (Horse and "7"), vert. 45d, Steeplechase. 100d, Hurdles. 115d, Bedouins on horseback.

1977, Oct. 10		*Perf. 14½*	
699 A203 5d multicolored		.20	.20
700 A203 10d multicolored		.20	.20
701 A203 15d multicolored		.35	.35
702 A203 45d multicolored		.90	.90
703 A203 115d multicolored		2.00	2.00
Nos. 699-703 (5)		3.65	3.65

Souvenir Sheet

704 A203 100d multicolored		4.50	4.50

7th Intl. Turf Championships, Tripoli, Oct. 1977.

Dome of the Rock, Jerusalem — A204

1977, Oct. 14		*Perf. 14½x14*	
705 A204 5d multicolored		.30	.20
706 A204 10d multicolored		.45	.20

Palestinian fighters and their families.

"The Green Book" — A205

35d, Hands with broken chain holding hook over citadel. 40d, Hands above chaos. 115d, Dove and Green Book rising from Africa, world map.

1977	**Litho.**	*Perf. 14*	
707 A205 Strip of 3		2.75	2.75
a. 35d multicolored		.35	.35
b. 40d multicolored		.50	.50
c. 115d multicolored		1.75	1.75

The Greek Book, by Khadafy outlines Libyan democracy. Green descriptive inscription on back beneath gum, in English on 35d, French on 40d, Arabic on 115d.

Emblems A206

1977		*Perf. 12½x13*	
708 A206 5d multicolored		.60	.20
709 A206 15d multicolored		.80	.20
710 A206 30d multicolored		1.10	.35
Nos. 708-710 (3)		2.50	.75

Standardization Day.

Elephant hunt. A207

Rock Carvings, Wadi Mathendous, c. 8000 B.C.: 10d, Crocodile and Young. 20d, Giraffe, vert. 30d, Antelope. 40d, Trumpeting elephant.

1978, Jan. 1		*Perf. 12½x13, 13x12½*	
711 A207 10d multicolored		.20	.20
712 A207 15d multicolored		.20	.20
713 A207 20d multicolored		.35	.35
714 A207 30d multicolored		.60	.60
715 A207 40d multicolored		1.00	1.00
Nos. 711-715 (5)		2.35	2.35

Silver Pendant — A208

Emblem, Compass and Lightning — A209

Silver Jewelry: 10d, Ornamental plate. 20d, Necklace with pendants. 25d, Crescent-shaped brooch. 115d, Armband.

1978, Mar. 1	**Litho.**	*Perf. 13x12½*	
716 A208 5d multicolored		.20	.20
717 A208 10d multicolored		.20	.20
718 A208 20d multicolored		.20	.20
719 A208 25d multicolored		.20	.20
720 A208 115d multicolored		1.50	1.50
Nos. 716-720 (5)		2.30	2.30

Tripoli International Fair.

1978, Mar. 10		*Perf. 13½*	
721 A209 30d multicolored		.50	.50
722 A209 115d multicolored		2.00	2.00

Arab Cultural Education Organization.

Children's Drawings and UNESCO Emblem A210

a, Dancing. b, Children with posters. c, Shopping street. d, Playground. e, Bride and attendants.

1978, Mar. 21			
723 A210 40d Strip of 5, #a.-e.		7.00	7.00

Children's Day.

Clenched Fist, Made of Bricks A211

1978, Mar. 22			
728 A211 30d multicolored		.65	.40
729 A211 115d multicolored		1.50	.70

Determination of Arab people.

Blood Pressure Gauge, WHO Emblem — A212

Games Emblem — A214

Antenna and ITU Emblem A213

1978, Apr. 7 *Perf. 13x12½*

730	A212	30d multicolored	.35	.35
731	A212	115d multicolored	1.75	.90

World Health Day, drive against hypertension.

1978, May 17 **Photo.** *Perf. 13½*

732	A213	30d silver & multi	.35	.20
733	A213	115d gold & multi	1.50	.65

10th World Telecommunications Day.

1978, July 13 **Litho.** *Perf. 12½*

734	A214	15d multicolored	.20	.20
735	A214	30d multicolored	.35	.35
736	A214	115d multicolored	1.50	1.50
		Nos. 734-736 (3)	2.05	2.05

3rd African Games, Algiers, 1978.

Inauguration of Tripoli International Airport — A215

1978, Aug. 10 **Litho.** *Perf. 13½*

737	A215	40d shown	.50	.50
738	A215	115d Terminal	2.00	.90

View of Ankara — A216

Soldiers, Jet, Ship — A217

1978, Aug. 17

739	A216	30d multicolored	.50	.20
740	A216	35d multicolored	.60	.35
741	A216	115d multicolored	1.60	1.60
		Nos. 739-741 (3)	2.70	2.15

Turkish-Libyan friendship.

1978, Sept. 1 *Perf. 14½*

35d, Tower, Green Book, oil derrick. 100d, View of Tripoli with mosque and modern buildings. 115d, View of Tripoli within cogwheel.

742	A217	30d multicolored	.50	.50
743	A217	35d org & multi	.35	.35
744	A217	115d blue & multi	1.50	1.25
		Nos. 742-744 (3)	2.35	2.10

Souvenir Sheet

745	A217	100d multicolored	2.75	2.75

9th anniversary of Sept. 1 Revolution. No. 745 contains one 50x41mm stamp.

Quarry and Symposium Emblem — A218

Designs: 40d, Oasis lake. 115d, Crater.

1978, Sept. 16 *Perf. 13½*

746	A218	30d multicolored	.50	.50
747	A218	40d multicolored	.60	.60
748	A218	115d multicolored	2.00	2.00
		Nos. 746-748 (3)	3.10	3.10

2nd Symposium on Libyan Geology.

Green Book and Three Races A219

1978, Oct. 18 *Perf. 12½*

749	A219	30d multicolored	.20	.20
750	A219	40d multicolored	.20	.50
751	A219	115d multicolored	1.25	1.25
		Nos. 749-751 (3)	1.95	1.95

International Anti-Apartheid Year.

Pilgrims, Minarets, Holy Kaaba A220

1978, Nov. 9 **Photo.** *Perf. 12*

752	A220	5d multicolored	.20	.20
753	A220	10d multicolored	.20	.20
754	A220	15d multicolored	.20	.20
755	A220	20d multicolored	.20	.20
		Nos. 752-755 (4)	.80	.80

Pilgrimage to Mecca.

Handclasp over Globe — A221

Fists, Guns, Map of Israel — A222

1978, Nov. 10 **Litho.** *Perf. 13½*

756	A221	30d multicolored	.40	.30
757	A221	40d multicolored	.50	.40
758	A221	115d multicolored	1.50	1.25
		Nos. 756-758 (3)	2.40	1.95

Technical Cooperation Among Developing Countries Conf., Buenos Aires, Argentina, Sept. 1978.

1978, Dec. 5 **Litho.** *Perf. 13½*

40d, 115d, Map of Arab countries and Israel, eagle and crowd. 145d, like 30d.

759	A222	30d multi	.35	.35
760	A222	40d multi, horiz.	.50	.50
761	A222	115d multi, horiz.	1.25	1.25
762	A222	145d multi	1.50	.90
		Nos. 759-762 (4)	3.60	3.00

Anti-Israel Summit Conf., Baghdad, Dec. 2-8.

Scales, Globe and Human Rights Flame — A223

Libyan Fort and Horse Racing — A224

1978, Dec. 10

763	A223	15d multicolored	.20	.20
764	A223	30d multicolored	.50	.50
765	A223	115d multicolored	1.25	1.25
		Nos. 763-765 (3)	1.95	1.95

Universal Declaration of Human Rights, 30th anniv.

1978, Dec. 11

766	A224	20d multicolored	.40	.20
767	A224	40d multicolored	.50	.50
768	A224	115d multicolored	1.50	1.50
		Nos. 766-768 (3)	2.40	2.20

Libyan Study Center.

Lilienthal's Glider, 1896 A225

Mounted Stag's Head — A226

25d, Spirit of St. Louis, 1927. 30d, Adm. Byrd's Polar flight, 1929. 50d, Graf Zeppelin, 1934, hydroplane and storks. 115d, Wilbur and Orville Wright and Flyer A. No. 774, Icarus falling. No. 775, Eagle and Boeing 727.

1978, Dec. 26 **Litho.** *Perf. 14*

769	A225	20d multicolored	.20	.20
770	A225	25d multicolored	.40	.40
771	A225	30d multicolored	1.25	1.25
772	A225	50d multicolored	1.50	1.50
773	A225	115d multicolored	1.25	1.25
		Nos. 769-773 (5)	4.60	4.60

Souvenir Sheets

774	A225	100d multicolored	2.75	2.75
775	A225	100d multicolored	2.75	2.75

75th anniversary of 1st powered flight.

Nos. 769-773 issued also in sheets of 4. Value, set $35.

Nos. 774-775 exist imperf. Value, pair $50.

Coil Stamps

1979, Jan. 15 **Photo.** *Perf. 14½x14*

776	A226	5d multicolored	.35	.35
777	A226	20d multicolored	.75	.75
778	A226	50d multicolored	1.50	1.50
		Nos. 776-778 (3)	2.60	2.60

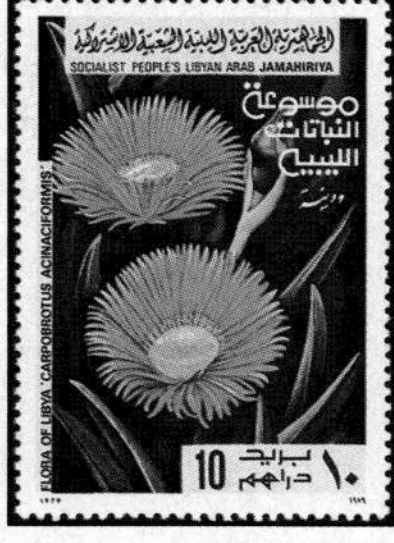

Carpobrotus Acinaciformis A227

Flora of Libya: 15d, Caralluma europaea. 20d, Arum cirenaicum. 35d, Lavatera arborea. 40d, Capparis spinosa. 50d, Ranunculus asiaticus.

1979, May 15 **Litho.** *Perf. 14*

779	A227	10d multicolored	.20	.20
780	A227	15d multicolored	.20	.20
781	A227	20d multicolored	.20	.20
782	A227	35d multicolored	.60	.60
783	A227	40d multicolored	.60	.60
784	A227	50d multicolored	.75	.75
		Nos. 779-784 (6)	2.55	2.55

People, Torch, Olive Branches — A228

1979 **Litho.** *Perf. 13x12½*

Size: 18x23mm

785	A228	5d multi	.20	.20
786	A228	10d multi	.20	.20
787	A228	15d multi	.20	.20
788	A228	30d multi	.35	.20
789	A228	50d multi	.50	.20
790	A228	60d multi	.60	.35
791	A228	70d multi	.75	.35
792	A228	100d multi	1.25	.60
793	A228	115d multi	1.25	.60

Perf. 13½

Size: 26½x32mm

794	A228	200d multi	1.90	1.25
795	A228	500d multi	4.75	2.50
796	A228	1000d multi	10.00	6.25
		Nos. 785-796 (12)	21.95	12.90

See Nos. 1053-1055.

Tortoise A229

Animals: 10d, Antelope. 15d, Hedgehog. 20d, Porcupine. 30d, Arabian camel. 35d, African wildcat. 45d, Gazelle. 115d, Cheetah. 10d, 30d, 35d, 45d, vert.

1979, Feb. 1 **Litho.** *Perf. 14½*

797	A229	5d multicolored	.20	.20
798	A229	10d multicolored	.20	.20
799	A229	15d multicolored	.60	.60
800	A229	20d multicolored	.60	.60
801	A229	30d multicolored	1.00	.60
802	A229	35d multicolored	1.40	.60
803	A229	45d multicolored	1.75	.75
804	A229	115d multicolored	3.50	1.25
		Nos. 797-804 (8)	9.25	4.80

Rug and Tripoli Fair Emblem — A230

Tripoli Fair emblem and various rugs.

1979, Mar. 1 Litho. *Perf. 11*

805 A230 10d multicolored .20 .20
806 A230 15d multicolored .20 .20
807 A230 30d multicolored .35 .35
808 A230 45d multicolored .50 .50
809 A230 115d multicolored 1.25 1.25
Nos. 805-809 (5) 2.50 2.50

17th Tripoli Fair.
Exist imperf. Value, set $30.

Children's Drawings and IYC Emblem A231

a, Families and planes. b, Shepherd, sheep and dog. c, Beach umbrellas. d, Boat in storm. e, Traffic policeman.

1979, Mar. 20 *Perf. 13½*

810 A231 20d Strip of 5, #a.-e. 5.00 3.50

Intl. Year of the Child.
Exists imperf. Value $30.

Book, World Map, Arab Achievements A232

1979, Mar. 22 *Perf. 13*

815 A232 45d multicolored .50 .50
816 A232 70d multicolored .75 .75

WMO Emblem, Weather Map and Tower — A233

1979, Mar. 23

817 A233 15d multicolored .20 .20
818 A233 30d multicolored .35 .35
819 A233 50d multicolored .60 .60
Nos. 817-819 (3) 1.15 1.15

World Meteorological Day.

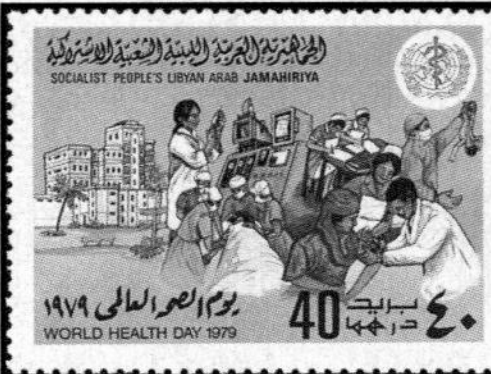

Medical Services, WHO Emblem — A234

1979, Apr. 7

820 A234 40d multicolored .60 .60

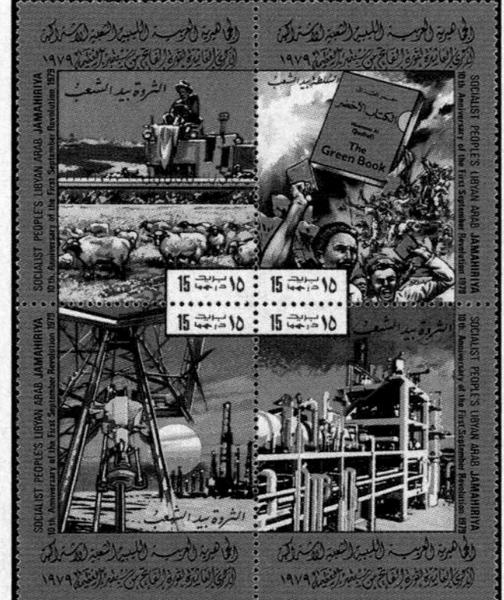

Farmer Plowing and Sheep — A235

1979, Sept. 1 Litho. *Perf. 14½*

821 Block of 4 1.00 1.00
a. A235 15d shown .20 .20
b. A235 15d Men holding Green Book .20 .20
c. A235 15d Oil field .20 .20
d. A235 15d Oil refinery .20 .20
822 Block of 4 2.00 2.00
a. A235 30d Dish antenna .40 .40
b. A235 30d Hospital .40 .40
c. A235 30d Doctor examining patient .40 .40
d. A235 30d Surgery .40 .40
823 Block of 4 3.00 3.00
a. A235 40d Street, Tripoli .50 .50
b. A235 40d Steel mill .50 .50
c. A235 40d Tanks .50 .50
d. A235 40d Tuareg horsemen .50 .50
824 Block of 4 4.00 4.00
a. A235 70d Revolutionaries, Green Book .90 .90
b. A235 70d Crowd, map of Libya .90 .90
c. A235 70d Mullah .90 .90
d. A235 70d Student .90 .90
Nos. 821-824 (4) 10.00 10.00

Souvenir Sheets

Imperf

825 A235 50d Revolution symbols, Green Book 2.50 2.50
826 A235 50d Monument 2.50 2.50

Sept. 1st revolution, 10th anniversary.

Volleyball A236

1979, Sept. 10

827 A236 45d shown .50 .50
828 A236 115d Soccer 1.25 1.25

Universiade '79 World University Games, Mexico City, Sept.
Exists imperf. Value, set $17.50.

Mediterranean Games, Split, Yugoslavia — A237

1979, Sept. 15 Litho. *Perf. 12x11½*

829 A237 15d multicolored .50 .50
830 A237 30d multicolored 1.40 .50
831 A237 70d multicolored 3.50 1.00
Nos. 829-831 (3) 5.40 2.00

Exhibition Emblem — A238

1979, Sept. 25 Photo. *Perf. 11½x11*

832 A238 45d multicolored .50 .50
833 A238 115d multicolored 1.50 1.50

TELECOM '79, 3rd World Telecommunications Exhibition, Geneva, Sept. 20-26.

A239

#834a, 10d, Seminar emblem, Green Book, crowd. #834b, 35d, Meeting hall (Size: 67x43½mm). #834c, 100d, Col. Khadafy. #835, Central portion of #834c.

1979, Oct. 1

834 A239 Strip of 3, #a.-c. 2.50 2.50

Size: 87x114mm

Imperf

835 A239 100d multicolored 3.50 3.50

Intl. Seminar of the Green Book, Benghazi, Oct. 1-3. No. 834 has continuous design.

Evacuation of Foreign Forces — A240

1979, Oct. 7

837 A240 30d shown .60 .40
838 A240 40d Tuareg horsemen .90 .50

Souvenir Sheet

Imperf

839 A240 100d Vignettes 3.00 3.00

Cyclist, Championship Emblem — A241

1979, Nov. 21

840 A241 15d shown .20 .20
841 A241 30d Cyclists, emblem, diff. .50 .50

Junior Cycling Championships, Tripoli, Nov. 21-23. Issued in sheetlets of 4.

Hurdles, Olympic Rings, Moscow '80 Emblem — A242

1979, Nov. 21

842 A242 45d Equestrian .50 .50
843 A242 60d Javelin .75 .75
844 A242 115d Hurdles 1.50 1.50
845 A242 160d Soccer 1.75 1.75
Nos. 842-845 (4) 4.50 4.50

Souvenir Sheets

846 A242 150d shown 3.50 3.50
847 A242 150d like #845 3.50 3.50

Pre-Olympics (Moscow '80 Olympic Games). Nos. 842-845 issued in sheetlets of 4 and sheets of 20 (4x5) with silver Moscow '80 Emblem covering background of every 20 stamps. Value, set of sheetlets of 4, $45.

Nos. 842-847 exist imperf. Values: set $55; souvenir sheets, $90.

Intl. Day of Cooperation with Palestinian People — A242a

1979, Nov. 29 Photo. *Perf. 12*

847A A242a 30d multicolored .25 .25
847B A242a 115d multicolored 1.75 1.75

Tug of War, Jumping — A243

National Games: No. 848, Polo, leap frog. No. 849, Racing, ball game, No. 850, Wrestling, log rolling. No. 852, Horsemen.

1980, Feb. 15

848 A243 Block of 4, #a.-d. 1.00 1.00
849 A243 Block of 4, #a.-d. 1.00 1.00
850 A243 Block of 4, #a.-d. 1.00 1.00
851 A243 Block of 4, #a.-d. 2.00 2.00
852 A243 Block of 4, #a.-d. 3.50 3.50
Nos. 848-852 (5) 8.50 8.50

Battles — A244

#853a, 20d, Gardabia, 1915. #853b, 35d, same. #854a, 20d, Shoghab, 1913. #854b, 35d, same. #855a, 20d, Fundugh Al-Shibani, 1922. #855b, 35d, same. #856a, 20d, Ghira. #856b, 35d, same.

Pairs have continuous design.

1980	Litho.		*Perf. 14½*	
853 A244	Pair, #a.-b.		*1.25*	*1.25*
854 A244	Pair, #a.-b.		*1.25*	*1.25*
855 A244	Pair, #a.-b.		*1.25*	*1.25*
856 A244	Pair, #a.-b.		*1.25*	*1.25*
	Nos. 853-856 (4)		*5.00*	*5.00*

Issued: #853, 4/28; #854, 5/25; #855, 6/1; #856, 8/15.

See Nos. 893-896, 921-932, 980-991, 1059-1070.

Girl Guides Examining Plant — A245

1980, Aug. 22		*Perf. 13½*	
861 A245	15d shown	.25	.25
862 A245	30d Guides cooking	.35	.35
863 A245	50d Scouts at camp-fire	.60	.60
864 A245	115d Scouts reading map	1.50	1.50
	Nos. 861-864 (4)	2.70	2.70

Souvenir Sheets

865 A245	100d like #861	2.25	2.25
866 A245	100d like #863	2.25	2.25

8th Pan Arab Girl Guide and 14th Pan Arab Scout Jamborees, Aug.

Men Holding OPEC Emblem A246

1980, Sept. 15		*Perf. 14½*	
867 A246	45d Emblem, globe	.50	.50
868 A246	115d shown	1.50	1.50

20th anniversary of OPEC.

Martyrdom of Omar Muktar, 1931 — A247

1980, Sept. 16			
869 A247	20d multicolored	.25	.25
870 A247	35d multicolored	.50	.50

Souvenir Sheet

870A A247	100d multicolored	2.50	2.50

UNESCO Emblem and Avicenna A248

1980, Sept. 20			
871 A248	45d Scientific symbols	.50	.50
872 A248	115d shown	1.50	1.50

School Scientific Exhibition, Sept. 20-24 and birth millenium of Arab physician Avicenna (115d).

18th Tripoli Fair A249

Various musical instruments. 15d vert.

1980	Litho.	*Perf. 13½*	
873 A249	5d multicolored	.25	.25
874 A249	10d multicolored	.25	.25
875 A249	15d multicolored	.25	.25
876 A249	20d multicolored	.25	.25
877 A249	25d multicolored	.40	.40
	Nos. 873-877 (5)	1.40	1.40

Souvenir Sheet

878 A249	100d Musicians	2.50	2.50

World Olive Oil Year A250

1980, Jan. 15	Litho.	*Perf. 13½*	
879 A250	15d multicolored	.25	.25
880 A250	30d multicolored	.35	.35
881 A250	45d multicolored	.50	.50
	Nos. 879-881 (3)	1.10	1.10

Intl. Year of the Child (1979) A251

Children's drawings: a, Riding horses. b, water sports. c, Fish. d, Gift sale. e, Preparing feast.

1980, Mar. 21			
882	Strip of 5	5.00	5.00
a.-e.	A251 20d any single	.50	.40

The Hegira, 1500th Anniv. A252

1980, Apr. 1			
883 A252	50d multicolored	.60	.60
884 A252	115d multicolored	1.50	1.50

Operating Room, Hospital — A253

1980, Apr. 7	Litho.	*Perf. 13½*	
885 A253	20d multicolored	.40	.40
886 A253	50d multicolored	.75	.75

World Health Day.

Sheik Zarruq Festival, Misurata, June 16-20 — A254

Arabian Towns Organization A255

1980, June 16			
887 A254	40d multicolored	.50	.50
888 A254	115d multicolored	1.50	1.50

Souvenir Sheet

889 A254	100d multicolored	2.75	2.75

1980, July 1		*Perf. 11½x12*	
890 A255	15d Ghadames	.25	.25
891 A255	30d Derna	.35	.35
892 A255	50d Tripoli	.60	.60
	Nos. 890-892 (3)	1.20	1.20

Battles Type of 1980

#893a, 20d, Yefren, 1915, #893b, 35d, same. #894a, 20d, El Hani, 1911, #894b, 35d, same. #895a, 20d, Sebha, 1914, #895b, 35d, same. #896a, 20d, Sirt, 1912, #896b, 35d, same.

Pairs have continuous design.

1980		*Perf. 13½*	
893 A244	Pair, #a.-b.	1.25	1.25
894 A244	Pair, #a.-b.	1.25	1.25
895 A244	Pair, #a.-b.	1.25	1.25
896 A244	Pair, #a.-b.	1.25	1.25
	Nos. 893-896 (4)	5.00	5.00

Issued: #893, 7/16; #894, 10/23; #895, 11/27; #896, 12/31.

Sept. 1 Revolution, 11th Anniv. — A256

Achievements of the Revolution.

1980, Sept. 1			
901 A256	5d Oil industry	.25	.25
902 A256	10d Youth festival	.25	.25
903 A256	15d Agriculture	.50	.50
904 A256	25d Transportation	1.25	.50
905 A256	40d Education	1.25	.50
906 A256	115d Housing	3.00	1.25
	Nos. 901-906 (6)	6.50	3.25

Souvenir Sheet

907 A256	100d Montage of achievements	2.75	2.75

No. 907 contains one stamp 30x50mm.

World Tourism Conference A257

1980, Sept. 10			
908 A257	45d multicolored	.50	.50
909 A257	115d multicolored	1.50	1.50

Intl. Year of the Disabled — A258

1981, Jan. 1		*Perf. 15*	
910 A258	20d multicolored	.25	.25
911 A258	45d multicolored	.35	.25
912 A258	115d multicolored	1.50	.50
	Nos. 910-912 (3)	2.10	1.00

Redrawn

1981, Nov. 21	Litho.	*Perf. 15*	
913 A258	45d multicolored	.35	.25
914 A258	115d multicolored	1.10	1.10

UPA Disabled Persons Campaign. Design redrawn to include Arab League Emblem.

Mosaics — A259

1981, Jan. 15		*Perf. 13½*	
915 A259	10d Horse	1.00	.25
916 A259	20d Sailing ship	1.00	.50
917 A259	30d Peacocks	2.00	.50
918 A259	40d Panther	2.00	.50
919 A259	50d Musician	2.50	.50
920 A259	115d Fish	6.50	1.00
	Nos. 915-920 (6)	15.00	3.25

Battles Type of 1980

#921a, 20d, Dernah, 1912, #921b, 35d, same. #922a, 20d, Bir Tagreft, 1928. #922b, 35d, same. #923a, 20d, Tawargha, 1923. #923b, 35d, same. #924a, 20d, .Funduk El-Jamel Misurata, 1915 #924b, 35d, same. #925a, 20d, Zuara, 1912. #925b, 35d, same. #926a, 20d, Sidi El-Khemri, 1915. #926b, 35d, same. #927a, 20d, El-Khoms, 1913. #927b, 35d, same. #928a, 20d, Roghdalin, 1912. #928b, 35d, same. #929a, 20d, Rughbat El-Naga, 1925. #929b, 35d, same. #930a, 20d, Tobruk. 1911. 1922, #930b, 35d, same. #931a, 20d, Bir Ikshadia, 1924. #931b, 35d, same. #932a, 20d, Ain Zara, 1924. #932b, 35d, same.

Pairs have continuous design.

1981	*Perf. 13½, 14½ (#926, 932)*		
921 A244	Pair, #a.-b.	1.25	1.25
922 A244	Pair, #a.-b.	1.25	1.25
923 A244	Pair, #a.-b.	1.25	1.25
924 A244	Pair, #a.-b.	1.25	1.25
925 A244	Pair, #a.-b.	1.25	1.25
926 A244	Pair, #a.-b.	1.25	1.25
927 A244	Pair, #a.-b.	1.25	1.25
928 A244	Pair, #a.-b.	1.25	1.25
929 A244	Pair, #a.-b.	1.25	1.25
930 A244	Pair, #a.-b.	1.25	1.25
931 A244	Pair, #a.-b.	1.25	1.25
932 A244	Pair, #a.-b.	1.25	1.25
	Nos. 921-932 (12)	15.00	15.00

Issued: #921, 1/17; #922, 2/25; #923, 3/20; #924, 4/13; #925, 5/26; #926, 6/4; #927, 7/27; #928, 8/15; #929, 9/16; #930, 10/27; #931, 11/19; #932, 12/4.

Tripoli Intl. Fair — A260

No. 707b, Crowd — A261

Ceramicware.

1981, Mar. 1 *Perf. 13½*

945 A260 5d Bowls, horiz. .25 .25
946 A260 10d Lamp .25 .25
947 A260 15d Vase .25 .25
948 A260 45d Water jar, horiz. .60 .25
949 A260 115d Spouted water jar, horiz. 1.75 .60
Nos. 945-949 (5) 3.10 1.60

1981, Mar. 2 *Perf. 15*

950 A261 50d multicolored .35 .35
951 A261 115d multicolored 1.50 .50

People's Authority Declaration, The Green Book.

Children's Day, IYC — A262

Children's illustrations: a, Desert camp. b, Women doing chores. c, Village scene. d, Airplane over playground. e, Minaret, camel, man.

1981, Mar. 21 **Litho.** *Perf. 13½*

952 Strip of 5 5.00 5.00
a.-e. A262 20d any single .50 .40

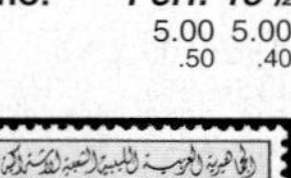

Bank of Libya, 25th Anniv. — A263

1981, Apr. 1 **Litho.** *Perf. 13½*

953 A263 45d multicolored .50 .35
954 A263 115d multicolored 1.75 1.10

Souvenir Sheet

955 A263 50d multicolored 1.50 1.50

World Health Day A264

1981, Apr. 7 *Perf. 14*

956 A264 45d multicolored .50 .50
957 A264 115d multicolored 1.50 .75

Intl. Year for Combating Racial Discrimination A265

1981, July 1 *Perf. 15*

958 A265 45d multicolored 1.10 .65
959 A265 50d multicolored 1.50 .75

September 1 Revolution, 12th Anniv. — A266

#960a-960b, Helicopter and jets. #960c-960d, Paratroopers. #961a-961b, Tanks. #961c-961d, Frogman parade. #962a-962b, Twelve-barrel rocket launchers. #962c-962d, Trucks with rockets. #963a-963b, Sailor parade. #963c-963d, Jeep and trucks with twelve-barrel rocket launchers. #964a-964b, Wheeled tanks and jeeps. #964c-964d, Tank parade. Nos. 960-962 vert. Pairs have continuous designs.

1981, Sept. 1 *Perf. 14½*

960 A266 5d Block of 4, #a.-d. 1.25 1.25
961 A266 10d Block of 4, #a.-d. 1.25 1.25
962 A266 15d Block of 4, #a.-d. 1.25 1.25
963 A266 20d Block of 4, #a.-d. 1.25 1.25
964 A266 25d Block of 4, #a.-d. 2.50 2.50
Nos. 960-964 (5) 7.50 7.50

Souvenir Sheet

Perf. 11

965 A266 50d Naval troop marching 6.50 6.50

No. 965 contains one 63x38mm stamp.

Miniature Sheet

Butterflies — A267

1981, Oct. 1 *Perf. 14½*

966 Sheet of 16 10.00
a.-d. A267 5d, any single .25 .25
e.-h. A267 10d, any single .60 .25
i.-l. A267 15d, any single .90 .40
m.-p. A267 25d, any single 1.25 .60

No. 966 printed in a continuous design, stamps of same denomination in blocks of 4. Sheetlets exist containing blocks of 4 for each denomination.

A268

A269

1981, Oct. 16 *Perf. 15*

967 A268 45d multicolored .50 .50
968 A268 200d multicolored 2.50 2.50

World Food Day.

1981, Nov. 17 *Perf. 13½*

969 A269 5d Grapes .25 .25
970 A269 10d Dates .25 .25
971 A269 15d Lemons .25 .25
972 A269 20d Oranges .40 .25
973 A269 35d Cactus fruit .80 .35
974 A269 55d Pomegranates 1.50 .60
Nos. 969-974 (6) 3.45 1.95

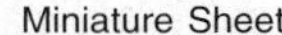

Miniature Sheet

A270

Mosaics: a, Animals facing right. b, Orpheus playing music. c, Animals facing left. d, Fish. e, Fishermen. f, Fish in basket. g, Farm yard. h, Birds eating fruit. i, Milking a goat. Illustration reduced.

1982, Jan. 1 *Perf. 13½*

975 A270 Sheet of 9 9.00 9.00
a.-i. 45d any single .75 .75

Nos. 975a-975c, shown in illustration, printed in continuous design.

3rd Intl. Koran Reading Contest — A271

Designs: 10d, Stone tablets, Holy Ka'aba, Mecca. 35d, Open Koran, creation of the world. 115d, Scholar, students.

1982, Jan. 7

976 A271 10d multicolored .20 .20
977 A271 35d multicolored .50 .25
978 A271 115d multicolored 1.50 .75
Nos. 976-978 (3) 2.20 1.20

Souvenir Sheet

979 A271 100d like 115d 3.50 3.50

Battles Type of 1980

#980a, 20d, Hun Gioffra, 1915. #980b, 35d, same. #981a, 20d, Gedabia, 1914. #981b, 35d, same. #982a, 20d, El-Asaba, 1913. #982b, 35d, same. #983a, 20d, El-Habela, 1917. #983b, 35d, same. #984a, 20d, Suk El-Ahad, 1915. #984b, 35d, same. #985a, 20d, El-Tangi, 1913. #985b, 35d, same. #986a, 20d, Sokna, 1913. #986b, 35d, same. #987a, 20d, Wadi Smalus, 1925. #987b, 35d, same. #988a, 20d, Sidi Abuagela, 1917. #988b, 35d, same. #989a, 20d, Sidi Surur, 1914. #989b, 35d, same. #990a, 20d, Kuefia, 1911. #990b, 35d, same. #991a, 20d, Abunjeim, 1940. #991b, 35d, same.

Pairs have continuous design.

1982 *Perf. 13½, 14½ (#985-988)*

980 A244 Pair, #a.-b. 1.25 1.25
981 A244 Pair, #a.-b. 1.25 1.25
982 A244 Pair, #a.-b. 1.25 1.25
983 A244 Pair, #a.-b. 1.25 1.25
984 A244 Pair, #a.-b. 1.25 1.25
985 A244 Pair, #a.-b. 1.25 1.25
986 A244 Pair, #a.-b. 1.25 1.25
987 A244 Pair, #a.-b. 1.25 1.25
988 A244 Pair, #a.-b. 1.25 1.25
989 A244 Pair, #a.-b. 1.25 1.25
990 A244 Pair, #a.-b. 1.25 1.25
991 A244 Pair, #a.-b. 1.25 1.25
Nos. 980-991 (12) 15.00 15.00

Issued: #980, 1/26; #981, 3/8; #982, 3/23; #983, 4/24; #984, 5/15; #985, 6/19; #986, 7/23; #987, 8/11; #988, 9/4; #989, 10/14; #990, 11/28; #991, 12/13.

Tripoli Intl. Fair — A272

1982, Mar. 1 *Perf. 13x12½*

1004 A272 5d Grinding stone .20 .20
1005 A272 10d Ox-drawn plow .20 .20
1006 A272 25d Pitching hay .25 .25
1007 A272 35d Tapestry weaving .50 .25
1008 A272 45d Traditional cooking .75 .35
1009 A272 100d Grain harvest 1.50 .75
Nos. 1004-1009 (6) 3.40 2.00

People's Authority Declaration, The Green Book — A273

1982, Mar. 2 *Perf. 13½*

1010 Strip of 3 7.50 7.50
a. A273 100d Harvester combine 1.25 .60
b. A273 200d Khadafy, scholar, rifles 2.50 2.25
c. A273 300d Govt. building, citizens 3.25 2.25

Scouting Movement, 75th Anniv. — A274

13th African Soccer Cup Championships A275

1982, Mar. 2

1011 Strip of 4 20.00 20.00
a. A274 100d Cub scout, blimp 1.50 .75
b. A274 200d Scouts, dog 3.00 1.50
c. A274 300d Scholar, scout 4.50 1.90
d. A274 400d Boy scout, rocket 7.00 3.50

Souvenir Sheets

1012 A274 500d Green Book 7.50 7.50
1013 A274 500d Khadafy, scouts 7.50 7.50

Nos. 1012-1013 each contain one stamp 39x42mm.

Nos. 1011-1013 exist imperf.

1982, Mar. 5

1014 A275 100d multi 1.50 .75
1015 A275 200d multi 3.00 1.50

1982 World Cup Soccer Championships, Spain — A276

World Cup trophy and various soccer plays.

1982, Mar. 15 *Perf. 14½*
1016 A276 45d multi .60 .60
1017 A276 100d multi 1.50 1.50
1018 A276 200d multi 2.75 2.75
1019 A276 300d multi 3.25 3.25
Nos. 1016-1019 (4) 8.10 8.10

Souvenir Sheets

1020 A276 500d like 45d 7.50 7.50
1021 A276 500d like 100d 7.50 7.50

Nos. 1016-1019 issued in sheets of 8 overprinted in silver with soccer ball in motion. Value $75. Sheetlets of 4 in each denomination exist without overprint.
Nos. 1020-1021 have Arabic text in green on reverse. Value $35.
Nos. 1016-1019 exist imperf. Value $15. Nos. 1020-1021 also exist imperf.

Palestinian Children's Day — A277

Designs: a, Two children. b, Girl with bowl. c, Girl with kaffiyeh. d, Girl hiding. e, Boy.

1982, Mar. 7 *Perf. 13½*
1022 Strip of 5 2.75 2.75
a.-e. A277 20d, any single .40 .40

Birds — A278

Arab Postal Union, 30th — A280

Teaching Hospitals Anniv. A279

Miniature Sheet

1982, Apr. 1 *Perf. 14½*
1023 Sheet of 16 18.00 18.00
a.-d. A278 15d, any single .40 .40
e.-h. A278 25d, any single .60 .50
i.-l. A278 45d, any single 1.00 .90
m.-p. A278 95d, any single 2.25 1.75

No. 1023a-1023p printed se-tenant in a continuous design; stamps of same denomination in blocks of 4.

1982, Apr. 7 *Perf. 13x12½*
1024 A279 95d multi 1.25 1.25
1025 A279 100d multi 1.25 1.25
1026 A279 205d multi 2.75 2.75
Nos. 1024-1026 (3) 5.25 5.25

1982, Apr. 12 *Perf. 13½*
1027 A280 100d multi 1.50 .75
1028 A280 200d multi 2.75 1.50

1982 World Chess Championships — A281

Board positions and chessmen: a, Chinese piece. b, African piece. c, Modern piece. d, European piece.

1982, May 1
1029 Block of 4 9.00 9.00
a.-d. A281 100d, any single 2.00 1.00

Souvenir Sheet

1030 A281 500d Overhead view of chessboard 10.00 10.00

No. 1030 contains one stamp 39x42mm.

World Telecommunications Day — A282

1982, May 17
1031 A282 100d multi 1.25 1.25
1032 A282 200d multi 2.50 2.50

Map of Libya, Green Book A283

1982, June 11
1033 A283 200d multi 2.50 1.50

Souvenir Sheet

1034 A283 300d multi 5.00 5.00

Post Day, FIP 51st anniv.

Organization of African Unity, 19th Summit A284

1982, Aug. 5 *Perf. 14*
1035 A284 50d OAU flag, Arab family .75 .75
1036 A284 100d Map of Africa, emblem 1.25 1.25

Size: 69x40mm

1037 A284 200d Khadafy, Green Book 2.50 2.50
Nos. 1035-1037 (3) 4.50 4.50

Souvenir Sheet

Perf. 13x13½

1038 A284 300d Fist, map 5.00 5.00

No. 1038 contains one stamp 29x42mm.

September 1 Revolution, 13th Anniv. — A285

Khadafy in uniforms and various armed forces' exercises.

1982, Sept. 1 *Perf. 11½*
1039 A285 15d multi .25 .25
1040 A285 20d multi .25 .25
1041 A285 30d multi 1.00 1.00
1042 A285 45d multi .60 .60
1043 A285 70d multi 1.00 1.00
1044 A285 100d multi 1.50 1.50
Nos. 1039-1044 (6) 4.60 4.60

Souvenir Sheet

Imperf

1045 A285 200d multi 4.00 4.00

Libyan Red Crescent, 25th Anniv. — A286

Intl. Day of Cooperation with Palestinian People — A287

1982, Oct. 5 *Perf. 13½*
1046 A286 100d Palm tree 1.75 1.25
1047 A286 200d "25," crescents 3.50 2.50

1982, Nov. 29
1048 A287 100d gray grn & blk 1.50 .75
1049 A287 200d brt bl, gray grn & blk 2.75 1.50

Al-Fateh University Symposium on Khadafy's Green Book — A288

1982, Dec. 1 *Perf. 12*
1050 A288 100d Khadafy in uniform 1.25 1.10
1051 A288 200d Khadafy, map, Green Book 2.50 2.50

Flowers — A289

Customs Cooperation Council, 30th Anniv. — A290

Miniature Sheet

Designs: a, Philadelphus. b, Hypericum. c, Antinhinum. d, Lily. e, Capparis. f, Tropaeolum. g, Rose. h, Chrysanthemum. i, Nigella damascena. j, Gaillardia lanceolata. k, Dahlia. l, Dianthus carophyllus. m, Notobasis syriaca. n, Nerium oleander. o, Iris histriodes. p, Scolymus hispanicus.

1983, Jan. 1 *Perf. 14½*
1052 Sheet of 16 10.00 10.00
a.-p. A289 25d, any single .50 .40

Torch Type of 1979

1983, Jan. 2 *Perf. 13½*

Size: 26½x32mm

1053 A228 250d multi 3.25 2.00
1054 A228 1500d multi 20.00 12.50
1055 A228 2500d multi 37.50 25.00
Nos. 1053-1055 (3) 60.75 39.50

1983, Jan. 15 *Perf. 14½x14*
1056 A290 25d Arab riding horse .25 .25
1057 A290 50d Riding camel .60 .60
1058 A290 100d Drawing sword 1.50 1.50
Nos. 1056-1058 (3) 2.35 2.35

Battles Type of 1980

#1059a, 1059b, Ghaser Ahmed, 1922. #1060a, 1060b, Sidi Abuarghub, 1923. #1061a, 1061b, Ghar Yunes, 1913. #1062a, 1062b, Bir Otman, 1926. #1063a, 1063b, Sidi Sajeh, 1922. #1064a, 1064b, Ras El-Hamam, 1915. #1065a, 1065b, Zawiet Ishghefa, 1913. #1066a, 1066b, Wadi Essania, 1930. #1067a, 1067b, El-Meshiashta, 1917. #1068a, 1068b, Gharara, 1925. #1069a, 1069b, Abughelan, 1922. #1070a, 1070b, Mahruka, 1913.
Pairs have continuous design.

1983 *Perf. 13½*
1059 A244 50d Pair, #a.-b. 2.00 2.00
1060 A244 50d Pair, #a.-b. 2.00 2.00
1061 A244 50d Pair, #a.-b. 2.00 2.00
1062 A244 50d Pair, #a.-b. 2.00 2.00
1063 A244 50d Pair, #a.-b. 2.00 2.00
1064 A244 50d Pair, #a.-b. 2.00 2.00
1065 A244 50d Pair, #a.-b. 2.00 2.00
1066 A244 50d Pair, #a.-b. 2.00 2.00
1067 A244 50d Pair, #a.-b. 2.00 2.00
1068 A244 50d Pair, #a.-b. 2.00 2.00
1069 A244 50d Pair, #a.-b. 2.00 2.00
1070 A244 50d Pair, #a.-b. 2.00 2.00
Nos. 1059-1070 (12) 24.00 24.00

Issued: #1059, 1/26; #1060, 2/2; #1061, 3/26; #1062, 4/9; #1063, 5/2; #1064, 6/24; #1065, 7/13; #1066, 8/8; #1067, 9/9; #1068, 10/22; #1069, 11/17; #1070, 12/24.

Miniature Sheet

Farm Animals — A291

Designs: a, Camel. b, Cow. c, Horse. d, Bull. e, Goat. f, Dog. g, Sheep. h, Ram. i, Goose. j, Turkey hen. k, Rabbit. l, Pigeon. m, Turkey. n, Rooster. o, Hen. p, Duck.

1983, Feb. 15 *Perf. 14½*
1083 Sheet of 16 10.00 10.00
a.-p. A291 25d any single .50 .40

Tripoli Intl. Fair A292

Libyans playing traditional instruments.

1983, Mar. 5 ***Perf. 14½x14, 14x14½***

1084	A292	40d multi, vert.	.60	.40
1085	A292	45d multicolored	.75	.50
1086	A292	50d multi, vert.	.75	.50
1087	A292	55d multicolored	1.00	.60
1088	A292	75d multi, vert.	1.25	.90
1089	A292	100d multi, vert.	1.60	1.10
		Nos. 1084-1089 (6)	5.95	4.00

Intl. Maritime Organization, 25th Anniv. — A293

Early sailing ships.

1983, Mar. 17 ***Perf. 14½***

1090	A293	100d Phoenician	2.00	.75
1091	A293	100d Viking	2.00	.75
1092	A293	100d Greek	2.00	.75
1093	A293	100d Roman	2.00	.75
1094	A293	100d Libyan	2.00	.75
1095	A293	100d Pharoah's ship	2.00	.75
		Nos. 1090-1095 (6)	12.00	4.50

Children's Day (1983) A294

Children's illustrations: a, Car. b, Tractor towing trailer. c, Children, dove. d, Boy Scouts. e, Dinosaur.

1983, Mar. 21 ***Perf. 14x14½***

1096	Strip of 5	2.75	2.75
a.-e.	A294 20d, any single	.40	.30

1st Intl. Symposium on Khadafy's Green Book — A295

1983, Apr. 1 ***Perf. 13½***

1097	A295	50d Khadafy, Green Book, map	.60	.40
1098	A295	70d Lecture hall, emblem	1.00	.50
1099	A295	80d Khadafy, Green Book, emblem	1.10	.75
		Nos. 1097-1099 (3)	2.70	1.65

Souvenir Sheet

Perf. 12½

1100	A295	100d Khadafy, Green Books	3.00	3.00

No. 1100 contains one stamp 57x48mm.

World Health Day A296

1983, Apr. 7 ***Perf. 12½***

1101	A296	25d Healthy children, vert.	.25	.25
1102	A296	50d Man in wheel-chair, vert.	.60	.40
1103	A296	100d Girl in hospital bed	1.25	.75
		Nos. 1101-1103 (3)	2.10	1.40

Pan-African Economic Committee, 25th Anniv. — A297

1983, Apr. 20 ***Perf. 13½***

1104	A297	50d multi	.60	.40
1105	A297	100d multi	1.25	.75
1106	A297	250d multi	3.00	2.00
		Nos. 1104-1106 (3)	4.85	3.15

Miniature Sheet

Fish A298

Designs: a, Labrus bimaculatus. b, Trigloporus lastoviza. c, Thalassoma pavo. d, Apogon imberbis. e, Scomber scombrus. f, Spondyliosoma cantharus. g, Trachinus draco. h, Blennius pavo. i, Scorpaena notata. j, Serranus scriba. k, Lophius piscatorius. l, Uranoscopus scaber. m, Auxis thazard. n, Zeus faber. o, Dactylopterus volitans. p, Umbrina cirrosa.

1983, May 15 ***Perf. 14½***

1107	Sheet of 16	10.00	10.00
a.-p.	A298 25d any single	.40	.30

Still-life by Gauguin (1848-1903) — A299

Paintings: No. 1108b, Abstract, unattributed. c, The Conquest of Tunis by Charles V, by Rubens. d, Arab Musicians in a Carriage, unattributed.

No. 1109a, Khadafy Glorified on Horseback, unattributed, vert. b, Triumph of David over the Syrians, by Raphael, vert. c, Laborers, unattributed, vert. d, Flower Vase, by van Gogh, vert.

1983, June 1 ***Perf. 11***

1108	Strip of 4	3.00	3.00
a.-d.	A299 50d, any single	.50	.35
1109	Strip of 4	3.00	3.00
a.-d.	A299 50d, any single	.50	.35

Souvenir Sheet

Ali Siala — A300

Scientists: No. 1110b, Ali El-Najar.

1983, June 1

1110	A300 Sheet of 2	3.50	3.50
a.-b.	100d, any single	1.50	1.50

1984 Summer Olympic Games, Los Angeles — A301

1983, June 15 ***Perf. 13½***

1111	A301	10d Basketball	.25	.20
1112	A301	15d High jump	.25	.20
1113	A301	25d Running	.25	.25
1114	A301	50d Gymnastics	.50	.40
1115	A301	100d Wind surfing	1.25	.75
1116	A301	200d Shot put	2.50	1.60
		Nos. 1111-1116 (6)	5.00	3.40

Souvenir Sheets

1117	A301	100d Equestrian	*3.00*	*3.00*
1118	A301	100d Soccer	*3.00*	*3.00*

#1111-1116 exist imperf. Value, set $22.50. Nos. 1117-1118 also exist imperf.

Nos. 1111-1116 exist printed together in a miniature sheet of 6. Values: perf $35; imperf $50. Each value was also printed in a miniature sheet of 4. Value, set of 6 sheets, $45.

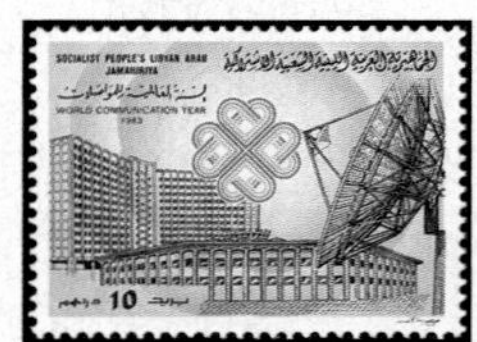

World Communications Year — A302

1983, July 1 ***Perf. 13***

1119	A302	10d multicolored	.40	.30
1120	A302	50d multicolored	.90	.60
1121	A302	100d multicolored	2.00	1.25
		Nos. 1119-1121 (3)	3.30	2.15

The Green Book, by Khadafy A303

Ideologies: 10d, The House is to be served by its residents. 15d, Power, wealth and arms are in the hands of the people. 20d, Masters in their own castles, vert. 35d, No democracy without popular congress. 100d, The authority of the people, vert. 140d, The Green Book is the guide of humanity for final release.

1983, Aug. 1 ***Perf. 13½***

1122	A303	10d multi	.25	.25
1123	A303	15d multi	.25	.25
1124	A303	20d multi	.25	.25
1125	A303	35d multi	.40	.25
1126	A303	100d multi	1.25	.75
1127	A303	140d multi	1.75	1.25
		Nos. 1122-1127 (6)	4.15	3.00

Souvenir Sheet

Litho. & Embossed

1128	A303	200d Khadafy in uniform	4.50	4.50

No. 1128 contains one gold embossed stamp 36x51mm.

2nd African Youth Sports Festival — A304

Designs: a, Team Handball. b, Basketball. c, Javelin. d, Running. e, Soccer.

1983, Aug. 22 **Litho.**

1129	Strip of 5	7.50	4.00
a.-e.	A304 100d, any single	1.25	.75

September 1 Revolution, 14th Anniv. — A305

Women in the Armed Forces.

1983, Sept. 1 ***Perf. 11½***

1130	A305	65d multi	.75	.75
1131	A305	75d multi	.90	.90
1132	A305	90d multi	1.00	1.00
1133	A305	100d multi	1.25	1.25
1134	A305	150d multi	1.75	1.75
1135	A305	250d multi	3.25	3.25
		Nos. 1130-1135 (6)	8.90	8.90

Souvenir Sheet

Perf. 11

1136	A305	200d multi	4.50	4.50

No. 1136 contains one stamp 63x38mm.

2nd Islamic Scout Jamboree — A306

1983, Sept. 2 ***Perf. 12½***

1137	A306	50d Saluting	.75	.75
1138	A306	100d Camping	2.00	2.00

Souvenir Sheet

1139	Sheet of 2	4.50	4.50
a.	A306 100d like 50d	2.00	2.00

No. 1139 contains Nos. 1138 and 1139a.

Traffic Day — A307

Saadun (1893-1923) A308

1983, Oct. 1 ***Perf. 14½x14***

1140	A307	30d Youth traffic monitors	1.25	.75
1141	A307	70d Traffic officer	2.50	1.00
1142	A307	200d Motorcycle police	8.00	3.50
		Nos. 1140-1142 (3)	11.75	5.25

1983, Oct. 11 ***Perf. 13½***

1143	A308	100d multicolored	1.50	.75

1st Manned Flight, Bicent. — A309

Early aircraft and historic flights: a, Americana, 1910. b, Nulli Secundus, 1907. c, J. B. Meusnier, 1785. d, Blanchard and Jeffries, 1785, vert. e, Pilatre de Rozier, 1784, vert. f, Montgolfiere, Oct. 19, 1783, vert.

1983, Nov. 1

1144 Strip of 6 10.00 10.00
a.-f. A309 100d, any single 1.50 .75

Intl. Day of Cooperation with Palestinian People — A310

1983, Nov. 29 ***Perf. 14½x14***

1145 A310 30d pale vio & lt bl grn .40 .25
1146 A310 70d lil & lt yel grn 1.25 .50
1147 A310 200d lt ultra & grn 3.50 1.75
Nos. 1145-1147 (3) 5.15 2.50

Miniature Sheet

Roman Mosaic — A311

Designs: Nos. 1148a-1148c, Gladiators. Nos. 1148d-1148f, Musicians, Nos. 1148g-1148i, Hunters. Illustration reduced.

1983, Dec. 1 ***Perf. 12***

1148 A311 Sheet of 9 7.00 7.00
a.-i. 50d, any single .75 .35

#1148a-1148c, 1148d-1148f and 1148g-1148i se-tenant in a continuous design.

Achievements of the Sept. 1 Revolution — A312

1983, Dec. 15 ***Perf. 13½***

1149 A312 10d Mosque .20 .20
1150 A312 15d Agriculture .20 .20
1151 A312 20d Industry .40 .25
1152 A312 35d Office building .50 .25
1153 A312 100d Health care 1.50 .60
1154 A312 140d Airport 2.25 1.10
Nos. 1149-1154 (6) 5.05 2.60

Souvenir Sheet

Litho. & Embossed

1155 A312 200d Khadafy 4.50 4.50

No. 1155 contains one gold embossed stamp 36x51mm.

Khadafy, Irrigation Project Survey Map A313

1983, Dec. 15

1156 A313 150d multicolored 2.25 1.25

A314

A315

Famous men: No. 1157a, Mahmud Burkis. No. 1157b, Ahmed El-Bakbak. No. 1157c, Mohamed El-Misurati. No. 1157d, Mahmud Ben Musa. No. 1157e, Abdulhamid Ben Ashiur. No. 1158a, Hosni Fauzi El-Amir. No. 1158b, Ali Haidar El-Saati. No. 1159, Mahmud Mustafa Dreza. No. 1160, Mehdi El-Sherif. No. 1161a, Ali El-Gariani. No. 1161b, Muktar Shakshuki. No. 1161c, Abdurrahman El-Busayri. No. 1161d, Ibbrahim Bakir. No. 1161e, Mahmud El-Janzuri. No. 1162a, Ahmed El-Feghi Hasan. No. 1162b, Bashir El Jawab.

1984 **Litho.** ***Perf. 13½***

1157 Strip of 5 6.00 6.00
a.-e. A314 100d any single 1.10 1.10
1158 Pair 3.50 1.50
a.-b. A314 100d any single 1.50 .60
1159 A314 100d multi 1.75 .60
1160 A315 100d multi 1.75 .60
1161 Strip of 5 15.00 15.00
a.-e. A314 200d any single 2.50 2.50
1162 Pair 6.00 6.00
a.-b. A315 200d any single 2.50 2.50
Nos. 1157-1162 (6) 34.00 29.70

Issued: #1157, 1161-1162, 1/1; #1158-1160, 2/20.

Miniature Sheet

Water Sports — A316

Designs: a, Two windsurfers. b, Two-man craft. c, Two-man craft, birds. d, Wind sailing, skis. e, Water skier facing front. f, Fisherman in boat. g, Power boating. h, Water skier facing right. i, Fisherman in surf. j, Kayaking. k, Surfing. l, Water skier wearing life jacket. m, Scuba diver sketching underwater. n, Diver. o, Snorkel diver removing fish from harpoon. p, Scuba diver surfacing.

1984, Jan. 10 ***Perf. 14½***

1164 Sheet of 16 8.50 8.50
a.-p. A316 25d any single .50 .50

African Children's Day — A317

Designs: a, Khadafy, girl scouts. b, Khadafy, children. c, Map, Khadafy, children (size: 63x44mm).

1984, Jan. 15 **Litho.** ***Perf. 14½***

1165 Strip of 3 3.50 3.50
a.-b. A317 50d, any single .80 .80
c. A317 100d multi 2.00 2.00

Women's Emancipation — A318

70d, Women, diff., vert. 100d, Soldiers, Khadafy.

1984, Jan. 20 ***Perf. 12***

1166 A318 55d multicolored .75 .40
1167 A318 70d multicolored 1.25 .45
1168 A318 100d multicolored 1.50 .75
Nos. 1166-1168 (3) 3.50 1.60

Irrigation A319

#1169: a, Desert, water. b, Produce, sheep grazing. c, Khadafy, irrigation of desert (size: 63x44mm). #1170-1171, Khadafy, map.

1984, Feb. 1 ***Perf. 14½***

1169 Strip of 3 2.50 2.50
a.-b. A319 50d any single .50 .25
c. A319 100d multicolored 1.50 .60

Size: 72x36mm

Perf. 13½

1170 A319 100d multicolored 1.50 .60

Souvenir Sheet

1171 A319 300d multicolored *7.00 7.00*

World Heritage — A320

Architectural ruins. No. 1174 vert.

1984, Feb. 10 ***Perf. 12***

1172 A320 50d Theater, Sabratha .60 .25
1173 A320 60d Temple, Cyrene .75 .30
1174 A320 70d Monument, Sabratha .90 .35
1175 A320 100d Arena, Leptis Magna 1.50 .60
1176 A320 150d Temple, Cyrene, diff. 2.00 .90
1177 A320 200d Basilica, Leptis Magna 2.75 1.40
Nos. 1172-1177 (6) 8.50 3.80

Silver Dirhams Minted A.D. 671-757 — A321

Designs: a, Hegira 115. b, Hegira 93. c, Hegira 121. d, Hegira 49. e, Hegira 135.

Litho. & Embossed

1984, Feb. 15 ***Perf. 13½***

1178 Strip of 5 15.00 15.00
a.-e. A321 200d, any single 2.75 1.25

Tripoli Intl. Fair A322

Tea served in various settings.

1984, Mar. 5 **Litho.** ***Perf. 12½***

1179 A322 25d multicolored .25 .25
1180 A322 35d multicolored .40 .25
1181 A322 45d multicolored .75 .25
1182 A322 55d multicolored .90 .40
1183 A322 75d multicolored 1.10 .40
1184 A322 100d multicolored 1.75 .95
Nos. 1179-1184 (6) 5.15 2.50

Musicians — A323

Designs: a, Muktar Shiaker Murabet. b, El-Aref El-Jamal. c, Ali Shiaalia. d, Bashir Fehmi.

1984, Mar. 15 ***Perf. 14½***

1185 Strip of 4 + label 9.00 9.00
a.-d. A323 100d, any single 1.90 1.00

Children's Day, IYC A324

Children's drawings: a, Recreation. b, Rainy day. c, Military strength. d, Playground. e, Porch swing, children, motorcycle.

1984, Mar. 21 ***Perf. 14***

1186 Strip of 5 2.75 2.75
a.-e. A324 20d, any single .45 .25

Arab League Constitution, 39th Anniv. A325

1984, Mar. 22 ***Perf. 13½***

1187 A325 30d multicolored .60 .60
1188 A325 40d multicolored .70 .70
1189 A325 50d multicolored 1.00 1.00
Nos. 1187-1189 (3) 2.30 2.30

Miniature Sheet

Automobiles, Locomotives — A326

1984, Apr. 1

1190 Sheet of 16 30.00 30.00
a.-h. A326 100d, Car, any single 1.75 .90
i.-p. A326 100d, Locomotive, any single 1.75 .90

No. 1190 pictures outline of two camels in gold. Size: 214x135mm.

World Health Day
A327

1984, Apr. 7 *Perf. 14½*

1191 A327 20d Stop Polio .25 .25
1192 A327 30d No. 910 .40 .25
1193 A327 40d Arabic text .90 .40
Nos. 1191-1193 (3) 1.55 .90

Crafts
A328

Designs: a, Shoemaker. b, Saddler. c, Women, wool. d, Spinner. e, Weaver. f, Tapestry weavers.

1984, May 1 *Perf. 12½*

1194 Strip of 6 15.00 15.00
a.-f. A328 150d, any single 2.25 1.25

Postal and Telecommunications Union Congress — A329

Designs: a, Telephones, mail. b, Computer operators. c, Emblem.

1984, May 15 *Perf. 14½*

1195 Strip of 3 3.50 3.50
a.-b. A329 50d, any single .75 .40
c. A329 100d multicolored 1.50 .75

Armed
Crowd — A330

Map, Fire,
Military — A331

Designs: No. 1197b, Soldiers. No. 1197c, Khadafy. No. 1198, Khadafy giving speech.

1984, May 17 *Perf. 12, 14½ (#1197)*

1196 A330 50d multi .90 .40
1197 Strip of 3 3.00 3.00
a.-b. A331 50d, any single .75 .25
c. A331 100d multi 1.75 .90
1198 A330 100d multi 1.50 .75
Nos. 1196-1198 (3) 5.40 4.15

Abrogation of the May 17 Treaty. Size of No. 1197c: 63x45mm.

Youth War
Casualties
A332

1984, June 4 *Perf. 10*

1199 A332 70d Damaged flag 1.00 .40
1200 A332 100d Children imprisoned 1.50 .75

Miniature Sheet

Green
Book
Quotations
A333

Designs: a, The Party System Aborts Democracy. b, Khadafy. c, Partners Not Wage-Workers. d, No Representation in Lieu of the People . . . e, Green Book. f, Committees Everywhere. g, Forming Parties Splits Societies. h, Party building, text on track. i, No Democracy without Popular Congresses.

1984, June 20 *Perf. 14*

1201 Sheet of 9 14.00 14.00
a.-i. A333 100d, any single 1.50 .75

See No. 1270.

Folk
Costumes — A334

Background colors: a, Green. b, Beige. c, Violet. d, Pale greenish blue. e, Salmon rose. f, Blue.

1984, July 1 *Perf. 14½x14*

1202 Strip of 6 12.50 12.50
a.-f. A334 100d, any single 1.75 1.00

Miniature Sheet

Natl. Soccer Championships — A335

Stadium, star, world cup and various action scenes.

1984, July 15 *Perf. 13½*

1203 Sheet of 16 20.00 20.00
a.-p. A335 70d, any single 1.10 .60

1984 Los
Angeles
Olympics — A336

World Food
Day — A337

1984, July 28

1204 A336 100d Soccer 1.75 1.00
1205 A336 100d Basketball 1.75 1.00
1206 A336 100d Swimming 1.75 1.00
1207 A336 100d Sprinting 1.75 1.00
1208 A336 100d Windsurfing 1.75 1.00
1209 A336 100d Discus 1.75 1.00
Nos. 1204-1209 (6) 10.50 6.00

Souvenir Sheets

1210 A336 250d Equestrian 6.00 6.00
1211 A336 250d Arab equestrian 6.00 6.00

1984, Aug. 1 *Perf. 12*

1212 A337 100d Forest scenes 1.75 .75
1213 A337 200d Men riding camels, oasis 3.50 1.25

Miniature Sheet

Sept. 1
Revolution, 15th
Anniv. — A338

Designs: a, Green books, building at right angle. b, Green book, building, minaret. c, Minaret, party building and grounds. d, Revolution leader. e, Eight-story building. f, Construction, dome. g, Highway, bridge. h, Green book, building at left angle. i, Shepherd, sheep. j, Harvester. k, Tractors. l, Industry. m, Khadafy. n, Irrigation pipe, man drinking. o, Silos, factory. p, Shipping.

1984, Sept. 15 *Perf. 14½*

1214 Sheet of 16 9.00 9.00
a.-p. A338 25d any single .50 .25

A339

Evacuation Day — A340

#1215b, Warrior facing left. #1215c, Khadafy leading battle (size: 63x45mm). #1216, Female rider. #1217, Battle scene. #1218, Italian whipping Libyan.

1984, Oct. 7

1215 Strip of 3 3.50 3.50
a.-b. A339 50d, any single .75 .40
c. A339 100d multi 1.50 .60

Perf. 11½

1216 A340 100d multicolored 1.50 .60
1217 A340 100d multicolored 1.50 .60
1218 A340 100d multicolored 1.50 .60
Nos. 1215-1218 (4) 8.00 5.30

Miniature Sheet

Equestrians — A341

Various jumping, racing and dressage exercises printed in a continuous design.

1984, Oct. 15 *Perf. 13½*

1219 Sheet of 16 9.00 .90
a.-p. A341 25d any single .50 .50

PHILAKOREA '84.

Agricultural
Traditions — A342

Designs: a, Farmer. b, Well, man, ox. c, Basket weaver. d, Shepherd, ram. e, Tanning hide. f, Coconut picker.

1984, Nov. 1 *Perf. 13½*

1220 Strip of 6 12.50 12.50
a.-f. A342 100d, any single 1.75 1.00

Union of Arab Pharmacists, 9th Congress — A343

1984, Nov. 6 *Perf. 12*

1221 A343 100d multicolored 1.75 1.75
1222 A343 200d multicolored 3.50 3.50

Arab-African Union — A344

1984, Nov. 15 *Perf. 12*

1223 A344 100d Map, banner, crowd 1.75 1.75
1224 A344 100d Men, flags 1.75 1.75

Nos.
1046,
1147
A345

1984, Nov. 29 *Perf. 12½*

1225 A345 100d pink & multi 3.50 3.50
1226 A345 150d brt yel grn & multi 4.50 4.50

Intl. Day of Cooperation with the Palestinian People.

Miniature Sheet

Intl. Civil Aviation Organization, 40th Anniv. — A346

Aircraft: a, Boeing 747 SP, 1975. b, Concorde, 1969. c, Lockheed L1011-500 Tristar, 1978. d, Airbus A310, 1982. e, Tupolev TU-134A, 1962. f, Shorts 360, 1981. g, Boeing 727, 1963. h, Caravelle 10, 1965. i, Fokker F27, 1955. j, Lockheed 749A Constellation, 1946. k, Martin 130, 1955. l, Douglas DC-3, 1936. m, Junkers JU-52, 1932. n, Lindbergh's Spirit of St. Louis, 1927 Ryan. o, De Havilland Moth, 1925. p, Wright Flyer, 1903.

1984, Dec. 7 *Perf. 13½*
1227 Sheet of 16 27.50 27.50
a.-p. A346 70d any single 1.50 .75

African Development Bank, 20th Anniv. — A347

UN Child Survival Campaign A348

"20" in different configurations and: 70d, Map, symbols of industry, education and agriculture. 100d, Symbols of research and development.

1984, Dec. 15
1228 A347 50d multicolored .90 .90
1229 A347 70d multicolored 1.25 1.25
1230 A347 100d multicolored 1.75 1.75
Nos. 1228-1230 (3) 3.90 3.90

1985, Jan. 1 *Perf. 12*
1231 A348 70d Mother, child 1.50 .75
1232 A348 70d Children 1.50 .75
1233 A348 70d Boys at military school 1.50 .75
1234 A348 70d Khadafy, children 1.50 .75
Nos. 1231-1234 (4) 6.00 3.00

Irrigation — A349

Drop of Water, Map — A350

1985, Jan. 15 *Perf. 14½x14*
1235 A349 100d shown 2.00 1.00
1236 A349 100d Flowers 2.00 1.00
1237 A349 100d Map, water 2.00 1.00
Nos. 1235-1237 (3) 6.00 3.00

Souvenir Sheet
Perf. 14x14½
1238 A350 200d shown 4.00 4.00

Musicians — A351

#1239a, Kamel El-Ghadi. #1239b, Lute. #1240a, Ahmed El-Khogia. #1240b, Violin. #1241a, Mustafa El-Fallah. #1241b, Zither. #1242a, Mohamed Hamdi. #1242b, Mask.

1985, Feb. 1 *Perf. 14½*
1239 A351 Pair 4.00 3.50
a.-b. 100d, any single 2.00 1.75
1240 A351 Pair 4.00 3.50
a.-b. 100d, any single 2.00 1.75
1241 A351 Pair 4.00 3.50
a.-b. 100d, any single 2.00 1.75
1242 A351 Pair 4.00 3.50
a.-b. 100d, any single 2.00 1.75
Nos. 1239-1242 (4) 16.00 14.00

Nos. 1239-1242 printed in sheets of 20, four strips of 5 consisting of two pairs each musician flanking center stamps picturing instruments.

Gold Dinars Minted A.D. 699-727 — A352

#1243a, Hegira 105. #1243b, Hegira 91. #1243c, Hegira 77. #1244, Dinar from Zuela.

Litho. and Embossed
1985, Feb. 15 *Perf. 13½*
1243 Strip of 3 12.50 12.50
a.-c. A352 200d, any single 4.00 2.50

Souvenir Sheet
1244 A352 300d multi 7.50 7.50

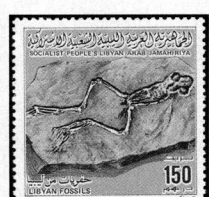

Fossils A353

1985, Mar. 1 **Litho.** *Perf. 13½*
1245 A353 150d Frog 6.00 3.00
1246 A353 150d Fish 6.00 3.00
1247 A353 150d Mammal 6.00 3.00
Nos. 1245-1247 (3) 18.00 9.00

People's Authority Declaration A354

Khadafy wearing: a, Folk costume. b, Academic robe. c, Khaki uniform. d, Black uniform. e, White uniform.

1985, Mar. 2 **Litho.** *Perf. 14½*
1248 Strip of 5 10.00 10.00
a.-e. A354 100d, any single 2.00 1.50

Tripoli Intl. Fair — A355

Musicians playing: a, Cymbals. b, Double flute, bongo. c, Wind instrument, drum. d, Drum. e, Tambourine.

1985, Mar. 5 *Perf. 14*
1249 Strip of 5 10.00 10.00
a.-e. A355 100d, any single 1.90 1.75

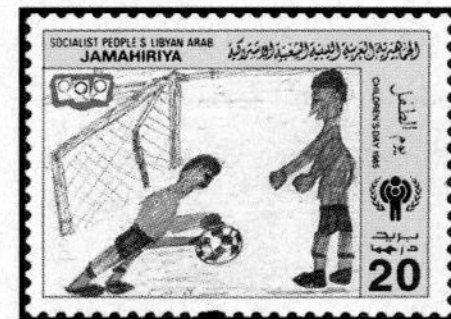

Children's Day, IYC A356

Children's drawings, various soccer plays: a, Goalie and player. b, Four players. c, Players as letters of the alphabet. d, Goalie save. e, Player heading the ball.

1985, Mar. 21 *Perf. 12*
1250 Strip of 5 7.50 7.50
a.-e. A356 20d, any single .40 .25

Intl. Program for Development of Telecommunications A357

World Health Day — A358

1985, Apr. 1
1251 A357 30d multicolored .40 .40
1252 A357 70d multicolored 1.00 1.00
1253 A357 100d multicolored 2.00 2.00
Nos. 1251-1253 (3) 3.40 3.40

1985, Apr. 7
1254 A358 40d Invalid, nurses 1.00 .60
1255 A358 60d Nurse, surgery 1.50 1.00
1256 A358 100d Nurse, child 2.50 1.60
Nos. 1254-1256 (3) 5.00 3.20

Miniature Sheet

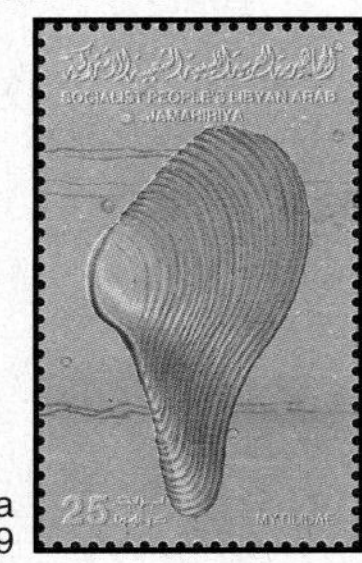

Sea Shells — A359

Designs: a, Mytilidae. b, Muricidae (white). c, Cardiidae. d, Corallophilidae. e, Muricidae. f, Muricacea. g, Turridae. h, Argonautidae. i, Tonnidae. j, Aporrhaidae. k, Trochidae. l, Cancellariidae. m, Epitoniidae. n, Turbnidae. o, Mitridae. p, Pectinidae.

1985, Apr. 20
1257 Sheet of 16 13.00 13.00
a.-p. A359 25d, any single .60 .25

Tripoli Intl. Book Fair — A360

Intl. Youth Year — A361

1985, Apr. 28 *Perf. 13½*
1258 A360 100d multi 2.00 1.50
1259 A360 200d multi 4.00 3.00

1985, May 1

Games: No. 1260a, Jump rope. No. 1260b, Board game. No. 1260c, Hopscotch. No. 1260d, Stickgame. No. 1260e, Tops. No. 1261a, Soccer. No. 1261b, Basketball.

1260 Strip of 5 6.00 6.00
a.-e. A361 20d, any single .40 .25

Souvenir Sheet
1261 Sheet of 2 9.00 9.00
a.-b. A361 100d, any single 3.00 1.00

No. 1261 contains 2 stamps 30x42mm.

Miniature Sheet

Mosque Minarets and Towers — A362

Mosques: a, Abdussalam Lasmar. b, Zaoviat Kadria. c, Zaoviat Amura. d, Gurgi. e, Mizran. f, Salem. g, Ghat. h, Ahmed Karamanli. i, Atya. j, El Kettani. k, Benghazi. l, Derna. m, El Derug. n, Ben Moussa. o, Ghadames. p, Abdulwahab.

1985, May 15 *Perf. 12*
1262 Sheet of 16 15.00 15.00
a.-p. A362 50d, any single .75 .60

A363

A364

1985, June 1 Litho. *Perf. 13½*

1263 A363 100d Hamida El-Anezi 2.00 1.50
1264 A363 100d Jamila Zemerli 2.00 1.50

Teachers' Day.

1985 June 12

Battle of the Philadelphia: a, Ship sinking. b, Militia. c, Hand-to-hand combat.

1265 Strip of 3 4.00 4.00
a.-b. A364 50d, any single 1.00 1.00
c. A364 100d multicolored 1.75 1.75

Size of No. 1265c: 60x48mm. Continuous design with No. 1265c in middle.

A365

Khadafy's Islamic Pilgrimage — A366

"The Holy Koran is the Law of Society" and Khadafy: a, Writing. b, Kneeling. c, With Holy Kaaba. d, Looking in window. e, Praying at pilgrimage ceremony.

1985, June 16

1266 Strip of 5 22.50 22.50
a.-e. A365 200d, any single 4.00 2.50

Souvenir Sheet

1267 A366 300d multicolored 6.50 6.50

Miniature Sheet

Mushrooms — A367

Designs: a, Leucopaxillus lepistoides. b, Amanita caesarea. c, Coriolus hirsutus. d, Cortinarius subfulgens. e, Dermocybe pratensis. f, Macrolepiota excoriata. g, Amanita curtipes. h, Trametes ljubarskyi. i, Pholiota aurivella. j, Boletus edulis. k, Geastrum sessile. l, Russula sanguinea. m, Cortinarius herculeus. n, Pholiota lenta. o, Amanita rubenscens. p, Scleroderma polyrhizum.

1985, July 15

1268 Sheet of 16 16.00 16.00
a.-p. A367 50d, any single .90 .40

No. 1268 exists imperf. Value $50.

Women's Folk Costumes — A368

Designs: a, Woman in violet. b, In white. c, In brown and blue. d, In blue. e, In red.

1985, Aug. 1 *Perf. 14½x14*

1269 Strip of 5 10.00 10.00
a.-e. A368 100d, any single 1.75 1.50

Green Book Quotations Type of 1984
Miniature Sheet

Designs: a, In Need Freedom Is Latent. b, Khadafy reading. c, To Make A Party You Split Society. d, Public Sport Is for All the Masses. e, Green Books, doves. f, Wage-Workers Are a Type of Slave . . . g, People Are Only Harmonious with Their Own Arts and Heritages. h, Khadafy orating. i, Democracy Means Popular Rule Not Popular Expression.

1985, Aug. 15 *Perf. 14*

1270 Sheet of 9 17.50 17.50
a.-i. A333 100d, any single 1.75 1.50

A369

September 1 Revolution, 16th Anniv. — A370

Designs: a, Food. b, Oil pipeline, refinery. c, Capital, olive branch. d, Mosque, modern buildings. e, Flag, mountains. f, Telecommunications apparatus.

1985, Sept. 1 *Perf. 12½*

1271 Strip of 6 12.50 12.50
a.-f. A369 100d, any single 2.00 1.50
1272 A370 200d multi 4.50 4.50

Mosque Entrances A371

Designs: a, Zauiet Amoura, Janzour. b, Shiaieb El-ain, Tripoli. c, Zauiet Abdussalam El-asmar, Zliten. d, Karamanli, Tripoli. e, Gurgi, Tripoli.

1985, Sept. 15 *Perf. 14*

1273 Strip of 5 10.00 10.00
a.-e. A371 100d, any single 2.00 1.50

Miniature Sheet

Basketball A372

Various players in action.

1985, Oct. 1 Litho. *Perf. 13x12½*

1274 Sheet of 16 9.00 9.00
a.-p. A372 25d any single .50 .40

Evacuation A373

Designs: a, Man on crutches, web, tree. b, Man caught in web held by disembodied hands. c, Three men basking in light.

1985, Oct. 7 *Perf. 15*

1275 Strip of 3 6.50 6.50
a.-c. A373 100d any single 1.75 1.50

Stamp Day — A374

Italia 85: a, Man sitting at desk, Type A228, Earth. b, Magnifying glass, open stock book, Type A228. c, Stamps escaping envelope.

1985, Oct. 25 *Perf. 12*

1276 Strip of 3 4.00 4.00
a.-c. A374 50d, any single 1.00 .60

1986 World Cup Soccer Championships — A375

1985, Nov. 1 *Perf. 13½*

1277 A375 100d Block, heading the ball 2.00 1.50
1278 A375 100d Kick, goalie catching ball 2.00 1.50
1279 A375 100d Goalie, block, dribble 2.00 1.50
1280 A375 100d Goalie, dribble, sliding block 2.00 1.50
1281 A375 100d Goalie catching the ball 2.00 1.50
1282 A375 100d Block 2.00 1.50
Nos. 1277-1282 (6) 12.00 9.00

Souvenir Sheet

1283 A375 200d Four players 8.50 8.50

Intl. Day of Cooperation with the Palestinian People A376

1985, Nov. 29 Litho. *Perf. 12½*

1284 A376 100d multi 1.75 1.50
1285 A376 150d multi 3.25 2.25

A set of 12 stamps picturing Khadafy was to be issued Jan. 1, 1986. Supposedly these were on sale for two hours. Value $175.

Importation Prohibited

Importation of the stamps of Libya was prohibited as of Jan. 7, 1986.

General Post and Telecommunications Co. — A378

1986, Jan. 15 *Perf. 12*

1298 A378 100d yel & multi 2.25 1.50
1299 A378 150d yel grn & multi 2.75 2.00

Peoples Authority Declaration — A379

Designs: b, Hand holding globe and paper. c, Dove, Khadafy's Green Book (size: 53x37mm).

1986, Mar. 2 *Perf. 12½x13*

1300 Strip of 3 4.50 4.50
a.-b. A379 50d, any single 1.00 .60
c. A379 100d multicolored 2.00 1.25

Musical Instruments — A380

Designs: a, Flute. b, Drums. c, Horn. d, Cymbals. e, Hand drum.

1986, Mar. 5

1301 Strip of 5 10.00 10.00
a.-e. A380 100d any single 2.00 1.50

Tripoli International Fair.

Intl. Children's Day — A381

Designs: a, Boy Scout fishing. b, Riding camel. c, Chasing butterflies. d, Beating drum. e, Soccer game.

1986, Mar. 21 ***Perf. 13½***

1302 Strip of 5 8.50 8.50
a.-e. A381 50d any single 1.25 .75

World Health Day — A382

1986, Apr. 7

1303 A382 250d sil & multi 5.00 3.00
1304 A382 250d gold & multi 5.00 3.00

Government Programs A383

Designs: a, Medical examinations. b, Education. c, Farming (size: 63x42mm).

1986, May 1 ***Perf. 14½***

1305 Strip of 3 3.75 3.75
a.-b. A383 50d any single .85 .60
c. A383 100d multicolored 1.75 1.25

Miniature Sheet

World Cup Soccer Championships, Mexico — A384

Designs: No. 1306a, 2 players. No. 1306b, 3 players in red and white shirts, one in green. No. 1306c, 2 players, referee. No. 1306d, Shot at goal. No. 1306e, 2 players with striped shirts. No. 1306f, 2 players with blue shirts, one with red. No. 1307, 7 players. No. 1308, 1st Libyan team, 1931.

1986, May 31 ***Perf. 13½***

1306 Sheet of 6 7.50 7.50
a.-f. A384 50d any single 1.10 .75

Souvenir Sheets

1307 A384 200d multicolored 6.50 6.50
1308 A384 200d multicolored 6.50 6.50

Nos. 1307-1308 each contain one 52x37mm stamp.

Miniature Sheet

Vegetables A385

Designs: a, Peas. b, Zucchini. c, Beans. d, Eggplant. e, Corn. f, Tomato. g, Red pepper. h, Cucumbers. i, Garlic. j, Cabbage. k, Cauliflower. l, Celery. m, Onions. n, Carrots. o, Potato. p, Radishes.

1986, June 1 ***Perf. 13x12½***

1309 Sheet of 16 15.00 15.00
a.-p. A385 50d any single .85 .75

No. 1309 has a continuous design.

Miniature Sheet

Khadafy and Irrigation Project A386

Khadafy and: a, Engineer reviewing plans, drill rig. b, Map. c, Well. d, Drought conditions. e, Water pipe. f, Pipes, pulleys, equipment. g, Lowering water pipe. h, Construction workers, trailer. i, Hands holding water. j, Opening water valve. k, Laying pipeline. l, Trucks hauling pipes. m, Khadafy holding green book, city. n, Giving vegetables to people. o, Boy drinking, man cultivating field. p, Men in prayer, irrigation. (Khadafy not shown on Nos. 1310h, 1310i, 1310k, 1310 l, 1310o.)

1986, July 1 ***Perf. 13½***

1310 Sheet of 16 35.00 35.00
a.-p. A386 100d any single 2.00 1.40

A387

A388

American Attack on Libya, Apr. 15 — A389

Designs: Nos. 1311a-1311p, Various scenes in Tripoli during and after air raid. No. 1312a. F14 aircraft. No. 1312b, Aircraft carrier, people. No. 1312c, Sinking of USS *Philadelphia,* 1801.
Illustration A389 is reduced.

1986, July 13

1311 A387 Sheet of 16, #a.-p. 26.00 26.00
1312 Strip of 3 3.50 3.50
a.-b. A388 50d multicolored .85 .65
c. A388 100d multicolored 1.75 1.25
1313 A389 100d multicolored 2.10 1.50

No. 1312 has a continuous design. Size of No. 1312b: 60x38mm.

Khadafy's Peace Methods A390

Khadafy: b, Reading Green Book. c, With old woman. d, Praying with children. e, Visiting sick. f, Driving tractor.

1986, July 13

1314 Sheet of 6 12.50 12.50
a.-f. A390 100d any single 2.00 1.40

Miniature Sheet

Green Book Quotations A391

Designs: a, The House Must be Served by its Own Tenant. b, Khadafy. c, The Child is Raised by His Mother. d, Democracy is the Supervision of the People by the People. e, Green Books. f, Representation is a Falsification of Democracy. g, The Recognition of Profit is an Acknowledgement of Exploitation. h, Flowers. i, Knowledge is a Natural Right of Every Human Being...

1986, Aug. 1 ***Perf. 14***

1315 Sheet of 9 19.00 19.00
a.-i. A391 100d any single 2.00 1.40

Sept. 1st Revolution, 17th Anniv. A392

a, Public health. b, Agriculture. c, Sunflowers by Vincent Van Gogh. d, Defense. e. Oil industry.

1986, Sept. 1

1316 Strip of 5 22.50 22.50
a.-e. A392 200d any single 4.00 2.75

A393

Arab-African Union, 1st Anniv. — A394

1986, Sept. 15 ***Perf. 12***

1317 A393 250d Libyan, Arab horsemen 5.00 4.00
1318 A394 250d Women in native dress 5.00 4.00

Evacuation Day — A395

Designs: a, Mounted warrior. b, Two horsemen, infantry. c, Cavalry charge.

1986, Oct. 7 ***Perf. 13½***

1319 Strip of 3 6.00 6.00
a. A395 50d multicolored 1.00 .60
b. A395 100d multicolored 2.00 1.10
c. A395 150d multicolored 2.75 2.40

Intl. Peace Year A396

1986, Oct. 24 ***Perf. 14½***

1320 A396 200d bl & multi 4.00 3.00
1321 A396 200d grn & multi 4.00 3.00

Solidarity with the Palestinians — A397

1986, Nov. 29 ***Perf. 12½***

1322 A397 250d pink & multi 5.00 4.00
1323 A397 250d blue & multi 5.00 4.00

Music and Dance — A398

Designs: a, Man beating drum. b, Masked dancer. c, Woman dancing with jugs on her head. d, Man playing bagpipe. e, Man beating hand drum.

1986, Dec. 1 ***Perf. 12***

1324 Strip of 5 8.00 8.00
a.-e. A398 70d any single 1.50 1.25

Gazella Leptoceros — A399

1987, Mar. 2 ***Perf. 13½***

1325 A399 100d Two adults 3.00 2.00
1326 A399 100d Fawn nursing 3.00 2.00
1327 A399 100d Adult sleeping 3.00 2.00
1328 A399 100d Adult drinking 3.00 2.00
Nos. 1325-1328 (4) 12.00 8.00

World Wildlife Fund.

Nos. 1325-1328 exist imperf. Value, set $27.50.

A400

A401

Crowd of People and: a, Oilfields. b, Buildings. c, Khadafy, buildings, globe.

1987, Mar. 2 ***Perf. 13½***

1329 Strip of 3 40.00 40.00
a.-b. A400 500d multicolored 10.00 8.00
c. A400 1000d multicolored 20.00 15.00

People's Authority declaration.

No. 1329 has a continuous design. Size of No. 1329c: 42x37mm.

1987, Sept. 1 *Perf. 13½*

Sept. 1st Revolution, 18th Anniv.: a, Shepherd, sheep. b, Khadafy. c, Mosque. d, Irrigation pipeline. e, Combine in field. f, Khadafy at microphones. g, Harvesting grain. h, Irrigation. i, Soldier. j, Militiaman. k, Fountain. l, Skyscrapers. m, House, women. n, Children. o, Assembly hall. p, Two girls.

Miniature Sheet

1330 Sheet of 16 65.00 65.00
a.-p. A401 150d any single 3.00 2.25

No. 1330 has a continuous design.

Libyan Freedom Fighters — A402

No. 1331: a, Omer Abed Anabi Al Mansuri. b, Ahmed Ali Al Emrayd. c, Khalifa Said Ben Asker. d, Mohamed Ben Farhat Azawi. e, Mohamed Souf Al Lafi Al Marmori.

1988, Feb. 15

1331 Strip of 5 29.00 29.00
a. A402 100d multicolored 2.00 1.25
b. A402 200d multicolored 5.75 4.25
c. A402 300d multicolored 8.00 4.50
d. A402 400d multicolored
e. A402 500d multicolored 9.00 6.50

Freedom Festival Day — A403

1988, June 1

1332 A403 100d yel & multi 1.75 1.25
1333 A403 150d grn & multi 3.00 2.00
1334 A403 250d brn org & multi 5.00 3.50
Nos. 1332-1334 (3) 9.75 6.75

Miniature Sheet

American Attack on Libya, 2nd Anniv. A404

Khadafy: a, With woman and children. b, Playing chess. c, Fleeing from bombing with children. d, Praying in desert. e, Praying with children. f, Visiting wounded child. g, With infants and children, horiz. h, Delivering speech, horiz. i, With family, horiz.

#1336, In desert, vert. #1337, Making speech.

1988, July 13

1335 Sheet of 9 25.00 25.00
a.-i. A404 150d any single 2.75 2.00

Souvenir Sheets

Litho. & Embossed

1336 A404 500d gold & multi 10.00 10.00
1337 A404 500d gold & multi 10.00 10.00

No. 1335 exists imperf.

September 1st Revolution, 19th Anniv. — A405

1988, Sept. 19 **Litho.**

1338 A405 100d brt bl & multi 1.75 1.25
1339 A405 250d gray & multi 4.50 3.00
1340 A405 300d cit & multi 5.00 4.25
1341 A405 500d bl grn & multi 10.00 7.00
Nos. 1338-1341 (4) 21.25 15.50

1988 Summer Olympics, Seoul — A406

1988, Sept. 17

1342 A406 150d Tennis 2.75 2.00
1343 A406 150d Equestrian 2.75 2.00
1344 A406 150d Relay race 2.75 2.00
1345 A406 150d Soccer 2.75 2.00
1346 A406 150d Distance race 2.75 2.00
1347 A406 150d Cycling 2.75 2.00
Nos. 1342-1347 (6) 16.50 12.00

Souvenir Sheet

1348 A406 750d Soccer, diff. 13.00 13.00

#1348 contains one 30x42mm stamp. Exists imperf. #1342-1347 exist in miniature sheets of 1. Value, set $37.50.

Miniature Sheet

1988 Summer Olympics, Seoul — A407

1988, Sept 17

1350 Sheet of 3 8.50 8.50
a. A407 100d Bedouin rider 2.00 2.00
b. A407 200d shown 3.00 3.00
c. A407 200d Show jumping, diff. 3.00 3.00

Olymphilex '88, Seoul.

A408 A409

Design: Libyan Palm Tree.

1988, Nov. 1

1351 A408 500d Fruit 10.00 6.50
1352 A408 1000d Palm tree 18.00 12.00

1988

1353 Strip of 3 11.50 11.50
a. A409 100d shown 2.00 1.40
b. A409 200d Boy with rocks 3.50 2.75
c. A409 300d Flag, map 5.75 4.25

Palestinian uprising. #1353b, size: 45x39mm.

People's Authority Declaration — A410

1989

1354 A410 260d dk grn & multi 5.00 3.00
1355 A410 500d gold & multi 10.00 6.00

Miniature Sheet

September 1 Revolution, 20th Anniv. — A411

Designs: a, Crowd, Green Books, emblem. b, Soldiers, Khadafy, irrigation pipeline. c, Military equipment, Khadafy, communication and transportation. d, Mounted warriors. e, Battle scenes.

1989 *Perf. 13½*

1356 A411 Sheet of 5 14.00 14.00
a.-e. 150d any single 2.75 2.00
f. Bklt. pane of 5, perf. 13½ horiz. 14.00 14.00

Souvenir Sheet

1357 A411 250d Khadafy 4.00 4.00

No. 1357 contains one 36x51mm stamp. Stamps from No. 1356f have gold border at right.

Libyans Deported to Italy — A412

#1359, Libyans in boats. #1360, Khadafy, crescent moon. #1361, Khadafy at left, in desert. #1362, Khadafy at right, soldiers. #1363, Khadafy in center, Libyans.

1989

1358 A412 100d shown 1.75 1.25
1359 A412 100d multicolored 1.75 1.25
1360 A412 100d multicolored 1.75 1.25
1361 A412 100d multicolored 1.75 1.25
1362 A412 100d multicolored 1.75 1.25
Nos. 1358-1362 (5) 8.75 6.25

Souvenir Sheet

1363 A412 150d multicolored 3.00 3.00

No. 1363 contains one 72x38mm stamp.

A413

A414

1989 *Perf. 12*

1364 A413 150d multicolored 2.75 2.75
1365 A413 200d multicolored 4.25 4.25

Demolition of Libyan-Tunisian border fortifications.

1989 *Perf. 12x11½*

1366 A414 100d shown 2.25 2.25
1367 A414 300d Man, flag, crowd 6.50 6.50
1368 A414 500d Emblem 10.00 10.00
Nos. 1366-1368 (3) 18.75 18.75

Solidarity with the Palestinians.

Ibn Annafis, Physician A415

1989 *Perf. 12*

1369 A415 100d multicolored 2.75 2.75
1370 A415 150d multicolored 4.00 4.00

A416

A417

1990, Oct. 18 **Litho.** *Perf. 14*

Granite Paper

1371 A416 100d multicolored 1.75 1.75
1372 A416 300d multicolored 8.00 8.00

Intl. Literacy Year.

1990, Oct. 18

Granite Paper

1373 A417 100d multicolored 1.75 1.75
1374 A417 400d multicolored 5.25 5.25

Organization of Petroleum Exporting Countries (OPEC), 30th anniv.

A418

A419

1990, June 28 *Perf. 11½x12*

1375 A418 100d brt org & multi 1.75 1.75
1376 A418 400d grn & multi 8.00 8.00

Evacuation of US military base, 20th anniv.

1990, Apr. 24

1377 A419 300d bl & multi 5.00 5.00
1378 A419 500d vio & multi 10.00 10.00

People's authority declaration.

A420

A421

Plowing Season in Libya: 2000d, Man on tractor plowing field.

1990, Dec. 4 *Perf. 14*

Granite Paper

1379 A420 500d multicolored 11.00 11.00
1380 A420 2000d multicolored 37.50 37.50

1990, Nov. 5 *Perf. 14*

Granite Paper

1381 A421 100d grn & multi 1.75 1.75
1382 A421 400d vio & multi 8.00 8.00
1383 A421 500d bl & multi 9.25 9.25
Nos. 1381-1383 (3) 19.00 19.00

Souvenir Sheet

Perf. 11½

1384 A421 500d Trophy, map, horiz. 11.00 11.00

World Cup Soccer Championships, Italy. No. 1384 contains one 38x33mm stamp.

Sept. 1st Revolution, 21st Anniv. A422

1990, Sept. 3 *Perf. 14*

Granite Paper

1385 A422 100d multicolored 2.00 2.00
1386 A422 400d multicolored 8.50 8.50
1387 A422 1000d multicolored 21.00 21.00
Nos. 1385-1387 (3) 31.50 31.50

Imperf

Size: 120x90mm

1388 A422 200d multi, diff. 8.50 8.50

Maghreb Arab Union, 2nd Anniv. — A423

1991, Mar. 10 **Litho.** *Perf. 13½*

1389 A423 100d multicolored 2.00 2.00
1390 A423 300d gold & multi 5.75 5.75

People's Authority Declaration — A424

1991, Mar. 10

1391 A424 300d multicolored 5.00 5.00
1392 A424 400d silver & multi 10.00 10.00

Children's Day — A425

World Health Day — A426

1991, Mar. 22

1393 A425 100d Butterflies, girl 2.75 2.75
1394 A425 400d Bird, boy 10.00 10.00

1991, Apr. 7

1395 A426 100d blue & multi 1.75 1.75
1396 A426 200d green & multi 3.50 3.50

Scenes from Libya A427

1991, June 20

1397 A427 100d Wadi el Hayat, vert. 1.75 1.75
1398 A427 250d Mourzuk 5.00 5.00
1399 A427 500d Ghadames 10.00 10.00
Nos. 1397-1399 (3) 16.75 16.75

Irrigation Project A428

a, Laborers, heavy equipment. b, Khadafy, heavy equipment. c, Livestock, fruit & vegetables.

1991, Aug. 28 *Perf. 12*

1400 A428 50d Strip of 3, #a.-c. 3.50 3.50

No. 1400 has a continuous design. Size of No. 1400b: 60x36mm.

Sept. 1st Revolution, 22nd Anniv. — A429

1991, Sept. 1 *Perf. 13½*

1401 A429 300d Chains, roses & "22" 5.75 5.75
1402 A429 400d Chains, "22" 7.25 7.25
a. Souv. sheet of 2, #1401-1402 16.00 16.00

Telecom '91 A430

1991, Oct. 7 **Litho.** *Perf. 13½*

1403 A430 100d Emblems, vert. 1.75 1.75
1404 A430 500d Buildings, satillite dish 9.25 9.25

Libyans Deported to Italy A431

1991, Oct. 26 **Litho.** *Perf. 13½*

1405 A431 100d Monument, soldier 1.75 1.75
1406 A431 400d Ship, refugees, soldiers 7.25 7.25
a. Souv. sheet of 2, #1405-1406 10.00 10.00

Arab Unity A432

1991, Nov. 15 *Perf. 12*

1407 A432 50d tan & multi 1.00 1.00
1408 A432 100d blue & multi 2.00 2.00

Miniature Sheet

Trucks, Automobiles and Motorcycles A433

Designs: a-d, Various trucks. e-h, Various off-road race cars. i-p, Various motorcycles.

1991, Dec. 28 *Perf. 14*

1409 A433 50d Sheet of 16, #a.-p. 17.50 17.50

Eagle — A434

Col. Khadafy — A434a

1992 *Perf. 11½*

Granite Paper (#1412-1419)

Background Colors

1412 A434 100d yellow 1.40 .85
1413 A434 150d blue gray 2.25 1.25
1414 A434 200d bright blue 2.75 1.75
1415 A434 250d orange 3.75 2.00
1416 A434 300d purple 4.25 2.50
1418 A434 400d bright pink 5.75 3.50
1419 A434 450d bright green 7.25 3.75

Perf. 13½

1420 A434a 500d yellow green 6.50 3.50
1421 A434a 1000d rose 13.00 7.00
1422 A434a 2000d blue 26.00 14.00
1423 A434a 5000d violet 65.00 37.50
1424 A434a 6000d yellow brown 80.00 45.00
Nos. 1412-1424 (12) 217.90 122.60

Issued: #1412-1416, 1418-1419, 1/1/92; #1420-1424, 9/1/92.

This is an expanding set. Numbers may change.

People's Authority Declaration A435

1992, Mar. **Litho.** *Perf. 12*

1425 A435 100d yellow & multi 1.50 1.50
1426 A435 150d blue & multi 2.25 2.25

African Tourism Year (in 1991) A436

1992, Apr. 5 *Perf. 14½*

Granite Paper

1427 A436 50d purple & multi .75 .75
1428 A436 100d pink & multi 1.40 1.40

1992 Summer Olympics, Barcelona A437

1992, June 15 *Perf. 12*

1429 A437 50d Tennis .75 .75
1430 A437 50d Long jump .75 .75
1431 A437 50d Discus .75 .75
Nos. 1429-1431 (3) 2.25 2.25

Size: 106x82mm

Imperf

1432 A437 100d Olympic torch, rings 1.50 1.50

Revolutionary Achievements — A438

Designs: 100d, Palm trees. 150d, Steel mill. 250d, Cargo ship. 300d, Libyan Airlines. 400d, Natl. Assembly, Green Books. 500d, Irrigation pipeline, Khadafy.

1992, June 30 *Perf. 14*

Granite Paper

1433 A438 100d multicolored 1.40 1.40
1434 A438 150d multicolored 2.25 2.25
1435 A438 250d multicolored 3.75 3.75
1436 A438 300d multicolored 4.25 4.25
1437 A438 400d multicolored 5.75 5.75
1438 A438 500d multicolored 7.25 7.25
Nos. 1433-1438 (6) 24.65 24.65

Tripoli Intl. Fair — A439

1992, Mar. ***Perf. 12***

1439 A439 50d Horse & buggy

1440 A439 100d Horse & sulky

Mahgreb Arab Union Philatelic Exhibition — A440

1992, Feb. 17 ***Perf. 14½***

1441 A440 75d blue green & multi	2.50	1.75
1442 A440 80d blue & multi	2.50	1.75

Miniature Sheet

Fish A441

Designs: a, Fish with spots near eye. b, Thin fish. d, Brown fish, currents. e, Fish, plants at LR. f, Fish, plants at LL.

1992, Apr. 15 ***Perf. 14***

1443 A441 100d Sheet of 6, #a.-f.	14.00	14.00

Miniature Sheet

Horsemanship — A442

Designs: a, Woman rider with gun. b, Man on white horse. c, Mongol rider. d, Roman officer. e, Cossack rider. f, Arab rider. 250d, Two Arab riders.

1992, Apr. 25 ***Perf. 13½x14***

1444 A442 100d Sheet of 6, #a.-f.	9.50	9.50

Souvenir Sheet

1445 A442 250d multicolored	5.00	5.00

Khadafy — A443

Designs: No. 1450a, like No. 1446. b, like No. 1447. c, like No. 1448. d, like No. 1449.

1992, Jan. 1 ***Perf. 14x13½***

1446 A443 100d blue green & multi	2.00	2.00
1447 A443 100d gray & multi	2.00	2.00
1448 A443 100d rose lake & multi	2.00	2.00
1449 A443 100d yellow & multi	2.00	2.00
Nos. 1446-1449 (4)	8.00	8.00

Souvenir Sheet

1450 A443 150d Sheet of 4, #a.-d.	11.00	11.00

Evacuation of Foreign Forces — A444

Costumes A445

1992, Oct. 7 **Litho.** ***Perf. 14***

1451 A444 75d Horse, broken chain	1.00	1.00
1452 A444 80d Flag, broken chain	1.00	1.00

1992, Dec. 15 **Litho.** ***Perf. 12***

Women wearing various traditional costumes.

Denomination color: a, green. b, black. c, violet blue. d, sky blue. e, yellow brown.

1453 A445 50d Strip of 5, #a.-e.	3.25	3.25

Sept. 1st Revolution, 23rd Anniv. — A446

1992, Sept. 1

1454 A446 50d Torch, "23"	.75	.75
1455 A446 100d Flag, "23"	1.40	1.40

Souvenir Sheet

1456 A446 250d Eagle, "23"	3.50	3.50

No. 1456 contains one 50x40mm stamp.

Libyans Deported to Italy — A447

1992, Oct. 26

1457 A447 100d tan & multi	1.40	1.40
1458 A447 250d blue & multi	3.00	3.00

Oasis A448

Designs: 100d, Gazelle drinking. 200d, Camels, palm trees, vert. 300d, Palm trees, camel and rider.

1992, Oct. 1 ***Perf. 14***

1459 A448 100d multicolored	1.50	1.50
1460 A448 200d multicolored	3.00	3.00
1461 A448 300d multicolored	5.00	5.00
Nos. 1459-1461 (3)	9.50	9.50

Palestinian Intifada — A449

Designs: 100d, Palestinian holding rock and flag. 300d, Map of Israel and Palestine, Dome of the Rock, Palestinian flag, olives, hand holding rock, vert.

1992, Nov. 26 **Litho.** ***Perf. 12***

1462-1463 A449 Set of 2	3.75	3.75

Doctors — A450

Designs: 40d, Dr. Mohamed Ali Imsek (1883-1945). 60d, Dr. Aref Adhani Arif (1884-1935).

1993, Feb. 1

1464-1465 A450 Set of 2	.95	.95

Intl. Conference on Nutrition, Rome — A451

Background colors: 70d, Blue. 80d, Green.

1993, Feb. 15

1466-1467 A451 Set of 2	1.50	1.50

People's Authority Declaration — A452

Col. Khadafy, map of Libya, crowd, eagle, oil rig, pipeline and tanker: 60d, 65d, 75d.

1993, Mar. 2 ***Perf. 14¾***

1468-1470 A452 Set of 3	1.90	1.90

Tripoli Intl. Fair A453

Various Fair participants, Fair emblem and panel color of: No. 1471, 60d, Pink. No. 1472, 60d, Yellow green. No. 1473, 60d, Blue, vert. No. 1474, 60d, Orange, vert. 100d, People on horses.

1993, Mar. 15 ***Perf. 14***

1471-1474 A453 Set of 4	2.10	2.10

Souvenir Sheet

Perf. 11¾

1475 A453 100d multi	1.10	1.10

No. 1475 contains one 38x32mm stamp.

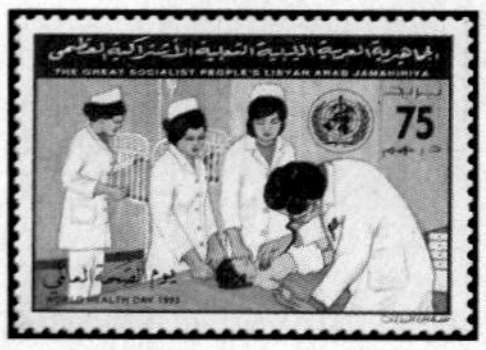

World Health Day A454

Designs: 75d, Doctor and three nurses examining child. 85d, Doctor and two nurses examining woman.

1993, Apr. 7 ***Perf. 13¼***

1476-1477 A454 Set of 2	1.60	1.60

Children's Day — A455

No. 1478 — Various girls with background of: a, Gray green (red headdress). b, Red curtains. c, Gray. d, Home furnishings. e, Beige.

1993, May 1 ***Perf. 13¾***

1478 Horiz. strip of 5	3.75	3.75
a.-e. A455 75d Any single	.75	.75

Miniature Sheet

Watercraft — A456

No. 1479: a, Ship with swan's head figurehead. b, Ship with triangular sail and oars. c, Ship with one large white sail. d, Ship with rectangular sail and oars. e, Ship with three triangular sails. f, Sailboat, map of Western Mediterranean area. g, Sailboat, map of Eastern Mediterranean area. h, Ship with two red triangular sails. i, Ship with four sails, red flag. j, Sailboat, map of Western Libya. k, Sailboat, map of Eastern Libya. l, Ship with three sails on main mast. m, Ocean liner with black hull. n, Ship with six tan sails. o, Ship with furled sails. p, Ocean liner with white hull.

1993, July 15 ***Perf. 13¼***

1479 A456 50d Sheet of 16, #a-p	8.50	8.50

Miniature Sheet

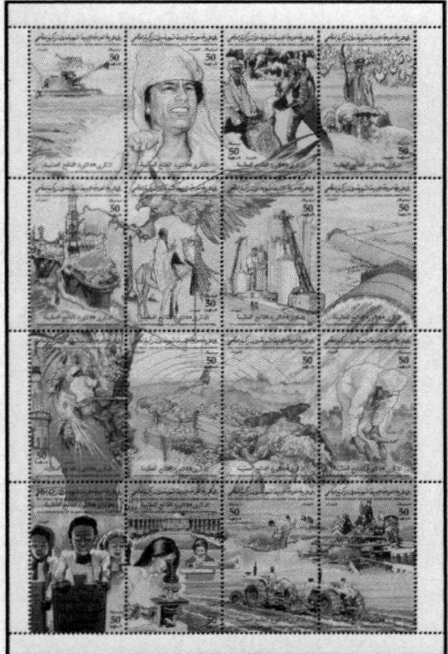

Sept. 1 Revolution, 24th Anniv. — A457

No. 1480: a, Grain combine. b, Col. Khadafy. c, Cows, man with feed bucket. d, Shepherd and sheep. e, Oil platform, map of Western Libya. f, Eagle, man on camel, map of Eastern Libya. g, Cranes lifting large tanks. h, Water pipeline. i, Man picking dates. j, Man in field, crates of vegetables. k, Crates of vegetables. l, Man picking vegetables. m, Three children. n, Building, women at typewriter and microscope. o, Man in field, tractor. p, Tractors in field.

1993, Dec. 10 ***Perf. 14***
1480 A457 50d Sheet of 16, #a-p 10.50 10.50

Miniature Sheet

Libyans Deported to Italy — A458

No. 1481: a, Guard tower, soldier with gun, woman tending to sick man. b, Soldier with gun and bayonet guarding Libyans. c, Col. Khadafy with headdress. d, Man holding box and walking stick. e, Soldiers whipping man. f, Man on horse. g, Four men. h, Soldier guarding people looking at hanged man. i, Soldier standing near wooden post, soldier guarding Libyans. j, Woman on camel, soldiers. k, Soldiers on horses among Libyans. l, Boat with deportees. m, Col. Khadafy without headdress. n, Libyan with arm raised, hand of Col. Khadafy. o, Soldier pointing gun at horseman with sword. p, Horseman carrying gun.

1993, Dec. 15 ***Perf. 14½***
1481 A458 50d Sheet of 16, #a-p 10.50 10.50

Miniature Sheet

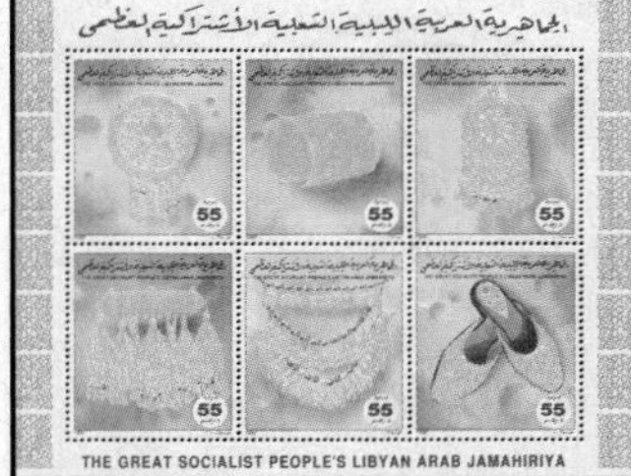

Items Made of Silver — A459

No. 1482: a, Medallion with five-pointed star and tassels. b, Wristband. c, Medallion with star with ten rays and tassels. d, Rod with tassels. e, Necklace. f, Slippers.

Litho. & Embossed With Foil Application

1994, Aug. 10 ***Perf. 13¼***
1482 A459 55d Sheet of 6, #a-f 3.75 3.75

A460

Sept. 1 Revolution, 25th Anniv. — A461

No. 1483: a, Jet, Col. Khadafy in robe (40x40mm). b, Warriors on horseback, mother and child, Col. Khadafy in military uniform (60x40mm). c, Ship, shepherd, man and woman, man on camel (40x40mm).
Illustration A460 reduced.

1994, Sept. 1 **Litho.** ***Perf. 12***
1483 A460 100d Horiz. strip of 3, #a-c 3.75 3.75

Souvenir Sheet

1484 A461 1000d multi 11.50 11.50

1994 World Cup Soccer Championships, United States — A462

World Cup, and various soccer players with horizontal stripes in: No. 1485, 100d, Red and brown. No. 1486, 100d, Red violet, purple, and green. No. 1487, 100d, Green and purple. No. 1488, 100d, Green, black and yellow. No. 1489, 100d, Orange, brown and red. No. 1490, 100d, Yellow orange, brown and orange.
No. 1491, 500d, Soccer players, World Cup, red violet background. No. 1492, 500d, Soccer player, ball, "1990," horiz.

1994, Oct. 15 ***Perf. 13¼***
1485-1490 A462 Set of 6 7.00 7.00

Souvenir Sheets

1491-1492 A462 Set of 2 11.50 11.50

No. 1491 contains one 42x51mm stamp; No. 1492 contains one 51x42mm stamp.

Miniature Sheet

Libyans Deported to Italy — A463

No. 1493: a, Col. Khadafy. b, Airplane, man with rifle. c, Two men, one with rifle, nose of airplane. d, Tail of airplane, man with rifle. e, Soldier with bayoneted rifle, Libyans looking at dead animal. f, Libyans with rifles, camel. g, Nose of camel, horsemen and soldiers. h, Man carrrying child, drawn swords, horsemen. i, Soldier with whip. j, Man with open mouth. k, Tank and soldiers. l, Soldiers on horseback, women. m, Woman tending to injured man, man with bound hands, rifles. n, Soldier bayoneting man. o, Building, women, soldiers on horseback. p, Deportees in boats.

1994, Oct. 26 ***Perf. 12***
1493 A463 95d Sheet of 16, #a-p 19.00 19.00

Mosques — A464

No. 1494 — Mosques in: a, Darghut. b, Benghazi. c, Kabao. d, Gouzgu. e, Siala. f, El Kettani.

1994, Nov. 15 **Litho.**
1494 Horiz. strip of 6 9.00 9.00
a.-f. A464 70d Any single 1.50 1.50

Miniature Sheet

People's Authority Declaration — A465

No. 1495: a, Navy ship, jet, women soldiers. b, Wheat, hand holding Green Book, tractor trailer cab. c, Family, water pipeline, tractor trailers. d, Fruit, vegetables, people holding Green Book. e, Col. Khadafy, butterfly, flowers. f, Young men, fruit and vegetables.

1994, Dec. 1 ***Perf. 14¾***
1495 A465 80d Sheet of 6, #a-f 10.50 10.50

Evacuation of Foreign Forces — A466

Denomination in: 65d, Blue. 95f, Green.

1994, Dec. 15 ***Perf. 14***
1496-1497 A466 Set of 2 2.10 2.10

Miniature Sheet

Khadafy Prize for Human Rights — A467

No. 1498: a, Helmeted soldiers, men with sticks, South African flag. b, Men with sticks, South African flag. c, South African Pres. Nelson Mandela. d, Col. Khadafy. e, Indian at fire, crescent moon. f, Armed Indians on horses. g, Indian chief. h, Indian dancer. i, Men with rifles, jets. j, Women, jet, open book. k, Open book. l, Surgeons. m, Palestinians with flag, denomination at left. n, Palestinians with flag, denomination at right. o, Palestinians throwing rocks. p, Palestinians, soldiers.

1994, Dec. 31 ***Perf. 13¼***
1498 A467 95d Sheet of 16, #a-p 20.00 20.00

No. 1498 exists with marginal inscription with correct spelling of "Prize."

People's Authority Declaration A468

Background color: No. 1499, 100d, Green. No. 1500, 100d, Blue. No. 1501, 100d, Yellow.

1995, July 1 ***Perf. 12***
1499-1501 A468 Set of 3 1.90 1.90

Arab League, 50th Anniv. A469

Background color: No. 1502, 200d, Green. No. 1503, 200d, Blue.
No. 1504: a, Emblem in silver. b, Emblem in gold.

1995, July 20 **Litho.** ***Perf. 13¼***
1502-1503 A469 Set of 2 6.50 6.50

Litho. & Embossed With Foil Application

1504 A469 1000d Sheet of 2, #a-b 11.50 11.50

Miniature Sheet

Libyan Soccer Players — A470

No. 1505: a, Messaud Zentuti. b, Salem Shermit. c, Ottoman Marfua. d, Ghaleb Siala. e, 1935 Libyan Team. f, Senussi Mresila.

1995, Aug. 1 **Litho.**
1505 A470 100d Sheet of 6, #a-f 7.50 7.50

Miniature Sheet

Zoo Animals — A471

No. 1506: a, Camel. b, Secretary bird. c, African wild dog. d, Oryx. e, Baboon. f, Golden jackal. g, Crowned eagle. h, Eagle owl. i, Desert hedgehog. j, Sand gerbil. k, Addax. l, Fennec. m, Lanner falcon. n, Desert wheatear. o, Pintailed sandgrouse. p, Jerboa.

1995, Aug. 15 ***Perf. 13¾x14***
1506 A471 100d Sheet of 16, #a-p 21.00 21.00

Miniature Sheet

Fruit — A472

No. 1507: a, Grapefruit. b, Wild cherries. c, Mulberries. d, Strawberry tree fruit (arbutus). e, Plums. f, Pears. g, Apricots. h, Almonds. i, Prickly pears. j, Lemons. k, Peaches. l, Dates. m, Olives. n, Oranges. o, Figs. p, Grapes.

1995, Aug. 20
1507 A472 100d Sheet of 16, #a-p 21.00 21.00

Miniature Sheet

Sept. 1 Revolution, 26th Anniv. — A473

No. 1508: a, Students and chemist. b, Minaret, fist of Col. Khadafy, men. c, Col. Khadafy. d, Scientists and buildings. e, Nurses, doctor and patients. f, Surgeons. g, Woman at keyboard, shoemakers. h, Audio technicians, musician. i, Crane, bulldozer and buildings. j, Grain elevator. k, Offshore oil rig, nose of airplane. l, Tail of airplane, ship. m, Goats and sheep. n, Water pipeline. o, Camels, vegetables, water. p, Fruit, grain combine.

1995, Sept. 1
1508 A473 100d Sheet of 16, #a-p 21.00 21.00

Scouts — A474

No. 1509 — Scouting emblem and: a, Antelope, Scout and butterflies (40x40mm). b, Scouts, butterflies, antelope and cat (60x40mm). c, Scouts, wheat, butterfly, flower.
Illustration reduced.

1995, Sept. 10 ***Perf. 12***
1509 A474 250d Horiz. strip of 3, #a-c 16.00 16.00

American Attack on Libya, 9th Anniv. — A475

No. 1510: a, Ships and people (40x50mm). b, Airplanes, helicopters and people, hand holding Green Book (60x50mm). c, Airplane, mother and child (40x50mm).
Illustration reduced.

1995, Sept. 15
1510 A475 100d Horiz. strip of 3, #a-c 4.25 4.25

Tripoli Intl. Fair — A476

Horsemen with background colors of: No. 1511, 100d, Light blue. No. 1512, 100d, Blue. No. 1513, 100d, Violet. No. 1514, 100d, Blue green, vert. No. 1515, 100d, Blue green with black stripes, vert. No. 1516, 100d, Orange, vert.
1000d, Col. Khadafy on horse.

1995, Sept. 20
1511-1516 A476 Set of 6 8.50 8.50

Souvenir Sheet

1517 A476 1000d multi 13.50 13.50

No. 1517 contains one 80x50mm stamp.

Miniature Sheet

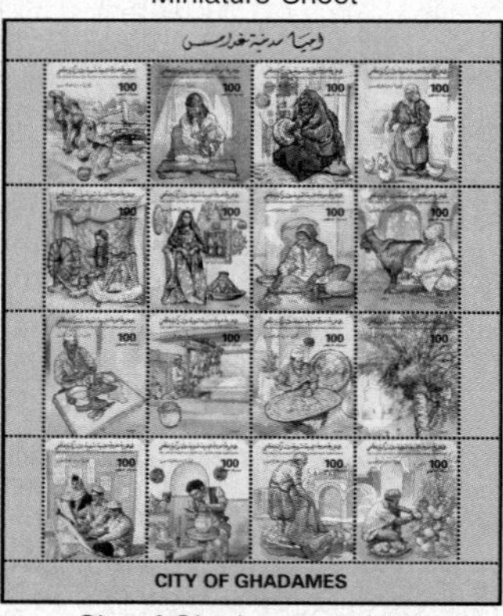

City of Ghadames — A477

No. 1518: a, Camel, woman with water jugs. b, Woman with bread on wooden board. c, Seated woman with vase. d, Woman feeding chickens. e, Woman at spinning wheel. f, Woman standing. g, Woman cooking. h, Woman milking goat. i, Shoemaker. j, Man at loom. k, Metalworker with hammer. l, Date picker. m, Men at religious school. n, Potter. o, Tanner. p, Man picking tomatoes.

Perf. 14½x14¼

1995, Sept. 30 **Litho.**
1518 A477 100d Sheet of 16, #a-p 21.00 21.00

Evacuation of Foreign Forces — A478

Panel color: 50d, Pink. 100d, Green. 200d, Lilac.

1995, Oct. 7 **Litho.** ***Perf. 14¾x14¼***
1519-1521 A478 Set of 3 4.75 4.75

Bees and Flowers A479

Panel color: No. 1522, 100d, Green. No. 1523, 100d, Pink. No. 1524, 100d, Purple.

1995, Oct. 10 ***Perf. 14¼x14¾***
1522-1524 A479 Set of 3 4.25 4.25

Dr. Mohamed Feituri — A480

1995, Oct. 20 ***Perf. 14¾x14¼***
1525 A480 200d multi 2.75 2.75

Campaign Against Smoking — A481

Color of central stripe: No. 1526, 100d, Orange. No. 1527, 100d, Yellow.

1995, Oct. 20
1526-1527 A481 Set of 2 2.75 2.75

Miniature Sheet

Libyans Deported to Italy — A482

No. 1528: a, Col. Khadafy. b, Horsemen. c, Battle scene with blue sky, denomination at LR. d, Battle scene with blue sky, airplane, denomination at LL. e, Battle scene, arch. f, Battle scene, red building at UR. g, Battle scene with red sky, soldier holding pistol. h, Battle scene with red sky, building at UR. i, Three Libyans in foreground. j, Battle scene with running soldiers. k, Battle scene of horsemen and riflemen facing right. l, Soldiers, Libyan man in foreground at LR. m, Two horesemen with arms raised. n, Man in foreground shooting at horsemen. o, Children. p, Child, deportees in boats.

1995, Oct. 26 ***Perf. 12***
1528 A482 100d Sheet of 16, #a-p 21.00 21.00

Miniature Sheet

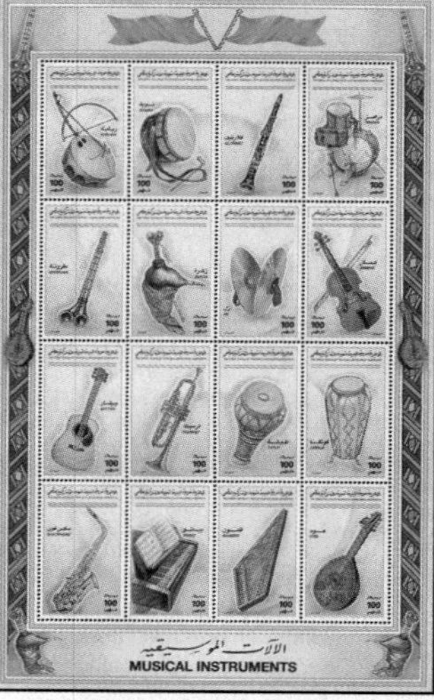

Musical Instruments — A483

No. 1529: a, Rababa. b, Nouba (drum). c, Clarinet. d, Drums. e, Magruna. f, Zukra. g, Zil (cymbals). h, Kaman (violin). i, Guitar. j, Trumpet. k, Tapla (drum). l, Gonga (drum). m, Saxophone. n, Piano. o, Gandon (zither). p, Ood.

1995, Nov. 1 ***Perf. 13¾x14***
1529 A483 100d Sheet of 16, #a-p 21.00 21.00

Doors of Mizda — A484

No. 1530: a, Blue door. b, Door with arched design in rectangular doorway. c, Log door. d, Door with rounded top in archway. e, Door of planks in rectangular doorway.

1995, Nov. 10 *Perf. 13¼*

1530 Horiz. strip of 5 3.00 3.00
a.-e. A484 100d Any single .60 .60

Intl. Olympic Committee, Cent. — A485

Denomination color: No. 1531, 100d, Red. No. 1532, 100d, Black.

1995, Nov. 15 *Perf. 13½*

1531-1532 A485 Set of 2 1.25 1.25

Prehistoric Animals — A486

No. 1533: a, Baryonyx. b, Oviraptor. c, Stenonychosaurus. d, Tenontosaurus. e, Yangchuanosaurus. f, Stegotetrabelodon, denomination at LR. g, Stegotetrabelodon, denomination at LL. h, Psittacosaurus. i, Heterodontosaurus. j, Loxodonta atlantica. k, Mammuthus. l, Erlikosaurus. m, Cynognathus. n, Plateosaurus. o, Staurikosaurus. p, Lystrosaurus.

500d, Stegotetrabelodon, horiz.

1995, Nov. 20 *Perf. 13½*

1533 Miniature sheet of 16 11.50 11.50
a.-p. A486 100d Any single .70 .70

Souvenir Sheet

Perf. 13¼

1534 A486 500d multi 3.75 3.75

No. 1534 contains one 53x49mm stamp.

Children's Day A487

No. 1535: a, Boy, dinosaur with cane. b, Boy on elephant. c, Boy, Scout emblem, turtle and mushroom. d, Dinosaur and soccer ball. e, Boy with gun, pteranodon.

1995, Nov. 25 *Perf. 13½*

1535 Horiz. strip of 5 14.00 14.00
a.-e. A487 100d Any single 2.75 2.75

Palestinian Intifada — A488

No. 1536: a, Boy throwing object at helicopter. b, Dome of the Rock, Palestinian with flag. c, People, Palestinian flag.

Illustration reduced.

1995, Nov. 29 *Perf. 14*

1536 A488 100d Horiz. strip of 3, #a-c 4.25 4.25

Intl. Civil Aviation Organization, 50th Anniv. — A489

Denomination color: No. 1537, 100d, Black. No. 1538, 100d, Blue.

1995, Dec. 7 *Perf. 13½x13¼*

1537-1538 A489 Set of 2 1.25 1.25

United Nations, 50th Anniv. — A490

Background color: No. 1539, 100d, Dark red lilac. No. 1540, 100d, Light red lilac.

1995, Dec. 20 *Perf. 13½*

1539-1540 A490 Set of 2 1.25 1.25

Miniature Sheet

Flowers — A491

No. 1541: a, Iris germanica. b, Canna edulis. c, Nerium oleander. d, Papaver rhoeas. e, Strelitzia reginae. f, Amygdalus communis.

1995, Dec. 31 *Perf. 14¾*

1541 A491 200d Sheet of 6, #a-f 10.50 10.50

People's Authority Declaration A492

Panel color: 100d, Pink. 150d, Light blue. 200d, Light green.

1996, Mar. 2 *Perf. 13¼*

1542-1544 A492 Set of 3 4.75 4.75

1996 Summer Olympics, Atlanta — A493

No. 1545: a, Soccer. b, Long jump. c, Tennis. d, Cycling. e, Boxing. f, Equestrian.

No. 1546, 500d, Runner. No. 1547, 500d, Equestrian, diff.

1996, Aug. 15 *Perf. 14½*

1545 A493 100d Sheet of 6, #a-f 6.25 6.25

Souvenir Sheets

1546-1547 A493 Set of 2 10.50 10.50

Miniature Sheet

Sept. 1 Revolution, 27th Anniv. — A494

No. 1548: a, Camel, man, fruits, water. b, Water pipeline, fruit. c, Tractor, water, women. d, Oil worker. e, Tailor. f, Seamstress, Col. Khadafy's fist. g, Col. Khadafy. h, Building, women with microscope. i, Nurses at anatomy lesson, man with microscope. j, School child. k, Woman with open book. l, Man playing zither. m, Airplanes. n, Dish antenna, ship, man on camel. o, Ship, television camera. p, Television actress, woman at microphone.

1996, Sept. 1 *Perf. 13¾x14*

1548 A494 100d Sheet of 16, #a-p 17.00 17.00

Miniature Sheet

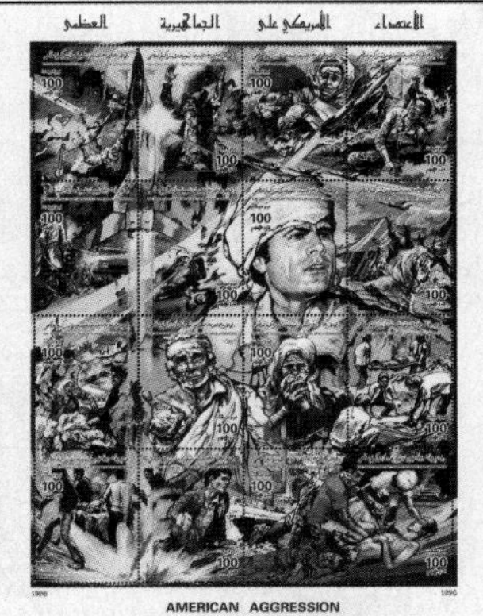

American Attack on Libya, 10th Anniv. — A495

No. 1549: a, Left side of missile, explosion. b, Right side of missile, man with raised arms. c, Casualties, airplanes. d, Airplane at left, man on ground. e, Firefighter spraying burning car. f, Damaged vehicles. g, Col. Khadafy. h, Casualties, airplane at top. i, Rescuers assisting casualties. j, Man with extended hand. k, Woman with hands to face. l, Stretcher bearers. m, Three men and casualty. n, Man with bloody hand. o, Woman and child casualties. p, Burning car, rescuers attending to bleeding casualty.

1996, Sept. 15 *Perf. 13¾*

1549 A495 100d Sheet of 16, #a-p 17.00 17.00

Miniature Sheet

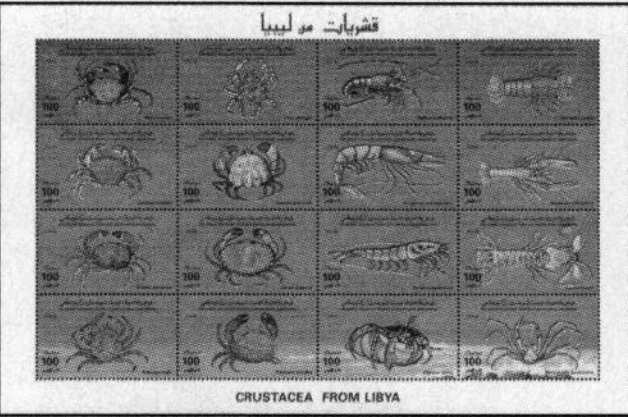

Crustaceans — A496

No. 1550: a, Necora puber. b, Lissa chiragra. c, Palinurus elephas. d, Scyllarus arctus. e, Carcinus maenas. f, Calappa granulata. g, Parapenaeus longirostris. h, Nephrops norvegicus. i, Eriphia verrucosa. j, Cancer pagurus. k, Penaeus kerathurus. l, Squilla mantis. m, Maja squinado. n, Pilumnus hirtellus. o, Pagurus alatus. p, Macropodia tenuirostris.

1996, Oct. 1 *Perf. 14x13¾*

1550 A496 100d Sheet of 16, #a-p 17.00 17.00

Miniature Sheet

Intl. Day of Maghreb Handicrafts — A497

Various handicrafts.

1996, Oct. 15 *Perf. 13¾x14*

1551 A497 100d Sheet of 16, #a-p 17.00 17.00

Miniature Sheet

Libyans Deported to Italy — A498

No. 1552: a, Guard tower, soldier with gun, woman tending to sick man. b, Soldier with gun and bayonet, soldier on horseback. c, Col. Khadafy with headdress. d, Man holding box and walking stick. e, Soldiers whipping man. f, Man on horse. g, Four men. h, Soldier guarding people looking at hanged man. i, Soldier standing near wooden post, soldier guarding Libyans. j, Woman on camel, soldiers. k, Soldiers on horses among Libyans. l, Boat with deportees. m, Col. Khadafy without headdress. n, Libyan with arm raised, hand of Col. Khadafy. o, Soldier pointing gun at horseman with sword. p, Horseman carrying gun.

1996, Oct. 26 **Litho.**
1552 A498 100d Sheet of 16, #a-p 17.00 17.00

Miniature Sheet

Horses — A499

No. 1553: a, Brown horse, lake at right. b, Brown horse in front of lake, tree at right. c, Brown horse in front of lake, tree at right. d, Dark brown horse, trees in background. e, Dark brown horse with raised leg. f, Horse at base of tree. g, Gray horse galloping. h, Piebald horse. i, Gray horse, palm tree at left. j, Head of black horse and tail of brown horse. k, Brown horse, palm fronds at upper right. l, Brown horse with gray mane, palm tree at right. m, Head of black horse, body of gray horse, tail of brown horse. n, Head of brown horse, body of black horse, hindquarters of two brown horses. o, Head of brown horse, parts of three other brown horses. p, Head of brown horse, chest of another brown horse, palm tree at right.

1996, Oct. 30 ***Perf. 14x13¾***
1553 A499 100d Sheet of 16, #a-p 17.00 17.00

Miniature Sheet

Camels — A500

No. 1554: a, Camelus dromedarius with head at right. b, Head of Camelus dromedarius. c, Camelus dromedarius with head at left. d, Camelus ferus bactrianus with head at right. e, Camelus ferus ferus. f, Camelus ferus bactrianus with head at left.

1996, Nov. 15 ***Perf. 12***
1554 A500 200d Sheet of 6, #a-f 12.50 12.50

Press and Information A501

Designs: 100d, Photographer, newspapers, computer. 200d, Musicians, video technician, computer, dish antenna.

1996, Nov. 20
1555-1556 A501 Set of 2 3.25 3.25

Miniature Sheet

Fossils and Prehistoric Animals — A502

No. 1557: a, Mene rhombea fossil. b, Mesodon macrocephalus fossil. c, Eyron arctiformis fossil. d, Stegosaurus. e, Pteranodon. f, Allosaurus.

1996, Nov. 25
1557 A502 200d Sheet of 6, #a-f 15.00 15.00

Palestinian Intifada — A503

Frame color: 100d, Yellow. 150d, Green. 200d, Blue.

1996, Nov. 29
1558-1560 A503 Set of 3 4.75 4.75

African Children's Day — A504

Designs: 50d, Child, beige frame. 150d, Child, blue frame. 200d, Mother, child, dove.

1996, Dec. 5 ***Perf. 13¼***
1561-1563 A504 Set of 3 2.10 2.10

Children's Day — A505

No. 1564 — Various cats with background colors of: a, Rose. b, Blue green. c, Blue. d, Yellow green. e, Gray green.

1996, Dec. 5
1564 Horiz. strip of 5 5.25 5.25
a.-e. A505 100d Any single 1.00 1.00

Intl. Family Day — A506

No. 1565 — Family and: a, 150d, Building (21x27mm). b, 150d, Automobile (21x27mm). c, 200d, Stylized globe (46x27mm). Illustration reduced.

1996, Dec. 10 ***Perf. 13x13¼***
1565 A506 Horiz. strip of 3, #a-c 2.60 2.60

Miniature Sheet

Teachers — A507

No. 1566: a, Mohamed Kamel El-Hammali. b, Mustafa Abdulla Ben-Amer. c, Mohamed Messaud Fesheka. d, Kairi Mustafa Serraj. e, Muftah El-Majri. f, Mohamed Hadi Arafa.

1996, Dec. 15 ***Perf. 13¼***
1566 A507 100d Sheet of 6, #a-f 3.25 3.25

Miniature Sheet

Singers — A508

No. 1567: a, Mohamed Salim and zither. b, Mohamed M. Sayed Bumedyen and flute. c, Otman Najim and ood. d, Mahmud Sherif and tapla. e, Mohamed Ferjani Marghani and piano. f, Mohamed Kabazi and violin.

1996, Dec. 15
1567 A508 100d Sheet of 6, #a-f 3.25 3.25

Miniature Sheet

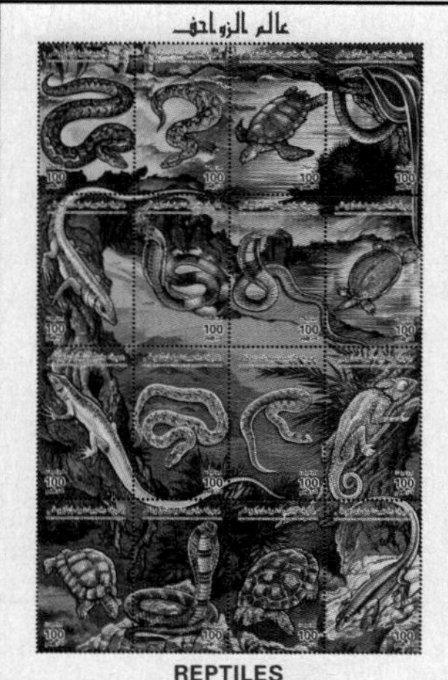

Reptiles — A509

No. 1568: a, Snake, leaves and building at top. b, Snake, building at top. c, Turtle, water and part of snake. d, Snake on tree branch. e, Brown lizard on rock. f, Cobra with head at left. g, Cobra and water. h, Turtle, water, tail of cobra. i, Green lizard on rock. j, Snake, foliage at bottom. k, Snake, foliage at bottom and right. l, Lizard with curled tail. m, Turtle on rock. n, Cobra with head at right. o, Turtle on grass. p, Gray lizard on rock.

1996, Dec. 20 ***Perf. 13¾x14***
1568 A509 100d Sheet of 16, #a-p 17.00 17.00

Miniature Sheet

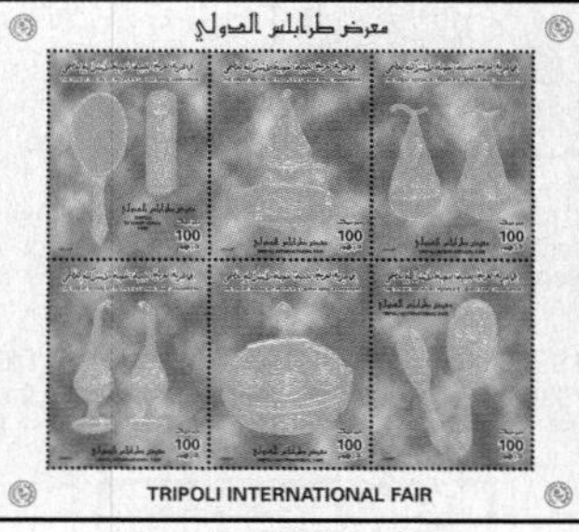

Tripoli Intl. Fair — A510

No. 1569: a, Mirror and brush. b, Container and plate. c, Two containers with rounded bases. d, Two containers on pedestals. e, Oval ornament. f, Brushes.

Litho. & Embossed with Foil Application

1996, Dec. 30 ***Perf. 13¾***
1569 A510 100d Sheet of 6, #a-f 6.25 6.25

A511

People's Authority Declaration, 20th Anniv. — A512

Frame color: 100d, Yellow. 200d, Blue. 300d, Green.

1997, Mar. 2 **Litho.** ***Perf. 12***
1570-1572 A511 Set of 3 7.50 7.50

Souvenir Sheet

Imperf

1573 A512 10,000d multi 90.00 90.00

No. 1573 has a perforated label that bears the denomination but lacks the country name.

Scouts and Philately — A513

No. 1574: a, 50d, Group of scouts, open album, wheat, flag. b, 50d, Two scouts, two albums, wheat. c, 100d, Butterflies, books, scouts and flags.

1997, Mar. 15 ***Perf. 14***
1574 A513 Horiz. strip of 3, #a-c 2.50 2.50

Health Care — A514

No. 1575: a, 50d, Doctor looking at test tube. b, 50d, Doctor, microscope. c, 100d, Doctor and nurse examining baby.

1997, Apr. 7

1575 A514 Horiz. strip of 3, #a-c 2.10 2.10

Buildings A515

Designs: 50d, Shown. 100d, Building with attached tower, vert. 200d, Tower, vert.

Perf. 14¼x14¾, 14¾x14¼

1997, Apr. 15

1576-1578 A515 Set of 3 4.75 4.75

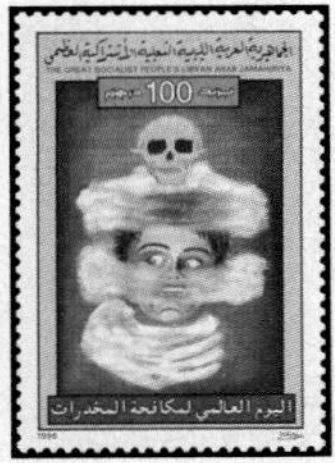

Campaign Against Smoking — A516

Frame color: 100d, Blue. 150d, Green. 200d, Pink.

1997, Apr. 30 ***Perf. 14¾x14¼***

1579-1581 A516 Set of 3 2.40 2.40

Arab National Central Library — A517

Building, map, open book, and olive branches with background in: 100d, Blue. 200d, Green.

1000d, Building, map, books, computer and Col. Khadafy, horiz.

1997, Aug. 10 ***Perf. 13¼***

1582-1583 A517 Set of 2 1.60 1.60

Souvenir Sheet

1584 A517 1000d multi 5.25 5.25

No. 1584 contains one 116x49mm stamp.

Arab Tourism Year — A518

Perf. 13¼x13½

1997, Aug. 20 **Litho.**

1585 Horiz. strip of 3 10.50 10.50

a. A518 100d Black denomination 2.00 2.00

b. A518 200d Red denomination 3.75 3.75

c. A518 250d Blue denomination 4.75 4.75

Miniature Sheet

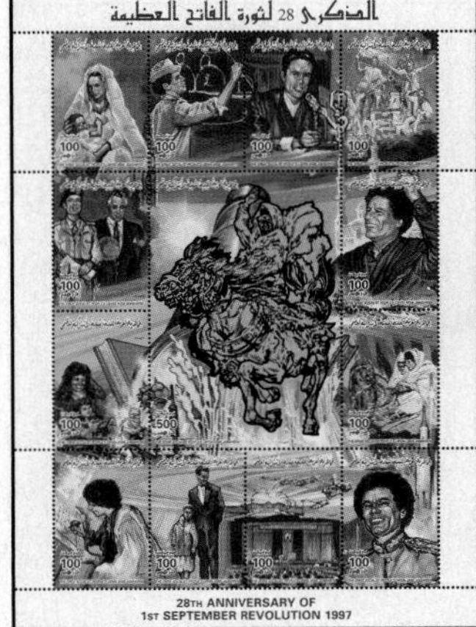

A519

Sept. 1 Revolution, 28th Anniv. — A520

No. 1586: a, 100d, Mother and child. b, 100d, Col. Khadafy as student. c, 100d, Khadafy at microphone. d, 100d, People on tank. e, 100d, Khadafy and man in suit. f, 100d, Khadafy with fist raised. g, 100d, Woman, child, corner of Green Book. h, 100d, Three people, corner of Green Book. i, 100d, Khadafy with pen. j, 100d, Man and child. k, 100d, Government buildings, helicopters. l, 100d, Khadafy in military uniform. m, 500d, Khadafy on horse. Size of Nos. 1586a-1586l: 28x43mm. Size of No. 1586m: 56x86mm.

Litho., Litho with Foil Application (#1586m)

1997, Sept. 1 ***Perf. 14***

1586 A519 Sheet of 13, #a-m 17.00 17.00

Souvenir Sheet

Perf. 13¾

1587 A520 500d multi 5.75 5.75

Miniature Sheet

Intl. Day of Maghreb Handicrafts — A521

No. 1588 — Various shoes with toes pointing to: a, LR corner. b, Bottom. c, LL corner. d, UR corner. e, Top. f, UL corner.

Litho. With Foil Application

1997, Sept. 20 ***Perf. 13¾***

1588 A521 300d Sheet of 6, #a-f 17.00 17.00

Miniature Sheet

Tripoli Intl. Fair — A522

No. 1589 — Items made of silver: a, Medallion with tassels. b, Round medallion. c, Diamond-shaped medallion with tassels. d, Curved medallion. e, Necklace. f, Ring.

Litho. & Embossed With Foil Application

1997, Sept. 20

1589 A522 500d Sheet of 6, #a-f 27.50 27.50

Evacuation of Foreign Forces — A523

Denominations: 100d, 150d, 250d.

1997, Oct. 7 **Litho.** ***Perf. 14¾x14¼***

1590-1592 A523 Set of 3 2.40 2.40

Miniature Sheet

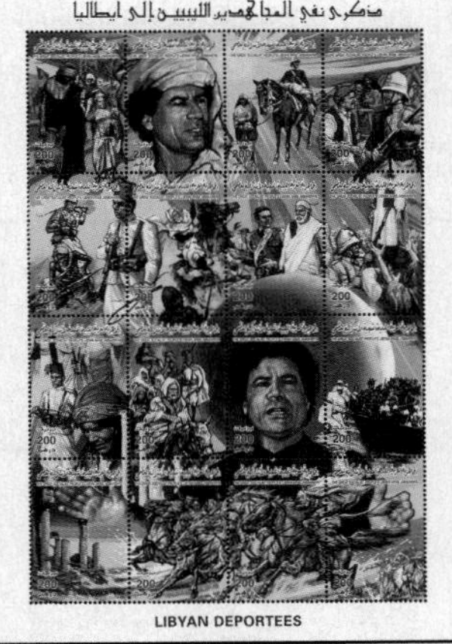

Libyans Deported to Italy — A524

No. 1593: a, Person carrying water jug. b, Col. Khadafy with headdress. c, Man, soldier on horse. d, Soldier and Libyans. e, Soldier whipping man. f, Soldier, man on horse. g, Libyan man and man in uniform. h, People at hanging. i, Man with purple fez, woman with red headdress. j, People, horse and camel. k, Col. Khadafy without headdress. l, Deportees on boats. m, Hand of Khadafy above pillars. n, Horsemen and pillars. o, Horsemen. p, Horsemen and hand of Khadafy.

1997, Oct. 26 ***Perf. 14***

1593 A524 200d Sheet of 16, #a-p 30.00 30.00

Worldwide Fund for Nature (WWF) A525

No. 1594 — Felis lybica: a, With prey at water. b, Adult and kittens. c, Under tree. d, Two adults.

1997, Nov. 1 ***Perf. 13¼***

1594 Horiz. strip of 4 7.50 7.50

a.-d. A525 200d Any single 1.75 1.75

Printed in sheets containing two strips.

Souvenir Sheet

Natl. Society for Wildlife Conservation — A526

No. 1595: a, Antelope facing forward. b, Ram. c, Antelope facing left.

1997, Nov. 1 ***Perf. 13¼***

1595 A526 100d Sheet of 3, #a-c 14.00 14.00

Miniature Sheet

American Attack on Libya, 11th Anniv. — A527

No. 1596: a, Explosion. b, Green Book, Libyan airplanes. c, Minarets, hand of Col. Khadafy. d, Col. Khadafy without headdress. e, Wing of American airplane. f, Nose of American airplane. g, Libyan airplanes. h, People looking at tail of American airplane. i, Rockets hitting American airplane. j, Arm of Col. Khadafy. k, Col. Khadafy with headdress. l, Man, fist of Col. Khadafy. m, Rockets and people. n, Col. Khadafy visiting injured person. o, Col. Khadafy kissing girl's hand. p, People with fists raised.

1997, Nov. 15 ***Perf. 14***

1596 A527 200d Sheet of 16, #a-p 32.50 32.50

Miniature Sheet

Great Man-Made River — A528

No. 1597: a, Fist, outline map of Libya. b, Col. Khadafy pointing to pipeline. c, Technicians reading paper, equipment. d, Col. Khadafy pointing to map. e, Col. Khadafy. f, Pipe, crane lifting cylinders. g, Col. Khadafy, pipe, vertical cylinder. h, Col. Khadafy, vertical cylinder. i, Col. Khadafy, construction trailer. j, Technician and equipment. k, Col. Khadafy, pipes lifted by crane. l, Col. Khadafy, line of trucks carrying pipe. m, Man with hand on spigot. n, Col. Khadafy with clasped hands. o, Hands under faucet, crops. p, Woman, child, flowers and fruit.

1997, Dec. 1 ***Perf. 14***
1597 A528 200d Sheet of 16, #a-p 32.50 32.50

People's Authority Declaration — A529

Panel color: 150d, Blue green. 250d, Purple. 300d, Blue.

1998, Mar. 2 ***Perf. 13¼***
1598-1600 A529 Set of 3 10.50 10.50

Miniature Sheet

Tripoli Intl. Fair — A530

No. 1601 — Items made of silver: a, Container with two spouts. b, Bowl on pedestal. c, Amphora. d, Container on tray. e, Lidded bowl. f, Three-legged container.

Litho. & Embossed With Foil Application

1998, Mar. 5 ***Perf. 13¾***
1601 A530 400d Sheet of 6, #a-f 22.50 22.50

Children's Day — A531

No. 1602 — Various girls in native dress with background colors of: a, Light blue. b, Yellow green. c, Red orange. d, Lilac. e, Yellow brown.

1998, Mar. 21 **Litho.** ***Perf. 13¼***
1602 Horiz. strip of 5 5.25 5.25
a.-e. A531 100d Any single 1.00 1.00

World Health Day — A532

Panel color: 150d, Buff. 250d, Light blue. 300d, Lilac.

1998, Apr. 7
1603-1605 A532 Set of 3 7.50 7.50

American Attack on Libya, 12th Anniv. — A533

No. 1606 — Airplanes, ships and: a, Helicopters, people with raised fists (28x48mm). b, Mother and child, Col. Khadafy (60x48mm). c, Man, boy and birds (28x48mm).
Illustration reduced.

1998, Apr. 15
1606 A533 100d Horiz. strip of 3, #a-c 3.25 3.25

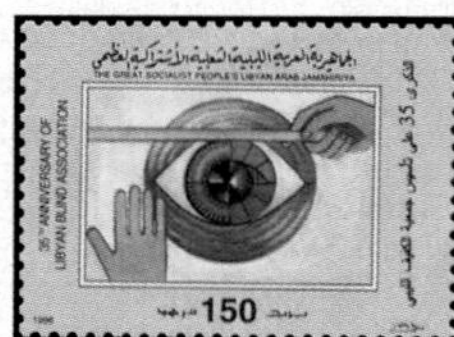

Libyan Blind Association, 35th Anniv. — A534

Designs: 150d, Eye, hand with cane, raised hand. 250d, Blind people, stringed instrument, books.

1998, May 1 ***Perf. 12***
1607-1608 A534 Set of 2 4.50 4.50

Arab Bee Union — A535

Frame color: 250d, Blue. 300d, Yellow. 400d, Light green.

1998, June 1
1609-1611 A535 Set of 3 12.50 12.50

1998 World Cup Soccer Championships, France — A536

No. 1612 — Soccer player with: a, Ball at LR, orange and white lines at bottom. b, Top of World Cup. c, Ball at left, orange and white lines at bottom. d, No visible uniform number, left part of stadium at bottom. e, Bottom of World Cup, stadium. f, Uniform No. 5, right part of stadium at bottom.

No. 1613, 1000d, Player, World Cup, denomination at LL. No. 1614, 1000d, Player, World Cup, denomination at LR.

1998, June 10 ***Perf. 13¼***
1612 A536 200d Sheet of 6, #a-f 16.00 16.00

Souvenir Sheets

1613-1614 A536 Set of 2 25.00 25.00

Nos. 1613-1614 each contain one 42x51mm stamp.

Miniature Sheet

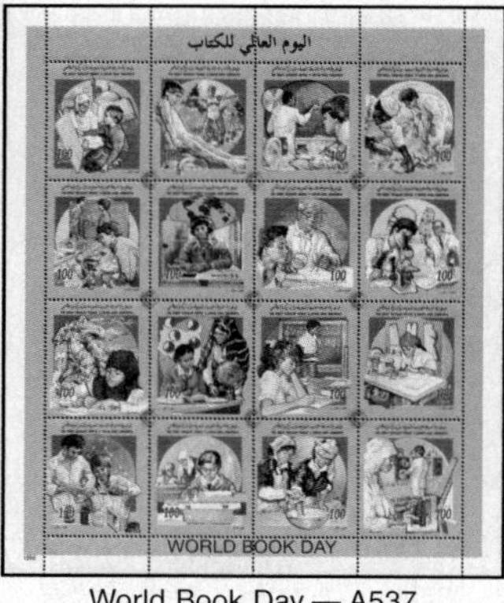

World Book Day — A537

No. 1615: a, Man, boy, mosque. b, Gymnasts. c, Science teacher at blackboard, student, ear. d, Men picking vegetables. e, Men at blackboard, man with machinery. f, Man with headset microphone, world map. g, Teacher with compass, student. h, Scientists with microscope. i, Girl writing, horseman. j, Teacher, student, map of Libya, globe. k, Music teacher at blackboard, student. l, Woman at sewing machine. m, Chemistry teacher and student. n, Teacher and women at typewriters. o, Cooks. p, Woman at computer keyboard, computer technician.

1998, June 23
1615 A537 100d Sheet of 16, #a-p 17.00 17.00

Map of the Great Man-Made River — A538

Denomination color: 300d, Green. 400d, Blue.
2000d, Bister.

Litho. & Embossed With Foil Application

1998, July 1
1616-1617 A538 Set of 2 8.00 8.00

Souvenir Sheet

1618 A538 2000d gold & multi 21.00 21.00

Miniature Sheet

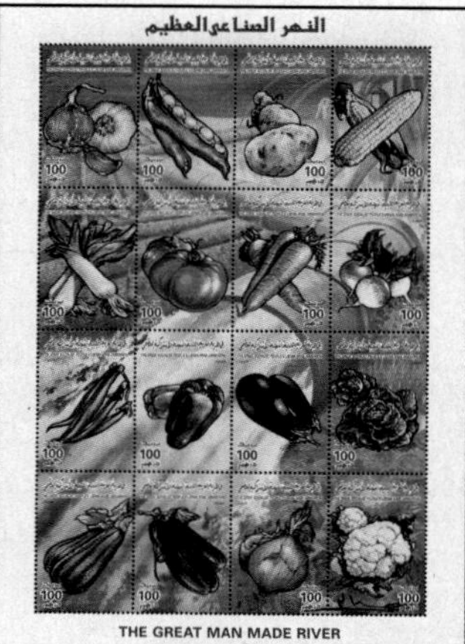

Great Man-Made River and Vegetables — A539

No. 1619: a, Garlic. b, Peas. c, Potatoes. d, Corn. e, Leeks. f, Tomatoes. g, Carrots. h, Radishes. i, Beans. j, Peppers. k, Eggplant. l, Lettuce. m, Squash. n, Cucumbers. o, Onions, p, Cauliflower.

1998, Sept. 1 **Litho.** ***Perf. 14***
1619 A539 100d Sheet of 16, #a-p 20.00 20.00

Miniature Sheet

Children's Day — A540

No. 1620 — Scouting trefoil and: a, Scouts, dog. b, Scouts saluting, birds. c, Scouts saluting, flags, tents. d, Scouts, sheep. e, Scouts playing musical instruments, tying down tent. f, Scouts at campfire, bird, boat.

1998, Aug. 1 ***Perf. 14¼***
1620 A540 400d Sheet of 6, #a-f 52.50 52.50

A541

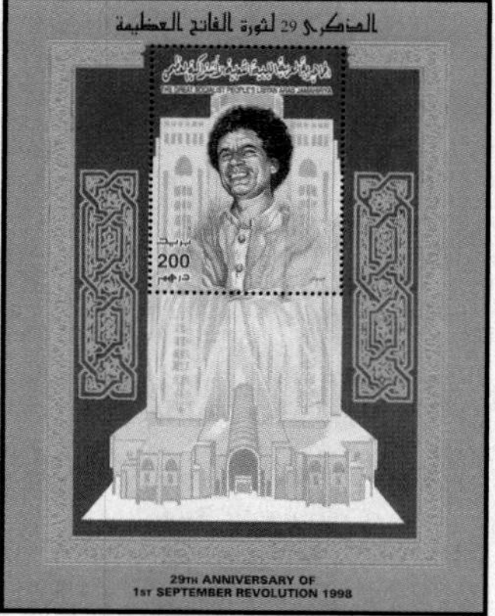

Sept. 1 Revolution, 29th Anniv. — A542

No. 1621: a, Col. Khadafy. b, Horseman, pipeline, vegetables. c, Fruit, pipeline, head of eagle. d, Tail of eagle, minaret. e, Surgeons, students. f, Book, map of Northwestern Africa. g, Book, men, map of Northeastern Africa and Arabian Peninsula. h, Mosque. i, People with flags, grain combine. j, Ship. k, Apartment buildings, l, Boy. m, People, irrigation rig, building. n, Building with flagpole at right. o, Building with flagpole at right, irrigation rig. p, Building, irrigation rig.

1998, Sept. 1 **Litho.** ***Perf. 14¼***
1621 A541 200d Sheet of 16, #a-p 37.50 37.50

Souvenir Sheet
Litho. & Embossed
Perf. 13½x13¾

1622 A542 200d shown 2.40 2.40

Evacuation of Foreign Forces — A543

Panel color: 100d, Pink. 150d, Light green. 200d, Light blue.

1998, Oct. 7 Litho. *Perf. 13¼*
1623-1625 A543 Set of 3 4.75 4.75

Stamp Day — A544

Panel color: 300d, Buff. 400d, Blue.

1998, Oct. 9 *Perf. 12*
1626-1627 A544 Set of 2 10.00 10.00

Miniature Sheet

Libyans Deported to Italy — A545

No. 1628: a, Ship, trucks. b, Bound woman, barbed wire. c, Man, barbed wire. d, Soldiers marching Libyans at gunpoint. e, Airplane, battle scene. f, Barbed wire, line of Libyans. g, Barbed wire, soldier and Libyan. h, Soldiers aiming rifles at Libyans, man with camel. i, Horseman, man ladling water. j, Soldier in boat. k, Boats with deportees. l, Boats with deportees, ships. m, Horsemen, man carrying woman. n, Horsemen raising rifles. o, Horseman and flag. p, Mother and child.

1998, Oct. 26 *Perf. 13¼*
1628 A545 150d Sheet of 16, #a-p 25.00 25.00

Miniature Sheet

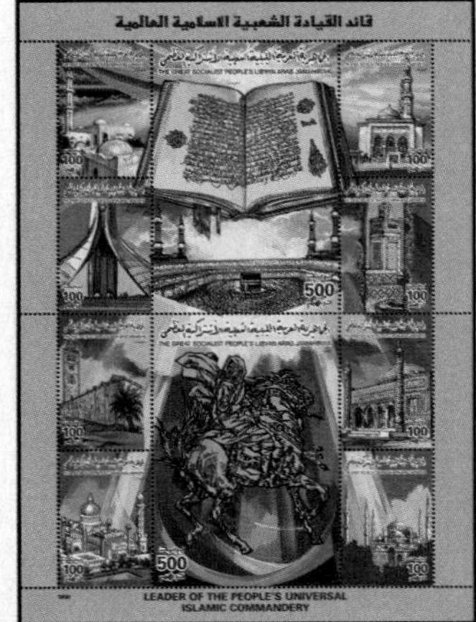

Leadership of Islam — A546

No. 1629: a, 100d, White mosque, minaret at left. b, 100d, White mosque, minaret at right. c, 100d, Modern mosque. d, 100d, Mosque seen through arch. e, 100d, Mosque and palm tree, minaret at left. f, 100d, Mosque with blue dome. g, 100d, Mosque with brown dome, six minarets. h, 100d, Mosque, five minarets. i, 500d, Koran, Holy Kaaba. j, 500d, Col. Khadafy on horse. Sizes: 100d stamps, 28x42mm; 500d stamps, 56x84mm.

Litho., Litho. With Foil Application (#1629j)

1998, Nov. 1 *Perf. 14*
1629 A546 Sheet of 10, #a-j 21.00 21.00

Miniature Sheet

Scouts and the Handicapped — A547

No. 1630: a, Scout reading to boy in wheelchair, butterfly. b, Scout leader instructing group of Scouts. c, Scout photographing bird, boy in wheelchair. d, Scout raising flag, boy in wheelchair. e, Scout sawing log, boy in wheelchair. f, Scout near campfire, boy in wheelchair. g, Scouts with pots in fire, crutches. h, Scouts with pad of paper and pencil. i, Wheelchair basketball player in purple uniform. j, Wheelchair basketball player making shot. k, Handicapped runners. l, Man in wheelchair playing table tennis. m, Man in wheelchair playing hockey. n, Man in wheelchair throwing shot put. o, Handicapped cyclist. p, Handicapped javelin thrower.

1998, Nov. 15 Litho. *Perf. 13¼*
1630 A547 100d Sheet of 16, #a-p 26.00 26.00

Miniature Sheet

A548

Sept. 1 Revolution, 30th Anniv. — A549

No. 1631: a, 100d, Antelopes and "30." b, 100d, Mosque. c, 100d, Woman playing stringed instrument. d, 100d, Horsemen in desert. e, 100d, Grain combine. f, 100d, Ship. g, 100d, Ship, horsemen, flag. h, 100d, Horsemen, flag. i, 100d, Water pipeline, fruit. j, 100d, Butterflies, shepherd and sheep. k, 100d, Building, ship, horse's legs. l, 100d, Dates. m, 200d, Col. Khadafy on horse. Sizes: 100d stamps; 28x42mm, 200d, 56x84mm.

Litho., Litho. With Foil Application (#1631m, 1632)

1999, Sept. 1 *Perf. 14*
1631 A548 Sheet of 13, #a-m 10.50 10.50

Souvenir Sheet
Perf. 13¾

1632 A549 200d shown 1.75 1.75

A550

Organization of African Unity Assembly of Heads of State and Government, Tripoli — A551

No. 1633: a, Pipeline worker, musicians, minarets. b, Surgeons, woman carrying jug. c, Artisan, camel rider, satellite. d, Col. Khadafy, butterflies. e, Pipeline worker, fruit picker. f, Fruit picker, grain combine.

1999, Sept. 8 Litho. *Perf. 14¼x14½*
1633 A550 300d Sheet of 6, #a-f 12.50 12.50

Souvenir Sheet
Perf. 13¾x14

1634 A551 500d shown 3.75 3.75

Evacuation of Foreign Forces — A552

Frame color: 150d, Pink. 250d, Beige. 300d, Light blue.

1999, Oct. 7 *Perf. 12*
1635-1637 A552 Set of 3 7.50 7.50

A553

People's Authority Declaration — A554

No. 1638: a, Col. Khadafy with fist raised, man on camel. b, People looking at book. c, Airplane, building, dish antenna. d, Antelope, weaver, tractor. e, Open faucet, pipeline. f, Pipleine, fruit pickers.

No. 1639, 300d, Map of Libya, Col. Khadafy with raised fist, building. No. 1640, 300d, Dove, people, Col. Khadafy.

2000, Mar. 2 Litho. *Perf. 14½x14¼*
1638 A553 100d Sheet of 6, #a-f 4.50 4.50

Souvenir Sheets
Perf. 13¾

Litho. & Embossed with Foil Application

1639-1640 A554 Set of 2 4.50 4.50

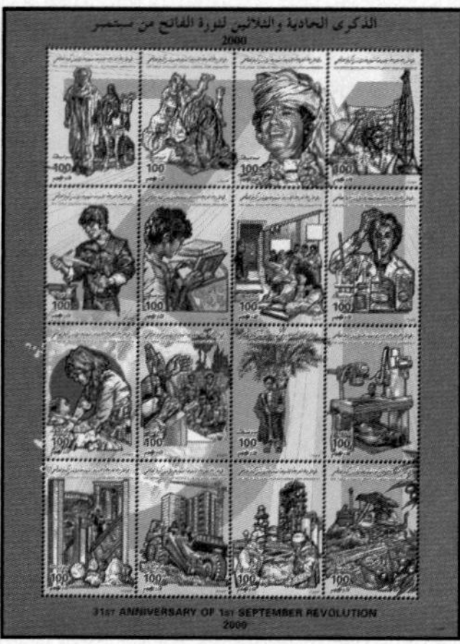
A555

Sept. 1 Revolution, 31st Anniv. — A556

No. 1641: a, Man walking, camel rider. b, Tea drinkers, camels. c, Col. Khadafy. d, Men with raised fists. e, Machinist with torch. f, Boy reading. g, Classroom. h, Scientist. i, Mother and child. j, People attending speech. k, Man and palm tree. l, Patient in X-ray machine. m, Mosque, n, Bulldozer, crane and building. o, Oil workers. p, Bulldozer.

No. 1642, 300d, Col. Khadafy, minaret. No. 1643, 300d, Col. Khadafy, boy and palm tree.

2000, Sept. 1 Litho. *Perf. 14*
1641 A555 100d Sheet of 16, #a-p 11.50 11.50

Souvenir Sheets
Litho. With Foil Application
Perf. 13¾
1642-1643 A556 Set of 2 4.25 4.25

El-Mujahed Mohamed Abdussalam Ahmeda Abouminiar El-Gaddafi — A557

No. 1644: a, Man holding box. b, Palm tree and horsemen. c, Horsemen and soldiers on horseback. d, Soldiers and armed horsemen. e, Horseman raising rifle above head. f, Men raising rifles, Col. Khadafy.

300d, Man reading book.

2000, Sept. 9 Litho. *Perf. 13¼*
1644 A557 200d Sheet of 6, #a-f 8.50 8.50

Souvenir Sheet
Litho. & Embossed With Foil Application
1645 A557 300d multi 2.10 2.10

Souvenir Sheet

España 2000 Intl. Philatelic Exhibition — A558

No. 1646: a, A. Castellano (1926-97). b, M. B. Karamanli (1922-95).

2000, Oct. 6 Litho. *Imperf.*
1646 A558 250d Sheet of 2, #a-b 3.75 3.75

People's Authority Declaration A559

Denomination color: 150d, Pink. 200d, Blue.

2001, Mar. 2 *Perf. 14*
1647-1648 A559 Set of 2 2.75 2.75

Miniature Sheet

Organization of African Unity Assemby of Heads of State and Government — A560

No. 1649: a, Heads of various states. b, Heads of state, horsemen. c, Men on camels. d, People with hands raised. e, Man holding picture of Col. Khadafy. f, Col. Khadafy at microphone.

2001, Mar. 2 Litho. *Perf. 13½x13¼*
1649 A560 200d Sheet of 6, #a-f 8.75 8.75

Souvenir Sheets

Organization of African Unity Assembly of Heads of State and Government — A561

Background colors: No. 1650, 500d, Gold. No. 1651, 500d, Silver.

Litho. & Embossed With Foil Application
2001, Mar. 2 *Perf. 13¼*
1650-1651 A561 Set of 2 7.50 7.50

Miniature Sheet

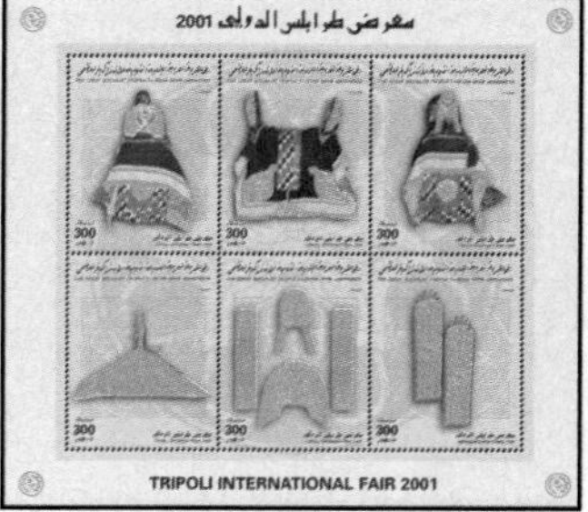

Tripoli Intl. Fair — A562

No. 1652: a, Rear view of saddle. b, Side view of saddle. c, Front view of saddle. d, Stirrup. e, Four pieces of tack. f, Two pieces of tack.

Litho. & Embossed with Foil Application
2001, Apr. 2 *Perf. 13¾*
1652 A562 300d Sheet of 6, #a-f 21.00 21.00

Miniature Sheet

Fight Against American Aggression — A563

No. 1653: a, Exploding jet. b, American jet. c, Pilot. d, American plane shooting missile. e, Parachute. f, Airplanes. g, Child crying. h, Palm tree, explosion. i, Missiles. j, Broken egg. k, Teddy bear. l, Clock. m, Explosion in city. n, Man rescuing casualty. o, Man holding child casualty. p, Family fleeing.

2001, Apr. 15 Litho. *Perf. 13¼*
1653 A563 100d Sheet of 16, #a-p 16.00 16.00

Desertification Project — A564

No. 1654: a, Man with hoe (30x39mm). b, Men near stream (60x39mm). c, Camels (30x39mm).

Illustration reduced.

2001, June 26 Litho. *Perf. 13¼*
1654 A564 250d Horiz. strip of 3, #a-c 12.00 12.00

Miniature Sheet

Great Man-Made River — A565

No. 1655: a, Smokestack. b, Pipeline and flags. c, Palm tree, fruit. d, Grapes. e, Clothed boy, rainbow. f, Bathing boy, rainbow. g, Woman carrying fruit. h, Woman holding jug. i, Woman with red and black headdress. j, Woman with green striped headdress. k, Duck, rainbow. l, Boy running. m, Drummer hitting drum with hand. n, Horn player. o, Drummer hitting drum with stick. p, Tractors in field.

2001, Sept. 15 Litho. *Perf. 11¾*
1655 A565 200d Sheet of 16, #a-p 32.50 32.50

A566

Sept. 1 Revolution, 32nd Anniv. — A567

No. 1656: a, Col. Khadafy in headdress. b, Buildings, water pipeline, helicopters, tank, horsemen. c, Ship, airplane, camel rider. d, Tea drinkers. e, Children. f, Pillars, antelopes, woman. g, Man walking, camel rider. h, Camels, birds. i, Woman with container. j, Sword fight. k, Man and camel rider. l, Camels, pipeline worker, fruit. m, Potter. n, Musicians and weaver. o, Artisan. p, Col. Khadafy with clasped hands.

No. 1657, 300d, Col. Khadafy, pipeline and fruit (gold background). No. 1658, 300d, Col. Khadafy, pipeline and fruit (silver background).

Litho. and Hologram
2001, Sept. 1 *Perf. 13¼*
1656 A566 100d Sheet of 16, #a-p 16.00 16.00
q. Booklet pane, #a-p, litho. 16.00 —
Complete booklet, #1656q 16.00

Souvenir Sheets
Litho. & Embossed With Foil Application

1657-1658 A567 Set of 2 4.25 4.25

Intl. Day of the Orphan — A568

Panel color: 100d, Blue. 200d, Red violet. 300d, Olive green.

2001, Oct. 1 Litho. *Perf. 14¾x14½*
1659-1661 A568 Set of 3 9.25 9.25

Health Care — A569

Arabic inscription color: 200d, Green. 300d, Yellow orange.

2001, Dec. 1 Litho. *Perf. 14*
1662-1663 A569 Set of 2 6.25 6.25

Miniature Sheet

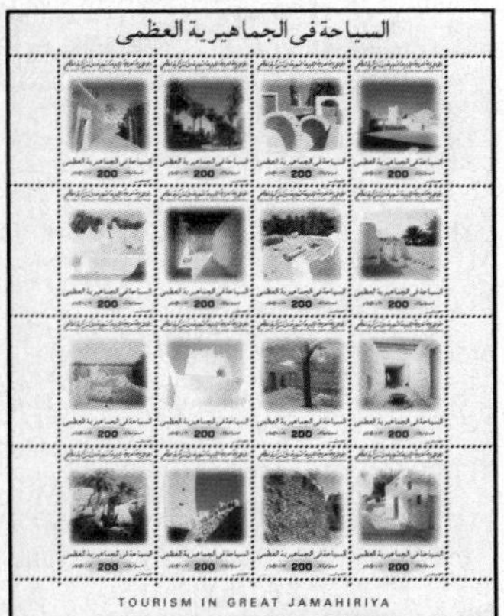

Tourism — A570

Various tourist attractions.

2002, May 1 *Perf. 11¾*
1664 A570 200d Sheet of 16, #a-p *47.50 47.50*

Intl. Customs Day — A571

Designs: 200d, 400d.

2002, July 1 *Perf. 14*
1665-1666 A571 Set of 2 8.00 8.00

A572

Sept. 1 Revolution, 33rd Anniv. — A573

No. 1667: a, Col. Khadafy. b, Airplanes. c, Camel rider, woman pouring tea. d, Artisans. e, Bulldozer, building. f, Chemist, oil rig. g, Ships. h, Doctors and patients. i, Technician at industrial plant. j, Man at computer, k, Man, spigot, water pipeline, crane. l, Chemist, man at microscope. m, Television camera and technician. n, Fruit, vegetables, grain combine. o, Spear carriers, musician. p, Map of Africa, musicians.

No. 1668, 300d, Col. Khadafy, map of Africa (gold background). No. 1669, 300d, Col. Khadafy, map of Africa (silver background).

Litho. & Hologram

2002, Sept. 1 *Perf. 13¼*
1667 A572 100d Sheet of 16, #a-p 19.00 19.00
q. Booklet pane, #a-p, litho. 19.00 —
Complete booklet, #1667q 19.00

Souvenir Sheets
Litho. & Embossed With Foil Application

1668-1669 A573 Set of 2 7.50 7.50

Universal Declaration of Human Rights, 50th Anniv. — A576

Panel color: 250d, Red orange. 500d, Blue green.

2002, Nov. 1 Litho. *Perf. 14*
1672-1673 A576 Set of 2 9.50 9.50

Universal Postal Union, 125th Anniv. — A577

Panel color: 200d, Blue. 250d, Red violet.

2002, Dec. 1
1674-1675 A577 Set of 2 5.25 5.25

A580

September 1 Revolution, 34th Anniv. — A581

No. 1679: a, 300d, Doctors and microscope (30x40mm). b, 300d, Nurses studying anatomy (30x40mm). c, 300d, Mother and child (30x40mm). d, 300d, Soldiers, white flag (30x40mm). e, 500d, Teachers, students, building (60x40mm). f, 500d, Helicopter, pilot, women, nurse and patients (60x40mm). g, 500d, Marching band, soldiers in vehicle (60x40mm). h, 1000d, Col. Khadafy, airplane, satellite dish.

2003, May 20 Litho. *Perf. 12*
1679 A580 Sheet of 8, #a-h 20.00 20.00

Souvenir Sheet
Litho. & Embossed With Foil Application

1680 A581 2000d multi 15.00 15.00

September 1 Revolution, 35th Anniv. A582

Background color: 750d, Gray green. 1000d, Yellow green.

2004 Litho. *Perf. 13*
1681-1682 A582 Set of 2 4.50 4.50

Khairi Khaled Nuri (1943-2004), Philatelist — A583

2004 Litho. & Hologram *Perf. 13¼*
1683 A583 500d multi 2.00 2.00

People's Authority Declaration, 27th Anniv. A584

Color of rays: 400d, Yellow brown. 1000d, Blue green.

2004 Litho. *Perf. 13*
1684-1685 A584 Set of 2 3.50 3.50

1st Communication and Information Technology Exhibition — A585

2005, July 29 *Perf. 13*
1686 A585 750d multi 2.40 2.40

Souvenir Sheet
Imperf

1687 A585 1000d multi 2.60 2.60

People's Authority Declaration, 28th Anniv. — A586

Delegates: 300d, Seated. 1000d, Voting.

2005 *Perf. 13*
1688-1689 A586 Set of 2 3.25 3.25

September 1 Revolution, 36th Anniv. A587

Background color: 750d, Yellow orange. 1000d, Blue.

2005
1690-1691 A587 Set of 2 4.50 4.50

Miniature Sheet

Total Solar Eclipse of March 29, 2006 — A588

No. 1692 — Eclipse and: a, Band of totality over map of Libya. b, Buildings, map of Libya. c, Altitude and duration figures. d, Stylized fish, camel, cactus, palm tree and Libyan. e, Saddled camel. f, Camels and riders.

2006, Mar. 29
1692 A588 250d Sheet of 6, #a-f 4.25 4.25

People's Authority Declaration, 29th Anniv. A589

Wheat ear, flag, fist and torch with background color of: 400d, Yellow. 1000d, Blue.

2006, Nov. 1
1693-1694 A589 Set of 2 3.50 3.50

September 1 Revolution, 37th Anniv. — A590

2006
1695 A590 1000d multi 2.50 2.50

Famous African Leaders — A591

Map of Africa and: No. 1696, 500d, Gamal Abdel Nasser (1918-70), Egyptian President. No. 1697, 500d, Kwame Nkrumah (1909-72), President of Ghana. No. 1698, 500d, Ahmed Ben Bella, President of Algeria. No. 1699, 500d, Patrice Lumumba (1925-61), Congolese Prime Minister. No. 1700, 500d, Kenneth Kaunda, President of Zambia. No. 1701, 500d, Julius Nyerere (1922-99), President of Tanzania. No. 1702, 500d, Modibo Keita (1915-77), President of Mali.

1000d, Map of Africa, Nasser, Nkrumah, Ben Bella, Lumumba, Kaunda, Nyerere and Keita, horiz.

2007, Mar. 6 ***Perf. 12¾***
1696-1702 A591 Set of 7 8.50 8.50
1702a Miniature sheet of 7, #1696-1702 8.50 8.50

Size: 98x75mm

Imperf

1703 A591 1000d multi 2.25 2.25

Third Communication and Information Technology Exhibition — A592

2007, May 27 ***Perf. 13***
1704 A592 750d multi 2.00 2.00

Tripoli, Capital of Islamic Culture A593

2007, June 16 **Litho.**
1705 A593 500d multi 1.40 1.40

Intl. Day Against Drug Abuse and Illicit Trafficking A594

2007, June 26
1706 A594 750d multi 2.00 2.00

People's Authority Declaration, 30th Anniv. A595

2007, July 4
1707 A595 750d multi 2.00 2.00

36th Tripoli Intl. Fair — A596

No. 1708: a, Ring (orange background). b, Pendant (green background). c, Ring (purple background).

Illustration reduced.

2007, July 4 ***Perf. 13x13x13¼***
1708 Strip of 3 3.75 3.75
a.-c. A596 500d Any single 1.25 1.25

Printed in sheets containing 2 strips + 2 labels.

September 1 Revolution, 38th Anniv. — A599

2007, Sept. 1 **Litho.** ***Perf. 13***
1711 A599 1000d multi 2.50 2.50
a. Souvenir sheet of 1 2.50 2.50

Khadafy Project for African Women, Children and Youth A600

2007, Sept. 9
1712 A600 500d multi 1.40 1.40

Libyan Red Crescent Society, 50th Anniv. A601

Red Crescent emblem and: 500d, Red Crescent volunteers. 1000d, 50th anniversary emblem.

2007 ***Perf. 13***
1713-1714 A601 Set of 2 4.00 4.00

SEMI-POSTAL STAMPS

Many issues of Italy and Italian Colonies include one or more semipostal denominations. To avoid splitting sets, these issues are generally listed as regular postage, semipostals or airmails, etc.

Semi-Postal Stamps of Italy Overprinted

1915-16 **Wmk. 140** ***Perf. 14***
B1 SP1 10c + 5c rose 4.25 *17.00*
a. Double overprint 650.00
B2 SP2 15c + 5c slate 17.00 *30.00*
B3 SP2 20c + 5c org ('16) 5.00 *32.50*
Nos. B1-B3 (3) 26.25 *79.50*

No. B2 with Additional Surcharge

1916, Mar.
B4 SP2 20c on 15c + 5c slate 17.00 *32.50*
a. Double surcharge 650.00

View of Port, Tripoli SP1

Designs: B5, B6, View of port, Tripoli. B7, B8, Arch of Marcus Aurelius. B9, B10, View of Tripoli.

1927, Feb. 15 **Litho.**
B5 SP1 20c + 5c brn vio & black 4.25 15.00
B6 SP1 25c + 5c bl grn & black 4.25 15.00
B7 SP1 40c + 10c blk brn & black 4.25 15.00
B8 SP1 60c + 10c org brn & black 4.25 15.00
B9 SP1 75c + 20c red & black 4.25 15.00
B10 SP1 1.25 l + 20c bl & blk 21.00 37.50
Nos. B5-B10 (6) 42.25 112.50

First Sample Fair, Tripoli. Surtax aided fair. See Nos. EB1-EB2.

View of Tripoli — SP2

Knights of Malta Castle SP3

Designs: 50c+20c, Date palm. 1.25 l+20c, Camel riders. 2.55 l+50c, View of Tripoli. 5 l+1 l, Traction well.

1928, Feb. 20 **Wmk. 140** ***Perf. 14***
B11 SP2 30c + 20c mar & blk 3.50 *17.00*
B12 SP2 50c + 20c bl grn & blk 3.50 *17.00*
B13 SP2 1.25 l + 20c red & blk 3.50 *17.00*
B14 SP3 1.75 l + 20c bl & blk 3.50 *17.00*
B15 SP3 2.55 l + 50c brn & blk 5.00 *21.00*
B16 SP3 5 l + 1 l pur & blk 8.50 *32.50*
Nos. B11-B16 (6) 27.50 *121.50*

2nd Sample Fair, Tripoli, 1928. The surtax was for the aid of the Fair.

Olive Tree — SP4

Herding SP5

Designs: 50c+20c, Dorcas gazelle. 1.25 l+20c, Peach blossoms. 2.55 l+50c, Camel caravan. 5 l+1 l, Oasis with date palms.

1929, Apr. 7
B17 SP4 30c + 20c mar & blk 10.00 *21.00*
B18 SP4 50c + 20c bl grn & blk 10.00 *21.00*
B19 SP4 1.25 l + 20c scar & blk 10.00 *21.00*
B20 SP5 1.75 l + 20c bl & blk 10.00 *21.00*
B21 SP5 2.55 l + 50c yel brn & blk 10.00 *21.00*
B22 SP5 5 l + 1 l pur & blk 125.00 *250.00*
Nos. B17-B22 (6) 175.00 *355.00*

3rd Sample Fair, Tripoli, 1929. The surtax was for the aid of the Fair.

Harvesting Bananas — SP6

Water Carriers SP7

Designs: 50c, Tobacco plant. 1.25 l, Venus of Cyrene. 2.55 l+45c, Black bucks. 5 l+1 l, Motor and camel transportation. 10 l+2 l, Rome pavilion.

1930, Feb. 20 **Photo.**

No.	Design	Value	Unused	Used
B23	SP6	30c dark brown	2.50	*12.50*
B24	SP6	50c violet	2.50	*12.50*
B25	SP6	1.25 l deep blue	2.50	*12.50*
B26	SP7	1.75 l + 20c scar	4.25	*21.00*
B27	SP7	2.55 l + 45c dp grn	13.50	*30.00*
B28	SP7	5 l + 1 l dp org	13.50	*42.50*
B29	SP7	10 l + 2 l dk vio	13.50	*47.50*
		Nos. B23-B29 (7)	52.25	*178.50*

4th Sample Fair at Tripoli, 1930. The surtax was for the aid of the Fair.

Statue of Ephebus — SP8

Exhibition Pavilion SP9

Designs: 25c, Arab musician. 50c, View of Zeughet. 1.25 l, Snake charmer. 1.75 l+25c, Windmill. 2.75 l+45c, "Zaptie." 5 l+1 l, Mounted Arab.

1931, Mar. 8

No.	Design	Value	Unused	Used
B30	SP8	10c black brown	4.25	*8.50*
B31	SP8	25c green	4.25	*8.50*
B32	SP8	50c purple	4.25	*8.50*
B33	SP8	1.25 l blue	4.25	*13.50*
B34	SP8	1.75 l + 25c car rose	4.25	*17.00*
B35	SP8	2.75 l + 45c org	4.25	*21.00*
B36	SP8	5 l + 1 l dl vio	12.50	*30.00*
B37	SP9	10 l + 2 l brn	42.50	*62.50*
		Nos. B30-B37 (8)	80.50	*169.50*
		Nos. B30-B37,C3,EB3 (10)	89.00	*207.00*

Fifth Sample Fair, Tripoli. Surtax aided fair.

Papaya Tree SP10

Dorcas Gazelle SP12

Ar Tower, Mogadiscio SP11

Designs: 10c, 50c, Papaya tree. 20c, 30c, Euphorbia abyssinica. 25c, Fig cactus. 75c, Mausoleum, Ghirza. 1.75 l+25c, Lioness. 5 l+1 l, Bedouin with camel.

1932, Mar. 8

No.	Design	Value	Unused	Used
B38	SP10	10c olive brn	5.00	*13.50*
B39	SP10	20c brown red	5.00	*13.50*
B40	SP10	25c green	5.00	*13.50*
B41	SP10	30c olive blk	5.00	*13.50*
B42	SP10	50c dk violet	5.00	*13.50*
B43	SP10	75c carmine	6.75	*13.50*
B44	SP11	1.25 l dk blue	6.75	*19.00*
B45	SP11	1.75 l + 25c ol brn	29.00	*65.00*
B46	SP11	5 l + 1 l dp bl	29.00	*130.00*
B47	SP12	10 l + 2 l brn violet	105.00	*260.00*
		Nos. B38-B47 (10)	201.50	*555.00*
		Nos. B38-B47,C4-C7 (14)	350.50	*887.00*

Sixth Sample Fair, Tripoli. Surtax aided fair.

Ostrich — SP13

Arab Musician SP14

Designs: 25c, Incense plant. 30c, Arab musician. 50c, Arch of Marcus Aurelius. 1.25 l, African eagle. 5 l+1 l, Leopard. 10 l+2.50 l, Tripoli skyline and fasces.

1933, Mar. 2 **Photo.** **Wmk. 140**

No.	Design	Value	Unused	Used
B48	SP13	10c dp violet	32.50	32.50
B49	SP13	25c dp green	17.50	*32.50*
B50	SP14	30c orange brn	17.50	*32.50*
B51	SP13	50c purple	16.00	*32.50*
B52	SP13	1.25 l dk blue	40.00	*60.00*
B53	SP14	5 l + 1 l ol brn	80.00	*130.00*
B54	SP13	10 l + 2.50 l car	80.00	*200.00*
		Nos. B48-B54 (7)	283.50	*520.00*
		Nos. B48-B54,C8-C13 (13)	383.00	*835.00*

Seventh Sample Fair, Tripoli. Surtax aided fair.

Pomegranate Tree — SP15

Designs: 50c+10c, 2 l+50c, Musician. 75c+15c, 1.25 l+25c, Tribesman.

1935, Feb. 16

No.	Design	Value	Unused	Used
B55	SP15	10c + 10c brown	1.25	*4.50*
B56	SP15	20c + 10c rose red	1.25	*4.50*
B57	SP15	50c + 10c purple	1.25	*4.50*
B58	SP15	75c + 15c car	1.25	*4.50*
B59	SP15	1.25 l + 25c dl blue	1.25	*4.50*
B60	SP15	2 l + 50c ol grn	1.25	*8.50*
		Nos. B55-B60 (6)	7.50	*31.00*
		Nos. B55-B60,C19-C24 (12)	20.25	*88.50*

Ninth Sample Fair, Tripoli. Surtax aided fair.

AIR POST STAMPS

Italy Nos. C3 and C5 Overprinted

1928-29 **Wmk. 140** ***Perf. 14***

No.	Design	Value	Unused	Used
C1	AP2	50c rose red	10.00	17.00
C2	AP2	80c brn vio & brn ('29)	32.50	*60.00*

Airplane AP1

1931, Mar. 8 **Photo.** **Wmk. 140**

No.	Design	Value	Unused	Used
C3	AP1	50c blue	1.75	*15.00*

See note after No. B37.

Seaplane over Bedouin Camp AP2

Designs: 50c, 1 l, Seaplane over Bedouin camp. 2 l+1 l, 5 l+2 l, Seaplane over Tripoli.

1932, Mar. 1 ***Perf. 14***

No.	Design	Value	Unused	Used
C4	AP2	50c dark blue	10.00	*36.00*
C5	AP2	1 l org brown	10.00	*36.00*
C6	AP2	2 l + 1 l dk gray	24.00	*80.00*
C7	AP2	5 l + 2 l car	105.00	*180.00*
		Nos. C4-C7 (4)	149.00	*332.00*

See note after No. B47.

Seaplane Arriving at Tripoli AP3

Designs: 50c, 2 l+50c, Seaplane arriving at Tripoli. 75c, 10 l+2.50 l, Plane over Tagiura. 1 l, 5 l+1 l, Seaplane leaving Tripoli.

1933, Mar. 1

No.	Design	Value	Unused	Used
C8	AP3	50c dp green	9.50	*20.00*
C9	AP3	75c carmine	9.50	*20.00*
C10	AP3	1 l dk blue	9.50	*20.00*
C11	AP3	2 l + 50c pur	16.00	*45.00*
C12	AP3	5 l + 1 l org brn	27.50	*65.00*
C13	AP3	10 l + 2.50 l gray blk	27.50	*145.00*
		Nos. C8-C13 (6)	99.50	*315.00*

See note after No. B54.

Seaplane over Tripoli Harbor AP4

Airplane and Camel — AP5

Designs: 50c, 5 l+1 l, Seaplane over Tripoli harbor. 75c, 10 l+2 l, Plane and minaret.

1934, Feb. 17 **Photo.** **Wmk. 140**

No.	Design	Value	Unused	Used
C14	AP4	50c slate bl	8.50	*26.00*
C15	AP4	75c red org	8.50	*26.00*
C16	AP4	5 l + 1 l dp grn	105.00	*175.00*
C17	AP4	10 l + 2 l dl vio	105.00	*175.00*
C18	AP5	25 l + 3 l org brn	125.00	*225.00*
		Nos. C14-C18 (5)	352.00	*627.00*

Eighth Sample Fair, Tripoli. Surtax aided fair. See Nos. CE1-CE2.

Plane and Ancient Tower — AP6

Camel Train AP7

Designs: 25c+10c, 3 l+1.50 l, Plane and ancient tower. 50c+10c, 2 l+30c, Camel train. 1 l+25c, 10 l+5 l, Arab watching plane.

1935, Apr. 12

No.	Design	Value	Unused	Used
C19	AP6	25c + 10c green	.85	*5.00*
C20	AP7	50c + 10c slate bl	.85	*5.00*
C21	AP7	1 l + 25c blue	.85	*5.00*
C22	AP7	2 l + 30c rose red	.85	*6.75*
C23	AP6	3 l + 1.50 l brn	.85	*6.75*
C24	AP7	10 l + 5 l dl vio	8.50	*29.00*
		Nos. C19-C24 (6)	12.75	*57.50*

See note after No. B60.

Cyrenaica No. C6 Overprinted in Black

1936, Oct.

No.	Design	Value	Unused	Used
C25	AP2	50c purple	10.00	.40
		Never hinged	25.00	

Same on Tripolitania Nos. C8 and C12

1937

No.	Design	Value	Unused	Used
C26	AP1	50c rose carmine	.40	.20
C27	AP2	1 l deep blue	2.10	1.00
		Set, never hinged	6.25	

See Nos. C45-C50.

Ruins of Odeon Theater, Sabrata AP8

1937, Mar. 15 **Photo.**

No.	Design	Value	Unused	Used
C28	AP8	50c dark violet	2.50	*6.75*
C29	AP8	1 l vio black	2.50	*10.00*
		Set, never hinged	12.50	

Opening of a coastal road to the Egyptian frontier.

Nos. C28-C29 Overprinted "XI FIERA DI TRIPOLI"

1937, Mar. 15

No.	Design	Value	Unused	Used
C30	AP8	50c dark violet	15.00	*37.50*
C31	AP8	1 l violet blk	15.00	*37.50*
		Set, never hinged	75.00	

11th Sample Fair, Tripoli.

View of Tripoli AP9

Eagle Attacking Serpent AP10

1938, Mar. 12 ***Perf. 14***

No.	Design	Value	Unused	Used
C32	AP9	50c dk olive grn	1.25	*2.50*
C33	AP9	1 l slate blue	1.25	*6.00*
		Set, never hinged	6.25	

12th Sample Fair, Tripoli.

1938, Apr. 25 **Wmk. 140**

No.	Design	Value	Unused	Used
C34	AP10	50c olive brown	.40	*2.10*
C35	AP10	1 l brn violet	1.25	*4.50*
		Set, never hinged	4.25	

Birth bimillenary Augustus Caesar (Octavianus), first Roman emperor.

Arab and Camel AP11

Design: 50c, Fair entrance.

1939, Apr. 12 **Photo.**

C36 AP11 25c green .40 *2.10*
C37 AP11 50c olive brown .65 *2.10*
C38 AP11 1 l rose violet .85 *2.50*
Nos. C36-C38 (3) 1.90 *6.70*
Set, never hinged 4.25

13th Sample Fair, Tripoli.

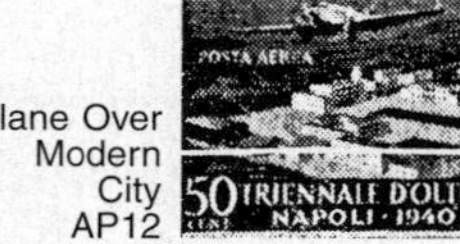

Plane Over Modern City AP12

Design: 1 l, 5 l+2.50 l, Plane over oasis.

1940, June 3

C39 AP12 50c brn blk .60 *1.00*
C40 AP12 1 l brn vio .60 *2.10*
C41 AP12 2 l + 75c indigo 1.25 *6.25*
C42 AP12 5 l + 2.50 l copper brn 1.25 *12.00*
Nos. C39-C42 (4) 3.70 *21.35*
Set, never hinged 8.50

Triennial Overseas Exposition, Naples.

Hitler, Mussolini and Inscription "Two Peoples, One War" AP13

1941, Apr. 24

C43 AP13 50c slate green 2.50 *35.00*
Never hinged 6.25

Rome-Berlin Axis.

Cyrenaica No. C9 Overprinted in Black Like No. C25

1941

C44 AP3 1 l black 8.50 *42.50*
Never hinged 21.00

Same Overprint on Tripolitania Nos. C9-C11, C13-C15

C45 AP1 60c red orange .85
C46 AP1 75c deep blue .85 32.50
C47 AP1 80c dull violet .85 60.00
C48 AP2 1.20 l dark brown .85 75.00
C49 AP2 1.50 l orange red .85 92.50
C50 AP2 5 l green .85
Nos. C45-C50 (6) 5.10
Set, never hinged 12.50

Catalogue values for unused stamps in this section, from this point to the end of the section, are for Never Hinged items.

United Kingdom of Libya

ICY Type of Regular Issue

Perf. 14½x14

1965, Jan. 1 **Litho.** **Unwmk.**

C51 A60 50m dp lil & gold 1.90 .90
a. Souvenir sheet 5.00 5.00

No. C51a exists imperf.; same value.

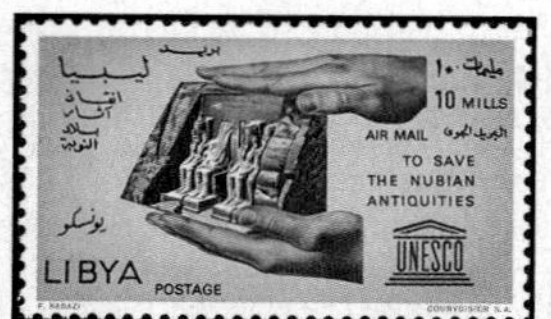

Hands Holding Facade of Abu Simbel — AP14

1966, Jan. 1 **Photo.** ***Perf. 11½***
Granite Paper

C52 AP14 10m bis & dk brn .40 .20
a. Souvenir sheet of 4 2.00 3.75
C53 AP14 15m gray grn & dk grn .50 .20
a. Souvenir sheet of 4 2.50 5.00
C54 AP14 40m dl sal & dk brn 1.60 .65
a. Souvenir sheet of 4 6.50 13.00
Nos. C52-C54 (3) 2.50 1.05

UNESCO world campaign to save historic monuments in Nubia.

Inauguration of WHO Headquarters, Geneva — AP15

Perf. 10x10½

1966, May 3 **Litho.** **Unwmk.**

C55 AP15 20m blk, yel & bl .20 .20
C56 AP15 50m blk, yel grn & red .90 .65
C57 AP15 65m blk, sal & brn red 1.40 1.40
Nos. C55-C57 (3) 2.50 2.25

Flag and Globe — AP16

1966, Oct. 1 **Photo.** ***Perf. 11½***
Granite Paper

C58 AP16 25m multicolored .50 .40
C59 AP16 60m multicolored 1.40 1.00
C60 AP16 85m gray & multi 1.90 1.40
Nos. C58-C60 (3) 3.80 2.80

Inauguration of Kingdom of Libya Airlines, 1st anniv.

AIR POST SPECIAL DELIVERY STAMPS

APSD1

Wmk. 140

1934, Feb. 17 **Photo.** ***Perf. 14***

CE1 APSD1 2.25 l olive blk 32.50 *55.00*
CE2 APSD1 4.50 l + 1 l gray blk 32.50 *55.00*
Set, never hinged 162.50

8th Sample Fair at Tripoli. The surtax was for the aid of the Fair.

SPECIAL DELIVERY STAMPS

Special Delivery Stamps of Italy Overprinted

1915, Nov. **Wmk. 140** ***Perf. 14***

E1 SD1 25c rose red 35.00 17.00
E2 SD2 30c blue & rose 8.00 *35.00*
Set, never hinged 105.00

Two types exist in the overprint applied to Nos. E1-E2. See note following Nos. 1-15.
For surcharges see Nos. E7-E8.

"Italia" SD3

1921-23 **Engr.** ***Perf. 13½***

E3 SD3 30c blue & rose 2.50 *7.50*
E4 SD3 50c rose red & brn 3.50 *12.00*
E5 SD3 60c dk red & brn ('23) 8.50 *19.00*
E6 SD3 2 l dk bl & red ('23) 12.00 *35.00*
Nos. E3-E6 (4) 26.50 *73.50*
Set, never hinged 65.00

30c, 2 l inscribed "EXPRES."
For surcharges see Nos. E9-E12.

Nos. E1-E2 Surcharged

1922, June 1

E7 SD1 60c on 25c rose red 13.50 *19.00*
E8 SD2 1.60 l on 30c bl & rose 15.00 *37.50*
Set, never hinged 72.50

Nos. E5-E6 Surcharged in Blue or Red:

No. E9

Nos. E10, E12

No. E11

1926-36

E9 SD3 70c on 60c 8.50 *19.00*
E10 SD3 2.50 l on 2 l (R) 12.00 *35.00*

Perf. 11

E11 SD3 1.25 l on 60c 6.00 2.00
a. Perf. 14 ('36) 22.00 4.25
Never hinged 55.00
b. Black surcharge *120,000.* *12,000.*
Never hinged *150,000.*
E12 SD3 2.50 l on 2 l (R) 160.00 *650.00*
Nos. E9-E12 (4) 186.50 *706.00*
Set, never hinged 475.00

Issued: #E9-E10, July 1926; #E11-E12, 1927.

Catalogue values for unused stamps in this section, from this point to the end of the section, are for Never Hinged items.

United Kingdom of Libya

Zuela Saracen Castle SD4

Perf. 11½

1966, Feb. 10 **Unwmk.** **Litho.**

E13 SD4 90m car rose & lt grn 2.75 1.60

Coat of Arms of Libya and "POLIGRAFICA & CARTEVALORI — NAPLES" printed on back in yellow green.

SEMI-POSTAL SPECIAL DELIVERY STAMPS

Camel Caravan SPSD1

Wmk. 140

1927, Feb. 15 **Litho.** ***Perf. 14***

EB1 SPSD1 1.25 l + 30c pur & blk 10.00 37.50
EB2 SPSD1 2.50 l + 1 l yel & blk 10.00 37.50
Set, never hinged 50.00

See note after No. B10.
No. EB2 is inscribed "EXPRES."

War Memorial SPSD2

1931, Mar. 8 **Photo.**

EB3 SPSD2 1.25 l + 20c car rose 6.75 *22.50*
Never hinged 17.00

See note after No. B37.

AUTHORIZED DELIVERY STAMPS

Italy No. EY1 Overprinted in Black

1929, May 11 **Wmk. 140** ***Perf. 14***

EY1 AD1 10c dull blue 30.00 50.00
Never hinged 75.00
a. Perf. 11 120.00 210.00
Never hinged 300.00

Italy No. EY2 Overprinted in Black

1941, May ***Perf. 14***

EY2 AD2 10c dark brown 12.00 42.50
Never hinged 30.00

A variety of No. EY2, with larger "LIBIA" and yellow gum, was prepared in 1942, but not issued. Value, unused 85 cents never hinged $2.10.

AD1

1942 **Litho.** **Wmk. 140**

EY3 AD1 10c sepia .85
Never hinged 2.10

No. EY3 was not issued.

POSTAGE DUE STAMPS

Italian Postage Due Stamps, 1870-1903 Overprinted in Black

1915, Nov. **Wmk. 140** ***Perf. 14***

J1	D3	5c buff & magenta	2.50	*10.00*
J2	D3	10c buff & magenta	2.50	*5.00*
J3	D3	20c buff & magenta	3.25	*8.50*
a.		Double overprint	550.00	
b.		Inverted overprint	550.00	
J4	D3	30c buff & magenta	4.25	*10.00*
J5	D3	40c buff & magenta	6.75	*12.50*
a.		"40" in black	*5,000.*	
		Never hinged	*7,500.*	
J6	D3	50c buff & magenta	4.25	*8.50*
J7	D3	60c buff & magenta	6.75	*17.00*
J8	D3	1 l blue & magenta	4.25	17.00
a.		Double overprint	*8,500.*	*10,500.*
J9	D3	2 l blue & magenta	65.00	*92.50*
J10	D3	5 l blue & magenta	75.00	*150.00*
		Nos. J1-J10 (10)	174.50	*331.00*

1926

J11	D3	60c buff & brown	120.00	*190.00*

Postage Due Stamps of Italy, 1934, Overprinted in Black

1934

J12	D6	5c brown	.25	*3.25*
J13	D6	10c blue	.25	*3.25*
J14	D6	20c rose red	1.75	1.75
J15	D6	25c green	1.75	1.75
J16	D6	30c red orange	1.75	*6.75*
J17	D6	40c black brn	1.75	*4.25*
J18	D6	50c violet	2.10	.40
J19	D6	60c black	2.10	*17.00*
J20	D7	1 l red orange	1.75	.40
J21	D7	2 l green	45.00	17.00
J22	D7	5 l violet	85.00	37.50
J23	D7	10 l blue	12.50	*50.00*
J24	D7	20 l carmine	12.75	*67.50*
		Nos. J12-J24 (13)	168.70	*210.80*

In 1942 a set of 11 "Segnatasse" stamps, picturing a camel and rider and inscribed "LIBIA," was prepared but not issued. Values for set: hinged $12; never hinged $30.

Catalogue values for unused stamps in this section, from this point to the end of the section, are for Never Hinged items.

United Kingdom of Libya

Postage Due Stamps of Cyrenaica, 1950 Surcharged in Black

For Use in Tripolitania

1951 **Unwmk.** ***Perf. 12½***

J25	D1	1mal on 2m dk brown	9.00	18.00
J26	D1	2mal on 4m dp grn	15.00	*30.00*
J27	D1	4mal on 8m scar	25.00	*50.00*
J28	D1	10mal on 20m org yel	50.00	*100.00*
a.		Arabic "20" for "10"		
J29	D1	20mal on 40m dp bl	80.00	*160.00*
		Nos. J25-J29 (5)	179.00	*358.00*

Cyrenaica Nos. J1-J7 Overprinted in Black

For Use in Cyrenaica

Overprint 13mm High

1952 **Unwmk.** ***Perf. 12½***

J30	D1	2m dark brown	10.00	*20.00*
J31	D1	4m deep green	10.00	*20.00*
J32	D1	8m scarlet	15.00	*30.00*
J33	D1	10m vermilion	20.00	*4.00*
J34	D1	20m orange yel	30.00	*60.00*
J35	D1	40m deep blue	42.50	*85.00*
J36	D1	100m dk gray	92.50	*180.00*
		Nos. J30-J36 (7)	220.00	*399.00*

D1

Castle at Tripoli — D2

1952 **Litho.** ***Perf. 11½***

J37	D1	2m chocolate	1.00	.35
J38	D1	5m blue green	1.60	.90
J39	D1	10m carmine	3.00	1.50
J40	D1	50m violet blue	11.00	4.00
		Nos. J37-J40 (4)	16.60	6.75

1964, Feb. 1 **Photo.** ***Perf. 14***

J41	D2	2m red brown	.25	.25
J42	D2	6m Prus green	.50	.50
J43	D2	10m rose red	1.00	1.00
J44	D2	50m brt blue	2.00	2.00
		Nos. J41-J44 (4)	3.75	3.75

Men in Boat, Birds, Mosaic — D3

Ancient Mosaics: 10d, Head of Medusa. 20d, Peacock. 50d, Fish.

1976, Nov. 15 **Litho.** ***Perf. 14***

J45	D3	5d bister & multi	.25	.25
J46	D3	10d orange & multi	.25	.25
J47	D3	20d blue & multi	.35	.35
J48	D3	50d emerald & multi	.80	.80
		Nos. J45-J48 (4)	1.65	1.65

Nos. J45-J48 have multiple coat of arms printed on back in pale green beneath gum.

OFFICIAL STAMPS

Catalogue values for unused stamps in this section are for Never Hinged items.

United Kingdom of Libya

Nos. 135-142 Overprinted in Black

1952 **Unwmk.** ***Perf. 11½***

O1	A27	2m yel brn	.90	.60
O2	A27	4m gray	1.50	.90
O3	A27	5m bl grn	7.50	3.00
O4	A27	8m vermilion	5.50	2.50
O5	A27	10m purple	7.00	3.00
O6	A27	12m lil rose	11.00	6.25
O7	A27	20m dp bl	19.00	9.50
O8	A27	25m chocolate	25.00	12.50
		Nos. O1-O8 (8)	77.40	38.25

PARCEL POST STAMPS

These stamps were used by affixing them to the way bill so that one half remained on it following the parcel, the other half staying on the receipt given the sender. Most used halves are right halves. Complete stamps were obtainable canceled, probably to order. Both unused and used values are for complete stamps.

Italian Parcel Post Stamps, 1914-22, Overprinted

1915-24 **Wmk. 140** ***Perf. 13½***

Q1	PP2	5c brown	3.25	*14.00*
a.		Double overprint	425.00	
Q2	PP2	10c deep blue	3.25	*14.00*
Q3	PP2	20c blk ('18)	4.00	*14.00*
Q4	PP2	25c red	4.00	*14.00*
Q5	PP2	50c orange	6.50	*14.00*
Q6	PP2	1 l violet	6.50	*20.00*
Q7	PP2	2 l green	8.00	*20.00*
Q8	PP2	3 l bister	14.00	*20.00*
Q9	PP2	4 l slate	14.00	*20.00*
Q10	PP2	10 l rose lil ('24)	80.00	*110.00*
Q11	PP2	12 l red brn ('24)	160.00	*250.00*
Q12	PP2	15 l ol grn ('24)	160.00	*350.00*
Q13	PP2	20 l brn vio ('24)	275.00	*450.00*
		Nos. Q1-Q13 (13)	738.50	*1,310.*

Halves Used

Q1	1.00
Q2	1.50
Q3	1.50
Q4	1.50
Q5	1.50
Q6	1.50
Q7	1.50
Q8	1.50
Q9	1.50
Q10	10.00
Q11	11.00
Q12	25.00
Q13	65.00

Same Overprint on Parcel Post Stamps of Italy, 1927-36

1927-38

Q14	PP3	10c dp bl ('36)	4.25	*9.50*
Q15	PP3	25c red ('36)	4.25	*9.50*
Q16	PP3	30c ultra ('29)	1.75	*4.75*
Q17	PP3	50c orange	75.00	275.00
a.		Overprint 8¾x2mm ('31)	125.00	*400.00*
Q18	PP3	60c red ('29)	1.75	*4.75*
Q19	PP3	1 l lilac ('36)	40.00	*120.00*
Q20	PP3	2 l grn ('38)	47.50	*120.00*
Q21	PP3	3 l bister	2.50	*12.00*
Q22	PP3	4 l gray	2.50	*16.00*
Q23	PP3	10 l rose lil ('36)	350.00	550.00
Q24	PP3	20 l brn vio ('36)	400.00	*675.00*
		Nos. Q14-Q24 (11)	929.50	*1,796.*

Halves Used

Q14	.50
Q15	.50
Q16	.50
Q17	12.50
Q17a	22.50
Q18	.50
Q19	7.50
Q20	7.50
Q21	1.50
Q22	2.50
Q23	30.00
Q24	35.00
Q15	.35
Q17	9.00
Q19-Q20	1.50
Q21-Q22	.50
Q23	18.00
Q24	19.00

The overprint measures 10x1½mm on No. Q17.

Same Overprint on Italy No. Q24

1939

Q25	PP3	5c brown	*16,000.*	
		Never hinged	20,000.	

The overprint was applied to the 5c in error. Few examples exist.

OCCUPATION STAMPS

Catalogue values for unused stamps in this section are for Never Hinged items.

Issued under French Occupation

Stamps of Italy and Libya were overprinted in 1943: "FEZZAN Occupation Française" and "R. F. FEZZAN" for use in this region when General Leclerc's forces 1st occupied it.

Fezzan-Ghadames

Sebha Fort — OS1

Mosque and Fort Turc Murzuch OS2

Map of Fezzan-Ghadames, Soldier and Camel — OS3

1946 **Unwmk.** **Engr.** ***Perf. 13***

1N1	OS1	10c black	.40	.40
1N2	OS1	50c rose	.40	.40
1N3	OS1	1fr brown	.50	.50
1N4	OS1	1.50fr green	.65	.65
1N5	OS1	2fr ultramarine	.85	.85
1N6	OS2	2.50fr violet	1.00	1.00
1N7	OS2	3fr rose carmine	1.40	1.40
1N8	OS2	5fr chocolate	1.40	1.40
1N9	OS2	6fr dark green	1.30	1.30
1N10	OS2	10fr blue	1.40	1.40
1N11	OS3	15fr violet	1.75	1.75
1N12	OS3	20fr red	1.90	1.90
1N13	OS3	25fr sepia	1.90	1.90
1N14	OS3	40fr dark green	2.50	2.50
1N15	OS3	50fr deep blue	2.75	2.75
		Nos. 1N1-1N15 (15)	20.10	20.10

FEZZAN

Catalogue values for unused stamps in this section are for Never Hinged items.

Monument, Djerma Oasis — OS1

Tombs of the Beni-Khettab — OS2

Well at Gorda OS3

Col. Colonna d'Ornano and Fort at Murzuch OS4

Philippe F. M. de Hautecloque (Gen. Jacques Leclerc) — OS5

1949 **Unwmk.** **Engr.** ***Perf. 13***

2N1	OS1	1fr black	1.25	1.25
2N2	OS1	2fr lil pink	1.25	1.25
2N3	OS2	4fr red brn	2.50	2.50
2N4	OS2	5fr emerald	2.50	2.50
2N5	OS3	8fr blue	3.00	3.00

2N6 OS3 10fr brown 4.50 4.50
2N7 OS3 12fr dk grn 7.25 7.25
2N8 OS4 15fr sal red 12.00 9.75
2N9 OS4 20fr brn blk 5.50 4.50
2N10 OS5 25fr dk bl 6.75 6.25
2N11 OS5 50fr cop red 11.00 10.00
Nos. 2N1-2N11 (11) 57.50 52.75

Camel Raising OS6

Agriculture OS7

Well Drilling — OS8

Ahmed Bey — OS9

1951
2N12 OS6 30c brown 1.50 1.50
2N13 OS6 1fr dp bl 1.50 1.50
2N14 OS6 2fr rose car 1.50 1.50
2N15 OS7 4fr red 2.25 2.25
2N16 OS7 5fr green 2.25 2.25
2N17 OS7 8fr dp bl 2.40 2.40
2N18 OS8 10fr sepia 6.25 6.00
2N19 OS8 12fr dp grn 7.50 7.25
2N20 OS8 15fr brt red 7.50 7.25
2N21 OS9 20fr blk brn & vio brn 7.50 7.25
2N22 OS9 25fr dk bl & bl 9.25 9.00
2N23 OS9 50fr ind & brn org 9.25 9.00
Nos. 2N12-2N23 (12) 58.65 57.15

OCCUPATION SEMI-POSTAL STAMPS

Catalogue values for unused stamps in this section are for Never Hinged items.

"The Unhappy Ones"
OSP1 OSP2

1950 **Unwmk.** **Engr.** ***Perf. 13***
2NB1 OSP1 15fr + 5fr red brn 3.50 3.50
2NB2 OSP2 25fr + 5fr blue 3.50 3.50

The surtax was for charitable works.

OCCUPATION AIR POST STAMPS

Catalogue values for unused stamps in this section are for Never Hinged items.

Airport in Fezzan OAP1

Plane over Fezzan — OAP2

1948 **Unwmk.** **Engr.** ***Perf. 13***
2NC1 OAP1 100fr red 8.50 8.50
2NC2 OAP2 200fr indigo 12.00 12.00

Oasis OAP3

Murzuch OAP4

1951
2NC3 OAP3 100fr dark blue 7.25 7.25
2NC4 OAP4 200fr vermilion 7.75 7.75

OCCUPATION POSTAGE DUE STAMPS

Catalogue values for unused stamps in this section are for Never Hinged items.

Oasis of Brak — D1

1950 **Unwmk.** **Engr.** ***Perf. 13***
2NJ1 D1 1fr brown black 1.75 1.75
2NJ2 D1 2fr deep green 1.75 1.75
2NJ3 D1 3fr red brown 2.10 2.10
2NJ4 D1 5fr purple 2.50 2.50
2NJ5 D1 10fr red 4.50 4.50
2NJ6 D1 20fr deep blue 6.75 6.75
Nos. 2NJ1-2NJ6 (6) 19.35 19.35

GHADAMES

Catalogue values for unused stamps in this section are for Never Hinged items.

Cross of Agadem — OS1

1949 **Unwmk.** **Engr.** ***Perf. 13***
3N1 OS1 4fr sep & red brn 5.25 5.00
3N2 OS1 5fr pck bl & dk grn 5.25 5.00
3N3 OS1 8fr sep & org brn 5.25 5.00
3N4 OS1 10fr blk & dk ultra 5.25 5.00
3N5 OS1 12fr vio & red vio 13.50 12.50
3N6 OS1 15fr brn & red brn 9.25 8.50
3N7 OS1 20fr sep & emer 12.00 10.00
3N8 OS1 25fr sepia & blue 12.50 12.00
Nos. 3N1-3N8 (8) 68.25 63.00

OCCUPATION AIR POST STAMPS

Catalogue values for unused stamps in this section are for Never Hinged items.

Cross of Agadem — OAP1

1949 **Unwmk.** **Engr.** ***Perf. 13***
3NC1 OAP1 50fr pur & rose 17.50 16.00
3NC2 OAP1 100fr sep & pur brn 21.00 21.00

LIECHTENSTEIN

'lik-tən-ˌshtin

LOCATION — Central Europe southeast of Lake Constance, between Austria and Switzerland
GOVT. — Principality
AREA — 61.8 sq. mi.
POP. — 31,320 (1997)
CAPITAL — Vaduz

The Principality of Liechtenstein is a sovereign state consisting of the two counties of Schellenberg and Vaduz. Since 1921 the post office has been administered by Switzerland.

100 Heller = 1 Krone
100 Rappen = 1 Franc (1921)

Catalogue values for unused stamps in this country are for Never Hinged items, beginning with Scott 368 in the regular postage section, Scott B22 in the semi-postal section, Scott C24 in the air post section, and Scott O30 in the offical section.

Watermarks

Greek Cross — Wmk. 183

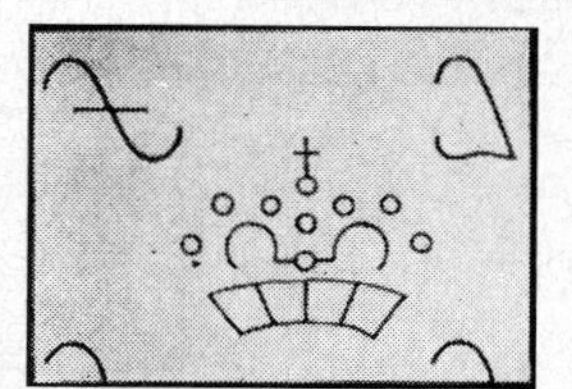
Crown and Initials — Wmk. 296

Austrian Administration of the Post Office

Prince Johann II — A1

1912 **Unwmk.** **Typo.** ***Perf. 12½x13***

Thick Chalky Paper

1 A1 5h yellow green 35.00 13.00
2 A1 10h rose 70.00 13.00
3 A1 25h dark blue 70.00 40.00
Nos. 1-3 (3) 175.00 66.00
Set, never hinged 725.00

1915

Thin Unsurfaced Paper

1a A1 5h yellow green 12.00 *15.00*
2a A1 10h rose 75.00 22.50
3a A1 25h dark blue 575.00 150.00
b. 25h ultramarine 350.00 350.00
#1a-3a, never hinged 2,500.
#3b, never hinged 1,300.

Coat of Arms — A2

Prince Johann II — A3

1917-18
4 A2 3h violet 1.40 1.50
5 A2 5h yellow green 1.40 1.50
6 A3 10h claret 1.40 1.50
7 A3 15h dull red 1.40 1.50
8 A3 20h dark green 1.40 1.50
9 A3 25h deep blue 1.40 1.50
Nos. 4-9 (6) 8.40 9.00
Set, never hinged 37.50

Exist imperf. Value, set $350.
For surcharges see Nos. 11-16.

Prince Johann II — A4

1918

Dates in Upper Corners

10 A4 20h dark green .45 *2.00*
Never hinged 3.25

Accession of Prince Johann II, 60th anniv. Exists imperf. Value $150.

National Administration of the Post Office

Stamps of 1917-18 Overprinted or Surcharged

a

b

c

1920
11 A2(a) 5h yellow green 1.90 *7.50*
a. Inverted overprint 75.00 *175.00*
Never hinged 200.00
b. Double overprint 15.00 *100.00*
Never hinged 40.00
12 A3(a) 10h claret 1.90 *7.50*
a. Inverted overprint 75.00 *175.00*
Never hinged 200.00
b. Double overprint 15.00 *100.00*
Never hinged 40.00
c. Overprint type "c" 15.00 *100.00*
Never hinged 35.00
13 A3(a) 25h deep blue 1.90 *7.50*
a. Inverted overprint 75.00 *175.00*
Never hinged 200.00
b. Double overprint 15.00 *100.00*
Never hinged 35.00

14 A2(b) 40h on 3h violet 1.90 *7.50*
a. Inverted surcharge 75.00 *175.00*
Never hinged 200.00
15 A3(c) 1k on 15h dull red 1.90 *7.50*
a. Inverted surcharge 75.00 *175.00*
Never hinged 200.00
b. Overprint type "a" 67.50 *150.00*
Never hinged 250.00
16 A3(c) 2½k on 20h dk grn 1.90 *7.50*
a. Inverted surcharge 75.00 *175.00*
Never hinged 200.00
Nos. 11-16 (6) 11.40 *45.00*
Set, never hinged 50.00

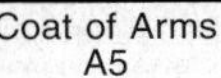
Coat of Arms A5

Chapel of St. Mamertus A6

Coat of Arms with Supporters A15

Designs: 40h, Gutenberg Castle. 50h, Courtyard, Vaduz Castle. 60h, Red Tower, Vaduz. 80h, Old Roman Tower, Schaan. 1k, Castle at Vaduz. 2k, View of Bendern. 5k, Prince Johann I. 7½k, Prince Johann II.

1920 **Engr.** ***Imperf.***
18 A5 5h olive bister .25 5.75
19 A5 10h deep orange .25 5.75
20 A5 15h dark blue .25 5.75
21 A5 20h deep brown .25 5.75
22 A5 25h dark green .25 5.75
23 A5 30h gray black .25 5.75
24 A5 40h dark red .25 5.75
25 A6 1k blue .25 5.75

Perf. 12½
32 A5 5h olive bister .25 *.50*
33 A5 10h deep orange .25 *.50*
34 A5 15h deep blue .25 *.50*
35 A5 20h red brown .25 *.50*
36 A6 25h olive green .25 *.50*
37 A5 30h dark gray .25 *.50*
38 A6 40h claret .25 *.50*
39 A6 50h yellow green .25 *.50*
40 A6 60h red brown .25 *.50*
41 A6 80h rose .25 *.50*
42 A6 1k dull violet .45 *.90*
43 A6 2k light blue .45 *1.00*
44 A6 5k black .45 *1.10*
45 A6 7½k slate .45 *1.50*
46 A15 10k ocher .45 *1.50*
Nos. 18-46 (23) 6.75 *57.00*
Set, never hinged 27.50

Used values for Nos. 18-46 are for canceled to order stamps. Value with postal cancels approximately $45.

Many denominations of Nos. 32-46 are found imperforate, imperforate vertically and imperforate horizontally.

For surcharges see Nos. 51-52.

Madonna and Child — A16

1920, Oct. 5
47 A16 50h olive green .45 *1.40*
48 A16 80h brown red .45 *1.40*
49 A16 2k dark blue .45 *2.10*
Nos. 47-49 (3) 1.35 *4.90*
Set, never hinged 7.50

80th birthday of Prince Johann II.

Imperf., Pairs
47a A16 50h 6.00 —
48a A16 80h 6.00 —
49a A16 2k 6.00 —
Set, never hinged 24.00

Swiss Administration of the Post Office
No. 19 Surcharged

No. 51

No. 52

1921 **Unwmk.** **Engr.** ***Imperf.***
51 A5 2rp on 10h dp org .90 *27.50*
Never hinged 3.50
a. Double surcharge 99.50 *140.00*
Never hinged 160.00
b. Inverted surcharge 80.00 *140.00*
Never hinged 140.00
c. Double surch., one inverted 100.00 *87.50*
Never hinged 175.00
52 A5 2rp on 10h dp org .60 *20.00*
Never hinged 1.40
a. Double surcharge 80.00 *175.00*
Never hinged 140.00
b. Inverted surcharge 80.00 *175.00*
Never hinged 140.00
c. Double surch., one inverted 92.50 *190.00*
Never hinged 160.00

Arms with Supporters A19

Chapel of St. Mamertus A20

View of Vaduz A21

Designs: 25rp, Castle at Vaduz. 30rp, View of Bendern. 35rp, Prince Johann II. 40rp, Old Roman Tower at Schaan. 50rp, Gutenberg Castle. 80rp, Red Tower at Vaduz.

1921 ***Perf. 12½, 9½ (2rp, 10rp, 15rp)***
Surface Tinted Paper (#54-61)
54 A19 2rp lemon 1.00 *10.00*
55 A19 2½rp black 1.10 *11.00*
a. Perf. 9½ 1.25 *57.50*
Never hinged 3.50
56 A19 3rp orange 1.10 *10.00*
a. Perf. 9½ 140.00 *3,750.*
Never hinged 350.00
57 A19 5rp olive green 11.50 1.75
a. Perf. 9½ 67.50 *13.00*
Never hinged 200.00
58 A19 7½rp dark blue 6.75 *35.00*
a. Perf. 9½ 275.00 *875.00*
Never hinged 675.00
59 A19 10rp yellow green 26.00 8.75
a. Perf. 12½ 35.00 6.00
Never hinged 90.00
60 A19 13rp brown 8.25 *77.50*
a. Perf. 9½ 95.00 *2,150.*
Never hinged 300.00
61 A19 15rp dark violet 22.50 20.00
a. Perf. 12½ 21.00 24.00
Never hinged 67.50
62 A20 20rp dull vio & blk 67.50 1.90
63 A20 25rp rose red & blk 3.50 3.00
64 A20 30rp dp grn & blk 75.00 17.00
65 A20 35rp brn & blk, *straw* 6.50 *13.50*
66 A20 40rp dk blue & blk 9.75 5.50
67 A20 50rp dk green & blk 17.00 6.75
68 A20 80rp gray & blk 30.00 *67.50*
69 A21 1fr dp claret & blk 57.50 45.00
Nos. 54-69 (16) 344.95 *334.15*
Set, never hinged 1,150.

Nos. 54-69 exist imperforate; Nos. 54-61, partly perforated. See Nos. 73, 81. For surcharges see Nos. 70-71.

Nos. 58, 60a Surcharged in Red

1924 ***Perf. 12½, 9½***
70 A19 5rp on 7½rp 1.25 2.00
Never hinged 3.50
a. Perf. 9½ 15.00 6.75
Never hinged 45.00
71 A19 10rp on 13rp .70 15.00
Never hinged 2.00
a. Perf. 12½ 19.00 40.00
Never hinged 35.00

Type of 1921
1924 **Wmk. 183** ***Perf. 11½***
Granite Paper
73 A19 10rp green 14.00 2.00
Never hinged 65.00

Peasant A28

Government Palace and Church at Vaduz A30

Design: 10rp, 20rp, Courtyard, Vaduz Castle.

1924-28 **Typo.** ***Perf. 11½***
74 A28 2½rp ol grn & red vio ('28) 1.25 *5.00*
75 A28 5rp brown & blue 2.25 .75
76 A28 7½rp bl grn & brn ('28) 1.90 *5.50*
77 A28 15rp red brn & bl grn ('28) 8.75 *27.50*

Engr.
78 A28 10rp yellow grn 11.50 .60
79 A28 20rp deep red 37.50 .90
80 A30 1½fr blue 82.50 87.50
Nos. 74-80 (7) 145.65 127.75
Set, never hinged 550.00

Bendern Type of 1921
1925
81 A20 30rp blue & blk 11.50 2.00
Never hinged 55.00

Prince Johann II — A31

Prince Johann II as Boy and Man A32

1928, Nov. 12 **Typo.** **Wmk. 183**
82 A31 10rp lt brn & ol grn 4.50 5.00
83 A31 20rp org red & ol grn 6.75 10.00
84 A31 30rp sl bl & ol grn 22.50 17.50
85 A31 60rp red vio & ol grn 45.00 *75.00*

Engr.
Unwmk.
86 A32 1.20fr ultra 37.50 *87.50*
87 A32 1.50fr black brown 67.50 *190.00*
88 A32 2fr deep carmine 67.50 *190.00*
89 A32 5fr dark green 67.50 *225.00*
Nos. 82-89 (8) 318.75 *800.00*
Set, never hinged 925.00

70th year of the reign of Prince Johann II.

Prince Francis I, as a Child — A33

Prince Francis I as a Man — A34

Princess Elsa — A35

Prince Francis and Princess Elsa — A36

1929, Dec. 2 **Photo.**
90 A33 10rp olive green .35 *3.00*
91 A34 20rp carmine .55 *5.00*
92 A35 30rp ultra .90 *17.50*
93 A36 70rp brown 16.00 *100.00*
Nos. 90-93 (4) 17.80 *125.50*
Set, never hinged 55.00

Accession of Prince Francis I, Feb. 11, 1929.

Grape Girl — A37

Chamois Hunter — A38

Mountain Cattle — A39

Courtyard, Vaduz Castle — A40

Mt. Naafkopf — A41

Chapel at Steg — A42

Rofenberg Chapel — A43

Chapel of St. Mamertus — A44

Alpine Hotel, Malbun — A45

Gutenberg Castle — A46

Schellenberg Monastery — A47

Castle at Vaduz — A48

Mountain Cottage — A49

Prince Francis and Princess Elsa — A50

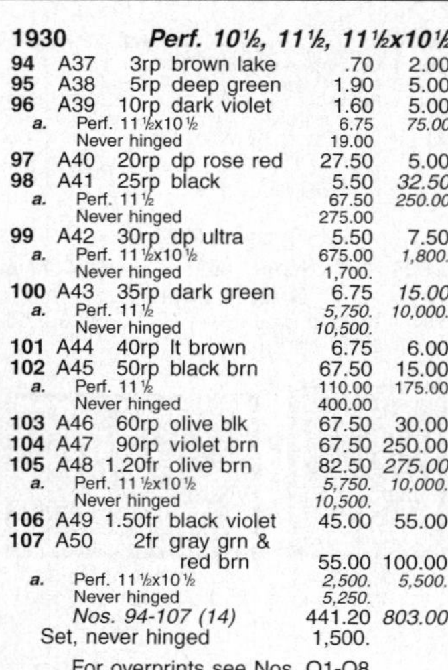

1930 ***Perf. 10½, 11½, 11½x10½***

94	A37	3rp brown lake	.70	2.00
95	A38	5rp deep green	1.90	5.00
96	A39	10rp dark violet	1.60	5.00
a.		Perf. 11½x10½	6.75	*75.00*
		Never hinged	19.00	
97	A40	20rp dp rose red	27.50	5.00
98	A41	25rp black	5.50	*32.50*
a.		Perf. 11½	67.50	*250.00*
		Never hinged	275.00	
99	A42	30rp dp ultra	5.50	7.50
a.		Perf. 11½x10½	675.00	*1,800.*
		Never hinged	1,700.	
100	A43	35rp dark green	6.75	*15.00*
a.		Perf. 11½	*5,750.*	*10,000.*
		Never hinged	*10,500.*	
101	A44	40rp lt brown	6.75	6.00
102	A45	50rp black brn	67.50	15.00
a.		Perf. 11½	110.00	175.00
		Never hinged	400.00	
103	A46	60rp olive blk	67.50	30.00
104	A47	90rp violet brn	67.50	250.00
105	A48	1.20fr olive brn	82.50	*275.00*
a.		Perf. 11½x10½	*5,750.*	*10,000.*
		Never hinged	*10,500.*	
106	A49	1.50fr black violet	45.00	55.00
107	A50	2fr gray grn & red brn	55.00	100.00
a.		Perf. 11½x10½	*2,500.*	*5,500.*
		Never hinged	*5,250.*	
		Nos. 94-107 (14)	441.20	*803.00*
		Set, never hinged	1,500.	

For overprints see Nos. O1-O8.

Mt. Naafkopf A51

Gutenberg Castle A52

Vaduz Castle — A53

1933, Jan. 23 ***Perf. 14½***

108	A51	25rp red orange	175.00	62.50
109	A52	90rp dark green	6.75	*75.00*
110	A53	1.20fr red brown	91.50	*250.00*
		Nos. 108-110 (3)	273.25	*387.50*
		Set, never hinged	825.00	

For overprints see Nos. O9-O10.

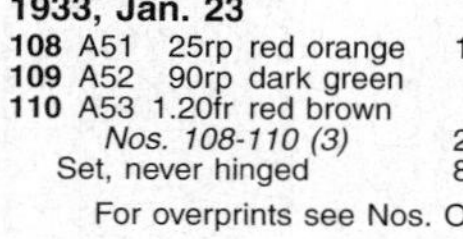

Prince Francis I
A54 A55

1933, Aug. 28 ***Perf. 11***

111	A54	10rp purple	18.00	35.00
112	A54	20rp brown carmine	18.00	35.00
113	A54	30rp dark blue	18.00	35.00
		Nos. 111-113 (3)	54.00	105.00
		Set, never hinged	160.00	

80th birthday of Prince Francis I.

1933, Dec. 15 **Engr.** ***Perf. 12½***

114	A55	3fr violet blue	82.50	175.00
		Never hinged	225.00	

See No. 152.

Agricultural Exhibition Issue
Souvenir Sheet

Arms of Liechtenstein — A56

1934, Sept. 29 ***Perf. 12***
Granite Paper

115	A56	5fr brown	*1,200.*	*2,100.*
		Never hinged	*2,450.*	
		Single stamp	*850.00*	1,700.
		Never hinged	*1,600.*	

See No. 131.

Coat of Arms A57

"Three Sisters" (Landmark) A58

Church of Schaan A59

Bendern A60

Rathaus, Vaduz — A61

Samina Valley — A62

Samina Valley in Winter A63

Ruin at Schellenberg — A64

Government Palace — A65

Vaduz Castle A66

Gutenberg Castle A68

Alpine Hut — A69

Princess Elsa — A70

Coat of Arms — A71

60rp, Vaduz castle, diff. 1.50fr, Valuna.

1934-35 **Photo.** ***Perf. 11½***

116	A57	3rp copper red	.25	.50
117	A58	5rp emerald	3.25	1.50
118	A59	10rp deep violet	.45	1.00
119	A60	15rp red org ('35)	.25	1.00
120	A61	20rp red ('35)	.45	1.00
121	A62	25rp brown ('35)	18.00	47.50
122	A63	30rp dk blue ('35)	3.75	1.50
123	A64	35rp gray grn ('35)	.90	*6.00*
124	A65	40rp brown ('35)	1.10	5.00
125	A66	50rp lt brown	16.00	15.00
126	A66	60rp claret	1.40	*6.50*
127	A68	90rp deep green	5.50	*21.00*
128	A69	1.20fr deep blue	2.25	*21.00*
129	A69	1.50fr brown car ('35)	2.75	*25.00*
		Nos. 116-129 (14)	56.30	*153.50*
		Set, never hinged	160.00	

Engr.
Perf. 12½

130	A70	2fr henna brn ('35)	55.00	*175.00*
		Never hinged	110.00	
131	A71	5fr dk violet ('35)	275.00	*850.00*
		Never hinged	525.00	

No. 131 has the same design as the 5fr in the souvenir sheet, No. 115. See #226, B14. For overprints see Nos. O11-O20.

Bridge at Malbun A72

Labor: 20rp, Constructing Road to Triesenberg. 30rp, Binnen Canal. 50rp, Bridge near Planken.

1937, June 30 **Photo.**

132	A72	10rp brt violet	1.10	1.50
133	A72	20rp red	1.10	2.00
134	A72	30rp brt blue	1.10	2.50
135	A72	50rp yellow brown	1.10	3.00
		Nos. 132-135 (4)	4.40	9.00
		Set, never hinged	16.00	

Ruin at Schalun — A76

Peasant in Rhine Valley A77

Ruin at Schellenberg — A78

Knight and Gutenberg Castle A79

Baron von Brandis and Vaduz Castle A80

Designs: 5rp, Chapel at Masescha. 10rp, Knight and Vaduz Castle. 15rp, Upper Valüna Valley. 20rp, Wooden Bridge over Rhine, Bendern. 25rp, Chapel at Steg. 90rp, "The Three Sisters". 1fr, Frontier stone. 1.20fr, Gutenberg Castle and Harpist. 1.50fr, Alpine View of Lawena and Schwartzhorn.

1937-38

136	A76	3rp yellow brown	.25	*.50*

Pale Buff Shading

137	A76	5rp emerald	.25	.25
138	A76	10rp violet	.25	.25
139	A76	15rp dk slate grn	.25	*.50*
140	A76	20rp brown orange	.25	.50
141	A76	25rp chestnut	.45	*2.50*
142	A77	30rp blue & gray	2.75	1.00
144	A78	40rp dark green	1.90	2.00
145	A79	50rp dark brown	.70	*2.50*
146	A80	60rp dp claret ('38)	1.90	2.50
147	A80	90rp gray vio ('38)	9.25	*15.00*
148	A80	1fr red brown	1.90	*12.50*
149	A80	1.20fr dp brown ('38)	6.75	*22.50*
150	A80	1.50fr slate bl ('38)	2.75	*22.50*
		Nos. 136-150 (14)	29.60	*85.00*
		Set, never hinged	87.50	

For overprints see Nos. O21-O29.

Souvenir Sheet

FÜRSTENTUM LIECHTENSTEIN

geb. Vaduz, 17. März 1839,
gest. München, 25. November 1901

DRITTE LIECHTENSTEINISCHE BRIEFMARKEN-AUSSTELLUNG
VADUZ, 30. JULI BIS 8. AUGUST 1938

Staatsdruckerei, Wien

Josef Rheinberger — A91

1938, July 30 **Engr.** ***Perf. 12***

151		Sheet of 4	18.00	20.00
		Never hinged	55.00	
	a.	A91 50rp slate gray	2.25	3.75
		Never hinged	5.50	

Third Philatelic Exhibition of Liechtenstein. Sheet size: 99¾x135mm.

See No. 153.

Francis Type of 1933
Thick Wove Paper

1938, Aug. 15 ***Perf. 12½***

152	A55	3fr black, *buff*	9.25	*80.00*
		Never hinged	19.00	

Issued in memory of Prince Francis I, who died July 25, 1938. Sheets of 20.

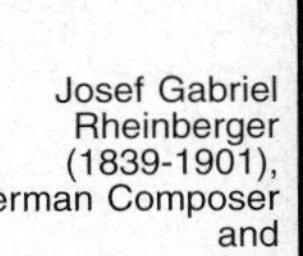

Josef Gabriel Rheinberger (1839-1901), German Composer and Organist — A92

1939, Mar. 31

153	A92	50rp slate green	.70	*4.50*
		Never hinged	1.90	

Issued in sheets of 20. See No. 151.

Scene of Homage, 1718 — A93

1939, May 29

154	A93	20rp green lake	.90	2.00
155	A93	30rp slate blue	.90	1.50
156	A93	50rp gray green	.90	2.00
		Nos. 154-156 (3)	2.70	5.50
		Set, never hinged	11.00	

Honoring Prince Franz Joseph II. Sheets of 20.

Cantonal Coats of Arms — A94

Prince Franz Joseph II — A96

Design: 3fr, Arms of Principality.

1939

157	A94	2fr dk green, *buff*	6.75	*37.50*
158	A94	3fr indigo, *buff*	4.50	*37.50*
159	A96	5fr brown, *buff*	13.50	*25.00*
	a.	Sheet of 4	85.00	*140.00*
		Never hinged	150.00	
		Nos. 157-159 (3)	24.75	*100.00*
		Set, never hinged	60.00	

2fr, 3fr issued in sheets of 12; 5fr in sheets of 4.

Prince Johann as a Child A100

Memorial Tablet A101

Prince Johann II — A102

30rp, Prince Johann and Tower at Vaduz. 50rp, Prince Johann and Gutenberg Castle. 1fr, Prince Johann in 1920 and Vaduz Castle.

1940 **Photo.** ***Perf. 11½.***

160	A100	20rp henna brown	.45	*2.00*
161	A100	30rp indigo	.45	*3.00*
162	A100	50rp dk slate grn	.90	*10.00*
163	A100	1fr brown vio	6.75	*65.00*
164	A101	1.50fr violet blk	6.50	*60.00*
165	A102	3fr brown	3.25	*20.00*
		Nos. 160-165 (6)	18.30	*160.00*
		Set, never hinged	45.00	

Birth centenary of Prince Johann II.

Nos. 160-164 issued in sheets of 25; No. 165 in sheets of 12.

Issue dates: 3fr, Oct. 5; others Aug. 10.

Gathering Corn A103

Wine Press A104

Sharpening Scythe — A105

Milkmaid and Cow A106

Native Costume A107

1941, Apr. 7

166	A103	10rp dull red brown	.75	.45
167	A104	20rp lake	.75	1.10
168	A105	30rp royal blue	.75	*2.50*
169	A106	50rp myrtle green	2.40	*14.00*
170	A107	90rp deep claret	2.40	*14.00*
		Nos. 166-170 (5)	7.05	*32.05*
		Set, never hinged	14.00	

Madonna and Child — A108

1941, July 7 **Engr.**

171	A108	10fr brown car	42.50	*97.50*
		Never hinged	80.00	

Issued in sheets of 4.

Johann Adam Andreas — A109

Designs: 30rp, Wenzel. 100rp, Anton Florian. 150rp, Joseph Adam.

1941, Dec. 18 **Photo.**

172	A109	20rp brown car	.50	*1.25*
173	A109	30rp royal blue	.70	*2.50*
174	A109	100rp violet blk	1.90	*13.00*
175	A109	150rp slate green	1.90	*13.00*
		Nos. 172-175 (4)	5.00	*29.75*
		Set, never hinged	11.00	

Saint Lucius A113

Designs: 30rp, Reconstruction of Vaduz Castle. 50rp, Signing the Treaty of May 3, 1342. 1fr, Battle of Gutenberg. 2fr, Scene of Homage, 1718.

1942, Apr. 22 **Engr.** ***Perf. 11½***

176	A113	20rp brn org, *buff*	1.40	.95
177	A113	30rp steel bl, *buff*	1.40	1.40
178	A113	50rp dk ol grn, *buff*	1.90	*5.50*
179	A113	1fr dull brn, *buff*	2.50	*13.50*
180	A113	2fr vio blk, *buff*	2.75	*14.00*
		Nos. 176-180 (5)	9.95	*35.35*
		Set, never hinged	20.00	

600th anniversary of the separation of Liechtenstein from the House of Monfort.

Johann Karl — A118

30rp, Franz Joseph I. 1fr, Alois I. 1.50fr, Johann I.

1942, Oct. 5 **Photo.**

181	A118	20rp rose	.50	1.25
182	A118	30rp brt blue	.50	*3.00*
183	A118	1fr rose lilac	1.75	*16.00*
184	A118	1.50fr deep brown	2.00	*16.00*
		Nos. 181-184 (4)	4.75	*36.25*
		Set, never hinged	11.00	

Prince Franz Joseph II — A122

Countess Georgina von Wilczek — A123

Prince and Princess — A124

1943, Mar. 5

185 A122 10rp dp rose violet .45 *1.10*
186 A123 20rp henna brown .45 *1.10*
187 A124 30rp slate blue .45 *1.10*
Nos. 185-187 (3) 1.35 3.30
Set, never hinged 3.25

Marriage of Prince Franz Joseph II and Countess Georgina von Wilczek.

Prince Johann II — A126

Princes: 20rp, Alois II. 100rp, Franz Joseph I. 150rp, Franz Joseph II.

Perf. 11½

1943, July 5 Unwmk. Photo.

188 A126 20rp copper brown .35 *.60*
189 A126 30rp deep ultra .60 *1.10*
190 A126 100rp olive gray 1.10 *7.00*
191 A126 150rp slate green 1.25 *7.00*
Nos. 188-191 (4) 3.30 *15.70*
Set, never hinged 7.25

Sheets of 20.

Terrain before Reclaiming A129

30rp, Draining the Canal. 50rp, Plowing Reclaimed Land. 2fr, Harvesting Crops.

1943, Sept. 6

192 A129 10rp violet black .30 *.55*
193 A129 30rp deep blue .85 *2.00*
194 A129 50rp slate green 1.10 *8.50*
195 A129 2fr olive brown 2.00 *12.50*
Nos. 192-195 (4) 4.25 *23.55*
Set, never hinged 8.75

Vaduz A133

Gutenberg A134

1943, Dec. 27

196 A133 10rp dark gray .45 .45
197 A134 20rp chestnut brown .50 *1.00*
Set, never hinged 2.00

Planken — A135

Bendern — A136

Designs: 10rp, Triesen. 15rp, Ruggell. 20rp, Vaduz. 25rp, Triesenberg. 30rp, Schaan. 40rp, Balzers. 50rp, Mauren. 60rp, Schellenberg. 90rp, Eschen. 1fr, Vaduz Castle. 120rp, Valuna Valley. 150rp, Lawena.

1944-45

198 A135 3rp dk brn & buff .25 .20
199 A136 5rp sl grn & buff .25 .20
200 A136 10rp gray & buff .25 .20
201 A136 15rp bl gray & buff .30 *.60*
202 A136 20rp org red & buff .30 .40
203 A136 25rp dk rose vio & buff .30 *.80*
204 A136 30rp blue & buff .35 .40
205 A136 40rp brown & buff .55 1.00
206 A136 50rp bluish blk & pale gray .70 1.60
207 A136 60rp green & buff 3.75 5.00
208 A136 90rp ol grn & buff 3.75 5.00
209 A136 1fr dp cl & buff 2.25 *5.00*
210 A136 120rp red brown 2.25 *5.75*
211 A136 150rp royal blue 2.25 *5.75*
Nos. 198-211 (14) 17.50 *31.90*
Set, never hinged 37.50

Issue years: 10rp, 15rp, 40rp-1fr, 1945; others, 1944. See No. 239. For surcharge and overprints see No. 236, O30-O36.

Crown and Rose — A149

1945, Apr. 9

212 A149 20rp multicolored .85 *.55*
213 A149 30rp multicolored .85 *1.40*
214 A149 1fr multicolored 1.00 *4.50*
Nos. 212-214 (3) 2.70 *6.45*
Set, never hinged 4.25

Birth of Prince Johann Adam Pius, Feb. 14, 1945. Sheets of 20.

Prince Franz Joseph II — A150

Arms of Liechtenstein and Vaduz Castle — A152

Design: 3fr, Princess Georgina.

1944-45 Photo.

215 A150 2fr brown, *buff* 6.00 *16.00*
216 A150 3fr dark green 3.50 *11.50*

Engr.

217 A152 5fr bl gray, *cr* ('45) 10.50 *32.50*
Nos. 215-217 (3) 20.00 *60.00*
Set, never hinged 40.00

Nos. 215-217 were issued in sheets of 8. See Nos. 222, 259-260.

Saint Lucius — A153

1946, Mar. 14 Unwmk. *Perf. 11½*

218 A153 10fr gray blk, *cr* 22.50 *30.00*
Never hinged 42.50
Sheet of 4 160.00 *200.00*
Never hinged 190.00

Issued in sheets measuring 105x130mm.

Red Deer — A154

Varying Hare — A155

Capercaillie A156

1946, Dec. 10 Photo.

219 A154 20rp henna brown 1.50 *2.50*
220 A155 30rp grnsh blue 1.50 *3.25*
221 A156 150rp olive brown 3.00 *11.50*
Nos. 219-221 (3) 6.00 *17.25*
Set, never hinged 12.00

Arms Type of 1945

1947, Mar. 20 Engr.

222 A152 5fr henna brn, *cream* 12.50 *37.50*
Never hinged 25.00

Issued in sheets of 8.

Chamois — A157

Alpine Marmot — A158

Golden Eagle — A159

1947, Oct. 15 Photo. Unwmk.

223 A157 20rp henna brown 1.60 *1.90*
224 A158 30rp grnsh blue 2.25 *3.25*
225 A159 150rp dark brown 4.25 *19.00*
Nos. 223-225 (3) 8.10 *24.15*
Set, never hinged 16.00

Elsa Type of 1935

1947, Dec. 10 Engr. *Perf. 14½*

226 A70 2fr black, *yelsh* 2.25 *12.50*
Never hinged 4.25

Issued in memory of Princess Elsa, who died Sept. 28, 1947. Sheets of 20.

Portrait of Ginevra dei Benci by Leonardo da Vinci — A160

Designs: 20rp, Girl, Rubens. 30rp, Self-portrait, Rembrandt. 40rp, Canon, Massys. 50rp, Madonna, Memling. 60rp, French Painter, 1456, Fouquet. 80rp, Lute Player, Gentileschi. 90rp, Man, Strigel. 120rp, Man, Raphael.

1949, Mar. 15 Photo. *Perf. 11½*

227 A160 10rp dark green .25 *.35*
228 A160 20rp henna brown .70 *.80*
229 A160 30rp sepia 1.40 .90
230 A160 40rp blue 3.50 .90
231 A160 50rp violet 2.75 *6.75*
232 A160 60rp grnsh gray 6.25 6.25
233 A160 80rp brown orange 1.40 *4.25*
234 A160 90rp olive bister 6.25 5.75
235 A160 120rp claret 1.40 *5.25*
Nos. 227-235 (9) 23.90 31.20
Set, never hinged 47.50

Issued in sheets of 12.
See No. 238.

No. 198 Surcharged with New Value and Bars in Dark Brown

1949, Apr. 14

236 A135 5rp on 3rp dk brn & buff .30 *.45*
Never hinged .65

Map, Post Horn and Crown A161

1949, May 23

237 A161 40rp blue & indigo 2.00 4.75
Never hinged 3.75

75th anniversary of the UPU.
For surcharge see No. 246.

Portrait Type of 1949
Souvenir Sheet
Unwmk.

1949, Aug. 6 Photo. *Imperf.*

238 Sheet of 3 65.00 *110.00*
a. A160 10rp dull green 5.25 *11.00*
b. A160 20rp lilac rose 32.50 *65.00*
c. A160 40rp blue 5.25 *11.00*
Never hinged 110.00

5th Philatelic Exhibition.
Sheet size: 121½x69½mm. Sold for 3fr.

Scenic Type of 1944

1949, Dec. 1 *Perf. 11½*

239 A136 5rp dk brown & buff 12.00 1.00
Never hinged 26.00

Rossauer Castle, Vienna A163

Church at Bendern A164

Prince Johann Adam Andreas — A165

1949, Nov. 15 Engr. *Perf. 14½*

240 A163 20rp dark violet 1.00 2.00
241 A164 40rp blue 3.50 6.25
242 A165 150rp brown red 5.50 9.25
Nos. 240-242 (3) 10.00 17.50
Set, never hinged 20.00

250th anniv. of the purchase of the former dukedom of Schellenberg. Sheets of 20.
For surcharge see No. 265.

Roe Deer — A166

Black Grouse — A167

Badger — A168

1950, Mar. 7 **Photo.** ***Perf. 11½***

243 A166 20rp red brown 4.75 4.50
244 A167 30rp Prus green 4.75 6.50
245 A168 80rp dark brown 19.00 45.00
Nos. 243-245 (3) 28.50 56.00
Set, never hinged 62.50

Issued in sheets of 20.

No. 237 Surcharged with New Value and Bars Obliterating Commemorative Inscriptions

1950, Nov. 7

246 A161 1fr on 40rp bl & ind 14.00 *45.00*
Never hinged 25.00

Boy Cutting Bread — A169

Designs: 10rp, Laborer. 15rp, Cutting hay. 20rp, Harvesting corn. 25rp, Load of hay. 30rp, Wine grower. 40rp, Farmer and scythe. 50rp, Cattle raising. 60rp, Plowing. 80rp, Woman with potatoes. 90rp, Potato cultivation. 1fr, Tractor with potatoes.

Perf. 11½

1951, May 3 **Unwmk.** **Photo.**

247 A169 5rp claret .25 .25
248 A169 10rp green .25 .45
249 A169 15rp yellow brown 2.50 5.00
250 A169 20rp olive brown .50 .65
251 A169 25rp rose brown 2.50 5.00
252 A169 30rp grnsh gray 1.25 .55
253 A169 40rp deep blue 4.00 6.50
254 A169 50rp violet brown 3.75 3.25
255 A169 60rp brown 3.75 3.00
256 A169 80rp henna brown 4.00 6.75
257 A169 90rp olive green 7.50 6.75
258 A169 1fr indigo 30.00 6.75
Nos. 247-258 (12) 60.25 44.90
Set, never hinged 125.00

Types of 1944, Redrawn

Perf. 12½x12

1951, Nov. 20 **Engr.** **Wmk. 296**

259 A150 2fr dark blue 9.00 *37.50*
a. Perf. 14½ 450.00 160.00
260 A150 3fr dk red brown 80.00 110.00
a. Perf. 14½ 50.00 *210.00*
Set, never hinged 175.00
Set, perf. 14½, never hinged 900.00

Issued in sheets of 20.

Portrait, Savolodo — A170

Madonna, Botticelli — A171

Design: 40rp St. John, Del Sarto.

Perf. 11½

1952, May 27 **Unwmk.** **Photo.**

261 A170 20rp violet brown 19.00 2.75
262 A171 30rp brown olive 12.50 7.00
263 A170 40rp violet blue 6.25 5.75
Nos. 261-263 (3) 37.75 15.50
Set, never hinged 75.00

Issued in sheets of 12.

Vaduz Castle — A172

Wmk. 296

1952, Sept. 25 **Engr.** ***Perf. 14½***

264 A172 5fr deep green 92.50 150.00
Never hinged 160.00

Issued in sheets of 9.

No. 241 Surcharged with New Value and Wavy Lines in Red

1952, Sept. 25 **Unwmk.**

265 A164 1.20fr on 40rp blue 12.50 *50.00*
Never hinged 24.00

Portrait of a Young Man — A173

St. Nicholas by Zeitblom — A174

Designs: 30rp, St. Christopher by Cranach. 40rp, Leonhard, Duke of Hag, by Kulmbach.

Perf. 11½

1953, Feb. 5 **Unwmk.** **Photo.**

266 A173 10rp dk olive green .50 .90
267 A174 20rp olive brown 8.25 2.40
268 A174 30rp violet brown 16.00 7.75
269 A173 40rp slate blue 18.00 *45.00*
Nos. 266-269 (4) 42.75 *56.05*
Set, never hinged 80.00

Issued in sheets of 12.

Lord Baden-Powell A175

1953, Aug. 4 **Engr.** ***Perf. 13x13½***

270 A175 10rp deep green .70 .90
271 A175 20rp dark brown 6.75 2.25
272 A175 25rp red 5.75 18.00
273 A175 40rp deep blue 5.50 6.00
Nos. 270-273 (4) 18.70 27.15
Set, never hinged 35.00

Intl. Scout Conf. Sheets of 20.

Alemannic Disc, 600 A. D. — A176

Prehistoric Settlement of Borscht A177

Design: 1.20fr, Rössen jug.

1953, Nov. 26 ***Perf. 11½***

274 A176 10rp orange brown 4.50 *11.50*
275 A177 20rp deep gray green 4.75 *11.50*
276 A176 1.20fr dark blue gray 24.00 *32.50*
Nos. 274-276 (3) 33.25 *55.50*
Set, never hinged 65.00

Opening of National Museum, Vaduz.

Soccer Players — A178

Designs: 20rp, Player kicking ball. 25rp, Goalkeeper. 40rp, Two opposing players.

1954, May 18 **Photo.**

277 A178 10rp dull rose & brn .95 .90
278 A178 20rp olive green 3.75 1.40
279 A178 25rp orange brown 10.50 *30.00*
280 A178 40rp lilac gray 8.50 9.00
Nos. 277-280 (4) 23.70 *41.30*
Set, never hinged 42.50

See #289-292, 297-300, 308-311, 320-323.

Nos. B19-B21 Surcharged with New Value and Bars in Color of Stamp

1954, Sept. 28 **Unwmk.** ***Perf. 11½***

281 SP15 35rp on 10rp+10rp 2.00 2.25
282 SP16 60rp on 20rp+10rp 10.00 10.50
283 SP15 65rp on 40rp+10rp 3.00 7.25
Nos. 281-283 (3) 15.00 20.00
Set, never hinged 27.50

Madonna in Wood, 14th Century — A179

1954, Dec. 16 **Engr.**

284 A179 20rp henna brown 1.50 1.90
285 A179 40rp gray 8.50 17.50
286 A179 1fr dark brown 8.50 17.00
Nos. 284-286 (3) 18.50 36.40
Set, never hinged 37.50

Prince Franz Joseph II — A180

Princess Georgina — A181

1955, Apr. 5 ***Perf. 14½***

Cream Paper

287 A180 2fr dark brown 47.50 47.50
288 A181 3fr dark green 47.50 47.50
Set, never hinged 160.00

Issued in sheets of 9.

Sports Type of 1954

Designs: 10rp, Slalom. 20rp, Mountain climbing. 25rp, Skiing. 40rp, Resting on summit.

1955, June 14 **Photo.** ***Perf. 11½***

289 A178 10rp aqua & brn vio .45 .80
290 A178 20rp green & ol bis 3.25 .80
291 A178 25rp lt ultra & sep 9.75 16.00
292 A178 40rp olive & pink 9.75 6.00
Nos. 289-292 (4) 23.20 23.60
Set, never hinged 42.50

Prince Johann Adam — A183

Eagle, Crown and Oak Leaves — A184

Portraits: 20rp, Prince Philipp. 40rp, Prince Nikolaus. 60rp, Princess Nora.

1955, Dec. 14

Granite Paper

Cross in Red

293 A183 10rp dull violet .75 .70
294 A183 20rp slate green 3.00 1.60
295 A183 40rp olive brown 3.00 7.25
296 A183 60rp rose brown 3.25 4.00
Nos. 293-296 (4) 10.00 13.55
Set, never hinged 18.00

Liechtenstein Red Cross, 10th anniversary.

Sports Type of 1954

Designs: 10rp, Javelin thrower. 20rp, Hurdling. 40rp, Pole vaulting. 1fr, Sprinters.

Perf. 11½

1956, June 21 **Unwmk.** **Photo.**

Granite Paper

297 A178 10rp lt red brn & ol grn .45 .40
298 A178 20rp lt ol grn & pur 1.90 .45
299 A178 40rp blue & vio brn 2.75 2.75
300 A178 1fr org ver & ol brn 6.50 9.75
Nos. 297-300 (4) 11.60 13.35
Set, never hinged 22.50

1956, Aug. 21

Granite Paper

301 A184 10rp dk brown & gold 1.10 1.00
302 A184 120rp slate blk & gold 5.75 5.00
Set, never hinged 14.00

150th anniversary of independence.

Prince Franz Joseph II — A185

Prince Johann Adam — A186

1956, Aug. 21

303 A185 10rp dark green .95 .45
304 A185 15rp bright ultra 1.40 3.00
305 A185 25rp purple 1.40 3.00
306 A185 60rp dark brown 4.75 2.75
Nos. 303-306 (4) 8.50 9.20
Set, never hinged 17.50

50th birthday of Prince Franz Joseph II.

1956, Aug. 21

Granite Paper

307 A186 20rp olive green 1.25 .70
Never hinged 3.00

Issued to publicize the 6th Philatelic Exhibition, Vaduz, Aug. 25-Sept. 2. Sheets of 9.

Sports Type of 1954

Designs: 10rp, Somersault on bar. 15rp, Jumping over vaulting horse. 25rp, Exercise on rings. 1.50fr, Somersault on parallel bars.

1957, May 14 **Photo.** ***Perf. 11½***

308 A178 10rp pale rose & ol grn .95 .95
309 A178 15rp pale grn & dl pur 2.75 *7.00*
310 A178 25rp ol bis & Prus grn 3.75 *8.25*
311 A178 1.50fr lemon & sepia 11.00 *19.00*
Nos. 308-311 (4) 18.45 35.20
Set, never hinged 32.50

Pine A187

Lord Baden-Powell A188

Designs: 20rp, Wild roses. 1fr, Birches.

1957, Sept. 10 ***Perf. 11½***

Granite Paper

312 A187 10rp dark violet 1.90 2.25
313 A187 20rp brown carmine 1.90 .95
314 A187 1fr green 3.25 8.00
Nos. 312-314 (3) 7.05 11.20
Set, never hinged 16.00

See Nos. 326-328, 332-334, 353-355.

1957, Sept. 10 **Unwmk.**

Design: 10rp, Symbolical torchlight parade.

315 A188 10rp blue black .75 1.50
316 A188 20rp dark brown .75 1.50
a. Sheet, 6 each #315-316 12.00 21.00
Never hinged 21.00
Set, never hinged 3.00

Cent. of the birth of Lord Baden-Powell and the 60th anniv. of the Boy Scout movement.

Chapel of St. Mamertus — A189

40rp, Madonna and saints. 1.50fr, Pieta.

1957, Dec. 16 ***Perf. 11½***

317 A189 10rp dark brown .35 .35
318 A189 40rp dark blue 1.10 *5.50*
319 A189 1.50fr brown lake 6.50 9.50
Nos. 317-319 (3) 7.95 15.35
Set, never hinged 15.00

Issued in sheets of 20. Sheet inscribed: "Furstentum Liechtenstein" and "Weihnacht 1957" (Christmas 1957).

Sports Type of 1954

Designs: 15rp, Girl swimmer. 30rp, Fencers. 40rp, Tennis. 90rp, Bicyclists.

1958, Mar. 18 **Photo.**

Granite Paper

320 A178 15rp lt blue & pur .65 1.00
321 A178 30rp pale rose lil & ol gray 3.25 6.00
322 A178 40rp sal pink & sl bl 3.25 6.00
323 A178 90rp lt ol grn & vio brn 1.65 4.00
Nos. 320-323 (4) 8.80 17.00
Set, never hinged 12.50

Relief Map of Liechtenstein A190

1958, Mar. 18

324 A190 25rp bister, vio & red .35 .75
325 A190 40rp blue, vio & red .35 .75
Set, never hinged 1.50

World's Fair, Brussels, Apr. 17-Oct. 19.
Sheets of 25. For surcharges see Nos. B22-B23.

Tree-Bush Design of 1957

Designs: 20rp, Maples at Lawena. 50rp, Holly at Schellenberg. 90rp, Yew at Maurerberg.

1958, Aug. 12 ***Perf. 11½***

Granite Paper

326 A187 20rp chocolate 1.75 .75
327 A187 50rp olive green 7.00 4.50
328 A187 90rp violet blue 1.75 2.75
Nos. 326-328 (3) 10.50 8.00
Set, never hinged 19.00

Sts. Moritz and Agatha A191

"The Good Shepherd" A192

Christmas: 35rp, St. Peter. 80rp, Chapel of St. Peter, Mals-Balzers.

1958, Dec. 4 **Photo.** **Unwmk.**

Granite Paper

329 A191 20rp dk slate green 1.90 2.50
330 A191 35rp dk blue violet 1.90 2.50
331 A191 80rp dark brown 1.90 2.50
Nos. 329-331 (3) 5.70 7.50
Set, never hinged 9.50

Issued in sheets of 20.

Tree-Bush Type of 1957

Designs: 20rp, Larch in Lawena. 50rp, Holly on Alpila. 90rp, Linden in Schaan.

1959, Apr. 15 ***Perf. 11½***

332 A187 20rp dark violet 2.50 2.00
333 A187 50rp henna brown 2.50 2.00
334 A187 90rp dark green 2.50 2.00
Nos. 332-334 (3) 7.50 6.00
Set, never hinged 14.00

1959, Apr. 15 **Unwmk.**

335 A192 30rp rose violet & gold .50 .85
Never hinged .85

Issued in memory of Pope Pius XII.

Flags and Rhine Valley — A193

Man Carrying Hay — A194

Apple Harvest A195

Designs: 5rp, Church at Bendern and sheaves. 20rp, Rhine embankment. 30rp, Gutenberg Castle. 40rp, View from Schellenberg. 50rp, Vaduz Castle. 60rp, Naafkopf, Falknis Range. 75rp, Woman gathering sheaves. 90rp, Woman in vineyard. 1fr, Woman in kitchen. 1.30fr, Return from the field. 1.50fr, Family saying grace.

1959-64

Granite Paper

336 A193 5rp gray olive ('61) .20 .20
337 A193 10rp dull violet .20 .20
338 A193 20rp lilac rose .20 .20
339 A193 30rp dark red .20 .20
340 A193 40rp olive grn ('61) 1.10 .55
341 A193 50rp deep blue .30 .35
342 A193 60rp brt grnsh bl .45 .55
343 A194 75rp deep ocher ('60) 1.10 1.00
344 A194 80rp olive grn ('61) .90 .90
345 A194 90rp red lilac ('61) .90 .90
346 A194 1fr chestnut ('61) .90 .90
347 A195 1.20fr orange ver ('60) 1.40 1.10
348 A195 1.30fr brt green ('64) 1.10 .90
349 A195 1.50fr brt blue ('60) 1.40 1.40
Nos. 336-349 (14) 10.35 9.35
Set, never hinged 12.50

Belfry, Bendern Church — A196

Christmas: 60rp, Sculpture, bell, St. Theodul's church. 1fr, Sculpture, tower of St. Lucius' church.

1959, Dec. 2 **Unwmk.** ***Perf. 11½***

350 A196 5rp dk slate green .55 .25
351 A196 60rp olive 3.50 4.25
352 A196 1fr deep claret 2.75 2.50
Nos. 350-352 (3) 6.80 7.00
Set, never hinged 11.00

Issued in sheets of 20.

Tree-Bush Type of 1957

Designs: 20rp, Beech tree on Gafadura. 30rp, Juniper on Alpila. 50rp, Pine on Sass.

1960, Sept. 19

353 A187 20rp brown 4.50 6.00
354 A187 30rp deep plum 4.50 6.00
355 A187 50rp Prus green 15.00 6.00
Nos. 353-355 (3) 24.00 18.00
Set, never hinged 40.00

Europa Issue, 1960

Honeycomb A197

1960, Sept. 19 ***Perf. 14***

356 A197 50rp multicolored *45.00 45.00*
Never hinged *90.00*

Issued to promote the idea of a united Europe. Sheets of 20.

Princess Gina A198

Heinrich von Frauenberg A199

Portraits: 1.70fr, Prince Johann Adam Pius. 3fr, Prince Franz Joseph II.

1960-64 **Engr.** ***Perf. 14***

356A A198 1.70fr violet ('64) 1.00 1.50
b. Imperf., pair *1,750. 1,750.*
357 A198 2fr dark blue 2.25 2.00
a. Imperf., pair *1,750. 1,750.*
358 A198 3fr deep brown 2.25 2.00
Nos. 356A-358 (3) 5.50 5.50
Set, never hinged 7.00

Issued in sheets of 16.

1961-62 **Photo.** ***Perf. 11½***

Minnesingers: 20rp, King Konradin. 25rp, Ulrich von Liechtenstein. 30rp, Kraft von Toggenburg. 35rp, Ulrich von Gutenberg. 40rp, Heinrich von Veldig. 1fr, Konrad von Alstetten. 1.50fr, Walther von der Vogelweide. 2fr, Tannhäuser. (Designs from 14th century Manesse manuscript.)

359 A199 15rp multi .60 .75
360 A199 20rp multi ('62) .30 .30
361 A199 25rp multi 1.25 1.65
362 A199 30rp multi ('62) .40 .40
363 A199 35rp multi 1.50 2.00
364 A199 40rp multi ('62) .65 .65
365 A199 1fr multi 2.50 2.00
366 A199 1.50fr multi 9.25 15.00
367 A199 2fr multi ('62) 1.65 1.65
Nos. 359-367 (9) 18.10 24.40
Set, never hinged 22.50

Issued in sheets of 20. See #381-384, 471.

Catalogue values for unused stamps in this section, from this point to the end of the section, are for Never Hinged items.

Europa Issue, 1961

Cogwheels A200

1961, Oct. 3 **Unwmk.** ***Perf. 13½***

368 A200 50rp multicolored *.35* .25

Printed in sheets of 20.

Souvenir Sheet

Prince Johann II — A201

Portraits: 10rp, Francis I. 25rp, Franz Joseph II.

1962, Aug. 2 **Photo.** ***Perf. 11½***

369 Sheet of 3 7.00 5.00
a. A201 5rp gray green 1.40 1.25
b. A201 10rp deep rose 1.40 1.25
c. A201 25rp blue 1.40 1.25

50th anniv. of Liechtenstein's postage stamps and in connection with the Anniv. Stamp Exhib., Vaduz, Aug. 4-12. No. 369 sold for 3fr.

Hands A202

1962, Aug. 2

370 A202 50rp indigo & red *.45* .45

Europa. Issued in sheets of 20.

Malaria Eradication Emblem — A203

Pietà — A204

1962, Aug. 2 **Engr.**

371 A203 50rp turquoise blue .35 .35

WHO drive to eradicate malaria. Sheets of 20.

1962, Dec. 6 **Photo.**

Designs: 50rp, Angel with harp, fresco. 1.20fr, View of Mauren.

372 A204 30rp magenta .60 .60
373 A204 50rp deep orange .85 .85
374 A204 1.20fr deep blue 1.10 1.10
Nos. 372-374 (3) 2.55 2.55

Issued in sheets of 20.

Prince Franz Joseph II A205

1963, Apr. 3 **Engr.** ***Perf. 13½x14***

375 A205 5fr dull green 4.00 3.00

Accession of Prince Franz Joseph II, 25th anniv.
Sheets of 8. Exists imperf. Value $1,500.

Angel of the Annunciation A206

Greek Architectural Elements A207

Perf. 11½

1963, Aug. 26 Unwmk. Photo.

376 A206 20rp shown .30 .30
377 A206 80rp Three Kings .70 .70
378 A206 1fr Family .70 .70
Nos. 376-378 (3) 1.70 1.70

Centenary of the International Red Cross.

Europa Issue, 1963

1963, Aug. 26

379 A207 50rp multicolored *1.00 1.00*

Bread and Milk — A208

1963, Aug. 26

380 A208 50rp dk red pur & brn .40 .40

FAO "Freedom from Hunger" campaign.

Minnesinger Type of 1961-62

Minnesingers: 25rp, Heinrich von Sax. 30rp, Kristan von Hamle. 75rp, Werner von Teufen. 1.70fr, Hartmann von Aue.

Perf. 11½

1963, Dec. 5 Unwmk. Photo.

381 A199 25rp multicolored .30 .30
382 A199 30rp multicolored .30 .30
383 A199 75rp multicolored .75 .75
384 A199 1.70fr multicolored 1.25 1.25
Nos. 381-384 (4) 2.60 2.60

Issued in sheets of 20.

Olympic Rings, Flags of Austria and Japan A209

1964, Apr. 15 ***Perf. 11½***

385 A209 50rp Prus bl, red & blk .40 .40

Olympic Games 1964. Sheets of 20.

Arms of Counts of Werdenberg-Vaduz A210

Coats of Arms: 30rp, Barons of Brandis. 80rp, Counts of Sulz. 1.50fr, Counts of Hohenems.

1964, Sept. 1 Photo.

386 A210 20rp multicolored .20 .20
387 A210 30rp multicolored .20 .20
388 A210 80rp multicolored .45 .45
389 A210 1.50fr multicolored .70 .70
Nos. 386-389 (4) 1.55 1.55

See Nos. 396-399.

Europa Issue, 1964

Roman Castle, Schaan A211

1964, Sept. 1 ***Perf. 13x14***

390 A211 50rp multicolored *2.00 .80*

Masescha Chapel — A212

Peter Kaiser — A213

40rp, Mary Magdalene, altarpiece. 1.30fr, Madonna with Sts. Sebastian & Roch, altarpiece.

1964, Dec. 9 Photo. ***Perf. 11½***

391 A212 10rp violet black .20 .20
392 A212 40rp dark blue .40 .40
393 A212 1.30fr deep claret 1.00 1.00
Nos. 391-393 (3) 1.60 1.60

Issued in sheets of 20.

1964, Dec. 9 Engr.

394 A213 1fr dk grn, *buff* .55 .55

Kaiser (1793-1864), historian. Sheets of 20.

Madonna, Wood Sculpture, 18th Century — A214

Perf. 11½

1965, Apr. 22 Unwmk. Engr.

395 A214 10fr orange red 7.00 6.00

Issued in sheets of 4.

Arms Type of 1965

Lords of: 20rp, Schellenberg. 30rp, Gutenberg. 80rp, Frauenberg. 1fr, Ramschwag.

Perf. 11½

1965, Aug. 31 Unwmk. Photo.

396 A210 20rp multicolored .20 .20
397 A210 30rp multicolored .20 .20
398 A210 80rp multicolored .50 .50
399 A210 1fr multicolored .55 .55
Nos. 396-399 (4) 1.45 1.45

Alemannic Ornament A215

Europa: The design is from a belt buckle, about 600 A.D., found in a man's tomb near Eschen.

1965, Aug. 31

400 A215 50rp vio bl, gray & brn *.45 .35*

The Annunciation by Ferdinand Nigg — A216

Princess Gina and Prince Franz Josef Wenzel — A217

Paintings by Nigg: 30rp, The Three Kings. 1.20fr, Jesus in the Temple, horiz.

1965, Dec. 7 Photo. ***Perf. 11½***

401 A216 10rp yel grn & dk grn .20 .20
402 A216 30rp orange & red brn .25 .25
403 A216 1.20fr ultra & grnsh bl .50 .50
Nos. 401-403 (3) .95 .95

Ferdinand Nigg (1865-1949), painter.

1965, Dec. 7

404 A217 75rp gray, buff & gold .40 .40

Communication Symbols — A218

1965, Dec. 7

405 A218 25rp multicolored .20 .20

Centenary of the ITU.

Soil Conservation, Tree — A219

20rp, Clean air, bird. 30rp, Unpolluted water, fish. 1.50fr, Nature preservation, sun.

1966, Apr. 26 Photo. ***Perf. 11½***

406 A219 10rp brt yellow & grn .20 .20
407 A219 20rp blue & dk blue .20 .20
408 A219 30rp brt green & ultra .20 .20
409 A219 1.50fr yellow & red .60 .60
Nos. 406-409 (4) 1.20 1.20

Issued to publicize nature conservation.

Prince Franz Joseph II A220

Arms of Barons of Richenstein A221

1966, Apr. 26

410 A220 1fr gray, gold, buff & dk brn .50 .50

60th birthday of Prince Franz Joseph II.

1966, Sept. 6 Photo. ***Perf. 11½***

Coats of Arms: 30rp, Vaistli knights. 60rp, Lords of Trisun. 1.20fr, von Schiel.

Light Gray Background

411 A221 20rp multicolored .20 .20
412 A221 30rp multicolored .20 .20
413 A221 60rp multicolored .20 .20
414 A221 1.20fr multicolored .45 .45
Nos. 411-414 (4) 1.05 1.05

Common Design Types pictured following the introduction.

Europa Issue, 1966

Common Design Type

1966, Sept. 6 Photo. ***Perf. 14x13***

Size: 25x32mm

415 CD9 50rp ultra, dp org & lt grn *.40 .35*

Vaduz Parish Church — A222

St. Florin — A223

30rp, Madonna. 1.70fr, God the Father.

1966, Dec. 6 Photo. ***Perf. 11½***

416 A222 5rp orange red & cit .20 .20
417 A223 20rp lemon & magenta .20 .20
418 A223 30rp dull rose & dp bl .20 .20
419 A223 1.70fr gray & red brown .65 .65
Nos. 416-419 (4) 1.25 1.25

Restoration of the Vaduz Parish Church.

Europa Issue, 1967

Common Design Type

1967, Apr. 20 Photo. ***Perf. 11½***

420 CD10 50rp multicolored .45 .40

The Man from Malans and his White Horse — A225

Fairy Tales of Liechtenstein: 30rp, The Treasure of Gutenberg. 1.20fr, The Giant of Guflina slaying the Dragon.

1967, Apr. 20

421 A225 20rp multicolored .20 .20
422 A225 30rp multicolored .20 .20
423 A225 1.20fr green & multi .70 .65
Nos. 421-423 (3) 1.10 1.05

See Nos. 443-445, 458-460.

Souvenir Sheet

Prince Hans Adam and Countess Kinsky — A226

1967, June 26 Engr. ***Perf. 14x13½***

424 A226 Sheet of 2 2.00 2.00
a. 1.50fr slate blue (Prince) 1.00 1.00
b. 1.50fr red brown (Countess) 1.00 1.00

Wedding of Prince Hans Adam of Liechtenstein and Marie Aglae Countess Kinsky of Wichnitz and Tettau, July 30, 1967.

EFTA Emblem
A227

1967, Sept. 28 Photo. *Perf. 11½*

425 A227 50rp multicolored .45 .45

European Free Trade Association. See note after Norway No. 501.

A228

A229

Christian Symbols: 20rp, Alpha and Omega. 30rp, Trophaeum (The Victorious Cross). 70rp, Chrismon.

1967, Sept. 28

426 A228 20rp rose cl, blk, & gold .20 .20
427 A228 30rp multicolored .20 .20
428 A228 70rp dp ultra, blk & gold .55 .45
Nos. 426-428 (3) .95 .85

1967, Sept. 28 Engr. & Litho.

429 A229 1fr rose claret & pale grn .75 .55

Johann Baptist Büchel (1853-1927), priest, educator, historian and poet. Printed on fluorescent paper.

Peter and Paul, Patron Saints of Mauren — A230

Patron Saints: 5rp, St. Joseph, Planken. 10rp, St. Laurentius, Schaan. 30rp, St. Nicholas, Balzers. 40rp, St. Sebastian, Nendeln. 50rp, St. George, Schellenberg Chapel. 60rp, St. Martin, Eschen. 70rp, St. Fridolin, Ruggell. 80rp, St. Gallus, Triesen. 1fr, St. Theodul, Triesenberg. 1.20fr, St. Ann, Vaduz Castle. 1.50fr, St. Mary, Bendern-Gamprin. 2fr, St. Lucius, patron saint of the Principality.

1967-71 Photo. *Perf. 11½*

430 A230 5rp multi ('68) .20 .20
431 A230 10rp multi ('68) .20 .20
432 A230 20rp blue & multi .20 .20
433 A230 30rp dark red & multi .25 .20
433A A230 40rp multi ('71) .45 .35
434 A230 50rp multi ('68) .40 .30
435 A230 60rp multi ('68) .45 .35
436 A230 70rp multi .50 .40
437 A230 80rp multi ('68) .55 .50
438 A230 1fr multi ('68) .75 .55
439 A230 1.20fr violet bl & multi .80 .90
440 A230 1.50fr multi ('68) 1.10 .95
441 A230 2fr multi ('68) 1.25 1.25
Nos. 430-441 (13) 7.10 6.35

Issued: 20rp, 30rp, 70rp, 1.20fr, 12/7/67; 5rp, 1.50fr, 8/29/68; 40rp, 6/11/71; 2fr, 12/5/68; others 4/25/68.

Europa Issue, 1968
Common Design Type

1968, Apr. 25
Size: 32½x23mm

442 CD11 50rp crimson, gold & ultra .45 .40

Fairy Tale Type of 1967

30rp, The Treasure of St. Mamerten. 50rp, The Goblin from the Bergerwald. 80rp, The Three Sisters. (Denominations at right.)

1968, Aug. 29

443 A225 30rp Prus blue, yel & red .20 .20
444 A225 50rp green, yel & bl .35 .30
445 A225 80rp brt bl, yel & lt bl .55 .55
Nos. 443-445 (3) 1.10 1.05

Arms of Liechtenstein and Wilczek
A231

1968, Aug. 29

446 A231 75rp multicolored .65 .65

Silver wedding anniversary of Prince Franz Joseph II and Princess Gina.

Sir Rowland Hill — A232

Coat of Arms — A233

Portraits: 30rp, Count Philippe de Ferrari. 80rp, Carl Lindenberg. 1fr, Maurice Burrus. 1.20fr, Théodore Champion.

1968-69 Engr. *Perf. 14x13½*

447 A232 20rp green .20 .20
448 A232 30rp red brown .25 .20
449 A232 80rp dark brown .55 .45
450 A232 1fr black .70 .65
451 A232 1.20fr dark blue .90 .70
Nos. 447-451 (5) 2.60 2.20

Issued to honor "Pioneers of Philately."
Issued: 80rp, 1.20fr, 8/28/69; others, 12/5/68.
See Nos. 509-511.

1969, Apr. 24 Engr. *Perf. 14x13½*

452 A233 3.50fr dark brown 2.50 1.60

Sheets of 16.

Europa Issue, 1969
Common Design Type

1969, Apr. 24 Photo. *Perf. 14*
Size: 33x23mm

453 CD12 50rp brn red, yel & grn *.45 .45*

"Biology" (Man and DNA Molecule) A234

30rp, "Physics" (man and magnetic field). 50rp, "Astronomy" (man and planets). 80rp, "Art" (artist and Prince Franz Joseph II and Princess Gina).

1969, Aug. 28 Photo. *Perf. 11½*

454 A234 10rp grn, dk bl & dp cl .20 .20
455 A234 30rp brown & multi .25 .20
456 A234 50rp ultra & green .45 .30
457 A234 80rp brn, dk brn & yel .70 .50
Nos. 454-457 (4) 1.60 1.20

250th anniv. of the Duchy of Liechtenstein.

Fairy Tale Type of 1967

20rp, The Cheated Devil. 50rp, The Fiery Red Goat. 60rp, The Grafenberg Treasure (toad). (Denominations at right.)

1969, Dec. 4 Photo. *Perf. 11½*

458 A225 20rp multicolored .20 .20
459 A225 50rp yellow & multi .40 .35
460 A225 60rp red & multi .55 .45
Nos. 458-460 (3) 1.15 1.00

"T" and Arms of Austria-Hungary, Liechtenstein and Switzerland — A235

1969, Dec. 4 *Perf. 13½*

461 A235 30rp gold & multi .30 .25

Cent. of the Liechtenstein telegraph system.

Arms of St. Lucius Monastery, Chur — A236

Prince Wenzel — A237

Arms of Ecclesiastic Patrons: 50rp, Pfäfers Abbey (dove). 1.50fr, Chur Bishopric (stag).

1969, Dec. 4 *Perf. 11½*

462 A236 30rp multicolored .25 .20
463 A236 50rp multicolored .40 .35
464 A236 1.50fr multicolored 1.00 1.00
Nos. 462-464 (3) 1.65 1.55

See Nos. 475-477, 486-488.

1970, Apr. 30 Photo. *Perf. 11½*

465 A237 1fr sepia & multi .80 .80

25th anniv. of the Liechtenstein Red Cross.

Orange Lily — A238

Native Flowers: 30rp, Bumblebee orchid. 50rp, Glacier crowfoot. 1.20fr, Buck bean.

1970, Apr. 30

466 A238 20rp multicolored .20 .20
467 A238 30rp green & multi .25 .25
468 A238 50rp olive & multi .55 .55
469 A238 1.20fr multicolored 1.10 1.10
Nos. 466-469 (4) 2.10 2.10

Issued to publicize the European Conservation Year 1970. See Nos. 481-484, 500-503.

Europa Issue, 1970
Common Design Type

1970, Apr. 30 Litho. *Perf. 14*
Size: 31½x20½mm

470 CD13 50rp emerald, dk bl & yel *.45 .45*

Minnesinger Type of 1961-62
Souvenir Sheet

Minnesingers: 30rp, Wolfram von Eschenbach. 50rp, Reinmar der Fiedler. 80rp, Hartmann von Starkenberg. 1.20fr, Friedrich von Hausen.

1970, Aug. 27 Photo. *Perf. 11½*

471 Sheet of 4 2.25 2.25
a. A199 30rp multicolored .20 .20
b. A199 50rp multicolored .30 .30
c. A199 80rp multicolored .50 .50
d. A199 1.20fr multicolored .65 .65

Wolfram von Eschenbach (1170-1220), German minnesinger (poet). Sold for 3fr.

Prince Franz Joseph II
A239

Mother & Child, Sculpture by Rudolf Schädler
A240

Portrait: 2.50fr, Princess Gina.

1970-71 Engr. *Perf. 14x13½*

472 A239 2.50fr violet blue ('71) 1.90 1.10
473 A239 3fr black 2.00 1.25

Issued: 2.50fr, 6/11; 3fr, 12/3. Sheets of 16.

1970, Dec. 3 Photo. *Perf. 11½*

474 A240 30rp dark red & multi .30 .30

Christmas.

Ecclesiastic Arms Type of 1969

Arms of Ecclesiastic Patrons: 20rp, Abbey of St. John in Thur Valley (Lamb of God). 30rp, Ladies' Abbey, Schänis (crown). 75rp, Abbey of St. Gallen (bear rampant).

1970, Dec. 3

475 A236 20rp lt blue & multi .20 .20
476 A236 30rp gray, red & gold .25 .25
477 A236 75rp green, yel & brn .60 .60
Nos. 475-477 (3) 1.05 1.05

Bronze Boar, La Tène Period
A241

30rp, Peacock, Roman, 2nd cent. 75rp, Decorated copper bowl, 13th cent.

1971, Mar. 11 Photo. *Perf. 11½*

478 A241 25rp dp ultra & bluish blk .25 .25
479 A241 30rp dk brown & green .25 .25
480 A241 75rp multicolored .60 .60
Nos. 478-480 (3) 1.10 1.10

Opening of the National Museum, Vaduz.

Flower Type of 1970

Flowers: 10rp, Cyclamen. 20rp, Moonwort. 50rp, Superb pink. 1.50fr, Alpine columbine.

1971, Mar. 11

481 A238 10rp multicolored .20 .20
482 A238 20rp multicolored .20 .20
483 A238 50rp multicolored .45 .45
484 A238 1.50fr multicolored 1.25 1.10
Nos. 481-484 (4) 2.10 1.95

Europa Issue, 1971
Common Design Type

1971, June 11 Photo. *Perf. 13½*
Size: 31x21mm

485 CD14 50rp grnsh bl, yel & blk *.45 .45*

Ecclesiastic Arms Type of 1969

Arms of Ecclesiastic Patrons: 30rp, Knights of St. John, Feldkirch (Latin and moline crosses). 50rp, Weingarten Abbey (grapes). 1.20fr, Ottobeuren Abbey (eagle and cross).

1971, Sept. 2 Photo. *Perf. 11½*

486 A236 30rp bister & multi .25 .25
487 A236 50rp multicolored .35 .35
488 A236 1.20fr gray & multi .90 .90
Nos. 486-488 (3) 1.50 1.50

Princely Crown
A242

Design: 70rp, Page from constitution.

1971, Sept. 2

489 A242 70rp grn, gold, blk & cop .55 .55
490 A242 80rp dk bl, gold, red & plum .65 .65

50th anniversary of the constitution.

Madonna, by Andrea della Robbia — A243

Long-distance Skiing — A244

1971, Dec. 9

491 A243 30rp multicolored .30 .25

Christmas 1971.

1971, Dec. 9

Olympic Rings and: 40rp, Ice hockey. 65rp, Downhill skiing, women's. 1.50fr, Figure skating, women's.

492 A244 15rp lemon & dk brn .20 .20
493 A244 40rp multicolored .35 .30
494 A244 65rp multicolored .55 .55
495 A244 1.50fr multicolored 1.25 1.10
Nos. 492-495 (4) 2.35 2.15

11th Winter Olympic Games, Sapporo, Japan, Feb. 3-13, 1972.

1972, Mar. 16 Photo. *Perf. 11*

10rp, Gymnast. 20rp, High jump. 40rp, Running, women's. 60rp, Discus. All horiz.

496 A244 10rp claret, brn & gray .20 .20
497 A244 20rp olive, brn & yel .20 .20
498 A244 40rp red, brn & gray .30 .30
499 A244 60rp brn, dk brn & bl .65 .50
Nos. 496-499 (4) 1.35 1.20

20th Olympic Games, Munich, Aug. 26-Sept. 10.

Flower Type of 1970

Flowers: 20rp, Anemone. 30rp, Turk's cap. 60rp, Alpine centaury. 1.20fr, Reed mace.

1972, Mar. 16

500 A238 20rp dk blue & multi .20 .20
501 A238 30rp olive & multi .25 .20
502 A238 60rp multicolored .55 .55
503 A238 1.20fr multicolored 1.00 1.00
Nos. 500-503 (4) 2.00 1.95

Europa Issue, 1972

Common Design Type

1972, Mar. 16

504 CD15 40rp dk ol, bl grn & rose red *.45 .45*

Souvenir Sheet

Bendern and Vaduz Castle — A246

1972, June 8 Engr. *Perf. 13½*

505 A246 Sheet of 2 2.75 2.75
a. 1fr violet blue .90 .90
b. 2fr carmine 1.75 1.75

8th Liechtenstein Philatelic Exhibition, LIBA 1972, Vaduz, Aug. 18-27.

Faun, by Rudolf Schädler A247

Madonna with Angels, by Ferdinand Nigg A248

1972, Sept. 7 Photo. *Perf. 11½*

506 A247 20rp shown .20 .20
507 A247 30rp Dancer .20 .20
508 A247 1.10fr Owl .85 .80
Nos. 506-508 (3) 1.25 1.20

Sculptures made of roots and branches by Rudolf Schädler.

Portrait Type of 1968-69

Portraits: 30rp, Emilio Diena. 40rp, André de Cock. 1.30fr, Theodore E. Steinway.

1972, Sept. 7 Engr. *Perf. 14x13½*

509 A232 30rp Prus green .20 .20
510 A232 40rp dk violet brn .30 .25
511 A232 1.30fr violet blue 1.00 .90
Nos. 509-511 (3) 1.50 1.35

Pioneers of Philately.

1972, Dec. 7 Photo. *Perf. 11½*

512 A248 30rp black & multi .30 .25

Christmas 1972.

Silum — A249

Nautilus Cup — A250

Landscapes: 10rp, Lawena Springs. 15rp, Ruggell Marsh. 25rp, Steg, Kirchlispitz. 30rp, Fields, Schellenberg. 40rp, Rennhof, Mauren. 50rp, Tidrüfe Vaduz. 60rp, Eschner Riet. 70rp, Mittagspitz. 80rp, Three Sisters, Schaan Forest. 1fr, St. Peter's and Tower House, Mäls. 1.30fr, Road, Frommenhaus. 1.50fr, Ox Head Mountain. 1.80fr, Hehlawangspitz. 2fr, Saminaschlucht.

1972-73 Engr. & Litho. *Perf. 11½*

513 A249 5rp brown, yel & mag .20 .20
514 A249 10rp slate grn & cit .20 .20
515 A249 15rp red brn & citron .20 .20
516 A249 25rp dk vio & pale grn .25 .20
517 A249 30rp purple & buff .25 .20
518 A249 40rp vio & pale salmon .30 .25
519 A249 50rp vio bl & rose .40 .35
520 A249 60rp green & yellow .50 .45
521 A249 70rp dk & lt blue .60 .50
522 A249 80rp Prus grn & cit .65 .55
523 A249 1fr red brn & lt grn .85 .65
524 A249 1.30fr ultra & lt grn 1.10 1.00
525 A249 1.50fr brn & lt blue 1.25 1.00
526 A249 1.80fr brown & buff 1.50 1.25
527 A249 2fr sepia & pale grn 1.65 1.40
Nos. 513-527 (15) 9.90 8.40

Issued: 10rp, 15rp, 80rp, 1fr, 1.50fr, 12/7; 30rp, 1.30fr, 1.80fr, 3/8/73; 50rp, 60rp, 70rp, 6/7/73; 5rp, 25rp, 40rp, 2fr, 12/6/73.

Europa Issue, 1973

Common Design Type

1973, Mar. 8 Photo. *Perf. 11½*

Size: 33x23mm

528 CD16 30rp purple & multi *.25 .25*
529 CD16 40rp blue & multi *.35 .35*

1973, June 7 Photo. *Perf. 11½*

70rp, Ivory tankard. 1.10fr, Silver goblet.

530 A250 30rp gray & multi .20 .20
531 A250 70rp multicolored .50 .50
532 A250 1.10fr dk blue & multi .90 .90
Nos. 530-532 (3) 1.60 1.60

Drinking vessels from the Princely Treasury.

Arms of Liechtenstein and Municipalities A251

Engraved & Photogravure

1973, Sept. 6 *Perf. 14x13½*

533 A251 5fr black & multi 4.00 3.00

Coenonympha Oedippus A252

Designs: 15rp, Alpine newt. 25rp, European viper (adder). 40rp, Common curlew. 60rp, Edible frog. 70rp, Dappled butterfly. 80rp, Grass snake. 1.10fr, Three-toed woodpecker.

1973-74 Photo. *Perf. 11½*

534 A252 15rp multicolored .20 .20
535 A252 25rp multicolored .30 .25
536 A252 30rp orange & multi .25 .25
537 A252 40rp brown & multi .35 .35
538 A252 60rp multicolored .60 .60
539 A252 70rp multicolored .65 .60
540 A252 80rp multicolored .70 .70
541 A252 1.10fr multicolored 1.00 1.00
Nos. 534-541 (8) 4.05 3.95

Issue dates: 30rp, 40rp, 60rp, 80rp, Dec. 6. Others, June 6, 1974.

Virgin and Child, by Bartolomeo di Tommaso — A253

The Vociferant Horseman, by Andrea Riccio — A254

Engraved & Lithographed

1973, Dec. 6 *Perf. 13½*

542 A253 30rp gold & multi .40 .30

Christmas 1973.

1974, Mar. 21 Photo. *Perf. 11½*

Europa: 40rp, Kneeling Venus, by Antonio Susini.

543 A254 30rp tan & multi *.35 .30*
544 A254 40rp ultra & multi *.50 .45*

Chinese Vase, 19th Century — A255

Soccer A256

Chinese vases from Princely Treasury.

1974, Mar. 21

545 A255 30rp shown .30 .25
546 A255 50rp from 1740 .45 .40
547 A255 60rp from 1830 .55 .55
548 A255 1fr circa 1700 .95 .95
Nos. 545-548 (4) 2.25 2.15

1974, Mar. 21

549 A256 80rp lemon & multi .80 .75

World Soccer Championships, Munich June 13-July 7.

Post Horn and UPU Emblem A257

1974, June 6 *Perf. 13½*

550 A257 40rp gold, green & blk .35 .30
551 A257 60rp gold, red & blk .55 .40

Centenary of Universal Postal Union.

Bishop F. A. Marxer — A258

Photogravure and Engraved

1974, June 6 *Perf. 14x13½*

552 A258 1fr multicolored .85 .85

Bicentenary of the death of Bishop Franz Anton Marxer (1703-1775).

Prince Constantin A259

Prince Hans Adam — A260

Princess Gina and Prince Franz Joseph II — A261

80rp, Prince Maximilian. 1.20fr, Prince Alois.

1974-75 Photo. *Perf. 11½*

553 A259 70rp dk green & gold .70 .55
554 A259 80rp dp claret & gold .75 .65
555 A259 1.20fr bluish blk & gold 1.10 1.00

Engr.
Perf. 14x13½

556 A260 1.70fr slate green 1.40 1.25

Photogravure and Engraved
Perf. 13½x14

557 A261 10fr gold & choc 8.00 8.00
Nos. 553-557 (5) 11.95 11.45

No. 557 printed in sheets of 4.
Issued: 1.70fr, 12/5; 10fr, 9/5/74; others, 3/13/75.

St. Florian — A262

50rp, St. Wendelin. 60rp, Virgin Mary with Sts. Anna and Joachim. 70rp, Nativity.

1974, Dec. 5 Photo. *Perf. 12*

560 A262 30rp multicolored .30 .25
561 A262 50rp multicolored .40 .35
562 A262 60rp multicolored .50 .50
563 A262 70rp multicolored .65 .65
Nos. 560-563 (4) 1.85 1.75

Designs are from 19th century devotional glass paintings. Christmas 1974.

"Cold Sun," by Martin Frommelt A263

Europa: 60rp, "Village," by Louis Jaeger.

1975, Mar. 13 *Perf. 11½*

564 A263 30rp multicolored *.25 .25*
565 A263 60rp multicolored *.50 .45*

Red Cross Activities — A264

Imperial Crown — A266

Coronation Robe — A265

1975, June 5 Photo. *Perf. 11½*

566 A264 60rp dk blue & multi .55 .55

30th anniv. of the Liechtenstein Red Cross.

1975 Engr. & Photo. *Perf. 14*

567 A266 30rp Imperial cross .45 .40
568 A266 60rp Imperial sword .70 .70
569 A266 1fr Orb 1.40 1.25
570 A265 1.30fr shown 2.75 2.75
571 A266 2fr shown 3.50 2.75
Nos. 567-571 (5) 8.80 7.85

Treasures of the Holy Roman Empire from the Treasury of the Hofburg in Vienna, Austria.
Issue dates: 1.30fr, Sept. 4; others, June 5.
See Nos. 617-620.

St. Mamerten, Triesen A267

Designs: 50rp, Red House, Vaduz, 14th century. 70rp, Prebendary House, Eschen, 14th century. 1fr, Gutenberg Castle.

1975, Sept. 4 Photo. *Perf. 11½*

572 A267 40rp multicolored .40 .35
573 A267 50rp multicolored .45 .35
574 A267 70rp plum & multi .85 .85
575 A267 1fr dk blue & multi 1.10 1.10
Nos. 572-575 (4) 2.80 2.65

European Architectural Heritage Year 1975.

Speed Skating A268

Designs (Olympic Rings and): 25rp, Ice hockey. 70rp, Downhill skiing. 1.20fr, Slalom.

1975, Dec. 4 Photo. *Perf. 11½*

576 A268 20rp multicolored .20 .20
577 A268 25rp multicolored .25 .20
578 A268 70rp multicolored .60 .50
579 A268 1.20fr yellow & multi 1.10 .95
Nos. 576-579 (4) 2.15 1.85

12th Winter Olympic Games, Innsbruck, Austria, Feb. 4-15, 1976.

Daniel in the Lions' Den — A269

River Crayfish — A270

Designs: 60rp, Virgin and Child. 90rp, St. Peter. All designs are after Romanesque sculptured capitals in Chur Cathedral, c. 1208.

Photogravure and Engraved

1975, Dec. 4 *Perf. 14*

580 A269 30rp gold & purple .25 .25
581 A269 60rp gold & green .40 .40
582 A269 90rp gold & claret .75 .75
Nos. 580-582 (3) 1.40 1.40

Christmas and Holy Year 1975.

1976, Mar. 11 Photo. *Perf. 11½*

World Wildlife Fund: 40rp, European pond turtle. 70rp, Old-world otter. 80rp, Lapwing.

583 A270 25rp multicolored .75 .75
584 A270 40rp multicolored 1.10 1.10
585 A270 70rp multicolored 1.60 1.60
586 A270 80rp multicolored 2.75 2.75
Nos. 583-586 (4) 6.20 6.20

Mouflon — A271

Europa: 80rp, Pheasant family. Ceramics by Prince Hans von Liechtenstein.

1976, Mar. 11

587 A271 40rp multicolored *.40 .35*
588 A271 80rp violet & multi *.80 .75*

Roman Fibula, 3rd Century A272

1976, Mar. 11

589 A272 90rp vio bl, grn & gold 1.00 .80

Historical Association of Liechtenstein, 75th anniversary.

Souvenir Sheet

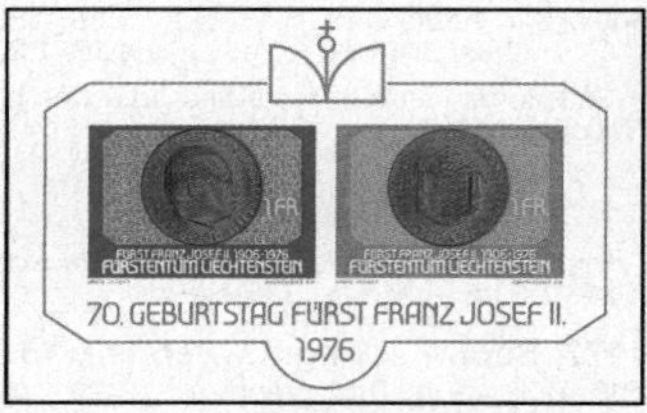

Franz Josef II 50fr-Memorial Coin — A273

1976, June 10 Photo. *Imperf.*

590 A273 Sheet of 2 1.75 1.75
a. 1fr blue & multi .85 .85
b. 1fr red & multi .85 .85

70th birthday of Prince Franz Joseph II of Liechtenstein.

Judo and Olympic Rings — A274

Rubens' Sons, Albrecht and Nikolas — A275

Designs (Olympic Rings and): 50rp, volleyball. 80rp, Relay race. 1.10fr, Long jump, women's.

1976, June 10 *Perf. 11½*

591 A274 35rp multicolored .25 .25
592 A274 50rp multicolored .45 .45
593 A274 80rp multicolored .65 .65
594 A274 1.10fr multicolored .90 .90
Nos. 591-594 (4) 2.25 2.25

21st Olympic Games, Montreal, Canada, July 17-Aug. 1.

1976, Sept. 9 Engr. *Perf. 13½x14*

Rubens Paintings: 50rp, Singing Angels. 1fr, The Daughters of Cecrops, horiz. (from Collection of Prince of Liechtenstein).

Size: 24x38mm

595 A275 50rp gold & multi 1.40 1.40
596 A275 70rp gold & multi 2.00 2.00

Size: 48x38mm

597 A275 1fr gold & multi 5.50 5.50
Nos. 595-597 (3) 8.90 8.90

400th anniversary of the birth of Peter Paul Rubens (1577-1640), Flemish painter. Sheets of 8 (2x4).

Zodiac Signs — A276

1976-78 Photo. *Perf. 11½*

598 A276 20rp Pisces .20 .20
599 A276 40rp Aries .35 .35
600 A276 40rp Cancer ('77) .40 .35
601 A276 40rp Scorpio ('78) .45 .45
602 A276 50rp Sagittarius ('78) .50 .45
603 A276 70rp Leo ('77) .65 .65
604 A276 80rp Taurus .75 .70
605 A276 80rp Virgo ('77) .75 .75
606 A276 80rp Capricorn ('78) .75 .70
607 A276 90rp Gemini 1.00 .75
608 A276 1.10fr Libra ('77) 1.10 1.10
609 A276 1.50fr Aquarius ('78) 1.25 1.25
Nos. 598-609 (12) 8.15 7.70

Flight into Egypt — A277

Ortlieb von Brandis, Sarcophagus A278

Monastic Wax Works: 20rp, Holy Infant of Prague, horiz. 80rp, Holy Family and Trinity. 1.50fr, Holy Family, horiz.

1976, Dec. 9 Photo. *Perf. 11½*

610 A277 20rp multicolored .20 .20
611 A277 50rp multicolored .40 .40
612 A277 80rp multicolored .55 .55
613 A277 1.50fr multicolored 1.25 1.25
Nos. 610-613 (4) 2.40 2.40

Christmas 1976.

Photogravure and Engraved

1976, Dec. 9 *Perf. 13½x14*

614 A278 1.10fr gold & dk brown .90 .70

Ortlieb von Brandis, Bishop of Chur (1458-1491).

Map of Liechtenstein, by J. J. Heber, 1721 — A279

Europa: 80rp, View of Vaduz, by Ferdinand Bachmann, 1815.

1977, Mar. 10 Photo. *Perf. 12½*

615 A279 40rp multicolored *.40 .40*
616 A279 80rp multicolored *.80 .80*

Treasure Type of 1975

40rp, Holy Lance and Particle of the Cross. 50rp, Imperial Evangel of St. Matthew. 80rp, St. Stephen's Purse. 90rp, Tabard of Imperial Herald.

Engraved and Photogravure

1977, June 8 *Perf. 14*

617 A266 40rp gold & multi .40 .30
618 A266 50rp gold & multi .50 .45
619 A266 80rp gold & multi .70 .65
620 A266 90rp gold & multi 1.00 .90
Nos. 617-620 (4) 2.60 2.30

Treasures of the Holy Roman Empire from the Treasury of the Hofburg in Vienna.

Emperor Constantius II Coin — A280

Coins: 70rp, Lindau bracteate, c. 1300. 80rp, Ortlieb von Brandis, 1458-1491.

1977, June 8 Photo. *Perf. 11½*

Granite Paper

621	A280	35rp gold & multi	.35	.30
622	A280	70rp silver & multi	.60	.55
623	A280	80rp silver & multi	.80	.65
		Nos. 621-623 (3)	1.75	1.50

Frauenthal Castle A281

Castles: 50rp, Gross Ullersdorf. 80rp, Liechtenstein Castle near Mödling, Austria. 90rp, Liechtenstein Palace, Vienna.

Engraved and Photogravure

1977, Sept. 8 *Perf. 13½x14*

624	A281	20rp slate grn & gold	.20	.20
625	A281	50rp magenta & gold	.50	.50
626	A281	80rp dk violet & gold	.80	.80
627	A281	90rp dk blue & gold	.90	.90
		Nos. 624-627 (4)	2.40	2.40

Children — A282

Traditional Costumes: 70rp, Two girls. 1fr, Woman in festival dress.

1977, Sept. 8 Photo. *Perf. 11½*

Granite Paper

628	A282	40rp multicolored	.50	.40
629	A282	70rp multicolored	.75	.70
630	A282	1fr multicolored	1.25	1.10
		Nos. 628-630 (3)	2.50	2.20

Princess Tatjana A283

1977, Dec. 7 Photo. *Perf. 11½*

631	A283	1.10fr brown & gold	.90	.85

Angel — A284

Liechtenstein Palace, Vienna A285

Sculptures by Erasmus Kern: 50rp, St. Rochus. 80rp, Virgin and Child. 1.50fr, God the Father.

1977, Dec. 7

632	A284	20rp multicolored	.20	.20
633	A284	50rp multicolored	.45	.45
634	A284	80rp multicolored	.75	.75
635	A284	1.50fr multicolored	1.50	1.50
		Nos. 632-635 (4)	2.90	2.90

Christmas 1977.

Photogravure and Engraved

1978, Mar. 2 *Perf. 14*

Europa: 80rp, Feldsberg Castle.

636	A285	40rp gold & slate blue	*.35*	*.30*
637	A285	80rp gold & claret	*.75*	*.70*

Farmhouse, Triesen — A286

Designs: 20rp, Houses, Upper Village, Triesen. 35rp, Barns, Balzers. 40rp, Monastery, Bendern. 50rp, Residential Tower, Balzers-Mäls. 70rp, Parish house. 80rp, Farmhouse, Schellenberg. 90rp, Parish house, Balzers. 1fr, Rheinberger House, Music School, Vaduz. 1.10fr, Street, Mitteldorf, Vaduz. 1.50fr, Town Hall, Triesenberg. 2fr, National Museum and Administrator's Residence, Vaduz.

1978 Photo. *Perf. 11½*

638	A286	10rp multicolored	.20	.20
639	A286	20rp multicolored	.20	.20
640	A286	35rp multicolored	.30	.30
641	A286	40rp multicolored	.30	.30
642	A286	50rp multicolored	.40	.40
643	A286	70rp multicolored	.55	.55
644	A286	80rp multicolored	.60	.60
645	A286	90rp multicolored	.70	.70
646	A286	1fr multicolored	.75	.75
647	A286	1.10fr multicolored	.90	.90
648	A286	1.50fr multicolored	1.10	1.10
649	A286	2fr multicolored	1.50	1.50
		Nos. 638-649 (12)	7.50	7.50

Vaduz Castle A287

Vaduz Castle: 50rp, Courtyard. 70rp, Staircase. 80rp, Triptych from High Altar, Castle Chapel.

Engraved and Photogravure

1978, June 1 *Perf. 13½x14*

650	A287	40rp gold & multi	.45	.45
651	A287	50rp gold & multi	.60	.60
652	A287	70rp gold & multi	.85	.85
653	A287	80rp gold & multi	1.10	1.10
		Nos. 650-653 (4)	3.00	3.00

40th anniversary of reign of Prince Franz Joseph II. Sheet of 8.

Prince Karl I, Coin, 1614 A288

Adoration of the Shepherds A289

Designs: 50rp, Prince Johann Adam, medal, 1694. 80rp, Prince Josef Wenzel, medal, 1773.

1978, Sept. 7 Photo. *Perf. 11½*

654	A288	40rp multicolored	.35	.35
655	A288	50rp multicolored	.50	.50
656	A288	80rp multicolored	.95	.95
		Nos. 654-656 (3)	1.80	1.80

1978, Dec. 7 Photo. *Perf. 11½*

Stained-glass Windows, Triesenberg: 50rp, Holy Family. 80rp, Adoration of the Kings.

657	A289	20rp multicolored	.20	.20
658	A289	50rp multicolored	.50	.50
659	A289	80rp multicolored	.80	.80
		Nos. 657-659 (3)	1.50	1.50

Christmas 1978.

Piebald, by Hamilton and Faistenberger A290

Golden Carriage of Prince Joseph Wenzel, by Martin von Meytens — A291

Design: 80rp, Black stallion, by Johann Georg von Hamilton.

Photo. & Engr.

1978, Dec. 7 *Perf. 13½x14*

660	A290	70rp multicolored	.60	.60
661	A290	80rp multicolored	.70	.70

Perf. 12

662	A291	1.10fr multicolored	.95	.95
		Nos. 660-662 (3)	2.25	2.25

Sheets of 8.

Mail Plane over Schaan A292

Europa: 80rp, Zeppelin over Vaduz Castle.

1979, Mar. 8 Photo. *Perf. 11½*

663	A292	40rp multicolored	*.50*	*.45*
664	A292	80rp multicolored	*.65*	*.60*

First airmail service, St. Gallen to Schaan, Aug. 31, 1930, and first Zeppelin flight to Liechtenstein, June 10, 1931.

Child Drinking — A293

90rp, Child eating. 1.10fr, Child reading.

1979, Mar. 8

665	A293	80rp silver & multi	.75	.70
666	A293	90rp silver & multi	.85	.85
667	A293	1.10fr silver & multi	.95	.95
		Nos. 665-667 (3)	2.55	2.50

International Year of the Child.

Ordered Wave Fields A294

Sun over Continents A296

Council of Europe A295

1979, June 7 Litho. *Perf. 11½*

668	A294	50rp multicolored	.35	.35

Photo.

669	A295	80rp multicolored	.75	.75
670	A296	100rp multicolored	.75	.75
		Nos. 668-670 (3)	1.85	1.85

Intl. Radio Consultative Committee (CCIR) of the Intl. Telecommunications Union, 50th anniv. (50rp); Entry into Council of Europe (80rp); aid to developing countries (100rp).

Heraldic Panel of Carl Ludwig von Sulz — A297

Heraldic Panels of: 70rp, Barbara von Sulz, née zu Staufen. 1.10fr, Ulrich von Ramschwag and Barbara von Hallwil.

Photogravure and Engraved

1979, June 1 *Perf. 13½*

671	A297	40rp multicolored	.30	.30
672	A297	70rp multicolored	.50	.50
673	A297	1.10fr multicolored	.95	.95
		Nos. 671-673 (3)	1.75	1.75

Sts. Lucius and Florin, Fresco in Waltensburg-Vuorz Church — A298

Photogravure and Engraved

1979, Sept. 6 *Perf. 13½*

674	A298	20fr multicolored	14.00	13.00

Patron saints of Liechtenstein. Printed in sheets of 4.

Annunciation, Embroidery — A299

Christmas (Ferdnand Nigg Embroideries): 50rp, Christmas. 80rp, Blessed Are the Peacemakers.

1979, Dec. 6 Engr. *Perf. 13½*

675 A299 20rp multicolored .20 .20
676 A299 50rp multicolored .40 .35
677 A299 80rp multicolored .60 .50
Nos. 675-677 (3) 1.20 1.05

Cross-Country Skiing A300

Olympic Rings and: 70rp, Oxhead Mountain. 1.50fr, Ski lift.

1979, Dec. 6 Photo. *Perf. 12*

678 A300 40rp multicolored .30 .25
679 A300 70rp multicolored .50 .45
680 A300 1.50fr multicolored 1.10 1.00
Nos. 678-680 (3) 1.90 1.70

13th Winter Olympic Games, Lake Placid, NY, Feb. 12-24, 1980.

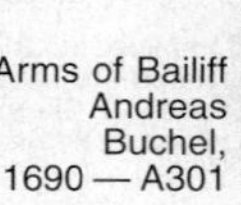

Arms of Bailiff Andreas Buchel, 1690 — A301

Designs: Various arms.

1980, Mar. 10 Photo. *Perf. 11½*
Granite Paper

681 A301 40rp shown .30 .25
682 A301 70rp Georg Marxer, 1745 .50 .45
683 A301 80rp Luzius Frick, 1503 .55 .50
684 A301 1.10fr Adam Oehri, 1634 .75 .70
Nos. 681-684 (4) 2.10 1.90

See Nos. 704-707, 729-732.

Princess Maria Leopoldine Esterhazy, by Antonio Canova — A302

Europa: 80rp, Maria Theresa, Duchess of Savoy, by Martin van Meytens.

1980, Mar. 10

685 A302 40rp multicolored *.40 .35*
686 A302 80rp multicolored *.60 .50*

Milking Pail — A303

Liechtenstein No. 94 — A304

Old Alpine Farm Tools: 50rp, Wooden heart, ceremonial cattle decoration. 80rp, Butter churn.

1980, Sept. 8

687 A303 20rp multicolored .20 .20
688 A303 50rp multicolored .40 .35
689 A303 80rp multicolored .65 .55
Nos. 687-689 (3) 1.25 1.10

1980, Sept 8

690 A304 80rp multicolored .65 .60

Postal Museum, 50th anniversary.

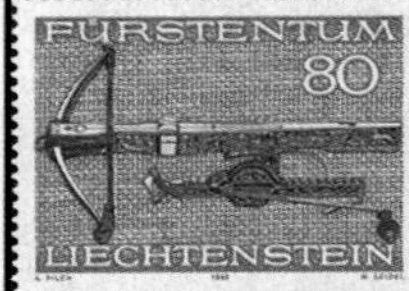

Crossbow with Spanning Device A305

1980, Sept. 8 Engr. *Perf. 13½x14*

691 A305 80rp shown .60 .55
692 A305 90rp Spear, knife .65 .60
693 A305 1.10fr Rifle, powderhorn .75 .65
Nos. 691-693 (3) 2.00 1.80

Triesenberg Family In Traditional Costumes A306

1980, Sept. 8 Photo. *Perf. 12*
Granite Paper

694 A306 40rp shown .30 .25
695 A306 70rp Folk dancers, Schellenberg .55 .50
696 A306 80rp Brass band, Mauren .65 .60
Nos. 694-696 (3) 1.50 1.35

Green Beeches, Matrula Forest — A307

Glad Tidings — A308

Photogravure and Engraved

1980, Dec. 9 *Perf. 14*

697 A307 40rp shown .35 .35
698 A307 50rp White firs, Valorsch Valley .45 .45
699 A307 80rp Beech forest, Schaan .65 .65
700 A307 1.50fr Forest, Oberplanken 1.25 1.25
Nos. 697-700 (4) 2.70 2.70

1980, Dec. 9 Photo. *Perf. 11½*
Granite Paper

701 A308 20rp shown .20 .20
702 A308 50rp Creche .45 .45
703 A308 80rp Epiphany .70 .70
Nos. 701-703 (3) 1.35 1.35

Christmas 1980.

Bailiff Arms Type of 1980

1981, Mar. 9 Photo. *Perf. 11½*
Granite Paper

704 A301 40rp Anton Meier, 1748 .30 .30
705 A301 70rp Kaspar Kindle, 1534 .50 .50
706 A301 80rp Hans Adam Negele, 1600 .60 .60
707 A301 1.10fr Peter Matt, 1693 .90 .90
Nos. 704-707 (4) 2.30 2.30

Fireworks at Vaduz Castle — A309

Europa: 80rp, National Day procession.

1981, Mar. 9 *Perf. 12½*
Granite Paper

708 A309 40rp multicolored *.35 .30*
709 A309 80rp multicolored *.65 .60*

Souvenir Sheet

Prince Alois, Princess Elisabeth and Prince Franz Joseph II — A310

1981, June 9 Photo. *Perf. 13*
Granite Paper

710 A310 Sheet of 3 2.50 2.50
a. 70rp shown .50 .50
b. 80rp Princes Alois and Franz Joseph II .55 .55
c. 150rp Prince Franz Joseph II 1.00 1.00

75th birthday of Prince Franz Joseph II.

Scout Emblems A311

Man in Wheelchair A312

1981, June 9

711 A311 20rp multicolored .20 .20

50th anniversary of Boy Scouts and Girl Guides.

1981, June 9

712 A312 40rp multicolored .25 .25

International Year of the Disabled.

St. Theodul, 1600th Birth Anniv. — A313

Mosses and Lichens A314

1981, June 9

713 A313 80rp multicolored .55 .55

Photogravure and Engraved

1981, Sept. 7 *Perf. 13½*

714 A314 40rp Xanthoria parietina .30 .30
715 A314 50rp Parmelia physodes .35 .35
716 A314 70rp Sphagnum palustre .50 .50
717 A314 80rp Amblystegium .60 .60
Nos. 714-717 (4) 1.75 1.75

Gutenberg Castle A315

1981, Sept. 7

718 A315 20rp shown .20 .20
719 A315 40rp Castle yard .30 .30
720 A315 50rp Parlor .35 .35
721 A315 1.10fr Great Hall .85 .85
Nos. 718-721 (4) 1.70 1.70

St. Charles Borromeo (1538-1584) A316

St. Nicholas — A317

Famous Visitors to Liechtenstein (Paintings): 70rp, Goethe (1749-1832), by Angelica Kauffmann. 80rp, Alexander Dumas (1824-1895). 1fr, Hermann Hesse (1877-1962), by Cuno Amiet.

Lithographed and Engraved

1981, Dec. 7 *Perf. 14*

722 A316 40rp multicolored .35 .35
723 A316 70rp multicolored .60 .60
724 A316 80rp multicolored .70 .70
725 A316 1fr multicolored .80 .80
Nos. 722-725 (4) 2.45 2.45

See Nos. 747-750.

1981, Dec. 7 Photo. *Perf. 11½*
Granite Paper

726 A317 20rp shown .20 .20
727 A317 50rp Adoration of the Kings .45 .45
728 A317 80rp Holy Family .70 .70
Nos. 726-728 (3) 1.35 1.35

Christmas 1981.

Bailiff Arms Type of 1980

1982, Mar. 8 Photo.
Granite Paper

729 A301 40rp Johann Kaiser, 1664 .35 .35
730 A301 70rp Joseph Anton Kaufmann, 1748 .55 .55
731 A301 80rp Christoph Walser, 1690 .70 .70
732 A301 1.10fr Stephan Banzer, 1658 1.00 1.00
Nos. 729-732 (4) 2.60 2.60

Europa 1982 — A318

1982, Mar. 8
Granite Paper

733 A318 40rp Peasants' Uprising, 1525 *.35 .30*
734 A318 80rp Imperial Direct Rule, 1396 *.65 .60*

Hereditary Prince Hans Adam — A319

1982, June 7 **Granite Paper**

735 A319 1fr shown .75 .75
736 A319 1fr Princess Marie Aglae .75 .75

LIBA '82, 10th Liechtenstein Philatelic Exhibition, Vaduz, July 31-Aug. 8.

1982 World Cup — A320

Designs: Sports arenas.

1982, June 7 **Granite Paper**

737 A320 15rp Triesenberg .20 .20
738 A320 25rp Mauren .20 .20
739 A320 1.80fr Balzers 1.25 1.25
Nos. 737-739 (3) 1.65 1.65

Farming A321

1982, Sept. 20 **Photo.** ***Perf. 11½***
Granite Paper

740 A321 30rp shown .25 .25
741 A321 50rp Horticulture .40 .40
742 A321 70rp Forestry .50 .50
743 A321 150rp Dairy farming 1.10 1.10
Nos. 740-743 (4) 2.25 2.25

View of Neu-Schellenberg, 1861, by Moriz Menzinger (1832-1914) — A322

Photogravure and Engraved

1982, Sept. 20 ***Perf. 13½x14***

744 A322 40rp shown .30 .30
745 A322 50rp Vaduz, 1860 .35 .35
746 A322 100rp Bendern, 1868 .85 .85
Nos. 744-746 (3) 1.50 1.50

Visitor Type of 1981

Paintings: 40rp, Emperor Maximilian I (1459-1519), by Bernhard Strigel. 70rp, Georg Jenatsch (1596-1639). 80rp, Angelika Kaufmann (1741-1807), self portrait. 1fr, Fidelis von Sigmaringen (1577-1622).

1982, Dec. 6 ***Perf. 14***

747 A316 40rp multicolored .30 .30
748 A316 70rp multicolored .50 .50
749 A316 80rp multicolored .60 .60
750 A316 1fr multicolored .75 .75
Nos. 747-750 (4) 2.15 2.15

Christmas 1982 — A323

Europa 1983 — A324

Designs: Chur Cathedral sculptures.

1982, Dec. 6 **Photo.** ***Perf. 11½***
Granite Paper

751 A323 20rp Angel playing lute .20 .20
752 A323 50rp Virgin and Child .40 .40
753 A323 80rp Angel playing organ .65 .65
Nos. 751-753 (3) 1.25 1.25

1983, Mar. 7 **Photo.**

Designs: 40rp, Notker Balbulus of St. Gall (840-912), Benedictine monk, poet and liturgical composer. 80rp, St. Hildegard of Bingen (1098-1179).

754 A324 40rp multicolored *.40 .30*
755 A324 80rp multicolored *.65 .55*

A325 A326

Shrovetide and Lenten customs: 40rp, Last Thursday before Lent. 70rp, Begging for eggs on Shrove Tuesday. 180fr, Bonfire, first Sunday in Lent.

Photogravure and Engraved

1983, Mar. 7 ***Perf. 14***

756 A325 40rp multicolored .35 .35
757 A325 70rp multicolored .60 .60
758 A325 1.80fr multicolored 1.50 1.50
Nos. 756-758 (3) 2.45 2.45

See Nos. 844-846, 915-917.

1983, June 6 **Photo.** ***Perf. 12***

Landscapes by Anton Ender (b. 1898).

759 A326 40rp Schaan, on the Zollstrasse .35 .35
760 A326 50rp Balzers with Gutenberg Castle .40 .40
761 A326 2fr Stag by the Reservoir 1.75 1.75
Nos. 759-761 (3) 2.50 2.50

Protection of Shores and Coasts — A327

1983, June 6

762 A327 20rp shown .25 .25
763 A327 40rp Manned flight bicentenary .35 .35
764 A327 50rp World communications year .45 .45
765 A327 80rp Humanitarian aid .70 .70
Nos. 762-765 (4) 1.75 1.75

Pope John Paul II A328

1983, Sept. 5 **Photo.**

766 A328 80rp multicolored 1.00 1.00

Princess Gina — A329

1983, Sept. 5 ***Perf. 12x11½***

767 A329 2.50fr shown 2.25 2.25
768 A329 3fr Prince Franz Joseph II 2.75 2.75

Christmas 1983 — A330

1983, Dec. 5 **Photo.** ***Perf. 12***
Granite Paper

769 A330 20rp Seeking shelter .20 .20
770 A330 50rp Child Jesus .40 .40
771 A330 80rp The Three Magi .70 .70
Nos. 769-771 (3) 1.30 1.30

1984 Winter Olympics, Sarajevo — A331

Snowflakes.

1983, Dec. 5 **Photo.** ***Perf. 11½x12***
Granite Paper

772 A331 40rp multicolored .40 .40
773 A331 80rp multicolored .80 .80
774 A331 1.80fr multicolored 1.65 1.65
Nos. 772-774 (3) 2.85 2.85

Famous Visitors to Liechtenstein A332

Paintings: 40rp, Count Alexander Wassiljewitsch Suworow-Rimnikski (1730-1800), Austro-Russian Army general. 70rp, Karl Rudolf Count von Buol-Schauenstein (1760-1833). 80rp, Carl Zuckmayer (1896-1977), playwright. 1fr, Curt Goetz (1888-1960), actor and playwright.

Photogravure and Engraved

1984, Mar. 12 ***Perf. 14***

775 A332 40rp multicolored .40 .40
776 A332 70rp multicolored .70 .70
777 A332 80rp multicolored .80 .80
778 A332 1fr multicolored 1.00 1.00
Nos. 775-778 (4) 2.90 2.90

A333

A334

1984, Mar. 12 **Photo.** ***Perf. 12***
Granite Paper

779 A333 50rp multicolored *.45 .40*
780 A333 80rp multicolored *.65 .60*

Europa (1959-1984).

Photogravure and Engraved

1984, June 12 ***Perf. 14***

The Destruction of Trisona Fairy Tale Illustrations: Root Carvings by Beni Gassner.

781 A334 35rp Warning messenger .35 .35
782 A334 50rp Buried town .50 .50
783 A334 80rp Spared family .80 .80
Nos. 781-783 (3) 1.65 1.65

1984 Summer Olympics A335

1984, June 12 **Photo.** ***Perf. 11½***
Granite Paper

784 A335 70rp Pole vault .65 .65
785 A335 80rp Discus .75 .75
786 A335 1fr Shot put 1.00 1.00
Nos. 784-786 (3) 2.40 2.40

Industries and Occupations — A336

1984, Sept. 10 **Photo.** ***Perf. 11½***

787 A336 5rp Banking & trading .20 .20
788 A336 10rp Construction, plumbing .20 .20
789 A336 20rp Production, factory worker .25 .25
790 A336 35rp Contracting, draftswoman .35 .35
791 A336 45rp Manufacturing, sales rep .45 .45
792 A336 50rp Catering .50 .50
793 A336 60rp Carpentry .60 .60
794 A336 70rp Public health .70 .70
795 A336 80rp Industrial research .80 .80
796 A336 1fr Masonry 1.00 1.00
797 A336 1.20fr Industrial management 1.25 1.25
798 A336 1.50fr Posta & communications 1.50 1.50
Nos. 787-798 (12) 7.80 7.80

Princess Marie Aglae — A337

Christmas 1984 — A338

Photogravure and Engraved

1984, Dec. 10 ***Perf. 14x13½***

799 A337 1.70fr shown 1.50 1.50
800 A337 2fr Prince Hans Adam 1.90 1.90

1984, Dec. 10 **Photo.** ***Perf. 11***

801 A338 35rp Annunciation .35 .35
802 A338 50rp Holy Family .55 .55
803 A338 80rp Three Kings .80 .75
Nos. 801-803 (3) 1.70 1.65

Europa 1985 A339

1985, Mar. 11 **Photo.** ***Perf. 11½***

804 A339 50rp Three Muses *.45 .40*
805 A339 80rp Pan and Muses *.70 .65*

Orders and Monestaries A340

Photogravure and Engraved

1985, Mar. 11 ***Perf. 13½x14***

806 A340 50rp St. Elisabeth .55 .55
807 A340 1fr Schellenberg Convent 1.10 1.10

808 A340 1.70fr Gutenberg Mission 1.90 1.90
Nos. 806-808 (3) 3.55 3.55

Cardinal Virtues — A341

1985, June 10 Photo. *Perf. 11½x12*
809 A341 35rp Justice .35 .35
810 A341 50rp Temperance .50 .50
811 A341 70rp Prudence .70 .70
812 A341 1fr Fortitude 1.00 1.00
Nos. 809-812 (4) 2.55 2.55

Princess Gina, President of Natl. Red Cross, 40th Anniv. A342

Portrait and: 20rp, Helping refugees, 1945. 50rp, Rescue service. 1.20fr, Child refugees, 1979.

1985, June 10 *Perf. 12x11½*
813 A342 20rp multicolored .20 .20
814 A342 50rp multicolored .55 .55
815 A342 1.20fr multicolored 1.40 1.40
Nos. 813-815 (3) 2.15 2.15

Souvenir Sheet

State Visit of Pope John Paul II — A343

Designs: 50rp, Papal coat of arms. 80rp, Chapel of St. Maria zum Trost, Dux, Schaan. 1.70fr, Our Lady of Liechtenstein, St. Mary the Comforter.

1985, Feb. 2 *Perf. 11½*
816 A343 Sheet of 3 4.25 4.25
a. 50rp multi 1.40 1.40
b. 80rp multi 1.40 1.40
c. 1.70fr multi 1.40 1.40

Paintings from the Princely Collections A344

Christmas 1985 — A345

50rp, Portrait of a Canon, by Quintin Massys (1466-1530). 1fr, Portrait of Clara Serena Rubens, by Peter Paul Rubens (1577-1640). 1.20fr, Portrait of the Duke of Urbino, by Raphael (1483-1520).

Photogravure and Engraved
1985, Sept. 2 *Perf. 14*
817 A344 50rp multicolored .50 .50
818 A344 1fr multicolored 1.10 1.10
819 A344 1.20fr multicolored 1.40 1.40
Nos. 817-819 (3) 3.00 3.00

1985, Dec. 9 Photo. *Perf. 11½x12*
820 A345 35rp Frankincense .35 .35
821 A345 50rp Gold .50 .50
822 A345 80rp Myrrh .85 .85
Nos. 820-822 (3) 1.70 1.70

Kirchplatz Theater, 15th Anniv. — A346

Photogravure and Engraved
1985, Dec. 9 *Perf. 14*
823 A346 50rp Tragedy .40 .40
824 A346 80rp Commedia dell'arte .55 .55
825 A346 1.50rp Opera buffa 1.75 1.75
Nos. 823-825 (3) 2.70 2.70

Weapons from the Prince's Armory A347

Designs: 35rp, Halberd, bodyguard of Prince Charles I. 50rp, German morion, 16th cent. 80rp, Halberd, bodyguard of Prince Carl Eusebius.

1985, Dec. 9 *Perf. 13½x14½*
826 A347 35rp multicolored .35 .35
827 A347 50rp multicolored .50 .50
828 A347 80rp multicolored .85 .85
Nos. 826-828 (3) 1.70 1.70

A348

A349

1986, Mar. 10 Photo. *Perf. 12*
829 A348 50rp Swallows *.45 .40*
830 A348 90rp Robin *.95 .90*

Europa 1986.

1986-89 Photo. *Perf. 11½x12*

Views of Vaduz Castle.

Granite Paper
832 A349 20rp Outer courtyard .20 .20
833 A349 25rp View from the south ('89) .35 .35
835 A349 50rp Castle, mountains .40 .40
838 A349 90rp Inner gate ('87) 1.10 1.10
840 A349 1.10fr Back view .90 .90
841 A349 1.40fr Inner courtyard ('87) 1.75 1.75
Nos. 832-841 (6) 4.70 4.70

This is an expanding set. Numbers will change if necessary.

Fasting Sacrifice — A350

A352

1986, Mar. 10 Photo. *Perf. 12*
843 A350 1.40fr multicolored 1.40 1.40

Type of 1983

Photogravure and Engraved
1986, June 9 *Perf. 13½*
844 A325 35rp Palm Sunday procession .40 .40
845 A325 50rp Wedding .60 .60
846 A325 70rp Rogation Day procession .80 .80
Nos. 844-846 (3) 1.80 1.80

1986, June 9 Photo. *Perf. 11½*

Karl Freiherr Haus von Hausen (1823-89), founder.

847 A352 50rp multicolored .55 .55

Natl. Savings Bank, Vaduz, 125th anniv.

A353

Hunting — A354

Photogravure and Engraved
1986, June 9 *Perf. 13½*
848 A353 3.50fr multicolored 4.50 4.50

Prince Franz Joseph II, 80th birthday.

1986, Sept. 9 *Perf. 13x13½*
849 A354 35rp Roebuck, Ruggeller Riet .40 .40
850 A354 50rp Chamois in winter, Rappenstein .60 .60
851 A354 1.70fr Rutting stag, Lawena 2.00 2.00
Nos. 849-851 (3) 3.00 3.00

Crops A355

1986, Sept. 9 Photo. *Perf. 12x11½*
852 A355 50rp White cabbage, beets .65 .65
853 A355 80rp Red cabbage 1.10 1.10
854 A355 90rp Potatoes, onions, garlic 1.25 1.25
Nos. 852-854 (3) 3.00 3.00

Christmas A356

Trees A357

Archangels.

1986, Dec. 9 *Perf. 11½*
855 A356 35rp Michael .45 .40
856 A356 50rp Gabriel .65 .65
857 A356 90rp Raphael 1.25 1.25
Nos. 855-857 (3) 2.35 2.30

1986, Dec. 9
858 A357 25rp Silver fir .30 .30
859 A357 90rp Spruce 1.10 1.10
860 A357 1.40fr Oak 1.65 1.65
Nos. 858-860 (3) 3.05 3.05

Europa 1987 — A358

Nicholas Among the Thorns — A359

Modern architecture: 50rp, Primary school, 1980, Gamprin. 90rp, Parish church, c. 1960, Schellenburg.

1987, Mar. 9 Photo. *Perf. 11½x12*
Granite Paper
861 A358 50rp multicolored *.60 .55*
862 A358 90rp multicolored *1.25 1.00*

1987, Mar. 9 *Perf. 11½*
Granite Paper
863 A359 1.10fr multicolored 1.50 1.50

Nicholas von der Flue (1417-1487), canonized in 1947.

Hereditary Prince Alois — A360

Fish — A361

Photo. & Engr.
1987, June 9 *Perf. 14*
864 A360 2fr multicolored 2.50 2.50

No. 864 printed in sheets of 8.

1987, June 9 Photo. *Perf. 11½*
865 A361 50rp Cottus gobio .60 .60
866 A361 90rp Salmo trutta fario 1.10 1.10
867 A361 1.10fr Thymallus thymallus 1.40 1.40
Nos. 865-867 (3) 3.10 3.10

A362

A363

Liechtenstein City Palace, Vienna.

1987, Sept. 7 Photo. *Perf. 11½*
Granite Paper

868 A362 35rp Arch .45 .45
869 A362 50rp Entrance .60 .60
870 A362 90rp Staircase 1.10 1.10
Nos. 868-870 (3) 2.15 2.15

1987, Sept. 7 *Perf. 11½*

871 A363 1.40fr House of Liechtenstein coat of arms 1.90 1.90

Purchase of County of Vaduz, 275th anniv.

Diet, 125th Anniv. A364

1987, Sept. 7 *Perf. 11½*

872 A364 1.70fr Constitution of 1862 2.25 2.25

Christmas — A365

The Evangelists, illuminated codices from the Golden Book, c. 1100, Abbey of Pfafers, purportedly made under the direction of monks from Reichenau Is.

Photo. & Engr.
1987, Dec. 7 *Perf. 14*

873 A365 35rp St. Matthew .30 .30
874 A365 50rp St. Mark .40 .40
875 A365 60rp St. Luke .50 .50
876 A365 90rp St. John .75 .75
Nos. 873-876 (4) 1.95 1.95

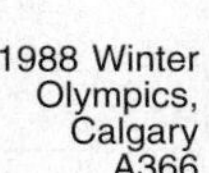

1988 Winter Olympics, Calgary A366

Humorous drawings by illustrator Paul Flora of Austria: 25rp, The Toil of the Cross-country Skier. 90rp, Courageous Pioneer of Skiing. 1.10fr, As Grandfather Used to Ride on a Bobsled.

1987, Dec. 7 *Perf. 14x13½*

877 A366 25rp multicolored .30 .30
878 A366 90rp multicolored 1.10 1.10
879 A366 1.10fr multicolored 1.40 1.40
Nos. 877-879 (3) 2.80 2.80

See Nos. 888-891.

Europa 1988 — A367

Modern communication & transportation.

1988, Mar. 7 Photo. *Perf. 11½x12*
Granite Paper

880 A367 50rp Satellite dish *.60 .55*
881 A367 90rp High-speed monorail *1.00 .90*

European Campaign to Protect Undeveloped and Developing Lands — A368

1988, Mar. 7 *Perf. 12*
Granite Paper

882 A368 80rp Forest preservation 1.00 1.00
883 A368 90rp Layout for village development 1.10 1.10
884 A368 1.70rp Traffic planning 2.00 2.00
Nos. 882-884 (3) 4.10 4.10

Balancing nature conservation with natl. development.

Souvenir Sheet

Succession to the Throne — A369

Portraits: a, Crown Prince Hans Adam. b, Prince Alois, successor to the crown prince. c, Prince Franz Josef II, ruler.

Photo. & Engr.
1988, June 6 *Perf. 14½x13½*

885 A369 Sheet of 3 4.00 4.00
  a. 50rp black, gold & bright blue .65 .65
  b. 50rp black, gold & sage green .65 .65
  c. 2fr black, gold & deep rose 2.50 2.50

North and South Campaign A370

1988, June 6 Photo. *Perf. 12x11½*
Granite Paper

886 A370 50rp Public radio .65 .65
887 A370 1.40fr Adult education 1.75 1.75

Cultural cooperation with Costa Rica. See Costa Rica Nos. 401-402.

Olympics Type of 1988

Humorous drawings by illustrator Paul Flora of Austria: 50rp, Cycling. 80rp, Gymnastics. 90rp, Running. 1.40fr, Equestrian.

Photo. & Engr.
1988, Sept. 5 *Perf. 14x13½*

888 A366 50rp multicolored .65 .65
889 A366 80rp multicolored 1.00 1.00
890 A366 90rp multicolored 1.10 1.10
891 A366 1.40fr multicolored 1.75 1.75
Nos. 888-891 (4) 4.50 4.50

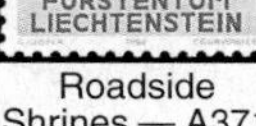

Roadside Shrines — A371

Christmas — A372

1988, Sept. 5 Photo. *Perf. 11½x12*
Granite Paper

892 A371 25rp Kaltweh Chapel, Balzers .35 .35
893 A371 35rp Oberdorf, Vaduz, c. 1870 .45 .45
894 A371 50rp Bangstrasse, Ruggell .65 .65
Nos. 892-894 (3) 1.45 1.45

1988, Dec. 5 Photo. *Perf. 11½x12*
Granite Paper

895 A372 35rp Joseph, Mary .40 .40
896 A372 50rp Christ child .55 .55
897 A372 90rp Adoration of the Magi 1.00 1.00
Nos. 895-897 (3) 1.95 1.95

The Letter — A373

Europa 1989 — A374

Details of Portrait of Marie-Therese de Lamballe (The Letter), by Anton Hickel (1745-1798): 90rp, Handkerchief and writing materials in open desk. 2fr, Entire painting.

Photo. & Engr.
1988, Dec. 5 *Perf. 13x13½*

898 A373 50rp shown .65 .65
899 A373 90rp multicolored 1.10 1.10
900 A373 2fr multicolored 2.50 2.50
Nos. 898-900 (3) 4.25 4.25

1989, Mar. 6 Photo. *Perf. 11½x12*

Traditional children's games.

Granite Paper

901 A374 50rp Cat and Mouse *.70 .65*
902 A374 90rp Stockleverband *1.40 1.25*

Josef Gabriel Rheinberger (1839-1901), Composer, and Score — A375

Photo. & Engr.
1989, Mar. 6 *Perf. 14x13½*

903 A375 2.90fr multicolored 3.50 3.50

Fish — A376

1989, June 5 Photo. *Perf. 12x11½*
Granite Paper

904 A376 50rp *Esox lucius* .65 .65
905 A376 1.10fr *Salmo trutta lacustris* 1.40 1.40
906 A376 1.40fr *Noemacheilus barbatulus* 1.75 1.75
Nos. 904-906 (3) 3.80 3.80

World Wildlife Fund — A377

1989, June 5 *Perf. 12*
Granite Paper

907 A377 25rp *Charadrius dubuis* .65 .65
908 A377 35rp *Hyla arborea* 1.10 1.10
909 A377 50rp *Libelloides coccajus* 1.50 1.50
910 A377 90rp *Putorius putorius* 2.75 2.75
Nos. 907-910 (4) 6.00 6.00

Mountains A378

1989, Sept. 4 Photo. *Perf. 11½*
Granite Paper

911 A378 50rp Falknis .60 .60
912 A378 75rp Plassteikopf .90 .90
913 A378 80rp Naafkopf .95 .95
914 A378 1.50fr Garselliturm 1.75 1.75
Nos. 911-914 (4) 4.20 4.20

See Nos. 930-939.

Folklore Type of 1983

Autumn activities: 35rp, Alpine herdsman and flock return from pasture. 50rp, Shucking corn. 80rp, Cattle market.

Photo. & Engr.
1989, Sept. 4 *Perf. 14*

915 A325 35rp multicolored .40 .40
916 A325 50rp multicolored .60 .60
917 A325 80rp multicolored .95 .95
Nos. 915-917 (3) 1.95 1.95

Christmas A379

Details of the triptych *Adoration of the Magi*, by Hugo van der Goes (50rp) and student (35rp, 90rp), late 15th cent.: 35rp, Melchior and Balthazar. 50rp, Caspar and holy family. 90rp, Donor with St. Stephen.

1989, Dec. 4 *Perf. 13½*
Size of 35rp and 90rp: 23x41mm

918 A379 35rp multicolored .45 .45
919 A379 50rp shown .60 .60
920 A379 90rp multicolored 1.10 1.10
Nos. 918-920 (3) 2.15 2.15

Minerals A380

1989, Dec. 4 *Perf. 13½x13*

921 A380 50rp Scepter quartz .55 .55
922 A380 1.10fr Pyrite ball 1.25 1.25
923 A380 1.50fr Calcite 1.65 1.65
Nos. 921-923 (3) 3.45 3.45

Europa 1990 — A381

Postage Stamps, 150th Anniv. — A382

Post offices.

1990, Mar. 5 Photo. *Perf. 11½x12*
Granite Paper

924 A381 50rp shown *.70 .60*
925 A381 90rp Modern p.o. *1.25 1.10*

1990, Mar. 5 ***Perf. 11½***

Granite Paper

926 A382 1.50fr Penny Black 1.65 1.65

1990 World Cup Soccer Championships, Italy — A383

1990, Mar. 5 Granite Paper ***Perf. 12***

927 A383 2fr multicolored 2.50 2.50

Princess Gina A384

1990, June 5 Litho. ***Perf. 11½***

Granite Paper

928 A384 2fr shown 2.75 2.75
929 A384 3fr Prince Franz Joseph II 4.00 4.00

1st anniv of death.

Mountains Type of 1989

1990-93

Granite Paper

930 A378 5rp Augstenberg .20 .20
931 A378 10rp Hahnenspiel .20 .20
933 A378 35rp Nospitz .50 .50
933A A378 40rp Ochsenkopf .50 .50
934 A378 45rp Drei Schwestern .60 .60
935 A378 60rp Kuhgrat .90 .90
936 A378 70rp Galinakopf .95 .95
938 A378 1fr Schonberg 1.25 1.25
939 A378 1.20fr Bleikaturm 1.75 1.75
940 A378 1.60fr Schwarzhorn 2.00 2.00
941 A378 2fr Scheienkopf 2.50 2.50
Nos. 930-941 (11) 11.35 11.35

Issued: 5, 45, 70rp, 1fr, 6/5; 10, 35, 60rp, 1.20fr, 9/3; 40rp, 6/3/91; 1.60fr, 3/2/92; 2fr, 3/1/93.

This is an expanding set. Numbers will change if neccessary.

A385

A386

Paintings by Benjamin Steck (1902-1981).

Photo. & Engr.

1990, June 5 ***Perf. 14***

942 A385 50rp shown .65 .65
943 A385 80rp Fruit, dish 1.00 1.00
944 A385 1.50fr Basket, fruit, stein 2.00 2.00
Nos. 942-944 (3) 3.65 3.65

Photo. & Engr.

1990, Sept. 3 ***Perf. 13x13½***

Game birds.

945 A386 25rp Pheasant .35 .35
946 A386 50rp Blackcock .65 .65
947 A386 2fr Mallard duck 2.75 2.75
Nos. 945-947 (3) 3.75 3.75

European Postal Communications, 500th Anniv. — A387

1990, Dec. 3 ***Perf. 13½x14***

948 A387 90rp multicolored 1.25 1.25

A388

A389

Christmas (Lenten Cloth of Bendern): 35rp, The Annunciation. 50rp, Birth of Christ. 90rp, Adoration of the Magi.

1990, Dec. 3 Photo. ***Perf. 12***

Granite Paper

949 A388 35rp multicolored .50 .50
950 A388 50rp multicolored .70 .70
951 A388 90rp multicolored 1.25 1.25
Nos. 949-951 (3) 2.45 2.45

Photo. & Engr.

1990, Dec. 3 ***Perf. 14***

Holiday Customs: 35rp, St. Nicholas Visiting Children on Feast of St. Nicholas. 50rp, Waking "sleepyheads" on New Year's Day. 1.50fr, Good wishes on New Year's Day.

952 A389 35rp multicolored .45 .45
953 A389 50rp multicolored .65 .65
954 A389 1.50fr multicolored 2.00 2.00
Nos. 952-954 (3) 3.10 3.10

Europa — A390

Designs: 50rp, Telecommunications satellite, Olympus I. 90rp, Weather satellite, Meteosat.

1991, Mar. 4 Photo. ***Perf. 11½***

Granite Paper

955 A390 50rp multicolored *.80* .60
956 A390 90rp multicolored *1.25* 1.10

St. Ignatius of Loyola (1491-1556), Founder of Jesuit Order — A391

90rp, Wolfgang Amadeus Mozart.

1991, Mar. 4 ***Perf. 11½***

Granite Paper

957 A391 80rp multicolored 1.10 1.10
958 A391 90rp multicolored 1.25 1.25

A392

A393

1991, Mar. 4 ***Perf. 11½***

Granite Paper

959 A392 2.50fr multicolored 3.50 3.50

UN membership, 1990.

1991, June 3 Photo. ***Perf. 11½***

Paintings: 50rp, Maloja, by Giovanni Giacometti. 80rp, Rheintal, by Ferdinand Gehr. 90rp, Bergell, by Augusto Giacometti. 1.10fr, Hoher Kasten, by Hedwig Scherrer.

Granite Paper

960 A393 50rp multicolored .60 .60
961 A393 80rp multicolored .95 .95
962 A393 90rp multicolored 1.00 1.00
963 A393 1.10fr multicolored 1.40 1.40
Nos. 960-963 (4) 3.95 3.95

Swiss Confederation, 700th anniv.

Military Uniforms A394

Designs: 50rp, Non-commissioned officer, private. 70rp, Uniform tunic, trunk. 1fr, Sharpshooters, officer and private.

Photo. & Engr.

1991, June 3 ***Perf. 13½x14***

964 A394 50rp multicolored .60 .60
965 A394 70rp multicolored .85 .85
966 A394 1fr multicolored .95 .95
Nos. 964-966 (3) 2.40 2.40

Last action of Liechtenstein's military, 1866 (70rp).

Princess Marie — A395

Photo. & Engr.

1991, Sept. 2 ***Perf. 13x13½***

967 A395 3fr shown 3.75 3.75
968 A395 3.40fr Prince Hans Adam II 4.25 4.25

LIBA 92, Natl. Philatelic Exhibition A396

1991, Sept. 2 Photo. ***Perf. 11½***

Granite Paper

969 A396 90rp multicolored 1.10 1.10

A397

A398

Christmas (Altar of St. Mamertus Chapel, Triesen): 50rp, Mary. 80rp, Madonna and Child. 90rp, Angel Gabriel.

Photo. & Engr.

1991, Dec. 2 ***Perf. 13½x14***

970 A397 50rp multicolored .70 .70
971 A397 80rp multicolored 1.10 1.10
972 A397 90rp multicolored 1.25 1.25
Nos. 970-972 (3) 3.05 3.05

1991, Dec. 2 Photo. ***Perf. 11½x12***

1992 Winter Olympics, Albertville: 70rp, Cross-country skiers, doping check. 80rp, Hockey players, good sportsmanship. 1.60rp, Downhill skier, safety precautions.

Granite Paper

973 A398 70rp multicolored .95 .95
974 A398 80rp multicolored 1.10 1.10
975 A398 1.60fr multicolored 2.25 2.25
Nos. 973-975 (3) 4.30 4.30

1992, Mar. 2 Photo. ***Perf. 11½***

1992 Summer Olympics, Barcelona: 50rp, Women's relay, drugs, broken medal. 70rp, Cycling, safety precautions. 2.50fr, Judo, good sportsmanship.

Granite Paper

976 A398 50rp multicolored .65 .65
977 A398 70rp multicolored .90 .90
978 A398 2.50fr multicolored 3.25 3.25
Nos. 976-978 (3) 4.80 4.80

Discovery of America, 500th Anniv. A400

1992, Mar. 2

Granite Paper

979 A400 80rp shown *1.10* *1.00*
980 A400 90rp New York skyline *1.40* *1.25*

Europa.

Postillion Blowing Horn — A401

Clown in Envelope A402

Designs: No. 982, Postillion delivering valentine. No. 984, Wedding violinist.

Photo. & Engr.

1992, June 1 ***Perf. 14x13½***

981 A401 50rp multicolored .65 .65
982 A401 50rp multicolored .65 .65

Photo.

Perf. 12½

Granite Paper

983 A402 50rp multicolored .65 .65
984 A402 50rp multicolored .65 .65
Nos. 981-984 (4) 2.60 2.60

Souvenir Sheet

Prince Hans-Adam and Princess Marie, 25th Wedding Anniv. — A403

Designs: a, 2fr, Coat of Arms of Liechtenstein-Kinsky Alliance. b, 2.50fr, Prince Hans-Adam and Princess Marie.

1992, June 1 ***Perf. 11½***

Granite Paper

985 A403 Sheet of 2, #a.-b. 5.75 5.75

Ferns — A404

40rp, Blechnum spicant. 50rp, Asplenium trichomanes. 70rp, Phyllitis scolopendrium. 2.50fr, Asplenium ruta-muraria.

Photo. & Engr.

1992, Sept. 7 *Perf. 14*

986 A404 40rp multicolored .65 .65
987 A404 50rp multicolored .75 .75
988 A404 70rp multicolored 1.10 1.10
989 A404 2.50fr multicolored 4.00 4.00
Nos. 986-989 (4) 6.50 6.50

Creation of Vaduz County, 650th Anniv. A405

1992, Sept. 7 *Perf. 13½x14*

990 A405 1.60fr multicolored 2.50 2.50

Christmas A406

Hereditary Prince Alois A407

Scenes in Triesen: 50rp, Chapel, St. Mamertus. 90rp, Nativity scene, St. Gallus Church. 1.60rp, St. Mary's Chapel.

1992, Dec. 7 **Photo.** *Perf. 11½*

Granite Paper

991 A406 50rp multicolored .60 .60
992 A406 90rp multicolored 1.10 1.10
993 A406 1.60fr multicolored 2.00 2.00
Nos. 991-993 (3) 3.70 3.70

Photo. & Engr.

1992, Dec. 7 *Perf. 13x13½*

994 A407 2.50fr multicolored 3.50 3.50

A408

A409

Europa (Contemporary paintings): 80rp, 910805, by Bruno Kaufmann. 1fr, The Little Blue, by Evi Kliemand.

1993, Mar. 1 **Photo.** *Perf. 11½x12*

Granite Paper

995 A408 80rp multicolored *.90* *.75*
996 A408 1fr multicolored *1.10* *.90*

1993, Mar. 1 *Perf. 11½*

Paintings by Hans Gantner (1853-1914): 50rp, Chalets in Steg and Naafkopf. 60rp, Sass Mountain with Hunting Lodge. 1.80fr, Red House in Vaduz.

Granite Paper

997 A409 50rp multicolored .65 .65
998 A409 60rp multicolored .75 .75
999 A409 1.80fr multicolored 2.25 2.25
Nos. 997-999 (3) 3.65 3.65

Tibetan Art — A410

60rp, Detail from Thangka painting, Tale of the Ferryman. 80rp, Religious dance mask. 1fr, Detail from Thangka painting, The Tale of the Fish.

1993, June 7 **Photo.** *Perf. 11½*

Granite Paper

1000 A410 60rp multicolored .75 .75
1001 A410 80rp multicolored 1.00 1.00
1002 A410 1fr multicolored 1.25 1.25
Nos. 1000-1002 (3) 3.00 3.00

A411

A412

1993, June 7 *Perf. 11½x12*

Granite Paper

1003 A411 1.80fr Tree of life 2.25 2.25

Church Missionary Work.

Photo. & Engr.

1993, June 7 *Perf. 14x13½*

Contemporary painting: Black Hatter, by Friedensreich Hundertwasser.

1004 A412 2.80fr multicolored 3.50 3.50

Souvenir Sheet

Marriage of Hereditary Prince Alois and Duchess Sophie of Bavaria, July 3 — A413

1993, June 7 **Photo.** *Perf. 11½*

Granite Paper

1005 A413 4fr multicolored 5.25 5.25

Wild Animals — A414

Meadow Plants — A415

Photo. & Engr.

1993, Sept. 6 *Perf. 13x13½*

1006 A414 60rp Badger .80 .80
1007 A414 80rp Marten 1.00 1.00
1008 A414 1fr Fox 1.25 1.25
Nos. 1006-1008 (3) 3.05 3.05

1993, Sept. 6

1009 A415 50rp Origanum vulgare .65 .65
1010 A415 60rp Salvia pratensis .80 .80
1011 A415 1fr Seseli annuum 1.25 1.25
1012 A415 2.50fr Prunella grandiflora 3.25 3.25
Nos. 1009-1012 (4) 5.95 5.95

See Nos. 1056-1059.

Christmas — A416

A417

Calligraphic Christmas texts by: 60rp, Rainer Maria Rilke. 80rp, Th. Friedrich. 1fr, Rudolph Alexander Schroder.

1993, Dec. 6 **Photo.** *Perf. 11½x12*

Granite Paper

1013 A416 60rp multicolored .80 .80
1014 A416 80rp multicolored 1.00 1.00
1015 A416 1fr multicolored 1.25 1.25
Nos. 1013-1015 (3) 3.05 3.05

1993, Dec. 6

Granite Paper

1016 A417 60rp Ski jump .80 .80
1017 A417 80rp Slalom skiing 1.00 1.00
1018 A417 2.40fr Bobsled 3.00 3.00
Nos. 1016-1018 (3) 4.80 4.80

1994 Winter Olympics, Lillehammer.

Anniversaries and Events A418

A419

A420

1994, Mar. 7 **Photo.** *Perf. 11½*

Granite Paper

1019 A418 60rp multicolored .75 .75
1020 A419 1.80fr multicolored 2.25 2.25
1021 A420 2.80fr multicolored 3.50 3.50
Nos. 1019-1021 (3) 6.50 6.50

Principality of Liechtenstein, 275th anniv. (#1019). Intl. Olympic Committee, cent. (#1020). 1994 World Cup Soccer Championships, US (#1021).

Alexander von Humboldt (1769-1859) A421

Europa: 80rp, Vultur gryphus. 1fr, Rhexia cardinalis.

Photo. & Engr.

1994, Mar. 7 *Perf. 13x13½*

1022 A421 80rp multicolored *1.10* *.90*
1023 A421 1fr multicolored *1.40* *1.00*

Mobile, by Jean Tinguely (1925-91) A422

Photo. & Engr.

1994, June 6 *Perf. 13½x14*

1024 A422 4fr multicolored 5.50 5.50

Letter Writing — A423

1994, June 6 **Photo.** *Perf. 12½*

Granite Paper

1025 A423 60rp Elephant .80 .80
1026 A423 60rp Cherub .80 .80
1027 A423 60rp Pig .80 .80
1028 A423 60rp Dog .80 .80
Nos. 1025-1028 (4) 3.20 3.20

Life Cycle of Grape Vine A424

Designs: No. 1029, Spring, vine beginning to flower. No. 1030, Summer, green grapes on vine. No. 1031, Autumn, ripe grapes ready for harvest. No. 1032, Winter, bare vine in snow.

1994, Sept 5 **Photo.** *Perf. 11½*

Granite Paper

1029 A424 60rp multicolored .80 .80
1030 A424 60rp multicolored .80 .80
1031 A424 60rp multicolored .80 .80
1032 A424 60rp multicolored .80 .80
a Block of 4, #1029-1032 3.25 3.25

No. 1032a is continuous design.

Minerals A425

Photo. & Engr.

1994, Sept. 5 *Perf. 13½x12½*

1033 A425 60rp Strontianite .80 .80
1034 A425 80rp Faden quartz 1.10 1.10
1035 A425 3.50fr Ferrous dolomite 4.75 4.75
Nos. 1033-1035 (3) 6.65 6.65

A426

A427

Christmas contemporary art, by Anne Frommelt: 60rp, The True Light. 80rp, Peace on Earth. 1fr, See the House of God.

1994, Dec. 5 Photo. *Perf. 11½*
Granite Paper

1036 A426 60rp multicolored .90 .90
1037 A426 80rp multicolored 1.25 1.25
1038 A426 1fr multicolored 1.50 1.50
Nos. 1036-1038 (3) 3.65 3.65

Photo. & Engr.
1994, Dec. 5 *Perf. 14*

The Four Elements, by Ernst Steiner.

1039 A427 60rp Earth .90 .90
1040 A427 80rp Water 1.25 1.25
1041 A427 1fr Fire 1.50 1.50
1042 A427 2.50fr Air 4.00 4.00
Nos. 1039-1042 (4) 7.65 7.65

Peace and Freedom A428

Europa: 80rp, 1fr, Excerpts from speeches of Prince Franz Josef II.

1995, Mar. 6 Photo. *Perf. 11½*
Granite Paper

1043 A428 80rp multicolored *1.10* .90
1044 A428 1fr multicolored *1.40 1.10*

A429

Anniversaries and Events
A430 A431

60rp, Princess Marie, Bosnian children.

1995, Mar. 6
Granite Paper

1045 A429 60rp multicolored .95 .95
1046 A430 1.80fr multicolored 3.00 3.00
1047 A431 3.50fr multicolored 5.50 5.50
Nos. 1045-1047 (3) 9.45 9.45

Liechtenstein Red Cross, 50th anniv. (#1045). UN, 50th anniv. (#1046). The Alps, European Landscape of the Year 1995-96 (#1047).

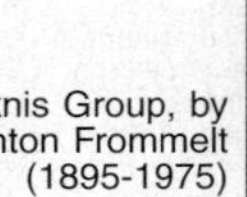

Falknis Group, by Anton Frommelt (1895-1975) A432

Paintings: 80rp, Three Oaks. 4.10fr, Rhine below Triesen.

1995, June 6 Photo. *Perf. 12*
Granite Paper

1048 A432 60rp multicolored 1.00 1.00
1049 A432 80rp multicolored 1.40 1.40
1050 A432 4.10fr multicolored 7.25 7.25
Nos. 1048-1050 (3) 9.65 9.65

Letter Writing — A433

No. 1051, Girl, boy building heart with bricks. No. 1052, Boy, girl bandaging sunflower. No. 1053, Girl, boy & rainbow. No. 1054, Boy in hot air balloon delivering letter to girl.

1995, June 6 *Perf. 12½*
Granite Paper

1051 A433 60rp multicolored 1.00 1.00
1052 A433 60rp multicolored 1.00 1.00
1053 A433 60rp multicolored 1.00 1.00
1054 A433 60rp multicolored 1.00 1.00
a. Vert. strip of 4, #1051-1054 + label 4.00 4.00

Liechtenstein-Switzerland Postal Relationship — A434

Litho. & Engr.
1995, Sept. 5 *Perf. 13½*

1055 A434 60rp multicolored 1.00 1.00

See Switzerland No. 960.

No. 1055 and Switzerland No. 960 are identical. This issue was valid for postage in both countries.

Plant Type of 1993
Photo. & Engr.
1995, Sept. 5 *Perf. 13x13½*

1056 A415 60rp Arnica montana 1.00 1.00
1057 A415 80rp Urtica dioica 1.40 1.40
1058 A415 1.80fr Valeriana officinalis 3.00 3.00
1059 A415 3.50fr Ranunculus ficaria 6.00 6.00
Nos. 1056-1059 (4) 11.40 11.40

A435

A436

Paintings by Lorenzo Monaco: 60rp, Angel kneeling, facing right. 80rp, Madonna and Child, two angels at her feet. 1fr, Angel kneeling, facing left.

Photo. & Engr.
1995, Dec. 4 *Perf. 14½x13½*

1060 A435 60rp multicolored 1.00 1.00
1061 A435 80rp multicolored 1.40 1.40
1062 A435 1fr multicolored 1.75 1.75
Nos. 1060-1062 (3) 4.15 4.15

Christmas.

1995, Dec. 4

Painting: 4fr, Lady with Lap Dog, by Paul Wunderlich.

1063 A436 4fr multicolored 6.75 6.75

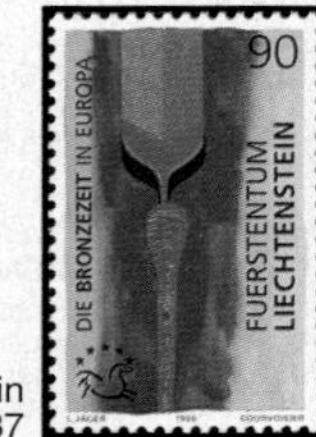

Bronze Age in Europe — A437

1996, Mar. 4 Photo. *Perf. 11½*
Granite Paper

1064 A437 90rp Crucible, pin 1.50 1.50

Countess Nora Kinsky (1888-1923), Nurse, Mother of Princess Gina — A438

Profile and: 90rp, Mar. 7, 1917 diary entry. 1.10fr, Feb. 28, 1917 diary entry.

1996, Mar. 4
Granite Paper

1065 A438 90rp multicolored *1.75* 1.00
1066 A438 1.10fr multicolored *2.25* 1.25

Paintings of Village Views, by Marianne Siegl, Based on Sketches by Otto Zeiller A439

10rp, Eschen. 20rp, Farmhouse, St. Joseph's Chapel, Planken. 80rp, Farmhouse, Ruggell. 1fr, Postal auxiliary office, Nendeln. 1.20fr, Buildings, Triesen. 1.30fr, Upper Village, Triesen. 1.70fr, St. Theresa's Church, Schaanwald. 2fr, Rural houses, barns, Gamprin. 4fr, Parish Church, center of village, Triesenberg. 5fr, Vaduz Castle.

1996-99 Photo. *Perf. 12*
Granite Paper

1068 A439 10rp multicolored .20 .20
1069 A439 20rp multicolored .40 .30
1070 A439 80rp multicolored 1.50 1.10
1071 A439 1fr multicolored 2.00 1.40
1072 A439 1.20fr multicolored 2.40 1.75
1073 A439 1.30fr multicolored 2.60 1.75
1074 A439 1.70fr multicolored 3.25 2.25
1075 A439 2fr multicolored 4.00 2.70
1076 A439 4fr multicolored 8.00 5.25
1077 A439 5fr multicolored 10.00 8.25
Nos. 1068-1077 (10) 34.35 24.95

Issued: 10rp, 5fr, 3/4/96; 20rp, 1.30fr, 1.70fr, 3/3/97; 2fr, 4fr, 6/2/98; 80rp, 1fr, 1.20fr, 3/1/99.

See Nos. 1167-1174.

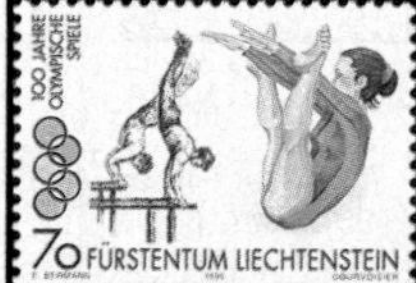

Modern Olympic Games, Cent. A440

1996, June 3 Photo. *Perf. 11½*
Granite Paper

1079 A440 70rp Gymnastics 1.40 1.10
1080 A440 90rp Hurdles 1.75 1.50
1081 A440 1.10fr Cycling 2.25 1.75
Nos. 1079-1081 (3) 5.40 4.35

Ferdinand Gehr, 100th Birthday A441

Various paintings of flowers.

1996, June 3
Granite Paper

1083 A441 70rp multicolored 1.40 1.10
1084 A441 90rp multicolored 1.75 1.50
1085 A441 1.10fr multicolored 2.25 1.75

Size: 33x23mm

1086 A441 1.80fr multicolored 3.50 3.00
Nos. 1083-1086 (4) 8.90 7.35

Austria, Millennium A442

Photo. & Engr.
1996, Sept. 2 *Perf. 13½*

1087 A442 90rp multicolored 1.75 1.75

New Constitution, 75th Anniv. — A443

Litho., Engr. & Embossed
1996, Sept. 2 *Perf. 14*

1088 A443 10fr Natl. arms 20.00 20.00

A444

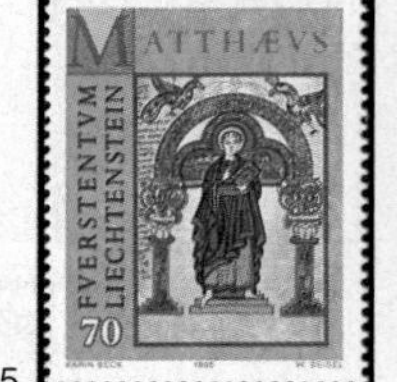

A445

Paintings by Russian Artist, Eugen Zotow (1881-1953): 70rp, "Country Estate in Poltava." 1.10fr, "Three Bathers in a Park in Berlin." 1.40fr, "View of Vaduz."

Photo. & Engr.
1996, Dec. 2 *Perf. 14*

1089 A444 70rp multicolored 1.40 1.10
1090 A444 1.10fr multicolored 2.25 1.75
1091 A444 1.40fr multicolored 2.75 2.25
Nos. 1089-1091 (3) 6.40 5.10

1996, Dec. 2

Christmas: Illuminated manuscripts, symbols of the Evangelists.

1092 A445 70rp Matthew 1.40 1.10
1093 A445 90rp Mark 1.75 1.40
1094 A445 1.10fr Luke 2.25 1.75
1095 A445 1.80fr John 3.50 3.00
Nos. 1092-1095 (4) 8.90 7.25

A446

A447

Photo. & Engr.

1997, Mar. 3 *Perf. 13½*

1096	A446 70rp multicolored		1.40	.95

Franz Schubert (1797-1828), composer.

1997, Mar. 3 **Photo.** *Perf. 12*

Europa, Liechtenstein Myths: 90rp, Wild Gnomes. 1.10fr, Foal of Planken.

Granite Paper

1097	A447	90rp multicolored	*1.75*	*1.00*
1098	A447	1.10fr multicolored	*2.25*	*1.10*

St. Lucius, Virgin Mary Holding Infant Jesus, St. Florin, by Gabriel Dreher A448

Photo. & Engr.

1997, June 2 *Perf. 13½x13*

1099	A448 20fr multicolored		40.00	40.00

A449

A450

Painting, "Jeune Fille en Fleur," by Enrico Baj.

1997, Aug. 22 **Photo.** *Perf. 11½*

Granite Paper

1100	A449 70rp multicolored		1.40	1.40

Photo. & Engr.

1997, Aug. 22 *Perf. 14*

Mushrooms: 70rp, Phaeolepiota aurea. 90rp, Helvella silvicola. 1.10fr, Aleuria aurantia.

1101	A450	70rp multicolored	1.40	.95
1102	A450	90rp multicolored	1.75	1.20
1103	A450	1.10fr multicolored	2.25	1.50
		Nos. 1101-1103 (3)	5.40	3.65

Railway in Liechtenstein, 125th Anniv. — A451

Train stations: 70rp, Schaanwald. 90rp, Nendeln. 1.80fr, Schaan-Vaduz.

1997, Aug. 22 **Photo.** *Perf. 11½*

Granite Paper

1104	A451	70rp multicolored	1.40	.95
1105	A451	90rp multicolored	1.75	1.20
1106	A451	1.80fr multicolored	3.50	2.40
		Nos. 1104-1106 (3)	6.65	4.55

Christmas Tree Decorations A452

Photo. & Engr.

1997, Dec. 1 *Perf. 14*

1107	A452	70rp shown	1.40	1.00
1108	A452	90rp Bell	1.75	1.25
1109	A452	1.10fr Oval with pointed ends	2.25	1.50
		Nos. 1107-1109 (3)	5.40	3.75

A453

A454

Skiing, 1998 Winter Olympic Games, Nagano.

1997, Dec. 1 *Perf. 12½*

Granite Paper

1110	A453	70rp Cross-country	1.40	1.00
1111	A453	90rp Slalom	1.75	1.25
1112	A453	1.80fr Downhill	3.50	2.50
		Nos. 1110-1112 (3)	6.65	4.75

1998, Mar. 2 **Photo.** *Perf. 12*

Contemporary Art, Paintings by Heinz Mack: No. 1113, Verano (Der Sommer). No. 1114, Hommage An Liechtenstein. No. 1115, Zwischen Tag Und Traum. No. 1116, Salute Chirico!.

Granite Paper

1113	A454	70rp multicolored	1.40	.95
1114	A454	70rp multicolored	1.40	.95
1115	A454	70rp multicolored	1.40	.95
1116	A454	70rp multicolored	1.40	.95
a.		Block or strip of 4, #1113-1116	6.00	3.80

Festivals A455

Europa: 90rp, National holiday. 1.10fr, Festival of the Musical Societies.

1998, Mar. 2

Granite Paper

1117	A455	90rp multicolored	*1.75*	*1.00*
1118	A455	1.10fr multicolored	*2.25*	*1.10*

Customs Treaty with Switzerland, 75th Anniv. — A456

1998, Mar. 2

Granite Paper

1119	A456 1.70fr multicolored		3.25	2.25

1998 World Cup Soccer Championships, France — A457

1998, Mar. 2

Granite Paper

1120	A457 1.80fr multicolored		3.50	2.50

Letter Writing — A458

Clown: No. 1121, With woman. No. 1122, Holding four leaf clovers. No. 1123, Tipping hat. No. 1124, Holding paper with heart.

Photo. & Engr.

1998, June 2 *Perf. 14*

1121	A458	70rp multicolored	1.40	.95
1122	A458	70rp multicolored	1.40	.95
1123	A458	70rp multicolored	1.40	.95
1124	A458	70rp multicolored	1.40	.95
a.		Strip of 4, #1121-1124	6.00	3.80

1848 Protest March A459

1998, Sept. 7 **Photo.** *Perf. 12*

Granite Paper

1125	A459 1.80fr multicolored		3.50	2.50

A460

A461

Traditional Crafts: 90rp, Cooper's tools, tub. 2.20fr, Wooden shoemaker's tools, clog. 3.50fr, Cartwright's tools, wheel.

1998, Sept. 7

Granite Paper

1126	A460	90rp multicolored	1.75	1.25
1127	A460	2.20fr multicolored	4.25	3.00
1128	A460	3.50fr multicolored	7.00	4.75
		Nos. 1126-1128 (3)	13.00	9.00

Photo. & Engr.

1998, Dec. 7 *Perf. 14*

Christmas (Nativity Scene in high relief): 70rp, Soldier, Virgin Mary. 90rp, Entire nativity scene. 1.10fr, Joseph, donkey.

1129	A461	70rp multicolored	1.40	1.00
1130	A461	90rp multicolored	1.75	1.25
1131	A461	1.10fr multicolored	2.25	1.60
		Nos. 1129-1131 (3)	5.40	3.85

No. 1130 is 34x26mm.

Preservation of Historic Sites — A462

Older buildings, Hinterschellengerg: 90rp, Guest house. 1.70fr, St. George's Chapel, vert. 1.80fr, Farmhouse.

1998, Dec. 7 **Photo.** *Perf. 11½*

Granite Paper

1132	A462	90rp multicolored	1.75	1.25
1133	A462	1.70fr multicolored	3.25	2.50
1134	A462	1.80fr multicolored	3.50	2.50
		Nos. 1132-1134 (3)	8.50	6.25

A463

A464

1998, Dec. 7

Granite Paper

1135	A463 2.80fr multicolored		5.50	4.00

Telephone in Liechtenstein, cent.

1999, Mar. 1 **Photo.** *Perf. 11½x12*

Europa (Conservation Areas): 90rp, Snake, Schwabbrünnen-Aescher marshland. 1.10fr, Bird, Ruggell marsh.

Granite Paper

1136	A464	90rp multicolored	*1.75*	*1.00*
1137	A464	1.10fr multicolored	*2.25*	*1.25*

Unterland, 300th Anniv. — A465

Continuous scene of villages: a, Schellenberg, buildings, fortress. b, Mauren, domed steeple on church. c, Eschen,, church, houses. d, Ruggell, road leading into village. e, Gamprin, gray-roofed buildings, church.

1999, Mar. 1 *Perf. 12*

Granite Paper

1138	A465	Sheet of 5 + label	9.00	6.25
a.-e.		90rp any single	1.75	1.25

Anniversaries A466

Stylized designs: No. 1139, Council of Europe 50th anniv. emblem. No. 1140, Bird holding letter. No. 1141, Hand holding heart.

1999, May 25 Photo. *Perf. 11½x12*
Granite Paper

1139	A466 70rp multicolored	1.40	.95
1140	A466 70rp multicolored	1.40	.95
1141	A466 70rp multicolored	1.40	.95
	Nos. 1139-1141 (3)	4.20	2.85

No. 1140, UPU, 125th anniv. No. 1141, Caritas Liechtenstein, 75th anniv.

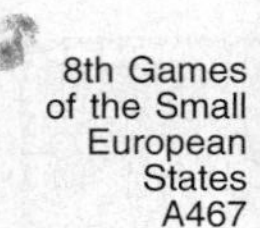

8th Games of the Small European States A467

1999, May 25
Granite Paper

1142	A467 70rp Judo	1.40	.95
1143	A467 70rp Swimming	1.40	.95
1144	A467 70rp Javelin	1.40	.95
1145	A467 90rp Volleyball	1.75	1.25
1146	A467 90rp Squash	1.75	1.25
1147	A467 90rp Tennis	1.75	1.25
1148	A467 90rp Table tennis	1.75	1.25
1149	A467 90rp Cycling	1.75	1.25
1150	A467 90rp Shooting	1.75	1.25
	Nos. 1142-1150 (9)	14.70	10.35

Johann Wolfgang von Goethe (1749-1832), Poet — A468

Quotations and scenes from Faust: 1.40fr, "Grey, dear friend, is all theory and green the golden tree of life." 1.70fr, "I'll take the wager!...Done! And again, and again!"

Photo. & Engr.
1999, Sept. 9 *Perf. 14*

1151	A468 1.40fr multicolored	2.75	1.90
1152	A468 1.70fr multicolored	3.25	2.25

Paintings by Eugen Verling (1891-1968) A469

Designs: 70rp, Herrengasse. 2fr, Old Vaduz with Castle. 4fr, House in Fürst-Franz-Josef-Strasse, Vaduz.

1999, Sept. 9

1153	A469 70rp multicolored	1.40	.95
1154	A469 2fr multicolored	4.00	2.75
1155	A469 4fr multicolored	8.00	5.50
	Nos. 1153-1155 (3)	13.40	9.20

A470

A471

Walser house identification marks.

1999, Dec. 6 Photo. *Perf. 11¾*
Granite Paper

1156	A470 70rp Door mark	1.40	.90
1157	A470 90rp Picture mark	1.75	1.10
1158	A470 1.80fr Axe mark	3.50	2.40
	Nos. 1156-1158 (3)	6.65	4.40

Photo. & Engr.
1999, Dec. 6 *Perf. 13½*

1159	A471 3.60fr multicolored	4.75	4.75

Johann Gutenberg, inventor of letterpress printing.

Christmas Paintings by Joseph Walser A472

1999, Dec. 6 *Perf. 13½x14¼*

1160	A472 70rp The Annunciation	1.40	.90
1161	A472 90rp Nativity	1.75	1.10
1162	A472 1.10fr Presentation of Jesus	2.25	1.40
	Nos. 1160-1162 (3)	5.40	3.40

Souvenir Sheet

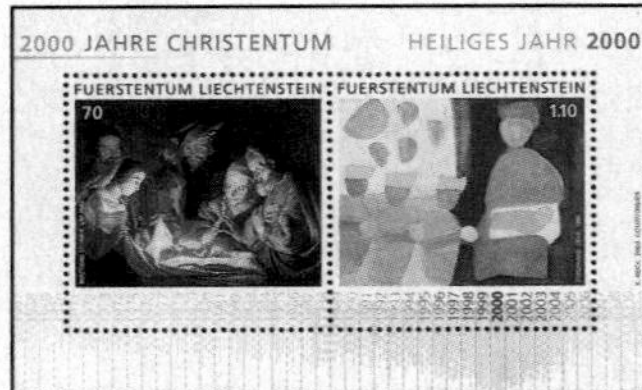

Millennium — A473

Designs: 70rp, The Adoration of the Shepherds, by Matthias Stomer. 1.10fr, The Magi, by Ferdinand Gehr.

2000, Jan. 1 Photo. *Perf. 12*
Granite Paper

1163	Sheet of 2	4.00	2.25
a.	A473 70rp multi	1.40	.85
b.	A473 1.10fr multi	2.25	1.40

Christianity, 2000th anniv.

Creation of Liechtenstein Post, Ltd. — A474

2000, Jan. 1 *Perf. 11¾*
Granite Paper

1164	A474 90rp multi	1.75	1.10

Village Views Type of 1996

Designs: 50rp, Church and vicarage, Ruggell. 60rp, Chapel of St. Peter, Balzers. 70rp, Parish church, Schellenberg. 1.10fr, Holy Cross Chapel, Eschen. 1.40fr, Farmhouse, parish church, Mauren. 1.80fr, Chapel of Peace, Malbun. 1.90fr, Tower of Church of St. Lawrence, Schaan. 2.20fr, Höfle District, Balzers. 4.50fr, Church mound, Bendern.

2000-01 Photo. *Perf. 11¾*
Granite Paper

1167	A439 50rp multi	1.00	.60
1168	A439 60rp multi	1.25	.75
1169	A439 70rp multi	1.40	.85
1171	A439 1.10fr multi	2.25	1.40
1172	A439 1.40fr multi	2.75	1.75
1173	A439 1.80fr multi	3.50	2.25
1174	A439 1.90fr multi	3.75	2.25
1175	A439 2.20fr multi	4.50	2.60
1175A	A439 4.50fr multi	9.00	5.50
	Nos. 1167-1175A (9)	29.40	17.95

Issued: 70rp, 1.80fr, 2.20fr, 4.50fr, 6/5/01.

This in an expanding set. Numbers may change.

"Gods Once Walked" Exhibition at Vaduz Museum of Art — A475

Designs: 70rp, Mars and Rhea Silvia, by Peter Paul Rubens. 1.80fr, Cupid With Soap Bubble, by Rembrandt.

Photo. & Engr.
2000, Mar. 6 *Perf. 13½x12¾*

1176	A475 70rp multi	1.40	.85
1177	A475 1.80fr multi	3.50	2.25

Europa, 2000
Common Design Type
2000, May 9 Photo. *Perf. 11½x11¾*
Granite Paper

1178	CD17 1.10fr multi	*2.25*	*1.75*

Expo 2000, Hanover — A476

Art by Friedensreich Hundertwasser: 70rp, Fragrance of Humus. 90rp, Do Not Wait Houses — Move. 1.10fr, The Car: A Drive Towards Nature and Creation.

Photo. & Engr.
2000, May 9 *Perf. 14¼x13½*

1179	A476 70rp multi	1.40	.80
1180	A476 90rp multi	1.75	1.00
1181	A476 1.10fr multi	2.25	1.25
	Nos. 1179-1181 (3)	5.40	3.05

Images of Peace A477

Art by mouth and foot painters: 1.40fr, Dove of Peace, by Antonio Martini. 1.70fr, Universal Peace, by Alberto Alvarez. 2.20fr, Rainbow, by Eiichi Minami.

2000, May 9 Photo. *Perf. 11¾x11½*

1182	A477 1.40fr multi	2.75	1.60
1183	A477 1.70fr multi	3.25	1.90
1184	A477 2.20fr multi	4.50	2.50
	Nos. 1182-1184 (3)	10.50	6.00

2000 Summer Olympics, Sydney A478

Designs: 80rp, Koalas on rings. 1fr, High jump by kangaroo joey. 1.30fr, Emus racing. 1.80fr, Platypuses swimming.

2000, Sept. 4 Photo. *Perf. 11¾*
Granite Paper

1185	A478 80rp multi	1.60	.95
1186	A478 1fr multi	2.00	1.10
1187	A478 1.30fr multi	2.50	1.50
1188	A478 1.80fr multi	3.50	2.10
	Nos. 1185-1188 (4)	9.60	5.65

Organization for Security and Co-operation In Europe, 25th Anniv. A479

2000, Sept. 4 Granite Paper

1189	A479 1.30fr multi	2.50	1.50

Issued in sheets of 20 stamps and 5 labels.

Opening Of Liechtenstein Art Museum — A480

Designs: 80rp, The Dreaming Bee, by Joan Miró. 1.20fr, Cube by Sol LeWitt. 2fr, A Bouquet of Flowers, by Roelant Savery.

2000, Sept. 4 Photo. *Perf. 11¾*
Granite Paper (#1190-1191)

1190	A480 80rp multi	1.60	.95
1191	A480 1.20fr multi	2.40	1.40

Size: 31x46mm
Photo. & Engr.
Perf. 13¾

1192	A480 2fr multi	4.00	2.40
	Nos. 1190-1192 (3)	8.00	4.75

Mushrooms A481

90rp, Mycena adonis. 1.10fr, Chalciporus amarellus. 2fr, Hygrocybe caylptriformis.

Photo. & Engr.
2000, Dec. 4 *Perf. 14¼*

1193-1195	A481 Set of 3	8.00	4.50

Christmas A482

Various creches: 80rp, 1.30fr, 1.80fr.

2000, Dec. 4 *Perf. 13¾x14*

1196-1198	A482 Set of 3	7.75	4.50

Europa — A483

2001, Mar. 5 Photo. *Perf. 11½x11¾*
Granite Paper

1199	A483 1.30fr multi	*2.50*	*2.25*

Liechtenstein's Presidency of Council of Europe — A484

2001, Mar. 5 *Perf. 11¾*
Granite Paper

1200	A484 1.80fr multi	3.50	2.10

Scratch-off Greetings A485

Postman in: No. 1201, 70rp, Red uniform (hidden flower bouquet). No. 1202, 70rp, Blue uniform (hidden envelope).

2001, Mar. 5 Granite Paper

1201-1202	A485 Set of 2 unscratched	3.00	1.75
	Set, scratched		1.75

Easter Eggs of the Russian Czars — A486

Designs: 1.20fr, Silver egg. 1.80fr, Cloisonné egg. 2fr, Porcelain egg.

Photo. & Engr.

2001, Mar. 5 ***Perf. 13¾***
1203-1205 A486 Set of 3 10.00 6.00

Liechtenstein Historical Association, Cent. — A487

Designs: No. 1206, 70rp, Mars of Gutenberg. No. 1207, Carolignian cruciform fibula.

2001, June 5 Photo. ***Perf. 11¾***
Granite Paper
1206-1207 A487 Set of 2 2.75 1.75

Josef Gabriel Rheinberger (1839-1901), Musician A488

Photo. & Engr.

2001, Sept. 3 ***Perf. 14***
1208 A488 3.50fr multi 7.00 4.25

Votive Pictures — A489

Designs: 70rp, 1733 picture, Chapel of Our Lady, Dux. 1.20fr, 1802 picture, St. George's Chapel, Schellenberg. 1.30fr, 1718 picture, Chapel of Our Lady, Dux.

2001, Sept. 3 ***Perf. 13½***
1209-1211 A489 Set of 3 6.50 4.00

Building Preservation A490

Designs: 70rp, St. Theresa's Chapel, Schaanwald. 90rp, St. Johann's winery, Mauren. 1.10fr, Pirsch transformer station, Schaanwald.

2001, Sept. 3 Photo. ***Perf. 11¾***
Granite Paper
1212-1214 A490 Set of 3 5.25 3.25

Traditional Crafts Type of 1998

Designs: 70rp, Blacksmith's tools, horseshoe, yoke bars. 90rp, Rakemaker's tools, rake. 1.20fr, Saddler's tools, horse collar.

2001, Dec. 3 Photo. ***Perf. 11¾***
Granite Paper
1215-1217 A460 Set of 3 5.50 3.50

Abstract Art by Gottfried Honegger A491

Untitled works: 1.80fr, 2.20fr.

2001, Dec. 3 ***Perf. 11½***
Granite Paper
1218-1219 A491 Set of 2 8.00 5.00

Christmas — A492

Medallions: 70rp, Annunciation. 90rp, Nativity. 1.30fr, The Presentation of the Lord.

2001, Dec. 3 ***Perf. 12x11¾***
Granite Paper
1220-1222 A492 Set of 3 4.00 3.50

Liechtenstein Students' Spice Bees Experiment on Space Shuttle A493

2002, Mar. 4 Photo. ***Perf. 13½x14¼***
1223 A493 90rp multi 1.75 1.10

LIBA.02 Stamp Exhibition, Vaduz — A494

2002, Mar. 4 ***Perf. 13¾***
1224 A494 1.20fr multi 2.40 1.40

Europa — A495

Designs: 90rp, Tightrope walker. 1.30fr, Juggler.

Photo. & Engr.

2002, Mar. 4 ***Perf. 14¼x14***
1225-1226 A495 Set of 2 *4.25 3.75*

Intl. Year of Mountains A496

Intl. Commision for Protection of the Alps A497

2002, Mar. 4 Photo. ***Perf. 13¾x13½***
1227 A496 70rp multi 1.40 .85
1228 A497 1.20fr multi 2.40 1.40

Paintings by Friedrich Kaufmann (1892-1972) A498

Views of: 70rp, Schellenberg. 1.30fr, Schaan. 1.80fr, Steg.

2002, Mar. 4 ***Perf. 13½x13¾***
1229-1231 A498 Set of 3 7.50 4.50

Building Preservation Type of 2001

Designs: 70rp, House, Popers, horiz. 1.20fr, House, Weiherring, horiz.

Perf. 13¾x13½

2002, June 3 **Photo.**
1232-1233 A490 Set of 2 3.75 2.40

2002 World Cup Soccer Championships, Japan and Korea — A499

2002, June 3 ***Perf. 13½x14¼***
1234 A499 1.80fr multi 3.50 2.25

Royalty A500

Designs: 3fr, Princess Marie. 3.50fr, Prince Hans Adam II.

2002, June 3 ***Perf. 13¾x13½***
1235-1236 A500 Set of 2 13.00 8.25

Liba.02 Stamp Exhibition, Vaduz — A501

Liechtenstein stamps depicting: 90rp, Various topics. 1.30fr, Royalty.

2002, Aug. 8 Photo. ***Perf. 13½***
1237-1238 A501 Set of 2 4.25 3.00

Royalty Type of 2002

Designs: 2fr, Hereditary Princess Sophie. 2.50fr, Hereditary Prince Alois.

2002, Aug. 8 ***Perf. 13¾x13½***
1239-1240 A500 Set of 2 9.00 6.00

Orchids — A502

Designs: 70rp, Epipogium aphyllum. 1.20fr, Ophrys insectifera. 1.30fr, Nigritella nigra.

2002, Aug. 8 ***Perf. 13½x13¾***
1241-1243 A502 Set of 3 6.25 4.25

Inn Sign Art — A503

Designs: 1.20fr, Eagle, Vaduz. 1.80fr, Angel, Balzers. 3fr, Eagle, Bendern.

Photo. & Engr.

2002, Nov. 25 ***Perf. 13½x14¼***
1244-1246 A503 Set of 3 12.00 8.25

Christmas — A504

Batik art by Sister Regina Hassler: 70rp, Search for Shelter. 1.20fr, Nativity. 1.80fr, Flight to Egypt.

Perf. 14¼x13½

2002, Nov. 25 **Photo.**
1247-1249 A504 Set of 3 7.50 5.25

Europa A505

2003, Mar. 3 Photo. ***Perf. 13½x12¾***
1250 A505 1.20fr multi *2.40 2.25*

Building Preservation Type of 2001

Designs: 70rp, St. Fridolin Church, Ruggell. 2.50fr, House, Spidach, horiz..

Perf. 13½x13¾, 13¾x3½

2003, Mar. 3
1251-1252 A490 Set of 2 6.25 4.75

Viticulture Throughout the Year — A506

Designs: 1.30fr, Pruning (February). 1.80fr, Tying vines to arbor (March). 2.20fr, Hoeing soil (April).

2003, Mar. 3 ***Perf. 14¼***
1253-1255 A506 Set of 3 10.50 7.75

2003, June 2 Photo. ***Perf. 14¼***

Designs: 1.20fr, Looping vines (May). 1.80fr, Leaf work (June). 3.50fr, Removing high growth (July).

1256-1258 A506 Set of 3 13.00 10.00

2003, Sept. 1 Photo. ***Perf. 14¼***

Designs: 70rp, Thinning out of vines (August). 90rp, Harvesting grapes (September). 1.10fr, Pressing grapes (October).

1259-1261 A506 Set of 3 5.25 4.00

2003, Nov. 24

Designs: 70rp, First tasting of wine (November). 90rp, Harvest of frozen grapes (December). 1.20fr, Bottling wine (January).

1262-1264 A506 Set of 3 5.50 4.25

Liechtenstein Association for the Disabled, 50th Anniv. — A507

2003, June 2 **Photo.** ***Perf. 14¼***
1265 A507 70rp multi 1.40 1.10

Reopening of National Museum — A508

Museum building and: 1.20fr, Ammonite fossil. 1.30fr, Shield of bailiff of Vaduz.

2003, June 2 ***Perf. 14***
1266-1267 A508 Set of 2 5.00 3.75

White Storks and Nest — A509

Photo. & Engr.

2003, Sept. 1 ***Perf. 12¾x13½***
1268 A509 2.20fr multi 4.50 3.25

Saints — A510

Designs: No. 1269, 1.20fr, St. Blasius. No. 1270, 1.20fr, St. George. No. 1271, 1.30fr, St. Erasmus. No. 1272, 1.30fr, St. Vitus.

2003, Sept. 1 ***Perf. 13½***
1269-1272 A510 Set of 4 10.00 7.25

Stamps of the same denomination were printed in sheets of 20 arranged in blocks of 10 of each stamp separated by a horizontal gutter.

See Nos. 1280-1285.

Children's Drawings A511

Designs: 70rp, Cow, by Laura Beck. No. 1274, 1.80fr, Apple Tree, by Patrick Marxer, vert. No. 1275, 1.80fr, Bee, by Laura Lingg.

Perf. 13½x14¼, 14¼x13½

2003, Nov. 24 **Photo.**
1273-1275 A511 Set of 3 8.50 6.25

Christmas — A512

Reverse glass paintings: 70rp, Archangel Gabriel. 90rp, Nativity. 1.30fr, Three Magi.

2003, Nov. 24 ***Perf. 14¼x13½***
1276-1278 A512 Set of 3 5.75 4.25

AHV Old Age and Survivor's Insurance, 50th Anniv. — A513

2004, Jan. 3 **Photo.** ***Perf. 14***
1279 A513 85rp multi 1.40 1.40

Saints Type of 2003

Designs: No. 1280, 1fr, St. Achatius. No. 1281, 1fr, St. Margareta. No. 1282, 1.20fr, St. Christophorus. No. 1283, 1.20fr, St. Pantaleon. No. 1284, 2.50fr, St. Aegidius. No. 1285, 2.50fr, St. Cyriakus.

Photo. & Engr.

2004, Mar. 1 ***Perf. 13½***
1280-1285 A510 Set of 6 19.00 15.50

Stamps of the same denomination were printed in sheets of 20 arranged in blocks of 10 of each stamp separated by a horizontal gutter.

Europa — A514

2004, Mar. 1 **Photo.** ***Perf. 13¾x13½***
1286 A514 1.30fr multi *2.50 2.25*

2004 Summer Olympics, Athens — A515

2004, June 1 **Photo.** ***Perf. 14¼***
1287 A515 85rp multi 1.75 1.40

Orchid Type of 2002

Designs: 85rp, Ophrys apifera. 1fr, Orchis ustulata. 1.20fr, Epipactis purpurata.

2004, June 1 ***Perf. 13½x13¾***
1288-1290 A502 Set of 3 6.00 4.75

Aerial Views A516

2004, June 1 ***Perf. 13½***

1291 A516	15rp Bendern	.30	.25
1292 A516	85rp Gross-Steg	1.75	1.40
1293 A516	1fr Tuass	2.00	1.60
1294 A516	6fr Gutenberg	12.00	9.25
	Nos. 1291-1294 (4)	16.05	12.50

See No. 1312.

Building Preservation Type of 2001

Designs: 2.20fr, House on Unterdorfstrasse, horiz. 2.50fr, Row of houses, Dorfstrasse, horiz.

Perf. 13¾x13½

2004, Sept. 6 **Photo.**
1295-1296 A490 Set of 2 9.50 7.50

Sciences — A517

Designs: 85rp, Mathematics. 1fr, Physics. 1.30fr, Chemistry. 1.80fr, Astronomy.

2004, Sept. 6 ***Perf. 13¾x14***
1297-1300 A517 Set of 4 10.00 8.00

Digital Palimpsest Research A518

Photo. & Engr.

2004, Nov. 22 ***Perf. 14¼***
1301 A518 2.50fr multi 5.00 4.25

Fossils — A519

Designs: 1.20fr, Ammonite. 1.30fr, Sea urchin. 2.20fr, Shark tooth.

2004, Nov. 22
1302-1304 A519 Set of 3 9.50 8.00

Christmas A520

Designs: 85rp, Annunciation. 1fr, Holy Family. 1.80fr, Adoration of the Magi.

2004, Nov. 22 **Photo.** ***Rouletted 6¾***
1305-1307 A520 Set of 3 7.25 6.25

Punched holes are in stamp frames to give stamps a lace-like appearance.

Saints Type of 2003

Designs: No. 1308, 85rp, St. Eustachius. No. 1309, 85rp, St. Dionysius. No. 1310, 1.80fr, St. Catharine. No. 1311, 1.80fr, St. Barbara.

Photo. & Engr.

2005, Mar. 7 ***Perf. 13½***
1308-1311 A510 Set of 4 10.50 9.25

Aerial Views Type of 2004

2005, Mar. 7 **Photo.**
1312 A516 3.60fr Triesenberg 7.25 6.25

Europa A521

2005, Mar. 7
1313 A521 1.30fr multi *2.50 2.25*

Venus at a Mirror, by Peter Paul Rubens A522

2005, Mar. 7 **Photo. & Engr.**
1314 A522 2.20fr multi 4.50 4.00

See Austria No. 1980.

Paintings of Flower Arrangements A523

Designs: No. 1315, 85rp, Magnolia Flowers, by Chen Hongshou (shown). No. 1316, 85rp, Flower Vase in a Windoe Niche, by Ambrosius Bosschaert the Elder.

2005, May 18 **Photo.** ***Perf. 14***
1315-1316 A523 Set of 2 3.25 3.00

See People's Republic of China Nos. 3433-3434.

Inn Signs — A524

Designs: 1fr, Stallion, Rössle Inn, Schaan. 1.40fr, Edelweiss Inn, Triesenberg. 2.50fr, Lion, Löwen Inn, Bendern.

Photo. & Engr.

2005, June 6 ***Perf. 14¼x13½***
1317-1319 A524 Set of 3 10.00 8.25

Postal Museum, 75th Anniv. A525

Designs: 1.10fr, Hermann E. Sieger, museum founder. 1.30fr, Liechtenstein stamps on stock page. 1.80fr, 1930 Zeppelin cover.

Perf. 13½x14¼

2005, June 6 **Photo.**
1320-1322 A525 Set of 3 8.25 7.00

Building Preservation Type of 2001

Designs: 85rp, Oberbendern. 2.20fr, Church Hill, Bendern.

Perf. 13¾x13½

2005, Sept. 5 **Photo.**
1323-1324 A490 Set of 2 6.00 5.00

Bats — A526

Designs: 1.80fr, Plecotus auritus. 2fr, Myotis myotis.

2005, Sept. 5 ***Perf. 14¼***
1325-1326 A526 Set of 2 7.50 6.25

Pastures A527

Designs: 85rp, Bargälla. 1fr, Pradamee. 1.30fr, Gritsch. 1.80fr, Valüna.

2005, Sept. 5 ***Perf. 13½x14¼***
1327-1330 A527 Set of 4 10.00 8.00

Aerial Views Type of 2004

2005, Nov. 21 **Photo.** ***Perf. 13½***
1331 A516 1.50fr Oberland 3.00 2.40
1332 A516 1.60fr Ruggeller Riet 3.25 2.50
1333 A516 3fr Naafkopf 6.00 4.75
Nos. 1331-1333 (3) 12.25 9.65

2006 Winter Olympics, Turin, Italy — A528

Designs: 1.20fr, Ski jumping. 1.30fr, Biathlon. 1.40fr, Slalom skiing.

2005, Nov. 21 ***Perf. 14¼x14***
1334-1336 A528 Set of 3 8.00 6.25

Christmas A529

Wood sculptures by Toni Gstöhl: 85rp, The Annunciation. 1fr, Holy Family. 1.30fr, Adoration of the Shepherds.

Photo. & Engr.

2005, Nov. 21 ***Perf. 14¼x13½***
1337-1339 A529 Set of 3 6.25 5.00

Aerial Views Type of 2004

2006, Mar. 6 **Photo.** ***Perf. 13½***
1340 A516 2.50fr Rhine Canal 5.00 4.00
1341 A516 3.50fr Rhine Valley 7.00 5.50

Lost in Her Dreams, by Friedrich von Amerling A530

2006, Mar. 6 **Photo. & Engr.**
1342 A530 2.20fr multi 4.50 3.50

See Austria No. 2041.

Paintings by Eugen Wilhelm Schüepp (1915-74) A531

Designs: 1fr, Peat Cutters, Ruggell Marsh. 1.80fr, Neugut, Schaan.

2006, Mar. 6 **Photo.** ***Perf. 13½x14¼***
1343-1344 A531 Set of 2 5.50 4.50

Europa A532

Winning designs from stamp design contest: 1.20fr, Bridge, by Nadja Beck. 1.30fr, Face of Integration, by Elisabeth Müssner.

2006, Mar. 6
1345-1346 A532 Set of 2 *5.00 4.00*

2006 World Cup Soccer Championships, Germany — A533

Perf. 13½x14¼

2006, June 6 **Photo.**
1347 A533 3.30fr multi 6.50 5.50

A534

A535

Designs: 85rp, Woman holding G clef. 1fr, Backpacker. 1.20fr, Restaurant patron. 1.80fr, Skier.

2006, June 6 ***Perf. 13¾***
1348-1351 A534 Set of 4 9.75 8.25

Tourism promotion.

2006, June 6 **Litho. & Engr.**

Designs: 85rp, Prince Johann I. 1fr, National flag. 1.30fr, Flag of the Princely House of Liechtenstein. 1.80fr, National arms.

1352-1355 A535 Set of 4 10.00 8.25

Full sovereignty, bicent.

Pastures Type of 2005

Designs: 85rp, Lawena. 1.30fr, Gapfahl. 2.40fr, Gafadura.

Perf. 13½x14¼

2006, Sept. 4 **Photo.**
1356-1358 A527 Set of 3 9.00 7.50

Wolfgang Amadeus Mozart (1756-91), Composer — A536

2006, Sept. 4 ***Perf. 13¾x14¼***
1359 A536 1.20fr multi 2.50 2.00

Miniature Sheet

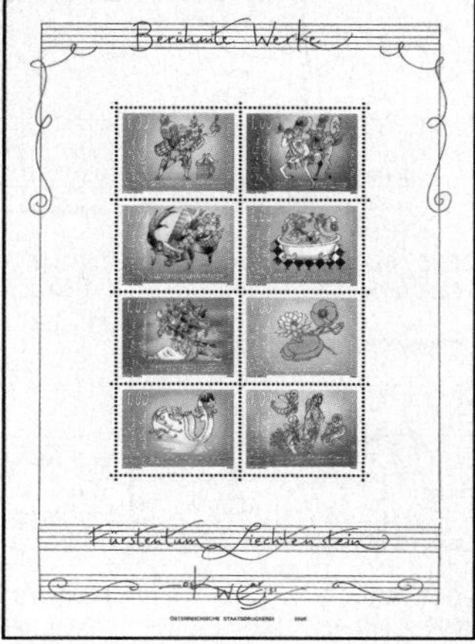

Classical Music — A537

No. 1360: a, The Magic Flute, by Wolfgang Amadeus Mozart. b, Radetzky March, by Johann Strauss. c, Rhapsody in Blue, by George Gershwin. d, Water Music, by George Frideric Handel. e, Pastoral Symphony, by Ludwig van Beethoven. f, Waltz of the Flowers, by Peter Ilich Tchaikovsky. g, The Swan, by Camille Saint-Saens. h, A Midsummer Night's Dream, by Felix Mendelssohn.

2006, Sept. 4 ***Perf. 13½x14¼***
1360 A537 Sheet of 8 16.00 13.00
a.-h. 1fr Any single 2.00 1.60

Building Preservation Type of 2001

Designs: 1.80fr, Governor's residence and Liechtenstein Institute, Bendern. 3.50fr, Bühl House, Gamprin, horiz.

Perf. 13½x13¾, 13¾x13½

2006, Nov. 20 **Photo.**
1361-1362 A490 Set of 2 10.50 8.50

Inventions A538

Designs: 1.30fr, Curta calculator. 1.40fr, Carena film camera. 2.40fr, PAV sliding caliper.

2006, Nov. 20 ***Perf. 14¼x14***
1363-1365 A538 Set of 3 10.00 8.25

Christmas A539

Frescos from Chapel of St. Mary, Dux: 85rp, The Annunciation. 1fr, Nativity. 1.30fr, Presentation at the Temple.

Photo. & Engr.

2006, Nov. 20 ***Perf. 13½***
1366-1368 A539 Set of 3 6.25 5.00

Scouting, Cent. — A540

2007, Mar. 5 **Photo.** ***Perf. 14¼***
1369 A540 1.30fr multi 2.50 2.10

Portrait of a Lady, by Bernardino Zaganelli da Cotignola A541

Litho. & Engr.

2007, Mar. 5 ***Perf. 13¾***
1370 A541 2.40fr multi 4.75 4.00

See Austria No. 2086.

Musical Terms A542

Designs: 85rp, Allegro. 1.80fr, Capriccio. 2fr, Crescendo. 3.50fr, Con fuoco.

2007, Mar. 5 **Photo.** ***Perf. 13½***
1371-1374 A542 Set of 4 16.00 13.50

Aerial Views Type of 2004

2007, June 4 **Photo.** ***Perf. 13½***
1375 A516 1.10fr Nendeln 1.90 1.90
1376 A516 1.80fr Malbun 3.00 3.00
1377 A516 2.60fr Ackerland 4.25 4.25
Nos. 1375-1377 (3) 9.15 9.15

Greeting Card Art — A543

Designs: 85rp, Boy delivering flower and letter to girl. 1fr, Two children carrying litter with cake, flowers and letter. 1.30fr, Bird carrying letter.

2007, June 4 ***Rouletted 6¾***
1378-1380 A543 Set of 3 5.25 5.25

Punched holes are in stamp frames to give stamps a lacelike appearance.

Paintings of Rhine Landscapes by Johann Ludwig Bleuler (1792-1850) A544

Designs: 1fr, Castle and Village of Vaduz. 1.30fr, Rätikon Mountain. 2.40fr, Confluence of the Ill and Rhine.

Perf. 13½x14¼

2007, June 4 **Photo. & Engr**
1381-1383 A544 Set of 3 7.75 7.75

Pastures Type of 2005

Designs: 1fr, Hintervalorsch. 1.40fr, Sücka. 2.20fr, Guschgfiel.

Perf. 13½x14¼

2007, Sept. 3 **Photo.**
1384-1386 A527 Set of 3 7.75 7.75

Technical Innovations From Liechtenstein A545

Designs: 1.30fr, Hilti hammer and drill. 1.80fr, Kaiser mobile walking excavator. 2.40fr, Hoval AluFer composite heating tube.

2007, Sept. 3 ***Perf. 14¼***
1387-1389 A545 Set of 3 9.25 9.25

Beetles A546

Designs: 85rp, Trichodes apiarius. 100rp, Cetania aurata. 130rp, Dytiscus marginalis.

2007, Sept. 3 **Litho.** ***Perf. 13¾x14***
1390-1392 A546 Set of 3 5.25 5.25

Panoramic View of Liechtenstein — A547

2007, Oct. 1 **Litho.** ***Perf. 14***
1393 A547 130rp multi 2.25 2.25

Building Preservation Type of 2001

Designs: 2fr, St. Martin's Church, Eschen. 2.70fr, Mill, Eschen, horiz.

Perf. 13½x13¾, 13¾x13½

2007, Nov. 19 **Photo.**
1394-1395 A490 Set of 2 8.25 8.25

New Parliament Building A548

2007, Nov. 19 ***Perf. 13¾***
1396 A548 130rp multi 2.25 2.25

Natural Phenomena A549

Designs: 85rp, Rainbow above Three Sisters Massif. 100rp, Lightning over Bendern. 180rp, Ice crystal halo around Moon over Malbun.

2007, Nov. 19 **Litho.** ***Perf. 14¼***
1397-1399 A549 Set of 3 6.50 6.50

Christmas A550

Designs: 85rp, Chapel of St. Mary, Gamprin-Oberbühl. 1fr, Büel Chapel, Eschen. 1.30fr, Chapel of St. Wolfgang, Triesen.

Perf. 13½x14¼

2007, Nov. 19 **Photo.**
1400-1402 A550 Set of 3 5.50 5.50

Pastures Type of 2005

Designs: 2.60fr, Guschg. 3fr, Güschgle.

2008, Mar. 3 **Photo.** ***Perf. 13½x14¼***
1403-1404 A527 Set of 2 11.00 11.00

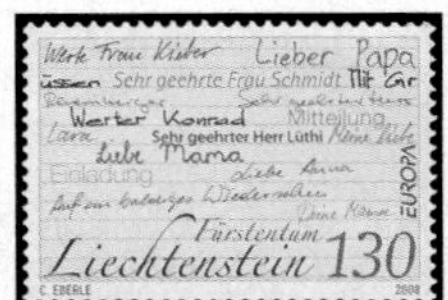

Europa A551

2008, Mar. 3 **Litho.** ***Perf. 13½x13¾***
1405 A551 130rp multi 2.60 2.60

Volunteer Fire Fighters A552

2008, Mar. 3 ***Perf. 13½***
1406 A552 1fr multi 2.00 2.00

Sleeping Princess Marie Franziska, by Friedrich von Amerling A553

2008, Mar. 3 **Photo. & Engr.**
1407 A553 2.40fr multi 4.75 4.75

See Austria No. 2144.

Spoerry-Areal, Vaduz — A554

Chapel of St. Mamertus, Triesen — A555

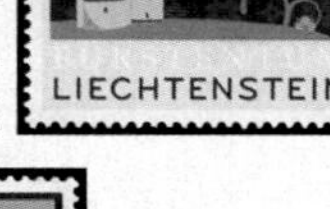

Vaduz Castle — A556

2008, Mar. 3 **Litho.** ***Perf. 14***
1408 A554 85rp multi 1.75 1.75
1409 A555 1fr multi 2.00 2.00
1410 A556 1.30fr multi 2.60 2.60
Nos. 1408-1410 (3) 6.35 6.35

Mother and Queen of the Precious Blood with Child, by Unknown Artist — A557

2008, June 2 **Litho.** ***Perf. 12¾x13½***
1411 A557 220rp multi 4.25 4.25

Schellenberg Convent, 150th anniv.

2008 Summer Olympics, Beijing — A558

Mascots involved in: 85rp, Martial arts. 100rp, Soccer.

2008, June 2 ***Perf. 14¼x13½***
1412-1413 A558 Set of 2 3.75 3.75

2008 Paralympics, Beijing — A559

Designs: 130rp, Marathon. 180rp, Table tennis.

2008, June 2 ***Perf. 13½x14¼***
1414-1415 A559 Set of 2 6.00 6.00

2008 European Soccer Championships, Austria and Switzerland — A560

Designs: No. 1416, 130rp, St. Stephen's Cathedral, Vienna, soccer player waltzing, violinist. No. 1417, 130rp, Soccer fans holding Liechtenstein flag, wearing Swiss hat, and Austrian scarf. No. 1418, 130rp, Alphorn player, Matterhorn, soccer player.

2008, June 2 ***Perf. 14***
1416-1418 A560 Set of 3 7.50 7.50

Nos. 1416-1418 printed in sheets containing 4 #1417 and 6 each #1416 and 1418.

Hymenopterans A561

Designs: 85rp, Osmia brevicornis. 1fr, Epeoloides coecutiens. 1.30fr, Odynerus spinipes.

2008, June 2 ***Perf. 14¼***
1419-1421 A561 Set of 3 6.25 6.25

Souvenir Sheet

Prince Karl I (1569-1627) — A562

Photo. & Engr.

2008, Sept. 1 ***Perf. 13¾x13½***
1422 A562 5fr multi 9.25 9.25

Princely house of Liechtenstein, 400th anniv.

Miniature Sheet

Drawings by Wilhelm Busch (1832-1908) — A563

No. 1423: a, Schoolmaster Lampel. b, Hans Huckebein. c, Max and Moritz. d, Widow Bolte. e, Pious Helene. f, Fipps the Monkey. g, Tailor Böck. h, Balduin Bählamm.

2008, Sept. 1 **Photo.** ***Perf. 14x13¾***
1423 A563 Sheet of 8 20.00 20.00
a.-h. 1.30fr Any single 2.50 2.50

Building Preservation Type of 2001

Design: Schädler Ceramics Building, Nendeln, horiz.

Perf. 13¾x13½

2008, Nov. 17 **Photo.**
1424 A490 3.80fr multi 6.50 6.50

Technical Innovations Type of 2007

Designs: 1.20fr, Neutrik NC3MX audio cable connectors. 1.40fr, Ivoclar Vivadent bluephase polymerization unit. 2.20fr, Presta DeltaValveControl variable valve-lift system.

2008, Nov. 17 ***Perf. 14¼***
1425-1427 A545 Set of 3 8.25 8.25

Christmas A564

Designs: 85rp, Candles, flowers and evergreen branches. 100rp, Children carrying holly, horiz. 130rp, Christmas tree and gifts.

Perf. 14¼x14½, 14½x14¼

2008, Nov. 17 **Litho.**
1428-1430 A564 Set of 3 5.50 5.50

Civil Protection Volunteers — A565

2009, Mar. 2 **Litho.** ***Perf. 13¾x13½***
1431 A565 1fr multi 1.75 1.75

Europa — A566

Litho. With Hologram Affixed

2009, Mar. 2 ***Perf. 14¼***
1432 A566 1.30fr multi 2.25 2.25

Land Registry, 200th Anniv. A567

2009, Mar. 2 **Litho.** ***Perf. 13¾***
1433 A567 330rp multi 5.75 5.75

Liechtenstein Post AG, 10th Anniv. — A568

Designs: 85rp, Counter clerk handling package. 100rp, Mail deliverer. 130rp, Mail sorter.

2009, Mar. 2 ***Perf. 13¾x13½***
1434-1436 A568 Set of 3 5.50 5.50

Linoleum Prints by Stephan Sude — A569

Designs: 1fr, Unfolding. 1.30fr, Awareness. 2.70fr, Fulfillment.

2009, Mar. 2 ***Perf. 14x13¼***
1437-1439 A569 Set of 3 8.50 8.50

SEMI-POSTAL STAMPS

Prince Johann II — SP1

Coat of Arms — SP2

Wmk. 183

1925, Oct. 5 **Engr.** ***Perf. 11½***
B1 SP1 10rp yellow green 27.50 14.00
B2 SP1 20rp deep red 20.00 14.00
B3 SP1 30rp deep blue 6.00 4.50
Nos. B1-B3 (3) 53.50 32.50
Set, never hinged 150.00

85th birthday of the Prince Regent. Sold at a premium of 5rp each, the excess being devoted to charities.

1927, Oct. 5 **Typo.**
B4 SP2 10rp multicolored 6.75 *15.00*
B5 SP2 20rp multicolored 6.75 *15.00*
B6 SP2 30rp multicolored 5.00 *12.50*
Nos. B4-B6 (3) 18.50 *42.50*
Set, never hinged 50.00

87th birthday of Prince Johann II.
These stamps were sold at premiums of 5, 10 and 20rp respectively. The money thus obtained was devoted to charity.

Railroad Bridge Demolished by Flood SP3

Designs: 10rp+10rp, Inundated Village of Ruggel. 20rp+10rp, Austrian soldiers rescuing refugees. 30rp+10rp, Swiss soldiers salvaging personal effects.

1928, Feb. 6 **Litho.** **Unwmk.**
B7 SP3 5rp + 5rp brn vio & brn 11.00 20.00
B8 SP3 10rp + 10rp bl grn & brn 15.00 22.50
B9 SP3 20rp + 10rp dl red & brn 15.00 22.50
B10 SP3 30rp + 10rp dp bl & brn 12.50 22.50
Nos. B7-B10 (4) 53.50 87.50
Set, never hinged 180.00

The surtax on these stamps was used to aid the sufferers from the Rhine floods.

Coat of Arms — SP7

Princess Elsa — SP8

Design: 30rp, Prince Francis I.

1932, Dec. 21 **Photo.**
B11 SP7 10rp (+ 5rp) olive grn 15.00 *25.00*
B12 SP8 20rp (+ 5rp) rose red 15.00 *25.00*
B13 SP8 30rp (+ 10rp) ultra 20.00 *30.00*
Nos. B11-B13 (3) 50.00 *80.00*
Set, never hinged 125.00

The surtax was for the Child Welfare Fund.

Postal Museum Issue
Souvenir Sheet

SP10

1936, Oct. 24 **Litho.** ***Imperf.***
B14 SP10 Sheet of 4 12.50 *37.50*
Never hinged 37.50

Sheet contains 2 each, #120, 122. Sold for 2fr.

"Protect the Child" — SP11

Designs: No. B16, "Take Care of the Sick." No. B17, "Help the Aged."

Perf. 11½

1945, Nov. 27 **Photo.** **Unwmk.**
B15 SP11 10rp + 10rp multi .65 *1.75*
B16 SP11 20rp + 20rp multi .65 *2.25*
B17 SP11 1fr + 1.40fr multi 4.75 *20.00*
Nos. B15-B17 (3) 6.05 *24.00*
Set, never hinged 11.00

Souvenir Sheet

Post Coach — SP14

1946, Aug. 10
B18 SP14 Sheet of 2 21.00 *32.50*
Never hinged 35.00
a. 10rp dark violet brown & buff 5.00 *15.00*
Never hinged 12.50

25th anniv. of the Swiss-Liechtenstein Postal Agreement. Sheet, size: 82x60½mm, sold for 3fr.

Canal by Albert Cuyp — SP15

Willem van Huythuysen by Frans Hals — SP16

40rp+10rp, Landscape by Jacob van Ruysdael.

1951, July 24 ***Perf. 11½***
B19 SP15 10rp + 10rp olive grn 5.00 7.00
B20 SP16 20rp + 10rp dk vio brn 5.00 *14.00*
B21 SP15 40rp + 10rp blue 5.00 7.00
Nos. B19-B21 (3) 15.00 *28.00*
Set, never hinged 30.00

Issued in sheets of 12. For surcharges see Nos. 281-283.

Catalogue values for unused stamps in this section, from this point to the end of the section, are for Never Hinged items.

Nos. 324-325 Surcharged with New Value and Uprooted Oak Emblem

1960, Apr. 7
B22 A190 30rp + 10rp on 40rp .55 *1.00*
B23 A190 50rp + 10rp on 25rp .90 *2.00*

World Refugee Year, July 1, 1959-June 30, 1960. The surtax was for aid to refugees.

Growth Symbol SP17

1967, Dec. 7 **Photo.** ***Perf. 11½***
B24 SP17 50rp + 20rp multi .50 .60

Surtax was for development assistance.

AIR POST STAMPS

Airplane over Snow-capped Mountain Peaks — AP1

Airplane above Vaduz Castle — AP2

Airplane over Rhine Valley — AP3

Perf. 10½, 10½x11½

1930, Aug. 12 **Photo.** **Unwmk.**
Gray Wavy Lines in Background
C1 AP1 15rp dark brown 6.00 *8.00*
C2 AP1 20rp slate 14.00 11.50
C3 AP2 25rp olive brown 8.00 *21.00*
C4 AP2 35rp slate blue 12.00 *20.00*
C5 AP3 45rp olive green 27.50 *40.00*
C6 AP3 1fr lake 32.50 30.00
Nos. C1-C6 (6) 100.00 *130.50*
Set, never hinged 350.00

For surcharge see No. C14.

Zeppelin over Naafkopf, Falknis Range AP4

Design: 2fr, Zeppelin over Valüna Valley.

1931, June 1 ***Perf. 11½***
C7 AP4 1fr olive black 37.50 *75.00*
C8 AP4 2fr blue black 72.50 *200.00*
Set, never hinged 325.00

Golden Eagle — AP6

15rp, Golden Eagle in flight, diff. 20rp, Golden Eagle in flight, diff. 30rp, Osprey. 50rp, Eagle.

1934-35
C9 AP6 10rp brt violet ('35) 4.50 13.00
C10 AP6 15rp red orange ('35) 12.00 30.00
C11 AP6 20rp red ('35) 14.00 30.00

C12 AP6 30rp brt blue ('35) 14.00 30.00
C13 AP6 50rp emerald 8.00 21.00
Nos. C9-C13 (5) 52.50 124.00
Set, never hinged 150.00

No. C6 Surcharged with New Value

1935, June 24 *Perf. 10½x11½*
C14 AP3 60rp on 1fr lake 25.00 37.50
Never hinged 75.00

Airship "Hindenburg" AP11

Design: 2fr, Airship "Graf Zeppelin."

1936, May 1 *Perf. 11½*
C15 AP11 1fr rose carmine 30.00 62.50
C16 AP11 2fr violet 20.00 62.50
Set, never hinged 125.00

AP13

AP20

10rp, Barn swallows. 15rp, Black-headed Gulls. 20rp, Gulls. 30rp, Eagle. 50rp, Northern Goshawk. 1fr, Lammergeier. 2fr, Lammergeier.

1939, Apr. 3 **Photo.**
C17 AP13 10rp violet .30 .20
C18 AP13 15rp red orange .80 1.65
C19 AP13 20rp dark red 1.00 .45
C20 AP13 30rp dull blue 1.00 .80
C21 AP13 50rp brt green 2.75 1.65
C22 AP13 1fr rose car 2.75 *12.00*
C23 AP13 2fr violet 2.00 *12.00*
Nos. C17-C23 (7) 10.60 *28.75*
Set, never hinged 20.00

Catalogue values for unused stamps in this section, from this point to the end of the section, are for Never Hinged items.

1948

Designs: 10rp, Leonardo da Vinci. 15rp, Joseph Montgolfier. 20rp, Jacob Degen. 25rp, Wilhelm Kress. 40rp, E. G. Robertson. 50rp, W. S. Henson. 1fr, Otto Lilienthal. 2fr, S. A. Andrée. 5fr, Wilbur Wright. 10fr, Icarus.

C24 AP20 10rp dark green .55 .20
C25 AP20 15rp dark violet .55 .80
C26 AP20 20rp brown .90 .20
a. 20rp reddish brown 32.50 2.75
Never hinged 65.00
C27 AP20 25rp dark red 1.10 1.25
C28 AP20 40rp violet blue 1.25 1.25
C29 AP20 50rp Prus blue 1.40 1.25
C30 AP20 1fr chocolate 8.00 2.75
C31 AP20 2fr rose lake 4.50 3.50
C32 AP20 5fr olive green 5.75 4.75
C33 AP20 10fr slate black 26.00 14.00
Nos. C24-C33 (10) 50.00 29.95

Issued in sheets of 9.
Exist imperf. Value, set $6,500.

Helicopter, Bell 47-J AP21

Planes: 40rp, Boeing 707 jet. 50rp, Convair 600 jet. 75rp, Douglas DC-8.

1960, Apr. 7 **Unwmk.** *Perf. 11½*
C34 AP21 30rp red orange 2.25 2.25
C35 AP21 40rp blue black 3.75 2.25
C36 AP21 50rp deep claret 9.50 4.00
C37 AP21 75rp olive green 2.00 2.25
Nos. C34-C37 (4) 17.50 10.75

30th anniv. of Liechtenstein's air post stamps.

POSTAGE DUE STAMPS

National Administration of the Post Office

D1

1920 **Unwmk.** **Engr.** *Perf. 12½*
J1 D1 5h rose red .20 .20
J2 D1 10h rose red .20 .20
J3 D1 15h rose red .20 .20
J4 D1 20h rose red .20 .20
J5 D1 25h rose red .20 .20
J6 D1 30h rose red .20 .20
J7 D1 40h rose red .20 .20
J8 D1 50h rose red .20 .20
J9 D1 80h rose red .20 .20
J10 D1 1k dull blue .20 .40
J11 D1 2k dull blue .20 .40
J12 D1 5k dull blue .20 .40
Nos. J1-J12 (12) 2.40 3.00
Set, never hinged 3.00

Nos. J1-J12 exist imperf. and part perf.

Swiss Administration of the Post Office

D2

Post Horn — D3

1928 **Litho.** **Wmk. 183** *Perf. 11½*
Granite Paper
J13 D2 5rp purple & orange .70 *1.75*
J14 D2 10rp purple & orange .85 *1.75*
J15 D2 15rp purple & orange 1.40 *8.50*
J16 D2 20rp purple & orange 1.40 *2.50*
J17 D2 25rp purple & orange 1.40 *5.00*
J18 D2 30rp purple & orange 4.00 *7.50*
J19 D2 40rp purple & orange 4.75 *8.50*
J20 D2 50rp purple & orange 5.50 *12.50*
Nos. J13-J20 (8) 20.00 *48.00*
Set, never hinged 57.50

Engraved; Value Typographed in Dark Red

1940 **Unwmk.** *Perf. 11½*
J21 D3 5rp gray blue 1.00 *2.10*
J22 D3 10rp gray blue .50 .40
J23 D3 15rp gray blue .75 *2.10*
J24 D3 20rp gray blue .75 *1.25*
J25 D3 25rp gray blue 1.25 *2.50*
J26 D3 30rp gray blue 2.00 *3.25*
J27 D3 40rp gray blue 2.00 *3.25*
J28 D3 50rp gray blue 2.00 *3.75*
Nos. J21-J28 (8) 10.25 *18.60*
Set, never hinged 25.00

OFFICIAL STAMPS

Regular Issue of 1930 Overprinted in Various Colors with Crown and:

Perf. 10½, 11½, 11½x10½

1932 **Unwmk.**
O1 A38 5rp dk grn (Bk) 5.50 9.00
O2 A39 10rp dark vio (R) 37.50 7.50
a. Perf. 11½x10½ *600.00* *1,000.*
Never hinged *950.00*
O3 A40 20rp dp rose red (Bl) 50.00 7.50
a. Perf. 10½ 160.00 40.00
Never hinged 375.00
O4 A42 30rp ultra (R) 10.00 10.00
a. Perf. 10½ 15.00 17.50
Never hinged 40.00
O5 A43 35rp dp grn (Bk) 8.00 20.00
a. Perf. 11½ *3,750.* *6,000.*
Never hinged *7,000.*
O6 A45 50rp blk brn (Bl) 37.50 12.50
a. Perf. 11½ 90.00 140.00
Never hinged 200.00
O7 A46 60rp olive blk (R) 7.50 32.50
O8 A48 1.20fr olive brn (G) 82.50 275.00
Nos. O1-O8 (8) 238.50 374.00
Set, never hinged 700.00

Nos. 108, 110 Overprinted in Black

1933 *Perf. 14½*
O9 A51 25rp red orange 30.00 35.00
O10 A53 1.20fr red brown 60.00 *175.00*
Set, never hinged 200.00

Same Overprint in Various Colors on Regular Issue of 1934-35

1934-36 *Perf. 11½*
O11 A58 5rp emerald (R) .50 1.25
O12 A59 10rp dp violet (Bk) .60 1.10
O13 A60 15rp red orange (V) .30 1.10
O14 A61 20rp red (Bk) .35 1.10
O15 A62 25rp brown (R) 27.50 *65.00*
O16 A62 25rp brown (Bk) 1.50 *6.75*
O17 A63 30rp dark blue (R) 1.90 3.50
O18 A66 50rp lt brown (V) .90 1.25
O19 A68 90rp dp green (Bk) 5.50 *20.00*
O20 A69 1.50fr brown car (Bl) 27.50 *110.00*
Nos. O11-O20 (10) 66.55 *211.05*
Set, never hinged 150.00

Regular Issue of 1937-38 Overprinted in Black, Red or Blue

1937-41
O21 A76 5rp emerald (Bk) .20 .20
O22 A76 10rp vio & buff (R) .20 .25
O23 A76 20rp brown org (Bl) .95 1.00
O24 A76 20rp brn org (Bk) ('41) .95 1.00
O25 A76 25rp chestnut (Bk) .50 1.25
O26 A77 30rp blue & gray (Bk) .75 .50
O27 A79 50rp dk brn & buff (R) .45 1.00
O28 A80 1fr red brown (Bk) .85 *4.25*
O29 A80 1.50fr slate bl (Bk) ('38) 2.75 *7.25*
Nos. O21-O29 (9) 7.60 *16.70*
Set, never hinged 15.00

Catalogue values for unused stamps in this section, from this point to the end of the section, are for Never Hinged items.

Stamps of 1944-45 Overprinted in Black

1947
O30 A136 5rp slate grn & buff 1.25 .75
O31 A136 10rp gray & buff 1.25 .75
O32 A136 20rp org red & buff 1.50 .75
O33 A136 30rp blue & buff 1.90 1.40
O34 A136 50rp bluish blk & pale gray 2.00 3.00
O35 A136 1fr dp cl & buff 9.00 9.00
O36 A136 150rp royal blue 9.00 9.00
Nos. O30-O36 (7) 25.90 24.65

Crown — O1

Government Building, Vaduz — O2

Engr.; Value Typo.

1950-68 **Unwmk.** *Perf. 11½*
Buff Granite Paper
Narrow Gothic Numerals
O37 O1 5rp red vio & gray .20 .20
O38 O1 10rp ol grn & mag .20 .20
O39 O1 20rp org brn & bl .20 .20
O40 O1 30rp dk red brn & org red .25 .25
O41 O1 40rp blue & hn brn .35 .35
O42 O1 55rp dk gray grn & red .70 1.10
a. White paper ('68) 45.00 *125.00*
O43 O1 60rp slate & mag .70 1.10
a. White paper ('68) 6.00 *22.50*
O44 O1 80rp red org & gray .70 .90
O45 O1 90rp choc & blue .90 1.25
O46 O1 1.20fr grnsh bl & org 1.10 1.25
Nos. O37-O46 (10) 5.30 6.80

1968-69 *Perf. 11½*
White Granite Paper
Broad Numerals, Varying Thickness
O47 O1 5rp olive brn & org .20 .20
O48 O1 10rp violet & car .20 .20
O49 O1 20rp ver & emer .20 .20
O50 O1 30rp green & red .20 .20
O51 O1 50rp ultra & red .35 .35
O52 O1 60rp orange & ultra .40 .40
O53 O1 70rp maroon & emer .50 .50
O54 O1 80rp bl grn & car .55 .55
O55 O1 95rp slate & red ('69) .65 .65
O56 O1 1fr rose cl & grn .70 .70
O57 O1 1.20fr lt red brn & grn .80 .80
O58 O1 2fr brn & org ('69) 1.25 1.25
Nos. O47-O58 (12) 6.00 6.00

Engr., Value Typo.

1976-89 *Perf. 14*
O59 O2 10rp yel brn & vio .20 .20
O60 O2 20rp car lake & bl .20 .20
O61 O2 35rp blue & red .25 .25
O62 O2 40rp dull pur & grn .30 .30
O63 O2 50rp slate & mag .40 .40
O64 O2 70rp vio brn & bl grn .55 .55
O65 O2 80rp green & mag .60 .60
O66 O2 90rp vio & bl grn .70 .70
O67 O2 1fr olive & mag .80 .80
O68 O2 1.10fr brown & ultra .85 .85
O69 O2 1.50fr dull grn & red 1.25 1.25
O70 O2 2fr orange & blue 1.60 1.60
O75 O2 5fr rose vio & brn org 5.75 5.75
Nos. O59-O75 (13) 13.45 13.45

Issued: 5fr, 9/4/89; others, 12/9/76.
This is an expanding set. Numbers will change if necessary.

LITHUANIA

ˌli-thə-ˈwā-nē-ə

(Lietuva)

LOCATION — Northern Europe bordering on the Baltic Sea
GOVT. — Independent republic
AREA — 25,170 sq. mi.
POP. — 3,584,966 (1999 est.)
CAPITAL — Vilnius

Lithuania was under Russian rule when it declared its independence in 1918. The League of Nations recognized it in 1922. In 1940 it became a republic in the Union of Soviet Socialist Republics.

Lithuania declared its independence on March 11, 1990. Lithuanian independence was recognized by the Soviet Union on Sept. 6, 1991.

100 Skatiku = 1 Auksinas
100 Centai = 1 Litas (1922, 1993)
100 Kopecks = 1 Ruble (1991)

Catalogue values for unused stamps in this country are for Never Hinged items, beginning with Scott 30, Scott B43 in the semi-postal section, Scott C1 in the air post section, Scott CB1 in the air post semi-postal section and Scott 2N9 in the Russian occupation section.

Nos. 1-26 were printed in sheets of 20 (5x4) which were imperf. at the outer sides, so that only 6 stamps in each sheet were fully perforated. Values are for the stamps partly imperf. The stamps fully perforated sell for at least double these values. There was also a printing of Nos. 19-26 in a sheet of 160, composed of blocks of 20 of each stamp. Pairs or blocks with different values se-tenant sell for considerably more than the values for the stamps singly.

Nos. 1-26 are without gum.

Watermarks

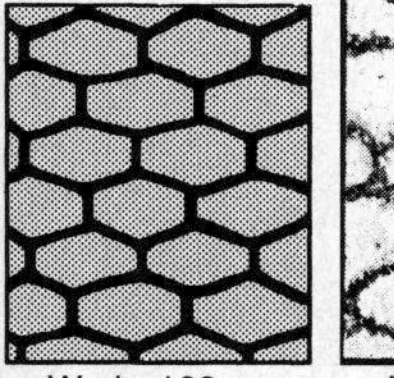

Wmk. 109 — Webbing

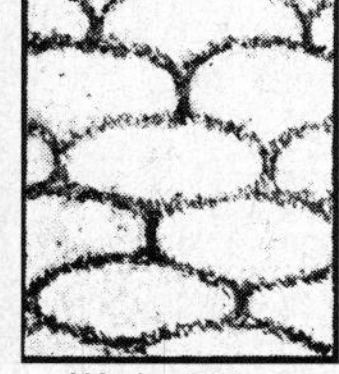

Wmk. 144 — Network

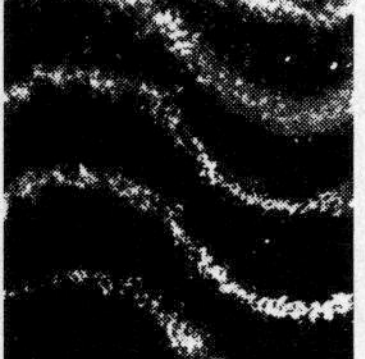

Wmk. 145 — Wavy Lines

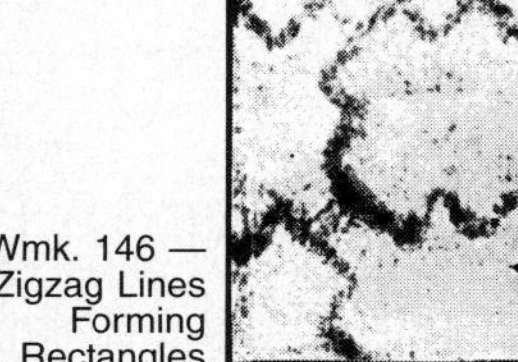

Wmk. 146 — Zigzag Lines Forming Rectangles

Wmk. 147 — Parquetry

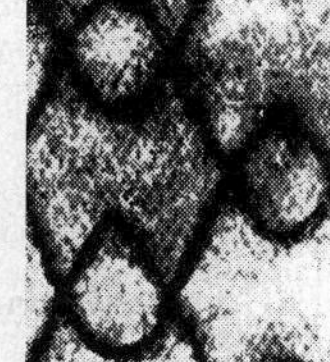

Wmk. 198 — Intersecting Diamonds

Wmk. 209 — Multiple Ovals

Wmk. 238 — Multiple Letters

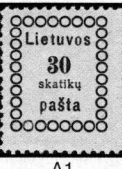

A1 A2

Perf. 11½

1918, Dec. 27 Unwmk. Typeset

First Vilnius Printing

Thin Figures

No.	Type	Description	Unused	Used
1	A1	10sk black	100.00	100.00
2	A1	15sk black	100.00	100.00

1918, Dec. 31

Second Vilnius Printing

Thick Figures

No.	Type	Description	Unused	Used
3	A1	10sk black	70.00	55.00
4	A1	15sk black	70.00	55.00
5	A1	20sk black	18.00	15.00
6	A1	30sk black	20.00	15.00
7	A1	40sk black	25.00	15.00
8	A1	50sk black	20.00	15.00
		Nos. 3-8 (6)	223.00	170.00

First Kaunas Issue

1919, Jan. 29

No.	Type	Description	Unused	Used
9	A2	10sk black	8.00	5.50
10	A2	15sk black	8.00	5.50
a.		"5" for "15"	90.00	70.00
11	A2	20sk black	8.00	5.50
12	A2	30sk black	8.00	5.50
		Nos. 9-12 (4)	32.00	22.00

A3

A4

Second Kaunas Issue

1919, Feb. 18

No.	Type	Description	Unused	Used
13	A3	10sk black	3.00	1.75
14	A3	15sk black	3.00	1.75
15	A3	20sk black	3.00	1.75
a.		"astas" for "pastas"	70.00	60.00
16	A3	30sk black	3.00	1.75
17	A3	40sk black	3.00	1.75
18	A3	50sk black	3.00	1.75
19	A3	60sk black	3.00	1.75
		Nos. 13-19 (7)	21.00	12.25

Third Kaunas Issue

1919, Mar. 1

No.	Type	Description	Unused	Used
20	A4	10sk black	4.00	1.75
21	A4	15sk black	4.00	1.75
22	A4	20sk black	4.00	1.75
23	A4	30sk black	4.00	1.75
24	A4	40sk black	4.00	1.75
25	A4	50sk black	4.00	1.75
26	A4	60sk black	4.00	1.75
		Nos. 20-26 (7)	28.00	12.25

Catalogue values for unused stamps in this section, from this point to the end of the section, are for Never Hinged items.

The White Knight "Vytis"
A5 A6

A7

A8

Perf. 10½ to 14 & Compound

1919 Litho. Wmk. 144

Gray Granite Paper

No.	Type	Description	Unused	Used
30	A5	10sk deep rose	1.00	.30
a.		Wmk. vert.	17.50	10.00
31	A5	15sk violet	1.00	.30
a.		Wmk. vert.	17.50	10.00
32	A5	20sk dark blue	1.25	.35
33	A5	30sk deep orange	1.25	.35
a.		Wmk. vert.	17.50	10.00
34	A5	40sk dark brown	1.25	.35
35	A6	50sk blue green	1.25	.50
36	A6	75sk org & dp rose	1.25	.35
37	A7	1auk gray & rose	2.50	.50
38	A7	3auk bis brn & rose	2.50	.50
39	A7	5auk blue grn & rose	2.50	.75
		Nos. 30-39 (10)	15.75	4.25

Nos. 30a, 31a and 33a are from the first printing with watermark vertical showing points to left; various perforations.

Nos. 30-39 exist imperf. Value in pairs, $50.

Issued: #30a, 31a, 33a, 2/17/19; #30-36, 3/20/19.

1919 Wmk. 145

Thick White Paper

No.	Type	Description	Unused	Used
40	A5	10sk dull rose	.35	.20
41	A5	15sk violet	.35	.20
42	A5	20sk dark blue	.35	.20
43	A5	30sk orange	.35	.20
44	A5	40sk red brown	.35	.20
45	A6	50sk green	.35	.20
46	A6	75sk yel & dp rose	.35	.20
47	A7	1auk gray & rose	.90	.20
48	A7	3auk yellow brn & rose, perf. 12½	.55	.25
49	A7	5auk bl grn & rose	.90	.35
		Nos. 40-49 (10)	4.80	2.20

Nos. 40-49 exist imperf. Value in pairs, $42.50.

Perf. 10½ to 14 & Compound

1919, May 8

Thin White Paper

No.	Type	Description	Unused	Used
50	A5	10sk red	.35	.20
51	A5	15sk lilac	.35	.20
52	A5	20sk dull blue	.35	.20
53	A5	30sk buff	.35	.20
54	A5	40sk gray brn	.35	.20
55	A6	50sk lt green	.35	.20
56	A6	60sk violet & red	.35	.20
57	A6	75sk bister & red	.35	.20
58	A8	1auk gray & red	.35	.20
59	A8	3auk lt brown & red	.35	.20
60	A8	5auk blue grn & red	.35	.20
		Nos. 50-60 (11)	3.85	2.20

Nos. 50-60 exist imperf. Value, pairs $70.

See Nos. 93-96. For surcharges see Nos. 114-115, 120-139, 149-150.

"Lithuania" Receiving Benediction — A9

The Spirit of Lithuania Rises — A10

"Lithuania" with Chains Broken — A11

White Knight — A12

1920, Feb. 16 Wmk. 146 *Perf. 11½*

No.	Type	Description	Unused	Used
70	A9	10sk dp rose	3.50	2.00
71	A9	15sk lt violet	3.50	2.00
72	A9	20sk gray blue	3.50	2.00
73	A10	30sk yellow brn	3.50	2.00
74	A11	40sk brown & grn	3.50	2.00
75	A10	50sk deep rose	3.50	2.00
76	A10	60sk lt violet	3.50	2.00
77	A11	80sk purple & red	3.50	2.00
78	A11	1auk green & red	3.50	2.00
79	A12	3auk brown & red	3.50	2.00
80	A12	5auk green & red	3.50	2.00
a.		Right "5" dbl., grn and red	90.00	90.00
		Nos. 70-80 (11)	38.50	22.00

Anniv. of natl. independence. The stamps were on sale only 3 days in Kaunas. The stamps were available in other cities after that. Only a limited number of stamps was sold at post offices but 40,000 sets were delivered to the bank of Kaunas.

All values exist imperforate.

White Knight — A13

Grand Duke Vytautas — A14

Grand Duke Gediminas A15

Sacred Oak and Altar A16

1920, Aug. 25

No.	Type	Description	Unused	Used
81	A13	10sk rose	.85	.40
a.		Imperf., pair	40.00	
82	A13	15sk dark violet	.85	.40
83	A14	20sk grn & lt grn	.85	.40
84	A13	30sk brown	.85	.40
a.		Pair, #82, 84	40.00	
85	A15	40sk gray grn & vio	.85	.40
86	A14	50sk brn & brn org	2.50	1.00
87	A14	60sk red & org	1.50	1.00
88	A15	80sk blk, db & red	1.50	1.00
89	A16	1auk orange & blk	1.50	1.00
90	A16	3auk green & blk	1.50	1.00
91	A16	5auk gray vio & blk	4.00	1.00
		Nos. 81-91 (11)	16.75	8.00

Opening of Lithuanian National Assembly. On sale for three days.

1920

No.	Type	Description	Unused	Used
92	A14	20sk green & lilac	150.00	
92A	A15	40sk gray grn, buff & vio	150.00	
92B	A14	50sk brown & gray lil	150.00	

92C A14 60sk red & green 150.00
92D A15 80sk black, grn & red 150.00
Nos. 92-92D (5) 750.00

Nos. 92 to 92D were trial printings. By order of the Ministry of Posts, 2,000 copies of each were placed on sale at post offices.

Type of 1919 Issue

1920 Unwmk. *Perf. 11½*
93 A5 15sk lilac 6.00 2.00
94 A5 20sk deep blue 6.00 2.00

Wmk. 109
95 A5 20sk deep blue 5.25 2.00
96 A5 40sk gray brown 12.00 3.00
Nos. 93-96 (4) 29.25 9.00

Watermark horizontal on Nos. 95-96.
No. 96 exists perf. 10½x11½.

Imperf., Pairs
93a A5 15sk 32.00 32.00
94a A5 20sk 32.00 32.00
95a A5 20sk 17.00 17.00
96a A5 40sk 48.00 48.00

Sower
A17

Peasant Sharpening Scythe
A18

Prince Kestutis
A19

Black Horseman
A20

Perf. 11, 11½ and Compound
1921-22
97 A17 10sk brt rose .85 .55
98 A17 15sk violet .35 *.70*
99 A17 20sk ultra .25 .20
100 A18 30sk brown 2.50 *1.10*
101 A19 40sk red .25 .20
102 A18 50sk olive .35 .20
103 A18 60sk grn & vio 2.50 *1.65*
104 A19 80sk brn org & car .35 .20
105 A19 1auk brown & grn .35 .20
106 A19 2auk gray bl & red .35 .20
107 A20 3auk yel brn & dk bl 1.00 .40
108 A17 4auk yel & dk bl ('22) .45 .20
109 A20 5auk gray blk & rose 1.00 *1.50*
110 A17 8auk grn & blk ('22) .45 .20
111 A20 10auk rose & vio 1.00 .55
112 A20 25auk bis brn & grn 1.25 .85
113 A20 100auk dl red & gray blk 12.50 8.00
Nos. 97-113 (17) 25.75 16.90

Imperf., Pairs
97a A17 10sk —
98a A17 15sk —
99a A17 20sk —
100a A18 30sk —
101a A19 40sk 25.00
102a A18 50sk 25.00
103a A18 60sk —
104a A19 80sk —
105a A19 1auk —
106a A19 2auk 120.00
107a A20 3auk 120.00
109a A20 5auk 120.00
110a A17 8auk 10.00 10.00
111a A20 10auk 50.00
112a A20 25auk 50.00
113a A20 100auk 50.00

For surcharges see Nos. 140-148, 151-160.

No. 57 Surcharged

Perf. 12½x11½
1922, May Wmk. 145
114 A6 4auk on 75sk bis & red .90 .20
a. Inverted surcharge 35.00 35.00

Same with Bars over Original Value
115 A6 4auk on 75sk bis & red 4.00 *8.00*
a. Double surcharge 30.00 30.00

Povilas Luksis
A20a

Justinas Staugaitis, Antanas Smetona, Stasys Silingas — A20b

Portraits: 40s, Lt. Juozapavicius. 50s, Dr. Basanavicius. 60s, Mrs. Petkeviciute. 1auk, Prof. Voldemaras. 2auk, Pranas Dovidaitis. 3auk, Dr. Slezevicius. 4auk, Dr. Galvanauskas. 5auk, Kazys Grinius. 6auk, Dr. Stulginskis. 8auk, Pres. Smetona.

1922 Litho. Unwmk.
116 A20a 20s blk & car rose 1.25 .90
116A A20a 40s bl grn & vio 1.25 .90
116B A20a 50s plum & grnsh bl 1.25 .90
117 A20a 60s pur & org 1.25 .90
117A A20a 1auk car & lt bl 1.25 .90
117B A20a 2auk dp bl & yel brn 1.25 .90
c. Center inverted 100.00 100.00
118 A20a 3auk mar & ultra 1.25 .90
118A A20a 4auk dk grn & red vio 1.25 .90
118B A20a 5auk blk brn & dp rose 1.25 .90
119 A20a 6auk dk bl & grnsh bl 1.25 .90
a. Cliché of 8auk in sheet of 6auk 100.00 100.00
119B A20a 8auk ultra & bis 1.25 .90
119C A20b 10auk dk vio & bl grn 1.25 .90
Nos. 116-119C (12) 15.00 10.80

League of Nations' recognition of Lithuania. Sold only on Oct. 1, 1922.

Forty sheets of the 6auk each included eight examples of the 8auk.

Stamps of 1919-22 Surcharged in Black, Carmine or Green

On Nos. 37-39

1922 Wmk. 144 *Perf. 11½x12*
Gray Granite Paper
120 A7 3c on 1auk 175.00 110.00
121 A7 3c on 3auk 175.00 110.00
122 A7 3c on 5auk 110.00 65.00
Nos. 120-122 (3) 460.00 285.00

White Paper
Wmk. 145
Perf. 14, 11½, 12½x11½
123 A5 1c on 10sk red 2.75 1.50
124 A5 1c on 15sk lilac 4.00 1.50
125 A5 1c on 20sk dull bl 2.50 1.50
126 A5 1c on 30sk orange 110.00 110.00
127 A5 1c on 30sk buff .40 .40
128 A5 1c on 40sk gray brn 2.00 1.50
129 A6 2c on 50sk green 3.00 1.50
130 A6 2c on 60sk vio & red .20 .20
131 A6 2c on 75sk bis & red 2.00 1.50
132 A8 3c on 1auk gray & red .45 .45
133 A8 3c on 3auk brn & red .25 .20
134 A8 3c on 5auk bl grn & red .25 .20
Nos. 123-125,127-134 (11) 17.80 10.45

On Stamps of 1920

1922 Unwmk. *Perf. 11*
136 A5 1c on 20sk dp bl (C) 4.00 2.00

Wmk. Webbing (109)
Perf. 11, 11½
138 A5 1c on 20sk dp bl (C) 3.75 2.00
139 A5 1c on 40sk gray brn (C) 8.00 1.25

On Stamps of 1921-22
140 A18 1c on 50sk ol (C) .25 .20
a. Imperf., pair 45.00
b. Inverted surcharge 40.00
c. Double surch., one invtd.
141 A17 3c on 10sk 12.00 8.00
142 A17 3c on 15sk .25 .20
143 A17 3c on 20sk .45 1.50
144 A18 3c on 30sk 17.50 12.00
145 A19 3c on 40sk .45 .45
a. Imperf., pair
146 A18 5c on 50sk .20 .20
147 A18 5c on 60sk 17.50 15.00
148 A19 5c on 80sk .60 .50
a. Imperf., pair 35.00 15.00

Wmk. Wavy Lines (145)
Perf. 12½x11½
149 A6 5c on 4auk on 75sk (No. 114) (G) 1.75 10.00
150 A6 5c on 4auk on 75sk (No. 115) (G) 17.50 17.50

Wmk. Webbing (109)
Perf. 11, 11½
151 A19 10c on 1auk .85 .20
a. Inverted surcharge 55.00
152 A19 10c on 2auk .25 .20
a. Inverted surcharge 50.00
b. Imperf., pair 45.00
153 A17 15c on 4auk .25 .20
a. Inverted surcharge 45.00
154 A20 25c on 3auk 17.50 17.50
155 A20 25c on 5auk 12.00 5.00
156 A20 25c on 10auk 2.50 1.50
a. Imperf., pair 45.00
157 A17 30c on 8auk (C) 1.25 .35
a. Inverted surcharge 45.00 25.00
158 A20 50c on 25auk 4.00 2.50
160 A20 1 l on 100auk 4.25 2.50
Nos. 136-160 (23) 127.05 100.75

A21

Ruin — A22

Seminary Church, Kaunas — A23

1923 Litho. Wmk. 109 *Perf. 11*
165 A21 10c violet 6.75 .20
166 A21 15c scarlet 2.50 .20
167 A21 20c olive brown 2.50 .20
168 A21 25c deep blue 2.50 .20
169 A22 50c yellow green 2.50 .20
170 A22 60c red 2.50 .20
171 A23 1 l orange & grn 11.00 .20
172 A23 3 l red & gray 15.00 .45
173 A23 5 l brown & blue 22.50 1.00
Nos. 165-173 (9) 67.75 2.85

See Nos. 189-209, 281-282. For surcharges see Nos. B1-B42.

Memel Coat of Arms — A24

Lithuanian Coat of Arms — A25

Biruta Chapel — A26

Kaunas, War Memorial
A27

Trakai Ruins
A28

Memel Lighthouse — A29

Memel Harbor
A30

Perf. 11, 11½, 12
1923, Aug. Unwmk.
176 A24 1c rose, grn & blk 2.25 1.60
177 A25 2c dull vio & blk 2.25 1.60
178 A26 3c yellow & blk 2.25 1.60
179 A24 5c bl, buff & blk 2.75 1.90
180 A27 10c orange & blk 2.75 1.90
181 A27 15c green & blk 3.00 2.50
182 A28 25c brt vio & blk 3.00 2.50
183 A25 30c red vio & blk 5.00 5.00
184 A29 60c ol grn & blk 4.00 2.75
185 A30 1 l bl grn & blk 4.00 2.75
186 A26 2 l red & black 10.00 7.50
187 A28 3 l blue & black 10.00 7.50
188 A29 5 l ultra & black 10.00 7.50
Nos. 176-188 (13) 61.25 46.60

This series was issued ostensibly to commemorate the incorporation of Memel with Lithuania.

Type of 1923 Issue

1923 Unwmk. *Perf. 11*
189 A21 5c pale green 4.00 .20
190 A21 10c violet 5.50 .20
a. Imperf., pair 50.00
191 A21 15c scarlet 7.00 .20
a. Imperf., pair 50.00
193 A21 25c blue 11.00 .20
Nos. 189-193 (4) 27.50 .80

1923 Wmk. 147
196 A21 2c pale brown 1.25 .25
197 A21 3c olive bister 1.40 .20
198 A21 5c pale green 1.40 .20
199 A21 10c violet 3.25 .20
202 A21 25c deep blue 7.00 .20
a. Imperf., pair 40.00
204 A21 36c orange brown 11.00 .75
Nos. 196-204 (6) 25.30 1.80

Perf. 11½, 14½, 11½x14½
1923-25 Wmk. 198
207 A21 25c deep blue 500.00 450.00
208 A22 50c deep green ('25) 4.00 .40
209 A22 60c carmine ('25) 4.50 .40

Double- barred Cross A31

Dr. Jonas Basanavicius A32

1927, Jan. *Perf. 11½, 14½*
210 A31 2c orange 1.75 .20
211 A31 3c deep brown 1.75 .20
212 A31 5c green 2.50 .20
a. Imperf., pair 25.00
213 A31 10c violet 4.00 .20
214 A31 15c red 3.50 .20
a. Imperf., pair 25.00
215 A31 25c blue 4.50 .20
Nos. 210-215 (6) 18.00 1.20

1927-29 Wmk. 147 *Perf. 14½*
216 A31 5c green 30.00 35.00
217 A31 30c blue ('30) 30.00 6.00
See Nos. 233-240, 278-280.

1927 Unwmk. *Perf. 11½, 14½x11½*
219 A32 15c claret & blk 2.50 1.25
220 A32 25c dull blue & blk 2.50 1.25
221 A32 50c dk green & blk 2.50 1.25
222 A32 60c dk violet & blk 5.00 2.00
Nos. 219-222 (4) 12.50 5.75

Dr. Jonas Basanavicius (1851-1927), patriot and folklorist.

National Arms — A33

1927, Dec. 23 Wmk. 109 *Perf. 14½*
223 A33 1 l blue grn & gray 2.25 .75
224 A33 3 l vio & pale grn 6.00 .75
225 A33 5 l brown & gray 7.50 1.25
Nos. 223-225 (3) 15.75 2.75

Pres. Antanas Smetona — A34

Decade of Independence A35

Dawn of Peace — A36

1928, Feb. Wmk. 109
226 A34 5c org brn & grn 1.00 .30
227 A34 10c violet & blk 1.25 .30
228 A34 15c orange & brn 1.25 .30
229 A34 25c blue & indigo 1.25 .30
230 A35 50c ultra & dl vio 1.50 .30
231 A35 60c carmine & blk 1.50 .55
232 A36 1 l blk brn & drab 2.00 .70
Nos. 226-232 (7) 9.75 2.75

10th anniv. of Lithuanian independence.

Type of 1926 Issue

1929-31
233 A31 2c orange ('31) 16.50 1.00
234 A31 5c green 3.75 .20
235 A31 10c violet ('31) 12.00 1.00
237 A31 15c red 4.50 .20
a. Tête bêche pair 45.00 35.00
239 A31 30c dark blue 7.00 .20

Unwmk.
240 A31 15c red ('30) 12.50 .60
Nos. 233-240 (6) 56.25 3.20

Grand Duke Vytautas A37

Grand Duke, Mounted A38

1930, Feb. 16 *Perf. 14*
242 A37 2c yel brn & dk brn .45 .20
243 A37 3c dk brn & vio .45 .20
244 A37 5c yel grn & dp org .45 .20
245 A37 10c vio & emer .45 .20
246 A37 15c dp rose & vio .45 .20
247 A37 30c dk bl & brn vio .85 .20
248 A37 36c brn vio & ol blk 1.25 .30
249 A37 50c dull grn & ultra .85 .35
250 A37 60c dk blue & rose .85 .40
251 A38 1 l bl grn, db & red brn 3.50 1.00
252 A38 3 l dk brn, sal & dk vio 4.75 1.75
253 A38 5 l ol brn, gray & red 11.50 2.75
254 A38 10 l multicolored 30.00 15.00
255 A38 25 l multicolored 60.00 52.50
Nos. 242-255 (14) 115.80 75.25

5th cent. of the death of the Grand Duke Vytautas.

Kaunas, Railroad Station A39

Cathedral at Vilnius A39a

Designs: 15c, 25c, Landscape on the Neman River. 50c, Main Post Office, Kaunas.

Perf. 14, Imperf.
1932, July 21 Wmk. 238
256 A39 10c dk red brn & ocher .45 .45
257 A39 15c dk brown & ol .80 .80
258 A39 25c dk blue & ol 1.25 1.25
259 A39 50c gray blk & ol 2.50 2.50
260 A39a 1 l dk blue & ol 5.00 5.00
261 A39a 3 l red brn & gray grn 6.50 6.50

Wmk. 198
262 A39 5c vio bl & ocher .45 .45
263 A39a 60c grnsh blk & lil 5.00 5.00
Nos. 256-263 (8) 21.95 21.95

Issued for the benefit of Lithuanian orphans.

In September, 1935, a red overprint was applied to No. 259: "ORO PASTAS / LITUANICA II / 1935 / NEW YORK-KAUNAS." Value, $250.

Vytautas Fleeing from Prison, 1382 A40

Designs: 15c, 25c, Conversion of Ladislas II Jagello and Vytautas (1386). 50c, 60c, Battle at Tannenberg (1410). 1 l, 3 l, Meeting of the Nobles (1429).

1932 Wmk. 209 *Perf. 14, Imperf.*
264 A40 5c red & rose lake .75 .35
265 A40 10c ol bis & org brn .85 .35
266 A40 15c rose lil & ol grn 1.00 .50
267 A40 25c dk vio brn & ocher 2.25 1.25
268 A40 50c dp grn & bis brn 2.25 1.75
269 A40 60c ol grn & brn car 5.50 2.50
270 A40 1 l ultra & ol grn 6.00 3.00
271 A40 3 l dk brn & dk grn 6.50 4.00
Nos. 264-271 (8) 25.10 13.70

15th anniversary of independence.

A. Visteliauskas A41

Mother and Child — A42

Designs: 15c, 25c, Petras Vileisis. 50c, 60c, Dr. John Sliupas. 1 l, 3 l, Jonas Basanavicius.

1933 *Perf. 14, Imperf.*
272 A41 5c yel grn & car .60 .30
273 A41 10c ultra & car .80 .40
274 A41 15c orange & red 1.00 .50
275 A41 25c dk bl & blk brn 1.50 .90
276 A41 50c ol gray & dk bl 2.50 1.50
277 A41 60c org brn & chnt 8.00 4.00
277A A41 1 l red & vio brn 10.00 4.75
277B A41 3 l turq grn & vio brn 11.00 6.00
Nos. 272-277B (8) 35.40 18.35

50th anniv. of the 1st newspaper, "Ausra," in lithuanian language.

1933, Sept. *Perf. 14, Imperf.*

Designs: 15c, 25c, Boy reading. 50c, 60c, Boy playing with blocks. 1 l, 3 l, Woman and boy at the Spinning Wheel.

277C A42 5c dp yel grn & org brn .25 .20
277D A42 10c rose brn & ultra .35 .20
277E A42 15c ol grn & plum .45 .25
277F A42 25c org & gray blk 1.50 .75
277G A42 50c ol grn & car 1.75 1.25
277H A42 60c blk & yel org 5.75 3.00
277I A42 1 l dk brn & ultra 6.75 3.25
277K A42 3 l rose lil & ol grn 7.25 *5.00*
Nos. 277C-277K (8) 24.05 *13.90*

Issued for the benefit of Lithuanian orphans.

Types of 1923-26 Issues

1933-34 Wmk. 238 *Perf. 14*
278 A31 2c orange 37.50 6.00
279 A31 10c dark violet 50.00 9.00
280 A31 15c red 37.50 4.50
281 A22 50c green 37.50 9.00
282 A22 60c red 37.50 9.00
Nos. 278-282 (5) 200.00 37.50

Pres. Antanas Smetona, 60th Birthday — A43

1934 Unwmk. Engr. *Perf. 11½*
283 A43 15c red 7.50 .20
284 A43 30c green 10.00 .25
285 A43 60c blue 12.50 .40
Nos. 283-285 (3) 30.00 .85

A44

A47

Arms — A45

Knight A48

Girl with Wheat — A46

Wmk. 198; Wmk. 209 (35c, 10 l)
1934-35 Litho. *Perf. 14*
286 A44 2c rose & dull org 1.25 .20
287 A44 5c bl grn & grn 1.25 .20
288 A45 10c chocolate 2.75 .20
289 A46 25c dk brn & emer 4.50 .20
290 A45 35c carmine 4.50 .20
291 A46 50c dk blue & blue 5.75 .20
292 A47 1 l sl & mar 70.00 .20
293 A47 3 l grn & gray grn .35 .20
294 A48 5 l maroon & gray bl .55 .45
295 A48 10 l choc & yel 3.00 3.75
Nos. 286-295 (10) 93.90 5.80

No. 290 exists imperf. Value, pair $35.
For overprint see No. 2N9.

1936-37 Wmk. 238 *Perf. 14*
Size: 17½x23mm
296 A44 2c orange ('37) .25 .20
297 A44 5c green .30 .20

Pres. Smetona A49

Arms A50

1936-37 Unwmk.
298 A49 15c carmine 9.00 .20
299 A49 30c green ('37) 12.00 .20
300 A49 60c ultra ('37) 11.00 .20
Nos. 298-300 (3) 32.00 .60

1937-39 Wmk. 238 *Perf. 14*
Paper with Gray Network
301 A50 10c green 1.60 .20
302 A50 25c magenta .25 .20
303 A50 35c red .85 .20
304 A50 50c brown .40 .20
305 A50 1 l dp vio bl ('39) .45 .45
Nos. 301-305 (5) 3.55 1.25

No. 304 exists in two types:
I — "50" is fat and broad, with "0" leaning to right.
II — "50" is thinner and narrower, with "0" straight.
For overprint see No. 2N10.

Jonas Basanavicius Reading Act of Independence A51

President Antanas Smetona A52

Perf. 13x13½

1939, Jan. 15 Engr. Unwmk.

306 A51 15c dark red .50 .30
307 A52 30c deep green .85 .30
308 A51 35c red lilac 1.25 .45
309 A52 60c dark blue 1.25 .60
a. Souvenir sheet of 2, #308-309 10.00 15.00
b. As "a," imperf. 60.00 60.00
Nos. 306-309 (4) 3.85 1.65

20th anniv. of Independence.
Nos. 309a, 309b sold for 2 l.

Same Overprinted in Blue

1939

310 A51 15c dark red .85 .90
311 A52 30c deep green .90 .90
312 A51 35c red lilac 2.00 1.00
313 A52 60c dark blue 2.25 1.00
Nos. 310-313 (4) 6.00 3.80

Recovery of Vilnius.

View of Vilnius A53

Gediminas — A54

Trakai Ruins A55

Unwmk.

1940, May 6 Photo. *Perf. 14*

314 A53 15c brn & pale brn .45 .25
315 A54 30c dk grn & lt grn .85 .85
316 A55 60c dk bl & lt bl 1.75 1.00
a. Souv. sheet of 3, #314-316, imperf. 16.00 16.00
Nos. 314-316 (3) 3.05 2.10

Return of Vilnius to Lithuania, Oct. 10, 1939. Exist imperf.
No. 316a has simulated perforations in gold. Sold for 2 l.

White Knight — A56

Angel — A57

Woman Releasing Dove A58

Mother and Children A59

Liberty Bell — A60

Mythical Animal — A61

1940

317 A56 5c brown carmine .20 .20
318 A57 10c green .85 .35
319 A58 15c dull orange .20 .20
320 A59 25c light brown .20 .20
321 A60 30c Prussian green .20 .20
322 A61 35c red orange .25 .25
Nos. 317-322 (6) 1.90 1.40

Nos. 317-322 exist imperf.
For overprints see Nos. 2N11-2N16.

Nos. 371-399 were issued before the Soviet Union recognized the independence of Lithuania on Sept. 6, 1991, but were available and valid for use after that date.

Angel and Map — A66

Colors: 5k, Green. 10k, Brown violet. 20k, Blue. 50k, Red.

1990, Oct. 7 Litho. *Imperf.*
Without Gum

371-374 A66 Set of 4 2.10 2.10

Simulated Perforations and Denomination in Brownish Gray

Denominations and colors as before.

1990, Dec. 22 Without Gum

375-378 A66 Set of 4 1.50 1.50

White Knight "Vytis" — A67

Hill With Crosses, Siauliai — A68

Design: 200k, Liberty Bell.

1991 Photo. *Perf. 14*

379 A67 10k multi .30 .20
380 A67 15k multi .30 .20
381 A67 20k multi .30 .20
382 A67 30k multi .30 .20
383 A68 50k multi .30 .20
384 A68 200k multi .40 .20

Litho.
Imperf
Without Gum

385 A67 15k dl grn & blk .30 .20
386 A67 25k brn & blk .30 .20
387 A67 30k plum & blk .30 .20
Nos. 379-387 (9) 2.80 1.80

Issued: 10k, 20k, #382, 50k, 200k, 1/10; #380, 3/15; #385, 3/13; 25k, #387, 7/23.
No. 385 has a simulated outline of a perforated stamp.

See Nos. 411-418.

Liberty Statue — A69

1991, Feb. 16 Photo. *Perf. 13¾x14*

388 A69 20k multi .25 .20

Declaration of Independence from Soviet Union, 1st Anniv. — A70

1991, Mar. 11 Litho. *Perf. 13¼x13*

389 A70 20k multi .25 .20

Religious Symbols — A71

Designs: 40k, Crosses. 70k, Madonna. 100k, Spires, St. Anne's Church, Vilnius.

1991, Mar. 15 Photo. *Perf. 13¾x14*

390-392 A71 Set of 3 1.25 .75

Resistance to Soviet and German Occupation, 50th Anniv. — A72

Designs: 20k, Candle, barbed wire. 50k, Heart, daggers. 70k, Sword, wreath.

1991, June 14 Litho. *Perf. 13¼*

393-395 A72 Set of 3 1.25 .75

Fourth World Lithuanian Games A73

Emblem and: 20k, Map. 50k+25k, Head.

1991, July 27 Photo. *Perf. 13¼x13*

396-397 A73 Set of 2 .85 .50

A74

A75

Denominations: 20k, 70k.

1991. Aug. 20 Litho. *Perf. 12½x13*

398-399 A74 Set of 2 1.25 .75

Expedition to Mt. Everest.

1991, Sept. 28 Litho. *Perf. 13x13½*

400 A75 30k Castle .30 .30
401 A75 50k Grand Duke .55 .55
402 A75 70k Early view of Vilnius .85 .85
Nos. 400-402 (3) 1.70 1.70

Grand Duke Gediminas, 650th dath anniv.

Ciconia Nigra — A76

Design: 50k, Grus grus.

1991, Nov. 21 Litho. *Perf. 14*

403 A76 30k +15k multi .65 .55
404 A76 50k multicolored .75 .65

White Knight Type of 1991

1991, Dec. 20 Photo. *Perf. 14*
Background Colors

411 A67 40k black .20 .20
412 A67 50k purple .20 .20
415 A67 100k dark green .25 .25
418 A67 500k blue .90 .55
Nos. 411-418 (4) 1.55 1.20

For surcharges see Nos. 450-452.

A78

OLIMPINIS KOMITETAS
TAUTINIS
LIETUVA
+25
50
LIETUVA

A79

1992, Mar. 15 Litho. *Perf. 13x13½*

421 A78 100k multicolored .30 .30

Lithuanian admission to UN.

1992, Mar. 22

Emblems.

422 A79 50k +25k Olympic Committee .25 .25
423 A79 130k Albertville .40 .40
424 A79 280k Barcelona 1.10 1.10
Nos. 422-424 (3) 1.75 1.75

Lithuanian Olympic participation. Surtax for Lithuanian Olympic Committee.

200
LIETUVA

A80

A81

1992, July 11 *Perf. 12½x13*

425 A80 200k Cypripedium .30 .30
426 A80 300k Eringium maritimum .50 .50

Litho. & Engr.

1992, Oct. 3 *Perf. 12½x13*

Birds of the Baltic Shores: No. 427, Pandion haliaetus. No. 428, Limosa limosa. No. 429, Mergus merganser. No. 430, Tadorna tadorna.

Booklet Stamps

427 A81 B grn & grnsh blk .70 .50
428 A81 B grn & red brn .70 .50
429 A81 B grn, red brn & brn .70 .50
430 A81 B grn & red brn .70 .50
a. Booklet pane of 4, #427-430 3.25

Sold for 15r on day of issue.
See Estonia Nos. 231-234a, Latvia Nos. 332-335a and Sweden Nos. 1975-1978a.

Coats of Arms — A82

19th Cent. Costumes — A83

1992, Oct. 11 **Litho.** *Perf. 14*

431 A82 2r Kedainiai .20 .20
432 A82 3r Vilnius .20 .20
433 A82 10r National .55 .55
Nos. 431-433 (3) .95 .95

See Nos. 454-456, 497-499, 521-522, 554-556, 586-588, 607-609, 642-644, 677-679, 704-706, 716-718, 736-740, 762-764, 788-789, 813-815, 833-835.

1992, Oct. 18 *Perf. 13x13½*

Couples in different traditional costumes of the Suwalki region.

434 A83 2r multicolored .20 .20
435 A83 5r multicolored .25 .25
436 A83 7r multicolored .40 .35
Nos. 434-436 (3) .85 .80

See #465-467, 493-495, 511-513, 539-541.

Churches — A84

300k, Zapishkis Church, 16th cent. 1000k, Saints Peter & Paul Church, Vilnius, 17th cent. 1500k, Christ Church of the Resurrection, Kaunas, 1934.

1993, Jan. 15 **Litho.** *Perf. 12*

437 A84 300k bister & blk .20 .20
438 A84 1000k blue green & blk .50 .35
439 A84 1500k gray & blk .85 .50
Nos. 437-439 (3) 1.55 1.05

See Nos. 502-504

Independence — A85

Designs: A, Jonas Basanavicius (1851-1927), journalist and politician. B, Jonas Vileisis (1872-1942), lawyer and politician.

1993, Feb. 16

440 A85 (A) red & multi .25 .20
441 A85 (B) green & multi .95 .65

No. 440 sold for 3r and No. 441 sold for 15r on day of issue.
See Nos. 479-480, 506-507, 536-537, 563-564, 592-593, 622-623, 660-661.

A86

Grand Duke Vytautas, 600th Birth Anniv. — A87

Designs: 500k, Royal Seal. 1000k, 5000k, Portrait. 1500k, Vytautas in Battle of Grunwald, by Jan Matejko.

1993, Feb. 27

442 A86 500k bister, red & blk .20 .20
443 A87 1000k citron, blk & red .40 .30
444 A87 1500k lem, blk & red .60 .50
Nos. 442-444 (3) 1.20 1.00

Souvenir Sheet

445 A87 5000k citron, black & red 1.60 1.60

Famous Lithuanians A88

Designs: 1000k, Simonas Daukantas (1793-1864), educator and historian. 2000k, Vydunas (1868-1953), preserver of Lithuanian traditional culture. 4500k, Vincas Mykolaitis Putinas (1893-1967), philosopher and psychologist.

1993, Mar. 13

446 A88 1000k multicolored .25 .25
447 A88 2000k multicolored .50 .50
448 A88 4500k multicolored 1.00 .90
Nos. 446-448 (3) 1.75 1.65

See Nos. 475-477, 514-516, 533-535, 560-562, 599-601, 624-626.

No. 382, 387 and 411 Surcharged

1993 **Photo, Litho. (#451)** *Perf. 14*

450 A67 100k on 30k magenta .20 .20
451 A67 100k on 30k magenta, imperf, without gum .20 .20
452 A67 300k on 40k #411 .20 .20
Nos. 450-452 (3) .60 .60

Issued: 300k, 1/19; #450, 1/26; #451, 3/10.
Nos. 450-451 without surcharge was issued prior to Soviet recognition of Lithuanian Independence.

Coat of Arms Type of 1992

Size: 24x31mm

1993, July 3 **Litho.** *Perf. 11*

454 A82 5c Skuodas .20 .20
a. Tete-beche pair .40 .40
455 A82 30c Telsiai .35 .30
a. Tete-beche pair 1.20 .60
456 A82 50c Klaipeda .55 .45
a. Tete-beche pair 1.70 .90
Nos. 454-456 (3) 1.10 .95

World Lithuanian Unity Day — A89

5c, The Spring, by M. K. Ciurlionis. 80c, Capts. Steponas Darius and Stasys Girenas.

1993, July 17 *Perf. 13*

457 A89 5c multicolored .20 .20
a. Tete-beche pair .30
458 A89 80c multicolored .75 .75
a. Tete-beche pair 2.40

Deaths of Darius and Girenas, 60th anniv. (#458).

Natl. Arms — A90

1993, July 21 **Litho.** *Perf. 13x12½*

459 A90 (A) bister & multi .30 .20
460 A90 (B) green & multi .80 .20

#459 sold for 5c; #460 for 80c on day of issue.
Dated 1992.

Visit of Pope John Paul II — A91

1993, Sept. 3 **Litho.** *Perf. 13½x13*

461 A91 60c Kryziu Kalnas .50 .30
462 A91 60c Siluva .50 .30
463 A91 80c Vilnius .70 .35
464 A91 80c Kaunas .70 .35
Nos. 461-464 (4) 2.40 1.30

Natl. Costumes Type of 1992

Couples in different traditional costumes of the Dzukai.

1993, Oct. 30 **Litho.** *Perf. 12*

Size: 23x36mm

465 A83 60c multicolored .40 .25
466 A83 80c multicolored .60 .35
467 A83 1 l multicolored 1.00 .45
Nos. 465-467 (3) 2.00 1.05

Lithuanian Postal System, 75th Anniv. — A92

Post offices: No. 468, Klaipeda. No. 469, Kaunas. 80c, Vilnius. 1 l, No. 1.

1993, Nov. 16

468 A92 60c multicolored .40 .20
469 A92 60c multicolored .40 .20
470 A92 80c multicolored .60 .30
471 A92 1 l multicolored .90 .40
Nos. 468-471 (4) 2.30 1.10

Europa — A93

Endangered Species — A94

80c, The Old Master, by A. Gudaitis, 1939.

1993, Dec. 24 **Litho.** *Perf. 12*

472 A93 80c multicolored 1.40 1.40
a. Tete-beche pair 3.50 3.50

1993, Dec. 30 **Litho.** *Perf. 12*

473 A94 80c Emys orbicularis .60 .30
474 A94 1 l Bufo calamita 1.00 .40

See Nos. 500-501, 519-520.

Famous Lithuanians Type of 1993

Designs: 60c, Kristijonas Donelaitis (1714-80), poet. 80c, Vincas Kudirka (1858-99), physician, writer. 1 l, Maironis (1862-1932), poet.

1994, Mar. 26 **Litho.** *Perf. 12*

475 A88 60c multicolored .35 .20
476 A88 80c multicolored .55 .30
477 A88 1 l multicolored .85 .40
Nos. 475-477 (3) 1.75 .90

1994 Winter Olympics, Lillehammer A95

1994, Feb. 11

478 A95 1.10 l multicolored .75 .40

Independence Type of 1993

#479, Pres. Antanas Smetona (1874-1944). #480, Aleksandras Stulginskis.

1994, Feb. 16

479 A85 1 l red brown & multi .80 .35
480 A85 1 l brown & multi .80 .35

A96

Natl. Arms — A96a

Perf. 12, 13½ (40c), 13½x13 (50c)

1994-97 **Litho.**

481 A96 5c dark brown .20 .20
482 A96 10c deep violet .20 .20
483 A96 20c dark green .20 .20
484 A96 40c deep rose mag .20 .20
485 A96 50c green blue .30 .20
486 A96a 1 l gray & multi .50 .25
a. Souvenir sheet of 4 3.00 3.00
487 A96a 2 l buff & multi 1.50 .50
488 A96a 3 l green & multi 2.00 .75
Nos. 481-488 (8) 5.10 2.50

Independence, 5th anniv. (#486a).
Issued: 5c, 10c, 4/9/94; 20c, 11/19/94; 2 l, 3 l, 7/23/94; 1 l, 3/11/95; 40c, 5/4/96; 50c, 4/5/97.
This is an expanding set. Numbers may change.

Europa — A97

1994, May 7 **Litho.** *Perf. 12*

491 A97 80c Artillery rockets, 17th cent. .70 .40

Souvenir Sheet

100th Postage Stamp — A98

Illustration reduced.

1994, May 21 Litho. *Perf. 12*
492 A98 10 l multicolored 8.00 8.00

No. 492 sold for 12 l.

Natl. Costumes Type of 1992

Couples in different traditional costumes of Samogitia.

1994, June 25 Litho. *Perf. 12*
493 A83 5c multicolored .30 .20
494 A83 80c multicolored .60 .25
495 A83 1 l multicolored .70 .30
Nos. 493-495 (3) 1.60 .75

Lithuanian World Song Festival — A99

1994, July 6
496 A99 10c multicolored .20 .20

Coat of Arms Type of 1992

1994, Sept. 10 Litho. *Perf. 12*
Size: 25x32mm
497 A82 10c Punia .25 .20
498 A82 60c Alytus .45 .20
499 A82 80c Perloja .60 .30
Nos. 497-499 (3) 1.30 .70

Endangered Species Type of 1993

1994, Oct. 22 Litho. *Perf. 12*
500 A94 20c Nyctalus noctula .30 .20
501 A94 20c Glis glis .30 .20

Church Type of 1993

1994, Nov. 12
502 A84 10c Kaunus, 16th cent. .25 .20
503 A84 60c Kedainiu, 17th cent. .45 .25
504 A84 80c Vilnius, 18th cent. .60 .35
Nos. 502-504 (3) 1.30 .80

Christmas A101

1994, Dec. 3 Litho. *Perf. 12*
505 A101 20c multicolored .25 .20

Independence Type of 1993

#506, Pranas Dovydaitis. #507, Steponas Kairys.

1995, Feb. 16 Litho. *Perf. 12*
506 A85 20c multicolored .20 .20
507 A85 20c multicolored .20 .20

Via Baltica Highway Project — A102

No. 509: a, Parnu. b, Bauska. c, Like #508.

1995, Apr. 20 Litho. *Perf. 14*
508 A102 20c multicolored .20 .20

Souvenir Sheet

509 A102 1 l Sheet of 3, #a.-c. 2.25 2.25

See Estonia Nos. 288-289, Latvia Nos. 394-395.

Sculpture, Mother's School — A103

1995, Apr. 29 Litho. *Perf. 12*
510 A103 1 l multicolored 1.40 1.40

Europa.

Natl. Costumes Type of 1992

Couples in traditional costumes of Aukstaiciai.

1995, May 20 Litho. *Perf. 12*
511 A83 20c multicolored .25 .20
512 A83 70c multicolored .60 .25
513 A83 1 l multicolored .75 .30
Nos. 511-513 (3) 1.60 .75

Europa.

Famous People Type of 1993

Writers: 30c, Motiejus Valancius (1801-75). 40c, Zemaite (1845-1921). 70c, Kipras Petrauskas (1885-1968).

1995, May 27 Litho. *Perf. 12*
514 A88 30c multicolored .20 .20
515 A88 40c multicolored .40 .20
516 A88 70c multicolored .60 .25
Nos. 514-516 (3) 1.20 .65

A104

A105

1995, June 14 Litho. *Perf. 12*
517 A104 20c multicolored .25 .20

Day of mourning & hope.

1995, July 30 Litho. *Perf. 12*
518 A105 30c multicolored .25 .20

5th World Sports Games.

Endangered Species Type of 1993

1995, Aug. 26 Litho. *Perf. 12*
519 A94 30c Arctia villica .25 .20
520 A94 30c Baptria tibiale .25 .20

Coat of Arms Type of 1992

Size: 25x32mm

Arms of villages in Suvalkija: 40c, Virbalis. 1 l, Kudirkos Naumiestis, horiz.

1995, Sept. 16 Litho. *Perf. 12*
521 A82 40c multicolored .30 .20
522 A82 1 l multicolored .90 .30

Valerie Mesalina, by Franciskus Smuglevicius — A106

1995, Oct. 6 Litho. *Perf. 12½*
523 A106 40c multicolored .35 .20

Castles — A107

1995, Nov. 18 *Perf. 11½x12*
524 A107 40c Vilnius .30 .20
525 A107 70c Trakai .60 .30
526 A107 1 l Birzai .90 .45
Nos. 524-526 (3) 1.80 .95

Christmas A108

Designs: 40c, People celebrating Christmas in outdoor snow scene. 1 l, People with lanterns walking toward church.

1995, Dec. 2 Litho. *Perf. 13*
527 A108 40c multicolored .30 .20
528 A108 1 l multicolored .90 .45

Bison Bonasus A109

1996, Jan. 20 *Perf. 13x13½*
529 A109 30c shown .25 .25
530 A109 40c Two adults .40 .25
531 A109 70c Adult, calf .75 .40
532 A109 1 l Two adults, calf 1.00 1.00
a. Miniature sheet, 2 each #529-532 4.50 4.50
Nos. 529-532 (4) 2.40 1.90

World Wildlife Fund.

Famous Lithuanians Type of 1993

Designs: 40c, Kazys Grinius (1866-1950). No. 534, Antanas Zmudzinavicius (1876-1966). No. 535, Balys Sruoga (1896-1947).

1996, Feb. 2 Litho. *Perf. 13x13½*
533 A88 40c multicolored .20 .20
534 A88 1 l multicolored .65 .30
535 A88 1 l multicolored .65 .30
Nos. 533-535 (3) 1.50 .80

Independence Type of 1993

#536, Vladas Mironas. #537, Jurgis Saulys.

1996, Feb. 16 Litho. *Perf. 13½x13*
536 A85 40c gray, blk & buff .30 .20
537 A85 40c olive, blk & buff .30 .20

Barbora Radvilaite (1520-51) — A110

1996, Apr. 27 Litho. *Perf. 13½x13*
538 A110 1 l multicolored 1.50 1.50

Europa.

19th Cent. Costumes Type of 1992

Couples in different traditional costumes of the Klaipeda region: #540, Man in blue coat. #541, Man wearing wooden shoes.

1996, May 25 Litho. *Perf. 13½*
539 A83 40c multicolored .35 .20
540 A83 1 l multicolored .75 .35
541 A83 1 l multicolored .75 .35
Nos. 539-541 (3) 1.85 .90

A116

A117

1996, June 14 Litho. *Perf. 13½*
547 A116 40c Christ .35 .20
548 A116 40c Angel .35 .20

Day of Mourning and Hope.

1996, July 19 *Perf. 13½x13*

Designs: No. 549, Greek discus thrower. No. 550, Basketball players.

549 A117 1 l multicolored 1.00 .50
550 A117 1 l multicolored 1.00 .50

1996 Summer Olympic Games, Atlanta.

Paintings, by M.K. Ciurlionis — A118

#551, Kapines, 1909. #552, Auka, 1909. #553: a, Andante, 1908. b, Allegro, 1908.

1996, Sept. 21 Litho. *Perf. 13½x13*
551 A118 40c multicolored .35 .20
552 A118 40c multicolored .35 .20

Souvenir Sheet

Perf. 12½x11½

553 A118 3 l Sheet of 2, #a.-b. 5.00 5.00

No. 553 contains 26x53mm stamps.

Coat of Arms Type of 1992

Size: 25x33mm

1996, Oct. 19 Litho. *Perf. 13½x13*
554 A82 50c Seduva .45 .20
555 A82 90c Panevezys .70 .35
556 A82 1.20 l Zarasai 1.00 .50
Nos. 554-556 (3) 2.15 1.05

Souvenir Sheet

Lithuanian Basketball Team, Bronze Medalists, 1996 Summer Olympic Games, Atlanta — A119

1996, Nov. 16 *Perf. 12½*
557 A119 4.20 l multicolored 3.50 3.50

Christmas A120

1996, Nov. 30 *Perf. 13½x13*
558 A120 50c Angels .35 .20
559 A120 1.20 l Santa on horse 1.00 .50

Famous Lithuanians Type of 1993

Designs: 50c, Ieva Simonaityte (1897-1978). 90c, Jonas Sliupas (1861-1944). 1.20 l, Vladas Jurgutis (1885-1966).

1997, Jan. 23 Litho. *Perf. 13x13½*
560 A88 50c brown & greem .40 .20
561 A88 90c gray & yellow .70 .35
562 A88 1.20 l blue green & orange .90 .45
Nos. 560-562 (3) 2.00 1.00

Independence Type of 1993

#563, Mykolas Birziska. #564, Kazimieras Saulys.

1997, Feb. 16 Litho. *Perf. 13½x13*
563 A85 50c multicolored .40 .25
564 A85 50c multicolored .40 .25

First Lithuanian Book, 450th Anniv. — A121

1997, Feb. 15 Litho. *Perf. 13½x13*
565 A121 50c gray & red .45 .25

Souvenir Sheet

566 A121 4.80 l like #565 3.50 3.50

No. 566 contains one 29x38mm stamp.

Souvenir Sheet

Flag on Mountain Top — A122

1997, Feb. 25 *Perf. 11½x12½*
567 A122 4.80 l multicolored 4.00 4.00

Expeditions to highest peaks on each continent.

Stories and Legends A123

Children's drawings: No. 568, Girl, horse. No. 569, King, moon, stars, bird, vert.

1997, Apr. 12 Litho. *Perf. 13*
568 A123 1.20 l multicolored 1.25 1.25
569 A123 1.20 l multicolored 1.25 1.25

Europa.

A124

A125

1997, May 9 Litho. *Perf. 13*
570 A124 50c multicolored .45 .25

First Lithuanian School, 600th Anniv.

1997, May 10 *Perf. 14x14½*

Old Ships of the Baltic Sea: 50c, Kurenas, 16th cent.

No. 572: a, Kurenas, 16th cent., diff. b, Maasilinn ship, 16th cent. c, Linijkugis, 17th cent.

571 A125 50c multicolored .45 .25
572 A125 1.20 l Sheet of 3, #a.-c. 3.00 3.00

See Estonia Nos. 322-323, Latvia Nos. 443-444.

Palanga Botanical Park, Cent. — A126

1997, June 1 Litho. *Perf. 13½x13*
573 A126 50c multicolored .45 .25
a. Tete-beche pair .90 .90

Numbers 574-577 are unassigned.

2nd Baltic Sea Games — A127

1997, June 25 Litho. *Perf. 13½*
578 A127 90c multicolored .75 .35

Museum Art A128

Designs: 90c, Animal face carved on ritual staff. 1.20 l, Coins, 15th cent.

1997, July 12 *Perf. 13½x13*
579 A128 90c multicolored .75 .35
580 A128 1.20 l multicolored 1.00 .50

Double Barred Crosses A129

Mushrooms A130

1997, Aug. 2 Litho. *Perf. 13½*
581 A129 20c olive .25 .20
582 A129 50c brown .35 .20

No. 582 exists dated 1998.
See Nos. 602, 604, 617-619.

1997, Sept. 20 Litho. *Perf. 13½x13*

Designs: No. 583, Morchella elata. No. 584, Boletus aereus.

583 A130 1.20 l multicolored 1.00 .50
a. Tete-beche pair 2.00 2.00
584 A130 1.20 l multicolored 1.00 .50
a. Tete-beche pair 2.00 2.00

Letters of Grand Duke Gediminas A131

1997, Oct. 4 *Perf. 14*
585 A131 50c multicolored .45 .25

Coat of Arms Type of 1992

Size: 25x33mm

1997, Oct. 18 Litho. *Perf. 13½x13*
586 A82 50c Neringa .40 .20
587 A82 90c Vilkaviskis .70 .35
588 A82 1.20 l Pasvalys .90 .45
Nos. 586-588 (3) 2.00 1.00

Christmas and New Year — A132

1997, Nov. 22 Litho. *Perf. 13*
589 A132 50c shown .40 .20
590 A132 1.20 l Snow on trees 1.00 .50

1998 Winter Olympic Games, Nagano — A133

1998, Jan. 17 Litho. *Perf. 14*
591 A133 1.20 l multicolored 1.00 .45
a. Tete-beche pair 2.00 2.00

Independence Type of 1993 and

Declaration of Independence — A134

Designs: 50c, Alfonsas Petrulis. 90c, Jokubas Sernas. Illustration reduced.

Perf. 13½x12½

1998, Feb. 16 Litho.
592 A85 50c olive and black .35 .20
593 A85 90c brown and black .85 .40

Souvenir Sheet

Perf. 12½x11½

594 A134 6.60 l multicolored 5.25 5.25

Independence, 80th anniv.

Souvenir Sheet

National Anthem, Cent. — A135

Illustration reduced.

1998, Feb. 16 *Perf. 12½*
595 A135 5.20 l multicolored 4.25 4.25

Antanas Gustaitis, Aviator, Birth Cent. A136

Designs: 2 l, Portrait of Gustaitis, ANBO 41. 3 l, Design drawings, ANBO-VIII.

1998, Mar. 27 Litho. *Perf. 14*
596 A136 2 l multicolored 1.75 .85
597 A136 3 l multicolored 2.25 1.10

Natl. Song Festival — A137

1998, Apr. 18 *Perf. 13½*
598 A137 1.20 l multicolored 1.75 1.75
a. Tete-beche pair 3.75 3.75

Europa.

Famous Lithuanians Type of 1993

50c, Tadas Ivanauskas (1882-1971), scientist. #600, Jurgis Baltrusaitis (1873-1944), writer, Jurgis Baltrusaitis (1903-88), historian. #601, Stasys Lozoraitis (1898-1983), Stasys Lozoraitis (1924-94), politicians.

1998, Apr. 25 *Perf. 13x13½*
599 A88 50c multicolored .40 .20

Size: 45x26mm

600 A88 90c multicolored .70 .35
601 A88 90c multicolored .70 .35
Nos. 599-601 (3) 1.80 .90

Double-Barred Crosses Type of 1997

1998, June 1 Litho. *Perf. 13½*
602 A129 70c yellow bister .60 .30

#602 exists dated 1999.

2nd Lithuanian Olympic Games, 6th World Lithuanian Games A138

1998, June 23 *Perf. 14*
603 A138 1.35 l multicolored 1.10 .55
a. Tete beche pair 2.25 2.25

Double-Barred Crosses Type of 1997

1998, July 4 Litho. *Perf. 13½*
604 A129 35c plum & pink .30 .20

Red Book of Lithuania A139

Fish: No. 605, Coregonus lavaretus holsatus. No. 606, Salmo salar.

1998, July 11 *Perf. 13x13½*
605 A139 1.40 l multicolored 1.10 .55
606 A139 1.40 l multicolored 1.10 .55

Coat of Arms Type of 1992

Size: 25x33mm

1998, Sept. 12 Litho. *Perf. 13*
607 A82 70c Kernave .55 .25
608 A82 70c Trakai .55 .25
609 A82 1.35 l Kaunas 1.10 .55
Nos. 607-609 (3) 2.20 1.05

Vilnius-Cracow Post Route Established, 1562 — A141

1998, Oct. 9 Litho. *Perf. 14*
611 A141 70c multicolored .60 .30

Souvenir Sheet

Lithuanian Post, 80th Anniv. — A142

Illustration reduced.

1998, Oct. 9 Litho. *Perf. 12*
612 A142 13 l multicolored 11.00 11.00

No. 612 contains a holographic image. Soaking in water may affect the hologram.

Museum Paintings — A143

70c, "Through the Night," by Antanas Zmuidzinavicius (1876-1966). 1.35 l, "The Garden of Bernardines, Vilnius," by Juozapas Marsevskis (1825-83).

1998, Oct. 17 Litho. *Perf. 13½x13*
613 A143 70c multicolored .60 .30
614 A143 1.35 l multicolored 1.00 .50

New Year — A144

Christmas: 1.35 l, Winter scene, people walking through giant tree, village.

1998, Nov. 14 Litho. *Perf. 12½*
615 A144 70c multicolored .50 .25
616 A144 1.35 l multicolored 1.10 .55

Double-Barred Crosses Type of 1997

1998, Nov. 14 Litho. *Perf. 13½*
617 A129 5c lt & dk citron .25 .20
618 A129 10c tan & brown .25 .20
619 A129 20c lt & dk olive green .25 .20
Nos. 617-619 (3) .75 .60

#617-619 exist dated 1999.

Adam Mickiewicz (1798-1855), Poet — A145

1998, Dec. 24 *Perf. 14*
620 A145 70c multicolored .60 .30
a. Tete beche pair 1.25 1.25

Souvenir Sheet

Publication of "Postile," by M. Dauksa (1527-1613), 400th Anniv. — A146

Illustration reduced.

1999, Jan. 23 Litho. *Perf. 12½*
621 A146 5.90 l brown & gray 5.00 5.00

Independence Type of 1993

Designs: No. 622, Petras Klimas. No. 623, Donatas Malinauskas.

Perf. 13½x12½

1999, Feb. 16 Litho.
622 A85 70c red & black .60 .30
623 A85 70c blue & black .60 .30

Famous Lithuanians Type of 1993

Designs: No. 624, Juozas Matulis (1899-1993). No. 625, Augustinas Gricius (1899-1972). 1.35 l, Pranas Skardzius (1899-1975).

1999, Mar. 19 Litho. *Perf. 13*
624 A88 70c multicolored .60 .30
625 A88 70c multicolored .60 .30
626 A88 1.35 l multicolored 1.10 .55
Nos. 624-626 (3) 2.30 1.15

NATO, 50th Anniv. — A147

1999, Mar. 27 Litho. *Perf. 13¾x14*
627 A147 70c multicolored .60 .30

National Parks — A148

Europa: No. 628, Traditional homes, lake, islands, Aukotaitija Natl. Park. No. 629, Sand dunes, amber, Curonian Spit Natl. Park.

1999, Apr. 10 Litho. *Perf. 13x13¼*
628 A148 1.35 l multicolored 1.40 1.40
629 A148 1.35 l multicolored 1.40 1.40

Council of Europe, 50th Anniv. — A149

1999, May 1 Litho. *Perf. 14*
630 A149 70c multicolored .60 .30

Melniai Windmill — A150

1999, May 8 Litho. *Perf. 14*
631 A150 70c shown .70 .35
632 A150 70c Pumpenai Windmill .70 .35

Bees — A151

Designs: 70c, Dasypoda argentata. 2 l, Bombus pomorum.

1999, June 12 *Perf. 13¼x13*
633 A151 70c multicolored .70 .35
634 A151 2 l multicolored 1.60 .80

UPU, 125th Anniv. A152

1999, July 3 Litho. *Perf. 14*
635 A152 70c multicolored .60 .30

Lithuanian Philatelic Society Emblems, No. 1, Pre-independence Stamp — A153

1999, July 31 Litho. *Perf. 14*
636 A153 1 l multicolored .90 .50
Complete booklet, 10 #636 10.00

Lithuanian Philatelic Society, 75th Anniv.

Souvenir Sheet

Centenary of First Performance of Play, "America in the Baths" — A154

Designs: a, Producers. b, Theater poster.

1999, Aug. 20 Litho. *Perf. 12½*
637 A154 4 l Sheet of 2, #a.-b. 5.50 5.50

A155

A156

Baltic Chain, 10th Anniv. — Family and flags: 1 l, No. 640a, Lithuanian. No. 640: b, Estonian. c, Latvian.

1999, Aug. 23 Litho. *Perf. 12¾*

639 A155 1 l multicolored	.75	.40

Souvenir Sheet

640 A155 2 l Sheet of 3, #a.-c.	4.00	4.00

See Estonia Nos. 366-367, Latvia Nos. 493-494.

1999, Aug. 28 Litho. *Perf. 14*

641 A156 70c multicolored	.50	.25

Freedom fight movement, 50th anniv.

Coat of Arms Type of 1992
Size: 25x33mm

1999, Sept. 18 *Perf. 13½x13*

642 A82 70c Marijampole	.50	.25
643 A82 1 l Siaulai	.75	.35
644 A82 1.40 l Rokiskis	1.00	.45
Nos. 642-644 (3)	2.25	1.05

Museum Pieces — A157

Designs: 70c, Sword of Gen. S. Zukauskas. 3 l, Hussar armor.

1999, Oct. 9 *Perf. 13¼x13½*

645 A157 70c multicolored	.50	.25
646 A157 3 l multicolored	2.00	1.00

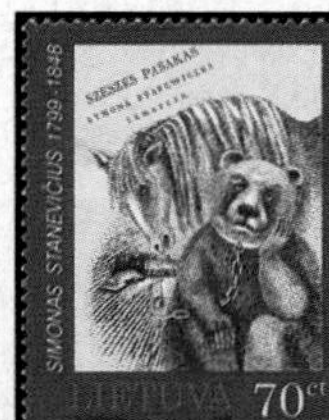

A158

A159

1999, Oct. 23 Litho. *Perf. 14*

647 A158 70c multicolored	.50	.25

Simonas Stanevicius (1799-1848), writer.

Perf. 12½x13½
1999, Nov. 13 Litho.

648 A159 70c shown	.50	.25
649 A159 1.35 l Buildings, candles	1.00	.50

Christmas and New Year's Day.

Forged Monument Tops — A160

Designs: 10c, Rietavas. 20c, Andriunal. 1 l, Veivirzenai. 1.30 l, Vaizgakiemis. 1.70 l, Baukai.

2000-06 Litho. *Perf. 13½x13¼*
Vignettes in Blue
Designs 22mm High

650 A160 10c tan	.30	.20
a. Perf. 11¼	.30	.20
651 A160 20c yellow	.35	.20
a. Perf. 11¼	.35	.20
652 A160 1 l pale rose	.90	.45
a. Perf. 11¼	1.00	.50
653 A160 1.30 l lt green	1.10	.55
654 A160 1.70 l lt blue	1.40	.70
Nos. 651-654 (4)	3.75	1.90

Perf. 13x12½
Designs 20mm High

655 A160 10c tan	.20	.20
656 A160 20c yellow	.20	.20

Designs 21mm High

657 A160 1 l pale rose	.75	.35
658 A160 1.30 l lt green	1.00	.50
Nos. 655-658 (4)	2.15	1.25

Issued: Nos. 650-654, 1/3/00; Nos. 650a, 651a, 652a, 5/4/02; Nos. 655-656, 10/8/05; Nos. 657-658, 5/27/06.
Nos. 650a, 651a exist dated "2003."
Nos. 650a, 651a exist dated "2004."
Nos. 655, 656 exist dated "2006."

Independence Type of 1993

Designs: 1.30 l, Jonas Vailokaitis (1886-1994), banker. 1.70 l, Jonas Smilgevicius (1870-1942), banker.

Perf. 13¼x12¾
2000, Feb. 16 Litho.

660 A85 1.30 l multi	1.00	.50
661 A85 1.70 l multi	1.50	.75

Souvenir Sheet

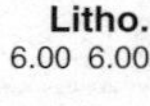

Declaration of Independence From Soviet Union, 10th Anniv. — A161

Perf. 12¼x11½
2000, Mar. 11 Litho.

662 A161 7.40 l multi	6.00	6.00

Famous Lithuanians A162

Designs: 1 l, Vincas Pietaris (1850-1902), writer. 1.30 l, Kanutas Ruseckas (1800-60), artist. 1.70 l, Povilas Visinskis (1875-1906), writer.

2000, Mar. 25 *Perf. 13x13¼*

663 A162 1 l multi	.80	.40
664 A162 1.30 l multi	1.00	.50
665 A162 1.70 l multi	1.40	.70
Nos. 663-665 (3)	3.20	1.60

Items From Klaipeda Clock Museum — A163

1 l, Sundial. 2 l, Renaissance-style clock.

2000, Apr. 15 *Perf. 12*

666 A163 1 l multi	1.00	.50
667 A163 2 l multi	1.50	.75

Europa, 2000
Common Design Type

2000, May 9 *Perf. 13¼x13*

668 CD17 1.70 l multi	3.00	3.00

Birds of Prey From Red Book of Lithuania — A164

1 l, Pandion haliaetus. 2 l, Milvus migrans.

2000, June 2 *Perf. 13¼x13*

669 A164 1 l multi	.90	.45
670 A164 2 l multi	1.60	.80

Sea Museum of Lithuania — A165

#671, Spheniscus magellanicus. #672, Halichoerus grypus.

2000, Aug. 26 Litho. *Perf. 12*

671-672 A165 1 l Set of 2	2.00	1.00
671a Tete beche pair	2.25	2.25
672a Tete beche pair	2.25	2.25

2000 Summer Olympics, Sydney A166

Designs: 1 l, Cycling. 3 l, Swimming.

2000, Sept. 2

673-674 A166 Set of 2	3.25	1.75

Souvenir Sheet

Mikalojus Konstantinas Ciurlionis (1875-1911), Artist — A167

2000, Sept. 22 Litho. *Perf. 12*

675 A167 4 l multi	3.25	3.25

Reappearance of Lithuanian Postage Stamps, 10th Anniv. — A168

2000, Oct. 7 Litho. *Perf. 12*

676 A168 1 l multi	.85	.40

Arms Type of 1992

Designs: No. 677, 1 l, Raseinai. No. 678, 1 l, Taurage. 1.30 l, Utena.

2000, Oct. 21 Litho. *Perf. 12*
Size: 25x33mm

677-679 A82 Set of 3	2.75	1.40

Christmas and New Year's Day — A169

Roadside shrines: 1 l, 1.70 l.

2000, Nov. 11

680-681 A169 Set of 2	2.10	1.00

Souvenir Sheet

Holy Year 2000 — A170

No. 682: a, Nativity. b, Jesus and disciples. c, Crucifixion. d, Resurrection.

2000, Nov. 25

682 A170 2 l Sheet of 4, #a-d	6.50	6.50

Advent of New Millennium A171

2000, Dec. 2

683 A171 1 l multi	.85	.40

Souvenir Sheet

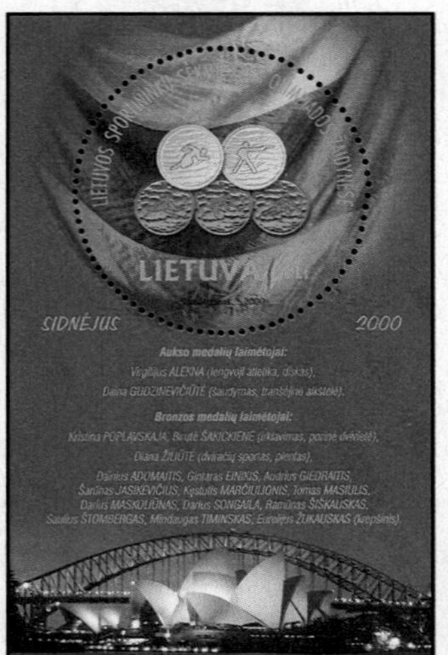

Medals Won at 2000 Summer Olympics, Sydney — A172

Illustration reduced.

2000, Dec. 9 Litho. *Perf.*
684 A172 4 l multi 3.25 3.25

Storming of TV Station by Soviet Troops, 10th Anniv. — A173

Illustration reduced.

2001, Jan. 13 *Perf. 12*
685 A173 1 l multi + label .85 .40

Independence Type of 1993

Designs: 1 l, Saliamonas Banaitis (1866-1933), newspaper publisher and politician. 2 l, Justinas Staugaitis (1863-1943), bishop and politician.

2001, Feb. 16 Litho. *Perf. 12*
686-687 A85 Set of 2 2.40 1.25

Famous Lithuanians Type of 2000

Designs: No. 688, 1 l, Juozas Mikenas (1901-64), artist. No. 689, 1 l, Pranas Vaicaitis (1876-1901), poet. 1.70 l, Petras Vileisis (1851-1926), civil engineer.

2001, Mar. 24 Litho. *Perf. 12*
688-690 A162 Set of 3 3.00 1.50

Europa A174

Designs: No. 691, 1.70 l, Neman River. No. 692, 1.70 l, Lake Galve.

2001, Apr. 14 *Perf. 13x13¼*
691-692 A174 Set of 2 3.75 3.75

Flowers From Red Book of Lithuania — A175

Designs: 2 l, Nymphoide peltata. 3 l, Erica tetralix.

2001, May 12 *Perf. 13¼x13*
693-694 A175 Set of 2 4.00 2.00

Bridges A176

Designs: 1 l, Papalauja Bridge. 1.30 l, Pakurojis Dam Bridge.

2001, June 9 *Perf. 12*
695-696 A176 Set of 2 1.90 .95

Souvenir Sheet

Lithuania, 1000th Anniv. (in 2009) — A177

Designs: a, Flag. b, Arms. c, Map of country. d, Map of Europe.

2001, June 23 *Perf. 11*
697 A177 2 l Sheet of 4, #a-d + 2 labels 6.50 6.50

Baltic Coast Landscapes A178

Designs: 1 l, No. 699a, Palanga. No. 699b, Lahemaa. No. 699c, Vidzeme.

2001, Sept. 15 Litho. *Perf. 13½*
698 A178 1 l multi .85 .40

Souvenir Sheet

699 Sheet of 3 4.75 4.75
a.-c. A178 2 l Any single 1.50 1.25

See Estonia Nos. 423-424, Latvia Nos. 534-535.

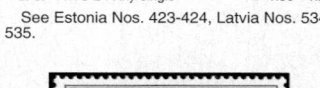

Ethnographic Open Air Museum Exhibits — A179

19th cent. dwellings from: 1 l, Kirdeikiai. 2 l, Darbenai.

2001, Sept. 22 *Perf. 12*
700-701 A179 Set of 2 2.40 1.25

Sculpture by Juozas Zikaras (1881-1944) A180

2001, Oct. 4
702 A180 3 l multi 2.40 1.25

Postal Regulations Enacted by Stefan Bathory, 1583 — A181

2001, Oct. 6
703 A181 1 l multi .85 .40

Coat of Arms Type of 1992
Size: 25x33mm

Designs: 1 l, Lazdijai. 1.30 l, Birzai. 1.70 l, Veliuona.

2001, Oct. 27 Litho. *Perf. 12*
704-706 A82 Set of 3 3.25 1.60

Christmas and New Year — A182

Birds on: 1 l, Covered tree. 1.70 l, Christ's cradle.

2001, Nov. 10 Litho. *Perf. 12*
707-708 A182 Set of 2 2.10 1.00

Souvenir Sheet

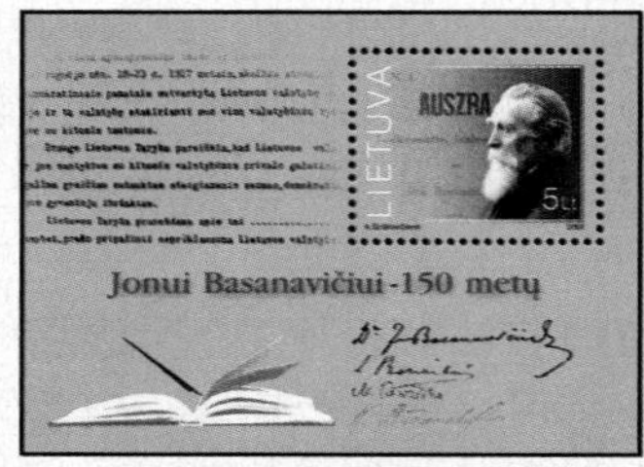

Dr. Jonas Basanavicius (1851-1927), Patriot, Folklorist — A183

2001, Nov. 17 *Perf. 12x11½*
709 A183 5 l multi 4.00 4.00

2002 Winter Olympics, Salt Lake City — A184

2002, Jan. 26 Litho. *Perf. 12*
710 A184 1.70 l multi 1.40 .70

Independence Type of 1993

Designs: No. 711, 1 l, Kazys Bizauskas (1892-1941), statesman. No. 712, 1 l, Stanislovas Narutavicius (1862-1932), politician.

2002, Feb. 16
711-712 A85 Set of 2 1.60 .80

Famous Lithuanians A185

Designs: 1 l, Antanas Salys (1902-72), linguist. 1.30 l, Satrijos Ragana (1877-1930), writer. 1.70 l, Oskaras Milasius (1877-1939), poet.

2002, Mar. 2 Litho. *Perf. 12*
713-715 A185 Set of 3 3.00 1.50

See Nos. 734-735, 759-761, 782-784, 805-807, 830-832, 858-860, 884-886.

Coat of Arms Type of 1992
Size: 25x33mm

Designs: No. 716, 1 l, Anyksciai. No. 717, 1 l, Birstonas. 1.70 l, Prienai.

2002, Mar. 23
716-718 A82 Set of 3 3.00 1.50

State Historical Archives, 150th Anniv. — A186

2002, Apr. 6
719 A186 1 l multi .85 .40

Mammals From Red Book of Lithuania A187

Designs: 1 l, Mustela erminea. 3 l, Lynx lynx.

2002, Apr. 13 *Perf. 13x13¼*
720-721 A187 Set of 2 3.25 1.60

Europa — A188

2002, May 4 Litho. *Perf. 13¼x13*
722 A188 1.70 l multi 1.50 1.50

Vilnius Fire ad Rescue Brigade, Bicent. A189

2002, May 25 *Perf. 12*
723 A189 1 l multi .85 .40

Narrow-gauge Railways — A190

Designs: 1.30 l, TU2 diesel locomotive. 2 l, PT4 steam engine.

2002, June 8
724-725 A190 Set of 2 2.75 1.40

Souvenir Sheet

Lithuania, 1000th Anniv. (in 2009) — A191

Designs: a, Artifact of first people in Lithuania, 10,000 B.C. b, Roman historian Tacitus mentions Aestii people, 98. c, Vikings attack

Apuole Castle, 853. d, First mention of Lithuania in Quedlinburg Annals, 1009.

2002, June 22 *Perf. 11*
726 A191 2 l Sheet of 4, #a-d, + 2 labels 6.50 6.50

Souvenir Sheet

Klaipeda, 750th Anniv. — A192

2002, Aug. 1 *Perf. 11½x12¼*
727 A192 5 l multi 4.00 4.00

Maironis Lithuanian Literature Museum, Kaunas A193

Designs: 1 l, Exhibits. 3 l, Museum exterior.

2002, Sept. 7 *Perf. 12*
728-729 A193 Set of 2 3.00 1.50

Establishment of Postal Service by King Sigismund III Vasa, 1620 — A194

2002, Oct. 5
730 A194 1 l multi .85 .40

Christmas and New Year's Day — A195

Cross and: 1 l, Clock, candles and holly. 1.70 l, Christmas tree and angels.

2002, Nov. 9
731-732 A195 Set of 2 2.10 1.00

European Children's Day — A196

2002, Nov. 16
733 A196 1 l multi .85 .40

Famous Lithuanians Type of 2002

Designs: 1 l, Laurynas Stuoka-Gucevicius (1753-98), architect. 1.30 l, Juozas Eretas (1896-1984), author and politician.

2003, Jan. 25 *Perf. 12*
734-735 A185 Set of 2 1.75 .85

Coat of Arms Type of 1992

Designs: No. 736, 1 l, Gargzdai. No. 737, 1 l, Kretinga. No. 738, 1 l, Palanga. No. 739, 1 l, Papile. No. 740, 1 l, Rietavas.

2003, Feb. 15 **Litho.** *Perf. 12*
Size: 25x33mm
736-740 A82 Set of 5 4.00 2.00

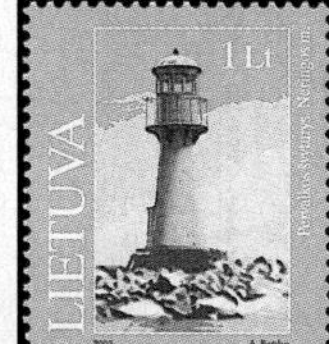

Lighthouses A198

Designs: 1 l, Pervalka. 3 l, Uostodvaris.

2003, Mar. 15
741-742 A198 Set of 2 3.00 1.50

Europa — A199

2003, Apr. 19 **Litho.** *Perf. 13½x13*
743 A199 1.70 l multi 1.40 1.40
a. Tete beche pair 3.00 3.00

Rebuilding of Palace of Lithuania's Rulers — A200

2003, Apr. 26 *Perf. 12*
744 A200 1 l multi .85 .40

Vilnius University Astronomical Observatory, 250th Anniv. — A201

2003, May 10 *Perf. 12*
745 A201 1 l multi .85 .40

Insects From Red Book of Lithuania A202

Designs: No. 746, 3 l, Lucanus cervus. No. 747, 3 l, Cerambyx cerdo.

2003, May 24 *Perf. 13x13½*
746-747 A202 Set of 2 5.00 2.50

Souvenir Sheet

Lithuania, 1000th Anniv. (in 2009) — A203

No. 748: a, Rise of Lithuania, 1183. b, Battle of Siauliai, 1236. c, Coronation of Mindaugas, 1253. d, Selection of Vilnius as capital of Lithuania, 1323.

2003, June 21 *Perf. 11*
748 A203 2 l Sheet of 4, #a-d, + 2 labels 6.50 3.25

Souvenir Sheet

Coronation of Mindaugas, 750th Anniv. — A204

2003, July 5 *Perf. 11½x12¼*
749 A204 5 l multi 4.00 2.00

13th European Hot Air Balloon Championships — A205

2003, Aug. 8 *Perf. 12*
750 A205 1.30 l multi 1.10 .55

Vincentas Cardinal Sladkevicius (1920-2000) A206

2003, Aug. 20
751 A206 1 l multi .85 .40

Panevezys, 500th Anniv. — A207

2003, Sept. 7
752 A207 1 l multi .85 .40

Map of Kaunas-Vilnius-Grodno Postal Route, 1664 — A208

2003, Oct. 4
753 A208 1 l multi .85 .40

Christmas and New Year's Day — A209

Villages at: 1 l, Christmas. 1.70 l, New Year's Eve.

2003, Nov. 8
754-755 A209 Set of 2 2.10 1.00

Souvenir Sheet

Lithuania, 2003 European Men's Basketball Champions — A210

2003, Dec. 6 **Litho.** *Perf. 12x11½*
756 A210 5 l multi 4.00 2.00

Gliders in Lithuanian Aviation Museum A211

Designs: No. 757, 1 l, BK-7. No. 758, 1 l, BRO-12.

2003, Dec. 17 *Perf. 12*
757-758 A211 Set of 2 1.60 .80

Famous Lithuanians Type of 2002

Designs: No. 759, 1 l, Jonas Aistis (1904-73), poet. No. 760, 1 l, Kazimieras Buga (1879-1924), philologist. No. 761, Adolfas Jucys (1904-74), physicist.

2004, Jan. 24 **Litho.** *Perf. 12*
759-761 A185 Set of 3 2.50 1.25

Coat of Arms Type of 1992

Designs: 1 l, Mazeikiai. 1.30 l, Radviliskis. 1.40 l, Ukmerge.

2004, Feb. 14
Size: 25x33mm
762-764 A82 Set of 3 3.00 1.50

Vilnius University, 425th Anniv. — A213

2004, Mar. 20
765 A213 1 l multi .85 .40

Europa — A214

Designs: No. 766, 1.70 l, Sailboat. No. 767, 1.70 l, Beach umbrella.

2004, Apr. 10 **Litho.** *Perf. 12*
766-767 A214 Set of 2 3.00 3.00

Return to Printing Lithuanian in Latin Letters, Cent. A215

2004, May 1 Litho. *Perf. 12*

768 A215 1.30 l multi 1.00 .50

Admission to European Union — A216

No. 769: a, Stars, flags of newly-added countries, map of Europe. b, Stars and Lithuanian flag, map and arms.

2004, May 1

769 A216 1.70 l Horiz. pair, #a-b 2.50 1.25

FIFA (Fédération Internationale de Football Association), Cent. A217

2004, May 15

770 A217 3 l multi 2.25 1.10

Chiune Sugihara (1900-86), Japanese Diplomat Who Issued Transit Visas to Jews in World War II — A218

2004, June 19 Litho. *Perf. 12*

771 A218 1 l multi .85 .40

Souvenir Sheet

Lithuania, 1000th Anniv. — A219

No. 772: a, Defense of Pilenai Castle, 1336. b, Battle at the Blue Waters, 1362. c, Christening of Lithuania, 1387. d, Battle of Zalgiris, 1410.

2004, July 3 *Perf. 11*

772 A219 2 l Sheet of 4, #a-d, + 2 labels 6.00 3.00

Exhibits in Tadas Ivanauskas Zoology Museum, Kaunas — A220

No. 773: a, Aquila chrysaetos. b, Iguana iguana.
Illustration reduced.

2004, July 10 *Perf. 12*

773 A220 1 l Horiz. pair, #a-b 1.60 .80

2004 Summer Olympics, Athens A221

2004 Olympic emblem and: 2 l, Pentathlon equestrian event. 3 l, Canoeing.

2004, July 31

774-775 A221 Set of 2 4.00 2.00

Owls From Red Book of Lithuania — A222

Designs: 1.30 l, Bubo bubo. 3 l, Asio flammeus.

2004, Oct. 2 Litho. *Perf. 12*

776-777 A222 Set of 2 3.50 1.75

Kaunas Funiculars A223

Designs: 1 l, Aleksotas Funicular. 1.30 l, Zaliakalnis Funicular.

2004, Oct. 16

778-779 A223 Set of 2 1.90 .95

Christmas A224

Stars and: 1 l, Christmas tree. 1.70 l, Bird.

2004, Nov. 6

780-781 A224 Set of 2 2.00 2.00

Famous Lithuanians Type of 2002

Designs: No. 782, 1 l, Kazys Boruta (1905-65), writer. No. 783, 1 l, Petras Kalpokas (1880-1945), painter. No. 784, 1 l, Jonas Puzinas (1905-78), archaeologist.

2005, Jan. 8 Litho. *Perf. 12*

782-784 A185 Set of 3 2.25 2.25

Congratulations A225

Designs: No. 785, 1 l, Gerbera daisies, freesias and scroll. No. 786, 1 l, Lilies, freesias and box.

Serpentine Die Cut 6¾

2005, Jan. 29 Litho.

Booklet Stamps

Self-Adhesive

785-786 A225 Set of 2 1.50 1.50

786a Booklet pane, 4 each #785-786 6.00

Sartai Horse Race, Cent. A226

2005, Feb. 5 *Perf. 12*

787 A226 1 l multi .75 .75

Coat of Arms Type of 1992

Designs: No. 788, 1 l, Druskininkai. No. 789, 1 l, Vabalninkas.

2005, Mar. 5 Size: 25x33mm

788-789 A82 Set of 2 1.60 1.60

Europa A227

Designs: No. 790, 1.70 l, Cow, cheese. No. 791, 1.70 l, Loaf of black bread.

2005, Apr. 9 Litho. *Perf. 12*

790-791 A227 Set of 2 2.60 2.60

National Museum, 150th Anniv. — A228

No. 792: a, Brass jewelry, 1st-2nd cent. b, Illustration of first exhibition in Aula Hall, Vilnius University.
Illustration reduced.

2005, May 7

792 A228 1 l Pair, #a-b 1.40 1.40

Train and Kaunas Railway Tunnel A229

2005, June 11

793 A229 3 l multi 2.10 2.10

Souvenir Sheet

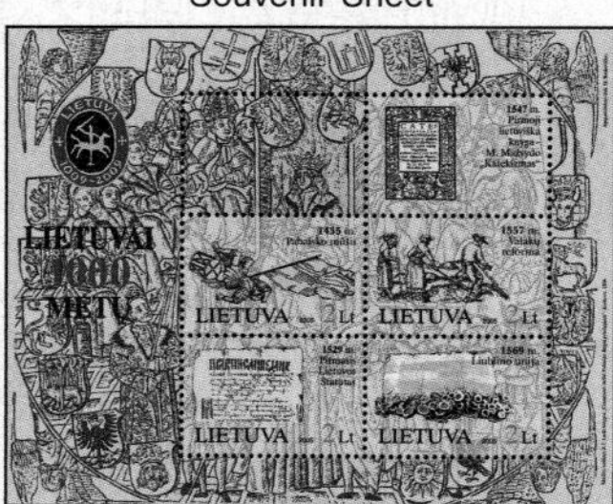

Lithuania, 1000th Anniv. — A230

No. 794: a, Battle of Pabaiskas, 1435. b, Valakai Reform, 1557. c, First Lithuanian statute, 1529. d, Union of Lublin, 1569.

2005, July 2 *Perf. 11*

794 A230 2 l Sheet of 4, #a-d, + 2 labels 6.00 6.00

90th World Esperanto Congress, Vilnius A231

2005, July 23 Litho. *Perf. 12*

795 A231 1 l multi .75 .75

Churches A232

Designs: 1 l, Vilnius Evangelical Lutheran Church. 1.30 l, St. Casimir Church, Vilnius.

2005, Sept. 3 *Perf. 13½*

796-797 A232 Set of 2 1.75 1.75

Flora and Fauna from Red Book of Lithuania — A233

No. 798: a, Gavia arctica. b, Trapa natans.
Illustration reduced.

2005, Sept. 10

798 A233 1 l Horiz. pair, #a-b 1.50 1.50

Souvenir Sheet

Mikolajus Konstantinas Ciurlionis (1875-1911), Painter and Composer — A234

No. 799 — Details from Sonata of the Sea triptych: a, Allegro. b, Andante. c, Finale.

2005, Sept. 24 *Perf. 14*

799 A234 2 l Sheet of 3, #a-c, + label 4.50 4.50

Map of St. Petersburg-Warsaw Post Road, 1830-36 — A235

2005, Oct. 8 Litho. *Perf. 14¼x14*

800 A235 1 l multi .75 .75

Christmas A236

Designs: 1 l, Candle and snow-covered evergreen branch. 1.70 l, Santa Claus in sleigh.

2005, Nov. 5 *Perf. 12¾x13*

801-802 A236 Set of 2 1.90 1.90

Dr. Jonas Basanavicius, Vilnius City Hall and Commemorative Medal — A237

2005, Dec. 3 ***Perf. 14¼x14***
803 A237 1 l multi .75 .75

Congress of Lithuanians, cent.

2006 Winter Olympics, Turin — A238

2006, Jan. 28 **Litho.** ***Perf. 14x14¼***
804 A238 1.70 l multi 1.25 1.25

Famous Lithuanians Type of 2002

Designs: No. 805, 1 l, Adolfas Sapoka (1906-61), historian. No. 806, 1 l, Petras Rimsa (1881-1961), sculptor. No. 807, 1 l, Antanas Vaiciulaitis (1906-92), writer.

2006, Feb. 11 ***Perf. 13½***
805-807 A185 Set of 3 2.10 2.10

Vilnius Album, by Jonas K. Vilcinskis, 160th Anniv. of Publication A239

2006, Feb. 25 ***Perf. 13x12¾***
808 A239 1 l multi .70 .70

Social Insurance System, 80th Anniv. A240

2006, Mar. 18 ***Perf. 14¼x14***
809 A240 1 l multi .70 .70

Lithuanian Theater, Music and Cinema Museum, 80th Anniv. — A241

No. 810: a, Parvo camera, 1930s. b, Music box, 1900.
Illustration reduced.

2006, Mar. 18 ***Perf. 13½***
810 A241 1 l Pair, #a-b 1.40 1.40

Printed in sheets containing 10 of each stamp + 5 labels. Each sheet contains se-tenant pairs of the same stamp.

Europa A242

Designs: No. 811, 1.70 l, Woman dancing with man in wheelchair. No. 812, 1.70 l, People in wheelchairs being pushed around track.

2006, Apr. 15
811-812 A242 Set of 2 2.50 2.50

Coat of Arms Type of 1992

Designs: No. 813, 1 l, Kupiskis. No. 814, 1 l, Sakiai. No. 815, 1 l, Silute.

2006, May 13 ***Perf. 14x14¼***
Size: 25x33mm
813-815 A82 Set of 3 2.25 2.25

Souvenir Sheet

Lithuania, 1000th Anniv. — A243

No. 816: a, Establishment of Vilnius University, 1579. b, Truce of Andrusov, 1667. c, Four-year Sejm, 1788. d, Uprising of 1794.

2006, July 1 ***Perf. 11***
816 A243 2 l Sheet of 4, #a-d, + 2 labels 6.00 6.00

Basilicas A244

Designs: 1 l, Vilnius Basilica. 1.70 l, Kaunas Basilica.

2006, Aug. 5 ***Perf. 12¾x13***
817-818 A244 Set of 2 2.00 2.00

Birds and Fish From Red Book of Lithuania A245

No. 819: a, Polysticta stelleri. b, Acipenser sturio.

2006, Sept. 16 ***Perf. 13½***
819 A245 1 l Vert. pair, #a-b 1.50 1.50

Establishment of Lithuania Post and First Postage Stamps, 1918 — A246

2006, Oct. 7 ***Perf. 14¼x14***
820 A246 1 l multi .75 .75

Premiere of Opera "Birute," Cent. — A247

2006, Nov. 4 **Litho.** ***Perf. 13¼x12¾***
821 A247 2 l multi 1.60 1.60

Christmas A248

Designs: 1 l, Birds, triangular window. 1.70 l, Trees, star, berries, straw.

2006, Nov. 18 ***Perf. 12¾x13¼***
822-823 A248 Set of 2 2.10 2.10

18th Century Wooden Church Belfries — A249

Belfries from churches in: 10c, Pasvalys. 20c, Rozalimas. 50c, Tryskiai. 1 l, Saukenai. 1.30 l, Vaiguva. 1.70 l, Vajasiskis.

Die Cut Perf. 12½
2007, Jan. 1 **Litho.**
Self-Adhesive

824 A249 10c blue & blk .20 .20
825 A249 20c org & blk .20 .20
826 A249 50c bl grn & blk .40 .40
827 A249 1 l brn & blk .80 .80
828 A249 1.30 l lil & blk 1.00 1.00
829 A249 1.70 l ol brn & blk 1.40 1.40
Nos. 824-829 (6) 4.00 4.00

See Nos. 842-846.

Famous Lithuanians Type of 2002

Designs: No. 830, 1 l, Bernardas Brazdzionis (1907-2002), writer. No. 831, 1 l, Vytautas Kazimieras Jonynas (1907-97), artist. 3 l, Leonas Sapiega (1557-1633), state chancellor of the Grand Duchy of Lithuania.

2007, Jan. 27 ***Perf. 13½***
830-832 A185 Set of 3 3.75 3.75

Coat of Arms Type of 1992

Designs: 1 l, Svencionys. 1.30 l, Kelme. 2 l, Moletai.

2007, Mar. 3 ***Perf. 14x14¼***
Size: 25x33mm
833-835 A82 Set of 3 3.25 3.25

Europa A250

Designs: No. 836, 1.70 l, Scouting flag, musical score. No. 837, 1.70 l, Symbols of Lithuanian Scouts.

2007, Apr. 14 **Litho.** ***Perf. 13½***
836-837 A250 Set of 2 2.75 2.75

Scouting, cent.

Churches A251

Designs: 1 l, St. Anne's and Bernardine Churches, Vilnius. 1.30 l, Church buildings, Pazaislis.

2007, May 12 ***Perf. 12¾x13***
838-839 A251 Set of 2 2.10 2.10

Souvenir Sheet

Lithuania, 1000th Anniv. — A252

No. 840: a, Publication of first Lithuanian newspaper, "Ausra," 1883. b, Abolition of the prohibition on printing in Latin characters, 1904. c, Great Seimas of Vilnius, 1905. d, Lithuanian Declaration of Independence, 1918.

2007, June 23 **Litho.** ***Perf. 11***
840 A252 3 l Sheet of 4, #a-d, + 2 labels 9.50 9.50

Trakai History Museum — A253

No. 841: a, Map of New Trakai in 1600, by J. Kamarauskas. b, Chess pieces, 15th cent.
Illustration reduced.

2007, July 28 **Litho.** ***Perf. 13½***
841 A253 2 l Pair, #a-b 3.25 3.25

Printed in sheets containing 10 of each stamp + 5 labels.

Wooden Church Belfries Type of 2007

Belfries from churches in: 5c, Vabalininkas, 19th cent. 35c, Varputenai, 18th cent. 1.35 l, Deguciai, 19th cent. 1.55 l, Geidziai, 19th cent. 2.15 l, Pavandenes, 17th cent.

Die Cut Perf. 12½
2007, Sept. 1 **Litho.**
Self-Adhesive

842 A249 5c yel grn & blk .20 .20
843 A249 35c gray & blk .30 .30
844 A249 1.35 l yel & blk 1.10 1.10
845 A249 1.55 l brn org & blk 1.25 1.25
846 A249 2.15 l rose lake & blk 1.75 1.75
Nos. 842-846 (5) 4.60 4.60

Juozas Miltinis (1907-94), Actor and Theater Founder A254

2007, Sept. 1 **Litho.** ***Perf. 12¾x13***
847 A254 2.45 l multi 2.00 2.00

Birds — A255

No. 848 — Birds of the Cepkeliai Nature Reserve, Lithuania and Katra Sanctuary, Belarus: a, Gallinago media. b, Crex crex.

2007, Oct. 3 *Perf. 14*
848 Horiz. pair + central label 5.00 5.00
a.-b. A255 2.90 l Either single 2.25 2.25

See Belarus No. 625.

Stamps and Covers From Establishment of Lithuania Post in 1992 — A256

2007, Oct. 6
849 A256 1.35 l multi 1.25 1.25

Christmas A257

Conifer sprigs and: 1.35 l, Snowflake, Christmas ornaments. 2.45 l, Stars, globe.

2007, Nov. 10 *Perf. 13x12¾*
850-851 A257 Set of 2 3.25 3.25

Famous Lithuanians Type of 2008

Designs: 2 l, Martynas Jankus (1858-1946), publisher. 2.15 l, Zenonas Ivinskis (1908-71), historian. 2.90 l, Antanas Maceina (1908-87), philosopher.

2008, Jan. 19 **Litho.** *Perf. 13½*
858-860 A185 Set of 3 6.00 6.00

Restoration of Independence, 90th Anniv. — A259

2008, Feb. 16
861 A259 1.35 l multi 1.25 1.25

State Awards of the Baltic Countries — A260

Designs: Nos. 862, 863a, Order of Vytautas the Great, Lithuania. No. 863b, Order of the National Coat of Arms, Estonia. No. 863c, Order of Three Stars, Latvia.

Perf. 13½x13¾

2008, Mar. 15 **Litho.**
862 A260 7 l multi 6.50 6.50

Souvenir Sheet

863 A260 5 l Sheet of 3, #a-c, + label 14.00 14.00

See Estonia Nos. 592-593, Latvia Nos. 701-702.

Items From Rokiskis Regional Museum — A261

No. 864: a, Wood carving, by Lionginas Sepka. b, 19th cent. women's clothing. Illustration reduced.

2008, Apr. 19 **Litho.** *Perf. 14*
864 A261 1.55 l Horiz. pair, #a-b 2.75 2.75

Europa A262

Designs: No. 865, 2.45 l, Grand Duke Gediminas and his letters of 1323. No. 866, 2.45 l, Vilnius, 2009 European Cultural Capital.

2008, May 3
865-866 A262 Set of 2 4.50 4.50

Sajudis Party, 20th Anniv. A263

2008, May 31
867 A263 1.35 l multi 1.25 1.25

Expo Zaragoza 2008 — A264

2008, June 7 *Die Cut Perf. 12½*
Self-Adhesive
868 A264 2.45 l multi 2.25 2.25

Miniature Sheet

Lithuania, 1000th Anniv. — A265

No. 869: a, First Lithuanian Cabinet of Ministers, 1918. b, Consitituent Assembly, 1920. c, Opening of Kaunas Museum, 1922. d, Occupation of Memel (Klaipeda) by Lithuania, 1923. e, Opening of Zemaiciai Road (man signing document, 1939). f, Assignation of Lithuania to Soviet Union, 1939.

2008, June 28 *Perf. 14*
869 A265 3 l Sheet of 6, #a-f 16.50 16.50

Crashed Transatlantic Flight of Captains Steponas Darius and Stasys Girenas, 75th Anniv. — A266

2008, July 12
870 A266 2.90 l multi 2.60 2.60

2008 Summer Olympics, Beijing — A267

Designs: 2.15 l, Women's marathon. 2.45 l, Yachting.

2008, July 26
871-872 A267 Set of 2 4.25 4.25

Apparitions of the Virgin Mary at Siluva, 400th Anniv. — A268

2008, Aug. 30 **Litho.** *Perf. 14*
873 A268 1.55 l multi 1.40 1.40

Worldwide Fund for Nature (WWF) A269

Coracias garrulus: Nos. 874, 878a, 1.35 l, On branch with beak closed, denomination at LR. Nos. 875, 878b, 1.35 l, In flight. Nos. 876, 878c, 1.35 l, On branch with beak open, denomination at LL. Nos. 877, 878d, 1.35 l, On branch with beak closed, denomination at LL.

2008, Sept. 6 *Perf. 14*
Stamps With White Frames
874-877 A269 Set of 4 4.50 4.50

Souvenir Sheet
Stamps Without White Frames
878 A269 1.35 l Sheet of 4, #a-d 4.50 4.50

Arms Type of 1992

Designs: No. 879, 1.35 l, Jurbarkas. No. 880, 1.35 l, Joniskis. 3 l, Sirvintos.

2008, Oct. 4 **Litho.**
Size: 26x31mm
879-881 A82 Set of 3 4.50 4.50

Christmas and New Year's Day A270

Designs: 1.35 l, Holiday lights. 2.45 l, Snow-covered evergreen branch.

2008, Nov. 8 *Perf. 14*
882-883 A270 Set of 2 3.00 3.00

Famous Lithuanians Type of 2002

Designs: 1.35 l, Jonas Zemaitas (1909-54), military officer. 2 l, Vaclovas Birziska (1884-1956), educator and library founder. 2.15 l, Mecislovas Reinys (1884-1953), archbishop.

2009, Jan. 17 **Litho.** *Perf. 14*
884-886 A185 Set of 3 4.25 4.25

SEMI-POSTAL STAMPS

Regular Issue of 1923-24 Surcharged in Blue, Violet or Black:

On A21

On A22

On A23

1924, Feb. **Wmk. 147** *Perf. 11*

B1	A21	2c + 2c pale brn (Bl)	1.25	1.50
B2	A21	3c + 3c ol bis (Bl)	1.25	1.50
B3	A21	5c + 5c pale grn (V)	1.25	1.50
B4	A21	10c + 10c vio (Bk)	3.00	3.00
B5	A21	36c + 34c org brn (V)	6.50	10.00

Wmk. Webbing (109)

B6	A21	10c + 10c vio (Bk)	6.50	7.50
B7	A21	15c + 15c scar (V)	1.50	1.50
B8	A21	20c + 20c ol brn (Bl)	3.00	3.50
B9	A21	25c + 25c bl (Bk)	18.00	18.00
B10	A22	50c + 50c yel grn (V)	7.00	8.00
B11	A22	60c + 60c red (V)	7.00	10.00
B12	A23	1 l + 1 l org & grn (V)	8.00	*11.00*
B13	A23	3 l + 2 l red & gray (V)	12.00	*15.00*
B14	A23	5 l + 3 l brn & bl (V)	16.00	*18.00*

Unwmk.

B15	A21	25c + 25c dp bl (Bk)	5.00	6.00
		Nos. B1-B15 (15)	97.25	116.00

For War Invalids

Semi-Postal Stamps of 1924 Surcharged

Surcharged in Gold or Copper

1926, Dec. 3 **Wmk. 147**

B16	A21	1 + 1c on #B1	1.00	1.25
a.		Inverted surcharge	40.00	
B17	A21	2 + 2c on #B2 (C)	1.00	1.25
B19	A21	2 + 2c on #B3	1.00	1.25
a.		Double surch., one inverted	40.00	
B20	A21	5 + 5c on #B4	2.00	2.00
B21	A21	14 + 14c on #B5	6.00	7.00

Wmk. Webbing (109)

B22	A21	5 + 5c on #B6	10.00	10.00
B23	A21	5 + 5c on #B7	2.00	2.00
B24	A21	10 + 10c on #B8	2.00	2.00
B25	A21	10 + 10c on #B9	65.00	65.00

Unwmk.

B26	A21	10 + 10c on #B15	4.00	5.00

Surcharged in Copper or Silver:

On A22

On A23

Wmk. Webbing (109)

B27 A22 20 + 20c on #B10 4.00 5.00
B28 A22 25 + 25c on #B11 6.00 7.00
B29 A23 30 + 30c on #B12 (S) 9.00 11.00
Nos. B16-B29 (13) 113.00 119.75

For War Orphans

Surcharged in Gold

1926, Dec. 3 **Wmk. 147**

B30 A21 1 + 1c on #B1 .90 .90
B31 A21 2 + 2c on #B2 .90 .90
a. Inverted surcharge 260.00
B32 A21 2 + 2c on #B3 .90 .90
a. Inverted surcharge 30.00
B33 A21 5 + 5c on #B4 2.00 2.25
B34 A21 19 + 19c on #B5 4.00 5.00

Wmk. Webbing (109)

B35 A21 5 + 5c on #B6 10.00 10.00
B36 A21 10 + 10c on #B7 1.75 2.00
B37 A21 15 + 15c on #B8 2.00 2.25
B38 A21 15 + 15c on #B9 65.00 65.00

Unwmk.

B39 A21 15 + 15c on #B15 3.00 3.00

Surcharged in Gold:

On A22

On A23

Wmk. 109

B40 A22 25c on #B10 5.00 6.00
B41 A22 30c on #B11 8.00 7.00
B42 A23 50c on #B12 10.00 11.00
Nos. B30-B42 (13) 113.45 116.20

Catalogue values for unused stamps in this section, from this point to the end of the section, are for Never Hinged items.

Javelin throwing — SP1

Natl. Olympiad, July 15-20: 5c+5c, Archery. 30c+10c, Diving. 60c+15c, Running.

Unwmk.

1938, July 13 **Photo.** ***Perf. 14***

B43 SP1 5c + 5c grn & dk grn 6.50 6.50
B44 SP1 15c + 5c org & red org 6.50 6.50
B45 SP1 30c + 10c bl & dk bl 12.00 12.00
B46 SP1 60c + 15c tan & brn 16.00 16.00
Nos. B43-B46 (4) 41.00 41.00

Same Overprinted in Red, Blue or Black:

Nos. B47, B50

Nos. B48-B49

1938, July 13

B47 SP1 5c + 5c (R) 12.00 7.50
B48 SP1 15c + 5c (Bl) 12.00 7.50
B49 SP1 30c + 10c (R) 15.00 7.50
B50 SP1 60c + 15c (Bk) 20.00 12.50
Nos. B47-B50 (4) 59.00 35.00

National Scout Jamboree, July 12-14. Forged cancellations exist.

Basketball Players
SP6 SP7

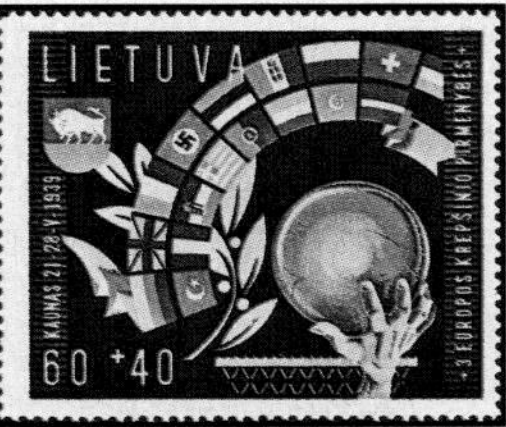

Flags of Competing Nations and Basketball — SP8

1939 **Photo.** ***Perf. 14***

B52 SP6 15c + 10c copper brn & brn 6.50 6.50
B53 SP7 30c + 15c myrtle grn & grn 6.50 6.50
B54 SP8 60c + 40c blue vio & gray vio 12.00 12.00
Nos. B52-B54 (3) 25.00 25.00

3rd European Basketball Championships held at Kaunas. The surtax was used for athletic equipment. Nos. B52-B54 exist imperf. Value, each pair, $175.

AIR POST STAMPS

Catalogue values for unused stamps in this section are for Never Hinged items.

Winged Posthorn AP1

Airplane over Neman River — AP2

Air Squadron AP3

Plane over Gediminas Castle — AP4

1921 **Litho.** **Wmk. 109** ***Perf. 11½***

C1 AP1 20sk ultra 1.60 .75
C2 AP1 40sk red orange 1.40 .75
C3 AP1 60sk green 1.40 .75
a. Imperf., pair 45.00
C4 AP1 80sk lt rose 1.40 .75
a. Horiz. pair, imperf. vert. 50.00 40.00
C5 AP2 1auk green & red 1.60 .50
a. Imperf., pair 40.00 40.00
C6 AP3 2auk brown & blue 1.75 .75
C7 AP4 5auk slate & yel 2.75 1.25
Nos. C1-C7 (7) 11.90 5.50

For surcharges see Nos. C21-C26, C29.

Allegory of Flight — AP5

1921, Nov. 6

C8 AP5 20sk org & gray bl 2.50 1.50
C9 AP5 40sk dl bl & lake 2.50 1.50
C10 AP5 60sk vio bl & ol grn 2.50 1.50
C11 AP5 80sk ocher & dp grn 2.50 1.50
a. Vert. pair, imperf. btwn. 35.00 35.00
C12 AP5 1auk bl grn & bl 2.50 1.50
C13 AP5 2auk gray & brn org 2.50 1.50
C14 AP5 5auk dl lil & Prus bl 2.50 1.50
Nos. C8-C14 (7) 17.50 10.50

Opening of airmail service.

Plane over Kaunas — AP6

Black Overprint

1922, July 16 ***Perf. 11, 11½***

C15 AP6 1auk ol brn & red 2.75 2.75
a. Imperf., pair 60.00
C16 AP6 3auk violet & grn 2.75 2.75
C17 AP6 5auk dp blue & yel 2.75 4.00
Nos. C15-C17 (3) 8.25 9.50

Nos. C15-C17, without overprint, were to be for the founding of the Air Post service but they were not put in use at that time. Subsequently the word "ZENKLAS" (stamp) was overprinted over "ISTEIGIMAS" (founding) and the date "1921, VI, 25" was obliterated by short vertical lines.

For surcharge see No. C31.

Plane over Gediminas Castle — AP7

1922, July 22

C18 AP7 2auk blue & rose 1.50 .85
C19 AP7 4auk brown & rose 1.50 .85
C20 AP7 10auk black & gray bl 1.75 1.40
Nos. C18-C20 (3) 4.75 3.10

For surcharges see Nos. C27-C28, C30.

Nos. C1-C7, C17-C20 Surcharged like Regular Issues in Black or Carmine

1922

C21 AP1 10c on 20sk 5.75 2.50
C22 AP1 10c on 40sk 3.00 1.50
C23 AP1 10c on 60sk 3.00 1.50
a. Inverted surcharge 45.00
C24 AP1 10c on 80sk 3.00 1.50
C25 AP2 20c on 1auk 12.00 6.00
C26 AP3 20c on 2auk 15.00 7.50
a. Without "CENT" 200.00 140.00
C27 AP7 25c on 2auk 1.75 1.00
a. Inverted surcharge 45.00 40.00
C28 AP7 30c on 4auk (C) 1.75 1.00
a. Double surcharge 50.00 45.00
C29 AP4 50c on 5auk 3.00 1.50
C30 AP7 50c on 10auk 1.75 1.00
a. Inverted surcharge 50.00 45.00
C31 AP6 1 l on 5auk 25.00 15.00
a. Double surcharge 50.00
Nos. C21-C31 (11) 75.00 40.00

"Flight" AP9

Map of Lithuania, Klaipeda and Vilnius — AP14

Airplane and Carrier Pigeons AP8

1924, Jan. 28 **Wmk. 147** ***Perf. 11***

C32 AP8 20c yellow 1.75 .75
C33 AP8 40c emerald 1.75 .75
a. Horiz. or vert. pair, imperf. between 60.00
C34 AP8 60c rose 1.75 .75
a. Imperf., pair 75.00
C35 AP9 1 l dk brown 3.50 .75
Nos. C32-C35 (4) 8.75 3.00

Most copies, if not all, of the "unwatermarked" varieties show faint traces of watermark, according to experts.

For surcharges see Nos. CB1-CB4.

Swallow — AP10

1926, June 17 **Wmk. 198** ***Perf. 14½***

C37 AP10 20c carmine rose 1.25 .75
a. Horiz. or vert. pair, imperf. between 55.00
C38 AP10 40c violet & red org 1.25 .75
a. Horiz. or vert. pair, imperf. between 55.00
C39 AP10 60c blue & black 2.50 .75
a. Horiz. or vert. pair, imperf. between 55.00
c. Center inverted 250.00 160.00
Nos. C37-C39 (3) 5.00 2.25

Juozas Tubelis — AP11

Vytautas and Airplane over Kaunas AP12

Vytautas and Antanas Smetona AP13

1930, Feb. 16 **Wmk. 109** ***Perf. 14***

C40 AP11 5c blk, bis & brn .70 .30
C41 AP11 10c dk bl, db & blk .70 .30
C42 AP11 15c mar, gray & bl .70 .30
C43 AP12 20c dk brn, org & dl red .70 .50
C44 AP12 40c dk bl, lt bl & vio 1.25 .50
C45 AP13 60c bl grn, lil & blk 2.00 .55
C46 AP13 1 l dl red, lil & blk 3.75 1.00
Nos. C40-C46 (7) 9.80 3.45

5th cent. of the death of the Grand Duke Vytautas.

15c, 20c, Airplane over Neman. 40c, 60c, City Hall, Kaunas. 1 l, 2 l, Church of Vytautas, Kaunas.

Wmk. Multiple Letters (238)

1932, July 21 ***Perf. 14, Imperf.***

C47 AP14 5c ver & ol grn .85 .60
C48 AP14 10c dk red brn & ocher .85 .60
C49 AP14 15c dk bl & org yel .85 .60
C50 AP14 20c sl blk & org 3.50 .75
C51 AP14 60c ultra & ocher 5.00 3.00
C52 AP14 2 l dk bl & yel 6.50 4.00

Wmk. 198

C53 AP14 40c vio brn & yel 4.50 5.00
C54 AP14 1 l vio brn & grn 8.50 3.50
Nos. C47-C54 (8) 30.55 18.05

Issued for the benefit of Lithuanian orphans.

Mindaugas in the Battle of Shauyai, 1236 — AP15

15c, 20c, Coronation of Mindaugas (1253). 40c, Grand Duke Gediminas and his followers. 60c, Founding of Vilnius by Gediminas (1332). 1 l, Gediminas capturing the Russian Fortifications. 2 l, Grand Duke Algirdas before Moscow (1368).

Perf. 14, Imperf.

1932, Nov. 28 **Wmk. 209**

C55 AP15 5c grn & red lil .90 .75
C56 AP15 10c emer & rose .90 .75
C57 AP15 15c rose vio & bis brn .90 .75
C58 AP15 20c rose red & blk brn 3.50 .50
C59 AP15 40c choc & dk gray 5.50 1.10
C60 AP15 60c org & gray blk 6.00 3.00
C61 AP15 1 l rose vio & grn 7.00 5.00
C62 AP15 2 l dp bl & brn 8.00 7.50
Nos. C55-C62 (8) 32.70 19.35

Anniv. of independence.

Nos. C58-C62 exist with overprint "DARIUS-GIRENAS / NEW YORK-1933- KAUNAS" below small plane. The overprint was applied in New York with the approval of the Lithuanian consul general. Lithuanian postal authorities seem not to have been involved in the creation or release of these overprints.

Trakai Castle, Home of the Grand Duke Kestutis — AP16

Designs: 15c, 20c, Meeting of Kestutís and the Hermit Birute. 40c, 60c, Hermit Birute. 1 l, 2 l, Kestutis and his Brother Algirdas.

1933, May 6 ***Perf. 14, Imperf.***

C63 AP16 5c ol gray & dp bl .80 .60
C64 AP16 10c gray vio & org brn .80 .60
C65 AP16 15c dp blue & lilac .80 .60
C66 AP16 20c org brn & lilac 2.50 1.00
C67 AP16 40c lt ultra & lilac 3.50 *1.75*
C68 AP16 60c brown & lt ultra 5.00 *3.50*
C69 AP16 1 l ol gray & dp bl 7.00 *4.00*
C70 AP16 2 l vio gray & yel grn 10.00 *8.00*
Nos. C63-C70 (8) 30.40 *20.05*

Reopening of air service to Berlin-Kaunas-Moscow, and 550th anniv. of the death of Kestutis.

Joseph Maironis — AP17

Joseph Tumas-Vaizgantas — AP17a

Designs: 40c, 60c, Vincas Kudirka. 1 l, 2 l, Julia A. Zemaite.

1933, Sept. 15 ***Perf. 14, Imperf.***

C71 AP17 5c crim & dp bl .65 .65
C72 AP17 10c bl vio & grn .65 .65
C73 AP17a 15c dk grn & choc .65 .65
C74 AP17a 20c brn car & ultra .90 .90
C75 AP17 40c red brn & ol grn 1.50 1.50
C76 AP17 60c dk bl & choc 2.50 2.50
C77 AP17 1 l citron & indigo 3.50 3.50
C78 AP17 2 l dp grn & red brn 5.75 5.75
Nos. C71-C78 (8) 16.10 16.10

Issued for the benefit of Lithuanian orphans.

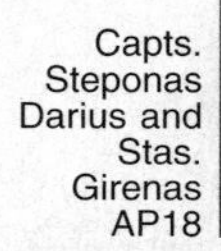

Capts. Steponas Darius and Stas. Girenas AP18

Ill-Fated Plane "Lituanica" AP19

The Dark Angel of Death — AP20

"Lituanica" over Globe — AP21

"Lituanica" and White Knight — AP22

Perf. 11½

1934, May 18 **Unwmk.** **Engr.**

C79 AP18 20c scarlet & blk .20 .20
C80 AP19 40c dp rose & bl .20 .20
C81 AP18 60c dk vio & blk .20 .20
C82 AP20 1 l black & rose .35 .20
C83 AP21 3 l gray grn & org .90 .50
C84 AP22 5 l dk brn & bl 3.50 3.25
Nos. C79-C84 (6) 5.35 4.55

Death of Capts. Steponas Darius and Stasys Girenas on their New York-Kaunas flight of 1933.

No. C80 exists with diagonal overprint: "F. VAITKUS / nugalejo Atlanta / 21-22-IX-1935." Value $300.

Felix Waitkus and Map of Transatlantic Flight — AP23

Wmk. 238

1936, Mar. 24 **Litho.** ***Perf. 14***

C85 AP23 15c brown lake 2.25 .75
C86 AP23 30c dark green 3.25 .75
C87 AP23 60c blue 4.25 2.00
Nos. C85-C87 (3) 9.75 3.50

Transatlantic Flight of the Lituanica II, Sept. 21-22, 1935.

AIR POST SEMI-POSTAL STAMPS

Catalogue values for unused stamps in this section are for Never Hinged items.

Nos. C32-C35 Surcharged like Nos. B1-B9 (No. CB1), Nos. B10-B11 (Nos. CB2-CB3), and Nos. B12-B14 (No. CB4) in Red, Violet or Black

1924 **Wmk. 147** ***Perf. 11***

CB1 AP8 20c + 20c yellow (R) 16.00 8.00
CB2 AP8 40c + 40c emerald (V) 16.00 8.00
CB3 AP8 60c + 60c rose (V) 16.00 8.00
CB4 AP9 1 l + 1 l dk brown 16.00 8.00
Nos. CB1-CB4 (4) 64.00 32.00

Surtax for the Red Cross. See note following No. C35.

SOUTH LITHUANIA

GRODNO DISTRICT

Russian Stamps of 1909-12 Surcharged in Black or Red

1919 **Unwmk.** ***Perf. 14, 14½x15***

L1 A14 50sk on 3k red 60.00 50.00
a. Double surcharge
L2 A14 50sk on 5k claret 60.00 50.00
a. Imperf., pair 300.00 275.00
L3 A15 50sk on 10k dk bl (R) 60.00 50.00
L4 A11 50sk on 15k red brn & bl 60.00 50.00
a. Imperf., pair 350.00 325.00
L5 A11 50sk on 25k grn & gray vio (R) 60.00 50.00
L6 A11 50sk on 35k red brn & grn 60.00 50.00
L7 A8 50sk on 50k vio & grn 60.00 50.00
L8 A11 50sk on 70k brn & org 60.00 50.00
Nos. L1-L8 (8) 480.00 400.00

Excellent counterfeits are plentiful.

This surcharge exists on Russia No. 119, the imperf. 1k orange of 1917. Value, unused $90, used $60.

OCCUPATION STAMPS

ISSUED UNDER GERMAN OCCUPATION

German Stamps Overprinted in Black

On Stamps of 1905-17

1916-17 **Wmk. 125** ***Perf. 14, 14½***

1N1 A22 2½pf gray .65 *1.00*
1N2 A16 3pf brown .25 .20
1N3 A16 5pf green .65 *1.00*
1N4 A22 7½pf orange .65 *1.00*
1N5 A16 10pf carmine .65 *1.00*
1N6 A22 15pf yel brn 3.00 2.00
1N7 A22 15pf dk vio ('17) .65 *1.00*
1N8 A16 20pf ultra 1.00 1.00
1N9 A16 25pf org & blk, *yel* .50 *.50*
1N10 A16 40pf lake & blk 1.00 *3.75*
1N11 A16 50pf vio & blk, *buff* 1.00 *1.50*
1N12 A17 1m car rose 12.00 3.50
Nos. 1N1-1N12 (12) 22.00 *17.45*
Set, never hinged 40.00

These stamps were used in the former Russian provinces of Suvalki, Vilnius, Kaunas, Kurland, Estland and Lifland.

ISSUED UNDER RUSSIAN OCCUPATION

Catalogue values for unused stamps in this section are for Never Hinged items.

Lithuanian Stamps of 1937-40 Overprinted in Red or Blue

1940 **Wmk. 238** ***Perf. 14***

2N9 A44 2c orange (Bl) .30 .40
2N10 A50 50c brown (Bl) .75 .50

Unwmk.

2N11 A56 5c brown car (Bl) .30 .40
2N12 A57 10c green (R) 10.00 10.00
2N13 A58 15c dull orange (Bl) .30 .40
2N14 A59 25c lt brown (R) .30 .40
2N15 A60 30c Prus green (R) .65 .50
2N16 A61 35c red orange (Bl) .90 1.00
Nos. 2N9-2N16 (8) 13.50 13.60

Values for used stamps are for CTOs. Postally used examples are considerably more.

The Lithuanian Soviet Socialist Republic was proclaimed July 21, 1940.

LOURENCO MARQUES

lə-ˈren,t-,sō-,mär-ˈkes

LOCATION — In the southern part of Mozambique in Southeast Africa
GOVT. — Part of Portuguese East Africa Colony
AREA — 28,800 sq. mi. (approx.)
POP. — 474,000 (approx.)
CAPITAL — Lourenço Marques

Stamps of Mozambique replaced those of Lourenço Marques in 1920. See Mozambique No. 360.

1000 Reis = 1 Milreis
100 Centavos = 1 Escudo (1913)

King Carlos — A1

Perf. 11½, 12½, 13½

1895 Typo. Unwmk.

1 A1 5r yellow .75 .25
2 A1 10r redsh violet .75 .35
3 A1 15r chocolate 1.00 .50
4 A1 20r lavender 1.00 .50
5 A1 25r blue green 1.00 .30
a. Perf. 11½ 3.50 1.00
6 A1 50r light blue 2.00 1.00
a. Perf. 13½ 15.00 5.00
b. Perf. 11½ — —
7 A1 75r rose 1.50 1.25
8 A1 80r yellow grn 4.75 3.00
9 A1 100r brn, *yel* 3.00 1.00
a. Perf. 12½ 5.00 3.25
10 A1 150r car, *rose* 5.00 3.00
11 A1 200r dk bl, *bl* 6.00 3.00
12 A1 300r dk bl, *sal* 7.50 4.00
Nos. 1-12 (12) 34.25 18.15

For surcharges and overprints see Nos. 29, 58-69, 132-137, 140-143, 156-157, 160.

Saint Anthony of Padua Issue

Regular Issues of Mozambique, 1886 and 1894, Overprinted in Black

1895 Without Gum Perf. 12½

On 1886 Issue

13 A2 5r black 20.00 12.00
14 A2 10r green 25.00 12.00
15 A2 20r rose 35.00 14.00
16 A2 25r lilac 40.00 14.00
17 A2 40r chocolate 35.00 15.00
18 A2 50r bl, perf. 13½ 30.00 14.00
a. Perf. 12½ 50.00 27.50
19 A2 100r yellow brn 110.00 90.00
20 A2 200r gray vio 42.50 32.50
21 A2 300r orange 70.00 40.00

On 1894 Issue

Perf. 11½

22 A3 5r yellow 35.00 25.00
23 A3 10r redsh vio 40.00 15.00
24 A3 50r light blue 50.00 32.50
a. Perf. 12½ 275.00 275.00
25 A3 75r rose, perf. 12½ 65.00 50.00
26 A3 80r yellow grn 80.00 65.00
27 A3 100r brown, *buff* 350.00 160.00
28 A3 150r car, *rose*, perf. 12½ 50.00 40.00
Nos. 13-28 (16) 1,077. 631.00

No. 12 Surcharged in Black

1897, Jan. 2

29 A1 50r on 300r 200.00 150.00

Most exmaples of No. 29 were issued without gum.

King Carlos — A2

1898-1903 Perf. 11½

Name, Value in Black except 500r

30 A2 2½r gray .35 .30
31 A2 5r orange .35 .30
32 A2 10r lt green .35 .30
33 A2 15r brown 1.25 .85
34 A2 15r gray green ('03) .75 .50
a. Imperf.
35 A2 20r gray violet .65 .40
a. Imperf.
36 A2 25r sea green .70 .40
a. Perf. 13½ 47.50 8.50
b. 25r light green (error) *32.50 32.50*
c. Perf. 12½ *70.00* 60.00
37 A2 25r car ('03) .35 .30
a. Imperf.
38 A2 50r blue 2.00 .50
39 A2 50r brown ('03) .90 .75
40 A2 65r dull bl ('03) 18.50 8.50
41 A2 75r rose 2.00 1.50
42 A2 75r lilac ('03) 1.25 .95
a. Imperf.
43 A2 80r violet 2.50 1.25
44 A2 100r dk blue, *blue* 1.75 .65
a. Perf. 13½ 14.50 5.00
45 A2 115r org brn, *pink* ('03) 6.00 5.00
46 A2 130r brn, *straw* ('03) 6.00 5.00
47 A2 150r brn, *straw* 2.25 1.40
48 A2 200r red lil, *pnksh* 2.75 1.25
49 A2 300r dk bl, *rose* 3.25 1.50
50 A2 400r dl bl, *straw* ('03) 7.00 5.00
51 A2 500r blk & red, *bl* ('01) 6.00 3.00
52 A2 700r vio, *yelsh* ('01) 12.00 7.00
Nos. 30-52 (23) 78.90 46.60

For surcharges and overprints see Nos. 57, 71-74, 76-91, 138, 144-155.

Coat of Arms — A3

Surcharged On Upper and Lower Halves of Stamp

1899 Imperf.

53 A3 5r on 10r grn & brn 20.00 7.00
54 A3 25r on 10r grn & brn 20.00 7.00
55 A3 50r on 30r grn & brn 30.00 11.00
a. Inverted surcharge
56 A3 50r on 800r grn & brn 40.00 20.00
Nos. 53-56 (4) 110.00 45.00

The lower half of No. 55 can be distinguished from that of No. 56 by the background of the label containing the word "REIS." The former is plain, while the latter is formed of white intersecting curved horizontal lines over vertical shading of violet brown.

Values are for undivided stamps. Halves sell for ¼ as much.

Most exmaples of Nos. 53-56 were issued without gum. Values are for stamps without gum.

No. 41 Surcharged in Black

1899 Perf. 11½

57 A2 50r on 75r rose 5.00 2.50

Most exmaples of No. 57 were issued without gum. Values are for stamps without gum.

Surcharged in Black

On Issue of 1895

1902 Perf. 11½, 12½

58 A1 65r on 5r yellow 4.00 2.50
59 A1 65r on 15r choc 4.00 2.50
60 A1 65r on 20r lav 5.00 2.50
a. Perf. 12½ 25.00 15.00
61 A1 115r on 10r red vio 5.00 3.00
62 A1 115r on 200r bl, *bl* 5.00 3.00
63 A1 115r on 300r bl, *sal* 5.00 3.00
64 A1 130r on 25r grn, perf. 12½ 2.00 2.00
a. Perf. 11½ 30.00 22.50
65 A1 130r on 80r yel grn 3.00 3.00
66 A1 130r on 150r car, *rose* 4.00 3.00
67 A1 400r on 50r lt bl 8.00 6.00
68 A1 400r on 75r rose 8.00 6.00
69 A1 400r on 100r brn, *buff* 7.00 6.00

On Newspaper Stamp of 1893

70 N1 65r on 2½ brn 4.00 2.00
Nos. 58-70 (13) 64.00 44.50

Surcharge exists inverted on Nos. 61, 70.

Nos. 64, 67 and 68 have been reprinted on thin white paper with shiny white gum and clean-cut perforation 13½. Value $6 each.

For overprints see Nos. 132-137, 140-143, 156-157, 160.

Issue of 1898-1903 Overprinted in Black

1903 Perf. 11½

71 A2 15r brown 2.00 .85
72 A2 25r sea green 1.50 .85
73 A2 50r blue 2.50 .85
74 A2 75r rose 3.00 1.40
a. Inverted overprint 50.00 50.00
Nos. 71-74 (4) 9.00 3.95

Surcharged in Black

1905

76 A2 50r on 65r dull blue 2.25 2.00

Regular Issues Overprinted in Carmine or Green

1911

77 A2 2½r gray .30 .25
78 A2 5r orange .30 .25
a. Double overprint 10.00 10.00
b. Inverted overprint 10.00 10.00
79 A2 10r lt grn .40 .35
80 A2 15r gray grn .40 .35
a. Inverted overprint 10.00 10.00
81 A2 20r dl vio .40 .40
82 A2 25r car (G) .90 .50
83 A2 50r brown .80 .50
84 A2 75r lilac 1.10 .50
85 A2 100r dk bl, *bl* .80 .55
86 A2 115r org brn, *pink* 9.00 3.50
87 A2 130r brn, *straw* .80 .60
88 A2 200r red lil, *pnksh* .85 .60
89 A2 400r dl bl, *straw* 1.25 1.10
90 A2 500r blk & red, *bl* 1.50 1.10
91 A2 700r vio, *yelsh* 1.75 1.25
Nos. 77-91 (15) 20.55 11.80

Vasco da Gama Issue of Various Portuguese Colonies Common Design Types Surcharged

1913 Perf. 12½-16

On Stamps of Macao

92 CD20 ¼c on ½a bl grn 2.25 2.25
93 CD21 ½c on 1a red 2.25 2.25
94 CD22 1c on 2a red vio 2.25 2.25
95 CD23 2½c on 4a yel grn 2.25 2.25
96 CD24 5c on 8a dk bl 2.25 2.25
97 CD25 7½c on 12a vio brn 4.25 4.25
98 CD26 10c on 16a bis brn 3.50 3.50
a. Inverted surcharge 40.00 40.00
99 CD27 15c on 24a bister 3.75 3.75
Nos. 92-99 (8) 22.75 22.75

On Stamps of Portuguese Africa

100 CD20 ¼c on 2½r bl grn 1.75 1.75
101 CD21 ½c on 5r red 1.75 1.75
102 CD22 1c on 10r red vio 1.75 1.75
103 CD23 2½c on 25r yel grn 1.75 1.75
104 CD24 5c on 50r dk bl 1.75 1.75
105 CD25 7½c on 75r vio brn 4.00 4.00
106 CD26 10c on 100r bis brn 2.75 2.75
107 CD27 15c on 150r bis 2.75 2.75
Nos. 100-107 (8) 18.25 18.25

On Stamps of Timor

108 CD20 ¼c on ½a bl grn 1.75 1.75
109 CD21 ½c on 1a red 1.75 1.75
110 CD22 1c on 2a red vio 1.75 1.75
111 CD23 2½c on 4a yel grn 1.75 1.75
112 CD24 5c on 8a dk bl 2.00 1.75
113 CD25 7½c on 12a vio brn 4.00 4.00
114 CD26 10c on 16a bis brn 2.75 2.75
115 CD27 15c on 24a bister 2.75 2.75
Nos. 108-115 (8) 18.50 18.25
Nos. 92-115 (24) 59.50 59.25

Ceres — A4

1914 Typo. Perf. 15x14

Name and Value in Black

116 A4 ¼c olive brn .25 .20
117 A4 ½c black .25 .20
a. Value omitted 15.00
118 A4 1c blue grn .25 .20
119 A4 1½c lilac brn .25 .20
a. Imperf.
120 A4 2c carmine .25 .20
121 A4 2½c lt vio .25 .20
122 A4 5c dp blue .25 .20
123 A4 7½c yellow brn .50 .40
124 A4 8c slate .50 .40
125 A4 10c orange brn 1.50 .85
126 A4 15c plum 1.00 .70
127 A4 20c yellow grn 2.50 .90
128 A4 30c brown, *green* 3.50 1.00
129 A4 40c brown, *pink* 9.00 4.00
130 A4 50c orange, *sal* 8.00 3.00
131 A4 1e green, *blue* 10.00 3.00
Nos. 116-131 (16) 38.25 15.65

Values of Nos. 116-124 are for stamps on ordinary paper. Those on chalky paper sell for 8 to 12 times as much. Nos. 127-131 issued only on chalky paper.

For surcharges see Nos. 139, 159, 161-162, B1-B12.

In 1921 Nos. 117 and 119 were surcharged 10c and 30c respectively, for use in Mozambique as Nos. 230 and 231. These same values, surcharged 5c and 10c respectively, with the addition of the word "PORTEADO," were used in Mozambique as postage dues, Nos. J44 and J45.

Provisional Issue of 1902 Overprinted Locally in Carmine

1914 Perf. 11½, 12½

132 A1 115r on 10r red vio 1.00 .45
a. "Republica" inverted 20.00
133 A1 115r on 200r bl, *bl* 1.00 .45
134 A1 115r on 300r bl, *sal* 1.10 .45
a. Double overprint 40.00 40.00
135 A1 130r on 25r grn 1.50 .70
a. Perf. 12½ 3.25 1.60
136 A1 130r on 80r yel grn 1.10 .35
137 A1 130r on 150r car, *rose* 1.10 .35
Nos. 132-137 (6) 6.80 2.75

No. 135a was issued without gum.

Nos. 78 and 117 Perforated Diagonally and Surcharged in Carmine

1915 ***Perf. 11½***

138 A2 ¼c on half of 5r org, pair 5.00 5.00
a. Pair without dividing perfs. 20.00 20.00

Perf. 15x14

139 A4 ¼c on half of ½c blk, pair 9.00 9.00

The added perforation on Nos. 138-139 runs from lower left to upper right corners, dividing the stamp in two. Values are for pairs, both halves of the stamp.

Provisional Issue of 1902 Overprinted in Carmine

1915 ***Perf. 11½, 12½***

140 A1 115r on 10r red vio .55 .40
141 A1 115r on 200r bl, *bl* .70 .40
142 A1 115r on 300r bl, *sal* .70 .40
143 A1 130r on 150r car, *rose* .75 .40
Nos. 140-143 (4) 2.70 1.60

Nos. 34 and 80 Surcharged

1915

On Issue of 1903

144 A2 2c on 15r gray grn .90 .80

On Issue of 1911

145 A2 2c on 15r gray grn .90 .80
a. New value inverted 22.50

Regular Issues of 1898-1903 Overprinted Locally in Carmine

1916

146 A2 15r gray grn 1.50 1.00
147 A2 50r brown 3.50 2.00
a. Inverted overprint
148 A2 75r lilac 3.50 2.00
149 A2 100r blue, *bl* 3.00 1.00
150 A2 115r org brn, *pink* 2.50 1.00
151 A2 130r brown, *straw* 10.00 5.00
152 A2 200r red lil, *pnksh* 7.00 2.00
153 A2 400r dull bl, *straw* 12.00 4.00
154 A2 500r blk & red, *bl* 7.00 3.00
155 A2 700r vio, *yelsh* 12.00 5.00
Nos. 146-155 (10) 62.00 26.00

Same Overprint on Nos. 67-68

1917

156 A1 400r on 50r lt blue 1.25 .65
a. Perf. 13½ 11.50 9.00
157 A1 400r on 75r rose 2.50 1.00

No. 69 exists with this overprint. It was not officially issued.

Type of 1914 Surcharged in Red

1920 ***Perf. 15x14***

159 A4 4c on 2½c violet 1.00 .30

Stamps of 1914 Surcharged in Green or Black

a

b

1921

160 A1(a) ¼c on 115r on 10r red vio (G) .80 .80
161 A4(b) 1c on 2½c vio (Bk) .60 .40
a. Inverted surcharge 40.00
162 A4(b) 1½c on 2½c vio (Bk) .80 .60
Nos. 160-162 (3) 2.20 1.80

Nos. 159-162 were postally valid throughout Mozambique.

SEMI-POSTAL STAMPS

Regular Issue of 1914 Overprinted or Surcharged:

a

b

c

1918 ***Perf. 15x14½***

B1 A4(a) ¼c olive brn 2.00 *3.00*
B2 A4(a) ½c black 2.00 4.00
B3 A4(a) 1c bl grn 2.00 *4.00*
B4 A4(a) 2½c violet 4.00 4.00
B5 A4(a) 5c blue 4.00 *6.00*
B6 A4(a) 10c org brn 5.00 *7.00*
B7 A4(b) 20c on 1½c lil brn 5.00 *8.00*
B8 A4(a) 30c brn, *grn* 5.00 *9.00*
B9 A4(b) 40c on 2c car 5.00 *10.00*
B10 A4(b) 50c on 7½c bis 8.00 *12.00*
B11 A4(b) 70c on 8c slate 10.00 *15.00*
B12 A4(c) $1 on 15c mag 10.00 *15.00*
Nos. B1-B12 (12) 62.00 *97.00*

Nos. B1-B12 were used in place of ordinary postage stamps on Mar. 9, 1918.

NEWSPAPER STAMPS

Numeral of Value — N1

Perf. 11½

1893, July 28 **Typo.** **Unwmk.**

P1 N1 2½r brown .25 *.65*
a. Perf. 12½ 20.00 17.50

For surcharge see No. 70.

Saint Anthony of Padua Issue

Mozambique No. P6 Overprinted

1895, July 1 ***Perf. 11½, 13½***

P2 N3 2½r brown 20.00 17.50
a. Inverted overprint 30.00 30.00

LUXEMBOURG

ˈlək-səm-ˌbərg

LOCATION — Western Europe between southern Belgium, Germany and France
GOVT. — Grand Duchy
AREA — 999 sq. mi.
POP. — 476,200 (2007)
CAPITAL — Luxembourg

12½ Centimes = 1 Silbergroschen
100 Centimes = 1 Franc
100 Cents = 1 Euro (2002)

Catalogue values for unused stamps in this country are for Never Hinged items, beginning with Scott 321 in the regular postage section, Scott B216 in the semi-postal section.

Watermarks

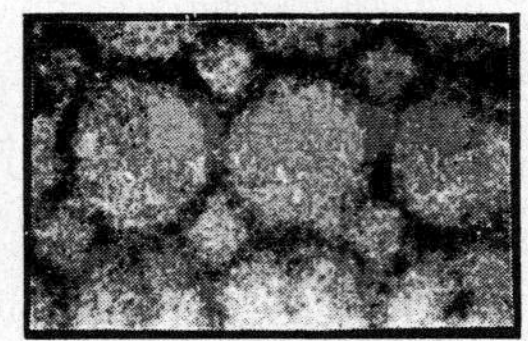

Wmk. 110 — Octagons

Wmk. 149 — W

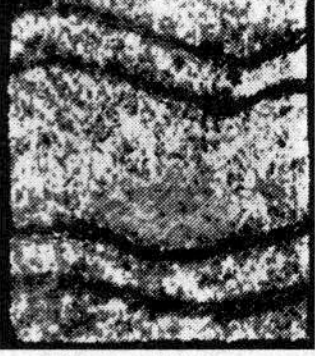

Wmk. 213 — Double Wavy Lines

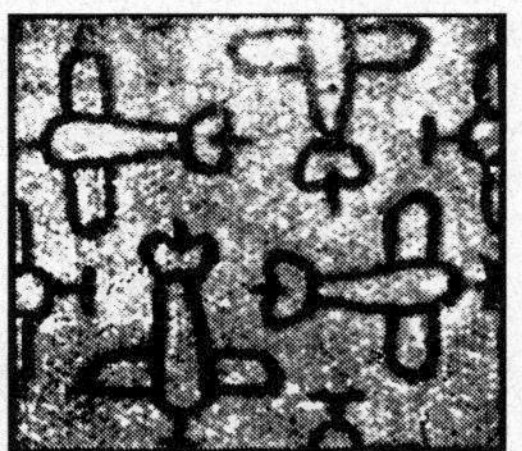

Wmk. 216 — Multiple Airplanes

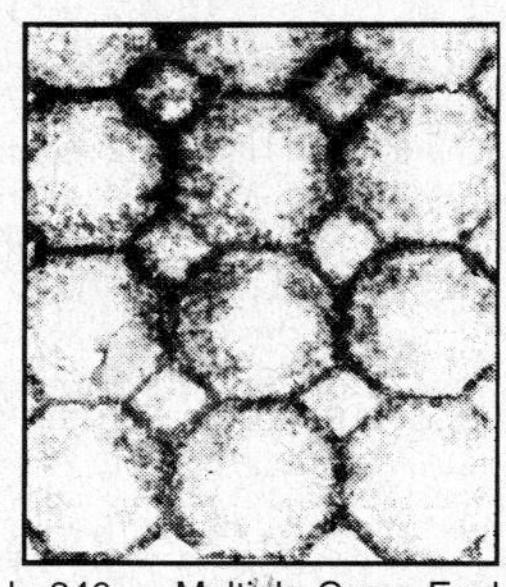

Wmk. 246 — Multiple Cross Enclosed in Octagons

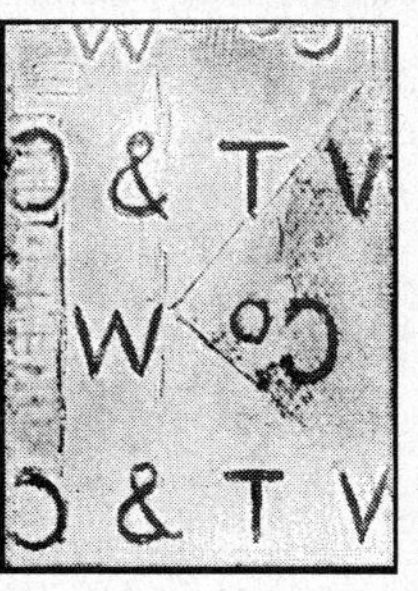

Wmk. 247 — Multiple Letters

Unused values of Nos. 1-47 are for stamps without gum. Though these stamps were issued with gum, most examples offered are without gum. Stamps with original gum sell for more.

Grand Duke William III — A1

Luxembourg Print

Wmk. 149

1852, Sept. 15 **Engr.** ***Imperf.***

1 A1 10c gray black *2,850.* 72.50
a. 10c greenish black ('53) *3,000.* 82.50
b. 10c intense black ('54) *3,650.* 160.00
2 A1 1sg brown red ('53) 1,950. 125.00
a. 1sg brick red 1,950. 125.00
b. 1sg orange red ('54) 1,950. 125.00
c. 1sg blood red 3,400. 625.00
3 A1 1sg rose ('55) 1,875. 100.00
a. 1sg carmine rose ('56) 1,875. 115.00
b. 1sg dark carmine rose, thin paper ('59) 1,950. 300.00
Nos. 1-3 (3) 297.50

Reprints of both values exist on watermarked paper. Some of the reprints show traces of lines cancelling the plates, but others can be distinguished only by an expert.

See Nos. 278-279, 603.

Coat of Arms
A2 A3

No. 26

No. 39

Frankfurt Print

1859-64 **Typo.** **Unwmk.**

4 A2 1c buff ('63) 175.00 *575.00*
5 A2 2c black ('60) 125.00 *700.00*
6 A2 4c yellow ('64) 240.00 225.00
a. 4c orange ('60) 250.00 250.00
7 A3 10c blue 250.00 25.00
8 A3 12½c rose 350.00 200.00
9 A3 25c brown 475.00 350.00
10 A3 30c rose lilac 400.00 300.00
11 A3 37½c green 400.00 250.00
12 A3 40c red orange 1,200. 300.00

Counterfeits of Nos. 1-12 exist.

See Nos. 13-25, 27-38, 40-47. For surcharges and overprints see Nos. 26, 39, O1-O51.

1865-71 ***Rouletted***

13 A2 1c red brown 225.00 325.00
14 A2 2c black ('67) 25.00 21.00
15 A2 4c yellow ('67) 775.00 225.00
16 A2 4c green ('71) 52.50 30.00
Nos. 13-16 (4) 1,077. 601.00

1865-74 ***Rouletted in Color***

17 A2 1c red brown ('72) 52.50 10.50
18 A2 1c orange ('69) 52.50 10.50
a. 1c brown orange ('67) 150.00 52.50
b. 1c red orange ('69) 1,825. 475.00
19 A3 10c rose lilac 175.00 5.25
a. 10c lilac 150.00 5.25
b. 10c gray lilac 150.00 5.25
20 A3 12½c carmine ('71) 225.00 10.50
a. 12½c rose 250.00 10.50
21 A3 20c gray brown ('72) 150.00 10.50
a. 20c yellow brown ('69) 175.00 10.50
22 A3 25c blue ('72) 1,050. 15.00
22A A3 25c ultra ('65) 1,050. 15.00
23 A3 30c lilac rose 1,150. 100.00
24 A3 37½c bister ('66) 1,050. 325.00
25 A3 40c pale orange ('74) 52.50 100.00
a. 40c orange red ('66) 1,400. 77.50
26 A3 1fr on 37½c bis ('73) 1,175. 100.00
a. Surcharge inverted *3,600.*

Luxembourg Print

1874 **Typo.** ***Imperf.***

27 A2 4c green 150.00 150.00

1875-79 ***Perf. 13***

Narrow Margins

29 A2 1c red brown ('78) 52.50 10.50
30 A2 2c black 175.00 35.00
31 A2 4c green 3.00 *13.00*

32 A2 5c yellow ('76) 225.00 35.00
a. 5c orange yellow 775.00 150.00
b. Imperf. 925.00 1,100.
33 A3 10c gray lilac 600.00 3.00
b. 10c lilac 1,700. 40.00
c. Imperf. 2,700. *3,250.*
34 A3 12½c lilac rose ('77) 775.00 26.00
35 A3 12½c car rose ('76) 550.00 35.00
36 A3 25c blue ('77) 1,050. 21.00
37 A3 30c dull rose ('78) 1,000. 600.00
38 A3 40c orange ('79) 3.00 *13.00*
39 A3 1fr on 37½c bis ('79) 10.50 *37.50*
a. "Pranc" 6,750. *7,800.*
b. Without surcharge 675.00
c. As "b," imperf. 825.00

In the Luxembourg print the perforation is close to the border of the stamp. Excellent forgeries of No. 39a are plentiful, as well as faked cancellations on Nos. 31, 38 and 39.

Nos. 32b and 33c are said to be essays; Nos. 39b and 39c printer's waste.

Haarlem Print

1880-81 ***Perf. 11½x12, 12½x12, 13½***

Wide Margins

40 A2 1c yellow brn ('81) 9.50 6.00
41 A2 2c black 8.50 1.75
42 A2 5c yellow ('81) 250.00 110.00
43 A3 10c gray lilac 190.00 1.00
44 A3 12½c rose ('81) 225.00 225.00
45 A3 20c gray brown ('81) 55.00 19.00
46 A3 25c blue 300.00 5.00
47 A3 30c dull rose ('81) 4.00 *22.50*

Gray Yellowish Paper

Perf. 12½

42a A2 5c 7.25
43a A3 10c 3.50
44a A3 12½c 9.50
46a A3 25c 5.00
Nos. 42a-46a (4) 25.25

Stamps on gray yellowish paper were not regularly issued.

"Industry" and "Commerce" A6

Grand Duke Adolphe A7

Perf. 11½x12, 12½x12, 12½, 13½

1882, Dec. 1 **Typo.**

48 A6 1c gray lilac .20 *.40*
49 A6 2c olive gray .20 *.40*
50 A6 4c olive bister .25 *2.50*
51 A6 5c lt green .50 .40
52 A6 10c rose 6.00 .40
53 A6 12½c slate 1.75 *30.00*
54 A6 20c orange 3.00 1.90
55 A6 25c ultra 190.00 1.90
56 A6 30c gray green 19.00 14.50
57 A6 50c bister brown .75 *11.00*
58 A6 1fr pale violet .75 *30.00*
59 A6 5fr brown orange 37.50 *190.00*
Nos. 48-59 (12) 259.90 *283.40*

For overprints see Nos. O52-O64.

Perf. 11, 11½, 11½x11 and 12½

1891-93 **Engr.**

60 A7 10c carmine .20 *.40*
a. Sheet of 25 100.00
61 A7 12½c slate grn ('93) .50 *.70*
62 A7 20c orange ('93) 12.00 *.70*
a. 20c brown, perf 11½ *110.00* 300.00
63 A7 25c blue .70 .60
a. Sheet of 25 *1,000.*
64 A7 30c olive grn ('93) 1.40 1.25
65 A7 37½c green ('93) 2.75 2.50
66 A7 50c brown ('93) 7.25 3.00
67 A7 1fr dp violet ('93) 14.50 6.50
68 A7 2½fr black ('93) 1.50 *25.00*
69 A7 5fr lake ('93) 37.50 80.00
Nos. 60-69 (10) 78.30 120.65

No. 62a was never on sale at any post office, but exists postally used.

Perf. 11½ stamps are from the sheets of 25.

For overprints see Nos. O65-O74.

Grand Duke Adolphe — A8

1895, May 4 **Typo.** ***Perf. 12½***

70 A8 1c pearl gray 2.10 .50
71 A8 2c gray brown .20 *.20*
72 A8 4c olive bister .20 *.50*
73 A8 5c green 2.10 .20
74 A8 10c carmine 8.25 .20
Nos. 70-74 (5) 12.85 1.60

For overprints see Nos. O75-O79.

Coat of Arms — A9

Grand Duke William IV — A10

1906-26 **Typo.** ***Perf. 12½***

75 A9 1c gray ('07) .20 .20
76 A9 2c olive brn ('07) .20 .20
77 A9 4c bister ('07) .20 *.40*
78 A9 5c green ('07) .20 .20
79 A9 5c lilac ('26) .20 .20
80 A9 6c violet ('07) .20 *.50*
81 A9 7½c orange ('19) .20 *3.50*

Engr.

Perf. 11, 11½x11

82 A10 10c scarlet 1.50 .20
a. Souvenir sheet of 10 450.00 *1,200.*
83 A10 12½c slate grn ('07) 1.75 .60
84 A10 15c orange brn ('07) 1.75 .70
85 A10 20c orange ('07) 2.50 .70
86 A10 25c ultra ('07) 60.00 .50
87 A10 30c olive grn ('08) 1.00 .70
88 A10 37½c green ('07) 1.00 .80
a. Perf. 12½ 30.00 14.50
89 A10 50c brown ('07) 5.00 1.25
90 A10 87½c dk blue ('08) 1.75 11.00
91 A10 1fr violet ('08) 6.00 2.10
92 A10 2½fr vermilion ('08) 55.00 92.50
93 A10 5fr claret ('08) 9.50 60.00
Nos. 75-93 (19) 148.15 176.25

No. 82a for accession of Grand Duke William IV to the throne.

For surcharges and overprints see Nos. 94-96, 112-117, O80-O98.

Nos. 90, 92-93 Surcharged in Red or Black

1912-15

94 A10 62½c on 87½c (R) 1.75 *2.50*
95 A10 62½c on 2½fr (Bk) ('15) 2.50 *5.00*
96 A10 62½c on 5fr (Bk) ('15) .70 *3.50*
Nos. 94-96 (3) 4.95 *11.00*

Grand Duchess Marie Adelaide A11

Grand Duchess Charlotte A12

1914-17 **Engr.** ***Perf. 11½, 11½x11***

97 A11 10c lake .20 .20
98 A11 12½c dull green .20 .20
99 A11 15c sepia .20 *.20*
100 A11 17½c dp brown ('17) .20 *.60*
101 A11 25c ultra .20 .20
102 A11 30c bister .20 *.70*
103 A11 35c dark blue .20 *.60*
104 A11 37½c black brn .20 *.60*
105 A11 40c orange .20 *.50*
106 A11 50c dark gray .20 *.70*
107 A11 62½c blue green .40 *3.50*
108 A11 87½c orange ('17) .30 *3.50*
109 A11 1fr orange brown 2.50 1.00
110 A11 2½fr red .60 *3.50*
111 A11 5fr dark violet 9.50 *55.00*
Nos. 97-111 (15) 15.30 *71.00*

For surcharges and overprints see Nos. 118-124, B7-B10, O99-O113. Nos. 97, 98, 101, 107, 109 and 111 overprinted "Droits de statistique" are revenue stamps.

Stamps of 1906-19 Surcharged with New Value and Bars in Black or Red

1916-24

112 A9 2½c on 5c ('18) .20 .20
a. Double surcharge 75.00
113 A9 3c on 2c ('21) .20 *.20*
114 A9 5c on 1c ('23) .20 *.20*
115 A9 5c on 4c ('23) .20 *.60*
116 A9 5c on 7½c ('24) .20 *.20*
117 A9 6c on 2c (R) ('22) .20 *.25*
118 A11 7½c on 10c ('18) .20 .20
119 A11 17½c on 30c .20 *.60*
120 A11 20c on 17½c ('21) .20 *.20*
121 A11 25c on 37½c ('23) .20 *.20*
a. Double surcharge 90.00
122 A11 75c on 62½c (R) ('22) .20 *.20*
123 A11 80c on 87½c ('22) .20 *.20*
124 A11 87½c on 1fr .60 *7.25*
Nos. 112-124 (13) 3.00 *10.50*

1921, Jan. 6 **Engr.** ***Perf. 11½***

125 A12 15c rose .20 *.40*
a. Sheet of 5, perf 11 150.00 *250.00*
b. Sheet of 25, perf. 11½, 11x11½, 12x11½ 5.50 *17.00*

Birth of Prince Jean, first son of Grand Duchess Charlotte, Jan. 5 (No. 125a). No. 125 was printed in sheets of 100.

See Nos. 131-150. For surcharges and overprints see Nos. 154-158, O114-O131, O136.

Vianden Castle — A13

Foundries at Esch — A14

Adolphe Bridge — A15

1921-34 ***Perf. 11, 11x11½, 11½***

126 A13 1fr carmine .20 *.45*
127 A13 1fr dk blue ('26) .20 *.55*

Perf. 11½x11; 11½ (#129)

128 A14 2fr indigo .20 *.65*
129 A14 2fr dk brown ('26) 2.50 2.25
130 A15 5fr dk violet 8.75 8.75
a. Perf. 12½ ('34) 14.00 11.00
Nos. 126-130 (5) 11.85 12.65

See No. B85. For overprints see Nos. O132-O135, O137-138, O140.

Charlotte Type of 1921

1921-26 ***Perf. 11½***

131 A12 2c brown .20 .20
132 A12 3c olive green .20 .20
a. Sheet of 25 10.00 25.00
133 A12 6c violet .20 .20
a. Sheet of 25 10.00 25.00
134 A12 10c yellow grn .20 .40
135 A12 10c olive brn ('24) .20 .20
136 A12 15c brown olive .20 .20
137 A12 15c pale green ('24) .20 .20
138 A12 15c dp orange ('26) .20 .40
139 A12 20c dp orange .20 .20
a. Sheet of 25 60.00 *110.00*
140 A12 20c yellow grn ('26) .20 .40
141 A12 25c dk green .20 .20
142 A12 30c carmine rose .20 .20
143 A12 40c brown orange .20 .20
144 A12 50c deep blue .20 .60
145 A12 50c red ('24) .20 .40
146 A12 75c red .20 1.50
a. Sheet of 25 325.00
147 A12 75c deep blue ('24) .20 .40
148 A12 80c black .20 1.25
a. Sheet of 25 325.00
Nos. 131-148 (18) 3.60 7.35

For surcharges and overprints see Nos. 154-158, O114-O131, O136.

Philatelic Exhibition Issue

1922, Aug. 27 ***Imperf.***

Laid Paper

149 A12 25c dark green 1.50 5.50
150 A12 30c carmine rose 1.50 5.50

Nos. 149 and 150 were sold exclusively at the Luxembourg Phil. Exhib., Aug. 1922.

Souvenir Sheet

View of Luxembourg — A16

1923, Jan. 3 ***Perf. 11***

151 A16 10fr dp grn, sheet 1,100. *1,800.*

Birth of Princess Elisabeth.

1923, Mar. ***Perf. 11½***

152 A16 10fr black 7.25 *12.50*
a. Perf. 12½ ('34) 7.25 *11.00*

For overprint see No. O141.

The Wolfsschlucht near Echternach — A17

1923-34 ***Perf. 11½***

153 A17 3fr dk blue & blue 1.10 1.10
a. Perf. 12½ ('34) .90 .65

For overprint see No. O139.

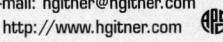

Stamps of 1921-26 Surcharged with New Values and Bars

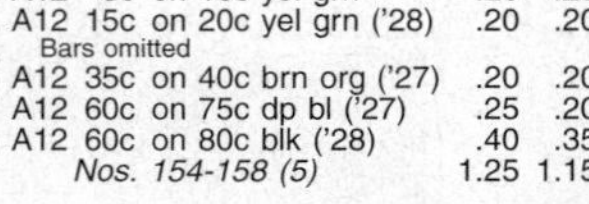

1925-28

154 A12 5c on 10c yel grn .20 .20
155 A12 15c on 20c yel grn ('28) .20 .20
a. Bars omitted
156 A12 35c on 40c brn org ('27) .20 .20
157 A12 60c on 75c dp bl ('27) .25 .20
158 A12 60c on 80c blk ('28) .40 .35
Nos. 154-158 (5) 1.25 1.15

Grand Duchess Charlotte — A18

1926-35 Engr. *Perf. 12*

159 A18 5c dk violet .20 .20
160 A18 10c olive grn .20 .20
161 A18 15c black ('30) .25 .25
162 A18 20c orange .40 .20
163 A18 25c yellow grn .50 .20
164 A18 25c vio brn ('27) .45 .20
165 A18 30c yel grn ('27) .45 .50
166 A18 30c gray vio ('30) .50 .40
167 A18 35c gray vio ('28) .25 .20
168 A18 35c yel grn ('30) .20 .20
169 A18 40c olive gray .20 .20
170 A18 50c red brown .20 .20
171 A18 60c blue grn ('28) .25 .20
172 A18 65c black brn .25 .50
173 A18 70c blue vio ('35) .20 .20
174 A18 75c rose .25 .25
175 A18 75c bis brn ('27) .20 .20
176 A18 80c bister brn .25 .60
177 A18 90c rose ('27) 1.50 .90
178 A18 1fr black 1.25 .60
179 A18 1fr rose ('30) .60 .50
180 A18 1¼fr dk blue .20 .45
181 A18 1¼fr yellow ('30) 7.25 .90
182 A18 1¼fr blue grn ('31) .60 .20
183 A18 1¼fr rose car ('34) 12.00 1.40
184 A18 1½fr dp blue ('27) 2.50 .90
185 A18 1¾fr dk blue ('30) .40 .50
Nos. 159-185 (27) 31.50 11.25
Set, never hinged 90.00

For surcharges and overprints see Nos. 186-193, N17-N29, O142-O178.

Stamps of 1926-35, Surcharged with New Values and Bars

1928-39

186 A18 10(c) on 30c yel grn ('29) .50 .20
187 A18 15c on 25c yel grn .40 .30
187A A18 30c on 60c bl grn ('39) .20 1.00
188 A18 60c on 65c blk brn .25 .25
189 A18 60c on 75c rose .25 .25
190 A18 60c on 80c bis brn .45 .50
191 A18 70(c) on 75c bis brn ('35) 6.00 .20
192 A18 75(c) on 90c rose ('29) 1.75 .20
193 A18 1¾(fr) on 1½fr dp bl ('29) 3.50 1.60
Nos. 186-193 (9) 13.30 4.50
Set, never hinged 30.00

The surcharge on No. 187A has no bars.

View of Clervaux — A19

1928-34 *Perf. 12½*

194 A19 2fr black ('34) 1.00 .50
Never hinged 3.50
a. Perf. 11½ ('28) 1.25 .60
Never hinged 6.00

See No. B66. For overprint see No. O179.

Coat of Arms — A20

1930, Dec. 20 Typo. *Perf. 12½*

195 A20 5c claret .40 .20
196 A20 10c olive green .60 .20
Set, never hinged 3.00

View of the Lower City of Luxembourg — A21

Gate of "Three Towers" — A22

1931, June 20 Engr.

197 A21 20fr deep green 3.25 9.50
Never hinged 5.50

For overprint see No. O180.

1934, Aug. 30 *Perf. 14x13½*

198 A22 5fr blue green 1.25 3.50
Never hinged 3.25

For surcharge and overprint see Nos. N31, O181.

Castle From Our Valley — A23

1935, Nov. 15 *Perf. 12½x12*

199 A23 10fr green 2.10 5.75
Never hinged 4.50

For surcharge and overprint see Nos. N32, O182.

Municipal Palace — A24

1936, Aug. 26 Photo. *Perf. 11½*
Granite Paper

200 A24 10c brown .20 .20
201 A24 35c green .20 .50
202 A24 70c red orange .20 *.70*
203 A24 1fr carmine rose 1.25 *5.50*
204 A24 1.25fr violet 2.10 *7.00*
205 A24 1.75fr brt ultra 1.25 *6.00*
Nos. 200-205 (6) 5.20 *19.90*
Set, never hinged 13.00

11th Cong. of Intl. Federation of Philately. See No. 859.

Arms of Luxembourg — A25

William I — A26

Designs: 70c, William II. 75c, William III. 1fr, Prince Henry. 1.25fr, Grand Duke Adolphe. 1.75fr, William IV. 3fr, Regent Marie Anne. 5fr, Grand Duchess Marie Adelaide. 10fr, Grand Duchess Charlotte.

1939, May 27 Engr. *Perf. 12½x12*

206 A25 35c brt green .25 .20
207 A26 50c orange .25 .25
208 A26 70c slate green .20 .20
209 A26 75c sepia .65 *1.25*
210 A26 1fr red 1.60 *3.25*
211 A26 1.25fr brown violet .20 .20
212 A26 1.75fr dark blue .20 .20
213 A26 3fr lt brown .25 .50
214 A26 5fr gray black .50 *1.00*
215 A26 10fr copper red .75 *2.75*
Nos. 206-215 (10) 4.85 *9.80*
Set, never hinged 7.75

Centenary of Independence.

Allegory of Medicinal Baths — A35

1939, Sept. 18 Photo. *Perf. 11½*

216 A35 2fr brown rose .50 1.40
Never hinged 1.00

Elevation of Mondorf-les-Bains to town status.

See No. B104. For surcharge see No. N30.

Souvenir Sheet

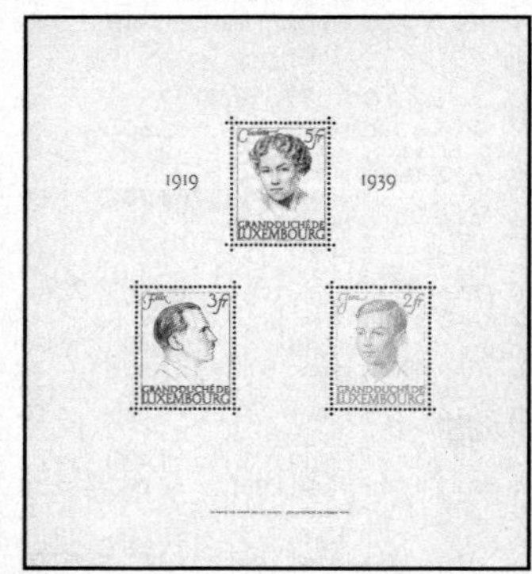

A36

1939, Dec. 20 Engr. *Perf. 14x13*

217 A36 Sheet of 3 35.00 *90.00*
Sheet, never hinged 90.00
a. 2fr vermilion, *buff* 5.75 *22.50*
b. 3fr dark green, *buff* 5.75 *22.50*
c. 5fr blue, *buff* 5.75 *22.50*

20th anniv. of the reign of Grand Duchess Charlotte (Jan. 15, 1919) and her marriage to Prince Felix (Nov. 6, 1919).

See Nos. B98-B103.

Grand Duchess Charlotte — A37

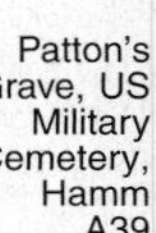

Lion from Duchy Arms — A38

1944-46 Unwmk. *Perf. 12*

218 A37 5c brown red .20 .20
219 A37 10c black .20 .20
219A A37 20c orange ('46) .20 .20
220 A37 25c sepia .20 .20
220A A37 30c carmine ('46) .20 .20
221 A37 35c green .20 .20
221A A37 40c dk blue ('46) .20 .20
222 A37 50c dk violet .20 .20
222A A37 60c orange ('46) 1.10 .20
223 A37 70c rose pink .20 .20
223A A37 70c dp green ('46) .35 *.90*
223B A37 75c sepia ('46) .20 .20
224 A37 1fr olive .20 .20
225 A37 1¼fr red orange .20 *.55*
226 A37 1½fr red orange ('46) .20 .20
227 A37 1¾fr blue .20 .25
228 A37 2fr rose car ('46) 1.60 .25
229 A37 2½fr dp violet ('46) 2.50 *4.50*
230 A37 3fr dp yel grn ('46) .35 .50
231 A37 3½fr brt blue ('46) .50 *.75*
232 A37 5fr dk blue grn .20 .20
233 A37 10fr carmine .20 .60
234 A37 20fr deep blue .35 *17.50*
Nos. 218-234 (23) 9.95 *28.60*
Set, never hinged 15.00

1945 Engr. *Perf. 14x13*

235 A38 20c black .20 .20
236 A38 30c brt green .20 .20
237 A38 60c deep violet .20 .20
238 A38 75c brown red .20 .20
239 A38 1.20fr red .20 .20
240 A38 1.50fr rose lilac .20 .20
241 A38 2.50fr lt blue .20 .20
Set, never hinged 1.00

Issued: 1.20fr, 5/15/45; 30c, 1.50fr, 2.50fr, 7/19; 20c, 75c, 10/1; 60c, 12/13.

Patton's Grave, US Military Cemetery, Hamm — A39

Gen. Patton, Broken Chain and Advancing Tanks — A40

1947, Oct. 24 Photo. *Perf. 11½*

242 A39 1.50fr dk carmine .20 *.20*
243 A40 3.50fr dull blue .70 *3.25*
244 A39 5fr dk slate grn .70 *3.25*
245 A40 10fr chocolate 3.25 *37.50*
Nos. 242-245 (4) 4.85 *44.20*
Set, never hinged 14.50

George S. Patton, Jr. (1885-1945), American general.

Esch-sur-Sûre Fortifications — A41

Luxembourg — A44

Moselle River — A42

Steel Mills — A43

Perf. 11½x11, 11x11½

1948, Aug. 5 Engr. Unwmk.

246 A41 7fr dark brown 5.50 .70
247 A42 10fr dark green .40 .20
248 A43 15fr carmine .40 .65
249 A44 20fr dark blue .55 .65
Nos. 246-249 (4) 6.85 2.20
Set, never hinged 22.50

Grand Duchess Charlotte — A45

1948-49 *Perf. 11½*

250 A45 15c olive brn ('49) .20 .20
251 A45 25c slate .20 .20
252 A45 60c brown ('49) .25 .20
253 A45 80c green ('49) .25 .20
254 A45 1fr red lilac .70 .20
255 A45 1.50fr grnsh bl .70 .20
256 A45 1.60fr slate gray ('49) .70 *1.40*
257 A45 2fr dk vio brn .70 .20
258 A45 4fr violet blue 1.40 .55
259 A45 6fr brt red vio ('49) 2.25 .70
260 A45 8fr dull green ('49) 2.25 1.40
Nos. 250-260 (11) 9.60 5.45
Set, never hinged 35.00

See Nos. 265-271, 292, 337-340, B151.

Self-Inking Canceller A46

1949, Oct. 6 **Photo.**

261 A46 80c blk, Prus grn & pale grn .20 .60
262 A46 2.50fr dk brn, brn red & sal rose 1.10 *1.60*
263 A46 4fr blk, bl & pale bl 3.00 *6.50*
264 A46 8fr dk brn, brn & buff 9.50 *30.00*
Nos. 261-264 (4) 13.80 38.70
Set, never hinged 27.50

UPU, 75th anniv.

Charlotte Type of 1948-49

1951, Mar. 15 **Engr.** **Unwmk.**

265 A45 5c red orange .20 .20
266 A45 10c ultra .20 .20
267 A45 40c crimson .20 .20
268 A45 1.25fr dk brown .70 .35
269 A45 2.50fr red .70 .20
270 A45 3fr blue 4.50 .35
271 A45 3.50fr rose lake 1.90 .45
Nos. 265-271 (7) 8.40 1.95
Set, never hinged 35.00

Agriculture and Industry A47

Globe and Scales A48

1fr, 3fr, People of Europe & Charter of Freedom.

1951, Oct. 25 **Photo.** ***Perf. 11½***

272 A47 80c deep green *4.00* *3.50*
273 A47 1fr purple *2.75* *.45*
274 A48 2fr black brown *11.00* *.45*
275 A47 2.50fr dk carmine *14.00* *10.00*
276 A47 3fr orange brn *20.00* *15.00*
277 A48 4fr blue *25.00* *20.00*
Nos. 272-277 (6) 76.75 49.40
Set, never hinged *125.00*

Issued to promote a united Europe.

Grand Duke William III — A49

Perf. 13½x13

1952, May 24 **Engr.** **Unwmk.**

Dates, Ornaments in Olive Green

278 A49 2fr black 22.50 *55.00*
Never hinged 32.50
279 A49 4fr red brown 22.50 *55.00*
Never hinged 32.50

Printed in sheets containing two panes of eight stamps each, alternating the two denominations. Centenary of Luxembourg's postage stamps. Price per set, 26fr, which included admission to the CENTILUX exhibition.

See Nos. C16-C20.

Hurdle Race — A50

Designs: 2fr, Football. 2.50fr, Boxing. 3fr, Water polo. 4fr, Bicycle racing. 8fr, Fencing.

1952, Aug. 20 **Photo.** ***Perf. 11½***

Designs in Black

280 A50 1fr pale green .20 .30
281 A50 2fr brown buff .65 .35
282 A50 2.50fr salmon pink 1.50 1.10
283 A50 3fr buff 1.90 1.75
284 A50 4fr lt blue 9.25 9.00
285 A50 8fr lilac 5.50 6.00
Nos. 280-285 (6) 19.00 18.50
Set, never hinged 37.50

15th Olympic Games, Helsinki; World Bicycling Championships of 1952.

Wedding of Princess Josephine-Charlotte of Belgium and Hereditary Grand Duke Jean — A51

1953, Apr. 1

286 A51 80c dull violet .20 .20
287 A51 1.20fr lt brown .20 .20
288 A51 2fr green .55 .20
289 A51 3fr red lilac .90 .65
290 A51 4fr brt blue 3.25 1.25
291 A51 9fr brown red 3.25 1.25
Nos. 286-291 (6) 8.35 3.75
Set, never hinged 16.00

Charlotte Type of 1948-49

1953, May 18 **Engr.**

292 A45 1.20fr gray .45 .30
Never hinged 1.00

Radio Luxembourg — A52

Victor Hugo's Home, Vianden A53

1953, May 18 ***Perf. 11½x11***

293 A52 3fr purple 2.75 1.50
294 A53 4fr Prussian blue 1.75 1.50
Set, never hinged 8.75

150th birth anniv. of Victor Hugo (No. 294).

St. Willibrord Basilica Restored — A54

Pierre d'Aspelt — A55

Design: 2.50fr, Interior view.

1953, Sept. 18 ***Perf. 13x13½***

295 A54 2fr red 1.60 .45
296 A54 2.50fr dk gray grn 2.75 7.25
Set, never hinged 8.75

Consecration of St. Willibrord Basilica at Echternach.

1953, Sept. 25

297 A55 4fr black 5.25 5.50
Never hinged 9.00

Pierre d'Aspelt (1250-1320), chancellor of the Holy Roman Empire and Archbishop of Mainz.

Fencing Swords, Mask and Glove — A56

Winged "L" Over Map — A57

1954, May 6 ***Perf. 13½x13***

298 A56 2fr red brn & blk brn, *gray* 2.25 .90
Never hinged 4.50

World Fencing Championship Matches, Luxembourg, June 10-22.

1954, May 6 **Photo.** ***Perf. 11½***

299 A57 4fr dp bl, yel & red 6.50 6.50
Never hinged 11.00

6th Intl. Fair, Luxembourg, July 10-25.

Flowers — A58

Artisan, Wheel and Tools — A59

1955, Apr. 1

300 A58 80c Tulips .20 .20
301 A58 2fr Daffodils .20 .20
302 A58 3fr Hyacinths 1.50 3.25
303 A58 4fr Parrot tulips 1.75 5.00
Nos. 300-303 (4) 3.65 8.65
Set, never hinged 8.75

Flower festival at Mondorf-les-Bains.
See Nos. 351-353.

1955, Sept. 1 **Engr.** ***Perf. 13***

304 A59 2fr dk gray & blk brn .70 .35
Never hinged 1.40

Natl. Handicraft Exposition at Luxembourg — Limpertsburg, Sept. 3-12.

Dudelange Television Station A60

1955, Sept. 1 **Unwmk.**

305 A60 2.50fr dk brn & redsh brn .65 .35
Never hinged 1.90

Installation of the Tele-Luxembourg station at Dudelange.

United Nations Emblem and Children Playing A61

UN, 10th anniv.: 80c, "Charter." 4fr, "Justice" (Sword and Scales). 9fr, "Assistance" (Workers).

1955, Oct. 24 ***Perf. 11x11½***

306 A61 80c black & dk bl .25 .65
307 A61 2fr red & brown 1.90 .35
308 A61 4fr dk blue & red 1.50 4.25
309 A61 9fr dk brn & sl grn .60 1.50
Nos. 306-309 (4) 4.25 6.75
Set, never hinged 11.00

A62

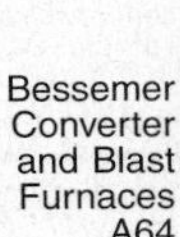

A63

2fr, Anemones. 2.50fr, 4fr, Roses. 3fr, Crocuses.

1956 **Photo.** ***Perf. 11½***

Flowers in Natural Colors

310 A62 2fr gray violet .25 .20
311 A62 2.50fr brt blue 2.50 5.00
312 A62 3fr red brown 1.00 1.60
313 A62 4fr purple 1.25 1.60
Nos. 310-313 (4) 5.00 8.40
Set, never hinged 10.00

Flower Festival at Mondorf-les-Bains (Nos. 310, 312). Nos. 311 and 313 are inscribed: "Luxembourg-Ville des Roses."

Issued: #310, 312, Apr. 27; #311, 313, May 30.

1956, May 30

Steel beam and city emblem.

314 A63 2fr brt grnsh bl, red & blk .70 .50
Never hinged 2.50

50th anniversary of Esch-sur-Alzette.

Bessemer Converter and Blast Furnaces A64

Steel Beam and Model of City of Luxembourg A65

"Rebuilding Europe" A66

Design: 4fr, 6-link chain, miner's lamp.

Perf. 11x11½, 11½x11

1956, Aug. 10 **Engr.**

315 A64 2fr dull red 12.00 .55
316 A65 3fr dark blue 12.00 *22.50*
317 A64 4fr green 3.25 *4.75*
Nos. 315-317 (3) 27.25 27.80
Set, never hinged 55.00

4th anniv. of the establishment in Luxembourg of the headquarters of the European Coal and Steel Community.

1956, Sept. 15 ***Perf. 13***

318 A66 2fr brown & black *55.00* *.25*
319 A66 3fr brick red & car *17.50* *17.50*
320 A66 4fr brt bl & dp bl *1.75* *3.75*
Nos. 318-320 (3) 74.25 21.50
Set, never hinged *200.00*

Cooperation among the six countries comprising the Coal and Steel Community.

Catalogue values for unused stamps in this section, from this point to the end of the section, are for Never Hinged items.

Central Station from Train Window
A67

1956, Sept. 29 ***Perf. 13x12½***

321	A67 2fr black & sepia	2.25	.45

Electrification of Luxembourg railways.

Ignace de la Fontaine
A68

Design: 7fr, Grand Duchess Charlotte.

1956, Nov. 7 ***Perf. 11½***

322	A68 2fr gray brown	1.25	.30
323	A68 7fr dull purple	2.50	.70

Centenary of the Council of State.

Lord Baden-Powell and Luxembourg Scout Emblems — A69

Designs: 2.50fr, Lord Baden-Powell and Luxembourg Girl Scout emblems.

1957, June 17 ***Perf. 11½x11***

324	A69 2fr ol grn & red brn	1.00	.50
325	A69 2.50fr dk vio & claret	2.50	*2.00*

Birth centenary of Robert Baden-Powell and 50th anniv. of the founding of the Scout movement.

Prince Henry — A70

Children's Clinic — A71

Design: 4fr, Princess Marie-Astrid.

1957, June 17 **Photo.** ***Perf. 11½***

326	A70 2fr brown	1.00	.25
327	A71 3fr bluish grn	3.25	*3.25*
328	A70 4fr ultra	2.25	*2.75*
	Nos. 326-328 (3)	6.50	*6.25*

Children's Clinic of the Prince Jean-Princess Josephine-Charlotte Foundation.

"United Europe" — A72

Fair Building and Flags — A73

1957, Sept. 16 **Engr.** ***Perf. 12½x12***

329	A72 2fr reddish brn	*5.50*	*1.75*
330	A72 3fr red	*37.50*	*10.00*
331	A72 4fr rose lilac	*35.00*	*8.00*
	Nos. 329-331 (3)	78.00	*19.75*
	Hinged	20.00	

A united Europe for peace and prosperity.

1958, Apr. 16 ***Perf. 12x11½***

332	A73 2fr ultra & multi	.25	.20

10th International Luxembourg Fair.

Luxembourg Pavilion, Brussels
A74

1958, Apr. 16 **Unwmk.**

333	A74 2.50fr car & ultra	.25	.20

International Exposition at Brussels.

St. Willibrord — A75

1fr, Sts. Willibrord & Irmina from "Liber Aureus." 5fr, St. Willibrord, young man & wine cask.

1958, May 23 **Engr.** ***Perf. 13x13½***

334	A75 1fr red	.25	.30
335	A75 2.50fr olive brn	.35	.20
336	A75 5fr blue	.90	*1.00*
	Nos. 334-336 (3)	1.50	*1.50*

1300th birth anniv. of St. Willibrord, apostle of the Low Countries and founder of Echternach Abbey.

Charlotte Type of 1948-49

1958 **Unwmk.** ***Perf. 11½***

337	A45 20c dull claret	.20	.20
338	A45 30c olive	.20	.20
339	A45 50c dp org	.35	.20
340	A45 5fr violet	8.25	.40
	Nos. 337-340 (4)	9.00	1.00

Issued: No. 337, 8/1; Nos. 338-340, 7/1.

Common Design Types pictured following the introduction.

Europa Issue, 1958
Common Design Type

1958, Sept. 13 **Litho.** ***Perf. 12½x13***
Size: 21x34mm

341	CD1 2.50fr car & bl	*.30*	.20
342	CD1 3.50fr green & org	*1.00*	*.35*
343	CD1 5fr blue & red	*1.10*	*.55*
	Nos. 341-343 (3)	2.40	1.10

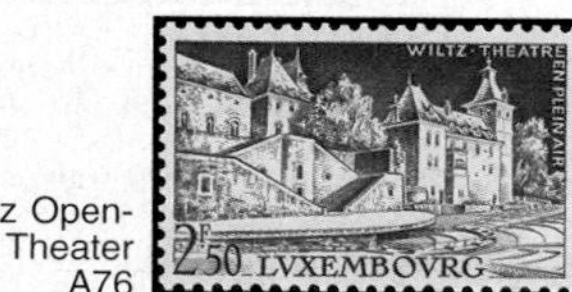

Wiltz Open-Air Theater
A76

Vintage, Moselle
A77

1958, Sept. 13 **Engr.** ***Perf. 11x11½***

344	A76 2.50fr slate & sepia	.50	.20
345	A77 2.50fr lt grn & sepia	.50	.20

No. 345 issued to publicize 2,000 years of grape growing in Luxembourg region.

Grand Duchess Charlotte — A78

NATO Emblem — A79

1959, Jan. 15 **Photo.** ***Perf. 11½***

346	A78 1.50fr pale grn & dk grn	1.00	.50
347	A78 2.50fr pink & dk brn	1.00	.50
348	A78 5fr lt bl & dk bl	1.65	*1.25*
	Nos. 346-348 (3)	3.65	*2.25*

40th anniv. of the accession to the throne of the Grand Duchess Charlotte.

1959, Apr. 3 ***Perf. 12½x12***

349	A79 2.50fr brt ol & bl	.20	.20
350	A79 8.50fr red brn & bl	.50	.35

NATO, 10th anniversary.

Flower Type of 1955, Inscribed "1959"

1fr, Iris. 2.50fr, Peonies. 3fr, Hydrangea.

1959, Apr. 3 ***Perf. 11½***
Flowers in Natural Colors

351	A58 1fr dk bl grn	.35	.35
352	A58 2.50fr deep blue	.50	.35
353	A58 3fr deep red lilac	.65	.65
	Nos. 351-353 (3)	1.50	1.35

Flower festival, Mondorf-les-Bains.

Europa Issue, 1959
Common Design Type
Perf. 12½x13½

1959, Sept. 19 **Litho.**
Size: 22x33mm

354	CD2 2.50fr olive	*1.75*	*.45*
355	CD2 5fr dk blue	*3.25*	*1.75*

Locomotive of 1859 and Hymn — A80

1959, Sept. 19 **Engr.** ***Perf. 13½***

356	A80 2.50fr red & ultra	1.60	.35

Centenary of Luxembourg's railroads.

Man and Child Knocking at Door — A81

Holy Family, Flight into Egypt
A82

Perf. 11½x11, 11x11½

1960, Apr. 7 **Unwmk.**

357	A81 2.50fr org & slate	.20	.20
358	A82 5fr pur & slate	.30	.30

World Refugee Year, July 1, 1959-June 30, 1960.

Steel Worker Drawing CECA Initials and Map of Member Countries
A83

1960, May 9 ***Perf. 11x11½***

359	A83 2.50fr dk car rose	.60	.20

10th anniv. of the Schumann Plan for a European Steel and Coal Community.

European School and Children
A84

1960, May 9

360	A84 5fr bl & gray blk	.90	.90

Establishment of the first European school in Luxembourg.

Heraldic Lion and Tools
A85

1960, June 14 **Photo.** ***Perf. 11½***

361	A85 2.50fr gray, red, bl & blk	1.40	.30

Natl. Exhibition of Craftsmanship, Luxembourg-Limpertsberg, July 9-18.

Grand Duchess Charlotte — A86

1960-64 **Engr.** **Unwmk.**

362	A86	10c claret ('61)	.20	.20
363	A86	20c rose red ('61)	.20	.20
363A	A86	25c org ('64)	.20	.20
364	A86	30c gray olive	.20	.20
365	A86	50c dull grn	.60	.20
366	A86	1fr vio blue	.75	.20
367	A86	1.50fr rose lilac	.75	.20
368	A86	2fr blue ('61)	.80	.20
369	A86	2.50fr rose vio	1.40	.20
370	A86	3fr vio brn ('61)	1.60	.20
371	A86	3.50fr aqua ('64)	2.25	1.90
372	A86	5fr lt red brn	2.25	.25
373	A86	6fr slate ('64)	2.75	.20
		Nos. 362-373 (13)	13.95	4.35

The 50c, 1fr and 3fr were issued in sheets and in coils. Every fifth coil stamp has control number on back.

Europa Issue, 1960
Common Design Type

1960, Sept. 19 ***Perf. 11x11½***
Size: 37x27mm

374	CD3 2.50fr indigo & emer	*.40*	*.40*
375	CD3 5fr maroon & blk	*1.10*	*.40*

Great Spotted Woodpecker
A87

Clervaux and Abbey of St. Maurice and St. Maur
A88

Designs: 1.50fr, Cat, horiz. 3fr, Filly, horiz. 8.50fr, Dachshund.

1961, May 15 Photo. *Perf. 11½*

No.	Type	Denomination	Description	Unused	Used
376	A87	1fr	multicolored	.20	.20
377	A87	1.50fr	multicolored	.20	.20
378	A87	3fr	gray, buff & red brn	.40	.40
379	A87	8.50fr	lt grn, blk & ocher	.80	.60
			Nos. 376-379 (4)	1.60	1.40

Issued to publicize animal protection.

1961, June 8 Engr. *Perf. 11½x11*

380 A88 2.50fr green .50 .25

General Patton Monument, Ettelbruck A89

1961, June 8 *Perf. 11x11½*

381 A89 2.50fr dark blue & gray .50 .25

The monument commemorates the American victory of the 3rd Army under Gen. George S. Patton, Jr., Battle of the Ardennes Bulge, 1944-45.

Europa Issue, 1961

Common Design Type

1961, Sept. 18 *Perf. 13x12½*

Size: 29½x27mm

382 CD4 2.50fr red *.35 .30*
383 CD4 5fr blue *.25 .25*

Cyclist Carrying Bicycle — A90

St. Laurent's Church, Diekirch — A91

Design: 5fr, Emblem of 1962 championship.

1962, Jan. 22 Photo. *Perf. 11½*

384 A90 2.50fr lt ultra, crim & blk .25 .20
385 A90 5fr multicolored .45 .40

Intl. Cross-country Bicycle Race, Esch-sur-Alzette, Feb. 18.

Europa Issue, 1962

Common Design Type

1962, Sept. 17 Unwmk. *Perf. 11½*

Size: 32½x23mm

386 CD5 2.50fr ol bis, yel grn & brn blk *.35 .30*
387 CD5 5fr rose lil, lt grn & brn blk *.50 .40*

1962, Sept. 17 Engr. *Perf. 11½x11*

388 A91 2.50fr brown & blk .40 .25

Bock Rock Castle, 10th Century A92

Gate of Three Towers, 11th Century — A93

Designs (each stamp represents a different century): No. 391, Benedictine Abbey, Munster. No. 392, Great Seal of Luxembourg, 1237. No. 393, Rham Towers. No. 394, Black Virgin, Grund. No. 395, Grand Ducal Palace. No. 396, The Citadel of the Holy Ghost. No. 397, Castle Bridge. No. 398, Town Hall. No. 399, Municipal theater, bridge and European Community Center.

Perf. 14x13 (A92), 11½ (A93)

Engr. (A92), Photo. (A93)

1963, Apr. 13

No.	Type	Denomination	Description	Unused	Used
389	A92	1fr	slate blue	.45	.45
390	A93	1fr	multicolored	.20	.20
391	A92	1.50fr	dl red brn	.45	.45
392	A93	1.50fr	multicolored	.20	.20
393	A92	2.50fr	gray grn	.45	.45
394	A93	2.50fr	multicolored	.20	.20
395	A92	3fr	brown	.45	.45
396	A93	3fr	multicolored	.20	.20
397	A92	5fr	brt violet	.60	.60
398	A93	5fr	multicolored	.60	.60
399	A92	11fr	multicolored	.90	.90
			Nos. 389-399 (11)	4.70	4.70

Millennium of the city of Luxembourg; MELUSINA Intl. Phil. Exhib., Luxembourg, Apr. 13-21. Set sold only at exhibition. Value of 62fr included entrance ticket. Nos. 390, 392, 394 and 396 however were sold without restriction.

Blackboard Showing European School Buildings — A94

1963, Apr. 13 Photo. *Perf. 11½*

400 A94 2.50fr gray, grn & mag .20 .20

10th anniv. of the European Schools in Luxembourg, Brussels, Varese, Mol and Karlsruhe.

Colpach Castle and Centenary Emblem A95

1963, May 8 Engr. *Perf. 13*

401 A95 2.50fr hn brn, gray & red .20 .20

Centenary of the Intl. Red Cross. Colpach Castle, home of Emile Mayrisch, was donated to the Luxembourg League of the Red Cross for a rest home.

Twelve Stars of Council of Europe — A96

Brown Trout Taking Bait — A97

1963, June 25 *Perf. 13x14*

402 A96 2.50fr dp ultra, *gold* .20 .20

10th anniv. of the European Convention of Human Rights.

Europa Issue, 1963

Common Design Type

1963, Sept. 16 Photo. *Perf. 11½*

Size: 32½x23mm

403 CD6 3fr bl grn, lt grn & org *.40 .35*
404 CD6 6fr red brn, org red & org *.60 .40*

1963, Sept. 16 Engr. *Perf. 13*

405 A97 3fr indigo .25 .20

World Fly-Fishing Championship, Wormeldange, Sept. 22.

Map of Luxembourg, Telephone Dial and Stars — A98

Power House — A99

1963, Sept. 16 Photo. *Perf. 11½*

406 A98 3fr ultra, brt grn & blk .25 .20

Completion of telephone automation.

1964, Apr. 17 Engr. *Perf. 13*

3fr, Upper reservoir, horiz. 6fr, Lohmuhle dam.

No.	Type	Denomination	Description	Unused	Used
407	A99	2fr	red brn & sl	.20	.20
408	A99	3fr	red, sl grn & lt bl	.20	.20
409	A99	6fr	choc, grn & bl	.25	.20
			Nos. 407-409 (3)	.65	.60

Inauguration of the Vianden hydroelectric station.

Barge Entering Lock at Grevenmacher Dam — A100

1964, May 26 Unwmk.

410 A100 3fr indigo & brt bl .35 .20

Opening of Moselle River canal system.

Europa Issue, 1964

Common Design Type

1964, Sept. 14 Photo. *Perf. 11½*

Size: 22x38mm

411 CD7 3fr org brn, yel & dk bl *.35 .25*
412 CD7 6fr yel grn, yel & dk brn *.55 .30*

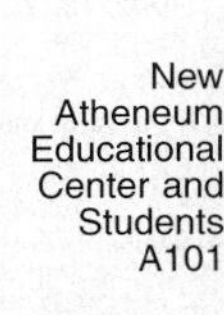

New Atheneum Educational Center and Students A101

1964, Sept. 14 Unwmk.

413 A101 3fr dk bl grn & blk .20 .20

Benelux Issue

King Baudouin, Queen Juliana and Grand Duchess Charlotte — A101a

1964, Oct. 12

Size: 45x26mm

414 A101a 3fr dull bl, yel & brn .25 .20

20th anniv. of the customs union of Belgium, Netherlands and Luxembourg.

Grand Duke Jean and Grand Duchess Josephine Charlotte A102

1964, Nov. 11 Photo. *Perf. 11½*

415 A102 3fr indigo .35 .20
416 A102 6fr dk brown .35 .30

Grand Duke Jean's accession to throne.

Rotary Emblem and Cogwheels A103

Grand Duke Jean A104

1965, Apr. 5 Photo. *Perf. 11½*

417 A103 3fr gold, car, gray & ultra .40 .20

Rotary International, 60th anniversary.

1965-71 Engr. Unwmk.

No.	Type	Denomination	Description	Unused	Used
418	A104	25c	olive bister ('66)	.20	.20
419	A104	50c	rose red	.25	.20
420	A104	1fr	ultra	.25	.20
421	A104	1.50fr	dk vio brn ('66)	.20	.20
422	A104	2fr	magenta ('66)	.20	.20
423	A104	2.50fr	orange ('71)	.35	.25
424	A104	3fr	gray	.50	.20
425	A104	3.50fr	brn org ('66)	.35	.40
426	A104	4fr	vio brn ('71)	.30	.20
427	A104	5fr	green ('71)	.35	.20
428	A104	6fr	purple	.95	.20
429	A104	8fr	bl grn ('71)	.80	.20
			Nos. 418-429 (12)	4.70	2.65

The 50c, 1fr, 2fr, 3fr, 4fr, 5fr and 6fr were issued in sheets and in coils. Every fifth coil stamp has control number on back.

See Nos. 570-576.

ITU Emblem, Old and New Communication Equipment — A105

1965, May 17 Litho. *Perf. 13½*

431 A105 3fr dk pur, claret & blk .20 .20

ITU, centenary.

Europa Issue, 1965

Common Design Type

Perf. 13x12½

1965, Sept. 27 Photo. Unwmk.

Size: 30x23½mm

432 CD8 3fr grn, maroon & blk .35 *.30*
433 CD8 6fr tan, dk bl & grn .55 *.45*

Inauguration of WHO Headquarters, Geneva — A106

1966, Mar. 7 Engr. *Perf. 11x11½*

434 A106 3fr green .20 .20

Torch and Banner — A107

Key and Arms of City of Luxembourg, and Arms of Prince of Chimay — A108

1966, Mar. 7 **Photo.** ***Perf. 11½***
435 A107 3fr gray & brt red .20 .20

50th anniversary of the Workers' Federation in Luxembourg.

1966, Apr. 28 **Engr.** ***Perf. 13x14***

Designs: 2fr, Interior of Cathedral of Luxembourg, painting by Juan Martin. 3fr, Our Lady of Luxembourg, engraving by Richard Collin. 6fr, Column and spandrel with sculptured angels from Cathedral.

436 A108 1.50fr green .20 .20
437 A108 2fr dull red .20 .20
438 A108 3fr dk blue .20 .20
439 A108 6fr red brown .25 .25
Nos. 436-439 (4) .85 .85

300th anniv. of the Votum Solemne (Solemn Promise) which made the Virgin Mary Patron Saint of the City of Luxembourg.

Europa Issue, 1966
Common Design Type
Perf. 13½x12½
1966, Sept. 26 **Litho.**
Size: 25x37mm
440 CD9 3fr gray & vio bl .40 *.30*
441 CD9 6fr olive & dk grn .70 *.50*

Diesel Locomotive A109

Design: 3fr, Electric locomotive.

1966, Sept. 26 **Photo.** ***Perf. 11½***
442 A109 1.50fr multicolored *.30* .20
443 A109 3fr multicolored *.60* .30

5th Intl. Philatelic Exhibition of Luxembourg Railroad Men, Sept. 30-Oct. 3.

Grand Duchess Charlotte Bridge A110

1966, Sept. 26 **Engr.** ***Perf. 13***
444 A110 3fr dk car rose .20 .20

Tower Building, Kirchberg, Seat of European Community — A111

Design: 13fr, Design for Robert Schuman monument, Luxembourg.

1966, Sept. 26
445 A111 1.50fr dk green .20 .20
446 A111 13fr deep blue .55 .25

"Luxembourg, Center of Europe."

View of Luxembourg, 1850, by Nicolas Liez — A112

Map of Luxembourg Fortress, 1850, by Theodore de Cederstolpe — A113

1967, Mar. 6 **Engr.** ***Perf. 13***
447 A112 3fr bl, vio brn & grn .20 .20
448 A113 6fr blue, brn & red .25 .20

Centenary of the Treaty of London, which guaranteed the country's neutrality after the dismantling of the Fortress of Luxembourg.

Europa Issue, 1967
Common Design Type
1967, May 2 **Photo.** ***Perf. 11½***
Size: 33x22mm
449 CD10 3fr cl brn, gray & buff *.50* *.35*
450 CD10 6fr dk brn, vio gray & lt bl *.75* *.50*

Lion, Globe and Lions Emblem — A115

NATO Emblem and European Community Administration Building — A116

1967, May 2 **Photo.** ***Perf. 11½***
451 A115 3fr multicolored .20 .20

Lions International, 50th anniversary.

Canceled to Order
Luxembourg's Office des Timbres, Direction des Postes, was offering, at least as early as 1967, to sell commemorative issues canceled to order.

1967, June 13 **Litho.** ***Perf. 13x12½***
452 A116 3fr lt grn & dk grn .25 .20
453 A116 6fr dp rose & dk car .40 .40

NATO Council meeting, Luxembourg, June 13-14.

Youth Hostel, Ettelbruck A117

Home Gardener A118

1967, Sept. 14 **Photo.** ***Perf. 11½***
454 A117 1.50fr multicolored .20 .20

Luxembourg youth hostels.

1967, Sept. 14
455 A118 1.50fr brt grn & org .20 .20

16th Congress of the Intl. Assoc. of Home Gardeners.

Shaving Basin with Wedding Scene, 1819 — A119

Design: 3fr, Ornamental vase, 1820, vert.

1967, Sept. 14
456 A119 1.50fr ol grn & multi .20 .20
457 A119 3fr ultra & lt gray .25 .20

Faience industry in Luxembourg, 200th anniv.

Wormeldange - Moselle River — A120

Mertert, Moselle River Port A121

1967, Sept. 14 **Engr.** ***Perf. 13***
458 A120 3fr dp bl, claret & ol .25 .20
459 A121 3fr violet bl & slate .25 .20

Swimming — A122

Sport: 1.50fr, Soccer. 2fr, Bicycling. 3fr, Running. 6fr, Walking. 13fr, Fencing.

1968, Feb. 22 **Photo.** ***Perf. 11½***
460 A122 50c bl & grnsh bl .20 .20
461 A122 1.50fr brt grn & emer .20 .20
462 A122 2fr yel grn & lt yel grn .20 .20
463 A122 3fr dp org & dl org .20 .20
464 A122 6fr grnsh bl & pale grn .30 .20
465 A122 13fr rose cl & rose .50 .50
Nos. 460-465 (6) 1.60 1.50

Issued to publicize the 19th Olympic Games, Mexico City, Oct. 12-27.

Europa Issue, 1968
Common Design Type
1968, Apr. 29 **Photo.** ***Perf. 11½***
Size: 32½x23mm
466 CD11 3fr ap grn, blk & org brn *.40* *.35*
467 CD11 6fr brn org, blk & ap grn *.70* *.50*

Kind Spring Pavilion A123

1968, Apr. 29 **Photo.** ***Perf. 11½***
468 A123 3fr multicolored .20 .20

Issued to publicize Mondorf-les-Bains.

Fair Emblem A124

1968, Apr. 29
469 A124 3fr dp vio, dl bl gold & red .20 .20

20th Intl. Fair, Luxembourg City, May 23-June 2.

Children's Village of Mersch A125

Orphan and Foster Mother — A126

1968, Sept. 18 **Engr.** ***Perf. 13***
470 A125 3fr slate grn & dk red brn .20 .20
471 A126 6fr slate bl, blk & brn .30 .20

Mersch children's village. (Modeled after Austrian SOS villages for homeless children.)

Red Cross and Symbolic Blood Transfusion — A127

1968, Sept. 18 **Photo.** ***Perf. 11½***
472 A127 3fr lt blue & car .20 .20

Voluntary Red Cross blood donors.

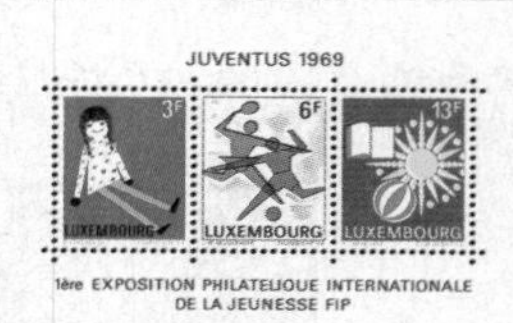

Luxair Plane over Luxembourg — A128

1968, Sept. 18 **Engr.** ***Perf. 13***
473 A128 50fr olive, bl & dk bl 1.65 .70

Issued for tourist publicity.

Souvenir Sheet

"Youth and Leisure" — A129

Designs, a, 3fr, Doll. b, 6fr, Ballplayers. c, 13fr, Book, compass rose and ball.

1969, Apr. 3 **Photo.** ***Perf. 11½***
Granite Paper
474 A129 Sheet of 3 4.00 3.25
a.-c. any single 1.25 1.00

1st Intl. Youth Phil. Exhib., JUVENTUS 1969, Luxembourg, Apr. 3-8.

No. 474 was on sale only at the exhibition. Sold only with entrance ticket for 40fr.

Europa Issue, 1969
Common Design Type
1969, May 19 **Photo.** ***Perf. 11½***
Size: 32½x23mm
475 CD12 3fr gray, brn & org *.50* *.35*
476 CD12 6fr vio gray, blk & yel *.60* *.35*

Boy on Hobbyhorse, by Joseph Kutter (1894-1941) — A130

Design: 6fr, View of Luxembourg, by Kutter.

1969, May 19 Engr. *Perf. 12x13*

477 A130 3fr multicolored .25 .20

a. Green omitted *150.00 150.00*

478 A130 6fr multicolored .35 .35

ILO, 50th Anniv. A131

Photo.; Gold Impressed (Emblem)

1969, May 19 *Perf. 14x14½*

479 A131 3fr brt grn, vio & gold .20 .20

Mobius Strip in Benelux Colors — A131a

1969, Sept. 8 Litho. *Perf. 12½x13½*

480 A131a 3fr multicolored .30 .20

25th anniv. of the signing of the customs union of Belgium, Netherlands and Luxembourg.

NATO, 20th Anniv. A132

Grain and Mersch Agricultural Center — A133

1969, Sept. 8 *Perf. 13½x12½*

481 A132 3fr org brn & dk brn .30 .20

1969, Sept. 8 Photo. *Perf. 11½*

482 A133 3fr bl grn, gray & blk .20 .20

Issued to publicize agricultural progress.

St. Willibrord's Basilica and Abbey, Echternach A134

#484, Castle and open-air theater, Wiltz.

1969, Sept. 8 Engr. *Perf. 13*

483 A134 3fr dark blue & indigo .25 .20

484 A134 3fr slate green & indigo .25 .20

Pasqueflower A135

Design: 6fr, Hedgehog and 3 young.

1970, Mar. 9 Photo. *Perf. 11½*

485 A135 3fr multicolored .25 .20

486 A135 6fr green & multi .45 .40

European Conservation Year.

Goldcrest A136

1970, Mar. 9 Engr. *Perf. 13*

487 A136 1.50fr org, grn & blk brn .20 .20

Luxembourg Society for the protection and study of birds, 50th anniv.

Traffic Sign and Street Scene A137

1970, May 4 Photo. *Perf. 11½*

488 A137 3fr rose mag, red & blk .25 .20

The importance of traffic safety.

Europa Issue, 1970

Common Design Type

1970, May 4

Size: 32½x23mm

489 CD13 3fr brown & multi *.50 .30*

490 CD13 6fr green & multi *.75 .45*

Empress Kunigunde and Emperor Henry II, Window, Luxembourg Cathedral — A138

1970, Sept. 14 Photo. *Perf. 12*

491 A138 3fr multicolored .20 .20

Centenary of the Diocese of Luxembourg.

Census Symbol A139

1970, Sept. 14 *Perf. 11½*

492 A139 3fr dk grn, grnsh bl & red .20 .20

Census of Dec. 31, 1970.

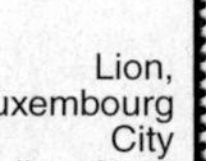

Lion, Luxembourg City Hall — A140

1970, Sept. 14

493 A140 3fr bister, lt bl & dk brn .20 .20

50th anniversary of the City of Luxembourg through the union of 5 municipalities.

UN Emblem A141

Perf. 12½x13½

1970, Sept. 14 Litho.

494 A141 1.50fr bl & vio bl .20 .20

25th anniversary of the United Nations.

Monks in Abbey Workshop A142

Olympic Rings, Arms of Luxembourg A143

Miniatures Painted at Echternach, about 1040: 3fr, Laborers going to the vineyard (Matthew 20:1-6). 6fr, Laborers toiling in vineyard. 13fr, Workers searching for graves of the saints.

1971, Mar. 15 Photo. *Perf. 12*

495 A142 1.50fr gold & multi .20 .20

496 A142 3fr gold & multi .20 .20

497 A142 6fr gold & multi .25 .20

498 A142 13fr gold & multi .50 .45

Nos. 495-498 (4) 1.15 1.05

1971, May 3 Photo. *Perf. 12½*

499 A143 3fr ultra & multi .25 .20

Intl. Olympic Committee, 71st session.

Europa Issue, 1971

Common Design Type

1971, May 3 *Perf. 12½x13*

Size: 34x25mm

500 CD14 3fr ver, brn & blk *.55 .30*

501 CD14 6fr brt grn, brn & blk *.80 .65*

A145

1971, May 3 Litho. *Perf. 13x13½*

502 A145 3fr org, dk brn & yel .20 .20

Christian Workers Union, 50th anniv.

Artificial Lake, Upper Sure A146

Designs: No. 504, Water treatment plant, Esch-sur-Sure. 15fr, ARBED Steel Corporation Headquarters, Luxembourg.

1971, Sept. 13 Engr. *Perf. 13*

503 A146 3fr ol, grnsh bl & indigo .20 .20

504 A146 3fr brn, sl grn & grnsh bl .25 .20

505 A146 15fr indigo & blk brn .70 .40

Nos. 503-505 (3) 1.15 .80

School Girl with Coin — A147

1971, Sept. 13 Photo. *Perf. 11½*

506 A147 3fr violet & multi .20 .20

School children's savings campaign.

Coins of Luxembourg and Belgium — A148

Bronze Mask — A149

1972, Mar. 6

507 A148 1.50fr lt grn, sil & blk .20 .20

Economic Union of Luxembourg and Belgium, 50th anniversary.

1972, Mar. 6

Archaeological Objects, 4th to 1st centuries, B.C.: 1fr, Bronze bowl, horiz. 8fr, Limestone head. 15fr, Glass jug in shape of head.

508 A149 1fr lemon & multi .20 .20

509 A149 3fr multicolored .20 .20

510 A149 8fr multicolored .60 .60

511 A149 15fr multicolored .80 .80

Nos. 508-511 (4) 1.80 1.80

Europa Issue 1972

Common Design Type

1972, May 2 Photo. *Perf. 11½*

Size: 22x33mm

512 CD15 3fr rose vio & multi .70 *.25*

513 CD15 8fr gray blue & multi 1.10 *.60*

Archer A150

1972, May 2

514 A150 3fr crimson, blk & olive .40 .20

3rd European Archery Championships.

Robert Schuman Medal — A151

The Fox Wearing Tails — A152

1972, May 2 Engr. *Perf. 13*

515 A151 3fr gray & slate green .50 .20

Establishment in Luxembourg of the European Coal and Steel Community, 20th anniv.

1972, Sept. 11 Photo. *Perf. 11½*

516 A152 3fr scarlet & multi .35 .20

Centenary of the publication of "Renert," satirical poem by Michel Rodange.

National Monument A153

Court of Justice of European Communities, Kirchberg — A154

1972, Sept. 11 Engr. *Perf. 13*

517 A153 3fr sl grn, olive & vio .20 .20
518 A154 3fr brn, bl & slate grn .30 .20

Epona on Horseback — A155

Archaeological Objects: 4fr, Panther killing swan, horiz. 8fr, Celtic gold stater inscribed Pottina. 15fr, Bronze boar, horiz.

1973, Mar. 14 Photo. *Perf. 11½*

519 A155 1fr salmon & multi .20 .20
520 A155 4fr beige & multi .20 .20
521 A155 8fr multicolored .65 .65
522 A155 15fr multicolored .65 .65
Nos. 519-522 (4) 1.70 1.70

Europa Issue 1973

Common Design Type

1973, Apr. 30 Photo. *Perf. 11½*

Size: 32x22mm

523 CD16 4fr org, dk vio & lt bl *.85 .35*
524 CD16 8fr ol, vio blk & yel *1.50 .70*

Bee on Honeycomb A156

Nurse Holding Child A157

1973, Apr. 30 Photo. *Perf. 11½*

525 A156 4fr ocher & multi .35 .20

Publicizing importance of beekeeping.

1973, Apr. 30

526 A157 4fr multicolored .30 .20

Publicizing importance of day nurseries.

Laurel Branch A158

1973, Sept. 10 Photo. *Perf. 11½*

527 A158 3fr violet bl & multi .25 .20

50th anniv. of Luxembourg Board of Labor.

Jerome de Busleyden A159

National Strike Memorial, Wiltz A160

1973, Sept. 10 Engr. *Perf. 13*

528 A159 4fr black, brn & pur .30 .20

Council of Mechelen, 500th anniv.

1973, Sept. 10

529 A160 4fr ol bis, sl & sl grn .25 .20

In memory of the Luxembourg resistance heroes who died during the great strike of 1942.

Capital, Byzantine Hall, Vianden — A161

St. Gregory the Great — A161a

Designs: No. 534, Sts. Cecilia and Valerian crowned by angel, Hollenfels Church. No. 535, Interior, Septfontaines Church. 8fr, Madonna and Child, St. Irmina's Chapel, Rosport. 12fr, St. Augustine Sculptures by Jean-Georges Scholtus from pulpit in Feulen parish church, c. 1734.

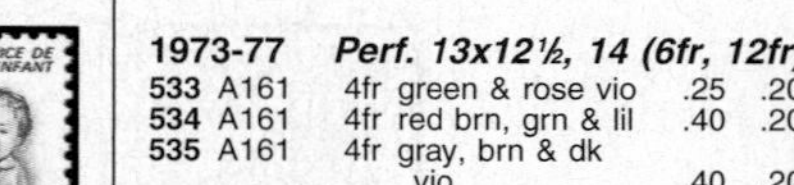

1973-77 *Perf. 13x12½, 14 (6fr, 12fr)*

533 A161 4fr green & rose vio .25 .20
534 A161 4fr red brn, grn & lil .40 .20
535 A161 4fr gray, brn & dk vio .40 .20
536 A161a 6fr maroon .30 .25
537 A161 8fr sepia & vio bl .70 .60
538 A161a 12fr slate blue .75 .65
Nos. 533-538 (6) 2.80 2.10

Architecture of Luxembourg: Romanesque, Gothic, Baroque.

Issued: #533, 8fr, 9/10/73; #534-535, 9/9/74; 6fr, 12fr, 9/16/77.

Princess Marie Astrid — A162

Torch — A163

1974, Mar. 14 Photo. *Perf. 11½*

540 A162 4fr blue & multi .65 .20

Princess Marie-Astrid, president of the Luxembourg Red Cross Youth Section.

1974, Mar. 14

541 A163 4fr ultra & multi .20 .20

50th anniversary of Luxembourg Mutual Insurance Federation.

Royal Seal of Henri VII — A164

Seals from 13th-14th Centuries: 3fr, Equestrian, seal of Jean, King of Bohemia. 4fr, Seal of Town of Diekirch. 19fr, Virgin and Child, seal of Convent of Marienthal.

1974, Mar. 14

542 A164 1fr purple & multi .20 .20
543 A164 3fr green & multi .30 .25
544 A164 4fr multicolored .45 .20
545 A164 19fr multicolored 1.50 1.25
Nos. 542-545 (4) 2.45 1.90

Hind, by Auguste Trémont — A165

Winston Churchill, by Oscar Nemon — A166

Europa: 8fr, "Growth," abstract sculpture, by Lucien Wercollier.

1974, Apr. 29 Photo. *Perf. 11½*

546 A165 4fr ocher & multi *3.00 .75*
547 A165 8fr brt blue & multi *6.00 2.25*

1974, Apr. 29

548 A166 4fr lilac & multi .30 .20

Sir Winston Churchill (1874-1965), statesman.

Fairground, Aerial View — A167

Theis, the Blind — A168

1974, Apr. 29

549 A167 4fr silver & multi .30 .20

Publicity for New International Fairground, Luxembourg-Kirchberg.

1974, Apr. 29

550 A168 3fr multicolored .30 .20

Mathias Schou, Theis the Blind (1747-1824), wandering minstrel.

UPU Emblem and "100" — A169

1974, Sept. 9 Photo. *Perf. 11½*

551 A169 4fr multicolored .30 .30
552 A169 8fr multicolored .80 .80

Centenary of Universal Postal Union.

"BENELUX" A170

1974, Sept. 9

553 A170 4fr bl grn, dk grn & lt bl .80 .20

30th anniversary of the signing of the customs union of Belgium, Netherlands and Luxembourg.

View of Differdange A171

1974, Sept. 9 Engr. *Perf. 13*

554 A171 4fr rose claret .20 .20

Bourglinster A172

Designs: 1fr, Fish Market, Old Luxembourg, vert. 4fr, Market Square, Echternach. 19fr, St. Michael's Square, Mersch, vert.

Perf. 14x13½, 13½x14

1975, Mar. 10 Engr.

555 A172 1fr olive green .75 .20
556 A172 3fr deep brown 1.40 .40
557 A172 4fr dark purple 1.50 .60
558 A172 19fr copper red 1.25 1.00
Nos. 555-558 (4) 4.90 2.20

European Architectural Heritage Year.

Joseph Kutter, Self-portrait A173

Moselle Bridge, Remich, by Nico Klopp — A174

Paintings: 8fr, Still Life, by Joseph Kutter. 20fr, The Dam, by Dominique Lang.

1975, Apr. 28 Photo. *Perf. 11½*
559 A173 1fr multicolored .25 .20
560 A174 4fr multicolored *1.75* *.40*
561 A174 8fr multicolored *2.75* *1.25*
562 A173 20fr multicolored 1.25 .50
Nos. 559-562 (4) 6.00 2.35

Cultural series. #560-561 are Europa Issue.

Robert Schuman, Gaetano Martino, Paul-Henri Spaak Medals A175

1975, Apr. 28
563 A175 4fr yel grn, gold & brn 1.10 .25

Robert Schuman's declaration establishing European Coal and Steel Community, 25th anniv.

Albert Schweitzer (1875-1965), Medical Missionary — A176

1975, Apr. 28 Engr. *Perf. 13*
564 A176 4fr bright blue .90 .20

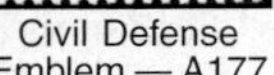

Civil Defense Emblem — A177

Figure Skating — A178

1975, Sept. 8 Photo. *Perf. 11½*
565 A177 4fr multicolored .65 .25

Civil Defense Org. for protection and rescue.

1975, Sept. 8 Engr. *Perf. 13*

4fr, Water skiing, horiz. 15fr, Mountain climbing.

566 A178 3fr green, bl & lilac .25 .20
567 A178 4fr dk brn, grn & lt brn .40 .30
568 A178 15fr brown, indigo & grn 1.25 .70
Nos. 566-568 (3) 1.90 1.20

Grand Duke Type of 1965-71

1975-91 Engr. *Perf. 11½*
Granite Paper (14fr, 22fr)

570 A104 7fr orange .45 .20
571 A104 9fr yellow green .65 .20
572 A104 10fr black .50 .20
573 A104 12fr brick red 1.00 .20
573A A104 14fr dark blue .65 .30
574 A104 16fr green 1.00 .25
574A A104 18fr brown olive .80 .40
575 A104 20fr blue .80 .20
576 A104 22fr orange brown 1.10 .80
Nos. 570-576 (9) 6.95 2.75

Issued: 10fr, 1/9; 9fr, 12fr, 20fr, 12/23; 16fr, 2/25/82; 7fr, 7/1/83; 18fr, 3/3/86; 14fr, 1/2/90; 22fr, 9/23/91.

Grand Duchess Charlotte A179

Design: No. 580, Prince Henri.

1976, Mar. 8 Litho. *Perf. 14x13½*
579 A179 6fr green & multi .40 .20
580 A179 6fr dull blue & multi .90 .25

80th birthday of Grand Duchess Charlotte and 21st birthday of Prince Henri, heir to the throne.

Gold Brooch — A180

5fr, Footless beaker, horiz. 6fr, Decorated vessel, horiz. 12fr, Gold coin. All designs show excavated items of Franco-Merovingian period.

Perf. 13½x12½, 12½x13½
1976, Mar. 8
581 A180 2fr blue & multi .20 .20
582 A180 5fr black & multi .30 .30
583 A180 6fr lilac & multi .45 .30
584 A180 12fr multicolored 1.00 1.10
Nos. 581-584 (4) 1.95 1.90

Soup Tureen A181

Europa: 12fr, Deep bowl. Tureen and bowl after pottery from Nospelt, 19th century.

1976, May 3 Photo. *Perf. 11½*
585 A181 6fr lt violet & multi *1.00* *.30*
586 A181 12fr yel grn & multi *1.75* *1.00*

Independence Hall, Philadelphia A182

Boomerang A183

1976, May 3
587 A182 6fr lt blue & multi .35 .25

American Bicentennial.

1976, May 3
588 A183 6fr brt rose lil & gold .35 .20

21st Olympic Games, Montreal, Canada, July 17-Aug. 1.

"Vibrations of Sound" A184

1976, May 3
589 A184 6fr red & multi .35 .20

Jeunesses Musicales (Young Music Friends), association to foster interest in music and art.

Alexander Graham Bell — A185

Virgin and Child with St. Anne — A186

1976, Sept. 9 Engr. *Perf. 13*
590 A185 6fr slate green .35 .25

Centenary of first telephone call by Alexander Graham Bell, Mar. 10, 1876.

1976, Sept. 9 Photo. *Perf. 11½*

Renaissance sculptures: 12fr, Grave of Bernard de Velbruck, Lord of Beaufort.

591 A186 6fr gold & multi .35 .20
592 A186 12fr gold, gray & blk .70 .70

Johann Wolfgang von Goethe A187

Old Luxembourg A188

Portraits: 5fr, J. M. William Turner. 6fr, Victor Hugo. 12fr, Franz Liszt.

1977, Mar. 14 Engr. *Perf. 13*
593 A187 2fr lake .20 .20
594 A187 5fr purple .30 .25
595 A187 6fr slate green .35 .30
596 A187 12fr violet blue .70 .65
Nos. 593-596 (4) 1.55 1.40

Famous visitors to Luxembourg.

1977, May 3 Photo. *Perf. 11½*

Europa: 12fr, Adolphe Bridge and European Investment Bank headquarters.

597 A188 6fr multicolored *1.00* *.25*
598 A188 12fr multicolored *2.00* *.60*

Esch-sur-Sure A189

Marguerite de Busbach A190

Design: 6fr, View of Ehnen.

1977, May 3 Engr. *Perf. 13*
599 A189 5fr Prus blue .40 .25
600 A189 6fr deep brown .35 .25

1977, May 3 Photo. *Perf. 11½*

#602, Louis Braille, by Lucienne Filippi.

601 A190 6fr multicolored .35 .20
602 A190 6fr multicolored .35 .20

Notre Dame Congregation, founded by Marguerite de Busbach, 350th anniversary; Louis Braille (1809-1852), inventor of the Braille system of writing for the blind.

Souvenir Sheet

Luxembourg Nos. 1-2 — A191

Engr. & Photo.
1977, Sept. 15 *Perf. 13½*
603 A191 40fr gray & red brown 5.25 5.25

125th anniv. of Luxembourg's stamps.

Head of Medusa, Roman Mosaic, Diekirch, 3rd Century A.D. — A192

1977, Sept. 15 Photo. *Perf. 11½*
604 A192 6fr multicolored .50 .30

Orpheus and Eurydice, by C. W. Gluck A193

1977, Sept. 15 *Perf. 11½x12*
605 A193 6fr multicolored .60 .25

Intl. Wiltz Festival, 25th anniv.

Europa Tamed, by R. Zilli, and Map of Europe A194

1977, Dec. 5 Photo. *Perf. 11½*
606 A194 6fr multicolored .60 .30

20th anniversary of the Treaties of Rome, setting up the European Economic Community and the European Atomic Energy Commission.

Souvenir Sheet

Grand Duke and Grand Duchess of Luxembourg — A195

Photogravure and Engraved
1978, Apr. 3 *Perf. 13½x14*
607 A195 Sheet of 2 2.00 2.00
a. 6fr dark blue & multi .90 .90
b. 12fr dark red & multi .90 .90

Silver wedding anniversary of Grand Duke Jean and Grand Duchess Josephine Charlotte.

Souvenir Sheet

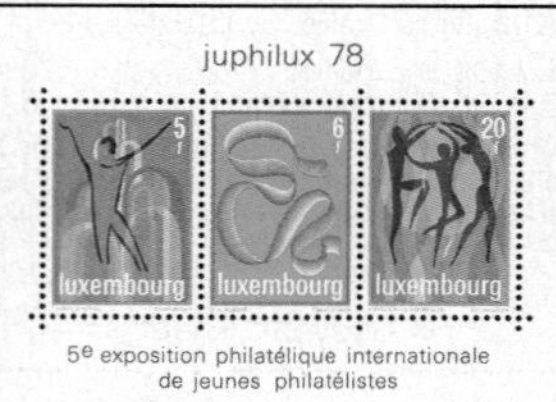

Youth Fountain, Streamer and Dancers — A196

1978, Apr. 3 Photo. *Perf. 11½*

608 A196 Sheet of 3		4.25	4.25
a. 5fr ultra & multi		1.40	1.40
b. 6fr orange & multi		1.40	1.40
c. 20fr yellow green & multi		1.40	1.40

Juphilux 78, 5th International Young Philatelists' Exhibition, Luxembourg, Apr. 6-10.

Charles IV, Statue, Charles Bridge, Prague A197

Emile Mayrish, by Theo Van Rysselberghe A198

Europa: 12fr, Pierre d'Aspelt, tomb, Mainz Cathedral.

1978, May 18 Engr. *Perf. 13½*

609 A197 6fr dark violet blue *1.40* .30
610 A197 12fr dull rose lilac *3.25* *.70*

Charles IV (1316-78), Count of Luxembourg, Holy Roman Emperor. Pierre d'Aspelt (c. 1250-1320), Archbishop of Mainz and Prince-Elector.

1978, May 18 *Perf. 11½*

611 A198 6fr multicolored .85 .30

Emile Mayrish (1862-1928), president of International Steel Cartel and promoter of United Europe.

Our Lady of Luxembourg A199

Trumpeters and Old Luxembourg A200

1978, May 18 Photo. *Perf. 11½*

612 A199 6fr multicolored .25 .25
613 A200 6fr multicolored .25 .25

Our Lady of Luxembourg, patroness, 300th anniv.; 135th anniv. of Grand Ducal Military Band.

Starving Child, Helping Hand, Millet — A201

League Emblem, Lungs, Open Window — A202

Open Prison Door — A203

1978, Sept. 11 Photo. *Perf. 11½*

614 A201 2fr multicolored .20 .20
615 A202 5fr multicolored .25 .25
616 A203 6fr multicolored .40 .30
Nos. 614-616 (3) .85 .75

"Terre des Hommes," an association to help underprivileged children; Luxembourg Anti-Tuberculosis League, 70th anniv.; Amnesty Intl. and 30th anniv. of Universal Declaration of Human Rights.

Squared Stone Emerging from Rock, City of Luxembourg — A204

1978, Sept. 11 Engr. *Perf. 13½x13*

617 A204 6fr violet blue .45 .25

Masonic Grand Lodge of Luxembourg, 175th anniversary.

Julius Caesar on Denarius, c. 44 B.C. A205

St. Michael's Church, Mondorf-les-Bains A206

Roman Coins, Found in Luxembourg: 6fr, Empress Faustina I on Sestertius, 141 A.D. 9fr, Empress Helena on Follis, c. 324-330. 26fr, Emperor Valens on Solidus, c. 367-375.

1979, Mar. 5 Photo. *Perf. 11½*

618 A205 5fr multicolored .20 .20
619 A205 6fr multicolored .20 .20
620 A205 9fr multicolored .65 .55
621 A205 26fr multicolored 1.25 1.00
Nos. 618-621 (4) 2.30 1.95

1979, Mar. 5 Engr. *Perf. 13*

Design: 6fr, Luxembourg Central Station.

622 A206 5fr multicolored .30 .20
623 A206 6fr rose claret .60 .30

Troisvierges Stagecoach A207

Europa: 12fr, Early wall telephone, vert.

1979, Apr. 30 Photo. *Perf. 11½*

624 A207 6fr multicolored *5.75* .35
625 A207 12fr multicolored *5.75* *1.50*

Michel Pintz Facing Jury A208

1979, Apr. 30 Engr. *Perf. 13*

626 A208 2fr rose lilac .30 .20

180th anniversary of peasant uprising against French occupation.

Antoine Meyer — A209

Abundance Crowning Work and Thrift, by Auguste Vinet — A210

Design: 6fr, Sidney Gilchrist Thomas.

1979, Apr. 30

627 A209 5fr carmine .30 .20
628 A209 6fr light blue .30 .25
629 A210 9fr black .50 .35
Nos. 627-629 (3) 1.10 .80

Antoine Meyer (1801-1857), mathematician and first national poet; centenary of acquisition of Thomas process for production of high-quality steel; 50th anniversary of Luxembourg Stock Exchange.

European Parliament A211

1979, June 7 Photo. *Perf. 11½*

630 A211 6fr multi 5.00 .90

European Parliament, first direct elections, June 7-10.

Angel with Chalice, by Barthelemy Namur — A212

Rococo Art: 12fr, Angel with anchor, by Namur, from High Altar, St. Michael's Church, Luxembourg.

Engraved and Photogravure

1979, Sept. 10 *Perf. 13½*

631 A212 6fr multi .35 .25
632 A212 12fr multi .65 .50

Road Safety for Children A213

1979, Sept. 10 Photo. *Perf. 11½*

633 A213 2fr multi .20 .20

International Year of the Child.

Radio Tele-Luxembourg Emblem — A214

1979, Sept. 10

634 A214 6fr ultra, blue & red .45 .25

50 years of broadcasting in Luxembourg.

John the Blind, Silver Coin, 1331 — A215

Ettelbruck Town Hall — A216

14th Century Coins: 2fr, Sts. Gervase and Protais, silver grosso. 6fr, Easter lamb, gold coin. 20fr, Crown and arms, silver grosso.

1980, Mar. 5 Photo. *Perf. 11½*

635 A215 2fr multi .20 .20
636 A215 5fr multi .25 .25
637 A215 6fr multi .35 .35
638 A215 20fr multi 1.20 1.20
Nos. 635-638 (4) 2.00 2.00

See Nos. 651-654.

1980, Mar. 5 Engr. *Perf. 13*

No. 640, State Archives Building, horiz.

639 A216 6fr brn & dk red .35 .25
640 A216 6fr multi .35 .25

Jean Monnet — A217

Sports for All — A218

Europa: 12fr, St. Benedict of Nursia.

1980, Apr. 28 *Perf. 13½*

641 A217 6fr dark blue *1.50* .35
642 A217 12fr olive green *2.50* .65

1980, Apr. 28 Photo. *Perf. 11½*

Granite Paper

643 A218 6fr multi .95 .20

Worker Pouring Molten Iron — A219

Mercury by Jean Mich — A220

Design: 6fr, Man, hand, gears, horiz.

1980, Apr. 28

644 A219 2fr multi .20 .20
645 A219 6fr multi .40 .20

9th World Congress on Prevention of Occupational Accidents & Diseases, Amsterdam, May 6-9.

1980, Sept. 10 Engr. *Perf. 14*

Art Nouveau Sculpture by Jean Mich.

646 A220 8fr shown .50 .40
647 A220 12fr Ceres .70 .55

Introduction of Postal Code — A221

1980, Sept. 10 Photo. *Perf. 11½*

648 A221 4fr multi .40 .20

Police Car and Officers A222

1980, Sept. 10

649 A222 8fr multi .50 .30

State control of police force, 50th anniv.

Grand Duke Jean, Personal Arms — A223

Photo. & Engr.

1981, Jan. 5 *Perf. 13½*

650 A223 Sheet of 3 2.50 2.50
a. 8fr multi .65 .65
b. 12fr multi .75 .75
c. 30fr multi 1.00 1.00

Grand Duke Jean, 60th birthday.

Coin Type of 1980

Silver Coins: 4fr, Philip IV patagon, 1635. 6fr, Empress Maria Theresa 12 sol, 1775. 8fr, Emperor Joseph II 12 sol, 1789. 30fr, Emperor Francois II 72 sol, 1795.

1981, Mar. 5 Photo. *Perf. 11½*

651 A215 4fr multi .20 .20
652 A215 6fr multi .25 .20
653 A215 8fr multi .30 .30
654 A215 30fr multi 1.25 1.10
Nos. 651-654 (4) 2.00 1.80

National Library A225

1981, Mar. 5 Engr. *Perf. 13*

655 A225 8fr shown .35 .20
656 A225 8fr European Hemicycle, Kirchberg .35 .20

Hammelsmarsch (Sheep Procession) A226

Europa: 12fr, Bird-shaped whistle, Eimaischen market.

1981, May 4 Photo. *Perf. 13½*

657 A226 8fr multi *1.00* .35
658 A226 12fr multi *2.25* .45

Knight on Chessboard A227

Savings Account Book, State Bank A228

First Bank Note, 1856 — A229

1981, May 4 *Perf. 11½*

Granite Paper

659 A227 4fr multi .25 .20
660 A228 8fr multi .35 .35
661 A229 8fr multi .35 .35

Luxembourg Chess Federation, 50th anniv.; State Savings Bank, 125th anniv.; Intl. Bank of Luxembourg, 125th anniv. of issuing rights.

Wedding of Prince Henri and Maria Teresa Mestre, Feb. 14 A230

Photo. & Engr.

1981, June 22 *Perf. 13½*

662 A230 8fr multi .50 .40

Sheets of 12.

Single-seater Gliders A231

Energy Conservation A232

1981, Sept. 28 Photo. *Perf. 11½*

Granite Paper

663 A231 8fr shown .30 .30
664 A231 16fr Propeller planes, horiz. .60 .60
665 A231 35fr Jet, Luxembourg Airport, horiz. 1.50 1.40
Nos. 663-665 (3) 2.40 2.30

1981, Sept. 28

Granite Paper

666 A232 8fr multi .35 .35

Apple Trees in Blossom, by Frantz Seimetz (1858-1914) A233

World War II Resistance — A234

Landscape Paintings: 6fr, Summer Landscape, by Pierre Blanc (1872-1946). 8fr, The Larger Hallerbach, by Guido Oppenheim (1862-1942). 16fr, Winter Evening, by Eugene Mousset (1877-1941).

1982, Feb. 25 Engr. *Perf. 11½*

667 A233 4fr multi .20 .20
668 A233 6fr multi .30 .30
669 A233 8fr multi .40 .40
670 A233 16fr multi .80 .80
Nos. 667-670 (4) 1.70 1.70

1982, Feb. 25

Design: Cross of Hinzert (Natl. Monument of the Resistance and Deportation) and Political Prisoner, by Lucien Wercollier.

671 A234 8fr multi .40 .35

Europa 1982 A235

St. Theresa of Avila (1515-1582) A236

1982, May 4 Photo.

Granite Paper

672 A235 8fr Treaty of London, 1867 *4.00* .45
673 A235 16fr Treaty of Paris, 1951 *6.00* 1.25

1982, May 4

Design: 8fr, Raoul Follereau (1903-1977), "Apostle of the Lepers."

Granite Paper

674 A236 4fr multi .20 .20
675 A236 8fr multi .40 .40

State Museums A237

1982, May 4 Photo. & Engr.

676 A237 8fr shown .45 .35
677 A237 8fr Synagogue of Luxembourg .45 .35

Bourscheid Castle — A238

Intl. Youth Hostel Federation, 50th Anniv. — A239

Designs: Restored castles.

1982, Sept. 9 Engr. *Perf. 11½*

Granite Paper

678 A238 6fr shown .30 .25
679 A238 8fr Vianden, horiz. .45 .35

1982, Sept. 9 Photo.

680 A239 4fr shown .30 .20
681 A239 8fr Scouting year, vert. .60 .35

Civilian and Military Deportation Monument — A240

1982, Sept. 9

682 A240 8fr multi .50 .35

Mercury, Sculpture by Auguste Tremond — A241

NATO Emblem, Flags — A242

1983, Mar. 7 Photo. *Perf. 11½*

Granite Paper

683 A241 4fr multi .20 .20

FOREX '83, 25th Intl. Assoc. of Foreign Exchange Dealers' Congress, June 2-5.

1983, Mar. 7

Granite Paper

684 A242 6fr multi .25 .25

25th anniv. of NAMSA (NATO Maintenance and Supply Agency).

Echternach Cross of Justice, 1236 — A243

Globe, CCC Emblem — A244

1983, Mar. 7

Granite Paper

685 A243 8fr multi .45 .35

30th Cong. of Intl. Union of Barristers, July 3-9.

1983, Mar. 7

Granite Paper

686 A244 8fr multi .45 .35

30th anniv. of Council of Customs Cooperation.

Natl. Federation of Fire Brigades Centenary A245

1983, Mar. 7

Granite Paper

687 A245 8fr Fire engine, 1983 .45 .35
688 A245 16fr Hand pump, 1740 .85 .65

Europa 1983 — A246

The Good Samaritan, Codex Aureus Escorialensis Miniatures, 11th Cent., Echternach.

1983, May 3 **Photo.**

689 A246 8fr Highway robbers *2.00 .45*
690 A246 16fr Good Samaritan *3.75 1.00*

Giant Bible, 11th Cent. — A247

World Communications Year — A248

Illuminated Letters.

Photo. & Engr.

1983, May 3 ***Perf. 14***

691 A247 8fr "h," Book of Baruch .45 .35
692 A247 35fr "B," letter of St. Jerome 2.00 1.50

1983, May 3 **Photo.** ***Perf. 11½***

693 A248 8fr Post code .40 .35
694 A248 8fr Satellite relay, horiz. .40 .35

Town Hall, Dudelange A249

7fr, St. Lawrence Church, Diekirch, vert.

1983, Sept. 7 **Photo. & Engr.**

695 A249 7fr multi .40 .25
696 A249 10fr multi .55 .35

Basketball Fed., 50th Anniv. A250

European Working Dog Championship A251

Tourism — A252

1983, Sept. 7 **Photo.**

Granite Paper

697 A250 7fr multi .40 .25
698 A251 10fr Alsatian sheepdog .55 .35
699 A252 10fr View of Luxembourg .55 .35
Nos. 697-699 (3) 1.50 .95

Environment Protection A253

1984, Mar. 6 **Photo.** ***Perf. 11½***

Granite Paper

700 A253 7fr Pedestrian zoning .35 .20
701 A253 10fr Water purification .50 .25

2nd European Parliament Election — A254

1984, Mar. 6

Granite Paper

702 A254 10fr Hands holding emblem .60 .40

A255

A256

1984, Mar. 6 **Engr.** ***Perf. 12½x13***

703 A255 10fr No. 1 .50 .35
704 A255 10fr Union meeting .50 .35
705 A255 10fr Mail bag .50 .35
706 A255 10fr Train .50 .35
Nos. 703-706 (4) 2.00 1.40

Philatelic Federation (1934); Civil Service Trade Union (1909); Postal Workers' Union (1909); Railroad (1859).

1984, May 7 **Photo.** ***Perf. 11½x12***

707 A256 10fr The Race, by Jean Jacoby (1891-1936) .55 .35

1984 Summer Olympics.

Europa (1959-84) A257

1984, May 7 ***Perf. 11½***

Granite Paper

708 A257 10fr green *3.00 .40*
709 A257 16fr orange *4.50 1.00*

Young Turk Caressing His Horse, by Delacroix A258

Paintings: 4fr, The Smoker, by David Teniers the Younger (1610-90). 10fr, Epiphany, by Jan Steen (1626-79). 50fr, The Lacemaker, by Pieter van Slingelandt (1640-91). 4fr, 50fr vert.

Photo. & Engr.

1984, May 7 ***Perf. 14***

710 A258 4fr multi .25 .20
711 A258 7fr multi .40 .25
712 A258 10fr multi .60 .35
713 A258 50fr multi 2.75 2.00
Nos. 710-713 (4) 4.00 2.80

Marine Life Fossils — A259

Restored Castles — A260

1984, Sept. 10 **Photo.** ***Perf. 11½***

714 A259 4fr Pecten sp. .20 .20
715 A259 7fr Gryphaea arcuata .40 .25
716 A259 10fr Coeloceras raqyinianum .55 .35
717 A259 16fr Daildius .90 .60
Nos. 714-717 (4) 2.05 1.40

1984, Sept. 10 **Engr.**

718 A260 7fr Hollenfels .40 .25
719 A260 10fr Larochette .55 .40

A261

A262

1984, Sept. 10 ***Perf. 12x12½***

720 A261 10fr Soldier, US flag .75 .35

40th Anniv. of D Day (June 6).

1985, Mar. 4 **Photo.** ***Perf. 11½***

Portrait medals in the state museum: 4fr, Jean Bertels (1544-1607), Historian, Abbott of Echternach. 7fr, Emperor Charles V (1500-1558). 10fr, King Philip II of Spain (1527-1598). 30fr, Prince Maurice of Orange-Nassau, Count of Vianden (1567-1625).

Granite Paper

721 A262 4fr multi .25 .20
722 A262 7fr multi .40 .20
723 A262 10fr multi .60 .30
724 A262 30fr multi 1.75 .90
Nos. 721-724 (4) 3.00 1.60

See Nos. 739-742.

Anniversaries A263

#725, Benz Velo, First automobile in Luxembourg, 1895. #726, Push-button telephone, sound waves. #727, Fencers.

1985, Mar. 4 ***Perf. 12x11½***

Granite Paper

725 A263 10fr multi .65 .40
726 A263 10fr multi .65 .40
727 A263 10fr multi .65 .40
Nos. 725-727 (3) 1.95 1.20

Centenary of the first automobile; Luxembourg Telephone Service, cent.; Luxembourg Fencing Federation, 50th anniv.

Visit of Pope John Paul II — A264

Europa 1985 — A265

1985, Mar. 4 ***Perf. 11½x12***

Granite Paper

728 A264 10fr Papal arms .75 .40

1985, May 8 ***Perf. 11½***

Designs: 10fr, Grand-Duke Adolphe Music Federation. 16fr, Luxembourg Music School.

729 A265 10fr multi *4.00 .45*
730 A265 16fr multi *5.00 .90*

Souvenir Sheet

End of World War II, 40th Anniv. — A266

Designs: a, Luxembourg resistance fighters, Wounded Fighters medal. b, Luxembourg War Cross. c, Badge of the Union of Luxembourg Resistance Movements. d, Liberation of the concentration camps.

1985, May 8 ***Perf. 11½x12***

Granite Paper

731 A266 Sheet of 4 2.75 2.75
a.-d. 10fr, any single .60 .40

Endangered Wildlife — A267

1985, Sept. 23 **Photo.** ***Perf. 12x11½***

732 A267 4fr Athene nocturna .20 .20
733 A267 7fr Felis silvestris .40 .20
734 A267 10fr Vanessa atalantica, vert. .55 .35
735 A267 50fr Hyla arborea, vert. 2.75 1.65
Nos. 732-735 (4) 3.90 2.40

Historic Monuments A268

1985, Sept. 23 **Engr.** ***Perf. 11½***

736 A268 7fr Echternach Orangery, 1750 .45 .20
737 A268 10fr Mohr de Waldt House, 17th cent. .65 .45

Natl. Art Collection A269

Photo. & Engr.

1985, Sept. 23 *Perf. 14*

738 A269 10fr 18th cent. book cover, Natl. Library .40 .20

Portrait Medals Type of 1985

1986, Mar. 3 Photo. *Perf. 11½*

Granite Paper

739 A262 10fr Count of Monterey, 1675 .65 .40
740 A262 12fr Louis XIV, 1684 .70 .45
741 A262 18fr Pierre de Weyms, c. 1700 1.10 .70
742 A262 20fr Duke of Marlborough, 1706 1.25 .80
Nos. 739-742 (4) 3.70 2.35

Federation of Luxembourg Beekeepers' Associations, Cent. A270

Mondorf State Spa, Cent. — A271

Natl. Table Tennis Federation, 50th Anniv. — A272

1986, Mar. 3 *Perf. 11½*

743 A270 12fr Bee collecting pollen .75 .50
744 A271 12fr Mosaic .75 .50
745 A272 12fr Boy playing table tennis .75 .50
Nos. 743-745 (3) 2.25 1.50

Europa 1986 A273

Fortifications A274

1986, May 5 Photo. *Perf. 12*

Granite Paper

751 A273 12fr Polluted forest, city *2.75* .50
752 A273 20fr Man, pollution sources *3.75 1.00*

1986, May 5

Granite Paper

753 A274 15fr Ft. Thungen, horiz. 1.60 .60
754 A274 18fr Invalid's Gate 1.60 .70
755 A274 50fr Malakoff Tower 3.00 2.00
Nos. 753-755 (3) 6.20 3.30

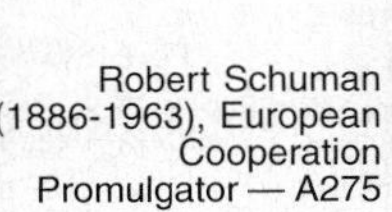

Robert Schuman (1886-1963), European Cooperation Promulgator — A275

1986, June 26 *Perf. 12 on 3 Sides*

Granite Paper

756 A275 2fr pink & blk .20 .20
a. Bklt. pane of 4 .30
757 A275 10fr lt bl & blk .50 .40
a. Bklt. pane of 4 2.75
b. Bklt. pane of 2, #756-757 + 2 labels 1.40

Nos. 756-757 issued in booklets only.

European Road Safety Year — A276

Countess Ermesinde (1186-1247), Ruler of Luxembourg A278

Bas-relief, Town Hall, Esch-Sur-Alzette — A277

1986, Sept. 15 Photo. *Perf. 11½*

758 A276 10fr multi .55 .40

Photogravure & Engraved

1986, Sept. 15 *Perf. 14x13½*

Design: No. 760, Stairs to the Chapel of the Cross, Grevenmacher.

759 A277 12fr shown .75 .50
760 A277 12fr multi .75 .50

1986, Sept. 15 *Perf. 13½x14*

Designs: No. 761, Presentation of the letter of freedom to Echternach inhabitants, 1236, engraving (detail) by P.H. Witkamp, c. 1873. 30fr, Charter seal, Marienthal Convent, 1238.

761 A278 12fr multi .70 .50
762 A278 30fr multi 1.65 1.20

A279

A280

A281

1987, Mar. 9 Photo. *Perf. 11½*

763 A279 6fr Eliomys quercinus, horiz. .65 .35
764 A279 10fr Calopteryx splendens 1.00 .50
765 A279 12fr Cinclus cinclus 1.60 .35
766 A279 25fr Salamandra salamandra terrestris, horiz. 2.25 1.25
Nos. 763-766 (4) 5.50 2.45

Wildlife conservation.

1987, Mar. 9

767 A280 12fr multi .60 .50

Natl. Home Amateur Radio Operators Network, 50th anniv.

1987, Mar. 9

768 A281 12fr multi .60 .50

Luxembourg Intl. Fair, 50th anniv.

Europa 1987 — A282

12fr, Aquatic Sports Center. 20fr, European Communities Court of Justice and abstract sculpture by Henry Moore (1898-1986).

1987, May 4 Photo. *Perf. 11½*

769 A282 12fr multi *3.00* .40
770 A282 20fr multi *5.00* .90

St. Michael's Church Millenary A283

Designs: 12fr, Consecration of the church by Archbishop Egbert of Trier, 987, stained glass window by Gustav Zanter. 20fr, Baroque organ-chest, 17th century.

Photogravure & Engraved

1987, May 4 *Perf. 14*

771 A283 12fr multi .75 .50
772 A283 20fr multi 1.25 .80

15th Century Paintings by Giovanni Ambrogio Bevilacqua A284

Polyptych panels in the State Museum: 10fr, St. Bernard of Sienna and St. John the Baptist. 18fr, St. Jerome and St. Francis of Assisi.

1987, May 4 *Perf. 11½*

773 A284 10fr multi .55 .40
774 A284 18fr multi 1.00 .70

Rural Architecture A285

Photo. & Engr.

1987, Sept. 14 *Perf. 13½*

775 A285 10fr Hennesbau Bark Mill, 1826, Niederfeulen .50 .40
776 A285 12fr Health Center, 18th cent., Mersch .60 .50
777 A285 100fr Post Office, 18th cent., Bertrange 5.00 4.00
Nos. 775-777 (3) 6.10 4.90

Chamber of Deputies (Parliament) 139th Anniv. — A286

Designs: 6fr, Charles Metz (1799-1853), first President. 12fr, Parliament, 1860, designed by Antoine Hartmann (1817-1891).

1987, Sept. 14 Engr. *Perf. 14*

778 A286 6fr violet brn .25 .25
779 A286 12fr blue black .50 .50

Flowers by Botanical Illustrator Pierre-Joseph Redoute (1759-1840) A287

1988, Feb. 8 Photo. *Perf. 11½x12*

780 A287 6fr Orange lily, water lily .40 .40
781 A287 10fr Primula, double narcissus .65 .65
782 A287 12fr Tulip .80 .80
783 A287 50fr Iris, gorteria 3.25 3.25
Nos. 780-783 (4) 5.10 5.10

European Conf. of Ministers of Transport A288

Eurocontrol, 25th Anniv. A289

1988, Feb. 8 *Perf. 12*

784 A288 12fr multi .70 .70
785 A289 20fr multi 1.25 1.25

Souvenir Sheet

Family of Prince Henri — A290

1988, Mar. 29 Photo. *Perf. 12*

786 A290 Sheet of 3 5.50 5.50
a. 12fr Maria Theresa .70 .70
b. 18fr Guillaume, Felix and Louis 1.00 1.00
c. 50fr Prince Henri 2.75 2.75

JUVALUX '88, 9th intl. youth philatelic exhibition, Mar. 29-Apr. 4.

Europa 1988 — A291

Communication.

1988, June 6 Photo. *Perf. 11½*

787 A291 12fr Automatic mail handling *3.75* .50
788 A291 20fr Electronic mail *4.00 1.25*

Tourism — A292

Designs: 10fr, Wiltz town hall and Cross of Justice Monument, c. 1502. 12fr, Castle, Differdange, 16th cent., vert.

Photo. & Engr.

1988, June 6 *Perf. 13½*

789 A292 10fr multi .60 .60
790 A292 12fr multi .70 .70

See Nos. 824-825, 841-842.

League of Luxembourg Student Sports Associations (LASEL), 50th Anniv. A293

1988, June 6 **Photo.** *Perf. 11½*

791 A293 12fr multi .70 .70

Doorways A294

Architectural drawings by Joseph Wegener (1895-1980) and his students, 1949-1951: 12fr, Septfontaines Castle main entrance, 1785. 25fr, National Library regency north-wing entrance, c. 1720. 50fr, Holy Trinity Church baroque entrance, c. 1740.

Litho. & Engr.

1988, Sept. 12 *Perf. 14*

792 A294 12fr black & buff .65 .65
793 A294 25fr blk & citron 1.25 1.25
794 A294 50fr blk & yel bister 2.60 2.60
Nos. 792-794 (3) 4.50 4.50

Jean Monnet (1888-1979), French Economist — A295

1988, Sept. 12 **Engr.**

795 A295 12fr multi .65 .65

European Investment Bank, 30th Anniv. A296

1988, Sept. 12 **Litho. & Engr.**

796 A296 12fr yel grn & blk .65 .65

A297

A298

1988, Sept. 12 **Photo.** *Perf. 11½*

797 A297 12fr multi .65 .65

1988 Summer Olympics, Seoul.

1989, Mar. 6 **Photo.** *Perf. 11½x12*

Design: 12fr, Portrait and excerpt from his speech to the Chamber of Deputies, 1896.

798 A298 12fr multi .60 .60

C.M. Spoo (1837-1914), advocate of Luxembourgish as the natl. language.

Book Workers' Fed., 125th Anniv. — A299

Natl. Red Cross, 75th Anniv. — A300

1989, Mar. 6

799 A299 18fr multi .95 .95

1989, Mar. 6

800 A300 20fr Henri Dunant 1.00 1.00

Independence of the Grand Duchy, 150th Anniv. — A301

Design: 12fr, Lion, bronze sculpture by Auguste Tremont (1892-1980) guarding the grand ducal family vault, Cathedral of Luxembourg.

Photo. & Engr.

1989, Mar. 6 *Perf. 14*

801 A301 12fr multi .60 .60

Astra Telecommunications Satellite — A302

1989, Mar. 6 **Photo.** *Perf. 11½*

802 A302 12fr multi .60 .60

Europa 1989 — A303

Tour de France — A304

Paintings (children at play): 12fr, *Three Children in a Park,* 19th cent., anonymous. 20fr, *Child with Drum,* 17th cent., anonymous.

1989, May 8 **Photo.** *Perf. 11½x12*

803 A303 12fr multi *2.00* .55
804 A303 20fr multi *3.00* .90

1989, May 8 *Perf. 11½*

805 A304 9fr multi .50 .50

Start of the bicycle race in Luxembourg City.

A305

A306

1989, May 8 *Perf. 11½x12*

806 A305 12fr multi .60 .60

Interparliamentary Union, cent.

1989, May 8

807 A306 12fr multi .60 .60

European Parliament 3rd elections.

Council of Europe, 40th Anniv. A307

1989, May 8 *Perf. 12x11½*

808 A307 12fr multi .60 .60

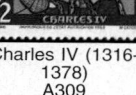

Reign of Grand Duke Jean, 25th Anniv. A308

Charles IV (1316-1378) A309

1989, Sept. 18 **Photo.** *Perf. 12x11½*

Booklet Stamps

810 A308 3fr black & orange .20 .20
a. Bklt. pane of 4 .55
811 A308 9fr black & blue green .40 .40
a. Bklt. pane of 4 1.70
b. Bklt. pane, 1 each #810, 811 + 2 labels .55
Booklet, 1 each #810a, 811a, 811b 2.85

Photo. & Engr.

1989, Sept. 18 *Perf. 13½x14*

Stained-glass windows by Joseph Oberberger in the Grand Ducal Loggia, Cathedral of Luxembourg: 20fr, John the Blind (1296-1346). 25fr, Wenceslas II (1361-1419).

821 A309 12fr shown .60 .60
822 A309 20fr multi .95 .95
823 A309 25fr multi 1.25 1.25
Nos. 821-823 (3) 2.80 2.80

Independence of the Grand Duchy, 150th anniv.

Tourism Type of 1988

Designs: 12fr, Clervaux Castle interior courtyard, circa 12th cent. 18fr, Bronzed wild boar of Titelberg, 1st cent., vert.

Litho. & Engr.

1989, Sept. 18 *Perf. 13½*

824 A292 12fr multi .60 .60
825 A292 18fr multi .90 .90

Views of the Former Fortress of Luxembourg, 1814-1815, Engravings by Christoph Wilhelm Selig (1791-1837) — A310

1990, Mar. 5 **Photo.** *Perf. 12x11½*

826 A310 9fr shown .40 .35
827 A310 12fr multi, diff. .45 .40
828 A310 20fr multi, diff. 1.10 .95
829 A310 25fr multi, diff. 1.50 .95
Nos. 826-829 (4) 3.45 2.65

Congress of Vienna, 1815, during which the Duchy of Luxembourg was elevated to the Grand Duchy of Luxembourg.

Schueberfouer Carnival, 650th Anniv. — A311

1990, Mar. 15 *Perf. 11½x12*

830 A311 9fr Carnival ride .65 .45

Batty Weber (1860-1940), Writer — A312

ITU, 125th Anniv. — A313

1990, Mar. 15

831 A312 12fr multi .50 .40

1990, Mar. 15

832 A313 18fr multicolored .85 .65

A314

A315

Europa (Post Offices): 12fr, Luxembourg City. 20fr, Esch-Sur-Alzette, vert.

Litho. & Engr.

1990, May 28 *Perf. 13½*

833 A314 12fr buff & blk *6.00* .40
834 A314 20fr lt bl & blk *9.00* *1.25*

Photo. & Engr.

1990, May 28 *Perf. 14x13½*

Prime Ministers: 9fr, Paul Eyschen (1841-1915). 12fr, Emmanuel Servais (1811-1890).

835 A315 9fr multicolored .45 .35
836 A315 12fr multicolored .55 .35

A316

A317

1990, May 28 **Photo.** ***Perf. 11½***
837 A316 12fr Psallus Pseudoplatani .55 .35

Luxembourg Naturalists' Society, cent.

Litho. & Engr.

1990, Sept. 24 ***Perf. 14***

Fountains: 12fr, Sheep's march by Will Lofy. 25fr, Fountain of Doves. 50fr, "Maus Ketty" by Lofy.

838 A317 12fr multicolored .50 .35
839 A317 25fr multicolored 1.10 .90
840 A317 50fr multicolored 2.10 2.25
Nos. 838-840 (3) 3.70 3.50

Tourism Type of 1988

1990, Sept. 24 ***Perf. 13½***
841 A292 12fr Mondercange .50 .25
842 A292 12fr Schifflange .50 .25

Souvenir Sheet

Nassau-Weilburg Dynasty, Cent. — A318

Designs: a, Grand Duke Adolphe. b, Grand Duchess Marie-Adelaide. c, Grand Ducal House arms. d, Grand Duchess Charlotte. e, Grand Duke Guillaume. f, Grand Duke Jean.
Illustration reduced.

Photo. & Engr.

1990, Nov. 26 ***Perf. 14x13½***
843 A318 Sheet of 6 8.00 8.00
a.-b. 12fr multicolored 1.00 1.00
c.-d. 18fr mulitcolored 1.00 1.00
e.-f. 20fr multicolored 1.00 1.00

View From the Trier Road by Sosthene Weis (1872-1941) — A319

Paintings: 18fr, Vauban Street and the Viaduct. 25fr, St. Ulric Street.

Perf. 12x11½, 11½x12

1991, Mar. 4 **Photo.**
844 A319 14fr multicolored .65 .40
845 A319 18fr multicolored .65 .65
846 A319 25fr multi, vert. 1.25 1.00
Nos. 844-846 (3) 2.55 2.05

Fungi — A320

1991, Mar. 4 ***Perf. 11½***
847 A320 14fr Geastrum varians .65 .45
848 A320 14fr Agaricus (Gymnopus) thiebautii .65 .45
849 A320 18fr Agaricus (lepiota) lepidocephalus .90 .90
850 A320 25fr Morchella favosa 1.40 .90
Nos. 847-850 (4) 3.60 2.70

Europa A321

1991, May 13 **Photo.** ***Perf. 12x11½***
851 A321 14fr Astra 1A, 1B satellites *3.75* *.50*
852 A321 18fr Betzdorf ground station *5.00* *1.40*

Natl. Miners' Monument, Kayl — A322

Art by Emile Kirscht — A323

Designs: No. 854, Magistrates' Court, Redange-Sur-Attert, horiz.

1991, May 23 ***Perf. 11½x12, 12x11½***
853 A322 14fr multicolored .70 .40
854 A322 14fr multicolored .70 .40

1991, May 23 ***Perf. 11½***

#856, Edmund de la Fontaine (1823-91), poet.

855 A323 14fr multicolored .70 .40
856 A323 14fr multicolored .70 .40

Labor Unions, 75th anniv. (No. 855).

Post and Telecommunications Museum — A324

Perf. 11½ on 3 sides

1991, Sept. 23 **Photo.**

Booklet Stamps

857 A324 4fr Old telephone 1.90 1.40
a. Bklt. pane of 1 + 3 labels 2.00
858 A324 14fr Old postbox .50 .45
a. Bklt. pane of 4 2.00

A325

A326

1991, Sept. 23 ***Perf. 11½***
859 A325 14fr Stamp of Type A24 .70 .40

Stamp Day, 50th anniv.

Photo. & Engr.

1991, Sept. 23 ***Perf. 14***

Designs: Gargoyles.

860 A326 14fr Young girl's head .65 .40
861 A326 25fr Woman's head 1.10 1.00
862 A326 50fr Man's head 2.00 1.60
Nos. 860-862 (3) 3.75 3.00

See Nos. 874-876.

Jean-Pierre Pescatore Foundation, Cent. A327

Buildings: No. 864, High Technology Institute. No. 865, New Fair and Congress Centre.

1992, Mar. 16 **Photo.** ***Perf. 11½***
863 A327 14fr lil rose & multi .70 .55
864 A327 14fr grn & multi .70 .55
865 A327 14fr brt bl & multi .70 .55
Nos. 863-865 (3) 2.10 1.65

Bettembourg Castle A328

1992, Mar. 16
866 A328 18fr shown .70 .65
867 A328 25fr Walferdange station 1.10 .90

Europa A329

Emigrants to US: 14fr, Nicholas Gonner (1835-1892), newspaper editor. 22fr, N. E. Becker (1842-1920), journalist.

Photo. & Engr.

1992, May 18 ***Perf. 13½x14½***
868 A329 14fr multicolored *3.50* *.50*
869 A329 22fr multicolored *4.50* *1.25*

Lions Clubs Intl., 75th Anniv. — A330

General Strike, 50th Anniv. — A331

1992, May 18 **Photo.** ***Perf. 11½***
870 A330 14fr multicolored .65 .40
871 A331 18fr sepia & lake .75 .70

1992 Summer Olympics, Barcelona A332

1992, May 18 ***Perf. 12x11½***
872 A332 14fr multicolored 1.25 .40

Expo '92, Seville A333

1992, May 18 ***Perf. 11½***
873 A333 14fr Luxembourg pavilion .60 .35

Gargoyle Type of 1991

Photo. & Engr.

1992, Oct. 5 ***Perf. 14***
874 A326 14fr Ram's head .60 .45
875 A326 22fr Lion's head 1.10 1.10
876 A326 50fr Satyr's head 1.90 1.75
Nos. 874-876 (3) 3.60 3.30

Stained Glass Windows, by Auguste Tremont — A334

1992, Oct. 5 **Photo.** ***Perf. 11½x12***
877 A334 14fr Post horn, letters .50 .40
878 A334 22fr Post rider 1.40 1.25
879 A334 50fr Insulators 1.75 1.60
Nos. 877-879 (3) 3.65 3.25

Luxembourg Post and Telecommunications, 150th anniv.

Single European Market A335

1992, Oct. 5 ***Perf. 11½x12***
880 A335 14fr multicolored .60 .35

Fountain of the Children with Grapes, Schwebsingen — A336

Design: No. 882, Old Ironworks Cultural Center, Steinfort.

1993, Mar. 8 **Photo.** ***Perf. 12x11½***
881 A336 14fr multicolored .70 .50
882 A336 14fr multicolored .70 .50

Grand Duke Jean — A337

Litho. & Engr.

1993-95 *Perf. 13½x13*

Background Color

No.	Design	Description	Unused	Used
883	A337	1fr yellow brown	.20	.20
883A	A337	2fr olive gray	.20	.20
884	A337	5fr yellow green	.20	.20
885	A337	7fr brick red	.30	.20
886	A337	10fr blue	.30	.25
887	A337	14fr pink	1.40	.30
888	A337	15fr green	.55	.45
889	A337	16fr orange	.60	.50
890	A337	18fr orange	.70	.35
891	A337	20fr red	.70	.55
892	A337	22fr dark green	.90	.75
893	A337	25fr gray blue	.90	.65
894	A337	100fr brown	3.25	2.40
		Nos. 883-894 (13)	10.20	7.00

Issued: 5, 7, 14, 18, 22, 25fr, 3/8/93; 1, 15, 20, 100fr, 3/7/94; 2, 10, 16fr, 1/30/95.

See Nos. 957, 1026.

New Technologies in Surgery A338

1993, May 10 Photo. *Perf. 11½*

No.	Design	Description	Unused	Used
895	A338	14fr multicolored	.60	.50

Contemporary Paintings — A339

Europa: 14fr, Rezlop, by Fernand Roda. 22fr, So Close, by Sonja Roef.

1993, May 10

No.	Design	Description	Unused	Used
896	A339	14fr multicolored	*1.25*	.40
897	A339	22fr multicolored	*1.75*	.80

A340

A341

Designs: 14fr, Burgundy Residence. 20fr, Simons House. 50fr, Cassal House.

Photo. & Engr.

1993, May 10 *Perf. 14*

No.	Design	Description	Unused	Used
898	A340	14fr multicolored	.50	.35
899	A340	20fr multicolored	.85	.65
900	A340	50fr multicolored	2.40	1.90
		Nos. 898-900 (3)	3.75	2.90

1993, Sept. 20 Photo. *Perf. 11½*

No.	Design	Description	Unused	Used
901	A341	14fr multicolored	.60	.35

Environmental protection.

A342

A343

1993, Sept. 20

No.	Design	Description	Unused	Used
902	A342	14fr multicolored	.60	.40
903	A343	14fr multicolored	.60	.40

Jean Schortgen (1880-1918), 1st worker elected to Parliament (#902); Artistic Circle of Luxembourg, cent.

Museum Exhibits A344

14fr, Electric tram, Tram & Bus Museum, City of Luxembourg. 22fr, Iron ore tipper wagon, Natl. Mining Museum, Rumelange. 60fr, Horse-drawn carriage, Wiltz Museum of Ancient Crafts.

Photo. & Engr.

1993, Sept. 20 *Perf. 14*

No.	Design	Description	Unused	Used
904	A344	14fr multicolored	.60	.35
905	A344	22fr multicolored	1.00	1.00
906	A344	60fr multicolored	2.40	1.75
		Nos. 904-906 (3)	4.00	3.10

See Nos. 933-935.

Snow-Covered Landscape, by Joseph Kutter (1894-1941) — A345

Design: No. 908, The Moselle, by Nico Klopp (1894-1930).

1994, Mar. 7 Photo. *Perf. 11½x12*

No.	Design	Description	Unused	Used
907	A345	14fr multicolored	.60	.40
908	A345	14fr multicolored	.60	.40

4th General Elections to European Parliament A346

1994, May 16 Photo. *Perf. 11½*

No.	Design	Description	Unused	Used
909	A346	14fr multicolored	.60	.40

European Inventions, Discoveries A347

1994, May 16

No.	Design	Description	Unused	Used
910	A347	14fr Armillary sphere	*1.75*	.40
911	A347	22fr Sail boats, map	*2.25*	1.00

Europa.

21st Intl. Congress of Genealogy & Heraldry — A348

14th World Congress of Intl. Police Assoc. — A349

Intl. Year of the Family A350

1994, May 16 *Perf. 11½*

No.	Design	Description	Unused	Used
912	A348	14fr multicolored	.60	.40
913	A349	18fr multicolored	.65	.60
914	A350	25fr multicolored	1.00	.85
		Nos. 912-914 (3)	2.25	1.85

Europe A351

1994, Sept. 19 *Perf. 11½*

No.	Design	Description	Unused	Used
915	A351	14fr Dove, stars	.50	.35
916	A351	14fr Circle of stars	.50	.35
917	A351	14fr Bronze Age bowl	2.00	.75
		Nos. 915-917 (3)	3.00	1.45

Western European Union, 40th anniv. (#915). Office for Official Publications of European Communities, 25th anniv. (#916). European Bronze Age Research Campaign (#917).

Liberation, 50th Anniv. A352

1994, Sept. 19 Photo. *Perf. 12x11½*

No.	Design	Description	Unused	Used
918	A352	14fr multicolored	.60	.45

Former Refuges in Luxembourg A353

Designs: 15fr, Munster Abbey. 25fr, Holy Spirit Convent. 60fr, St. Maximine Abbey of Trier.

Photo. & Engr.

1994, Sept. 19 *Perf. 14*

No.	Design	Description	Unused	Used
919	A353	15fr multicolored	.75	.75
920	A353	25fr multicolored	1.00	1.00
921	A353	60fr multicolored	2.25	1.75
		Nos. 919-921 (3)	4.00	3.50

A354

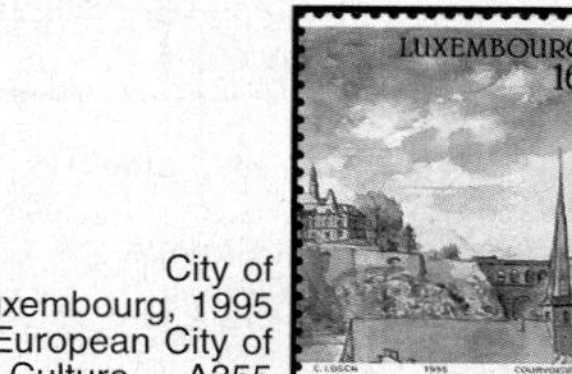

City of Luxembourg, 1995 European City of Culture — A355

A356

Paintings by Hundertwasser A357

Panoramic view of city showing buildings and: No. 923a, Steeples, trees. b, Gateway through fortress wall. c, Angles in fortress wall. d, Roof of church.

Designs: No. 924, The King of the Antipodes. No. 925, The House with the Arcades and the Yellow Tower. No. 926, Small Path.

1995, Mar. 6 *Perf. 12x11½, 11½x12* **Photo.**

No.	Design	Description	Unused	Used
922	A354	16fr multicolored	.75	.60
923		Strip of 4	3.25	3.00
a.-d.		A355 16fr any single	.75	.50

Photo. & Engr.

Perf. 14

No.	Design	Description	Unused	Used
924	A356	16fr gold, silver & multi	1.00	.60
925	A357	16fr black & multi	1.00	.60
926	A357	16fr yellow & multi	1.00	.60
		Nos. 922-926 (5)	7.00	5.40

No. 923 is a continuous design.

Liberation of the Concentration Camps, 50th Anniv. — A358

Europa: 25fr, Barbed wire, cracked plaster.

1995, May 15 Photo. *Perf. 11½x12*

No.	Design	Description	Unused	Used
927	A358	16fr multicolored	*1.00*	*.50*
928	A358	25fr multicolored	*1.25*	*.80*

European Nature Conservation Year — A359

1995, May 15 Litho. *Perf. 13½*

No.	Design	Description	Unused	Used
929	A359	16fr multicolored	.70	.50

A360

A362

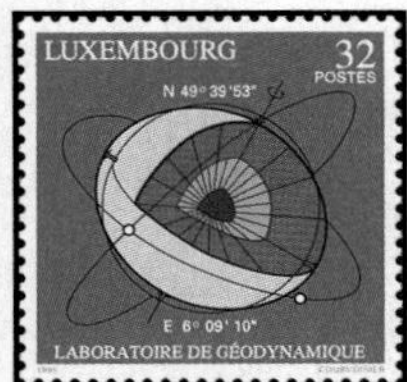

European Geodynamics and Seismology Center
A361

1995, May 15 Photo. *Perf. 11½x12*
930 A360 16fr multicolored .75 .60

Small States of Europe Games, Luxembourg.

1995, May 15 *Perf. 11½*
931 A361 32fr multicolored 1.40 1.10

1995, May 15 *Perf. 11½x12*
932 A362 80fr multicolored 3.25 2.50

UN, 50th anniv.

Museum Exhibits Type of 1993

Designs, vert: 16fr, Churn, Country Art Museum, Vianden. 32fr, Wine press, Wine Museum, Ehnen. 80fr, Sculpture of a Potter, by Leon Nosbusch, Pottery Museum, Nospelt.

Photo. & Engr.
1995, Sept. 18 *Perf. 14*
933 A344 16fr multicolored .65 .40
934 A344 32fr multicolored 1.10 .90
935 A344 80fr multicolored 3.25 2.25
Nos. 933-935 (3) 5.00 3.55

Luxembourg-Reykjavik, Iceland Air Route, 40th Anniv. — A363

1995, Sept. 18 Litho. *Perf. 13*
936 A363 16fr multicolored .70 .55

See Iceland No. 807.

Tourism
A364

1995, Sept. 18 Photo. *Perf. 11½*
937 A364 16fr Erpeldange .65 .50
938 A364 16fr Schengen .65 .50

Portrait of Emile Mayrisch (1862-1928), by Théo Van Rysselberghe (1862-1926) — A365

1996, Mar. 2 Photo. *Perf. 11½*
939 A365 (A) multicolored 1.25 .50

On day of issue No. 939 was valued at 16fr. See Belgium No. 1602.

National Railway, 50th Anniv. — A366

Passenger train: a, Cab facing left. b, Hooked together. c, Cab facing right.

1996, Mar. 4 Photo. *Perf. 11½*
940 Strip of 3 2.25 2.25
a.-c. A366 16fr Any single .70 .60

No. 940 is a continuous design.

Grand Duchess Charlotte (1896-1985) — A367

Design: Statue, Luxembourg City.

1996, Mar. 4
Booklet Stamp
941 A367 16fr multicolored .65 .40
a. Booklet pane of 8 5.00
Complete booklet, #941a 5.00

Mihály Munkácsy (1844-1900), Hungarian Painter — A368

Designs: No. 942, Portrait of Munkácsy, by Edouard Charlemont, 1884. No. 943, Portrait of Marie Munchen, by Munkácsy, 1885, vert.

1996, May 20 Photo. *Perf. 11½*
942 A368 16fr multicolored .70 .50
943 A368 16fr multicolored .70 .50

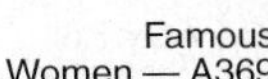

Famous Women — A369

Europa: 16fr, Marie de Bourgogne (1457-82), duchess of Luxembourg. 25fr, Empress Maria-Theresa of Austria (1717-80), duchess of Luxembourg.

Photo. & Engr.
1996, May 20 *Perf. 14x13½*
944 A369 16fr multicolored *1.40 .70*
945 A369 25fr multicolored *1.75 .90*

Luxembourg Confederation of Christian Trade Unions, 75th Anniv.
A370

Radio, Cent. — A371

Modern Olympic Games, Cent. — A372

Motion Pictures, Cent. — A373

Perf. 12x11½, 11½x12
1996, May 20 Photo.
946 A370 16fr multicolored .75 .60
947 A371 20fr multicolored .80 .70
948 A372 25fr multicolored 1.25 1.25
949 A373 32fr multicolored 1.40 1.25
Nos. 946-949 (4) 4.20 3.80

Registration and Property Administration, Bicent. — A374

1996, Sept. 23 Photo. *Perf. 11½*
950 A374 16fr multicolored .75 .60

Let Us Live Together
A375

#951, Four children. #952, "L'Abbraccio," bronze statue by M.J. Kerschen, vert.

1996, Sept. 23
951 A375 16fr multicolored .70 .50
952 A375 16fr multicolored .70 .50

Mustelidae
A376

Litho. & Engr.
1996, Sept. 23 *Perf. 13½*
953 A376 16fr Meles meles .80 .50
954 A376 20fr Mustela putorius .80 .60
955 A376 80fr Lutra lutra 3.50 2.75
Nos. 953-955 (3) 5.10 3.85

John the Blind (1296-1346), King of Bohemia, Count of Luxembourg
A377

Litho. & Engr.
1996, Dec. 9 *Perf. 13½*
956 A377 32fr multicolored 1.40 1.25

Grand Duke Jean Type of 1993
Litho. & Engr.
1997, Jan. 2 *Perf. 13½x13*
957 A337 8fr green & black .35 .30

Treaties of Rome, 40th Anniv.
A378

Belgian-Luxembourg Economic Union, 75th Anniv. — A379

1997, Mar. 3 Photo. *Perf. 11½*
958 A378 16fr multicolored .65 .50
959 A379 20fr multicolored .85 .55

Tourism
A380

Designs: No. 960, Servais House, Mersch. No. 961, Baroque Church, Koerich, vert.

1997, Mar. 3
960 A380 16fr multicolored .65 .50
961 A380 16fr multicolored .65 .50

11th World Congress of Rose Societies — A381

Roses: 16fr, Grand Duchess Charlotte. 20fr, Beautiful Sultana. 80fr, In Memory of Jean Soupert.

1997, Mar. 3 *Perf. 11½*
962 A381 16fr multicolored .75 .60

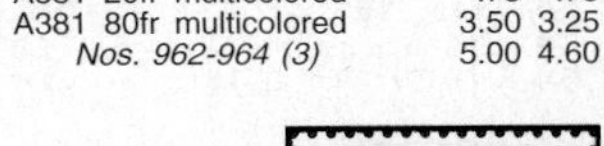

Size: 33x25mm
963 A381 20fr multicolored .75 .75
964 A381 80fr multicolored 3.50 3.25
Nos. 962-964 (3) 5.00 4.60

Stories and Legends — A382

Europa: 16fr, Melusina of Luxembourg. 25fr, Hunter of Hollenfels.

1997, May 12
965 A382 16fr multicolored *1.25 .60*
966 A382 25fr multicolored *1.75 .80*

A383

A384

Mondorf Spa, 150th Anniv. A385

1997, May 12

967 A383 16fr multicolored .75 .55
968 A384 16fr multicolored .75 .55
969 A385 16fr multicolored .75 .55
Nos. 967-969 (3) 2.25 1.65

Grand-Ducal Gendarmerie, bicent. (#967). Union of Small Domestic Animals Farming Societies, 75th anniv. (#968).

JUVALUX 98 — A386

1997, May 12

970 A386 16fr Emblem .85 .60
971 A386 80fr Postal history 3.25 2.75

Saar-Lorraine-Luxembourg Summit — A387

1997, Oct. 16 **Photo.** ***Perf. 11½***

972 A387 16fr multicolored .75 .50

See Germany #1982 & France #2613.

Mills — A388

Clocks — A389

Litho. & Engr.

1997, Oct. 16 ***Perf. 13½***

973 A388 16fr Kalborn Mill, horiz. .80 .60
974 A388 50fr Ramelli Mill 2.00 1.75

Photo. & Engr.

1997, Oct. 16 ***Perf. 13x13½***

Designs: 16fr, Oak wall clock, 1816. 32fr, Astronomic clock with walnut case, mid 19th cent. 80fr, Pear tree wood wall clock, 1815.

975 A389 16fr multicolored .85 .60
976 A389 32fr multicolored 1.40 1.25
977 A389 80fr multicolored 3.50 3.00
Nos. 975-977 (3) 5.75 4.85

Henry V, the Blonde (1247-81), Count of Luxembourg A390

1997, Dec. 8 **Photo.** ***Perf. 11½***

978 A390 32fr multicolored 1.50 1.25

Tourism A391

#979, Hesperange. #980, Rodange Church, vert.

1998, Mar. 23 **Photo.** ***Perf. 11½***

979 A391 16fr multicolored .70 .50
980 A391 16fr multicolored .70 .50

See Nos. 1023-1024.

Freshwater Fish A392

Designs: 16fr, Salmo trutta. 25fr, Cottus gobio. 50fr, Alburnoides bipunctatus.

Litho. & Engr.

1998, Mar. 23 ***Perf. 13½x13***

981 A392 16fr multicolored 1.00 .50
982 A392 25fr multicolored 1.60 1.40
983 A392 50fr multicolored 2.25 2.00
Nos. 981-983 (3) 4.85 3.90

NGL (Independent Luxembourg Trade Union), 50th Anniv. — A393

Broom Festival, Wiltz, 50th Anniv. — A394

Jean Antoine Zinnen (1827-98), Composer A395

Abolition of Censorship, 150th Anniv. A396

1998, Mar. 23 **Photo.** ***Perf. 11½***

984 A393 16fr multicolored .85 .60
985 A394 16fr multicolored .85 .60
986 A395 20fr multicolored .85 .80
987 A396 50fr multicolored 2.00 2.00
Nos. 984-987 (4) 4.55 4.00

King Henri VII (1275?-1313) of Luxembourg, King of Germany, Holy Roman Emperor — A397

1998, June 18 **Photo.** ***Perf. 11½***

988 A397 (A) multicolored 1.25 .60

Granting of the Right to hold a Luxembourg Fair, 700th anniv.

No. 988 was valued at 16fr on the day of issue.

Natl. Holidays and Festivals — A398

Juvalux 98 — A399

A400

Europa: 16fr, Fireworks over bridge, National Day. 25fr, Flame, stained glass window, National Remembrance Day.

1998, June 18

989 A398 16fr multicolored *1.40* *.50*
990 A398 25fr multicolored *1.60* *.65*

1998, June 18 **Photo. & Engr.**

16fr, Town postman, 1880. 25fr, Letter, 1590, horiz. 50fr, Country postman, 1880.

#994, Engraving showing 1861 view of Luxembourg.

991 A399 16fr multicolored .80 .60
992 A399 25fr multicolored 1.00 1.00
993 A399 50fr multicolored 2.00 1.75
Nos. 991-993 (3) 3.80 3.35

Souvenir Sheet

994 Sheet of 2 5.25 5.25
a. A400 16fr multicolored .80 .80
b. A400 80fr multicolored 3.50 3.50

St. Jean de L'Esperance, Grand Lodge of Luxembourg, 150th Anniv. — A401

1998, Sept. 21 **Litho.** ***Perf. 13½***

995 A401 16fr multicolored .75 .50

Abbey of Echternach, 1300th Anniv. A402

Various architectural drawings.

1998, Sept 21 **Photo.** ***Perf. 11½***

996 A402 16fr multicolored .75 .60
997 A402 48fr multicolored 2.25 1.90
998 A402 60fr multicolored 2.25 1.90
Nos. 996-998 (3) 5.25 4.40

Museum Exhibits A403

City of Luxembourg History Museum: 16fr, Spanish army helmet, 16th cent. 80fr, Wayside Cross, Hollerich, 1718.

Litho. & Engr.

1998, Sept. 21 ***Perf. 13½***

999 A403 16fr multicolored .85 .60
1000 A403 80fr multicolored 3.25 2.75

NAMSA (NATO Maintenance and Supply Organization), 40th Anniv. — A404

1998, Dec. 7 **Photo.** ***Perf. 11½***

1001 A404 36fr multicolored 1.60 1.25

Introduction of the Euro A405

1999, Mar. 8 **Photo.** ***Perf. 11½***

1002 A405 (A) multicolored 1.25 .60

No. 1002 was valued at 16fr on the day of issue.

Council of Europe, 50th Anniv. — A406

1999, Mar. 8

1003 A406 16fr multicolored .85 .65

Owls A407

1999, Mar. 8 ***Perf. 12***

1004 A407 (A) Strix aluco, vert. 1.25 .65
1005 A407 32fr Bubo bubo 1.60 1.75
1006 A407 60fr Tyto alba 3.25 2.50
Nos. 1004-1006 (3) 6.10 4.90

No. 1004 was valued at 16fr on the day of issue.

NATO, 50th Anniv. A408

1999, Mar. 8 ***Perf. 11½***

1007 A408 80fr multicolored 4.25 3.50

Europa — A409

National Parks: 16fr, Haute-Sûre. 25fr, Ardennes-Eifel.

1999, May 17 **Photo.** ***Perf. 11½x12***

1008 A409 16fr multicolored *1.00* *.50*
1009 A409 25fr multicolored *1.25* *.80*

Natl. Federation of Mutuality, 75th Anniv. — A410

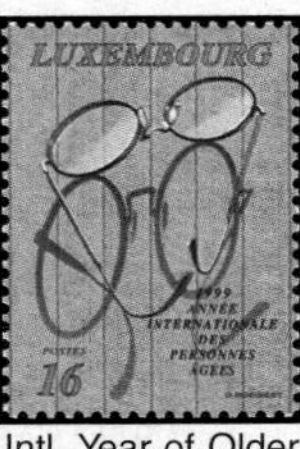

Intl. Year of Older Persons — A411

UPU, 125th Anniv. A412

A413 A414

1999, May 17 *Perf. 11½*

1010 A410 16fr multicolored .85 .65
1011 A411 16fr multicolored .85 .65
1012 A412 16fr multicolored .85 .65
1013 A413 32fr multicolored 1.75 1.60
1014 A414 80fr multicolored 4.25 3.25
Nos. 1010-1014 (5) 8.55 6.80

Luxembourg Federation of Amateur Photographers, 50th anniv. (#1013). Luxembourg Gymnastics Federation, cent. (#1014).

Aline Mayrisch-de Saint-Hubert (1874-1947), President of Luxembourg Red Cross — A416

18th Birthday of Prince Guillaume A415

Photo. & Engr.

1999, Sept. 21 *Perf. 13½*

1015 A415 16fr multicolored .85 .65

1999, Sept. 21 **Litho. & Engr.**

1016 A416 20fr multicolored 1.00 .90

Travelling Into the Future A417

1999, Sept. 21 **Photo.** *Perf. 11¾*

1017 A417 16fr Communication by road .85 .70
1018 A417 20fr Information age 1.00 1.00
1019 A417 80fr Conquering space 4.25 3.25
Nos. 1017-1019 (3) 6.10 4.95

Johann Wolfgang von Goethe (1749-1832), German Poet — A418

1999, Nov. 30 **Photo.** *Perf. 11¾*

1020 A418 20fr henna & dk brn 1.00 .90

Year 2000 — A419

No. 1021: a, Large white area under A and 2000. b, Large blue area under A. c, Large blue area under A and URG. d, Large blue area under LUX.

Illustration reduced.

Serpentine Die Cut 8 Vert.

2000, Jan. 3 **Photo.**

Self-Adhesive

Booklet Stamps

1021 A419 Booklet pane of 4 5.00
a.-d. (A) Any single 1.25 .60
Booklet, 2 #1021 10.00

Nos. 1021a-1021d sold for 16fr on day of issue.

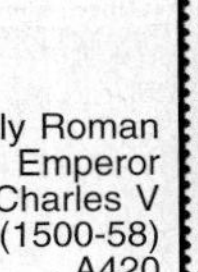

Holy Roman Emperor Charles V (1500-58) A420

Litho. & Engr.

2000, Mar. 7 *Perf. 13½*

1022 A420 A multi 1.25 .50

Sold for 16fr on day of issue.

Tourism Type of 1998

Designs: No. 1023, Walferdange Castle. No. 1024, Wasserbillig railway station, vert.

Perf. 11¾x11½, 11½x11¾

2000, Mar. 7 **Photo.**

Granite Paper

1023 A391 A multi 1.25 .50
1024 A391 A multi 1.25 .50

Sold for 16fr on day of issue.

World Mathematics Year A421

2000, Mar. 7 *Perf. 11½x11¾*

1025 A421 80fr multi 3.00 2.75

Grand Duke Jean Type of 1993

Litho. & Engr.

2000, Mar. 31 *Perf. 13¼x13*

Background Color

1026 A337 9fr pink .40 .30

Musical Instruments — A422

Perf. 11½x11¾

2000, Mar. 31 **Photo.**

Granite Paper

1027 A422 3fr French horn .20 .20
1028 A422 12fr Saxophone .55 .45
1029 A422 21fr Violin .95 .65
1030 A422 30fr Piano 1.40 1.10
Nos. 1027-1030 (4) 3.10 2.40

See Nos. 1045-1046.

Ducks A423

Designs: 18fr, Anas platyrhynchos. 24fr, Aythya ferina, vert. 30fr, Aythya fuligula.

2000, May 9 *Perf. 11¾x11½*

Granite Paper

1031 A423 18fr multi .80 .60

Perf. 11½x11¾

1032 A423 24fr multi 1.10 .90
1033 A423 30fr multi 1.40 1.25
Nos. 1031-1033 (3) 3.30 2.75

Esch-sur-Alzette Gas Works, Cent. (in 1999) — A424

2000, May 9 *Perf. 11¾x11½*

Granite Paper

1034 A424 18fr multi .80 .60

Europa, 2000

Common Design Type

2000, May 9 *Perf. 11½x11¾*

Granite Paper

1035 CD17 21fr multi *2.00 1.00*

Robert Schuman's European Unity Plan, 50th Anniv. A425

2000, May 9 *Perf. 11½x11¾*

1036 A425 21fr multi .95 .75

Art Collection of Luxembourg Posts & Telecommunications — A426

Art by: 21fr, Will Kesseler. 24fr, Joseph Probst, vert. 36fr, Mett Hoffmann.

Perf. 11¾x11½, 11½x11¾

2000, Sept. 27 **Photo.**

Granite Paper

1037 A426 21fr multi .95 .50
1038 A426 24fr multi 1.10 .75
1039 A426 36fr multi 1.60 1.25
Nos. 1037-1039 (3) 3.65 2.50

Towers on Historic Walking Trails A427

Designs: 18fr, Tower of Jacob, Wenzel trail. 42fr, Bons Malades Gate, Vauban trail.

Photo. & Engr.

2000, Sept. 27 *Perf. 13½x14¼*

1040 A427 18fr multi .80 .60
1041 A427 42fr multi 1.90 1.75

Blast Furnace "B," Esch-Belval A428

2000, Sept. 27 *Perf. 11¾x11½*

1042 A428 A multi .80 .60

No. 1042 sold for 18fr on day of issue.

Accession of Grand Duke Henri — A429

Designs: 18fr, Prince Henri in uniform, Princess Maria Teresa in pink suit. 100fr, Prince in suit, Princess in red blouse.

2000, Sept. 27 **Photo.** *Perf. 11¾*

Granite Paper (18fr)

1043 A429 18fr multi .80 .70

Souvenir Sheet

Photo. (margin Photo. & Engr.)

Perf. 11½

1044 A429 100fr multi 4.25 4.25

No. 1043 issued in sheets of 12, five of which (positions 6, 8, 9, 10 and 11) have a red and blue "ribbon" running diagonally through stamp margin. No. 1044 contains one 46x35mm stamp.

Musical Instruments Type of 2000

2000, Dec. 5 **Photo.** *Perf. 11½x11¾*

Granite Paper

1045 A422 9fr Electric guitar .40 .30
1046 A422 24fr Accordion 1.00 .80

Treaty Establishing European Coal and Steel Community, 50th Anniv. — A430

Perf. 11¼x11½

2001, Mar. 20 **Photo.**

1047 A430 21fr multi 1.25 .75

Tourism Type of 1998

Designs: No. 1048, 18fr, Bestgen Mill, Schifflange. No. 1049, 18fr, Chapel, Wormeldange, and millstone, Ahn, vert.

Perf. 11¾x11½, 11½x11¾

2001, Mar. 20

Granite Paper

1048-1049 A391 Set of 2 2.10 1.25

Writers — A431

Designs: 18fr, Nik Welter (1871-1951). 24fr, André Gide (1869-1951). 30fr, Michel Rodange (1827-76).

Perf. 13½x13¼

2001, Mar. 20 **Litho. & Engr.**
1050-1052 A431 Set of 3 4.25 2.40

Europa A432

Designs: A (18fr), Stream, Mullerthal region. 21fr, Pond and Kaltreis water tower, Luxembourg-Bonnevoie.

Perf. 11¾x11½, 11½x11¾

2001, May 22 **Photo.**
Granite Paper
1053-1054 A432 Set of 2 2.00 1.60

Rescue Workers — A433

Designs: 18fr, Air rescue. 30fr, Rescue divers. 45fr, Fire fighters.

2001, May 22 *Perf. 11½x11¾*
Granite Paper
1055-1057 A433 Set of 3 5.50 4.00

Humanitarian Services — A434

Designs: 18fr, Humanitarian aid. 24fr, Intl. Organization for Migration, 50th anniv.

2001, May 22 *Perf. 11½*
1058-1059 A434 Set of 2 2.50 1.75

Old Postal Vehicles — A435

Designs: 3fr, Citroen 2CV Mini-van, 1960s. 18fr, Volkswagen Beetle, 1970s.

Serpentine Die Cut 8¼ Vert.

2001, May 22
Booklet Stamps
Granite Paper
1060 A435 3fr multi .20 .20
1061 A435 18fr multi 1.10 .75
a. Booklet, 6 each #1060-1061 8.00

European Year of Languages A436

2001, Oct. 1 **Photo.** *Perf. 11¾x11½*
Granite Paper
1062 A436 A multi 1.10 .80

Luxembourg postal officials state that No. 1062 sold for 45 eurocents on the day of issue, though euro currency was not in circulation on the day of issue. On the day of issue, 45 eurocents was the equivalent of approximately 18fr.

Nos. 1063-1071, 1074, 1076, 1078, 1080, 1084, and B425-B429 are denominated solely in euro currency though euro currency would not circulate until Jan. 1, 2002. From their date of issue until Dec. 31, 2001, these stamps could be purchased for Luxembourg francs. The official pegged rate of 40.3399 francs to the euro made rounding the franc purchase price a necessity for such purchases. The approximate franc equivalent of the euro denominations is shown in parentheses in the listings.

Traveling Into the Future Type of 1999

Designs: 45c (18fr), Renewable energy. 59c (24fr), Waste recycling. 74c (30fr), Biological research.

2001, Oct. 1 *Perf. 11¾*
Granite Paper
1063-1065 A417 Set of 3 4.50 3.25

Euro Coinage A437

Designs : Coin obverses with values of stamp denominations.

2001, Oct. 1 *Perf. 11½*

1066	A437	5c (2fr) multi	.20	.20
1067	A437	10c (4fr) multi	.25	.20
1068	A437	20c (8fr) multi	.50	.40
1069	A437	50c (20fr) multi	1.25	.90
1070	A437	€1 (40fr) multi	2.50	1.75
1071	A437	€2 (80fr) multi	5.25	3.75
		Nos. 1066-1071 (6)	9.95	7.20

Grand Duke Henri — A438

Photo. & Engr.

2001-03 *Perf. 11¾x11½*
Vignette Color

1072	A438	1c blue	.20	.20
1073	A438	3c green	.20	.20
1074	A438	7c (3fr) blue	.20	.20
1075	A438	22c (9fr) brown	.55	.40
1076	A438	30c (12fr) green	.75	.45
1077	A438	45c (18fr) violet	1.10	.65
1078	A438	52c brown	1.40	.90
1079	A438	59c blue	1.50	.90
1080	A438	74c brown	1.90	1.10
1081	A438	89c red violet	2.25	1.25
		Nos. 1072-1081 (10)	10.05	6.25

Issued: 7c, 22c, 30c, 45c, 10/1/01. 52c, 59c, 74c, 89c, 3/5/02. 1c, 3c, 10/1/03.

Kiwanis International A439

2001, Dec. 6 **Photo.** *Perf. 11½*
1084 A439 52c (21fr) multi 1.40 .95

100 Cents = 1 Euro (€)

Art Collection of Luxembourg Posts & Telecommunications — A440

Art by: 22c, Moritz Ney, vert. 45c, Dany Prüm. 59c, Christiane Schmit, vert.

Perf. 14¼x14, 14x14¼

2002, Mar. 5 **Photo.**
1085-1087 A440 Set of 3 3.25 2.25

European Court Anniversaries A441

Designs: 45c, European Court of Auditors, 25th anniv. 52c, Court of Justice of the European communities, 50th anniv.

2002, Mar. 5 **Litho.** *Perf. 13½*
1088-1089 A441 Set of 2 2.50 1.75

Sports — A442

No. 1090: a, Snowboarding. b, Skateboarding. c, Rollerblading. d, Bicycling. e, Volleyball. f, Basketball.

Die Cut Perf. 10 on 3 Sides

2002, Mar. 5
Booklet Stamps
Self-Adhesive
1090 Booklet pane of 6 4.00
a.-c. A442 7c Any single .20 .20
d.-f. A442 45c Any single 1.10 .80
Booklet, 2 #1090 8.00

Europa — A443

Designs: 45c, Tightrope walker. 52c, Clown.

2002, May 14 **Litho.** *Perf. 13½*
1091-1092 A443 Set of 2 *3.00 1.75*

Cultural Anniversaries — A444

Designs: A, 50th Wiltz Festival. €1.12, Victor Hugo (1802-85), writer.

2002, May 14 *Perf. 13¼*
1093-1094 A444 Set of 2 4.00 3.00

No. 1093 sold for 45c on day of issue.

Start of Tour de France in Luxembourg A445

Designs: 45c, Stylized bicycle. 52c, François Faber (1887-1915), 1909 champion. €2.45, The Champion, by Joseph Kutter.

Litho. (45c), Litho. & Engr.
Perf. 13¼x13½, 13½x13¼

2002, May 14
1095-1097 A445 Set of 3 9.00 6.25

Grevenmacher Charter of Freedom, 750th Anniv. — A446

2002, Sept. 14 **Litho.** *Perf. 13¼x13*
1098 A446 74c multi 1.90 1.50

Nature Museum, Museum of Natural History A447

No. 1099: a, Water drop on spruce needle. b, Butterfly. c, Leaf rosette of *Echeveria* plant. d, Berries.

Serpentine Die Cut 8 Vert.

2002, Sept. 14 **Photo.**
Self-Adhesive
1099 Booklet pane of 4 4.50
a.-d. A447 A Any single 1.10 .80
Booklet, 2 #1099 9.00

Nos. 1099a-1099d had franking value of 45c on day of issue, but booklet sold for discounted price of €3.35.

Souvenir Sheet

Luxembourg Stamps, 150th Anniv. — A448

No. 1100: a, Grand Duke William II, man and woman, 1852 (47x27mm). b, Grand Duke Adolphe, woman, 1902 (47x27mm). c, Grand Duchess Charlotte, street scene, 1952 (47x27mm). d, Grand Duke Henri, hot air balloons in street, 2002 (71x27mm).

Photo. & Engr.

2002, Sept. 14 *Perf. 11¾*
1100 A448 45c Sheet of 4, #a-d 4.75 4.75

The Post in 50 Years A449

Designs: 22c, Postmen in spacecraft, buildings, vert. A, Spacecraft in flight, cell phone, letter and "@" in orbit around planet.

Perf. 14x14½, 14½x14

2002, Oct. 19 **Litho.**
1101-1102 A449 Set of 2 1.75 1.40

No. 1102 sold for 45c on day of issue.

Grand Duke Jean and Princess Joséphine-Charlotte, 50th Wedding Anniv. — A450

Perf. 14¼x14½

2003, Mar. 18 **Litho.**
1103 A450 45c multi 1.10 .95

Official Journal of the European Communities, 50th Anniv. — A451

2003, Mar. 18 ***Perf. 14½x14***
1104 A451 52c multi 1.40 1.10

Famous Women A452

Designs: No. 1105, 45c, Catherine Schleimer-Kill (1884-1973), feminist leader. No. 1106, 45c, Lou Koster (1889-1973), composer.

2003, Mar. 18 **Photo.** ***Perf. 11½***
1105-1106 A452 Set of 2 2.40 1.90

Tourism A453

Designs: 50c, Fontaine Marie Convent, Differdange. €1, Castle, Mamer. €2.50, St. Joseph Church, Esch-sur-Alzette, vert.

Perf. 14½x14, 14x14½

2003, Mar. 18 **Litho.**
1107-1109 A453 Set of 3 10.50 9.50

Luxembourg Athénée, 400th Anniv. A454

2003, May 20 **Litho.** ***Perf. 14¼x14½***
1110 A454 45c multi 1.10 1.00

Europa A455

Poster art: 45c, 1952 poster for National Lottery, by Roger Gerson. 52c, 1924 poster for Third Commercial Fair, by Auguste Trémont.

2003, May 20 ***Perf. 13¼x13***
1111-1112 A455 Set of 2 *2.75 1.75*

Bridges — A456

Designs: 45c, Adolphe Bridge, 1903. 59c, Stierchen Bridge, 14th cent. (36x26mm). 89c, Victor Bodson Bridge, 1994 (36x26mm).

Photo. & Engr.

2003, May 20 ***Perf. 11½***
1113-1115 A456 Set of 3 5.00 4.25

Electrification of Luxembourg, 75th Anniv. — A457

Litho. & Embossed

2003, Sept. 23 ***Perf. 13¼x13***
1116 A457 A multi 1.25 1.25

Sold for 50c on day of issue.

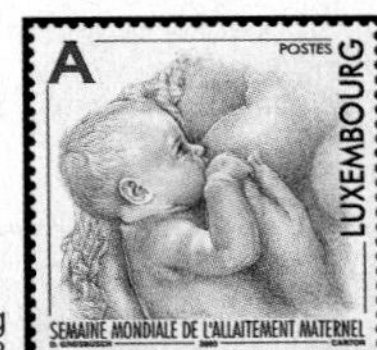

Breastfeeding A458

2003, Sept. 23 **Litho.** ***Perf. 13½***
1117 A458 A multi 1.25 1.25

Sold for 50c on day of issue.

Gaart an Heem Agricultural Cooperatives, 75th Anniv. — A459

Gardeners with: 25c, Spade. A, Basket and rake. €2, Watering can.

2003, Sept. 23 ***Perf. 14½x14***
1118-1120 A459 Set of 3 7.00 6.50

No. 1119 sold for 50c on day of issue.

Industrial Products Made in Luxembourg A460

Designs: 60c, Steel. 70c, Medical valve. 80c, Polyester film.

2003, Oct. 1 **Photo.** ***Perf. 11½***
1121-1123 A460 Set of 3 5.00 5.00

Grand Duke Henri Type of 2001-03

Photo. & Engr.

2004-2006 ***Perf. 11¾x11½***

Vignette Color

1126	A438	25c claret	.65	.65
1129	A438	50c black	1.25	1.25
1130	A438	60c blue	1.50	1.50
1131	A438	70c purple	1.75	1.75
1132	A438	80c olive black	2.10	2.00
1133	A438	90c brown	2.25	2.25
1133A	A438	€1 blue	2.60	2.60
	Nos. 1126-1133A (7)		12.10	12.00

Issued: 25c, 50c, 60c, 80c, 3/16/04; 70c, 90c, €1, 9/26/06.

Emigrants to the United States A461

Designs: 50c, Edward Steichen (1879-1973), photographer. 70c, Hugo Gernsbach (1884-1967), science fiction writer.

Photo. & Engr.

2004, Mar. 16 ***Perf. 11½***
1134-1135 A461 Set of 2 3.25 3.00

Anniversaries of Commercial Events A462

Designs: No. 1136, 50c, Commercial Union of Esch-sur-Alzette, cent. No. 1137, 50c, Luxembourg City Annual Street Market, 75th anniv.

2004, Mar. 16 **Litho.** ***Perf. 14¼***
1136-1137 A462 Set of 2 2.60 2.60

Mushrooms — A463

No. 1138: a, Cantharellus tubaeformis. b, Ramaria flava. c, Stropharia cyanea. d, Helvella lacunosa. e, Anthurus archeri. f, Clitopilus prunulus.

Die Cut Perf. 10

2004, Mar. 16 **Litho.**

Self-Adhesive

1138	Booklet pane of 6	4.50	
a.-c.	A463 10c Any single	.25	.25
d.-f.	A463 50c Any single	1.25	1.25
	Complete booklet, 2 #1138	9.00	

European Parliament Elections A464

2004, May 9 **Litho.** ***Perf. 13¼x13***
1139 A464 50c multi 1.25 1.25

2004 Summer Olympics, Athens A465

European Sports Education Year A466

2004, May 9 **Photo.** ***Perf. 11½x11¾***
1140 A465 50c multi 1.25 1.25
1141 A466 60c multi 1.40 1.40

European School, 50th Anniv. A467

2004, May 9 **Litho.** ***Perf. 14¼x14½***
1142 A467 70c multi 1.75 1.75

Europa A468

Designs: 50c, Stone bridge over Schiessentuempel. 60c, Bourscheid Beach, Bourscheid Castle.

2004, May 9 ***Perf. 13¼x13***
1143-1144 A468 Set of 2 *3.00 3.00*

Luxembourg Stock Exchange, 75th Anniv. — A469

Perf. 11¼x11½

2004, Sept. 28 **Litho. & Engr.**
1145 A469 50c multi 1.25 1.25

Food Products Made in Luxembourg — A470

Designs: 35c, Baked goods, beer. 60c, Meats, wine. 70c, Dairy products.

Perf. 13½x13¾

2004, Sept. 28 **Litho.**
1146-1148 A470 Set of 3 4.00 4.00

National Museum of History and Art — A471

Designs: 50c, Museum building. €1.10, Young Woman with a Fan, by Luigi Rubio. €3, Charity, by Lucas Cranach the Elder or Lucas Cranach the Younger.

2004, Sept. 28 **Photo.** ***Perf. 11¾***
1149-1151 A471 Set of 3 11.50 11.50

World War II Liberation, 60th Anniv. A472

2004, Dec. 7 **Litho.** ***Perf. 14x13½***
1152 A472 70c multi 1.90 1.90

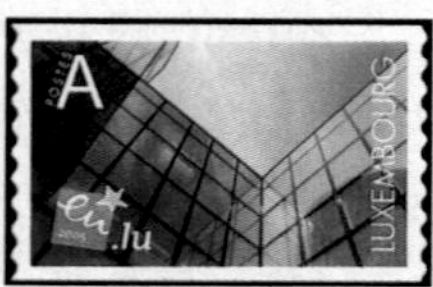

Luxembourg's Presidency of European Union — A473

No. 1153: a, Building with glass facade. b, Arch, Echternach Basilica. c, Vineyard along Moselle River. d, Rusted iron girder.

Serpentine Die Cut 8¼ Vert.

2005, Jan. 25 **Photo.**

Self-Adhesive

1153 Booklet pane of 4 5.00
a.-d. A473 A any single 1.25 1.25
Complete booklet, 2 #1153 10.00

On the day of issue, Nos. 1153a-1153d each had a franking value of 50c, but complete booklet sold for €3.80.

Rotary International, Cent. — A474

2005, Mar. 15 **Litho.** ***Perf. 13½x13***
1154 A474 50c multi 1.40 1.40

Ettelbrück Neuro-psychiatric Medical Center, 150th Anniv. — A475

2005, Mar. 15 ***Perf. 13½***
1155 A475 50c multi 1.40 1.40

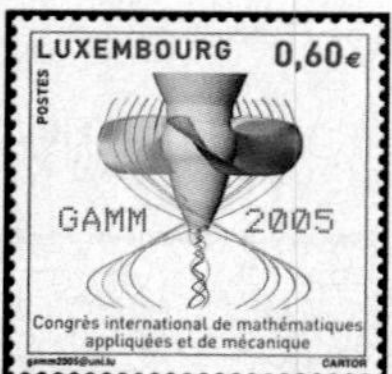

76th Intl. Congress of Applied Mathematics and Mechanics A476

2005, Mar. 15
1156 A476 60c multi 1.60 1.60

Benelux Parliament, 50th Anniv. — A477

2005, Mar. 15 ***Perf. 13¼x12¾***
1157 A477 60c multi 1.60 1.60

Tourism A478

Designs: 50c, Shoe factory, Kayl-Tétange. 60c, Village scene and website address of National Tourist Office (44x31mm). €1, Statue of St. Eloi, Rodange, and foundry worker.

Perf. 14x13¼, 12¾ (60c)

2005, Mar. 15
1158-1160 A478 Set of 3 5.50 5.50

Opening of Grand Duchess Joséphine-Charlotte Concert Hall — A479

2005, May 24 ***Perf. 13¼x13¾***
1161 A479 50c multi 1.25 1.25

Europa A480

Designs: 50c, Judd mat Gaardebounen (pork and beans). 60c, Feirstengszalot (beef, egg and pickle salad).

2005, May 24 ***Perf. 13½***
1162-1163 A480 Set of 2 2.75 2.75

Railways A481

Designs: 50c, Niederpallen Station, CVE 357 car of De Jhangeli narrow-gauge railway. 60c, AL-T3 locomotive. €2.50, PH 408 passenger car.

2005, May 24 **Photo.** ***Perf. 11½***
1164-1166 A481 Set of 3 9.00 9.00

Hand Lifting Self-Adhesive Paper From Backing — A482

Serpentine Die Cut 11x11¼

2005, May 24

Self-Adhesive

Coil Stamps

1167 Vert. strip of 4 2.50
a. A482 25c dark red & multi .60 .60
b. A482 25c red orange & multi .60 .60
c. A482 25c orange & multi .60 .60
d. A482 25c yellow & multi .60 .60
1168 Vert. strip of 4 5.00
a. A482 50c dark green & multi 1.25 1.25
b. A482 50c green & multi 1.25 1.25
c. A482 50c emerald & multi 1.25 1.25
d. A482 50c yellow green & multi 1.25 1.25

Rolls of 100 of the 25c stamps sold for €24, and rolls of 100 of the 50c stamps sold for €48.

Famous People A483

Designs: 50c, Jean-Pierre Pescatore (1793-1855), philanthropist. 90c, Marcel Reuland (1905-56), writer. €1, Marie-Henriette Steil (1898-1930), writer, vert.

Photo. & Engr.

2005, Sept. 27 ***Perf. 11½***
1169-1171 A483 Set of 3 6.00 6.00

Butterflies A484

Designs: 35c, Papilio machaon. 70c, Argynnis paphia, vert. €1.80, Lysandra coridon.

2005, Sept. 27 **Litho.**
1172-1174 A484 Set of 3 7.25 7.25

Rocks A485

No. 1175: a, Schist. b, Rocks with iron (minerai de fer). c, Luxembourg sandstone. d, Conglomerate rocks.

Serpentine Die Cut 12¾ Vert.

2005, Sept. 27

Self-Adhesive

1175 Booklet pane of 4 4.75
a.-d. A485 A Any single 1.10 1.10
Complete booklet, 2 #1175 9.50

The complete booklet sold for €3.80, but each stamp had a franking value of 50c on the day of issue.

Seeing Eye Dog A486

Litho. & Embossed

2005, Dec. 6 ***Perf. 13x13¼***
1176 A486 70c dk blue & lemon 1.75 1.75

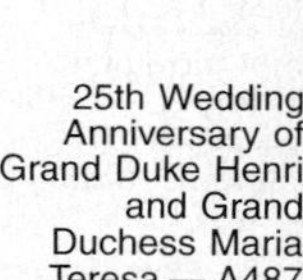

25th Wedding Anniversary of Grand Duke Henri and Grand Duchess Maria Teresa — A487

2006, Feb. 7 **Litho.** ***Perf. 13¼x13¾***
1177 A487 50c multi 1.25 1.25

Souvenir Sheet

Perf. 13¼x13
1178 A487 €2.50 multi 6.25 6.25

No. 1178 contains one 26x37mm stamp.

Blood Donation A488

2006, Mar. 14 **Litho.** ***Perf. 13¼***
1179 A488 50c multi 1.25 1.25

Tourism A489

Designs: No. 1180, 50c, Parc Merveilleux, Bettembourg. No. 1181, 50c, Birelerhaff Pigeon Tower, Sandweiler, vert.

2006, Mar. 14 ***Perf. 11½***
1180-1181 A489 Set of 2 2.40 1.25

Electrification of Railway Network, 50th Anniv. — A490

Designs: 50c, Train passing station. 70c, Train on bridge. €1, Railway workers repairing electrical wires, vert.

2006, Mar. 14 ***Perf. 13¼x13, 13x13¼***
1182-1184 A490 Set of 3 5.25 5.25

Personalized Stamp Website "meng.post.lu" — A491

2006, May 16 **Litho.** ***Perf. 11½***
1185 A491 A multi + label 1.40 1.40

No. 1185 sold for 50c on day of issue. Labels could be personalized for a fee.

Esch-sur-Alzette, Cent. — A492

2006, May 16 ***Perf. 13½***
1186 A492 50c multi 1.40 1.40

Soccer Teams in Luxembourg, Cent. — A493

2006 World Cup Soccer Championships, Germany — A494

2006, May 16 ***Perf. 13x13¼***
1187 A493 50c multi 1.40 1.40
1188 A494 90c multi 2.40 2.40

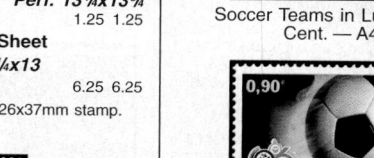

Europa A495

Contest-winning cell phone photos: 50c, Hands making heart. 70c, People holding globe.

2006, May 16 ***Perf. 12½***
1189-1190 A495 Set of 2 3.25 3.25

State Council, 150th Anniv. — A496

Litho. & Embossed

2006, Sept. 26 ***Perf. 13½***
1191 A496 50c multi 1.25 1.25

Luxembourg Chess Federation, 75th Anniv. — A497

2006, Sept. 26
1192 A497 90c multi 2.25 2.25

Bank Sesquicentenaries — A498

Designs: No. 1193, 50c, State Savings Bank (Spuerkeess). No. 1194, 50c, Dexia-BIL Bank.

2006, Sept. 26 **Litho.** ***Perf. 13¼x13***
1193-1194 A498 Set of 2 2.60 2.60

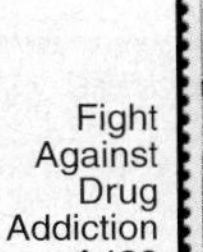

Fight Against Drug Addiction A499

Designs: 50c, Children's drawing of man and "No Drugs" sign. €1, Ashtray with vegetables and cheese, vert.

2006, Sept. 26 ***Perf. 11½***
1195-1196 A499 Set of 2 3.75 3.75

Luxembourg Horticultural Federation, 75th Anniv. — A500

No. 1197: a, Flowers. b, Fruits and vegetables.
Illustration reduced.

2006, Dec. 5 **Litho.** ***Perf. 13¼x13¾***
1197 A500 Horiz. pair 3.75 3.75
a.-b. 70c Either single 1.75 1.75

Luxembourg, 2007 European Cultural Capital — A501

No. 1198 — Silhouettes of deer and men with deer heads with background color of: a, Blue. b, Orange. c, Bright yellow green. d, Red violet.

Serpentine Die Cut 8½ Vert.

2007, Jan. 30 **Litho.**
1198 Booklet pane of 4 5.25
a.-d. A501 A Any single 1.25 1.25
Complete booklet, 2 #1198 10.50

Nos. 1198a-1198d each sold for 50c on day of issue.

Luxembourg Caritas, 75th Anniv. A502

2007, Mar. 20 **Litho.** ***Perf. 11½***
1199 A502 50c multi 1.40 1.40

Luxembourg Automobile Club, 75th Anniv. A503

2007, Mar. 20
1200 A503 50c multi 1.40 1.40

Treaty of Rome, 50th Anniv. A504

Designs: 70c, Delegates. €1, Text and stars.

2007, Mar. 20 ***Perf. 13x13¼***
1201-1202 A504 Set of 2 4.75 4.75

"Postes" A505

Denomination A506

Serpentine Die Cut 11x11¼

2007, Mar. 20 **Photo.**

Self-Adhesive

Coil Stamps

1203 A505 25c pur & multi .70 .70
1204 A506 25c brn & multi .70 .70
1205 A505 25c dk bl & multi .70 .70
1206 A506 25c dk grn & multi .70 .70
a. Vert. strip of 4, #1203-1206 2.80
1207 A505 50c red vio & multi 1.40 1.40
1208 A506 50c red & multi 1.40 1.40
1209 A505 50c bl & multi 1.40 1.40
1210 A506 50c grn & multi 1.40 1.40
a. Vert. strip of 4, #1207-1210 5.60
Nos. 1203-1210 (8) 8.40 8.40

Europa A507

Designs: 50c, Scout campground. 70c, Scouts, globe, knot.

2007, May 22 **Litho.** ***Perf. 13x13¼***
1211-1212 A507 Set of 2 3.25 3.25

Scouting, cent.

Town Centenaries — A508

Designs: No. 1213, 50c, Differdange. No. 1214, 50c, Dudelenge. No. 1215, 50c, Ettelbruck. No. 1216, 50c, Rumelange.

2007, May 22 **Photo.** ***Perf. 11½***
1213-1216 A508 Set of 4 5.50 5.50

Places of Culture A509

Designs: 50c, Rockhal. 70c, Grand Duke Jean Museum of Modern Art. €1, Neumünster Abbey.

2007, May 22 ***Perf. 12½***
1217-1219 A509 Set of 3 6.00 6.00

"Transborderism" A510

2007, Sept. 3 **Photo.** ***Perf. 11½***
1220 A510 50c multi 1.40 1.40

Rotunda of Luxembourg Train Station — A511

2007, Sept. 3 **Photo. & Engr.**
1221 A511 70c multi 1.90 1.90

See Belgium No. 2253.

Casa Luxemburg, Sibiu, Romania — A512

2007, Sept. 3 **Litho.** ***Perf. 13x13¼***
1222 A512 70c multi 1.90 1.90

See Romania Nos. 4993-4994.

Luxembourg Army Peace-keeping Missions — A513

2007, Sept. 3 **Photo.** ***Perf. 11½***
1223 A513 70c multi 1.90 1.90

Souvenir Sheet

Roman Mosaic, Vichten — A514

No. 1224: a, Thalia and Euterpe. b, Terpsichore and Melpomene. c, Clio and Urania. d, Polymnia and Erato. e, Calliope and Homer. Nos. 1224a-1224d are 58x29mm octagonal stamps, No. 1224e is a 55x55mm diamond-shaped stamp.

2007, Sept. 3 **Litho.** ***Perf. 14¼***
1224 A514 Sheet of 5 8.25 8.25
a.-d. 50c Any single 1.40 1.40
e. €1 multi 2.60 2.60

Esch-sur-Sure Dam — A515

Uewersauer Stauséi — A516

Serpentine Die Cut 12½x13½

2007, Dec. 4 **Litho.**

Self-Adhesive

1225 Horiz. pair 4.25
a. A515 70c multi 2.10 2.10
b. A516 70c multi 2.10 2.10

St. Willibrord (658-739) A517

2008, Mar. 18 **Litho.** ***Perf. 13***
1226 A517 50c multi 1.60 1.60

European Investment Bank, 50th Anniv. A518

2008, Mar. 18 ***Perf. 13x13¼***

1227 A518 70c purple & silver 2.25 2.25

Eurosystem, 10th Anniv. — A519

2008, Mar. 18 ***Perf. 13½x13¾***

1228 A519 €1 multi 3.25 3.25

Luxembourg Philharmonic Orchestra, 75th Anniv. — A520

Henri Pensis (1900-58), Conductor — A521

2008, Mar. 18

1229 A520 50c multi 1.60 1.60
1230 A521 70c multi 2.25 2.25

2008 Summer Olympics, Beijing A522

2008, May 20 **Litho.** ***Perf. 14x13½***

1231 A522 70c multi 2.25 2.25

Luxembourg Basketball Federation, 75th Anniv. — A523

Luxembourg Soccer Federation, Cent. — A524

2008, May 20 ***Perf. 12½***

1232 A523 A multi 1.60 1.60
1233 A524 A multi 1.60 1.60

Nos. 1232 and 1233 each sold for 50c on day of issue.

Europa A525

Smiling letter with wings: 50c, Standing on hand. 70c, Flying.

2008, May 20

1234-1235 A525 Set of 2 4.00 4.00

Tourism A526

Designs: No. 1236, A, Bridge, Diekirch, and city arms. No. 1237, A, Building, Leudelange, and city arms. No. 1238, A, Rindschleiden Church, Wahl, vert.

2008, May 20 ***Perf. 11½***

1236-1238 A526 Set of 3 4.75 4.75

Diekirch, 125th anniv., Leudelange, 150th anniv. Nos. 1236-1238 each sold for 50c on day of issue.

Medico-social League, Cent. — A527

2008, Sept. 30 **Litho.** ***Perf. 13¾***

1239 A527 A multi 1.40 1.40

Sold for 50c on day of issue.

Agricultural Technical School, Ettelbruck, 125th Anniv. A528

2008, Sept. 30

1240 A528 A multi 1.40 1.40

Sold for 50c on day of issue.

Federation of Popular Education Associations, Cent. — A529

2008, Sept. 30 ***Perf. 13x13¼***

1241 A529 A multi 1.40 1.40

Sold for 50c on day of issue.

Natl. League for the Protection of Animals, Cent. A530

2008, Sept. 30

1242 A530 A multi 1.40 1.40

Sold for 50c on day of issue.

NATO Maintenance and Supply Agency, 50th Anniv. — A531

2008, Sept. 30

1243 A531 70c multi 2.00 2.00

Greetings A532

Winning art from children's stamp design contest by: 70c, A. Wainer. €1, S. Rauschenberger.

2008, Sept. 30 ***Perf. 11½***

1244-1245 A532 Set of 2 4.75 4.75

A533 A534

Different shapes of colored background lines with "ATR" at: No. 1246, LR. No. 1247, UL. No. 1248, LL. No. 1249, UR.

Different shapes of colored background lines with "A" at: No. 1250, LL. No. 1251, UL. No. 1252, LR. No. 1253, UR.

Serpentine Die Cut 11

2008, Sept. 30

Coil Stamps

Self-Adhesive

1246 A533 ATR blue .70 .70
1247 A533 ATR purple .70 .70
1248 A533 ATR green .70 .70
1249 A533 ATR red .70 .70
a. Vert. strip of 4, #1246-1249 2.80
1250 A534 A multi 1.40 1.40
1251 A534 A multi 1.40 1.40
1252 A534 A multi 1.40 1.40
1253 A534 A multi 1.40 1.40
a. Vert. strip of 4, #1250-1253 5.60
Nos. 1246-1253 (8) 8.40 8.40

On day of issue, Nos. 1246-1249 each sold for 25c, Nos. 1250-1253, for 50c.

Happiness — A535

No. 1254: a, Bowling pins, denomination over red violet. b, Gift, denomination over yellow green. c, Wrapped candies, denomination over green. d, Wrapped candies, denomination over blue. e, Gift, denomination over green. f, Bowling pins, denomination over yellow green. g, Dice, "A" over red violet. h, Drum and sticks, "A" over yellow green. i, Four-leaf clovers, "A" over green. j, Four-leaf clovers, "A" over blue. k, Drum and sticks, "A" over green. l, Dice, "A" over yellow green.

Die Cut Perf. 10 on 3 Sides

2008, Sept. 30

Self-Adhesive

1254 Booklet pane of 12 12.00
a.-f. A535 20c Any single .55 .55
g.-l. A535 A Any single 1.40 1.40

Nos. 1254g-1254l each sold for 50c on day of issue.

New Courthouse of Court of Justice of the European Communities — A536

2008, Dec. 2 **Litho.** ***Perf. 14x13¼***

1255 A536 70c multi 1.90 1.90

Election of Holy Roman Emperor Henry VII (c. 1269-1313), 700th Anniv. — A537

2008, Dec. 2 ***Perf. 13¼x13***

1256 A537 €1 multi 2.60 2.60

Introduction of the Euro, 10th Anniv. — A538

2009, Mar. 17 **Litho.** ***Perf. 12½***

1257 A538 A multi 1.25 1.25

No. 1257 sold for 50c on day of issue.

Luxembourg Aero Club, Cent. — A539

New Airport Terminal A540

No. 1258: a, Satellite, airplane, hang glider, left half of balloon. b, Right half of balloon, glider, parachutist, jet plane.

Illustration A539 reduced.

2009, Mar. 17 ***Perf. 11½***

1258 A539 50c Horiz. pair, #a-b 2.60 2.60
1259 A540 90c multi 2.25 2.25

Natl. Federation of Fire Fighters, 125th Anniv. A541

Designs: 20c, Modern fire truck. A, Fire fighter rescuing child. €2, Antique fire truck.

2008, Mar. 17 ***Perf. 13x13¼***

1260-1262 A541 Set of 3 7.00 7.00

No. 1261 sold for 50c on day of issue.

Postmen's Federation, Cent. A542

General Confederation of the Civil Service, Cent. — A543

Natl. Federation of Railroad and Transportation Workers, Cent. — A544

2009, Mar. 17 *Perf. 14x13¼*

1263 A542 50c multi 1.25 1.25
1264 A543 A multi 1.25 1.25
1265 A544 A multi 1.25 1.25
Nos. 1263-1265 (3) 3.75 3.75

On day of issue, Nos. 1264-1265 each sold for 50c.

SEMI-POSTAL STAMPS

Clervaux Monastery SP1

Designs: 15c+10c, View of Pfaffenthal. 25c+10c, View of Luxembourg.

Engr.; Surcharge Typo. in Red

1921, Aug. 2 **Unwmk.** *Perf. 11½*

B1 SP1 10c + 5c green .20 *4.50*
B2 SP1 15c + 10c org red .20 *5.75*
B3 SP1 25c + 10c dp grn .20 *4.50*
Nos. B1-B3 (3) .60 *14.75*
Set, never hinged 2.25

The amount received from the surtax on these stamps was added to a fund for the erection of a monument to the soldiers from Luxembourg who died in World War I.

Nos. B1-B3 with Additional Surcharge in Red or Black

1923, May 27

B4 SP1 25c on #B1 (R) 1.10 *14.50*
B5 SP1 25c on #B2 1.10 *17.50*
B6 SP1 25c on #B3 1.10 *14.50*
Nos. B4-B6 (3) 3.30 *46.50*
Set, never hinged 8.75

Unveiling of the monument to the soldiers who died in World War I.

Regular Issue of 1914-15 Surcharged in Black or Red

1924, Apr. 17 *Perf. 11½x11*

B7 A11 12½c + 7½c grn .20 *2.75*
B8 A11 35c + 10c dk bl (R) .20 *2.75*
B9 A11 2½fr + 1fr red 1.10 *27.50*
B10 A11 5fr + 2fr dk vio .55 *17.50*
Nos. B7-B10 (4) 2.05 *50.50*
Set, never hinged 3.50

Nurse and Patient SP4

Prince Jean SP5

1925, Dec. 21 **Litho.** *Perf. 13*

B11 SP4 5c (+ 5c) dl vio .20 .70
B12 SP4 30c (+ 5c) org .20 3.00
B13 SP4 50c (+ 5c) red brn .20 *5.50*
B14 SP4 1fr (+ 10c) dp bl .40 *14.00*
Nos. B11-B14 (4) 1.00 *23.20*
Set, never hinged 1.75

1926, Dec. 15 **Photo.** *Perf. 12½x12*

B15 SP5 5c (+ 5c) vio & blk .20 .55
B16 SP5 40c (+ 10) grn & blk .20 .90
B17 SP5 50c (+ 15c) lem & blk .20 .95
B18 SP5 75c (+ 20c) lt red & blk .25 *11.00*
B19 SP5 1.50fr (+ 30c) gray bl & blk .35 *12.00*
Nos. B15-B19 (5) 1.20 *25.40*
Set, never hinged 2.50

Grand Duchess Charlotte and Prince Felix — SP6

1927, Sept. 4 **Engr.** *Perf. 11½*

B20 SP6 25c dp vio 1.10 *10.00*
B21 SP6 50c green 1.50 *16.00*
B22 SP6 75c rose lake 1.10 *10.00*
B23 SP6 1fr gray blk 1.10 *10.00*
B24 SP6 1½fr dp bl 1.10 *10.00*
Nos. B20-B24 (5) 5.90 *56.00*
Set, never hinged 17.00

Introduction of postage stamps in Luxembourg, 75th anniv. These stamps were sold exclusively at the Luxembourg Philatelic Exhibition, September 4-8, 1927, at a premium of 3 francs per set, which was donated to the exhibition funds.

Princess Elisabeth SP7

Princess Marie Adelaide SP8

1927, Dec. 1 **Photo.** *Perf. 12½*

B25 SP7 10c (+ 5c) turq bl & blk .20 *.55*
B26 SP7 50c (+ 10c) dk brn & blk .20 *.95*
B27 SP7 75c (+ 20c) org & blk .20 *1.50*
B28 SP7 1fr (+ 30c) brn lake & blk .25 *11.00*
B29 SP7 1½fr (+ 50c) ultra & blk .20 *11.00*
Nos. B25-B29 (5) 1.05 *25.00*
Set, never hinged 2.25

The surtax was for Child Welfare societies.

1928, Dec. 12 *Perf. 12½x12*

B30 SP8 10c (+ 5c) ol grn & brn vio .20 *1.10*
B31 SP8 60c (+ 10c) brn & ol grn .40 *2.75*
B32 SP8 75c (+ 15c) vio rose & bl grn .70 *7.25*
B33 SP8 1fr (+ 25c) dk grn & brn 1.75 *22.50*
B34 SP8 1½fr (+ 50c) cit & bl 1.75 *22.50*
Nos. B30-B34 (5) 4.80 *56.10*
Set, never hinged 11.00

Princess Marie Gabrielle SP9

Prince Charles SP10

1929, Dec. 14 *Perf. 13*

B35 SP9 10c (+ 10c) mar & dp grn .20 *1.10*
B36 SP9 35c (+ 15c) dk grn & red brn 1.50 *7.25*
B37 SP9 75c (+ 30c) ver & blk 1.75 *9.00*
B38 SP9 1¼fr (+ 50c) mag & bl grn 2.25 *22.50*
B39 SP9 1¾fr (+ 75c) Prus bl & sl 2.75 *27.50*
Nos. B35-B39 (5) 8.45 *67.35*
Set, never hinged 20.00

The surtax was for Child Welfare societies.

1930, Dec. 10 *Perf. 12½*

B40 SP10 10c (+ 5c) bl grn & ol brn .20 1.10
B41 SP10 75c (+ 10c) vio brn & bl grn 1.10 *4.75*
B42 SP10 1fr (+ 25c) car rose & vio 2.50 *17.50*
B43 SP10 1¼fr (+ 75c) ol bis & dk brn 4.00 *22.50*
B44 SP10 1¾fr (+ 1.50fr) ultra & red brn 4.50 *22.50*
Nos. B40-B44 (5) 12.30 *68.35*
Set, never hinged 50.00

The surtax was for Child Welfare societies.

Princess Alix SP11

Countess Ermesinde SP12

1931, Dec. 10

B45 SP11 10c (+ 5c) brn org & gray .40 1.10
B46 SP11 75c (+ 10c) claret & bl grn 4.00 *14.50*
B47 SP11 1fr (+ 25c) dp grn & gray 7.25 *29.00*
B48 SP11 1¼fr (+ 75c) dk vio & bl grn 7.25 *29.00*
B49 SP11 1¾fr (+ 1.50fr) bl & gray 11.00 *55.00*
Nos. B45-B49 (5) 29.90 *128.60*
Set, never hinged 110.00

The surtax was for Child Welfare societies.

1932, Dec. 8

B50 SP12 10c (+ 5c) ol bis .40 1.10
B51 SP12 75c (+ 10c) dp vio 2.75 *14.50*
B52 SP12 1fr (+ 25c) scar 11.00 *32.50*
B53 SP12 1¼fr (+ 75c) red brn 11.00 *32.50*
B54 SP12 1¾fr (+ 1.50fr) dp bl 11.00 *32.50*
Nos. B50-B54 (5) 36.15 *113.10*
Set, never hinged 92.50

The surtax was for Child Welfare societies.

Count Henry VII — SP13

John the Blind — SP14

1933, Dec. 12

B55 SP13 10c (+ 5c) yel brn .40 1.10
B56 SP13 75c (+ 10c) dp vio 4.75 *14.50*
B57 SP13 1fr (+ 25c) car rose 11.00 *35.00*
B58 SP13 1¼fr (+ 75c) org brn 14.50 *47.50*
B59 SP13 1¾fr (+ 1.50fr) brt bl 14.50 *50.00*
Nos. B55-B59 (5) 45.15 *148.10*
Set, never hinged 125.00

1934, Dec. 5

B60 SP14 10c (+ 5c) dk vio .20 1.10
B61 SP14 35c (+ 10c) dp grn 2.50 *9.00*
B62 SP14 75c (+ 15c) rose lake 2.50 *9.00*
B63 SP14 1fr (+ 25c) dp rose 14.50 *47.50*
B64 SP14 1¼fr (+ 75c) org 14.50 *47.50*
B65 SP14 1¾fr (+ 1.50fr) brt bl 14.50 *47.50*
Nos. B60-B65 (6) 48.70 *161.60*
Set, never hinged 125.00

Teacher SP15

Sculptor and Painter — SP16

Journalist SP17

Engineer SP18

Scientist SP19

Lawyer — SP20

Savings Bank and Adolphe Bridge — SP21

Surgeon SP22

1935, May 1 **Unwmk.** *Perf. 12½*

B65A SP15 5c violet .20 *1.10*
B65B SP16 10c brn red .25 *1.10*
B65C SP17 15c olive .40 *1.75*
B65D SP18 20c orange .55 *3.50*
B65E SP19 35c yel grn .70 *3.25*
B65F SP20 50c gray blk .95 *4.75*
B65G SP21 70c dk green 1.40 *5.50*
B65H SP22 1fr car red 1.75 *7.25*
B65J SP19 1.25fr turq 7.25 *50.00*

B65K SP18 1.75fr blue 9.00 *52.50*
B65L SP16 2fr lt brown 27.50 *110.00*
B65M SP17 3fr dk brown 37.50 *150.00*
B65N SP20 5fr lt blue 65.00 *275.00*
B65P SP15 10fr red vio 160.00 *450.00*
B65Q SP22 20fr dk green 175.00 *550.00*
Nos. B65A-B65Q (15) 487.45 *1,665.*
Set, never hinged 1,000.

Sold at double face, surtax going to intl. fund to aid professional people.

Philatelic Exhibition Issue

Type of Regular Issue of 1928

Wmk. 246

1935, Aug. 15 Engr. *Imperf.*
B66 A19 2fr (+ 50c) blk 4.75 *16.00*
Never hinged 13.00

Philatelic exhibition held at Esch-sur-Alzette.

Charles I — SP23

Perf. 11½

1935, Dec. 2 Photo. Unwmk.
B67 SP23 10c (+ 5c) vio .20 .40
B68 SP23 35c (+ 10c) grn .40 *.55*
B69 SP23 70c (+ 20c) dk brn .95 *1.50*
B70 SP23 1fr (+ 25c) rose lake 14.50 *37.50*
B71 SP23 1.25fr (+ 75c) org brn 14.50 *37.50*
B72 SP23 1.75fr (+ 1.50fr) bl 14.50 *47.50*
Nos. B67-B72 (6) 45.05 *124.95*
Set, never hinged 110.00

Wenceslas I, Duke of Luxembourg — SP24

1936, Dec. 1 *Perf. 11½x13*
B73 SP24 10c + 5(c) blk brn .20 .25
B74 SP24 35c + 10(c) bl grn .20 *.55*
B75 SP24 70c + 20(c) blk .40 *.90*
B76 SP24 1fr + 25(c) rose car 2.50 *14.50*
B77 SP24 1.25fr + 75(c) vio 2.25 *29.00*
B78 SP24 1.75fr + 1.50(fr) saph 1.60 *17.50*
Nos. B73-B78 (6) 7.15 *62.70*
Set, never hinged 32.50

Wenceslas II — SP25

1937, Dec. 1 *Perf. 11½x12½*
B79 SP25 10c + 5c car & blk .20 .40
B80 SP25 35c + 10c red vio & grn .20 .55
B81 SP25 70c + 20c ultra & red brn .25 .55
B82 SP25 1fr + 25c dk grn & scar 1.60 *17.00*
B83 SP25 1.25fr + 75c dk brn & vio 2.25 *17.00*
B84 SP25 1.75fr + 1.50fr blk & ultra 2.75 *17.50*
Nos. B79-B84 (6) 7.25 *53.00*
Set, never hinged 17.50

Souvenir Sheet

SP26

Wmk. 110

1937, July 25 Engr. *Perf. 13*
B85 SP26 Sheet of 2 4.00 *11.50*
Never hinged 11.00
a. 2fr red brown, single stamp 1.50 *5.50*

National Philatelic Exposition at Dudelange on July 25-26.

Sold for 5fr per sheet, of which 1fr was for the aid of the exposition.

Portrait of St. Willibrord — SP28

St. Willibrord, after a Miniature SP29

Abbey at Echternach — SP30

Designs: No, B87, The Rathaus at Echternach. No. B88, Pavilion in Abbey Park, Echternach. No. B91, Dancing Procession in Honor of St. Willibrord.

Perf. 14x13, 13x14

1938, June 5 Engr. Unwmk.
B86 SP28 35c + 10c dk bl grn .40 *.55*
B87 SP28 70c + 10c ol gray .70 *.55*
B88 SP28 1.25fr + 25c brn car 1.50 *2.50*
B89 SP29 1.75fr + 50c sl bl 2.50 *2.75*
B90 SP30 3fr + 2fr vio brn 5.50 *9.00*
B91 SP30 5fr + 5fr dk vio 6.50 *7.25*
Nos. B86-B91 (6) 17.10 22.60
Set, never hinged 60.00

12th centenary of the death of St. Willibrord. The surtax was used for the restoration of the ancient Abbey at Echternach.

Duke Sigismond SP32

Prince Jean SP33

1938, Dec. 1 Photo. *Perf. 11½*
B92 SP32 10c + 5c lil & blk .20 .40
B93 SP32 35c + 10c grn & blk .20 .55
B94 SP32 70c + 20c buff & blk .25 *.55*
B95 SP32 1fr + 25c red org & blk 1.90 *14.50*
B96 SP32 1.25fr + 75c gray bl & blk 1.90 *14.50*
B97 SP32 1.75fr + 1.50fr bl & blk 3.25 *22.50*
Nos. B92-B97 (6) 7.70 *53.00*
Set, never hinged 22.50

1939, Dec. 1 Litho. *Perf. 14x13*

Designs: Nos. B99, B102, Prince Felix. Nos. B100, B103, Grand Duchess Charlotte.

B98 SP33 10c + 5c red brn, *buff* .20 .40
B99 SP33 35c + 10c sl grn, *buff* .20 1.10
B100 SP33 70c + 20c blk, *buff* .95 *1.50*
B101 SP33 1fr + 25c red org, *buff* 4.00 *32.50*
B102 SP33 1.25fr + 75c vio brn, *buff* 4.75 *50.00*
B103 SP33 1.75fr + 1.50fr lt bl, *buff* 5.50 *65.00*
Nos. B98-B103 (6) 15.60 *150.50*
Set, never hinged 45.00

See No. 217 (souvenir sheet).

Allegory of Medicinal Baths — SP36

1940, Mar. 1 Photo. *Perf. 11½*
B104 SP36 2fr + 50c gray, blk & slate grn 1.10 *20.00*
Never hinged 4.00

Stamps of 1944, type A37, surcharged "+50C," "+5F" or "+15F" in black, were sold only in canceled condition, affixed to numbered folders. The surtax was for the benefit of Luxembourg evacuees. Value for folder, $15.

Homage to France SP37

Thanks to: No. B118, USSR. No. B119, Britannia. No. B120, America.

1945, Mar. 1 Engr. *Perf. 13*
B117 SP37 60c + 1.40fr dp grn .20 .20
B118 SP37 1.20fr + 1.80fr red .20 .20
B119 SP37 2.50fr + 3.50fr dp bl .20 .20
B120 SP37 4.20fr + 4.80fr dp vio .20 .20
Nos. B117-B120 (4) .80 .80
Set, never hinged .95

Issued to honor the Allied Nations. Exist imperf. Value, set $60.

Statue Carried in Procession SP41

Statue of Our Lady "Patrona Civitatis" SP42

"Our Lady of Luxembourg" SP43

Cathedral Façade SP44

Altar with Statue of Madonna — SP45

1945, June 4
B121 SP41 60c + 40c grn .20 1.10
B122 SP42 1.20fr + 80c red .20 1.10
B123 SP43 2.50fr + 2.50fr dp bl .20 *5.50*
B124 SP44 5.50fr + 6.50fr dk vio .65 *77.50*
B125 SP45 20fr + 20fr choc .65 *80.00*
Nos. B121-B125 (5) 1.90 *165.20*
Set, never hinged 4.00

Exist imperf. Value, set $250.

Souvenir Sheet

"Our Lady of Luxembourg" — SP46

1945, Sept. 30 Engr. *Imperf.*
B126 SP46 50fr + 50fr blk 1.10 *55.00*
Never hinged 2.10

Young Fighters — SP47

Refugee Mother and Children — SP48

Political Prisoner — SP49 Executed Civilian — SP50

1945, Dec. 20 Photo. *Perf. 11½*

B127 SP47 20c + 30c sl grn & buff .20 *1.10*
B128 SP48 1.50fr + 1fr brn red & buff .20 *1.10*
B129 SP49 3.50fr + 3.50fr bl, dp bl & buff .20 *10.50*
B130 SP50 5fr + 10fr brn, dk brn & buff .20 *10.50*
Nos. B127-B130 (4) .80 *23.20*
Set, never hinged 1.40

Souvenir Sheet

1946, Jan. 30 Unwmk. *Perf. 11½*

B131 Sheet of 4 8.75 *300.00*
Never hinged 25.00
a. SP47 2.50fr + 2.50fr sl grn & buff 2.25 *50.00*
b. SP48 3.50fr + 6.50fr brown red & buff 2.25 *50.00*
c. SP49 5fr + 15fr bl, dp bl & buff 2.25 *50.00*
d. SP50 20fr + 20fr brown, dark brown & buff 2.25 *50.00*

Tribute to Luxembourg's heroes and martyrs.
The surtax was for the National Welfare Fund.

Souvenir Sheet

Old Rolling Mill, Dudelange — SP52

1946, July 28 Engr. & Typo.

B132 SP52 50fr brn & dk bl, *buff* 5.50 *35.00*
Never hinged 13.00

National Postage Stamp Exhibition, Dudelange, July 28-29, 1946. The sheets sold for 55fr.

Jean l'Aveugle — SP53

1946, Dec. 5 Photo.

B133 SP53 60c + 40c dk grn .20 *1.75*
B134 SP53 1.50fr + 50c brn red .20 *3.00*
B135 SP53 3.50fr + 3.50fr dp bl .60 *27.50*
B136 SP53 5fr + 10fr sepia .40 *22.50*
Nos. B133-B136 (4) 1.40 *54.75*
Set, never hinged 2.50

600th anniv. of the death of Jean l'Aveugle (John the Blind), Count of Luxembourg.

Ruins of St. Willibrord Basilica — SP54

Twelfth Century Miniature of St. Willibrord SP59

Designs: #B138, Statue of Abbot Jean Bertels. #B139, Emblem of Echternach Abbey. #B140, Ruins of the Basilica's Interior. #B141, St. Irmine and Pepin of Hersta Holding Model of the Abbey.

Perf. 13x14, 14x13

1947, May 25 Engr.

B137 SP54 20c + 10c blk .20 .25
B138 SP54 60c + 10c dk grn .40 .55
B139 SP54 75c + 25c dk car .55 .75
B140 SP54 1.50fr + 50c dk brn .70 .75
B141 SP54 3.50fr + 2.50fr dk bl 2.25 *4.75*
B142 SP59 25fr + 25fr dk pur 15.00 *25.00*
Nos. B137-B142 (6) 19.10 *32.05*
Set, never hinged 50.00

The surtax was to aid in restoring the Basilica of Saint Willibrord at Echternach.

Michel Lentz — SP60

Edmond de La Fontaine (Dicks) — SP61

1947, Dec. 4 Photo. *Perf. 11½*

B143 SP60 60c + 40c sep & buff .25 1.10
B144 SP60 1.50fr + 50c dp plum & buff .25 1.10
B145 SP60 3.50fr + 3.50fr dp bl & gray 2.75 *17.50*
B146 SP60 10fr + 5fr dk grn & gray 2.40 *17.50*
Nos. B143-B146 (4) 5.65 *37.20*
Set, never hinged 17.00

1948, Nov. 18

B147 SP61 60c + 40c brn & pale bis .25 .95
B148 SP61 1.50fr + 50c brn car & buff .45 .95
B149 SP61 3.50fr + 3.50fr dp bl & gray 5.50 *19.00*
B150 SP61 10fr + 5fr dk grn & gray 4.50 *19.00*
Nos. B147-B150 (4) 10.70 *39.90*
Set, never hinged 19.00

125th anniversary of the birth of Edmond de La Fontaine, poet and composer.

Type of Regular Issue of 1948
Souvenir Sheet

1949, Jan. 8 Unwmk. *Perf. 11½*

B151 Sheet of 3 50.00 55.00
Never hinged 100.00
a. A45 8fr + 3fr blue gray 14.00 17.00
b. A45 12fr + 5fr green 14.00 17.00
c. A45 15fr + 7fr brown 14.00 17.00

30th anniversary of Grand Duchess Charlotte's ascension to the throne. Border and dates "1919-1949" in gray.

Michel Rodange — SP62

1949, Dec. 5

B152 SP62 60c + 40c ol grn & gray .40 .55
B153 SP62 2fr + 1fr dk vio & rose 2.75 *5.00*
B154 SP62 4fr + 2fr sl blk & gray 4.50 *7.50*
B155 SP62 10fr + 5fr brn & buff 4.50 *17.50*
Nos. B152-B155 (4) 12.15 *30.55*
Set, never hinged 22.50

Wards of the Nation
SP63 SP64

1950, June 24 Engr. *Perf. 12½x12*

B156 SP63 60c + 15c dk sl bl 1.25 1.50
B157 SP64 1fr + 20c dk car rose 3.25 1.50
B158 SP63 2fr + 30c red brn 2.25 1.50
B159 SP64 4fr + 75c dk bl 7.50 *17.00*
B160 SP63 8fr + 3fr blk 21.00 *45.00*
B161 SP64 10fr + 5fr lil rose 22.50 *45.00*
Nos. B156-B161 (6) 57.75 *111.50*
Set, never hinged 90.00

The surtax was for child welfare.

Jean A. Zinnen SP65

Laurent Menager SP66

1950, Dec. 5 Photo. *Perf. 11½*

B162 SP65 60c + 10c ind & gray .35 .25
B163 SP65 2fr + 15c cer & buff .35 .40
B164 SP65 4fr + 15c vio bl & bl gray 3.25 *6.50*
B165 SP65 8fr + 5fr dk brn & buff 9.25 *25.00*
Nos. B162-B165 (4) 13.20 *32.15*
Set, never hinged 27.50

1951, Dec. 5

Gray Background

B166 SP66 60c + 10c sepia .25 .40
B167 SP66 2fr + 15c dl ol grn .25 .40
B168 SP66 4fr + 15c blue 2.50 *4.00*
B169 SP66 8fr + 5fr vio brn 10.50 *30.00*
Nos. B166-B169 (4) 13.50 *34.80*
Set, never hinged 29.00

50th anniversary of the death of Laurent Menager, composer.

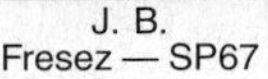

J. B. Fresez — SP67

Candlemas Singing — SP68

1952, Dec. 3

B170 SP67 60c + 15c dk bl grn & pale bl .25 .40
B171 SP67 2fr + 25c chnt brn & buff .25 .40
B172 SP67 4fr + 25c dk vio bl & gray 1.90 *4.00*
B173 SP67 8fr + 4.75fr dp plum & lil gray 13.00 *35.00*
Nos. B170-B173 (4) 15.40 *39.80*
Set, never hinged 32.50

1953, Dec. 3

Designs: 80c+20c, 4fr+50c, Procession with ratchets. 1.20fr+30c, 7fr+3.35fr, Breaking Easter eggs.

B174 SP68 25c + 15c red org & dp car .25 .40
B175 SP68 80c + 20c vio brn & bl gray .25 .40
B176 SP68 1.20fr + 30c bl grn & ol grn .50 .95
B177 SP68 2fr + 25c brn car & brn .40 .40
B178 SP68 4fr + 50c grnsh bl & vio bl 3.00 *9.00*
B179 SP68 7fr + 3.35fr vio & pur 9.00 *22.50*
Nos. B174-B179 (6) 13.40 *33.65*
Set, never hinged 27.50

The surtax was for the National Welfare Fund of Grand Duchess Charlotte.

Clay Censer and Whistle — SP69

Toys for St. Nicholas Day — SP70

Designs: 80c+20c, 4fr+50c, Sheep and bass drum. 1.20fr+30c, 7fr+3.45fr, Merry-go-round horses. 2fr+25c, As No. B180.

1954, Dec. 3

B180 SP69 25c + 5c car lake & cop brn .25 .55
B181 SP69 80c + 20c dk gray .25 .55
B182 SP69 1.20fr + 30c dk bl grn & cr .60 1.90
B183 SP69 2fr + 25c brn & ocher .35 .55
B184 SP69 4fr + 50c brt bl 3.00 *6.50*
B185 SP69 7fr + 3.45fr pur 8.75 *25.00*
Nos. B180-B185 (6) 13.20 *35.05*
Set, never hinged 32.50

1955, Dec. 5 Unwmk. *Perf. 11½*

Designs: 80c+20c, 4fr+50c, Christ child and lamb (Christmas). 1.20fr+30c, 7fr+3.45fr, Star, crown and cake (Epiphany).

B186 SP70 25c + 5c sal & dk car .20 .40
B187 SP70 80c + 20c gray & gray blk .20 .40
B188 SP70 1.20fr + 30c ol grn & sl grn .35 .95
B189 SP70 2fr + 25c buff & dk brn .40 .40
B190 SP70 4fr + 50c lt bl & brt bl 3.25 *11.00*
B191 SP70 7fr + 3.45fr rose vio & claret 6.50 *15.00*
Nos. B186-B191 (6) 10.90 *28.15*
Set, never hinged 22.50

Arms of Echternach — SP71

Arms: 80c+20c, 4fr+50c, Esch-sur-Alzette. 1.20fr+30c, 7fr+3.45fr, Grevenmacher.

1956, Dec. 5 Photo.

Arms in Original Colors

B192 SP71 25c + 5c blk & sal pink .20 .40
B193 SP71 80c + 20c ultra & yel .20 .40
B194 SP71 1.20fr + 30c ultra & gray .20 1.10
B195 SP71 2fr + 25c blk & buff .20 .40
B196 SP71 4fr + 50c ultra & lt bl 1.90 *5.50*
B197 SP71 7fr + 3.45fr ultra & pale vio 3.50 *11.50*
Nos. B192-B197 (6) 6.20 *19.30*
Set, never hinged 14.50

1957, Dec. 4 Unwmk. *Perf. 11½*

25c+5c, 2fr+25c, Luxembourg. 80c+20c, 4fr+50c, Mersch. 1.20fr+30c, 7fr+3.45fr, Vianden.

Arms in Original Colors

B198 SP71 25c + 5c ultra & org .20 *.40*
B199 SP71 80c + 20c blk & lem .20 *.40*
B200 SP71 1.20fr + 30c ultra & lt bl grn .20 *.70*

B201 SP71 2fr + 25c ultra & pale brn .20 *.40*
B202 SP71 4fr + 50c blk & pale vio bl .50 *5.50*
B203 SP71 7fr + 3.45fr ultra & rose lil 3.25 *8.00*
Nos. B198-B203 (6) 4.55 15.40
Set, never hinged 11.00

1958, Dec. 3 ***Perf. 11½***

30c+10c, 2.50fr+50c, Capellen. 1fr+25c, 5fr+50c, Diekirch. 1.50fr+25c, 8.50fr+4.60fr, Redange.

Arms in Original Colors

B204 SP71 30c + 10c blk & pink .20 *.40*
B205 SP71 1fr + 25c ultra & buff .20 *.40*
B206 SP71 1.50fr + 25c ultra & pale grn .20 *.55*
B207 SP71 2.50fr + 50c blk & gray .20 *.40*
B208 SP71 5fr + 50c ultra 2.25 *5.50*
B209 SP71 8.50fr + 4.60fr ultra & lil 2.50 *8.00*
Nos. B204-B209 (6) 5.55 *15.25*
Set, never hinged 11.00

1959, Dec. 2

30c+10c, 2.50fr+50c, Clervaux. 1fr+25c, 5fr+50c, Remich. 1.50fr+25c, 8.50fr+4.60fr, Wiltz.

Arms in Original Colors

B210 SP71 30c + 10c ultra & pink .20 .40
B211 SP71 1fr + 25c ultra & pale lem .20 .40
B212 SP71 1.50fr + 25c blk & pale grn .20 .55
B213 SP71 2.50fr + 50c ultra & pale fawn .20 .40
B214 SP71 5fr + 50c ultra & lt bl .65 *2.25*
B215 SP71 8.50fr + 4.60fr blk & pale vio 2.75 *11.00*
Nos. B210-B215 (6) 4.20 *15.00*
Set, never hinged 9.25

Catalogue values for unused stamps in this section, from this point to the end of the section, are for Never Hinged items.

Princess Marie-Astrid SP72

Prince Jean SP73

1fr+25c, 5fr+50c, Princess in party dress. 1.50fr+25c, 8.50fr+4.60fr, Princess with book.

1960, Dec. 5 **Photo.** ***Perf. 11½***

B216 SP72 30c + 10c brn & lt bl .35 .20
B217 SP72 1fr + 25c brn & pink .35 .20
B218 SP72 1.50fr + 25c brn & lt bl .65 .50
B219 SP72 2.50fr + 50c brn & yel .50 .35
B220 SP72 5fr + 50c brn & pale lil 1.00 *2.50*
B221 SP72 8.50fr + 4.60fr brn & pale ol 9.25 *11.50*
Nos. B216-B221 (6) 12.10 15.25

Type of 1960

Prince Henri: 30c+10c, 2.50fr+50c, Infant in long dress. 1fr+25c, 5fr+50c, Informal portrait. 1.50fr+25c, 8.50fr+ 4.60fr, In dress suit.

1961, Dec. 4 **Unwmk.** ***Perf. 11½***

B222 SP72 30c + 10c brn & brt pink .35 .25
B223 SP72 1fr + 25c brn & lt vio .35 .25
B224 SP72 1.50fr + 25c brn & sal .50 .50
B225 SP72 2.50fr + 50c brn & pale grn .50 .25
B226 SP72 5fr + 50c brn & cit 3.00 2.50
B227 SP72 8.50fr + 4.60fr brn & gray 5.00 *6.50*
Nos. B222-B227 (6) 9.70 10.25

1962, Dec. 3 **Photo.** ***Perf. 11½***

Designs: Different portraits of the twins Prince Jean and Princess Margaretha. Nos. B228 and B233 are horizontal.

Inscriptions and Portraits in Dark Brown

B228 SP73 30c + 10c org yel .25 .20
B229 SP73 1fr + 25c lt bl .25 .20
B230 SP73 1.50fr + 25c pale ol .35 .35
B231 SP73 2.50fr + 50c rose .35 .25
B232 SP73 5fr + 50c lt yel grn 1.25 *2.25*
B233 SP73 8.50fr + 4.60fr lil gray 3.25 *4.50*
Nos. B228-B233 (6) 5.70 7.75

St. Roch, Patron of Bakers — SP74

Three Towers — SP75

Patron Saints: 1fr+25c, St. Anne, tailors. 2fr+25c, St. Eloi, smiths. 3fr+50c, St. Michael, shopkeepers. 6fr+50c, St. Bartholomew, butchers. St. Theobald, seven crafts.

1963, Dec. 2 **Unwmk.** ***Perf. 11½***

Multicolored Design

B234 SP74 50c + 10c pale lil .20 .20
B235 SP74 1fr + 25c tan .20 .20
B236 SP74 2fr + 25c lt grnsh bl .20 .20
B237 SP74 3fr + 50c lt bl .20 .25
B238 SP74 6fr + 50c buff 1.00 *1.60*
B239 SP74 10fr + 5.90fr pale yel grn 1.60 *3.00*
Nos. B234-B239 (6) 3.40 5.45

1964, Dec. 7 **Photo.** ***Perf. 11½***

Children's paintings: 1fr+25c, 6fr+50c, Grand Duke Adolphe Bridge, horiz. 2fr+25c, 10fr+5.90fr, The Lower City.

B240 SP75 50c + 10c multi .20 .20
B241 SP75 1fr + 25c multi .20 .20
B242 SP75 2fr + 25c multi .20 .30
a. Value omitted *300.00*
B243 SP75 3fr + 50c multi .20 .30
B244 SP75 6fr + 50c multi 1.00 1.50
B245 SP75 10fr + 5.90fr multi 1.25 *2.50*
Nos. B240-B245 (6) 3.05 5.00

The Roman Lady of Titelberg — SP76

Fairy Tales of Luxembourg: 1fr+25c, Schäppchen, the Huntsman. 2fr+25c, The Witch of Koerich. 3fr+50c, The Gnomes of Schoenfels. 6fr+50c, Tollchen, Watchman of Hesperange. 10fr+5.90fr, The Old Spinster of Heispelt.

1965, Dec. 6 **Photo.** ***Perf. 11½***

B246 SP76 50c + 10c multi .20 .20
B247 SP76 1fr + 25c multi .20 .20
B248 SP76 2fr + 25c multi .20 .20
B249 SP76 3fr + 50c multi .20 .20
B250 SP76 6fr + 50c multi .50 *1.25*
B251 SP76 10fr + 5.90fr multi 1.25 *3.00*
Nos. B246-B251 (6) 2.55 5.05

Fairy Tale Type of 1965

Fairy Tales of Luxembourg: 50c+10c, The Veiled Matron of Wormeldange. 1.50fr+25c, Jekel, Warden of the Wark. 2fr+25c, The Black Man of Vianden. 3fr+50c, The Gracious Fairy of Rosport. 6fr+1fr, The Friendly Shepherd of Donkolz. 13fr+6.90fr, The Little Sisters of Trois-Vièrges.

1966, Dec. 6 **Photo.** ***Perf. 11½***

B252 SP76 50c + 10c multi .20 .20
B253 SP76 1.50fr + 25c multi .20 .20
B254 SP76 2fr + 25c multi .20 .20
B255 SP76 3fr + 50c multi .20 .30
B256 SP76 6fr + 1fr multi .50 *1.00*
B257 SP76 13fr + 6.90fr multi .85 *2.25*
Nos. B252-B257 (6) 2.15 4.15

Prince Guillaume SP77

Castle of Berg SP78

Portraits: 1.50fr+25c, Princess Margaretha. 2fr+25c, Prince Jean. 3fr+50c, Prince Henri as Boy Scout. 6fr+1fr, Princess Marie-Astrid.

1967, Dec. 6 **Photo.** ***Perf. 11½***

B258 SP77 50c + 10c yel & brn .20 .20
B259 SP77 1.50fr + 25c gray bl & brn .20 .20
B260 SP77 2fr + 25c pale rose & brn .20 .20
B261 SP77 3fr + 50c lt ol & brn .65 .20
B262 SP77 6fr + 1fr lt vio & brn .50 *1.00*
B263 SP78 13fr + 6.90fr multi .65 *3.00*
Nos. B258-B263 (6) 2.40 4.80

Medico-professional Institute at Cap — SP79

Deaf-mute Child Imitating Bird — SP80

Handicapped Children: 2fr+25c, Blind child holding candle. 3fr+50c, Nurse supporting physically handicapped child. 6fr+1fr, Cerebral palsy victim. 13fr+6.90fr, Mentally disturbed child.

1968, Dec. 5 **Photo.** ***Perf. 11½***

Designs and Inscriptions in Dark Brown

B264 SP79 50c + 10c lt bl .20 .20
B265 SP80 1.50fr + 25c lt grn .20 .20
B266 SP80 2fr + 25c yel .25 .25
B267 SP80 3fr + 50c bl .25 .25
B268 SP80 6fr + 1fr buff .50 1.10
B269 SP80 13fr + 6.90fr pink 1.60 *3.00*
Nos. B264-B269 (6) 3.00 5.00

Vianden Castle SP81

Children of Bethlehem SP82

Luxembourg Castles: 1.50fr+25c, Lucilinburhuc. 2fr+25c, Bourglinster. 3fr+50c, Hollenfels. 6fr+1fr, Ansembourg. 13fr+6.90fr, Beaufort.

1969, Dec. 8 **Photo.** ***Perf. 11½***

B270 SP81 50c + 10c multi .20 .20
B271 SP81 1.50fr + 25c multi .20 .20
B272 SP81 2fr + 25c multi .20 .20
B273 SP81 3fr + 50c multi .20 .20
B274 SP81 6fr + 1fr multi .60 *1.25*
B275 SP81 13fr + 6.90fr multi 1.00 *3.00*
Nos. B270-B275 (6) 2.40 5.05

1970, Dec. 7 **Photo.** ***Perf. 11½***

Luxembourg Castles: 50c+10c, Clervaux. 1.50fr+25c, Septfontaines. 2fr+25c, Bourscheid. 3fr+50c, Esch-sure-Sure. 6fr+1fr, Larochette. 13fr+6.90fr, Brandenbourg.

B276 SP81 50c + 10c multi .20 .20
B277 SP81 1.50fr + 25c multi .20 .20
B278 SP81 2fr + 25c multi .20 .20
B279 SP81 3fr + 50c multi .20 .20
B280 SP81 6fr + 1fr multi .60 *1.25*
B281 SP81 13fr + 6.90fr multi 1.00 *3.00*
Nos. B276-B281 (6) 2.40 5.05

The surtax on Nos. B180-B281 was for charitable purposes.

1971, Dec. 6 **Photo.** ***Perf. 11½***

Wooden Statues from Crèche of Beaufort Church: 1.50fr+25c, Shepherds. 3fr+50c, Nativity. 8fr+1fr, Herdsmen. 18fr+6.50fr, King offering gift.

Sculptures in Shades of Brown

B282 SP82 1fr + 25c lilac .25 .20
B283 SP82 1.50fr + 25c olive .25 .20
B284 SP82 3fr + 50c gray .35 .20
B285 SP82 8fr + 1fr lt ultra 1.10 *2.25*
B286 SP82 18fr + 6.50fr grn 1.90 *4.50*
Nos. B282-B286 (5) 3.85 7.35

The surtax was for various charitable organizations.

Angel — SP83

Sts. Anne and Joachim — SP84

Stained Glass Windows, Luxembourg Cathedral: 1.50fr+25c, St. Joseph. 3fr+50c, Virgin and Child. 8fr+1fr, People of Bethlehem. 18fr+6.50fr, Angel facing left.

1972, Dec. 4

B287 SP83 1fr + 25c multi .20 .20
B288 SP83 1.50fr + 25c multi .20 .20
B289 SP83 3fr + 50c multi .20 .20
B290 SP83 8fr + 1fr multi 1.00 *2.25*
B291 SP83 18fr + 6.50fr multi 2.75 *6.00*
Nos. B287-B291 (5) 4.35 8.85

Surtax was for charitable purposes.

1973, Dec. 5 **Photo.** ***Perf. 11½***

Sculptures: 3fr+25c, Mary meeting Elizabeth. 4fr+50c, Virgin and Child and a King. 8fr+1fr, Shepherds. 15fr+7fr, St. Joseph holding candle. Designs from 16th century reredos, Hermitage of Hachiville.

B292 SP84 1fr + 25c multi .20 .20
B293 SP84 3fr + 25c multi .20 .20
B294 SP84 4fr + 50c multi .25 .20
B295 SP84 8fr + 1fr multi 1.10 *2.25*
B296 SP84 15fr + 7fr multi 3.00 *6.00*
Nos. B292-B296 (5) 4.75 8.85

Annunciation — SP85

Crucifixion — SP86

Designs: 3fr+25c, Visitation. 4fr+50c, Nativity. 8fr+1fr, Adoration of the King. 15fr+7fr, Presentation at the Temple. Designs of Nos. B297-B301 are from miniatures in the "Codex Aureus Epternacensis" (Gospel from Echternach Abbey). The Crucifixion is from the carved ivory cover of the Codex, by the Master of Echternach, c. 983-991.

1974, Dec. 5 **Photo.** ***Perf. 11½***

B297 SP85 1fr + 25c multi .20 .20
B298 SP85 3fr + 25c multi .20 .20
B299 SP85 4fr + 50c multi .20 .20

B300 SP85 8fr + 1fr multi 1.10 3.00
B301 SP85 15fr + 7fr multi 2.00 5.50
Nos. B297-B301 (5) 3.70 9.10

Souvenir Sheet
Photogravure & Engraved
Perf. 13½

B302 SP86 20fr + 10fr multi 3.50 8.00

50th anniversary of Caritas issues. No. B302 contains one 34x42mm stamp.

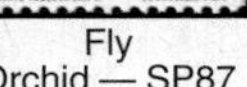
Fly Orchid — SP87

Lilies of the Valley — SP88

Flowers: 3fr+25c, Pyramidal orchid. 4fr+50c, Marsh hellebore. 8fr+1fr, Pasque-flower. 15fr+7fr, Bee orchid.

1975, Dec. 4 Photo. *Perf. 11½*

B303 SP87 1fr + 25c multi .20 .20
B304 SP87 3fr + 25c multi .35 .25
B305 SP87 4fr + 50c multi .50 .20
B306 SP87 8fr + 1fr multi 1.00 1.60
B307 SP87 15fr + 7fr multi 2.75 5.00
Nos. B303-B307 (5) 4.80 7.25

The surtax on Nos. B303-B317 was for various charitable organizations.

1976, Dec. 6

Flowers: 2fr+25c, Gentian. 5fr+25c, Narcissus. 6fr+50c, Red hellebore. 12fr+1fr, Late spider orchid. 20fr+8fr, Two-leafed squill.

B308 SP87 2fr + 25c multi .20 .30
B309 SP87 5fr + 25c multi .25 .30
B310 SP87 6fr + 50c multi .30 .30
B311 SP87 12fr + 1fr multi 1.00 2.00
B312 SP87 20fr + 8fr multi 2.75 5.50
Nos. B308-B312 (5) 4.50 8.40

1977, Dec. 5 Photo. *Perf. 11½*

Flowers: 5fr+25c, Columbine. 6fr+50c, Mezereon. 12fr+1fr, Early spider orchid. 20fr+8fr, Spotted orchid.

B313 SP88 2fr + 25c multi .20 .20
B314 SP88 5fr + 25c multi .25 .25
B315 SP88 6fr + 50c multi .50 .25
B316 SP88 12fr + 1fr multi 1.40 2.75
B317 SP88 20fr + 8fr multi 2.25 5.50
Nos. B313-B317 (5) 4.60 8.95

St. Matthew — SP89

Spring — SP90

Behind-glass Paintings, 19th Century: 5fr+25c, St. Mark. 6fr+50c, Nativity. 12fr+1fr, St. Luke. 20fr+8fr, St. John.

1978, Dec. 5 Photo. *Perf. 11½*

B318 SP89 2fr + 25c multi .20 .20
B319 SP89 5fr + 25c multi .25 .30
B320 SP89 6fr + 50c multi .35 .30
B321 SP89 12fr + 1fr multi 1.25 .90
B322 SP89 20fr + 8fr multi 1.90 4.00
Nos. B318-B322 (5) 3.95 5.70

Surtax was for charitable organizations.

1979, Dec. 5 Photo. *Perf. 12*

Behind-glass Paintings, 19th Century: 5fr+25c, Summer. 6fr+50c, Charity. 12fr+1fr, Autumn. 20fr+8fr, Winter.

B323 SP90 2fr + 25c multi .20 .20
B324 SP90 5fr + 25c multi .25 .25
B325 SP90 6fr + 50c multi .35 .25
B326 SP90 12fr + 1fr multi .85 1.25
B327 SP90 20fr + 8fr multi 1.75 4.50
Nos. B323-B327 (5) 3.40 6.45

St. Martin — SP91

Behind-glass Paintings, 19th Century: 6fr+50c, St. Nicholas. 8fr+1fr, Madonna and Child. 30fr+1fr, St. George the Martyr.

1980, Dec. 5 Photo. *Perf. 11½*

B328 SP91 4fr + 50c multi .20 .20
B329 SP91 6fr + 50c multi .25 .25
B330 SP91 8fr + 1fr multi .45 .45
B331 SP91 30fr + 10fr multi 1.75 1.75
Nos. B328-B331 (4) 2.65 2.65

Surtax was for charitable organizations.

Arms of Petange SP92

Nativity, by Otto van Veen (1556-1629) SP93

1981, Dec. 4 Photo.

Granite Paper

B332 SP92 4fr + 50c shown .25 .30
B333 SP92 6fr + 50c Larochette .30 .35
B334 SP93 8fr + 1fr shown .50 .60
B335 SP92 16fr + 2fr Stadtbredimus .90 1.10
B336 SP92 35fr + 12fr Weiswampach 2.25 2.75
Nos. B332-B336 (5) 4.20 5.10

Surtax was for charitable organizations.

1982, Dec. 6 Photo. *Perf. 11½*

Design: 8fr+1fr, Adoration of the Shepherds, stained-glass window, by Gust Zanter, Hoscheid Parish Church.

Granite Paper

B337 SP92 4fr + 50c Bettembourg .25 .25
B338 SP92 6fr + 50c Frisange .35 .35
B339 SP93 8fr + 1fr multi .45 .45
B340 SP92 16fr + 2fr Mamer .90 .90
B341 SP92 35fr + 12fr Heinerscheid 2.25 2.25
Nos. B337-B341 (5) 4.20 4.20

Surtax was for charitable organizations.

1983, Dec. 5 Photo.

B342 SP92 4fr + 1fr Winseler .20 .20
B343 SP92 7fr + 1fr Beckerich .40 .40
B344 SP93 10fr + 1fr Nativity .50 .50
B345 SP92 16fr + 2fr Feulen .85 .85
B346 SP92 40fr + 13fr Mertert 3.00 3.00
Nos. B342-B346 (5) 4.95 4.95

Surtax was for charitable organizations.

Inquisitive Child — SP94

Children Exhibiting Various Moods.

1984, Dec. 5 Photo.

B347 SP94 4fr + 1fr shown .20 .20
B348 SP94 7fr + 1fr Daydreaming .45 .45
B349 SP94 10fr + 1fr Nativity .55 .55
B350 SP94 16fr + 2fr Sulking .95 .95
B351 SP94 40fr + 13fr Admiring 3.25 3.25
Nos. B347-B351 (5) 5.40 5.40

Surtax was for charitable organizations.

1985, Dec. 5 Photo.

B352 SP94 4fr + 1fr Girl drawing .20 .20
B353 SP94 7fr + 1fr Two boys .30 .30
B354 SP94 10fr + 1fr Adoration of the Magi .40 .40
B355 SP94 16fr + 2fr Fairy tale characters 1.00 1.00
B356 SP94 40fr + 13fr Embarrassed girl 2.75 2.75
Nos. B352-B356 (5) 4.65 4.65

Surtax was for charitable organizations.

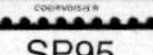
SP95

SP96

Book of Hours, France, c. 1550, Natl. Library — SP97

Christmas: illuminated text.

1986, Dec. 8 Photo. *Perf. 11½*

B357 SP95 6fr + 1fr Annunciation .45 .45
B358 SP95 10fr + 1fr Angel appears to the Shepherds .55 .55
B359 SP95 12fr + 2fr Nativity .70 .70
B360 SP95 18fr + 2fr Adoration of the Magi 1.00 1.00
B361 SP95 20fr + 8fr Flight into Egypt 1.40 1.40
Nos. B357-B361 (5) 4.10 4.10

1987, Dec. 1 *Perf. 12*

B362 SP96 6fr + 1fr Annunciation .40 .40
B363 SP96 10fr + 1fr Visitation .65 .65
B364 SP96 12fr + 2fr Adoration of the Magi .85 .85
B365 SP96 18fr + 2fr Presentation in the Temple 1.10 1.10
B366 SP96 20fr + 8fr Flight into Egypt 1.60 1.60
Nos. B362-B366 (5) 4.60 4.60

1988, Dec. 5 *Perf. 11½*

B367 SP97 9fr +1fr Annunciation to the Shepherds .55 .55
B368 SP97 12fr +2fr Adoration of the Magi .75 .75
B369 SP97 18fr +2fr Virgin and Child 1.10 1.10
B370 SP97 20fr +8fr Pentecost 1.50 1.50
Nos. B367-B370 (4) 3.90 3.90

Surtax for charitable organizations.

Christmas SP98

Chapels: No. B371, St. Lambert and St. Blase, Fennange, vert. No. B372, St. Quirinus, Luxembourg. No. B373, St. Anthony the Hermit, Reisdorf, vert. No. B374, The Hermitage, Hachiville.

1989, Dec. 11 Photo. *Perf. 12x11½*

B371 SP98 9fr +1fr multi .50 .50
B372 SP98 12fr +2fr multi .70 .70
B373 SP98 18fr +3fr multi 1.10 1.10
B374 SP98 25fr +8fr multi 1.60 1.60
Nos. B371-B374 (4) 3.90 3.90

Surtax for social work.

1990, Nov. 26 Photo. *Perf. 11½*

Chapels: No. B375, Congregation of the Blessed Virgin Mary, Vianden, vert. No. B376, Our Lady, Echternach. No. B377, Our Lady, Consoler of the Afflicted, Grentzingen. B378, St. Pirmin, Kaundorf, vert.

B375 SP98 9fr +1fr multi .60 .60
B376 SP98 12fr +2fr multi .85 .85
B377 SP98 18fr +3fr multi 1.25 1.25
B378 SP98 25fr +8fr multi 2.00 2.00
Nos. B375-B378 (4) 4.70 4.70

Surtax for charitable organizations.

1991, Dec. 9 Photo. *Perf. 11½*

Chapels: No. B379, St. Donatus, Arsdorf, vert. No. B380, Our Lady of Sorrows, Brandenbourg. No. B381, Our Lady, Luxembourg. No. B382, The Hermitage, Wolwelange, vert.

B379 SP98 14fr +2fr multi .95 .95
B380 SP98 14fr +2fr multi .95 .95
B381 SP98 18fr +3fr multi 1.25 1.25
B382 SP98 22fr +7fr multi 1.75 1.75
Nos. B379-B382 (4) 4.90 4.90

Surtax used for philanthropic work.

Endangered Birds — SP99

Designs: No. B383, Hazel grouse. No. B384, Golden oriole, vert. 18fr+3fr, Black stork. 22fr+7fr, Red kite, vert.

1992, Dec. 7 Photo. *Perf. 11½*

B383 SP99 14fr +2fr multi 1.00 1.00
B384 SP99 14fr +2fr multi 1.00 1.00
B385 SP99 18fr +3fr multi 1.25 1.25
B386 SP99 22fr +7fr multi 1.75 1.75
Nos. B383-B386 (4) 5.00 5.00

Surtax for Luxembourg charitable organizations.

1993, Dec. 6 Photo. *Perf. 11½*

Designs: No. B387, Snipe. No. B388, Kingfisher, vert. 18fr+3fr, Little ringed plover. 22fr+7fr, Sand martin, vert.

B387 SP99 14fr +2fr multi .90 .90
B388 SP99 14fr +2fr multi .90 .90
B389 SP99 18fr +3fr multi 1.25 1.25
B390 SP99 22fr +7fr multi 1.60 1.60
Nos. B387-B390 (4) 4.65 4.65

Surtax for Luxembourg charitable organizations.

1994, Sept. 19 Photo. *Perf. 11½*

Designs: No. B391, Partridge. No. B392, Stonechat, vert. 18fr+3fr, Blue-headed wagtail. 22fr+7fr, Great grey shrike, vert.

B391 SP99 14fr +2fr multi 1.00 1.00
B392 SP99 14fr +2fr multi 1.00 1.00
B393 SP99 18fr +3fr multi 1.25 1.25
B394 SP99 22fr +7fr multi 1.90 1.90
Nos. B383-B394 (12) 14.80 14.80

Christmas SP100

Trees SP101

Design: 16fr + 2fr, Stained glass window, parish church of Alzingen.

1995, Dec. 4 Photo. *Perf. 11½*

B395 SP100 16fr +2fr multi 1.25 1.25

Surtax for Luxembourg charitable organizations.

1995, Dec. 4

Designs: No. B396, Tilia platyphyllos. No. B397, Aesculus hippocastanum, horiz. 20fr+3fr, Quercus pedunculata, horiz. 32fr+7fr, Betula pendula.

B396 SP101 16fr +2fr multi 1.25 1.25
B397 SP101 16fr +2fr multi 1.25 1.25
B398 SP101 20fr +3fr multi 1.50 1.50
B399 SP101 32fr +7fr multi 2.75 2.75
Nos. B396-B399 (4) 6.75 6.75

Surtax for Luxembourg charitable organizations.

See Nos. B400-B403, B405-B408.

1996, Dec. 9

Designs: No. B400, Fraxinus excelsior. No. B401, Salix SSP, horiz. 20fr+3fr, Sorbus domestica, horiz. 32fr+7fr, Fagus silvatica.

B400 SP101 16fr +2fr multi 1.00 1.00
B401 SP101 16fr +2fr multi 1.00 1.00
B402 SP101 20fr +3fr multi 1.25 1.25
B403 SP101 32fr +7fr multi 2.25 2.25
Nos. B400-B403 (4) 5.50 5.50

Surtax for Luxembourg charitable organizations.

Christmas SP102

1996, Dec. 9
B404 SP102 16fr +2fr multi 1.00 1.00

Surtax for Luxembourg charitable organizations.

Tree Type of 1995

Designs: No. B405, Ulmus glabra. No. B406, Acer platanoides. 20fr+3fr, Prunus avium. 32fr+7fr, Juglans regia, horiz.

1997, Dec. 8 Photo. *Perf. 11½*
B405 SP101 16fr +2fr multi 1.00 1.00
B406 SP101 16fr +2fr multi 1.00 1.00
B407 SP101 20fr +3fr multi 1.25 1.25
B408 SP101 32fr +7fr multi 2.25 2.25
Nos. B405-B408 (4) 5.50 5.50

Christmas SP103

1997, Dec. 8
B409 SP103 16fr +2fr multi 1.00 1.00

Christmas SP104

1998, Dec. 7 Photo. *Perf. 11½*
B410 SP104 16fr +2fr multi 1.00 1.00

Charity Stamps SP105

Drawings of villages by Abbot Jean Bertels, 16th cent.: No. B411, Bech. No. B412, Ermesturf (Ermsdorf). 20fr+3fr, Itsich (Itzig). 32fr+7fr, Steinhem (Steinheim).

1998, Dec. 7
B411 SP105 16fr +2fr green & multi 1.00 1.00
B412 SP105 16fr +2fr brown & multi 1.00 1.00
B413 SP105 20fr +3fr red & multi 1.25 1.25
B414 SP105 32fr +7fr blue & multi 2.25 2.25
Nos. B411-B414 (4) 5.50 5.50

See #B415-B418, B420-B423.

Perf. 11¾x11½

1999, Nov. 30 Photo.

Drawings of villages by Abbot Jean Bertels, 16th cent.: No. B415, Oswiler (Osweiler). No. B416, Bettemburch (Bettembourg). 20fr+3fr, Cruchte auf der Alset (Cruchten). 32fr+7fr, Berchem.

B415 SP105 16fr +2fr red vio & multi 1.00 1.00
B416 SP105 16fr +2fr blue & multi 1.00 1.00
B417 SP105 20fr +3fr bl grn & multi 1.25 1.25
B418 SP105 32fr +7fr brown & multi 2.00 2.00
Nos. B415-B418 (4) 5.25 5.25

Surtax for Luxembourg charitable organizations.

Christmas SP106

1999, Nov. 30 *Perf. 11¾*
B419 SP106 16fr +2fr multi 1.00 1.00

Surtax for Luxembourg charitable organizations.

Village Drawings Type of 1998

By Abbot Jean Bertels, 16th cent.: 18fr+2fr, Lorentzwiler (Lorentzweiler). 21fr+3fr, Costurf (Consdorf). 24fr+3fr, Elfingen (Elvange). 36fr+7fr, Sprenckigen (Sprinkange).

2000, Dec. 5 Photo. *Perf. 11¾x11½*
Granite Paper
B420 SP105 18fr +2fr grn & multi .85 .85
B421 SP105 21fr +3fr brn & multi 1.00 1.00
B422 SP105 24fr +3fr red & multi 1.10 1.10
B423 SP105 36fr +7fr bl & multi 1.90 1.90
Nos. B420-B423 (4) 4.85 4.85

Surtax for Luxembourg charitable organizations.

Christmas SP107

2000, Dec. 5 *Perf. 11¾*
Granite Paper
B424 SP107 18fr +2fr multi .85 .85

Surtax for Luxembourg charitable organizations.

Christmas SP108

2001, Dec. 6 Photo. *Perf. 14*
B425 SP108 45c +5c (18fr+2fr) multi 1.25 1.25

See note before No. 1063. A star-shaped hole is found at the UL portion of the design.

Fauna SP109

Designs: 45c+5c (18fr+2fr), Squirrel. 52c+8c (21fr+3fr), Wild boar. 59c+11c (24fr+4fr), Hare, vert. 89c+21c (36fr+8fr), Wood pigeon, vert.

Perf. 11¾x11½, 11½x11¾
2001, Dec. 6
Granite Paper
B426-B429 SP109 Set of 4 6.25 6.25

Christmas SP110

2002, Dec. 10 Photo. *Perf. 13¾*
B430 SP110 45c +5c multi 1.25 1.25

Surtax for Grand Duchess Charlotte charities.

Fauna SP111

Designs: 45c+5c, Red fox. 52c+8c, Hedgehog and snail, vert. 59c+11c, Pheasant. 89c+21c, Deer, vert.

2002, Dec. 10 *Perf. 11½*
B431-B434 SP111 Set of 4 6.25 6.25

Christmas — SP112

No. B435: a, Round Church of Ehnen, Christmas tree. b, Wormer Koeppchen Chapel.
Illustration reduced.

2003, Dec. 9 Litho. *Perf. 14¼*
B435 SP112 50c +5c Pair, #a-b 2.75 2.75

Surtax for Luxembourg charitable organizations.

Fauna SP113

Designs: 50c+5c, Roe deer, vert. 60c+10c, Raccoons. 70c+10c, Weasel, vert. €1+25c, Goshawk.

2003, Dec. 9 Photo. *Perf. 11½*
B436-B439 SP113 Set of 4 8.00 8.00

Surtax for Luxembourg charitable organizations.

Christmas SP114

Litho. & Embossed

2004, Dec. 7 *Perf. 13*
B440 SP114 50c +5c multi 1.50 1.50

Sports SP115

Designs: 50c+5c, Skiing. 60c+10c, Running, vert. 70c+10c, Swimming. €1+25c, Soccer, vert.

Perf. 13x13½, 13½x13
2004, Dec. 7 Litho.
B441-B444 SP115 Set of 4 8.75 8.75

Christmas SP116

2005, Dec. 6 Litho. *Perf. 13¼*
B445 SP116 50c +5c multi 1.40 1.40

Sports Type of 2004

Designs: 50c+5c, Figure skating, vert. 70c+10c, Basketball, vert. 90c+10c, Judo, vert. €1+25c, Tennis, vert.

2005, Dec. 6 *Perf. 13½x13*
B446-B449 SP115 Set of 4 8.50 8.50

Christmas SP117

2006, Dec. 5 Litho. *Perf. 12½*
B450 SP117 50c +5c multi 1.40 1.40

Modern Pipe Organs SP118

Organ from: 50c+5c, Grand Auditorium of the Luxembourg Music Conservatory. 70c+10c, Bridel. 90c+10c, Mondercange Parish Church. €1+25c, Luxembourg-Grund.

2006, Dec. 5 *Perf. 13¼x13*
B451-B454 SP118 Set of 4 9.25 9.25

Christmas SP119

2007, Dec. 4 Litho. *Perf. 12½*
B455 SP119 50c +5c multi 1.60 1.60

Modern Pipe Organs Type of 2006

Organ from: 50c+5c, Church of Niederwiltz. 70c+10c, Sandweiler, horiz. 90c+10c, Echternacht Basilica, horiz. €1+25c, St. Joseph's Church, Esch-sur-Alzette.

2007, Dec. 4 *Perf. 13½x13, 13x13½*
B456-B459 SP118 Set of 4 10.50 10.50

Christmas SP120

2008, Dec. 2 Litho. *Perf. 12½*

B460	SP120	50c +5c multi	1.40	1.40

Modern Pipe Organs Type of 2006

Organ from: 50c+5c, Junglinster. 70c+10c, Church, Mondorf-les-Bains, horiz. 90c+10c, Church, Vianden. €1+25c, Notre Dame Cathedral, Luxembourg.

2008, Dec. 2 *Perf. 13½x13, 13x13½*

B461-B464	SP118	Set of 4	9.25	9.25

AIR POST STAMPS

Airplane over Luxembourg — AP1

1931-33 Unwmk. Engr. *Perf. 12½*

C1	AP1	50c green ('33)	.55	*1.10*
C2	AP1	75c dark brown	.55	*1.50*
C3	AP1	1fr red	.55	*1.50*
C4	AP1	1¼fr dark violet	.55	*1.50*
C5	AP1	1¾fr dark blue	.55	*1.50*
C6	AP1	3fr gray black ('33)	1.10	*6.00*
		Nos. C1-C6 (6)	3.85	*13.10*
		Set, never hinged	8.25	

Aerial View of Moselle River — AP2

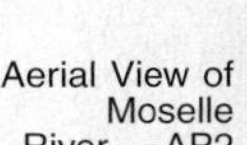

Wing and View of Luxembourg AP3

Vianden Castle — AP4

1946, June 7 Photo. *Perf. 11½*

C7	AP2	1fr dk ol grn & gray	.20	.20
C8	AP3	2fr chnt brn & buff	.20	*.25*
C9	AP4	3fr sepia & brown	.20	*.25*
C10	AP2	4fr dp vio & gray vio	.25	*.40*
C11	AP3	5fr dp mag & buff	.20	*.40*
C12	AP4	6fr dk brown & gray	.25	*.55*
C13	AP2	10fr henna brn & buff	.40	*.55*
C14	AP3	20fr dk blue & cream	.90	*1.50*
C15	AP4	50fr dk green & gray	1.75	1.75
		Nos. C7-C15 (9)	4.35	5.85
		Set, never hinged	8.75	

1852 and 1952 AP5

1952, May 24

Stamps in Gray and Dark Violet Brown

C16	AP5	80c olive grn	.40	.55
C17	AP5	2.50fr brt car	.80	1.40
C18	AP5	4fr brt blue	1.60	3.00
C19	AP5	8fr brown red	30.00	*55.00*
C20	AP5	10fr dull brown	22.50	*47.50*
		Nos. C16-C20 (5)	55.30	*107.45*
		Set, never hinged	100.00	

Centenary of Luxembourg's postage stamps. Nos. C16-C18 were available at face, but complete sets sold for 45.30fr, which included admission to the CENTILUX exhibition.

POSTAGE DUE STAMPS

Coat of Arms — D1

1907 Unwmk. Typo. *Perf. 12½*

J1	D1	5c green & black	.20	*.25*
J2	D1	10c green & black	1.40	*.25*
J3	D1	12½c green & black	.45	*.90*
J4	D1	20c green & black	.70	*.80*
J5	D1	25c green & black	17.50	1.50
J6	D1	50c green & black	.65	*4.25*
J7	D1	1fr green & black	.35	*3.50*
		Nos. J1-J7 (7)	21.25	11.45

See Nos. J10-J22.

Nos. J3, J5 Surcharged

1920

J8	D1	15c on 12½c	2.25	*7.25*
J9	D1	30c on 25c	2.25	*9.00*

Arms Type of 1907

1921-35

J10	D1	5c green & red	.20	*.40*
J11	D1	10c green & red	.20	*.35*
J12	D1	20c green & red	.20	*.35*
J13	D1	25c green & red	.20	*.35*
J14	D1	30c green & red	.55	*.60*
J15	D1	35c green & red ('35)	.55	.35
J16	D1	50c green & red	.55	*.60*
J17	D1	60c green & red ('28)	.45	*.50*
J18	D1	70c green & red ('35)	.55	.35
J19	D1	75c green & red ('30)	.55	.25
J20	D1	1fr green & red	.55	*1.10*
J21	D1	2fr green & red ('30)	.55	*6.50*
J22	D1	3fr green & red ('30)	1.60	*18.00*
		Nos. J10-J22 (13)	6.70	29.70
		Set, never hinged	27.50	

D2

D3

1946-48 Photo. *Perf. 11½*

J23	D2	5c bright green	.20	*.65*
J24	D2	10c bright green	.20	*.50*
J25	D2	20c bright green	.20	*.50*
J26	D2	30c bright green	.20	*.50*
J27	D2	50c bright green	.20	*.40*
J28	D2	70c bright green	.20	*.70*
J29	D2	75c brt green ('48)	.70	.25
J30	D3	1fr carmine	.20	*.25*
J31	D3	1.50fr carmine	.20	*.25*
J32	D3	2fr carmine	.20	*.25*
J33	D3	3fr carmine	.20	*.35*
J34	D3	5fr carmine	.55	.45
J35	D3	10fr carmine	.95	*4.00*
J36	D3	20fr carmine	2.75	*22.50*
		Nos. J23-J36 (14)	6.95	31.55
		Set, never hinged	13.00	

OFFICIAL STAMPS

Forged overprints on Nos. O1-O64 abound.

Unused values of Nos. O1-O51 are for stamps without gum. Though these stamps were issued with gum, most examples offered are without gum. Stamps with original gum sell for somewhat more.

Regular Issues Overprinted Reading Diagonally Up or Down

Frankfurt Print

Rouletted in Color except 2c

1875 Unwmk.

O1	A2	1c red brown	27.50	37.50
O2	A2	2c black	27.50	37.50
O3	A3	10c lilac	2,100.	2,100.
O4	A3	12½c rose	475.00	575.00
O5	A3	20c gray brn	37.50	57.50
O6	A3	25c blue	250.00	140.00
O7	A3	25c ultra	1,900.	1,400.
O8	A3	30c lilac rose	32.50	*75.00*
O9	A3	40c pale org	160.00	225.00
a.		40c org red, thick paper	250.00	325.00
c.		As "a," thin paper	1,650.	1,400.
O10	A4	1fr on 37½c bis	150.00	22.50

Double overprints exist on Nos. O1-O6, O8-O10.

Overprints reading diagonally down sell for more.

Inverted Overprint

O1a	A2	1c	190.00	225.00
O2a	A2	2c	190.00	225.00
O3a	A3	10c	2,500.	2,500.
O4a	A3	12½c	650.00	925.00
O5a	A3	20c	55.00	75.00
O6a	A3	25c	1,100.	1,300.
O7a	A3	25c	2,100.	1,500.
O8a	A3	30c	650.00	925.00
O9b	A3	40c pale orange	325.00	450.00
O10a	A4	1fr on 37½c	175.00	75.00

Luxembourg Print

1875-76 *Perf. 13*

O11	A2	1c red brown	11.00	27.50
O12	A2	2c black	14.00	32.50
O13	A2	4c green	100.00	190.00
O14	A2	5c yellow	65.00	85.00
a.		5c orange yellow	75.00	110.00
O15	A3	10c gray lilac	92.50	100.00
O16	A3	12½c rose	85.00	100.00
O17	A3	12½c lilac rose	225.00	275.00
O18	A3	25c blue	11.00	*32.50*
O19	A5	1fr on 37½c bis	42.50	65.00
		Nos. O11-O19 (9)	646.00	907.50

Double overprints exist on Nos. O11-O15.

Inverted Overprint

O11a	A2	1c	92.50	*110.00*
O12a	A2	2c	150.00	190.00
O13a	A2	4c	160.00	190.00
O14b	A2	5c	500.00	650.00
O15a	A3	10c	500.00	190.00
O16a	A3	12½c	400.00	550.00
O17a	A3	12½c	450.00	525.00
O18a	A3	25c	125.00	175.00
O19a	A5	1fr on 37½c	190.00	250.00
		Nos. O11a-O19a (9)	2,567.	2,830.

Haarlem Print

1880 *Perf. 11½x12, 12½x12, 13½*

O22	A3	25c blue	2.25	2.75

Overprinted

Frankfurt Print

1878 *Rouletted in Color*

O23	A2	1c red brown	140.00	160.00
O25	A3	20c gray brn	190.00	225.00
O26	A3	30c lilac rose	750.00	575.00
O27	A3	40c orange	325.00	450.00
O28	A4	1fr on 37½c bis	550.00	110.00
		Nos. O23-O28 (5)	1,955.	1,520.

Inverted Overprint

O23a	A2	1c	225.00	300.00
O25a	A3	20c	325.00	400.00
O26a	A3	30c	925.00	700.00
O27a	A3	40c	875.00	925.00
O28a	A4	1fr on 37½c	650.00	150.00

Luxembourg Print

1878-80 *Perf. 13*

O29	A2	1c red brown	750.00	925.00
O30	A2	2c black	190.00	225.00
O31	A2	4c green	190.00	225.00
O32	A2	5c yellow	375.00	450.00
O33	A3	10c gray lilac	375.00	400.00
O34	A3	12½c rose	65.00	110.00
O35	A3	25c blue	525.00	550.00
		Nos. O29-O35 (7)	2,470.	2,885.

Inverted Overprint

O29a	A2	1c	140.00	160.00
O30a	A2	2c	14.50	27.50
O31a	A2	4c	150.00	190.00
O32a	A2	5c	1,500.	1,500.
O33a	A3	10c	92.50	110.00
O34a	A3	12½c	525.00	600.00
O35a	A3	25c	850.00	1,000.

Overprinted

Frankfurt Print

1881 *Rouletted in Color*

O39	A3	40c orange	37.50	65.00
a.		Inverted overprint	210.00	275.00

"S.P." are initials of "Service Public."

Luxembourg Print

Perf. 13

O40	A2	1c red brown	140.00	160.00
O41	A2	4c green	210.00	210.00
a.		Inverted overprint	250.00	
O42	A2	5c yellow	600.00	750.00
O43	A5	1fr on 37½c bis	32.50	47.50
		Nos. O40-O43 (4)	982.50	1,167.

Haarlem Print

Perf. 11½x12, 12½x12, 13½

O44	A2	1c yellow brn	8.50	9.25
O45	A2	2c black	9.25	9.25
O46	A2	5c yellow	140.00	190.00
a.		Inverted overprint	225.00	
O47	A3	10c gray lilac	125.00	160.00
O48	A3	12½c rose	225.00	250.00
O49	A3	20c gray brown	65.00	92.50
O50	A3	25c blue	72.50	92.50
O51	A3	30c dull rose	75.00	110.00
		Nos. O44-O51 (8)	720.25	913.50

Stamps of the 1881 issue with the overprint of the 1882 issue shown below were never issued.

Overprinted

Perf. 11½x12, 12½x12, 12½, 13½

1882

O52	A6	1c gray lilac	.25	.50
O53	A6	2c ol gray	.25	.50
a.		"S" omitted	110.00	
O54	A6	4c ol bister	.35	.65
O55	A6	5c lt green	.55	.80
O56	A6	10c rose	12.00	20.00
O57	A6	12½c slate	1.90	4.75
O58	A6	20c orange	1.90	4.00
O59	A6	25c ultra	19.00	27.50
O60	A6	30c gray grn	4.25	10.00
O61	A6	50c bis brown	1.10	2.75
O62	A6	1fr pale vio	1.10	2.75
O63	A6	5fr brown org	12.00	27.50
		Nos. O52-O63 (12)	54.65	101.70

Nos. O52-O63 exist without one or both periods, also with varying space between "S" and "P." Nine denominations exist with double overprint, six with inverted overprint.

Overprinted ***S. P.***

1883 *Perf. 13½*

O64	A6	5fr brown org	*2,200.*	*2,200.*

Overprinted

1891-93 *Perf. 11, 11½, 11½x11, 12½*

O65 A7 10c carmine .20 .50
a. Sheet of 25 55.00
O66 A7 12½c slate grn 6.50 8.75
O67 A7 20c orange 12.00 8.50
O68 A7 25c blue .35 .50
a. Sheet of 25 65.00
O69 A7 30c olive grn 8.25 8.50
O70 A7 37½c green 8.25 10.00
O71 A7 50c brown 6.50 10.00
O72 A7 1fr dp vio 6.50 11.50
O73 A7 2½fr black 37.50 72.50
O74 A7 5fr lake 32.50 55.00
Nos. O65-O74 (10) 118.55 185.75

1895 *Perf. 12½*

O75 A8 1c pearl gray 1.90 1.90
O76 A8 2c gray brn 1.40 1.90
O77 A8 4c olive bis 1.40 1.90
O78 A8 5c green 4.00 5.00
O79 A8 10c carmine 32.50 35.00
Nos. O75-O79 (5) 41.20 45.70

Nos. O66-O79 exist without overprint and perforated "OFFICIEL" through the stamp. Value for set, $25.

Nos. O65a and O68a were issued to commemorate the coronation of Grand Duke Adolphe.

Regular Issue of 1906-26 Overprinted

1908-26 *Perf. 11x11½, 12½*

O80 A9 1c gray .20 .20
a. Inverted overprint 125.00
O81 A9 2c olive brn .20 .20
O82 A9 4c bister .20 .20
a. Double overprint 140.00
O83 A9 5c green .20 .20
O84 A9 5c lilac ('26) .20 .20
O85 A9 6c violet .20 .20
O86 A9 7½c org ('19) .20 .20
O87 A10 10c scarlet .25 *.45*
O88 A10 12½c slate grn .25 *.55*
O89 A10 15c orange brn .40 *.70*
O90 A10 20c orange .40 *.70*
O91 A10 25c ultra .40 *.70*
O92 A10 30c olive grn 4.00 *6.50*
O93 A10 37½c green .65 .65
O94 A10 50c brown 1.10 *1.50*
O95 A10 87½c dk blue 2.75 *3.25*
O96 A10 1fr violet 3.25 *4.00*
O97 A10 2½fr vermilion 65.00 65.00
O98 A10 5fr claret 55.00 47.50
Nos. O80-O98 (19) 134.85 132.90

On Regular Issue of 1914-17

1915-17

O99 A11 10c lake .35 *.65*
O100 A11 12½c dull grn .35 *.65*
O101 A11 15c olive blk .35 *.65*
O102 A11 17½c dp brn ('17) .35 *.65*
O103 A11 25c ultra .35 *.65*
O104 A11 30c bister 1.40 *5.00*
O105 A11 35c dk blue .35 *1.10*
O106 A11 37½c blk brn .35 *1.50*
O107 A11 40c orange .45 *1.10*
O108 A11 50c dk gray .45 *.95*
O109 A11 62½c blue grn .45 *1.50*
O110 A11 87½c org ('17) .45 *1.75*
O111 A11 1fr orange brn .45 *1.50*
O112 A11 2½fr red .45 *2.75*
O113 A11 5fr dk violet .45 *3.25*
Nos. O99-O113 (15) 7.00 23.65

On Regular Issues of 1921-26 in Black

1922-26 *Perf. 11½, 11½x11, 12½*

O114 A12 2c brown .20 .20
O115 A12 3c olive grn .20 .20
O116 A12 6c violet .20 .20
O117 A12 10c yellow grn .20 .35
O118 A12 10c ol grn ('24) .20 .35
O119 A12 15c brown ol .20 .35
O120 A12 15c pale grn ('24) .20 .35
O121 A12 15c dp org ('26) .20 .25
O122 A12 20c dp orange .20 .35
O123 A12 20c yel grn ('26) .20 .25
O124 A12 25c dk green .20 .35
O125 A12 30c car rose .20 .35
O126 A12 40c brown org .20 .35
O127 A12 50c dp blue .20 .45
O128 A12 50c red ('24) .20 .35
O129 A12 75c red .20 .45
O130 A12 75c dp bl ('24) .20 .45
O131 A12 80c black 4.75 11.00
O132 A13 1fr carmine .40 .90
O133 A14 2fr indigo 3.00 6.50
O134 A14 2fr dk brn ('26) 1.75 5.00
O135 A15 5fr dk vio 17.50 42.50
Nos. O114-O135 (22) 30.80 71.50

On Regular Issues of 1921-26 in Red

1922-34 *Perf. 11, 11½, 11½x11, 12½*

O136 A12 80c blk, perf. 11½ .20 .35
O137 A13 1fr dk bl, perf. 11½ ('26) .20 .55
O138 A14 2fr ind, perf. 11½x11 .45 1.25
O139 A17 3fr dk bl & bl, perf. 11 2.75 2.75
a. Perf. 11½ .90 1.40
b. Perf. 12½ 1.60 2.25
O140 A15 5fr dk vio, perf. 11½x11 4.00 7.50
a. Perf. 12½ ('34) 27.50 27.50
O141 A16 10fr blk, perf. 11½ 10.00 21.00
a. Perf. 12½ 27.50 27.50
Nos. O136-O141 (6) 17.60 33.40

On Regular Issue of 1926-35

1926-27 *Perf. 12*

O142 A18 5c dk violet .20 .20
O143 A18 10c olive grn .20 .20
O144 A18 20c orange .20 .20
O145 A18 25c yellow grn .20 .20
O146 A18 25c blk brn ('27) .35 .55
O147 A18 30c yel grn ('27) .65 1.10
O148 A18 40c olive gray .20 .20
O149 A18 50c red brown .20 .20
O150 A18 65c black brn .20 .20
O151 A18 75c rose .20 .20
O152 A18 75c bis brn ('27) .45 .70
O153 A18 80c bister brn .20 .40
O154 A18 90c rose ('27) .35 .55
O155 A18 1fr black .20 .40
O156 A18 1¼fr dk blue .20 .20
O157 A18 1½fr dp blue ('27) .55 .95
Nos. O142-O157 (16) 4.55 6.45

Type of Regular Issue, 1926-35, Overprinted

1928-35 Wmk. 213

O158 A18 5c dk violet .20 .20
O159 A18 10c olive grn .20 .20
O160 A18 15c black ('30) .20 .65
O161 A18 20c orange .45 .65
O162 A18 25c violet brn .45 .65
O163 A18 30c yellow grn .50 .70
O164 A18 30c gray vio ('30) .20 .65
O165 A18 35c yel grn ('30) .20 .65
O166 A18 35c gray vio .50 .70
O167 A18 40c olive gray .50 .70
O168 A18 50c red brown .45 .65
O169 A18 60c blue grn .45 .65
O170 A18 70c blue vio ('35) 3.50 7.25
O171 A18 75c bister brn .45 .65
O172 A18 90c rose .50 .70
O173 A18 1fr black .50 .70
O174 A18 1fr rose ('30) .20 .65
O175 A18 1¼fr yel ('30) 1.75 4.50
O176 A18 1¼fr bl grn ('31) 1.75 4.50
O177 A18 1½fr deep blue .50 .70
O178 A18 1¾fr dk blue ('30) .20 .65
Nos. O158-O178 (21) 13.65 27.35

Type of Regular Issues of 1928-31 Overprinted Like Nos. O80-O98

1928-31 Wmk. 216 *Perf. 11½*

O179 A19 2fr black .50 1.00

Wmk. 110 *Perf. 12½*

O180 A21 20fr dp green ('31) 2.25 5.00

No. 198 Overprinted Like Nos. O80-O98

1934 Unwmk. *Perf. 14x13½*

O181 A22 5fr blue green 2.25 3.25

Type of Regular Issue of 1935 Overprinted Like Nos. O158-O178 in Red

1935 Wmk. 247 *Perf. 12½x12*

O182 A23 10fr green 1.60 4.00

OCCUPATION STAMPS

Issued under German Occupation

Stamps of Germany, 1933-36, Overprinted in Black

1940, Oct. 1 Wmk. 237 *Perf. 14*

N1 A64 3pf olive bis .25 *.50*
N2 A64 4pf dull blue .25 *.55*
N3 A64 5pf bright green .25 *.50*
N4 A64 6pf dark green .25 *.50*
N5 A64 8pf vermilion .25 *.50*
N6 A64 10pf chocolate .25 *.50*
N7 A64 12pf deep carmine .25 *.50*
N8 A64 15pf maroon .25 *.70*
a. Inverted overprint 450.00 *1,300.*
N9 A64 20pf bright blue .25 *1.25*
N10 A64 25pf ultra .35 *1.75*
N11 A64 30pf olive green .35 *1.75*
N12 A64 40pf red violet .50 *1.90*
N13 A64 50pf dk green & blk .50 *2.00*
N14 A64 60pf claret & blk .50 *2.75*
N15 A64 80pf dk blue & blk 1.00 *3.75*
N16 A64 100pf orange & blk 1.25 *5.75*
Nos. N1-N16 (16) 6.70 *25.15*
Set, never hinged 20.00

Nos. 159-162, 164, 168-171, 173, 175, 179, 182, 216, 198-199 Surcharged in Black

b

a

c

d

Perf. 12, 14x13½, 12½x12, 11½

1940, Dec. 5 Unwmk.

N17 A18(a) 3rpf on 15c .20 *.35*
N18 A18(a) 4rpf on 20c .20 *.40*
N19 A18(a) 5rpf on 35c .20 *.40*
N20 A18(a) 6rpf on 10c .20 *.40*
N21 A18(a) 8rpf on 25c .20 *.40*
N22 A18(a) 10rpf on 40c .20 *.40*
N23 A18(a) 12rpf on 60c .20 *.40*
N24 A18(a) 15rpf on 1fr rose .20 *.40*
N25 A18(a) 20rpf on 50c .20 *.75*
N26 A18(a) 25rpf on 5c .20 *1.25*
N27 A18(a) 30rpf on 70c .20 *.60*
N28 A18(a) 40rpf on 75c .20 *1.00*
N29 A18(a) 50rpf on 1¼fr .20 *.60*
N30 A35(b) 60rpf on 2fr 1.40 *12.50*
N31 A22(c) 80rpf on 5fr .40 *2.25*
N32 A23(d) 100rpf on 10fr .50 *3.00*
Nos. N17-N32 (16) 4.90 *25.10*
Set, never hinged 7.00

OCCUPATION SEMI-POSTAL STAMPS

Semi-Postal Stamps of Germany, 1940 Overprinted in Black

1941, Jan. 12 Unwmk. *Perf. 14*

NB1 SP153 3pf + 2pf dk brn .20 *.85*
NB2 SP153 4pf + 3pf bluish blk .20 *.85*
NB3 SP153 5pf + 3pf yel grn .20 *.85*
NB4 SP153 6pf + 4pf dk grn .20 *.85*
NB5 SP153 8pf + 4pf dp org .20 *.85*
NB6 SP153 12pf + 6pf carmine .20 *.85*
NB7 SP153 15pf + 10pf dk vio brn .30 *1.90*
NB8 SP153 25pf + 15pf dp ultra .85 *3.75*
NB9 SP153 40pf + 35pf red lil 1.50 *6.25*
Nos. NB1-NB9 (9) 3.85 *17.00*
Set, never hinged 7.50

MACAO

mə-'kau

LOCATION — Off the Chinese coast at the mouth of the Canton River
GOVT. — Special Administrative Area of China (PRC) (as of 12/20/99)
AREA — 8 sq. mi.
POP. — 415,850 (1998)
CAPITAL — Macao

Formerly a Portuguese overseas territory. The territory includes the two small adjacent islands of Coloane and Taipa.

1000 Reis = 1 Milreis
78 Avos = 1 Rupee (1894)
100 Avos = 1 Pataca (1913)

Catalogue values for unused stamps in this country are for Never Hinged items, beginning with Scott 339 in the regular postage section, Scott C16 in the air post section, Scott J50 in the semi-postal section, and Scott RA11 in the postal tax section.

Watermark

Wmk. 232 — Maltese Cross

Portuguese Crown — A1

Perf. 12½, 13½

1884-85 Typo. Unwmk.

1 A1 5r black 13.00 9.00
2 A1 10r orange 25.00 12.00
3 A1 10r green ('85) 30.00 9.00
4 A1 20r bister 32.50 22.50
5 A1 20r rose ('85) 45.00 18.00
6 A1 25r rose 22.50 5.25
7 A1 25r violet ('85) 30.00 13.50
8 A1 40r blue 115.00 40.00
9 A1 40r yellow ('85) 42.50 20.00
10 A1 50r green 250.00 75.00
11 A1 50r blue ('85) 57.50 25.00
12 A1 80r gray ('85) 57.50 30.00
13 A1 100r red lilac 75.00 24.00
a. 100r lilac 75.00 24.00
14 A1 200r orange 70.00 20.00
15 A1 300r chocolate 100.00 25.00
Nos. 1-15 (15) 965.50 348.25

All values exist both perf 12½ and 13½. The cheaper variety is listed above. For detailed listings, see the Scott Specialized Catalogue of Stamps and Covers.

The reprints of the 1885 issue are printed on smooth, white chalky paper, ungummed and on thin white paper with shiny white gum and clean-cut perforation 13½.

For surcharges see Nos. 16-28, 108-109.

No. 13a Surcharged in Black

1884

Without Gum

No.	Type	Description	Unused	Used
16	A1	80r on 100r lilac	90.00	45.00
a.		Inverted surcharge	*200.00*	*75.00*
b.		Without accent on "e" of "reis"	80.00	47.50
c.		Perf. 13½	125.00	55.00
d.		As "b," perf. 13½	140.00	62.50

Nos. 6 and 10 Surcharged in Black, Blue or Red:

b

c

1885

Without Gum

No.	Type	Description	Unused	Used
17	A1(b)	5r on 25r rose, perf. 12½ (Bk)	21.00	6.50
a.		With accent on "e" of "Reis"	35.00	12.00
b.		Double surcharge	200.00	150.00
c.		Inverted surcharge	175.00	110.00
d.		Perf. 13½	125.00	100.00
18	A1(b)	10r on 25r rose (Bl)	47.50	18.00
a.		Accent on "e" of "Reis"		
b.		Pair, one without surcharge		—
19	A1(b)	10r on 50r grn, perf. 13½ (Bl)	625.00	225.00
a.		Perf. 12½	625.00	260.00
20	A1(b)	20r on 50r green (Bk)	47.50	10.00
a.		Double surcharge		150.00
b.		Accent on "e" of "Reis"	—	—
21	A1(b)	40r on 50r grn, perf. 12½ (R)	175.00	50.00
a.		Perf. 13½	240.00	50.00
		Nos. 17-21 (5)	916.00	309.50

1885

Without Gum

No.	Type	Description	Unused	Used
22	A1(c)	5r on 25r rose (Bk)	32.50	18.00
a.		Original value not obliterated		
23	A1(c)	10r on 50r green (Bk)	32.50	18.00
a.		Inverted surcharge		
b.		Perf. 12½	32.50	18.00

Nos. 12, 13a and 14 Surcharged in Black

1887

Without Gum

No.	Type	Description	Unused	Used
24	A1	5r on 80r gray	32.50	9.00
a.		"R" of "Reis" 4mm high	125.00	50.00
b.		Perf. 12½	150.00	45.00
25	A1	5r on 100r lilac	125.00	90.00
a.		Perf. 12½	95.00	60.00
26	A1	10r on 80r gray	65.00	20.00
a.		"R" 4mm high	140.00	47.50
27	A1	10r on 200r orange	140.00	62.50
a.		"R" 4mm high, "e" without accent	200.00	80.00
b.		Perf. 13½	140.00	62.50
28	A1	20r on 80r gray	100.00	35.00
a.		"R" 4mm high	175.00	47.50
b.		Perf. 12½	100.00	50.00
c.		"R" 4mm high, "e" without accent	160.00	47.50
		Nos. 24-28 (5)	462.50	216.50

The surcharges with larger "R" (4mm) have accent on "e." Smaller "R" is 3mm high.

Occasionally Nos. 24, 26 and 28 may be found with original gum. Values the same.

Coat of Arms — A6

Red Surcharge

1887, Oct. 20 ***Perf. 12½***

Without Gum

No.	Type	Description	Unused	Used
32	A6	5r green & buff	15.00	7.00
a.		With labels, 5r on 10r	77.50	65.00
b.		With labels, 5r on 20r	90.00	65.00
c.		With labels, 5r on 60r	77.50	65.00
33	A6	10r green & buff	22.50	9.00
a.		With labels, 10r on 10r	95.00	75.00
b.		With labels, 10r on 60r	110.00	75.00
34	A6	40r green & buff	37.50	*14.00*
a.		With labels, 40r on 20r	150.00	*110.00*
		Nos. 32-34 (3)	75.00	30.00

Nos. 32-34 were local provisionals, created by perforating contemporary revenue stamps to remove the old value inscriptions and then surcharging the central design portion. The unused portion of the design was normally removed prior to use. For simplicity's sake, we refer to these extraneous portions of the original revenue stamps as "labels."

The 10r also exists with 20r labels, and 40r with 10r labels. Value, $250 each.

King Luiz — A7

King Carlos — A9

Typographed and Embossed

1888, Jan. ***Perf. 12½, 13½***

Chalk-surfaced Paper

No.	Type	Description	Unused	Used
35	A7	5r black	21.00	4.00
36	A7	10r green	21.00	6.00
a.		Perf. 13½	75.00	37.50
37	A7	20r carmine	35.00	13.00
38	A7	25r violet	35.00	13.00
39	A7	40r chocolate	35.00	18.00
a.		Perf. 13½	60.00	26.00
40	A7	50r blue	60.00	13.50
41	A7	80r gray	95.00	22.50
a.		Imperf., pair	—	
42	A7	100r brown	45.00	22.50
43	A7	200r gray lilac	90.00	45.00
44	A7	300r orange	72.50	45.00
		Nos. 35-44 (10)	509.50	202.50

Nos. 37-44 were issued without gum.

For surcharges and overprints see Nos. 45, 58-66B, 110-118, 164-170, 239.

No. 43 Surcharged in Red

1892

Without Gum

No.	Type	Description	Unused	Used
45	A7	30r on 200r gray lilac	60.00	24.00
a.		Inverted surcharge	275.00	165.00

1894, Nov. 15 **Typo.** ***Perf. 11½***

No.	Type	Description	Unused	Used
46	A9	5r yellow	8.25	3.75
47	A9	10r redsh violet	8.25	3.75
48	A9	15r chocolate	12.50	5.25
49	A9	20r lavender	14.00	6.00
50	A9	25r green	35.00	11.25
51	A9	50r lt blue	37.50	22.50
a.		Perf. 13½	*500.00*	*300.00*
52	A9	75r carmine	70.00	30.00
53	A9	80r yellow green	37.50	22.50
54	A9	100r brown, *buff*	40.00	22.50
55	A9	150r carmine, *rose*	45.00	22.50
56	A9	200r dk blue, *blue*	62.50	34.00
57	A9	300r dk blue, *sal*	82.50	45.00
		Nos. 46-57 (12)	453.00	229.00

Nos. 49-57d were issued without gum, No. 49 with or without gum.

For surcharges and overprints see Nos. 119-130, 171-181, 183-186, 240, 251, 257-258.

Stamps of 1888 Surcharged in Red, Green or Black

1894 **Without Gum** ***Perf. 12½***

No.	Type	Description	Unused	Used
58	A7	1a on 5r black (R)	11.00	4.50
a.		Short "1"	11.00	4.50
b.		Inverted surcharge	100.00	100.00
c.		Double surcharge	*400.00*	
d.		Surch. on back instead of face	*200.00*	*200.00*
59	A7	3a on 20r carmine (G)	19.00	4.50
a.		Inverted surcharge	—	—
60	A7	4a on 25r violet (Bk)	19.00	9.00
a.		Inverted surcharge	60.00	50.00
61	A7	6a on 40r choc (Bk)	25.00	6.75
a.		Perf. 13½	19.00	12.00
62	A7	8a on 50r blue (R)	55.00	18.00
a.		Double surch., one inverted	—	—
b.		Inverted surcharge	125.00	60.00
c.		Perf. 13½	62.50	40.00
63	A7	13a on 80r gray (Bk)	22.50	7.00
a.		Double surcharge	—	—
64	A7	16a on 100r brown (Bk)	45.00	18.00
a.		Inverted surcharge	—	—
b.		Perf. 13½	115.00	110.00
65	A7	31a on 200r gray lil (Bk)	72.50	25.00
a.		Inverted surcharge	150.00	125.00
b.		Perf. 13½	75.00	25.00
66	A7	47a on 300r orange (G)	72.50	11.00
a.		Double surcharge	—	—
		Nos. 58-66 (9)	341.50	103.75

The style of type used for the word "PROVISORIO" on Nos. 58 to 66 differs for each value.

A 2a on 10r green was unofficially surcharged and denounced by the authorities.

On No. 45

No.	Type	Description	Unused	Used
66B	A7	5a on 30r on 200r	150.00	50.00

Common Design Types pictured following the introduction.

Vasco da Gama Issue

Common Design Types

1898, Apr. 1 **Engr.** ***Perf. 12½ to 16***

No.	Type	Description	Unused	Used
67	CD20	½a blue green	10.00	2.25
68	CD21	1a red	10.00	3.75
69	CD22	2a red violet	10.00	5.25
70	CD23	4a yellow green	10.00	7.50
71	CD24	8a dark blue	19.00	12.00
72	CD25	12a violet brown	30.00	22.00
73	CD26	16a bister brown	26.00	22.00
74	CD27	24a bister	30.00	22.00
		Nos. 67-74 (8)	145.00	96.75

For overprints and surcharges see Nos. 187-194.

King Carlos — A11

1898-1903 **Typo.** ***Perf. 11½***

Name and Value in Black except #103

No.	Type	Description	Unused	Used
75	A11	½a gray	4.50	1.00
a.		Perf. 12½	15.00	7.50
76	A11	1a orange	4.50	1.00
a.		Perf. 12½	15.00	7.50
77	A11	2a yellow green	5.75	1.50
78	A11	2a gray green ('03)	6.25	1.50
79	A11	2½a red brown	7.50	2.25
80	A11	3a gray violet	7.50	2.25
81	A11	3a slate ('03)	6.25	1.65
82	A11	4a sea green	9.00	5.00
83	A11	4a carmine ('03)	6.25	1.50
84	A11	5a gray brn ('00)	14.00	3.75
85	A11	5a pale yel brn ('03)	9.00	2.25
86	A11	6a red brown ('03)	10.00	2.00
87	A11	8a blue	12.50	3.75
88	A11	8a gray brn ('03)	15.00	4.00
89	A11	10a slate blue ('00)	15.00	3.75
90	A11	12a rose	15.00	6.50
91	A11	12a red lilac ('03)	62.50	15.00
92	A11	13a violet	18.00	6.50
93	A11	13a gray lilac ('03)	22.50	6.00
94	A11	15a pale ol grn ('00)	90.00	23.00
95	A11	16a dk blue, *bl*	17.00	7.50
96	A11	18a org brn, *pink* ('03)	32.50	11.50
97	A11	20a brn, *yelsh* ('00)	45.00	11.50
98	A11	24a brown, *buff*	27.50	7.50
99	A11	31a red lilac	27.50	9.00
100	A11	31a red lil, *pink* ('03)	32.50	11.50
101	A11	47a dk blue, *rose*	50.00	11.50
102	A11	47a dull bl, *straw* ('03)	60.00	13.00
103	A11	78a blk & red, *bl* ('00)	77.50	17.50
		Nos. 75-103 (29)	710.50	194.65

Issued without gum: Nos. 76a, 77, 79-80, 82, 84, 89, 94, 97 and 103.

For surcharges and overprints see Nos. 104-107, 132-136, 141, 147-157D, 159-161, 182, 195-209, 253-255, 258A.

Nos. 92, 95, 98-99 Surcharged in Black

1900

No.	Type	Description	Unused	Used
104	A11	5a on 13a violet	20.00	3.50
105	A11	10a on 16a dk bl, *bl*	22.50	5.00
106	A11	15a on 24a brn, *buff*	22.50	8.25
107	A11	20a on 31a red lilac	25.00	13.50
		Nos. 104-107 (4)	90.00	30.25

Nos. 106-107 were issued without gum.

Regular Issues Surcharged

On Stamps of 1884-85

1902 ***Perf. 11½***

Black Surcharge

No.	Type	Description	Unused	Used
108	A1	6a on 10r orange	30.00	9.75
a.		Double surcharge	*300.00*	*175.00*
109	A1	6a on 10r green	21.00	6.00

On Stamps of 1888

Red Surcharge

Perf. 12½, 13½

110 A7 6a on 5r black 10.00 3.50
a. Inverted surcharge 110.00 60.00

Black Surcharge

111 A7 6a on 10r green 8.25 3.50
112 A7 6a on 40r choc 8.25 3.50
a. Double surcharge 125.00 50.00
b. Perf. 13½ 30.00 10.00
113 A7 18a on 20r rose 17.00 4.50
a. Double surcharge 160.00 70.00
114 A7 18a on 25r violet 175.00 60.00
115 A7 18a on 80r gray 190.00 67.50
a. Double surcharge 225.00 175.00
116 A7 18a on 100r brown 42.50 26.00
a. Perf. 13½ 90.00 35.00
117 A7 18a on 200r gray lil 175.00 67.50
a. Perf. 12½ 190.00 60.00
118 A7 18a on 300r orange 30.00 10.00
a. Perf. 13½ 57.50 25.00

Issued without gum: Nos. 110-118.

Nos. 109 to 118 inclusive, except No. 111, have been reprinted. The reprints have white gum and clean-cut perforation 13½ and the colors are usually paler than those of the originals.

On Stamps of 1894

1902-10 ***Perf. 11½, 13½***

119 A9 6a on 5r yellow 7.75 2.75
a. Inverted surcharge 82.50 65.00
120 A9 6a on 10r red vio 26.00 5.25
121 A9 6a on 15r choc 26.00 5.25
122 A9 6a on 25r green 7.75 2.75
123 A9 6a on 80r yel grn 7.75 2.75
124 A9 6a on 100r brn, *buff* 15.00 6.00
a. Perf. 11½ 26.00 10.00
125 A9 6a on 200r bl, *bl* 10.00 2.75
a. Vert. half used as 3a on cover ('10) 40.00
126 A9 18a on 20r lavender 21.00 6.75
127 A9 18a on 50r lt blue 26.00 6.75
a. Perf. 13½ 77.50 17.00
128 A9 18a on 75r carmine 21.00 6.75
129 A9 18a on 150r car, *rose* 21.00 7.50
130 A9 18a on 300r bl, *salmon* 26.00 6.75

On Newspaper Stamp of 1893

Perf. 12½

131 N3 18a on 2½r brown 10.00 3.25
a. Perf. 13½ 27.50 9.00
b. Perf. 11½ 45.00 14.00
Nos. 108-131 (24) 932.25 327.00

Issued without gum: Nos. 122-130, 131b.

Stamps of 1898-1900 Overprinted in Black

1902 ***Perf. 11½***

132 A11 2a yellow green 21.00 4.00
133 A11 4a sea green 32.50 10.00
134 A11 8a blue 21.00 7.00
135 A11 10a slate blue 26.00 8.00
136 A11 12a rose 70.00 26.00
Nos. 132-136 (5) 170.50 55.00

Issued without gum: Nos. 133, 135.

Reprints of No. 133 have shiny white gum and clean-cut perforation 13½. Value $1.

No. 91 Surcharged

1905

141 A11 10a on 12a red lilac 30.00 12.50

Nos. J1-J3 Overprinted

1910, Oct. ***Perf. 11½x12***

144 D1 ½a gray green 12.50 6.75
a. Inverted overprint 30.00 25.00
145 D1 1a yellow green 15.00 6.75
a. Inverted overprint 30.00 25.00
146 D1 2a slate 20.00 7.50
a. Inverted overprint 60.00 25.00
Nos. 144-146 (3) 47.50 21.00

Stamps of 1898-1903 Overprinted in Carmine or Green

Lisbon Overprint

Overprint 24½mm long. "A" has flattened top.

1911, Apr. 2 ***Perf. 11½***

147 A11 ½a gray 2.10 .75
a. Inverted overprint 20.00 20.00
147B A11 1a orange 2.00 .75
c. Inverted overprint 20.00 20.00
148 A11 2a gray green 2.00 .75
149 A11 3a slate 6.25 .75
150 A11 4a carmine (G) 6.25 2.00
a. 4a pale yel brn (error) 55.00 50.00
151 A11 5a pale yel brn 6.25 4.00
152 A11 6a red brown 6.25 4.00
153 A11 8a gray brown 6.25 4.00
154 A11 10a slate blue 6.25 4.00
155 A11 13a gray lilac 10.00 5.00
156 A11 16a dk blue, *bl* 10.00 5.00
157 A11 18a org brn, *pink* 16.00 6.00
157A A11 20a brown, *straw* 16.00 6.00
157B A11 31a red lil, *pink* 30.00 8.00
157C A11 47a dull bl, *straw* 50.00 10.00
157D A11 78a blk & red, *bl* 82.50 12.00
Nos. 147-157D (16) 258.10 73.00

Issued without gum: Nos. 153-157D.

Coat of Arms — A14

1911 ***Perf. 11½x12***

Red Surcharge

158 A14 1a on 5r brn & buff 32.50 12.50
a. "1" omitted 67.50 50.00
b. Inverted surcharge 52.50 26.50

Stamps of 1900-03 Surcharged

Diagonal Halves

1911 **Without Gum** ***Perf. 11½***

Black Surcharge

159 A11 2a on half of 4a car 32.50 32.50
a. "2" omitted 80.00 80.00
b. Inverted surcharge 150.00 82.50
d. Entire stamp 67.50 65.00
159C A11 5a on half of 10a sl bl (#89) 4,000. —
e. Entire stamp 8,500. —

Red Surcharge

160 A11 5a on half of 10a sl bl (#89) 4,500. 1,500.
a. Inverted surcharge 5,000. 1,750.
b. Entire stamp 11,000. 5,000.
161 A11 5a on half of 10a sl bl (#135) 125.00 80.00
a. Inverted surcharge 350.00 200.00
b. Entire stamp 275.00 165.00

A15

1911 ***Perf. 12x11½***

Laid or Wove Paper

162 A15 1a black 525.00 —
a. "Corrieo" 1,900. —
163 A15 2a black 600.00 —
a. "Corrieo" 1,900. —

The vast majority of used stamps were not canceled.

Surcharged Stamps of 1902 Overprinted in Red or Green

Local Overprint

Overprint 23mm long. "A" has pointed top.

1913 **Without Gum** ***Perf. 11½***

164 A1 6a on 10r green (R) 37.50 12.00

Perf. 12½, 13½

165 A7 6a on 5r black (G) 15.00 3.50
166 A7 6a on 10r green (R) 31.00 8.00
167 A7 6a on 40r choc (R) 10.50 3.00
a. Perf. 13½ 50.00 20.00
168 A7 18a on 20r car (G) 21.00 6.00
169 A7 18a on 100r brown (R) 82.50 40.00
a. Perf. 13½ 100.00 50.00
170 A7 18a on 300r org (R) 32.50 9.00
a. Perf. 13½ 50.00 10.00
Nos. 164-170 (7) 230.00 81.50

"Republica" overprint exists inverted on Nos. 164-170.

"Republica" overprint exists double on No. 164.

1913 **Without Gum** ***Perf. 11½, 13½***

171 A9 6a on 10r red vio (G) 14.50 4.50
172 A9 6a on 10r red vio (R) 175.00 26.00
173 A9 6a on 15r choc (R) 14.50 5.00
174 A9 6a on 25r green (R) 16.00 5.00
175 A9 6a on 80r yel grn (R) 14.50 5.00
176 A9 6a on 100r brn, *buff*(R) 30.00 7.00
a. Perf. 11½ 32.50 8.00
177 A9 18a on 20r lav (R) 19.00 5.00
178 A9 18a on 50r lt bl (R) 19.00 5.00
a. Perf. 13½ 21.00 6.00
179 A9 18a on 75r car (G) 19.00 5.50
180 A9 18a on 150r car, *rose* (G) 21.00 6.00
181 A9 18a on 300r dk bl, *buff* (R) 32.50 10.00

On No. 141

182 A11 10a on 12a red lil (R) 13.00 4.50
Nos. 171-182 (12) 388.00 88.50

"Republica" overprint exists inverted on Nos. 171-181.

Stamps of Preceding Issue Surcharged

1913 **Without Gum** ***Perf. 11½***

183 A9 2a on 18a on 20r (R) 10.00 4.00
184 A9 2a on 18a on 50r (R) 10.00 4.00
a. Perf. 13½ 11.00 4.25
185 A9 2a on 18a on 75r (G) 10.00 4.00
186 A9 2a on 18a on 150r (G) 10.00 4.00
Nos. 183-186 (4) 40.00 16.00

"Republica" overprint exists inverted on Nos. 183-186. Value, each $20.

The 2a surcharge exists inverted or double on Nos. 183-186. For values, see Classic Specialized Catalogue.

Vasco da Gama Issue Overprinted or Surcharged:

j

k

187 CD20 (j) ½a blue green 7.75 2.00
188 CD21 (j) 1a red 8.50 2.00
189 CD22 (j) 2a red violet 8.50 2.00
a. Double ovpt., one inverted 100.00
190 CD23 (j) 4a yellow grn 7.75 2.00
191 CD24 (j) 8a dk blue 13.00 2.00
192 CD25 (k) 10a on 12a vio brn 24.00 5.00
193 CD26 (j) 16a bister brn 17.00 4.00
194 CD27 (j) 24a bister 27.50 5.00
Nos. 187-194 (8) 114.00 24.00

Stamps of 1898-1903 Overprinted in Red or Green

1913 **Without Gum** ***Perf. 11½***

195 A11 4a carmine (G) 250.00 100.00
196 A11 5a yellow brn 27.50 20.00
a. Inverted overprint 50.00 40.00
197 A11 6a red brown 77.50 40.00
198 A11 8a gray brown 625.00 300.00
198A A11 10a dull blue —
199 A11 13a violet 77.50 32.50
a. Inverted overprint 95.00
200 A11 13a gray lilac 37.50 20.00
201 A11 16a blue, *bl* 45.00 20.00
202 A11 18a org brn, *pink* 45.00 20.00
203 A11 20a brown, *yelsh* 45.00 20.00
204 A11 31a red lil, *pink* 67.50 30.00
205 A11 47a dull bl, *straw* 100.00 40.00

Only 20 copies of No. 198A were sold by the Post Office.

Stamps of 1911-13 Surcharged

On Stamps of 1911 With Lisbon "Republica"

1913

206 A11 ½a on 5a yel brn (R) 15.00 3.00
a. "½ Avo" inverted 125.00 70.00
207 A11 4a on 8a gray brn (R) 30.00 4.00
a. "4 Avos" inverted 150.00 70.00

On Stamps of 1913 With Local "Republica"

208 A11 1a on 13a violet (R) 125.00 30.00
209 A11 1a on 13a gray lil (R) 15.00 3.00
Nos. 206-209 (4) 185.00 40.00

Issued without gum: Nos. 207-209.

"Ceres" — A16

1913-24 ***Perf. 12x11½, 15x14***

Name and Value in Black

210 A16 ½a olive brown 1.75 .20
a. Inscriptions inverted 50.00
211 A16 1a black 1.75 .20
a. Inscriptions inverted 50.00
b. Inscriptions double 50.00
212 A16 1½a yel grn ('24) 1.75 .20
213 A16 2a blue green 1.75 .20
a. Inscriptions inverted 40.00
214 A16 3a orange ('23) 10.00 3.00
215 A16 4a carmine 6.75 1.00
216 A16 4a lemon ('24) 14.00 2.25
217 A16 5a lilac brown 7.75 3.00
218 A16 6a lt violet 7.75 3.00
219 A16 6a gray ('23) 47.50 7.50
220 A16 8a lilac brown 7.75 3.00
221 A16 10a deep blue 7.75 3.00
222 A16 10a pale blue ('23) 27.50 6.00
223 A16 12a yellow brn 11.00 3.00
224 A16 14a lilac ('24) 42.50 12.00
225 A16 16a slate 20.00 5.00

226 A16 20a orange brn 20.00 5.00
227 A16 24a slate grn ('23) 25.00 7.00
228 A16 32a orange brn ('24) 25.00 8.00
229 A16 40a plum 21.00 5.00
230 A16 56a dull rose ('24) 50.00 15.00
231 A16 58a brown, *grn* 35.00 12.00
232 A16 72a brown ('23) 67.50 20.00
233 A16 76a brown, *pink* 50.00 14.00
234 A16 1p orange, *sal* 67.50 20.00
235 A16 1p orange ('24) 200.00 30.00
236 A16 3p green, *bl* 200.00 55.00
237 A16 3p pale turq ('24) 425.00 95.00
238 A16 5p car rose ('24) 350.00 82.50
Nos. 210-238 (29) 1,753. 421.05

For surcharges see Nos. 256, 259-267.

Preceding Issues and No. P4 Overprinted in Carmine

On Stamps of 1902

Perf. 11½, 12, 12½, 13½, 11½x12

1915

239 A7 6a on 10r green 14.50 4.00
240 A9 6a on 5r yellow 14.50 4.00
241 A9 6a on 10r red vio 14.50 4.00
242 A9 6a on 15r choc 12.50 3.25
243 A9 6a on 25r green 12.00 4.00
244 A9 6a on 80r yel grn 12.00 4.00
245 A9 6a on 100r brn, *buff* 21.00 4.00
246 A9 6a on 200r bl, *bl* 11.00 6.00
247 A9 18a on 20r lav 21.00 6.00
248 A9 18a on 50r lt bl 45.00 6.75
249 A9 18a on 75r car 40.00 6.75
250 A9 18a on 150r car, *rose* 45.00 8.00
251 A9 18a on 300r bl, *sal* 40.00 10.00
252 N3 18a on 2½r brn 32.50 6.00

With Additional Overprint

253 A11 8a blue 14.50 8.25
254 A11 10a slate blue 14.50 6.00
a. "Provisorio" double 110.00

On Stamp of 1905

255 A11 10a on 12a red lilac 19.00 9.75
Nos. 239-255 (17) 383.50 100.75

Issued without gum: Nos. 243-251 and 255.

No. 217 Surcharged

1919-20

Without Gum

256 A16 ½a on 5a lilac brn 100.00 32.50

Nos. 243 and 244 Surcharged

257 A9 2a on 6a on 25r green 500.00 125.00
258 A9 2a on 6a on 80r yel grn 100.00 70.00

No. 152 Surcharged

258A A11 2a on 6a red brown 175.00 70.00
Nos. 256-258A (4) 875.00 297.50

Issued without gum: Nos. 256-258A.

Stamps of 1913-24 Surcharged

1931-33

259 A16 1a on 24a slate grn ('33) 14.50 4.00
260 A16 2a on 32a org brn ('33) 14.50 4.00
261 A16 4a on 12a bis brn ('33) 14.50 4.00
262 A16 5a on 6a lt gray ('33) 57.50 20.00
263 A16 5a on 6a lt vio ('33) 30.00 11.00
264 A16 7a on 8a lil brn 24.00 5.00
265 A16 12a on 14a lil 24.00 5.00
266 A16 15a on 16a dk gray ('33) 24.00 5.00
267 A16 20a on 56a dl rose ('33) 50.00 11.00
Nos. 259-267 (9) 253.00 69.00

"Portugal" and Vasco da Gama's Flagship "San Gabriel" — A17

Wmk. 232

1934, Feb. 1 Typo. *Perf. 11½*

268 A17 ½a bister .45 .40
269 A17 1a olive brown .45 .20
270 A17 2a blue green 1.10 .50
271 A17 3a violet 1.40 .50
272 A17 4a black 1.75 .50
273 A17 5a gray 1.75 .80
274 A17 6a brown 1.75 .80
275 A17 7a brt rose 3.25 1.00
276 A17 8a brt blue 3.25 1.00
277 A17 10a red orange 7.25 2.00
278 A17 12a dark blue 7.25 2.00
279 A17 14a olive green 7.25 2.00
280 A17 15a maroon 7.25 2.00
281 A17 20a orange 7.25 2.00
282 A17 30a apple green 14.00 3.50
283 A17 40a violet 14.00 3.50
284 A17 50a olive bister 21.00 5.00
285 A17 1p lt blue 110.00 27.50
286 A17 2p brown org 140.00 35.00
287 A17 3p emerald 225.00 40.00
288 A17 5p dark violet 350.00 87.50
Nos. 268-288 (21) 925.40 217.70

See Nos. 316-323. For overprints and surcharges see Nos. 306-315, C1-C6, J43-J49.

Common Design Types

Perf. 13½x13

1938, Aug. 1 Engr. Unwmk.

Name and Value in Black

289 CD34 1a gray green 1.00 .35
290 CD34 2a orange brown 1.25 .55
291 CD34 3a dk vio brn 1.25 .55
292 CD34 4a brt green 1.25 .55
293 CD35 5a dk carmine 1.25 .55
294 CD35 6a slate 1.25 .55
295 CD35 8a rose violet 2.10 2.25
296 CD37 10a brt red vio 2.50 2.25
297 CD37 12a red 3.25 2.60
298 CD37 15a orange 3.25 2.60
299 CD36 20a blue 16.50 2.90
300 CD36 40a gray black 16.50 3.50
301 CD36 50a brown 16.50 3.75
302 CD38 1p brown car 50.00 7.25
303 CD38 2p olive green 100.00 11.00
304 CD38 3p blue violet 125.00 22.50
305 CD38 5p red brown 250.00 37.50
Nos. 289-305 (17) 592.85 101.20

For surcharge see No. 315A.

Stamps of 1934 Surcharged in Black:

a

b

1941 Wmk. 232 *Perf. 11½x12*

306 A17(a) 1a on 6a brown 7.50 3.00
307 A17(b) 2a on 6a brown 3.00 1.50
308 A17(b) 3a on 6a brown 3.00 1.50
309 A17(a) 5a on 7a brt rose 120.00 50.00
310 A17(b) 5a on 7a brt rose 17.50 8.25
311 A17(a) 5a on 8a brt blue 19.50 9.75
312 A17(b) 5a on 8a brt blue 12.00 8.25
313 A17(b) 8a on 30a apple grn 9.00 4.00
314 A17(b) 8a on 40a violet 9.00 4.00
315 A17(b) 8a on 50a olive bis 9.00 4.50
Nos. 306-315 (10) 209.50 94.75

No. 294 Surcharged in Black:

1941 Unwmk. *Perf. 13½x13*

315A CD35 3a on 6a slate 70.00 32.50

Counterfeits exist.

"Portugal" Type of 1934

1942 Litho. *Rough Perf. 12*

Thin Paper Without Gum

316 A17 1a olive brown 1.90 .75
317 A17 2a blue green 1.90 .75
318 A17 3a vio, perf. 11 22.50 2.50
a. Perf. 12 27.50 3.25
319 A17 6a brown 27.50 3.00
a. Perf. 10 55.00 7.00
b. Perf. 11 47.50 6.00
320 A17 10a red orange 15.00 1.50
321 A17 20a orange 15.00 1.50
a. Perf. 11 47.50 5.00
322 A17 30a apple green 27.50 2.50
323 A17 40a violet 37.50 3.25
Nos. 316-323 (8) 148.80 15.75

Macao Dwelling A18

Pagoda of Barra — A19

Designs: 2a, Mountain fort. 3a, View of Macao. 8a, Praia Grande Bay. 10a, Leal Senado Square. 20a, Sao Jeronimo Hill. 30a, Marginal Ave. 50a, Relief of Goddess Ma. 1p, Gate of Cerco. 3p, Post Office. 5p, Solidao Walk.

1948, Dec. 20 Litho. *Perf. 10½*

324 A18 1a dk brn & org 2.25 .50
325 A19 2a rose brn & rose 1.60 .50
326 A18 3a brn vio & lil 3.75 .75
327 A18 8a rose car & rose 2.25 .90
328 A18 10a lilac rose & rose 3.75 1.25
329 A18 20a dk blue & gray 4.75 1.50
330 A18 30a black & gray 9.25 2.50
331 A18 50a brn & pale bis 14.00 5.00
332 A19 1p emer & pale grn 110.00 15.00
333 A19 2p scarlet & rose 92.50 15.00
334 A19 3p dl grn & gray grn 140.00 16.00
335 A18 5p vio bl & gray 275.00 22.50
Nos. 324-335 (12) 659.10 81.40

See Nos. 341-347A.

Catalogue values for unused stamps in this section, from this point to the end of the section, are for Never Hinged items.

Lady of Fatima Issue

Common Design Type

1949, Feb. 1 Unwmk. *Perf. 14½*

336 CD40 8a scarlet 40.00 12.00

Symbols of the UPU — A20

Dragon — A21

1949, Dec. 24 Litho. Unwmk.

337 A20 32a claret & rose 50.00 15.00

75th anniv. of the formation of the UPU.

Holy Year Issue

Common Design Types

1950, July 26 *Perf. 13x13½*

339 CD41 32a dk slate gray 27.50 6.00
340 CD42 50a carmine 27.50 6.50

Scenic Types of 1948

Designs as before.

1950-51 *Perf. 14*

341 A18 1a violet & rose 2.75 .75
342 A19 2a ol bis & yel 2.75 .75
343 A18 3a org red & buff 8.50 1.25
344 A18 8a slate & gray 11.00 1.25
345 A18 10a red brn & org 15.00 3.25
346 A18 30a vio bl & bl 17.50 3.25
347 A18 50a ol grn & yel grn 42.50 4.00
347A A19 1p dk org brn & org brn 110.00 24.00
Nos. 341-347A (8) 210.00 38.50

A 1p ultra & vio, perf. 11, was not sold in Macao. Value $100.

#341-347 issued in 1951, the 1p in 1950.

1951 *Perf. 11½x12*

348 A21 1a org yel, *lemon* 2.25 .50
349 A21 2a dk grn, *blue* 2.25 .50
350 A21 10a vio brn, *blue* 8.00 2.50
351 A21 10a brt pink, *blue* 7.50 2.50
Nos. 348-351 (4) 20.00 6.00

Nos. 348-351 were isuued without gum. For overprints see Nos. J50-J52.

Holy Year Extension Issue

Common Design Type

1951, Dec. 3 Litho. *Perf. 14*

352 CD43 60a magenta & pink + label *50.00* 9.00

Stamp without label sells for much less.

Fernao Mendes Pinto — A22

Portraits: 2a and 10a, St. Francis Xavier. 3a and 50a, Jorge Alvares. 6a and 30a, Luis de Camoens.

1951, Aug. 27 *Perf. 11½*

353 A22 1a steel bl & gray bl .90 .50
354 A22 2a dk brown & ol grn 1.90 .50
355 A22 3a deep grn & grn 2.25 .75
356 A22 6a purple 3.00 1.00
357 A22 10a red brn & org 7.25 1.50
358 A22 20a brown car 14.00 3.25
359 A22 30a dk brn & ol grn 21.00 4.50
360 A22 50a red & orange 57.50 11.00
Nos. 353-360 (8) 107.80 23.00

Sampan — A23 Junk — A24

Design: 5p, Junk.

1951, Nov. 1 Unwmk.

361 A23 1p vio bl & bl 37.50 2.25
362 A24 3p black & vio 140.00 15.00
363 A23 5p henna brown 175.00 24.00
Nos. 361-363 (3) 352.50 41.25

Medical Congress Issue
Common Design Type

Design: Sao Rafael Hospital.

1952, June 16 Unwmk. *Perf. 13½*
364 CD44 6a black & purple 9.75 3.50

Statue of St. Francis Xavier — A25

Statue of Virgin Mary — A26

St. Francis Xavier Issue

16a, Arm of St. Francis. 40a, Tomb of St. Francis.

1952, Nov. 28 Litho. *Perf. 14*
365 A25 3a blk, *grnsh gray* 4.00 .90
366 A25 16a choc, *buff* 17.00 3.00
367 A25 40a blk, *blue* 21.00 5.25
Nos. 365-367 (3) 42.00 9.15

400th anniv. of the death of St. Francis Xavier.

1953, Apr. 28 Unwmk. *Perf. 13½*
368 A26 8a choc & dull ol 3.75 1.00
369 A26 10a blue blk & buff 15.00 4.00
370 A26 50a slate grn & ol grn 26.00 6.00
Nos. 368-370 (3) 44.75 11.00

Exhibition of Sacred Missionary Art, held at Lisbon in 1951.

Stamp of Portugal and Arms of Colonies — A27

1954, Mar. 9 Photo. *Perf. 13*
371 A27 10a multicolored 10.00 2.00

Cent. of Portugal's first postage stamps.

Firecracker Flower — A28

Map of Colony — A29

Flowers: 3a, Forget-me-not. 5a, Dragon claw. 10a, Nunflower. 16a, Narcissus. 30a, Peach flower. 39a, Lotus flower. 1p, Chrysanthemum. 3p, Cherry blossoms. 5p, Tangerine blossoms.

1953, Sept. 22 *Perf. 11½*
Flowers in Natural Colors
372 A28 1a dark red .60 .25
373 A28 3a dark green .60 .25
374 A28 5a dark brown .60 .25
375 A28 10a dp grnsh blue .60 .35
376 A28 16a yellow brown 1.25 .35
377 A28 30a dk olive grn 2.75 .40
378 A28 39a violet blue 3.25 .40
379 A28 1p deep plum 7.25 .90
380 A28 3p dark gray 16.50 2.00
381 A28 5p deep carmine 27.50 3.25
Nos. 372-381 (10) 60.90 8.40

For surcharges see #443-444.

Sao Paulo Issue
Common Design Type

1954, Aug. 4 Litho. *Perf. 13½*
382 CD46 39a org, cream & blk 14.00 2.75

Sao Paulo founding, 400th anniversary.
For surcharge see #445.

Perf. 12½x13½
1956, May 10 Photo.
Inscriptions and design in brown, red, green, ultra & yellow (buff on 10a, 40a, 90a)
383 A29 1a gray .50 .40
384 A29 3a pale gray 1.10 .50
385 A29 5a pale pink 1.50 .75
386 A29 10a buff 3.00 .90
387 A29 30a lt blue 7.50 1.25
388 A29 40a pale green 10.00 1.50
389 A29 90a pale gray 14.00 2.75
390 A29 1.50p pink 25.00 3.75
Nos. 383-390 (8) 62.60 11.80

Exhibition Emblems and View — A30

Armillary Sphere — A31

1958, Nov. 8 Litho. *Perf. 14½*
391 A30 70a multicolored 6.00 1.75

World's Fair, Brussels, Apr. 17-Oct. 19.

Tropical Medicine Congress Issue
Common Design Type

Design: Cinnamomum camphora.

1958, Nov. 15 *Perf. 13½*
392 CD47 20a multicolored 8.00 2.50

1960, June 25 Litho. *Perf. 13½*
393 A31 2p multicolored 11.50 3.50

500th anniversary of the death of Prince Henry the Navigator.

Sports Issue
Common Design Type

Sports: 10a, Field hockey. 16a, Wrestling. 20a, Table tennis. 50a, Motorcycling. 1.20p, Relay race. 2.50p, Badminton.

1962, Feb. 9 *Perf. 13½*
Multicolored Design
394 CD48 10a blue & yel grn 2.00 .40
395 CD48 16a brt pink 2.50 .60
396 CD48 20a orange 3.50 .80
397 CD48 50a rose 6.00 .80
398 CD48 1.20p blue & beige 25.00 2.75
399 CD48 2.50p gray & brown 35.00 6.25
Nos. 394-399 (6) 74.00 11.60

Anti-Malaria Issue
Common Design Type

Design: Anopheles hyrcanus sinensis.

1962, Apr. 7 Litho. *Perf. 13½*
400 CD49 40a multicolored 7.00 2.00

Bank Building — A32

1964, May 16 Unwmk. *Perf. 13½*
401 A32 20a multicolored 10.00 2.25

Centenary of the National Overseas Bank of Portugal.

ITU Issue
Common Design Type

1965, May 17 Litho. *Perf. 14½*
402 CD52 10a pale grn & multi *5.50* 1.50

National Revolution Issue
Common Design Type

Design: 10a, Infante D. Henrique School and Count de S. Januario Hospital.

1966, May 28 Litho. *Perf. 11½*
403 CD53 10a multicolored 5.00 1.50

Drummer, 1548 — A32a

Designs: 15a, Soldier with sword, 1548. 20a, Harquebusier, 1649. 40a, Infantry officer, 1783. 50a, Infantry soldier, 1783. 60a, Colonial infantry soldier (Indian), 1902. 1p, Colonial infantry soldier (Chinese), 1903. 3p, Colonial infantry soldier (Chinese) 1904.

1966, Aug. 8 Litho. *Perf. 13*
404 A32a 10a multicolored 1.25 .40
405 A32a 15a multicolored 2.25 .75
406 A32a 20a multicolored 2.50 .75
407 A32a 40a multicolored 4.50 .85
408 A32a 50a multicolored 5.00 1.50
409 A32a 60a multicolored 12.00 1.75
410 A32a 1p multicolored 15.00 3.00
411 A32a 3p multicolored 27.50 6.25
Nos. 404-411 (8) 70.00 15.25

Navy Club Issue, 1967
Common Design Type

Designs: 10a, Capt. Oliveira E. Carmo and armed launch Vega. 20a, Capt. Silva Junior and frigate Dom Fernando.

1967, Jan. 31 Litho. *Perf. 13*
412 CD54 10a multicolored 3.25 1.00
413 CD54 20a multicolored 6.25 2.75

Arms of Pope Paul VI and Golden Rose — A33

Cabral Monument, Lisbon — A34

1967, May 13 *Perf. 12½x13*
414 A33 50a multicolored 5.75 2.00

50th anniversary of the apparition of the Virgin Mary to three shepherd children at Fatima.

Cabral Issue

Design: 70a, Cabral monument, Belmonte.

1968, Apr. 22 Litho. *Perf. 14*
415 A34 20a multicolored 4.25 1.00
416 A34 70a multicolored 6.00 2.25

500th anniversary of the birth of Pedro Alvares Cabral, navigator who took possession of Brazil for Portugal.

Admiral Coutinho Issue
Common Design Type

Design: 20a, Adm. Coutinho with sextant, vert.

1969, Feb. 17 Litho. *Perf. 14*
417 CD55 20a multicolored 3.75 1.50

Church of Our Lady of the Relics, Vidigueira A35

Bishop D. Belchior Carneiro A36

Vasco da Gama Issue

1969, Aug. 29 Litho. *Perf. 14*
418 A35 1p multicolored 11.00 1.50

Vasco da Gama (1469-1524), navigator.

Administration Reform Issue
Common Design Type

1969, Sept. 25 Litho. *Perf. 14*
419 CD56 90a multicolored 5.00 1.00

1969, Oct. 16 Litho. *Perf. 13*
420 A36 50a multicolored 3.25 .75

4th centenary of the founding of the Santa Casa da Misericordia in Macao.

King Manuel I Issue

Portal of Mother Church, Golega — A37

1969, Dec. 1 Litho. *Perf. 14*
421 A37 30a multicolored 6.25 .90

500th anniversary of the birth of King Manuel I.

Marshal Carmona Issue
Common Design Type

5a, Antonio Oscar Carmona in general's uniform.

1970, Nov. 15 Litho. *Perf. 14*
422 CD57 5a multicolored 1.50 .75

Dragon Mask — A38

1971, Sept. 30 *Perf. 13½*
423 A38 5a lt blue & multi 1.10 .20
424 A38 10a Lion mask 2.25 .50

Lusiads Issue

Portuguese Delegation at Chinese Court — A39

1972, May 25 Litho. *Perf. 13*
425 A39 20a citron & multi 13.00 3.75

4th centenary of publication of The Lusiads by Luiz Camoens.

Olympic Games Issue
Common Design Type

Design: Hockey and Olympic emblem.

1972, June 20 *Perf. 14x13½*
426 CD59 50a multicolored 3.50 1.00

Lisbon-Rio de Janeiro Flight Issue
Common Design Type

Design: "Santa Cruz" landing in Rio de Janeiro.

1972, Sept. 20 Litho. *Perf. 13½*
427 CD60 5p multicolored 22.50 7.50

Pedro V Theater and Lyre — A42

1972, Dec. 25 **Litho.** ***Perf. 13½***
428 A42 2p multicolored 10.00 2.50

Centenary of Pedro V Theater, Macao.

WMO Centenary Issue
Common Design Type

1973, Dec. 15 **Litho.** ***Perf. 13***
429 CD61 20a blue grn & multi 6.25 1.00

Viscount St. Januario A44

Design: 60a, Hospital, 1874 and 1974.

1974, Jan. 25 **Litho.** ***Perf. 13½***
430 A44 15a multicolored .85 .50
431 A44 60a multicolored 3.75 .90

Viscount St. Januario Hospital, Macao, cent.
For surcharge see No. 457.

George Chinnery, Self-portrait A45

1974, Sept. 23 **Litho.** ***Perf. 14***
432 A45 30a multicolored 3.50 1.25

George Chinnery (1774-1852), English painter who lived in Macao.

Macao-Taipa Bridge — A46

Design: 2.20p, Different view of bridge.

1974, Oct. 7 **Litho.** ***Perf. 14x13½***
433 A46 20a multicolored 1.50 .40
434 A46 2.20p multicolored 12.50 1.25

Inauguration of the Macao-Taipa Bridge.
For surcharge see #446.

Man Raising Banner A47

1975, Apr. 25 ***Perf. 12***
435 A47 10a ocher & multi 2.00 .75
436 A47 1p multicolored 13.50 3.25

Revolution of Apr. 25, 1974, 1st anniv.

Pou Chai Pagoda — A48

Design: 20p, Tin Hau Pagoda.

1976, Jan. 30 **Litho.** ***Perf. 13½x13***
437 A48 10p multicolored 15.00 1.75
438 A48 20p multicolored 32.50 3.75

A 1p stamp for the 400th anniv. of the Macao Diocese was prepared but not issued. Some copies were sold in Lisbon. Value $100.

"The Law" — A50

1978 **Litho.** ***Perf. 13½***
440 A50 5a blk, dk & lt blue 3.00 1.00
441 A50 2p blk, org brn & buff 125.00 5.00
442 A50 5p blk, ol & yel grn 25.00 4.50
Nos. 440-442 (3) 153.00 10.50

Legislative Assembly, Aug. 9, 1976.

Nos. 376, 378, 382, 434 Surcharged

1979, Nov.
443 A28 10a on 16a 7.50 2.00
444 A28 30a on 39a (#378) 9.50 2.00
445 CD46 30a on 39a (#382) 65.00 9.00
446 A46 2p on 2.20p 11.00 3.00
Nos. 443-446 (4) 93.00 16.00

Luis de Camoens (1524-80), Poet — A51

Buddha, Macao Cathedral — A52

1981, June **Litho.** ***Perf. 13½***
447 A51 10a multicolored .70 .25
448 A51 30a multicolored 1.40 .35
449 A51 1p multicolored 3.25 .60
450 A51 3p multicolored 4.75 1.25
Nos. 447-450 (4) 10.10 2.45

1981, Sept.
451 A52 15a multicolored .25 .20
452 A52 40a multicolored .50 .20
453 A52 50a multicolored 1.00 .20
454 A52 60a multicolored 1.50 .20
455 A52 1p multicolored 2.00 .50
456 A52 2.20p multicolored 5.00 .95
Nos. 451-456 (6) 10.25 2.25

Transcultural Psychiatry Symposium.

No. 431 Surcharged

1981 **Litho.** ***Perf. 13½***
457 A44 30a on 60a multi 6.00 1.00

Health Services Building A53

Designs: Public Buildings and Monuments.

1982, June 10 **Litho.** ***Perf. 12x12½***
458 A53 30a shown .65 .20
459 A53 40a Guia Lighthouse 1.90 .20
460 A53 1p Portas do Cerco 2.50 .25
461 A53 2p Luis de Camoes Museum 3.25 .50
462 A53 10p School Welfare Service Building 7.50 2.50
Nos. 458-462 (5) 15.80 3.65

See Nos. 472-476, 489-493.

Autumn Festivals A54

Designs: Painted paper lanterns.

1982, Oct. 1 ***Perf. 12x11½***
463 A54 40a multicolored 1.75 .50
464 A54 1p multicolored 4.75 .75
465 A54 2p multicolored 5.50 1.25
466 A54 5p multicolored 14.00 2.50
Nos. 463-466 (4) 26.00 5.00

Geographical Position — A55

1982, Dec. 1 **Litho.** ***Perf. 13***
467 A55 50a Aerial view 4.00 .50
468 A55 3p Map 15.00 1.75

World Communications Year — A56

1983, Feb. 16 ***Perf. 13½***
469 A56 60a Telephone operators 1.10 .20
470 A56 3p Mailman, mailbox 2.25 .95
471 A56 6p Globe, satellites 4.50 2.00
Nos. 469-471 (3) 7.85 3.15

Architecture Type of 1982

1983, May 12 **Litho.** ***Perf. 13***
472 A53 10a Social Welfare Institute .85 .20
473 A53 80a St. Joseph's Seminary 1.75 .40
474 A53 1.50p St. Dominic's Church 2.25 .75
475 A53 2.50p St. Paul's Church ruins 3.50 1.40
476 A53 7.50p Senate House 8.50 3.25
Nos. 472-476 (5) 16.85 6.00

Medicinal Plants A57

1983, July 14 **Litho.** ***Perf. 13½x14***
477 A57 20a Asclepias curassavica 1.00 .70
478 A57 40a Acanthus ilicifolius 1.50 .70
479 A57 60a Melastoma sanguineum 2.00 .70
480 A57 70a Nelumbo nucifera 3.00 1.40
481 A57 1.50p Bombax malabaricum 4.00 2.00
482 A57 2.50p Hibiscus mutabilis 7.25 4.00
a. Souvenir sheet of 6, #477-482 45.00
Nos. 477-482 (6) 18.75 9.50

No. 482a sold for 6.50p.

16th Century Discoveries — A58

1983, Nov. 15 **Litho.** ***Perf. 13½x14***
483 A58 4p multicolored 5.00 2.00
484 A59 4p multicolored 5.00 2.00
a. Pair, #483-484 10.00 5.00

A60

A61

1984, Jan. 25 **Litho.** ***Perf. 13½***
485 A60 60a multicolored 3.50 .75
a. Booklet pane of 5 21.00

New Year 1984 (Year of the Rat).
No. 485a has straight edges.
See Nos. 504, 522, 540, 560, 583, 611, 639, 662, 684, 718, 757, 804.

1984, Mar. 1 **Litho.** ***Perf. 12½***

Design of First Stamp Issue, 1884.

486 A61 40a orange & blk 1.00 .20
487 A61 3p gray & blk 2.10 .60
488 A61 5p sepia & blk 4.75 1.10
a. Souvenir sheet of 3, #486-488 18.00
Nos. 486-488 (3) 7.85 1.90

Centenary of Macao postage stamps.

Architecture Type of 1982

1984, May 18 **Litho.** ***Perf. 13½***
489 A53 20a Holy House of Mercy .35 .20
490 A53 60a St. Lawrence Church .70 .20
491 A53 90a King Peter V Theater 1.10 .20
492 A53 3p Palace of St. Sancha 2.10 .25
493 A53 15p Moorish barracks 4.25 1.25
Nos. 489-493 (5) 8.50 2.10

Birds, Ausipex '84 Emblem A62

1984, Sept. 21 **Litho.** ***Perf. 13***
494 A62 30a Kingfishers .85 .40
495 A62 40a European jay .90 .40
496 A62 50a White eyes 1.75 .40
497 A62 70a Hoopoe 2.50 .40
498 A62 2.50p Peking nightingale 7.00 1.10
499 A62 6p Wild duck 8.75 2.25
Nos. 494-499 (6) 21.75 4.95

Philakorea '84 Emblem, Fishing Boats A63

1984, Oct. 22 **Litho.**

500 A63 20a Hok lou t'eng .85 .25
501 A63 60a Tai t'ong 1.75 .65
502 A63 2p Tai mei chai 4.25 1.10
503 A63 5p Ch'at pong t'o 8.50 2.00
Nos. 500-503 (4) 15.35 4.00

New Year Type of 1984

1985, Feb. 13 **Litho.** ***Perf. 13½***

504 A60 1p Buffalo 3.00 .60
a. Booklet pane of 5 *20.00*

Intl. Youth Year — A65

1985, Apr. 19 **Litho.** ***Perf. 13½***

505 A65 2.50p shown *1.75* .25
506 A65 3p Clasped hands *2.25* .75

Visit of President Eanes of Portugal A66

1985, May 27 **Litho.**

507 A66 1.50p multicolored 2.10 .30

Luis de Camoens Museum, 25th Anniv. — A67

Silk paintings by Chen Chi Yun.

1985, June 27 **Litho.**

508 A67 2.50p Two travelers, hermit 3.25 .85
509 A67 2.50p Traveling merchant 3.25 .85
510 A67 2.50p Conversation in a garden 3.25 .85
511 A67 2.50p Veranda of a house 3.25 .85
a. Block or strip of 4, #508-511 20.00 7.00
Nos. 508-511 (4) 13.00 3.40

Butterflies, World Tourism Assoc. Emblem — A68

1985, Sept. 27 **Litho.**

512 A68 30a Euploea midamus 1.40 .20
513 A68 50a Hebomoia glaucippe 1.40 .20
514 A68 70a Lethe confusa 2.10 .30
515 A68 2p Heliophorus epicles 2.75 .70
516 A68 4p Euthalia phemius seitzi 5.50 2.00
517 A68 7.50p Troides helena 7.75 3.00
a. Sheet of 6, #512-517 *60.00*
Nos. 512-517 (6) 20.90 6.40

World Tourism Day.

Cargo Boats A69

Designs: 50a, Tou. 70a, Veng Seng Lei motor junk. 1p, Tong Heng Long No. 2 motor junk. 6p, Fong Vong San cargo ship.

1985, Oct. 25 ***Perf. 14***

518 A69 50a multicolored .75 .20
519 A69 70a multicolored 2.25 .50
520 A69 1p multicolored 3.75 1.00
521 A69 6p multicolored 6.00 2.50
Nos. 518-521 (4) 12.75 4.20

New Year Type of 1984

1986, Feb. 3 ***Perf. 13½***

522 A60 1.50p Tiger 3.00 .50
a. Booklet pane of 5 19.00

No. 522a has straight edges.

City of Macau, 400th Anniv. A71

1986, Apr. 10 **Litho.** ***Perf. 13½***

523 A71 2.20p multicolored *4.50* 1.50

Musical Instruments A72

1986, May 22

524 A72 20a Suo-na 1.75 .50
525 A72 50a Sheng 2.10 .65
526 A72 60a Er-hu 2.50 .65
527 A72 70a Ruan 4.25 1.25
528 A72 5p Cheng 10.00 1.90
529 A72 8p Pi-pa 12.50 4.00
a. Souvenir sheet of 6, #524-529 *55.00*
Nos. 524-529 (6) 33.10 8.95

AMERIPEX '86.

Ferries A73

1986, Aug. 28 **Litho.** ***Perf. 13***

530 A73 10a Hydrofoil .35 .20
531 A73 40a Hovermarine 3.25 .60
532 A73 3p Jetfoil 3.50 1.25
533 A73 7.5p High-speed ferry 8.50 2.50
Nos. 530-533 (4) 15.60 4.55

Fortresses — A74

1986, Oct. 3 **Litho.** ***Perf. 12½***

534 A74 2p Taipa 10.00 2.00
535 A74 2p Sao Paulo do Monte 10.00 2.00
536 A74 2p Our Lady of Guia 10.00 2.00
537 A74 2p Sao Francisco 10.00 2.00
a. Block or strip of 4, #534-537 65.00 12.00
Nos. 534-537 (4) 40.00 8.00

Macao Security Forces, 10th anniv. No. 537a has continuous design.

A75

Dr. Sun Yat-sen — A76

1986, Nov. 12 **Litho.** ***Perf. 12½***

538 A75 70a multicolored *1.40* *.50*

Souvenir Sheet

539 A76 1.30p shown *12.00* *9.00*

New Year Type of 1984

1987, Jan. 21 ***Perf. 13½***

540 A60 1.50p Hare 3.25 .60
a. Booklet pane of 5 22.50

No. 540a has straight edges.

Shek Wan Ceramic Figures in the Luis de Camoens Museum — A78

1987, Apr. 10 **Litho.** ***Perf. 13½***

541 A78 2.20p Medicine man (4/1) 3.00 1.00
542 A78 2.20p Choi San, god of good fortune (4/2) 3.00 1.00
543 A78 2.20p Yi, sun god (4/3) 3.00 1.00
544 A78 2.20p Chung Kuei, conqueror of demons (4/4) 3.00 1.00
a. Block or strip of 4, #541-544 17.50 10.00
Nos. 541-544 (4) 12.00 4.00

Dragon Boat Festival A79

1987, May 29 **Litho.** ***Perf. 13½***

545 A79 50a Dragon boat race 2.25 .45
546 A79 5p Figurehead 5.50 1.50

Decorated Fans — A80

Casino Gambling — A81

1987, July 29 **Litho.** ***Perf. 12½***

547 A80 30a multicolored 2.25 1.00
548 A80 70a multi, diff. 4.75 1.50
549 A80 1p multi, diff. 12.50 1.75
550 A80 6p multi, diff. 12.50 4.75
a. Souvenir sheet of 4, #547-550 *125.00*
Nos. 547-550 (4) 32.00 9.00

1987, Sept. 30 ***Perf. 13½***

551 A81 20a Fan-tan 7.00 2.00
552 A81 40a Cussec 7.00 2.00
553 A81 4p Baccarat 7.00 2.25
554 A81 7p Roulette 7.00 2.25
Nos. 551-554 (4) 28.00 8.50

Traditional Transportation — A82

1987, Nov. 18 **Litho.** ***Perf. 13½***

555 A82 10a Market wagon .50 .20
556 A82 70a Sedan chair 1.60 .20
557 A82 90a Rickshaw 3.00 .50
558 A82 10p Tricycle rickshaw 7.75 2.00
Nos. 555-558 (4) 12.85 2.90

Souvenir Sheet

559 A82 7.50p Sedan chair, diff. *21.00*

New Year Type of 1984

1988, Feb. 10 **Litho.** ***Perf. 13½***

560 A60 2.50p Dragon 4.25 1.25
a. Booklet pane of 5 25.00

No. 560a has straight edges.

Wildlife Protection A84

1988, Apr. 14 **Litho.** ***Perf. 12½x12***

561 A84 3p Erinaceus europaeus 3.25 1.00
562 A84 3p Meles meles 3.25 1.00
563 A84 3p Lutra lutra 3.25 1.00
564 A84 3p Manis pentadactyla 3.25 1.00
a. Block or strip of 4, #561-564 20.00 7.50
Nos. 561-564 (4) 13.00 4.00

World Health Organization, 40th Anniv. — A85

1988, June 1 **Litho.** ***Perf. 13½***

565 A85 60a Breast-feeding 2.50 .50
566 A85 80a Immunization 3.75 .50
567 A85 2.40p Blood donation 7.75 1.75
Nos. 565-567 (3) 14.00 2.75

Modes of Transportation — A86

1988, July 15 **Litho.**

568 A86 20a Bicycles .60 .25
569 A86 50a Vespa, Lambretta 1.25 .50
570 A86 3.30p 1907 Rover 20hp 3.25 .75
571 A86 5p 1912 Renault delivery truck 4.75 1.50
Nos. 568-571 (4) 9.85 3.00

Souvenir Sheet

572 A86 7.50p 1930s Sedan *16.00*

1988 Summer Olympics, Seoul A87

1988, Sept. 19 Litho.

573	A87 40a	Hurdles	.75	.25
574	A87 60a	Basketball	1.25	.25
575	A87 1p	Soccer	2.25	.70
576	A87 8p	Table tennis	4.25	1.40
		Nos. 573-576 (4)	8.50	2.60

Souvenir Sheet

577	Sheet of 5, #573-576, 577a	*20.00*	
a.	A87 5p Tae kwon do	*10.00*	

World Post Day — A88

35th Macao Grand Prix — A89

1988, Oct. 10 Litho. Perf. 14

578	A88 13.40p	Electronic mail	5.25	.50
579	A88 40p	Express mail	10.50	2.50

1988, Nov. 24 Litho. Perf. 12½

580	A89 80a	Sedan	1.00	.20
581	A89 2.80p	Motorcycle	3.25	.40
582	A89 7p	Formula 3	7.75	1.40
a.		Souvenir sheet of 3, #580-582	*25.00*	
		Nos. 580-582 (3)	12.00	2.00

New Year Type of 1984

1989, Jan. 20 Litho. Perf. 13½

583	A60 3p	Snake	6.25	.75
a.		Booklet pane of 5	32.50	

No. 583a has straight edges. Value for No. 583 is for stamp perfed on 4 sides.

Occupations A91

1989, Mar. 1 Litho. Perf. 12x12½

584	A91 50a	Water carrier	.60	.20
585	A91 1p	Tan-kya woman	1.40	.40
586	A91 4p	Tin-tin (junk) man	2.75	.65
587	A91 5p	Tofu peddler	4.00	1.25
		Nos. 584-587 (4)	8.75	2.50

See Nos. 612-615, 640-643.

Watercolors by George Smirnoff in the Luis de Camoens Museum — A92

1989, Apr. 10 Litho. Perf. 12½x12

588	A92 2p	multi (4-1)	2.10	.60
589	A92 2p	multi (4-2)	2.10	.60
590	A92 2p	multi (4-3)	2.10	.60
591	A92 2p	multi (4-4)	2.10	.60
a.		Block or strip of 4, #588-591	12.75	3.25
		Nos. 588-591 (4)	8.40	2.40

Snakes A93

1989, July 7 Litho.

592	A93 2.50p	*Naja naja*	2.10	.60
593	A93 2.50p	*Bungarus fasciatus*	2.10	.60
594	A93 2.50p	*Trimeresurus albolabris*	2.10	.60
595	A93 2.50p	*Elaphe radiata*	2.10	.60
a.		Block or strip of 4, #592-595	12.75	3.25
		Nos. 592-595 (4)	8.40	2.40

Traditional Games — A94

1989, July 31 Litho. Perf. 13½

596	A94 10a	Talu	.65	.20
597	A94 60a	Triol	1.90	.20
598	A94 3.30p	Chiquia	3.75	.85
599	A94 5p	Xadrez Chines	5.00	1.40
		Nos. 596-599 (4)	11.30	2.65

Airplanes A95

1989, Oct. 9 Litho.

600	A95 50a	Over church	.50	.20
601	A95 70a	American over lighthouse	1.00	.20
602	A95 2.80p	Over wharf	1.50	.70
603	A95 4p	Over junk	3.00	1.00
		Nos. 600-603 (4)	6.00	2.10

Souvenir Sheet

604	A95 7.50p	Over harbor	*12.00*	4.00

No. 604 contains one 40x30mm stamp.

World Stamp Expo '89, Washington, DC — A96

1989, Nov. 17 Litho. Perf. 12½

605	A96 40a	Malacca	.45	.25
606	A96 70a	Thailand	.90	.25
607	A96 90a	India	1.40	.50
608	A96 2.50p	Japan	2.25	.65
609	A96 7.50p	China	4.50	1.60
		Nos. 605-609 (5)	9.50	3.25

Souvenir Sheet

610	Sheet of 6, #605-609, 610a	*14.00*	8.00
a.	A96 3p Macao	*4.00*	4.00

Influence of the Portuguese in the Far East.

New Year Type of 1984

1990, Jan. 19 Litho. Perf. 13½

611	A60 4p	Horse	3.50	1.00
a.		Booklet pane of 5	19.00	

No. 611a has straight edges. Value for No. 611 is for stamp perfed on 4 sides.

Occupations Type of 1989

1990, Mar. 1 Litho. Perf. 12x12½

612	A91 30a	Long chau singer	.90	.45
613	A91 70a	Cobbler	1.75	.85
614	A91 1.50p	Scribe	2.75	.85
615	A91 7.50p	Net fisherman	8.00	2.10
		Nos. 612-615 (4)	13.40	4.25

Souvenir Sheet

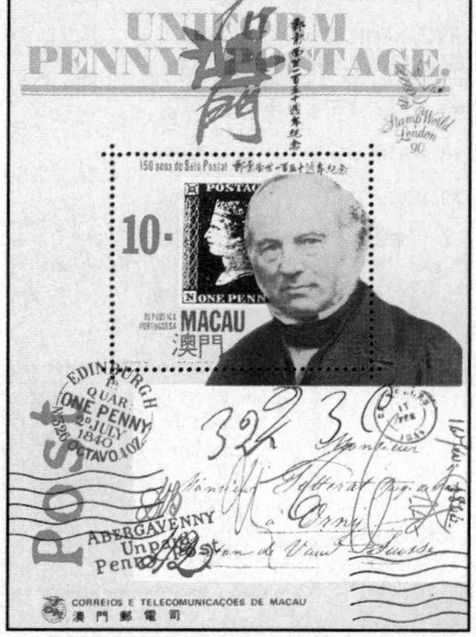
Penny Black, 150th Anniv. — A99

1990, May 3 Litho. Perf. 12

616	A99 10p	multicolored	*12.50*	4.00

Stamp World London 90.

Lutianus Malabaricus — A100

1990, June 8 Perf. 12x12½

617	A100 2.40p	shown	1.90	.90
618	A100 2.40p	Epinephelus megachir	1.90	.90
619	A100 2.40p	Macropodus opercularis	1.90	.90
620	A100 2.40p	Ophiocephalus maculatus	1.90	.90
a.		Block or strip of 4, #617-620	10.50	3.50
		Nos. 617-620 (4)	7.60	3.60

Decorative Porcelain A101

1990, Aug. 24 Litho. Perf. 12½

621	A101 3p	shown	2.10	1.00
622	A101 3p	Furniture	2.10	1.00
623	A101 3p	Toys	2.10	1.00
624	A101 3p	Artificial flowers	2.10	1.00
a.		Souvenir sheet of 4, #621-624	*25.00*	*8.00*
b.		Block or strip of 4, #621-624	12.50	5.00
		Nos. 621-624 (4)	8.40	4.00

Asian Games, Beijing — A102

1990, Sept. 22 Litho. Perf. 13½

625	A102 80a	Cycling	.65	.20
626	A102 1p	Swimming	1.10	.25
627	A102 3p	Judo	3.25	1.00
628	A102 4.20p	Shooting	5.00	1.40
		Nos. 625-628 (4)	10.00	2.85

Souvenir Sheet

629	Sheet of 5, #625-628, 629a	*18.00*	*9.00*
a.	A102 6p Martial arts	*5.00*	*5.00*

Compass Roses from Portuguese Charts — A103

Charts by 16th century cartographers: Lazaro Luis, Diogo Homem, Fernao Vaz Dourado, and Luiz Teixeira.

1990, Oct. 9 Litho. Perf. 13½

630	A103 50a	shown	.90	.40
631	A103 1p	multi, diff.	1.75	.40
632	A103 3.50p	multi, diff.	3.50	1.10
633	A103 6.50p	multi, diff.	8.00	1.50
		Nos. 630-633 (4)	14.15	3.40

Souvenir Sheet

634	A103 5p	multi, diff.	*18.00*	*6.00*

Games with Animals A104

1990, Nov. 15 Litho. Perf. 14

635	A104 20a	Cricket fight	.60	.20
636	A104 80a	Bird fight	1.75	.45
637	A104 1p	Greyhound race	2.25	.60
638	A104 10p	Horse race	7.00	1.25
		Nos. 635-638 (4)	11.60	2.50

New Year Type of 1984

1991, Feb. 8 Litho. Perf. 13½

639	A60 4.50p	Sheep	3.75	.75
b.		Booklet pane of 5	*22.50*	

No. 639b has straight edges.

Occupations Type of 1987

1991, Mar. 1 Perf. 14

640	A91 80a	Knife grinder	.85	.45
641	A91 1.70p	Flour puppet vender	1.75	.45
642	A91 3.50p	Street barber	4.25	.90
643	A91 4.20p	Fortune teller	6.75	1.75
		Nos. 640-643 (4)	13.60	3.55

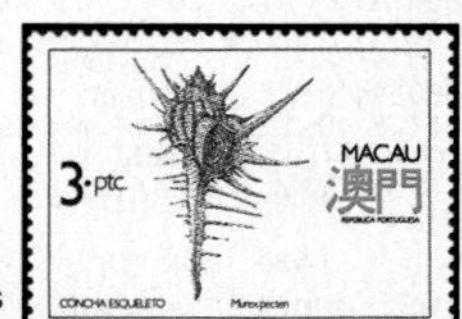
Shells A106

1991, Apr. 18 Litho. Perf. 14

644	A106 3p	Murex pecten	1.90	.90
645	A106 3p	Harpa harpa	1.90	.90
646	A106 3p	Chicoreus rosarius	1.90	.90
647	A106 3p	Tonna zonata	1.90	.90
a.		Strip of 4, #644-647	10.50	7.00
		Nos. 644-647 (4)	7.60	3.60

Chinese Opera — A107

Various performers in costume.

1991, June 5 Litho. *Perf. 13½*
648 A107 60a multicolored 1.50 .35
649 A107 80a multicolored 2.25 .35
650 A107 1p multicolored 3.75 .70
651 A107 10p multicolored 11.00 2.10
Nos. 648-651 (4) 18.50 3.50

Flowers A108

Designs: 1.70p, Delonix regia. 3p, Ipomoea cairica. 3.50p, Jasminum mesnyi. 4.20p, Bauhinia variegata.

1991, Oct. 9 Litho. *Perf. 13½*
652 A108 1.70p multicolored 1.50 .50
653 A108 3p multicolored 2.25 1.00
654 A108 3.50p multicolored 3.75 1.50
655 A108 4.20p multicolored 4.50 2.00
a. Souvenir sheet of 4, #652-655 32.50 12.50
Nos. 652-655 (4) 12.00 5.00

Cultural Exchange A109

Namban screen: No. 656, Unloading boat.

1991, Nov. 16 Litho. *Perf. 12*
656 A109 4.20p multicolored 2.50 .80
657 A109 4.20p shown 2.50 .80
a. Souvenir sheet of 2, #656-657 27.50 12.50

Holiday Greetings A110

1991, Nov. 29 Litho. *Perf. 14½*
658 A110 1.70p Lunar New Year .80 .25
659 A110 3p Santa Claus, Christmas 1.25 .25
660 A110 3.50p Old man 2.10 .50
661 A110 4.20p Girl at New Year party 4.25 1.00
Nos. 658-661 (4) 8.40 2.00

New Year Type of 1984

1992, Jan. 28 Litho. *Perf. 13½*
662 A60 4.50p Monkey 4.25 1.00
a. Booklet pane of 5 22.50

No. 662a has straight edges.

Paintings of Doors and Windows A111

1992, Mar. 1 *Perf. 14*
663 A111 1.70p multicolored 1.00 .45
664 A111 3p multi, diff. 2.00 1.00
665 A111 3.50p multi, diff. 3.00 1.00
666 A111 4.20p multi, diff. 4.25 1.75
Nos. 663-666 (4) 10.25 4.20

Mythological Chinese Gods — A112

1992, Apr. 3 Litho. *Perf. 14*
667 A112 3.50p T'it Kuai Lei (4-1) 5.50 2.50
668 A112 3.50p Chong Lei Kun (4-2) 5.50 2.50
669 A112 3.50p Cheong Kuo Lou (4-3) 5.50 2.50
670 A112 3.50p Loi Tong Pan (4-4) 5.50 2.50
a. Block or strip of 4, #667-670 25.00 12.50
Nos. 667-670 (4) 22.00 10.00

See Nos. 689-692.

Lion Dance Costume A113

Designs: 2.70p, Lion, diff. 6p, Dragon.

1992, May 18
671 A113 1p multicolored 1.00 .50
672 A113 2.70p multicolored 2.00 .50
673 A113 6p multicolored 3.75 1.00
Nos. 671-673 (3) 6.75 2.00

World Columbian Stamp Expo '92, Chicago.

1992 Summer Olympics, Barcelona — A114

1992, July 1 Litho. *Perf. 13*
674 A114 80a High jump .65 .40
675 A114 4.20p Badminton 1.25 .40
676 A114 4.70p Roller hockey 1.90 .50
677 A114 5p Yachting 2.50 1.25
a. Souvenir sheet of 4, #674-677 12.00 5.75
Nos. 674-677 (4) 6.30 2.55

Temples A115

1992, Oct. 9 *Perf. 14*
678 A115 1p Na Cha .85 .45
679 A115 1.50p Kun Iam 1.25 .45
680 A115 1.70p Hong Kon 1.75 .85
681 A115 6.50p A Ma 3.50 1.75
Nos. 678-681 (4) 7.35 3.50

See Nos. 685-688.

Portuguese-Chinese Friendship — A116

1992, Nov. 1 Litho. *Perf. 14*
682 A116 10p multicolored 3.00 1.00
a. Souv. sheet, perf. 13½ 13.50 5.50

Tung Sin Tong Charity Organization, Cent. — A117

1992, Nov. 27 *Perf. 12x11½*
683 A117 1p multicolored 1.75 .40

New Year Type of 1984

1993, Jan. 18 Litho. *Perf. 13½*
684 A60 5p Rooster 2.40 1.00
a. Booklet pane of 5 17.00

No. 684a has straight edges.

Temple Type of 1992

1993, Mar. 1 Litho. *Perf. 14*
685 A115 50a T'am Kong .50 .20
686 A115 2p T'in Hau 1.00 .30
687 A115 3.50p Lin Fong 1.50 .50
688 A115 8p Pau Kong 2.00 1.00
Nos. 685-688 (4) 5.00 2.00

Mythological Chinese Gods Type of 1992

Designs: No. 689, Lam Ch'oi Wo seated on crane in flight. No. 690, Ho Sin Ku, seated on peach flower.No. 691, Hon Seong Chi throwing peonies from basket. No. 692, Ch'ou Kuok K'ao seated on gold plate.

1993, Apr. 1 Litho. *Perf. 14*
689 A112 3.50p multi (4-1) *3.50 2.00*
690 A112 3.50p multicolored (4-2) *3.50 2.00*
691 A112 3.50p multicolored (4-3) *3.50 2.00*
692 A112 3.50p multicolored (4-4) *3.50 2.00*
a. Strip of 4, #689-692 *14.00 8.00*

Chinese Wedding — A118

#693, Three children celebrating. #694, Bride. #695, Groom. #696, Woman with parasol, person being carried. 8p, Bride & groom.

1993, May 19 *Perf. 14*
693 A118 3p multicolored *1.00 .75*
694 A118 3p multicolored *1.00 .75*
695 A118 3p multicolored *1.00 .75*
696 A118 3p multicolored *1.00 .75*
a. Strip of 4, #693-696 *5.00 4.00*

Souvenir Sheet

Perf. 14½x14

697 A118 8p multicolored *6.75 5.50*

No. 697 contains one 50x40mm stamp.

World Environment Day — A119

Birds — A120

1993, June 5 Litho. *Perf. 14*
698 A119 1p multicolored 1.25 .40

1993, June 27
699 A120 3p Falco peregrinus 1.25 .90
700 A120 3p Aquila obrysaetos 1.25 .90
701 A120 3p Asio otus 1.25 .90
702 A120 3p Tyto alba 1.25 .90
a. Block or strip of 4, #699-702 5.00 3.60
b. Souvenir sheet of 4, #699-702 *12.50 8.00*

Union of Portuguese Speaking Capitals — A121

1993, July 30 Litho. *Perf. 13½*
703 A121 1.50p multicolored 1.00 .50

Portuguese Arrival in Japan, 450th Anniv. A122

50a, Japanese using musket. 3p, Catholic priests. 3.50p, Exchanging items of trade.

1993, Sept. 22 Litho. *Perf. 12x11½*
704 A122 50a multicolored .60 .20
705 A122 3p multicolored 1.25 .30
706 A122 3.50p multicolored 1.75 .75
Nos. 704-706 (3) 3.60 1.25

See Portugal Nos. 1964-1966.

Flowers A123

Designs: 1p, Spathodea campanulata. 2p, Tithonia diversifolia. 3p, Rhodomyrtus tomentosa. 8p, Passiflora foetida.

1993, Oct. 9 *Perf. 14½*
707 A123 1p multicolored .55 .40
708 A123 2p multicolored 1.10 .65
709 A123 3p multicolored 1.10 .90
710 A123 8p multicolored 2.25 2.50
a. Souvenir sheet of 4, #707-710 *12.50 8.00*
Nos. 707-710 (4) 5.00 4.45

Portuguese Ships A124

1993, Nov. 5 Litho. *Perf. 14*
711 A124 1p Caravel .50 .25
712 A124 2p Round caravel 1.00 .50
713 A124 3.50p Nau 1.00 .60
714 A124 4.50p Galleon 1.50 1.25
a. Souvenir sheet of 4, #711-714 *7.75 4.50*
Nos. 711-714 (4) 4.00 2.60

Macao Grand Prix, 40th Anniv. A125

1993, Nov. 16 Litho. *Perf. 13½*
715 A125 1.50p Stock car .50 .50
716 A125 2p Motorcycle 1.00 .50
717 A125 4.50p Formula 1 race car 2.00 1.50
Nos. 715-717 (3) 3.50 2.50

New Year Type of 1984

1994, Feb. 3 Litho. *Perf. 13½*
718 A60 5p Dog 2.10 1.00
a. Booklet pane of 5 14.50

New Year 1994 (Year of the Dog).
No. 718a has straight edges.

Prince Henry the Navigator (1394-1460) — A126

Illustration reduced.

1994, Mar. 4 Litho. *Perf. 12*
719 A126 3p multicolored 2.10 1.00

See Portugal No. 1987.

Scenes of Macao, by George Chinnery (1774-1852) — A127

Designs: No. 720, Hut, natives. No. 721, S. Tiago Fortress. No. 722, Overview of Praia Grande. No. 723, S. Francisco Church.

1994, Mar. 21 *Perf. 14*
720 A127 3.50p multi (4-1) 1.25 .75
721 A127 3.50p multi (4-2) 1.25 .75
722 A127 3.50p multi (4-3) 1.25 .75
723 A127 3.50p multi (4-4) 1.25 .75
a. Block or strip of 4, #720-723 5.00 3.00
b. Souvenir sheet of 4, #720-723 *11.00 6.50*

Spring Festival of New Lunar Year A128

Designs: 1p, Girl, woman shopping. 2p, Celebration. 3.50p, Couple preparing food at table. 4.50p, Old man making decorations.

1994, Apr. 6
724 A128 1p multicolored .50 .25
725 A128 2p multicolored 1.00 .50
726 A128 3.50p multicolored 1.00 .60
727 A128 4.50p multicolored 1.75 1.25
Nos. 724-727 (4) 4.25 2.60

Mythological Chinese Gods — A129

Statuettes: No. 728, Happiness. No. 729. Prosperity. No. 730, Longevity.

1994, May 9 Litho. *Perf. 12*
728 A129 3p multi (3-1) *2.25 1.25*
729 A129 3p multi (3-2) *2.25 1.25*
730 A129 3p multi (3-3) *2.25 1.25*
a. Strip of 3, #728-730 *8.25 3.75*
b. Souvenir sheet of 3, #728-730 *13.50 6.00*

A130

A131

1994 World Cup Soccer Championships, US: Various soccer players.

1994, June 1
731 A130 2p multicolored .70 .55
732 A130 3p multicolored 1.00 .80
733 A130 3.50p multicolored 1.25 .95
734 A130 4.50p multicolored 1.60 1.25
a. Souvenir sheet of 4, #731-734 *13.50 7.50*
Nos. 731-734 (4) 4.55 3.55

1994, June 27 Litho. *Perf. 12*

Traditional Chinese shops.

735 A131 1p Rice shop .55 .25
736 A131 1.50p Medicinal drink shop .85 .40
737 A131 2p Salt fish shop 1.25 .55
738 A131 3.50p Pharmacy 2.10 .95
Nos. 735-738 (4) 4.75 2.15

Navigation Instruments A132

1994, Sept. 13 Litho. *Perf. 12*
739 A132 3p Astrolabe 1.25 .80
740 A132 3.50p Quadrant 1.40 .95
741 A132 4.50p Sextant 1.75 1.25
Nos. 739-741 (3) 4.40 3.00

12th Asian Games, Hiroshima 1994 A133

1994, Sept. 30 Litho. *Perf. 12*
742 A133 1p Fencing .40 .30
743 A133 2p Gymnastics .85 .55
744 A133 3p Water polo 1.25 .80
745 A133 3.50p Pole vault 1.50 .95
Nos. 742-745 (4) 4.00 2.60

Bridges A134

1994, Oct. 8
746 A134 1p Nobre de Carvalho .35 .30
747 A134 8p Friendship 2.25 2.00

Fortune Symbols — A135

Designs: 3p, Child, carp, water lily. 3.50p, Basket of peaches, child, bats. 4.50p, Flower, child playing mouth organ.

1994, Nov. 7 Litho. *Perf. 12*
748 A135 3p multicolored 1.50 1.00
749 A135 3.50p multicolored 1.65 1.25
750 A135 4.50p multicolored 2.25 1.50
Nos. 748-750 (3) 5.40 3.75

Religious Art — A136

Designs: 50a, Stained glass, angel's head. 1p, Stained glass, Holy Ghost. 1.50p, Silver sacrarium. 2p, Silver salver. 3p, Ivory sculpture, Escape to Egypt. 3.50p, Gold & silver chalice.

1994, Nov. 30
751 A136 50a multicolored .20 .20
752 A136 1p multicolored .40 .25
753 A136 1.50p multicolored .65 .40
754 A136 2p multicolored .90 .55
755 A136 3p multicolored 1.25 .80
756 A136 3.50p multicolored 1.50 .95
Nos. 751-756 (6) 4.90 3.15

New Year Type of 1984

1995, Jan. 23 Litho. *Perf. 13½*
757 A60 5.50p Boar 3.00 1.50

Tourism A138

Scenes of Macao, by Lio Man Cheong: 50a, Walkway beside pond. 1p, Lighthouse. 1.50p, Temple. 2p, Buildings along coast. 2.50p, Columns, temple. 3p, Ruins on hill overlooking city. 3.50p, Bridge. 4p, Trees in park.

1995, Mar. 1 Litho. *Perf. 12*
758 A138 50a multicolored .25 .20
759 A138 1p multicolored .50 .30
760 A138 1.50p multicolored .65 .40
761 A138 2p multicolored .90 .55
762 A138 2.50p multicolored 1.10 .65
763 A138 3p multicolored 1.25 .80
764 A138 3.50p multicolored 1.50 .95
765 A138 4p multicolored 1.75 1.10
Nos. 758-765 (8) 7.90 4.95

World Day of the Consumer A139

1995, Mar. 15
766 A139 1p multicolored 1.00 .30

Asian Pangolin — A140

1995, Apr. 10
767 A140 1.50p Facing left (4-1) *2.25* .50
768 A140 1.50p Hanging by tail (4-2) *2.25* .50
769 A140 1.50p On tree limb (4-3) *2.25* .50
770 A140 1.50p On tree stump (4-4) *2.25* .50
a. Block or strip of 4, #767-770 *9.50* 6.50

World wildlife Fund.
Issued in sheets of 16 stamps.

Legend of Buddhist Goddess Kun Iam — A141

#772, Seated atop dragon, holding flower. #773, Meditating. #774, Holding infant.
8p, Goddess with many faces, hands.

1995, May 5 Litho. *Perf. 12*
771 A141 3p multicolored 3.00 .80
772 A141 3p multicolored 3.00 .80
773 A141 3p multicolored 3.00 .80
774 A141 3p multicolored 3.00 .80
a. Block or strip of 4, #771-774 14.50 11.00

Souvenir Sheet

775 A141 8p multicolored *11.00 9.00*

Senado Square — A142

Designs: No. 776, Street, bell tower. No. 777, Street, plaza, shops. No. 778, Fountain, plaza. No. 779, Plaza, buildings.
8p, Bell tower, building, horiz.

1995, June 24 Litho. *Perf. 12*
776 A142 2p multicolored 1.25 .65
777 A142 2p multicolored 1.25 .65
778 A142 2p multicolored 1.25 .65
779 A142 2p multicolored 1.25 .65
a. Strip of 4, #776-779 5.00 2.75

Souvenir Sheet

780 A142 8p multicolored 10.00 6.00

Temple Type of 1992

1995, July 17 Litho. *Perf. 12*
781 A115 50a Kuan Tai .20 .20
782 A115 1p Pak Tai .40 .25
783 A115 1.50p Lin K'ai .65 .40
784 A115 3p Sek Kam Tong 1.25 .80
785 A115 3.50p Fok Tak 1.60 .95
Nos. 781-785 (5) 4.10 2.60

Singapore '95 — A143

Birds: No. 786, Gurrulax canorus. No. 787, Serinus canarius. No. 788, Zosterops japonica. No. 789, Leiothrix lutea. 10p, Copsychus saularis.

1995, Sept. 1 Litho. *Perf. 12*
786 A143 2.50p multicolored 2.25 .65
787 A143 2.50p multicolored 2.25 .65
788 A143 2.50p multicolored 2.25 .65
789 A143 2.50p multicolored 2.25 .65
a. Strip of 4, #786-789 9.00 2.60

Souvenir Sheet

790 A143 10p multicolored *10.00 5.50*

Intl. Music Festival — A144

1995, Oct. 9 **Litho.** ***Perf. 12***

791 A144 1p Pipa (6-1) 1.00 .25
792 A144 1p Erhu (6-2) 1.00 .25
793 A144 1p Gongo (6-3) 1.00 .25
794 A144 1p Sheng (6-4) 1.00 .25
795 A144 1p Xiao (6-5) 1.00 .25
796 A144 1p Tambor (6-6) 1.00 .25
a. Block of 6, #791-796 6.00 1.50

Souvenir Sheet

797 A144 8p Musicians, horiz. *10.00* *5.00*

UN, 50th Anniv. A145

1995, Oct. 24 **Litho.** ***Perf. 12***

798 A145 4.50p multicolored 1.75 1.25

Macao Intl. Airport A146

Designs: 1p, Airplane above terminal. 1.50p, Boeing 747 on ground, terminal. 2p, Hangars, 747 with boarding ramp at door. 3p, Airplane, control tower. 8p, Boeing 747 over runway.

1995, Dec. 8 **Litho.** ***Perf. 12***

799 A146 1p multicolored .50 .25
800 A146 1.50p multicolored .80 .40
801 A146 2p multicolored 1.00 .50
802 A146 3p multicolored 1.50 .75
Nos. 799-802 (4) 3.80 1.90

Souvenir Sheet

Perf. 12½

803 A146 8p multicolored *10.00* *5.00*

No. 803 contains one 51x38mm stamp.

New Year Type of 1984
Miniature Sheet of 12

Designs: a, like #485. b, like #504. c, like #522. d, like #540. e, like #560. f, like #583. g, like #611. h, like #639. i, like #662. j, like #684. k, like #718. l, like #757.

1995, Dec. 15 **Litho.** ***Perf. 13½***

804 A60 1.50p #a.-l. + label *15.00* *5.00*

New Year 1996 (Year of the Rat) A147

1996, Feb. 12 **Litho.** ***Perf. 12***

805 A147 5p multicolored 4.75 1.25

Souvenir Sheet

806 A147 10p like No. 805 *8.00* *5.00*

Traditional Chinese Bird Cages — A148

Various styles.

1996, Mar. 1 **Litho.** ***Perf. 12***

807 A148 1p multi (4-1) .35 .25
808 A148 1.50p multi (4-2) .55 .40
809 A148 3p multi (4-3) 1.00 .75
810 A148 4.50p multi (4-4) 1.60 1.10
Nos. 807-810 (4) 3.50 2.50

Souvenir Sheet

811 A148 10p purple & multi *6.00* 2.50

Paintings, by Herculano Estorninho A149

Scenes of Macao: 50a, Boats. 1.50p, Street, buildings at night, vert. 3p, Fronts of buildings during day, vert. 5p, Townhouse complex.
10p, Entrance to building, vert.

1996, Apr. 1

812 A149 50a multi (4-1) .20 .20
813 A149 1.50p multi (4-2) .55 .40
814 A149 3p multi (4-3) 1.00 .75
815 A149 5p multi (4-4) 1.75 1.25
Nos. 812-815 (4) 3.50 2.60

Souvenir Sheet

816 A149 10p multi *6.00* 2.50

Myths and Legends — A150

Designs: No. 817, Man holding staff. No. 818, Man riding tiger. No. 819, Man on top of fireplace.

1996, Apr. 30 **Litho.** ***Perf. 12***

817 A150 3.50p Tou Tei (3-1) .95 .60
818 A150 3.50p Choi San (3-2) .95 .60
819 A150 3.50p Chou Kuan (3-3) .95 .60
a. Strip of 3, #817-819 3.00 3.00
b. Souvenir sheet of 3, #817-819 *9.25* 3.00

Traditional Chinese Tea Houses A151

Designs: No. 820, Two men seated at table. No. 821, Cook holding steaming tray of food, woman, baby. No. 822, Woman holding up papers. No. 823, Waiter pouring tea, man seated.
8p, Food, serving bowl.

1996, May 17 ***Perf. 12***

820 A151 2p multi (4-1) 1.60 .55
821 A151 2p multi (4-2) 1.60 .55
822 A151 2p multi (4-3) 1.60 .55
823 A151 2p multi (4-4) 1.60 .55
a. Block of 4, #820-823 6.50 2.25

Souvenir Sheet

824 A151 8p multi *9.00* 2.25

No. 823a is a continuous design. China '96 (#824).

Greetings Stamps A152

Designs: 50a, Get well. 1.50p, Congratulations on new baby. 3p, Happy birthday. 4p, Marriage congratulations.

1996, June 14 **Litho.** ***Perf. 12***

825 A152 50a multi (4-1) .20 .20
826 A152 1.50p multi (4-2) .65 .40
827 A152 3p multi (4-3) 1.25 .75
828 A152 4p multi (4-4) 1.60 1.00
Nos. 825-828 (4) 3.70 2.35

1996 Summer Olympic Games, Atlanta A153

1996, July 19

829 A153 2p Swimming (4-1) .50 .35
830 A153 3p Soccer (4-2) .80 .55
831 A153 3.50p Gymnastics (4-3) .90 .60
832 A153 4.50p Sailboarding (4-4) 1.10 .80
Nos. 829-832 (4) 3.30 2.30

Souvenir Sheet

833 A153 10p Boxing *6.00* 2.50

Civil and Military Emblems A154

#834, Bird looking left. #835, Dragon. #836, Bird looking right. #837, Leopard.

1996, Sept. 18

834 A154 2.50p bl & multi (4-1) 1.25 .65
835 A154 2.50p grn & multi (4-2) 1.25 .65
836 A154 2.50p grn & multi (4-3) 1.25 .65
837 A154 2.50p pur & multi (4-4) 1.25 .65
a. Block of 4, #834-837 5.00 2.60

See Nos. 947-951.

Fishing with Nets — A155

Boats, fish in sea: No. 838, Six small nets extended from mast of boat. No. 839, Modern trawler. No. 840, Junk trawling. No. 841, Sailboat with nets extended from both sides.

1996, Oct. 9 **Litho.** ***Perf. 12***

838 A155 3p multi (4-1) 1.50 1.00
839 A155 3p multi (4-2) 1.50 1.00
840 A155 3p multi (4-3) 1.50 1.00
841 A155 3p multi (4-4) 1.50 1.00
a. Strip of 4, #838-841 6.00 5.00

Legislative Assembly, 20th Anniv. — A156

Illustration reduced.

1996, Oct. 15 **Litho.** ***Perf. 12x12½***

842 A156 2.80p multicolored .75 .50

Souvenir Sheet

843 A156 8p like No. 842 *6.00* 3.00

Paper Kites A157

1996, Oct. 21 **Litho.** ***Perf. 12***

844 A157 3.50p Dragonfly (4-1) 1.60 1.00
845 A157 3.50p Butterfly (4-2) 1.60 1.00
846 A157 3.50p Owl in flight (4-3) 1.60 1.00
847 A157 3.50p Standing owl (4-4) 1.60 1.00
a. Block of 4, #844-847 9.00 6.50

Souvenir Sheet

Perf. 12½

848 A157 8p Dragon *10.00* 7.50

No. 848 contains one 51x38mm stamp.

Traditional Chinese Toys — A158

1996, Nov. 13 **Litho.** ***Perf. 12***

849 A158 50a shown .20 .20
850 A158 1p Fish .45 .25
851 A158 3p Doll 1.40 .80
852 A158 4.50p Dragon 2.10 1.25
Nos. 849-852 (4) 4.15 2.50

New Year 1997 (Year of the Ox) A159

1997, Jan. 23 **Litho.** ***Perf. 12***

853 A159 5.50p multicolored *3.00* *2.00*

Souvenir Sheet

854 A159 10p multicolored *6.00* *4.00*

No. 854 is a continuous design.

Lucky Numbers A160

1996 **Litho.** ***Perf. 12***

855 A160 2p "2," Simplicity .70 .50
856 A160 2.80p "8," Prosperity .90 .60
857 A160 3p "3," Progress 1.00 .65
858 A160 3.90p "9," Longevity 1.40 1.00
Nos. 855-858 (4) 4.00 2.75

Souvenir Sheet

859 A160 9p Man outside house *6.00* *4.00*

Hong Kong '97 (#859).

Paintings of Macao, by Kwok Se — A161

2p, Junks. 3p, Fortress on side of mountain. 3.50p, Retreat house. 4.50p, Cerco Gate.
8p, Rooftop of building, horiz.

1997, Mar. 1 **Litho.** ***Perf. 12***

860 A161 2p multicolored .60 .60
861 A161 3p multicolored .90 .90
862 A161 3.50p multicolored 1.10 1.10
863 A161 4.50p multicolored 1.40 1.40
Nos. 860-863 (4) 4.00 4.00

Souvenir Sheet

864 A161 8p multicolored 5.00 4.00

A162

A163

Boat People: 1p, Old woman seated. 1.50p, Woman wearing hat. 2.50p, Woman carrying baby. 5.50p, Man, boy.

1997, Mar. 26 Litho. *Perf. 12*

865	A162	1p multicolored	.60	.40
866	A162	1.50p multicolored	.70	.50
867	A162	2.50p multicolored	1.10	.80
868	A162	5.50p multicolored	2.60	1.75
a.		Block of 4, #865-868	5.00	4.00

1997, Apr. 29 Litho. *Perf. 12*

Temple A-Ma: No. 869, Steps leading to entrance. No. 870, People strolling past temple, one with umbrella. No. 871, People outside pagoda, pedicab. No. 872, Towers from temple, one emiting smoke.

869	A163	3.50p multicolored	.50	.35
870	A163	3.50p multicolored	.50	.35
871	A163	3.50p multicolored	.50	.35
872	A163	3.50p multicolored	.50	.35
a.		Strip of 4, #869-872	3.00	3.00

Souvenir Sheet

873	A163	8p Boat	*4.50*	*4.50*

Drunken Dragon Festival — A164

Stylized designs: 2p, Two men, one holding dragon. 3p, Man holding up dragon. 5p, Two men, one holding horn.
9p, Dragon, man, horiz.

1997, May 14

874	A164	2p multicolored	.55	.55
875	A164	3p multicolored	.80	.80
876	A164	5p multicolored	1.25	1.25
a.		Strip of 3, #874-876	2.60	2.60

Souvenir Sheet

877	A164	9p multicolored	*5.00*	*5.00*

Father Luís Fróis, 400th Death Anniv. A165

No. 879, Father Fróis, cathedral, vert.

1997, June 9 Litho. *Perf. 12*

878	A165	2.50p multi (2-1)	.65	.65
879	A165	2.50p multi (2-2)	.65	.65

See Portugal Nos. 2165-2167.

Legends and Myths — A166

Gods of Protection: #880, Wat Lot. #881, San Su. #882, Chon Keng. #883, Wat Chi Kong.
10p, Chon Keng and Wat Chi Kong.

1997, June 18 Litho. *Perf. 12*

880	A166	2.50p multicolored	.60	.60
881	A166	2.50p multicolored	.60	.60
882	A166	2.50p multicolored	.60	.60
883	A166	2.50p multicolored	.60	.60
a.		Block of 4, #880-883	3.00	3.00
		Nos. 880-883 (4)	2.40	2.40

Souvenir Sheet

884	A166	10p multicolored	4.00	4.00

No. 884 contains one 40x40mm stamp.

Macao Red Cross, 77th Anniv. — A167

1997, July 12 *Perf. 12½*

885	A167	1.50p multicolored	.40	.40

No. 885 is printed se-tenant with label.

Verandas A168

Various architectural styles.
8p, Close up of veranda, vert.

1997, July 30 Litho. *Perf. 12*

886	A168	50a multi (6-1)	.20	.20
887	A168	1p multi (6-2)	.25	.25
888	A168	1.50p multi (6-3)	.40	.40
889	A168	2p multi (6-4)	.50	.50
890	A168	2.50p multi (6-5)	.65	.65
891	A168	3p multi (6-6)	.75	.75
a.		Block of 6, #886-891	2.75	2.75

Souvenir Sheet

892	A168	8p multicolored	2.10	2.10

Traditional Chinese Fans — A169

Fong Soi (Chinese Geomancy) A170

1997, Sept. 24 Litho. *Perf. 12*

893	A169	50a Planta (4-1)	.20	.20
894	A169	1p Papel (4-2)	.25	.25
895	A169	3.50p Seda (4-3)	.95	.95
896	A169	4p Pluma (4-4)	1.10	1.10
a.		Block of 4, #893-896	2.40	2.40

Souvenir Sheet

897	A169	9p Sandalo	5.00	4.00

1997, Oct. 9 Litho. *Perf. 12*

Chinese principles of Yin and Yang related to the five elements of the ancient Zodiac.

898	A170	50a green & multi	.20	.20
899	A170	1p orange & multi	.25	.25
900	A170	1.50p brown & multi	.40	.40
901	A170	2p yellow & multi	.55	.55
902	A170	2.50p blue & multi	.65	.65
a.		Strip of 5, #898-902	2.00	2.00

Souvenir Sheet

903	A170	10p green & multi	2.60	2.60

Martial Arts — A171

1997, Nov. 19

904	A171	1.50p Kung Fu	.40	.40
905	A171	3.50p Judo	.95	.95
906	A171	4p Karate	1.10	1.10
a.		Strip of 3, #904-906	2.40	2.40

New Year 1998 (Year of the Tiger) A172

1998, Jan. 18 Litho. *Perf. 12*

907	A172	5.50p multicolored	1.50	1.50

Souvenir Sheets

908	A172	10p multicolored	2.75	2.75
a.		Ovptd. in sheet margin	2.75	2.75

No. 908 is a continuous design.
No. 908a overprinted in Gold in Sheet Margin with "Amizade Luso-Chinesa / Festival de Macao" & Chinese Text

Street Vendors A173

Vendors at stands, carts: No. 909, 1p, Frying foods. 1.50p, Food products, eggs. 2p, Clothing items. 2.50p, Balloons. 3p, Flowers. 3.50p, Fruits and vegetables.
6p, Vendor at fruit and vegetable stand, diff.

1998, Feb. 13 Litho. *Perf. 12*

909	A173	1p multi (6-1)	.25	.25
910	A173	1.50p multi (6-2)	.40	.40
911	A173	2p multi (6-3)	.55	.55
912	A173	2.50p multi (6-4)	.65	.65
913	A173	3p multi (6-5)	.80	.80
914	A173	3.50p multi (6-6)	.95	.95
a.		Block of 6, #909-914	3.60	3.60

Souvenir Sheets

915	A173	6p multicolored	1.60	1.60
a.		Ovptd. in sheet margin	1.60	1.60

No. 915a overprinted in Gold in Sheet Margin with "Amizade Luso-Chinesa / Festival de Macao" & Chinese Text

Traditional Gates A174

Inscriptions: 50a, "Beco da Sé." 1p, "Pátio da Ilusao." 3.50p, "Travessa da galinhas." 4p, "Beco das Felicidades."
9p, "Seminário d S. José," vert.

1998, Mar. 1

916	A174	50a multi (4-1)	.20	.20
917	A174	1p multi (4-2)	.25	.25
918	A174	3.50p multi (4-3)	.95	.95
919	A174	4p multi (4-4)	1.10	1.10
		Nos. 916-919 (4)	2.50	2.50

Souvenir Sheets

920	A174	9p multicolored	2.40	2.40
a.		Ovptd. in sheet margin	2.40	2.40

No. 920a overprinted in Gold in Sheet Margin with "Amizade Luso-Chinesa / Festival de Macao" & Chinese Text

Myths and Legends — A175

Gods of Ma Chou: No. 921, Holding baby. No. 922, Watching image appear in smoke. No. 923, With cherubs. No. 924, Hovering over junks.
10p, Face.

1998, Apr. 23 Litho. *Perf. 12*

921	A175	4p multi (4-1)	1.10	1.10
922	A175	4p multi (4-2)	1.10	1.10
923	A175	4p multi (4-3)	1.10	1.10
924	A175	4p multi (4-4)	1.10	1.10
a.		Strip of 4, #921-924	4.40	4.40

Souvenir Sheets

925	A175	10p multicolored	2.60	2.60
a.		Ovptd. in sheet margin	2.60	2.60

No. 925a overprinted in Gold in Sheet Margin with "Amizade Luso-Chinesa / Festival de Macao" & Chinese Text

Voyage to India by Vasco da Gama, 500th Anniv. A176

Designs: 1p, Sailing ship. 1.50p, Vasco da Gama. 2p, Map, sailing ship.
8p, Compass rose.

1998, May 20 Litho. *Perf. 12*

926	A176	1p multi (3-1)	*.35*	*.35*
927	A176	1.50p multi (3-2)	*.50*	*.50*
928	A176	2p multi (3-3)	*.65*	*.65*
a.		Strip of 3, #926-928	*1.50*	*1.50*

Souvenir Sheet

929	A176	8p multicolored	*3.75*	*3.75*

Nos. 926-929 are inscribed "1598" instead of "1498," and were withdrawn after two days. For corrected version, see Nos. 943-946.

Oceans A177

Stylized designs: 2.50p, Mermaid, shells, sailing ship, compass rose. 3p, Compass rose, fish, oil derrick.
9p, Sailing ship, seagull, fish, cloud, sun.

1998, May 22

930	A177	2.50p multi (2-1)	.65	.65
931	A177	3p multi (2-2)	.75	.75
a.		Pair, #930-931	1.40	1.40

Souvenir Sheets

932	A177	9p multicolored	2.25	2.25
a.		Ovptd. in sheet margin	2.25	2.25

No. 932a overprinted in Gold in Sheet Margin with "Amizade Luso-Chinesa / Festival de Macao" & Chinese Text

1998 World Cup Soccer Championships, France — A178

Various soccer plays.

1998, June 10 Litho. *Perf. 12*

933 A178 3p multicolored .80 .80
934 A178 3.50p multicolored .95 .95
935 A178 4p multicolored 1.00 1.00
936 A178 4.50p multicolored 1.25 1.25
Nos. 933-936 (4) 4.00 4.00

Souvenir Sheets

937 A178 9p multicolored 2.40 2.40
a. Ovptd. in sheet margin 2.40 2.40

No. 937a overprinted in Gold in Sheet Margin with "Amizade Luso-Chinesa / Festival de Macao" & Chinese Text

Chinese Opera Masks A179

1998, July 28 Litho. *Perf. 12*

938 A179 1.50p Lio, Seak Chong (4-1) .40 .40
939 A179 2p Wat, Chi Kong (4-2) .55 .55
940 A179 3p Kam, Chin Pao (4-3) .80 .80
941 A179 5p Lei, Kwai (4-4) 1.25 1.25
a. Strip of 4, #938-941 3.00 3.00

Souvenir Sheets

942 A179 8p Masked player 2.00 2.00
a. Ovptd. in sheet margin 2.00 2.00

No. 942a overprinted in Gold in Sheet Margin with "Amizade Luso-Chinesa / Festival de Macao" & Chinese Text

Vasco da Gama Type of 1998 Inscribed "1498"

1998, Sept. 4 Litho. *Perf. 12*

943 A176 1p like #926 .25 .25
944 A176 1.50p like #927 .40 .40
945 A176 2p like #928 .55 .55
a. Strip of 3, #943-945 1.25 1.25

Souvenir Sheets

946 A176 8p like #929 2.00 2.00
a. Ovptd. in sheet margin 2.00 2.00

Issued to correct the error on #926-929.
No. 946a overprinted in Gold in Sheet Margin with "Amizade Luso-Chinesa / Festival de Macao" & Chinese Text

Civil and Military Emblems Type of 1996

Designs: 50a, Lion. 1p, Dragon. 1.50p, Bird looking right. 2p, Bird looking left.
9p, Bird flying.

1998, Sept. 9

947 A154 50a multi (4-1) .20 .20
948 A154 1p multi (4-2) .25 .25
949 A154 1.50p multi (4-3) .40 .40
950 A154 2p multi (4-4) .55 .55
a. Strip of 4, #947-950 1.25 1.25

Souvenir Sheets

951 A154 9p multicolored 2.50 2.50
a. Ovptd. in sheet margin 2.50 2.50

No. 951a overprinted in Gold in Sheet Margin with "Amizade Luso-Chinesa / Festival de Macao" & Chinese Text

Kun Iam Temple A180

Scenes inside temple compound: No. 952, Buddha figure standing. No. 953, Entrance gate, man running, benches. No. 954, Entrance to building, people. No. 955, People, stream, pagoda, flowers.
10p, Table, chairs, top of incense burner.

1998 Litho. *Perf. 12*

952 A180 3.50p multicolored .90 .90
953 A180 3.50p multicolored .90 .90
954 A180 3.50p multicolored .90 .90
955 A180 3.50p multicolored .90 .90
a. Block of 4, #952-955 3.60 3.60

Souvenir Sheets

956 A180 10p multicolored 2.50 2.50
a. Ovptd. in sheet margin 2.50 2.50

No. 956a overprinted in Gold in Sheet Margin with "Amizade Luso-Chinesa / Festival de Macao" & Chinese Text

Paintings of Macao, by Didier Rafael Bayle A181

Designs: 2p, Street scene, buggy, vert. 3p, People standing outside of buildings. 3.50p, Building atop wall. 4.50p, Buildings, house along street, vert.
8p, Top of building.

1998, Nov. 11 Litho. *Perf. 12*

957 A181 2p multi (4-1) .50 .50
958 A181 3p multi (4-2) .75 .75
959 A181 3.50p multi (4-3) .90 .90
960 A181 4.50p multi (4-4) 1.10 1.10
Nos. 957-960 (4) 3.25 3.25

Souvenir Sheets

961 A181 8p multicolored 2.00 2.00
a. Ovptd. in sheet margin 2.00 2.00

No. 961a overprinted in Gold in Sheet Margin with "Amizade Luso-Chinesa / Festival de Macao" & Chinese Text

Tiles A182

Designs: 1p, Dragon. 1.50p, Sailing ship. 2.50p, Chinese junk. 5.50p, Peacock.
10p, Building, lighthouse.

1998, Dec. 8

962 A182 1p multi (4-1) .25 .25
963 A182 1.50p multi (4-2) .40 .40
964 A182 2.50p multi (4-3) .65 .65
965 A182 5.50p multi (4-4) 1.40 1.40
a. Block of 4, #962-965 2.75 2.75

Souvenir Sheets

966 A182 10p multicolored 2.50 2.50
a. Ovptd. in sheet margin 2.50 2.50

No. 966a overprinted in Gold in Sheet Margin with "Amizade Luso-Chinesa / Festival de Macao" & Chinese Text

New Year 1999 (Year of the Rabbit) A183

1999, Feb. 8 Litho. *Perf. 12*

967 A183 5.50p multicolored 1.40 1.40

Souvenir Sheet

968 A183 10p multicolored 2.75 2.75
a. Ovptd. in sheet margin 2.75 2.75

No. 968 is a continuous design.
No. 968a overprinted in gold in sheet margin with "Amizade Luso-Chinesa / Transferencia da Soberania de / MACAU 1999 / Sichuan Chengdu," dates and Chinese text.

Characters from Novel, "Dream of the Red Mansion," by Cao Xuequin — A184

1999, Mar. 1 Litho. *Perf. 12*

969 A184 2p Bao Yu (6-1) .55 .55
970 A184 2p Dayiu (6-2) .55 .55
971 A184 2p Bao Chai (6-3) .55 .55
972 A184 2p Xi Feng (6-4) .55 .55
973 A184 2p San Jie (6-5) .55 .55
974 A184 2p Qing Wen (6-6) .55 .55
a. Block of 6, #969-974 3.25 3.25

Souvenir Sheet

975 A184 8p Bao Yu & Dayiu 2.00 2.00
a. Ovptd. in sheet margin 2.10 2.10

No. 975a overprinted in gold in sheet margin with "Amizade Luso-Chinesa / Transferencia da Soberania de / MACAU 1999 / Sichuan Chengdu," dates and Chinese text.

Maritime Heritage A185

1999, Mar. 19 Litho. *Perf. 12*

976 A185 1.50p Sailing ships .40 .40
977 A185 2.50p Marine life .60 .60
a. Pair, #976-977 1.00 1.00

Souvenir Sheet

978 A185 6p Whale, vert. 1.60 1.60
a. Ovptd. in sheet margin 1.60 1.60

Australia '99, World Stamp Expo.
No. 978a overprinted in gold in sheet margin with "Amizade Luso-Chinesa / Transferencia da Soberania de / MACAU 1999 / Sichuan Chengdu," dates and Chinese text.

First Portugal-Macao Flight, 75th Anniv. — A186

Airplanes: No. 979, Breguet 16 Bn2, "Patria." No. 980, DH9.

1999, Apr. 19 Litho. *Perf. 12*

979 A186 3p multicolored .80 .80
980 A186 3p multicolored .80 .80
a. Souvenir sheet, #979-980 1.60 1.60
b. As "a," ovptd. in sheet margin 1.60 1.60

See Portugal Nos. 2289-2290.
No. 980a is a continuous design.
No. 980b overprinted in gold in sheet margin with "Amizade Luso-Chinesa / Transferencia da Soberania de / MACAU 1999 / Sichuan Chengdu," dates and Chinese text.

A187

A188

Traditional Water Carrier: a, 1p, Woman carrying container (4-1). b, 1.50p, Filling container from pump (4-2). c, 2p, Drawing water from well (4-3). d, 2.50p, Filling container from faucet (4-4).
7p, Woman carrying containers up stairs.

1999, Apr. 28 *Perf. 12*

Horiz. Strip or Block of 4

981 A187 #a.-d. 1.75 1.75

Souvenir Sheet

982 A187 7p multicolored 1.90 1.90
a. Ovptd. in sheet margin 1.90 1.90

No. 981 was issued in sheets of 4 strips or blocks, each in a different order.
No. 982a overprinted in gold in sheet margin with "Amizade Luso-Chinesa / Transferencia de Soberania de / MACAU 1999 / China Shanghai," date and Chinese text.

1999, May 5 Litho. *Perf. 12*

Telecommunications — #983: a, 50a, Sea-Me-We cable. b, 1p, Satellite dishes. c, 3.50p, Cellular phones. d, 4p, Television. e, 4.50p, Internet.
8p, Computer mouse.

983 A188 Strip of 5, #a.-e. 3.50 3.50

Souvenir Sheet

984 A188 8p multi 2.00 2.00
a. Ovptd. in sheet margin 2.00 2.00

No. 984 has a holographic image. Soaking in water may affect hologram.
No. 984a is overprinted in gold in sheet margin with "Amizade Luso-Chinesa / Transferencia de Soberania de / MACAU 1999 / China Shanghai," date and Chinese text.

Modern Buildings, Construction — A189

1p, Cultural Center. 1.50p, Museum of Macao. 2p, Maritime Museum. 2.50p, Maritime Terminal. 3p, University of Macao. 3.50p, Public Administration Building. 4.50p, World Trade Center. 5p, Coloane Go-kart Track. 8p, Bank of China. 12p, Ultramarine National Bank.

1999, June 2 Litho. *Perf. 12*

989 A189 1p multi .25 .25
990 A189 1.50p multi .40 .40
991 A189 2p multi .55 .55
992 A189 2.50p multi .65 .65
993 A189 3p multi .80 .80
994 A189 3.50p multi, vert. .90 .90
995 A189 4.50p multi, vert. 1.25 1.25
996 A189 5p multi, vert. 1.25 1.25
997 A189 8p multi, vert. 2.00 2.00
998 A189 12p multi, vert. 2.50 2.50
Nos. 989-998 (10) 10.55 10.55

TAP SEAC Buildings — A190

#999 — Various buildings with enominations in: a, Greenish blue. b, Orange. c, Dull yellow. d, Blue green (blue door).
10p, Orange.

1999, June 24

999 A190 1.50p Strip of 4, #a.-d. 1.50 1.50

Souvenir Sheet

1000 A190 10p multicolored 2.50 2.50
a. Ovptd. in sheet margin 2.50 2.50

#1000 overprinted in gold in sheet margin with "Amizade Luso-Chinesa / Transferencia de Soberania de / MACAU 1999 / Guangdong Cantao," date and Chinese text.

Dim Sum — A191

#1001 — Table settings with: a, Brown teapot. b, Two food platters. c, Two bamboo steamers. d, Flowered teapot.
9p, Various platters.

1999, Aug. 21

1001 A191 2.50p Strip of 4, #a.-d. 2.50 2.50

Souvenir Sheet

1002 A191 9p multicolored 2.25 2.25
a. Ovptd. in sheet margin 2.25 2.25

China 1999 World Philatelic Exhibition (No. 1002).
#1002 overprinted in gold in sheet margin with "Amizade Luso-Chinesa / Transferencia

de Soberania de / MACAU 1999 / Guangdong Cantao," date and Chinese text.

Modern Sculpture A192

Various unidentified sculptures.

1999, Oct. 9 Litho. *Perf. 12*

Background Color

1003 A192	1p red violet		.25	.25
1004 A192	1.50p brown, vert.		.40	.40
1005 A192	2.50p gray brn, vert.		.65	.65
1006 A192	3.50p blue grn		.90	.90
	Nos. 1003-1006 (4)		2.20	2.20

Souvenir Sheet

1007 A192	10p blue gray	2.50	2.50
a.	Ovptd. in sheet margin	2.50	2.50

No. 1007a overprinted in gold in sheet margin with "Amizade Luso-Chinesa / Transferencia da Soberania de / MACAU 1999 / Zhejiang Hangzhou," date and Chinese text.

Meeting of Portuguese and Chinese Cultures — A193

No. 1008: a, 1p, Ships. b, 1.50p, Building. c, 2p, Bridge. d, 3p, Fort.
10p, Fort, diff.

1999, Nov. 19 Litho. *Perf. 12¼*

1008 A193	Strip of 4, #a.-d.	1.90	1.90

Souvenir Sheet

1009 A193	10p multi	2.50	2.50
a.	Ovptd. in sheet margin	2.50	2.50

Perforations in corners of stamps on Nos. 1008-1009 are star-shaped.

No. 1009a overprinted in gold in sheet margin with "Amizade Luso-Chinesa / Transferencia da Soberania de / MACAU 1999 / Zhejiang Hangzhou," date and Chinese text.

See Portugal No. 2339.

Retrospective of Macao's Portuguese History — A194

No. 1010: a, 1p, Globe. b, 1.50p, Fort. c, 2p, Chinese, Portuguese people. d, 3.50p, Skyline, Nobre de Carvalho bridge.
9p, Arms.

1999, Dec. 19

1010 A194	Block or strip of 4, #a.-d.	2.00	2.00

Souvenir Sheet

1011 A194	9p multi	2.25	2.25
a.	Ovptd. in sheet margin	2.25	2.25

No. 1011a overprinted in gold in sheet margin with "Amizade Luso-Chinesa / Transferencia da Soberania de / MACAU 1999 / Macau," date and Chinese text.

Perforations in corners of stamps on Nos. 1010-1011 are star-shaped.

See Portugal No. 2340.

Special Administrative Region of People's Republic of China

Establishment of Special Administrative Region — A195

No. 1012: a, 1p, Temple, dragon. b, 1.50p, Friendship Bridge, dragon boats. c, 2p, Cathedral, Santa Claus, Christmas tree. d, 2.50p, Lighthouse, race cars. e, 3p, Building, dragons. f, 3.50p, Building, crowd.
8p, Flower.

1999, Dec. 20 Litho. *Perf. 12*

1012 A195	Block of 6, #a.-f.	3.50	3.50

Souvenir Sheet

1013 A195	8p multi	2.00	2.00
a.	Ovptd. in sheet margin	2.00	2.00

No. 1013a overprinted in gold in sheet margin with "Amizade Luso-Chinesa / Transferencia da Soberania de / MACAU 1999 / China — Macau," dte, "O futuro de Macau será melhor" and Chinese text.

Souvenir Sheet

Millennium — A196

Illustration reduced.

2000, Jan. 1 Litho. *Perf. 12¼*

1014 A196	8p multi	2.00	2.00

Perforations in corners of stamp are star-shaped.

New Year 2000 (Year of the Dragon) A197

2000, Jan. 28 *Perf. 12¼*

1015 A197	5.50p multi	1.40	1.40

Souvenir Sheet

1016 A197	10p multi	2.50	2.50

Perforations in corners of stamps on Nos. 1015-1016 are star-shaped.

Historic Buildings — A198

2000, Mar. 1 Litho. *Perf. 12¼*

1017	Strip of 4	1.90	1.90
a.	A198 1p green circles	.25	.25
b.	A198 1.50p pink circles	.40	.40
c.	A198 2p brown circles	.50	.50
d.	A198 3p blue circles	.75	.75

Souvenir Sheet

1018 A198	9p Brown circles	2.25	2.25

Perforations in corners of stamps are star-shaped.

Chinese Calligraphy A199

#1019 — Characters: a, Rectangle with bisecting line. b, Rectangle with lines inside. c, 8 horizontal lines, 3 vertical lines. d, 3 spots to left of 6 touching lines.
8p, Characters shown on #1019a-1019d.

2000, Mar. 23

1019	Block of 4	3.00	3.00
a.-d.	A199 3p any single	.75	.75

Souvenir Sheet

1020 A199	8p multi	2.00	2.00

Bangkok 2000 Stamp Exhibition (#1020).

Perforations in corners of stamps are star-shaped.

Scenes From "A Journey to the West" — A200

No. 1021: a, 1p, Monkey and tiger. b, 1.50p, Monkey on tree. c, 2p, Monkey and spear carrier. d, 2.50p, Spear carrier and dog. e, 3p, Man in robe. f, 3.50p, Monkey in palm of hand.
9p, Monkey with stick, horiz.

2000, May 5 Litho. *Perf. 12¼*

1021 A200	Block of 6, #a-f	3.50	3.50

Souvenir Sheet

1022 A200	9p multi	2.25	2.25

Perforations in corners of stamps are star-shaped.

Board Games A201

Designs: 1p, Chinese chess. 1.50p, Chess. 2p, Go. 2.50p, Parcheesi.

2000, June 8

1023-1026 A201	Set of 4	1.75	1.75

Souvenir Sheet

1027 A201	9p Chinese checkers	2.25	2.25

Perforations in corners of stamps are star-shaped.

Tea Rituals A202

2000, July 7

1028	Horiz. strip of 4	3.25	3.25
a.	A202 2p Square table, 4 people	.50	.50
b.	A202 3p Round table, 5 people	.75	.75
c.	A202 3.50p Round table, 3 people	.90	.90
d.	A202 4.50p Square table, 3 people	1.10	1.10

Souvenir Sheet

1029 A202	8p Woman pouring tea	2.10	2.10

Perforations in corners are star-shaped.

World Stamp Expo 2000, Anaheim (#1029).

Tricycle Drivers — A203

No. 1030: a, Driver pointing. b, Driver wearing yellow cap. c, Driver sitting on saddle. d, Driver with feet on saddle. e, Driver with crossed legs. f, Driver repairing tricycle.
8p, Driver standing next to tricycle, vert.
Illustration reduced.

2000, Sept. 1 Granite Paper

1030 A203	2p Block of 6, #a-f	3.00	3.00

Souvenir Sheet

1031 A203	8p multi	2.10	2.10

Perforations in corners of stamps are star-shaped.

Sculpture Type of 1999 Inscribed "Macau, China"

Various unidentified sculptures with background colors of: 1p, Brown. 2p, Green, vert. 3p, Purple, vert. 4p, Purple.
10p, Gray blue.

2000, Oct. 9 Granite Paper

1032-1035 A192	Set of 4	2.50	2.50

Souvenir Sheet

1036 A192	10p multi	2.60	2.60

Perforations in corners of stamps are star-shaped.

Ceramics and Chinaware — A204

No. 1037; a, Style. b, Color. c, Form. d, Function. e, Design. f, Export.
Illustration reduced.

2000, Oct. 31 Granite Paper

1037 A204	2.50p Sheet of 6, #a-f	3.75	3.75

Souvenir Sheet

1038 A204	8p Plate design	2.10	2.10

No. 1038 contains one 38mm diameter stamp. Perforations in corners of No. 1037 are star-shaped.

Jade Ornaments A205

Various ornaments. Colors of country name: 1.50p, Purple. 2p, Green, vert. 2.50p, Red, vert. 3p, Blue.
9p, Red, vert.

2000, Nov. 22 Granite Paper

1039-1042 A205	Set of 4	2.25	2.25

Souvenir Sheet

1043 A205	9p multi	2.25	2.25

Perforations in corners of stamps are star-shaped.

Special Administrative Region, 1st Anniv. — A206

No. 1044: a, 2p, Dancers, flags. b, 3p, Monument, dragon.

2000, Dec. 20 Litho. *Perf. 12¼*

Granite Paper (#1044)

1044 A206 Horiz. pair, #a-b 1.25 1.25

Souvenir Sheet

Litho. & Embossed

Perf. 13½x13

1045 A206 18p Flags, monument 4.50 4.50

No. 1045 contains one 60x40mm stamp. Perforations in corners of No. 1044 are star-shaped.

New Year 2001 (Year of the Snake) A207

2001, Jan. 18 Litho. *Perf. 13x13¼*

1046 A207 5.50p multi 1.40 1.40

Souvenir Sheet

Granite Paper

1047 A207 10p multi 2.50 2.50

Seng-Yu Proverbs — A208

Designs: No. 1048, Sleeping on a woodpile and tasting gall (4-1). No. 1049, Watching over a stump waiting for a rabbit (4-2). No. 1050, The fox making use of the tiger's fierceness (4-3). No. 1051, Meng Mu moving house three times (4-4).
8p, Man and bell.

2001, Feb. 1 Photo. *Perf. 11¾*

Granite Paper

1048 A208 2p multi .50 .50
a. Booklet pane of 1, plain paper 2.25
1049 A208 2p multi .50 .50
a. Booklet pane of 1, plain paper 2.25
1050 A208 2p multi .50 .50
a. Booklet pane of 1, plain paper 2.25
1051 A208 2p multi .50 .50
a. Booklet pane of 1, plain paper 2.25
Booklet, #1048a-1051a 9.00
Nos. 1048-1051 (4) 2.00 2.00

Souvenir Sheet

1052 A208 8p multi 2.10 2.10

Hong Kong 2001 Stamp Exhibition (#1052). Booklet containing Nos. 1048a-1051a sold for 35p.

Traditional Implements A209

Designs: 1p, Abacus. 2p, Plane. 3p, Iron. 4p, Balance scale.
8p, Abacus, plane, iron, balance scale.

2001, Mar. 1 Litho. *Perf. 14½x14*

1053-1056 A209 Set of 4 2.50 2.50

Souvenir Sheet

1057 A209 8p multi 2.10 2.10

Religious Beliefs A210

No. 1058: a, Buddha. b, People in prayer. c, Re-enactment of Christ carrying cross. d, People in procession.
8p, Symbols.

2001, Apr. 12 Litho. *Perf. 14½x14*

1058 Horiz. strip of 4 1.75 1.75
a. A210 1p multi .25 .25
b. A210 1.50p multi .35 .35
c A210 2p multi .50 .50
d. A210 2.50p multi .65 .65

Souvenir Sheet

Photo.

Perf.

1059 A210 8p multi 2.10 2.10

No. 1059 contains one 60mm diameter stamp.

Rescue Workers A211

No. 1060: a, Fireman. b, Hazardous materials worker. c, Fireman, diff. d, Ambulance crew.
8p, Firemen, diff

2001, May 2 Litho. *Perf. 14½x14*

1060 Horiz. strip of 4 2.75 2.75
a. A211 1.50p multi .35 .35
b. A211 2.50p multi .65 .65
c. A211 3p multi .75 .75
d. A211 4p multi 1.00 1.00

Souvenir Sheet

Perf. 14x14½

1061 A211 8p multi 2.10 2.10

No. 1061 contains one 60x40mm stamp.

Internet and E-Commerce — A212

Designs: 1.50p, Keys. 2p, Envelope with "@" symbol. 2.50p, Hand-held computer. 3p, Computer.
6p, Linked computers.

2001, June 30 Litho. *Perf. 14½x14*

1062-1065 A212 Set of 4 2.25 2.25

Souvenir Sheet

1066 A212 6p multi 1.50 1.50

Emblem of 2008 Summer Olympics, Beijing — A213

2001, July 14 Photo. *Perf. 13x13¼*

1067 A213 1p multi + label .25 .25

No. 1067 printed in sheets of 12 stamp + label pairs with one large central label. See People's Republic of China No. 3119, Hong Kong No. 940. No. 1067 with different label is from People's Republic of China No. 3119a.

The Romance of Three Kingdoms — A214

Designs: a, Men praying (4-1). b, Man with spear (4-2). c, Men at outdoors table (4-3). d, Man on horseback (4-4).
7p, Man with sword, horiz.

2001, Aug. 1 Litho. *Perf. 14x14½*

1068 A214 3p Block of 4, #a-d 3.00 3.00

Souvenir Sheet

Perf. 14½x14

1069 A214 7p multi 1.75 1.75

2001 Census — A215

Designs: 1p, Buildings, students, child health care. 1.50p, Buildings, street scene. 2.50p, Bridge, people.
6p, Buildings, students, child health care, street scene, bridge, people.

2001, Aug. 23 Litho. *Perf. 14x14½*

1070-1072 A215 Set of 3 1.25 1.25

Souvenir Sheet

1073 A215 6p multi 1.50 1.50

No. 1073 contains one 89x39mm stamp.

Stores — A216

No. 1074: a, 1.50p, Municipal market. b, 2.50p, Store with red window frames. c, 3.50p, Store, parked bicycles. d, 4.50p, Store, parked cars.
7p, Store tower and windows.
Illustration reduced.

2001, Sept. 13 *Perf. 14½x14*

1074 A216 Block of 4, #a-d 3.00 3.00

Souvenir Sheet

Perf. 14x14½

1075 A216 7p multi 1.75 1.75

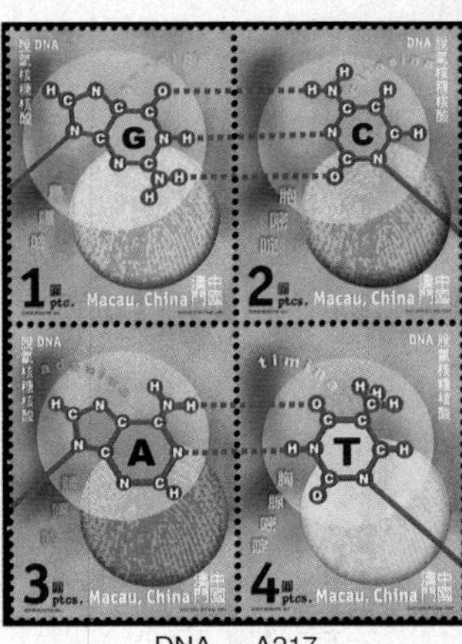

DNA — A217

Fingerprint and: a, 1p, Guanine. b, 2p, Cytosine. c, 3p, Adenine. d, 4p, Thymine.
8p, Adenine, horiz.

2001, Oct. 9 Photo. *Perf. 14x13½*

Granite Paper

1076 A217 Block of 4, #a-d 2.50 2.50

Souvenir Sheet

Perf. 13½x14

1077 A217 8p multi 2.00 2.00

No. 1077 contains one 44x29mm stamp.

Parks and Gardens — A218

No. 1078: a, 1.50p, Comendador Ho Yin Garden. b, 2.50p, Mong Há Hill Municipal Park. c, 3p, City of Flowers Garden. 4.50p, Taipa Grande Nature Park.
8p, Art Garden.

2001, Nov. 30 Litho. *Perf. 13½x14*

Granite Paper

1078 A218 Block of 4, #a-d 3.00 3.00

Souvenir Sheet

1079 A218 8p multi 2.00 2.00

I Ching A219

A219a

No. 1080 — Position of broken bars in trigrams (pa kua): a, No broken bars. b, First and second. c, Second and third. d, Second. e, First and third. f, First. g, Third. h, First, second and third.

2001, Dec. 10 Photo. *Perf. 13*
Granite Paper

1080 A219 2p Sheet of 8, #a-h 4.00 4.00

Souvenir Sheet
Perf. 13½x13¼

1081 A219a 8p shown 2.00 2.00

No. 1080 contains eight 39x34mm hexagonal stamps.

New Year 2002 (Year of the Horse) A220

Horse's head: 5.50p, With frame. 10p, With continuous design.

2002, Jan. 28 Litho. *Perf. 14½x14*

1082 A220 5.50p multi 1.40 1.40

Souvenir Sheet

1083 A220 10p multi 2.50 2.50

Characters From Novel "Dream of the Red Mansion II," by Cao Xuequin — A221

No. 1084: a, Lao Lao (6/1). b, Jin Chuan (6/2). c, Zi Juan (6/3). d, Xiang Yun (6/4). e, Liu Lang (6/5). f, Miao Yu (6/6).
8d, Woman reading book.
Illustration reduced.

2002, Mar. 1 *Perf. 14x14½*

1084 A221 2p Block of 6, #a-f 3.00 3.00

Souvenir Sheet

1085 A221 8p multi 2.00 2.00

Tou-tei Festival — A222

No. 1086: a, 1.50p, Opera. b, 2.50p, Dinner in appreciation of the elderly. c, 3.50p, Burning of religious objects. d, 4.50p, Preparing roasted pork.
8p, People watching performance, vert.
Illustration reduced.

2002, Mar. 15 *Perf. 14½x14*

1086 A222 Block of 4, #a-d 3.00 3.00

Souvenir Sheet
Perf. 14x14½

1087 A222 8p multi 2.00 2.00

Church of St. Paul, 400th Anniv. — A223

Various church statues: 1p, 3.50p.
8p, Statue in niche.

2002, Apr. 12 *Perf. 14½x14*

1088-1089 A223 Set of 2 1.10 1.10

Souvenir Sheet
Perf. 14x14½

1090 A223 8p multi 2.00 2.00

No. 1090 contains one 30x40mm stamp.

Participation of Chinese Team in 2002 World Cup Soccer Championships — A224

No. 1091: a, 1p, Goalie. b, 1.50p, Two players.
Illustration reduced.

Perf. 12 Syncopated

2002, May 16 Photo.

1091 A224 Horiz. pair, #a-b .65 .65

A souvenir sheet containing Nos. 1091a-1091b, People's Republic of China No. 3198 and Hong Kong Nos. 978a-978b exists.

Environmental Protection — A225

Designs: 1p, Conservation of maritime resources. 1.50p, Reforestation. 2p, Recycling. 2.50p, Protection of swamps. 3p, Reuse of resources. 3.50p, Municipal cleaning. 4p, Air purification. 4.50p, Health and hygiene. 8p, Quiet and comfort.

2002, June 5 Litho. *Perf. 13x13¼*

1092-1100 A225 Set of 9 7.50 7.50

Zheng Guanying (1842-1921), Reformer and Author — A226

Zheng and: a, 1p, Another man. b, 2p, Harbor scene. c, 3p, Men at table. d, 3.50p, Chinese text.
6p, Zheng seated at table.

2002, July 24 *Perf. 14*

1101 A226 Block of 4, #a-d 2.40 2.40

Souvenir Sheet

1102 A226 6p multi 1.50 1.50

No. 1102 contains one 40x60mm stamp.

Honesty and Equality A227

Various buildings: 1p, 3.50p.

2002, Sept. 13 Litho. *Perf. 14½x14*

1103-1104 A227 Set of 2 1.10 1.10

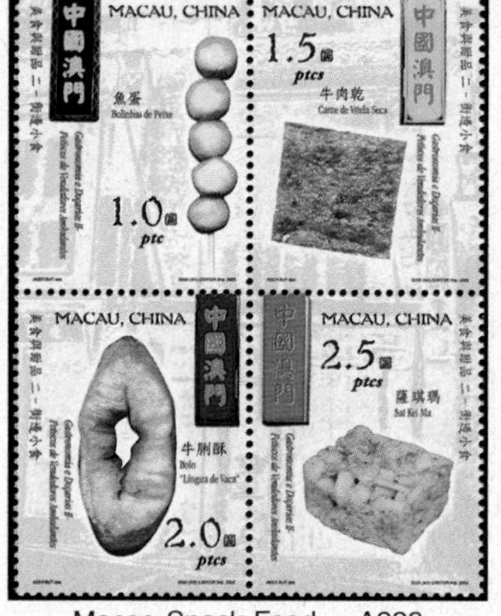

Macao Snack Food — A228

No. 1105: a, 1p, Bolinhas de peixe (fish balls). b, 1.50p, Carne de vitela seca (dried veal). c, 2p, Bolo (cake). d, 2.50p, Sat Kei Ma.
7p, Pastry.

2002, Sept. 26 Litho. *Perf. 13¼x13*

1105 A228 Block of 4, #a-d 1.75 1.75

Souvenir Sheet

1106 A228 7p multi 1.75 1.75

Portions of Nos. 1105-1106 were applied by a thermographic process, producing a raised, shiny effect. No. 1106 contains one 50x50mm diamond-shaped stamp.

Filial Love — A229

No. 1107: a, 1p, Farmer and elephant (O amor filial comove a Deus). b, 1.50p, Man and woman (Abanar a almofada e aquecer a manta). c, 2p, Man and bamboo plants (Chorar sobre o bambu fez crescer rebentos). d, 2.50p, Man and fish (Pescar para a mae deitado no gelo).
No. 1107E: f, Man with arms extended (Mal agasalhado mas tolerante com a madrasta). g, Man and woman (Saltaram carpas da nascente). h, Man with hat (Quem tem amor filial é também fiel). i, Man (Lealdade de pai, amor filial do filho).
7p, Man wearing deer's head (Dar leite de veado aos pais).

2002, Oct. 9 Litho. *Perf. 14*

1107 A229 Block of 4, #a-d 1.75 1.75
1107E Souvenir booklet 4.50
f.-i. A229 4.50p Any booklet pane of 1 1.10 1.10

Souvenir Sheet
Perf. 13½x13

1108 A229 7p multi 1.75 1.75

Particle Physics — A230

No. 1109: a, Unified electroweak interaction theory developed by Steven Weinberg, Sheldon Lee Glashow and Abdus Salam. b, Discovery of W and Z subatomic particles by Carlo Rubbia, 1983. c, Higgs diagram, developed by Richard Feynman and Peter Higgs. d, CERN large electron positron collider, 1989. e, Classification of particles and prediction of quarks by Murray Gell-Mann and George Zweig. f, Unification theory of Albert Einstein.
8p, Detection of positive and negative W particles, CERN LEP, 1996.

2002, Nov. 22 *Perf. 14x14½*

1109 A230 1.50p Block of 6, #a-f 2.25 2.25

Souvenir Sheet

1110 A230 8p multi 2.00 2.00

I Ching Type of 2001 and

A231

Peace Dance> — A231a

No. 1111 — Position of broken bars in trigrams (pa kua): a, Fourth. b, First, second and fourth. c, Second, third and fourth. d, Second and fourth. e, First, third and fourth. f, First and fourth. g, Third and fourth. h, First, second, third and fourth.

2002, Dec. 13 *Perf. 14*
Granite Paper

1111 A231 2p Sheet of 8, #a-h 4.00 4.00

Souvenir Sheet
Perf. 114x13½

1112 A231a 8p multi 2.00 2.00

No. 1111 contains eight 39x34 hexagonal stamps. Stamps from No. 1111 have Roman numeral II below "I Ching" and "Pa Kua."

New Year 2003 (Year of the Ram) A232

2003, Jan. 2 *Perf. 14½x14*

1113 A232 5.50p multi 1.40 1.40

Souvenir Sheet

1113A A232 10p multi 2.50 2.50

Legend of Liang Shanbo and Zhu Yingtai
A233

No. 1114: a, People seated and reading. b, People on bridge. c, People, tea pot and cups. d, Man holding red paper.
9p, People with butterfly wings.

2003, Feb. 15 Litho. *Perf. 13x13½*

1114	Horiz. strip of 4	3.50	3.50
a.-d.	A233 3.50p Any single	.85	.85

Souvenir Sheet

1115	A233 9p multi	2.25	2.25

No. 1115 contains one 40x60mm stamp.

The Outlaws of the Marsh — A234

No. 1116: a, Song Jiang. b, Lin Chong. c, Wu Song. d, Lu Zhishen. e, Wu Yong. f, Hua Rong.
8p, Heróis do Monte Liang Shan.
Illustration reduced.

2003, Mar. 1 *Perf. 13½x14*
Granite Paper (#1116)

1116	A234 2p Block of 6, #a-f	3.00	3.00

Souvenir Sheet
Perf. 14x14½

1117	A234 8p multi	2.00	2.00

Basic Law of Macao, 10th Anniv.
A235

Designs: 1p, Building, doves, cover of book of laws. 4.50p, Children, dove, flags of Macao and People's Republic of China, law book

2003, Mar. 31 *Perf. 14*

1118-1119	A235 Set of 2	1.40	1.40

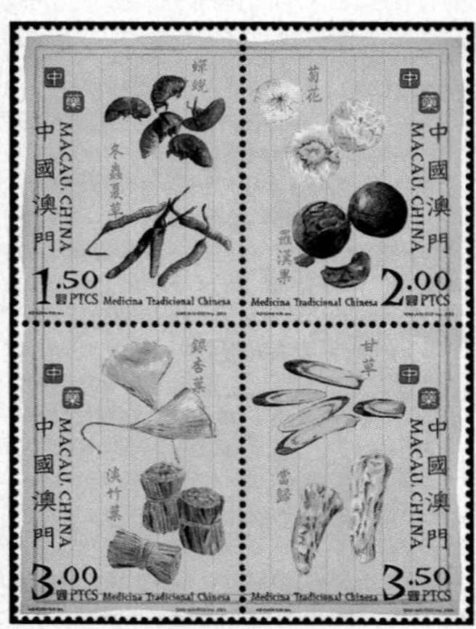

Traditional Chinese Medicine — A236

No. 1120 — Various medicines: a, 1.50p. b, 2p. c, 3p. d, 3.50p.
8p, Man holding bowl of medicine, horiz.

2003, May 28

1120	A236 Block of 4, #a-d	2.50	2.50

Souvenir Sheet

1121	A236 8p multi	2.00	2.00

Historic Buildings on Taipa and Coloane Islands — A237

Various buildings.

2003, June 18

1122	Horiz. strip of 4	2.00	2.00
a.	A237 1p multi	.25	.25
b.	A237 1.50p multi	.40	.40
c.	A237 2p multi	.50	.50
d.	A237 3.50p multi	.85	.85

Souvenir Sheet

1123	A237 9p multi	2.25	2.25

Everyday Life in the Past — A238

No. 1124: a, Calligrapher at table. b, Puppet maker. c, Man with food cart. d, Washerwoman. e, Woman with decorative lanterns. f, Man carrying food tray above head, man with baskets. g, Photographer. h, Man in chicken costume playing horn.
8p, Barber.

2003, July 30 *Perf. 13½x13*

1124	Block of 8	3.00	3.00
a.-h.	A238 1.50p Any single	.35	.35

Souvenir Sheet
Perf. 14x14½

1125	A238 8p multi	2.00	2.00

I Ching Type of 2001 and

Woman and Child — A239

No. 1126 — Position of broken bars in trigrams (pa kua): a, Second. b, Second, fifth and sixth. c, Second, fourth and fifth. d, Second and fifth. e, Second, fourth and sixth. f, Second and sixth. g, Second and fourth. h, Second, fourth, fifth and sixth.

2003, Sept. 10 *Perf. 14*
Granite Paper

1126	A219 2p Sheet of 8, #a-h	4.00	4.00

Souvenir Sheet
Perf. 14x13½

1127	A239 8p multi	2.00	2.00

No. 1126 contains eight 39x34mm hexagonal stamps. Stamps from No. 1126 have Roman numeral III below text "Pa Kua" and "I Ching."

Launch of First Manned Chinese Spacecraft
A240

No. 1128: a, 1p, Astronaut. b, 1.50p, Ship, Shenzhou spacecraft.

2003, Oct. 16 *Perf. 13x13½*

1128	A240 Pair, #a-b	.65	.65

A booklet containing No. 1128, People's Republic of China No. 3314 and Hong Kong No. 1062 exists. The booklet sold for a premium over face value.

50th Grand Prix of Macao — A241

No. 1129: a, 1p, Race car #5. b, 1.50p, Yellow race car #11. c, 2p, Red race car #11. d, 3p, Motorcycle #5. e, 3.50p, Race car #15. f, 4.50p, Race car #3.
12p, Race car and motorcycle.

Litho. & Embossed
2003, Oct. 29 *Perf. 14*

1129	A241 Sheet of 6, #a-f	4.00	4.00

Souvenir Sheet
Litho. With Hologram Applied
Perf.

1130	A241 12p multi	3.00	3.00

No. 1129 contains six 36x27mm stamps that have varnish applied to raised portions.

Macao Museum of Art — A242

No. 1131 — Artwork depicting: a, 1p, Man in hooded cloak. b, 1.50p, Hill overlooking harbor. c, 2p, Ruins of St. Paul's Church. d, 2.50p, Two men.
7p, Waterfront buildings, boats in harbor.
Illustration reduced.

2003, Dec. 1 Litho. *Perf. 14½x14*

1131	A242 Block of 4 #a-d	1.75	1.75

Souvenir Sheet

1132	A242 7p multi	1.75	1.75

No. 1132 contains one 57x55mm stamp.

New Year 2004 (Year of the Monkey)
A243

2004, Jan. 8 *Perf. 14½x14*

1133	A243 5.50p shown	1.40	1.40

Souvenir Sheet

1134	A243 10p Monkey, diff.	2.50	2.50

I Ching Type of 2001 and

Man Chiseling Stone — A244

No. 1135 — Position of broken bars in trigrams (pa kua): a, Second and third. b, Second, third, fifth and sixth. c, Second, third, fourth and fifth. d, Second, third and fifth. e, Second, third, fourth and sixth. f, Second, third and sixth. g, Second, third and fourth. h, Second, third, fourth, fifth and sixth.

2004, Mar. 1 *Perf. 14*
Granite Paper

1135	A219 2p Sheet of 8, #a-h	4.00	4.00

Souvenir Sheet
Perf. 14x13½

1136	A244 8p multi	2.00	2.00

No. 1135 contains eight 39x34mm hexagonal stamps. Stamps from No. 1135 have Roman numeral IV below text "Pa Kua" and "I Ching."

Li Sao — A245

No. 1137: a, Orientaçao. b, Cultivo. c, Aconselhamento pela Irma. d, Transmissao de esperança pela fénix. e, Viagens e reflexoes. f, Local da vida eterna.
8p, Li Sao, horiz.
Illustration reduced.

2004, May 28 *Perf. 13½x14*
Granite Paper

1137	A245 1.50p Block of 6, #a-f	2.25	2.25

Souvenir Sheet
Perf. 14x13½

1138	A245 8p multi	2.00	2.00

God of Guan Di — A246

2004, June 30 *Perf. 13½x14*
Granite Paper

1139	Horiz. strip of 4	3.00	3.00
a.	A246 1.50p shown	.35	.35
b.	A246 2.50p God, diff.	.65	.65
c.	A246 3.50p God, diff.	.90	.90
d.	A246 4.50p God, diff.	1.10	1.10

Souvenir Sheet
Perf. 14x13½

1140	A246 9p God, diff.	2.25	2.25

No. 1140 contains one 40x40mm stamp.

2004 Summer Olympics, Athens — A247

Designs: 1p, Woman runner. 1.50p, Long jump. 2p, Discus. 3.50p, Javelin.

2004, July 30 ***Perf. 13¼***

Granite Paper

1141-1144 A247 Set of 4 2.00 2.00

Deng Xiaoping (1904-97), Chinese Leader A248

Designs: 1p, Saluting. 1.50p, Wearing white shirt.
8p, As young man.

2004, Aug. 22 Litho. ***Perf. 13x13¼***

1145-1146 A248 Set of 2 .65 .65

Souvenir Sheet

Litho. & Embossed

Perf.

1147 A248 8p multi 2.00 2.00

No. 1147 contains one 40mm diameter stamp.

Intl. Fireworks Display Contest — A249

No. 1148 — Various landmarks and fireworks displays: a, 1p. b, 1.50p. c, 2p. d, 4.50p.
9p, Statue and fireworks, vert.
Illustration reduced.

Litho. & Silk Screened

2004, Sept. 2 ***Perf. 13¼***

Granite Paper

1148 A249 Block of 4, #a-d 2.25 2.25

Souvenir Sheet

Perf. 13x13¼

1149 A249 9p multi 2.25 2.25

No. 1149 contains one 40x60mm stamp.

People's Republic of China, 55th Anniv. — A250

No. 1150 — Buildings and: a, 1p, Flag of People's Republic of China. b, 1.50p, Flag of Macao. c, 2p, Arms of People's Republic of China. d, 3p, Arms of Macao.
7p, Buildings.
Illustration reduced.

2004, Oct. 1 Litho. ***Perf. 13x13¼***

Granite Paper

1150 A250 Block of 4, #a-d 1.90 1.90

Souvenir Sheet

Perf. 13¼x13

1151 A250 7p multi 1.75 1.75

No. 1151 contains one 60x40mm stamp.

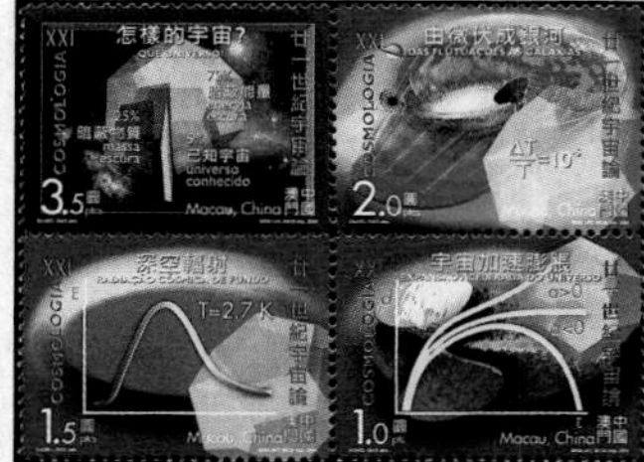

Cosmology — A251

No. 1152: a, 1p, Expansion and acceleration of the Universe. b, 1.50p, Cosmic radiation. c, 2p, Fluctuations of galaxies. d, 3.50p, What is the Universe?
8p, Big Bang Theory.
Illustration reduced.

2004, Oct. 9 ***Perf. 12¼***

1152 A251 Block of 4, #a-d 2.00 2.00

Souvenir Sheet

1153 A251 8p multi 2.00 2.00

Macao Garrison of the People's Liberation Army — A252

No. 1154 — Flag and, in foreground: a, 1p, Soldier holding sword. b, 1p, Soldier in tank. c, 1.50p, Soldiers in car. d, 1.50p, Soldiers giving blood. e, 3.50p, Soldier at attention holding gun. f, 3.50p, Soldier with helmet and rifle with bayonet.
8p, Soldiers in car, vert.
Illustration reduced.

2004, Dec. 1 ***Perf. 13x13¼***

1154 A252 Block of 6, #a-f 3.00 3.00

Souvenir Sheet

1155 A252 8p multi 2.00 2.00

No. 1155 contains one 40x60mm stamp.

Establishment of Special Administrative District, 5th Anniv. — A253

Lotus flowers and various buildings.

2004, Dec. 20 Litho. ***Perf. 14½x14***

1156 Horiz. strip of 4 2.25 2.25
- ***a.*** A253 1.50p multi .40 .40
- ***b.*** A253 2p multi .50 .50
- ***c.*** A253 2.50p multi .60 .60
- ***d.*** A253 3p multi .75 .75

Souvenir Sheet

Litho. & Embossed

1157 A253 10p multi 2.50 2.50

Souvenir Sheet

Air Macau, 10th Anniv. — A254

2004, Dec. 28 Litho. ***Perf. 14***

1158 A254 8p multi 2.00 2.00

New Year 2005 (Year of the Rooster) A255

2005, Jan. 13 Litho. ***Perf. 14½x14***

1159 A255 5.50p shown 1.40 1.40

Souvenir Sheet

1160 A255 10p Rooster, diff. 2.50 2.50

Everyday Life in the Past — A256

No. 1161: a, Cook (8/1). b, Man holding pole with hanging bottles (8/2). c, Man at work at small table (8/3). d, Textile worker (8/4). e, Man cutting coconuts (8/5). f, Cook at cart (8/6). g, Cook under lantern (8/7). h, Seamstress (8/8).
8p, Mailman on bicycle.

2005, Mar. 1 ***Perf. 12¼***

1161 Block of 8 3.00 3.00
- ***a.-h.*** A256 1.50p Any single .35 .35

Souvenir Sheet

1162 A256 8p multi 2.00 2.00

Sai Van Bridge A257

Designs: 1p, Bridge. 3.50p, Bridge and approaches.
8p, Bridge tower, vert.

2005, Mar. 23 ***Perf. 14***

1163-1164 A257 Set of 2 1.10 1.10

Souvenir Sheet

1165 A257 8p multi 2.00 2.00

Libraries A258

2005, Apr. 15

1166 Horiz. strip of 4 2.00 2.00
- ***a.*** A258 1p Central Library .25 .25
- ***b.*** A258 1.50p Sir Robert Ho Tung Library .35 .35
- ***c.*** A258 2p Coloane Library .50 .50
- ***d.*** A258 3.50p Mong Há Library .90 .90

Souvenir Sheet

1167 A258 8p Public Commercial Assoc. Library 2.00 2.00

No. 1167 contains one 60x40mm stamp.

Mothers and Offspring — A259

2005, May 8 ***Perf. 14½x14***

1168 Horiz. strip of 4 + 4 alternating labels 2.00 2.00
- ***a.*** A259 1p Humans + label .25 .25
- ***b.*** A259 1.50p Kangaroos + label .35 .35
- ***c.*** A259 2p Birds and nest + label .50 .50
- ***d.*** A259 3.50p Ducks + label .90 .90

Labels could be personalized, with sheets containing 5 strips and 20 labels selling for 60p.

The Romance of the Western Chamber — A260

No. 1169 — Inscriptions: a, Espreitando a Beldade à Luz da Lua (6/1). b, Ying Ying Ouvindo Música (6/2). c, O Amor e Ansiedade de Zhang Sheng (6/3). d, A Interrogaçao da Dama (6/4). e, Sonhando com Ying Ying na Pensao (6/5). f, A Uniao dos Amados (6/6).
8p, A Espera da Lua.

2005, June 10 ***Perf. 13¼x14***

Granite Paper

1169 A260 2p Block of 6, #a-f 3.00 3.00

Souvenir Sheet

Perf. 14x13¼

1170 A260 8p multi 2.00 2.00

Voyages of Admiral Zheng He, 600th Anniv. A261

No. 1171: a, Admiral Zheng He. b, Giraffe. c, Ship and map.
8p, Ships.

2005, June 28 Litho. ***Perf. 13x13½***

1171 Horiz. strip of 3 1.00 1.00
- ***a.*** A261 1p multi .25 .25
- ***b.-c.*** A261 1.50p Either single .35 .35

Souvenir Sheet

Perf. 13¼

1172 A261 8p multi 2.00 2.00

No. 1172 contains one 50x30mm stamp.

UNESCO World Heritage Sites — A262

Various buildings in Historical Center of Macao World Heritage Site with background colors of: a, 1p, White. b, 1.50p, Red. c, 2p, Orange. d, 3.50p, Dark green.
8p, Green.
Illustration reduced.

2005, July 16 ***Perf. 14***
1173 A262 Block of 4, #a-d 2.00 2.00

Souvenir Sheet

1174 A262 8p multi 2.00 2.00

4th East Asian Games, Macao — A263

No. 1175 — Stylized athletes and: a, 1p, Olympic Swimming Pool of Macao. b, 1.50p, Nautical Center, Praia Grande. c, 2p, Tennis Academy. d, 2.50p, IPM Sports Pavilion. e, 3.50p, Macao Stadium. f, 4.50p, Tap Seac Sports Pavilion.
8p, Sports Arena.
Illustration reduced.

2005, Aug. 30 ***Perf. 14x13¼***

Granite Paper

1175 A263 Block of 6, #a-f 3.75 3.75

Souvenir Sheet

Perf.

1176 A263 8p multi 2.00 2.00

No. 1176 contains one 55x38mm oval stamp.

Macao Bank Notes, Cent. — A264

Designs: 1p, 1 pataca note. 1.50p, 5 pataca note. 3p, 10 pataca note. 4.50p, 50 pataca note.
8p, 100 pataca note.

2005, Sept. 2 ***Perf. 13½x14***

Granite Paper

1177-1180 A264 Set of 4 2.50 2.50

Souvenir Sheet

1181 A264 8p multi 2.00 2.00

Great Chinese Inventions — A265

No. 1182: a, 1p, Textile loom. b, 1.50p, Paper. c, 2p, Metal smelting. d, 4.50p, Calendar.
8p, Seismograph.
Illustration reduced.

2005, Oct. 9 ***Perf. 14x13½***

Granite Paper

1182 A265 Block of 4, #a-d 2.25 2.25

Souvenir Sheet

1183 A265 8p multi 2.00 2.00

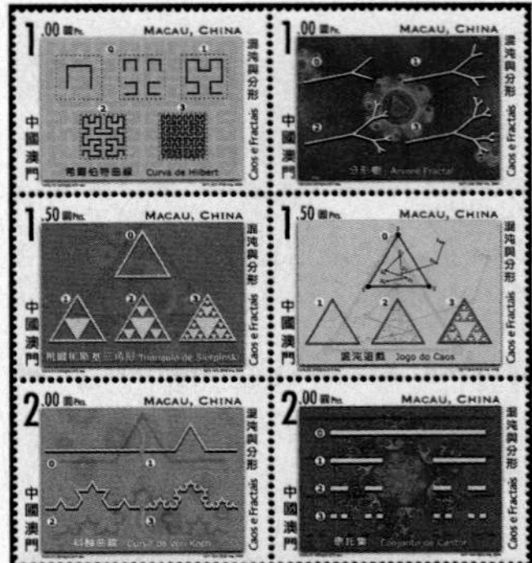

Chaos and Fractal Mathematics — A266

No. 1184: a, 1p, Hilbert's Curve. b, 1p, Tree Fractal. c, 1.50p, Sierpinski Triangle. d, 1.50p, Chaos Game. e, 2p, Von Koch Curve. f, 2p, Cantor Set.
8p, Julia Set.
Illustration reduced.

2005, Nov. 16 ***Perf. 14***
1184 A266 Block of 6, #a-f 2.25 2.25

Souvenir Sheet

1185 A266 8p multi 2.00 2.00

New Year 2006 (Year of the Dog) A267

2006, Jan. 9 **Litho.** ***Perf. 13x13¼***
1186 A267 5.50p multi 1.40 1.40

Souvenir Sheet

1187 A267 10p multi 2.50 2.50

Lanterns — A268

No. 1188 — Various lanterns: a, (4/1). b, (4/2). c, (4/3). d, (4/4).

2006, Feb. 12 ***Perf. 13¼x13***
1188 Horiz. strip of 4 1.25 1.25
a.-b. A268 1p Either single .25 .25
c.-d. A268 1.50p Either single .35 .35

Souvenir Sheet

Perf. 13x13¼

1189 A268 8p multi 2.00 2.00

Everyday Life in the Past — A269

No. 1190: a, Cook (8/1). b, Food vendor (8/2). c, Man holding scissors (8/3). d, Man with small round table (8/4). e, Cobbler (8/5). f, Man with pots (8/6). g, Man hammering pails (8/7). h, Man carrying goods suspended from stick (8/8).
8p, Man looking at kettle.

2006, Mar. 1 ***Perf. 14***
1190 Block of 8 3.00 3.00
a.-h. A269 1.50p Any single .35 .35

Souvenir Sheet

1191 A269 8p multi 2.00 2.00

Items from Communications Museum — A270

No. 1192: a, Rubber stamp (8/1). b, Scale (8/2). c, Mail box (8/3). d, Mail sorting boxes (8/4). e, Telephone (8/5). f, Telephone switching equipment (8/6). g, Radio (8/7). h, Submarine cable (8/8).
10p, Macao #1, horiz.

2006, May 18 ***Perf. 13¼x14***

Granite Paper

1192 Block of 8 3.00 3.00
a.-h. A270 1.50p Any single .35 .35

Souvenir Sheet

1193 A270 10p multi 2.50 2.50

2006 World Cup Soccer Championships, Germany — A271

Various soccer players.

Litho. & Embossed

2006, June 9 ***Perf. 13¼***
1194 Block of 4 3.00 3.00
a. A271 1.50p multi .35 .35
b. A271 2.50p multi .65 .65
c. A271 3.50p multi .90 .90
d. A271 4p multi 1.00 1.00

Fans — A272

No. 1195 — Various pictures on fans: a, (5/1). b, (5/2). c, (5/3). d, (5/4). e, (5/5).
10p, Three children.

2006, June 28 **Litho.** ***Perf. 14x13¼***

Granite Paper

1195 Vert. strip of 5 3.00 3.00
a.-b. A272 1.50p Either single .35 .35
c.-d. A272 2.50p Either single .65 .65
e. A272 3.50p multi .90 .90

Souvenir Sheet

1196 A272 10p multi 2.50 2.50

No. 1196 contains one 40x30mm stamp.

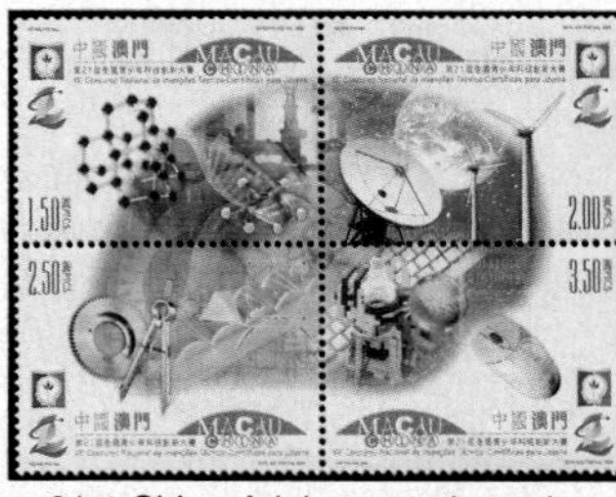

21st China Adolescents Invention Contest — A273

No. 1197: a, 1.50p, Models of molecules, laboratory equipment (4/1). b, 2p, Dish antenna, Earth, windmills (4/2). c, 2.50p, Gear, compass, pyramid and diagrams (4/3). d, 3.50p, Invention, computer keyboard and mouse (4/4).
10p, Atomic model, contest venue, vert.
Illustration reduced.

2006, July 28 ***Perf. 14***
1197 A273 Block of 4, #a-d 2.40 2.40

Souvenir Sheet

1198 A273 10p multi 2.50 2.50

No. 1198 contains one 40x60mm stamp.

Street Scenes — A274

No. 1199: a, Rua de S. Domingos (4/1). b, Rua de Camilo Pessanha (4/2). c, Calcada de S. Francisco Xavier (4/3). d, Travessa da Paixao (4/4).
10p, Largo de Santo Agostinho.

2006, Sept. 13 ***Perf. 13½x14***

Granite Paper

1199 Block of 4 2.25 2.25
a.-b. A274 1.50p Either single .35 .35
c. A274 2.50p multi .65 .65
d. A274 3.50p multi .90 .90

Souvenir Sheet

Perf. 14x13½

1200 A274 10p multi 2.50 2.50

University of Macao, 25th Anniv. A275

No. 1201 — Inscriptions for Faculty of: a, Social Sciences and Humanities (5/1). b, Law (5/2). c, Science and Education (5/3). d, Science and Technology (5/4). e, Business Management (5/5).
10p, University emblem.

2006, Sept. 28 ***Perf. 13x13½***
1201 Horiz. strip of 5 1.90 1.90
a.-e. A275 1.50p Any single .35 .35

Souvenir Sheet

1202 A275 10p multi 2.50 2.50

I Ching Type of 2001 and

Two Women — A276

No. 1203 — Position of broken bars in trigrams (pa kua): a, Sixth. b, First, second and sixth. c, Second, third and sixth. d, Second and sixth. e, First, third and sixth. f, First and sixth. g, Third and sixth. h, First, second, third and sixth.

2006, Oct. 9 ***Perf. 13***
1203 A219 2p Sheet of 8, #a-h 4.00 4.00

Souvenir Sheet

1204 A276 10p shown 2.50 2.50

No. 1204 contains eight 39x34mm hexagonal stamps. Stamps from No. 1135 have Roman numeral "V" below text "Pa Kua" and "I Ching."

Jesuits — A277

Designs: No. 1205, 1.50p, Matteo Ricci (1552-1610), missionary, and red Chinese chop. No. 1206, 1.50p, St. Francis Xavier (1506-52), missionary, and cross. No. 1207, 3.50p, Allesandro Valignano (1539-1606), missionary, and capital. No. 1208, 3.50p, Melchior Carneiro (c. 1516-83), in red bishop's stole.
10p, St. Ignatius Loyola (1491-1556), founder of Society of Jesus.

2006, Nov. 30 Litho. *Perf. 13½x14*
1205-1208 A277 Set of 4 2.50 2.50

Souvenir Sheet
Perf. 14x13½
1209 A277 10p multi 2.50 2.50

New Year 2007 (Year of the Pig) A278

2007, Jan. 8 Litho. *Perf. 13x13¼*
1210 A278 5.50p multi 1.40 1.40

Souvenir Sheet
1211 A278 10p multi 2.50 2.50

Shek Wan Ceramics — A279

No. 1212: a, 1.50p, Lao Zi (4/1). b, 1.50p, Lu Yu (4/2). c, 1.50p, Philosopher (4/3). d, 2.50p, Luo Han Seated (4/4).
8p, Concubine After Bath.
Illustration reduced.

2007, Feb. 3
1212 A279 Block of 4, #a-d 1.75 1.75

Souvenir Sheet
1213 A279 8p multi 2.00 2.00

Everyday Life in the Past — A280

No. 1214: a, Man carrying tray on head (8/1). b, Man pouring tea into bowls (8/2). c, Rickshaw (8/3). d, People around table looking into bowl (8/4). e, Seamstress (8/5). f, Shoemaker (8/6). g, Ceramics artists (8/7). h, Embroiderer at booth (8/8).
10p, Festival dragon.

2007, Mar. 1 *Perf. 14*
1214 Block of 8 3.00 3.00
a.-h. A280 1.50p Any single .35 .35

Souvenir Sheet
1215 A280 10p multi 2.50 2.50

Traditional Chinese Shops — A281

No. 1216: a, 1.50p, Seamstress's shop (4/1). b, 1.50p, Acupuncturist and herbalist (4/2). c, 2.50p, Print shop (4/3). d, 3.50p, Restaurant (4/4).
10p, Street scene with man carting sign from shop.

2007, May 8 *Perf. 14½x14*
1216 A281 Block of 4, #a-d 2.25 2.25

Souvenir Sheet
1217 A281 10p multi 2.50 2.50

Seng Yu Proverbs — A282

Designs: Nos. 1218, 1223a, 1.50p, The Foolish Old Man Moved a Mountain (pink frame, 4/1). Nos. 1219, 1223b, 1.50p, The Friendship Between Guan and Bao (blue green frame, 4/2). Nos. 1220, 1223c, 3.50p, Calling Black White (lilac frame, 4/3). Nos. 1221, 1223d, 3.50p, The Quarrel Between Snipe and Clam (orange frame, 4/4).
10p, Horses and riders before riderless horse pulling cart, horiz.

2007, June 1 *Perf. 14*
1218-1221 A282 Set of 4 2.50 2.50

Souvenir Sheet
1222 A282 10p multi 2.50 2.50

Self-Adhesive
Booklet Stamps
Serpentine Die Cut 14
1223 Booklet pane, #1223a-1223d 2.50 2.50
Complete booklet, 2 #1223 5.00

No. 1222 contains one 60x40mm stamp.

A Journey to the West — A283

No. 1224: a, 1.50p, King and entourage, sprite with stick on cloud (6/1). b, 1.50p, Sprite on cloud, woman dreaming of horned spirit (6/2). c, 2p, Man with foot pierced by spear tip, woman, sprite without stick on cloud (6/3). d, 2p, Sprite on cloud battling other sprites (6/4). e, 2.50p, Sprite with stick, sprite with rake, sprite with swords (6/5). f, 2.50p, Sprite with rake on cloud, spirit with eight hands, spider (6/6).
10p, Sprite and sun.
Illustration reduced.

2007, June 18 *Perf. 14*
1224 A283 Block of 6, #a-f 3.00 3.00

Souvenir Sheet
1225 A283 10p multi 2.50 2.50

Scouting, Cent. A284

Lord Robert Baden-Powell, Macao Scouting emblem, flag ceremony and: 1.50p, Scout with semaphore flags. 2p, Scouts saluting. 2.50p, Scouts setting up campfire. No. 1229, 3.50p, Scouts lashing sticks together. No. 1230, 3.50p, Scout giving directions to other Scout.
10p, Flag, cannon and buildings, vert.

2007, July 9 *Perf. 13x13¼*
1226-1230 A284 Set of 5 3.25 3.25

Souvenir Sheet
Perf. 13¼x13
1231 A284 10p multi 2.50 2.50

Arrival of Robert Morrison (1782-1834), First Protestant Missionary in China, Bicent. — A285

Morrison and: 1.50p, Lilac panel. 3.50p, Yellow panel.

2007, Sept. 28 Litho. *Perf. 13x13¼*
1232-1233 A285 Set of 2 1.25 1.25

Souvenir Sheet

Mount Kangrinboqe, Tibet — A286

2007, Oct. 9 *Perf. 14*
1234 A286 10p multi 2.50 2.50

Applications of the Golden Ratio — A287

No. 1235: a, 1.50p, Fibonacci sequence. b, 2p, Sunflower spirals. c, 2.50p, Penrose tiling. d, 3.50p, Nautilus shell.
10p, Phi and equation.

2007, Oct. 26 *Perf. 13¼x13*
1235 A287 Block of 4, #a-d 2.40 2.40

Souvenir Sheet
1236 A287 10p multi 2.50 2.50

Chinese Philosophers — A288

No. 1237 Chinese character and: a, 1.50p, Lao Tzu (Lao Zi). b, 2.50p, Chuang Tzu (Zhuang Zi). c, 3.50p, Confucius (Confúcio). d, 4p, Meng Tzu (Méncio).
10p, Lao Tzu, Chuang Tzu, Confucius, Meng Tzu.
Illustration reduced.

Litho. & Embossed
2007, Nov. 30 *Perf. 13x13¼*
1237 A288 Block of 4, #a-d 3.00 3.00

Souvenir Sheet
Perf.
1238 A288 10p multi 2.50 2.50

No. 1238 contains one 42mm diameter stamp.

New Year 2008 (Year of the Rat) — A289

No. 1239: a, Metal sculpture of rat. b, Wood carving of rat. c, Watercolor painting of rat. d, Fireworks and laser light image of rat. e, Clay teapot depicting rat.
10p, Clay teapot depicting rat and 2008 Beijing Summer Olympics emblem.

Litho., Litho. & Embossed with Foil and Hologram Application (#1239e, 1240)

2008, Jan. 23 *Perf. 14¼*
1239 Horiz. strip of 5 2.75 2.75
a.-d. A289 1.50p Any single .35 .35
e. A289 5p multi 1.25 1.25

Souvenir Sheet
1240 A289 10p multi 2.50 2.50

No. 1240 contains one 50x50mm diamond-shaped stamp.

I Ching Type of 2001 and

Man Steering Raft — A290

No. 1241 — Position of broken bars in trigrams (pa kua): a, Fourth and sixth. b, First, second, fourth and sixth. c, Second, third, fourth and sixth. d, Second, fourth and sixth. e, First, third, fourth and sixth. f, First, fourth and sixth. g, Third, fourth and sixth. h, First, second, third, fourth and sixth.

2008, Mar. 1 Litho. *Perf. 14*
Granite Paper
1241 A219 2p Sheet of 8, #a-h 4.00 4.00

Souvenir Sheet
1242 A290 10p multi 2.50 2.50

No. 1241 contains eight 39x34mm hexagonal stamps. Stamps from No. 1241 have Roman numeral "VI" below text "Pa Kua" and "I Ching."

Olympic Torch Relay A291

Designs: 1.50p, Man holding Olympic torch, Parthenon. 3.50p, Mascot holding Olympic torch, lotus flower.
10p, Olympic torch, doves, vert.

2008, May 3 *Perf. 13x13¼*
1243-1244 A291 Set of 2 1.25 1.25

Souvenir Sheet
Perf. 13
1245 A291 10p multi 2.50 2.50

No. 1245 contains one 40x70mm stamp.

Western Legends — A292

No. 1246: a, The Golden Apple. b, The Gordian Knot. c, The Trojan Horse. d, The Riddle of the Sphinx.
10p, Cupid and Psyche, horiz.

2008, June 2 ***Perf. 13¼x14***

Granite Paper

1246 Horiz. strip of 4 3.00 3.00
a. A292 1.50p multi .35 .35
b. A292 2.50p multi .65 .65
c. A292 3.50p multi .90 .90
d. A292 4.00p multi 1.00 1.00

Souvenir Sheet

Perf. 14x13¼

1247 A292 10p multi 2.50 2.50

Native Cuisine of Macao and Singapore A293

No. 1248: a, Panqueca Indiana. b, Arroz de Frango à Hainan. c, Carne de Porco à Alentejana. d, Lombo de Bacalhau Braseado em Lascas. e, Laksa. f, Saté. g, Arroz Frito à Yangzhou. h, Frango Frito.
No. 1249, vert.: a, Arroz no Tacho de Porcelana. b, Caranguejo con Piri-piri.

2008, July 4 ***Perf. 13¼x14***

Granite Paper

1248 Block of 8 5.00 5.00
a.-d. A293 1.50p Any single .35 .35
e.-h. A293 3.50p Any single .90 .90

Souvenir Sheet

1249 Sheet of 2 2.50 2.50
a.-b. A293 5p Either single 1.25 1.25

See Singapore Nos. 1318-1320.

Historic Center of Macau UNESCO World Heritage Site A294

Designs: 1.50p, Fortaleza do Monte. 2p, Largo do Lilau. 2.50p, Lou Kau House. 3p, Largo do Senado. 3.50p, Sam Kai Vui Kun. 4p, Igreja da Sé. 4.50p, Quartel dos Mouros. 5p, St. Anthony's Church.

2008, July 31 **Litho.** ***Perf. 13x13½***

1250 A294 1.50p multi .35 .35
1251 A294 2p multi .50 .50
1252 A294 2.50p multi .65 .65
1253 A294 3p multi .75 .75
1254 A294 3.50p multi .90 .90
1255 A294 4p multi 1.00 1.00
1256 A294 4.50p multi 1.10 1.10
1257 A294 5p multi 1.25 1.25
Nos. 1250-1257 (8) 6.50 6.50

2008 Summer Olympics, Beijing A295

Designs: 5p, National Aquatics Center. 10p, National Stadium.

2008, Aug. 8 ***Perf. 13x13½***

1258 A295 5p multi 1.25 1.25

Souvenir Sheet

Perf. 13

1259 A295 10p multi 2.50 2.50

No. 1259 contains one 54x74mm irregular, six-sided stamp.

20th Macao Intl. Fireworks Display Contest — A296

No. 1260 — Fireworks displays over various sections of Macao: a, 1.50p. b, 2.50p. c, 3.50p. d, 5p.

2008, Oct. 1 **Litho.** ***Perf. 14x13½***

Granite Paper

1260 A296 Sheet of 4, #a-d 3.25 3.25

Souvenir Sheet

1261 A296 10p shown 2.50 2.50

Celebration — A297

No. 1262: a, 1.50p, "Celebration" in many languages. b, 3.50p, UPU emblem.
Illustration reduced.

2008, Oct. 9 ***Perf. 14***

1262 A297 Horiz. pair, #a-b 1.25 1.25

Souvenir Sheet

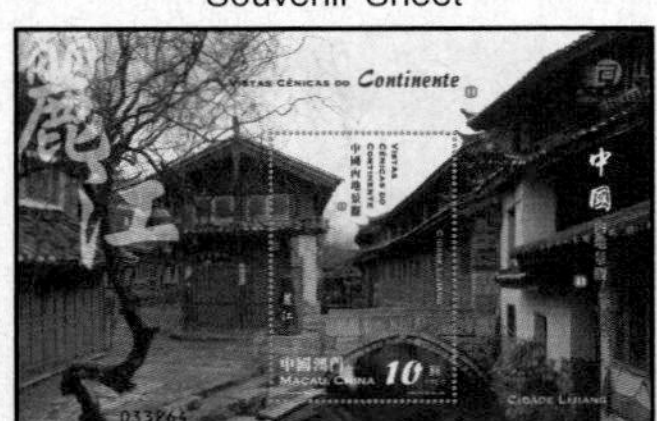

Lijiang, People's Republic of China — A298

2008, Nov. 7

1263 A298 10p multi 2.50 2.50

Traditional Handicrafts A299

Designs: 1.50p, Ivory carving. 2p, Ceramic painting. 2.50p, Basket weaving. 3.50p, Wood carving.
10p, Beaded embroidery.

2008, Dec. 1 ***Perf. 13x13¼***

1264-1267 A299 Set of 4 2.40 2.40

Souvenir Sheet

Perf. 13¼x13

1268 A299 10p multi 2.50 2.50

No. 1268 contains one 60x40mm stamp.

Louis Braille (1809-52), Educator of the Blind — A300

2009, Jan. 4 **Litho.** ***Perf. 13¼***

1269 A300 5p black 1.25 1.25

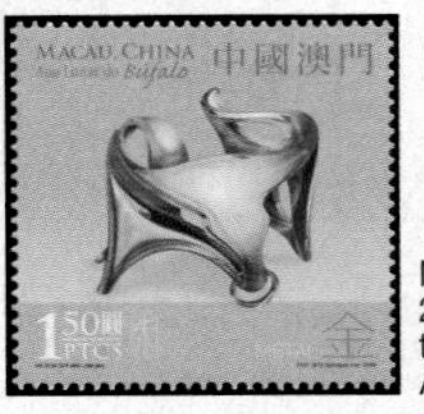

New Year 2009 (Year of the Buffalo) A301

No. 1270: a, Metal sculpture of buffalo head. b, Wood carving of buffalo head. c, Watercolor drawing of buffalo head. d, Fireworks display of buffalo head. e, Clay teapot with buffalo design.
10p, Clay teapot with buffalo design, diff.

Litho. (1.50p), Litho. & Embossed With Foil Application (5p, 10p)

2009, Jan. 8 ***Perf. 14¼***

1270 Horiz. strip of 5 2.75 2.75
a.-d. A301 1.50p Any single .35 .35
e. A301 5p multi 1.25 1.25

Souvenir Sheet

1271 A301 10p multi 2.50 2.50

No. 1271 contains one 50x50mm diamond-shaped stamp.

AIR POST STAMPS

Stamps of 1934 Overprinted or Surcharged in Black

a

b

1936 **Wmk. 232** ***Perf. 11½***

C1 A17 (a) 2a blue green 2.50 .75
C2 A17 (a) 3a violet 4.25 .75
C3 A17 (b) 5a on 6a brown 4.25 .75
C4 A17 (a) 7a brt rose 4.25 .75
C5 A17 (a) 8a brt blue 11.00 1.00
C6 A17 (a) 15a maroon 27.50 4.00
Nos. C1-C6 (6) 53.75 8.00

Common Design Type
Name and Value in Black

Perf. 13½x13

1938, Aug. 1 **Engr.** **Unwmk.**

C7 CD39 1a red orange .90 .50
C8 CD39 2a purple 1.10 .50
C9 CD39 3a orange 1.60 .90
C10 CD39 5a ultra 3.25 1.25
C11 CD39 10a lilac brn 5.50 1.25
C12 CD39 20a dk green 11.00 3.00
C13 CD39 50a red brown 18.00 4.00
C14 CD39 70a rose car 22.50 5.00
C15 CD39 1p magenta 45.00 18.00
Nos. C7-C15 (9) 108.85 34.40

No. C13 exists with overprint "Exposicao Internacional de Nova York, 1939-1940" and Trylon and Perisphere. Value $325.

Catalogue values for unused stamps in this section, from this point to the end of the section, are for never hinged items.

Plane over Bay of Grand Beach — AP1

1960, Dec. 11 **Litho.** ***Perf. 14***

C16 AP1 50a shown 3.00 .40
C17 AP1 76a Penha Chapel 5.00 1.25
C18 AP1 3p Macao 16.00 2.00
C19 AP1 5p Bairro de Mong Ha 20.00 2.00
C20 AP1 10p Penha and Bay 32.50 2.25
Nos. C16-C20 (5) 76.50 7.90
Set, hinged 40.00

No. C17 Surcharged

1979, Aug. 3 **Litho.** ***Perf. 14***

C21 AP1 70a on 76a multi *37.50* 3.25

POSTAGE DUE STAMPS

Numeral of Value — D1

Perf. 11½x12

1904, July **Typo.** **Unwmk.**

Name and Value in Black

J1 D1 ½a gray green 1.50 1.25
a. Name & value inverted 125.00 60.00
J2 D1 1a yellow grn 2.00 1.25
J3 D1 2a slate 2.00 1.25
J4 D1 4a pale brown 2.75 1.25
J5 D1 5a red orange 3.50 2.00
J6 D1 8a gray brown 4.00 2.00
J7 D1 12a red brown 6.00 2.00
J8 D1 20a dull blue 10.00 4.50
J9 D1 40a carmine 20.00 6.00
J10 D1 50a orange 26.50 12.00
J11 D1 1p gray violet 52.50 25.00
Nos. J1-J11 (11) 130.75 58.50

Issued without gum: Nos. J7-J11. Issued with or without gum: No. J4. Others issued with gum.
For overprints see Nos. 144-146, J12-J32.

Issue of 1904 Overprinted in Carmine or Green

Lisbon Overprint

Overprint 24½mm long. "A" has flattened top.

1911

J12 D1 ½a gray green .50 .30
J13 D1 1a yellow green 1.00 .50
J14 D1 2a slate 1.25 .65
J15 D1 4a pale brown 1.50 .75
J16 D1 5a orange 2.00 1.00
J17 D1 8a gray brown 4.00 1.75
J18 D1 12a red brown 7.00 2.00
J19 D1 20a dull blue 9.50 3.00
J20 D1 40a carmine (G) 12.50 4.00
J21 D1 50a orange 16.00 5.00
J22 D1 1p gray violet 30.00 7.50
Nos. J12-J22 (11) 85.25 26.45

Issued without gum: Nos. J19-J22.

Issue of 1904 Overprinted in Red or Green

Local Overprint

Overprint 23mm long. "A" has pointed top.

1914

J22A D1 ½a gray green *1,600. 600.00*
J23 D1 1a yellow green 3.00 .50
J24 D1 2a slate 3.00 .50
J25 D1 4a pale brown 3.00 .75
J26 D1 5a orange 3.50 .75
J27 D1 8a gray brown 3.50 .90
J28 D1 12a red brown 3.50 .80
J29 D1 20a dull blue 12.50 3.00
J30 D1 40a car (G) 35.00 5.00
a. Double ovpt., red and green 100.00 27.50
J31 D1 50a orange 35.00 8.00
J32 D1 1p gray violet 70.00 10.00
Nos. J23-J32 (10) 172.00 30.20

Issued without gum: Nos. J28, J30-J32.

D2

Name and Value in Black

1947 Typo. *Perf. 11½x12*

J33 D2 1a red violet 1.00 1.00
J34 D2 2a purple 1.50 1.00
J35 D2 4a dark blue 2.50 1.00
J36 D2 5a chocolate 3.50 1.00
J37 D2 8a red violet 4.50 1.00
J38 D2 12a orange brown 7.50 1.00
J39 D2 20a yellow green 8.50 3.00
J40 D2 40a brt carmine 10.00 3.50
J41 D2 50a orange yellow 19.00 7.75
J42 D2 1p blue 30.00 9.00
Nos. J33-J42 (10) 88.00 29.25

Stamps of 1934 Surcharged "PORTEADO" and New Values in Carmine

1949, May 1 Wmk. 232

J43 A17 1a on 4a black 3.75 .85
J44 A17 2a on 6a brown 3.75 .85
J45 A17 4a on 8a brt blue 4.25 .85
J46 A17 5a on 10a red org 4.75 .85
J47 A17 8a on 12a dk blue 4.75 1.40
J48 A17 12a on 30a apple grn 6.50 1.50
J49 A17 20a on 40a violet 6.50 1.50
Nos. J43-J49 (7) 34.25 7.80

Catalogue values for unused stamps in this section, from this point to the end of the section, are for Never Hinged items.

Nos. 348, 349 and 351 Overprinted or Surcharged in Black or Carmine

1951, June 6 Unwmk.

J50 A21 1a org yel, *lem* 1.40 .20
J51 A21 2a dk grn, *bl* (C) 1.40 .20
J52 A21 7a on 10a brt pink, *bl* 1.40 .20
Nos. J50-J52 (3) 4.20 .60

Common Design Type

1952 Photo. & Typo. *Perf. 14*
Numeral in Red; Frame Multicolored

J53 CD45 1a violet blue .75 .20
J54 CD45 3a chocolate .75 .20
J55 CD45 5a indigo .75 .20
J56 CD45 10a dark red 3.00 .40
J57 CD45 30a indigo 3.75 .50
J58 CD45 1p chocolate 11.50 1.50
Nos. J53-J58 (6) 20.50 3.00

WAR TAX STAMPS

Victory WT1

1919, Aug. 11 Unwmk. *Perf. 15x14*
Overprinted in Black or Carmine

MR1 WT1 2a green 2.25 1.00
MR2 WT1 11a green (C) 3.50 1.40

Nos. MR1-MR2 were also for use in Timor.

A 9a value was issued for revenue use. Value $10.

NEWSPAPER STAMPS

Nos. P1-P2

No. P3

Typographed and Embossed
1892-93 Unwmk. *Perf. 12½*
Black Surcharge
Without Gum

P1 A7 2½r on 40r choc 6.00 2.50
  a. Inverted surcharge 45.00 30.00
  b. Perf. 13½ 7.00 4.50
P2 A7 2½r on 80r gray 9.00 4.00
  a. Inverted surcharge 60.00 50.00
  b. Double surcharge
  c. Perf. 13½ 45.00 35.00
P3 A7 2½r on 10r grn ('93) 6.00 4.00
  a. Double surcharge
  b. Perf. 13½ 7.00 5.75
Nos. P1-P3 (3) 21.00 10.50

N3

N4

1893-94 Typo. *Perf. 11½*

P4 N3 2½r brown 3.25 2.00
  a. Perf. 11½ 3.25 2.25
  b. Perf. 13½ 3.50 2.00
P5 N4 ½a on 2½r brn (Bk) ('94) 4.50 2.75
  a. Double surcharge

For surcharges see Nos. 131, 252.

POSTAL TAX STAMPS

Pombal Commemorative Issue
Common Design Types
Perf. 12½

1925, Nov. 3 Engr. Unwmk.

RA1 CD28 2a red org & blk 3.25 .70
RA2 CD29 2a red org & blk 3.25 .70
RA3 CD30 2a red org & blk 3.25 .70
Nos. RA1-RA3 (3) 9.75 2.10

Symbolical of Charity
PT1 PT2

1930, Dec. 25 Litho. *Perf. 11*

RA4 PT1 5a dk brown, *yel* 7.00 5.00

1945-47 *Perf. 11½, 12, 10*

RA5 PT2 5a blk brn, *yel* 10.50 7.50
RA6 PT2 5a bl, *bluish* ('47) 30.00 6.75
RA7 PT2 10a grn, *citron* 10.00 3.75
RA8 PT2 15a org, *buff* 1.50 3.75
RA9 PT2 20a rose red, *sal* 60.00 6.75
RA10 PT2 50a red vio, *pnksh* 3.00 3.00
Nos. RA5-RA10 (6) 115.00 31.50

Catalogue values for unused stamps in this section, from this point to the end of the section, are for Never Hinged items.

1953-56 *Perf. 10½x11½*

RA11 PT2 10a bl, *pale grn* ('56) 2.00 1.50
RA12 PT2 20a chocolate, *yel* 11.00 5.00
RA13 PT2 50a car, *pale rose* 10.00 4.50
Nos. RA11-RA13 (3) 23.00 11.00

1958 *Perf. 12x11½*

RA14 PT2 1a gray grn, *grnsh* .75 .35
RA15 PT2 2a rose lilac, *grysh* 1.50 .75

Type of 1945-47 Redrawn
Imprint: "Lito. Imp. Nac.-Macau"

1961-66 *Perf. 11*

RA16 PT2 1a gray grn, *grnsh* 1.50 .80
RA17 PT2 2a rose lil, *grysh* 1.50 .80
RA18 PT2 10a bl, *pale grn* ('62) 1.50 .80
RA19 PT2 20a brn, *yel* ('66) 1.75 1.00
Nos. RA16-RA19 (4) 6.25 3.40

Nos. RA16-RA19 have accent added to "E" in "Assistencia."

Nos. RA4-RA19 were issued without gum.

Type of 1945-47 Redrawn and Surcharged

1979 Litho. *Perf. 11x11½*

RA20 PT2 20a on 1p yel grn, *cream* 5.00

No. RA20 has no accent above "E," no imprint and was not issued without surcharge.

No. RA17 Surcharged

Methods and Perfs As Before
1981
Without Gum

RA21 PT2 20a on 2a #RA17 — —

POSTAL TAX DUE STAMPS

Pombal Commemorative Issue
Common Design Types

1925 Unwmk. *Perf. 12½*

RAJ1 CD28 4a red orange & blk 3.25 .70
RAJ2 CD29 4a red orange & blk 3.25 .70
RAJ3 CD30 4a red orange & blk 3.25 .70
Nos. RAJ1-RAJ3 (3) 9.75 2.10

MACEDONIA

ˌma-sə-ˈdō-nē-ə

LOCATION — Central Balkans, bordered by on the north by Serbia, to the east by Bulgaria, on the south by Greece and by Albania on the west.
GOVT. — Republic
AREA — 9,928 sq. mi.
POP. — 2,022,604 (1999 est.)
CAPITAL — Skopje

Formerly a constituent republic in the Socialist Federal Republic of Yugoslavia. Declared independence on Nov. 21, 1991.

100 Deni (de) = 1 Denar (d)

Catalogue values for all unused stamps in this country are for Never Hinged items.

Watermark

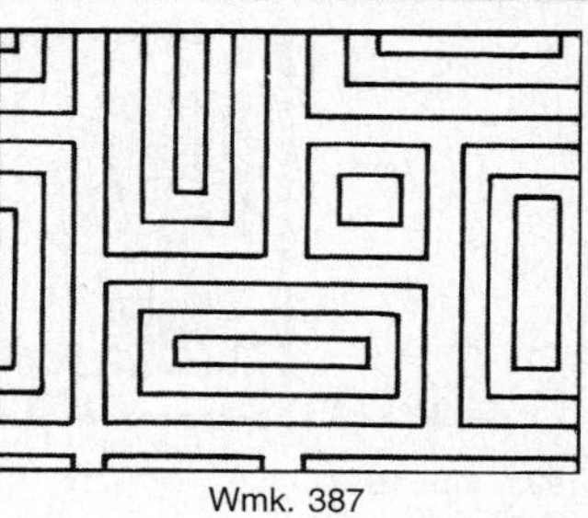
Wmk. 387

Bas Relief — A1

1992-93 Litho. *Perf. 13½x13*

1 A1 30d multicolored *.50 .35*

Perf. 10

2 A1 40d multicolored *.55 .25*

Issued: 30d, 9/8/92; 40d, 3/15/93.

For surcharges see Nos. 21, 42.

Christmas — A2

Frescoes: 100d, Nativity Scene, 16th cent. 500d, Virgin and Child, 1422.

1992, Dec. 10 Litho. *Perf. 13x13½*

3 A2 100d multicolored *1.25 1.25*
4 A2 500d multicolored *2.50 2.50*

Natl. Flag — A3

1993, Mar. 15 *Perf. 13½x13*

5 A3 10d multicolored *.75 .30*
6 A3 40d multicolored *1.25 .30*
7 A3 50d multicolored *1.25 .60*
Nos. 5-7 (3) *3.25 1.20*

For surcharges see Nos. 23, 40-41.

Fish — A4

Designs: 50d, 1000d, Rutilus macedonicus. 100d, 2000d, Salmothymus achridanus.

1993, Mar. 15 *Perf. 10*

8 A4 50d multicolored *.35 .20*
9 A4 100d multicolored *.35 .20*
10 A4 1000d multicolored *4.00 2.10*
11 A4 2000d multicolored *5.00 3.25*
Nos. 8-11 (4) *9.70 5.75*

Easter — A5

1993, Apr. 16
12 A5 300d multicolored 2.25 1.75

Trans-Balkan Telecommunications Network — A6

1993, May 6
13 A6 500d multicolored 1.25 .75

Admission to the UN, Apr. 8, 1993 — A7

1993, July 28
14 A7 10d multicolored 1.50 .95

A8

A9

1993, Aug. 2
15 A8 10d multicolored 1.50 .95

Souvenir Sheet
Imperf

16 A8 30d multicolored 4.25 4.25

Ilinden Uprising, 90th anniv.

1993, Nov. 4
17 A9 4d multicolored .50 .50

Size: 85x67mm
Imperf

18 A9 40d multicolored 3.75 3.75

Macedonian Revolutionary Organization, cent.

Christmas A10

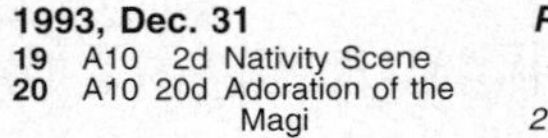

1993, Dec. 31 ***Perf. 10***
19 A10 2d Nativity Scene .75 .75
20 A10 20d Adoration of the Magi 2.75 2.10

Nos. 1, 5, RA1 Surcharged

1994, Apr. 2 ***Perfs., Etc. as Before***
21 A1 2d on 30d multi .25 .25
22 PT1 8d on 2.50d multi 1.10 1.10
23 A3 15d on 10d multi 2.50 2.50
Nos. 21-23 (3) 3.85 3.85

Size and location of surcharge varies.

Easter — A11

Revolutionaries — A12

1994, Apr. 29 **Litho.** ***Perf. 10***
24 A11 2d multicolored .50 .30

1994, May 23

Designs: 8d, Kosta Racin (1908-43), writer. 15d, Grigor Prlicev (1830-93), writer. 20d, Nikola Vapzarov (1909-42), poet. 50d, Goce Delchev (1872-1903), politician.

25 A12 8d multicolored .85 .60
26 A12 15d multicolored 1.25 1.10
27 A12 20d multicolored 2.50 1.50
28 A12 50d multicolored 3.00 2.10
Nos. 25-28 (4) 7.60 5.30

Intl. Year of the Family — A13

1994, June 21
29 A13 2d multicolored .40 .20

Liberation Day, 50th Anniv. — A14

Swimming Marathon, Ohrid Lake — A15

Designs: 5d, St. Prohor Pcinski Monastery, up close. 50d, View of entire grounds.

1994, Aug. 2 **Litho.** ***Perf. 10***
30 A14 5d multicolored .45 .45

Size: 108x73mm
Imperf

31 A14 50d multicolored 4.00 3.25

1994, Aug. 22
32 A15 8d multicolored .65 .40

Stamp Day — A16

1994, Sept. 12
33 A16 2d multicolored .90 .65

Nova Makedonija, Mlad Boretz, & Makedonka Newspapers, 50th Anniv. — A17

1994, Sept. 13 **Litho.** ***Perf. 10***
34 A17 2d multicolored .90 .65

St. Kliment of Ohrid Library, 50th Anniv. A18

Manuscripts: 2d, 15th cent. 10d, 13th cent.

1994, Sept. 29 **Litho.** ***Perf. 10***
35 A18 2d multi .25 .20
36 A18 10d multi, vert. 1.75 1.40

Macedonian Radio, 50th Anniv. — A19

1994, Dec. 26 **Litho.** ***Perf. 10***
37 A19 2d multicolored .40 .30

Wildlife Conservation — A20

1994, Dec. 26 **Litho.** ***Perf. 10***
38 A20 5d Pinus peluse .50 .40
39 A20 10d Lynx lynx martinoi 1.25 1.00

Nos. 2, 6 Surcharged in Black or Gold

a

b

Perfs., Etc. as Before

1995, Mar. 13 **Litho.**
40 A3(a) 2d on 40d #6 2.10 2.10
41 A3(b) 2d on 40d #6 1.10 1.10
42 A1(a) 5d on 40d #2 (G) .75 .75
Nos. 40-42 (3) 3.95 3.95

Easter — A21

1995, Apr. 23 **Litho.** ***Perf. 10***
43 A21 4d multicolored .50 .35

End of World War II, 50th Anniv. A22

1995, May 9 **Litho.** ***Perf. 10***
44 A22 2d multicolored 1.00 .65

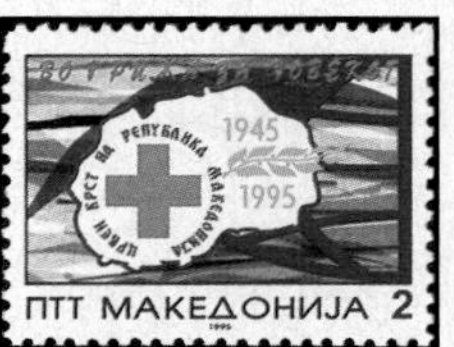

Macedonian Red Cross, 50th Anniv. — A23

1995, May 20 **Litho.** ***Perf. 10***
45 A23 2d multicolored 1.00 .65

Wilhelm Röntgen (1845-1923), Discovery of the X-Ray, Cent. — A24

1995, May 20
46 A24 2d multicolored 1.00 .65

Vojdan Cernodrinski (1875-1951), Theater Festival, 50th Anniv. — A25

1995, June 8

47 A25 10d multicolored *1.00 .65*

Death of Prince Marko Kraljevic, 600th Anniv. A26

1995, June 22

48 A26 20d multicolored *1.75 1.25*

Gorgi Puleski (1818-95), Writer A27

1995, July 8

49 A27 2d multicolored *.85 .55*

Writer's Festival, Struga A28

1995, Aug. 23 Litho. *Perf. 10*

50 A28 2d multicolored *1.50 1.00*

A29

A30

1995, Oct. 4

51 A29 15d Mosque of Tetovo *1.50 1.25*

1995, Oct. 4 Litho. *Perf. 10*

Architecture.

52 A30 2d Malesevija *.20 .20*
53 A30 20d Krakornica *1.50 1.10*

See #81-83 and design A63a.

Motion Pictures, Cent. A31

Film strip of early movie and: No. 54, Auguste and Louis Lumiére. No. 55, Milton and Janaki Manaki, Macedonian cinematographers.

1995, Oct. 6 *Perf. 10 on 3 Sides*

54 A31 10d multicolored *1.50 1.50*
55 A31 10d multicolored *1.50 1.50*
a. Pair, #54-55 *3.00 3.00*

UN, 50th Anniv. A32

1995, Oct. 24

56 A32 20d Blocks, globe in nest *1.50 1.50*
57 A32 50d Blocks, sun *3.00 3.00*

Christmas A33

1995, Dec. 13

58 A33 15d multicolored *1.10 1.10*

Birds A34

15d, Pelecanus crispus. 40d, Gypaetus barbatus.

1995, Dec. 14

59 A34 15d multicolored *1.75 1.75*
60 A34 40d multicolored *3.00 3.00*

Reform of Macedonian Language, 50th Anniv. — A35

1995, Dec. 18

61 A35 5d multicolored *.45 .45*

St. Bogorodica Church, Ohrid, 700th Anniv. — A36

Designs: 8d, Detail of fresco, exterior view, St. Kliment of Ohrid (840-916). 50d, Portion of fresco inside church, #62.

1995, Dec. 19

62 A36 8d multicolored *.60 .60*

Size: 80x61mm

Imperf

62A A36 50d multicolored *72.50 72.50*

Macedonia's Admission to UPU, 1st Anniv. — A37

1995, Dec. 27

62B A37 10d Post office, Skopje *.70 .70*

Admission to Council of Europe (CE) and Organization for Security and Cooperation in Europe (OSCE) — A37a

1995, Dec. 27

62C A37a 20d multicolored *1.25 1.25*

Modern Olympic Games, Cent., 1996 Summer Olympic Games, Atlanta A38

1996, May 20 Litho. *Perf. 10*

63 A38 2d Kayak race *.40 .40*
64 A38 8d Basketball, vert. *.50 .50*
65 A38 15d Swimming *1.10 1.10*
66 A38 20d Wrestling *1.60 1.60*
67 A38 40d Boxing, vert. *2.75 2.75*
68 A38 50d Running, vert *3.50 3.50*
Nos. 63-68 (6) 9.85 9.85

Intl. Decade to Fight Illegal Drugs — A39

1996, July 11 Litho. *Perf. 10*

69 A39 20d multicolored *1.50 1.50*

Children's Paintings — A40

1996, July 15

70 A40 2d Boy *.20 .20*
71 A40 8d Girl *.60 .60*

Peak of Czar Samuel of Bulgaria's Power, 1000th Anniv. A41

1996, July 19

72 A41 40d multicolored *3.00 3.00*

G. Petrov (1865-1921), Revolutionary A42

1996, Aug. 2

73 A42 20d multicolored *1.40 1.40*

Independence, 5th Anniv. — A43

1996, Sept. 8

74 A43 10d multicolored *.70 .70*

Vera Ciriviri-Trena (1920-44), Freedom Fighter — A44

Mother Teresa (1910-97) — A45

1996, Nov. 22 Litho. *Perf. 13x13½*

75 A44 20d multicolored *4.75 3.00*
76 A45 40d multicolored *9.50 6.50*

Europa.

Christmas — A46

Terra Cotta Tiles — A47

Designs: No. 77, Tree, children caroling in snow. No. 78, Candle, nuts, apples.

1996, Dec. 14 Litho. *Perf. 10*

77 A46 10d multicolored *.70 .70*
78 A46 10d multicolored *.70 .70*
a. Pair, #77-78 *1.40 1.40*

1996, Dec. 19

#79a, 80a, 4d, Daniel in lions den. #79b, 80b, 8d, Sts. Christopher & George. #79c, 80c, 20d, Joshua, Caleb. #79d, 80d, 50d, Unicorn.

Blocks of 4, #a.-d.

79 A47 bl grn & multi *5.00 5.00*
80 A47 yel grn & multi *5.00 5.00*

Traditional Architecture Type of 1995

1996

81 A30 2d House, Nistrovo *.20 .20*
82 A30 8d House, Brodets *.65 .65*
83 A30 10d House, Niviste *.75 .75*
Nos. 81-83 (3) 1.60 1.60

Issued: 8d, 12/20; 2d, 10d, 12/25.

See Nos. 112-116.

Butterflies A49

4d, Pseudochazara cingovskii. 40d, Colias balcanica.

1996, Dec. 21

84 A49 4d multicolored *.25 .25*
85 A49 40d multicolored *3.75 3.75*

UNICEF, 50th Anniv. A50

1996, Dec. 31 *Perf. 14½*

86 A50 20d shown *1.50 1.50*
87 A50 40d UNESCO, 50th anniv. *2.50 2.50*

Alpine Skiing Championships, 50th Anniv. — A51

1997, Feb. 7 *Perf. 10*

88 A51 20d multicolored *1.25 1.25*

Alexander Graham Bell (1847-1922) — A52

1997, Mar. 12

89 A52 40d multicolored *2.50 2.50*

Ancient Roman Mosaics, Heraklia and Stobi A53

1997, Mar. 26 *Perf. 10*

90 A53 2d Wild dog *.25 .25*
91 A53 8d Bull *.45 .45*
92 A53 20d Lion *1.25 1.25*
93 A53 40d Leopard with prey *2.25 2.25*
Nos. 90-93 (4) 4.20 4.20

Size: 79x56mm

Imperf

94 A53 50d Deer, peacocks *4.00 4.00*

No. 94 has simulated perforations within the design.

Cyrilic Alphabet, 1100th Anniv. A54

Cyrillic inscriptions and: No. 95, Gold embossed plate. No. 96, St. Cyril (827-69), St. Methodius (825-84), promulgators of Cyrillic alphabet.

1997, May 2 *Perf. 10*

95 A54 10d multicolored *.65 .65*
96 A54 10d multicolored *.65 .65*
a. Pair, #95-96 *1.40 1.40*

A55

A56

Europa (Stories and Legends): 20d, Man kneeling down, another seated in background. 40d, Man, tree, bird dressed as man.

1997, June 6 *Perf. 15x14*

97 A55 20d multicolored *2.25 2.00*
98 A55 40d multicolored *5.00 3.50*

1997, June 5 *Perf. 10*

99 A56 15d multicolored *.95 .95*

5th Natl. Ecology Day.

St. Naum A57

1997, July 3 *Perf. 10*

100 A57 15d multicolored *.95 .95*

Mushrooms — A58

2d, Cantharellus cibarius. 15d, Boletus aereus. 27d, Amanita caesarea. 50d, Morchella conica.

1997, Nov. 7 Litho. *Perf. 10*

101 A58 2d multicolored *.50 .50*
102 A58 15d multicolored *1.00 1.00*
103 A58 27d multicolored *1.75 1.75*
104 A58 50d multicolored *3.00 3.00*
Nos. 101-104 (4) 6.25 6.25

Week of the Child — A59

Minerals — A60

1997, Oct. 11

105 A59 27d multicolored *1.50 1.50*

1997, Oct. 10

106 A60 27d Stibnite *1.50 1.50*
107 A60 40d Lorandite *2.25 2.25*

Mahatma Gandhi (1869-1948) A61

1998, Feb. 4 Litho. *Perf. 13½*

108 A61 30d multicolored *1.50 1.50*

Pythagoras (c. 570-c. 500 BC), Greek Philosopher, Mathematician — A62

1998, Feb. 6

109 A62 16d multicolored *.90 .90*

1998 Winter Olympic Games, Nagano — A63

1998, Feb. 7

110 A63 4d Slalom skier + label *.20 .20*
111 A63 30d Cross country skiers + label *1.50 1.50*

Nos. 110-111 were each printed with a se-tenant label.

Traditional Architecture A63a

Location of home: 2d, Novo Selo. 4d, Jablanica. 16d, Kiselica. 20d, Konopnica. 30d, Ambar. 50d, Galicnik.

1998

112 A63a 2d multicolored *.20 .20*
113 A63a 4d multicolored *.20 .20*
113A A63a 16d multicolored *.80 .80*
114 A63a 20d multicolored *1.00 1.00*
115 A63a 30d multicolored *1.50 1.50*
116 A63a 50d multicolored *2.50 2.50*
Nos. 112-116 (6) 6.20 6.20

Issued: 2d, 4d, 30d, 2/9; 20d, 50d, 2/12; 16d, 6/10.

See Nos. 146-148.

Painting, "Exodus," by Kole Manev A64

1998, Feb. 11

117 A64 30d multicolored *1.50 1.50*

Exodus from Aegean Macedonia, 50th anniv.

Neolithic Artifacts A65

Designs: 4d, Water flasks. 18d, Animal-shaped bowl. 30d, Woman figure. 60d, Bowl.

1998, Apr. 29 Litho. *Perf. 13½*

118 A65 4d multicolored *.20 .20*
119 A65 18d multicolored *.90 .90*
120 A65 30d multicolored *1.50 1.50*
121 A65 60d multicolored *3.00 3.00*
Nos. 118-121 (4) 5.60 5.60

1998 World Cup Soccer Championships, France — A66

4d, Looking down at soccer field, ball. 30d, Soccer field with world map in center.

1998, Apr. 30

122 A66 4d multicolored *.20 .20*
123 A66 30d multicolored *1.50 1.50*

Natl. Festivals A67

Europa: 30d, Dancers, Strumica. 40d, People wearing masks, Vevcani.

1998, May 5 Litho. *Perf. 13½*

124 A67 30d multicolored *1.75 1.00*
125 A67 40d multicolored *2.25 1.50*

Carnival Cities Congress, Strumica — A68

1998, May 10 Litho. *Perf. 13½*

126 A68 30d multicolored *1.50 1.50*

World Ecology Day — A69

4d, Stylized flower. 30d, Smokestack uprooting tree.

1998, June 5 Litho. *Perf. 13½*

127 A69 4d multicolored .25 .25
128 A69 30d multicolored 1.50 1.50

Dimitri Cupovski, 120th Birth Anniv. — A70

1998, June 30

129 A70 16d multicolored .80 .80

Railroads in Macedonia, 125th Anniv. — A72

30d, Document, building, early steam locomotive, vert. 60d, Locomotive, 1873.

1998, Aug. 9 Litho. *Perf. 13½*

130 A72 30d multicolored 1.50 1.50
131 A72 60d multicolored 3.00 3.00

Fossil Skulls Found in Macedonia A73

Designs: 4d, Ursus spelaeus. 8d, Mesopithecus pentelici. 18d, Tragoceros. 30d, Aceratherium incisivum.

1998, Sept. 17

132 A73 4d multicolored .25 .25
133 A73 8d multicolored .40 .40
134 A73 18d multicolored .90 .90
135 A73 30d multicolored 1.50 1.50
Nos. 132-135 (4) 3.05 3.05

Music Fair, Zlatoustova, Cent. — A74

Design: Atanas Badev, composer.

1998, Sept. 21

136 A74 25d multicolored 1.25 1.25

Children's Day — A75

1998, Oct. 5

137 A75 30d multicolored 1.50 1.50

Beetles A76

4d, Cerambyx cerdo. 8d, Rosalia alpina. 20d, Oryctes nasicornis. 40d, Lucanus cervus.

1998, Oct. 20

138 A76 4d multicolored .25 .25
139 A76 8d multicolored .50 .50
140 A76 20d multicolored 1.10 1.10
141 A76 40d multicolored 2.25 2.25
Nos. 138-141 (4) 4.10 4.10

A77

Christmas and New Year A77a

1998, Nov. 20

142 A77 4d multicolored .20 .20
143 A77a 30d multicolored 1.50 1.50

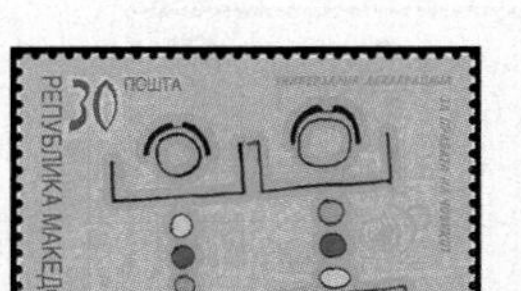

Universal Declaration of Human Rights, 50th Anniv. — A78

1998, Dec. 10

144 A78 30d multicolored 1.50 1.50

Sharplaninec Dog — A79

1999, Jan. 20 Litho. *Perf. 13¼*

145 A79 15d multi .75 .75

Architecture Type of 1998

"Republica Macedonia" in Cyrillic

Location of home: 1d, Bogomila. 4d, Svekani. 5d, Teovo.

1999 Litho. *Perf. 13¼*

146 A63A 1d multi .20 .20
147 A63A 4d multi .20 .20
148 A63A 5d multi .25 .25
Nos. 146-148 (3) .65 .65

Issued: 4d, 2/1; 5d, 2/25; 1d, 11/5.

Icons — A80

Designs: 4d, 1535 Slepche Monastery Annunciation icon, Demir Hisar, by Dimitar Zograf. 8d, 1862 St. Nicholas Church icon, Ohrid. 18d, 1535 Slepche Monastery Madonna and Child icon, Demir Hisar. 30d, 1393-94 Zrze Monastery Jesus icon, Prilep.

50d, 1626 Lesnovo Monastery Jesus icon, Probishtip.

1999, Mar. 3 *Perf. 11¾*

149 A80 4d multi .20 .20
150 A80 8d multi .40 .40
151 A80 18d multi .90 .90
152 A80 30d multi 1.50 1.50
Nos. 149-152 (4) 3.00 3.00

Souvenir Sheet

153 A80 50d multi 2.50 2.50

Dimitar A. Pandilov (1899-1963), Painter — A81

1999, Mar. 14 *Perf. 13¼*

154 A81 4d multi .25 .25

Telegraphy in Macedonia, Cent. A82

1999, Apr. 22

155 A82 4d multi .25 .25

Saints Cyril and Methodius University, Skopje, 50th Anniv. A83

1999, Apr. 24

156 A83 8d multi .40 .40

Issued in sheets of 8 + label.

Council of Europe, 50th Anniv. A84

1999, May 5

157 A84 30d multi 1.50 1.50

Europa A85

Natl. Parks: 30d, Pelister. 40d, Mavrovo.

1999, May 5

158 A85 30d multi *2.00 1.00*
159 A85 40d multi *2.50 1.50*

Ecology — A86

1999, June 5

160 A86 30d multi 1.50 1.50

Macedonian Leaders from the Middle Ages — A87

Designs: a, 30d, Strez (1204-14). b, 8d, Gorgi Voytech (1072-1073). c, 18d, Dobromir Hrs (1195-1203). d, 4d, Petar Deljan (1040-41).

1999, June 25

161 A87 Block of 4, #a.-d. 3.00 3.00

Kuzman Sapkarev (1834-1909), Folklorist — A88

1999, Sept. 1 Litho. *Perf. 13¼*

162 A88 4d multi .25 .25

Flowers — A89

Designs: 4d, Crocus scardicus. 8d, Astragalus mayeri. 18d, Campanula formanekiana. 30d, Viola kosaninii.

1999, Sept. 16

163 A89 4d multi .25 .25
164 A89 8d multi .50 .50
165 A89 18d multi 1.00 1.00
166 A89 30d multi 1.50 1.50
Nos. 163-166 (4) 3.25 3.25

Children's Day — A90

1999, Oct. 4

167 A90 30d multi 1.50 1.50

UPU, 125th Anniv. A91

1999, Oct. 9

168 A91 5d Post horn, emblem .25 .25
169 A91 30d Emblem, post horn 1.50 1.50

Krste Petkov Misirkov (1875-1926), Writer — A92

1999, Nov. 18

170 A92 5d multi .25 .25

Christmas — A93

1999, Nov. 24

171 A93 30d multi 1.50 1.50

New Year's Day — A94

1999, Nov. 24 ***Perf. 13¼***

172 A94 5d multi .25 .25

Slavic Presence in Macedonia, 1400th Anniv. — A95

1999, Oct. 27 **Litho.** ***Perf. 13¼***

173 A95 5d multi .25 .25

Christianity, 2000th Anniv. — A96

Icons and frescoes: 5d, Altar cross, St. Nikita Monastery, vert. 10d, Fresco of Holy Mother of God, St. Mark's Monastery. 15d, St. Clement of Ohrid, vert. 30d, Fresco of Apostle Paul St. Andrew's Monastery, vert.

50d, St. Sophia's Cathedral, Ohrid, vert.

2000, Jan. 19

174-177 A96 Set of 4 3.00 3.00

Souvenir Sheet

178 A96 50d multi 2.50 2.50

No. 178 contains one 30x31mm stamp.

Millennium A97

No. 179: a, 5d, "2000." b, 30d, Religious symbols.

2000, Feb. 16

179 A97 Vert. pair, #a-b 1.75 1.75

Silver Jewelry — A98

Designs: 5d, Pin with icon, Ohrid, 19th cent. 10d, Bracelet, Bitola, 20th cent. 20d, Earrings, Ohrid, 18th cent. 30d, Brooch, Bitola, 19th-20th cent.

2000, Mar. 1 **Litho.** ***Perf. 13¼***

180-183 A98 Set of 4 3.50 3.50

Macedonian Philatelic Society, 50th Anniv. — A99

2000, Mar. 19

184 A99 5d multi .30 .30

World Meteorological Organization, 50th Anniv. — A100

2000, Mar. 23 **Litho.** ***Perf. 13¼***

185 A100 30d multi 1.50 1.50

Easter — A101

2000, Apr. 21 **Litho.** ***Perf. 13¼***

186 A101 5d multi .30 .30

Europa, 2000

Common Design Type

2000, May 9 ***Perf. 14***

187 CD17 30d multi *2.25 2.25*

2000 Summer Olympics, Sydney A102

Designs: 5d: Runners. 30d, Wrestlers.

2000, May 17 ***Perf. 13¼***

188-189 A102 Set of 2 1.90 1.90

Ecology — A103

2000, June 5 **Litho.** ***Perf. 13¼***

190 A103 5d multi .25 .25

Architecture Type of 1998

2000, July 28

191 A63a 6d House, Zdunje .30 .30

Printing Pioneers — A104

Designs: 6d, Theodosius Sinaitski. 30d, Johannes Gutenberg.

2000, July 28

192-193 A104 Set of 2 1.90 1.90

Mother Teresa (1910-97) A105

2000, Aug. 26

194 A105 6d multi .30 .30

Birds — A106

Designs: 6d, Egretta garzeta. 10d, Ardea cinerea. 20d, Ardea purpurea. 30d, Plegadis falcinellus.

2000, Sept. 14

195-198 A106 Set of 4 3.50 3.50

Children's Week A107

2000, Oct. 2 **Litho.** ***Perf. 13¼***

199 A107 6d multi .30 .30

Duke Dimo Hadi Dimov (1875-1924) A108

2000, Oct. 20

200 A108 6d multi .30 .30

Economics Faculty of Sts. Cyril & Methodius Univ., 50th Anniv. — A109

2000, Nov. 1

201 A109 6d multi .30 .30

Joachim Krchovski, 250th Anniv. of Birth A110

2000, Nov. 8

202 A110 6d multi .30 .30

Christmas A111

2000, Nov. 22

203 A111 30d multi 1.50 1.50

UN High Commissioner For Refugees, 50th Anniv. — A112

Designs: 6d, Handprints. 30d, Globe, hands.

2001, Jan. 10 **Litho.** ***Perf. 13¼***

204-205 A112 Set of 2 1.75 1.75

Worldwide Fund for Nature (WWF) — A113

Imperial eagle: a, 6d, Facing right. b, 8d, With chick. c, 10d, In flight, and close-up of head. d, 30d, Close-up of head.

2001, Feb. 1 **Litho.** ***Perf. 14***
206 A113 Block of 4, #a-d 3.00 3.00

Partenija Zografski (1818-1876) A114

2001, Feb. 6 **Litho.** ***Perf. 13¼***
207 A114 6d multi .30 .30

A115

Native Costumes — A116

Designs: 6d, Dolmi Polog. 12d, Albanian. 18d, Reka. 30d, Skopska Crna Gora.
50d, Women, men in costumes, house, vegetables.

2001, Mar. 1 ***Perf. 13¼***
208-211 A115 Set of 4 3.25 3.25

Souvenir Sheet
Imperf
Granite Paper

212 A116 50d multi 2.50 2.50

Lazar Licenoski (1901-64), Painter — A117

2001, Mar. 23 ***Perf. 13¼***
213 A117 6d multi .30 .30

National Archives, 50th Anniv. — A118

2001, Apr. 1
214 A118 6d multi .30 .30

Easter A119

2001, Apr. 15
215 A119 6d multi .30 .30

Europa — A120

No. 216, Boat on lake: a, 18d. b, 36d.
Illustration reduced.

2001, May 16 **Granite Paper**
216 A120 Horiz. pair, #a-b *3.50 3.50*

Revolt Against Ottoman Rule, 125th Anniv. A121

2001, May 20 **Litho.** ***Perf. 13¼***
217 A121 6d multi .30 .30

2nd Individual European Chess Championships A122

2001, June 1 **Litho.** ***Perf. 13¼***
218 A122 36d multi 1.90 1.90
a. Booklet pane of 4 7.75 —
Booklet, #218a 7.75

Booklet sold for 145d.

Boats in Lake Dojran A123

2001, June 5 **Litho.** ***Perf. 13¼***
219 A123 6d multi .30 .30

Architecture Type of 1998
Perf. 13¼

2001, June 25 **Litho.** **Unwmk.**
220 A63a 6d House, Mitrasinci .30 .30

Independence, 10th Anniv. — A124

2001, Sept. 8 **Wmk. 387**
221 A124 6d multi .30 .30

Trees A125

Designs: 6d, Juniperus excelsa. 12d, Quercus macedonica. 24d, Arbutus andrachne. 36d, Quercus coccifera.

Perf. 13¼

2001, Sept. 12 **Litho.** **Unwmk.**
222-225 A125 Set of 4 4.00 4.00

Children's Day — A126

Perf. 13¼

2001, Oct. 1 **Litho.** **Unwmk.**
226 A126 6d multi .30 .30

Year of Dialogue Among Civilizations A127

2001, Oct. 9 **Granite Paper**
227 A127 36d multi 1.90 1.90

Nature Museum, 75th Anniv. A128

2001, Oct. 26
228 A128 6d multi .30 .30

Christmas — A129

2001, Nov. 22
229 A129 6d multi .30 .30

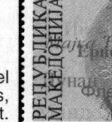

Nobel Prizes, Cent. A130

2001, Dec. 10 **Litho.** ***Perf. 13¼***
230 A130 36d multi 1.90 1.90

2002 Winter Olympics, Salt Lake City — A131

Designs: 6d, Skier. 36d, Skier, diff.

2002, Jan. 16 **Litho.** ***Perf. 14***
231-232 A131 Set of 2 2.10 2.10

Ancient Coins A132

Designs: 6d, King Lykkeios of Paeonia obol, 359-340 B.C. 12d, Alexander III tetradrachm. 24d, Kings of Macedon tetrobol, 185-165 B.C. 36d, Philip II of Macedon gold stater.
50d, Kings of Macedon coin.

2002, Mar. 1
233-236 A132 Set of 4 4.00 4.00

Souvenir Sheet

237 A132 50d multi 2.50 2.50

Petar Mazev (1927-93), Painter A133

2002, Apr. 15
238 A133 6d multi .30 .30

Dimitar Kondovski (1927-93), Painter A134

2002, Apr. 15
239 A134 6d multi .30 .30

Leonardo da Vinci (1452-1519) and Mona Lisa A135

2002, Apr. 15
240 A135 36d multi 1.90 1.90

Easter — A136

2002, Apr. 24
241 A136 6d multi .30 .30

Europa
A137

Designs: 6d, Acrobat, bicycle on wire, seal. 36d, Ball on wire, bicycle.

2002, May 9
242-243 A137 Set of 2 *2.25 2.00*

2002 World Cup Soccer Championships, Japan and Korea — A138

2002, May 15
244 A138 6d multi .30 .30

Environmental Protection — A139

2002, June 5
245 A139 6d multi .30 .30

National Arms — A140

Background colors: 10d, Blue. 36d, Greenish blue.

2002, June 18
246-247 A140 Set of 2 2.40 2.40

Architecture A141

Buildings in: 36d, Krushevo. 50d, Bitola.

2002, June 26 ***Perf. 13¼***
248-249 A141 Set of 2 4.50 4.50

Metodija Andonov Cento (1902-57), 1st President of Antifascist Council for the Natl. Liberation of Macedonia
A142

2002, Aug. 18 Litho. ***Perf. 13¼***
250 A142 6d multi .30 .30

Nikola Karev (1877-1905), President of Krushevo Republic, Aug. 1903 — A143

2002, Aug. 18
251 A143 18d multi .90 .90

Fauna — A144

No. 252: a, 6d, Perdix perdix. b, 12d, Sus scrofa. c, 24d, Rupicapra rupicapra. d, 36d, Alectoris graeca.

2002, Sept. 11 ***Perf. 14***
252 A144 Block of 4, #a-d 4.00 4.00

Children's Day — A145

2002, Oct. 1
253 A145 6d multi .30 .30

Architecture Type of 1998

2002, Nov. 5 ***Perf. 13¼***
254 A63a 3d House, Jachince .20 .20
255 A63a 9d House, Ratevo .45 .45

Christmas — A146

2002, Nov. 20
256 A146 9d multi .45 .45

Andreja Damjanov (1813-78), Builder of Churches A147

2003, Jan. 21
257 A147 36d multi 1.90 1.90

Musical Instruments A148

Designs: 9d, Gajda. 10d, Tambura. 20d, Kemene. 50d, Tapan.

2003, Feb. 19 Litho. ***Perf. 13¼***
258-261 A148 Set of 4 4.00 4.00

Scouting In Macedonia, 50th Anniv. A149

2003, Feb. 22
262 A149 9d multi .45 .45

Krste Petkov Misirkov Macedonian Language Institute, 50th Anniv. A150

2003, Mar. 5
263 A150 9d multi .45 .45

Europa — A151

Poster art: No. 264, 36d, 1966 poster. No. 265, 36d, 1994 Intl. Triennial of Graphic Art poster.

2003, May 9 ***Perf. 13¼x13½***
Granite Paper
264-265 A151 Set of 2 *3.75 3.00*

Ursus Arctos A152

2003, June 5 ***Perf. 13½x13¼***
266 A152 9d multi .55 .55

Building, Skopje A153

Building, Resen A154

2003, June 16
267 A153 10d multi .50 .50
268 A154 20d multi 1.00 1.00

Macedonian Arms — A155

Designs: 9d, Latin lettering. 36d, Cyrillic lettering.

2003, June 23 ***Perf. 13¼x13½***
269-270 A155 Set of 2 2.25 2.25

World Youth Handball Championships A156

2003, July 30
271 A156 36d multi 1.90 1.90

Printed in sheets of 8 + label.

Ilinden Uprising, Cent. A157

Uprising participants and: 9d, Seal. 36d, Memorial.
50d, Seal, diff.

2003, Aug. 2 ***Perf. 13½x13¼***
272-273 A157 Set of 2 2.25 2.25

Souvenir Sheet

274 A157 50d multi + label 2.50 2.50

Paintings — A158

Paintings by: 9d, Nikola Martinovski (1903-73), vert. 36d, Vincent van Gogh (1853-90)

Perf. 13½x13¼, 13¼x13½
2003, Aug. 18
275-276 A158 Set of 2 2.25 2.25

Flowers — A159

Designs: 9d, Colchicum macedonicum. 20d, Viola allchariensis. 36d, Tulipa mariannae. 50d, Thymus oehmianus.

Perf. 13¼x13½
2003, Sept. 25 Litho.
277-280 A159 Set of 4 6.00 6.00

Writers A160

Designs: No. 281, 9d, Jeronim de Rada (1814-1903). No. 282, 9d, Said Najdeni (1864-1903).

2003, Sept. 30 ***Perf. 13½x13¼***
281-282 A160 Set of 2 .90 .90

Children's Day — A161

2003, Oct. 6 ***Perf. 13¼x13½***
283 A161 9d multi .45 .45

Kresnensko Uprising, 125th Anniv. A162

2003, Oct. 17 ***Perf. 13½x13¼***
284 A162 9d multi .45 .45

Dimitar Vlahov (1878-1953), Politician — A163

2003, Nov. 8 **Litho.** ***Perf. 13½x13¼***
285 A163 9d multi .45 .45

Christmas A164

2003, Nov. 19
286 A164 9d multi .45 .45

Handicrafts A165

DesignsL 5d, Tassels. 9d, Pitcher. 10d, Kettle. 20d, Ornament.

2003-04 **Litho.** ***Perf. 13¼x13½***
287 A165 3d multi .20 .20
288 A165 5d multi .25 .25
289 A165 9d multi .45 .45
290 A165 10d multi .50 .50
291 A165 12d multi .60 .60
292 A165 20d multi 1.00 1.00
Nos. 287-292 (6) 3.00 3.00

Issued: 9d, 12/16; 10d, 1/21/04; 5d, 20d, 6/4/04; 3d, 12d, 6/4/04.

Powered Flight, Cent. A166

Perf. 13½x13¼
2003, Dec. 17 **Litho.**
293 A166 50d multi 3.00 3.00

Paintings Type of 2003

Designs: No. 294, 9d, Street and Buildings, by Tomo Vladimirski (1904-71), vert. No. 295, 9d, Street Scene, by Vangel Kodzoman (1904-94).

Perf. 13½x13¼, 13¼x13½
2004, Feb. 14
294-295 A158 Set of 2 1.00 1.00

Decorated Weapons — A167

Designs: 10d, Sword, 1806. 20d, Saber, 19th cent. 36d, Gun, 18th cent. 50d, Rifle, 18th cent.
Illustration reduced.

2004, Mar. 10 ***Perf. 13¼x13½***
Stamps + Labels
296-299 A167 Set of 4 6.50 6.50

Rugs — A168

Various rugs: 36d, 50d.

2004, Mar. 24
300-301 A168 Set of 2 4.75 4.75

Konstandin Kristoforidhi, Publisher of First Albanian Dictionary in Macedonia A169

2004, Apr. 19
302 A169 36d multi 2.00 2.00

House, Kratovo A170

2004, Apr. 23 ***Perf. 13½x13¼***
303 A170 20d multi 1.10 1.10

Macedonian Intention to Enter European Union — A171

2004, May 4
304 A171 36d multi 2.00 2.00

Europa — A172

No. 305 — People at beach: a, Denomination at left. b, Denomination at right.
Illustration reduced.

Perf. 13¼x13½
2004, May 7 **Wmk. 387**
305 A172 50d Horiz. pair, #a-b 5.00 4.50

Prespa Ecopark — A173

Perf. 13¼x13½
2004, June 5 **Litho.** **Unwmk.**
306 A173 36d multi 2.00 2.00

2004 Summer Olympics, Athens — A174

No. 307 — Map of Europe, Olympic rings with flags and 2004 Summer Olympics emblem at: a, Left. b, Right.
Illustration reduced.

Perf. 13½x13¼
2004, June 16 **Wmk. 387**
307 A174 50d Horiz. pair, #a-b 5.25 5.25

Sami Frasheri (1850-1904), Writer — A175

Perf. 13½x13¼
2004, June 18 **Litho.** **Unwmk.**
308 A175 12d multi .60 .60

FIFA (Fédération Internationale de Football Association), Cent. — A176

2004, July 3
309 A176 100d multi 5.25 5.25

Marko Cepenkov (1829-1920), Writer — A177

2004, Sept. 1
310 A177 12d multi .60 .60

Vasil Glavinov (1869-1929), Politician — A178

2004, Sept. 1 ***Perf. 13¼x13½***
311 A178 12d multi .60 .60

Birds — A179

Designs: 12d, Bombycilla garrulus. 24d, Lanius senator. 36d, Monticola saxatilis. 48d, Pyrrhula pyrrhula.
60d, Tichodroma muraria.

Perf. 13¼x13½
2004, Sept. 25 **Litho.**
312-315 A179 Set of 4 6.75 6.75

Souvenir Sheet
Imperf
316 A179 60d multi 3.50 3.50

No. 316 contains one 27x36mm stamp.

Children's Day A180

2004, Oct. 4 **Litho.** ***Perf. 13½x13¼***
317 A180 12d multi .60 .60

Information Technology Society Summit A181

2004, Oct. 16
318 A181 36d multi 1.75 1.75

Aseman Gospel, 1000th Anniv. A182

2004, Oct. 27 **Litho.** ***Perf. 13½x13¼***
319 A182 12d multi .60 .60

Marco Polo (1254-1324), Explorer — A183

2004, Nov. 10

320 A183 36d multi 1.75 1.75

Christmas A184

2004, Nov. 24 ***Perf. 13¼x13½***

321 A184 12d multi .60 .60

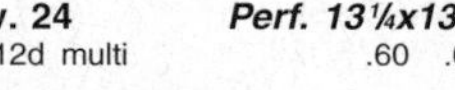

Konstantin Miladinov (1830-62), Poet A185

2005, Feb. 4 ***Perf. 13½x13¼***

322 A185 36d multi 1.75 1.75

Illuminated Manuscripts A186

Designs: 12d, Manuscript from 16th-17th cent. 24d, Manuscript from 16th cent.

2005, Mar. 9 ***Perf. 13¼x13½***

323-324 A186 Set of 2 1.75 1.75

A187

Embroidery — A188

2005, Mar. 23 ***Perf. 13½x13¼***

325 A187 36d multi 2.00 2.00
326 A188 50d multi 2.75 2.75

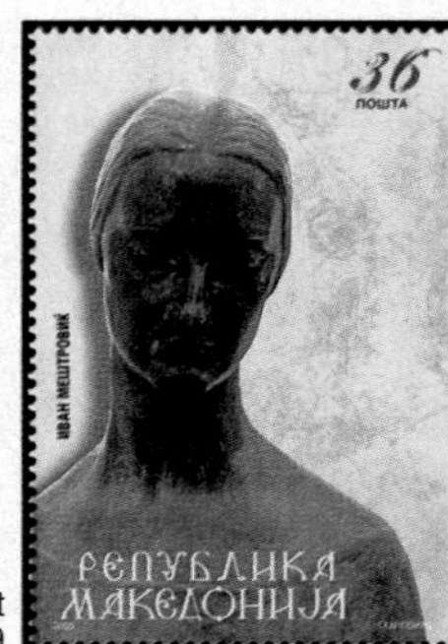

Art A189

Designs: 36d, Sculpture by Ivan Mestrovic. 50d, Painting by Paja Jovanovic, horiz.

Perf. 13½x13¼, 13¼x13½

2005, Apr. 6

327-328 A189 Set of 2 4.75 4.75

First Book in Albanian Language, 450th Anniv. — A190

2005, Apr. 27 ***Perf. 13¼x13½***

329 A190 12d multi .60 .60

Skanderbeg (1405-68), Albanian National Hero — A191

2005, Apr. 27

330 A191 36d multi 1.75 1.75

Europa — A192

Designs: a, 36d, Wheat, bread. b, 60d, Peppers, plate of food.
Illustration reduced.

2005, May 9 ***Perf. 13½x13¼***

331 A192 Horiz. pair, #a-b 5.00 5.00

Vlachs' Day, Cent. A193

2005, Apr. 27 Litho. ***Perf. 13½x13¼***

332 A193 12d multi .60 .60

Environmental Protection A194

2005, June 4 ***Perf. 13¼x13½***

333 A194 36d multi 1.75 1.75

Friezes — A195

Frieze from: 3d, 16th cent. 4d, 15th cent. 6d, 16th cent., diff. 8d, 1883-84. 12d, 16th cent., diff.

2005, June 8 Litho. ***Perf. 13¼x13½***

334-338 A195 Set of 5 1.60 1.60

First Automobile in Macedonia, Cent. — A196

First Glider in Macedonia, 50th Anniv. — A197

Perf. 13½x13¼

2005, June 15 **Litho.**

339 A196 12d multi .60 .60
340 A197 36d multi 1.75 1.75

Intl. Year of Physics A198

2005, June 30

341 A198 60d multi 3.00 3.00

Fruit A199

Designs: 12d, Malus Miller (apples). 24d, Prunus persica (peaches). 36d, Prunus avium (cherries). 48d, Prunus sp. (plums).
100d, Pyrus sp. (pears), vert.

Perf. 13½x13¼

2005, Sept. 14 Litho. Wmk. 387

342-345 A199 Set of 4 7.00 7.00

Souvenir Sheet

Perf. 13¼x13½

346 A199 100d multi 6.00 6.00

Smolar Waterfall — A200

Perf. 13¼x13½

2005, Sept. 28 Unwmk.

347 A200 24d multi 1.25 1.25

Hans Christian Andersen (1805-75), Author A201

2005, Oct. 3 Litho. ***Perf. 13½x13¼***

348 A201 12d multi .60 .60

Kozjak Dam A202

2005, Oct. 25

349 A202 12d multi .60 .60

Brsjac Rebellion, 125th Anniv. A203

2005, Oct. 28

350 A203 12d multi .60 .60

Rila Congress, Cent. — A204

2005, Oct. 28 ***Perf. 13¼x13½***

351 A204 12d multi .60 .60

Europa Stamps, 50th Anniv. (in 2006) — A205

Emblems and Europa stamps: Nos. 352a, 353a, 60d, #243. Nos. 352b, 353b, 170d, #158. Nos. 352c, 353c, 250d, #97. Nos. 352d, 353d, 350d, #76.
Illustration reduced.

2005, Nov. 14 *Perf. 13½x13¼*
352 A205 Block of 4, #a-d 45.00 45.00

Souvenir Sheet

353 A205 Sheet of 4, #a-d 45.00 45.00

Stamp sizes: Nos. 352a-352d, 40x30mm; Nos. 353a-353d, 40x29mm.

Whitewater Kayaker A206

2005, Nov. 23
354 A206 36d multi 1.75 1.75

Christmas A207

2005, Nov. 23 *Perf. 13¼x13½*
355 A207 12d multi .60 .60

Macedonia Post Emblem — A208

Perf. 13¼x13½

2005, Dec. 14 **Litho.**
356 A208 12d multi .60 .60

2006 Winter Olympics, Turin — A209

Designs: 36d, Skiing. 60d, Ice hockey.

2006, Jan. 26
357-358 A209 Set of 2 4.75 4.75

Fresco and Matejce Monastery A210

Isaac Celebi Mosque — A211

2006, Mar. 8
359 A210 12d multi .60 .60
360 A211 24d multi 1.25 1.25

Léopold Sédar Senghor (1906-2001), First President of Senegal — A212

2006, Mar. 20 *Perf. 13½x13¼*
361 A212 36d multi 1.75 1.75

Handicrafts With Inlaid Mother-of-Pearl A213

Designs: 12d, Wooden shoes. 24d, Decorative objects.

2006, Mar. 22 *Perf. 13¼x13½*
362-363 A213 Set of 2 1.75 1.75

Wood Carving by Makarie Negriev Frckovski A214

Cupola of St. Peter's Basilica, Vatican City, 450th Anniv. A215

2006, Apr. 5 *Perf. 13½x13¼*
364 A214 12d multi .60 .60
365 A215 36d multi 1.75 1.75

Zivko Firfov (1906-84), Composer A216

2006, Apr. 26 *Perf. 13¼x13½*
366 A216 24d multi 1.25 1.25

Wolfgang Amadeus Mozart (1756-91), Composer A217

2006, Apr. 26
367 A217 60d multi 3.00 3.00

Europa A218

Designs: 36d, Lettered balls. 60d, Lettered blocks.

2006, May 9 *Perf. 13½x13¼*
368-369 A218 Set of 2 5.00 5.00

Souvenir Sheet

Macedonian Europa Stamps, 10th Anniv. — A219

No. 370: a, Pope John Paul II (1920-2005). b, Mother Teresa (1910-97).

2006, May 9 *Perf. 13¼x13½*
370 A219 60d Sheet of 2, #a-b 6.50 6.50

Fight Against Desertification — A220

2006, June 5 **Litho.** *Perf. 13½x13¼*
371 A220 12d multi .50 .50

Grand Prix Racing, Cent. A221

Perf. 13½x13¼

2006, June 14 **Litho.**
372 A221 36d multi 1.75 1.75

Nikola Tesla (1856-1943), Electrical Engineer — A222

Perf. 13½x13¼

2006, June 28 **Litho.**
373 A222 24d multi 1.00 1.00

Christopher Columbus (1451-1506), Explorer — A223

2006, June 28
374 A223 36d multi 1.50 1.50

Containers — A224

2006, Aug. 30 **Litho.** *Perf. 12¾x13*
375 A224 3d Carafe .20 .20
376 A224 6d Pitcher, bowl .30 .30

Shells — A225

Designs: 12d, Ancylus scalariformis. 24d, Macedopyrgula pavlovici. 36d, Gyraulus trapezoides. 48d, Valvata hirsutecostata. 72d, Ochridopyrgula macedonica.

2006, Sept. 6 **Litho.** *Perf. 13¼x13½*
377-380 A225 Set of 4 6.75 6.75

Souvenir Sheet

381 A225 72d multi 4.00 4.00

UNICEF, 60th Anniv. A226

2006, Oct. 2 *Perf. 13½x13¼*
382 A226 12d multi .50 .50

Lynx and Galicica Natl. Park A227

2006, Oct. 2
383 A227 24d multi 1.00 1.00

World Senior Men's and Women's Bowling Championships — A228

2006, Oct. 20
384 A228 36d multi 1.50 1.50

Bishop Frang Bardhi (1606-43) A229

Pres. Boris Trajkovski (1956-2004) A230

Kemal Ataturk (1881-1938), Turkish Statesman A231

Archbishop Dositheus, 100th Anniv. of Birth — A232

2006, Oct. 25 *Perf. 13¼x13½*

385 A229 12d multi	.50	.50
386 A230 12d multi	.50	.50
387 A231 24d multi	1.00	1.00
388 A232 24d multi	1.00	1.00
Nos. 385-388 (4)	3.00	3.00

Christmas A233

2006, Nov. 22 *Perf. 13½x13¼*
389 A233 12d multi .55 .55

Metal Objects — A234

Designs: 4d, Handled container, Bitola, 19th cent. 5d, Wine flask, Skopje, 20th cent., vert. 10d, Bell, Skopje, 18th cent., vert. 12d, Lidded container, Prilep, 18th-19th cent., vert.

Perf. 13x12¾, 12¾x13

2006, Nov. 30

390 A234 4d multi	.20	.20
391 A234 5d multi	.20	.20
392 A234 10d multi	.45	.45
393 A234 12d multi	.55	.55
Nos. 390-393 (4)	1.40	1.40

Kokino Megalithic Observatory A235

Designs: 12d, Mold for amulet. 36d, Sunrise over observatory.

2007, Jan. 31 *Perf. 13¼x13½*
394-395 A235 Set of 2 2.10 2.10

Nos. 394-395 each were printed in sheets of 8 + label.

Monastery Anniversaries — A236

Designs: 12d, Slivnica Monastery, 400th anniv. 36d, St. Nikita Monastery, 700th anniv., vert.

Perf. 13½x13¼, 13¼x13½

2007, Jan. 31
396-397 A236 Set of 2 2.10 2.10

Handicrafts A237

Designs: 12d, Tepelak, Kicevo, 18th-19th cent. 36d, Casket, Ohrid, 19th cent.

2007, Feb. 14 *Perf. 13½x13¼*
398-399 A237 Set of 2 2.10 2.10

Fish A238

Designs: 12d, Cobitis vardarensis. 36d, Zingel balcanicus. 60d, Chondrostoma vardarense. No. 403, 100d, Barbus macedonicus.
No. 404, 100d, Leuciscus cephalus.

2007, Feb. 28
400-403 A238 Set of 4 11.50 11.50

Souvenir Sheet

404 A238 100d multi 5.50 5.50

Epos of Freedom, Mosaic by Borko Lazeski A239

Head of a Woman, by Pablo Picasso — A240

2007, Mar. 14 *Perf. 13½x13¼*
405 A239 36d multi 1.60 1.60

Perf. 13¼x13½

406 A240 100d multi 4.50 4.50

Cubism, cent.

Intl. Francophone Day — A241

2007, Mar. 20 *Perf. 13½x13¼*
407 A241 12d multi .55 .55

Cat — A242

2007, Apr. 9 *Perf. 13¼x13½*
408 A242 12d multi .65 .65

Europa A243

Macedonian Scouting emblem and: 60d, Scout camp. 100d, Scout, tent, vert.

Perf. 13½x13¼, 13¼x13½

2007, May 9 **Litho.**
409-410 A243 Set of 2 7.00 7.00

Souvenir Sheet

Europa — A243a

2007, May 9 **Litho.** *Perf. 13½x13¼*
411 A243a 160d multi *35.00 35.00*

Scouting, cent.

Discovery of St. Cyril's Grave, 150th Anniv. — A244

2007, May 23 *Perf. 13¼x13½*
412 A244 50d multi 2.25 2.25

Smokestacks and Clock — A245

2007, June 5 **Litho.** *Perf. 13¼x13½*
413 A245 12d multi .55 .55

Carl von Linné (1707-78), Botanist — A246

Notes of Dmitri Mendeleev (1834-1907), Chemist — A247

2007, June 20 *Perf. 13¼x13½*
414 A246 36d multi 1.60 1.60

Perf. 13½x13¼

415 A247 36d multi 1.60 1.60

Euro-Atlantic Partnership Council Security Forum, Ohrid — A248

2007, June 28 *Perf. 13½x13¼*
416 A248 60d multi 2.60 2.60

Intl. Sailing Federation, Cent. A249

2007, July 31 **Litho.** *Perf. 13½x13¼*
417 A249 35d multi 1.60 1.60

Maminska River Waterfall — A250

Perf. 13¼x13½

2007, Sept. 19 **Litho.**
418 A250 12d multi .55 .55

Mitrush Kuteli (1907-67), Writer — A251

Fan S. Noli (1882-1965), Albanian Prime Minister — A252

2007, Sept. 25

419	A251	12d multi	.55	.55
420	A252	12d multi	.55	.55

Children's Day A253

2007, Oct. 1 Litho. ***Perf. 13½x13¼***

421	A253	12d multi	.55	.55

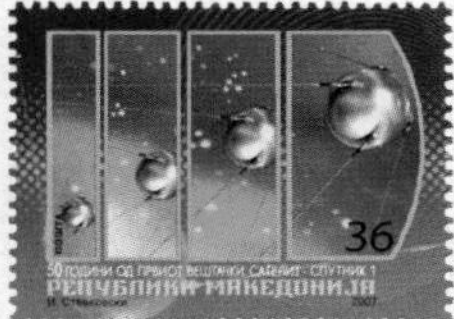

Launch of Sputnik 1, 50th Anniv. A254

2007, Oct. 4 Litho. ***Perf. 13½x13¼***

422	A254	36d multi	1.75	1.75

Petre Prlicko (1905-95), Actor A255

2007, Oct. 31 Litho. ***Perf. 13½x13¼***

423	A255	12d multi	.60	.60

Jordan Hadzi Konstantinov-Dzinot (1821-82), Educator — A256

2007, Oct. 31

424	A256	12d multi	.60	.60

Handbag — A257

2007, Nov. 9 Litho. ***Perf. 12¾x13***

425	A257	12d multi	.60	.60

Christmas A258

Perf. 13½x13¼

2007, Nov. 21 **Litho.**

426	A258	12d multi	.60	.60

Tose Proeski (1981-2007), Singer — A259

2007, Dec. 15 ***Perf. 13¼x13½***

427	A259	12d multi	.60	.60

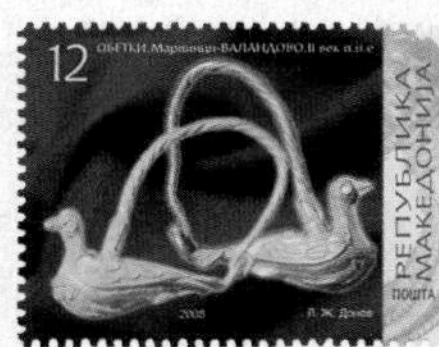

Earrings A260

Designs: 12d, Earrings with pigeon design, 2nd cent. B.C. 24d, Earring with lion design, 4th cent. B.C., vert.

Perf. 13½x13¼, 13¼x13½

2008, Jan. 23 **Litho.**

428-429	A260	Set of 2	1.75	1.75

Launch of Explorer 1 Satellite, 50th Anniv. — A261

2008, Jan. 31 Litho. ***Perf. 13¼x13½***

430	A261	24d multi	1.25	1.25

High-speed Train — A262

2008, Feb. 27 ***Perf. 13½x13¼***

431	A262	100d multi	5.00	5.00

Worldwide Fund for Nature (WWF) — A263

No. 432 — Upupa epops: a, 12d, In flight. b, 24d, Head. c, 48d, On branch, facing left with insect in beak. d, 60d, On branch, facing right.
Illustration reduced.

Perf. 13½x13¼

2008, Mar. 28 **Litho.**

432	A263	Block of 4, #a-d	7.50	7.50

Bulldog — A264

2008, Apr. 16 Litho. ***Perf. 13¼x13½***

433	A264	30d multi	1.50	1.50

Europa — A265

No. 434 — Envelopes over: a, 50d, Western Hemisphere, dark blue panel at top, country name in yellow. b, 100d, Asia, Eastern Europe and Africa, dark blue panel at top, country name in pink.

No. 435, 50d: a, As No. 434a, green panel at top. b, As No. 434b, green panel at top. c, As No. 434a, blue panel at top, country name in orange. d, As No. 434b, blue panel at top, country name in orange.
Illustration reduced.

2008, May 7 Litho. ***Perf. 13½x13¼***

434	A265	Horiz. pair, #a-b	7.50	7.50

Miniature Sheet

435	A265	50d Sheet of 4, #a-d	*15.00*	*15.00*

No. 435 was sold with, but not attached to, a booklet cover.

Robert Schuman, Macedonian and European Union Flags — A266

Macedonian and European Union Flags, Eiffel Tower, Paris — A267

Macedonian and European Union Flags, Ljubljana, Slovenia — A268

Perf. 13¼x13½, 13½x13¼

2008, May 22

436	A266	36d multi	1.90	1.90
437	A267	50d multi	2.60	2.60
438	A268	50d multi	2.60	2.60
		Nos. 436-438 (3)	7.10	7.10

Environmental Protection — A269

2008, June 5 Litho. ***Perf. 13½x13¼***

439	A269	12d multi	.60	.60

Rudolf Diesel (1858-1918), Inventor — A270

2008, June 18 ***Perf. 13¼x13½***

440	A270	30d multi	1.60	1.60

Eqrem Cabej (1908-80), Linguist A272

2008, Aug. 6 Litho. ***Perf. 13½x13¼***

445	A272	12d multi	.60	.60

14th Intl. Congress of Slavists, Ohrid A273

2008, Sept. 10

446	A273	12d multi	.55	.55

Flowers — A274

Designs: 1d, Helichrysum zivojinii. 12d, Pulsatilla halleri, horiz. 50d, Stachys iva, horiz. No. 450, 72d, Fritillaria macedonica.
No. 451, 72d, Centaurea grbavacensis.

Perf. 13¼x13½, 13½x13¼

2008, Sept. 10

447-450	A274	Set of 4	6.25	6.25

Souvenir Sheet

451	A274	72d multi	3.50	3.50

Matka Cave A275

2008, Sept. 24 ***Perf. 13½x13¼***

452	A275	12d multi	.55	.55

Children's Day A276

2008, Oct. 6

453	A276	12d multi	.55	.55

European Women's Handball Championships — A277

2008, Oct. 15
454 A277 30d multi 1.25 1.25

POSTAL TAX STAMPS

Men Blowing Horns — PT1

1991, Dec. 30 Litho. ***Perf. 13½***
RA1 PT1 2.50d multicolored *.75 .75*

No. RA1 was required on mail Dec. 31, 1991-Sept. 8, 1992. For surcharge see No. 22.

Anti-Cancer Week — PT2

Designs: Nos. RA2, RA6, Emblems, inscriptions. Nos. RA3, RA7, Magnetic resonance imaging scanner. Nos. RA4, RA8, Overhead scanner, examination table. No. RA5, RA9c, Mammography imager. No. RA9, Ultra sound computer.

1992, Mar. 1 Litho. ***Perf. 10***
RA2 PT2 5d multicolored *1.00 1.00*
RA3 PT2 5d multicolored *1.00 1.00*
RA4 PT2 5d multicolored *1.00 1.00*
RA5 PT2 5d multicolored *1.00 1.00*
a. Block of 4, #RA2-RA5 *4.00 4.00*
RA6 PT2 5d multicolored *.30 .30*
RA7 PT2 5d multicolored *.30 .30*
RA8 PT2 5d multicolored *.30 .30*
RA9 PT2 5d multicolored *.30 .30*
a. Block of 4, #RA6-RA9 *1.25 1.25*
b. Souv. sheet of 3, #RA7-RA9, RA9c *22.50 22.50*
c. PT2 5d multicolored *.40 .40*
Nos. RA2-RA9 (8) 5.20 5.20

Inscription at right reads up on No. RA2 and down on No. RA6. Designs on Nos. RA7-RA8, RA9c are without red cross symbol.

Souvenir folders with perf. and imperf. sheets of RA9b sold for 40d. Value for both sheets in folder, $50.

Obligatory on mail Mar. 1-8.

See Nos. RA28-RA31.

Red Cross Week PT3

Designs: RA10, Slogans. No. RA11, Airplanes dropping supplies. No. RA12, Aiding traffic accident victim. No. RA13, Evacuating casualties from building.

1992, May 8 ***Perf. 10***
RA10 PT3 10d multicolored *.20 .20*
RA11 PT3 10d multicolored *.20 .20*
RA12 PT3 10d multicolored *.20 .20*
RA13 PT3 10d multicolored *.20 .20*
a. Block of 4, #RA10-RA13 *.65 .65*

Nos. RA10-RA13 exist with silver-colored borders in perf. and imperf. miniature sheets that sold for 80d. Value for both sheets $7.50.

Obligatory on mail May 8-15.

PT4

PT5

Solidarity Week: #RA14, Skopje earthquake. #RA15, Woman holding girl. #RA16, Mother carrying infant. #RA17, Mother, children, airplane.

130d, Woman, child, airport control tower.

1992, June 1 ***Perf. 10***
RA14 PT4 20d multicolored *.20 .20*
RA15 PT4 20d multicolored *.20 .20*
RA16 PT4 20d multicolored *.20 .20*
RA17 PT4 20d multicolored *.20 .20*
a. Block of 4 *.65 .65*

Size: 74x97mm

Imperf

RA18 PT4 130d multicolored *3.25 3.25*

No. RA18 also exists with perf. vignette. Same value.

Obligatory on mail June 1-7.

See No. RA55.

1992, Sept. 14 ***Perf. 10***

Anti-Tuberculosis Week: No. RA20, Nurse, infant. No. RA21, Nurse giving oxygen to patient. No. RA22, Infant in bed.

200d, Child being treated by nurse.

RA19 PT5 20d multicolored *.20 .20*
RA20 PT5 20d multicolored *.20 .20*
RA21 PT5 20d multicolored *.20 .20*
RA22 PT5 20d multicolored *.20 .20*
a. Block of 4, #RA19-RA22 *.65 .65*

Size: 74x97mm

Imperf

RA23 PT5 200d vermilion & multi *2.75 2.75*

No. RA23 exists with magenta inscriptions, and also with perf. vignette and either magenta or vermilion inscriptions. Obligatory on mail Sept. 14-21.

Red Cross Fund PT6

1993, Feb. 1 Litho. ***Perf. 10***
RA24 PT6 20d Shown *.20 .20*
RA25 PT6 20d Marguerites *.20 .20*
RA26 PT6 20d Carnations *.20 .20*
RA27 PT6 20d Mixed bouquet *.20 .20*
a. Block of 4, #RA24-RA27 *.65 .65*

Nos. RA24-RA27 exist in perf. or imperf. miniature sheets with either gold or silver backgrounds and inscriptions, that sold for 500d each. Value for both sheets $7.50.

Obligatory on mail Feb. 1-28.

Cancer Therapy Type of 1992

Designs: No. RA28, Nuclear medicine caduceus, inscriptions. No. RA29, Radiographic equipment. No. RA30, Radiology machine. No. RA31, Scanner.

1993, Mar. 1 Litho. ***Perf. 10***
RA28 PT2 20d multicolored *.20 .20*
RA29 PT2 20d multicolored *.20 .20*
RA30 PT2 20d multicolored *.20 .20*
RA31 PT2 20d multicolored *.20 .20*
a. Block of 4, #RA28-RA31 *.65 .65*

#RA28-RA31 exist in perf. & imperf. miniature sheets with gold background or inscription, that sold for 500d each. Value for both sheets $3.50.

Obligatory on mail Mar. 1-8.

Red Cross Week PT7

1993, May 8 Litho. ***Perf. 10***
RA32 PT7 50d Inscriptions *.20 .20*
RA33 PT7 50d Man holding baby *.20 .20*
RA34 PT7 50d Patient in wheelchair *.20 .20*
RA35 PT7 50d Carrying stretcher *.20 .20*
a. Block of 4, #RA32-RA35 *.65 .65*

Perf. & imperf. miniature sheets of Nos. RA32-RA35 exist with yellow inscription tablets that sold for 700d each. Value for both sheets $3.50.

Obligatory on mail May 8-15.

1993, June 1 ***Perf. 10***
RA36 PT7 50de Skopje earthquake *.20 .20*
RA37 PT7 50de Unloading boxes *.20 .20*
RA38 PT7 50de Labeling boxes *.20 .20*
RA39 PT7 50de Boxes, fork lift *.20 .20*
a. Block of 4, #RA36-RA39 *.65 .65*

Perf. & imperf. miniature sheets of Nos. RA36-RA39 exist with gold inscription tablets that sold for 7d each. Value for both sheets $3.50.

Obligatory on mail June 1-7.

1993, Sept. 14 ***Perf. 10***

Designs: Nos. RA40, Inscriptions. Nos. RA41, Children in meadow. Nos. RA42, Bee on flower. No. RA43, Goat behind rock.

RA40 PT7 50de black, gray & red *.20 .20*
RA41 PT7 50de green & multi *.20 .20*
RA42 PT7 50de green & multi *.20 .20*
RA43 PT7 50de green & multi *.20 .20*
a. Block of 4, #RA40-RA43 *.65 .65*

Nos. RA41-RA43 exist in perf. & imperf. miniature sheets that sold for 15d each. Values for both sheets $3.25. Nos. RA40-RA43 exist with yellow omitted, resulting in blue stamps Value of the blue set $2.25.

Obligatory on mail Sept. 14-21.

See Nos. RA52-RA54.

Anti-Cancer Week — PT8

1994, Mar. 1 ***Perf. 10***
RA44 PT8 1d Inscription, emblem *.20 .20*
RA45 PT8 1d Lily *.20 .20*
RA46 PT8 1d Mushroom *.20 .20*
RA47 PT8 1d Swans *.20 .20*
a. Block of 4, #RA44-RA47 *.65 .65*

Nos. RA44-RA47 without silver color exist in perf. & imperf. miniature sheets and sold for 20d. Value for both sheets $3.25.

Obligatory on mail Mar. 1-8.

Red Cross Type of 1993 and

PT9

1994, May 8 Litho. ***Perf. 10***
RA51 PT9 1d shown *.20 .20*
RA52 PT7 1d like #RA41 *.20 .20*
RA53 PT7 1d like #RA39 *.20 .20*
RA54 PT7 1d like #RA33 *.20 .20*
a. Block of 4, #RA51-RA54 *.65 .65*

Nos. RA51-RA54 exist without denomination in perf. & imperf. miniature sheets and sold for 30d each. Value for both sheets $3.75.

Obligatory on mail May 8-15, 1994.

Skopje Earthquake Type of 1993

1994, June 1
RA55 PT4 1d like #RA14 *.45 .45*

Obligatory on mail June 1-7, 1994.

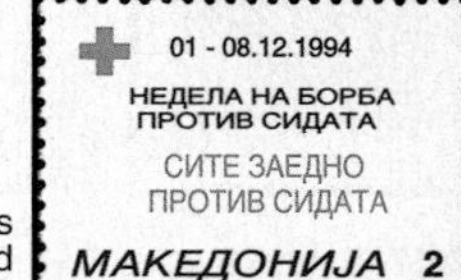

Red Cross Fund PT10

1994, Dec. 1 Litho. ***Perf. 10***
RA56 PT10 2d shown *.20 .20*
RA57 PT10 2d Globe *.20 .20*
RA58 PT10 2d AIDS awareness *.20 .20*
RA59 PT10 2d Condoms *.20 .20*
a. Block of 4, No. RA56-RA59 *.80 .80*

Size: 80x95mm

Imperf

RA60 PT10 40d like RA57 *4.50 4.50*

Country name and value omitted from vignette on No. RA60, which also exists with perf. vignette. Obligatory on mail Dec. 1-8.

Anti-Cancer Week — PT11

Red Cross Fund — PT12

1995, Mar. 1
RA61 PT11 1d shown *.20 .20*
RA62 PT11 1d White lilies *.20 .20*
RA63 PT11 1d Red lilies *.20 .20*
RA64 PT11 1d Red roses *.20 .20*
a. Block of 4, Nos. RA61-RA64 *.70 .70*

Size: 97x74mm

Imperf

RA65 PT11 30d like #RA61, RA64 *3.75 3.75*

Blue inscriptions, country name, and value omitted from vignette on No. RA65, which also exists with perf. vignette. Obligatory on mail Mar. 1-8.

1995, May 8

Designs: No. RA66, Red Cross emblem. No. RA67, Red Cross volunteers holding clipboards. No. RA68, Young volunteers wearing white shirts. No. RA69, RA70, Red Cross, Red Crescent symbols, globe.

RA66 PT12 1d multicolored *.20 .20*
RA67 PT12 1d multicolored *.20 .20*
RA68 PT12 1d multicolored *.20 .20*
RA69 PT12 1d blue & multi *.20 .20*
a. Strip of 4, Nos. RA70-RA73 *.80 .80*

Size: 68x85mm

Imperf

RA70 PT12 30d multicolored *3.75 3.75*

No. RA70 also exists with perf. vignette. Obligatory on mail May 8-15.

Solidarity Week PT13

1995, June 1
RA71 PT13 1d shown *.45 .45*

Size: 85x70

Imperf

RA72 PT13 30d like No. RA75 *3.00 3.00*

No. RA72 also exists with perf. vignette. Obligatory on mail June 1-7.

Robert Koch (1843-1910), Bacteriologist — PT14

1995, Sept. 14 Litho. *Perf. 10*

RA73 PT14 1d shown *.20 .20*

Size: 90x73mm

Imperf

RA74 PT14 30d like No. RA73 *2.50 2.50*

No. RA74 exists with perf. vignette. Obligatory on mail Sept. 14-21.

PT15

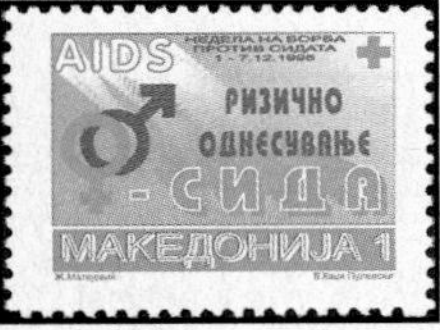

PT16

1995, Oct. 2 Litho. *Die Cut*

Self-Adhesive

RA75 PT15 2d blue violet & red *.45 .45*

Children's Week. Obligatory on mail 10/2-8.

1995, Nov. 1 Litho. *Perf. 10*

RA76 PT16 1d multicolored *.40 .40*

Size: 90x72mm

Imperf

RA77 PT16 30d like #RA76 *2.50 2.50*

Red Cross, AIDS awareness. No. RA77 also exists with perf. vignette. Obligatory on mail Nov. 1-7.

Red Cross PT17

1996, Mar. 1 Litho. *Perf. 10*

RA78 PT17 1d multicolored *.45 .45*

Size: 98x76mm

Imperf

RA79 PT17 30d like #RA78 *3.00 3.00*

No. RA79 also exists with perf. vignette. Obligatory on mail Mar. 1-8.

PT18

Red Cross Week — PT19

Fundamental principles of Red Cross, Red Crescent Societies, inscriptions in: No. RA81, Macedonian. No. RA82, English. No. RA83, French. RA84, Spanish.

1996, May 8 Litho. *Perf. 10*

RA80 PT18 1d multicolored *.20 .20*
RA81 PT19 1d multicolored *.20 .20*
RA82 PT19 1d multicolored *.20 .20*
RA83 PT19 1d multicolored *.20 .20*
RA84 PT19 1d multicolored *.20 .20*
a. Strip of 5, #RA80-RA84 *.65 .65*

Obligatory on mail May 8-15.

Red Cross, Solidarity Week — PT20

1996, June 1 Litho. *Perf. 10*

RA86 PT20 1d multicolored *.25 .25*

No. RA86 exists without country name or denomination in perf. & imperf. miniature sheets and sold for 30d each. Value for both sheets $5.50. Obligatory on mail June 1-7, 1996.

Red Cross, Fight Tuberculosis Week — PT21

1996, Sept. 14 Litho. *Perf. 10*

RA87 PT21 1d multicolored *.65 .65*

Size: 80x90mm

Imperf

RA88 PT21 30d like #RA87 *2.75 2.75*

No. RA88 also exists with perf. vignette. Obligatory on mail Sept. 14-21.

Red Cross, AIDS Awareness PT22

1996, Dec. 6

RA89 PT22 1d multicolored *.40 .40*

Size: 90x73mm

Imperf

RA90 PT22 30d like #RA89 *2.75 2.75*

No. RA90 also exists with perf. vignette. Obligatory on mail Dec. 1-7.

Red Cross, Cancer Week — PT23

Red Cross — PT24

1997, Apr. 1

RA91 PT23 1d Cross in pale org *.35 .35*
a. Cross in red *.70 .70*

No. RA91 obligatory on mail Apr. 1-8. No. RA91a issued 5/8.

1997, May 8

RA92 PT24 1d multicolored *1.75 1.75*

Obligatory on mail May 8-15.

Children's Day — PT25

Red Cross, Anti-Tuberculosis PT26

1997, June 1

RA93 PT25 1d Cross in deep vermilion *.25 .25*
a. Cross in red *.60 .60*

Obligatory on mail June 1-8.

1997, Sept. 14

RA94 PT26 1d multicolored *.30 .30*

Obligatory on mail, Sept. 14-21.

Red Cross — PT27

1997, Dec. 1 Litho. *Perf. 10*

RA95 PT27 1d multicolored *.30 .30*

Obligatory on mail Dec. 1-7.

Red Cross Fight Against Cancer PT28

1998, Mar. 1 *Perf. 13½*

RA96 PT28 1d multicolored *.25 .25*

Obligatory on mail Mar. 1-8.

Red Cross, Humanity PT29

1998, May 8

RA97 PT29 2d multicolored *.25 .25*

Obligatory on mail May 8-15.

Red Cross — PT30

PT31

1998, June 1 Litho. *Perf. 13½*

RA98 PT30 2d multicolored *.25 .25*

Obligatory on mail June 1-7, 1998.

1998, Sept. 14 Litho. *Perf. 13½*

RA99 PT31 2d multicolored *.25 .25*

Fight tuberculosis. Obligatory on mail Sept. 14-21, 1998.

PT32

PT33

1998, Dec. 1
RA100 PT32 2d multicolored .25 .25

AIDS awareness. Obligatory on mail Dec. 1-7, 1998.

1999, Mar. 1 **Litho.** ***Perf. 13¼***
RA101 PT33 2d multi .25 .25

Red Cross fight against cancer. Obligatory on mail Mar. 1-7, 1999.

Red Cross PT34

1999, May 8
RA102 PT34 2d multi .25 .25

Obligatory on mail May 8-15, 1999.

PT35

PT36

1999, June 1
RA103 PT35 2d multi .25 .25

Red Cross, solidarity week. Obligatory on mail June 1-7, 1999.

1999, Sept. 14 **Litho.** ***Perf. 13¼***
RA104 PT36 2d multi .25 .25

Fight tuberculosis. Obligatory on mail Sept. 14-21.

AIDS Awareness PT37

1999, Dec. 1
RA105 PT37 2.50d multi .30 .30

Obligatory on mail Dec. 1-7.

Anti-Cancer Week — PT38

2000, Mar. 1 **Litho.** ***Perf. 13¼***
RA106 PT38 2.50d multi .25 .25

Obligatory on mail Mar. 1-8.

Red Cross PT39

2000, May 8
RA107 PT39 2.50d multi .25 .25

Obligatory on mail May 8-15.

Red Cross — PT40

2000, June 1
RA108 PT40 2.50d multi .25 .25

Obligatory on mail June 1-7.

Red Cross — PT41

2000 Sept. 14 **Litho.** ***Perf. 13¼***
RA109 PT41 3d multi .30 .30

Obligatory on mail Sept. 14-21.

Fight Against AIDS — PT42

2000 Dec. 1
RA110 PT42 3d multi .30 .30

Obligatory on mail Dec. 1-7.

Fight Against Cancer — PT43

2001, Mar. 1 **Litho.** ***Perf. 13¼***
RA111 PT43 3d multi .30 .30

Obligatory on mail Mar. 1-8.

Red Cross PT44

2001, May 8
RA112 PT44 3d multi .30 .30

Obligatory on mail May 8-15.

Red Cross Solidarity Week — PT45

2001, June 1
RA113 PT45 3d multi .30 .30

Obligatory on mail June 1-7.

Fight Against Tuberculosis PT46

2001, Sept. 14
RA114 PT46 3d multi .30 .30

Obligatory on mail Sept. 14-21.

Campaign Against AIDS — PT47

2001, Dec. 1 **Litho.** ***Perf. 13¼***
RA115 PT47 3d multi .30 .30

Obligatory on mail Dec. 1-7.

Campaign Against Cancer PT48

2002, Mar. 1
RA116 PT48 3d multi .30 .30

Obligatory on mail Mar. 1-8.

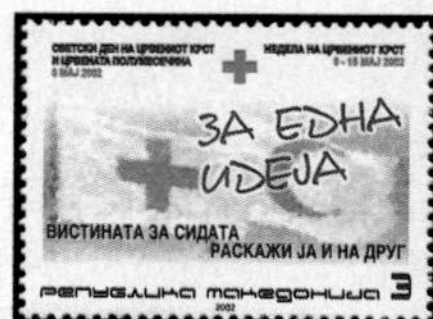

Red Cross Week PT49

2002, May 8 **Litho.** ***Perf. 13¼***
RA117 PT49 3d multi .30 .30

Obligatory on mail May 8-15.

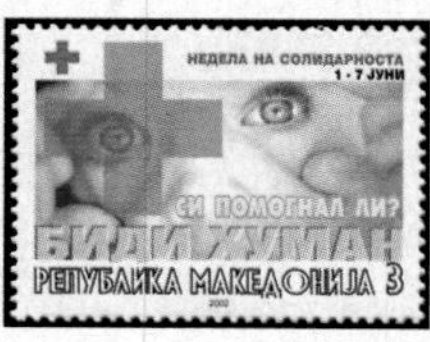

Red Cross Solidarity Week PT50

2002, June 1
RA118 PT50 3d multi .30 .30

Obligatory on mail June 1-7.

Tuberculosis Prevention PT51

2002, Sept. 14
RA119 PT51 3d multi .30 .30

Obligatory on mail Sept. 14-21.

Campaign Against AIDS PT52

2002, Dec. 1
RA120 PT52 3d multi .30 .30

Campaign Against Cancer — PT53

2003, Mar. 1 **Litho.** ***Perf. 13¼***
RA121 PT53 4d multi .30 .30

Obligatory on mail Mar. 1-8.

Campaign Against AIDS — PT54

2003, May 8
RA122 PT54 4d multi .30 .30

Obligatory on mail May 8-15.

Red Cross Solidarity — PT55

2003, June 1 ***Perf. 13¼x13½***

RA123 PT55 4d multi .30 .30

Obligatory on mail June 1-7.

Tuberculosis Prevention PT56

Perf. 13½x13¼

2003, Sept. 14 **Litho.**

RA124 PT56 4d multi .30 .30

Obligatory on mail Sept. 14-21.

Campaign Against AIDS — PT57

2003, Dec. 1 **Litho.** ***Perf. 13¼x13½***

RA125 PT57 4d multi .30 .30

Obligatory on mail Dec. 1-7.

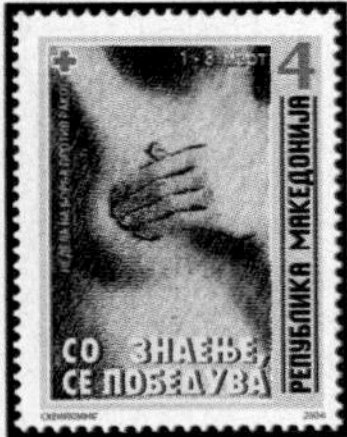

Campaign Against Cancer — PT58

2004, Mar. 1

RA126 PT58 4d multi .30 .30

Obligatory on mail Mar. 1-8.

Red Cross Week — PT59

2004, May 8

RA127 PT59 4d multi .30 .30

Obligatory on mail May 8-15.

Red Cross Solidarity Week — PT60

2004, June 1 **Litho.** ***Perf. 13¼x13½***

RA128 PT60 6d multi .45 .45

Obligatory on mail June 1-7.

Tuberculosis Week — PT61

2004, Sept. 14 ***Perf. 13½x13¼***

RA129 PT61 6d multi .45 .45

Obligatory on mail Sept. 14-21.

Campaign Against AIDS PT62

2004, Dec. 1 **Litho.** ***Perf. 13½x13¼***

RA130 PT62 6d multi .45 .45

Obligatory on mail Dec. 1-7.

Campaign Against Cancer — PT63

2005, Mar. 1 ***Perf. 13¼x13½***

RA131 PT63 6d multi .40 .40

Obligatory on mail Mar. 1-8.

Red Cross PT64

2005, May 8 **Litho.** ***Perf. 13½x13¼***

RA132 PT64 6d multi .40 .40

Obligatory on mail May 8-15.

Campaign Against Tuberculosis — PT65

Perf. 13½x13¼

2005, Sept. 14 **Litho.**

RA133 PT65 6d multi .40 .40

Obligatory on mail Sept. 14-21.

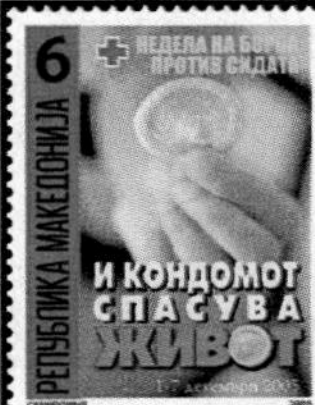

Campaign Against AIDS — PT66

2005, Dec. 1 ***Perf. 13¼x13½***

RA134 PT66 6d multi .40 .40

Obligatory on mail Dec. 1-7.

Campaign Against Breast Cancer — PT67

2006, Mar. 1 **Litho.** ***Perf. 13¼x13½***

RA135 PT67 6d multi .40 .40

Obligatory on mail Mar. 1-7.

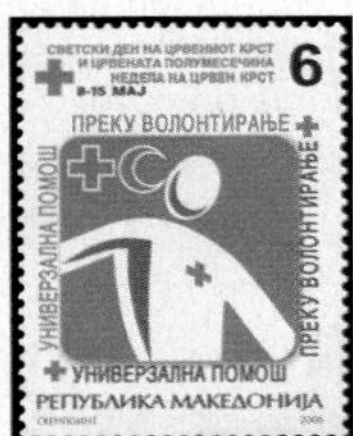

Red Cross Week — PT68

2006, May 18 **Litho.** ***Perf. 13¼x13½***

RA136 PT68 6d multi .40 .40

Obligatory on mail May 8-15.

Campaign Against Tuberculosis — PT69

2006, Sept. 14 ***Perf. 13½x13¼***

RA137 PT69 6d multi .40 .40

Obligatory on mail Sept. 14-21.

Campaign Against AIDS PT70

2006, Dec. 1

RA138 PT70 6d multi .40 .40

Obligatory on mail Dec. 1-7.

Campaign Against Cancer — PT71

2007, Mar. 1 **Litho.** ***Perf. 13¼x13½***

RA139 PT71 6d multi .25 .25

Obligatory on mail Mar. 1-8.

Red Cross Week — PT72

2007, May 8

RA140 PT72 6d multi .30 .30

Obligatory on mail May 8-15.

Campaign Against Tuberculosis PT73

2007, Sept. 14

RA141 PT73 6d multi .30 .30

Obligatory on mail Sept. 14-21.

Campaign Against AIDS PT74

2007, Dec. 1 ***Perf. 13½x13¼***

RA142 PT74 6d multi .30 .30

Obligatory on mail Dec. 1-8.

ISSUED UNDER GERMAN OCCUPATION

During World War II, Yugoslav Macedonia was annexed by Bulgaria. From April 1941 until Sept. 8, 1944, Bulgarian stamps were used in the region. On Sept. 8, 1944, Bulgaria signed an armistace with the Allies, and Macedonia was occupied by German forces. A puppet state was created, which collapsed upon the German withdrawal on Nov. 13.

Catalogue values for all unused stamps in this section are for Never Hinged examples. Hinged stamps are worth approximately 60% of the values shown.

Bulgaria Nos 364//413 Overprinted in Black or Red (R)

Ovpt. I

Ovpt. II

Photo., Typo. (#N1, N2)

1944, Oct. 28 ***Perf. 13***

Overprinted I

N1	A177	1 l on 10st red org (#364)	4.00	*16.00*
N2	A178	3 l on 15st blue (#365) (R)	4.00	*16.00*

Overprinted II

N3	A201	6 l on 10st dk blue (#398) (R)	6.00	*26.00*
N4	A201	9 l on 15st Prus blue (#399) (R)	6.00	*26.00*
N5	A201	9 l on 15st dk ol brn (#400) (R)	9.00	*30.00*
N6	A209	15 l on 4 l ol gray (#411) (R)	30.00	*60.00*
N7	A210	20 l on 7 l dp blue (#412) (R)	45.00	*60.00*
N8	A211	30 l on 14 l fawn (#413)	52.50	*110.00*
		Nos. N1-N8 (8)	156.50	*344.00*

There are two types of both overprints, differing in the font of the "9" in the year date. Values for the more common types are given above.

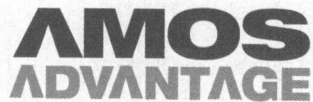

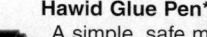

MADAGASCAR

ˌmad-ə-ˈgas-kər

British Consular Mail

Postage stamps issued by the British Consulate in Madagascar were in use for a short period until the British relinquished all claims to this territory in favor of France in return for which France recognized Great Britain's claims in Zanzibar.

See Malagasy Republic for stamps inscribed "Madagascar."

12 Pence = 1 Shilling

> British Consular Mail stamps of Madagascar were gummed only in one corner. Unused values are for stamps without gum. Examples having the original corner gum will command higher prices. Most used examples of these stamps have small faults and values are for stamps in this condition. Used stamps without faults are scarce and are worth more. Used stamps are valued with the commonly used crayon or pen cancellations.

"B C M" and Arms — A1

Handstamped "British Vice-Consulate"

1884 Unwmk. Typo. *Rouletted*

Black Seal Handstamped

1	A1	1p violet	500.	400.
b.	Seal omitted		5,500.	5,500.
2	A1	2p violet	325.	290.
3	A1	3p violet	350.	300.
4	A1	4p violet 1 oz.	4,250.	4,250.
a.	"1 oz." corrected to "4 oz." in mss.		800.	700.
b.	Seal omitted		*5,500.*	5,500.
5	A1	6p violet	450.	*500.*
6	A1	1sh violet	425.	*475.*
7	A1	1sh6p violet	500.	*500.*
8	A1	2sh violet	700.	*700.*
9	A1	1p on 1sh vio		
10	A1	4½ on 1sh vio		
11	A1	6p red	900.	800.

1886

Violet Seal Handstamped

12	A1	4p violet	1,350.	—
13	A1	6p violet	2,400.	—

Handstamped "British Consular Mail" as on A3

Black Seal Handstamped

14	A1	4p violet	1,850.	—

Violet Seal Handstamped

15	A1	4p violet	5,500.	—

The 1, 2, 3 and 4 pence are inscribed "POSTAL PACKET," the other values of the series are inscribed "LETTER."

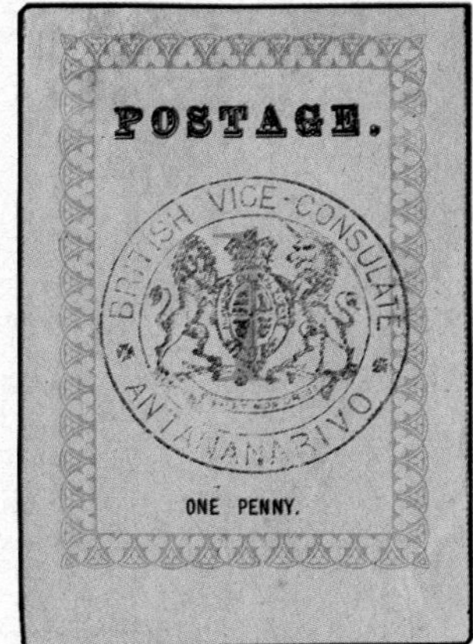

"British Vice-Consulate" — A2

Three types of A2 and A3:
I — "POSTAGE" 29½mm. Periods after "POSTAGE" and value.
II — "POSTAGE" 29½mm. No periods.
III — "POSTAGE" 24½mm. Period after value.

1886

Violet Seal Handstamped

16	A2	1p rose, I	325.	—
a.	Type II		1,050.	—
17	A2	1½p rose, I	1,050.	*875.*
a.	Type II		1,950.	—
18	A2	2p rose, I	350.	—
19	A2	3p rose, I	450.	*375.*
a.	Type II		1,150.	—
20	A2	4p rose, III	500.	—
21	A2	4½p rose, I	550.	*350.*
a.	Type II		1,750.	—
22	A2	6p rose, II	1,350.	—
23	A2	8p rose, I	1,250.	*1,250.*
a.	Type III		600.	—
24	A2	9p rose	1,100.	—
24A	A2	1sh rose, III	—	
24B	A2	1sh6p rose, III	4,250.	—
25	A2	2sh rose, III	2,600.	—

Black Seal Handstamped

Type I

26	A2	1p rose	125.	*150.*
27	A2	1½p rose	2,000.	*1,150.*
28	A2	2p rose	160.	—
29	A2	3p rose	2,000.	*1,100.*
30	A2	4½p rose	1,750.	*575.*
31	A2	8p rose	3,250.	*2,600.*
32	A2	9p rose	3,250.	*2,900.*
32A	A2	2sh rose, III	—	—

"British Consular Mail" — A3

1886

Violet Seal Handstamped

33	A3	1p rose, II	110.	—
34	A3	1½p rose, II	175.	—
35	A3	2p rose, II	185.	—
36	A3	3p rose, II	160.	—
37	A3	4p rose, III	475.	—
38	A3	4½p rose, II	160.	—
39	A3	6p rose, II	375.	—
40	A3	8p rose, III	650.	—
a.	Type I		1,500.	—
41	A3	9p rose, I	300.	—
42	A3	1sh rose, III	1,350.	—
43	A3	1sh6p rose, III	1,500.	—
44	A3	2sh rose, III	1,750.	—

Black Seal Handstamped

45	A3	1p rose, I	90.	—
a.	Type II		90.	*140.*
46	A3	1½p rose, I	95.	—
a.	Type II		87.50	*130.*
47	A3	2p rose, I	115.	—
a.	Type II		82.50	*130.*
48	A3	3p rose, I	110.	*160.*
a.	Type II		95.	*140.*
49	A3	4p rose, III	225.	—
50	A3	4½p rose, I	110.	*150.*
a.	Type II		95.	*140.*
51	A3	6p rose, II	95.	*140.*
52	A3	8p rose, I	140.	—
a.	Type III		750.	—
53	A3	9p rose, I	150.	*210.*
54	A3	1sh rose, III	525.	—
55	A3	1sh6p rose, III	625.	—
56	A3	2sh rose, III	700.	—

Seal Omitted

45b	A3	1p rose, II	3,000.
46b	A3	1½p rose, II	3,000.
48b	A3	3p rose, II	4,500.
49a	A3	4p rose, III	3,500.
50b	A3	4½p rose, II	5,000.
51a	A3	6p rose, II	5,500.
52b	A3	8p rose, III	3,750.
53a	A3	9p rose, I	4,000.
54a	A3	1sh rose, III	4,500.
55a	A3	1sh6p rose, III	4,000.
56a	A3	2sh rose, III	4,500.

Some students of these issues doubt that the 1886 "seal omitted" varieties were regularly issued.

Red Seal Handstamped

57	A3	3p rose, I		*12,000.*
58	A3	4½p rose, I		*7,000.*

MADEIRA

mə-ˈdir-ə

LOCATION — A group of islands in the Atlantic Ocean northwest of Africa
GOVT. — Part of the Republic of Portugal
AREA — 314 sq. mi.
POP. — 150,574 (1900)
CAPITAL — Funchal

These islands are considered an integral part of Portugal and since 1898 postage stamps of Portugal have been in use. See Portugal for issues also inscribed Madeira, starting in 1980.

1000 Reis = 1 Milreis
100 Centavos = 1 Escudo (1925)

> It is recommended that the rare overprinted 1868-81 stamps be purchased accompanied by certificates of authenticity from competent experts.

King Luiz
A1 A2

Stamps of Portugal Overprinted

1868, Jan. 1 Unwmk. *Imperf.*

Black Overprint

2	A1	20r bister	200.00	120.00
a.	Inverted overprint		—	
b.	Rouletted			—
3	A1	50r green	200.00	120.00
4	A1	80r orange	225.00	125.00
a.	Double overprint		—	
5	A1	100r lilac	225.00	125.00
	Nos. 2-5 (4)		850.00	490.00

The 5r black does not exist as a genuinely imperforate original.

Reprints of 1885 are on stout white paper, ungummed. (Also, 5r, 10r and 25r values were overprinted.) Reprints of 1905 are on ordinary white paper with shiny gum and have a wide "D" and "R." Value, $12 each.

Lozenge Perf.

2c	A1	20r		—
3a	A1	50r		—
4b	A1	80r		—
5a	A1	100r		—

Overprinted in Red or Black

1868-70 *Perf. 12½*

6	A1	5r black (R)	55.00	37.50
8	A1	10r yellow	90.00	80.00
9	A1	20r bister	140.00	110.00
10	A1	25r rose	57.50	12.00
a.	Inverted overprint			
11	A1	50r green	200.00	140.00
a.	Inverted overprint		—	
12	A1	80r orange	180.00	140.00
13	A1	100r lilac	190.00	140.00
a.	Inverted overprint		—	
14	A1	120r blue	110.00	80.00
15	A1	240r violet ('70)	500.00	425.00
	Nos. 6-15 (9)		1,522.	1,164.

Two types of 5r differ in the position of the "5" at upper right.

The reprints are on stout white paper, ungummed, with rough perforation 13½, and on thin white paper with shiny white gum and clean-cut perforation 13½. The overprint has the wide "D" and "R" and the first reprints included the 5r with both black and red overprint. Value $10 each.

Overprinted in Red or Black

1871-80 *Perf. 12½, 13½*

16	A2	5r black (R)	11.00	8.00
a.	Inverted overprint		—	
b.	Double overprint		55.00	55.00
c.	Perf. 14		90.00	55.00
18	A2	10r yellow	35.00	22.50
19	A2	10r bl grn ('79)	140.00	110.00
a.	Perf. 13½		160.00	140.00
20	A2	10r yel grn ('80)	65.00	52.50
21	A2	15r brn ('75)	19.00	11.50
22	A2	20r bister	37.50	22.50
23	A2	25r rose	13.50	4.50
a.	Inverted overprint		40.00	40.00
b.	Double overprint		40.00	40.00
24	A2	50r green ('72)	67.50	30.00
a.	Double overprint		—	
b.	Inverted overprint		200.00	200.00
25	A2	50r blue ('80)	125.00	55.00
26	A2	80r orange ('72)	77.50	67.50
27	A2	100r pale lil ('73)	90.00	60.00
a.	Perf. 14		200.00	85.00
b.	Perf. 13½		160.00	75.00
28	A2	120r blue	110.00	80.00
29	A2	150r blue ('76)	160.00	140.00
a.	Perf. 13½		175.00	150.00
30	A2	150r yel ('79)	300.00	240.00
31	A2	240r vio ('74)	700.00	500.00
32	A2	300r vio ('76)	75.00	67.50
	Nos. 16-32 (16)		2,026.	1,471.

There are two types of the overprint, the second one having a broad "D."

The reprints have the same characteristics as those of the 1868-70 issues.

A3

A4

King Luiz — A5

1880-81

33	A3	5r black	35.00	21.00
34	A4	25r pearl gray	40.00	21.00
a.	Inverted overprint		75.00	75.00
35	A5	25r lilac	42.50	11.00
a.	25r purple brown		32.50	11.00
b.	25r gray		35.00	10.00
	Nos. 33-35 (3)		117.50	53.00

Nos. 33, 34 and 35 have been reprinted on stout white paper, ungummed, and the last three on thin white paper with shiny white gum. The perforations are as previously described.

Common Design Types pictured following the introduction.

Vasco da Gama Issue

Common Design Types

1898, Apr. 1 Engr. *Perf. 14-15*

37	CD20	2½r blue grn	2.40	1.25
38	CD21	5r red	2.40	1.25
39	CD22	10r red violet	3.00	1.50
40	CD23	25r yel green	2.75	1.25
41	CD24	50r dk blue	8.50	3.25
42	CD25	75r vio brown	10.00	7.00
43	CD26	100r bister brn	10.00	7.00
44	CD27	150r bister	15.00	11.50
	Nos. 37-44 (8)		54.05	34.00

Nos. 37-44 with "REPUBLICA" overprint and surcharges are listed as Portugal Nos. 199-206.

Ceres — A6

1928, May 1 Engr. *Perf. 13½*

Value Typographed in Black

45	A6	3c deep violet	.30	*.60*
46	A6	4c orange	.30	*.60*
47	A6	5c light blue	.30	*.60*
48	A6	6c brown	.30	*.60*
49	A6	10c red	.30	*.60*
50	A6	15c yel green	.30	*.60*
51	A6	16c red brown	.35	*.60*
52	A6	25c violet rose	.75	.60
53	A6	32c blue grn	.75	.60
54	A6	40c yel brown	1.50	*1.75*
55	A6	50c slate	1.50	*1.75*
56	A6	64c Prus blue	1.50	*3.00*
57	A6	80c dk brown	1.50	*5.00*
58	A6	96c carmine rose	7.50	*3.00*
59	A6	1e black	1.25	3.00
a.		Value omitted	42.50	*45.00*
		Never hinged	75.00	
60	A6	1.20e light rose	1.25	*3.00*
61	A6	1.60e ultra	1.25	*3.00*
62	A6	2.40e yellow	2.00	*3.50*
63	A6	3.36e dull green	3.00	*5.75*
64	A6	4.50e brown red	4.00	*9.00*
65	A6	7e dark blue	5.00	*17.50*
		Nos. 45-65 (21)	34.90	*64.65*

It was obligatory to use these stamps in place of those in regular use on May 1, June 5, July 1 and Dec. 31, 1928, Jan. 1 and 31, May 1 and June 5, 1929. The amount obtained from this sale was donated to a fund for building a museum.

Less than very fine examples sell for much less.

NEWSPAPER STAMP

Numeral of Value — N1

Newspaper Stamp of Portugal Overprinted in Black

Perf. 12½, 13½

1876, July 1 Unwmk.

P1	N1	2½r olive	11.00	4.25
a.		Inverted overprint	30.00	

The reprints have the same papers, gum, perforations and overprint as the reprints of the regular issues.

POSTAL TAX STAMPS

Pombal Commemorative Issue

Common Design Types

1925 Unwmk. Engr. *Perf. 12½*

RA1	CD28	15c gray & black	.60	.65
RA2	CD29	15c gray & black	.60	.65
RA3	CD30	15c gray & black	.60	.65
		Nos. RA1-RA3 (3)	1.80	1.95

POSTAL TAX DUE STAMPS

Pombal Commemorative Issue

Common Design Types

1925 Unwmk. *Perf. 12½*

RAJ1	CD28	30c gray & black	.85	3.50
RAJ2	CD29	30c gray & black	.85	3.50
RAJ3	CD30	30c gray & black	.85	3.50
		Nos. RAJ1-RAJ3 (3)	2.55	10.50

MALAGASY REPUBLIC

ˌmal-lə-ˈgə-sē

Madagascar (French)

Malagasy Democratic Republic

Republic of Madagascar

LOCATION — Large island off the coast of southeastern Africa
GOVT. — Republic
AREA — 226,658 sq. mi.
POP. — 14,062,000 (1995 est.)
CAPITAL — Antananarivo

Madagascar became a French protectorate in 1885 and a French colony in 1896 following several years of dispute among France, Great Britain, and the native government. The colony administered the former protectorates of Anjouan, Grand Comoro, Mayotte, Diego-Suarez, Nossi-Be and Sainte-Marie de Madagascar. Previous issues of postage stamps are found under these individual headings. The Malagasy Republic succeeded the colony in 1958 and became the Democratic Republic of Malagasy in 1975. The official name was again changed in 1993 to Republic of Madagascar.

For British Consular Mail stamps of 1884-1886, see Madagascar.

100 Centimes = 1 Franc
100 Centimes = 1 Ariary (1976)

See France No. 2767 for stamp inscribed "Madagascar."

Catalogue values for unused stamps in this country are for Never Hinged items, beginning with Scott 241 in the regular postage section, Scott B15 in the semi-postal section, Scott C37 in the airpost section, and Scott J31 in the postage due section.

French Offices in Madagascar

The general issues of French Colonies were used in these offices in addition to the stamps listed here.

Stamps of French Colonies Surcharged in Black:

a

b

5

c

1889 Unwmk. *Perf. 14x13½*

Overprint Type "a"

1	A9	05c on 10c blk, *lav*	*650.*	*190.*
a.		Inverted surcharge	*1,500.*	*1,100.*
2	A9	05c on 25c blk, *rose*	*650.*	*190.*
a.		Inverted surcharge	*1,500.*	*1,100.*
b.		25c on 10c lav (error)	*9,000.*	*7,250.*
3	A9	25c on 40c red, *straw*	*575.*	*160.*
a.		Inverted surcharge	*1,200.*	*925.*

1891

Overprint Type "b"

4	A9	05c on 40c red, *straw*	*200.00*	*90.00*
5	A9	15c on 25c blk, *rose*	*200.00*	*100.00*
a.		Surcharge vertical	*210.00*	*125.00*

Overprint Type "c"

6	A9	5c on 10c blk, *lav*	*225.00*	*110.00*
a.		Double surcharge	*750.00*	*725.00*
7	A9	5c on 25c blk, *rose*	*240.00*	*125.00*

See Senegal Nos. 4, 8 for similar surcharge on 20c, 30c.

Forgeries of Nos. 1-7 exist.

A4

1891 Type-set *Imperf.*

Without Gum

8	A4	5c blk, *green*	150.00	30.00
9	A4	10c blk, *lt bl*	100.00	30.00
10	A4	15c ultra, *pale bl*	100.00	32.50
11	A4	25c brn, *buff*	21.00	14.00
12	A4	1fr blk, *yellow*	1,000.	275.00
13	A4	5fr vio & blk, *lil*	2,000.	1,000.

Ten varieties of each. Nos. 12-13 have been extensively forged.

Stamps of France 1876-90, Overprinted in Red or Black

1895 *Perf. 14x13½*

14	A15	5c grn, *grnsh* (R)	15.00	7.25
15	A15	10c blk, *lav* (R)	47.50	28.00
16	A15	15c bl (R)	70.00	18.00
17	A15	25c blk, *rose* (R)	100.00	20.00
18	A15	40c red, *straw* (Bk)	80.00	28.00
19	A15	50c rose, *rose* (Bk)	100.00	42.50
20	A15	75c dp vio, *org* (R)	110.00	50.00
21	A15	1fr brnz grn, *straw* (Bk)	130.00	65.00
22	A15	5fr vio, *lav* (Bk)	175.00	80.00
		Nos. 14-22 (9)	827.50	338.75

Majunga Issue

Stamps of France, 1876-86, Surcharged with New Value

1895

Manuscript Surcharge in Red

22A	A15	0,15c on 25c blk, *rose*		*6,500.*
22B	A15	0,15c on 1fr brnz grn, *straw*		*5,250.*

Handstamped in Black

22C	A15	15c on 25c blk, *rose*		*6,000.*
22D	A15	15c on 1fr brnz grn, *straw*		*5,500.*

On most of #22C and all of #22D the manuscript surcharge of #22A-22B was washed off. Three types of "15" were used for No. 22C.

Stamps of France, 1876-84, Surcharged with New Value

1896

23	A15	5c on 1c blk, *bl*	*5,500.*	*2,100.*
24	A15	15c on 2c brn, *buff*	*2,100.*	*875.*
25	A15	25c on 3c gray, *grysh*	*2,750.*	*950.*
26	A15	25c on 4c cl, *lav*	*5,500.*	*1,600.*
27	A15	25c on 40c red, *straw*	*1,350.*	*700.*

The oval of the 5c and 15c surcharges is smaller than that of the 25c, and it does not extend beyond the edges of the stamp as the 25c surcharge does.

Excellent counterfeits of the surcharges on Nos. 22A to 27 exist.

Issues of the Colony

Navigation and Commerce — A7

1896-1906 Typo. *Perf. 14x13½*

Colony Name in Blue or Carmine

28	A7	1c blk, *lil bl*	1.00	.80
29	A7	2c brn, *buff*	1.75	.95
a.		Name in blue black	3.75	3.75
30	A7	4c claret, *lav*	1.90	1.25
31	A7	5c grn, *grnsh*	6.50	1.25
32	A7	5c yel grn ('01)	1.60	.70
33	A7	10c blk, *lav*	6.50	1.75
34	A7	10c red ('00)	2.50	.70
35	A7	15c blue, quadrille paper	12.50	1.25
36	A7	15c gray ('00)	2.25	1.25
37	A7	20c red, *grn*	6.25	1.60
38	A7	25c blk, *rose*	9.00	4.00
39	A7	25c blue ('00)	21.50	20.00
40	A7	30c brn, *bis*	8.00	3.00
41	A7	35c blk, *yel* ('06)	36.00	6.00
42	A7	40c red, *straw*	9.50	4.75
43	A7	50c car, *rose*	11.50	2.40
44	A7	50c brn, *az* ('00)	27.50	25.00
45	A7	75c dp vio, *org*	5.00	3.75
46	A7	1fr brnz grn, *straw*	12.50	2.25
a.		Name in blue ('99)	24.00	18.50
47	A7	5fr red lil, *lav* ('99)	32.50	27.50
		Nos. 28-47 (20)	215.75	110.15

Perf. 13½x14 stamps are counterfeits.

For surcharges see Nos. 48-55, 58-60, 115-118, 127-128.

Nos. 32, 43, 44 and 46, affixed to pressboard with animals printed on the back, were used as emergency currency in the Comoro Islands in 1920.

Surcharged in Black

1902

48	A7	05c on 50c car, *rose*	6.00	4.00
a.		Inverted surcharge	90.00	90.00
49	A7	10c on 5fr red lil, *lav*	19.50	14.50
a.		Inverted surcharge	110.00	110.00
50	A7	15c on 1fr ol grn, *straw*	8.00	6.00
a.		Inverted surcharge	97.50	97.50
b.		Double surcharge	290.00	290.00
		Nos. 48-50 (3)	33.50	24.50

Surcharged in Black

51	A7	0,01 on 2c brn, *buff*	8.00	8.00
a.		Inverted surcharge	57.50	57.50
b.		"00,1" instead of "0,01"	115.00	115.00
c.		As "b" inverted	—	—
d.		Comma omitted	160.00	160.00
e.		Name in blue black	8.25	8.25
52	A7	0,05 on 30c brn, *bis*	8.50	8.50
a.		Inverted surcharge	57.50	57.50
b.		"00,5" instead of "0,05"	72.50	72.50
c.		As "b" inverted	350.00	350.00
d.		Comma omitted	160.00	160.00
53	A7	0,10 on 50c car, *rose*	8.00	8.00
a.		Inverted surcharge	57.50	57.50
b.		Comma omitted	160.00	160.00
54	A7	0,15 on 75c vio, *org*	6.25	6.25
a.		Inverted surcharge	62.50	62.50
b.		Comma omitted	160.00	160.00
55	A7	0,15 on 1fr ol grn, *straw*	12.50	12.50
a.		Inverted surcharge	80.00	80.00
b.		Comma omitted	1,050.	1,050.

Surcharged On Stamps of Diego-Suarez

56	A11	0,05 on 30c brn, *bis*	132.50	110.00
a.		"00,5" instead of "0,05"	775.00	775.00
b.		Inverted surcharge	1,050.	1,050.
57	A11	0,10 on 50c car, *rose*	*4,100.*	*4,100.*
		Nos. 51-55 (5)	43.25	43.25

Counterfeits of Nos. 56-57 exist with surcharge both normal and inverted.

Surcharged in Black

58	A7	0,01 on 2c brn, *buff*	8.00	8.00
a.		Inverted surcharge	57.50	57.50
b.		Comma omitted	160.00	160.00
59	A7	0,05 on 30c brn, *bis*	7.25	7.25
a.		Inverted surcharge	57.50	57.50
b.		Comma omitted	160.00	160.00
60	A7	0,10 on 50c car, *rose*	6.25	6.25
a.		Inverted surcharge	57.50	57.50
b.		Comma omitted	160.00	160.00
		Nos. 58-60 (3)	21.50	21.50

Surcharged On Stamps of Diego-Suarez

61 A11 0,05 on 30c brn, *bis* 110.00 110.00
a. Inverted surcharge 1,050. 1,050.
62 A11 0,10 on 50c car, *rose* *4,100.* *4,100.*

BISECTS

During alleged stamp shortages at several Madagascar towns in 1904, it is claimed that bisects were used. After being affixed to letters, these bisects were handstamped "Affranchissement - exceptionnel - (faute de timbres)" and other inscriptions of similar import. The stamps bisected were 10c, 20c, 30c and 50c denominations of Madagascar type A7 and Diego-Suarez type A11. The editors believe these provisionals were unnecessary and speculative.

Zebu, Traveler's Tree and Lemur — A8

Transportation by Sedan Chair — A9

1903 Engr. *Perf. 11½*

63 A8 1c dk violet 1.00 1.00
a. On bluish paper 6.75 5.50
64 A8 2c olive brn 1.00 1.00
65 A8 4c brown 1.10 1.10
66 A8 5c yellow grn 5.75 1.40
67 A8 10c red 10.00 1.00
68 A8 15c carmine 14.00 1.25
a. On bluish paper *140.00* *140.00*
69 A8 20c orange 4.75 2.25
70 A8 25c dull blue 25.00 4.25
71 A8 30c pale red 36.00 13.50
72 A8 40c gray vio 25.00 5.00
73 A8 50c brown org 45.00 24.00
74 A8 75c orange yel 55.00 25.00
75 A8 1fr dp green 55.00 26.00
76 A8 2fr slate 70.00 27.50
77 A8 5fr gray black 72.50 *80.00*
Nos. 63-77 (15) 421.10 214.25

Nos. 63-77 exist imperf. Value of set, $600.
For surcharges see Nos. 119-124, 129.

1908-28 Typo. *Perf. 13½x14*

79 A9 1c violet & ol .20 .20
80 A9 2c red & ol .20 .20
81 A9 4c ol brn & brn .20 .20
82 A9 5c bl grn & ol .85 .20
83 A9 5c blk & rose ('22) .20 .20
84 A9 10c rose & brown .85 .20
85 A9 10c bl grn & ol grn ('22) .50 .30
86 A9 10c org brn & vio ('25) .20 .20
87 A9 15c dl vio & rose ('16) .20 .20
88 A9 15c dl grn & lt grn ('27) .40 .35
89 A9 15c dk bl & rose red ('28) 1.40 .80
90 A9 20c org & brn .45 .25
91 A9 25c blue & blk 2.50 .60
92 A9 25c vio & blk ('22) .25 .20
93 A9 30c brown & blk 2.50 1.10
94 A9 30c rose red & brn ('22) .45 .30
95 A9 30c grn & red vio ('25) .40 .20
96 A9 30c dp grn & yel grn ('27) 1.25 .80
97 A9 35c red & black 1.75 .90
98 A9 40c vio brn & blk 1.00 .50
99 A9 45c bl grn & blk .80 .50
100 A9 45c red & ver ('25) .40 .35
101 A9 45c gray lil & mag ('27) 1.25 .80
102 A9 50c violet & blk .85 .50
103 A9 50c blue & blk ('22) .75 .50
104 A9 50c blk & org ('25) .80 .20
105 A9 60c vio, *pnksh* ('25) .60 .50
106 A9 65c black & bl ('25) .80 .70
107 A9 75c rose red & blk .80 .50
108 A9 85c grn & ver ('25) 1.25 .80
109 A9 1fr brown & ol .80 .50
110 A9 1fr dull blue ('25) .95 .95
111 A9 1fr rose & grn ('28) 5.25 4.25
112 A9 1.10fr bis & bl grn ('28) 1.75 1.75
113 A9 2fr blue & olive 3.50 1.40
114 A9 5fr vio & vio brn 12.00 5.25
Nos. 79-114 (36) 48.30 27.35

75c violet on pinkish stamps of type A9 are No. 138 without surcharge.

For surcharges and overprints see Nos. 125-126, 130-146, 178-179, B1, 212-214.

Preceding Issues Surcharged in Black or Carmine

1912, Nov. *Perf. 14x13½*

115 A7 5c on 15c gray (C) 1.00 1.00
116 A7 5c on 20c red, *grn* .90 .90
a. Inverted surcharge 125.00
117 A7 5c on 30c brn, *bis* (C) 1.00 1.00
118 A7 10c on 75c vio, *org* 8.50 8.50
a. Double surcharge 250.00
119 A8 5c on 2c ol brn (C) .50 .50
120 A8 5c on 20c org .80 .80
121 A8 5c on 30c pale red 1.00 1.00
122 A8 10c on 40c gray vio (C) 1.40 1.40
123 A8 10c on 50c brn org 2.75 2.75
124 A8 10c on 75c org yel 5.25 5.25
a. Inverted surcharge 190.00
Nos. 115-124 (10) 23.10 23.10

Two spacings between the surcharged numerals are found on Nos. 115 to 118. For detailed listings, see the *Scott Classic Specialized Catalogue of Stamps and Covers.*

Stamps of Anjouan, Grand Comoro Island, Mayotte and Mohéli with similar surcharges were also available for use in Madagascar and the entire Comoro archipelago.

Preceding Issues Surcharged in Red or Black

g

h

1921

On Nos. 98 & 107

125 A9 (g) 30c on 40c (R) 1.75 1.75
126 A9 (g) 60c on 75c 2.75 2.75

On Nos. 45 & 47

127 A7 (g) 60c on 75c (R) 6.50 6.50
a. Inverted surcharge 175.00 175.00
128 A7 (h) 1fr on 5fr .75 .75

On No. 77

129 A8 (h) 1fr on 5fr (R) 70.00 70.00
Nos. 125-129 (5) 81.75 81.75

Stamps and Type of 1908-16 Surcharged in Black or Red

130 A9 1c on 15c dl vio & rose .70 .70
131 A9 25c on 35c red & blk 5.00 5.00
132 A9 25c on 35c red & blk (R) 15.00 15.00
133 A9 25c on 40c brn & blk 4.25 4.25
134 A9 25c on 45c grn & blk 2.75 2.75
Nos. 130-134 (5) 27.70 27.70
Nos. 125-134 (10) 109.45 109.45

Stamps and Type of 1908-28 Surcharged with New Value and Bars

1922-27

135 A9 25c on 15c dl vio & rose .25 .20
a. Double surcharge 72.50
136 A9 25c on 2fr bl & ol .30 .20
137 A9 25c on 5fr vio & vio brn .55 .20
138 A9 60c on 75c vio, *pnksh* .45 .35
139 A9 65c on 75c rose red & blk .80 .80
140 A9 85c on 45c bl grn & blk 1.25 1.00
141 A9 90c on 75c dl red & rose red .80 .80
142 A9 1.25fr on 1fr lt bl (R) .60 .25
143 A9 1.50fr on 1fr dp bl & dl bl .60 .25
144 A9 3fr on 5fr grn & vio 1.60 1.00
145 A9 10fr on 5fr org & rose lil 7.50 4.75
146 A9 20fr on 5fr rose & sl bl 8.50 6.75
Nos. 135-146 (12) 23.20 16.55

Years of issue: #138, 1922; #136, 137, 1924; #135, 139-140, 1925; #142, 1926; #141, 142-146, 1927.

See Nos. 178-179.

Sakalava Chief — A10

Hova Woman — A12

Hova with Oxen A11

Bétsiléo Woman A13

Perf. 13½x14, 14x13½

1930-44 Typo.

147 A11 1c dk bl & bl grn ('33) .20 .20
148 A10 2c brn red & dk brn .20 .20
149 A10 4c dk brn & vio .20 .20
150 A11 5c lt grn & red .25 .20
151 A12 10c ver & dp grn .40 .20
152 A13 15c dp red .25 .20
153 A11 20c yel brn & dk bl .25 .20
154 A12 25c vio & dk brn .25 .20
155 A13 30c Prus blue .65 .45
156 A10 40c grn & red .75 .50
157 A13 45c dull violet .90 .55
158 A11 65c ol grn & vio 1.10 .80
159 A13 75c dk brown .85 .50
160 A11 90c brn red & dk red 1.40 .90
161 A12 1fr yel brn & dk bl 1.75 1.10
162 A12 1fr dk red & car rose ('38) .95 .90
163 A12 1.25fr dp bl & dk brn ('33) 1.60 .90
164 A10 1.50fr dk & dp bl 5.50 1.10
165 A10 1.50fr brn & dk red ('38) .75 .50
165A A10 1.50fr dk red & brn ('44) .50 .50
166 A10 1.75fr dk brn & dk red ('33) 4.25 1.60
167 A10 5fr vio & dk brn 1.25 .70
168 A10 20fr yel brn & dk bl 2.00 1.75
Nos. 147-168 (23) 26.20 14.35

For surcharges and overprints see #211, 215, 217-218, 222-223, 228-229, 233, 235, 239, 257 and note after #B10.

Common Design Types pictured following the introduction.

Colonial Exposition Issue
Common Design Types

1931 Engr. *Perf. 12½*
Name of Country in Black

169 CD70 40c deep green 1.40 1.00
170 CD71 50c violet 2.00 1.25
171 CD72 90c red orange 2.00 1.25
172 CD73 1.50fr dull blue 2.50 1.50
Nos. 169-172 (4) 7.90 5.00

General Joseph Simon Galliéni — A14

1931 Engr. *Perf. 14*
Size: 21½x34½mm

173 A14 1c ultra .50 .45
174 A14 50c orange brn 1.40 .35
175 A14 2fr deep red 5.75 4.25
176 A14 3fr emerald 4.75 2.50
177 A14 10fr dp orange 4.00 2.50
Nos. 173-177 (5) 16.40 10.05

See Nos. 180-190. For overprints and surcharges see Nos. 216, 219, 221, 224, 232, 258.

Nos. 113 and 109 Surcharged

1932 *Perf. 13½x14*

178 A9 25c on 2fr bl & ol .75 .50
179 A9 50c on 1fr brn & ol .75 .50

No. 178 has numerals in thick block letters. No. 136 has thin shaded numerals.

Galliéni Type of 1931

1936-40 Photo. *Perf. 13½, 13x13½*
Size: 21x34mm

180 A14 3c sapphire ('40) .25 .20
181 A14 45c brt green ('40) .50 .40
182 A14 50c yellow brown .25 .20
183 A14 60c brt red lil ('40) .40 .20
184 A14 70c brt rose ('40) .60 .40
185 A14 90c copper brn ('39) .50 .40
186 A14 1.40fr org yel ('40) .90 .50
187 A14 1.60fr purple ('40) .90 .60
188 A14 2fr dk carmine .50 .20
189 A14 3fr green 4.50 2.25
190 A14 3fr olive blk ('39) .90 .70
Nos. 180-190 (11) 10.20 6.05

For overprint see note after #B10.

Paris International Exposition Issue
Common Design Types

1937, Apr. 15 Engr. *Perf. 13*

191 CD74 20c dp violet .95 .95
192 CD75 30c dk green .95 .95
193 CD76 40c car rose 1.00 1.00
194 CD77 50c dk brn & blk 1.40 1.40
195 CD78 90c red 1.40 1.40
196 CD79 1.50fr ultra 1.40 1.40
Nos. 191-196 (6) 7.10 7.10

Colonial Arts Exhibition Issue
Common Design Type
Souvenir Sheet

1937 *Imperf.*

197 CD74 3fr orange red 5.00 *5.50*

Jean Laborde A15

1938-40 *Perf. 13*

198 A15 35c green .65 .40
199 A15 55c dp purple .65 .40
200 A15 65c orange red .90 .40

201 A15 80c violet brn .65 .40
202 A15 1fr rose car .90 .40
203 A15 1.25fr rose car ('39) .40 .20
204 A15 1.75fr dk ultra 1.75 .70
205 A15 2.15fr yel brn 2.50 1.75
206 A15 2.25fr dk ultra ('39) .60 .50
207 A15 2.50fr blk brn ('40) .65 .50
208 A15 10fr dk green ('40) 1.25 .80
Nos. 198-208 (11) 10.90 6.45

Nos. 198-202, 204, 205 commemorate the 60th anniv. of the death of Jean Laborde, explorer.

For overprints and surcharges see Nos. 220, 225-227, 230-231, 234, 236-237.

New York World's Fair Issue

Common Design Type

1939, May 10 Engr. *Perf. 12½x12*
209 CD82 1.25fr car lake 1.00 1.00
210 CD82 2.25fr ultra 1.10 1.10

For surcharge see No. 240.

Porters Carrying Man in Chair, and Marshal Petain — A15a

1941 Engr. *Perf. 12x12½*
210A A15a 1fr bister brn .75
210B A15a 2.50fr blue .75

Nos. 210A-210B were issued by the Vichy government and were not placed on sale in the colony.

For overprints see #B13-B14.

Type of 1930-44 Surcharged in Black with New Value

1942 *Perf. 14x13½*
211 A11 50c on 65c dk brn & mag 2.25 .50

French Explorers de Hell, Passot & Jehenne — A15b

1942 Engr. *Perf. 13x13½*
211A A15b 1.50fr blue & red brn 1.10

Centenary of French colonies of Mayotte and Nossi Bé.

No. 211A was issued by the Vichy government in France, but was not placed on sale in Madagascar.

Nos. 143, 145-146 with Additional Overprint in Red or Black

1942 Unwmk. *Perf. 14x13½*
212 A9 1.50fr on 1fr (R) 1.75 1.75
213 A9 10fr on 5fr (Bk) 10.00 10.00
214 A9 20fr on 5fr (R) 12.50 12.50

Stamps of 1930-40 Overprinted Like Nos. 212-214 in Black or Red or:

215 A10 2c brn red & dk brn 1.10 1.10
216 A14 3c sapphire (R) 115.00 115.00
217 A13 15c deep red 10.00 10.00
218 A11 65c dk brn & mag .80 .80
219 A14 70c brt rose 1.10 1.10
220 A15 80c violet brn 3.25 3.25
221 A14 1.40fr orange yel 1.40 1.40
222 A10 1.50fr dk bl & dp bl (R) 2.50 2.25
223 A10 1.50fr brn & dk red 2.75 2.75
224 A14 1.60fr purple 1.40 1.40
225 A15 2.25fr dk ultra (R) 1.00 1.00
226 A15 2.50fr black brn (R) 5.00 5.000
227 A15 10fr dk green 6.25 6.25
228 A10 20fr yel brn & dk bl (R) *675.00 750.00*

Stamps of 1930-40 Surcharged in Black or Red

229 A11 5c on 1c dk bl & bl grn .65 .65
230 A15 10c on 55c dp pur 1.60 1.60
231 A15 30c on 65c org red 1.00 1.00
232 A14 50c on 90c cop brn 1.00 1.00
233 A12 1fr on 1.25fr dp bl & dk brn 3.25 3.25
234 A15 1fr on 1.25fr rose car 12.50 12.50
235 A10 1.50fr on 1.75fr dk brn & dk red .95 .95
236 A15 1.50fr on 1.75fr ultra (R) .95 .95
237 A15 2fr on 2.15fr yel brn 1.60 1.60

No. 211 with additional Overprint Like Nos. 217-218 in Black

239 A11 50c on 65c dk brn & mag .50 .50

New York World's Fair Stamp Overprinted Like #217-218 in Red

Perf. 12½x12
240 CD82 2.25fr ultra 1.00 1.00
Nos. 212-227,229-240 (27) 200.80 200.55

Catalogue values for unused stamps in this section, from this point to the end of the section, are for Never Hinged items.

Traveler's Tree — A16

1943 Unwmk. Photo. *Perf. 14x14½*
241 A16 5c ol gray .20 .20
242 A16 10c pale rose vio .20 .20
243 A16 25c emerald .20 .20
244 A16 30c dp orange .20 .20
245 A16 40c slate bl .20 .20
246 A16 80c dk red brn .20 .20
247 A16 1fr dull blue .20 .20
248 A16 1.50fr crim rose .35 .30
249 A16 2fr dull yel .35 .30
250 A16 2.50fr brt ultra .35 .30
251 A16 4fr aqua & red .55 .45
252 A16 5fr green & blk .55 .45
253 A16 10fr sal pink & dk bl .95 .75
254 A16 20fr dl vio & brn 1.10 .90
Nos. 241-254 (14) 5.60 4.85

For surcharges see Nos. 255-256, 261-268.

Types of 1930-44 without "RF"

1943-44
254A A11 20c yel brn & dk bl .40
254B A14 60c lilac rose .65
254C A12 1fr dk red & car rose 1.40
254D A10 1.50fr brn & dk red .95
254E A10 5fr vio & dk brn 2.50
Nos. 254A-254E (5) 5.90

On type A10, the two panels at the top of the frame have been reversed, with the value at the left and a blank (RF removed) panel at right.

Nos. 254A-254E were issued by the Vichy government in France, but were not placed on sale in Madagascar.

Nos. 241 and 242 Surcharged with New Values and Bars in Red or Blue

1944
255 A16 1.50fr on 5c (R) .65 .55
256 A16 1.50fr on 10c (Bl) 1.00 .85

Nos. 229 and 224 Surcharged with New Values and Bars in Red or Black

Perf. 14x13½, 14
257 A11 50c on 5c on 1c (R) .85 .70
258 A14 1.50fr on 1.60fr (Bk) 1.10 .95
Nos. 255-258 (4) 3.60 3.05

Eboue Issue

Common Design Type

1945 Engr. *Perf. 13*
259 CD91 2fr black .60 .50
260 CD91 25fr Prus green 1.10 .95

Nos. 241, 243 and 250 Surcharged with New Values and Bars in Carmine or Black

1945 *Perf. 14x14½*
261 A16 50c on 5c ol gray (C) .40 .35
262 A16 60c on 5c ol gray (C) .60 .50
263 A16 70c on 5c ol gray (C) .60 .50
264 A16 1.20fr on 5c ol gray (C) .60 .50
265 A16 2.40fr on 25c emer .60 .50
266 A16 3fr on 25c emer .60 .50
267 A16 4.50fr on 25c emer .85 .70
268 A16 15fr on 2.50fr brt ultra (C) .85 .70
Nos. 261-268 (8) 5.10 4.25

Southern Dancer — A17

Gen. J. S. Galliéni — A20

Herd of Zebus A18

Sakalava Man and Woman A19

Betsimisaraka Mother and Child — A21

General Jacques C. R. A. Duchesne A22

Marshal Joseph J. C. Joffre A23

Perf. 13x13½, 13½x13

1946 Photo. Unwmk.
269 A17 10c green .20 .20
270 A17 30c orange .20 .20
271 A17 40c brown ol .20 .20
272 A17 50c violet brn .20 .20
273 A18 60c dp ultra .25 .20
274 A18 80c blue grn .40 .20
275 A19 1fr brown .25 .20
276 A19 1.20fr green .25 .20
276A A20 1.50fr dk red .25 .20
277 A20 2fr slate blk .25 .20
278 A20 3fr dp claret .40 .20
278A A21 3.60fr dk car rose .85 .65
279 A21 4fr dp ultra .40 .20
280 A21 5fr red orange .65 .20
281 A22 6fr dk grnsh bl .40 .20
282 A22 10fr red brn .65 .20
283 A23 15fr violet brn 1.00 .30
284 A23 20fr dk vio bl 1.40 .65
285 A23 25fr brown 2.25 1.00
Nos. 269-285 (19) 10.45 5.60

Military Medal Issue

Common Design Type

Engraved and Typographed

1952, Dec. 1 Unwmk. *Perf. 13*
286 CD101 15fr multicolored 3.75 2.50

Creation of the French Military Medal, cent.

Tropical Flowers — A24

Long-tailed Ground Roller A25

1954 Engr.
287 A24 7.50fr ind & gray grn 1.25 .20
288 A25 8fr brown carmine .90 .35
289 A25 15fr dk grn & dp ultra 2.25 .35
Nos. 287-289 (3) 4.40 .90

Colonel Lyautey and Royal Palace, Tananarive A26

1954-55
290 A26 10fr vio bl, ind & bl ('55) .90 .20
291 A26 40fr dk sl bl & red brn 1.60 .20

FIDES Issue

Common Design Type

Designs: 3fr, Tractor and modern settlement. 5fr, Gallieni school. 10fr, Pangalanes Canal. 15fr, Irrigation project.

1956, Oct. 22 Engr. *Perf. 13x12½*
292 CD103 3fr gray vio & vio brn .40 .20
293 CD103 5fr org brn & dk vio brn .40 .35
294 CD103 10fr indigo & lilac .60 .35
295 CD103 15fr grn & bl grn .85 .20
Nos. 292-295 (4) 2.25 1.10

Coffee
A26a

1956, Oct. 22 ***Perf. 13***
296 A26a 20r red brn & dk brn .55 .20

Manioc — A27 Vanilla — A28

Design: 4fr, Cloves.

1957, Mar. 12 **Unwmk.** ***Perf. 13***
297 A27 2fr bl, grn & sepia .20 .20
298 A28 4fr dp grn & red .55 .20
299 A28 12fr dk vio, dl grn & sepia .75 .35
Nos. 297-299 (3) 1.50 .75

Malagasy Republic
Human Rights Issue
Common Design Type

1958, Dec. 10 **Engr.** ***Perf. 13***
300 CD105 10fr brn & dk bl .80 .40

Universal Declaration of Human Rights, 10th anniversary.
"CF" stands for "Communauté française."

> Imperforates
> Most Malagasy stamps from 1958 onward exist imperforate in issued and trial colors, and also in small presentation sheets in issued colors.

Flower Issue
Common Design Type
Perf. 12½x12, 12x12½

1959, Jan. 31 **Photo.**
301 CD104 6fr Datura, horiz. .60 .20
302 CD104 25fr Poinsettia .90 .30

Flag and
Assembly
Building
A29

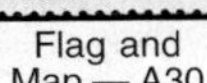

Flag and Map — A30 French and Malagasy Flags and Map — A31

1959, Feb. 28 **Engr.** ***Perf. 13***
303 A29 20fr brn vio, car & emer .30 .20
304 A30 25fr gray, red & emer .45 .20

Proclamation of the Malagasy Republic.

1959, Feb. 28
305 A31 60fr multi 1.60 .50

Issued to honor the French Community.

Chionaema
Pauliani
A32

Ylang-ylang — A33

Designs: 30c, 40c, 50c, 3fr, Various butterflies. 5fr, Sisal. 8fr, Pepper. 10fr, Rice. 15fr, Cotton.

1960 **Unwmk.** ***Perf. 13***
306 A32 30c multicolored .50 .20
307 A32 40c emer, sep & red brn .50 .20
308 A32 50c vio brn, blk & stl bl .50 .20
309 A32 1fr ind, red & dl pur .50 .20
310 A32 3fr ol, vio blk & org .50 .20
311 A32 5fr red, brn & emer .50 .20
312 A33 6fr dk grn & brt yel .55 .20
313 A32 8fr crim rose, emer & blk .55 .20
314 A33 10fr dk grn, yel grn & lt brn 1.00 .20
315 A32 15fr brown & grn 1.10 .20
Nos. 306-315 (10) 6.20 2.00

Family Planting
Trees — A34

1960, Feb. 1 **Engr.** ***Perf. 13***
316 A34 20fr red brn, buff & grn .90 .30

Issued for the "Week of the Tree," Feb. 1-7.

C.C.T.A. Issue
Common Design Type

1960, Feb. 22
317 CD106 25fr lt bl grn & plum .60 .30

Pres.
Philibert
Tsiranana
and
Map — A36

1960, Mar. 25 **Unwmk.** ***Perf. 13***
318 A36 20fr green & brn .35 .20

Athletes of Two Races — A37 Pres. Philibert Tsiranana — A38

1960 **Engr.** ***Perf. 13***
319 A37 25fr choc, org brn & ultra .60 .30

First Games of the French Community, Apr. 13-18, at Tananarive.

1960, July 29 **Unwmk.** ***Perf. 13***
320 A38 20fr red, blk & brt grn .35 .20

Issued to honor Pres. Tsiranana, "Father of Independence." For surcharge see No. B18.

Gray Lemur — A39

Designs: 4fr, Ruffed lemur, horiz. 12fr, Mongoose lemur.

1961, Dec. 9 ***Perf. 13***
321 A39 2fr brn & grnsh bl .25 .20
322 A39 4fr brn, grn & blk .45 .20
323 A39 12fr grn & red brn 1.10 .20
Nos. 321-323,C67-C69 (6) 16.80 5.05

Pres.
Tsiranana
Bridge,
Sofia River
A40

1962, Jan. 4 **Unwmk.** ***Perf. 13***
324 A40 25fr bright blue 1.00 .20

First Train
Built at
Tananarive
A41

1962, Feb. 1
325 A41 20fr dk grn 1.10 .30

UN and
Malagasy Flags
over Government
Building,
Tananarive
A42

1962, Mar. 14 ***Perf. 13***
326 A42 25fr multicolored .45 .20
327 A42 85fr multicolored 1.90 .55

Malagasy Republic's admission to the UN.
For surcharge see No. 409.

Ranomafana Village — A43

Designs: 30fr, Tritriva crater lake. 50fr, Foulpointe shore. 60fr, Fort Dauphin.

1962, May 7 **Engr.** ***Perf. 13***
328 A43 10fr sl grn, grnsh bl & cl .25 .20
329 A43 30fr sl grn, cl & grnsh bl .65 .20
330 A43 50fr ultra, cl & sl grn .90 .30
331 A43 60fr cl, ultra & sl grn 1.10 .40
Nos. 328-331,C70 (5) 4.65 1.70

African and Malgache Union Issue
Common Design Type

1962, Sept. 8 **Photo.** ***Perf. 12½x12***
332 CD110 30fr grn, bluish grn, red & gold .80 .80

First anniversary of the African and Malgache Union.

Arms of
Republic
and
UNESCO
Emblem
A44

1962, Sept. 3 **Unwmk.**
333 A44 20fr rose, emer & blk .60 .20

First Conference on Higher Education in Africa, Tananarive, Sept. 3-12.

Power
Station — A45

Designs: 8fr, Atomic reactor and atom symbol, horiz. 10fr, Oil derrick. 15fr, Tanker, horiz.

Perf. 12x12½, 12½x12
1962, Oct. 18 **Litho.**
334 A45 5fr blue, yel & red .20 .20
335 A45 8fr blue, red & yel .30 .20
336 A45 10fr multicolored .40 .20
337 A45 15fr bl, red brn & blk .50 .20
Nos. 334-337 (4) 1.40 .80

Industrialization of Madagascar.

Factory and
Globe
A46

1963, Jan. 7 **Typo.** ***Perf. 14x13½***
338 A46 25fr dp org & blk .55 .20

International Fair at Tamatave.

Hertzian Cable, Tananarive-
Fianarantsoa — A47

1963, Mar. 7 **Photo.** ***Perf. 12½x12***
339 A47 20fr multi .55 .20

Madagascar Blue Pigeon — A48 Gastrorchis Humblotii — A49

Birds: 2fr, Blue coua. 3fr, Red fody. 6fr, Madagascar pigmy kingfisher.
Orchids: 10fr, Eulophiella roempleriana. 12fr, Angraecum sesquipedale.

1963 **Unwmk.** ***Perf. 13***
340 A48 1fr multi .45 .30
341 A48 2fr multi .45 .30
342 A48 3fr multi .60 .30
343 A48 6fr multi .75 .30
344 A49 8fr multi 1.00 .30
345 A49 10fr multi 1.90 .45
346 A49 12fr multi 2.10 .50
Nos. 340-346,C72-C74 (10) 21.50 6.60

Arms — A50

Arms of: 1.50fr, Antsirabe. 5fr, Antalaha. 10fr, Tulear. 15fr, Majunga. 20fr, Fianarantsoa. 25fr, Tananarive. 50fr, Diégo-Suarez.

Imprint: "R. Louis del. So. Ge. Im."

1963-65 Litho. *Perf. 13*
Size: 23½x35½mm

347 A50 1.50fr multi ('64) .20 .20
348 A50 5fr multi ('65) .20 .20
349 A50 10fr multi ('64) .20 .20
350 A50 15fr multi ('64) .35 .20
351 A50 20fr multi .50 .20
352 A50 25fr multi .55 .20
353 A50 50fr multi ('65) 1.25 .50
Nos. 347-353 (7) 3.25 1.70

See Nos. 388-390, 434-439.
For surcharge see No. 503.

Map and Centenary Emblem — A51

Globe and Hands Holding Torch — A52

1963, Sept. 2 *Perf. 12x12½*
354 A51 30fr multi 1.00 .50

Centenary of the International Red Cross.

1963, Dec. 10 Engr. *Perf. 12½*
355 A52 60fr ol, ocher & car .85 .40

Universal Declaration of Human Rights, 15th anniv.

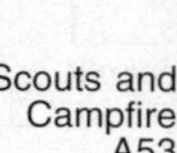
Scouts and Campfire A53

1964, June 6 Engr. *Perf. 13*
356 A53 20fr dk red, org & car .70 .30

40th anniv. of the Boy Scouts of Madagascar.

Europafrica Issue, 1964

Dove and Globe A54

1964, July 20 Engr.
357 A54 45fr ol grn, brn red & blk 1.00 .35

First anniversary of economic agreement between the European Economic Community and the African and Malgache Union.

Carved Statue of Woman — A55

University Emblem — A56

Malagasy Art: 30fr, Statue of sitting man.

1964, Oct. 20 Unwmk. *Perf. 13*
358 A55 6fr dk bl, brt bl & sepia .45 .20
359 A55 30fr dp grn, ol bis & dk brn .80 .30
Nos. 358-359,C79 (3) 3.50 1.40

Cooperation Issue
Common Design Type

1964, Nov. 7 Engr. *Perf. 13*
360 CD119 25fr blk, dk brn & org brn .60 .25

1964, Dec. 5 Litho. *Perf. 13x12½*
361 A56 65fr red, blk & grn .70 .35

Founding of the University of Madagascar, Tannanarive. The inscription reads: "Foolish is he who does not do better than his father."

Jejy — A57

Valiha Player A58

Musical instruments: 3fr, Kabosa (lute). 8fr, Hazolahy (sacred drum).

1965 Engr. *Perf. 13*
Size: 22x36mm
362 A57 3fr mag, vio bl & dk brn .50 .20
363 A57 6fr emer, rose lil & dk brn .60 .20
364 A57 8fr brn, grn & blk .90 .20

Photo. *Perf. 12½x13*
365 A58 25fr multi 1.75 .60
Nos. 362-365,C80 (5) 9.25 3.20

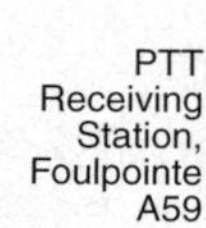
PTT Receiving Station, Foulpointe A59

1965, May 8 Engr. *Perf. 13*
366 A59 20fr red org, dk grn & ocher .50 .25

Issued for Stamp Day, 1965.

ITU Emblem, Old and New Telecommunication Equipment — A60

1965, May 17
367 A60 50fr ultra, red & grn 1.00 .40

ITU, centenary.

Jean Joseph Rabearivelo A61

Pres. Philibert Tsiranana A62

1965, June 22 Photo. *Perf. 13x12½*
368 A61 40fr dk brn & org .60 .30

Issued to honor the poet Jean Joseph Rabearivelo, pen name of Joseph Casimir, (1901-37).

1965, Oct. 18 *Perf. 13x12½*
369 A62 20fr multi .25 .20
a. Souv. sheet of 4 1.00 1.00
370 A62 25fr multi .40 .20
a. Souv. sheet of 4 2.00 2.00

55th birthday of President Philibert Tsiranana.

Mail Coach A63

History of the Post: 3fr, Early automobile. 4fr, Litter. 10fr, Mail runner, vert. 12fr, Mail boat. 25fr, Oxcart. 30fr, Old railroad mail car. 65fr, Hydrofoil.

1965-66 Engr. *Perf. 13*
371 A63 3fr vio, dp bis & sky bl ('66) .40 .25
372 A63 4fr ultra, grn & dk brn ('66) .35 .25
373 A63 10fr multi .35 .25
374 A63 12fr multi .40 .25
375 A63 20fr bis, grn & red brn .90 .30
376 A63 25fr sl grn, dk brn & org .85 .30
377 A63 30fr pck bl, red & sep ('66) 2.50 .50
378 A63 65fr vio, brn & Prus bl ('66) 2.00 .50
Nos. 371-378 (8) 7.75 2.60

Leper's Crippled Hands A64

1966, Jan. 30
379 A64 20fr dk grn, dk brn & red .70 .30

Issued for the 13th World Leprosy Day.

Couple Planting Trees A65

1966, Feb. 21
380 A65 20fr dk brn, pur & bl grn .60 .20

Reforestation as a national duty.

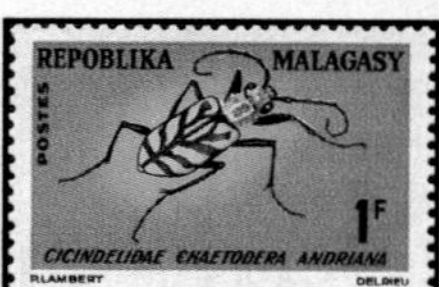

Tiger Beetle A66

Insects: 6fr, Mantis. 12fr, Long-horned beetle. 45fr, Weevil.

1966 Photo. *Perf. 12½x12*
Insects in Natural Colors
381 A66 1fr brick red 1.25 .20
382 A66 6fr rose claret 1.25 .20
383 A66 12fr Prus blue 3.00 .30
384 A66 45fr lt yel grn 4.25 .50
Nos. 381-384 (4) 9.75 1.20

Stamp of 1903 — A67

1966, May 8 Engr. *Perf. 13*
385 A67 25fr red & sepia .75 .30

Issued for Stamp Day 1966.

Betsileo Dancers A68

1966, June 13 Photo. *Perf. 12½x13*
Size: 36x23mm
386 A68 5fr multi .55 .20

See No. C83.

Symbolic Tree and Emblems — A69

1966, June 26
387 A69 25fr multi .60 .25

Conference of the Organisation Commune Africaine et Malgache (OCAM), Tananarive.

No. 387 dated "JUIN 1966," original date "Janvier 1966" obliterated with bar. Exists without overprint "JUIN 1966" and bar. Value $100.

Arms Type of 1963-65
Imprint: "S. Gauthier So. Ge. Im."

20fr, Mananjary. 30fr, Nossi-Bé. 90fr, Antsohihy.

1966-68 Litho. *Perf. 13*
Size: 23½x35½mm
388 A50 20fr multi ('67) .40 .20
389 A50 30fr multi .45 .20
390 A50 90fr multi ('68) 1.50 .40
Nos. 388-390 (3) 2.35 .80

For surcharge see No. 503.

Singers and Map of Madagascar — A70

1966, Oct. 14 Engr. *Perf. 13*
392 A70 20fr red brn, grn & dk car rose .60 .20

Issued in honor of the National Anthem.

UNESCO Emblem A71

1966, Nov. 4
393 A71 30fr red, yel & slate .60 .20

UNESCO, 20th anniv.

Lions Emblem — A72

1967, Jan. 14 Photo. *Perf. 13x12½*
394 A72 30fr multi .60 .30

50th anniversary of Lions International.

Rice Harvest A73

1967, Jan. 27 *Perf. 12½x13*
395 A73 20fr multi .60 .20

FAO International Rice Year.

Adventist Temple, Tanambao-Tamatave — A74

Designs: 5fr, Catholic Cathedral, Tananarive, vert. 10fr, Mosque, Tamatave.

1967, Feb. 20 Engr. *Perf. 13*
396 A74 3fr lt ultra, grn & bis .25 .20
397 A74 5fr brt rose lil, grn & vio .25 .20
398 A74 10fr dp bl, brn & grn .30 .20
Nos. 396-398 (3) .80 .60

Norbert Raharisoa at Piano A75

1967, Mar. 23 Photo. *Perf. 12½x12*
399 A75 40fr citron & multi .85 .35

Norbert Raharisoa (1914-1963), composer.

Jean Raoult Flying Blériot Plane, 1911 A76

45fr, Barnard-Bougault and hydroplane, 1926.

1967, Apr. 28 Engr. *Perf. 13*
Size: 35½x22mm
400 A76 5fr gray bl, brn & grn .85 .25
401 A76 45fr brn, stl bl & blk 1.75 .50
Nos. 400-401,C84 (3) 13.60 3.75

History of aviation in Madagascar.

Ministry of Equipment and Communications — A77

1967, May 8 Engr. *Perf. 13*
402 A77 20fr ocher, ultra & grn .60 .20

Issued for Stamp Day, 1967.

Lutheran Church, Tananarive, Madagascar Map — A78

1967, Sept. 24 Photo. *Perf. 12x12½*
403 A78 20fr multi .70 .25

Lutheran Church in Madagascar, cent.

Map of Madagascar and Emblems — A79

1967, Oct. 16 Engr. *Perf. 13*
404 A79 90fr red brn, bl & dk red 1.10 .40

Hydrological Decade (UNESCO), 1965-74.

Dance of the Bilo Sakalavas — A80

Design: 30fr, Atandroy dancers.

1967, Nov. 25 Photo. *Perf. 13x12½*
Size: 22x36mm
405 A80 2fr lt grn & multi .30 .20
406 A80 30fr multi .60 .20
Nos. 405-406,C86-C87 (4) 7.65 2.40

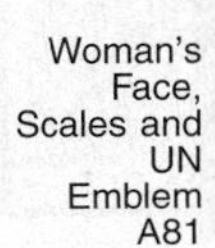

Woman's Face, Scales and UN Emblem A81

1967, Dec. 16 *Perf. 12½x13*
407 A81 50fr emer, dk bl & brn .70 .30

UN Commission on the Status of Women.

Human Rights Flame — A82

1968, Mar. 16 Litho. *Perf. 13x12½*
408 A82 50fr blk, ver & grn .70 .30

International Human Rights Year.

No. 327 Surcharged with New Value and 3 Bars

1968, June 4 Engr. *Perf. 13*
409 A42 20fr on 85fr multi .70 .40

"Industry" A83

Designs: 20fr, "Agriculture" (mother and child carrying fruit and grain, and cattle), vert. 40fr, "Communications and Investments," (train, highway, factory and buildings).

1968, July 15
410 A83 10fr rose car, grn & dk pur .25 .20
411 A83 20fr dp car, grn & blk .30 .20
412 A83 40fr brn, vio & sl bl .60 .25
Nos. 410-412 (3) 1.15 .65

Completion of Five-year Plan, 1964-68.

Church, Translated Bible, Cross and Map of Madagascar — A84

1968, Aug. 18 Photo. *Perf. 12½x12*
413 A84 20fr multi .55 .20

Sesquicentennial of Christianity in Madagascar.

Isotry-Fitiavana Protestant Church — A85

12fr, Catholic Cathedral, Fianarantsoa. 50fr, Aga Khan Mosque, Tananarive.

1968, Sept. 10 Engr. *Perf. 13*
414 A85 4fr red brn, brt grn & dk brn .25 .20
415 A85 12fr plum, bl & hn brn .30 .20
416 A85 50fr brt grn, bl & indigo .60 .25
Nos. 414-416 (3) 1.15 .65

President and Mrs. Tsiranana A86

1968, Oct. 14 Photo. *Perf. 12½x12*
417 A86 20fr car, org & blk .30 .20
418 A86 30fr car, grnsh bl & blk .50 .20
a. Souv. sheet of 4, 2 each #417-418 2.00 1.10

10th anniv. of the Republic.

Madagascar Map and Cornucopia with Coins — A87

Striving Mankind — A88

1968, Nov. 3 Photo. *Perf. 12x12½*
419 A87 20fr multi .60 .20

50th anniversary of the Malagasy Savings Bank.

1968, Dec. 3 Photo. *Perf. 12½x12*

15fr, Mother, child and physician, horiz.

420 A88 15fr ultra, yel & crim .30 .20
421 A88 45fr vio bl & multi .55 .20

Completion of Five-Year Plan, 1964-68.

Queen Adelaide Receiving Malagasy Delegation, London, 1836 — A89

1969, Mar. 29 Photo. *Perf. 12x12½*
422 A89 250fr multi 5.75 2.50

Malagasy delegation London visit, 1836-37.

Cogwheels, Wrench and ILO Emblem A90

1969, Apr. 11 *Perf. 12½x12*
423 A90 20fr grn & multi .50 .20

ILO, 50th anniv.

Telecommunications and Postal Building, Tananarive — A91

1969, May 8 Engr. *Perf. 13*
424 A91 30fr bl, brt grn & car lake .60 .20

Issued for Stamp Day 1969.

Steering Wheel, Map, Automobiles — A92

1969, June 1 Photo. *Perf. 12*
425 A92 65fr multi 1.00 .30

Automobile Club of Madagascar, 20th anniv.

Pres. Philibert Tsiranana — A93

Banana Plants — A94

1969, June 26 Photo. ***Perf. 12x12½***
426 A93 20fr multi .45 .20

10th anniversary of the inauguration of Pres. Philibert Tsiranana.

1969, July 7 Engr. ***Perf. 13***
427 A94 5fr shown .65 .20
428 A94 15fr Lichi tree 1.25 .20

Runners A95

1969, Sept. 9 Engr. ***Perf. 13***
429 A95 15fr yel grn, brn & red .55 .20

Issued to commemorate the 19th Olympic Games, Mexico City, Oct. 12-27, 1968.

Malagasy House, Highlands A96

Carnelian A97

Malagasy Houses: #430, Betsileo house, Highlands. #431, Tsimihety house, West Coast, horiz. 60fr, Malagasy house, Highlands.

1969-70 Engr. ***Perf. 13***
430 A96 20fr bl, ol & ver .30 .20
431 A96 20fr sl, brt grn & red .30 .20
432 A96 40fr blk, bl & dk red .60 .25
433 A96 60fr vio bl, dp grn & brn .90 .30
Nos. 430-433 (4) 2.10 .95

Issued: 40fr, 60fr, 11/25/69; others, 11/25/70.

Arms Type of 1963-65

1fr, Maintirano. 10fr, Ambalavao. #436, Morondava. #437, Ambatondrazaka. #438, Fenerive-Est. 80fr, Tamatave.

1970-72 Photo. ***Perf. 13***
434 A50 1fr multi ('72) .25 .20
435 A50 10fr multi ('72) .35 .20
436 A50 25fr multi ('71) .55 .20
437 A50 25fr multi ('71) .55 .20
438 A50 25fr multi ('72) .70 .20
439 A50 80fr pink & multi 1.10 .30
Nos. 434-439 (6) 3.50 1.30

The 10fr, 80fr are dated "1970." #437 is dated "1971." #434, 438 are dated "1972."

Sizes: #434, 438, 22x37mm; others, 25½x36mm.

Imprints: "S. Gauthier" on Nos. 434, 438; "S. Gauthier Delrieu" on others.

Perf. 12x12½ (5, 20fr), 13 (12, 15fr)
1970-71 Photo.

Semi-precious Stones: 12fr, Yellow calcite. 15fr, Quartz. 20fr, Ammonite.

440 A97 5fr brn, dl rose & yel 4.25 1.00
441 A97 12fr multi ('71) 4.75 1.00
442 A97 15fr multi ('71) 6.25 1.50
443 A97 20fr grn & multi 17.50 2.00
Nos. 440-443 (4) 32.75 5.50

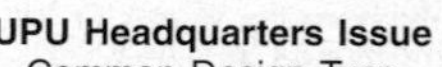

UPU Headquarters Issue
Common Design Type

1970, May 20 Engr. ***Perf. 13***
444 CD133 20fr lil rose, brn & ultra .55 .20

UN Emblem and Symbols of Justice A98

1970, June 26 Engr. ***Perf. 13***
445 A98 50fr blk, ultra & org .70 .30

25th anniversary of the United Nations.

Fruits of Madagascar — A99

1970, Aug. 18 Photo. ***Perf. 13***
446 A99 20fr multi 1.75 .25

Volute Delessertiana — A100

Shells: 10fr, Murex tribulus. 20fr, Spondylus.

1970, Sept. 9 Photo. ***Perf. 13***
447 A100 5fr Prus bl & multi .90 .25
448 A100 10fr vio & multi 1.10 .25
449 A100 20fr multi 3.00 .30
Nos. 447-449 (3) 5.00 .80

Aye-aye — A101

1970, Oct. 7 Photo. ***Perf. 12½***
450 A101 20fr multi .45 .25

Intl. Conference for Nature Conservation, Tananarive, Oct. 7-10.

Pres. Tsiranana A102

1970, Dec. 30 Photo. ***Perf. 12½***
451 A102 30fr grn & lt brn .60 .20

60th birthday of Pres. Philibert Tsiranana.

Tropical Soap Factory, Tananarive A103

Designs: 15fr, Comina chromium smelting plant, Andriamena. 50fr, Textile mill, Majunga.

1971, Apr. 14 Photo. ***Perf. 12½x12***
452 A103 5fr multi .30 .20

Engr. ***Perf. 13***
453 A103 15fr vio bl, blk & ocher .35 .20

Photo. ***Perf. 13***
454 A103 50fr multi .65 .20
Nos. 452-454 (3) 1.30 .60

Economic development.

Globe, Agriculture, Industry, Science A104

1971, Apr. 22 Photo. ***Perf. 12½x12***
455 A104 5fr multi .25 .20

Extraordinary meeting of the Council of the C.E.E.-E.A.M.A. (Communauté Economique Européen-Etats Africains et Malgache Associés).

Mobile Rural Post Office A105

1971, May 8 ***Perf. 13***
456 A105 25fr multi .55 .20

Stamp Day.

Gen. Charles de Gaulle — A106

Madagascar Hilton, Tananarive A107

1971, June 26 Engr. ***Perf. 13***
457 A106 30fr ultra, blk & rose 1.00 .35

In memory of Charles de Gaulle (1890-1970), President of France.

For surcharge see No. B24.

1971, July 23 Photo.

Design: 25fr, Hotel Palm Beach, Nossi-Bé.

458 A107 25fr multi .50 .20

Engr.
459 A107 65fr vio bl, brn & lt grn .85 .30

Trees and Post Horn — A108

1971, Aug. 6 Photo. ***Perf. 12½x12***
460 A108 3fr red, yel & grn .30 .20

Forest preservation campaign.

House, South West Madagascar — A109

10fr, House from Southern Madagascar.

1971, Nov. 25 ***Perf. 13x12½***
461 A109 5fr lt bl & multi .25 .20
462 A109 10fr lt bl & multi .35 .20

Children Playing, and Cattle A110

1971, Dec. 11 Litho. ***Perf. 13***
463 A110 50fr grn & multi 1.00 .30

UNICEF, 25th anniv.

Cable-laying Railroad Car, PTT Emblem — A111

1972, Apr. 8 Engr. ***Perf. 13***
464 A111 45fr slate grn, red & choc 1.50 .40

Coaxial cable connection between Tananarive and Tamatave.

Philibert Tsiranana Radar Station — A112

1972, Apr. 8 Photo. ***Perf. 13½***
465 A112 85fr bl & multi 1.00 .40

A113

A114

Voters and Pres. Tsiranana.

1972, May 1 ***Perf. 12½x13***
466 A113 25fr yel & multi .55 .35

Presidential election, Jan. 30, 1972.

1972, May 30 Photo. ***Perf. 12x12½***
467 A114 10fr Mail delivery .60 .20

Stamp Day 1972.

Emblem and Stamps of Madagascar A115

Stamps shown are #352, 410, 429, 449.

1972, June 26 ***Perf. 13***
468 A115 25fr org & multi .50 .20
469 A115 40fr org & multi .60 .30
470 A115 100fr org & multi 1.50 .50
a. Souv. sheet of 3, #468-470 3.50 3.50
Nos. 468-470 (3) 2.60 1.00

2nd Malgache Philatelic Exhibition, Tananarive, June 26-July 9.

Andapa-Sambava Road and Monument — A116

1972, July 6 ***Perf. 12½x12***
471 A116 50fr multi .60 .30

Opening of the Andapa-Sambava road.

Diesel Locomotive A117

1972, July 6 Engr. ***Perf. 13***
472 A117 100fr multicolored 4.50 .50

Razafindrahety College — A118

1972, Aug. 6
473 A118 10fr choc, bl & red brn .25 .20

Razafindrahety College, Tananarive, sesqui.

Volleyball A119

1972, Aug. 6 Typo. ***Perf. 12½x13***
474 A119 12fr orange, blk & brn .45 .20

African volleyball championship.

Oil Refinery, Tamatave A120

1972, Sept. 18 Engr. ***Perf. 13***
475 A120 2fr bl, bister & slate grn .45 .20

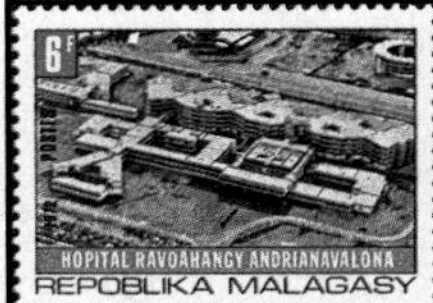

Ravoahangy Andrianavalona Hospital — A121

1972, Oct. 14 Photo. ***Perf. 13x12½***
476 A121 6fr multi .25 .20

Plowing A122

1972, Nov. 15 Photo. ***Perf. 13½x14***
477 A122 25fr gold & multi .70 .30

Betsimisaraka Costume — A123

Design: 15fr, Merina costume.

1972, Dec. 30 Photo. ***Perf. 13x12½***
478 A123 10fr blue & multi .20 .20
479 A123 15fr brown & multi .45 .20

Farmer and Produce — A124

1973, Feb. 6 Photo. ***Perf. 13***
480 A124 25fr lt blue & multi .45 .20

10th anniversary of the Malagasy Committee of "Freedom from Hunger Campaign."
For surcharge see No. 499.

Volva Volva A125

Shells: 10fr, 50fr, Lambis chiragra. 15fr, 40fr, Harpa major. 25fr, Like 3fr.

1973, Apr. 5 Litho. ***Perf. 13***
481 A125 3fr olive & multi .35 .20
482 A125 10fr blue grn & multi .55 .25
483 A125 15fr brt blue & multi 1.00 .25
484 A125 25fr lt blue & multi 1.40 .30
485 A125 40fr multicolored 1.75 .30
486 A125 50fr red lilac & multi 3.00 .40
Nos. 481-486 (6) 8.05 1.70

Tsimandoa Mail Carrier — A126

Builders and Map of Africa — A127

1973, May 13 Engr. ***Perf. 13***
487 A126 50fr ind, ocher & sl grn .75 .30

Stamp Day 1973.

1973, May 25 Photo. ***Perf. 13***
488 A127 25fr multicolored .60 .25

Organization for African Unity, 10th anniversary.

Campani Chameleon A128

Various Chameleons: 5fr, 40fr, Male nasutus. 10fr, 85fr, Female nasutus. 60fr, Like 1fr.

1973, June 15 Photo. ***Perf. 13x12½***
489 A128 1fr dp car & multi .35 .20
490 A128 5fr brown & multi .35 .20
491 A128 10fr green & multi .50 .20
492 A128 40fr red lilac & multi 1.40 .25
493 A128 60fr dk blue & multi 1.90 .40
494 A128 85fr brown & multi 3.00 .60
Nos. 489-494 (6) 7.50 1.85

Lady's Slipper A129

Orchids: 25fr, 40fr, Pitcher plant.

1973, Aug. 6 Photo. ***Perf. 12½***
495 A129 10fr multicolored .90 .20
496 A129 25fr rose & multi 1.10 .30
497 A129 40fr lt blue & multi 2.50 .35
498 A129 100fr multicolored 5.50 .70
Nos. 495-498 (4) 10.00 1.55

No. 480 Surcharged with New Value, 2 Bars, and Overprinted in Ultramarine: "SECHERESSE / SOLIDARITE AFRICAINE"

1973, Aug. 16 ***Perf. 13***
499 A124 100fr on 25fr multi 1.40 .50

African solidarity in drought emergency.

African Postal Union Issue
Common Design Type

1973, Sept. 12 Engr. ***Perf. 13***
500 CD137 100fr vio, red & slate grn 1.00 .35

Greater Dwarf Lemur A131

Design: 25fr, Weasel lemur, vert.

1973, Oct. 9 Engr. ***Perf. 13***
501 A131 5fr brt green & multi .75 .30
502 A131 25fr ocher & multi 1.75 .60
Nos. 501-502,C117-C118 (4) 10.25 3.20

Lemurs of Madagascar.

No. 389 Surcharged

1974, Feb. 9 Litho. ***Perf. 13***
503 A50 25fr on 30fr multi .35 .20

Scouts Helping to Raise Cattle — A132

Mother with Children and Clinic — A133

Design: 15fr, Scouts building house; African Scout emblem.

1974, Feb. 14 Engr. ***Perf. 13***
504 A132 4fr blue, slate & emer .20 .20
505 A132 15fr chocolate & multi .30 .25
Nos. 504-505,C122-C123 (4) 5.85 1.80

Malagasy Boy Scouts.

1974, May 24 Photo. ***Perf. 13***
506 A133 25fr multicolored .35 .20

World Population Year.

Rainibetsimisaraka — A134

1974, July 26 Photo. ***Perf. 13***
507 A134 25fr multicolored .65 .30

In memory of Rainibetsimisaraka, independence leader.

Marble Blocks A135

Design: 25fr, Marble quarry.

1974, Sept. 27 Photo. ***Perf. 13***
508 A135 4fr multicolored .80 .25
509 A135 25fr multicolored 2.10 .45

Malagasy marble.

Europafrica Issue, 1974

Links, White and Black Faces, Map of Europe and Africa — A136

1974, Oct. 17 Engr. *Perf. 13*
510 A136 150fr dk brown & org 1.75 .60

Grain and Hand A137

1974, Oct. 29
511 A137 80fr light blue & ocher 1.00 .35

World Committee against Hunger.

Tuléar Dog A138

Design: 100fr, Hunting dog.

1974, Nov. 26 Photo. *Perf. 13x13½*
512 A138 50fr multicolored 2.50 .50
513 A138 100fr multicolored 3.50 .90

Malagasy Citizens — A139

1974, Dec. 9 *Perf. 13½x13*
514 A139 5fr blue grn & multi .25 .20
515 A139 10fr multicolored .25 .20
516 A139 20fr yellow grn & multi .35 .20
517 A139 60fr orange & multi .90 .25
Nos. 514-517 (4) 1.75 .85

Introduction of "Fokonolona" community organization.

Symbols of Development — A140

1974, Dec. 16 Photo. *Perf. 13x13½*
518 A140 25fr ultra & multi .30 .20
519 A140 35fr blue grn & multi .50 .25

National Council for Development.

Woman, Rose, Dove and Emblem — A141

1975, Jan. 21 Engr. *Perf. 13*
520 A141 100fr brown, emer & org 1.10 .40

International Women's Year 1975.

Col. Richard Ratsimandrava — A142

1975, Apr. 25 Photo. *Perf. 13*
521 A142 15fr brown & salmon .20 .20
522 A142 25fr black, bl & brn .35 .25
523 A142 100fr black, lt grn & brn 1.25 .30
Nos. 521-523 (3) 1.80 .75

Ratsimandrava (1933-1975), head of state.

Sofia Bridge A143

1975, May 29 Litho. *Perf. 12½*
524 A143 45fr multicolored .80 .30

Count de Grasse and "Randolph" — A144

Design: 50fr, Marquis de Lafayette, "Lexington" and HMS "Edward."

1975, June 30 Litho. *Perf. 11*
525 A144 40fr multicolored .60 .25
526 A144 50fr multicolored .80 .30
Nos. 525-526,C137-C139 (5) 8.90 2.45

American Bicentennial.
For overprints see Nos. 564-565, C164-C167.

Euphorbia Viguieri A145

Tropical Plants: 25fr, Hibiscus. 30fr, Plumieria rubra acutitolia. 40fr, Pachypodium rosulatum.

1975, Aug. 4 Photo. *Perf. 12½*
527 A145 15fr lemon & multi .30 .25
528 A145 25fr black & multi .50 .25
529 A145 30fr orange & multi .70 .30
530 A145 40fr dk red & multi 1.10 .30
Nos. 527-530,C141 (5) 5.10 2.00

Brown, White, Yellow and Black Hands Holding Globe — A146

1975, Aug. 26 Litho. *Perf. 12*
531 A146 50fr multicolored .70 .25

Namibia Day (independence for South-West Africa.)

Woodpecker — A147

1975, Sept. 16 Litho. *Perf. 14x13½*
532 A147 25fr shown .60 .25
533 A147 40fr Rabbit 1.00 .25
534 A147 50fr Frog 1.40 .30
535 A147 75fr Tortoise 2.50 .45
Nos. 532-535,C145 (5) 7.40 1.70

International Exposition, Okinawa.

Lily Waterfall A148

Design: 40fr, Lily Waterfall, different view.

1975, Sept. 17 Litho. *Perf. 12½*
536 A148 25fr multicolored .45 .25
537 A148 40fr multicolored .65 .25

4-man Bob Sled — A149

100fr, Ski jump. 140fr, Speed skating.

1975, Nov. 19 Litho. *Perf. 14*
538 A149 75fr multicolored .80 .25
539 A149 100fr multicolored 1.10 .30
540 A149 140fr multicolored 1.60 .40
Nos. 538-540,C149-C150 (5) 9.00 2.15

12th Winter Olympic games, Innsbruck, 1976.
For overprints see Nos. 561-563, C161-C163.

Pirogue A150

Designs: 45fr, Boutre (Arabian coastal vessel).

1975, Nov. 20 Photo. *Perf. 12½*
541 A150 8fr multicolored .50 .25
542 A150 45fr ultra & multi 1.75 .40

Canadian Canoe and Kayak — A151

Design: 50fr, Sprint and Hurdles.

1976, Jan. 21 Litho. *Perf. 14x13½*
543 A151 40fr multicolored .45 .25
544 A151 50fr multicolored .55 .25
Nos. 543-544,C153-C155 (5) 7.50 2.30

21st Summer Olympic games, Montreal.
For overprints see Nos. 571-572, C168-C171.

Count Zeppelin and LZ-127 over Fujiyama, Japan — A152

Designs (Count Zeppelin and LZ-127 over): 50fr, Rio. 75fr, NYC. 100fr, Sphinx.

1976, Mar. 3 *Perf. 11*
545 A152 40fr multicolored .50 .25
546 A152 50fr multicolored .70 .25
547 A152 75fr multicolored 1.25 .30
548 A152 100fr multicolored 1.50 .35
Nos. 545-548,C158-C159 (6) 11.20 2.65

75th anniversary of the Zeppelin.

Aragonite A154

50fr, Petrified wood. 150fr, Celestite.

Worker, Globe, Eye Chart and Eye — A153

1976, Apr. 7 Photo. *Perf. 12½*
549 A153 100fr multicolored 1.75 .50

World Health Day: "Foresight prevents blindness."

1976, May 7 Photo. *Perf. 12½*

550	A154	25fr blue & multi	2.75	.50
551	A154	50fr blue grn & multi	3.50	1.00
552	A154	150fr orange & multi	14.00	2.00
		Nos. 550-552 (3)	20.25	3.50

Alexander Graham Bell and First Telephone — A155

50fr, Telephone lines, 1911. 100fr, Central office, 1895. 200fr, Cable ship, 1925. 300fr, Radio telephone. 500fr, Telstar satellite and globe.

1976, May 13 Litho. *Perf. 14*

553	A155	25fr multicolored	.25	.20
554	A155	50fr multicolored	.45	.25
555	A155	100fr multicolored	.80	.30
556	A155	200fr multicolored	1.75	.55
557	A155	300fr multicolored	2.75	.75
		Nos. 553-557 (5)	6.00	2.05

Souvenir Sheet

558	A155	500fr multicolored	5.25	1.40

Cent. of 1st telephone call by Alexander Graham Bell, Mar. 10, 1876.

Children with Books A156

Design: 25fr, Children with books, vert.

1976, May 25 Litho.

559	A156	10fr multicolored	.25	.20
560	A156	25fr multicolored	.50	.25

Books for children.

Nos. 538-540 Overprinted

a. VAINQUEUR ALLEMAGNE FEDERALE
b. VAINQUEUR KARL SCHNABL AUTRICHE
c. VAINQUEUR SHEILA YOUNG ETATS-UNIS

1976, June 17

561	A149 (a)	75fr multi	.80	.30
562	A149 (b)	100fr multi	1.25	.45
563	A149 (c)	140fr multi	1.75	.60
		Nos. 561-563,C161-C162 (5)	8.30	2.75

12th Winter Olympic games winners.

Nos. 525-526 Overprinted "4 Juillet / 1776-1976"

1976, July 4

564	A144	40fr multicolored	.60	.30
565	A144	50fr multicolored	.80	.40
		Nos. 564-565,C164-C166 (5)	7.40	2.50

American Bicentennial.

Graph of Projected Landing Spots on Mars — A157

Viking project to Mars: 100fr, Viking probe in flight. 200fr, Viking probe on Mars. 300fr, Viking probe over projected landing spot. 500fr, Viking probe approaching Mars.

1976, July 17 Litho. *Perf. 14*

566	A157	75fr multicolored	.60	.25
567	A157	100fr multicolored	.85	.30
568	A157	200fr multicolored	1.75	.40
569	A157	300fr multicolored	2.50	.60
		Nos. 566-569 (4)	5.70	1.55

Souvenir Sheet

570	A157	500fr multicolored	5.25	1.00

Nos. 543-544 Overprinted

a. A. ROGOV / V. DIBA
b. H. CRAWFORD / J. SCHALLER

1977, Jan.

571	A151 (a)	40fr multi	.45	.25
572	A151 (b)	50fr multi	.60	.30
		Nos. 571-572,C168-C170 (5)	6.80	2.40

21st Summer Olympic games winners.

Rainandriamampandry — A158

Portrait: No. 574, Rabezavana.

1976-77 Litho. *Perf. 12x12½*

573	A158	25fr multicolored	.50	.25
574	A158	25fr multicolored	.25	.25

Rainandriamampandry was Malagasy Foreign Minister who signed treaties in 1896.
Issued: #73, Oct. 15; #74, Mar. 29, 1977.

"Indian Ocean - Zone of Peace." A159

Design: 60fr, Globe with Africa and Indian Ocean, doves, vert. 160fr, Doves, Indian Ocean on Globe.

Perf. 12½x12, 12x12½

1976, Nov. 18

575	A159	60fr multicolored	.60	.25
576	A159	160fr shown	1.40	.50

Coat of Arms — A160

1976, Dec. 30 Litho. *Perf. 12*

577	A160	25fr multicolored	.30	.20

Democratic Republic of Malagasy, 1st anniv.

Lt. Albert Randriamaromanana — A161

Portrait: #578, Avana Ramanantoanina.

1977, Mar. 29

578	A161	25fr multicolored	.25	.20
579	A161	25fr multicolored	.25	.20

National Mausoleum — A162

1977, Mar. 29 *Perf. 12½x12*

580	A162	100fr multicolored	1.25	.40

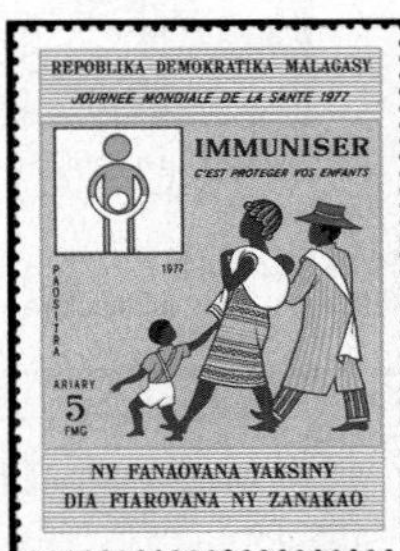

Family A163

1977, Apr. 7 *Perf. 12x12½*

581	A163	5fr yellow & multi	.25	.20

World Health Day: Immunization protects the children.

Tananarive Medical School — A164

1977, June 30 Litho. *Perf. 12½x12*

582	A164	250fr multicolored	2.50	.80

80th anniversary of Tananarive Medical School.

Mail Bus — A165

1977, Aug. 18 Litho. *Perf. 12½x12*

583	A165	35fr multicolored	.40	.25

Rural mail delivery.

Telegraph Operator — A166

1977, Sept. 13 Litho. *Perf. 12½x12*

584	A166	15fr multicolored	.25	.25

Telegraph service Tananarive-Tamatave, 90th anniv.

Malagasy Art — A167

1977, Sept. 29 *Perf. 12x12½*

585	A167	10fr multicolored	.25	.20

Malagasy Academy, 75th anniversary.

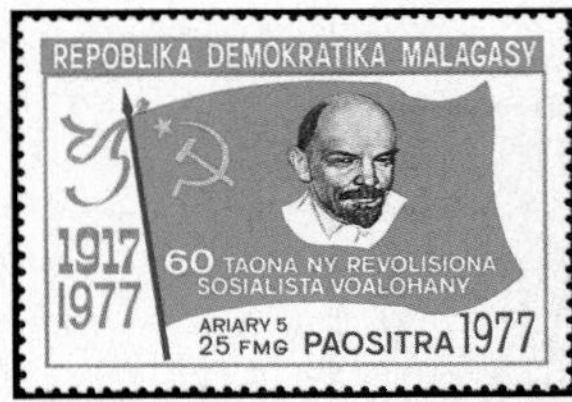

Lenin and Russian Flag — A168

1977, Nov. 7 Litho. *Perf. 12½x12*

586	A168	25fr multicolored	2.00	.35

60th anniversary of Russian October Revolution.

Raoul Follereau, Map of Malagasy A169

1978, Jan. 28 Litho. *Perf. 12x12½*

587	A169	5fr multicolored	1.10	.30

25th anniversary of Leprosy Day.

Antenna, ITU Emblem A170

1978, May 17 Litho. *Perf. 12x12½*

588	A170	20fr multicolored	.25	.25

10th World Telecommunications Day.

Black and White Men Breaking Chains of Africa — A171

1978, June 22 Photo. ***Perf. 12½x12***

589 A171 60fr multicolored .60 .25

Anti-Apartheid Year.

Boy and Girl, Arch: Pen, Gun and Hoe A172

Farm Workers, Factory, Tractor A173

1978, July 28 Litho. ***Perf. 12½x12***

590 A172 125fr multicolored 1.00 .40

Youth, the pillar of revolution.

1978, Aug. 24

591 A173 25fr multicolored .25 .20

Socialist cooperation.

Women — A174

Children Bringing Gifts — A175

1979, Mar. 8 Litho. ***Perf. 12½x12***

592 A174 40fr multicolored .35 .20

Women, supporters of the revolution.

1979, June 1 Litho. ***Perf. 12x12½***

593 A175 10fr multicolored .25 .20

International Year of the Child.

Lemur Macaco A176

Fauna: 25fr, Lemur catta, vert. 1000fr, Foussa.

Perf. 12½x12, 12x12½

1979, July 6 Litho.

594 A176 25fr multi .70 .20

595 A176 125fr multi 2.75 .35

596 A176 1000fr multi 9.75 2.50

Nos. 594-596,C172-C173 (5) 15.45 3.50

Jean Verdi Salomon A177

1979, July 25 ***Perf. 12x12½***

597 A177 25fr multicolored .25 .20

Jean Verdi Salomon (1913-1978), poet.

Talapetraka (Medicinal Plant) — A178

1979, Sept. 27 Litho. ***Perf. 12½***

598 A178 25fr multicolored .90 .25

Map of Magagascar, Dish Antenna — A179

1979, Oct. 12

599 A179 25fr multicolored .25 .20

Stamp Day 1979 A180

1979, Nov. 9

600 A180 500fr multicolored 4.50 1.40

Jet, Map of Africa A181

1979, Dec. 12 ***Perf. 12½***

601 A181 50fr multicolored .60 .25

ASECNA (Air Safety Board), 20th anniversary.

Lenin Addressing Workers in the Winter Palace A182

1980, Apr. 22 Litho. ***Perf. 12x12½***

602 A182 25fr multicolored .60 .25

Lenin's 110th birth anniversary.

Bus and Road in Madagascar Colors A183

Flag and Map under Sun — A184

1980, June 15 Litho. ***Perf. 12x12½***

603 A183 30fr multicolored .35 .20

Socialist Revolution, 5th anniversary.

1980, June 26 ***Perf. 12½x12***

604 A184 75fr multicolored .60 .25

Independence, 20th anniversary.

Armed Forces Day — A185

1980, Aug. Litho. ***Perf. 12½x12***

605 A185 50fr multicolored .45 .25

Dr. Joseph Raseta (1886-1979) A186

1980, Oct. 15 Litho. ***Perf. 12x12½***

606 A186 30fr multicolored .30 .20

Anatirova Temple Centenary — A187

1980, Nov. 27 Litho. ***Perf. 12½x12***

607 A187 30fr multicolored .35 .25

Hurdles, Olympic Torch, Moscow '80 Emblem — A188

1980, Dec. 29

608 A188 30fr shown .45 .20

609 A188 75fr Boxing .85 .30

Nos. 608-609,C175-C176 (4) 8.05 2.70

22nd Summer Olympic Games, Moscow, July 19-Aug. 3.

Democratic Republic of Madagascar, 5th Anniversary A189

1980, Dec. 30 ***Perf. 12x12½***

610 A189 30fr multicolored .35 .20

Downhill Skiing — A190

1981, Jan. 26 Litho. ***Perf. 12½x12***

611 A190 175fr multicolored 1.75 .60

13th Winter Olympic Games, Lake Placid, Feb. 12-24, 1980.

Angraecum Leonis A191

1981, Mar. 23 Litho. ***Perf. 11½***

612 A191 5fr shown .50 .20

613 A191 80fr Angraecum ramosum 1.75 .30

614 A191 170fr Angraecum sesquipedale 2.75 .65

Nos. 612-614 (3) 5.00 1.15

For surcharge, see No. 1474B.

A192

A193

1981, June 12 Litho. *Perf. 12*

615 A192 25fr Student at desk .30 .20
616 A192 80fr Carpenter .75 .30

Intl. Year of the Disabled.

1981, July 10 Litho. *Perf. 12½x12*

617 A193 15fr multi .25 .20
618 A193 45fr multi .55 .25

13th World Telecommunications Day.

Neil Armstrong on Moon (Apollo 11) — A194

Space Anniversaries.

1981, July 23 *Perf. 11½*

619 A194 30fr Valentina Tereshkova .30 .20
620 A194 80fr shown .80 .25
621 A194 90fr Yuri Gagarin .90 .25
Nos. 619-621 (3) 2.00 .70

Brother Raphael Louis Rafiringa (1854-1919) A195

1981, Aug. 10 Litho. *Perf. 12*

622 A195 30fr multi .35 .20

World Literacy Day — A196

1981, Sept. 8

623 A196 30fr multi .35 .20

World Food Day — A197

1981, Oct. 16 Litho. *Perf. 12x12½*

624 A197 200fr multi 1.90 .60

See No. 635.

Oaths of Magistracy Renewal — A198

1981, Oct. 30 *Perf. 12½x12*

625 A198 30fr blk & lil rose .35 .20

Dove, by Pablo Picasso (1881-1973) — A199

1981, Nov. 18 Photo. *Perf. 11½x12*

626 A199 80fr multi 1.00 .30

20th Anniv. of UPU Membership — A200

Design: Nos. C76, C77, emblem.

1981, Nov. 19 Litho. *Perf. 12*

627 A200 5fr multi .20 .20
628 A200 30fr multi .35 .20

TB Bacillus Centenary A201

1982, June 21 Litho. *Perf. 12*

629 A201 30fr multi .45 .20

Jeannette Mpihira (1903-1981), Actress and Singer — A202

1982, June 24 *Perf. 12½*

630 A202 30fr multi .35 .25

Haliaeetus Vociferoides A203

1982, July

631 A203 25fr Vanga curvirostris, horiz. 1.10 .20
632 A203 30fr Leptostomus discolor, horiz. 1.40 .20
633 A203 200fr shown 4.75 .70
Nos. 631-633 (3) 7.25 1.10

Pierre Louis Boiteau (1911-1980), Educator A204

1982, Sept. 13

634 A204 30fr multi .35 .20

World Food Day Type of 1981

1982, Oct. 16 *Perf. 12x12½*

635 A197 80fr multi .75 .25

No. 635 is overprinted "EFA POLO ARIARY" on the text.

25th Anniv. of Launching of Sputnik I — A205

1982, Oct. 4 Litho. *Perf. 12*

636 A205 10fr Sputnik I .25 .20
637 A205 80fr Yuri Gagarin, Vostok I .80 .25
638 A205 100fr Soyuz-Salyut 1.00 .30
Nos. 636-638 (3) 2.05 .75

1982 World Cup — A206

Designs: Various soccer players.

1982, Oct. 14 *Perf. 12x12½*

639 A206 30fr multi .30 .20
640 A206 40fr multi .40 .20
641 A206 80fr multi .80 .25
Nos. 639-641 (3) 1.50 .65

Souvenir Sheet

Perf. 11½x12½

642 A206 450fr multi 4.50 1.60

Scene at a Bar, by Edouard Manet (1832-1883) — A207

1982, Nov. 25 *Perf. 12½x12*

643 A207 5fr shown .55 .25
644 A207 30fr Lady in a White Dress .75 .30
645 A207 170fr Portrait of Mallarme 3.50 .70
Nos. 643-645 (3) 4.80 1.25

Souvenir Sheet

Perf. 11½x12½

646 A207 400fr The Fifer, vert. 8.00 2.00

For surcharge, see No. 1475B.

Local Fish — A208

1982, Dec. 14 *Perf. 11½*

647 A208 5fr Lutianus sebae .30 .20
648 A208 20fr Istiophorus platypterus .35 .20
649 A208 30fr Pterois volitans .55 .25
650 A208 50fr Thunnus albacares 1.25 .25
651 A208 200fr Epinephelus fasciatus 3.75 .60
Nos. 647-651 (5) 6.20 1.50

Souvenir Sheet

Perf. 12½x12

652 A208 450fr Latimeria chalumnae 7.00 2.00

No. 652 contains one stamp 38x26mm.

Fort Mahavelona Ruins — A209

1982, Dec. 22 *Perf. 12½x12*

653 A209 10fr shown .20 .20
654 A209 30fr Ramena Beach .25 .20
655 A209 400fr Flowering jacaranda trees 3.00 1.00
Nos. 653-655 (3) 3.45 1.40

60th Anniv. of USSR — A210

1982, Dec. 29

656 A210 10fr Tractors .20 .20
657 A210 15fr Pylon .20 .20
658 A210 30fr Kremlin, Lenin .25 .20
659 A210 150fr Arms 1.25 .50
Nos. 656-659 (4) 1.90 1.10

World Communications Year — A211

80fr, Stylized figures holding wheel.

1983, May 17 Litho. *Perf. 12*

660 A211 30fr multi .25 .20
661 A211 80fr multi .80 .30

United African Organization, 20th Anniv. A212

1983, May 25 Litho. *Perf. 12*

662 A212 30fr multi .25 .20

Henri Douzon, Lawyer and Patriot — A213

1983, June 27 Litho. *Perf. 12*

663 A213 30fr multi .25 .20

Souvenir Sheet

Manned Flight Bicentenary — A214

1983, July 20 Litho. *Perf. 12*

664 A214 500fr Montgolfiere balloon 5.75 2.00

Souvenir Sheet

Raphael, 500th Birth Anniv. — A215

1983, Aug. 10 Litho. *Perf. 12*

665 A215 500fr The Madonna Connestable 5.75 2.00

Lemur — A216

Various lemurs. Nos. 668-669, 671 vert.

Perf. 12½x12, 12x12½

1983, Dec. 6 Litho.

666 A216 30fr Daubentonia madagascariensis .55 .25
667 A216 30fr Microcebus murinus .55 .25
668 A216 30fr Lemur variegatus .55 .25
669 A216 30fr Propithecus verreauxi .55 .25
670 A216 200fr Indri indri 3.50 .80
Nos. 666-670 (5) 5.70 1.80

Souvenir Sheet

671 A216 500fr Perodicticus potto 8.00 2.00

1984 Winter Olympics A217

1984, Jan. 20 Litho. *Perf. 11½*

672 A217 20fr Ski jumping .20 .20
673 A217 30fr Speed skating .25 .20
674 A217 30fr Downhill skiing .25 .20
675 A217 30fr Hockey .25 .20
676 A217 200fr Figure skating 2.00 .60
Nos. 672-676 (5) 2.95 1.40

Souvenir Sheet

677 A217 500fr Cross-country skiing 4.75 2.00

No. 677 contains one stamp 48x32mm.

Vintage Cars — A218

1984, Jan. 27 *Perf. 12½x12*

678 A218 15fr Renault, 1907 .25 .20
679 A218 30fr Benz, 1896 .30 .20
680 A218 30fr Baker, 1901 .30 .20
681 A218 30fr Blake, 1901 .30 .20
682 A218 200fr FIAL, 1908 2.40 .60
Nos. 678-682 (5) 3.55 1.40

Souvenir Sheet

Perf. 12½x11½

683 A218 450fr Russo-Baltique, 1909 5.50 2.00

Pastor Ravelojaona (1879-1956), Encyclopedist A219

1984, Feb. 14 *Perf. 12x12½*

684 A219 30fr multi .25 .20

See No. 704.

Madonna and Child, by Correggio (1489-1534) A220

Various Correggio paintings.

1984, May 5 Litho. *Perf. 12x12½*

685 A220 5fr multi .20 .20
686 A220 20fr multi .25 .20
687 A220 30fr multi .35 .20
688 A220 80fr multi .75 .30
689 A220 200fr multi 2.10 .60
Nos. 685-689 (5) 3.65 1.50

Souvenir Sheet

690 A220 400fr multi 5.50 2.00

A221

A222

1984, July 27

691 A221 5fr Paris landmarks .20 .20
692 A221 20fr Wilhelm Steinitz .30 .20
693 A221 30fr Champion, cup .50 .25
694 A221 30fr Vera Menchik .50 .25
695 A221 215fr Champion, cup, diff. 3.00 .80
Nos. 691-695 (5) 4.50 1.70

Souvenir Sheet

696 A221 400fr Children playing chess 5.50 2.00

World Chess Federation, 60th anniv.

1984, Aug. 10

697 A222 100fr Soccer 1.00 .35

1984 Summer Olympics.

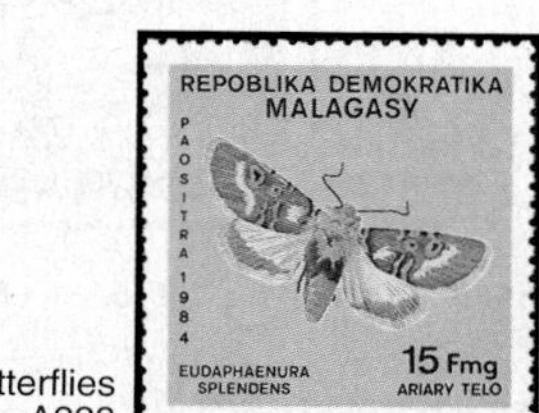

Butterflies A223

1984, Aug. 30 Litho. *Perf. 11½*

698 A223 15fr Eudaphaenura splendens .45 .20
699 A223 50fr Othreis boseae 1.40 .25
700 A223 50fr Pharmacophagus antenor 1.40 .25
701 A223 50fr Acraea hova 1.40 .25
702 A223 200fr Epicausis smithii 5.50 .65
Nos. 698-702 (5) 10.15 1.60

Miniature Sheet

Perf. 11½x12½

703 A223 400fr Papilio delandii 7.50 2.00

No. 703 contains one stamp 37x52mm.

Famous People Type

Jean Ralaimongo (1884-1944).

1984, Oct. 4 *Perf. 12x12½*

704 A219 50fr Portrait .60 .20

Children's Rights A225

1984, Nov. 20 Litho. *Perf. 12½x12*

705 A225 50fr Youths in school bag .50 .20

Malagasy Orchids — A226

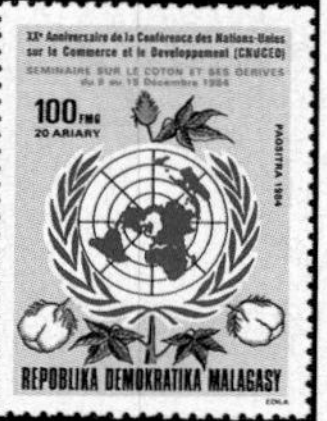

Cotton Seminar, UN Trade and Development Conference A227

1984, Nov. 20 Litho. *Perf. 12*

706 A226 20fr Disa incarnata .30 .20
707 A226 235fr Eulophiella roempleriana 3.25 .70
Nos. 706-707,C180-C182 (5) 6.55 1.50

Miniature Sheet

Perf. 12x12½

708 A226 400fr Gastrorchis tuberculosa 7.50 2.00

No. 708 contains one stamp 30x42mm.

1984, Dec. 15 Litho. *Perf. 13x12½*

709 A227 100fr UN emblem, cotton bolls 1.00 .30

Malagasy Language Bible, 150th Anniv. A228

1985, Feb. 11 Litho. *Perf. 12½x12*

710 A228 50fr multi .50 .20

1985 Agricultural Census — A229

1985, Feb. 21 Litho. *Perf. 12x12½*

711 A229 50fr Census taker, farmer .50 .20

Allied Defeat of Nazi Germany, 40th Anniv. — A230

20fr, Russian flag-raising, Berlin, 1945. 50fr, Normandy-Niemen squadron shooting down German fighter planes. #714, Soviet Victory Parade, Red Square, Moscow. #715, Victorious French troops marching through Arc de Triomphe, vert.

1985 ***Perf. 12½x12, 12x12½***

712 A230 20fr multi .30 .20
713 A230 50fr multi .30 .35
714 A230 100fr multi .90 .35
715 A230 100fr multi 3.00 .70
Nos. 712-715 (4) 4.50 1.60

Issue dates: #712-714, May 9; #715, Oct.

Cats and Dogs A231

1985, Apr. 25 ***Perf. 12x12½, 12½x12***

716 A231 20fr Siamese .30 .20
717 A231 20fr Bichon .30 .20
718 A231 50fr Abyssinian, vert. .75 .25
719 A231 100fr Cocker spaniel, vert. 1.40 .35
720 A231 235fr Poodle 3.50 .80
Nos. 716-720 (5) 6.25 1.80

Souvenir Sheet

721 A231 400fr Kitten 6.00 2.00

No. 721 contains one stamp 42x30mm, perf. 12½x12.

Gymnastic Event, Natl. Stadium, Atananarivo — A232

1985, July 9 ***Perf. 12½x12***

722 A232 50fr multi .45 .20

Natl. Socialist Revolution, 10th anniv.

Commemorative Medal, Memorial Stele — A233

1985, July 9

723 A233 50fr multi 1.25 .25

Independence, 25th anniv.

Intl. Youth Year — A234

Natl. Red Cross, 70th Anniv. — A235

1985, Sept. 18 ***Perf. 12***

724 A234 100fr Emblem, map 1.00 .25

1985, Oct. 3 ***Perf. 12x12½***

725 A235 50fr multi .90 .20

Indira Gandhi — A236

22nd World Youth and Student's Festival, Moscow — A237

1985, Oct. 31 ***Perf. 13½***

726 A236 100fr multi 1.10 .35

1985, Nov. ***Perf. 12***

727 A237 50fr multi .50 .20

Rouen Cathedral at Night, by Monet — A238

UN, 40th Aniv. — A239

Impressionist paintings: No. 729, View of Sea at Sainte-Marie, by van Gogh, horiz. 45fr, Young Women in Black, by Renoir. 50fr, The Red Vineyard at Arles, by van Gogh, horiz. 100fr, Boulevard des Capucines in Paris, by Monet, horiz. 400fr, In the Garden, by Renoir.

1985, Oct. 25 **Litho.** ***Perf. 12***

728 A238 20fr multi .50 .20
729 A238 20fr multi .50 .20
730 A238 45fr multi .90 .20
731 A238 50fr multi 1.10 .20
732 A238 100fr multi 2.40 .50
Nos. 728-732 (5) 5.40 1.30

Souvenir Sheet

Perf. 12x12½

733 A238 400fr multi 6.00 2.75

No. 733 contains one 30x42mm stamp.

1985, Oct. 31 ***Perf. 12***

734 A239 100fr multi 1.00 .30

Orchids A240

1985, Nov. 8

735 A240 20fr Aeranthes grandiflora 1.00 .20
736 A240 45fr Angraecum magdalanae 1.50 .25
737 A240 50fr Aerangis stylosa 1.75 .30
738 A240 100fr Angraecum eburneum longicalcar 3.25 .50
739 A240 100fr Angraecum sesquipedale 3.25 .50
Nos. 735-739 (5) 10.75 1.75

Souvenir Sheet

Perf. 12x12½

740 A240 400fr Angraecum aburneum superbum 8.00 2.50

Nos. 735, 737-740 vert. No. 740 contains one 30x42mm stamp.

INTERCOSMOS — A241

Cosmonauts, natl. flags, rockets, satellites and probes.

1985, Nov. ***Perf. 12x12½***

741 A241 20fr USSR, Czechoslovakia .25 .20
742 A241 20fr Soyuz-Apollo emblem .25 .20
743 A241 50fr USSR, India .55 .25
744 A241 100fr USSR, Cuba 1.00 .30
745 A241 200fr USSR, France 1.90 .65
Nos. 741-745 (5) 3.95 1.60

Souvenir Sheet

746 A241 400fr Halley's Comet, probe 5.50 1.75

No. 746 contains one stamp 42x30mm.

Independence, 10th Anniv. — A242

1985, Dec. 30 **Litho.** ***Perf. 12½x12***

747 A242 50fr Industrial symbols .45 .20

Natl. Insurance and Securities Co. (ARO), 10th Anniv. — A243

1986, Jan. 20 ***Perf. 12x12½***

748 A243 50fr dk brn, yel org & gray brn .45 .25

Paintings in the Tretyakov Gallery, Moscow — A244

Designs: 20fr, Still-life with Flowers and Fruit, 1839, by I. Chroutzky. No. 750, Portrait of Alexander Pushkin, 1827, by O. Kiprenski, vert. No. 751, Portrait of an Unknown Woman, 1883, by I. Kramskoi. No. 752, The Crows Have Returned, 1872, by A. Sakrassov, vert. 100fr, March, 1895, by I. Levitan. 450fr, Portrait of Pavel Tretyakov, 1883, by I. Repin, vert.

Perf. 12½x12, 12x12½

1986, Apr. 26 **Litho.**

749 A244 20fr multi .25 .20
750 A244 50fr multi .80 .25
751 A244 50fr multi .80 .25
752 A244 50fr multi .80 .25
753 A244 100fr multi 2.25 .40
Nos. 749-753 (5) 4.90 1.35

Souvenir Sheet

754 A244 450fr multi 4.50 2.00

1986 World Cup Soccer Championships, Mexico — A245

1986, May 31 ***Perf. 13½***

755 A245 150fr multi 1.40 .45

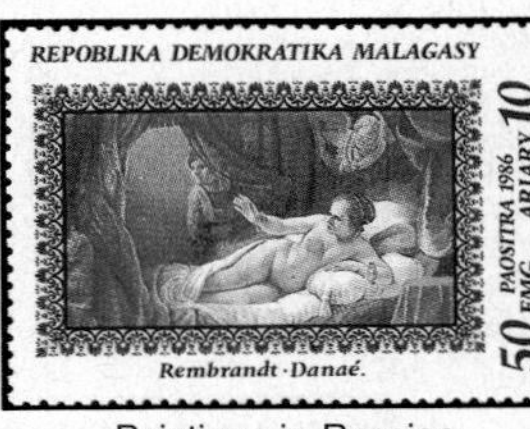

Paintings in Russian Museums — A246

#756, David and Urie, by Rembrandt, vert. #757, Danae, by Rembrandt. #758, Portrait of the Nurse of the Infant Isabella, by Rubens, vert. #759, The Alliance of Earth and Water, by Rubens, vert. #760, Portrait of an Old Man in Red, by Rembrandt. #761, The Holy Family, by Raphael.

Perf. 12x12½, 12½x12

1986, Mar. 24 **Litho.**

756 A246 20fr multi .25 .20
757 A246 50fr multi .70 .25
758 A246 50fr multi .70 .25
759 A246 50fr multi .70 .25
760 A246 50fr multi .75 .25
Nos. 756-760 (5) 3.10 1.20

Souvenir Sheet

Perf. 11½x12½

761 A246 450fr multi 3.50 2.50

UN Child Survival Campaign A247

A248

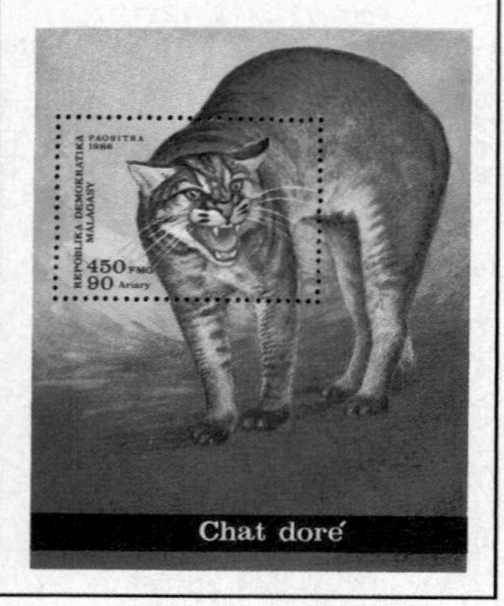

Wildcats — A249

1986, June 1 Litho. *Perf. 12x12½*

762 A247 60fr multi .60 .25

1986, July 17

763 A248 10fr Sable .25 .20
764 A248 10fr Chaus .25 .20
765 A248 60fr Serval .70 .25
766 A248 60fr Caracal .70 .25
767 A248 60fr Bengal .70 .25
Nos. 763-767 (5) 2.60 1.15

Souvenir Sheet

Perf. 12½x12

768 A249 450fr Golden 4.75 2.00

Intl. Peace Year A249a

1986, Sept. 12 *Perf. 12*

769 A249a 60fr shown .55 .25
770 A249a 150fr Hemispheres, emblem, vert. 1.25 .40

World Post Day — A250

1986, Oct. 9 Litho. *Perf. 13x12½*

771 A250 60fr multi .60 .25
772 A250 150fr multi 1.40 .40

No. 772 is airmail.

A251

Birds — A252

Perf. 12x12½, 12½x12

1986, Dec. 23 Litho.

773 A251 60fr Xenopirostris daimi, vert. .80 .25
774 A251 60fr Falculea palliata .80 .25
775 A251 60fr Coua gigas .80 .25
776 A251 60fr Coua cristata .80 .25
777 A251 60fr Cianolanius madagascariensis, vert. .80 .25
Nos. 773-777 (5) 4.00 1.25

Souvenir Sheet

778 A252 450fr Bubulcus ibis ibis 6.00 2.00

A253

Endangered Species — A254

Perf. 12x12½, 12½x12

1987, Mar. 13 Litho.

779 A253 60fr Lophotibis cristata, vert. 1.10 .25
780 A253 60fr Coracopsis nigra 1.10 .25
781 A254 60fr Crocodylus niloticus 1.10 .25
782 A254 60fr Geochelone yniphora 1.10 .25
Nos. 779-782 (4) 4.40 1.00

Souvenir Sheet

783 A253 450fr Centropus toulou, vert. 6.25 2.00

Anti-Colonial Revolt, 40th Anniv. — A255

A256

1987, Mar. 29 *Perf. 12*

784 A255 60fr multi .50 .20
785 A256 60fr multi .50 .20

1st Games of Indian Ocean Towns A257

1987, Apr. 15 *Perf. 13½*

786 A257 60fr multi .55 .25
787 A257 150fr multi 1.25 .40

Le Sarimanok — A258

1987, Apr. 15

788 A258 60fr Port side .60 .25
789 A258 150fr Starboard side 1.40 .40

African and Madagascar Coffee Organization, 25th Anniv. — A259

1987, Apr. 24 Litho. *Perf. 12*

790 A259 60fr Coffee plant .55 .25
791 A259 150fr Map 1.40 .40

Halley's Comet — A260

Space probes.

1987, May 13 *Perf. 13½*

792 A260 60fr Giotto, ESA .40 .20
793 A260 150fr Vega 1, Russia .90 .25
794 A260 250fr Vega 2, Russia 1.75 .40
795 A260 350fr Planet-A1, Japan 2.50 .60
796 A260 400fr Planet-A2, Japan 2.75 .65
797 A260 450fr ICE, US 3.25 .70
Nos. 792-797 (6) 11.55 2.80

Souvenir Sheet

798 A260 600fr Halley, Giotto 4.50 1.00

Litho. & Embossed 'Gold Foil' Stamps
These stamps generally are of a different design format than the rest of the issue. Since there is a commemorative inscription tying them to the issue a separate illustration is not being shown.

1988 Calgary Winter Olympics — A261

Jean-Joseph Rabearivelo (d. 1937), Poet — A263

Men's Downhill — A262

1987, May 13

799 A261 60fr Biathlon .40 .20
800 A261 150fr shown .90 .25
801 A261 250fr Luge 1.75 .40
802 A261 350fr Speed skating 2.50 .60
803 A261 400fr Hockey 2.75 .65
804 A261 450fr Pairs figure skating 3.25 .70
Nos. 799-804 (6) 11.55 2.80

Litho. & Embossed

804A A261 1500fr Speed skating 11.00

Souvenir Sheets

Litho.

805 A262 600fr shown 4.75 1.25

Litho. & Embossed

805A A262 1500fr Slalom skiing 7.50

No. 804A exists in souvenir sheet of 1.

1987, June 22 *Perf. 13½*

806 A263 60fr multi .40 .25

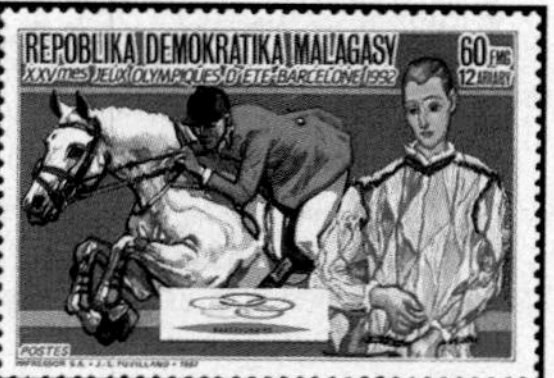

1992 Summer Olympics, Barcelona — A264

Athletes, emblem and art or architecture: 60fr, Equestrian, and the Harlequin, by Picasso. 150fr, Weight lifting, church. 250fr, Hurdles, Canaletas Fountain. 350fr, High jump, amusement park. 400fr, Men's gymnastics, abbey. 450fr, Rhythmic gymnastics, Arc de Triomphe. 600fr, Equestrian, Columbus monument.

1987, Oct. 7 Litho. *Perf. 13½*

807 A264 60fr multi .25 .20
808 A264 150fr multi .80 .25
809 A264 250fr multi 1.40 .40
810 A264 350fr multi 2.00 .60
811 A264 400fr multi 2.25 .65
812 A264 450fr multi 2.50 .70
Nos. 807-812 (6) 9.20 2.80

Souvenir Sheet

813 A264 600fr multi 3.75 1.25

Nos. 811-813 are airmail.

A265

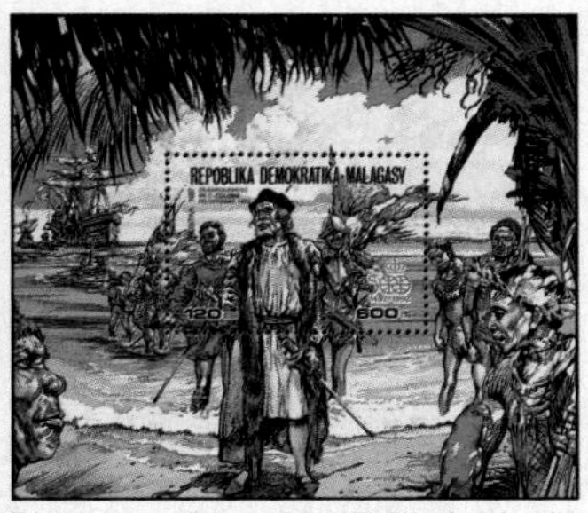

Discovery of America, 500th Anniv. (in 1992) — A266

Anniv. emblem and: 60fr, Bartolomeu Dias (c. 1450-1500), Portuguese navigator, departure from De Palos, 1492. 150fr, Henry the Navigator (1394-1460), prince of Portugal, Samana Cay. 250fr, A. De Marchena landing, 1492. 350fr, Paolo Toscanelli dal Pozzo (1397-1482), Italian physician and cosmographer, La Navidad Fort. 400fr, Queen Isabella I, Barcelona, 1493. 450fr, Christopher Columbus, the Nina. 600fr, Landing in New World, 1492.

1987, Sept. 24 Litho. *Perf. 13½*

814 A265 60fr multi .30 .20
815 A265 150fr multi .80 .30
816 A265 250fr multi 1.25 .55
817 A265 350fr multi 1.90 .85
818 A265 400fr multi 2.25 1.00
819 A265 450fr multi 2.50 1.10
Nos. 814-819 (6) 9.00 4.00

Souvenir Sheet

820 A266 600fr multi 4.00 1.50

A267

A268

1987, July 27 *Perf. 12½x12*

821 A267 60fr multi .40 .25

Natl. telecommunications research laboratory.

1987, Aug. 14

822 A268 60fr lt blue, blk & brt ultra .40 .25

Rafaravavy Rasalama (d. 1837), Christian martyr.

Antananarivo-Tamatave Telegraph Link, Cent. — A269

1987, Sept. 15 *Perf. 12x12½*

823 A269 60fr multi .40 .25

Pasteur Institute, Paris, Cent. — A270

1987, Oct. 26 *Perf. 13½*

824 A270 250fr multi 1.10 .50

City of Berlin, 750th Anniv. — A271

Design: Anniv. emblem, television tower and the Interhotel in East Berlin.

1987, Oct. 18 Litho. *Perf. 12½x12*

825 A271 150fr multi .40 .30

Schools Festival — A272

1987, Oct. 23 *Perf. 12x12½*

826 A272 60fr multi .25 .20

Paintings in the Pushkin Museum, Moscow — A273

Designs: 10fr, After the Shipwreck (1847), by Eugene Delacroix (1798-1863). No. 828, Still-life with Swan (c. 1620), by Frans Snyders (1579-1647). No. 829, Jupiter and Callisto (1744), by Francois Boucher (1703-1770), vert. No. 830, Chalet in the Mountains (1874), by Jean Desire Gustav Courbet (1819-1877). 150fr, At the Market (1564), by Joachim Bueckelaer. 1000fr, Minerva (1560), by Paolo Veronese (1528-1588), vert.

Perf. 12½x12, 12x12½

1987, Nov. 10

827 A273 10fr multi .30 .20
828 A273 60fr multi .45 .20
829 A273 60fr multi .45 .20
830 A273 60fr multi .45 .20
831 A273 150fr multi 1.00 .25
Nos. 827-831 (5) 2.65 1.05

Souvenir Sheet

832 A273 1000fr multi 7.00 2.75

Pan-African Telecommunications Union, 10th Anniv. — A274

1987, Dec. 28 *Perf. 13x12½*

833 A274 250fr multi .60 .45

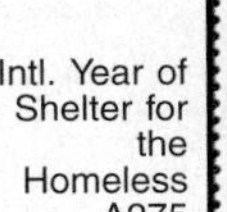

Intl. Year of Shelter for the Homeless — A275

1988, Feb. 15 Litho. *Perf. 12*

834 A275 80fr shown .20 .20
835 A275 250fr Family in shelter, rain, vert. .55 .25

Fauna — A276

1988, Apr. 18 Litho. *Perf. 13½*

836 A276 60fr Hapalemur simus 1.75 .75
837 A276 150fr Propithecus diadema diadema 2.25 .75
838 A276 250fr Indri indri 3.25 1.00
839 A276 350fr Varecia variegata variegata 5.00 1.25
840 A276 550fr Madagascar young heron 1.50 .60
841 A276 1500fr Nossi-Be chameleon 3.50 1.60
Nos. 836-841 (6) 17.25 5.95

Souvenir Sheet

842 A276 1500fr Uratelornis (bird) 6.50 6.50

Conservation and service organization emblems: World Wildlife Fund (60fr, 150fr, 250fr and 350fr); Rotary Intl. (550fr and No. 842); and Scouting trefoil (No. 841).

Nos. 840-841 exist in souvenir sheet of 2.

For overprints see Nos. 1134, 1154.

October Revolution, Russia, 70th Anniv. — A277

1988, Mar. 7 Litho. *Perf. 12x12½*

843 A277 60fr Lenin .60 .20
844 A277 60fr Revolutionaries .60 .20
845 A277 150fr Lenin, revolutionaries 1.25 .20
Nos. 843-845 (3) 2.45 .60

1988 Winter Olympics, Calgary — A278

1988, May 11 *Perf. 11½*

846 A278 20fr Pairs figure skating .20 .20
847 A278 60fr Slalom .20 .20
848 A278 60fr Speed skating .20 .20
849 A278 100fr Cross-country skiing .30 .20
850 A278 250fr Ice hockey .70 .30
Nos. 846-850 (5) 1.60 1.10

Souvenir Sheet

851 A278 800fr Ski jumping 2.50 1.75

Discovery of Radium by Pierre and Marie Curie, 90th Anniv. — A279

1988, July 14 Litho. *Perf. 12*

852 A279 150fr blk & rose lil .50 .20

OAU, 25th Anniv. — A280

1988, May 25 Litho. *Perf. 13*

853 A280 80fr multi .25 .20

Natl. Telecommunications and Posts Institute, 20th Anniv. — A281

1988, June 22 *Perf. 13½*

854 A281 80fr multi .25 .20

Saint-Michel College, Cent. — A282

1988, July 9

855 A282 250fr multi .55 .30

Alma-Ata Declaration, 10th Anniv. — A283

WHO, 40th Anniv. — A284

1988, Aug. 11 Litho. *Perf. 12*

856 A283 60fr multi .30 .20

1988, Aug. 11

857 A284 150fr multi .30 .20

Tsimbazaza Botanical and Zoological Park, 150th Anniv. — A285

Perf. 12x12½, 12½x12

1988, Aug. 22

858 A285 20fr Lemur habitat .55 .25
859 A285 80fr Lemur and young .55 .25
860 A285 250fr shown 1.50 .40
Nos. 858-860 (3) 2.60 .90

Souvenir Sheet

861 A285 1000fr Lemur and mate 3.50 2.25

Size of No. 859: 25x37mm.

Boy Scouts Studying Birds and Butterflies A286

Designs: 80fr, Upupa epops maginata, Coua caerulea and scout photographing bird. 250fr, Chrysiridia croesus and comparing butterfly to a sketch. 270fr, Nelicurvius nelicourvi, Foudia omissa and constructing bird feeder. 350fr, Papilio dardanus and studying butterflies with magnifying glass. 550fr, Coua critata and tagging bird. No. 867, Argema mittrei and writing observations. No. 868, Merops superciliosus and recording bird calls. No. 868A, Euchloron megaera. No. 868B, Rhynchee.

1988, Sept. 29

862 A286 80fr multi .20 .20
863 A286 250fr multi .55 .30
864 A286 270fr multi .60 .30
865 A286 350fr multi .80 .40
866 A286 550fr multi 1.25 .60
867 A286 1500fr multi 3.75 1.60
Nos. 862-867 (6) 7.15 3.40

Souvenir Sheet

868 A286 1500fr multi 3.50 2.25

Litho. & Embossed

Perf. 13½

868A A286 5000fr gold & multi 8.00

Souvenir Sheet

868B A286 5000fr gold & multi 8.00

No. 868 contains one stamp 36x51mm.
Nos. 868A-868B dated 1989. Nos. 868A-868B exist imperf.

Composers and Entertainers A287

Designs: 80fr, German-made clavier and Carl Philipp Emanuel Bach (1714-1788), organist and composer. 250fr, Piano and Franz Peter Schubert (1797-1828), Austrian composer. 270fr, Scene from opera Carmen, 1875, and Georges Bizet (1838-1875), French composer. 350fr, Scene from opera Pelleas et Melisande, 1902, and Claude Debussy (1862-1918), French composer. 550fr, George Gershwin (1898-1937), American composer. No. 874, Elvis Presley (1935-1977), American entertainer. No. 875, Rimsky-Korsakov (1844-1908), Russian composer, and Le Coq d'Or from the opera of the same name.

1988, Oct. 28 ***Perf. 12x12½, 12½x12***

869 A287 80fr multi .20 .20
870 A287 250fr multi .55 .30
871 A287 270fr multi .60 .30
872 A287 350fr multi .80 .40
873 A287 550fr multi 1.25 .60
874 A287 1500fr multi 3.50 1.60
Nos. 869-874 (6) 6.90 3.40

Souvenir Sheet

875 A287 1500fr multi 3.25 3.25

For overprints see Nos. 1135-1136.

Intl. Fund for Agricultural Development (IFAD), 10th Anniv. — A288

1988, Sept. 4 **Litho.** ***Perf. 12***

876 A288 250fr multi .50 .25

School Feast — A289

1988, Nov. 22

877 A289 80fr multi .25 .20

A290

Ships — A291

Paintings: 20fr, The Squadron of the Sea, Black Feodossia, by Ivan Aivazovski, vert. No. 879, Seascape with Sailing Ships, by Simon de Vlieger, vert. No. 880, The Ship Lesnoie, by N. Semenov, vert. 100fr, The Merchantman, Orel, by N. Golitsine. 250fr, Naval Exercises, by Adam Silo, vert. 550fr, On the River, by Abraham Beerstraten.

1988, Dec. 5 ***Perf. 12x12½, 12½x12***

878 A290 20fr multi .20 .20
879 A290 80fr multi .25 .20
880 A290 80fr multi .25 .20
881 A290 100fr shown .35 .20
882 A290 250fr multi .80 .25
Nos. 878-882 (5) 1.85 1.05

Souvenir Sheet

Perf. 11½x12½

883 A291 550fr shown 2.00 1.00

World Wildlife Fund — A292

Insect species in danger of extinction: 20fr, Tragocephala crassicornis. 80fr, Polybothris symptuosa-gema. 250fr, Euchroea auripigmenta. 350fr, Stellognata maculata.

1988, Dec. 13 ***Perf. 12***

884 A292 20fr multi *1.00* —
885 A292 80fr multi *6.50* —
886 A292 250fr multi *22.50* —
887 A292 350fr multi *30.00* —
Nos. 884-887 (4) *60.00*

Intl. Red Cross and Red Crescent Organizations, 125th Annivs. — A293

1988, Dec. 27 **Litho.** ***Perf. 12***

888 A293 80fr Globe, stretcher-bearers, vert. .20 .20
889 A293 250fr Emblems, Dunant .55 .30

UN Declaration of Human Rights, 40th Anniv. (in 1988) — A294

1989, Jan. 10

890 A294 80fr shown .25 .20
891 A294 250fr Hands, "4" and "0" .60 .30

Dated 1988.

Transportation — A295

Designs: 80fr, 1909 Mercedes-Benz Blitzen Benz. 250fr, Micheline ZM 517 Tsikirity, Tananarive-Moramanga line. 270fr, Bugatti Coupe Binder 41. 350fr, Electric locomotive 1020-DES OBB, Germany. 1500fr, Souleze Autorail 701 DU CFN, Madagascar. No. 897, 1913 Opel race car. No. 898, Bugatti Presidential Autorail locomotive and Bugatti Type 57 Atalante automobile.

1989, Jan. 24 ***Perf. 13½***

892 A295 80fr multi .20 .20
893 A295 250fr multi .50 .25
894 A295 270fr multi .60 .25
895 A295 350fr multi 1.00 .35
896 A295 1500fr multi 3.50 1.40
897 A295 2500fr multi 5.50 2.40
Nos. 892-897 (6) 11.30 4.85

Souvenir Sheet

898 A295 2500fr multi 5.00 3.50

Nos. 893-897 exist imperf. Value, set $13.

Dinosaurs — A296

1989, Feb. 1 **Litho.** ***Perf. 12½x12***

899 A296 20fr Tyrannosaurus .25 .20
900 A296 80fr Stegosaurus 1.10 .20
901 A296 250fr Arsinoitherium 3.25 .50
902 A296 450fr Triceratops 4.50 1.00
Nos. 899-902 (4) 9.10 1.90

Souvenir Sheet

Perf. 11½x12½

903 A296 600fr Sauralophus, vert. 2.75 1.25

Women as the Subject of Paintings — A297

Designs: 20fr, *Tahitian Pastorales*, by Gauguin. No 905, *Portrait of a Young Woman*, by Titian, vert. No. 906, *Portrait of a Little Girl*, by Jean-Baptiste Greuze (1725-1805), vert. 100fr, *Woman in Black*, by Renoir, vert. 250fr, *Lacemaker*, by Vassili Tropinine, vert. 550fr, *The Annunciation*, by Cima Da Conegliano (c. 1459-1517), vert.

1989, Feb. 10 ***Perf. 12½x12, 12x12½***

904 A297 20fr multi .20 .20
905 A297 80fr multi .25 .20
906 A297 80fr multi .25 .20
907 A297 100fr multi .35 .20
908 A297 250fr multi .75 .30
Nos. 904-908 (5) 1.80 1.10

Souvenir Sheet

Perf. 11½x12½

909 A297 550fr multi 1.60 1.00

Orchids A298

1989, Feb. 28 **Litho.** ***Perf. 12***

910 A298 5fr *Sobennikoffia robusta*, vert. .45 .20
911 A298 10fr *Grammangis fallax* .45 .20
912 A298 80fr *Cymbidiella humblotii*, vert. 1.25 .20
913 A298 80fr *Angraecum sororium*, vert. 1.25 .20
914 A298 250fr *Oenia oncidiiflora*, vert. 3.00 .35
Nos. 910-914 (5) 6.40 1.15

Souvenir Sheet

915 A298 1000fr *Aerangis curnowiana* 5.50 2.75

Jawaharlal Nehru (1889-1964), 1st Prime Minister of Independent India — A299

1989, Mar. 7 **Litho.** ***Perf. 13***

916 A299 250fr multi .50 .25

Ornamental Mineral Industry A300

1989, Apr. 12 **Litho.** ***Perf. 13½***

917 A300 80fr Rose quartz .30 .20
918 A300 250fr Petrified wood .90 .30

Views of Antananarivo A301

Designs: 5fr, Mahamasina Sports Complex, Ampefiloha Quarter. 20fr, Andravoahangy and Anjanahary Quarters. No. 921, Zoma Market and Faravohitra Quarter. No. 922, Andohan'Analakely Quarter and March 29th monument. 250fr, Independence Avenue and Jean Ralaimongo monument. 550fr, Queen's Palace and Andohalo School on Lake Anosy.

1989, Mar. 31 Litho. *Perf. 13½*

No.	Type	Value	Description	Unused	Used
919	A301	5fr	multi	.20	.20
920	A301	20fr	multi	.20	.20
921	A301	80fr	multi	.25	.25
922	A301	80fr	multi	.25	.25
923	A301	250fr	multi	.50	.25
924	A301	550fr	multi	.90	.35
			Nos. 919-924 (6)	2.30	1.50

Visit of Pope John Paul II — A302

1989, Apr. 28 *Perf. 12x12½*

No.	Type	Value	Description	Unused	Used
925	A302	80fr	shown	.30	.20
926	A302	250fr	Pope, map	1.00	.25

French Revolution, Bicent. A303

1989, July 7 Litho. *Perf. 12½*

No.	Type	Value	Description	Unused	Used
927	A303	250fr	Storming of the Bastille	.60	.25

Phobos Space Program for the Exploration of Mars — A304

1989, Aug. 29 Litho. *Perf. 12½x12*

No.	Type	Value	Description	Unused	Used
928	A304	20fr	Mars 1	.20	.20
929	A304	80fr	Mars 3	.25	.20
930	A304	80fr	Sond 2	.25	.20
931	A304	250fr	Mariner 9	.55	.25
932	A304	270fr	Viking 2	.65	.30
			Nos. 928-932 (5)	1.90	1.15

Souvenir Sheet

No.	Type	Value	Description	Unused	Used
933	A304	550fr	Phobos	1.50	.60

PHILEXFRANCE '89 and French Revolution, Bicent. — A305

Exhibition emblems, key people and scenes from the revolution: 250fr, Honore-Gabriel Riqueti (1749-1791), Count of Mirabeau, at the meeting of Estates-General, June 23, 1789. 350fr, Camille Desmoulins (1760-1794), call to arms, July 12, 1789. 1000fr, Lafayette (1757-1834), women's march on Versailles, Oct. 5, 1789. 1500fr, King tried by the National Convention, Dec. 26, 1792. 2500fr, Charlotte Corday (1768-1793), assassination of Marat, July 13, 1793. 3000fr, Bertrand Barere de Vieuzac, Robespierre, Jean-Marie Collot D'Herbois, Lazare Nicolas Carnot, George Jacques Danton, Georges Auguste Couthon, Pierre-Louis Prieur, Antoine Saint-Just and Marc Guillaume Vadiez, Committee of Public Safety, July, 1793. No. 939A, Family saying farewell to Louis XVI. No. 939B, Danton and the Club of the Cordeliers.

Illustration reduced.

1989, July 14 Litho. *Perf. 13½*

No.	Type	Value	Description	Unused	Used
934	A305	250fr	multicolored	.45	.20
935	A305	350fr	multicolored	.65	.25
936	A305	1000fr	multicolored	1.60	.65
937	A305	1500fr	multicolored	2.50	1.00
938	A305	2500fr	multicolored	4.25	1.60
			Nos. 934-938 (5)	9.45	3.70

Souvenir Sheet

No.	Type	Value	Description	Unused	Used
939	A305	3000fr	multicolored	4.50	4.50

Litho. & Embossed

No.	Type	Value	Description	Unused	Used
939A	A305	5000fr	gold & multi	8.00	

Souvenir Sheet

No.	Type	Value	Description	Unused	Used
939B	A305	5000fr	gold & multi	8.00	

Nos. 939A-939B exist imperf.

For overprints see #1161-1165, 1166A-1166B.

French Revolution, Bicent. — A306

Paintings and sculpture: 5fr, *Liberty Guiding the People,* by Eugene Delacroix. 80fr, "La Marseillaise" from *Departure of the Volunteers in 1792,* high relief on the Arc de Triomphe, 1833-35, by Francois Rude. 250fr, *The Tennis Court Oath,* by David.

1989, Oct. 25 *Perf. 12½x12*

No.	Type	Value	Description	Unused	Used
940	A306	5fr	multicolored	.20	.20
941	A306	80fr	multicolored	.45	.25
942	A306	250fr	multicolored	.90	.25
			Nos. 940-942 (3)	1.55	.70

No. 942 is airmail.

Rene Cassin (1887-1976), Nobel Peace Prize Winner and Institute Founder — A307

1989, Nov. 21 *Perf. 12*

No.	Type	Value	Description	Unused	Used
943	A307	250fr	multicolored	.40	.20

Intl. Law Institute of the French-Speaking Nations, 25th anniv.

Hapalemur aureus A308

1989, Dec. 5 Litho. *Perf. 12*

No.	Type	Value	Description	Unused	Used
944	A308	250fr	multicolored	1.10	.35

A309

A309a

Various athletes, cup and: 350fr, Cavour Monument, Turin. 1000fr, Christopher Columbus Monument, Genoa, 1903. 1500fr, Michelangelo's *David.* 2500fr, *Abduction of Prosperina,* by Bernini, Rome. 3000fr, Statue of Leonardo da Vinci, 1903. 5000fr, Castel Nuovo, Naples.

1989, Dec. 12 Litho. *Perf. 13½*

No.	Type	Value	Description	Unused	Used
945	A309	350fr	multicolored	.65	.25
946	A309	1000fr	multicolored	1.60	.65
947	A309	1500fr	multicolored	2.25	1.00
948	A309	2500fr	multicolored	4.00	1.60
			Nos. 945-948 (4)	8.50	3.50

Souvenir Sheet

No.	Type	Value	Description	Unused	Used
949	A309	3000fr	multicolored	4.25	2.00

Litho. & Embossed

No.	Type	Value	Description	Unused	Used
949A	A309a	5000fr	gold & multi	8.00	

1990 World Cup Soccer Championships, Italy.

For overprints see Nos. 1137-1140.

A310

1989, Oct. 7 Litho. *Perf. 13½*

No.	Type	Value	Description	Unused	Used
950	A310	80fr	Long jump	.20	.20
951	A310	250fr	Pole vault	.35	.20
952	A310	550fr	Hurdles	.80	.40
953	A310	1500fr	Cycling	2.25	1.10
954	A310	2000fr	Baseball	3.00	1.45
955	A310	2500fr	Tennis	3.75	1.75
			Nos. 950-955 (6)	10.35	5.10

Souvenir Sheet

No.	Type	Value	Description	Unused	Used
956	A310	3000fr	Soccer	4.50	2.10

1992 Summer Olympics, Barcelona.

Scenic Views and Artifacts A311

1990, May 29

Size: 47x33mm (#958, 960)

No.	Type	Value	Description	Unused	Used
957	A311	70fr	Queen Isalo Rock	.20	.20
958	A311	70fr	Sakalava pipe	.20	.20
959	A311	150fr	Sakalava combs	.30	.20
960	A311	150fr	Lonjy Is., Diego Suarez Bay	.30	.20
			Nos. 957-960 (4)	1.00	.80

Fish A312

1990, Apr. 26 Litho. *Perf. 12*

No.	Type	Value	Description	Unused	Used
961	A312	5fr	Heniochus acuminatus	.35	.20
962	A312	20fr	Simenhelys dofleinl	.35	.20
963	A312	80fr	Phinobatos perceli	.35	.20
964	A312	250fr	Epinephelus fasciatus	1.50	.25
965	A312	320fr	Sphurna zygaena	1.90	.35
			Nos. 961-965 (5)	4.45	1.20

Souvenir Sheet

No.	Type	Value	Description	Unused	Used
966	A312	550fr	Latimeria chalumnae	3.50	1.50

Nos. 962-963 vert. Nos. 961-966 inscribed 1989.

Moon Landing, 20th Anniv. — A314

Designs: 80fr, Voyager 2, Neptune. 250fr, Hydro 2000 flying boat. 550fr, NOAA satellite. 1500fr, Magellan probe, Venus. 2000fr, Concorde. 2500fr, Armstrong, Aldrin, Collins, lunar module. 3000fr, Apollo 11 astronauts, first step on moon.

1990, June 19 Litho. *Perf. 13½*

No.	Type	Value	Description	Unused	Used
967	A314	80fr	multicolored	.20	.20
968	A314	250fr	multicolored	.35	.20
969	A314	550fr	multicolored	.80	.40
970	A314	1500fr	multicolored	2.25	1.10
971	A314	2000fr	multicolored	3.00	1.50
972	A314	2500fr	multicolored	3.75	1.90
			Nos. 967-972 (6)	10.35	5.30

Souvenir Sheet

No.	Type	Value	Description	Unused	Used
973	A314	3000fr	multicolored	4.75	2.25

For overprint see No. 1304.

Nos. 967-972 exist in souvenir sheets of 1, and se-tenant in a sheet of 6.

A315

A316

1990, July 17

No.	Type	Value	Description	Unused	Used
974	A315	350fr	Bobsled	.50	.25
975	A315	1000fr	Speed skating	1.50	.75
976	A315	1500fr	Nordic skiing	2.25	1.10
977	A315	2500fr	Super giant slalom	3.75	1.90
			Nos. 974-977 (4)	8.00	4.00

Souvenir Sheet

No.	Type	Value	Description	Unused	Used
978	A315	3000fr	Giant slalom	4.50	2.25

Litho. & Embossed

978A A315 5000fr Pairs figure skating 8.00

Souvenir Sheet

978B A315 5000fr Ice hockey 8.00

1992 Winter Olympics, Albertville. Nos. 978A-978B exist imperf.
For overprints see Nos. 1141-1145.

1990, June 19 Litho. *Perf. 12*

979 A316 250fr blk, ultra & bl .45 .20

Intl. Maritime Organization, 30th anniv.

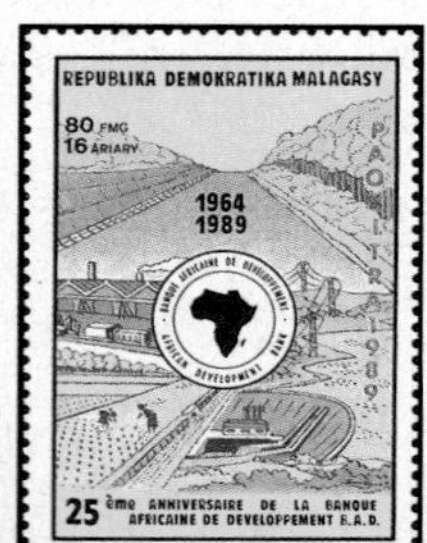

African Development Bank, 25th Anniv. A317

1990, June 19

980 A317 80fr multicolored .30 .20

A318 A319

1990, June 28

981 A318 150fr multicolored .30 .20

Campaign against polio.

1990, Aug. 22

982 A319 100fr multicolored .30 .20

Independence, 30th anniv.

A320 A322

1990, Aug. 24 *Perf. 12½x12*

983 A320 100fr yellow & multi .35 .20
984 A320 350fr lil rose & multi .65 .30

3rd Indian Ocean Games.

1990, Oct. 19 Litho. *Perf. 12*

986 A322 350fr multicolored .65 .30

Ho Chi Minh (1890-1969), Vietnamese leader.

Lemurs A323

1990, Nov. 23 Litho. *Perf. 11½*

987 A323 10fr Avahi laniger .35 .20
988 A323 20fr Lemur fulvus sanfordi .35 .20
989 A323 20fr Lemur fulvus albifrons .35 .20
990 A323 100fr Lemur fulvus collaris 1.25 .20
991 A323 100fr Lepulemur ruficaudatus 1.25 .20
Nos. 987-991 (5) 3.55 1.00

Souvenir Sheet

992 A323 350fr Lemur fulvus fulvus 3.00 .50

Shells A324

1990, Dec. 21 *Perf. 12½*

993 A324 40fr Tridacna squamosa .80 .20
994 A324 50fr Terebra demidiata, Terebra subulata .80 .20

Anniversaries and Events A325

100fr, Charles de Gaulle, liberation of Paris, 1944. 350fr, Galileo probe orbiting Jupiter. 800fr, Apollo 11 crew & Columbia command module, 1st Moon landing, 1969. 900fr, De Gaulle, 1942. 1250fr, Concorde jet, TGV high-speed train. 2500fr, De Gaulle as head of provisional government, 1944. 3000fr, Apollo 11 crew, Eagle lunar module. #1001A, De Gaulle with Roosevelt & Churchill. #1001B, Charles de Gaulle.

1990, Dec. 28 Litho. *Perf. 13½*

995 A325 100fr multi .20 .20
996 A325 350fr multi .60 .30
997 A325 800fr multi 1.40 .70
998 A325 900fr multi 1.60 .80
999 A325 1250fr multi 2.25 1.10
1000 A325 2500fr multi 4.50 2.25
Nos. 995-1000 (6) 10.55 5.35

Souvenir Sheet

1001 A325 3000fr multi 5.25 2.75

Litho. & Embossed

1001A A325 5000fr gold & multi 7.50

Souvenir Sheet

1001B A325 5000fr gold & multi 7.50

Nos. 995-1000, 1001A exist in souvenir sheets of 1. A souvenir sheet containing Nos. 996-997 exists.

Mushrooms — A325b

Designs: 25fr, Boletus edulis. 100fr, Suillus luteus. 350fr, Amanita muscaria. 450fr, Boletus calopus. 680fr, Boletus erythropus. 800fr, Leccinum scabrum. 900fr, Leccinum testaceoscabrum.
1500fr, Lycoperdon perlatum.

1990, Dec. 28 Litho. *Perf. 12*

1001C A325b 25fr multi .25 .20
1001D A325b 100fr multi .40 .20
1001E A325b 350fr multi .85 .25
1001F A325b 450fr multi 1.25 .30
1001G A325b 680fr multi 1.75 .45
1001H A325b 800fr multi 1.90 .50
1001I A325b 900fr multi 2.10 .60

Imperf

Size: 71x91mm

1001J A325b 1500fr multi 4.50 4.50
Nos. 1001C-1001J (8) 13.00 7.00

Intl. Literacy Year A326

1990, Dec. 30 *Perf. 12*

1002 A326 20fr Book, guiding hands, vert. .25 .20
1003 A326 100fr Open Book, hand holding pencil .25 .20

Dogs — A326a

1991, Mar. 20 Litho. *Perf. 12*

1003A A326a 30fr Greyhound .25 .20
1003B A326a 50fr Japanese spaniel .25 .20
1003C A326a 140fr Toy terrier .60 .20
1003D A326a 350fr Chow .90 .25
1003E A326a 500fr Miniature pinscher 1.25 .30
1003F A326a 800fr Afghan 2.10 .50
1003G A326a 1140fr Papillon 3.00 .75

Imperf

Size: 70x90mm

1003H A326a 1500fr Shih tzu 4.00 1.40
Nos. 1003A-1003H (8) 12.35 3.80

Nos. 1003D-1003H are airmail.

Democratic Republic of Madagascar, 15th Anniv. (in 1990) — A327

1991, Apr. 8 Litho. *Perf. 12*

1004 A327 100fr multicolored .25 .20

Dated 1990.

Trees — A328

1991, June 20 Litho. *Perf. 13½*

1005 A328 140fr Adansonia fony .55 .20
1006 A328 500fr Didierea madagascariensis 1.25 .40

Scouts, Insects and Mushrooms A329

Insects: 140fr, Helictopleurus splendidicollis. 640fr, Cocles contemplator. 1140fr, Euchroea oberthurii.
Mushrooms: 500fr, Russula radicans. 1025fr, Russula singeri. 3500fr, Lactariopsis pandani.
4500fr, Euchroea spinnasuta fairmaire and Russula aureotacta.

1991, Aug. 2 Litho. *Perf. 13½*

1007 A329 140fr multicolored .35 .20
1008 A329 500fr multicolored .90 .30
1009 A329 640fr multicolored 1.00 .40
1010 A329 1025fr multicolored 1.75 .65
1011 A329 1140fr multicolored 2.10 .70
1012 A329 3500fr multicolored 5.25 2.25
Nos. 1007-1012 (6) 11.35 4.50

Souvenir Sheet

1013 A329 4500fr multicolored 7.00 5.75

#1007-1012 exist in souvenir sheets of 1.
For overprints see Nos. 1149-1156.

Discovery of America, 500th Anniv. A330

Designs: 15fr, Ship, 9th cent.. 65fr, Clipper ship, 1878. 140fr, Golden Hind. 500fr, Galley, 18th cent. 640fr, Galleon Ostrust, 1721, vert. 800fr, Caravel Amsterdam, 1539, vert. 1025fr, Santa Maria, 1492. 1500fr, Map.

1991, Sept. 10 Litho. *Perf. 12*

1014 A330 15fr multicolored .20 .20
1015 A330 65fr multicolored .25 .20
1016 A330 140fr multicolored .55 .20
1017 A330 500fr multicolored 1.25 .30
1018 A330 640fr multicolored 1.50 .40
1019 A330 800fr multicolored 1.60 .50
1020 A330 1025fr multicolored 1.75 .65

Size: 90x70mm

1021 A330 1500fr multicolored 3.50 1.50
Nos. 1014-1021 (8) 10.60 3.95

No. 1021 contains one 40x27mm perf. 12 label in center of stamp picturing ships and Columbus.

Domesticated Animals A331

Designs: 140fr, Dog. 500fr, Arabian horse. 640fr, House cats. 1025fr, Himalayan cats. 1140fr, Draft horse. 5000fr, German shepherd. 10,000fr, Horse, cat & dog.

1991, Sept. 27 Litho. *Perf. 13½*

1022 A331 140fr multicolored .25 .20
1023 A331 500fr multicolored .90 .30
1024 A331 640fr multicolored 1.00 .40
1025 A331 1025fr multicolored 1.75 .65
1026 A331 1140fr multicolored 2.25 .70
1027 A331 5000fr multicolored 7.25 3.25
Nos. 1022-1027 (6) 13.40 5.50

Souvenir Sheet

1028 A331 10,000fr multicolored 13.00 6.50

Nos. 1022-1028 exist imperf. and in souvenir sheets of 1.

Birds — A332

Designs: 40fr, Hirundo rustica. 55fr, Circus melanoluecos, vert. 60fr, Cuculas canorus, vert. 140fr, Threskiornis aethiopicus. 210fr, Porphyrio poliocephalus. 500fr, Coracias garrulus. 2000fr, Oriolus oriolus. 1500fr, Upupa epops.

Perf. 12½x12, 12x12½

1991, Dec. 10 **Litho.**

1029 A332 40fr multicolored .20 .20
1030 A332 55fr multicolored .20 .20
1031 A332 60fr multicolored .25 .20
1032 A332 140fr multicolored .45 .20
1033 A332 210fr multicolored .70 .25
1034 A332 500fr multicolored 1.00 .35
1035 A332 2000fr multicolored 3.00 1.10

Size: 70x90mm

Imperf

1036 A332 1500fr multicolored 3.00 1.40
Nos. 1029-1036 (8) 8.80 3.90

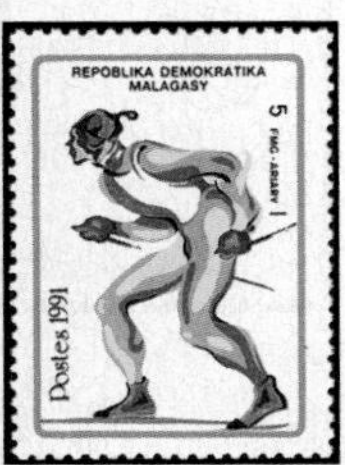

1992 Winter Olympics, Albertville A333

1991, Dec. 30 **Litho.** ***Perf. 12x12½***

1037 A333 5fr Cross-country skiing .20 .20
1038 A333 15fr Biathlon .20 .20
1039 A333 60fr Ice hockey .25 .20
1040 A333 140fr Downhill skiing .45 .25
1041 A333 640fr Figure skating 1.25 .40
1042 A333 1000fr Ski jumping 1.60 .70
1043 A333 1140fr Speed skating 2.00 .75

Imperf

Size: 90x70mm

1044 A333 1500fr Three hockey players 3.00 1.40
Nos. 1037-1044 (8) 8.95 4.10

For surcharge see #1478.

Paul Minault College, 90th Anniv. A333a

1991 **Litho.** ***Perf. 13½***

1044A A333a 140fr multicolored .65 .30

Space Program A334

Designs: 140fr, Astronaunts repairing space telescope. 500fr, Soho solar observation probe. 640fr, Topex-Poseidon, observing oceans. 1025fr, Hipparcos probe, Galaxy 3C75. 1140fr, Voyager II surveying Neptune. 5000fr, Adeos, ETS VI, earth observation and communications satellites. 7500fr, Crew of Apollo 11.

1992, Apr. 22 ***Perf. 13½***

1045 A334 140fr multi .25 .20
1046 A334 500fr multi .70 .30
1047 A334 640fr multi .90 .40
1048 A334 1025fr multi 1.40 .65
1049 A334 1140fr multi 1.60 .70
1050 A334 5000fr multi 6.75 3.25
a. Souvenir sheet of 6, #1045-1050 19.00 19.00
Nos. 1045-1050 (6) 11.60 5.50

Souvenir Sheet

1051 A334 7500fr multi 12.00 9.75

Nos. 1045-1050 exist in souvenir sheets of one.

Entertainers A335

1992, Apr. 29

1052 A335 100fr Ryuichi Sakamoto .20 .20
1053 A335 350fr John Lennon .60 .25
1054 A335 800fr Bruce Lee 1.50 .50
1055 A335 900fr Sammy Davis, Jr. 1.75 .60
1056 A335 1250fr John Wayne 1.90 .80
1057 A335 2500fr James Dean 3.50 1.60
Nos. 1052-1057 (6) 9.45 3.95

Souvenir Sheet

1058 A335 3000fr Clark Gable & Vivien Leigh 5.25 2.00

Nos. 1052-1057 exist in souvenir sheets of one.

Fight Against AIDS — A336

1990 Sports Festival — A338

Reforestation — A337

1992, July 29 **Litho.** ***Perf. 12***

1059 A336 140fr lil rose & black .40 .20

Dated 1991.

1992, July 29 **Litho.** ***Perf. 12***

1060 A337 140fr black & green .30 .20

Dated 1991.

1992, Aug. 20

1061 A338 140fr multicolored .35 .20

Dated 1991.

Meteorology in Madgascar, Cent. A339

1992, Nov. 10 **Litho.** ***Perf. 12x12½***

1062 A339 140fr multicolored .40 .20

Fruit — A341

Perf. 12½x12, 12x12½

1992, May 27 **Litho.**

1064 A341 10fr Litchis .30 .20
1065 A341 50fr Oranges .30 .20
1066 A341 60fr Apples .35 .20
1067 A341 140fr Peaches .50 .25
1068 A341 555fr Bananas, vert. 1.25 .45
1069 A341 800fr Avocados, vert. 1.75 .60
1070 A341 1400fr Mangoes, vert. 3.00 1.25

Size: 89x70mm

Imperf

1071 A341 1600fr Mixed fruit 3.25 1.40
Nos. 1064-1071 (8) 10.70 4.55

For surcharges, see Nos. 1473A, 1486.

1992 Summer Olympics, Barcelona A342

1992, June 30 ***Perf. 11½***

1072 A342 65fr Women's gymnastics .20 .20
1073 A342 70fr High jump .20 .20
1074 A342 120fr Archery .25 .20
1075 A342 140fr Cycling .30 .20
1076 A342 675fr Weight lifting 1.10 .45
1077 A342 720fr Boxing 1.10 .50
1078 A342 1200fr Canoeing 1.75 .75

Imperf

Size: 90x70mm

1078A A342 1600fr Volleyball 3.00 1.40
Nos. 1072-1078A (8) 7.90 3.90

Litho. & Embossed

Perf. 13½

1079 A342 5000fr Judo 8.00

For surcharge, see No. 1477.

Butterflies — A344

Designs: 15fr, Eusemia bisma. 35fr, Argema mittrei, vert. 65fr, Alcidis aurora. 140fr, Agarista agricola. 600fr, Trogonoptera croesus. 850fr, Trogonodtera priamus. 1300fr, Pereute leucodrosime. 1500fr, Chrysirridia madagaskariensis.

Perf. 12½x12, 12x12½

1992, June 24 **Litho.**

1080 A344 15fr multicolored .20 .20
1081 A344 35fr multicolored .20 .20
1082 A344 65fr multicolored .45 .20
1083 A344 140fr multicolored .70 .20
1084 A344 600fr multicolored 1.50 .45
1085 A344 850fr multicolored 2.00 .60
1086 A344 1300fr multicolored 2.50 .85

Imperf

Size: 70x90mm

1087 A344 1500fr multicolored 4.75 1.50
Nos. 1080-1087 (8) 12.30 4.20

Anniversaries and Events — A345

Designs: 500fr, Jean-Henri Dunant, delivery of Red Cross supplies. 640fr, Charles de Gaulle, battle of Bir Hacheim. 1025fr, Brandenburg Gate, people on Berlin wall. 1500fr, Village health clinic, Rotary, Lions emblems. 3000fr, Konrad Adenauer. 3500fr, Dirigible LZ4, hanger on Lake Constance, Ferdinand von Zeppelin. 7500fr, Wolfgang Amadeus Mozart at piano, palace, cathedral in Salzburg.

1992, Dec. 8 **Litho.** ***Perf. 13½***

1088 A345 500fr multicolored .70 .30
1089 A345 640fr multicolored .90 .45
1090 A345 1025fr multicolored 1.50 .75
1091 A345 1500fr multicolored 2.00 1.00
1092 A345 3000fr multicolored 4.25 2.00
1093 A345 3500fr multicolored 5.00 2.50
Nos. 1088-1093 (6) 14.35 7.00

Souvenir Sheet

1094 A345 7500fr multicolored 10.00 5.00

Intl. Red Cross (#1088). Battle of Bir Hacheim, 50th anniv. (#1089). Brandenburg Gate, bicent. and destruction of Berlin Wall, 3rd anniv. (#1090). Konrad Adenauer, 25th death anniv. (#1092). Ferdinand von Zeppelin, 75th death anniv. (#1093). Mozart, death bicent. (in 1991), (#1094).

For overprint see No. 1146.

1994 World Cup Soccer Championships, U.S. — A346

Soccer players, Georgia landmarks: 140fr, Ficklin Home, Macon. 640fr, Herndon Home, Atlanta. 1025fr, Cultural Center, Augusta. 5000fr, Old Governor's Mansion, Milledgeville. 7500fr, Player, stars, stripes.

1992, Dec. 15 **Litho.** ***Perf. 13½***

1095 A346 140fr multicolored .20 .20
1096 A346 640fr multicolored .90 .45
1097 A346 1025fr multicolored 1.40 .75
1098 A346 5000fr multicolored 7.00 3.50
Nos. 1095-1098 (4) 9.50 4.90

Souvenir Sheet

1099 A346 7500fr multicolored 10.25 5.25

Miniature Sheet

Inventors and Inventions — A347

No. 1100: a, Gutenberg (1394?-1468), printing press. b, Newton (1642-1727), telescope. c, John Dalton (1766-1844), atomic theory. d, Louis-Jacques-Mande Daguerre (1789-1851), photographic equipment. e, Faraday (1791-1867), electric motor. f, Orville (1871-1948), Wilbur Wright (1867-1912), motor-powered airplane. g, Bell (1847-1922), telephone. h, Edison (1847-1931), phonograph. i, Benz (1844-1929), motor-driven vehicle. j, Charles Parsons (1854-1931), steam turbine. k, Diesel (1858-1913), Diesel engine. l, Marconi, radio. m, Auguste-Marie-Louis Lumiere (1862-1954), Louis-Jean Lumiere (1864-1948), motion pictures. n, Oberth (1894-1989), rocketry. o, John W. Mauchly (1907-1980), John P. Eckert, electronic computer. p, Arthur Schawlow, laser.

1993, Apr. 27

1100 A347 500fr Sheet of 16, #a.-p. 11.00 5.50

Dated 1990.

Transportation — A348

No. 1101 — Race cars: a, 20fr, 1956 Bugatti. b, 20fr, 1968 Ferrari. c, 140fr, 1962 Lotus MK25. d, 140fr, 1970 Matra. e, 1250fr, 1963 Porsche. f, 1250fr, 1980 Ligier JS11. g, 3000fr, 1967 Honda. h, 3000fr, 1992 B192 Benetton.

No. 1102 — Locomotives: a, 20fr, C62, Japan, 1948. b, 20fr, SZD, USSR, 1975. c, 140fr, MU A1A-A1A, Norway, 1954. d, 140fr, Series 26 2-D-2, Africa, 1982. e, 1250fr, Amtrak Metroliner, US, 1967. f, 1250fr, VIA, Canada, 1982. g, 3000fr, Diesel, Union Pacific RR, US, 1969. h, 3000fr, Atlantic, TGV, France, 1990.

1993, Mar. 23

1101 A348 Block of 8, #a.-h. 12.00 6.00
1102 A348 Block of 8, #a.-h. 12.00 6.00

Dated 1990.

Wildlife — A349

No. 1103 — Birds: a, 45fr, Coua verreauxi. b, 45fr, Asio helvola hova. c, 60fr, Coua cristata. d, 60fr, Euryceros prevostii. e, 140fr, Coua gigas. f, 140fr, Foudia madagascariensis. g, 3000fr, Falculea palliata. h, 3000fr, Eutriorchis astur.

No. 1104 — Butterflies: a, 45fr, Chrysiridia madagascariensis. b, 45fr, Hypolimnas misippus. c, 60fr, Charaxes antamboulou. d, 60fr, Papilio antenor. e, 140fr, Hypolimnas dexithea. f, 140fr, Charaxes andranodorus. g, 3000fr, Euxanthe madagascariensis. h, 3000fr, Papilio grosesmithi.

1993, May 27

1103 A349 Block of 8, #a.-h. 8.75 4.25
1104 A349 Block of 8, #a.-h. 8.75 4.25

Dated 1991.

Intl. Conference on Nutrition, Rome — A350

1992, Nov. 3

1105 A350 500fr multicolored 1.00 .40

Automobiles — A351

1993, Jan. 28 Litho. *Perf. 12*

1106	A351	20fr BMW	.20	.20
1107	A351	40fr Toyota	.20	.20
1108	A351	60fr Cadillac	.20	.20
1109	A351	65fr Volvo	.20	.20
1110	A351	140fr Mercedes Benz	.20	.20
1111	A351	640fr Ford	1.00	.50
1112	A351	3000fr Honda	5.00	2.50

Size: 90x70mm

Imperf

1113	A351	2000fr Renault	3.00	1.50
		Nos. 1106-1113 (8)	10.00	5.50

Birds — A352

Designs: 50fr, Anodorhynchus hiacinthinus. 60fr, Nymphicus hollandicus. 140fr, Melopsittacus undulatus. 500fr, Aratinga jandya. 675fr, Melopsittacus undulatus, diff. 800fr, Cyanoramphus novaezelandiae. 1750fr, Nestor notabilis. 2000fr, Ara militaris.

1993, Feb. 24

1114	A352	50fr multicolored	.40	.20
1115	A352	60fr multicolored	.40	.20
1116	A352	140fr multicolored	.50	.20
1117	A352	500fr multicolored	1.75	.45
1118	A352	675fr multicolored	2.50	.65
1119	A352	800fr multicolored	2.75	.70
1120	A352	1750fr multicolored	6.00	1.50

Size: 71x91mm

Imperf

1121	A352	2000fr multicolored	5.00	2.00
		Nos. 1114-1121 (8)	19.30	5.90

For surcharge, see No. 1473B.

Mollusks A353

1993, Feb. 3

1122	A353	40fr Turbo marmoratus	.20	.20
1123	A353	60fr Mitra mitra	.20	.20
1124	A353	65fr Argonauta argo	.20	.20
1125	A353	140fr Conus textile	.30	.20
1126	A353	500fr Aplysia depilans	1.10	.45
1127	A353	675fr Harpa amouretta	1.50	.70
1128	A353	2500fr Cypraea tigris	4.50	2.25

Size: 70x90mm

Imperf

1129	A353	2000fr Architectonica maxima	5.00	1.75
		Nos. 1122-1129 (8)	13.00	5.95

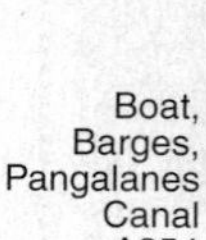

Boat, Barges, Pangalanes Canal A354

1993, Jan. 29 Litho. *Perf. 12*

1130 A354 140fr multicolored .40 .25

Miniature Sheet

Ships A355

No. 1131: a, 5fr, Egyptian ship. b, 5fr, Mediterranean galley. c, 5fr, Great Western, England, 1837. d, 5fr, Mississippi River sidewheeler, US, 1850. e, 15fr, Bireme, Phoenicia. f, 15fr, Viking long ship. g, 15fr, Clermont, US, 1806. h, 15fr, Pourquoi-pas, France, 1936. i, 140fr, Santa Maria, Spain, 1492. j, 140fr, HMS Victory, England, 1765. k, 140fr, Fast motor yacht, Monaco. l, 140fr, Bremen, Germany, 1950. m, 10,000fr, Sovereign of the Seas, England, 1637. n, 10,000fr, Cutty Sark, England, 1869. o, 10,000fr, Savannah, US, 1959. p, 10,000fr, Condor, Australia.

1993, Apr. 6 Litho. *Perf. 13½*

1131 A355 Sheet of 16, #a.-p. 50.00 25.00

Miniature Sheet

Nobel Prize Winners in Physics, Chemistry and Medicine A356

No. 1132: a, Albert Einstein, Niels Bohr. b, Wolfgang Pauli, Max Born. c, Joseph Thomson, Johannes Stark. d, Otto Hahn, Hideki Yukawa. e, Owen Richardson, William Shockley. f, Albert Michelson, Charles Townes. g, Wilhelm Wien, Lev Landau. h, Karl Braun, Sir Edward Appleton. i, Percy Bridgman, Nikolai Semenov. j, Sir William Ramsay, Glenn Seaborg. k, Otto Wallach, Hermann Staudinger. l, Richard Synge, Alex Theorell. m, Thomas Morgan, Hermann Muller. n, Allvar Gullstrand, Willem Einthoven. o, Sir Charles Sherrington, Otto Loewi. p, Jules Bordet, Sir Alexander Fleming.

1993, Mar. 11

1132 A356 500fr Sheet of 16, #a.-p. 11.00 5.50

Alex misspelled on No. 1132l.

Miniature Sheet

Lemurs — A357

No. 1133: a, 60fr, Hapalemur simus. b, 150fr, Propithecus diadema. c, 250fr Indri indri. d, 350fr, Varecia variegata.

1992, Oct. 9 Litho. *Perf. 13½*

1133 A357 Sheet of 4, #a.-d. 5.50 2.00

World Post Day.

No. 840 Ovptd. in Silver

1993, Sept. 28 Litho. *Perf. 13½*

1134 A276 550fr multicolored *3.75 1.90*

Exists in souvenir sheet of 1.

No. 874 Ovptd. in Silver with Guitar and "THE ELVIS'S GUITAR / 15th ANNIVERSARY OF HIS DEATH / 1977-1992" in English or French

1993, Sept. 28

1135	A287	1500fr English ovpt.	2.50	1.10
1136	A287	1500fr French ovpt.	2.50	1.10
a.		Pair, #1135-1136	5.00	2.25

No. 1135 exists in souvenir sheet of 1.

Nos. 945-948 Ovptd. in Gold

1993, Sept. 28

1137	A309	350fr multicolored	.50	.30
1138	A309	1000fr multicolored	1.50	.75
1139	A309	1500fr multicolored	2.25	1.25
1140	A309	2500fr multicolored	3.75	1.90
		Nos. 1137-1140 (4)	8.00	4.20

Nos. 974-978 Ovptd. in Gold

1993, Sept. 28

1141	A315	350fr multicolored	.50	.25
1142	A315	1000fr multicolored	1.50	.75
1143	A315	1500fr multicolored	2.25	1.10
1144	A315	2500fr multicolored	3.75	1.90
		Nos. 1141-1144 (4)	8.00	4.00

Souvenir Sheet

1145 A315 3000fr multicolored 4.75 2.50

No. 1088 Overprinted in Red

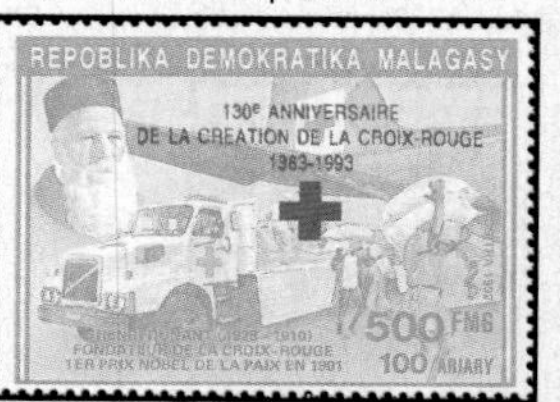

1993, Sept. 28

1146 A345 500fr multicolored 3.50 1.75

Exists in souvenir sheet of 1, overprinted in red or green.

Miniature Sheet

Commercial Airlines — A358

No. 1147: a, 10fr, Lufthansa, Germany. b, 10fr, Air France. c, 10fr, Air Canada. d. 10fr, ANA, Japan. e, 60fr, British Airways. f, 60fr, DO-X, Germany. g, 60fr, Shinmeiwa, Japan. h, 60fr, Royal Jordanian. i, 640fr, Alitalia, Italy. j, 640fr, Hydro 2000, France-Europe. k, 640fr, Boeing 314 Clipper, US. l, 640fr, Air Madagascar. m, 5000fr, Emirates Airlines, United Arab Emirates n, 5000fr, Scandinavian Airways. o, 5000fr, KLM, Netherlands. p, 5000fr, Air Caledonia.

1993, Nov. 22 Litho. *Perf. 13½*

1147 A358 Sheet of 16, #a.-p. 30.00 15.00

Dated 1990.

Miniature Sheet

Painters — A359

No. 1148: a, 50fr, Da Vinci. b, 50fr, Titian. c, 50fr, Rembrandt. d, 50fr, J.M.W. Turner (1775-1851). e, 640fr, Michelangelo. f, 640fr, Rubens. g, 640fr, Goya. h, 640fr, Delacroix (1798-1863). i, 1000fr, Monet. j, 1000fr, Gauguin. k, 1000fr, Toulouse Lautrec (1864-1901). l, 1000fr, Dali (1904-89). m, 2500fr, Renoir. n, 2500fr, Van Gogh. o, 2500fr, Picasso. p, 2500fr, Andy Warhol.

1993, May 10

1148 A359 Sheet of 16, #a.-p. 22.50 11.50

The local currency on Nos. 1148m-1148p is obliterated by a black overprint.

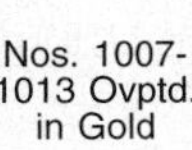

Nos. 1007-1013 Ovptd. in Gold

No. 841 Ovptd. in Metallic Green

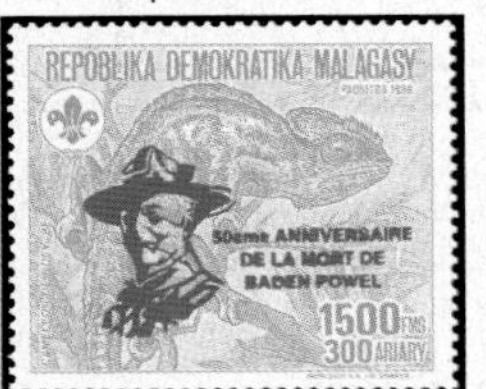

1993, Sept. 28 Litho. *Perf. 13½*

1149	A329	140fr multicolored	.20	.20
1150	A329	500fr multicolored	.65	.30
1151	A329	640fr multicolored	.90	.40
1152	A329	1025fr multicolored	1.25	.60
1153	A329	1140fr multicolored	1.50	.75
1154	A276	1500fr multicolored	2.00	1.00
1155	A329	3500fr multicolored	4.50	2.25
		Nos. 1149-1155 (7)	11.00	5.50

Souvenir Sheet

1156 A329 4500fr multicolored 6.00 3.00

Fauna A360

No. 1157 — Dogs: a, 40fr, Golden retriever. b, 140fr, Fox terrier. c, 40fr, Coton de tulear. d, 140fr, Langhaar.

No. 1158 — Cats: a, 40fr, Birman. b, 140fr, Egyptian. c, 40fr, European creme. d, 140fr, Rex du Devon.

No. 1159 — Reptiles: a, 1000fr, Phelsuma madagascariensis. b, 2000fr, Cameleon de parson. c, 1000fr, Laticauda laticaudate. d, 2000fr, Testudo radiata.

No. 1160 — Beetles: a, 1000fr, Euchroea spininasuta. b, 2000fr, Orthophagus minnulus klug. c, 1000fr, Helictopleurus radicollis. d, 2000fr, Euchroea coelestis.

1993, Dec. 7 Litho. *Perf. 13½*

1157	A360	Block of 4, #a.-d.	.50	.25
1158	A360	Block of 4, #a.-d.	.50	.25
1159	A360	Block of 4, #a.-d.	8.00	4.00
1160	A360	Block of 4, #a.-d.	8.00	4.00
e.		Sheet of 16, #1157-1160	18.00	8.50

Dated 1991.

Nos. 934-938 Ovptd. in Metallic Blue, Nos. 939-939B Ovptd. in Metallic Red Lilac

Illustration reduced.

1993, Sept. 28

1161	A305	250fr multicolored	.35	.20
1162	A305	350fr multicolored	.50	.25
1163	A305	1000fr multicolored	1.50	.75
1164	A305	1500fr multicolored	2.25	1.10
1165	A305	2500fr multicolored	3.75	1.90
		Nos. 1161-1165 (5)	8.35	4.20

Souvenir Sheet

1166 A305 3000fr multi 4.50

Litho. & Embossed

Perf. 13½

1166A A305a 5000fr gold & multi 8.00

Souvenir Sheet

1166B A305a 5000fr gold & multi 8.00

Nos. 1161-1165 exist in souvenir sheets of 1, and in a sheet containing Nos. 1161-1165 plus label.

A number has been reserved for an additional value in this set.

Marine Life — A361

No. 1167 — Shells: a, 15fr, Chicoreus torrefactus. b, 15fr, Fasciolaria filamentosa. c, 30fr, Stellaria solaris. d, 30fr, Harpa ventricosa lamarck.

No. 1168 — Crustaceans: a, 1250fr, Panulirus (#1167c). b, 1250fr, Stenopus hispidus (#1167d). c, 1500fr, Pagure. d, 1500fr, Bernard l'hermite (#1168b).

No. 1169 — Fish: a, 15fr, Pigopytes diacanthus. b, 15fr, Coelacanth latimeria chalumnae. c, 30fr, Ostracion cyanurus. d, 30fr, Coris gaimardi. e, 1250fr, Balistapus undulatus. f, 1250fr, Forcipiger longirostris. g, 1500fr, Adioryx diadema. h, 1500fr, Pterois lunulata.

1993, Nov. 26 *Perf. 13½*

1167	A361	Block of 4, #a.-d.	.20	.20
1168	A361	Block of 4, #a.-d.	7.25	3.50
1169	A361	Block of 8, #a.-h.	7.25	3.50
i.		Sheet of 16, #1167-1169	16.50	7.50

Dated "1991."

Flora — A362

No. 1170 — Orchids: a, 45fr, Oceonia oncidiflora. b, 60fr, Cymbidella rhodochica. c, 140fr, Vanilla planifolia. d, 3000fr, Phaius humblotii.

No. 1171 — Fruits: a, 45fr, Artocarpus altilis. b, 60fr, Eugenia malaceensis. c, 140fr, Jambosa domestica. d, 3000fr, Papaya.

No. 1172 — Mushrooms: a, 45fr, Russula annulata. b, 60fr, Lactarius claricolor. c, 140fr, Russula tuberculosa. d, 3000fr, Russula fistulosa.

No. 1173 — Vegetables: a, 45fr, Sweet potatoes. b, 60fr, Yams. c, 140fr, Avocados. d, 3000fr, Mangoes.

1993, Dec. 15 Litho. *Perf. 13*

1170	A362	Strip of 4, #a.-d.	4.25	2.25
1171	A362	Strip of 4, #a.-d.	4.25	2.25
1172	A362	Strip of 4, #a.-d.	4.25	2.25
1173	A362	Strip of 4, #a.-d.	4.25	2.25
e.		Sheet of 16, #1170-1173	18.00	9.00

1994 Winter Olympics, Lillehammer A362a

Designs: 140fr, Biathlon. 1250fr, Ice hockey. 2000fr, Figure skating. 2500fr, Slalom skiing. 5000fr, Downhill skiing. #1173K, Ski jumping. #1173L, Speed skating.

1994, Jan. 19 Litho. *Perf. 13*

1173F-1173I A362a Set of 4 *18.50 9.25*

Souvenir Sheet

1173J A362a 5000fr multi *7.25 3.50*

Litho. & Embossed

1173K A362a 10,000fr gold & multi 13.00

Souvenir Sheet

1173L A362a 10,000fr gold & multi 13.00

No. 1173K exists in a souvenir sheet of 1.

For overprints see # 1288A-1288E.

1996 Summer Olympics, Atlanta — A362b

Scene in Atlanta, event: 640fr, 1892 Windsor Hotel Americus, dressage. 1000fr, Covington Courthouse, women's shot put. 1500fr, Carolton Community Activities Center, table tennis. 3000fr, Newman Historic Commercial Court Square, soccer. 7500fr, Relay race runner. No. 1173R, Pole vault, vert. No. 1173S, Hurdles, vert.

1994, Jan. 19

1173M-1173P A362b Set of 4 *19.50 9.50*

Souvenir Sheet

1173Q A362b 7500fr multi *27.00 13.50*

Litho. & Embossed

1173R A362b 5000fr gold & multi 7.50

Souvenir Sheet

1173S A362b 5000fr gold & multi 8.00

Prehistoric Animals A363

Designs: 35fr, Dinornis maximus, vert. 40fr, Ceratosaurus, vert. 140fr, Mosasavrus, vert. 525fr, Protoceratops. 640fr, Styvacosaurus. 755fr, Smilodon. 1800fr, Uintatherium.

2000fr, Tusks of mammuthus, trees, vert.

1995, Feb. 23 Litho. *Perf. 12*

1174-1180 A363 Set of 7 4.50 4.50

Souvenir Sheet

1181 A363 2000fr multicolored 3.50 1.50

For surcharge see #1474.

Wild Animals A364

Designs: 10fr, Panthera pardus. 30fr, Martes. 60fr, Vulpes vulpes. 120fr, Canis lupus. 140fr (No. 1186), Fennecus zerda. 140fr (No. 1187), Panthera leo. 3500fr, Uncia uncia.

2000fr, Panthera onca.

1995, Mar. 21

1182-1188 A364 Set of 7 5.00 5.00

Souvenir Sheet

1189 A364 2000fr multicolored 3.50 3.50

D-Day Landings, Normandy, 50th Anniv. — A365

No. 1190: a, 3000fr, American troops, flamethrower. b, 1500fr, Coming ashore. c, 3000fr, Explosion, German commander pointing.

No. 1191 — Liberation of Paris, 50th anniv. : a, 3000fr, Notre Dame, resistance fighters, crowd. b, 1500fr, Arch de Triomphe, woman cheering. c, 3000fr, Eiffel Tower, parade, French troops.

1994 *Perf. 13½*

1190	A365	Strip of 3, #a.-c.	6.75	3.50
1191	A365	Strip of 3, #a.-c.	6.75	3.50

Nos. 1190b, 1191b are 30x47mm. Nos. 1190-1191 are continuous design.

Aquarium Fish A366

Designs: 10fr, Pomacanthus imperator. 30fr, Betta splendens. 45fr, Trichogaster leeri. 95fr, Labrus bimaculatus. No. 1196, 140fr, Synodontis nigreventris. No. 1197, 140fr, Cichlasoma biocellatum. 3500fr, Fudulus heteroclitus.
2000fr, Carassius auratus, vert.

1994, June 28 Litho. *Perf. 12½x12*
1192-1198 A366 Set of 7 5.75 5.75

Souvenir Sheet
Perf. 12x12½
1199 A366 2000fr multicolored 3.25 3.25

Modern Locomotives — A367

Designs: 5fr, Superviem Odoriko. 15fr, Morrison Knudsen Corporation. 140fr, ER-200. 265fr, General Motors. 300fr, New Jersey Transit. 575fr, Siemens Inter-City Express. 2500fr, Sweden's Fast Train.
2000fr, Alstham T60.

1993, Nov. 10 *Perf. 12*
1200-1206 A367 Set of 7 5.00 4.50

Souvenir Sheet
1207 A367 2000fr multicolored 3.25 1.50

For surcharge, see No. 1477A.

Cathedrals A368

Cathedral, location: 10fr, Antwerp, Belgium. 100fr, Cologne, Germany. 120fr, Antsirabe, Masdagascar. 140fr, Kremlin, Moscow. 525fr, Notre Dame, Paris. 605fr, Toledo, Spain. 2500fr, St. Stephens, Vienna.
2000fr, Westminster Abbey, London.

1995, Feb. 14 *Perf. 12x12½*
1208-1214 A368 Set of 7 4.50 4.50

Souvenir Sheet
1215 A368 2000fr multicolored 2.75 2.75

Dated 1994.
No. 1215 is inscribed with country name only in the sheet margin.
For overprint, see No. 1475.

Insects — A369

Designs: 20fr, Necrophorus tomentosus. 60fr, Dynastes tityus. 140fr, Megaloxantha bicolor. 605fr, Calosoma sycophanta. 720fr, Chrysochroa mirabilis. 1000fr, Crioceris asparaqi. 1500fr, Cetonia aurata.
2000fr, Goliathus goliathus.

1994, Feb. 2 *Perf. 12*
1216-1222 A369 Set of 7 5.50 5.50

Size: 85x58mm
Imperf
1223 A369 2000fr multicolored 2.25 1.25

Miniature Sheet

PHILAKOREA '94 — A370

No. 1224: a, 100fr, John Lennon, Ella Fitzgerald. b, 140fr, Marilyn Monroe, Elvis Presley. c, 550fr, U.S. Pres. Bill Clinton, Louis Armstrong.

1995, Feb. 23 *Perf. 12*
1224 A370 Sheet of 2 each, #a.-c. + 3 labels 4.75 2.25

Ancient Art & Architecture — A371

Designs: No. 1225, 350fr, Statue of Augustus, vert. No. 1226, 350fr, Statue, Land Surveyor, vert. No. 1227, 350fr, Painting, "Child of Thera," vert. No. 1228, 350fr, Sarcophagous, Cerveteri and Wife, vert. No. 1229, 350fr, Statue, Athena of Fidia, vert. No. 1230, 405fr, Colosseum, Rome. No. 1231, 405fr, Mask of Agamemnon, vert. No. 1232, 405fr, Forum of Caesar. No. 1233, 405fr, She-Wolf suckling Romulus & Remus. No. 1234, 405fr, Parthenon, Athens. No. 1235, 525fr, Carthaginian mask, vert. No. 1236, 525fr, Bust of Emperor Tiberius, vert. No. 1237, 525fr, Statue of Alexandar the Great, vert. No. 1238, 525fr, Detail, Taormina Theater, vert. No. 1239, 525fr, Denarius of Caesar. No. 1240, 605fr, Forum, Pompeii, vert. No. 1241, 605fr, Bronze statue, Riace, vert. No. 1242, 605fr, Venus de Milo, vert. No. 1243, 605fr, Bronze statue, Archer, vert. No. 1244, 605fr, Pont Du Gard Aqueduct, Nimes.

1994 Litho. *Perf. 13½*
1225-1244 A371 Set of 20 6.50 3.25

Elvis Presley (1935-77) A371a

Design: No. 1244B, "The King," "Presley," Elvis wearing black.

Litho. & Embossed
1994, June 8 *Perf. 13½*
1244A A371a 10,000fr gold & multi 12.00

Souvenir Sheet
1244B A371a 10,000fr gold & multi 12.00

Exists in sheets of 4.

The Stuff of Heroes, by Philip Kaufman — A372

No. 1245: a, 140fr, Astronaut. b, 140fr, Astronaut up close, walking. c, 5000fr, Spacecraft, astronaut.

1994
1245 A372 Strip of 3, #a.-c. 3.75 1.90

Motion pictures, cent. No. 1245 is a continuous design and exists in souvenir sheet of 1 with scenes from the film "Blade Runner."
No. 1245c is 60x47mm.

Intl. Olympic Committee, Cent. — A373

No. 1246: a, 2500fr, Flag. b, 2500fr, Olympic flame. c, 3500fr, Pierre de Coubertin.

1994
1246 A373 Strip of 3, #a.-c. 5.75 2.75

No. 1246 is a continuous design and exists in souvenir sheet of 1. No. 1246c is 60x47mm.

ILO, 75th Anniv. — A374

1994 Litho. *Perf. 13½*
1247 A374 140fr multicolored .25 .20

A374a

Designs: 30fr, Mahafaly jewelry. 60fr, Sakalava fork and spoon. 140fr, Antandroy jewelry. 430fr, Sakalava jewelry. 580fr, Antaimoro Ambalavao paper. 1250fr Sakalava jewelry, diff. 1500fr, Inlaid cabinet.
2000fr, Ampanihy tapestry.

1995, Feb. 2 Litho. *Perf. 11¼*
1247A A374a 30fr multi
1247B A374a 60fr multi
1247C A374a 140fr multi
1247D A374a 430fr multi
1247E A374a 580fr multi
1247F A374a 1250fr multi
1247G A374a 1500fr multi

Souvenir Sheet
Imperf
1247H A374a 2000fr multi

Modern Ships — A375

Ships: 45fr, Russian car ferry. 50fr, Australian cargo. 100fr, Japanese cruise. 140fr, US cruise. 300fr, English hovercraft. 350fr, Danish cargo. 3000fr, Korean container ship.
2000fr, Finnish car ferry, vert.

1994 Litho. *Perf. 12*
1248-1254 A375 Set of 7 4.50 4.50

Souvenir Sheet
1255 A375 2000fr multicolored 3.25 3.25

1994 World Cup Soccer Championships, U.S. — A375a

Player at: No. 1255A, Left. No. 1255B, Right.

Litho. & Embossed
1994, Aug. 24 *Perf. 13½*
1255A A375a 10,000fr gold & multi 12.00

Souvenir Sheet
1255B A375a 10,000fr gold & multi 12.00

A377 A378

Sports: 5fr, Hurdles. 140fr, Boxing. 525fr, Gymnastics. 550fr, Weight lifting. 640fr, Swimming. 720fr, Equestrian. 1500fr, Soccer.
2000fr, Race walking, horiz.

1995, Apr. 4 Litho. *Perf. 12*
1264-1270 A377 Set of 7 5.00 2.50

Souvenir Sheet
1271 A377 2000fr multicolored 3.25 1.25

1993, Nov. 10 Litho. *Perf. 12*

Orchids: 50fr, Paphiopedilum siamense. 65fr, Cypripedium calceolus. 70fr, Ophrys oestrifera. 140fr, Cephalanthera rubra. 300fr, Cypripedium macranthon. 640fr, Calanthe vestita. 2500fr, Cypripedium guttatum. 2000fr, Oncidium tigrinum.

1272-1278 A378 Set of 7 6.00 2.50

Size: 90x70mm
Imperf
1279 A378 2000fr multicolored 3.25 1.25

Sharks A379

Designs: 10fr, Galeocerdo cuvieri. 45fr, Pristiophorus japonicus. 140fr, Rincodon typus. 270fr, Sphyrna zygaena. 600fr, Carcharhinus longimanus. 1200fr, Stegostoma tigrinum. 1500fr, Scapanorhynchus owstoni. 2000fr, Galeoshinas zyopterus.

1993, Sept. 22 *Perf. 12*
1280-1286 A379 Set of 7 5.00 2.50

Size: 70x90mm
Imperf
1287 A379 2000fr multicolored 3.25 1.25

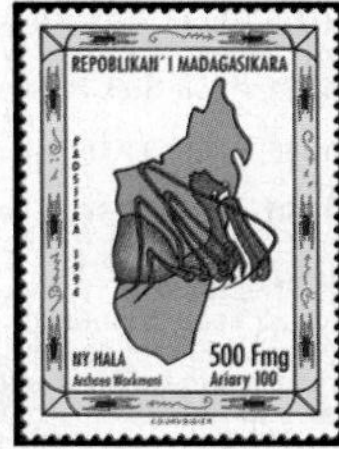

Archaea Workmani A380

1994 ***Perf. 15***

1288 A380 500fr multicolored 1.00 .75

Nos. 1173F-1173J Ovptd. With Names of Winners in Silver or Gold

1994, Aug. 30 Litho. ***Perf. 13***

1288A-1288D A362a Set of 4 *18.50 9.25*

Souvenir Sheet

1288E A362a 5000fr multi *7.25 3.50*

Overprinted in silver: 140fr, "M. BEDARD / CANADA." 1250fr, "MEDAILLE D'OR / SUEDE." 2000fr, "O. BAYUL / UKRAINE." 2500fr, "M. WASMEIER / ALLEMAGNE." 5000fr,

Overprinted in gold: 5000fr, "D. COMPAGNONI / ITALIE."

Marilyn Monroe (1926-62), Elvis Presley (1935-77) — A381

Scenes from films: No. 1289, 100fr, Gentlemen Prefer Blondes. No. 1290, 100fr, Clambake, Roustabout, Viva Las Vegas. 550fr, Some Like it Hot. 1250fr, Girls, Girls, Girls, King Creole. 5000fr, Niagara. 10,000fr, Double Trouble, Kid Gallahad, Speedway.

Illustration reduced.

1995, Aug. 15 Litho. ***Perf. 13½***

1289-1294 A381 Set of 6 12.50 12.50

#1289-1294 exist in souvenir sheets of 1.

Motion Pictures, Cent. A382

Actor, film: No. 1295, 140fr, James Dean, Rebel Without a Cause. No. 1296, 140fr, Burt Lancaster, Vera Cruz. 5000fr, Elvis Presley, Speedway. 10,000fr, Marilyn Monroe, How to Marry a Millionaire.

1995, Aug. 16 Litho. ***Perf. 13½***

1295-1298 A382 Set of 4 11.00 11.00

a. Miniature sheet of 4, #1295-1298 *17.50 17.50*

#1295-1298 exist in souvenir sheets of 1.

Locusts A383

Designs: No. 1299, Assylidae, natural enemy of the locust. No. 1300, Locust eating corn, vert. No. 1301, Gathering locusts for consumption.

1995, Sept. 26 Litho. ***Perf. 13½***

1299 A383 140fr multicolored .90 .20

1300 A383 140fr multicolored .90 .20

1301 A383 140fr multicolored .90 .20

Nos. 1299-1301 (3) 2.70 .60

Malagasyan Bible, 160th Anniv. — A384

World Post Day — A385

1995, June 21 Litho. ***Perf. 15***

1302 A384 140fr multicolored .25 .20

1995, Oct. 9 ***Perf. 13½***

1303 A385 500fr multicolored .80 .35

Nos. 967-972 Ovptd. in Silver

1996, Jan. 21 Litho. ***Perf. 13½***

1304 A314 2000fr on No. 971 *3.50 1.75*

1304A A314 Sheet of 6, #b-g, 1304

No. 1304 exists in souvenir sheet of 1, overprinted in gold or silver. No. 1304A exists with gold overprint.

Death of Charles de Gaulle, 25th Anniv. A386

No. 1305: a, 100fr, World War I battle. b, 100fr, As President of France. c, 100fr, Brazzaville, 1940. d, 500fr, Pierre Brossolette, Churchill, De Gaulle. e, 500fr, Young woman. f, 500fr, Yak 9T, Gen. Leclerc. g, 1500fr, Liberation of Paris. h, 1500fr, De Gaulle as younger man. i, 1500fr, Jean Moulin, Free French barricade in Paris. j, 7500fr, Writing Tourbillon de L'Histoire, Colombey Les Deux Eglises. k, 7500fr, Giving speech as older diplomat. l, 7500fr, Doves, French flag, older De Gaulle standing on hilltop.

1996, Apr. 28 Litho. ***Perf. 13½***

1305 A386 Sheet of 12, #a.-l. 21.50 10.75

See design A390.

Famous People A387

Designs: 1500fr, Wilhelm Steinitz (1836-1900), American chess master. 1750fr, Emmanuel Lasker (1868-1941), German chess master. 2000fr, Enzo Ferrari (1898-1988), automobile designer. 2500fr, Thomas Stafford, American astronaut, A.A. Leonov, Russian cosmonaut. 3000fr, Jerry Garcia (d. 1995), musician. 3500fr, Ayrton Senna (1960-94), race car driver. 5000fr, Paul-Emile Victor (1907-95), polar explorer. 7500fr, Paul Harris (1868-1947), founder of Rotary Intl.

1996, Feb. 20

1306-1313 A387 Set of 8 20.00 10.00

#1306-1313 exist in souvenir sheets of 1.

UN and UNICEF, 50th Anniv. A388

Designs: No. 1314, 140fr, Hand holding shaft of grain, UN emblem. No. 1315, 140fr, UN building, flags, map, woman feeding child. No. 1316, 140fr, Child holding plate of food, child holding UNICEF emblem. 7500fr, Two children, UNICEF emblem.

1996, Aug. 30

1314-1317 A388 Set of 4 5.25 2.50

#1314-1317 exist in souvenir sheets of 1.

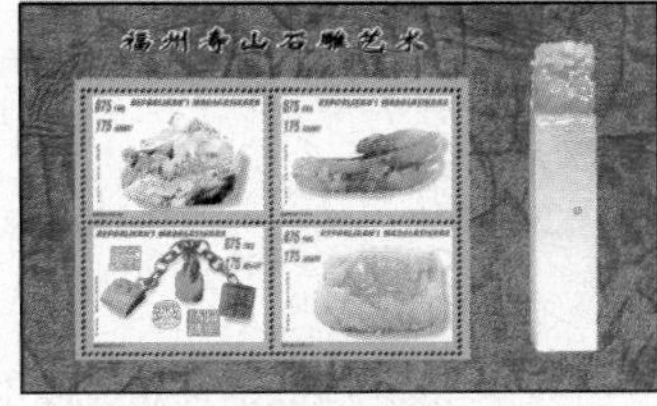

Jade — A389

No. 1318, 175fr: a, People on mountain. b, Carving of insect, leaves. c, Chops on a chain. d, Insect in stone.

1996, Apr. 20 Litho. ***Perf. 13½***

1318 A389 Sheet of 4, #a.-d. 2.50 1.25

A390

No. #1319: Bruce Lee (1940-73), various portraits.

No. #1320: John Lennon (1940-80), various portraits.

No. 1321: Locomotives: a, Train going left. b, Train going right. c, ICE Train, Germany. d, Eurostar.

No. 1322: Louis Pasteur (1822-95), various portraits.

No. 1323: Francois Mitterrand (1916-96), various portraits.

No. 1324: Intl. Space Station: a, Shuttle Atlantis, MIR Space Station. b, MIR. c, Intl. Space Station. d, Shuttle, Alpha section of station.

1996 Litho. ***Perf. 13½***

1319 A390 500fr Sheet of 4, #a.-d. 2.25 1.10

1320 A390 1500fr Sheet of 4, #a.-d. 3.75 1.90

1321 A390 1500fr Sheet of 4, #a.-d. 3.75 1.90

1322 A390 1750fr Sheet of 4, #a.-d. 4.25 2.10

1323 A390 2000fr Sheet of 4, #a.-d. 5.00 2.50

1324 A390 2500fr Sheet of 4, #a.-d. 6.25 3.00

Post Day — A396

Various local post offices: a, 500fr. b, 1000fr. c, 3500fr. d, 5000fr.

1996, Oct. 16 Litho. ***Perf. 13½***

1325 A396 Sheet of 4, #a.-d. 6.25 3.00

Sports Cars — A397

No. 1326: a, Mercedes W196 driven by Juan Manuel Fangio. b, Porsche 911 Carrera. c, Porsche 917-30. d, Mercedes 600 SEC.

1996

1326 A397 3000fr Sheet of 4, #a.-d. 7.50 3.75

1996 Olympic Games, Atlanta

Perf. 11¾x11½

1996, Dec. 27 Litho.

Granite Paper

1326E A397a 140fr Judo

1326F A397a 140fr Tennis

UN, 50th Anniv. — A398

1995, Oct. 24 Litho. ***Perf. 11½x11¾***

1327 A398 140fr Private sector promotion

1328 A398 500fr Lemur, tortoise

1330 A398 1500fr Grain stalks

An additional stamp exists in this set. The editors would like to examine it.

1998 Winter Olympics, Nagano A399

Designs: 160fr, Ice hockey. 350fr, Pairs figure skating. 5000fr, Biathlon. 7500fr, Freestyle skiing.
12,500fr, Speed skating.

1997 Litho. *Perf. 13½*
1331-1334 A399 Set of 4 6.75 3.50

Souvenir Sheet

1335 A399 12,500fr multicolored 6.50 3.25

No. 1335 contains one 42x60mm stamp.

1998 World Cup Soccer Championships, France — A400

Various soccer plays: 300fr, 1350fr, 3000fr, 10,000fr.

1997
1336-1339 A400 Set of 4 7.75 4.00

Souvenir Sheet

1340 A400 12,500fr Player, ball 6.50 3.25

No. 1340 contains one 42x60mm stamp.

Greenpeace, 25th Anniv. — A401

Views of Rainbow Warrior I: 1500fr, At anchor. 3000fr, Under sail. 3500fr, Going left, small raft. 5000fr, Going forward at full speed.
12,500fr, Under sail, vert.

1996, Apr. 16 Litho. *Perf. 13½*
1341-1344 A401 Set of 4 5.50 2.75

Souvenir Sheet

1345 A401 12,500fr multicolored 5.50 2.75

Dinosaurs — A402

No. 1346: a, Herrerasaurus, archaeopteryx. b, Segnosaurus, dimorphodon. c, Sauropelta, proavis.
No. 1347: a, Eudimorphodon, eustreptospondylus. b, Triceratops, rhamphorychus. c, Pteranodon, segnosaurus.
12,500fr, Tenontosaurus, deinonychus, vert.

1998, Feb. 25
1346 A402 1350fr Sheet of 3, #a.-c. 2.25 1.10
1347 A402 5000fr Sheet of 3, #a.-c. 8.00 4.00

Souvenir Sheet

1348 A402 12,500fr multicolored 6.50 3.25

Dated 1997.

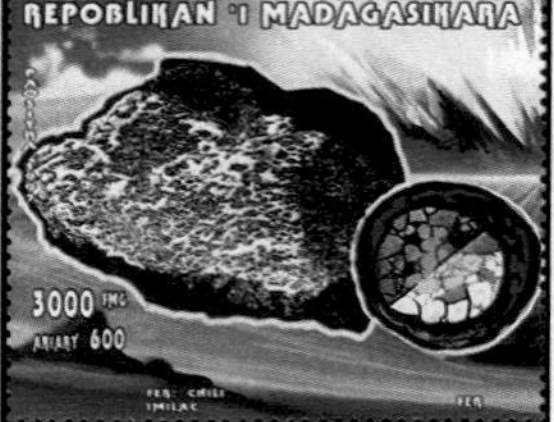

Meteorites and Minerals — A403

No. 1349 — Meteorites: a, Iron, found in Chile. b, Iron, found in Alvord, Iowa. c, Silicate in lunar meteorite, found in Antarctica.
No. 1350 — Minerals: a, Agate, dioptase. b, Malachite, garnet. c, Chrysolile, wulfenite.
12,500fr, Mars meterorite, found in Antarctica.

1998, Feb. 25
1349 A403 3000fr Sheet of 3, #a.-c. 5.00 2.50
1350 A403 7500fr Sheet of 3, #a.-c. 12.00 6.00

Souvenir Sheet

1351 A403 12,500fr multicolored 6.50 3.25

Dated 1997.

World Post Day — A404

1997, Oct. 21 Litho. *Perf. 13½*
1352 A404 300fr multicolored 5.50 2.75

Radio Nederland in Madagascar, 25th Anniv. — A404a

Perf. 11¾x11½
1997, Sept. 18 Litho.
Granite Paper
1352A A404a 500fr multi — —

Third Francophone Games — A404b

Background colors: 300fr, Light blue. 1850fr, Beige.

1997, Oct. 9 Litho. *Perf. 11½x11¾*
Granite Paper
1352B-1352C A404b Set of 2 1.75 1.75

For surcharge, see No. 1490.

Diana, Princess of Wales (1961-97) A405

No. 1353 — Diana wearing: a, High-collared white dress. b, Halter-style dress. c, Choker necklace, purple dress. d, Wide-brimmed hat. e, Jeweled choker necklace. f, White dress, no necklace. g, Black dress. h, White dress, pearls. i, Red dress.
No. 1354 — Portraits of Diana: a, Wearing jeweled necklace. b, With Pope John Paul II. c, Wearing beaded jacket. d, With Nelson Mandela. e, With man from India. f, With Emperor Akihito. g, Holding infant. h, Receiving flowers from child. i, Visiting sick child.
No. 1355, 12,500fr, With Mother Teresa (in margin). No. 1356, 12,500fr, With Princess Grace (in margin). No. 1357, 12,500fr, With land mine victim. No. 1358, 12,500fr, Rose-colored dress, hat.

1998, Feb. 18 Litho. *Perf. 13½*
1353 A405 1350fr Sheet of 9, #a.-i. 6.50 3.25
1354 A405 1750fr Sheet of 9, #a.-i. 8.50 4.25

Souvenir Sheets

1355-1358 A405 Set of 4 27.00 14.00

Nos. 1355-1358 each contain one 42x60mm stamp.

Pasteur Institute of Madagascar, Cent. — A405a

1998 Litho. *Perf. 11¾x11½*
1358A A405a 500fr multi — —
1358B A405a 2500fr multi —

An additional stamp was issued in this set. The editors would like to examine it.

1998 World Cup Soccer Championships, France — A406

No. 1359 — Group A: a, Brazil. b, Scotland. c, Morocco. d, Norway.
No. 1360 — Group B: a, Italy. b, Chile. c, Cameroun. d, Austria.
No. 1361 — Group C: a, France. b, South Africa. c, Saudi Arabia. d, Denmark.
No. 1362 — Group D: a, Spain. b, Nigeria. c, Paraguay. d, Bulgaria.
No. 1363 — Group E: a, Netherlands. b, Belgium. c, South Korea. d, Mexico.
No. 1364 — Group F: a, Germany. b, US. c, Yugoslavia. d, Iran.
No. 1365 — Group G: a, Romania. b, Colombia. c, England. d, Tunisia.
No. 1366 — Group H: a, Argentina. b, Japan. c, Jamaica. d, Croatia.

1998, July 10 Litho. *Perf. 13½*
1359 A406 1350fr Sheet of 4, #a.-d. 2.75 1.40
1360 A406 1500fr Sheet of 4, #a.-d. 3.00 1.50
1361 A406 1700fr Sheet of 4, #a.-d. 3.50 1.75
1362 A406 2000fr Sheet of 4, #a.-d. 4.00 2.00
1363 A406 2500fr Sheet of 4, #a.-d. 5.00 2.50
1364 A406 3000fr Sheet of 4, #a.-d. 6.00 3.00
1365 A406 3500fr Sheet of 4, #a.-d. 7.00 3.50
1366 A406 5000fr Sheet of 4, #a.-d. 10.00 5.00

Sheets exist without Group A-Group H inscriptions. Stamps on these sheets have different denominations, and some design details differ. These sheets were allegedly on sale for a brief time before withdrawal.

Antsirabe Military Academy, 30th Anniv. — A406a

1998 Litho. *Perf. 11½x11¾*
1366E A406a 500fr multi — —
1366F A406a 2500fr multi —

Insects, Butterflies, Mushrooms, Minerals — A407

No. 1367 — Insects: a, Batocera wallacei, heliocopris antenor. b, Carabus auratus, calosome.
No. 1368 — Butterflies: a, Catopsilia thauruma. b, Iphiclides podalirius.
No. 1369 — Mushrooms: a, Hygrocybe punicea. b, Lepista nuda.
No. 1370 — Insects: a, Euchroma gigantea, goliathus goliathus. b, Pyrrbocor apterus, Acroninus longimanus.
No. 1371 — Butterflies: a, Hypolimnas dexithea. b, Colotis zoe.
No. 1372 — Mushrooms: a, Boletus edulis bull. b, Hygrophorus hypotheium.
No. 1373 — Minerals: a, Vanadinite. b, Carnotite.
No. 1374, 12,500fr, Papilio dardanus. No. 1375, 12,500fr, Albatrellus ovinus.

1998 Litho. *Perf. 13½*
Sheets of 2
1367 A407 1350fr Sheet of 2, #a.-b. 1.60 .70
1368 A407 2500fr Sheet of 2, #a.-b. 3.00 1.25
1369 A407 3000fr Sheet of 2, #a.-b. 3.50 1.50
1370 A407 3500fr Sheet of 2, #a.-b. 4.00 1.75
1371 A407 5000fr Sheet of 2, #a.-b. 5.75 2.50
1372 A407 7500fr Sheet of 2, #a.-b. 8.25 3.75
1373 A407 10,000fr Sheet of 2, #a.-b. 11.00 5.00

Souvenir Sheets

1374-1375 A407 Set of 2 14.00 6.50

Nos. 1374-1375 each contain one 36x42mm stamp.

Personalities A408

Designs: No. 1376, Andrianary Ratianarivo (1895-1949). No. 1377, Odeam Rakoto (1922-73). No. 1378, Fredy Rajaofera (1902-68).

1997, Aug. 21

1376-1378	A408 140fr Set of 3		.45	.25

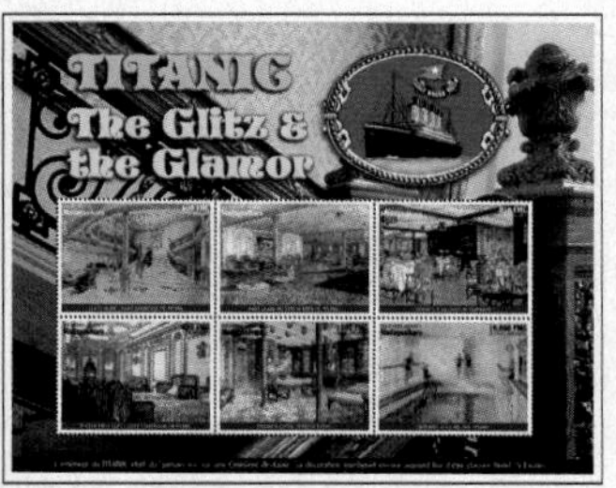

The Titanic — A409

No. 1379 — Faces of the Titanic: a, 1300fr, J. Pierpont Morgan, owner, White Star Line. b, 1300fr, J. Bruce Ismay, director, White Star Line. c, 1300fr, Lord James Pirrie, builder, Harland & Wolff. d, 1300fr, Alexander Carlisle, designer, Harland & Wolff. e, 1300fr, Edward John Smith, Captain of Titanic. f, 1750fr, Arthur Rostron, Captain of Carpathia.

No. 1380 — Rescue: a, 1350fr, Women and children first. b, 1350fr, Lifeboats lowered. c, 1350fr, Lifeboats called back. d, 1350fr, Captain Smith hands child to safety. e, 1700fr, Few saved from water. f, 1700fr, Reaching Carpathia.

No. 1381, vert. — Various pictures of ship taken from period postcards: a, 300fr. b, 5000fr. c, 1200fr. d, 7500fr.

No. 1382 — Interior of ship: a, 800fr, Grand staircase. b, 800fr, Reception area. c, 850fr, Restaurant. d, 850fr, Stateroom. e, 1300fr, Turkish baths. f, 10.000fr, Swimming pool.

No. 1383 — Building the ship: a, 1450fr, Drafting room, 1907-08. b, 2050fr, Hull constructed, 1909-11. c, 5000fr, Launch, Belfast, May 31, 1911. d, 7500fr, Fitting out, 1911-12.

No. 1384 — The aftermath: a, 300fr, "The Sun" post lastest bulletins. b, 450fr, Paperboys on street. c, 1050fr, Hearses, coffins at dock. d, 5000fr, Wallace Hartley, "The Last Tune." e, 10,000fr, Engineers Monument, 1914.

1998, Sept. 10 Litho. *Perf. 13½*

1379	A409	Sheet of 6, #a.-f.	3.50	1.50
1380	A409	Sheet of 6, #a.-f.	3.75	1.60
1381	A409	Sheet of 4, #a.-d.	6.25	2.50
1382	A409	Sheet of 6, #a.-f.	6.50	2.75
1383	A409	Sheet of 4, #a.-d.	7.00	3.00
1384	A409	Sheet of 5, #a.-e.	7.25	3.25

No. 1381 contains four 37½x49mm stamps. No. 1382 contains six 49x38mm stamps. No. 1384, five 28x35mm stamps.

Famous Disasters at Sea — A410

No. 1385: a, 160fr, Sinking of the Titanic, 1912. b, 160fr, Torpedoing of the Lusitania, 1915. c, 1350fr, Burning of the Atlantique, 1933. d, 1350fr, Burning of the Normandie, 1942. e, 1350fr, Wilhelm Gustloff being torpedoed, 1945. f, 1350fr, Sinking of the Andrea Doria, 1956. g, 3500fr, Burning of the Queen Elizabeth, 1972. h, 3500fr, Sinking of the Amoco Cadiz, 1978. i, 3500fr, Sinking of the Estonia, 1994.

No. 1386, Various scenes of Titanic disaster.

1998, Nov. 6 Litho. *Perf. 13½*

1385	A410	Sheet of 9, #a.-i.	7.75	3.75

Souvenir Sheet

1386	A410	12,500fr multicolored	6.25	3.00

No. 1386 contains one 120x51mm stamp.

Trains, Sports Cars, Airplanes — A411

No. 1387 — Trains: a, Steam locomotive, 477.043, China. b, Kruckenberg Zeppelin Train, Germany. c, Mountain 498, China. d, Gottardo tram, Switzerland. e, TGV 001, France. f, ET-403, Germany. g, Le Shuttle, France. h, Shinkansen, Japan. i, TGV Alexander Dumas, France.

No. 1388 — Sports cars: a, Opel Kapitan, Germany. b, Volkswagen Beetle, Germany. c, Fiat Topolino, Italy. d, Facel Delahaye, France-England. e, Bristol Series 407, England. f, Alfa Romeo 2500, Italy. g, Chrysler Viper GTS, US. h, McLaren FI, England. i, Mercedes Brabus SLK, Germany.

No. 1389 — Airplanes: a, Aerospatiale STS 2000, France. b, Piggyback Space Shuttle, US. c, Hermes Rocket, France, Germany, Italy. d, Northrop B-35, US. e, Airbus A310, A321, A340, Europe. f, Armstrong Whitworth A.W52, Great Britain. g, Concorde, UK, France, going right. h, Tupolev, Russia. i, Concorde, France, UK, going left.

1998, Nov. 6

1387	A411	1700fr Sheet of 9, #a.-i.	7.50	3.75
1388	A411	2000fr Sheet of 9, #a.-i.	9.00	4.50
1389	A411	3000fr Sheet of 9, #a.-i.	13.50	6.75

Balloons A412

No. 1390: a, 300fr, "Pilatre de Rozier," Montgolfier, 1783. b, 300fr, Charles and Robert, 1783. c, 300fr, Blanchard and Jeffries, 1785. d, 350fr, "Pilatre de Rozier," 1785. e, 350fr, "Testu-Brissy," 1798. f, 350fr, "Atlantic," 1858. g, 5000fr, "Small World," 1959. h, 5000fr, "Strato-lab High 5", 1961. i, 5000fr, "Double Eagle II", 1978.

10,000fr, Auguste Piccard (1884-1962), balloon.

1998, Nov. 6

1390	A412	Sheet of 9, #a.-i.	8.50	4.25

Souvenir Sheet

1391	A412	10,000fr multicolored	5.00	2.50

No. 1391 contains one 42x51mm stamp.

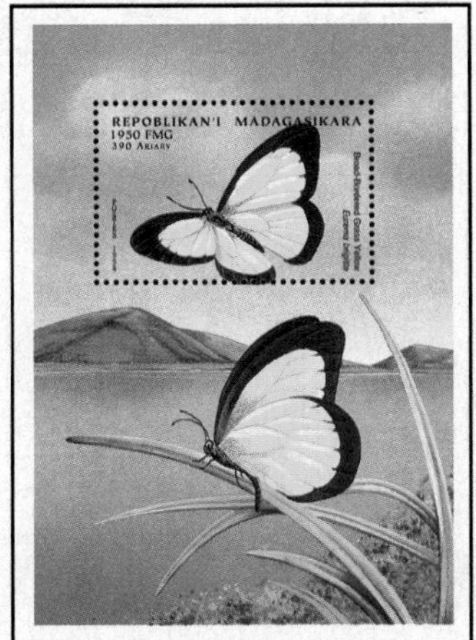

Butterflies and Moths — A413

No. 1392: a, 1950fr, Citrus swallowtail. b, 1950fr, Mocker swallowtail. c, 1950fr, Striped policeman. d, 1950fr, Golden piper. e, 1950fr, Painted lady. f, 1950fr, Monarch. g, 250fr, Gold-banded forester. h, 250fr, Madagascan sunset moth. i, 250fr, Palla butterfly. j, 250fr, Blue pansy. k, 250fr, Common grass blue. l, 250fr, Crimson tip.

1800fr, Cabbage butterfly, vert. No. 1394, Broad-bordered grass yellow. 2250fr, Figtree blue. 3500fr, African migrant, vert.

1999, Mar. 24

1392	A413	Sheet of 12, #a.-l.	7.50	3.50

Souvenir Sheets

1393	A413	1800fr multicolored	1.25	.55
1394	A413	1950fr multicolored	1.40	.60
1395	A413	2250fr multicolored	1.50	.65
1396	A413	3500fr multicolored	2.50	1.00

Birds — A414

No. 1397: a, 250fr, Madagascar blue pigeon. b, 250fr, White-tailed tropicbird. c, 1350fr, Madagascan red fody. d, 1350fr, Crested drongo. e, 250fr, Namaqua dove. f, 250fr, Helmet bird. g, 1350fr, Blue-crowned roller. h, 1350fr, Red-eyed roller. i, 250fr, Coral-billed nuthatch. j, 250fr, Wattled false sunbird. k, 1350fr, Short-legged ground roller. l, 1350fr, Pied crow.

No. 1398, 4000fr, Barn owl. No. 1399, 4000fr, Goliath heron.

No. 1400, 7200fr, Marah harrier hawk, horiz. No. 1401, 7200fr, Vasa parrot, horiz.

1999, Feb. 17 Litho. *Perf. 13½*

1397	A414	Sheet of 12, #a.-l.	4.75	1.75

Souvenir Sheets

1398-1399	A414	Set of 2	4.25	1.50
1400-1401	A414	Set of 2	7.75	2.75

New Year 1999 (Year of the Rabbit) — A415

No. 1402 — Stylized rabbits: a, Facing right. b, Looking right over shoulder. c, Looking left over shoulder. d, Facing left.

10,000fr, Facing forward.

1999, Apr. 7 Litho. *Perf. 14*

1402	A415	1500fr Block of 4, #a.-d.	3.00	1.25

Souvenir Sheet

1403	A415	10,000fr multi	4.75	3.75

Grain and Map — A415a

1999 Litho. *Perf. 13½*

1403A	A415a	450fr brn & multi	—	—
1403B	A415a	900fr red & multi		
1403C	A415a	900fr green & multi	—	—
1403D	A415a	1500fr (300a) blue & multi	—	—
1403E	A415a	5600fr multi	—	—

No. 1403B is airmail. Denomination is at bottom on No. 1403A. Nos. 1403A and 1403C are dated "2000." On No. 1403D, the denomination is at the bottom with large capital and lower case letters.

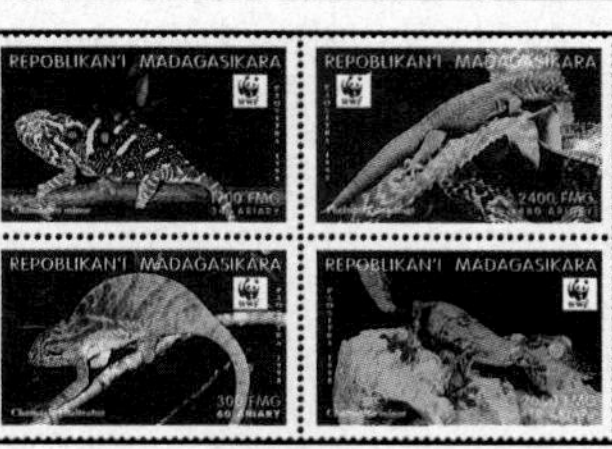

Lizards — A416

World Wildlife Fund: a, 1700fr, Chamaeleo minor (on branch). b, 2400fr, Phelsuma standingi. c, 300fr, Chamaeleo balteatus. d, 2050fr, Chamaeleo minor (on rock). e, 2050fr, as "d," inscribed "Urplatus fimbriatus."

1999, Apr. 7

1404	A416	Block of 4, #a.-d.	8.75	8.75
f.		Block of 4, #1404a-1404c, 1404e	5.25	5.25

Issued in sheets of 16 stamps.
Issued: No. 1404e, 7/23.

Fauna A417

Designs: No. 1405, 1950fr, Toucan. No. 1406, 1950fr, Hummingbird. No. 1407, 1950fr, Dendrobates pumilis. No. 1408, 1950fr, Jaguar, vert. No. 1409, 1950fr, Dendrobate (frog). No. 1410, 1950fr, Pangolin.

No. 1411: a, Three-toed sloth (d). b, Chameleon (e). c, Loris (f). d, Tree frog. e, Tarsier. f, Civet (i). g, Cicada. h, Callicore butterfly. i, Python (f).

No. 1412: a, Flying fox (bat). b, Galago (a, d, e). c, Squirrel monkey (f). d, Red kingfisher. e, Blue parrot (h). f, Heliconide butterfly. g, Oranutan (d). h, Tamarin. i, Ocelot (h).

No. 1413, 10,000fr, Tiger. No. 1414, 10,000fr, Leopard.

1999, Apr. 7

1405-1410	A417	Set of 6	4.50	4.50
1411	A417	2250fr Sheet of 9, #a.-i.	7.50	7.50
1412	A417	2450fr Sheet of 9, #a.-i.	7.75	7.75

Souvenir Sheets

1413-1414	A417	Set of 2	7.50	7.50

Film Stars — A418

No. 1414A: b, Antonio Banderas. c, Glenn Close. d, Harrison Ford. e, Pamela Anderson. f, Tom Hanks. g, Michelle Pfeiffer. h, Leonardo Di Caprio. i, Sharon Stone. j, Tom Cruise.

No. 1415: a. Catherine Deneuve. b, Gérard Depardieu. c, John-Paul Belmondo. d, John Reno. e, Johnny Hallyday. f, Christopher Lambert. g, Jean Gabin. h, Alain Delon. i, Brigitte Bardot.

1999 Litho. *Perf. 13½*

1414A	A418	2500fr Sheet of 9, #b.-j.	12.00	12.00
1415	A418	3500fr Sheet of 9, #a.-i.	11.50	11.50

Fauna A419

No. 1416: a, Rotary International emblem and Hapalemur gris, satellite. b, Rotary International emblem and Lemur vari, satellite. c, Rotary International emblem and Hanka. d, Scouting emblem, comet ,and Sifaka de verreaux. e, Scouting emblem, comet, and Euplere de goudot. f, Scouting emblem, comet, and Potamochere. g, Lions International emblem and Rousette geante, satellite. h, Lions International emblem, Lampira, comet. i, Lions International emblem, Maki catta, satellite.

No. 1416J - Butterfly and : k, Gibbon lar. l, Macaque rhesus. m, Maki macaco. n, Gélada. o, Maki brun. p, Nasique. q, Maki vari. r, Mandrill. s, Hapalémur gris.

1999

Sheets of 9 + 3 Labels

1416 A419 2500fr Sheets of 9, #a.-i., + 3 labels 10.00 10.00
1416J A419 3500fr Sheets of 9, #k.-s., + 3 labels 14.00 14.00

Intl. Year of the Ocean A420

Designs: No. 1417, Scarus gibbus. No, 1418, Gramma loreto. No. 1419, Arusetta asfur. No. 1420, Daseyllus trimaculatus.

No. 1421: a, Hyporhamphus unifasciatus. b, Delphinus delphis. c, Cetorhinus maximus. d, Manta birostris. e, Chactodon capistratus. f, Microspathodon chysurus.

No. 1422: a, Coryphaena hippurus. b, Diodon holacanthus. c, Aequorea aequorea. d, Sphyraena barracuda. e, Octopus vulgaris. f, Acanthurus bahianus. g, Gymnothorax moringa. h, Limulus polyphemus. i, Pristis pictinata.

No. 1423: a, 1350fr, Balistoides niger. b, 1350fr, Isiophorus platypterus. c, 2750fr, Carcharhinus limbatus. d, 2750fr, Carcharodon carcharias. e, 1350fr, Zanclus cornutus. f, 1350fr, Mermaid's face. g, 2750fr, Gramma loreto. h, 2750fr, Rhinecanthus aculeatus. i, 1350fr, Lactoria cornuta. j, 1350fr, Hippocampus kuda. k, 2750fr, Pygoplites diancanthus. l, 2750fr, Epinephelus lanceolatus. m, 1350fr, Echinaster sepositus. n, 1350fr, Ocypede quadrata. o, 2750fr, Amphiprion clarkii. p, 2750fr, Cyphoma gibbosum.

No. 1424, 7200fr, Odontaspis taurus, vert. No. 1425, 7200fr, Stenalla plagiodon.

1999, June 10 ***Perf. 14***

1417-1420 A420 550fr Set of 4 1.75 1.75

Sheets of 6, 9 or 16

1421 A420 550fr Sheet of 6, #a.-f. 1.60 1.60
1422 A420 3500fr Sheet of 9, #a.-i. 15.00 15.00
1423 A420 Sheet of 16, #a.-p. 15.00 15.00

Souvenir Sheets

1424-1425 A420 Set of 2 7.25 7.25

No. 1423a-1423p are each 33x52mm. Dated 1998.

Trains — A421

No. 1426, 4000fr: a, Danish State Railways, 1950-59. b, France, 1963. c, East Germany, 1980. d, Finnish State Railways, 1950. e, Canada, 1949. f, West Germany, 1952.

No. 1427, 4000fr: a, Light Branch 4-4-0 locomotive, Ireland, 1948. b, 4-8-0 locomotive, Argentina, 1949. c, 2-8-0 locomotive, US, 1943. d, Gold rush steam engine, US, 1870. e, Royal Blue, US, 1870-80. f, Queensland Railways, Australia, 1952.

No. 1428, 4000fr: a, 0-4-0 Lightning, England, 1829. b, Grampton, Namur, Belgium, 1848. c, Lion, England, 1838. d, Borsig, Germany, 1841. e, Baldwin "Eight-coupled" locomotive, US, 1846. f, Crampton, England, 1848.

No. 1429, 10,000fr, Diesel multiple-unit express train, Japan. No. 1430, 10,000fr, 4-8-0 steam locomotive, US, 19th cent.

1999, June 22

Sheets of 6, #a-f

1426-1428 A421 Set of 3 27.00 27.00

Souvenir Sheets

1429-1430 A421 Set of 2 7.50 7.50

Nos. 1429-1430 each contain one 76x50mm stamp. No. 1426c is incorrectly inscribed with date, "1930."

A422

Dinosaurs A423

Designs: No. 1431, 500fr, Stenonychosaurus, vert. No. 1432, 500fr, Iguanodon, vert. No. 1433, 500fr, Staurikosaurus, vert. No. 1434, 500fr, Plateosaurus, vert.

No. 1435, 500fr, Antrodemus. No. 1436, 500fr, Corythosaurus, vert. No. 1437, 500fr, Stegosaurus, vert. No. 1438, 500fr, Lambeosaurus, vert. No. 1439, 500fr, Hypsilophodon, vert.

No. 1440: a, Psittacosaurus. b, Allosaurus. c, Stegosaurus. d, Hypsilophodon. e, Triceratops. f, Camptosaurus. g, Compsognathus. h, Carnotaurus.

No. 1441, vert: a, Brachiosaurus. b, Tyrannosaurus. c, Plateosaurus. d, Hadrosaurus. e, Triceratops. f, Iguanodon.

No. 1442, 12,500fr, Styracosaurus. No. 1443, 12,500fr, Brachiosaurus, vert. No. 1444, 12,500fr, Tyrannosaurus rex, vert.

1999, July 6 **Litho.** ***Perf. 14***

1431-1434 A422 Set of 4 1.10 1.10
1435-1439 A423 Set of 5 1.40 1.40
1440 A422 1850fr Sheet of 8, #a.-h. 5.50 5.50
1441 A422 1950fr Sheet of 6, #a.-f. 4.50 4.50

Souvenir Sheets

1442-1444 A422 Set of 3 13.50 13.50

Nos. 1431-1439 dated 1998. Numbers have been reserved for additional values in this set.

Princess Diana — A424

1999, Aug. 10 **Litho.** ***Perf. 13½***

1446 A424 1950fr multicolored 1.00 1.00

Issued in sheets of six stamps. Compare with Type A434.

Picasso Paintings A425

Designs: 2750fr, Bacchanalia, 1955. 7200fr, Picador, 1971, vert. 7500fr Seated Nude, 1906-07, vert.

12,500fr, The Two Saltimbanques, 1901, vert.

1999, Aug. 10 **Litho.** ***Perf. 13x13¼***

1447-1449 A425 Set of 3 6.75 6.75

Souvenir Sheet

1450 A425 12,500fr multi 4.75 4.75

Dated 1998.

Mahatma Gandhi — A426

Perf. 13½x13¼

1999, Aug. 10 **Litho.**

1451 A426 2250fr Profile 1.25 1.25

Souvenir Sheet

1452 A426 12,500fr Gandhi shirtless 4.75 4.75

No. 1451 issued in sheets of four stamps. Dated 1998.

Indian Ocean Commission, 15th Anniv. A427

1999 **Litho.** ***Perf. 13¼***

1453 A427 500fr multicolored .60 .60

Fire Fighting Apparatus — A429

No. 1456, 2500fr: a, Pumper Boat "Dauphin," Africa. b, 60T Pumper, US. c, Fire train, Switzerland.

No. 1457, 2500fr: a, Gillois amphibian engine, Germany. b, Ford FMC pumper. c, Cherry picker pumper, Iraq.

1999 **Sheets of 3, #a-c**

1456-1457 A429 Set of 2 7.00 7.00

Trains — A430

No. 1458, 3500fr: a, Pen-y-Darren, England. b, Pennsylvania Railroad locomotive. c, Norfolk and Western locomotive.

No. 1459, 3500fr: a, TGV Postal, France. b, TGV, Sweden. c, Magnetic train "Europa."

1999 **Sheets of 3, #a-c**

1458-1459 A430 Set of 2 9.50 9.50

Airplanes — A431

No. 1460, 5000fr: a, Short-Mayo Composite. b, Boeing 747. c, Concorde, Air France poster.

No. 1461, 5000fr: a, Concorde, KLM poster. b, 1931 Curtiss F9C. c, Macchi-Castoldi MC72.

1999 **Sheets of 3, #a-c**

1460-1461 A431 Set of 2 13.00 13.00

Space Achievements — A432

No. 1462, 7500fr: a, Viking. b, Voyager. c, Apollo 11.

No. 1463, 7500fr: a, Dog Laika. b, Yuri Gagarin, Vostok spacecraft. c, Mir space station.

1999 **Sheets of 3, #a-c**

1462-1463 A432 Set of 2 20.00 20.00

Boy Scouts — A433

Scouts, No. 1464: a, Bandaging thigh. b, Splinting arm. c, Making sling. d, Pulling tape from roll.

No. 1464E: f, Oeniella polystachys. g, Cynorkis lowiana. h, Oeceoclades saundersiana. i, Cynorkis purpurascens.

No. 1465: a, Upupa epops. b, Nettapus auritus. c, Leptosomus discolor. d, Brachypteracias squamigera.

No. 1465E: f, Euchraca spinnasuta. g, Cricket. h, Scorpion. i, Euchroea nigrostellata.

No. 1466: a, Charaxes antamboulou. b, Hypolimnas misippus. c, Papilio demodocus. d, Papilio antenor.

No. 1467: a, Eucalyptoboletus. b, Cantharllus congolensis. c, Gomphus. d, Russula.

No. 1468: a, Jasper. b, Granite. c, Rhodonite. d, Morganite.

No. 1469: a, Soccer. b, Chess. c, Table tennis. d, Cycling.

1999 Litho. *Perf. 13¼*

1464	A433	1350fr Sheet of 4, #a.-d.	2.25	2.75
1464E	A433	1500fr Sheet of 4, #f.-i.	3.00	3.00
1465	A433	1950fr Sheet of 4, #a.-d.	4.00	4.00
1465E	A433	2000fr Sheet of 4, #f.-i.	4.00	4.00
1466	A433	2500fr Sheet of 4, #a.-d.	4.75	4.75
1467	A433	3000fr Sheet of 4, #a.-d.	5.50	5.50
1468	A433	5000fr Sheet of 4, #a.-d.	8.75	8.75
1469	A433	7500fr Sheet of 4, #a.-d.	13.50	13.50
		Nos. 1464-1469 (8)	45.75	46.25

No. B27 Handstamp Surcharged in Violet

Printing Methods and Perfs as before

1999 (?)

1471 SP7 60fr on 350fr+20fr on 250fr+20fr

Nos. 1001G, 1043, 1068, 1076, 1179, 1213, 1352C Surcharged

#1472B

No. 1118 Surcharged

No. 1473A

300 Fmg 60 Ariary

#1474A

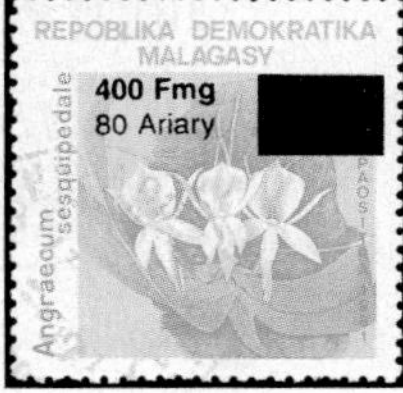

#1474B

No. 1477

Printing Methods and Perfs as Before

1999 (?)

1472B	A368	300fr on 605fr #1213	—	—
1473A	A342	300fr on 675fr #1076		—
1473B	A352	300fr on 675fr #1118	—	—
1474A	A363	300fr on 755fr #1179	—	—
1474B	A191	400fr on 170fr #614	—	—
1475B	A207	500fr on 170fr #645	—	—
1477	A341	500fr on 555fr #1068		—
1477A	A367	500fr on 575fr #1205	—	—
1478A	A325b	500fr on 680fr #1001G	—	—
1482	A333	500fr on 1140fr #1043	—	—
1486	A341	500fr on 1400fr #1070	—	—
1490	A404b	500fr on 1850fr #1352C	—	—

Many additional surcharges have been reported. The editors would like to examine them. This is an expanding set. Numbers may change.

20th Century Celebrities — A434

No. 1491: a, Princess Diana. b, Kwame Nkrumah. c, Gen. Georgy Zhukov. d, Samora Machel. e, Gen. Moshe Dayan. f, Mahatma Gandhi. g, Jacqueline Kennedy. h, Gen. John Pershing.

1999 Litho. *Perf. 13½*

1491 A434 1950fr Sheet of 8, #a.-h. 7.25 7.25

Famous People — A435

Designs: No. 1492, 900fr, Razafindrakotohasina Rahantavololona. No. 1493, 900fr, Gen. Gabriel Ramanantsoa. No. 1494, 900fr, Rasalama. No. 1495, 900fr, Dr. Ralivao Ramiaramanana. No. 1496, 900fr, Jérôme-Henri Cardinal Rakotomalala. No. 1497, 900fr, Rakotovao Razakaboana.

2000, Jan. 12 Litho. *Perf. 14*

1492-1497 A435 Set of 6 3.00 3.00

UPU, 125th Anniv. — A436

UPU emblem, postmen of various eras and: 1000fr, Mailbox. 1200fr, Postmen, space shuttle, airplane, cargo. 1800fr, Cable-laying ships. 3200fr, 19th century diligence, modern mail truck. 3500fr, balloon, Apollo 15 astronaut. 5000fr, Stentor satellite, Claude Chappe's semaphore. 5600fr, Micheline ZM 517, Autorail Bouleze 701. 7500fr, Old and modern mail trains.

1999 Litho. *Perf. 13¼*

1498-1505 A436 Set of 8 13.00 13.00

Nos. 1498-1505 exist in souvenir sheets of 1.

The Incredible Hulk — A437

No. 1506: a, Hulk with gray skin, wearing white shirt. b, Head of Hulk, red background. c, Hulk with fist raised, blue background. d, Hulk with red violet pants, lilac background. e, Hulk with ripped shirt, orange background. f, Hulk wearing sunglasses. g, Hulk shirtless, orange and red background. h, Hulk holding shirt, red violet and orange background. i, Hulk, multicolored striped background.

12,500fr, Hulk, yellow and orange background.

1999, Apr. 29 Litho. *Perf. 13¼*

1506 A437 1800fr Sheet of 9, #a-i 7.00 7.00

Souvenir Sheet

1507 A437 12,500fr multi 6.00 6.00

No. 1507 contains one 36x42mm stamp.

Silver Surfer — A438

No. 1509: a, Silver Surfer at left, dark blue green background. b, Head of Silver Surfer, red brown background. c, Silver Surfer at right, black background with large star. d, Silver Surfer on surfboard, purple background. e, Head of Silver Surfer, green background. f, Silver Surfer carrying surfboard, purple background. g, Silver Surfer, Earth and outer space in background. h, Silver Surfer, multicolored striped background. i, Silver Surfer on surfboard, outer space background with red and blue spots.

12,500fr, Silver Surfer, diff.

1999, Apr. 29

1508 A438 1800fr Sheet of 9, #a-i 7.00 7.00

Souvenir Sheet

1509 A438 12,500fr multi 6.00 6.00

No. 1509 contains one 36x42mm stamp.

Spiderman — A439

No. 1510: a, Peter Parker turning into Spiderman. b, Spiderman with fist at upper right. c, Spiderman crouching. d, Spiderman holding silk at top. e, Head of Spiderman. f, Spiderman with rays around head. g, Spiderman with arms together, on silk. h, Spiderman with two strands of silk. i, Spiderman with large black spider on front of costume, and netting under arms.

12,500fr, Spiderman with arms raised.

1999, Apr. 29

1510 A439 3200fr Sheet of 9, #a-i 11.50 11.50

Souvenir Sheet

1511 A439 12,500fr multi 6.00 6.00

No. 1511 contains one 30x42mm stamp.

Garfield — A440

No. 1512: a, Garfield sitting. b, Garfield looking between legs. c, Garfield holding teddy bear. d, Garfield climbing wall. e, Garfield sticking out tongue. f, Garfield with legs crossed. g, Garfield asleep. h, Garfield standing. i, Odie.

1999, Apr. 29

1512 A440 3200fr Sheet of 9, #a-i 11.50 11.50

Miniature Sheets

Trains — A441

No. 1513, 800fr: a, Locomotive PK 102 on Brickaville to Fonavana line. b, Locomotive in Diego-Suarez region, 1904. c, 030T locomotive, 1922. d, BBB Alsthom Diesel-electric, 1937.

No. 1514, 1500fr: a, Locomotive 42104, 1906. b, Decauville 60 gauge locomotive. c, Mallet 020+020T locomotive, 1916. d, Garratt No. 101 locomotive, 1925.

No. 1515, 2000fr: a, Billard ZM 111 rail car, 1938. b, BB AD16 locomotive. c, Brissoneau Diesel-electric rail car, 1958. d, BBB 2nd Series 106-112, 1958.

No. 1516, 3500fr: a, Train at Fianarantsoa Station. b, AD 12 Alsthom locomotive. c, Mallet 131+131 St. Leonard. d, Micheline ZM 514.

No. 1517, 4000fr: a, Decauville 0.20 gauge 1m locomotive. b, BB235 Diesel. c, Baldwin 031 T locomotive. d, BBB Alsthom Diesel locomotive, 1935.

No. 1518, 4400fr: a, Decauville 60 gauge Montagne d'Ambre locomotive. b, Brissoneau & Lotz Diesel, 1938. c, Mallet 120+020 T locomotive, 1902. d, Corpet-Louvet locomotive.

No. 1519, 5200fr: a, Adiz BB229 locomotive. b, 030T Weidnecht locomotive, 1901. c, Jung locomotive, 1922. d, Billard rail car, 1934.

No. 1520, 10,000fr: a, Mallet 020+020 locomotive, 1925. b, Decauville 030 locomotive, 1907. c, Garratt 130+031 locomotive, 1925. d, Nosy Be 030N1, 1868.

2000, July 21 *Perf. 13¼*

Sheets of 4, #a-d

1513-1520 A441 Set of 8 45.00 45.00

Miniature Sheets

2000 Summer Olympics, Sydney — A442

No. 1521, 500fr: a, Soccer. b, Handball. c, Judo. d, Kayaking.

No. 1522, 1350fr: a, Cycling. b, Swimming. c, Boxing. d, Fencing.

No. 1523, 2500fr: a, Basketball. b, Cycling, diff. c, Equestrian. d, Running.

No. 1524, 3200fr: a, Weight lifting. b, Javelin. c, Equestrian, diff. d, Yachting.

No. 1525, 5000fr: a, Shot put. b, Women's gymnastics. c, Men's tennis. d, High jump.

No. 1526, 7500fr: a, Diving. b, Wrestling. c, Table tennis. d, Pole vault.

12,500fr, Kayaking and equestrian, horiz.

2000, Aug. 2 **Litho.**

Sheets of 4, #a-d

1521-1526 A442 Set of 6 25.00 25.00

Souvenir Sheet

1527 A442 12,500fr multi 4.00 4.00

No. 1527 contains one 57x51mm stamp and exists imperf.

Space Achievements A443

Launches of: No. 1528, 1500fr, Gemini 1. No. 1529, 1500fr, Saturn 1. No. 1530, 1500fr, Apollo 6. No. 1531, 1500fr, Mariner 3. No. 1532, 1500fr, Mariner 4. No. 1533, 1500fr, Titan IIIC. No. 1534, 1500fr, Discovery. No. 1535, 1500fr, Soyuz 19.

No. 1536, 3500fr — Spacecraft: a, Cassini-Huygens. b, Exosat. c, ICE. d, Solar Mesosphere Explorer. e, Mir Space Station. f, Observer.

No. 1537, 3500fr — Spacecraft: a, Mars 1. b, Solar Max. c, Venera 4. d, Skylab. e, Space Shuttle Challenger. f, Mars 3.

No. 1538, 4400fr — Spacecraft: a, Ranger 1. b, Mariner 4. c, Gemini 9. d, Gemini 2. e, Apollo 15. f, Gemini 12.

No. 1539, 5000fr — Spacecraft: a, Agena. b, Syncom 1. c, Olympus 1. d, FLT Satcom. e, Skynet 4B. f, COBE.

No. 1540, 6800fr, horiz.: a, Skylab. b, Agena 1. c, Agena 2. d, X-36. e, Space Shuttle. f, Dale Gardner spacewalking.

No. 1541, 6800fr, horiz.: a, Hermes prototype. b, Pioneeer 10. c, Venture Star. d, Viking. e, Spacecraft landing on Mars. f, Mars Rover.

No. 1542, 10,000fr, Apollo 1 mission patch. No. 1543, 10,000fr, Apollo 9 mission patch. No. 1544, 10,000fr, Apollo 11 mission patch. No. 1545, 10,000fr, Apollo-Soyuz mission patch. No. 1546, 10,000fr, Columbia Space Shuttle mission patch. No. 1547, 12,500fr, Gemini 4 mission patch. No. 1548, 12,500fr, Gemini 12 mission patch. No. 1549, 12,500fr, Gemini 9 mission patch, horiz. No. 1550, 12,700fr, Huygens Probe approaching Titan. No. 1551, 12,700fr, Space Shuttle at Space Station, horiz.

Perf. 14, 14¾ (#1540-1541, 1550-1551)

2000, Sept. 22

1528-1535 A443 Set of 8 3.75 3.75

Sheets of 6, #a-f

1536-1541 A443 Set of 6 55.00 55.00

Souvenir Sheets

1542-1551 A443 Set of 10 35.00 35.00

June 21, 2001 Solar Eclipse A444

2001, June 21 *Perf. 13x13¼*

1552 A444 5600fr multi — —

Dialogue Among Civilizations — A445

2001, Oct. 12 *Perf. 13½x13¼*

1553 A445 3500fr multi 2.50 2.50

Miniature Sheets

Flora and Fauna — A446

No. 1554, 250fr — Turtles: a, Tortue geante des Seychelles. b, Tortue luth. c, Tortue panthere. d, Caouanne. e, Cistude d'Europe. f, Chelonee.

No. 1555, 400fr — Fish: a, Astronotus ocellatus. b, Cyphotilapia frontosa. c, Bothriolepis. d, Pseudanthias tuka. e, Cleidopus gloriamaris. f, Ablabys taenionotus.

No. 1556, 500fr — Owls: a, Grand duc de Virginie. b, Chouette cheveche Brahmans. c, Grand duc du cap. d, Grand duc d'Afrique. e, Hibou moyen duc. f, Petit duc Choliba.

No. 1557, 1500fr, vert. — Turtles: a, Tortue à cou cache d'Afrique. b, Tortue à dos diamante. c, Tortue d'Hermann. d, Tortue Grecque. e, Tortue caret. f, Geochelone denticulata.

No. 1558, 2500fr, vert. — Parrots: a, Ara militaire. b, Ara vert. c, Ara macao. d, Ara hyacinthe. e, Perroquet de Meyer. f, Ara ararauna.

No. 1559, 3400fr, vert. — Bears and pandas: a, Ours lippu. b, Ours noir. c, Ours polaire. d, Petit panda. e, Ours des cocotiers. f, Ours à collier.

No. 1560, 3500fr — Insects and spiders: a, Xylocopa violacea. b, Triatoma infestans. c, Myrmecia gulosa. d, Mantis religiosa. e, Atrax robustus. f, Euglosse.

No. 1561, 4000fr, vert. — Primates: a, Ouistiti mignon. b, Tamarin lion d'ore. c, Singe de nuit. d, Magot. e, Vervet. f, Ouakari.

No. 1562, 4200fr — Flowers: a, Stapelia wilmaniae. b, Centaurea montana. c, Pagonia suffruticosa. d, Acanthosicyos horrida. e, Erimophila colorhabdos. f, Amaryllis belladonna.

No. 1563, 4400fr — Orchids: a, Cattleya amethystoglossa. b, Vanda coerulea. c, Orchis robusta. d, Orchis papilionacea. e, Orchis fragrans. f, Orchis italica.

Perf. 13½x13¼, 13¼x13½

2001, Oct. 25

Sheets of 6, #a-f

1554-1563 A446 Set of 10 47.50 47.50

The following items inscribed "Repoblikan'i Madigaskara" have been declared "illegal" by Madagascar postal officials:

Sheets of nine 2000fr stamps: Motorbikes; Concorde; Elephants; Birds (2 different).

Sheets of nine stamps: Dinosaurs.

Sheet of six 5600fr stamps: Mars Exploration.

Sheets of four 5600fr stamps: Chess; Prehistoric horses; Mushrooms and eagles; Mushrooms and cats; Mushrooms and butterflies; Mushrooms and owls (2 different).

Sheet of three 5600fr stamps: Nude females (3 different).

Sheet of four 5000fr stamps: Monet paintings.

Souvenir sheets of one 1750fr stamp: Marilyn Monroe (8 different).

Souvenir sheets of two 7500fr stamps: Marilyn Monroe.

Souvenir sheet of one 12,500fr stamp: J. Baptiste Simeon Chardin.

Souvenir sheets of one: Actors Robert De Niro, Robert Redford and Leonardo DiCaprio; Actress Michelle Pfeiffer; Concorde (2 different); Fire fighting (4 different).

Famous Men — A447

Designs: No. 1564, 1500fr, Rakoto Frah (1925-2001), flutist. No. 1565, 1500fr, Albert Rakoto Ratsimamanga (1907-2001), ambassador.

2002, Oct. 9 **Litho.** *Perf. 13x12¾*

1564-1565 A447 Set of 2 2.75 2.75

Primates — A448

Design: 1000fr, Verreaux's sifaka (prophiteque de Verreauxi). 2500fr, Lemur catta.

2002, Oct. 9 **Litho.** *Perf. 13x12¾*

1566 A448 1000fr multi —

1567 A448 2500fr multi 1.75 1.75

Furcifer Pardalis — A448a

2002, Oct. 9 **Litho.** *Perf. 12¾x13*

1568 A448a 3000fr multi —

Flora A449

Designs: 100fr, Chorisia ventricosa. 350fr, Eichhornia crassipes, vert. 400fr, Didieraceae. 500fr, Palm tree, Nosy Iranja, vert. 900fr, Ravinala, vert. 4400fr, Takhtajania perrieri. 6800fr, Ravinala, diff., vert.

Perf. 12¾x13, 13x12¾

2002, Oct. 9 **Litho.**

1569-1575 A449 Set of 7 12.50 12.50

Diplomatic Relations Between Madagascar and People's Republic of China, 30th Anniv. — A450

2002, Nov. 6 *Perf. 12*

1576 A450 2500fr multi 1.90 1.90

5 Iraimbilanja = 1 Ariary

Establishment of Japan International Cooperation Agency Bureau in Madagascar — A451

2003, Dec. 4 **Litho.** *Perf. 13x13¼*

1577 A451 300a multi 2.25 2.25

The ariary officially replaced the franc on Aug. 1, 2003.

Indri Indri — A452

Denomination color: 500a, Bister. 3000a, White.

2003, Dec. 4 **Litho.** *Perf. 13¼x13*

1578 A452 500a multi 1.75 1.75

1579 A452 3000amulti — —

House, Falafa A454

House in High Plateaus A455

2003, Dec. 4 Litho. ***Perf. 13¼x13½***

1581	A454	900a multi	3.00 3.00
1582	A455	1100a multi	—

Two additional stamps were issued in this set. The editors would like to examine any examples.

Indian Ocean Commission, 20th Anniv. — A457

2003, Dec. 4 Litho. ***Perf. 13¼x13***

1584	A457	1200a multi	—

Flowers — A458

Designs: 100a, Megistostegium microphyllum. 120a, Tambourissa, horiz. 200a, Leptolaena diospyroidea. 1500a, Schizolaena tampoketsana.

Perf. 13¼x13, 13x13¼

2003, Dec. 4 Litho.

1586	A458	100a multi	—
1587	A458	120a multi	—
1588	A458	200a multi	—
1590	A458	1500a multi	—

Two additional stamps were issued in this set. The editors would like to examine any examples.

World Health Day — A459

2004, Oct. 9 Litho. ***Perf. 13½x13***

1591	A459	300a multi	1.75 1.75

Isalo Wolf Rock Formation A460

Nosy Mitsio — A461

Fort Dauphin A462

Tamatave A463

Dancers at Rova of Ambohimanga — A464

Red Tsingy, Irodo A465

Lemur and Ostriches A466

Perf. 13¼x13, 13x13¼

2004, Nov. 15 Litho.

1592	A460	400a multi	1.25	.50
1593	A461	600a multi		.60
1594	A462	1000a multi	2.75	1.00
1595	A463	1200a multi		1.25
1596	A464	2000a multi	5.25	1.50
1597	A465	5000a multi	13.00	3.25
1598	A466	10,000a multi	30.00	6.00

Royalty — A467

Designs: 20a, Ranavalona I, 1828-61. 80a, Ranavalona III, 1883-96. 100a, Radama I, 1810-28. 200a, Radama II, 1861-63. 500a, Rasoherina, 1863-68. 800a, Andrianampoinimerina, 1787-1810. 1500a, Ranavalona II, 1863-83.

2004, Nov. 15 Litho. ***Perf. 13¼x13***

1599-1605	A467	Set of 7	15.00 15.00

Rotary International, Cent. — A468

2005, Feb. 23 ***Perf. 13x13¼***

1606	A468	2100a multi	2.60 2.60

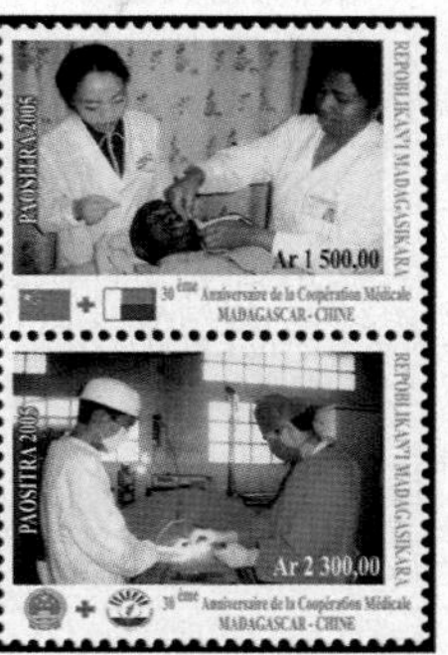

Medical Cooperation Between Madagascar and People's Republic of China, 30th Anniv. — A469

No. 1607 — Medical workers, patients and Chinese and Madagascar: a, 1500a, Flags. b, 2300a, Arms.

2005, Dec. 8 ***Perf. 12***

1607	A469	Pair, #a-b	3.50 3.50

Miniature Sheet

Orchids — A470

No. 1608, 1500a: a, Aerangis cryptodon. b, Aeranthes grandiflora. c, Aeranthes henrici. d, Aeranthes peyrotii. e, Oeccoclades spathulifera. f, Angraecum sesquipedale. g, Cynorchis elata. h, Angraecum viguieri. i, Gastrochis humblotii. j, Gastrorchis lutea. k, Gastrorchis pulcher. l, Jumellea sagittata. m, Microcoelia gilpinae. n, Angraecum praestans.

2005, Dec. 29 ***Perf. 13¼x13***

1608	A470	Sheet of 14, #a-n, + 2 labels	19.50 19.50

Campaign Against AIDS — A471

2006, Feb. 10

1609	A471	300a multi	.40 .40

Mpitandrina Rainimamonjisoa (1805-82) A472

2006, Mar. 1

1610	A472	300a blk & lt blue	.40 .40

Madagascar Philatelists Association, 20th Anniv. (in 2004) — A473

2006, Mar. 1

1611	A473	300a multi	.40 .40

Léopold Sédar Senghor (1906-2001), First President of Senegal — A474

2006, Mar. 20

1612	A474	2000a multi	2.00 2.00

Seventh Indian Ocean Islands Games — A475

2007, June 22 Litho. ***Perf. 13***

1613	A475	300a multi	.40 .40

Ile Sainte Marie Whale Festival A476

Designs: 1100a, Two whales. 3000a, Whale and two fish, vert.

Perf. 13x13¼, 13¼x13

2007, Aug. 2 Litho.

1614-1615	A476	Set of 2	8.50 8.50

Régis Rajemisa-Raolison (1913-90), Linguist, Founder of Havatsa Upem — A477

2008, May 15 Litho. *Perf. 13*
1616 A477 300a red & black .40 .40

SEMI-POSTAL STAMPS

No. 84 Surcharged in Red

1915, Feb. Unwmk. *Perf. 13½x14*
B1 A9 10c + 5c rose & brn 1.25 1.25

Curie Issue
Common Design Type

1938, Oct. 24 *Perf. 13*
B2 CD80 1.75fr + 50c brt ultra 9.00 9.00

French Revolution Issue
Common Design Type
Name and Value Typographed in Black

1939, July 5 Photo.
B3 CD83 45c + 25c grn 8.75 8.75
B4 CD83 70c + 30c brn 8.75 8.75
B5 CD83 90c + 35c red org 8.75 8.75
B6 CD83 1.25fr + 1fr rose pink 8.75 8.75
B7 CD83 2.25fr + 2fr blue 8.75 8.75
Nos. B3-B7 (5) 43.75 43.75

Common Design Type and

Malgache Sharpshooter — SP1

Tank Corpsman SP2

1941 Photo. *Perf. 13½*
B8 SP1 1fr + 1fr red 1.50
B9 CD86 1.50fr + 3fr maroon 1.50
B10 SP2 2.50fr + 1fr blue 1.75
Nos. B8-B10 (3) 4.75

Nos. B8-B10 were issued by the Vichy government in France, but were not placed on sale in Madagascar.

Nos. 162, 190 Surcharged "SECOURS +50c NATIONAL"

1942
B11 A12 1fr + 50c dk red & car rose .40
B12 A14 3fr + 50c olive black .40

Nos. B11-B12 were issued by the Vichy government in France, but were not placed on sale in Madagascar.

Petain Type of 1941
Surcharged in Black or Blue (Bl)

1944 Engr. *Perf. 12½x12*
B13 50c + 1.50fr on 2.50fr deep blue (Bl) .80
B14 + 2.50fr on 1fr bister brown .80

Colonial Development Fund.

Nos. B13-B14 were issued by the Vichy government in France, but were not placed on sale in Madagascar.

Catalogue values for unused stamps in this section, from this point to the end of the section, are for Never Hinged items.

Red Cross Issue
Common Design Type

1944 Unwmk. *Perf. 14½x14*
B15 CD90 5fr + 20fr dk grn .90 .90

The surtax was for the French Red Cross and national relief.

Gen. J. S. Galliéni and Malagasy Plowing — SP3

1946, Nov. Engr. *Perf. 13*
B16 SP3 10fr + 5fr dk vio brn .60 .60

50th anniv. of Madagascar's as a French Colony.

Tropical Medicine Issue
Common Design Type

1950, May 15
B17 CD100 10fr + 2fr dk Prus grn & brn vio 5.50 5.50

The surtax was for charitable work.

Malagasy Republic
No. 320 Surcharged in Ultramarine with New Value and: "FETES DE L'INDEPENDANCE"

1960, July 29 Engr. *Perf. 13*
B18 A38 20fr + 10fr red, blk & brt grn .60 .35

Anti-Malaria Issue
Common Design Type

1962, Apr. 7 *Perf. 12½x12*
B19 CD108 25fr + 5fr yel grn .90 .50

Post Office, Tamatave SP4

1962, May 8 Engr. *Perf. 13*
B20 SP4 25fr + 5fr sl grn, bl & lt red brn .70 .35

Issued for Stamp Day, 1962.

Freedom from Hunger Issue
Common Design Type

1963, Mar. 21 *Perf. 13*
B21 CD112 25fr + 5fr red org, plum & brn .70 .45

FAO "Freedom from Hunger" campaign.

Type of 1962

20fr+5fr, Central Parcel P. O., Tananarive.

1963, May 8 Engr.
B22 SP4 20fr + 5fr bl grn & red brn .60 .35

Issued for Stamp Day, 1963.

Postal Savings and Checking Accounts Building, Tananarive — SP5

1964, May 8 Unwmk. *Perf. 13*
B23 SP5 25fr + 5fr bl, bis & dk grn .90 .50

Issued for Stamp Day, 1964.

No. 457 Surcharged in Violet Blue

1972, June 26 Engr. *Perf. 13*
B24 A106 30fr + 20fr multi .90 .50

Charles de Gaulle memorial.

SP6 SP7

1989, June 15 Litho.
B25 SP6 80fr +20fr Torch bearer .25 .20

Village games.

1990, Aug. 7 Litho. *Perf. 12*
B26 SP7 100fr+20fr on 80fr+20fr .45 .20
B27 SP7 350fr+20fr on 250fr+20fr .80 .35

3rd Indian Ocean Games. Nos. B26-B27 were not issued without surcharge.

For surcharge see No. 1471.

AIR POST STAMPS

Airplane and Map of Madagascar — AP1

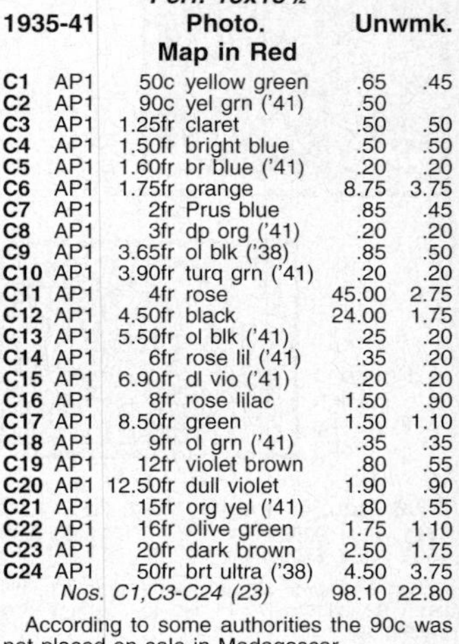

1935-41 *Perf. 13x13½* Photo. Unwmk.
Map in Red

C1	AP1	50c	yellow green	.65	.45
C2	AP1	90c	yel grn ('41)	.50	
C3	AP1	1.25fr	claret	.50	.50
C4	AP1	1.50fr	bright blue	.50	.50
C5	AP1	1.60fr	br blue ('41)	.20	.20
C6	AP1	1.75fr	orange	8.75	3.75
C7	AP1	2fr	Prus blue	.85	.45
C8	AP1	3fr	dp org ('41)	.20	.20
C9	AP1	3.65fr	ol blk ('38)	.85	.50
C10	AP1	3.90fr	turq grn ('41)	.20	.20
C11	AP1	4fr	rose	45.00	2.75
C12	AP1	4.50fr	black	24.00	1.75
C13	AP1	5.50fr	ol blk ('41)	.25	.20
C14	AP1	6fr	rose lil ('41)	.35	.20
C15	AP1	6.90fr	dl vio ('41)	.20	.20
C16	AP1	8fr	rose lilac	1.50	.90
C17	AP1	8.50fr	green	1.50	1.10
C18	AP1	9fr	ol grn ('41)	.35	.35
C19	AP1	12fr	violet brown	.80	.55
C20	AP1	12.50fr	dull violet	1.90	.90
C21	AP1	15fr	org yel ('41)	.80	.55
C22	AP1	16fr	olive green	1.75	1.10
C23	AP1	20fr	dark brown	2.50	1.75
C24	AP1	50fr	brt ultra ('38)	4.50	3.75
			Nos. C1,C3-C24 (23)	98.10	22.80

According to some authorities the 90c was not placed on sale in Madagascar.

Airplane and Map of Madagascar — AP1a

Type of 1935-41 without "RF"

1942-44
Map in Red,
Tablet & Value in Blue (except #C25)

C25	AP1a	50c	yel grn	.20
C25A	AP1a	90c	yel grn	.55
C25B	AP1a	1.25fr	claret	.30
C25C	AP1a	1.50fr	bright blue	.50
C25D	AP1a	2fr	Prus blue	.50
C25E	AP1a	3.65fr	olive black	.65
C25F	AP1a	4fr	rose	.65
C25G	AP1a	4.50fr	black	.50
C25H	AP1a	5fr	red brown	.90
C25I	AP1a	8fr	rose lilac	.90
C25J	AP1a	8.50fr	green	.90
C25K	AP1a	10fr	green	.65
C25L	AP1a	12.50fr	dull violet	.70
C25M	AP1a	16fr	olive green	.70
C25N	AP1a	20fr	dark brown	1.25
C25O	AP1a	50fr	brt ultra	1.75
			Nos. C25-C25O (16)	11.60

Nos. C25-C25O were issued by the Vichy government in France, but were not placed on sale in Madagascar.

Airplane Over Farm — AP1b

1942-44 Engr. *Perf. 13*
C26 AP1b 100fr red brown .65

No. C26 was issued by the Vichy government in France, but was not placed on sale in Madagascar.

Air Post Stamps of 1935-38 Overprinted in Black

1942 *Perf. 13x13½*

C27 AP1 1.50fr brt bl & red 6.50 6.50
C28 AP1 1.75fr org & red 92.50 92.50
C29 AP1 8fr rose lil & red 2.10 2.10
C30 AP1 12fr vio brn & red 4.00 4.00
C31 AP1 12.50fr dl vio & red 2.50 2.50
C32 AP1 16fr ol grn & red 6.50 6.50
C33 AP1 50fr brt ultra & red 4.00 4.00

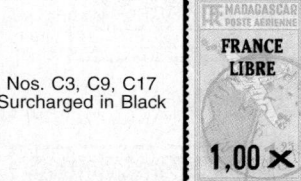

Nos. C3, C9, C17 Surcharged in Black

C34 AP1 1fr on 1.25fr 4.75 4.75
C35 AP1 3fr on 3.65fr 1.25 1.25
C36 AP1 8fr on 8.50fr 1.40 1.40
Nos. C27-C36 (10) 125.50 125.50

Catalogue values for unused stamps in this section, from this point to the end of the section, are for Never Hinged items.

Common Design Type

1943 **Photo.** *Perf. 14½x14*

C37 CD87 1fr dk orange .25 .20
C38 CD87 1.50fr brt red .25 .20
C39 CD87 5fr brown red .40 .35
C40 CD87 10fr black .40 .35
C41 CD87 25fr ultra .90 .55
C42 CD87 50fr dk green 1.40 .80
C43 CD87 100fr plum 2.00 1.25
Nos. C37-C43 (7) 5.60 3.70

Victory Issue

Common Design Type

Perf. 12½

1946, May 8 **Unwmk.** **Engr.**

C44 CD92 8fr brown red .90 .35

European victory of the Allied Nations in World War II.

Chad to Rhine Issue

Common Design Types

1946, June 6

C45 CD93 5fr brt blue 1.50 1.25
C46 CD94 10fr dk car rose 1.60 1.25
C47 CD95 15fr gray grn 1.60 1.25
C48 CD96 20fr brown olive 1.75 1.40
C49 CD97 25fr dk violet 1.75 1.50
C50 CD98 50fr brown org 2.10 1.75
Nos. C45-C50 (6) 10.30 8.40

Tamatave — AP2

Allegory of Air Mail — AP3

Plane over Map of Madagascar — AP4

Perf. 13½x12½, 12½x13½

1946 **Photo.** **Unwmk.**

C51 AP2 50fr bl vio & car 1.50 .50
C52 AP3 100fr brn & car 4.00 .90
C53 AP4 200fr bl grn & brn 7.50 2.00
Nos. C51-C53 (3) 13.00 3.40

No. C52 Overprinted in Carmine

1948, Oct. 26 *Perf. 12½x13½*

C54 AP3 100fr brn & car 45.00 *65.00*

Issued to publicize the French claim to Antarctic Adelie Land, discovered by Jules S. C. Dumont d'Urville in 1840.

UPU Issue

Common Design Type

1949, July 4 **Engr.** *Perf. 13*

C55 CD99 25fr multi 4.00 2.75

Scene Near Bemananga — AP5

1952, June 30 **Unwmk.** *Perf. 13*

C56 AP5 500fr brn, blk brn & dk grn 25.00 6.50

Liberation Issue

Common Design Type

1954, June 6

C57 CD102 15fr vio & vio brn 3.25 2.00

Pachypodes — AP6

Designs: 100fr, Antsirabé viaduct, grey-headed gull. 200fr, Ring-tailed lemurs.

1954, Sept. 20

C58 AP6 50fr dk bl grn & dk grn 3.50 .70
C59 AP6 100fr dp ultra, blk & choc 5.75 1.40
C60 AP6 200fr dk grn & sep 19.00 4.50
Nos. C58-C60 (3) 28.25 6.60

Malagasy Republic

Sugar Cane Harvest — AP7

Charaxes Antamboulou — AP8

Designs: 40fr, Tobacco field. 100fr, Chrysiridia Madagascariensis. 200fr, Argema mittrel, vert. 500fr, Mandrare bridge.

1960 **Unwmk.** **Engr.** *Perf. 13*

C61 AP7 30fr grn, vio brn & pale brn 2.00 .20
C62 AP7 40fr Prus grn & ol gray 2.25 .20
C63 AP8 50fr multi 4.00 .35
C64 AP8 100fr sl grn, emer & org 6.50 .50
C65 AP8 200fr pur & yel 8.50 1.40
C66 AP7 500fr Prus grn, bis & ultra 16.00 2.50
Nos. C61-C66 (6) 39.25 5.15

Diademed Sifakas — AP9

Lemurs: 85fr, Indri. 250fr, Verreaux's sifaka.

1961, Dec. 9 **Unwmk.** *Perf. 13*

C67 AP9 65fr slate grn & red brn 2.75 .70
C68 AP9 85fr olive, blk & brn 3.25 1.00
C69 AP9 250fr Prus grn, blk & mar 9.00 2.75
Nos. C67-C69 (3) 15.00 4.45

For surcharge see No. C90.

Plane over Nossi-Bé AP10

1962, May 7 **Engr.** *Perf. 13*

C70 AP10 100fr red brn, bl & dk grn 1.75 .60
a. Souv. sheet of 5, #328-331, C70 5.00 1.50

1st Malagasy Philatelic Exhibition, Tananarive, May 5-13.

Turbojet Airliner, Emblem — AP11

1963, Apr. 18 **Unwmk.** *Perf. 13*

C71 AP11 500fr dk bl, red & grn 8.00 3.25

Madagascar commercial aviation.

Helmet Bird — AP12

Birds: 100fr, Pitta-like ground roller. 200fr, Crested wood ibis.

1963, Aug. 12 **Photo.** *Perf. 13x12½*

C72 AP12 40fr multi 2.25 .65
C73 AP12 100fr multi 4.00 1.25
C74 AP12 200fr multi 8.00 2.25
Nos. C72-C74 (3) 14.25 4.15

African Postal Union Issue

Common Design Type

1963, Sept. 8 *Perf. 12½*

C75 CD114 85fr grn, ocher & red 1.25 .80

Map of Madagascar, Jet Plane and UPU Emblem — AP13

1963, Nov. 2 **Engr.** *Perf. 13*

C76 AP13 45fr dk car, grnsh bl & ultra .65 .20
C77 AP13 85fr dk car, vio & bl 1.10 .50

Malagasy Republic's admission to the UPU, Nov. 2, 1961.

Meteorological Center, Tananarive and Tiros Satellite — AP14

1964, Mar. 23 **Unwmk.**

C78 AP14 90fr org brn, ultra & grn 1.50 .90

UN 4th World Meteorological Day, Mar. 23.

Zebu, Wood Sculpture AP15

1964, Oct. 20 **Engr.** *Perf. 13*

C79 AP15 100fr lil rose, dk vio & brn 2.25 .90

Musical Instrument Type of Regular Issue

200fr, Lokanga bara (stringed instrument).

1965, Feb. 16 **Unwmk.** *Perf. 13*

Size: 26x47mm

C80 A57 200fr grn, org & choc 5.50 2.00

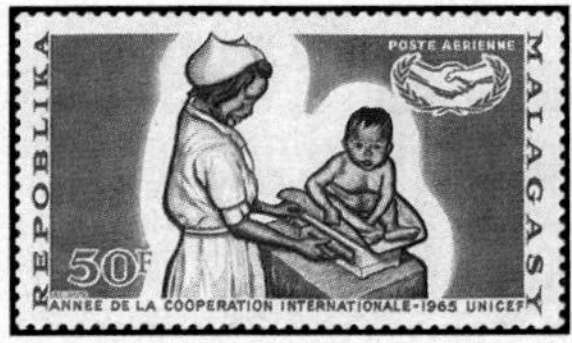

Nurse Weighing Infant, and ICY Emblem — AP16

Design: 100fr, Small boy and girl, child care scenes and ICY emblem.

1965, Sept. 20 **Engr.** *Perf. 13*

C81 AP16 50fr multi .55 .25
C82 AP16 100fr multi 1.10 .55

International Cooperation Year.

Dance Type of Regular Issue

250fr, Dance of a young girl, Sakalava, vert.

1966, June 13 Photo. *Perf. 13*
Size: 27x49mm

C83 A68 250fr multi 5.50 2.00

Aviation Type of Regular Issue

Design: 500fr, Dagnaux-Dufert and his Bréguet biplane, 1927.

1967, Apr. 28 Engr. *Perf. 13*
Size: 48x27mm

C84 A76 500fr Prus bl, blk & brn 11.00 3.00

No. C84 for the 40th anniv. of the 1st Majunga-Tananarive flight.

African Postal Union Issue, 1967
Common Design Type

1967, Sept. 9 Engr. *Perf. 13*

C85 CD124 100fr ol bis, red brn & brt pink 1.25 .60

Dancer Type of Regular Issue

Designs: 100fr, Tourbillon dance, horiz. 200fr, Male dancer from the South.

1967-68 Photo. *Perf. 11½*
Size: 38x23mm

C86 A80 100fr multi ('68) 2.00 .60

Perf. 13
Size: 27x48mm

C87 A80 200fr multi 4.75 1.40

Issue dates: 100fr, Nov. 25; 200fr, Nov. 25.

WHO Emblem, Bull's Head Totem and Palm Fan — AP17

1968, Apr. 7 Photo. *Perf. 12½x13*

C88 AP17 200fr bl, yel brn & red 2.00 .90

WHO, 20th anniv.; Intl. Congress of Medical Science, Apr. 2-12.

Tananarive-Ivato International Airport — AP18

1968, May 8 Engr. *Perf. 13*

C89 AP18 500fr lt red brn, dl bl & dl grn 6.75 3.00

Issued for Stamp Day.

No. C68 Surcharged in Vermilion with New Value and 2 Bars

1968, June 24 Engr. *Perf. 13*

C90 AP9 20fr on 85fr multi .75 .25

PHILEXAFRIQUE Issue

Lady Sealing Letter, by Jean Baptiste Santerre AP19

1968, Dec. 30 Photo. *Perf. 12½x12*

C91 AP19 100fr lilac & multi, with label 3.25 .70

Issued to publicize PHILEXAFRIQUE Philatelic Exhibition in Abidjan, Feb. 14-23. Printed with alternating lilac label.

2nd PHILEXAFRIQUE Issue
Common Design Type

Design: 50fr, Madagascar No. 274, map of Madagascar and Malagasy emblem.

1969, Feb. 14 Engr. *Perf. 13*

C92 CD128 50fr gray, brn red & sl grn 1.75 .85

Sunset over Madagascar Highlands, by Henri Ratovo — AP20

Painting: 100fr, On the Seashore of the East Coast of Madagascar, by Alfred Razafinjohany.

1969, Nov. 5 Photo. *Perf. 12x12½*

C93 AP20 100fr brn & multi 1.90 .65
C94 AP20 150fr multi 3.75 1.25

Lunar Landing Module and Man on the Moon — AP21

1970, July 20 Engr. *Perf. 13*

C95 AP21 75fr ultra, dk gray & sl grn 1.25 .40

1st anniv. of man's 1st landing on the moon.

Boeing 737 — AP22

1970, Dec. 18 Engr. *Perf. 13*

C96 AP22 200fr bl, red brn & grn 3.25 .90

Jean Ralaimongo (1884-1944) AP23

Portraits: 40fr, René Rakotobe (1918-71). 65fr, Albert Sylla (1909-67). 100fr, Joseph Ravoahangy Andrianavalona (1893-1970).

1971-72 Photo. *Perf. 12½; 13 (40fr)*

C97 AP23 25fr red brn, org & blk .40 .20
C98 AP23 40fr dp cl, ocher & blk .60 .20
C99 AP23 65fr grn, lt grn & blk .50 .25
C100 AP23 100fr vio bl, lt bl & blk 1.25 .35
Nos. C97-C100 (4) 2.75 1.00

Famous Malagasy men.
Issued: #C98, 7/25/72; others, 10/14/71.

African Postal Union Issue, 1971

"Mpisikidy" by G. Rakotovao and UAMPT Building, Brazzaville, Congo — AP24

1971, Nov. 13 Photo. *Perf. 13x13½*

C105 AP24 100fr bl & multi 1.25 .45

10th anniv. of African and Malagasy Posts and Telecommunications Union (UAMPT).

Running, Olympic Village AP25

Design: 200fr, Judo, Olympic Stadium.

1972, Sept. 11 Photo. *Perf. 13½*

C106 AP25 100fr multi 1.40 .60
C107 AP25 200fr multi 2.50 .85

20th Olympic Games, Munich, 8/26-9/11.

Mohair Goat AP26

1972, Nov. 15

C108 AP26 250fr multi 5.50 1.60

Adoration of the Kings, by Andrea Mantegna — AP27

Christmas: 85fr, Virgin and Child, Florentine School, 15th century, vert.

1972, Dec. 15 Photo. *Perf. 13*

C109 AP27 85fr gold & multi 1.00 .45
C110 AP27 150fr gold & multi 2.25 .70

Landing Module, Astronauts and Lunar Rover AP28

1973, Jan. 25 Engr. *Perf. 13*

C111 AP28 300fr dp cl, gray & brn 4.50 1.40

Apollo 17 moon mission, Dec. 7-19, 1972.

The Burial of Christ, by Grunewald — AP29

Easter: 200fr, Resurrection, by Mattias Grunewald, horiz. Both paintings from panels of Issenheim altar.

1973, Mar. 22 Photo. *Perf. 13*

C112 AP29 100fr gold & multi 1.25 .45
C113 AP29 200fr gold & multi 2.75 .70

Early Excursion Car — AP30

Design: 150fr, Early steam locomotive.

1973, July 25 Photo. *Perf. 13x12½*

C114 AP30 100fr multi 1.90 .70
C115 AP30 150fr multi 3.00 1.00

WMO Emblem, Radar, Map of Madagascar, Hurricane AP31

Pres. John F. Kennedy, US Flag — AP32

1973, Sept. 3 **Engr.** ***Perf. 13***
C116 AP31 100fr blk, ultra & org 1.50 .50

Cent. of intl. meteorological cooperation.

Lemur Type of Regular Issue

Designs: 150fr, Lepilemur mustelinus, vert. 200fr, Cheirogaleus major.

1973, Oct. 9 **Engr.** ***Perf. 13***
C117 A131 150fr multi 3.00 .90
C118 A131 200fr multi 4.75 1.40

1973, Nov. 22 **Photo.** ***Perf. 13***
C119 AP32 300fr multi 9.25 1.40

10th anniv. of the death of John F. Kennedy.

Soccer — AP33

1973, Dec. 20 **Engr.** ***Perf. 13***
C120 AP33 500fr lil rose, dk brn & org brn 7.00 2.00

World Soccer Cup, Munich, 1974.
For overprint see No. C130.

Copernicus, Ranger and Heliocentric System — AP34

1974, Jan. 22
C121 AP34 250fr multi 4.00 1.10

500th anniversary of the birth of Nicolaus Copernicus (1473-1543), Polish astronomer.

Scout Type of Regular Issue

Designs (African Scout Emblem and): 100fr, Scouts bringing sick people to Red Cross tent, horiz. 300fr, Scouts fishing and fish, horiz.

1974, Feb. 14 **Engr.** ***Perf. 13***
C122 A132 100fr multi 1.10 .35
C123 A132 300fr multi 4.25 1.00

Camellia, Hummingbird, Table Tennis Player — AP35

100fr, Girl player, flower and bird design.

1974, Mar. 19 **Engr.** ***Perf. 13***
C124 AP35 50fr bl & multi 1.00 .30
C125 AP35 100fr multi 1.75 .60

Table Tennis Tournament, Peking.

Autorail Micheline — AP36

Malagasy Locomotives: 85fr, Track inspection trolley. 200fr, Garratt (steam).

1974, June 7 **Engr.** ***Perf. 13***
C126 AP36 50fr multi 1.00 .35
C127 AP36 85fr multi 1.40 .45
C128 AP36 200fr multi 3.75 .95
Nos. C126-C128 (3) 6.15 1.75

Letters and UPU Emblem — AP37

1974, July 9 **Engr.** ***Perf. 13***
C129 AP37 250fr multi 4.00 1.10

Centenary of Universal Postal Union.
For overprint see No. C133.

No. C120 Overprinted: "R.F.A. 2 / HOLLANDE 1"

1974, Aug. 20 **Engr.** ***Perf. 13***
C130 AP33 500fr multi 6.25 2.00

World Cup Soccer Championship, 1974, victory of German Federal Republic.

Link-up in Space, Globe, Emblem — AP38

250fr, Link-up, globe and emblem, diff.

1974, Sept. 12
C131 AP38 150fr org, bl & slate grn 1.25 .65
C132 AP38 250fr bl, brn & slate grn 2.75 .90

Russo-American space cooperation.
For overprints see Nos. C142-C143.

No. C129 Overprinted

1974, Oct. 9 **Engr.** ***Perf. 13***
C133 AP37 250fr multi 2.00 .70

100 years of international collaboration.

Adoration of the Kings, by J. L. David AP39

Christmas: 300fr, Virgin of the Cherries and Child, by Quentin Massys.

1974, Dec. 20 **Photo.** ***Perf. 13***
C134 AP39 200fr gold & multi 2.75 .60
C135 AP39 300fr gold & multi 4.00 1.10

UN Emblem and Globe — AP40

1975, June 24 **Litho.** ***Perf. 12½***
C136 AP40 300fr grn, bl & blk 3.00 .90

United Nations Charter, 30th anniversary.

American Bicentennial Type, 1975

Designs: 100fr, Count d'Estaing and "Languedoc." 200fr, John Paul Jones, "Bonhomme Richard" and "Serapis." 300fr, Benjamin Franklin, "Millern" and "Montgomery." 500fr, George Washington and "Hanna."

1975, June 30 **Litho.** ***Perf. 11***
C137 A144 100fr multi 1.25 .30
C138 A144 200fr multi 2.50 .70
C139 A144 300fr multi 3.75 .90
Nos. C137-C139 (3) 7.50 1.90

Souvenir Sheet

C140 A144 500fr multi 7.00 1.50

For overprints see Nos. C164-C167.

Flower Type of 1975

Design: 85fr, Turraea sericea.

1975, Aug. 4 **Photo.** ***Perf. 12½***
C141 A145 85fr dp grn, yel & org 2.50 .90

Nos. C131-C132 Overprinted

1975, Aug. 5 **Engr.** ***Perf. 13***
C142 AP38 150fr multi 1.25 .45
C143 AP38 250fr multi 2.75 .75

Apollo Soyuz link-up in space, July 17, 1975.

Bas-relief and Stupas — AP41

1975, Aug. 10 **Engr.** ***Perf. 13***
C144 AP41 50fr bl, car & bister 1.25 .35

UNESCO campaign to save Borobudur Temple, Java.

Exposition Type, 1975

1975, Sept. 16 **Litho.** ***Perf. 14x13½***
C145 A147 125fr Deer 1.90 .45

Souvenir Sheet

C146 A147 300fr Jay 4.75 1.00

Hurdling and Olympic Rings — AP42

200fr, Weight lifting and Olympic rings, vert.

1975, Oct. 9 **Litho.** ***Perf. 12½***
C147 AP42 75fr multi 1.00 .25
C148 AP42 200fr multi 2.75 .70

Pre-Olympic Year 1975.

12th Winter Olympics Type, 1975

Designs: 200fr, Cross-country skiing. 245fr, Down-hill skiing. 450fr, Figure skating, pairs.

1975, Nov. 19 ***Perf. 14***
C149 A149 200fr multi 2.75 .55
C150 A149 245fr multi 2.75 .65

Souvenir Sheet

C151 A149 450fr multi 4.50 1.40

For overprints see Nos. C161-C163.

Landing Module, Apollo 14 Emblem — AP43

1976, Jan. 18 **Engr.** ***Perf. 13***
C152 AP43 150fr red, grn & ind 1.75 .50

Apollo 14 moon landing, 5th anniversary.
For overprint see No. C157.

21st Summer Olympics Type, 1976

Designs: 100fr, Shot-put and long jump. 200fr, Gymnastics, horse and balance bar. 300fr, Diving, 3-meter and platform. 500fr, Swimming, free-style and breast stroke.

1976, Jan. 21 **Litho.** ***Perf. 13½***
C153 A151 100fr multi 1.00 .30
C154 A151 200fr multi 2.25 .60
C155 A151 300fr multi 3.25 .90
Nos. C153-C155 (3) 6.50 1.80

Souvenir Sheet

C156 A151 500fr multi 5.25 1.40

For overprints see Nos. C168-C171.

No. C152 Overprinted: "5e Anniversaire / de la mission / APOLLO XIV"

1976, Feb. 5 **Engr.** ***Perf. 13***
C157 AP43 150fr red, grn & indigo 1.75 .70

Apollo 14 moon landing, 5th anniversary.

Zeppelin Type of 1976

Designs (Count Zeppelin and LZ-127 over): 200fr, Brandenburg Gate, Berlin 300fr, Parliament, London. 450fr, St. Peter's Cathedral, Rome.

1976, Mar. 3 Litho. *Perf. 11*

C158 A152 200fr multi 3.00 .60
C159 A152 300fr multi 4.25 .90

Souvenir Sheet

C160 A152 450fr multi 5.50 1.40

Nos. C149-C151 Overprinted

a. VAINQUEUR IVAR FORMO NORVEGE
b. VAINQUEUR ROSI MITTERMAIER ALLEMAGNE DE L'OUEST
c. VAINQUEUR IRINA RODNINA ALEXANDER ZAITSEV URSS

1976, June 17

C161 A149 (a) 200fr multi 2.00 .60
C162 A149 (b) 245fr multi 2.50 .80

Souvenir Sheet

C163 A149 (c) 450fr multi 5.25 2.75

12th Winter Olympic games winners.

Nos. C137-C140 Overprinted "4 Juillet / 1776-1976"

1976, July 4

C164 A144 100fr multi 1.00 .30
C165 A144 200fr multi 2.25 .60
C166 A144 300fr multi 2.75 .90
Nos. C164-C166 (3) 6.00 1.80

Souvenir Sheet

C167 A144 500fr multi 5.25 2.75

American Bicentennial.

Nos. C153-C156 Overprinted

a. U. BEYER / A. ROBINSON
b. N. ANDRIANOV / N. COMANECI
c. K. DIBIASI / E. VAYTSEKHOVSKAIA,
d. J. MONTGOMERY / H. ANKE

1977, Jan.

C168 A151 (a) 100fr multi 1.00 .30
C169 A151 (b) 200fr multi 2.00 .65
C170 A151 (c) 300fr multi 2.75 .90
Nos. C168-C170 (3) 5.75 1.85

Souvenir Sheet

C171 A151 (d) 500fr multi 5.25 2.75

21st Summer Olympic Games winners.

Fauna Type of 1979

1979, July 6

C172 A176 20fr Tortoises .75 .20
C173 A176 95fr Macaco lemurs 1.50 .25

International Palestinian Solidarity Day — AP44

1979, Nov. 29 Litho. *Perf. 12x12½*

C174 AP44 60fr multi .50 .20

Olympic Type of 1980

1980, Dec. 29 Litho. *Perf. 12½x12*

C175 A188 250fr Judo 2.25 .70
C176 A188 500fr Swimming 4.50 1.50

Stamp Day — AP45

1981, Dec. 17 Litho. *Perf. 12x12½*

C177 AP45 90fr multi .90 .25

20th Anniv. of Pan-African Women's Org. — AP46

1982, Aug. 6 Litho. *Perf. 12*

C178 AP46 80fr dk brn & lt brn .70 .25

Hydroelectric Plant, Andekaleka — AP47

1982, Sept. 13 *Perf. 12½x12*

C179 AP47 80fr multi .70 .25

Orchid Type of 1984

1984, Nov. 20 Litho. *Perf. 12*

C180 A226 50fr Eulophiella elisabethae, horiz. 1.00 .20
C181 A226 50fr Grammangis ellisii, horiz. 1.00 .20
C182 A226 50fr Grammangis spectabilis 1.00 .20
Nos. C180-C182 (3) 3.00 .60

Solar Princess, by Sadiou Diouf AP48

1984, Dec. 22 Litho. *Perf. 12*

C183 AP48 100fr multi .90 .25

Intl. Civil Aviation Org., 40th anniv.

Halley's Comet AP49

1986, Apr. 5 Litho. *Perf. 12½x13*

C184 AP49 150fr multi 1.25 .50

Admission of Madagascar into the UPU, 25th Anniv. AP50

1986, Dec. 23 Litho. *Perf. 11½*

C185 AP50 150fr multi 1.25 .40

Air Madagascar, 25th Anniv. — AP51

1987, June 17 Litho. *Perf. 12x12½*

C186 AP51 60fr Piper Aztec .55 .20
C187 AP51 60fr Twin Otter .55 .20
C188 AP51 150fr Boeing 747 1.10 .30
Nos. C186-C188 (3) 2.20 .70

Socialist Revolution, 15th Anniv. — AP52

1990, June 16 Litho. *Perf. 13½*

C189 AP52 100fr Map .20 .20
C190 AP52 350fr Architecture .60 .30

Madagascan Bible Society, 25th Anniv. — AP53

1990, Sept. 17 *Perf. 12½*

C191 AP53 25fr lt bl & multi .20 .20
C192 AP53 100fr bl, blk & grn, vert. .20 .20

Stamp Day — AP54

1990, Oct. 9 Litho. *Perf. 13x12½*

C193 AP54 350fr multicolored 1.25 .30

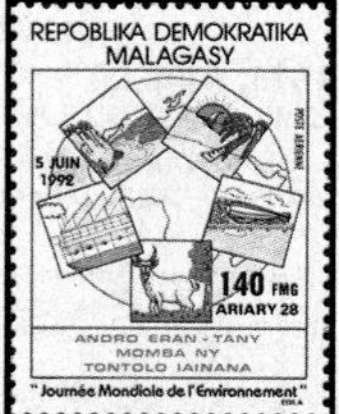

AP55

AP56

1992, June 5 Litho. *Perf. 12½*

C194 AP55 140fr multicolored .25 .20

World Environment Day.

1992, Oct. 9 Litho. *Perf. 13½*

C195 AP56 500fr multicolored .70 .35

World Post Day.

Girl Guides, 50th Anniv. AP57

1993, Aug. Litho. *Perf. 11½*

C196 AP57 140fr multicolored .25 .20

AP58

AP59

1993, Nov. 20 Litho. *Perf. 12*

C197 AP58 500fr multicolored .80 .40

African Industrialization Day.

1994 Litho. *Perf. 11½x11, 11x11½*

C198 AP59 140fr shown .20 .20
C199 AP59 500fr Logo, vert. .70 .40

Zone A conference.

Madagascar Hilton, 25th Anniv.—AP60

1995, Oct. 8 Litho. *Perf. 13½*

C200 AP60 500fr black, blue & bister .80 .60

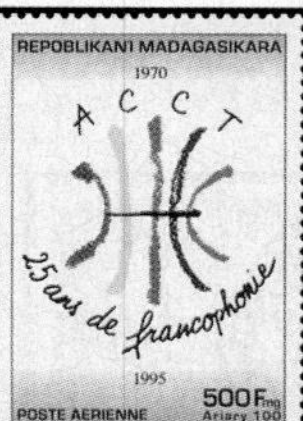

ACCT, 25th Anniv. — AP60a

1996, Aug. 9 Litho. *Perf. 14¾x15*

C200A AP60a 500fr multi .60

FAO, 50th Anniv. — AP60b

Designs: 140fr, Map, FAO emblem, grains. 500fr, FAO emblem, map, grains, diff.

1995, Aug. 16 Litho. *Perf. 15*

C200B AP60b 140fr multi — —
C200C AP60b 500fr multi — —
Set of 2 125.00

UN Industrial Development Organization, 30th Anniv. — AP60c

Perf. 11¾x11½

1996, June 17 Litho.

Granite Paper

C200D AP60c 140fr multi .25 .20

Souvenir Sheet

Zheng He, Chinese Navigator — AP61

Illustration reduced.

1998 Litho. *Perf. 13½*

C201 AP61 5700fr multicolored 3.00 1.50

AIR POST SEMI-POSTAL STAMPS

French Revolution Issue

Common Design Type

Unwmk.

1939, July 5 Photo. *Perf. 13*

Name and Value in Orange

CB1 CD83 4.50fr + 4fr brn blk 16.00 16.00

"Maternity" Statue at Tannarive City Hall — SPAP1

Manankavaly Free Milk Station — SPAP2

Mother & Children — SPAP3

1942, June 22 Engr. *Perf. 13*

CB2 SPAP1 1.50fr + 3.50fr lt grn .65
CB3 SPAP2 2fr + 6fr yel brn .65
CB4 SPAP3 3fr + 9fr car red .65
Nos. CB2-CB4 (3) 1.95

Native children's welfare fund.

Nos. CB2-CB4 were issued by the Vichy government in France, but were not placed on sale in Madagascar.

Colonial Education Fund

Common Design Type

1942, June 22

CB5 CD86a 1.20fr + 1.80fr blue & red .65

No. CB5 was issued by the Vichy government in France, but was not placed on sale in Madagascar.

POSTAGE DUE STAMPS

D1

Governor's Palace — D2

Postage Due Stamps of French Colonies Overprinted in Red or Blue

1896 Unwmk. *Imperf.*

J1 D1 5c blue (R) 9.75 8.00
J2 D1 10c brown (R) 9.00 6.50
J3 D1 20c yellow (Bl) 8.00 6.00
J4 D1 30c rose red (Bl) 8.00 7.00
J5 D1 40c lilac (R) 65.00 42.50
J6 D1 50c gray vio (Bl) 12.00 8.25
J7 D1 1fr dk grn (R) 70.00 57.50
Nos. J1-J7 (7) 181.75 135.75

1908-24 Typo. *Perf. 13½x14*

J8 D2 2c vio brn .20 .20
J9 D2 4c violet .20 .20
J10 D2 5c green .20 .20
J11 D2 10c deep rose .20 .20
J12 D2 20c olive green .40 .40
J13 D2 40c brn, *straw* .45 .45
J14 D2 50c brn, *bl* .60 .60
J15 D2 60c orange ('24) .60 .60
J16 D2 1fr dark blue 1.10 1.10
Nos. J8-J16 (9) 3.95 3.95

Type of 1908 Issue Surcharged

1924-27

J17 D2 60c on 1fr org 1.90 1.90

Surcharged

J18 D2 2fr on 1fr lil rose ('27) .90 .90
J19 D2 3fr on 1fr ultra ('27) .90 .90

Postage Due Stamps of 1908-27 Overprinted or Surcharged in Black

1943 *Perf. 13½x14*

J20 D2 10c dp rose .95 .95
J21 D2 20c olive grn .95 .95
J22 D2 30c on 5c green .95 .95
J23 D2 40c brn, *straw* 1.00 1.00
J24 D2 50c brn, *blue* 1.40 1.40
J25 D2 60c orange .95 .95
J26 D2 1fr dark blue .95 .95
J27 D2 1fr on 2c vio brn 4.50 4.50
J28 D2 2fr on 1fr lil rose 1.10 1.10
J29 D2 2fr on 4c vio 2.10 2.10
J30 D2 3fr on 1fr ultra 1.25 1.25
Nos. J20-J30 (11) 16.10 16.10

Catalogue values for unused stamps in this section, from this point to the end of the section, are for Never Hinged items.

D3

Independence Monument — D4

1947 Photo. *Perf. 13*

J31 D3 10c dk violet .20 .20
J32 D3 30c brown .20 .20
J33 D3 50c dk bl grn .20 .20
J34 D3 1fr dp orange .20 .20
J35 D3 2fr red violet .45 .45
J36 D3 3fr red brown .45 .45
J37 D3 4fr blue .50 .50
J38 D3 5fr henna brown .55 .55
J39 D3 10fr slate green .70 .70
J40 D3 20fr vio blue 1.75 1.75
Nos. J31-J40 (10) 5.20 5.20

Malagasy Republic

Engraved; Denomination Typographed

1962, May 7 Unwmk. *Perf. 13*

J41 D4 1fr brt green .20 .20
J42 D4 2fr copper brn .20 .20
J43 D4 3fr brt violet .20 .20
J44 D4 4fr slate .20 .20
J45 D4 5fr red .20 .20
J46 D4 10fr yellow grn .20 .20
J47 D4 20fr dull claret .25 .25
J48 D4 40fr blue .55 .55
J49 D4 50fr rose red .85 .85
J50 D4 100fr black 1.60 1.60
Nos. J41-J50 (10) 4.45 4.45

MALAWI

mə-'lä-wē

LOCATION — Southeast Africa
GOVT. — Republic in British Commonwealth
AREA — 36,100 sq. mi.
POP. — 10,000,416 (1999 est.)
CAPITAL — Lilongwe

The British Protectorate of Nyasaland became the independent state of Malawi on July 6, 1964, and a republic on July 6, 1966.

12 Pence = 1 Shilling
20 Shillings = 1 Pound
100 Tambalas = 1 Kwacha (1970)

Catalogue values for all unused stamps in this country are for Never Hinged items.

Watermark

Wmk. 357 — Multiple Cockerel

Dr. H. Kamuzu Banda and Independence Monument — A1

Prime Minister Banda and: 6p, Sun rising from lake. 1sh3p, National flag. 2sh6p, Coat of Arms.

Perf. 14½

1964, July 6 Unwmk. Photo.

1 A1 3p dk gray & lt ol green .20 .20
2 A1 6p car rose, red, gold & bl .20 .20
3 A1 1sh3p dull vio, blk, red & grn .55 .20
4 A1 2sh6p multicolored .85 .85
Nos. 1-4 (4) 1.80 1.45

Malawi's independence, July 6, 1964.

Mother and Child — A2

Designs: 1p, Chambo fish. 2p, Zebu bull. 3p, Peanuts. 4p, Fishermen in boat. 6p, Harvesting tea. 9p, Tung nut, flower and leaves. 1sh, Lumber and tropical pine branch. 1sh3p, Tobacco drying and Turkish tobacco plant. 2sh6p, Cotton industry. 5sh, Monkey Bay, Lake Nyasa. 10sh, Afzelia tree (pod mahogany). £1, Nyala antelope, vert.

1964, July 6

Size: 23x19mm

5 A2 ½p lilac .20 *.30*
6 A2 1p green & black .20 .20
7 A2 2p red brown .20 .20
8 A2 3p pale brn, brn red & grn .20 .20
9 A2 4p org yel & indigo .95 .20

Size: 41½x25, 25x41½mm

10 A2 6p bl, vio bl & brt yel grn .85 .20
11 A2 9p grn, yel & brn .35 .20
12 A2 1sh yel, brn & dk green .30 .20
13 A2 1sh3p red brn & olive .55 *.70*
14 A2 2sh6p blue & brown 1.25 1.10
15 A2 5sh "Monkey Bay-Lake Nyasa" .75 *3.25*
16 A2 10sh org brn, grn & gray 1.75 *2.25*
17 A2 £1 yel & dk brn 7.50 6.25
Nos. 5-17 (13) 15.05 15.25

See #26, 41-51. For surcharges see #27-28.

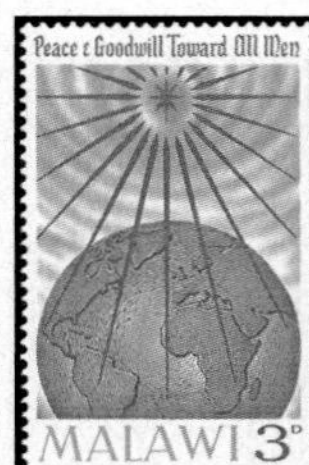

Star of Bethlehem over World — A3

1964, Dec. 1 Photo. *Perf. 14½*

18 A3 3p brt green & gold .20 .20
19 A3 6p lilac rose & gold .20 .20
20 A3 1sh3p lilac & gold .20 .20
21 A3 2sh6p ultra & gold .20 .30
a. Souvenir sheet of 4 1.25 *1.50*
Nos. 18-21 (4) .80 .90

Christmas. No. 21a contains Nos. 18-21 with simulated perforations.

Sixpence, Shilling, Florin and Half-Crown Coins — A4

1965, Mar. 1 Unwmk. *Perf. 13x13½*

Coins in Silver and Black

22 A4 3p green .20 .20
23 A4 9p rose .20 .20
a. Silver omitted
24 A4 1sh6p rose violet .25 .25
25 A4 3sh dark blue .45 *.75*
a. Souvenir sheet of 4 1.90 1.75
Nos. 22-25 (4) 1.10 1.40

First coinage of Malawi. No. 25a contains Nos. 22-25 with simulated perforations. Sold for 6sh.

Type of 1964 Redrawn

1965, June 1 Photo. *Perf. 14½*

26 A2 5sh "Monkey Bay-Lake Malawi" 8.50 1.25

Nos. 13-14 Surcharged with New Value and Two Bars

1965, June 14

27 A2 1sh6p on 1sh3p .30 .25
28 A2 3sh on 2sh6p .30 .25

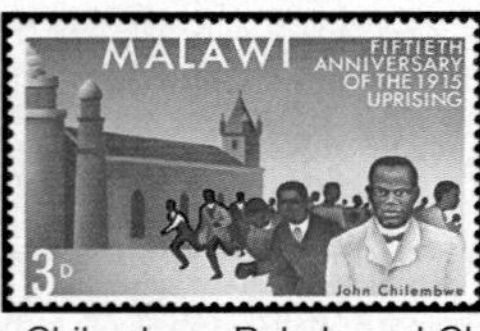

John Chilembwe, Rebels and Church at Mbwombwe — A5

1965, Aug. 20 Photo. *Perf. 14½*

29 A5 3p yel grn & purple .20 .20
30 A5 9p red org & olive .20 .20
31 A5 1sh6p dk blue & red brn .20 .20
32 A5 3sh dull bl & green .25 .25
a. Souvenir sheet of 4, #29-32 7.50 7.50
Nos. 29-32 (4) .85 .85

50th anniversary of the revolution of Jan. 23, 1915, led by John Chilembwe (1871-1915), missionary.

Microscope and Open Book — A6

1965, Oct. 6 *Perf. 14*

33 A6 3p emer & slate .20 .20
34 A6 9p brt rose & slate .20 .20
35 A6 1sh6p purple & slate .20 .20
36 A6 3sh ultra & slate .20 .30
a. Souvenir sheet of 4, #33-36 5.00 5.00
Nos. 33-36 (4) .80 .90

Opening of the University of Malawi in temporary quarters in Chichiri secondary school, Blantyre. The University will be located in Zomba.

African Danaine A7

Designs: Various butterflies.

Perf. 13x13½

1966, Feb. 15 Unwmk.

37 A7 4p multicolored 1.25 .20
38 A7 9p multicolored 2.00 .20
39 A7 1sh6p lil, blk & blue 2.75 .45
40 A7 3sh blue, dk brn & bis 4.25 *6.75*
a. Souvenir sheet of 4, #37-40 25.00 25.00
Nos. 37-40 (4) 10.25 7.60

See No. 51.

Type of 1964

Designs: 1sh6p, Curing tobacco and Burley tobacco plant. £2, Cyrestis camillus sublineatus (butterfly). Other designs as in 1964.

Wmk. 357

1966-67 Photo. *Perf. 14½*

Size: 23x19mm

41 A2 ½p lilac .20 .20
42 A2 1p green & black .20 .20
43 A2 2p red brown ('67) .20 .20
44 A2 3p multi ('67) .25 .20

Size: 41½x25mm

45 A2 6p blue, vio bl & brt yel grn ('67) 2.00 .80
46 A2 9p grn, yel & brn ('67) 1.00 .20
47 A2 1sh yel, brn & dk green .30 .20
48 A2 1sh6p choc & emer .40 .20
49 A2 5sh multi ('67) 9.00 2.75
50 A2 10sh org brn, grn & gray ('67) 17.50 *18.50*
51 A2 £2 dl vio, yel & blk 35.00 27.50
Nos. 41-51 (11) 66.05 50.95

British Central Africa Stamp 1891 — A8

President Kamuzu Banda — A9

1966, May 4 *Perf. 14½*

54 A8 4p yel grn & sl blue .20 .20
55 A8 9p dull rose & sl blue .20 .20
56 A8 1sh6p lil & slate blue .25 .25
57 A8 3sh blue & slate blue .35 .35
a. Souvenir sheet of 4, #54-57 6.50 4.00
Nos. 54-57 (4) 1.00 1.00

Postal service, 75th anniv.

Perf. 14x14½

1966, July 6 Wmk. 357

58 A9 4p green, sil & brn .20 .20
59 A9 9p magenta, sil & brn .20 .20
60 A9 1sh6p violet, sil & brn .20 .20
61 A9 3sh blue, sil & brn .30 .30
a. Souvenir sheet of 4, #58-61 2.75 2.75
Nos. 58-61 (4) .90 .90

Republic Day, July 6, 1966; 2nd anniv. of Independence.

Star over Bethlehem — A10

1966, Oct. 12 Photo. *Perf. 14½x14*

63 A10 4p deep green & gold .20 .20
64 A10 9p plum & gold .20 .20
65 A10 1sh6p orange & gold .20 .20
66 A10 3sh deep blue & gold .35 .35
Nos. 63-66 (4) .95 .95

Christmas.

Ilala I, 1875 A11

Steamers on Lake Malawi: 9p, Dove, 1892. 1sh6p, Chauncey Maples, 1901. 3sh, Guendolen, 1899.

1967, Jan. 4 *Perf. 14½x14*

67 A11 4p emer, black & yel .45 .25
a. Yellow omitted *500.00*
68 A11 9p car rose, blk & yellow .50 .35
69 A11 1sh6p lt vio, blk & red .75 .60
70 A11 3sh ultra, black & red 1.75 1.75
Nos. 67-70 (4) 3.45 2.95

Pseudotropheus Auratus — A12

Fish of Lake Malawi: 9p, Labeotropheus trewavasae. 1sh6p, Pseudotropheus zebra. 3sh, Pseudotropheus tropheops.

1967, May 3 Photo. *Perf. 12½x12*

71 A12 4p green & multi .45 .20
72 A12 9p ocher & multi .65 .20
73 A12 1sh6p multicolored .80 .30
74 A12 3sh ultra & multi 1.90 1.90
Nos. 71-74 (4) 3.80 2.60

Rising Sun and Cogwheel — A13

Perf. 13½x13

1967, July 5 Litho. Unwmk.

75 A13 4p black & brt grn .20 .20
76 A13 9p black & car rose .20 .20
77 A13 1sh6p black & brt pur .20 .20
78 A13 3sh black & brt ultra .30 .30
a. Souvenir sheet of 4, #75-78 1.25 1.25
Nos. 75-78 (4) .90 .90

Malawi industrial development.

Nativity A14

Perf. 14x14½

1967, Oct. 12 Photo. Wmk. 357

79 A14 4p vio blue & green .20 .20
80 A14 9p vio blue & red .20 .20
81 A14 1sh6p vio blue & yel .20 .20
82 A14 3sh bright blue .30 .30
a. Souvenir sheet of 4, #79-82, perf. 14x13½ 1.40 1.40
Nos. 79-82 (4) .90 .90

Christmas.

Calotropis Procera — A15

Wild Flowers: 9p, Borreria dibrachiata. 1sh6p, Hibiscus rhodanthus. 3sh, Bidens pinnatipartita.

1968, Apr. 24 Litho. *Perf. 13½x13*

83 A15 4p green & multi .20 .20
84 A15 9p pale green & multi .20 .20
85 A15 1sh6p lt green & multi .25 .20
86 A15 3sh brt blue & multi .45 .65
a. Souvenir sheet of 4, #83-86 3.00 3.00
Nos. 83-86 (4) 1.10 1.25

Thistle No. 1, 1902 A16

Locomotives: 9p, G-class steam engine, 1954. 1sh6p, "Zambesi" diesel locomotive No. 202, 1963. 3sh, Diesel rail car No. 1, 1955.

1968, July 24 Photo. *Perf. 14x14½*

87 A16 4p gray grn & multi .25 .20
88 A16 9p red & multi .55 .50
89 A16 1sh6p cream & multi 1.10 1.00
90 A16 3sh lt ultra & multi 2.25 2.25
a. Souv. sheet of 4, #87-90, perf. 14 5.25 5.25
Nos. 87-90 (4) 4.15 3.95

Nativity, by Piero della Francesca A17

Paintings: 9p, Adoration of the Shepherds, by Murillo. 1sh6p, Adoration of the Shepherds, by Guido Reni. 3sh, Nativity with God the Father and the Holy Ghost, by Giovanni Batista Pittoni.

1968, Nov. 6 Photo. Wmk. 357

91 A17 4p black & multi .20 .20
92 A17 9p multicolored .20 .20
93 A17 1sh6p multicolored .20 .20
94 A17 3sh blue & multi .30 .30
a. Souvenir sheet of 4, #91-94, perf. 14x13½ .80 .80
Nos. 91-94 (4) .90 .90

Christmas.

Scarlet-chested Sunbird — A18

Nyasa Lovebird — A19

Birds: 2p, Violet-backed starling. 3p, White-browed robin-chat. 4p, Red-billed firefinch. 9p, Yellow bishop. 1sh, Southern carmine bee-eater. 1sh6p, Grayheaded bush shrike. 2sh, Paradise whydah. 3sh, African paradise flycatcher. 5sh, Bateleur. 10sh, Saddlebill. £1, Purple heron. £2, Livingstone's lorie.

1968, Nov. 13 *Perf. 14½*

Size: 23x19, 19x23mm

95 A18 1p multicolored .20 .25
96 A18 2p multicolored .20 .25
97 A18 3p multicolored .20 .25
98 A18 4p multicolored .40 .40
99 A19 6p multicolored .50 .25
100 A19 9p multicolored .55 .60

Perf. 14

Size: 42x25, 25x42mm

101 A18 1sh multicolored .65 .25
102 A18 1sh6p multicolored 5.50 *6.25*
103 A18 2sh multicolored 5.75 *6.25*
104 A19 3sh multicolored 6.00 4.25
105 A19 5sh multicolored 8.00 4.50
106 A19 10sh multicolored 8.50 8.50
107 A19 £1 multicolored 15.00 *20.00*
109 A18 £2 multicolored 40.00 *50.00*
Nos. 95-109 (14) 91.45 *102.00*

No. 104 was surcharged "30t Special United Kingdom Delivery Service" in 5 lines and issued Feb. 8, 1971, during the British postal strike. The 30t was to pay a private postal service. Values: unused 50c, used $2.25.

See #136-137. For overprint see #131.

ILO Emblem A20

Photo., Gold Impressed (Emblem)

Perf. 14x14½

1969, Feb. 5 Wmk. 357

110 A20 4p deep green .20 .20
111 A20 9p dk rose brown .20 .20
112 A20 1sh6p dark gray .20 .20
113 A20 3sh dark blue .30 .30
a. Souvenir sheet of 4, #110-113 2.50 2.50
Nos. 110-113 (4) .90 .90

ILO, 50th anniversary.

White Fringed Ground Orchid A21

Malawi Orchids: 9p, Red ground orchid. 1sh6p, Leopard tree orchid. 3sh, Blue ground orchid.

1969, July 9 Litho. *Perf. 13½*

114 A21 4p gray & multi .25 .25
115 A21 9p gray & multi .40 .40
116 A21 1sh6p gray & multi .60 .60
117 A21 3sh gray & multi 1.25 1.25
a. Souvenir sheet of 4, #114-117 4.00 4.00
Nos. 114-117 (4) 2.50 2.50

African Development Bank Emblem — A22

1969, Sept. 10 *Perf. 14*

118 A22 4p multicolored .20 .20
119 A22 9p multicolored .20 .20
120 A22 1sh6p multicolored .20 .20
121 A22 3sh multicolored .20 .20
a. Souvenir sheet of 4, #118-121 1.10 1.10
Nos. 118-121 (4) .80 .80

African Development Bank, 5th anniv.

"Peace on Earth" A23

1969, Nov. 5 Photo. *Perf. 14x14½*

122 A23 2p citron & blk .20 .20
123 A23 4p Prus blue & blk .20 .20
124 A23 9p scarlet & blk .20 .20
125 A23 1sh6p purple & blk .20 .20
126 A23 3sh ultra & blk .30 .30
a. Souvenir sheet of 5, #122-126 1.50 1.50
Nos. 122-126 (5) 1.10 1.10

Christmas.

Bean Blister Beetle — A24

Runner — A25

Insects: 4p, Elegant grasshopper. 1sh6p, Pumpkin ladybird. 3sh, Praying mantis.

1970, Feb. 4 Litho. *Perf. 14x14½*

127 A24 4p multicolored .30 .25
128 A24 9p multicolored .30 .25
129 A24 1sh6p multicolored .55 .50
130 A24 3sh multicolored 1.00 1.00
a. Souvenir sheet of 4, #127-130 2.50 2.50
Nos. 127-130 (4) 2.15 2.00

No. 102 Overprinted: "Rand Easter Show / 1970"

1970, Mar. 18 Photo. *Perf. 14*

131 A18 1sh6p multicolored .70 *1.50*

75th Anniversary Rand Easter Show, Johannesburg, South Africa, Mar. 24-Apr. 6.

1970, June 3 Litho. *Perf. 13*

132 A25 4p green & dk blue .20 .20
133 A25 9p rose & dk bl .20 .20
134 A25 1sh6p dull yel & dk bl .20 .20
135 A25 3sh blue & dk blue .30 .30
a. Souvenir sheet of 4, #132-135 1.10 1.10
Nos. 132-135 (4) .90 .90

9th Commonwealth Games, Edinburgh, Scotland, July 16-25.

Dual Currency Issue

Bird Type of 1968 with Denominations in Tambalas

Designs: 10t/1sh, Southern carmine bee-eater. 20t/2sh, Paradise whydah.

1970, Sept. 2 Photo. *Perf. 14½*
Size: 42x25mm

136 A18 10t/1sh multicolored 1.50 .35
137 A18 20t/2sh multicolored 2.25 1.40

Aegocera Trimenii A26

Moths of Malawi: 9p, Epiphora bauhiniae. 1sh6p, Parasa karschi. 3sh, Teracotona euprepia.

Perf. 11x11½

1970, Sept. 30 **Wmk. 357**

138 A26 4p multicolored .35 .35
139 A26 9p multicolored .50 .50
140 A26 1sh6p multicolored 1.00 1.00
141 A26 3sh multicolored 2.25 2.25
a. Souvenir sheet of 4, #138-141 8.50 8.50
Nos. 138-141 (4) 4.10 4.10

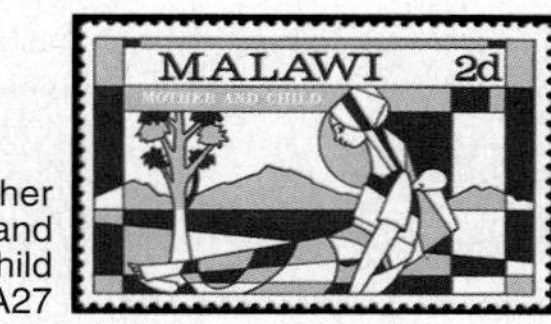

Mother and Child A27

1970, Nov. 4 Litho. *Perf. 14½*

142 A27 2p black & yel .20 .20
143 A27 4p black & emer .20 .20
144 A27 9p black & dp org .20 .20
145 A27 1sh6p black & red lil .20 .20
146 A27 3sh black & ultra .20 .20
a. Souv. sheet of 5, #142-146 + label 1.40 1.40
Nos. 142-146 (5) 1.00 1.00

Christmas.

Decimal Currency

Greater Kudu — A28

Eland — A29

Antelopes: 2t, Nyala. 3t, Reedbuck. 5t, Puku. 8t, Impala. 15t, Klipspringer. 20t, Livingstone's suni. 30t, Roan antelope. 50t, Waterbuck. 1k, Bushbuck. 2k, Red duiker. 4k, Gray bush duiker.

Perf. 13½x14 (A28), 14x14½ (A29)

1971, Feb. 15 Litho. Wmk. 357

148 A28 1t dull vio & multi .20 .20
a. Perf. 14½x14, coil .20 .20
b. Perf. 14 ('74) .20 .20
149 A28 2t dp yel & multi .20 .20
150 A28 3t ap grn & multi .20 .20
a. Perf. 14 ('74) .30 .30
151 A28 5t multicolored .20 .20
a. Perf. 14 ('74) .40 .30
152 A28 8t org red & multi .35 .20
153 A29 10t green & multi .40 .35
154 A29 15t brt pur & multi .65 .40
155 A29 20t bl gray & multi .85 .70
156 A29 30t dull blue & multi 5.75 .70
157 A29 50t multicolored 1.10 .90
158 A29 1k multicolored 4.00 2.00
159 A29 2k gray & multi 8.00 4.00
160 A29 4k multicolored 25.00 22.00
Nos. 148-160 (13) 46.90 32.05

Decimal Coins A30

1971, Feb. 15 *Perf. 14½*

161 A30 3t multicolored .20 .20
162 A30 8t dull red & multi .20 .20
163 A30 15t purple & multi .35 .30
164 A30 30t brt blue & multi .50 .50
a. Souvenir sheet of 4, #161-164 1.80 1.80
Nos. 161-164 (4) 1.25 1.20

Introduction of decimal currency and coinage.

Engravings by Albrecht Dürer — A31

Design: Nos. 165, 167, 169, 171, Christ on the Cross. Nos. 166, 168, 170, 172, The Resurrection.

1971, Apr. 7 Litho. *Perf. 14x13½*

165 3t emerald & black .20 .20
166 3t emerald & black .20 .20
a. A31 Pair, #165-166 .20 .20
167 8t orange & black .20 .20
168 8t orange & black .20 .20
a. A31 Pair, #167-168 .20 .20
169 15t red lilac & black .20 .20
170 15t red lilac & black .20 .20
a. A31 Pair, #169-170 .40 .40
171 30t blue & black .30 .30
a. Souv. sheet of 4, #165, 167, 169, 171 2.00 2.00
172 30t blue & black .30 .30
a. Souv. sheet of 4, #166, 168, 170, 172 2.00 2.00
b. A31 Pair, #171-172 .60 .60
Nos. 165-172 (8) 1.80 1.80

Easter. Printed checkerwise in sheets of 25.

Holarrhena Febrifuga — A32

Drum Major — A33

Flowering Shrubs and Trees: 8t, Brachystegia spiciformis. 15t, Securidaca longepedunculata. 30t, Pterocarpus rotundifolius.

1971, July 14 Litho. Wmk. 357

173 A32 3t gray & multi .20 .20
174 A32 8t gray & multi .20 .20
175 A32 15t gray & multi .35 .30
176 A32 30t gray & multi .60 .60
a. Souvenir sheet of 4, #173-176 2.00 2.00
Nos. 173-176 (4) 1.35 1.30

1971, Oct. 5 *Perf. 14x14½*

177 A33 30t lt blue & multi .90 .90

50th anniversary of Malawi Police Force.

Madonna and Child, by William Dyce — A34

Paintings of Holy Family by: 8t, Martin Schongauer. 15t, Raphael. 30t, Bronzino.

1971, Nov. 10 *Perf. 14½*

178 A34 3t green & multi .20 .20
179 A34 8t carmine & multi .20 .20
180 A34 15t dp claret & multi .35 .35
181 A34 30t dull blue & multi .70 .70
a. Souvenir sheet of 4, #178-181 2.25 2.25
Nos. 178-181 (4) 1.45 1.45

Christmas.

Vickers Viscount — A35

Airplanes: 8t, Hawker Siddeley 748. 15t, Britten Norman Islander. 30t, B.A.C. One Eleven.

1972, Feb. 9 Litho. *Perf. 13½x14*

182 A35 3t brt grn, blk & red .35 .20
183 A35 8t red org & black .55 .25
184 A35 15t dp rose lil, red & black .85 .75
185 A35 30t vio blue & multi 1.50 1.50
a. Souvenir sheet of 4, #182-185 10.00 10.00
Nos. 182-185 (4) 3.25 2.70

Publicity for Air Malawi.

Figures, Chencherere Hill — A36

Rock Paintings: 8t, Lizard and cat, Chencherere Hill. 15t, Symbols, Diwa Hill. 30t, Sun behind rain, Mikolongwe Hill.

1972, May 10 *Perf. 13½*

186 A36 3t black & yel grn .35 .20
187 A36 8t black & dp car .40 .20
188 A36 15t black, vio & car .60 .45
189 A36 30t black, blue & yel 1.10 1.10
a. Souv. sheet of 4, #186-189, perf. 15 5.00 5.00
Nos. 186-189 (4) 2.45 1.95

Athlete and Olympic Rings — A37

1972, Aug. 9 *Perf. 14x14½*

190 A37 3t gray, black & green .20 .20
191 A37 8t gray, black & scar .20 .20
192 A37 15t gray, black & lilac .25 .25
193 A37 30t gray, black & blue .50 .50
a. Souvenir sheet of 4, #190-193 2.25 2.25
Nos. 190-193 (4) 1.15 1.15

20th Olympic Games, Munich, 8/26-9/10.

Malawi Coat of Arms — A38

1972, Oct. 20 Litho. *Perf. 13½x14*

194 A38 15t blue & multi .65 .65

18th Commonwealth Parliamentary Conference, Malawi, Oct. 1972.

Adoration of the Kings, by Orcagna — A39

Paintings of the Florentine School: 8t, Madonna and Child Enthroned, anonymous. 15t, Madonna and Child with Sts. Bonaventura and Louis of Toulouse, by Carlo Crivelli. 30t, Madonna and Child with St. Anne, by Jean de Bruges.

Perf. 14½x14

1972, Nov. 8 Wmk. 357

195	A39	3t lt olive & multi	.20	.20
196	A39	8t carmine & multi	.20	.20
197	A39	15t purple & multi	.25	.25
198	A39	30t blue & multi	.60	.60
a.		Souvenir sheet of 4, #195-198	1.60	1.60
		Nos. 195-198 (4)	1.25	1.25

Christmas.

Charaxes Bohemani — A40

1973 ***Perf. 13½x14***

199	A40	3t shown	.60	.30
200	A40	8t Uranothauma crawshayi	1.00	.80
201	A40	15t Charaxes acuminatus	2.00	1.60
202	A40	30t "Euphaedra zaddachi"	6.00	6.00
a.		Souvenir sheet of 4, #199-202	18.00	17.00
203	A40	30t Amauris ansorgei	5.25	*6.00*
		Nos. 199-203 (5)	14.85	14.70

Issued: #199-202, Feb. 7; #203, Apr. 5.

Dr. Livingstone and Map of West Africa — A41

Livingstone Choosing Site for Mission — A42

1973 Litho. ***Perf. 13½x14***

204	A41	3t apple grn & multi	.20	.20
205	A41	8t red orange & multi	.20	.20
206	A41	15t multicolored	.30	.30
207	A41	30t blue & multi	.55	.55
a.		Souvenir sheet of 4, #204-207	1.40	1.40
208	A42	50t black & multi	.60	.60
a.		Souvenir sheet of 1	1.25	1.25
		Nos. 204-208 (5)	1.85	1.85

Dr. David Livingstone (1813-73), medical missionary and explorer.

Issued: #204-207, 207a, 5/1; #208, 208a, 12/12.

Thumb Dulcitone (Kalimba) A43

African Musical Instruments: 8t, Hand zither (bangwe; vert.). 15t, Hand drum (ng'oma; vert.). 30t, One-stringed fiddle (kaligo).

1973, Aug. 8 Wmk. 357 ***Perf. 14***

209	A43	3t brt green & multi	.20	.20
210	A43	8t red & multi	.20	.20
211	A43	15t violet & multi	.25	.25
212	A43	30t blue & multi	.35	.35
a.		Souvenir sheet of 4, #209-212	3.50	3.50
		Nos. 209-212 (4)	1.00	1.00

The Three Kings A44

1973, Nov. 8 ***Perf. 13½x14***

213	A44	3t blue & multi	.20	.20
214	A44	8t ver & multi	.20	.20
215	A44	15t multicolored	.20	.20
216	A44	30t orange & multi	.30	.30
a.		Souvenir sheet of 4, #213-216	1.25	1.25
		Nos. 213-216 (4)	.90	.90

Christmas.

Largemouth Black Bass — A45

Designs: Game fish.

1974, Feb. 20 Litho. ***Perf. 14x14½***

217	A45	3t shown	.30	.25
218	A45	8t Rainbow trout	.35	.30
219	A45	15t Lake salmon	.80	.75
220	A45	30t Triggerfish	1.50	1.50
a.		Souvenir sheet of 4, #217-220	4.50	4.50
		Nos. 217-220 (4)	2.95	2.80

30th anniv. of Angling Society of Malawi.

UPU Emblem, Map of Africa with Malawi A46

1974, Apr. 24 ***Perf. 13½***

221	A46	3t green & bister	.20	.20
222	A46	8t ver & bister	.20	.20
223	A46	15t lilac & bister	.25	.25
224	A46	30t gray & bister	.50	.50
a.		Souvenir sheet of 4, #221-224	1.75	1.75
		Nos. 221-224 (4)	1.15	1.15

Centenary of Universal Postal Union.

Capital Hill, Lilongwe and Pres. Kamuzu Banda A47

1974, July 3 Litho. ***Perf. 14***

225	A47	3t emerald & multi	.20	.20
226	A47	8t red & multi	.20	.20
227	A47	15t lilac & multi	.20	.20
228	A47	30t vio blue & multi	.25	.25
a.		Souvenir sheet of 4, #225-228	.90	.90
		Nos. 225-228 (4)	.85	.85

10th anniversary of independence.

Madonna of the Meadow, by Giovanni Bellini — A48

Paintings: 8t, Holy Family, by Jacob Jordaens. 15t, Nativity, by Peter F. de Grebber. 30t, Adoration of the Shepherds, by Lorenzo di Credi.

1974, Dec. 4 Litho. ***Perf. 13½x14***

229	A48	3t dk green & multi	.20	.20
230	A48	8t multicolored	.20	.20
231	A48	15t purple & multi	.20	.20
232	A48	30t dk blue & multi	.40	.40
a.		Souvenir sheet of 4, #229-232	1.00	1.00
		Nos. 229-232 (4)	1.00	1.00

Christmas.

African Snipe A49

Double-banded Sandgrouse A50

Malawi Coat of Arms — A51

Birds: 3t, Blue quail. 5t, Red-necked francolin. 8t, Harlequin quail. 10t, Spurwing goose. 15t, Denham's bustard. 20t, Knob-billed duck. 30t, Helmeted guinea fowl. 50t, Pigmy goose. 1k, Garganey. 2k, White-faced tree duck. 4k, Green pigeon.

Wmk. 357

1975, Feb. 19 Litho. ***Perf. 14***

Size: 17x21, 21x17mm

233	A49	1t multicolored	.20	.40
234	A50	2t multicolored	.35	.40
235	A50	3t multicolored	1.40	1.60
236	A49	5t multicolored	4.00	2.00
237	A50	8t multicolored	6.00	1.60

Perf. 14½

Size: 25x41, 41x25mm

238	A49	10t multicolored	8.50	.80
239	A49	15t multicolored	3.50	5.00
240	A49	20t multicolored	1.10	1.60
241	A49	30t multicolored	1.40	1.25
242	A50	50t multicolored	2.25	2.00
243	A50	1k multicolored	6.00	5.25
244	A49	2k multicolored	14.00	11.50
245	A50	4k multicolored	25.00	22.50
		Nos. 233-245 (13)	73.70	55.90

See #270-279. For overprints see #263, 294.

Coil Stamps

1975-85 ***Perf. 14½x14***

246	A51	1t dark violet blue	.35	.20
247	A51	5t red ('85)	1.00	.25

"Mpasa" A52

Designs: Lake Malawi ships.

1975, Mar. 12 Wmk. 357 ***Perf. 13½***

251	A52	3t shown	.35	.30
252	A52	8t "Ilala II"	.55	.45
253	A52	15t "Chauncy Maples"	1.00	1.00
254	A52	30t "Nkwazi"	2.00	*2.50*
a.		Souvenir sheet of 4, #251-254, perf. 14½	5.00	5.00
		Nos. 251-254 (4)	3.90	4.25

Habenaria Splendens — A53

Bush Baby — A54

Orchids of Malawi: 10t, Eulophia cucullata. 20t, Disa welwitschii. 40t, Angraecum conchiferum.

1975, June 6 Litho. ***Perf. 14½***

255	A53	3t lt green & multi	.60	.25
256	A53	10t red orange & multi	.70	.50
257	A53	20t dull vio & multi	1.10	.90
258	A53	40t multicolored	1.75	*2.25*
a.		Souvenir sheet of 4, #255-258	12.00	12.00
		Nos. 255-258 (4)	4.15	3.90

1975, Sept. 3 Litho. ***Perf. 14***

259	A54	3t shown	.25	.20
260	A54	10t Leopard	.40	.30
261	A54	20t Roan antelope	.80	.80
262	A54	40t Burchell's zebra	1.60	*2.00*
a.		Souvenir sheet of 4, #259-262	6.00	6.00
		Nos. 259-262 (4)	3.05	3.30

Animals of Malawi.

No. 242 Overprinted: "10th ACP / Ministerial / Conference / 1975"

1975, Dec. 9 Litho. ***Perf. 14½***

263	A50	50t multicolored	1.75	1.75

10th African, Caribbean and Pacific Ministerial Conference.

Adoration of the Kings, French A55

Christmas: 10t, Nativity, 16th century, Spanish. 20t, Nativity, by Pierre Raymond, 16th century. 40t, Angel Appearing to the Shepherds, 14th century, English.

1975, Dec. 12 ***Perf. 13x13½***

264	A55	3t multicolored	.20	.20
265	A55	10t multicolored	.20	.20
266	A55	20t purple & multi	.25	.25
267	A55	40t blue & multi	.35	.35
a.		Souv. sheet of 4, #264-267, perf. 14	2.60	2.60
		Nos. 264-267 (4)	1.00	1.00

Bird Types of 1975

1975 Litho. Unwmk. ***Perf. 14***

Size: 21x17mm

270	A50	3t multicolored	5.00	3.50

Perf. 14½

Size: 25x41mm

273	A49	10t multicolored	3.00	3.75
274	A49	15t multicolored	3.00	4.25
279	A49	2k multicolored	8.00	*15.00*
		Nos. 270-279 (4)	19.00	26.50

For overprint see No. 293.

Alexander Graham Bell — A56

President Kamuzu Banda — A57

Perf. 14x14½

1976, Mar. 24 Litho. Wmk. 357

281	A56	3t green & black	.20	.20
282	A56	10t dp lilac rose & blk	.20	.20
283	A56	20t brt purple & blk	.30	.30
284	A56	40t brt blue & blk	.60	.60
a.		Souvenir sheet of 4, #281-284	2.00	2.00
		Nos. 281-284 (4)	1.30	1.30

Centenary of first telephone call by Alexander Graham Bell, Mar. 10, 1876.

1976, July 1 Photo. *Perf. 13*

285 A57 3t brt green & multi .20 .20
286 A57 10t multicolored .20 .20
287 A57 20t violet & multi .30 .30
288 A57 40t dull blue & multi .65 .65
a. Souvenir sheet of 4, #285-288 1.75 1.75
Nos. 285-288 (4) 1.35 1.35

10th anniversary of the Republic.

Bagnall Diesel No. 100 A58

Diesel Locomotives: 10t, Shire class No. 503. 20t, Nippon Sharyo No. 301. 40t, Hunslet No. 110.

1976, Oct. 1 Litho. *Perf. 14½*

289 A58 3t emerald & multi .50 .30
290 A58 10t red & multi 1.00 .40
291 A58 20t lilac & multi 2.00 .90
292 A58 40t blue & multi 3.50 3.50
a. Souvenir sheet of 4, #289-292 7.50 7.50
Nos. 289-292 (4) 7.00 5.10

Malawi Railways.

Nos. 274 and 241 Overprinted:

1976, Oct. 22 Litho. Unwmk.

293 A49 15t multicolored 2.75 1.40

Wmk. 357

294 A49 30t multicolored 3.25 3.25

Blantyre Mission centenary.

Christ Child on Straw Bed — A59

Ebony Ancestor Figures — A60

1976, Dec. 6 Wmk. 357 *Perf. 14*

295 A59 3t green & multi .20 .20
296 A59 10t magenta & multi .20 .20
297 A59 20t purple & multi .25 .25
298 A59 40t dk blue & multi .35 .35
a. Souvenir sheet of 4, #295-298 2.25 2.25
Nos. 295-298 (4) 1.00 1.00

Christmas.

1977, Apr. 1 Litho. Wmk. 357

Handicrafts: 10t, Ebony elephant, horiz. 20t, Ebony rhinoceros, horiz. 40t, Wooden antelope.

299 A60 4t yellow & multi .20 .20
300 A60 10t black & multi .20 .20
301 A60 20t ocher & multi .25 .25
302 A60 40t ver & multi .35 .35
a. Souvenir sheet of 4, #299-302 2.25 2.25
Nos. 299-302 (4) 1.00 1.00

Chileka Airport, Blantyre, and VC10 A61

Transportation in Malawi: 10t, Leyland bus on Blantyre-Lilongwe Road. 20t, Ilala II on Lake Malawi. 40t, Freight train of Blantyre-Nacala line on overpass.

1977, July 12 Litho. *Perf. 14½*

303 A61 4t multicolored .50 .25
304 A61 10t multicolored .50 .40
305 A61 20t multicolored 1.25 .95
306 A61 40t multicolored 2.00 *2.75*
a. Souvenir sheet of 4, #303-306 4.50 4.50
Nos. 303-306 (4) 4.25 4.35

Pseudotropheus Johanni — A62

Lake Malawi Fish: 10t, Pseudotropheus livingstoni. 20t, Pseudotropheus zebra. 40t, Genyochromis mento.

Wmk. 357, Unwmkd.

1977, Oct. 4 Litho. *Perf. 13½x14*

307 A62 4t multicolored .40 .20
308 A62 10t multicolored .60 .30
309 A62 20t multicolored 1.50 .60
310 A62 40t multicolored 1.75 1.50
a. Souvenir sheet of 4, #307-310 4.50 4.50
Nos. 307-310 (4) 4.25 2.60

Virgin and Child, by Bergognone A63

Entry into Jerusalem, by Giotto A64

Virgin and Child: 10t, with God the Father and Angels, by Ambrogio Bergognone. 20t, detail from Bottigella altarpiece, by Vincenzo Foppa. 40t, with the fountain, by Jan Van Eyck.

Perf. 14x13½

1977, Nov. 21 Unwmk.

311 A63 4t multicolored .20 .20
312 A63 10t red & multi .20 .20
313 A63 20t lilac & multi .25 .25
314 A63 40t vio blue & multi .50 .50
a. Souvenir sheet of 4, #311-314 3.50 3.50
Nos. 311-314 (4) 1.15 1.15

Christmas.

1978, Mar. 1 Litho. *Perf. 12x12½*

Giotto Paintings: 10t, Crucifixion. 20t, Descent from the Cross. 40t, Jesus Appearing to Mary.

315 A64 4t multicolored .20 .20
316 A64 10t multicolored .20 .20
317 A64 20t multicolored .35 .25
318 A64 40t multicolored .65 .65
a. Souvenir sheet of 4, #315-318 2.75 2.75
Nos. 315-318 (4) 1.40 1.30

Easter.

Lions, Wildlife Fund Emblem A65

Animals and Wildlife Fund Emblem: 4t, Nyala, vert. 20t, Burchell's zebras. 40t, Reedbuck, vert.

1978, June 1 Unwmk. *Perf. 13x13½*

319 A65 4t multicolored *5.00* *1.00*
320 A65 10t multicolored *12.00* *2.00*
321 A65 20t multicolored *20.00* *3.00*
322 A65 40t multicolored *27.50* *12.00*
a. Souvenir sheet of 4, #319-322, perf. 13½ *100.00* 60.00
Nos. 319-322 (4) *64.50* *18.00*

Malamulo Seventh Day Adventist Church — A66

Virgin and Child and: 10t, Likoma Cathedral. 20t, St. Michael's and All Angel's, Blantyre. 40t, Zomba Catholic Cathedral.

1978, Nov. 15 Wmk. 357 *Perf. 14*

323 A66 4t multicolored .20 .20
324 A66 10t multicolored .20 .20
325 A66 20t multicolored .30 .30
326 A66 40t multicolored .50 .50
a. Souvenir sheet of 4, #323-326 1.40 1.40
Nos. 323-326 (4) 1.20 1.20

Christmas.

Vanilla Polylepis — A67

Brachystegia Spiciformis A68

Orchids of Malawi: 2t, Cirrhopetalum umbellatum. 5t, Calanthe natalensis. 7t, Ansellia gigantea. 8t, Tridactyle bicaudata. 10t, Acampe pachyglossa. 15t, Eulophia quartiniana. 20t, Cyrtorchis arcuata. 30t, Eulophia tricristata. 50t, Disa hamatopetala. 75t, Cynorchis glandulosa. 1k, Aerangis kotschyana. 1.50k, Polystachya dendrobiiflora. 2k, Disa ornithantha. 4k, Cytorchis praetermissa.

1979, Jan. 2 Litho. *Perf. 13½*

327 A67 1t multicolored .60 .30
328 A67 2t multicolored .60 .30
329 A67 5t multicolored .60 .30
330 A67 7t multicolored .60 .50
331 A67 8t multicolored .60 .30
332 A67 10t multicolored .60 .30
333 A67 15t multicolored .60 .40
334 A67 20t multicolored .70 .55
335 A67 30t multicolored 1.50 .40
336 A67 50t multicolored 1.25 .60
337 A67 75t multicolored 2.50 *4.00*
338 A67 1k multicolored 2.25 1.75
339 A67 1.50k multicolored 3.00 *4.75*
340 A67 2k multicolored 4.00 2.75
341 A67 4k multicolored 9.00 8.50
Nos. 327-341 (15) 28.40 25.70

1979, Jan. 21 *Perf. 14x13½*

Trees: 10t, Widdringtonia nodiflora. 20t, Sandalwood. 40t, African mahogany.

342 A68 5t multicolored .30 .25
343 A68 10t multicolored .40 .35
344 A68 20t multicolored .80 .75
345 A68 40t multicolored 1.25 *2.00*
a. Souvenir sheet of 4, #342-345 3.25 3.25
Nos. 342-345 (4) 2.75 3.35

National Tree Planting Day.

Railroad Bridge A69

Designs: 10t, Station and train. 20t, 40t, Train passing through man-made pass, diff.

1979, Feb. 17 Litho. *Perf. 14½*

346 A69 5t multicolored .30 .25
347 A69 10t multicolored .50 .35
348 A69 20t multicolored .90 .75
349 A69 40t multicolored 1.50 *2.00*
a. Souvenir sheet of 4, #346-349 6.25 6.25
Nos. 346-349 (4) 3.20 3.35

Inauguration of Salima-Lilongwe Railroad.

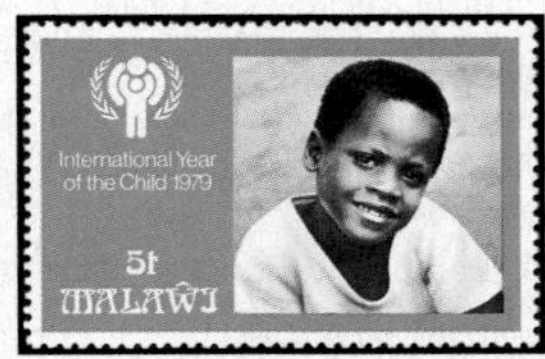

Malawi Boy and IYC Emblem — A70

Designs: Malawi children and IYC emblem.

1979, July 10 Wmk. 357 *Perf. 14*

350 A70 5t multicolored .25 .25
351 A70 10t multicolored .25 .25
352 A70 20t multicolored .35 .30
353 A70 40t multicolored .55 .55
Nos. 350-353 (4) 1.40 1.35

International Year of the Child.

Malawi No. 1 A71

Stamps of Malawi: 10t, #2. 20t, #3. 40t, #4.

1979, Sept. 17 Litho. *Perf. 13½x14*

354 A71 5t multicolored .20 .20
355 A71 10t multicolored .20 .20
356 A71 20t multicolored .20 .20
357 A71 40t multicolored .30 .30
a. Souvenir sheet of 4, #354-357 1.25 1.25
Nos. 354-357 (4) .90 .90

Sir Rowland Hill (1795-1879), originator of penny postage.

Christmas — A72

Designs: Landscapes.

1979, Nov. 15 Litho. *Perf. 13½x14*

358 A72 5t multicolored .25 .25
359 A72 10t multicolored .25 .25
360 A72 20t multicolored .30 .30
361 A72 40t multicolored .60 .60
Nos. 358-361 (4) 1.40 1.40

Limbe Rotary Club Emblem — A73

Malawi Rotary Club Emblems: 10t, Blantyre. 20t, Lilongwe. 40t, Rotary Intl.

1980, Feb. 23 Litho. *Perf. 13½*

362 A73 5t multicolored .20 .20
363 A73 10t multicolored .20 .20
364 A73 20t multicolored .35 .35
365 A73 40t multicolored .85 .85
a. Souvenir sheet of 4, #362-365 2.50 2.50
Nos. 362-365 (4) 1.60 1.60

Rotary International, 75th anniversary.

Mangochi District Post Office, 1976, London 1980 Emblem — A74

London 1980 Emblem and: 10t, New Blantyre sorting office, 1979. 20t, Mail transfer hut, Walala. 1k, Nyasaland Post Office, Chiromo, 1891.

1980, May 6 Wmk. 357 *Perf. 14½*

366 A74 5t blue green & blk .20 .20
367 A74 10t red & black .20 .20
368 A74 20t dp violet & black .20 .20
369 A74 1k dk blue & black .65 .65
a. Souvenir sheet of 4, #366-369 2.25 2.25
Nos. 366-369 (4) 1.25 1.25

London 1980 International Stamp Exhibition, May 6-14.

Agate Nodule — A75

1980, Aug. 20 Litho. *Perf. 13½*

370 A75 5t shown 1.25 .25
371 A75 10t Sunstone 1.75 .25
372 A75 20t Smoky Quartz 3.00 .60
373 A75 1k Kyanite crystal 6.75 *8.00*
Nos. 370-373 (4) 12.75 9.10

Elephants Drinking (Christmas) A76

1980, Nov. 10 Litho. *Perf. 13*

374 A76 5t shown .50 .45
375 A76 10t Flowers .45 .35
376 A76 20t Train 1.25 .90
377 A76 1k Bird 2.10 2.10
Nos. 374-377 (4) 4.30 3.80

Livingstone's Suni — A77

1981, Feb. 4 Litho. *Perf. 14½*

378 A77 7t shown .25 .25
379 A77 10t Blue duikers .30 .25
380 A77 20t African buffalo .50 .40
381 A77 1k Lichtenstein's hartebeests 1.75 1.75
Nos. 378-381 (4) 2.80 2.65

Standard A Earth Station A78

1981, Apr. 24 Litho. *Perf. 14½*

382 A78 7t shown .20 .20
383 A78 10t Blantyre International Gateway Exchange .25 .20
384 A78 20t Standard B Earth Station .35 .25
385 A78 1k Satellite and earth 1.75 1.75
a. Souvenir sheet of 4, #382-385 2.75 2.75
Nos. 382-385 (4) 2.55 2.40

International communications.

World Food Day A79

1981, Sept. 11 Litho. *Perf. 14*

386 A79 7t Corn .20 .20
387 A79 10t Rice .25 .20
388 A79 20t Finger millet .50 .25
389 A79 1k Wheat 1.60 1.60
Nos. 386-389 (4) 2.55 2.25

Holy Family, by Lippi A80

Christmas: 7t, Adoration of the Shepherds, by Murillo, vert. 20t, Adoration of the Shepherds, by Louis Le Nain. 1k, Virgin and Child, St. John the Baptist and Angel, by Paolo Morando, vert.

Perf. 13½x13, 13x13½

1981, Nov. 26 Litho.

390 A80 7t multicolored .25 .25
391 A80 10t multicolored .30 .25
392 A80 20t multicolored .60 .55
393 A80 1k multicolored 1.50 1.50
Nos. 390-393 (4) 2.65 2.55

Wildlife in Natl. Parks A81

1982, Mar. 15 Litho. *Perf. 14½x14*

394 A81 7t Impalas .25 .20
395 A81 10t Lions .45 .20
396 A81 20t Kudus .75 .25
397 A81 1k Flamingos 3.00 3.00
Nos. 394-397 (4) 4.45 3.65

Kamuzu Academy — A82

Designs: Academy views.

1982, July 1 Litho. *Perf. 14½*

398 A82 7t multicolored .25 .25
399 A82 20t multicolored .30 .25
400 A82 30t multicolored .45 .40
401 A82 1k multicolored 1.50 1.50
Nos. 398-401 (4) 2.50 2.40

1982 World Cup — A83

1982, Sept. *Perf. 14x14½*

402 A83 7t Players 1.25 1.00
403 A83 20t World Cup 2.25 2.25
404 A83 30t Stadium 2.75 2.75
Nos. 402-404 (3) 6.25 6.00

Souvenir Sheet

405 A83 1k Emblem on field 2.75 2.75

Remembrance Day — A84

Designs: War Memorials.

1982, Nov. 5 *Perf. 14½*

406 A84 7t Blantyre .20 .20
407 A84 20t Zomba .20 .20
408 A84 30t Chichiri, badges .30 .30
409 A84 1k Lilongwe 1.00 1.50
Nos. 406-409 (4) 1.70 2.20

A85

1983, Mar. 14 Wmk. 357 *Perf. 14*

410 A85 7t Kwacha Intl. Conf. Ctr. .20 .20
411 A85 20t Tea picking, Mulanje .20 .20
412 A85 30t Map .35 .25
413 A85 1k Pres. Banda, flag .75 *.85*
Nos. 410-413 (4) 1.50 1.50

Commonwealth Day.

The Miraculous Draught of Fishes, by Raphael (1483-1517) — A86

Designs: 7t, 20t, 30t, Details. 1k, Entire painting. 7t, 20t vert.

1983, Apr. 4 Litho. Wmk. 357

414 A86 7t multicolored .40 .30
415 A86 20t multicolored 1.00 1.00
416 A86 30t multicolored 1.40 1.40
Nos. 414-416 (3) 2.80 2.70

Souvenir Sheet

417 A86 1k multicolored 3.25 3.25

Fish Eagles — A87

Designs: a, Lakeside sentinel. b, Gull-like, far-carrying call. c, Diving on its fish prey. d, Prey captured. e, Feeding on its catch. Nos. 418a-418e in continuous design.

1983, July 11 Wmk. 357 *Perf. 14½*

418 Strip of 5 17.00 17.00
a.-e. A87 30t multicolored 1.90 1.90

Manned Flight Bicentenary — A88

Kamuzu Intl. Airport.

1983, Aug. 31 Litho. *Perf. 14*

419 A88 7t multicolored .20 .20
420 A88 20t multi, diff. .45 .35
421 A88 30t multi, diff. .65 .65
422 A88 1k multi, diff. 2.00 2.00
a. Souvenir sheet of 4, #419-422 3.50 3.50
Nos. 419-422 (4) 3.30 3.20

Christmas — A89

Local flowers.

1983, Nov. 1 Wmk. 357 *Perf. 14*

423 A89 7t Clerodendium myricoides .60 .35
424 A89 20t Gloriosa superba 1.40 1.00
425 A89 30t Gladiolus laxiflorus 1.75 1.40
426 A89 1k Aframomum angustifolium 4.75 4.75
Nos. 423-426 (4) 8.50 7.50

Aquarium Species, Lake Malawi A90

Perf. 14½x14

1984, Feb. 2 Wmk. 373

427 A90 1t Melanochromis auratus .45 *1.00*
428 A90 2t Haplochromis compressiceps .45 *1.00*
429 A90 5t Labeotropheus fuelleborni .45 *1.00*
430 A90 7t Pseudotropheus lombardoi .45 .40
431 A90 8t Gold pseudotropheus zebra .45 .40
432 A90 10t Trematocranus jacobfreibergi .45 .30
433 A90 15t Melanochromis crabro .45 .30
434 A90 20t Marbled pseadotropheus .55 .30
435 A90 30t Labidochromis caeruleus .65 .50
436 A90 40t Haplochromis venustus 1.10 .65
437 A90 50t Aulonacara of Thumbi 2.75 2.50
438 A90 75t Melanochromis vermivorus 4.00 4.00
439 A90 1k Pseudotropheus zebra 4.50 4.50
440 A90 2k Trematocranus spp. 6.50 6.50
441 A90 4k Aulonacara of Mbenje 9.25 9.25
Nos. 427-441 (15) 32.45 32.60

Nos. 427, 430-436 exist inscribed "1986." Value, set $23.

Nyika Red Hare A91

1984, Feb. 2 Wmk. 357 *Perf. 14*

442 A91 7t shown .70 .20
443 A91 20t Sun squirrel 1.40 .45
444 A91 30t Hedgehog 1.90 1.00
445 A91 1k Genet 2.50 *3.75*
Nos. 442-445 (4) 6.50 *5.40*

1984 Summer Olympics A92

Local Butterflies A93

1984, June 1 Litho. *Perf. 14*

446 A92 7t Running .25 .20
447 A92 20t Boxing .60 .30
448 A92 30t Bicycling 1.00 1.00
449 A92 1k Long jump 1.75 1.75
a. Souvenir sheet of 4, #446-449 5.00 5.00
Nos. 446-449 (4) 3.60 3.25

1984, Aug. 1 Photo. *Perf. 11½*
Granite Paper

450 A93 7t Euphaedra neophron 1.75 .40
451 A93 20t Papilio dardanus 4.25 .65
452 A93 30t Antanartia schaeneia 4.75 1.50
453 A93 1k Spindasis *6.75 9.50*
Nos. 450-453 (4) 17.50 12.05

Christmas — A94

Virgin and Child Paintings.

Wmk. 357
1984, Oct. 15 Litho. *Perf. 14½*

454 A94 7t Duccio .75 .30
455 A94 20t Raphael 2.00 .40
456 A94 30t Lippi 2.75 1.25
457 A94 1k Wilton diptych *5.50 7.50*
Nos. 454-457 (4) 11.00 9.45

Fungi A94a

1985, Jan. 23 *Perf. 14½x14*

458 A94a 7t Leucopaxillus gracillimus 1.75 .50
459 A94a 20t Limacella guttata 3.75 .65
460 A94a 30t Termitomyces eurhizles 4.75 1.75
461 A94a 1k Xerulina asprata 9.00 *10.00*
Nos. 458-461 (4) 19.25 *12.90*

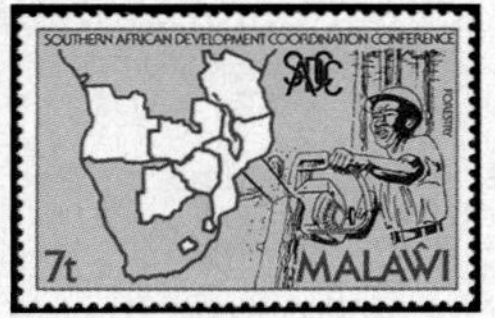

Southern African Development Coordination Conference — A95

1985, Apr. 1 Litho. *Perf. 14*

462 A95 7t Forestry 1.25 .35
463 A95 15t Communications 2.00 .40
464 A95 20t Transportation 5.75 1.50
465 A95 1k Fishing 6.75 6.75
Nos. 462-465 (4) 15.75 9.00

Ships on Lake Malawi A96

1985, June 3 *Perf. 13½x13*

466 A96 7t Ufulu 1.25 .40
467 A96 15t Chauncy Maples 2.50 .40
468 A96 20t Mtendere 3.25 1.00
469 A96 1k Ilala 6.00 6.00
a. Souvenir sheet of 4, #466-469, perf. 13x12 14.00 14.00
Nos. 466-469 (4) 13.00 7.80

Audubon Birth Bicent. — A97

1985, Aug. 1 Litho. *Perf. 14*

470 A97 7t Stierling's woodpecker 1.75 .50
471 A97 15t Lesser seed-cracker 3.00 .50
472 A97 20t Gunning's akalat 3.30 1.00
473 A97 1k Boehm's bee-eater 5.50 5.50
a. Souvenir sheet of 4, #470-473 17.00 17.00
Nos. 470-473 (4) 13.55 7.50

Christmas A98

Halley's Comet A99

Paintings: 7t, The Virgin of Humility, by Jaime Serra. 15t, Adoration of the Magi, by Stefano da Zevio. 20t, Madonna and Child, by Gerard van Honthorst. 1k, Virgin of Zbraslav, by a Master of Vissi Brod.

Perf. 11½x12
1985, Oct. 14 Unwmk.

474 A98 7t multicolored .45 .30
475 A98 15t multicolored 1.25 .35
476 A98 20t multicolored 1.75 .55
477 A98 1k multicolored 4.25 4.25
Nos. 474-477 (4) 7.70 5.45

1986, Feb. 10 Wmk. 357 *Perf. 14½*

478 A99 8t Earth, comet and Giotto trajectories 1.00 .35
479 A99 15t Comet over Earth 1.10 .35
480 A99 20t Over Malawi 1.75 .45
481 A99 1k Giotto probe *3.50 5.00*
Nos. 478-481 (4) 7.35 6.15

1986 World Cup Soccer Championships, Mexico — A100

Various soccer plays.

Perf. 12x11½
1986, May 26 Unwmk.
Granite Paper

482 A100 8t multicolored 1.00 .30
483 A100 15t multicolored 1.50 .35
484 A100 20t multicolored 2.25 .85
485 A100 1k multicolored 5.50 5.50
a. Souvenir sheet of 4, #482-485 14.00 14.00
Nos. 482-485 (4) 10.25 7.00

Natl. Independence, 20th Anniv. — A101

1986, June 30 Litho. *Perf. 14*

486 A101 8t Pres. Banda 2.25 2.25
487 A101 15t Natl. flag 1.25 .25
488 A101 20t Natl. crest 1.40 .35
489 A101 1k Natl. airline 5.25 5.25
Nos. 486-489 (4) 10.15 8.10

Christmas — A102

1986, Dec. 15 Litho. *Perf. 11½*

Paintings: 8t, Virgin and Child, by Botticelli (1445-1510). 15t, Adoration of the Shepherds, by Guido Reni (1575-1642). 20t, Madonna of the Veil, by Carlo Dolci (1616-86). 1k, Adoration of the Magi, by Jean Bourdichon.

490 A102 8t multicolored .75 .25
491 A102 15t multicolored 1.25 .25
492 A102 20t multicolored 2.00 .50
493 A102 1k multicolored *6.00 7.50*
Nos. 490-493 (4) 10.00 8.50

World Wildlife Fund A103

Bugeranus carunculatus.

1987, Jan. 30 Wmk. 357 *Perf. 14½*

494 A103 8t Wattled crane 2.75 .45
495 A103 15t Two cranes 4.00 .60
496 A103 20t Nesting 4.75 .90
497 A103 75t Crane in water 8.75 8.75
Nos. 494-497 (4) 20.25 10.70

1988, Oct. Wmk. 373

494a A103 8t 7.75 1.75
495a A103 15t 11.00 3.25
496a A103 20t 12.00 3.75
497a A103 75t 16.50 15.00
Nos. 494a-497a (4) 47.25 23.75

British Steam Locomotives — A104

1987, May 25 Litho. *Perf. 14x13½*

498 A104 10t Shamrock No. 2, 1902 3.25 .45
499 A104 25t D Class No. 8, 1914 4.50 .60
500 A104 30t Thistle No. 1, 1902 5.00 1.00
501 A104 1k Kitson No. 6, 1903 9.00 9.00
Nos. 498-501 (4) 21.75 11.05

Hippopotamus A105

1987, Aug. 24 Photo. *Perf. 12½*
Granite Paper

502 A105 10t Feeding 2.00 .35
503 A105 25t Swimming, roaring 3.75 .50
504 A105 30t Mother and young swimming 3.75 .85
505 A105 1k At rest, egret 9.50 8.75
a. Souvenir sheet of 4, #502-505 20.00 20.00
Nos. 502-505 (4) 19.00 10.45

Wild Flowers — A106

Locally Carved and Staunton Chessmen A107

Unwmk.
1987, Oct. 19 Litho. *Perf. 14*

506 A106 10t Stathmostelma spectabile 1.25 .25
507 A106 25t Pentanisia schweinfurthii 2.50 .35
508 A106 30t Chironia krebsii 3.00 .70
509 A106 1k Ochna macrocalyx 5.00 5.00
Nos. 506-509 (4) 11.75 6.30

1988, Feb. 8 Wmk. 384 *Perf. 14½*

510 A107 15t Knights 2.00 .30
511 A107 35t Bishops 3.00 .90
512 A107 50t Rooks 3.50 1.75
513 A107 2k Queens 9.25 9.25
Nos. 510-513 (4) 17.75 12.20

1988 Summer Olympics, Seoul — A108

Birds — A109

1988, June 13 Unwmk. *Perf. 14*

514 A108 15t High jump .60 .25
515 A108 35t Javelin 1.00 .40
516 A108 50t Women's tennis 1.50 .70
517 A108 2k Shot put 3.00 3.00
a. Souvenir sheet of 4, #514-517 7.00 7.00
Nos. 514-517 (4) 6.10 4.35

Perf. 11½x12, 15x14½ (10k)
1988 Photo.
Granite Paper (1t-4k)

518 A109 1t Eastern forest scrub-warbler .60 .60
519 A109 2t Yellow-throated warbler .60 .60
520 A109 5t Moustached green tinkerbird .60 .60
521 A109 7t Waller's chest-nut-wing starling .60 .60
522 A109 8t Oriole finch .60 .60
523 A109 10t Starred robin 1.50 1.00
524 A109 15t Bar-tailed trogon .60 .25
525 A109 20t Green twinspot .60 .25
526 A109 30t Gray cuckoo shrike .60 .25
527 A109 40t Black-fronted bush shrike .65 .40
528 A109 50t White-tailed crested fly-catcher 1.50 1.00
529 A109 75t Green barbet 1.10 1.00
530 A109 1k Cinnamon dove 1.50 1.10
531 A109 2k Silvery-cheeked hornbill 2.50 2.00
532 A109 4k Crowned eagle 5.25 3.75
533 A109 10k Red-and-blue sunbird 13.50 9.75
Nos. 518-533 (16) 32.30 23.75

Issue dates: 10k, Oct. 3, others, July 25.

1994 *Perf. 11½x12*

533A A109 10k Starred robin 10.00 5.00

Common Design Types pictured following the introduction.

Lloyds of London, 300th Anniv.

Common Design Type

15t, Royal Exchange, 1844. 35t, Opening of the Nkula Falls hydroelectric power station, horiz. 50t, Air Malawi passenger jet, horiz. 2k, Cruise ship Queen Elizabeth (Seawise University) on fire, Hong Kong, 1972.

Wmk. 373

1988, Oct. 24 Litho. ***Perf. 14***

534 CD341 15t multicolored .60 .30
535 CD341 35t multicolored 1.25 .50
536 CD341 50t multicolored 3.75 .80
537 CD341 2k multicolored 7.00 7.00
Nos. 534-537 (4) 12.60 8.60

Christmas — A110

Paintings: 15t, Madonna in the Church, by Jan Van Eyck (d. 1441). 35t, Virgin, Infant Jesus and St. Anne, by Leonardo da Vinci. 50t, Virgin and Angels, by Cimabue (c. 1240-1302). 2k, Virgin and Child, by Alesso Baldovinetti (c. 1425-1499).

1988, Nov. 28 Unwmk. ***Perf. 14***

538 A110 15t multicolored 1.00 .30
539 A110 35t multicolored 1.75 .40
540 A110 50t multicolored 2.25 .90
541 A110 2k multicolored 5.25 5.25
Nos. 538-541 (4) 10.25 6.85

Angling Soc. of Malawi, 50th Anniv. A111

1989, Apr. 11

542 A111 15t Tsungwa 1.25 .25
543 A111 35t Mpasa 2.25 .40
544 A111 50t Yellow fish 3.00 1.75
545 A111 2k Tiger fish 7.75 7.75
Nos. 542-545 (4) 14.25 10.15

Natl. Independence, 25th Anniv. — A112

1989, June 26

546 A112 15t Independence Arch 1.25 .30
547 A112 35t Grain silos 2.75 .50
548 A112 50t Capital Hill 3.75 1.75
549 A112 2k Reserve Bank Headquarters 8.75 8.75
Nos. 546-549 (4) 16.50 11.30

African Development Bank, 25th Anniv. — A113

1989, Oct. 30

550 A113 15t Blantyre Digital Telex Exchange 1.25 .30
551 A113 40t Dzalanyama steer 2.25 .50
552 A113 50t Mikolongwe heifer 2.75 1.75
553 A113 2k Zebu bull 7.75 7.75
Nos. 550-553 (4) 14.00 10.30

Cooperation with the UN, 25th Anniv. — A114

1989, Dec. 1 ***Perf. 14***

554 A114 15t shown 1.25 .30
555 A114 40t House, diff. 2.25 .45
556 A114 50t Thatched dwelling, house 3.00 1.75
557 A114 2k Tea Plantation 7.50 7.50
Nos. 554-557 (4) 14.00 10.00

Rural Housing Program.

Christmas A115

Designs: 15t, St. Michael and All Angels Church. 40t, Limbe Cathedral. 50t, Nkhoma CCAP Church. 2k, Likoma Is. Cathedral.

1989, Dec. 15

558 A115 15t multicolored 1.25 .30
559 A115 40t multicolored 2.25 .45
560 A115 50t multicolored 3.00 1.75
561 A115 2k multicolored 7.50 7.50
Nos. 558-561 (4) 14.00 10.00

Classic Cars A116

Perf. 14x13½

1990, Apr. 2 Litho. Unwmk.

562 A116 15t Ford Sedan, 1915 1.50 .40
563 A116 40t Two-seater Ford, 1915 3.00 1.00
564 A116 50t Ford, 1915 4.00 2.00
565 A116 2k Chevrolet Luxury Bus, 1930 9.50 9.50
a. Souvenir sheet of 4, #562-565, perf. 13x12 28.00 28.00
Nos. 562-565 (4) 18.00 12.90

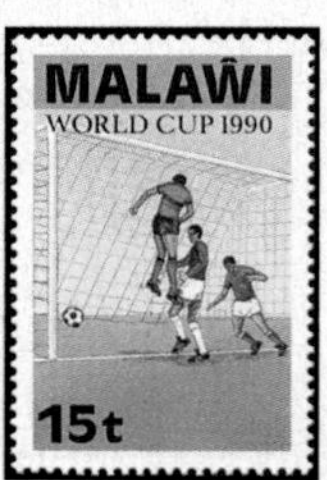

World Cup Soccer Championships, Italy — A117

1990, June 14 Litho. ***Perf. 14***

566 A117 15t shown 1.50 .30
567 A117 40t Two players 3.00 .75
568 A117 50t Shot on goal 4.00 2.00
569 A117 2k World Cup Trophy 9.50 9.50
a. Souvenir sheet of 4, #566-569 19.00 19.00
Nos. 566-569 (4) 18.00 12.55

SADCC, 10th Anniv. A118

1990, Aug. 24 Litho. ***Perf. 14***

570 A118 15t Map 1.50 .40
571 A118 40t Chambo 2.50 .55
572 A118 50t Cedar trees 3.50 2.00
573 A118 2k Nyala 9.50 9.50
a. Souvenir sheet of 4, #570-573 18.50 18.50
Nos. 570-573 (4) 17.00 12.45

Christmas A119

Orchids A120

Paintings by Raphael: 15t, Virgin and Child. 40t, The Transfiguration, detail. 50t, St. Catherine of Alexandrie. 2k, The Transfiguration.

1990, Nov. 26 ***Perf. 13½x14***

574 A119 15t multicolored 1.50 .40
575 A119 40t multicolored 2.75 .60
576 A119 50t multicolored 3.75 2.00
577 A119 2k multicolored 9.25 9.25
a. Souvenir sheet of 4, #574-577, perf. 12x13 19.00 19.00
Nos. 574-577 (4) 17.25 12.25

1990, Dec. 7

578 A120 15t Aerangis kotschyana 2.00 .40
579 A120 40t Angraecum eburneum 3.75 1.00
580 A120 50t Aerangis luteo alba 4.00 2.00
581 A120 2k Cyrtorchis arcuata 12.50 12.50
a. Souvenir sheet of 4, #578-581, perf. 12x13 23.00 23.00
Nos. 578-581 (4) 22.25 15.90

Wild Animals A121

1991, Apr. 23 Litho. ***Perf. 14x13½***

582 A121 20t Buffalo 1.50 .40
583 A121 60t Cheetah 3.50 1.50
584 A121 75t Greater kudu 3.50 1.50
585 A121 2k Black rhinoceros 13.00 10.00
a. Souvenir sheet of 4, #582-585, perf. 13x12 23.50 23.50
Nos. 582-585 (4) 21.50 13.40

Malawi Postal Services, Cent. A122

20t, Chiromo Post Office, 1891. 60t, Mail exchange hut, Walala. 75t, Mangochi Post Office. 2k, Standard A Earth station, 1981.

1991, July 2 ***Perf. 14x13½***

586 A122 20t multicolored 2.00 .40
587 A122 60t multicolored 2.75 1.00
588 A122 75t multicolored 3.00 1.25
589 A122 2k multicolored 9.50 8.00
a. Souvenir sheet of 4, #586-589, perf. 13x12 18.00 18.00
Nos. 586-589 (4) 17.25 10.65

Insects — A123

Christmas — A124

1991, Sept. 21 ***Perf. 13½x14***

590 A123 20t Red locust 2.00 .40
591 A123 60t Weevil 3.75 1.50
592 A123 75t Cotton stainer bug 3.75 1.75
593 A123 2k Pollen beetle 9.50 7.50
Nos. 590-593 (4) 19.00 11.15

1991, Nov. 26 Litho. ***Perf. 13½x14***

594 A124 20t Christ Child in manger 1.00 .35
595 A124 60t Adoration of the Magi 3.00 .60
596 A124 75t Nativity 3.50 1.00
597 A124 2k Virgin and Child 8.00 8.00
Nos. 594-597 (4) 15.50 9.95

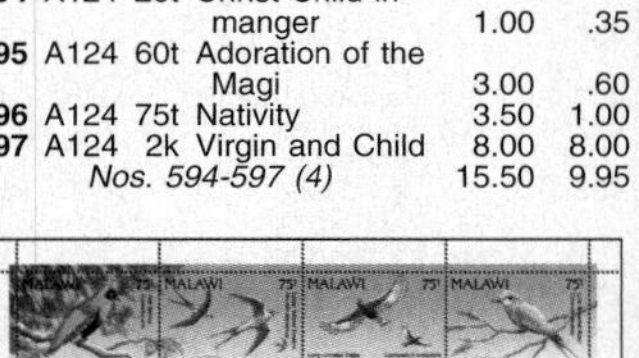

Birds — A125

Designs: a, Red bishop. b, Lesser striped swallow. c, Long-crested eagle. d, Lilac-breasted roller. e, African paradise flycatcher. f, White-fronted bee-eater. g, White-winged black tern. h, Brown-backed fire-finch. i, White-browed robin-chat. j, African fish eagle. k, Malachite kingfisher. l, Cabani's masked weaver. m, African barn owl. n, Yellow-bellied sunbird. o, Lesser flamingo. p, Crowned crane. q, African pitta. r, African darter. s, White-faced tree duck. t, African pied wagtail.

1992, Apr. 7 Litho. ***Perf. 14***

598 A125 75t Sheet of 20, #a.-t. 57.50 57.50

A number has been reserved for an additional value in this set.

1992 Summer Olympics, Barcelona — A126

1992, July 28 Litho. ***Perf. 13½***

600 A126 20t Long jump 1.40 .35
601 A126 60t High jump 2.00 .80
602 A126 75t Javelin 2.50 1.10
603 A126 2k Running 5.00 5.00
a. Souvenir sheet of 4, #600-603 13.00 13.00
Nos. 600-603 (4) 10.90 7.25

Christmas — A127

Details from paintings: 20t, Angel from The Annunciation, by Philippe de Champaigne. 75t, Virgin and Child, by Bernardino Luini. 95t, Virgin and Child, by Sassoferrato. 2k, Mary from The Annunciation, by Champaigne.

1992, Nov. 9 Litho. ***Perf. 14***

604 A127 20t multicolored .80 .25
605 A127 75t multicolored 1.90 .50
606 A127 95t multicolored 2.40 .80
607 A127 2k multicolored 5.75 5.50
Nos. 604-607 (4) 10.85 7.05

Intl. Space Year A128

Designs: 20t, Voyager II, Saturn. 75t, Center of a galaxy. 95t, Kanjedza II ground station. 2k, Communication satellite.

1992, Dec. 7 Litho. *Perf. 13½*

608 A128 20t multicolored 1.00 .35
609 A128 75t multicolored 2.25 .85
610 A128 95t multicolored 2.50 1.00
611 A128 2k multicolored 5.50 5.00
Nos. 608-611 (4) 11.25 7.20

Fruit — A129

Butterflies A130

1993, Mar. 21 Litho. *Perf. 13½x14*

612 A129 20t Strychnos spinosa 1.00 .30
613 A129 75t Adansonia digitata 2.50 1.00
614 A129 95t Ximenia caffra 2.75 1.10
615 A129 2k Uapaca kirkiana 4.75 4.75
Nos. 612-615 (4) 11.00 7.15

1993, June 28 Litho. *Perf. 13*

616 A130 20t Apaturopsis cleocharis 1.25 .40
617 A130 75t Euryphura achlys 2.75 1.00
618 A130 95t Cooksonia aliciae 3.25 1.60
619 A130 2k Charaxes protoclea azota 4.75 4.50
Nos. 616-619 (4) 12.00 7.50

A131

Dinosaurs — A132

Designs: No. 623a, Tyrannosaurus Rex. b, Dilophosaurus. c, Brachiosaurus. d, Gallimimus. e, Triceratops. f, Velociraptor.

1993, Dec. 30 Litho. *Perf. 13*

620 A131 20t Kentrosaurus 1.10 .75
621 A131 75t Stegosaurus 2.50 2.25
622 A131 95t Sauropod 3.00 2.50
Nos. 620-622 (3) 6.60 5.50

Miniature Sheet

623 A132 2k Sheet of 6, #a.-f. 21.00 21.00

Christmas — A133

1993, Nov. 30 Photo. *Perf. 11½*

Granite Paper

624 A133 20t Holy family .45 .45
625 A133 75t Shepherds .55 .45
626 A133 95t Wise men .70 .70
627 A133 2k Adoration of the magi 2.00 2.25
Nos. 624-627 (4) 3.70 3.85

Fish of Lake Malawi — A134

Designs: 20t, Pseudotropheus socolofi. 75t, Melanochromis auratus. 95t, Pseudotropheus lombardoi. 1k, Labeotropheus trewavasae. 2k, Pseudotropheus zebra. 4k, Pseudotropheus elongatus.

1994, Mar. 21 Litho. *Perf. 14x15*

628 A134 20t multicolored .45 .35
629 A134 75t multicolored 1.10 .45
630 A134 95t multicolored 1.25 .55
631 A134 1k multicolored 1.25 .90
632 A134 2k multicolored 2.50 2.25
633 A134 4k multicolored 4.25 3.75
Nos. 628-633 (6) 10.80 8.25

Ships of Lake Malawi — A135

1994, Oct. 19 Litho. *Perf. 13x13½*

634 A135 20t Ilala .70 .55
635 A135 75t MV Ufulu 1.10 .55
636 A135 95t The Pioneer 1.40 .65
637 A135 2k Dove 2.25 2.25
Nos. 634-637 (4) 5.45 4.00

Souvenir Sheet

638 A135 5k Monteith 9.00 9.00

Christmas — A136

Details or entire paintings: 20t, Virgin and Child, by Durer, vert. 75t, Magi Present Gifts to Infant Jesus, Franco-Flemish Book of Hours, vert. 95t, The Nativity, by Fra Filippo Lippi. 2k, Nativity with Magi, by Rogier van der Weyden.

1994, Nov. 30 Litho. *Perf. 14½*

639 A136 20t multicolored .55 .55
640 A136 75t multicolored .65 .55
641 A136 95t multicolored .80 .55
642 A136 2k multicolored 2.40 2.75
Nos. 639-642 (4) 4.40 4.40

Pres. Bakili Muluzi — A137

1995, Apr. 10 Litho. *Perf. 11½x12*

643 A137 40t red & multi .50 .50
644 A137 1.40k green & multi .50 .50
645 A137 1.80k blue & multi .60 .60
646 A137 2k brn org & multi .85 .85
Nos. 643-646 (4) 2.45 2.45

Establishment of COMESA (Common Market for Eastern & Southern African States).

Christmas A138

1995, Nov. 13 Litho. *Perf. 11½*

Granite Paper

647 A138 40t Pre-schoolers .70 .70
648 A138 1.40k Dispensing medicine .70 .70
649 A138 1.80k Water supply .90 .90
650 A138 2k Voluntary return 1.25 1.25
Nos. 647-650 (4) 3.55 3.55

Butterflies A139

1996, Dec. 5 Photo. *Perf. 11½*

Granite Paper

651 A139 60t Precis tugela .60 .60
652 A139 3k Papilo pelodorus 1.40 .75
653 A139 4k Acrea acrita 1.50 .90
654 A139 10k Malantis leda 3.25 3.00
Nos. 651-654 (4) 6.75 5.25

Christmas — A140

Designs: 10t, Instructor, children raising hands. 20t, Children enacting nativity scene. 30t, Children standing with hands clasped. 60t, Mother and child.

1996, Dec. 12

Granite Paper

655 A140 10t multicolored 1.00 1.00
656 A140 20t multicolored 1.00 1.00
657 A140 30t multicolored 1.25 1.00
658 A140 60t multicolored 2.50 2.00
Nos. 655-658 (4) 5.75 5.00

UN, 50th Anniv. A141

40t, Telecommunications & training. 1.40k, Clean water is essential for health. 1.80k, Protecting the environment, Mt. Mulanje. 2k, Food security.

1995, Oct. 30 Litho. *Perf. 11½*

659 A141 40t multicolored .80 .80
660 A141 1.40k multicolored .80 .80
661 A141 1.80k multicolored 1.00 1.00
662 A141 2k multicolored 1.00 1.00
a. Souvenir sheet, #659-662 4.50 4.50
Nos. 659-662 (4) 3.60 3.60

Paul Harris (1868-1947), Founder of Rotary, Intl. — A142

Rotary, Intl. emblem and: 60t, Map of Malawi. 3k, Eagle. 4.40k, Leopard.

1997, Oct. 6 Litho. *Perf. 11½*

663 A142 60t multicolored .55 .55
664 A142 3k multicolored .95 .95
665 A142 4.40k multicolored 1.40 1.40
666 A142 5k shown 1.50 1.50
Nos. 663-666 (4) 4.40 4.40

UNICEF, 50th Anniv. A143

Designs: 60t, Care and protection. 3k, Education. 4.40k, Nutrition. 5k, Immunization.

1997, Oct. 31 Litho. *Perf. 11¾x11½*

667 A143 60t multi .80 .80
668 A143 3k multi .80 .80
669 A143 4.40k multi 1.25 1.25
670 A143 5k multi 1.60 1.60
Nos. 667-670 (4) 4.45 4.45

A144

A145

Christmas: 60t, Holy Night, by Carlo Maratta. 3k, The Nativity, by Bernardino Luini. 4.40k, Adoration of the Magi, by Luini. 5k, Holy Family.

1997, Dec. 15 *Perf. 11¾*

671 A144 60t multi .80 .80
672 A144 3k multi .80 .80
673 A144 4.40k multi 1.25 1.25
674 A144 5k multi 1.60 1.60
Nos. 671-674 (4) 4.45 4.45

1998, Nov. 30 Litho. *Perf. 14½*

Diana, Princess of Wales (1961-97): Various portraits.

675 A145 60t multicolored .30 .30
676 A145 6k multicolored .40 .40
677 A145 7k multicolored .45 .45
678 A145 8k multicolored .55 .55
a. Souvenir sheet, Nos. 675-678 2.25 2.25
Nos. 675-678 (4) 1.70 1.70

Tourism A146

60t, Tattooed Rock, Mwalawamphini, Cape Maclear, vert. 6k, War Memorial Tower, Zomba, vert. 7k, Mtengatenga Postal hut, Walala. 8k, Original P.I.M. Church, Chiradzulu.

1998, Dec. 2 Litho. *Perf. 13*

679 A146 60t multicolored .50 .50
680 A146 6k multicolored .60 .60
681 A146 7k multicolored .75 .75
682 A146 8k multicolored .85 .85
Nos. 679-682 (4) 2.70 2.70

Universal Declaration of Human Rights, 50th Anniv. A147

Basic rights: 60t, Voting. 6k, Education. 7k, Equal justice. 8k, Owning property.

1998, Dec. 10

683 A147 60t multicolored .50 .50
684 A147 6k multicolored .60 .60
685 A147 7k multicolored .75 .75
686 A147 8k multicolored .85 .85
Nos. 683-686 (4) 2.70 2.70

Christmas — A148

Design: 60t, Madonna and Child.

1998, Dec. 15 Photo. ***Perf. 11¾***
Granite Paper

687 A148 60t multi .25 .25
688 A148 6k multi .25 .25
689 A148 7k Angel .25 .25
690 A148 8k multi .25 .25

Christmas — A149

60t, Madonna & Child. 6k, Nativity. 7k, Adoration of the Magi. 8k, Flight into Egypt.

1999, Dec. 13 Photo. ***Perf. 11¾***

691 A149 60t multi .55 .55
692 A149 6k multi .55 .55
693 A149 7k multi .70 .70
694 A149 8k multi .85 .85
Nos. 691-694 (4) 2.65 2.65

Southern African Development Community — A150

60t, Map of Africa. 6k, Malambe fruit juice bottles. 7k, Fishing resources research boat R/V Ndunduma. 8k, Locomotive.

Perf. 13¼x13½, 13½x13¼
2000, Feb. 22 Litho.

695 A150 60t multi, vert. .55 .55
696 A150 6k multi, vert. .55 .55
697 A150 7k multi .70 .70
698 A150 8k multi .85 .85
Nos. 695-698 (4) 2.65 2.65

Modern British Commonwealth, 50th Anniv. — A151

African musical instruments: 60t, Ng'oma. 6k, Kaligo. 7k, Kalimba. 8k, Chisekese.

2000, Feb. 22 ***Perf. 13¼x13½***

699 A151 60t multi .55 .55
700 A151 6k multi .55 .55
701 A151 7k multi .70 .70
702 A151 8k multi .85 .85
Nos. 699-702 (4) 2.65 2.65

Christmas — A152

Designs: 5k, Madonna and Child. 18k, Nativity. 20k, Madonna and Child, diff.

2000, Dec. 12 Photo. ***Perf. 11¾***

703-705 A152 Set of 3 2.75 2.75

Butterflies — A153

Designs: 1k, Euxanthe wakefieldi. 2k, Psuedacraea boisdurali. 4k, Catacroptera cloanthe. 5k, Myrina silenus ficedula. 10k, Cymothoe zombana. 20k, Charaxes castor. 50k, Charaxes pythoduras ventersi. 100k, Iolaus lalos.

2002 ? Litho. ***Perf. 14½x13¾***

706 A153 1k multi .25 .25
707 A153 2k multi .25 .25
708 A153 4k multi .25 .25
709 A153 5k multi .25 .25
710 A153 10k multi .25 .25
711 A153 20k multi .60 .60
712 A153 50k multi 1.75 1.75
713 A153 100k multi 3.25 3.25
Nos. 706-713 (8) 6.85 6.85

Worldwide Fund for Nature (WWF) A154

Kobus vardonii: a, Male. b, Two males butting heads. c, Male and female. d, Herd.

Perf. 13¼x13½
2003, Nov. 10 Litho.

714 Strip of 4 5.25 5.25
a.-d. A154 50k Any single 1.10 1.10
e. Souvenir sheet, 2 #714 11.50 11.50

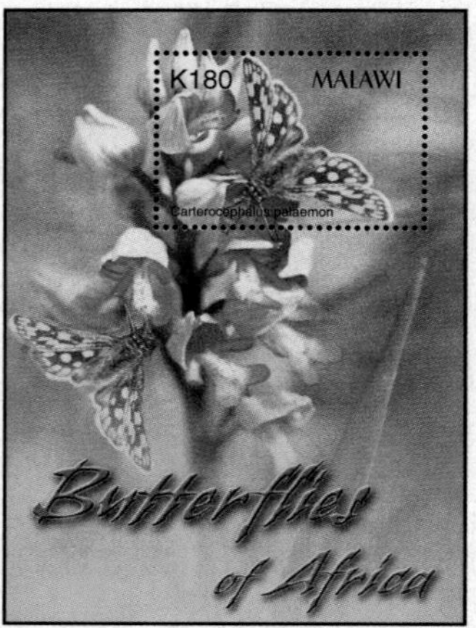

Butterflies, Birds, Orchids and Mushrooms — A155

No. 715, 50k — Butterflies: a, Bebearia octogramma. b, Charaxes nobilis. c, Cymothoe beckeri. d, Salamis anteva. e, Charaxes xiphares. f, Bebearia arcadius Fabricius.

No. 716, 50k, vert. — Birds: a, Upupa epops. b, Psittacus erithacus. c, Terathopus ecaudatus. d, Polemaetus bellicosus. e, Agapornis personatus. f, Scotopelia peli.

No. 717, 50k, vert. — Orchids: a, Angraecum eburneum. b, Ancistrochilus rothschildianus. c, Angraecum infundibulare. d, Ansellia africana. e, Disa veitchii. f, Angraecum compactum.

No. 718, 50k — Mushrooms: a, Pleurotus ostreatus. b, Macrolepiota procera. c, Amanita vaginata. d, Cantharellus tubaeformis. e, Hydnum repandum. f, Trametes versicolor.

No. 719, 180k, Carterocephalus palaemon. No. 720, 180k, Ardea cinerea. No. 721, 180k, Aerangis kotschyana. No. 722, 180k, Auricularia auricula, vert.

Perf. 13¼x13½, 13½x13¼
2003, Nov. 10
Sheets of 6, #a-f

715-718 A155 Set of 4 22.50 22.50

Souvenir Sheets

719-722 A155 Set of 4 13.50 13.50

Tour de France Bicycle Race, Cent. (in 2003) — A156

No. 723: a, Joop Zoetemelk, 1980. b, Bernard Hinault, 1981. c, Hinault, 1982. d, Laurent Fignon, 1983.

180k, Miguel Indurain, 1991-95.

2004, Feb. 6 ***Perf. 13¼***

723 A156 75k Sheet of 4, #a-d 5.75 5.75

Souvenir Sheet

724 A156 180k multi 3.50 3.50

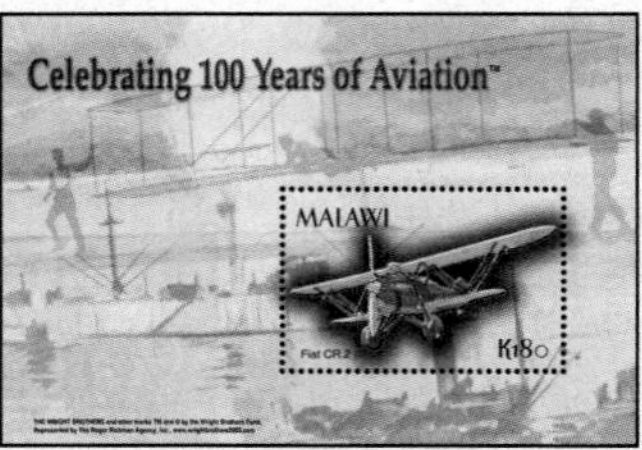

Powered Flight, Cent. (in 2003) — A157

No. 725: a, Vickers Vimy. b, D.H. 9A. c, Messerschmidt Bf. d, Mitsubishi A6M3.

180k, Fiat CR-2.

2004, Feb. 6 ***Perf. 14***

725 A157 75k Sheet of 4, #a-d 5.75 5.75

Souvenir Sheet

726 A157 180k multi 3.50 3.50

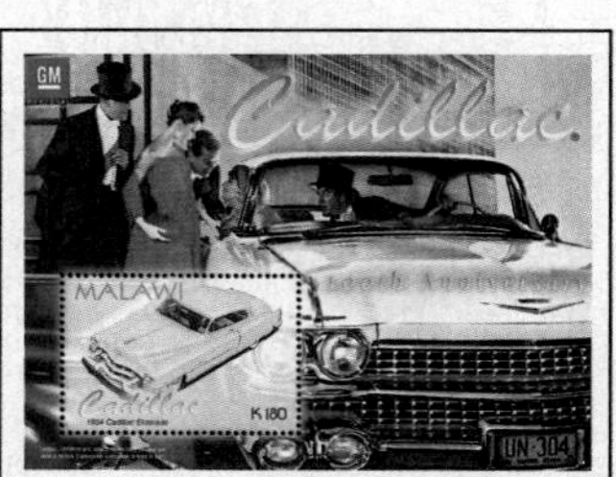

General Motors Automobiles — A158

No. 727, 75k — Cadillacs: a, 1959 Eldorado. b, 1962 Series 62. c, 1961 Sedan De Ville. d, 1930 V-16.

No. 728, 75k — Corvettes: a, 1965 convertible. b, 1965 Stingray. c, 1979. d, 1998.

No. 729, 180k, 1954 Cadillac Eldorado. No. 730, 180k, 1998 Corvette, diff.

2004, Feb. 6 Litho. ***Perf. 14***
Sheets of 4, #a-d

727-728 A158 Set of 2 11.50 11.50

Souvenir Sheets

729-730 A158 Set of 2 6.75 6.75

The following items inscribed "Malawi" have been declared "illegal" by Malawi postal officials:

Souvenir sheets of three 80k stamps depicting Birds of prey; cats; locomotives; Ferrari Formula 1 cars.

Miniature Sheet

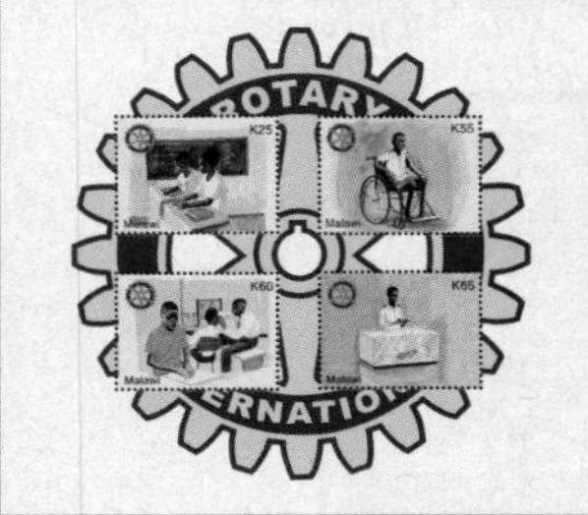

Rotary International, Cent. — A159

No. 731: a, 25k, Boys in classroom. b, 55k, Boy in wheelchair. c, 60k, Doctor examining patient. d, 65k, Nurse monitoring baby in incubator.

2005, July 25 Litho. ***Perf. 13¼***

731 A159 Sheet of 4, #a-d 3.50 3.50

POSTAGE DUE STAMPS

D1

Wmk. 357
1967, Sept. 1 Litho. ***Perf. 11½***

J1 D1 1p deep lilac rose .20 *4.50*
J2 D1 2p sepia .20 *4.50*
J3 D1 4p lilac .25 *5.00*
J4 D1 6p dark blue .35 *5.50*
J5 D1 8p emerald .50 *6.00*
J6 D1 1sh black .60 *6.00*
Nos. J1-J6 (6) 2.10 *31.50*

Values in Decimal Currency

1971, Feb. 15
Size: 18x23mm

J7 D1 2t sepia .20 *4.25*
J8 D1 4t lilac .40 *4.25*
J9 D1 6t dark blue .65 *4.50*
J10 D1 8t green .85 *4.50*
J11 D1 10t black 1.10 *4.50*
Nos. J7-J11 (5) 3.20 *22.00*

Type of 1971 Redrawn

1975 Wmk. 357 ***Perf. 14***
Size: 17x21mm

J12 D1 2t brown 1.75 *3.25*

No. J12 has accent mark over "W."

1977-78 Litho. Unwmk. ***Perf. 14***
Size: 18x21mm

J13 D1 2t sepia 8.00 4.50
J14 D1 4t rose lilac 8.00 4.50
J15 D1 8t brt green ('78) 3.50 *4.50*
J16 D1 10t black 8.00 5.25
Nos. J13-J16 (4) 27.50 18.75

1982 Wmk. 357, Sideways

J13a D1 2t .50 *1.00*
J14a D1 4t .50 *1.00*
J16a D1 10t .50 *1.00*
Nos. J13a-J16a (3) 1.50 *3.00*

1989 Litho. Unwmk. ***Perf. 15x14***
Size: 18x20½mm

J13b D1 2t .40 *.50*
J14b D1 4t .40 *.50*
J15a D1 8t .40 *.50*
J16b D1 10t .40 *.50*
Nos. J13b-J16b (4) 1.60 *2.00*

MALAYA

mə-'lā-ə

Federated Malay States

LOCATION — Malay peninsula
GOVT. — British Protectorate
AREA — 27,585 sq. mi.
CAPITAL — Kuala Lumpur

The Federated Malay States consisted of the sultanates of Negri Sembilan, Pahang, Perak and Selangor.

Stamps of the Federated Malay States replaced those of the individual states and were used until 1935, when individual issues were resumed.

100 Cents = 1 Dollar

Catalogue values for unused stamps in this country are for Never Hinged items, beginning with Scott 80 in the regular postage section, Scott J20 in the postage due section, Scott 128 in Johore, Scott 55 in Kedah, Scott 44 in Kelantan, Scott 1 in Malacca, Scott 36 in Negri Sembilan, Scott 44 in Pahang, Scott 1 in Penang, Scott 99 in Perak, Scott 1 in Perlis, Scott 74 in Selangor, and Scott 47 in Trengganu.

Watermarks

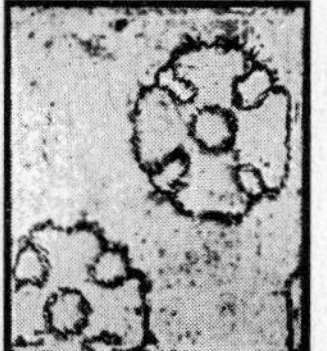

Wmk. 47 — Multiple Rosettes

Wmk. 71 — Rosette

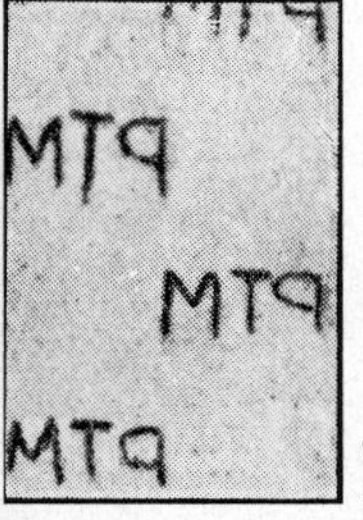

Wmk. 338 — PTM Multiple

(PTM stands for Persekutuan Tanah Melayu, or Federation of Malaya.)

Stamps of Straits Settlements overprinted "BMA MALAYA" are listed in Straits Settlements.

Stamps and Type of Negri Sembilan Overprinted in Black

1900 Wmk. 2 *Perf. 14*

No.	Type	Description	Unused	Used
1	A2	1c lilac & green	3.50	*9.00*
2	A2	2c lilac & brown	35.00	*77.50*
3	A2	3c lilac & black	3.25	*4.75*
4	A2	5c lilac & olive	85.00	*200.00*
5	A2	10c lilac & org	11.50	*35.00*
6	A2	20c green & olive	100.00	*125.00*
7	A2	25c grn & car rose	300.00	*425.00*
8	A2	50c green & black	110.00	*160.00*
		Nos. 1-8 (8)	648.25	*1,036.*

Overprinted on Perak Nos. 51, 53, 57-58, 60-61

1900

No.	Type	Description	Unused	Used
9	A9	5c lilac & olive	24.00	*65.00*
10	A9	10c lilac & org	90.00	*80.00*

Wmk. 1

No.	Type	Description	Unused	Used
11	A10	$1 green & lt grn	210.00	275.00
12	A10	$2 green & car rose	175.00	275.00
13	A10	$5 green & ultra	500.00	*725.00*
13A	A10	$25 green & org	*11,500.*	
		Revenue cancel		275.00
		Nos. 9-13 (5)	999.00	*1,420.*

No. 10 with bar omitted is an essay.

Elephants and Howdah — A3

Tiger — A4

Stamps of type A4 are watermarked sideways.

1900 Typo.

No.	Type	Description	Unused	Used
14	A3	$1 green & lt green	150.00	160.00
15	A3	$2 grn & car rose	160.00	175.00
16	A3	$5 green & ultra	350.00	400.00
17	A3	$25 grn & orange	3,750.	1,950.
		Nos. 14-17 (4)	4,410.	2,685.

High values with revenue cancellations are plentiful and inexpensive.

1901 Wmk. 2

No.	Type	Description	Unused	Used
18a	A4	1c green & gray	4.75	1.25
19b	A4	3c brn & gray brn	7.75	.25
20a	A4	4c carmine & gray	10.00	5.75
21	A4	5c scar & grn, *yel*	3.00	3.75
22a	A4	8c ultra & gray	24.00	8.50
23a	A4	10c violet & gray	90.00	10.00
24	A4	20c black & gray vio	26.00	12.00
25b	A4	50c brn org & gray brn	110.00	50.00
		Nos. 18a-25b (8)	275.50	91.50

1904-10 Wmk. 3

No.	Type	Description	Unused	Used
26a	A4	1c grn & gray brn	45.00	.85
27	A4	3c brown & gray	77.50	1.25
28	A4	4c rose & black	7.75	1.00
29	A4	5c scar & grn, *yel*	13.00	3.25
30c	A4	8c ultra & gray brn ('07)	11.00	5.75
31c	A4	10c claret & black	32.50	.75
32	A4	20c blk & gray vio ('05)	11.50	1.50
33b	A4	50c org brn & gr brn ('06)	18.00	9.25

The 1c and 4c are on ordinary paper, the other values on both ordinary and chalky papers. The least expensive varieties are shown. For comprehensive listing, see *Scott Classic Specialized Catalogue.*

Chalky Paper

No.	Type	Description	Unused	Used
34	A3	$1 green & lt green ('07)	90.00	57.50
35	A3	$2 green & car rose ('06)	105.00	140.00
36	A3	$5 grn & ultra ('06)	225.00	*160.00*
		Revenue cancellation		22.50
37	A3	$25 grn & org ('10)	1,600.	975.00
		Revenue cancellation		42.50
		Nos. 26a-37 (12)	2,236.	*1,356.*

High values with revenue cancellations are plentiful and inexpensive.

1906-22 Ordinary Paper

Two dies for Nos. 38 and 44:
I — Thick line under "Malay."
II — Thin line under "Malay."

No.	Type	Description	Unused	Used
38	A4	1c dull grn, die II	6.00	.20
b.		Die I	15.00	.55
39	A4	1c brown ('19)	3.50	1.50
40	A4	2c green ('19)	2.50	.55
41	A4	3c brown	10.50	.20
42	A4	3c carmine ('09)	3.50	.20
43	A4	3c dp gray ('19)	2.25	.20
44	A4	4c scar, die II	2.25	.20
b.		Die I ('19)	3.75	5.50
45	A4	6c orange ('19)	3.50	3.00
46	A4	8c ultra ('09)	21.00	1.60
47	A4	10c ultra ('19)	10.50	2.25
48	A4	35c red, *yellow*	9.00	*20.00*
		Nos. 38-48 (11)	74.50	29.90

1922-32 Wmk. 4

Ordinary Paper

No.	Type	Description	Unused	Used
49	A4	1c brown ('22)	2.75	3.00
50	A4	1c black ('23)	.85	.25
51	A4	2c dk brown ('25)	5.75	3.00
52	A4	2c green ('26)	.95	.20
53	A4	3c dp gray ('23)	4.25	7.00
54	A4	3c green ('24)	3.50	2.75
55	A4	3c brown ('27)	.95	.50
56	A4	4c scar (II) ('23)	3.50	.60
57	A4	4c orange ('26)	.80	.20
c.		Unwatermarked	*475.00*	*300.00*
58	A4	5c vio, *yel* ('22)	1.25	.20
59	A4	5c dk brown ('32)	2.40	.20
60	A4	6c orange ('22)	.80	.55
61	A4	6c scarlet ('26)	1.25	.20
62	A4	10c ultra ('23)	1.90	*7.75*
63	A4	10c ultra & blk ('23)	2.75	.80
64	A4	10c vio, *yel* ('31)	9.00	.55
65	A4	12c ultra ('22)	1.90	.20
66	A4	20c blk & vio ('23)	7.00	.25

Chalky Paper

No.	Type	Description	Unused	Used
67	A4	25c red vio & ol vio ('29)	3.50	1.25
68	A4	30c yel & dl vio ('29)	4.75	2.40
69	A4	35c red, *yel* ('28)	9.00	*21.00*
70	A4	35c dk vio & car ('31)	19.00	17.50
71	A4	50c org & blk ('24)	19.00	5.75
72	A4	50c blk, *bl grn* ('31)	6.25	1.90
73	A3	$1 gray grn & yel grn ('26)	19.00	*42.50*
a.		$1 green & blue green	24.00	*60.00*
74	A3	$2 grn & car ('26)	24.00	*87.50*
75	A3	$5 grn & ultra ('25)	95.00	*160.00*
76	A3	$25 grn & org ('28)	1,200.	875.00
		Nos. 49-75 (27)	251.05	*368.00*

#64 is on chalky paper; #66 exists on both ordinary and chalky paper; #69 is on ordinary paper.

1931-34

No.	Type	Description	Unused	Used
77	A4	$1 red & blk, *blue*	17.50	4.75
78	A4	$2 car & green, *yel* ('34)	55.00	50.00
79	A4	$5 car & green, *emer* ('34)	225.00	*240.00*
		Nos. 77-79 (3)	297.50	*294.75*

FEDERATION OF MALAYA

GOVT. — Sovereign state in British Commonwealth of Nations
AREA — 50,700 sq. mi.
POP. — 7,139,000 (est. 1961)
CAPITAL — Kuala Lumpur

The Federation comprised the nine states of Johore, Pahang, Negri Sembilan, Selangor, Perak, Kedah, Perlis, Kelantan and Trengganu and the settlements of Penang and Malacca.

Malaya joined the Federation of Malaysia in 1963.

100 Sen (Cents) = 1 Dollar (1957)

Catalogue values for unused stamps in this section are for Never Hinged items.

The Peace Issue of 1946 8c stamp inscribed "MALAYAN UNION" was not issued.

Rubber Tapping — A5

Map of Federation — A6

Designs: 12c, Federation coat of arms. 25c, Tin dredge and flag.

Perf. 13x12½, 12½

Engr., Litho.

1957, May 5 Wmk. 314

No.	Type	Description	Unused	Used
80	A5	6c blue, red & yel	1.00	.30
a.		Yellow omitted	45.00	
81	A5	12c car & multi	1.75	1.10
82	A5	25c multicolored	3.75	.40
83	A6	30c dp claret & red org	1.40	.30
		Nos. 80-83 (4)	7.90	2.10

Chief Minister Tunku Abdul Rahman and People of Various Races — A7

Perf. 12½

1957, Aug. 31 Wmk. 4 Engr.

No.	Type	Description	Unused	Used
84	A7	10c brown	.70	.70

Independence Day, Aug. 31.

United Nations Emblem — A8

Design: 30c, UN emblem, vert.

Perf. 13½, 12½

1958, Mar. 5 Wmk. 314

No.	Type	Description	Unused	Used
85	A8	12c rose red	.45	*1.00*
86	A8	30c plum	.65	*1.00*

Conf. of the Economic Commission for Asia and the Far East (ECAFE), Kuala Lumpur, Mar. 5-15.

Merdeka Stadium and Flag — A9

Tuanku Abdul Rahman, Paramount Ruler of Malaya — A10

Perf. 13½x14½, 14½x13½

1958, Aug. 31 Photo. Wmk. 314

No.	Type	Description	Unused	Used
87	A9	10c multicolored	.30	.30
88	A10	30c multicolored	.75	*1.10*

1st anniv. of the Independence of the Federation of Malaya.

A11

Torch of Freedom and Broken Chain — A12

Perf. 12½x13, 13x12½

1958, Dec. 10 Litho. Wmk. 314

89 A11 10c multicolored .25 .25

Photo.

90 A12 30c green .80 .80

10th anniv. of the signing of the Universal Declaration of Human Rights.

Mace and People — A13

WRY Emblem A14

Perf. 12½x13½

1959, Sept. 12 Photo. Unwmk.

91 A13 4c rose red .30 .30
92 A13 10c violet .30 .30
93 A13 25c yellow green .60 .40
Nos. 91-93 (3) 1.20 1.00

1st Federal Parliament of Malaya, inauguration.

Perf. 13½, 13

1960, Apr. 7 Engr. Wmk. 314

Design: 30c, Similar to 12c, vert.

94 A14 12c lilac .30 *.95*
95 A14 30c dark green .30 .30

World Refugee Year, 7/1/59-6/30/60.

Rubber Tree Seedling on Map of Malaya — A15

Tuanku Syed Putra — A16

Perf. 13x13½

1960, Sept. 19 Litho. Unwmk.

96 A15 6s red brn, grn & blk .20 *1.10*
97 A15 30s ultra, yel grn & blk .70 .70

15th meeting of the Intl. Rubber Study Group and the Natural Rubber Research Conference, Kuala Lumpur, Sept. 26-Oct. 1.

Perf. 13½x14½

1961, Jan. 4 Photo. Wmk. 314

98 A16 10s blue & black .50 .50

Installation of Tuanku Syed Putra of Perlis as Paramount Ruler (Yang di-Pertuan Agong.)

Colombo Plan Emblem — A17

Malaria Eradication Emblem — A18

1961, Oct. 30 Unwmk. *Perf. 13½*

99 A17 12s rose pink & black .55 *3.50*
100 A17 25s brt yellow & black 1.40 *3.50*
101 A17 30s brt blue & black 1.10 .80
Nos. 99-101 (3) 3.05 7.80

13th meeting of the Consultative Committee for Technical Co-operation in South and South East Asia, Kuala Lumpur, Oct. 30-Nov. 18.

Wmk. PTM Multiple (338)

1962, Apr. 7 *Perf. 14x14½*

102 A18 25s orange brown .35 *.70*
103 A18 30s dull violet .35 .30
104 A18 50s ultramarine .70 .70
Nos. 102-104 (3) 1.40 1.70

WHO drive to eradicate malaria.

Palmyra Leaf A19

1962, July 21 Photo. *Perf. 13½*

105 A19 10s violet & gldn brown .35 .35
106 A19 20s bluish grn & gldn brn .80 *1.25*
107 A19 50s car rose & gldn brn 2.25 *2.40*
Nos. 105-107 (3) 3.40 4.00

National Language Month. Watermark inverted on alternating stamps.

Children and their Future Shadows — A20

1962, Oct. 1 Wmk. 338 *Perf. 13½*

108 A20 10s bright rose lilac .20 .20
109 A20 25s ocher .70 .95
110 A20 30s bright green 3.00 .20
Nos. 108-110 (3) 3.90 1.35

Free primary education introduced Jan. 1962.

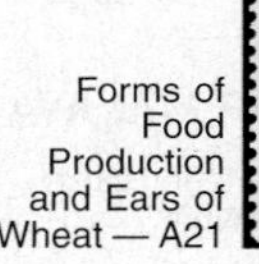

Forms of Food Production and Ears of Wheat — A21

1963, Mar. 21 Unwmk. *Perf. 11½*

Granite Paper

111 A21 25s lt ol grn & lilac rose 3.00 *4.00*
112 A21 30s dk car & lilac rose 3.25 1.75
113 A21 50s ultra & lilac rose 3.25 *4.00*
Nos. 111-113 (3) 9.50 9.75

FAO "Freedom from Hunger" campaign.

Cameron Highlands Dam and Pylon — A22

1963, June 26 Wmk. 338 *Perf. 14*

114 A22 20s purple & brt green .80 .25
115 A22 30s ultra & brt green 1.25 1.25

Opening of the Cameron Highlands hydroelectric plant.

Check listings for individual states for additional stamps inscribed "Malaya."

POSTAGE DUE STAMPS

D1

D2

Perf. 14½x14

1924-26 Typo. Wmk. 4

J1 D1 1c violet 4.25 7.75
J2 D1 2c black 2.50 3.50
J3 D1 4c green ('26) 4.75 *12.00*
J4 D1 8c red 8.75 *19.00*
J5 D1 10c orange 10.00 *17.50*
J6 D1 12c ultramarine 14.50 *25.00*
Nos. J1-J6 (6) 44.75 *84.75*

1936-38 *Perf. 14½x14*

J7 D2 1c dk violet ('38) 7.00 1.50
J8 D2 4c yellow green 19.00 1.90
J9 D2 8c scarlet 9.00 *7.50*
J10 D2 10c yel orange 12.00 .65
J11 D2 12c blue violet 15.00 *22.50*
J12 D2 50c black ('38) 47.50 *12.00*
Nos. J7-J12 (6) 109.50 *46.05*

#J7-J12 were also used in Straits Settlements.

For overprints see #NJ1-NJ20, Malacca #NJ1-NJ6.

1945-49

J13 D2 1c reddish violet 4.00 2.40
J14 D2 3c yel green 9.25 16.00
J15 D2 5c org scarlet 9.25 *19.00*
J16 D2 8c yel org ('49) 17.50 16.00
J17 D2 9c yel orange 55.00 55.00
J18 D2 15c blue vio 140.00 55.00
J19 D2 20c dk blue ('48) 12.50 19.00
Nos. J13-J19 (7) 247.50 182.40

For surcharge see No. J34.

Catalogue values for unused stamps in this section, from this point to the end of the section, are for Never Hinged items.

1951-62 Wmk. 4 *Perf. 14*

J20 D2 1c dull violet ('52) .40 1.75
J21 D2 2c dk gray ('53) .95 2.25
J22 D2 3c green ('52) 24.00 13.00
J23 D2 4c dk brown ('53) .50 5.00
J24 D2 5c vermilion 52.50 13.00
J25 D2 8c yel orange 2.50 4.50
J26 D2 12c magenta ('54) 1.25 6.50
J27 D2 20c deep blue 3.75 6.75
Nos. J20-J27 (8) 85.85 52.75

Nos. J13-J27 were used throughout the Federation and in Singapore, later in Malaysia.

1957-62 *Perf. 12½*

J21a D2 2c ('60) .50 *12.00*
J23a D2 4c ('60) .95 *16.00*
J26a D2 12c ('62) 2.25 *26.00*
J27a D2 20c 8.25 *32.50*
Nos. J21a-J27a (4) 11.95 *86.50*

1965 Wmk. 314 *Perf. 12*

J28 D2 1c plum .35 *3.50*
J29 D2 2c bluish black 1.10 *9.00*
J30 D2 4c brown 1.60 *13.50*
J31 D2 8c yel orange 3.00 *18.00*
J32 D2 12c magenta 2.25 *35.00*
J33 D2 20c dark blue 4.00 *50.00*
Nos. J28-J33 (6) 12.30 *129.00*

Nos. J28-J33 were used in Malaysia.

1964, Apr. 14 *Perf. 12½*

J28a D2 1c .50 *13.00*
J29a D2 2c 1.00 *16.00*
J30a D2 4c .75 *13.00*
J32a D2 12c 4.25 *26.00*
J33a D2 20c 6.50 *42.50*
Nos. J28a-J33a (5) 13.00 *110.50*

No. J16 Surcharged

1965, Jan. Wmk. 4

J34 D2 10c on 8c yel orange .45 *2.50*

OCCUPATION STAMPS

Issued Under Japanese Occupation

Malayan Fruit and Fronds OS1

Tin Dredging OS2

Monument to Japanese War Dead OS3

Malayan Plowman OS4

1943 Unwmk. Litho. *Perf. 12½*

N30 OS1 2c emerald .20 .20
a. Rouletted 2.25 2.25
b. Imperf., pair 6.50 6.50
N31 OS2 4c rose red .25 .20
a. Rouletted 2.25 2.25
b. Imperf., pair 6.50 6.50
N32 OS3 8c dull blue .20 .20
Nos. N30-N32 (3) .65 .60

1943, Sept. 1

N33 OS4 8c violet 11.00 4.25
N34 OS4 15c carmine red 9.75 4.25

Publicity for Postal Savings which had reached a $10,000,000 total in Malaya.

Rubber Tapping OS5

Seaside Houses OS6

Japanese Shrine, Singapore OS7

Sago Palms OS8

Johore Bahru and Strait of Johore OS9

Malay Mosque, Kuala Lumpur OS10

1943, Oct. 1

N35 OS5 1c gray green .40 .80
N36 OS5 3c olive gray .40 .25
N37 OS6 10c red brown .40 .25
N38 OS7 15c violet .70 2.00
N39 OS8 30c olive green .70 .70
N40 OS9 50c blue 1.60 1.60
N41 OS10 70c dull blue 22.50 18.00
Nos. N35-N41 (7) 26.70 23.60

Rice Planting and Map of Malaysia — OS11

1944, Feb. 15

N42	OS11	8c carmine	9.75	4.50
N43	OS11	15c violet	5.75	4.50

Issued on the anniversary of the fall of Singapore to commemorate the "Birth of New Malaya".

OCCUPATION POSTAGE DUE STAMPS

Stamps and Type of Postage Due Stamps of 1936-38 Handstamped in Black, Red or Brown

No. NJ7

1942 Wmk. 4 *Perf. 14½x14*

NJ1	D2	1c violet	15.00	*26.00*
NJ2	D2	3c yellow green	62.50	*70.00*
NJ3	D2	4c yellow green	42.50	32.50
NJ4	D2	8c red	85.00	72.50
NJ5	D2	10c yellow orange	27.50	*42.50*
NJ6	D2	12c blue violet	27.50	*52.50*
NJ7	D2	50c black	70.00	*85.00*
		Nos. NJ1-NJ7 (7)	330.00	381.00

Overprinted in Black

DAI NIPPON
2602
MALAYA

1942

NJ8	D2	1c violet	2.00	*10.50*
NJ9	D2	3c yel green	14.50	*21.00*
NJ10	D2	4c yel green	13.00	*13.50*
NJ11	D2	8c red	18.00	*19.00*
NJ12	D2	10c yel orange	2.00	*13.50*
NJ13	D2	12c blue violet	2.00	*29.00*
		Nos. NJ8-NJ13 (6)	51.50	106.50

The 9c and 15c with this overprint were not regularly issued.

Postage Due Stamps of 1936-45 Overprinted

1943

NJ14	D2	1c reddish vio	1.25	*4.00*
NJ15	D2	3c yel green	1.25	*4.00*
NJ15A	D2	4c yel green	50.00	*52.50*
NJ16	D2	5c scarlet	1.25	*4.75*
NJ17	D2	9c yel orange	.90	*6.75*
NJ18	D2	10c yel orange	1.00	*6.75*
NJ19	D2	12c blue violet	1.60	*13.50*
NJ20	D2	15c blue violet	1.60	*6.75*
		Nos. NJ14-NJ20 (8)	58.85	99.00

#NJ15A is said to have been extensively forged.

ISSUED UNDER THAI OCCUPATION

For use in Kedah, Kelantan, Perlis and Trengganu

War Memorial — OS1

Perf. 12½

1943, Dec. Unwmk. Litho.

2N1	OS1	1c pale yellow	42.50	*45.00*
2N2	OS1	2c buff	16.00	*29.00*
2N3	OS1	3c pale green	27.50	*52.50*
a.		Imperf., pair	975.00	
2N4	OS1	4c dull lilac	20.00	*40.00*
2N5	OS1	8c rose	20.00	*29.00*
2N6	OS1	15c lt blue	52.50	*85.00*
		Nos. 2N1-2N6 (6)	178.50	*280.50*

These stamps, in cent denominations, were for use only in the four Malayan states ceded to Thailand by the Japanese. The states reverted to British rule in September, 1945.

JOHORE

jə-'hōr

LOCATION — At the extreme south of the Malay Peninsula.
AREA — 7,330 sq. mi.
POP. — 1,009,649 (1960)
CAPITAL — Johore Bahru

Stamps of the Straits Settlements Overprinted in Black

Overprinted

1876 Wmk. 1 *Perf. 14*

1	A2	2c brown	20,000.	5,750.

Overprinted

Overprint 13 to 14mm Wide

1884-86 Wmk. 2

1A	A2	2c rose	210.00	*225.00*
c.		Double overprint	1,200.	

Without Period

Overprint 16 to 17x2mm

2	A2	2c rose	2,200.	725.00
a.		Double overprint		2,275.

Overprinted

Overprint 11x2½mm

3	A2	2c rose	115.00	*125.00*

Overprinted JOHORE

Overprint 17½x2¾mm

4	A2	2c rose	*9,000.*	—

Overprinted

Overprint 12½ to 15x2¾mm

5	A2	2c rose	17.00	*22.50*

Overprinted

Overprint 9x2½mm

6	A2	2c brown		
7	A2	2c rose	67.50	*67.50*
a.		Double overprint	900.00	

Overprinted

Overprint 9x3mm

8	A2	2c rose	57.50	60.00

Overprinted

Overprint 14 to 15x3mm

9	A2	2c rose	16.00	12.00

Tall "J" 3½mm high

10	A2	2c rose	140.00	*125.00*

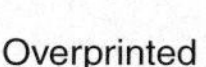

Overprinted

Overprint 15 to 15½x3mm

11	A2	2c rose	175.00	72.50

Overprinted

1891

Overprint 12½ to 13x2½mm

12	A2	2c rose	20.00	20.00

Overprint 12x2¾mm

13	A2	2c rose	*11,000.*	

Surcharged in Black:

JOHOR Two CENTS
a

JOHOR Two CENTS
b

c

JOHOR Two CENTS
d

1891

14	A3(a)	2c on 24c green	50.00	*67.50*
15	A3(b)	2c on 24c green	160.00	175.00
16	A3(c)	2c on 24c green	32.50	47.50
a.		"CENST"	1,100.	575.00
17	A3(d)	2c on 24c green	150.00	160.00
		Nos. 14-17 (4)	392.50	450.00

Sultan Abubakar — A5

1892-94 Typo. Unwmk.

18	A5	1c lilac & vio ('94)	.85	.60
19	A5	2c lilac & yellow	.75	*1.75*
20	A5	3c lil & car rose ('94)	.75	.60
21	A5	4c lilac & black	3.25	*22.50*
22	A5	5c lilac & green	8.50	*25.00*
23	A5	6c lilac & blue	9.50	*25.00*
24	A5	$1 green & car rose	90.00	*200.00*
		Nos. 18-24 (7)	113.60	*275.45*

For surcharges and overprints see #26-36.

Stamps of 1892-94 Surcharged in Black

1894

26	A5	3c on 4c lilac & blk	3.00	.65
a.		No period after "Cents"	115.00	85.00
27	A5	3c on 5c lilac & grn	2.40	4.25
a.		No period after "Cents"	275.00	175.00
28	A5	3c on 6c lilac & bl	4.25	5.00
a.		No period after "Cents"	210.00	240.00
29	A5	3c on $1 green & car	14.50	85.00
a.		No period after "Cents"	500.00	900.00
		Nos. 26-29 (4)	24.15	94.90

Coronation Issue

Stamps of 1892-94 Overprinted "KEMAHKOTAAN"

1896

30	A5	1c lilac & violet	.70	1.25
31	A5	2c lilac & yellow	.60	1.40
32	A5	3c lilac & car rose	1.60	1.40
33	A5	4c lilac & black	1.40	3.00
34	A5	5c lilac & green	7.75	10.00
35	A5	6c lilac & blue	7.25	*8.75*
36	A5	$1 green & car rose	60.00	125.00
		Nos. 30-36 (7)	79.30	150.80

Overprinted "KETAHKOTAAN"

30a	A5	1c	4.50	*6.00*
31a	A5	2c	5.75	*8.50*
32a	A5	3c	11.00	*13.00*
33a	A5	4c	4.00	*14.50*
34a	A5	5c	5.00	*10.50*
35a	A5	6c	9.00	*13.00*
36a	A5	$1	45.00	*190.00*
		Nos. 30a-36a (7)	84.25	*255.50*

Coronation of Sultan Ibrahim.

Sultan Ibrahim — A7

1896-99 Typo. Wmk. 71

37	A7	1c green	1.00	1.75
38	A7	2c green & blue	.60	.50
39	A7	3c green & vio	4.75	3.00
40	A7	4c grn & car rose	1.25	2.40
41	A7	4c yel & red ('99)	1.75	1.25
42	A7	5c green & brn	2.40	3.50
43	A7	6c green & yel	2.40	5.00
44	A7	10c green & black	10.50	*57.50*
45	A7	25c green & vio	11.50	*50.00*
46	A7	50c grn & car rose	21.00	*55.00*
47	A7	$1 lilac & green	37.50	*90.00*
48	A7	$2 lilac & car rose	47.50	*100.00*
49	A7	$3 lilac & blue	42.50	*140.00*
50	A7	$4 lilac & brn	42.50	*100.00*
51	A7	$5 lilac & orange	92.50	*160.00*
		Nos. 37-51 (15)	319.65	*769.90*

On Nos. 44-46 the numerals are on white tablets. Numerals of Nos. 48-51 are on tablets of solid color.

Stamps of 1896-1926 with revenue cancellations sell for a fraction of those used postally.

For surcharges see Nos. 52-58.

Nos. 40-41 Surcharged in Black

1903

52	A7	3c on 4c yel & red	1.25	1.25
a.		Without bars	4.00	*6.50*
53	A7	10c on 4c grn & car rose	3.50	4.75
a.		Without bars	35.00	*55.00*

Bars on Nos. 52-53 were handruled with pen and ink.

Surcharged

54 A7 50c on $3 lilac & blue 35.00 *87.50*

Surcharged

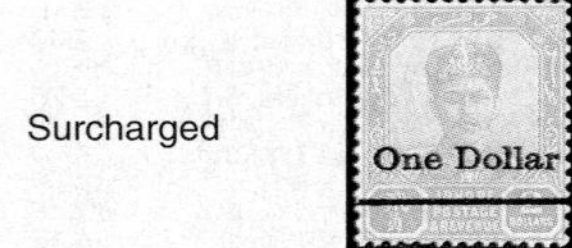

55 A7 $1 on $2 lilac & car rose 75.00 *140.00*
a. Inverted "e" in "one" 1,600.

Surcharged

1904

56 A7 10c on 4c yel & red 29.00 42.50
a. Double surcharge 9,800.
57 A7 10c on 4c grn & car rose 10.50 *40.00*
58 A7 50c on $5 lil & org 65.00 125.00
Nos. 56-58 (3) 104.50 207.50

Sultan Ibrahim — A8

The 10c, 21c, 25c, 50c, and $10 to $500 denominations of type A8 show the numerals on white tablets. The numerals of the 8c, 30c, 40c, and $2 to $5 demonimations are shown on tablets of solid colors.

1904-08 Typo. Wmk. 71

59 A8 1c violet & green .80 .20
60 A8 2c vio & brn org 1.50 2.40
61 A8 3c violet & black 1.50 .25
62 A8 4c violet & red 9.25 1.50
63 A8 5c violet & ol grn 1.10 3.00
64 A8 8c violet & blue 3.00 6.25
65 A8 10c violet & black 40.00 11.00
66 A8 25c violet & green 40.00 *24.00*
67 A8 50c violet & red 40.00 17.50
68 A8 $1 green & vio 19.00 *72.50*
69 A8 $2 green & car 27.50 *62.50*
70 A8 $3 green & blue 32.50 *87.50*
71 A8 $4 green & brn 35.00 *125.00*
72 A8 $5 green & org 47.50 *100.00*
73 A8 $10 green & blk 65.00 *150.00*
74 A8 $50 green & blue *225.00* *300.00*
75 A8 $100 green & scar *425.00* *625.00*
Revenue cancel 47.50
Nos. 59-73 (15) 363.65 *663.60*

The 1c, 2c and 10c also exist on chalky paper.

Nos. 74 and 75 were theoretically available for postage but were mostly used for revenue purposes.

For surcharge see No. 86.

1910-18 Wmk. 47

Chalky Paper

76 A8 1c violet & green .25 .20
77 A8 2c violet & orange 5.50 .80
78 A8 3c violet & black 4.00 .80
79 A8 4c violet & red 3.00 .95
80 A8 5c violet & ol grn 2.75 .80
81 A8 8c violet & blue 5.00 5.50
82 A8 10c violet & black 30.00 3.00
83 A8 25c violet & green 5.50 *27.50*
84 A8 50c violet & red 72.50 *92.50*
85 A8 $1 green & vio 77.50 *87.50*
Nos. 76-85 (10) 206.00 *219.55*

#78-79, 82 exist with horizontal watermark.

No. 64 Surcharged

1912 Wmk. 71

86 A8 3c on 8c vio & blue 2.40 4.75
a. "T" of "CENTS" omitted 475.00

1918-19 Typo. Wmk. 3

Chalky Paper

87 A8 2c violet & orange .95 1.90
88 A8 2c vio & grn ('19) .60 .85
89 A8 4c violet & red .70 .20
90 A8 5c vio & olive grn ('19) 1.90 2.75
91 A8 10c violet & blue 1.90 1.90
92 A8 21c violet & orange 3.50 5.50
93 A8 25c vio & grn ('19) 10.00 19.00
94 A8 50c vio & red ('19) 24.00 40.00
95 A8 $1 grn & red vio 14.00 55.00
96 A8 $2 green & scar 30.00 55.00
97 A8 $3 green & blue 35.00 92.50
98 A8 $4 green & brn 55.00 125.00
99 A8 $5 green & org 72.50 125.00
100 A8 $10 green & blk 150.00 *240.00*
Nos. 87-100 (14) 400.05 *764.60*

1921-40 Wmk. 4

101 A8 1c vio & blk .20 .20
102 A8 2c violet & brn .85 1.60
103 A8 2c green & dk grn ('28) .20 .20
104 A8 3c green ('25) 2.25 4.25
105 A8 3c dull vio & brn ('28) 1.40 1.50
106 A8 4c vio & red 2.25 .20
107 A8 5c vio & ol grn .50 .20
108 A8 6c vio & red brn .25 .20
109 A8 10c vio & blue 24.00 40.00
110 A8 10c vio & yel ('22) .50 .20
111 A8 12c vio & blue 1.50 1.90
111A A8 12c ultra ('40) 42.50 7.75
112 A8 21c dull vio & org ('28) 3.50 3.50
113 A8 25c vio & green 1.90 1.25
114 A8 30c dull vio & org ('36) 3.50 3.00
115 A8 40c dull vio & brn ('36) 3.50 *5.00*
116 A8 50c violet & red 3.50 1.50
117 A8 $1 grn & red vio 3.50 1.10
118 A8 $2 grn & red 7.75 5.50
119 A8 $3 grn & blue 55.00 72.50
120 A8 $4 grn & brn ('26) 92.50 150.00
121 A8 $5 grn & org 62.50 *72.50*
122 A8 $10 grn & blk 190.00 *240.00*
123 A8 $50 grn & ultra 775.00
124 A8 $100 grn & red 1,900.
125 A8 $500 ultra & org brn ('26) *26,500.*
Revenue cancel 190.00
Nos. 101-122 (23) 503.55 *614.05*

Nos. 123, 124 and 125 were available for postage but were probably used only fiscally.

A9

A10

1935, May 15 Engr. *Perf. 12½*

126 A9 8c Sultan Ibrahim, Sultana 5.00 1.50
Never hinged 8.00

1940, Feb. *Perf. 13½*

127 A10 8c Sultan Ibrahim 18.00 .35
Never hinged 27.50

Catalogue values for unused stamps in this section, from this point to the end of the section, are for Never Hinged items.

Silver Wedding Issue

Common Design Types

Inscribed: "Malaya Johore"

Perf. 14x14½

1948, Dec. 1 Wmk. 4 Photo.

128 CD304 10c purple .20 .20

Perf. 11½x11

Engr.; Name Typo.

129 CD305 $5 green 32.50 *55.00*

Common Design Types
Pictured following the introduction.

Sultan Ibrahim — A11

1949-55 Wmk. 4 Typo. *Perf. 18*

130 A11 1c black .45 .30
131 A11 2c orange .45 .30
132 A11 3c green 1.25 .65
133 A11 4c chocolate .45 .30
134 A11 5c rose vio ('52) .55 .30
135 A11 6c gray .70 .30
a. Wmk. 4a (error) 425.00
136 A11 8c rose red 2.25 1.60
137 A11 8c green ('52) 1.25 1.90
138 A11 10c plum .70 .30
a. Imperf., pair *925.00*
139 A11 12c rose red ('52) 1.40 3.50
140 A11 15c ultra 2.25 .90
141 A11 20c dk grn & blk 2.25 1.25
142 A11 20c ultra ('52) 1.50 .40
143 A11 25c org & rose lil 1.75 .30
144 A11 30c plum & rose red ('55) 4.50 3.00
145 A11 35c dk vio & rose red ('52) 3.50 2.75
146 A11 40c dk vio & rose red 4.50 9.00
147 A11 50c ultra & blk 3.25 .40
148 A11 $1 vio brn & ultra 6.25 2.50
149 A11 $2 rose red & emer 22.50 8.00
150 A11 $5 choc & emer 47.50 16.00
Nos. 130-150 (21) 109.20 53.95

UPU Issue

Common Design Types

Inscribed: "Malaya-Johore"

Engr.; Name Typo. on 15c, 25c

1949, Oct. 10 *Perf. 13½, 11x11½*

151 CD306 10c rose violet .50 .20
152 CD307 15c indigo 1.50 1.25
153 CD308 25c orange 1.10 1.90
154 CD309 50c slate 1.90 2.75
Nos. 151-154 (4) 5.00 6.10

Coronation Issue

Common Design Type

1953, June 2 Engr. *Perf. 13½x13*

155 CD312 10c magenta & black 1.40 .35

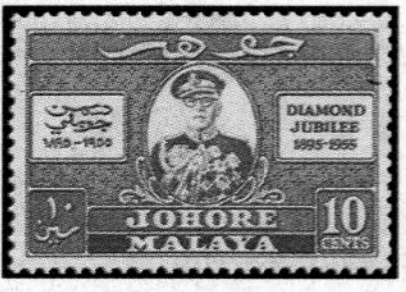

Sultan Ibrahim A12

1955, Nov. 1 Wmk. 4 *Perf. 14*

156 A12 10c carmine lake .50 .35

Sultan Ibrahim's Diamond Jubilee.

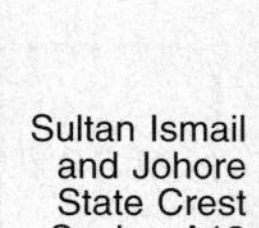

Sultan Ismail and Johore State Crest Seal — A13

Perf. 11½

1960, Feb. 10 Unwmk. Photo.

Granite Paper

157 A13 10c multicolored .45 .35

Coronation of Sultan Ismail.

Types of Kedah 1957 with Portrait of Sultan Ismail

1960 Wmk. 314 Engr. *Perf. 13*

158 A8 1c black .20 .20
159 A8 2c red orange .20 .20
160 A8 4c dark brown .20 .20
161 A8 5c dk car rose .20 .20
162 A8 8c dark green 2.00 *3.00*
163 A7 10c violet brown .40 .20
164 A7 20c blue 2.40 .75
165 A7 50c ultra & black .70 .30
166 A8 $1 plum & ultra 2.10 *3.50*
167 A8 $2 red & green 10.00 *16.00*
168 A8 $5 ol, grn & brn 35.00 *35.00*
Nos. 158-168 (11) 53.40 *59.55*

Starting in 1965, issues of Johore are listed with Malaysia.

POSTAGE DUE STAMPS

D1

Perf. 12½

1938, Jan. 1 Typo. Wmk. 4

J1 D1 1c rose red 10.50 *40.00*
J2 D1 4c green 40.00 *50.00*
J3 D1 8c dull yellow 42.50 *160.00*
J4 D1 10c bister brown 42.50 *62.50*
J5 D1 12c rose violet 62.50 *150.00*
Nos. J1-J5 (5) 198.00 *462.50*

OCCUPATION POSTAGE DUE STAMPS

Issued under Japanese Occupation

Johore Nos. J1-J5 Overprinted in Black, Brown or Red

1942 Wmk. 4 *Perf. 12½*

NJ1 D1 1c rose red 55.00 90.00
NJ2 D1 4c green 72.50 90.00
NJ3 D1 8c dull yellow 85.00 100.00
NJ4 D1 10c bister brown 20.00 60.00
NJ5 D1 12c rose violet 32.50 60.00
Nos. NJ1-NJ5 (5) 265.00 400.00

Johore Nos. J1-J5 Overprinted in Black

1943

NJ6 D1 1c rose red 2.50 *13.00*
NJ7 D1 4c green 2.50 *13.00*
NJ8 D1 8c dull yellow 9.00 *16.00*
NJ9 D1 10c bister brown 6.50 *20.00*
NJ10 D1 12c rose violet 6.50 *26.00*
Nos. NJ6-NJ10 (5) 27.00 *88.00*

Nos. NJ6-NJ10 exist with second character sideways.

KEDAH

'ke-də

LOCATION — On the west coast of the Malay Peninsula.
AREA — 3,660 sq. mi.
POP. — 752,706 (1960)
CAPITAL — Alor Star

Sheaf of Rice — A1

Native Plowing — A2

Council Chamber — A3

1912-21 Engr. Wmk. 3 *Perf. 14*

No.	Type	Description	Unused	Used
1	A1	1c green & black	.70	.30
2	A1	1c brown ('19)	.65	.60
3	A1	2c green ('19)	.60	.35
4	A1	3c car & black	5.50	.35
5	A1	3c dk violet ('19)	.80	1.75
6	A1	4c slate & car	12.00	.30
7	A1	4c scarlet ('19)	5.00	.35
8	A1	5c org brown & grn	2.75	*3.75*
9	A1	8c ultra & blk	4.50	*4.25*
10	A2	10c black brn & bl	2.75	1.25
11	A2	20c yel grn & blk	5.75	*4.75*
12	A2	21c red vio & vio ('19)	6.75	*72.50*
13	A2	25c red vio & bl ('21)	2.10	*32.50*
14	A2	30c car & black	3.75	*13.00*
15	A2	40c lilac & blk	4.25	*18.00*
16	A2	50c dull bl & brn	11.00	*16.00*
17	A3	$1 scar & blk, *yel*	19.00	*26.50*
18	A3	$2 dk brn & dk grn	26.50	*105.00*
19	A3	$3 dk bl & blk, *bl*	90.00	*200.00*
20	A3	$5 car & black	110.00	*210.00*
		Nos. 1-20 (20)	314.35	*711.50*

There are two types of No. 7, one printed from separate plates for frame and center, the other printed from a single plate.

Overprints are listed after No. 45.

Stamps of 1912 Surcharged

1919

No.	Type	Description	Unused	Used
21	A3	50c on $2 dk brn & dk grn	90.00	*90.00*
a.		"C" of ovpt. inserted by hand	1,575.	1,700.
22	A3	$1 on $3 dk bl & blk, *blue*	25.00	*110.00*

1921-36 Wmk. 4

Two types of 1c:

I — The 1's have rounded corners, small top serif. Small letters "c."

II — The 1's have square-cut corners, large top serif. Large letters "c."

Two types of 2c:

I — The 2's have oval drops. Letters "c" are fairly thick and rounded.

II — The 2's have round drops. Letters "c" thin and slightly larger.

No.	Type	Description	Unused	Used
23	A1	1c brown	.90	.20
24	A1	1c blk (I) ('22)	.35	.20
a.		1c black (II) ('39)	42.50	6.30
25	A1	2c green (I)	1.00	.20
a.		2c green (II) ('40)	90.00	13.00
26	A1	3c dk violet	1.60	1.40
27	A1	3c green ('22)	2.75	1.60
28	A1	4c carmine	10.50	.20
29	A1	4c dull vio ('26)	1.90	.20
30	A1	5c yellow ('22)	2.75	.20
31	A1	6c scarlet ('26)	1.40	1.40
32	A1	8c gray ('36)	18.00	.20
33	A2	10c blk brn & bl	3.50	1.60
34	A2	12c dk ultra & blk ('26)	4.50	*8.50*
35	A2	20c green & blk	5.25	4.50
36	A2	21c red vio & vio	4.50	*27.50*
37	A2	25c red vio & bl	4.50	*8.50*
38	A2	30c red & blk ('22)	6.00	*6.00*
39	A2	35c claret ('26)	10.00	*52.50*
40	A2	40c red vio & blk	6.00	*45.00*
41	A2	50c dp blue & brn	4.50	9.75
42	A3	$1 scar & blk, *yel* ('22)	13.50	15.00
43	A3	$2 brn & green	27.50	*150.00*
44	A3	$3 dk bl & blk, *bl*	75.00	*110.00*
45	A3	$5 car & black	97.50	*225.00*
		Nos. 23-45 (23)	303.40	*669.65*

For overprints see Nos. N1-N6.

Stamps of 1912-21 Overprinted in Black: "MALAYA-BORNEO EXHIBITION." in Three Lines

1922 Wmk. 3

No.	Type	Description	Unused	Used
3a	A1	2c green	9.25	*27.50*
12a	A2	21c red vio & vio	32.50	*110.00*
13a	A2	25c red vio & blue	32.50	*125.00*
b.		Inverted overprint	1,200.	
16a	A2	50c dull blue & brn	35.00	*150.00*

Wmk. 4

No.	Type	Description	Unused	Used
23a	A1	1c brown	3.25	*22.50*
26a	A1	3c dark violet	4.75	*42.50*
28a	A1	4c carmine	4.75	*42.50*
33a	A2	10c blk brn & blue	9.25	*57.50*
		Nos. 3a-33a (8)	131.25	*577.50*

Industrial fair at Singapore, Mar. 31-Apr. 15, 1922.

On Nos. 12a, 13a and 16a, "BORNEO" exists both 14mm and 15mm wide.

Sultan of Kedah, Sir Abdul Hamid Halim Shah — A4

1937, July Wmk. 4 *Perf. 12½*

No.	Type	Description	Unused	Used
46	A4	10c sepia & ultra	3.25	.60
47	A4	12c gray vio & blk	27.50	*14.50*
48	A4	25c brn vio & ultra	9.00	*5.50*
49	A4	30c dp car & yel grn	10.00	*11.50*
50	A4	40c brn vio & blk	3.25	*16.00*
51	A4	50c dp blue & sepia	4.75	*5.50*
52	A4	$1 dk green & blk	3.50	*12.00*
53	A4	$2 dk brn & yel grn	125.00	95.00
54	A4	$5 dp car & black	42.50	*100.00*
		Nos. 46-54 (9)	228.75	*260.60*
		Set, never hinged	300.00	

For overprints see Nos. N7-N15.

Catalogue values for unused stamps in this section, from this point to the end of the section, are for Never Hinged items.

Silver Wedding Issue

Common Design Types

Inscribed: "Malaya Kedah"

1948, Dec. 1 Photo. *Perf. 14x14½*

No.	Type	Description	Unused	Used
55	CD304	10c purple	.20	.25

Perf. 11½x11

Engraved; Name Typographed

No.	Type	Description	Unused	Used
56	CD305	$5 rose car	40.00	55.00

UPU Issue

Common Design Types

Inscribed: "Malaya-Kedah"

Engr.; Name Typo. on 15c, 25c

1949, Oct. 10 *Perf. 13½, 11x11½*

No.	Type	Description	Unused	Used
57	CD306	10c rose violet	.20	.20
58	CD307	15c indigo	2.25	1.90
59	CD308	25c orange	1.40	1.90
60	CD309	50c slate	2.10	2.75
		Nos. 57-60 (4)	5.95	6.75

Sheaf of Rice A5

Sultan Tungku Badlishah A6

1950-55 Wmk. 4 Typo. *Perf. 18*

No.	Type	Description	Unused	Used
61	A5	1c black	.30	.20
62	A5	2c orange	.30	.20
63	A5	3c green	.70	.60
64	A5	4c chocolate	.30	*.20*
65	A5	5c rose vio ('52)	.30	.20
66	A5	6c gray	.30	.20
67	A5	8c rose red	1.00	*2.00*
68	A5	8c green ('52)	.70	*2.00*
69	A5	10c plum	.30	.20
70	A5	12c rose red ('52)	.55	*4.00*
71	A5	15c ultramarine	2.10	*1.40*
72	A5	20c dk green & blk	2.10	*4.00*
73	A5	20c ultra ('52)	.90	.35
74	A6	25c org & rose lilac	1.10	.70
75	A6	30c plum & rose red ('55)	4.50	*1.50*
76	A6	35c dk vio & rose red ('52)	1.40	*2.50*
77	A6	40c dk vio & rose red	2.75	*9.25*
78	A6	50c ultra & black	1.50	.20
79	A6	$1 vio brown & ultra	10.50	2.50
80	A6	$2 rose red & emer	37.50	*35.00*
81	A6	$5 choc & emerald	50.00	*47.50*
		Nos. 61-81 (21)	119.10	*114.70*

Coronation Issue

Common Design Type

1953, June 2 Engr. *Perf. 13½x13*

No.	Type	Description	Unused	Used
82	CD312	10c magenta & black	1.40	.35

Fishing Craft — A7

Weaving and Sultan — A8

Portrait of Sultan Tungku Badlishah and: 1c, Copra. 2c, Pineapples. 4c, Rice field. 5c, Mosque. 8c, East Coast Railway. 10c, Tiger. 50c, Aborigines with blowpipes. $1, Government offices. $2, Bersilat.

Perf. 13x12½, 12½x13

1957 Engr. Wmk. 314

No.	Type	Description	Unused	Used
83	A8	1c black	.35	.30
84	A8	2c red orange	.35	.30
85	A8	4c dark brown	.35	.30
86	A8	5c dk car rose	.35	.30
87	A8	8c dark green	3.50	*12.00*
88	A7	10c chocolate	1.00	.50
89	A7	20c blue	4.00	3.25

Perf. 12½, 13½ ($1)

No.	Type	Description	Unused	Used
90	A7	50c ultra & black	3.25	*4.25*
91	A8	$1 plum & ultra	5.75	*13.50*
92	A8	$2 red & green	32.50	*35.00*
		Revenue cancel		.20
93	A8	$5 ol grn & brown	57.50	47.50
		Revenue cancel		.35
		Nos. 83-93 (11)	108.90	117.20

See Nos. 95-105.

Sultan Abdul Halim — A9

Perf. 14x14½

1959, Feb. 20 Photo. Wmk. 314

No.	Type	Description	Unused	Used
94	A9	10c ultra, red & yellow	.40	.40

Installation of the Sultan of Kedah, Abdul Halim.

Types of 1957

Designs as before with portrait of Sultan Abdul Halim.

Perf. 13x12½, 12½x13, 12½, 13½

1959-62 Engr. Wmk. 314

No.	Type	Description	Unused	Used
95	A8	1c black	.20	.95
96	A8	2c red orange	.20	1.90
97	A8	4c dark brown	.20	.95
98	A8	5c dk car rose	.20	.30
99	A8	8c dark green	4.00	5.00
100	A7	10c chocolate	.85	.30
101	A7	20c blue	.70	.85
102	A7	50c ultra & blk, perf. 12½x13 ('60)	.35	.45
a.		Perf. 12½	.35	.35
103	A8	$1 plum & ultra	2.00	*3.25*
104	A8	$2 red & green	15.00	*26.50*
105	A8	$5 ol grn & brn, perf. 13x12½ ('62)	25.00	19.00
a.		Perf. 12½	25.00	*25.00*
		Nos. 95-105 (11)	48.70	59.45

Starting in 1965, issues of Kedah are listed with Malaysia.

OCCUPATION STAMPS

Issued Under Japanese Occupation

Stamps of Kedah 1922-36, Overprinted in Red or Black

1942, May 13 Wmk. 4 *Perf. 14*

No.	Type	Description	Unused	Used
N1	A1	1c black (R)	2.40	2.75
N2	A1	2c green (R)	40.00	35.00
N3	A1	4c dull violet (R)	3.25	4.00
N4	A1	5c yellow (R)	3.00	4.00
a.		Black overprint	350.00	400.00
N5	A1	6c scarlet (Bk)	2.40	4.75
N6	A1	8c gray (R)	3.75	3.75

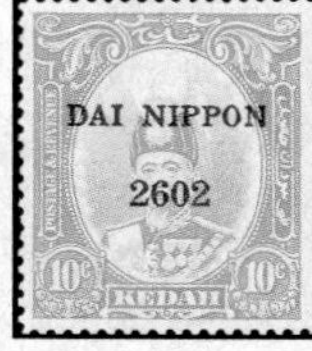

Nos. 46 to 54 Overprinted in Red

Perf. 12½

No.	Type	Description	Unused	Used
N7	A4	10c sepia & ultra	6.75	7.50
N8	A4	12c gray vio & blk	17.50	20.00
N9	A4	25c brn vio & ultra	8.75	11.00
a.		Black overprint	140.00	140.00
N10	A4	30c dp car & yel grn	80.00	87.50
N11	A4	40c brn vio & blk	35.00	40.00
N12	A4	50c dp blue & sep	35.00	35.00
N13	A4	$1 dk grn & blk	160.00	160.00
a.		Inverted overprint	350.00	350.00
N14	A4	$2 dk brn & yel green	275.00	190.00
N15	A4	$5 dp car & blk	125.00	125.00
a.		Black overprint	300.00	300.00
		Nos. N1-N15 (15)	797.80	730.25

KELANTAN

kə-ˈlan-ˌtan

LOCATION — On the eastern coast of the Malay Peninsula.

AREA — 5,750 sq. mi.

POP. — 545,620 (1960)

CAPITAL — Kota Bharu

Symbols of Government — A1

1911-15 Typo. Wmk. 3 *Perf. 14*

Ordinary Paper

No.	Type	Description	Unused	Used
1	A1	1c gray green	8.50	1.25
a.		1c green	7.25	.35
2	A1	3c rose red	5.00	.20
3	A1	4c black & red	1.90	.20
4	A1	5c grn & red, *yel*	12.00	1.25
5	A1	8c ultramarine	6.75	1.25
6	A1	10c black & violet	37.50	.90

Chalky Paper

No.	Type	Description	Unused	Used
7	A1	30c violet & red	13.50	3.00
8	A1	50c black & org	10.00	3.00
9	A1	$1 green & emer	57.50	*55.00*
10	A1	$1 grn & brn ('15)	72.50	2.40
11	A1	$2 grn & car rose	1.90	*4.75*
12	A1	$5 green & ultra	4.75	*8.75*
13	A1	$25 green & org	55.00	*105.00*
		Nos. 1-13 (13)	286.80	*186.95*

For overprints see listings after No. 26. For surcharges see Nos. N20-N22.

1921-28 Wmk. 4

Ordinary Paper

No.	Type	Description	Unused	Used
14	A1	1c green	6.50	.90
15	A1	1c black ('23)	.70	.70
16	A1	2c brown	6.50	*5.75*
17	A1	2c green ('26)	1.50	.60
18	A1	3c brown ('27)	4.00	2.25
19	A1	4c black & red	1.25	.20
20	A1	5c grn & red, *yel*	1.10	.20
21	A1	6c claret	3.50	*3.00*
22	A1	6c rose red ('28)	6.00	8.00
23	A1	10c black & violet	3.00	.20

Chalky Paper

24 A1 30c dull vio & red ('26) 6.00 *8.00*
25 A1 50c black & orange 7.25 *57.50*
26 A1 $1 green & brown 42.50 *90.00*
Nos. 14-26 (13) 89.80 *177.30*

Stamps of 1911-21 Overprinted in Black: "MALAYA BORNEO EXHIBITION" in Three Lines

1922 **Wmk. 3**

3a A1 4c black & red 4.50 *42.50*
4a A1 5c green & red, *yel* 7.00 *45.00*
7a A1 30c violet & red 9.00 *80.00*
8a A1 50c black & orange 11.50 *90.00*
10a A1 $1 green & brown 35.00 *125.00*
11a A1 $2 green & car rose 90.00 *225.00*
12a A1 $5 green & ultra 225.00 *550.00*

Wmk. 4

14a A1 1c green 3.25 *42.50*
23a A1 10c black & violet 7.75 *72.50*
Nos. 3a-23a (9) 393.00

Industrial fair at Singapore. Mar. 31-Apr. 15, 1922.

Sultan Ismail
A2 A2a

1928-33 **Engr.** ***Perf. 12***
Size: 21½x30mm

27 A2 $1 ultramarine 20.00 *50.00*

Perf. 14

28 A2 $1 blue ('33) 50.00 *47.50*

1937-40 ***Perf. 12***
Size: 22½x34½mm

29 A2a 1c yel & ol green .20 .65
30 A2a 2c deep green 1.50 .20
31 A2a 4c brick red 3.00 .80
32 A2a 5c red brown 3.00 .20
33 A2a 6c car lake 7.75 5.75
34 A2a 8c gray green 3.00 .20
35 A2a 10c dark violet 14.50 4.00
36 A2a 12c deep blue 1.90 *6.00*
37 A2a 25c vio & red org 3.00 *5.50*
38 A2a 30c scar & dk vio 27.50 *24.00*
39 A2a 40c blue grn & org 5.75 *32.50*
40 A2a 50c org & ol grn 35.00 *7.25*
41 A2a $1 dp grn & dk vio 32.50 *18.00*
42 A2a $2 red & red brn ('40) 275.00 *275.00*
43 A2a $5 rose lake & org ('40) 450.00 *650.00*
Nos. 29-43 (15) 863.60 *1,030.*
Set, never hinged 1,200.

For overprints see Nos. N1-N19.

Catalogue values for unused stamps in this section, from this point to the end of the section, are for Never Hinged items.

Silver Wedding Issue

Common Design Types
Inscribed: "Malaya Kelantan"

Perf. 14x14½

1948, Dec. 1 **Wmk. 4** **Photo.**

44 CD304 10c purple .30 .40

Perf. 11½x11

Engraved; Name Typographed

45 CD305 $5 rose car 40.00 *70.00*

Common Design Types pictured following the introduction.

UPU Issue

Common Design Types
Inscribed: "Malaya-Kelantan"

Engr.; Name Typo. on 15c, 25c

1949, Oct. 10 ***Perf. 13½, 11x11½***

46 CD306 10c rose violet .50 .50
47 CD307 15c indigo 1.90 .95
48 CD308 25c orange .80 2.40
49 CD309 50c slate 1.75 2.40
Nos. 46-49 (4) 4.95 6.25

Sultan Ibrahim — A3

Perf. 18

1951, July 11 **Wmk. 4** **Typo.**

50 A3 1c black .25 .40
51 A3 2c orange .75 .40
52 A3 3c green 5.25 2.10
53 A3 4c chocolate .25 .30
54 A3 6c gray .25 .30
55 A3 8c rose red 1.10 *4.75*
56 A3 10c plum .25 .30
57 A3 15c ultramarine 4.00 1.00
58 A3 20c dk green & blk .70 7.00
59 A3 25c orange & plum .80 1.00
60 A3 40c vio brn & rose red 6.75 15.00
61 A3 50c dp ultra & blk 1.60 .60
62 A3 $1 vio brown & ultra 10.50 6.00
63 A3 $2 rose red & emer 37.50 35.00
64 A3 $5 choc & emer 82.50 72.50

1952-55

65 A3 5c rose violet .70 .50
66 A3 8c green 1.10 *2.40*
67 A3 12c rose red 1.10 *3.25*
68 A3 20c ultramarine 1.25 *.25*
69 A3 30c plum & rose red ('55) 1.90 2.40
70 A3 35c dk vio & rose red 1.40 *1.90*
Nos. 50-70 (21) 159.90 157.35

Compare with Pahang A8, Perak A16, Selangor A15, Trengganu A5.

Coronation Issue

Common Design Type

1953, June 2 **Engr.** ***Perf. 13½x13***

71 CD312 10c magenta & black 1.60 *1.60*

Aborigines with Blowpipes
A4

Government Offices and Sultan
A5

Portrait of Sultan Ibrahim and: 1c, Copra. 2c, Pineapples. 4c, Rice field. 5c, Mosque. 8c, East Coast Railway. 10c, Tiger. 20c, Fishing craft. 50c, Aborigines with blowpipes. $1, Government Offices and Sultan. $2, Bersilat. $5, Weaving.

Perf. 13x12½, 12½x13, 13½ ($1)

1957-63 **Engr.** **Wmk. 314**

72 A5 1c black .20 .45
73 A5 2c red orange .90 1.25
74 A5 4c dark brown .45 .20
75 A5 5c dk car rose .45 .20
76 A5 8c dark green 1.40 3.25
77 A4 10c chocolate 2.50 .20
78 A4 20c blue 2.50 .45
79 A4 50c ultra & blk ('60) .70 .75
a. Perf 12½ 2.25 .60
80 A5 $1 plum & ultra 7.00 2.25
81 A5 $2 red & grn ('63) 15.00 *8.75*
a. Perf. 12½ 26.00 *30.00*
82 A5 $5 ol grn & brn ('63) 30.00 *32.50*
a. Perf. 12½ 27.50 *20.00*
Nos. 72-82 (11) 61.10 *50.25*

Sultan Yahya Petra — A6

1961, July 17 **Photo.** ***Perf. 14½x14***

83 A6 10s multicolored .55 .55

Installation of Sultan Yahya Petra.

Types of 1957 with Portrait of Sultan Yahya Petra

Designs as before.

Perf. 13x12½, 12½x13

1961-62 **Engr.** **Wmk. 338**

84 A5 1c black .20 *1.90*
85 A5 2c red orange .20 *1.90*
86 A5 4c dark brown .80 *.90*
87 A5 5c dk car rose .65 .30
88 A5 8c dark green 9.00 *11.50*
89 A4 10c violet brown ('61) 1.50 .35
90 A4 20c blue 5.50 1.25
Nos. 84-90 (7) 17.85 18.10

Starting in 1965, issues of Kelantan are listed with Malaysia.

OCCUPATION STAMPS

Issued Under Japanese Occupation

Kelantan No. 35 Handstamped in Black

1942 **Wmk. 4** ***Perf. 12***

N1 A2a 10c dark violet 400.00 500.00

Some authorities believe No. N1 was not regularly issued.

Kelantan Nos. 29-40 Surcharged in Black or Red and Handstamped with Oval Seal "a" in Red

1 Cents

Sunakawa — a

Handa — b

1942

N2 1c on 50c org & ol green 200.00 200.00
a. With "b" seal 65.00 65.00
N3 2c on 40c bl grn & orange 350.00 350.00
a. With "b" seal 55.00 65.00
N4 5c on 12c dp bl (R) 200.00 200.00
N5 8c on 5c red brn (R) 225.00 225.00
a. With "b" seal (R) 160.00 190.00
N6 10c on 6c car lake 95.00 150.00
a. With "b" seal 95.00 150.00
N7 12c on 8c gray green (R) 60.00 140.00
N8 30c on 4c brick red 1,100. 1,200.
N9 40c on 2c dp grn (R) 60.00 100.00
N10 50c on 1c yel & ol green 850.00 800.00

Kelantan Nos. 29-40, 19-20, 22 Surcharged in Black or Red and Handstamped with Oval Seal "a" in Red

2 CENTS

N10A 1c on 50c org & ol green 125.00 110.00
N11 2c on 40c bl grn & orange 125.00 125.00
N11A 4c on 30c scar & dark vio 1,200. 1,200.
N12 5c on 12c dp bl (R) 200.00 200.00
N13 6c on 25c vio & red org 200.00 200.00
N14 8c on 5c red brown (R) 110.00 87.50
N15 10c on 6c car lake 110.00 125.00
N16 12c on 8c gray grn (R) 225.00 250.00
a. With "b" seal (R) 75.00 100.00
N17 25c on 10c dk vio 1,200. *1,250.*
N17A 30c on 4c brick red 1,600. *1,800.*
N18 40c on 2c dp grn (R) 60.00 100.00
N19 50c on 1c yel & ol green *1,200.* 1,100.

Perf. 14

N20 $1 on 4c blk & red (R) 65.00 87.50
N21 $2 on 5c grn & red, *yel* 65.00 87.50
N22 $5 on 6c rose red 65.00 87.50

Examples of Nos. N2-N22 without handstamped seal are from the remainder stocks sent to Singapore after Kelantan was ceded to Thailand. Some authorities believe stamps without seals were used before June 1942.

ISSUED UNDER THAI OCCUPATION

OS1

1943, Nov. 15 ***Perf. 11***

2N1 OS1 1c violet & black *240.00* *375.00*
2N2 OS1 2c violet & black *300.00* *300.00*
2N3 OS1 4c violet & black *300.00* *375.00*
2N4 OS1 8c violet & black *300.00* *300.00*
2N5 OS1 10c violet & black *425.00* *550.00*
Nos. 2N1-2N5 (5) *1,565.* *1,900.*

Stamps with centers in red are revenues.

MALACCA

mə-'la-kə

Melaka

LOCATION — On the west coast of the Malay peninsula.
AREA — 640 sq. mi.
POP. — 318,110 (1960)
CAPITAL — Malacca

Catalogue values for unused stamps in this section are for Never Hinged items.

Silver Wedding Issue

Common Design Types
Inscribed: "Malaya Malacca"

Perf. 14x14½

1948, Dec. 1 **Wmk. 4** **Photo.**

1 CD304 10c purple .40 *3.00*

Engraved; Name Typographed

Perf. 11½x11

2 CD305 $5 lt brown 37.50 *50.00*

Type of Straits Settlements, 1937-41, Inscribed "Malacca"

Perf. 18

1949, Mar. 1 **Wmk. 4** **Typo.**

3 A29 1c black .40 *.95*
4 A29 2c orange 1.10 .60
5 A29 3c green .40 *2.40*
6 A29 4c chocolate .40 .20
7 A29 6c gray 1.00 *1.25*
8 A29 8c rose red 1.00 *8.50*
9 A29 10c plum .40 .20
10 A29 15c ultramarine 3.50 .85
11 A29 20c dk green & blk .60 *.95*
12 A29 25c org & rose lil .60 .95
13 A29 40c dk vio & rose red 1.50 *13.00*
14 A29 50c ultra & black 1.25 *1.50*
15 A29 $1 vio brn & ultra 11.50 *24.00*
16 A29 $2 rose red & emer 27.50 *27.50*
17 A29 $5 choc & emer 60.00 *50.00*
Nos. 3-17 (15) 111.15 *132.85*

See Nos. 22-26.

UPU Issue
Common Design Types
Inscribed: "Malaya-Malacca"
Engr.; Name Typo. on 15c, 25c
Perf. 13½, 11x11½

1949, Oct. 10 **Wmk. 4**
18 CD306 10c rose violet .35 *.55*
19 CD307 15c indigo 2.40 *2.00*
20 CD308 25c orange .50 *5.50*
21 CD309 50c slate 1.25 *5.50*
Nos. 18-21 (4) 4.50 *13.55*

Type of Straits Settlements, 1937-41, Inscribed "Malacca"

1952, Sept. 1 **Wmk. 4** ***Perf. 18***
22 A29 5c rose violet .75 *1.75*
23 A29 8c green 1.25 *5.75*
24 A29 12c rose red 2.25 *.90*
25 A29 20c ultramarine 3.75 3.25
26 A29 35c dk vio & rose red 1.75 *3.75*
Nos. 22-26 (5) 9.75 *15.40*

Coronation Issue
Common Design Type

1953, June 2 **Engr.** ***Perf. 13½x13***
27 CD312 10c magenta & black 1.10 .50

Queen Elizabeth II — A1

1954-55 **Wmk. 4** **Typo.** ***Perf. 18***
29 A1 1c black .20 .75
30 A1 2c orange .40 1.25
31 A1 4c chocolate .50 .20
32 A1 5c rose violet .40 2.75
33 A1 6c gray .20 .40
34 A1 8c green .55 3.00
35 A1 10c plum .65 .20
36 A1 12c rose red .40 3.25
37 A1 20c ultramarine .25 1.25
38 A1 25c orange & plum .25 1.75
39 A1 30c plum & rose red ('55) .25 *.40*
40 A1 35c vio brn & rose red .25 *1.25*
41 A1 50c ultra & black .40 *2.75*
42 A1 $1 vio brn & ultra 7.50 *9.00*
43 A1 $2 rose red & grn 32.50 *42.50*
44 A1 $5 choc & emerald 32.50 *47.50*
Nos. 29-44 (16) 77.20 118.20

Types of Kedah with Portrait of Queen Elizabeth II
Perf. 13x12½, 12½x13

1957 **Engr.** **Wmk. 314**
45 A8 1c black .20 *.55*
46 A8 2c red orange .20 *.55*
47 A8 4c dark brown .20 *.20*
48 A8 5c dark car rose .20 *.20*
49 A8 8c dark green 1.60 *3.25*
50 A7 10c chocolate .45 *.20*
51 A7 20c blue .45 *.55*

Perf. 12½, 13½ ($1)
52 A7 50c ultra & black .45 *.80*
53 A8 $1 plum & ultra 3.00 *3.25*
54 A8 $2 red & green 14.50 *25.00*
55 A8 $5 olive grn & brn 19.00 *40.00*
Nos. 45-55 (11) 40.25 74.55

Types of Kedah, 1957, With Melaka Tree and Mouse Deer Replacing Portrait of Queen Elizabeth II
Perf. 13x12½, 12½x13, 13½ ($1)

1960, Mar. 15 **Engr.** **Wmk. 314**
56 A8 1c black .20 *.50*
57 A8 2c red orange .20 *.70*
58 A8 4c dark brown .20 *.20*
59 A8 5c dark car rose .20 *.20*
60 A8 8c dark green 3.50 *3.75*
61 A7 10c violet brown .45 *.20*
62 A7 20c blue .75 *1.00*
63 A7 50c ultra & black .65 *1.00*
64 A8 $1 plum & ultra 3.25 *3.75*
65 A8 $2 red & green 7.50 *12.00*
66 A8 $5 ol grn & brn 13.00 *19.00*
Nos. 56-66 (11) 29.90 42.30

Starting in 1965, issues of Malacca (Melaka) are listed with Malaysia.

OCCUPATION STAMPS

Issued Under Japanese Occupation
Stamps of Straits Settlements, 1937-41 Handstamped in Carmine

The handstamp covers four stamps. Values are for single stamps. Blocks of four showing complete handstamp sell for six times the price of singles.

1942 **Wmk. 4** ***Perf. 14***
N1 A29 1c black 125.00 100.00
N2 A29 2c brown orange 90.00 80.00
N3 A29 3c green 100.00 90.00
N4 A29 5c brown 175.00 175.00
N5 A29 8c gray 275.00 150.00
N6 A29 10c dull violet 125.00 125.00
N7 A29 12c ultramarine 140.00 150.00
N8 A29 15c ultramarine 100.00 125.00
N9 A29 30c org & vio *3,500.* —
N10 A29 40c dk vio & rose red 800.00 800.00
N11 A29 50c blk, *emerald* 1,100. 1,100.
N12 A29 $1 red & blk, *bl* 1,350. 1,250.
N13 A29 $2 rose red & gray grn *3,500.* —
N14 A29 $5 grn & red, *grn* *3,500.* —

Some authorities believe Nos. N9, N13, and N14 were not regularly issued.

OCCUPATION POSTAGE DUE STAMPS

Malaya Postage Due Stamps and Type of 1936-38, Handstamped Like Nos. N1-N14 in Carmine

1942 **Wmk. 4** ***Perf. 14½x14***
NJ1 D2 1c violet *250.00* *225.00*
NJ2 D2 4c yel green *275.00* *275.00*
NJ3 D2 8c red *3,500.* *2,250.*
NJ4 D2 10c yel orange *550.00* *525.00*
NJ5 D2 12c blue violet *800.00* *725.00*
NJ6 D2 50c black *3,000.* *1,950.*
Nos. NJ1-NJ6 (6) *8,375.* *5,950.*

Pricing note above No. N1 also applies to Nos. NJ1-NJ6.

NEGRI SEMBILAN

'ne-grē səm-'bē-lən

LOCATION — South of Selangor on the west coast of the Malay Peninsula, bordering on Pahang on the east and Johore on the south.
AREA — 2,580 sq. mi.
POP. — 401,742 (1960)
CAPITAL — Seremban

Stamps of the Straits Settlements Overprinted in Black

1891 **Wmk. 2** ***Perf. 14***
Overprint 14½ to 15mm Wide
1 A2 2c rose 4.00 *8.00*

Tiger — A1

Tiger Head — A2

1891-94 **Typo.**
2 A1 1c green ('93) 4.00 1.25
3 A1 2c rose 4.00 *11.00*
4 A1 5c blue ('94) 37.50 *47.50*
Nos. 2-4 (3) 45.50 *59.75*

For surcharges see Nos. 17-18.

1895-99
5 A2 1c lilac & green 18.00 8.50
6 A2 2c lilac & brown 42.50 *140.00*
7 A2 3c lilac & car rose 18.00 1.50
8 A2 5c lilac & olive 10.00 11.50
9 A2 8c lilac & blue 35.00 20.00
10 A2 10c lilac & orange 32.50 17.00
11 A2 15c green & vio 50.00 *90.00*
12 A2 20c grn & ol ('99) 80.00 *45.00*
13 A2 25c grn & car rose 85.00 *110.00*
14 A2 50c green & black 90.00 80.00
Nos. 5-14 (10) 461.00 *523.50*

For surcharges see Nos. 15-16, 19-20.

Stamps of 1891-99 Surcharged

1899 **Green Surcharge**
15 A2 4c on 8c lil & blue 8.00 5.25
a. Double surcharge 2,750. 2,750.
b. Pair, one without surcharge 7,250. 4,800.
c. Double surch., 1 grn, 1 red 975.00 1,000.

Black Surcharge
16 A2 4c on 8c lil & blue 1,450. *1,600.*

Same Surcharge and Bar in Black
17 A1 4c on 1c green 3.00 *20.00*
18 A1 4c on 5c blue 1.50 *18.00*
19 A2 4c on 3c lil & car rose 4.00 *24.00*
a. Double surcharge 2,750. 1,200.
b. Pair, one without surcharge 12,000. *6,000.*
d. Bar double 975.00

Bar at bottom on #17-18, at top on #19.

No. 11 Surcharged in Black

1900
20 A2 1c on 15c grn & vio 125.00 *375.00*
a. Inverted period 525.00 *1,350.*

Arms of Negri Sembilan
A4 A5

1935-41 **Typo.** **Wmk. 4**
21 A4 1c black ('36) 2.10 .20
22 A4 2c dp green ('36) 1.40 .20
22A A4 2c brown org ('41) .20 *75.00*
22B A4 3c green ('41) .20 *11.00*
23 A4 4c brown orange 1.40 .20
24 A4 5c chocolate 1.40 .20
25 A4 6c rose red 7.75 1.90
25A A4 6c gray ('41) 5.00 *140.00*
26 A4 8c gray 3.25 .40
27 A4 10c dull vio ('36) 3.25 .20
28 A4 12c ultra ('36) 4.00 .95
28A A4 15c ultra ('41) 5.50 *97.50*
29 A4 25c rose red & dull vio ('36) 4.00 4.00
30 A4 30c org & dull vio ('36) 5.50 7.50
31 A4 40c dull vio & car 2.50 *9.75*
32 A4 50c blk, *emer* ('36) 10.00 1.50
33 A4 $1 red & blk, *bl* ('36) 4.00 5.50
34 A4 $2 rose red & grn ('36) 55.00 72.50
35 A4 $5 brn red & grn, *emer* ('36) 40.00 *97.50*
Nos. 21-35 (19) 156.45 *526.00*
Set, never hinged 290.00

For overprints see Nos. N1-N31.

Catalogue values for unused stamps in this section, from this point to the end of the section, are for Never Hinged items.

Silver Wedding Issue
Common Design Types
Inscribed: "Malaya Negri Sembilan"

1948, Dec. 1 **Photo.** ***Perf. 14x14½***
36 CD304 10c purple .75 .85

Perf. 11½x11
Engraved; Name Typographed
37 CD305 $5 green 29.00 40.00

Common Design Types pictured following the introduction.

1949-55 **Wmk. 4** **Typo.** ***Perf. 18***
38 A5 1c black .20 .20
39 A5 2c orange .20 .20
40 A5 3c green .50 .55
41 A5 4c chocolate .20 .20
42 A5 5c rose violet .20 .20
43 A5 6c gray .40 .20
44 A5 8c rose red .75 1.10
45 A5 8c green 3.00 3.75
46 A5 10c plum .40 .20
47 A5 12c rose red 3.00 3.75
48 A5 15c ultramarine 2.25 .75
49 A5 20c dk green & blk 1.25 1.50
50 A5 20c ultramarine 1.50 .55
51 A5 25c org & rose lilac .60 .35
52 A5 30c plum & rose red ('55) 3.50 2.75
53 A5 35c dk vio & rose red 1.50 3.75
54 A5 40c dk vio & rose red 1.60 *7.75*
55 A5 50c ultra & black 1.60 .75
56 A5 $1 vio brn & ultra 3.50 2.00
57 A5 $2 rose red & emer 15.00 15.00
58 A5 $5 choc & emerald 65.00 55.00
Nos. 38-58 (21) 106.15 100.50

UPU Issue
Common Design Types
Inscribed: "Malaya-Negri Sembilan"
Engr.; Name Typo. on 15c, 25c

1949, Oct. 10 ***Perf. 13½, 11x11½***
59 CD306 10c rose violet .20 .20
60 CD307 15c indigo .75 .75
61 CD308 25c orange 1.50 1.50
62 CD309 50c slate 2.25 4.25
Nos. 59-62 (4) 4.70 6.70

Coronation Issue
Common Design Type

1953, June 2 **Engr.** ***Perf. 13½x13***
63 CD312 10c magenta & black 1.60 .65

Types of Kedah with Arms of Negri Sembilan
Perf. 13x12½, 12½x13, 13½ ($1)

1957-63 **Engr.** **Wmk. 314**
64 A8 1c black .20 .20
65 A8 2c red orange .20 .20
66 A8 4c dark brown .20 .20
67 A8 5c dk car rose .20 .20
68 A8 8c dark green 1.00 *1.60*
69 A7 10c chocolate 1.50 *.20*
70 A7 20c blue .70 *.20*
71 A7 50c ultra & blk ('60) .60 *.20*
a. Perf. 12½ 1.75 *1.50*
72 A8 $1 plum & ultra 1.75 *2.25*
73 A8 $2 red & grn ('63) 17.00 *27.50*
a. Perf. 12½ 17.00 *27.50*
74 A8 $5 ol grn & brn ('62) 25.00 20.00
a. Perf. 12½ 32.50 *27.50*
Nos. 64-74 (11) 48.35 52.75

Negri Sembilan State Crest and Tuanku Munawir
A6

1961, Apr. 17 **Unwmk.** ***Perf. 14x13***
75 A6 10s blue & multi .45 *.65*

Installation of Tuanku Munawir as ruler (Yang di-Pertuan Besar) of Negri Sembilan.

Starting in 1965, issues of Negri (Negeri) Sembilan are listed with Malaysia.

OCCUPATION STAMPS

Issued under Japanese Occupation

Stamps and Type of Negri Sembilan, 1935-41, Handstamped in Red, Black, Brown or Violet

1942 Wmk. 4 *Perf. 14*

N1 A4 1c black 25.00 16.00
N2 A4 2c brown org 16.00 17.50
N3 A4 3c green 21.00 21.00
N4 A4 5c chocolate 29.00 27.50
N5 A4 6c rose red 600.00 600.00
N6 A4 6c gray 150.00 150.00
N7 A4 8c gray 87.50 87.50
N8 A4 8c rose red 55.00 47.50
N9 A4 10c dark violet 110.00 110.00
N10 A4 12c ultramarine 900.00 900.00
N11 A4 15c ultramarine 20.00 11.00
N12 A4 25c rose red & dk vio 35.00 40.00
N13 A4 30c org & dk vio 175.00 190.00
N14 A4 40c dk vio & car 750.00 750.00
N15 A4 $1 red & blk, *bl* 140.00 140.00
N16 A4 $5 brn red & grn, *emerald* 325.00 350.00

The 8c rose red is not known to have been issued without overprint.
Some authorities believe Nos. N5 and N7 were not regularly issued.

Stamps of Negri Sembilan, 1935-41, Overprinted in Black

N17 A4 1c black 1.40 1.40
 a. Inverted overprint 17.00 27.50
 b. Dbl. ovpt., one invtd. 47.50 67.50
N18 A4 2c brown orange 1.60 1.40
N19 A4 3c green 1.40 1.00
N20 A4 5c chocolate .90 .90
N21 A4 6c gray 2.00 2.00
 a. Inverted overprint 1,000.
N22 A4 8c rose red 2.75 2.75
N23 A4 10c dk violet 5.50 5.50
N24 A4 15c ultramarine 8.00 4.75
N25 A4 25c rose red & dk vio 2.00 6.75
N26 A4 30c org & dk vio 4.00 5.00
N27 A4 $1 red & blk, *bl* 140.00 175.00
 Nos. N17-N27 (11) 169.55 206.45

The 8c rose red is not known to have been issued without overprint.

Negri Sembilan, Nos. 21, 24 and 29, Overprinted or Surcharged in Black:

a

b

c

1943

N28 A4 1c black .65 .65
 a. Inverted overprint 17.00 24.00
N29 A4 2c on 5c choc .55 .65
N30 A4 6c on 5c choc .65 .90
 a. "6 cts." inverted 350.00 400.00
N31 A4 25c rose red & dk violet 2.00 2.75
 Nos. N28-N31 (4) 3.85 4.95

The Japanese characters read: "Japanese Postal Service."

PAHANG

pə-ˈhaŋ

LOCATION — On the east coast of the Malay Peninsula.
AREA — 13,820 sq. mi.
POP. — 338,210 (1960)
CAPITAL — Kuala Lipis

Stamps of the Straits Settlements Overprinted in Black

Overprinted

Overprint 16x2¾mm

1889 Wmk. 2 *Perf. 14*

1 A2 2c rose 140.00 60.00
2 A3 8c orange 2,175. 2,175.
3 A7 10c slate 275.00 300.00

Overprinted

Overprint 12½x2mm

4 A2 2c rose 8.50 *10.00*

Overprinted **PAHANG**

1890 Overprint 15x2½mm

5 A2 2c rose 8,000. 2,500.

Overprinted

Overprint 16x2¾mm

6 A2 2c rose 140.00 17.00

Surcharged in Black:

PAHANG
Two
CENTS

a

b

c

d

1891

7 A3 (a) 2c on 24c green 1,100. *1,325.*
8 A3 (b) 2c on 24c green 425.00 *500.00*
9 A3 (c) 2c on 24c green 225.00 *275.00*
10 A3 (d) 2c on 24c green 1,100. *1,325.*
 Nos. 7-10 (4) 2,850. 3,425.

A5

A6

1892-95 Typo.

11 A5 1c green 5.00 4.50
12 A5 2c rose 5.50 4.00
13 A5 5c blue 13.50 *47.50*
 Nos. 11-13 (3) 24.00 *56.00*

For surcharges see Nos. 21-22.

1895-99

14 A6 3c lilac & car rose 9.75 3.25
14A A6 4c lil & car rose ('99) 20.00 14.50
15 A6 5c lilac & olive 35.00 *25.00*
 Nos. 14-15 (3) 64.75 *42.75*

For surcharge see No. 28.

Stamps of Perak, 1895-99, Overprinted

1898-99

16 A9 10c lilac & orange 25.00 *30.00*
17 A9 25c grn & car rose 100.00 *190.00*
18 A9 50c green & black 500.00 *575.00*
18A A9 50c lilac & black 350.00 425.00

Overprinted

Wmk. 1

19 A10 $1 green & lt grn 450.00 600.00
20 A10 $5 green & ultra 1,700. 2,700.
 Nos. 16-20 (6) 3,125. 4,520.

No. 13 Cut in Half and Surcharged With New Value and Initials in ms.

1897 Wmk. 2

Red Surcharge

21 A5 2c on half of 5c blue *1,950.* *450.00*
 a. Black surcharge *10,000.* *3,600.*
22 A5 3c on half of 5c blue *1,800.* *450.00*
 a. Black surcharge *10,000.* *3,600.*

Perak No. 52 Surcharged

1899

25 A9 4c on 8c lilac & blue 6.75 6.75
 b. Inverted surcharge 4,250. 1,800.

Same Surcharge on pieces of White Paper

1898 Without Gum *Imperf.*

26 4c black 4,500.
27 5c black 3,000.

Pahang No. 15 Surcharged

1899 *Perf. 14*

28 A6 4c on 5c lilac & olive 22.50 *72.50*

Sultan Abu Bakar
A7 A8

1935-41 Typo. Wmk. 4 *Perf. 14*

29 A7 1c black ('36) .20 .20
30 A7 2c dp green ('36) 2.00 .20
30A A7 3c green ('41) .20 *5.50*
31 A7 4c brown orange 1.00 .20
32 A7 5c chocolate 1.20 .20
33 A7 6c rose red ('36) 4.50 *9.50*
34 A7 8c gray 3.25 .20
34A A7 8c rose red ('41) 1.00 *30.00*
35 A7 10c dk violet ('36) 1.00 .20
36 A7 12c ultra ('36) 4.25 3.00
36A A7 15c ultra ('41) 2.50 *40.00*
37 A7 25c rose red & pale vio ('36) 3.25 1.10
38 A7 30c org & dk vio ('36) 2.00 1.60
39 A7 40c dk vio & car 2.50 2.40
40 A7 50c black, *emer* ('36) 10.50 2.25
41 A7 $1 red & blk, *blue* ('36) 6.00 6.00
42 A7 $2 rose red & green ('36) 52.50 *87.50*
43 A7 $5 brn red & grn, *emer* ('36) 19.00 *87.50*
 Nos. 29-43 (18) 116.85 *277.55*

The 3c was printed on both ordinary and chalky paper; the 15c only on ordinary paper; other values only on chalky paper.
A 2c brown orange and 6c gray, type A7, exist, but are not known to have been regularly issued.
For overprints see Nos. N1-N21.

Catalogue values for unused stamps in this section, from this point to the end of the section, are for Never Hinged items.

Silver Wedding Issue

Common Design Types
Inscribed: "Malaya Pahang"

Perf. 14x14½

1948, Dec. 1 Photo. Wmk. 4

44 CD304 10c purple .50 .55

Perf. 11½x11

Engraved; Name Typopgraphed

45 CD305 $5 green 37.50 65.00

UPU Issue

Common Design Types
Inscribed: "Malaya-Pahang"

Engr.; Name Typo. on 15c, 25c

1949, Oct. 10 *Perf. 13½, 11x11½*

46 CD306 10c rose violet .20 .20
47 CD307 15c indigo .50 .50
48 CD308 25c orange 1.50 1.50
49 CD309 50c slate 2.50 2.50
 Nos. 46-49 (4) 4.70 4.70

Perf. 18

1950, June 1 Wmk. 4 Typo.

50 A8 1c black .30 .35
51 A8 2c orange .30 .35
52 A8 3c green .30 .70
53 A8 4c chocolate .30 .35
54 A8 6c gray .30 .35
55 A8 8c rose red .30 *3.50*
56 A8 10c plum .30 .35
57 A8 15c ultramarine .35 .35
58 A8 20c dk green & blk .35 *3.50*
59 A8 25c org & rose lilac .35 .35
60 A8 40c dk vio & rose red 1.40 *13.00*
61 A8 50c dp ultra & black 1.25 .35
62 A8 $1 vio brn & ultra 3.75 3.50
63 A8 $2 rose red & emer 21.00 37.50
64 A8 $5 choc & emer 65.00 *57.50*

1952-55

65 A8 5c rose violet .30 .30
66 A8 8c green 1.40 1.50
67 A8 12c rose red 1.40 2.50
68 A8 20c ultramarine 1.25 .35
69 A8 30c plum & rose red ('55) 2.00 .70
70 A8 35c dk vio & rose red 1.00 .45
 Nos. 50-70 (21) 102.90 *127.80*

Coronation Issue

Common Design Type

1953, June 2 Engr. *Perf. 13½x13*

71 CD312 10c magenta & black 1.75 .20

Types of Kedah with Portrait of Sultan Abu Bakar

Perf. 13x12½, 12½x13, 13½ ($1)

1957-62 Engr. Wmk. 314

72 A8 1c black .20 .20
73 A8 2c red orange .20 .20
74 A8 4c dark brown .20 .20
75 A8 5c dark car rose .20 .20
76 A8 8c dark green 1.25 *2.50*
77 A7 10c chocolate 1.10 .20
78 A7 20c blue 3.00 .25
79 A7 50c ultra & blk ('60) .80 .25
 a. Perf. 12½ .70 *1.75*
80 A8 $1 plum & ultra 8.50 3.00
81 A8 $2 red & green ('62) 8.50 *20.00*
 a. Perf. 12½ 7.25 *18.00*

82 A8 $5 ol grn & brn ('60) 16.00 *19.00*
a. Perf. 12½ 20.00 *27.50*
Nos. 72-82 (11) 39.95 46.00

Starting in 1965, issues of Pahang are listed with Malaysia.

OCCUPATION STAMPS

Issued under Japanese Occupation

Stamps of Pahang, 1935-41, Handstamped in Black, Red, Brown or Violet

1942 Wmk. 4 *Perf. 14*
N1 A7 1c black 35.00 40.00
N1A A7 3c green 125.00 140.00
N2 A7 5c chocolate 15.00 9.50
N3 A7 8c rose red 26.00 11.00
N3A A7 8c gray 240.00 240.00
N4 A7 10c dk violet 60.00 60.00
N5 A7 12c ultramarine 1,200. 1,200.
N6 A7 15c ultramarine 87.50 87.50
N7 A7 25c rose red & pale vio 21.00 37.50
N8 A7 30c org & dk vio 17.00 32.50
N9 A7 40c dk vio & car 17.50 35.00
N10 A7 50c blk, *emerald* 300.00 350.00
N11 A7 $1 red & blk, *bl* 100.00 125.00
N12 A7 $5 brown red & grn, *emer* 575.00 625.00

Some authorities claim the 2c green, 4c brown orange, 6c rose red and $2 rose red and green were not regularly issued with this overprint.

Stamps of Pahang, 1935-41, Overprinted in Black

N13 A7 1c black 2.00 1.10
N14 A7 5c chocolate 2.00 2.00
N15 A7 8c rose red 35.00 3.75
N16 A7 10c violet brown 20.00 9.00
N17 A7 12c ultramarine 2.00 3.00
N18 A7 25c rose red & pale vio 7.50 *10.50*
N19 A7 30c org & dk vio 2.75 *5.50*
Nos. N13-N19 (7) 71.25 *34.85*

Pahang No. 32 Overprinted and Surcharged in Black

e

f

1943
N20 A7(e) 6c on 5c chocolate 1.40 1.40
N21 A7(f) 6c on 5c chocolate 2.00 1.50

The Japanese characters read: "Japanese Postal Service."

PENANG

pə-naŋ

LOCATION — An island off the west coast of the Malay Peninsula, plus a coastal strip called Province Wellesley.
AREA — 400 sq. mi.
POP. — 616,254 (1960)
CAPITAL — Georgetown

Catalogue values for unused stamps in this section are for Never Hinged items.

Common Design Types pictured following the introduction.

Silver Wedding Issue
Common Design Types
Inscribed: "Malaya Penang"

Perf. 14x14½
1948, Dec. 1 Wmk. 4 Photo.
1 CD304 10c purple 1.50 1.50

Perf. 11½x11
Engraved; Name Typographed
2 CD305 $5 lt brown 42.50 37.50

Type of Straits Settlements, 1937-41, Inscribed "Penang"

1949-52 *Perf. 18*
3 A29 1c black .30 .30
4 A29 2c orange 1.25 .30
5 A29 3c green .30 1.50
6 A29 4c chocolate .30 .20
7 A29 5c rose vio ('52) 2.75 4.00
8 A29 6c gray .40 .30
9 A29 8c rose red .85 *4.50*
10 A29 8c green ('52) 2.10 2.25
11 A29 10c plum .30 .20
12 A29 12c rose red ('52) 2.75 7.00
13 A29 15c ultramarine .70 *.40*
14 A29 20c dk grn & blk .70 1.25
15 A29 20c ultra ('52) .75 1.50
16 A29 25c org & rose lilac 2.25 .30
17 A29 35c dk vio & rose red ('52) 1.25 1.75
18 A29 40c dk vio & rose red 2.10 *13.00*
19 A29 50c ultra & black 3.50 .30
20 A29 $1 vio brn & ultra 20.00 2.75
21 A29 $2 rose red & emer 30.00 2.75
22 A29 $5 choc & emerald 65.00 4.25
Nos. 3-22 (20) 137.55 *48.80*

UPU Issue
Common Design Types
Inscribed: "Malaya-Penang"

Engr.; Name Typo. on 15c, 25c
1949, Oct. 10 *Perf. 13½, 11x11½*
23 CD306 10c rose violet .25 *.20*
24 CD307 15c indigo 2.40 *3.25*
25 CD308 25c orange .70 *3.25*
26 CD309 50c slate 1.75 *4.00*
Nos. 23-26 (4) 5.10 10.70

Coronation Issue
Common Design Type

1953, June 2 Engr. *Perf. 13½x13*
27 CD312 10c magenta & black 2.00 .35

Type of Malacca, 1954

1954-55 Wmk. 4 Typo. *Perf. 18*
29 A1 1c black .20 .85
30 A1 2c orange .60 .45
31 A1 4c chocolate .80 .20
32 A1 5c rose violet 2.25 4.00
33 A1 6c gray .20 1.25
34 A1 8c green .25 *4.50*
35 A1 10c plum .25 .20
36 A1 12c rose red .35 4.50
37 A1 20c ultramarine .60 .20
38 A1 25c orange & plum .35 .20
39 A1 30c plum & rose red ('55) .35 .20
40 A1 35c vio brn & rose red .80 .95
41 A1 50c ultra & black .60 .20
42 A1 $1 vio brn & ultra 2.50 .35
43 A1 $2 rose red & grn 9.25 4.75
44 A1 $5 choc & emerald 47.50 4.75
Nos. 29-44 (16) 66.85 27.55

Types of Kedah with Portrait of Queen Elizabeth II

Perf. 13x12½, 12½x13
1957 Engr. Wmk. 314
45 A8 1c black .30 1.25
46 A8 2c red orange .30 1.25
47 A8 4c dark brown .30 .20
48 A8 5c dk car rose .30 .50
49 A8 8c dark green 2.00 2.75
50 A7 10c chocolate .50 .20
51 A7 20c blue .75 .75

Perf. 12½, 13½ ($1)
52 A7 50c ultra & black .50 .85
53 A8 $1 plum & ultra 8.50 .95
54 A8 $2 red & green 22.50 16.00
55 A8 $5 ol green & brown 30.00 16.00
Nos. 45-55 (11) 65.95 40.70

Types of Kedah, 1957 with Penang State Crest and Areca-nut Palm Replacing Portrait of Elizabeth II

Perf. 13x12½, 12½x13, 13½ ($1)
1960, Mar. 15 Engr. Wmk. 314
56 A8 1c black .20 *1.90*
57 A8 2c red orange .20 *1.90*
58 A8 4c dark brown .20 .20
59 A8 5c dk car rose .20 .20
60 A8 8c dark green 3.25 *5.75*
61 A7 10c violet brown .35 .20
62 A7 20c blue .50 .20
63 A7 50c ultra & black .35 .20
64 A8 $1 plum & ultra 5.00 1.90
65 A8 $2 red & green 5.00 7.25
Revenue cancel .20
66 A8 $5 ol green & brown 11.50 10.50
Nos. 56-66 (11) 26.75 30.20

Starting in 1965, issues of Penang (Pulau Pinang) are listed with Malaysia.

OCCUPATION STAMPS

Issued under Japanese Occupation

Stamps of Straits Settlements, 1937-41, Overprinted in Red or Black

1942 Wmk. 4 *Perf. 14*
N1 A29 1c black (R) 6.75 3.75
N2 A29 2c brown orange 5.75 4.75
N3 A29 3c green (R) 5.75 5.50
N4 A29 5c brown (R) 3.25 9.75
N5 A29 8c gray (R) 2.75 1.75
N6 A29 10c dull vio (R) 2.00 2.75
N7 A29 12c ultra (R) 4.50 *20.00*
N8 A29 15c ultra (R) 2.25 4.50
N9 A29 40c dk vio & rose red 5.75 *20.00*
N10 A29 50c black, *emer* (R) 5.25 *35.00*
N11 A29 $1 red & blk, *bl* 14.00 *47.50*
N12 A29 $2 rose red & gray grn 67.50 *100.00*
N13 A29 $5 grn & red, *grn* 675.00 800.00
Nos. N1-N13 (13) 800.50 1,055.

Stamps of Straits Settlements Handstamped in Red

Okugawa Seal

1942 Wmk. 4 *Perf. 14*
N14 A29 1c black 14.00 13.50
N15 A29 2c brown orange 29.00 27.50
N16 A29 3c green 24.00 27.50
N17 A29 5c brown 35.00 32.50
N18 A29 8c gray 32.50 42.50
N19 A29 10c dull violet 60.00 60.00
N20 A29 12c ultramarine 47.50 60.00
N21 A29 15c ultramarine 60.00 60.00
N22 A29 40c dk vio & rose red 125.00 140.00
N23 A29 50c blk, *emerald* 275.00 275.00
N24 A29 $1 red & blk, *bl* 300.00 325.00
N25 A29 $2 rose red & gray grn 1,000. 850.00
N26 A29 $5 grn & red, *grn* 2,750. 1,800.
Nos. N14-N26 (13) 4,752. 3,713.

Handstamped in Red

Uchibori Seal

N14a A29 1c 200.00 160.00
N15a A29 2c 200.00 140.00
N16a A29 3c 125.00 125.00
N17a A29 5c 2,750. 2,750.
N18a A29 8c 110.00 125.00
N19a A29 10c 200.00 200.00
N20a A29 12c 125.00 150.00
N21a A29 15c 150.00 160.00
Nos. N14a-N21a (8) 3,860. 3,810.

PERAK

'per-ə-,ak

LOCATION — On the west coast of the Malay Peninsula.
AREA — 7,980 sq. mi.
POP. — 1,327,120 (1960)
CAPITAL — Taiping

Straits Settlements No. 10 Handstamped in Black

1878 Wmk. 1 *Perf. 14*
1 A2 2c brown 2,400. 1,950.

Overprinted

Overprint 17x3½mm Wide

1880
2 A2 2c brown 40.00 *80.00*

Overprinted

Overprint 10 to 14½mm Wide
3 A2 2c brown 190.00 *200.00*

Same Overprint on Straits Settlements Nos. 40, 41a

1883 Wmk. 2
4 A2 2c brown 24.00 *72.50*
5 A2 2c rose 32.50 *60.00*

Overprinted

Overprint 14 to 15½mm Wide
6 A2 2c rose 5.50 4.00
a. Inverted overprint 525.00 675.00
b. Double overprint 800.00 800.00

Overprinted

Overprint 12¾ to 14mm Wide

1886-90
7 A2 2c rose 2.75 *8.50*
a. "FERAK" corrected by pen 450.00 *575.00*

Overprinted

Overprint 10x1¾mm
8 A2 2c rose 20.00 *60.00*

Overprinted

Overprint 13x2¾mm
10 A2 2c rose 9.00 *32.50*
a. Double overprint 1,950.

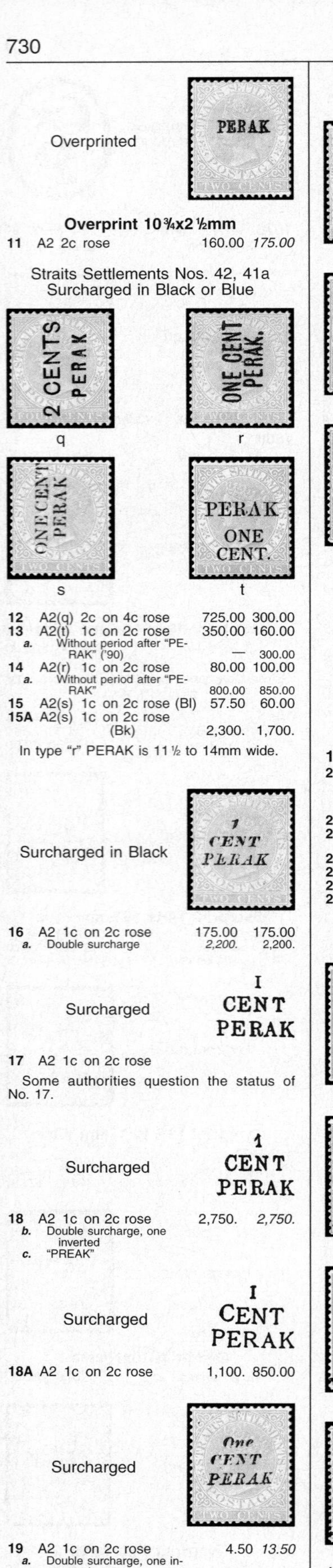

Overprinted

Overprint 10¾x2½mm

11 A2 2c rose 160.00 *175.00*

Straits Settlements Nos. 42, 41a Surcharged in Black or Blue

q r s t

12 A2(q) 2c on 4c rose 725.00 300.00
13 A2(t) 1c on 2c rose 350.00 160.00
a. Without period after "PERAK" ('90) — 300.00
14 A2(r) 1c on 2c rose 80.00 100.00
a. Without period after "PERAK" 800.00 850.00
15 A2(s) 1c on 2c rose (Bl) 57.50 60.00
15A A2(s) 1c on 2c rose (Bk) 2,300. 1,700.

In type "r" PERAK is 11½ to 14mm wide.

Surcharged in Black

16 A2 1c on 2c rose 175.00 175.00
a. Double surcharge *2,200.* 2,200.

Surcharged

I
CENT
PERAK

17 A2 1c on 2c rose

Some authorities question the status of No. 17.

Surcharged

1
CENT
PERAK

18 A2 1c on 2c rose 2,750. *2,750.*
b. Double surcharge, one inverted
c. "PREAK"

Surcharged

I
CENT
PERAK

18A A2 1c on 2c rose 1,100. 850.00

Surcharged

19 A2 1c on 2c rose 4.50 *13.50*
a. Double surcharge, one inverted
b. Inverted surcharge
c. "One" inverted *3,600.*
d. Double surcharge *1,500.*

No. 6 surcharged "1 CENT" in Italic Serifed Capital Letters

1886

19E A2 1c on 2c rose 3,300. 2,750.

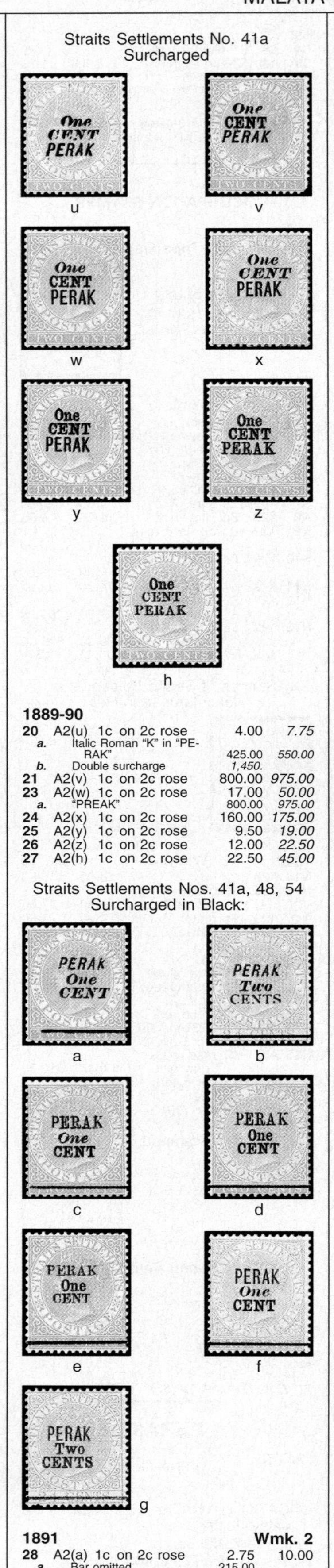

Straits Settlements No. 41a Surcharged

u v w x y z h

1889-90

20 A2(u) 1c on 2c rose 4.00 *7.75*
a. Italic Roman "K" in "PERAK" 425.00 *550.00*
b. Double surcharge *1,450.*
21 A2(v) 1c on 2c rose 800.00 *975.00*
23 A2(w) 1c on 2c rose 17.00 *50.00*
a. "PREAK" 800.00 *975.00*
24 A2(x) 1c on 2c rose 160.00 *175.00*
25 A2(y) 1c on 2c rose 9.50 *19.00*
26 A2(z) 1c on 2c rose 12.00 *22.50*
27 A2(h) 1c on 2c rose 22.50 *45.00*

Straits Settlements Nos. 41a, 48, 54 Surcharged in Black:

a b c d e f g

1891 **Wmk. 2**

28 A2(a) 1c on 2c rose 2.75 10.00
a. Bar omitted 215.00
29 A2(a) 1c on 6c violet 60.00 42.50
30 A3(b) 2c on 24c green 22.50 14.50
31 A2(c) 1c on 2c rose 9.75 37.50
a. Bar omitted *1,000.*
32 A2(d) 1c on 2c rose 2.75 14.50
a. Bar omitted 425.00

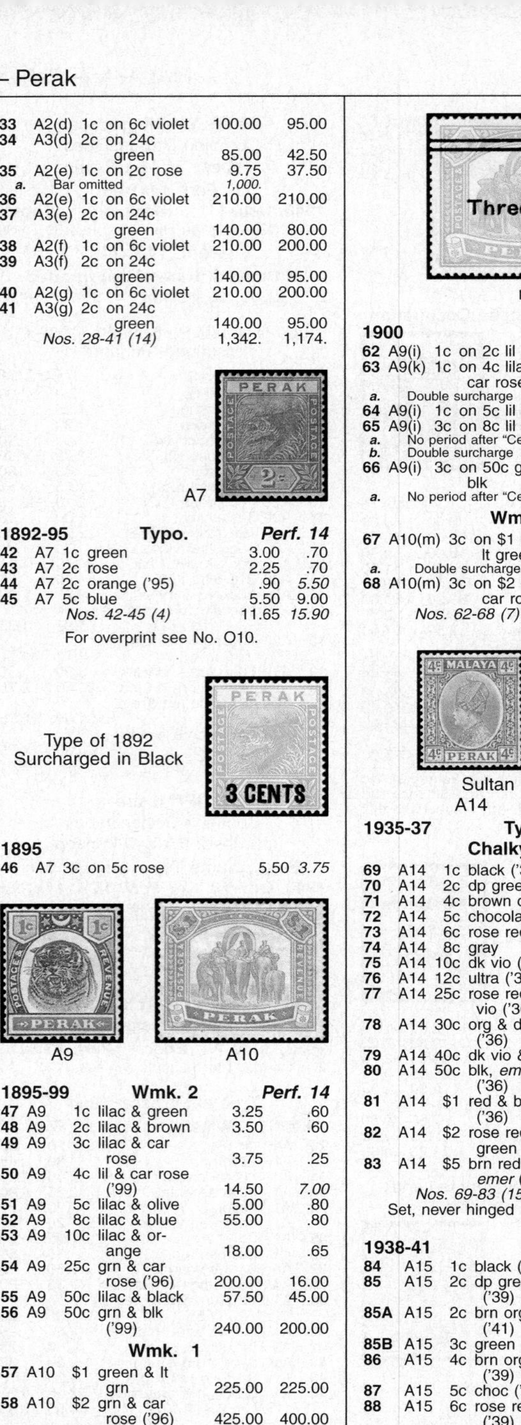

33 A2(d) 1c on 6c violet 100.00 95.00
34 A3(d) 2c on 24c green 85.00 42.50
35 A2(e) 1c on 2c rose 9.75 37.50
a. Bar omitted *1,000.*
36 A2(e) 1c on 6c violet 210.00 210.00
37 A3(e) 2c on 24c green 140.00 80.00
38 A2(f) 1c on 6c violet 210.00 200.00
39 A3(f) 2c on 24c green 140.00 95.00
40 A2(g) 1c on 6c violet 210.00 200.00
41 A3(g) 2c on 24c green 140.00 95.00
Nos. 28-41 (14) 1,342. 1,174.

A7

1892-95 **Typo.** ***Perf. 14***

42 A7 1c green 3.00 .70
43 A7 2c rose 2.25 .70
44 A7 2c orange ('95) .90 *5.50*
45 A7 5c blue 5.50 9.00
Nos. 42-45 (4) 11.65 *15.90*

For overprint see No. O10.

Type of 1892 Surcharged in Black

1895

46 A7 3c on 5c rose 5.50 *3.75*

A9 A10

1895-99 **Wmk. 2** ***Perf. 14***

47 A9 1c lilac & green 3.25 .60
48 A9 2c lilac & brown 3.50 .60
49 A9 3c lilac & car rose 3.75 .25
50 A9 4c lil & car rose ('99) 14.50 *7.00*
51 A9 5c lilac & olive 5.00 .80
52 A9 8c lilac & blue 55.00 .80
53 A9 10c lilac & orange 18.00 .65
54 A9 25c grn & car rose ('96) 200.00 16.00
55 A9 50c lilac & black 57.50 45.00
56 A9 50c grn & blk ('99) 240.00 200.00

Wmk. 1

57 A10 $1 green & lt grn 225.00 225.00
58 A10 $2 grn & car rose ('96) 425.00 400.00
59 A10 $3 green & ol ('96) 475.00 500.00
60 A10 $5 green & ultra 600.00 600.00
61 A10 $25 grn & org ('96) 11,000. 4,000.
Nos. 47-57 (11) 825.50 496.70

For surcharges and overprint see #62-68, O11, Malaya 9-13A.

Stamps of 1895-99 Surcharged in Black:

i k

m

1900 **Wmk. 2**

62 A9(i) 1c on 2c lil & brn .75 2.75
63 A9(k) 1c on 4c lilac & car rose 1.25 14.50
a. Double surcharge 1,325.
64 A9(i) 1c on 5c lil & ol 3.00 14.50
65 A9(i) 3c on 8c lil & bl 6.00 6.00
a. No period after "Cent" 200.00 *300.00*
b. Double surcharge 600.00 675.00
66 A9(i) 3c on 50c grn & blk 4.00 8.50
a. No period after "Cent" 160.00 *240.00*

Wmk. 1

67 A10(m) 3c on $1 grn & lt green 67.50 *175.00*
a. Double surcharge 1,800.
68 A10(m) 3c on $2 grn & car rose 40.00 *100.00*
Nos. 62-68 (7) 122.50 *321.25*

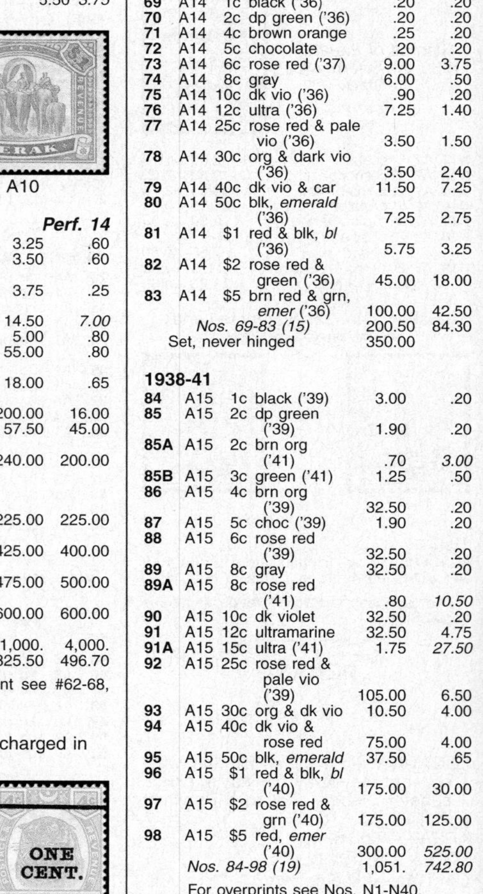

Sultan Iskandar
A14 A15

1935-37 **Typo.** **Wmk. 4**

Chalky Paper

69 A14 1c black ('36) .20 .20
70 A14 2c dp green ('36) .20 .20
71 A14 4c brown orange .25 .20
72 A14 5c chocolate .20 .20
73 A14 6c rose red ('37) 9.00 3.75
74 A14 8c gray 6.00 .50
75 A14 10c dk vio ('36) .90 .20
76 A14 12c ultra ('36) 7.25 1.40
77 A14 25c rose red & pale vio ('36) 3.50 1.50
78 A14 30c org & dark vio ('36) 3.50 2.40
79 A14 40c dk vio & car 11.50 7.25
80 A14 50c blk, *emerald* ('36) 7.25 2.75
81 A14 $1 red & blk, *bl* ('36) 5.75 3.25
82 A14 $2 rose red & green ('36) 45.00 18.00
83 A14 $5 brn red & grn, *emer* ('36) 100.00 42.50
Nos. 69-83 (15) 200.50 84.30
Set, never hinged 350.00

1938-41

84 A15 1c black ('39) 3.00 .20
85 A15 2c dp green ('39) 1.90 .20
85A A15 2c brn org ('41) .70 *3.00*
85B A15 3c green ('41) 1.25 .50
86 A15 4c brn org ('39) 32.50 .20
87 A15 5c choc ('39) 1.90 .20
88 A15 6c rose red ('39) 32.50 .20
89 A15 8c gray 32.50 .20
89A A15 8c rose red ('41) .80 *10.50*
90 A15 10c dk violet 32.50 .20
91 A15 12c ultramarine 32.50 4.75
91A A15 15c ultra ('41) 1.75 *27.50*
92 A15 25c rose red & pale vio ('39) 105.00 6.50
93 A15 30c org & dk vio 10.50 4.00
94 A15 40c dk vio & rose red 75.00 4.00
95 A15 50c blk, *emerald* 37.50 .65
96 A15 $1 red & blk, *bl* ('40) 175.00 30.00
97 A15 $2 rose red & grn ('40) 175.00 125.00
98 A15 $5 red, *emer* ('40) 300.00 *525.00*
Nos. 84-98 (19) 1,051. *742.80*

For overprints see Nos. N1-N40.

Catalogue values for unused stamps in this section, from this point to the end of the section, are for Never Hinged items.

Silver Wedding Issue
Common Design Types
Inscribed: "Malaya Perak"

1948, Dec. 1 Photo. *Perf. 14x14½*
99 CD304 10c purple 2.00 .20

Perf. 11½x11
Engraved; Name Typographed
100 CD305 $5 green 30.00 37.50

Common Design Types pictured following the introduction.

UPU Issue
Common Design Types
Inscribed: "Malaya-Perak"
Engr.; Name Typo. on 15c, 25c
Perf. 13½, 11x11½

1949, Oct. 10 Wmk. 4
101 CD306 10c rose violet .20 .20
102 CD307 15c indigo .70 .65
103 CD308 25c orange 1.10 1.25
104 CD309 50c slate 2.40 2.75
Nos. 101-104 (4) 4.40 4.85

Sultan Yussuf Izuddin Shah — A16

1950, Aug. 17 Typo. *Perf. 18*
105 A16 1c black .25 .40
106 A16 2c orange .25 .40
107 A16 3c green 2.00 1.40
108 A16 4c chocolate .25 .40
109 A16 6c gray .25 .40
110 A16 8c rose red .30 1.10
111 A16 10c plum .25 .40
112 A16 15c ultramarine .30 .50
113 A16 20c dk grn & blk .30 1.25
114 A16 25c org & plum .30 .40
115 A16 40c vio brn & rose red 2.00 7.50
116 A16 50c dp ultra & blk .75 .40
117 A16 $1 vio brn & ultra 10.00 1.10
118 A16 $2 rose red & emer 19.00 7.50
119 A16 $5 choc & emerald 67.50 22.50

1952-55
120 A16 5c rose violet .50 .40
121 A16 8c green 1.60 1.40
122 A16 12c rose red 1.60 3.50
123 A16 20c ultramarine 1.10 .40
124 A16 30c plum & rose red ('55) 1.90 .40
125 A16 35c dk vio & rose red 1.00 .50
Nos. 105-125 (21) 111.40 52.25

Coronation Issue
Common Design Type

1953 Engr. *Perf. 13½x13*
126 CD312 10c magenta & black 2.00 .20

Types of Kedah with Portrait of Sultan Yussuf Izuddin Shah
Perf. 13x12½, 12½x13, 13½ ($1)

1957-61 Engr. Wmk. 314
127 A8 1c black .25 .30
128 A8 2c red orange .45 .90
129 A8 4c dark brown .25 .25
130 A8 5c dk car rose .25 .25
131 A8 8c dark green 3.00 4.50
132 A7 10c chocolate 1.10 .25
133 A7 20c blue 2.25 .25
134 A7 50c ultra & blk ('60) .45 .25
a. Perf. 12½ .80 .80
135 A8 $1 plum & ultra 9.00 .55
136 A8 $2 red & grn ('61) 5.50 3.00
a. Perf. 12½ 6.00 5.75
137 A8 $5 ol grn & brn ('60) 13.50 10.50
a. Perf. 12½ 15.00 15.00
Nos. 127-137 (11) 36.00 21.00

Starting with 1963, issues of Perak are listed with Malaysia.

OFFICIAL STAMPS

Stamps and Types of Straits Settlements Overprinted in Black

1890 Wmk. 1 *Perf. 14*
O1 A3 12c blue 240.00 300.00
O2 A3 24c green 900.00 *1,000.*

Wmk. 2
O3 A2 2c rose 5.50 7.25
a. No period after "S" 85.00 105.00
b. Double overprint 1,800. 1,800.
O4 A2 4c brown 16.00 27.50
a. No period after "S" 200.00 *215.00*
O5 A2 6c violet 32.50 60.00
O6 A3 8c orange 42.50 90.00
O7 A7 10c slate 90.00 95.00
O8 A3 12c vio brown 300.00 400.00
O9 A3 24c green 225.00 *275.00*

P.G.S. stands for Perak Government Service.

Perak No. 45 Overprinted

1894
O10 A7 5c blue 85.00 1.25
a. Inverted overprint 1,150. 650.00

Same Overprint on No. 51

1897
O11 A9 5c lilac & olive 3.50 .60
a. Double overprint 725.00 500.00

OCCUPATION STAMPS

Issued under Japanese Occupation

Stamps of Perak, 1938-41, Handstamped in Black, Red, Brown or Violet

1942 Wmk. 4 *Perf. 14*
N1 A15 1c black 50.00 35.00
N2 A15 2c brn orange 35.00 21.00
N3 A15 3c green 35.00 37.50
N4 A15 5c chocolate 11.50 11.00
N5 A15 8c gray 55.00 37.50
N6 A15 8c rose red 25.00 35.00
N7 A15 10c dk violet 22.50 27.50
N8 A15 12c ultramarine 150.00 150.00
N9 A15 15c ultramarine 30.00 35.00
N10 A15 25c rose red & pale vio 27.50 30.00
N11 A15 30c org & dk vio 35.00 40.00
N12 A15 40c dk vio & rose red 175.00 190.00
N13 A15 50c blk, *emerald* 57.50 *60.00*
N14 A15 $1 red & blk, *bl* 275.00 300.00
N15 A15 $2 rose red & grn *1,500.* *1,500.*
N16 A15 $5 red, *emerald* 750.00 750.00

Some authorities claim No. N6 was not regularly issued. This overprint also exists on No. 85

Stamps of Perak, 1938-41, Overprinted in Black

N16A A15 1c black 40.00 40.00
N17 A15 2c brn org 1.60 1.60
a. Inverted overprint 27.50 29.00
N18 A15 3c green 1.25 1.40
a. Inverted overprint 27.50 30.00
N18B A15 5c chocolate 40.00
N19 A15 8c rose red 1.25 .65
a. Inverted overprint 10.00 10.00
b. Dbl. ovpt., one invtd. 250.00 275.00
c. Pair, one without ovpt. 500.00 475.00
N20 A15 10c dk violet 8.50 9.50
N21 A15 15c ultramarine 6.00 6.75
N21A A15 30c org & dk vio 35.00 35.00
N22 A15 50c blk, *emerald* 4.00 6.00
N23 A15 $1 red & blk, *bl* 350.00 *375.00*
N24 A15 $5 red, *emerald* 60.00 67.50
a. Inverted overprint 350.00 *400.00*

Some authorities claim Nos. N16A, N18B and N21A were not regularly issued.

Overprinted on Perak No. 87 and Surcharged in Black "2 Cents"
N25 A15 2c on 5c chocolate 2.00 1.40

Perak Nos. 84 and 89A Overprinted in Black

N26 A15 1c black 3.25 4.00
a. Inverted overprint 35.00 40.00
N27 A15 8c rose red 3.25 2.00
a. Inverted overprint 20.00 24.00

Overprinted on Perak No. 87 and Surcharged in Black "2 Cents"
N28 A15 2c on 5c chocolate 5.00 5.00
a. Inverted overprint 35.00 47.50
b. As "a," "2 Cents" omitted 50.00 57.50

Stamps of Perak, 1938-41, Overprinted or Surcharged in Black:

n

No. N31

No. N32

1943
N29 A15 1c black .65 .65
N30 A15 2c brn orange 35.00 35.00
N31 A15 2c on 5c choc 1.00 1.00
a. "2 Cents" inverted 35.00 40.00
b. Entire surcharge inverted 35.00 40.00
N32 A15 2c on 5c choc 1.40 1.40
a. Vertical characters invtd. 35.00 40.00
b. Entire surcharge inverted 35.00 40.00
N33 A15 3c green 37.50 37.50
N34 A15 5c chocolate 1.00 1.00
a. Inverted overprint 50.00 60.00
N35 A15 8c gray 35.00 35.00
N36 A15 8c rose red 1.00 1.00
a. Inverted overprint 35.00 40.00
N37 A15 10c dk violet 1.25 1.25
N38 A15 30c org & dk vio 2.75 4.00
N39 A15 50c blk, *emerald* 5.50 9.50
N40 A15 $5 red, *emerald* 75.00 85.00
Nos. N29-N40 (12) 197.05 212.30

No. N34 was also used in the Shan States of Burma. The Japanese characters read: "Japanese Postal Service."

Some authorities claim Nos. N30, N33 and N35 were not regularly issued.

PERLIS

'per-ləs

LOCATION — On the west coast of the Malay peninsula, adjoining Siam and Kedah.
AREA — 310 sq. mi.
POP. — 97,645 (1960)
CAPITAL — Kangar

Catalogue values for unused stamps in this section are for Never Hinged items.

Silver Wedding Issue
Common Design Types
Inscribed: "Malaya Perlis"
Perf. 14x14½

1948, Dec. 1 Photo. Wmk. 4
1 CD304 10c purple 2.50 *3.25*

Engraved; Name Typographed
Perf. 11½x11
2 CD305 $5 lt brown 37.50 *62.50*

UPU Issue
Common Design Types
Inscribed: "Malaya-Perlis"
Engr.; Name Typo. on 15c, 25c

1949, Oct. 10 *Perf. 13½, 11x11½*
3 CD306 10c rose violet .40 *1.50*
4 CD307 15c indigo 1.50 *4.00*
5 CD308 25c orange .95 *2.50*
6 CD309 50c slate 2.10 *4.50*
Nos. 3-6 (4) 4.95 12.50

Raja Syed Putra — A1

Perf. 18
1951, Mar. 26 Wmk. 4 Typo.
7 A1 1c black .25 *.40*
8 A1 2c orange .25 *.40*
9 A1 3c green 1.75 *6.00*
10 A1 4c chocolate .30 .50
11 A1 6c gray .30 1.00
12 A1 8c rose red 1.25 6.00
13 A1 10c plum .70 .40
14 A1 15c ultramarine 2.25 9.50
15 A1 20c dk green & blk 5.00 11.50
16 A1 25c org & rose lilac 1.75 3.00
17 A1 40c dk vio & rose red 5.00 *12.50*
18 A1 50c ultra & black 4.25 3.25
19 A1 $1 vio brn & ultra 13.00 13.00
20 A1 $2 rose red & emer 18.00 *45.00*
21 A1 $5 choc & emerald 57.50 *97.50*

1952-55
22 A1 5c rose violet .25 1.00
23 A1 8c green .85 *6.00*
24 A1 12c rose red .85 *7.00*
25 A1 20c ultramarine 1.25 2.25
26 A1 30c plum & rose red ('55) 8.75 *15.00*
27 A1 35c dk vio & rose red 2.25 *9.50*
Nos. 7-27 (21) 125.75 *250.70*

Coronation Issue
Common Design Type

1953, June 2 Engr. *Perf. 13½x13*
28 CD312 10c magenta & black 1.75 *5.50*

Types of Kedah with Portrait of Raja Syed Putra
Perf. 13x12½, 12½x13, 12½ ($2, $5), 13½ ($1)

1957-62 Engr. Wmk. 314
29 A8 1c black .25 .50
30 A8 2c red orange .25 *.50*
31 A8 4c dark brown .25 .25
32 A8 5c dk car rose .25 .25
33 A8 8c dark green 3.50 3.00
34 A7 10c chocolate 1.25 *3.00*
35 A7 20c blue 2.75 *5.00*
36 A7 50c ultra & blk ('62) 4.25 *5.50*
a. Perf. 12½ .50 *3.50*
37 A8 $1 plum & ultra 9.50 *14.75*
38 A8 $2 red & green 9.50 *11.00*
39 A8 $5 ol green & brown 17.50 *16.00*
Nos. 29-39 (11) 49.25 *59.75*

Starting in 1965, issues of Perlis are listed with Malaysia.

SELANGOR

sə-'laŋ-ər

LOCATION — South of Perak on the west coast of the Malay Peninsula.
AREA — 3,160 sq. mi.
POP. — 1,012,891 (1960)
CAPITAL — Kuala Lumpur

Stamps of the Straits Settlements Overprinted

Handstamped in Black or Red

1878 Wmk. 1 *Perf. 14*
1 A2 2c brown (Bk)
2 A2 2c brown (R) — 375.00

The authenticity of Nos. 1-2 and the 2c brown, watermarked Crown and CA, is questioned.

S.

Overprinted in Black

1882 **Wmk. 2**
3 A2 2c brown — 3,300.
4 A2 2c rose

Overprinted

Overprint 16 to 16¾mm Wide

1881 **Wmk. 1**
5 A2 2c brown 140.00 140.00
a. Double overprint

Overprint 16 to 17mm Wide

1882-83 **Wmk. 2**
6 A2 2c brown 200.00 160.00
7 A2 2c rose 160.00 125.00

Overprinted

Overprint 14¼x3mm

8 A2 2c rose 11.50 *24.00*
a. Double overprint 975.00 850.00

Overprinted

Overprint 14½ to 15½mm Wide

1886-89
9 A2 2c rose 42.50 *55.00*

Overprinted

Overprint 16½x1¾mm

9A A2 2c rose 67.50 72.50
b. Double overprint 1,000.

Overprinted

Overprint 15½ to 17mm Wide With Period

10 A2 2c rose 140.00 90.00

Without Period

11 A2 2c rose 14.50 3.25

Same Overprint, but Vertically

12 A2 2c rose 22.50 *37.50*

Overprinted

12A A2 2c rose 150.00 3.75

Overprinted *Selangor*

Overprint 17mm Wide

13 A2 2c rose 1,800. *1,950.*

Overprinted

14 A2 2c rose 425.00 190.00

Overprinted Vertically

1889
15 A2 2c rose 800.00 37.50

Overprinted Vertically

Overprint 19 to 20¾mm Wide

16 A2 2c rose 300.00 100.00

Similar Overprint, but Diagonally

17 A2 2c rose 2,750.

Overprinted Vertically

18 A2 2c rose 100.00 7.25

Same Overprint Horizontally

18A A2 2c rose 4,500.

Surcharged in Black:

a

b

c

d

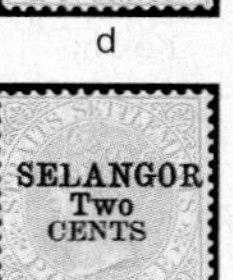

e

1891
19 A3 (a) 2c on 24c green 37.50 *75.00*
20 A3 (b) 2c on 24c green 225.00 *275.00*
21 A3 (c) 2c on 24c green 225.00 *150.00*
22 A3 (d) 2c on 24c green 125.00 *150.00*
23 A3 (e) 2c on 24c green 225.00 *275.00*
Nos. 19-23 (5) 837.50 925.00

A6

1891-95 **Typo.** **Wmk. 2**
24 A6 1c green 1.75 .30
25 A6 2c rose 4.25 1.25
26 A6 2c orange ('95) 3.00 1.00
27 A6 5c blue 30.00 5.75
Nos. 24-27 (4) 39.00 8.30

Type of 1891 Surcharged

1894
28 A6 3c on 5c rose 5.00 .70

A8

A9

1895-99 **Wmk. 2** ***Perf. 14***
29 A8 3c lilac & car rose 8.00 .35
30 A8 5c lilac & olive 8.50 .35
31 A8 8c lilac & blue 65.00 8.50
32 A8 10c lilac & orange 13.50 2.00
33 A8 25c grn & car rose 100.00 60.00
34 A8 50c lilac & black 80.00 29.00
35 A8 50c green & black 500.00 150.00

Wmk. 1
36 A9 $1 green & lt grn 70.00 160.00
37 A9 $2 grn & car rose 275.00 300.00
38 A9 $3 green & olive 675.00 500.00
39 A9 $5 green & ultra 300.00 400.00
40 A9 $10 grn & brn vio 850.00 1,000.
41 A9 $25 green & org 4,000. 4,000.

High values with revenue cancellations are plentiful and inexpensive.

Surcharged in Black:

1900 **Wmk. 2**
42 A8 1c on 5c lilac & olive 80.00 *125.00*
43 A8 1c on 50c grn & blk 1.60 16.00
a. Double surcharge 1,900.
44 A8 3c on 50c grn & blk 10.50 *16.00*
Nos. 42-44 (3) 92.10 *157.00*

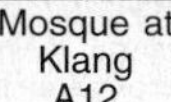

Mosque at Klang
A12

Sultan Sulaiman
A13

1935-41 **Typo.** **Wmk. 4** ***Perf. 14***
45 A12 1c black ('36) .30 .20
46 A12 2c dp green ('36) .95 .20
46A A12 2c org brn ('41) 4.00 1.90
46B A12 3c green ('41) 1.25 *2.10*
47 A12 4c orange brown .30 .20
48 A12 5c chocolate .95 .20
49 A12 6c rose red 7.75 .20
50 A12 8c gray .80 .20
51 A12 10c dk violet ('36) .80 .20
52 A12 12c ultra ('36) 2.25 .20
52A A12 15c ultra ('41) 12.50 *37.50*
53 A12 25c rose red & pale vio ('36) 2.25 *1.10*
54 A12 30c org & dk vio ('36) 2.10 *1.60*
55 A12 40c dk vio & car 2.75 1.90
56 A12 50c blk, *emer* ('36) 2.25 .80
57 A13 $1 red & black, *blue* ('36) 8.50 1.25
58 A13 $2 rose red & green ('36) 30.00 8.25
59 A13 $5 brn red & grn, *emer* ('36) 85.00 *50.00*
Nos. 45-59 (18) 164.70 *108.00*

Nos. 46A-46B were printed on both ordinary and chalky paper; 15c only on ordinary paper; other values only on chalky paper.

An 8c rose red was prepared but not issued.

For overprints see #N1-N15, N18A-N24, N26-N39.

Sultan Hisam-ud-Din Alam Shah
A14 A15

1941
72 A14 $1 red & blk, *blue* 10.50 7.00
73 A14 $2 car & green 65.00 *40.00*
Set, never hinged 100.00

A $5 stamp of type A14, issued during the Japanese occupation with different overprints (Nos. N18, N25A, N42), also exists without overprint. The unoverprinted stamp was not issued. Value $125.

For overprints see #N16-N17, N24A, N25, N40-N41.

Catalogue values for unused stamps in this section, from this point to the end of the section, are for Never Hinged items.

Silver Wedding Issue
Common Design Types
Inscribed: "Malaya Selangor"
Perf. 14x14½

1948, Dec. 1 **Photo.** **Wmk. 4**
74 CD304 10c purple .20 .20

Perf. 11½x11
Engraved; Name Typographed
75 CD305 $5 green 37.50 35.00

Common Design Types pictured following the introduction.

UPU Issue
Common Design Types
Inscribed: "Malaya-Selangor"
Engr.; Name Typo. on Nos. 77 & 78

1949, Oct. 10 ***Perf. 13½, 11x11½***
76 CD306 10c rose violet .50 .50
77 CD307 15c indigo .70 .70
78 CD308 25c orange 1.10 1.10
79 CD309 50c slate 2.50 2.50
Nos. 76-79 (4) 4.80 4.80

1949, Sept. 12 **Typo.** ***Perf. 18***
80 A15 1c black .25 .35
81 A15 2c orange .25 .35
82 A15 3c green .55 2.25
83 A15 4c chocolate .25 .35
84 A15 6c gray .35 .35
85 A15 8c rose red .55 2.25
86 A15 10c plum .25 .35
87 A15 15c ultramarine 1.75 .35
88 A15 20c dk grn & black 3.00 1.25
89 A15 25c orange & rose lil 1.50 .35
90 A15 40c dk vio & rose red 4.00 9.50
91 A15 50c ultra & black 1.10 .35
92 A15 $1 vio brn & ultra 4.50 .35
93 A15 $2 rose red & emer 13.50 2.25
94 A15 $5 choc & emerald 72.50 3.50

1952-55
95 A15 5c rose violet .25 .35
96 A15 8c green .35 .35
97 A15 12c rose red 1.10 .75
98 A15 20c ultramarine 2.25 .35
99 A15 30c plum & rose red ('55) 3.00 .75
100 A15 35c dk vio & rose red 1.75 1.25
Nos. 80-100 (21) 113.00 27.95

Coronation Issue
Common Design Type

1953, June 2 **Engr.** ***Perf. 13½x13***
101 CD312 10c magenta & black 1.75 .20

A16

Sultan Hisam-ud-Din Alam Shah — A17

Designs as in Kelantan, 1957.

Perf. 13x12½, 12½x13, 13½ ($1)

1957-60 Engr. Wmk. 314

102 A17 1c black .25 *2.75*
103 A17 2c red orange .50 *1.00*
104 A17 4c dark brown .25 .25
105 A17 5c dark car rose .25 .25
106 A17 8c dark green 2.10 *4.50*
107 A16 10c chocolate 1.00 .25
108 A16 20c blue 3.25 .25
109 A16 50c ultra & blk ('60) .50 .25
a. Perf. 12½ .40 .20
110 A17 $1 plum & ultra 3.50 .25
111 A17 $2 red & grn ('60) 4.50 3.25
a. Perf. 12½ 3.00 1.40
112 A17 $5 ol grn & brn ('60) 10.50 2.40
a. Perf. 12½ 10.00 4.25
Nos. 102-112 (11) 26.60 15.40

See Nos. 114-120.

Sultan Salahuddin Abdul Aziz Shah — A18

1961, June 28 Photo. *Perf. 14½x14*
113 A18 10s multicolored .40 .20

Sultan Salahuddin Abdul Aziz Shah, installation.

Types of 1957 with Portrait of Sultan Salahuddin Abdul Aziz Shah

Designs as before.

Perf. 13x12½, 12½x13

1961-62 Engr. Wmk. 338

114 A17 1c black .40 *2.75*
115 A17 2c red orange .40 *3.00*
116 A17 4c dark brown 1.00 .20
117 A17 5c dark car rose 1.00 .20
118 A17 8c dark green 4.25 *6.50*
119 A16 10c vio brown ('61) .90 .20
120 A16 20c blue 7.00 1.25
Nos. 114-120 (7) 14.95 14.10

Starting in 1965, issues of Selangor are listed with Malaysia.

OCCUPATION STAMPS

Issued under Japanese Occupation

Stamps of Selangor 1935-41 Handstamped Vertically or Horizontally in Black, Red, Brown or Violet

1942, Apr. 3 Wmk. 4 *Perf. 14*

N1 A12 1c black 15.00 21.00
N2 A12 2c deep green 600.00 600.00
N3 A12 2c orange brown 55.00 55.00
N4 A12 3c green 35.00 17.00
N5 A12 5c chocolate 10.00 10.00
N6 A12 6c rose red 200.00 200.00
N7 A12 8c gray 27.50 27.50
N8 A12 10c dark violet 22.50 27.50
N9 A12 12c ultramarine 47.50 47.50
N10 A12 15c ultramarine 17.00 20.00
N11 A12 25c rose red & pale vio 80.00 95.00
N12 A12 30c org & dk vio 15.00 30.00
N13 A12 40c dk vio & car 100.00 140.00
N14 A12 50c blk, *emerald* 40.00 47.50
N15 A13 $5 brn red & grn, *emer* 275.00 275.00

Some authorities believe No. N15 was not issued regularly.

Handstamped Vertically on Stamps and Type of Selangor 1941 in Black or Red

N16 A14 $1 red & blk, *bl* 67.50 80.00
N17 A14 $2 car & green 80.00 110.00
N18 A14 $5 brn red & grn, *emer* 110.00 110.00

Stamps and Type of Selangor, 1935-41, Overprinted in Black

1942, May

N18A A12 1c black 110.00 110.00
N19 A12 3c green 1.00 1.00
N19A A12 5c chocolate 110.00 110.00
N20 A12 10c dark violet 35.00 35.00
N21 A12 12c ultramarine 2.75 5.00
N22 A12 15c ultramarine 5.50 4.00
N23 A12 30c org & dk vio 35.00 35.00
N24 A12 40c dk vio & car 4.00 4.00
N24A A14 $1 red & blk, *bl* 35.00 35.00
N25 A14 $2 car & green 24.00 30.00
N25A A14 $5 red & grn, *emer* 55.00 55.00
Nos. N18A-N25A (11) 417.25 424.00

Overprint is horizontal on $1, $2, $5.

On Nos. N18A and N19 the overprint is known reading up, instead of down.

Some authorities claim Nos. N18A, N19A, N20, N23, N24A and N25A were not regularly issued.

Selangor No. 46B Overprinted in Black

DAI NIPPON
YUBIN

1942, Dec.
N26 A12 3c green 400.00 400.00

Stamps and Type of Selangor, 1935-41, Overprinted or Surcharged in Black or Red:

i

k

l

m

1943

N27 A12(i) 1c black 1.40 1.40
N28 A12(k) 1c black (R) .90 .90
N29 A12(l) 2c on 5c choc (R) .90 .90
N30 A12(i) 3c green 1.00 1.00
N31 A12(l) 3c on 5c choc .65 1.00
N32 A12(k) 5c choc (R) .65 1.00
N33 A12(l) 6c on 5c choc .25 *.90*
N34 A12(m) 6c on 5c choc .25 *1.00*
N35 A12(i) 12c ultra 1.40 1.60
N36 A12(i) 15c ultra 6.75 10.00
N37 A12(k) 15c ultra 13.50 13.50
N38 A12(m) $1 on 10c dk vio .50 *1.40*
N39 A12(m) $1.50 on 30c org & dk vio .50 *1.40*
N40 A14(i) $1 red & blk, *blue* 6.75 8.50
N41 A14(i) $2 car & grn 24.00 24.00
N42 A14(i) $5 brn red & grn, *emer* 50.00 55.00
Nos. N27-N42 (16) 109.40 123.50

The "i" overprint is vertical on Nos. N40-N42 and is also found reading in the opposite direction on Nos. N30, N35 and N36.

The overprint reads: "Japanese Postal Service."

Singapore is listed following Sierra Leone.

SUNGEI UJONG

'suŋə ü-juŋ

Formerly a nonfederated native state on the Malay Peninsula, which in 1895 was consolidated with the Federated State of Negri Sembilan.

Stamps of the Straits Settlements Overprinted in Black

Overprinted

1878 Wmk. 1 *Perf. 14*
2 A2 2c brown 3,600. 3,900.

Overprinted

SUNGEI
UJONG

4 A2 2c brown 400.00
5 A2 4c rose *1,950.* *2,000.*

No. 5 is no longer recognized by some experts.

Overprinted

1882-83 Wmk. 2
6 A2 2c brown 375.00 —
7 A2 4c rose 4,250. 4,800.

This overprint on the 2c brown, wmk. 1, is probably a trial printing.

Overprinted

11 A2 2c brown 325.00 *400.00*

Overprinted

1881-84

14 A2 2c brown 1,200. 550.00
15 A2 2c rose 140.00 140.00
a. "Ujong" printed sideways
b. "Sungei" printed twice
16 A2 4c brown 325.00 425.00
17 A3 8c orange 2,250. 1,700.
18 A7 10c slate 725.00 625.00

Overprinted

19 A2 2c brown 57.50 *160.00*

Overprinted

1885-90

Without Period
20 A2 2c rose 45.00 *77.50*

With Period
21 A2 2c rose 125.00 90.00
a. "UNJOG" 5,750. 4,000.

Overprinted

22 A2 2c rose 95.00 110.00
a. Double overprint 775.00 775.00

Overprinted

23 A2 2c rose 125.00 *150.00*

Overprinted

24 A2 2c rose 30.00 *47.50*
a. Double overprint

Overprinted

25 A2 2c rose 110.00 *125.00*

Overprinted

26 A2 2c rose 175.00 *175.00*
c. Double overprint

Overprinted

Overprint 14-16x3mm
26A A2 2c rose 12.00 *16.00*

Overprinted

26B A2 2c rose 50.00 21.00

Stamp of 1883-91 Surcharged:

a

b

c

SUNGEI
UJONG
Two
CENTS
d

1891

27 A3 (a) 2c on 24c green 240.00 *275.00*
28 A3 (b) 2c on 24c green 1,100. *1,200.*
29 A3 (c) 2c on 24c green 425.00 *500.00*

30	A3 (d)	2c on 24c green	1,100.	*1,200.*
		Nos. 27-30 (4)	2,865.	3,175.

On Nos. 27-28, SUNGEI is 14½mm, UJONG 12¾x2½mm.

A3

A4

1891-94 Typo. *Perf. 14*

31	A3	2c rose	40.00	35.00
32	A3	2c orange ('94)	2.25	5.50
33	A3	5c blue ('93)	6.50	7.75
		Nos. 31-33 (3)	48.75	48.25

Type of 1891 Surcharged in Black

1894

34	A3	1c on 5c green	1.40	.90
35	A3	3c on 5c rose	3.25	*6.00*

1895

36	A4	3c lilac & car rose	15.00	4.75

Stamps of Sungei Ujong were superseded by those of Negri Sembilan in 1895.

TRENGGANU

treŋ-'gä-ˌnü

LOCATION — On the eastern coast of the Malay Peninsula.
AREA — 5,050 sq. mi.
POP. — 302,171 (1960)
CAPITAL — Kuala Trengganu

A1

Sultan Zenalabidin — A2

1910-19 Typo. Wmk. 3 *Perf. 14*

Ordinary Paper

1a	A1	1c blue green	2.10	1.25
2	A1	2c red vio & brn ('15)	1.25	1.10
3	A1	3c rose red	2.75	2.75
4	A1	4c brn orange	4.25	*6.75*
5	A1	4c grn & org brn ('15)	2.50	*5.75*
6	A1	4c scarlet ('19)	1.50	*2.10*
7	A1	5c gray	1.75	*4.50*
8	A1	5c choc & gray ('15)	3.00	2.40
9	A1	8c ultramarine	1.75	11.00
10	A1	10c red & grn, *yel* ('15)	1.75	2.75

Chalky Paper

11a	A1	10c violet, *pale yel*	4.00	9.00
12	A1	20c red vio & vio	4.25	*5.75*
13	A1	25c dl vio & grn ('15)	9.75	*42.50*
14	A1	30c blk & dl vio ('15)	8.50	*65.00*
15	A1	50c blk & sep, *grn*	5.75	*11.50*
16	A1	$1 red & blk, *blue*	22.50	*29.00*
17	A1	$3 red & grn, *grn* ('15)	225.00	*500.00*
18	A2	$5 lil & blue grn	225.00	*675.00*
19	A2	$25 green & car	1,200.	*2,750.*
		Revenue Cancel		300.00
		Nos. 1a-19 (19)	1,727.	*4,128.*

On No. 19 the numerals and Arabic inscriptions at top, left and right are in color on a colorless background.

Overprints are listed after No. 41. For surcharges see Nos. B1-B4.

Sultan Badaru'l-alam
A3 A4

1921-38 Wmk. 4 *Perf. 14*

Chalky Paper

20	A3	1c black ('25)	2.75	1.75
21	A3	2c deep green	1.75	2.40
22	A3	3c dp grn ('25)	3.00	1.10
23	A3	3c lt brn ('38)	32.50	*22.50*
24	A3	4c rose red	2.40	2.00
25	A3	5c choc & gray	3.25	8.00
26	A3	5c vio, *yel* ('25)	2.75	2.00
27	A3	6c orange ('24)	6.00	.85
28	A3	8c gray ('38)	42.50	9.50
29	A3	10c ultramarine	3.25	1.50
30	A3	12c ultra ('25)	7.00	*7.25*
31	A3	20c org & dl vio	3.50	*2.40*
32	A3	25c dk vio & grn	3.75	*5.00*
33	A3	30c blk & dl vio	5.50	6.00
34	A3	35c red, *yel* ('25)	7.75	*12.50*
35	A3	50c car & green	11.50	5.25
36	A3	$1 ultra & vio, *bl* ('29)	15.00	6.00
37	A3	$3 red & green, *emer* ('25)	87.50	*240.00*
38	A4	$5 red & grn, *yel* ('38)	500.00	*2,800.*
39	A4	$25 blue & lil	750.00	*1,250.*
40	A4	$50 org & green	1,850.	*3,200.*
41	A4	$100 red & green	5,750.	7,500.
		Nos. 20-37 (18)	241.65	*336.00*

On Nos. 39 to 41 the numerals and Arabic inscriptions at top, left and right are in color on a colorless background.

A 2c orange, 6c gray, 8c rose red and 15c ultramarine, type A3, exist, but are not known to have been regularly issued.

For surcharges and overprints see Nos. 45-46, N1-N60.

Stamps of 1910-21 Overprinted in Black: "MALAYA BORNEO EXHIBITION" in THREE LINES

1922, Mar. Wmk. 3

8a	A1	5c chocolate & gray	4.75	*37.50*
10a	A1	10c red & green, *yel*	4.75	*37.50*
12a	A1	20c red vio & violet	4.25	*50.00*
13a	A1	25c dull vio & green	4.25	*50.00*
14a	A1	30c black & dull vio	4.25	*50.00*
15a	A1	50c blk & sepia, *grn*	4.25	*50.00*
16a	A1	$1 red & blk, *blue*	20.00	*95.00*
17a	A1	$3 red & grn, *green*	210.00	*575.00*
18a	A2	$5 lil & blue green	300.00	*575.00*

Wmk. 4

21a	A3	2c deep green	2.75	*47.50*
24a	A3	4c rose red	7.75	*47.50*
		Nos. 8a-24a (11)	567.00	*1,615.*

Industrial fair at Singapore, Mar. 31-Apr. 15.

1921 Wmk. 3

Chalky Paper

42	A3	$1 ultra & vio, *bl*	30.00	*40.00*
43	A3	$3 red & grn, *emer*	160.00	*160.00*
44	A4	$5 red & green, *yel*	160.00	*150.00*
		Nos. 42-44 (3)	350.00	*350.00*

Types of 1921-25 Surcharged in Black

1941, May 1 Wmk. 4 *Perf. 13½x14*

45	A3	2c on 5c magenta, *yel*	8.00	*6.50*
46	A3	8c on 10c lt ultra	13.00	*6.50*

For overprints see #N30-N33, N46-N47, N59-N60.

Catalogue values for unused stamps in this section, from this point to the end of the section, are for Never Hinged items.

Silver Wedding Issue

Common Design Types
Inscribed: "Malaya Trengganu"

1948, Dec. 1 Photo. *Perf. 14x14½*

47	CD304	10c purple	.20	.20

Engraved; Name Typographed

Perf. 11½x11

48	CD305	$5 rose car	37.50	62.50

Common Design Types pictured following the introduction.

UPU Issue

Common Design Types
Inscribed: "Malaya-Trengganu"

Engr.; Name Typo. on 15c, 25c

Perf. 13½, 11x11½

1949, Oct. 10 Wmk. 4

49	CD306	10c rose violet	.65	.65
50	CD307	15c indigo	.80	2.10
51	CD308	25c orange	1.40	3.50
52	CD309	50c slate	2.10	3.50
		Nos. 49-52 (4)	4.95	9.75

Sultan Ismail Nasiruddin Shah — A5

1949, Dec. 27 Typo. *Perf. 18*

53	A5	1c black	.40	.45
54	A5	2c orange	.40	.50
55	A5	3c green	1.25	1.50
56	A5	4c chocolate	.60	.50
57	A5	6c gray	1.25	1.25
58	A5	8c rose red	1.60	1.90
59	A5	10c plum	.60	.50
60	A5	15c ultramarine	1.75	1.60
61	A5	20c dk grn & black	2.40	5.00
62	A5	25c org & rose lilac	2.25	3.25
63	A5	40c dk vio & rose red	4.50	27.50
64	A5	50c dp ultra & black	2.75	2.75
65	A5	$1 vio brn & ultra	5.50	10.00
66	A5	$2 rose red & emer	30.00	24.50
67	A5	$5 choc & emerald	80.00	67.50

1952-55

68	A5	5c rose violet	.40	.50
69	A5	8c green	1.60	3.25
70	A5	12c rose red	1.60	*6.75*
71	A5	20c ultramarine	1.60	1.50
72	A5	30c plum & rose red ('55)	3.00	6.75
73	A5	35c dk vio & rose red	3.50	6.75
		Nos. 53-73 (21)	146.95	174.20

Coronation Issue

Common Design Type

1953, June 2 Engr. *Perf. 13½x13*

74	CD312	10c magenta & blk	1.75	1.00

Types of Kedah with Portrait of Sultan Ismail

Perf. 13x12½, 12½x13, 13½ ($1), 12½ ($2)

1957-63 Engr. Wmk. 314

75	A8	1c black	.30	.50
76	A8	2c red orange	1.00	.50
77	A8	4c dark brown	.30	.50
78	A8	5c dark car rose	.30	.50
79	A8	8c dark green	9.00	.50
80	A7	10c chocolate	.40	.50
81	A7	20c blue	.85	.60
82	A7	50c blue & blk	.40	2.40
a.		Perf. 12½	.50	2.25
83	A8	$1 plum & ultra	9.50	9.50
84	A8	$2 red & green	18.00	12.00
85	A8	$5 ol grn & brn, perf. 12½	27.50	25.00
a.		Perf. 13x12½	32.50	30.00
		Nos. 75-85 (11)	67.55	52.50

Issued: 20c, #85, 6/26/57; 2c, 50c, $1, 7/25/57; 10c, 8/4/57; 1c, 4c, 5c, 8c, $2, 8/21/57; #82a, 5/17/60; #85a, 8/13/63.

Starting in 1965, issues of Trengganu are listed with Malaysia.

SEMI-POSTAL STAMPS

Nos. 3, 4 and 9 Surcharged

1917, Oct. Wmk. 3 *Perf. 14*

B1	A1	3c + 2c rose red	1.50	*8.00*
a.		"CSOSS"	65.00	*100.00*
b.		Comma after "2c"	4.00	*10.50*
c.		Pair, one without surcharge	2,900.	2,900.
B2	A1	4c + 2c brn org	2.25	*12.50*
a.		"CSOSS"	275.00	*275.00*
b.		Comma after "2c"	16.00	*42.50*
B3	A1	8c + 2c ultra	3.50	*24.00*
a.		"CSOSS"	175.00	*210.00*
b.		Comma after "2c"	13.00	*45.00*
		Nos. B1-B3 (3)	7.25	*44.50*

Same Surcharge on No. 5

1918

B4	A1	4c + 2c grn & org brn	4.25	*11.50*
a.		Pair, one without surcharge	*2,300.*	

POSTAGE DUE STAMPS

D1

Perf. 14

1937, Aug. 10 Typo. Wmk. 4

J1	D1	1c rose red	8.25	*65.00*
J2	D1	4c green	9.00	*72.50*
J3	D1	8c lemon	47.50	*400.00*
J4	D1	10c light brown	92.50	*115.00*
		Nos. J1-J4 (4)	157.25	*652.50*
		Set, never hinged	275.00	

For overprints see Nos. NJ1-NJ4.

OCCUPATION STAMPS

Issued under Japanese Occupation

Stamps of Trengganu, 1921-38, Handstamped in Black or Brown

1942 Wmk. 4 *Perf. 14*

N1	A3	1c black	110.00	110.00
N2	A3	2c deep green	190.00	275.00
N3	A3	3c lt brown	140.00	110.00
N4	A3	4c rose red	275.00	190.00
N5	A3	5c violet, *yel*	17.50	19.00
N6	A3	6c orange	13.50	20.00
N7	A3	8c gray	17.50	25.00
N8	A3	10c ultramarine	13.50	27.50
N9	A3	12c ultramarine	15.00	25.00
N10	A3	20c org & dl vio	15.00	22.50
N11	A3	25c dk vio & grn	13.50	27.50
N12	A3	30c blk & dl vio	13.50	25.00
N13	A3	35c red, *yel*	22.50	27.50
N14	A3	50c car & grn	125.00	95.00
N15	A3	$1 ultra & vio, *blue*	1,650.	1,750.
N16	A3	$3 red & grn, *emerald*	125.00	140.00
N17	A4	$5 red & grn, *yellow*	240.00	240.00
N17A	A4	$25 blue & lil	1,500.	
N17B	A4	$50 org & grn	*8,800.*	
N17C	A4	$100 red & grn	950.00	

Handstamped in Red

N18	A3	1c black	275.00	225.00
N19	A3	2c dp green	140.00	160.00
N20	A3	5c violet, *yel*	35.00	20.00
N21	A3	6c orange	20.00	20.00
N22	A3	8c gray	275.00	240.00
N23	A3	10c ultramarine	275.00	275.00
N24	A3	12c ultramarine	55.00	55.00

N25	A3	20c org & dl vio	35.00	35.00
N26	A3	25c dk vio & grn	40.00	40.00
N27	A3	30c blk & dl vio	35.00	35.00
N28	A3	35c red, *yellow*	35.00	20.00
N29	A3	$3 red & grn, *emerald*	100.00	40.00
N29A	A3	$25 blue & lil	500.00	500.00

Handstamped on Nos. 45 and 46 in Black or Red

N30	A3	2c on 5c (Bk)	140.00	140.00
N31	A3	2c on 5c (R)	100.00	100.00
N32	A3	8c on 10c (Bk)	25.00	35.00
N33	A3	8c on 10c (R)	35.00	40.00

Stamps of Trengganu, 1921-38, Overprinted in Black

1942

N34	A3	1c black	15.00	17.00
N35	A3	2c deep green	100.00	*140.00*
N36	A3	3c light brown	16.00	29.00
N37	A3	4c rose red	15.00	20.00
N38	A3	5c violet, *yel*	10.00	20.00
N39	A3	6c orange	10.00	17.00
N40	A3	8c gray	67.50	20.00
N41	A3	12c ultramarine	10.00	13.50
N42	A3	20c org & dl vio	13.50	25.00
N43	A3	25c dk vio & grn	13.50	17.00
N44	A3	30c blk & dl vio	13.50	20.00
N45	A3	$3 red & grn, *emer*	100.00	140.00

Overprinted on Nos. 45 and 46 in Black

N46	A3	2c on 5c mag, *yel*	13.50	17.00
N47	A3	8c on 10c lt ultra	11.50	20.00
		Nos. N34-N47 (14)	409.00	*515.50*

Stamps of Trengganu, 1921-38, Overprinted in Black

1943

N48	A3	1c black	13.50	19.00
N49	A3	2c deep green	13.50	27.50
N50	A3	5c violet, *yel*	11.50	27.50
N51	A3	6c orange	15.00	27.50
N52	A3	8c gray	95.00	67.50
N53	A3	10c ultramarine	100.00	175.00
N54	A3	12c ultramarine	19.00	*35.00*
N55	A3	20c org & dl vio	20.00	*35.00*
N56	A3	25c dl vio & grn	19.00	*35.00*
N57	A3	30c blk & dl vio	20.00	*35.00*
N58	A3	35c red, *yellow*	20.00	*40.00*

Overprinted on Nos. 45 and 46 in Black

N59	A3	2c on 5c mag, *yel*	11.00	*35.00*
N60	A3	8c on 10c lt ultra	27.50	*35.00*
		Nos. N48-N60 (13)	385.00	*594.00*

The Japanese characters read: "Japanese Postal Service."

OCCUPATION POSTAGE DUE STAMPS

Trengganu Nos. J1-J4 Handstamped in Black or Brown

1942 Wmk. 4 *Perf. 14*

NJ1	D1	1c rose red	67.50	*95.00*
NJ2	D1	4c green	125.00	*125.00*
NJ3	D1	8c lemon	25.00	*67.50*
NJ4	D1	10c light brown	25.00	*67.50*
		Nos. NJ1-NJ4 (4)	242.50	*355.00*

The handstamp reads: "Seal of Post Office of Malayan Military Department."

MALAYSIA

mə-'lā-zhē-ə

LOCATION — Malay peninsula and northwestern Borneo

GOVT. — Federation within the British Commonwealth

AREA — 127,317 sq. mi.

POP. — 21,376,066 (1999 est.)

CAPITAL — Putrajaya (administrative); Kuala Lumpur (financial)

The Federation of Malaysia was formed Sept. 16, 1963, by a merger of the former Federation of Malaya, Singapore, Sarawak, and North Borneo (renamed Sabah), totaling 14 states. Singapore withdrew in 1965.

Sabah and Sarawak, having different rates than mainland Malaysia, continued to issue their own stamps after joining the federation. The system of individual state issues was extended to Perak in Oct. 1963, and to the 10 other members in Nov. 1965.

100 Cents (Sen) = 1 Dollar (Ringgit)

Catalogue values for all unused stamps in this country are for Never Hinged items.

Watermarks

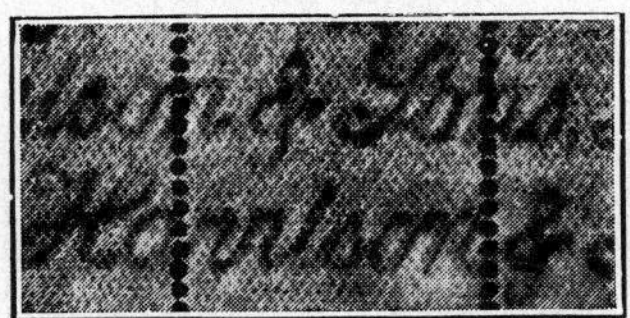

Wmk. 233 — "Harrison & Sons, London" in Script

Wmk. 338 — PTM Multiple

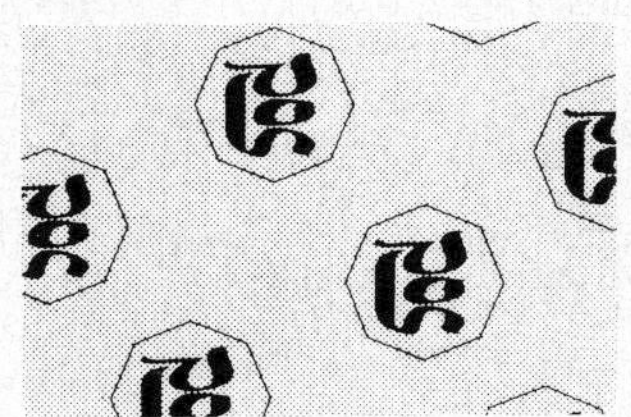

Wmk. 378 — Multiple POS in Octagonal Frame

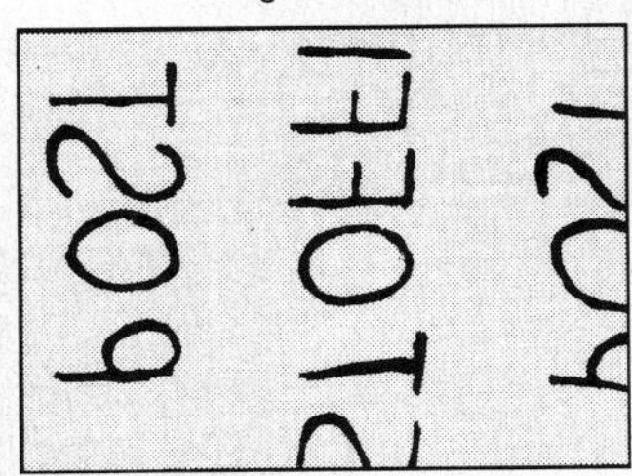

Wmk. 380 — "POST OFFICE"

Wmk. 388 — Multiple "SPM"

Map of Malaysia and 14-point Star — A1

Wmk. PTM Multiple (338)

1963, Sept. 16 Photo. *Perf. 14*

1	A1	10s violet & yellow	.30	.25
a.		Yellow omitted	100.00	75.00
2	A1	12s green & yellow	2.50	.80
3	A1	50s dk red brown & yel	2.00	.55
		Nos. 1-3 (3)	4.80	1.60

Formation of the Federation of Malaysia.

Orchids — A2

1963, Oct. 3 Unwmk. *Perf. 13x14*

4	A2	6s red & multi	1.50	.35
5	A2	25s black & multi	4.00	2.75

4th World Orchid Conf., Singapore, Oct. 8-11.

Parliament and Commonwealth Parliamentary Association Emblem — A4

1963, Nov. 4 *Perf. 13½*

7	A4	20s dk car rose & gold	.60	.30
8	A4	30s dk green & gold	1.90	.90

9th Commonwealth Parliamentary Assoc. Conf.

Globe, Torch, Snake and Hands — A5

1964, Oct. 10 Photo. *Perf. 14x13*

9	A5	25s Prus grn, red & blk	.25	.40
10	A5	30s lt violet, red & blk	.40	.30
11	A5	50s dull yellow, red & blk	.60	.30
		Nos. 9-11 (3)	1.25	1.00

Eleanor Roosevelt, 1884-1962.

ITU Emblem and Radar Tower — A6

1965, May 17 Photo. *Perf. 11½*

Granite Paper

12	A6	2c violet, blk & org	.70	.70
13	A6	25c brown, blk & org	3.50	3.50
14	A6	50c emerald, blk & brn	3.00	.55
		Nos. 12-14 (3)	7.20	4.75

Cent. of the ITU.

National Mosque, Kuala Lumpur — A7

1965, Aug. 27 Wmk. 338 *Perf. 14½*

15	A7	6c dark car rose	.25	.20
16	A7	15c dark red brown	.45	.20
17	A7	20c Prussian green	.75	.35
		Nos. 15-17 (3)	1.45	.75

Natl. Mosque at Kuala Lumpur, opening.

Control Tower and Airport — A8

Crested Wood Partridge — A9

1965, Aug. 30 *Perf. 14½x14*

18	A8	15c blue, blk & grn	.35	.20
a.		Green omitted	55.00	55.00
19	A8	30c brt pink, blk & grn	1.10	.30

Intl. Airport at Kuala Lumpur, opening.

1965, Sept. 9 Photo. *Perf. 14½*

Birds: 30c, Fairy bluebird. 50c, Blacknaped oriole. 75c, Rhinoceros hornbill. $1, Zebra dove. $2, Argus pheasant. $5, Indian paradise flycatcher. $10, Banded pitta.

20	A9	25c orange & multi	.75	.20
21	A9	30c tan & multi	.85	.20
a.		Blue omitted	140.00	
22	A9	50c rose & multi	1.40	.20
a.		Rose omitted	60.00	
23	A9	75c yel grn & multi	1.50	.20
24	A9	$1 ultra & multi	2.50	.35
25	A9	$2 maroon & multi	4.75	.65
26	A9	$5 dk grn & multi	25.00	2.50
27	A9	$10 brt red & multi	60.00	9.25
		Nos. 20-27 (8)	96.75	13.55

Soccer and Sepak Raga (Ball Game) — A10

National Monument, Kuala Lumpur — A11

1965, Dec. 14 Unwmk. *Perf. 13*

28	A10	25c shown	.60	.30
29	A10	30c Runner	.60	.60
30	A10	50c Diver	.80	.30
		Nos. 28-30 (3)	2.00	1.20

3rd South East Asia Peninsular Games, Kuala Lumpur, Dec. 14-21.

1966, Feb. 8 Wmk. 338 *Perf. 13½*

31	A11	10c yellow & multi	.25	.20
a.		Blue omitted	60.00	
32	A11	20c ultra & multi	1.50	.45

The National Monument by US sculptor Felix W. de Weldon commemorates the struggle of the people of Malaysia for peace and for freedom from communism.

Tuanku Ismail Nasiruddin — A12

Penang Free School — A13

1966, Apr. 11 Unwmk. *Perf. 13½*

33 A12 15c yellow & black .25 .20
34 A12 50c blue & black 1.25 .35

Installation of Tuanku Ismail Nasiruddin of Trengganu as Paramount Ruler (Yang di-Pertuan Agong).

Perf. 13x12½

1966, Oct. 21 Photo. Wmk. 338

Design: 50c, like 20c with Malayan inscription and school crest added.

35 A13 20c multicolored .50 .30
36 A13 50c multicolored 1.50 .40

Penang Free School, 150th anniversary.

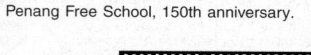

Mechanized Plowing and Palms — A14

No. 38, Rural health nurse, mother and child, dispensary. No. 39, Communication: train, plane, ship, cars and radio tower. No. 40, School children. No. 41, Dam and rice fields.

1966, Dec. 1 Unwmk. *Perf. 13*

37 A14 15c bister brn & multi .80 .30
38 A14 15c blue & multi .80 .30
39 A14 15c crimson & multi .80 .30
40 A14 15c ol green & multi .80 .30
41 A14 15c yellow & multi .80 .30
Nos. 37-41 (5) 4.00 1.50

Malaysia's First Development Plan.

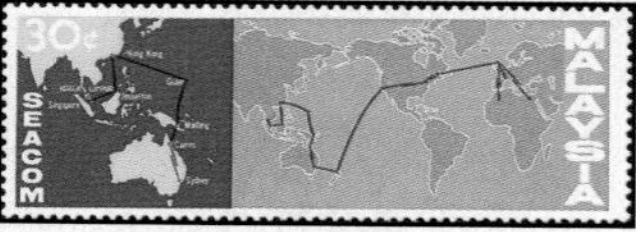

Maps Showing International and South East Asia Telephone Links — A15

1967, Mar. 30 Photo. *Perf. 13*

42 A15 30c multicolored .75 .30
43 A15 75c multicolored 5.25 4.50

Completion of the Hong Kong-Malaysia link of the South East Asia Commonwealth Cable, SEACOM.

Hibiscus and Rulers of Independent Malaysia — A16

1967, Aug. 31 Wmk. 338 *Perf. 14*

44 A16 15c yellow & multi .40 .30
45 A16 50c blue & multi 1.60 .60

10th anniversary of independence.

Arms of Sarawak and Council Mace — A17

1967, Sept. 8 Photo.

46 A17 15c yel green & multi .25 .20
47 A17 50c multicolored .65 .35

Representative Council of Sarawak, cent.

Straits Settlements No. 13 and Malaysia No. 20 — A18

30c, Straits Settlements #15, Malaysia #21. 50c, Straits Settlements #17, Malaysia #22.

1967, Dec. 2 Unwmk. *Perf. 11½*

48 A18 25c brt blue & multi 1.90 1.25
49 A18 30c dull green & multi 2.25 1.50
50 A18 50c yellow & multi 3.25 2.25
Nos. 48-50 (3) 7.40 5.00

Cent. of the Malaysian (Straits Settlements) postage stamps.

Tapped Rubber Tree and Molecular Unit — A20

Tapped Rubber Tree and: 30c, Rubber packed for shipment. 50c, Rubber tires for Vickers VC 10 plane.

Wmk. 338

1968, Aug. 29 Litho. *Perf. 12*

53 A20 25c brick red, blk & org .30 .25
54 A20 30c yellow, black & org .45 .30
55 A20 50c ultra, black & org .75 .30
Nos. 53-55 (3) 1.50 .85

Natural Rubber Conference, Kuala Lumpur.

Olympic Rings, Mexican Hat and Cloth — A21

Tunku Abdul Rahman Putra Al-Haj — A22

75c, Olympic rings & Malaysian batik cloth.

1968, Oct. 12 Wmk. 338 *Perf. 12*

56 A21 30c rose red & multi .50 .60
57 A21 75c ocher & multi 1.00 .25

19th Olympic Games, Mexico City, 10/12-27.

Perf. 13½

1969, Feb. 8 Photo. Unwmk.

Various portraits of Prime Minister Tunku Abdul Rahman Putra Al-Haj with woven pandanus patterns as background. 50c is horiz.

58 A22 15c gold & multi .40 .20
59 A22 20c gold & multi 1.00 .75
60 A22 50c gold & multi 1.25 .50
Nos. 58-60 (3) 2.65 1.45

Issued for Solidarity Week, 1969.

Malaysian Girl Holding Sheaves of Rice — A23

1969, Dec. 8 Wmk. 338 *Perf. 13½*

61 A23 15c silver & multi .35 .20
62 A23 75c gold & multi 1.90 .65

International Rice Year.

Kuantan Radar Station — A24

Intelsat III Orbiting Earth A25

Perf. 14x13

1970, Apr. 6 Photo. Unwmk.

63 A24 15c multicolored .60 .20
64 A25 30c multicolored 1.90 .85
65 A25 30c gold & multi 1.90 .95
Nos. 63-65 (3) 4.40 2.00

Satellite Communications Earth Station at Kuantan, Pahang, Malaysia.

No. 63 was printed tete beche (50 pairs) in sheet of 100 (10x10).

Blue-branded King Crow — A26

ILO Emblem — A27

Butterflies: 30c, Saturn. 50c, Common Nawab. 75c, Great Mormon. $1, Orange albatross. $2, Raja Brooke's birdwing. $5, Centaur oakblue. $10, Royal Assyrian.

1970, Aug. 31 Litho. *Perf. 13x13½*

66 A26 25c multicolored 1.10 .20
67 A26 30c multicolored 1.00 .20
68 A26 50c multicolored 1.50 .20
69 A26 75c multicolored 1.25 .20
70 A26 $1 multicolored 2.25 .25
71 A26 $2 multicolored 3.75 .35
72 A26 $5 multicolored 9.00 2.00
73 A26 $10 multicolored 18.00 5.00
Nos. 66-73 (8) 37.85 8.40

1970, Sept. 7 *Perf. 14½x13½*

74 A27 30c gray & blue .35 .30
75 A27 75c rose & blue .90 .30

50th anniv. of the ILO.

UN Emblem and Doves — A28

Sultan Abdul Halim — A29

Designs: 25c, Doves in elliptical arrangement. 30c, Doves arranged diagonally.

1970, Oct. 24 Litho. *Perf. 13x12½*

76 A28 25c lt brown, blk & yel .40 .25
77 A28 30c lt blue, yel & black .60 .25
78 A28 50c lt ol green & black 1.00 .40
Nos. 76-78 (3) 2.00 .90

25th anniversary of the United Nations.

Perf. 14½x14

1971, Feb. 20 Photo. Unwmk.

79 A29 10c yellow, blk & gold .50 .35
80 A29 15c purple, blk & gold .50 .35
81 A29 50c blue, blk & gold 1.75 .75
Nos. 79-81 (3) 2.75 1.45

Installation of Sultan Abdul Halim of Kedah as Paramount Ruler.

Bank Building and Crescent A30

1971, May 15 Photo. *Perf. 14*

82 A30 25c silver & black 3.00 1.00
83 A30 50c gold & brown 5.00 1.50

Opening of Main office of the Negara Malaysia Bank. Nos. 82-83 have circular perforations around vignette set within a white square of paper, perf. on 4 sides.

Malaysian Parliament — A31

Malaysian Parliament, Kuala Lumpur — A32

1971, Sept. 13 Litho. *Perf. 13½*

84 A31 25c multicolored 1.90 .40

Perf. 12½x13

85 A32 75c multicolored 4.75 .95

17th Commonwealth Parliamentary Conference, Kuala Lumpur.

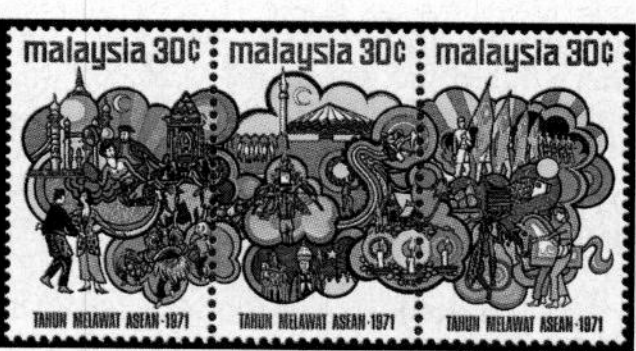

Malaysian Festival — A33

1971, Sept. 18 *Perf. 14½*

86 A33 Strip of 3 9.00 5.50
a. 30c Dancing couple 2.50 .75
b. 30c Dragon 2.50 .75
c. 30c Flags and stage horse 2.50 .75

Visit ASEAN (Association of South East Asian Nations) Year.

Elephant and Tiger — A34

Children's Drawings: No. 88, Cat and kittens. No. 89, Sun, flower and chick. No. 90, Monkey, elephant and lion in jungle. No. 91, Butterfly and flowers.

1971, Oct. 2 *Perf. 12½*

Size: 35x28mm

87 A34 15c pale yellow & multi 3.00 .25
88 A34 15c pale yellow & multi 3.00 .25

Size: 21x28mm

89 A34 15c pale yellow & multi 3.00 .25

Size: 35x28mm

90	A34	15c pale yellow & multi	3.00	.25
91	A34	15c pale yellow & multi	3.00	.25
a.		Strip of 5, #87-91	18.00	3.00

25th anniv. of UNICEF.

Track and Field — A35

30c, Sepak Raga (a ball game). 50c, Hockey.

1971, Dec. 11 ***Perf. 14½***

92	A35	25c orange & multi	1.10	.35
93	A35	30c violet & multi	1.40	.45
94	A35	50c green & multi	1.90	.95
		Nos. 92-94 (3)	4.40	1.75

6th South East Asia Peninsular Games. Kuala Lumpur, Dec. 11-18.

South East Asian Tourist Attractions — A36

Designs include stylized map.

1972, Jan. 31 **Litho.** ***Perf. 14½***

95	A36	Strip of 3	12.50	8.75
a.		30c Flag at left	3.25	.55
b.		30c High rise building	3.25	.55
c.		30c Horse & rider	3.25	.55

Pacific Area Tourist Assoc. Conference.

Secretariat Building — A37

50c, Kuala Lumpur Secretariat Building by night.

1972, Feb. 1 ***Perf. 14½x14***

96	A37	25c lt blue & multi	1.40	.40
97	A37	50c black & multi	3.25	.75

Achievement of city status by Kuala Lumpur.

Social Security Emblem — A38

WHO Emblem — A39

1973, July 2 **Litho.** ***Perf. 14½x13½***

98	A38	10c orange & multi	.25	.20
99	A38	15c yellow & multi	.35	.20
100	A38	50c gray & multi	.90	.50
		Nos. 98-100 (3)	1.50	.90

Introduction of Social Security System.

1973, Aug. 1 ***Perf. 13x12½, 12½x13***

Design: 30c, WHO emblem, horiz.

101	A39	30c yellow & multi	.75	.20
102	A39	75c blue & multi	1.75	.75

25th anniv. of World Health Org.

Flag of Malaysia, Fireworks, Hibiscus — A40

1973, Aug. 31 **Litho.** ***Perf. 14½***

103	A40	10c olive & multi	.85	.30
104	A40	15c brown & multi	.65	.30
105	A40	50c gray & multi	3.00	1.25
		Nos. 103-105 (3)	4.50	1.85

10th anniversary of independence.

INTERPOL and Malaysian Police Emblems A41

Design: 75c, "50" with INTERPOL and Malaysian police emblems.

1973, Sept. 15 ***Perf. 12½***

106	A41	25c brown org & multi	1.50	.40
107	A41	75c deep violet & multi	3.50	1.25

50th anniv. of the Intl. Criminal Police Organization (INTERPOL).

MAS Emblem and Plane A42

1973, Oct. 1 **Litho.** ***Perf. 14½***

108	A42	15c green & multi	.25	.20
109	A42	30c blue & multi	.75	.30
110	A42	50c brown & multi	1.75	.85
		Nos. 108-110 (3)	2.75	1.35

Inauguration of Malaysian Airline System.

View of Kuala Lumpur — A43

1974, Feb. 1 **Litho.** ***Perf. 12½x13***

111	A43	25c multicolored	1.00	.40
112	A43	50c multicolored	2.00	1.25

Establishment of Kuala Lumpur as a Federal Territory.

Development Bank Emblem and Projects — A44

1974, Apr. 25 **Litho.** ***Perf. 13½***

113	A44	30c gray & multi	.75	.30
114	A44	75c bister & multi	1.25	1.00

7th annual meeting of the Board of Governors of the Asian Development Bank.

Map of Malaysia and Scout Emblem — A45

Scout Saluting, Malaysian and Scout Flags — A46

Design: 50c, Malaysian Scout emblem.

Perf. 14x13½, 13x13½ (15c)

1974, Aug. 1 **Litho.**

115	A45	10c multicolored	.70	.20
116	A46	15c multicolored	1.10	.20
117	A45	50c multicolored	3.25	.90
		Nos. 115-117 (3)	5.05	1.30

Malaysian Boy Scout Jamboree.

Power Installations, NEB Emblem — A47

National Electricity Board Building A48

Perf. 14x14½, 13½x14½

1974, Sept. 1 **Litho.**

118	A47	30c multicolored	.85	.30
119	A48	75c multicolored	1.25	1.00

National Electricity Board, 25th anniversary.

"100," UPU and P.O. Emblems A49

1974, Oct. 9 **Litho.** ***Perf. 14½x13½***

120	A49	25c olive, red & yel	.50	.35
121	A49	30c blue, red & yel	.50	.25
122	A49	75c ocher, red & yel	1.00	.50
		Nos. 120-122 (3)	2.00	1.10

Centenary of Universal Postal Union.

Gravel Pump Tin Mine A50

Designs: 20c, Open cast mine. 50c, Silver tin ingot and tin dredge.

1974, Oct. 31 **Litho.** ***Perf. 14***

123	A50	15c silver & multi	.55	.30
124	A50	20c silver & multi	3.75	.50
125	A50	50c silver & multi	7.75	.80
		Nos. 123-125 (3)	12.05	1.60

4th World Tin Conference, Kuala Lumpur.

Hockey, Cup and Emblem A51

1975, Mar. 1 **Litho.** ***Perf. 14***

126	A51	30c yellow & multi	1.50	.30
127	A51	75c blue & multi	3.50	1.00

Third World Cup Hockey Tournament, Kuala Lumpur, Mar. 1-15.

Trade Union Emblem and Workers — A52

1975, May 1 **Litho.** ***Perf. 14x14½***

128	A52	20c orange & multi	.40	.25
129	A52	25c lt green & multi	.60	.25
130	A52	30c ultra & multi	.60	.30
		Nos. 128-130 (3)	1.60	.80

Malaysian Trade Union Cong., 25th anniv.

National Women's Organization Emblem and Heads — A53

1975, Aug. 25 **Litho.** ***Perf. 14***

131	A53	10c emerald & multi	.80	.30
132	A53	15c lilac rose & multi	.80	.30
133	A53	50c blue & multi	2.25	.70
		Nos. 131-133 (3)	3.85	1.30

International Women's Year.

Ubudiah Mosque, Perak — A54

b, Zahir Mosque, Kedah. c, National Mosque, Kuala Lumpur. d, Sultan Abu Bakar Mosque, Johore. e, Kuching State Mosque, Sarawak.

1975, Sept. 22 **Litho.** ***Perf. 14½x14***

134		Strip of 5	18.00	12.00
a.-e.	A54	15c single stamp	3.00	.50

Koran reading competition 1975, Malaysia.

Rubber Plantation and Emblem A55

Designs: 30c, "50" in form of latex cup and tire with emblem. 75c, Six test tubes showing various aspects of natural rubber.

1975, Oct. 22 **Litho.** ***Perf. 14x14½***

135	A55	10c gold & multi	.55	.30
136	A55	30c gold & multi	1.50	.60
137	A55	75c gold & multi	3.75	1.50
		Nos. 135-137 (3)	5.80	2.40

Rubber Research Institute of Malaysia, 50th anniversary.

Butterflies A55a

Coil Stamps

1976, Feb. 6 ***Perf. 14***

137A	A55a	10c Hebomoia glaucippe aturia	1.50	1.50
137B	A55a	15c Precis orithya wallacei	1.50	1.50

Scrub Typhus — A56

Sultan Jahya Petra — A57

Designs: 25c, Malaria (microscope, blood cells, slides). $1, Beri-beri (grain and men).

1976, Feb. 6 Litho. *Perf. 14*

138 A56 20c red orange & multi	.95	.30
139 A56 25c ultra & multi	1.10	.30
140 A56 $1 yellow & multi	2.25	1.00
Nos. 138-140 (3)	4.30	1.60

Institute for Medical Research, Kuala Lumpur, 75th anniversary.

Perf. 14½x13½

1976, Feb. 28 Photo.

141 A57 10c yel, black & bis	.40	.25
142 A57 15c lilac, black & bis	.60	.25
143 A57 50c blue, black & bis	3.50	1.40
Nos. 141-143 (3)	4.50	1.90

Installation of Sultan Jahya Petra of Kelantan as Paramount Ruler (Yang di-Pertuan Agong).

Council and Administrative Buildings — A58

1976, Aug. 17 Litho. *Perf. 12½*

144 A58 15c orange & black	.50	.20
145 A58 20c brt red lilac & black	.65	.25
146 A58 50c blue & black	1.25	.60
Nos. 144-146 (3)	2.40	1.05

Opening of the State Council Complex and Administrative Building, Sarawak.

Provident Fund Building A59

Provident Fund Emblems — A60

50c, Provident Fund Building at night.

Perf. 13½x14½, 14½ (A60)

1976, Oct. 18 Litho.

147 A59 10c blue & multi	.60	.35
148 A60 25c gray & multi	.55	.20
149 A59 50c violet & multi	.80	.55
Nos. 147-149 (3)	1.95	1.10

Employees' Provident Fund, 25th anniv.

Rehabilitation of the Blind — A61

75c, Blind man casting large shadow.

1976, Nov. 20 *Perf. 13½x14½*

150 A61 10c multicolored	.60	.30
151 A61 75c multicolored	1.90	1.25

25th anniv. of the Malaysian Assoc. for the Blind.

Abdul Razak and Crowd — A62

Designs: b, Abdul Razak in cap and gown at lectern. c, Abdul Razak pointing to new roads and bridges on map. d, New constitution. e, Abdul Razak addressing Association of Southeast Asian Countries.

1977, Jan. 14 Photo. *Perf. 14x14½*

152 Strip of 5	12.50	10.50
a.-e. A62 15c single stamp	1.50	.50

Prime Minister Tun Haji Abdul Razak bi Dato Hussein (1922-1976).

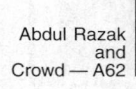

FELDA Housing Development A63

Design: 30c, View of oil palm settlement area and FELDA emblem.

1977, July 7 Litho. *Perf. 13½x14½*

153 A63 15c multicolored	.75	.30
154 A63 30c multicolored	1.25	.55

Federal Land Development Authority (FELDA), 21st anniversary.

"10" — A64

ASEAN, 10th anniv.: 75c, Flags of ASEAN members: Malaysia, Philippines, Singapore, Thailand and Indonesia.

1977, Aug. 8 Litho. *Perf. 13½x14½*

155 A64 10c multicolored	.75	.20
156 A64 75c multicolored	1.25	.75

SEA Games Emblems A65

Designs: 20c, Ball, symbolic of 9 participating nations. 75c, Running.

Perf. 13½x14½

1977, Nov. 19 Litho.

157 A65 10c multicolored	.40	.25
158 A65 20c multicolored	.40	.25
159 A65 75c multicolored	1.00	.40
Nos. 157-159 (3)	1.80	.90

9th South East Asia Games, Kuala Lumpur.

Bank Emblem A66

1978, Mar. 15 Litho. *Perf. 14*

160 A66 30c multicolored	.50	.20
161 A66 75c multicolored	1.00	.40

2nd annual meeting of Islamic Development Bank Governors, Kuala Lumpur, Mar. 1978.

Government Building A67

Designs: Views of Shah Alam.

1978, Dec. 7 Litho. *Perf. 13½x14½*

162 A67 10c multicolored	.25	.25
163 A67 30c multicolored	.35	.20
164 A67 75c multicolored	1.00	.40
Nos. 162-164 (3)	1.60	.85

Inauguration of Shah Alam as state capital of Selangor.

Mobile Post Office in Village — A68

Designs: 25c, General Post Office, Kuala Lumpur. 50c, Motorcyclist, rural mail delivery.

1978, July 10 *Perf. 13*

165 A68 10c multicolored	1.25	.40
166 A68 25c multicolored	1.40	.85
167 A68 50c multicolored	1.75	1.40
Nos. 165-167 (3)	4.40	2.65

4th Conf. of Commonwealth Postal Administrators.

Jamboree Emblem A69

Bees and Honeycomb A70

1978, July 26 Litho. *Perf. 13½*

168 A69 15c multicolored	1.25	.30
169 A70 $1 multicolored	4.75	1.40

4th Boy Scout Jamboree, Sarawak.

Globe, Crest and WHO Emblem A71

1978, Sept. 30 *Perf. 13½x14½*

170 A71 15c blue, red & black	.50	.35
171 A71 30c green, red & black	.90	.45
172 A71 50c pink, red & black	1.50	.70
Nos. 170-172 (3)	2.90	1.50

Global eradication of smallpox.

Dome of the Rock A72

1978, Aug. 21 Litho. *Perf. 12½*

173 A72 15c red & multi	1.25	.35
174 A72 30c blue & multi	3.25	1.40

For Palestinian fighters and their families.

Tiger — A73

Designs: 40c, Cobego. 50c, Chevrotain. 75c, Pangolin. $1, Leatherback turtle. $2, Tapir. $5, Gaur. $10, Orangutan, vert.

Perf. 15x14½, 14½x15

1979, Jan. 4 Litho. Wmk. 378

175 A73 30c multicolored	.60	.20
176 A73 40c multicolored	.70	.20
177 A73 50c multicolored	1.10	.20
178 A73 75c multicolored	1.25	.20
179 A73 $1 multicolored	1.60	.20
180 A73 $2 multicolored	2.50	.75
181 A73 $5 multicolored	7.25	2.00
182 A73 $10 multicolored	13.00	3.00
Nos. 175-182 (8)	28.00	6.75

1983-87

Unwmk.

175a A73 30c ('84)	1.40	.70
176a A73 40c ('84)	1.60	.55
177a A73 50c ('84)	1.90	.55
178a A73 75c ('87)	11.00	8.50
179a A73 $1	5.25	.55
180a A73 $2	7.00	.85
181a A73 $5 ('85)	20.00	7.00
182a A73 $10 ('86)	32.50	10.50
Nos. 175a-182a (8)	80.65	29.20

Central Bank of Malaysia — A74

Year of the Child Emblem — A75

10c, Central Bank of Malaysia & emblem.

Perf. 13½

1979, Jan. 26 Litho. Unwmk.

183 A74 10c multicolored, horiz.	.35	.35
184 A74 75c multicolored	1.40	.80

Central Bank of Malaysia, 20th anniv.

1979, Feb. 24 *Perf. 14*

Intl. Year of the Child: 15c, Children of the world, globe and ICY emblem. $1, Children at play, ICY emblem.

185 A75 10c multicolored	.60	.20
186 A75 15c multicolored	.50	.20
187 A75 $1 multicolored	4.00	1.40
Nos. 185-187 (3)	5.10	1.80

Symbolic Rubber Plant — A76

Designs: 10c, Symbolic palm. 75c, Symbolic rubber products.

1979, Apr. 30 Litho. *Perf. 13*

188 A76 10c brt green & gold	.25	.20
189 A76 20c multicolored	.60	.20
190 A76 75c brt green & gold	.75	.40
Nos. 188-190 (3)	1.60	.80

Centenary of rubber production (in 1977).

Rafflesia Hasseltii A77

Flowers: 2c, Pterocarpus indicus. 5c, Lagerstroemia speciosa. 10c, Durio zibethinus. 15c, Hibiscus. 20c, Rhododendron scortechinii. 25c, Phaeomeria speciosa.

Perf. 15x14½

1979, Apr. 30 Wmk. 378

191 A77 1c multicolored	.20	.20
192 A77 2c multicolored	.20	.20
193 A77 5c multicolored	.20	.20
a. Unwmkd. ('84)		
194 A77 10c multicolored	.20	.20
a. White flowers, unwmkd. ('84)	.20	.20
195 A77 15c multicolored	.25	.20
a. 15c yel & multi, unwmkd. ('83)	.20	.20
196 A77 20c multicolored	.30	.20
a. 20c greenish & multi, unwmkd. ('83)	.25	.20
197 A77 25c multicolored	.35	.20
a. Unwmkd. ('85)	5.00	
Nos. 191-197 (7)	1.70	1.40

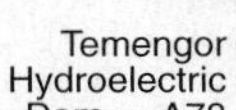

Temengor Hydroelectric Dam — A78

Designs: 25c, 50c, Dam and river, diff.

Perf. 13½x14½

1979, Sept. 19 **Litho.** **Unwmk.**

198 A78 15c multicolored .40 .30
199 A78 25c multicolored .85 .30
200 A78 50c multicolored 1.25 .40
Nos. 198-200 (3) 2.50 1.00

"TELECOM 79" — A79

Telecom Emblem and: 15c, Telephone receiver and globes. 50c, Modes of communication.

1979, Sept. 20 *Perf. 13½*

Size: 34x25mm

201 A79 10c multicolored .40 .25
202 A79 15c multicolored .30 .20

Perf. 14

Size: 29x28mm

203 A79 50c multicolored .90 .30
Nos. 201-203 (3) 1.60 .75

3rd World Telecommunications Exhibition, Geneva, Sept. 20-26.

Haji Ahmad Shah — A80

1980, July 10 **Litho.** *Perf. 14½*

204 A80 10c multicolored .35 .20
205 A80 15c multicolored .25 .20
206 A80 50c multicolored .80 .30
Nos. 204-206 (3) 1.40 .70

Installation of Sultan Haji Ahmad Shah of Pahang as Paramount Ruler (Yang di-Pertuan Agong).

Pahang-Sarawak Cable — A81

Designs: 15c, Dial with views of Kuantan and Kuching. 50c, Telephone and maps.

1980, Aug. 31 **Litho.** *Perf. 13½*

207 A81 10c shown .40 .20
208 A81 15c multicolored .30 .20
209 A81 50c multicolored .70 .25
Nos. 207-209 (3) 1.40 .65

National University of Malaysia, 10th Anniversary A82

15c, Jalan Pantai Baru campus. 75c, Great Hall & Tun Haji Abdul Razak (1st chancellor).

1980, Sept. 2 **Litho.** *Perf. 13½*

210 A82 10c shown .35 .20
211 A82 15c multicolored .25 .20
212 A82 75c multicolored .75 .30
Nos. 210-212 (3) 1.35 .70

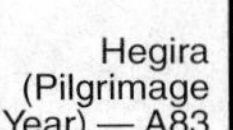

Hegira (Pilgrimage Year) — A83

1980, Nov. 9

213 A83 15c multicolored .35 .20
214 A83 50c multicolored .70 .25

International Year of the Disabled A84

Sultan Mahmud of Trengganu A85

1981, Feb. 14 **Litho.** *Perf. 13½*

215 A84 10c Child learning to walk .75 .20
216 A84 15c Seamstress .65 .20
217 A84 75c Athlete 3.25 .65
Nos. 215-217 (3) 4.65 1.05

1981, Mar. 21 **Litho.** *Perf. 14½*

218 A85 10c multicolored .20 .20
219 A85 15c multicolored .30 .20
220 A85 50c multicolored 1.10 .30
Nos. 218-220 (3) 1.60 .70

Industrial Training Seminar A86

Designs: Various workers.

1981, May 2 **Litho.** *Perf. 13½*

221 A86 10c multicolored .40 .20
222 A86 15c multicolored .25 .20
223 A86 30c multicolored .40 .20
224 A86 75c multicolored .70 .25
Nos. 221-224 (4) 1.75 .85

World Energy Conference, 25th anniv. — A87

1981, June 17 **Litho.** *Perf. 13½*

225 A87 10c "25" .55 .30
226 A87 15c Sources of Energy .45 .30
227 A87 75c Non-renewable energy 1.90 .55
Nos. 225-227 (3) 2.90 1.15

Centenary of Sabah — A88

1981, Aug. 31 **Litho.** *Perf. 12*

228 A88 15c Views, 1881 and 1981 .75 .30
229 A88 80c Traditional and modern farming 3.75 .75

Rain Tree A89

1981, Dec. 16 **Litho.** *Perf. 14*

230 A89 15c shown .65 .20
231 A89 50c Simber tree, vert. 2.00 .75
232 A89 80c Borneo camphorwood, vert. 3.50 .90
Nos. 230-232 (3) 6.15 1.85

Scouting Year and Jamboree, Apr. 9-16 A90

1982, Apr. 10 **Litho.** *Perf. 13½x13*

233 A90 15c Jamboree emblem .50 .30
234 A90 50c Flag, emblem 1.25 .35
235 A90 80c Emblems, knot 2.25 .55
Nos. 233-235 (3) 4.00 1.20

15th Anniv. of Assoc. of South East Asian Nations (ASEAN) A91

1982, Aug. 8 **Litho.** *Perf. 14*

236 A91 15c Meeting Center .50 .25
237 A91 $1 Flags 1.25 .95

Dome of the Rock, Jerusalem A92

1982, Aug. 21 *Perf. 13½*

238 A92 15c multicolored 1.50 .35
239 A92 $1 multicolored 7.50 1.10

For the freedom of Palestine.

25th Anniv. of Independence — A93

1982, Aug. 31 **Litho.** *Perf. 14*

240 A93 10c Kuala Lumpur .20 .20
241 A93 15c Independence celebration .25 .20
242 A93 50c Parade .70 .25
243 A93 80c Independence ceremony 1.00 .35
a. Souvenir sheet of 4, #240-243 16.00 16.00
b. Souvenir sheet of 4, #240-243 11.00 11.00
Nos. 240-243 (4) 2.15 1.00

No. 243a has a narrow silver frame around the center vignette of the 10c value. This frame was removed for the second printing, No. 243b.

Traditional Games — A94

1982, Oct. 30 *Perf. 13½*

244 A94 10c Shadow play 1.25 .35
245 A94 15c Cross top 1.25 .35
246 A94 75c Kite flying 6.50 .55
Nos. 244-246 (3) 9.00 1.25

Handicrafts — A95

1982, Nov. 26 **Litho.** *Perf. 13x13½*

247 A95 10c Sabah hats .65 .45
248 A95 15c Gold-threaded cloth .65 .45
249 A95 75c Sarawak pottery 3.25 .65
Nos. 247-249 (3) 4.55 1.55

Commonwealth Day — A96

1983, Mar. 14 **Litho.** *Perf. 14*

250 A96 15c Flag .40 .25
251 A96 20c Seri Paduka Baginda .40 .25
252 A96 40c Oil palm refinery .55 .35
253 A96 $1 Globe 1.10 .75
Nos. 250-253 (4) 2.45 1.60

First Shipment of Natural Gas, Bintulu, Sarawak — A97

1983, Jan. 22 **Litho.** *Perf. 12*

254 A97 15c Bintulu Port Authority emblem 1.40 .70
a. Perf. 13½ 35.00 3.25
255 A97 20c LNG Tanker Tenaga Satu 1.75 1.90
a. Perf. 13½ 40.00 3.50
256 A97 $1 Gas plant 5.50 1.50
a. Perf. 13½ 70.00 12.50
Nos. 254-256 (3) 8.65 4.10
Nos. 254a-256a (3) 145.00 19.25

Freshwater Fish — A98

1983, June 15 *Perf. 12x12½*

257 Pair 5.50 2.25
a. A98 20c Tilapia nilotica 1.40 .30
b. A98 20c Cyprinus carpio 1.40 .30
c. As #257, perf. 13½x14 10.00 10.00
258 Pair 6.50 2.75
a. A98 40c Puntius gonionotus 1.60 .35
b. A98 40c Ctenopharyngodon idellus 1.60 .35
c. As #258, perf. 13½x14 10.50 10.50

Opening of East-West Highway — A99

1983, July 1 *Perf. 14x13½*

259 A99 15c Lower Sungei Pergau Bridge 1.50 .40
260 A99 20c Sungei Perak Reservoir Bridge 1.50 .40
261 A99 $1 Map 6.75 1.25
Nos. 259-261 (3) 9.75 2.05

Armed Forces, 50th Anniv. — A100

Designs: 15c, Royal Malaysian Aircraft. 20c, Navy vessel firing missile. 40c, Battle at Pasir Panjang. 80c, Trooping of the Royal colors.

1983, Sept. 16 Litho. *Perf. 13½*

262 A100 15c multicolored .90 .40
263 A100 20c multicolored 1.25 .40
264 A100 40c multicolored 2.50 .40
265 A100 80c multicolored 5.50 .75
a. Souvenir sheet of 4, #262-265 17.00 17.00
Nos. 262-265 (4) 10.15 1.95

Helmeted Hornbill — A101

1983, Oct. 26 Litho. *Perf. 13½*

266 A101 15c shown 2.25 .40
267 A101 20c Wrinkled Hornbill 2.25 .40
268 A101 50c White crested Hornbill 2.75 .55
269 A101 $1 Rhinoceros Hornbill 4.75 1.10
Nos. 266-269 (4) 12.00 2.45

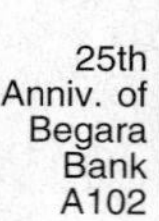

25th Anniv. of Begara Bank A102

Branch offices.

1984, Jan. 26 Litho. *Perf. 13½x14*

270 A102 20c Ipoh 1.50 .35
271 A102 $1 Alor Setar 2.75 .65

10th Anniv. of Federal Territory A103

Views of Kuala Lumpur. 20c, 40c vert.

Perf. 14x13½, 13½x14

1984, Feb. 1 Litho.

272 A103 20c multicolored 1.25 .50
273 A103 40c multicolored 1.75 .50
274 A103 80c multicolored 5.00 .85
Nos. 272-274 (3) 8.00 1.85

Labuan Federal Territory A104

Traditional Weapons A105

1984, Apr. 16 Litho. *Perf. 13½x14*

275 A104 20c Development symbols, map, arms 1.90 .65
276 A104 $1 Flag, map 6.00 .95

1984, May 30 *Perf. 13x14*

277 A105 40c Keris Semenanjung 1.50 .30
278 A105 40c Keris Pekakak 1.50 .30
279 A105 40c Keris Jawa 1.50 .30
280 A105 40c Tumbuk Lada 1.50 .30
a. Block of 4, #277-280 7.50 7.50

Asia-Pacific Broadcasting Union, 20th Anniv. — A106

1984, June 23 *Perf. 14x14½*

281 A106 20c Map, waves 2.00 .65
282 A106 $1 "20" 4.00 1.10

Kuala Lumpur Post Office Opening A107

1984, Oct. 29 *Perf. 12x11½*

283 A107 15c Facsimile transmission 1.00 .35
284 A107 20c Building 1.00 .30
285 A107 $1 Mail bag conveyor 2.50 .45
Nos. 283-285 (3) 4.50 1.10

Installation of Sultan of Johore as 8th Paramount Ruler of Malaysia — A108

Sultan Mahmood, Arms A109

1984, Nov. 15 Litho. *Perf. 12*

286 A108 15c multicolored 1.25 .40
287 A108 20c multicolored 1.25 .35
288 A109 40c multicolored 1.75 .50
289 A109 80c multicolored 3.00 .70
Nos. 286-289 (4) 7.25 1.95

A110

A111

Malaysian hibiscus.

1984, Dec. 12 Litho. *Perf. 13½*

290 A110 10c White hibiscus 1.25 .40
291 A110 20c Red hibiscus 1.25 .35
292 A110 40c Pink hibiscus 2.50 .40
293 A110 $1 Orange hibiscus 4.25 .90
Nos. 290-293 (4) 9.25 2.05

Perf. 13½x14, 14x13½

1985, Mar. 30 Litho.

294 A111 20c Badge, vert. 1.25 .30
295 A111 $1 Parliament, Kuala Lumpur 2.75 .45

Parliament, 25th anniv.

Protected Wildlife A112

1985, Apr. 25 *Perf. 14*

296 A112 10c Prionodon linsang 2.25 .55
297 A112 40c Nycticebus coucang, vert. 2.75 .45
298 A112 $1 Petaurista elegans, vert. 6.50 .45
Nos. 296-298 (3) 11.50 1.45

Intl. Youth Year — A113

1985, May 15 *Perf. 13*

299 A113 20c Youth solidarity 1.50 .40
300 A113 $1 Participation in natl. development 5.00 .65

Malaya Railways Centenary A114

Locomotives.

1985, June 1 *Perf. 13*

301 A114 15c Steam engine, 1885 2.50 .50
302 A114 20c Diesel-electric, 1957 2.75 .50
303 A114 $1 Diesel, 1963 6.75 .55
Nos. 301-303 (3) 12.00 1.55

Souvenir Sheet

Perf. 14x13

304 A114 80c Train leaving Kuala Lumpur Station, 1938 13.00 13.00

No. 304 contains one stamp 48x32mm.

Proton Saga A115

1985, July 9 *Perf. 14*

305 A115 20c multicolored 1.50 .50
306 A115 40c multicolored 2.25 .50
307 A115 $1 multicolored 4.75 .75
Nos. 305-307 (3) 8.50 1.75

Inauguration of natl. automotive industry.

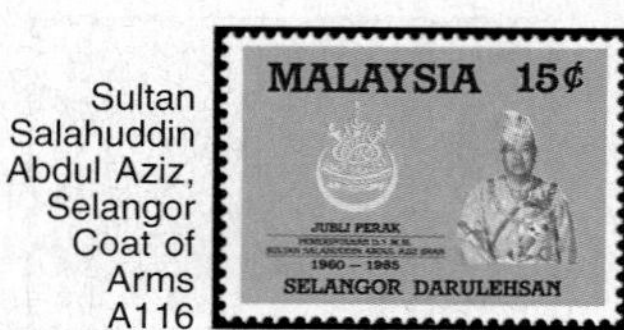

Sultan Salahuddin Abdul Aziz, Selangor Coat of Arms A116

1985, Sept. 5 *Perf. 13*

308 A116 15c multicolored .75 .75
309 A116 20c multicolored .90 .75
310 A116 $1 multicolored 4.00 1.50
Nos. 308-310 (3) 5.65 3.00

25th anniv. of coronation.

Penang Bridge Opening A117

1985, Sept. 15 Litho. *Perf. 13½x13*

311 A117 20c shown 1.75 .45
312 A117 40c Bridge, map 3.50 .45

Size: 44x28mm

Perf. 12½

313 A117 $1 Map 5.25 .65
Nos. 311-313 (3) 10.50 1.55

Natl. Oil Industry A118

1985, Nov. 4 *Perf. 12½*

314 A118 15c Offshore rig, vert. 1.75 .45
315 A118 20c 1st refinery 1.75 .45
316 A118 $1 Map of oil and gas fields 6.25 .65
Nos. 314-316 (3) 9.75 1.55

Coronation of Paduka Seri, Sultan of Perak A119

1985, Dec. 9 *Perf. 14*

317 A119 15c lt blue & multi .70 .40
318 A119 20c lilac & multi 1.00 .40
319 A119 $1 gold & multi 4.75 .75
Nos. 317-319 (3) 6.45 1.55

Birds A120

Wmk. 388

1986, Mar. 11 Litho. *Perf. 13¼*

320 A120 20c Lophura ignita, vert. 1.50 .25
a. Perf. 12 3.00 .75
321 A120 20c Pavo malacense, vert. 1.50 .25
a. Pair, #320-321 3.50 1.10
b. Perf. 12 4.75 1.25
c. Pair, #320a, 321b 7.75 5.25
322 A120 40c Lophura bulweri 2.25 .30
a. Perf. 12 7.00 1.25
323 A120 40c Argusianus argus 3.00 .30
a. Pair, #322-323 8.50 1.75
b. Perf. 12 6.00 1.25
c. Pair, #322a, 323b 11.50 9.75
Nos. 320-323 (4) 8.25 1.10

PATA '86, Pacific Area Travel Assoc. Conference, Persidangan — A121

No. 324: a, Two women dancing. b, Woman in red. c, Man and woman.

No. 325: a, Woman in gold. b, Woman holding fan. c, Woman in violet.

Perf. 15x14½

1986, Apr. 14 Litho. Unwmk.

324 Strip of 3 3.75 3.75
a.-c. A121 20c any single .65 .20
325 Strip of 3 5.00 5.00
a.-c. A121 40c any single .80 .20

Malaysia Games A122

Games Emblem — A123

Flags — A124

Wmk. 388

1986, Apr. 14 Litho. *Perf. 12*

326 A122 20c multicolored 2.00 .50
327 A123 40c multicolored 5.50 .50
328 A124 $1 multicolored 7.50 .80
Nos. 326-328 (3) 15.00 1.80

Nephelium Lappaceum A125

Averrhoa Carambola A126

Litho. (#329-332), Photo. (#333-336)
Perf. 12 (#329-332)

1986-2000 Wmk. 388

329 A125 40c shown .40 .20
a. Perf. 13½x14 .65
330 A125 50c Ananas comosus .60 .20
a. Perf. 13½x14 .65
331 A125 80c Durio zibethinus .95 .35
a. Perf. 13½x14 1.00
332 A125 $1 Garcinia mangostana 1.00 .35
a. Perf. 13½x14 1.00

Perf. 13½x14

332C A125 $5 Musa sapientum ('00) 1.75 .80

Perf. 13½
Wmk. 233

333 A126 $2 shown 2.10 .65
334 A126 $5 Musa sapientum 4.00 1.10
335 A126 $10 Mangifera odorata 6.75 3.75
336 A126 $20 Carica papaya 15.00 5.50
Nos. 329-336 (9) 32.55 12.90

No. 332C issued 2000; balance of set issued 6/5/86.

Two additional stamps were issued in this set. The editors would like to examine any examples.

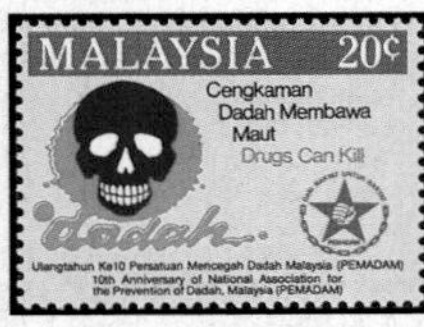

Natl. Assoc. for the Prevention of Drug Abuse, 10th Anniv. A127

1986, June 26 Wmk. 388 *Perf. 13*

337 A127 20c Skull 1.10 .50
338 A127 40c Dove 1.75 .50
339 A127 $1 Addict, vert. 5.75 .85
Nos. 337-339 (3) 8.60 1.85

Malaysian Airlines Kuala Lumpur-Los Angeles Inaugural Flight — A128

1986, July 31 *Perf. 14x13½*

340 A128 20c Flight routes map 2.50 .70
341 A128 40c MAS emblem, new route 3.50 .70
342 A128 $1 Emblem, stops 7.00 .90
Nos. 340-342 (3) 13.00 2.30

Industrial Productivity A129

1986, Nov. 3 Litho. *Perf. 14*

343 A129 20c Construction, vert. 1.25 .40
344 A129 40c Industry 2.50 .40
345 A129 $1 Automobile factory 6.50 .40
Nos. 343-345 (3) 10.25 1.20

Historic Buildings A130

15c, Istana Lama Seri Menanti, Negri Sembilan. 20c, Istana Kenangan, Perak. 40c, Bangunan Stadthuys, Malacca. $1, Istana Kuching, Sarawak.

1986, Dec. 20 *Perf. 13*

346 A130 15c multicolored 1.10 .60
347 A130 20c multicolored 1.10 .60
348 A130 40c multicolored 2.50 .60
349 A130 $1 multicolored 3.75 .95
Nos. 346-349 (4) 8.45 2.75

See design A146.

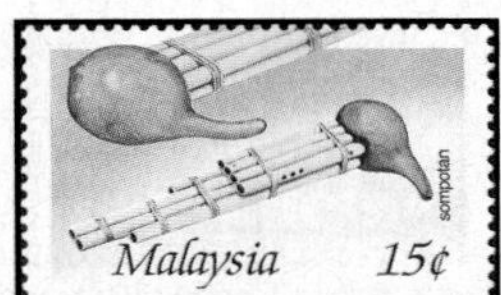

Folk Music Instruments — A131

1987, Mar. 7 Litho. *Perf. 12*

350 A131 15c Sompotan 1.10 .65
351 A131 20c Sapih 1.10 .65
352 A131 50c Serunai, vert. 3.00 .65
353 A131 80c Rebab, vert. 5.25 1.00
Nos. 350-353 (4) 10.45 2.95

Intl. Year of Shelter for the Homeless — A132

1987, Apr. 6 Litho. *Perf. 12*

354 A132 20c Model village 1.00 .60
355 A132 $1 Symbols of family, shelter 5.00 1.00

UN Anti-Drug Campaign and Congress, Vienna A133

1987, June 8 Litho. *Perf. 13½x13*

356 20c Health boy, family, rainbow .80 .20
357 20c Holding drugs .80 .20
a. A133 Pair, #356-357 3.25 1.50
358 40c Child warding off drugs 1.90 .20
359 40c Drugs, damaged body in capsule 1.90 .20
a. A133 Pair, #358-358 8.25 2.75
Nos. 356-359 (4) 5.40 .80

Nos. 357a, 359a have continuous designs.

Kenyir Hydroelectric Power Station Inauguration — A134

1987, July 13 *Perf. 12*

360 A134 20c Power facility, dam 2.00 .40
361 A134 $1 Side view 4.25 .55

33rd Commonwealth Parliamentary Conference — A135

1987, Sept. 1 Litho. *Perf. 12*

362 A135 20c Maces, parliament .65 .20
363 A135 $1 Parliament, maces, diff. 1.75 .35

Transportation and Communications Decade in Asia and the Pacific (1985-94) — A136

Designs: 15c, Satellites, Earth, satellite dish. 20c, Car, diesel train, Kuala Lumpur Station. 40c, MISC container ship. $1, Malaysia Airlines jet, Kuala Lumpur Airport.

1987, Oct. 26 *Perf. 13½x13*

364 A136 15c multicolored 1.40 .60
365 A136 20c multicolored 1.40 .60
366 A136 40c multicolored 2.75 .60
367 A136 $1 multicolored 5.50 .95
Nos. 364-367 (4) 11.05 2.75

Protected Wildcats A137

1987, Nov. 14

368 A137 15c Felis temminckii 3.00 .70
369 A137 20c Felis planiceps 3.00 .70
370 A137 40c Felis marmorata 6.75 .70
371 A137 $1 Neofelis nebulosa 9.50 1.40
Nos. 368-371 (4) 22.25 3.50

ASEAN, 20th Anniv. A138

1987, Dec. 14 Litho. *Perf. 13*

372 A138 20c "20," flags .40 .25
373 A138 $1 Flags, Earth 2.00 .50

Opening of Sultan Salahuddin Abdul Aziz Shah Mosque, Selangor A139

Dome, minarets and: 15c, Arches. 20c, Sultan Abdul Aziz Shah, Selangor crest. $1, Interior, vert.

1988, Mar. 11 Litho. *Perf. 12*

374 A139 15c multicolored .60 .35
375 A139 20c multicolored .60 .35
376 A139 $1 multicolored 1.75 .50
Nos. 374-376 (3) 2.95 1.20

Opening of Sultan Ismail Power Station, Trengganu A140

1988, Apr. 4 *Perf. 13*

377 A140 20c shown .50 .30
378 A140 $1 Station, diff. 2.50 .50

Wildlife Protection — A141

Birds.

1988, June 30 Litho. *Perf. 13*

379 20c Hypothymis azurea .90 .20
380 20c Dicaeum cruentatum .90 .20
a. A141 Pair, #379-380 4.75 1.10
381 50c Aethopyga siparaja 1.75 .20
382 50c Cymbirhynchus macrorhynchos 1.75 .20
a. A141 Pair, #381-382 8.25 1.75
Nos. 379-382 (4) 5.30 .80

Independence of Sabah and Sarawak, 25th Anniv.

A142 A143

1988, Aug. 31 Litho. *Perf. 13x13½*

383 A142 20c Sabah .85 .35
384 A142 20c Sarawak .85 .35
a. Pair, #383-384 1.60 .35
385 A143 $1 State and natl. symbols 2.75 .65
Nos. 383-385 (3) 4.45 1.35

A144

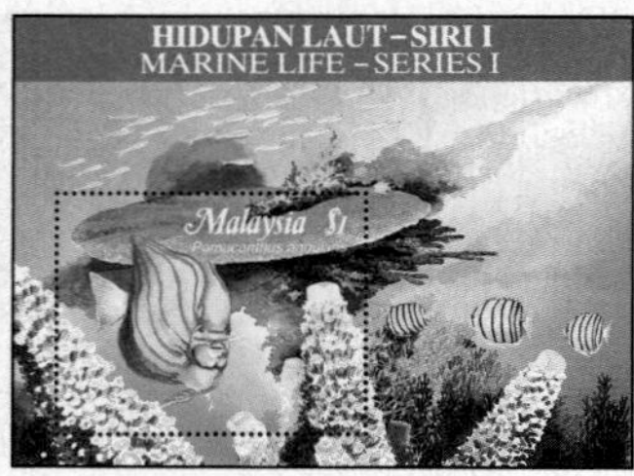

Marine Life — A145

Nudibranchs: No. 386: a, Glossodoris atromarginata. b, Phyllidia ocellata. c, Chromodoris annae. d, Flabellina macassarana. e, Fryeria ruppelli.

1988, Dec. 17 **Litho.** ***Perf. 12***

386 Strip of 5 7.00 7.00
a.-e. A144 20c any single .75 .25

Souvenir Sheet

Perf. 14

387 A145 $1 Pomacanthus annularis 6.00 6.00

No. 387 contains one stamp 50x40mm.

Historic Buildings, Malacca A146

#388, Perisytiharan Kemerdekaan Memorial. #389, Istana Kesultanan. $1, Porta da Santiago.

Perf. 13½x13, 13x13½

1989, Apr. 15 **Litho.**

388 A146 20c multicolored .50 .35
389 A146 20c multicolored .50 .35
390 A146 $1 multicolored, vert. 2.50 .70
Nos. 388-390 (3) 3.50 1.40

See design A130.

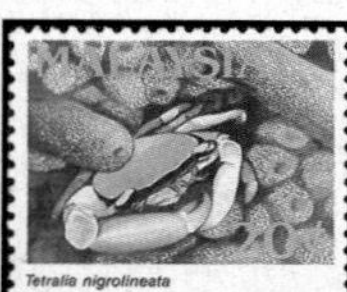

Crustaceans A147

Wmk. 388

1989, June 29 **Litho.** ***Perf. 12***

391 A147 20c *Tetralia nigrolineata* .45 .20
392 A147 20c *Neopetrolisthes maculatus* .45 .20
a. Pair, #391-392 1.50 .55
393 A147 40c *Periclimenes holthuisi* .85 .20
394 A147 40c *Synalpheus neomeris* .85 .20
a. Pair, #393-394 2.50 .85
Nos. 391-394 (4) 2.60 .80

7th Natl. Scout Jamboree A148

1989, July 26 ***Perf. 13½x13, 13x13½***

395 A148 10c Map, badges .65 .45
396 A148 20c Scout salute, natl. flag .65 .45
397 A148 80c Camping out 3.50 .75
Nos. 395-397 (3) 4.80 1.65

Nos. 395-396 vert.

15th SEA Games, Kuala Lumpur — A149

Installation of Sultan Azlan as Supreme Ruler — A150

Designs: 10c, Cycling, horiz. 20c, Track events, horiz. 50c, Swimming. $1, Torchbearer, stadium and flags.

Perf. 13½x13, 13x13½

1989, Aug. 20 **Litho.** **Wmk. 388**

398 A149 10c multicolored .55 .40
399 A149 20c multicolored .55 .40
400 A149 50c multicolored 1.50 .40
401 A149 $1 multicolored 2.75 .75
Nos. 398-401 (4) 5.35 1.95

1989, Sept. 18 ***Perf. 13x13½***

402 A150 20c multicolored .35 .20
403 A150 40c multicolored .70 .20
404 A150 $1 multicolored 1.75 .45
Nos. 402-404 (3) 2.80 .85

Commonwealth Heads of Government Meeting — A151

1989, Oct. 18 ***Perf. 13½x13, 13x13½***

405 A151 20c Conference center .45 .30
406 A151 50c Folk dancers, vert. .95 .35
407 A151 $1 Map, flag 1.90 .60
Nos. 405-407 (3) 3.30 1.25

Malaysia Airlines Inaugural Non-stop Flight to London, Dec. 2 A152

#408, Passenger jet, Malaysian clock tower, Big Ben. #409, Passenger jet, Malaysian skyscraper, Westminster Palace. $1, Map, passenger jet.

1989, Dec. 2 **Wmk. 388** ***Perf. 13***

408 A152 20c shown 2.25 2.25
409 A152 20c multicolored 2.25 2.25
a. Pair, #408-409 5.00 5.00
410 A152 $1 multicolored 7.00 7.00
Nos. 408-410 (3) 11.50 11.50

National Park, 50th Anniv. — A153

1989, Dec. 28 ***Perf. 13x13½***

411 A153 20c Map, sloth 2.00 .40
412 A153 $1 Crested arguses 5.50 .65

Visit Malaysia.

Visit Malaysia Year — A154

1990, Jan. 11 ***Perf. 12***

413 A154 20c Map .75 .50
414 A154 50c Drummers 1.75 .55
415 A154 $1 Yachts, scuba divers 2.75 .95
Nos. 413-415 (3) 5.25 2.00

Wildflowers A155

1990, Mar. 12

416 A155 15c *Dillenia suffruticosa* .35 .30
417 A155 20c *Mimosa pudica* .35 .30
418 A155 50c *Ipomoea carnea* .95 .30
419 A155 $1 *Nymphaea pubescens* 1.60 .45
Nos. 416-419 (4) 3.25 1.35

Kuala Lumpur A156

Wmk. 388

1990, May 14 **Litho.** ***Perf. 12***

420 A156 20c Flag, rainbow, vert. .45 .40
421 A156 40c shown .85 .40
422 A156 $1 Cityscape 1.90 .65
Nos. 420-422 (3) 3.20 1.45

South-South Consultation and Cooperation Conference — A157

1990, June 1 ***Perf. 13***

423 A157 20c shown .50 .35
424 A157 80c Emblem 2.25 .50

Alor Setar, 250th Anniv. A158

1990, June 2 ***Perf. 12***

425 A158 20c shown .45 .30
426 A158 40c Musicians, vert. .80 .30
427 A158 $1 Government bldg., vert. 1.75 .40
Nos. 425-427 (3) 3.00 1.00

Intl. Literacy Year A159

1990, Sept. 8 ***Perf. 12***

428 A159 20c Letters, sign language .40 .40
a. Perf. 13 20.00
429 A159 40c People reading .85 .40
430 A159 $1 Globe, pen nib, vert. 1.75 .45
Nos. 428-430 (3) 3.00 1.25

Turtles A160

1990, Nov. 17

431 A160 15c Dermochelys coriacea 1.40 .45
432 A160 20c Chelonia mydas 1.40 .45
433 A160 40c Eretmochelys imbricata 1.60 .45
434 A160 $1 Lepidochelys olivacea 3.50 .90
Nos. 431-434 (4) 7.90 2.25

MARA (Council of Indigenous People), 25th Anniv. A161

1991, Apr. 25

435 A161 20c Construction .40 .35
436 A161 40c Education .75 .35
437 A161 $1 Banking & industry 1.10 .50
Nos. 435-437 (3) 2.25 1.20

Wasps — A162

Designs: 15c, Eustenogaster calyptodoma. 20c, Vespa affinis indonensis. 50c, Sceliphorn javanum. $1, Ampulex compressa.

1991, July 29

438 A162 15c multicolored .45 .40
439 A162 20c multicolored .45 .40
440 A162 50c multicolored 1.00 .40
441 A162 $1 multicolored 2.10 .55
a. Souvenir sheet of 4, #438-441, perf. 14½x14 5.50 5.75
Nos. 438-441 (4) 4.00 1.75

Prime Ministers — A163

#442, Tunku Abdul Rahman Putra Al-Haj (1903-90). #443, Tun Hussein Onn (1922-90). #444, Tun Abdul Razak Hussein (1922-76).

1991, Aug. 30

442 A163 $1 multicolored 1.10 .35
443 A163 $1 multicolored 1.10 .35
444 A163 $1 multicolored 1.10 .35
Nos. 442-444 (3) 3.30 1.05

Historic Buildings A164

Designs: 15c, Istana Maziah, Trengganu. 20c, Istana Besar, Johore. 40c, Istana Bandar, Kuala Langat, Selangor. $1, Istana Jahar, Kelantan.

1991, Nov. 7

445 A164 15c multicolored .40 .30
446 A164 20c multicolored .40 .30
447 A164 40c multicolored .75 .30
448 A164 $1 multicolored 1.75 .55
Nos. 445-448 (4) 3.30 1.45

Sarawak Museum, Cent. A165

Museum buildings, fabric pattern and: 30c, Brass lamp. $1, Vase.

1991, Dec. 21

449 A165 30c multicolored .50 .30
450 A165 $1 multicolored 1.75 .65

Malaysian Postal Service — A166

Designs: No. 451a, Postman on bicycle. b, Postman on motorcycle. c, Mail truck. d, Mail truck, diff., oil tank. e, Globe, airplane.

1992, Jan. 1

451 A166 30c Strip of 5, #a.-e. 4.25 1.10

Malaysian Tropical Forests A167

Designs: 20c, Hill Dipterocarp Forest, Dyera costulata. 50c, Mangrove Swamp Forest, Rhizophora apiculata. $1, Lowland Dipterocarp Forest, Neobalanocarpus heimii.

1992, Mar. 23

452 A167 20c multicolored .40 .40
453 A167 50c multicolored 1.10 .40
454 A167 $1 multicolored 1.60 .65
Nos. 452-454 (3) 3.10 1.45

Installation of Yang di-Pertuan Besar of Negri Sembilan, Silver Jubilee A168

1992, Apr. 18

455 A168 30c Portrait, arms .40 .20
456 A168 $1 Building 1.60 .50

1992 Thomas Cup Champions in Badminton — A169

1992, July 25 *Perf. 12*

457 A169 $1 Cup, flag 1.10 .35
458 A169 $1 Players 1.10 .35

Souvenir Sheet

459 A169 $2 multicolored 3.00 3.00

No. 459 contains one 75x28mm stamp.

ASEAN, 25th Anniv. A170

1992, Aug. 8

460 A170 30c shown .70 .40
461 A170 50c Flora 1.25 .40
462 A170 $1 Architecture 2.10 .70
Nos. 460-462 (3) 4.05 1.50

Postage Stamps in Malaysia, 125th Annv. A171

#463, Straits Settlements #1, Malaya #84. #464, Straits Settlements #2, Malaysia #2. #465, Straits Settlements #11, Malaysia #421. #466, Straits Settlements #14, Malaysia #467. #467, Flag, simulated stamp.

1992, Sept. 1

463 A171 30c multicolored .60 .25
464 A171 30c multicolored .60 .25
a. Pair #463-464 1.75 1.75
465 A171 50c multicolored 1.00 .25
466 A171 50c multicolored 1.00 .25
a. Pair #465-466 2.25 2.25
Nos. 463-466 (4) 3.20 1.00

Souvenir Sheet

467 A171 $2 multicolored 4.00 4.00

Kuala Lumpur '92.

A173

Coral — A174

No. 471: a, Acropora. b, Dendronephthya. c, Dendrophyllia. d, Sinularia. e, Melithaea.
No. 472, Subergorgia.

1992, Dec. 21

471 A173 30c Strip of 5, #a.-e. 7.00 1.50

Souvenir Sheet

472 A174 $2 multicolored 5.50 5.50

16th Asian-Pacific Dental Congress A175

Children from various countries: #473, 4 girls. #474, 4 girls, 1 holding koala.
Dentists, flags of: No. 475, Japan, Malaysia, South Korea. No. 476, New Zealand, Thailand, People's Republic of China, Indonesia.

1993, Apr. 24

473 A175 30c multicolored .60 .25
474 A175 30c multicolored .60 .25
a. Pair, #473-474 1.50 .45
475 A175 50c multicolored .90 .25
476 A175 $1 multicolored 1.75 .50
a. Pair, #475-476 3.50 1.00
Nos. 473-476 (4) 3.85 1.25

A176

A177

1993, June 24

477 A176 30c Fairway, vert. 1.00 .55
478 A176 50c Old, new club houses, vert. 2.00 .55
479 A176 $1 Sand trap 3.00 .90
Nos. 477-479 (3) 6.00 2.00

Royal Selangor Golf Club, cent.

1993, Aug. 2

Wildflowers.

480 A177 20c Alpinia rafflesiana .65 .50
481 A177 30c Achasma megalocheilos .65 .50
482 A177 50c Zingiber spectabile 1.75 .55
483 A177 $1 Costus speciosus 3.00 1.00
Nos. 480-483 (4) 6.05 2.55

14th Commonwealth Forestry Conference — A178

1993, Sept. 13

484 A178 30c Globe, forest .90 .50
485 A178 50c Hand holding trees 1.40 .50
486 A178 $1 Trees under dome, vert. 2.50 .90
Nos. 484-486 (3) 4.80 1.90

Nos. 484-486 with Bangkok '93 Emblem Added

Wmk. 388

1993, Oct. 1 **Litho.** *Perf. 12*

486A A178 30c multicolored *4.50 4.00*
486B A178 50c multicolored *5.50 5.00*
486C A178 $1 multicolored *10.00 8.50*
Nos. 486A-486C (3) *20.00 17.50*

Kingfishers — A179

1993, Oct. 23

487 30c Halcyon smyrnensis .90 .40
488 30c Alcedo meninting .90 .40
a. A179 Pair, #487-488 2.25 .70
489 50c Halcyon concreta 1.50 .40
490 50c Ceyx erithacus 1.50 .40
a. A179 Pair, #489-490 3.75 .90
Nos. 487-490 (4) 4.80 1.60

A180

1993, Dec. 7

491 A180 30c SME MD3-160 airplane .75 .55
492 A180 50c Eagle X-TS airplane 1.50 .55
493 A180 $1 Patrol boat KD Kasturi 2.25 .75
Nos. 491-493 (3) 4.50 1.85

Souvenir Sheet

494 A180 $2 Map of Malaysia 3.75 3.75

Langkawi Intl. Maritime and Aerospace Exhibition (LIMA '93).

Visit Malaysia Year — A181

1994, Jan. 1

495 A181 20c Jeriau Waterfalls .50 .50
496 A181 30c Flowers .65 .55
497 A181 50c Marine life 1.25 .55
498 A181 $1 Wildlife 2.10 .85
Nos. 495-498 (4) 4.50 2.45

See Nos. 527A-527D.

Kuala Lumpur Natl. Planetarium A182

Designs: 30c, Exterior. 50c, Interior displays. $1, Theater auditorium.

1994, Feb. 7

499 A182 30c multicolored .80 .50
500 A182 50c multicolored 1.40 .50
501 A182 $1 multicolored 2.75 .80
Nos. 499-501 (3) 4.95 1.80

Orchids — A183

Designs: 20c, Spathoglottis aurea. 30c, Paphiopedilum barbatum. 50c, Bulbophyllum lobbii. $1, Aerides odorata. $2, Grammatophyllum speciosum.

1994, Feb. 17

502 A183 20c multicolored .70 .45
503 A183 30c multicolored .70 .45
504 A183 50c multicolored 1.10 .45
505 A183 $1 multicolored 2.10 .70
Nos. 502-505 (4) 4.60 2.05

Souvenir Sheet

506 A183 $2 multicolored 4.50 4.50

Hong Kong '94 (#506).

A184

A185

1994, June 17

507 A184 20c Decorative bowl .40 .30
508 A184 30c Celestial sphere .45 .30
509 A184 50c Dinar coins .65 .30
510 A184 $1 Decorative tile 1.50 .50
Nos. 507-510 (4) 3.00 1.40

World Islamic Civilization Festival '94.
See Nos. 528-531.

1994, July 26

511 A185 30c shown .85 .60
512 A185 50c Meat processing 1.25 .60
513 A185 $1 Cattle, laboratory 2.40 .85
Nos. 511-513 (3) 4.50 2.05

Veterinary Services, cent.

Electrification, Cent. — A186

1994, Sept. 3

514 A186 30c Laying cable .65 .40
515 A186 30c Lighted city .65 .40
a. Pair, #514-515 1.50 .50
516 A186 $1 Futuristic city 1.75 .70
Nos. 514-516 (3) 3.05 1.50

North-South Expressway A187

1994, Sept. 8

517 A187 30c shown .50 .35
518 A187 50c Interchange .70 .35
519 A187 $1 Bridge 1.40 .50
Nos. 517-519 (3) 2.60 1.20

A188

A189

1994, Sept. 22

520 A188 30c pink & multi .50 .30
521 A188 50c yellow & multi .65 .30
522 A188 $1 green & multi 1.25 .50
Nos. 520-522 (3) 2.40 1.10

Installation of 10th Yang Di-Pertuan Agong (Head of State).

Wmk. 388

1994, Oct. 29 Litho. *Perf. 12*

523 A189 $1 shown 1.25 .50
524 A189 $1 Mascot 1.25 .50
a. Pair, #523-524 + label 3.00 1.25

1998 Commonwealth Games, Kuala Lumpur.

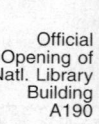

Official Opening of Natl. Library Building A190

1994, Dec. 16

525 A190 30c Library building .55 .40
526 A190 50c Computer terminal .75 .40
527 A190 $1 Manuscript 1.50 .55
Nos. 525-527 (3) 2.80 1.35

Nos. 495-498 with Added Inscription

Wmk. 388

1994, Nov. 8 Litho. *Perf. 12*

527A A181 20c multicolored *.75 .85*
527B A181 30c multicolored *1.25 .95*
527C A181 50c multicolored *1.75 1.50*
527D A181 $1 multicolored *3.00 2.75*
Nos. 527A-527D (4) *6.75 6.05*

Nos. 507-510 with Added Inscription

Wmk. 388

1994, Aug. 16 Litho. *Perf. 12*

528 A184 20c multicolored 1.50 1.50
529 A184 30c multicolored 1.25 1.25
530 A184 50c multicolored 3.00 3.00
531 A184 $1 multicolored 6.00 6.00
Nos. 528-531 (4) 11.75 11.75

A191

1994, Nov. 10 Unwmk. *Perf. 14½*

532 A191 30c shown .80 .45
533 A191 $1 Building complex 1.60 .70

Memorial to Tunku Abdul Rahman Putra Al-Haj (1903-1990), former Prime Minister.

Fungi — A192

1995, Jan. 18 *Perf. 14½x14*

534 A192 20c Bracket fungus .40 .30
535 A192 30c Cup fungus .45 .30
536 A192 50c Veil fungus .70 .30
537 A192 $1 Coral fungus 1.40 .45
Nos. 534-537 (4) 2.95 1.35

Neofelis Nebulosa A193

1995, Apr. 18 Wmk. 373 *Perf. 13½*

538 A193 20c shown .40 .25
539 A193 30c With young .60 .35
540 A193 50c With mouth open 1.00 .45
541 A193 $1 Lying on rock 2.00 .55
a. Strip of 4, #538-541 5.50 3.50

Nos. 538-541 were issued in sheets of 16 stamps.
World Wildlife Fund.

Marine Life — A194

1995, Apr. 10 Wmk. 388 *Perf. 12*

542 A194 20c Feather stars .90 .35
543 A194 20c Sea fans .90 .35
a. Pair, #542-543 2.25 .90
544 A194 30c Soft coral 1.75 .40
545 A194 30c Cup coral 1.75 .40
a. Pair, #544-545 3.75 1.10
Nos. 542-545 (4) 5.30 1.50

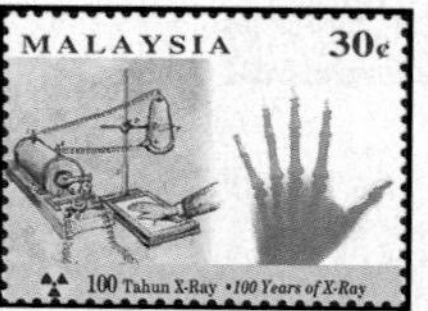

X-Ray, Cent. A195

#546, Early machine x-raying hand. #547, CAT scan machine. $1, Chest x-ray.

1995, May 29

546 A195 30c multicolored .30 .20
547 A195 30c multicolored .30 .20
a. Pair, #546-547 1.10 .35
548 A195 $1 multicolored 1.50 .50
Nos. 546-548 (3) 2.10 .90

1998 Commonwealth Games, Kuala Lumpur — A196

Various sporting events: No. 549, Badminton, cricket, shooting, tennis, weight lifting, hurdles, field hockey. No. 550, Cycling, lawn bowling, boxing, basketball, rugby, gymnastics.

Wmk. 388

1995, Sept. 10 Litho. *Perf. 14*

549 A196 $1 multicolored 2.40 .60
550 A196 $1 multicolored 2.40 .60
a. Pair, #549-550 + label 5.50 2.10

Traditional Weapons A197

1995, Sept. 1 Litho. *Perf. 14*

551 A197 20c Jemblah .35 .25
552 A197 30c Keris panjang .35 .25
553 A197 50c Kerambit .50 .25
554 A197 $1 Keris sundang 1.00 .30
Nos. 551-554 (4) 2.20 1.05

Souvenir Sheet

555 A197 $2 Lading terus 4.00 4.00

Singapore '95.

UN, 50th Anniv. A198

1995, Oct. 24 *Perf. 13½*

556 A198 30c shown .45 .30
557 A198 $1 UN emblem 1.25 .35

Intl. Assoc. of Travel Agents (IATA), 50th Anniv. — A199

Jet, globe and: No. 558, Historic buildings. No. 559, Sydney Opera House, Great Wall of China. No. 560, Eiffel Tower, Tower Bridge. No. 561, Hollywood Walk of Fame, Latin American pyramid.

1995, Oct. 30 *Perf. 14*

558 30c multicolored .65 .45
559 30c multicolored .65 .45
a. A199 Pair, #558-559 1.75 .65
560 50c multicolored .90 .45
561 50c multicolored .90 .45
a. A199 Pair, #560-561 2.25 .75
Nos. 558-561 (4) 3.10 1.80

Turtles A200

Perf. 14x14½

1995, Sept. 26 Litho. Wmk. 388

Booklet Stamps

562 A200 30c Chelonia mydas 2.50 .40
563 A200 30c Dermochelys coriacea 2.50 .40
a. Booklet pane, 5 each #562-563 27.50 16.00
Complete booklet, #563a 30.00

Proton Cars, 10th Anniv. — A201

#564, 1985 Saga 1.5. #565, 1992 Iswara 1.5 aeroback. #566, 1992, Iswara 1.5 sedan. #567, 1993 Wira 1.6 sedan. #568, 1993 Wira 1.6 aeroback. #569, 1994 Rally. #570, 1994 Satria 1.6. #571, 1995 Perdana 2.0. #572, 1995 Wira 1.6 aeroback. #573, 1995 Wira 1.8 sedan.

1995, Dec. Litho. *Perf. 14*

Booklet Stamps

564 A201 30c multicolored 1.25 .20
565 A201 30c multicolored 1.25 .20
566 A201 30c multicolored 1.25 .20
567 A201 30c multicolored 1.25 .20
568 A201 30c multicolored 1.25 .20
569 A201 30c multicolored 1.25 .20
570 A201 30c multicolored 1.25 .20
571 A201 30c multicolored 1.25 .20
572 A201 30c multicolored 1.25 .20
573 A201 30c multicolored 1.25 .20
a. Booklet pane, Nos. 564-573 12.50 8.00
Complete booklet, No. 573a 12.50

A202

A203

Malaysia East Asia Satellite: 30c, Ariane 4 being launched. 50c, Satellite in Earth orbit over East Asia. $1, Satellite Control Center, Langkawai.
$5, Satellite entering orbit, horiz.

1996, Jan. 13 *Perf. 13½*

574 A202 30c multicolored .45 .30
575 A202 50c multicolored .70 .30
576 A202 $1 multicolored 1.25 .45
Nos. 574-576 (3) 2.40 1.05

Souvenir Sheet

Perf. 14

577 A202 $5 multicolored 9.00 9.00

No. 577 contains a holographic image. Soaking in water may affect the hologram.

Wmk. 388

1996, Apr. 16 Litho. *Perf. 13½*

Pitcher Plants: #578, Nepenthes sanguinea. #579, Nepenthes macfarlanei. #580, Nepenthes rajah. #581, Nepenthes lowii.

578 A203 30c multicolored .35 .25
579 A203 30c multicolored .35 .25
a. Pair, Nos. 578-579 .85 .35
580 A203 50c multicolored .55 .25
581 A203 50c multicolored .55 .25
a. Pair, Nos. 580-581 1.40 .60
Nos. 578-581 (4) 1.80 1.00

Birds of Prey A204

Designs: 20c, Haliastur indus. 30c, Spilornis cheela. 50c, Haliaeetus leucogaster. $1, Spizaetus cirrhatus.
$2, Spizaetus alboniger, vert.

Wmk. 388

1996, May 18 Litho. *Perf. 14*

582	A204	20c multicolored	.45	.45
583	A204	30c multicolored	.55	.45
584	A204	50c multicolored	.75	.45
585	A204	$1 multicolored	1.75	.65
		Nos. 582-585 (4)	3.50	2.00

Souvenir Sheet

586	A204	$2 multicolored	5.00	5.00

CHINA '96 (#586).

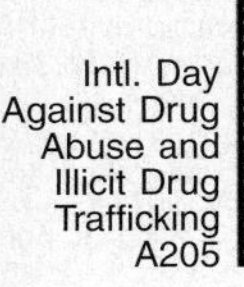
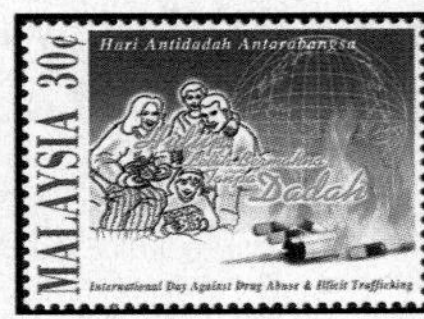

Intl. Day Against Drug Abuse and Illicit Drug Trafficking A205

Designs: No. 587, Family, drugs burning. No. 588, Various sporting activities, marajuana plants. $1, Family, rainbow.

Wmk. 388

1996, June 26 Litho. *Perf. 14*

587	A205	30c multicolored	.30	.25
588	A205	30c multicolored	.30	.25
a.		Pair, #587-588	.75	.30
589	A205	$1 multicolored	1.25	.45
		Nos. 587-589 (3)	1.85	.95

Butterflies — A206

#590, Graphium sarpedon. #591, Melanocyma faunula. #592, Delias hyparete. #593, Trogonoptera brookiana. #594, Terinos terpander.

1996, Sept. 27 Litho. *Perf. 14½x14*

Booklet Stamps

590	A206	30c multicolored	2.10	1.00
591	A206	30c multicolored	2.10	1.00
592	A206	30c multicolored	2.10	1.00
593	A206	30c multicolored	2.10	1.00
594	A206	30c multicolored	2.10	1.00
a.		Pane of 10, 2 each #590-594	21.00	17.50

Kuala Lumpur Tower A207

30c, Artist's impression. 50c, Tower head diagram. $1, Tower head, city at night. $2, Kuala Lumpur Tower, vert.

Perf. 13½

1996, Oct. 1 Litho. Unwmk.

595	A207	30c multicolored	.40	.20
596	A207	50c multicolored	.60	.20
597	A207	$1 multicolored	1.25	.35
		Nos. 595-597 (3)	2.25	.75

Souvenir Sheet

598	A207	$2 multicolored	2.75	2.75
a.		With added inscription in sheet margin	2.50	2.50

No. 598a inscribed with TAIPEI '96 emblem, issued 10/16/96.

14th Conference of Confederation of Asian and Pacific Accountants — A208

1996, Oct. 7 *Perf. 13½x14*

599	A208	30c CAPA logo	.60	.45
600	A208	$1 Globe	1.40	.65

Natl. Science Center A209

30c, Model of molecular structure. 50c, Model of atom, Science Center. $1, Natl. Science Center.

Unwmk.

1996, Nov. 29 Litho. *Perf. 14*

601	A209	30c multicolored	.50	.40
602	A209	50c multicolored	.70	.40
603	A209	$1 multicolored	1.40	.60
		Nos. 601-603 (3)	2.60	1.40

Souvenir Sheet

Stamp Week — A210

Wildlife: a, 20c, Nycticebus coucang. b, 30c, Callosciurus prevostil. c, 50c, Attacus atlas. d, $1, Hylobates lar. e, $1, Buceros rhinoceros. f, $2, Hemigalus derbyanus.

1996, Dec. 2

604	A210	Sheet of 6, #a.-f.	5.25	5.25

No. 604d is 30x60mm. Nos. 605e-605f are 60x30mm.

Birds — A211

Designs: 20c, Muscicapella hodgsoni. 30c, Leiothrix argentauris. 50c, Dicaeum celibicum. $1, Aethopyga mystacalis.

Perf. 13½x14

1997, Jan. 4 Litho. Unwmk.

605	A211	20c multicolored	.40	.40
606	A211	30c multicolored	.50	.40
607	A211	50c multicolored	.75	.40
608	A211	$1 multicolored	1.60	.65
		Nos. 605-608 (4)	3.25	1.85

16th Commonwealth Games, Kuala Lumpur '98 — A212

1996, Dec. 21 *Perf. 12*

609	A212	30c Running	.45	.20
610	A212	30c Hurdles	.45	.20
a.		Pair, #609-610	1.10	.50
611	A212	50c High jump	.75	.35
612	A212	50c Javelin	.75	.35
a.		Pair, #611-612	1.75	1.10
		Nos. 609-612 (4)	2.40	1.10

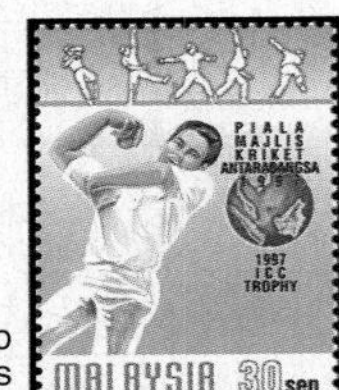

Intl. Cricket Cup Champions A213

1997, Mar. 24 Litho. *Perf. 14*

613	A213	30c shown	.35	.35
614	A213	50c Batsman	.65	.40
615	A213	$1 Wicket keeper	1.40	.55
		Nos. 613-615 (3)	2.40	1.30

Aviation in Malaysia, 50th Anniv. A214

Designs: 30c, Jet, world map. 50c, Jet approaching Kuala Lumpur. $1, Airplane tailfins of four Malaysian airlines.

Perf. 14, 13½ (#617)

1997, Apr. 2 Wmk. 388

616	A214	30c multicolored	.65	.65
617	A214	50c multicolored	1.10	.85
618	A214	$1 multicolored	2.50	1.00
a.		Perf. 13½	5.00	2.00
		Nos. 616-618 (3)	4.25	2.50

A215

A216

Light Rail Transit System: No. 620, Two trains, one on bridge, Kuala Lumpur skyline.

Perf. 14x14½

1997, Mar. 1 Litho. Unwmk.

Booklet Stamps

619	A215	30c shown	2.25	.60
620	A215	30c multicolored	2.25	.60
a.		Booklet pane, 5 each #619-620	25.00	22.50
		Complete booklet, #620a	25.00	

1997, May 7 *Perf. 14½x14*

Highland Flowers: No. 621, Schima wallichi. No. 622, Aeschynanthus longicalyx. No. 623. Aeschynanthus speciosa. No. 624, Phyllagathis tuberculata. No. 625, Didymocarpus quinquevulnerus.

Booklet Stamps

621	A216	30c multicolored	.70	.25
622	A216	30c multicolored	.70	.25
623	A216	30c multicolored	.70	.25
624	A216	30c multicolored	.70	.25
625	A216	30c multicolored	.70	.25
a.		Booklet pane, 2 each #621-625	7.50	6.00
		Complete booklet, #625a	8.00	
		Nos. 621-625 (5)	3.50	1.25

Ruler's Council, Cent. A217

Unwmk.

1997, July 31 Litho. *Perf. 14*

626	A217	30c Photo, 1897	.40	.30
627	A217	50c Emblem, arms	.60	.30
628	A217	$1 Emblem	1.00	.45
		Nos. 626-628 (3)	2.00	1.05

ASEAN, 30th Anniv. A218

1997, Aug. 8 Wmk. 388 *Perf. 13½*

629	A218	30c shown	.55	.40
630	A218	50c "30," emblem	.75	.40
631	A218	$1 Emblem, color bars	1.50	.65
		Nos. 629-631 (3)	2.80	1.45

A219

A220

Coral: 20c, Tubastrea. 30c, Melithaea. 50c, Aulostomus chinensis. $1, Symphillia.

1997, Aug. 23 Unwmk. *Perf. 14½*

632	A219	20c multicolored	.30	.30
633	A219	30c multicolored	.40	.30
634	A219	50c multicolored	.55	.30
635	A219	$1 multicolored	1.10	.45
		Nos. 632-635 (4)	2.35	1.35

1997, Aug. 25 *Perf. 13x13½*

Booklet Stamps

636	A220	30c Career women	.75	.20
637	A220	30c Family	.75	.20
a.		Booklet pane, 5 each #636-637	7.50	6.00
		Complete booklet, #637a	7.50	

20th Intl. Conf. of Pan-Pacific and Southeast Asia Women's Assoc., Kuala Lumpur.

9th World Youth Soccer Championships A221

30c, Mascot. 50c, Soccer ball, players, flag. $1, Map of Malaysia, silhouettes of players, soccer ball.

Perf. 13½x13

1997, June 16 Unwmk.

638	A221	30c multicolored	.40	.40
639	A221	50c multicolored	.55	.40

Perf. 13x12½

640	A221	$1 multicolored	1.00	.45
		Nos. 638-640 (3)	1.95	1.25

Souvenir Sheet

Chelonia Mydas — A222

Illustration reduced.

1997, Aug. 23 Litho. *Perf. 14½*

641	A222	$2 multicolored	3.50	3.50

Year of the Coral Reef.

7th Summit Level of the Group of 15 — A223

$1, Emblem, natl. flags of member nations.

Perf. 12, 13½ (#643)

1997, Nov. 3 Litho. Unwmk.

642 A223 30c shown .40 .40
643 A223 $1 multicolored 1.40 .65

Stamp Week A224

Protected wildlife: a, 20c, Tomistoma schlegelli. b, 30c, Tarsius bancanus, vert. c, 50c, Cervus unicolor, vert. d, $2, Rollulus rouloul. e, $2, Scleropages formosus.

1997, Dec. 1 ***Perf. 14½***

644 A224 Sheet of 5, #a.-e. 5.00 5.00

Philately in Malaysia, 50th Anniv. — A225

Malpex '97: a, 20c, Straits Settlements #7. b, 30c, #605-608. c, 50c, #604. d, $1, Early cover from Straits Settlements.

1997, Sept. 9 ***Perf. 12½***

645 A225 Sheet of 4, #a.-d. 3.75 3.75
e. Ovptd. in sheet margin in gold 2.50 2.50

No. 645e is inscribed in sheet margin with INDEPEX '97 exhibition emblem.

Rare Fruit — A226

1998, Jan. 10 ***Perf. 13½***

646 A226 20c Bouea macrophylla .25 .25
647 A226 30c Sandoricum koetjape .40 .30
648 A226 50c Nephelium ramboutan-ake .60 .30
649 A226 $1 Garcinia atroviridis .75 .45
Nos. 646-649 (4) 2.00 1.30

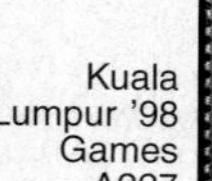

Kuala Lumpur '98 Games A227

1998, Feb. 23 ***Perf. 12***

650 A227 30c Field hockey .35 .25
651 A227 30c Women's netball .35 .25
a. Pair, #650-651 + label .75 .25
652 A227 50c Cricket .45 .25
653 A227 50c Rugby .45 .25
a. Pair, #652-653 + label 1.25 .50
Nos. 650-653 (4) 1.60 1.00

Kuala Lumpur '98 Games — A228

Stadiums for the venues: a, 1r, Utama Bukit Jalil. b, 50c, Tertutup. c, 30c, Hoki. d, 20c, Renang Complex.

Wmk. 388

1998, Feb. 23 Litho. ***Perf. 13⅓***

654 A228 Sheet of 4, #a.-d. 2.00 2.00

Early Coins A229

Coin's region, date: 20c, Trengganu, 1793-1808. 30c, Kedah, 1661-87. 50c, Johore, 1597-1615. $1, Kelantan, 1400-1780.

Wmk. 388

1998, Apr. 11 Litho. ***Perf. 13½***

655 A229 20c multicolored .30 .30
a. Perf. 14¼ 3.00 .25
656 A229 30c multicolored .40 .30
657 A229 50c multicolored .50 .30
a. Perf. 14¼ 4.25 .35
658 A229 $1 multicolored .80 .40
Nos. 655-658 (4) 2.00 1.30

Kuala Lumpur International Airport — A230

Designs: 30c, Tower, tramway, airplanes. 50c, Tower, airplanes at terminal. $1, Tower, airplane in air, airport below.
$2, Tower, globe overhead.

1998, June 27 ***Perf. 12***

659 A230 30c multicolored .35 .30
a. Perf. 12½ 5.00
660 A230 50c multicolored .65 .30
661 A230 $1 multicolored 1.00
a. Perf. 12½ 6.00 3.75
Nos. 659-661 (3) 2.00 .60

Souvenir Sheet

Perf. 14

662 A230 $2 multicolored 2.75 2.75

No. 662 contains one 26x36mm stamp.

Malaysian Red Crescent Society, 50th Anniv. — A231

1998, May 8 ***Perf. 13½***

663 A231 30c Rescue boat .50 .40
a. Perf. 14¼ 2.75 2.75
664 A231 $1 Mobile rescue unit 1.50 .60
a. Perf. 14¼ 21.00 21.00

Medicinal Plants — A234

20c, Solanum torvum. 30c, Tinospora crispa. 50c, Jatropha podagrica. $1, Hibiscus rosa-sinensis.

Wmk. 388

1998, July 18 Litho. ***Perf. 13¾***

671 A234 20c multicolored .25 .25
672 A234 30c multicolored .35 .30

Perf. 14¼

673 A234 50c multicolored .50 .30
674 A234 $1 multicolored .70 .35
Nos. 671-674 (4) 1.80 1.20

1998 Commonwealth Games, Kuala Lumpur — A235

a, 20c, Weight lifting. b, 20c, Badminton. c, 30c, Field hockey goalie. d, 30c, Field hockey. e, 20c, Netball. f, 20c, Shooting. g, 30c, Cycling. h, 30c, Lawn bowling. i, 50c, Gymnastics. j, 50c, Cricket. k, $1, Swimming. l, $1, Squash. m, 50c, Rugby. n, 50c, Running. o, $1, Boxing. p, $1, Bowling.

Perf. 14½x15

1998, Sept. 11 Litho. Wmk. 388

675 A235 Sheet of 16, #a.-p. 8.50 8.50

Modernization of Rail Transport — A236

Designs: 30c, Putra-LRT, 1998. 50c, Star-LRT, 1996. $1, KTM Commuter, 1995.

1998, Oct. 3 ***Perf. 13¾, 14¼***

676 A236 30c multicolored .35 .35
a. Perf. 14¼ 3.25
677 A236 50c multicolored .65 .35
a. Perf. 14¼ 1.25 .30
678 A236 $1 multicolored (Perf. 14¼) 1.25 .45
Nos. 676-678 (3) 2.25 1.15

1998 APEC (Asia-Pacific Economic Cooperation) Conference A237

Design: $1, Petronas Towers, people working with computers, office workers.

1998, Nov. 14

679 A237 30c shown .85 .40
a. Perf. 14¼ 1.40 1.40
680 A237 $1 multicolored .95 .85
a. Perf. 14¼ 4.25 4.25

Insects A238

Designs: a, 20c, Xylotrupes gideon, vert. b, 30c, Pomponia imperatoria, vert. c, 50c, Phyllium pulchrifolium, vert. d, $2, Hymenopus coronatus. e, $2, Macrolyristes corporalis.

Wmk. 388

1998, Nov. 28 Litho. ***Perf. 12½***

681 A238 Sheet of 5, #a.-e. 4.00 4.00

Stamp Week.
Nos. 681a-681c are each 30x40mm.

Gold Medal Winners at 16th Commonwealth Games — A238a

No. 681F: h, 30c, Air rifle. i, 30c, 48kg boxing. j, 30c, 50km walk. k, 30c, 69kg clean and jerk weight lifting. l, 50c, Men's doubles, bowling. m, 50c, Men's singles, bowling. n, 50c, Men's doubles, badminton. o, 50c, Men's singles, badminton. p, $1, Rhythmic gymnastics (64x26mm).
$2, Team photograph.

Perf. 13¾x14

1998, Dec. 12 Litho. Wmk. 388

681F A238a Sheet of 9, #h.-p., + 2 labels 12.00 12.00

Souvenir Sheet

681G A238a $2 multi 5.00 5.00

No. 681G contains one 128x80mm stamp.

Intl. Year for Older Persons A239

Wmk. 388

1999, Jan. 28 Litho. ***Perf. 14***

682 A239 $1 shown 1.00 .45
683 A239 $1 World map, people, diff. 1.00 .45

Fruit — A240

Designs: 20c, Syzgium malaccense. 30c, Garcinia prainiana. 50c, Mangifera caesia. $1, Salacca glabrescens.

1999, Feb. 27 ***Perf. 12***

684 A240 20c multicolored .20 .20
685 A240 30c multicolored .35 .20
686 A240 50c multicolored .50 .20
687 A240 $1 multicolored .85 .35
a. Strip of 4, #684-687 2.00 1.75
Nos. 684-687 (4) 1.90 .95

Domestic Cats — A241

Designs: 30c, Kucing Malaysia. 50c, Siamese. $1, Abyssinian.
No. 691: a, British shorthair. b, Scottish fold.
No. 692: a, Birman. b. Persian.

1999, Apr. 1 Litho. ***Perf. 12***

688 A241 30c multicolored .40 .30
689 A241 50c multicolored .65 .30
690 A241 $1 multicolored .95 .40
Nos. 688-690 (3) 2.00 1.00

Sheets of 2

691 A241 $1 #a.-b. 1.50 1.50
692 A241 $1 #a.-b. 1.50 1.50

Protected Mammals A242

Wmk. 388

1999, May 28 **Litho.** ***Perf. 12***

693 A242 20c Rhinoceros .20 .20
694 A242 30c Panther .20 .20
695 A242 50c Bear .25 .20
696 A242 1r Elephant .50 .25
697 A242 2r Orangutan 1.00 .35
a. Strip of 5, #693-697 2.50 2.50
b. Souvenir sheet, #697 1.00 1.00

Nos. 693-697 were issued in sheet containing 4 each. No. 697b is a continuous design.

Intl. Congress on AIDS in Asia and the Pacific, Kuala Lumpur A244

Perf. 14, 13½ (#700, 701)

1999, June 19 **Litho.** **Wmk. 388**

699 A244 30c shown .40 .40
700 A244 50c Emblems, hearts .50 .40
701 A244 1r Emblem as heart 1.10 .40
Nos. 699-701 (3) 2.00 1.20

P. Ramlee (1929-73), Actor, Director — A245

Designs: 20c, Wearing chain around neck. 30c, Wearing bow tie. 50c, Holding gun. No. 705, Behind camera.

No. 706: a, Wearing cap. b, With hands in air. c, Holding microphone. d, Wearing army uniform.

No. 707, Wearing patterned hat. No. 708, Wearing plaid shirt.

Perf. 13½x13¾

1999, July 24 **Litho.** **Wmk. 388**

702 A245 20c multicolored .50 .50
703 A245 30c multicolored .50 .50
704 A245 50c multicolored .65 .50
705 A245 $1 multicolored 1.40 .65
a. Perf. 14¼ .55 .25
Nos. 702-705 (4) 3.05 2.15

Strip of 4

706 A245 30c #a.-d. .65 .65

Souvenir Sheets

Perf. 14¼

707 A245 $1 multicolored .50 .50
708 A245 $1 multicolored .50 .50

No. 706 printed in sheets of 16 stamps.

Water Plants and Fish — A246

#709, Monochoria hastata. #710, Trichopsis vittatus. #711, Limnocharis flava. #712, Betta imbellis. #713, Nymphaea pubescens. #714, Trichogaster trichopterus. #715, Ipomea aquatica. #716, Helostoma temmincki. #717, Eichhornia crassipes. #718, Sphaerichthys osphronemoides.

Perf. 13¾x14

1999, July 31 **Litho.** **Wmk. 388**

709 A246 10c multi .20 .20
710 A246 10c multi .20 .20
a. Pair, #709-710 .50 .50
711 A246 15c multi .20 .20
712 A246 15c multi .20 .20
a. Pair, #711-712 .50 .50
713 A246 25c multi .20 .20
714 A246 25c multi .20 .20
a. Pair, #713-714 .60 .60
715 A246 50c multi .25 .20
716 A246 50c multi .25 .20
a. Pair, #715-716 1.25 1.25
717 A246 50c multi .25 .20
718 A246 50c multi .25 .20
a. Pair, #717-718 1.25 1.25
b. Block of 10 with bottom row of perforations perf 14½ 4.00 1.90
Nos. 709-718 (10) 2.20 2.00

Trees — A247

Designs: No. 719, Dryobalanops aromatica. No. 720, Alstonia angustiloba. No. 721, Fagraea fragrans. No. 722, Lagerstroemia floribunda. No. 723, Elateriospermum tapos.

Perf. 14x13½

1999, Aug. 14 **Litho.** **Wmk. 388**

719 A247 30c multicolored .20 .20
720 A247 30c multicolored .20 .20
721 A247 30c multicolored .20 .20
722 A247 30c multicolored .20 .20
723 A247 30c multicolored .20 .20
a. Strip of 5, #719-723 1.00 1.00
Complete bklt., 4 ea #719-723 4.00

Petronas Towers — A248

Designs: 30c, Daytime view. 50c, Architectural drawing. $1, Nighttime view.
$5, Hologram.

Perf. 14x14¼

1999, Aug. 30 **Litho.** **Unwmk.**

724 A248 30c multicolored .40 .40
725 A248 50c multicolored .55 .40
726 A248 $1 multicolored 1.00 .55
Nos. 724-726 (3) 1.95 1.35

Souvenir Sheet

Perf. 14½x14¼

727 A248 $5 multicolored 4.50 4.50

No. 727 contains one 30x50mm stamp with a holographic image. Soaking in water may affect hologram. No. 727 exists imperf.

Taiping, 125th Anniv. A249

Designs: 20c, Rickshaw, Peace Hotel. 30c, Automobile, building. 50c, Train, train station. $1, Airplanes, airport building.
$2, Building, horse-drawn carriage.

Unwmk.

1999, Sept. 1 **Litho.** ***Perf. 12***

728 A249 20c multi .55 .55
729 A249 30c multi .55 .55
730 A249 50c multi .65 .55
731 A249 $1 multi 1.25 .65
Nos. 728-731 (4) 3.00 2.30

Souvenir Sheet

732 A249 $2 multi 5.25 5.25

Tenaga Nasional, 50th Anniv. A250

Designs: 30c, Power station at night. 50c, High tension wire towers, control room. No. 735, Kuala Lumpur at night.

No. 736, Van, vert. No. 737, High tension wire towers, vert.

Perf. 14¼x14½

1999, Sept. 9 **Litho.** **Unwmk.**

733 A250 30c multicolored .60 .60
734 A250 50c multicolored .80 .60
735 A250 $1 multicolored 1.60 .80
Nos. 733-735 (3) 3.00 2.00

Souvenir Sheets

Perf. 13½x13¾

736 A250 $1 multicolored 1.00 1.00
737 A250 $1 multicolored 1.00 1.00

National Theater — A251

Various performers and views of building.

1999 **Litho.** **Wmk. 388** ***Perf. 12¼***

Panel Colors

738 A251 30c red .40 .40
739 A251 50c green .50 .40
740 A251 $1 violet 1.00 .50
Nos. 738-740 (3) 1.90 1.30

Installation of 11th Yang Di-Pertuan Agong (Head of State A252

Tuanku Salehuddin Abdul Aziz Shah ibni al-Marhum Hisamuddin Alam Shah and: 30c, Flag. 50c, Old building. $1, Modern building.

No. 744: a, Purple background. b, Yellow background. c, Blue background.

Perf. 13¾x13½

1999, Sept. 23 **Litho.** **Wmk. 388**

741 A252 30c multicolored .20 .20

Perf. 14¼

742 A252 50c multicolored .25 .20
743 A252 $1 multicolored .50 .25

Perf. 14x13¾

744 A252 30c Strip of 3, #a.-c. .50 .25
Nos. 741-744 (4) 1.45 .90

Size of Nos. 744a-744c: 24x30mm.

21st World Road Congress — A253

Unwmk.

1999, Oct. 3 **Litho.** ***Perf. 12***

745 A253 30c Entrance ramp .35 .35
746 A253 50c Bridge .45 .35
747 A253 $1 Interchange 1.00 .45
Nos. 745-747 (3) 1.80 1.15

A254

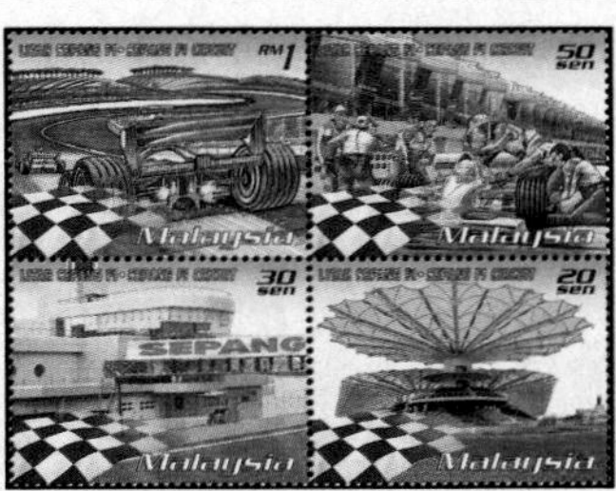

1999 Malaysia Grand Prix — A255

Racing helmets and: 20c, Canopy over track's stands. 30c, Stands. 50c, Car on track. $1, side view of car.

No. 752: a, 20c, Stands b, 30c, Race control building. c, 50c, Pits. d, $1, Track.

Unwmk.

1999, Oct. 16 **Litho.** ***Perf. 12***

748 A254 20c multi .45 .45
749 A254 30c multi .45 .45
750 A254 50c multi .60 .45
751 A254 $1 multi 1.10 .60
Nos. 748-751 (4) 2.60 1.95

Perf. 12½

752 A255 Strip or block of 4, #a.-d. 2.50 2.50

No. 752 printed in sheets of 16 stamps.

UPU, 125th Anniv. A256

Designs: 20c, Computer, envelopes. 30c, Globe, stamps. 50c, World map, airplane. $1, Malaysian Post Office emblem.

Perf. 13¾x13½

1999, Dec. 18 **Litho.** **Wmk. 388**

753 A256 20c multi .50 .50
754 A256 30c multi .50 .50

Perf. 14¼

755 A256 50c multi .60 .50
756 A256 $1 multi 1.10 .60
Nos. 753-756 (4) 2.70 2.10

Sultan of Perak, 25th Anniv. of Reign A257

Sultan and: a, Flowers. b, Butterfly, flower, highway. c, Divers, beach. d, Automobile plant. e, Palace.

Wmk. 388

1999, Oct. 23 **Litho.** ***Perf. 14¼***

757 A257 30c Strip of 5, #a.-e. .80 .40

Malaysia '99 World Cup Golf Tournament — A258

20c, World Cup. 30c, Ball on tee. 50c, Fairway and green. $1, Clubhouse and flag.

Perf. 14x13¾ Syncopated

1999, Nov. 18

758 A258 20c multi .45 .45
759 A258 30c multi .45 .45
760 A258 50c multi .50 .45
761 A258 $1 multi 1.00 .50
a. Sheet, 5 each #758-761 12.00 12.00
Nos. 758-761 (4) 2.40 1.85

Flowers — A259

No. 762: a, Strelitzia augusta. b, Heliconia rostrata. c, Heliconia psittacorum (yellow petals). d, Heliconia stricta. e, Musa violescens. f, Strelitzia reginae. g, Heliconia colgantea. h, Heliconia psittacorum (pink and blue petals). i, Heliconia latispatha. j, Phaeomeria speciosa.

1999, Nov. 29 Wmk. 388 *Perf. 12¼*

762 A259 30c Block or strip of 10, #a.-j. 3.00 1.75
k. Sheet, 2 blocks #762 6.00 6.00

Millennium A260

Stamp number in parentheses.

No. 763: a, Vine, bird (1). b, Pottery, waterfall (2). c, Frog, forest (3). d, People and machine, cultivated land (4). e, Fish, boat and lighthouse (5). f, Chevrotain, house (6). g, Elephant, forest (7). h, Dagger, ship (8). i, Clock tower, archway (9). j, Boat with sail, palm trees (10).

No. 764: a, Man with musical instrument, native people (11). b, Lantern and nautilus shell, native people (12). c, Doctor and patient, native people (13). d, Badminton player, native people (14). e, Dancer, native women (15). f, Motorcycle, automobile and highway (16). g, Butterfly, race car, airplane and tower (17). h, Train, satellite and city buildings (18). i, Computer operator, mosque (19). j, Truck, ship (20).

No. 765, $1, Sailing ship, horiz. No. 766, $1, Airplane, horiz.

1999-2000 *Perf. 12¾x12½*

763 A260 30c Block of 10, #a.-j. 6.00 3.25
k. Sheet, 2 #763 12.00 12.00
764 A260 30c Block or strip of 10, #a.-j. 6.00 3.25
k. Sheet, 2 #764 blocks 12.00 12.00

Perf. 12½x12¾

Wmk. 388

765-766 A260 Set of 2 6.00 6.00

Issued: No. 763, 12/31/99; No. 764, 1/1/00. No. 765, 12/31/99; No. 766, 1/1/00.

Fruit Type of 1986 Redrawn With "Sen" Instead of "C" and "RM" Instead of "$"

Perf. 13¾x14

2002-04 Litho. Wmk. 388

766A A125 40sen Like #329 — —
766B A125 50sen Like #330 — —
766D A125 1r Like #332 ('04) — —
766E A126 2r Like #333 ('04) — —
766G A126 10r Like #335 — —
766H A126 20r Like #336 — —

New Year 2000 (Year of the Dragon) — A261

No. 767 — Artifacts depicting dragons from: a, New stone age. b, 100 B.C. c, 800. d, 200 B.C. e, 700.

No. 768 — Fish: a, Osteoglossum bicirrhosum. b, Scleropages leichardti. c, Scleropages formosus (Prussian blue background). d, Osteoglossum ferreirai. e, Scleropages formosus (bister background).

No. 768G, Dragon on boat prow (square orientation). No. 768H, Dragon in parade (square orientation).

Wmk. 388

2000, Jan. 6 Litho. *Perf. 13¼*

767 A261 30c Strip of 5, #a.-e. .70 .70
f. Sheet, 4 #767 3.50 3.50
768 A261 30c Strip of 5, #a.-e. .70 .70
f. Sheet, 4 #768 3.50 3.50

Souvenir Sheets

768G A261 $1 multi 1.50 1.50
768H A261 $1 multi 1.50 1.50

Dawei 2000 World Team Table Tennis Championships — A262

20c, Paddles, globe. 50c, Tiger mascot playing table tennis. No. 771, Paddles, ball.

No. 772: a, Mascot, table and net. b, Paddles and table.

2000, Feb. 19 *Perf. 13½*

769 A262 30c multi .35 .35
770 A262 50c multi .50 .35
771 A262 $1 multi .95 .50
Nos. 769-771 (3) 1.80 1.20

Souvenir Sheet

Perf. 14¼

772 A262 $1 Sheet, #a.-b. 2.00 2.00

Souvenir Sheets

Millennium — A263

No. 773, Man, sailboat.

No. 774: a, Mt. Everest climbers with Malaysian flag. b, People with backpacks. c, Parchutist, people with flag, automobile.

Illustration reduced.

2000, Feb. 26 Wmk. 388 *Perf. 12*

773 A263 50c Sheet of 1 1.00 1.00
774 A263 50c Sheet of 3, #a.-c. 3.00 3.00

2nd Global Knowledge Conference — A264

No. 775: a, Finger pointing. b, Eye, globe.

No. 776: a, Head facing right. b, Head facing left.

Illustration reduced.

2000, Mar. 7 *Perf. 13½*

775 A264 30c Pair, a.-b., + central label .90 .60

Perf. 14x14¼

776 A264 50c Pair, a.-b., + central label 1.50 .75

Islamic Arts Museum, Kuala Lumpur — A265

20c, Inverted dome. 30c, Main dome. No. 778A, Like No. 778 but with central design element entirely in gold. 50c, Ottoman panel. $1, Art of the mosque.

Perf. 13¾x13½ Syncopated

2000, Apr. 6 Wmk. 388

777 A265 20c multi .40 .40
778 A265 30c multi .40 .40
778A A265 30c multi .40 .40
779 A265 50c multi .50 .40
780 A265 $1 multi 1.00 .50
Nos. 777-780 (5) 2.70 2.10

Boats — A266

No. 781: a, Perahu Buatan Barat. b, Perahu Payang (red and blue). c, Perahu Burung. d, Perahu Payang (red, white and green).

Illustration reduced.

Perf. 14x13½

2000, Apr. 15 Litho. Wmk. 388

781 A266 Block of 4 2.25 2.25
a.-d. 30c Any single .20 .20
Booklet, 5 each #a-d 12.00

Unit Trust Investment Week — A267

30c, Emblem, women with flags. 50c, People, Kuala Lumpur skyline. $1, People, globe.

Perf. 13½x13¾

2000, Apr. 20 Litho. Unwmk.

782 A267 30c multi .50 .50
783 A267 50c multi .65 .50
784 A267 $1 multi 1.25 .65
Nos. 782-784 (3) 2.40 1.65

Thomas and Uber Cup Badminton Championships — A268

No. 785: a, Male player. b, Flags, Thomas Cup (with handles). c, Mascot. d, Flags, Uber Cup. e, Female player.

$1, Thomas Cup, vert.

Perf. 12½x12¾

2000, May 11 Wmk. 388

785 Horiz. strip of 5 2.25 2.25
a.-e. A268 30c Any single .20 .20

Souvenir Sheet

Perf. 12¾x12½x12x12½

786 A268 $1 multi 2.25 2.25

No. 785 printed in sheets of 10 strips and ten labels.

Children's Games — A269

No. 787: a, Hopscotch. b, Tarik Upih. c, Kite flying. d, Marbles. e, Hoops and sticks.

2000, June 24 *Perf. 13½x13¾*

787 Horiz. strip of 5 4.00 4.00
a.-e. A269 30c Any single .50 .50
f. Miniature sheet, 4 #787 17.50 17.50

Islamic Conference of Foreign Ministers, 27th Session A270

No. 788: a, Red globe, electronic circuitry. b, Blue globe, Islamic design. c, Emblem, flower, bird. d, Green globe, Islamic design, diff. e, Purple globe, pens.

2000, June 26 *Perf. 13¾x13½*

788 Horiz. strip of 5 2.25 2.25
a.-e. A270 30c Any single .25 .25

National Census A271

No. 789: a, Family, map. b, Family in house, appliances. c, People on pie chart. d, Map, diplomas, mortarboard, workers. e, Male and female symbols.

2000, July 5 *Perf. 14¼*

789 Horiz. strip of 5 2.25 2.25
a.-e. A271 30c Any single .20 .20

Birds — A272

Designs: 20c, Polyplectron inopinatum. 30c, Rheinardia ocellata. 50c, Argisianus argus. $1, Lophura erythropthalma.

$2, Rheinardia ocellata, diff.

2000, July 22 *Perf. 13x13¼*

790 A272 20c multi .55 .55
791 A272 30c multi .55 .55
a. Sheet of 20 11.00
792 A272 50c multi .70 .55
793 A272 $1 multi 1.50 .70
Nos. 790-793 (4) 3.30 2.35

Souvenir Sheet

Perf. 13¾x14

794 A272 $2 multi 3.00 3.00

No. 794 contains one 32x27mm stamp.

A273

Intl. Union of Forestry Research World Congress — A274

No. 795: a, Shorea macrophylla. b, Dyera costulata. c, Alstonia angustiloba. d, Hopea odorata. e, Adenanthera pavonina.

No. 796 — Trees, 10c: a, Fagraea fragrans. b, Dryobalanops aromatica. c, Terminalia catappa. d, Samanea saman. e, Dracontomelon dao.

No. 797 — Leaves, 15c: a, Heritiera javanica. b, Johannesteijsmannia altifrons. c, Macaranga gigantea. d, Licuala grandis. e, Endospermum diadenum.

No. 798 — Tree barks, 25c: a, Pterocymbium javanicum. b, Dryobalanops aromatica. c, Dipterocarpus costulatus. d, Shorea leprosula. e, Ochanostachys amentacea.

No. 799 — Fauna, 50c: a, Muscicapa indigo. b, Nycticebus coucang. c, Felis marmorata. d, Cyprinus carpio. e, Trimerisurus wagleri.

Illustration A274 reduced.

Wmk. 388

2000, Aug. 7 Litho. *Perf. 12*

795 Horiz. strip of 5 4.00 4.00
a.-e. A273 30c Any single .25 .25
f. Sheet of 4 each #a-e 2.75 2.75

Sheets of 5, #a-e, + label

796-799 A274 Set of 4 9.00 9.00

Medical Research Institute, Cent. A275

Designs: 30c, Institute in 1901, Brugia malayi, Beri-beri. 50c, Institute in 1953, Clostridium bifermentans malaysia, Anophelese campestris. $1, Institute in 1976, chromatograph of DNA sequence, Eurycoma longifolia.

Perf. 13¾x13½, 14¼ (50c, $1, $2)

2000, Aug. 24 Unwmk.

800-802 A275 Set of 3 2.40 1.25

Souvenir Sheet

Wmk. 388

803 A275 $2 Molecular model 2.50 2.50

Protected Mammals A276

Designs: 20c, Cynogale bennettii (mouth open). No. 805, 30c, Cynogale bennettii (mouth closed). 50c, Arctictis binturong. $1, Arctictis binturong, diff.

No. 808: a, Hemigalus hosei. b, Paradoxurus hermaphroditus. c, Paguma larvata. d, Viverra tangalunga. e, Arctogalidia trivirgata.

No. 809: a, Hemigalus derbyanus. b, Prionodon linsang.

2000, Aug. 26 Wmk. 388 *Perf. 13¼*

804-807 A276 Set of 4 1.25 .55
808 Horiz. strip of 5 1.50 1.50
a.-e. A276 30c Any single .25 .20

Souvenir Sheet

809 A276 $1 Sheet of 2, #a-b 2.75 2.75

Rural and Industrial Development Authority, Trust Council for Indiginous People, 50th Anniv. — A277

Designs: 30c, Gear wheels. 50c, Compass, stethoscope. $1, Computer mouse and diskette.

2000, Sept. 14 *Perf. 14¼*

810-812 A277 Set of 3 2.25 2.25
810a Sheet of 20 2.50 2.50

Children's Games — A278

No. 813, 20c: a, Gasing. b, Baling tin.
No. 814, 30c: a, Letup-letup. b, Sepak raga.
Illustration reduced.

Perf. 14¼, 13¾x13½ (#814)

2000, Sept. 16

Horiz. Pairs, #a-b

813-814 A278 Set of 2 2.25 1.25

World Heart Day — A279

No. 815: a, People walking, cyclist. b, People jumping rope, playing with hula hoop and ball. c, Boy flying kite, children playing soccer. d, People exercising. e, Man gardening.

2000, Sept. 24 *Perf. 12¼*

815 Horiz. strip of 5 2.25 1.25
a.-e. A279 30c Any single .25 .25

Rhododendrons — A280

No. 816: a, Brookeanum. b, Jasminiflorum. c, Scortechinii. d, Pauciflorum.

No. 817: a, Crassifloium. b, Longiflorum. c, Javanicum. d, Variolosum. e, Acuminatum. f, Praetervisum. g, Himantodes. h, Maxwellii. i, Erocoides. j, Fallacinum.

$1, Malayanum.

2000, Oct. 9

816 A280 30c Block of 4, #a-d 1.50 .80
817 A280 30c Block of 10, #a-j 3.50 1.50

Souvenir Sheet

818 A280 $1 multi 1.60 1.60

A281

Dragonflies and Damselflies A282

No. 819: a, Vestalis gracilis. b, Crocothemis s. servilia male. c, Trithemis auraora. d, Pseudothemis jorina. e, Diplacodes nebulosa. f, Crocothemis s. servilia female. g, Neurobasis c. chinensis male. h, Burmagomphus divaricatus. i, Ictinogomphus d. melanops. j, Orthetrum testaceum. k, Trithemis festiva. l, Brachythemis contaminata. m, Neurobasis c. chinensis female. n, Neurothemis fluctuans. o, Acisoma panorpoides. p, Orthetrum s. sabina. q, Rhyothemis p. phyllis. r, Rhyothemis obsolescens. s, Neurothemis t. tulia. t, Lathrecista a. asiatica. u, Aethriamanta gracilis. v, Diplacodes trivialis. w, Neurothemis fulvia. x, Rhyothemis triangularis. y, Orthetrum glaucum.

No. 820: a, Neurobasis c. chinensis. b, Aristocypha fenestrella (with blue sky). c, Vestalis gracilis. d, Nannophya pymaea. e, Aristocypha fenestrella (no sky). f, Rhyothemis p. phyllis. g, Crocothemis s. servilia. h, Euphaea ochracea male. i, Euphaea ochracea female. j, Ceriagrion cerinorubellum.

2000, Nov. 25 *Perf. 14¼x13¾ Sync.*

819 Sheet of 25 12.00 12.00
a.-y. A281 (30c) Any single .25 .25

Booklet Stamps

Perf. 13½x14 Syncopated

820 Block of 10 4.50 4.50
a.-j. A282 30c Any single .25 .25
k. Booklet pane, 2# 820 3.75
Booklet, #820k 3.75

Quails and Partridges A283

Designs: 30c, Cotumix chinensis. 50c, Arborophila campbelli. $1, Turnix suscitator.

No. 824: a, Arborophila charltonii. b, Haematortyx sanguiniceps.

Wmk. 388, Unwmkd. (#822-823)

Perf. 13¾x13½, 14¼ (30c)

2001, Jan. 22 Litho.

821-823 A283 Set of 3 3.25 1.40

Souvenir Sheet

Perf. 14¼x14¼x13¾x14¼

824 A283 $2 Sheet of 2, #a-b 4.50 4.50

Creation of Putrajaya Federal Territory A284

Designs: 30c, Perdana Putra Building (Prime Minister's office building). $1, Perdana Putra Building, highway, government office buildings.

Perf. 13¾x13½, 14¼ ($1)

2001, Feb. 1 Litho. Wmk. 388

825-826 A284 Set of 2 2.50 1.25

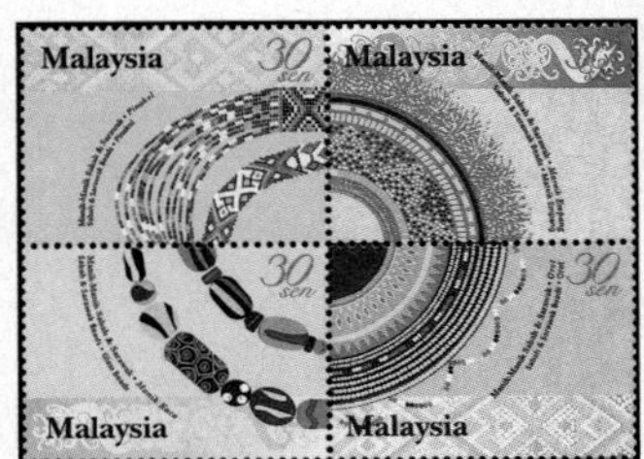

Sabah and Sarawak Beads — A285

No. 827: a, Pinakol. b, Mareik Empang. c, Glass beads. d, Orot.

Illustration reduced.

Wmk. 388

2001, Feb. 17 Litho. *Perf. 13¾*

827 A285 30c Block of 4, #a-d 2.25 1.25

Flowers — A286

Designs: 30c, Cananga odorata. 50c, Mimusops elengi. $1, Mesua ferrea.

$2, Michelia champaca.

2001, Mar. 27 *Perf. 13¾, 14¼ ($1)*

828-830 A286 Set of 3 2.50 1.25

Souvenir Sheet

Perf. 13¾x14¼x13¾x13¾

831 A286 $2 multi 2.50 2.50

Cutltural Items — A287

No. 832, 30c: a, Sireh Junjung. b, Penggendong Anak.

No. 833, 50c: a, Jebak Puyuh. b, Bekas Bara.

2001, June 11 *Perf. 13¾*

Horiz. pairs, #a-b

832-833 A287 Set of 2 2.40 1.10

Automobiles A288

No. 834: a, 1995 Perodua Kancil. b, 1995 Proton Tiara. c, 1995 Perodua Rusa. d, 1997 Proton Putra. e, 1999 Inokom Permas. f, 1999 Perodua Kembara. g, 2000 Proton GTi. h, 2000 TD2000. i, 2000 Perodua Kenari. j, 2000 Proton Waja.

2001, July 9

834 Block of 10 5.50 2.50
a.-j. A288 30c Any single .25 .25
Booklet, #834 5.50

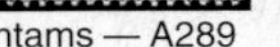

Bantams — A289

21st South East Asia Games — A290

Designs: 30c, Ayam Serama. 50c, Ayam Kapan. $1, Ayam Serama and chicks.

$3, Ayam Hutan, horiz.

Perf. 12¾x12½, 12 (50c)

2001, Aug. 1

835-837 A289 Set of 3 2.40 1.25

Souvenir Sheet

Perf. 12½

838 A289 $3 multi 5.00 5.00
a. As #838, with PhilaNippon '01 Emblem in margin 1.50 1.50

No. 838 contains one 45x35mm stamp.

2001, Sept. 8 *Perf. 13½x13¾*

Designs: 20c, Diving. 30c, Gymnastics. 50c, Bowling. $1, Weight lifting. $2, Cycling.

$5, Running.

839-843 A290 Set of 5 5.50 2.75

Souvenir Sheet

844 A290 $5 multi 6.50 6.50

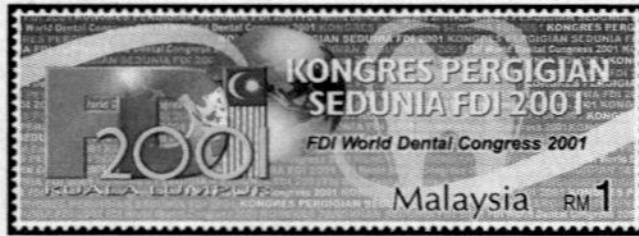

2001 World Dental Federation Congress — A291

Illustration reduced.

2001, Sept. 27 *Perf. 14¼*
845 A291 $1 multi 1.75 .80

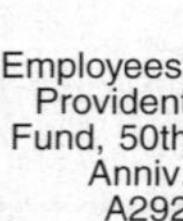

Employees' Provident Fund, 50th Anniv. A292

Designs: 30c, Headquarters. 50c, Bar graph. $1, Emblem, man and woman.

Perf. 14¼, 13¾x13½ ($1)
2001, Oct. 1
846-848 A292 Set of 3 2.75 1.25

Forestry Dept., Cent. — A293

Designs: 30c, Satellite, map, trees. 50c, Trees, leaf. $1, Seedlings and forest.

2001, Nov. 10 *Perf. 14¼*
849-851 A293 Set of 3 3.00 1.50

Stamp Week A294

Marine life: 20c, Tridacna gigas. 30c, Hippocampus sp. 50c, Oreaster occidentalis. $1, Cassis cornuta.
$3, Dugong dugon.

2001, Nov. 10 *Perf. 13¾x13½*
852-855 A294 Set of 4 3.00 1.40

Souvenir Sheet

Perf. 14¼

856 A294 $3 multi 3.50 3.50

No. 856 exists imperf. with a slightly larger, numbered margin. Value $5.50.

2002 KL Field Hockey World Cup — A295

Designs: 30c, Player with ball. 50c, Goaltender. $1, Player with ball, diff.
$3, Player, stadium playing field.

Perf. 13½x13¾
2002, Jan. 2 **Wmk. 388**
857-859 A295 Set of 3 3.00 1.40

Souvenir Sheet

Perf. 12¾x12½x12x12½

860 A295 $3 multi 3.50 3.50

No. 860 exists imperf. with a numbered margin.

Flowers — A296 Snakes — A297

Designs: 30c, Couroupita guianensii. No. 862, $1, Camellia nitidissima. No. 863, $1, Couroupita guianensis, diff.
No. 864: a, Schima brevifolia, horiz. b, Schima brevifolia.

2002, Feb. 5 **Wmk. 380** *Perf. 12¾*
861-863 A296 Set of 3 3.00 1.40

Souvenir Sheet

864 A296 $2 Sheet of 2, #a-b 3.50 3.50

See People's Republic of China No. 3180.

2002, Mar. 9 **Wmk. 388** *Perf. 14¼*

Designs: No. 865, 30c, Gonyophis margaritatus. No. 866, 30c, Python reticulatus. 50c, Bungarus candidus. $1, Maticora bivirgata.
No. 869: a, Ophiophagus hannah (brown). b, Ophiophagus hannah (black and white striped).

865-868 A297 Set of 4 3.50 1.60

Souvenir Sheet

Perf. 13¼

869 A297 $2 Sheet of 2, #a-b 4.00 4.00

Nos. 865-868 were each printed in sheets of 20 + 5 labels. No. 869 exists imperf. Value $5.50.

Express Rail Link A298

Designs: 30c, Kuala Lumpur Central Station.
No. 871: a, Train and station. b, Train, airplane and control tower.
No. 872: a, Train with red violet stripe, train with red stripe. b, Yellow and blue train, train with blue, orange and red stripes.
$2, Train with red violet stripe.

2002, Apr. 13 **Wmk. 388** *Perf. 12*
870 A298 30c multi 1.00 1.00
871 A298 50c Horiz. pair, #a-b 2.50 1.10

Souvenir Sheets

Perf. 12½x12¾

872 A298 $1 Sheet of 2, #a-b 3.00 3.00

Perf. 12½x12¾x12½x12

873 A298 $2 multi 3.00 3.00

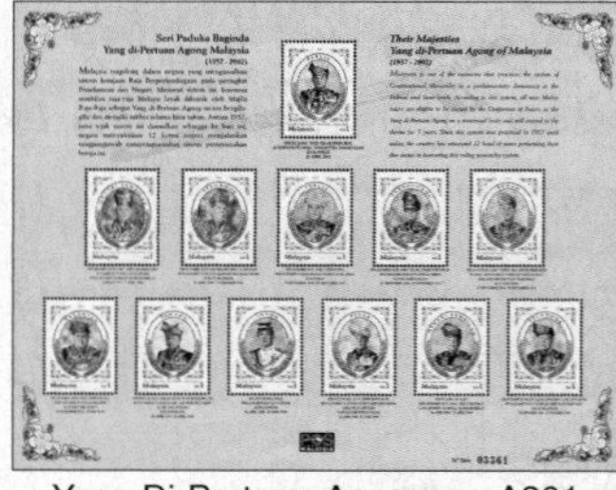

17th World Orchid Congress — A299

No. 874: a, Paraphalenopsis labukensis. b, Renanthera bella.
50c, Paphiopedilum sanderianum.
No. 876: a, Coelogyne pandurata. b, Phalaenopsis amabilis.
$5, Cleisocentron merillianum.

2002, Apr. 24 **Wmk. 380** *Perf. 12¾*
874 A299 30c Horiz. pair, #a-b 1.25 .80
875 A299 50c multi 1.00 .80
876 A299 $1 Horiz. pair, #a-b 3.25 1.25
Nos. 874-876 (3) 5.50 2.85

Souvenir Sheet

Perf. 13

Unwmk.

877 A299 $5 multi 8.00 8.00

No. 877 contains one 45x40mm stamp and exists imperf.

Installation of 12th Yang Di-Pertuan Agong — A300

Yang Di-Pertuan Agongs — A301

Background colors: 30c, Green. 50c, Red violet. $1, Yellow.
No. 881 — Ordinal number of Yang Di-Pertuan Agong: a, 1st. b, 2nd. c, 3rd. d, 4th. e, 5th. f, 6th. g, 7th. h, 8th. i, 9th. j, 10th. k, 11th. l, 12th.

2002, Apr. 25 **Wmk. 380** *Perf. 12¾*
878-880 A300 Set of 3 .80 .35

Miniature Sheet

881 A301 $1 Sheet of 12, #a-l 5.25 5.25

Aquatic Plants A302

Designs: 30c, Cryptocoryne purpurea. 50c, Barclaya kunstleri.
No. 884: a, Neptunia oleracea. b, Monochoria hastata.
No. 885: a, $1, Eichhornia crassipes, vert. b, $2, Nymphaea pubescens.

Perf. 12, 12½x12¾ (#884)
2002, May 11 **Wmk. 388**
882 A302 30c multi .60 .60
883 A302 50c multi 1.00 .60
884 A302 $1 Horiz. pair, #a-b 3.25 1.60
Nos. 882-884 (3) 4.85 2.80

Souvenir Sheet

Perf. 12¾x12½x12x12½, 12 (#885b)

885 A302 Sheet of 2, #a-b 6.50 6.50

Tropical Birds — A303

No. 886, 30c: a, Dryocopus javnesis. b, Oriolus chinensis.
No. 887, $1: a, Anthreptes rhodolaema. b, Irena puella.
$5, Dicaeum trigonostigma.

2002, June 27 *Perf. 12¾x12½*

Horiz. Pairs, #a-b

886-887 A303 Set of 2 5.50 2.75

Souvenir Sheet

Perf. 12¾x12½x12x12½

888 A303 $5 multi 8.00 8.00

No. 888 contains one 60x40mm stamp.
See Singapore Nos. 1014-1017.

Islands and Beaches — A304

No. 889, 30c: a, Pulau Sibu, Johore. b, Pulau Perhentian, Trengganu.
No. 890, 50c: a, Pulau Manukan, Sabah. b, Pulau Tioman, Pahang.
No. 891, $1: a, Pulau Singa Besar, Kedah. b, Pulau Pangkor, Perak.
No. 892: a, Batu Ferringhi, Penang. b, Port Dickson, Negri Sembilan.
Illustration reduced.

Wmk. 380
2002, July 31 **Litho.** *Perf. 12¾*

Horiz. Pairs, #a-b

889-891 A304 Set of 3 6.00 2.75

Souvenir Sheet

892 A304 $1 Sheet of 2, #a-b 4.00 1.75

Malaysian Unity — A305

No. 893: a, Musicians. b, Children at play.
50c, Seven people (80x29mm).
$2, People pulling rope.
Illustration reduced.

Wmk. 380
2002, Aug. 24 **Litho.** *Perf. 12¾*
893 A305 30c Horiz. pair, #a-b 1.40 .80
894 A305 50c multi 1.00 .80

Souvenir Sheet

895 A305 $2 multi 2.75 1.40

Zainal Abidin bin Ahmad (1895-1973), Academic — A306

Abidin bin Ahmad: 30c, And blackboard.
No. 897: a, And typewriter. b, And building.
$1, In library, vert.

Perf. 13½x13¼
2002, Sept. 17 **Wmk. 388**
896 A306 30c multi .85 .85
897 A306 50c Horiz. pair, #a-b 2.40 1.10

Souvenir Sheet

Perf. 13¼x13½

898 A306 $1 multi 3.00 1.50

Clothing — A307

Designs: No. 899, 30c, Green blouse. No. 900, 30c, Red blouse. No. 901, 50c, Yellow blouse. No. 902, 50c, Red blouse, diff.
$2, Blouse and skirt.

Perf. 12¾ (30c), 12¾x13¼ (50c)
2002, Nov. 2
899-902 A307 Set of 4 3.50 1.60

Souvenir Sheet

903 A307 $2 multi 3.50 1.60

No. 903 contains one 35x70mm stamp.

Sultan Idris University, 80th Anniv. A308

Designs: 30c, Suluh Budiman Building.
No. 905: a, Tadahan Selatan. b, Chancellory Building.

2002, Nov. 29 ***Perf. 12x12x13½x12***

904 A308 30c multi		.60	.60
a. Perf. 12		.20	.20

Perf. 12

905 A308 50c Horiz. pair, #a-b		2.50	1.10
c. As "a," perf. 12x12x13½x12		.40	.20
d. As "b," perf. 12x12x13½x12		.40	.20
e. Pair, #905c-905d		.85	.40

Wild and Tame Animals — A309

No. 906, 30c: a, Felis bengalensis. b, Felis catus.
No. 907, $1: a, Cacatua sulphurea. b, Ketupa ketupu.
No. 908, $1: a, Ratufa affinis. b, Oryctolagus cuniculus.
No. 909, $1, horiz.: a, Carassius auratus. b, Diodon liturosus.

2002, Dec. 17 ***Perf. 12½***

Horiz. pairs, #a-b

906-907 A309 Set of 2 5.00 2.40

Souvenir Sheets of 2, #a-b

Perf. 13½x12x13¼x13½, 13½x13½x12x13¼ (#909)

908-909 A309 Set of 2 6.00 3.00

Stamp Week.

Endangered Animals — A310

Southern serow: 30c, Head.
No. 911: a, Serow laying down. b, Serow walking.

2003, Jan. 25 ***Perf. 12¾x12½***

910 A310 30c multi	.75	.75
911 A310 50c Horiz. pair, #a-b	2.25	1.00

13th Conference of Heads of State or Government of Non-Aligned Countries — A311

No. 912, 30c — Malaysian flag, world map, conference emblem and: a, Doves, years of previous conferences (1961-1979). b, Hands, years of conferences (1983-2003).
No. 913, 50c — Globe, conference emblem and: a, Map of Malaysia. b, Dove, "2003," Malaysian flag.

2003, Feb. 6 ***Perf. 12½x12¾***

Horiz. pairs, #a-b

912-913 A311 Set of 2 2.25 1.10

Roses — A312

Designs: No. 914, Pink Rosa hybrida. No. 915, Red Rosa hybrida.
No. 916: a, Yellow Rosa hybrida. b, Floribunda.
No. 917: a, 1r, Floribunda miniature (29x40mm). b, 2r, Rosa centifolia (29x81mm).

Wmk. 380

2003, Feb. 22 **Litho.** ***Perf. 13¾***

914 A312 30c shown	.50	.50
915 A312 30c multi	.50	.50
916 A312 50c Horiz. pair, #a-b	1.40	.60
Nos. 914-916 (3)	2.40	1.60

Souvenir Sheet

Perf. 12¾

917 A312 Sheet of 2, #a-b 3.00 1.40

Nos. 914-917 are impregnated with a rose scent.

Tunku Abdul Rahman Putra Al-Haj (1903-90), Prime Minister — A313

Designs: 30c, Wearing brown hat. 50c, Wearing suit and tie.
No. 920: a, Wearing dark robe. b, Wearing light robe.
No. 921, With arm raised.

Perf. 12¾x12½

2003, Mar. 4 **Wmk. 388**

918 A313 30c multi	.50	.50
919 A313 50c multi	.60	.50
920 A313 $1 Horiz. pair, #a-b	2.75	1.40
Nos. 918-920 (3)	3.85	2.40

Souvenir Sheet

Perf. 13½

921 A313 $1 multi 2.25 1.10

Fighting Fish A314

Designs: 30c, Red and blue Betta splendens. No. 923, Yellow Betta splendens.
No. 924: a, Blue Betta splendens. b, Red Betta splendens.
No. 925: a, Betta imbellis. b, Betta coccina.

Perf. 12½x12¾, 13½x13¼ (#923)

2003, Apr. 26

922 A314 30c multi	.55	.55
923 A314 50c multi	.65	.55
924 A314 $1 Horiz. pair, #a-b	2.75	1.40
Nos. 922-924 (3)	3.95	2.50

Souvenir Sheet

Perf. 13½x13¾ Syncopated

925 A314 50c Sheet of 2, #a-b 3.00 1.40

No. 925 contains two 33x28mm stamps.

Clock Towers — A315

Designs: No. 926, 30c, Malacca, 1650. No. 927, 30c, Penang, 1897. No. 928, 30c, Sungai Petani, 1936. No. 929, 30c, Teluk Intan, 1885.
No. 930, 30c, Sarawak State Council Monument, 1967.
No. 931: a, Sultan Abdul Samad Building, 1897. b, Taiping Clock Tower, Perak, 1881.

2003, May 24 ***Perf. 12¾x12½***

926-930 A315 Set of 5	2.40	1.10
930a Booklet pane, 2 each #926-930	5.00	—
Complete booklet, #930a	5.00	

Souvenir Sheet

Perf. 12x12½x12¾x12½

931 A315 $1 Sheet of 2, #a-b 2.75 1.50

Beaches and Islands — A316

No. 932, 30c: a, Beach, Ligitan Island, Sabah. b, Map of Ligitan Island.
No. 933, 50c: a, Beach, Sipadan Island, Sabah. b, Map of Sipadan Island.
No. 934, vert.: a, Aerial view of Sipadan Island. b, Map of Ligitan Island.
Illustration reduced.

Litho. (#932a-943a), Litho. & Embossed (#932b-934b)

2003, June 28 **Wmk. 380** ***Perf. 13¼***

Horiz. Pairs, #a-b

932-933 A316 Set of 2 2.40 1.10

Souvenir Sheet

Perf. 12¾

934 A316 50c Sheet of 2, #a-b 2.40 1.10

Independence, 46th Anniv. — A317

Designs: 30c, Flag and clock tower. No. 936, $1, Flag (59x40mm).
No. 937, Tunku Abdul Rahman Putra in motorcade, horiz.

2003, Aug. 19 **Litho.** ***Perf. 12¾***

935-936 A317 Set of 2 2.00 .95

Souvenir Sheet

937 A317 $1 black 2.40 1.10

No. 937 contains one 59x40mm stamp.

Motorcycles and Scooters Made in Malaysia A318

Designs: 30c, Modenas Jaguh 175.
No. 939: a, Modenas Kriss 2. b, Modenas Kriss SG.
No. 940: a, Modenas Karisma 125. b, Modenas Kriss 1.
No. 941, $1: a, Comel Turbulence RG125. b, Comel Cyclone GP150.
No. 942, $1: a, MZ 125SM. b, MZ Perintis 1205 Classic.
No. 943, $1: a, Caviga Momos 125R. b, Nitro NE150 Windstar.
No. 944, $1: a, Demak Adventurer. b, Demak Beetle.

2003, Aug. 27 ***Perf. 12¾***

938 A318 30c multi	.60	.60
939 A318 50c Horiz. pair, #a-b	1.60	.70
940 A318 50c Horiz. pair, #a-b	1.60	.70
Nos. 938-940 (3)	3.80	2.00

Souvenir Sheets of 2, #a-b

941-944 A318 Set of 4 8.00 3.75

10th Islamic Summit Conference — A319

No. 945, 30c: a, Putrajaya Convention Center. b, Arabic text.
No. 946, 50c: a, Mosque at left, field of flag. b, Mosque at right, flag stripes.

2003, Oct. 3 ***Perf. 12¾***

Horiz. Pairs, #a-b

945-946 A319 Set of 2 2.25 1.10

50th World Children's Day — A320

Designs: 20c, World map, children in ring.
No. 948: a, Family, house, car, flag. b, Children with kite, graduate, man at computer, rocket, airplane.
No. 949: a, Text. b, Book, school, flag, kite, rainbow, soccer ball, automobile and flower.

Perf. 13½x13¼

2003, Oct. 11 **Wmk. 388**

947 A320 20c multi	.65	.65
a. Perf. 12½x12¾	.20	.20

Perf. 12

948 A320 30c Horiz. pair, #a-b	1.50	.95
c. As "a," perf. 12½x12¾	.30	.30
d. As "b," perf. 12½x12¾	.30	.30
949 A320 30c Horiz. pair, #a-b	1.50	.95
c. As "a," perf. 12½x12¾	.30	.30
d. As "b" perf. 12½x12¾	.30	.30
e. Booklet pane 2 each #947a, 948c, 948d, 949c, 949d	2.25	—
Complete booklet, #949e	2.25	

Nos. 938-940 with Bangkok 2003 Emblem Added at Upper Right

Wmk. 380

2003, Oct. 4 **Litho.** ***Perf. 12¾***

950 A318 30c Like #938	.50	.50
951 A318 50c Like #939, horiz. pair, #a-b	1.25	.60
952 A318 50c Like #940, horiz. pair, #a-b	1.25	.60
Nos. 950-952 (3)	3.00	1.70

Monkeys — A321

Designs: No. 953, Red leaf monkey, tail above branch. No. 954, Red leaf monkey, tail below branch.
No. 955: a, Proboscis monkey sitting on branch. b, Proboscis monkey reaching for branch.

2003, Dec. 16

953 A321 30c multi	.20	.20
954 A321 30c multi	.20	.20
955 A321 50c Horiz. pair, #a-b	1.10	.50
Nos. 953-955 (3)	1.50	.90

Lighthouses A322

Designs: No. 956, 30c, Muka Head Lighthouse. No. 957, 30c, One Fathom Bank Lighthouse. No. 958, 30c, Althingsburg Lighthouse. No. 959, 30c, Pulau Undan Lighthouse.
$1, Tanjung Tuan Lighthouse.

Perf. 12¾x12½

2004, Jan. 31 Wmk. 388

956-959 A322 Set of 4 2.00 .90

Souvenir Sheet

Perf. 13½

960 A322 $1 multi 3.00 1.40

Convention on Biological Diversity — A323

Designs; 30c, Flora and fauna. No. 962, 50c, DNA molecule, leaf, laboratory equipment, model showing human organs. No. 963, 50c, Convention emblem, world map.

2004, Feb. 9 Wmk. 380 *Perf. 12¾*

961-963 A323 Set of 3 2.00 1.00

Commonwealth Tourism Ministers' Meeting — A324

Emblem and: 30c, World map, city skyline, golf ball. 50c, World map, rocky shoreline. $1, Malaysian tourist attractions, vert.

2004, Mar. 19

964-966 A324 Set of 3 1.75 .80

National Service Program — A325

Designs: 30c, Emblem. 50c, Emblem, people on ropes. $1, Emblem, people with flag.
$2, Emblem, man saluting.

2004, May 22 Wmk. 380 *Perf. 12¾*

967-969 A325 Set of 3 1.75 .80

Souvenir Sheet

Perf. 13½

Wmk. 388

970 A325 $2 multi 1.75 .85

Malaysia - People's Republic of China Diplomatic Relations, 30th Anniv. — A326

No. 971, 30c: a, Malaysian flag, ship. b, Chinese flag, ship.
No. 972, $1: a, Ship, handshake. b, Flags, ship, world map.
$2, Malaysian and Chinese buildings, horiz.

Perf. 12¾x12½

2004, May 31 Wmk. 388

Horiz. pairs, #a-b

971-972 A326 Set of 2 1.75 .85

Souvenir Sheet

973 A326 $2 multi 1.75 .85
a. World Stamp Championship emblem added in margin in blue and black 1.75 .85

No. 973 contains one 60x40mm stamp.
No. 973a issued 8/28.

Mammals — A327

No. 974, 30c: a, Bos javanicus. b, Bos gaurus.
No. 975, $1: a, Panthera tigris. b, Elephas maximusp.
$2, Tapirus indicus, vert.
Illustration reduced.

Perf. 13½x13¼

2004, June 14 Wmk. 388

Horiz. pairs, #a-b

974-975 A327 Set of 2 1.75 .85

Souvenir Sheet

Perf. 12¾

Wmk. 380

976 A327 $2 multi 1.75 .85

Multimedia Super Corridor A328

Emblem and: 30c, MSC Building, flags. 50c, Globe, Petronas Towers, binary code. $1, Hand with identity card, people using computers, butterfly, cross-section of brain.
$2, Map of Multimedia Super Corridor, vert.

Horizontal Pairs

2004, July 11 Wmk. 380 *Perf. 12¾*

977-979 A328 Set of 3 .95 .45

Souvenir Sheet

Perf. 12¾x12½

Wmk. 388

980 A328 $2 multi 1.10 .55

Ports A329

No. 981: a, Johore. b, Kota Kinabalu.
No. 982: a, Kuantan. b, Penang.
$1, Bintulu. $2, Northport.

12, 13½ (#983)

2004, July 24 Wmk. 388

981 A329 30c Horiz. pair, #a-b .30 .20
982 A329 50c Horiz. pair, #a-b .55 .25
983 A329 $1 multi .55 .25
Nos. 981-983 (3) 1.40 .70

Souvenir Sheet

984 A329 $2 multi 1.10 .55

Transportation — A330

Designs: 30c, Trishaw. 50c, Rickshaw. $1, Padi horse.
$2, Bullock cart, vert.

Perf. 12, 13½x13¼ (1r)

2004, Aug. 18 Litho. Wmk. 388

985-987 A330 Set of 3 .95 .45

Souvenir Sheet

Perf. 14

988 A330 $2 multi 1.10 .55
a. Kuala Lumpur Stamp Show emblem in sheet margin 1.10 .55

No. 988 contains one 40x50mm stamp and exists imperf.
No. 988a issued 9/3/04.

Matang Mangroves, Perak, Cent. — A331

No. 989, 30c: a, Monkey on mangrove tree root. b, Insect on plant.
No. 990, $1: a, Boat, shells. b, Birds, tree.
$2, Young trees.

2004, Oct. 4 Wmk. 380 *Perf. 12¾*

Horiz. pairs, #a-b

989-990 A331 Set of 2 1.40 .70

Souvenir Sheet

991 A331 $2 multi 1.10 .55

Marine Life A332

Designs: 30c, Humpback whale. 50c, Octopus. $1, Bottlenose dolphin.
$2, Thornback ray.

Wmk. 380

2004, Oct. 9 Litho. *Perf. 12¾*

992-994 A332 Set of 3 .95 .45

Souvenir Sheet

995 A332 $2 multi 1.10 .55
a. Stamp Week emblem in sheet margin 1.10 .55

Medicinal Plants A333

Designs: 30c, Eurycoma longifolia. 50c, Labisia pumila.
No. 998: a, Pithecellobium bubalinum benth. b, Alleurites moluccana.
$2, Ficus deltoidea jack.

Wmk. 380

2004, Dec. 11 Litho. *Perf. 12¾*

996 A333 30c multi .20 .20
997 A333 50c multi .25 .20
998 A333 $1 Horiz. pair, #a-b 1.10 .55
Nos. 996-998 (3) 1.55 .95

Souvenir Sheet

999 A333 $2 multi 1.10 .55

Rare Rhododendrons A334

Designs: No. 1000, 30c, Rhododendron nervulosum. No. 1001, 30c, Rhododendron stenophyllum. 50c, Rhododendron rugosum. $1, Rhododendron stapfianum.
$2, Rhododendron lowii, horiz.

2005, Jan. 11 Wmk. 380 *Perf. 12¾*

1000-1003 A334 Set of 4 1.10 .55

Souvenir Sheet

1004 A334 $2 multi 1.10 .55

Fifth Minister's Forum on Infrastructure Development in the Asia-Pacific Region, Kuala Lumpur — A335

Emblems and: 30c, Kuala Lumpur skyline. 50c, Train and buildings. $1, Train station and airplane.

2005, Jan. 24 Wmk. 388 *Perf. 12*

1005-1007 A335 Set of 3 .95 .45

Birds A336

Designs: 30c, Crested honey buzzard. 50c, Purple heron. $1, Lesser crested tern.
$2, Dunlin.

2005, Feb. 3 Wmk. 388 *Perf. 13½*

1008-1010 A336 Set of 3 .95 .45

Souvenir Sheet

1011 A336 $2 multi 1.10 .55
a. Like #1011, with Pacific Explorer World Stamp Expo emblem in margin 1.10 .55

No. 1011a issued 4/21.

Proton Gen-2 Automobile A337

2005, Feb. 7 Wmk. 388 *Perf. 13½*

Color of Automobile

1012 A337 30c beige .20 .20
a. Perf. 12 .20 .20
b. Booklet pane, 10 #1012a 1.60 —
Complete booklet, #1012b 1.60
1013 A337 50c bright blue .25 .20
1014 A337 $1 red .55 .25
Nos. 1012-1014 (3) 1.00 .65

Souvenir Sheet

1015 A337 $2 dark blue, vert. 1.10 .55

Dances A338

Designs: 30c, Bharata Natyam and Kathak. 50c, Kipas and Payaung. $1, Zapin and Asyik.
$2, Datun Julud and Sumazau.

2005, Apr. 9 Wmk. 388 *Perf. 12*

1016 A338 30c multi .20 .20
a. Perf. 13½ .20 .20
1017 A338 50c multi .25 .20
1018 A338 $1 multi .55 .25
Nos. 1016-1018 (3) 1.00 .65

Souvenir Sheet

Perf. 13½

1019 A338 $2 multi 1.10 .55

Songkets
A339

Designs: 30c, Pucuk Rebung Gigi Yu. 50c, Bunga Bertabur Pecah Lapan.
No. 1022: a, Pucuk Rebung Gigi Yu dan Bunga Kayoban. b, Teluk Berantai Bunga Pecah Empat.
$2, Potong Wajik Bertabur.

Perf. 12¾x12½

2005, Apr. 29 Wmk. 388

1020 A339 30c multi .20 .20
1021 A339 50c multi .25 .20
1022 A339 $1 Horiz. pair, #a-b 1.10 .55
Nos. 1020-1022 (3) 1.55 .95

Souvenir Sheet

1023 A339 $2 multi 1.10 .55

Birds — A340

Designs: 20c, Spotted dove. 30c, Ochraceous bulbul. 40c, Long-tailed parakeet. 50c, White-rumped shama. 75c, Olive-backed sunbird. $1, Green-winged pigeon. $2, Banded pitta. $5, Imperial pigeon.

2005, May 14 *Perf. 13½x14*

1024 A340 20c multi .20 .20
1025 A340 30c multi .20 .20
1026 A340 40c multi .20 .20
1027 A340 50c multi .25 .20
1028 A340 75c multi .40 .20
1029 A340 $1 multi .55 .25
1030 A340 $2 multi 1.10 .55
1031 A340 $5 multi 2.60 1.25
Nos. 1024-1031 (8) 5.50 3.05

University of Malaysia, Cent.
A341

Designs: 30c, Dewan Tunku Canselor. 50c, Perpustakaan. No. 1034, Pusat Perubatan.
No. 1035: a, Rimba Ilmu. b, Koleksi Muzium Seni Asia.

2005, June 9 Wmk. 388 *Perf. 12*

1032 A341 30c multi .20 .20
a. Perf. 13½ .20 .20
b. Booklet pane, 10 #1032a 1.60 —
Complete booklet, #1032b 1.60
1033 A341 50c multi .25 .20

Perf. 13½

1034 A341 $1 multi .55 .25
Nos. 1032-1034 (3) 1.00 .65

Souvenir Sheet

Perf. 12½

1035 A341 $1 Sheet of 2, #a-b 1.10 .55

Malaysia — China Relations, 600th Anniv. — A342

Designs: No. 1036, 30c, Chinese chop. No. 1037, 30c, Ship. 50c, Malaysian and Chinese men talking. $1, Decorated plate.
$2, Ornament and coin.

Perf. 12¾x12½

2005, July 21 Litho. Wmk. 388

1036-1039 A342 Set of 4 1.10 .55

Souvenir Sheet

1040 A342 $2 multi 1.10 .55

Mammals Type of 2004

Endangered mammals: No. 1041, 30c, Malay weasel. No. 1042, 30c, Yellow-throated marten. 50c, Hairy-nosed otter. $1, Large spotted civet.
$2, Long-tailed porcupine, vert.

Perf. 13½, 12 (50c, $1)

2005, July 27

1041-1044 A327 Set of 4 1.10 .55
1042a Perf. 12 .20 .20

Souvenir Sheet

Perf. 12¾x12½

1045 A327 $2 multi 1.10 .55
a. As #1045, with Taipei 2005 emblem in sheet margin 1.10 .55

No. 1045a issued 8/19.

Water Transport
A343

Designs: 30c, Perahu kotak. 50c, Sampan. $1, Rakit buluh.
$2, Perahu batang, vert.

2005, Aug. 9 *Perf. 13½*

1046-1048 A343 Set of 3 .95 .50

Souvenir Sheet

Perf. 14x13½

1049 A343 $2 multi 1.10 .55

No. 1049 contains one 40x55mm stamp.

Malay College, Kuala Kangsar, Cent.
A344

Designs: 30c, School building. No. 1051, 50c, Tree. No. 1052, 50c, Prep school.
No. 1053, vert.: a, Sultan Idris Murshidul 'Adzam Shah. b, Sultan Alaiddin Sulaiman Shah. c, Yam Tuan Tuanku Muhamad Shah. d, Sultan Ahmad Al-Mu'adzam Shah.

2005, Aug. 30 *Perf. 13½*

1050-1052 A344 Set of 3 .70 .35

Souvenir Sheet

Perf. 12x11¾

1053 A344 50c Sheet of 4, #a-d 1.10 .55

No. 1053 contains four 22x51mm stamps.

Reptiles
A345

Designs: No. 1054, 30c, Varanus rudicollis. No. 1055, 30c, Varanus dumerilii. 50c, Gonocephalus grandis. $1, Crocodylus porosus.
$2, Draco quinquefasciatus, vert.

2005, Sept. 28 *Perf. 13½*

1054-1057 A345 Set of 4 1.10 .55

Souvenir Sheet

Perf. 14x13½

1058 A345 $2 multi 1.10 .55

No. 1058 contains one 40x50mm stamp.

Kites
A346

Designs: 30c, Wau Jala Budi. 50c, Wau Bulan. $1, Wau Kucing.
$2, Wau Merak.

2005, Oct. 10 *Perf. 13½, 12 ($1)*

1059-1061 A346 Set of 3 .95 .50
1060a Perf. 12 .30 .20

Souvenir Sheet

1062 A346 $2 multi 1.10 .55

Batik — A347

Designs: 30c, Binaan Asasi. 50c, Pesona Sutera. $1, Malaysia Bersatu.
$2, Penyatuan.

2005, Dec. 2 *Perf. 12¾x12½*

1063-1065 A347 Set of 3 .95 .50

Souvenir Sheet

1066 A347 $2 multi 1.10 .55

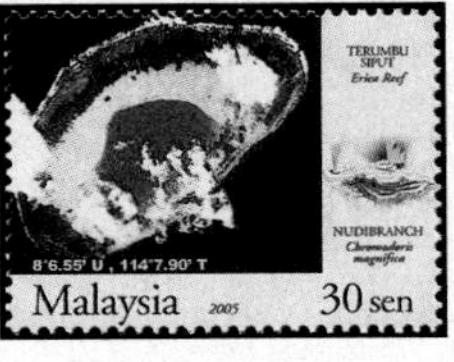

11th ASEAN Summit, Kuala Lumpur
A348

Emblem and: 30c, Flags of participating nations. 50c, Motto. $1, Aerial view of Kuala Lumpur.

2005, Dec. 12 *Perf. 12½x12¾*

1067-1069 A348 Set of 3 .95 .50

Islands and Marine Life
A349

Designs: No. 1070, 30c, Erica Reef, Nudibranch. No. 1071, 30c, Mariveles Reef, Sea cucumber. No. 1072, $1, Swallow Island, Sea star. No. 1073, $1, Investigator Reef, bivalve.
$2, Erica Reef, Mariveles Reef, Swallow Island, Investigator Reef, and Ubi Reef.

Perf. 12½x12¾, 13½ ($1)

2005, Dec. 22

1070-1073 A349 Set of 4 1.40 .70

Souvenir Sheet

Perf. 14

1074 A349 $2 multi 1.10 .55

No. 1074 contains one 50x40mm stamp.

Ducks
A350

Designs: No. 1075, 30c, Anas crecca. No. 1076, 30c, Cairina scutulata. No. 1077, 50c, Anas acuta. No. 1078, 50c, Anas clypeata.
$2, Phalacrocorax carbo.

Perf. 13½x13¼

2006, Jan. 26 Litho. Wmk. 388

1075-1078 A350 Set of 4 .85 .45
1076a Perf. 12 .20 .20

Souvenir Sheet

1079 A350 $2 multi 1.10 .55

Negara Audit Institute, Cent.
A351

Designs: 30c, Building. No. 1081, 50c, Documents. No. 1082, 50c, Emblems.

2006, Feb. 14 *Perf. 12½x12¾*

1080-1082 A351 Set of 3 .70 .35

Fruits — A352

Designs: 30c, Artocarpus sericicarpus. 50c, Phyllanthus acidus. No. 1085, $1, Garcinia hombroniana.
No. 1086, $1: a, Lepisanthes alata. b, Baccaurea polyneura.

Perf. 13¾x13½ Syncopated

2006, Mar. 28

1083-1085 A352 Set of 3 1.00 .50

Souvenir Sheet

Perf. 13¾ Syncopated

1086 A352 $1 Sheet of 2, #a-b 1.10 .55

Mountains — A353

No. 1087, 30c: a, Mt. Kinabalu and orchid. b, Gunung Ledang (Mt. Ophir) and flower.
No. 1088, 50c: a, Mt. Jerai and orchid. b, Mt. Mulu.
$2, Mt. Tahan.
Illustration reduced.

Litho. & Embossed

Perf. 13½x13¼

2006, Apr. 26 Wmk. 388

Horiz. Pairs, #a-b

1087-1088 A353 Set of 2 .90 .45

Souvenir Sheet

Perf. 14

Litho.

1088C A353 $2 multi 1.10 .55

No. 1088C contains one 50x40mm stamp.

Malaysia 30sen

Fish
A354

Designs: 30c, Leptobarbus hoevenii. No. 1090, 50c, Hampala macrolepidota. No. 1091, 50c, Pangasius sp. $1, Probarbus jullieni.
$5, Clarias batrachus, Mystus nemurus.

Perf. 12½x12¾

2006, May 25 Litho. Wmk. 388

1089-1092 A354 Set of 4 1.25 .60

Souvenir Sheet

Litho. With Hologram Applied

Perf. 13¼

1093 A354 $5 multi 2.75 1.40

No. 1093 contains one 70x33mm stamp.

Dewan Bahasa Dan Pustaka (Malay Language Governing Board), 50th Anniv.
A355

Designs: No. 1094, 50c, Emblem and leaf. No. 1095, 50c, Anniversary emblem and people reading. $1, Emblem, books and electronic devices.

2006. June 22 ***Perf. 12½x12¾***
1094-1096 A355 Set of 3 1.10 .55

Federal Land Development Authority, 50th Anniv. — A356

Designs: 30c, Palm plantation, fruit. 50c, Buildings. $1, Globe and buildings.

2006, July 7 Litho. ***Perf. 12½x12¾***
1097-1099 A356 Set of 3 1.00 .50

Sultan Azlan Shah Gallery
A357

Designs: 30c, Gallery emblem, sword and sheath. 50c, Gallery building. $1, Gallery emblem, headdress.

2006, July 18 ***Perf. 12***
1100-1102 A357 Set of 3 1.00 .50

Festivals
A358

Designs: 30c, Eid al-Fitr. 50c, Tahun Baru Cina (Chinese New Year). No. 1105, $1, Deepavali.

No. 1106, $1, vert.: a, Tadau Kaamatan. b, Pesta Gawai.

2006, Aug. 15 ***Perf. 12***
1103-1105 A358 Set of 3 1.00 .50

Souvenir Sheet

Perf. 12½

1106 A358 $1 Sheet of 2, #a-b 1.10 .55

Men's and Women's Traditional Costumes
A359

Designs: No. 1107, 50c, Malaysian (blue green background). No. 1108, 50c, Indian (orange background). No. 1109, 50c, Chinese (red background).

No. 1110, $1, vert.: a, Iban (blue background). b, Kadazan (tan background).

2006, Aug. 29 ***Perf. 12¾x12½***
1107-1109 A359 Set of 3 .85 .40

Souvenir Sheet

Perf. 13¼x13½

1110 A359 $1 Sheet of 2, #a-b 1.10 .55

Semi-aquatic Animals — A360

Designs: 30c, Periophthalmodon schlosseri. 50c, Pagurus bernhardus. No. 1113, $1, Cuora amboinensis.

No. 1114, $1, vert.: a, Polypedates leucomystax. b, Varanus salvator. c, Cynogale bennettii. d, Xenochrophis trianguligera.

Perf. 13½x13¼

2006, Oct. 9 Litho. Wmk. 388
1111-1113 A360 Set of 3 1.00 .50

Souvenir Sheet

Perf. 13¾x14¼ Syncopated

1114 A360 $1 Sheet of 4, #a-d 2.25 1.25

Stamp Week. No. 1114 contains four 29x34mm stamps.

18th Intl. Federation of Gynecology and Obstetrics Congress — A361

"FIGO" and: 30c, Woman and tree leaves. No. 1116, 50c, Map, woman's torso. No. 1117, 50c, Map, fetus.

2006, Nov. 6 ***Perf. 12½x12¾***
1115-1117 A361 Set of 3 .75 .45

2006 Far East & South Pacific Games for the Disabled, Kuala Lumpur — A362

Designs: 30c, Wheelchair racing. 50c, Swimming. $1, Wheelchair tennis.
$2, Wheelchair basketball.

2006, Nov. 25 ***Perf. 12¾x12½***
1118-1120 A362 Set of 3 1.00 .50

Souvenir Sheet

Perf. 13½

1121 A362 $2 multi 1.10 .60

ASEAN Dialogue with People's Republic of China, 15th Anniv.
A363

Designs: 30c, ASEAN emblem, Chinese flag, map with flags. 50c, Great Wall of China, flasks, port, highway, ASEAN emblem and Chinese flag. $1, Bow with ASEAN emblem and Chinese flag.

Perf. 12, 13½x13¼ ($1)

2006, Nov. 30
1122-1124 A363 Set of 3 1.00 1.00

25th General Assembly of World Veterans Federation, Kuala Lumpur
A364

Emblem and: 30c, Map. 50c, "25," Kuala Lumpur buildings. $1, Malaysian flag, sculpture of soldiers.

Perf. 13½x13¼, 12 (50c)

2006, Dec. 4 Litho. Wmk. 388

1125	A364 30c multi		.20	.20
1126	A364 50c multi		.30	.20
1127	A364 $1 multi		.55	.30
a.	Perf. 12		.55	.30
	Nos. 1125-1127 (3)		1.05	.70

South Pole Expedition
A365

Designs: 30c, Mountains, sled, tent. 50c, Man on skis pulling sled. $1, Man on skis pulling sled with parasail.

2006, Dec. 28 ***Perf. 13½x13¼***
1128-1130 A365 Set of 3 1.10 .55

Marine Life
A373

Designs: No. 1139, Leaf scorpionfish. No. 1140, Orange-striped triggerfish.

No. 1141: a, Chambered nautilus. b, Spotted boxfish.

Perf. 13½x13¼

2007, Feb. 6 Litho. Wmk. 388

1139	A373 50c multi	.30	.20
a.	Perf. 12	.30	.20
1140	A373 50c multi	.30	.20
a.	Perf. 12	.30	.20

Souvenir Sheet

1141 A373 $1 Sheet of 2, #a-b 1.25 .60

Dated 2006. See Brunei Nos. 588-590.

Tourism — A374

No. 1142: a, Hornbill, forest and flower. b, Diver and coral reef.

No. 1143: a, Buildings. b, Handicrafts.

No. 1144: a, Woman with red dress, with arms raised. b, Woman with red dress holding fan. c, Woman with blue dress. d, Woman with black dress. e, Woman with red and black dress with geometric patterns. f, Satay, Ketupat dan Aie Sirap. g, Yee Sang. h, Banana leaf rice dan Teh Tarik. i, Hinava. j, Manok Pansuh.

$2, Flag and buildings, vert.

Illustration reduced.

2007, Mar. 19 ***Perf. 13½x13¼***
1142 A374 30c Horiz. pair, #a-b .35 .20

Perf. 12

1143 A374 50c Horiz. pair, #a-b .60 .30

Booklet Stamps

Perf. 13½x13½

1144 A374 30c Booklet pane of 10, #a-j 1.75 .85
Compete booklet, #1144 1.75

Souvenir Sheet

Perf. 13¼x13½

1145 A374 $2 multi 1.25 .60

No. 1145 contains one 30x50mm stamp.

Installation of 13th Yang Di-Pertuan Agong — A375

13th Yang Di-Pertuan Agong and background colors of: 30c, Yellow. 50c, Green. $1, Purple.

2007, Apr. 26 ***Perf. 12½***
1146-1148 A375 Set of 3 1.10 .55

Amphibians
A376

Designs: 30c, Pedostibes hosii. No. 1150, 50c, Megophrys nasuta. No. 1151, 50c, Nyctixalus pictus.

$1, Rana laterimaculata.

2007, May 3 ***Perf. 12***
1149-1151 A376 Set of 3 .80 .40

Souvenir Sheet

Perf. 13¼

1152 A376 $1 multi .60 .30

No. 1152 contains one 35x33mm stamp.

Airplanes
A377

Designs: 30c, Shorts SC-7 Skyvan. No. 1154, 50c, GAF N22 Nomad. No. 1155, 50c, De Havilland Canada DHC 7-110.

No. 1156: a, Airspeed Consul. b, Douglas DC-3.

2007, May 24 ***Perf. 12***
1153-1155 A377 Set of 3 .80 .40

Souvenir Sheet

Perf. 13½x13¼

1156 A377 $1 Sheet of 2, #a-b 1.25 .60

Clock Towers — A378

Designs: 30c, J. W. W. Birch Clock Tower, 1917. 50c, Atkinson Clock Tower, 1905. $1, Alor Setar Clock Tower, 1912.

Perf. 13¼x14x13¼x13½

2007, June 6
1157-1159 A378 Set of 3 1.10 .55

Children's Folk Tales
A379

Designs: Nos. 1160a, 1161a, Bawang Putah Bawang Merah. Nos. 1160b, 1161b, Badang.

Nos. 1160c, 1162a, Sang Kancil Dengan Buaya. Nos. 1160d, 1162b, Sang Kancil Menolong Kerbau. No. 1160e, Mat Jenin.
$5, Si Tanggang.

Perf. 13½x13¼

2007, June 26 Litho. Wmk. 388

1160 Horiz. strip of 5 .90 .45
a.-e. A379 30c Any single .20 .20
f. Booklet pane, 2 each #1160a-1160e 1.90 —
Complete booklet, #1160f 1.90
1161 Horiz. pair .60 .30
a.-b. A379 50c Any single .30 .20
1162 Horiz. pair .60 .30
a.-b. A379 50c Any single .30 .20

Souvenir Sheet
Litho. With Foil Application
Perf. 14

1163 A379 $5 multi 3.00 1.50

No. 1163 contains one 50x38mm stamp.

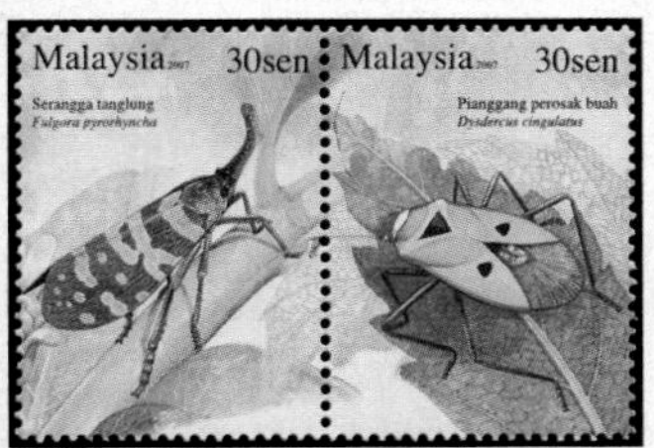

Insects — A380

No. 1164, 30c: a, Fulgora pyrorhyncha. b, Dysdercus cingulatus.
No. 1165, 50c: a, Valanga nigricornis. b, Rhaphipodus hopei.
$5, Antheraea helferi, horiz.

2007, July 7 ***Perf. 12¾x12½***
Horiz. Pairs, #a-b

1164-1165 A380 Set of 2 .95 .45

Souvenir Sheet
Perf. 14

1166 A380 $5 multi 3.00 1.50

No. 1166 contains one 50x38mm stamp.

Police Force, 200th Anniv. A381

Designs: 30c, Police and building. No. 1168, 50c, Police near jeep and in river, policeman wearing shorts. No. 1169, 50c, Police officers, cars, motorcycles, building and computer operator.

2007, July 24 ***Perf. 13½x13¼***

1167-1169 A381 Set of 3 .75 .40

Association of South East Asian Nations (ASEAN), 40th Anniv. — A382

No. 1170: a, Secretariat Building, Bandar Seri Begawan, Brunei. b, National Museum of Cambodia. c, Fatahillah Museum, Jakarta, Indonesia. d, Typical house, Laos. e, Malayan Railway Headquarters Building, Kuala Lumpur. f, Yangon Post Office, Myanmar (Burma). g, Malacañang Palace, Philippines. h, National Museum of Singapore. i, Vimanmek Mansion, Bangkok, Thailand. j, Presidential Palace, Hanoi, Viet Nam.

2007, Aug. 8 ***Perf. 13¾x14¼***

1170 Block of 10 3.00 1.50
a.-j. A382 50c Any single .30 .20

See Brunei No. 607, Burma No. 370, Cambodia No. 2339, Indonesia Nos. 2120-2121, Laos Nos., Philippines Nos. 3103-3105, Singapore No. 1265, Thailand No. 2315, Viet Nam Nos. 3302-3311.

Malaysian Independence, 50th Anniv. — A383

No. 1171 — Anniversary emblem, flag and: a, Dato' Onn Jaafar. b, Tunku Abdul Rahman Putra Al-Haj. c, Tun Abdul Razak. d, Tun Tan Cheng Lock. e, Tun V. T. Sambantahan.
No. 1172 — Anniversary emblem and: a, Tunku Abdul Rahman Putra Al-Haj, buildings, people, flag, statue. b, Petronas Twin Towers, government building, automobile and bridge.
No. 1173: a, Tunku Abdul Rahman Putra Al-Haj signing declaration of independence and anniversary emblem. b, Anniversary emblem.
$5, Flag.

2007, Aug. 31 ***Perf. 13½x13¼***

1171 Horiz. strip of 5 .90 .45
a.-e. A383 30c any single .20 .20
1172 Horiz. pair .35 .20
a.-b. A383 30c any single .20 .20
1173 Horiz. pair .60 .30
a.-b. A383 50c any single .30 .20

Souvenir Sheet
Perf. 13¼

1174 A383 $5 multi 3.00 1.50

No. 1174 contains one 70x33mm stamp and has foil application in margin.

Petronas Twin Towers, Kuala Lumpur, 2007 Recipient of Aga Khan Award for Architecture A384

2007, Sept. 4 ***Perf. 13¼x13½***

1175 A384 50c multi .30 .20

National and State Arms — A385

No. 1176: a, Malaysia. b, Kedah. c, Negri Sembilan. d, Pahang. e, Kelantan. f, Johore. g, Perak. h, Perlis. i, Selangor. j, Trengganu. k, Sarawak. l, Penang. m, Sabah. n, Malacca.

2007, Sept. 25 ***Perf. 13¾x14***

1176 Block of 14 4.25 2.10
a.-n. A385 50c Any single .30 .20

Vegetables A386

Designs: No. 1177, 50c, Solanum ferox. No. 1178, 50c, Etlingera elatior. No. 1179, 50c, Momordica charantia.
No. 1180: a, Luffa aegyptiaca. b, Psophocarpus tetragonolobus. c, Sesbania grandiflora. d, Solanum torvum.

Perf. 13¾x13½ Syncopated

2007, Nov. 26

1177-1179 A386 Set of 3 .90 .45

Souvenir Sheet
Perf. 13¾x14 Syncopated

1180 A386 $1 Sheet of 4, #a-d 2.40 1.25

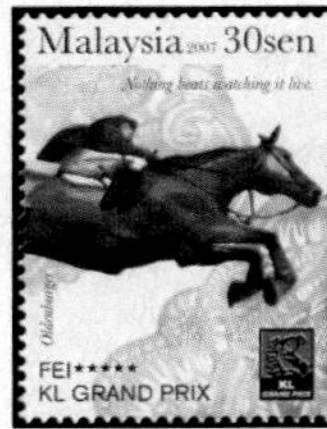

Kuala Lumpur Equestrian Grand Prix — A387

Horses: 30c, Oldenburger. No. 1182, 50c, Dutch Warmblood. No. 1183, 50c, Hanonverian.

2007, Dec. 13 ***Perf. 13½***

1181-1183 A387 Set of 3 .80 .40

Bridges — A388

Designs: 30c, Merdeka Bridge, Kedah. No. 1185, 50c, Kota Bridge, Selangor. No. 1186, 50c, Victoria Bridge, Perak. $1, Sungai Segamat Bridge, Johore.

Perf. 13¾x13¼

2008, Feb. 28 Litho. Wmk. 388

1184-1187 A388 Set of 4 1.50 .75

Nocturnal Animals A389

Designs: No. 1188, 30c, Mydaus javanensis. No. 1189, 30c, Echinosorex gymnurus. 50c, Catopuma temminckii. $1, Pteropas vampyrus.
No. 1192: a, $2, Tarsius bancanus (30x40mm). b, $3, Nycticebus coucang (60x40mm).

2008, Mar. 13 ***Perf. 13½x13¼***

1188-1191 A389 Set of 4 1.40 .70

Souvenir Sheet
Perf. 12¾x12½

1192 A389 Sheet of 2, #a-b 3.25 1.60

Butterflies A390

No. 1193: a, Smaller wood nymph. b, Malaysian lacewing.
50c, Malay red harlequin. $1, Glorious begum.
$5, Five-bar swordtail.

2008, Apr. 24 ***Perf. 13½x13¼***

1193 A390 30c Horiz. pair, #a-b .40 .20
d. As #1193, perf. 12 .40 .20
e. As #1193a, perf. 12 .20 .20
f. As#1193b, perf. 12 .20 .20
1194 A390 50c multi .35 .20
1195 A390 $1 multi .65 .30
Nos. 1193-1195 (3) 1.40 .70

Souvenir Sheet
Perf. 14

1196 A390 $5 multi 3.25 1.60

No. 1196 contains one 50x38mm stamp and has die cut slits in the sheet margin.

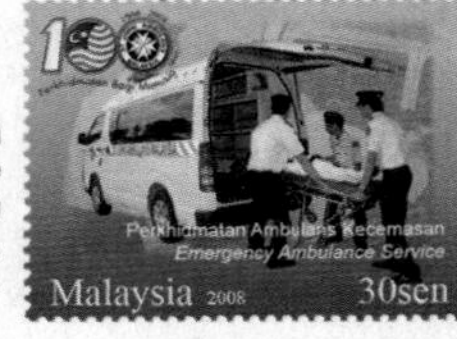

St. John Ambulance in Malaysia, Cent. A391

Centenary emblem and: 30c, Emergency ambulance service. 50c, First aid. $1, Cardiopulmonary resuscitation.

2008, May 22 ***Perf. 13½x13¼***

1197-1199 A391 Set of 3 1.10 .55

A392

Cultural Items — A393

Illustration A393 reduced.

2008, June 10 ***Perf. 13½x13¼***

1200 A392 30c Batu Giling .20 .20
1201 A392 50c Supu .30 .20

Perf. 13¼x13¾

1202 A393 50c Kukur Kelapa .30 .20
Nos. 1200-1202 (3) .80 .60

Intl. Dragon Boat Federation Club Crew World Championships — A394

Designs: 30c, Boats 6 and 3. 50c, Boats 5 and 2. $1, Boats 4 and 1.
$2, Boat 5.

Perf. 13½x13¼

2008, Aug. 1 Litho. Wmk. 388

1203-1205 A394 Set of 3 1.10 .55

Souvenir Sheet

1206 A394 $2 multi 1.25 .65
a. Imperf. 1.25 .65

No. 1206 contains one 80x30mm stamp.

Malaysian Scouting Association, Cent. — A395

Centenary emblem, scouting emblems and: 30c, Scouts reading map, Lord Robert Baden-Powell. No. 1208, 50c, Scout water activities. No. 1209, 50c, Scouts on monkey bridge.

2008, Aug. 14 ***Perf. 13½x13¼***

1207-1209 A395 Set of 3 .80 .40

Art A396

Designs: 30c, Semangat Ledang, by Syed Ahmad Jamal. 50c, Musim Buah, by Chuah Thean Teng, vert. $1, Pago-pago, by Latiff Mohidin.

2008, Aug. 28 ***Perf. 12½x12¾***
1210 A396 30c multi .20 .20
Perf. 12¾x12½
1211 A396 50c multi .30 .20
Size:35x35mm
Perf. 13¼
1212 A396 $1 multi .60 .30
Nos. 1210-1212 (3) 1.10 .70

Miniature Sheet

Royal Headgear — A397

No. 1213 — Headgear for: a, Leaders of Eight states and Yang Di-Pertuan Agong. b, Yang Di-Pertuan Agong. c, Sultan of Kedah. d, Yang Di-Pertuan Agong of Negri Sembilan. e, Sultan of Pahang. f, Sultan of Kelantan. g, Sultan of Perak. h, Raja of Perlis. i, Sultan of Selangor. j, Sultan of Trengganu.

2008, Sept. 16 ***Perf. 13¾x14***
1213 A397 50c Sheet of 10, #a-j 3.00 1.50

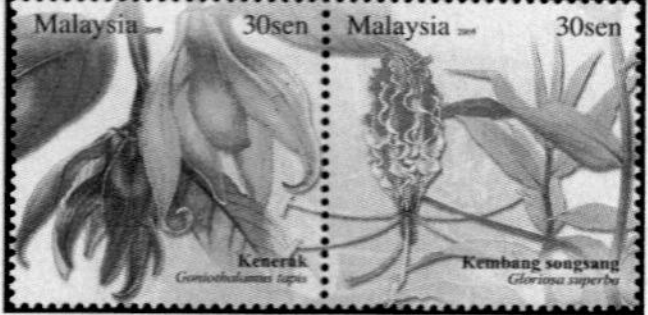

Flowers — A398

No. 1214, 30c: a, Goniothalamus tapis. b, Gloriosa superba.
No. 1215, 50c: a, Quisqualis indica. b, Michelia figo.
$5, Epiphyllum oxypetalum, vert.

Wmk. 388
2008, Oct. 9 Litho. ***Perf. 13¼***
Horiz. Pairs, #a-b
1214-1215 A398 Set of 2 .95 .45
Souvenir Sheet
Perf. 14
1216 A398 $5 multi 3.00 1.50

No. 1216 contains one 39x50mm stamp.

National Space Program — A399

Designs: 30c, Soyuz-TMA II rocket on launch pad. No. 1218, 50c, Malaysian astronaut. No. 1219, 50c, Intl. Space Station.
No. 1220: a, Rocket lifting off from launch pad. b, Rocket above Earth.

2008, Oct. 21 ***Perf. 13¼x13¾***
1217-1219 A399 Set of 3 .75 .35
Souvenir Sheet
1220 A399 $1 Sheet of 2, #a-b 1.25 .60

Shells — A400

Designs: No. 1221, 30c, Burnt murex. No. 1222, 30c, Horned helmet. No. 1223, 50c, Triton's trumpet. No. 1224, 50c, Frog shell.

2008, Nov. 11 ***Perf. 11¾***
1221-1224 A400 Set of 4 .90 .45

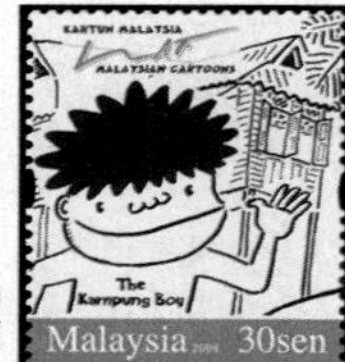

The Kampung Boy, Cartoons by Lat — A401

Designs: Nos. 1225a, 1226a, The Kampung Boy (29x33mm). Nos. 1225b, 1226b, Permainan Anak Kampung (58x33mm). Nos. 1225c, 1226c, Guru Sekolah Yang Garang (58x33mm). Nos. 1225d, 1226d, Town Boy (29x33mm). No. 1225e, Kampung Boy drawing picture (29x33mm).
$5, Malaysian daily life (60x40mm).

Perf. 13¾x14 Syncopated
2008, Dec. 1
1225 Horiz. strip of 5 .85 .45
a.-e. A401 30c Any single .20 .20
Complete booklet, 2 #1225 1.75
1226 Horiz. strip of 4 1.10 .55
a.-d. A401 50c Any single .25 .20
Souvenir Sheet
Perf. 12¾x12½
1227 A401 $5 silver & blk 2.75 1.40

Schools — A402

Designs: No. 1228, 50c, SMK Convent Bukit Nanas, Kuala Lumpur. No. 1229, 50c, SMK St. Thomas, Kuching, Sarawak. No. 1230, 50c, SMK Victoria (Victoria Institution), Kuala Lumpur. No. 1231, 50c, SM All Saints, Kota Kinabalu, Sabah.

2008, Dec. 16 ***Perf. 13½x13¼***
1228-1231 A402 Set of 4 1.25 .60

POSTAGE DUE STAMPS

Until 1966 Malaysia used postage due stamps of the Malayan Postal Union. See listings under Malaya.

D1

D2

Wmk. 338 Upright
1966, Aug. 15 Litho. ***Perf. 14½x14***
J1 D1 1c pink .20 .20
J2 D1 2c slate .60 .60
J3 D1 4c lt yellow green .65 .50
J4 D1 8c bright green 2.10 3.25
J5 D1 10c ultramarine 1.50 1.60
J6 D1 12c purple 1.50 1.50
J7 D1 20c brown 1.50 2.50
J8 D1 50c olive bister 3.50 4.25
Nos. J1-J8 (8) 11.55 14.40

Wmk. 338 Sideways
J4a D1 8c bright green 7.75 9.75
J5a D1 10c ultramarine 7.75 6.50
J7a D1 20c brown 10.50 8.50
J8a D1 50c olive bister 11.50 13.00
Nos. J4a-J8a (4) 37.50 37.75

Perf. 15x14
1981-84 Litho. Unwmk.
J9 D1 2c slate .35 .20
J10 D1 8c bright green .35 .20
J11 D1 10c blue .35 .20
J11A D1 12c maroon ('84) *14.00* *8.00*
J12 D1 20c brown .45 .20
J13 D1 50c olive bister 1.10 .30
Nos. J9-J13 (6) *16.60* *9.10*

1988, Sept. 15 Litho. ***Perf. 12***
J14 D2 5c brt rose & lil rose .20 .20
J15 D2 10c black & gray .20 .20
J16 D2 20c deep org & yel org .25 .25
J17 D2 50c blue grn & lt bl grn .45 .45
J18 D2 $1 brt blue & lt ultra .90 .90
Nos. J14-J18 (5) 2.00 2.00

JOHORE

Vanda Hookeriana and Sultan Ismail — A14

Orchids: 2c, Arundina graminifolia. 5c, Paphiopedilum niveum. 6c, Spathoglottis plicata. 10c, Arachnis flosaeris. 15c, Rhyncostylis retusa. 20c, Phalaenopsis violacea.

Wmk. 338
1965, Nov. 15 Photo. ***Perf. 14½***
Flowers in Natural Colors
169 A14 1c blk & lt grnsh bl .20 .20
a. Black omitted 100.00
b. Watermark sideways ('70) 1.00 1.00
170 A14 2c black, red & gray .20 .20
171 A14 5c black & Prus bl .20 .20
a. Yellow omitted 40.00
172 A14 6c black & lt lil .55 .20
173 A14 10c black & lt ultra .55 .20
a. Watermark sideways ('70) 5.00 2.50
174 A14 15c blk, lil rose & grn 1.90 .35
175 A14 20c black & brown 1.90 .60
Nos. 169-175 (7) 5.50 1.95

Malayan Jezebel and Sultan Ismail — A15

Butterflies: 2c, Black-veined tiger. 5c, Clipper. 6c, Lime butterfly. 10c, Great orange tip. 15c, Blue pansy. 20c, Wanderer.

Perf. 13½x13
1971, Feb. 1 Litho. Unwmk.
176 A15 1c multicolored .55 .55
177 A15 2c multicolored 1.50 1.50
178 A15 5c multicolored 1.90 .40
179 A15 6c multicolored 1.90 *2.50*
180 A15 10c multicolored 1.90 .55
181 A15 15c multicolored 1.90 .70
182 A15 20c multicolored 1.90 1.25
Nos. 176-182 (7) 11.55 7.45

1977 Photo.
176a A15 1c 3.50 2.75
177a A15 2c 3.50 *4.00*
178a A15 5c 3.50 .70
180a A15 10c 5.50 .35
181a A15 15c 11.00 .35
182a A15 20c 13.50 .80
Nos. 176a-182a (6) 40.50 8.95

Differentiating the lithograph and photogravure printings of the Butterflies issues:

Denominations and inscriptions have straight edges on the lithographed printings and broken edges on the photogravure printings.

Background colors and portrait show prominent screen dots on the lithographed stamps, but these features appear almost solid on the photogravure stamps except under high magnification.

Rafflesia Hasseltii and Sultan Ismail — A16

Flowers: 2c, Pterocarpus indicus. 5c, Lagerstroemia speciosa. 10c, Durio zibethinus. 15c, Hibiscus. 20c, Rhododendron scortechinii. 25c, Phaeomeria speciosa.

Wmk. 378
1979, Apr. 30 Litho. ***Perf. 14½***
183 A16 1c multicolored .25 .25
184 A16 2c multicolored .25 .25
185 A16 5c multicolored .25 .25
186 A16 10c multicolored .25 .25
187 A16 15c multicolored .25 .25
188 A16 20c multicolored .25 .25
189 A16 25c multicolored .75 .25
Nos. 183-189 (7) 2.25 1.75

1984
"Johor" in round type
185a A16 5c .65 .50
186a A16 10c .65 .50
187a A16 15c .50 .20
188a A16 20c .70 .20
Nos. 185a-188a (4) 2.50 1.40

Agriculture, State Arms and Sultan Mahmood Iskandar Al-Haj, Regent — A19

Wmk. 388
1986, Oct. 25 Litho. ***Perf. 12***
190 A19 1c Coffea liberica .40 .40
191 A19 2c Cocos nucifera .40 .40
192 A19 5c Theobroma cacao .40 .40
193 A19 10c Piper nigrum .40 .40
194 A19 15c Hevea brasiliensis .40 .40
195 A19 20c Elaeis guineensis .40 .40
196 A19 30c Oryza sativa .60 .60
Nos. 190-196 (7) 3.00 3.00

1986?
192a A19 5c Perf. 14 3.00
192b A19 5c Perf. 15x14½ 7.50
192c A19 5c Perf. 14x13½
193a A19 10c Perf. 14 3.00
193b A19 10c Perf. 14x13½
195a A19 20c Perf. 14 6.00
195b A19 20c Perf. 15x14½ 1.00
196a A19 30c Perf. 14 3.00
196b A19 30c Perf. 14x13½
196c A19 30c Perf. 14x14½ — —

Flowers, Arms and Sultan Mahmood Iskandar Ibni Al-Marhum Sultan Ismail — A20

Designs: 5c, Nelumbium nelumbo. 10c, Hydrangea macrophylla. 20c, Hippeastrum reticulatum. 30c, Bougainvillea. 40c, Ipomoea indica. 50c, Hibiscus rosa-sinensis.

Perf. 14¾x14½
2007, Dec. 31 Litho. Wmk. 388
197 A20 5c multi .20 .20
198 A20 10c multi .20 .20
Perf. 14x13¾
199 A20 20c multi .20 .20
200 A20 30c multi .20 .20
201 A20 40c multi .25 .20
202 A20 50c multi .30 .20
Nos. 197-202 (6) 1.35 1.20

KEDAH

Orchid Type of Johore, 1965, with Portrait of Sultan Abdul Halim

Wmk. 338
1965, Nov. 15 Photo. ***Perf. 14½***
Flowers in Natural Colors
106 A14 1c blk & lt grnsh bl .30 .30
a. Black omitted 90.00
b. Watermark sideways ('70) 1.00 1.00
107 A14 2c black, red & gray .30 .30
108 A14 5c black & Prus bl .30 .30

109 A14 6c black & lt lil .30 .30
110 A14 10c black & lt ultra .50 .30
a. Watermark sideways ('70) 4.00 3.00
111 A14 15c blk, lil rose & grn 2.25 .30
112 A14 20c black & brown 2.75 .45
Nos. 106-112 (7) 6.70 2.25

Butterfly Type of Johore, 1971, with Portrait of Sultan Abdul Halim

Perf. 13½x13

1971, Feb. 1 Litho. Unwmk.

113 A15 1c multicolored .45 .30
114 A15 2c multicolored .55 .30
115 A15 5c multicolored 1.40 .30
116 A15 6c multicolored 1.40 *1.75*
117 A15 10c multicolored 1.00 .30
118 A15 15c multicolored 1.40 .30
119 A15 20c multicolored 1.75 .50
Nos. 113-119 (7) 7.95 3.75

1977 Photo. Same Designs

114a A15 2c *29.00 17.00*
115a A15 5c 6.50 1.25
117a A15 10c 14.50 .75
118a A15 15c 4.50 .50
119a A15 20c 7.00 2.25
Nos. 114a-119a (5) *61.50 21.75*

For differentiating the lithograph and photogravure printings of the Butterflies issues, see notes after Johore No. 182a.

Flower Type of Johore, 1979, with Portrait of Sultan Abdul Halim

Wmk. 378

1979, Apr. 30 Litho. *Perf. 14½*

120 A16 1c multicolored .20 .20
121 A16 2c multicolored .20 .20
122 A16 5c multicolored .20 .20
123 A16 10c multicolored .20 .20
a. Unwmkd. ('85)
124 A16 15c multicolored .25 .20
a. Unwmkd. ('84) 3.25
125 A16 20c multicolored .40 .20
a. Pale yellow flowers ('84) .40 .20
126 A16 25c multicolored .45 .20
Nos. 120-126 (7) 1.90 1.40

25th Anniv. of Installation of Sultan Abdul Halim — A10

1983, July 15 Litho. *Perf. 13½*

127 A10 20c Portrait, vert. 1.50 .35
128 A10 40c View from Mt. Gunung Jerai 3.00 .45
129 A10 50c Rice fields, Mt. Gunung Jerai 3.25 .55
Nos. 127-129 (3) 7.75 1.35

Agriculture and State Arms Type of Johore with Sultan Abdul Halim

Wmk. 388

1986, Oct. 25 Litho. *Perf. 12*

130 A19 1c multicolored .35 .35
131 A19 2c multicolored .35 .35
132 A19 5c multicolored .35 .35
133 A19 10c multicolored .35 .35
134 A19 15c multicolored .35 .35
135 A19 20c multicolored .35 .35
136 A19 30c multicolored .35 .35
Nos. 130-136 (7) 2.45 2.45

1986?

132a A19 5c Perf. 15x14½ 4.00 .40
132b A19 5c Perf. 14 1.00 .20
133a A19 10c Perf. 14 3.00 .30
133b A19 10c Perf. 14x13¾, unwmk. 8.00
135a A19 20c Perf. 14 1.00 .20
136a A19 30c Perf. 14x14½ 2.00 .20
136b A19 30c Perf. 14x13½ 3.00 .25
136c A19 30c Perf. 15x14½ 3.00 .25

Flowers and Arms Type of Johore of 2007 With Portrait of Sultan Abdul Halim

Perf. 14x13¾

2007, Dec. 31 Litho. Wmk. 388

137 A20 5c multi .20 .20
138 A20 10c multi .20 .20
139 A20 20c multi .20 .20
140 A20 30c multi .20 .20
141 A20 40c multi .25 .20
142 A20 50c multi .30 .20
Nos. 137-142 (6) 1.35 1.20

Reign of Sultan Abdul Halim, 50th Anniv. A11

Sultan and: 30c, Buildings, farm field. 50c, Buildings. $1, Buildings and anniversary emblem.

Perf. 13½x13¼x12x13¼

2008, July 15

143-145 A11 Set of 3 1.10 1.10

KELANTAN

Orchid Type of Johore, 1965, with Portrait of Sultan Yahya Petra

Wmk. 338

1965, Nov. 15 Photo. *Perf. 14½*

Flowers in Natural Colors

91 A14 1c blk & lt grnsh bl .80 .80
a. Watermark sideways ('70) .60 .60
92 A14 2c black, red & gray .20 .20
93 A14 5c black & Prus bl .20 .20
94 A14 6c black & lt lil 1.00 .60
95 A14 10c black & lt ultra .45 .20
a. Watermark sideways ('70) 4.75 2.75
96 A14 15c blk, lil rose & grn 2.25 .20
97 A14 20c black & brown 2.25 .70
Nos. 91-97 (7) 7.15 2.90

Butterfly Type of Johore, 1971, with Portrait of Sultan Yahya Petra

Perf. 13½x13

1971, Feb. 1 Litho. Unwmk.

98 A15 1c multicolored .30 .20
99 A15 2c multicolored .30 .20
100 A15 5c multicolored .80 .20
101 A15 6c multicolored .90 .55
102 A15 10c multicolored 1.40 .20
103 A15 15c multicolored 2.75 .20
104 A15 20c multicolored 3.25 .55
Nos. 98-104 (7) 9.70 2.10

1977 Photo.

98a A15 1c 1.50 *3.75*
100a A15 5c 11.00 2.50
102a A15 10c 12.50 2.25
103a A15 15c 22.50 1.40
Nos. 98a-103a (4) 47.50 9.90

For differentiating the lithograph and photogravure printings of the Butterflies issues, see notes after Johore No. 182a.

Flower Type of Johore, 1979, with Portrait of Sultan Yahya Petra

Wmk. 378

1979, Apr. 30 Litho. *Perf. 14½*

105 A16 1c multicolored .20 .20
106 A16 2c multicolored .20 .20
107 A16 5c multicolored .20 .20
a. Unwmkd. ('86) .75 .20
108 A16 10c multicolored .20 .20
a. White flowers ('84) .30 .20
109 A16 15c multicolored .20 .20
110 A16 20c multicolored .20 .20
a. Pale yellow flowers ('84) .35 .20
111 A16 25c multicolored .80 .20
Nos. 105-111 (7) 2.00 1.40

Sultan Tengku Ismail Petra, Installation — A7

1980, Mar. 30 Litho. *Perf. 14½*

112 A7 10c multicolored .35 .35
113 A7 15c multicolored .50 .35
114 A7 50c multicolored 1.60 .95
Nos. 112-114 (3) 2.45 1.65

Agriculture and State Arms Type of Johore with Sultan Ismail Petra

Wmk. 388

1986, Oct. 25 Litho. *Perf. 12*

115 A19 1c multicolored .35 .35
116 A19 2c multicolored .35 .35
117 A19 5c multicolored .35 .35
118 A19 10c multicolored .35 .35
119 A19 15c multicolored .35 .35
120 A19 20c multicolored .35 .35
121 A19 30c multicolored .35 .35
Nos. 115-121 (7) 2.45 2.45

1986?

116a A19 2c Perf. 15x14½ 3.00 .50
118a A19 10c Perf. 14 3.00 .50
120a A19 20c Perf. 14 3.00 .50
121a A19 30c Perf. 14 1.00 .25

Reign of Sultan Tengku Ismail Petra, 25th Anniv. A8

Sultan and various buildings: 30c, 50c, $1.

Perf. 13½, 12 (50c)

2004, Feb. 29 Litho. Wmk. 388

122-124 A8 Set of 3 .95 .45

Flowers and Arms Type of Johore of 2007 With Portrait of Sultan Ismail Petra

Perf. 14x13¾

2007, Dec. 31 Litho. Wmk. 388

125 A20 5c multi .20 .20
126 A20 10c multi .20 .20
127 A20 20c multi .20 .20
128 A20 30c multi .20 .20
129 A20 40c multi .25 .20
130 A20 50c multi .30 .20
Nos. 125-130 (6) 1.35 1.20

MALACCA

(Melaka)

Orchid Type of Johore, 1965, with State Crest

Wmk. 338

1965, Nov. 15 Photo. *Perf. 14½*

Flowers in Natural Colors

67 A14 1c blk & lt grnsh blue .20 .20
a. Watermark sideways ('70) 1.10 1.10
68 A14 2c blk, red & gray .20 .20
69 A14 5c black & Prus bl .20 .20
70 A14 6c black & lt lilac .40 .40
71 A14 10c black & lt ultra .30 .20
a. Watermark sideways ('70) 7.25 5.25
72 A14 15c blk, lil rose & grn 2.40 .30
73 A14 20c black & brown 3.00 .95
Nos. 67-73 (7) 6.70 2.45

Butterfly Type of Johore, 1971, with State Crest

Perf. 13½x13

1971, Feb. 1 Litho. Unwmk.

74 A15 1c multicolored .60 .60
75 A15 2c multicolored 1.00 .60
76 A15 5c multicolored 1.50 .40
77 A15 6c multicolored 1.50 1.50
78 A15 10c multicolored 1.50 .65
79 A15 15c multicolored 2.75 1.25
80 A15 20c multicolored 2.75 1.40
Nos. 74-80 (7) 11.60 6.40

1977 Photo.

74a A15 1c 9.00 *11.50*
76a A15 5c 3.50 3.25
78a A15 10c 9.00 3.00
79a A15 15c 24.50 .85
80a A15 20c 8.50 5.50
Nos. 74a-80a (5) 54.50 24.10

For differentiating the lithograph and photogravure printings of the Butterflies issues, see notes after Johore No. 182a.

Flower Type of Johore, 1979, with State Crest

Wmk. 378

1979, Apr. 30 Litho. *Perf. 14½*

81 A16 1c multicolored .25 .25
82 A16 2c multicolored .25 .25
83 A16 5c multicolored .25 .25
84 A16 10c multicolored .25 .25
85 A16 15c multicolored .25 .25
86 A16 20c multicolored .40 .25
87 A16 25c multicolored .55 .25
Nos. 81-87 (7) 2.20 1.75

1983-86 Unwmk.

84a A16 10c ('85) 1.25 —
85a A16 15c ('86) .75 .50
86a A16 20c .75 —
Nos. 84a-86a (3) 2.75

Agriculture and State Arms Type of Johore

Wmk. 388

1986, Oct. 25 Litho. *Perf. 12*

88 A19 1c multicolored .35 .35
89 A19 2c multicolored .35 .35
90 A19 5c multicolored .35 .35
91 A19 10c multicolored .35 .35
92 A19 15c multicolored .35 .35
93 A19 20c multicolored .35 .35
94 A19 30c multicolored .40 .35
Nos. 88-94 (7) 2.50 2.45

1986? Litho.

90a A19 5c Perf. 14 1.00 .20
91a A19 10c Perf. 14 1.00 .20
91b A19 10c Perf. 15x14½ 1.50 .20
93a A19 20c Perf. 14 1.00 .20
94a A19 30c Perf. 14 3.00 .25
94b A19 30c Perf. 15x14½ 5.00 .35

Flowers and Arms Type of Johore of 2007

Perf. 14x13¾, 14¾x14½ (20c)

2007, Dec. 31 Litho. Wmk. 388

95 A20 5c multi .20 .20
96 A20 10c multi .20 .20
97 A20 20c multi .20 .20
98 A20 30c multi .20 .20
99 A20 40c multi .25 .20
100 A20 50c multi .30 .20
Nos. 95-100 (6) 1.35 1.20

NEGRI SEMBILAN

(Negeri Sembilan)

Orchid Type of Johore, 1965, with State Crest

Wmk. 338

1965, Nov. 15 Photo. *Perf. 14½*

Flowers in Natural Colors

76 A14 1c blk & lt grnsh blue .25 .20
a. Watermark sideways ('70) 4.00 1.60
77 A14 2c black, red & gray .25 .20
78 A14 5c black & Prus blue .50 .20
79 A14 6c black & lt lilac .75 .20
80 A14 10c black & lt ultra 1.00 .20
81 A14 15c blk, lil rose & grn 1.40 .20
82 A14 20c black & brown 2.00 .30
Nos. 76-82 (7) 6.15 1.50

Tuanku Ja'afar and Crest of Negri Sembilan — A7

1968, Apr. 8 Photo. *Perf. 13½*

83 A7 15c brt blue & multi .20 .20
84 A7 50c yellow & multi .60 .50

Installation of Tuanku Ja'afar ibni Al-Marhum as ruler (Yang di-Pertuan Besar) of Negri Sembilan.

Butterfly Type of Johore, 1971, with State Crest

Perf. 13½x13

1971, Feb. 1 Litho. Unwmk.

85 A15 1c multicolored .40 .30
86 A15 2c multicolored .40 .30
87 A15 5c multicolored .75 .30
88 A15 6c multicolored 1.00 .30
89 A15 10c multicolored 1.50 .30
90 A15 15c multicolored 2.50 .30
91 A15 20c multicolored 3.25 .35
Nos. 85-91 (7) 9.80 2.15

1977 Photo.

86a A15 2c 4.50 .30
87a A15 5c 4.50 .30
89a A15 10c 10.00 .80
90a A15 15c 19.00 1.50
91a A15 20c 24.00 2.00
Nos. 86a-91a (5) 62.00 4.90

For differentiating the lithograph and photogravure printings of the Butterflies issues, see notes after Johore No. 182a.

Flower Type of Johore, 1979, with State Crest

Wmk. 378

1979, Apr. 30 Litho. *Perf. 14½*

92 A16 1c multicolored .20 .20
93 A16 2c multicolored .20 .20
94 A16 5c multicolored .20 .20
a. Unwmkd. ('85) 1.10
95 A16 10c multicolored .20 .20
a. White flowers ('84) .20 .20
96 A16 15c multicolored .35 .20
a. Unwmkd. ('84) 3.25

97 A16 20c multicolored .40 .20
a. Pale yellow flowers ('84) .35 .20
98 A16 25c multicolored .55 .20
Nos. 92-98 (7) 2.10 1.40

Agriculture and State Arms Type of Johore

Wmk. 388

1986, Oct. 25 Litho. *Perf. 12*

99 A19 1c multicolored .35 .35
100 A19 2c multicolored .35 .35
101 A19 5c multicolored .35 .35
102 A19 10c multicolored .35 .35
103 A19 15c multicolored .35 .35
104 A19 20c multicolored .50 .35
105 A19 30c multicolored .35 .35
Nos. 99-105 (7) 2.60 2.45

1986? Litho.

101a A19 5c Perf. 14
102a A19 10c Perf. 14 1.00
102b A19 10c Perf. 15x14½ 7.50
104a A19 20c Perf. 14 2.50
105a A19 30c Perf. 14 3.00
105b A19 30c Perf. 14x14½ — —

Royal Heritage of Negri Sembilan — A8

Designs: 30c, Eight long keris. 50c, Audience Hall. $1, Tuanku Ja'afar Ibni Al-Marhum Tuanku Abdul Rahman, ruler of Negri Sembilan
$2, Tuanku Ja'afar and wife.

Perf. 12¾x12½

2007, Aug. 2 Litho. Wmk. 388

106-108 A8 Set of 3 1.10 .55

Souvenir Sheet

109 A8 $2 multi 1.25 .60

Flowers and Arms Type of Johore of 2007 With Portrait of Tuanku Jaafar Ibni Al-Marhum Tuanku Abdul Rahman

Perf. 14x13¾, 14¾x14½ (30c)

2007, Dec. 31 Litho. Wmk. 388

110 A20 5c multi .20 .20
111 A20 10c multi .20 .20
112 A20 20c multi .20 .20
113 A20 30c multi .20 .20
114 A20 40c multi .25 .20
115 A20 50c multi .30 .20
Nos. 110-115 (6) 1.35 1.20

PAHANG

Orchid Type of Johore, 1965, with Portrait of Sultan Abu Bakar

Wmk. 338

1965, Nov. 15 Photo. *Perf. 14½*

Flowers in Natural Colors

83 A14 1c blk & lt grnsh bl .20 .20
a. Watermark sideways ('70) .50 .50
84 A14 2c black, red & gray .20 .20
a. Unwmkd. ('85)
85 A14 5c black & Prus bl .45 .20
86 A14 6c black & lt lil .70 .20
87 A14 10c black & lt ultra 1.10 .20
a. Watermark sideways ('70) 4.50 2.50
88 A14 15c blk, lil rose & grn 1.50 .20
89 A14 20c black & brown 2.00 .25
Nos. 83-89 (7) 6.15 1.45

Butterfly Type of Johore, 1971, Portrait of Sultan Abu Bakar

Perf. 13½x13

1971, Feb. 1 Litho. Unwmk.

90 A15 1c multicolored .30 .30
91 A15 2c multicolored .30 .30
92 A15 5c multicolored .30 .30
93 A15 6c multicolored 1.00 .30
94 A15 10c multicolored 1.75 .30
95 A15 15c multicolored 2.75 .30
96 A15 20c multicolored 3.25 .35
Nos. 90-96 (7) 9.65 2.15

In 1973 booklet panes of 4 of the 5c, 10c, 15c were made from sheets.

Sultan Haji Ahmad Shah — A9

1975, May 8 Litho. *Perf. 14x14½*

97 A9 10c lilac, gold & black .35 .30
98 A9 15c yellow, green & black .80 .30
99 A9 50c ultra, dk blue & black 2.50 .85
Nos. 97-99 (3) 3.65 1.45

Installation of Sultan Haji Ahmad Shah as ruler of Pahang.

Black-veined Tiger and Sultan Haji Ahmad Shah — A18

1977-78

100 A18 2c multi ('78) *15.00 15.00*
101 A18 5c multicolored .95 .95
102 A18 10c multi ('78) 1.60 1.60
103 A18 15c multi ('78) 3.25 3.25
104 A18 20c multi ('78) 6.00 6.00
Nos. 100-104 (5) *26.80 26.80*

Flower Type of Johore, 1979, with Portrait of Sultan Haji Ahmad Shah

Wmk. 378

1979, Apr. 30 Litho. *Perf. 14½*

105 A16 1c multicolored .20 .20
106 A16 2c multicolored .20 .20
107 A16 5c multicolored .20 .20
a. 5c brt rose pink & yel flowers ('84) .20 .20
108 A16 10c multicolored .20 .20
a. Unwmkd. ('85) 2.25
109 A16 15c multicolored .35 .20
110 A16 20c multicolored .40 .20
a. Unwmkd. ('84) .45 .20
111 A16 25c multicolored .55 .20
Nos. 105-111 (7) 2.10 1.40

Agriculture and State Arms Type of Johore with Sultan Haji Ahmad Shah

Wmk. 388

1986, Oct. 25 Litho. *Perf. 12*

112 A19 1c multicolored .35 .35
113 A19 2c multicolored .35 .35
114 A19 5c multicolored .35 .35
115 A19 10c multicolored .35 .35
116 A19 15c multicolored .35 .35
117 A19 20c multicolored .35 .35
118 A19 30c multicolored .65 .35
Nos. 112-118 (7) 2.75 2.45

1986?

112a A19 1c Perf. 13½x14 6.00
115a A19 10c Perf. 15x14½
115b A19 10c Perf. 14x13½
118b A19 30c Perf. 15x14½
117a A19 20c Perf. 14 1.00
118a A19 30c Perf. 14 3.00

Flowers and Arms Type of Johore of 2007 With Portrait of Sultan Haji Ahmad Shah

Perf. 14x13¾

2007, Dec. 31 Litho. Wmk. 388

119 A20 5c multi .20 .20
120 A20 10c multi .20 .20
121 A20 20c multi .20 .20
122 A20 30c multi .20 .20
123 A20 40c multi .25 .20
124 A20 50c multi .30 .20
Nos. 119-124 (6) 1.35 1.20

PENANG

(Pulau Pinang)

Orchid Type of Johore, 1965, with State Crest

Wmk. 338

1965, Nov. 15 Photo. *Perf. 14½*

Orchids in Natural Colors

67 A14 1c black & lt grnsh bl .25 .20
a. Watermark sideways ('70) 1.90 1.90

68 A14 2c black, red & gray .30 .20
69 A14 5c black & Prus blue .60 .20
a. Prussian blue omitted
b. Yellow omitted
70 A14 6c black & lt lilac .65 .20
71 A14 10c black & lt ultra 1.10 .20
a. Watermark sideways ('70) 8.25 6.50
72 A14 15c black, lil rose & grn 1.40 .20
73 A14 20c black & brown 2.00 .20
Nos. 67-73 (7) 6.30 1.40

Butterfly Type of Johore, 1971, with State Crest

Perf. 13½x13

1971, Feb. 1 Litho. Unwmk.

74 A15 1c multicolored .40 .30
75 A15 2c multicolored .50 .30
76 A15 5c multicolored .85 .30
77 A15 6c multicolored .95 .30
78 A15 10c multicolored 1.40 .30
79 A15 15c multicolored 2.50 .30
80 A15 20c multicolored 3.00 .35
Nos. 74-80 (7) 9.60 2.15

1977 Photo.

74a A15 1c 32.50 2.10
76a A15 5c 2.75 .35
78a A15 10c 3.75 .35
79a A15 15c 11.00 .65
80a A15 20c 13.00 .80
Nos. 74a-80a (5) 63.00 4.25

For differentiating the lithograph and photogravure printings of the Butterflies issues, see notes after Johore No. 182a.

Flower Type of Johore, 1979, with State Crest

Wmk. 378

1979, Apr. 30 Litho. *Perf. 14½*

81 A16 1c multicolored .20 .20
82 A16 2c multicolored .20 .20
83 A16 5c multicolored .20 .20
84 A16 10c multicolored .20 .20
85 A16 15c multicolored .30 .20
86 A16 20c multicolored .35 .20
87 A16 25c multicolored .45 .20
Nos. 81-87 (7) 1.90 1.40

1984-85 Unwmk.

83a A16 5c .40 .20
84a A16 10c ('85)
85a A16 15c 3.25
86a A16 20c .40 .20

The State arms are larger on Nos. 83a-86a.

Agriculture and State Arms Type of Johore

Wmk. 388

1986, Oct. 25 Litho. *Perf. 12*

88 A19 1c multicolored .30 .30
89 A19 2c multicolored .30 .30
90 A19 5c multicolored .30 .30
91 A19 10c multicolored .30 .30
92 A19 15c multicolored .30 .30
93 A19 20c multicolored .30 .30
94 A19 30c multicolored .55 .30
Nos. 88-94 (7) 2.35 2.10

1986?

90a A19 5c Perf. 14 2.50
90b A19 5c Perf. 15x14½ 7.50
91a A19 10c Perf. 14 1.00
91b A19 10c Perf. 14x14½ 3.00
91c A19 10c Perf. 15x14½ 7.50
93a A19 20c Perf. 14 1.00
93b A19 20c Perf. 14x14½ 2.00
93c A19 20c Perf. 15x14½ 4.00
94a A19 30c Perf. 14 1.00
94b A19 30c Perf. 14x14½ 7.50
94c A19 30c Perf. 15x14½ 7.50

Flowers and Arms Type of Johore of 2007

Perf. 14x13¾

2007, Dec. 31 Litho. Wmk. 388

95 A20 5c multi .20 .20
96 A20 10c multi .20 .20
97 A20 20c multi .20 .20
98 A20 30c multi .20 .20
99 A20 40c multi .25 .20
100 A20 50c multi .30 .20
Nos. 95-100 (6) 1.35 1.20

PERAK

Sultan Idris Shah — A17

Wmk. 338

1963, Oct. 26 Photo. *Perf. 14*

138 A17 10c yel, blk, blue & brn .40 .20

Installation of Idris Shah as Sultan of Perak.

Orchid Type of Johore, 1965, with Portrait of Sultan Idris Shah

1965, Nov. 15 Wmk. 338 *Perf. 14½*

Flowers in Natural Colors

139 A14 1c blk & lt grnsh bl .25 .20
a. Watermark sideways ('70) 2.50 2.50
140 A14 2c black, red & gray .25 .20
141 A14 5c black & Prus blue .50 .20
a. Yellow omitted 20.00
142 A14 6c black & lt lilac .65 .20
143 A14 10c black & lt ultra 1.00 .20
a. Watermark sideways ('70) 9.50 9.00
144 A14 15c blk, lil rose & grn 1.25 .20
a. Lilac rose omitted 80.00
145 A14 20c black & brown 1.90 .25
Nos. 139-145 (7) 5.80 1.45

Butterfly Type of Johore, 1971, with Portrait of Sultan Idris Shah

Perf. 13½x13

1971, Feb. 1 Litho. Unwmk.

146 A15 1c multicolored .20 .20
147 A15 2c multicolored .35 .20
148 A15 5c multicolored .75 .20
149 A15 6c multicolored .90 .20
150 A15 10c multicolored 1.40 .20
151 A15 15c multicolored 2.50 .35
152 A15 20c multicolored 2.75 .35
Nos. 146-152 (7) 8.85 1.70

In 1973 booklet panes of 4 of the 5c, 10c, 15c were made from sheets.

1977 Photo.

146a A15 1c 2.75 .65
148b A15 5c 4.00 .65
150b A15 10c 4.50 .80
151b A15 15c 11.00 1.60
152a A15 20c 14.50 1.90
Nos. 146a-152a (5) 36.75 5.60

For differentiating the lithograph and photogravure printings of the Butterflies issues, see notes after Johore No. 182a.

Flower Type of Johore, 1979, with Portrait of Sultan Idris Shah

Wmk. 378

1979, Apr. 30 Litho. *Perf. 14½*

153 A16 1c multicolored .20 .20
154 A16 2c multicolored .20 .20
155 A16 5c multicolored .20 .20
a. Brt rose pink & yel flowers ('84) .20 .20
156 A16 10c multicolored .20 .20
a. White flowers ('84) .20 .20
157 A16 15c multicolored .30 .20
a. Unwmkd. ('85) 3.25
158 A16 20c multicolored .35 .20
a. Unwmkd. ('84) .45 .20
159 A16 25c multicolored .45 .20
Nos. 153-159 (7) 1.90 1.40

Agriculture and State Arms Type of Johore with Tun Azlan Shah, Raja

Wmk. 388

1986, Oct. 25 Litho. *Perf. 12*

160 A19 1c multicolored .30 .30
161 A19 2c multicolored .30 .30
162 A19 5c multicolored .30 .30
163 A19 10c multicolored .30 .30
164 A19 15c multicolored .30 .30
165 A19 20c multicolored .30 .30
166 A19 30c multicolored .45 .30
Nos. 160-166 (7) 2.25 2.10

1986?

161a A19 2c Perf. 15x14½ 3.00
162a A19 5c Perf. 14 3.00
162b A19 5c Perf. 15x14½ 7.50
163a A19 10c Perf. 14 1.00
165a A19 20c Perf. 14 1.50
165b A19 20c Perf. 14x14½
165c A19 20c Perf. 14¾x14½
166a A19 30c Perf. 14 8.00
166b A19 30c Perf. 15x14½ 7.50
166c A19 30c Perf. 14x13½

Flowers and Arms Type of Johore of 2007 With Portrait of Sultan Azlan Shah

Perf. 14x13¾

2007, Dec. 31 Litho. Wmk. 388

167 A20 5c multi .20 .20
168 A20 10c multi .20 .20
169 A20 20c multi .20 .20
170 A20 30c multi .20 .20
171 A20 40c multi .25 .20
172 A20 50c multi .30 .20
Nos. 167-172 (6) 1.35 1.20

PERLIS

Orchid Type of Johore, 1965, with Portrait of Regent Yang Teramat Mulia

Wmk. 338

1965, Nov. 15 Photo. *Perf. 14½*

Flowers in Natural Colors

40	A14	1c black & lt grnsh bl	.30	.20
41	A14	2c black, red & gray	.35	.20
42	A14	5c black & Prus blue	.50	.20
43	A14	6c black & lt lilac	.55	.20
44	A14	10c black & ultra	.85	.25
45	A14	15c blk, lil rose & grn	1.50	.50
46	A14	20c black & brown	2.50	.80
		Nos. 40-46 (7)	6.55	2.35

Butterfly Type of Johore, 1971, with Portrait of Sultan Syed Putra

Perf. 13½x13

1971, Feb. 1 Litho. Unwmk.

47	A15	1c multicolored	.25	.25
48	A15	2c multicolored	.30	.25
49	A15	5c multicolored	.65	.25
50	A15	6c multicolored	.85	.25
51	A15	10c multicolored	2.10	.30
52	A15	15c multicolored	2.10	.50
53	A15	20c multicolored	2.50	.70
		Nos. 47-53 (7)	8.75	2.50

In 1973 booklet panes of 4 of the 5c, 10c, 15c were made from sheets.

1977 Photo.

51b	A15	10c	*20.00*	*20.00*
52b	A15	15c	*4.00*	*3.00*
53a	A15	20c	*17.00*	*17.00*
		Nos. 51b-53a (3)	*41.00*	*40.00*

For differentiating the lithograph and photogravure printings of the Butterflies issues, see notes after Johore No. 182a.

Sultan Syed Putra — A2

1971, Mar. 28 Litho. *Perf. 13½x13*

54	A2	10c silver, yel & black	.30	.30
55	A2	15c silver, blue & blk	.35	.35
56	A2	50c silver, lt vio & blk	1.25	1.25
		Nos. 54-56 (3)	1.90	1.90

25th anniversary of the installation of Syed Putra as Raja of Perlis. Sold throughout Malaysia on Mar. 28, then only in Perlis.

Flower Type of Johore, 1979, with Portrait of Sultan Syed Putra

Wmk. 378

1979, Apr. 30 Litho. *Perf. 14½*

57	A16	1c multicolored	.20	.20
58	A16	2c multicolored	.20	.20
59	A16	5c multicolored	.20	.20
60	A16	10c multicolored	.20	.20
61	A16	15c multicolored	.35	.20
62	A16	20c multicolored	.45	.20
a.		Unwmk. ('85)	4.25	
63	A16	25c multicolored	.55	.20
		Nos. 57-63 (7)	2.15	1.40

Agriculture and State Arms Type of Johore with Tuanku Syed Putra, Raja

Wmk. 388

1986, Oct. 25 Litho. *Perf. 12*

64	A19	1c multicolored	.35	.35
65	A19	2c multicolored	.35	.35
66	A19	5c multicolored	.35	.35
67	A19	10c multicolored	.35	.35
68	A19	15c multicolored	.35	.35
69	A19	20c multicolored	.35	.35
70	A19	30c multicolored	.50	.35
		Nos. 64-70 (7)	2.60	2.45

1986?

67a	A19	10c Perf. 15x14½	4.00
70a	A19	30c Perf. 14	7.50

Reign of Tuanku Syed Putra Jamalullail, Raja of Perlis, 50th Anniv. A3

30c, Industry and produce. $1, Palace.

Wmk. 388

1995, Dec. 4 Litho. *Perf. 14*

71	A3	30c green & multi	1.00	1.00
72	A3	$1 blue & multi	3.00	3.00

Installation of Raja Tuanku Syed Sirajuddin Putra Jamalullail — A4

Denomination color: 30c, Blue. 50c, Green. $1, Purple.
$2, Raja and wife, horiz.

Perf. 13½x13¾

2001, May 7 Litho. Wmk. 388

73-75	A4	Set of 3	.95	.45

Souvenir Sheet

Perf. 14¼x13½x13¾x13½

76	A4	$2 multi	1.10	1.10

Flowers and Arms Type of Johore of 2007 With Portrait of Raja Tuanku Syed Sirajuddin Putra Jamalullail

Perf. 14x13¾

2007, Dec. 31 Litho. Wmk. 388

77	A20	5c multi	.20	.20
78	A20	10c multi	.20	.20
79	A20	20c multi	.20	.20
80	A20	30c multi	.20	.20
81	A20	40c multi	.25	.20
82	A20	50c multi	.30	.20
		Nos. 77-82 (6)	1.35	1.20

SABAH

North Borneo Nos. 280-295 Overprinted:

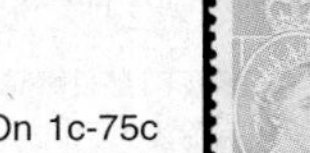

On 1c-75c

On $1-$10

Perf. 13x12½, 12½x13

1964, July 1 Engr. Wmk. 314

1	A92	1c lt red brn & grn	.25	.35
2	A92	4c orange & olive	.25	.35
3	A92	5c violet & sepia	.25	.35
4	A92	6c bluish grn & sl	.25	.35
5	A92	10c rose red & lt grn	.25	.35
6	A92	12c dull green & brn	.25	.35
7	A92	20c ultra & blue grn	.25	.35
8	A92	25c rose red & gray	.65	.45
9	A92	30c gray ol & sepia	.80	.65
10	A92	35c redsh brn & stl bl	1.00	.75
11	A92	50c brn org & blue grn	1.40	.90
12	A92	75c red vio & sl blue	2.00	1.25
13	A93	$1 yel green & brn	3.00	1.75
14	A93	$2 slate & brown	6.00	5.50
15	A93	$5 brown vio & grn	18.00	13.00
16	A93	$10 blue & carmine	40.00	26.50
		Nos. 1-16 (16)	74.60	53.20

Orchid Type of Johore, 1965, with State Crest

Wmk. 338

1965, Nov. 15 Photo. *Perf. 14½*

Flowers in Natural Colors

17	A14	1c black & lt grnsh bl	.30	.20
18	A14	2c black, red & gray	.30	.20
19	A14	5c black & Prus bl	.45	.20
20	A14	6c black & lt lilac	.65	.20
21	A14	10c black & lt ultra	1.25	.20
a.		Watermark sideways ('70)	8.00	2.75
22	A14	15c black, lil rose & grn	2.00	.20
23	A14	20c black & brown	3.00	.60
		Nos. 17-23 (7)	7.95	1.80

Butterfly Type of Johore, 1971, with State Crest

Perf. 13½x13

1971, Feb. 1 Litho. Unwmk.

24	A15	1c multicolored	.20	.20
25	A15	2c multicolored	.35	.20
26	A15	5c multicolored	.50	.20
27	A15	6c multicolored	.70	.20
28	A15	10c multicolored	1.50	.20
29	A15	15c multicolored	1.75	.20
30	A15	20c multicolored	3.00	.30
		Nos. 24-30 (7)	8.00	1.50

In 1973 booklet panes of 4 of the 5c, 10c, 15c were made from sheets.

1977 Photo.

24a	A15	1c	1.75	.20
25a	A15	2c	1.75	.20
26b	A15	5c	10.00	.20
28b	A15	10c	2.50	.20
29b	A15	15c	2.50	.30
		Nos. 24a-29b (5)	18.50	1.10

For differentiating the lithograph and photogravure printings of the Butterflies issues, see notes after Johore No. 182a.

Flower Type of Johore, 1979, with State Crest

Wmk. 378

1979, Apr. 30 Litho. *Perf. 14½*

32	A16	1c multicolored	.35	.35
33	A16	2c multicolored	.35	.35
34	A16	5c multicolored	.35	.35
35	A16	10c multicolored	.35	.35
36	A16	15c multicolored	.50	.35
37	A16	20c multicolored	.60	.35
38	A16	25c multicolored	.75	.35
		Nos. 32-38 (7)	3.25	2.45

1983-85 Unwmk.

35a	A16	10c ('85)	7.50
36a	A16	15c	6.00
37a	A16	20c	

Agriculture and State Arms Type of Johore

Wmk. 388

1986, Oct. 25 Litho. *Perf. 12*

39	A19	1c multicolored	.30	.30
40	A19	2c multicolored	.30	.30
41	A19	5c multicolored	.30	.30
42	A19	10c multicolored	.30	.30
43	A19	15c multicolored	.30	.30
44	A19	20c multicolored	.30	.30
45	A19	30c multicolored	.45	.30
		Nos. 39-45 (7)	2.25	2.10

1986?

40a	A19	2c Perf. 15x14½	3.00
45a	A19	30c Perf. 14	1.00
45b	A19	30c Perf. 15x14½	4.00

Sarawak

Stamps of types A14, A16 and A19 issued for Sarawak are listed in the "S" section.

Flowers and Arms Type of Johore of 2007

Perf. 14x13¾

2007, Dec. 31 Litho. Wmk. 388

46	A20	5c multi	.20	.20
47	A20	10c multi	.20	.20
48	A20	20c multi	.20	.20
49	A20	30c multi	.20	.20
50	A20	40c multi	.25	.20
51	A20	50c multi	.30	.20
		Nos. 46-51 (6)	1.35	1.20

SELANGOR

Orchid Type of Johore, 1965, with Portrait of Sultan Salahuddin Abdul Aziz Shah

Wmk. 338

1965, Nov. 15 Photo. *Perf. 14½*

Flowers in Natural Colors

121	A14	1c blk & lt grnsh bl	.20	.20
a.		Watermark sideways ('70)	1.50	.30
122	A14	2c black, red & gray	.30	.20
a.		Rose carmine omitted		
123	A14	5c black & Prus blue	.50	.20
124	A14	6c black & lt lilac	.65	.20
125	A14	10c black & lt ultra	1.00	.20
a.		Watermark sideways ('70)	5.50	.60
126	A14	15c blk, lil rose & grn	1.25	.20
127	A14	20c black & brown	2.25	.25
a.		Watermark sideways ('70)	9.50	.95
		Nos. 121-127 (7)	6.15	1.45

Butterfly Type of Johore, 1971, with Portrait of Sultan Salahuddin

Perf. 13½x13

1971, Feb. 1 Litho. Unwmk.

128	A15	1c multicolored	.30	.30
129	A15	2c multicolored	.45	.30
130	A15	5c multicolored	.75	.30
131	A15	6c multicolored	1.10	.20
132	A15	10c multicolored	1.60	.30
133	A15	15c multicolored	2.50	.30
134	A15	20c multicolored	3.25	.30
		Nos. 128-134 (7)	9.95	2.00

In 1973 booklet panes of 4 of the 5c, 10c, 15c were made from sheets.

1977 Photo.

128a	A15	1c	3.25	.75
130b	A15	5c	4.75	.75
132b	A15	10c	5.75	.95
133b	A15	15c	12.50	1.90
134a	A15	20c	15.00	2.50
		Nos. 128a-134a (5)	41.25	6.85

For differentiating the lithograph and photogravure printings of the Butterflies issues, see notes after Johore No. 182a.

Flower Type of Johore, 1979, with Portrait of Sultan Salahuddin Abdul Aziz Shah

Wmk. 378

1979, Apr. 30 Litho. *Perf. 14½*

135	A16	1c multicolored	.20	.20
136	A16	2c multicolored	.20	.20
137	A16	5c multicolored	.20	.20
a.		brt rose pink & yel flowers ('84)	.20	.20
138	A16	10c multicolored	.20	.20
a.		Unwmkd. ('85)	2.25	
139	A16	15c multicolored	.30	.20
a.		Unwmkd. ('84)	3.25	
140	A16	20c multicolored	.45	.20
a.		pale yellow flowers ('84)	.35	.20
141	A16	25c multicolored	.60	.20
		Nos. 135-141 (7)	2.15	1.40

Agriculture and State Arms Type of Johore with Sultan Salahuddin Abdul Aziz Shah

Wmk. 388

1986, Oct. 25 Litho. *Perf. 12*

142	A19	1c multicolored	.30	.30
143	A19	2c multicolored	.30	.30
144	A19	5c multicolored	.30	.30
145	A19	10c multicolored	.30	.30
146	A19	15c multicolored	.30	.30
147	A19	20c multicolored	.30	.30
148	A19	30c multicolored	.45	.30
		Nos. 142-148 (7)	2.25	2.10

1986?

144a	A19	5c Perf. 14	1.00
144b	A19	5c Perf. 15x14½	4.00
144c	A19	5c Perf. 14x13½	
145a	A19	10c Perf. 14	3.00
145b	A19	10c Perf. 15x14½	7.50
147a	A19	20c Perf. 14	1.00
148a	A19	30c Perf. 14	1.00
148b	A19	30c Perf. 14x14½	2.50
148c	A19	30c Perf. 15x14½	7.50

Coronation of Sultan Sharafuddin Idris Shah — A19

Designs: 30c, Wearing yellow hat. 50c, Wearing naval uniform. 1r, Wearing crown.

Perf. 12 (30c), 12¾x12½

2003, Mar. 8 Litho. Wmk. 388

149-151	A19	Set of 3	.95	.45

Flowers and Arms Type of Johore of 2007 With Portrait of Sultan Sharafuddin Idris Shah

Perf. 14¾x14½

2007, Dec. 31 Litho. Wmk. 388

152	A20	5c multi	.20	.20
153	A20	10c multi	.20	.20

Perf. 14x13¾

154	A20	20c multi	.20	.20
155	A20	30c multi	.20	.20
156	A20	40c multi	.25	.20
157	A20	50c multi	.30	.20
		Nos. 152-157 (6)	1.35	1.20

TRENGGANU

Orchid Type of Johore, 1965, with Portrait of Sultan Ismail

Wmk. 338

1965, Nov. 15 Photo. *Perf. 14½*

Flowers in Natural Colors

No.	Type	Denom.	Description	Unused	Used
86	A14	1c	black & lt grnsh bl	.20	.20
87	A14	2c	black, red & gray	.35	.20
88	A14	5c	black & Prus blue	.55	.20
89	A14	6c	black & lt lilac	.70	.20
90	A14	10c	black & lt ultra	.95	.20
91	A14	15c	blk, lil rose & grn	1.40	.20
92	A14	20c	black & brown	2.00	.30
			Nos. 86-92 (7)	6.15	1.50

Tuanku Ismail Nasiruddin — A6

Perf. 14½x13½

1970, Dec. 16 Photo. Unwmk.

No.	Type	Denom.	Description	Unused	Used
93	A6	10c	multicolored	.30	.30
94	A6	15c	brt yellow multi	.70	.70
95	A6	50c	dp plum & multi	2.25	2.25
			Nos. 93-95 (3)	3.25	3.25

Installation of Tuanku Ismail Nasiruddin Shah as Sultan of Trengganu, 25th anniv.

Butterfly Type of Johore, 1971, with Portrait of Sultan Ismail Nasiruddin

Perf. 13½x13

1971, Feb. 1 Litho. Unwmk.

No.	Type	Denom.	Description	Unused	Used
96	A15	1c	multicolored	.35	.35
97	A15	2c	multicolored	.40	.35
98	A15	5c	multicolored	.90	.35
99	A15	6c	multicolored	1.25	.35
100	A15	10c	multicolored	1.75	.40
101	A15	15c	multicolored	3.50	.65
102	A15	20c	multicolored	4.25	.70
			Nos. 96-102 (7)	12.40	3.15

In 1973 booklet panes of 4 of the 5c, 10c, 15c were made from sheets.

1977 Photo.

No.	Type	Denom.	Description	Unused	Used
98b	A15	5c		*10.00*	*10.00*
100b	A15	10c		*8.00*	*8.00*
101b	A15	15c		*8.00*	*8.00*
			Nos. 98b-101b (3)	*26.00*	*26.00*

For differentiating the lithograph and photogravure printings of the Butterflies issues, see notes after Johore No. 182a.

Flower Type of Johore, 1979, with Portrait of Sultan Ismail Nasiruddin

Wmk. 378

1979, Apr. 30 Litho. *Perf. 14½*

No.	Type	Denom.	Description	Unused	Used
103	A16	1c	multicolored	.20	.20
104	A16	2c	multicolored	.20	.20
105	A16	5c	multicolored	.20	.20
106	A16	10c	multicolored	.20	.20
107	A16	15c	multicolored	.35	.20
108	A16	20c	multicolored	.45	.20
109	A16	25c	multicolored	.55	.20
			Nos. 103-109 (7)	2.15	1.40

1983-86 Unwmk.

No.	Type	Denom.	Description	Unused	Used
106a	A16	10c	('86)	13.00	.20
107a	A16	15c	('85)	2.00	
108a	A16	20c		4.00	
109a	A16	25c	Pale salmon flowers	.75	.20
			Nos. 106a-109a (4)	19.75	

The portrait and State arms are smaller.

Agriculture and State Arms Type of Johore with Sultan Mahmud Al Marhum

Wmk. 388

1986, Oct. 25 Litho. *Perf. 12*

No.	Type	Denom.	Description	Unused	Used
110	A19	1c	multicolored	.35	.35
111	A19	2c	multicolored	.35	.35
112	A19	5c	multicolored	.35	.35
113	A19	10c	multicolored	.35	.35
114	A19	15c	multicolored	.35	.35
115	A19	20c	multicolored	.35	.35
116	A19	30c	multicolored	.50	.35
			Nos. 110-116 (7)	2.60	2.45

1986?

No.	Type	Denom.	Description	Unused	Used
110a	A19	1c	Perf. 13½x14	4.00	
115a	A19	20c	Perf. 14	7.50	
116a	A19	30c	Perf. 14	2.50	

Installation of HRH Sultan Mizan Zainal Abidin A7

Sultan Abidin and: 30c, Istana Maziah. 50c, Istana Maziah, 1903. $1, Masjid Tengku Tengah Zaharah.

Wmk. 388

1999, Mar. 4 Litho. *Perf. 14¼*

No.	Type	Denom.	Description	Unused	Used
117	A7	30c	multicolored	.20	.20
			Perf. 14½		
118	A7	50c	multicolored	.30	.20
			Perf. 13¾		
119	A7	$1	multicolored	.55	.25
			Nos. 117-119 (3)	1.05	.65

Flowers and Arms Type of Johore of 2007 With Portrait of Sultan Mizan Zainal Abidin

Perf. 14x13¾

2007, Dec. 31 Litho. Wmk. 388

No.	Type	Denom.	Description	Unused	Used
120	A20	5c	multi	.20	.20
121	A20	10c	multi	.20	.20
122	A20	20c	multi	.20	.20
123	A20	30c	multi	.20	.20
124	A20	40c	multi	.25	.20
125	A20	50c	multi	.30	.20
			Nos. 121-125 (5)	1.15	1.00

WILAYAH PERSEKUTUAN

Agriculture and State Arms Type of Johore

Wmk. 388

1986, Oct. 25 Litho. *Perf. 12*

No.	Type	Denom.	Description	Unused	Used
1	A19	1c	multicolored	.20	.20
2	A19	2c	multicolored	.20	.20
3	A19	5c	multicolored	.20	.20
4	A19	10c	multicolored	.20	.20
5	A19	15c	multicolored	.20	.20
6	A19	20c	multicolored	.25	.20
7	A19	30c	multicolored	.40	.20
			Nos. 1-7 (7)	1.65	1.40

1986?

No.	Type	Denom.	Description	Unused	Used
3a	A19	5c	Perf. 14	3.00	
3b	A19	5c	Perf. 15x14½	7.50	
4a	A19	10c	Perf. 14	3.00	
4b	A19	10c	Perf. 14x14½	7.50	
4c	A19	10c	Perf. 14¾x14½	—	—
6a	A19	20c	Perf. 14	1.00	
7a	A19	30c	Perf. 14	1.00	
7b	A19	30c	Perf. 15x14½	4.00	
7c	A19	30c	Perf. 14x14½		—

Agriculture and State Arms Type of Johore of 1986 Redrawn With "Sen" Instead of "C"

Designs as before.

Perf. 14¾x14½

2002 ? Litho. Wmk. 388

No.	Type	Denom.	Description	Unused	Used
10	A19	5sen	multi	—	—
			Perf. 14x14¾		
11	A19	10sen	multi	—	—
			Perf. 14x13¾		
13	A19	20sen	multi		—
14	A19	30sen	multi		—
a.			Perf. 14x13¾		—

Additional stamps were released in this set and also for other states. The editors would like to examine any examples.

Flowers and Arms Type of Johore of 2007

2007, Dec. 31 Litho. *Perf. 14x13¾*

No.	Type	Denom.	Description	Unused	Used
15	A20	5c	multi	.20	.20
16	A20	10c	multi	.20	.20
17	A20	20c	multi	.20	.20
18	A20	30c	multi	.20	.20
19	A20	40c	multi	.25	.20
20	A20	50c	multi	.30	.20
			Nos. 15-20 (6)	1.35	1.20

MALDIVE ISLANDS

'mol-ˌdīv 'ī-lənds

LOCATION — A group of 2,000 islands in the Indian Ocean about 400 miles southwest of Ceylon.
GOVT. — Republic
AREA — 115 sq. mi.
POP. — 300,220 (1999 est.)
CAPITAL — Male

Maldive Islands was a British Protectorate, first as a dependency of Ceylon, then from 1948 as an independent sultanate, except for a year (1953) as a republic. The islands became completely independent on July 26, 1965, and became a republic again on November 11, 1968.

100 Cents = 1 Rupee
100 Larees = 1 Rufiyaa (1951)

Catalogue values for unused stamps in this country are for Never Hinged items, beginning with Scott 20.

Watermarks

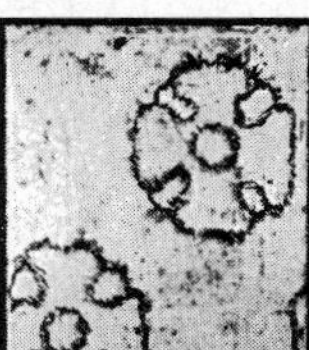

Wmk. 47 — Multiple Rosette

Wmk. 233 — "Harrison & Sons, London" in Script

Stamps of Ceylon, 1904-05, Overprinted

1906, Sept. 9 Wmk. 3 *Perf. 14*
1 A36 2c orange brown 16.00 *25.00*
2 A37 3c green 17.50 *25.00*
3 A37 4c yellow & blue 32.50 *60.00*
4 A38 5c dull lilac 5.00 *6.50*
5 A40 15c ultramarine 62.50 *100.00*
6 A40 25c bister 72.50 *100.00*
Nos. 1-6 (6) 206.00 *316.50*

Minaret of Juma Mosque, near Male — A1

1909 Engr. Wmk. 47
7 A1 2c orange brown 2.00 2.25
8 A1 3c green .50 .70
9 A1 5c red violet .30 .30
10 A1 10c carmine 7.50 .80
Nos. 7-10 (4) 10.30 4.05

Type of 1909 Issue Redrawn
Perf. 14½x14
1933 Photo. Wmk. 233
11 A1 2c gray 2.75 1.75
12 A1 3c yellow brown .75 1.50
13 A1 5c brown lake 17.50 10.00
14 A1 6c brown red 1.75 5.00
15 A1 10c green 1.00 .50
16 A1 15c gray black 6.50 11.00
17 A1 25c red brown 6.50 11.00
18 A1 50c red violet 6.50 11.00
19 A1 1r blue black 12.50 5.00
Nos. 11-19 (9) 55.75 56.75

On the 6c, 15c, 25c and 50c, the right hand panel carries only the word "CENTS."

Nos. 11-19 exist with watermark vert. or horiz. The 5c with vert. watermark sells for twice the price of the horiz. watermark.

Catalogue values for unused stamps in this section, from this point to the end of the section, are for Never Hinged items.

Palm Tree and Seascape — A2

Maldive Fish — A3

Unwmk.
1950, Dec. 24 Engr. *Perf. 13*
20 A2 2 l olive green 1.75 .50
21 A2 3 l deep blue 12.50 .85
22 A2 5 l dp blue green 12.50 .85
23 A2 6 l red brown .95 .70
24 A2 10 l red .95 .70
25 A2 15 l orange .95 .40
26 A2 25 l rose violet .95 .40
27 A2 50 l violet blue .95 .40
28 A2 1r dark brown 12.50 35.00
Nos. 20-28 (9) 44.00 39.80

1952
29 A3 3 l shown 1.90 2.25
30 A3 5 l Urns 1.10 1.60

Harbor of Male — A4

Fort and Governor's Palace — A5

Perf. 13½ (A4), 11½x11 (A5)
1956 Engr. Unwmk.
31 A4 2 l lilac .25 .25
32 A4 3 l gray green .25 .25
33 A4 5 l reddish brown .25 .25
34 A4 6 l blue violet .25 .25
35 A4 10 l light green .25 .25
36 A4 15 l brown .25 .25
37 A4 25 l rose red .25 .25
38 A4 50 l orange .25 .25
39 A5 1r light green .40 .30
40 A5 5r ultramarine 1.00 .70
41 A5 10r magenta 2.10 1.40
Nos. 31-41 (11) 5.50 4.40

Bicyclists and Olympic Emblem — A6

Design: 25 l, 50 l, 1r, Basketball, vert.

Perf. 11½x11, 11x11½
1960, Aug. 20 Engr.
42 A6 2 l rose violet & green .20 .20
43 A6 3 l grnsh gray & plum .20 .20
44 A6 5 l vio brn & dk blue .20 .20
45 A6 10 l brt green & brn .20 .20
46 A6 15 l brown & blue .20 .20
47 A6 25 l rose red & olive .20 .20
48 A6 50 l orange & dk vio .30 .30
49 A6 1r brt green & plum .50 .50
Nos. 42-49 (8) 2.00 2.00

17th Olympic Games, Rome, 8/25-9/11.

World Refugee Year Emblem A7

1960, Oct. 15 *Perf. 11½x11*
50 A7 2 l orange, vio & grn .20 .20
51 A7 3 l green, brn & red .20 .20
52 A7 5 l sepia, grn & red .20 .20
53 A7 10 l dull pur, grn & red .20 .20
54 A7 15 l gray grn, pur & red .20 .25
55 A7 25 l redsh brn, ultra & olive .20 .25
56 A7 50 l rose, olive & blue .20 .30
57 A7 1r gray, car rose & vio .35 .75
Nos. 50-57 (8) 1.75 2.35

WRY, July 1, 1959-June 30, 1960.

Tomb of Sultan — A8

Designs: 3 l, Custom house. 5 l, Cowry shells. 6 l, Old royal palace. 10 l, Road to Minaret, Juma Mosque, Male. 15 l, Council house. 25 l, Government secretariat. 50 l, Prime minister's office. 1r, Tomb and sailboats. 5r, Tomb by the sea. 10r, Port.

1960, Oct. 15 *Perf. 11½x11*
Various Frames
58 A8 2 l lilac .30 .30
59 A8 3 l green .30 .30
60 A8 5 l brown orange 2.75 2.50
61 A8 6 l bright blue .30 .30
62 A8 10 l carmine rose .30 .30
63 A8 15 l sepia .30 .30
64 A8 25 l dull violet .30 .30
65 A8 50 l slate .30 .30
66 A8 1r orange .30 .30
67 A8 5r dark blue 2.50 .75
68 A8 10r dull green 7.00 1.50
Nos. 58-68 (11) 14.65 7.15

Stamps in 25r, 50r and 100r denominations were also issued, but primarily for revenue purposes. Value for the three stamps, $350.

Coconuts — A9

Map of Male Showing Population Distribution A10

Perf. 14x14½, 14½x14
1961, Apr. 20 Photo. Unwmk.
Coconuts in Ocher
69 A9 2 l green .20 .20
70 A9 3 l ultramarine .20 .20
71 A9 5 l lilac rose .20 .20
72 A9 10 l red orange .20 .20
73 A9 15 l black .20 .20
74 A10 25 l multicolored .20 .20
75 A10 50 l multicolored .20 .20
76 A10 1r multicolored .25 .30
Nos. 69-76 (8) 1.65 1.70

Pigeon and 5c Stamp of 1906 A11

Designs: 10 l, 15 l, 20 l, Post horn and 3c stamp of 1906. 25 l, 50 l, 1r, Laurel branch and 2c stamp of 1906.

1961, Sept. 9 *Perf. 14½x14*
77 A11 2 l violet blue & mar .20 .20
78 A11 3 l violet blue & mar .20 .20
79 A11 5 l violet blue & mar .20 .20
80 A11 6 l violet blue & mar .20 .20
81 A11 10 l maroon & green .20 .20
82 A11 15 l maroon & green .20 .20
83 A11 20 l maroon & green .20 .20
84 A11 25 l green, mar & blk .20 .20
85 A11 50 l green, mar & blk .20 .20
86 A11 1r green, mar & blk .35 .35
a. Souvenir sheet of 4 2.40 3.00
Nos. 77-86 (10) 2.15 2.15

55th anniv. of the 1st postage stamps of the Maldive Islands.

No. 86a contains 4 No. 86, with simulated perforations.

Malaria Eradication Emblem — A12

1962, Apr. 7 Engr. *Perf. 13½x13*
87 A12 2 l orange brown .20 .20
88 A12 3 l green .20 .20
89 A12 5 l blue .20 .20
90 A12 10 l vermilion .20 .20
91 A12 15 l black .20 .20
92 A12 25 l dark blue .20 .20
93 A12 50 l green .25 .25
94 A12 1r purple .45 .45
Nos. 87-94 (8) 1.90 1.90

WHO drive to eradicate malaria.

Children and Map of Far East and Americas A13

UNICEF, 15th Anniv.: 25 l, 50 l, 1r, 5r, Children and Map of Africa, Europe and Asia.

Perf. 14½x14
1962, Sept. 9 Photo. Unwmk.
Children in Multicolor
95 A13 2 l sepia .20 .20
96 A13 6 l violet .20 .20
97 A13 10 l dark green .20 .20
98 A13 15 l ultramarine .20 .20
99 A13 25 l blue .20 .20
100 A13 50 l bright green .20 .20
101 A13 1r rose claret .20 .20
102 A13 5r emerald .90 .90
Nos. 95-102 (8) 2.30 2.30

Sultan Mohamed Farid Didi — A14

1962, Nov. 29 *Perf. 14x14½*
Portrait in Orange Brown and Sepia
103 A14 3 l bluish green .25 .25
104 A14 5 l slate .25 .25
105 A14 10 l blue .40 .40
106 A14 20 l olive .40 .40
107 A14 50 l dk carmine rose .40 .40
108 A14 1r dark purple .75 .75
Nos. 103-108 (6) 2.45 2.45

9th anniv. of the enthronement of Sultan Mohamed Farid Didi.

Regal Angelfish, Sultan's Crest and Skin Diver — A15

Tropical Fish: 10 l, 25 l, Moorish idol. 50 l, Diadem squirrelfish. 1r, Surgeonfish. 5r, Orange butterflyfish.

1963, Feb. 2 ***Perf. 13½***
109 A15 2 l multicolored .30 .30
110 A15 3 l multicolored .30 .30
111 A15 5 l multicolored .35 .35
112 A15 10 l multicolored .35 .35
113 A15 25 l multicolored .50 .50
114 A15 50 l multicolored .95 .95
115 A15 1r multicolored 1.90 1.90
116 A15 5r multicolored 12.00 12.00
Nos. 109-116 (8) 16.65 16.65

Fish in Net — A16

Design: 5 l, 10 l, 50 l, Wheat emblem and hand holding rice, vert.

1963, Mar. 21 **Photo.** ***Perf. 12***
117 A16 2 l green & lt brown 1.00 1.00
118 A16 5 l dull rose & lt brn 1.00 1.00
119 A16 7 l grnsh blue & lt brn 1.00 1.00
120 A16 10 l blue & lt brown 1.00 1.00
121 A16 25 l brn red & lt brn 2.50 2.50
122 A16 50 l violet & lt brown 5.00 5.00
123 A16 1r rose cl & lt brn 10.00 10.00
Nos. 117-123 (7) 21.50 21.50

FAO "Freedom from Hunger" campaign.

Centenary Emblem A17

1963, Oct. **Unwmk.** ***Perf. 14x14½***
124 A17 2 l dull purple & red .75 .75
125 A17 15 l slate green & red .75 .75
126 A17 50 l brown & red .95 .95
127 A17 1r dk blue & red 1.90 1.90
128 A17 4r dk ol grn & red 6.50 6.50
Nos. 124-128 (5) 10.85 10.85

Centenary of the International Red Cross.

Scout Emblem and Knot — A18

1963, Dec. 7 **Unwmk.** ***Perf. 13½***
129 A18 2 l purple & dp green .30 .30
130 A18 3 l brown & dp green .30 .30
131 A18 25 l dk blue & dp green .45 .45
132 A18 1r dp car & dp grn .95 .95
Nos. 129-132 (4) 2.00 2.00

11th Boy Scout Jamboree, Marathon, Aug. 1963. Printed in sheets of 12 (3x4) with ornamental borders and inscriptions.

Mosque at Male — A19

Wmk. 314
1964, Aug. 10 **Engr.** ***Perf. 11½***
133 A19 2 l rose violet .25 .25
134 A19 3 l green .25 .25
135 A19 10 l carmine rose .50 .50
136 A19 40 l black brown .50 .50
137 A19 60 l blue .60 .60
138 A19 85 l orange brown .85 .85
Nos. 133-138 (6) 2.95 2.95

Conversion of the Maldive Islanders to Mohammedanism in 1733 (1153 by Islamic calendar).

Shot Put and Maldive Arms A20

15 l, 25 l, 50 l, 1r, Runner, Maldive arms.

Perf. 14x13½
1964, Oct. 6 **Litho.** **Wmk. 314**
139 A20 2 l grnsh bl & dull vio .25 .25
140 A20 3 l red brn & maroon .25 .25
141 A20 5 l dk green & gray .25 .25
142 A20 10 l plum & indigo .40 .40
143 A20 15 l bis brn & dk brn .40 .40
144 A20 25 l dk bl & bluish blk .40 .40
145 A20 50 l olive & black .55 .55
146 A20 1r gray & dk purple 1.10 1.10
a. Souvenir sheet of 3 4.00 4.00
Nos. 139-146 (8) 3.60 3.60

18th Olympic Games, Tokyo, Oct. 10-25. #146a contains 3 imperf. stamps similar to #144-146.

General Electric Observation Communication Satellite — A21

Perf. 14½
1965, July 1 **Photo.** **Unwmk.**
147 A21 5 l dark blue .20 .20
148 A21 10 l brown .20 .20
149 A21 25 l green .45 .45
150 A21 1r magenta 1.75 1.75
Nos. 147-150 (4) 2.60 2.60

Quiet Sun Year, 1964-65. Printed in sheets of 9 (3x3) with ornamental borders and inscriptions.

Queen Nefertari Holding Sistrum and Papyrus — A22

Designs: 3 l, 10 l, 25 l, 1r, Ramses II.

1965, Sept. 1 **Litho.** **Wmk. 314**
151 A22 2 l dull bl grn & mar .30 .30
152 A22 3 l lake & green .30 .30
153 A22 5 l green & lake .30 .30
154 A22 10 l dk blue & ocher .30 .30
155 A22 15 l redsh brn & ind .45 .30
156 A22 25 l dull lil & indigo .75 .30
157 A22 50 l green & brown .95 .45
158 A22 1r brown & green 1.50 .90
Nos. 151-158 (8) 4.85 3.15

UNESCO world campaign to save historic monuments in Nubia.

John F. Kennedy and Doves A23

Design: 1r, 2r, President Kennedy and hands holding olive branches.

Unwmk.
1965, Oct. 1 **Photo.** ***Perf. 12***
159 A23 2 l slate & brt pink .20 .20
160 A23 5 l brown & brt pink .20 .20
161 A23 25 l blue blk & brt pink .20 .20
162 A23 1r red lil, yel & grn .30 .30
163 A23 2r sl green, yel & grn .55 .55
a. Souvenir sheet of 4 2.75 2.75
Nos. 159-163 (5) 1.45 1.45

#163a contains 4 imperf. stamps similar to #163.

UN Flag — A24

1965, Nov. 24 **Photo.** ***Perf. 12***
Flag in Aquamarine
164 A24 3 l red brown .30 .30
165 A24 10 l violet .30 .30
166 A24 1r dark olive brown .60 .45
Nos. 164-166 (3) 1.20 1.05

20th anniversary of the United Nations.

ICY Emblem A25

1965, Dec. 20 **Photo.** ***Perf. 12***
167 A25 5 l bister & dk brn .25 .25
168 A25 15 l dull vio & dk brn .25 .25
169 A25 50 l olive & dk brn .50 .30
170 A25 1r orange & dk brn 1.40 1.10
171 A25 2r blue & dk brn 2.00 2.25
a. Souvenir sheet of 3 8.50 8.50
Nos. 167-171 (5) 4.40 4.15

Intl. Cooperation Year. No. 171a contains three imperf. stamps with simulated perforation similar to Nos. 169-171.

Sea Shells A26

A27

Coat of Arms and: 2 l, 10 l, 30 l, No. 181, Conus alicus and cymatium maldiviensis (shells). 5 l, 10r, Conus litteratus and distorsia reticulata (shells). 7 l, No. 182, 2r, India-rubber vine flowers. 15 l, 50 l, 5r, Crab plover and gull. 3 l, 20 l, 1.50r, Reinwardtia trigynia.

1966, June 1 **Unwmk.** ***Perf. 12***
172 A26 2 l multicolored .20 .45
173 A27 3 l multicolored .20 .45
174 A26 5 l multicolored .40 .30
175 A27 7 l multicolored .40 .30
176 A26 10 l multicolored .75 .30
177 A26 15 l multicolored 3.25 .40
178 A27 20 l multicolored 1.00 .40
179 A26 30 l multicolored 2.40 .40
180 A26 50 l multicolored 5.75 .65
181 A26 1r multicolored 3.75 .65
182 A27 1r multicolored 3.75 .65
183 A27 1.50r multicolored 4.50 2.25
184 A27 2r multicolored 6.25 2.50
185 A26 5r multicolored 20.00 11.50
186 A26 10r multicolored 22.50 15.00
Nos. 172-186 (15) 75.10 36.20

Flag A28

1966, July 26 ***Perf. 14x14½***
187 A28 10 l grnsh blue, red & grn 1.75 .60
188 A28 1r ocher, brn, red & grn 6.25 1.25

1st anniv. of full independence from Great Britain.

Luna 9 on Moon — A29

Designs: 25 l, 1r, 5r, Gemini 6 and 7, rendezvous in space. 2r, Gemini spaceship as seen from second Gemini spaceship.

1966, Nov. 1 **Litho.** ***Perf. 15x14***
189 A29 10 l gray bl, lt brn & ultramarine .25 .25
190 A29 25 l car rose & green .30 .25
191 A29 50 l green & dp org .45 .25
192 A29 1r org brn & grnsh bl .75 .40
193 A29 2r violet & green 1.60 .60
194 A29 5r Prus blue & pink 2.75 1.60
a. Souvenir sheet of 3 7.25 6.75
Nos. 189-194 (6) 6.10 3.35

Rendezvous in space of Gemini 6 and 7 (US), Dec. 4, 1965, and the soft landing on Moon by Luna 9 (USSR), Feb. 3, 1966. No. 194a contains 3 imperf. stamps similar to Nos. 192-194 with simulated perforations.

UNESCO Emblem, Owl and Book — A30

20th anniv. of UNESCO: 3 l, 1r, Microscope, globe and communication waves. 5 l, 5r, Palette, violin and mask.

1966, Nov. 15 **Litho.** ***Perf. 15x14***
195 A30 2 l green & multi .50 .60
196 A30 3 l lt violet & multi .50 .60
197 A30 5 l orange & multi .75 .50
198 A30 50 l rose & multi 4.25 .75
199 A30 1r citron & multi 7.00 1.00
200 A30 5r multicolored 22.50 14.00
Nos. 195-200 (6) 35.50 17.45

Winston Churchill and Coffin on Gun Carriage — A31

10 l, 25 l, 1r, Churchill and catafalque.

1967, Jan. 1 ***Perf. 14½x13½***
201 A31 2 l ol grn, red & dk blue .50 .45
202 A31 10 l Prus grn, red & dk blue 2.25 .35
203 A31 15 l grn, red & dk bl 4.00 .35
204 A31 25 l vio, red & dk bl 5.00 .40
205 A31 1r brn, red & dk bl 10.00 1.00
206 A31 2.50r brn lake, red & dk blue 35.00 12.00
Nos. 201-206 (6) 56.75 14.55

Sir Winston Spencer Churchill (1874-1965), statesman and World War II leader.

Soccer and Jules Rimet Cup — A32

Designs: 3 l, 5 l, 25 l, 50 l, 1r, Various scenes from soccer and Jules Rimet Cup. 2r, British flag, Games' emblem and Big Ben Tower, London.

Perf. 14x13½

1967, Mar. 22 Photo. Unwmk.

207 A32 2 l ver & multi .35 .55
208 A32 3 l olive & multi .35 .55
209 A32 5 l brt purple & multi .35 .55
210 A32 25 l brt green & multi 1.25 .35
211 A32 50 l orange & multi 1.90 .35
212 A32 1r brt blue & multi 3.25 .75
213 A32 2r brown & multi 5.75 3.75
a. Souvenir sheet of 3 12.50 12.50
Nos. 207-213 (7) 13.20 6.85

England's victory in the World Soccer Cup Championship. No. 213a contains 3 imperf. stamps similar to Nos. 211-213.

Clown Butterflyfish — A33

Tropical Fish: 3 l, 1r, Four-saddled puffer. 5 l, Indo-Pacific blue trunkfish. 6 l, Striped triggerfish. 50 l, 2r, Blue angelfish.

1967, May 1 Photo. *Perf. 14*

214 A33 2 l brt violet & multi .25 .35
215 A33 3 l emerald & multi .25 .35
216 A33 5 l org brn & multi .25 .25
217 A33 6 l brt blue & multi .25 .25
218 A33 50 l olive & multi 4.75 .40
219 A33 1r rose red & multi 6.75 .80
220 A33 2r orange & multi 12.00 9.00
Nos. 214-220 (7) 24.50 11.40

Plane at Hulule Airport — A34

Designs: 5 l, 15 l, 50 l, 10r, Plane over administration building, Hulule Airport.

1967, July 26 *Perf. 14x13½*

221 A34 2 l citron & lil .25 .40
222 A34 5 l violet & green .25 .25
223 A34 10 l lt green & lilac .35 .25
224 A34 15 l yel bister & grn .55 .25
225 A34 30 l sky blue & vio bl 1.25 .25
226 A34 50 l brt pink & brn 2.25 .30
227 A34 5r org & vio blue 6.50 5.00
228 A34 10r lt ultra & dp brn 9.50 8.50
Nos. 221-228 (8) 20.90 15.20

For overprints see Nos. 235-242.

Man and Music Pavilion and EXPO '67 Emblem — A35

Designs: 5 l, 50 l, 2r, Man and his Community Pavilion and EXPO '67 emblem.

Perf. 14x13½

1967, Oct. 1 Photo. Unwmk.

EXPO '67 Emblem in Gold

229 A35 2 l ol gray, ol & brt rose .25 .25
230 A35 5 l ultra, grnsh blue & brn .25 .25
231 A35 10 l brn red, lt grn & red org .25 .25
232 A35 50 l brn, grnsh blue & org .45 .25
233 A35 1r vio, grn & rose lil .85 .45
234 A35 2r dk grn, emer & red brn 1.75 1.10
a. Souvenir sheet of 2 5.50 5.50
Nos. 229-234 (6) 3.80 2.55

EXPO '67 Intl. Exhibition, Montreal, Apr. 28-Oct. 27. No. 234a contains 2 imperf. stamps similar to Nos. 233-234 with simulated perforations.

Nos. 221-228 Overprinted in Gold: "International Tourist Year 1967"

1967, Dec. 1 Photo. *Perf. 14x13½*

235 A34 2 l citron & lilac .30 .35
236 A34 5 l violet & green .30 .30
237 A34 10 l lt green & lilac .30 .30
238 A34 15 l yel bister & grn .30 .30
239 A34 30 l sky blue & vio bl .35 .30
240 A34 50 l brt pink & brn .65 .35
241 A34 5r org & vio blue 4.50 3.75
242 A34 10r lt ultra & dp brn 6.75 6.00
Nos. 235-242 (8) 13.45 11.65

The overprint is in 3 lines on the 2 l, 10 l, 30 l, 5r; one line on the 5 l, 15 l, 50 l, 10r.

Lord Baden-Powell, Wolf Cubs, Campfire and Flag Signals — A36

Boy Scouts: 3 l, 1r, Lord Baden-Powell, Boy Scout saluting and drummer.

1968, Jan. 1 Litho. *Perf. 14x14½*

243 A36 2 l yel, brown & green .20 .20
244 A36 3 l lt bl, ultra & rose car .20 .20
245 A36 25 l dp org, red brn & vio blue 1.60 .30
246 A36 1r yel grn, grn & red brn 3.70 1.40
Nos. 243-246 (4) 5.70 2.10

Sheets of 12 (4x3) with decorative border. For overprints see Nos. 278-281.

French Satellites D-1 and A-1 — A37

3 l, 25 l, Luna 10, USSR. 7 l, 1r, Orbiter & Mariner, US. 10 l, 2r, Edward White, Virgil Grissom & Roger Chaffee, US. 5r, Astronaut V. M. Komarov, USSR.

1968, Jan. 27 Photo. *Perf. 14*

247 A37 2 l dp ultra & brt pink .20 .20
248 A37 3 l dk ol bis & vio .20 .20
249 A37 7 l rose car & ol .30 .20
250 A37 10 l blk, gray & dk bl .30 .20
251 A37 25 l purple & brt grn .30 .20
252 A37 50 l brown org & blue .50 .25
253 A37 1r dk sl grn & vio brn 1.00 .30
254 A37 2r blk, bl & dk brn 1.60 1.00
a. Souvenir sheet of 2 5.75 5.75
255 A37 5r blk, tan & lil rose 4.00 2.50
Nos. 247-255 (9) 8.40 5.05

International achievements in space and to honor American and Russian astronauts, who gave their lives during space explorations in 1967. No. 254a contains 2 imperf. stamps similar to Nos. 253-254.

Shot Put — A38

Design: 6 l, 15 l, 2.50r, Discus.

1968, Feb. Litho. *Perf. 14½*

256 A38 2 l emerald & multi .25 .25
257 A38 6 l dull yel & multi .25 .25
258 A38 10 l multicolored .25 .25
259 A38 15 l orange & multi .25 .25
260 A38 1r blue & multi .60 .30
261 A38 2.50r rose & multi 1.60 1.25
Nos. 256-261 (6) 3.20 2.55

19th Olympic Games, Mexico City, 10/12-27.

On the Adria, by Charles P. Bonington — A39

Seascapes: 1r, Ulysses Deriding Polyphemus (detail), by Joseph M. W. Turner. 2r, Sailboat at Argenteuil, by Claude Monet. 5r, Fishing Boats at Saintes-Maries, by Vincent Van Gogh.

1968, Apr. 1 Photo. *Perf. 14*

262 A39 50 l ultra & multi 1.00 .30
263 A39 1r dk green & multi 1.50 .40
264 A39 2r multicolored 2.50 1.50
265 A39 5r multicolored 6.75 4.00
Nos. 262-265 (4) 11.75 6.20

Montgolfier Balloon, 1783, and Zeppelin LZ-130, 1928 — A40

History of Aviation: 3 l, 1r, Douglas DC-3, 1933, and Boeing 707, 1958. 5 l, 50 l, Lilienthal's glider, 1892, and Wright brothers' plane, 1905. 7 l, 2r, British-French Concorde and Supersonic Boeing 733, 1968.

1968, June 1 Photo. *Perf. 14x13*

266 A40 2 l yel grn, ultra & bis brn .25 .35
267 A40 3 l org brn, greenish bl & lil .25 .35
268 A40 5 l grnsh bl, sl grn & lilac .30 .25
269 A40 7 l org, cl & ultra 1.25 .50
270 A40 10 l rose lil, bl & brn .75 .30
271 A40 50 l ol, sl grn & mag 2.50 .35
272 A40 1r ver, blue & emer 4.00 .75
273 A40 2r ultra, ol & brn vio 20.00 10.00
Nos. 266-273 (8) 29.30 12.85

Issued in sheets of 12.

WHO Headquarters, Geneva — A41

1968, July 15 Litho. *Perf. 14½x13*

274 A41 10 l grnsh bl, bl grn & vio .85 .25
275 A41 25 l org, ocher & green 1.25 .25
276 A41 1r emer, brt grn & brown 4.25 .70
277 A41 2r rose lil, dp rose lil & dk blue 8.25 4.75
Nos. 274-277 (4) 14.60 5.95

20th anniv. of WHO.

Nos. 243-246 Overprinted: "International / Boy Scout Jamboree, / Farragut Park, Idaho, / U.S.A. / August 1-9, 1967"

1968, Aug. 1 *Perf. 14x14½*

278 A36 2 l multicolored .25 .35
279 A36 3 l multicolored .25 .35
280 A36 25 l multicolored 1.75 .35
281 A36 1r multicolored 6.00 1.75
Nos. 278-281 (4) 8.25 2.80

1st anniv. of the Intl. Boy Scout Jamboree in Farragut State Park, ID.

Marine Snail Shells — A42

2 l, 50 l, Common curlew & redshank. 1r, Angel wings (clam shell) & marine snail shell.

1968, Sept. 24 Photo. *Perf. 14x13*

282 A42 2 l ultra & multi .70 .70
283 A42 10 l brown & multi 1.50 .30
284 A42 25 l multicolored 1.75 .30
285 A42 50 l multicolored 8.00 1.25
286 A42 1r multicolored 6.50 1.25
287 A42 2r multicolored 7.00 6.00
Nos. 282-287 (6) 25.45 9.80

Discus A43

50 l, Runner. 1r, Bicycling. 2r, Basketball.

1968, Oct. 12 *Perf. 14*

288 A43 10 l ultra & multi .35 .35
289 A43 50 l multicolored .35 .35
290 A43 1r plum & multi 2.75 .45
291 A43 2r violet & multi 4.25 1.40
Nos. 288-291 (4) 7.70 2.55

19th Olympic Games, Mexico City, 10/12-27. For overprints see Nos. 302-303.

Republic

Dhow A44

Republic Day: 1r, Coat of arms, map and flag of Maldive Islands.

Perf. 14x14½

1968, Nov. 11 Unwmk.

292 A44 10 l yel grn, ultra & dk brn 1.25 .30
293 A44 1r ultra, red & emerald 5.00 .85

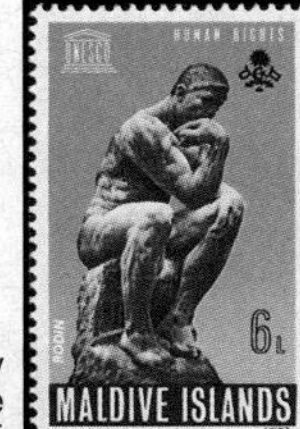

The Thinker, by Auguste Rodin — A45

Rodin Sculptures and UNESCO Emblem: 10 l, Hands. 1.50r, Sister and Brother. 2.50r, The Prodigal Son.

1969, Apr. 10 Photo. *Perf. 13½*

294 A45 6 l emerald & multi .40 .40
295 A45 10 l multicolored .45 .45
296 A45 1.50r brt blue & multi 2.50 2.50
297 A45 2.50r multicolored 3.50 3.50
a. Souvenir sheet of 2 9.50 10.00
Nos. 294-297 (4) 6.85 6.85

Intl. Human Rights Year and honoring UNESCO.

No. 297a contains 2 imperf. stamps similar to Nos. 296-297.

Astronaut Gathering Rock Samples on Moon A46

Designs: 6 l, Lunar landing module. 1.50r, Astronaut on steps of module. 2.50r, Astronaut with television camera.

1969, Sept. 25 Litho. *Perf. 14*

298 A46 6 l multicolored .25 .25
299 A46 10 l multicolored .25 .25
300 A46 1.50r multicolored 3.00 1.40
301 A46 2.50r multicolored 3.25 2.25
a. Souvenir sheet of 4 4.00 4.00
Nos. 298-301 (4) 6.75 4.15

Man's 1st moon landing. See note after US #C76.
Exist imperf.
No. 301a contains stamps similar to Nos. 298-301, with designs transposed on 10 l and 2.50r. Simulated perfs.
For overprints see Nos. 343-345.

Nos. 289-290 Overprinted: "REPUBLIC OF MALDIVES" and Commemorative Inscriptions

Designs: 50 l, overprinted "Gold Medal Winner / Mohamed Gammoudi / 5000m. run / Tunisia." 1r, overprinted "Gold Medal Winner / P. Trentin—Cycling / France."

1969, Dec. 10 Photo. *Perf. 14*

302 A43 50 l multicolored .85 .70
303 A43 1r multicolored 1.40 1.25

Columbia Daumon Victoria, 1899 — A47

Automobiles (pre-1908): 5 l, 50 l, Duryea Phaeton, 1902. 7 l, 1r, Packard S.24, 1906. 10 l, 2r, Autocar Runabout, 1907. 25 l, like 2 l.

1970, Feb. 1 Litho. *Perf. 12*

304 A47 2 l multicolored .20 .20
305 A47 5 l brt pink & multi .30 .20
306 A47 7 l ultra & multi .40 .20
307 A47 10 l ver & multi .45 .20
308 A47 25 l ocher & multi 1.25 .30
309 A47 50 l olive & multi 2.75 .40
310 A47 1r orange & multi 4.00 .70
311 A47 2r multicolored 6.25 4.50
a. Souvenir sheet of 2, #310-311, perf. 11½ 8.00 *8.00*
Nos. 304-311 (8) 15.60 6.70

Exist imperf.

Orange Butterflyfish — A48

Fish: 5 l, Spotted triggerfish. 25 l, Spotfin turkeyfish. 50 l, Forceps fish. 1r, Imperial angelfish. 2r, Regal angelfish.

1970, Mar. 1 Litho. *Perf. 10½*

312 A48 2 l blue & multi 1.10 .60
313 A48 5 l orange & multi 1.10 .60
314 A48 25 l emerald & multi 1.10 .60
315 A48 50 l brt pink & multi 1.75 .75
316 A48 1r lt vio bl & multi 3.50 1.40
317 A48 2r olive & multi 7.25 3.00
Nos. 312-317 (6) 15.80 6.95

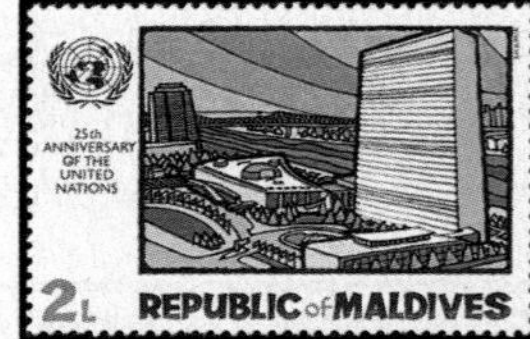

UN Headquarters, New York and UN Emblem — A49

25th anniv. of the UN: 10 l, Surgeons, nurse and WHO emblem. 25 l, Student, performer, musician and UNESCO emblem. 50 l, Children reading and playing, and UNICEF emblem. 1r, Lamb, cock, fish, grain and FAO emblem. 2r, Miner and ILO emblem.

1970, June 26 Litho. *Perf. 13½*

318 A49 2 l multicolored .35 .25
319 A49 10 l multicolored .60 .25
320 A49 25 l multicolored 1.75 .25
321 A49 50 l multicolored 2.40 .30
322 A49 1r multicolored 4.00 .65
323 A49 2r multicolored 6.00 1.25
Nos. 318-323 (6) 15.10 2.95

IMCO Emblem, Buoy and Ship — A50

EXPO Emblem and Australian Pavilion — A51

Design: 1r, Lighthouse and ship.

1970, July 26 Litho. *Perf. 13½*

324 A50 50 l multicolored .75 .30
325 A50 1r multicolored 4.50 .75

10th anniv. of the Intergovernmental Maritime Consultative Organization (IMCO).

1970, Aug. 1 *Perf. 13½x14*

EXPO Emblem and: 3 l, West German pavilion. 10 l, US pavilion. 25 l, British pavilion. 50 l, Russian pavilion. 1r, Japanese pavilion.

326 A51 2 l green & multi .25 .25
327 A51 3 l violet & multi .25 .25
328 A51 10 l brown & multi .40 .25
329 A51 25 l multicolored .95 .25
330 A51 50 l claret & multi 1.60 .35
331 A51 1r ultra & multi 2.10 .70
Nos. 326-331 (6) 5.55 2.05

EXPO '70 International Exhibition, Osaka, Japan, Mar. 15-Sept. 13, 1970.

Guitar Player, by Watteau — A52

Paintings: 7 l, Guitar Player in Spanish Costume, by Edouard Manet. 50 l, Guitar-playing Clown, by Antoine Watteau. 1r, Mandolin Player and Singers, by Lorenzo Costa (inscribed Ercole Roberti). 2.50r, Guitar Player and Lady, by Watteau. 5r, Mandolin Player, by Frans Hals.

1970, Aug. 1 Litho. *Perf. 14*

332 A52 3 l gray & multi .25 .25
333 A52 7 l yellow & multi .25 .25
334 A52 50 l multicolored .60 .60
335 A52 1r multicolored 1.00 1.00
336 A52 2.50r multicolored 2.50 2.50
337 A52 5r multicolored 4.75 4.75
a. Souvenir sheet of 2 8.50 8.00
Nos. 332-337 (6) 9.35 9.35

No. 337a contains 2 stamps similar to Nos. 336-337 but rouletted 13 and printed se-tenant.

Education Year Emblem and Adult Education — A53

Education Year Emblem and: 10 l, Teacher training. 25 l, Geography class. 50 l, Classroom. 1r, Instruction by television.

1970, Sept. 7 Litho. *Perf. 14*

338 A53 5 l multicolored .35 .35
339 A53 10 l multicolored .60 .35
340 A53 25 l multicolored 1.10 .35
341 A53 50 l multicolored 1.40 .60
342 A53 1r multicolored 2.50 1.40
Nos. 338-342 (5) 5.95 3.05

Issued for International Education Year.

Nos. 299-301 Overprinted in Silver: "Philympia / London 1970"

1970, Sept. 18

343 A46 10 l multicolored .30 .30
344 A46 1.50r multicolored 1.00 1.25
345 A46 2.50r multicolored 1.60 2.00
Nos. 343-345 (3) 2.90 3.55

Issued to commemorate Philympia 1970, London Philatelic Exhibition, Sept. 18-26.
This overprint was also applied to No. 301a. Value $10.

Soccer Play, Rimet Cup — A54

Boy Holding UNICEF Flag — A55

Various Soccer Scenes, and Rimet Cup.

1970 Litho. *Perf. 13½*

346 A54 3 l emerald & multi .25 .25
347 A54 6 l rose lilac & multi .40 .25
348 A54 7 l dp orange & multi .40 .25
349 A54 25 l blue & multi .40 .25
350 A54 1r olive & multi 4.50 1.00
Nos. 346-350 (5) 5.95 2.00

Jules Rimet 9th World Soccer Championships, Mexico City, May 30-June 21.

1971, Apr. 1 Litho. *Perf. 12*

UNICEF, 25th. Anniv.: 10 l, 2r, Girl holding balloon with UNICEF emblem.

351 A55 5 l pink & multi .30 .25
352 A55 10 l lt blue & multi .30 .25
353 A55 1r yellow & multi 2.25 .70
354 A55 2r pale lilac & multi 4.00 1.10
Nos. 351-354 (4) 6.85 2.30

Astronauts Swigert, Lovell and Haise — A56

Flowers Symbolizing Races and World — A57

Safe return of Apollo 13: 20 l, Spacecraft and landing module. 1r, Capsule and boat in Pacific Ocean.

1971, Apr. 27 *Perf. 14*

355 A56 5 l dull purple & multi .25 .25
356 A56 20 l multicolored .25 .25
357 A56 1r brt blue & multi 1.40 .70
Nos. 355-357 (3) 1.90 1.20

1971, May 3

358 A57 10 l multicolored .30 .30
359 A57 25 l gray & multi .30 .30

Intl. year against racial discrimination.

Mother and Child, by Auguste Renoir A58

Mother and Child Paintings by: 7 l, Rembrandt. 10 l, Titian. 20 l, Degas. 25 l, Berthe Morisot. 1r, Rubens. 3r, Renoir.

1971, Sept. Litho. *Perf. 12*

360 A58 5 l multicolored .25 .25
361 A58 7 l multicolored .35 .25
362 A58 10 l multicolored .35 .25
363 A58 20 l multicolored 1.25 .25
364 A58 25 l multicolored 1.40 .25
365 A58 1r multicolored 3.75 .70
366 A58 3r multicolored 7.75 5.00
Nos. 360-366 (7) 15.10 6.95

Capt. Alan B. Shepard, Jr. — A59

10 l, Maj. Stuart A. Roosa. 1.50r, Com. Edgar D. Mitchell. 5r, Apollo 14 shoulder patch.

1971, Nov. 11 Photo. *Perf. 12½*

367 A59 6 l dp green & multi .30 .30
368 A59 10 l claret & multi .45 .30

369 A59 1.50r ultra & multi 5.25 3.00
370 A59 5r multicolored 10.50 9.00
Nos. 367-370 (4) 16.50 12.60

Apollo 14 US moon landing mission, 1/31-2/9.

Ballerina, by Degas
A60

Paintings: 10 l, Dancing Couple, by Auguste Renoir. 2r, Spanish Dancer, by Edouard Manet. 5r, Ballerinas, by Degas. 10r, Moulin Rouge, by Henri Toulouse-Lautrec.

1971, Nov. 19 Litho. *Perf. 14*

371 A60 5 l plum & multi .25 .25
372 A60 10 l green & multi .25 .25
373 A60 2r org brn & multi 2.75 2.10
374 A60 5r dk blue & multi 5.50 4.25
375 A60 10r multicolored 7.75 7.75
Nos. 371-375 (5) 16.50 14.60

Nos. 371-375 Overprinted Vertically: "ROYAL VISIT 1972"

1972, Mar. 13 Litho. *Perf. 14*

376 A60 5 l plum & multi .20 .20
377 A60 10 l green & multi .20 .20
378 A60 2r org brn & multi 5.00 3.00
379 A60 5r dk blue & multi 9.00 6.00
380 A60 10r multicolored 10.00 8.50
Nos. 376-380 (5) 24.40 17.90

Visit of Elizabeth II and Prince Philip.

Book Year Emblem
A61

1972, May 1 *Perf. 13x13½*

381 A61 25 l orange & multi .35 .20
382 A61 5r multicolored 2.50 1.50

International Book Year.

National Costume of Scotland
A62

National Costumes: 15 l, Netherlands. 25 l, Norway. 50 l, Hungary. 1r, Austria. 2r, Spain.

1972, May 15 *Perf. 12*

383 A62 10 l gray & multi .65 .25
384 A62 15 l lt brown & multi .70 .25
385 A62 25 l multicolored 1.25 .25
386 A62 50 l lt brown & multi 2.10 .40
387 A62 1r gray & multi 3.00 .70
388 A62 2r lt olive & multi 5.00 2.40
Nos. 383-388 (6) 12.70 4.25

Stegosaurus — A63

Designs: Prehistoric reptiles.

1972, May 31 *Perf. 14*

389 A63 2 l shown .65 .50
390 A63 7 l Edaphosaurus 1.10 .45
391 A63 25 l Diplodocus 2.25 .45
392 A63 50 l Triceratops 2.25 .75
393 A63 2r Pteranodon 6.00 6.00
394 A63 5r Tyrannosaurus 12.00 12.00
Nos. 389-394 (6) 24.25 20.15

A souvenir sheet has two stamps similar to Nos. 393-394 with simulated perforations. It was not regularly issued. Value, $50.

Sapporo '72 Emblem, Cross Country Skiing
A64

1972, June Litho. *Perf. 14*

395 A64 3 l shown .25 .25
396 A64 6 l Bobsledding .25 .25
397 A64 15 l Speed skating .25 .25
398 A64 50 l Ski jump 1.00 .40
399 A64 1r Figure skating 1.75 .85
400 A64 2.50r Ice hockey 6.25 2.75
Nos. 395-400 (6) 9.75 4.75

11th Winter Olympic Games, Sapporo, Japan, Feb. 3-13.

Boy Scout Saluting — A65

Olympic Emblems, Bicycling — A66

Scout: 15 l, with signal flags. 50 l, Bugler. 1r, Drummer.

1972, Aug. 1

401 A65 10 l Prus green & multi .70 .25
402 A65 15 l dk red & multi 1.00 .25
403 A65 50 l dp green & multi 3.50 1.00
404 A65 1r purple & multi 5.00 1.75
Nos. 401-404 (4) 10.20 3.25

13th International Boy Scout Jamboree, Asagiri Plain, Japan, Aug. 2-11, 1971.

1972, Oct. Litho. *Perf. 14½x14*

405 A66 5 l shown .30 .30
406 A66 10 l Running .30 .30
407 A66 25 l Wrestling .30 .30
408 A66 50 l Hurdles, women's .40 .40
409 A66 2r Boxing 1.60 1.60
410 A66 5r Volleyball 4.00 4.00
Nos. 405-410 (6) 6.90 6.90

Souvenir Sheet

Perf. 15

411 Sheet of 2 7.50 7.50
a. A66 3r like 50 l 2.40 2.40
b. A66 4r like 10 l 3.00 3.00

20th Olympic Games, Munich, 8/26-9/11.
For overprints see Nos. 417-419.

Globe, Environment Emblem — A67

1972, Nov. 15 Litho. *Perf. 14½*

412 A67 2 l violet & multi .25 .25
413 A67 3 l brown & multi .25 .25
414 A67 15 l blue & multi .35 .35
415 A67 50 l red & multi .90 .90
416 A67 2.50r green & multi 4.00 4.00
Nos. 412-416 (5) 5.75 5.75

UN Conference on Human Environment, Stockholm, June 5-16.

Nos. 409-411 Overprinted in Violet Blue:
a. LEMECHEV / MIDDLE-WEIGHT /GOLD MEDALLIST
b. JAPAN / GOLD MEDAL / WINNER
c. EHRHARDT / 100 METER / HURDLES / GOLD MEDALLIST
d. SHORTER / MARATHON / GOLD MEDALLIST

1973, Feb. Litho. *Perf. 14½x14*

417 A66(a) 2r multicolored 4.25 3.50
418 A66(b) 5r multicolored 6.00 5.25

Souvenir Sheet

419 Sheet of 2 10.00 *10.00*
a. A66(c) 3r multicolored 3.25 *3.25*
b. A66(d) 4r multicolored 3.50 *3.50*

Gold medal winners in 20th Olympic Games: Viatschesiav Lemechev, USSR, middleweight boxing; Japanese team, volleyball. Annelie Ehrhardt, Germany, 100m. hurdles; Frank Shorter, US, marathon.

Flowers, by Vincent Van Gogh — A68

Paintings of Flowers by: 2 l, 3 l, 1r, 3r, 5r, Auguste Renoir (each different). 50 l, 5 l, Ambrosius Bosschaert.

1973, Feb. *Perf. 13½*

420 A68 1 l blue & multi .35 .35
421 A68 2 l tan & multi .35 .35
422 A68 3 l lilac & multi .35 .35
423 A68 50 l ultra & multi .90 .45
424 A68 1r emerald & multi 1.40 .45
425 A68 5r magenta & multi 4.50 4.50
Nos. 420-425 (6) 7.85 6.45

Souvenir Sheet

Perf. 15

426 Sheet of 2 9.50 *11.00*
a. A68 2r black & multi 2.00 *2.25*
b. A68 3r black & multi 2.50 *2.75*

Scouts Treating Injured Lamb
A69

Designs: 2 l, 1r, Lifesaving. 3 l, 5r, Agricultural training. 4 l, 2r, Carpentry. 5 l, Leapfrog.

1973, Aug. Litho. *Perf. 14½*

427 A69 1 l black & multi .25 .25
428 A69 2 l black & multi .25 .25
429 A69 3 l black & multi .25 .25
430 A69 4 l black & multi .25 .25
431 A69 5 l black & multi .25 .25
432 A69 1r black & multi 2.50 .60
433 A69 2r black & multi 5.00 3.75
434 A69 3r black & multi 6.25 6.25
Nos. 427-434 (8) 15.00 11.85

Souvenir Sheet

435 A69 5r black & multi 10.00 *11.50*

24th Boy Scout World Conference (1st in Africa), Nairobi, Kenya, July 16-21.
For overprints see Nos. 571-574.

Herschel's Marlin
A70

Fish and Ships: 2 l, 4r, Skipjack tuna. 3 l, Bluefin tuna. 5 l, 2.50r, Dolphinfish. 60 l, 75 l, Red snapper. 1.50r, Yellow crescent tail. 3r, Plectropoma maculatum. 5r, Like 1 l. 10r, Spanish mackerel.

1973, Aug. *Perf. 14½*

Size: 38½x24mm

436 A70 1 l lt green & multi .25 .25
437 A70 2 l dull org & multi .25 .25
438 A70 3 l brt red & multi .25 .25
439 A70 5 l multicolored .25 .25

Size: 28x22mm

440 A70 60 l yellow & multi .80 .40
441 A70 75 l purple & multi 1.00 .40

Size: 38½x24mm

442 A70 1.50r violet & multi 1.60 1.40
443 A70 2.50r blue & multi 2.00 2.00
444 A70 3r multicolored 2.50 2.50
445 A70 10r orange & multi 6.00 6.50
Nos. 436-445 (10) 14.90 14.20

Souvenir Sheet

Perf. 15

446 Sheet of 2 18.50 18.50
a. A70 4r carmine & multi 5.00 5.00
b. A70 5r bright green & multi 6.00 6.00

Nos. 436-445 exist imperf.

Goldenfronted Leafbird — A71

2 l, 3r, Fruit bat. 3 l, 50 l, Indian starred tortoise. 4 l, 5r, Kallima inachus (butterfly).

1973, Oct. Litho. *Perf. 14½*

447 A71 1 l brt pink & multi .25 .25
448 A71 2 l brt blue & multi .25 .25
449 A71 3 l ver & multi .35 .35
450 A71 4 l citron & multi .50 .35
451 A71 50 l emerald & multi .90 .50
452 A71 2r lt violet & multi 4.75 4.25
453 A71 3r multicolored 3.50 3.25
Nos. 447-453 (7) 10.50 9.20

Souvenir Sheet

454 A71 5r yellow & multi 22.50 22.50

Lantana Camara — A72

Native Flowers: 2 l, Nerium oleander. 3 l, 2r, Rosa polyantha. 4 l, Hibiscus manihot. 5 l, Bougainvillea glabra. 10 l, 3r, Plumera alba. 50 l, Poinsettia pulcherrima. 5r, Ononis natrix.

1973, Dec. 19 Litho. *Perf. 14*

No.	Type	Description	Unused	Used
455	A72	1 l ultra & multi	.30	.30
456	A72	2 l dp orange & multi	.30	.30
457	A72	3 l emerald & multi	.30	.30
458	A72	4 l blue grn & multi	.30	.30
459	A72	5 l lemon & multi	.30	.30
460	A72	10 l lilac & multi	.30	.30
461	A72	50 l yel grn & multi	.30	.30
462	A72	5r red & multi	3.00	3.00
		Nos. 455-462 (8)	5.10	5.10

Souvenir Sheet

No.	Type	Description	Unused	Used
463		Sheet of 2	5.75	6.50
a.	A72	2r lilac & multi	1.25	1.50
b.	A72	3r blue & multi	2.00	2.25

Tiros Weather Satellite A73

Designs: 2 l, 10r, Nimbus satellite. 3 l, 3r, Nomad weather ("weater") station. 4 l, A.P.T. instant weather picture (radar). 5 l, Richard's electrical wind speed recorder. 2r, like 1 l.

1974, Jan. 10 *Perf. 14½*

No.	Type	Description	Unused	Used
464	A73	1 l olive & multi	.25	.25
465	A73	2 l multicolored	.25	.25
466	A73	3 l brt blue & multi	.35	.35
467	A73	4 l ocher & multi	.35	.35
468	A73	5 l ocher & multi	.35	.35
469	A73	2r ultra & multi	2.75	3.50
470	A73	3r orange & multi	4.50	3.00
		Nos. 464-470 (7)	8.80	8.05

Souvenir Sheet

No.	Type	Description	Unused	Used
471	A73	10r lilac & multi	10.50	*10.50*

World Meteorological Cooperation, cent.

Apollo Spacecraft, John F. Kennedy — A74

Designs: 2 l, 3r, Mercury spacecraft and John Glenn. 3 l, Vostok 1 and Yuri Gagarin. 4 l, Vostok 6 and Valentina Tereshkova. 5 l, Soyuz 11 and Salyut spacecrafts. 2r, Skylab. 10r, Like 1 l.

1974, Feb. 1 Litho. *Perf. 14½*

No.	Type	Description	Unused	Used
472	A74	1 l multicolored	.25	.25
473	A74	2 l multicolored	.25	.25
474	A74	3 l multicolored	.35	.35
475	A74	4 l multicolored	.35	.35
476	A74	5 l multicolored	.35	.35
477	A74	2r multicolored	3.50	3.50
478	A74	3r multicolored	5.50	5.50
		Nos. 472-478 (7)	10.55	10.55

Souvenir Sheet

No.	Type	Description	Unused	Used
479	A74	10r multicolored	13.50	*13.50*

Space explorations of US and USSR.

Skylab and Copernicus — A75

Copernicus, Various Portraits and: 2 l, 1.50r, Futuristic orbiting station. 3 l, 5r, Futuristic flight station. 4 l, Mariner 2 on flight to Venus. 5 l, Mariner 4 on flight to Mars. 25 l, like 1 l. 10r, Copernicus Orbiting Observatory.

1974, Apr. 10 Litho. *Perf. 14½*

No.	Type	Description	Unused	Used
480	A75	1 l multicolored	.20	.20
481	A75	2 l multicolored	.20	.20
482	A75	3 l multicolored	.20	.20
483	A75	4 l multicolored	.40	.40
484	A75	5 l multicolored	.40	.40
485	A75	25 l multicolored	1.40	1.40
486	A75	1.50r multicolored	4.75	4.75
487	A75	5r multicolored	9.50	9.50
		Nos. 480-487 (8)	17.05	17.05

Souvenir Sheet

No.	Type	Description	Unused	Used
488	A75	10r multicolored	21.00	*22.50*

"Motherhood," by Picasso — A76

Picasso Paintings: 2 l, Harlequin and his Companion. 3 l, Pierrot Sitting. 20 l, 2r, Three Musicians. 75 l, L'Aficionada. 3r, 5r, Still life.

1974, May *Perf. 14*

No.	Type	Description	Unused	Used
489	A76	1 l multicolored	.30	.30
490	A76	2 l multicolored	.30	.30
491	A76	3 l multicolored	.30	.30
492	A76	20 l multicolored	.30	.30
493	A76	75 l multicolored	.70	.70
494	A76	5r multicolored	4.75	4.75
		Nos. 489-494 (6)	6.65	6.65

Souvenir Sheet

No.	Type	Description	Unused	Used
495		Sheet of 2	8.50	8.50
a.	A76	2r multicolored	1.90	1.90
b.	A76	3r multicolored	3.00	3.00

Pablo Picasso (1881-1973), painter.

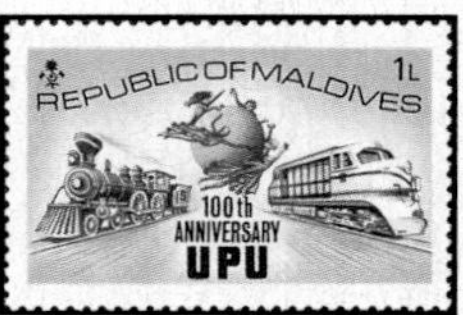

UPU Emblem, Old and New Trains A77

UPU Emblem and: 2 l, 2.50r, Old and new ships. 3 l, Zeppelin and jet. 1.50r, Mail coach and truck. 4r, 5r, Like 1 l.

1974, May Litho. *Perf. 14½, 13½*

No.	Type	Description	Unused	Used
496	A77	1 l lt green & multi	.30	.30
497	A77	2 l yellow & multi	.30	.30
498	A77	3 l rose & multi	.30	.30
499	A77	1.50r yel green & multi	1.00	1.00
500	A77	2.50r blue & multi	1.75	1.75
501	A77	5r ocher & multi	3.00	3.00
		Nos. 496-501 (6)	6.65	6.65

Souvenir Sheet

No.	Type	Description	Unused	Used
502	A77	4r ver & multi	*6.00*	6.00

UPU cent. No. 502 exists imperf.

Nos. 496-501 were printed in sheets of 50, perf. 14½, and also in sheets of 5 plus label, perf. 13½. The label shows UPU emblem, post horn, globe and carrier pigeon.

Capricorn A78

Designs: Zodiac signs and constellations.

1974, July 3

No.	Type	Description	Unused	Used
503	A78	1 l shown	.25	.25
504	A78	2 l Aquarius	.25	.25
505	A78	3 l Pisces	.25	.25
506	A78	4 l Aries	.25	.25
507	A78	5 l Taurus	.25	.25
508	A78	6 l Gemini	.25	.25
509	A78	7 l Cancer	.25	.25
510	A78	10 l Leo	.25	.25
511	A78	15 l Virgo	.25	.25
512	A78	20 l Libra	.25	.25
513	A78	25 l Scorpio	.25	.25
514	A78	5r Sagittarius	7.50	7.50
		Nos. 503-514 (12)	10.25	10.25

Souvenir Sheet

No.	Type	Description	Unused	Used
515	A78	10r Sun	21.00	*21.00*

Stamp size of 10r: 50x37mm.

Soccer and Games' Emblem — A79

Various soccer scenes & games' emblem.

1974, July 31 Litho. *Perf. 14½*

No.	Type	Description	Unused	Used
516	A79	1 l brown & multi	.25	.25
517	A79	2 l green & multi	.25	.25
518	A79	3 l ultra & multi	.25	.25
519	A79	4 l red & multi	.25	.25
520	A79	75 l lt blue & multi	1.25	.75
521	A79	4r olive & multi	3.00	2.50
522	A79	5r lilac & multi	3.50	3.00
		Nos. 516-522 (7)	8.75	7.25

Souvenir Sheet

No.	Type	Description	Unused	Used
523	A79	10r rose & multi	12.50	12.50

World Cup Soccer Championship, Munich, June 13-July 7.

Churchill and WWII Plane A80

Churchill: 2 l, As pilot. 3 l, First Lord of the Admiralty and battleship. 4 l, 10r, Aircraft carrier. 5 l, RAF fighters. 60 l, Anti-aircraft unit. 75 l, Tank. 5r, Seaplane.

1974, Nov. 30 Litho. *Perf. 14½*

No.	Type	Description	Unused	Used
524	A80	1 l multicolored	.25	.25
525	A80	2 l multicolored	.25	.25
526	A80	3 l multicolored	.30	.30
527	A80	4 l multicolored	.30	.30
528	A80	5 l multicolored	.30	.30
529	A80	60 l multicolored	3.00	3.00
530	A80	75 l multicolored	3.50	3.50
531	A80	5r multicolored	12.00	12.00
		Nos. 524-531 (8)	19.90	19.90

Souvenir Sheet

No.	Type	Description	Unused	Used
532	A80	10r multicolored	20.00	20.00

Sir Winston Churchill (1874-1965).

Cassis Nana — A81

Cypraea Diliculum — A82

1975, Jan. 25 *Perf. 14½, 14 (A82)*

No.	Type	Description	Unused	Used
533	A81	1 l shown	.25	.25
534	A81	2 l Murex triremus	.25	.25
535	A81	3 l Harpa major	.30	.30
536	A81	4 l Lambis chiragra	.30	.30
537	A81	5 l Conus pennaceus	.30	.30
538	A82	60 l shown	2.75	2.75
539	A82	75 l Clanculus pharaonis	3.25	3.25
540	A81	5r Chicoreus ramosus	7.25	*7.25*
		Nos. 533-540 (8)	14.65	*14.65*

Souvenir Sheet

Perf. 13½

No.	Type	Description	Unused	Used
541		Sheet of 2	14.50	14.50
a.	A81	2r like 3 l	3.75	3.75
b.	A81	3r like 2 l	4.75	4.75

Sea shells, including cowries.

Throne — A83

Eid-Miskith Mosque — A84

Designs: 10 l, Ornamental candlesticks (dul-lisa). 25 l, Tree-shaped lamp. 60 l, Royal umbrellas. 3r, Tomb of Al-Hafiz Abu-al Barakath al-Barubari.

1975, Feb. 22 Litho. *Perf. 14*

No.	Type	Description	Unused	Used
542	A83	1 l multicolored	.20	.20
543	A83	10 l multicolored	.20	.20
544	A83	25 l multicolored	.20	.20
545	A83	60 l multicolored	.30	.30
546	A84	75 l multicolored	.40	.40
547	A84	3r multicolored	1.60	1.60
		Nos. 542-547 (6)	2.90	2.90

Historic relics and monuments.

Tropical Fruit — A85

1975, Mar. Litho. *Perf. 14½*

No.	Type	Description	Unused	Used
548	A85	2 l Guava	.25	.25
549	A85	4 l Maldive mulberry	.25	.25
550	A85	5 l Mountain apples	.25	.25
551	A85	10 l Bananas	.25	.25
552	A85	20 l Mangoes	.25	.25
553	A85	50 l Papaya	.90	.60
554	A85	1r Pomegranates	1.40	.65
555	A85	5r Coconut	8.25	8.75
		Nos. 548-555 (8)	11.80	11.25

Souvenir Sheet

Perf. 13½

No.	Type	Description	Unused	Used
556		Sheet of 2	10.00	*11.00*
a.	A85	2r like 10 l	2.50	*3.00*
b.	A85	3r like 2 l	3.00	*3.50*

Phyllangia — A86

Designs: Corals, sea urchins and starfish.

1975, June 6 Litho. *Perf. 14½*

No.	Type	Description	Unused	Used
557	A86	1 l shown	.25	.25
558	A86	2 l Madrepora oculata	.25	.25
559	A86	3 l Acropora gravida	.25	.25
560	A86	4 l Stylotella	.25	.25
561	A86	5 l Acropora cervicornis	.25	.25
562	A86	60 l Strongylocentrotus pupuratus	.75	.65
563	A86	75 l Pisaster ochraceus	.90	.75
564	A86	5r Marthasterias glacialis	4.50	5.25
		Nos. 557-564 (8)	7.40	7.90

Souvenir Sheet

Imperf

No.	Type	Description	Unused	Used
565	A86	4r shown	14.00	14.00

"10," Clock Tower and Customs House
A87

"10" and: 5 l, Government offices. 7 l, North Eastern waterfront, Male. 15 l, Mosque and Minaret. 10r, Sultan Park and Museum.

1975, July 26 Litho. *Perf. 14½*

566 A87 4 l salmon & multi .25 .25
567 A87 5 l lt blue & multi .25 .25
568 A87 7 l bister & multi .25 .25
569 A87 15 l lilac & multi .25 .25
570 A87 10r lt green & multi 3.50 *5.75*
Nos. 566-570 (5) 4.50 *6.75*

10th anniversary of independence.

Nos. 432-435 Overprinted: "14th Boy Scout Jamboree / July 29-Aug. 7, 1975"

1975, July 26 Litho. *Perf. 14½*

571 A69 1r multicolored .65 .65
572 A69 2r multicolored 1.00 1.00
573 A69 3r multicolored 3.00 3.00
Nos. 571-573 (3) 4.65 4.65

Souvenir Sheet

574 A69 5r multicolored 10.50 10.50

Nordjamb 75, 14th World Boy Scout Jamboree, Lillehammer, Norway, July 29-Aug. 7.

Madura-Prau Bedang — A88

Sailing ships, except 5r: 2 l, Ganges patile. 3 l, Indian palla, vert. 4 l, "Odhi," vert. 5 l, Maldivian schooner. 25 l, Cutty Sark. 1r, 10r, Maldivian baggala, vert. 5r, Freighter Maldive Courage.

1975, July 26 *Perf. 14½*

575 A88 1 l multicolored .25 .25
576 A88 2 l multicolored .25 .25
577 A88 3 l multicolored .25 .25
578 A88 4 l multicolored .25 .25
579 A88 5 l multicolored .25 .25
580 A88 25 l multicolored .65 .30
581 A88 1r multicolored 1.25 .75
582 A88 5r multicolored 3.75 *5.75*
Nos. 575-582 (8) 6.90 8.05

Souvenir Sheet

Perf. 13½

583 A88 10r multicolored 12.50 *12.50*

Brahmaea Wallichii
A89

Designs: Butterflies.

1975, Sept. 7 Litho. *Perf. 14½*

584 A89 1 l shown .25 .25
585 A89 2 l Teoinopalpus imperialis .25 .25
586 A89 3 l Cethosia biblis .30 .30
587 A89 4 l Hestia jasonia .30 .30
588 A89 5 l Apatura .30 .30
589 A89 25 l Kallima horsfieldi 1.50 1.50
590 A89 1.50r Hebomoia leucippe 4.00 4.00
591 A89 5r Papilio memnon 10.00 10.00
Nos. 584-591 (8) 16.90 16.90

Souvenir Sheet

Perf. 13½

592 A89 10r like 25 l 27.50 27.50

Dying Slave by Michelangelo
A90

Cup and Vase
A91

Works by Michelangelo: 2 l, 4 l, 1r, 5r, paintings from Sistine Chapel. 3 l, Apollo. 5 l, Bacchus. 2r, 10r, David.

1975, Oct. 9 Litho. *Perf. 14½*

593 A90 1 l blue & multi .25 .25
594 A90 2 l multicolored .25 .25
595 A90 3 l red & multi .25 .25
596 A90 4 l multicolored .25 .25
597 A90 5 l emerald & multi .25 .25
598 A90 1r multicolored .70 .70
599 A90 2r red & multi 1.50 1.50
600 A90 5r multicolored 4.00 4.00
Nos. 593-600 (8) 7.45 7.45

Souvenir Sheet

Perf. 13½

601 A90 10r multicolored 7.50 7.50

Michelangelo Buonarotti (1475-1564), Italian sculptor, painter and architect.

1975, Dec. Litho. *Perf. 14*

Designs: 4 l, Boxes. 50 l, Vase with lid. 75 l, Bowls with covers. 1r, Worker finishing vases.

602 A91 2 l ultra & multi .20 .20
603 A91 4 l rose & multi .20 .20
604 A91 50 l multicolored .30 .30
605 A91 75 l blue & multi .45 .45
606 A91 1r multicolored .55 .55
Nos. 602-606 (5) 1.70 1.70

Maldivian lacquer ware.

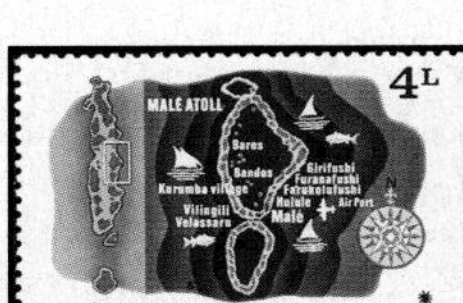

Map of Islands and Atolls
A92

Designs: 5 l, Yacht at anchor. 7 l, Sailboats. 15 l, Deep-sea divers and corals. 3r, Hulule Airport. 10r, Cruising yachts.

1975, Dec. 25 Litho. *Perf. 14*

607 A92 4 l multicolored .30 .30
608 A92 5 l multicolored .30 .30
609 A92 7 l multicolored .30 .30
610 A92 15 l multicolored .30 .30
611 A92 3r multicolored 2.40 2.40
612 A92 10r multicolored 6.50 7.00
Nos. 607-612 (6) 10.10 10.60

Tourist publicity.

Cross-country Skiing — A93

Gen. Burgoyne, by Joshua Reynolds — A94

Winter Olympic Games' Emblem and: 2 l, Speed skating. 3 l, Figure skating, pair. 4 l, Bobsled. 5 l, Ski jump. 25 l, Figure skating, woman. 1.15r, Slalom. 4r, Ice hockey. 10r, Skiing.

1976, Jan. 10 Litho. *Perf. 14½*

613 A93 1 l multicolored .30 .30
614 A93 2 l multicolored .30 .30
615 A93 3 l multicolored .30 .30
616 A93 4 l multicolored .30 .30
617 A93 5 l multicolored .30 .30
618 A93 25 l multicolored .40 .30
619 A93 1.15r multicolored .75 .75
620 A93 4r multicolored 2.25 2.25
Nos. 613-620 (8) 4.90 4.80

Souvenir Sheet

Perf. 13½

621 A93 10r multicolored 8.00 *9.00*

12th Winter Olympic Games, Innsbruck, Austria, Feb. 4-15. Exist imperf.

1976, Feb. 15 *Perf. 14½*

Paintings: 2 l, John Hancock, by John S. Copley. 3 l, Death of Gen. Montgomery, by John Trumbull, horiz. 4 l, Paul Revere, by Copley. 5 l, Battle of Bunker Hill, by Trumbull, horiz. 2r, Crossing of the Delaware, by Thomas Sully, horiz. 3r, Samuel Adams, by Copley. 5r, Surrender of Cornwallis, by Trumbull, horiz. 10r, Washington at Dorchester Heights, by Gilbert Stuart.

622 A94 1 l multicolored .25 .25
623 A94 2 l multicolored .25 .25
624 A94 3 l multicolored .25 .25
625 A94 4 l multicolored .25 .25
626 A94 5 l multicolored .25 .25
627 A94 2r multicolored 1.50 1.50
628 A94 3r multicolored 2.10 2.10
629 A94 5r multicolored 3.50 3.50
Nos. 622-629 (8) 8.35 8.35

Souvenir Sheet

Perf. 13½

630 A94 10r multicolored 17.00 *17.00*

American Bicentennial.

For overprints see Nos. 639-642.

Thomas Alva Edison
A95

Designs: 2 l, Alexander Graham Bell and his telephone. 3 l, Telephones of 1919, 1937 and 1972. 10 l, Cable tunnel. 20 l, Equalizer circuit assembly. 1r, Ships laying underwater cable. 4r, Telephones of 1876, 1890 and 1879 Edison telephone. 10r, Intelsat IV-A over earth station.

1976, Mar. 10 Litho. *Perf. 14½*

631 A95 1 l multicolored .25 .25
632 A95 2 l multicolored .25 .25
633 A95 3 l multicolored .25 .25
634 A95 10 l multicolored .25 .25
635 A95 20 l multicolored .25 .25
636 A95 1r multicolored .65 .65
637 A95 10r multicolored 6.50 6.50
Nos. 631-637 (7) 8.40 8.40

Souvenir Sheet

Perf. 13½

638 A95 4r multicolored 11.50 *11.50*

Centenary of first telephone call by Alexander Graham Bell, Mar. 10, 1876.

Nos. 627-630 Overprinted in Silver or Black: MAY 29TH-JUNE 6TH "INTERPHIL" 1976

1976, May 29 Litho. *Perf. 14½*

639 A94 2r multicolored (S) 1.75 1.75
640 A94 3r multicolored (S) 2.25 2.25
641 A94 5r multicolored (B) 3.50 3.50
Nos. 639-641 (3) 7.50 7.50

Souvenir Sheet

Perf. 13½

642 A94 10r multicolored (S) 13.50 13.50

Interphil 76 Intl. Philatelic Exhibition, Philadelphia, Pa., May 29-June 6. Overprint on 3r and 10r vertical. Same overprint in one horizontal silver line in margin of No. 642.

Wrestling — A96

Bonavist Beans — A97

Olympic Rings and: 2 l, Shot put. 3 l, Hurdles. 4 l, Hockey. 5 l, Women running. 6 l, Javelin. 1.50r, Discus. 5r, Team handball. 10r, Hammer throw.

1976, June 1 *Perf. 14½*

643 A96 1 l multicolored .20 .20
644 A96 2 l multicolored .20 .20
645 A96 3 l salmon & multi .20 .20
646 A96 4 l multicolored .20 .20
647 A96 5 l pink & multi .20 .20
648 A96 6 l multicolored .20 .20
649 A96 1.50r bister & multi 1.10 1.00
650 A96 5r lilac & multi 3.50 3.75
Nos. 643-650 (8) 5.80 5.95

Souvenir Sheet

Perf. 13½

651 A96 10r lemon & multi 9.25 *10.00*

21st Olympic Games, Montreal, Canada, July 17-Aug. 1.

1976-77 Litho. *Perf. 14*

Designs: 4 l, 20 l, Beans. 10 l, Eggplant. 50 l, Cucumber. 75 l, 2r, Snake gourd. 1r, Balsam pear.

652 A97 2 l green & multi .25 .25
653 A97 4 l lt blue & multi .60 .60
654 A97 10 l ocher & multi .60 .60
655 A97 20 l blue & multi ('77) .60 .60
656 A97 50 l multicolored .75 .75
657 A97 75 l bister & multi 1.00 1.00
658 A97 1r lilac & multi 1.40 1.40
659 A97 2r bis & multi ('77) 2.50 2.50
Nos. 652-659 (8) 7.70 7.70

1976 stamps issued July 26.

Viking I and Mars
A98

Design: 20r, Landing craft on Mars.

1976, Dec. 2 Litho. *Perf. 14*

660 A98 5r multicolored 3.00 3.00

Souvenir Sheet

661 A98 20r multicolored 13.00 *13.00*

Viking I US Mars Mission.

Coronation Ceremony — A99

Designs: 2 l, Elizabeth II and Prince Philip. 3 l, Queen, Prince Philip, Princes Edward and Andrew. 1.15r, Queen in procession. 3r, State coach. 4r, Queen, Prince Philip, Princess Anne and Prince Charles. 10r, Queen and Prince Charles.

1977, Feb. 6 *Perf. 14x13½, 12*

662 A99 1 l multicolored .40 .40
663 A99 2 l multicolored .40 .40
664 A99 3 l multicolored .40 .40
665 A99 1.15r multicolored .55 .50
666 A99 3r multicolored 1.10 *1.25*
667 A99 4r multicolored 1.10 *1.40*
Nos. 662-667 (6) 3.95 *4.35*

Souvenir Sheet

668 A99 10r multicolored 5.75 5.75

25th anniv. of the reign of Elizabeth II.

Nos. 662-667 were printed in sheets of 40 (4x10), perf. 14x13½, and sheets of 5 plus label, perf. 12, in changed colors.

Beethoven in Bonn, 1785 — A100

Designs: 2 l, Moonlight Sonata and portrait, 1801. 3 l, Goethe and Beethoven, Teplitz, 1811. 4 l, Beethoven, 1815, and his string instruments. 5 l, Beethoven House, Heiligenstadt, 1817. 25 l, Composer's hands, gold medal. 2r, Missa Solemnis, portrait, 1823. 4r,

Piano, room where Beethoven died, death mask. 5r, Portrait, 1825, hearing aids.

1977, Mar. 26 Litho. *Perf. 14*

669 A100 1 l multicolored .25 .25
670 A100 2 l multicolored .25 .25
671 A100 3 l multicolored .40 .40
672 A100 4 l multicolored .40 .40
673 A100 5 l multicolored .40 .40
674 A100 25 l multicolored 1.40 1.40
675 A100 2r multicolored 4.00 4.00
676 A100 5r multicolored 7.75 7.75
Nos. 669-676 (8) 14.85 14.85

Souvenir Sheet

677 A100 4r multicolored 10.50 *10.50*

Ludwig van Beethoven (1770-1827), composer, 150th death anniversary.

Electronic Tree and ITU Emblem A101

90 l, Central Telegraph Office, Maldives. 5r, Intelsat IV over map. 10r, Parabolic antenna, satellite communications earth station.

1977, May 17 Litho. *Perf. 14*

678 A101 10 l multicolored .25 .25
679 A101 90 l multicolored .50 .50
680 A101 10r multicolored 6.50 6.50
Nos. 678-680 (3) 7.25 7.25

Souvenir Sheet

681 A101 5r multicolored 6.25 6.25

Inauguration of Satellite Earth Station and for World Telecommunications Day.

Portrait by Gainsborough A102

Lesser Frigate Birds A103

Paintings: 2 l, 5 l, 10r, Rubens. 3 l, 95 l, 5r, Titian. 4 l, 1r, Gainsborough.

1977, May 20

682 A102 1 l multicolored .25 .25
683 A102 2 l multicolored .25 .25
684 A102 3 l multicolored .25 .25
685 A102 4 l multicolored .25 .25
686 A102 5 l multicolored .25 .25
687 A102 95 l multicolored .80 .60
688 A102 1r multicolored .80 .65
689 A102 10r multicolored 4.00 *6.00*
Nos. 682-689 (8) 6.85 *8.50*

Souvenir Sheet

690 A102 5r multicolored 5.25 *5.25*

Birth annivs. of Thomas Gainsborough; Peter Paul Rubens; Titian.

1977, July 26 Litho. *Perf. 14½*

Birds: 2 l, Crab plovers. 3 l, Long-tailed tropic bird. 4 l, Wedge-tailed shearwater. 5 l, Gray heron. 20 l, White tern. 95 l, Cattle egret. 1.25r, Blacknaped terns. 5r, Pheasant coucals. 10r, Striated herons.

691 A103 1 l multicolored .25 .25
692 A103 2 l multicolored .25 .25
693 A103 3 l multicolored .30 .30
694 A103 4 l multicolored .30 .30
695 A103 5 l multicolored .30 .30
696 A103 20 l multicolored 1.25 1.25
697 A103 95 l multicolored 2.50 2.50
698 A103 1.25r multicolored 3.50 3.50
699 A103 5r multicolored 6.50 *6.50*
Nos. 691-699 (9) 15.15 *15.15*

Souvenir Sheet

700 A103 10r multicolored 35.00 35.00

Charles A. Lindbergh — A104

Designs: 2 l, Lindbergh and Spirit of St. Louis. 3 l, Mohawk plane, horiz. 4 l, Lebaudy I airship, 1902, horiz. 5 l, Count Ferdinand von Zeppelin, and Zeppelin in Pernambuco. 1r, Los Angeles, U. S. Navy airship, 1924, horiz. 3r, Henry Ford and Lindbergh, 1942. 5r, Spirit of St. Louis, Statue of Liberty and Eiffel Tower, horiz. 7.50r, German naval airship over battleship, horiz. 10r, Vickers airship, 1917.

Perf. 13x13½, 13½x13

1977, Oct. 31 Litho.

701 A104 1 l multicolored .25 .25
702 A104 2 l multicolored .25 .25
703 A104 3 l multicolored .25 .25
704 A104 4 l multicolored .25 .25
705 A104 5 l multicolored .25 .25
706 A104 1r multicolored .60 .30
707 A104 3r multicolored 1.50 1.60
708 A104 10r multicolored 3.50 *4.75*
Nos. 701-708 (8) 6.85 *7.90*

Souvenir Sheet

709 Sheet of 2 17.00 17.00
a. A104 5r multicolored 4.00 4.00
b. A104 7.50r multicolored 5.00 5.00

Charles A. Lindbergh's solo transatlantic flight from New York to Paris, 50th anniv., and 75th anniv. of first navigable airship.

Boat Building A105

Maldivian Occupations: 15 l, High sea fishing. 20 l, Cadjan weaving. 90 l, Mat weaving. 2r, Lacemaking, vert.

1977, Dec. 12

710 A105 6 l multicolored .85 .85
711 A105 15 l multicolored 1.50 1.50
712 A105 20 l multicolored 1.75 1.75
713 A105 90 l multicolored 4.25 4.25
714 A105 2r multicolored 7.25 *7.25*
Nos. 710-714 (5) 15.60 *15.60*

Rheumatic Heart — A106

X-Ray Pictures: 50 l, Shoulder. 2r, Hand. 3r, Knee.

1978, Feb. 9 *Perf. 14*

715 A106 1 l multicolored .20 .20
716 A106 50 l multicolored .30 .30
717 A106 2r multicolored 1.25 1.25
718 A106 3r multicolored 1.75 1.75
Nos. 715-718 (4) 3.50 3.50

World Rheumatism Year.

Otto Lilienthal's Glider, 1890 — A107

Designs: 2 l, Chanute's glider, 1896. 3 l, Wright brothers testing glider, 1900. 4 l, A. V. Roe's plane with paper-covered wings, 1908. 5 l, Wilbur Wright showing his plane to King Alfonso of Spain, 1909. 10 l, Roe's second biplane. 20 l, Alexander Graham Bell and Wright brothers in Washington D.C., 1910. 95 l, Clifton Hadley's triplane, 1910. 5r, British B.E.2 planes, Upavon Field, 1914. 10r, Wilbur Wright flying first motorized plane, 1903.

1978, Feb. 27 Litho. *Perf. 13x13½*

719 A107 1 l multicolored .30 .35
720 A107 2 l multicolored .30 .35
721 A107 3 l multicolored .30 .35
722 A107 4 l multicolored .35 .35
723 A107 5 l multicolored .35 .35
724 A107 10 l multicolored .75 .75
725 A107 20 l multicolored 1.50 1.50
726 A107 95 l multicolored 3.50 3.50
727 A107 5r multicolored 9.50 9.50
Nos. 719-727 (9) 16.85 17.00

Souvenir Sheet

Perf. 14

728 A107 10r multicolored 16.00 *16.00*

75th anniversary of first motorized airplane.

Edward Jenner, Vaccination Discoverer A108

TV with Maldives Broadcasting Symbol — A109

Designs: 15 l, Foundling Hospital, London, where children were first inoculated, 1743, horiz. 50 l, Newgate Prison, London, where first experiments were carried out, 1721.

1978, Mar. 15 *Perf. 14*

729 A108 15 l multicolored .65 .30
730 A108 50 l multicolored 1.25 .65
731 A108 2r multicolored 3.25 3.25
Nos. 729-731 (3) 5.15 4.20

World eradication of smallpox.

1978, Mar. 29

Designs: 25 l, Circuit pattern. 1.50r, Station control panel, horiz.

732 A109 15 l multicolored .65 .65
733 A109 25 l multicolored .90 .90
734 A109 1.50r multicolored 4.00 4.00
Nos. 732-734 (3) 5.55 5.55

Inauguration of Maldive Islands television.

Sailing Ship — A110

The Ampulla — A111

Ships: 1 l, Phoenician. 2 l, Two-master. 5 l, Freighter Maldive Trader. 1r, Trading schooner. 1.25r, 4r, Sailing boat. 3r, Barque Bangala. (1 l, 2 l, 5 l, 1.25r, 4r, horiz.)

1978, Apr. 27 Litho. *Perf. 14½*

735 A110 1 l multicolored .25 .25
736 A110 2 l multicolored .25 .25
737 A110 3 l multicolored .25 .25
738 A110 5 l multicolored .25 .25
739 A110 1r multicolored .50 .50
740 A110 1.25r multicolored .95 .95
741 A110 3r multicolored 1.60 1.60
742 A110 4r multicolored 1.60 1.60
a. Souvenir sheet of 2 4.50 4.50
Nos. 735-742 (8) 5.65 5.65

No. 742a contains No. 742 and a 1r stamp in the design of No. 736.

1978, May 15 *Perf. 14*

Designs: 2 l, Scepter with dove. 3 l, Orb with cross. 1.15r, St. Edward's crown. 2r, Scepter with cross. 5r, Queen Elizabeth II. 10r, Anointing spoon.

743 A111 1 l multicolored .30 .30
744 A111 2 l multicolored .30 .30
745 A111 3 l multicolored .30 .30
746 A111 1.15r multicolored .30 .30
747 A111 2r multicolored .40 .40
748 A111 5r multicolored .70 .70
Nos. 743-748 (6) 2.30 2.30

Souvenir Sheet

749 A111 10r multicolored 2.25 2.25

Coronation of Elizabeth II, 25th anniv.

#743-748 were printed in sheets of 40 and in sheets of 3 + label, in changed colors. Labels show coronation regalia.

Capt. James Cook — A112

Designs: 2 l, Kamehameha I statue, Honolulu. 3 l, "Endeavour" and boat. 25 l, Capt. Cook and route of his 3rd voyage. 75 l, "Discovery" and "Resolution," map of Hawaiian Islands, horiz. 1.50r, Capt. Cook's first meeting with Hawaiians, horiz. 5r, "Endeavour." 10r, Capt. Cook's death, horiz.

1978, July 15 Litho. *Perf. 14½*

750 A112 1 l multicolored .25 .25
751 A112 2 l multicolored .25 .25
752 A112 3 l multicolored .25 .25
753 A112 25 l multicolored .50 .35
754 A112 75 l multicolored 1.25 1.25
755 A112 1.50r multicolored 1.75 1.75
756 A112 10r multicolored 6.50 *9.00*
Nos. 750-756 (7) 10.75 *13.10*

Souvenir Sheet

757 A112 5r multicolored 20.00 *20.00*

Schizophrys Aspera — A113

Maldivian Crabs and Lobster: 2 l, Atergatis floridus. 3 l, Percnon planissimum. 90 l, Portunus granulatus. 1r, Carpilius maculatus. No. 763, Huenia proteus. No. 765, Panulirus longipes, vert. 25r, Etisus laevimanus.

1978, Aug. 30 Litho. *Perf. 14*

758 A113 1 l multicolored .25 .25
759 A113 2 l multicolored .25 .25
760 A113 3 l multicolored .25 .25
761 A113 90 l multicolored .60 .40
762 A113 1r multicolored .60 .40
763 A113 2r multicolored .90 *1.25*
764 A113 25r multicolored 7.75 *9.50*
Nos. 758-764 (7) 10.60 *12.30*

Souvenir Sheet

765 A113 2r multicolored 3.50 3.50

Four Apostles, by Dürer — A114

Paintings by Albrecht Dürer (1471-1528): 20 l, Self-portrait, age 27. 55 l, Virgin and Child with Pear. 1r, Rhinoceros, horiz. 1.80r, Hare. 3r, The Great Piece of Turf. 10r, Columbine.

1978, Oct. 28 Litho. *Perf. 14*

No.	Type	Value	Color	Unused	Used
766	A114	10 l	multicolored	.25	.25
767	A114	20 l	multicolored	.25	.25
768	A114	55 l	multicolored	.25	.25
769	A114	1r	multicolored	.30	.30
770	A114	1.80r	multicolored	.60	.60
771	A114	3r	multicolored	.90	.90
			Nos. 766-771 (6)	2.55	2.55

Souvenir Sheet

No.	Type	Value	Color	Unused	Used
772	A114	10r	multicolored	5.75	5.75

Palms and Fishing Boat A115

Designs: 5 l, Montessori School. 10 l, TV tower and ITU emblem, vert. 25 l, Island with beach. 50 l, Boeing 737 over island. 95 l, Walk along the beach. 1.25r, Fishing boat at dawn. 2r, Presidential residence. 3r, Fishermen preparing nets. 5r, Afeefuddin Mosque.

1978, Nov. 11 Litho. *Perf. 14½*

No.	Type	Value	Color	Unused	Used
773	A115	1 l	multicolored	.20	.20
774	A115	5 l	multicolored	.20	.20
775	A115	10 l	multicolored	.20	.20
776	A115	25 l	multicolored	.20	.20
777	A115	50 l	multicolored	.25	.20
778	A115	95 l	multicolored	.35	.25
779	A115	1.25r	multicolored	.60	.50
780	A115	2r	multicolored	.75	1.00
781	A115	5r	multicolored	1.50	2.00
			Nos. 773-781 (9)	4.25	4.75

Souvenir Sheet

No.	Type	Value	Color	Unused	Used
782	A115	3r	multicolored	3.00	3.00

10th anniversary of Republic.

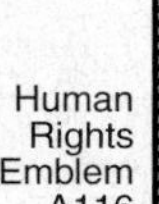

Human Rights Emblem A116

1978, Dec. 10 *Perf. 14*

No.	Type	Value	Color	Unused	Used
783	A116	30 l	multicolored	.25	.25
784	A116	90 l	multicolored	.40	.50
785	A116	1.80r	multicolored	.85	1.00
			Nos. 783-785 (3)	1.50	1.75

Universal Declaration of Human Rights, 30th anniversary.

Rare Spotted Cowrie — A117

Bellman Delivering Mail — A118

Sea Shells: 2 l, Imperial cone. 3 l, Green turban. 10 l, Giant spider conch. 1r, Leucodon cowrie. 1.80r, Fig cone. 3r, Glory of the sea. 5r, Top vase.

1979, Jan. Litho. *Perf. 14*

No.	Type	Value	Color	Unused	Used
786	A117	1 l	multicolored	.25	.25
787	A117	2 l	multicolored	.25	.25
788	A117	3 l	multicolored	.35	.35
789	A117	10 l	multicolored	.55	.55
790	A117	1r	multicolored	2.25	2.25
791	A117	1.80r	multicolored	3.00	3.00
792	A117	3r	multicolored	5.00	5.00
			Nos. 786-792 (7)	11.65	11.65

Souvenir Sheet

No.	Type	Value	Color	Unused	Used
793	A117	5r	multicolored	14.00	14.00

1979, Feb. 28 Litho. *Perf. 14*

Designs: 2 l, Royal mail coach, 1840, horiz. 3 l, First London letter box, 1855. 1.55r, Great Britain No. 1 and post horn. 5r, Maldive Islands No. 5 and carrier pigeon. 10r, Rowland Hill.

No.	Type	Value	Color	Unused	Used
794	A118	1 l	multicolored	.30	.30
795	A118	2 l	multicolored	.30	.30
796	A118	3 l	multicolored	.30	.30
797	A118	1.55r	multicolored	.45	.45
798	A118	5r	multicolored	1.60	1.60
			Nos. 794-798 (5)	2.95	2.95

Souvenir Sheet

No.	Type	Value	Color	Unused	Used
799	A118	10r	multicolored	3.00	3.75

Sir Rowland Hill (1795-1879), originator of penny postage.

For overprints see Nos. 853-855.

Girl with Teddy Bear — A119

IYC Emblem, Boy and: 1.25r, Model boat. 2r, Rocket launcher. 3r, Blimp. 5r, Train.

1979, May 10 Litho. *Perf. 14*

No.	Type	Value	Color	Unused	Used
800	A119	5 l	multicolored	.20	.20
801	A119	1.25r	multicolored	.45	.45
802	A119	2r	multicolored	.55	.55
803	A119	3r	multicolored	.75	.75
			Nos. 800-803 (4)	1.95	1.95

Souvenir Sheet

No.	Type	Value	Color	Unused	Used
804	A119	5r	multicolored	1.75	1.75

International Year of the Child.

White Feathers, by Matisse A120

Paintings by Henri Matisse (1869-1954): 25 l, Joy of Life. 30 l, Eggplants. 1.50r, Harmony in Red. 4r, Water Pitcher. 5r, Still-life.

1979, Aug. 20 Litho. *Perf. 14*

No.	Type	Value	Color	Unused	Used
805	A120	20 l	multicolored	.55	.55
806	A120	25 l	multicolored	.55	.55
807	A120	30 l	multicolored	.55	.55
808	A120	1.50r	multicolored	1.10	1.10
809	A120	5r	multicolored	3.00	3.00
			Nos. 805-809 (5)	5.75	5.75

Souvenir Sheet

No.	Type	Value	Color	Unused	Used
810	A120	4r	multicolored	4.00	4.00

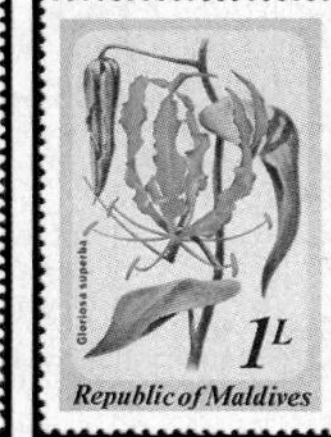

Sari and Mosque — A121

Gloriosa Superba — A122

National Costumes: 75 l, Sashed apron dress. Male Harbor. 90 l, Serape with necklace, radar station. 95 l, Flowered dress, mosque and minaret.

1979, Aug. 22 Litho. *Perf. 14*

No.	Type	Value	Color	Unused	Used
811	A121	50 l	multicolored	.20	.20
812	A121	75 l	multicolored	.20	.20
813	A121	90 l	multicolored	.35	.35
814	A121	95 l	multicolored	.40	.40
			Nos. 811-814 (4)	1.15	1.15

1979, Oct. 29 Litho. *Perf. 14*

No.	Type	Value	Color	Unused	Used
815	A122	1 l	shown	.20	.20
816	A122	3 l	Hibiscus	.20	.20
817	A122	50 l	Barringtonia asiatica	.20	.20
818	A122	1r	Abutilon indicum	.40	.40
819	A122	5r	Guettarda speciosa	1.75	1.75
			Nos. 815-819 (5)	2.75	2.75

Souvenir Sheet

No.	Type	Value	Color	Unused	Used
820	A122	4r	Pandanus odoratissimus	2.50	2.50

Maldive wildflowers.

Handicraft Exhibition A123

1979, Nov. 11

No.	Type	Value	Color	Unused	Used
821	A123	5 l	shown	.20	.20
822	A123	10 l	Jar and cup	.20	.20
823	A123	1.30r	Tortoise-shell jewelry	.55	.55
824	A123	2r	Wooden boxes	.75	.75
			Nos. 821-824 (4)	1.70	1.70

Souvenir Sheet

No.	Type	Value	Color	Unused	Used
825	A123	5r	Bracelets, necklace	1.75	1.75

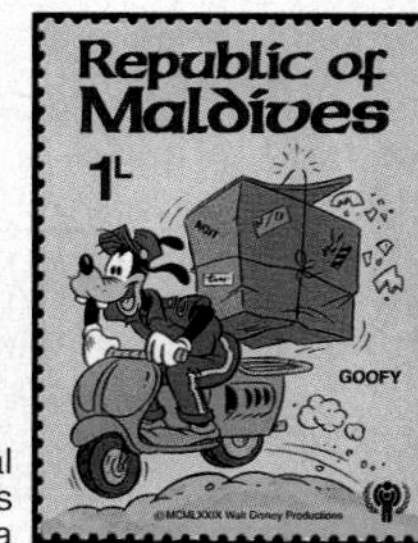

Postal Scenes A123a

1 l, Goofy delivering package. 2 l, Mickey at mailbox. 3 l, Goofy buried in letters. 4 l, Minnie Mouse, Pluto. 5 l, Mickey Mouse on skates. 10 l, Donald Duck at mailbox. 15 l, Chip and Dale carrying letter. 1.50r, Donald Duck on unicycle. 4r, Pluto at mailbox. 5r, Donald Duck wheeling crate.

1979, Dec. Litho. *Perf. 11*

No.	Type	Value	Color	Unused	Used
826	A123a	1 l	multicolored	.25	.25
827	A123a	2 l	multicolored	.25	.25
828	A123a	3 l	multicolored	.25	.25
829	A123a	4 l	multicolored	.25	.25
830	A123a	5 l	multicolored	.25	.25
831	A123a	10 l	multicolored	.25	.25
832	A123a	15 l	multicolored	.25	.25
833	A123a	1.50r	multicolored	.85	.85
834	A123a	5r	multicolored	2.40	*2.75*
			Nos. 826-834 (9)	5.00	*5.35*

Souvenir Sheet

Imperf

No.	Type	Value	Color	Unused	Used
835	A123a	4r	multicolored	7.50	7.50

National Day A124

Designs: 5 l, Post Ramadan dancing. 15 l, Festival of Eeduu. 95 l, Sultan's ceremonial band. 2r, Music festival. 5r, Sword dance.

1980, Jan. 19 Litho. *Perf. 14*

No.	Type	Value	Color	Unused	Used
836	A124	5 l	multicolored	.20	.20
837	A124	15 l	multicolored	.20	.20
838	A124	95 l	multicolored	.45	.45
839	A124	2r	multicolored	.90	.90
			Nos. 836-839 (4)	1.75	1.75

Souvenir Sheet

No.	Type	Value	Color	Unused	Used
840	A124	5r	multicolored	2.00	2.00

Leatherback Turtle — A125

1980, Feb. 17 Litho. *Perf. 14*

No.	Type	Value	Color	Unused	Used
841	A125	1 l	shown	.20	.20
842	A125	2 l	Flatback turtle	.20	.20
843	A125	5 l	Hawksbill turtle	.20	.20
844	A125	10 l	Loggerhead turtle	.20	.20
845	A125	75 l	Olive ridley	.40	.40
846	A125	10r	Atlantic ridley	5.00	5.00
			Nos. 841-846 (6)	6.20	6.20

Souvenir Sheet

No.	Type	Value	Color	Unused	Used
847	A125	4r	Green turtle	2.75	2.75

Paul Harris in Rotary Emblem — A126

1980, Mar. Litho. *Perf. 14*

No.	Type	Value	Color	Unused	Used
848	A126	75 l	shown	.40	.40
849	A126	90 l	Family	.45	.45
850	A126	1r	Grain	.50	.50
851	A126	10r	Caduceus	4.00	4.00
			Nos. 848-851 (4)	5.35	5.35

Souvenir Sheet

No.	Type	Value	Color	Unused	Used
852	A126	5r	Anniversary emblem	2.00	2.00

Rotary International, 75th anniversary.

Nos. 797-799 Overprinted "LONDON 1980"

1980, May 6 Litho. *Perf. 14*

No.	Type	Value	Color	Unused	Used
853	A118	1.55r	multicolored	2.00	1.75
854	A118	5r	multicolored	5.50	5.00

Souvenir Sheet

No.	Type	Value	Color	Unused	Used
855	A118	10r	multicolored	9.00	9.00

London 1980 International Stamp Exhibition, May 6-14. Sheet margin overprinted "Earls Court—London 6-14 May 1980."

Swimming, Moscow '80 Emblem — A127

1980, June 4 Litho. *Perf. 14*

No.	Type	Value	Color	Unused	Used
856	A127	10 l	shown	.20	.20
857	A127	50 l	Sprinting	.25	.25
858	A127	3r	Shot put	1.25	1.25
859	A127	4r	High jump	1.50	1.50
			Nos. 856-859 (4)	3.20	3.20

Souvenir Sheet

No.	Type	Value	Color	Unused	Used
860	A127	5r	Weight lifting	2.50	2.50

22nd Summer Olympic Games, Moscow, July 19-Aug. 3.

White-tailed Tropic Bird — A128

1980, July 10 Litho. *Perf. 14*

No.	Type	Value	Color	Unused	Used
861	A128	75 l	shown	.30	.25
862	A128	95 l	Sooty tern	.40	.35
863	A128	1r	Brown noddy	.40	.35
864	A128	1.55r	Eurasian curlew	.75	.75
865	A128	2r	Wilson's petrel	.85	.85
866	A128	4r	Caspian tern	1.75	1.75
			Nos. 861-866 (6)	4.45	4.30

Souvenir Sheet

867	A128	5r Red-footed & brown boobies	10.00	*10.00*

Seal of Sultan Ibrahim II (1720-1750) — A129

Sultans' Seals: 2 l, Mohamed Imadudeen II (1704-1720). 5 l, Mohamed Bin Haji Ali (1692-1701). 1r, Kuda Mohamed Rasgefaanu (1687-1691). 2r, Ibrahim Iskander I (1648-1687). 3r, Ibrahim Iskander, second seal.

1980, July 26

868	A129	1 l violet brn & blk	.20	.20
869	A129	2 l violet brn & blk	.20	.20
870	A129	5 l violet brn & blk	.20	.20
871	A129	1r violet brn & blk	.50	.50
872	A129	2r violet brn & blk	.60	.60
		Nos. 868-872 (5)	1.70	1.70

Souvenir Sheet

873	A129	3r violet brn & blk	1.25	1.25

Queen Mother Elizabeth, 80th Birthday A130

1980, Sept. 29 *Perf. 14*

874	A130	4r multicolored	2.00	2.00

Souvenir Sheet

Perf. 12

875	A130	5r multicolored	2.25	2.25

Munnaaru Tower A131

1980, Nov. 9 **Litho.** *Perf. 15*

876	A131	5 l shown	.20	.20
877	A131	10 l Hukuru Miskiiy Mosque	.20	.20
878	A131	30 l Medhuziyaaraiy Shrine	.20	.20
879	A131	55 l Koran verses on wooden tablets	.30	.30
880	A131	90 l Mother teaching son	.45	.45
		Nos. 876-880 (5)	1.35	1.35

Souvenir Sheet

881	A131	2r Map and arms of Maldives	1.00	1.00

Hegira (Pilgrimage Year).

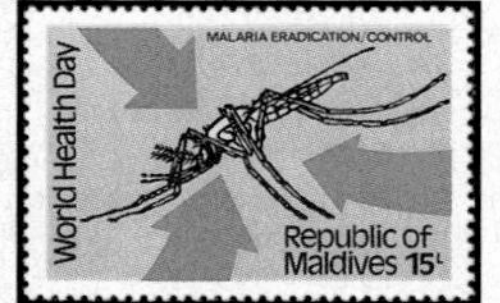

Malaria Eradication Control — A132

1980, Nov. 30 *Perf. 14*

882	A132	15 l shown	.30	.30
883	A132	25 l Balanced diet	.30	.30
884	A132	1.50r Oral hygiene	1.00	1.00
885	A132	5r Clinic visit	3.50	3.50
		Nos. 882-885 (4)	5.10	5.10

Souvenir Sheet

886	A132	4r like #885	2.50	2.50

World Health Day. No. 886 shows design of No. 885 in changed colors.

The Cheshire Cat — A133

Designs: Scenes from Walt Disney's Alice in Wonderland. 5r, vert.

1980, Dec. 22 *Perf. 11*

887	A133	1 l multicolored	.25	.25
888	A133	2 l multicolored	.25	.25
889	A133	3 l multicolored	.25	.25
890	A133	4 l multicolored	.30	.30
891	A133	5 l multicolored	.30	.30
892	A133	10 l multicolored	.30	.30
893	A133	15 l multicolored	.30	.30
894	A133	2.50r multicolored	1.75	1.75
895	A133	4r multicolored	3.00	3.00
		Nos. 887-895 (9)	6.70	6.70

Souvenir Sheet

896	A133	5r multicolored	6.75	*6.75*

Ridley Turtle A134

1980, Dec. 29 **Litho.** *Perf. 14*

897	A134	90 l shown	2.50	.50
898	A134	1.25r Angel flake fish	3.25	1.10
899	A134	2r Spiny lobster	4.00	1.50
		Nos. 897-899 (3)	9.75	3.10

Souvenir Sheet

900	A134	4r Fish	5.00	5.00

Tomb of Ghaazee Muhammad Thakurufaan — A135

National Day (Furniture and Palace of Muhammad Thakurufaan): 20 l, Hanging lamp, 16th century, vert. 30 l, Chair, vert. 95 l, Utheem Palace. 10r, Couch, vert.

1981, Jan. 7 *Perf. 15*

901	A135	10 l multicolored	.20	.20
902	A135	20 l multicolored	.20	.20
903	A135	30 l multicolored	.20	.20
904	A135	95 l multicolored	.40	.40
905	A135	10r multicolored	4.00	4.00
		Nos. 901-905 (5)	5.00	5.00

Common Design Types pictured following the introduction.

Royal Wedding Issue

Common Design Type

1981, June 22 **Litho.** *Perf. 14*

906	CD331a	1r Couple	.30	.30
907	CD331a	2r Buckingham Palace	.30	.30
908	CD331a	5r Charles	.40	.40
		Nos. 906-908 (3)	1.00	1.00

Souvenir Sheet

909	CD331	10r Royal state coach	1.00	1.00

Nos. 906-908 also printed in sheets of 5 plus label, perf. 12, in changed colors.

Majlis Chamber, 1932 A136

50th Anniv. of Citizens' Majlis (Grievance Rights); 1r, Sultan Muhammed Shamsuddin III (instituted system, 1932), vert. 4r, Constitution, 1932.

1981, June 27 *Perf. 15*

910	A136	95 l multicolored	.45	.45
911	A136	1r multicolored	.50	.50

Souvenir Sheet

912	A136	4r multicolored	3.00	3.00

Self-portrait with Palette, by Picasso (1881-1973) A137

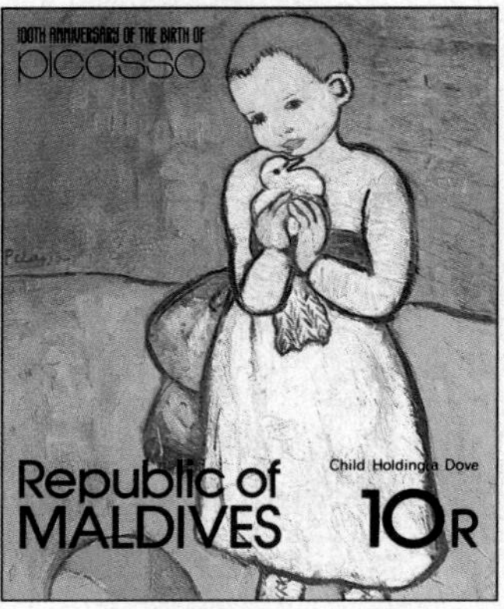

Child Holding a Dove — A138

1981, Aug. 26 **Litho.** *Perf. 14*

913	A137	5 l shown	.40	.40
914	A137	10 l Woman in Blue	.40	.40
915	A137	25 l Boy with a Pipe	.40	.40
916	A137	30 l Card Player	.40	.40
917	A137	90 l Sailor	.50	.50
918	A137	3r Self-portrait	1.50	1.50
919	A137	5r Harlequin	2.50	2.50

Imperf

920	A138	10r shown	4.75	4.75
		Nos. 913-920 (8)	10.85	10.85

No. 5 on Airmail Cover A139

1981, Sept. 9 **Litho.** *Perf. 14*

921	A139	25 l multicolored	.20	.20
922	A139	75 l multicolored	.30	.30
923	A139	5r multicolored	1.25	1.25
		Nos. 921-923 (3)	1.75	1.75

Postal service, 75th anniv.

Hulule Intl. Airport Opening A140

1981, Nov. 11

924	A140	5 l Jet taking off	.20	.20
925	A140	20 l Passengers leaving jet	.20	.20
926	A140	1.80r Refueling	1.00	1.00
927	A140	4r shown	1.50	*2.00*
		Nos. 924-927 (4)	2.90	*3.40*

Souvenir Sheet

928	A140	5r Terminal	3.50	3.50

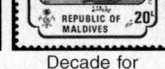

Intl. Year of the Disabled — A141

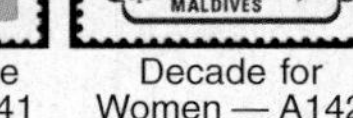

Decade for Women — A142

1981, Nov. 18 **Litho.** *Perf. 14½*

929	A141	2 l Homer	.25	.25
930	A141	5 l Cervantes	.30	.30
931	A141	1r Beethoven	2.25	2.25
932	A141	5r Van Gogh	4.00	*4.00*
		Nos. 929-932 (4)	6.80	*6.80*

Souvenir Sheet

933	A141	4r Helen Keller, Anne Sullivan	4.75	*4.75*

1981, Nov. 25 *Perf. 14*

934	A142	20 l Preparing fish	.20	.20
935	A142	90 l 16th cent. woman	.45	.45
936	A142	1r Tending yam crop	.50	.50
937	A142	2r Making coir rope	.75	.75
		Nos. 934-937 (4)	1.90	1.90

Fishermen's Day — A143

1981, Dec. 10

938	A143	5 l Collecting bait	.60	.25
939	A143	15 l Fishing boats	1.10	.25
940	A143	90 l Fisherman holding catch	1.60	.55
941	A143	1.30r Sorting fish	2.25	.85
		Nos. 938-941 (4)	5.55	1.90

Souvenir Sheet

942	A143	3r Loading fish for export	2.25	2.25

World Food Day A144

1981, Dec. 30 **Litho.** *Perf. 14*

943	A144	10 l Breadfruit	.35	.25
944	A144	25 l Hen, chicks	.90	.25
945	A144	30 l Corn	.90	.25
946	A144	75 l Skipjack tuna	2.10	.45
947	A144	1r Pumpkins	2.50	.60
948	A144	2r Coconuts	3.00	1.75
		Nos. 943-948 (6)	9.75	3.55

Souvenir Sheet

949	A144	5r Eggplants	3.50	3.50

50th Anniv. of Walt Disney's Pluto (1980) A145

1982, Mar. 29 **Litho.** *Perf. 13½x14*

950	A145	4r Scene from Chain Gang, 1930	3.75	3.50

Souvenir Sheet

951	A145	6r The Pointer, 1939	5.25	5.25

Princess Diana Issue
Common Design Type

1982, July 15 Litho. *Perf. 14½x14*

952 CD332 95 l Balmoral .50 .50
953 CD332 3r Honeymoon 1.50 1.50
954 CD332 5r Diana 2.50 2.50
Nos. 952-954 (3) 4.50 4.50

Souvenir Sheet

955 CD332 8r Diana, diff. 3.50 3.50

#952-954 also issued in sheetlets of 5 plus label.
For overprints and surcharges see Nos. 966-969, 1050, 1052, 1054, 1056.

Scouting Year
A146

1982, Aug. 9 Litho. *Perf. 14*

956 A146 1.30r Saluting .50 .50
957 A146 1.80r Fire building .75 .75
958 A146 4r Lifesaving 1.50 1.50
959 A146 5r Map reading 2.00 2.00
Nos. 956-959 (4) 4.75 4.75

Souvenir Sheet

960 A146 10r Flag, emblem 3.50 3.50

1982 World Cup — A147

TB Bacillus Cent. — A148

Various soccer players.

1982, Oct. 4 Litho. *Perf. 14*

961 A147 90 l multicolored 1.50 .65
962 A147 1.50r multicolored 2.00 1.10
963 A147 3r multicolored 3.00 2.25
964 A147 5r multicolored 3.75 3.75
Nos. 961-964 (4) 10.25 7.75

Souvenir Sheet

965 A147 10r multicolored 6.00 6.00

Nos. 952-955 Overprinted: "ROYAL BABY/21.6.82"

1982, Oct. 18 *Perf. 14½x14*

966 CD332 95 l multicolored .50 .50
967 CD332 3r multicolored 1.50 1.50
968 CD332 5r multicolored 2.50 2.50
Nos. 966-968 (3) 4.50 4.50

Souvenir Sheet

969 CD332 8r multicolored 5.00 5.00

Birth of Prince William of Wales, June 21.
#966-968 also issued in sheetlets of 5 + label.
For surcharges see #1051, 1053, 1055, 1057.

1982, Nov. 22 *Perf. 14½*

970 A148 5 l Koch isolating bacillus .20 .20
971 A148 15 l Slide, microscope .20 .20
972 A148 95 l Koch, 1905 .20 .20
973 A148 3r Koch, book illus. plates 1.25 1.25
Nos. 970-973 (4) 1.85 1.85

Souvenir Sheet

974 A148 5r Koch in lab 1.75 1.75

Natl. Education — A149

Designs: 90 l, Basic education scheme, 1980-85. 95 l, Formal primary education. 1.30r, Teacher training. 2.50r, Educational materials production. 6r, Thanna typewriter.

1982, Nov. 15

975 A149 90 l multicolored .25 .25
976 A149 95 l multicolored .25 .25
977 A149 1.30r multicolored .35 .35
978 A149 2.50r multicolored .60 .60
Nos. 975-978 (4) 1.45 1.45

Souvenir Sheet

979 A149 6r multicolored 1.75 1.75

Manned Flight Bicentenary — A150

1983, July 28 Litho. *Perf. 14*

980 A150 90 l Blohm & Voss Ha-139 1.00 1.00
981 A150 1.45r Macchi Castoldi MC-72 1.90 1.90
982 A150 4r Boeing F4B-3 5.00 5.00
983 A150 5r Le France 6.25 6.25
Nos. 980-983 (4) 14.15 14.15

Souvenir Sheet

984 A150 10r Nadar's Le Geant 4.75 4.75

For overprints see Nos. 1020-1022.

Roughtooth Dolphin — A151

1983, Sept. 6 Litho. *Perf. 14*

985 A151 30 l shown .60 .60
986 A151 40 l Indopacific humpback dolphin .60 .60
987 A151 4r Finless porpoise 6.00 6.00
988 A151 6r Pygmy sperm whale 9.00 9.00
Nos. 985-988 (4) 16.20 16.20

Souvenir Sheet

989 A151 5r Striped dolphins 7.75 7.75

Classic Cars
A152

1983, Aug. 15 Litho. *Perf. 14½x15*

990 A152 5 l Curved Dash Oldsmobile, 1902 .30 .30
991 A152 30 l Aston Martin Tourer, 1932 .30 .30
992 A152 40 l Lamborghini Miura, 1966 .30 .30
993 A152 1r Mercedes-Benz 300sl, 1954 .75 .75
994 A152 1.45r Stutz Bearcat, 1913 1.10 1.10
995 A152 5r Lotus Elite, 1958 3.75 3.75
Nos. 990-995 (6) 6.50 6.50

Souvenir Sheet

996 A152 10r Grand Prix Sunbeam, 1924 9.00 9.00

World Communications Year — A153

50 l, Dish antenna. 1r, Mail transport. 2r, Ship-to-shore communications. 10r, Land-air communications. 20r, Telephone calls.

1983, Oct. 9 *Perf. 14*

997 A153 50 l multicolored .30 .30
998 A153 1r multicolored .60 .60
999 A153 2r multicolored 1.10 1.10
1000 A153 10r multicolored 6.00 6.00
Nos. 997-1000 (4) 8.00 8.00

Souvenir Sheet

1001 A153 20r multicolored 6.00 6.00

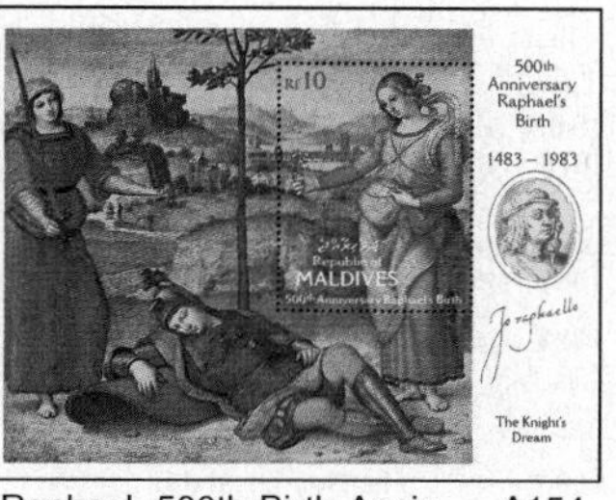

Raphael, 500th Birth Anniv. — A154

1983, Oct. 25 Litho. *Perf. 13½x14*

1002 A154 90 l La Donna Gravida .50 .50
1003 A154 3r Jean of Aragon 1.50 1.50
1004 A154 4r The Woman with the Unicorn 2.00 2.00
1005 A154 6r La Muta 3.00 3.00
Nos. 1002-1005 (4) 7.00 7.00

Souvenir Sheet

1006 A154 10r The Knights Dream 4.75 4.75

Intl. Palestinian Solidarity Day — A155

Various refugees, mosque.

1983, Nov. 29 Litho. *Perf. 14*

1007 A155 4r multicolored 2.00 2.00
1008 A155 5r multicolored 2.50 2.50
1009 A155 6r multicolored 3.00 3.00
Nos. 1007-1009 (3) 7.50 7.50

Natl. Development Programs — A156

1983, Dec. 10 Litho. *Perf. 13½x14*

1010 A156 7 l Education .20 .20
1011 A156 10 l Health care .20 .20
1012 A156 5r Food production 2.50 2.50
1013 A156 6r Fishing industry 3.00 3.00
Nos. 1010-1013 (4) 5.90 5.90

Souvenir Sheet

1014 A156 10r Inter-atoll transportation 3.00 3.00

A157

Tourism — A158

1984, Feb. *Perf. 14*

1015 A157 50 l Baseball .25 .25
1016 A157 1.55r Swimming .80 .80
1017 A157 3r Judo 1.50 1.50
1018 A157 4r Shot put 2.00 2.00
Nos. 1015-1018 (4) 4.55 4.55

Souvenir Sheet

1019 A157 10r Handball 4.75 4.75

23rd Olympic Games, Los Angeles, 7/28-8/12.
For overprints see Nos. 1090-1094.

Nos. 982-984 Overprinted: "19th UPU/CONGRESS HAMBURG"

1984 Litho. *Perf. 14*

1020 A150 4r multicolored 2.00 2.00
1021 A150 5r multicolored 2.50 2.50

Souvenir Sheet

1022 A150 10r multicolored 4.75 4.75

1984, Sept. 21 Litho. *Perf. 14½*

1023 A158 7 l Island resorts .40 .40
1024 A158 15 l Cruising .40 .40
1025 A158 20 l Snorkelling .40 .40
1026 A158 2r Wind surfing 1.00 1.00
1027 A158 4r Scuba diving 2.10 2.10
1028 A158 6r Night fishing 3.25 3.25
1029 A158 8r Big game fishing 4.25 4.25
1030 A158 10r Nature (turtle) 5.25 5.25
Nos. 1023-1030 (8) 17.05 17.05

50th Anniv. of Donald Duck — A160

Scenes from various cartoons and movies.

1984, Nov. Litho. *Perf. 14*

1040 A160 3 l multi .25 .25
1041 A160 4 l multi .25 .25
1042 A160 5 l multi .25 .25
1043 A160 10 l multi .25 .25
1044 A160 15 l multi .25 .25
1045 A160 25 l multi .25 .25
1045A A160 5r multi, perf. 12x12½ 2.00 2.00
1046 A160 8r multi 3.00 3.00
1047 A160 10r multi 4.00 4.00
Nos. 1040-1047 (9) 10.50 10.50

Souvenir Sheets

1048 A160 15r multi 5.00 5.00
1049 A160 15r multi 5.00 5.00

Nos. 952-955, 966-969 Surcharged

1984, July Litho. *Perf. 14½x14*

1050 CD332 1.45r on 95 l #952 *2.50 2.00*
1051 CD332 1.45r on 95 l #966 *2.50 2.00*
1052 CD332 1.45r on 3r #953 *2.50 2.00*
1053 CD332 1.45r on 3r #967 *2.50 2.00*
1054 CD332 1.45r on 5r #954 *2.50 2.00*
1055 CD332 1.45r on 5r #968 *2.50 2.00*
Nos. 1050-1055 (6) 15.00 12.00

Souvenir Sheet

1056 CD332 1.45r on 8r #955 *10.00 8.00*
1057 CD332 1.45r on 8r #969 *10.00 8.00*

Namibia Day
A161

1984, Aug. 26 *Perf. 15*

1058 A161 6r Breaking chain 1.75 1.75
1059 A161 8r Family, rising sun 2.25 2.25

Souvenir Sheet

1060 A161 10r Map, sun 3.50 3.50

Ausipex '84
A162

1984, Sept. 21
1061 A162 5r Frangipani 2.50 2.50
1062 A162 10r Cooktown orchid 5.25 5.25

Souvenir Sheet

1063 A162 15r Sun orchids 12.00 12.00

150th Birth Anniv. of Edgar Degas — A163

1984, Oct. Litho. *Perf. 14*
1064 A163 75 l Portrait of Edmond Iduranty .20 .20
1065 A163 2r Portrait of James Tissot .55 .55
1066 A163 5r Portrait of Achille Degas 1.40 1.40
1067 A163 10r Lady with Chrysanthemums 2.75 2.75
Nos. 1064-1067 (4) 4.90 4.90

Souvenir Sheet

1068 A163 15r Self-Portrait 5.00 5.00

Opening of Islamic Center A164

1984, Nov. 11 Litho. *Perf. 15*
1069 A164 2r Mosque .70 .70
1070 A164 5r Mosque, minaret, vert. 1.75 1.75

40th Anniv., International Civil Aviation Organization — A165

1984, Nov. 19 Litho. *Perf. 14*
1071 A165 7 l Boeing 737 .35 .35
1072 A165 4r Lockheed L-1011 2.40 2.40
1073 A165 6r McDonnell Douglas DC-10 3.25 3.25
1074 A165 8r Lockheed L-1011 4.00 4.00
Nos. 1071-1074 (4) 10.00 10.00

Souvenir Sheet

1075 A165 15r Shorts SC7 Skyvan 5.75 5.75

450th Anniv. of the Death of Correggio — A166

1984, Dec. 10 Litho. *Perf. 14*
1076 A166 5r Detail from The Day 1.40 1.40
1077 A166 10r Detail from The Night 2.75 2.75

Souvenir Sheet

1078 A166 15r Portrait of a Man 5.25 5.25

John J. Audubon A167

Illustrations from Audubon's Birds of America.

1985, Mar. 9 Litho. *Perf. 14*
1079 A167 3r Flesh-footed shearwater, vert. 2.25 1.25
1080 A167 3.50r Little grebe 2.75 1.40
1081 A167 4r Great cormorant, vert. 2.75 1.50
1082 A167 4.50r White-faced storm petrel 2.75 1.60
Nos. 1079-1082 (4) 10.50 5.75

Souvenir Sheet

1083 A167 15r Red-necked phalarope 5.50 5.50

See Nos. 1195-1204.

Natl. Security Services — A168

1985, June 6 Litho. *Perf. 14*
1084 A168 15 l Drill .50 .30
1085 A168 20 l Combat training .50 .30
1086 A168 1r Fire fighting 2.25 .45
1087 A168 2r Coast guard 2.75 .90
1088 A168 10r Parade, vert. 3.50 *4.50*
Nos. 1084-1088 (5) 9.50 6.45

Souvenir Sheet

1089 A168 10r Badge, cannon 4.00 4.00

Nos. 1015-1019 Ovptd. with Country or "Gold Medalist," Winner and Nation in 3 Lines

1985, July 17
1090 A157 50 l Japan .30 .30
1091 A157 1.55r Theresa Andrews .60 .60
1092 A157 3r Frank Wieneke 1.25 1.25
1093 A157 4r Claudia Loch 1.75 1.75
Nos. 1090-1093 (4) 3.90 3.90

Souvenir Sheet

1094 A157 10r US 3.00 3.00

Queen Mother, 85th Birthday A169

Johann Sebastian Bach, Composer A170

1985-86 *Perf. 14, 12 (1r, 4r, 10r)*
1095 A169 1r Wearing tiara .50 .50
1096 A169 3r like 1r .60 .60
1097 A169 4r At Middlesex Hospital, horiz. .70 .70
1098 A169 5r like 4r .95 .95
1099 A169 7r Wearing fur stole 1.25 1.25
1100 A169 10r like 7r 1.90 1.90
Nos. 1095-1100 (6) 5.90 5.90

Souvenir Sheet

1101 A169 15r With Prince of Wales 3.50 3.50

Issued: 1r, 4r, 10r, 1/4/86; 3r, 5r, 7r, 15r, 8/20/85. #1095, 1097, 1100 printed in sheets of 5 + label.

1985, Sept. 3 *Perf. 14*

Portrait, Invention No. 1 in C Major and: 15 l, Lira da Braccio. 2r, Tenor oboe. 4r, Serpent. 10r, Table organ.

1102 A170 15 l multi .25 .25
1103 A170 2r multi .70 .70
1104 A170 4r multi 1.25 1.25
1105 A170 10r multi 2.75 2.75
Nos. 1102-1105 (4) 4.95 4.95

Souvenir Sheet

1106 A170 15r Portrait 4.50 4.50

Ships A171

1985, Sept. 23
1107 A171 3 l Masodi .25 .25
1108 A171 5 l Naalu Batheli .25 .25
1109 A171 10 l Addu Odi .30 .30
1110 A171 2.60r Masdhoni, 2nd generation 1.40 1.40
1111 A171 2.70r Masdhoni 1.40 1.40
1112 A171 3r Baththeli Dhoni 1.60 1.60
1113 A171 5r Inter 1 2.50 2.50
1114 A171 10r Yacht Dhoni 5.00 5.00
Nos. 1107-1114 (8) 12.70 12.70

World Tourism Org., 10th Anniv. A172

1985, Oct. 2
1115 A172 6r Wind surfing 2.10 2.10
1116 A172 8r Scuba diving 3.00 3.00

Souvenir Sheet

1117 A172 15r Kuda Hithi Resort 5.00 5.00

Maldives Admission to UN, 20th Anniv. — A173

1985, Oct. 24
1118 A173 20 l shown .25 .25
1119 A173 15r Flags, UN building 3.75 3.75

UN 40th Anniv., Intl. Peace Year A174

1985, Oct. 24 Litho. *Perf. 14*
1120 A174 15 l UN Building .25 .25
1121 A174 2r IPY emblem .65 .65
1122 A174 4r Security Council 1.10 1.10
1123 A174 10r Lion, lamb 1.90 1.90
Nos. 1120-1123 (4) 3.90 3.90

Souvenir Sheet

1124 A174 15r UN Building, diff. 3.50 3.50

Nos. 1120-1121, 1123-1124, vert.

Intl. Youth Year A175

1985, Nov. 20 *Perf. 15*
1125 A175 90 l Culture .35 .35
1126 A175 6r Games 1.40 1.40
1127 A175 10r Community service, vert. 2.00 *2.75*
Nos. 1125-1127 (3) 3.75 4.50

Souvenir Sheet

1128 A175 15r Youth camp, vert. 3.50 3.50

Summit Nations Flags, Dedication by Pres. Maumoon — A176

1985, Dec. 8 *Perf. 14*
1129 A176 3r multicolored 2.50 2.50

South Asian Regional Cooperation, SARC, 1st Summit, Dec. 7-8, 1985.

Tuna A177

1985, Dec. 10
1130 A177 25 l Frigate .45 .45
1131 A177 75 l Little tuna .90 .90
1132 A177 3r Dogtooth 2.75 2.75
1133 A177 5r Yellowfin 3.25 3.25
Nos. 1130-1133 (4) 7.35 7.35

Souvenir Sheet

1134 A177 15r Skipjack 7.50 7.50

Fisherman's Day.

Mark Twain, American Novelist A178

Disney characters and Twain quotes.

1985, Dec. 21
1135 A178 2 l multicolored .25 .25
1136 A178 3 l multicolored .25 .25
1137 A178 4 l multicolored .30 .30
1138 A178 20 l multicolored .50 .50
1139 A178 4r multicolored 1.60 1.60
1140 A178 13r multicolored 6.00 6.00
Nos. 1135-1140 (6) 8.90 8.90

Souvenir Sheet

1141 A178 15r multicolored 8.00 8.00

Intl. Youth Year. 4r issued in sheet of 8.

The Brothers Grimm — A179

Disney characters in Doctor Knowall.

1985, Dec. 21
1142 A179 1 l multicolored .25 .25
1143 A179 5 l multicolored .25 .25
1144 A179 10 l multicolored .30 .30
1145 A179 15 l multicolored .30 .30

1146 A179 3r multicolored 1.40 1.40
1147 A179 14r multicolored 6.75 6.75
Nos. 1142-1147 (6) 9.25 9.25

Souvenir Sheet

1148 A179 15r multicolored 7.50 7.50

3r issued in sheets of 8.

World Disarmament Day — A180

1986, Feb. 10 ***Perf. 14½x14***

1149 A180 1.50r shown — —
1150 A180 10r Dove — —

Halley's Comet A181

Designs: 20 l, NASA space telescope. 1.50r, Giotto space probe. 2r, Plant-A probe, Japan. 4r, Edmond Halley, Stonehenge. 5r, Vega probe, USSR. 15r, Comet over Male.

1986, Apr. 29

1151 A181 20 l multicolored .65 .65
1152 A181 1.50r multicolored 1.40 1.40
1153 A181 2r multicolored 1.75 1.75
1154 A181 4r multicolored 2.50 2.50
1155 A181 5r multicolored 2.50 2.50
Nos. 1151-1155 (5) 8.80 8.80

Souvenir Sheet

1156 A181 15r multicolored 9.00 9.00

See Nos. 1210-1215.

Statue of Liberty, Cent. A182

Detail of statue and: 50 l, Walter Gropius (1883-1969), architect. 70 l, John Lennon (1940-1980), musician. 1r, George Balanchine (1904-1983), choreographer. 10r, Franz Werfel (1890-1945), writer. 15r, Close-up of statue, vert.

1986, May 5

1157 A182 50 l multicolored .45 .45
1158 A182 70 l multicolored 1.60 1.60
1159 A182 1r multicolored 1.75 1.75
1160 A182 10r multicolored 4.00 4.00
Nos. 1157-1160 (4) 7.80 7.80

Souvenir Sheet

1161 A182 15r multicolored 8.00 8.00

AMERIPEX '86 — A183

US stamps and Disney portrayals of American legends: 3 l, No. 1317, Johnny Appleseed. 4 l, No. 1122, Paul Bunyan. 5 l, No. 1381, Casey at the Bat. 10 l, No. 1548, Tales of Sleepy Hollow. 15 l, No. 922, John Henry. 20 l, No. 1061, Windwagon Smith. 13r, No. 1409, Mike Fink. 14r, No. 993, Casey Jones. No. 1170, Remember the Alamo, No. 1330. No. 1171, Pocahontas, Nos. 328-330.

1986, May 22 ***Perf. 11***

1162 A183 3 l multicolored .25 .25
1163 A183 4 l multicolored .25 .25
1164 A183 5 l multicolored .30 .30
1165 A183 10 l multicolored .30 .30
1166 A183 15 l multicolored .30 .30
1167 A183 20 l multicolored .30 .30
1168 A183 13r multicolored 8.75 8.75
1169 A183 14r multicolored 10.00 10.00
Nos. 1162-1169 (8) 20.45 20.45

Souvenir Sheets

Perf. 14

1170 A183 15r multicolored 8.50 8.50
1171 A183 15r multicolored 8.50 8.50

Queen Elizabeth II, 60th Birthday

Common Design Type

1986, May 29 ***Perf. 14***

1172 CD339 1r Girl Guides' rally, 1938 .25 .25
1173 CD339 2r Canada visit, 1985 .50 .50
1174 CD339 12r At Sandringham, 1970 2.75 2.75
Nos. 1172-1174 (3) 3.50 3.50

Souvenir Sheet

1175 CD339 15r Royal Lodge, 1940 4.50 4.50

For overprints see Nos. 1288-1291.

1986 World Cup Soccer Championships, Mexico — A184

Various soccer plays.

1986, June 18 **Litho.** ***Perf. 14***

1176 A184 15 l multicolored .85 .85
1177 A184 2r multicolored 2.50 2.50
1178 A184 4r multicolored 4.50 4.50
1179 A184 10r multicolored 8.00 8.00
Nos. 1176-1179 (4) 15.85 15.85

Souvenir Sheet

1180 A184 15r multicolored 7.50 7.50

For overprints see Nos. 1205-1209.

Royal Wedding Issue, 1986

Common Design Type

Designs: 10 l, Prince Andrew and Sarah Ferguson. 2r, Andrew. 12r, Andrew on ship's deck in uniform. 15r, Couple, diff.

1986, July 23

1181 CD340 10 l multi .25 .25
1182 CD340 2r multi .70 .70
1183 CD340 12r multi 4.00 4.00
Nos. 1181-1183 (3) 4.95 4.95

Souvenir Sheet

1184 CD340 15r multi 5.25 5.25

Marine Life A185

1986, Sept. 22 **Litho.** ***Perf. 15***

1185 A185 50 l Sea fan, moorish idol 1.50 1.50
1186 A185 90 l Regal angelfish 2.25 2.25
1187 A185 1r Anemone fish 2.25 2.25
1188 A185 2r Stinging coral, tiger cowrie 3.00 3.00
1189 A185 3r Emperor angelfish, staghorn coral 3.00 3.00
1190 A185 4r Black-naped tern 3.00 3.00
1191 A185 5r Fiddler crab, staghorn coral 3.00 3.00
1192 A185 10r Hawksbill turtle 3.75 3.75
Nos. 1185-1192 (8) 21.75 21.75

Souvenir Sheets

1193 A185 15r Trumpet fish 7.50 7.50
1194 A185 15r Long-nosed butterflyfish 7.50 7.50

Nos. 1185-1187, 1189 and 1193 show the World Wildlife Fund emblem.

Audubon Type of 1985

1986, Oct. 9 **Litho.** ***Perf. 14***

1195 A167 3 l Little blue heron .40 .40
1196 A167 4 l White-tailed kite, vert. .40 .40
1197 A167 5 l Greater shearwater .40 .40
1198 A167 10 l Magnificent frigatebird, vert. .45 .45
1199 A167 15 l Eared grebe, vert. .90 .90
1200 A167 20 l Common merganser, vert. .95 .95
1201 A167 13r Great-footed hawk 5.75 5.75
1202 A167 14r Greater prairie chicken 5.75 5.75
Nos. 1195-1202 (8) 15.00 15.00

Souvenir Sheets

1203 A167 15r White-fronted goose 12.00 12.00
1204 A167 15r Northern fulmar, vert. 12.00 12.00

Nos. 1197, 1199-1201 printed se-tenant with labels picturing a horned puffin, gray kingbird, downy woodpecker and water pipit, respectively.

Nos. 1176-1180 Ovptd. "WINNERS / Argentina 3 / W. Germany 2" in Gold

1986, Oct. 25

1205 A184 15 l multicolored .55 .55
1206 A184 2r multicolored 1.50 1.50
1207 A184 4r multicolored 2.40 2.40
1208 A184 10r multicolored 4.00 4.00
Nos. 1205-1208 (4) 8.45 8.45

Souvenir Sheet

1209 A184 15r multicolored 5.25 5.25

Nos. 1151-1156 Printed with Halley's Comet Symbol in Silver

1986, Oct. 30

1210 A181 20 l multicolored .70 .70
1211 A181 1.50r multicolored 1.40 1.40
1212 A181 2r multicolored 1.60 1.60
1213 A181 4r multicolored 2.25 2.25
1214 A181 5r multicolored 2.25 2.25
Nos. 1210-1214 (5) 8.20 8.20

Souvenir Sheet

1215 A181 15r multicolored 6.75 6.75

UNESCO, 40th Anniv. — A186

1986, Nov. 4 ***Perf. 15***

1216 A186 1r Aviation .30 .30
1217 A186 2r Boat-building .75 .75
1218 A186 3r Education 1.10 1.10
1219 A186 5r Research 2.00 2.00
Nos. 1216-1219 (4) 4.15 4.15

Souvenir Sheet

1220 A186 15r Ocean exploration 4.00 4.00

Mushrooms — A187

1986, Dec. 31 **Litho.** ***Perf. 15***

1221 A187 15 l Hypholoma fasciculare .75 .75
1222 A187 50 l Kuehneromyces mutabilis 1.60 1.60
1223 A187 1r Amanita muscaria 2.00 2.00
1224 A187 2r Agaricus campestris 2.75 2.75
1225 A187 3r Amanita pantherina 2.75 2.75
1226 A187 4r Coprinus comatus 2.75 2.75
1227 A187 5r Pholiota spectabilis 2.75 2.75
1228 A187 10r Pluteus cervinus 4.25 4.25
Nos. 1221-1228 (8) 19.60 19.60

Souvenir Sheets

1229 A187 15r Armillaria mellea 8.50 8.50
1230 A187 15r Stropharia aeruginosa 8.50 8.50

Nos. 1222-1223, 1225-1226 vert.

Flowers — A188

1987, Jan. 29 **Litho.** ***Perf. 15***

1231 A188 10 l Ixora .25 .25
1232 A188 20 l Frangipani .25 .25
1233 A188 50 l Crinum .25 .25
1235 A188 2r Pink rose .85 .85
1236 A188 4r Flamboyant 1.60 1.60
1238 A188 10r Ground orchid 4.00 4.00
Nos. 1231-1238 (6) 7.20 7.20

Souvenir Sheet

1239 A188 15r Gardenia 3.25 3.25
1240 A188 15r Oleander 3.25 3.25

Girl Guides, 75th Anniv. (in 1985) A189

1987, Apr. 4 **Litho.** ***Perf. 15***

1241 A189 15 l Nature study .25 .25
1242 A189 2r Guides, rabbits .65 .65
1243 A189 4r Bird-watching 2.10 2.10
1244 A189 12r Lady Baden-Powell, flag 2.40 2.40
Nos. 1241-1244 (4) 5.40 5.40

Souvenir Sheet

1245 A189 15r Sailing 3.75 3.75

Indigenous Trees and Plants — A190

1987, Apr. 22 **Litho.** ***Perf. 14***

1246 A190 50 l Thespesia populnea, vert. .20 .20
1247 A190 1r Cocos nucifera, vert. .20 .20
1248 A190 2r Calophyllum mophyllum, vert. .40 .40
1249 A190 3r Xyanthosoma indica .60 .60
1250 A190 5r Ipomoea batatas 1.10 1.10
1251 A190 7r Artocarpus altilis, vert. 1.40 1.40
Nos. 1246-1251 (6) 3.90 3.90

Souvenir Sheet

1252 A190 15r Cocos nucifera, diff., vert. 3.75 3.75

A191

America's Cup — A192

1987, May 4 Litho. *Perf. 15*

1253 A191 15 l Intrepid, 1970 .25 .25
1254 A191 1r France II, 1974 .35 .35
1255 A191 2r Gretel, 1962 .60 .60
1256 A191 12r Volunteer, 1887 3.75 3.75
Nos. 1253-1256 (4) 4.95 4.95

Souvenir Sheet

1257 A192 15r Defender Vs. Valkyrie III, 1895 4.00 4.00

Butterflies — A193 Scientists — A194

1987, Dec. 16 Litho. *Perf. 15*

1258 A193 15 l Precis octavia .50 .50
1259 A193 20 l Pachliopta hector .50 .50
1260 A193 50 l Teinopalpus imperialis .90 .90
1261 A193 1r Kallima horsfieldi 1.10 1.10
1262 A193 2r Cethosia biblis 2.00 2.00
1263 A193 4r Hestia jasonia 2.75 2.75
1264 A193 7r Papilio memnon 4.25 4.25
1265 A193 10r Meneris tulbaghia 4.75 4.75
Nos. 1258-1265 (8) 16.75 16.75

Souvenir Sheets

1266 A193 15r Acraea violae acraeinae 6.00 6.00
1267 A193 15r Hebomoia leucippe 6.00 6.00

1988, Jan. 10 *Perf. 14*

Designs: 1.50r, Sir Isaac Newton using prism to demonstrate his Theory of Light, horiz. 3r, Euclid (c. 300 B.C.), mathematician. 4r, Gregor Johann Mendel (1822-1884), botanist; father of genetics. 5r, Galileo, 1st man to observe 4 moons of Jupiter, horiz. 15r, Apollo spacecraft orbiting the moon.

1268 A194 1.50r multicolored 1.50 1.50
1269 A194 3r multicolored 2.10 2.10
1270 A194 4r multicolored 2.40 2.40
1271 A194 5r multicolored 4.00 4.00
Nos. 1268-1271 (4) 10.00 10.00

Souvenir Sheet

1272 A194 15r multicolored 7.25 *7.25*

Disney Characters, Space Exploration — A195

1988, Feb. 15

1273 A195 3 l Weather satellite .25 .25
1274 A195 4 l Navigation satellite .25 .25
1275 A195 5 l Communication satellite .25 .25
1276 A195 10 l Moon rover .25 .25
1277 A195 20 l Space shuttle .25 .25
1278 A195 13r Space docking 5.75 5.75
1279 A195 14r Voyager 2 5.75 5.75
Nos. 1273-1279 (7) 12.75 12.75

Souvenir Sheets

1280 A195 15r 1st Man on Moon 6.50 6.50
1281 A195 15r Space station colony 6.50 6.50

Nos. 1276-1278 and 1281 vert.

WHO, 40th Anniv. A196

1988, Apr. 7 Litho. *Perf. 14*

1282 A196 2r Immunization .60 .60
1283 A196 4r Clean water 1.10 1.10

For overprints see Nos. 1307-1308.

World Environment Day — A197

1988, May 9 *Perf. 15*

1284 A197 15 l Save water .25 .25
1285 A197 75 l Protect the reef .30 .30
1286 A197 2r Conserve nature .75 .75
Nos. 1284-1286 (3) 1.30 1.30

Souvenir Sheet

1287 A197 15r Banyan tree, vert. 4.25 4.25

Nos. 1172-1175 Ovptd. "40th WEDDING ANNIVERSARY/ H.M. QUEEN ELIZABETH II/ H.R.H. THE DUKE OF EDINBURGH" in Gold

1988, July 7 Litho. *Perf. 14*

1288 CD339 1r multicolored .35 .35
1289 CD339 2r multicolored .65 .65
1290 CD339 12r multicolored 4.00 4.00
Nos. 1288-1290 (3) 5.00 5.00

Souvenir Sheet

1291 CD339 15r multicolored 5.25 5.25

Transportation and Communication Decade for Asia and the Pacific — A198

Globe and: 2r, Postal communications. 3r, Earth satellite telecommunications technology. 5r, Space telecommunications technology. 10r, Automobile, aircraft and ship.

1988, May 31 Litho. *Perf. 14*

1292 A198 2r multicolored 1.50 1.50
1293 A198 3r multicolored 2.00 2.00
1294 A198 5r multicolored 3.00 3.00
1295 A198 10r multicolored 6.00 6.00
Nos. 1292-1295 (4) 12.50 12.50

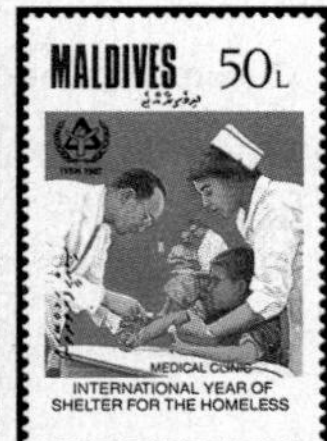

1988 Summer Olympics, Seoul — A199 Intl. Year of Shelter for the Homeless — A200

1988, July 16

1296 A199 15 l Discus .20 .20
1297 A199 2r 100-Meter sprint .60 .60
1298 A199 4r Gymnastics, horiz. 1.10 1.10
1299 A199 12r Steeplechase, horiz. 3.50 3.50
Nos. 1296-1299 (4) 5.40 5.40

Souvenir Sheet

1300 A199 20r Tennis, horiz. 5.25 5.25

For overprints see Nos. 1311-1315.

1988, July 20

1301 A200 50 l Medical clinic .35 .35
1302 A200 3r Prefab housing 1.60 1.60

Souvenir Sheet

1303 A200 15r Construction site 4.25 4.25

Intl. Fund for Agricultural Development (IFAD), 10th Anniv. — A201

1988, July 30

1304 A201 7r Breadfruit 2.00 2.00
1305 A201 10r Mango, vert. 2.75 2.75

Souvenir Sheet

1306 A201 15r Coconut palm, yellowtail tuna 4.25 4.25

Nos. 1282-1283 Ovptd.

1988, Dec. 1 Litho. *Perf. 14*

1307 A196 2r multicolored .60 .60
1308 A196 4r multicolored 1.10 1.10

Intl. Day for the Fight Against Aids.

John F. Kennedy (1917-1963), 35th US President — A202

Space achievements: a, Apollo launch. b, 1st Man on the Moon. c, Earth and astronaut driving moon rover. d, Space module and Kennedy. 15r, Kennedy addressing the nation.

1989, Feb. 19

1309 Strip of 4 9.50 9.50
a.-d. A202 5r any single 2.00 2.00

Souvenir Sheet

1310 A202 15r multicolored 5.00 5.00

Nos. 1296-1300 Overprinted for Olympic Winners

1989, Apr. 29 Litho. *Perf. 14*

1311 A199 15 l "J. SCHULT / DDR" .25 .25
1312 A199 2r "C. LEWIS / USA" .75 .75
1313 A199 4r "MEN'S ALL AROUND / V. ARTEMOV USSR" 1.40 1.40
1314 A199 12r "TEAM SHOW JUMPING / W. GERMANY" 4.50 4.50
Nos. 1311-1314 (4) 6.90 6.90

Souvenir Sheet

1315 A199 20r multi 6.50 6.50

No. 1315 has marginal ovpt. "OLYMPIC WINNERS / MEN'S SINGLES / GOLD M. MECIR / CZECH. / SILVER T. MAYOTTE / USA / BRONZE B. GILBERT / USA."

Paintings by Titian (b. 1489) A203

Designs: 15 l, Portrait of Benedetto Varchi, c. 1540. 1r, Portrait of a Young Man in a Fur, 1515. 2r, King Francis I of France, 1538. 5r, Portrait of Pietro Aretino, 1545. 15r, The Bravo, c. 1520. 20r, The Concert, 1512. No. 1322, An Allegory of Prudence, c. 1565. No. 1323, Portrait of Francesco Maria Della Rovere.

1989, May 15 Litho. *Perf. 13½x14*

1316 A203 15 l multicolored .25 .25
1317 A203 1r multicolored .30 .30
1318 A203 2r multicolored .70 .70
1319 A203 5r multicolored 1.60 1.60
1320 A203 15r multicolored 4.75 4.75
1321 A203 20r multicolored 6.25 6.25
Nos. 1316-1321 (6) 13.85 13.85

Souvenir Sheets

1322 A203 20r multicolored 5.00 5.00
1323 A203 20r multicolored 5.00 5.00

"Thirty-six Views of Mt. Fuji" — A204

Prints by Hokusai (1760-1849): 15 l, Fuji from Hodogaya. 50 l, Fuji from Lake Kawaguchi. 1r, Fuji from Owari. 2r, Fuji from Tsukudajima in Edo. 4r, Fuji from a Teahouse at Yoshida. 6r, Fuji from Tagonoura. 10r, Fuji from Mishima-goe. 12r, Fuji from the Sumida River in Edo. No. 1332, Fuji from Fukagawa in Edo. No. 1333, Fuji from Inume Pass.

1989 *Perf. 14*

1324 A204 15 l multicolored .20 .20
1325 A204 50 l multicolored .20 .20
1326 A204 1r multicolored .30 .30
1327 A204 2r multicolored .55 .55
1328 A204 4r multicolored 1.10 1.10
1329 A204 6r multicolored 1.60 1.60
1330 A204 10r multicolored 2.75 2.75
1331 A204 12r multicolored 3.25 3.25
Nos. 1324-1331 (8) 9.95 9.95

Souvenir Sheets

1332 A204 18r multicolored 5.00 5.00
1333 A204 18r multicolored 5.00 5.00

Hirohito (1901-1989) and enthronement of Akihito as emperor of Japan.

Issue dates: #1332, Oct. 16, others, Sept. 2.

Tropical Fish A205

1989, Oct. 16 Litho. *Perf. 14*

1334	A205	20 l	Clown triggerfish	.25	.25
1335	A205	50 l	Blue surgeonfish	.25	.25
1336	A205	1r	Bluestripe snapper	.30	.30
1337	A205	2r	Oriental sweetlips	.65	.65
1338	A205	3r	Wrasse	.95	.95
1339	A205	8r	Treadfin butterflyfish	2.50	2.50
1340	A205	10r	Bicolor parrotfish	3.25	3.25
1341	A205	12r	Saber squirrelfish	3.75	3.75
			Nos. 1334-1341 (8)	11.90	11.90

Souvenir Sheet

1342	A205	15r	Butterfly perch	7.50	7.50
1343	A205	15r	Semicircle angelfish	7.50	7.50

Nos. 1293-1294 Ovptd. "ASIA-PACIFIC / TELECOMMUNITY / 10 YEARS" in Silver

1989, July 5 Litho. *Perf. 14*

1344	A198 3r	multicolored	1.90	1.90
1345	A198 5r	multicolored	3.00	3.00

World Stamp Expo '89 Emblem, Disney Characters and Japanese Automobiles — A206

Designs: 15 l, 1907 Takuri Type 3. 50 l, 1917 Mitsubishi Model A. 1r, 1935 Datsun Roadstar. 2r, 1940 Mazda. 4r, 1959 Nissan Bluebird 310. 6r, 1958 Subaru 360. 10r, 1966 Honda 5800. 12r, 1966 Daihatsu Fellow. No. 1354, 1981 Isuzu Trooper II. No. 1355, 1985 Toyota Supra.

1989, Nov. 17 Litho. *Perf. 14x13½*

1346	A206	15 l	multicolored	.25	.25
1347	A206	50 l	multicolored	.25	.25
1348	A206	1r	multicolored	.40	.40
1349	A206	2r	multicolored	.75	.75
1350	A206	4r	multicolored	1.50	1.50
1351	A206	6r	multicolored	2.40	2.40
1352	A206	10r	multicolored	4.00	4.00
1353	A206	12r	multicolored	4.50	4.50
			Nos. 1346-1353 (8)	14.05	14.05

Souvenir Sheets

1354	A206	20r	multicolored	7.00	7.00
1355	A206	20r	multicolored	7.00	7.00

Souvenir Sheet

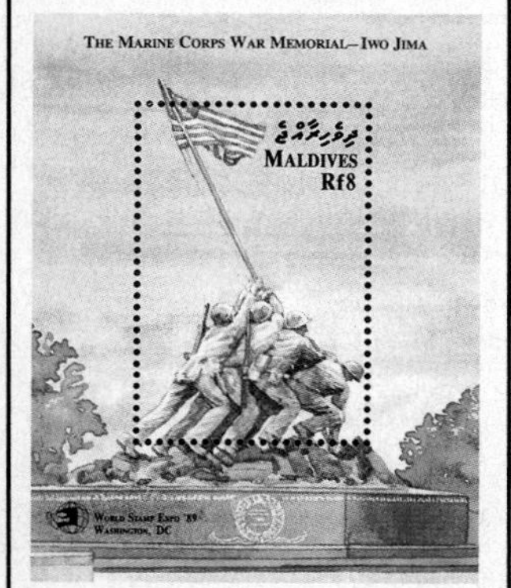

The Marine Corps War Memorial, Arlington, VA — A207

1989, Nov. 17 Litho. *Perf. 14*

1356	A207 8r	multicolored	2.00	2.00

World Stamp Expo '89.

1st Moon Landing, 20th Anniv. A208

1989, Nov. 24 *Perf. 14*

1357	A208	1r	*Eagle* lunar module	.30	.30
1358	A208	2r	Aldrin taking soil samples	.60	.60
1359	A208	6r	Solar wind experiment	1.75	1.75
1360	A208	10r	Nixon, astronauts	3.00	3.00
			Nos. 1357-1360 (4)	5.65	5.65

Souvenir Sheet

1361	A208	18r	Armstrong descending ladder	9.50	9.50

Railway Pioneers — A209

Designs: 10 l, Sir William Cornelius Van Horne (1843-1915), chairman of Canadian Pacific Railway, map and locomotive, 1894. 25 l, Matthew Murray, built rack locomotives for Middleton Colliery. 50 l, Louis Favre (1826-1879), built the St. Gotthard (spiral) Tunnel, 1881. 2r, George Stephenson (1781-1848), locomotive, 1825. 6r, Richard Trevithick (1771-1833), builder of 1st rail locomotive, 1804. 8r, George Nagelmackers, Orient Express dining car, 1869. 10r, William Jessop, Surrey horse-drawn cart on rails, 1770. 12r, Isambard Kingdom Brunel (1806-1859), chief engineer of Great Western Railway, introduced broad gauge, 1830's. No. 1370, George Pullman (1831-1897), *Pioneer* passenger car. No. 1371, Rudolf Diesel (1858-1913), inventor of the diesel engine, 1892, and diesel train.

1989, Dec. 26 Litho. *Perf. 14*

1362	A209	10 l	multicolored	.25	.25
1363	A209	25 l	multicolored	.25	.25
1364	A209	50 l	multicolored	.25	.25
1365	A209	2r	multicolored	.65	.65
1366	A209	6r	multicolored	2.00	2.00
1367	A209	8r	multicolored	2.50	2.50
1368	A209	10r	multicolored	3.25	3.25
1369	A209	12r	multicolored	3.75	3.75
			Nos. 1362-1369 (8)	12.90	12.90

Souvenir Sheets

1370	A209	18r	multicolored	5.00	5.00
1371	A209	18r	multicolored	5.00	5.00

Anniversaries and Events (in 1989) — A210

Designs: 20 l, Flag of India, Jawaharlal Nehru, Mahatma Gandhi. 50 l, Syringe, opium poppies, vert. 1r, William Shakespeare, birthplace, Stratford-on-Avon. 2r, Flag of France, storming of the Bastille, Paris, 1789, vert. 3r, Concorde jet, flags of France, Britain. 8r, George Washington, Mount Vernon estate, Virginia. 10r, Capt. William Bligh, the *Bounty.* 12r, Ships in port. No. 1380, 1st Televised baseball game, 1939, vert. No. 1381, Franz von Taxis (1458-1517), vert.

1990, Feb. 15 Litho. *Perf. 14*

1372	A210	20 l	multicolored	.25	.25
1373	A210	50 l	multicolored	.25	.25
1374	A210	1r	multicolored	.60	.60
1375	A210	2r	multicolored	1.10	1.10
1376	A210	3r	multicolored	1.60	1.60
1377	A210	8r	multicolored	4.50	4.50
1378	A210	10r	multicolored	5.75	5.75
1379	A210	12r	multicolored	7.00	7.00
			Nos. 1372-1379 (8)	21.05	21.05

Souvenir Sheets

1380	A210	18r	multicolored	8.75	8.75
1381	A210	18r	multicolored	8.75	8.75

Birth cent. of Nehru (20 l); SAARC Year for Combatting Drug Abuse (50 l); 425th birth anniv. of Shakespeare (1r); French Revolution, bicent. (2r); first test flight of the Concorde supersonic jet, 20th anniv. (3r); American presidency, bicent. (8r); Mutiny on the *Bounty,* bicent. (10r); Hamburg, 800th anniv. (12r); 1st televised baseball game, 50th anniv. (No. 1380); and European postal communications, 500th anniv. (No. 1381).

Johann von Taxis was the first postmaster of Thurn & Taxis in 1489, not Franz, who is credited on No. 1381.

Natl. Independence, 25th Anniv. — A211

Designs: 20 l, Bodu Thakurufaanu Memorial Center, Utheemu. 25 l, Islamic Center, Male. 50 l, Natl. flag, UN, Islamic Conf., Commonwealth and SAARC emblems. 2r, Muleeaage, Male. 5r, Natl. Security Service, Maldives. 10r, Natl. crest, emblem of the Citizens' Majlis (parliament).

1990, Jan. 1 Litho. *Perf. 14*

1382	A211	20 l	multicolored	.20	.20
1383	A211	25 l	multicolored	.20	.20
1384	A211	50 l	multicolored	.20	.20
1385	A211	2r	multicolored	.50	.50
1386	A211	5r	multicolored	1.25	1.25
			Nos. 1382-1386 (5)	2.35	2.35

Souvenir Sheet

1387	A211	10r	multicolored	4.50	4.50

French Revolution, Bicent. (in 1989) A212

Paintings: 15 l, *Louis XVI in Coronation Robes,* by Duplessis. 50 l, *Monsieur Lavoisier and His Wife,* by David. 1r, *Madame Pastoret,* by David. 2r, *Oath of Lafayette at the Festival of Federation,* artist unknown. 4r, *Madame Trudaine,* by David. 6r, *Chenard Celebrating the Liberation of Savoy,* by Boilly. 10r, *An Officer Swears Allegiance to the Constitution,* artist unknown. 12r, *Self-portrait,* by David. No. 1396, *The Tennis Court Oath, June 20, 1789,* by David, horiz. No. 1397, *Jean-Jacques Rousseau and the Symbols of the Revolution,* by Jeaurat.

1990, Jan. 11 Litho. *Perf. 14*

1388	A212	15 l	multicolored	.25	.25
1389	A212	50 l	multicolored	.25	.25
1390	A212	1r	multicolored	.40	.40
1391	A212	2r	multicolored	.85	.85
1392	A212	4r	multicolored	1.50	1.50
1393	A212	6r	multicolored	2.40	2.40
1394	A212	10r	multicolored	4.00	4.00
1395	A212	12r	multicolored	4.50	4.50
			Nos. 1388-1395 (8)	14.15	14.15

Souvenir Sheets

1396	A212	20r	multicolored	6.00	6.00
1397	A212	20r	multicolored	6.00	6.00

Stamp World London '90 — A213

Walt Disney characters demonstrating sports popular in Britain.

1990 Litho. *Perf. 14x13½*

1398	A213	15 l	Rugby	.25	.25
1399	A213	50 l	Curling	.25	.25
1400	A213	1r	Polo	.40	.40
1401	A213	2r	Soccer	.85	.85
1402	A213	4r	Cricket	1.50	1.50
1403	A213	6r	Horse racing, Ascot	2.50	2.50
1404	A213	10r	Tennis	4.00	4.00
1405	A213	12r	Lawn bowling	4.50	4.50
			Nos. 1398-1405 (8)	14.25	14.25

Souvenir Sheets

1406	A213	20r	Fox hunting	8.00	8.00
1407	A213	20r	Golf, St. Andrews, Scotland	8.00	8.00

Penny Black, 150th Anniv. A214

1990, May 3 Litho. *Perf. 15x14*

1408	A214	8r	Silhouettes	2.50	2.50
1409	A214	12r	Silhouettes, diff.	3.75	3.75

Souvenir Sheet

1410	A214	18r	Penny Black	5.25	5.25

Queen Mother 90th Birthday
A215 A216

1990, July 8 *Perf. 14*

1411	A215	6r	shown	1.25	1.25
1412	A216	6r	shown	1.25	1.25
1413	A215	6r	As Lady Bowes-Lyon, diff.	1.25	1.25
			Nos. 1411-1413 (3)	3.75	3.75

Souvenir Sheet

1414	A216	18r	On Wedding Day, diff.	4.00	4.00

Nos. 1411-1413 printed in sheets of 9.

A217

A218

A219

Islamic Heritage Year A220

1990, July 22 Litho. *Perf. 14*

1415	A217	1r	blue & black	.25	.25
1416	A218	1r	blue & black	.25	.25
1417	A218	1r	Building, diff.	.25	.25
1418	A219	2r	blue & black	.50	.50
1419	A220	2r	blue & black	.50	.50
1420	A219	2r	Building, diff.	.50	.50
a.			Block of 6, #1415-1420	3.00	3.00

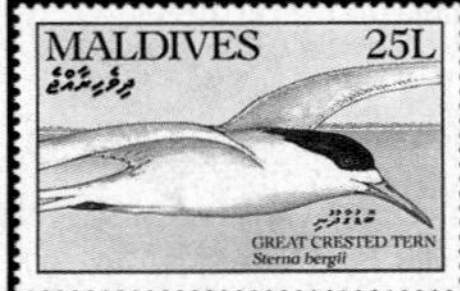

Great Crested Tern A221

1990, Aug. 9 Litho. *Perf. 14*

1421 A221 25 l shown .20 .20
1422 A221 50 l Koel .20 .20
1423 A221 1r White tern .25 .25
1424 A221 3.50r Cinnamon bittern .90 .90
1425 A221 6r Sooty tern 1.50 1.50
1426 A221 8r Audubon's shearwater 2.00 2.00
1427 A221 12r Brown noddy 3.00 3.00
1428 A221 15r Lesser frigatebird 3.75 3.75
Nos. 1421-1428 (8) 11.80 11.80

Souvenir Sheets

1429 A221 18r White-tailed tropicbird 6.25 6.25
1430 A221 18r Grey heron 6.25 6.25

World War II Milestones — A222

Designs: 15 l, US Marines repulse Japanese invasion of Wake Island, Dec. 11, 1941. 25 l, Gen. Stilwell begins offensive in Burma, Mar. 4, 1944. 50 l, US begins offensive in Normandy, July 3, 1944. 1r, US forces secure Saipan, July 9, 1944. 2.50r, D-Day, June 6, 1944. 3.50r, Allied forces land in Norway, Apr. 14, 1940. 4r, Adm. Mountbatten named Chief of Combined Operations, Mar. 18, 1942. 6r, Gen. MacArthur accepts Japanese surrender, Sept. 2, 1945. 10r, Potsdam Conference, July 16, 1945. 12r, Allied invade Sicily, July 10, 1943. 18r, Atlantic convoys.

1990, Aug. 9 Litho. *Perf. 14*

1431 A222 15 l multicolored .20 .20
1432 A222 25 l multicolored .20 .20
1433 A222 50 l multicolored .20 .20
1434 A222 1r multicolored .25 .25
1435 A222 2.50r multicolored .60 .60
1436 A222 3.50r multicolored 1.10 1.10
1437 A222 4r multicolored 1.25 1.25
1438 A222 6r multicolored 2.00 2.00
1439 A222 10r multicolored 3.25 3.25
1440 A222 12r multicolored 4.00 4.00
Nos. 1431-1440 (10) 13.05 13.05

Souvenir Sheet

1441 A222 18r multicolored 7.75 7.75

A223

5th SAARC Summit — A224

1990, Nov. 21 Litho. *Perf. 14*

1442 A223 75 l Satellite communications .40 .40
1443 A223 3.50r Flags 1.50 1.50

Souvenir Sheet

1444 A224 20r Map 6.75 6.75

Flowers — A225

Bonsai — A226

1990, Dec. 9 Litho. *Perf. 14*

1445 A225 20 l Spathoglottis plicata .25 .25
1446 A225 75 l Hippeastrum puniceum .25 .25
1447 A225 2r Tecoma stans .65 .65
1448 A225 3.50r Catharanthus roseus 1.10 1.10
1449 A225 10r Ixora coccinea 3.25 3.25
1450 A225 12r Clitoria ternatea 4.00 4.00
1451 A225 15r Caesalpinia pulcherrima 4.75 4.75
Nos. 1445-1451 (7) 14.25 14.25

Souvenir Sheets

1452 A225 20r Rosa sp. 5.00 5.00
1453 A225 20r Plumeria obtusa 5.00 5.00
1454 A225 20r Jasminum grandiflorum 5.00 5.00
1455 A225 20r Hibiscus tiliaceous 5.00 5.00

Expo '90, Intl. Garden and Greenery Exposition, Osaka, Japan.
2r, 3.50r, 10r, 12r are horiz.

1990-91

1456 A226 20 l Winged Euonymus .25 .25
1457 A226 50 l Japanese black pine .25 .25
1458 A226 1r Japanese five needle pine .30 .30
1459 A226 3.50r Flowering quince 1.25 1.25
1460 A226 5r Chinese elm 1.60 1.60
1461 A226 8r Japanese persimmon 2.75 2.75
1462 A226 10r Japanese wisteria 3.25 3.25
1463 A226 12r Satsuki azalea 4.00 4.00
Nos. 1456-1463 (8) 13.65 13.65

Souvenir Sheets

1464 A226 20r Sargent juniper 6.25 6.25
1465 A226 20r Trident maple 6.25 6.25

Expo '90, Intl. Garden and Greenery Exposition, Osaka, Japan.
Issued: 50 l, 1r, 8r, 10r, #1464, 12/9/90; 20 l, 3.50r, 5r, 12r, #1465, 1/29/91.

Aesop's Fables — A227

Walt Disney characters: 15 l, Tortoise and the Hare. 50 l, Town Mouse and Country Mouse. 1r, Fox and the Crow. 3.50r, Travellers and the Bear. 4r, Fox and the Lion. 6r, Mice and the Cat. 10r, Fox and the Goat. 12r, Dog in the Manger. No. 1474, Miller, his Son and the Ass, vert. No. 1475. Miser's Gold, vert.

1990, Dec. 11 Litho. *Perf. 14*

1466 A227 15 l multicolored .20 .20
1467 A227 50 l multicolored .20 .20
1468 A227 1r multicolored .35 .35
1469 A227 3.50r multicolored 1.25 1.25
1470 A227 4r multicolored 1.50 1.50
1471 A227 6r multicolored 2.25 2.25
1472 A227 10r multicolored 3.75 3.75
1473 A227 12r multicolored 4.25 4.25
Nos. 1466-1473 (8) 13.75 13.75

Souvenir Sheets

1474 A227 20r multicolored 7.50 7.50
1475 A227 20r multicolored 7.50 7.50

Intl. Literacy Year.

A228

A229

Steam Locomotives: 20 l, "31" Class, East African Railways. 50 l, Mikado, Sudan Railways. 1r, Beyer-Garratt GM Class, South African Railways. 3r, "7th" Class, Rhodesia Railways. 5r, Central Pacific 229. 8r, Reading 415. 10r, Porter Narrow-guage. 12r, Great Northern 515. No. 1484, American Standard 315. No. 1485, East African Railways 5950.

1990, Dec. 15

1476 A228 20 l multicolored .20 .20
1477 A228 50 l multicolored .20 .20
1478 A228 1r multicolored .40 .40
1479 A228 3r multicolored 1.25 1.25
1480 A228 5r multicolored 2.00 2.00
1481 A228 8r multicolored 3.50 3.50
1482 A228 10r multicolored 4.25 4.25
1483 A228 12r multicolored 5.00 5.00
Nos. 1476-1483 (8) 16.80 16.80

Souvenir Sheets

1484 A228 20r multicolored 8.25 8.25
1485 A228 20r multicolored 8.25 8.25

1990, Dec. 27

Various players from participating countries.

1486 A229 1r Holland .35 .35
1487 A229 2.50r England .90 .90
1487A A229 3.50r Argentina 1.40 1.40
1488 A229 5r Brazil 1.90 1.90
1488A A229 7r Italy 2.50 2.50
1489 A229 10r Russia 3.75 3.75
1489A A229 15r West Germany 5.75 5.75
Nos. 1486-1489A (7) 16.55 16.55

Souvenir Sheets

1490 A229 18r Austria 4.50 4.50
1491 A229 18r South Korea 4.50 4.50
1492 A229 20r Italy (dk blue shirt) 5.00 5.00
1493 A229 20r Argentina (blue & white shirt) 5.00 5.00

World Cup Soccer Championships, Italy.

No. 1111 Surcharged

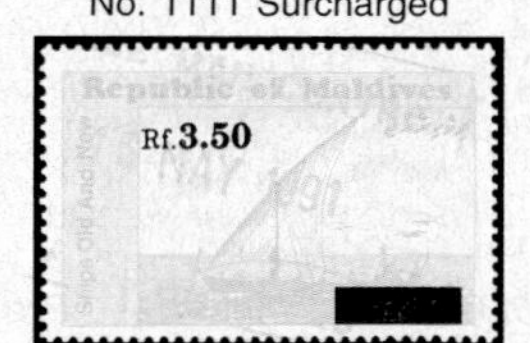

Methods and Perfs As Before

1990

1493B A171 3.50r on 2.70r #1111 —

An additional stamp was issued in this set. The editors would like to examine any examples.

Peter Paul Rubens (1577-1640), Painter — A230

Entire works or details from paintings by Rubens: 20 l, Summer. 50 l, Landscape with Rainbow. 1r, Wreckage of Aeneas. 2.50r, Chateau de Steen. 3.50r, Landscape with Herd of Cows. 7r, Ruins of Palantine. 10r, Landscape with Peasants and Cows. 12r, Wagon Fording a Stream. No. 1502, Landscape with a Sunset. No. 1503, Peasants with Cattle by a Stream in a Woody Landscape. No. 1504, Shepherd with his Flock in a Wooded Landscape. No. 1505, Stuck Wagon.

1991, Feb. 7 Litho. *Perf. 14x13½*

1494 A230 20 l multicolored .20 .20
1495 A230 50 l multicolored .20 .20
1496 A230 1r multicolored .35 .35
1497 A230 2.50r multicolored .80 .80
1498 A230 3.50r multicolored 1.10 1.10
1499 A230 7r multicolored 2.25 2.25
1500 A230 10r multicolored 3.50 3.50
1501 A230 12r multicolored 4.00 4.00
Nos. 1494-1501 (8) 12.40 12.40

Souvenir Sheets

1502-1505 A230 20r each 5.00 5.00

First Marathon Run, 490 B.C. — A231

Events and anniversaries (in 1990): 1r, Anthony Fokker (1890-1939), aircraft builder. 3.50r, Launch of first commercial satellite, 25th anniv. 7r, East, West German foreign ministers sign re-unification documents, Oct. 3, 1990, horiz. 8r, Magna Carta, 775th anniv. 10r, Dwight D. Eisenhower. 12r, Winston Churchill. 15r, Pres. Reagan destroying Berlin Wall, horiz. No. 1514, Brandenburg Gate, horiz. No. 1515, Battle of Britain, 50th anniv., horiz.

1991, Mar. 11 *Perf. 14*

1506 A231 50 l multicolored .25 .25
1507 A231 1r multicolored .30 .30
1508 A231 3.50r multicolored 1.25 1.25
1509 A231 7r multicolored 2.50 2.50
1510 A231 8r multicolored 2.75 2.75
1511 A231 10r multicolored 3.50 3.50
1512 A231 12r multicolored 4.25 4.25
1513 A231 15r multicolored 5.25 5.25
Nos. 1506-1513 (8) 20.05 20.05

Souvenir Sheets

1514 A231 20r multicolored 7.50 7.50
1515 A231 20r multicolored 7.50 7.50

Global Warming A232

1991, Apr. 10

1516 A232 3.50r Dhoni 2.00 2.00
1517 A232 7r Freighter 3.75 3.75

Year of the Girl Child — A233

1991, Apr. 14

1518 A233 7r multicolored 2.50 2.50

Year of the Child A234

Children's drawings: 3.50r, Beach scene. 5r, City scene. 10r, Visualizing fruit. 25r, Scuba diver.

1991, May 10

1519 A234 3.50r multicolored 1.25 1.25
1520 A234 5r multicolored 1.90 1.90
1521 A234 10r multicolored 3.75 3.75
1522 A234 25r multicolored 9.25 9.25
Nos. 1519-1522 (4) 16.15 16.15

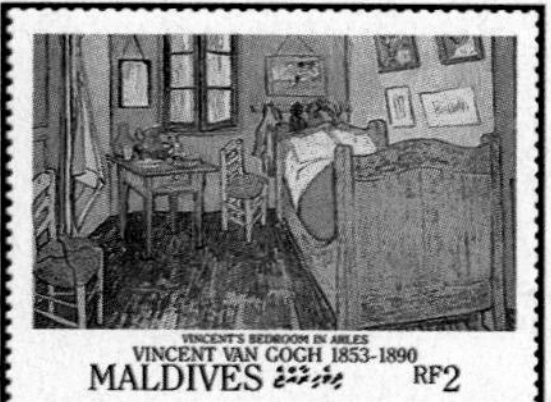

Paintings by Vincent Van Gogh — A235

Designs: 15 l, Japanese Vase with Roses and Anemones, vert. 20 l, Still Life: Red Poppies and Daisies, vert. 2r, Vincent's Bedroom in Arles. 3.50r, The Mulberry Tree. 7r, Blossoming Chestnut Branches. 10r, Morning: Peasant Couple Going to Work. 12r, Still Life: Pink Roses. 15r, Child with Orange, vert. No. 1531, Courtyard of the Hospital at Arles. No. 1532, Houses in Auvers, vert.

1991, June 6 Litho. *Perf. 13½*

1523 A235 15 l multicolored .30 .30
1524 A235 20 l multicolored .30 .30
1525 A235 2r multicolored .75 .75
1526 A235 3.50r multicolored 1.40 1.40
1527 A235 7r multicolored 2.75 2.75
1528 A235 10r multicolored 4.00 4.00
1529 A235 12r multicolored 4.50 4.50
1530 A235 15r multicolored 5.75 5.75
Nos. 1523-1530 (8) 19.75 19.75

Sizes: 100x75mm, 75x100mm

Imperf

1531 A235 25r multicolored 8.25 8.25
1532 A235 25r multicolored 8.25 8.25

Royal Family Birthday, Anniversary

Common Design Type

1991, July 4 Litho. *Perf. 14*

1533 CD347 1r multi .30 .30
1534 CD347 2r multi .60 .60
1535 CD347 3.50r multi 1.10 1.10
1536 CD347 5r multi 1.50 1.50
1537 CD347 7r multi 2.10 2.10
1538 CD347 8r multi 2.50 2.50
1539 CD347 12r multi 3.75 3.75
1540 CD347 15r multi 4.25 4.25
Nos. 1533-1540 (8) 16.10 16.10

Souvenir Sheets

1541 CD347 25r Elizabeth, Philip 7.25 7.25
1542 CD347 25r Charles, Diana, sons 7.25 7.25

1r, 3.50r, 7r, 15r, No. 1542, Charles and Diana, 10th wedding anniversary. Others, Queen Elizabeth II, 65th birthday.

Hummel Figurines — A236

Designs: 10 l, No. 1552a, Child painting. 25 l, No. 1552b, Boy reading at table. 50 l, No. 1552c, Boy with back pack. 2r, No. 1551a, School Girl. 3.50r, No. 1551b, The Bookworm (boy sitting and reading). 8r, No. 1551c, Little Brother's Lesson. 10r, No. 1551d, School Girls. 25r, No. 1552d, Three school boys.

1991, July 25 Litho. *Perf. 14*

1543 A236 10 l multicolored .20 .20
1544 A236 25 l multicolored .20 .20
1545 A236 50 l multicolored .20 .20
1546 A236 2r multicolored .60 .60
1547 A236 3.50r multicolored 1.10 1.10
1548 A236 8r multicolored 2.40 2.40
1549 A236 10r multicolored 3.00 3.00
1550 A236 25r multicolored 7.25 7.25
Nos. 1543-1550 (8) 14.95 14.95

Souvenir Sheets

1551 A236 5r Sheet of 4, #a.-d. 5.50 5.50
1552 A236 8r Sheet of 4, #a.-d. 9.00 9.00

Japanese Steam Locomotives — A237

1991, Aug. 25 Litho. *Perf. 14*

1553 A237 15 l C 57, vert. .20 .20
1554 A237 25 l Series 6250 .20 .20
1555 A237 1r D 51, vert. .35 .35
1556 A237 3.50r Series 8620 1.25 1.25
1557 A237 5r Class 10 1.90 1.90
1558 A237 7r C 61, vert. 2.75 2.75
1559 A237 10r Series 9600 3.75 3.75
1560 A237 12r D 52 4.75 4.75
Nos. 1553-1560 (8) 15.15 15.15

Souvenir Sheets

1561 A237 20r Class 1080 6.00 6.00
1562 A237 20r C 56 6.00 6.00

Phila Nippon '91.

Butterflies A238

1991, Dec. 2 Litho. *Perf. 14*

1563 A238 10 l Blue salamis .25 .25
1564 A238 25 l Mountain beauty .25 .25
1565 A238 50 l Lucerne blue .35 .35
1566 A238 2r Monarch .95 .95
1567 A238 3.50r Common rose 1.75 1.75
1568 A238 5r Black witch 2.50 2.50
1569 A238 8r Oriental swallowtail 4.00 4.00
1570 A238 10r Gaudy commodore 5.00 5.00
Nos. 1563-1570 (8) 15.05 15.05

Souvenir Sheets

1571 A238 20r Pearl crescent 7.25 7.25
1572 A238 20r Friar 7.25 7.25

No. 1570 inscribed "guady."

Japanese Space Program A239

Designs: 15 l, H-11 Launch Vehicle. 20 l, H-II Orbiting plane. 2r, Geosynchronous satellite 5. 3.50r, Marine observation satellite-1. 7r, Communications satellite 3. 10r, Broadcasting satellite-2. 12r, H-1 Launch Vehicle, vert. 15r, Space flier unit, space shuttle. No. 1581, Katsura tracking and data acquisition station. No. 1582, M-3S II Launch vehicle, vert.

1991, Dec. 11

1573 A239 15 l multicolored .25 .25
1574 A239 20 l multicolored .25 .25
1575 A239 2r multicolored .60 .60
1576 A239 3.50r multicolored 1.10 1.10
1577 A239 7r multicolored 2.10 2.10
1578 A239 10r multicolored 3.00 3.00
1579 A239 12r multicolored 3.75 3.75
1580 A239 15r multicolored 4.75 4.75
Nos. 1573-1580 (8) 15.80 15.80

Souvenir Sheets

1581 A239 20r multicolored 7.25 7.25
1582 A239 20r multicolored 7.25 7.25

Miniature Sheet

Franklin D. Roosevelt A240

World War II Leaders of the Pacific Theater: b, Douglas MacArthur. c, Chester Nimitz. d, Jonathan Wainwright. e, Ernest King. f, Claire Chennault. g, William Halsey. h, Marc Mitscher. i, James Doolittle. j, Raymond Spruance.

1991, Dec. 30 Litho. *Perf. 14½x15*

1583 A240 3.50r Sheet of 10, #a.-j. 16.00 16.00

Grand Prix Race Cars A241

Designs: 20 l, Williams FW-07. 50 l, Brabham BT50 BMW Turbo. 1r, Williams FW-11 Honda. 3.50r, Ferrari 312 T3. 5r, Lotus Honda 99T. 7r, Benetton Ford B188. 10r, Tyrrell P34 Six-wheeler. 21r, Renault RE-30B Turbo. No. 1592, Ferrari F189. No. 1593, Brabham BT50 BMW Turbo, diff.

1991, Dec. 28 Litho. *Perf. 14*

1584 A241 20 l multicolored .25 .25
1585 A241 50 l multicolored .25 .25
1586 A241 1r multicolored .30 .30
1587 A241 3.50r multicolored 1.10 1.10
1588 A241 5r multicolored 1.60 1.60
1589 A241 7r multicolored 2.25 2.25
1590 A241 10r multicolored 3.25 3.25
1591 A241 21r multicolored 6.75 6.75
Nos. 1584-1591 (8) 15.75 15.75

Souvenir Sheets

1592 A241 25r multicolored 8.25 8.25
1593 A241 25r multicolored 8.25 8.25

Miniature Sheet

Enzo Ferrari (1898-1988) — A242

Ferrari Race cars: a, 1957 Testa Rossa. b, 1966 275GTB. c, 1951 "Aspirarta." d, Testarossa. f, 1958 Dino 246. g, 1952 Type 375. h, Mansell's Formula One. i, 1975 312T.

1991, Dec. 28

1594 A242 5r Sheet of 9, #a.-i. 18.00 18.00

17th World Scout Jamboree A243

Designs: 10r, Scouts diving on reef. 11r, Hand making scout sign, emblem, vert. 18r, Lord Robert Baden-Powell, vert. 20r, Czechoslovakian scout (local) stamp, vert.

1991, Dec. 30

1595 A243 10r multicolored 2.50 2.50
1596 A243 11r multicolored 3.00 3.00

Souvenir Sheets

1597 A243 18r multicolored 4.50 4.50
1598 A243 20r multicolored 5.00 5.00

Wolfgang Amadeus Mozart, Death Bicent. A244

Portrait of Mozart and: 50 l, Schwarzenberg Palace. 1r, Spa at Baden. 2r, Royal Palace, Berlin. 5r, Viennese Masonic seal. 7r, St. Marx. No. 1604, Josepsplatz, Vienna.

1991, Dec. 30

1599 A244 50 l multicolored .20 .20
1600 A244 1r multicolored .25 .25
1601 A244 2r multicolored .55 .55
1602 A244 5r multicolored 1.25 1.25
1603 A244 7r multicolored 1.75 1.75
1604 A244 20r multicolored 5.00 5.00
Nos. 1599-1604 (6) 9.00 9.00

Souvenir Sheet

1605 A244 20r Bust of Mozart, vert. 5.00 5.00

Brandenburg Gate, Bicent. — A245

Designs: 20 l, Flag. 1.75 l, Man embracing child, Berlin wall. 4r, Soldiers behind barricade, demonstrator. 15r, World War I Iron Cross. No. 1610, Helmet. No. 1611, 1939 helmet. No. 1612, Studded helmet.

1991, Dec. 30

1606 A245 20 l multicolored .20 .20
1607 A245 1.75r multicolored .45 .45
1608 A245 4r multicolored 1.00 1.00
1609 A245 15r multicolored 3.75 3.75
Nos. 1606-1609 (4) 5.40 5.40

Souvenir Sheets

1610 A245 18r multicolored 4.50 4.50
1611 A245 18r multicolored 4.50 4.50
1612 A245 18r multicolored 4.50 4.50

Anniversaries and Events — A246

Designs: No. 1613, Otto Lilienthal, glider No. 16. No. 1614, "D-Day," Normandy 1944, Charles de Gaulle. 7r, Front of locomotive, vert. 8r, Kurt Schwitters, artist and Landesmuseum. 9r, Map, man in Swiss costume. 10r, Charles de Gaulle in Madagascar, 1958. 12r, Steam locomotive. 15r, Portrait of Charles de Gaulle, vert. 20r, Locomotive and coal car.

1991, Dec. 30 Litho. *Perf. 14*

1613 A246 6r multicolored 2.00 2.00
1614 A246 6r multicolored 1.50 1.50
1615 A246 7r multicolored 1.75 1.75
1616 A246 8r multicolored 2.00 2.00
1617 A246 9r multicolored 2.25 2.25
1618 A246 10r multicolored 2.50 2.50
1619 A246 12r multicolored 3.00 3.00
Nos. 1613-1619 (7) 15.00 15.00

Souvenir Sheets

1620 A246 15r multicolored 4.50 4.50
1621 A246 20r multicolored 5.00 5.00

First glider flight, cent. (#1613). Charles de Gaulle, birth cent. in 1990 (#1614, #1618, & #1620). Trans-Siberian Railway, cent. (#1615, #1619 & #1621). Hanover, 750th anniv. (#1616). Swiss Confederation, 700th anniv. (#1617).

No. 1621 contains one 58x43mm stamp.

Birds — A247

Perf. 14½, 13 (6.50r+50 l, 30r, 40r)

1992-94

1624 A247 10 l Numenius phaeopus .25 .25
1625 A247 25 l Egretta alba .25 .25
1626 A247 50 l Ardea cinerea .25 .25
1627 A247 2r Phalacrocorax aristotelis .60 .60
1628 A247 3.50r Sterna dougallii 1.10 1.10
1629 A247 5r Tringa nebularia 1.50 1.50
1630 A247 6.50r +50 l Neophron percnopterus 1.75 1.75
1631 A247 8r Upupa epops 2.40 2.40
1632 A247 10r Elanus caeruleus 3.00 3.00
1633 A247 25r Eudocimus ruber 4.75 4.75
1634 A247 30r Falco peregrinus 6.00 6.00
1635 A247 40r Milvus migrans 8.50 8.50
1636 A247 50r Pluvialis squatarola 10.50 10.50
Nos. 1624-1636 (13) 40.85 40.85

Issued: 10 l, 25 l, 50 l, 2r, 3.50r, 5r, 8r, 10r, 25r, 2/17/92; 6.50r+50 l, 30r, 11/93; 40r, 1994(?).

See No. 2323.

Queen Elizabeth II's Accession to the Throne, 40th Anniv.

Common Design Type

1992, Feb. 6 ***Perf. 14***

1637 CD348 1r multicolored .30 .30
1638 CD348 3.50r multicolored 1.10 1.10
1639 CD348 7r multicolored 2.25 2.25
1640 CD348 10r multicolored 3.25 3.25
Nos. 1637-1640 (4) 6.90 6.90

Souvenir Sheets

1641 CD348 18r Queen, palm trees 5.50 5.50
1642 CD348 18r Queen, boat 5.50 5.50

This set differs from the common design in that the Queen's portrait and local view are separated by a curved line rather than with a cypher outline.

Disney Characters on World Tour A248

Designs: 25 l, Mickey on Flying Carpet Airways. 50 l, Goofy at Big Ben, London. 1r, Mickey in Holland. 2r, Pluto eating pasta, Italy. 3r, Mickey, Donald do sombero stomp in Mexico. 3.50r, Mickey, Goofy, and Donald form Miki Tiki, Polynesia. 5r, Goofy's Alpine antics, Austria. 7r, Mickey Maus, Germany. 10r, Donald as Samurai Duck. 12r, Mickey in Russia. 15r, Mickey's Oom-pah Band in Germany. No. 1654, Mickey, globe. No. 1655, Donald in Ireland chasing leprechaun with pot of gold at end of rainbow, horiz. No. 1655A, Pluto, kangaroo with joey, Australia.

1992, Feb. 4 ***Perf. 13x13½***

1643 A248 25 l multi .20 .20
1644 A248 50 l multi .20 .20
1645 A248 1r multi .35 .35
1646 A248 2r multi .65 .65
1647 A248 3r multi .90 .90
1648 A248 3.50r multi .90 .90
1649 A248 5r multi 1.25 1.25
1650 A248 7r multi 1.75 1.75
1651 A248 10r multi 2.50 2.50
1652 A248 12r multi 3.25 3.25
1653 A248 15r multi 5.00 5.00
Nos. 1643-1653 (11) 16.95 16.95

Souvenir Sheets

1654 A248 25r multi 6.25 6.25
1655 A248 25r multi 5.00 5.00
1655A A248 25r multi 5.00 5.00

While the rest of the set has the same issue date as Nos. 1644-1645, 1647, 1653-1654, their dollar value was lower when they were released.

Fish A249

1992, Mar. 23 **Litho.** ***Perf. 14***

1656 A249 7 l Blue surgeonfish .30 .30
1657 A249 20 l Bigeye .30 .30
1658 A249 50 l Yellowfin tuna .30 .30
1659 A249 1r Two-spot red snapper .30 .30
1660 A249 3.50r Sabre squirrelfish 1.00 1.00
1661 A249 5r Picasso triggerfish 1.40 1.40
1662 A249 8r Bennet's butterfly fish 2.25 2.25
1663 A249 10r Parrotfish 3.00 3.00
1664 A249 12r Grouper 3.50 3.50
1665 A249 15r Skipjack tuna 4.25 4.25
Nos. 1656-1665 (10) 16.60 16.60

Souvenir Sheets

1666 A249 20r Clownfish 4.00 4.00
1667 A249 20r Sweetlips 4.00 4.00
1667A A249 20r Threadfin butterflyfish 4.00 4.00
1667B A249 20r Clown triggerfish 4.00 4.00

World Columbian Stamp Expo '92, Chicago A250

Walt Disney characters in Chicago: 1r, Mickey as Indian with Jean Baptiste Pointe du Sable, founder of Chicago. 3.50r, Donald at old Chicago post office, 1831. 7r, Donald in old Fort Dearborn. 15r, Goofy, mastodon at Museum of Science and Industry. 25r, Minnie and Mickey at Ferris wheel midway, Columbian Exposition, 1893, horiz.

1992, Apr. 15 ***Perf. 13½x14***

1668 A250 1r multicolored .30 .30
1669 A250 3.50r multicolored 1.10 1.10
1670 A250 7r multicolored 2.25 2.25
1671 A250 15r multicolored 4.75 4.75
Nos. 1668-1671 (4) 8.40 8.40

Souvenir Sheet

Perf. 14x13½

1672 A250 25r multicolored 7.50 7.50

No. 1671 identifies Field Museum as Museum of Science and Industry.

Granada '92 — A251

Disney characters in old Alhambra, Granada: 2r, Minnie in Court of Lions. 5r, Goofy bathing in Lions Fountain. 8r, Mickey walking near Gate of Justice. 12r, Donald Duck serenading Daisy in Vermilion Towers. No. 1682, Goofy and Mickey outside Towers of the Alhambra.

1992, Apr. 15 ***Perf. 13½x14***

1678 A251 2r multicolored .60 .60
1679 A251 5r multicolored 1.50 1.50
1680 A251 8r multicolored 2.50 2.50
1681 A251 12r multicolored 4.00 4.00
Nos. 1678-1681 (4) 8.60 8.60

Souvenir Sheet

1682 A251 25r multicolored 7.50 7.50

A252

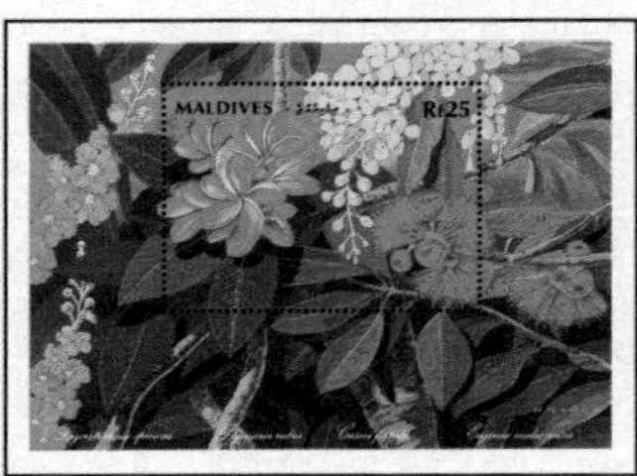

Flowers of the World — A253

1992, Apr. 26 **Litho.** ***Perf. 14½***

1688 A252 25 l United States .25 .25
1689 A252 50 l Australia .25 .25
1690 A252 2r England .70 .70
1691 A252 3.50r Brazil 1.25 1.25
1692 A252 5r Holland 1.75 1.75
1693 A252 8r France 2.75 2.75
1694 A252 10r Japan 3.50 3.50
1695 A252 15r Africa 5.25 5.25
Nos. 1688-1695 (8) 15.70 15.70

Souvenir Sheets

Perf. 14

1696 A253 25r org, yel & red vio flowers 6.75 6.75
1696A A253 25r red, pink & yel flowers 6.75 6.75

No. 1696 contains one 57x43mm stamp. No. 1696A contains one 57x34mm stamp.

Natl. Security Service, Cent. A254

1992, Apr. 21 ***Perf. 14***

1697 A254 3.50r Coast Guard 1.25 1.25
1698 A254 5r Infantry 2.25 2.25
1699 A254 10r Aakoatey 4.75 4.75
1700 A254 15r Fire department 7.00 7.00
Nos. 1697-1700 (4) 15.25 15.25

Souvenir Sheet

1701 A254 20r Sultan in procession 7.50 7.50

A255

A256

Mushrooms: 10 l, Laetiporus sulphureus. 25 l, Coprinus atramentarius. 50 l, Gandoderma lucidum. 3.50r, Russula aurata. 5r, Polyporus umbellatus. 8r, Suillus grevillei. 10r, Clavaria zollingeri. No. 1709, Boletus edulis. No. 1710, Trametes cinnabarina. No. 1711, Marasmius oreades.

1992, May 14 **Litho.** ***Perf. 14***

1702 A255 10 l multicolored .20 .20
1703 A255 25 l multicolored .20 .20
1704 A255 50 l multicolored .20 .20
1705 A255 3.50r multicolored 1.00 1.00
1706 A255 5r multicolored 1.40 1.40
1707 A255 8r multicolored 2.40 2.40
1708 A255 10r multicolored 2.75 2.75
1709 A255 25r multicolored 7.50 7.50
Nos. 1702-1709 (8) 15.65 15.65

Souvenir Sheets

1710 A255 25r multicolored 7.00 7.00
1711 A255 25r multicolored 7.00 7.00

1992, June 1

1712 A256 10 l Hurdles .25 .25
1713 A256 1r Boxing .25 .25
1714 A256 3.50r Women's running .90 .90
1715 A256 5r Discus 1.25 1.25
1716 A256 7r Basketball 1.75 1.75
1717 A256 10r Running 2.50 2.50
1718 A256 12r Rhythmic gymnastics 3.25 3.25
1719 A256 20r Fencing 5.25 5.25
Nos. 1712-1719 (8) 15.40 15.40

Souvenir Sheets

1720 A256 25r Torch 5.00 5.00
1721 A256 25r Olympic rings, flags 5.00 5.00

1992 Summer Olympics, Barcelona.

A256a

Dinosaurs — A257

1992 Winter Olympics, Albertville: 5r, Two-man bobsled. 8r, Free-style ski jump. 10r, Women's cross-country skiing. No. 1725, Women's slalom skiing, horiz. No. 1726, Men's figure skating.

1992, June 1 **Litho.** ***Perf. 14***

1722 A256a 5r multicolored 1.00 1.00
1723 A256a 8r multicolored 1.60 1.60
1724 A256a 10r multicolored 2.00 2.00
Nos. 1722-1724 (3) 4.60 4.60

Souvenir Sheets

1725 A256a 25r multicolored 5.00 5.00
1726 A256a 25r multicolored 5.00 5.00

1992, Sept. 15 **Litho.** ***Perf. 14***

1727 A257 5 l Deinonychus .20 .20
1728 A257 10 l Styracosaurus .20 .20
1729 A257 25 l Mamenchisaurus .20 .20
1730 A257 50 l Stenonychosaurus .20 .20
1731 A257 1r Parasaurolophus .20 .20

No.	Type	Value	Description	Unused	Used
1732	A257	1.25r	Scelidosaurus	.30	.30
1733	A257	1.75r	Tyrannosaurus	.40	.40
1734	A257	2r	Stegosaurus	.45	.45
1735	A257	3.50r	Iguanodon	.80	.80
1736	A257	4r	Anatosaurus	.90	.90
1737	A257	5r	Monoclonius	1.10	1.10
1738	A257	7r	Tenontosaurus	1.60	1.60
1739	A257	8r	Brachiosaurus	1.90	1.90
1740	A257	10r	Euoplocephalus	2.25	2.25
1741	A257	25r	Triceratops	5.75	5.75
1742	A257	50r	Apatosaurus	11.50	11.50
			Nos. 1727-1742 (16)	27.95	27.95

Souvenir Sheets

No.	Type	Value	Description	Unused	Used
1743	A257	25r	Iguanodon, allosaurus	5.00	5.00
1744	A257	25r	Hadrosaur	5.00	5.00
1745	A257	25r	Tyrannosaurus, triceratops	5.00	5.00
1746	A257	25r	Brachiosaurus, iguanodons	5.00	5.00

Genoa '92.

1992 Summer Olympics, Barcelona A258

1992, June 1 Litho. *Perf. 14*

No.	Type	Value	Description	Unused	Used
1747	A258	10 l	Pole vault, vert.	.25	.25
1748	A258	25 l	Pommel horse	.25	.25
1749	A258	50 l	Shot put, vert.	.25	.25
1750	A258	1r	Horizontal bar	.25	.25
1751	A258	2r	Triple jump	.50	.50
1752	A258	3.50r	Table tennis, vert.	.90	.90
1753	A258	7r	Wrestling	1.90	1.90
1754	A258	9r	Baseball, vert.	2.25	2.25
1755	A258	12r	Swimming	3.25	3.25
			Nos. 1747-1755 (9)	9.80	9.80

Souvenir Sheet

No.	Type	Value	Description	Unused	Used
1756	A258	25r	Decathlon (high jump)	10.00	10.00

Souvenir Sheets

Mysteries of the Universe — A259

#1757, Loch Ness monster. #1758, Explosion of the Hindenburg. #1759, Crystal skulls. #1760, Black holes. #1761, UFO over Washington State. #1762, UFO near Columbus, Ohio. #1763, Explosion at Chernobyl, 1986. #1764, Crop circles of Great Britain. #1765, Ghosts of English castles and mansions. #1766, Drawings of Plain of Nasca, Peru, vert. #1767, Stonehenge, England, vert. #1768, Bust of Plato, the disappearance of Atlantis. #1769, Footprint of Yeti (abominable snowman), vert. #1770, Pyramids of Giza. #1771, Bermuda Triangle. #1772, The Mary Celeste, vert.

1992, Oct. 28

No.	Type	Description	Unused	Used
1757-1772	A259	25r each	5.00	5.00

1994 World Cup Soccer Championships, US — A260

Players of 1990 German team: 10 l, Jurgen Klinsmann. 25 l, Pierre Littbarski. 50 l, Lothar Matthaus. 1r, Rudi Voller. 2r, Thomas Hassler. 3.50r, Thomas Berthold. 4r, Jurgen Kohler. 5r, Berti Vogts, trainer. 6r, Bodo Illgner. 7r, Klaus Augenthaler. 8r, Franz Beckenbauer, coach. 10r, Andreas Brehme. 12r, Guido Buchwald.

No. 1786, Team members, horiz. No. 1787, Unidentified player in action, horiz.

1992, Aug. 10 Litho. *Perf. 14*

No.	Type	Value	Description	Unused	Used
1773	A260	10 l	multicolored	.20	.20
1774	A260	25 l	multicolored	.20	.20
1775	A260	50 l	multicolored	.20	.20
1776	A260	1r	multicolored	.20	.20
1777	A260	2r	multicolored	.40	.40
1778	A260	3.50r	multicolored	.70	.70
1779	A260	4r	multicolored	.80	.80
1780	A260	5r	multicolored	1.00	1.00
1781	A260	6r	multicolored	1.25	1.25
1782	A260	7r	multicolored	1.40	1.40
1783	A260	8r	multicolored	1.60	1.60
1784	A260	10r	multicolored	2.00	2.00
1785	A260	12r	multicolored	2.40	2.40
			Nos. 1773-1785 (13)	12.35	12.35

Souvenir Sheets

No.	Type	Value	Description	Unused	Used
1786	A260	35r	multicolored	7.00	7.00
1787	A260	35r	multicolored	7.00	7.00

Souvenir Sheet

New York Public Library — A261

1992, Oct. 28 Litho. *Perf. 14*

No.	Type	Value	Description	Unused	Used
1788	A261	20r	multicolored	5.25	5.25

Postage Stamp Mega Event '92, New York City.

Walt Disney's Goofy, 60th Anniv. — A262

Scenes from Disney cartoon films: 10 l, Father's Weekend, 1953. 50 l, Symphony Hour, 1942. 75 l, Frank Duck Brings 'Em Back Alive, 1946. 1r, Crazy with the Heat, 1947. 2r, The Big Wash, 1948. 3.50r, How to Ride a Horse, 1950. 5r, Two Gun Goofy, 1952. 8r, Saludos Amigos, 1943, vert. 10r, How to Be a Detective, 1952. 12r, For Whom the Bulls Toil, 1953. 15r, Double Dribble, 1946, vert.

No. 1801, Mickey and the Beanstalk, 1947. No. 1802, Double Dribble, 1946, vert., diff. No. 1803, The Goofy Success Story, 1955.

Perf. 14x13½, 13½x14

1992, Dec. 7 Litho.

No.	Type	Value	Description	Unused	Used
1789	A262	10 l	multicolored	.25	.25
1791	A262	50 l	multicolored	.25	.25
1792	A262	75 l	multicolored	.25	.25
1793	A262	1r	multicolored	.25	.25
1794	A262	2r	multicolored	.50	.50
1795	A262	3.50r	multicolored	.90	.90
1796	A262	5r	multicolored	1.25	1.25
1797	A262	8r	multicolored	2.00	2.00
1798	A262	10r	multicolored	2.50	2.50
1799	A262	12r	multicolored	3.00	3.00
1800	A262	15r	multicolored	3.75	3.75
			Nos. 1789-1800 (11)	14.90	14.90

Souvenir Sheets

No.	Type	Value	Description	Unused	Used
1801	A262	20r	multicolored	4.50	4.50
1802	A262	20r	multicolored	4.50	4.50
1803	A262	20r	multicolored	4.50	4.50

A number has been reserved for an additional value in this set.

A263

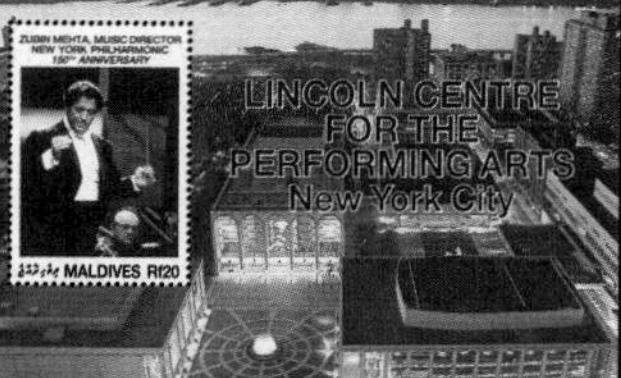

Anniversaries and Events — A264

Designs: 1r, Zeppelin on bombing raid over London during World War I. No. 1805, German, French flags, Konrad Adenauer, Charles de Gaulle. No. 1806, Radio telescope. No. 1807, Columbus studying globe. No. 1808, Indian rhinoceros. 7r, WHO, ICN, and FAO emblems. 8r, Green sea turtle. No. 1822, Scarlet macaw. No. 1811, Lion's Intl. emblem and Melvin Jones, founder. No. 1812, Yacht America, first America's Cup winner, 1851. 12r, Columbus claiming San Salvador for Spain. No. 1814, Voyager 1 approaching Saturn. No. 1815, NATO flag, airplanes, Adenauer. 20r, Graf Zeppelin over New York City. No. 1817, Landsat satellite. No. 1818, Count Zeppelin. No. 1819, Santa Maria. No. 1820, Konrad Adenauer. No. 1821, Zubin Mehta, music director, NY Philharmonic, vert. No. 1823, Friedrich Schmiedl (b. 1902), rocket mail pioneer.

1992-93 Litho. *Perf. 14*

No.	Type	Value	Description	Unused	Used
1804	A263	1r	multicolored	.30	.30
1805	A263	3.50r	multicolored	.90	.90
1806	A263	3.50r	multicolored	.70	.70
1807	A263	6r	multicolored	1.50	1.50
1808	A263	6r	multicolored	1.25	1.25
1809	A263	7r	multicolored	1.40	1.40
1810	A263	8r	multicolored	1.60	1.60
1811	A263	10r	multicolored	2.00	2.00
1812	A263	10r	multicolored	2.00	2.00
1813	A263	12r	multicolored	3.00	3.00
1814	A263	15r	multicolored	3.00	3.00
1815	A263	15r	multicolored	4.00	4.00
1816	A263	20r	multicolored	6.00	6.00
			Nos. 1804-1816 (13)	27.65	27.65

Souvenir Sheets

No.	Type	Value	Description	Unused	Used
1817	A263	20r	multicolored	6.00	6.00
1818	A263	20r	multicolored	6.25	6.25
1819	A263	20r	multicolored	6.25	6.25
1820	A263	20r	multicolored	6.00	6.00
1821	A264	20r	multicolored	6.75	6.75
1822	A263	20r	multicolored	6.00	4.60
1823	A263	25r	multicolored	6.50	6.50
			Nos. 1817-1823 (7)	43.75	42.35

Count Zeppelin, 75th anniv. of death (#1804, 1816, 1818). Konrad Adenauer, 25th anniv. of death (#1805, 1815, 1820). Intl. Space Year (#1806, 1814, 1817). Columbus' discovery of America, 500th anniversary (#1807, 1813, 1819). Earth Summit, Rio de Janeiro (#1808, 1810, 1822). Intl. Conference on Nutrition, Rome (#1809). Lions Intl., 75th anniversary (#1811). America's Cup yacht race (#1812). New York Philharmonic, 150th anniv. (#1821).

No. 1823 contains one 27x35mm stamp.

Issue dates: Nos. 1805, 1808, 1810, 1815, 1820, 1822, Jan. 1993. Others, Nov. 1992.

Miniature Sheet

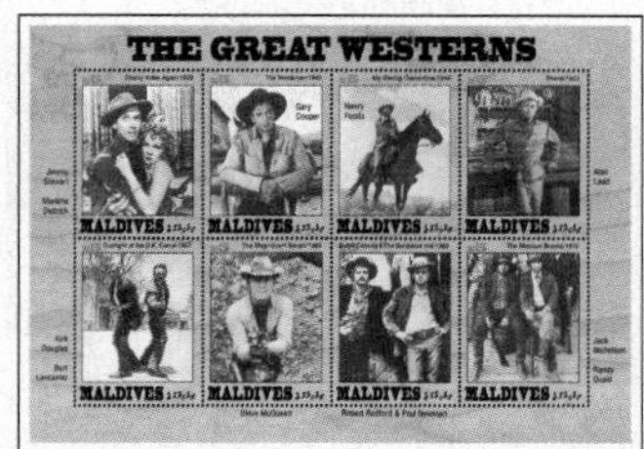

Western Films — A265

Actors and film: No. 1824a, Jimmy Stewart and Marlene Dietrich, Destry Rides Again, 1939. b, Gary Cooper, The Westerner, 1940. c, Henry Fonda, My Darling Clementine, 1940. d, Alan Ladd, Shane, 1953. e, Kirk Douglas and Burt Lancaster, Gunfight at the O.K. Coral, 1957. f, Steve McQueen, The Magnificent Seven, 1960. g, Robert Redford and Paul Newman, Butch Cassidy & The Sundance Kid, 1969. h, Jack Nicholson and Randy Quaid, The Missouri Breaks, 1976.

No. 1825, Clint Eastwood, Pale Rider. No. 1826, John Wayne, The Searchers, 1956.

1992-93 Litho. *Perf. 13½x14*

No.	Type	Value	Description	Unused	Used
1824	A265	5r	Sheet of 8, #a.-h.	12.00	12.00

Souvenir Sheets

No.	Type	Value	Description	Unused	Used
1825	A265	20r	multicolored	5.25	5.25
1826	A265	20r	multicolored	5.25	5.25

Issued: #1824-1825, 1992; #1826, Jan. 1993.

Miniature Sheet

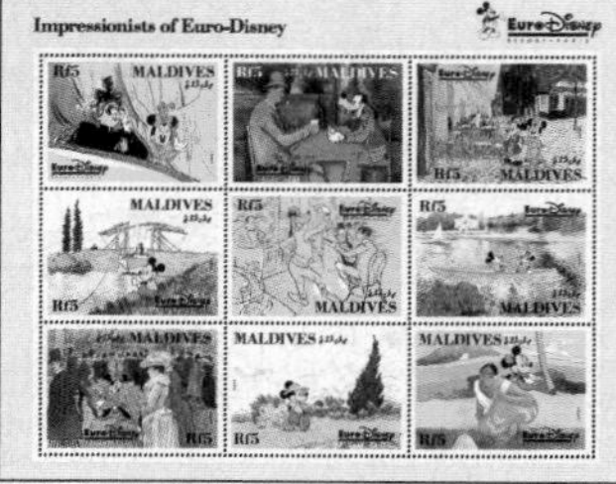

Opening of Euro Disney Resort, Paris — A266

Disney characters in paintings by French impressionists — #1827: a, Minnie on theater balcony. b, Goofy playing cards. c, Mickey and Minnie walking by outdoor cafe. d, Mickey fishing. e, Goofy dancing to music of harp player. f, Mickey and Minnie in boat. g, Minnie on dance floor. h, Mickey strolling through country. i, Minnie standing behind Polynesian woman.

1992, Dec. *Perf. 14x13½*

No.	Type	Value	Description	Unused	Used
1827	A266	5r	Sheet of 9, #a.-i.	15.00	15.00

Souvenir Sheets

No.	Type	Value	Description	Unused	Used
1828	A266	20r	Goofy	4.00	4.00
1829	A266	20r	Minnie	4.00	4.00
1830	A266	20r	Mickey	4.00	4.00

Perf. 13½x14

No.	Type	Value	Description	Unused	Used
1831	A266	20r	Donald Duck, vert.	4.00	4.00

SAARC Year of the Environment — A267

Designs: 25 l, Waterfall, drought area. 50 l, Clean, polluted beaches. 5r, Clean, polluted ocean. 10r, Clean island with vegetation, island polluted with trees dying.

1992, Dec. 30 Litho. *Perf. 14*

No.	Type	Value	Description	Unused	Used
1832	A267	25 l	multicolored	.20	.20
1833	A267	50 l	multicolored	.20	.20
1834	A267	5r	multicolored	1.00	1.00
1835	A267	10r	multicolored	2.00	2.00
			Nos. 1832-1835 (4)	3.40	3.40

Elvis Presley (1935-1977) A268

a, Portrait. b, With guitar. c, With microphone.

1993, Jan. 7

No.	Type	Value	Description	Unused	Used
1836	A268	3.50r	Strip of 3, #a.-c.	2.50	2.50

A set of 4 stamps commemorating South Asia Tourism year, formerly listed as Nos. 1837-1840, were prepared but not issued.

Miniature Sheets

Madame Seriziat A270

Louvre Museum, Bicent.

Details or entire paintings, by Jacques-Louis David:

#1841: b, Pierre Seriziat. c, Madame de Verninac. d, Madame Recamier. e, Self-portrait. f, General Bonaparte. g-h, The Lictors Returning to Brutus the Bodies of his Sons (left, right).

#1842: a, Self-portrait. b, The Woman in Blue. c, The Jeweled Woman. d, Young Girl in her Dressing Room. e, Haydee. f, Chartres Cathedral. g, The Belfry at Douai. h, The Bridge at Mantes.

Paintings by Jean-Honore Fragonard (1732-1806):

#1843: a, The Study. b, Denis Diderot. c, Marie-Madeleine Guimard. d, The Inspiration. e, Tivoli Cascades. f, The Music Lesson. g, The Bolt. h, Blindman's Buff.

#1844, The Gardens of the Villa D'Este, Tivoli, by Jean-Baptiste-Camille Corot, horiz.

#1845, Young Tiger Playing with its Mother, by Delacroix.

1993, Jan. 7 Litho. *Perf. 12*

Sheets of 8

1841 A270 8r #a.-h. + label 13.00 13.00
1842 A270 8r #a.-h. + label 13.00 13.00
1843 A270 8r #a.-h. + label 13.00 13.00

Souvenir Sheets

Perf. 14½

1844 A270 20r multicolored 6.25 6.25
1845 A270 20r multicolored 6.25 6.25

Nos. 1844-1845 contains one 88x55mm stamp.

Miniature Sheet

Coronation of Queen Elizabeth II, 40th Anniv. A271

Designs: a, 3.50r, Official coronation photograph. b, 5r, St. Edward's crown. c, 10r, Dignataries viewing ceremony. d, 10r, Queen, Prince Philip examining banknote.

1993, June 2 *Perf. 13½x14*

1846 A271 Sheet, 2 ea #a.-d. 13.50 13.50

A number has been reserved for an additional value in this set.

Shells — A272

Endangered Animals — A273

1993, July 15 Litho. *Perf. 14*

1848 A272 7 l Precious wentletrap .25 .25
1849 A272 15 l Purple sea snail .25 .25
1850 A272 50 l Arabian cowrie .25 .25
1850A A272 3.50r Major harp .90 .90
1850B A272 4r Royal paper bubble 1.00 1.00
1851 A272 5r Sieve cowrie 1.25 1.25
1852 A272 6r Episcopal miter 1.60 1.60
1852A A272 7r Camp pitarvenus 1.75 1.75
1853 A272 8r Eyed auger 2.10 2.10
1854 A272 10r Onyx cowrie 2.50 2.50
1854A A272 12r Map cowrie 3.00 3.00
1855 A272 20r Caltrop murex 5.25 5.25
Nos. 1848-1855 (12) 20.10 20.10

Souvenir Sheets

1856 A272 25r Scorpion spider conch 8.00 8.00
1857 A272 25r Black striped triton 8.00 8.00
1857A A272 25r Bull's-mouth helmet 8.00 8.00

1993, July 20 Litho. *Perf. 14*

1857B A273 7 l Sifaka lemur .25 .25
1858 A273 10 l Snow leopard .25 .25
1859 A273 15 l Numbat .25 .25
1859A A273 25 l Gorilla .25 .25
1860 A273 2r Koalas .55 .55
1860A A273 3.50r Cheetah .95 .95
1861 A273 5r Yellow-footed rock wallaby 1.40 1.40
1862 A273 7r Orangutan 2.00 2.00
1863 A273 8r Black lemur 2.25 2.25
1864 A273 10r Black rhinoceros 2.75 2.75
1865 A273 15r Humpback whale 4.25 4.25
1865A A273 20r Mauritius parakeet 5.50 5.50
Nos. 1857B-1865A (12) 20.65 20.65

Souvenir Sheets

1866 A273 25r Asian elephant 8.00 8.00
1867 A273 25r Tiger 8.00 8.00
1867A A273 25r Giant panda 8.00 8.00

Miniature Sheets

Fish A274

#1868: b, Black pyramid butterflyfish. c, Bird wrasse. d, Checkerboard wrasse. e, Blue face angelfish. f, Bannerfish. g, Threadfin butterflyfish. h, Picasso triggerfish. i, Pennantfish. j, Grouper. k, Black back butterflyfish. l, Redfin triggerfish. m, Redfin butterflyfish.

#1868A: n, Yellow goatfish. o, Emperor angelfish. p, Madagascar butterflyfish. q, Empress angelfish. r, Longnose butterfly. s, Racoon butterflyfish. t, Harlequin filefish. u, Wedgetailed triggerfish. v, Clark's anemonefish. w, Clown triggerfish. x, Zebra lionfish. y, Maldive clownfish.

#1869, Goldbelly anemone, vert. #1869A, Klein's butterflyfish, vert.

1993, June 30 *Perf. 14x13½*

Sheets of 12

1868 A274 3.50r #b.-m. 9.50 9.50
1868A A274 3.50r #n.-y. 9.50 9.50

Souvenir Sheets

Perf. 12x13

1869 A274 25r multicolored 6.00 6.00
1869A A274 25r multicolored 6.00 6.00

Miniature Sheets

Birds — A275

No. 1870: a, Pallid harrier. b, Cattle egret. c, Koel (b). d, Tree pipit. e, Short-ear owl. f, European kestrel. g, Yellow wagtail. h, Common heron. i, Black bittern. j, Common snipe. k, Little egret. l, Little stint.

No. 1871: a, Gull-billed tern. b, Long-tailed tropicbird (a). c, Frigate bird. d, Wilson's petrel. e, White tern. f, Brown booby. g, Marsh harrier. h, Common noddy. i, Little heron. j, Turnstone. k, Curlew. l, Crab plover.

No. 1872, Caspian tern, horiz. No. 1873, Audubon's shearwater, horiz.

1993, July 5 *Perf. 13½x14*

1870 A275 3.50r Sheet of 12, #a.-l. 9.50 9.50
1871 A275 3.50r Sheet of 12, #a.-l. 9.50 9.50

Souvenir Sheet

Perf. 13x12

1872 A275 25r multicolored 6.00 6.00
1873 A275 25r multicolored 6.00 6.00

No. 1871 is horiz.

Year of Productivity
A276 A277

1993, July 25 *Perf. 14*

1874 A276 7r multicolored 1.60 1.60
1875 A277 10r multicolored 2.40 2.40

A278 A279

Picasso (1881-1973): 3.50r, Still Life with Pitcher and Apples, 1919. 5r, Bowls and Jug, 1908. 10r, Bowls of Fruit and Loaves, 1908. 20r, Green Still Life, 1914, horiz.

1993, Oct. 11 Litho. *Perf. 14*

1876 A278 3.50r multicolored .90 .90
1877 A278 5r multicolored 1.25 1.25
1878 A278 10r multicolored 2.50 2.50
Nos. 1876-1878 (3) 4.65 4.65

Souvenir Sheet

1879 A278 20r multicolored 5.25 5.25

1993, Oct. 11

Copernicus (1473-1543): 3.50r, Early astronomical instrument. 15r, Astronaut wearing Manned Maneuvering Unit. 20r, Copernicus.

1880 A279 3.50r multicolored 1.00 1.00
1881 A279 15r multicolored 4.25 4.25

Souvenir Sheet

1882 A279 20r multicolored 5.25 5.25

Royal Wedding of Crown Prince Naruhito, Princess Masako — A280

3.50r, Crown Prince Naruhito. 10r, Princess Masako, horiz. 25r, Princess Masako.

1993, Oct. 11

1883 A280 3.50r multicolored .75 .75
1884 A280 10r multicolored 2.25 2.25

Souvenir Sheet

1885 A280 25r multicolored 6.25 6.25

1994 Winter Olympics, Lillehammer, Norway — A281

1993, Oct. 11

8r, Marina Kiehl, gold medalist, women's downhill, 1988. 15r, Vegard Ulvang, gold medalist, cross-country skiing, 1992. 25r, Soviet ice hockey goalie, 1980.

1886 A281 8r multicolored 2.00 2.00
1887 A281 15r multicolored 4.00 4.00

Souvenir Sheet

1888 A281 25r multicolored 6.50 6.50

Polska '93 — A282

Fine arts: 3.50r, Zolte Roze, by Menasze Seidenbeurel, 1932. 5r, Cracow Historical Museum. 18r, Apples and Curtain, by Waclaw Borowski. 25r, Seascape, by Roman Sielski, 1931, horiz.

1993, Oct. 11 Litho. *Perf. 14*

1889 A282 3.50r multicolored .90 .90
1890 A282 5r multicolored 1.25 1.25
1891 A282 8r multicolored 2.00 2.00
Nos. 1889-1891 (3) 4.15 4.15

Souvenir Sheet

1892 A282 25r multicolored 5.00 5.00

Butterflies A283

1993, Oct. 25

1893 A283 7 l Commander .25 .25
1894 A283 20 l Blue tiger .25 .25
1895 A283 25 l Centaur oak-blue .25 .25
1896 A283 50 l Common banded peacock .25 .25
1897 A283 5r Glad-eye bushbrown 1.40 1.40
1898 A283 6.50r + 50 l Common tree nymph 2.00 2.00
1899 A283 7r Lemon emigrant 2.00 2.00
1900 A283 10r Blue pansy 2.75 2.75
1901 A283 12r Painted lady 3.50 3.50
1902 A283 15r Blue mormon 4.25 4.25
1903 A283 18r Tamil yeoman 5.00 5.00
1904 A283 20r Crimson rose 5.50 5.50
Nos. 1893-1904 (12) 27.40 27.40

Souvenir Sheets

1905 A283 25r Common imperial 7.50 7.50
1906 A283 25r Great orange tip 7.50 7.50
1907 A283 25r Black prince 7.50 7.50

Nos. 1905-1907 are vert.

Aviation Anniversaries — A284

Designs: 3.50r, Zeppelin on bombing raid caught in British search lights, vert. 5r, Homing pigeon. 10r, Dr. Hugo Eckener, vert. 15r, Airmal service medal, Jim Edgerton's Jenny, mail truck. 20r, USS Macon approaching mooring mast, vert.

Each 25r: #1913, Blanchard's balloon, 1793, vert. #1914, Santos-Dumont's flight around Eiffel Tower, 1901, vert.

1993, Nov. 22 **Litho.** ***Perf. 14***

1908-1912 A284 Set of 5 14.00 14.00

Souvenir Sheets

1913-1914 A284 Set of 2 10.00 10.00

Dr. Hugo Eckener, 125th birth anniv. (3.50r, 10r, 20r, No. 1913).

Miniature Sheets

First Ford Engine, First Benz Four-Wheeled Car, Cent. — A285

#1915: a, 1915 Model T (b, d-e). b, Henry Ford (e). c, Drawing of 1st Ford engine (b, e-f). d, 1993 Ford Probe GT (e). e, 1947 Ford Sportsman, front (f). f, As "f," rear (e). g, 1915 Ford advertisement (j). h, 1955 Ford Thunderbird (g, i). i, Ford emblem (f, h). j, 1958 Edsel Citation. k, 1941 Ford half-ton pickup. l, Model T.

#1916: a, 1937 Daimler-Benz Straight 8 (b). b, Karl Benz (e). c, Mercedes-Benz advertisement (f). d, 1929 Mercedes 38-250SS (e). e, 1893 Benz Viktoria (f, h). f, Mercedes star emblem (i). g, WWI Mercedes engine. h, 1957 Mercedes-Benz 300SL Gullwing (g). i, 1993 Mercedes Benz SL coupe/roadster (h). j, 1906 Benz 4-cylinder car (k). k, Early Benz advertisement. l, Benz Viktoria, 1893.

1993, Nov. 22

1915 A285 3.50r Sheet of 12, #a.-l. 12.00 12.00
1916 A285 3.50r Sheet of 12, #a.-l. 12.00 12.00

Souvenir Sheets

1917 A285 25r 1933 Ford Model Y 6.50 6.50
1918 A285 25r 1955 Mercedes 300S 6.50 6.50

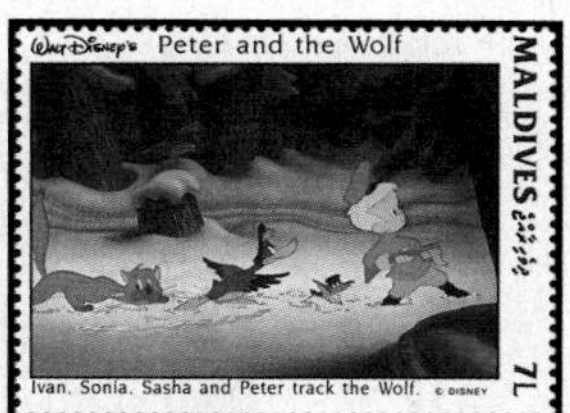

Peter and the Wolf — A286

Characters and scenes from Disney animated film: 7 l, 15 l, 20 l, 25 l, 50 l, 1r.
Nos. 1925a-1925i: Part 1.
Nos. 1926a-1926i: Part 2.

1993, Dec. 20

1919-1924 A286 Set of 6 1.00 1.00

Miniature Sheets of 9

1925 A286 3.50r #a.-i. 7.50 7.50
1926 A286 3.50r #a.-i. 7.50 7.50

Souvenir Sheets

1927 A286 25r Sonia 5.00 5.00
1928 A286 25r Ivan 5.00 5.00

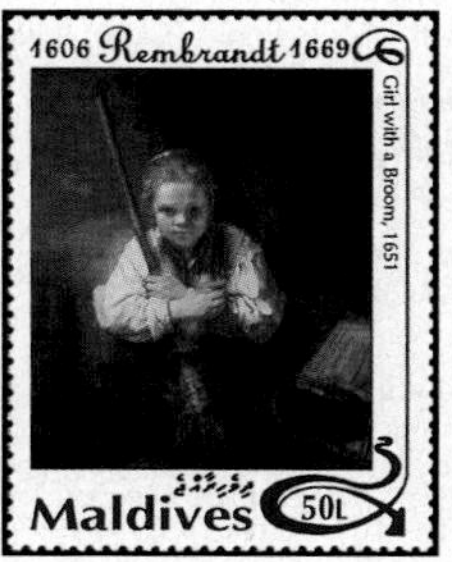

Fine Art — A287

Paintings by Rembrandt: 50 l, Girl with a Broom. No. 1931, 3.50r, Young Girl at half-open Door. 5r, The Prophetess Hannah (Rembrandt's Mother). 7r, Woman with a Pink Flower. 12r, Lucretia. No. 1939, 15r, Lady with an Ostich Feather Fan.

Paintings by Matisse: 2r, Girl with Tulips (Jeanne Vaderin). No. 1932, 3.50r. Portrait of Greta Moll. 6.50r, The Idol. 9r, Mme. Matisse in Japanese Robe. 10r, Portrait of MMe Matisse (The Green Line). No. 1940, 15r, The Woman with the Hat.

Each 25r: No. 1941, Married Couple with 3 Children (A Family Group), by Rembrandt, horiz. No. 1942, The Painter's Family, by Matisse. No. 1942A: The Music Makers, by Rembrandt.

1994, Jan. 11 **Litho.** ***Perf. 13***

1929-1940 A287 Set of 12 21.00 21.00

Souvenir Sheets

1941-1942A A287 Set of 3 22.50 22.50

No. 1942A issued Feb. 2.

1994 World Cup Soccer US — A288

Players, country: 7 l, Windischmann, US; Giannini, Italy. 20 l, Carnevale, Gascoigne. 25 l, Platt & teammates, England. 3.50r, Koeman, Holland; Klinsmann, Germany. 5r, Quinn, Ireland; Maldini, Italy. 7r, Lineker, England. 15r, Hassam, Egypt; Moran, Ireland. 18r, Canniggia, Argentina.

Each 25r: No. 1951, Conejo, Costa Rica; Mozer, Brazil, horiz. No. 1952, Armstrong & Barboa, US; Orgis, Austria.

1994, Jan. 11 ***Perf. 14***

1943-1950 A288 Set of 8 12.50 12.50

Souvenir Sheets

1951-1952 A288 Set of 2 12.00 12.00

A289

Hong Kong '94 — A290

Stamps, Moon-Lantern Festival, Hong Kong: No. 1953, Hong Kong #416, girls, lanterns. No. 1954, Lanterns, #660.

Cloisonne Enamel, Qing Dynasty: No. 1955a, Vase. b, Flower holder. c, Elephant with vase on back. d, Pot (Tibetan-style lama's milk-tea pot. e, Fo-dog. f, Pot with swing handle.

1994, Feb. 18 **Litho.** ***Perf. 14***

1953 A289 4r multicolored .80 .80
1954 A289 4r multicolored .80 .80
a. Pair, #1953-1954 1.60 1.60

Miniature Sheet

1955 A290 2r Sheet of 6, #a.-f. 6.00 6.00

Nos. 1953-1954 issued in sheets of 5 pairs. No. 1954a is a continuous design.

New Year 1994 (Year of the Dog) (#1955e).

Sierra Club, Cent. A290a

Various animals, each 6.50r:

Nos. 1956a-1956b, Prairie dog. c.-e, Woodland caribou. f, Galapagos penguin.

No. 1957, vert: a, Humpback whale. b.-c, Ocelot. d, Snow monkey. e, Prairie dog. f, Golden lion tamarin.

No. 1958: a.-b, Golden lion tamarin. c.-d, Humpback whale. e, Bengal tiger. f, Ocelot. g.-h, Snow monkey.

No. 1959, vert: a.-b, Galapagos penguin. c.-d, Bengal tiger. e.-g, Philippine tarsier. h, Sierra Club centennial emblem.

1994, May 20 **Litho.** ***Perf. 14***

Miniature Sheets of 6, #a-f

1956-1957 A290a Set of 2 18.50 18.50

Miniature Sheets of 8, #a-h

1958-1959 A290a Set of 2 22.50 22.50

Dome of the Rock, Jerusalem — A291

1994, June 10 ***Perf. 13½***

1960 A291 8r multicolored 1.50 1.50

A292

Designs: 25 l, Elasmosaurus. 50 l, Dilophosaurus. 1r, Avimimus. 5r, Chasmosaurus. 8r, Edmontonia. 10r, Anatosaurus. 15r, Velociraptor. 20r, Spinosaurus.

No. 1969, each 3r: a, Dimorphodon. b, Megalosaurus. c, Kuehneosaurus. d, Dryosaurus. e, Kentrosaurus. f, Baraposaurus (c). g, Tenontosaurus. h, Elaphrosaurus (i). i, Maiasaura. j, Huayangosaurus. k, Rutiodon. l, Pianitzkysaurus.

No. 1970, each 3r: a, Quetzalcoatlus. b, Daspletosaurus. c, Pleurocoelus. d, Baryonyx. e, Pentaceratops. f, Kritosaurus. g, Microvenator (h). h, Nodosaurus. i, Montanaceratops. j, Dromiceiomimus. k, Dryptosaurus. l, Parkosaurus.

Each 25r: #1971, Gallimimus. #1972, Plateosaurus, vert.

1994, June 20 ***Perf. 14***

1961-1968 A292 Set of 8 16.50 16.50

Miniature Sheets of 12, #a-l

1969-1970 A292 Set of 2 19.50 19.50

Souvenir Sheets

1971-1972 A292 Set of 2 10.00 10.00

Nos. 1969-1970 are continuous design.

Locomotives A293

Domestic Cats — A294

Designs: 25 l, 2-6-6-0 Mallet, Indonesia, horiz. 50 l, C62, Japan, horiz. 1r, D51, Japan. 5r, 4-6-0 Steam, India. 8r, Class 485 electric, Japan, horiz. 10r, Class WP Pacific, India. 15r, "People" class RM 4-6-2, China. 20r, C57, Japan, horiz.

No. 1981: a, W Class 0-6-2, India. b, C53 Class, Indonesia. c, C-10, Japan. d, Hanomag 4-8-0, India. e, Hakari bullet train, Japan. f, C-55, Japan.

Each 25r: No. 1982, 4-4-0, Indonesia. No. 1983, Series 8620, Japan.

1994, July 4

1973-1980 A293 Set of 8 11.00 11.00

Miniature Sheet of 6

1981 A293 6.50r +50 l, #a.-f. 7.50 7.50

Souvenir Sheets

1982-1983 A293 Set of 2 10.00 10.00

1994, July 11

Designs: 7 l, Japanese bobtail, horiz. 20 l, Siamese. 25 l, Persian longhair, horiz. 50 l, Somali. 3.50r, Oriental shorthair, horiz. 5r, Burmese, horiz. 7r, Bombay, horiz. 10r, Turkish van. 12r, Javanese. 15r, Singapura, horiz. 18r, Turkish angora. 20r, Egyptian mau.

Each 25r: #1996, Birman. #1997, Korat. #1998, Abyssinian.

1984-1995 A294 Set of 12 17.00 17.00

Souvenir Sheets

1996-1998 A294 Set of 3 15.00 15.00

Miniature Sheets of 6

1994 World Cup Soccer Championships, US — A295

No. 1999a, 10 l, Franco Baresi, Italy, Stuart McCall, Scotland. b, 25 l, McCarthy, Great Britain, Lineker, Ireland. c, 50 l, J. Helt, Denmark, R. Gordillo, Spain. d, 5r, Martin Vasquez, Spain, Enzo Scifo, Belgium. e, 10r, Emblem. f, 12f, Tomas Brolin, Sweden, Gordon Durie, Scotland.

No. 2000a, Bebeto, Brazil. b, Lothar Matthaus, Great Britain. c, Diego Maradona, Argentina. d, Stephane Chapuasti, Switzerland. e, George Hagi, Romania. f, Carlos Valderama, Colombia.

No. 2001, Hossam Hassan, 2nd Egyptian player.

1994, Aug. 4 Litho. *Perf. 14*

1999 A295 #a.-f. 5.00 5.00
2000 A295 6.50r #a.-f, vert. 7.00 7.00

Souvenir Sheet

2001 A295 10r multicolored 3.75 3.75

D-Day, 50th Anniv. A296

Designs: 2r, Amphibious DUKW approaches Utah Beach. 4r, Landing craft tank, Sword Beach. 18r, Landing craft infantry damaged at Omaha Beach.

No. 2006, Canadian commandos, Juno Beach.

1994, Aug. 8

2003-2005 A296 Set of 3 4.50 4.50

Souvenir Sheet

2006 A296 25r multicolored 5.50 5.50

A297

Intl. Olympic Committee, Cent. — A298

Designs: 7r, Linford Christie, Great Britain, track 1988. 12r, Koji Gushiken, Japan, gymnastics, 1984.

25r, George Hackl, Germany, single luge, 1994.

1994, Aug. 8

2007 A297 7r multicolored 1.25 1.25
2008 A297 12r multicolored 2.25 2.25

Souvenir Sheet

2009 A298 25r multicolored 5.25 5.25

A299

PHILAKOREA '94 — A300

Designs: 50 l, Suwan Folk Village duck pond. 3.50r, Youngduson Park. 20r, Ploughing, Hahoe Village, Andong region.

Ceramics, Choson & Koryo Dynasties: No. 2013a, Pear-shaped bottle. b, Vase. c, Vase with repaired lip. d, Labed vase, stoneware. e, Vase, celadon-glazed. f, Vase, unglazed stone. g, Ritual water sprinkler. h, Celadon-glazed vase.

25r, Hunting (detail from eight-panel screen, Choson Dynasty), vert.

1994, Aug. 8 *Perf. 14, 13½ (#2013)*

2010-2012 A299 Set of 3 5.00 5.00

Miniature Sheet of 8

2013 A300 3r #a.-h. 5.00 5.00

Souvenir Sheet

2014 A299 25r multicolored 5.25 5.25

First Manned Moon Landing, 25th Anniv. A301

No. 2015, each 5r: a, Apollo 11 crew. b, Apollo 11 patch, signatures of crew. c, "Buzz" Aldrin, lunar module, Eagle. d, Apollo 12 crew. e, Apollo 12 patch, signatures of crew. f, Alan Bean transporting ALSEP.

No. 2016, each 5r: a, Apollo 16 crew. b, Apollo 16 patch, signatures of crew. c, John Young gives a "Navy salute." d, Apollo 17 crew. e, Apollo 17 patch, signatures of crew. f, Night launch of Apollo 17.

25r, Launch at Baikonur.

1994, Aug. 8 *Perf. 14*

Miniature Sheets of 6, #a-f

2015-2016 A301 Set of 2 13.50 13.50

Souvenir Sheet

2017 A301 25r multicolored 5.25 5.25

UN Development Plan — A302

1r, Woman, baby, undernourished man, city on island. 8r, Island native, case worker, island, ship.

1994 Litho. *Perf. 14*

2018 A302 1r multicolored .20 .20
2019 A302 8r multicolored 1.90 1.90

Miniature Sheet of 12

Space Exploration A304

#2020: a, Voyager 2. b, Sputnik. c, Apollo-Soyuz. d, Apollo 10 descent. e, Apollo 11 mission insignia. f, Hubble space telescope. g, Buzz Aldrin. h, RCA lunar cam. i, Lunar rover. j, Jim Irwin. k, Apollo 12 lunar module. l, Lunar soil extraction.

Each 25r: #2021, David Scott in open hatch of Apollo 9 command module. #2022, Alan Shepard, Jr. waving salute from moon, Apollo 14, horiz.

1994, Aug. 8 Litho. *Perf. 14*

2020 A304 5r #a.-l. 17.50 17.50

Souvenir Sheets

2021-2022 A304 Set of 2 13.50 13.50

Aminiya School, 50th Anniv. A305

15 l, Discipline. 50 l, Arts. 1r, Emblem, hand holding book, vert. 8r, Girls carrying books, vert. 10r, Sports. 11r, Girls cheering, vert. 13r, Science.

1994, Nov. 28

2023-2029 A305 Set of 7 8.50 8.50

ICAO, 50th Anniv. A306

Designs: 50 l, Boeing 747. 1r, De Havilland Comet 4. 2r, Male Intl. Airport, Maldives. 3r, Lockheed 1649 Super Star. 8r, European Airbus. 10r, Dornier Do228. 25r, Concorde.

1994, Dec. 31

2030-2035 A306 Set of 6 8.25 8.25

Souvenir Sheet

2036 A306 25r multicolored 5.50 5.50

Miniature Sheets of 9

Water Birds A307

Designs: No. 2037a, Northern pintail (b, d). b, Comb duck (c). c, Ruddy duck. d, Garganey (a, e, g, h). e, Lesser whistling duck (b, c, f). f, Green winged teal. g, Fulvous whistling duck. h, Northern shoveler (e). i, Cotton pygmy goose (h).

No. 2038, vert.: a, Pochard (b). b, Mallard (c, e, f). c, Wigeon. d, Northern shoveler (e, g). e, Northern pintail (h). f, Garganey (e, i). g, Tufted duck. h, Ferruginous duck (i). i, Red-crested pochard.

Each 25r: No. 2039, Cotton pygmy goose, vert. No. 2040, Garganey, diff.

1995, Feb. 27 Litho. *Perf. 14*

2037 A307 5r #a.-i. 8.25 8.25
2038 A307 6.50r + 50 l #a.-i. 11.50 11.50

Souvenir Sheets

2039-2040 A307 Set of 2 9.00 9.00

Monuments of the World — A308

Designs: 7 l, Taj Mahal. 10 l, Washington Monument. 15 l, Mt. Rushmore Memorial. 25 l, Arc de Triomphe, vert. 50 l, Sphinx, vert. 5r, El Castillo Monument of the Toltec, Chichen Itza, Yucatan, Mexico. 8r, Toltec monument, Tula, Mexico, vert. 12r, Victory Column, Berlin, vert.

Each 25r: No. 2049, Moai statues, Easter Island. No. 2050, Stonehenge.

1995, Feb. 28

2041-2048 A308 Set of 8 6.00 6.00

Souvenir Sheets

2049-2050 A308 Set of 2 9.00 9.00

No. 2049 contains one 43x57mm stamp, No. 2050 one 85x28mm stamp.

Donald Duck, 50th Birthday (in 1994) — A309

Scenes from "Donald and the Wheel:" 3 l, Racing chariot. 4 l, Standing on log. 5 l, Operating steam locomotive. 10 l, Looking at cave drawing, vert. 20 l, Sitting in "junked" car, vert. 25 l, Listening to phonograph. 5r, Climbing on mammoth. 20r, Pushing old car.

Disney Duck family orchestra, vert, each 5r: No. 2059a, Donald Duck, saxophone. b, Moby Duck, violin. c, Feathry Duck, banjo. d, Daisy Duck, harp. e, Gladstone Gander, clarinet. f, Dewey, Louie, Huey, oboe. g, Gus Goose, flute. h, Ludwig von Drake, trombone.

Donald Duck family portraits, vert, each 5r: No. 2060a, Daisy. b, Donald. c, Grandma. d, Gus Goose. e, Gyro Gearloose, f, Huey, Dewey, Louie. g, Ludwig von Drake. h, Scrooge McDuck.

Each 25r: No. 2061, Dixieland band, vert. No. 2062, Donald conducting symphony orchestra. No. 2063, Donald being photographed, vert. No. 2064, Huey, Dewey, Louie in family portrait.

Perf. 13½x13, 13x13½

1995, Mar. 22 Litho.

2051-2058 A309 Set of 8 5.50 5.50

Miniature Sheets of 8, #a-h

2059-2060 A309 Set of 2 14.50 14.50

Souvenir Sheets

2061-2064 A309 Set of 4 18.00 18.00

EID Greetings — A310

1r, Mosque. 1r, Rose. 8r, Hibiscus. 10r, Orchids.

1995, May 1 Litho. *Perf. 14*

2065-2068 A310 Set of 4 3.75 3.75

Whales, Dolphins, & Porpoises A311

Nos. 2069-2072: 1r, Killer whale. 2r, Bottlenose dolphin. 8r, Humpback whale. 10r, Common dolphin.

No. 2073, each 3r: a, Hourglass dolphin. b, Bottlenose dolphin. c, Dusky dolphin. d, Spectacled porpoise. e, Fraser's dolphin. f, Commerson's dolphin. g, Spinner dolphin. h, Dalls dolphin. i, Spotted dolphin. j, Indus river dolphin. k, Hector's dolphin. l, Amazon river dolphin.

No. 2074, each 3r: a, Right whale (d). b, Killer whale (a). c, Humpback whale (f). d, Beluga. e, Narwhale. f, Blue whale (e, g). g, Bowhead whale (h, k). h, Fin whale (d, e, g). i, Pilot whale. j, Grey whale. k, Sperm whale (l). l, Goosebeaked whale.

Each 25r: No. 2075, Hourglass dolphin. No. 2076, Sperm whale.

1995, May 16

2069-2072 A311 Set of 4 4.00 4.00

Miniature Sheets of 12, #a-l

2073-2074 A311 Set of 2 15.50 15.50

Souvenir Sheets

2075-2076 A311 Set of 2 11.00 11.00

Singapore '95.

UN, 50th Anniv. A311a

Designs: 30 l, Emblem, security of small states. 8r, Women in development. 11r, Peace keeping, peace making operations. 13r, Disarmament.

1995, July 6 Litho. *Perf. 14*

2076A-2076D A311a Set of 4 5.75 5.75

UN, 50th Anniv. — A312

No. 2077: a, 6.50r+50 l, Child, dove flying left. b, 8r, Earth from space. c, 10r, Child, Dove flying right.

25r, UN emblem, dove.

1995, July 6 Litho. *Perf. 14*

2077 A312 Strip of 3, #a.-c. 4.50 4.50

Souvenir Sheet

2078 A312 25r multicolored 4.50 4.50

No. 2077 is a continuous design.

FAO, 50th Anniv. — A313

A312a A313

1995 Litho. *Perf. 14*

2078A A312a 7r Food for all 1.25 1.25

2078B A312a 8r Dolphin-friendly fishing 1.40 1.40

1995, July 6

No. 2079: a, 6.50r+50 l, Child eating. b, 8r, FAO emblem. c, 10r, Mother, child.

25r, Food emblem, child, horiz.

2079 A313 Strip of 3, #a.-c. 4.50 4.50

Souvenir Sheet

2080 A313 25r multicolored 4.50 4.50

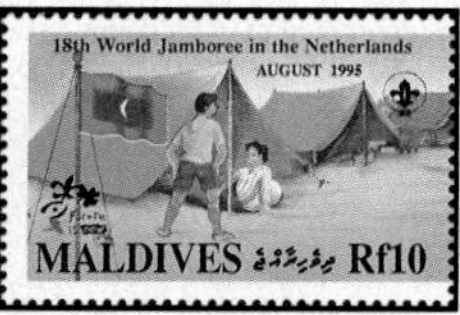

1995 Boy Scout Jamboree, Holland — A314

No. 2081: a, 10r, Natl. flag, scouts, tents. b, 12r, Scout cooking. c, 15r, Scouts sitting before tents.

25r, Scout playing flute, camp at night, vert.

1995, July 6

2081 A314 Strip of 3, #a.-c. 6.75 6.75

Souvenir Sheet

2082 A314 25r multicolored 4.50 4.50

No. 2081 is a continuous design.

Queen Mother, 95th Birthday — A315

No. 2083: a, Drawing. b, Blue print dress, pearls. c, Formal portrait. d, Blue outfit.

25r, Pale violet hat, violet & blue dress.

1995, July 6 *Perf. 13½x14*

2083 A315 5r Block or strip of 4, #a.-d. 4.00 4.00

Souvenir Sheet

2084 A315 25r multicolored 4.50 4.50

No. 2083 was issued in sheets of 2.

Sheets of Nos. 2083-2084 exist overprinted in margin with black frame and text "In Memoriam 1900-2002."

Natl. Library, 50th Anniv. A316

Designs: 2r, Boys seated at library table. 8r, Two people standing, two at table.

10r, Library entrance.

1995, July 12 *Perf. 14*

2085 A316 2r multicolored .35 .35

2086 A316 8r multicolored 1.40 1.40

Size: 100x70mm

Imperf

2087 A316 10r multicolored 1.75 1.75

Miniature Sheets of 6 or 8

End of World War II, 50th Anniv. A317

No. 2088: a, 203mm Red Army howitzer. b, Ruins of Hitler's residence, Berchtesgaden. c, Operation Manna, Allies drop food to starving Dutch. d, Soviet IL-1 fighter. e, Inmates, British troops burn last hut at Belsen. f, Last V1 Buzz Bomb launched against London. g, US 3rd Armored Division passes through ruins of Cologne. h, Gutted Reichstag, May 7, 1946.

No. 2089: a, Grumman F6F-3 Hellcat. b, F4-U1 attacking with rockets. c, Douglas Dauntless. d, Guadalcanal, Aug. 7, 1942. e, US Marines in Alligator landing craft. f, US Infantry landing craft.

Each 25r: No. 2090, Allied soldiers with smiling faces. No. 2091, Corsair fighters.

1995, July 6 Litho. *Perf. 14*

2088 A317 5r #a.-h. + label 7.25 7.25

2089 A317 6.50r +50 l #a.-f. + label 7.50 7.50

Souvenir Sheets

2090-2091 A317 Set of 2 9.00 9.00

Turtles A318

Hawksbill turtle: No. 2092a, Crawling. b, Two in water. c, One crawling out of water. d, Swimming.

No. 2093: a, Spur-thighed tortoise. b, Aldabra turtle. c, Loggerhead turtle. d, Olive ridley. e, Leatherback turtle. f, Green turtle. g, Atlantic ridley. h, Hawsbill turtle.

25r, Chelonia mydas.

1995, Aug. 22

2092 A318 10r Strip of 4, #a.-d. 8.00 8.00

Miniature Sheet of 8

2093 A318 3r #a.-h. 4.50 4.50

Souvenir Sheet

2094 A318 25r multicolored 7.00 7.00

World Wildlife Fund (#2092). No. 2092 was printed in sheets of 12 stamps.

Miniature Sheets

Singapore '95 — A319

Mushrooms, butterflies, each 2r: No. 2095a, Russula aurata, papilio demodocus. b, Kallimoides rumia, lepista saeva. c, Lapista nuda, hypolimnas salmacis. d, Precis octavia, boletus subtomentosus.

No. 2096: a, 5r, Gyroporus castaneus, hypolimnas salmacis. b, 8r, Papilio dardanus, Gomphidius glutinosus. c, 10r, Russula olivacea, precis octavia. d, 12r, Prepona praeneste, boletus edulis.

Each 25r: No. 2097, Hypolimnas salmacis, boletus rhodoxanthus, vert. No. 2098, Amanita muscaria, kallimoides rumia, vert.

1995, Oct. 18 Litho. *Perf. 14*

2095 A319 Sheet of 4, #a.-d. 1.50 1.50

2096 A319 Sheet of 4, #a.-d. 7.50 7.50

Souvenir Sheets

2097-2098 A319 Set of 2 10.00 10.00

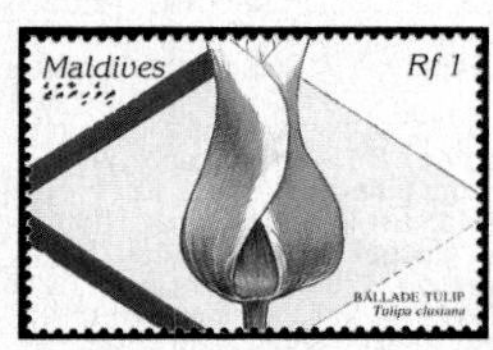

Flowers A320

Designs: 1r, Ballade tulip. 3r, White mallow. 5r, Regale trumpet lily. 7r, Lilactime dahlia. 8r, Blue ideal iris. 10r, Red crown imperial.

No. 2105, a, Dendrobium waipahu beauty. b, Brassocattleya Jean Murray "Allan Christenson." c, Cymbidium Fort George "Lewes." d, Paphiopedilum malipoense. e, Cycnoches chlorochilon. f, Rhyncholaelia digbgana. g, Lycaste deppei. h, Masdevallia constricta. i, Paphiopedilum Clair de Lune "Edgard Van Belle."

Each 25r: No. 2106, Psychopsis krameriana. No. 2107, Cockleshell orchid.

1995, Dec. 4 Litho. *Perf. 14*

2099-2104 A320 Set of 6 7.25 7.25

Miniature Sheet

2105 A320 5r Sheet of 9, #a.-i. 9.25 9.25

Souvenir Sheets

2106-2107 A320 Set of 2 9.00 9.00

Miniature Sheet

Elvis Presley (1935-77) A321

Various portraits.

1995, Dec. 8 *Perf. 13½x14*

2108 A321 5r Sheet of 9, #a.-i. 8.00 8.00

Souvenir Sheet

Perf. 14x13½

2109 A321 25r multi, horiz. 4.50 4.50

Miniature Sheets

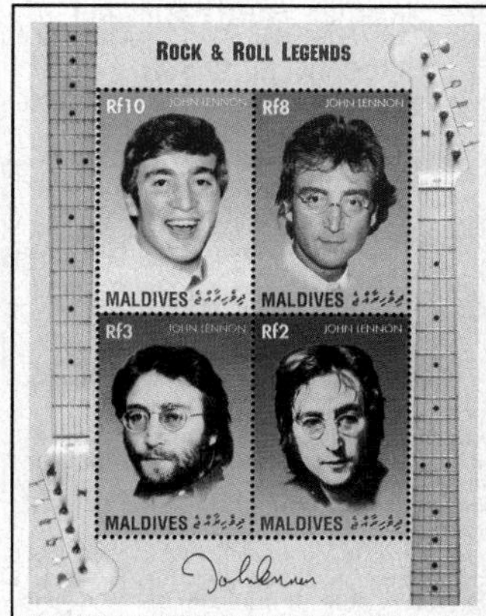

John Lennon (1940-80), Entertainer — A322

No. 2110, Various portraits.

No. 2111: a, 10r, As young man. b, 8r, Younger man with glasses. c, 3r, With beard. d, 2r, Older picture without beard.

No. 2112, Standing at microphone.

1995, Dec. 8

2110 A322 5r Sheet of 6, #a.-f. 8.75 8.75

2111 A322 Sheet of 4, #a.-d. 6.75 6.75

Souvenir Sheet

2112 A322 25r multicolored 7.00 7.00

Nobel Prize Fund Established, Cent. — A323

Recipients: No. 2113, each 5r: a, Bernardo A. Houssay, medicine, 1947. b, Paul H. Müller, medicine, 1948. c, Walter R. Hess, medicine, 1949. d, Sir MacFarlane Burnet, medicine, 1960. e, Baruch S. Blumberg, medicine, 1976. f, Daniel Nathans, medicine, 1978. g, Glenn T. Seaborg, chemistry, 1951. h, Ilya Prigogine, chemistry, 1977. i, Kenichi Fukui, chemistry, 1981.

No. 2114, each 5r: a, Johannes Van Der Waals, physics, 1910. b, Charles Édouard Guillaume, physics, 1920. c, Sir James Chadwick, physics, 1935. d, Willem Einthoven, medicine, 1924. e, Henrik Dam, medicine, 1943. f, Sir Alexander Fleming, medicine, 1945. g, Hermann J. Muller, medicine, 1946. h, Rodney R. Porter, medicine, 1972. i, Werner Arber, medicine, 1978.

No. 2115, each 5r: a, Dag Hammarskjold, peace, 1961. b, Alva R. Myrdal, peace, 1982. c, Archbishop Desmond M. Tutu, peace, 1984. d, Rudolf C. Eucken, literature, 1908. e, Aleksandr Solzhenitsyn, literature, 1970. f, Gabriel Garcia Márquez, literature, 1982. g, Chen N. Yang, physics, 1957. h, Karl A. Müller, physics, 1987. i, Melvin Schwartz, physics, 1988.

No. 2116, each 5r: a, Niels Bohr, physics, 1922. b, Ben R. Mottelson, physics, 1975. c, Patrick White, literature, 1973. d, Elias Canetti, literature, 1981. e, Theodor Kocher, medicine, 1909. f, August Krogh, medicine, 1920. g, William P. Murphy, medicine, 1934. h, John H. Northrop, chemistry, 1946. i, Luis F. Leloir, chemistry, 1970.

No. 2117, each 5r: a, Carl Spitteler, literatue, 1919. b, Henri Bergson, literature, 1927. c, Johannes V. Jensen, literature, 1944. d, Antoine-Henri Becquerel, physics, 1903. e, Sir William H. Bragg, physics, 1915. f, Sir William L. Bragg, physics, 1915. g, Fredrik Bajer, peace, 1908. h, Léon Bourgeois, peace, 1920. i, Karl Branting, peace, 1921.

No. 2118, each 5r: a, Robert A. Millikan, physics, 1923. b, Louis V. de Broglie, physics, 1929. c, Ernest Walton, physics, 1951. d, Richard Willstätter, chemistry, 1915. e, Lars Onsager, chemistry, 1968. f, Gerhard Herzberg, chemistry, 1971. g, William B. Yeats, literature, 1923. h, George B. Shaw, literature, 1925. i, Eugene O'Neill, literature, 1936.

Each 25r: No. 2119, Eisaku Sato, peace, 1974. No. 2120, Robert Koch, medicine, 1905. No. 2121, Otto Wallach, chemistry, 1910. No. 2122, Konrad Bloch, medicine, 1964. No. 2123, Samuel Beckett, literature, 1969. No. 2124, Hideki Yukawa, physics, 1949.

1995, Dec. 28 Litho. *Perf. 14*

Miniature Sheets of 9, #a-i

2113-2118 A323 Set of 6 48.00 48.00

Souvenir Sheets

2119-2124 A323 Set of 6 27.00 27.00

1996 Summer Olympics, Atlanta A324

Designs: 1r, Rhythmic gymnastics, Tokyo, 1964. 3r, Archery, Moscow, 1980. 5r, Diving, Stockholm, 1912. 7r, High jump, London, 1948. 10r, Track and field, Berlin, 1936. 12r, Hurdles, Amsterdam 1928.

No. 2131: a, Montreal 1976. b, Decathlon. c, Olympic pin, Moscow, 1980. d, Fencing. e, Olympic medal. f, Equestrian. g, Sydney, 2000. h, Track and field. i, Seoul, 1988.

Each 25r: No. 2132, Olympic torch, vert. No. 2133, Olympic flame, vert.

1996, Jan. 25 Litho. *Perf. 14*

2125-2130 A324 Set of 6 7.00 7.00

Miniature Sheet

2131 A324 5r Sheet of 9, #a.-i. 8.25 8.25

Souvenir Sheets

2132-2133 A324 Set of 2 9.00 9.00

Paintings from Metropolitan Museum of Art — A325

No. 2134, each 4r: a, Self-portrait, by Degas. b, Andromache & Astyanax, by Prud'hon. c, René Grenier, by Toulouse-Lautrec. d, The Banks of the Biéve Near Bicetre, by Rousseau. e, The Repast of the Lion, by Rousseau. f, Portrait Yves Gobillard-Morisot, by Degas. g, Sunflowers, by Van Gogh. h, The Singer in Green, by Degas.

No. 2135, each 4r: a, Still Life, by Fantin-Latour. b, Portrait of a Lady in Gray, by Degas. c, Apples & Grapes, by Monet. d, The Englishman, by Toulouse-Lautrec. e, Cypresses, by Van Gogh. f, Flowers in Chinese Vase, by Redon. g, The Gardener, by Seurat. h, Large Sunflowers I, by Nolde.

By Manet: No. 2136, each 4r: a, The Spanish Singer. b, Young Man in Costume of Majo. c, Mademoisselle Victorine. d, Boating. e, Peonies. f, Woman with a Parrot. g, George Moore. h, The Monet Family in Their Garden.

No. 2137, each 4r7: a, Goldfish, by Matisse. b, Spanish Woman: Harmony in Blue, by Matisse. c, Nasturtiums & the "Dance" II, by Matisse. d, The House Behind Trees, by Braque. e, Māda Primavesi, by Klimt. f, Head of a Woman, by Picasso. g, Woman in White, by Picasso. h, Harlequin, by Picasso.

Each 25r: No. 2138, Northeaster, by Homer. No. 2139, The Fortune Teller, by Georges de la Tour. No. 2140, Santi (Sanzio), Ritratto di Andrea Navagero E Agostino Beazzano, by Raphael. No. 2141, Portrait of a Woman, by Rubens.

1996, Apr. 22 Litho. *Perf. 13½x14*

Sheets of 8, #a-h + label

2134-2137 A325 Set of 4 32.50 32.50

Souvenir Sheets

Perf. 14

2138-2141 A325 Set of 4 21.00 21.00

Nos. 2138-2141 each contain one 85x57mm stamp.

Nos. 2140-2141 are not in the Metropolitan Museum.

Disney Characters Visit China — A326

No. 2142, each 2r: a, Mickey at the Great Wall. b, Pluto's encounter in the Temple Garden. c, Minnie saves the pandas. d, Mickey sails with the junks. e, Goofy at the grottoes. f, Donald, Daisy at the marble boat.

No. 2143, each 2r: a, Mickey leads terra cotta statues. b, Goofy's masks. c, Traditional fishing with Donald, Goofy. d, Mickey, Minnie in dragon boat. e, Donald at Peking Opera. f, Mickey, Minnie, in Chinese Garden.

No. 2144, vert: a, Mickey, Minnie snowballing at ice pagoda. b, Donald, Mickey fly Chinese kites. c, Goofy plays anyiwu. d, Mickey, Goofy, origami. e, Donald, Mickey in dragon dance.

No. 2145, 5r, Mickey viewing Guilin. No. 2146, 7r, Mickey, Minnie at Moon Festival. No. 2147, 8r, Donald enjoying traditional Chinese food.

1996, May 10 *Perf. 14x13½, 13½x14*

Sheets of 6, #a-f

2142-2143 A326 Set of 2 9.50 9.50

Sheet of 5, #a-e

2144 A326 3r #a.-e. + label 5.50 5.50

Souvenir Sheets

2145 A326 5r multicolored 1.50 1.50
2146 A326 7r multicolored 2.10 2.10
2147 A326 8r multicolored 2.40 2.40

CHINA '96, 9th Asian Intl. Philatelic Exhibition.

1996 Summer Olympic Games, Atlanta A327

Gold medalists: 1r, Stella Walsh, 100-meters, 1932. 3r, Emil Zatopek, 10,000-meters, 1952, vert. 10r, Olga Fikotova, discus throw, 1956. 12r, Joan Benoit, women's marathon, 1984.

No. 2152: a, Ethel Catherwood, high jump, 1928. b, Mildred "Babe" Didrikson, javelin, 1932. c, Francina (Fanny) Blankers-Koen, hurdles, 1948. d, Tamara Press, shot put, 1960. e, Lia Manoliu, discus, 1968. f, Rosa Mota, women's marathon, 1988.

Gold medalists in weight lifting, vert: No. 2153a, Yanko Rusev, lightweight, 1980. b, Peter Baczako, middle heavyweight, 1980. c, Leonid Taranenko, heavyweight, 1980. d, Aleksandr Kurlovich, heavyweight, 1988. e, Assen Zlateu, middleweight, 1980. f, Zeng Guoqiang, flyweight, 1984. g, Yurik Vardanyan, heavyweight, 1980. h, Sultan Rakhmanov, super heavyweight, 1980. i, Vassily Alexeev, super heavyweight, 1972.

Each 25r: No. 2154, Irena Szewinska, gold medal winner, 400-meters, 1976. No. 2155, Naim Suleymanoglu, gold medal winner, weight lifting, 1988, vert.

1996, May 27 Litho. *Perf. 14*

2148-2151 A327 Set of 4 4.75 4.75

Miniature Sheets

2152 A327 5r Sheet of 6, #a.-f. 5.50 5.50
2153 A327 5r Sheet of 9, #a.-i. 8.00 8.00

Souvenir Sheets

2154-2155 A327 Set of 2 9.00 9.00

Olymphilex '96 (#2155).

Queen Elizabeth II, 70th Birthday A329

Designs: a, Portrait. b, As younger woman wearing hat, pearls. c, Younger picture seated at desk.

25r, On balcony with Queen Mother.

1996, June 21 Litho. *Perf. 13½x14*

2164 A329 8r Strip of 3, #a.-c. 5.25 5.25

Souvenir Sheet

2165 A329 25r multicolored 4.50 4.50

No. 2164 was issued in sheets of 9 stamps.

UNICEF, 50th Anniv. — A330

Designs: 5r (#2166), 7r (#2167), 7r (#2167A), girl, blue margin, 10r (#2168), Girls of different races.

25r, Baby girl.

1996, July 10 *Perf. 14*

2166-2168 A330 Set of 4 4.50 4.50

Souvenir Sheet

2169 A330 25r multicolored 4.50 4.50

Butterflies — A331

No. 2170, vert: a, Cymothoe cocccinata. b, Morpho rhetenor. c, Callicore lidwina (b, d). d, Heliconius erato.

No. 2171: a, Epiphora albida. b, Satyrus dryas. c, Satyrus lena. d, Papilio tynderaeus. e, Urota Suraka. f, Satyrus nercis.

No. 2172, vert: a, Spicebush swallowtail. b, Giant swallowtail. c, Lime swallowtail caterpillar (b). d, Painted beauty (c). e, Monarch caterpillar. f, Monarch (e, g). g, Monarch caterpillar & pupa. h, Harris' checkerspot.

Each 25r: No. 2173, Heliconius cydno, vert. No. 2174, Zebra, vert.

1996, July 10

2170 A331 7r Strip of 4, #a.-d. 5.00 5.00
2171 A331 7r Sheet of 6, #a.-f. 7.50 7.50
2172 A331 7r Sheet of 8, #a.-h. 10.00 10.00

Souvenir Sheets

2173-2174 A331 Set of 2 10.00 10.00

No. 2170 was issued in sheets of 8 stamps.

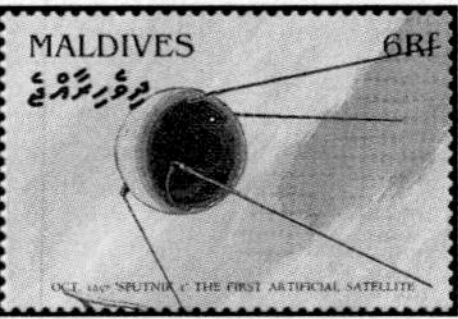

Space Exploration — A332

Designs: No. 2175a, Sputnik I, 1957. b, Apollo 11 Command Module returns to earth, 1969. c, Skylab, 1973. d, Edward White, 1st US astronaut to walk in space, 1965. e, Mariner 9, 1st artificial satellite of Mars, 1971. f, Apollo and Soviet Soyuz dock together, 1975.

25r, Apollo 8 being launched, 1968, vert.

1996, July 10 *Perf. 14*

2175 A332 6r Sheet of 6, #a.-f. 6.50 6.50

Souvenir Sheet

2176 A332 25r multicolored 5.25 5.25

Trains A333

No. 2177, each 3r: a, Electric container train, Germany. b, John Blenkinsop's rack locomotive. c, DB Diesel electric, West Germany. d, Timothy Hackworth's "Royal George," 1827. e, Robert Stephenson (1803-59). f, Trevithick's "New Castle" locomotive. g, Deltic locomotives, British Rail. h, Stockton No. 5, 1826. i, Passenger shuttle, English Channel Tunnel.

No. 2178, each 3r: a, Southern Pacific's "Daylight," San Francisco, US, 1952. b, Timothy Hackworth's "Sans Pareil." c, Chicago & North Western, US. d, Richard Trevithick's "Pen-Y-Darran" locomotive. e, Isambard Kingdom Brunel (1806-59). f, Great Western engine of 1838. g, Passenger train, Canada. h, Mohawk & Hudson Railroad "Experiment," 1832. i, "The ICE," Germany.

No. 2179, each 3r: a, F4 OPH Diesel locomotives, US. b, Stephenson's "Experiment." c, Indian Pacific Intercontinental, Australia. d, George Stephenson's engine, 1815. e, George Stephenson (1781-1848). f, Stephenson's "Rocket," 1829. g, British Rail 125 HST. h, First rail passenger coach, "Experiment," 1825. i, TOFAC, US.

Each 25r: No. 2180, Tom Thumb, 1830. No. 2181, The DeWitt Clinton, 1831. No. 2182, The General, 1855.

1996, Sept. 2 Litho. *Perf. 14*

Sheets of 9, #a-i

2177-2179 A333 Set of 3 21.00 21.00

Souvenir Sheets

2180-2182 A333 Set of 3 15.00 15.00

Fauna A334

Endangered animals:

No. 2183, each 5r: a, Shoebill stork. , Red-billed hornbill. c, Hippopotamus. d, Gorilla. e, Lion. f, Gray-crowned crane.

No. 2184, each 5r: a, Giant panda. b, Indian elephant. c, Arrow poison frog. d, Mandrill. e, Snow leopard. f, California condor.

Wildlife:

No. 2185, vert, each 5r: a, Yellow baboon. b, Zebra duiker. c, Yellow-backed duiker. d, Pygmy hippopotamus. e, Large-spotted genet. f, African spoonbill. g, White-faced whistling duck. h, Helmeted gunieafowl.

No. 2186, vert, each 5r: a, Bongo. b, Bushback. c, Namaqua dove. d, Hoopoe. e, African fish eagle. f, Egyptian goose. g, Saddle-billed stork. h, Blue-breasted kingfisher.

Each 25r: No. 2187, Tiger, vert. No. 2188, Leopard.

1996, Sept. 9

Sheet of 6

2183-2184 A334 Set of 2 11.00 11.00

Sheet of 8

2185-2186 A334 Set of 2 14.50 14.50

Souvenir Sheets

2187-2188 A334 Set of 2 9.00 9.00

Motion Pictures, Cent. — A335

Progressive scenes from "Pluto and the Flypaper, each 4r:": Nos. 2189a-2189h, Scenes 1-8. No. 2191a-2191i, Scenes 9-17.
Progressive scenes from "Mickey Mouse in The Little Whirlwind, each 4r:" Nos. 2190a-2190h, Scenes 1-8. Nos. 2192a-2192i, Scenes 9-17.
Each 25r: No. 2193, Scene from "Pluto and the Flypaper." No. 2194, Scene from "Mickey Mouse in The Little Whirlwind."

1996, Dec. 2 Litho. *Perf. 13½x14*

Sheets of 8, #a-h, + Label

2189-2190 A335 Set of 2 21.00 21.00

Sheets of 9, #a-i

2191-2192 A335 Set of 2 22.50 22.50

Souvenir Sheets

2193-2194 A335 Set of 2 17.00 17.00

Fauna A336

Designs: a, Saguinus oedipus. b, Bison bonasus. c, Panthera tigris. d, Tetrao urogallus. e, Ailuropoda melanoleuca. f, Trogonoptera brookiana. g, Castor canadensis. h, Leiopelma hamiltoni. i, Trichechus manatus latirostris.
25r, Pan troglodytes.

1996 Litho. *Perf. 14*

2195 A336 7r Sheet of 9, #a.-i. 11.50 11.50

Souvenir Sheet

2196 A336 25r multicolored 4.50 4.50

Turtle Preservation — A336a

1996 ? Litho. *Perf. 12¾*

2196A Horiz. strip of 3 — —
b. A336a 1r Turtle's head — —
c. A336a 7r Turtle's plastron — —
d. A336a 8r Two turtles — —

Hong Kong '97 — A337

Chinese motifs inside letters: No. 2197a, "H." b, "O." c, "N." d, "G" (birds). e, "K." f, "O," diff. g, "N." h, "G" (junk).
25r, "Hong Kong."

1997, Feb. 12 Litho. *Perf. 14*

2197 A337 5r Sheet of 8, #a.-h. 8.25 8.25

Souvenir Sheet

2198 A337 25r multicolored 5.00 5.00

No. 2198 contains one 77x39mm stamp.

Birds — A338

a, Gymnogyps californianus. b, Larus audouinii. c, Fratercula artica. d, Pharomachrus mocinno. e, Amazona vittata. f, Paradisaea minor. g, Nipponia nippon. h, Falco punctatus. i, Strigops habroptilus.
25r, Campephilus principalis.

1997, Feb. 12

2199 A338 5r Sheet of 9, #a.-i. 10.00 10.00

Souvenir Sheet

2200 A338 25r multicolored 6.00 6.00

Eagles

A339 A340

Designs: 1r, Crowned solitary eagle. 2r, African hawk eagle, horiz. 3r, Lesser spotted eagle. 5r, Stellar's sea eagle. 8r, Spanish imperial eagle, horiz. 10r, Harpy eagle. 12r, Crested serpent eagle, horiz.
Bald eagles: No. 2208: a, Wings upward in flight. b, Looking backward on limb. c, Up close, head left. d, Up close, head right. e, On limb. f, In flight.
No. 2209, American bald eagle, horiz. No. 2210, Bald eagle.

1997, Mar. 20 Litho. *Perf. 14*

2201-2207 A339 Set of 7 7.50 7.50
2208 A340 5r Sheet of 6, #a.-f. 5.50 5.50

Souvenir Sheets

2209 A339 25r multicolored 4.50 4.50
2210 A340 25r multicolored 4.50 4.50

Automobiles — A341

No. 2211, each 5r: a, 1911 Blitzer Benz, Germany. b, 1917 Datsun, Japan. c, 1929 Auburn 8-120, US. d, 1996 Mercedes-Benz C280, Germany. e, Suzuki UR-1, Japan. f, Chrysler Atlantic, US.
No. 2212, each 5r: a, 1961 Mercedes-Benz 190SL, Germany. b, 1916 Kwaishinha DAT, Japan. c, 20/25 Rolls-Royce Roadster, England. d, 1997 Mercedes-Benz SLK, Germany. e, 1996 Toyota Camry, Japan. f, 1959 Jaguar MK2, England.
Each 25r: No. 2213, 1939 VW built by Dr. Porsche. No. 2214, Mazda RX-01.

1997, Mar. 27

Sheets of 6, #a-f

2211-2212 A341 Set of 2 11.00 11.00

Souvenir Sheets

2213-2214 A341 Set of 2 9.00 9.00

1998 Winter Olympics, Nagano — A342

Medalists: 2r, Ye Qiabo, 1992 speed skating. 3r, Leonhard Stock, 1980 downhill. 8r, Bjorn Daehlie, 1992 cross-country skiing. 12r, Wolfgang Hoppe, 1984 bobsledding.
No. 2219: a, Herma Von Szabo-Planck, 1924 figure skating. b, Katarina Witt, 1988 figure skating. c, Natalia Bestemianova, Andrei Bukin, 1988 ice dancing. d, Jayne Torvill, Christopher Dean, 1984 ice dancing.
Each 25r: No. 2220, Sonja Henie, 1924 figure skating. No. 2221, Andree Joly, Pierre Brunet, 1932 figure skating.

1997, Mar. 13 Litho. *Perf. 14*

2215-2218 A342 Set of 4 4.50 4.50
2219 A342 5r Block of 4, #a.-d. 3.50 3.50

Souvenir Sheets

2220-2221 A342 Set of 2 9.00 9.00

No. 2219 was issued in sheets of 8 stamps.

Ships A343

Designs: 1r, SS Patris II, 1926, Greece. 2r, MV Infanta Beatriz, 1928, Spain. 8r, SS Stavangerjord, 1918, Norway. 12r, MV Baloeran, 1929, Holland.
No. 2226, each 3r: a, SS Vasilefs Constantinos, 1914, Greece. b, SS Cunene, 1911, Portugal. c, MV Selandia, 1912, Denmark. d, SS President Harding, 1921, US. e, MV Ulster Monarch, 1929, Great Britain. f, SS Matsonia, 1913, US. g, SS France, 1911, France. h, SS Campania, 1893, Great Britain. i, SS Klipfontein, 1922, Holland.
No. 2227, each 3r: a, MV Eridan, 1929, France. b, SS Mount Clinton, 1921, US. c, SS Infanta Isabel, 1912, Spain. d, SS Suwa Maru, 1914, Japan. e, SS Yorkshire, 1920, Great Britain. f, MV Highland Chieftan, 1929, Great Britain. g, MV Sardinia, 1920, Norway. h, SS San Guglielmo, 1911, Italy. i, SS Avila, 1927, Great Britain.
Each 25r: No. 2228, SS Mauritania, 1907, Great Britain. No. 2229, SS United States, 1952, US. No. 2230, SS Queen Mary, 1930, Great Britain. No. 2231, Royal Yacht Brittania sailing into Hong Kong harbor.

1997, Apr. 1

2222-2225 A343 Set of 4 5.50 5.50

Sheets of 9, #a-i

2226-2227 A343 Set of 2 12.00 12.00

Souvenir Sheets

2228-2231 A343 Set of 4 21.00 21.00

No. 2231 contains one 57x42mm stamp.

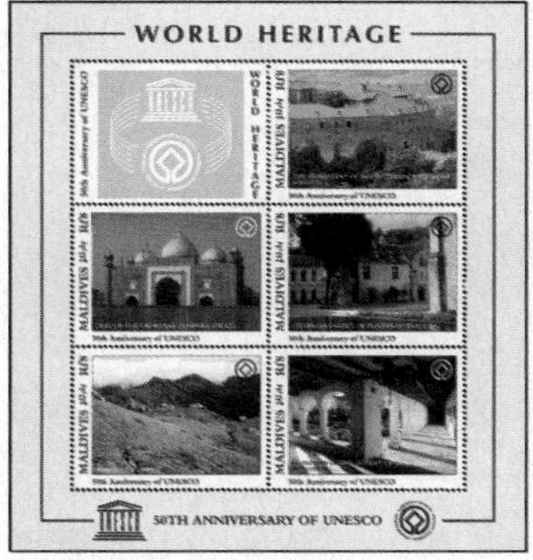

UNESCO, 50th Anniv. — A344

1r, Prayer wheels, Lhasa, vert. 2r, Roman ruins, Temple of Diana, Portugal. 3r, Cathedral of Santa Maria Hildesheim, Germany. 7r, Monument of Nubia at Abu Simbel, Egypt, vert. 8r, Entrance to Port of Mandraki, Rhodes, Greece. 10r, Nature Reserve of Scandola, France. 12r, Temple on the Lake, China.
No. 2232, vert, each 5r: a, Virunga Natl. Park, Zaire. b, Valley of Mai Nature Reserve, Seychelles. c, Kandy, Sri Lanka. d, Taj Mahal, India. e, Istanbul, Turkey. f, Sana'a, Yemen. g, Blenheim Palace, Oxfordshire, England. h, Grand Canyon Natl. Park, US.
No. 2233, vert, each 5r: a, Gondar, Ethiopia. b, Bwindi Natl. Park, Uganda. c, Bemaraha Nature Reserve, Madagascar. d, Buddhist ruins of Takht-i-Bahi, Pakistan. e, Anuradhapura, Sri Lanka. f, Cairo, Egypt. g, Ruins at Petra, Jordan. h, Natl. Park of Ujung Kulon, Indonesia.
Sites in China, vert: No. 2234, each 5r: a-f, Mount Taishan. g-h, Terracotta warriors.
Sites in Japan: No. 2235, each 8r: a-e, Horyu-Ji.
No. 2236, each 8r: a, Monastery of Agios Stefanos Meteora, Greece. b, Taj Mahal, India. c, Cistercian Abbey of Fontenay, France. d, Yakushima, Japan. e, Cloisters of the Convent, San Gonzalo, Portugal.
No. 2237, each 8r: a, Olympic Natl. Park, US. b, Nahanni Waterfalls, Canada. c, Los Glaciares Natl. Park, Argentina. d, Bonfin Salvador Church, Brazil. e, Convent of the Companions of Jesus, Morelia, Mexico.
Each 25r: No. 2238, Temple, Chengde, China. No. 2239, Serengeti Natl. Park, Tanzania. No. 2240, Anuradhapura, Sri Lanka. No. 2241, Monument to Fatehpur Sikri, India.

1997, Apr. 7

2231A-2231G A344 Set of 7 5.75 5.75

Sheets of 8, #a-h, + Label

2232-2234 A344 Set of 3 22.00 22.00

Sheets of 5, #a-e, + Label

2235-2237 A344 Set of 3 22.00 22.00

Souvenir Sheets

2238-2241 A344 Set of 4 18.00 18.00

Queen Elizabeth II, Prince Philip, 50th Wedding Anniv. A345

No. 2242: a, Queen. b, Royal Arms. c, Queen, Prince seated on thrones. d, Queen, Prince holding baby. e, Buckingham Palace. f, Prince.
25r, Queen wearing crown.

1997, June 12 Litho. *Perf. 14*

2242 A345 5r Sheet of 6, #a.-f. 5.50 5.50

Souvenir Sheet

2243 A345 25r multicolored 4.50 4.50

Paintings by Hiroshige (1797-1858) A346

No. 2244: a, Dawn at Kanda Myojin Shrine. b, Kiyomizu Hall & Shinobazu Pond at Ueno. c, Ueno Yamashita. d, Moon Pine, Ueno. e, Flower Pavilion, Dango Slope, Sendagi. f, Shitaya Hirokoji.
Each 25r: No. 2245, Seido and Kanda River from Shohei Bridge. No. 2246, Hilltop View, Yushima Tenjin Shrine.

1997, June 12 *Perf. 13½x14*

2244 A346 8r Sheet of 6, #a.-f. 8.25 8.25

Souvenir Sheets

2245-2246 A346 Set of 2 9.00 9.00

Heinrich von Stephan (1831-97) A347

a, Early mail messenger, India. b, Von Stephan, UPU emblem. c, Autogiro, Washington DC.

1997, June 12 *Perf. 14*

2247 A347 2r Sheet of 3, #a.-c. 3.75 3.75

PACIFIC 97.

A number has been reserved for a souvenir sheet with this set.

South Asian Assoc. for Regional Cooperation (SAARC) Summit — A348

1997, May 12 Litho. *Perf. 13*

2249 A348 3r shown .55 .55
2250 A348 5r Flags, "SAARC" .90 .90

A349

A350

Birds: 30 l, Anous stolidus. 1r, Spectacled owl. 2r, Buffy fish owl. 3r, Peregrine falcon. 5r, Golden eagle. 8r, Bateleur. No. 2257, 10r, Crested caracara. No. 2258, 10r, Childonias hybrida. 15r, Sula sula.

No. 2260: a, Rueppell's parrot. b, Blue-headed parrot. c, St. Vincent parrot. d, Gray parrot. e, Masked lovebird. f, Sun parakeet.

Each 25r: No. 2261, Secretary bird. No. 2262, Bald eagle.

1997 *Perf. 14*

2251-2259 A349 Set of 9 9.75 9.75
2260 A349 7r Sheet of 6, #a.-f. 7.50 7.50

Souvenir Sheets

2261-2262 A349 Set of 2 11.00 11.00

1997, June 24 Litho. *Perf. 14½x14*

Flowers: 1r, Canarina eminii. 2r, Delphinium macrocentron. 3r, Leucadendron discolor. 5r, Nymphaea caerulea. 7r, Rosa multiflora. 8r, Bulbophyllum barbigerum. 12r, Hibiscus vitifolius.

No. 2270, horiz: a, Acacia seyal. b, Gloriosa superba. c, Gnidia subcordata. d, Platycelphium voense. e, Aspilia mossambicensis. f, Adenium obesum.

Each 25r: No. 2271, Aerangis rhodosticta, horiz. No. 2272, Dichrostachys cinerea, horiz.

2263-2269 A350 Set of 6 7.25 7.25

Perf. 14x14½

2270 A350 8r Sheet of 6, #a.-f. 11.50 11.50

Souvenir Sheets

2271-2272 A350 Set of 2 17.00 17.00

No. 2267 is 16x20mm.

A351

Dinosaurs A352

5r, Archaeopteryx. 8r, Mosasaurus. 12r, Deinonychus. 15r, Triceratops.

No. 2277, each 7r: a, Diplodocus (b, c, d, e, f). b. Tyrannosaurus rex (c, e, f). c, Pteranodon. d, Montanaceratops. e, Dromaeosaurus (d). f, Oviraptor (e).

No. 2278, each 7r: a, Euoplocephalus. b, Compsognathus. c, Herrerasaurus. d, Styracosaurus. e, Baryonyx. f, Lesothosaurus.

No. 2279, each 7r: a, Triceratops. b, Pachycephalosaurus. c, Iguanodon. d, Tyrannosaurus. e, Corythosaurus. f, Stegosaurus.

No. 2280, each 7r: a, Troodon (d). b, Brachosaurus (c). c, Saltasaurus (a, b, d, e, f). d, Oviraptor. e, Parasaurolophus (f). f, Psittacosaurus.

No. 2281, Tyrannosaurus rex. No. 2282, Archaeopteryx.

1997, Nov. 20 Litho. *Perf. 14*

2273-2276 A351 Set of 4 7.25 7.25

Sheets of 6, #a-f

2277 A351 7r #a.-f. 7.50 7.50
2278-2280 A352 Set of 3 22.50 22.50

Souvenir Sheets

2281 A351 25r multicolored 11.00 11.00
2282 A352 25r multicolored 11.00 11.00

1998 World Cup Soccer Championships, France — A353

Past winners: 1r, Brazil, 1994. 2r, West Germany, 1954. 3r, Argentina, 1986. 7r, Argentina, 1978. 8r, England, 1966. 10r, Brazil, 1970.

Various scenes from 1966 finals, England v. West Germany, each 3r: Nos. 2289a-2289h.

Italian tournament winners, each 3r: No. 2290: a, Raulo Rossi, Italy, 1982. b, Zoff & Gentile, Italy, 1982. c, Angelo Schiavio, Italy. d, 1934 team. e, 1934 team entering stadium. f, 1982 team. g, San Paolo Stadium, Italy. h, 1938 team.

Brazilian teams, players, each 3r: No. 2291: a, 1958 team pictue. b, Luis Bellini, 1958. c, 1962 team. d, Carlos Alberto, 1970. e, Mauro, 1962. f, 1970 team. g, Dunga, 1994. h, 1994 team.

Each 25r: No. 2292, Klinsmann, Germany. No. 2293, Ronaldo, Brazil, vert. No. 2294, Schmeichel, Denmark, vert.

Perf. 14x13½, 13½x14

1997, Dec. 10 Litho.

2283-2288 A353 Set of 6 5.60 5.60

Sheets of 8 + Label

2289-2291 A353 Set of 3 13.00 13.00

Souvenir Sheets

2292-2294 A353 Set of 3 15.00 15.00

Diana, Princess of Wales (1961-97) — A354

Various portraits, color of sheet margin, each 7r: No. 2295, Pale pink. No. 2296, Pale yellow. No. 2297, Pale blue.

Each 25r: No. 2298, Diana on ski lift. No. 2299, In polka dot dress. No. 2300, Wearing lei.

1998, Feb. 9 Litho. *Perf. 13½*

Sheets of 6, #a-f

2295-2297 A354 Set of 3 22.50 22.50

Souvenir Sheets

2298-2300 A354 Set of 3 13.50 13.50

John F. Kennedy (1917-63) A355

Various portraits.

1998 Litho. *Perf. 13½x14*

2301 A355 5r Sheet of 9, #a.-i. 8.00 8.00

Nelson Mandela, Pres. of South Africa — A356

1998 *Perf. 14*

2302 A356 4r multicolored 1.50 1.50

Classic Airplanes A357

No. 2303: a, Yakovlev Yak 18. b, Beechcraft Bonanza. c, Piper Cub. d, Tupolev Tu-95. e, Lockheed C-130 Hercules. f, Piper PA-28 Cherokee. g, Mikoyan-Gurevich MiG-21. h, Pilatus PC-6 Turbo Porter. i, Antonov An-2.

25r, KC-135E.

1998

2303 A357 5r Sheet of 9, #a.-i. 8.00 8.00

Souvenir Sheet

2304 A357 25r multicolored 4.50 4.50

No. 2304 contains one 85x28mm stamp.

Cats A358

Designs, vert: 5r, White American shorthair. 8r, Sphinx. 10r, Tabby American shorthair. 12r, Scottish fold.

No. 2309, each 7r: a, American curl, Maine coon (d). b, Maine coon (a, d, e). c, Siberian (f). d, Somali. e, European Burmese (d). f, Nebelung.

No. 2310, each 7r: a, Bicolor British shorthair (b). b, Manx. c, Tabby American shorthair (b, e, f). d, Silver tabby Persian (e). e, Oriental white. f, Norwegian forest cat (e).

Each 30r: No. 2311, Snowshoe, vert. No. 2312, Norwegian forest cat, vert.

1998, June 1 Litho. *Perf. 14*

2305-2308 A358 Set of 4 6.25 6.25

Sheets of 6, #a-f

2309-2310 A358 Set of 2 15.00 15.00

Souvenir Sheets

2311-2312 A358 Set of 2 11.00 11.00

Airplanes A359

Designs: 2r, Boeing 737 HS. 7r, Boeing 727. 8r, Boeing 747, 1970. 10r, Boeing 737.

No. 2317, each 5r: a, FSW Fighter. b, V-Jet II. c, Pilatus PC-12. d, Citation Exel. e, Stutz Bearcat. f, Cessna T-37 (B). g, Peregrine business jet. h, Beech Baron 53.

No. 2318, each 5r: a, CL-215. b, P-3 Orion. c, Yak 54. d, Cessna float plane. e, CL-215 Amphibian. f, CL-215 SAR Amphibian. g, Twin Otter. h, Rockwell Quail.

Each 25r: No. 2319, Falcon Jet. No. 2320, Beechcraft Model 18.

1998, Aug. 10 Litho. *Perf. 14*

2313-2316 A359 Set of 4 4.75 4.75

Sheets of 8, #a-h

2317-2318 A359 Set of 2 14.50 14.50

Souvenir Sheets

2319-2320 A359 Set of 2 10.00 10.00

The Titanic A360

No. 2321: a, Capt. Edward J. Smith's cap. b, Deck chair. c, Fifth Officer Harold Lowe's coat button. d, Lifeboat. e, Steering wheel. f, Lifejacket.

25r, Newpaper picture of the Titanic at sea.

1998, Sept. 27 Litho. *Perf. 14*

2321 A360 7r Sheet of 6, #a.-f. 8.50 8.50

Souvenir Sheet

2322 A360 25r multicolored 5.50 5.50

Bird Type of 1992

1998, Oct. 26 Litho. *Perf. 14½*

2323 A247 100r Anas clypeata 14.00 14.00

IFAD, 20th Anniv. — A361

Designs: 1r, Papaya tree. 5r, Fruits. 7r, Fishermen on boat. 8r, Coconut tree. 10r, Vegetables.

1998, Nov. 30 Litho. *Perf. 14*

2324-2328 A361 Set of 5 5.50 5.50

Ferrari Automobiles — A361a

No. 2328A: c, 250 TR. d, 1957 250 GT TDF. e, 250 GT.

25r, 365 GTC 2+2.

Illustration reduced.

1998, Dec. 15 Litho. *Perf. 14*

2328A A361a 10r Sheet of 3, #c-e 5.25 5.25

Souvenir Sheet

Perf. 13¾x14¼

2328B A361a 25r multi 4.25 4.25

No. 2328A contains three 39x25mm stamps.

1998 World Scout Jamboree, Chile — A362

a, Robert Baden-Powell inspecting Scouts, Amesbury, c. 1909. b, Lord, Lady Baden-Powell, children, South Africa Tour, 1927. c, Robert Baden-Powell pins merit badges on Chicago Scouts, 1926.

1998, Dec. 15
2329 A362 12r Sheet of 3, #a.-c. 6.50 6.50

A363

Diana, Princess of Wales (1961-97) — A364

Illustration A364 reduced.

1998, Dec. 15 ***Perf. 14½x14***
2330 A363 10r multicolored 1.75 1.75

Size: 95x56mm

Litho. & Embossed

Die Cut Perf. 7½

2331 A364 50r shown
2332 A364 50r Rose, Diana

No. 2330 was issued in sheets of 6.

Fish A365

Designs: No. 2333, 50 l, Threadfin butterfly fish. No. 2334, 50 l, Queen angelfish. 1r, Oriental sweetlips. No. 2336, 7r, Bandit angelfish. No. 2337, 7r, Achilles tang. 8r, Red-headed butterfly fish. 50r, Blue striped butterfly fish.

No. 2340: a, Mandarinfish. b, Copper-banded butterfly fish. c, Harlequin tuskfish. d, Yellow-tailed demoiselle. e, Wimplefish. f, Red emperor snapper. g, Clown triggerfish. h, Common clown. i, Regal tang.

No. 2341: a, Emperor angelfish. b, Common squirrelfish. c, Lemonpeel angelfish. d, Powderblue surgeon. e, Moorish idol. f, Bicolor cherub. g, Scribbled angelfish. h, Two-banded anemonefish. i, Yellow tang.

Each 25r: No. 2342, Porkfish. No. 2343, Long-nosed butterfly fish.

1998, Dec. 10 **Litho.** ***Perf. 14***
2333-2339 A365 Set of 7 13.50 13.50
2340 A365 3r Sheet of 9, #a.-i. 4.75 4.75
2341 A365 5r Sheet of 9, #a.-i. 8.25 8.25

Souvenir Sheets

2342-2343 A365 Set of 2 9.00 9.00

Intl. Year of the Ocean A366

Marine life: No. 2344, Skipjack tuna.

No. 2345: a, 25 l, Triton. b, 50 l, Napoleon wrasse. c, 1r, Whale shark. d, 3r, Gray reef shark. e, 7r, Blue whale.

No. 2346: a, Harp seal. b, Killer whale. c, Sea otter. d, Beluga. e, Narwhal. f, Walrus. g, Sea lion. h, Humpback salmon. i, Emperor penguin.

No. 2347: a, Ocean sunfish. b, Opalescent squid. c, Electric eel. d, Corded neptune.

Each 25r: No. 2348, Horseshoe crab. No. 2349, Blue whale. No. 2350, Triton, diff.

1999, Apr. 1 **Litho.** ***Perf. 14***
2344 A366 7r multicolored 1.25 1.25

Sheets of 6, 9, 4

2345 A366 #a.-e. + 1 #2344 3.50 3.50
2346 A366 5r #a.-i. 8.00 8.00
2347 A366 8r #a.-d. 5.75 5.75

Souvenir Sheets

2348-2350 A366 Set of 3 13.50 13.50

No. 2344 was issued in sheets of 6.
No. 2350 incorrectly inscribed Coral Reef.

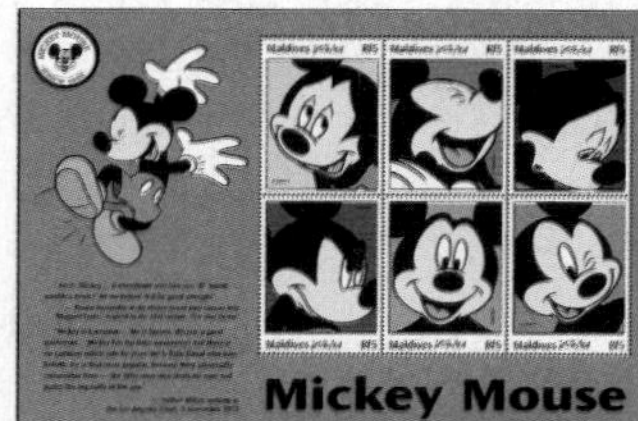

Mickey Mouse, 70th Anniv. (in 1998) — A367

#2351, each 5r: Various pictures of Mickey Mouse.
#2352, each 5r: Various pictures of Minnie Mouse.
#2353, each 7r: Various pictures of Donald Duck.
#2354, each 7r: Various pictures of Daisy Duck.
#2355, each 7r: Various pictures of Goofy.
#2356, each 7r: Various pictures of Pluto.
Each 25r: #2357, Minnie sipping drink. #2358, Minnie looking backward. #2359, Mickey grabbing Donald's hand, horiz. #2360, Minnie wearing pearls. #2361, Mickey with hand on head. #2362, Mickey after throwing ball.

Perf. 13½x14, 14x13½ (#2359)

1999, May 27 **Litho.**

Sheets of 6, #a-f

2351-2352 A367 Set of 2 11.00 11.00
2353-2356 A367 Set of 4 30.00 30.00

Souvenir Sheets

2357-2362 A367 Set of 6 27.00 27.00

Stamp in No. 2358 is printed se-tenant with label.
Sheets similar to #2351-2352 with "5Rs" denomination and #2353-2356 with "25Rs" exist.

Butterflies A368

50 l, Great orange tip. 1r, Large green aporandria. 2r, Common mormon. 3r, African migrant. 5r, Common pierrot. 10r, Giant redeye.

No. 2369, vert, each 7r: a, Common red flash. b, Burmese lascar. c, Common peirrot. d, Baron. e, Leaf blue. f, Great orange tip.

No. 2370, vert, each 7r: a, Crimson tip. b, Tawny rajah. c, Leafwing butterfly. d, Great egg-fly. e, Blue admiral. f, African migrant.

Each 25r: No. 2371, Crimson tip. No. 2372, Large oak blue.

1999, June 8 **Litho.** ***Perf. 14***
2363-2368 A368 Set of 6 3.75 3.75

Sheets of 6, #a-f

2369-2370 A368 Set of 2 15.00 15.00

Souvenir Sheets

2371-2372 A368 Set of 2 9.00 9.00

Dinosaurs A369

Designs: 1r, Scelidosaurus. 3r, Yansudaurus. 5r, Ornitholestes. 8r, Astrodon.

No. 2377, vert, each 7r: a, Archisaurus. b, Pterenodon. c, Barosaurus. d, Iguanodon. e, Archaeopteryx. f, Ceratosaurus.

No. 2378, each 7r: a, Stegosaurus. b, Corythosaurus. c, Celiosaurus. d, Avimimus. e, Styracosaurus. f, Massospondylus.

No. 2379, vert, each 7r: a, Dimorphodon. b, Rhamphorhynchus. c, Allosaurus. d, Leaellynasaura. e, Troodon. f, Syntarsus.

Each 25r: No. 2380, Brachiosaurus. No. 2381, Megalosaurus.

1999, June 22
2373-2376 A369 Set of 4 3.00 3.00

Sheets of 6, #a-f

2377-2379 A369 Set of 3 22.50 22.50

Souvenir Sheets

2380-2381 A369 Set of 2 9.00 9.00

Marine Environment Wildlife — A370

30 l, Broderip's cowrie. 1r, Fairy tern. 3r, Darker Maldivian green heron. 7r, Blackflag sandperch. 8r, Coral hind. 10r, Olive ridley turtle.

No. 2388, each 5r: a, Brown booby. b, Red-tailed tropicbird. c, Sooty tern. d, Striped dolphin. e, Long-snouted spinner dolphin. f, Crab plover. g, Hawksbill turtle. h, Indo-Pacific sergeant. i, Yellowfin tuna.

No. 2389, each 5r: a, Manta ray. b, Green turtle. c, Pan-tropical spotted dolphin. d, Moorish idols. e, Threadfin anthias. f, Goldbar wrasse. g, Palette surgeonfish. h, Three spot angelfish. i, Oriental sweetlips.

Each 25r: No. 2390, Cinnamon bittern. No. 2391, Blue-faced angelfish.

1999, Oct. 26 **Litho.** ***Perf. 14***
2382-2387 A370 Set of 6 5.00 5.00

Sheets of 9, #a-i

2388-2389 A370 Set of 2 15.50 15.50

Souvenir Sheets

2390-2391 A370 Set of 2 8.50 8.50

Trains A371

Designs: 50 l, 2-2-2 locomotive, Egypt. 1r, Le Shuttle, France. 2r, 4-4-0 Gowan & Marx, US. 3r, TGV, France. 5r, Ae 6/6 electric locomotive, Switzerland. 8r, Stephenson's Long-boilered 2-4-0 locomotive, Great Britain. 10r, The Philadelphia, Austria. 15r. E class, Great Britain.

No. 2400, each 7r: a, Stephenson's Long-boilered locomotive, diff. b, 4-2-2 Cornwall, Great Britain. c, First locomotive, Germany. d, Great Western, Great Britain. e, Standard Stephenson 2-4-0, France. f, 2-2-2 Meteor, Great Britain.

No. 2401, each 7r: a, Type 4 class 4t, Great Britain. b, 1500 horsepower Diesel-electric locomotive, Malaysia. c, Co-Co 7000 Class, France. d, Diesel-hydraulic passenger locomotive, Thailand. e, Diesel-hydraulic locomotive, Burma. f, Hikari, Japan.

Each 25r: No. 2402, 2-2-2, Passenger locomotive, France. No. 2403, King Arthur class, Great Britain.

1999, Oct. 26
2392-2399 A371 Set of 8 7.50 7.50

Sheets of 6, #a-f

2400-2401 A371 Set of 2 14.50 14.50

Souvenir Sheets

2402-2403 A371 Set of 2 10.00 10.00

A372

Queen Mother (b. 1900) — A373

No. 2404: a, With King George VI, 1936. b, In 1941. c, In 1960. d, In 1981.
25r, At Order of the Garter Service.
Illustration A373 reduced.

Gold Frames

1999, Dec. 1 **Litho.** ***Perf. 14***
2404 A372 7r Sheet of 4, #a.-d., + label 6.00 6.00

Souvenir Sheet

Perf. 13¾

2405 A372 25r multi 6.00 6.00

Litho. & Embossed

Die Cut Perf. 8¾

Without Gum

2406 A373 50r gold & multi

No. 2405 contains one 38x51mm stamp.
See Nos. 2605-2606.

Hokusai Paintings — A374

No. 2407, each 7r: a, A Coastal view. b, Bath House by a Lake. c, Drawings (horse). d, Drawings (two birds). e, Evening Cool at Ryogoku. f, Girls Boating.

No. 2408, each 7r: a, Haunted House. b, Juniso Shrine at Yotsuya. c, Drawings (one bird). d, Drawings (two people). e, Lover in the Snow. f, Mountain Tea House.

Each 25r: No. 2409, Girls Gathering Spring Herbs, vert. No. 2410, Scene in the Yoshiwara, vert.

1999, Dec. 23 ***Perf. 13¾***

Sheets of 6, #a.-f.

2407-2408 A374 Set of 2 16.50 16.50

Souvenir Sheets

2409-2410 A374 Set of 2 10.00 10.00

IBRA '99, Nuremberg — A375

Trains (as described): 12r, Drache, 1848. 15r, Der Adler, 1833.
Illustration reduced.

1999, Dec. 23 ***Perf. 14x14½***
2411-2412 A375 Set of 2 6.00 6.00

The illustrations of the two stamps were switched.

Souvenir Sheets

PhilexFrance '99 — A376

Trains: No. 2413, Standard Stephenson 2-4-0, 1837. No. 2414, Long-boilered Stephenson, 1841.
Illustration reduced.

1999, Dec. 23 *Perf. 13¾*
2413-2414 A376 25r each 4.50 4.50

Rights of the Child — A377

No. 2415: a, Black denomination in UL. b, White denomination in UL. c, Black denomination in UR.
25r, Peter Ustinov, UNICEF goodwill ambassador.

1999, Dec. 23 *Perf. 14*
2415 A377 10r Sheet of 3, #a.-c. 6.00 6.00

Souvenir Sheet

2416 A377 25r multi 4.25 4.25

Mars Colony of the Future A378

No. 2417, each 5r: a, Phobos and Deimos. b, Improved Hubble Telescope. c, Passenger shuttle. d, Skyscrapers. e, Taxi cab. f, Landing facilities. g, Vegetation. h, Walking on Mars. i, Mars rover.
No. 2418, each 5r: a, Russian Phobos 25. b, Earth and moon. c, Space shuttle. d, Lighthouse. e, Excursion space liner. f, Inner-city shuttle. g, Viking lander. h, Air and water purification plants. i, Life in a Mars city.
Each 25r: No. 2419, Mars, vert. No. 2420, Astronaut, vert.

2000, Jan. 24 Litho. *Perf. 14*

Sheets of 9, #a.-i.

2417-2418 A378 Set of 2 17.50 17.50

Souvenir Sheets

2419-2420 A378 Set of 2 10.00 10.00

Millennium — A379

Highlights of 1750-1800: a, American Declaration of Independence, 1776. b, Hot air balloon flight by Montgolfier brothers, 1783. c, French Revolution begins with storming of the Bastille, 1789. d, James Watt patents steam engine, 1769. e, Wolfgang Amadeus Mozart born, 1756. f, Ts'ao Hsueh-ch'in publishes "Dream of the Red Chamber," 1791. g, Napoleon conquers Egypt, 1798. h, Catherine the Great becomes Empress of Russia, 1762. i, Joseph Priestley discovers oxygen, 1774. j, Benjamin Franklin publishes studies on electricity, 1751. k, Edward Jenner develops vaccination against smallpox, 1796. l, French and Indian War, 1754. m, Jean Honoré Fragonard paints "The Swing," c. 1766. n, Ludwig van Beethoven born, 1770. o, Louis marries Marie Antoinette, 1770. p, Capt. James Cook explores in South Pacific, discovers east coast of Australia, 1770 (60x40mm). q, Luigi Galvani experiments with electricity on nerves and muscles, c. 1780.

2000, Feb. 1 *Perf. 12¾x12½*
2421 A379 3r Sheet of 17, #a.-q., + label 10.00 10.00

Destination 2000 Tourism Campaign — A380

Designs: a, Yellow flowers. b, School of fish. c, Airplane, boat prow. d, White flowers. e, Lionfish. f, Windsurfers.

2000, Feb. 1 *Perf. 13¾*
2422 A380 7r Sheet of 6, #a.-f. 9.00 9.00

Solar Eclipse, Aug. 11, 1999 — A381

No. 2423 (Sky background), each 7r: a, First contact. b, Second contact. c, Totality. d, Third contact. e, Fourth contact. f, Observatory.
No. 2424 (Outer space background), each 7r: a, First contact. b, Second contact. c, Totality. d, Third contact. e, Fourth contact. f, Solar and heliospheric observatory.

2000, Mar. 8 Litho. *Perf. 14*

Sheets of 6, #a.-f.

2423-2424 A381 Set of 2 14.50 14.50

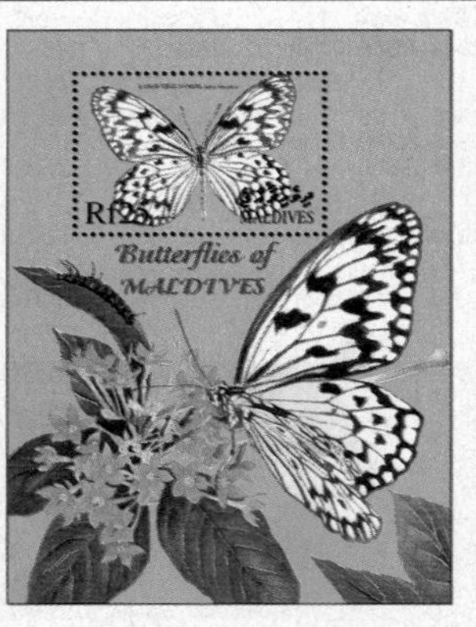

Butterflies — A382

No. 2425, each 5r: a, Red lacewing. b, Large oak blue. c, Yellow coster. d, Great orange tip. e, Common pierrot. f, Cruiser. g, Hedge blue. h, Great egg-fly. i, Common tiger.
No. 2426, each 5r: a, Common wall. b, Koh-i-noor. c, Indian red admiral. d, Tawny rajah. e, Blue triangle. f, Orange albatross. g, Common rose swallowtail. h, Jeweled nawab. i, Striped blue crow.
Each 25r: No. 2427, Large tree nymph. No. 2428, Blue pansy.
Illustration reduced.

2000, Apr. 10 Litho. *Perf. 13¼x13½*

Sheets of 9, #a-i

2425-2426 A382 Set of 2 17.50 17.50

Souvenir Sheets

2427-2428 A382 Set of 2 10.00 10.00

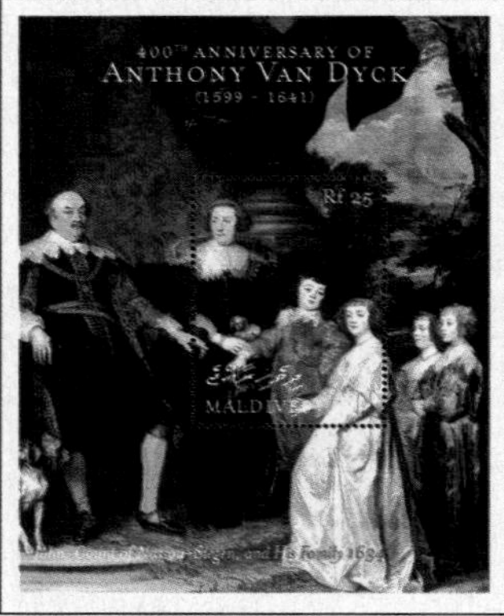

Paintings of Anthony Van Dyck — A383

No. 2429, each 5r: a, Martin Rijckaert. b, Frans Snyders. c, Quentin Simons. d, Lucas van Uffel, 1622. e, Nicolaes Rockox. f, Nicholas Lanier.
No. 2430, each 5r: a, Inigo Jones. b, Lucas van Uffel, (actually detail from John, Count of Nassau-Sieger and his Family) c. 1622-25. c, Margaretha de Vos, Wife of Frans Snyders. d, Peter Breughel the Younger. e, Cornelis van der Geest. f, Francois Langlois as a Savoyard.
No. 2431, each 5r: a, Portrait of a Family. b, Earl and Countess of Denby and Their Daughter. c, Family Portrait. d, A Genoese Nobleman with his Children. e, Thomas Howard, Earl of Arundel, and His Grandson. f, The Woman in Gold (Battonia Balbi with her Children).
Each 25r: No. 2432, John, Count of Nassau-Siegen, and His Family. No. 2433, The Lomellini Family. No. 2434, Lucas and Cornelis de Wael. No. 2435, The Painter Jan de Wael and His Wife Gertrude de Jode. No. 2436, Sir Kenelm and Lady Digby with Their Two Eldest Sons. No. 2437, Sir Philip Herbert, 4th Earl of Pembroke, and His Family.
Illustration reduced.

2000, May 1 *Perf. 13¾*

Sheets of 6, #a-f

2429-2431 A383 Set of 3 40.00 40.00

Souvenir Sheets

2432-2437 A383 Set of 6 25.00 25.00

Trains A384

Designs: 5r, Shinkansen, Japan. 8r, Super Azusa, Japan. No. 2440, 10r, Spacia, Japan. 15r, Nozomi, Japan.
No. 2442, each 10r: a, 1909 Shanghai-Nanking Railway 4-6-2. b, 1910 Shanghai-Nanking Railway 4-2-2. c, 1914 Manchurian Railway 4-6-2. d, 1934 Chinese National Railway Hankow Line 4-8-4. e, 1949 Chinese National Railway 2-8-2. f, 1949 Chinese National Railway 2-10-0.
No. 2443, each 10r: a, 1856 East Indian Railway "Fawn" 2-2-2. b, 1893 East Indian Railway 4-4-0. c, 1909 Bengal-Nagpur Railway 4-4-2. d, 11924 Great Peninsular Railway 4-6-0. e, 1932 North Western Railway 4-6-2. f, 1949 Indian National Railway 4-6-2.
Each 25r: No. 2444, Chinese National Railways Class JS 2-8-2. No. 2445, Indian National Railway Class WP 4-6-2.

2000, June 8 Litho. *Perf. 14*
2438-2441 A384 Set of 4 6.50 6.50

Sheets of 6, #a-f

2442-2443 A384 Set of 2 20.00 20.00

Souvenir Sheets

2444-2445 A384 Set of 2 10.00 10.00

The Stamp Show 2000, London (Nos. 2442-2445). Nos. 2444-2445 each contain one 57x42mm stamp.

Millennium A385

Designs: 10 l, Republic Monument. 30 l, Bodu Thakurufaanu Memorial Center. 1r, Health services. No. 2449, 7r, Hukuru Miskiiy. No. 2450, 7r, Male Intl. Airport. 10r, Educational development.
No. 2452, 25r, People's Majlis. No. 2453, 25r, Economic development. No. 2454, 25r, Islamic Center.

2000, Aug. 31 Litho. *Perf. 14*
2446-2451 A385 Set of 6 6.00 6.00

Souvenir Sheets

Perf. 13¼

2452-2454 A385 Set of 3 13.00 13.00

Souvenir Sheets

First Public Railways, 175th Anniv. — A386

No. 2455: a, Locomotion No. 1, George Stephenson. b, William Hedley's Puffing Billy.
Illustration reduced.

2000, Sept. 13 *Perf. 14*
2455 A386 10r Sheet of 2, #a-b 4.50 4.50

2000 Summer Olympics, Sydney — A387

No. 2456: a, Suzanne Lenglen. b, Fencing. c, Olympic Stadium, Tokyo, and Japanese flag. d, Ancient Greek long jumper.
Illustration reduced.

2000, Sept. 13
2456 A387 10r Sheet of 4, #a-d 7.50 7.50

First Zeppelin Flight, Cent. — A388

No. 2457, horiz.: a, Graf Zeppelin. b, Graf Zeppelin II. c, LZ-9.
Illustration reduced.

2000, Sept. 13 ***Perf. 14***
2457 A388 13r Sheet of 3, #a-c 6.75 6.75

Souvenir Sheet
Perf. 13¾
2458 A388 25r LZ-88 6.00 6.00

No. 2457 contains three 39x25mm stamps.

Apollo-Soyuz Mission, 25th Anniv. — A389

No. 2459, vert.: a, Apollo 18 and Soyuz 19. b, Soyuz 19. c, Apollo 18.
Illustration reduced.

2000, Sept. 13 ***Perf. 14***
2459 A389 13r Sheet of 3, #a-c 6.75 6.75

Souvenir Sheet
2460 A389 25r Soyuz 19 5.25 5.25

Orchids — A390

Designs: 50 l, Dendrobium crepidatum. 1r, Eulophia guineensis. 2.50r, Cymbidium finlaysonianum. 3.50r, Paphiopedilum druryi.

No. 2465, 10r: a, Aerides odorata. b, Dendrobium chrysotoxum. c, Dendrobium anosmum. d, Calypso bulbosa. e, Paphiopedilum fairrieanum. f, Cynorkis fastigiata.

No. 2466, 10r: a, Angraecum germinyanum. b, Phalaenopsis amabilis. c, Thrixspermum cantipeda. d, Phaius tankervilleae. e, Rhynchostylis gigantea. f, Papilionanthe teres.

No. 2467, 25r, Cymbidium dayanum. No. 2468, 25r, Spathoglottis plicata.

2000, Sept. 13
2461-2464 A390 Set of 4 1.25 1.25

Sheets of 6, #a-f
2465-2466 A390 Set of 2 21.00 21.00

Souvenir Sheets
2467-2468 A390 Set of 2 10.00 10.00

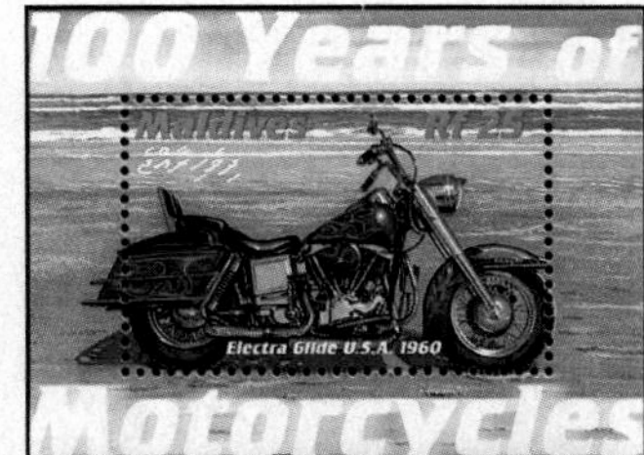

Birds A391

Designs: 15 l, White tern. 25 l, Brown booby. 30 l, White-collared kingfisher, vert. 1r, Black-winged stilt, vert.

No. 2473, 10r: a, Great frigatebird. b, Common noddy. c, Common tern. d, Sula sula. e, Sooty tern. f, Phaeton leturus.

No. 2474, 10r, vert.: a, White-collared kingfisher. b, Island thrush. c, Red-tailed tropicbird. d, Peregrine falcon. e, Night heron. f, Great egret.

No. 2475, 13r: a, Ringed plover. b, Turnstone. c, Thicknee. d, Black-bellied plover. e, Crab plover. f, Curlew.

No. 2476, 25r, Great cormorant, vert. No. 2477, 25r, Cattle egret, vert.

2000, Sept. 13 ***Perf. 13¾***
2469-2472 A391 Set of 4 .30 .30

Sheets of 6, #a-f
2473-2475 A391 Set of 3 32.50 32.50

Souvenir Sheets
2476-2477 A391 Set of 2 8.50 8.50

Motorcycles — A392

No. 2478, 7r: a, 1907 Matchless. b, 1966 Manch 4 1200 TTS. c, 1957 Lambretta LD-150. d, 1990 Yamaha XJP 1200. e, 1885 Daimler. f, 1950-60 John Player Norton.

No. 2479, 7r: a, 1969 Honda CB 750. b, 1913 Harley-Davidson. c, 1925 Bohmerland. d, 1910 American Indian. e, 1993 Triumph Trophy 1200. f, 1928, Moto Guzzi 500S.

No. 2480, 25r, 1960 Electra Glide. No. 2481, 25r, 1950 Harley-Davidson.
Illustration reduced.

2000, Oct. 30 ***Perf. 13¼x13½***

Sheets of 6, #a-f
2478-2479 A392 Set of 2 16.50 16.50

Souvenir Sheets
2480-2481 A392 Set of 2 10.00 10.00

A393

Marine Life — A394

No. 2482: a, Longnosed filefish. b, Hawaiian squirrelfish. c, Freckled hawkfish. d, McCosker's flasher wrasse. e, Pygoplites diacanthus. f, Paraeentzopyge venusta.

No. 2483, 5r: a, Chaetodon lunula. b, Stethojulis albovittata. c, Green turtle. d, Jobfish. e, Damsel fish. f, Chaetodon meyeri. g, Cirrhilabrus exquistus. h, Anemonefish.

No. 2484, 5r: a, Coris aygula. b, Snapper. c, Sea bass. d, Chaetodon bennetti. e, Pelagic snapper. f, Cardinalfish. g, Thalassoma hardwicke. h, Surgeonfish.

No. 2485, 5r: a, Grouper. b, Pygoplites diacanthus. c, Forcipiger flavissimus. d, Goatfish. e, Trumpet fish. f, Anthias. g, Centropyge bispinosus. h, Sweetlips.

No. 2486, 25r, H. aberrans. No. 2487, 25r, Angelfish. No. 2488, 25r, Moray eel. No. 2489, 25r, Spiny butterflyfish.
Illustration reduced.

2000, Nov. 15 **Litho.** ***Perf. 14***
2482 A393 5r Sheet of 6, #a-f 5.00 5.00

Sheets of 8, #a-h
2483-2485 A394 Set of 3 21.00 21.00

Souvenir Sheets
2486 A393 25r multi 4.25 4.25
2487-2489 A394 Set of 3 13.00 13.00

Flowers — A395

No. 2490, 5r: a, Corn lily. b, Clivia. c, Red hot poker. d, Crown of thorns. e, Cape daisy. f, Geranium.

No. 2491, 5r, horiz.: a, Fringed hibiscus. b, Erica vestita. c, Bird-of-paradise. d, Peacock orchid. e, Mesembryanthemums. f, African violets.

No. 2492, 25r, Gladiolus. No. 2493, 25r, Calla lily, horiz.
Illustration reduced.

2000, Nov. 15

Sheets of 6, #a-f
2490-2491 A395 Set of 2 13.50 13.50

Souvenir Sheets
2492-2493 A395 Set of 2 10.00 10.00

Airplanes, Automobiles and Trains — A396

Designs: 2.50r, Papyrus, vert. 3r, Hiawatha. 12r, Supermarine SGB. 13r, MLX01.

No. 2498, 5r: a, Thrust SSC. b, Curtiss R3C-2. c, Rocket. d, BB-9004. e, Mallard. f, TGV.

No. 2499, 5r: a, Lockheed XP-80. b, Mikoyan MiG-23. c, Tempest. d, Bluebird. e, Blue Flame. f, Thrust 2.

No. 2500, 25r, Bell X-1. No. 2501, 25r, Lockheed SR-71 Blackbird, vert.

2000, Nov. 29
2494-2497 A396 Set of 4 5.25 5.25

Sheets of 6, #a-f
2498-2499 A396 Set of 2 10.00 10.00

Souvenir Sheets
2500-2501 A396 Set of 2 8.50 8.50

Paintings from the Prado — A397

No. 2502, 7r: a, The Nobleman with the Golden Chain, by Tintoretto. b, Triumphal Arch, by Domenichino. c, Don Garcia de Medici, by Bronzino. d, Micer Marsilio from Micer Marsilio and His Wife, by Lorenzo Lotto. e, La Infanta Maria Antoinetta Fernanda, by Jacopo Amigoni. f, Wife from Micer Marsilio and his Wife.

No. 2503, 7r: a, Two women with headdresses. b, Woman in red. c, Men. d, The Duke of Lerma on Horseback, by Rubens. e, The Death of Seneca, by the Workshop of Rubens. f, Marie de Medici by Rubens. a-c from Achilles Amongst the Daughters of Lycomedes, by Peter Paul Rubens and Anthony Van Dyck.

No. 2504, 7r: a, Self-portrait, by Albrecht Dürer. b, A Woman and Her Daughter, by Adriaen van Cronenburch. c, Portrait of a man, by Dürer. d, Woman and children. e, Artemisia, by Rembrandt. f, The Artist. d, f from The Artist and His Family, by Jacob Jordaens.

No. 2505, 7r: a, The Painter Andrea Sacchi, by Carlo Maratta. b, Two men. c, Charles Cecil Roberts, by Pompeo Girolamo Batoni. d, Francesco Albani, by Sacchi. e, Three men. f, William Hamilton, by Batoni. b, e from The Turkish Ambassador to the Court of Naples, by Giuseppe Bonito

No. 2506, 7r: a, The Marquesa of Villafranca, by Francisco de Goya. b, Maria Ruthven, by Van Dyck. c, Cardinal-Infante Ferdinand, by Van Dyck. d, Frederik Hendrik, Prince of Orange, by Van Dyck. e, Van Dyck from Self-portrait with Endymion Porter. f, Porter from Self-portrait with Endymion Porter.

No. 2507, 7r: a, Philip V, by Hyacinthe Rigaud. b, Louis XIV, by Rigaud. c, Don Luis, Prince of Asturias, by Michel-Ange Houasse. d, Duke Carlo Emanuele II of Savoy with His Wife and Son, by Charles Dauphin. e, Kitchen Maid by Charles-François Hutin. f, Hurdy-gurdy Player, by Georges de La Tour.

No. 2508, 25r, Elizabeth of Valois, by Sofonisba Anguisciola. No. 2509, 25r, Camilla Gonzaga, Countess of San Segundo with Her Three Children, by Parmigianino. No. 2510, 25r, The Turkish Ambassador to the Court of Naples. No. 2511, 25r, Duke Carlo Emanuele of Savoy with His Wife and Son. No. 2512, 25r, The Artist and His Family, horiz. No. 2513, 25r, The Devotion of Rudolf I, by Rubens and Jan Wildens, horiz.
Illustration reduced.

Perf. 12x12¼, 12¼x12
2000, Nov. 29

Sheets of 6, #a-f
2502-2507 A397 Set of 6 42.50 42.50

Souvenir Sheets
2508-2513 A397 Set of 6 26.00 26.00

España 2000 Intl. Philatelic Exhibition.

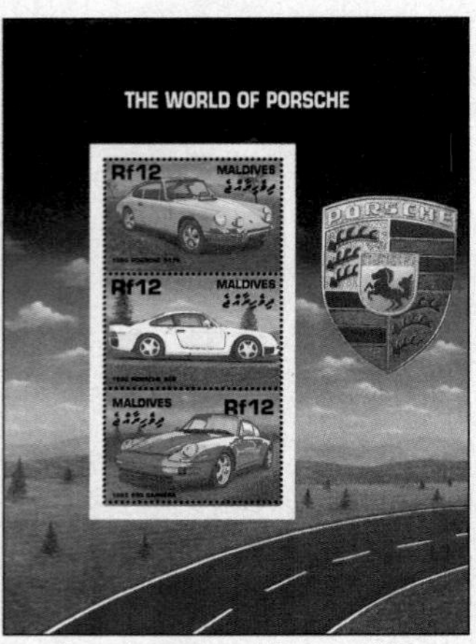

Porsche Automobiles — A398

No. 2514, 12r: a, 1966 911S. b, 1988 959. c, 1995 993 Carrera.
No. 2515, 12r: a, 1963 356 SC. b, 1975 911 Turbo. c, Unidentified.

2000, Nov. 30 Litho. *Perf. 14*
Sheets of 3, #a-c

2514-2515 A398 Set of 2 12.50 12.50

Souvenir Sheet

2516 A398 25r 2000 Boxter 4.25 4.25

No. 2516 contains one 56x42mm stamp.

Mushrooms A399

Designs: 30 l, Cortinarius collinitus. 50 l, Russula ochroleuca. 2r, Lepiota acutesquamosa. 3r, Hebeloma radicosum. 13r, Amanita echinocephala. 15r, Collybia iocephala.
No. 2523, 7r: a, Tricholoma aurantium. b, Pholiota spectabilis. c, Russula caerulea. d, Amanita phalloides. e, Mycena strobilinoides. f, Boletus satanas.
No. 2524, 7r: a, Amanita muscaria. b, Mycena lilacifolia. c, Coprinus comatus. d, Morchella crassipes. e, Russula nigricans. f, Lepiota procera.
No. 2525, 25r, Tricholoma aurantium, diff. No. 2526, 25r, Lepiota procera, diff.

2001, Jan. 2

2517-2522 A399 Set of 6 5.75 5.75

Sheets of 6, #a-f

2523-2524 A399 Set of 2 14.50 14.50

Souvenir Sheets

2525-2526 A399 Set of 2 8.50 8.50

Battle of Britain, 60th Anniv. — A400

No. 2527, 5r: a, German commanders look across the English Channel. b, The armorers make ready. c, The German attack begins. d, Germany bombs the British coast. e, Germany bombs British cities. f, Luftwaffe sets St. Paul's Cathedral ablaze. g, Aerial dogfight. h, A British Spitfire is shot down.
No. 2528, 5r: a, Leaders of Great Britain. b, British pilots prepare to confront the Luftwaffe. c, RAF planes take off. d, British aircraft meet the enemy. e, Luftwaffe meets tough resistance. f, Dogfight above English Channel. g, German planes fall short of their objective. h Many German planes are shot down.
No. 2529, 25r, Hawker Hurricane. No. 2530, 25r, Messerschmitt ME 109.

2001, Jan. 2 *Perf. 14*
Sheets of 8, #a-h

2527-2528 A400 Set of 2 13.50 13.50

Souvenir Sheets

2529-2530 A400 Set of 2 8.50 8.50

Rijksmuseum, Amsterdam, Bicent. (in 2000) — A401

No. 2531, 7r: a, Donkey's head and rider from Donkey Riding on the Beach, by Isaac Lazarus Israels. b, The Paternal Admonition, by Gerard Terborch, the Younger. c, The Sick Woman, by Jan Havicksz Steen. d, Girls with red hats from Donkey Riding on the Beach. e, Pompeius Occo, by Dirck Jacobsz. f, Woman With a Child in a Pantry, by Pieter de Hooch.
No. 2532, 7r: a, The Holy Kinship, by Geertgen tot Sint Jans. b, Sir Thomas Gresham, by Anthonis Mor. c, Self-portrait as St. Paul, by Rembrandt. d, Cleopatra's Banquet, by Gerard Lairesse. e, Still Life With Flowers in a Glass, by Jan Breughel, the Elder. f, Portrait of a Man, Possibly Nicolaes Hasselaer, by Frans Hals.
No. 2533, 7r: a, Rembrandt's Mother, by Gerard Dou. b, Portrait of a Girl Dressed in Blue, by Jan Cornelisz Verspronck. c, Old Woman at Prayer, by Nicolaes Maes. d, Feeding the Hungry from The Seven Works of Charity, by the Master of Alkmaar. e, The Threatened Swan, by Jan Asselyn. f, The Daydreamer, by Maes.
No. 2534, 7r: a, Woman seated in doorway, from The Little Street, by Jan Vermeer. b, Two women from The Love Letter, by Vermeer. c, Woman in Blue Reading a Letter, by Vermeer. d, Woman and pillar from The Love Letter. e, The Milkmaid, by Vermeer. f, Arched doorway, from The Little Street.
No. 2535, 25r, Johannes Wtenbogaert, by Rembrandt. No. 2536, 25r, The Staalmeesters (The Syndics), by Rembrandt. No. 2537, 25r, The Night Watch, by Rembrandt. No. 2538, 25r, Shipwreck on a Rocky Coast, by Wijnandus Johannes Joseph Nuyen, horiz.

2001, Jan. 15 *Perf. 13¾*
Sheets of 6, #a-f

2531-2534 A401 Set of 4 30.00 30.00

Souvenir Sheets

2535-2538 A401 Set of 4 17.00 17.00

Ill-fated Ships — A402

No. 2539, 5r: a, Milton Iatrides, 1970. b, Cyclops, 1918. c, Marine Sulphur Queen, 1963. d, Rosalie, 1840. e, Mary Celeste, 1872. f, Atlanta, 1880.
No. 2540, 5r: a, Windfall, 1962. b, Kobenhavn, 1928. c, Pearl, 1874. d, HMS Bulwark, 1914. e, Patriot, 1812. f, Lusitania, 1915.
No. 2541, 25r, La Baussole and L'Astrolabe, 1789. No. 2542, 25r, Titanic, 1912.

2001, Feb. 12 *Perf. 14*
Sheets of 6, #a-f

2539-2540 A402 Set of 2 10.00 10.00

Souvenir Sheets

2541-2542 A402 Set of 2 8.50 8.50

Flower Type of 1997

2001, Mar. 1 *Perf. 14¾x14*
Size: 16x20mm

2543 A350 10r Like #2267 1.75 1.75

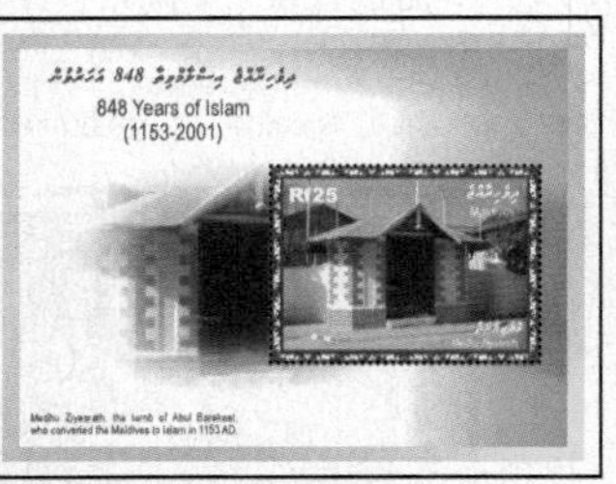

Islam in Maldive Islands, 848th Anniv. — A403

No. 2544: a, Dharumavantha Rasgefaanu Mosque. b, Plaque of Hukurumiskiiy. c, Learning the Holy Koran. d, Institute of Islamic Studies. e, Center for the Holy Koran. f, Islamic Center.

2001, July 9 Litho. *Perf. 13¾*

2544 A403 10r Sheet of 6, #a-f 10.00 10.00

Souvenir Sheet

2545 A403 25r Medhu Ziyaarath 4.25 4.25

Fish — A404

Designs: No. 2546, 10r, Pterois miles. No. 2547, 10r, Pomacanthus imperator.

2001, July 16 *Perf. 14x14¾*

2546-2547 A404 Set of 2 3.50 3.50

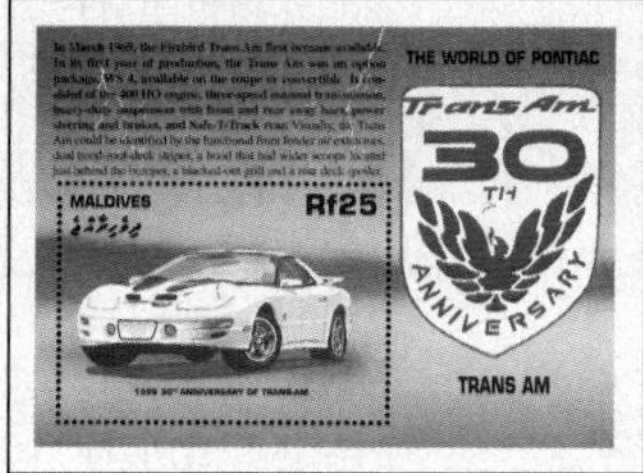

Pontiac Trans-Am Automobiles — A405

No. 2548, 12r: a, 1970. b, 1989. c, 1994.
No. 2549, 12r: a, 1976. b, 1988. c, 1988 Coupe.

2001 *Perf. 14*
Sheets of 3, #a-c

2548-2549 A405 Set of 2 12.50 12.50

Souvenir Sheet
Perf. 14¼

2550 A405 25r 1999 4.25 4.25

Nos. 2548-2549 each contain three 42x28mm stamps.

Automobiles — A406

Designs: 1r, 1930 Pierce-Arrow. 2r, 1938 Mercedes-Benz 540K. 8r, 1934 Duesenberg J. 10r, 1931 Bugatti Royale.
No. 2555, 7r: a, 1931 Auburn convertible sedan. b, 1931 Mercedes SSKL. c, 1929 Packard roadster. d, 1940 Chevrolet. e, 1915 Mercer. f, 1941 Packard sedan.
No. 2556, 7r: a, 1932 Chevrolet roadster. b, 1929 Cadillac Fleetwood roadster. c, 1928 Bentley Speed Six. d, 1930 Cadillac Fleetwood. e, 1936 Ford convertible. f, 1929 Hudson Phaeton.
No. 2557, 25r, 1930 Cord Brougham. No. 2558, 25r, 1931 Rolls-Royce P-1.

2001 *Perf. 14*

2551-2554 A406 Set of 4 3.50 3.50

Sheets of 6, #a-f

2555-2556 A406 Set of 2 14.50 14.50

Souvenir Sheets

2557-2558 A406 Set of 2 8.50 8.50

Phila Nippon '01, Japan — A407

No. 2559, 7r (28x42mm) — Prints of women by Utamaro: a, Reed Blind, Model Young Women Woven in Mist. b, Woman with Parasol. c, High-ranked Courtesan, Five Shades of Ink in the Northern Quarter. d, Comparison of Beauties of the Southern Quarter. e, The Barber.
No. 2560, 7r — Actors by Shunsho Katsukawa: a, Danjuro Ichikawa V (black kimono, 28x85mm). b, Danjuro Ichikawa V (arm raised, 28x85mm). c, Danjuro Ichikawa V (arms crossed on chest, 28x85mm). d, Danjuro Ichikawa V (wrapped in kimono, 28x85mm). e, Tomoeman Otani I and Mitsugaro Bando I (56x85mm).
No. 2561, 25r, The Courtesan Hinazuru of the House Called Keizetsuro, by Utamaro. No. 2562, 25r, Jomyo Tsutsui and the Priest Ichirai on the Uji Bridge, by Kiyomasu Torii.

2001, July 18 Litho. *Perf. 14*
Sheets of 5, #a-e

2559-2560 A407 Set of 2 12.00 12.00

Souvenir Sheets
Perf. 13¾

2561-2562 A407 Set of 2 8.50 8.50

Giuseppe Verdi (1813-1901), Opera Composer — A408

No. 2563: a, Alfred Piccaver. b, Rigoletto costume, Heinrich. c, Rigoletto costume, Cologne. d, Cornell MacNeil.
25r, Matteo Manugerra.

2001, Aug. 26 *Perf. 14*
2563 A408 10r Sheet of 4, #a-d 6.75 6.75

Souvenir Sheet

2564 A408 25r multi 4.25 4.25

Mao Zedong (1893-1976) — A409

No. 2565: a, Red background. b, Blue background. c, Gray background.
25r, Wearing cap.

2001, Aug. 26 *Perf. 13¾*
2565 A409 15r Sheet of 3, #a-c 7.75 7.75

Souvenir Sheet

2566 A409 25r multi 4.25 4.25

Queen Victoria (1819-1901) — A410

No. 2567: a, Earring at right. b, Earring at left. c, As old woman. d, In black dress.
25r, With hand on chin.

2001, Aug. 26 *Perf. 14*
2567 A410 10r Sheet of 4, #a-d 6.75 6.75

Souvenir Sheet

2568 A410 25r multi 4.25 4.25

Queen Elizabeth II, 75th Birthday — A411

No. 2569: a, Without hat. b, Wearing large crown. c, Wearing tiara. d, Wearing red uniform. e, Wearing black cape and hat. f, Wearing tan hat.
25r, Wearing crown, diff.

2001, Aug. 26
2569 A411 7r Sheet of 6, #a-f 7.25 7.25

Souvenir Sheet

2570 A411 25r multi 4.25 4.25

Nobel Prizes, Cent. — A412

No. 2571 — Economics laureates: a, Simon Kuznets, 1971. b, Wassily Leontief, 1973. c, Lawrence R. Klein, 1980. d, Friedrich A. von Hayek, 1974. e, Leonid V. Kantorovich, 1975.

No. 2572, 7r — Peace laureates: a, Ernesto T. Moneta, 1907. b, Albert J. Luthuli, 1960. c, Henri Dunant, 1901. d, Charles Albert Gobat, 1902. e, Sean MacBride, 1974. f, Elie Ducommun, 1902.

No. 2573, 7r — Peace laureates: a, Adolfo Pérez Esquivel, 1980. b, Mikhail S. Gorbachev, 1990. c, Betty Williams, 1976. d, Alfonso Garcia Robles, 1982. e, Paul D'Estournelles de Constant, 1909. f, Louis Renault, 1907.

No. 2574, 25r, Trygve Haavelmo, Economics, 1989. No. 2575, 25r, Vicente Aleixandre, Literature, 1977. No. 2576, 25r, Octavio Paz, Literature, 1990.

2001, Sept. 29 **Litho.** *Perf. 14*
2571 A412 7r Sheet of 5, #a-e 6.00 6.00

Sheets of 6, #a-f

2572-2573 A412 Set of 2 14.50 14.50

Souvenir Sheets

2574-2576 A412 Set of 3 13.00 13.00

Mercedes-Benz Automobiles, Cent. — A413

Designs: 2.50r, 1939 W165 Grand Prix. 5r, 1928 460 Nürburg Sport Roadster. 8r, 1928 Boattail Speedster. 15r, 1909 Blitzen Benz.

No. 2581, 7r: a, 1927 680S. b, 1934 150. c, 1936 540K Roadster. d, 1933 770 Grosser Mercedes. e, 1958 220SE. f, 1990 500SL.

No. 2582, 7r: a, 1933 290. b, 1927 Model S. c, 1953 300SL Coupe. d, 1911 Benz Victoria. e, 1968 280SL. f, 1937 W125 Grand Prix.

No. 2583, 25r, 1931 370S. No. 2584, 25r, 1955 300SLR.

2001, Oct. 30 **Litho.** *Perf. 14*
2577-2580 A413 Set of 4 5.25 5.25

Sheets of 6, #a-f

2581-2582 A413 Set of 2 14.50 14.50

Souvenir Sheets

2583-2584 A413 Set of 2 8.50 8.50

2002 World Cup Soccer Championships, Japan and Korea — A414

World Cup Trophy and: 1r, Eusebio, Portugal, Portuguese flag. 3r, Johan Cruyff, Netherlands, Netherlands flag. 7r, French player and flag. 10r, Japanese player and flag. 12r, Seoul World Cup Stadium, horiz. 15r, 1930 World Cup poster.

25r, Gerd Müller's winning goal for West Germany, 1974, vert.

2001, Nov. 28
2585-2590 A414 Set of 6 8.25 8.25

Souvenir Sheet

2591 A414 25r multi 4.25 4.25

No. 2591 contains one 42x56mm stamp.

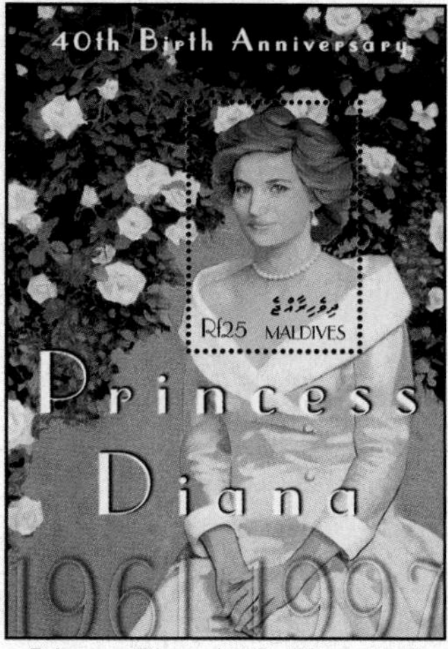

Princess Diana (1961-97) — A415

No. 2592: a, Pink rose. b, White rose. c, Yellow rose. d, Beige rose.
25r, Wearing pearl necklace.

2001, Dec. 26
2592 A415 10r Sheet of 4, #a-d 6.75 6.75

Souvenir Sheet

2593 A415 25r multi 4.25 4.25

New Year 2002 (Year of the Horse) — A416

No. 2594 — Paintings by Xu Beihong: a, Running Horse (painting 45mm tall). b, Standing Horse. c, Running Horse (painting 49mm tall). d, Horse (painting 44mm tall). e, Horse (painting 48mm tall).
15r, Horse, horiz.

2001, Dec. 26 *Perf. 14*
2594 A416 5r Sheet of 5, #a-e 4.25 4.25

Souvenir Sheet

Perf. 14x14½

2595 A416 15r multi 2.60 2.60

No. 2594 contains five 31x63mm stamps.

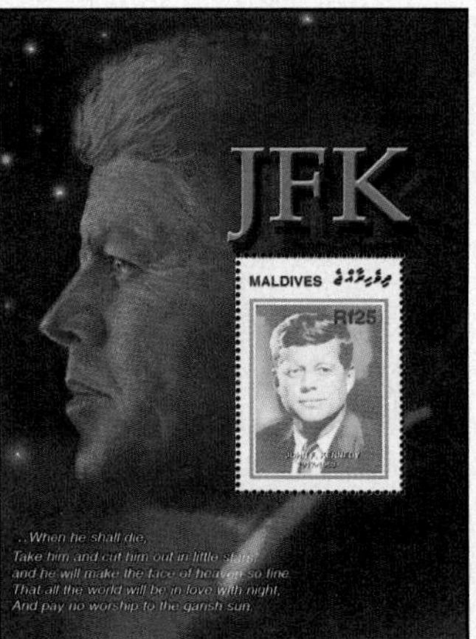

Pres. John F. Kennedy — A417

No. 2596, 5r: a, At Dexter, 1927. b, At Harvard, 1935. c, In Navy, 1943. d, At wedding, 1953. e, With brother Robert, 1956. f, At Presidential inauguration, 1961.

No. 2597, 5r: a, With Nikita Khrushchev, 1961. b, With Harold Macmillan. c, With Charles de Gaulle, 1961. d, With Jawaharlal Nehru, 1962. e, With Konrad Adenauer, 1963. f, With Dr. Martin Luther King, Jr., 1963.

No. 2598, 25r, Portrait. No. 2599, 25r, With wife, 1961.

2001, Dec. 26 *Perf. 14*

Sheets of 6, #a-f

2596-2597 A417 Set of 2 10.50 10.50

Souvenir Sheets

2598-2599 A417 Set of 2 8.50 8.50

Moths — A418

No. 2600, 7r: a, Cymothoe lucasi. b, Milionia grandis. c, Ornithoptera eroesus. d, Hyantis hodeva. e, Ammobiota festiva. f, Blue salamis.

No. 2601, 7r: a, Zygaena occitanica. b, Campyloes desgodinsi. c, Bhutanitis thaidina. d, Six-tailed helicopsis. e, Parnassius charltonius. f, Acraea ecucogiap.

No. 2602: a, Papilio dardanus. b, Baomisa hieroglyphica. c, Troides prattorum. d, Funonia rhadama.

No. 2603, 25r, Hypolera cassotis. No. 2604, 25r, Euphydryas maturna, vert.

2001, Dec. 26 **Litho.**

Sheets of 6, #a-f

2600-2601 A418 Set of 2 14.50 14.50
2602 A418 10r Sheet of 4, #a-d 6.75 6.75

Souvenir Sheets

2603-2604 A418 Set of 2 8.50 8.50

Queen Mother Type of 1999 Redrawn

No. 2605: a, With King George VI, 1936. b, In 1941. c, In 1960. d, In 1981.
25r, At Order of the Garter Service.

2001, Dec. *Perf. 14*

Yellow Orange Frames

2605 A372 7r Sheet of 4, #a-d, + label 4.75 4.75

Souvenir Sheet

Perf. 13¾

2606 A372 25r multi 4.25 4.25

Queen Mother's 101st birthday. No. 2606 contains one 38x51mm stamp slightly darker than that found on No. 2405. Sheet margins of Nos. 2605-2606 lack embossing and gold arms and frames found on Nos. 2404-2405.

Reign of Queen Elizabeth II, 50th Anniv. — A419

No. 2607: a, With Princess Margaret. b, Wearing white hat. c, Wearing tiara. d, Holding flowers.

25r, At coronation.

2002, Feb. 6 Litho. *Perf. 14¼*

2607 A419 10r Sheet of 4, #a-d 7.00 7.00

Souvenir Sheet

2608 A419 25r multi 4.25 4.25

Cats — A420

Designs: 3r, Havana brown. 5r, American wirehair. 8r, Norwegian forest cat. 10r, Seal point Siamese.

No. 2613, 7r: a, British blue. b, Red mackerel Manx. c, Scottish fold. d, Somali. e, Balinese. f, Exotic shorthair.

No. 2614, 7r, horiz.: a, Persian. b, Exotic shorthair, diff. c, Ragdoll. d, Manx. e, Tonkinese. f, Scottish fold, diff.

25r, Blue mackerel tabby Cornish rex.

2002, Apr. 8 *Perf. 14*

2609-2612 A420 Set of 4 4.50 4.50

Sheets of 6, #a-f

2613-2614 A420 Set of 2 14.50 14.50

Souvenir Sheet

2615 A420 25r multi 4.25 4.25

Birds A421

Designs: 1r, Swinhoe's snipe. 2r, Oriental honey buzzard. 3r, Asian koel. No. 2619, 5r, Red-throated pipet. No. 2620, 7r, Short-eared owl. 10r, Eurasian spoonbill. 12r, Pied wheatear. 15r, Oriental pratincole.

No. 2624, 5r: a, Lesser noddy. b, Roseate tern. c, Frigate minor. d, Saunder's tern. e, White-bellied storm petrel. f, Red-footed booby.

No. 2625, 5r: a, Cattle egret. b, Barn swallow. c, Osprey. d, Little heron. e, Ruddy turnstone. f, Sooty tern.

No. 2626, 7r: a, Rose-ringed parakeet. b, Common swift. c, Lesser kestrel. d, Golden oriole. e, Asian paradise flycatcher. f, Indian roller.

No. 2627, 7r: a, Pallid harrier. b, Gray heron. c, Blue-tailed bee-eater. d, White-breasted water hen. e, Cotton pygmy goose. f, Maldivian pond heron.

No. 2628, 25r, White-tailed tropicbird. No. 2629, 25r, Greater flamingo. No. 2630, 25r, Cinnamon bittern. No. 2631, 25r, White tern.

2002, Apr. 8

2616-2623 A421 Set of 8 9.50 9.50

Sheets of 6, #a-f

2624-2627 A421 Set of 4 25.00 25.00

Souvenir Sheets

2628-2631 A421 Set of 4 17.00 17.00

Prehistoric Animals — A422

No. 2632, 7r: a, Sivatherium. b, Flat-headed peccary. c, Shasta ground sloth. d, Harlan's ground sloth. e, European woolly rhinoceros. f, Dwarf pronghorn.

No. 2633, 7r: a, Macrauchenia. b, Gyptodon. c, Nesodon. d, Imperial tapir. e, Short-faced bear. f, Mammoth.

No. 2634, 25r, Saber-toothed cat. No. 2635, 25r, Woolly mammoth, vert.

2002, May 21

Sheets of 6, #a-f

2632-2633 A422 Set of 2 14.50 14.50

Souvenir Sheets

2634-2635 A422 Set of 2 8.50 8.50

2002 Winter Olympics, Salt Lake City — A423

Designs: No. 2636, 12r, Freestyle skiing. No. 2637, 12r, Downhill skiing.

2002, July 11 Litho. *Perf. 13½x13¼*

2636-2637 A423 Set of 2 4.00 4.00

a. Souvenir sheet, #2636-2637 4.00 4.00

Intl. Year of Mountains — A424

No. 2638: a, Mt. Ama Dablam, Nepal. b, Mt. Clements, US. c, Mt. Artesonraju, Peru. d, Mt. Cholatse, Nepal.

25r, Balloon and Mt. Jefferson, US.

2002, July 11 *Perf. 14*

2638 A424 15r Sheet of 4, #a-d 10.50 10.50

Souvenir Sheet

2639 A424 25r multi 4.25 4.25

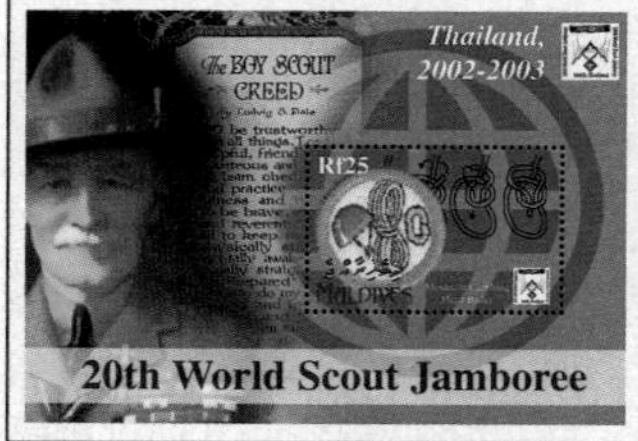

20th World Scout Jamboree, Thailand — A425

No. 2640, vert.: a, Temple. b, Thailand Scout. c, Merit badges.

25r, Mountain climbing merit badge.

2002, July 11

2640 A425 15r Sheet of 3, #a-c 7.75 7.75

Souvenir Sheet

2641 A425 25r multi 4.25 4.25

Souvenir Sheet

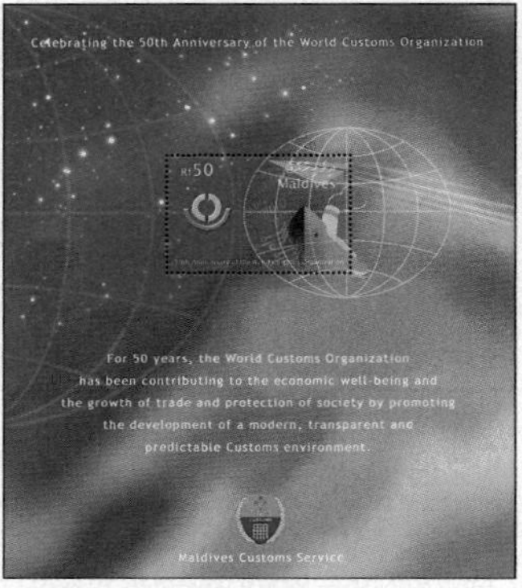

World Customs Organization, 50th Anniv. — A426

2002, Aug. 12 *Perf. 13¾*

2642 A426 50r multi 8.50 8.50

Elvis Presley (1935-77) A427

2002, Oct. 7

2643 A427 5r multi .80 .80

Printed in sheets of 9.

Flowers and Butterflies — A428

No. 2644, 7r — Flowers: a, Morning glory. b, Wedding bell anemone. c, Barrett Browning narcissus. d, Persian jewel nigella. e, Whirligig pink osteospermum. f, Brown lasso iris.

No. 2645, 7r — Orchids: a, Laelia gouldiana. b, Cattleya Louise Georgiana. c, Laeliocattleya Christopher Gubler. d, Miltoniopsis Bert Field Crimson Glow. e, Lemboglossum bictoniense. f, Derosara Divine Victor.

No. 2646, 7r — Butterflies: a, Morpho menelus. b, Small postman. c, Hewitson's blue hairstreak. d, Green swallowtail. e, Cairns birdwing. f, Queen.

No. 2647, 25r, Little pink beauty aster. No. 2648, 25r, Angraecum veitchii, vert. No. 2649, 25r, Cymothoe lurida butterfly.

2002, Nov. 4 Litho. *Perf. 14*

Sheets of 6, #a-f

2644-2646 A428 Set of 3 20.00 20.00

Souvenir Sheets

2647-2649 A428 Set of 3 12.00 12.00

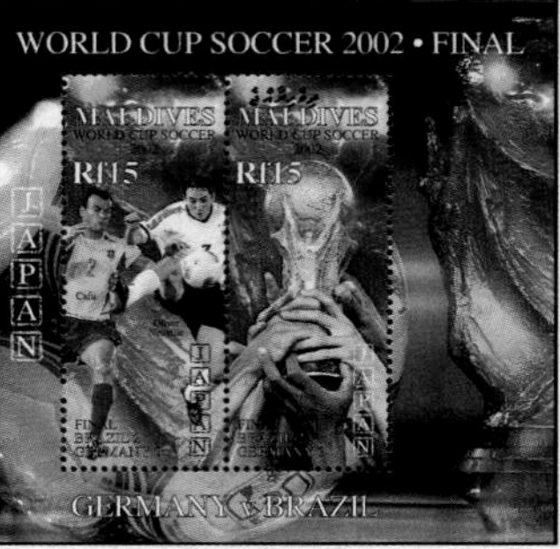

2002 World Cup Soccer Championships, Japan and Korea — A429

No. 2650, 7r: a, Torsten Frings sliding. b, Roberto Carlos. c, Frings kicking. d, Ronaldo pointing. e, Oliver Neuville. f, Ronaldo with ball.

No. 2651, 7r: a, Eul Yong Lee, Alpay Ozalan. b, Myung Bo Hong, Hakan Sukur. c, Emre Belozoglu, Chong Gug Song. d, Ergun Penbe, Chong Gug Song. e, Ergun Penbe, Ki Hyeon Seol. f, Chong Gug Song, Hakan Unsal.

No. 2652, 15r: a, Cafu and Neuville. b, Hands holding World Cup.

No. 2653, 15r: a, Dietmar Hamann. b, Cafu holding World Cup.

No. 2654, 15r: a, Ilhan Mansiz. b, Young Pyo Lee.

No. 2655, 15r: a, Hakan Sukur. b, Sang Chul Yoo.

2002, Nov. 12 *Perf. 13½*

Sheets of 6, #a-f

2650-2651 A429 Set of 2 13.00 13.00

Souvenir Sheets of 2, #a-b

2652-2655 A429 Set of 4 19.00 19.00

Teddy Bears, Cent. — A430

No. 2656: a, Hairdresser. b, Construction worker. c, Gardener. d, Chef.

No. 2657, 12r: a, Mother. b, Sister and brother. c, Father.

No. 2658, 12r: a, Nurse. b, Doctor. c, Dentist.

No. 2659, 30r, Soccer player. No. 2660, 30r, Golfer. No. 2661, 30r, Snow boarder.

2002, Nov. 18 *Perf. 14*

2656 A430 8r Sheet of 4, #a-d 5.00 5.00

Sheets of 3, #a-c

2657-2658 A430 Set of 2 11.50 11.50

Souvenir Sheets

2659-2661 A430 Set of 3 14.00 14.00

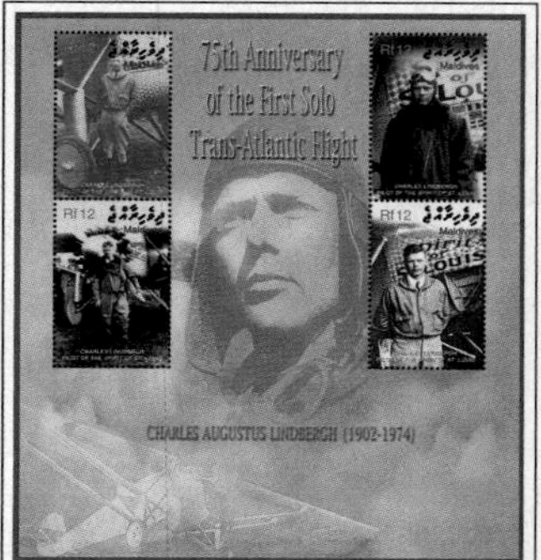

First Non-Stop Solo Transatlantic Flight, 75th Anniv. — A430a

No. 2661A, 12r — Various photos of Charles Lindbergh and Spirit of St. Louis: c, Blue. d, Brown. e, Gray. f, Red violet.

No. 2661B, 12r: g, Donald Hall, designer of Spirit of St. Louis. h, Charles Lindbergh. i, Lindbergh, Spirit of St. Louis (Lindbergh distorted). j, Lindbergh, Hall and President Mahoney of Ryan Aircraft.

2002, Dec. 2 Litho. *Perf. 14*

2661A	A430a 12r Sheet of 4, #c-f	7.50	7.50
2661B	A430a 12r Sheet of 4, #g-j	7.50	7.50

Princess Diana (1961-97)
A431 A432

2002, Dec. 2

2662	A431 12r multi	1.90	1.90
2663	A432 12r multi	1.90	1.90

Nos. 2662-2663 were each printed in sheets of 4.

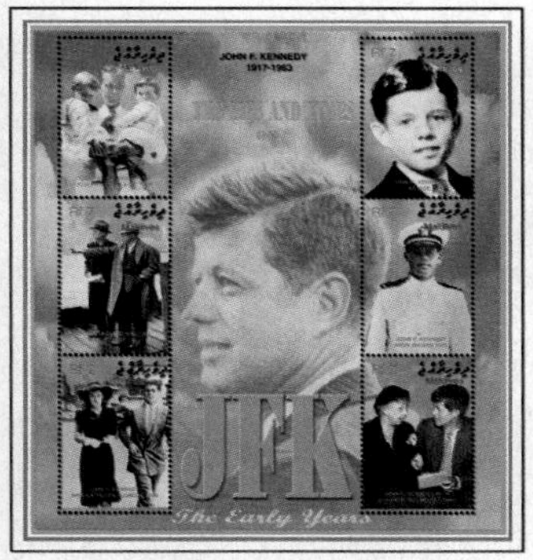

Pres. John F. Kennedy (1917-63) — A432a

No. 2663A: b, With father Joseph P., and brother Joseph, Jr. c, At age 11. d, Inspecting Boston waterfront, 1951. e, As Navy Ensign, 1941. f, With sister Kathleen in London, 1939. g, With Eleanor Roosevelt, 1951.

2002, Dec. 2 Litho. *Perf. 14*

2663A	A432a 7r Sheet of 6, #b-g	6.75	6.75

Pres. Ronald Reagan — A433

Designs: No. 2664, Green background. No. 2665, Blue background.

No. 2666: a, Wearing brown suit. b, Wearing black suit with red tie.

2002, Dec. 2

2664	A433 12r multi	1.90	1.90
2665	A433 12r multi	1.90	1.90
a.	Horiz. pair, #2664-2665	4.00	4.00
2666	A433 12r Horiz. pair, #a-b	4.00	4.00
	Nos. 2664-2666 (3)	7.80	7.80

Nos. 2664-2665 were printed in sheets containing two of each stamp. No. 2666 was printed in sheets containing two pairs.

Amphilex 2002 Intl. Stamp Exhibition, Amsterdam — A434

No. 2667, 7r — Life of Queen Mother Juliana and Prince Bernhard: a, Wedding, 1937. b, Birth of Princess Beatrix, 1938. c, Exile in Canada, 1940-45. d, Installation of Juliana as queen, 1948. e, Zeeland flood, 1953. f, Royal couple.

No. 2668, 7r — Portraits depicting Queen Beatrix by: a, Pauline Hille. b, John Klinkenberg. c, Beatrice Filius. d, Will Kellermann. e, Graswinckel. f, Marjolijn Spreeuwenberg.

2002, Dec. 8 *Perf. 14*
Sheets of 6, #a-f

2667-2668	A434 Set of 2	13.00	13.00

Fish A435

Birds and Sharks — A436

Designs: 10 l, Flame basslet. 15 l, Teardrop butterflyfish. 20 l, Hamburg damselfish. 25 l, Bridled tern. 50 l, Blue-lined surgeonfish. 1r, Common tern. 2r, Common noddy. No. 2676, Yellow-breasted wrasse. No. 2677, Blue shark. 4r, Harlequin filefish. 5r, Orangespine unicornfish. 10r, Emperor angelfish. 12r, Bullseye. 20r, Scalloped hammerhead shark.

Perf. 14 (A435), 10¾x13 (25 l, 1r, 2r), 13¼x14 (#2677, 20r)

2002, Dec. 24

2669	A435	10 l multi	.20	.20
2670	A435	15 l multi	.20	.20
2671	A435	20 l multi	.20	.20
2672	A436	25 l multi	.20	.20
2673	A435	50 l multi	.20	.20
2674	A436	1r multi	.20	.20
2675	A436	2r multi	.30	.30
2676	A435	2.50r multi	.40	.40
2677	A436	2.50r multi	.40	.40
2678	A435	4r multi	.60	.60
2679	A435	5r multi	.75	.75
2680	A435	10r multi	1.50	1.50
2681	A435	12r multi	1.90	1.90
2682	A436	20r multi	3.00	3.00
		Nos. 2669-2682 (14)	10.05	10.05

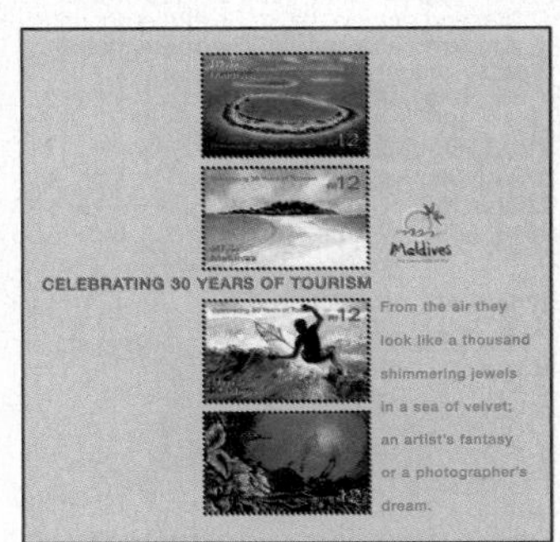

Tourism, 30th Anniv. — A437

No. 2683: a, Atolls. b, Sand spit. c, Surfer. d, Underwater scene.

2002, Dec. 25 *Perf. 13½*

2683	A437 12r Sheet of 4, #a-d	7.50	7.50

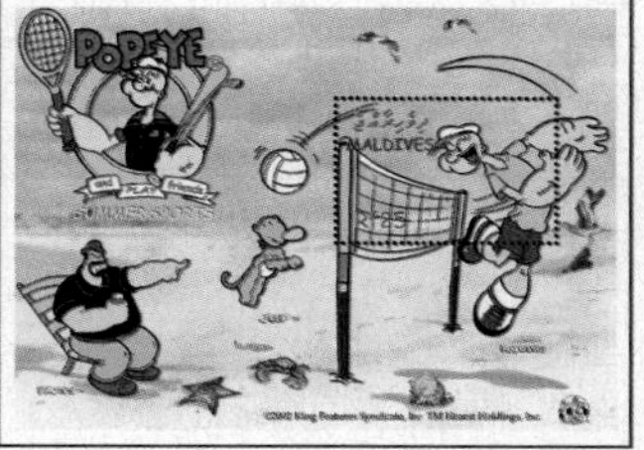

Popeye — A438

No. 2684, vert: a, Diving. b, Surfing. c, Sailboarding. d, Baseball. e, Hurdles. f, Tennis.

25r, Volleyball.

2003, Jan. 27 *Perf. 14*

2684	A438 7r Sheet of 6, #a-f	6.50	6.50

Souvenir Sheet

2685	A438 25r multi	4.00	4.00

National Museum, 50th Anniv. A439

Various museum items: 3r, 3.50r, 6.50r, 22r.

2003, Jan. 31 Litho.

2686-2689	A439 Set of 4	5.50	5.50

UNICEF — A440

Designs: 2.50r, Father and child. 5r, Mother kissing child. 20r, Child learning to walk.

2003, Jan. 31 *Perf. 15x14*

2690-2692	A440 Set of 3	4.25	4.25

Shells — A441

Designs: No. 2693, 10r, Sundial shell. No. 2694, 10r, Cardita clam. No. 2695, 10r, Corn shell. No. 2696, 10r, Cowrie shell.

2003, Mar. 25 Litho. *Perf. 13¼*

2693-2696	A441 Set of 4	6.25	6.25

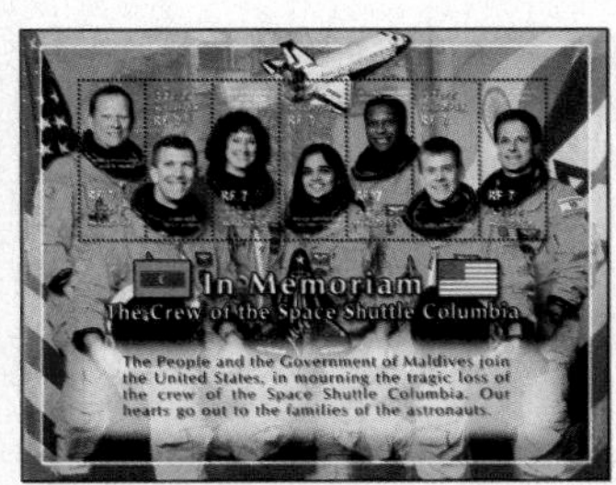

Astronauts Killed in Space Shuttle Columbia Accident — A442

No. 2697: a, Mission Specialist 1 David M. Brown. b, Commander Rick D. Husband. c, Mission Specialist 4 Laurel Blair Salton Clark. d, Mission Specialist 4 Kalpana Chawla. e, Payload Commander Michael P. Anderson. f, Pilot William C. McCool. g, Payload Specialist 4 Ilan Ramon.

2003, Apr. 7 *Perf. 13½x13¼*

2697	A442 7r Sheet of 7, #a-g	7.75	7.75

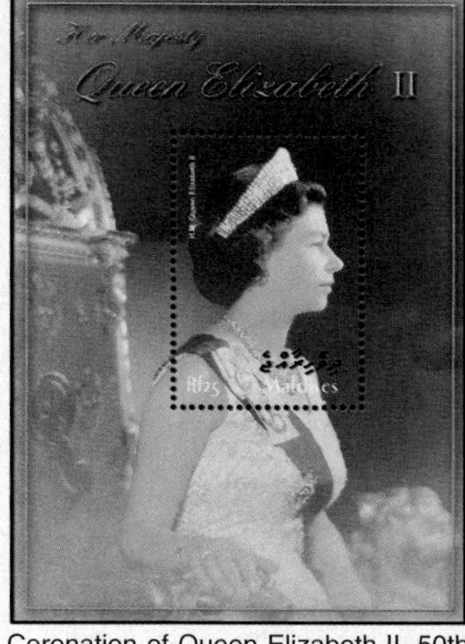

Coronation of Queen Elizabeth II, 50th Anniv. — A443

No. 2698: a, Wearing hat. b, Wearing crown. c, Wearing tiara.

25r, Wearing tiara, diff.

2003, May 26 *Perf. 14*

2698	A443 15r Sheet of 3, #a-c	7.00	7.00

Souvenir Sheet

2699	A443 25r multi	4.00	4.00

Prince William, 21st Birthday — A444

No. 2700: a, As toddler. b, Wearing red and blue tie. c, Wearing tie with blue squares.

25r, As toddler, wearing cap.

2003, May 26

2700	A444 15r Sheet of 3, #a-c	7.00	7.00

Souvenir Sheet

2701	A444 25r multi	4.00	4.00

Paintings by Albrecht Dürer (1471-1528) A445

Designs: 3r, Drummer and Piper from wing of the Jabach Altarpiece. 5r, Portrait of a Young Man. 7r, Wire-drawing Mill, horiz. 10r, Innsbruck from the North, horiz.

No. 2706: a, Portrait of Jacob Muffel. b, Portrait of Hieronymus Holzschuher. c, Portrait of Johannes Kleberger. d, Self-portrait.
25r, The Weiden Mill, horiz.

2003, June 17 ***Perf. 14¼***

2702-2705 A445 Set of 4 4.00 4.00
2706 A445 12r Sheet of 4, #a-d 7.50 7.50

Souvenir Sheet

2707 A445 25r multi 4.00 4.00

Japanese Art — A446

Designs: 2r, Detail from The Actor Sojuro Nakamura as Mitsukuni, by Yoshitaki Utagawa. 5r, Detail from The Actor Sojuro Nakamura as Mitsukuni, by Yoshitaki Utagawa, diff. 7r, The Ghost of Koheiji Kohada, by Hokuei Shunkosai. 15r, Ariwara no Narihira as Seigen, by Kunisada Utagawa.
No. 2712: a, The Ghost of Mitsumune Shikibunojo, by Kunisada Utagawa. b, Fuwa Bansakui, by Yoshitoshi Tsukioka. c, The Lantern Ghost of Oiwa, by Shunkosai. d, The Greedy Hag, by Tsukioka.
25r, The Spirit of Sogoro Sakura Haunting Koszuke Hotta.

2003, June 17

2708-2711 A446 Set of 4 4.50 4.50
2712 A446 10r Sheet of 4, #a-d 6.25 6.25

Souvenir Sheet

2713 A446 25r multi 4.00 4.00

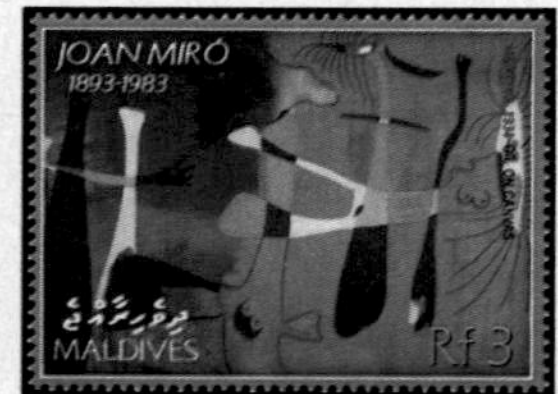

Paintings by Joan Miró (1893-1983) — A447

Designs: 3r, Untitled painting, 1934. 5r, Hirondelle Amour. 10r, Two Women. 15r, Women Listening to Music.
No. 2718: a, Woman and Birds. b, Nocturne. c, Morning Star. d, The Escape Ladder.
No. 2719, 25r, Rhythmic Personages, vert. No. 2720, 25r, Women Encircled by the Flight of a Bird, vert.

2003, June 17 ***Perf. 14¼***

2714-2717 A447 Set of 4 5.25 5.25
2718 A447 12r Sheet of 4, #a-d 7.50 7.50

Size: 83x104mm

Imperf

2719-2720 A447 Set of 2 8.00 8.00

Tour de France Bicycle Race, Cent. — A448

No. 2721, 10r: a, Maurice Garin, 1903. b, Henri Cornet, 1904. c, Louis Trousselier, 1905. d, René Pottier, 1906.
No. 2722, 10r: a, Lucien Petit-Breton on Bicycle, 1907. b, Head of Petit-Breton, 1907. c, François Faber, 1909. d, Octave Lapize, 1910.
No. 2723, 10r: a, Eddy Merckx, 1974. b, Bernard Thévenet, 1975. c, Lucien Van Impe, 1976. d, Thévenet, 1977.

No. 2724, 25r, Bernard Hinault, 1979. No. 2725, 25r, Henri Desgranges. No. 2726, 25r, Le Réveil Matin Cafe, Montgeron, France.

2003, July 3 ***Perf. 13¼***

Sheets of 4, #a-d

2721-2723 A448 Set of 3 19.00 19.00

Souvenir Sheets

2724-2726 A448 Set of 3 12.00 12.00

Powered Flight, Cent. — A449

No. 2727, 10r — Alberto Santos-Dumont's: a, Airship No. 1. b, Airship No. 4, c, Airship with 14bis airplane. d, Airship No. 16.
No. 2728, 10r: a, Santos Dumont with Demoiselle airplane. b, Demoiselle airplane. c, Voisin-Farman No. 1 biplane. d, Gold Bug, built by Glenn Curtiss.
No. 2729, 25r, Santos-Dumont's Airship No. 6. No. 2730, 25r, Santos-Dumont's 14bis Airplane.

2003, July 14 ***Perf. 14***

Sheets of 4, #a-d

2727-2728 A449 Set of 2 12.50 12.50

Souvenir Sheets

2729-2730 A449 Set of 2 8.00 8.00

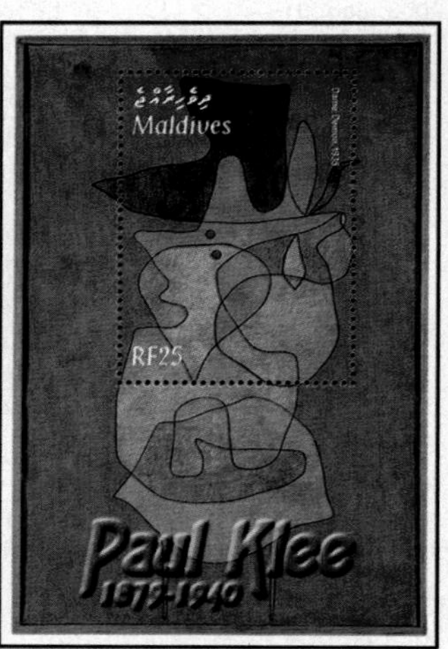

Paintings of Paul Klee (1879-1940) — A450

No. 2731, horiz.: a, Near Taormina, Scirocco. b, Small Town Among the Rocks. c, Still Life with Props. d, North Room.
25r, Dame Demon.

2003, Dec. 4 ***Perf. 13½***

2731 A450 10r Sheet of 4, #a-d 6.25 6.25

Souvenir Sheet

2732 A450 25r multi 4.00 4.00

Maumoon Abdul Gayoom, 25th Anniv. as President — A451

Illustration reduced.

Litho. & Embossed

2003 ***Die Cut Perf. 8***

Without Gum

2733 A451 200r gold & multi 32.50 32.50

Norman Rockwell (1894-1978) — A452

No. 2734 — Four Seasons Calendar: Man and Boy, 1948: a, Winter (ice skating). b, Spring (resting amidst flowers). c, Summer (fishing). d, Autumn (raking leaves).
25r, Illustration for Hallmark Cards, 1937.

2003, Dec. 4 **Litho.** ***Perf. 13¼***

2734 A452 10r Sheet of 4, #a-d 6.25 6.25

Imperf

2735 A452 25r shown 4.00 4.00

No. 2734 contains four 38x50mm stamps.

Intl. Year of Fresh Water — A453

No. 2736: a, Ari Atoll. b, Fresh water for all. c, Desalination plant, Malé.
25r, Community rain water tank.

2003, Dec. 22 ***Perf. 14***

2736 A453 15r Sheet of 3, #a-c 7.00 7.00

Souvenir Sheet

2737 A453 25r multi 4.00 4.00

Fish A454

Designs: 1r, Clown triggerfish. 7r, Sixspot grouper. 10r, Long-nosed butterflyfish. 15r, Longfin bannerfish.
No. 2742: a, Goldtail demoiselle. b, Queen coris. c, Eight-banded butterflyfish. d, Meyer's butterflyfish. e, Exquisite butterflyfish. f, Yellowstripe snapper. g, Yellowback anthias. h, Black-spotted moray. i, Clown anemonefish.
No. 2743: a, Bluestreak cleaner wrasse. b, Threeband demoiselle. c, Palette surgeonfish. d, Emperor snapper. e, Bicolor angelfish. f, Picasso triggerfish.
25r, Chevron butterflyfish.

2003, Dec. 22

2738-2741 A454 Set of 4 5.25 5.25
2742 A454 4r Sheet of 9, #a-i 5.75 5.75
2743 A454 7r Sheet of 6, #a-f 6.75 6.75

Souvenir Sheet

2744 A454 25r multi 4.00 4.00

Nos. 2738-2741 were each printed in sheets of four.

Butterflies — A455

Designs: 3r, Yamfly. 5r, Striped blue crow. 8r, Indian red admiral. 15r, Great eggfly.
No. 2749, horiz.: a, Blue triangle. b, Monarch. c, Broad-bordered grass yellow. d, Red lacewing. e, African migrant. f, Plain tiger.
25r, Beak butterfly.

2003, Dec. 22

2745-2748 A455 Set of 4 5.00 5.00
2749 A455 7r Sheet of 6, #a-f 6.75 6.75

Souvenir Sheet

2750 A455 25r multi 4.00 4.00

Birds A456

Designs: 15 l, Great frigatebird. 20 l, Ruddy turnstone. 25 l, Hoopoe. 1r, Cattle egret.
No. 2755: a, Red-billed tropicbird. b, Red-footed booby. c, Common tern. d, Caspian tern. e, Common curlew. f, Black-bellied plover.
25r, Gray heron.

2003, Dec. 22

2751-2754 A456 Set of 4 .25 .25
2755 A456 7r Sheet of 6, #a-f 6.75 6.75

Souvenir Sheet

2756 A456 25r multi 4.00 4.00

Paintings by Pablo Picasso (1881-1973) — A457

No. 2757: a, Portrait of Jaime Sabartés, 1901. b, Portrait of the Artist's Wife (Olga), 1923. c, Portrait of Olga, 1923. d, Portrait of Jaime Sabartés, 1904.
30r, The Tragedy, 1903.

2003, Dec. 4 **Litho.** ***Perf. 13¼***

2757 A457 10r Sheet of 4, #a-d 6.25 6.25

Imperf

2758 A457 30r multi 4.75 4.75

No. 2757 contains four 37x50mm stamps.

Flowers — A458

Designs: 30 l, Coelogyne asperata. 75 l, Calanthe rosea. 2r, Eria javanica. 10r, Spathoglottis affinis.
No. 2763, horiz.: a, Bird of paradise. b, Flamingo flower. c, Red ginger. d, Cooktown orchid. e, Vanda tricolor. f, Chinese hibiscus.
25r, Morning glory.

2003, Dec. 22 ***Perf. 14***
2759-2762 A458 Set of 4 2.00 2.00
2763 A458 7r Sheet of 6, #a-f 6.75 6.75

Souvenir Sheet

2764 A458 25r multi 4.00 4.00

FIFA (Fédération Internationale de Football Association) Cent. — A459

World Cup winning teams: No. 2765, 5r, Germany, 1974. No. 2766, 5r, Argentina, 1978. No. 2767, 5r, Italy, 1982. No. 2768, 5r, Argentina, 1986. No. 2769, 5r, Germany, 1990. No. 2770, 5r, Brazil, 1994. No. 2771, 5r, France, 1998. No. 2772, 5r, Brazil, 2002.

2004, Mar. 8 ***Perf. 13½***
2765-2772 A459 Set of 8 6.25 6.25

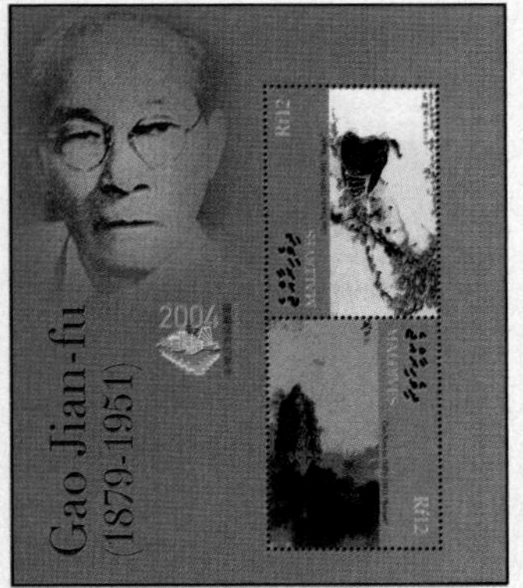
Paintings by Gao Jian-fu (1879-1951) — A460

No. 2773: a, Landscape. b, Moon Night. c, Fox. d, Spider web. e, Woman with mirror. f, Man sitting on ground.
No. 2774: a, Eagle. b, Sunset.

2004, Mar. 8 ***Perf. 13¼***
2773 A460 7r Sheet of 6, #a-f 6.75 6.75
2774 A460 12r Sheet of 2, #a-b 3.75 3.75

2004 Hong Kong Stamp Expo.

Cessation of Concorde Flights — A461

No. 2775: a, F-BVFD, Rio de Janeiro. b, F-BVFC, New York. c, F-BTSD, Honolulu. d, F-BTSD, Lisbon. e, F-BVFA, Washington. f, F-BVFD, Dakar, Senegal. g, G-BOAC, Singapore. h, G-BOAA, Sydney. i, G-BOAD, Hong Kong. j, G-BOAD, Amsterdam. k, G-BOAE, Tokyo. l, G-BOAF, Madrid.
No. 2776, 25r, 214 G-BOAG, Museum of Flight, Seattle. No. 2777, 25r, 214 G-BOAG, horizon. No. 2778, 25r, 204 G-BOAC, British flag.

2004, Mar. 8 ***Perf. 13¼x13½***
2775 A461 1r Sheet of 12, #a-l 1.90 1.90

Souvenir Sheets

2776-2778 A461 Set of 3 12.00 12.00

Paintings in the Hermitage, St. Petersburg, Russia A462

Designs: 1r, Self-portrait, by Anthony van Dyck. 3r, Self-portrait, by Michael Sweerts. 7r, Anna Dalkeith, Countess of Morton, by van Dyck. 12r, Lady Anna Kirk, by van Dyck.
No. 2783: a, Portrait of Prince Alexander Kurakin, by Marie-Louise-Elisabeth Vigée-Lebrun. b, Portrait of a Lady in Waiting to the Infanta Isabella, by Peter Paul Rubens. c, Portrait of a Lady in Blue, by Thomas Gainsborough. d, The Actor Pierre Jéliolte in the Role of Apollo, by Louis Tocqué.
No. 2784, 25r, The Stolen Kiss, by Jean-Honoré Fragonard, horiz. No. 2785, 25r, A Scene from Corneille's Tragedy "La Comte d'Essex," by Nicolas Lancret, horiz.

2004, Mar. 29 ***Perf. 14¼***
2779-2782 A462 Set of 4 3.75 3.75
2783 A462 10r Sheet of 4, #a-d 6.25 6.25

Souvenir Sheets

2784-2785 A462 Set of 2 7.75 7.75

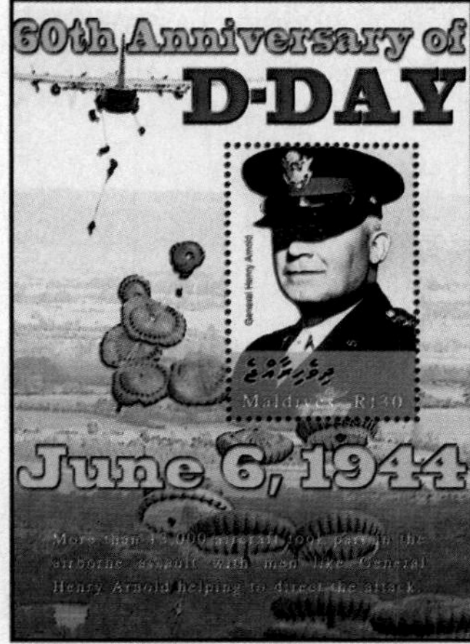
D-Day, 60th Anniv. — A463

No. 2786, 6r: a, Gen. Dwight Eisenhower. b, Field Marshal Guenther von Kluge. c, Air Marshal Sir Trafford Leigh-Mallory. d, Field Marshal Walter Model. e, Field Marshal Gerd von Rundstedt. f, Sir Arthur Tedder.
No. 2787, 6r: a, Maj. Gen. Clarence Huebner. b, Brig. Gen. Anthony McAuliffe. c, Maj. Gen. Leonard Gerow. d, Gen. Adolf Galland. e, Brig. Gen. W. M. Hoge. f, Maj. Gen. Sir Percy Hobart.
No. 2788, 6r: a, Rear Admiral Kirk. b, Field Marshal Erwin Rommel. c, Gen. George Marshall. d, Gen. Jan Smuts. e, Gen. Lt. Gunther Blumentritt. f. Maj. Gen. J. Lawton Collins.
No. 2789, 6r: a, Winston Churchill. b, Adm. Sir Bertram Ramsay. c, Gen. Lt. Dietrich Kraiss. d, Maj. Gen. Richard Gale. e, Gen. George Patton. f, Maj. Gen. Maxwell Taylor.
No. 2790, 6r, horiz.: a, Lt. Gen. Omar Bradley. b, Rear Admiral Hall. c, Maj. Gen. Huebner, diff. d, Adm. Karl Dönitz. e, Rear Admiral Wilkes. f, Capt. Chauncey Camp.
No. 2791, 30r, Gen. Henry Arnold. No. 2792, 30r, Rear Adm. Donald Moon. No. 2793, 30r, Lt. Gen. Sir Frederick Morgan. No. 2794, 30r, Gen. Sir Bernard Montgomery. No. 2795, 30r, Rear Adm. Carlton Bryant, horiz.

Perf. 13½x13¼, 13¼x13½

2004, May 19

Sheets of 6, #a-f

2786-2790 A463 Set of 5 28.00 28.00

Souvenir Sheets

2791-2795 A463 Set of 5 24.00 24.00

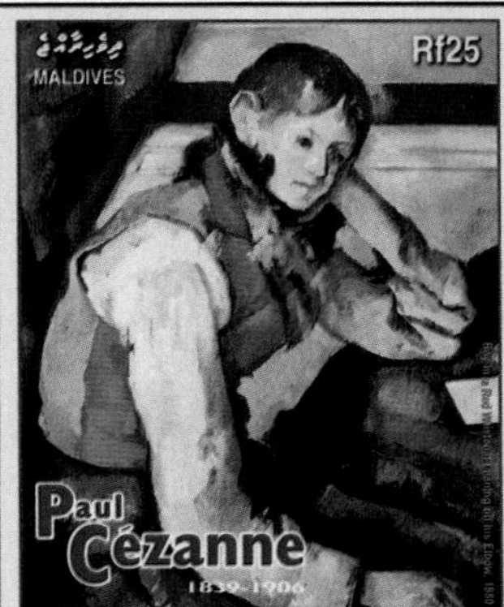
Paintings by Paul Cézanne (1839-1906) — A464

No. 2796, horiz.: a, Still Life with Peppermint Bottle and Blue Rug. b, House in Provence. c. Le Château Noir. d, Basket of Apples.
25r, Boy in a Red Waistcoat Leaning on his Elbow.

2004, July 6 ***Perf. 13¼***
2796 A464 10r Sheet of 4, #a-d 6.25 6.25

Imperf

2797 A464 25r multi 4.00 4.00

No. 2796 contains four 50x37mm stamps.

Paintings by Henri Rousseau (1844-1910) — A465

No. 2798, horiz.: a, Nègre Attaqué par un Jaguar. b, Paysage Exotique. c. La Cascade. d, Le Repas du Lion.
25r, Le Rêve.

2004, July 6 ***Perf. 13¼***
2798 A465 10r Sheet of 4, #a-d 6.25 6.25

Imperf

2799 A465 25r multi 4.00 4.00

No. 2798 contains four 50x37mm stamps.

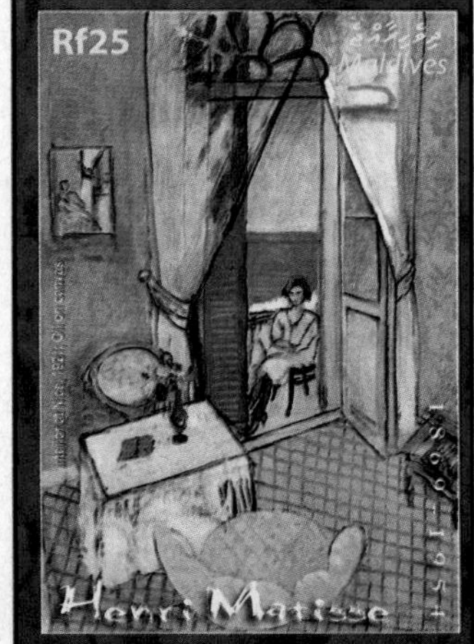
Paintings by Henri Matisse (1869-1954) — A466

No. 2800, horiz.: a, Conversation. b, Still Life with a Blue Tablecloth. c. Seville Still Life II. d, Woman Before an Aquarium.
25r, Interior at Nice.

2004, July 6 ***Perf. 13¼***
2800 A466 10r Sheet of 4, #a-d 6.25 6.25

Imperf

2801 A466 25r multi 4.00 4.00

No. 2800 contains four 50x37mm stamps.

Steam Locomotives, 200th Anniv. — A467

No. 2802, 12r: a, Planet Class 2-2-0. b, American 4-4-0. c, Newmar. d, Class 500 4-6-0.

No. 2803, 12r: a, Firefly Class 2-2-2. b, French "Single." c, Medoc Class 2-4-0. d, German 4-4-0.

No. 2804, 12r: a, Adler 2-2-2. b, Beuth 2-2-2. c, Northumbrian 0-2-2. d, Class 4-6-2.

No. 2805, 12r: a, Woodburning Beyer Garratt 4-8-2+2-8-4. b, Double headed train over Kaaiman River, Africa. c, Garratt 4-8-2+2-8-4. d, Class 15 Garratt.

No. 2806, 12r: a, East African Railways Garratt. b, Rhodesian Railways 12th Class. c, Class 2-6-2. d, Class 19D 4-8-2.

No. 2807, 12r: a, Evening Star. b, Britannia. c, The George Stephenson. d, Sudan Railways 310 2-8-2.

No. 2808, 30r, Claud Hamilton Class 4-4-0. No. 2809, 30r, Class P8 4-6-0. No. 2810, 30r, Vauxhall 2-2-0. No. 2811, 30r, American, diff. No. 2812, 30r, The Lord Nelson. No. 2813, 30r, Flying Scotsman.

2004, July 6 ***Perf. 13¼x13½***

Sheets of 4, #a-d

2802-2807 A467 Set of 6 45.00 45.00

Souvenir Sheets

2808-2813 A467 Set of 6 28.00 28.00

Jules Verne (1828-1905), Writer — A468

No. 2814, 12r: a, Archipelago on Fire. b, Clovis Dardentor. c, The Golden Volcano. d, Le Superbe Orénoque.

No. 2815, 12r — Michael Strogoff, Courier of the Czar: a, People (pink background). b, People in grass (green background). c, People (blue background). d, Animal and head in grass (green background).

No. 2816, 12r — Family Without a Name: a, Woman. b, Soldier. c, Crowd. d, Soldiers and Indian with guns.

No. 2817, 12r — César Cascabel: a, Men pushing train car (blue green background). b, Man (brown background). c, Crevasse (blue green background). d, Crowd and sign (pink background).

No. 2818, 12r — The Lighthouse at the End of the World: a, Men on ship. b, Man with arm extended. c, Rocks. d, Fisherman with hat.

No. 2819, 25r, The Survivors of the Chancellor. No. 2820, 25r, Keraban the Inflexible. No. 2821, 25r, Family Without a Name, diff. No. 2822, 25r, César Cascabel, diff. No. 2823, 25r, The Lighthouse at the End of the World, diff.

2004, July 29 ***Perf. 13¼x13½***

Sheets of 4, #a-d

2814-2818 A468 Set of 5 37.00 37.00

Souvenir Sheets

2819-2823 A468 Set of 5 19.00 19.00

Marilyn Monroe — A469

2004, Aug. 16 ***Perf. 13½x13¼***

2824 A469 7r multi 1.10 1.10

Printed in sheets of 6.

George Herman "Babe" Ruth (1895-1948), Baseball Player — A470

No. 2826: a, Swinging bat. b, Wearing cap, striped uniform. c, Holding two bats. d, Profile of Ruth.

2004

2825 A470 3r shown .45 .45

2826 A470 10r Sheet of 4, #a-d 6.25 6.25

No. 2825 printed in sheets of 16. World Series, 100th anniv.

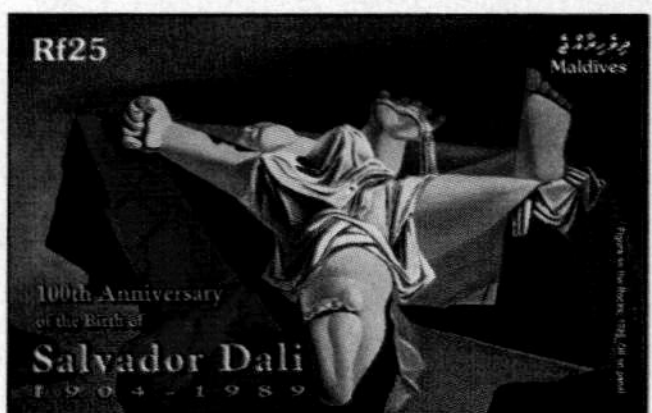

Paintings by Salvador Dali (1904-89) — A471

No. 2827: a, The Endless Enigma. b, The Persistence of Memory. c, Soft Construction with Boiled Beans — Premonition of Civil War. d, Still Life — Fast Moving.

25r, Figure on the Rocks.

2004, July 6 **Litho.** ***Perf. 13½***

2827 A471 10r Sheet of 4, #a-d 6.25 6.25

Imperf

2828 A471 25r multi 4.00 4.00

No. 2827 contains four 50x37mm stamps.

2004 Summer Olympics, Athens A472

Designs: 2r, Gold medal, 1904 St. Louis Olympics. 5r, Krater depicting Olympic athletes. 7r, Count Jean de Beaumont, Intl. Olympic Committee member. 12r, Pommel horse, horiz.

2004, Sept. 30 ***Perf. 14¼***

2829-2832 A472 Set of 4 4.00 4.00

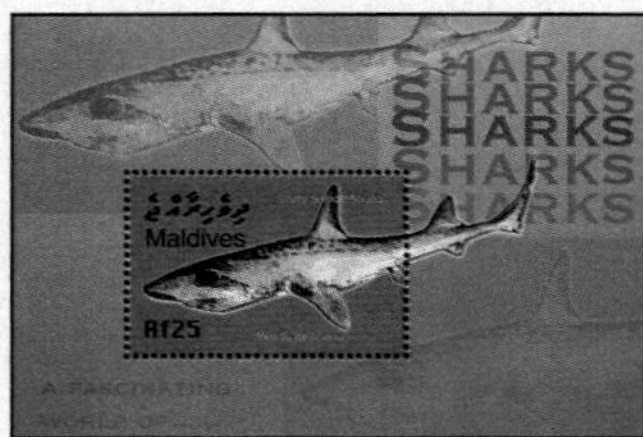

Sharks — A473

No. 2833: a, Silvertip shark. b, Silky shark. c, Great white shark. d, Gray reef shark.

$25, Starry smoothhound shark.

2004, Nov. 4

2833 A473 10r Sheet of 4, #a-d 6.25 6.25

Souvenir Sheet

2834 A473 25r multi 4.00 4.00

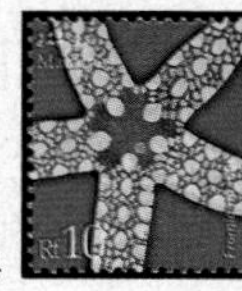

Starfish — A474

Designs: No. 2835, 10r, Fromia monilis (green background). No. 2836, 10r, Linckia laevigata. No. 2837, 10r, Nardoa novaecalidoniae. No. 2838, 10r, Fromia monilis (red background).

2004, Nov. 4 ***Perf. 15x14***

2835-2838 A474 Set of 4 6.25 6.25

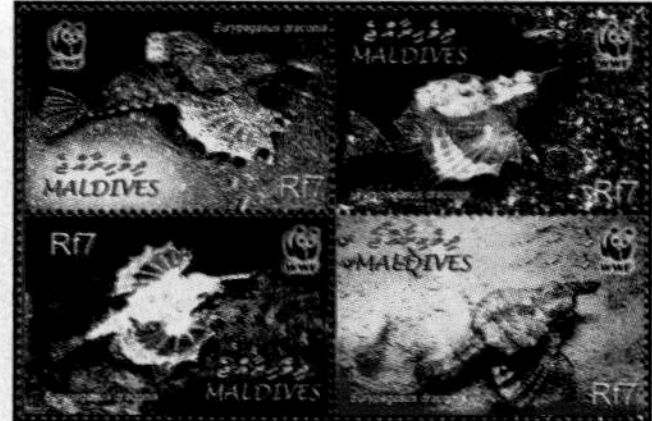

Worldwide Fund for Nature (WWF) — A475

No. 2839 — Eurypegasus draconis and: a, Country name at LL, denomination at LR. b, Country name at UL, denomination at LR, dark background. c, Country name at LR, denomination at UL. d, Country name at UL, denomination at LR, light background.

Illustration reduced.

2004, Dec. 15 **Litho.** ***Perf. 14***

2839 A475 7r Block of 4, #a-d 4.50 4.50

e. Miniature sheet, 2 each #2839a-2839d 9.00 9.00

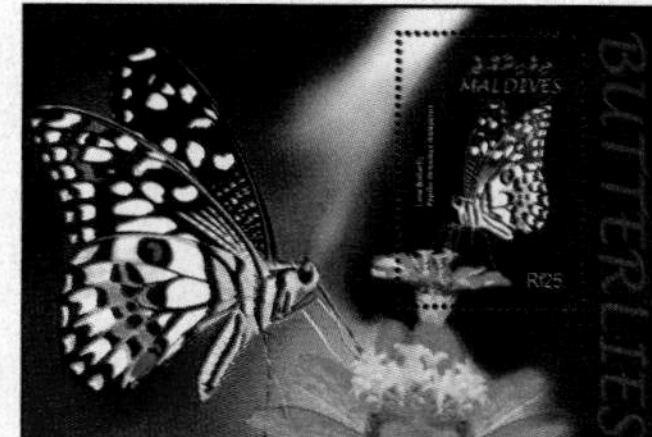

Butterflies — A476

No. 2840, horiz.: a, Red lacewing. b, Amesia sanguiflua. c, Pericallia galactina. d, Limenitis dudu dudu.

25r, Lime butterfly.

2004, Dec. 15

2840 A476 10r Sheet of 4, #a-d 6.25 6.25

Souvenir Sheet

2841 A476 25r multi 4.00 4.00

Dolphins — A477

No. 2842: a, Striped dolphin. b, Amazon River dolphin. c, Bottlenose dolphin. d, Spinner dolphin.

25r, Long-snouted spinner dolphin.

2004, Dec. 15 **Litho.** ***Perf. 14***

2842 A477 10r Sheet of 4, #a-d 6.25 6.25

Souvenir Sheet

2843 A477 25r multi 4.00 4.00

Reptiles and Amphibians — A478

No. 2844, horiz.: a, Eyelash pit viper. b, Basilisk lizard. c, Calico snake. d, Maki frog.

25r, Naja melanoleuca.

2004, Dec. 15

2844 A478 10r Sheet of 4, #a-d 6.25 6.25

Souvenir Sheet

2845 A478 25r multi 4.00 4.00

Mushrooms — A479

No. 2846, horiz.: a, Parrot mushroom. b, Hygrocybe miniata. c, Aleuria aurantia. d, Thaxterogaster porphyreum.

25r, Galerina autumnalis.

2004, Dec. 15

2846 A479 10r Sheet of 4, #a-d 6.25 6.25

Souvenir Sheet

2847 A479 25r multi 4.00 4.00

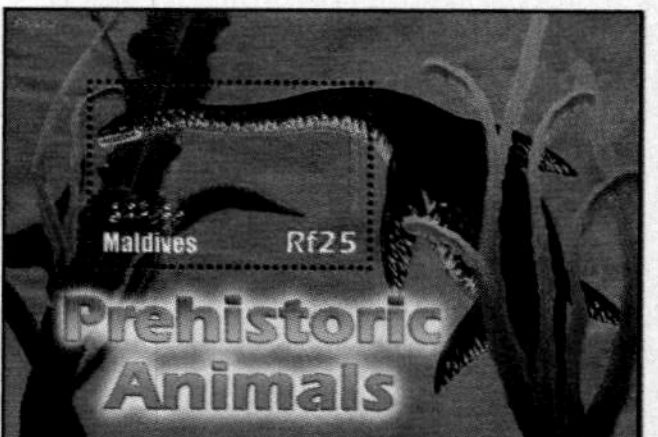

Prehistoric Animals — A480

No. 2848, 10r: a, Macroplata. b, Ichthyosaurus. c, Shonisaurus. d, Archelon.

No. 2849, 10r, vert.: a, Albertosaurus. b, Iguanodon. c, Deinonychus, name at right. d, Baryonyx.

No. 2850, 10r, vert.: a, Deinonychus, name at left. b, Styracosaurus. c, Ornitholestes. d, Euoplocephalus.

No. 2851, 10r, vert.: a, Pterodactylus. b, Cearadactylus. c, Pterosaur. d, Sordes.

No. 2852, 25r, Muraeonosaurus. No. 2853, 25r, Styracosaurus, diff. No. 2854, 25r, Leptoceratops. No. 2855, 25r, Archaeopteryx.

2004, Dec. 15 *Perf. 14*

Sheets of 4, #a-d

2848-2851 A480 Set of 4 25.00 25.00

Souvenir Sheets

2852-2855 A480 Set of 4 16.00 16.00

Souvenir Sheet

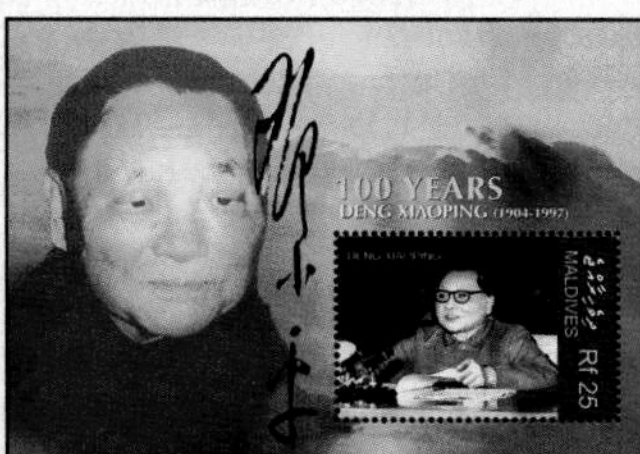

Deng Xiaoping (1904-97), Chinese Leader — A481

2005, Jan. 26

2856 A481 25r multi 4.00 4.00

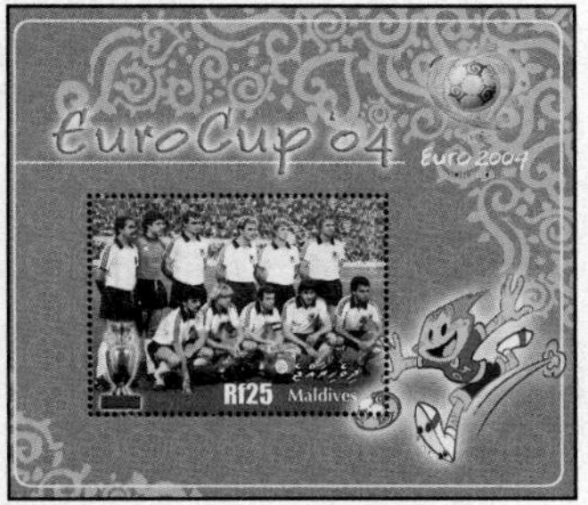

2004 European Soccer Championships, Portugal — A482

No. 2857, vert.: a, Jupp Derwall. b, René Vandereycke. c, Horst Hrubesch. d, Stadio Olimpico.

25r, 1980 Germany team.

2005, Jan. 26 *Perf. 14*

2857 A482 12r Sheet of 4, #a-d 7.50 7.50

Souvenir Sheet

2858 A482 25r multi 4.00 4.00

No. 2857 contains four 28x42mm stamps.

Rotary International, Cent. — A483

No. 2859 — Chicago skyline: a, Part of Sears Tower at R. b, Sears Tower at L. c, CNA Tower (red brick building) at L.

25r, Telecommunications tower.

2005, July 12 **Litho.** *Perf. 12¾*

2859 A483 15r Sheet of 3, #a-c 7.00 7.00

Souvenir Sheet

2860 A483 25r multi 4.00 4.00

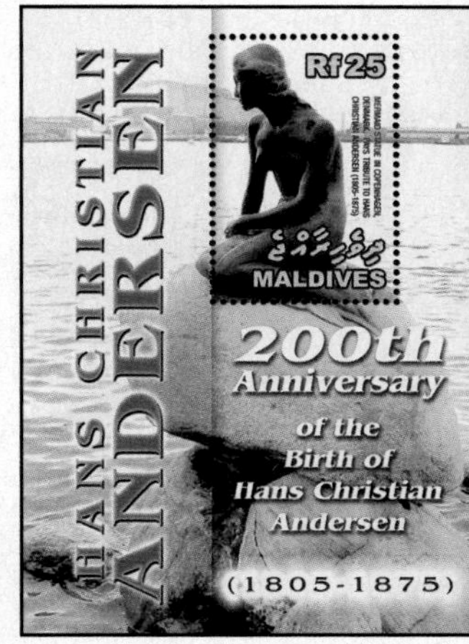

Hans Christian Andersen (1805-75), Author — A484

No. 2861: a, Statue of Andersen wearing hat. b, Photograph of Andersen. c, Statue of Andersen without hat.

25r, Little Mermaid Statue, Copenhagen.

2005, Sept. 20

2861 A484 15r Sheet of 3, #a-c 7.00 7.00

Souvenir Sheet

2862 A484 25r multi 4.00 4.00

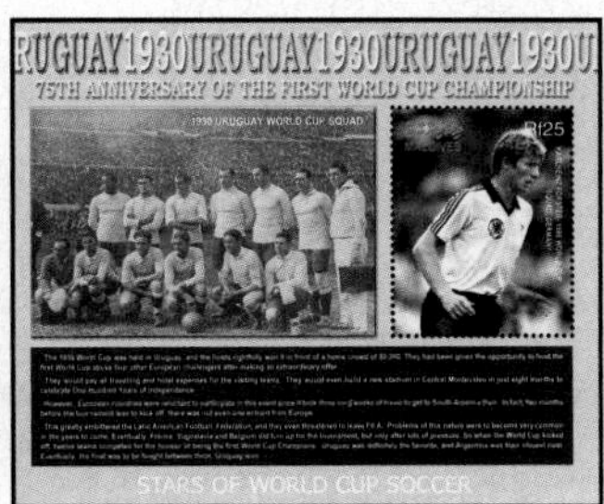

World Cup Soccer Championships, 75th Anniv. — A485

No. 2863: a, Oscar. b, Karl-Heinz Rummenigge. c, Oliver Kahn.

25r, Karlheinz Forster..

2005, Sept. 20 *Perf. 13¼*

2863 A485 15r Sheet of 3, #a-c 7.00 7.00

Souvenir Sheet

Perf. 12¼x12

2864 A485 25r multi 4.00 4.00

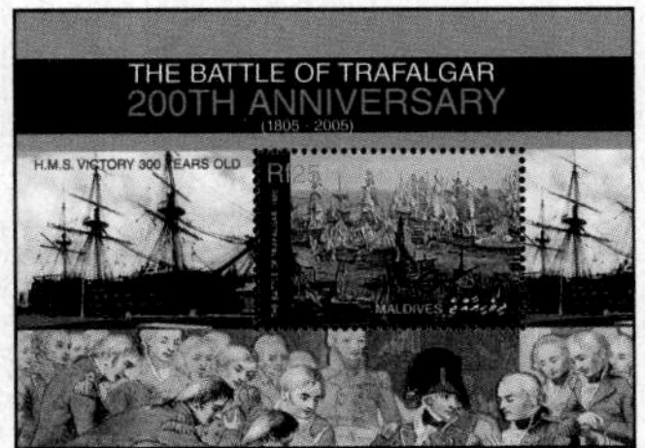

Battle of Trafalgar, Bicent. — A486

No. 2865, vert.: a, Admiral Cuthbert Collingwood. b, Napoleon Bonaparte. c, Admiral Horatio Nelson. d, Capt. Thomas Masterman Hardy.

25r, Ships at battle.

2005, Sept. 20 *Perf. 12¾*

2865 A486 10r Sheet of 4, #a-d 6.25 6.25

Souvenir Sheet

2866 A486 25r multi 4.00 4.00

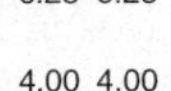

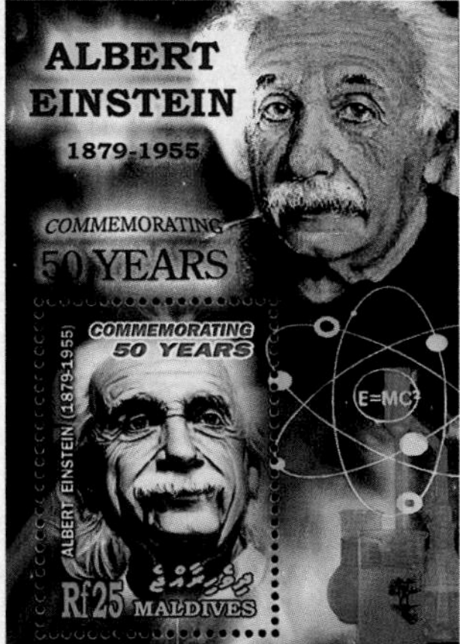

Albert Einstein (1879-1955), Physicist — A487

No. 2867, horiz. — Portraits of Einstein in: a, Red brown (denomination at R). b, Pink & blue (denomination at L). c, Green & pink (denomination at R). d, Brown (denomination at L).

25r, Einstein, diff.

2005, Sept. 20

2867 A487 10r Sheet of 4, #a-d 6.25 6.25

Souvenir Sheet

2868 A487 25r multi 4.00 4.00

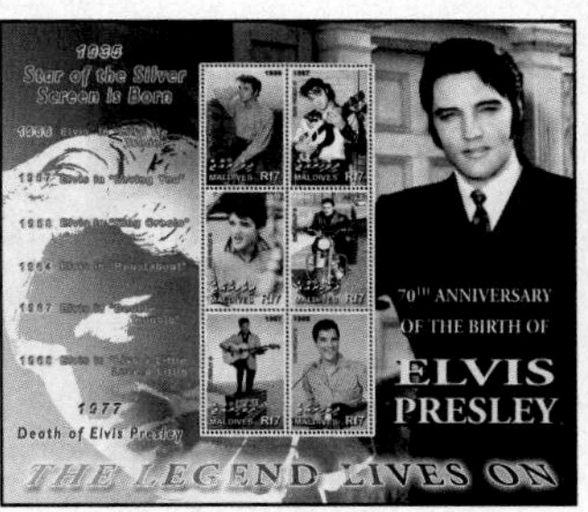

Elvis Presley (1935-77) — A488

No. 2869, 7r — Photographs of Presley from: a, 1956 (sepia). b, 1957. c, 1958. d, 1964. e, 1967. f, 1968.

No. 2870, 7r — Photographs of Presley from: a, 1956 (black and white). b, 1960. c, 1962. d, 1969. e, 1973. f, 1975.

2005, Nov. 15 *Perf. 13¾x13¼*

Sheets of 6, #a-f

2869-2870 A488 Set of 2 13.00 13.00

Elvis Presley (1935-77) — A489

Illustration reduced.

Lihto. & Embossed

2006, Jan. 17 ***Die Cut Perf 7½***

Without Gum

2871 A489 85r gold & multi 13.50 13.50

Miniature Sheets

Children's Drawings — A490

No. 2872, 10r — Sea Life: a, Bubbles, by Raquel Bobolia. b, Bubble Fish, by Sarah Bowen. c, Lipfish, by Elsa Fleisher. d, Flounder, by Erica Malchowski.

No. 2873, 10r — Birds: a, Purple Bird, by Anna Badger. b, Parrots, by Nick Abrams. c, Pretty Bird, by Jessie Abrams. d, Royal Parrot, by Ashley Mondfrans.

No. 2874, 10r — Flowers: a, Orange Sunflower, by Brett Walker. b, Red Flower, by Jessica Shutt. c, Flower Pot, by Nick Abrams. d, Blue Flower Vase, by Trevor Nielsen.

2006, Jan. 24 **Litho.** *Perf. 13¼*

Sheets of 4, #a-d

2872-2874 A490 Set of 3 19.00 19.00

Skates and Rays — A491

Designs: 20 l, Himantura uamak. 1r, Manta birostris. 2r, Taeniura lymma. 20r, Aetobatus narinari.

2006, Feb. 27 *Perf. 13¾x14¼*

2875-2878 A491 Set of 4 3.75 3.75

Souvenir Sheet

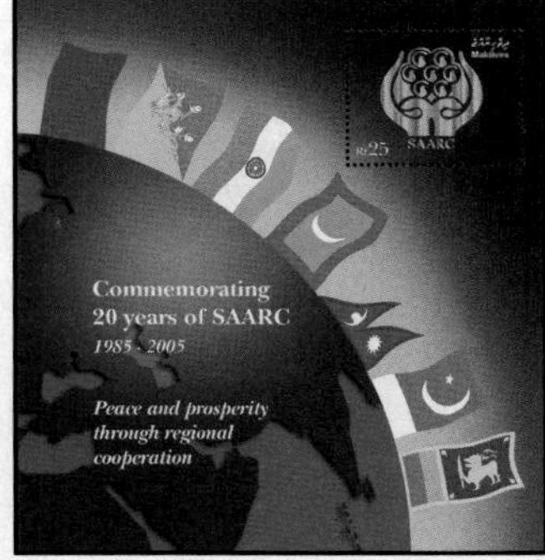

South Asian Association for Regional Cooperation, 20th Anniv. — A492

2006, Mar. 9 *Perf. 13¼*

2879 A492 25r multi 4.00 4.00

2006 Winter Olympics, Turin — A493

Designs: 7r, Norway #B52. 8r, Poster for 1952 Oslo Winter Olympics, vert. 10r, Poster for 1936 Garmisch-Partenkirchen Winter Olympics, vert. 12r, Germany #B79, vert.

2006, May 9 *Perf. 14¼*

2880-2883 A493 Set of 4 5.75 5.75

Miniature Sheet

Wolfgang Amadeus Mozart (1756-91), Composer — A494

No. 2884: a, Portrait in oval frame. b, Mozart looking left. c, Mozart as child. d, Bust.

2006, June 29 ***Perf. 12¾***

2884 A494 12r Sheet of 4, #a-d 7.50 7.50

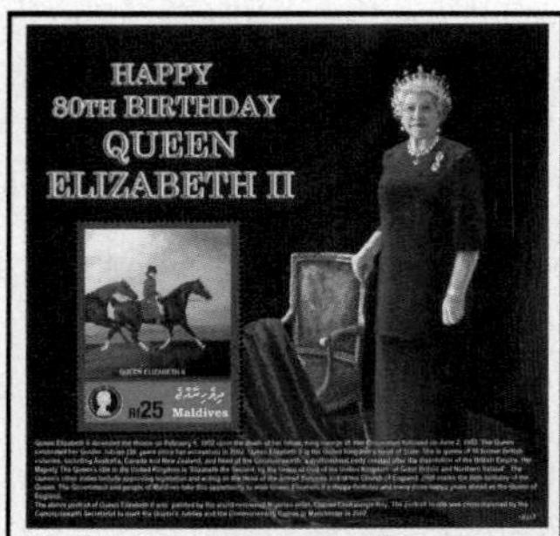

Queen Elizabeth II, 80th Birthday — A495

No. 2885 — Queen and: a, Pres. John F. Kennedy. b, Pres. Ronald Reagan. c, Pres. Gerald R. Ford. d, Pres. George W. Bush.

25r, Portrait of Queen on horse by Chinwe Chukwuogo-Roy.

2006 ***Perf. 14¼***

2885 A495 15r Sheet of 4, #a-d 9.50 9.50

Souvenir Sheet

2886 A495 25r multi 4.00 4.00

Souvenir Sheet

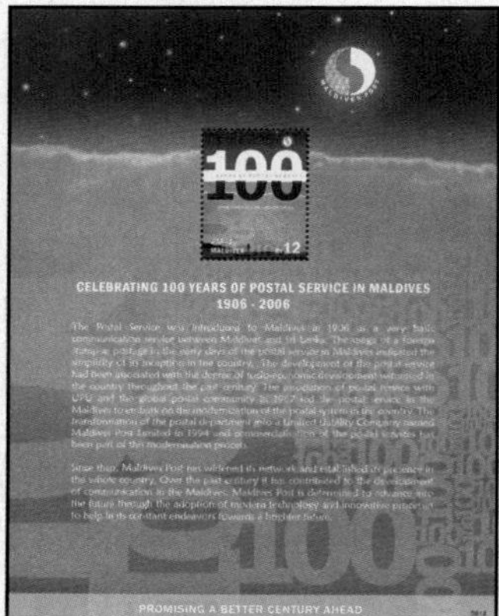

Maldive Islands Postal Service, Cent. — A496

2006, Nov. 1 **Litho.** ***Perf. 12½***

2887 A496 12r multi 1.90 1.90

Souvenir Sheet

Ludwig Durr (1878-1956), Zeppelin Engineer — A497

No. 2888 — Durr and: a, Zeppelin over Frankfurt. b, Balloons and Festhalle, Frankfurt. c, Hindenburg.

2006, Nov. 15 ***Perf. 13¼***

2888 A497 15r Sheet of 3, #a-c 7.00 7.00

Fish — A498

Designs: No. 2889, 10r, Dascyllus aruanus. No. 2890, 10r, Balistoides conspicillum. No. 2891, 10r, Pomacanthus imperator. No. 2892, 10r, Chaetodon meyeri.

2006, Nov. 1 **Litho.** ***Perf. 12¾***

2889-2892 A498 Set of 4 6.25 6.25

Miniature Sheet

Elvis Presley (1935-77) — A499

No. 2893 — Presley with: a, Microphone at left, denomination in pink. b, Microphone at center, denomination in white. c, Microphone at center, denomination in light blue. d, Microphone at left, denomination in light green.

2006, Nov. 15 ***Perf. 13¼***

2893 A499 12r Sheet of 4, #a-d 7.50 7.50

Space Achievements — A500

No. 2894: a, R-7 missile (Sputnik 1 launcher). b, Sputnik 1. c, Inside Sputnik 1. d, Sputnik 2. e, Map of Earth showing Sputnik 1 orbits. f, Sputnik 3.

No. 2895, 12r: a, Calipso satellite. b, Cloud-Sat satellite. c, Aqua satellite. d, Aura satellite.

No. 2896, 12r: a, Nucleus of Halley's Comet. b, Halley's Comet. c, Giotto Space Probe. d, Close-up image of Halley's Comet taken by Giotto.

No. 2897, 25r, Apollo spacecraft. No. 2898, 25r, Giotto. No. 2899, 25r, Stardust satellite.

2006, Nov. 15 ***Perf. 13¼***

2894 A500 8r Sheet of 6, #a-f 7.50 7.50

Sheets of 4, #a-d

2895-2896 A500 Set of 2 15.00 15.00

Souvenir Sheets

2897-2899 A500 Set of 3 12.00 12.00

Birds A501

Designs: 1r, Bar-tailed godwit. 2r, Black-headed gull. No. 2902, 10r, Masked booby, vert. 20r, Kentish plover.

No. 2904, 10r: a, Common swifts. b, Sooty tern. c, Yellow wagtail. d, House sparrow.

No. 2905, 10r: a, Tufted duck. b, Caspian tern. c, Southern giant petrel. d, Glossy ibis.

No. 2906, 30r, Purple herons. No. 2907, 30r, Osprey, vert. No. 2908, 30r, Golden-throated barbet, vert.

2007, Feb. 8 ***Perf. 14***

2900-2903 A501 Set of 4 5.25 5.25

Sheets of 4, #a-d

2904-2905 A501 Set of 2 12.50 12.50

Souvenir Sheets

2906-2908 A501 Set of 3 14.00 14.00

Fish A502

Designs: 1r, Ragged-finned lionfish. 2r, Vlaming's unicornfish. No. 2911, 10r, White-spotted grouper. 20r, Maldive anemonefish.

No. 2913, 10r: a, Bicolor parrotfish. b, Blue-barred parrotfish. c, Bullethead parrotfish. d, Dusky parrotfish.

No. 2914, 10r: a, Imperial angelfish. b, Clown triggerfish. c, Black-saddled coral trout. d, Slender grouper.

No. 2915, 30r, Shadow soldierfish. No. 2916, 30r, Picasso triggerfish. No. 2917, 30r, Blue-faced angelfish.

2007, Feb. 8

2909-2912 A502 Set of 4 5.25 5.25

Sheets of 4, #a-d

2913-2914 A502 Set of 2 12.50 12.50

Souvenir Sheets

2915-2917 A502 Set of 3 14.00 14.00

Flowers A503

Designs: 1r, Ranunculus eschscholtzii. 2r, Ratibida columnaris. No. 2920, 10r, Mentzelia laevicaulis. 20r, Clintonia unifloria.

No. 2922, 10r: a, Machaeranthera tanacetifolia. b, Aquilegia coerulea. c, Gentiana detonsa. d, Linum perenne.

No. 2923, 10r: a, Ipomopsis aggregata. b, Rosa woodsii. c, Lewisia rediviva. d, Penstemon rydbergii.

No. 2924, 30r, Ipomoea purpurea. No. 2925, 30r, Encelia farinosa. No. 2926, 30r, Epilobium angustifolium.

2007, Feb. 8

2918-2921 A503 Set of 4 5.25 5.25

Sheets of 4, #a-d

2922-2923 A503 Set of 2 12.50 12.50

Souvenir Sheets

2924-2926 A503 Set of 3 14.00 14.00

Orchids — A504

Designs: 1r, Dendrobium formosum. 2r, Bulbophyllum Elizabeth Ann. No. 2929, 10r, Dendrobium bigibbum. 20r, Spathoglottis gracilis.

No. 2931, 10r: a, Bulbophyllum lasiochilum. b, Phaius Microburst. c, Coelogyne mooreana. d, Bulbophyllum nasseri.

No. 2932, 10r: a, Cymbidium erythrostylum. b, Phaius humboldtii x Phaius tuberculosis. c, Dendrobium farmeri. d, Dendrobium junceum.

No. 2933, 30r, Coelogyne cristata, horiz. No. 2934, 30r, Bulbophyllum graveolens, horiz. No. 2935, 30r, Dendrobium crocatum.

2007, Feb. 8

2927-2930 A504 Set of 4 5.25 5.25

Sheets of 4, #a-d

2931-2932 A504 Set of 2 12.50 12.50

Souvenir Sheets

2933-2935 A504 Set of 3 14.00 14.00

Scouting, Cent. A505

2007, Feb. 21 ***Perf. 13¼***

Color of Denomination

2936 A505 15r purple 2.40 2.40

Souvenir Sheet

2937 A505 25r blue 4.00 4.00

No. 2936 was printed in sheets of 3.

Intl. Polar Year — A506

No. 2938 — King penguins with background color of: a, Light blue. b, Lilac. c, Yellow green. d, Blue green. e, Red violet. f, Green.

25r, African penguin with party hat.

2007, May 1 **Litho.** ***Perf. 13¼***

2938 A506 12r Sheet of 6, #a-f 11.50 11.50

Souvenir Sheet

2939 A506 25r multi 4.00 4.00

Miniature Sheet

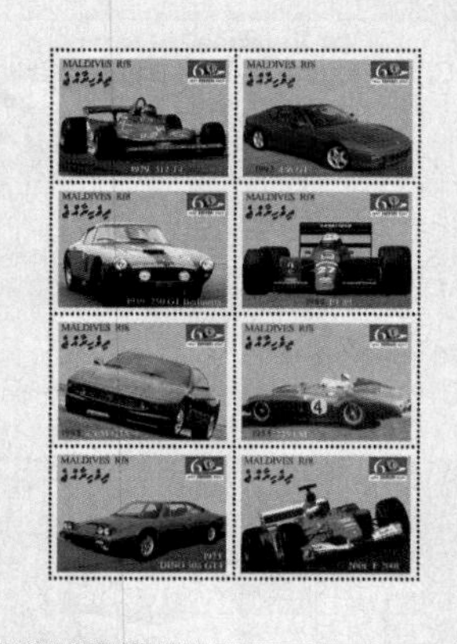

Ferrari Automobiles, 60th Anniv. — A507

No. 2940: a, 1979 312 T4. b, 1992 456 GT. c, 1959 250 GT Berlinetta. d, 1989 F1 89. e, 1998 456M GTA. f, 1955 735 LM. g, 1973 Dino 308 GT4. h, 2001 F 2001.

2007, Aug. 12

2940 A507 8r Sheet of 8, #a-h 10.00 10.00

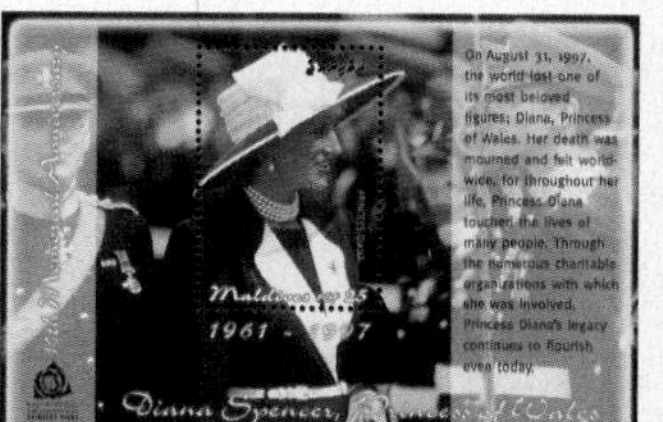

Princess Diana (1961-97) — A508

No. 2941 — Diana with white hat and: a, Gray jacket, close-up. b, Green dress, close-up. c, White striped jacket, close-up. d, Green dress. e, White striped jacket. f, Gray jacket. 25r, Black and white jacket.

2007, Aug. 12
2941 A508 8r Sheet of 6, #a-f 7.50 7.50

Souvenir Sheet

2942 A508 25r multi 4.00 4.00

Fish — A509

Designs: 10 l, Chaetodon triangulum. 50 l, Chaetodon kleinii. 12r, Chaetodon trifasciatus. 15r, Chaetodon madagascariensis. 20r, Chaetodon lunula.

2007, Oct. 9 Litho. *Perf. 13¼*
2943-2947 A509 Set of 5 7.50 7.50

2008 Summer Olympics, Beijing — A510

No. 2948: a, Rie Mastenbroek, swimming gold medalist, 1936. b, Poster for 1936 Summer Olympics. c, Jesse Owens, long jump gold medalist, 1936. d, Jack Beresford, rowing gold medalist, 1936.

2008, Jan. 8 Litho. *Perf. 13¼*
2948 Horiz. strip of 4 4.50 4.50
a.-d. A510 7r Any single 1.10 1.10
e. Souvenir sheet, #2948a-2948d 4.50 4.50

Miniature Sheet

Elvis Presley (1935-77) — A511

No. 2949 — Presley wearing: a, Brown jacket. b, Blue shirt, holding guitar. c, Red jacket and white shirt. d, Gray jacket and black shirt. e, Blue shirt, holding guitar behind microphone. f, Red shirt, holding microphone.

2008, Jan. 8 Litho. *Perf. 13¼*
2949 A511 8r Sheet of 6, #a-f 7.50 7.50

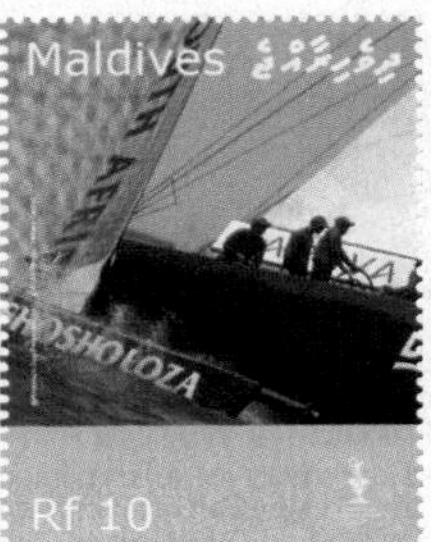

America's Cup Yachting Championships — A512

No. 2950 — Various yachts with panel colors of: a, Yellow orange. b, Red. c, Dark blue. d, Blue green.

2008, Jan. 8
2950 Strip of 4 9.25 9.25
a. A512 10r multi 1.60 1.60
b. A512 12r multi 1.90 1.90
c. A512 15r multi 2.40 2.40
d. A512 20r multi 3.25 3.25

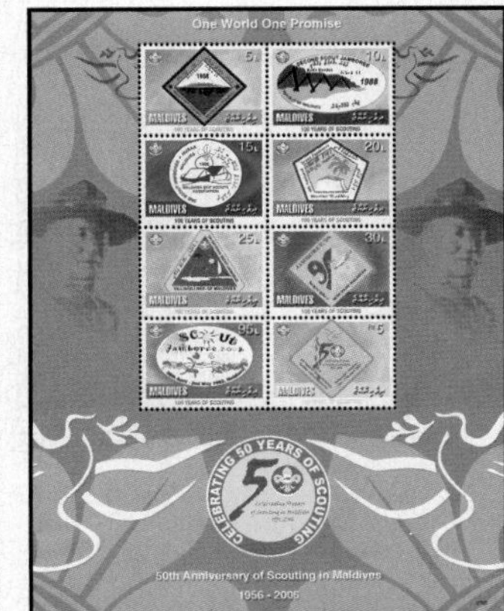

Scouting In Maldive Islands, 50th Anniv. — A513

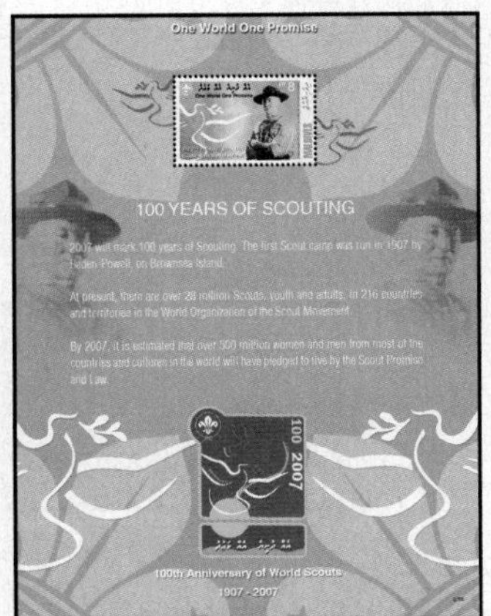

Scouting, Cent. (in 2007) — A514

No. 2951 — Emblems of national jamborees from: a, 5 l, 1986. b, 10 l, 1988. c, 15 l, 1990. d, 20 l, 1992. e, 25 l, 1995. f, 30 l, 1998. g, 95 l, 2002. h, 5r, 2007.

2008, Feb. 19
2951 A513 Sheet of 8, #a-h 1.10 1.10

Souvenir Sheet

2952 A514 8r multi 1.25 1.25

Miniature Sheet

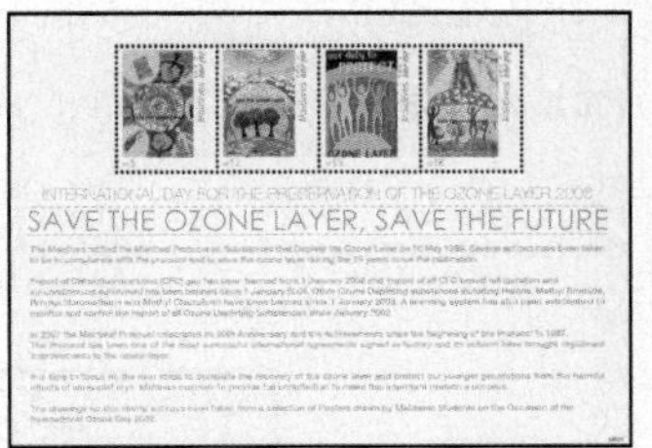

Intl. Day for the Preservation of the Ozone Layer — A515

No. 2953 — Various "Save the Ozone Layer" posters by Maldivian students: a, 5r. b, 12r. c, 15r. d, 18r.

2008, Sept. 10 Litho. *Perf. 12½*
2953 A515 Sheet of 4, #a-d 8.00 8.00

Miniature Sheet

Elvis Presley (1935-77) — A516

No. 2954 — Presley: a, Playing guitar. b, With hand in foreground at right. c, Singing, with legs shown. d, Facing right, holding microphone. e, Singing, with microphone at left. f, Beside car, wearing hat.

2008, Sept. 11 *Perf. 13¼*
2954 A516 8r Sheet of 6, #a-f 7.50 7.50

Miniature Sheet

Royal Air Force, 90th Anniv. — A517

No. 2955: a, Sopwith F-1 Camel. b, Aerospatiale Puma HC1 helicopter. c, Wessex helicopter. d, Armstrong Whitworth Atlas.

2008, Sept. 11 *Perf. 11½*
2955 A517 12r Sheet of 4, #a-d 7.50 7.50

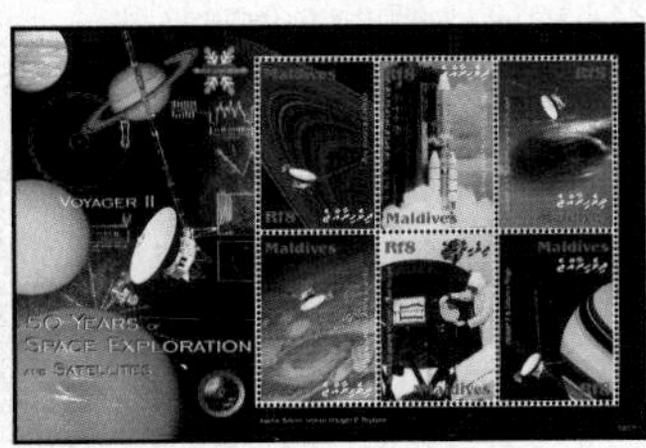

A518

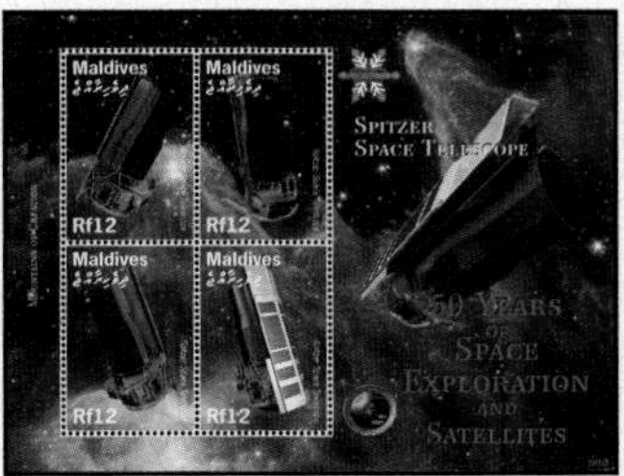

Space Exploration, 50th Anniv. (in 2007) — A519

No. 2956: a, Voyager 2 and rings of Uranus. b, Titan 3E Centaur rocket launching Voyager 2. c, Voyager 2 and Neptune's Great Dark Spot. d, Voyager 2 and Jupiter's Great Red Spot. e, Technician placing gold record into Voyager 2. f, Voyager 2 and rings of Saturn.

No. 2957, 12r — Spitzer Space Telescope: a, Top of telescope pointing to UR corner. b, Top of telescope pointing to top margin. c, Top of telescope pointing to UL corner. d, Solar panels of telescope shown.

No. 2958, 12r — Sputnik 1: a, With black background, denomination at LL. b, With orange background. c, And technician. d, With Moon in background.

No. 2959, 12r — Explorer 1: a, Atop Juno 1 rocket. b, With Earth in background. c, With clouds in background. d, And Dr. James Van Allen.

No. 2960, 12r — Vanguard 1: a, With Earth at top. b, And technicians. c, And rocket. d, With Earth at bottom.

2008, Sept. 11 *Perf. 13¼*
2956 A518 8r Sheet of 6, #a-f 7.50 7.50

Sheets of 4, #a-d

2957-2960 A519 Set of 4 30.00 30.00

MALI

'mä-lē

(Federation of Mali)

LOCATION — West Africa
GOVT. — Republic within French Community
AREA — 482,077 sq. mi.
POP. — 5,862,000 (est.)
CAPITAL — Dakar and Bamako

The Federation of Mali, founded Jan. 17, 1959, consisted of the Republic of Senegal and the French Sudan. It broke up in June, 1960. See Senegal.

100 Centimes = 1 Franc

Catalogue values for all unused stamps in this country are for Never Hinged items.

Flag and Map of Mali A1

Unwmk.

1959, Nov. 7 Engr. *Perf. 13*

1	A1	25fr grn, car & dp claret	1.00	.50

Founding of the Federation of Mali.

Imperforates

Most Mali stamps exist imperforate in issued and trial colors, and also in small presentation sheets in issued colors.

Parrotfish A2

Fish: 10fr, Triggerfish. 15fr, Psetta. 20fr, Blepharis crinitus. 25fr, Butterflyfish. 30fr, Surgeonfish. 85fr, Dentex.

1960, Mar. 5

Fish in Natural Colors

2	A2	5fr olive	.40	.20
3	A2	10fr brt grnsh blue	.40	.20
4	A2	15fr dark blue	.55	.20
5	A2	20fr gray green	.90	.40
6	A2	25fr slate green	1.10	.55
7	A2	30fr dark blue	2.00	.90
8	A2	85fr dark green	3.75	2.00
		Nos. 2-8 (7)	9.10	4.45

For overprints see Nos. 10-12.

Common Design Types pictured following the introduction.

C.C.T.A. Issue

Common Design Type

1960, May 21 *Perf. 13*

9	CD106	25fr lt violet & magenta	1.40	.50

REPUBLIC OF MALI

GOVT. — Republic
AREA — 463,500 sq. mi.
POP. — 10,429,124 (1999 est.)
CAPITAL — Bamako

The Republic of Mali, formerly the French Sudan, proclaimed its independence on June 20, 1960, when the Federation of Mali ceased to exist.

Nos. 5, 6 and 8 Overprinted "REPUBLIQUE DU MALI" and Bar

Unwmk.

1961, Jan. 15 Engr. *Perf. 13*

Fish in Natural Colors

10	A2	20fr gray green	1.60	.65
11	A2	25fr slate green	2.00	.65
12	A2	85fr dark green	3.50	1.60
		Nos. 10-12 (3)	7.10	2.90

Pres. Mamadou Konate — A3

Design: 25fr, Pres. Modibo Keita.

1961, Mar. 18

13	A3	20fr green & baclk	.40	.20
14	A3	25fr maroon & black	.50	.20

For miniature sheet see No. C11a.

Reading Class, Bullock Team and Factory — A4

1961, Sept. 22 Unwmk. *Perf. 13*

15	A4	25fr multi	.90	.40

First anniversary of Independence.

Shepherd and Sheep A5

Designs: 1fr, 10fr, 40fr, Cattle. 2fr, 15fr, 50fr, Mali Arts Museum. 3fr, 20fr, 60fr, Plowing. 4fr, 25fr, 85fr, Harvester.

Unwmk.

1961, Dec. 24 Engr. *Perf. 13*

16	A5	50c car rose, blk & dk grn	.20	.20
17	A5	1fr grn, bl & bister	.20	.20
18	A5	2fr ultra, grn & org red	.20	.20
19	A5	3fr bl, grn & brn	.20	.20
20	A5	4fr bl grn, indigo & bis	.20	.20
21	A5	5fr bl, olive & maroon	.20	.20
22	A5	10fr ol blk, bl & sepia	.20	.20
23	A5	15fr ultra, grn & bis brn	.45	.20
24	A5	20fr bl, grn & org red	.45	.20
25	A5	25fr dk bl & yel grn	.50	.20
26	A5	30fr vio, grn & dk brn	.60	.30
27	A5	40fr sl grn, bl & org red	.80	.30
28	A5	50fr ultra, grn & rose car	1.00	.30
29	A5	60fr blue, green & brown	1.25	.30
30	A5	85fr bl, bis & dk red brn	1.90	.45
		Nos. 16-30 (15)	8.35	3.65

King Mohammed V of Morocco and Map of Africa — A6

1962, Jan. 4 Photo. *Perf. 12*

31	A6	25fr multicolored	.45	.20
32	A6	50fr multicolored	.55	.20

1st anniv. of the conference of African heads of state at Casablanca.

Patrice Lumumba A7

1962, Feb. 12 Unwmk. *Perf. 12*

33	A7	25fr choc & brn org	.70	.20
34	A7	100fr choc & emerald	1.00	.45

Issued in memory of Patrice Lumumba, Premier of the Congo (Democratic) Republic.

Pegasus and UPU Monument, Bern — A8

1962, Apr. 21 *Perf. 12½x12*

35	A8	85fr red brn, yel & brt grn	1.75	.75

1st anniv. of Mali's admission to the UPU.

Map of Africa and Post Horn — A8a

1962, Apr. 23 *Perf. 13½x13*

36	A8a	25fr dk red brn & dp grn	.60	.20
37	A8a	85fr dp green & org	1.10	.40

Establishment of African Postal Union.

Sansanding Dam — A9

Cotton Plant A10

1962, Oct. 27 Photo. *Perf. 12*

38	A9	25fr dk gray, ultra & grn	.45	.20
39	A10	45fr multicolored	1.60	.40

Telstar, Earth and Television Set — A10a

1962, Nov. 24 Engr. *Perf. 13*

40	A10a	45fr dk car, vio & brn	1.00	.45
41	A10a	55fr green, vio & ol	1.40	.55

1st television connection of the US and Europe through the Telstar satellite, 7/11-12.

Bull, Chemical Equipment, Chicks — A11

1963, Feb. 23 Unwmk. *Perf. 13*

42	A11	25fr red brn & grnsh bl	.50	.20

Sotuba Zootechnical Institute. See No. C15.

Tractor A12

1963, Mar. 21 Engr.

43	A12	25fr vio bl, dk brn & blk	.65	.20
44	A12	45fr bl grn, red brn & grn	1.10	.30

FAO "Freedom from Hunger" campaign.

High Altitude Balloon and WMO Emblem A13

Winners, 800-meter Race — A14

1963, June 12 Photo. *Perf. 12½*

Green Emblem; Yellow and Black Balloon

45	A13	25fr ultra	.45	.20
46	A13	45fr carmine rose	.80	.30
47	A13	60fr red brown	1.00	.40
		Nos. 45-47 (3)	2.25	.90

Studies of the atmosphere.

1963, Aug. 10 Unwmk. *Perf. 12*

20fr, Acrobatic dancers. 85fr, Soccer.

48	A14	5fr multi	.20	.20
49	A14	10fr multi	.20	.20
50	A14	20fr multi, horiz.	.70	.25
51	A14	85fr multi, horiz.	2.10	.60
		Nos. 48-51 (4)	3.20	1.25

Issued to publicize Youth Week.

Centenary Emblem — A15

Kaempferia Aethiopica — A16

1963, Sept. 1 *Perf. 13½x13*
Emblem in Gray, Yellow and Red

52	A15	5fr lt ol grn & blk	.55	.20
53	A15	10fr yellow & blk	.65	.20
54	A15	85fr red & blk	1.50	.75
		Nos. 52-54 (3)	2.70	1.15

Centenary of the International Red Cross.

1963, Dec. 23 **Unwmk.** *Perf. 13*

Tropical plants: 70fr, Bombax costatum. 100fr, Adenium Honghel.

55	A16	30fr multicolored	.55	.20
56	A16	70fr multicolored	1.75	.45
57	A16	100fr multicolored	3.75	.60
		Nos. 55-57 (3)	6.05	1.25

Plane Spraying, Locust and Village A17

Designs (each inscribed "O.I.C.M.A."): 5fr, Head of locust and map of Africa, vert. 10fr, Locust in flight over map of Mali, vert.

1964, June 15 **Engr.** *Perf. 13*

58	A17	5fr org brn, dl cl & grn	.50	.20
59	A17	10fr org brn, ol & bl grn	.75	.25
60	A17	20fr bis, org brn & yel grn	1.10	.30
		Nos. 58-60 (3)	2.35	.75

Anti-locust campaign.

Soccer Player and Tokyo Stadium — A18

Designs (stadium in background): 10fr, Boxer, vert. 15fr, Runner, vert. 85fr, Hurdler.

1964, June 27 **Unwmk.**

61	A18	5fr red, brt grn & dk pur	.20	.20
62	A18	10fr blk, dl bl & org brn	.35	.20
63	A18	15fr violet & dk red	.55	.25
64	A18	85fr vio, dk brn & sl grn	2.50	1.00
a.		Min. sheet of 4, #61-64	4.50	4.50
		Nos. 61-64 (4)	3.60	1.65

18th Olympic Games, Tokyo, Oct. 10-25.

IQSY Emblem and Eclipse of Sun — A19

1964, July 27 **Engr.** *Perf. 13*

65	A19	45fr multicolored	1.00	.40

International Quiet Sun Year, 1964-65.

Map of Viet Nam A20

Defassa Waterbuck A21

1964, Nov. 2 **Photo.** *Perf. 12x12½*

66	A20	30fr multicolored	.60	.20

Issued to publicize the solidarity of the workers of Mali and those of South Viet Nam.

1965, Apr. 5 **Engr.**

Designs: 5fr, Cape buffalo, horiz. 10fr, Scimitar-horned oryx. 30fr, Leopard, horiz. 90fr, Giraffe.

67	A21	1fr choc, brt bl & grn	.20	.20
68	A21	5fr grn, ocher & choc	.20	.20
69	A21	10fr grn, brt pink & bis brn	.55	.20
70	A21	30fr dk red, grn & choc	1.00	.35
71	A21	90fr bis brn, sl & yel grn	3.00	.75
		Nos. 67-71 (5)	4.95	1.70

Abraham Lincoln A22

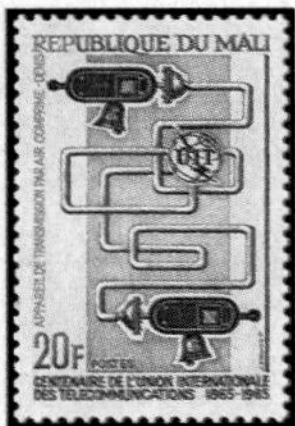

Denis Compressed Air Transmitter A23

1965, Apr. 15 **Photo.** *Perf. 13x12½*

72	A22	45fr black & multi	.75	.50
73	A22	55fr dp green & multi	1.50	.60

Centenary of the death of Lincoln.

1965, May 17 **Engr.** *Perf. 13*

Designs: 30fr, Hughes telegraph system, horiz. 50fr, Lescurre heliograph.

74	A23	20fr orange, blk & bl	.55	.20
75	A23	30fr org, ocher & sl grn	.85	.30
76	A23	50fr org, dk brn & sl grn	1.25	.50
		Nos. 74-76 (3)	2.65	1.00

Centenary of the ITU.

Mother and infants — A24

Designs: 5fr, Mobile X-ray Unit and Lungs. 25fr, Examination of patient at Marchoux Institute and slide. 45fr, Biology laboratory.

1965, July 5 **Unwmk.** *Perf. 13*

77	A24	5fr lake, red & vio	.20	.20
78	A24	10fr brn ol, red & sl grn	.35	.20
79	A24	25fr dk brn, red & grn	.65	.25
80	A24	45fr dk brn, red & sl grn	1.25	.50
		Nos. 77-80 (4)	2.45	1.15

Issued to publicize the Health Service.

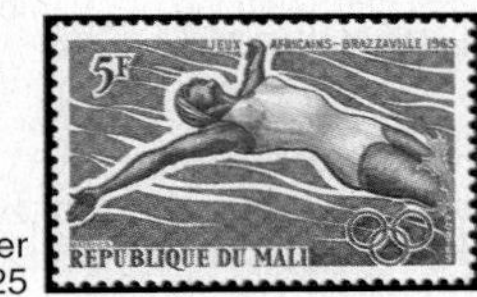

Swimmer A25

1965, July 19 **Engr.**

81	A25	5fr shown	.20	.20
82	A25	15fr Judo	.80	.30

1st African Games, Brazzaville, July 18-25.

Globe, Vase, Quill, Trumpet A26

55fr, Mask, palette and microphones. 90fr, Dancers, mask and printed cloth.

1966, Apr. 4 **Engr.** *Perf. 13*

83	A26	30fr black, red & ocher	.45	.20
84	A26	55fr car rose, emer & blk	1.00	.30
85	A26	90fr ultra, org & dk brn	1.60	.45
		Nos. 83-85 (3)	3.05	.95

International Negro Arts Festival, Dakar, Senegal, Apr. 1-24.

WHO Headquarters, Geneva — A27

1966, May 3 **Photo.** *Perf. 12½x13*

86	A27	30fr org yel, bl & ol grn	.70	.20
87	A27	45fr org yel, bl & dl red	.90	.30

Inauguration of the WHO Headquarters.

Fishermen with Nets — A28

River Fishing: 4fr, 60fr, Group fishing with large net. 20fr, 85fr, Commercial fishing boats.

1966, May 30 **Engr.** *Perf. 13*

88	A28	3fr ultra & brn	.20	.20
89	A28	4fr Prus bl & org brn	.20	.20
90	A28	20fr dk brn, ultra & grn	.55	.20
91	A28	25fr dk brn, bl & brt grn	.70	.20
92	A28	60fr mag, brn & brt grn	1.10	.30
93	A28	85fr dk pur, dl bl & grn	1.60	.60
		Nos. 88-93 (6)	4.35	1.70

Initiation of Pioneers A29

Design: 25fr, Dance and Pioneer emblem.

1966, July 25 **Engr.** *Perf. 13*

94	A29	5fr multicolored	.20	.20
95	A29	25fr multicolored	.80	.25

Issued to honor the pioneers of Mali.

Inoculation of Zebu A30

1967, Jan. 16 **Photo.** *Perf. 12½x13*

96	A30	10fr dp grn, yel grn & brn	.35	.20
97	A30	30fr Prus bl, bl & brn	1.00	.30

Campaign against cattle plague.

View of Timbuktu and Tourist Year Emblem A31

1967, May 15 **Engr.** *Perf. 13*

98	A31	25fr Prus bl, red lil & org	.70	.20

International Tourist Year, 1967.

Ugada Grandicollis A32

Insects: 5fr, Chelorrhina polyphemus, vert. 50fr, Phymateus cinctus.

1967, Aug. 14 **Engr.** *Perf. 13*

99	A32	5fr brt bl, sl grn & brn	.65	.20
100	A32	15fr sl grn, dk brn & red	1.10	.25
101	A32	50fr sl grn, dk brn & dp org	2.75	.45
		Nos. 99-101 (3)	4.50	.90

Teacher and Adult Class A33

1967, Sept. 8 **Photo.** *Perf. 12½x13*

102	A33	50fr black, grn & car	1.00	.25

International Literacy Day, Sept. 8.

Europafrica Issue

Birds, New Buildings and Map A34

1967, Sept. 18 *Perf. 12½x12*

103	A34	45fr multicolored	1.25	.35

Lions Emblem and Crocodile — A35

1967, Oct. 16 **Photo.** *Perf. 13x12½*

104	A35	90fr yellow & multi	1.75	.75

50th anniversary of Lions International.

Water Cycle and UNESCO Emblem A36

1967, Nov. 15 **Photo.** *Perf. 13*

105	A36	25fr multicolored	.70	.20

Hydrological Decade (UNESCO), 1965-74.

WHO Emblem A37

1968, Apr. 8 Engr. *Perf. 13*

106 A37 90fr sl grn, dk car rose & bl 1.40 .40

20th anniv. of the World Health Organization.

Linked Hearts and People A38

1968, Apr. 28 Engr. *Perf. 13*

107 A38 50fr sl grn, red & vio bl .90 .25

International Day of Sister Communities.

Books, Student, Chart, and Map of Africa A39

1968, Aug. 12 Engr. *Perf. 13*

108 A39 100fr carmine, ol & blk 1.25 .40

10th anniv. of the Intl. Assoc. for the Development of Libraries and Archives in Africa.

Michaux bicycle, 1861 A40

Designs: 2fr, Draisienne, 1809. 5fr, De Dion-Bouton automobile, 1894, horiz. 45fr, Panhard & Levassor automobile, 1914, horiz.

1968, Aug. 12

109 A40 2fr grn, olive & magenta .40 .20
110 A40 5fr lemon, indigo & red .75 .20
111 A40 10fr brt grn, indigo & brn 1.25 .20
112 A40 45fr ocher, gray grn & blk 2.25 .30
Nos. 109-112,C60-C61 (6) 8.65 1.90

Tourist Emblem with Map of Africa and Dove A41

1969, May 12 Photo. *Perf. 12½x13*

113 A41 50fr lt ultra, grn & red .70 .20

Year of African Tourism.

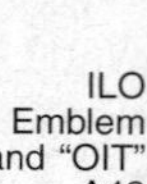

ILO Emblem and "OIT" A42

1969, May 12 Engr. *Perf. 13*

114 A42 50fr vio, slate grn & brt bl .50 .20
115 A42 60fr slate, red & ol brn .90 .25

Intl. Labor Organization, 50th anniv.

Panhard, 1897, and Citroen 24, 1969 — A43

30fr, Citroen, 1923, Citroen DS 21, 1969.

1969, May 30 Engr. *Perf. 13*

116 A43 25fr blk, maroon & lemon .95 .20
117 A43 30fr blk, brt grn & dk grn 1.60 .20
Nos. 116-117,C71-C72 (4) 6.40 1.35

Play Blocks A44

Toys: 10fr, Mule on wheels. 15fr, Ducks. 20fr, Racing car and track.

1969 Photo. *Perf. 12½x13*

118 A44 5fr red, gray & yel .20 .20
119 A44 10fr red, yel & olive .25 .20
120 A44 15fr red, salmon & yel grn .35 .20
121 A44 20fr red, indigo & org .45 .20
Nos. 118-121 (4) 1.25 .80

Intl. Toy Fair in Nuremberg, Germany.

Ram A45

1969, Aug. 18 Engr. *Perf. 13*

122 A45 1fr shown .20 .20
123 A45 2fr Goat .20 .20
124 A45 10fr Donkey .35 .20
125 A45 35fr Horse 1.00 .30
126 A45 90fr Dromedaries 1.75 .50
Nos. 122-126 (5) 3.50 1.40

Development Bank Issue
Common Design Type

1969, Sept. 10

127 CD130 50fr brt lil, grn & ocher .40 .20
128 CD130 90fr ol brn, grn & ocher .85 .20

Boy Being Vaccinated A46

1969, Nov. 10 Engr. *Perf. 13*

129 A46 50fr brn, indigo & brt grn .90 .25

Campaign against smallbox and measles.

ASECNA Issue
Common Design Type

1969, Dec. 12 Engr. *Perf. 13*

130 CD132 100fr dark slate green 1.00 .30

African and Japanese Women A47

150fr, Flags and maps of Mali and Japan.

1970, Apr. 13 Engr. *Perf. 13*

131 A47 100fr brown, bl & ocher 1.00 .30
132 A47 150fr dk red, yel grn & org 1.50 .40

Issued to publicize EXPO '70 International Exhibition, Osaka, Japan, Mar. 15-Sept. 13.

Satellite Telecommunications, Map of Africa and ITU Emblem — A48

1970, May 17 Engr. *Perf. 13*

133 A48 90fr car rose & brn 1.00 .30

World Telecommunications Day.

UPU Headquarters Issue
Common Design Type

1970, May 20 Engr. *Perf. 13*

134 CD133 50fr dk red, bl grn & ol .55 .20
135 CD133 60fr red lil, ultra & red brn .70 .20

Post Office, Bamako A49

Public Buildings: 40fr, Chamber of Commerce, Bamako. 60fr, Public Works Ministry, Bamako. 80fr, City Hall, Segou.

1970, Nov. 23 Engr. *Perf. 13*

136 A49 30fr brn, brt grn & olive .45 .20
137 A49 40fr brn, sl grn & dp claret .55 .20
138 A49 60fr brn red, sl grn & gray .70 .20
139 A49 80fr brn, brt grn & emer 1.00 .25
Nos. 136-139 (4) 2.70 .85

Gallet 030T, 1882 A50

Old Steam Locomotives: 40fr, Felou 030T, 1882. 50fr, Bechevel 230T, 1882. 80fr, Type 231, 1930. 100fr, Type 141, 1930.

1970, Dec. 14 Engr. *Perf. 13*

140 A50 20fr brt grn, dk car & blk 1.75 .50
141 A50 40fr blk, dk grn & ocher 2.25 .60
142 A50 50fr bis brn, bl grn & blk 3.00 .80
143 A50 80fr car rose, blk & bl grn 4.00 1.00
144 A50 100fr ocher, bl grn & blk 6.75 1.60
Nos. 140-144 (5) 17.75 4.50

Scout Sounding Retreat — A51

Bambara Mask, San — A52

Boy Scouts: 5fr, Crossing river, horiz. 100fr, Canoeing, horiz.

Perf. 13x12½, 12½x13

1970, Dec. 28 Litho.

145 A51 5fr multicolored .20 .20
146 A51 30fr multicolored .55 .20
147 A51 100fr multicolored 1.40 .40
Nos. 145-147 (3) 2.15 .80

1971, Jan. 25 Photo. *Perf. 12x12½*

Designs: 25fr, Dogon mask, Bandiagara. 50fr, Kanaga ideogram. 80fr, Bambara ideogram.

148 A52 20fr orange & multi .25 .20
149 A52 25fr brt green & multi .45 .20
150 A52 50fr dk purple & multi .70 .20
151 A52 80fr blue & multi 1.00 .25
Nos. 148-151 (4) 2.40 .85

Boy, Medical and Scientific Symbols A53

1971, Mar. 22 Engr. *Perf. 13*

152 A53 100fr dp car, ocher & grn 1.40 .40

B.C.G. inoculation (Bacillus-Calmette-Guerin) against tuberculosis, 50th anniv.

Boy Scouts, Mt. Fuji, Japanese Print — A54

1971, Apr. 19

153 A54 80fr lt ultra, dp plum & brt grn .90 .25

13th Boy Scout World Jamboree, Asagiri Plain, Japan, Aug. 2-10.

UNICEF Emblem, Hands and Rose A55

60fr, UNICEF emblem, women & children, vert.

1971, May 24 Engr. *Perf. 13*

154 A55 50fr brn org, car & dk brn .55 .20
155 A55 60fr vio bl, grn & red brn .70 .20

25th anniv. of UNICEF.

Mali Farmer — A56

Map of Africa with Communications Network — A57

Costumes of Mali: 10fr, Mali farm woman. 15fr, Tuareg. 60fr, Embroidered robe, Grand Boubou. 80fr, Ceremonial robe, woman.

1971, June 14 Photo. *Perf. 13*

156 A56 5fr gray & multi .20 .20
157 A56 10fr vio bl & multi .35 .20
158 A56 15fr yellow & multi .45 .20
159 A56 60fr gray & multi .70 .20
160 A56 80fr tan & multi 1.00 .30
Nos. 156-160 (5) 2.70 1.10

1971, Aug. 16 Photo. *Perf. 13*

161 A57 50fr bl, vio bl & org .50 .20

Pan-African telecommunications system.

Hibiscus A58

Flowers: 50fr, Poinsettia. 60fr, Adenium obesum. 80fr, Dogbane. 100fr, Satanocrater berhautii.

1971, Oct. 4 Litho. *Perf. 14x13½*

162 A58 20fr multicolored .55 .20
163 A58 50fr multicolored 1.00 .25
164 A58 60fr multicolored 1.40 .30
165 A58 80fr multicolored 1.75 .40
166 A58 100fr multicolored 2.25 .50
Nos. 162-166 (5) 6.95 1.65

For surcharge see No. 204.

Mother, Child and Bird (Sculpture) A59

1971, Dec. 27 Engr. *Perf. 13x12½*

167 A59 70fr mag, sepia & bl grn .90 .25

Natl. Institute of Social Security, 15th anniv.

ITU Emblem A60

1972, May 17 Photo. *Perf. 13x13½*

168 A60 70fr blue, maroon & blk .90 .25

4th World Telecommunications Day.

Clay Funerary Statuette — A61

Mali Art: 40fr, Female torso, wood. 50fr, Masked figure, painted stone. 100fr, Animals and men, wrought iron.

1972, May 29 *Perf. 12½x13*

169 A61 30fr org red & multi .35 .20
170 A61 40fr yellow & multi .55 .20
171 A61 50fr red & multi .70 .20
172 A61 100fr lt green & multi 1.40 .40
Nos. 169-172 (4) 3.00 1.00

Morse and Telegraph A62

1972, June 5 Engr. *Perf. 13*

173 A62 80fr red, emer & choc 1.10 .35

Centenary of the death of Samuel F. B. Morse (1791-1872), inventor of the telegraph.

Weather Balloon over Africa — A63

1972, July 10 Photo. *Perf. 12½x13*

174 A63 130fr multicolored 1.75 .50

12th World Meteorology Day.

Sarakolé Dance, Kayes — A64

People, Book, Pencil — A65

Designs: Folk dances.

1972, Aug. 21 Photo. *Perf. 13*

175 A64 10fr shown .35 .20
176 A64 20fr LaGomba, Bamako .55 .20
177 A64 50fr Hunters' dance, Bougouni .70 .20
178 A64 70fr Koré Duga, Ségou .90 .25
179 A64 80fr Kanaga, Sanga 1.00 .30
180 A64 120fr Targui, Timbuktu 1.60 .40
Nos. 175-180 (6) 5.10 1.55

1972, Sept. 8 Typo. *Perf. 12½x13*

181 A65 80fr black & yel grn .90 .20

World Literacy Day, Sept. 8.

"Edison Classique," Mali Instruments A66

1972, Sept. 18 Engr. *Perf. 13*

182 A66 100fr multicolored 1.25 .35

First Anthology of Music of Mali.

Aries — A67

Signs of the Zodiac: No. 184, Taurus. No. 185, Gemini. No. 186, Cancer. No. 187, Leo. No. 188, Virgo. No. 189, Libra. No. 190, Scorpio. No. 191, Sagittarius. No. 192, Capricorn. No. 193, Aquarius. No. 194, Pisces.

1972, Oct. 23 Engr. *Perf. 11*

183 A67 15fr lilac & bis brn .40 .20
184 A67 15fr bister brn & blk .40 .20
a. Pair #183-184 .80 .40
185 A67 35fr maroon & indigo .65 .20
186 A67 35fr emerald & mar .65 .20
a. Pair ,#185-186 1.40 .40
187 A67 40fr blue & red brn .70 .20
188 A67 40fr dk pur & red brn .70 .20
a. Pair, #187-188 1.40 .40
189 A67 45fr dk blue & mar .80 .30
190 A67 45fr maroon & brt grn .80 .30
a. Pair, #189-180 1.60 .60
191 A67 65fr dk violet & ind 1.00 .35
192 A67 65fr dk vio & gray ol 1.00 .35
a. Pair, #191-192 2.00 .70
193 A67 90fr brt pink & ind 1.60 .60
194 A67 90fr brt pink & grn 1.60 .60
a. Pair, #193-194 3.25 1.25
Nos. 183-194 (12) 10.30 3.70

Arrival of First Locomotive in Bamako, 1906 A68

Designs (Locomotives): 30fr, Thies-Bamako, 1920. 60fr, Thies-Bamako, 1927. 120fr, Two Alsthom BB, 1947.

1972, Dec. 11 Engr. *Perf. 13*

195 A68 10fr ind, brn & sl grn 1.75 .50
196 A68 30fr sl grn, ind & brn 3.50 1.00
197 A68 60fr sl grn, ind & brn 5.25 1.50
198 A68 120fr sl grn & choc 7.25 2.00
Nos. 195-198 (4) 17.75 5.00

2nd African Games, Lagos, Nigeria, Jan. 7-18 — A69

1973, Jan. 15 Photo. *Perf. 12½*

199 A69 70fr High jump .55 .20
200 A69 270fr Discus 1.40 .50
201 A69 280fr Soccer 1.60 .75
Nos. 199-201 (3) 3.55 1.45

INTERPOL Emblem and Headquarters — A70

1973, Feb. 28 Photo. *Perf. 13*

202 A70 80fr multi .90 .20

50th anniversary of International Criminal Police Organization (INTERPOL).

Blind Man and Disabled Boy — A71

Cora — A72

1973, Apr. 24 Engr. *Perf. 12½x13*

203 A71 70fr dk car, brick red & blk .70 .20

Help for the handicapped.

No. 166 Surcharged with New Value, 2 Bars, and Overprinted: "SECHERESSE / SOLIDARITE AFRICAINE"

1973, Aug. 16 Litho. *Perf. 13½*

204 A58 200fr on 100fr multi 2.25 .65

African solidarity in drought emergency.

Perf. 12½x13, 13x12½

1973, Dec. 10 Engr.

Musical Instruments: 10fr, Balafon, horiz. 15fr, Djembe. 20fr, Guitar. 25fr, N'Djarka. 30fr, M'Bolon. 35fr, Dozo N'Goni. 40fr, N'Tamani.

205 A72 5fr mar, dk grn & brn .35 .20
206 A72 10fr bl & choc .45 .20
207 A72 15fr brn, dk red & yel .55 .20
208 A72 20fr mar & brn ol .65 .20
209 A72 25fr org, yel & blk .70 .20
210 A72 30fr vio bl & blk .80 .20
211 A72 35fr dk red & brn .90 .35
212 A72 40fr dk red & choc 1.10 .35
Nos. 205-212 (8) 5.50 1.90

Farmer with Newspaper, Corn — A73

Soccer, Goalkeeper, Symbolic Globe and Net — A74

1974, Mar. 11 Engr. *Perf. 12½x13*

213 A73 70fr multi .70 .20

"Kibaru," rural newspaper, 2nd anniv.

1974, May 6 Engr. *Perf. 13*

280fr, Games' emblem, soccer and ball.

214 A74 270fr multi 2.00 .90
215 A74 280fr multi 2.25 .90

World Cup Soccer Championships, Munich, June 13-July 7.

For surcharges see Nos. 219-220.

Old and New Ships, UPU Emblem — A75

Artisans of Mali — A76

90fr, Old and new planes, UPU emblem. 270fr, Old and new trains, UPU emblem.

1974, June 2 Engr. *Perf. 12½x13*

216 A75 80fr brn & multir .55 .25
217 A75 90fr ultra & multi .80 .30
218 A75 270fr lt grn & multi 2.25 .75
Nos. 216-218 (3) 3.60 1.30

Centenary of Universal Postal Union.

For surcharges see Nos. 229-230.

Nos. 214-215 Surcharged and Overprinted in Black or Red: "R.F.A. 2 / HOLLANDE 1"

1974, Aug. 28 Engr. *Perf. 13*

219 A74 300fr on 270fr multi 2.50 .90
220 A74 330fr on 280fr multi (R) 2.75 .90

World Cup Soccer Championship, 1974, victory of German Federal Republic.

1974, Sept. 16 Photo. ***Perf. 12½x13***

221 A76 50fr Weaver .55 .20
222 A76 60fr Potter .65 .20
223 A76 70fr Smiths .70 .20
224 A76 80fr Sculptor .80 .25
Nos. 221-224 (4) 2.70 .85

Niger River near Gao — A77

Landscapes: 20fr, The Hand of Fatma (rock formation), vert. 40fr, Gouina Waterfall. 70fr, Dogon houses, vert.

Perf. 13x12½, 12½x13

1974, Sept. 23

225 A77 10fr multi .20 .20
226 A77 20fr multi .25 .20
227 A77 40fr multi .55 .20
228 A77 70fr multi .80 .30
Nos. 225-228 (4) 1.80 .90

Nos. 216 and 218 Surcharged and Overprinted in Black or Red: "9 OCTOBRE 1974"

1974, Oct. 9 Engr. ***Perf. 13***

229 A75 250fr on 80fr multi 2.00 .90
230 A75 300fr on 270fr multi (R) 2.50 .90

UPU Day.

Mao Tse-tung, Flags, Great Wall — A78

1974, Oct. 21 Engr. ***Perf. 13***

231 A78 100fr multi 2.25 .55

People's Republic of China, 25th anniv.

Artisans and Lions Emblem — A79

100fr, View of Samanko and Lions emblem.

1975, Feb. 3 Photo. ***Perf. 13***

232 A79 90fr red & multi .70 .20
233 A79 100fr blue & multi .90 .25

5th anniv. of lepers' rehabilitation village, Samanko, sponsored by Lions Intl.

For surcharges see Nos. 303-304.

Tetrodon Fahaka A80

Designs: Fish.

1975, May 12 Engr. ***Perf. 13***

234 A80 60fr *shown* 1.10 .30
235 A80 70fr *Malopterurus electricus* 1.25 .35
236 A80 80fr *Citharinus latus* 1.50 .40
237 A80 90fr *Hydrocyon forskali* 1.75 .45
238 A80 110fr *Lates niloticus* 2.25 .50
Nos. 234-238 (5) 7.85 2.00

See Nos. 256-260.

Woman and IWY Emblem — A81

1975, June 9 Engr. ***Perf. 13***

239 A81 150fr red & grn 1.25 .35

International Women's Year 1975.

Morris "Oxford," 1913 A82

Automobiles: 130fr, Franklin "E," 1907. 190fr, Daimler, 1900. 230fr, Panhard & Levassor, 1895.

1975, June 16

240 A82 90fr blk, ol & lil .75 .30
241 A82 130fr vio bl, gray & red 1.25 .35
242 A82 190fr bl, grn & indigo 1.75 .50
243 A82 230fr red, ultra & brn ol 2.00 .50
Nos. 240-243 (4) 5.75 1.65

Carthaginian Tristater, 500 B.C. — A83

Ancient Coins: 170fr, Decadrachma, Syracuse, 413 B.C. 190fr, Acanthe tetradrachma, 400 B.C. 260fr, Didrachma, Eritrea, 480-445 B.C.

1975, Oct. 13 Engr. ***Perf. 13***

244 A83 130fr bl, cl & blk .70 .25
245 A83 170fr emer, brn & blk 1.00 .45
246 A83 190fr grn, red & blk 1.40 .65
247 A83 260fr dp bl, org & blk 2.00 .90
Nos. 244-247 (4) 5.10 2.25

UN Emblem and "ONU" — A84

1975, Nov. 10 Engr. ***Perf. 13***

248 A84 200fr emer & brt bl 1.25 .45

30th anniversary of UN.

A. G. Bell, Waves, Satellite, Telephone — A85

1976, Mar. 8 Litho. ***Perf. 12x12½***

249 A85 180fr brn, ultra & ocher 1.25 .35

Centenary of first telephone call by Alexander Graham Bell, Mar. 10, 1876.

Chameleon A86

1976, Mar. 31 Litho. ***Perf. 12½***

250 A86 20fr shown .35 .20
251 A86 30fr Lizard .55 .20
252 A86 40fr Tortoise .70 .20
253 A86 90fr Python 1.60 .45
254 A86 120fr Crocodile 2.10 .60
Nos. 250-254 (5) 5.30 1.65

Konrad Adenauer and Cologne Cathedral — A87

1976, Apr. 26 Engr. ***Perf. 13***

255 A87 180fr mag & dk brn 1.40 .40

Konrad Adenauer (1876-1967), German Chancellor.

Fish Type of 1975

1976, June 28 Engr. ***Perf. 13***

256 A80 100fr *Heterotis niloticus* .75 .20
257 A80 120fr *Synodontis budgetti* 1.00 .20
258 A80 130fr *Heterobranchus bidorsalis* 1.00 .25
259 A80 150fr *Tilapia monodi* 1.25 .35
260 A80 220fr *Alestes macrolepidotus* 1.75 .45
Nos. 256-260 (5) 5.75 1.45

Page from Children's Book — A88

"Le Roi de l'Air" — A89

1976, July 19

261 A88 130fr red & multi .90 .30

Books for children.

1976, July 26 Litho. ***Perf. 12½x13***

262 A89 120fr multi 1.40 .40

First lottery, sponsored by L'Essor newspaper.

"Do not overload scaffold" — A90

1976, Aug. 16 Litho. ***Perf. 13***

263 A90 120fr multi .70 .20

National Insurance Institute, 20th anniv.

Letters, UPU and UN Emblems — A91

1976, Oct. 4 Engr. ***Perf. 13***

264 A91 120fr lil, org & grn .90 .30

UN Postal Administration, 25th anniv.

Moto-Guzzi 254, Italy — A92

Motorcycles: 120fr, BMW 900, Germany. 130fr, Honda-Egli, Japan. 140fr, Motobecane LT-3, France.

1976, Oct. 18 Engr. ***Perf. 13***

265 A92 90fr multi 1.00 .20
266 A92 120fr multi 1.25 .25
267 A92 130fr multi 1.25 .35
268 A92 140fr multi 1.50 .35
Nos. 265-268 (4) 5.00 1.15

Fishing Boat, Masgat — A93

180fr, Coaster, Cochin China. 190fr, Fireboat, Dunkirk, 1878. 200fr, Nile river boat.

1976, Dec. 6 Engr. ***Perf. 13***

269 A93 160fr multi .80 .30
270 A93 180fr multi .90 .30
271 A93 190fr multi 1.00 .35
272 A93 200fr multi 1.00 .45
Nos. 269-272 (4) 3.70 1.40

Indigo Finch A94

Birds: 25fr, Yellow-breasted barbet. 30fr, Vitelline masked weaver. 40fr, Bee-eater. 50fr, Senegal parrot.

1977, Apr. 18 Photo. *Perf. 13*

273	A94	15fr multi	.25	.20
274	A94	25fr multi	.45	.20
275	A94	30fr multi	.55	.20
276	A94	40fr multi	.70	.25
277	A94	50fr multi	.90	.30
		Nos. 273-277 (5)	2.85	1.15

See Nos. 298-302.

Braille Statue, Script and Reading Hands — A95

1977, Apr. 25 Engr. *Perf. 13*

278 A95 200fr multi 1.40 .45

Louis Braille (1809-1852), inventor of the reading and writing system for the blind.

Electronic Tree, ITU Emblem — A96

1977, May 17 Photo.

279 A96 120fr dk brn & org .50 .20

World Telecommunications Day.

Dragonfly A97

Insects: 10fr, Praying mantis. 20fr, Tropical wasp. 35fr, Cockchafer. 60fr, Flying stag beetle.

1977, June 15 Photo. *Perf. 13x12½*

280	A97	5fr multi	.35	.20
281	A97	10fr multi	.45	.20
282	A97	20fr multi	.55	.20
283	A97	35fr multi	.80	.20
284	A97	60fr multi	1.00	.25
		Nos. 280-284 (5)	3.15	1.05

Knight and Rook A98

Chess Pieces: 130fr, Bishop and pawn, vert. 300fr, Queen and King.

1977, June 27 Engr. *Perf. 13*

285	A98	120fr multi	1.60	.40
286	A98	130fr multi	1.75	.50
287	A98	300fr multi	3.75	1.10
		Nos. 285-287 (3)	7.10	2.00

Europafrica Issue

Symbolic Ship, White and Brown Persons — A99

1977, July 18 Litho. *Perf. 13*

288 A99 400fr multi 2.50 .70

Horse, by Leonardo da Vinci A100

Drawings by Leonardo da Vinci: 300fr, Head of Young Woman. 500fr, Self-portrait.

1977, Sept. 5 Engr. *Perf. 13*

289	A100	200fr dk brn & blk	1.25	.55
290	A100	300fr dk brn & ol	1.75	.55
291	A100	500fr dk brn & red	2.75	.90
		Nos. 289-291 (3)	5.75	2.00

Hotel de l'Amitié, Bamako — A101

1977, Oct. 15 Litho. *Perf. 13x12½*

292 A101 120fr multi .70 .20

Opening of the Hotel de l'Amitié, Oct. 15.

Dome of the Rock Jerusalem A102

1977, Oct. 17 *Perf. 12½*

293	A102	120fr multi	.90	.20
294	A102	180fr multi	1.10	.30

Palestinian fighters and their families.

Black Man, Chains and UN Emblem A103

130fr, Statue of Liberty, people & UN emblem. 180fr, Black children & horse behind fence.

1978, Mar. 13 Engr. *Perf. 13*

295	A103	120fr multi	.65	.20
296	A103	130fr multi	.70	.20
297	A103	180fr multi	1.10	.35
		Nos. 295-297 (3)	2.45	.75

International Year against Apartheid.

Bird Type of 1977

Birds: 20fr, Granatine bengala. 30fr, Lagonosticta vinacea. 50fr, Lagonosticta. 70fr, Turtle dove. 80fr, Buffalo weaver.

1978, Apr. 10 Litho. *Perf. 13*

298	A94	20fr multi	.65	.20
299	A94	30fr multi	.80	.20
300	A94	50fr multi	1.00	.25
301	A94	70fr multi	1.50	.35
302	A94	80fr multi	2.00	.45
		Nos. 298-302 (5)	5.95	1.45

Nos. 232-233 Surcharged with New Value, Bar and: "XXe ANNIVERSAIRE DU LIONS CLUB DE BAMAKO 1958-1978"

1978, May 8 Photo.

303	A79	120fr on 90fr multi	.80	.20
304	A79	130fr on 100fr multi	1.00	.20

20th anniversary of Bamako Lions Club.

Wall and Desert — A105

1978, May 18 Litho. *Perf. 13*

306 A105 200fr multi 1.25 .35

Hammamet Conference for reclamation of the desert.

Mahatma Gandhi and Roses — A106

1978, May 29 Engr.

307 A106 140fr blk, brn & red 1.50 .25

Mohandas K. Gandhi (1869-1948), Hindu spiritual leader.

Dermestes — A107

Insects: 25fr, Ground beetle. 90fr, Cricket. 120fr, Ladybird. 140fr, Goliath beetle.

1978, June 12 Photo. *Perf. 13*

308	A107	15fr multi	.55	.20
309	A107	25fr multi	.70	.20
310	A107	90fr multi	1.25	.20
311	A107	120fr multi	1.25	.25
312	A107	140fr multi	1.75	.30
		Nos. 308-312 (5)	5.50	1.15

Bridge — A108

Design: 100fr, Dominoes, vert.

1978, June 26 Engr.

313	A108	100fr multi	.90	.20
314	A108	130fr multi	1.25	.30

Aristotle — A109

1978, Oct. 16 Engr. *Perf. 13*

315 A109 200fr multi 1.40 .30

Aristotle (384-322 B.C.), Greek philosopher.

Human Rights and UN Emblems — A110

1978, Dec. 11 Engr. *Perf. 13*

316 A110 180fr red, bl & brn 1.25 .25

Universal Declaration of Human Rights, 30th anniversary.

Manatee — A111

Endangered Wildlife: 120fr, Chimpanzee. 130fr, Damaliscus antelope. 180fr, Oryx. 200fr, Derby's eland.

1979, Apr. 23 Litho. *Perf. 12½*

317	A111	100fr multi	.90	.20
318	A111	120fr multi	1.00	.20
319	A111	130fr multi	1.10	.20
320	A111	180fr multi	1.60	.30
321	A111	200fr multi	1.75	.30
		Nos. 317-321 (5)	6.35	1.20

Boy Praying and IYC Emblem — A112

IYC emblem and: 200fr, Girl and Boy Scout holding bird. 300fr, IYC emblem, boys with calf.

1979, May 7 Engr. *Perf. 13*

322	A112	120fr multi	.70	.20
323	A112	200fr multi	1.00	.30
324	A112	300fr multi	1.75	.45
		Nos. 322-324 (3)	3.45	.95

International Year of the Child.

Judo and Notre Dame, Paris — A113

1979, May 14 Engr. *Perf. 13*

325 A113 200fr multi 1.40 .40

World Judo Championship, Paris.

Telecommunications A114

Wood Carving A115

1979, May 17 **Litho.**

326 A114 120fr multi .70 .20

11th Telecommunications Day.

1979, May 18 ***Perf. 13x12½***

Sculptures from National Museum: 120fr, Ancestral figures. 130fr, Animal heads, and kneeling woman.

327 A115 90fr multi .55 .20
328 A115 120fr multi .70 .20
329 A115 130fr multi .90 .25
Nos. 327-329 (3) 2.15 .65

International Museums Day.

Rowland Hill and Mali No. 15 — A116

130fr, Zeppelin & Saxony #1. 180fr, Concorde & France #3. 200fr, Stagecoach & US #2. 300fr, UPU emblem & Penny Black.

1979, May 21 **Engr.** ***Perf. 13***

330 A116 120fr multi .65 .20
331 A116 130fr multi .70 .20
332 A116 180fr multi .90 .30
333 A116 200fr multi 1.00 .30
334 A116 300fr multi 1.75 .55
Nos. 330-334 (5) 5.00 1.55

Sir Rowland Hill (1795-1879), originator of penny postage.

Cora Players — A117

1979, June 4 **Litho.** ***Perf. 13***

335 A117 200fr multi 1.75 .45

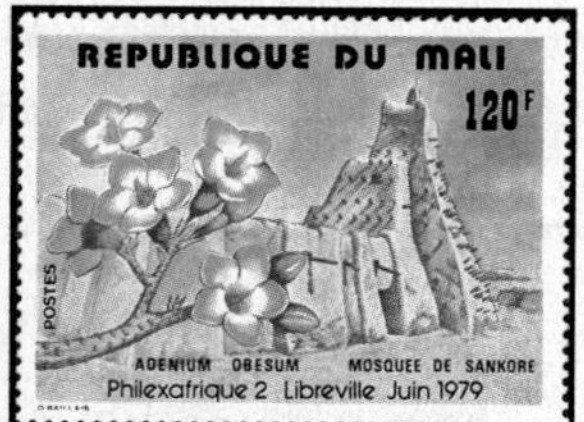

Adenium Obesum and Sankore Mosque — A118

Design: 300fr, Satellite, mounted messenger, globe and letter, vert.

1979, June 8 **Photo.**

336 A118 120fr multi 1.75 .65

Engr.

337 A118 300fr multi 3.00 1.40

Philexafrique II, Libreville, Gabon, June 8-17. Nos. 336, 337 printed in sheets of 10 and 5 labels showing exhibition emblem.

Map of Mali — A119

Design: 300fr, Men planting trees.

1979, June 18 **Litho.** ***Perf. 13x12½***

338 A119 200fr multi 1.25 .35
339 A119 300fr multi 2.00 .60

Operation Green Sahel.

Lemons — A120

Sigmund Freud — A121

1979, June 25 ***Perf. 12½x13***

340 A120 10fr shown .25 .20
341 A120 60fr Pineapple .55 .20
342 A120 100fr Papayas .90 .20
343 A120 120fr Soursops 1.00 .20
344 A120 130fr Mangoes 1.10 .25
Nos. 340-344 (5) 3.80 1.05

1979, Sept. 17 **Engr.** ***Perf. 13***

345 A121 300fr vio bl & sepia 1.75 .55

Sigmund Freud (1856-1939), founder of psychoanalysis.

Timbuktu, Man and Camel A122

Design: 130fr, Caillié, Map of Sahara.

1979, Sept. 27 ***Perf. 13x12½***

346 A122 120fr multi .90 .25
347 A122 130fr multi 1.00 .30

René Caillié (1799-1838), French explorer, 180th birth anniversary.

Eurema Brigitta A123

1979, Oct. 15 **Litho.** ***Perf. 13***

348 A123 100fr *shown* 1.60 .20
349 A123 120fr *Papilio pylades* 1.75 .25
350 A123 130fr *Melanitis leda satyridae* 2.25 .30
351 A123 180fr *Gonimbrasia belina occidentalis* 2.75 .40
352 A123 200fr *Bunaea alcinoe* 3.00 .45
Nos. 348-352 (5) 11.35 1.60

Greyhound A124

Designs: Dogs.

1979, Nov. 12 **Litho.** ***Perf. 12½***

353 A124 20fr multi .35 .20
354 A124 50fr multi .45 .20
355 A124 70fr multi .55 .20
356 A124 80fr multi .65 .20
357 A124 90fr multi .70 .25
Nos. 353-357 (5) 2.70 1.05

Wild Donkey — A125

1980, Feb. 4 **Litho.** ***Perf. 13x13½***

358 A125 90fr shown .70 .20
359 A125 120fr Addax .90 .20
360 A125 130fr Cheetahs 1.00 .25
361 A125 140fr Mouflon 1.00 .30
362 A125 180fr Buffalo 1.60 .30
Nos. 358-362 (5) 5.20 1.25

Photovoltaic Cell Pumping Station, Koni — A126

Solar Energy Utilization: 100fr, Sun shields, Dire. 120fr, Solar stove, Bamako. 130fr, Heliodynamic solar energy generating station, Dire.

1980, Mar. 10 **Litho.** ***Perf. 13***

363 A126 90fr multi .45 .20
364 A126 100fr multi .55 .20
365 A126 120fr multi .65 .20
366 A126 130fr multi .80 .20
Nos. 363-366 (4) 2.45 .80

For surcharge see No. 511.

Horse Breeding, Mopti A127

1980, Mar. 17

367 A127 100fr shown .80 .20
368 A127 120fr Nioro .90 .20
369 A127 130fr Koro 1.00 .20
370 A127 180fr Coastal zone 1.25 .30
371 A127 200fr Banamba 1.25 .55
Nos. 367-371 (5) 5.20 1.45

Alexander Fleming (Discoverer of Penicillin) A128

1980, May 5 **Engr.** ***Perf. 13***

372 A128 200fr multi 1.50 .45

Avicenna and Medical Instruments A129

Design: 180fr, Avicenna as teacher (12th century manuscript illustration)

1980, May 12 ***Perf. 13x12½***

373 A129 120fr multi .60 .20
374 A129 180fr multi .75 .30

Avicenna (980-1037), Arab physician and philosopher, 1000th birth anniversary.

Pilgrim at Mecca — A130

Guavas — A131

1980, May 26 **Litho.** ***Perf. 13***

375 A130 120fr shown .55 .20
376 A130 130fr Praying hands, stars, Mecca .55 .20
377 A130 180fr Pilgrims, camels, horiz. .80 .30
Nos. 375-377 (3) 1.90 .70

Hegira, 1500th Anniversary.

1980, June 9

378 A131 90fr shown .65 .20
379 A131 120fr Cashews .70 .20
380 A131 130fr Oranges .80 .20
381 A131 140fr Bananas 1.00 .25
382 A131 180fr Grapefruit 1.10 .30
Nos. 378-382 (5) 4.25 1.15

League of Nations, 60th Anniversary A132

1980, June 23 **Engr.** ***Perf. 13***

383 A132 200fr multi .90 .30

Festival Emblem, Mask, Xylophone A133

1980, July 5 **Litho.** ***Perf. 12½***

384 A133 120fr multi .60 .20

6th Biennial Arts and Cultural Festival, Bamako, July 5-15.

Sun Rising over Map of Africa — A134

1980, July 7 Engr. *Perf. 13*

385	A134	300fr multi	1.25	.45

Afro-Asian Bandung Conference, 25th anniversary.

Market Place, Conference Emblem A135

1980, Sept. 15 Litho. *Perf. 13*

386	A135	120fr View of Mali, vert.	.65	.20
387	A135	180fr shown	1.00	.30

World Tourism Conf., Manila, Sept. 27.

Hydro-electric Dam and Power Station — A136

20th Anniversary of Independence: 120fr, Pres. Traore, flag of Mali, National Assembly building. 130fr, Independence monument, Bamako, Political Party badge, vert.

1980, Sept. 15 *Perf. 13x12½*

388	A136	100fr multi	.55	.20
389	A136	120fr multi	.70	.20
390	A136	130fr multi	.90	.25
		Nos. 388-390 (3)	2.15	.65

Utetheisa Pulchella A137

1980, Oct. 6 *Perf. 13½*

391	A137	50fr *shown*	1.10	.20
392	A137	60fr *Mylothis chloris pieridae*	1.25	.20
393	A137	70fr *Hypolimnas misippus*	1.40	.25
394	A137	80fr *Papilio demodocus*	1.75	.30
		Nos. 391-394,C402 (5)	11.50	1.95

Fight Against Cigarette Smoking — A138

1980, Oct. 13 Litho. *Perf. 12½x12*

395	A138	200fr multi	1.25	.40

European-African Economic Convention — A139

1980, Oct. 20 *Perf. 12½*

396	A139	300fr multi	2.25	.55

Agricultural Map of West Africa A140

West African Economic Council, 5th anniversary (Economic Maps): 120fr, Transportation. 130fr, Industry. 140fr, Communications.

1980, Nov. 5 *Perf. 13½x13*

397	A140	100fr multi	.55	.20
398	A140	120fr multi	.65	.20
399	A140	130fr multi	.70	.20
400	A140	140fr multi	.80	.25
		Nos. 397-400 (4)	2.70	.85

African Postal Union, 5th Anniv. — A141

Senuofo Fertility Statue — A142

1980, Dec. 24 Photo. *Perf. 13½*

401	A141	130fr multi	.90	.25

1981, Jan. 12 Litho. *Perf. 13*

Designs: Fertility statues.

402	A142	60fr Nomo dogon	.35	.20
403	A142	70fr shown	.45	.20
404	A142	90fr Bamanan	.65	.20
405	A142	100fr Spirit	.70	.20
406	A142	120fr Dogon	.90	.25
		Nos. 402-406 (5)	3.05	1.05

Mambi Sidibe — A143

Hegira (Pilgrimage Year) — A144

Designs: Philosophers.

1981, Feb. 16 *Perf. 12½x13*

407	A143	120fr shown	.70	.20
408	A143	130fr Amadou Hampate	.70	.20

1981, Feb. 23 *Perf. 13*

409	A144	120fr multi	.65	.20
410	A144	180fr multi	1.10	.30

Maure Zebu A145

Designs: Cattle breeds.

1981, Mar. 9 *Perf. 12½*

411	A145	20fr Kaarta zebu	.70	.20
412	A145	30fr Peul du Macina zebu	.85	.20
413	A145	40fr Maure zebu	1.10	.20
414	A145	80fr Touareg zebu	1.60	.25
415	A145	100fr N'Dama cow	1.75	.30
		Nos. 411-415 (5)	6.00	1.15

See Nos. 433-437.

Hibiscus Double Rose — A146

Designs: Flowers.

1981, Mar. 16

416	A146	50fr Crinum de Moore	.45	.20
417	A146	100fr Double Rose Hibiscus	.90	.20
418	A146	120fr Pervenche	1.10	.20
419	A146	130fr Frangipani	1.25	.25
420	A146	180fr Orgueil de Chine	1.75	.45
		Nos. 416-420 (5)	5.45	1.30

See Nos. 442-446.

Wrench Operated by Artificial Hand A147

Perf. 13x12½, 12x13

1981, May 4 Engr.

421	A147	100fr Heads, vert.	.65	.20
422	A147	120fr shown	.70	.20

Intl. Year of the Disabled.

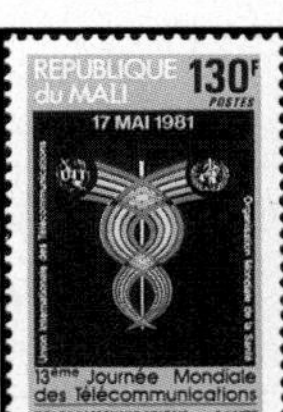

13th World Telecommunications Day — A148

1981, May 17 Litho. *Perf. 13x12½*

423	A148	130fr multi	1.00	.20

Pierre Curie, Lab Equipment A149

1981, May 25 Engr.

424	A149	180fr multi	2.25	.50

Curie (1859-1906), discoverer of radium.

Scouts at Water Hole — A150

1981, June 8 Litho. *Perf. 13*

425	A150	110fr shown	1.50	.25
426	A150	160fr Sending signals	2.25	.40
427	A150	300fr Salute, vert.	4.00	.60
		Nos. 425-427 (3)	7.75	1.25

Souvenir Sheet

428	A150	500fr Lord Baden-Powell	8.50	5.00

4th African Scouting Conf., Abidjan, June.

Nos. 425-428 Overprinted in Red in 2 or 3 Lines: "DAKAR 8 AOUT 1981/28e CONFERENCE MONDIALE DU SCOUTISME"

1981, June 29

429	A150	110fr multi	1.50	.25
430	A150	160fr multi	2.25	.40
431	A150	300fr multi	4.00	.60
		Nos. 429-431 (3)	7.75	1.25

Souvenir Sheet

432	A150	500fr multi	8.50	5.00

28th World Scouting Conf., Dakar, Aug. 8.

Cattle Type of 1981

Various goats.

1981, Sept. 14 Litho. *Perf. 13x13½*

433	A145	10fr Maure	.25	.20
434	A145	25fr Peul	.35	.20
435	A145	140fr Sahel	1.25	.20
436	A145	180fr Tuareg	1.60	.25
437	A145	200fr Djallonke	1.90	.30
		Nos. 433-437 (5)	5.35	1.15

World UPU Day — A151

1981, Oct. 9 Engr. *Perf. 13*

438	A151	400fr multi	3.00	.60

World Food Day — A152

1981, Oct. 16

439	A152	200fr multi	1.50	.35

Europafrica Economic Convention — A153

1981, Nov. 23 Engr. *Perf. 13*

440	A153	700fr multi	4.00	.95

60th Anniv. of Tuberculosis Inoculation — A154

1981, Dec. 7 *Perf. 13x12½*
441 A154 200fr multi 1.50 .45

Flower Type of 1981

1982, Jan. 18 **Litho.** *Perf. 13*
442 A146 170fr White water lilies 1.10 .20
443 A146 180fr Red kapok bush 1.10 .20
444 A146 200fr Purple mimosa 1.40 .25
445 A146 220fr Pobego lilies 1.40 .35
446 A146 270fr Satan's chalices 1.75 .45
Nos. 442-446 (5) 6.75 1.45

Ceremonial Mask — A155

25th Anniv. of Sputnik I Flight — A156

Designs: Various masks.

1982, Feb. 22 **Litho.** *Perf. 12½*
447 A155 5fr multi .20 .20
448 A155 35fr multi .30 .20
449 A155 180fr multi 1.25 .30
450 A155 200fr multi 1.40 .35
451 A155 250fr multi 1.75 .35
Nos. 447-451 (5) 4.90 1.40

1982, Mar. 29 **Litho.** *Perf. 13*
452 A156 270fr multi 1.60 .40

Fight Against Polio — A157

1982, May 3
453 A157 180fr multi 1.10 .30

Lions Intl. and Day of the Blind A158

1982, May 10 **Engr.**
454 A158 260fr multi 1.60 .25

"Good Friends" Hairstyle — A159

Designs: Various hairstyles.

1982, May 24 **Litho.**
455 A159 140fr multi .60 .20
456 A159 150fr multi .80 .20
457 A159 160fr multi 1.10 .30
458 A159 180fr multi 1.50 .30
459 A159 270fr multi 2.25 .55
Nos. 455-459 (5) 6.25 1.55

Zebu A160

Designs: Various breeds of zebu.

1982, July 5 *Perf. 12½*
460 A160 10fr multi .45 .20
461 A160 60fr multi .90 .20
462 A160 110fr multi 1.25 .20
463 A160 180fr multi 2.00 .30
464 A160 200fr multi 2.25 .35
Nos. 460-464 (5) 6.85 1.25

Wind Surfing (New Olympic Class) — A161

Pres. John F. Kennedy — A162

Designs: Various wind surfers.

1982, Nov. 22 **Litho.** *Perf. 12½x13*
465 A161 200fr multi 1.25 .30
466 A161 270fr multi 1.75 .45
467 A161 300fr multi 2.00 .55
Nos. 465-467 (3) 5.00 1.30

1983, Apr. 4 **Engr.** *Perf. 13*
468 A162 800fr shown 4.25 1.10
469 A162 800fr Martin Luther King 4.25 1.10

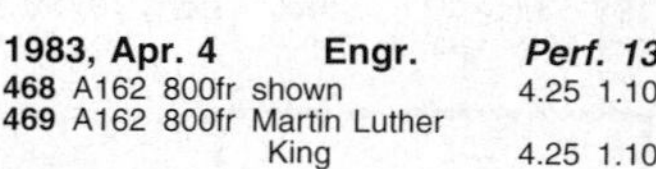

Oua Traditional Hairstyle — A163

1983, Apr. 25 **Litho.**
470 A163 180fr shown 1.25 .20
471 A163 200fr Nation 1.40 .20
472 A163 270fr Rond point 1.75 .30
473 A163 300fr Naamu-Naamu 2.00 .35
474 A163 500fr Bamba-Bamba 3.50 .60
Nos. 470-474 (5) 9.90 1.65

World Communications Year — A164

1983, May 17 **Litho.** *Perf. 13*
475 A164 180fr multi 1.25 .35

Bicent. of Lavoisier's Water Analysis — A165

Musicians — A166

1983, May 27 **Engr.** *Perf. 13*
476 A165 300fr multi 1.75 .45

1983, June 13 **Litho.** *Perf. 13x13½*
477 A166 200fr Banzoumana Sissoko 1.00 .20
478 A166 300fr Batourou Sekou Kouyate 1.60 .30

Nicephore Niepce, Photography Pioneer, (1765-1833) A167

1983, July 4 **Engr.** *Perf. 13*
479 A167 400fr Portrait, early camera 2.25 .40

2nd Pan African Youth Festival — A168

Palestinian Solidarity A169

14th World UPU Day — A170

1983, Aug. 22 **Litho.** *Perf. 12½*
480 A168 240fr multi 1.50 .25
481 A169 270fr multi 1.75 .35

1983, Oct. 10 **Engr.** *Perf. 12½*
482 A170 240fr multi 1.50 .30

For surcharge see No. 500.

Sahel Goat A171

1984, Jan. 30 **Litho.** *Perf. 13*
483 A171 20fr shown .25 .20
484 A171 30fr Billy goat .45 .20
485 A171 50fr Billy goat, diff. .70 .20
486 A171 240fr Kaarta goat 2.25 .30
487 A171 350fr Southern goats 3.25 .45
Nos. 483-487 (5) 6.90 1.35

For surcharges see Nos. 497-499, 501-502.

Rural Development A172

Fragrant Trees A173

1984, June 1 **Litho.** *Perf. 13*
488 A172 5fr Crop disease prevention .25 .20
489 A172 90fr Carpenters, horiz. 1.00 .20
490 A172 100fr Tapestry weaving, horiz. 1.10 .25
491 A172 135fr Metal workers, horiz. 1.40 .40
Nos. 488-491 (4) 3.75 1.05

1984, June 1
492 A173 515fr Borassus flabelifer 5.00 1.75
493 A173 1225fr Vitelaria paradoxa 12.00 3.50

For surcharge see No. 583.

UN Infant Survival Campaign — A174

1984, June 12 **Engr.**
494 A174 120fr Child, hearts 1.50 .35
495 A174 135fr Children 1.75 .40

1984 UPU Congress — A175

1984, June 18

496 A175 135fr Anchor, UPU emblem, view of Hamburg 1.60 .35

Nos. 482-487 Surcharged

1984

497 A171 10fr on 20fr #483 .30 .20
498 A171 15fr on 30fr #484 .30 .20
499 A171 25fr on 50fr #485 .40 .20
500 A170 120fr on 240fr #482 1.60 .30
501 A171 120fr on 240fr #486 2.00 .30
502 A171 175fr on 350fr #487 2.75 .50
Nos. 497-502 (6) 7.35 1.70

West African Economic Community, CEAO, 10th Anniv. A176

1984, Oct. 22 **Litho.** ***Perf. 13½***

503 A176 350fr multi 3.50 1.75

For surcharge see No. 588.

Prehistoric Animals A177

1984, Nov. 5 **Litho.** ***Perf. 12½***

504 A177 10fr Dimetrodon .25 .20
505 A177 25fr Iguanodon, vert. .55 .20
506 A177 30fr Archaeopteryx, vert. .80 .20
507 A177 120fr Like 10fr 2.50 .40
508 A177 175fr Like 25fr 4.00 .60
509 A177 350fr Like 30fr 7.50 1.50
510 A177 470fr Triceratops 11.00 4.00
Nos. 504-510 (7) 26.60 7.10

For surcharges see Nos. 579, 593.

No. 366 Overprinted "Aide au Sahel 84" and Surcharged

1984 **Litho.** ***Perf. 13***

511 A126 470fr on 130fr 6.00 2.00

Issued to publicize drought relief efforts.

Mali Horses A178

1985, Jan. 21 **Litho.** ***Perf. 13½***

512 A178 90fr Modern horse 1.25 .30
513 A178 135fr Horse from Beledougou 1.75 .40
514 A178 190fr Horse from Nara 2.75 .60
515 A178 530fr Horse from Trait 7.75 1.75
Nos. 512-515 (4) 13.50 3.05

For surcharges see Nos. 586, 591.

Fungi — A179

1985, Jan. 28 **Litho.** ***Perf. 12½***

516 A179 120fr Clitocybe nebularis 1.60 .90
517 A179 200fr Lepiota cortinarius 2.50 .90
518 A179 485fr Agavicus semotus 6.75 1.60
519 A179 525fr Lepiota procera 7.00 1.60
Nos. 516-519 (4) 17.85 5.00

For surcharges see Nos. 589-590.

Health — A180

Designs: 120fr, 32nd World Leprosy Day, Emile Marchoux (1862-1943), Marchoux Institute, 150th anniv. 135fr, Lions Intl., Samanko Convalescence Village, 15th anniv. 470fr, Anti-polio campaign, research facility, victim.

1985, Feb. 18 **Litho.** ***Perf. 13***

520 A180 120fr multi 1.50 .35
521 A180 135fr multi 1.75 .40
522 A180 470fr multi 5.00 1.50
Nos. 520-522 (3) 8.25 2.25

For surcharges see Nos. 580, 584. No. 522 is airmail.

Cultural and Technical Cooperation Agency, 15th Anniv. — A181

1985, Mar. 20

523 A181 540fr brn & brt bl grn 5.25 1.50

Intl. Youth Year A182

Youth activities.

1985, May 13 ***Perf. 12½x13***

524 A182 120fr Natl. Pioneers Movement emblem 1.00 .40
525 A182 190fr Agricultural production 2.00 .60
526 A182 500fr Sports 5.00 1.50
Nos. 524-526 (3) 8.00 2.50

For surcharge see No. 587.

PHILEXAFRICA '85, Lome, Togo — A183

1985, June 24 ***Perf. 13***

527 A183 250fr Education, telecommunications 2.75 2.00
528 A183 250fr Road, dam, computers 2.75 2.00
a. Pair, #527-528 7.50 2.75
Nos. 527-528,C517-C518 (4) 10.00 6.20

Nos. 527-528 show the UPU emblem.

Cats A184

1986, Feb. 15 **Litho.** ***Perf. 13½***

529 A184 150fr Gray 2.75 .50
530 A184 200fr White 3.75 .75
531 A184 300fr Tabby 4.50 1.00
Nos. 529-531 (3) 11.00 2.25

For surcharge see No. 582.

Fight Against Apartheid — A185

1986, Feb. 24 ***Perf. 13***

532 A185 100fr shown 1.50 .30
533 A185 120fr Map, broken chain 1.60 .40

Telecommunications and Agriculture — A186

1986, May 17 **Litho.** ***Perf. 13***

534 A186 200fr multi 2.50 .60

1986 World Cup Soccer Championships, Mexico — A187

Various soccer plays.

1986, May 24 **Litho.** ***Perf. 12½***

535 A187 160fr multi 1.50 .45
536 A187 225fr multi 2.50 .65

Souvenir Sheet

537 A187 500fr multi 5.25 2.25

For overprints surcharges see #539-541, 585.

James Watt (1736-1819), Inventor, and Steam Engine — A188

1986, May 26 ***Perf. 12½x12***

538 A188 110fr multi 2.00 .35

For surcharge see No. 581.

Nos. 535-537 Ovptd. "ARGENTINE 3 / R.F.A. 2" in Red

1986, July 30 **Litho.** ***Perf. 12½***

539 A187 160fr multi 2.25 .60
540 A187 225fr multi 3.50 .80

Souvenir Sheet

541 A187 500fr multi 6.50 2.50

World Wildlife Fund — A189

Derby's Eland, Taurotragus derbianus.

1986, Aug. 11 **Litho.** ***Perf. 13***

542 A189 5fr Adult head 2.00 .25
543 A189 20fr Adult in brush 3.75 .25
544 A189 25fr Adult walking 3.75 .25
545 A189 200fr Calf suckling 30.00 4.00
Nos. 542-545 (4) 39.50 4.75

Henry Ford (1863-1947), Auto Manufacturer, Inventor of Mass Production — A190

1987, Feb. 16 **Litho.** ***Perf. 13***

546 A190 150fr Model A, 1903 2.10 .45
547 A190 200fr Model T, 1923 2.75 .90
548 A190 225fr Thunderbird, 1968 3.00 1.00
549 A190 300fr Lincoln Continental, 1963 3.25 1.10
Nos. 546-549 (4) 11.10 3.45

Bees A191

1987, May 11 **Litho.** ***Perf. 13½***

550 A191 100fr Apis florea, Asia 2.00 .50
551 A191 150fr Apis dorsata, Asia 2.40 .60
552 A191 175fr Apis adansonii, Africa 2.50 .75
553 A191 200fr Apis mellifica, worldwide 2.75 .90
Nos. 550-553 (4) 9.65 2.75

Lions Club Activities — A192

1988, Jan. 13 Litho. *Perf. 12½*
554 A192 200fr multi 2.50 .85

World Health Organization, 40th Anniv. — A193

1988, Feb. 22 Litho. *Perf. 12½x12*
555 A193 150fr multi 1.60 .55

For surcharge see No. 557.

John F. Kennedy (1917-1963), 35th US President A194

1988, June 6 Litho. *Perf. 13*
556 A194 640fr multi 6.25 2.50

For surcharge see No. 592.

No. 555 Surcharged in Dark Red

1988, June 13 *Perf. 12½x12*
557 A193 300fr on 150fr multi 3.00 1.40

Mali Mission Hospital in Mopti and World Medicine organization.

Organization of African Unity, 25th Anniv. — A194a

1988, June 27 Litho. *Perf. 12½*
558 A194a 400fr multi 3.75 1.60

Universal Immunization Campaign — A195

1989, May 2 Litho. *Perf. 13½*
559 A195 20fr shown .25 .20
560 A195 30fr Inoculating woman .35 .20
561 A195 50fr Emblem, needles, diff. .55 .20
562 A195 175fr Inoculating boy 1.90 .80
Nos. 559-562 (4) 3.05 1.40

Intl. Law Institute of the French-Speaking Nations — A196

1989, May 15 *Perf. 12½*
563 A196 150fr multi 1.60 .60
564 A196 200fr multi 2.00 .80

World Post Day — A197

1989, Oct. 9 Litho. *Perf. 13*
565 A197 625fr multicolored 7.25 3.00

For surcharge see No. 594.

Visit of Pope John Paul II — A198

1990, Jan. 28 Litho. *Perf. 13x12½*
566 A198 200fr multicolored 3.00 .90

Multinational Postal School, 20th Anniv. — A199

1990, May 31 Litho. *Perf. 12½*
567 A199 150fr multicolored 1.60 .65

Independence, 30th Anniv. — A200

1990, Sept. 20 Litho. *Perf. 13x12½*
568 A200 400fr multicolored 4.25 1.75

Intl. Literacy Year A201

1990, Sept. 24 Litho. *Perf. 13½*
569 A201 150fr grn & multi 1.40 .65
570 A201 200fr org & multi 2.10 .90

A202

A203

Lions Intl. Water Project, 6th anniv.: No. 572, Rotary Club fight against polio, 30th anniv.

1991, Feb. 25 Litho. *Perf. 13x12½*
571 A202 200fr multicolored 2.25 1.00
572 A202 200fr multicolored 2.25 1.00

1991, Apr. 29 Litho. *Perf. 12½*

Designs: Tribal dances of Mali.

573 A203 50fr Takamba .55 .30
574 A203 100fr Mandiani 1.00 .60
575 A203 150fr Kono 1.60 .90
576 A203 200fr Songho 2.10 1.10
Nos. 573-576 (4) 5.25 2.90

A204

A205

1991, Dec. 2 Litho. *Perf. 12½*
577 A204 200fr multicolored 2.00 1.00

Central Fund for Economic Cooperation, 50th anniv.

1992, Mar. 26 Litho. *Perf. 12½*
578 A205 150fr multicolored 1.60 .75

National Women's Movement.

Various Stamps of 1984-89 Surcharged in Black or Black and Silver

1992, June Litho. *Perfs. as Before*
579 A177 25fr on 470fr #510 .40 .20
580 A180 25fr on 470fr #522 .40 .20
581 A188 30fr on 110fr #538 .50 .20
582 A184 50fr on 300fr #531 .80 .20
583 A173 50fr on 1225fr #493 .80 .20
584 A180 150fr on 135fr #521 (Bk & S) 2.50 .60
585 A187 150fr on 160fr #535 2.50 .60
586 A178 150fr on 190fr #514 2.50 .60
587 A182 150fr on 190fr #525 2.50 .60
588 A176 150fr on 350fr #503 2.50 .60
589 A179 150fr on 485fr #518 2.50 .60
590 A179 150fr on 525fr #519 2.50 .60
591 A178 150fr on 530fr #515 2.50 .60
592 A194 200fr on 640fr #556 3.25 .80
593 A177 240fr on 350fr #509 3.75 1.00
594 A197 240fr on 625fr #565 3.75 1.00
Nos. 579-594 (16) 33.65 8.60

No. 580 is airmail. Size and location of surcharge varies. No. 585 also overprinted "Euro '92."

New Constitution, 1st Anniv. — A205a

1993, Jan. 12 Litho. *Perf. 11½x12*
594A A205a 150fr multi *45.00*
594B A205a 225fr multi *65.00*

Martyr's Day, 2nd Anniv. — A206

1993, Mar. 26 Litho. *Perf. 11½*
595 A206 150fr blue & multi 55.00 55.00
596 A206 160fr yellow & multi 55.00 55.00

Rotary Intl. and World Health Organization (WHO) — A206a

Designs: 150fr, Polio victims, Rotary emblem. 200fr, WHO emblem, pregnant woman receiving vaccination.

1993, Apr. 16 Litho. *Perf. 14*
596A A206a 150fr multi *45.00*
596B A206a 200fr multi *65.00*

Lions Club in Mali, 35th Anniv. A207

1993, Dec. 20 Litho. *Perf. 14½*

597 A207 200fr blue & multi 55.00 55.00
598 A207 225fr red & multi 55.00 55.00

Monument, Liberty Place — A207a

1993, Dec. 20 Photo. *Perf. 11¾*

Granite Paper

598A A207a 20fr multicolored
598B A207a 25fr multicolored
598C A207a 50fr multi
598D A207a 100fr multicolored
598E A207a 110fr multicolored
598F A207a 150fr multicolored
598G A207a 200fr multicolored
598H A207a 225fr multicolored
598I A207a 240fr multicolored
598J A207a 260fr multicolored

1994 Winter Olympics, Lillehammer A208

1994, Feb. 12 Litho. *Perf. 13*

599 A208 150fr Pairs figure skating .90 .50
600 A208 200fr Giant slalom 1.25 .75
601 A208 225fr Ski jumping 1.75 1.00
602 A208 750fr Speed skating 3.00 1.75
Nos. 599-602 (4) 6.90 4.00

Souvenir Sheet

603 A208 2000fr Downhill skiing 9.00 9.00

No. 603 contains one 36x36mm stamp.
For overprints see Nos. 671-676.

1994 World Cup Soccer Championships, US — A209

Designs: 200fr, Juan Schiaffino, Uruguay. 240fr, Diego Maradona, Argentina. 260fr, Paolo Rossi, Italy. 1000fr, Franz Beckenbauer, Germany. 2000fr, Just Fontaine, France.

1994, Mar. 15 Litho. *Perf. 13*

604 A209 200fr multicolored .90 .90
605 A209 240fr multicolored 1.40 .80
606 A209 260fr multicolored 1.60 .90
607 A209 1000fr multicolored 5.00 2.75
Nos. 604-607 (4) 8.90 5.35

Souvenir Sheet

608 A209 2000fr multicolored 9.00 9.00

For overprints see Nos. 677-681.

Miniature Sheet

Dinosaurs A210

a, 5fr, Scaphonyx. b, 10fr, Cynognathus. c, 15fr, Lesothosaurus. d, 20fr, Scutellosaurus. e, 25fr, Ceratosaurus. f, 30fr, Dilophosaurus. g, 40fr, Dryosaurus. h, 50fr, Heterodontosaurus. i, 60fr, Anatosaurus. j, 70fr, Saurornithoides. k, 80fr, Avimimus. l, 90fr, Saltasaurus. m, 300fr, Dromaeosaurus. n, 400fr, Tsintaosaurus. o, 600fr, Velociraptor. p, 700fr, Ouranosaurus.
2000fr, Daspletosaurus, iguanodon.

1994, Mar. 28

609 A210 Sheet of 16, #a.-p. 15.00 8.00

Souvenir Sheet

610 A210 2000fr multicolored 12.00 12.00

Insects A211

Designs: 40fr, Sternuera castanea, vert. 50fr, Eudicella gralli. 100fr, Homoderus mellyi, vert. 200fr, Kraussaria angulifera.

1994, Mar. 30 Litho. *Perf. 13*

611 A211 40fr multicolored .40 .20
612 A211 50fr multicolored .70 .35
613 A211 100fr multicolored 1.10 .60
614 A211 200fr multicolored 2.00 1.00
Nos. 611-614 (4) 4.20 2.15

Vaccination Campaign Against Measles — A212

1994, Apr. 7 Litho. *Perf. 13½*

615 A212 150fr black & green .90 .50
616 A212 200fr black & blue 1.60 .90

Birds A213

1994, Apr. 25

617 A213 25fr Pigeons .30 .20
618 A213 30fr Turkeys .30 .20
619 A213 150fr Crowned cranes, vert. 1.40 .70
620 A213 200fr Chickens, vert. 1.50 .80
Nos. 617-620 (4) 3.50 1.90

Intl. Year of the Family — A213a

1994, May 2

620A A213a 220fr multicolored 1.25 .60

Jazz Musicians A214

1994, May 23 Litho. *Perf. 13*

621 A214 200fr Ella Fitzgerald .80 .60
622 A214 225fr Lionel Hampton 1.00 .70
623 A214 240fr Sarah Vaughan 1.25 .85
624 A214 300fr Count Basie 1.75 1.25
625 A214 400fr Duke Ellington 2.25 1.50
626 A214 600fr Miles Davis 3.00 2.00
Nos. 621-626 (6) 10.05 6.90

Souvenir Sheet

627 A214 1500fr Louis Armstrong 8.00 8.00

No. 627 contains one 45x45mm stamp.

Ancient Art — A215

#628-637: 15fr, Venus of Brassempoury, vert. 25fr, Petroglyphs, Tanum, vert. 45fr, Prehistoric cave drawings, vert. 50fr, Cave paintaings, Lascaux. 55fr, Tomb of Amonherkhopeshef, vert. 65fr, Goddess Anubis and the pharaoh. 75fr, Sphinx. 85fr, Bust of Nefertiti, vert. 95fr, Statue of Shibum, vert. 100fr, Standard of Ur. 130fr, Mesopotamian bull's head harp, vert.
#638-647: 135fr, Mesopotamian scroll. 140fr, Assyrian dignitary, vert. 180fr, Enameled horse, Babylon. 190fr, Assyrian carving of hunters, vert. 200fr, Mona Lisa of Nimrud, vert. 225fr, Carthaginian coin. 250fr, Phoenician sphinx, vert. 275fr, Persian archer, vert. 280fr, Ceramic and glass mask, vert.

1994, Aug. 24 Litho. *Perf. 13½*

628-647 A215 Set of 20 15.00 15.00

D-Day Landings, Normandy, 50th Anniv. — A216

Villiers-Bocage, June 12: No. 648a, Explosion, men being killed. b, Tank firing. c, Tank, men with weapons.
Beaumont-Sur-Sarthe, June 6: No. 649a, Explosion, airplanes. b, British airplanes, tanks. c, German tanks, soldier firing machine gun.
Utah Beach, June 6: No. 650a, Explosion, bow of landing craft. b, Stern of landing craft, soldiers. c, Landing craft filled with troops.
Aerial battle: No. 651a, British planes dropping bombs. b, British, German planes. c, British, German planes, explosion.
Sainte-Mere-Eglise, June 5: No. 652a, German troops firing on paratroopers. b, Church tower. c, Paratroopers, German troops.

1994, June 6

Strips of 3

648 A216 200fr #a.-c. 3.25 1.75
649 A216 300fr #a.-c. 4.00 2.25
650 A216 300fr #a.-c. 4.00 2.25
651 A216 400fr #a.-c. 5.25 3.00
652 A216 400fr #a.-c. 5.25 3.00
Nos. 648-652 (5) 21.75 12.25

Nos. 648-652 are each continuous designs. Nos. 648b, 649b, 650b, 651b, 652b are each 30x47mm.

Orchids, Vegetables, & Mushrooms A217

Orchids: 25fr, Disa kewensis. 50fr, Angraecum eburneum. 100fr, Ansellia africana.
Vegetables: 140fr, Sorghum. 150fr, Onions. 190fr, Corn.
Mushrooms: 200fr, Lepiota (clitocybe) nebularis. 225fr, Macrolepiota (lepiota) procera. 500fr, Lepiota aspera.

1994, Sept. 12

653 A217 25fr multicolored .20 .20
654 A217 50fr multicolored .35 .20
655 A217 100fr multicolored .65 .35
a. Souvenir sheet of 3, #653-655 *11.00 7.50*
656 A217 140fr multicolored .70 .40
657 A217 150fr multicolored .80 .45
658 A217 190fr multicolored 1.00 .60
a. Souvenir sheet of 3, #656-658 *11.00 7.50*
659 A217 200fr multicolored 1.10 .65
660 A217 225fr multicolored 1.25 .75
661 A217 500fr multicolored 2.75 1.50
a. Souvenir sheet of 3, #659-661 *11.00 7.50*
Nos. 653-661 (9) 8.80 5.10

Moths, Butterflies & Insects A218

Designs: 20fr, Polyptychus roseus. 30fr, Elymniopsis bammakoo. 40fr, Deilephila nerii. 150fr, Utetheisa pulchella. 180fr, Charaxes jasius. 200fr, Mylothris chloris.
Insects: 225fr, Goliath beetle. 240fr, Locust. 350fr, Praying mantis.

1994, Sept. 12

662 A218 20fr multicolored .20 .20
663 A218 30fr multicolored .20 .20
664 A218 40fr multicolored .20 .20
665 A218 150fr multicolored .90 .50
666 A218 180fr multicolored 1.00 .55
667 A218 200fr multicolored 1.00 .60
a. Souv. sheet of 6, #662-667 *22.50 12.50*
668 A218 225fr multicolored 1.10 .65
669 A218 240fr multicolored 1.25 .70
670 A218 350fr multicolored 1.60 .90
a. Souv. sheet of 3, #668-670 *11.00 6.50*
Nos. 662-670 (9) 7.45 4.50

Nos. 599-603 Ovptd. in Silver or Gold with Name of Olympic Medalist, Country

Overprints in silver: No. 671a, "Y. GORDEYEVA / S. GRINKOV / RUSSIE." No. 671b, "O. GRISHCHUK / Y. PLATOV / RUSSIE." No. 672a, "D. COMPAGNONI / ITALIE." No. 672b, "M. WASMEIER / ALLEMAGNE." No. 673a, "E. BREDESEN /NORVEGE." No. 673b, "J. WEISSFLOG / ALLEMAGNE." No. 674a, "B. BLAIR, U.S.A." No. 674b, "J.O. KOSS / NORVEGE."
Overprint in gold: No. 675, "L. KJUS / NORVEGE." No. 676, "P. WIBERG / SUEDE."

1994, Sept. 12 Litho. *Perf. 13*

671 A208 150fr Pair, #a.-b. 1.75 1.00
672 A208 200fr Pair, #a.-b. 2.75 1.50
673 A208 225fr Pair, #a.-b. 3.50 2.00
674 A208 750fr Pair, #a.-b. 10.00 5.50
Nos. 671-674 (4) 18.00 10.00

Souvenir Sheet

675 A208 2000fr multicolored 9.00 5.00
676 A208 2000fr multicolored 9.00 5.00

Nos. 604-608 Ovptd. in Metallic Red

1994, Sept. 15 Litho. *Perf. 13*

677 A209 200fr multicolored .90 .50
678 A209 240fr multicolored 1.25 .70
679 A209 260fr multicolored 1.40 .80
680 A209 1000fr multicolored 5.25 3.00
Nos. 677-680 (4) 8.80 5.00

Souvenir Sheet

681 A209 2000fr multicolored 9.00 5.00

Intl. Olympic Committee, Cent. — A218a

1994, June 23 Litho. *Perf. 13½*

681A A218a 150fr multicolored 1.10 .60
681B A218a 200fr multicolored 1.60 .90

Exist in imperf souvenir sheets of 1.

Intl. Olympic Committee, Cent. — A219

Pierre de Coubertin and: 225fr, Woman carrying flame, vert. 240fr, Olympic rings, vert. 300fr, Torch bearer. 500fr, Gold medal of Olympic rings.

600fr, Flame, statue of flag bearer.

1994, June 23 *Perf. 13½*

682 A219 225fr multicolored .90 .50
683 A219 240fr multicolored 1.00 .60
684 A219 300fr multicolored 1.60 .90
685 A219 500fr multicolored 2.75 1.50
Nos. 682-685 (4) 6.25 3.50

Souvenir Sheet

686 A219 600fr multicolored 3.50 2.00

Anniversaries & Events A220

Designs: 150fr, Erst Julius Opik, Galileo probe, impact of comet on Jupiter. 200fr, Clyde Tombaugh, probe moving toward Pluto. 500fr, Intl. Red Cross, Henri Dunant. 650fr, Crew of Apollo 11, 1st manned moon landing. 700fr, Lions Intl., Rotary Intl. 800fr, Gary Kasparov chess champion.

1994, Apr. 10 Litho. *Perf. 13½*

687 A220 150fr multicolored .60 .30
688 A220 200fr multicolored .90 .45
689 A220 500fr multicolored 2.25 1.10
690 A220 650fr multicolored 2.75 1.40
691 A220 700fr multicolored 3.00 1.50
692 A220 800fr multicolored 3.50 1.75
Nos. 687-692 (6) 13.00 6.50

Nos. 687-692 exist in souvenir sheets of 1.

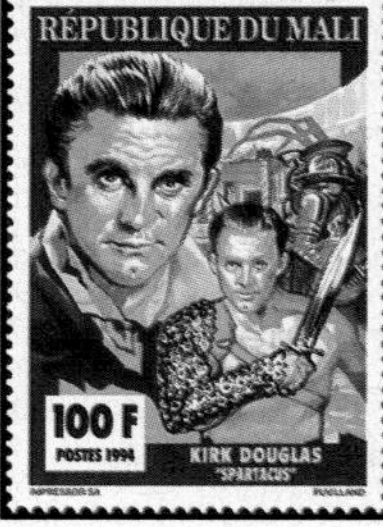

Motion Picture, Cent. — A221

Movie star, movie: 100fr, Kirk Douglas, Spartacus. 150fr, Elizabeth Taylor, Cleopatra. 200fr, Clint Eastwood, Sierra Torrid. 225fr, Marilyn Monroe, The River of No Return. 500fr, Arnold Schwarzenegger, Conan the Barbarian. 1000fr, Elvis Presley, Loving You. 1500fr, Charlton Heston, The Ten Commandments.

1994, May 23 Litho. *Perf. 13½*

693-698 A221 Set of 6 16.00 8.75

Souvenir Sheet

699 A221 1500fr multicolored 8.25 4.50

No. 695 is airmail.

Fight Against AIDS A222

Designs: 150fr, Woman, man holding condoms. 225fr, Nurse with AIDS patient, researcher looking into microscope.

1994, June 30

700 A222 150fr multicolored 1.10 .60
701 A222 225fr multicolored 1.60 .90

Tourism A223

Designs: 150fr, Traditional buildings, statue, vert. 200fr, Sphinx, pyramids, ruins.

1994, Dec. 5

702 A223 150fr multicolored 1.10 .60
703 A223 200fr multicolored 1.60 .90

1996 Summer Olympics, Atlanta — A224

Designs: 25fr, Reiner Klimke, dressage. 50fr, Kristin Otto, swimming. 100fr, Hans-Gunther Winkler, equestrian. 150fr, Birgit Fischer-Schmidt, kayak. 200fr, Nicole Uphoff, dressage, vert. 225fr, Renate Stecher, track, vert. 230fr, Michael Gross, swimming. 240fr, Karin Janz, gymnastics. 550fr, Anja Fichtel, fencing, vert. 700fr, Heide Rosendahl-Ecker, track, vert.

1995, Mar. 27

704-713 A224 Set of 10 12.50 7.00

Dated 1994.

Rotary Intl., 90th Anniv. — A225

1995, Oct. 18 Litho. *Perf. 14*

714 A225 1000fr Paul Harris, logo 6.50 3.50

Souvenir Sheet

715 A225 1500fr 1905, 1995 Logos 8.00 4.50

Miniature Sheets

Birds, Butterflies — A226

No. 716: a, Campephilos imperialis. b, Momotus momota. c, Ramphastos sulfuratus. d, Halcyon malimbica. e, Trochilus polytmus. f, Cardinalis cardinalis. g, Pharomachrus mocinno. h, Aratinga solstitialis. i, Amazona arausiaca. j, Eudocimus ruber. k, Carduelis cucullatus. l, Anodorhynchus hyacinthinus. m, Passerina leclancherii. n, Pipra mentalis. o, Rupicola rupicola. p, Sicalis flaveola.

No. 717: a, Carito niger. b, Chloroceryle amazona. c, Tersina virdis. d, Momotus momota. e, Campephilus menaloleucos. f, Leistes militaris. g, Sarcoramphus papa. h, Pilherodius pileatus. i, Tityra cayana. j, Tangara chilinsis. k, Amazona ochrocephala. l, Saltator maximus. m, Paroaria dominicana. n, Egretta tricolor. o, Piaya melano gaster. p, Thamnophilus doliatus.

No. 718: a, Paradise whydah (g). b, Red-necked francolin. c, Whale-headed stork (i). d, Ruff (j). e, Marabou stork (k). f, White pelican. g, Western curlew. h, Scarlet ibis. i, Great crested crebe. j, White spoonbill. k, African jacana. l, African pygmy goose.

No. 719: a, Ruby-throated hummingbird. b, Grape shoemaker, blue morpho butterflies. c, Northern hobby. d, Cuvier toucan (g). e, Black-necked red cotinga (h). f, Green-winged macaws (i). g, Flamingo (j). h, Malachite kingfisher. i, Bushy-crested hornbill (l). j, Purple swamphen (k). k, Striped body (j, l). l, Painted lady butterfly.

Each 1000fr: No. 720, Topaza pella. No. 721, Sporophila lineola.

1995, Oct. 20 Litho. *Perf. 14*

Sheets of 16 & 12

716 A226 50fr #a.-p. 6.50 3.50
717 A226 100fr #a.-p. 11.00 6.00
718 A226 150fr #a.-l. 12.00 6.50
719 A226 200fr #a.-l. 16.00 8.50
Nos. 716-719 (4) 45.50 24.50

Souvenir Sheets

720-721 A226 Set of 2 12.00 6.75

John Lennon (1940-80) A227

1995 Litho. *Perf. 14*

722 A227 150fr multicolored 1.25 .70

No. 722 was issued in sheets of 16.

Miniature Sheets

Motion Pictures, Cent. A228

Western actors: No. 723:a, Justus D. Barnes (misidentified as George Barnes). b, William S. Hart. c, Tom Mix. d, Wallace Beery. e, Gary Cooper. f, John Wayne.

Actresses and their directors: No. 724: a, Marlene Dietrich, Josef Von Sternberg. b, Jean Harlow, George Cukor. c, Mary Astor, John Huston (Houston on stamp). d, Ingrid Bergman, Alfred Hitchcock. e, Claudette Colbert, Cecil B. De Mille. f, Marilyn Monroe, Billy Wilder.

Musicals and their stars: No. 725: a, Singin' in the Rain, Gene Kelly. b, The Bandwagon, Anne Miller, Ray Bolger. c, Cabaret, Liza Minnelli, Joel Gray. d, The Sound of Music, Julie Andrews. e, Top Hat, Ginger Rogers, Fred Astaire. f, Saturday Night Fever, John Travolta.

Each 1000fr: No. 726, Robert Redford as the Sundance Kid. No. 727, Liv Ullman, actress, Ingmar Bergman, director. No. 728, Judy Garland in the Wizard of Oz.

1995, Dec. 8 Litho. *Perf. 13½x14*

Sheets of 6

723 A228 150fr #a.-f. 5.25 3.00
724 A228 200fr #a.-f. 7.25 4.00
725 A228 240fr #a.-f. 9.00 5.00
Nos. 723-725 (3) 21.50 12.00

Souvenir Sheets

726-728 A228 Set of 3 16.00 9.00

Nos. 723-728 have various styles of lettering.

Miniature Sheet

Stars of Rock and Roll — A229

No. 729: a, Connie Francis. b, The Ronettes. c, Janis Joplin. d, Debbie Harry of Blondie. e, Cyndi Lauper. f, Carly Simon.

No. 730, Bette Midler.

1995, Dec. 8

729 A229 225fr Sheet of 6, #a.-f. 8.00 4.50

Souvenir Sheet

730 A229 1000fr multicolored 5.25 3.00

Traditional Cooking Utensils A230

5fr, Canaris, vert. 50fr, Mortier, calebasse, vert. 150fr, Fourneau. 200fr, Vans, vert. 500fr, Vans.

1995, Nov. 20 Litho. *Perf. 14*

731-734 A230 Set of 4 2.75 1.50

Souvenir Sheet

735 A230 500fr multicolored 3.00 1.75

18th World Scout Jamboree, Holland — A231

Scout examining butterfly or mushroom: 150fr, Saturnia pyri. 225fr, Gonepteryx rhamni. 240fr, Myrina silenus. 500fr, Clitocybe nebularis. 650fr, Agaricus semotus. 725fr, Lepiota procera.
1500fr, Morpho cypris.

1995, Aug. 1 Litho. *Perf. 13½*

736-741	A231	Set of 6	11.50	5.75

Souvenir Sheet

742	A231	1500fr multicolored	9.25	4.50

Nos. 736-741 exist in souvenir sheets of 1.

UN, 50th Anniv. A232

Designs: 20fr, 170fr, UN emblem, scales of justice, doves, vert. 225fr, 240fr, Doves, UN emblem, four men of different races.

1995, Oct. 24 Litho. *Perf. 13*

743	A232	20fr light blue & multi	.20	.20
744	A232	170fr light grn & multi	1.00	.55
745	A232	225fr light pur & multi	1.25	.55
746	A232	240fr light org & multi	1.50	.85
		Nos. 743-746 (4)	3.95	2.15

Ayrton Senna (1960-94), F-1 Race Car Driver — A233

1000fr, Jerry Garcia (1942-95), entertainer.

1995 *Perf. 13½*

747	A233	500fr multicolored	2.25	1.10
748	A233	1000fr multicolored	4.50	2.25

Nos. 747-748 exist in souvenir sheets of one.

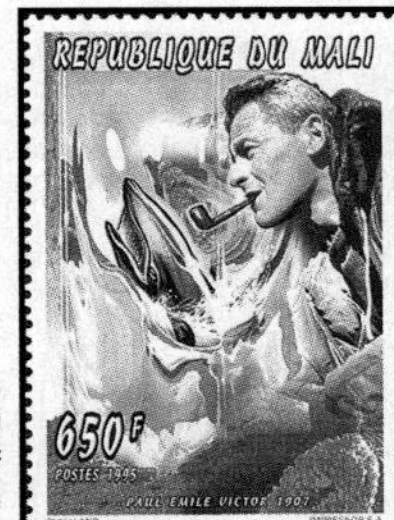

1945-49 Greenland Expeditions of Paul Emile Victor — A234

1995

749	A234	150fr Charles de Gaulle	.70	.35
750	A234	200fr De Gaulle, liberation of Paris	.90	.45
751	A234	240fr Enzo Ferrari	1.10	.55
752	A234	650fr multicolored	3.00	1.50
753	A234	725fr Paul Harris	3.25	1.60
754	A234	740fr Michael Schumacher	3.50	1.75
		Nos. 749-754 (6)	12.45	6.20

Nos. 749-754 exist in souvenir sheets of 1.

A235

A236

Designs: 150fr, Second election party emblems, horiz. 200fr, Pres. Alpha Oumar Konare. 225fr, First election party emblems, horiz. 240fr, Natl. flag, map, party representations.

1995 Litho. *Perf. 13½*

755	A235	150fr multicolored	.70	.35
756	A235	200fr multicolored	.90	.45
757	A235	225fr multicolored	1.00	.50
758	A235	240fr multicolored	1.10	.55
		Nos. 755-758 (4)	3.70	1.85

Second Presidential elections.

1995

Economic Community of West African States (ECOWAS): 150fr, Regional integration, horiz. 200fr, Cooperation. 220fr, Prospect of creating one currency, horiz. 225fr, Peace and security, horiz.

759	A236	150fr multicolored	.70	.35
760	A236	200fr multicolored	.90	.45
761	A236	220fr multicolored	1.00	.50
762	A236	225fr multicolored	1.00	.50
		Nos. 759-762 (4)	3.60	1.80

Mushrooms — A237

Genus Russula: No. 763: a, Emetica. b, Laurocerasi. c, Rosacea. d, Occidentalis. e, Fragilis. f, Mariae. g, Eeruginea. h, Compacta.
Genus Boletus: No. 764: a, Felleus. b, Elegans. c, Castaneus. d, Edulis. e, Aereus. f, Granulatus. g, Cavipes. h, Badius.
Genus Lactarius: No. 765: a, Deliciosus. b, Luculentus. c, Pseudomucidus. d, Scrobiculatus. e, Deceptivus. f, Indigo. g, Peckii. h, Lignyotus.
Genus Amanita: No. 766a, Caesarea. b, Muscaria. c, Solitaria. d, Verna. e, Malleata. f. Phalloides. g, Citrina. h, Pantherina.
Each 1000fr: No. 767, Coprinus atramentarius. No. 768, Panaeolus subbalteatus.

1996, Mar. 15 Litho. *Perf. 14*

763	A237	25fr Sheet of 8, #a.-h.	1.60	.85
764	A237	150fr Sheet of 8, #a.-h.	9.00	5.00
765	A237	200fr Sheet of 8, #a.-h.	12.00	6.50
766	A237	225fr Sheet of 8, #a.-h.	14.00	7.50

Souvenir Sheets

767-768	A237	Set of 2	14.00	8.00

Sites in Beijing — A238

No. 769: a, Bridge, Gateway to Hall of Supreme Harmony. b, Temple of Heaven. c, Great Wall. d, Hall of Supreme Harmony. e, Courtyard, Gate of Heavenly Purity, f, Younghe Gong Temple. g, Lang Ru Ting, Bridge of Seventeen Arches. h, Meridian Gate (Wu Men). i, Corner Tower.
Each 500fr: No. 770, Pagoda, vert. No. 771, Li Peng.

1996, May 13

769	A238	100fr Sheet of 9, #a.-i.	7.50	4.25

Souvenir Sheets

770-771	A238	Set of 2	7.00	4.25

No. 771 contains one 47x72mm stamp. CHINA '96 (Nos. 769, 771).

Trains A239

Historic: No. 772: a, "Novelty," 1829. b, Premiere class Liverpool & Manchester Line, 1830. c, William Norris, 1843. d, Trevithick, 1808. e, Robert Stephenson "Rocket," 1829. f, "Puffing Billy," William Hedley, 1813.
No. 773: a, Subway Train, London. b, San Francisco cable car. c, Japanese monorail. d, Pantograph car, Stockholm. e, Double-decker tram, Hong Kong. f, Sacre-Coeur Cog Train, Montmartre, France.
No. 774: a, Docklands Light Railway, London. b, British Railway's high-speed diesel train. c, Japanese Bullet Train. d, Germany Inter-City Electric high speed train. e, French TGV high-speed electric train. f, German "Wuppertal" monorail.
Trains of China: No. 775: a, RM Class Pacific. b, Manchurian steam engine. c, SY Class 2-8-2, Tangshan. d, SL Class 4-6-2 Pacific. e, Chengtu-Kunming steam. f, Lanchow passenger train.
Each 500fr: No. 776, Rheingold Express, 1925. No. 777, Matterhorn cable car, vert. No. 778, Superchief, best long-distance diesel, US. No. 779, Shanghai-Nanking Railway.

1996, July 29

772	A239	180fr Sheet of 6, #a.-f.	8.00	4.50
773	A239	250fr Sheet of 6, #a.-f.	12.00	6.50
774	A239	310fr Sheet of 6, #a.-f.	14.00	7.75
775	A239	320fr Sheet of 6, #a.-f.	15.00	8.25

Souvenir Sheets

776-779	A239	Set of 4	16.00	9.00

Nos. 776-779 each contain one 57x43mm stamp.

Express Mail Service, 10th Anniv. A240

Designs: 30fr, Man with package, vert. 40fr, Bird holding package, letter, vert. 90fr, World map, woman with letter holding telephone receiver. 320fr, 320fr, Mail van, hands holding letters, map.

1996, Sept. 1 Litho. *Perf. 14*

780	A240	30fr multicolored	.20	.20
781	A240	40fr multicolored	.30	.20
782	A240	90fr multicolored	.55	.30
783	A240	320fr multicolored	1.75	1.00
		Nos. 780-783 (4)	2.80	1.70

Queen Elizabeth II, 70th Birthday A241

Designs: a, Portrait. b, Wearing blue & red hat. c, Portrait as young woman.
1000fr, Portrait as young girl.

1996, Sept. 9 *Perf. 13½x14*

784	A241	370fr Strip of 3, #a.-c.	5.50	2.25

Souvenir Sheet

785	A241	1000fr multicolored	5.25	2.00

No. 784 was issued in sheets of 9 stamps.

Nanking Bridge — A242

1996 Litho. *Perf. 13½*

786	A242	270fr multicolored	2.50	1.25

Mosques A243

1996

787	A243	250fr Djenne	3.50	2.00
788	A243	310fr Sankore	4.50	2.50

Pandas, Dogs, and Cats — A244

Panda, vert: No. 789: a, Climbing on branch. b, On bare limb. c. Closer view. d, Lying in branch with leaves.
Dogs, cats: No. 790: a, Azawakh. b, Basenji. c, Javanais. d, Abyssin.

1996

789	A244	150fr Sheet of 4, #a.-d.	3.25	1.60
790	A244	310fr Sheet of 4, #a.-d.	6.00	3.00

Nos. 789a-789d are 39x42mm.

Marilyn Monroe (1926-62) A245

Various portraits.

1996

791	A245	320fr Sheet of 9, #a.-i.	14.00	7.00

Souvenir Sheet

792	A245	2000fr multicolored	9.50	4.75

No. 792 contains one 42x60mm stamp.

Entertainers A246

#793: a, Frank Sinatra. b, Johnny Mathis. c, Dean Martin. d, Bing Crosby. e, Sammy Davis, Jr. f, Elvis Presley. g, Paul Anka. h, Tony Bennett. i, Nat "King" Cole.

No. 794, Various portraits of John Lennon.

1996

Sheets of 9

793 A246 250fr #a.-i. 10.00 5.00
794 A246 310fr #a.-i. 12.50 6.25

U.S. Space Shuttle, Challenger A247

Designs: a, Halley's Comet, Andromeda Galaxy. b, Mars. c, Challenger, Saturn. d, Moon, Jupiter.

1000fr, Shuttle Challenger.

1996, Oct. 14 *Perf. 14*

795 A247 320fr Sheet of 4, #a.-d. 5.75 3.00

Souvenir Sheet

796 A247 1000fr multicolored 5.25 3.00

No. 796 contains one 85x29mm stamp.

Mickey's ABC's A248

Disney characters in various scenes with: No. 797: a, "MICKEY." b, "A." c, "B." d, "C." e, "D." f, "E." g, "F." h, "G." i, "H."

No. 798: a, "I." b, "J." c, "K." d, "L." e, "M." f, "N." g, "O." h, "P." i, "Q."

No. 799: a, "R." b, "S." c, "T." d, "U." e, "V." f, "W." g, "X." h, "Y." i, "Z."

Each 1000fr: No. 800, Mouse child holding "DE MICKEY" sign, horiz. No. 801, Mouse children with various letters.

1996, Oct. 15 Litho. *Perf. 13½x14*

797 A248 50fr Sheet of 9, #a.-i. 2.25 1.25
798 A248 100fr Sheet of 9, #a.-i. 4.50 2.50
799 A248 200fr Sheet of 9, #a.-i. 9.00 5.00

Souvenir Sheets

800-801 A248 Set of 2 10.50 6.00

Sites in Beijing A249

#802, Hall of Supreme Harmony. #803, Great Wall. #804, Hall of Prayers for Good Harvests, Temple of Heaven.

1996 *Perf. 13½*

802 A249 180fr multicolored 1.75 1.00
803 A249 180fr multicolored 1.75 1.00
804 A249 180fr multicolored 1.75 1.00
Nos. 802-804 (3) 5.25 3.00

Cotton Production A250

Designs: 20fr, Cotton plant, vert. 25fr, People working in cotton fields. 50fr, Holding plant, vert. 310fr, Dumping cotton into cart.

1996 *Perf. 13½*

805 A250 20fr multicolored .20 .20
806 A250 25fr multicolored .20 .20
807 A250 50fr multicolored .25 .20
808 A250 310fr multicolored 1.40 .70
Nos. 805-808 (4) 2.05 1.30

Birds and Snakes A251

a, Crowned eagle in flight. b, Tufted eagle. c, Python. d, Gabon viper.

Songbirds: No. 810: a, Choucador splendide. b, Astrid ondulé. c, Martin chasseur. d, Coucou didric.

Butterflies: No. 811a, Salamis parhassus. b, Charaxes bohemani. c, Coeliades forestan. d, Mimacrea marshalli.

1996

809 A251 180fr Sheet of 4, #a.-d. 3.25 1.60
810 A251 250fr Sheet of 4, #a.-d. 4.50 2.25
811 A251 320fr Sheet of 4, #a.-d. 5.75 3.00

Third World — A252

Design: 250fr, Hot air balloon in flight.

1996

812 A252 180fr shown 2.50 1.25
813 A252 250fr multicolored 3.00 1.50

A253

A254

1996

814 A253 180fr green & multi 1.00 .50
815 A253 250fr bister & multi 1.50 .75

Death of Abdoul Karim Camara (Cabral), 16th anniv.

1997, Jan. 10 Litho. *Perf. 14*

Dogs: #816, Airdale terrier. #817, Briard. #818, Schnauzer. #819, Chow chow.

Cats: #820, Turkish van. #821, Sphynx. #822, Korat. #823, American curl.

Dogs, horiz.: #824: a, Basset hound. b, Dachshund. c, Brittany spaniel. d, Saint Bernard. e, Bernese mountain. f, Irish setter. g, Gordon setter. h, Poodle. i, Pointer.

Cats, horiz: #825: a, Scottish fold. b, Javanese. c, Norwegian forest. d, American shorthair. e, Turkish angora. f, British shorthair. g, Egyptian mau. h, Maine coon. i, Burmese.

Each 1000fr: #826, Newfoundland. #827, Flame point Himalayan Persian.

816-819 A254 100fr Set of 4 2.50 1.25
820-823 A254 150fr Set of 4 3.25 1.10
824 A254 150fr Sheet of 9, #a.-i. 7.50 3.75
825 A254 180fr Sheet of 9, #a.-i. 8.50 4.25

Souvenir Sheets

826-827 A254 Set of 2 11.00 6.00

Environmental Protection A255

Fauna: No. 828: a, Dolphin. b, Ok, Rhea. d, Black rhinochrinoceros. e, Malayan tapir. f, Galapagos tortoise. g, Walrus. h, Gray wolf. i, Giraffe.

1000fr, Koala.

1997, Feb. 3

828 A255 250fr Sheet of 9, #a.-i. 14.00 7.75

Souvenir Sheet

829 A255 1000fr multicolored 6.00 3.25

Ships A256

Warships: No. 830: a, Bellerophon, England, 1867. b, Chen Yuan, China 1882. c, Hiei, Japan, 1877. d, Kaiser, Austria, 1862. e, King Wilhelm, Germany, 1869. f, Re D'Italia, Italy, 1864.

Paddle steamers: No. 831: a, Arctic, US, 1849. b, Washington, France, 1847. c, Esploratore, Italy, 1863. d, Fuad, Turkey, 1864. e, Hope, Confederate States of America, 1864. f, Britannia, England, 1840.

Each 1000fr: No. 832, Arabia, England, 1851. No. 833, Northumberland, England, 1867.

1996, Dec. 20 Litho. *Perf. 14*

830 A256 250fr Sheet of 6, #a.-f. 6.00 3.00
831 A256 320fr Sheet of 6, #a.-f. 10.00 3.75

Souvenir Sheets

832-833 A256 Set of 2 12.00 6.75

Wildlife — A257

Designs: a, Hippotragus niger. b, Damaliscus hunter. c, G. demidovii. d, Chimpanzee.

1996 Litho. *Perf. 13½*

834 A257 250fr Sheet of 4, #a.-d. 5.00 2.50

UNESCO, 50th anniv.

Red Cross — A258

Dogs: a, Rottweiler. b, Newfoundland. c, German shepherd. d, Bobtail (English sheepdog).

1996

835 A258 250fr Sheet of 4, #a.-d. 4.25 2.10

African Education Year — A259

100fr, Student with book, map, vert. 150fr, Classroom. 180fr, Families watching video program on farming techniques. 250fr, African people being educated, map, vert.

1996, Apr. 4 *Perf. 14*

836 A259 100fr multicolored .45 .45
837 A259 150fr multicolored .65 .65
838 A259 180fr multicolored .80 .80
839 A259 250fr multicolored 1.10 1.10
Nos. 836-839 (4) 3.00 3.00

Nos. 836-839 were not available until March 1997.

Folk Dances — A260

1996 *Perf. 13½*

840 A260 150fr Dounouba .65 .65
841 A260 170fr Gomba .75 .75
842 A260 225fr Sandia 1.40 1.40
843 A260 230fr Sabar 1.50 1.50
Nos. 840-843 (4) 4.30 4.30

Service Organizations — A261

No. 844: a, Man carrying bags. b, Man drinking water. c, Child holding bowl of food. d, Mother feeding infant.

No. 845: a, Girl with food. b, Man holding rice bowl. c, Woman holding bowl of food. d, Child opening box of food.

1996

844 A261 500fr Sheet of 4, #a.-d. 8.50 4.25
845 A261 650fr Sheet of 4, #a.-d. 11.50 5.75

79th Lions Intl. Convention (#844). 91st Rotary Intl. Convention (#845).

City of Canton, 2210th Anniv. A262

Designs: a, Statue of goats. b, Seal. c, Boat. d, Fruits, tea pot. e, Buildings. f, Dragon.

1996

846 A262 50fr Sheet of 6, #a.-f. 1.40 .70

FAO, 50th Anniv. A264

Space satellite, fauna: a, MOP.2, grasshopper. b, Meteosat P.2, lion. c, Envisat, dolphins. d, Radar satellite, whale.

1996 **Litho.** *Perf. 13½*

847 A264 310fr Sheet of 4, #a.-d. 5.00 2.50

Artifacts from Natl. Museum — A265

1996

848 A265 5fr Kara .20 .20
849 A265 10fr Hambe .20 .20
850 A265 180fr Pinge .80 .40
851 A265 250fr Merenkun 1.10 .55
Nos. 848-851 (4) 2.30 1.35

Nos. 848-851 exist in souvenir sheets of 1.

1998 Winter Olympics, Nagano A266

250fr, Speed skating. 310fr, Slalom skiing. 750fr, Figure skating. 900fr, Hockey.
2000fr, Downhill skiing.

1996

852 A266 250fr multicolored 1.25 .60
853 A266 310fr multicolored 1.50 .75
854 A266 750fr multicolored 3.50 1.75
855 A266 900fr multicolored 4.00 2.00
Nos. 852-855 (4) 10.25 5.10

Souvenir Sheet

856 A266 2000fr multicolored 10.00 5.00

Fauna, Mushrooms A267

a, Ploceus ocularis. b, Hemiolaus coecolus. c, Hebeloma radicosum. d, Sparassus dufouri simon.

1996

857 A267 750fr Sheet of 4, #a.-d. 13.00 6.50

New Year 1997 (Year of the Ox) — A268

1997

858 A268 500fr shown 2.00 1.00

Size: 53x35mm

859 A268 500fr Black porcelain ox 2.00 1.00

Nos. 858-859 exist in souvenir sheets of 1.

Butterflies A269

#860, Black-lined eggar. #861, Common opae. #862, Veined tiger. #863, The basker.

No. 864: a, Natal barred blue. b, Common grass blue. c, Fire grid. d, Mocker swallowtail. e, Azure hairstreak. f, Mother-of-pearl butterfly. g, Boisduval's false asraea. h, Pirate butterfly. i, African moon moth.

No. 865, vert.: a, Striped policeman. b, Mountain sandman. c, Brown-veined white. d, Bowker's widow. e, Foxy charaxes. f, Pirate. g, African clouded yellow. h, Garden inspector.

Each 1000fr: No. 866, Plain tiger. No. 867, Beautiful tiger. No. 868, African clouded yellow, vert. No. 869, Zebra white, vert.

1997, Jan. 27 *Perf. 14*

860-863 A269 180fr Set of 4 3.50 1.75
864 A269 150fr Sheet of 9, #a.-i. 6.25 3.00
865 A259 210fr Sheet of 8, #a.-h. 9.50 4.75

Souvenir Sheets

866-869 A269 Set of 4 24.00 12.00

Disney Characters A270

Greetings stamps: 25fr, Goofy, Bon Voyage. 50fr, Mickey, Happy New Year. 100fr, Goofy, Happy Birthday. 150fr, Donald writing. 180fr, Minnie writing. 250fr, Mickey, Minnie, anniversary. 310fr, Mickey, Minnie going on vacation. 320fr, Mickey, Minnie kissing.

Each 1500fr: No. 878, Daisy Duck, horiz. No. 879, Huey, Dewey, Louie throwing school books in air, horiz.

1997, Mar. 1 *Perf. 13½x14*

870-877 A270 Set of 8 7.00 3.50

Souvenir Sheets

878-879 A270 Set of 2 15.00 7.50

Bridges — A271

1997 **Litho.** *Perf. 14*

880 A271 100fr Mahina .50 .25
881 A271 150fr Selingue Dam .80 .40
882 A271 180fr King Fahd 1.00 .50
883 A271 250fr Martyrs 1.50 .75
Nos. 880-883 (4) 3.80 1.90

Dated 1996.

1998 World Cup Soccer Championships, France — A272

Various action scenes.

1997 *Perf. 13½*

884 A272 180fr multicolored 1.00 .50
885 A272 250fr multicolored 1.25 .60
886 A272 320fr multicolored 1.50 .75
887 A272 1060fr multicolored 4.50 2.25
Nos. 884-887 (4) 8.25 4.10

Souvenir Sheet

888 A272 2000fr multicolored 9.00 4.25

Dated 1996. No. 888 contains one 36x42mm stamp.

Formula I Race Car Drivers A273

Designs: a, Michael Schumacher. b, Damon Hill. c, Jacques Villeneuve. d, Gerhard Berger.

1996 **Litho.** *Perf. 13½*

889 A273 650fr Sheet of 4, #a.-d. 11.00 5.50

John F. Kennedy (1917-63) A274

Various portraits.

1997

890 A274 390fr Sheet of 9, #a.-i. 15.00 7.50

John Lennon (1940-80) A275

Various portraits.

1997

891 A275 250fr Sheet of 9, #a.-i. 9.50 4.75

Deng Xiaoping (1904-97), Chinese Leader A276

Designs: a, As young man. b, Without hat. c, With hat. d, As middle-aged man.
250fr, Being kissed by child.

1997 *Perf. 13½*

892 A276 250fr Sheet of 4, #a.-d. 4.00 2.00

Souvenir Sheet

Perf. 13x13½

893 A276 250fr multicolored 4.00 2.00

No. 893 contains 69x50mm stamp.

Elvis Presley, 20th Death Anniv. A277

No. 894, Various portraits. No. 895, Portrait, Elvis on motorcycle.

1997 **Litho.** *Perf. 13½*

894 A277 310fr Sheet of 9, #a.-i. 12.00 6.00

Souvenir Sheet

895 A277 2000fr multicolored 9.00 4.50

No. 895 contains one 42x51mm stamp.

Marine Life A278

No. 896: a, Chaetodon auriga. b, Balistoides conspicillum. c, Forcipiger longirostris. d, Chelmon rostratus. e, Plectorhinchus diagrammus. f, Stegastes leucostictus. g, Chaetodon kleinii. h, Synchiropus splendidus. i, Platax orbicularis.

No. 897: a, Amphiprion percula. b, Holacanthus ciliaris. c, Chaetodon reticulatus. d, Pomacanthus imperator. e, Heniochus acuminatus. f, Lienardella fasciata. g, Zanclus cornutus. h, Scarus guacamaia. i, Lutjanus sebae.

No. 898: a, Tursiops truncatus. b, Phaethon lepturus. c, Istiophorus platypterus. d, Sphyma zygaena. e, Reinhardtius hippoglossoides. f, Manta birostris. g, Thunnus albacares. h, Himantolophus groenlandicus. i, Tridacana gigas.

No. 899: a, Cypselurus heterurus. b, Sailboat. c, Delphinus delphis. d, Cacharodon carcharias. e, Orcinus orca (b, f). f, Salmo salar. g, Conger conger. h, Pomatomus saltatrix. i, Sphyraena barracuda.

Each 1000r: No. 900, Balaenoptera musculus. No. 901, Megaptera novaengliae, vert.

1997, Mar. 2 Litho. *Perf. 14*

896 A278 150fr Sheet of 9, #a.-i. 6.00 6.00
897 A278 180fr Sheet of 9, #a.-i 7.00 7.00
898 A278 250fr Sheet of 9, #a.-i. 9.75 9.75
899 A278 310fr Sheet of 9, #a.-i. 11.50 11.50

Souvenir Sheets

900-901 A278 Set of 2 9.00 9.00

Transportation — A279

Cyclists: No. 902: a, Rudolph Lewis, 1912. b, Jacques Anquetil, 4-time Tour de France winner. c, Miguel Indurain, hour record holder.

Sailing ships: No. 903: a, Lightning, by Donald McKay, 1856. b, Olivier de Kersauson, winner of Jules Verne trophy. c. Lockheed Sea Shadow, US.

Motorcycles, cyclists: No. 904: a, Coventry Eagle-Jap 998cm3. b, Michael Doohan, Honda 500 NSRV4. c, Harley-Davidson, Heritage Softail classic FLSTC.

Airships: No. 905: a, "Gifford," steam-powered dirigible, 1852. b, Count Ferdinand von Zeppelin, Zeppelin NT LZ N07. c, Nobile N1, "Norge," 1926.

Trains: No. 906: a, Locomotive G 4/5 2-8-0, Switzerland. b, W.V. Siemens, ICE train, Germany. c, Maglev HSST-5, Japan.

Race cars: No. 907: a, 1949 Ferrari Type 166/MM. b, Michael Schumacher, F1 310B Ferrari. c, Ferrari F50.

Sled dogs: No. 908: a, Eskimo. b, Alaskan malamute. c, Siberian husky.

Aircraft: No. 909: a, Wright Brothers' first flight at Kitty Hawk. b, Andre Turcat, Concorde. c, X34 space vehicle.

1997 Litho. *Perf. 13½*

902 A279 180fr Strip of 3, #a.-c. 2.10 1.00
903 A279 250fr Strip of 3, #a.-c. 3.00 1.50
904 A279 320fr Strip of 3, #a.-c. 3.75 2.00
905 A279 370fr Strip of 3, #a.-c. 4.25 2.25
906 A279 460fr Strip of 3, #a.-c. 5.50 2.75
907 A279 490fr Strip of 3, #a.-c. 5.75 3.00
908 A279 530fr Strip of 3, #a.-c. 6.50 3.25
909 A279 750fr Strip of 3, #a.-c. 8.75 4.50

Movie Stars — A281

Designs: a, John Wayne. b, Frank Sinatra. c, Rita Hayworth. d, Sammy Davis, Jr. e, Marilyn Monroe. f, Eddie Murphy. g, Elizabeth Taylor. h, James Dean. i, Robert Mitchum.

1997

910 A281 320fr Sheet of 9, #a.-i. 11.00 5.50

A282

A283

Diana, Princess of Wales (1961-97) — A284

Designs: No. 911, Various close-up portraits. No. 912, Pictures of various times in Diana's life.

Each 1500fr: No. 913, In pink dress with Pres. Clinton (in margin). No. 914, Wearing strapless evening dress. No. 915, Wearing hat and veil. No. 916, In blue dress with Nelson Mandela (in margin).

1997 Litho. *Perf. 13½*

911 A282 250fr Sheet of 9, #a.-i. 8.75 4.50
912 A283 370fr Sheet of 9, #a.-i. 13.00 6.50

Souvenir Sheets

913-916 A284 Set of 4 26.00 13.00

Mars Pathfinder A285

Dr. Cheick M. Diarra: a, blue & multi background. b, green & multi background. c, Part of Mars in background. d, violet black & multi background.

1997

917 A285 180fr Sheet of 4, #a.-d. 5.50 2.50

Crested Porcupine A286

World Wildlife Fund: a, Two adults. b, One adult crawling right. c, Mother with young. d, Adult with quills raised.

1998

918 A286 250fr Block of 4, #a.-d. 6.75 3.00

Churches A287

Pieces from Natl. Museum — A288

1997 Litho. *Perf. 13½*

919 A287 5fr Kita Basilica .20 .20
920 A287 10fr San Cathedral .20 .20
921 A287 150fr Bamako Cathedral .70 .35
922 A287 370fr Mandiakuy Church 1.75 .85
Nos. 919-922 (4) 2.85 1.60

1997

20fr, Bamanan. 25fr, Dogon couple. 250fr, Tasmasheq. 310fr, Oil lamp, Boo.

923 A288 20fr multicolored .20 .20
924 A288 25fr multicolored .20 .20
925 A288 250fr multicolored 1.25 .60
926 A288 310fr multicolored 1.50 .75
Nos. 923-926 (4) 3.15 1.75

Cotton Industry — A289

1997

927 A289 30fr Spools of threads .20 .20
928 A289 50fr Clothing .20 .20
929 A289 180fr Towels 1.00 .50
930 A289 320fr Textile production 1.50 .75
Nos. 927-930 (4) 2.90 1.65

"Star Wars" Motion Pictures A290

Various scenes from: No. 931, "The Return of the Jedi." No. 932, "Star Wars." No. 933: "The Empire Strikes Back."

1997 Litho. *Perf. 13½*

Sheets of 9

931 A290 180fr #a.-i. 7.00 7.00
932 A290 310fr #a.-i. 12.00 12.00
933 A290 320fr #a.-i. 13.00 13.00

Wild Animals A291

Lions Intl. — #934: a, Lion. b, Cheetah standing. c, Cheetah lying down. d, Leopard.

Rotary Intl. — #935: a, Giraffe. b, Addax. c, Kob. d, Okapi.

1997

934 A291 310fr Sheet of 4, #a.-d. 5.00 2.50
935 A291 320fr Sheet of 4, #a.-d. 5.75 2.75

Mars Pathfinder — A292

Insignia and various scenes of Pathfinder mission.

1997

936 A292 370fr Sheet of 9, #a.-i. 15.00 7.50

Cats — A293

No. 937: a, Sphynx. b, Siberian brown tabby. c, Somali creme. d, Java cream point. 1500fr, Chartreux.

1997 Litho. *Perf. 13½*

937 A293 530fr Sheet of 4, #a.-d. 9.00 4.50

Souvenir Sheet

938 A293 1500fr multicolored 6.50 3.25

No. 938 contains one 36x42mm stamp.

Scouts and Birds A294

1997

Color of Bird

939 A294 180fr yellow & black .90 .45
940 A294 490fr black & white 2.75 1.40
941 A294 530fr gray & yel org 3.00 1.50
Nos. 939-941 (3) 6.65 3.35

Souvenir Sheets

942 A294 Sheet of 3, #a.-c. + 3 labels 10.00 5.00
943 A294 1500fr multicolored 7.00 7.00

No. 942 sold for 2200fr. Nos. 942a-942c have the same designs and denominations as Nos. 939-941 but have continuous background showing portion of scouting emblem.

No. 943 contains 42x50mm stamp.

1997

Various mushrooms, scout: 250fr, Frying mushrooms. 320fr, Grilling mushrooms. 1060fr, Gathering mushrooms, placing in bag.

944 A294 250fr multicolored 1.25 .60
945 A294 320fr multicolored 1.50 .75
946 A294 1060fr multicolored 5.00 2.50
Nos. 944-946 (3) 7.75 3.85

Souvenir Sheet

947 A294 Sheet of 3, #a.-c. + 3 labels 11.00 5.50

#947 sold for 2600fr. #947a-947c have the same designs and denominations as #944-946 but have continuous background showing portion of scouting emblem. A number has been reserved for an additional souvenir sheet with this set.

1998

Various minerals, scout: 150fr, Looking at minerals with magnifying glass. 750fr, Reading book. 900fr, Using chisel.

949 A294 150fr multicolored .70 .35
950 A294 750fr multicolored 3.50 1.75
951 A294 900fr multicolored 4.50 2.25
Nos. 949-951 (3) 8.70 4.35

Souvenir Sheet

952 A294 Sheet of 3, #a.-c. + 3 labels 12.00 6.00

No. 952 sold for 2800fr. Nos. 952a-952c have the same designs and denominations as Nos. 949-951 but have continuous background showing portion of scouting emblem.

1998 Litho. *Perf. 13½*

Various butterflies, scout: 310fr, Photographing butterfly. 430fr, Using book to identify butterfly. 460fr, Holding and looking at butterfly.

954 A294 310fr multicolored 1.40 .70
955 A294 430fr multicolored 2.25 1.10
956 A294 460fr multicolored 2.40 1.25
Nos. 954-956 (3) 6.05 3.05

Souvenir Sheet

957 A294 Sheet of 3, #a.-c. + 3 labels 10.00 5.00

No. 957 sold for 2200fr. Nos. 957a-957c have same designs and denominations as Nos. 954-956 but have continuous background showing portion of scouting emblem. A number has been reserved for an additional souvenir sheet with this set.

Flame of Peace, Timbuktu — A295

Pan-African Postal Union, 18th anniv. — A296

1997

959 A295 180fr yellow & multi 2.00 1.00
960 A295 250fr dull red & multi 3.00 1.50

Dated 1996.

1998

961 A296 250fr Addax 1.50 .75

Local Views — A297

5fr, Mosque, Mopti. 10fr, Fertility doll, Mopti. 15fr, Fishermen. 20fr, Woman carrying bowls on head, Macina. 25fr, Friendship Hotel. 30fr, Sikasso Hill. 40fr, Camel caravan, Azalai. 50fr, Women's hair style, Kayes. 60fr, Old Dogon man. 70fr, Shepherd. 80fr, Playing musical instrument, Wassoulou. 90fr, Crest, Ciwara Bamanan.

1998

962 A297 5fr multi .20 .20
963 A297 10fr multi, vert. .20 .20
964 A297 15fr multi .20 .20
966 A297 20fr multi, vert. .20 .20
966 A297 25fr multi, vert. .30 .30
967 A297 30fr multi, vert. .30 .30
968 A297 40fr multi, vert. .30 .30
969 A297 50fr multi, vert. .30 .30
970 A297 60fr multi, vert. .40 .40
971 A297 70fr multi, vert. .40 .40
972 A297 80fr multi, vert. .40 .40
973 A297 90fr multi, vert. .40 .40
Nos. 962-973 (12) 3.60 3.60

Travels of Pope John Paul II — A298

#974: a, Looking at book with Fidel Castro, Cuba. b, Walking with Castro, Cuba. c, With girl, Castro, Cuba. d, With boy, Nigeria. e, With three nuns, Cuba. f, Reading inscription on monument, Cuba. g, Holding crucifix, blessing child, Nigeria. h, Standing before monument, Nigeria. i, Giving blessing, people in traditional costumes, Nigeria.

Nos. 975a, 975c, 975d, 975e, 975f, 975g, 975i: Various portraits of Mother Teresa with Pope John Paul II. No. 975b, Pope John Paul II. No. 975h, Mother Teresa.

1998 Litho. *Perf. 13½*

Sheets of 9

974 A298 310fr #a.-i. 12.00 6.00
975 A298 320fr #a.-i. 12.00 6.00

Animal Type of 1997

Dogs — #976: a, Dachshund. b, Persian hound. c, Chihuahua. d, Pug.
1500fr, Dalmatian.

1998 Litho. *Perf. 13½*

976 A293 390fr Sheet of 4, #a.-d. 6.50 3.25

Souvenir Sheet

977 A293 1500fr multicolored 6.25 3.00

No. 977 contains one 36x42mm stamp.

Entertainers A299

No. 978, Various portraits of James Dean.

No. 979, opera singers: a, Placido Domingo. b, Luciano Pavarotti. c, Jose Carreras. d, Andrea Bocelli. e, Maria Callas. f, Jose Van Dam. g, Renata Tebaldi. h, Montserrat Caballe. i, Kiri Te Kanawa.

No. 980, actresses: a, Audrey Hepburn. b, Greta Garbo. c, Elizabeth Taylor. d, Grace Kelly. e, Jean Harlow. f, Ava Gardner. g, Lana Turner. h, Marilyn Monroe. i, Vivien Leigh.

1998 Litho. *Perf. 13½*

Sheets of 9

978 A299 250fr #a.-i. 9.50 4.75
979 A299 310fr #a.-i. 13.00 6.50
980 A299 320fr #a.-i. 13.00 6.50

Chess Masters A300

Portraits: a, Adolf Anderssen, 1818-79. b, Wilhelm Steinitz, 1836-1900. c, Emmanuel Lasker, 1868-1941. d, Alexandre Alekhine, 1892-1946. e, Tigran Petrossian, 1929-84. f, Boris Spassky, 1937. g, Bobby Fischer, 1943. h, Garry Kasparov, 1963. i, Anatoli Karpov, 1951.

1998

981 A300 370fr Sheet of 9, #a.-i. 15.00 7.50

Eric Tabarly (1931-98), French Sailor — A301

Designs: a, Portrait. b, Tabarly at helm, yachts Pen Duick, Pen Duick VI. c, Tabarly, Charles de Gaulle.

1998

982 A301 390fr Sheet of 3, #a.-c. 5.00 2.50

No. 982b is 60x50mm.

France, 1998 World Cup Soccer Champions — A302

No. 983: a, Laurent Blanc. b, Lilian Thurman. c, David Trezeguet.

No. 984: a, Marcel Desailly. b, Fabien Barthez. c, Christian Karembeu.

No. 985: a, Didier Deschamps. b, Emmanuel Petit. c, Bixente Lizarazu.

No. 986: a, Youri Djorkaeff. b, Zinedine Zidane. c, Aime Jacquet.

2000fr, Team picture.

1998 Litho. *Perf. 13½*

Sheets of 3

983 A302 250fr #a.-c. 4.00 2.00
984 A302 370fr #a.-c. 5.00 2.75
985 A302 390fr #a.-c. 6.00 3.00
986 A302 750fr #a.-c. 10.50 5.25

Souvenir Sheet

987 A302 2000fr multicolored 10.00 10.00

No. 987 contains one 57x51mm stamp.

Jacques-Yves Cousteau (1910-97), Underwater Explorer, Environmentalist A303

No. 988: a, Cousteau, ship Calypso. b, Divers, underwater submersibles. c, Diver looking into submarine habitat, man playing chess.

No. 989: a, Portrait, Cousteau with Pres. John F. Kennedy. b, Divers retrieving amphora. c, Hard hat diver, Cousteau wearing early aqualung.

1998

Sheets of 3

988 A303 460fr #a.-c. 6.50 3.25
989 A303 490fr #a.-c. 7.00 3.50

Nos. 988b, 989b are each 60x51mm.

History of Chess A304

Chess pieces, boards — #990: a, India, 18th cent. b, Italy, 1700. c, Siam, 18th cent. d, France, 1880. e, Austria, 1872. f, Germany, 1925. g, Yugoslavia, 20th cent. h, China, 20th cent. i, Russia, 20th cent.

No. 991, Albert V of Bavaria playing chess with his wife, Anne of Austria. No. 992, Arabian chess. No. 993, Japanese chess. No. 994, Nefertari, Ramses II playing chess.

1998 Litho. *Perf. 13½*

990 A304 370fr Sheet of 9, #a.-i. 12.50 6.25

Souvenir Sheets

991-994 A304 1500fr each 5.75 3.00

Nos. 991-994 each contain one 57x51mm stamp.

Pope John Paul II — A305

No. 995: Various portraits of John Paul II portrayed with events, popes depicting papal history.

Pope John Paul II, famous cathedrals — #996: a, Chartres. b, Santiago de Compostela. c, St. Sophie, Novgorod, Russia. d, St. Peter's Basilica, Vatican City. e, Our Lady of Peace Basilica, Yamoussoukro, Ivory Coast. f, Milan.

Pope John Paul II, famous cathedrals — #997: a, Sacred Family, Barcelona. b, Saint Sophie, Kiev. c, Notre Dame, Lausanne. d, Cathedral of Mexico. e, Cathedral of Cologne. f, Burgos Cathedral.

1998 Litho. *Perf. 13½*

Sheets of 6 or 9

995 A305 250fr #a.-i. 8.00 4.00
996 A305 370fr #a.-f. 7.50 3.75
997 A305 750fr #a.-f. 15.00 7.50

Granaries A306

1998 Litho. *Perf. 13½*

998 A306 25fr Sénoufo, vert. .20 .20
999 A306 180fr Sarakolé .70 .35
1000 A306 310fr Minianka, vert. 1.40 .70
1001 A306 320fr Boo, vert. 1.40 .70
Nos. 998-1001 (4) 3.70 1.95

Trees A307

1998

1002 A307 100fr Tamarindus indica .50 .25
1003 A307 150fr Adansonia digitata .70 .35
1004 A307 180fr Acacia senegal .80 .40
1005 A307 310fr Parkia biglobosa 1.50 .75
Nos. 1002-1005 (4) 3.50 1.75

National Museum Pieces — A308

1998

1006 A308 50fr Bamanan .20 .20
1007 A308 150fr Dogon .60 .30
1008 A308 250fr Bamanan, diff. 1.00 .50
1009 A308 320fr Minianka 1.40 .70
Nos. 1006-1009 (4) 3.20 1.70

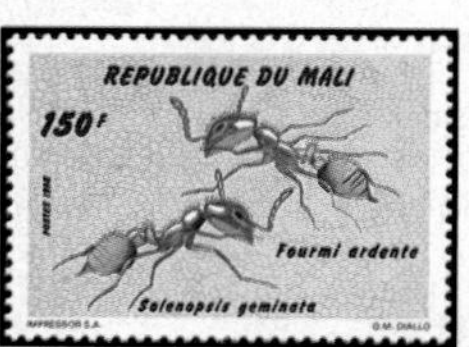

Ants A309

150fr, Solenopsis geminata. 180fr, Camponotus pennsylvanicus. 250fr, Monorium minimum. 310fr, Lasius niger.

1998

1010 A309 150fr multi .60 .30
1011 A309 180fr multi, vert. .80 .40
1012 A309 250fr multi 1.25 .60
1013 A309 310fr multi 1.50 .75
Nos. 1010-1013 (4) 4.15 2.05

Baladji Cisse (1924-77), Boxer — A309a

1999, May 12 Litho. *Perf. 13½*

1013B A309a 250fr shown —

An additional stamp was issued in this set. The editors would like to examine any example.

World Teachers' Day A310

Various views of teachers working.

1999 Litho. *Perf. 13½*

1014 A310 150fr multi, vert. .60 .30
1015 A310 250fr multi, vert. 1.00 .50
1016 A310 370fr multi, vert. 1.50 .75
1017 A310 390fr multi 1.75 .85
Nos. 1014-1017 (4) 4.85 2.40

Fight Against Poverty A311

1999 Litho. *Perf. 13¼*

1018 A311 150fr Agriculture .70 .35
1019 A311 180fr Labor projects .90 .45
1020 A311 750fr Food, vert. 3.25 1.60
1021 A311 1000fr Potable water 4.25 2.10
Nos. 1018-1021 (4) 9.10 4.50

UPU, 125th Anniv. A312

UPU emblem and: 150fr, Airplane, train, boat. 250fr, Stick figures with letters. 310fr, Eagles, antelopes with letters. 320fr, Eagle with letter on mud structure, vert.

1999

1022 A312 150fr multi .60 .30
1023 A312 250fr multi 1.00 .50
1024 A312 310fr multi 1.25 .60
1025 A312 320fr multi 1.40 .70
Nos. 1022-1025 (4) 4.25 2.10

Flora and Fauna A313

No. 1026 — Reptiles: a, Pseudonaja textilis. b, Litoria chloris. c, Imantodes inornata. d, Pyton arboricole. e, Pachydactylus bibroni. f, Trimeresurus wagleri.

No. 1027 — Orchids: a, Epidendrum ellipticum. b, Oncidium macranthum. c, Miltoniopsis roezlii. d, Oncidium barbatum. e, Miltonia warscewiczii. f, Lockhartia oerstedii.

No. 1028 — Birds: a, Amandava subflava. b, Ploceus bojeri. c, Lagonostica senegala. d, Uraeginthus bengalus. e, Monticola saxatilis. f, Saxicola torquata.

No. 1028G — Birds: a, Tyto alba. b, Pernis apivorus. c, Bubo africanus. d, Gypaetus barbatus meridionalis. e, Strix aluco. f, Milvus migrans.

No. 1029 — Butterflies: a, Cymothoe hypatha. b, Cymothoe sangaris. c, Top view, Charaxes fournierae. d, Male Catopsilia thauruma. e, Bottom view, Charaxes fournierae. f, Female Catopsilia thauruma.

No. 1030 — Mushrooms: a, Amanita muscaria. b, Amanita spissa. c, Helvella acetabulum. d, Pleurotus ostreatus. e, Phallus duplicatus. f, Cortinarius salor.

1999

Sheets of 6

1026 A313 350fr #a.-f. 9.00 4.50
1027 A313 390fr #a.-f. 10.00 5.00
1028 A313 430fr #a.-f. 11.00 5.50
1028G A313 460fr #h-m 12.00 6.00
1029 A313 490fr #a.-f. 13.00 6.50
1030 A313 530fr #a.-f. 14.00 7.00
Nos. 1026-1030 (6) 69.00 34.50

Rocks, Dinosaurs and Volcanoes A314

No. 1031 — Dinosaurs and rocks: a, Edmontonia, Ensisheim meteorite. b, Iguanodon, Saint-Mesmin meteorite. c, Allosaurus, Pallasite meteorite. d, Troodon, Lunar meteorite. e, Lesothosaurus, rock from Bouvant. f, Carnotaurus, Axtell meteorite. g, Deinonychus, Orgueil meteorite. h, Dilophosaurus, rock from Douar Mghila. i. Psittacosaurus, L'Aigle meteorite.

No. 1032 — Volcanic eruptions and rocks: a, Popocatepetl, 1519, Peekskill meteorite. b, Santorin, 1645, Tamentit meteorite. c, Mt. Pelee, 1902, Ouallen meteorite. d, Herculaneum during Vesuvius eruption, 79, Chinguetti meteorite. e, Krakatoa, 1883, Pultush meteorite. f, Soufriere, 1979, rock from Sienne. g, Mt. St. Helens, 1980, Allende meteorite. h, Kilauea, 1984, Parnallee meteorite. i, Mt. Etna, 1986, Tamentit meteorite.

1500fr, Pompeii during Vesuvius eruption, 79.

1999 *Perf. 13¼*

Sheets of 9

1031 A314 250fr #a.-i. 9.00 4.50
1032 A314 310fr #a.-i. 12.00 6.00

Souvenir Sheet

Perf. 13½

1033 A314 1500fr multi 6.75 3.25

No. 1033 contains one 39x56mm stamp.

Space A315

No. 1034: a, Hubble Space Telescope. b, Venera 12. c, Space shuttle. d, Ariane 5.

No. 1035: a, Apollo-Soyuz mission. b, Carl Sagan, Viking 1. c, Voyager 1. d, Giotto probe, Edmond Halley.

1999 *Perf. 13¼*

Sheets of 4

1034 A315 250fr #a.-d. 4.50 2.25
1035 A315 310fr #a.-d. 5.50 2.75

The Malian government declared that sheets of 9 stamps containing 100, 150, 200, 250, 300, 350, 400, 450 and 500fr stamps with the following topics are "illegal": Trains, Chess, Prehistoric Animals, Ferdinand Magellan, Christopher Columbus, Mushrooms, Computers, Wolves, Minerals, International Red Cross, Composers, Horses, and Wild Animals (tiger, lion, eagle, etc.)

Space Type of 1999

No. 1036: a, Frank Borman, Apollo 8. b, Neil Armstrong, Apollo 11. c, Luna 16 and Lunokhod 2. d, Surveyor 3.

No. 1037: a, Konstantin Tsiolkovsky. b, Robert H. Goddard. c, Hermann Oberth. d, Theodor von Kármán.

No. 1038: a, Laika, Sputnik 2. b, Yuri Gagarin, Vostok 1. c, Edward White, Gemini 4. d, John Glenn, Friendship 7.

No. 1039: a, Apollo 15 Lunar Rover. b, Pioneer 10. c, Skylab. d, Mariner 10.

1999 Litho. *Perf. 13¼*

Sheets of 4

1036 A315 320fr #a-d 5.50 2.75
1037 A315 500fr #a-d 8.75 4.25
1038 A315 750fr #a-d 13.00 6.50
1039 A315 900fr #a-d 15.00 7.50
Nos. 1036-1039 (4) 42.25 21.00

Garfield the Cat — A319

No. 1048: a, With eyes half shut, pink background. b, With eyes open, pink background. c, Touching chin. d, With eyes open and open mouth. e, Showing tongue. f, With eyes open, showing teeth. g, With eyes open, blue background. h, With eyes half shut, blue background. i, Odie.

1000fr, As mailman.

1999, May 20 Litho. *Perf. 13¼*

1048 A319 250fr Sheet of 9, #a-i 10.00 5.00

Souvenir Sheet

1049 A319 1000fr multi 4.50 2.25

No. 1049 contains one 36x42mm stamp.

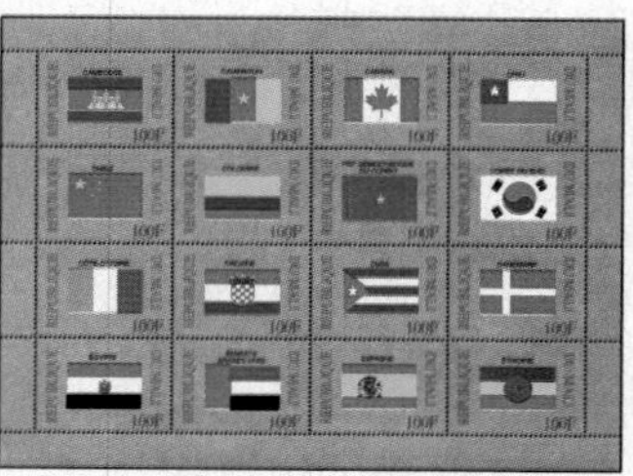
Flags of the World — A321

No. 1058: a, Myanmar. b, Namibia. c, Nepal. d, Niger. e, Nigeria. f, Norway. g, Uganda. h, Pakistan. i, Netherlands. j, Peru. k, Philippines. l, Poland. m, New Zealand. n, Portugal. o, North Korea. p, Romania.

No. 1059: a, Russia. b, Rwanda. c, Singapore. d, Slovakia. e, Sudan. f, Sri Lanka. g, Sweden. h, Switzerland. i, Syria. j, Tanzania. k, Czech Republic. l, Thailand. m, Somalia. n, Tunisia. o, Turkey. p, Ukraine.

No. 1060: a, Finland. b, France. c, Great Britain. d, Greece. e, Guinea. f, Hungary. g, India. h, Indonesia. i, Iran. j, Iraq. k, Ireland. l, Iceland. m, Israel. n, Italy. o, Libya. p, Japan.

No. 1061: a, Cambodia. b, Cameroun. c, Canada. d, Chile. e, People's Republic of China. f, Colombia. g, Democratic Republic of the Congo. h, South Korea. i, Ivory Coast. j, Croatia. k, Cuba. l, Denmark. m, Egypt. n, United Arab Emirates. o, Spain. p, Ethiopia.

No. 1062: a, Afghanistan. b, South Africa. c, Albania. d, Algeria. e, Germany. f, United States. g, Angola. h, Saudi Arabia. i, Argentina. j, Australia. k, Austria. l, Bangladesh. m, Belgium. n, Bolivia. o, Brazil. p, Bulgaria.

No. 1063: a, Jordan. b, Kenya. c, Kuwait. d, Laos. e, Lebanon. f, Lithuania. g, Luxembourg. h, Madagascar. i, Malaysia. j, Mali. k, Viet Nam. l, Morocco. m, Mauritius. n, Mexico. o, Monaco. p, Mongolia.

1999, Aug. 2 Litho. *Perf. 13¼*

1058 A321 20fr Sheet of 16, #a-p — —
1059 A321 25fr Sheet of 16, #a-p — —
1060 A321 50fr Sheet of 16, #a-p — —
1061 A321 100fr Sheet of 16, #a-p 5.00 2.50
q. Cameroun, flag with green star — —
r. Sheet of 16, #1061a, 1061c-1061q — —
1063 A321 100fr Sheet of 16, #a-p — —

No. 1061b has a Cameroun flag with a yellow star.

Sikasso Cathedral — A322

No. 1065: a, Photograph. b, Drawing. Illustration reduced.

1999, Dec. 25 Litho. ***Perf. 13¼***

1065 A322 150fr Horiz. pair, #a-b 1.40 .70

Christianity, 2000th Anniv. — A323

No. 1066, 100fr: a, St. Louis. b, Construction of Amiens Cathedral, 13th cent. c, Joan of Arc. d, Pope John Paul II.

No. 1067, 180fr: a, Jesus Christ. b, Persecution of Christians by Nero. c, St. Peter. d, Charlemagne.

1999, Dec. 25

Sheets of 4, #a-d

1066-1067 A323 Set of 2 5.00 2.50

Religious Paintings — A324

No. 1068, 250fr: a, Heller Madonna, by Albrecht Dürer. b, Virgin and Child, by Dürer. c, Madonna with Sts. Francis and Liberale, by Giorgione. d, Virgin and Child, by Giorgione.

No. 1069, 310fr: a, Virgin and Child, by Fra Filippo Lippi. b, Virgin and Child with Two Angels, by Lippi. c, Virgin and Sleeping Child, by Andrea Mantegna. d, Madonna of Victory, by Mantegna.

No. 1070, 320fr: a, Virgin and Child, by Hugo van der Goes. b, Virgin and Child and landscape, by van der Goes. c, Madonna and Child with St. Peter and a Martyred Saint, by Paolo Veronese. d, Adoration of the Magi, by Veronese.

No. 1071, 370fr: a, Madonna and Child Between St. Peter and St. Sebastian, by Giovanni Bellini. b, Madonna and Child with Cherubim, by Bellini. c, Madonna and Child with Two Angels, by Sandro Botticelli. d, Bardi Madonna, by Botticelli.

No. 1072, 390fr: a, Rest During the Flight to Egypt, with St. Francis, by Corregio. b, The Night, by Corregio. c, Senigallia Madonna, by Piero della Francesca. d, Virgin and Child and Four Angels, by della Francesca.

No. 1073, 750fr: a, Virgin and Child (rectangular), by Quentin Massys. b, Virgin and Child (curved top) by Massys. c, Madonna and Saint Sixtus, by Raphael. d, Madonna of the Duke of Alba, by Raphael.

1999, Dec. 25

Sheets of 4, #a-d

1068-1073 A324 Set of 6 40.00 20.00

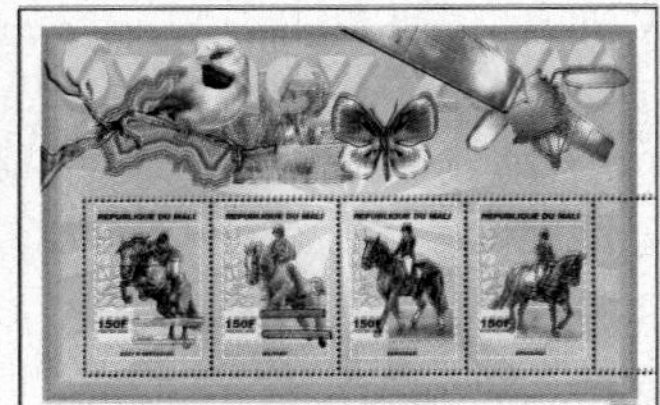

2000 Summer Olympics, Sydney — A325

No. 1074, 150fr — Equestrian events: a, Show jumping. b, Military jumping. c, Dressage, horse facing left. d, Dressage, horse facing right.

No. 1075, 460fr — Tennis: a, Woman with green trim on dress. b, Man with red trim on shirt. c, Woman, diff. d, Man, diff.

No. 1076, 530fr — Table tennis: a, Green and red shirt and shorts. b, White shirt, red shorts. c, White and red shirt, black shorts. d, Yellow and green shirt, black shorts.

No. 1077, 750fr — Basketball: a, Red and yellow uniform. b, Green uniform. c, White and red uniform. d, Yellow and green uniform.

1000fr, Hurdler, horse and rider, horiz.

2000, June 30

Sheets of 4, #a-d

1074-1077 A325 Set of 4 45.00 22.50

Souvenir Sheet

1078 A325 1000fr multi 6.00 3.00

No. 1078 contains one 57x51mm stamp.

2002 World Cup Soccer Championships, Japan and Korea — A326

No. 1079, 150fr: a, Pedro Cea. b, Schiavo. c, Luigi Colaussi. d, Juan Schiaffino.

No. 1080, 250fr: a, Fritz Walter. b, Pelé. c, Amarildo. d, Bobby Moore.

No. 1081, 320fr: a, Jairzinho. b, Franz Beckenbauer. c, Mario Kempes. d, Paolo Rossi.

No. 1082, 750fr: a, Diego Maradona. b, Jurgen Klinsmann. c, Romario. d, Zinedine Zidane.

2000, June 30

Sheets of 4, #a-d

1079-1082 A326 Set of 4 35.00 17.50

Fauna, Mushrooms and Prehistoric Animals — A327

No. 1083, 150fr — Birds: a, Ganga de Liechtenstein. b, Guepier à gorge blanche. c, Moineau domestique. d, Euplecte de feu. e, Irrisor namaquois. f, Pique-boeuf à bec jaune.

No. 1084, 180fr — Dogs: a, Dalmatian. b, Hungarian Kuvasz. c, Swedish shepherd. d, Ibiza dog. e, Golden retriever. f, Dachshund.

No. 1085, 250fr — Cats: a, White cat with orange eyes. b, Somali. c, Himalayan blue tortie point. d, Korat. e, Bombay. f, La Perm.

No. 1086, 310fr — Butterflies: a, Paralethe dendrophilis. b, Papilio ophidicephalus. c, Kallima jacksoni. d, Hypolimnas antevorta. e, Papilio nobilis. f, Euxanthe wakefieldi.

No. 1087, 320fr — Butterflies: a, Euxanthe eurinome. b, Euryphura chalcis. c, Dira mintha. d, Euphaedra zaddachi. e, Euphaedra neophron. f, Euxanthe tiberius.

No. 1088, 370fr — Mushrooms: a, Volvariella acystidiata. b, Leucopricus birnbaumii. c, Cystoderma elegans. d, Leucoprinus elaidis. e, Leucoprinus discoideus. f, Leucoagaricus carminescens.

No. 1089, 370fr — Birds: a, Pririt du cap. b, Petit duc scops. c, Ouette d'Egypte. d, Rollier d'Europe. e, Promerops du cap. f, Sauteur du cap.

No. 1090, 390fr — Mushrooms: a, Volvariella parvispora. b, Volvariella surrecta. c, Lentinus similis. d, Leucoagaricus holosericeus. e, Leucoagaricus pepinus. f, Agrocybe elegantior.

No. 1091, 460fr — Prehistoric animals: a, Psittacosaurus. b, Phororhacos. c, Coelophysis. d, Saurornithoides. e, Acanthopholis. f, Varannosaurus.

No. 1092, 490fr — Prehistoric animals: a, Dromiceiomimus. b, Placodus. c, Ceratosaurus. d, Heterodontosaurus. e, Diatryma. f, Ouranosaurus.

2000, Sept. 25

Sheets of 6, #a-f

1083-1092 A327 Set of 10 110.00 55.00

Campaign Against Malaria A328

Designs: No. 1093, 150fr, Doctor, mother and child. No. 1094, 150fr, Man with briefcase, man with crutch, syringe. No. 1095, 150fr, Doctor, syringe. 430fr, Mother, child, syringe, quinine tablets.

2000

1093-1096 A328 Set of 4 3.25 1.60

Intl. Volunteers Year (in 2001) — A329

2000

1097 A329 250fr multi .80 .40

Independence, 40th Anniv. — A330

Designs: 20fr, Provincial map. 375fr, Flag-raising ceremony, front and back of 50-franc banknote, vert.

2001 Litho. ***Perf. 13***

1099 A330 20fr multi — —

1100 A330 375fr multi — —

An additional stamp was issued in this set. The editors would like to examine it.

Senegal River Regional Organization — A331

2001 Litho. ***Perf. 12¾***

1101 A331 30fr multi — —

1102 A331 100fr multi — —

1103 A331 5000frmulti — —

No. 1102 exists dated "2003."

A332

A333

Perf. 13¼, 13x12¾ (#1105)

2002 Litho.

1104 A332 195fr multi — —

1105 A333 255fr multi — —

1106 A332 385fr multi — —

23rd African Cup Soccer Tournament

Nos. 1104-1106 dated "2001." Three additional stamps exist in this set. The editors would like to examine any examples.

Bobo Mask — A334

Dogon Mask — A335

Sénoufo Sanctuary Door — A336

Bamanan Fertility Statue — A337

2001-03 Litho. ***Perf. 12¾***

1110	A334	5fr multi ('02)		—	—
1111	A335	10fr multi ('02)		—	—
1112	A336	25fr multi ('02)		—	—
1113	A334	40fr multi ('02)		—	—
1114	A335	75fr multi ('02)		—	—
1115	A334	195fr multi		—	—
1116	A335	195fr multi ('03)		1.00	.50
1117	A334	235fr multi		—	—
1118	A335	255fr multi		—	—
1119	A337	255fr multi ('03)		1.40	.70
1120	A335	325fr multi		—	—
1121	A336	385fr multi		—	—
1123	A337	500fr multi		—	—

Issued: Nos. 1115, 1117, 1118, 1120, 1121, 1123, 2001; Nos. 1110, 1111, 1112-1114, 2002. Nos. 1116, 1119, 2003. Nos. 1111, 1114 exist dated "2004." No. 1116 exists dated "2005." Three additional stamps exist in this set. The editors would like to examine any examples.

AIDS Prevention A338

2002, Jan. 10 Litho. ***Perf. 12¾***

1125 A338 195fr multi —

Five additional stamps were issued in this set. The editors would like to examine any examples.

Songhoi Woman's Hairstyle — A340

Peulh Woman — A341

Badiangara Cliffs A342

Perf. 12¾, 13x12¾ (#1131)

2003, Mar. 7 **Litho.**

1131 A340 50fr multi .25 .25
1132 A341 385fr multi 2.25 2.25
1133 A342 485fr multi 2.75 2.75

Balaphone Festival A343

2003, Mar. 7 **Litho.** ***Perf. 12¾***

1134 A343 565fr multi 3.00 .300

An additional stamp was issued in this set. The editors would like to examine any examples.

Djenné Fair — A345

2005, Aug. 18 **Litho.** ***Perf. 12¾***

1136 A345 20fr multi .50 .50

Map of Africa, Water Drop, Lions International Emblem — A346

2005, Aug. 18 **Litho.** ***Perf. 12¾***

1137 A346 465fr multi 3.25 3.25

SEMI-POSTAL STAMPS

Anti-Malaria Issue

Common Design Type

Perf. 12½x12

1962, Apr. 7 **Engr.** **Unwmk.**

B1 CD108 25fr + 5fr pale vio bl 1.25 .60

Algerian Family — SP1

1962, Dec. 24 **Photo.** ***Perf. 12x12½***

B2 SP1 25fr + 5fr multi .70 .30

Issued for the national campaign to show the solidarity of the peoples of Mali and Algeria.

AIR POST STAMPS

Federation

Composite View of St. Louis, Senegal — AP1

Unwmk.

1959, Dec. 11 **Engr.** ***Perf. 13***

C1 AP1 85fr multi 2.75 1.00

Founding of St. Louis, Senegal, tercentenary, and opening of the 6th meeting of the executive council of the French Community.

Birds — AP2

100fr, Amethyst starling. 200fr, Bateleur eagle, horiz. 500fr, Barbary shrike.

Perf. 12½x13, 13x12½

1960, Feb. 13 **Photo.**

C2 AP2 100fr multi 3.50 2.00
C3 AP2 200fr multi 9.00 2.50
C4 AP2 500fr multi 24.00 11.50
Nos. C2-C4 (3) 36.50 16.00

Republic

Nos. C2-C4 Overprinted or Surcharged "REPUBLIQUE DU MALI" and Bars

1960, Dec. 18

C5 AP2 100fr multi 5.25 1.60
C6 AP2 200fr multi 8.00 2.75
C7 AP2 300fr on 500fr multi 11.50 5.25
C8 AP2 500fr multi 20.00 8.25
Nos. C5-C8 (4) 44.75 17.85

Pres. Modibo Keita — AP3

1961, Mar. 18 **Engr.** ***Perf. 13***

Designs: 200fr, Mamadou Konate.

C9 AP3 200fr claret & gray brn 3.75 .85
C10 AP3 300fr grn & blk 5.50 1.10

Flag, Map, UN Emblem — AP4

1961, Mar. 18

C11 AP4 100fr multicolored 2.25 .75
a. Min. sheet of 3, #13, 14, C11 3.00 3.00

Proclamation of independence and admission to UN.

Sankore Mosque, Timbuktu — AP5

200fr, View of Timbuktu. 500fr, Bamako & arms.

1961, Apr. 15 **Unwmk.** ***Perf. 13***

C12 AP5 100fr Prus bl, red brn & gray 2.75 .50
C13 AP5 200fr grn, brn & red 5.25 1.50
C14 AP5 500fr red brn, Prus bl & dk grn 13.50 3.00
Nos. C12-C14 (3) 21.50 5.00

Inauguration of Timbuktu airport and Air Mali.

Bull, Chemical Equipment and Chicks — AP6

1963, Feb. 23 **Engr.**

C15 AP6 200fr bis, mar & grnsh bl 5.00 1.25

Sotuba Zootechnical Institute.

Air Ambulance — AP7

Designs: 55fr, National Line plane loading. 100fr, Intl. Line Vickers Viscount in flight.

1963, Nov. 2 **Unwmk.** ***Perf. 13***

C16 AP7 25fr dk bl, emer & red brn .45 .20
C17 AP7 55fr bis, bl & red brn 1.10 .30
C18 AP7 100fr dk bl, red brn & yel grn 2.10 .60
Nos. C16-C18 (3) 3.65 1.10

Issued to publicize Air Mali.

Crowned Crane and Giant Tortoise — AP8

1963, Nov. 23 **Unwmk.** ***Perf. 13***

C19 AP8 25fr sepia, org & ver 1.60 .60
C20 AP8 200fr multi 7.00 2.25

Animal protection.

UN Emblem, Flag, Doves — AP9

1963, Dec. 10 **Engr.**

C21 AP9 50fr lt grn, yel & red 1.40 .40

15th anniversary of the Universal Declaration of Human Rights.

Cleopatra and Ptolemy at Kôm Ombo — AP10

1964, Mar. 9 **Unwmk.** ***Perf. 12***

C22 AP10 25fr dp claret & bister 1.00 .35
C23 AP10 55fr dp claret & lt ol grn 2.00 .75

UNESCO world campaign to save historic monuments in Nubia.

Pres. John F. Kennedy — AP11

1964, Oct. 26 **Photo.** ***Perf. 12½***

C24 AP11 100fr sl, red brn & blk 2.50 1.00
a. Souv. sheet of 4 10.00 10.00

Touracos — AP12

200fr, Abyssinian ground hornbills, vert. 300fr, Egyptian vultures, vert. 500fr, Goliath herons.

1965, Feb. 15 **Engr.** ***Perf. 13***

C25 AP12 100fr grn, dk bl & red 2.75 .90
C26 AP12 200fr blk, red & brt bl 8.00 1.25
C27 AP12 300fr blk, sl grn & yel 12.50 2.25
C28 AP12 500fr sl grn, dk brn & claret 20.00 3.50
Nos. C25-C28 (4) 43.25 7.90

UN Headquarters, New York, and ICY Emblem — AP13

1965, Mar. 15 Unwmk. *Perf. 13*
C29 AP13 55fr bis, dk bl & vio brn 1.25 .40

International Cooperation Year.

Pope John XXIII AP14

Perf. 12½x13
1965, Sept. 14 Photo. Unwmk.
C30 AP14 100fr multi 2.50 1.00

Winston Churchill — AP15

1965, Oct. 11 Engr. *Perf. 13*
C31 AP15 100fr brn & indigo 2.50 1.00

Dr. Albert Schweitzer and Sick Child — AP16

1965, Dec. 20 Photo. *Perf. 12½*
C32 AP16 100fr multi 2.75 1.00
a. Souv. sheet of 4 11.00 11.00

Major Edward H. White and Gemini 4 — AP17

#C34, Lt. Col. Alexei A. Leonov. 300fr, Gordon Cooper, Charles Conrad, Alexei Leonov & Pavel Belyayev, Parthenon, Athens, & vase, vert.

1966, Jan. 10
C33 AP17 100fr vio, yel, lt bl & blk 1.75 1.10
C34 AP17 100fr bl, red, yel & blk 1.75 1.10
C35 AP17 300fr multi 5.25 3.00
Nos. C33-C35 (3) 8.75 5.20

Achievements in space research and 16th Intl. Astronautical Congress, Athens, Sept. 12-18, 1965.

Papal Arms and UN Emblem — AP18

1966, July 11 Engr. *Perf. 13*
C36 AP18 200fr brt bl, grnsh bl & grn 3.50 1.75

Visit of Pope Paul VI to the UN, NYC, Oct. 4, 1965.

People and UNESCO Emblem — AP19

1966, Sept. 5 Engr. *Perf. 13*
C37 AP19 100fr dk car rose, sl grn & ultra 2.50 1.25

20th anniv. of UNESCO.

Soccer Players, Ball, Globe, and Jules Rimet Cup — AP20

1966, Oct. 31 Photo. *Perf. 13*
C38 AP20 100fr multi 2.75 1.40

8th International Soccer Championship Games, Wembley, England, July 11-30.

Crab and Mt. Fuji — AP21

UNICEF Emblem and Children — AP22

1966, Nov. 30 Photo. *Perf. 13*
C39 AP21 100fr multi 2.25 .90

9th Intl. Anticancer Cong., Tokyo, Oct. 23-29.

1966, Dec. 10 Engr.
C40 AP22 45fr dp bl, bis brn & red lil 1.00 .40

20th anniv. of UNICEF.

Land Cruisers in Hoggar Mountain Pass — AP23

1967, Mar. 20 Engr. *Perf. 13*
C41 AP23 200fr multi 6.25 2.00

"Black Cruise 1924," which crossed Africa from Beni-Abbes, Algeria to the Indian Ocean and on to Tananarive, Madagascar, Oct. 28, 1924-June 26, 1925.

Diamant Rocket and Francesco de Lana's 1650 Flying Boat — AP24

Designs: 100fr, A-1 satellite and rocket launching adapted from Jules Verne. 200fr, D-1 satellite and Leonardo da Vinci's bird-borne flying machine.

1967, Apr. 17 Engr. *Perf. 13*
C42 AP24 50fr brt bl, pur & grn .90 .25
C43 AP24 100fr dk Prus bl, dk car & lil 1.75 .50
C44 AP24 200fr sl bl, ol & pur 3.50 1.00
Nos. C42-C44 (3) 6.15 1.75

Honoring French achievements in space.

Amelia Earhart and Map of Mali — AP25

1967, May 29 Photo. *Perf. 13*
C45 AP25 500fr bl & multi 11.00 3.00

Amelia Earhart's stop at Gao, West Africa, 30th anniv.

Paul as Harlequin, by Picasso AP26

Picasso Paintings: 50fr, Bird Cage. 250fr, The Flutes of Pan.

1967, June 16 *Perf. 12½*
C46 AP26 50fr multi 1.25 .40
C47 AP26 100fr multi 2.75 .75
C48 AP26 250fr multi 5.75 1.60
Nos. C46-C48 (3) 9.75 2.75

See No. C82.

Jamboree Emblem, Scout Knots and Badges — AP27

Design: 100fr, Scout with portable radio transmitter, tents and Jamboree badge.

1967, July 10 Engr. *Perf. 13*
C49 AP27 70fr dk car, emer & bl grn .90 .25
C50 AP27 100fr dk car lake, sl grn & blk 1.25 .30
a. Strip of 2, #C49-C50 + label 3.00 1.75

12th Boy Scout World Jamboree, Farragut State Park, Idaho, Aug. 1-9.

Head of Horse, by Toulouse-Lautrec — AP28

300fr, Cob-drawn gig, by Toulouse-Lautrec.

Perf. 12x12½, 12½x12
1967, Dec. 11 Photo.
C51 AP28 100fr multi 3.25 1.25
C52 AP28 300fr multi, vert. 8.00 2.50

See Nos. C66-C67.

Grenoble AP29

Design: 150fr, Bobsled course on Huez Alp.

1968, Jan. 8 Engr. *Perf. 13*
C53 AP29 50fr bl, yel brn & grn .90 .25
C54 AP29 150fr brn, vio bl & stl bl 2.25 .75

10th Winter Olympic Games, Grenoble, France, Feb. 6-18.

Roses and Anemones, by Van Gogh — AP30

Paintings: 150fr, Peonies in Vase, by Edouard Manet (36x49mm). 300fr, Bouquet, by Delacroix (41x42mm). 500fr, Daisies in Vase, by Jean François Millet (49x37mm).

Perf. 13, 12½x12, 12x12½

1968, June 24 **Photo.**

C55 AP30 50fr multi 1.00 .50
C56 AP30 150fr grn & multi 2.40 .65
C57 AP30 300fr grn & multi 4.75 1.40
C58 AP30 500fr car & multi 7.00 2.00
Nos. C55-C58 (4) 15.15 4.55

Martin Luther King, Jr. — AP31

Long Jumper and Satellite — AP32

1968, July 22 ***Perf. 12½***

C59 AP31 100fr rose lil, sal pink & blk 1.40 .40

Bicycle Type of Regular Issue

Designs: 50fr, Bicyclette, 1918. 100fr, Mercedes Benz, 1927, horiz.

1968, Aug. 12 **Engr.** ***Perf. 13***

C60 A40 50fr gray, dk grn & brick red 1.25 .30
C61 A40 100fr lemon, indigo & car 2.75 .70

1968, Nov. 25 **Photo.** ***Perf. 12½***

100fr, Soccer goalkeeper and satellite.

C62 AP32 100fr multi, horiz. 1.40 .60
C63 AP32 150fr multi 2.50 .80

19th Olympic Games, Mexico City, 10/12-27.

PHILEXAFRIQUE Issue

Editorial Department, by François Marius Granet — AP33

1968, Dec. 23 **Photo.** ***Perf. 12½x12***

C64 AP33 200fr multi 3.50 1.75

Issued to publicize PHILEXAFRIQUE Philatelic Exhibition in Abidjan, Feb. 14-23. Printed with alternating light green label.

See Nos. C85-C87, C110-C112, C205-C207, C216-C217.

2nd PHILEXAFRIQUE Issue

Common Design Type

100fr, French Sudan #64, sculpture.

1969, Feb. 14 **Engr.** ***Perf. 13***

C65 CD128 100fr pur & multi 2.00 1.00

Painting Type of 1967

Paintings: 150fr, Napoleon as First Consul, by Antoine Jean Gros, vert. 2000fr, Bivouac at Austerlitz, by Louis François Lejeune.

Perf. 12½x12, 12x12½

1969, Feb. 25 **Photo.**

C66 AP28 150fr multi 4.00 1.25
C67 AP28 250fr multi 5.75 1.75

Napoleon Bonaparte (1769-1821).

Montgolfier's Balloon — AP34

Designs: 150fr, Ferber 5, experimental biplane. 300fr, Concorde.

1969, Mar. 10 **Photo.** ***Perf. 13***

C68 AP34 50fr multi .70 .30
C69 AP34 150fr multi 2.25 .60
C70 AP34 300fr multi 4.50 1.40
a. Strip of 3, #C68-C70 9.00 4.50

1st flight of the prototype Concorde plane at Toulouse, France, Mar. 1, 1969.

For overprints see Nos. C78-C80.

Auto Type of Regular Issue

55fr, Renault, 1898, Renault 16, 1969. 90fr, Peugeot, 1893, Peugeot 404, 1969.

1969, May 30 **Engr.** ***Perf. 13***

C71 A43 55fr rose car, blk & brt pink 1.60 .35
C72 A43 90fr blk, dp car & indigo 2.25 .60

Ronald Clarke, Australia, 10,000-meter Run, 1965 — AP35

World Records: 90fr, Yanis Lusis, USSR, Javelin, 1968. 120fr, Yoshinobu Miyake, Japan, weight lifting, 1967. 140fr, Randy Matson, US, shot put, 1968. 150fr, Kipchoge Keino, Kenya, 3,000-meter run, 1965.

1969, June 23 **Engr.** ***Perf. 13***

C73 AP35 60fr bl & ol brn .45 .20
C74 AP35 90fr car rose & red brn .70 .30
C75 AP35 120fr emer & gray ol 1.00 .55
C76 AP35 140fr gray & brn 1.00 .60
C77 AP35 150fr red org & blk 1.25 .65
Nos. C73-C77 (5) 4.40 2.30

Issued to honor sports world records.

Nos. C68-C70 Overprinted in Red with Lunar Landing Module and: "L'HOMME SUR LA LUNE / JUILLET 1969 / APOLLO 11"

1969, July 25 **Photo.** ***Perf. 13***

C78 AP34 50fr multi .90 .60
C79 AP34 150fr multi 2.25 1.25
C80 AP34 300fr multi 3.50 2.00
a. Strip of 3, #C78-C80 9.00 4.50

Man's 1st landing on moon, July 20, 1969. US astronauts Neil A. Armstrong and Col. Edwin E. Aldrin, Jr., with Lieut. Col. Michael Collins piloting Apollo 11.

Apollo 8, Moon and Earth — AP35a

Embossed on Gold Foil

1969, July 24 ***Die-cut perf 10½***

C81 AP35a 2000fr gold 27.00 27.00

US Apollo 8 mission, the 1st men in orbit around the moon, Dec. 21-27, 1968.

Painting Type of 1967

500fr, Mona Lisa, by Leonardo da Vinci.

1969, Oct. 20 **Photo.** ***Perf. 12½***

C82 AP26 500fr multi 7.25 2.25

Mahatma Gandhi — AP36

1969, Nov. 24 **Engr.** ***Perf. 13***

C83 AP36 150fr brt bl, ol brn & red brn 3.00 .70

Map of West Africa, Post Horns and Lightning Bolts — AP37

1970, Feb. 23 **Photo.** ***Perf. 12½***

C84 AP37 100fr multi 1.00 .40

11th anniversary of the West African Postal Union (CAPTEAO).

Painting Type of 1968

Paintings: 100fr, Madonna and Child, from Rogier van der Weyden school. 150fr, Nativity, by the master of Flemalle. 250fr, Madonna and Child with St. John, from the Dutch School.

1970, Mar. 2

C85 AP33 100fr multi 1.00 .40
C86 AP33 150fr multi 1.60 .80
C87 AP33 250fr multi 3.50 1.40
Nos. C85-C87 (3) 6.10 2.60

Roosevelt AP38

Lenin — AP39

1970, Mar. 30 **Photo.** ***Perf. 12½***

C88 AP38 500fr red, lt ultra & blk 5.00 2.50

Pres. Franklin D. Roosevelt (1882-1945).

1970, Apr. 22

C89 AP39 300fr pink, grn & blk 4.50 1.25

Jules Verne and Firing of Moon Rockets — AP40

150fr, Jules Verne, rockets, landing modules & moon. 300fr, Jules Verne & splashdown.

1970, May 4

C90 AP40 50fr multi .90 .30
C91 AP40 150fr multi 2.25 .80
C92 AP40 300fr multi 4.00 1.60
Nos. C90-C92 (3) 7.15 2.70

Nos. C90-C92 Overprinted in Red or Blue: "APOLLO XIII / EPOPEE SPATIALE / 11-17 AVRIL 1970"

1970, June **Photo.** ***Perf. 12½***

C93 AP40 50fr multi (Bl) .55 .25
C94 AP40 150fr multi (R) 1.60 .80
C95 AP40 300fr multi (Bl) 3.25 1.60
Nos. C93-C95 (3) 5.40 2.65

Flight and safe return of Apollo 13, Apr. 11-13, 1970.

Intelsat III — AP41

Telecommunications Through Space: 200fr, Molniya I satellite. 300fr, Radar. 500fr, "Project Symphony" (various satellites).

1970, July 13 **Engr.** ***Perf. 13***

C96 AP41 100fr gray, brt bl & org .90 .40
C97 AP41 200fr bl, gray & red lil 1.75 .50
C98 AP41 300fr org, dk brn & gray 2.75 1.40
C99 AP41 500fr dk brn, sl & grnsh bl 4.50 2.25
Nos. C96-C99 (4) 9.90 4.55

For surcharges see Nos. C108-C109.

Auguste and Louis Lumière, Jean Harlow and Marilyn Monroe AP42

1970, July 27 Photo. *Perf. 12½x12*
C100 AP42 250fr multi 5.25 2.00

Issued to honor Auguste Lumière (1862-1954), and his brother Louis Jean Lumière (1864-1948), inventors of the Lumière process of color photography and of a motion picture camera.

Soccer — AP43

1970, Sept. 7 Engr. *Perf. 13*
C101 AP43 80fr bl, dp car & brn ol .90 .30
C102 AP43 200fr dp car, bl grn & ol brn 2.25 .80

9th World Soccer Championships for the Jules Rimet Cup, Mexico City, May 30-June 21, 1970.

Rotary Emblem, Map of Mali and Ceremonial Antelope Heads — AP44

Men Holding UN Emblem, and Doves — AP45

1970, Sept. 21 Photo. *Perf. 12½*
C103 AP44 200fr multi 2.75 1.25

Issued to honor Rotary International.

1970, Oct. 5 Engr. *Perf. 13*
C104 AP45 100fr dk pur, red brn & dk bl 1.25 .50

25th anniversary of the United Nations.

Koran Page, Baghdad, 11th Century AP46

Moslem Art: 200fr, Tree, and lion killing deer, mosaic, Jordan, c. 730, horiz. 250fr, Scribe, miniature, Baghdad, 1287.

1970, Oct. 26 Photo. *Perf. 12½x12*
C105 AP46 50fr multi .90 .30
C106 AP46 200fr multi 1.75 .65
C107 AP46 250fr multi 2.75 .95
Nos. C105-C107 (3) 5.40 1.90

Nos. C97-C98 Surcharged and Overprinted: "LUNA 16 / PREMIERS PRELEVEMENTS AUTOMATIQUES / SUR LA LUNE / SEPTEMBRE 1970"

1970, Nov. 9 Engr. *Perf. 13*
C108 AP41 150fr on 200fr multi 1.25 .65
C109 AP41 250fr on 300fr multi 2.25 .95

Unmanned moon probe of the Russian space ship Luna 16, Sept. 12-24.

Painting Type of 1968

100fr, Nativity, Antwerp School, c. 1530. 250fr, St. John the Baptist, by Hans Memling. 300fr, Adoration of the Kings, Flemish School, 17th cent.

1970, Dec. 1 Photo. *Perf. 12½x12*
C110 AP33 100fr brown & multi 1.00 .40
C111 AP33 250fr brown & multi 2.75 .95
C112 AP33 300fr brown & multi 3.50 1.25
Nos. C110-C112 (3) 7.25 2.60

Christmas 1970.

Gamal Abdel Nasser — AP47

Embossed on Gold Foil

1970, Nov. 25 *Perf. 12½*
C113 AP47 1000fr gold 15.00 15.00

In memory of Gamal Abdel Nasser (1918-1970), President of Egypt.

Charles de Gaulle AP48

Embossed on Gold Foil

1971, Feb. 8 *Die-cut Perf. 10*
C114 AP48 2000fr gold, red & dp ultra 70.00 70.00

In memory of Gen. Charles de Gaulle (1890-1970), President of France.

Alfred Nobel — AP49

Tennis, Davis Cup — AP50

1971, Feb. 22 Engr. *Perf. 13*
C115 AP49 300fr multi 3.50 1.00

Alfred Nobel (1833-1896), inventor of dynamite, sponsor of Nobel Prize.

1971, Mar. 8

Designs: 150fr, Derby at Epsom, horiz. 200fr, Racing yacht, America's Cup.

C116 AP50 100fr bl, lil & slate 1.75 .60
C117 AP50 150fr brn, brt grn & ol 2.75 .90
C118 AP50 200fr brt bl, ol & brn 3.50 1.25
Nos. C116-C118 (3) 8.00 2.75

The Arabian Nights — AP51

Designs: 180fr, Ali Baba and the 40 Thieves. 200fr, Aladdin's Lamp.

1971, Apr. 5 Photo. *Perf. 13*
C119 AP51 120fr gold & multi 1.75 .60
C120 AP51 180fr gold & multi 2.50 .90
C121 AP51 200fr gold & multi 3.00 1.00
Nos. C119-C121 (3) 7.25 2.50

Olympic Rings and Sports — AP52

1971, June 28 Photo. *Perf. 12½*
C122 AP52 80fr ultra, yel grn & brt mag .90 .30

Pre-Olympic Year.

Mariner 4 — AP53

Design: 300fr, Venera 5 in space.

1971, Sept. 13 Engr. *Perf. 13*
C123 AP53 200fr multi 1.75 .70
C124 AP53 300fr multi 2.75 .95

Space explorations of US Mariner 4 (200fr); and USSR Venera 5 (300fr).

Santa Maria, 1492 — AP54

Famous Ships: 150fr, Mayflower, 1620. 200fr, Potemkin, 1905. 250fr, Normandie, 1935.

1971, Sept. 27
C125 AP54 100fr brn, bluish grn & pur 1.25 .40
C126 AP54 150fr sl grn, brn & pur 2.00 .70
C127 AP54 200fr car, bl & dk ol 2.50 .80
C128 AP54 250fr blk, bl & red 3.25 1.00
Nos. C125-C128 (4) 9.00 2.90

Symbols of Justice and Maps — AP55

1971, Oct. 18
C129 AP55 160fr mar, ocher & dk brn 1.40 .50

25th anniversary of the International Court of Justice in The Hague, Netherlands.

Statue of Zeus, by Phidias — AP56

Nat "King" Cole — AP57

The Seven Wonders of the Ancient World: 80fr, Cheops Pyramid and Sphinx. 100fr, Temple of Artemis, Ephesus, horiz. 130fr, Lighthouse at Alexandria. 150fr, Hanging Gardens of Babylon, horiz. 270fr, Mausoleum of Halicarnassus. 280fr, Colossus of Rhodes.

1971, Dec. 13
C130 AP56 70fr ind, dk red & pink .70 .25
C131 AP56 80fr brn, bl & blk .90 .25
C132 AP56 100fr org, ind & pur 1.00 .30
C133 AP56 130fr rose lil, blk & grnsh bl 1.25 .40
C134 AP56 150fr brn, brt grn & bl 1.50 .50
C135 AP56 270fr sl, brn & plum 2.50 .70
C136 AP56 280fr sl lil & ol 2.75 .80
Nos. C130-C136 (7) 10.60 3.20

1971, Dec. 6 Photo. *Perf. 13x12½*

Famous American Black Musicians: 150fr, Erroll Garner. 270fr, Louis Armstrong.

C137 AP57 130fr blk, brn & yel 2.75 .40

C138 AP57 150fr blk, bl & yel 3.00 .50

C139 AP57 270fr blk, rose car & yel 5.00 .70

Nos. C137-C139 (3) 10.75 1.60

Slalom and Japanese Child AP58

200fr, Ice hockey & character from Noh play.

1972, Jan. 10 Engr. *Perf. 13*

C140 AP58 150fr multicolored 1.25 .50

C141 AP58 200fr multicolored 1.75 .70

a. Souv. sheet of 2, #C140-C141 3.50 3.50

11th Winter Olympic Games, Sapporo, Japan, Feb. 3-13.

Santa Maria della Salute, by Ippolito Caffi — AP59

Paintings of Venice, by Ippolito Caffi: 270fr, Rialto Bridge. 280fr, St. Mark's Square, vert.

1972, Feb. 21 Photo. *Perf. 13*

C142 AP59 130fr gold & multi 1.25 .45

C143 AP59 270fr gold & multi 2.00 .70

C144 AP59 280fr gold & multi 2.10 .75

Nos. C142-C144 (3) 5.35 1.90

UNESCO campaign to save Venice.

Hands of 4 Races Holding Scout Flag — AP60

1972, Mar. 27 Engr. *Perf. 13*

C145 AP60 200fr dk red, ocher & ol gray 2.25 .60

World Boy Scout Seminar, Cotonou, Dahomey, March, 1972.

"Your Heart is your Health" — AP61

1972, Apr. 7 Engr. *Perf. 13*

C146 AP61 150fr brt bl & red 1.75 .50

World Health Day.

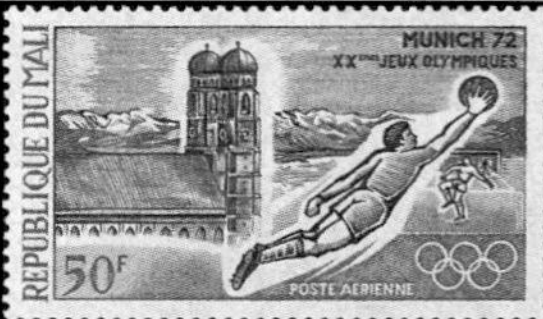

Soccer Player and Frauenkirche, Munich — AP62

Designs (Sport and Munich Landmarks): 150fr, Judo and TV Tower, vert. 200fr, Steeplechase and Propylaeum, vert. 300fr, Runner and Church of the Theatines.

1972, Apr. 17

C147 AP62 50fr ocher, dk bl & grn .45 .20

C148 AP62 150fr dk bl, ocher & grn 1.25 .45

C149 AP62 200fr grn, dk bl & ocher 1.60 .60

C150 AP62 300fr dk bl, grn & ocher 2.25 .75

a. Min. sheet of 4, #C147-C150 5.75 5.75

Nos. C147-C150 (4) 5.55 2.00

20th Olympic Games, Munich, 8/26-9/10. For overprints see Nos. C165-C166, C168.

Apollo 15, Lunar Rover, Landing Module — AP63

Design: 250fr, Cugnot's steam wagon and Montgolfier's Balloon.

1972, Apr. 27

C151 AP63 150fr multicolored 1.75 .60

C152 AP63 250fr multicolored 3.50 1.25

Development of transportation.

Cinderella AP64

Fairy Tales: 80fr, Puss in Boots. 150fr, Sleeping Beauty.

1972, June 19 Engr. *Perf. 13x12½*

C153 AP64 70fr multicolored 1.10 .30

C154 AP64 80fr multicolored 1.25 .35

C155 AP64 150fr multicolored 2.00 .60

Nos. C153-C155 (3) 4.35 1.25

Charles Perrault (1628-1703), French writer.

Astronauts and Lunar Rover on Moon — AP65

1972, July 24 Engr. *Perf. 13*

C156 AP65 500fr multicolored 4.00 1.40

US Apollo 16 moon mission, Apr. 15-27.

Book Year Emblem — AP66

1972, Aug. 7 Litho. *Perf. 12½*

C157 AP66 80fr bl, gold & grn 1.75 .60

International Book Year 1972.

Bamako Rotary Emblem with Crocodiles AP67

1972, Oct. 9 Engr. *Perf. 13*

C158 AP67 170fr dk brn, red & ultra 1.75 .60

10th anniv. of the Bamako Rotary Club.

Hurdler, Olympic Rings, Melbourne Cathedral, Kangaroo — AP68

Designs (Olympic Rings and): 70fr, Boxing, Helsinki Railroad Station, arms of Finland, vert. 140fr, Running, Colosseum, Roman wolf. 150fr, Weight lifting, Tokyo stadium, phoenix, vert. 170fr, Swimming, University Library, Mexico City; Aztec sculpture. 210fr, Javelin, Munich Stadium, Arms of Munich. Stamps inscribed with name of gold medal winner of event shown.

1972, Nov. 13 Engr. *Perf. 13*

C159 AP68 70fr red, ocher & ind .45 .20

C160 AP68 90fr red brn, bl & sl .55 .25

C161 AP68 140fr brn, brt grn & ol gray .90 .30

C162 AP68 150fr dk car, emer & gray ol 1.00 .35

C163 AP68 170fr red lil, brn & Prus bl 1.10 .40

C164 AP68 210fr ultra, emer & brick red 1.25 .50

Nos. C159-C164 (6) 5.25 2.00

Retrospective of Olympic Games 1952-1972. For overprint see No. C167.

Nos. C148-C150 and C164 Overprinted:

a. JUDO / RUSKA / 2 MEDAILLES D'OR
b. STEEPLE / KEINO / MEDAILLE D'OR
c. MEDAILLE D'OR / 90m. 48
d. 100m.-200m. / BORZOV / 2 MEDAILLES D'OR

1972, Nov. 27 Engr. *Perf. 13*

C165 AP62 150fr multi (a) 1.00 .40

C166 AP62 200fr multi (b) 1.40 .50

C167 AP68 210fr multi (c) 1.60 .55

C168 AP62 300fr multi (d) 2.25 .70

Nos. C165-C168 (4) 6.25 2.15

Gold medal winners in 20th Olympic Games: Wim Ruska, Netherlands, heavyweight judo (#C165); Kipchoge Keino, Kenya, 3000m. steeplechase (#C166); Klaus Wolfermann, Germany, javelin (#C167); Valery Borzov, USSR, 100m., 200m. race (#C168).

Emperor Haile Selassie AP69

1972, Dec. 26 Photo. *Perf. 12½*

C169 AP69 70fr grn & multi .70 .25

80th birthday of Emperor Haile Selassie of Ethiopia.

Plane, Balloon, Route Timbuktu to Bamako — AP70

300fr, Balloon, jet & route Timbuktu to Bamako.

1972, Dec. 29 *Perf. 13½*

C170 AP70 200fr multi 1.25 .50

C171 AP70 300fr bl & multi 2.25 .80

First postal balloon flight in Mali.

Bishop of 14th Century European Chess Set — AP71

Design: 200fr, Knight (elephant), from 18th century Indian set.

1973, Feb. 19 Engr. *Perf. 13*

C172 AP71 100fr dk car, bl & ind 1.75 .60

C173 AP71 200fr blk, red & brn 3.50 1.25

World Chess Championship, Reykjavik, Iceland, July-Sept., 1972.

Postal Union Emblem, Letter and Dove AP72

1973, Mar. 9 Photo. *Perf. 11½x11*

C174 AP72 70fr bl, blk & org .70 .25

10th anniv. (in 1971) of African Postal Union. This stamp was to be issued Dec. 8, 1971. It was offered by the agency on Mar. 9, 1973. Copies were sold in Mali as early as July or August, 1972.

No. C20, Collector's Hand and Philatelic Background AP73

1973, Mar. 12 Engr. *Perf. 13*

C175 AP73 70fr multi 1.75 .50

Stamp Day, 1973.

Astronauts and Lunar Rover on Moon AP74

1973, Mar. 26
C176 AP74 250fr bl, indigo & bis 2.75 1.00

Souvenir Sheet

C177 AP74 350fr choc, vio bl & ultra 2.75 1.60

Apollo 17 US moon mission, 12/7-19/72.

Nicolaus Copernicus — AP75

1973, Apr. 9 **Engr.** ***Perf. 13***
C178 AP75 300fr brt bl & mag 3.50 1.25

500th anniversary of the birth of Nicolaus Copernicus (1473-1543), Polish astronomer.

Dr. Armauer G. Hansen and Leprosy Bacillus — AP76

1973, May 7 **Engr.** ***Perf. 13***
C179 AP76 200fr blk, yel grn & red 2.25 .85

Centenary of the discovery of the Hansen bacillus, the cause of leprosy.

Bentley and Alfa Romeo, 1930 — AP77

Designs: 100fr, Jaguar and Talbot, 1953. 200fr, Matra and Porsche, 1972.

1973, May 21 **Engr.** ***Perf. 13***
C180 AP77 50fr bl, org & grn .50 .25
C181 AP77 100fr grn, ultra & car .90 .30
C182 AP77 200fr ind, grn & car 2.50 .60
Nos. C180-C182 (3) 3.90 1.15

50th anniversary of the 24-hour automobile race at Le Mans, France.

Camp Fire, Fleur-de-Lis AP78

Designs (Fleur-de-Lis and): 70fr, Scouts saluting flag, vert. 80fr, Scouts with flags. 130fr, Lord Baden-Powell, vert. 270fr, Round dance and map of Africa.

1973, June 4
C183 AP78 50fr dk red, ultra & choc .35 .25
C184 AP78 70fr sl grn, dk brn & red .55 .25

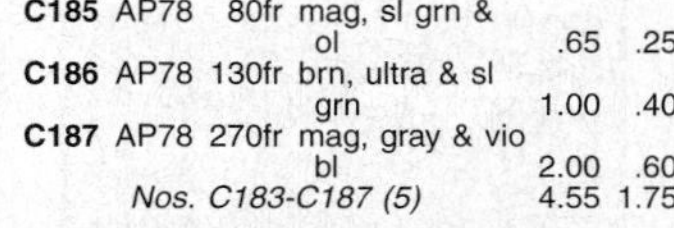
C185 AP78 80fr mag, sl grn & ol .65 .25
C186 AP78 130fr brn, ultra & sl grn 1.00 .40
C187 AP78 270fr mag, gray & vio bl 2.00 .60
Nos. C183-C187 (5) 4.55 1.75

Mali Boy and Girl Scouts and International Scouts Congress.
For surcharges see Nos. C222-C223.

Swimming, US and "Africa" Flags — AP79

80fr, Discus, javelin, vert. 330fr, Runners.

1973, July 30 **Engr.** ***Perf. 13***
C188 AP79 70fr red, sl grn & bl .50 .25
C189 AP79 80fr vio bl, dk ol & red .60 .25
C190 AP79 330fr red & vio bl 2.50 .80
Nos. C188-C190 (3) 3.60 1.30

First African-United States sports meet.

Head and City Hall, Brussels AP80

Perseus, by Benvenuto Cellini — AP81

1973, Sept. 17 **Engr.** ***Perf. 13***
C191 AP80 70fr brt ultra, ol & vio .70 .25

Africa Weeks, Brussels, Sept. 15-30, 1973.

1973, Sept. 24

Famous Sculptures: 150fr, Pietá, by Michelangelo. 250fr, Victory of Samothrace, Greek 1st century B.C.

C192 AP81 100fr dk car & sl grn 1.00 .30
C193 AP81 150fr dk car & dp cl 1.60 .50
C194 AP81 250fr dk car & dk ol 2.75 .80
Nos. C192-C194 (3) 5.35 1.60

Stephenson's Rocket and Buddicom Engine — AP82

Locomotives: 150fr, Union Pacific, 1890, and Santa Fe, 1940. 200fr, Mistral and Tokaido, 1970.

1973, Oct. 8 **Engr.** ***Perf. 13***
C195 AP82 100fr brn, bl & blk 1.10 .40
C196 AP82 150fr red, brt ultra & dk car 1.75 .70
C197 AP82 200fr ocher, bl & ind 2.50 .90
Nos. C195-C197 (3) 5.35 2.00

Apollo XI on Moon AP83

75fr, Landing capsule, Apollo XIII. 100fr, Astronauts & equipment on moon, Apollo XIV. 280fr, Rover, landing module % astronauts on moon, Apollo XV. 300fr, Lift-off from moon, Apollo XVII.

1973, Oct. 25
C198 AP83 50fr vio, org & sl grn .35 .25
C199 AP83 75fr slate, red & bl .55 .25
C200 AP83 100fr slate, bl & ol brn .70 .30
C201 AP83 280fr vio bl, red & sl grn 1.75 .55
C202 AP83 300fr slate, red & sl grn 2.00 .80
Nos. C198-C202 (5) 5.35 2.15

Apollo US moon missions.
For surcharges see Nos. C224-C225.

Pablo Picasso — AP84

John F. Kennedy — AP85

1973, Nov. 7 **Litho.** ***Perf. 12½***
C203 AP84 500fr multi 5.50 2.00

Pablo Picasso (1881-1973), painter.

1973, Nov. 12
C204 AP85 500fr gold, brt rose lil & blk 4.75 1.75

Painting Type of 1968

100fr, Annunciation, by Vittore Carpaccio, horiz. 200fr, Virgin of St. Simon, by Federigo Baroccio. 250fr, Flight into Egypt, by Andrea Solario.

Perf. 13x12½, 12½x12, 12½x13

1973, Nov. 30 **Litho.**
C205 AP33 100fr blk & multi .90 .25
C206 AP33 200fr blk & multi 1.75 .60
C207 AP33 250fr blk & multi 2.25 .80
Nos. C205-C207 (3) 4.90 1.65

Christmas 1973.

Soccer Player and Ball — AP86

250fr, Goalkeeper & ball. 500fr, Frauenkirche, Munich, Arms of Munich & soccer ball, horiz.

1973, Dec. 3 **Engr.** ***Perf. 13***
C208 AP86 150fr emer, ol brn & red 1.25 .50
C209 AP86 250fr emer, vio bl & ol brn 2.25 .70

Souvenir Sheet

C210 AP86 500fr bl & multi 4.50 4.50

World Soccer Cup, Munich.

Musicians, Mosaic from Pompeii — AP87

Designs (Mosaics from Pompeii): 250fr, Alexander the Great in battle, vert. 350fr, Bacchants, vert.

1974, Jan. 21 **Engr.** ***Perf. 13***
C211 AP87 150fr sl bl, ol & rose 1.50 .30
C212 AP87 250fr mag, ol & ocher 2.00 .50
C213 AP87 350fr ol, dp brn & ocher 2.50 .70
Nos. C211-C213 (3) 6.00 1.50

Winston Churchill — AP88

1974, Mar. 18 **Engr.** ***Perf. 13***
C214 AP88 500fr black 3.75 1.25

Chess Game — AP89

1974, Mar. 25 **Engr.** ***Perf. 13***
C215 AP89 250fr multi 5.25 1.75

21st Chess Olympic Games, Nice 1974.

Painting Type of 1968

Paintings: 400fr, Crucifixion, Alsatian School, c. 1380, vert. 500fr, Burial of Christ, by Titian.

Perf. 12½x13, 13x12½

1974, Apr. 12 **Photo.**
C216 AP33 400fr multi 2.75 .90
C217 AP33 500fr multi 3.50 1.25

Easter 1974.

Lenin — AP90

1974, Apr. 22 **Engr.** ***Perf. 13***
C218 AP90 150fr vio bl & lake 2.75 .60

50th anniversary of the death of Lenin.

Women's Steeplechase — AP91

1974, May 20 **Engr.** ***Perf. 13***
C219 AP91 130fr bl, lil & brn 2.25 .60

World Horsewomen's Championship, La Baule, France, June 30-July 7.

Skylab Docking in Space — AP92

250fr, Skylab over globe with Africa.

1974, July 1 **Engr.** ***Perf. 13***
C220 AP92 200fr bl, sl & org 1.40 .50
C221 AP92 250fr lil, sl & org 2.40 .70

Skylab's flight over Africa, 1974.

Nos. C184-C185 Surcharged in Violet Blue with New Value, Two Bars and:

a. 11e JAMBOREE ARABE / AOUT 1974 LIBAN
b. CONGRES PANARABE LIBAN / AOUT 1974

1974, July 8 **Engr.** ***Perf. 13***
C222 AP78 130fr on 70fr (a) 1.50 .50
C223 AP78 170fr on 80fr (b) 1.90 .60

11th Pan-Arab Jamboree and Pan-Arab Congress, Batrun, Lebanon, Aug. 1974.

Nos. C200-C201 Surcharged in Red with New Value, Two Bars and:

c. Ier DEBARQUEMENT / SUR LA LUNE / 20-VII-69
d. Ier PAS SUR LA / LUNE 21-VII-69

1974, July 15
C224 AP83 130fr on 100fr (c) 1.00 .40
C225 AP83 300fr on 280fr (d) 3.00 1.25

First manned moon landing, July 20, 1969, and first step on moon, July 21, 1969.

1906 and 1939 Locomotives — AP93

Locomotives: 120fr, Baldwin, 1870, and Pacific, 1920. 210fr, Al., 1925, and Buddicom, 1847. 330fr, Hudson, 1938, and La Gironde, 1839.

1974, Oct. 7 **Engr.** ***Perf. 13***
C226 AP93 90fr dk car & multi 1.10 .40
C227 AP93 120fr ocher & multi 1.50 .50
C228 AP93 210fr org & multi 2.40 .70
C229 AP93 330fr grn & multi 3.50 1.10
Nos. C226-C229 (4) 8.50 2.70

Skier, Winter Sports and Olympic Rings AP94

1974, Oct. 7
C230 AP94 300fr multi 2.75 .80

Holy Family, by Hans Memling AP95

310fr, Virgin & Child, Bourgogne School. 400fr, Adoration of the Kings, by Martin Schongauer.

1974, Nov. 4 **Photo.** ***Perf. 12½***
C231 AP95 290fr multi 2.10 .60
C232 AP95 310fr multi 2.50 .70
C233 AP95 400fr multi 3.25 1.10
Nos. C231-C233 (3) 7.85 2.40

Christmas 1974.
See Nos. C238-C240, C267-C269.

Raoul Follereau — AP96

1974, Nov. 18 **Engr.** ***Perf. 13***
C234 AP96 200fr brt bl 2.75 .85

Raoul Follereau (1903-1977), apostle to the lepers and educator of the blind. See No. C468.

Europafrica Issue

Train, Jet, Cogwheel, Grain, Maps of Africa and Europe — AP97

1974, Dec. 27 **Engr.** ***Perf. 13***
C235 AP97 100fr brn, grn & indigo 1.00 .30
C236 AP97 110fr ocher, vio bl & pur 1.10 .40

Painting Type of 1974

Designs: 200fr, Christ at Emmaus, by Philipe de Champaigne, horiz. 300fr, Christ at Emmaus, by Paolo Veronese, horiz. 500fr, Christ in Majesty, Limoges, 13th century.

Perf. 13x12½, 12½x13
1975, Mar. 24 **Litho.**
C238 AP95 200fr multi 1.50 .50
C239 AP95 300fr multi 2.50 .70
C240 AP95 500fr multi 4.50 1.25
Nos. C238-C240 (3) 8.50 2.45

Easter 1975.

"Voyage to the Center of the Earth" — AP99

Jules Verne's Stories: 170fr, "From Earth to Moon" and Verne's portrait. 190fr, "20,000 Leagues under the Sea." 220fr, "A Floating City."

1975, Apr. 7 **Engr.** ***Perf. 13***
C241 AP99 100fr multi .75 .25
C242 AP99 170fr multi 1.40 .45
C243 AP99 190fr multi 1.40 .50
C244 AP99 220fr multi 1.75 .55
Nos. C241-C244 (4) 5.30 1.75

Dawn, by Michelangelo — AP100

Design: 500fr, Moses, by Michelangelo.

1975, Apr. 28 **Photo.** ***Perf. 13***
C245 AP100 400fr multi 3.00 .90
C246 AP100 500fr multi 3.75 1.25

Michelangelo Buonarroti (1475-1564), Italian sculptor, painter and architect.

Astronaut on Moon — AP101

Designs: 300fr, Constellations Virgo and Capricorn. 370fr, Statue of Liberty, Kremlin, Soyuz and Apollo spacecraft.

1975, May 19 **Engr.** ***Perf. 13***
C247 AP101 290fr multi 1.40 .60
C248 AP101 300fr multi 1.40 .60
C249 AP101 370fr multi 2.40 .90
Nos. C247-C249 (3) 5.20 2.10

Soviet-American space cooperation.
For overprints see Nos. C264-C266.

Boy Scout, Globe, Nordjamb 75 Emblem AP103

150fr, Boy Scout giving Scout sign. 290fr, Scouts around campfire.

1975, June 23 **Engr.** ***Perf. 13***
C251 AP103 100fr claret, brn & bl .75 .25
C252 AP103 150fr red, brn & grn 1.10 .30
C253 AP103 290fr bl, grn & claret 2.10 .65
Nos. C251-C253 (3) 3.95 1.20

Nordjamb 75, 14th Boy Scout Jamboree, Lillehammer, Norway, July 29-Aug. 7.

Battle Scene and Marquis de Lafayette — AP104

300fr, Battle scene & George Washington. 370fr, Battle of Chesapeake Bay & Count de Grasse.

1975, July 7 **Engr.** ***Perf. 13***
C254 AP104 290fr lt bl & indigo 1.75 .60
C255 AP104 300fr lt bl & indigo 1.75 .60
C256 AP104 370fr lt bl & indigo 2.25 .90
a. Strip of 3, #C254-C256 8.50 3.50

Bicentenary of the American Revolution. No. C256a has continuous design.

Schweitzer, Bach and Score AP105

Designs: No. C257, Albert Einstein (1879-1955), theoretical physicist. No. No. C258, André-Marie Ampère (1775-1836), French physicist. 100fr, Clément Ader (1841-1925), French aviation pioneer. No. C260, Dr. Albert Schweitzer (1875-1965), Medical missionary and musician. No. C261, Sir Alexander Fleming (1881-1955), British bacteriologist, discoverer of penicillin.

1975 **Engr.** ***Perf. 13***
C257 AP105 90fr multi 1.10 .40
C258 AP105 90fr pur, org & bister 1.10 .40
C259 AP105 100fr bl, red & lilac 1.10 .40
C260 AP105 150fr grn, bl & dk grn 1.60 .60
C261 AP105 150fr lil, bl & brick red 1.25 .45
Nos. C257-C261 (5) 6.15 2.25

Issued: #C257, May 26; #C258, Sept. 23; 100fr, Dec. 8; #C260, Jan. 14; #C261, July 21.
For surcharge see No. C358.

Olympic Rings and Globe — AP106

400fr, Montreal Olympic Games' emblem.

1975, Oct.
C262 AP106 350fr pur & bl 2.50 .75
C263 AP106 400fr blue 3.00 .85

Pre-Olympic Year 1975.

Nos. C247-C249 Overprinted: "ARRIMAGE / 17 Juil. 1975"

1975, Oct. 20 **Engr.** ***Perf. 13***
C264 AP101 290fr multi 2.10 .60
C265 AP101 300fr multi 2.25 .65
C266 AP101 370fr multi 3.25 1.00
Nos. C264-C266 (3) 7.60 2.25

Apollo-Soyuz link-up in space, July 17, 1975.

Painting Type of 1974

Designs: 290fr, Visitation, by Ghirlandaio. 300fr, Nativity, Fra Filippo Lippi school. 370fr, Adoration of the Kings, by Velazquez.

1975, Nov. 24 **Litho.** ***Perf. 12½x13***
C267 AP95 290fr multi 2.10 .60
C268 AP95 300fr multi 2.25 .70
C269 AP95 370fr multi 3.25 1.10
Nos. C267-C269 (3) 7.60 2.40

Christmas 1975.

Concorde — AP107

1976, Jan. 12 Litho. *Perf. 13*

C270 AP107 500fr multi 5.25 1.50

Concorde supersonic jet, first commercial flight, Jan. 21, 1976.
For overprint see No. C315.

AP108

AP109

1976, Feb. 16 Litho. *Perf. 13*

C271 AP108 120fr Figure skating .70 .25
C272 AP108 420fr Ski jump 2.25 .70
C273 AP108 430fr Slalom 2.25 .70
Nos. C271-C273 (3) 5.20 1.65

12th Winter Olympic Games, Innsbruck, Austria, Feb. 4-15.

1976, Apr. 5 Litho. *Perf. 12½*

Eye examination, WHO emblem.

C274 AP109 130fr multi 1.00 .25

World Health Day: "Foresight prevents blindness."

Space Ship with Solar Batteries — AP110

Design: 300fr, Astronaut working on orbital space station, vert.

1976, May 10 Engr. *Perf. 13*

C275 AP110 300fr org, dk & lt bl 2.00 .60
C276 AP110 400fr mag, dk bl & org 3.00 .90

Futuristic space achievements.

American Eagle, Flag and Liberty Bell — AP111

Designs: 400fr, Revolutionary War naval battle and American eagle. 440fr, Indians on horseback and American eagle, vert.

1976, May 24 Litho. *Perf. 12½*

C277 AP111 100fr multi .70 .25
C278 AP111 400fr multi 3.00 .75
C279 AP111 440fr multi 3.00 .80
Nos. C277-C279 (3) 6.70 1.80

American Bicentennial. Nos. C278-C279 also for Interphil 76, International Philatelic Exhibition, Philadelphia, Pa, May 29-June 6.

Running AP112

Designs (Olympic Rings and): 250fr, Swimming. 300fr, Field ball. 440fr, Soccer.

1976, June 7 Engr. *Perf. 13*

C280 AP112 200fr red brn & blk 1.10 .30
C281 AP112 250fr multi 1.40 .40
C282 AP112 300fr multi 2.00 .50
C283 AP112 440fr multi 2.75 .75
Nos. C280-C283 (4) 7.25 1.95

21st Olympic Games, Montreal, Canada, July 17-Aug. 1.

Cub Scout and Leader — AP113

Designs: 180fr, Scouts tending sick animal, horiz. 200fr, Night hike.

1976, June 14 Engr. *Perf. 13*

C284 AP113 140fr ultra & red brn 1.00 .35
C285 AP113 180fr dk brn & multi 1.40 .45
C286 AP113 200fr brn org & vio bl 1.50 .50
Nos. C284-C286 (3) 3.90 1.30

First African Boy Scout Jamboree, Nigeria.

Mohenjo-Daro, Bull from Wall Relief — AP114

Design: 500fr, Man's head, animals, wall and UNESCO emblem.

1976, Sept. 6 Engr. *Perf. 13*

C287 AP114 400fr blk, bl & pur 2.40 .60
C288 AP114 500fr dk red, bl & grn 3.25 1.10

UNESCO campaign to save Mohenjo-Daro excavations.

Europafrica Issue

Freighter, Plane, Map of Europe and Africa — AP115

1976, Sept. 20

C289 AP115 200fr vio brn & bl 2.00 .70

Nativity, by Taddeo Gaddi — AP116

Paintings: 300fr, Adoration of the Kings, by Hans Memling. 320fr, Nativity, by Carlo Crivelli.

1976, Nov. 8 Litho. *Perf. 13x12½*

C290 AP116 280fr multi 2.00 .50
C291 AP116 300fr multi 2.25 .60
C292 AP116 320fr multi 2.40 .75
Nos. C290-C292 (3) 6.65 1.85

Christmas 1976.

Viking Flying to Mars — AP117

1000fr, Viking landing craft on Mars.

1976, Dec. 8 Engr. *Perf. 13*

C293 AP117 500fr red, brn & bl 3.00 1.25
C294 AP117 1000fr multi 5.00 1.75
a. Miniature sheet of 2 10.00 3.50

Operation Viking, US Mars mission, No. C294a contains 2 stamps similar to Nos. C293-C294 in changed colors.

Pres. Giscard d'Estaing, Village and Bambara Antelope — AP118

1977, Feb. 13 Photo. *Perf. 13*

C295 AP118 430fr multi 4.25 .90

Visit of Pres. Valéry Giscard d'Estaing of France, Feb. 13-15.

Elizabeth II and Prince Philip — AP119

Designs: 200fr, Charles de Gaulle. vert. 250fr, Queen Wilhelmina, vert. 300fr, King Baudouin and Queen Fabiola. 480fr, Coronation of Queen Elizabeth II, vert.

1977, Mar. 21 Litho. *Perf. 12*

C296 AP119 180fr multi 1.10 .45
C297 AP119 200fr multi 1.25 .45
C298 AP119 250fr multi 1.60 .55
C299 AP119 300fr multi 2.00 .65
C300 AP119 480fr multi 3.00 1.00
Nos. C296-C300 (5) 8.95 3.10

Personalities involved in de-colonization.

Newton, Rocket and Apple — AP120

1977, May 7 Engr. *Perf. 13*

C301 AP120 400fr grn, brn & red 3.25 .90

Isaac Newton (1643-1727), natural philosopher and mathematician, 250th death anniversary.

Charles Lindbergh and Spirit of St. Louis — AP121

430fr, Spirit of St. Louis flying over clouds.

1977, Apr. 4 Litho. *Perf. 12*

C302 AP121 420fr org & pur 2.75 .80
C303 AP121 430fr multi 2.75 .80

Charles A. Lindbergh's solo transatlantic flight from New York to Paris, 50th anniversary.

Sassenage Castle, Grenoble — AP122

1977, May 21 Litho. *Perf. 12½*

C304 AP122 300fr multi 2.00 .60

Intl. French Language Council, 10th anniv.

Zeppelin No. 1, 1900 — AP123

Designs: 130fr, Graf Zeppelin, 1924. 350fr, Hindenburg aflame at Lakehurst, NJ, 1937. 500fr, Ferdinand von Zeppelin and Graf Zeppelin.

1977, May 30 Engr. *Perf. 13*

C305 AP123 120fr multi .70 .25
C306 AP123 130fr multi .90 .25
C307 AP123 350fr multi 2.25 .65
C308 AP123 500fr multi 3.25 .75
Nos. C305-C308 (4) 7.10 1.90

History of the Zeppelin.

Martin Luther King, American and Swedish Flags — AP124

Design: 600fr, Henri Dunant, Red Cross, Swiss and Swedish flags.

1977, July 4 Engr. *Perf. 13*

C309 AP124 600fr multi 2.25 .70
C310 AP124 700fr multi 2.75 .75

Nobel Peace Prize recipients.

Soccer — AP125

Designs: 200fr, 3 soccer players, vert. 420fr, 3 soccer players.

1977, Oct. 3 Engr. *Perf. 13*

C311 AP125 180fr multi .70 .30
C312 AP125 200fr multi .90 .35
C313 AP125 420fr multi 2.00 .75
Nos. C311-C313 (3) 3.60 1.40

World Soccer Cup Elimination Games.

Mao Tse-tung and COMATEX Hall, Bamako — AP126

1977, Nov. 7 Engr. *Perf. 13*

C314 AP126 300fr dull red 5.00 .90

Chairman Mao Tse-tung (1893-1976).

No. C270 Overprinted in Violet Blue: "PARIS NEW-YORK 22.11.77"

1977, Nov. 22 Litho. *Perf. 13*

C315 AP107 500fr multi 11.50 5.50

Concorde, first commerical transatlantic flight, Paris to New York.

Virgin and Child, by Rubens AP127

Rubens Paintings: 400fr, Adoration of the Kings. 600fr, Detail from Adoration of the Kings, horiz.

1977, Dec. 5 *Perf. 12½x12, 12x12½*

C316 AP127 400fr gold & multi 1.75 .60
C317 AP127 500fr gold & multi 2.25 .80
C318 AP127 600fr gold & multi 3.00 1.00
Nos. C316-C318 (3) 7.00 2.40

Christmas 1977, and 400th birth anniversary of Peter Paul Rubens (1577-1640).

Battle of the Amazons, by Rubens — AP128

Rubens Paintings: 300fr, Return from the fields. 500fr, Hercules fighting the Nemean Lion, vert.

Perf. 12x12½, 12½x12

1978, Jan. 16 Litho.

C319 AP128 200fr multi 1.00 .30
C320 AP128 300fr multi 1.60 .50
C321 AP128 500fr multi 2.75 .80
Nos. C319-C321 (3) 5.35 1.60

Peter Paul Rubens, 400th birth anniversary.

Schubert Composing "Winterreise" — AP129

Design: 300fr, Schubert and score, vert.

1978, Feb. 13

C322 AP129 300fr multi 1.60 .50
C323 AP129 420fr multi 2.25 .70

Franz Schubert (1797-1828), Austrian composer.

Capt. Cook Receiving Hawaiian Delegation — AP130

Design: 300fr, Cook landing on Hawaii. Designs after sketches by John Weber.

1978, Feb. 27 Engr. *Perf. 13*

C324 AP130 200fr multi 1.50 .40
C325 AP130 300fr multi 2.50 .55

Capt. James Cook (1728-1779), bicentenary of his arrival in Hawaii.

Soccer — AP131

250fr, One player. 300fr, Two players, horiz.

1978, Mar. 20

C326 AP131 150fr multi 1.00 .30
C327 AP131 250fr multi 1.60 .50
a. "REPUPLIQUE" 3.25 .90
C328 AP131 300fr multi 2.10 .60
a. Min. sheet of 3, #C326-C328 + label 6.00 4.00
b. As "a," #C326, C327a, C328 9.00 6.00
Nos. C326-C328 (3) 4.70 1.40

World Soccer Cup Championships, Argentina, 1978, June 1-25.

Nos. C327 and C328a were issued in July to correct the spelling error.

For overprints see Nos. C338-C340.

Jesus with Crown of Thorns, by Dürer AP132

430fr, Resurrection, by Albrecht Dürer.

1978, Mar. 28

C329 AP132 420fr multi 3.00 .60
C330 AP132 430fr multi 3.25 .60

Easter 1978. See Nos. C359-C361.

Citroen, C3-Trefle, 1922 — AP133

Citroen Cars: 130fr, Croisiere Noire, 1924, tractor. 180fr, B14G, 1927. 200fr, "11" Tractor Avant, 1934.

1978, Apr. 24 Engr. *Perf. 13*

C331 AP133 120fr multi 1.10 .25
C332 AP133 130fr multi 1.25 .25
C333 AP133 180fr multi 1.60 .40
C334 AP133 200fr multi 1.75 .45
Nos. C331-C334 (4) 5.70 1.35

Andre Citroen (1878-1935), automobile designer and manufacturer.

UPU Emblem, World Map, Country Names — AP133a

Design: 130fr, UPU emblem, globe and names of member countries.

1978, May 15

C334A AP133a 120fr multi .80 .25
C335 AP133a 130fr red, grn & emer 1.10 .25

Centenary of Congress of Paris where General Postal Union became the Universal Postal Union.

Europafrica Issue

Zebra, Miniature by Mansur, Jehangir School, 1620 — AP134

Design: 100fr, Ostrich Incubating Eggs, Syrian Manuscript, 14th Century.

1978, July 24 Litho. *Perf. 13x12½*

C336 AP134 100fr multi 3.00 .60
C337 AP134 110fr multi 3.00 .60

Nos. C326-C328a Overprinted in Black:

a. CHAMPION / 1978 / ARGENTINE
b. 2e HOLLANDE
c. 3e BRESIL / 4e ITALIE

1978, Aug. 7 Engr. *Perf. 13*

C338 AP131 150fr multi (a) 1.25 .35
C339 AP131 250fr multi (b) 1.60 .50
C340 AP131 300fr multi (c) 2.25 .60
a. Souvenir sheet of 3 6.50 2.50
Nos. C338-C340 (3) 5.10 1.45

Winners, World Soccer Cup Championship, Argentina. Overprints on No. C340a are green including label overprint: FINALE / ARGENTINA 3 HOLLANDE 1.

Elizabeth II in Coronation Robes AP135

Design: 500fr, Coronation coach.

1978, Sept. 18 Litho. *Perf. 12½x12*

C341 AP135 500fr multi 2.40 .65
C342 AP135 1000fr multi 5.25 1.50

Coronation of Queen Elizabeth II, 25th anniv.

US No. C3a and Douglas DC-3 AP136

History of Aviation: 100fr, Belgium No. 252 and Stampe SV-4. 120fr, France No. C48 and Ader's plane No. 3. 130fr, Germany No. C2 and Junker Ju-52. 320fr, Japan No. C25 and Mitsubishi A-6M "Zero."

1978, Oct. 16 Engr. *Perf. 13*

C343 AP136 80fr multi .45 .20
C344 AP136 100fr multi .55 .20
C345 AP136 120fr multi .65 .20
C346 AP136 130fr multi .70 .20
C347 AP136 320fr multi 1.75 .55
Nos. C343-C347 (5) 4.10 1.35

Annunciation, by Dürer — AP137

Etchings by Dürer: 430fr, Virgin and Child. 500fr, Adoration of the Kings.

1978, Nov. 6

C348 AP137 420fr blk & rose car 1.60 .50
C349 AP137 430fr ol grn & brn 1.75 .60
C350 AP137 500fr blk & red 2.40 .70
Nos. C348-C350 (3) 5.75 1.80

Christmas 1978 and 450th death anniversary of Albrecht Dürer (1471-1528), German painter.

Rocket and Trajectory Around Moon — AP138

Design: 300fr, Spaceship circling moon.

1978, Nov. 20 Engr. *Perf. 13*

C351 AP138 200fr multi 1.50 .60
C352 AP138 300fr multi 2.25 .70
a. Pair, #C351-C352 + label 4.75 2.00

10th anniversary of 1st flight around moon.

Ader's Plane and Concorde — AP139

Designs: 130fr, Wright Flyer A and Concorde. 200fr, Spirit of St. Louis and Concorde.

1979, Jan. 25 Litho. *Perf. 13*

C353 AP139 120fr multi .80 .25
C354 AP139 130fr multi 1.00 .30
C355 AP139 200fr multi 1.75 .55
Nos. C353-C355 (3) 3.55 1.10

1st supersonic commercial flight, 3rd anniv.
For surcharges see Nos. C529-C531.

Philexafrique II-Essen Issue

Common Design Types

Designs: No. C356, Dromedary and Mali No. C26. No. C357, Bird and Lubeck No. 1.

1979, Jan. 29 Litho. *Perf. 13x12½*

C356 CD138 200fr multi 3.00 1.00
C357 CD139 200fr multi 3.00 1.00
a. Pair, #C356-C357 + label 7.50 3.00

No. C257 Surcharged

1979, Mar. 26 Engr. *Perf. 13*

C358 AP105 130fr on 90fr multi 1.50 .50

Albert Einstein (1879-1955).

Easter Type of 1978

Dürer Etchings: 400fr, Jesus Carrying Cross. 430fr, Crucified Christ. 480fr, Pietà.

1979, Apr. 9

C359 AP132 400fr bl & blk 2.50 .75
C360 AP132 430fr red & blk 2.75 .85
C361 AP132 480fr ultra & blk 3.00 .95
Nos. C359-C361 (3) 8.25 2.55

Easter 1979.

Basketball and Cathedral, Moscow AP140

430fr, Soccer and St. Basil's Cathedral.

1979, Apr. 17 Litho. *Perf. 13*

C362 AP140 420fr multi 2.25 .80
C363 AP140 430fr multi 2.25 .80

Pre-Olympic Year.

Mali #C92, Apollo Spacecraft AP141

Design: 500fr, Mali No. C176, lift-off.

1979, Oct. 22 Litho. *Perf. 12½x13*

C364 AP141 430fr multi 2.25 .70
C365 AP141 500fr multi 2.40 .80

Apollo 11 moon landing, 10th anniversary.

Capt. Cook, Ship, Kerguelen Island — AP142

Design: 480fr, Capt. Cook, Ship, Hawaii.

1979, Oct. 29 *Perf. 13x12½*

C366 AP142 300fr multi 1.75 .60
C367 AP142 480fr multi 2.40 .85

Capt. James Cook (1728-1779).

David Janowski (1868-1927), Chess Pieces — AP143

Chess Pieces and Grand Masters: 140fr, Alexander Alekhine (1892-1946). 200fr, W. Schlage. 300fr, Effim D. Bogoljubow (1889-1952).

1979, Nov. 30 Engr. *Perf. 13*

C368 AP143 100fr red & brn 1.00 .25
C369 AP143 140fr multi 1.40 .25
C370 AP143 200fr multi 2.00 .40
C371 AP143 300fr multi 2.75 .55
Nos. C368-C371 (4) 7.15 1.45

For overprints see Nos. C441-C442.

Adoration of the Kings, by Dürer AP144

Christmas 1979: 400fr, 500fr, Adoration of the Kings by Dürer, diff.

1979, Dec. 10 *Perf. 13x13½*

C372 AP144 300fr brn org & brn 1.60 .50
C373 AP144 400fr bl & brn 2.25 .70
C374 AP144 500fr dk grn & brn 2.75 .90
Nos. C372-C374 (3) 6.60 2.10

Jet, Map of Africa AP145

1979, Dec. 27 Litho. *Perf. 12½*

C375 AP145 120fr multi .90 .30

ASECNA (Air Safety Board), 20th anniv.

Train, Globe, Rotary Emblem AP146

Rotary Intl., 75th Anniv.: 250fr, Jet. 430fr, Bamako Club emblem, meeting hall.

1980, Jan. 28 Litho. *Perf. 12½*

C376 AP146 220fr multi 1.10 .40
C377 AP146 250fr multi 1.10 .40
C378 AP146 430fr multi 2.00 .70
Nos. C376-C378 (3) 4.20 1.50

Speed Skating, Lake Placid '80 Emblem, Snowflake AP147

1980, Feb. 11 *Perf. 13*

C379 AP147 200fr shown .90 .25
C380 AP147 300fr Ski jump 1.25 .50
a. Souvenir sheet of 2 3.25 2.00

13th Winter Olympic Games, Lake Placid, NY, Feb. 12-24. No. C380a contains Nos. C379-C380 in changed colors.

Stephenson's Rocket, Mali No. 196 — AP148

Liverpool-Manchester Railroad, 150th Anniversary: 300fr, Stephenson's Rocket, Mali No. 142.

1980, Feb. 25 Engr.

C381 AP148 200fr multi 1.10 .25
C382 AP148 300fr multi 1.75 .50

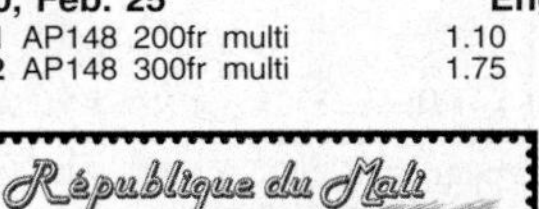

Equestrian, Moscow '80 Emblem — AP149

1980, Mar. 10 Engr. *Perf. 13*

C383 AP149 200fr shown 1.00 .30
C384 AP149 300fr Yachting 1.40 .50
C385 AP149 400fr Soccer 2.25 .70
a. Souvenir sheet of 3, #C383-C385 5.00 5.00
Nos. C383-C385 (3) 4.65 1.50

22nd Summer Olympic Games, Moscow, July 19-Aug. 3.
For overprints see Nos. C399-C401.

Jesus Carrying Cross, by Maurice Denis AP150

Easter: 500fr, Jesus before Pilate, by Dürer.

1980, Mar. 31

C386 AP150 480fr brn & org red 2.50 .80
C387 AP150 500fr org red & brn 2.50 .80

Kepler, Copernicus and Solar System Diagram — AP151

200fr, Kepler & diagram of earth's orbit.

1980, Apr. 7 Engr. *Perf. 13*

C388 AP151 200fr multi, vert. 1.25 .30
C389 AP151 300fr multi 1.75 .50

Discovery of Pluto, 50th Anniversary — AP152

1980, Apr. 21

C390 AP152 420fr multi 2.10 .75

Lunokhod I, Russian Flag — AP153

Design: 500fr, Apollo and Soyuz spacecraft, flags of US and Russia.

1980, Apr. 28

C391 AP153 480fr multi 2.25 .70
C392 AP153 500fr multi 2.25 .70

Lunokhod I, 10th anniversary; Apollo-Soyuz space test program, 5th anniversary.

Rochambeau, French Fleet Landing at Newport, R.I. — AP154

French Cooperation in American Revolution: 430fr, Rochambeau and George Washington, eagle.

1980, June 16 Engr. *Perf. 13*
C393 AP154 420fr multi 2.25 .75
C394 AP154 430fr multi 2.25 .75

Jet Flying Around Earth — AP155

Designs: No. C396, Ship, people, attack. No. C397, Astronaut on moon. No. C398, Space craft, scientists, moon. Nos. C395-C396 from "Around the World in 80 Days;" Nos. C397-C398 from "From Earth to Moon."

1980, June 30 Engr. *Perf. 11*
C395 AP155 100fr multi + label .80 .25
C396 AP155 100fr multi + label .80 .25
C397 AP155 150fr multi + label 1.10 .30
C398 AP155 150fr multi + label 1.10 .30
Nos. C395-C398 (4) 3.80 1.10

Jules Verne (1828-1905), French science fiction writer. Nos. C395-C398 each printed se-tenant with label showing various space scenes.

Nos. C383-C385a Overprinted:

200fr — CONCOURS COMPLET/ INDIVIDUEL/ROMAN (It.)/ BLINOV (Urss) /SALNIKOV (Urss)
300fr — FINN/RECHARDT (Fin.)/ MAYRHOFER (Autr.)/ BALACHOV (Urss)
400fr — TCHECOSLOVAQUIE/ ALLEMAGNE DE L'EST/URSS

1980, Sept. 8 Engr. *Perf. 13*
C399 AP149 200fr multi 1.00 .30
C400 AP149 300fr multi 1.40 .50
C401 AP149 400fr multi 2.25 .75
a. Souvenir sheet of 3 5.00 5.00
Nos. C399-C401 (3) 4.65 1.55

Butterfly Type of 1980

1980, Oct. 6 Litho. *Perf. 13x12½*
Size: 48x36mm
C402 A137 420fr *Denaus chrysippus* 6.00 1.00

Charles De Gaulle, Map and Colors of France — AP156

1980, Nov. 9 Litho. *Perf. 13½x13*
C403 AP156 420fr shown 3.50 .90
C404 AP156 430fr De Gaulle, cross 3.50 .90

Charles De Gaulle, 10th anniv. of death.

Mali No. 140, Amtrak Train — AP157

Mali Stamps and Trains: 120fr, No. 195, Tokaido, Japan, vert. 200fr, No. 144, Rembrandt, Germany. 480fr, No. 143, TGV-001 France, vert.

1980, Nov. 17 Engr. *Perf. 13*
C405 AP157 120fr multi .70 .25
C406 AP157 130fr multi .80 .25
C407 AP157 200fr multi 1.10 .40
C408 AP157 480fr multi 2.75 .90
Nos. C405-C408 (4) 5.35 1.80

For overprint see No. C425.

Holy Family, by Lorenzo Lotto — AP158

Christmas 1980 (Paintings): 400fr, Flight to Egypt, by Rembrandt, vert. 500fr, Christmas Night, by Gauguin.

1980, Dec. 1 Litho. *Perf. 13x12½*
C409 AP158 300fr multi 1.60 .55
C410 AP158 400fr multi 2.10 .70
C411 AP158 500fr multi 2.50 .80
Nos. C409-C411 (3) 6.20 2.05

Self-portrait, by Picasso — AP159

1981, Jan. 26 Litho. *Perf. 12½x13*
C412 AP159 1000fr multi 7.50 2.00

Pablo Picasso (1881-1973).

Soccer Players — AP160

Designs: Soccer players.

1981, Feb. 28 *Perf. 13*
C413 AP160 100fr multi .65 .25
C414 AP160 200fr multi 1.10 .35
C415 AP160 300fr multi 1.75 .50
Nos. C413-C415 (3) 3.50 1.10

Souvenir Sheet

C416 AP160 600fr multi 3.75 1.75

World Cup Soccer preliminary games.

Mozart and Instruments — AP161

225th Birth Anniversary of Wolfgang Amadeus Mozart: 430fr, Mozart and instruments, diff.

1981, Mar. 30 Litho. *Perf. 13*
C417 AP161 420fr multi 3.00 .70
C418 AP161 430fr multi 3.00 .70

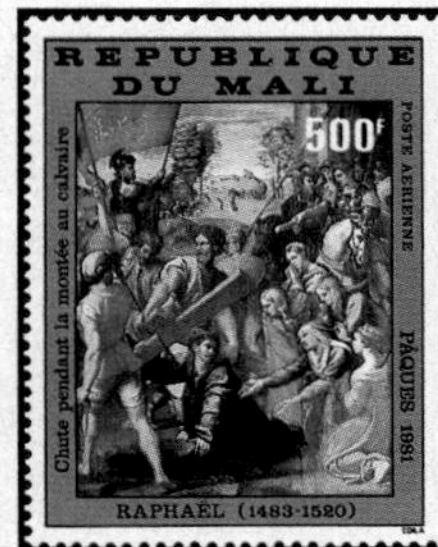

Jesus Falls on the Way to Calvary, by Raphael AP162

Easter 1981: 600fr, Ecce Homo, by Rembrandt.

1981, Apr. 6 *Perf. 12½x13*
C419 AP162 500fr multi 2.50 .80
C420 AP162 600fr multi 2.75 .90

Alan B. Shepard AP163

Exploration of Saturn — AP164

Space Anniversaries: No. C422, Yuri Gagarin's flight, 1961. 430fr, Uranus discovery bicentennial, horiz.

1981, Apr. 21 Litho. *Perf. 13*
C421 AP163 200fr multi 1.00 .30
C422 AP163 200fr multi 1.00 .30
C423 AP164 380fr multi 2.00 .55
C424 AP163 430fr multi 2.10 .65
Nos. C421-C424 (4) 6.10 1.80

No. C408 Overprinted:
"26 fevrier 1981
Record du monde de/vitesse-380 km/h."

1981, June 15 Engr.
C425 AP157 480fr multi 3.50 .90

New railroad speed record.

US No. 233, Columbus and His Fleet — AP165

475th Death Anniversary of Christopher Columbus (Santa Maria and): 200fr, Spain No. 418, vert. 260fr, Spain No. 421, vert. 300fr, US No. 232.

1981, June 22
C426 AP165 180fr multi 1.00 .30
C427 AP165 200fr multi 1.25 .35
C428 AP165 260fr multi 1.75 .55
C429 AP165 300fr multi 2.10 .65
Nos. C426-C429 (4) 6.10 1.85

Columbia Space Shuttle — AP166

Designs: Space shuttle.

1981, July 6 Litho. *Perf. 13*
C430 AP166 200fr multi 1.25 .30
C431 AP166 500fr multi 3.00 .90
C432 AP166 600fr multi 3.50 1.00
Nos. C430-C432 (3) 7.75 2.20

Souvenir Sheet
Perf. 12

C433 AP166 700fr multi 5.75 2.00

For overprint see No. C440.

Harlequin on Horseback AP167

Picasso Birth Cent.: 750fr, Child Holding a Dove.

1981, July 15 *Perf. 12½x13*
C434 AP167 600fr multi 4.00 1.00
C435 AP167 750fr multi 5.00 1.10

Prince Charles and Lady Diana, St. Paul's Cathedral AP168

1981, July 20 *Perf. 12½*
C436 AP168 500fr shown 2.25 .70
C437 AP168 700fr Couple, coach 3.50 1.00

Royal wedding.

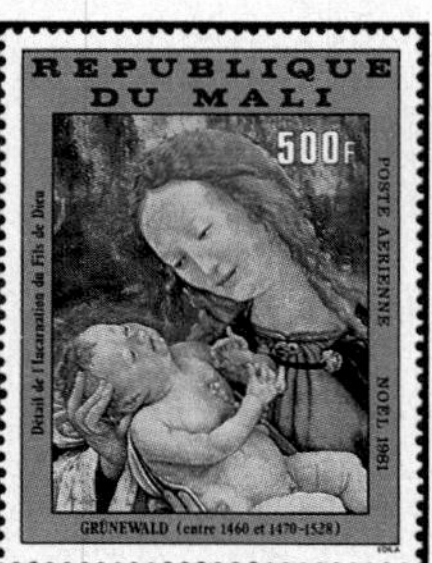

Christmas 1981 AP169

Designs: Virgin and Child paintings.

1981, Nov. 9 Litho. *Perf. 12½x13*
C438 AP169 500fr Grunewald 2.75 .70
C439 AP169 700fr Correggio 3.50 1.00

See Nos. C451-C452, C464-C466, C475-C477, C488-C489, C511.

No. C433 Overprinted In Blue: "JOE ENGLE / RICHARD TRULY / 2 eme VOL SPATIAL"

1981, Nov. 12 Litho. *Perf. 12*
C440 AP166 700fr multi 5.00 1.50

Nos. C369, C371 Overprinted with Winners' Names and Dates

1981, Dec. Engr. *Perf. 13*
C441 AP143 140fr multi 1.25 .35
C442 AP143 300fr multi 2.75 .60

Lewis Carroll (1832-1908) — AP170

Designs: Scenes from Alice in Wonderland.

1982, Jan. 30 Litho. *Perf. 12½*
C443 AP170 110fr multi 2.50 .60
C444 AP170 130fr multi 2.50 .80
C445 AP170 140fr multi 2.50 1.00
Nos. C443-C445 (3) 7.50 2.40

AP171

AP172

1982, Feb. 8 *Perf. 13*
C446 AP171 700fr Portrait, by Gilbert Stuart 4.50 1.10

George Washington's Birth, 250th anniv. Incorrectly inscribed "Stuart Gilbert."

1982, Mar. 15 Litho. *Perf. 13*

1982 World Cup: Various soccer players.

C447 AP172 220fr multi 1.00 .30
C448 AP172 420fr multi 2.00 .50
C449 AP172 500fr multi 2.25 .75
Nos. C447-C449 (3) 5.25 1.55

Souvenir Sheet

Perf. 12½

C450 AP172 680fr multi 4.50 2.00

For overprints see Nos. C458-C461.

Art Type of 1981

Paintings: 680fr, Transfiguration, by Fra Angelico. 1000fr, Pieta, by Bellini, horiz.

Perf. 12½x13, 13x12½

1982, Apr. 19 Litho.
C451 AP169 680fr multi 3.25 1.75
C452 AP169 1000fr multi 4.25 1.25

Mali No. O30, France No. 1985 — AP174

1982, June 1 *Perf. 13*
C453 AP174 180fr shown 1.00 .25
C454 AP174 200fr No. C356 1.25 .35
a. Pair, #C453-C454 + label 2.75 1.40

PHILEXFRANCE '82 Intl. Stamp Exhibition, Paris, June 11-21.

Fire Engine, France, 1850 — AP175

Designs: French fire engines.

1982, June 14
C455 AP175 180fr shown 1.10 .25
C456 AP175 200fr 1921 1.25 .30
C457 AP175 270fr 1982 1.75 .45
Nos. C455-C457 (3) 4.10 1.00

Nos. C447-C450 Overprinted with Finalists' and Scores in Brown, Black, Blue or Red

1982, Aug. 16 Litho. *Perf. 13*
C458 AP172 220fr multi (Brn) 1.25 .25
C459 AP172 420fr multi 1.75 .55
C460 AP172 500fr multi (Bl) 2.25 .75
Nos. C458-C460 (3) 5.25 1.55

Souvenir Sheet

Perf. 12½

C461 AP172 680fr multi (R) 3.50 1.75

Italy's victory in 1982 World Cup.

Scouting Year — AP176

1982 *Perf. 12½*
C462 AP176 300fr Tent, Baden-Powell 1.25 .45
C463 AP176 500fr Salute, emblem 2.25 .80

Art Type of 1981

Boy with Cherries, by Edouard Manet (1832-83).

1982, Oct. 28 Litho. *Perf. 12½x13*
C464 AP169 680fr multi 4.50 1.25

Art Type of 1981

Madonna and Child Paintings.

1982, Nov. 10
C465 AP169 500fr Titian 2.25 .75
C466 AP169 1000fr Bellini 4.50 1.25

Johann von Goethe (1749-1832), Poet — AP179

1982, Dec. 13 Engr. *Perf. 13*
C467 AP179 500fr multi 3.25 .85

Follereau Type of 1974

1983, Jan. 24
C468 AP96 200fr dk brn 1.40 .35

Vostok VI, 20th Anniv. — AP180

Manned Flight, 200th Anniv. — AP181

1983, Feb. 14 Litho. *Perf. 12½*
C469 AP180 400fr Valentina Tereshkova 2.00 .60

1983, Feb. 28 *Perf. 13*
C470 AP181 500fr Eagle transatlantic balloon 3.25 .75
C471 AP181 700fr Montgolfiere 4.25 1.10

Pre-Olympic Year — AP182

1983, Mar. 14 Litho. *Perf. 13*
C472 AP182 180fr Soccer .90 .25
C473 AP182 270fr Hurdles 1.25 .45
C474 AP182 300fr Wind surfing 1.75 .55
Nos. C472-C474 (3) 3.90 1.25

Art Type of 1981

Raphael paintings.

1983, Mar. 28 *Perf. 12½x13*
C475 AP169 400fr Deposition 2.00 .60
C476 AP169 600fr Transfiguration 3.00 .85

Art Type of 1981

Design: Family of Acrobats with Monkey, by Picasso (1881-1973).

1983, Apr. 30 Litho. *Perf. 12½x13*
C477 AP169 680fr multi 3.75 1.25

Lions Intl. — AP185

1983, May 9 *Perf. 12½*
C478 Pair 15.00 6.50
a. AP185 700fr shown 4.00 1.10
b. AP185 700fr Rotary Intl. 4.00 1.10

Challenger Spacecraft AP186

1983, July 29 Litho. *Perf. 13*
C479 AP186 1000fr multi 4.75 1.25

Printed se-tenant with orange red label showing astronaut Sally Ride.

Paris-Dakar Auto Race — AP187

1983, Sept. 5 Litho. *Perf. 12½*
C480 AP187 240fr Mercedes, 1914 1.60 .35
C481 AP187 270fr SSK, 1929 1.75 .45
C482 AP187 500fr W196, 1954 3.50 .75
Nos. C480-C482 (3) 6.85 1.55

Souvenir Sheet

C483 AP187 1000fr Mercedes van 8.50 2.00

For surcharge see No. C506.

Chess Game — AP188

1983, Oct. 24 Engr. *Perf. 13*
C484 AP188 300fr Pawn, bishop 2.25 .40
C485 AP188 420fr Knight, castle 2.75 .70
C486 AP188 500fr King, Queen 3.75 .80
Nos. C484-C486 (3) 8.75 1.90

Souvenir Sheet

C487 AP188 700fr Various chess pieces 5.75 1.75

Art Type of 1981

Raphael Paintings.

1983, Nov. 7 Litho. *Perf. 12½x13*
C488 AP169 700fr Canigiani Madonna 3.50 .90
C489 AP169 800fr Madonna with Lamb 3.75 1.00

Portrait of Leopold Zborowski, by Amedeo Modigliani (1884-1920) — AP190

1984, Feb. 13 Litho. *Perf. 12½x13*
C490 AP190 700fr multi 4.75 1.25

Abraham Lincoln — AP191

Duke Ellington AP192

1984, Feb. 27 *Perf. 12½*
C491 AP191 400fr Henri Dunant 2.00 .50
C492 AP191 540fr shown 2.50 .60

1984, Mar. 12 *Perf. 13½x13*
C493 AP192 470fr Sidney Bechet 5.00 .90
C494 AP192 500fr shown 6.00 .90

Glider — AP193

1984, Mar. 26
C495 AP193 270fr shown 1.60 .35
C496 AP193 350fr Hang glider 2.00 .55

1984 Summer Olympics — AP194

1984, Apr. 9 *Perf. 13*
C497 AP194 265fr Weight lifting 1.60 .35
C498 AP194 440fr Equestrian 2.50 .55
C499 AP194 500fr Hurdles 3.00 .60

Souvenir Sheet

Perf. 12½

C500 AP194 700fr Wind surfing 5.50 1.75

For surcharges see Nos. C507-C510.

Easter 1984 — AP195

Paintings; 940fr, Crucifixion, by Rubens, vert. 970fr, Resurrection, by Mantegna.

1984, Apr. 24 **Engr.**
C501 AP195 940fr multi 6.25 1.25
C502 AP195 970fr multi 6.25 1.25

Gottlieb Daimler Birth Sesquicentenary — AP196

1984, June 1 **Engr.** *Perf. 13*
C503 AP196 350fr Mercedes Simplex 3.50 1.00
C504 AP196 470fr Mercedes-Benz 370-S 4.75 1.25
C505 AP196 485fr 500-SEC 5.00 1.25
Nos. C503-C505 (3) 13.25 3.50

No. C480 Overprinted and Surcharged

1984 **Litho.** *Perf. 12½*
C506 AP187 120fr on 240fr #C480 1.75 .40

Nos. C497-C500 Overprinted and Surcharged

1984, Oct. **Litho.** *Perf. 13*
C507 AP194 135fr on 265fr 1.00 .50
C508 AP194 220fr on 440fr 1.75 1.00
C509 AP194 250fr on 500fr 2.50 1.25
Nos. C507-C509 (3) 5.25 2.75

Souvenir Sheet

C510 AP194 350fr on 700fr 5.25 3.00

Overprints refer to the winners of the events depicted.

Art Type of 1981

Painting: Virgin and Child, by Lorenzo Lotto.

1984, Nov. 20 **Litho.** *Perf. 12½x13*
C511 AP169 500fr multi 5.00 2.00

Audubon Birth Bicentenary — AP198

1985, Apr. 15 **Litho.** *Perf. 13*
C512 AP198 180fr Kingfisher 2.00 .70
C513 AP198 300fr Bustard, vert. 3.25 1.25
C514 AP198 470fr Ostrich, vert. 5.50 2.00
C515 AP198 540fr Buzzard 6.00 2.10
Nos. C512-C515 (4) 16.75 6.05

For surcharge see No. C560, C562, C567.

ASECNA Airlines, 25th Anniv. — AP199

1985, June 10 *Perf. 12½*
C516 AP199 700fr multi 6.25 2.50

For surcharge see No. C559.

PHILEXAFRICA Type of 1985

1985, June 24 *Perf. 13*
C517 A183 200fr Boy Scouts, lion 2.25 1.10
C518 A183 200fr Satellite communications 2.25 1.10
a. Pair, #C517-C518 5.75 2.00

Halley's Comet — AP200

1986, Mar. 24 **Litho.** *Perf. 12½*
C519 AP200 300fr multi 2.75 1.10

For surcharge see No. C558.

Statue of Liberty, Cent. — AP201

1986, Apr. 7 *Perf. 13*
C520 AP201 600fr multi 6.50 2.25

Gottlieb Daimler Motorcycle — AP202

1986, Apr. 14
C521 AP202 400fr multi 4.75 1.40

1st Internal combustion automotive engine, cent.

Paul Robeson (1898-1976), American Actor, Singer — AP203

1986, May 10
C522 AP203 500fr Portrait, Show Boat 5.75 1.75

Karl Eberth (1835-1926), Bacteriologist, and Typhoid Bacilli — AP204

World Chess Championships AP205

1986, June 7 **Litho.** *Perf. 12x12½*
C523 AP204 550fr multi 5.25 2.50

1986, June 16 *Perf. 12½*
C524 AP205 400fr Chessmen 4.50 1.40
C525 AP205 500fr Knight 5.25 1.75

Disappearance of Jean Mermoz, 50th Anniv. — AP206

Mermoz and: 150fr, Latecoere-300 seaplane. 600fr, Cams 53 Oiseau Tango, seaplane. 625fr, Flight map, Le Comte de La Vaulx aircraft.

1986, Aug. 18 **Litho.** *Perf. 13*
C526 AP206 150fr multi 1.75 .50
C527 AP206 600fr multi 5.25 1.75
C528 AP206 625fr multi 5.25 2.00
Nos. C526-C528 (3) 12.25 4.25

Nos. C353-C355 Surcharged "1986-10e Anniversaire du ler Vol/Commercial Supersonique" and New Value

1986, Sept. 29
C529 AP139 175fr on 120fr 2.00 .60
C530 AP139 225fr on 130fr 2.50 .80
C531 AP139 300fr on 200fr 3.75 1.00
Nos. C529-C531 (3) 8.25 2.40

Hansen, Leprosy Bacillus, Follereau and Lepers — AP207

1987, Jan. 26 **Litho.** *Perf. 13*
C532 AP207 500fr multi 5.50 1.60

Gerhard Hansen (1841-1912), Norwegian physician who discovered the leprosy bacillus (1869); Raoul Follereau (1903-1977), philanthropist.

Konrad Adenauer (1876-1967), West German Chancellor AP208

1987, Mar. 9 **Litho.** *Perf. 13*
C533 AP208 625fr org, buff & blk 6.25 2.25

Pre-Olympics Year — AP209

Buddha and: 400fr, Runners. 500fr, Soccer players.

1987, Apr. 6 **Engr.**
C534 AP209 400fr blk & red brn 4.00 1.40
C535 AP209 500fr lil rose, ol grn & ol 5.00 1.75

25th Summer Olympics, Seoul, 1988.

Al Jolson in The Jazz Singer — AP210

1987, Apr. 20

C536 AP210 550fr dk red brn & car rose 7.75 2.25

Sound films, 60th anniv.

Albert John Luthuli (1899-1967), 1960 Nobel Peace Prize Winner — AP211

1987, May 26 Engr. *Perf. 13*

C537 AP211 400fr multi 3.75 1.10

Service Organizations AP212

1987, June 8 Litho. *Perf. 13*

C538 AP212 500fr Rotary Int'l. 5.00 1.60
C539 AP212 500fr Lions Int'l. 5.00 1.60

Coubertin, Ancient Greek Runners, Contemporary Athletes — AP213

1988, Feb. 14 Litho. *Perf. 13*

C540 AP213 240fr shown 2.25 .80
C541 AP213 400fr 5-ring emblem, stadium 4.00 1.40

125th birth anniv. of Baron Pierre de Coubertin (1863-1937), French educator and sportsman who promulgated revival of the Olympic Games; 1988 Summer Olympics, Seoul.

For surcharge see No. C565

Harlequin, by Pablo Picasso (1881-1973) — AP214

1988, Apr. 4 Litho. *Perf. 13*

C542 AP214 600fr multi 6.25 2.00

For surcharge see No. C563.

1st Scheduled Transatlantic Flight of the Concorde (London-New York), 15th Anniv. — AP215

1988, May 2 *Perf. 13*

C543 AP215 500fr multi 6.00 2.00

Home Improvement for a Verdant Mali — AP216

1989, Feb. 6 Litho. *Perf. 12½*

C544 AP216 5fr shown .20 .20
C545 AP216 10fr Furnace, tree, field .25 .20
C546 AP216 25fr like 5fr .35 .25
C547 AP216 100fr like 10fr 1.25 .45
Nos. C544-C547 (4) 2.05 1.10

1st Man on the Moon, 20th Anniv. — AP217

1989, Mar. 13 Engr. *Perf. 13*

C548 AP217 300fr multi. 3.00 1.00
C549 AP217 500fr multi, vert. 5.00 1.60

For surcharges see Nos. C561, C564.

French Revolution, Bicent. AP218

1989, July 3 Engr. *Perf. 13*

C550 AP218 400fr Women's march on Versailles 4.50 1.40
C551 AP218 600fr Storming of the Bastille 6.25 1.90

For surcharges see Nos. C566, C568.

World Cup Soccer Championships, Italy — AP219

1990, June 4 Litho. *Perf. 13*

C552 AP219 200fr multi 2.10 .70
C553 AP219 225fr multi, diff. 2.25 .80

Souvenir Sheet

C554 AP219 500fr like #C552 5.25 2.50

No. C552 overprinted in red "ITALIE : 2 / ANGLETERRE : 1"

No. C553 overprinted in red "R.F.A. : 1 / ARGENTINE : 0"

No. C554 overprinted in red in margin "1er : R.F.A. 2eme : ARGENTINE 3eme : ITALIE"

1990

C555 AP219 200fr on #C552 2.10 .85
C556 AP219 225fr on #C553 2.25 .85

Souvenir Sheet

C557 AP219 500fr on #C554 5.25 2.75

#C512-C513, C515-C516, C519, C541-C542, C548-C551 Surcharged Like #579-594

1992, June *Perfs. as Before*

Printing Methods as Before

C558 AP200 20fr on 300fr .35 .25
C559 AP199 20fr on 700fr .35 .25
C560 AP198 30fr on 180fr .90 .25
C561 AP217 30fr on 500fr .90 .25
C562 AP198 100fr on 540fr 3.00 .50
C563 AP214 100fr on 600fr 3.00 .50
C564 AP217 150fr on 300fr 4.50 .75
C565 AP213 150fr on 400fr 4.50 .75
C566 AP218 150fr on 400fr 4.50 .75
C567 AP198 200fr on 300fr 5.75 1.00
C568 AP218 240fr on 600fr 7.00 1.25
Nos. C558-C568 (11) 34.75 6.50

Size and location of surcharge varies. No. C565 also overprinted "BARCELONE 92."

POSTAGE DUE STAMPS

Bambara Headpiece — D1

Perf. 14x13½

1961, Mar. 18 Engr. Unwmk.

J1 D1 1fr black .25 .20
J2 D1 2fr bright ultra .25 .20
J3 D1 5fr red lilac .30 .20
J4 D1 10fr orange .50 .25
J5 D1 20fr bright green .75 .25
J6 D1 25fr red brown .95 .30
Nos. J1-J6 (6) 3.00 1.40

Polyptychus Roseus — D2

No. J8, Deilephila Nerii. No. J9, Gynanisa maja. No. J10, Bunaea alcinoe. No. J11, Teracolus eris. No. J12, Colotis antevippe. No. J13, Charaxes epijasius. No. J14, Manatha microcera. No. J15, Hypokopelates otraeda. No. J16, Lipaphnaeus leonina. No. J17, Gonimbrasia hecate. No. J18, Lobounaea christyi. No. J19, Hypolimnas misippus. No. J20, Catopsilia florella.

1964, June 1 Photo. *Perf. 11*

Butterflies and Moths in Natural Colors

J7 1fr olive green .30 .20
J8 1fr org & brn .30 .20
a. D2 Pair, #J7-J8 .60 .20
J9 2fr emer & brn .40 .20
J10 2fr emer & brn .40 .20
a. D2 Pair, #J9-J10 .80 .20
J11 3fr rose lil & brn .40 .20
J12 3fr rose lil & brn .40 .20
a. D2 Pair, #J11-J12 .80 .20
J13 5fr blk & rose .40 .20
J14 5fr green .40 .20
a. D2 Pair, #J13-J14 .80 .20
J15 10fr yel, org & blk .85 .35
J16 10fr blue .85 .35
a. D2 Pair, #J15-J16 1.75 .70
J17 20fr lt bl & brn 1.60 .70
J18 20fr lt bl & brn 1.60 .70
a. D2 Pair, #J17-J18 3.25 1.40
J19 25fr grn & yel 2.25 1.00
J20 25fr dp grn & blk 2.25 1.00
a. D2 Pair, #J19-J20 4.50 2.00
Nos. J7-J20 (14) 12.40 5.70

Nos. J7-J20 Surcharged

1984 Photo. *Perf. 11*

J21 5fr on 1fr #J7 .30 .20
J22 5fr on 1fr #J8 .30 .20
a. D2 Pair, #J21-J22 .60 .20
J23 10fr on 2fr #J9 .30 .20
J24 10fr on 2fr #J10 .30 .20
a. D2 Pair, #J23-J24 .60 .20
J25 15fr on 3fr #J11 .30 .20
J26 15fr on 3fr #J12 .30 .20
a. D2 Pair, #J25-J26 .60 .20
J27 25fr on 5fr #J13 .40 .20
J28 25fr on 5fr #J14 .40 .20
a. Pair, #J27-J28 .80 .20
J29 50fr on 10fr #J15 .70 .30
J30 50fr on 10fr #J16 .70 .30
a. D2 Pair, #J29-J30 1.40 .60
J31 100fr on 20fr #J17 1.60 .70
J32 100fr on 20fr #J18 1.60 .70
a. D2 Pair, #J31-J32 3.25 1.40
J33 125fr on 25fr #J19 2.00 .85
J34 125fr on 25fr #J20 2.00 .85
a. Pair, #J33-J34 4.00 1.75
Nos. J21-J34 (14) 11.20 5.30

OFFICIAL STAMPS

Dogon Mask — O1

Mali Coat of Arms — O2

Perf. 14x13½

1961, Mar. 18 Engr. Unwmk.

O1 O1 1fr gray .30 .20
O2 O1 2fr red orange .30 .20
O3 O1 3fr black .30 .20
O4 O1 5fr light blue .30 .20
O5 O1 10fr bister brown .35 .20
O6 O1 25fr brt ultra .75 .20
O7 O1 30fr car rose .90 .20
O8 O1 50fr Prus green 1.40 .20
O9 O1 85fr red brown 2.25 .65
O10 O1 100fr emerald 2.75 .65
O11 O1 200fr red lilac 5.50 1.25
Nos. O1-O11 (11) 15.10 4.15

1964, June 1 Photo. *Perf. 12½*

National Colors and Arms in Multicolor, Background in Light Green

O12 O2 1fr green .30 .20
O13 O2 2fr light vio .30 .20
O14 O2 3fr gray .30 .20
O15 O2 5fr lilac rose .30 .20
O16 O2 10fr bright blue .30 .20
O17 O2 25fr ocher .35 .20
O18 O2 30fr dark green .50 .20
O19 O2 50fr orange .75 .20
O20 O2 85fr dark brown 1.10 .60
O21 O2 100fr red 1.40 .60
O22 O2 200fr dk vio bl 2.75 1.10
Nos. O12-O22 (11) 8.35 3.90

City Coats of Arms — O3

1981, Sept. **Photo.** ***Perf. 12½x13***

O23 O3 5fr Gao .30 .20
O24 O3 15fr Timbuktu .35 .20
O25 O3 50fr Mopti .45 .20
O26 O3 180fr Segou 1.25 .25
O27 O3 200fr Sikasso 1.50 .35
O28 O3 680fr Koulikoro 4.00 .90
O29 O3 700fr Kayes 4.75 1.10
O30 O3 1000fr Bamako 6.25 1.40
Nos. O23-O30 (8) 18.85 4.60

Nos. O23-O30 Surcharged

1984 **Photo.** ***Perf. 12½x13***

O31 O3 15fr on 5fr .30 .20
O32 O3 50fr on 15fr .55 .25
O33 O3 120fr on 50fr 1.25 .25
O34 O3 295fr on 180fr 3.25 .60
O35 O3 470fr on 200fr 4.50 .85
O36 O3 515fr on 680fr 5.00 1.00
O37 O3 845fr on 700fr 8.25 1.75
O38 O3 1225fr on 1000fr 13.00 2.25
Nos. O31-O38 (8) 36.10 7.15

MALTA

'mol-tə

LOCATION — A group of islands in the Mediterranean Sea off the coast of Sicily
GOVT. — Republic within the British Commonwealth
AREA — 122 sq. mi.
POP. — 376,513 (1998)
CAPITAL — Valletta

The former colony includes the islands of Malta, Gozo, and Comino. It became a republic Dec. 13, 1974.

4 Farthings = 1 Penny
12 Pence = 1 Shilling
20 Shillings = 1 Pound
10 Mils = 1 Cent (1972)
100 Cents = 1 Pound (1972)
100 Cents = 1 Euro (2008)

Catalogue values for unused stamps in this country are for Never Hinged items, beginning with Scott 206 in the regular postage section, Scott B1 in the semi-postal section, Scott C2 in the air post section, and Scott J21 in the postage due section.

Watermark

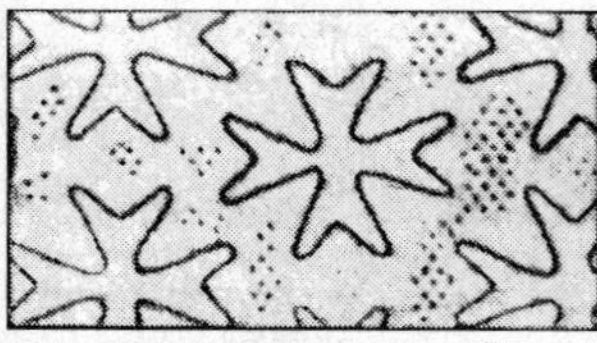
Wmk. 354 — Maltese Cross, Multiple

Values for unused stamps are for examples with original gum as defined in the catalogue introduction. Very fine examples of Nos. 1-7 will have perforations touching the frameline on one or more sides due to the narrow spacing of the stamps on the plate. Stamps with perfs clear of the frameline are scarce and will command higher prices.

Queen Victoria
A1 A2

A3

A4

1860-61 **Unwmk.** **Typo.** ***Perf. 14***

1 A1 ½p buff ('61) 775. 375.
2 A1 ½p buff, *bluish* 1,125. 550.
a. Imperf. *11,000.*

1863-80 **Wmk. 1**

3 A1 ½p yellow buff ('75) 80.00 65.00
a. ½p buff 100.00 65.00
b. ½p brown orange ('67) 400.00 110.00
c. ½p orange yel ('80) 200.00 110.00
4 A1 ½p golden yel (aniline) ('74) 325.00 375.00

1865 ***Perf. 12½***

5 A1 ½p buff 160.00 110.00
a. ½p yellow buff 325.00 190.00

1878 ***Perf. 14x12½***

6 A1 ½p buff 190.00 100.00
a. Perf. 12½x14 —

No. 6a used is believed to be unique. It has a small fault.

1882 **Wmk. 2** ***Perf. 14***

7 A1 ½p orange 21.00 *57.50*

1885, Jan. 1

8 A1 ½p green 3.25 .60
9 A2 1p car rose 5.75 .40
a. 1p rose 100.00 30.00
10 A3 2p gray 6.50 1.75
11 A4 2½p ultramarine 47.50 1.25
a. 2½p bright ultramarine 47.50 1.25
b. 2½p dull blue 65.00 3.00
12 A3 4p brown 13.00 3.50
a. Imperf., pair *6,000.* *6,000.*
13 A3 1sh violet 45.00 11.00
Nos. 8-13 (6) 121.00 18.50

For surcharge see No. 20.

Queen Victoria within Maltese Cross — A5

1886 **Wmk. 1**

14 A5 5sh rose 125.00 95.00

Gozo Fishing Boat — A6

Ancient Galley — A7

1899, Feb. 4 **Engr.** **Wmk. 2**

15 A6 4½p black brown 21.00 15.00
16 A7 5p brown red 40.00 17.50

See Nos. 42-45.

"Malta" — A8

St. Paul after Shipwreck — A9

1899 **Wmk. 1**

17 A8 2sh6p olive gray 47.50 14.00
18 A9 10sh blue black 105.00 75.00

See No. 64. For overprint see No. 85.

Valletta Harbor — A10

1901, Jan. 1 **Wmk. 2**

19 A10 1f red brown 1.75 .55

See Nos. 28-29.

No. 11 Surcharged in Black

1902, July 4

20 A4 1p on 2½p ultra 1.25 1.60
a. "Pnney" 32.50 *65.00*
b. Double surcharge 17,500. 4,500.

King Edward VII — A12

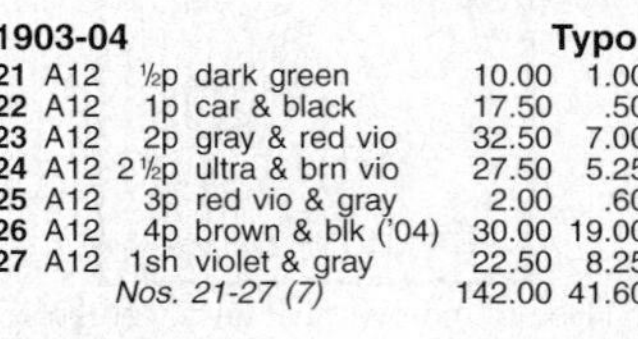

1903-04 **Typo.**

21 A12 ½p dark green 10.00 1.00
22 A12 1p car & black 17.50 .50
23 A12 2p gray & red vio 32.50 7.00
24 A12 2½p ultra & brn vio 27.50 5.25
25 A12 3p red vio & gray 2.00 .60
26 A12 4p brown & blk ('04) 30.00 19.00
27 A12 1sh violet & gray 22.50 8.25
Nos. 21-27 (7) 142.00 41.60

1904-11 **Wmk. 3**

28 A10 1f red brown ('05) 7.00 .95
29 A10 1f dk brown ('10) 3.50 .20
30 A12 ½p green 6.00 .35
31 A12 1p car & blk ('05) 11.00 .25
32 A12 1p carmine ('07) 3.00 .20
33 A12 2p gray & red vio ('05) 12.00 2.50
34 A12 2p gray ('11) 3.75 6.50
35 A12 2½p ultra & brn vio 25.00 .70
36 A12 2½p ultra ('11) 6.50 3.75
37 A12 4p brn & blk ('06) 13.00 6.50
38 A12 4p scar & blk, *yel* ('11) 4.75 4.00
39 A12 1sh violet & gray 57.50 2.40
40 A12 1sh blk, *grn* ('11) 8.75 3.75
41 A12 5sh scar & grn, *yel* ('11) 75.00 87.50

Engr.

42 A6 4½p black brn ('05) 32.50 6.50
43 A6 4½p orange ('11) 5.25 4.00
44 A7 5p red ('04) 32.50 5.75
45 A7 5p ol green ('10) 5.00 4.00
Nos. 28-45 (18) 312.00 139.80

A13

A15

King George V — A16

1914-21 **Typo.**

Ordinary Paper

49 A13 ¼p brown 1.25 .20
50 A13 ½p green 2.50 .35
51 A13 1p scarlet ('15) 1.75 .45
a. 1p carmine ('14) 1.75 .20
52 A13 2p gray ('15) 11.00 4.75
53 A13 2½p ultramarine 2.50 .60

Chalky Paper

54 A15 3p vio, *yel* 3.00 *11.50*
58 A13 6p dull vio & red vio 13.00 *21.00*
59 A15 1sh black, *green* 14.00 *20.00*
a. 1sh black, *bl grn*, ol back 22.50 27.50
b. 1sh black, *emerald* ('21) 37.50 *82.50*
c. As "b," olive back 10.00 *27.50*
60 A16 2sh ultra & dl vio, *bl* 57.50 35.00
61 A16 5sh scar & grn, *yel* 105.00 *115.00*

Surface-colored Paper

62 A15 1sh blk, *grn* ('15) 16.00 *30.00*
Nos. 49-54,58-62 (11) 227.50 238.85

See Nos. 66-68, 70-72. For overprints see Nos. 77-82, 84.

Valletta Harbor — A17

1915 **Engr.**

Ordinary Paper

63 A17 4p black 17.50 4.75

St. Paul A18

George V A19

1919

64 A8 2sh6p olive green 70.00 *95.00*
65 A18 10sh black 3,500. *4,400.*
Revenue cancel 85.00

For overprint see No. 83.

1921-22 **Typo.** **Wmk. 4**

Ordinary Paper

66 A13 ¼p brown 2.75 *32.50*
67 A13 ½p green 3.50 *22.50*
68 A13 1p rose red 3.25 1.90
69 A19 2p gray 5.25 2.00
70 A13 2½p ultramarine 4.25 *32.50*

Chalky Paper

71 A13 6p dull vio & red vio 32.50 80.00
72 A16 2sh ultra & dull vio, *bl* 70.00 *225.00*

Engr.

Ordinary Paper

73 A18 10sh black 400.00 *750.00*
Nos. 66-73 (8) 521.50 1,146.

For overprints and surcharge see Nos. 86-93, 97.

Stamps of 1914-19 Overprinted in Red or Black

1922 **Wmk. 3**

Ordinary Paper

Overprint 21mm

77 A13 ½p green 1.10 2.00
78 A13 2½p ultra 9.75 32.50

Chalky Paper

79 A15 3p violet, *yel* 3.50 19.00
80 A13 6p dull lil & red vio 2.75 18.00
81 A15 1sh black, *emer* 4.00 18.00

Overprint 28mm

82 A16 2sh ultra & dull vio, *bl* (R) 250.00 525.00

Ordinary Paper

83 A8 2sh6p olive grn 25.00 52.50

Chalky Paper

84 A16 5sh scar & grn, *yel* 57.50 92.50
Nos. 77-84 (8) 353.60 759.50

Wmk. 1

Ordinary Paper

85 A9 10sh blue black (R) 225.00 *400.00*

Same Overprint on Stamps of 1921

1922 Ordinary Paper Wmk. 4

Overprint 21mm

86 A13 ¼p brown .35 *.85*
87 A13 ½p green 2.25 *7.00*
88 A13 1p rose red 1.10 .20
89 A19 2p gray 2.50 .50
90 A13 2½p ultramarine 1.25 1.10

Chalky Paper

91 A13 6p dull vio & red vio 12.50 *37.50*

Overprint 28mm

92 A16 2sh ultra & dull vio, *bl* (R) 45.00 *100.00*

Ordinary Paper

93 A18 10sh black (R) 160.00 *225.00*
Nos. 86-93 (8) 224.95 372.15

No. 69 Surcharged

1922, Apr. 15

97 A19 1f on 2p gray .75 .50

"Malta" — A20

Britannia and Malta — A21

1922-26 Typo.

Chalky Paper

98 A20 ¼p brown 3.00 .70
99 A20 ½p green 3.00 .20
100 A20 1p buff & plum 3.75 .20
101 A20 1p violet ('24) 3.75 .90
102 A20 1½p org brn ('23) 4.75 .20
103 A20 2p ol brn & turq 3.25 1.40
104 A20 2½p ultra ('26) 3.25 *8.00*
105 A20 3p ultramarine 4.25 1.75
a. 3p blue 3.75 1.75
106 A20 3p blk, *yel* ('26) 3.50 *15.00*
107 A20 4p yel & ultra 2.25 *2.75*
108 A20 6p ol grn & vio 3.75 2.50
109 A21 1sh ol brn & blue 8.00 2.75
110 A21 2sh ultra & ol brn 11.50 11.50
111 A21 2sh6p blk & red vio 12.50 *17.50*
112 A21 5sh ultra & org 24.00 *47.50*
113 A21 10sh ol brn & gray 62.50 *175.00*

Engr.

Ordinary Paper

114 A20 £1 car red & blk ('25) 140.00 *350.00*
a. £1 rose car & blk ('22) 140.00 *350.00*
Nos. 98-114 (17) 297.00 637.85

No. 114a has watermark sideways.

For overprints and surcharges see Nos. 115-129.

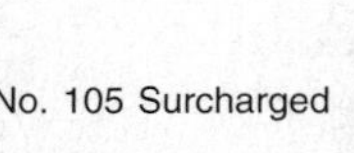

No. 105 Surcharged

1925, Dec.

115 A20 2½p on 3p ultramarine 2.00 *4.00*

Stamps of 1922-26 Overprinted

1926

116 A20 ¼p brown .80 *4.50*
117 A20 ½p green .80 .20
118 A20 1p violet 1.10 .25
119 A20 1½p orange brown 1.10 .70
120 A20 2p ol brn & turq .85 1.10
121 A20 2½p ultramarine 1.40 .90
122 A20 3p black, *yel* .85 .90
a. Inverted overprint 200.00 *550.00*
123 A20 4p yel & ultra 11.00 *25.00*
124 A20 6p ol grn & vio 3.25 4.00
125 A21 1sh ol brn & bl 6.25 16.00
126 A21 2sh ultra & ol brown 60.00 *160.00*
127 A21 2sh6p blk & red vio 18.50 *47.50*
128 A21 5sh ultra & org 11.00 *47.50*
129 A21 10sh ol brn & gray 8.50 *21.00*
Nos. 116-129 (14) 125.40 329.55

George V — A22

Valletta Harbor — A23

St. Publius — A24

Notabile (Mdina) — A25

Gozo Fishing Boat — A26

Statue of Neptune — A27

Ruins at Mnaidra — A28

St. Paul — A29

1926-27 Typo. *Perf. 14½x14*

131 A22 ¼p brown .90 .20
132 A22 ½p green .70 .20
133 A22 1p red 3.50 1.10
134 A22 1½p orange brn 2.25 .20
135 A22 2p gray 5.25 *11.00*
136 A22 2½p blue 4.50 1.10
137 A22 3p dark violet 5.00 3.00
138 A22 4p org red & blk 3.75 *11.00*
139 A22 4½p yel buff & vio 4.00 3.25
140 A22 6p red & violet 5.00 4.25

Engr. *Perf. 12½*

Inscribed: "Postage"

141 A23 1sh black 7.50 5.25
142 A24 1sh6p green & blk 7.50 *15.00*
143 A25 2sh dp vio & blk 7.50 *17.00*
144 A26 2sh6p ver & black 17.00 *55.00*
145 A27 3sh blue & blk 20.00 *35.00*
146 A28 5sh green & blk 25.00 *70.00*
147 A29 10sh car & blk 62.50 *110.00*
Nos. 131-147 (17) 181.85 *342.55*

See #167-183. For overprints see #148-166.

Stamps and Type of 1926-27 Overprinted in Black

1928 *Perf. 14½x14*

148 A22 ¼p brown 1.75 .20
149 A22 ½p green 1.75 .20
150 A22 1p red 2.00 *3.75*
151 A22 1p orange brown 5.25 .20
152 A22 1½p yel brown 2.25 1.00
153 A22 1½p red 5.00 .20
154 A22 2p gray 5.00 *10.50*
155 A22 2½p blue 2.25 .20
156 A22 3p dark violet 2.25 1.00
157 A22 4p org red & blk 2.25 2.00
158 A22 4½p yel & violet 2.50 1.10
159 A22 6p red & violet 2.50 1.75

Overprinted in Red

Perf. 12½

160 A23 1sh black 6.25 3.00
161 A24 1sh6p green & blk 7.50 *11.00*
162 A25 2sh dp vio & blk 27.50 *62.50*
163 A26 2sh6p ver & black 20.00 *26.00*
164 A27 3sh ultra & blk 22.50 *35.00*
165 A28 5sh yel grn & blk 32.50 *75.00*
166 A29 10sh car rose & black 62.50 *100.00*
Nos. 148-166 (19) 213.50 334.60

Issued: #151, 153, Dec. 5; others, Oct. 1.

Types of 1926-27 Issue

1930, Oct. 20 Typo. *Perf. 14½x14*

Inscribed: "Postage & Revenue"

167 A22 ¼p brown .70 .20
168 A22 ½p green .70 .20
169 A22 1p yel brown .70 .20
170 A22 1½p red .80 .20
171 A22 2p gray 1.40 .60
172 A22 2½p blue 2.25 .20
173 A22 3p dark violet 1.75 .20
174 A22 4p org red & blk 1.40 *4.50*
175 A22 4½p yel & violet 3.75 1.40
176 A22 6p red & violet 3.25 1.40

Engr. *Perf. 12½*

177 A23 1sh black 11.00 16.00
178 A24 1sh6p green & blk 9.75 22.50
179 A25 2sh dp vio & blk 11.00 22.50
180 A26 2sh6p ver & black 20.00 55.00
181 A27 3sh ultra & blk 30.00 62.50
182 A28 5sh yel grn & blk 37.50 75.00
183 A29 10sh car rose & blk 65.00 140.00
Nos. 167-183 (17) 200.95 402.60

Common Design Types pictured following the introduction.

Silver Jubilee Issue

Common Design Type

1935, May 6 *Perf. 11x12*

184 CD301 ½p green & blk .40 *.60*
185 CD301 2½p ultra & brn 2.50 *4.50*
186 CD301 6p ol grn & lt bl 6.75 4.50
187 CD301 1sh brn vio & ind 11.00 *17.00*
Nos. 184-187 (4) 20.65 *26.60*
Set, never hinged 42.50

Coronation Issue

Common Design Type

1937, May 12 Wmk. 4 *Perf. 13½x14*

188 CD302 ½p deep green .20 .20
189 CD302 1½p carmine .25 .20
190 CD302 2½p bright ultra .55 .50
Nos. 188-190 (3) 1.00 .90
Set, never hinged 2.50

Valletta Harbor — A30

Fort St. Angelo — A31

Verdala Palace — A32

Neolithic Ruins — A33

Victoria and Citadel, Gozo — A34

De l'Isle Adam Entering Mdina — A35

St. John's Co-Cathedral A36

Mnaidra Temple — A37

Statue of Antonio Manoel de Vilhena — A38

Woman in Faldetta — A39

St. Publius — A40

Mdina Cathedral A41

Palace Square — A43

Statue of Neptune — A42

St. Paul — A44

1938-43 Wmk. 4 *Perf. 12½*

No.	Type	Denomination / Color	Unused	Used
191	A30	1f brown	.20	.20
192	A31	½p green	.40	.20
192A	A31	½p chnt ('43)	.20	.20
193	A32	1p chestnut	3.50	.20
193A	A32	1p grn ('43)	.20	.20
194	A33	1½p rose red	.25	.20
194A	A33	1½p dk gray ('43)	.20	.20
195	A34	2p dark gray	.90	.75
195A	A34	2p rose red ('43)	.40	.25
196	A35	2½p blue	.90	.60
196A	A35	2½p violet ('43)	.35	.35
197	A36	3p violet	.75	.55
197A	A36	3p blue ('43)	.40	.20
198	A37	4½p ocher & ol green	.30	.30
199	A38	6p rose red & ol green	.60	.30
200	A39	1sh black	.60	.55
201	A40	1sh6p sage grn & black	7.50	1.00
202	A41	2sh dk bl & lt grn	1.10	1.10
203	A42	2sh6p rose red & black	5.00	4.00
204	A43	5sh bl grn & blk	4.75	4.75
205	A44	10sh dp rose & blk	15.00	14.00
		Nos. 191-205 (21)	43.50	30.10
		Never hinged	72.50	

See #236a. For overprints see #208-222.

Catalogue values for unused stamps in this section, from this point to the end of the section, are for Never Hinged items.

Peace Issue

Common Design Type

Inscribed: "Malta" and Crosses

Perf. 13½x14

1946, Dec. 3 Engr. Wmk. 4

No.	Type	Denomination / Color	Unused	Used
206	CD303	1p bright green	.20	.20
207	CD303	3p dark ultra	.35	.90

Stamps of 1938-43 Overprinted in Black or Carmine

a

1948, Nov. 25 *Perf. 12½*

No.	Type	Denomination / Color	Unused	Used
208	A30	1f brown	.35	.20
209	A31	½p chestnut	.35	.20
210	A32	1p green	.35	.20
211	A33	1½p dk gray (C)	1.40	.20
212	A34	2p rose red	1.40	.30
213	A35	2½p violet (C)	.90	.30
214	A36	3p blue (C)	1.40	.20
215	A37	4½p ocher & ol grn	2.25	1.75
216	A38	6p rose red & ol green	3.50	.45
217	A39	1sh black	3.25	.70
218	A40	1sh6p sage grn & blk	2.75	1.25
219	A41	2sh dk bl & lt grn (C)	5.75	2.75
220	A42	2sh6p rose red & blk	14.00	2.75
221	A43	5sh bl grn & blk (C)	22.50	5.00
222	A44	10sh dp rose & blk	22.50	25.00
		Nos. 208-222 (15)	82.65	41.25

The overprint is smaller on No. 208. It reads from lower left to upper right on Nos. 209 and 221.

See Nos. 235-240.

Silver Wedding Issue

Common Design Types

Inscribed: "Malta" and Crosses

1949, Jan. 4 Photo. *Perf. 14x14½*

No.	Type	Denomination / Color	Unused	Used
223	CD304	1p dark green	.55	.20

Perf. 11½x11

Engr.

No.	Type	Denomination / Color	Unused	Used
224	CD305	£1 dark blue	50.00	47.50

UPU Issue

Common Design Types

Inscribed: "Malta" and Crosses

Perf. 13½, 11x11½

1949, Oct. 10 Engr. Wmk. 4

No.	Type	Denomination / Color	Unused	Used
225	CD306	2½p violet	.35	.20
226	CD307	3p indigo	3.75	1.25
227	CD308	6p dp carmine	.75	1.10
228	CD309	1sh slate	.75	*2.75*
		Nos. 225-228 (4)	5.60	5.30

Princess Elizabeth — A45

Madonna and Child — A46

1950, Dec. 1 Engr. *Perf. 12x11½*

No.	Type	Denomination / Color	Unused	Used
229	A45	1p emerald	.20	.20
230	A45	3p bright blue	.25	.25
231	A45	1sh gray black	.75	1.40
		Nos. 229-231 (3)	1.20	1.85

Visit of Princess Elizabeth.

1951, July 12

No.	Type	Denomination / Color	Unused	Used
232	A46	1p green	.20	.20
233	A46	3p purple	.55	.20
234	A46	1sh slate black	1.25	1.00
		Nos. 232-234 (3)	2.00	1.40

700th anniv. of the presentation of the scapular to St. Simon Stock.

Types of 1938-43 Overprinted Type "a" in Red or Black

1953, Jan. 8 Wmk. 4 *Perf. 12½*

No.	Type	Denomination / Color	Unused	Used
235	A32	1p gray (R)	.45	.20
236	A33	1½p green	.45	.20
a.		Overprint omitted		*11,500.*
237	A34	2p ocher	.45	.20
238	A35	2½p rose red	.80	*2.25*
239	A36	3p violet (R)	.80	.20
240	A37	4½p ultra & ol grn (R)	.85	*1.25*
		Nos. 235-240 (6)	3.80	4.30

Coronation Issue

Common Design Type

Inscribed: "Malta" and Crosses

1953, June 3 Engr. *Perf. 13½x13*

No.	Type	Denomination / Color	Unused	Used
241	CD312	1½p dk green black	.55	.20

Type of 1938-43 with Portrait of Queen Elizabeth II Inscribed: "Royal Visit 1954."

1954, May 3 *Perf. 12½*

No.	Type	Denomination / Color	Unused	Used
242	A36	3p violet	.35	.20

Visit of Elizabeth II and the Duke of Edinburgh, 1954.

Central Altarpiece, Collegiate Parish Church, Cospicua — A47

Perf. 14½x13½

1954, Sept. 8 Photo. Wmk. 4

No.	Type	Denomination / Color	Unused	Used
243	A47	1½p bright green	.20	.20
244	A47	3p ultramarine	.20	.20
245	A47	1sh gray black	.40	.40
		Nos. 243-245 (3)	.80	.80

Cent. of the promulgation of the Dogma of the Immaculate Conception.

Monument of the Great Siege, 1565 — A48

Auberge de Castille — A49

Designs: ¼p, Wignacourt Aqueduct Horse-trough. 1p, Victory Church. 1½p, War Memorial. 2p, Mosta Dome. 3p, King's Scroll. 4½p, Roosevelt's Scroll. 6p, Neolithic Temples at Tarxien. 8p, Vedette. 1sh, Mdina Gate. 1sh6p, Les Gavroches. 2sh, Monument of Christ the King. 2sh6p, Monument of Nicolas Cottoner. 5sh, Raymond Perellos Monument. 10sh, St. Paul. £1, Baptism of Christ.

1956-57 Engr. *Perf. 11½*

No.	Type	Denomination / Color	Unused	Used
246	A48	¼p violet	.20	.20
247	A48	½p yel orange	.55	.20
248	A48	1p black	.55	.20
249	A48	1½p brt green	.35	.20
250	A48	2p brown	1.75	.20
251	A49	2½p orange brown	1.75	.35
252	A48	3p rose red	1.75	.20
253	A48	4½p blue	2.75	.25
254	A49	6p slate blue	.85	.20
255	A48	8p olive bister	4.00	*1.10*
256	A48	1sh purple	1.10	.30
257	A48	1sh6p Prus green	14.00	.40
258	A48	2sh olive green	14.00	2.75

Perf. 13½x13

No.	Type	Denomination / Color	Unused	Used
259	A48	2sh6p cop brown	10.50	2.50
260	A48	5sh emerald	17.00	3.25
261	A48	10sh dk carmine	42.50	14.00
262	A48	£1 yel brn ('57)	42.50	29.00
		Nos. 246-262 (17)	156.10	55.30

See Nos. 296-297.

First George Cross Issue

Symbol of Malta's War Effort — A50

Searchlights over Malta — A51

Design: 1sh, Bombed houses.

Perf. 14x14½, 14½x14

1957, Apr. 15 Photo.

Cross in Silver

No.	Type	Denomination / Color	Unused	Used
263	A50	1½p green	.20	.20
264	A51	3p bright red	.20	.20
265	A50	1sh dark red brown	.20	.20
		Nos. 263-265 (3)	.60	.60

Award of the George Cross to Malta for its war effort.

See Nos. 269-274.

Symbols of Architecture — A52

Designs: 3p, Symbols of Industry, vert. 1sh, Symbols of electronics and chemistry and Technical School, Paola.

Perf. 14½x14, 14x14½

1958, Feb. 15 Wmk. 314

No.	Type	Denomination / Color	Unused	Used
266	A52	1½p dp green & blk	.20	.20
267	A52	3p rose red, blk & gray	.20	.20
268	A52	1sh gray, blk & lilac	.25	.25
		Nos. 266-268 (3)	.65	.65

Technical education on Malta.

Second George Cross Issue

Types of 1957

1½p, Bombed-out family & searchlights. 3p, Convoy entering harbor. 1sh, Searchlight battery.

1958, Apr. 15 *Perf. 14½x14, 14x14½*

Cross in Silver

No.	Type	Denomination / Color	Unused	Used
269	A51	1½p black & brt green	.20	.20
270	A50	3p black & vermilion	.20	.20
271	A51	1sh black & brt lilac	.25	.25
		Nos. 269-271 (3)	.65	.65

Third George Cross Issue

Types of 1957

Designs: 1½p, Air Raid Precautions Organization helping wounded. 3p, Allegory of Malta. 1sh, Mother and child during air raid.

1959, Apr. 15 *Perf. 14x14½, 14½x14*

No.	Type	Denomination / Color	Unused	Used
272	A50	1½p gold, green & black	.20	.20
273	A51	3p gold, lilac & black	.20	.20
274	A50	1sh gold, gray & black	.80	1.10
		Nos. 272-274 (3)	1.20	1.50

St. Paul's Shipwreck, Painting in St. Paul's Church, Valletta — A53

Statue of St. Paul, St. Paul's Grotto, Rabat — A54

Designs: 3p, Consecration of St. Publius. 6p, St. Paul leaving Malta; painting, St. Paul's Church, Valletta. 1sh, Angel holding tablet with quotations from Acts of the Apostles. 2sh6p, St. Paul and St. Paul's Bay islets.

Wmk. 314

1960, Feb. 9 Photo. *Perf. 13*

No.	Type	Denomination / Color	Unused	Used
275	A53	1½p bister, brt bl & gold	.25	.20
a.		Gold dates & crosses omitted	*65.00*	*57.50*
276	A53	3p lt blue, red lil & gold	.30	.20
277	A53	6p car, gray & gold	.40	.20

Perf. 14x14½

No.	Type	Denomination / Color	Unused	Used
278	A54	8p black & gold	.60	*.75*
279	A54	1sh brt cl & gold	.60	.50
280	A54	2sh6p brt grnsh bl & gold	2.25	2.25
a.		Gold omitted	*375.00*	
		Nos. 275-280 (6)	4.40	4.10

19th centenary of St. Paul's shipwreck on Malta.

Stamp of 1860 — A55

Perf. 13x13½

1960, Dec. 1 Engr. Wmk. 314

281	A55	1½p multi	.20	.20
282	A55	3p multi	.35	.20
283	A55	6p multi	.50	1.10
		Nos. 281-283 (3)	1.05	1.50

Centenary of Malta's first postage stamp.

Fourth George Cross Issue

George Cross A56

Background designs: 3p, Sun and water. 1sh, Maltese crosses.

1961, Apr. 15 Photo. *Perf. 14½x14*

284	A56	1½p gray, bister & buff	.20	.20
285	A56	3p ol gray, lt & dk grnsh blue	.35	.20
286	A56	1sh ol green, vio & lil	.85	2.00
		Nos. 284-286 (3)	1.40	2.40

19th anniv. of the award of the George Cross to Malta.

Madonna Damascena A57

David Bruce and Themistocles Zammit A58

Designs: 3p, Great Siege Monument by Antonio Sciortino. 6p, Grand Master La Valette (1557-1568). 1sh, Assault on Fort Elmo (old map).

Perf. 12½x12

1962, Sept. 7 Wmk. 314

287	A57	2p ultramarine	.20	.20
288	A57	3p dark red	.20	.20
289	A57	6p olive green	.25	.25
290	A57	1sh rose lake	.25	.45
		Nos. 287-290 (4)	.90	1.10

Great Siege of 1565 in which the knights of the Order of St. John and the Maltese Christians defeated the Turks.

Freedom from Hunger Issue
Common Design Type

1963, June 4 *Perf. 14x14½*

291	CD314	1sh6p sepia	2.25	2.75

Red Cross Centenary Issue
Common Design Type

1963, Sept. 2 Litho. *Perf. 13*

292	CD315	2p black & red	.25	.25
293	CD315	1sh6p ultra & red	3.00	4.75

Type of 1956

Designs as before.

1963-64 Engr. *Perf. 11½*

296	A48	1p black	1.00	.70
297	A48	2p brown ('64)	2.10	*2.40*

Perf. 14x13½

1964, Apr. 14 Photo. Wmk. 314

1sh6p, Goat and laboratory equipment.

298	A58	2p dl grn, blk & brn	.20	.20
a.		Black omitted	*250.00*	
299	A58	1sh6p rose lake & blk	1.00	1.00

Anti-Brucellosis (Malta fever) Congress of the UN FAO, Valletta, June 8-13.

Nicola Cottoner Attending Sick Man and Congress Emblem — A59

6p, Statue of St. Luke & St. Luke's Hospital. 1sh6p, Sacra Infermeria, Valletta.

Perf. 13½x14

1964, Sept. 5 Wmk. 354

300	A59	2p multicolored	.20	.20
301	A59	6p multicolored	.55	.55
302	A59	1sh6p multicolored	1.25	2.10
		Nos. 300-302 (3)	2.00	2.85

1st European Cong. of Catholic Physicians, Malta, Sept. 6-10.

Independent State

Dove, Maltese Cross and British Crown — A60

Nativity — A61

Dove, Maltese Cross and: 3p, 1sh6p, Pope's tiara. 6p, 2sh6p, UN Emblem.

Perf. 14½x13½

1964, Sept. 21 Photo.

Gold and

303	A60	2p gray ol & red	.40	.20
304	A60	3p dk red brn & red	.45	.20
305	A60	6p sl blue & red	1.00	.30
306	A60	1sh ultra & red	1.00	.40
307	A60	1sh6p bl blk & red	2.75	1.50
308	A60	2sh6p vio bl & red	3.00	3.00
		Nos. 303-308 (6)	8.60	5.60

Malta's independence.

Perf. 13x13½

1964, Nov. 3 Wmk. 354

309	A61	2p magenta & gold	.20	.20
310	A61	4p ultra & gold	.25	.25
311	A61	8p dp green & gold	1.25	1.10
		Nos. 309-311 (3)	1.70	1.55

Cippus, Phoenician and Greek Inscriptions — A62

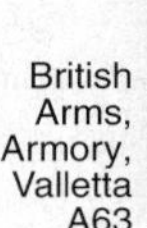

British Arms, Armory, Valletta A63

Designs (History of Malta): ½p, Neolithic (sculpture of sleeping woman). 1½p, Roman (sculpture). 2p, Proto-Christian (lamp, Roman temple, Chrismon). 2½p, Saracen (tomb, 12th cent.). 3p, Siculo Norman (arch, Palazzo Gatto-Murina, Notabile). 4p, Knights of Malta (lamp base, cross, and armor of knights). 4½p, Maltese navy (16th cent. galleons). 5p, Fortifications. 6p, French occupation (Cathedral of Notabile, cap, fasces). 10p, Naval Arsenal.

1sh, Maltese Corps of the British Army (insignia). 1sh3p, International Eucharistic Congress, 1913 (angels adoring Eucharist and map of Malta). 1sh6p, Self Government, 1921 (Knights of Malta Hall, present assembly seat). 2sh, Civic Council, Gozo (Statue of Livia, Gozo City Hall). 2sh6p, State of Malta (seated woman and George Cross). 3sh, Independence (doves, UN emblem, British crown, and Pope's tiara).

5sh, "HAFMED," (headquarters and insigne of Allied Forces, Mediterranean). 10sh, Map of Mediterranean. £1, Catholicism (Sts. Paul, Publius and Agatha).

Perf. 14x14½, 14½ (A63)

1965-70 Photo. Wmk. 354

312	A62	½p violet & yel	.20	.20
313	A62	1p multi	.20	.20
a.		Booklet pane of 6 ('70)	.35	
314	A62	1½p multi	.20	.20
315	A62	2p multi	.20	.20
a.		Gold omitted	25.00	
b.		Booklet pane of 6 ('70)	.40	
316	A62	2½p multi	.20	.20
a.		Gold ("SARACENIC") omitted	55.00	
317	A62	3p multi	.20	.20
a.		Imperf., pair	250.00	
b.		Gold (windows) omitted	37.50	
318	A62	4p multi	.20	.20
a.		Black (arms shading) omitted	47.50	
b.		Silver omitted	45.00	
319	A62	4½p multi	.20	.20
319A	A62	5p multi ('70)	.25	.20
b.		Booklet pane of 6 ('71)	1.75	
320	A62	6p multi	.20	.20
a.		Black omitted	60.00	
b.		Silver ("MALTA") omitted	60.00	
321	A63	8p multi	.20	.20
321A	A63	10p multi ('70)	.30	.20
322	A63	1sh multi	.30	.20
323	A63	1sh3p multi	.65	.45
324	A63	1sh6p multi	.50	.25
a.		Queen's head omitted	*225.00*	
325	A63	2sh multi	.65	.45
326	A63	2sh6p multi	.75	.50
327	A63	3sh multi	.95	.60
328	A63	5sh multi	1.60	1.00
329	A63	10sh multi	3.25	2.50
330	A63	£1 multi	6.00	4.50
a.		Pink (shading on figures) omitted	30.00	
		Nos. 312-330 (21)	17.20	12.85

Issued: 5p, 10p, 8/1/70; others 1/7/65.

For surcharges see Nos. 447-449, 521.

Dante, by Raphael — A64

1965, July 7 Unwmk. *Perf. 14*

331	A64	2p dark blue	.20	.20
332	A64	6p olive green	.20	.20
333	A64	2sh chocolate	.80	.70
		Nos. 331-333 (3)	1.20	1.10

700th birth anniv. of Dante Alighieri.

Turkish Encampment and Fort St. Michael A65

Blockading Turkish Armada — A66

Designs: 3p, Knights and Turks in battle. 8p, Arrival of relief force. 1sh, Trophy, arms of Grandmaster Jean de La Valette. 1sh6p, Allegory of Victory, mural by Calabrese from St. John's Co-Cathedral. 2sh6p, Great Siege victory medal; Jean de La Valette on obverse, David slaying Goliath on reverse.

Perf. 14½x14, 13

1965, Sept. 1 Photo. Wmk. 354

334	A65	2p multicolored	.20	.20
335	A65	3p multicolored	.20	.20
336	A66	6p multicolored	.30	.25
a.		Black omitted	*140.00*	
b.		Gold omitted	*165.00*	
337	A65	8p multicolored	.45	.35
338	A66	1sh multicolored	1.10	.90
339	A65	1sh6p multicolored	1.40	1.10
340	A65	2sh6p multicolored	3.50	3.00
		Nos. 334-340 (7)	7.15	6.00

Great Siege (Turks against Malta), 4th cent.

The Three Wise Men A67

Perf. 11x11½

1965, Oct. 7 Photo. Wmk. 354

341	A67	1p dk purple & red	.20	.20
342	A67	4p dk pur & blue	.90	.80
343	A67	1sh3p dk pur & dp mag	1.00	.90
		Nos. 341-343 (3)	2.10	1.90

Winston Churchill, Map and Cross of Malta — A68

Winston Churchill: 3p, 1sh6p, Warships in Valletta Harbor and George Cross.

1966, Jan. 24 *Perf. 14½x14*

344	A68	2p blk, gold & red	.20	.20
345	A68	3p dk grn, gold & blk	.20	.20
346	A68	1sh dp cl, gold & red	.30	.30
a.		Gold omitted	225.00	
347	A68	1sh6p dk bl, gold & vio	.50	.45
		Nos. 344-347 (4)	1.20	1.15

Grand Master Jean Parisot de la Valette — A69

3p, Pope St. Pius V. 6p, Map of Valletta. 1sh, Francesco Laparelli, Italian architect. 2sh6p, Girolamo Cassar, Maltese architect.

1966, Mar. 28 Unwmk. *Perf. 12*

348	A69	2p gold & multi	.20	.20
349	A69	3p gold & multi	.20	.20
350	A69	6p gold & multi	.20	.20
351	A69	1sh gold & multi	.20	.20
352	A69	2sh6p gold & multi	.55	.55
		Nos. 348-352 (5)	1.35	1.35

400th anniversary of Valletta.

Kennedy — A70

Trade Fair — A71

Perf. 15x14

1966, May 28 Photo. Wmk. 354

353	A70	3p ol gray, blk & gold	.20	.20
354	A70	1sh6p dull bl, blk & gold	.35	.35

President John F. Kennedy (1917-1963).

1966, June 16 *Perf. 13x13½*

355	A71	2p multicolored	.20	.20
356	A71	8p gray & multi	.25	.25
357	A71	2sh6p tan & multi	.70	.70
		Nos. 355-357 (3)	1.15	1.15

The 10th Malta Trade Fair.

Nativity — A72

George Cross — A73

1966, Oct. 7 Photo. Wmk. 354

358 A72 1p multicolored .20 .20
359 A72 4p multicolored .20 .20
360 A72 1sh3p multicolored .20 .20
Nos. 358-360 (3) .60 .60

1967, Mar. 1 ***Perf. 14½x14***

361 A73 2p multicolored .20 .20
362 A73 4p multicolored .20 .20
363 A73 3sh slate & multi .30 .30
Nos. 361-363 (3) .70 .70

25th anniv. of the award of the George Cross to Malta and Gozo for the war effort.

Crucifixion of St. Peter — A74

Keys, Tiara, Bible, Cross and Sword — A75

Design: 3sh, Beheading of St. Paul.

Perf. 14½, 13½x14

1967, June 28 Photo. Wmk. 354

364 A74 2p black & brn orange .20 .20
365 A75 8p blk, gold & lt ol grn .20 .20
366 A74 3sh black & brt blue .40 .35
Nos. 364-366 (3) .80 .75

1900th anniv. of the martyrdom of the Apostles Peter and Paul.

St. Catherine of Siena by Melchior Gafá — A76

Sculptures by Gafá: 4p, St. Thomas from Villanova. 1sh6p, Christ's baptism. 2sh6p, St. John the Baptist.

1967, Aug. 1 ***Perf. 13½***

367 A76 2p black, gold, buff & ultra .20 .20
368 A76 4p gold, buff, blk & grn .20 .20
369 A76 1sh6p gold, buff, blk & org brown .20 .20
370 A76 2sh6p black, gold, buff & dp car .30 .30
Nos. 367-370 (4) .90 .90

Melchior Gafá (1635-67), Maltese sculptor.

Ruins of Megalithic Temples, Tarxien — A77

Designs: 6p, Facade of Palazzo Falzon, Notabile. 1sh, Facade of Old Parish Church, Birkirkara. 3sh, Entrance to Auberge de Castille.

1967, Sept. 12 Photo. ***Perf. 14½***

371 A77 2p gold, Prus bl & blk .20 .20
372 A77 6p org brn, blk, gray & gold .20 .20
373 A77 1sh gold, ol, ind & blk .20 .20
374 A77 3sh dk car, rose, blk, gray & gold .30 .30
Nos. 371-374 (4) .90 .90

Issued to publicize the 15th Congress of the History of Architecture, Malta, Sept. 12-16.

Nativity — A78

Design: 1sh4p, Angels facing left.

1967, Oct. 20 ***Perf. 13½x14***

375 A78 1p slate, gold & red .20 .20
a. Red omitted (stars) 50.00
376 A79 8p slate, gold & red .20 .20
377 A78 1sh4p slate, gold & red .30 .30
a. Triptych, #375-377 .55 .50
Nos. 375-377 (3) .70 .70

Sheets of Nos. 375-377 were arranged in 2 ways: sheets containing 60 stamps of the same denomination arranged tête bêche, and sheets containing 20 triptychs.

Arms of Malta — A80

Designs: 4p, Queen Elizabeth II in the robes of the Order of St. Michael and St. George, vert. 3sh, Queen and map of Malta.

Perf. 14½x14, 14x14½

1967, Nov. 13 Photo. Wmk. 354

378 A80 2p slate & multi .20 .20
379 A80 4p dp claret, blk & gold .20 .20
380 A80 3sh black & gold .30 .30
Nos. 378-380 (3) .70 .70

Visit of Queen Elizabeth II, Nov. 14-17.

Human Rights Flame and People A81

1968, May 2 Photo. ***Perf. 14½***

Size: 40x19mm

381 A81 2p sepia, dp car, blk & gold .20 .20

Perf. 12x12½

Size: 24x24mm

382 A81 6p gray, dk blue, blk & gold .20 .20

Perf. 14½

Size: 40x19mm

383 A81 2sh gray, grnsh blue, blk & gold .25 .20
Nos. 381-383 (3) .65 .60

International Human Rights Year.

Fair Emblem — A82

Perf. 14x14½

1968, June 1 Photo. Wmk. 354

384 A82 4p black & multi .20 .20
385 A82 8p Prus blue & multi .20 .20
386 A82 3sh dp claret & multi .40 .40
Nos. 384-386 (3) .80 .80

12th Malta Intl. Trade Fair, July 1-15.

La Valette in Battle Dress — A83

La Valette's Tomb, Church of St. John, Valletta — A84

Designs: 1p, Arms of Order of St. John of Jerusalem and La Valette's arms, horiz. 2sh6p, Putti bearing shield with date of La Valette's death, and map of Malta.

Perf. 13x14, 14x13

1968, Aug. 1 Photo. Wmk. 354

387 A83 1p black & multi .20 .20
388 A83 8p dull blue & multi .20 .20
389 A84 1sh6p blue grn & multi .20 .20
390 A83 2sh6p dp claret & multi .30 .30
Nos. 387-390 (4) .90 .90

400th anniv. of the death of Grand Master Jean de La Valette (1494-1568).

Star of Bethlehem, Shepherds and Angel A85

8p, Nativity. 1sh4p, The Three Wise Men.

Perf. 14½x14

1968, Oct. 3 Wmk. 354

391 A85 1p multicolored .20 .20
392 A85 8p gray & multi .20 .20
393 A85 1sh4p tan & multi .25 .25
Nos. 391-393 (3) .65 .65

Christmas. Printed in sheets of 60 with alternate rows inverted.

"Agriculture" A86

Mahatma Gandhi A87

1sh, Greek medal and FAO emblem. 2sh6p, Woman symbolizing soil care.

1968, Oct. 21 Photo. ***Perf. 12½x12***

394 A86 4p ultra & multi .20 .20
395 A86 1sh gray & multi .20 .20
396 A86 2sh6p multicolored .45 .45
Nos. 394-396 (3) .85 .85

6th Regional Congress for Europe of the FAO, Malta, Oct. 28-31.

Perf. 12x12½

1969, Mar. 24 Photo. Wmk. 354

397 A87 1sh6p gold, blk & sepia .35 .35

Birth cent. of Mohandas K. Gandhi (1869-1948), leader in India's struggle for independence.

ILO Emblem A88

1969, May 26 ***Perf. 13½x14½***

398 A88 2p indigo, blue grn & gold .20 .20
399 A88 6p brn blk, red brn & gold .20 .20

50th anniv. of the ILO.

Sea Bed, UN Emblem and Dove — A89

Designs: 2p, Robert Samut, bar of music and coat of arms. 10p, Map of Malta and homing birds. 2sh, Grand Master Pinto and arms of Malta University.

1969, July 26 Photo. ***Perf. 13½***

400 A89 2p vio blk, blk, gold & red .20 .20
401 A89 5p gray, Prus blue, gold & blk .20 .20
402 A89 10p olive, blk & gold .20 .20
403 A89 2sh dk olive, blk, red & gold .30 .30
Nos. 400-403 (4) .90 .90

Cent. of the birth of Robert Samut, composer of Natl. Anthem (2p); UN resolution on peaceful uses of the sea bed (5p); convention of Maltese emigrants (10p), Aug. 3-16; bicent. of the founding of Malta University (2sh).

June 17, 1919, Uprising Monument A90

"Tourism" A91

Designs: 5p, Maltese flag and 5 doves, horiz. 1sh6p, Dove and emblems of Malta, UN and Council of Euorpe. 2sh6p, Dove and symbols of trade and industry.

Perf. 13x12½

1969, Sept. 20 Photo. Wmk. 354

404 A90 2p black, gray, buff & gold .20 .20
405 A91 5p gray, blk, red & gold .20 .20
406 A91 10p gold, Prus blue, gray & blk .20 .20
407 A91 1sh6p gold, olive & multi .20 .20
408 A91 2sh6p gold, brn ol, gray & blk .40 .40
Nos. 404-408 (5) 1.20 1.20

Fifth anniversary of independence.

St. John the Baptist in Robe of Knight of Malta A92

Mortar and Jars from Infirmary — A93

Designs: 1p, The Beheading of St. John By Caravaggio. 5p, Interior of St. John's Co-

Cathedral. 6p, Allegory depicting functions of the Order. 8p, St. Jerome, by Caravaggio. 1sh6p, St. Gerard Receiving Godfrey de Bouillon, 1093, by Antoine de Favray. 2sh, Sacred vestments.

Perf. 14x13 (1p, 8p); 13½x14 (2p, 6p, 1sh6p); 13½ (5p) 12x12½ (10p, 2sh)

1970, Mar. 21 Photo. Wmk. 354

409 A92 1p black & multi .20 .20
410 A92 2p black & multi .20 .20
411 A92 5p black & multi .20 .20
412 A92 6p black & multi .20 .20
413 A92 8p black & multi .20 .20
414 A93 10p black & multi .20 .20
415 A92 1sh6p black & multi .35 .35
416 A93 2sh black & multi .45 .45
Nos. 409-416 (8) 2.00 2.00

13th Council of Europe Art Exhibition in honor of the Order of St. John in Malta, Apr. 2-July 1.

Sizes: 1p, 8p, 54x38mm; 2p, 6p, 44x30mm; 5p, 37x37mm; 10p, 2sh, 60x19mm; 1sh6p, 44x33mm.

EXPO '70 Emblem — A94

1970, May 29 ***Perf. 15***

417 A94 2p gold & multi .20 .20
418 A94 5p gold & multi .20 .20
419 A94 3sh gold & multi .45 .45
Nos. 417-419 (3) .85 .85

Issued to publicize EXPO '70 International Exhibition, Osaka, Japan, Mar. 15-Sept. 13.

UN Emblem, Dove, Scales and Symbolic Figure — A95

Perf. 14x14½

1970, Sept. 30 Litho. Wmk. 354

420 A95 2p brown & multi .20 .20
421 A95 5p purple & multi .20 .20
422 A95 2sh6p vio blue & multi .50 .50
Nos. 420-422 (3) .90 .90

25th anniversary of the United Nations.

Books and Quill — A96

Dun Karm, Books and Pens — A97

Perf. 13x14

1971, Mar. 20 Litho. Wmk. 354

423 A96 1sh6p multicolored .20 .20
424 A97 2sh black & multi .30 .30

No. 423 issued in memory of Canon Gian Pietro Francesco Agius Sultana (De Soldanis; 1712-1770), historian and writer; No. 424 for the centenary of the birth of Mgr. Karm Psaila (Dun Karm, 1871-1961), Maltese poet.

Europa Issue, 1971

Common Design Type

1971, May 3 ***Perf. 13½x14½***

Size: 32x22mm

425 CD14 2p olive, org & blk .20 .20
426 CD14 5p ver, org & black .20 .20
427 CD14 1sh6p gray, org & blk *.30 .30*
Nos. 425-427 (3) .70 *.70*

St. Joseph, by Giuseppe Cali — A98

Design: 5p, 1sh6p, Statue of Our Lady of Victory. 10p, Like 2p.

Perf. 13x13½

1971, July 24 Litho. Wmk. 354

428 A98 2p dk blue & multi .20 .20
429 A98 5p gray & multi .20 .20
430 A98 10p multicolored .30 .30
431 A98 1sh6p multicolored .45 .45
Nos. 428-431 (4) 1.15 1.15

Centenary (in 1970) of the proclamation of St. Joseph as patron of the Universal Church (2p, 10p), and 50th anniversary of the coronation of the statue of Our Lady of Victory in Senglea, Malta.

Blue Rock Thrush — A99

Design: 2p, 1sh6p, Thistle, vert.

Perf. 14x14½, 14½x14

1971, Sept. 18

432 A99 2p multicolored .20 .20
433 A99 5p bister & multi .20 .20
434 A99 10p orange & multi .30 .30
435 A99 1sh6p bister & multi .55 .55
Nos. 432-435 (4) 1.25 1.25

Heart and WHO Emblem A100

1972, Mar. 20 ***Perf. 14***

436 A100 2p yel green & multi .20 .20
437 A100 10p lilac & multi .20 .20
438 A100 2sh6p lt blue & multi .50 .50
Nos. 436-438 (3) .90 .90

World Health Day, Apr. 7.

Coin Showing Mnara (Lampstand) A101

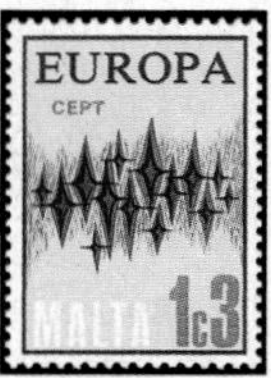

Sparkles, Symbolic of Communications CD15

Decimal Currency Coins: 2m, Maltese Cross. 3m, Bee and honeycomb. 1c, George Cross. 2c, Penthesilea. 5c, Altar, Megalithic Period. 10c, Grandmaster's Barge, 18th century. 50c, Great Siege Monument, by Antonio Sciortino.

Perf. 14 (16x21mm), 2m, 3m, 2c; Perf. 14½x14 (21x26mm), 5m, 1c, 5c

1972, May 16

439 A101 2m rose red & multi .20 .20
440 A101 3m pink & multi .20 .20
441 A101 5m lilac & multi .20 .20
442 A101 1c multicolored .20 .20
443 A101 2c orange & multi .20 .20
444 A101 5c multicolored .30 .30

Perf. 13½

Size: 27x35mm

445 A101 10c yellow & multi .55 .55
446 A101 50c multicolored 2.75 2.75
Nos. 439-446 (8) 4.60 4.60

Coins to mark introduction of decimal currency.

Nos. 319A, 321 and 323 Surcharged with New Value and 2 Bars

Perf. 14x14½, 14½

1972, Sept. 30 Photo. Wmk. 354

447 A62 1c3m on 5p multi .20 .20
448 A63 3c on 8p multi .20 .20
449 A63 5c on 1sh3p multi .30 .30
Nos. 447-449 (3) .70 .70

Europa Issue 1972

1972, Nov. 11 Litho. ***Perf. 13x13½***

450 CD15 1c3m yellow & multi .20 .20
451 CD15 3c multicolored .20 .20
452 CD15 5c pink & multi *.25 .25*
453 CD15 7c5m multicolored *.40 .40*
Nos. 450-453 (4) 1.05 1.05

Issued in sheets of 10 plus 2 labels (4x3). Labels are in top row.

Archaeology A103

Woman with Grain, FAO Emblem A104

1973, Mar. 31 Litho. ***Perf. 13½***

Size: 22x24mm

454 A103 2m shown .20 .20
455 A103 4m History (knights) .20 .20
456 A103 5m Folklore .20 .20
457 A103 8m Industry .20 .20
458 A103 1c Fishing .20 .20
459 A103 1c3m Pottery .20 .20
460 A103 2c Agriculture .20 .20
461 A103 3c Sport .20 .20
462 A103 4c Marina .20 .20
463 A103 5c Fiesta .30 .30
464 A103 7c5m Regatta .40 .40
465 A103 10c Charity (St. Martin) .55 .55
466 A103 50c Education 2.75 2.75
467 A103 £1 Religion 5.75 5.75

Perf. 13½x14

Size: 32x27mm

468 A103 £2 Arms of Malta 11.00 11.00
Nos. 454-468 (15) 22.55 22.55

Europa Issue 1973

Common Design Type

1973, June 2 Unwmk. ***Perf. 14***

Size: 36½x19½mm

469 CD16 3c multicolored .20 .20
470 CD16 5c multicolored *.30 .30*
471 CD16 7c5m dk bl & multi *.50 .50*
Nos. 469-471 (3) 1.00 1.00

1973, Oct. 6 Wmk. 354 ***Perf. 13½***

7c5m, Mother and child, WHO emblem. 10c, Two heads, Human Rights flame.

472 A104 1c3m yel grn, blk & gold .20 .20
473 A104 7c5m ultra, blk & gold .40 .40
474 A104 10c claret, blk & gold .60 .60
Nos. 472-474 (3) 1.20 1.20

World Food Program, 10th anniv.; WHO, 25th anniv.; Universal Declaration of Human Rights, 25th anniv.

Girolamo Cassar, Architect — A105

3c, Giuseppe Barth, opthalmologist. 5c, Nicolo' Isouard, composer. 7c5m, John Borg, botanist. 10c, Antonio Sciortino, sculptor.

1974, Jan. 12 Litho. ***Perf. 14***

475 A105 1c3m slate green & gold .20 .20
476 A105 3c indigo & gold .20 .20
477 A105 5c olive gray & gold .30 .30
478 A105 7c5m slate blue & gold .40 .40
479 A105 10c brn vio & gold .55 .55
Nos. 475-479 (5) 1.65 1.65

Prominent Maltese.

Statue of Goddess, 3rd Millenium B.C. A106

Europa (CEPT Emblem and): 3c, Carved door, Cathedral, Mdina, 11th cent, vert. 5c, Silver monstrance, 1689. 7c5m, "Vettina" (statue of nude woman), by Antonio Sciortino (1879-1947), vert.

1974, July 13 ***Perf. 13½x14, 14x13½***

480 A106 1c3m gray blue, blk & gold .20 .20
481 A106 3c ol brn, blk & gold .20 .20
482 A106 5c lilac, blk & gold *.30 .30*
483 A106 7c5m dull grn, blk & gold *.55 .55*
Nos. 480-483 (4) 1.25 1.25

Heinrich von Stephan, Coach and Train, UPU Emblem A107

UPU Emblem, von Stephan and: 5c, Paddle steamer and ocean liner. 7c5m, Balloon and jet. 50c, UPU Congress Building, Lausanne, and UPU Headquarters, Bern.

Wmk. 354

1974, Sept. Litho. ***Perf. 13½***

484 A107 1c3m multicolored .20 .20
485 A107 5c multicolored .30 .30
486 A107 7c5m multicolored .40 .40
487 A107 50c multicolored 2.75 2.75
a. Souvenir sheet of 4, #484-487 3.75 3.75
Nos. 484-487 (4) 3.65 3.65

Centenary of Universal Postal Union.

President, Prime Minister, Minister of Justice at Microphone — A108

1c3m, President, Prime Minister, Speaker at Swearing-in ceremony. 5c, Flag of Malta.

1975, Mar. 31 ***Perf. 14***

488 A108 1c3m red & multi .20 .20
489 A108 5c gray, red & black .30 .30
490 A108 25c red & multi 1.40 1.40
Nos. 488-490 (3) 1.90 1.90

Proclamation of the Republic, Dec. 13, 1974.

IWY Emblem, Mother and Child A109

Designs: 3c, 20c, Secretary (woman in public life), IWY emblem. 5c, Like 1c3m.

Wmk. 354

1975, May 30 Litho. ***Perf. 13***

491 A109 1c3m violet & gold .20 .20
492 A109 3c blue gray & gold .40 .20
493 A109 5c olive & gold .80 .50
494 A109 20c red brown & gold 3.75 2.50
Nos. 491-494 (4) 5.15 3.40

International Women's Year.

Allegory of Malta, by Francesco de Mura — A110

Europa: 15c, Judith and Holofernes, by Valentin de Boulogne.

1975, July 15 Litho. *Perf. 14*

495 A110 5c multicolored *.30 .30*
496 A110 15c multicolored *.80 .80*

Floor Plan of Ggantija Complex, 3000 B.C. — A111

Designs: 3c, View of Mdina. 5c, Typical Maltese town. 25c, Fort St. Angelo.

1975, Sept. 16 *Perf. 14*

497 A111 1c3m black & org .20 .20
498 A111 3c org, pur & black .25 .20
499 A111 5c gray, black & org .45 .35
500 A111 25c org, tan & black 2.75 1.75
Nos. 497-500 (4) 3.65 2.50

European Architectural Heritage Year.

"Right to Work" — A112

Designs: 5c, Protection of the Environment (Landscape). 25c, Maltese flags.

1975, Dec. 12 Litho. Wmk. 354

501 A112 1c3m multicolored .20 .20
502 A112 5c multicolored .30 .20
503 A112 25c multicolored 1.40 .75
Nos. 501-503 (3) 1.90 1.15

First anniversary of Malta Republic.

Republic Coat of Arms — A113

Perf. 13½x14

1976, Jan. 28 Litho. Wmk. 354

504 A113 £2 black & multi 11.00 10.00

Feast of Sts. Peter and Paul — A114

Designs: 1c3m, "Festa" (flags and fireworks), vert. 7c5m, Carnival. 10c, Good Friday (Christ carrying cross), vert.

1976, Feb. 26 Litho. *Perf. 14*

505 A114 1c3m multicolored .20 .20
506 A114 5c multicolored .30 .20
507 A114 7c5m multicolored .40 .25
508 A114 10c multicolored 1.25 .85
Nos. 505-508 (4) 2.15 1.50

Maltese folk festivals.

Water Polo, Olympic Rings A115

Olympic Rings and: 5c, Yachting. 30c, Running.

1976, Apr. 28 Litho. *Perf. 13½x14*

509 A115 1c7m sl green & red .20 .20
510 A115 5c dp blue & red .30 .20
511 A115 30c sepia & red 1.75 1.25
Nos. 509-511 (3) 2.25 1.65

21st Olympic Games, Montreal, Canada, July 17-Aug. 1.

Europa A116

1976, July 8 Litho. Wmk. 354

512 A116 7c Lace-making *.35 .35*
513 A116 15c Stone carving *.70 .70*

Grandmaster Nicola Cotoner, Founder — A117

5c, Dissected arm & hand. 7c, Dr. Fra Giuseppe Zammit, 1st professor. 11c, School & balustrade.

1976, Sept. 14 Litho. *Perf. 13½*

514 A117 2c multicolored .20 .20
515 A117 5c multicolored .30 .20
516 A117 7c multicolored .40 .20
517 A117 11c multicolored .80 .65
Nos. 514-517 (4) 1.70 1.25

School of Anatomy and Surgery, Valletta, 300th anniversary.

Armor of Grand Master Jean de La Valette — A118

Suits of Armor: 7c, Grand Master Aloph de Wignacourt. 11c, Grand Commander Jean Jacques de Verdelin.

1977, Jan. 20 Litho. Wmk. 354

518 A118 2c green & multi .20 .20
519 A118 7c brown & multi .40 .25
520 A118 11c ultra & multi .60 .40
Nos. 518-520 (3) 1.20 .85

No. 318 Surcharged with New Value and Bar

1977, Mar. 24 Photo. *Perf. 14x14½*

521 A62 1c7m on 4p multi .35 .20

Annunciation, Tapestry after Rubens — A119

Crucifixion — A120

Tapestries after Designs by Rubens: 7c, The Four Evangelists. 11c, Nativity. 20c, Adoration of the Kings.

Flemish tapestries commissioned for St. John's Co-Cathedral, Valletta.

Wmk. 354

1977, Mar. 30 Litho. *Perf. 14*

522 A119 2c multicolored .20 .20
523 A119 7c multicolored .40 .25
524 A120 11c multicolored .60 .55
525 A120 20c multicolored 1.10 1.10

1978, Jan. 26

Flemish Tapestries: 2c, Jesus' Entry into Jerusalem, by unknown painter. 7c, Last Supper, by Nicholas Poussin. 11c, Crucifixion, by Rubens. 25c, Resurrection, by Rubens.

526 A120 2c multicolored .20 .20
527 A120 7c multicolored .40 .25
528 A120 11c multicolored .60 .45
529 A120 25c multicolored 1.40 1.10

1979, Jan. 24

Tapestries after Designs by Rubens (Triumph of): 2c, Catholic Church. 7c, Charity. 11c, Faith. 25c, Truth.

530 A119 2c multicolored .20 .20
531 A119 7c multicolored .40 .25
532 A119 11c multicolored .60 .40
533 A119 25c multicolored 1.40 .95
Nos. 522-533 (12) 7.50 5.90

Consecration of St. John's Co-Cathedral, Valetta, 400th anniv. (#522-533). Peter Paul Rubens (1577-1640; #522-525).

See Nos. 567-569.

Malta Map, Telecommunication — A121

Designs: 1c, 6c, Map of Italy, Sicily, Malta and North Africa, telecommunication tower and waves, vert. 17c, like 8c.

Perf. 14x13½, 13½x14

1977, May 17 Litho. Wmk. 354

535 A121 1c green, red & blk .20 .20
536 A121 6c multicolored .35 .35
537 A121 8c multicolored .45 .45
538 A121 17c purple, red & blk .95 .95
Nos. 535-538 (4) 1.95 1.95

World Telecommunication Day.

View of Ta' L-Isperanza — A122

Europa: 20c, Harbor, Is-Salini.

1977, July Litho. *Perf. 13½*

539 A122 7c multicolored *.30 .30*
540 A122 20c multicolored *.90 .90*

Issued in sheets of 10.

Help Given Handicapped Worker — A123

7c, Stonemason & shipbuilder. 20c, Mother holding dead son, & Service to the Republic order, horiz. Sculptures from Workers' Monument.

1977, Oct. 12 Litho. Wmk. 354

541 A123 2c red brown & brn .20 .20
542 A123 7c brown & dk brn .40 .40
543 A123 20c multicolored 1.10 1.10
Nos. 541-543 (3) 1.70 1.70

Tribute to Maltese workers.

Lady on Horseback and Soldier, by Dürer A124

Grand Master Nicola Cotoner Monument A125

Dürer Engravings: 8c, Bagpiper. 17c, Madonna with Long-tailed Monkey.

1978, Mar. 7 *Perf. 14*

544 A124 1c7m dk blue, blk & red .20 .20
545 A124 8c gray, blk & red .45 .45
546 A124 17c dk grn, blk & red .95 .95
Nos. 544-546 (3) 1.60 1.60

Albrecht Dürer (1471-1528), German painter and engraver.

1978, Apr. 26 *Perf. 14x13½*

Europa: 25c, Grand Master Ramon Perellos monument, by Giusepe Mazzuoli. The monument on 7c is believed to be the work of Giovanni Batista Foggini.

547 A125 7c multicolored *.30 .30*
548 A125 25c multicolored *1.10 1.10*

Goalkeeper — A126

Argentina '78 Emblem and: 11c, 15c, different soccer scenes.

Perf. 14x13½

1978, June 6 Litho. Wmk. 354

549 A126 2c multicolored .20 .20
550 A126 11c multicolored .60 .60
551 A126 15c multicolored .85 .85
a. Souvenir sheet of 3, #549-551 1.75 1.75
Nos. 549-551 (3) 1.65 1.65

11th World Cup Soccer Championship, Argentina, June 1-25.

Fishing Boat — A127

Maltese Speronara and AirMalta Fuselage — A128

Designs: 5c, 17c Changing of colors. 7c, 20c, British soldier and oranges. 8c, like 2c.

1979, Mar. 31 *Perf. 14*

552 A127 2c claret & multi .20 .20
553 A127 5c claret & multi .30 .30
554 A127 7c claret & multi .40 .40
555 A127 8c dk blue & multi .45 .45
556 A127 17c dk blue & multi .95 .95
557 A127 20c dk blue & multi 1.10 1.10
Nos. 552-557 (6) 3.40 3.40

End of military agreement between Malta and Great Britain.

1979, May 9

Europa: 25c, Coastal watch tower and radio link tower.

558 A128 7c multicolored *.30 .30*
559 A128 25c multicolored *1.00 1.00*

Children and Globe — A129

Designs: 7c, Children flying kites. 11c, Children in a circle holding hands.

1979, June 13 ***Perf. 14x13½, 14***

Size: 20x38mm

560 A129 2c multicolored .20 .20

Size: 27x33mm

561 A129 7c multicolored .40 .40
562 A129 11c multicolored .60 .60
Nos. 560-562 (3) 1.20 1.20

International Year of the Child.

Loggerhead Turtle — A130

Marine Life: 2c, Gibbula nivosa. 7c, Dolphinfish. 25c, Noble pen shell.

1979, Oct. 10 **Litho.** ***Perf. 13½***
563 A130 2c multicolored .20 .20
564 A130 5c multicolored .30 .30
565 A130 7c multicolored .40 .40
566 A130 25c multicolored 1.40 1.40
Nos. 563-566 (4) 2.30 2.30

Tapestry Type of 1977-79

Tapestries after Designs by Rubens: 2c, The Institution of Corpus Domini. 8c, The Destruction of Idolatry. 50c, Portrait of Grand Master Perellos, vert.

1980, Jan. 30 **Wmk. 354** ***Perf. 14***
567 A120 2c multicolored .20 .20
568 A120 8c multicolored .45 .45

Souvenir Sheet

569 A119 50c multicolored 2.75 2.75

Victoria Citadel, Gozo A131

Monument Restoration (UNESCO Emblem and): 2c5m, Hal Saflieni Catacombs, Paola, 2500 B.C., vert. 6c, Vilhena Palace, Mdina, 18th century, vert. 12c, St. Elmo Fort, Valletta, 16th century.

1980, Feb. 15
570 A131 2c5m multicolored .20 .20
571 A131 6c multicolored .35 .35
572 A131 8c multicolored .45 .45
573 A131 12c multicolored .70 .70
Nos. 570-573 (4) 1.70 1.70

Don Gorg Preca (1880-1962), Founder of Soc. of Christian Doctrine — A132

1980, Apr. 12 **Litho.** ***Perf. 14x13½***
574 A132 2c5m gray violet .20 .20

Ruzar Briffa (1906-1963), Poet, by Vincent Apap — A133

Europa (Vincent Apap Sculpture): 30c, Mikiel Anton Vassalli (1764-1829), freedom fighter and scholar.

1980, Apr. 29 ***Perf. 13½x14***
575 A133 8c slate green & dp bis .30 .30
576 A133 30c brown red & olive 1.00 1.00

Chess Pieces A134

Designs: Chess pieces. 30c, vert.

1980, Nov. **Litho.** ***Perf. 14***
577 A134 2c5m multicolored .20 .20
578 A134 8c multicolored .45 .45
579 A134 30c multicolored 1.75 1.75
Nos. 577-579 (3) 2.40 2.40

Chess Olympiad, Valletta, Nov. 20-Dec. 8.

Barn Owl — A135

1981, Jan. 20 **Wmk. 354** ***Perf. 13½***
580 A135 3c shown .25 .25
581 A135 8c Sardinian warbler .50 .50
582 A135 12c Woodchat shrike .75 .75
583 A135 23c Stormy petrel 1.40 1.40
Nos. 580-583 (4) 2.90 2.90

Europa Issue 1981

Climbing the Gostra (Greasy Pole) — A136

1981, Apr. 28 **Litho.** ***Perf. 14***
584 A136 8c Horse race .30 .30
585 A136 30c shown 1.00 1.00

25th Intl. Fair of Malta, Naxxar, July 1-15 — A137

1981, June 12 ***Perf. 13½***
586 A137 4c multicolored .20 .20
587 A137 25c multicolored 1.40 1.40

Disabled Artist — A138

World Food Day — A139

1981, July 17 **Litho.** ***Perf. 13½***
588 A138 3c shown .20 .20
589 A138 35c Boy on crutches 2.00 2.00

Intl. Year of the Disabled.

1981, Oct. 16 **Litho.** ***Perf. 14***
590 A139 8c multicolored .45 .45
591 A139 23c multicolored 1.25 1.25

Men Hauling Building Stone — A140

1981, Oct. 31 **Wmk. 354** ***Perf. 14***
592 A140 5m shown .20 .20
593 A140 1c Growing cotton .20 .20
594 A140 2c Ship building .20 .20
595 A140 3c Minting coins .20 .20
596 A140 5c Artistic achievements .30 .30
597 A140 6c Fishing .35 .35
598 A140 7c Farming .40 .40
599 A140 8c Quarrying .45 .45
600 A140 10c Grape pressing .55 .55
601 A140 12c Ship repairing .70 .70
602 A140 15c Energy .85 .85
603 A140 20c Communications 1.10 1.10
604 A140 25c Factories 1.40 1.40
605 A140 50c Water drilling 2.75 2.75
606 A140 £1 Sea transport 5.75 5.75
607 A140 £3 Air transport 17.00 17.00
Nos. 592-607 (16) 32.40 32.40

Shipbuilding and Repairing, Tarznar Shipyards — A141

1982, Jan. 29 **Litho.** ***Perf. 13½x14***
608 A141 3c Assembly sheds .20 .20
609 A141 8c Ships in dry dock .45 .45
610 A141 13c Tanker .75 .75
611 A141 27c Tanker, diff. 1.50 1.50
Nos. 608-611 (4) 2.90 2.90

Man and Home for the Elderly A142

1982, Mar. 16 **Litho.** ***Perf. 14***
612 A142 8c shown .45 .45
613 A142 30c Woman, hospital 1.75 1.75

Europa Issue 1982

Redemption of the Islands, 1428 — A143

1982, Apr. 29 **Litho.** ***Perf. 14***
614 A143 8c shown .30 .30
615 A143 30c Declaration of Rights, 1802 1.25 1.25

1982 World Cup — A144

Designs: Various soccer players.

1982, June 11 **Litho.** ***Perf. 14***
616 A144 3c multicolored .20 .20
617 A144 12c multicolored .70 .70
618 A144 15c multicolored .90 .90
a. Souvenir sheet of 3, #616-618 4.00 4.00
Nos. 616-618 (3) 1.80 1.80

Brigantine — A145

1982, Nov. 13 **Litho.**
619 A145 3c shown .20 .20
619A A145 8c Tartana .70 .70
619B A145 12c Xebec .95 .95
619C A145 20c Speronara 1.75 1.75
Nos. 619-619C (4) 3.60 3.60

See #637-640, 670-673, 686-689, 703-706.

Malta Railway Centenary — A146

1983, Jan. 21 **Wmk. 354** ***Perf. 14***
620 A146 3c Manning Wardle, 1883 .25 .25
621 A146 13c Black Hawthorn, 1884 .95 .95
622 A146 27c Beyer Peacock, 1895 2.00 2.00
Nos. 620-622 (3) 3.20 3.20

Commonwealth Day — A147

1983, Mar. 14
623 A147 8c Map .45 .45
624 A147 12c Transportation .70 .70
625 A147 15c Beach, vert. .85 .85
626 A147 23c Industry, vert. 1.25 1.25
Nos. 623-626 (4) 3.25 3.25

Europa Issue 1983

Megalithic Temples, Ggantija — A148

Wmk. 354

1983, May 5 **Litho.** ***Perf. 14***
627 A148 8c shown .40 .40
628 A148 30c Fort St. Angelo 1.60 1.60

World Communications Year — A149

Perf. 13½x14

1983, July 14 **Litho.** **Wmk. 354**
629 A149 3c Dish antennas .25 .25
630 A149 7c Ships .45 .45
631 A149 13c Trucks .80 .80
632 A149 20c Games emblem 1.25 1.25
Nos. 629-632 (4) 2.75 2.75

25th anniv. of Intl. Maritime Org. (7c); 30th anniv. of Customs Cooperation Council (13c); 9th Mediterranean Games, Casablanca, 9/3-17 (20c).

Monsignor Giuseppe De Piro (1877-1933), Founder of Missionary Society of St. Paul — A150

1983, Sept. 1 Litho. *Perf. 14*
633 A150 3c multicolored .30 .30

40th Anniv. of General Workers' Union — A151

1983, Oct. 5 Litho. *Perf. 14x13½*
634 A151 3c Founding rally .25 .25
635 A151 8c Family, workers .50 .50
636 A151 27c Headquarters 1.60 1.60
Nos. 634-636 (3) 2.35 2.35

Maltese Ship Type of 1982

1983, Nov. 17 Litho. *Perf. 14x13½*
637 A145 2c Strangier, 1813 .30 .30
638 A145 12c Tigre 1839 .95 .95
639 A145 13c La Speranza, 1844 1.00 1.00
640 A145 20c Wignacourt 1844 1.75 1.75
Nos. 637-640 (4) 4.00 4.00

Europa (1959-1984) A152

1984, Apr. 27 Wmk. 354 *Perf. 14*
641 A152 8c multicolored *.40 .40*
642 A152 30c multicolored *1.60 1.60*

Police Force, 170th Anniv. A153

1984 Summer Olympics A154

1984, June 14 Litho. *Perf. 14x13½*
643 A153 3c Officer, 1880 .25 .25
644 A153 8c Mounted policeman 1.00 1.00
645 A153 11c Officer on motorcycle 1.25 1.25
646 A153 25c Traffic duty, firemen 3.00 3.00
Nos. 643-646 (4) 5.50 5.50

1984, July 26 Litho. *Perf. 13½x14*
647 A154 7c Running .40 .40
648 A154 12c Gymnastics .70 .70
649 A154 23c Swimming 1.25 1.25
Nos. 647-649 (3) 2.35 2.35

10th Anniv. of Republic — A155

Malta Post Office Cent. — A156

1984, Dec. 12 Litho. Wmk. 354
650 A155 3c Dove on map .30 .30
651 A155 8c Fortress .70 .70
652 A155 30c Hands, flag 2.50 2.50
Nos. 650-652 (3) 3.50 3.50

1985, Jan. 2 Litho. *Perf. 14*
653 A156 3c No. 8 .25 .25
654 A156 8c No. 9 .50 .50
655 A156 12c No. 11 .90 .90
656 A156 20c No. 12 1.50 1.50
a. Souvenir sheet of 4, #653-656 3.50 3.50
Nos. 653-656 (4) 3.15 3.15

International Youth Year — A157

1985, Mar. 7 *Perf. 14x13½, 13½x14*
657 A157 2c shown .25 .25
658 A157 13c Three youths, vert. .80 .80
659 A157 27c Female holding flame 1.60 1.60
Nos. 657-659 (3) 2.65 2.65

Composers A158

Europa: 8c, Nicolo Baldacchino (1895-1971). 30c, Francesco Azopardi (1748-1809).

1985, Apr. 25 Litho. *Perf. 14*
660 A158 8c multicolored *.65 .65*
661 A158 30c multicolored *2.40 2.40*

Guzeppi Bajada and Manwel Attard, Martyrs A159

7c, Karmnu Abela, Wenzu Dyer. 35c, June 7 Uprising Memorial Monument, vert.

1985, June 7 *Perf. 14x14½, 14½x14*
662 A159 3c multicolored .25 .25
663 A159 7c multicolored .45 .45
664 A159 35c multicolored 2.10 2.10
Nos. 662-664 (3) 2.80 2.80

June 7 Uprising, 66th anniv.

UN, 40th Anniv. A160

1985, July 26 *Perf. 13½x14*
665 A160 4c Stylized birds .25 .25
666 A160 11c Arrows .65 .65
667 A160 31c Human figures 1.90 1.90
Nos. 665-667 (3) 2.80 2.80

Famous Men — A161

Portraits: 8c, George Mitrovich (1794-1885), politician and author, novel frontispiece, The Cause of the People of Malta Now Before Parliament. 12c, Pietru Caxaru (1438-1485), scholar, manuscript.

1985, Oct. 3 *Perf. 14*
668 A161 8c multicolored .85 .85
669 A161 12c multicolored 1.25 1.25

Ships Type of 1982

1985, Nov. 27
670 A145 3c Scotia paddle steamer, 1844 .35 .35
671 A145 7c Tagliaferro, 1882 .70 .70
672 A145 15c Gleneagles, 1885 1.75 1.75
673 A145 23c L'Isle Adam, 1886 3.00 3.00
Nos. 670-673 (4) 5.80 5.80

Intl. Peace Year A162

Perf. 14x14½, 13½x14 (#675)
1986, Jan. 28 Litho. Wmk. 354
674 A162 8c John XXIII Peace Laboratory .85 .85
675 A162 11c Unity 1.25 1.25
676 A162 27c Peaceful coexistence 3.00 3.00
Nos. 674-676 (3) 5.10 5.10

Size of No. 675: 43x27mm.

Europa Issue 1986

Butterflies A163

1986, Apr. 3 *Perf. 14½x14*
677 A163 8c shown *.60 .60*
678 A163 35c Earth, air, fire and water *2.75 2.75*

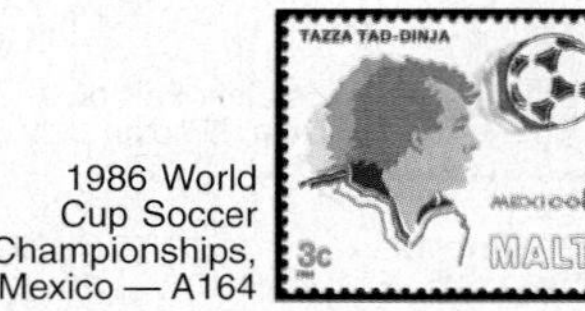

1986 World Cup Soccer Championships, Mexico — A164

1986, May 30 Wmk. 354 *Perf. 14*
679 A164 3c Heading the ball .40 .40
680 A164 7c Goalie catching ball 1.10 1.10
681 A164 23c Dribbling 3.50 3.50
a. Souvenir sheet of 3, #679-681 6.00 6.00
Nos. 679-681 (3) 5.00 5.00

Philanthropists A165

Designs: 2c, Fra Diegu (1831-1902). 3c, Adelaide Cini (1838-1885). 8c, Alfonso Maria Galea (1861-1941). 27c, Vincenzo Bugeja (1820-1890).

1986, Aug. 28 *Perf. 14½x14*
682 A165 2c multicolored .40 .40
683 A165 3c multicolored .50 .50
684 A165 8c multicolored 1.10 1.10
685 A165 27c multicolored 4.00 4.00
Nos. 682-685 (4) 6.00 6.00

Ships Type of 1982

1986, Nov. 19 Wmk. 354 *Perf. 14*
686 A145 7c San Paul 1.00 1.00
687 A145 10c Knight of Malta 1.25 1.25
688 A145 12c Valetta City 1.75 1.75
689 A145 20c Saver 2.75 2.75
Nos. 686-689 (4) 6.75 6.75

Malta Ornithological Society, 25th Anniv. — A166

1987, Jan. 26 Litho. *Perf. 14*
690 A166 3c Erithacus rubecula .90 .45
691 A166 8c Falco peregrinus 2.10 .75
692 A166 13c Upupa epops 2.75 3.00
693 A166 23c Calonectris diomedea 3.25 4.50
Nos. 690-693 (4) 9.00 8.70

Nos. 691-692 vert.

Europa Issue 1987

Limestone Buildings A167

1987, Apr. 15 Litho. *Perf. 14½x14*
694 A167 8c Aquasun Lido *.50 .50*
695 A167 35c St. Joseph's Church, Manikata *2.90 2.90*

Military Uniforms — A168

Uniforms of the Order of St. John of Jerusalem (1530-1798).

1987, June 10 Wmk. 354 *Perf. 14*
696 A168 3c Soldier, 16th cent. .40 .40
697 A168 7c Officer, 16th cent. .90 .90
698 A168 10c Flag bearer, 18th cent. 1.25 1.25
699 A168 27c General of the galleys, 18th cent 3.50 3.50
Nos. 696-699 (4) 6.05 6.05

See #723-726, 739-742, 764-767, 774-777.

European Environment Year — A169

Anniversaries and events: 8c, Esperanto movement, cent. 23s, Intl. Year of Shelter for the Homeless.

Perf. 14½x14

1987, Aug. 18 **Wmk. 354**

700 A169 5c shown .85 .85
701 A169 8c multicolored 1.40 1.40
702 A169 23c multicolored 3.75 3.75
Nos. 700-702 (3) 6.00 6.00

Ships Type of 1982

1987, Oct. 16 **Litho.** ***Perf. 14***

703 A145 2c Medina, 1969 .40 .40
704 A145 11c Rabat, 1974 1.60 1.60
705 A145 13c Ghawdex, 1979 2.00 2.00
706 A145 20c Pinto, 1987 2.75 2.75
Nos. 703-706 (4) 6.75 6.75

A170

Designs: 8c, Dr. Arvid Pardo, representative to UN from Malta who proposed the resolution. 12c, UN emblem.

Wmk. 354

1987, Dec. 18 **Litho.** ***Perf. 14½***

707 A170 8c multicolored 1.40 1.40
708 A170 12c multicolored 2.10 2.10

Souvenir Sheet

Perf. 13x13½

709 Sheet of 2 3.50 3.50
a. A170 8c multicolored 1.25 1.25
b. A170 12c multicolored 1.90 1.90

UN resolution for peaceful use of marine resources, 20th anniv. Nos. 709a-709b printed in a continuous design.

Nazju Falzon (1813-1865), Clergyman A171

Famous men: 3c, Monsignor Sidor Formosa (1851-1931), benefactor of the poor. 4c, Sir Luigi Preziosi (1888-1965), opthalmologist who developed an operation for the treatment of glaucoma. 10c, Father Anastasju Cuschieri (1876-1962), theologian, poet. 25c, Monsignor Pietru Pawl Saydon (1895-1971), translator, commentator on scripture.

Perf. 14½x14

1988, Jan. 23 **Wmk. 354**

710 A171 2c shown .35 .35
711 A171 3c multicolored .35 .35
712 A171 4c multicolored .40 .40
713 A171 10c multicolored .80 .80
714 A171 25c multicolored 2.10 2.10
Nos. 710-714 (5) 4.00 4.00

Anniversaries and Events — A172

10c, Statue of youth and St. John Bosco in the chapel at St. Patrick's School, Sliema. 12c, Assumption of Our Lady, main altarpiece at Ta' Pinu Sanctuary, Gozo, completed in 1619 by Amodeo Bartolomeo Perugino. 14c, Christ the King monument at the Mall, Floriana, by Antonio Sciortino (1879-1947).

1988, Mar. 5 **Litho.** ***Perf. 14***

715 A172 10c multicolored .95 .95
716 A172 12c multicolored 1.25 1.25
717 A172 14c multicolored 1.40 1.40
Nos. 715-717 (3) 3.60 3.60

St. John Bosco (1815-88), educator (10c); Marian Year (12c); Intl. Eucharistic Congress, Malta, Apr. 24-28, 1913, 75th anniv. (14c).

Land, Sea and Air Transportation A173

Europa (Transport and communication): 35c, Telecommunications.

1988, Apr. 9 ***Perf. 14***

718 A173 10c multicolored *.65 .65*
719 A173 35c multicolored *2.40 2.40*

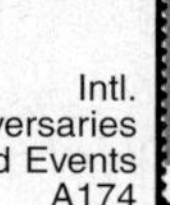

Intl. Anniversaries and Events A174

Globe picturing hemispheres and: 4c, Red Cross, Red Crescent emblems. 18c, Symbolic design dividing world into north and south regions. 19c, Caduceus, EKG readout.

1988, May 25 **Litho.** ***Perf. 14***

720 A174 4c multicolored .35 .35
721 A174 18c multicolored 1.50 1.50
722 A174 19c multicolored 1.75 1.75
Nos. 720-722 (3) 3.60 3.60

Intl. Red Cross and Red Crescent Organizations, 125th annivs. (4c); European Public Campaign on North-South Interdependence and Solidarity (18c); WHO, 40th anniv. (19c).

Military Uniforms Type of 1987

Designs: 3c, Light Infantry private, 1800. 4c, Coast Artillery gunner, 1802. 10c, Ist Maltese Provincial Battalion field officer, 1805. 25c, Royal Malta Regiment subaltern, 1809.

1988, July 23 **Litho.** **Wmk. 354**

723 A168 3c multicolored .30 .30
724 A168 4c multicolored .35 .35
725 A168 10c multicolored .95 .95
726 A168 25c multicolored 2.40 2.40
Nos. 723-726 (4) 4.00 4.00

A175

A176

Perf. 14x13½

1988, Sept. 17 **Wmk. 354**

727 A175 4c Running .30 .30
728 A175 10c Women's diving .65 .65
729 A175 35c Basketball 2.10 2.10
Nos. 727-729 (3) 3.05 3.05

1988 Summer Olympics, Seoul.

1989, Jan. 28 **Litho.** ***Perf. 13½***

730 A176 2c Commonwealth .25 .25
731 A176 3c Council of Europe .25 .25
732 A176 4c United Nations .30 .30
733 A176 10c Labor .70 .70
734 A176 12c Justice .80 .80

Size: 41x32mm

Perf. 14

735 A176 25c Liberty 1.75 1.75
Nos. 730-735 (6) 4.05 4.05

Natl. independence, 25th anniv.

New Natl. Emblem — A177

1989, Mar. 25 ***Perf. 14***

736 A177 £1 multicolored 5.75 5.75

Children's Toys — A178

Europa.

1989, May 6

737 A178 10c Kite *.75 .75*
738 A178 35c Dolls *2.75 2.75*

Military Uniforms Type of 1987

3c, Officer of the Maltese Veterans, 1815. 4c, Subaltern of the Royal Malta Fencibles, 1839. 10c, Militia private, 1856. 25c, Royal Malta Fencibles Artillery colonel, 1875.

1989, June 24 **Litho.** **Wmk. 354**

739 A168 3c multicolored .30 .30
740 A168 4c multicolored .55 .55
741 A168 10c multicolored 1.25 1.25
742 A168 25c multicolored 3.00 3.00
Nos. 739-742 (4) 5.10 5.10

Anniversaries and Events — A179

1989, Oct. 17 **Litho.** **Wmk. 354**

743 A179 3c multicolored .25 .25
744 A179 4c multi, diff. .35 .35
745 A179 10c multi, diff. .75 .75
746 A179 14c multi, diff. 1.00 1.00
747 A179 25c multi, diff. 1.75 1.75
Nos. 743-747 (5) 4.10 4.10

UN Declaration on Social Progress and Development, 20th anniv. (3c); signing of the European Social Charter by Malta (4c); Council of Europe, 40th anniv. (10c); Natl. Teachers' Union, 70th anniv. (14c); assembly of the Knights of the Sovereign Military Order of Malta (25c).

Pres. Bush, Map and Gen.-Sec. Gorbachev — A180

1989, Dec. 2 **Litho.** **Wmk. 354**

748 A180 10c chalky blue, org & brn 1.25 1.25

US-Soviet summit, Malta, Dec. 2-3.

Europa 1990 — A181

Post offices: 10c, Auberge d'Italie, Valletta, 1574, vert. 35c, Branch P.O., Zebbug, 1987.

1990, Feb. 9

749 A181 10c multicolored *.60 .60*
750 A181 35c multicolored *2.25 2.25*

Anniversaries & Events — A182

1990, Apr. 7

751 A182 3c multi, vert. .35 .35
752 A182 4c shown .45 .45
753 A182 19c multicolored 1.60 1.60
754 A182 20c multi, vert. 1.60 1.60
Nos. 751-754 (4) 4.00 4.00

UNESCO World Literacy Year (3c); subjection of Malta to Count Roger the Norman and subsequent rulers of Sicily, 900th anniv. (4c); 25th anniv. of Malta's membership in the ITU (19c); and 20th Congress of the Union of European Soccer Associations, Malta (20c).

British Poets and Novelists — A183

1990, May 3 ***Perf. 13½***

755 A183 4c Samuel Taylor Coleridge .35 .35
756 A183 10c Lord Byron .80 .80
757 A183 12c Sir Walter Scott .95 .95
758 A183 25c William Makepeace Thackeray 1.90 1.90
Nos. 755-758 (4) 4.00 4.00

Visit of Pope John Paul II, May 25-27 — A184

1990, May 25 ***Perf. 14***

759 A184 4c St. Paul .25 .25
760 A184 25c Pope John Paul II 1.75 1.75
a. Pair, #759-760 2.10 2.10

World Cup Soccer Championships, Italy — A185

Soccer ball &: 5c, flags. 10c, hands & goal net.

1990, June 8 **Wmk. 354**

761 A185 5c multicolored .40 .40
762 A185 10c multicolored .70 .70
763 A185 14c multicolored 1.10 1.10
a. Souvenir sheet of 3, #761-763 2.50 2.50
Nos. 761-763 (3) 2.20 2.20

Military Uniforms Type of 1987

Designs: 3c, Captain, Royal Malta Militia, 1889. 4c, Field Officer, Royal Malta Artillery, 1905. 10c, Laborer, Malta Labor Corps, 1915. 25c, Lieutenant, King's Own Malta Regiment of Militia, 1918.

1990, Aug. 25 ***Perf. 14***

No.	Type	Description	Unused	Used
764	A168	3c multicolored	.35	.35
765	A168	4c multicolored	.60	.60
766	A168	10c multicolored	1.40	1.40
767	A168	25c multicolored	3.25	3.25
		Nos. 764-767 (4)	5.60	5.60

Maltese Philatelic Society, 25th Anniv. A186

1991, Mar. 6 **Litho.** **Wmk. 354**

No.	Type	Description	Unused	Used
768	A186	10c multicolored	.85	.85

Europa — A187

1991, Mar. 16

No.	Type	Description	Unused	Used
769	A187	10c Eurostar	*.70*	*.70*
770	A187	35c Ariane 4, space plane	*2.40*	*2.40*

St. Ignatius of Loyola (1491-1556), Founder of Jesuit Order — A188

Designs: 4c, Marie Therese Pisani (1806-1865), Benedictine Nun, vert. 30c, St. John of the Cross (1542-1591), Christian mystic.

1991, Apr. 29 **Litho.** ***Perf. 14***

No.	Type	Description	Unused	Used
771	A188	3c multicolored	.25	.25
772	A188	4c multicolored	.30	.30
773	A188	30c multicoloed	2.00	2.00
		Nos. 771-773 (3)	2.55	2.55

Military Uniforms Type of 1987

Colors Officers: 3c, Royal Malta Fencibles, 1860. 10c, Royal Malta Regiment of Militia, 1903. 19c, King's Own Malta Regiment, 1968. 25c, Armed Forces of Malta, 1991.

Wmk. 354

1991, Sept. 23 **Litho.** ***Perf. 14***

No.	Type	Description	Unused	Used
774	A168	3c multicolored	.30	.30
775	A168	10c multicolored	.80	.80
776	A168	19c multicolored	1.50	1.50
777	A168	25c multicolored	1.90	1.90
		Nos. 774-777 (4)	4.50	4.50

Union Haddiema Maghqudin, 25th Anniv. — A189

1991, Sept. 23 ***Perf. 14x13½***

No.	Type	Description	Unused	Used
778	A189	4c multicolored	.30	.30

Birds of Prey — A190

1991, Oct. 3 ***Perf. 14***

No.	Type	Description	Unused	Used
779	A190	4c Pernis apivorus	*2.00*	*1.00*
780	A190	4c Circus aeruginosus	*2.00*	*1.00*
781	A190	10c Falco eleonorae	*3.50*	*1.75*
782	A190	10c Falco naumanni	*3.50*	*1.75*
a.		Strip of 4, #779-782	*14.00*	*14.00*

World Wildlife Fund.

Tourism A191

Designs: 1c, Ta' Hagrat neolithic temples, Mgarr. 2c, Cottoner Gate. 3c, St. Michael's Bastion, Valletta. 4c, Spinola Palace, St. Julian's. 5c, Old church, Birkirkara. 10c, Wind surfing, Mellieha Bay. 12c, Boat anchored at Wied iz-Zurrieq. 14c, Mgarr Harbor, Gozo. 20c, Yacht Marina. 50c, Gozo Channel. £1, Statue of Arab Horses, by Sciortino. £2, Independence Monument, by Bonnici, vert.

1991, Dec. 9 ***Perf. 13½***

No.	Type	Description	Unused	Used
783	A191	1c multicolored	.20	.20
784	A191	2c multicolored	.20	.20
785	A191	3c multicolored	.20	.20
786	A191	4c multicolored	.25	.25
787	A191	5c multicolored	.30	.30
788	A191	10c multicolored	.65	.65
789	A191	12c multicolored	.75	.75
790	A191	14c multicolored	.85	.85
791	A191	20c multicolored	1.25	1.25
792	A191	50c multicolored	3.25	3.25
793	A191	£1 multicolored	6.25	6.25
794	A191	£2 multicolored	12.50	12.50
		Nos. 783-794 (12)	26.65	26.65

Malta Intl. Airport A192

1992, Feb. 8 ***Perf. 14***

No.	Type	Description	Unused	Used
795	A192	4c shown	.50	.50
796	A192	10c Flags, airport	1.25	1.25

Discovery of America, 500th Anniv. — A193

1992, Feb. 20 ***Perf. 14x14½***

No.	Type	Description	Unused	Used
797	A193	10c Columbus' fleet	*.65*	*.65*
798	A193	35c Columbus, map	*2.25*	*2.25*

Europa.

George Cross, 1942 — A194

George Cross and: 4c, Royal Malta Artillery. 10c, Siege Bell. 50c, Santa Maria convoy entering Grand Harbor.

1992, Apr. 15 ***Perf. 14***

No.	Type	Description	Unused	Used
799	A194	4c multicolored	.55	.55
800	A194	10c multicolored	1.25	1.25
801	A194	50c multicolored	6.00	6.00
		Nos. 799-801 (3)	7.80	7.80

1992 Summer Olympics, Barcelona — A195

1992, June 24

No.	Type	Description	Unused	Used
802	A195	3c Runners	.25	.25
803	A195	10c High jump	.85	.85
804	A195	30c Swimmer	2.50	2.50
		Nos. 802-804 (3)	3.60	3.60

Historic Buildings A196

Designs: 3c, Church of the Flight of the Holy Family into Egypt, vert. 4c, St. John's Co-Cathedral. 19c, Church of the Madonna del Pilar, vert. 25c, Auberge de Provence.

1992, July 5

No.	Type	Description	Unused	Used
805	A196	3c blk, gray & buff	.35	.35
806	A196	4c blk, salmon & buff	.45	.45
807	A196	19c blk, green & buff	1.75	1.75
808	A196	25c blk, pink & buff	2.25	2.25
		Nos. 805-808 (4)	4.80	4.80

University of Malta, 400th Anniv. — A197

1992, Nov. 11

No.	Type	Description	Unused	Used
809	A197	4c Early building, vert.	.40	.40
810	A197	30c Modern complex	2.75	2.75

Lions Intl., 75th Anniv. — A198

1993, Feb. 4

No.	Type	Description	Unused	Used
811	A198	4c We serve	.40	.40
812	A198	50c Sight first campaign	3.50	3.50

Europa A199

Contemporary paintings by: 10c, Pawl Carbonaro, vert. 35c, Alfred Chircop.

1993, Apr. 7

No.	Type	Description	Unused	Used
813	A199	10c multicolored	*.60*	*.60*
814	A199	35c multicolored	*2.00*	*2.00*

5th Games of Small States of Europe A200

1993, May 4 ***Perf. 13½x14***

No.	Type	Description	Unused	Used
815	A200	3c Torchbearer	.25	.25
816	A200	4c Cycling	.40	.40
817	A200	10c Tennis	.90	.90
818	A200	35c Sailing	3.25	3.25
a.		Souvenir sheet of 4, #815-818	5.00	5.00
		Nos. 815-818 (4)	4.80	4.80

Boy Scouts and Girl Guides of Malta — A201

1993, July 21 ***Perf. 14***

No.	Type	Description	Unused	Used
819	A201	3c Leader bandaging girl	.25	.25
820	A201	4c Bronze Cross	.25	.25
821	A201	10c Scout at camp fire	.75	.75
822	A201	35c Scout recieving Bronze Cross	2.75	2.75
		Nos. 819-822 (4)	4.00	4.00

Girl Guides in Malta, 70th anniv. (#819). Award of Bronze Cross for Gallantry to Boy Scouts of Malta, 50th anniv. (#820-822).

A202

A203

1993, Sept. 23 ***Perf. 14½x14***

No.	Type	Description	Unused	Used
823	A202	5c Papilio machaon	.55	.55
824	A202	35c Vanessa atalanta	2.75	2.75

1993, Oct. 5 ***Perf. 13½***

No.	Type	Description	Unused	Used
825	A203	4c multicolored	.40	.40

General Worker's Union, 50th anniv.

Souvenir Sheet

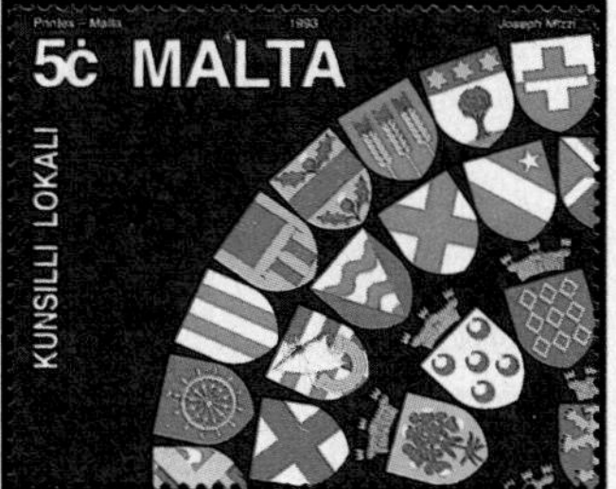

Local Councils — A204

Designs showing various local flags with denominations at: a, UL. b, UR. c, LL. d, LR.

1993, Nov. 20 ***Perf. 14½***

No.	Type	Description	Unused	Used
826		Sheet of 4	2.00	2.00
a.-d.		A204 5c any single	.40	.40

Dental Assoc. of Malta, 50th Anniv. — A205

Design: 44c, Dental instrument, teeth.

1994, Feb. 12

827 A205 5c multicolored .50 .50
828 A205 44c multicolored 3.50 3.50

Europa — A206

Designs: 14c, Sir Themistocles Zammit (1864-1935), discoverer of micro-organism causing undulant fever. 30c, Marble candelabrum, 2nd cent. B.C., Natl. Museum of Archaeology, Valletta.

1994, Mar. 29 *Perf. 14*

829 A206 14c multicolored *.85 .85*
830 A206 30c multicolored *1.90 1.90*

Anniversaries and Events — A207

1994, May 10

831 A207 5c shown .45 .45
832 A207 9c Crosses .70 .70
833 A207 14c Farm animals 1.10 1.10
834 A207 20c Factory worker 1.60 1.60
835 A207 25c Cathedral, vert. 2.00 2.00
Nos. 831-835 (5) 5.85 5.85

Intl. Year of the Family (#831). Malta Red Cross Society, 3rd anniv. (#832). Agrarian Society, 150th anniv. (#833). ILO, 75th anniv. (#834). St. Paul's Anglican Cathedral, 150th anniv. (#835).

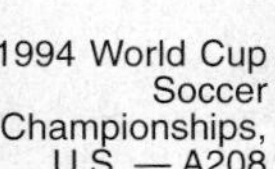

1994 World Cup Soccer Championships, U.S. — A208

1994, June 9

836 A208 5c shown .35 .35
837 A208 14c Ball, net, map 1.00 1.00
838 A208 30c Ball, field, map 2.25 2.25
a. Souvenir sheet of 3, #836-838 4.00 4.00
Nos. 836-838 (3) 3.60 3.60

Aviation Anniversaries & Events — A209

Aircraft, related objects: 5c, Trophy, map, Twin Comanche. 14c, Airshow emblem, Phantom jet, demonstration team in silhouette, Alouette helicopter, flag. 20c, Emblem, Avro York, old terminal building, DeHavilland Dove. 25c, Emblem, DeHavilland Comet, new terminal, Airbus 320.

1994, July 2

839 A209 5c multicolored .45 .45
840 A209 14c multicolored 1.25 1.25
841 A209 20c multicolored 1.90 1.90
842 A209 25c multicolored 2.25 2.25
Nos. 839-842 (4) 5.85 5.85

Intl. Air Rally of Malta, 25th anniv. (#839). Malta Intl. Airshow (#840). ICAO, 50th anniv. (#841-842).

First Manned Moon Landing, 25th Anniv. — A210

1994, July 20

843 A210 14c multicolored 1.25 1.25

Christmas — A211

1994, Oct. 26

844 A211 5c shown .30 .30

Size: 28x40mm

845 A211 9c +2c Angel in pink .65 .65
846 A211 14c +3c Madonna & child 1.00 1.00
847 A211 20c +3c Angel in green 1.40 1.40
Nos. 844-847 (4) 3.35 3.35

Antique Maltese Silver — A212

Designs: 5c, Ewer, Vilhena period. 14c, Balsamina, Pinto period. 20c, Coffee pot, Pinto period. 25c, Sugar box, Pinto period.

Wmk. 354

1994, Dec. 12 **Litho.** *Perf. 14*

848 A212 5c multicolored .40 .40
849 A212 14c multicolored 1.00 1.00
850 A212 20c multicolored 1.50 1.50
851 A212 25c multicolored 1.75 1.75
Nos. 848-851 (4) 4.65 4.65

Anniversaries & Events — A213

1995, Feb. 27

852 A213 2c multicolored .25 .25
853 A213 5c multicolored .35 .35
854 A213 14c multicolored .85 .85
855 A213 20c multicolored 1.25 1.25
856 A213 25c multicolored 1.50 1.50
Nos. 852-856 (5) 4.20 4.20

Natl. Assoc. of Pensioners, 25th anniv. (#852). Natl. Youth Council of Malta, 10th anniv. (#853). 4th World Conf. on Women, Beijing (#854). Malta Memorial District Nursing Assoc., 50th anniv. (#855). Louis Pasteur (1822-95) (#856).

Peace & Freedom A214

Europa: 14c, Hand with olive twig, rainbow, vert. 30c, Doves.

1995, Mar. 29

857 A214 14c multicolored *.75 .75*
858 A214 30c multicolored *1.60 1.60*

50th Anniversaries — A215

Designs: 5c, End of World War II, ships, planes. 14c, Formation of UN, people joining hands. 35c, FAO, hands holding bowl of wheat, FAO emblem.

1995, Apr. 21

859 A215 5c multicolored .35 .35
860 A215 14c multicolored .85 .85
861 A215 35c multi, vert. 2.10 2.10
Nos. 859-861 (3) 3.30 3.30

Telecommunications & Electricity — A216

1995, June 15

862 A216 2c Light bulb .25 .25
863 A216 5c Cable, binary numbers .35 .35
864 A216 9c Satellite dish .55 .55
865 A216 14c Sun's rays, trees .85 .85
866 A216 20c Telephone, satellite 1.25 1.25
Nos. 862-866 (5) 3.25 3.25

European Nature Conservation Year — A217

1995, July 24

867 A217 5c Ruins, Girna .50 .50
868 A217 14c Podarcis filfolensis 1.25 1.25
869 A217 44c Pina halepensis 4.25 4.25
Nos. 867-869 (3) 6.00 6.00

Antique Clocks — A218

Designs: 1c, Pinto's turret clock. 5c, Michelangelo Sapiano, long case & smaller clock. 14c, Arlogg tal-lira (case) clock. 25c, Maltese sundials.

1995, Oct. 5

870 A218 1c multicolored .40 .40
871 A218 5c multicolored .60 .60
872 A218 14c multicolored 1.40 1.40
873 A218 25c multicolored 2.40 2.40
Nos. 870-873 (4) 4.80 4.80

Christmas — A219

Designs: 5c, Christmas Eve children's procession. 5c+2c, Children carrying manger. 14c+3c, Boy carrying manger, boy with lamp. 25c+3c, Boy with lamp, balcony.
Illustration reduced.

Wmk. 354

1995, Nov. 15 **Litho.** *Perf. 14*

874 A219 5c multi .35 .35

Size: 26x32mm

875 A219 5c +2c multi .45 .45
876 A219 14c +3c multi 1.10 1.10
877 A219 25c +3c multi 1.75 1.75
Nos. 874-877 (4) 3.65 3.65

Surtax for child welfare organizations.

Child and Youth Welfare Organizations — A220

Silhouettes of youth, children, and: 5c, Maltese cross, Palace of the President. 14c, Fr. Nazzareno Camilleri, St. Patricks' School. 20c, St. Maria of St. Euphrasia Pelletier, convent building. 25c, Globe, children looking at pool.

1996, Feb. 29

878 A220 5c multicolored .35 .35
879 A220 14c multicolored .85 .85
880 A220 20c multicolored 1.25 1.25
881 A220 25c multicolored 1.50 1.50
Nos. 878-881 (4) 3.95 3.95

President's Award, 35th anniv. (#878). Fr. Camilleri, 90th death anniv. (#879). St. Maria, death bicent. (#880). UNICEF, 50th anniv. (#881).

Prehistoric Art — A221

Sculptures, pottery from 5000-2500BC: 5c, People, animals. 14c, Two people seated, one with missing head. 20c, Venus figure, vert. 35c, Pitcher, vert.

1996, Mar. 29

882 A221 5c multicolored .35 .35
883 A221 14c multicolored .85 .85
884 A221 20c multicolored 1.25 1.25
885 A221 35c multicolored 2.10 2.10
Nos. 882-885 (4) 4.55 4.55

Famous Women — A222

Europa: 14c, Mabel Strickland (1899-1988). 30c, Inez Soler (1910-1974).

1996, Apr. 24

886 A222 14c multicolored *.80 .80*
887 A222 30c multicolored *1.75 1.75*

Anniversaries and Events — A223

Designs: No. 888, UN, decade against drug abuse. No. 889, Malta Federation of Industry, 50th anniv. 14c, Self-government, 75th anniv. 44c, Guglielmo Marconi, radio, cent.

1996, June 5

888	A223	5c multicolored	.35	.35
889	A223	5c multicolored	.35	.35
890	A223	14c multicolored	.85	.85
891	A223	44c multicolored	2.75	2.75
		Nos. 888-891 (4)	4.30	4.30

1996 Summer Olympic Games, Atlanta A224

1996, July 10

892	A224	2c Judo	.25	.25
893	A224	5c Running	.35	.35
894	A224	14c Swimming	.85	.85
895	A224	25c Shooting	1.50	1.50
		Nos. 892-895 (4)	2.95	2.95

Paintings, by or of Giuseppe Calì — A225

Designs: 5c, Boy cutting wheat. 14c, Dog. 20c, Woman with hoe standing on hillside, vert. 25c, Portrait of Calì, by Dingli, vert.

1996, Aug. 22

896	A225	5c multicolored	.35	.35
897	A225	14c multicolored	.85	.85
898	A225	20c multicolored	1.25	1.25
899	A225	25c multicolored	1.50	1.50
		Nos. 896-899 (4)	3.95	3.95

Buses A226

2c, Tal-Gallarija "Diamond Star" No. 1990. 5c, Stewart "Tom Mix" No. 434. 14c, Diamond T "Verdala" No. 1764. 30c, Front control No. 3495.

Wmk. 354

1996, Sept. 26 Litho. *Perf. 14*

900	A226	2c multicolored	.30	.30
901	A226	5c multicolored	.45	.45
902	A226	14c multicolored	1.10	1.10
903	A226	30c multicolored	2.50	2.50
		Nos. 900-903 (4)	4.35	4.35

Christmas — A227

Stained glass windows: 5c+2c, Madonna and Child. 14c+3c, Angel flying right. 25c+3c, Angel flying left.

1996, Nov. 7

904	A227	5c shown	.30	.30

Size: 26x31mm

905	A227	5c +2c multi	.45	.45
906	A227	14c +3c multi	1.00	1.00
907	A227	25c +3c multi	1.75	1.75
		Nos. 904-907 (4)	3.50	3.50

City Bicentennials A228

1997, Feb. 20

908	A228	6c Hompesch	.40	.40
909	A228	16c Ferdinand	1.00	1.00
910	A228	26c Beland	1.60	1.60
a.		Souvenir Sheet of 3, #908-910	4.00	4.00
		Nos. 908-910 (3)	3.00	3.00

Treasures of Malta — A229

1997, Apr. 11

911	A229	2c Suggetta	.20	.20
912	A229	6c Suggetta, diff.	.45	.45
913	A229	16c Sedan chair, vert.	1.00	1.00
914	A229	27c Sedan chair, diff., vert.	1.60	1.60
		Nos. 911-914 (4)	3.25	3.25

A230

A231

Europa (Stories and Legends): 16c, Man carrying door, figure in front of house (Gahan). 35c, Woman kneeling in prayer, knight on white horse (St. Dimitri).

1997, May 5

915	A230	16c multicolored	*.90*	*.90*
916	A230	35c multicolored	*2.00*	*2.00*

1997, July 10

917	A231	1c multicolored	.20	.20
918	A231	16c multicolored	.90	.90

Antonio Sciortino (1879-1947), sculptor.

Gozo Cathedral, 300th Anniv. — A232

1997, July 10

919	A232	6c multi	.35	.35
920	A232	11c multi, diff.	.60	.60

Joseph Caleia (1897-1975), Actor — A233

1997, July 10

921	A233	6c multicolored	.35	.35
922	A233	22c multi, diff.	1.25	1.25

Pioneers of Freedom — A234

Designs: 6c, Dr. Albert V. Laferla (1887-1943). 16c, Sister Emilie de Vialar (1797-1856). 19c, Msgr. Paolo Pullicino (1815-90). 26c, Msgr. Tommaso Gargallo (c. 1544-1614).

Wmk. 354

1997, Sept. 24 Litho. *Perf. 14*

923	A234	6c multicolored	.35	.35
924	A234	16c multicolored	.90	.90
925	A234	19c multicolored	1.10	1.10
926	A234	26c multicolored	1.40	1.40
		Nos. 923-926 (4)	3.75	3.75

Christmas — A235

Designs: 6c, Nativity. 6c+2c, Madonna and Child, vert. 16c+3c, Joseph with donkey, vert. 26c+3c, Shepherd, sheep, vert.

1997, Nov. 12

927	A235	6c multi	.35	.35
928	A235	6c +2c multi	.45	.45
929	A235	16c +3c multi	1.10	1.10
930	A235	26c +3c multi	1.60	1.60
		Nos. 927-930 (4)	3.50	3.50

Victoria Lines, Cent. A236

Designs: 2c, Fort, soldiers in front of wall. 16c, Soldiers with cannon, fort.

1997, Dec. 5

931	A236	2c multicolored	.20	.20
932	A236	16c multicolored	.90	.90

Self-government, 50th Anniv. — A237

Designs: 6c, Man looking at paper, group of people. 37c, People in line waiting to vote.

1997, Dec. 5

933	A237	6c multicolored	.35	.35
934	A237	37c multicolored	2.10	2.10

Treasures of Malta — A238

Designs: No. 935, Vest. No. 936, Portrait of a Woman, by Antoine de Favray (1706-98). No. 937, Portrait of Woman Holding Girl, by de Favray. No. 938, Early woman's costume. 26c, Valletta, city of culture.

1998, Feb. 26

935	A238	6c multicolored	.40	.40
936	A238	6c multicolored	.40	.40
937	A238	16c multicolored	.95	.95
938	A238	16c multicolored	.95	.95
		Nos. 935-938 (4)	2.70	2.70

Souvenir Sheet

Perf. 13x13½

939	A238	26c multicolored	1.75	1.75

No. 939 contains one 39x48mm stamp.

French Occupation of Malta, Bicent. — A239

Designs: No. 940, Ferdinand von Hompesch, commander of Knights of St. John. No. 941, French fleet, map. No. 942, French coming ashore. No. 943, Napoleon Bonaparte.

Wmk. 239

1998, Mar. 28 Litho. *Perf. 14*

940	A239	6c multicolored	.40	.40
941	A239	6c multicolored	.40	.40
a.		Pair, #940-941	.95	.95
942	A239	16c multicolored	.95	.95
943	A239	16c multicolored	.95	.95
a.		Pair, #942-943	2.40	2.40
		Nos. 940-943 (4)	2.70	2.70

National Festivals A240

Europa: 16c, 35c, Various boats at annual regatta.

Wmk. 354

1998, Apr. 22 Litho. *Perf. 14*

944	A240	16c multicolored	*.90*	*.90*
945	A240	35c multicolored	*2.00*	*2.00*

Intl. Year of the Ocean A241

Designs: 2c, Diver, dolphin, vert. 6c, Diver, hand holding sea urchin, vert. 16c, Diver, Jacques Cousteau (1910-97), deep sea explorer. 27c, Two divers.

Wmk. 354

1998, May 27 Litho. *Perf. 14*

946	A241	2c multicolored	.25	.25
947	A241	6c multicolored	.60	.60
948	A241	16c multicolored	1.40	1.40
949	A241	27c multicolored	2.40	2.40
		Nos. 946-949 (4)	4.65	4.65

1998 World Cup Soccer Championship, France — A242

Various soccer plays, flags from participating teams.

1998, June 10

950	A242	6c multicolored	.55	.55
951	A242	16c multicolored	1.10	1.10
952	A242	22c multicolored	1.75	1.75
a.		Souvenir sheet, #950-952	3.50	3.50
		Nos. 950-952 (3)	3.40	3.40

Anniversaries and Events — A243

1c, Intl. Maritime Organization, 50th anniv. 6c, Symbolic people, emblem, Universal Declaration of Human Rights. 11c, Cogs in wheels, Assoc. of General Retailers & Traders, 50th anniv. 19c, Roman god Mercury, Malta Chamber of Commerce, 150th anniv. 26c, Stylized planes, Air Malta, 25th anniv.

Wmk. 354

1998, Sept. 17 Litho. *Perf. 14*

953	A243	1c multicolored	.25	.25
954	A243	6c multicolored	.40	.40
955	A243	11c multicolored	.65	.65
956	A243	19c multicolored	1.25	1.25
957	A243	26c multicolored	1.60	1.60
		Nos. 953-957 (5)	4.15	4.15

Christmas A244

Paintings by Mattia Preti (1613-99): 6c, Rest on the Flight to Egypt. 6c+2c, Virgin and Child with Saints Anthony the Abbot and John the Baptist. 16c+3c, Virgin and Child with Saints Raphael, Nicholas and Gregory. 26c+3c, Virgin and Child with Saints John the Baptist and Nicholas.

Wmk. 354

1998, Nov. 19 Litho. *Perf. 14*

958	A244	6c multicolored	.40	.40
959	A244	6c +2c multi	.50	.50
960	A244	16c +3c multi	1.25	1.25
961	A244	26c +3c multi	1.75	1.75
		Nos. 958-961 (4)	3.90	3.90

Knights Hospitaller, Order of St. John of Jerusalem, 900th Anniv. — A245

2c, Fort St. Angelo. 6c, Grandmaster L'Isle Adam, vert. 16c, Grandmaster La Valette, vert. 27c, Auberge de Castille.

Wmk. 354

1999, Feb. 26 Litho. *Perf. 14*

962	A245	2c multicolored	.25	.25
963	A245	6c multicolored	.40	.40
964	A245	16c multicolored	.95	.95
965	A245	27c multicolored	1.60	1.60
		Nos. 962-965 (4)	3.20	3.20

Council of Europe, 50th Anniv. — A246

Designs: 6c, European Parliament in session. 16c, Human Rights Building.

1999, Apr. 6

966	A246	6c multicolored	.60	.60
967	A246	16c multicolored	1.40	1.40

Nature Reserves — A247

Europa: 16c, Charadrius dubius, Ghadira Nature Reserve. 35c, Alcedo atthis, Simar Nature Reserve.

Unwmk.

1999, Apr. 6 Litho. *Perf. 14*

968	A247	16c multicolored	*.90*	*.90*
969	A247	35c multicolored	*2.00*	*2.00*

UPU, 125th Anniv. — A248

UPU emblem and: a, 6c, Sailing ship, Valletta Bastions, Marsamxett Harbor. b, 16c, IBRA '99 emblem, Nuremberg, Germany. c, 22c, Philexfrance emblem, Eiffel Tower, Paris. d, 27c, Beijing '99 emblem, Beijing. e, 37c, Australia '99 emblem, Melbourne.

1999, June 2 *Perf. 13¾x14*

970	A248	Strip of 5, #a.-e.	7.50	7.50

Tourism — A249

Sun shining and: 6c, Man, woman in boat, vert. 16c, Man taking picture of family posed with Knight of Malta, vert. 22c, Man basking in sun while frying egg on stomach. 27c, Girl with flowers, man pushing woman in horse-drawn carriage. 37c, Cave man among ruins pulling luggage, reading travel guide.

Perf. 14x13¾, 13¾x14

1999, June 16

971	A249	6c multicolored	.40	.40
972	A249	16c multicolored	.95	.95
973	A249	22c multicolored	1.40	1.40
974	A249	27c multicolored	1.60	1.60
975	A249	37c multicolored	2.25	2.25
		Nos. 971-975 (5)	6.60	6.60

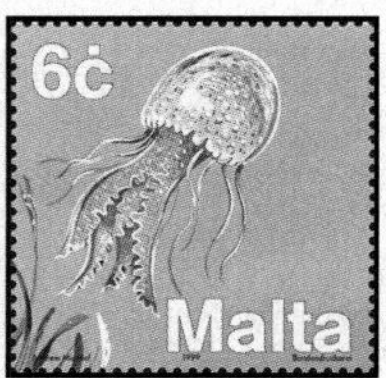

Marine Life — A250

No. 976: a, Pelagia noctiluca (jellyfish). b, Thalassoma pavo (fish with green stripes). c, Sepia officinalis (squid.) d, Sphaerechinus granularis (sea urchin). e, Epinephelus guaza (large fish). f, Diplodus vulgaris (fish with black stripes). g, Astroides calycularis (corals). h, Maia squinado (crab). i, Coris julis (fish with orange stripes). j, Octopus vulgaris (octopus). k, Charonia variegata (shell). l, Sparisoma cretense (red, green and blue fish). m, Hippocampus ramulosus (seahorse). n, Dardanus arrosor (hermit crab). o, Muraena helena (moray eel). p, Echinaster sepositus (starfish).

Perf. 13¾

1999, Aug. 25 Litho. Unwmk.

976		Sheet of 16	10.00	10.00
a.-p.		A250 6c Any single	.55	.55

Animal names are on sheet margin only.

Uprising Against France, 200th Anniv. A251

#977, Father Mikiel Scerri. #978, Sculpture. #979, French Gen. Belgrand de Vaubois. #980, British Capt. Alexander Ball.

1999, Oct. 6 Litho. *Perf. 14*

977	A251	6c multicolored	.40	.40
978	A251	6c multicolored	.40	.40
a.		Pair, #977-978	1.25	1.25
979	A251	16c multicolored	.95	.95
980	A251	16c multicolored	.95	.95
a.		Pair, #979-980	3.25	3.25
		Nos. 977-980 (4)	2.70	2.70

Crowning of Painting of Our Lady of Mellieha, Cent. — A252

1999, Oct. 6

981	A252	35c shown	2.10	2.10

Souvenir Sheet

982	A252	6c Crowned Madonna, vert.	.90	.90

Flowers A253

Designs: 2c, Pancratium maritimum. 4c, Iris pseudopumila. 6c, Narcissus tazetta. 16c, Crocus longiflorus. 25c, Ornithogalum arabicum. 46c, Tulipa sylvestris.

1999, Oct. 20 Litho. *Perf. 13¾*

983	A253	2c multi	.20	.20
984	A253	4c multi	.20	.20
985	A253	6c multi	.35	.35
986	A253	16c multi	.90	.90
987	A253	25c multi	1.40	1.40
988	A253	46c multi	2.50	2.50
		Nos. 983-988 (6)	5.55	5.55

See Nos. 1022-1027, 1061-1066, 1102-1107, 1139-1140, 1213-1214.

Christmas A254

6c, Madonna & Child. 6c+3c, Carolers. 16c+3c, Santa Claus. 26c+3c, Tree, ornament.

1999, Nov. 27

989	A254	6c multi	.40	.40
990	A254	6c + 3c multi	.55	.55
991	A254	16c + 3c multi	1.25	1.25
992	A254	26c + 3c multi	1.75	1.75
		Nos. 989-992 (4)	3.95	3.95

Republic of Malta, 25th Anniv. — A255

6c, Legislative meeting room. 11c, Chambers of House of Representatives. 16c, Central Bank of Malta. 19c, Flags, aerial view of Valletta. 26c, Computer, airplane, port facilities.

1999, Dec. 10 Litho. *Perf. 14*

993	A255	6c multi	.40	.40
994	A255	11c multi	.65	.65
995	A255	16c multi	.95	.95
996	A255	19c multi	1.25	1.25
997	A255	26c multi	1.60	1.60
		Nos. 993-997 (5)	4.85	4.85

Greetings — A256

Designs: 3c, Gift, roses. 6c, Roses, letter, picture frame. 16c, Heart, tulips. 20c, Clock, champagne bottle, glass. 22c, Roses, wedding rings.

Unwmk.

2000, Feb. 9 Litho. *Perf. 14*

998	A256	3c multi	.25	.25
999	A256	6c multi	.40	.40
1000	A256	16c multi	.95	.95
1001	A256	20c multi	1.25	1.25
1002	A256	22c multi	1.40	1.40
		Nos. 998-1002 (5)	4.25	4.25

Malta in the 20th Century — A257

Designs: 6c, Cruise ship, small boat. 16c, Festival, musicians. 22c, Family walking, view of harbor. 27c, Farm family, Victoria Citadel, Gozo.

2000, Mar. 7 *Perf. 13¾x14*

1003	A257	6c multi	.40	.40
1004	A257	16c multi	.95	.95
1005	A257	22c multi	1.40	1.40
1006	A257	27c multi	1.60	1.60
		Nos. 1003-1006 (4)	4.35	4.35

Sports A258

Designs: 6c, Soccer players, trophy. 16c, Swimmer, sailboats. 26c, Judo, shooting, runners. 37c, Soccer players.

2000, Mar. 28 *Perf. 14*

1007	A258	6c multi	.35	.35
1008	A258	16c multi	.90	.90
1009	A258	26c multi	1.50	1.50
1010	A258	37c multi	2.10	2.10
		Nos. 1007-1010 (4)	4.85	4.85

Malta Soccer Assoc., cent. (6c); 2000 Summer Olympics, Sydney (16c, 26c); European Soccer Championships (37c).

Europa, 2000
Common Design Type

2000, May 9 ***Perf. 14***
Color of Large "E"

1011 CD17 16c green *.95 .95*
1012 CD17 46c blue *2.75 2.75*

Air Transportation, Cent. — A259

#1013, D. H. 66 Hercules, 1928. #1014, Zeppelin LZ-127, 1933. #1015, Douglas DC-3 Dakota, 1949. #1016, Airbus A320.

2000, July 28
1013 A259 6c multi .40 .40
1014 A259 6c multi .40 .40
a. Pair, #1013-1014 1.25 1.25
1015 A259 16c multi .95 .95
1016 A259 16c multi .95 .95
a. Pair, #1015-1016 3.25 3.25
b. Souvenir sheet, #1013-1016 4.00 4.00
Nos. 1013-1016 (4) 2.70 2.70

Fireworks — A260

Denominations: 2c, 6c, 16c, 20c, 50c.

2000, July 19 **Litho.** ***Perf. 13¾x14***
1017-1021 A260 Set of 5 6.25 6.25

Flower Type of 1999

Designs: 1c, Helichrysum melitense. 3c, Cistus creticus. 10c, Rosa sempervirens. 12c, Cynara cardunculus. 20c, Anacamptis pyramidalis. £2, Adonis microcarpa.

2000, Sept. 13 **Litho.** ***Perf. 13¾***
1022 A253 1c multi .20 .20
1023 A253 3c multi .20 .20
1024 A253 10c multi .55 .55
1025 A253 12c multi .70 .70
1026 A253 20c multi 1.10 1.10
1027 A253 £2 multi 11.00 11.00
Nos. 1022-1027 (6) 13.75 13.75

Stampin' the Future Children's Stamp Design Contest Winners A261

Artwork by: #1028, Bettina Paris. #1029, Roxana Caruana. #1030, Jean Paul Zammit. #1031, Chiara Borg.

2000, Oct. 18 ***Perf. 14x13¾***
1028-1031 A261 6c Set of 4 1.90 1.90

See also Nos. 1250, B85.

Christmas — A262

Designs: 6c, Children, Holy Family. 6c+3c, Magi. 16c+3c, Christmas tree, Santa Claus, family. 26c, Christmas tree, church, family.

2000, Nov. 18 **Litho.** ***Perf. 14***
1032-1035 A262 Set of 4 4.25 4.25
1035a Souv. sheet, #1032-1035 4.50 4.50

Size of No. 1033: 23x27mm.

Carnival — A263

Various scenes and cartoon mascots at LL with: 6c, Horn. 11c, Guitar, vert. 16c, Drum, vert. 19c, Tambourine, vert. 27c, Flute.

No. 1041: a, 12c, Clowns (black and white photo), mascot with tambourine, b, 37c, Clowns (color photo), mascot with drum.

Perf. 13¾x14, 14x13¾
2001, Feb. 23 **Litho.**
1036-1040 A263 Set of 5 5.25 5.25

Souvenir Sheet
Perf. 13¾
1041 A263 Sheet of 2, #a-b 3.00 3.00

No. 1041 contains two 34x34mm stamps.

Lighthouses A264

Designs: 6c, Sant'lermu. 16c, Gurdan. 22c, Delimara.

2001, Mar. 21 ***Perf. 14x13¾***
1042-1044 A264 Set of 3 3.75 3.75

Paintings by Edward Caruana Dingli — A265

Denominations: 2c, 4c, 6c, 10c, 26c.

2001, Apr. 18
1045-1049 A265 Set of 5 4.00 4.00

Visit of Pope John Paul II A266

Designs: 6c, Nazju Falzon, Gorg Preca, and Adeodata Pisani, Maltese beatified by Pope. 16c, Pope, statue.
75c, Falzon, Preca, Pisani and Pope.

2001, May 4 ***Perf. 14***
1050-1051 A266 Set of 2 2.25 2.25

Souvenir Sheet
1052 A266 75c multi 4.50 4.50

Europa A267

Designs: 16c, Discoglossus pictus. 46c, Sympetrum fonscolombii.

2001, May 23 **Litho.** ***Perf. 14x14¼***
1053-1054 A267 Set of 2 *3.50 3.50*

Birds — A268

No. 1055: a, Larus cachinnans. b, Falco tinnunculus. c, Oriolus oriolus, d, Fringilla coelebs. e, Monticola solitarius. f, Merops apiaster. g, Hirundo rustica. h, Passer hispaniolensis. i, Sylvia conspicillata. j, Streptopelia turtur. k, Anas acuta. l, Ixobrychus minutus. m, Scolopax rusticola. n, Asio flammeus. o, Vanellus vanellus. p, Gallinula chloropus.

2001, June 22 **Litho.** ***Perf. 13¾***
1055 A268 6c Sheet of 16, #a-p 8.50 8.50

Musical Instruments A269

Designs: 1c, Whistle flute. 3c, Reed pipe. 14c, Maltese bagpipe. 20c, Friction drum. 25c, Frame drum.

2001, Aug. 22 **Litho.** ***Perf. 13¾***
1056-1060 A269 Set of 5 3.75 3.75

Flower Type of 1999

Designs: 5c, Papaver rhoeas. 11c, Silene colorata. 19c, Anthemis arvensis. 27c, Borago officinalis. 50c, Chrysanthemum coronarium. £1, Malva sylvestris.

2001, Sept. 19
1061-1066 A253 Set of 6 12.00 12.00

See No. 1269A.

Dogs A270

Designs: 6c, Kelb tal-Fenek. 16c, Kelb tal-Kacca. 19c, Maltese. 35c, Kelb tal-But.

2001, Oct. 20 **Litho.** ***Perf. 14***
1067-1070 A270 Set of 4 5.25 5.25

Worldwide Fund for Nature (WWF) — A271

Seahorses: No. 1071, 6c, Hippocampus guttulatus. No. 1072, 6c, Hippocampus hippocampus. No. 1073, 16c, Hippocampus guttulatus, diff. No. 1074, 16c, Hippocampus hippocampus, diff.

2002 **Litho.** ***Perf. 14¼x14***
1071-1074 A271 Set of 4 3.50 3.50

Antique Furniture — A272

Designs: 2c, Credenza. 4c, Bureau, vert. 11c, Table, vert. 26c, Armoire, vert. 60c, Credenza, diff.

2002, Mar. 27 **Litho.** ***Perf. 14***
1075-1079 A272 Set of 5 5.75 5.75

Europa — A273

2002, May 9 **Litho.** ***Perf. 14***
1080 A273 16c multi *.95 .95*

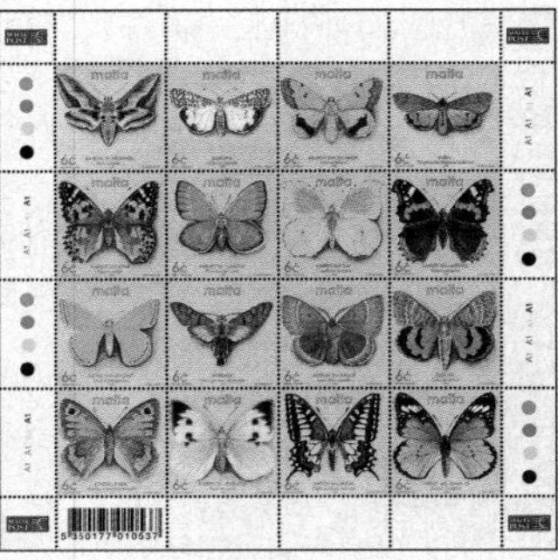
Butterflies and Moths — A274

No. 1081: a, Hyles sammuii. b, Utetheisa pulchella. c, Ophiusa tirhaca. d, Phragmatobia fulginosa melitensis. e, Vanessa cardui. f, Polyommatus icarus. g, Gonepteryx cleopatra. h, Vanessa atalanta. i, Eucrostes indigenata. j, Macroglossum stellatarum. k, Lasiocampa quercus. l, Catoeala elocata. m, Maniola jurtina hyperhispulla. n, Pieris brassicae. o, Papilio machaon melitensis. p, Danaus chrysippus.

2002, June ***Perf. 13¾***
1081 A274 6c Sheet of 16, #a-p 7.00 7.00

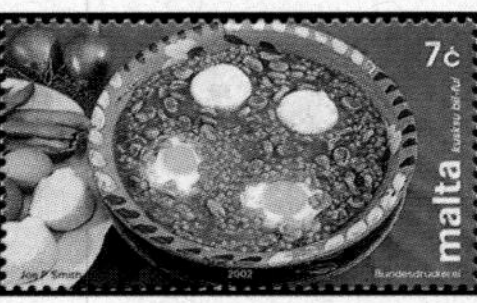

Maltese Cuisine A275

Designs: 7c, Kusksu bil-ful. 12c, Qaqocc mimli. 16c, Lampuki. 27c, Qaghqa tal-kavatelli. 75c, Stuffat tal-fenek.

2002, Aug. 13 **Litho.** ***Perf. 14***
1082-1085 A275 Set of 4 4.50 4.50

Souvenir Sheet
1086 A275 75c multi 6.25 6.25

Succulent Plants — A276

Designs: 1c, Yavia cryptocarpa. 7c, Aztekium hintonii, vert. 28c, Pseudolithos migiurtinus. 37c, Pierrebraunia brauniorum, vert. 76c, Euphorbia turbiniformis.

2002, Sept. 25
1087-1091 A276 Set of 5 8.75 8.75

Famous Men — A277

Designs: 3c, Adrian Dingli (1817-1900), legislator. 7c, Oreste Kirkop (1923-98), opera singer. 15c, Father Athanasius Kircher (1602-80), vulcanologist. 35c, Father Saverio Cassar (1746-1805), Gozo Uprising leader. 50c, Emmanuele Vitale (1759-1802), commander in uprising against the French.

2002, Oct. 18 **Litho.** ***Perf. 14***
1092-1096 A277 Set of 5 6.25 6.25

Christmas A278

Designs: 7c, Mary and Joseph in donkey cart. 16c, Angels, Magi, Holy Family in bus. 22c, Holy Family and Angels on boat. 37c, Shepherds in field, Holy family in horse-drawn carriage. 75c, Angel, Magi, Holy Family and animals on galley.

2002, Nov. 20
1097-1101 A278 Set of 5 8.75 8.75

Flower Type of 1999

Designs: 7c, Vitex agnus-castus. 22c, Spartium junceum. 28c, Crataegus azalorus. 37c, Cercis siliquastrum. 45c, Myrtus communis. 76c, Pistacia lentiscus.

2003, Jan. 30 ***Perf. 13¾***

1102 A253 7c multi	.40	.40
1103 A253 22c multi	1.25	1.25
1104 A253 28c multi	1.60	1.60
1105 A253 37c multi	2.25	2.25
1106 A253 45c multi	2.75	2.75
1107 A253 76c multi	4.50	4.50
Nos. 1102-1107 (6)	12.75	12.75

Automobiles — A279

Designs: 2c, 1965 Vanden Plas Princess. 7c, 1948 Allard "M" Type. 10c, 1904 Cadillac Model B. 26c, 1936 Fiat Cinquecento Model A Topolino. 35c, 1965 Ford Anglia Super.

2003, Feb. 26 **Litho.** ***Perf. 14***
1108-1112 A279 Set of 5 4.50 4.50

Military Architecture — A280

Designs: 1c, Fort St. Elmo. 4c, Rinella Battery. 11c, Fort St. Angelo. 16c, Reserve Post R15. 44c, Fort Tigné.

2003, Mar. 21 **Litho.** ***Perf. 14***
1113-1117 A280 Set of 5 4.50 4.50

Martyrdom of St. George, 1700th Anniv. — A281

Various paintings depicting St. George: 3c, 7c, 14c, 19c, 27c.

2003, Apr. 23
1118-1122 A281 Set of 5 3.75 3.75

Europa — A282

Poster art: 16c, Cisk Beer. 46c, 1939 Carnival.

2003, May 9
1123-1124 A282 Set of 2 *3.50 3.50*

Games of Small European States A283

Designs: 25c, Track and field. 50c, Shooting. 75c, Volleyball. £3, Swimming.

2003, May 21 **Litho.** ***Perf. 14x14¼***
1125-1128 A283 Set of 4 25.00 25.00

Coronation of Queen Elizabeth II, 50th Anniv. — A284

Queen Elizabeth II: 12c, With woman. 15c, Seated in limousine. 22c, With Prince Philip, reading book. 60c, With Prince Philip, receiving book from man.
£1, Queen and crowd of people.

2003, June 3
1129-1132 A284 Set of 4 6.00 6.00

Souvenir Sheet

1133 A284 £1 multi 6.75 6.75

Souvenir Sheet

Valletta Bastions — A285

2003, July 1 **Litho.** ***Perf. 14x13¾***
1134 A285 £1.50 multi + 4 labels 9.00 9.00

Elton John concert, July 6, 2003.

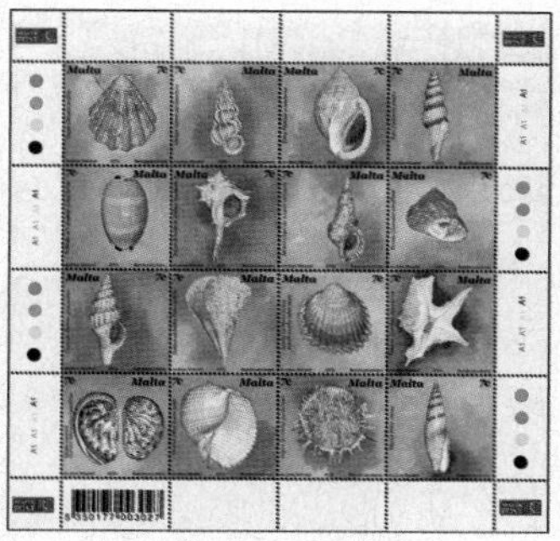

Shells — A286

No. 1135: a, Chlamys pesfelis. b, Gyroscala lamellosa. c, Phalium granulatum. d, Fusiturris similis. e, Luria lurida. f, Bolinus brandaris. g, Charonia tritonis variegata. h, Clanculus corallinus. i, Fusinus syracusanus. j, Pinna nobilis. k, Acanthocardia tuberculata. l, Aporrhais pespelcani. m, Haliotis tuberculata lamellosa. n, Tonna galea. o, Spondylus gaederopus. p, Mitra zonata.

2003, Aug. 20 **Litho.** ***Perf. 13¾***
1135 A286 7c Sheet of 16, #a-p 7.50 7.50

Sailboats A287

Designs: 8c, Malta-Syracuse Race. 22c, Middle Sea Race, vert. 35c, Royal Malta Yacht Club, vert.

2003, Sept. 30 **Litho.** ***Perf. 14***
1136-1138 A287 Set of 3 3.75 3.75

Flower Type of 1999

Designs: 7c, Vitex agnus-castus.16c, Crocus longiflorus.

Serpentine Die Cut 12½ on 2 or 3 Sides

2003, Oct. 22

Booklet Stamps
Self-Adhesive
Size: 23x23mm

1139 A253 7c multi	.40	.40
a. Booklet pane of 12	5.00	
1140 A253 16c multi	.90	.90
a. Booklet pane of 6	5.50	

Windmills — A288

Designs: 11c, Is-Sur ta'San Mikiel, Valletta. 27c, Ta'Kola, Xaghra, vert. 45c, Tax-Xarolla, Zurrieq, vert.

2003, Oct. 29 ***Perf. 14***
1141-1143 A288 Set of 3 5.25 5.25

Christmas — A289

Designs: 7c, The Annunciation, vert. 16c, Holy Family, vert. 22c, Adoration of the Magi. 50c, Adoration of the Magi.

2003, Nov. 12
1144-1147 A289 Set of 4 6.75 6.75

Letter Boxes — A290

Boxes from era of: 1c, Queen Victoria. 16c, King Edward VII. 22c, King George V, King George VI. 37c, Queen Elizabeth II. 76c, Independent Malta (Malta Post).

2004, Mar. 12
1148-1152 A290 Set of 5 10.50 10.50

Cats — A291

Various cats with denominations and country name in: 7c, Golden brown. 27c, Dark brown. 28c, Lilac. 50c, Red brown. 60c, Green.

2004, Mar. 26 ***Perf. 13¾***
1153-1157 A291 Set of 5 10.00 10.00

Souvenir Sheet

Salesians in Malta, Cent. — A292

2004, Apr. 7 ***Perf. 14***
1158 A292 75c multi 4.25 4.25

Fauna — A293

No. 1159: a, Pipistrellus pygmaeus. b, Myotis blythi punicus. c, Mustela nivalis. d, Atelerix algirus fallax. e, Chamaeleo chamaeleon. f, Crocidura sicula. g, Chalcides ocellatus. h, Podarcis filfolensis filfolensis. i, Tarentola mauritanica. j, Hemidactylus turcicus. k, Elaphe situla. l, Coluber viridiflavus. m, Delphinus delphis. n, Stenella coeruleoalba. o, Monachus monachus. p, Chelonia mydas.

2004, Apr. 21 ***Perf. 13¾***
1159 A293 16c Sheet of 16, #a-p 14.50 14.50

Admission to European Union — A294

Stars, map of Europe and: 16c, Flags of newly-admitted countries. 28c, Officials signing treaty.

2004, May 1 ***Perf. 14***
1160-1161 A294 Set of 2 2.50 2.50

Europa — A295

Designs: 16c, Youths jumping into water. 51c, People at archaeological site.

2004, May 19 ***Perf. 13¾x14***
1162-1163 A295 Set of 2 *3.75 3.75*

Wayside Chapels A296

Designs: 3c, Lunzjata-Hal Milliere, Zurrieq. 7c, San Basilju, Mqabba. 39c, San Cir, Rabat. 48c, Santa Lucija, Mtarfa. 66c, Ta' Santa Marija, Kemmuna.

2004, June 16 **Litho.** ***Perf. 14***
1164-1168 A296 Set of 5 10.50 10.50

Trams A297

Designs: 19c, Side view of tram. 37c, Tram and conductor (22x40mm). 50c, Ticket (22x40mm). 75c, Tram and archway.

Perf. 13¾, 14 (37c, 50c)
2004, July 14
1169-1172 A297 Set of 4 10.50 10.50

2004 Summer Olympics, Athens A298

Designs: 11c, Discus thrower. 16c, Doric column, olive wreath. 76c, Javelin thrower.

Perf. 14¼
2004, Aug. 13 **Litho.** **Unwmk.**
1173-1175 A298 Set of 3 6.00 6.00

Religious Festivals — A299

Designs: 5c, Ascension Day. 15c, St. Gregory's Day. 27c, Pilgrimage on First Sunday in Lent. 51c, St. Martin's Day, vert. £1, Feast of Sts. Peter and Paul, vert.

Perf. 14x14¼, 14¼x14
2004, Sept. 15 **Wmk. 354**
1176-1180 A299 Set of 5 11.50 11.50

Works of Art A300

Designs: 2c, Church of St. Mary, Attard. 20c, Mdina Cathedral organ, music by Benignon Zerafa, vert. 57c, Statue of St. Agatha, vert. 62c, Books, illustration for poem "The Turkish Galleon," by Gian Antonio Vassallo, vert.
72c, Icon of St. Paul, vert.

Perf. 14x14¼, 14¼x14
2004, Oct. 13 **Litho.** **Wmk. 354**
1181-1184 A300 Set of 4 10.50 10.50

Souvenir Sheet

1185 A300 72c multi 5.00 5.00

Christmas — A301

Various effigies of Infant Jesus: 7c, 16c, 22c, 50c. Nos. 1187-1189 vert.

Perf. 14x14¼, 14¼x14
2004, Nov. 10 **Litho.** **Wmk. 354**
1186-1189 A301 Set of 4 5.75 5.75

Historic Maps A302

Designs: 1c, Map of Malta by Abbé Jean Quintin, 1536. 12c, Map of Malta by Antonio Lafreri, 1551. 37c, Fresco map of Malta, by Matteo Perez d'Aleccio, 1565. £1.02, Map of Gozo, Comino, Cominotto and Marfa Peninsula, by Fr. Luigi Bartolo, 1745.

Wmk. 354
2005, Jan. 19 **Litho.** ***Perf. 14***
1190-1193 A302 Set of 4 9.25 9.25

Rotary International, Cent. — A303

Rotary emblem and: 27c, Dar il-Kaptan Home, Mtarfa, woman, man. 76c, Map of Malta.

Perf. 14x14¼
2005, Feb. 23 **Litho.** **Wmk. 354**
1194-1195 A303 Set of 2 6.50 6.50

Hans Christian Andersen (1805-75), Author A304

Paper Cutting by Andersen, Scissors — A305

Designs: 60c, Pen, inkwell, illustration of duckling, manuscript handwritten by Andersen. 75c, Andersen's drawing of Casino dell'Orlogio, Rome, and boots.

Perf. 14x13¾
2005, Mar. 3 **Litho.** **Wmk. 354**
1196 A304 7c gray & black .45 .45
1197 A305 22c blue & black 1.40 1.40
1198 A305 60c multi 3.75 3.75
1199 A305 75c multi 4.75 4.75
Nos. 1196-1199 (4) 10.35 10.35

See Denmark Nos. 1323-1326.

Pope John Paul II (1920-2005) A306

2005, Apr. 15 ***Perf. 14***
1200 A306 51c multi 3.25 3.25

Miniature Sheet

Insects — A307

No. 1201: a, Coccinella septempunctata. b, Chrysoperla carnea. c, Apis mellifera. d, Crocothermis erythraea. e, Anax imperator. f, Lampyris pallida. g, Henosepilachna elaterii. h, Forficula decipiens. i, Mantis religiosa. j, Eumenes lunulatus. k, Cerambyx cerdo. l, Gryllus bimaculatus. m, Xylocopa violacea. n, Cicada orni. o, Acrida ungarica. p, Oryctes nasicornis.

2005, Apr. 20 ***Perf. 14¼***
1201 A307 16c Sheet of 16, #a-p 15.50 15.50

Europa — A308

Designs: 16c, Stuffed peppers, zucchini and eggplant. 51c, Fried rabbit in wine and garlic.

2005, May 9 ***Perf. 14¼x14***
1202-1203 A308 Set of 2 *4.00 4.00*

Paintings Depicting St. Catherine — A309

Designs: No. 1204, 28c, The Beheading of St. Catherine, by unknown artist. No. 1205, 28c, The Martyrdom of St. Catherine, by Mattia Preti, vert. No. 1206, 45c, St. Catherine Disputing the Philosophers, by Francesco Zahra. No. 1207, 45c, Mystic Marriage, by Sahra, vert.

Perf. 14x14¼, 14¼x14
2005, June 15 **Litho.** **Wmk. 354**
1204-1207 A309 Set of 4 8.25 8.25

Famous People A310

Designs: 3c, Monsignor Michael Azzopardi (1910-87), religious educator. 19c, Egidio Lapira (1897-1970), dental surgeon. 20c, Petition of Guzeppi Callus (1505-61), doctor executed for taxation opposition. 46c, Hand and quill pen of Geronimo Matteo Abos (1715-60), composer. 76c, Gio Francesco Abela (1592-1655), historian, ambassador.

Wmk. 354
2005, July 13 **Litho.** ***Perf. 14¼***
1208-1212 A310 Set of 5 9.50 9.50

Flower Type of 1999 Redrawn

Design: 7c, Vitex agnus-castus. 16c, Crocus longiflorus.

2005 **Litho.** ***Perf. 14¼***
1213 A253 7c multi + label .40 .40
1214 A253 16c multi + label .95 .95

Nos. 1213-1214 have "2005" year date and "Printex Ltd" inscription at lower right. Additionally, No. 1213 has wider distance between denomination and country name than No. 1102, and No. 1214 has denomination and country name in a different font than No. 986. Nos. 1213-1214 were issued in sheets of 10 stamps and 10 labels. Labels could be personalized for an additional fee.

Horses and Mules at Work A311

Designs: 11c, Horse-drawn hearse. 15c, Mule pulling plow. 62c, Mule at grindstone. 66c, Horse pulling cart.

Perf. 14x14¼
2005, Aug. 19 **Litho.** **Wmk. 354**
1215-1218 A311 Set of 4 9.00 9.00

End of World War II, 60th Anniv. A312

Scenes from Battle of Malta: 2c, Civilians on food line. 5c, Royal Navy ships under attack. 25c, Anti-aircraft gunners. 51c, Aviators and planes. £1, Tanker "Ohio."

2005, Sept. 23
1219-1223 A312 Set of 5 10.50 10.50

Christmas — A313

Mosaics of paintings by Envin Cremona from National Sanctuary of Our Lady of Ta' Pinu, Gozo: 7c, Nativity. 16c, Annunciation, vert. 22c, Adoration of the Magi. 50c, Flight into Egypt (68x27mm).

Perf. 14¼, 13¾x14 (50c)
2005, Oct. 12 Litho. Wmk. 354
1224-1227 A313 Set of 4 5.50 5.50

Souvenir Sheets

Commonwealth Heads of Governments Meeting — A314

Flags of Malta, British Commonwealth and: 14c, Commonwealth Heads of Government flag. 28c, Doves. 37c, Maltese cross. 75c, People.

Perf. 14x14¼
2005, Nov. 23 Litho. Wmk. 354
1228-1231 A314 Set of 4 8.50 8.50

Souvenir Sheet

Europa Stamps, 50th Anniv. — A315

No. 1232: a, 5c, #677. b, 13c, #628. c, 23c, #540. d, 24c, #738.

2006, Jan. 3 ***Perf. 13¾x14***
1232 A315 Sheet of 4, #a-d 3.75 3.75

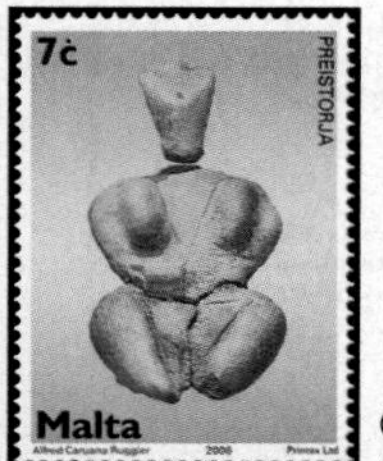

Ceramics A316

Designs: 7c, Neolithic terra-cotta female figurine. 16c, Roman terra-cotta head. 28c, Terra-cotta oil lamp holder. 37c, Sicilian maiolica plate. 60c, Stylized figure in traditional Maltese costume, by Ianni Bonnici.

Wmk. 354
2006, Feb. 25 Litho. ***Perf. 14¼***
1233-1237 A316 Set of 5 8.25 8.25

Miniature Sheet

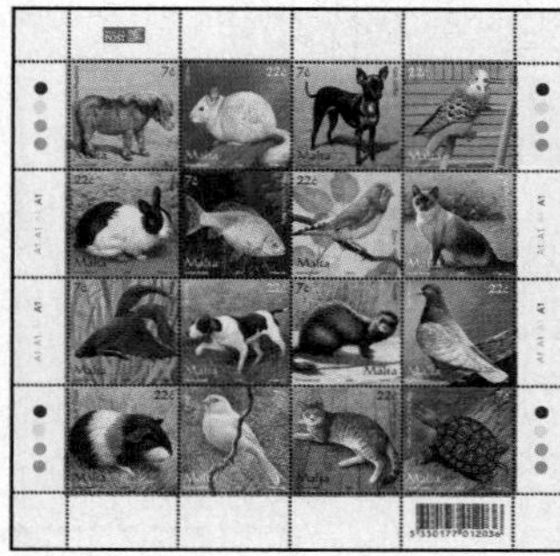

Pets — A317

No. 1238: a, Shetland pony. b, Chihuahua. c, Goldfish. d, Siamese cat. e, Siamese fighting fish. f, Ferret. g, Canary. h, Turtle. i, Chinchilla. j, Parakeet. k, Rabbit. l, Zebra finch. m, Pointer. n, Pigeon. o, Guinea pig. p, House cat.

Wmk. 354
2006, Mar. 14 Litho. ***Perf. 14¼***
1238 A317 Sheet of 16 13.50 13.50
a.-h. 7c Any single .40 .40
i.-p. 22c Any single 1.25 1.25

Traditional Holy Week Celebrations A318

Designs: 7c, Men carrying crosses. 15c, Men carrying crucifixion scene. 22c, Float. 27c, Men pulling statue of Jesus. 82c, Decorated altar.

2006, Apr. 12 ***Perf. 14¼x14***
1239-1243 A318 Set of 5 9.25 9.25

Europa A319

Designs: 16c, Shown. 51c, Stick figures, diff. (28x41mm).

Perf. 14¼, 14¼x14 (51c)
2006, May 9
1244-1245 A319 Set of 2 4.00 4.00

2006 World Cup Soccer Championships, Germany A320

Designs: 7c, Bobby Charlton. 16c, Pelé. 27c, Franz Beckenbauer. 76c, Dino Zoff.

2006, June 2 ***Perf. 14¼x14***
1246-1249 A320 Set of 4 7.75 7.75
1249a Souvenir sheet, #1246-1249 7.75 7.75

Stampin' The Future Type of 2000 Souvenir Sheet

2006, June 5 ***Perf. 14***
1250 A261 £1.50 Like #1028 9.00 9.00

Ten percent of the sale went to the Rainforest Foundation.

Naval Vessels A321

Designs: 8c, Gran Carraca di Rodi. 29c, Guillaume Tell (HMS Malta). 51c, USS Constitution. 76c, HMS Dreadnought. £1, Slava and USS Belknap.

Wmk. 354
2006, Aug. 18 Litho. ***Perf. 14¼***
1251-1255 A321 Set of 5 16.00 16.00

Greetings A322

Inscriptions: 8c, Happy Birthday. 16c, Happy Anniversary. 27c, Congratulations. 37c, Best Wishes.

2006, Sept. 18
1256-1259 A322 Set of 4 5.25 5.25

Castles and Towers A323

Designs: 7c, Wignacourt Tower. 16c, Verdala Castle. 27c, San Lucjan Tower. 37c, Kemmuna Tower. £1, Selmun Castle.

Perf. 14x14¼
2006, Sept. 29 Litho. Wmk. 354
1260-1264 A323 Set of 5 11.00 11.00

Christmas — A324

Designs: 8c, Paolino Vassallo (1856-1923), composer of "Inno per Natale," Nativity. 16c, Carmelo Pace (1906-93), composer of "They Heard the Angels," Magi on camels. 22c, Paul Nani (1906-86), composer of "Maltese Christmas," angels. 27c, Carlo Diacono (1876-1942), composer of "Notte di Natale," shepherds and angel.

50c, Wolfgang Amadeus Mozart (1756-91), composer of "Alma Dei Creatoris."

2006, Nov. 6 ***Perf. 14¼***
1265-1268 A324 Set of 4 4.50 4.50

Souvenir Sheet
Perf. 13¾
1269 A324 50c multi 3.25 3.25

No. 1269 contains one 40x30mm stamp.

Flower Type of 1999 Redrawn

2006 Litho. Wmk. 354 ***Perf. 14¼***
1269A A253 1c Like #1022 .20 .20

No. 1269A has a "2006" year date and "Printex Ltd." inscription at lower right. Additionally, the country name has a different font than No. 1022, with the lines in the lettering being of equal thickness throughout the letter on No. 1269A. Other differences in the vignette exist.

Due to the scheduled conversion to the euro on Jan. 1, 2008, Nos. 1270-1274 and all stamps issued in 2007 will show denominations in pounds and the not-yet-circulating euros.

Crafts A325

Designs: 8c, Wrought iron window guard, blacksmith and anvil. 16c, Glass ornamental objects, glassblower. 22c, Filigree pendant, silversmith. 37c, Pottery, potter. 60c, Reed baskets, basket maker.

2006, Dec. 29 ***Perf. 14¼***
1270-1274 A325 Set of 5 8.75 8.75

Sculptures from 3000-2500 B.C. — A326

Designs: 15c, Human head. 29c, Animals, horiz. 60c, Spirals, horiz. £1.50, Headless nude female.

Wmk. 354
2007, Feb. 28 Litho. ***Perf. 14¼***
1275-1278 A326 Set of 4 16.00 16.00

Miniature Sheet

Fruit — A327

No. 1279: a, Opuntia ficus-indica (prickly pears). b, Viris vinifera (grapes). c, Eriobotrya japonica (loquats). d, Morus nigra (black mulberries). e, Ficus carica (figs). f, Citrus limonum (lemons). g, Pyrus communis (pear). h, Prunus persica (peaches). i, Punica granatum (pomegranates). j, Prunus salicina (plums). k, Citrullus vulgaris (watermelons). l, Citrus sinensis (orange). m, Olea europaea (olives). n, Lycopersicon esculentum (tomatoes). o, Malus domestica (apples). p, Cucumis melo (cantaloupe).

2007, Apr. 16
1279 A327 8c Sheet of 16, #a-p 8.00 8.00

Balconies
A328

Designs: 8c, Wrought iron balcony. 22c, Stone balcony. 27c, Balustraded balcony, National Library. 29c, Closed wooden balcony. 46c, Art Deco balcony by Silvio Mercieca.

51c, Ornamented balcony, Hostel de Verdelin, Valletta, horiz.

Wmk. 354

2007, Apr. 28 Litho. ***Perf. 14¼***

1280-1284 A328 Set of 5 8.50 8.50

Souvenir Sheet

Perf. 13¾

1285 A328 51c multi 3.25 3.25

No. 1285 contains one 37x28mm stamp.

Europa
A329

Emblems of Scout Association of Malta, Scouting Centenary and: 16c, Lord Robert Baden-Powell. 51c, Maltese scouts at 1957 Jamboree.

2007, May 9 ***Perf. 14¼***

1286-1287 A329 Set of 2 4.25 4.25

Canonization of St. George Preca (1880-1962)
A330

Background color: 8c, Blue. £1, Orange.

Wmk. 354

2007, May 28 Litho. ***Perf. 14¼***

1288-1289 A330 Set of 2 6.75 6.75

Toys — A331

Photographs of children and: 2c, Rocking horse, tricycle, car. 3c, Baby carriage, drums and tops. 16c, Boats, beach pails and shovel. 22c, Dolls. 50c, Truck, motorcycle and race car.

2007, July 11 ***Perf. 14¼x14***

1290-1294 A331 Set of 5 6.00 6.00

Paintings by Caravaggio — A332

Designs: 5c, St. Jerome. 29c, The Beheading of St. John the Baptist (48x40mm). £2, The Beheading of St. John the Baptist, vert.

2007, July 20 ***Perf. 14¼***

1295-1296 A332 Set of 2 2.25 2.25

Souvenir Sheet

1297 A332 £2 multi 13.00 13.00

Arrival of Caravaggio on Malta, 400th anniv.

Motorcycles — A333

Designs: 1c, 1954 Royal Enfield. 16c, 1941 Matchless G3/L. 27c, 1903 Minerva. 50c, 1965 Triumph Speed Twin.

Perf. 14x14¼

2007, Sept. 12 Litho. Wmk. 354

1298-1301 A333 Set of 4 6.25 6.25

Greetings Stamps
A334

2007, Sept. 28 ***Perf. 14¼***

1302 A334 8c Hearts .55 .55
 a. Sheet of 5 + 5 labels 13.50 13.50
1303 A334 8c Stars .55 .55
 a. Sheet of 5 + 5 labels 13.50 13.50
1304 A334 8c Roses .55 .55
 a. Sheet of 5 + 5 labels 13.50 13.50
1305 A334 8c Balloons .55 .55
 a. Sheet of 5 + 5 labels 13.50 13.50
1306 A334 8c Champagne flutes .55 .55
 a. Sheet of 5 + 5 labels 13.50 13.50
1307 A334 8c Teddy bears .55 .55
 a. Sheet of 5 + 5 labels 13.50 13.50
 Nos. 1302-1307 (6) 3.30 3.30

Labels on Nos. 1302a-1307a were personalizable, with full sheets each selling for £2, with a minimum purchase of two sheets of any stamp.

Paintings by John Martin Borg
A335

Designs: 11c, Mdina Skyline. 16c, Qrendi. 37c, Vittoriosa Waterfront. 46c, Mgarr Harbor, Gozo. 76c, Xlendi Bay, Gozo.

2007, Oct. 1 ***Perf. 14¼***

1308-1312 A335 Set of 5 12.50 12.50

Fruit Type of 2007

Souvenir Sheet

2007, Oct. 18

1313 A327 75c Like #1279m 5.00 5.00

National Tree Planting Weekend. An unspecified portion of the proceeds of the sale went to the 34U Campaign.

Bands
A336

Various bands: 4c, 15c, 21c, 22c, £1.

2007, Nov. 13

1314-1318 A336 Set of 5 11.00 11.00

Christmas
A337

Maltese arms and nave paintings in St. Andrew's Church, Luqa, by Giuseppe Calì: 8c, Madonna and Child. 16c, Holy Family with Women and Young Girl. 21c, Infant Jesus and Young Girl.

2007, Nov. 20

1319-1321 A337 Set of 3 3.50 3.50

See Vatican City Nos. 1370-1372.

Youth Soccer Association, 25th Anniv. — A338

Society of Christian Doctrine Museum, Cent. — A339

Religious Figures — A340

Treaty of Rome, 50th Anniv. — A341

Designs: 16c, Monsignor Frangisk Bonnici (1852-1905), founder of St. Joseph Institute, Hamrun. 43c, Father Manwel Magri (1851-1907), ethnographer and archaeologist. 86c, Carolina Cauchi (1824-1907), founder of Dominican Sisters of Malta.

Wmk. 354

2007, Dec. 1 Litho. ***Perf. 14¼***

1322 A338 4m multi .20 .20
1323 A339 9c multi .60 .60
1324 A340 16c multi 1.10 1.10
1325 A340 43c multi 3.00 3.00
1326 A340 86c multi 6.00 6.00
 Nos. 1322-1326 (5) 10.90 10.90

Souvenir Sheet

Perf. 13¾

1327 A341 76c multi 5.25 5.25

No. 1327 contains one 40x30mm stamp.

Souvenir Sheet

Obverse and Reverse of Maltese Pound Coin — A342

Wmk. 354

2007, Dec. 31 Litho. ***Perf. 14¼***

1328 A342 £1 multi 7.00 7.00

Last day of use of pound currency.

100 Cents = 1 Euro

Souvenir Sheet

Introduction of Euro Currency — A343

No. 1329: a, Statue of Aphrodite, map of Cyprus. b, Sleeping Lady statue.

Wmk. 354

2008, Jan. 1 Litho. ***Perf. 14¼***

1329 A343 €1 Sheet of 2, #a-b 6.00 6.00

See Cyprus No. 1088.

Souvenir Sheet

Obverse and Reverse of Maltese Euro Coin — A344

2008, Jan. 1

1330 A344 €1 multi 3.00 3.00

Door Knockers
A345

Various door knockers with background color of: 26c, Blue. 51c, Red. 63c, Brown. €1.77, Green.

2008, Mar. 5 ***Perf. 14¼x14***

1331-1334 A345 Set of 4 9.75 9.75

2008 Summer Olympics, Beijing — A346

Designs: 5c, Shooting. 12c, Swimming. €1.57, Running.

2008, Mar. 7		*Perf. 14x14¼*	
1335-1337 A346	Set of 3	5.50	5.50

Europa — A347

Mail room, postman with bicycle in: 37c, Sepia. €1.19, Black.

Wmk. 354

2008, May 9	**Litho.**	*Perf. 14¼*	
1338-1339 A347	Set of 2	5.00	5.00

Birth of St. Paul, 2000th Anniv. — A348

Statues depicting St. Paul from: 19c, Conversion of St. Paul Church, Safi. 68c, St. Paul's Shipwreck Church, Munxar. €1.08, St. Paul's Shipwreck Church, Rabat.
€3, St. Paul's Shipwreck Church, Valletta.

2008, June 28			
1340-1342 A348	Set of 3	6.25	6.25

Souvenir Sheet

1343 A348	€3 multi	9.50	9.50

Intl. Year of Planet Earth A349

Emblem and: 7c, Sand dune. 86c, Tree in field. €1, Earth. €1.77, Sea coast.

Wmk. 354

2008, Aug. 11	**Litho.**	*Perf. 14¼*	
1344-1347 A349	Set of 4	11.00	11.00

Cruise Liners A350

Designs: 63c, MSC Musica. €1.16, M.S. Voyager of the Seas. €1.40, M. S. Westerdam. €3, RMS Queen Elizabeth 2.

Perf. 14x14¼

2008, Nov. 18	**Litho.**	**Wmk. 354**	
1348-1351 A350	Set of 4	16.00	16.00

Christmas — A351

Paintings: 19c, Madonna and Child with the Infant St. John the Baptist, by Francesco Trevisani. 26c, Nativity, by Master Alberto. 37c, Virgin and Child with the Infant St. John the Baptist, by Carlo Maratta.

2008, Nov. 27		*Perf. 14¼*	
1352-1354 A351	Set of 3	2.10	2.10

SEMI-POSTAL STAMPS

All semi-postal issues are for Christmas.

Catalogue values for unused stamps in this section are for Never Hinged items.

Two Peasants with Tambourine and Bagpipe SP1

Star of Bethlehem and: 5p+1p, Angels with Trumpet and Harp, Star of Bethlehem and Mdina Cathedral. 1sh6p+3p, Choir boys singing Christmas carols.
The background of the 3 stamps together shows the Cathedral of Mdina, Malta, and surrounding countryside.

Wmk. 354

1969, Nov. 8	**Litho.**	*Perf. 12½*	
B1 SP1	1p +1p multi	.20	.20
B2 SP1	5p +1p multi	.20	.20
B3 SP1	1sh6p +3p multi	.20	*.30*
a.	Triptych, #B1-B3	.50	.50
	Nos. B1-B3 (3)	.60	.70

Nos. B1-B3 were printed each in sheets of 60, and in sheets containing 20 triptychs.

Christmas Eve Procession — SP2

10p+2p, Nativity & Cathedral. 1sh6p+3p, Adoration of the Shepherds & Mdina Cathedral.

1970, Nov. 7	**Photo.**	*Perf. 14x13½*	
B4 SP2	1p +½p multi	.20	.20
B5 SP2	10p +2p multi	.20	.20
B6 SP2	1sh6p +3p multi	.30	*.45*
	Nos. B4-B6 (3)	.70	*.85*

Surtax for child welfare organizations.

Angel — SP3

#B8, Madonna & Child. #B9, Shepherd.

1971, Nov. 8		*Perf. 14*	
B7 SP3	1p +½p multi	.20	.20
B8 SP3	10p +2p multi	.25	.25
B9 SP3	1sh6p +3p multi	.40	.40
a.	Souv. sheet, #B7-B9, perf. 15	1.00	*1.25*
	Nos. B7-B9 (3)	.85	.85

1972, Dec.	**Litho.**	*Perf. 13½*	

Designs: 3c+1c, Angel playing tambourine. 7c5m+1c5m, Angel singing.

B10 SP3	8m +2m dk gray & gold	.20	.20
B11 SP3	3c +1c dk purple & gold	.20	.20
B12 SP3	7c5m +1c5m slate & gold	.50	*.50*
a.	Souvenir sheet of 3, #B10-B12	2.00	*2.50*
	Nos. B10-B12 (3)	.90	.90

1973, Nov. 10	**Litho.**	*Perf. 13½*	

8m+2m, Singers, organ pipes. 3c+1c, Virgin & Child with star. 7c5m+1c5m, Star, candles, buildings, tambourine.

B13 SP3	8m +2m multi	.20	.20
B14 SP3	3c +1c multi	.30	.30
B15 SP3	7c5m +1c5m multi	.80	.80
a.	Souvenir sheet of 3, #B13-B15	5.00	*6.00*
	Nos. B13-B15 (3)	1.30	1.30
	Nos. B7-B15 (9)	3.05	3.05

Star and Holy Family — SP4

Designs: 3c+1c, Star and two shepherds. 5c+1c, Star and three shepherds. 7c5m+1c5m, Star and Three Kings.

1974, Nov. 22	**Litho.**	*Perf. 14*	
B16 SP4	8m +2m multi	.20	.20
B17 SP4	3c +1c multi	.20	.20
B18 SP4	5c +1c multi	.35	.35
B19 SP4	7c5m +1c5m multi	.50	.50
	Nos. B16-B19 (4)	1.25	1.25

Nativity, by Maestro Alberto — SP5

8m+2m, Shepherds. 7c5m+1c5m, Three Kings.

1975, Nov. 4 *Perf. 13½*
Size: 24x23mm (#B20, B22); 49x23mm (#B21)

B20 SP5	8m +2m multi	.20	.20
B21 SP5	3c +1c multi	.50	.40
B22 SP5	7c5m +1c5m multi	2.00	*2.50*
a.	Triptych, #B20-B22	3.50	*4.00*
	Nos. B20-B22 (3)	2.70	*3.10*

Printed singly and as triptychs. Surtax for child welfare.

SP6

Madonna and Saints, by Domenico di Michelino — SP7

Details of Painting: 5c+1c, Virgin & Child. 7c+1c5m, St. Christopher & Bishop.

1976, Nov. 23	**Litho.**	*Perf. 13½*	
B23 SP6	1c +5m multi	.20	.20
B24 SP6	5c +1c multi	.40	.30
B25 SP6	7c +1c5m multi	.70	.65

Perf. 13½x14

B26 SP7	10c +2c multi	1.50	1.50
	Nos. B23-B26 (4)	2.80	2.65

Nativity SP8

Crèche Figurines: 1c+5m, Annunciation to the Shepherds. 11c+1c5m, Shepherds.

Perf. 13½x14

1977, Nov. 16		**Wmk. 354**	
B27 SP8	1c +5m multi	.20	.20
B28 SP8	7c +1c multi	.45	.45
B29 SP8	11c +1c5m multi	.80	.80
a.	Triptych, #B27-B29	1.50	1.50
	Nos. B27-B29 (3)	1.45	1.45

Nos. B27-B29 printed singly and as triptychs. Surtax was for child welfare.

Christmas Decorations, People and Church — SP9

Designs: 5c+1c, Decorations and angels. 7c+1c5m, Decorations and carolers. 11c+3c, Combined designs of #B30-B32.

1978, Nov. 9 **Litho.** *Perf. 14*
Size: 24x30mm

B30 SP9	1c +5m multi	.20	.20
B31 SP9	5c +1c multi	.35	.35
B32 SP9	7c +1c5m multi	.50	.50

Perf. 13½
Size: 58x22½mm

B33 SP9	11c +3c multi	.80	.80
	Nos. B30-B33 (4)	1.85	1.85

Nativity, by Giuseppe Cali — SP10

Designs (Cali Paintings): 5c+1c, 11c+3c, Flight into Egypt. 7c+1c5m, Nativity.

1979, Nov. 14	**Litho.**	*Perf. 14x13½*	
B34 SP10	1c +5m multi	.20	.20
B35 SP10	5c +1c multi	.35	.35
B36 SP10	7c +1c5m multi	.50	.50
B37 SP10	11c +3c multi	.80	.80
	Nos. B34-B37 (4)	1.85	1.85

Nativity, by Anton Inglott (1915-1945) — SP11

Details of Painting: 2c+5m, Annunciation. 6c+1c, Angel. 8c+1c5m, Holy Family.

1980, Oct. 7 **Litho.** *Perf. 14x13½*
Size: 20x47mm

B38 SP11	2c +5m multi	.20	.20
B39 SP11	6c +1c multi	.40	.40
B40 SP11	8c +1c5m multi	.55	.55

Perf. 14½x14
Size: 47x39mm

B41 SP11	12c +3c shown	.85	.85
	Nos. B38-B41 (4)	2.00	2.00

SP12

1981, Nov. 18	**Wmk. 354**	*Perf. 14*	
B42 SP12	2c +1c Children, vert.	.20	.20
B43 SP12	8c +2c Procession	.55	.55
B44 SP12	20c +3c Service, vert.	1.25	1.25
	Nos. B42-B44 (3)	2.00	2.00

SP13

Three Kings Following Star: 2c+1c, Star. 8c+2c, Three Kings. 20c+3c, Entire design.

1982, Oct. 8 Litho. *Perf. 13½*

B45 SP13 2c +1c multi .20 .20
B46 SP13 8c +2c multi .55 .55

Perf. 14

Size: 45x36mm

B47 SP13 20c +3c multi 1.25 1.25
Nos. B45-B47 (3) 2.00 2.00

SP14

Illuminated Manuscripts, Book of Hours, 15th Cent.: 2c+1c, Annunciation. 8c+2c, Nativity. 20c+3c, Three Kings bearing gifts. Surtax was for child welfare.

1983, Sept. 6 Litho. *Perf. 14*

B48 SP14 2c +1c multi .25 .25
B49 SP14 8c +2c multi .60 .60
B50 SP14 20c +3c multi 1.40 1.40
Nos. B48-B50 (3) 2.25 2.25

SP15

Paintings by Peter-Paul Caruana, Church of Our Lady of Porto Salvo, Valletta, 1850: 2c+1c, Visitation, vert. 8c+2c, Epiphany. 20c+3c, Jesus Among the Doctors.

1984, Oct. 5 Litho. *Perf. 14*

B51 SP15 2c +1c multi .30 .30
B52 SP15 8c +2c multi .85 .85
B53 SP15 20c +3c multi 2.00 2.00
Nos. B51-B53 (3) 3.15 3.15

SP16

1985, Oct. 10 Litho. *Perf. 14*

B54 SP16 2c +1c Adoration of the Magi .35 .35
B55 SP16 8c +2c Nativity .90 .90
B56 SP16 20c +3c Trumpeter Angels 1.90 1.90
Nos. B54-B56 (3) 3.15 3.15

Surtax for child welfare organizations.

SP17

Paintings by Giuseppe D'Arena (1633-1719).

1986, Oct. 10 Wmk. 354 *Perf. 14½*

B57 SP17 2c +1c The Nativity .55 .55
B58 SP17 8c +2c The Nativity, detail, vert. 1.75 1.75
B59 SP17 20c +3c The Epiphany 4.00 4.00
Nos. B57-B59 (3) 6.30 6.30

Surtax for child welfare organizations.

SP18

Illuminated text from choral books of the Veneranda Assemblea of St. John's Conventual Church, Valletta.

1987, Nov. 6 Litho. *Perf. 14*

B60 SP18 2c +1c Mary's Visit to Elizabeth .50 .50
B61 SP18 8c +2c Nativity 1.50 1.50
B62 SP18 20c +3c Adoration of the Magi 3.50 3.50
Nos. B60-B62 (3) 5.50 5.50

Surtax for child welfare organizations and the handicapped.

SP19

1988, Nov. 5 Litho. *Perf. 14½x14*

B63 SP19 3c +1c Shepherd .30 .30
B64 SP19 10c +2c Nativity .75 .75
B65 SP19 25c +3c Magi 1.75 1.75
Nos. B63-B65 (3) 2.80 2.80

Surtax for child welfare organizations and the handicapped.

SP20

Various angels from frescoes by Mattia Preti in the vault of St. John's Co-Cathedral, Valletta, 1666.

1989, Nov. 11 *Perf. 14*

B66 SP20 3c +1c multi .30 .30
B67 SP20 10c +2c multi 1.10 1.10
B68 SP20 20c +3c multi 2.10 2.10
Nos. B66-B68 (3) 3.50 3.50

Surtax for child welfare organizations and the handicapped.

SP21

SP22

Creche figures.

1990, Nov. 10

Size: #B70, 41x27mm

B69 SP21 3c +1c Carrying water .30 .30
B70 SP21 10c +2c Nativity .85 .85
B71 SP21 25c +3c Shepherd 1.90 1.90
Nos. B69-B71 (3) 3.05 3.05

Surtax for child welfare organizations.

1991, Nov. 6

B72 SP22 3c +1c Wise men .30 .30
B73 SP22 10c +2c Mary, Joseph, Jesus .80 .80
B74 SP22 25c +3c Shepherds 1.90 1.90
Nos. B72-B74 (3) 3.00 3.00

Surtax for child welfare organizations.

SP23

Paintings from dome spandrels of Mosta Parish Church by Giuseppe Cali (1846-1930): 3c+1c, Nativity scene. 10c+2c, Adoration of the Magi. 25c+3c, Christ among the Elders in the Temple.

1992, Oct. 22

B75 SP23 3c +1c multi .35 .35
B76 SP23 10c +2c multi 1.40 1.40
B77 SP23 25c +3c multi 3.25 3.25
Nos. B75-B77 (3) 5.00 5.00

Surtax for child welfare organizations.

SP24

Designs: 3c+1c, Christ Child in manger. 10c+2c, Christmas tree. 25c+3c, Star.

1993, Nov. 20

B78 SP24 3c +1c multi .40 .40
B79 SP24 10c +2c multi .85 .85
B80 SP24 25c +3c multi 1.90 1.90
Nos. B78-B80 (3) 3.15 3.15

Beginning with No. 845, semi-postal stamps are included with the postage portion of the set.

Christmas — SP25

Children's art: 6c+2c, Man with net chasing star. 15c+2c, People, Chirstmas tree. 16c+2c, People hugging. 19c+3c, Woman with shopping bags.

2001, Nov. 29 Litho. *Perf. 14*

B81-B84 SP25 Set of 4 4.00 4.00

Stampin' the Future Type of 2000

Souvenir Sheet

Wmk. 354

2006, Dec. 22 Litho. *Perf. 14*

B85 A261 £1.50 + (16c) Like #1029 10.00 10.00

Surtax was for the Valletta YMCA.

AIR POST STAMPS

No. 140 Overprinted

Perf. 14½x14

1928, Apr. 1 Typo. Wmk. 4

C1 A22 6p red & violet 5.50 6.75

Catalogue values for unused stamps in this section, from this point to the end of the section, are for Never Hinged items.

Jet over Valletta AP1

Designs: 3c, 5c, 20c, 35c, Winged emblem. 7c5m, 25c, like 4c.

Wmk. 354

1974, Mar. Litho. *Perf. 13½*

Cross Emblem in Red and Blue

C2 AP1 3c ol brown & gold .20 .20
C3 AP1 4c dk blue & gold .20 .20
C4 AP1 5c dk vio bl & gold .30 .30
C5 AP1 7c5m sl green & gold .40 .40
C6 AP1 20c vio brn & gold 1.10 1.10
C7 AP1 25c slate & gold 1.40 1.40
C8 AP1 35c brown & gold 2.00 2.00
Nos. C2-C8 (7) 5.60 5.60

Jet and Megalithic Temple — AP2

Designs: 7c, 20c, Air Malta Boeing 720B approaching Malta. 11c, 75c, Jumbo jet landing at Luqa Airport. 17c, like 5c.

1978, Oct. 3 Litho. *Perf. 13½*

C9 AP2 5c multicolored .30 .30
C10 AP2 7c multicolored .40 .40
C11 AP2 11c multicolored .60 .60
C12 AP2 17c multicolored .95 .95
C13 AP2 20c multicolored 1.10 1.10
C14 AP2 75c multicolored 4.25 4.25
Nos. C9-C14 (6) 7.60 7.60

Boeing 737, 1984 AP3

1984, Jan. 26 Wmk. 354 *Perf. 14*

C15 AP3 7c shown .45 .45
C16 AP3 8c Boeing 720B, 1974 .50 .50
C17 AP3 16c Vickers Vanguard, 1964 .95 .95
C18 AP3 23c Vickers Viscount, 1958 1.40 1.40
C19 AP3 27c Douglas DC3 Dakota, 1948 1.60 1.60
C20 AP3 38c AW Atlanta, 1936 2.40 2.40
C21 AP3 75c Dornier Wal, 1929 4.50 4.50
Nos. C15-C21 (7) 11.80 11.80

POSTAGE DUE STAMPS

D1

Maltese Cross — D2

1925 Typeset Unwmk. *Imperf.*

No.	Type	Denom.	Color	Unused	Used
J1	D1	½p	black, *white*	1.40	8.00
J2	D1	1p	black, *white*	3.75	3.50
J3	D1	1½p	black, *white*	3.50	4.25
J4	D1	2p	black, *white*	8.50	*15.00*
J5	D1	2½p	black, *white*	3.25	3.25
a.			"2" of "½" omitted	1,200.	1,400.
J6	D1	3p	black, *gray*	10.50	*17.00*
J7	D1	4p	black, *orange*	5.75	*11.00*
J8	D1	6p	black, *orange*	5.75	*20.00*
J9	D1	1sh	black, *orange*	8.50	*25.00*
J10	D1	1sh6p	black, *orange*	16.00	*62.50*
			Nos. J1-J10 (10)	66.90	*169.50*
			Set, never hinged	130.00	

These stamps were typeset in groups of 42. In each sheet there were four impressions of a group, two of them being inverted and making tete beche pairs.

Forged examples of No. J5a are known.

Wmk. 4 Sideways

1925 Typo. *Perf. 12*

No.	Type	Denom.	Color	Unused	Used
J11	D2	½p	blue green	1.40	.70
J12	D2	1p	violet	1.40	.50
J13	D2	1½p	yellow brown	1.75	1.00
J14	D2	2p	gray	12.50	1.25
J15	D2	2½p	orange	2.25	1.40
J16	D2	3p	dark blue	4.00	1.40
J17	D2	4p	olive green	14.00	*18.00*
J18	D2	6p	claret	3.50	4.75
J19	D2	1sh	gray black	7.50	*14.00*
J20	D2	1sh6p	deep rose	9.75	*32.50*
			Nos. J11-J20 (10)	58.05	*75.50*
			Set, never hinged	85.00	

In 1953-57 six values (½p-2p, 3p, 4p) were reissued on chalky paper in slightly different colors.

Catalogue values for unused stamps in this section, from this point to the end of the section, are for Never Hinged items.

1966 Wmk. 314 *Perf. 12*

No.	Type	Denom.	Color	Unused	Used
J21	D2	2p	sepia	22.50	*26.00*

Wmk. 354 Sideways

1968 *Perf. 12½*

No.	Type	Denom.	Color	Unused	Used
J22	D2	½p	green	.20	.20
J23	D2	1p	rose violet	.20	.20
J24	D2	1½p	bister brn	.30	.30
J25	D2	2p	brown black	.45	.45
J26	D2	2½p	orange	.50	.50
J27	D2	3p	Prus blue	.60	.60
J28	D2	4p	olive	.90	.90
J29	D2	6p	purple	1.50	1.50
J30	D2	1sh	black	1.60	1.60
J31	D2	1sh6p	rose car	3.75	3.75
			Nos. J22-J31 (10)	10.00	10.00

1967, Nov. 9 *Perf. 12*

No.	Type	Denom.	Unused	Used
J22a	D2	½p	3.25	3.25
J23a	D2	1p	4.50	4.50
J25a	D2	2p	6.75	6.75
J28a	D2	4p	82.50	*110.00*
		Nos. J22a-J28a (4)	97.00	*124.50*

Numeral — D3

Scroll — D4

Perf. 13x13½

1973, Apr. 28 Litho. Wmk. 354

No.	Type	Denom.	Color	Unused	Used
J32	D3	2m	brown	.20	.20
J33	D3	3m	brown orange	.20	.20
J34	D3	5m	carmine	.20	.20
J35	D3	1c	deep green	.20	.20
J36	D3	2c	black	.20	.20
J37	D3	3c	olive	.20	.20
J38	D3	5c	violet blue	.30	.30
J39	D3	10c	deep magenta	.60	.60
			Nos. J32-J39 (8)	2.10	2.10

Wmk. 354

1993, Jan. 4 Litho. *Perf. 14*

No.	Type	Denom.	Color	Unused	Used
J40	D4	1c	brt pink & lt pink	.20	.20
J41	D4	2c	brt blue & lt blue	.20	.20
J42	D4	5c	brt grn & lt grn	.30	.30
J43	D4	10c	org yel & brt yel	.55	.55
			Nos. J40-J43 (4)	1.25	1.25

WAR TAX STAMPS

Nos. 50, 25 Overprinted

1918 Wmk. 3 *Perf. 14*

No.	Type	Denom.	Color	Unused	Used
MR1	A13	½p	green	.30	.30

Wmk. 2

No.	Type	Denom.	Color	Unused	Used
MR2	A12	3p	red violet & gray	3.00	4.00

MANCHUKUO

'man-'chü-'kwō

LOCATION — Covering Manchuria, or China's three northeastern provinces —Fengtien, Kirin and Heilungkiang—plus Jehol province.

GOVT. — Independent state under Japanese influence

AREA — 503,013 sq. mi. (estimated)

POP. — 43,233,954 (est. 1940)

CAPITAL — Hsinking (Changchun)

Manchukuo was formed in 1932 with the assistance of Japan. In 1934 Henry Pu-yi, Chief Executive, was enthroned as Emperor Kang Teh. In 1945, when Japan surrendered to the Allies, the terms included the return of Manchukuo to China. The puppet state was dissolved.

100 Fen = 1 Yuan

Watermarks

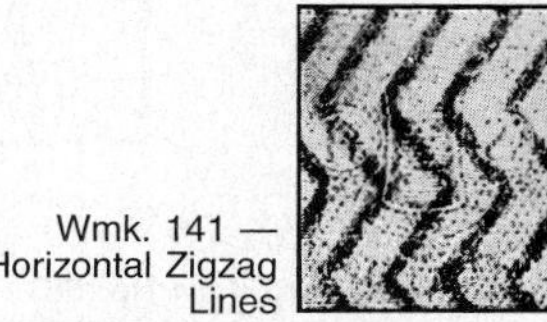
Wmk. 141 — Horizontal Zigzag Lines

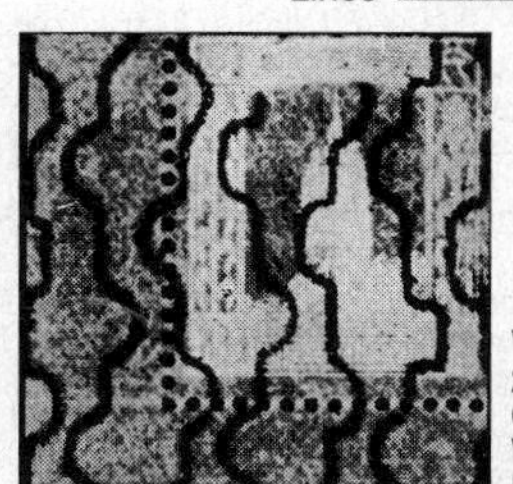
Wmk. 239 — Curved Wavy Lines

Wmk. 242 — Characters

Pagoda at Liaoyang A1

Chief Executive Henry Pu-yi A2

Five characters in top label.

Inscription reads "Manchu State Postal Administration."

Lithographed

Perf. 13x13½

1932, July 26 Unwmk.

White Paper

No.	Type	Denom.	Color	Unused	Used
1	A1	½f	gray brown	1.25	.70
2	A1	1f	dull red	1.60	.35
3	A1	1½f	lilac	5.50	5.00
4	A1	2f	slate	6.00	1.00
5	A1	3f	dull brown	7.50	7.50
6	A1	4f	olive green	2.25	.50
7	A1	5f	green	3.50	.55
8	A1	6f	rose	9.50	3.50
9	A1	7f	gray	3.00	1.00
10	A1	8f	ocher	15.00	12.50
11	A1	10f	orange	5.50	.50
12	A2	13f	dull brown	11.00	7.00
13	A2	15f	rose	20.00	3.00
14	A2	16f	turquoise grn	27.50	9.00
15	A2	20f	gray brown	8.00	1.75
16	A2	30f	orange	8.50	2.25
17	A2	50f	olive green	20.00	3.25
18	A2	1y	violet	37.50	9.00
			Nos. 1-18 (18)	193.10	68.35
			Set, never hinged	275.00	

A local provisional overprint of a horizontal line of four characters in red or black, reading "Chinese Postal Administration," was applied to Nos. 1-18 by followers of Gen. Su Ping-wen, who rebelled against the Manchukuo government in September, 1932. Many counterfeits exist.

See #23-31. For surcharges see #36, 59-61.

See note on local handstamps at the end of the Manchukuo listing.

Flags, Map and Wreath — A3

Old State Council Building — A4

1933, Mar. 1 *Perf. 12½*

No.	Type	Denom.	Color	Unused	Used
19	A3	1f	orange	4.00	4.00
20	A4	2f	dull green	12.00	12.00
21	A3	4f	light red	4.50	4.50
22	A4	10f	deep blue	30.00	30.00
			Nos. 19-22 (4)	50.50	50.50
			Set, never hinged	75.00	

1st anniv. of the establishing of the State. Nos. 19-22 were printed in sheets of 100 with a special printing in sheets of 20.

Type of 1932

Perf. 13x13½

1934, Feb. Engr. Wmk. 239

Granite Paper

No.	Type	Denom.	Color	Unused	Used
23	A1	½f	dark brown	2.50	1.65
24	A1	1f	red brown	2.50	.90
25	A1	1½f	dark violet	5.50	3.00
26	A1	2f	slate	5.00	1.50
27	A1	3f	brown	2.75	.60
28	A1	4f	olive brown	25.00	5.00
29	A1	10f	deep orange	10.00	1.00
30	A2	15f	rose	450.00	200.00
31	A2	1y	violet	30.00	11.00
			Nos. 23-31 (9)	533.25	224.65

For surcharge see No. 60.

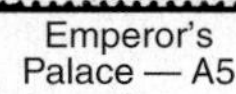
Emperor's Palace — A5

Phoenix — A6

1934, Mar. 1 *Perf. 12½*

No.	Type	Denom.	Color	Unused	Used
32	A5	1½f	orange brown	4.25	3.75
33	A6	3f	carmine	3.25	2.25
34	A5	6f	green	9.00	7.50
35	A6	10f	dark blue	20.00	17.50
			Nos. 32-35 (4)	36.50	31.00
			Set, never hinged	50.00	

Enthronement of Emperor Kang Teh. Nos. 32-35 were printed in sheets of 100, with a special printing in sheets of 20.

No. 6 Surcharged in Black

Perf. 13x13½

1934 Unwmk. White Paper

No.	Type	Denom.	Color	Unused	Used
36	A1	1f	on 4f olive grn	5.50	2.50
			Never hinged	7.00	
a.			Brown surcharge	37.50	37.50
b.			Upper left character of surcharge omitted		
c.			Inverted surcharge	110.00	110.00

Pagoda at Liaoyang A7

Emperor Kang Teh A8

Six characters in top label instead of five as in 1932-34 issues.

Inscription reads "Manchu Empire Postal Administration."

Perf. 13x13½

1934-36 Wmk. 239 Engr.

Granite Paper

37 A7 ½f brown .50 .35
38 A7 1f red brown 1.00 .30
39 A7 1½f dk violet 1.00 .50
 a. Booklet pane of 6 90.00
41 A7 3f brown ('35) .75 .35
 a. Booklet pane of 6 80.00
42 A7 5f dk blue ('35) 10.00 2.00
43 A7 5f gray ('36) 5.00 2.00
44 A7 6f rose ('35) 3.00 .60
45 A7 7f dk gray ('36) 2.50 2.00
47 A7 9f red orange ('35) 2.50 .75
50 A8 15f ver ('35) 2.50 .85
51 A8 18f Prus grn ('35) 25.00 5.00
52 A8 20f dk brown ('35) 4.00 .90
53 A8 30f orange brn ('35) 4.50 .90
54 A8 50f ol grn ('35) 6.00 2.00
55 A8 1y dk violet ('35) 20.00 6.00
 a. 1y violet 20.00 8.00
 Nos. 37-55 (15) 88.25 24.50
 Set, never hinged 110.00

4f and 8f, type A7, were prepared but not issued. Values $45 and $15, respectively.

1935 Wmk. 242 *Perf. 13x13½*

57 A7 10f deep blue 8.50 1.25
58 A8 13f light brown 11.50 5.75
 Set, never hinged 27.50

Nos. 6 and 28 Surcharged in Black

1935, March Unwmk.

White Paper

59 A1 3f on 4f ol grn 65.00 60.00
 Never hinged 90.00

Wmk. 239

Granite Paper

60 A1 3f on 4f olive brn 8.00 4.00
 Never hinged 15.00

Similar Surcharge on No. 14

1935, Feb. 13 Unwmk.

White Paper

61 A2 3f on 16f turq grn 14.00 9.00
 Never hinged 18.00
 Nos. 59-61 (3) 87.00 73.00

Orchid Crest of Manchukuo A9

Sacred White Mountains and Black Waters A10

1935, Jan. 1 Litho. Wmk. 141

Granite Paper

62 A9 2f green 4.00 1.75
63 A10 4f dull ol grn 2.00 1.50
64 A9 8f ocher 3.50 4.00
65 A10 12f brown red 10.00 *17.50*
 Nos. 62-65 (4) 19.50 24.75
 Set, never hinged 27.50

Nos. 62-65 exist imperforate.

1935 Wmk. 242

66 A9 2f yellow green 3.50 .75
68 A9 8f ocher 5.00 3.00
70 A10 12f brown red 11.00 8.00
 Nos. 66-70 (3) 19.50 11.75
 Set, never hinged 29.00

Nos. 62-70 issued primarily to pay postage to China, but valid for any postal use.

See Nos. 75-78, 113, 115, 158. For surcharges see Nos. 101, 103-104, 106-109, People's Republic of China No. 2L19.

Mt. Fuji — A11

Phoenix — A12

Perf. 11, 12½ and Compound

1935, Apr. 2 Engr. Wmk. 242

71 A11 1½f dull green 2.25 1.60
72 A12 3f orange 2.50 2.50
 a. 3f red orange 6.00 5.00
73 A11 6f dk carmine 5.50 4.75
 a. Horiz. pair, imperf. btwn. 250.00
 b. Perf. 11x12½ 45.00 37.50
74 A12 10f dark blue 6.00 6.00
 a. Perf. 12½x11 40.00 37.50
 b. Perf. 12½ 22.50 25.00
 Nos. 71-74 (4) 16.25 14.85
 Set, never hinged 23.00

Visit of the Emperor of Manchukuo to Tokyo.

Orchid Crest — A13

Types of A9 & A10

Redrawn and Engraved

1936 Wmk. 242 *Perf. 13x13½*

75 A13 2f lt green .80 .30
76 A10 4f olive green 2.75 .75
77 A13 8f ocher 2.25 1.25
78 A10 12f orange brn 37.50 27.50
 Nos. 75-78 (4) 43.30 29.80
 Set, never hinged 57.50

Unbroken lines of shading in the background of Nos. 76 and 78. Shading has been removed from right and left of the mountains. Nearly all lines have been removed from the lake. There are numerous other alterations in the design.

Issued primarily to pay postage to China, but valid for any postal use.

See #112. For surcharges see #102-106.

Wild Goose over Sea of Japan — A14

Communications Building at Hsinking — A15

Perf. 12x12½, 12½x12

1936, Jan. 26 Wmk. 242

79 A14 1½f black brown 2.50 2.00
80 A15 3f rose lilac 2.50 1.60
81 A14 6f carmine rose 5.75 5.75
82 A15 10f blue 8.00 6.00
 Nos. 79-82 (4) 18.75 15.35
 Set, never hinged 40.00

Postal convention with Japan.

New State Council Building A16

Carting Soybeans A17

North Mausoleum at Mukden A18

Summer Palace at Chengteh A19

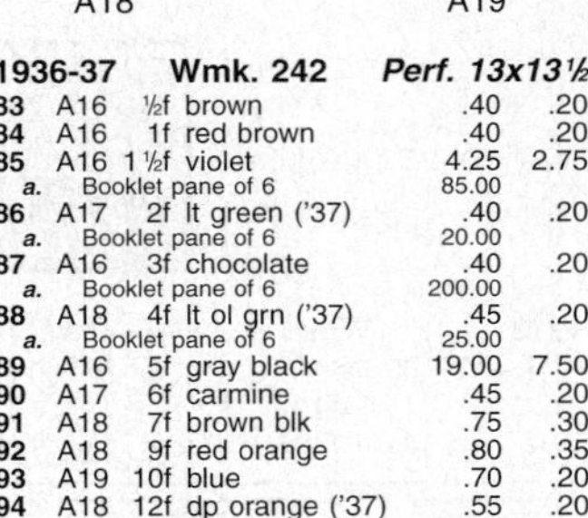

1936-37 Wmk. 242 *Perf. 13x13½*

83 A16 ½f brown .40 .20
84 A16 1f red brown .40 .20
85 A16 1½f violet 4.25 2.75
 a. Booklet pane of 6 85.00
86 A17 2f lt green ('37) .40 .20
 a. Booklet pane of 6 20.00
87 A16 3f chocolate .40 .20
 a. Booklet pane of 6 200.00
88 A18 4f lt ol grn ('37) .45 .20
 a. Booklet pane of 6 25.00
89 A16 5f gray black 19.00 7.50
90 A17 6f carmine .45 .20
91 A18 7f brown blk .75 .30
92 A18 9f red orange .80 .35
93 A19 10f blue .70 .20
94 A18 12f dp orange ('37) .55 .20
95 A18 13f brown 30.00 35.00
96 A18 15f carmine 3.00 .55
97 A17 20f dk brown 1.10 .35
98 A19 30f chestnut brn 1.10 .35
99 A17 50f olive green 1.60 .50
100 A19 1y violet 4.25 .60
 Nos. 83-100 (18) 69.60 49.85
 Set, never hinged 110.00

Nos. 83, 84, 86, 88 and 93 are known imperforate but were not regularly issued.

See Nos. 159-163. For overprints see Nos. 140-141, 148-151. For surcharges see People's Republic of China Nos. 2L1-2L2, 2L11-2L18, 2L20-2L37, 2L40-2L52.

a

b

c

d

1937

Surcharged on No. 66

101 A9 (a) 2½f on 2f 2.50 2.50

Surcharged on Nos. 75, 76 and 78

102 A13 (a) 2½f on 2f 2.50 2.50
103 A10 (b) 5f on 4f 3.75 3.75
104 A10 (c) 13f on 12f 10.50 10.00

Surcharged in Black on Nos. 75, 76 and 70

Space between bottom characters of surcharge 4½mm

105 A13 (d) 2½f on 2f 2.00 1.90
 a. Inverted surcharge 200.00 *225.00*
 b. Vert. pair, one without surch. 95.00
106 A10 (b) 5f on 4f 3.50 2.75
107 A10 (c) 13f on 12f 11.00 9.50

Surcharged on No. 70

Space between characters 6½mm

108 A10 (c) 13f on 12f 175.00 175.00

Same Surcharge on No. 63

Space between characters 4½mm

Wmk. 141

109 A10 (b) 5f on 4f 6.50 5.25
 Nos. 101-109 (9) 217.25 213.15
 Set, never hinged 310.00

Nos. 101-109 were issued primarily to pay postage to China, but were valid for any postal use.

Rising Sun over Manchurian Plain — A20

Composite Picture of Manchurian City — A21

Perf. 12½

1937, Mar. 1 Litho. Unwmk.

110 A20 1½f carmine rose 3.00 3.00
111 A21 3f blue green 2.50 1.75
 Set, never hinged 7.50

5th anniv. of the founding of the State of Manchukuo.

Types of 1936

Perf. 13x13½

1937 Wmk. 242 Engr.

112 A13 2½f dk violet .75 .40
113 A10 5f black .25 .25
115 A10 13f dk red brown .80 .60
 Nos. 112-115 (3) 1.80 1.25
 Set, never hinged 2.40

Issued primarily to pay postage to China, but were valid for any postal use.

Pouter Pigeon — A22

National Flag and Buildings — A23

Perf. 12x12½

1937, Sept. 16 Unwmk.

116 A22 2f dark violet 2.50 1.60
117 A23 4f rose carmine 2.50 1.25
118 A22 10f dark green 5.75 3.25
119 A23 20f dark blue 7.50 5.25
 Nos. 116-119 (4) 18.25 11.35
 Set, never hinged 22.50

Completion of the national capital, Hsinking, under the first Five-Year Construction Plan.

Map — A24

Dept. of Justice Building — A27

Japanese Residents' Association Building — A25

Postal Administration Building — A26

Perf. 12x12½, 13

1937, Dec. 1 Litho. Unwmk.

121 A24 2f dark carmine 1.25 .90
122 A25 4f green 2.25 1.10
123 A25 8f orange 4.75 3.25
124 A26 10f blue 5.25 3.75
125 A27 12f lt violet 6.25 5.00
126 A26 20f lilac brown 8.25 6.00
Nos. 121-126 (6) 28.00 20.00
Set, never hinged 30.00

Issued in commemoration of the abolition of extraterritorial rights within Manchukuo.

New Year Greetings — A28

Map and Cross — A29

1937, Dec. 15 Engr. *Perf. 12x12½*

127 A28 2f dk blue & red 1.90 .55
Never hinged 2.40
a. Double impression of border 12.50

Issued to pay postage on New Year's greeting cards.

Wmk. 242

1938, Oct. 15 Litho. *Perf. 13*

128 A29 2f lake & scarlet 1.20 1.10
129 A29 4f slate grn & scar 1.25 1.10
Set, never hinged 3.75

Founding of the Red Cross Soc. in Manchukuo.

Network of State Railroads in Manchukuo A30

Express Train "Asia" A31

1939, Oct. 21

130 A30 2f dk org, blk & dp bl 1.75 1.40
131 A31 4f dp blue & indigo 1.75 1.40
Set, never hinged 4.50

Attainment of 10,000 kilometers in the railway mileage in Manchuria.

Stork Flying above Mast of Imperial Flagship — A32

1940 Photo. Unwmk.

132 A32 2f brt red violet .70 .70
133 A32 4f brt green .70 .70
Set, never hinged 1.75

Second visit of Emperor Kang Teh to Emperor Hirohito of Japan.

Census Taker and Map of Manchukuo A33

Census Form A34

1940, Sept. 10 Litho. Wmk. 242

134 A33 2f vio brn & org .55 .55
135 A34 4f black & green .60 .60
a. Double impression of green 50.00
Set, never hinged 1.50

National census starting Oct. 1.

Message of Congratulation from Premier Chang Ching-hui — A35

Dragon Dance A36

1940, Sept. 18 Engr.

136 A35 2f carmine .55 .55
137 A36 4f indigo .60 .60
a. Imperf., pair 90.00
Set, never hinged 1.75

2600th anniversary of the birth of the Japanese Empire.

Soldier — A37

1941, May 25 Photo. Unwmk.

138 A37 2f deep carmine .60 .60
139 A37 4f bright ultra .60 .60
Set, never hinged 2.00

Conscription Law, effective June 1, 1941.

Nos. 86 and 88 Overprinted in Red or Blue

Perf. 13x13½

1942, Feb. 16 Wmk. 242

140 A17 2f lt green (R) .60 .60
141 A18 4f lt olive grn (Bl) .60 .60
Set, never hinged 2.00

"Return of Singapore to East Asia, 9th year of Kang Teh."

Kengoku Shrine A38

Map of Manchukuo A39

Flag of Manchukuo A40

Perf. 12x12½, 12½x12

1942, Mar. 1 Engr.

142 A38 2f carmine .40 .40
143 A38 4f lilac .40 .40
144 A39 10f red, *yel* 1.10 1.50
145 A40 20f indigo, *yel* 2.25 2.00
Nos. 142-145 (4) 4.15 4.30
Set, never hinged 5.00

"10th anniv. of Manchukuo, Mar. 1, 1942."

Allegory of National Harmony — A41

Women of Five Races, Dancing — A42

1942, Sept. 15

146 A41 3f orange .50 .40
147 A42 6f light green .75 *1.00*
Set, never hinged 1.75

"10th anniv. of the founding of Manchukuo, Sept. 15, 1942."

Nos. 87 and 90 Overprinted in Green or Blue

1942, Dec. 8 *Perf. 13x13½*

148 A16 3f chocolate (G) .40 .40
149 A17 6f carmine (Bl) .40 .40
Set, never hinged 1.10

1st anniv. of the "Greater East Asia War." The overprint reads "Asiatic Prosperity Began This Day December 8, 1941."

Nos. 87 and 90 Overprinted in Red or Blue

1943, May 1

150 A16 3f chocolate (R) .40 .40
151 A17 6f carmine (Bl) .40 .40
Set, never hinged 1.10

Proclamation of the labor service law.

Red Cross Nurse Carrying Stretcher A43

Smelting Furnace A44

1943, Oct. 1 Photo.

152 A43 6f green .60 .60
Never hinged .90

5th anniv. of the founding of the Red Cross Society of Manchukuo, Oct. 1, 1938.

1943, Dec. 8 Unwmk. *Perf. 13*

153 A44 6f red brown .40 .40
Never hinged .55

2nd anniv. of the "Greater East Asia War."

Chinese Characters A45

Japanese Characters A46

Perf. 13x13½

1944 Wmk. 242 Litho.

154 A45 10f rose .75 *1.25*
a. Imperf., vert. pair #154, 155 10.00
b. Vert. pair #154, 155 1.50 *2.50*
155 A46 10f rose .75 *1.25*
156 A45 40f gray green 3.25 3.25
a. Imperf., vert. pair #156, 157 15.00
b. 40f with 10f vignette, perf. 140.00 140.00
c. 40f with 10f vignette, imperf. 200.00
d. Vert. pair #156, 157 6.50 6.50
157 A46 40f gray green 3.25 3.25
Nos. 154-157 (4) 8.00 *9.00*
Set, never hinged 10.00

"Japan's Progress Is Manchukuo's Progress." Issued as propaganda for the close relationship of Japan and Manchukuo.

Frames of the 10f vignettes have rounded corners, those of the 40f vignettes have indented corners.

Types of 1935 and 1936-37

1944-45 Litho.

158 A10 5f gray black 1.00 *1.75*
a. Imperf., pair 10.00
159 A17 6f crimson rose 2.25 *3.50*
160 A19 10f light blue 5.00 *6.50*
161 A17 20f brown 1.75 *2.50*
162 A19 30f buff ('45) 1.90 *2.50*
163 A19 1y dull lilac 2.50 *2.75*
Nos. 158-163 (6) 14.40 *19.50*
Set, never hinged 20.00

For surcharges see People's Republic of China Nos. 2L1, 2L14, 2L19, 2L24, 2L27, 2L30-2L31, 2L35, 2L37, 2L49, 2L52.

"One Heart, One Soul" — A47

1945, May 2

164 A47 10f red .60 *1.50*
Never hinged .90
a. Imperf., pair 4.00 *5.00*

Emperor's edict of May 2, 1935, 10th anniv.

AIR POST STAMPS

Sheep Grazing AP1

Railroad Bridge AP2

Wmk. Characters (242)

1936-37 Engr. *Perf. 13x13½*

Granite Paper

C1 AP1 18f green 15.00 12.50
C2 AP1 19f blue green ('37) 5.00 3.50
C3 AP2 38f blue 16.00 15.00
C4 AP2 39f deep blue ('37) 1.60 1.75
Nos. C1-C4 (4) 37.60 32.75
Set, never hinged 45.00

With the end of World War II and the collapse of Manchukuo, the Northeastern Provinces reverted to China. In many Manchurian towns and cities, the Manchukuo stamps were locally handstamped in ideograms: "Republic of China," "China Postal Service" or "Temporary Use for China." A typical example is shown above. Many of these local issues also were surcharged.

MARIANA ISLANDS

ˌmar-ē-ˈa-nə ˈī-lənds

LOCATION — A group of 14 islands in the West Pacific Ocean, about 1500 miles east of the Philippines.
GOVT. — Possession of Spain, then of Germany
AREA — 246 sq. mi.
POP. — 44,025 (1935)
CAPITAL — Saipan

Until 1899 this group belonged to Spain but in that year all except Guam were ceded to Germany.

100 Centavos = 1 Peso
100 Pfennig = 1 Mark (1899)

Values for unused stamps are for examples with original gum as defined in the catalogue introduction. Very fine examples of Nos. 1-6 will have perforations touching or just cutting into the design. Stamps with perfs clear on all sides and well centered are rare and sell for substantially more.

Issued under Spanish Dominion

King Alfonso XIII — A1

Stamps of the Philippines Handstamped Vertically in Blackish Violet Reading Up or Down

1899, Sept. Unwmk. *Perf. 14*

No.	Type	Description	Unused	Used
1	A1	2c dark blue green	875.00	325.00
2	A1	3c dark brown	675.00	225.00
3	A1	5c car rose	1,000.	350.00
4	A1	6c dark blue	6,500.	5,000.
5	A1	8c gray brown	500.00	200.00
6	A1	15c slate green	2,500.	1,300.

Overprint forgeries of Nos. 1-6 exist.

Issued under German Dominion

Stamps of Germany, 1889-90, Overprinted in Black at 56 degree Angle

1900, May Unwmk. *Perf. 13½x14½*

No.	Type	Description	Unused	Used
11	A9	3pf dark brn	12.00	*30.00*
12	A9	5pf green	16.00	*32.50*
13	A10	10pf carmine	19.00	*45.00*
14	A10	20pf ultra	25.00	*125.00*
15	A10	25pf orange	62.50	*160.00*
b.		Inverted overprint	*2,400.*	
16	A10	50pf red brn	65.00	*210.00*
		Nos. 11-16 (6)	199.50	*602.50*

Forged cancellations exist on Nos. 11-16, 17-29.

Stamps of Germany, 1889-90, Overprinted in Black at 48 degree Angle

1899, Nov. 18

No.	Type	Description	Unused	Used
11a	A9	3pf light brown	*2,000.*	*2,000.*
12a	A9	5pf green	*2,500.*	*1,700.*
13a	A10	10pf carmine	190.00	*200.00*
14a	A10	20pf ultra	190.00	*200.00*
15a	A10	25pf orange	*2,750.*	*2,750.*
16a	A10	50pf red brown	*2,750.*	*2,750.*

Kaiser's Yacht "Hohenzollern"
A4 A5

1901, Jan. Typo. *Perf. 14*

No.	Type	Description	Unused	Used
17	A4	3pf brown	1.10	*1.75*
18	A4	5pf green	1.10	*1.90*
19	A4	10pf carmine	1.10	*4.25*
20	A4	20pf ultra	1.25	*7.25*
21	A4	25pf org & blk, *yel*	1.75	*12.50*
22	A4	30pf org & blk, *sal*	1.75	*13.50*
23	A4	40pf lake & blk	1.75	*13.50*
24	A4	50pf pur & blk, *sal*	2.00	*15.00*
25	A4	80pf lake & blk, *rose*	2.50	*25.00*

Engr.

Perf. 14½x14

No.	Type	Description	Unused	Used
26	A5	1m carmine	3.50	*72.50*
27	A5	2m blue	5.50	*92.50*
28	A5	3m blk vio	7.25	*140.00*
29	A5	5m slate & car	140.00	*500.00*
		Nos. 17-29 (13)	170.55	*899.65*

Wmk. Lozenges (125)

1916-19 Typo. *Perf. 14*

No.	Type	Description	Unused
30	A4	3pf brown ('19)	1.00

Engr.

Perf. 14½x14

No.	Type	Description	Unused
31	A5	5m slate & carmine	30.00

Nos. 30 and 31 were never placed in use.

MARIENWERDER

mä-'rē-ən-ˌveˌərd-ər

LOCATION — Northeastern Germany, bordering on Poland
GOVT. — A district of West Prussia

By the Versailles Treaty the greater portion of West Prussia was ceded to Poland but the district of Marienwerder was allowed a plebiscite which was held in 1920 and resulted in favor of Germany.

100 Pfennig = 1 Mark

Plebiscite Issues

Symbolical of Allied Supervision of the Plebiscite — A1

1920 Unwmk. Litho. *Perf. 11½*

1 A1 5pf green .75 1.40
2 A1 10pf rose red .75 1.25
3 A1 15pf gray .75 1.75
4 A1 20pf brn org .75 1.10
5 A1 25pf deep blue .75 1.10
6 A1 30pf orange .95 1.10
7 A1 40pf brown .75 1.10
8 A1 50pf violet .75 1.10
9 A1 60pf red brown 4.25 2.50
10 A1 75pf chocolate .95 1.10
11 A1 1m brn & grn .75 1.10
12 A1 2m dk vio 2.10 3.00
13 A1 3m red 5.00 4.25
14 A1 5m blue & rose 24.00 22.00
Nos. 1-14 (14) 43.25 43.85
Set, never hinged 92.50

These stamps occasionally show parts of two papermakers' watermarks, consisting of the letters "O. B. M." with two stars before and after, or "P. & C. M."

Nos. 1-14 exist imperf.; value for set, $700. Nearly all exist part perf.

Stamps of Germany, 1905-19, Overprinted

1920 Wmk. 125 *Perf. 14, 14½*

24 A16 5pf green 15.00 *30.00*
a. Inverted overprint 125.00
Never hinged 210.00
26 A16 20pf bl vio 6.00 *25.00*
a. Inverted overprint 62.50
Never hinged 125.00
b. Double overprint 85.00
Never hinged 150.00
28 A16 50pf vio & blk, *buff* 375.00 *850.00*
29 A16 75pf grn & blk 4.25 *7.50*
a. Inverted overprint 62.50
Never hinged 125.00
30 A16 80pf lake & blk, *rose* 75.00 *120.00*
31 A17 1m car rose 85.00 *160.00*
a. Inverted overprint 425.00
Never hinged 850.00
Nos. 24-31 (6) 560.25 *1,192.*
Set, never hinged 1,200.

Trial impressions were made in red, green and lilac, and with 2½mm instead of 3mm space between the lines of the overprint. These were printed on the 75pf and 80pf. The 1 mark was overprinted with the same words in 3 lines of large sans-serif capitals. All these are essays. Some were passed through the post, apparently with speculative intent.

Stamps of Germany, 1905-18, Surcharged

32 A22 1m on 2pf gray 22.50 *45.00*
33 A22 2m on 2½pf gray 8.50 *17.00*
a. Inverted surcharge 55.00 *100.00*
Never hinged 100.00
34 A16 3m on 3pf brown 12.00 *17.00*
a. Double surcharge 55.00 *100.00*
Never hinged 100.00
b. Inverted surcharge 55.00 *100.00*
Never hinged 100.00
35 A22 5m on 7½pf org 8.50 *21.00*
a. Inverted surcharge 55.00 *100.00*
Never hinged 100.00
b. Double surcharge 55.00 *100.00*
Never hinged 100.00
Nos. 32-35 (4) 51.50 *100.00*
Set, never hinged 125.00

There are two types of the letters "M," "C," "i" and "e" and of the numerals "2" and "5" in these surcharges.

Counterfeits exist of Nos. 24-35.

Stamps of Germany, 1920, Overprinted

1920, July *Perf. 15x14½*

36 A17 1m red 2.50 *4.25*
37 A17 1.25m green 3.25 *5.00*
38 A17 1.50m yellow brown 4.25 *6.75*
39 A21 2.50m lilac rose 2.50 *5.00*
Nos. 36-39 (4) 12.50 *21.00*
Set, never hinged 30.00

A2

1920 Unwmk. *Perf. 11½*

40 A2 5pf green 2.50 1.75
41 A2 10pf rose red 2.50 1.75
42 A2 15pf gray 11.00 11.00
43 A2 20pf brn org 1.10 1.75
44 A2 25pf dp bl 12.50 *17.00*
45 A2 30pf orange 1.00 .85
46 A2 40pf brown .80 .80
47 A2 50pf violet 1.50 1.00
48 A2 60pf red brn 6.00 3.50
49 A2 75pf chocolate 6.00 5.00
50 A2 1m brn & grn .85 .70
51 A2 2m dk vio 1.25 1.00
52 A2 3m light red 1.75 1.00
53 A2 5m blue & rose 2.75 1.25
Nos. 40-53 (14) 51.50 48.35
Set, never hinged 120.00

MARSHALL ISLANDS

'mär-shəl 'ī-ləndz

LOCATION — Two chains of islands in the West Pacific Ocean, about 2,500 miles southeast of Tokyo
GOVT. — Republic
AREA — 70 sq. mi.
POP. — 65,507 (1999 est.)
CAPITAL — Majuro Atoll

The Marshall Islands were German possession from 1885 to 1914. Seized by Japan in 1914, the islands were taken by the US in WW II and became part of the US Trust Territory of the Pacific in 1947. By agreement with the USPS, the islands began issuing their own stamps in 1984, with the USPS continuing to carry the mail to and from the islands.

On Oct. 21, 1986 Marshall Islands became a Federation as a Sovereign State in Compact of Free Association with the US.

100 Pfennig = 1 Mark
100 Cents = 1 Dollar

Catalogue values for unused stamps in this country are for Never Hinged items, beginning with Scott 31 in the regular postage section, and Scott C1 in the airpost section.

Watermark

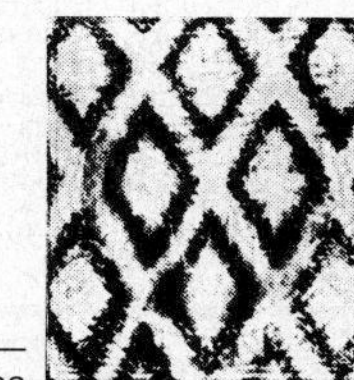

Wmk. 125 — Lozenges

Issued under German Dominion

Stamps of Germany Overprinted "Marschall-Inseln" in Black

1897 Unwmk. *Perf. 13½x14½*

1 A9 3pf dk brn 140.00 *725.00*
a. 3pf light brown *4,250.* *2,200.*
2 A9 5pf green 120.00 *550.00*
3 A9 10pf carmine 50.00 *150.00*
4 A10 20pf ultra 50.00 *150.00*
5 A10 25pf orange 140.00 *925.00*
6 A10 50pf red brown 140.00 *925.00*
Nos. 1-6 (6) 640.00 3,425.

Nos. 5 and 6 were not placed in use, but canceled stamps exist.

A small quantity of the 3pf, 5pf, 10pf and 20pf were issued at Jaluit. These have yellowish, dull gum. Later overprintings of Nos. 1-6 were sold only at Berlin, and have white, smooth, shiny gum. No. 1a belongs to the Jaluit issue. For detailed listings, see the *Scott Specialized Catalogue of Stamps and Covers.*

Forged cancellations are found on almost all Marshall Islands stamps.

Overprinted "Marshall-Inseln"

1899-1900

7 A9 3pf dk brn ('00) 4.50 *5.50*
a. 3pf light brown 250.00 *775.00*
8 A9 5pf green 9.25 *12.50*
9 A10 10pf car ('00) 11.25 *16.00*
10 A10 20pf ultra ('00) 16.00 *25.00*
11 A10 25pf orange 19.00 *42.50*
12 A10 50pf red brown 30.00 *47.50*
Nos. 7-12 (6) 90.00 *149.00*

Kaiser's Yacht "Hohenzollern"
A3 A4

1901 Unwmk. Typo. *Perf. 14*

13 A3 3pf brown .65 1.75
14 A3 5pf green .65 1.75
15 A3 10pf carmine .65 *5.00*
16 A3 20pf ultra .95 *9.25*
17 A3 25pf org & blk, *yel* 1.00 *16.00*
18 A3 30pf org & blk, *sal* 1.00 *16.00*
19 A3 40pf lake & blk 1.00 *16.00*
20 A3 50pf pur & blk, *sal* 1.40 *25.00*
21 A3 80pf lake & blk, *rose* 2.50 *35.00*

Engr.
Perf. 14½x14

22 A4 1m carmine 3.75 *85.00*
23 A4 2m blue 5.50 *120.00*
24 A4 3m blk vio 8.50 *200.00*
25 A4 5m slate & car 125.00 *500.00*
Nos. 13-25 (13) 152.55 *1,030.*

Wmk. Lozenges (125)

1916 Typo. *Perf. 14*

26 A3 3pf brown .85

Engr.
Perf. 14½x14

27 A4 5m slate & carmine 35.00

Nos. 26 and 27 were never placed in use.

The stamps of Marshall Islands overprinted "G. R. I." and new values in British currency were all used in New Britain and are listed among the issues for that country.

Two unauthorized issues appeared in 1979. The 1st, a set of five for the "Establishment of Government, May 1, 1979," consists of 8c, 15c, 21c, 31c and 75c labels. The 75c is about the size of a postcard. The 2nd, a set of four se-tenant blocks of four 10c labels for the Intl. Year of the Child. This set also exists imperf. and with specimen overprints.

Catalogue values for unused stamps in this section, from this point to the end of the section, are for Never Hinged items.

Inauguration of Postal Service — A5

1984, May 2 Litho. *Perf. 14x13½*

31 A5 20c Outrigger canoe .50 .50
32 A5 20c Fishnet .50 .50
33 A5 20c Navigational stick chart .50 .50
34 A5 20c Islet .50 .50
a. Block of 4, #31-34 2.00 2.00

Mili Atoll, Astrolabe — A6

Maps and Navigational Instruments.

1984-85 Litho. *Perf. 15x14*

35 A6 1c shown .20 .20
36 A6 3c Likiep, Azimuth compass .20 .20
37 A6 5c Ebon, 16th cent. compass .20 .20
38 A6 10c Jaluit, anchor buoys .20 .20
39 A6 13c Ailinginae, Nocturnal .25 .25
a. Booklet pane of 10 *8.00* —
40 A6 14c Wotho Atoll, navigational stick chart .30 .30
a. Booklet pane of 10 *7.50* —
41 A6 20c Kwajalein and Ebeye, stick chart .40 .40
a. Booklet pane of 10 *10.00* —
b. Bklt. pane, 5 each 13c, 20c *9.25* —
42 A6 22c Eniwetok, 18th cent. lodestone storage case .45 .45
a. Booklet pane of 10 *9.50* —
b. Bklt. pane, 5 each 14c, 22c *8.50* —
43 A6 28c Ailinglaplap, printed compass .55 .55
44 A6 30c Majuro, navigational stick-chart .60 .60
45 A6 33c Namu, stick chart .65 .65
46 A6 37c Rongelap, quadrant .75 .75
47 A6 39c Taka, map compass, 16th cent. sea chart .80 .80
48 A6 44c Ujelang, chronograph .90 .90
49 A6 50c Maloelap and Aur, nocturlabe 1.00 1.00
49A A6 $1 Arno, 16th cent. sector compass 2.00 2.00
Nos. 35-49A (16) 9.45 9.45

Issued: 1c, 3c, 10c, 30c, $1, 6/12; 13c, 20c, 28c, 37c, 12/19/84; 14c, 22c, 33c, 39c, 44c, 50c, 6/5/85.

See Nos. 107-109.

No. 7 — A7

1984, June 19 ***Perf. 14½x15***

50 A7 40c shown .60 .60
51 A7 40c No. 13 .60 .60
52 A7 40c No. 4 .60 .60
53 A7 40c No. 25 .60 .60
a. Block of 4, #50-53 2.40 2.40

Philatelic Salon, 19th UPU Congress, Hamburg, June 19-26.

Ausipex '84 — A8

Dolphins.

1984, Sept. 5 **Litho.** ***Perf. 14***

54 A8 20c Common .40 .40
55 A8 20c Risso's .40 .40
56 A8 20c Spotter .40 .40
57 A8 20c Bottlenose .40 .40
a. Block of 4, #54-57 1.60 1.60

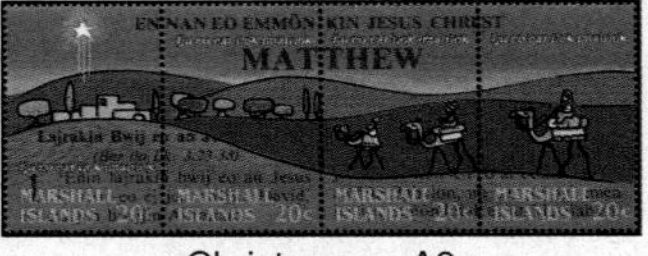

Christmas — A9

Illustration reduced.

1984, Nov. 7 **Litho.** ***Perf. 14***

58 Strip of 4 2.25 2.25
a.-d. A9 20c any single .50 .50
e. Sheet of 16 9.00

Sheet background shows text from Marshallese New Testament, giving each stamp a different background.

Marshall Islands Constitution, 5th Anniv. — A10

1984, Dec. 19 **Litho.** ***Perf. 14***

59 A10 20c Traditional chief .40 .40
60 A10 20c Amata Kabua .40 .40
61 A10 20c Chester Nimitz .40 .40
62 A10 20c Trygve Lie .40 .40
a. Block of 4, #59-62 1.60 1.60

Audubon Bicentenary — A11

1985, Feb. 15 **Litho.** ***Perf. 14***

63 A11 22c Forked-tailed Petrel .60 .60
64 A11 22c Pectoral Sandpiper .60 .60
a. Pair, #63-64 1.20 1.20
Nos. 63-64,C1-C2 (4) 3.00 3.00

Sea Shells — A12

1985, Apr. 17 **Litho.** ***Perf. 14***

65 A12 22c Cymatium lotorium .45 .45
66 A12 22c Chicoreus cornucervi .45 .45
67 A12 22c Strombus aurisdanae .45 .45
68 A12 22c Turbo marmoratus .45 .45
69 A12 22c Chicoreus palmarosae .45 .45
a. Strip of 5, #65-69 2.25 2.25

See Nos. 119-123, 152-156, 216-220.

Decade for Women A13

1985, June 5 **Litho.** ***Perf. 14***

70 A13 22c Native drum .40 .40
71 A13 22c Palm branches .40 .40
72 A13 22c Pounding stone .40 .40
73 A13 22c Ak bird .40 .40
a. Block of 4, #70-73 1.65 1.65

Reef and Lagoon Fish A14

1985, July 15 **Litho.** ***Perf. 14***

74 A14 22c Acanthurus dussumieri .45 .45
75 A14 22c Adioryx caudimaculatus .45 .45
76 A14 22c Ostracion meleacaris .45 .45
77 A14 22c Chaetodon ephippium .45 .45
a. Block of 4, #74-77 1.80 1.80

Intl. Youth Year A15

IYY and Alele Nautical Museum emblems and: No. 78, Marshallese youths and Peace Corps volunteers playing basketball. No. 79, Legend teller reciting local history, girl listening to recording. No. 80, Islander explaining navigational stick charts. No. 81, Jabwa stick dance.

1985, Aug. 31 **Litho.** ***Perf. 14***

78 A15 22c multicolored .45 .45
79 A15 22c multicolored .45 .45
80 A15 22c multicolored .45 .45
81 A15 22c multicolored .45 .45
a. Block of 4, #78-81 1.80 1.80

1856 American Board of Commissions Stock Certificate for Foreign Missions — A16

Missionary ship Morning Star I: 22c, Launch, Jothan Stetson Shipyard, Chelsea, MA, Aug. 7, 1857. 33c, First voyage, Honolulu to the Marshalls, 1857. 44c, Marshall islanders pulling Morning Star I into Ebon Lagoon, 1857.

1985, Oct. 21 **Litho.** ***Perf. 14***

82 A16 14c multicolored .25 .25
83 A16 22c multicolored .45 .45
84 A16 33c multicolored .65 .65
85 A16 44c multicolored .90 .90
Nos. 82-85 (4) 2.25 2.25

Christmas.

US Space Shuttle, Astro Telescope, Halley's Comet — A17

Comet tail and research spacecraft: No. 87, Planet A Space Probe, Japan. No. 88, Giotto spacecraft, European Space Agency. No. 89, INTERCOSMOS Project Vega spacecraft, Russia, France, etc. No. 90, US naval tracking ship, NASA observational aircraft, cameo portrait of Edmond Halley (1656-1742), astronomer. Se-tenant in continuous design.

1985, Nov. 21

86 A17 22c multicolored 1.00 1.00
87 A17 22c multicolored 1.00 1.00
88 A17 22c multicolored 1.00 1.00
89 A17 22c multicolored 1.00 1.00
90 A17 22c multicolored 1.00 1.00
a. Strip of 5, #86-90 5.00 5.00

Medicinal Plants A18

1985, Dec. 31 **Litho.** ***Perf. 14***

91 A18 22c Sida fallax .45 .45
92 A18 22c Scaevola frutescens .45 .45
93 A18 22c Guettarda speciosa .45 .45
94 A18 22c Cassytha filiformis .45 .45
a. Block of 4, #91-94 1.90 1.90

Maps Type of 1984

1986-87 ***Perf. 15x14, 14 ($10)***

107 A6 $2 Wotje and Erikub, terrestrial globe, 1571 4.50 4.50
108 A6 $5 Bikini, Stick chart 9.50 9.50

Size: 31x31mm

109 A6 $10 Stick chart of the atolls 16.00 16.00
Nos. 107-109 (3) 30.00 30.00

Issued: $2, $5, 3/7/86; $10, 3/31/87.

Marine Invertebrates — A19

1986, Mar. 31 **Litho.** ***Perf. 14½x14***

110 A19 14c Triton's trumpet 1.50 1.50
111 A19 14c Giant clam 1.50 1.50
112 A19 14c Small giant clam 1.50 1.50
113 A19 14c Coconut crab 1.50 1.50
a. Block of 4, #110-113 8.00 8.00

Souvenir Sheet

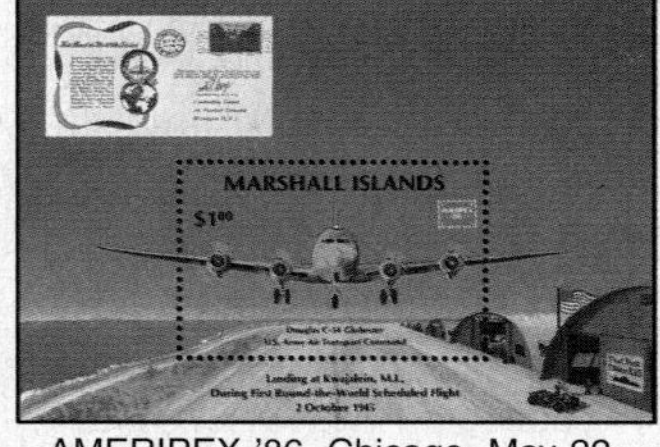

AMERIPEX '86, Chicago, May 22-June 1 — A20

1986, May 22 **Litho.** ***Perf. 14***

114 A20 $1 Douglas C-54 Globester 2.75 2.75

1st Around-the-world scheduled flight, 40th anniv. No. 114 has multicolored margin continuing the design and picturing US Air Transport Command Base, Kwajalein Atoll and souvenir card.

See Nos. C3-C6.

Operation Crossroads, Atomic Bomb Tests, 40th Anniv. — A21

Designs: No. 115, King Juda, Bikinians sailing tibinal canoe. No. 116, USS Sumner, amphibious DUKW, advance landing. No. 117, Evacuating Bikinians. No. 118, Land reclamation, 1986.

1986, July 1 **Litho.** ***Perf. 14***

115 A21 22c multicolored .45 .45
116 A21 22c multicolored .45 .45
117 A21 22c multicolored .45 .45
118 A21 22c multicolored .45 .45
a. Block of 4, #115-118 1.90 1.90

See No. C7.

Seashells Type of 1985

1986, Aug. 1 **Litho.** ***Perf. 14***

119 A12 22c Ramose murex .45 .45
120 A12 22c Orange spider .45 .45
121 A12 22c Red-mouth frog shell .45 .45
122 A12 22c Laciniate conch .45 .45
123 A12 22c Giant frog shell .45 .45
a. Strip of 5, #119-123 2.25 2.25

Game Fish A22

1986, Sept. 10 **Litho.**

124 A22 22c Blue marlin .40 .40
125 A22 22c Wahoo .40 .40
126 A22 22c Dolphin fish .40 .40
127 A22 22c Yellowfin tuna .40 .40
a. Block of 4, #124-127 1.60 1.60

Christmas, Intl. Peace Year — A23

1986, Oct. 28 **Litho.** ***Perf. 14***

128 A23 22c United Nations UR .60 .60
129 A23 22c United Nations UL .60 .60
130 A23 22c United Nations LR .60 .60
131 A23 22c United Nations LL .60 .60
a. Block of 4, #128-131 2.50 2.50

See No. C8.

US Whaling Ships A24

1987, Feb. 20 **Litho.** ***Perf. 14***

132 A24 22c James Arnold, 1854 .50 .50
133 A24 22c General Scott, 1859 .50 .50
134 A24 22c Charles W. Morgan, 1865 .50 .50
135 A24 22c Lucretia, 1884 .50 .50
a. Block of 4, #132-135 2.00 2.00

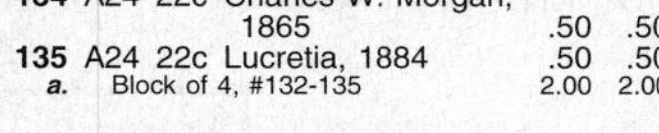

Historic and Military Flights A25

Designs: No. 136, Charles Lindbergh commemorative medal, Spirit of St. Louis crossing the Atlantic, 1927. No. 137, Lindbergh flying in the Battle of the Marshalls, 1944. No. 138, William Bridgeman flying in the Battle of Kwajalein, 1944. No. 139, Bridgeman testing the Douglas Skyrocket, 1951. No. 140, John Glenn flying in the Battle of the Marshalls. No. 141, Glenn, the first American to orbit the Earth, 1962.

1987, Mar. 12 Litho. *Perf. 14½*

136 A25 33c multicolored .70 .70
137 A25 33c multicolored .70 .70
a. Pair, #136-137 1.40 1.40
138 A25 39c multicolored .75 .75
139 A25 39c multicolored .75 .75
a. Pair, #138-139 1.50 1.50
140 A25 44c multicolored .80 .80
141 A25 44c multicolored .80 .80
a. Pair, #140-141 1.60 1.60
Nos. 136-141 (6) 4.50 4.50

Souvenir Sheet

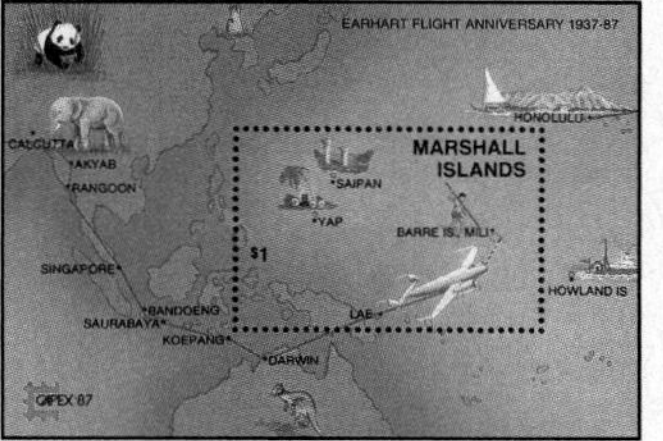

CAPEX '87 — A26

1987, June 15 Litho. *Perf. 14*

142 A26 $1 Map of flight 2.50 2.50

Amelia Earhart (1897-1937), American aviator who died during attempted round-the-world flight, 50th anniv. No. 142 has multicolored margin picturing Earhart's flight pattern from Calcutta, India, to the crash site near Barre Is., Marshall Is.

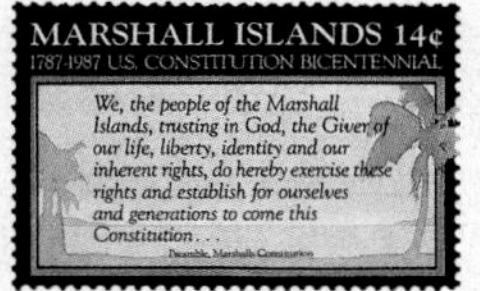

US Constitution Bicentennial — A27

Excerpts from the Marshall Islands and US Constitutions.

1987, July 16 Litho. *Perf. 14*

143 A27 14c We,... Marshall .30 .30
144 A27 14c National seals .30 .30
145 A27 14c We,... United States .30 .30
a. Triptych, #143-145 1.00 1.00
146 A27 22c All we have... .40 .40
147 A27 22c Flags .40 .40
148 A27 22c to establish... .40 .40
a. Triptych, #146-148 1.25 1.25
149 A27 44c With this Constitution... .80 .80
150 A27 44c Stick chart, Liberty Bell .80 .80
151 A27 44c to promote... .80 .80
a. Triptych, #149-151 2.50 2.50
Nos. 143-151 (9) 4.50 4.50

Triptychs printed in continuous designs.

Seashells Type of 1985

1987, Sept. 1 Litho. *Perf. 14*

152 A12 22c Magnificent cone .40 .40
153 A12 22c Partridge tun .40 .40
154 A12 22c Scorpion spider conch .40 .40
155 A12 22c Hairy triton .40 .40
156 A12 22c Chiragra spider conch .40 .40
a. Strip of 5, #152-156 2.00 2.00

Copra Industry A28

Contest-winning crayon drawings by Amram Enox; design contest sponsored by the Tobular Copra Processing Co.

1987, Dec. 10 Litho. *Perf. 14*

157 A28 44c Planting coconut .65 .65
158 A28 44c Making copra .65 .65
159 A28 44c Bottling coconut oil .65 .65
a. Triptych, #157-159 2.00 2.00

Biblical Verses A29

1987, Dec. 10

160 A29 14c Matthew 2:1 .25 .25
161 A29 22c Luke 2:14 .40 .40
162 A29 33c Psalms 33:3 .60 .60
163 A29 44c Pslams 150:5 .75 .75
Nos. 160-163 (4) 2.00 2.00

Christmas.

Marine Birds A30

1988, Jan. 27

164 A30 44c Pacific reef herons .75 .75
165 A30 44c Bar-tailed godwit .75 .75
166 A30 44c Masked booby .75 .75
167 A30 44c Northern shoveler .75 .75
a. Block of 4, #164-167 3.00 3.00

Fish — A31

Perf. 14½x14, 14 (#187)

1988-89 Litho.

168 A31 1c Damselfish .20 .20
169 A31 3c Blackface butterflyfish .20 .20
170 A31 14c Hawkfish .25 .25
a. Booklet pane of 10 3.75 —
171 A31 15c Balloonfish .25 .25
a. Booklet pane of 10 4.50 —
172 A31 17c Trunk fish .30 .30
173 A31 22c Lyretail wrasse .35 .35
a. Booklet pane of 10 5.00 —
b. Bklt. pane, 5 each 14c, 22c 5.00 —
174 A31 25c Parrotfish .35 .35
a. Booklet pane of 10 7.25 —
b. Bklt. pane, 5 each 15c, 25c 7.25 —
175 A31 33c White-spotted boxfish .60 .60
176 A31 36c Spotted boxfish .65 .65
177 A31 39c Surgeonfish .75 .75
178 A31 44c Long-snouted butterflyfish .80 .80
179 A31 45c Trumpetfish .80 .80
180 A31 56c Sharp-nosed puffer 1.00 1.00
181 A31 $1 Seahorse 1.90 1.90
182 A31 $2 Ghost pipefish 3.50 3.50
183 A31 $5 Big-spotted triggerfish 8.00 8.00
184 A31 $10 Blue jack ('89) 16.00 16.00
Nos. 168-184 (17) 35.90 35.90

Issued: #170a, 173a, 173b, 3/31/88; 15c, 25c, 36c, 45c, 7/19/; #171a, 174a, 174b, 12/15; $10, 3/31/89; others, 3/17/88.

A32

1988 Summer Olympics, Seoul — A33

Athletes in motion: 15c, Javelin thrower. 25c, Runner. Illustrations reduced.

1988, June 30 Litho. *Perf. 14*

188 A32 15c Strip of 5, #a-e 1.65 1.65
189 A33 25c Strip of 5, #a-e 2.25 2.25

Souvenir Sheet

Pacific Voyages of Robert Louis Stevenson — A34

Stick chart of the Marshalls and: a, *Casco* sailing through the Golden Gate. b, At the Needles of Ua-Pu, Marquesas. c, *Equator* departing from Honolulu and Kaiulani, an Hawaiian princess. d, Chief's canoe, Majuro Lagoon. e, Bronze medallion, 1887, by Augustus St. Gaudens in the Tate Gallery, London. f, Outrigger canoe and S.S. *Janet Nicoll* in Majuro Lagoon. g, View of Apemama, Gilbert Is. h, Samoan outrigger canoe, Apia Harbor. i, Stevenson riding horse Jack at his estate, Vailima, Samoa.

1988, July 19 Litho. *Perf. 14*

190 Sheet of 9 6.25 4.50
a.-i. A34 25c any single .50 .50

Robert Louis Stevenson (1850-1894), Scottish novelist, poet and essayist.

Colonial Ships and Flags A35

Designs: No. 191, Galleon *Santa Maria de La Victoria*, 1526, and Spanish "Ragged Cross" ensign in use from 1516 to 1785. No. 192, Transport ships *Charlotte* and *Scarborough*, 1788, and British red ensign, 1707-1800. No. 193, Schooner *Flying Fish*, sloop-of-war *Peacock*, 1841, and U.S. flag, 1837-1845. No. 194, Steamer *Planet*, 1909, and German flag, 1867-1919.

1988, Sept. 2 Litho. *Perf. 14*

191 A35 25c multicolored .50 .50
192 A35 25c multicolored .50 .50
193 A35 25c multicolored .50 .50
194 A35 25c multicolored .50 .50
a. Block of 4, #191-194 2.00 2.00

Christmas — A36

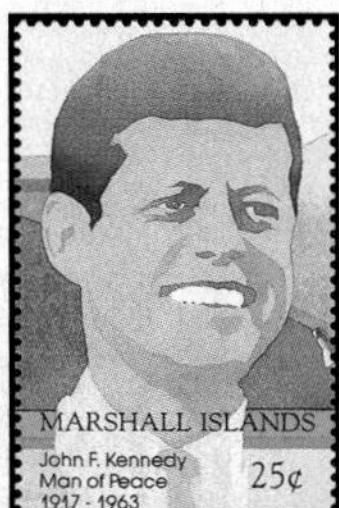

A37

No. 195, Santa Claus riding in sleigh. No. 196, Reindeer, hut and palm trees. No. 197, Reindeer and palm trees. No. 198, Reindeer, palm tree, fish. No. 199, Reindeer and outrigger canoe.

1988, Nov. 7 Litho. *Perf. 14*

195 A36 25c multicolored .50 .50
196 A36 25c multicolored .50 .50
197 A36 25c multicolored .50 .50
198 A36 25c multicolored .50 .50
199 A36 25c multicolored .50 .50
a. Strip of 5, #195-199 2.50 2.50

No. 199a has a continuous design.

1988, Nov. 22 Litho. *Perf. 14*

200 A37 25c Nuclear threat diminished .55 .55
201 A37 25c Signing the Test Ban Treaty .55 .55
202 A37 25c Portrait .55 .55
203 A37 25c US-USSR Hotline .55 .55
204 A37 25c Peace Corps enactment .55 .55
a. Strip of 5, #200-204 2.75 2.75

Tribute to John F. Kennedy. No. 204a has a continuous design.

US Space Shuttle Program and Kwajalein — A38

#205, Launch of *Prime* from Vandenberg Air Force Base downrange to the Kwajalein Missile Range. #206, *Prime* X023A/SV-5D lifting body reentering atmosphere. #207, Parachute landing and craft recovery off Kwajalein Is. #208, Shuttle over island.

1988, Dec. 23 Litho. *Perf. 14*

205 25c multicolored .50 .50
206 25c multicolored .50 .50
207 25c multicolored .50 .50
208 25c multicolored .50 .50
a. A38 Strip of 4, #205-208 2.00 2.00

NASA 30th anniv. and 25th anniv. of the Project PRIME wind tunnel tests.

See No. C21.

Links to Japan A39

Designs: No. 209, Typhoon Monument, Majuro, 1918. No. 210, Seaplane base and railway depot, Djarrej Islet, c. 1940. No. 211, Fishing boats. No. 212, Japanese honeymooners scuba diving, 1988.

1989, Jan. 19 Litho. *Perf. 14*

209 A39 45c multicolored .75 .75
210 A39 45c multicolored .75 .75
211 A39 45c multicolored .75 .75
212 A39 45c multicolored .75 .75
a. Block of 4, #209-212 3.00 3.00

Links to Alaska A40

Paintings by Claire Fejes.

1989, Mar. 31 Litho. *Perf. 14*

213 A40 45c Island Woman .85 .85
214 A40 45c Kotzebue, Alaska .85 .85
215 A40 45c Marshallese Madonna .85 .85
a. Strip of 3, #213-215 2.55 2.55

Printed in sheets of 9.

Seashell Type of 1985

1989, May 15 Litho. *Perf. 14*

216 A12 25c Pontifical miter .50 .50
217 A12 25c Tapestry turban .50 .50
218 A12 25c Flame-mouthed helmet .50 .50
219 A12 25c Prickly Pacific drupe .50 .50
220 A12 25c Blood-mouthed conch .50 .50
a. Strip of 5, #216-220 2.50 2.50

Souvenir Sheet

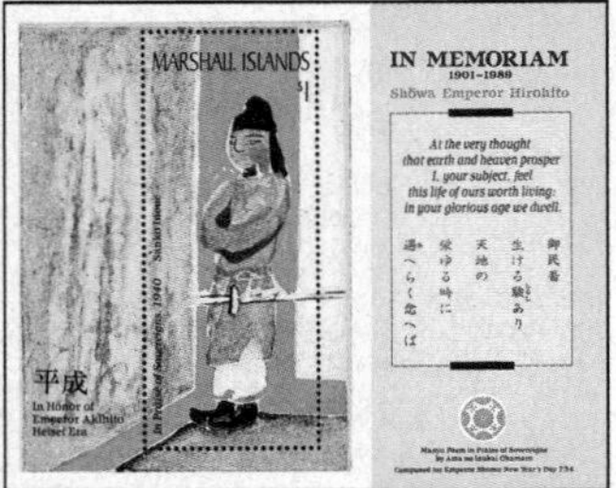

In Praise of Sovereigns, 1940, by Sanko Inoue — A41

1989, May 15 Litho. *Perf. 14*

221 A41 $1 multicolored 2.00 2.00

Hirohito (1901-89) and enthronement of Akihito as emperor of Japan.

Migrant Birds A42

1989, June 27 Litho. *Perf. 14*

222 A42 45c Wandering tattler .85 .85
223 A42 45c Ruddy turnstone .85 .85
224 A42 45c Pacific golden plover .85 .85
225 A42 45c Sanderling .85 .85
a. Block of 4, #222-225 3.40 3.40

Postal History A43

PHILEXFRANCE '89 — A44

Designs: No. 226, Missionary ship *Morning Star V,* 1905, and Marshall Isls. #15 canceled. No. 227, Marshall Isls. #15-16 on registered letter, 1906. No. 228, *Prinz Eitel Friedrich,* 1914, and German sea post cancel. No. 229, Cruiser squadron led by SMS *Scharnhorst,* 1914, and German sea post cancel.

No. 230: a, SMS *Bussard* and German sea post cancel and Germany #32. b, US Type A924 and Marshall Isls. #34a on FDC. c, LST 119 FPO, 1944, US Navy cancel and pair of US #853. d, Mail boat, 1936, cancel and Japan #222. e, Majuro PO f, Marshall Isls. cancel, 1951, and four US #803.

No. 231, Germany #32 and Marshall Isls. cancel, 1889.

1989, July 7

226 A43 45c multicolored .80 .80
227 A43 45c multicolored .80 .80
228 A43 45c multicolored .80 .80
229 A43 45c multicolored .80 .80
a. Block of 4, #226-229 3.25 3.25

Souvenir Sheets

230 Sheet of 6 10.00 10.00
a.-f. A44 25c any single 1.50 1.50
231 A43 $1 multicolored 10.00 3.00

Nos. 230b and 230e are printed in a continuous design.

1st Moon Landing, 20th Anniv. A45

Apollo 11: No. 232, Liftoff. No. 233, Neil Armstrong. No. 234, Lunar module *Eagle.* No. 235, Michael Collins. No. 236, Raising the American flag on the Moon. No. 237, Buzz Aldrin. $1, 1st step on the Moon and "We came in peace for all mankind."

1989, Aug. 1 Litho. *Perf. 13½*

Booklet Stamps

232 A45 25c multicolored 1.25 1.25
233 A45 25c multicolored 1.25 1.25
234 A45 25c multicolored 1.25 1.25
235 A45 25c multicolored 1.25 1.25
236 A45 25c multicolored 1.25 1.25
237 A45 25c multicolored 1.25 1.25

Size: 75x32mm

238 A45 $1 multicolored 7.00 5.00
a. Booklet pane of 7, #232-238 15.00
Nos. 232-238 (7) 14.50 12.50

Decorative inscribed selvage separates No. 238 from Nos. 232-237 and surrounds it like a souvenir sheet margin. Selvage around Nos. 232-237 is plain.

World War II

A46

A47

Anniversaries and events, 1939: #239, Invasion of Poland. #240, Sinking of HMS *Royal Oak.* #241, Invasion of Finland.

Battle of the River Plate: #242, HMS *Exeter,.* #243, HMS *Ajax,.* #244, *Admiral Graf Spee,.* #245, HMNZS *Achilles,.*

1989 Litho. *Perf. 13½*

239 A46 25c W1 (1-1) .60 .45
240 A46 45c W2 (1-1) 1.00 .75
241 A46 45c W3 (1-1) 1.00 .75
242 A46 45c W4 (4-1) .80 .75
243 A46 45c W4 (4-2) .80 .75
244 A46 45c W4 (4-3) .80 .75
245 A46 45c W4 (4-4) .80 .75
a. Block of 4, #242-245 3.25 3.00

Issued: #239, 9/1; #240, 10/13; #241, 11/30; #245a, 12/13.

1990

1940: #246, Invasion of Denmark. #247, Invasion of Norway. #248, Katyn Forest Massacre. #249, Bombing of Rotterdam. #250, Invasion of Belgium. #251, Winston Churchill becomes prime minister of England. #252, Evacuation of the British Expeditionary Force at Dunkirk. #253, Evacuation at Dunkirk. #254, Occupation of Paris.

246 A46 25c W5 (2-1) .60 .50
247 A46 25c W5 (2-2) .60 .50
a. Pair, #246-247 1.25 1.00
248 A47 25c W6 (1-1) .50 .50
249 A46 25c W8 (2-1) .50 .50
250 A46 25c W8 (2-2) .50 .50
a. Pair, #249-250 1.00 1.00
251 A46 45c W7 (1-1) 1.00 .90
252 A46 45c W9 (2-1) 1.00 .90
253 A46 45c W9 (2-2) 1.00 .90
a. Pair, #252-253 2.00 1.80
254 A47 45c W10 (1-1) 1.00 .90

Issued: #247a, 4/9; #248, 4/16; #249-251, 5/10; #252-253, 6/4; #254, 6/14.

1990

#255, Battle of Mers-el-Kebir, 1940. #256, Battles for the Burma Road, 1940-45.

US Destroyers for British bases: #257, HMS Georgetown (ex-USS Maddox). #258, HMS Banff (ex-USCGC Saranac). #259, HMS Buxton (ex-USS Edwards). #260, HMS Rockingham (ex-USS Swasey).

Battle of Britain: #261, Supermarine Spitfire Mark IA. #262, Hawker Hurricane Mark I. #263, Messerschmitt Bf109E. #264, Junkers JU87B-2. #265, Tripartite Pact Signed 1940.

255 A46 25c W11 (1-1) .60 .50
256 A47 25c W12 (1-1) .60 .50
257 A46 45c W13 (4-1) 1.00 .90
258 A46 45c W13 (4-2) 1.00 .90
259 A46 45c W13 (4-3) 1.00 .90
260 A46 45c W13 (4-4) 1.00 .90
a. Block of 4, #257-260 4.00 3.60
261 A46 45c W14 (4-1) 1.00 .90
262 A46 45c W14 (4-2) 1.00 .90
263 A46 45c W14 (4-3) 1.00 .90
264 A46 45c W14 (4-4) 1.00 .90
a. Block of 4, #261-264 4.00 3.60
265 A46 45c W15 1.10 .90

Issued: #255, 7/3; #256, 7/18; #260a, 9/9; #264a, 9/15; #265, 9/27.

1990-91

Designs: #266, Roosevelt elected to third term, 1940. Battle of Taranto: #267, HMS Illustrious. #268, Fairey Swordfish. #269, RM Andrea Doria. #270, RM Conte di Cavour.

Roosevelt's Four Freedoms Speech: #271, Freedom of Speech. #272, Freedom from Want. #273, Freedom of Worship. #274, Freedom From Fear. #275, Battle of Beda Fomm, Feb. 5-7, 1941.

Germany Invades the Balkans: #276, Invasion of Greece. #277, Invasion of Yugoslavia.

Sinking of the Bismarck: #278, HMS Prince of Wales. #279, HMS Hood. #280, Bismarck. #281, Fairey Swordfish. #282, German Invasion of Russia, 1941.

266 A47 25c W16 .60 .50
267 A46 25c W17 (4-1) .60 .50
268 A46 25c W17 (4-2) .60 .50
269 A46 25c W17 (4-3) .60 .50
270 A46 25c W17 (4-4) .60 .50
a. Block of 4, #266-270 2.50 2.00
271 A46 30c W18 (4-1) .65 .60
272 A46 30c W18 (4-2) .65 .60
273 A46 30c W18 (4-3) .65 .60
274 A46 30c W18 (4-4) .65 .60
a. Block of 4, #271-274 2.60 2.40
275 A46 30c Tanks, W19 .60 .60
276 A47 29c W20 (2-1) .60 .60
277 A47 29c W20 (2-2) .60 .60
a. Pair, #276-277 1.25 1.25
278 A46 50c W21 (4-1) 1.00 1.00
279 A46 50c W21 (4-2) 1.00 1.00
280 A46 50c W21 (4-3) 1.00 1.00
281 A46 50c W21 (4-4) 1.00 1.00
a. Block of 4, #278-281 4.00 4.00
282 A46 30c Tanks, W22 .60 .60

Issued: #266, 11/5/90; #270a, 11/11/90; #274a, 1/6/91; #275, 2/5/91; #277a, 4/6/91; #281a, 5/27/91; #282, 6/22/91.

1991

1941 — Declaration of the Atlantic Charter: #283, Pres. Roosevelt and USS Augusta. #284, Churchill and HMS Prince of Wales. #285, Siege of Moscow.

Sinking of USS Reuben James: #286, Reuben James hit by torpedo. #287, German U-562 submarine.

Japanese attack on Pearl Harbor: #288, American warplanes. # 289, Japanese warplanes. #290, USS Arizona. #291, Japanese aircraft carrier Akagi.

283 A47 29c W23 (2-1) .60 .60
284 A47 29c W23 (2-2) .60 .60
a. Pair, #283-284 1.25 1.25
285 A46 29c W24 .60 .60
286 A46 30c W25 (2-1) .60 .60
287 A46 30c W25 (2-1) .60 .60
a. Pair, #286-287 1.25 1.25
288 A47 50c W26 (4-1) 1.00 1.00
a. Revised inscription 4.75 1.00
289 A47 50c W26 (4-2) 1.00 1.00
290 A47 50c W26 (4-3) 1.00 1.00
291 A47 50c W26 (4-4) 1.00 1.00
a. Block of 4, #288-291 4.00 4.00
b. Block of 4, #288a, 289-291 8.50 4.00

Inscriptions read "Peal" on No. 288 and "Pearl" on No. 288a.

Issued: #284a, 8/14; #285, 10/2; #287a, 10/31; #291a, 12/7.

1991-92

1941-42: #292, Japanese capture Guam. #293, Fall of Singapore.

First combat of the Flying Tigers: #294, Curtiss Tomahawk. #295, Mitsubishi Ki-21 on fire. #296, Fall of Wake Island.

#297, Roosevelt and Churchill at Arcadia Conference. #298, Japanese tank entering Manila. #299, Japanese take Rabaul. #300, Battle of the Java Sea. #301, Rangoon falls to Japanese. #302, Japanese land on New Guinea. #303, MacArthur evacuated from Corregidor. #304, Raid on Saint-Nazaire. #305, Surrender of Bataan / Death March. #306, Doolittle Raid on Tokyo. #307, Fall of Corregidor.

292 A47 29c W27 .60 .60
293 A46 29c W28 .60 .60
294 A46 50c W29 (2-1) 1.00 1.00
295 A46 50c W29 (2-2) 1.00 1.00
a. Pair, #294-295 2.00 2.00
296 A46 29c W30 .60 .60
297 A46 29c W31 .60 .60
298 A46 50c W32 1.00 1.00
299 A46 29c W33 .60 .60
300 A46 29c W34 .60 .60
301 A47 50c W35 1.00 1.00
302 A46 29c W36 .60 .60
303 A46 29c W37 .60 .60
304 A46 29c W38 .60 .60
305 A47 29c W39 .60 .60
306 A47 50c W40 1.00 1.00
307 A46 29c W41 .60 .60

Issued: #292-293, 12/10/91; #295a, 12/20/91; #296, 12/23/91; #297, 1/1/92; #298, 1/2/92; #299, 1/23/92; #300, 2/15/92; #301-302, 3/8/92; #303, 3/11/92; #304, 3/27/92; #305, 4/9/92; #306, 4/18/92; #307, 5/6/92.

1992

1942 — Battle of the Coral Sea: #308, USS Lexington. #309, Japanese Mitsubishi A6M2 Zeros. #310, Douglas SBD Dauntless dive bombers. #311, Japanese carrier Shoho.

Battle of Midway: #312, Japanese aircraft carrier Akagi. #313, U.S. Douglas SBD Dauntless dive bombers. #314, USS Yorktown. #315, Nakajima B5N2 Kate torpedo planes.

#316, Village of Lidice destroyed. #317, Fall of Sevastopol.

Convoy PQ17 destroyed: #318, British merchant ship in convoy. #319, German U-boats.

#320, Marines land on Guadalcanal. #323, Battle of Stalingrad. #324, Battle of Eastern Solomons.

#321, Battle of Savo Island. #322, Dieppe Raid. #325, Battle of Cape Esperance. #326, Battle of El Alamein.

Battle of Barents Sea: #327, HMS Sheffield. #328, Admiral Hipper.

308 A46 50c W42 (4-1) 1.00 1.00
a. Revised inscription 2.00 1.00
309 A46 50c W42 (4-2) 1.00 1.00
a. Revised inscription 2.00 1.00
310 A46 50c W42 (4-3) 1.00 1.00
a. Revised inscription 2.00 1.00
311 A46 50c W42 (4-4) 1.00 1.00
a. Block of 4, #308-311 4.00 4.00
b. Revised inscription 2.00 1.00
c. Block of 4, #308a-310a, 311b 8.50 4.00
312 A46 50c W43 (4-1) 1.00 1.00
313 A46 50c W43 (4-3) 1.00 1.00
314 A46 50c W43 (4-2) 1.00 1.00
315 A46 50c W43 (4-4) 1.00 1.00
a. Block of 4, #312-315 4.00 4.00
316 A46 29c W44 .60 .60
317 A47 29c W45 .60 .60
318 A46 29c W46 (2-1) .60 .60
319 A46 29c W46 (2-2) .60 .60
a. Pair, #318-319 1.25 1.25
320 A46 29c W47 .60 .60
321 A47 29c W48 .60 .60
322 A46 29c W49 .60 .60
323 A47 50c W50 1.25 1.00
324 A46 29c W51 .60 .60
325 A46 50c W52 1.25 1.00
326 A46 29c W53 .60 .60
327 A46 29c W54 (2-1) .60 .60
328 A46 29c W54 (2-2) .60 .60
a. Pair, #327-328 1.25 1.25

Inscription reads "U.S.S. Lexington/Grumman F4F-3 Wildcat" on No. 308a, "Japanese Aichi D3A1 Vals/Nakajima B5N2 Kate" on No. 309a, "U.S. Douglas TBD-1 Devastators" on No. 310a, "Japanese Carrier Shoho/Mitsubishi A6M2 Zeros" on No. 311b.

Issued: #311a, 5/8/92; #315a, 6/4; #316, 6/9/92; #317, 7/4; #319a, 7/5; #320, 8/7; #321, 8/9; #322-323, 8/19; #324, 8/24; #325, 10/11; #326, 10/23; #328a, 12/31.

Vertical pairs, Nos. 312-313 and Nos. 314-315 have continuous designs.

No. 310 incorrectly identifies Douglas TBD torpedo bombers.

1993 Litho. *Perf. 13½*

1943 — #329, Casablanca Conf. #330, Liberation of Kharkov.

Battle of Bismarck Sea: #331, Japanese A6M Zeroes, destroyer Arashio. #332, U.S. P38 Lightnings, Australian Beaufighter. #333, Japanese destroyer Shirayuki. #334, U.S. A-20 Havoc, B-25 Mitchell.

#335, Interception of Admiral Yamamoto.

Battle of Kursk: #336, German Tiger I. #337, Soviet T-34.

329 A46 29c W55 .65 .60
330 A46 29c W56 .65 .60
331 A46 50c W57 (4-1) 1.00 1.00
332 A46 50c W57 (4-2) 1.00 1.00
333 A46 50c W57 (4-3) 1.00 1.00
334 A46 50c W57 (4-4) 1.00 1.00
a. Block of 4, #331-334 4.00 4.00
335 A46 50c W58 1.00 1.00
336 A46 29c W59 (2-1) .85 .60
337 A46 29c W59 (2-2) .85 .60
a. Pair, #336-337 1.70 1.25
Nos. 239-337 (99) 78.50 74.05

Issued: #329, 1/14; #330, 2/16; #334a, 3/3; #335, 4/18; #337a, 7/5.

See #467-524, 562-563.

Christmas A57

Angels playing musical instruments.

1989, Oct. 25 *Perf. 13½*

341 A57 25c Horn .80 .80
342 A57 25c Singing carol .80 .80
343 A57 25c Lute .80 .80
344 A57 25c Lyre .80 .80
a. Block of 4, #341-344 3.25 3.25

Miniature Sheet

Milestones in Space Exploration A58

Designs: a, Robert Goddard and 1st liquid fuel rocket launch, 1926. b, *Sputnik,* 1st manmade satellite, 1957. c, 1st American satellite, 1958. d, Yuri Gagarin, 1st man in space, 1961. e, John Glenn, 1st American to orbit Earth, 1962. f, Valentina Tereshkova, 1st woman in space, 1963. g, Aleksei Leonov, 1st space walk, 1965. h, Edward White, 1st American to walk in space, 1965. i, Gemini-Titan 6A, 1st rendezvous in space, 1965. j, 1st Soft landing on the Moon, 1966. k, Gemini 8, 1st docking in space, 1966. l, 1st probe of Venus, 1967. m, Apollo 8, 1st manned orbit of the Moon, 1968. n, Apollo 11, 1st man on the Moon, 1969. o, Soyuz 11, 1st space station crew, 1971. p, Apollo 15, 1st manned lunar vehicle, 1971. q, *Skylab 2,* 1st American manned space station, 1973. r, 1st Flyby of Jupiter, 1973. s, Apollo-Soyuz, 1st joint space flight, 1975. t, 1st Landing on Mars, 1976. u, 1st flyby of Saturn, 1979. v, *Columbia,* 1st space shuttle flight, 1981. w, 1st probe beyond the solar system, 1983. x, 1st untethered space walk, 1984. y, Launch of space shuttle *Discovery,* 1988.

1989, Nov. 24 Litho. *Perf. 13½*

345 Sheet of 25 25.00 25.00
a.-y. A58 45c any single .90 .90

No. 345 contains World Stamp Expo '89 emblem on selvage.

Birds

A59 A59a

1990-92 Litho. *Perf. 13½*

346 A59 1c Black noddy .20 .20
347 A59 5c Red-tailed tropic bird .20 .20
348 A59 10c Sanderling .20 .20
349 A59 12c Black-naped tern .25 .25
350 A59 15c Wandering tattler .30 .30
351 A59 20c Bristle-thighed curlew .40 .40
352 A59 23c Northern shoveler .45 .45
353 A59 25c Brown noddy .50 .50
354 A59 27c Sooty tern .55 .55
355 A59 29c Wedge-tailed shearwater .60 .60
356 A59a 29c Northern pintail .60 .60
357 A59 30c Pacific golden plover .60 .60
358 A59 35c Brown booby .70 .70
359 A59 36c Red footed booby .75 .75
360 A59 40c White tern .80 .80
361 A59 50c Great frigate bird 1.00 1.00
a. Min. sheet of 4 (#347, 350, 353, 361) 2.25 2.00
362 A59 52c Great crested tern 1.00 1.00
363 A59 65c Lesser sand plover 1.25 1.25
364 A59 75c Little tern 1.50 1.50
365 A59 $1 Pacific reef heron 2.00 2.00
365A A59 $2 Masked booby 4.00 4.00
Nos. 346-365A (21) 17.85 17.85

No. 361a for ESSEN '90, Germany Apr. 19-22.

Issued: 5c, 15c, 25c, 50c, 3/8; 30c, 36c, 40c, $1, 10/11; #361a, 4/19; #355, 20c, 52c, 2/22/91; 27c, 3/8/91; 1c, 12c, 35c, $2, 11/6/91; #356, 2/3/92; 10c, 23c, 65c, 75c, 4/24/92.

See Nos. 430-433.

Children's Games A60

1990, Mar. 15

366 A60 25c Lodidean .80 .75
367 A60 25c Lejonjon .80 .75
368 A60 25c Etobobo .80 .75
369 A60 25c Didmakol .80 .75
a. Block of 4, #366-369 3.25 3.00

Penny Black, 150th Anniv. A61

Designs: No. 370, Penny Black, 1840. No. 371, Essay by James Chalmers. No. 372, Essay by Robert Sievier. No. 373, Essay by Charles Whiting. No. 374, Essay by George Dickinson. No. 375, Medal engraved by William Wyon to celebrate Queen Victoria's first visit to London. $1, Engraver Charles Heath, engraving for master die.

1990, Apr. 6 Booklet Stamps

370 A61 25c multicolored 1.00 1.00
371 A61 25c multicolored 1.00 1.00
372 A61 25c multicolored 1.00 1.00
373 A61 25c multicolored 1.00 1.00
374 A61 25c multicolored 1.00 1.00
375 A61 25c multicolored 1.00 1.00

Size: 73x31mm

376 A61 $1 multicolored 4.00 4.00
a. Booklet pane of 7, #370-376 10.00 —
Nos. 370-376 (7) 10.00 10.00

Decorative inscribed selvage picturing part of a Penny Black proof sheet separates No. 376 from Nos. 370-375 in pane and surrounds it like a souvenir sheet margin. Selvage around Nos. 370-375 is plain.

Endangered Wildlife — A62

Sea Turtles: No. 377, Pacific green turtle hatchlings entering ocean. No. 378, Pacific great turtle under water. No. 379, Hawksbill hatchling, eggs. No. 380, Hawksbill turtle in water.

1990, May 3

377 A62 25c multicolored .80 .75
378 A62 25c multicolored .80 .75
379 A62 25c multicolored .80 .75
380 A62 25c multicolored .80 .75
a. Block of 4, #377-380 3.25 3.00

Stick Chart, Canoe and Flag of the Republic of the Marshall Islands A63

1990, Sept. 28 *Perf. 11x10½*

381 A63 25c multicolored .95 .60

See #615, US #2507, Micronesia #124-126.

German Reunification — A64

1990, Oct. 3 *Perf. 13½*

382 A64 45c multicolored 1.25 1.00

Christmas A65

1990, Oct. 25 Litho. *Perf. 13½*

383 A65 25c Canoe, stick chart .75 .75
384 A65 25c Missionary preaching .75 .75
385 A65 25c Sailors dancing .75 .75
386 A65 25c Youths dancing .75 .75
a. Block of 4, #383-386 3.00 3.00

Breadfruit — A66

1990, Dec. 15 Litho. *Perf. 12x12½*

387 A66 25c Harvesting .75 .75
388 A66 25c Peeling, slicing .75 .75
389 A66 25c Preserving .75 .75
390 A66 25c Kneading dough .75 .75
a. Block of 4, #387-390 3.00 3.00

US Space Shuttle Flights, 10th Anniv. A67

1991, Apr. 12 Litho. *Perf. 13½*

391 A67 50c 747 ferry .90 .90
392 A67 50c Orbital release of LDEF .90 .90
393 A67 50c Lift-off .90 .90
394 A67 50c Landing .90 .90
a. Block of 4, #391-394 3.75 3.75

Flowers — A68

1991, June 10 Litho. *Perf. 13½*

395 A68 52c Ixora carolinensis 1.10 1.00
396 A68 52c Clerodendrum inerme 1.10 1.00
397 A68 52c Messerchmidia argentea 1.10 1.00
398 A68 52c Vigna marina 1.10 1.00
a. Miniature sheet of 4, #395-398 4.75 4.00
b. Block of 4, #395-398, without inscription 4.50 4.00

Phila Nippon '91 (No. 398a). Stamps from miniature sheets inscribed C53A.

Operation Desert Storm — A69

1991, July 4 Litho. *Perf. 13½*

399	A69	29c	multicolored	.80	.60

Birds — A70

1991, July 16 Booklet Stamps

400	A70	29c	Red-footed booby	1.25	.60
401	A70	29c	Great frigate bird (7-2)	1.25	.60
402	A70	29c	Brown booby	1.25	.60
403	A70	29c	White tern	1.25	.60
404	A70	29c	Great frigate bird (7-5)	1.25	.60
405	A70	29c	Black noddy	1.25	.60

Size: 75x33mm

406	A70	$1	White-tailed tropic bird	6.50	2.00
a.			Booklet pane of 7, #400-406	14.00	—
			Nos. 400-406 (7)	14.00	5.60

Decorative selvage separates No. 406 from Nos. 400-405 and surrounds it like a souvenir sheet margin.

Aircraft of Air Marshall Islands — A71

1991, Sept. 10 Litho. *Perf. 13½*

407	A71	12c	Dornier 228	.25	.20
408	A71	29c	Douglas DC-8	.65	.50
409	A71	50c	Hawker Siddeley 748	1.10	.85
410	A71	50c	Saab 2000	1.10	.85
			Nos. 407-410 (4)	3.10	2.40

Admission to United Nations A72

1991, Sept. 24 Litho. *Perf. 11x10½*

411	A72	29c	multicolored	.70	.65

Christmas — A73

1991, Oct. 25 *Perf. 13½*

412	A73	30c	multicolored	.75	.75

Peace Corps in Marshall Islands, 25th Anniv. A74

1991, Nov. 26 Litho. *Perf. 11x10½*

413	A74	29c	multicolored	.75	.60

Ships A75

#414, Bulk cargo carrier, Emlain. #415, Tanker, CSK Valiant. #416, Patrol boat, Ionmeto. #417, Freighter, Micro Pilot.

1992, Feb. 15 Litho. *Perf. 11x10½*

414	A75	29c	multicolored	.80	.45
415	A75	29c	multicolored	.80	.45
416	A75	29c	multicolored	.80	.45
417	A75	29c	multicolored	.80	.45
a.			Strip of 4, #414-417	3.25	2.00

Voyages of Discovery A76

Designs: No. 418, Traditional tipnol. No. 419, Reconstructed Santa Maria. No. 420, Constellation Argo Navis. No. 421, Marshallese sailor, tipnol. No. 422, Columbus, Santa Maria. No. 423, Astronaunt, Argo Navis. $1, Columbus, sailor, and astronaunt.

1992, May 23 Litho. *Perf. 13½*

Booklet Stamps

418	A76	50c	multicolored	1.00	1.00
419	A76	50c	multicolored	1.00	1.00
420	A76	50c	multicolored	1.00	1.00
421	A76	50c	multicolored	1.00	1.00
422	A76	50c	multicolored	1.00	1.00
423	A76	50c	multicolored	1.00	1.00

Size: 75x32mm

424	A76	$1	multicolored	4.00	2.00
a.			Booklet pane of 7, #418-424	10.00	—

Decorative selvage separates No. 424 from Nos. 418-423 and surrounds it like a souvenir sheet margin.

Traditional Handicrafts — A77

1992, Sept. 9 Litho. *Perf. 13½*

425	A77	29c	Basket weaving	.60	.60
426	A77	29c	Canoe models	.60	.60
427	A77	29c	Wood carving	.60	.60
428	A77	29c	Fan making	.60	.60
a.			Strip of 4, #425-428	2.40	2.40

Christmas A78

1992, Oct. 29 Litho. *Perf. 11x10½*

429	A78	29c	multicolored	.70	.60

Bird Type of 1990

1992, Nov. 10 Litho. *Perf. 13½*

430	A59	9c	Whimbrel	.20	.20
431	A59	22c	Greater scaup	.45	.45
432	A59	28c	Sharp-tailed sandpiper	.55	.55
433	A59	45c	Common teal	.90	.90
			Nos. 430-433 (4)	2.10	2.10

Reef Life — A79

1993, May 26 Litho. *Perf. 13½*

434	A79	50c	Butterflyfish	1.40	1.00
435	A79	50c	Soldierfish	1.40	1.00
436	A79	50c	Damselfish	1.40	1.00
437	A79	50c	Filefish	1.40	1.00
438	A79	50c	Hawkfish	1.40	1.00
439	A79	50c	Surgeonfish	1.40	1.00

Size: 75x33mm

440	A79	$1	Parrotfish	5.50	2.00
a.			Booklet pane of 7, #434-440	13.00	—
			Nos. 434-440 (7)	13.90	8.00

Decorative selvage separates No. 440 from Nos. 434-439 and surrounds it like a souvenir sheet margin.

Ships A80

Marshallese Sailing Vessels — A81

Designs: 10c, Spanish galleon San Jeronimo. 14c, USCG Fisheries Patrol vessel Cape Corwin. 15c, British merchant ship Britannia. 19c, Island transport Micro Palm. 20c, Dutch ship Eendracht. 23c, Frigate HMS Cornwallis. 24c, U.S. naval schooner Dolphin. 29c, Missionary packet Morning Star. 30c, Russian brig Rurick. 32c, Spanish sailing ship Santa Maria de la Vittoria. 35c, German warship SMS Nautilus. 40c, British brig Nautilus. 45c, Japanese warships Nagara, Isuzu. 46c, Trading schooner Equator. 50c, Aircraft carrier USS Lexington CV-16. 52c, HMS Serpent. 55c, Whaling ship Potomac. 60c, Coast Guard cutter Assateague. 75c, British transport Scarborough. 78c, Whaler Charles W. Morgan. 95c, US steam vessel Tanager. $1, Walap, Eniwetok. $1, Barkentine hospital ship Tole Mour. $2, Walap, Jaluit. $2.90, Marshall Islands fishing vessels. $3, Schooner Victoria. $5, Tipnol, Ailuk. $10, Racing canoes.

Perf. 11x10½ (A80), 13½ (A81)

1993-95 Litho.

441	A80	10c	multicolored	.20	.20
442	A80	14c	multicolored	.30	.30
443	A80	15c	multicolored	.30	.30
444	A80	19c	multicolored	.40	.40
445	A80	20c	multicolored	.40	.40
446	A80	23c	multicolored	.45	.45
447	A80	24c	multicolored	.50	.50
448	A80	29c	multicolored	.60	.60
449	A80	30c	multicolored	.60	.60
450	A80	32c	multicolored	.65	.65
451	A80	35c	multicolored	.70	.70
452	A80	40c	multicolored	.80	.80
453	A80	45c	multicolored	.90	.90
454	A80	46c	multicolored	.95	.95
455	A80	50c	multicolored	1.00	1.00
456	A80	52c	multicolored	1.10	1.10
457	A80	55c	multicolored	1.10	1.10
458	A80	60c	multicolored	1.25	1.25
459	A80	75c	multicolored	1.50	1.50
460	A80	78c	multicolored	1.65	1.65
461	A80	95c	multicolored	1.90	1.90
462	A80	$1	multicolored	2.00	2.00
463	A81	$1	multicolored	2.00	2.00
464	A81	$2	multicolored	4.00	4.00
465	A80	$2.90	multicolored	5.75	5.75
466	A80	$3	multicolored	6.00	6.00
466A	A81	$5	multicolored	10.00	10.00
466B	A81	$10	multicolored	20.00	20.00
			Nos. 441-466B (28)	67.00	67.00

Souvenir Sheet

Stamp Size: 46x26mm

466C	A81		Sheet of 4, #d.-g.	3.75	3.50

No. 466C contains 15c, 23c, 52c and 75c stamps. Inscription reads "Hong Kong '94 Stamp Exhibition" in Chinese on Nos. 466Cd, 466Cg, and in English on Nos. 466Ce-466Cf.

Issued: 15c, 24c, 29c, 50c, 6/24/93; 19c, 23c, 52c, 75c, 10/14/93; #463, 5/29/93; $2, 8/26. 10c, 30c, 35c, $2.90, 4/19/94; $5, 3/15/94; $10, 8/18/94; 20c, 40c, 45c, 55c, 9/23/94; #466C, 2/18/94; 14c, 46c, 95c, #462, 9/25/95; 32c, 60c, 78c, $3, 5/5/95.

See #605.

World War II Type of 1989

1943 — Invasion of Sicily: #467, Gen. George S. Patton, Jr. #468, Gen. Bernard L. Montgomery. #469, Americans landing at at Licata. #470, British landing south of Syracuse.

Allied bomber raids on Schweinfurt: #471, B-17F Flying Fortresses and Bf-109 fighter. #472, Liberation of Smolensk. #473, Landings at Bougainville. #474, Invasion of Tarawa, 1943. #475, Teheran Conference, 1943.

Battle of North Cape: #476, HMS Duke of York. #477, Scharnhorst.

1944 — #478, Gen. Dwight D. Eisenhower, SHAEF Commander. #479, Invasion of Anzio. #480, Siege of Leningrad lifted. #481, U.S. liberates Marshall Islands. #482, Japanese defeated at Truk. #483, Big Week, US bombing of Germany.

1993-94 Litho. *Perf. 13½*

467	A46	52c	W60 (4-1)	1.10	1.10
468	A46	52c	W60 (4-2)	1.10	1.10
469	A46	52c	W60 (4-3)	1.10	1.10
470	A46	52c	W60 (4-4)	1.10	1.10
a.			Block of 4, #467-470	4.50	4.50
471	A46	50c	W61	1.00	1.00
472	A47	29c	W62	.60	.60
473	A46	29c	W63	.60	.60
474	A46	50c	W64	1.00	1.00
475	A47	52c	W65	1.10	1.10
476	A46	29c	W66 (2-1)	.60	.60
477	A46	29c	W66 (2-2)	.60	.60
a.			Pair, #476-477	1.25	1.25
478	A46	29c	W67	.60	.60
479	A46	50c	W68	1.00	1.00
480	A46	52c	W69	1.10	1.10
481	A46	29c	W70	.60	.60
482	A47	29c	W71	.60	.60
483	A46	52c	W72	1.10	1.10
			Nos. 467-483 (17)	14.90	14.90

Issued: #467-470, 7/10/93; #471, 8/17/93; #472, 9/25/93; #473, 11/1/93; #474, 11/20/93; #475, 12/1/93; #476-477, 12/26/93; #478, 1/16/94; #479, 1/22/94; #480, 1/27/94; #481, 2/4/94; #482, 2/17/94; #483, 2/20/94.

1994 Litho. *Perf. 13½*

1944 — #484, Lt. Gen. Mark Clark, Rome falls to the Allies.

D-Day-Allied landings in Normandy: #485, Horsa gliders. #486, U.S. P-51B Mustangs, British Hurricanes. #487, German gun defenses. #488, Allied amphibious landing.

#489, V-1 flying bombs strike England. #490, U.S. Marines land on Saipan.

First Battle of the Philippine Sea: #491, Grumman F6F-3 Hellcat.

#492, U.S. liberates Guam. #493, Warsaw uprising. #494, Liberation of Paris. #495, U.S. Marines land on Peliliu. #496, MacArthur returns to the Philippines. #497, Battle of Leyte Gulf.

German battleship Tirpitz sunk: #498, Avro Lancaster. #499, Tirpitz.

Battle of the Bulge: #500, Infantry. #501, Armor. #502, Aviation. #503, Lt. Col. Creighton W. Abrams, Brig. Gen. Anthony C. McAuliffe.

484	A47	50c	W73	1.00	1.00
485	A46	75c	W74 (4-1)	1.60	1.50
a.			Revised inscription	3.25	1.50
486	A46	75c	W74 (4-2)	1.60	1.50
a.			Revised inscription	3.25	1.50
487	A46	75c	W74 (4-3)	1.60	1.50
a.			Revised inscription	3.25	1.50
488	A46	75c	W74 (4-4)	1.60	1.50
a.			Block of 4, #485-488	6.50	6.00
b.			Block of 4, #485a-487a, 488	12.00	6.00
489	A46	50c	W75	1.00	1.00
490	A46	29c	W76	.60	.60
491	A46	50c	W77	1.00	1.00
492	A46	29c	W78	.60	.60
493	A46	50c	W79	1.00	1.00
494	A46	50c	W80	1.00	1.00
495	A46	29c	W81	.60	.60
496	A46	52c	W82	1.00	1.00
497	A46	52c	multicolored	1.00	1.00
498	A46	50c	W84 (2-1)	1.00	1.00
499	A46	50c	W84 (2-2)	1.00	1.00
a.			Pair, #498-499	2.00	2.00
500	A47	50c	W85 (4-1)	1.00	1.00
501	A47	50c	W85 (4-2)	1.00	1.00
502	A47	50c	W85 (4-3)	1.00	1.00
503	A47	50c	W85 (4-4)	1.00	1.00
a.			Block of 4, #500-503	5.00	4.00
			Nos. 484-503 (20)	21.20	20.80

Inscription reads "Horsa Gliders, Parachute Troops" on #485a, "British Typhoon-1B, U.S. P51B Mustangs" on #486a, "German Gun Defenses, Pointe du Hoc" on #487a.

Issued: #484, 6/4; #485-488, 6/6; #489, 6/13; #490, 6/15; #491, 6/19; #492, 7/21; #493, 8/1; 494, 8/25; #495, 9/15; #496, 10/20; #497, 10/24; #498-499, 11/12; #500-503, 12/16.

1995 Litho. *Perf. 13½*

1945 — #504, Stalin, Churchill, Roosevelt, Yalta Conference. #505, Meissen porcelain, bombing of Dresden, 1945. #506, Iwo Jima invaded by US Marines.

#507, Remagen Bridge taken by US forces. #508, Okinawa invaded by US forces. #509, Death of Franklin D. Roosevelt.

#510, US/USSR troops meet at Elbe River. #511, Russian troops capture Berlin. #512, Allies liberate concentration camps.

VE Day: #513, German surrender, Rheims. # 514, Times Square, New York. #515, Victory Parade, Moscow. #516, Buckingham Palace, London.

UN Charter signed: #517, 563, U.S. Pres. Harry S Truman, Veteran's Memorial Hall, San Francisco.

#518, Potsdam Conference Convenes. #519, Churchill resigns. #520, B-29 Enola Gay drops atomic bomb on Hiroshima.

V-J Day: #521, Mt. Fuji, ships in Tokyo Bay. #522, USS Missouri. #523, Adm. Nimitz signs surrender document. #524, Japanese delegation.

504 A47 32c W86 .65 .65
505 A47 55c W87 1.10 1.10
506 A47 $1 W88 2.25 2.00
507 A47 32c W89 .65 .65
508 A47 55c W90 1.10 1.10
509 A46 50c W91 1.00 1.00
510 A46 32c W92 .65 .65
511 A46 60c W93 1.25 1.25
512 A46 55c W94 1.10 1.10
513 A46 75c W95 (4-1) 1.60 1.50
514 A46 75c W95 (4-2) 1.60 1.50
515 A46 75c W95 (4-3) 1.60 1.50
516 A46 75c W95 (4-4) 1.60 1.50
a. Block of 4, #513-516 6.50 6.00
517 A46 32c W96 .65 .65
518 A46 55c W97 1.10 1.10
519 A47 60c W98 1.25 1.25
520 A46 $1 W99 2.25 2.00
521 A46 75c W100 (4-1) 1.75 1.50
522 A46 75c W100 (4-2) 1.75 1.50
523 A46 75c W100 (4-3) 1.75 1.50
524 A46 75c W100 (4-4) 1.75 1.50
a. Block of 4, #521-524 7.25 6.00
Nos. 504-524 (21) 28.40 26.50

Issued: #504, 2/4/95; #505, 2/13/95; #506, 2/19/95; #507, 3/7/95; #508, 4/1/95; #509, 4/12/95; #516a, 5/8/95; #517, 6/26/95; #518, 7/7/95; #519, 7/26/95; #520, 8/6/95; #524a, 9/2/95.

Souvenir Sheets

#562a, like #303. #562b, like #496.

1994-95 ***Imperf.***
562 Sheet of 2 2.00 2.00
a.-b. A46 50c any single 1.00 1.00
563 A46 $1 like #517 2.00 2.00

No. 563 contains one 80x50mm stamp with UN 50th anniv. emblem.
Issued: #562, 10/20/94; #563, 6/26/95.
Nos. 525-561, 564-566 are unassigned.

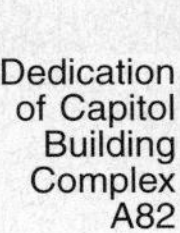

Dedication of Capitol Building Complex A82

Designs: No. 567, Capitol building. No. 568, Nitijela (parliament) building. No. 569, Natl. seal, vert. No. 570, Flag over complex, vert.

1993, Aug. 11 Litho. ***Perf. 11x10½***
567 A82 29c multi (4-1) .50 .50
568 A82 29c multi (4-2) .50 .50

Perf. 10½x11
569 A82 29c multi (4-3) .50 .50
570 A82 29c multi (4-4) .50 .50
Nos. 567-570 (4) 2.00 2.00

Souvenir Sheet

Christening of Mobil Super Tanker Eagle — A83

1993, Aug. 25 ***Perf. 13½***
571 A83 50c multicolored .85 .85

Marshallese Life in 1800's — A84

1993, Sept. 15 Litho. ***Perf. 13½***
572 A84 29c Woman, breadfruit (4-1) .60 .60
573 A84 29c Canoes, warrior (4-2) .60 .60
574 A84 29c Young chief (4-3) .60 .60
575 A84 29c Drummer, dancers (4-4) .60 .60
a. Block of 4, #572-575 2.40 2.40

Christmas A85

1993, Oct. 25 Litho. ***Perf. 13½***
576 A85 29c multicolored .60 .60

Souvenir Sheet

Constitution, 15th Anniv. — A86

1994, May 1 Litho. ***Perf. 13½***
577 A86 $2.90 multicolored 4.50 4.50

Souvenir Sheet

Marshall Islands Postal Service, 10th Anniv. — A87

1994, May 2
578 A87 29c multicolored .60 .60

1994 World Cup Soccer Championships, U.S. — A88

Design: No. 580, Soccer players, diff.

1994, June 17 Litho. ***Perf. 13½***
579 A88 50c red & multi (2-1) 1.60 1.00
580 A88 50c blue & multi (2-2) 1.60 1.00
a. Pair, #579-580 3.25 2.00

No. 580a has a continuous design.

Miniature Sheet

Solar System — A89

Mythological characters, symbols: a, Solar system. b, Sun. c, Moon. d, Mercury. e, Venus. f, Earth. g, Mars. h, Jupiter. i, Saturn. j, Uranus. k, Neptune. l, Pluto.

1994, July 20 Litho. ***Perf. 13½***
582 A89 50c Sheet of 12, #a.-l. 12.00 12.00

First Manned Moon Landing, 25th Anniv. — A90

Designs: No. 583, First step onto Moon's surface. No. 584, Planting US flag on Moon. No. 585, Astronaut's salute to America, flag. No. 586, Astronaut stepping onto Moon, John F. Kennedy.

1994, July 20
583 A90 75c multi (4-1) 1.10 1.10
584 A90 75c multi (4-2) 1.10 1.10
585 A90 75c multi (4-3) 1.10 1.10
586 A90 75c multi (4-4) 1.10 1.10
a. Block of 4, #583-586 4.50 4.50
b. Souvenir sheet of 4, #583-586 4.50 4.50

Souvenir Sheet

Butterflies A91

1994, Aug. 16 Litho. ***Perf. 13½***
587 A91 Sheet of 3 3.75 3.75
a. 29c Meadow argus .60 .60
b. 52c Brown awl 1.10 1.10
c. $1 Great eggfly 2.00 2.00

PHILAKOREA '94.

Christmas — A92

1994, Oct. 28 Litho. ***Perf. 13½***
588 A92 29c multicolored .60 .60

Souvenir Sheet

New Year 1995 (Year of the Boar) — A93

Illustration reduced.

1995, Jan. 2 Litho. ***Perf. 13½***
589 A93 50c multicolored 1.00 1.00

Marine Life — A94

Designs: a, Meyer's butterflyfish, achilles tang, scuba diver. b, Scuba diver, moorish idols (a, d). c, Pacific green turtle, fairy basslets. d, Fairy basslets, emperor angelfish, orange-fin anemonefish.

1995, Mar. 20 Litho. ***Perf. 13½***
590 A94 55c Block of 4, #a.-d. 4.50 4.50

See Nos. 614, 644.

John F. Kennedy (1917-63), 35th Pres. of US — A95

Designs: a, PT-109. b, Taking presidential oath. c, Peace Corps volunteers. d, US aircraft, naval vessels, Cuban Missile Crisis. e, Signing Nuclear Test Ban Treaty. f, Eternal flame, Arlington Natl. Cemetery.

1995, May 29 Litho. ***Perf. 13½***
591 A95 55c Strip of 6, #a.-f. 5.25 5.25

Marilyn Monroe (1926-1962), Actress — A96

Various portraits with background color: a, red. b, green. c, orange. d, violet.

1995, June 1 Litho. ***Perf. 13½***
592 A96 75c Block of 4, #a.-d. 5.75 5.75

No. 592 was issued in sheets of three blocks.

Cats — A97

Designs: a, Siamese, exotic shorthair. b, American shorthair, Persian. c, Maine coon, Burmese. d, Abyssinian, Himalayan.

1995, July 5 Litho. ***Perf. 13½***
593 A97 32c Block of 4, #a.-d. 2.50 2.50

Mir-Space Shuttle Docking & Apollo-Soyuz Link-Up — A98

a, Space station Mir. b, Space shuttle Atlantis. c, Apollo command module. d, Soyuz spacecraft.

1995, June 29 Litho. ***Perf. 13½***
594 A98 75c Block of 4, #a.-d. 4.75 4.75

Nos. 594 is a continuous design.

Pacific Game Fish — A99

a, Pacific sailfish. b, Albacore. c, Wahoo. d, Pacific blue marlin. e, Yellowfin tuna. f, Giant trevally. g, Dolphin fish. h, Mako shark.

1995, Aug. 21 Litho. ***Perf. 13½***
595 A99 60c Block of 8, #a.-h. 11.00 11.00

Island Legends — A100

Designs: a, Inedel's Magic Kite. b, Lijebake Rescues Her Granddaughter. c, Jebro's Mother Invents the Sail. d, Limajnon Escapes to the Moon.

1995, Aug. 25 Litho. ***Perf. 13½***
596 A100 32c Block of 4, #a.-d. + 4 labels 2.50 2.50

See Nos. 612, 643.

Miniature Sheet

Singapore '95 World Stamp Exhibition A101

Orchids: a, Paphiopedilum armeniacum. b, Masdevallia veitchiana. c, Cattleya francis. d, Cattleya x guatemalensis.

1995, Sept. 1 Litho. ***Perf. 13½***
597 A101 32c Sheet of 4, #a.-d. 2.25 2.25

Souvenir Sheet

Intl. Stamp & Coin Expo, Beijing '95 — A102

Illustration reduced.

1995, Sept. 12
598 A102 50c Suzhou Gardens .85 .85

Christmas A103

1995, Oct. 31 Litho. ***Perf. 13½***
599 A103 32c multicolored .55 .55

Miniature Sheet

Jet Fighter Planes — A104

a, Me 262-1a Schwalbe. b, Meteor F.MK8. c, F-80 Shooting Star. d, F-86 Sabre. e, F9F-2 Panther. f, MiG-15. g, F-100 Super Sabre. h, F-102A Delta Dagger. i, F-104 Starfighter. j, MiG-21 MT. k, F8U Crusader. l, F-105 Thunderbird. m, Saab J35 Draken. n, Fiat G91Y. o, F-4 Phantom II. p, Saab JA37 Viggen. q, Mirage F1C. r, F-14 Tomcat. s, F-15 Eagle. t, F-16 Fighting Falcon. u, Tornado F.MK3. v, Sukhoi Su-27UB. w, Mirage 2000C. x, Sea Harrier FRS.MK1. y, F-117 Nighthawk.

1995, Nov. 10
600 A104 32c Sheet of 25, #a.-y. 16.00 16.00

No. 600 was sold in uncut sheets of 6 panes.

See Nos. 617, 641, 666, 708, 728.

Yitzhak Rabin (1922-95), Israeli Prime Minister — A105

1995, Nov. 10 Litho. ***Perf. 14***
601 A105 32c multicolored .55 .55

No. 601 was issued in sheets of 8.

Souvenir Sheet

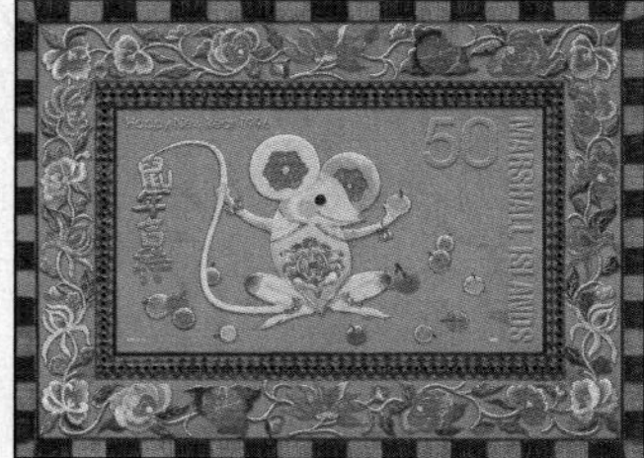

New Year 1996 (Year of the Rat) — A106

Illustration reduced.

1996, Jan. 5 Litho. ***Perf. 13½***
602 A106 50c multicolored .85 .85

Native Birds A107

Designs: a, Blue-gray noddy. b, Gray-backed tern. c, Masked booby. d, Black-footed albatross.

1996, Feb. 26 Litho. ***Perf. 13½***
603 A107 32c Block of 4, #a.-d. 2.50 2.50

Wild Cats — A108

a, Cheetah. b, Tiger. c, Lion. d, Jaguar.

1996, Mar. 8 Litho. ***Perf. 13½***
604 A108 55c Block of 4, #a.-d. 3.75 3.75

Sailing Ship Type of 1993
Miniature Sheet

Designs: a, like #443. b, like #447. c, like #448. d, like #455. e, like #444. f, like #446. g, like #456. h, like #459. i, like #441. j, like #449. k, like #451. l, like #465. m, Malmel outrigger sailing canoe. n, like #445. o, like #452. p, like #453. q, like #457. r, like #450. s, like #458. t, like #460. u, like #466. v, like #442. w, like #454. x, like #459A. y, like #462.

1996, Apr. 18 Litho. ***Perf. 11x10½***
605 A80 32c Sheet of 25, #a.-y. 16.00 16.00

Olympic Games, Cent. — A109

First Olympic stamps, Greece: a, #119. b, #124. c, #123. d, #125.

1996, Apr. 27 Litho. ***Perf. 12***
606 A109 60c Block of 4, #a.-d. 4.00 4.00

Issued in sheets of 4. A small number were were overprinted in gold in the margin for Olymphilex '96.

Miniature Sheet

History of the Marshall Islands A110

a, Undersea eruptions form island bases. b, Coral reefs grow. c, Storms bring birds & seeds. d, Early human inhabitants arrive. e, Seen by Spanish explorers, 1527. f, Capt. John Marshall, RN, charts islands, 1788. g, Islands become German protectorate, 1885. h, Japan seizes islands, 1914. i, US troops liberate islands, 1944. j, Bikiniatoll evacuated for nuclear testing, 1946. k, Islands become UN Trust Territory, 1947. l, Independence, 1986.

1996, May 2 Litho. ***Perf. 13x12***
607 A110 55c Sheet of 12, #a.-l. 10.50 10.50

Elvis Presley's First #1 Hit, "Heartbreak Hotel," 40th Anniv. — A111

1996, May 5 ***Perf. 10½x11***
608 A111 32c multicolored .65 .65

Issued in sheets of 20.

Souvenir Sheet

China '96, 9th Asian Intl. Philatelic Exhibition — A112

Design: The Palance Museum, Shenyang. Illustration reduced.

1996, May 17 ***Perf. 13½***
609 A112 50c multicolored 1.00 1.00

James Dean (1931-55), Actor — A113

1996, June 1 Litho. ***Perf. 10½x11***
610 A113 32c multicolored .65 .65

No. 610 was issued in sheets of 20.

First Ford Automobile, Cent. — A114

Designs: a, 1896 Quadricycle. b, 1903 Model A Roadster. c, 1909 Model T Touring Car. d, 1929 Model A Station Wagon. e, 1955 Thunderbird. f, 1964 ½ Mustang convertible. g, 1995 Explorer. h, 1996 Taurus.

1996, June 4 Litho. ***Perf. 13½***
611 A114 60c Sheet of 8, #a.-h. 6.00 6.00

Island Legends Type of 1995

Designs: a, Kijeek An Letao. b, Mennin Jobwodda. c, Wa Kone, Waan Letao. d, Kouj.

1996, July 19
612 A100 32c Block of 4, #a.-d. + 4 labels 2.25 2.25

Steam Locomotives — A115

Designs: a, Pennsylvania K4, U.S. b, "Big Boy," US. c, Mallard, Great Britain. d, RENFE Class 242, Spain. e, DB Class 01, Germany. f, FS Group 691, Italy. g, "Royal Hudson," Canada. h, Evening Star, Great Britain. i, SAR 520 Class, Australia. j, SNCF 232.U1, France. k, QJ "Advance Forward," China. l, C62 "Swallow," Japan.

1996, Aug. 23 Litho. *Perf. 13½*
613 A115 55c Sheet of 12, #a.-l. 11.00 11.00

Marine Life Type of 1995

Designs: a, like #590a. b, like #590b. c, like #590c. d, like #590d.

1996, Oct. 21 Litho. *Perf. 13½*
614 A94 32c Block of 4, #a.-d. 1.75 1.75

Taipei '96, 10th Asian Intl. Philatelic Exhibition. Nos. 614a-614b have Chinese inscription, Nos. 614c-614d English.

Stick Chart, Canoe and Flag of the Republic Type of 1990

1996, Oct. 21 *Perf. 11x10½*
615 A63 $3 like No. 381 6.00 6.00

No. 615 inscribed "Free Association United States of America."

Angels from "Madonna and Child with Four Saints," by Rosso Fiorentino A116

1996, Oct. 31 Litho. *Perf. 13½*
616 A116 32c multicolored .55 .55

Christmas.

Legendary Planes Type of 1995

Biplanes: a, JN-3 Jenny. b, SPAD XIII. c, Albatros D.III. d, DH-4 LIberty. e, Fokker Dr.1. f, F-1 Camel. g, Martin MB-2. h, MB-3A Tommy. i, Curtiss TS-1. j, P-1 Hawk. k, Boeing PW-9. l, Douglas 0-2H. m, LB-5 Pirate. n, 02U-1 Corsair. o, F8C Heldiver. p, Boeing F4B-4. q, J6B Gerfalcon. r, Martin BM. s, FF-1 Fifi. t, C.R. 32 Cricket. u, Polikarpov I-15 Gull. v, Mk.1 Swordfish. w, Aichi D1A2. x, Grumman F3F. y, SOC-3 Seagull.

1996, Nov. 1
617 A104 32c Sheet of 25, #a.-y. 16.00 16.00

Native Crafts A117

Designs: a, Fan making. b, Canoe models. c, Carving. d, Basketmaking.

1996, Nov. 7 Litho. *Perf. 11x10½*
618 A117 32c Block of 4, #a.-d. 1.60 1.60

See Nos. 629-630.

Souvenir Sheet

New Year 1997 (Year of the Ox) — A118

Illustration reduced.

1997, Jan. 7 Litho. *Perf. 13x13½*
619 A118 60c multicolored 1.25 1.25

Amata Kabua (1928-96), President of Marshall Islands — A119

1997, Jan. 27 Litho. *Perf. 13½*
620 A119 32c multicolored .65 .65
621 A119 60c multicolored 1.25 1.25

No. 621 has vertical inscriptions in English.

Elvis Presley (1935-77) A120

Designs: a, "Rocking 50's." b, "Soaring 60's." c, "Sensational 70's."

1997, Jan. 8 Litho. *Perf. 13½*
622 A120 32c Strip of 3, #a.-c. 2.00 2.00

Hong Kong '97 — A121

Hong Kong at sunrise, ships: No. 623: a, Walap. b, Junk.
Hong Kong at night, ships: No. 624: a, Canoe. b, Junk, diff.
Illustration reduced.

1997, Feb. 12 *Perf. 12*
Sheets of 2
623 A121 32c #a.-b. + 3 labels 1.25 1.25
624 A121 32c #a.-b. + 3 labels 1.25 1.25

Christianity in Marshall Islands, 140th Anniv. — A122

Apostles: No. 625: a, Andrew. b, Matthew. c, Philip. d, Simon. e, Thaddeus. f, Thomas. g, Bartholomew. h, John. i, James, the Lesser. j, James, the Greater. k, Paul. l, Peter.
$3, The Last Supper, by Peter Paul Rubens.

1997, Mar. 28 *Perf. 13½*
625 A122 60c Sheet of 12, #a.-l. 14.50 14.50

Souvenir Sheet
Perf. 13x13½
626 A122 $3 multicolored 6.00 6.00

No. 626 contains one 80x50mm stamp.

First Decade of 20th Century — A123

Designs: a, Family of immigrants. b, Dowager Empress, Boxers, China. c, Photography for every man. d, Dr. Walter Reed, mosquito. e, Sigmund Freud. f, Marconi, wireless transmitter. g, Enrico Caruso, phonograph. h, Wright Brothers, Flyer. i, Einstein. j, HMS Dreadnought. k, San Francisco earthquake, 1906. l, Gandhi, non-violent protestors. m, Picasso. n, Dawn of the automobile age. o, Man, camels, oil derrick amid sand dunes.

1997, Apr. 15 Litho. *Perf. 13½*
627 A123 60c Sheet of 15, #a.-o. 18.00 18.00

See Nos. 646, 654, 657, 679, 702, 711, 723, 726 and 730.

Deng Xiaoping (1904-97), Chinese Leader — A124

1997, Apr. 21
628 A124 60c multicolored 1.25 1.25

Crafts Type of 1996

Designs: Nos. 629a, 630a, Fan making. Nos. 629b, 630b, Canoe models. Nos. 629c, 630c, Wood carving. Nos. 629d, 630d, Basket making.

1997, May 29 Litho. *Perf. 11x10½*
Self-Adhesive
629 A117 32c Block of 4, #a.-d. 2.50 2.50

Serpentine Die Cut Perf. 11
Self-Adhesive
630 A117 32c Strip of 4, #a.-d. 2.50 2.50

No. 629 was issued in sheets of 20 stamps. No. 630 was issued in sheets of 16 stamps. Die cutting does not extend through backing paper on No. 630.

Marshall Islands Stamps, Cent., US Stamps, 150th Anniv. A126

1997, May 29 Litho. *Perf. 13½*
Booklet Stamps
631 A126 50c No. 1 1.00 1.00
632 A126 50c No. 2 1.00 1.00
633 A126 50c No. 3 1.00 1.00
634 A126 50c No. 4 1.00 1.00
635 A126 50c No. 5 1.00 1.00
636 A126 50c No. 6 1.00 1.00
a. Booklet pane, #631-636 6.00

Size: 75x32mm
637 A126 $1 US Nos. 1 & 2 2.00 2.00
a. Booklet pane of 1 2.00
Complete booklet, #636a, #637a 8.00

PACIFIC 97.

Bristle-thighed Curlew — A127

World Wildlife Fund: a, Walking right. b, On tree branch. c, Standing with mouth open. d, In flight.

1997, June 6
638 A127 16c Block or strip of 4, #a.-d. 4.00 4.00

Souvenir Sheet

Bank of China, Hong Kong — A128

Illustration reduced.

1997, July 1 Litho. *Perf. 13½*
639 A128 50c multicolored 1.00 1.00

Canoes A129

Designs: a, Pacific Arts Festival canoe, Walap of Enewetak. b, Large Voyaging canoe, Walap of Jaluit. c. Racing canoe. d, Sailing canoe, Tipnol of Ailuk.

1997, July 10 Litho. *Perf. 13½*
640 A129 32c Block or strip of 4, #a.-d. 2.50 2.50

Legendary Aircraft Type of 1995

Designs: a, C-54 Skymaster. b, B-36 Peacemaker. c, F-86 Sabre. d, B-47 Stratojet. e, C-124 Globemaster II. f, C-121 Constellation. g, B-52 Stratofortress. h, F-100 Super Sabre. i, F-104 Starfighter. j, C-130 Hercules. k, F-105 Thunderchief. l, KC-135 Stratotanker. m, B-58 Hustler. n, F-4 Phanton II. o, T-38 Talon. p, C-141 Star Lifter. q, F-111 Aardvark. r, SR-71 "Blackbird." s, C-5 Galaxy. t, A-10 Thunderbolt II. u, F-15 Eagle. v, F-16 Fighting Falcon. w, F-117 Nighthawk. x, B-2 Spirit. y, C-17 Globemaster III.

1997, July 19
641 A104 32c Sheet of 25, #a.-y. 16.00 16.00

USS Contstitution, Bicent. — A130

1997, July 21
642 A130 32c multicolored .65 .65

Island Legends Type of 1995

Designs: a, The Large Pool of Mejit. b, The Beautiful Woman of Kwajalein. c, Sharks and Lowakalle Reef. d, The Demon of Adrie.

1997, Aug. 15 Litho. *Perf. 13½*
643 A100 32c Block of 4, #a.-d. +4 labels 2.50 2.50

Marine Life Type of 1995

Designs: a, Watanabe's angelfish, gray reef shark. b, Raccoon butterflyfish. c, Flame angelfish. d, Square-spot fairy basslets.

1997, Aug. 21
644 A94 60c Block of 4, #a.-d. 4.75 4.75

Diana, Princess of Wales (1961-97) A131

Various portraits, background color: a, violet. b, blue. c, yellow orange.

1997, Sept. 30 Litho. *Perf. 13½*
645 A131 60c Strip of 3, #a.-c. 3.75 3.75

No. 645 printed in sheets with two vertical strips flanking three horizontal strips.

Events of the 20th Century Type

1910-19: a, Women mobilize for equal rights. b, Ernest Rutherford, model of atom. c, Sun Yat-sen. d, Sinking of the Titanic. e, Igor Stravinsky, The Rite of Spring. f, Ford begins assembly line production of autos. g, Archduke Franz Ferdinand, wife Sophie. h, German U-boat sinks Lusitania. i, Soldiers in trenches at Battle of Verdun. j, Patrick Pearse proclaims Irish Republic. k, Jews praying at Wailing Wall. l, Cruiser Aurora. m, Baron Manfred von Richtofen. n, German revolutionary troops, 1918. o, Negotiators write Treaty of Versailles.

1997, Oct. 15 Litho. *Perf. 13½*
646 A123 60c Sheet of 15, #a.-o. 18.00 18.00

Christmas A132

Cherubs from Sistine Madonna, by Raphael: No. 647, With hand under chin. No. 648, With arms folded under chin.

1997, Oct. 25
647 A132 32c multicolored .60 .60
648 A132 32c multicolored .60 .60
a. Pair, #647-648 1.25 1.25

US State-Named Warships — A133

Designs: a.-z., aa.-ax.: USS Alabama-USS Wyoming in alphabetical order. USS Honolulu shown for Hawaii.

1997, Nov. 1
649 A133 20c Sheet of 50 20.00 20.00

Souvenir Sheet

Shanghai 97, Intl. Stamp and Coin Expo — A134

Treasure ship, Ming Dynasty. Illustration reduced.

1997, Nov. 19 Litho. *Perf. 13x13½*
650 A134 50c multicolored 1.00 1.00

Souvenir Sheet

New Year 1998 (Year of the Tiger) — A135

Illustration reduced.

1998, Jan. 2 Litho. *Perf. 13x13½*
651 A135 60c multicolored 1.25 1.25

Elvis Presley's 1968 Television Special A136

Scenes from special: a, shown. b, Red background. c, Elvis in white suit.

1998, Jan. 8 *Perf. 13½*
652 A136 32c Strip of 3, #a.-c. 1.75 1.75

Sea Shells A137

a, Chicoreus brunneus. b, Cypraea aurantium. c, Lambis chiragra. d, Tridanca squamosa.

1998, Feb. 13 Litho. *Perf. 13½*
653 A137 32c Strip of 4, #a.-d. 2.50 2.50

Events of the 20th Century Type

1920-29: a, Radio broadcasting reaches the world. b, Quest for peace lurches forward. c, Architects reshape the world. d, Funerary mask of King Tutankhamen. e, USSR emerges as a Communist State. f, Nations emerge from Ottoman Empire, Kemal Ataturk. g, Arrival of the Jazz Age. h, Age of the rocket launched, Robert Goddard. i, Talkies arrive at the movie theater. j, Scourge of Fascism arrives. k, Man's universe expands. l, Penicillin launches antibiotic revolution. m, First glimmers of television. n, Aviation shrinks the world, Graf Zeppelin. o, World suffers economic depression.

1998, Mar. 16 Litho. *Perf. 13½*
654 A123 60c Sheet of 15, #a.-o. 18.00 18.00

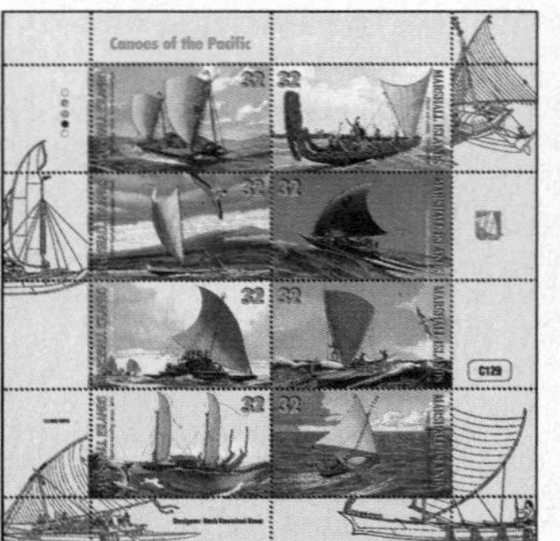

Canoes of the Pacific — A138

a, Pahi Sailing canoe, Tuamotu Archipelago. b, Maori war canoe, New Zealand. c, Wa'a Kaukahi fishing canoe, Hawaii. d, Amatasi sailing canoe, Samoa. e, Ndrua sailing canoe, Fiji. f, Tongiaki voyaging canoe, Tonga. g, Tipairua traveling canoe, Tahiti. h, Walap sailing canoe, Marshall Islands.

1998, May 21 Litho. *Perf. 13½*
655 A138 32c Sheet of 8, #a.-h. 5.00 5.00

See Nos. 690-698.

Berlin Airlift, 50th Anniv. — A139

Designs: a, Douglas C-54/R4D-5. b, Avro York. c, Watching the flights of freedom. d, Berliners welcoming supplies.

1998, June 26 Litho. *Perf. 13½*
656 A139 60c Block of 4, #a.-d. 4.75 4.75

Events of the 20th Century Type

1930-39: a, Economic depression engulfs the world. b, Scientists split the atom. c, Stalin's terror reigns in Soviet Union. d, Fascism becomes rampant. e, Engineers harness nature (Dneproges Dam). f, Streamlined design symbolizes bright future. g, Passengers travel airways in comfort. h, Artists protest the scourges of war. i, Media create indelible memories. j, Japanese agression arouses world opinion. k, Era of appeasement. l, Inventions pave way to future. m, Persecution of Jews portends holocaust. n, World War II begins in Europe. o, Movies cheer audiences.

1998, July 15
657 A123 60c Sheet of 15, #a.-o. 17.50 17.50

Czar Nicholas II — A140

#658, Coronation Czar Nicholas II, 1896. #659, Russo-Japanese War and the Cruiser Varyag, 1904-05. #660, Czar's Manifesto, 1905. #661, Peasant sower, Rasputin, 1905. #662, Czar with soldiers at the front, 1915. #663, Ipateva House, Ekaterinburg, 1917. $3, Family portrait.

1998, July 17 *Perf. 13½*

Booklet Stamps

658 A140 60c multicolored 1.25 1.25
659 A140 60c multicolored 1.25 1.25
660 A140 60c multicolored 1.25 1.25
661 A140 60c multicolored 1.25 1.25
662 A140 60c multicolored 1.25 1.25
663 A140 60c multicolored 1.25 1.25

Size: 60x54mm

Perf. 13½ at Top

664 A140 $3 multicolored 6.00 6.00
a. Booklet pane, #658-664 13.50
Complete booklet, #664a 13.50

George Herman "Babe" Ruth (1895-1948) A141

1998, Aug. 16 Litho. *Perf. 13½*
665 A141 32c multicolored .65 .65

Legendary Aircraft Type of 1995

US Navy aircraft: a, NC-4. b, PBY-5 Catalina. c, TBD Devastator. d, SB2U Vindicator. e, F4F Wildcat. f, OS2U Kingfisher. g, SBD Dauntless. h, F4U Corsair. i, SB2C Helldiver. j, PV-Ventura. k, TBM Avenger. l, F6F Hellcat. m, PB4Y-2 Privateer. n, A-1J Skyraider. o, F2H Banshee. p, F9F-2B Panther. q, P5M Marlin. r, F-8 Crusader. s, F-4 Phantom II. t, A-6 Intruder. u, P-3 Orion. v, A-7 Corsair II. w, A-4 Skyhawk. x, S-3 Viking. y, F/A-18 Hornet.

1998, Aug. 28
666 A104 32c Sheet of 25, #a.-y. 16.00 16.00

Chevrolet Automobiles — A142

Designs: a, 1912 Classic Six. b, 1931 Sports Roadster. c, 1941 Special Deluxe. d, 1955 Cameo Carrier Fleetside. e, 1957 Corvette. f, 1957 Bel Air. g, 1967 Camaro. h, 1970 Chevelle SS 454.

1998, Sept. 1
667 A142 60c Sheet of 8, #a.-h. 9.50 9.50

Marshallese Language and Alphabet — A143

Letter, example of Marshallese word beginning with letter: a, "A," Amata Kabua, first president. b, "A," Aj, to weave. c, "B," butterfly. d, "D," beautiful lady. e, "E," fish. f, "I," Rainbow. g, "J," mat. h, "K," house of government. i, "L," stars. j, "L," Tropicbird. k, "M," breadfruit. l, "M," Arrowroot plant. m, "N," Coconut tree. n, "N," Ocean wave. o, "N," shark tooth. p, "O," Fish net. q, "O," Tattoo. r, "O," Lionfish. s, "P," Visitor's hut. t, "R," Whale. u, "T," outrigger canoe. v, "U," Fire. w, "U," Dorsal fin of whale. x, "W," Woven sail.

1998, Sept. 14
668 A143 33c Sheet of 24, #a.-x. 16.00 16.00

New Buildings in Marshall Islands — A144

a, Trust Company of the Marshall Islands, 1998. b, Embassy of the People's Republic of China, 1996. c, Outrigger Marshall Islands Resort, 1996.

1998, Oct. 12
669 A144 33c Strip of 3, #a.-c. 2.00 2.00

Christmas A145

1998, Oct. 26

670 A145 32c Midnight angel .65 .65

John Glenn's Return to Space A146

#671, Friendship 7 launch, 1962. #672, Glenn in spacesuit, 1962. #673, Mercury capsule in space, 1962. #674, Shuttle Discovery Launch, 1998. #675, Astronaut and US Senator Glenn, 1998. #676, Shuttle Discovery in space, 1998.

$3, US #1193, astrological drawings.

1998, Oct. 29

Booklet Stamps

671	A146 60c multicolored	1.25	1.25
672	A146 60c multicolored	1.25	1.25
673	A146 60c multicolored	1.25	1.25
674	A146 60c multicolored	1.25	1.25
675	A146 60c multicolored	1.25	1.25
676	A146 60c multicolored	1.25	1.25

Size: 75x32mm

677	A146 $3 multicolored	6.00	6.00
a.	Booklet pane, #671-677	13.50	
	Complete booklet, #677a	13.50	

Souvenir Sheet

Antonov An-124 Delivering Drought Relief Supplies — A147

Illustration reduced.

1998, Nov. 3 Litho. *Perf. 13½*

678 A147 $3.20 multicolored 6.50 6.50

Events of the 20th Century Type

1940-49: a, Aviation assumes strategic importance. b, State of war becomes global. c, Missiles announce new age of warfare. d, Music raises spirits. e, Determined peoples fight for survival. f, The Holocaust. g, Mankind faces Atomic Age. h, War's end brings hope. i, Computer age dawns. j, Nations unite for peace. k, World demands justice from war criminals. l, A time for rebuilding. m, Transistor opens door to miniaturization. n, World divided by cold war. o, New China is proclaimed.

1998, Nov. 16 Litho. *Perf. 13½*

679 A123 60c Sheet of 15, #a.-o. 17.50 17.50

Warships — A148

Designs: a, Trireme Galley. b, Trireme Romano. c, Viking Longship. d, Ming Treasure ship. e, The Mary Rose. f, Nuestra Señora del Rosario. g, Korean Turtle ship. h, Brederode. i, Galera Veneziana. j, Santisima Trinidad. k, Ville de Paris. l, HMS Victory. m, Bonhomme Richard. n, USS Constellation. o, USS Hartford. p, Fijian Ndrua. q, HMS Dreadnought. r, HMAS Australia. s, HMS Dorsetshire. t, Graf Spee. u, Yamato. v, USS Tautog. w, Bismarck. x, USS Hornet. y, USS Missouri.

1998, Dec. 1

680 A148 33c Sheet of 25, #a.-y. 16.00 16.00

Souvenir Sheet

New Year 1999 (Year of the Rabbit) — A149

Illustration reduced.

1999, Jan. 2 Litho. *Perf. 13x13½*

681 A149 60c multicolored 1.25 1.25

Birds — A150

1c, Lesser golden plover. 3c, Siberian tattler. 20c, Brown noddy. 22c, Common fairy tern. 33c, Micronesian pigeon. 55c, Long-tailed cuckoo. $1, Christmas shearwater. $10, Eurasian tree sparrow.

1999, Jan. 9 *Perf. 13½*

682	A150 1c multicolored	.20	.20
683	A150 3c multicolored	.20	.20
684	A150 20c multicolored	.40	.40
685	A150 22c multicolored	.45	.45
686	A150 33c multicolored	.65	.65
687	A150 55c multicolored	1.10	1.10
688	A150 $1 multicolored	2.00	2.00
689	A150 $10 multicolored	15.00	15.00
	Nos. 682-689 (8)	20.00	20.00

See Nos. 714-721.

Canoes of the Pacific Type

Designs: a, like #655a. b, like #655b. c, like #655c. d, like #655f. e, like #655e. f, like #655d. g, like #655g. h, like #655h.

1999, Jan. 25 Litho. *Perf. 13½*

690 A138 33c Sheet of 8, #a.-h. 5.25 5.25

Self-Adhesive

Size: 40x25mm

Perf. 11x10½

691	A138 33c like #690a	.65	.65
692	A138 33c like #690b	.65	.65
693	A138 33c like #690c	.65	.65
694	A138 33c like #690d	.65	.65
695	A138 33c like #690e	.65	.65
696	A138 33c like #690f	.65	.65
697	A138 33c like #690g	.65	.65
698	A138 33c like #690h	.65	.65
a.	Block of 10, #691-697, 3 #698	6.50	

Issued in sheets of 20.

Great American Indian Chiefs — A151

Designs: a, Tecumseh. b, Powhatan. c, Hiawatha. d, Dull knife. e, Sequoyah. f, Sitting Bull. g, Cochise. h, Red Cloud. i, Geronimo. j, Chief Joseph. k, Pontiac. l, Crazy Horse.

1999, Feb. 1 *Perf. 13½*

699 A151 60c Sheet of 12, #a.-l. 14.50 14.50

National Flag A152

1999, Feb. 5 *Perf. 14*

700 A152 33c multicolored .65 .65

Flowers of the Pacific A153

Designs: a, Plumeria. b, Vanda. c, Ilima. d, Tiare. e, White ginger. f, Hibiscus.

1999, Feb. 18 *Perf. 13½*

701 A153 33c Block of 6, #a.-f. 4.00 4.00

Events of the 20th Century Type

1950-59: a, World enters age of television. b, Cold war battles erupt. c, Vaccines conquer scourge of polio. d, U.S., USSR engage in arms race. e, Science begins to unravel genetic code. f, Conquests reach unconquered heights. g, Pageantry reassures commonwealth. h, Rock 'n' roll reshapes music beat. i, Suns sets on Colonial Empires. j, World condemns racial discrimination. k, Unrest challenges Communism's march. l, Vision of European Union takes form. m, Space race opens space age. n, Jets shrink time and distance. o, Microchip presages computer revolution.

1999, Mar. 15

702 A123 60c Sheet of 15, #a.-o. 18.00 18.00

Souvenir Sheet

HMAS Australia — A154

1999, Mar. 19

703 A154 $1.20 multicolored 2.50 2.50

Australia '99, World Stamp Expo.

Elvis Presley — A155

1999, Apr. 6 Litho. *Perf. 13½*

704 A155 33c multicolored .65 .65

IBRA '99 World Stamp Exhibition, Nuremberg, Germany A156

Designs: a, #25. b. #24. c. #23. d, #22.

1999, Apr. 27 Litho. *Perf. 13½*

705 A156 60c Sheet of 4, #a.-d. 4.75 4.75

Marshall Islands Constitution, 20th Anniv. — A157

1999, May 1 Litho. *Perf. 13½*

706 A157 33c Constitution Committee .65 .65

Marshall Islands Postal Service, 15th Anniv. — A158

Portions of No. 607 and, clockwise: a, #572, 644, 689, 597d (b). b, #668c, 595c, 655h, 597a. c, #381, 570, 574, 668d. d, #597b, 643b, 621.

1999, May 2

707 A158 33c Block of 4, #a.-d. 2.50 2.50

Legendary Aircraft Type of 1995

a, Martin B-10B. b, Northrop A-17A Nomad. c, Douglas B-18 Bolo. d, Boeing B-17F Flying Fortress. e, Douglas A-20 Havoc. f, North American B-25B Mitchell. g, Consolidated B-24D Liberator. h, North American P-51B Mustang. i, Martin B-26 Marauder. j, Douglas A-26B Invader. k, Bell P-59 Airacomet. l, Boeing KC-97 Stratofreighter. m, Douglas A-1J Skyraider. n, Lockheed P2V-7 Neptune. o, North American B-45 Tornado. p, Boeing B-50 Superfortress. q, North American AJ-2 Savage. r, Grumman F9F Cougar. s, Douglas A-3 Skywarrior. t, Martin B-57E Canberra. u, Douglas EB-66 Destroyer. v, Grumman E-2A Hawkeye. w, Northrop F-5E Tiger II. x, McDonnell Douglas AV-8B Harrier II. y, Rockwell B-1B Lancer.

1999, June 1

708 A104 33c Sheet of 25, #a.-y. 16.00 16.00

Souvenir Sheet

PhilexFrance 99 — A159

Illustration reduced.

1999, July 2 Litho. *Perf. 13½*

709 A159 $1 Astronaut, lunar rover 2.00 2.00

Souvenir Sheet

Tanker Alrehab — A160

1999, July 15 Litho. *Perf. 13x13½*
710 A160 60c multi 1.25 1.25

Events of the 20th Century Type

1960-69: a, Invention of the laser. b, Pill revolutionizes family planning. c, Gagarin becomes the Columbus of the cosmos. d, Communism advertizes failures. e, Planet Earth endangered. f, Superpowers totter on precipice of war. g, Spirit of ecumenism renews Christianity. h, Railways achieve record speeds. i, Cultural Revolution stuns China. j, Arab-Israeli War unsettles Middle East. k, Organ transplants repair human body. l, America engulfed in Vietnam War. m, Political assassinations shock world. n, Supersonic travel becomes a reality. o, Mankind leaps from Earth to Moon.

1999, July 15 *Perf. 13½*
711 A123 60c Sheet of 15, #a.-o. 18.00 18.00

First Manned Moon Landing, 30th Anniv. — A161

Designs: a, Saluting astronaut, Earth. b, Flag. c, Astronaut.

1999, July 20
712 A161 33c Sheet of 3, #a.-c. 2.00 2.00

Ships — A162

Designs: a, Galleon Los Reyes, Spain, 1568. b, Frigate Dolphin, Great Britain, 1767. c, Bark Scarborough, Great Britain, 1788. d, Brig Rurick, Russia, 1817.

1999, Aug. 26
713 A162 33c Block of 4, #a.-d. 2.75 2.75

Bird Type of 1999

Designs: 5c, Black-tailed godwit. 40c, Franklin's gull. 45c, Rufous-necked stint. 75c, Kermadec petrel. $1.20, Purple-capped fruit dove. $2, Mongolian plover. $3.20, Cattle egret. $5, Dunlin.

1999, Sept. 16 Litho. *Perf. 13½*

714	A150	5c	multi	.20	.20
715	A150	40c	multi	.80	.80
716	A150	45c	multi	.90	.90
717	A150	75c	multi	1.50	1.50
718	A150	$1.20	multi	2.40	2.40
719	A150	$2	multi	4.00	4.00
720	A150	$3.20	multi	6.50	6.50
721	A150	$5	multi	10.00	10.00
	Nos. 714-721 (8)			26.30	26.30

Christmas A163

1999, Oct. 26 Litho. *Perf. 13½*
722 A163 33c multi .65 .65

Events of the 20th Century Type

1970-79: a, Jumbo jets enter transatlantic service. b, China advances on world stage. c, Terrorists range the world. d, Space stations orbit earth. e, Oil crisis strangles world. f, China unearths underground army. g, Reign of death devastates Cambodia. h, Superpowers proclaim era of détente. i, America celebrates bicentennial. j, Personal computers reach markets. k, Diagnostic tools revolutionize medicine. l, Automobiles transport millions. m, Prospect of peace in Middle East. n, Compact disc revolutionizes recording. o, Islam's prophets resurgent.

1999, Nov. 15
723 A123 60c Sheet of 15, #a.-o. 18.00 18.00

Millennium — A164

Earth and inscriptions: No. 724, "December 31, 1999." No. 725, "January 1, 2000."

1999, Dec. 31 Litho. *Perf. 13½*
724 33c multi .65 .65
725 33c multi .65 .65
a. A164 Pair, #724-725 1.30 1.30

Events of the 20th Century Type

1980-89: a, People unite in freedom's quest. b, Mankind confronts new diseases. c, Royal romance captivates the world. d, Information age begins. e, Armed conflicts upset peace. f, Cell phone revolutionizes communication. g, Every man a movie maker. h, Space exploration makes headlines. i, Disaster alerts public to nuclear risks. j, Perestroika signals change. k, Technology of war advances. l, Terrorism claims innocent victims. m, World's oceans endangered. n, Eys of the world on Tiananmen. o, Events signal "end of history."

2000, Jan. 15
726 A123 60c Sheet of 15, #a.-o. 18.00 18.00

Souvenir Sheet

New Year 2000 (Year of the Dragon) — A165

Illustration reduced.

2000, Jan. 20 *Perf. 13x13½*
727 A165 60c multi 1.25 1.25

Legendary Aircraft Type of 1995

Designs: a, P-26 Peashooter. b, N2S-1 Kaydet. c, P-35A. d, P-36A Hawk. e, P-40B Warhawk. f, P-38 Lightning. g, P-39D Airacobra. h, C-46 Commando. i, P-47D Thunderbolt. j, P-61B Black Widow. k, B-29 Superfortress. l, F7F-3N Tigercat. m, F8F-2 Bearcat. n, F-82, Twin Mustang. o, F-84G Thunderjet. p, FJ-1 Fury. q, C-119C Flying Boxcar. r, F3D-2 Skynight. s, F-89D Scorpion. t, F-94B Starfire. u, F4D Skyray. v, F3H-2 Demon. w, RF-101A/C Voodoo. x, U-2F Dragon Lady. y, OV-10 Bronco.

2000, Feb. 10 *Perf. 13½*
728 A104 33c Sheet of 25, #a.-y. 16.00 16.00

Roses — A166

Rose varieties: a, Masquerade. b, Tuscany Superb. c, Frau Dagmar Hastrup. d, Ivory Fashion. e, Charles De Mills. f, Peace.

2000, Feb. 23
729 A166 33c Block of 6, #a.-f. 4.00 4.00

Events of the 20th Century Type

1990-99: a, Free markets and trade reshape world economy. b, Coalition expels Iraq from Kuwait. c, South Africans freed from apartheid. d, WWW revolutionizes information superhighway. e, Era of Soviet power ends. f, A lasting peace in Middle East is promised. g, Engineering triumphs alter landscape. h, Ethnic conflicts stun world. i, Athletes celebrate peaceful world competition. j, Scientists probe secrets of life. k, Hong Kong and Macao return to China. l, Space exploration captivates millions. m, World mourns global heroines. n, Architecture shows confidence in the future. o, World population soars to new record.

2000, Mar. 15 Litho. *Perf. 13½*
730 A123 60c Sheet of 15, #a-o 18.00 18.00

Pandas — A167

a, Adult seated. b, Adult, seated, facing away, & cub. c, Adult holding cub. d, Two adults. e, Adult climbing. f, Adult & cub seated.

Illustration reduced.

2000, Mar. 31 *Perf. 11¾*
731 A167 33c Block of 6, #a-f 4.00 4.00

American Presidents — A168

No. 732: a, 1c, George Washington. b, 2c, John Adams. c, 3c, Thomas Jefferson. d, 4c, James Madison. e, 5c, James Monroe. f, 6c, John Quincy Adams.

No. 733: a, 7c, Andrew Jackson. b, 8c, Martin Van Buren. c, 9c, William Henry Harrison. d, 10c, John Tyler. e, 11c, James K. Polk. f, 12c, Zachary Taylor.

No. 734: a, 13c, Millard Fillmore. b, 14c, Franklin Pierce. c, 15c, James Buchanan. d, 16c, Abraham Lincoln. e, 17c, Andrew Johnson. f, 18c, Ulysses S. Grant.

No. 735: a, 19c, Rutherford B. Hayes. b, 20c, James A. Garfield. c, 21c, Chester A. Arthur. d, 22c, Grover Cleveland. e, 23c, Benjamin Harrison. f, 24c, White House.

No. 736: a, 25c, William McKinley. b, 26c, Theodore Roosevelt. c, 27c, William H. Taft. d, 28c, Woodrow Wilson. e, 29c, Warren G. Harding. f, 30c, Calvin Coolidge.

No. 737: a, 31c, Herbert C. Hoover. b, 32c, Franklin D. Roosevelt. c, 33c, Harry S Truman. d, 34c, Dwight D. Eisenhower. e, 35c, John F. Kennedy. f, 36c, Lyndon B. Johnson.

No. 738: a, 37c, Richard M. Nixon. b, 38c, Gerald R. Ford. c, 39c, James E. Carter. d, 40c, Ronald W. Reagan. e, 41c, George H. W. Bush. f, 42c, William J. Clinton.

Illustration reduced.

2000, Apr. 18 *Perf. 13½*

732	A168	Sheet of 6, #a-f	.45	.45
733	A168	Sheet of 6, #a-f	1.25	1.25
734	A168	Sheet of 6, #a-f	1.90	1.90
735	A168	Sheet of 6, #a-f	2.60	2.60
736	A168	Sheet of 6, #a-f	3.25	3.25
737	A168	Sheet of 6, #a-f	4.00	4.00
738	A168	Sheet of 6, #a-f	4.75	4.75
		Nos. 732-738 (7)	18.20	18.20

First Zeppelin Flight, Cent. — A169

Designs: a, Original Zeppelin, 1900. b, Graf Zeppelin I, 1928. c, Hindenburg, 1936. d, Graf Zeppelin II, 1937.

Illustration reduced.

2000, May 11 *Perf. 13½*
739 A169 33c Block of 4, #a-d 2.75 2.75

Sir Winston Churchill — A170

#740, War correspondent in South Africa, 1899-1900. #741, Engagement and marriage to Clementine Hozier, 1908. #742, Young statesman, 1900-14. #743, Writer and academic, 1898-1960. #744, First Lord of the Admiralty, 1939-40. #745, Prime Minister, 1940-45. $1, Appointed knight, Nobel Prize for Literature, 1946-65.

2000, June 16 Litho. *Perf. 13½*

Booklet Stamps

740	A170	60c	multi	1.25	1.25
741	A170	60c	multi	1.25	1.25
742	A170	60c	multi	1.25	1.25
743	A170	60c	multi	1.25	1.25
744	A170	60c	multi	1.25	1.25
745	A170	60c	multi	1.25	1.25

Size: 87x67mm

Perf. 13½ at Top

746 A170 $1 multi 2.00 2.00
a. Booklet pane, #740-746 9.50
Booklet, #746a 9.50

US Military, 225th Anniv. A171

No. 747: a, Army. b, Navy, c, Marines.

2000, June 22 *Perf. 13½*
747 Horiz. strip of 3 2.00 2.00
a.-c. A171 33c Any single .65 .65

National Government — A172

No. 748: a, National seal. b, Nitijela, horiz. c, National flag. d, Capitol buildijng, horiz.
Illustration reduced.

2000, July 4 Litho. *Perf. 13½*
748 A172 33c Block of 4, #a-d 2.75 2.75

Ships — A173

No. 749: a, Half Moon. b, La Grande Hermine. c, Golden Hind. d, Mathew. e, Victoria. f, Sao Gabriel.
Illustration reduced.

2000, July 20
749 A173 60c Block of 6, #a-f 7.25 7.25

Queen Mother, 100th Birthday — A174

No. 750: a, As child. b, As young wife. c, As Queen. d, As Queen Mother.

2000, Aug. 4
750 A174 60c Block of 4, #a-d 5.00 5.00

Reef Life A175

No. 751: a, Green sea turtle. b, Blue-girdled angelfish. c, Clown triggerfish. d, Harlequin tuskfish. e, Lined butterflyfish. f, White-bonnet anemonefish. g, Longnose filefish. h, Emperor angelfish.

2000, Aug. 24
751 Sheet of 8 5.50 5.50
a.-h. A175 33c Any single .65 .65

Butterflies — A176

No. 752: a, Holly blue. b, Swallowtail. c, Clouded yellow. d, Small tortoiseshell. e, Nettle tree. f, Long-tailed blue. g, Cranberry blue. h, Small heath. i, Pontic blue. j, Lapland fritillary k, Large blue. l, Monarch.
Illustration reduced.

2000, Sept. 14 *Perf. 11¾*
752 A176 60c Sheet of 12, #a-l 14.50 14.50

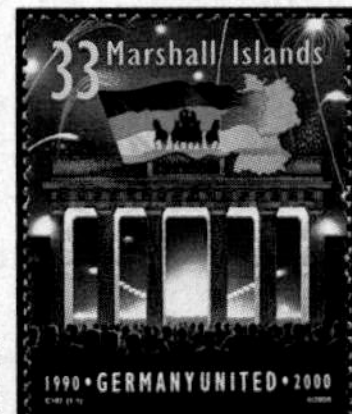

Reunification of Germany, 10th Anniv. — A177

2000, Oct. 3 *Perf. 13½*
753 A177 33c multi .65 .65

Submarines — A178

No. 754: a, USS S-44, 1925. b, USS Gato, 1941. c, USS Wyoming, 1996. d, USS Cheyenne, 1997.
Illustration reduced.

2000, Oct. 12
754 Block of 4 2.75 2.75
a.-d. A178 33c Any single .65 .65

Christmas — A179

2000, Oct. 26 *Perf. 10¼x11¼*
755 A179 33c multi .65 .65

Sun Yat-sen — A180

No. 756: a, As youth in Cuiheng village, 1866. b, As student in Honolulu and Hong Kong, 1879. c, As President of Tong Meng Hui, 1905. d, Revolution, 1911. e, President of the Republic of China, 1912. f, Principles of Democracy. g, Sun Yat-sen Memorial, Nanjing and Great Wall of China (87x62mm).

2000, Nov. 12 Litho. *Perf. 13½*
756 Booklet pane of 7 9.50
a.-f. A180 60c Any single 1.25 1.25
g. A180 $1 multi, perf. 13½ at top 2.00 2.00
Booklet, #756 9.50

Souvenir Sheet

New Year 2001 (Year of the Snake) — A181

2001, Jan. 2 Litho. *Perf. 13x13¾*
757 A181 80c multi 1.60 1.60

Flowers of the Month — A182

2001 *Perf. 11¾*

Stamp + label

758	A182 34c	Carnations	.70	.70
759	A182 34c	Violets	.70	.70
760	A182 34c	Jonquil	.70	.70
761	A182 34c	Sweet pea	.70	.70
762	A182 34c	Lily of the valley	.70	.70
763	A182 34c	Rose	.70	.70
764	A182 34c	Larkspur	.70	.70
765	A182 34c	Poppy	.70	.70
766	A182 34c	Aster	.70	.70
767	A182 34c	Marigold	.70	.70
768	A182 34c	Chrysanthemum	.70	.70
769	A182 34c	Poinsettia	.70	.70
		Nos. 758-769 (12)	8.40	8.40

Issued: No. 758, 1/5; No. 759, 2/1; No. 760, 3/1; No. 761, 4/3; No. 762, 5/1; No. 763, 6/1; No. 764, 7/3; No. 765, 8/1; No. 766, 9/5; No. 767, 10/1; No. 768, 11/1; No. 769, 12/1.

Sailing Canoes A183

Walaps of: $5, Jaluit. $10, Eniwetok.

2001, Jan. 19 Engr. *Perf. 12¼*
770 A183 $5 green 10.00 10.00
771 A183 $10 blue 20.00 20.00

Famous People — A184

Designs: 34c, Pres. Amata Kabua. 55c, Robert Reimers, entrepreneur. 80c, Leonard Hacker, S. J., humanitarian. $1, Dwight Heine, educator.

2001, Jan. 22 Litho. *Perf. 10¼x11¼*
772 A184 34c multi .70 .70
773 A184 55c multi 1.10 1.10
774 A184 80c multi 1.60 1.60
775 A184 $1 multi 2.00 2.00
Nos. 772-775 (4) 5.40 5.40

See No. 784.

Butterflies Type of 2000

No. 776: a, Red admiral. b, Moroccan orange tip. c, Silver-studded blue. d, Marbled white. e, False Apollo. f, Ringlet. g, Map. h, Fenton's wood white. i, Grecian copper. j, Pale Arctic clouded yellow. k, Great banded greyling. l, Cardinal.

2001, Feb. 22 *Perf. 11¾*
776 A176 80c Sheet of 12, #a-l 20.00 20.00

Fairy Tales A185

No. 777: a, Tom Thumb. b, Three Little Pigs. c, Gulliver's Travels. d, Cinderella. e, Gallant John. f, Ugly Duckling. g, Fisher and the Goldfish.

2001, Mar. 22 Litho. *Perf. 13½*
777 Vert. strip of 7 5.00 5.00
a.-g. A185 34c Any single .70 .70

Watercraft Racing — A186

No. 778: a, Canoeing. b, Windsurfing. c, Cruising yachts. d, Sailing dinghy.
Illustration reduced.

2001, Apr. 6
778 A186 34c Block of 4, #a-d 2.75 2.75

Manned Spaceflight, 40th Anniv. A187

No. 779: a, Yuri A. Gagarin. b, Alan B. Shepard, Jr. c, Virgil I. Grissom. d, Gherman S. Titov.

2001, Apr. 12
779 Block of 4 + 4 labels 6.50 6.50
a.-d. A187 80c Any single 1.60 1.60

Stamp Day — A188

2001, May 2
780 A188 34c multi .70 .70
a. Tete-beche pair 1.40 1.40

American Achievements in Space — A189

No. 781: a, First U.S. astronaut in space, 1962. b, First US space walk, 1965. c, First man on the Moon, 1969. d, First space shuttle, 1977.

Illustration reduced.

2001, May 15
781 A189 80c Block of 4, #a-d 6.50 6.50

Marine Life — A190

No. 782: a, Longnose butterflyfish, star puffer, starfish. b, Nautilus. c, Raccoon butterflyfish. d, Porkfish, grouper.
Illustration reduced.

2001, June 7
782 A190 34c Block of 4, #a-d 2.75 2.75

Sports — A191

No. 783: a, Basketball. b, Bowling. c, Table tennis. d, Kayaking.
Illustration reduced.

2001, June 26 ***Perf. 11¾***
783 A191 34c Block of 4, #a-d 2.75 2.75

Famous People Type of 2001

Design: 57c, Atlan Anien, legislator.

2001, July 9 ***Perf. 10¼x11¼***
784 A184 57c multi 1.10 1.10

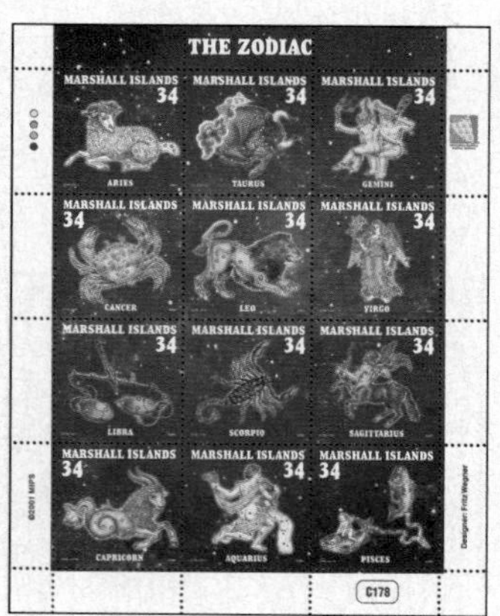

Zodiac Signs — A192

No. 785: a, Aries. b, Taurus. c, Gemini. d, Cancer. e, Leo. f, Virgo. g, Libra. h, Scorpio. i, Sagittarius. j, Capricorn. k, Aquarius. l, Pisces.

2001, July 17 ***Perf. 11¾***
785 A192 34c Sheet of 12, #a-l 8.25 8.25

Phila Nippon '01 — A193

No. 786: a, Black Cat, by Tan Axi. b, Brown Cat, by Tan Axi. c, Cliffs, by Wang Xinhai. d, Boat and Bridge, by Li Yan. e, Rooster, by Wang Xinlan. f, Great Wall, by Liu Zhong. g, Crane, by Wang Lynn. h, Baboon With Basket, by Wang Yani. i, Baboon in Tree, by Wang Yani. j, Umbrella, by Sun Yuan. k, Baboon With Fruit, by Wang Yani. l, Baboon on Ox, by Wang Yani.

2001, Aug. 1 **Litho.** ***Perf. 11¾***
786 A193 80c Sheet of 12, #a-l 20.00 20.00

US Naval Heroes in WWII Pacific Theater — A194

No. 787: a, Adm. Raymond A. Spruance. b, Adm. Arleigh A. Burke. c, Adm. Ernest A. King. d, Adm. Richmond K. Turner. e, Adm. Marc A. Mitscher. f, Adm. Chester W. Nimitz. g, Lt. Edward H. O'Hare. h, Adm. William F. Halsey, Jr. i, The Sullivan Brothers.

2001, Aug. 24 ***Perf. 13½***
787 A194 80c Sheet of 9, #a-i 14.50 14.50

Classic Cars — A195

No. 788: a, 1916 Stutz Bearcat. b, 1909 Stanley Steamer. c, 1934 Citroen 7CV. d, 1910 Rolls-Royce Silver Ghost. e, 1927 Daimler. f, 1935 Hispano-Suiza Type 68V-12. g, 1928 Lancia Lambda V4. h, 1927 Volvo OV4.

2001, Sept. 11
788 A195 34c Block of 8, #a-h 5.50 5.50

Remembrance of Victims of Sept. 11, 2001 Terrorist Attacks — A196

No. 789: a, U.S. flag, "Blessed are those. . ." b, Statue of Liberty, "United we stand. . ." c, U.S. flag, "An attack on freedom. . ." d, U.S. flag, "In the great struggle. . ." e, Statue of Freedom, "We go forward. . ." f, U.S. flag, "In the face of terrorism. . ." g, American people (75x32mm)

2001, Oct. 11 **Litho.** ***Perf. 13½***

789	Booklet pane of 7	6.25	—
a.-f.	A196 34c Any single	.70	.70
g.	A196 $1 multi	2.00	2.00
	Booklet, #789	6.25	

Christmas A197

No. 790: a, Angel on high. b, Adoration of the Magi. c, Nativity scene. d, Adoration of the shepherds.

2001, Oct. 26

790	Vert. strip of 4	2.80	2.80
a.-d.	A197 34c Any single	.70	.70

Airplanes — A198

No. 791: a, Supermarine Sea Eagle. b, Gloster Sea Gladiator. c, DHC-6 Twin Otter. d, Shorts 330. e, Sandringham Flying Boat. f, De Havilland DHC-7. g, Beech Duke B60. h, Fokker Friendship F27. i, Consolidated B-24J Liberator. j, Vickers 953C Merchantman.
Illustration reduced.

Perf. 11¼x10¼
2001, Nov. 13 **Litho.**
791 A198 80c Block of 10, #a-j 16.00 16.00

Souvenir Sheet

New Year 2002 (Year of the Horse) — A199

2002, Jan. 2 ***Perf. 13x13½***
792 A199 80c multi 1.60 1.60

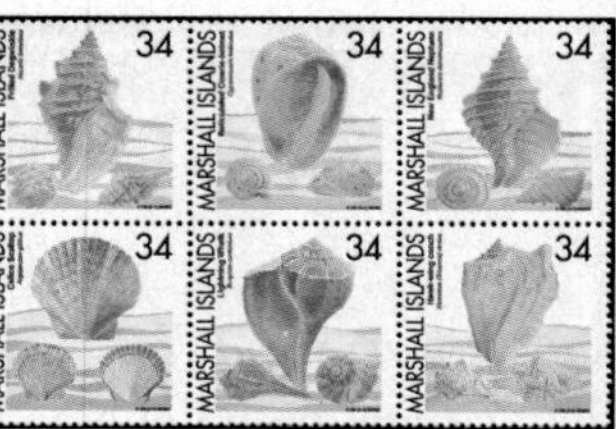

Shells — A200

No. 793: a, Frilled dogwinkle. b, Reticulated cowrie-helmet. c, New England neptune. d, Calico scallop. e, Lightning whelk. f, Hawk-wing conch.
Illustration reduced.

2002, Jan. 22 ***Perf. 11¾***
793 A200 34c Block of 6, #a-f 4.25 4.25

Souvenir Sheet

Reign of Queen Elizabeth II, 50th Anniv. — A201

2002, Feb. 6 **Litho.** ***Perf. 13x13½***
794 A201 80c multi 1.60 1.60

United We Stand — A202

2002, Feb. 11 ***Perf. 13½***
795 A202 34c multi .70 .70

Classic Cars Type of 2001

No. 796: a, 1909 Le Zebre. b, 1886 Hammel. c, 1902 Wolseley. d, 1899 Eysink. e, 1903 Dansk. f, 1907 Spyker. g, 1913 Fiat Model Zero. h, 1902 Weber.

2002, Feb. 26
796 A195 34c Block of 8, #a-h 5.50 5.50

Corals — A203

No. 797: a, Mixed. b, Chalice. c, Elkhorn. d, Finger.
Illustration reduced.

2002, Mar. 13
797 A203 34c Block of 4, #a-d 2.75 2.75

Butterflies Type of 2000

No. 798: a, Grayling. b, Eastern festoon. c, Speckled wood. d, Cranberry fritillary. e, Bath white. f, Meadow brown. g, Two-tailed pasha. h, Scarce swallowtail. i, Dusky grizzled skipper. j, Provençal short-tailed blue. k, Dryal. l, Comma.

2002, Mar. 25 *Perf. 11¾*

798 A176 80c Sheet of 12, #a-l 20.00 20.00

Horses in Art — A204

No. 799: a, Horses, by Giorgio de Chirico. b, Tartar Envoys Give Horse to Qianlong, by Father Giuseppe Castiglione. c, Gathering Seaweed, by Anton Mauve. d, Mares and Foals, by George Stubbs. e, A Mare and Her Foal in a Spring Meadow, by Wilson Hepple. f, Horse with Child and a Dog, by Natale Attanasio. g, The Horse, by Waterhouse Hawkins. h, Attendants and a Horse, by Edgar Degas. i, Mares and Foals in a Landscape, by Stubbs. j, The Horse, by Guglielmo Ciardi. k, Little Blue Horse, by Franz Marc. l, Sketch for the Set of "Fire Bird," by Pavel Kuznetsov.

80c, Emperor Qianlong Leaving for his Summer Residence, by Castiglione.

2002, Apr. 15 Litho. *Perf. 13½*

799 A204 34c Sheet of 12, #a-l 8.25 8.25

Souvenir Sheet

Perf. 13x13½

800 A204 80c multi 1.60 1.60

No. 800 contains one 80x50mm stamp.

Miniature Sheet

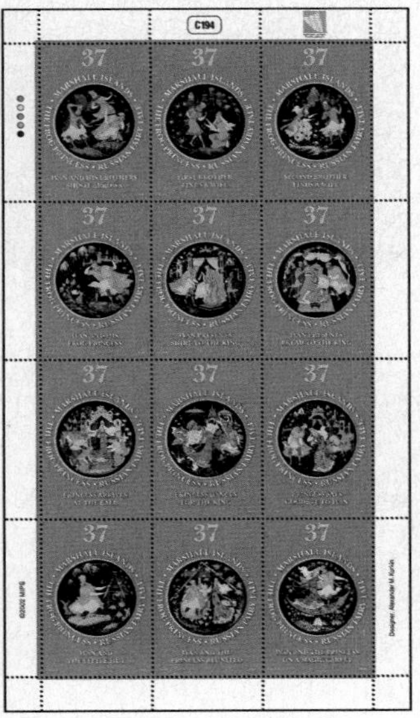

Russian Fairy Tale, "The Frog Princess" — A205

No. 801: a, Ivan and his brothers shoot arrows. b, First brother finds a wife. c, Second brother finds a wife. d, Ivan and his Frog Princess. e, Ivan presents shirt to the king. f, Ivan presents bread to the king. g, Princess arrives at the ball. h, Princess dances for the king. i, Princess says goodbye to ivan. j, Ivan and the little hut. k, Ivan and the Princess reunited. l, Ivan and the Princess on a magic carpet.

2002, Apr. 26 Litho. *Perf. 12½x12¼*

801 A205 37c Sheet of 12, #a-l 9.00 9.00

Carousel Figures — A206

No. 802: a, Armored horse and rabbit. b, Zebra and camel. c, Horse, reindeer and angel. d, Horse, frog and tiger.
Illustration reduced.

2002, May 13 Litho. *Perf. 13½*

802 A206 80c Block of 4, #a-d 6.50 6.50

Birds — A207

No. 803: a, Lesser golden plover. b, Siberian tattler. c, Brown noddy. d, Common fairy tern. e, Micronesian pigeon. f, Long-tailed cuckoo. g, Christmas shearwater. h, Eurasian tree sparrow. i, Black-tailed godwit. j, Franklin's gull. k, Rufous-necked stint. l, Kermadec petrel. m, Purple-capped fruit dove. n, Mongolian plover. o, Cattle egret. p, Dunlin.

2002, May 29

803 A207 37c Sheet of 16, #a-p 12.00 12.00

Benjamin Franklin (1706-90) — A208

No. 804: a, Inventor. b, Scholar.
Illustration reduced.

2002, June 10 Litho. *Perf. 13½*

804 A208 80c Horiz. pair, #a-b 3.25 3.25

Sea Turtles — A209

No. 805: a, Loggerhead. b, Leatherback. c, Hawksbill. d, Green.
Illustration reduced.

2002, June 25

805 A209 37c Block of 4, #a-d 3.00 3.00

Intl. Federation of Stamp Dealers' Associations, 50th Anniv. — A210

No. 806: a, Stamp collector. b, First day of issue. c, Father and daughter collectors. d, Young collector. e, Sharing Dad's stamp collection. f, The new generation.
Illustration reduced.

2002, July 2

806 A210 80c Block of 6, #a-f 9.75 9.75

US Navy Ships — A211

No. 807: a, USS Hartford. b, Bon Homme Richard. c, Prince de Neufchatel. d, USS Ohio. e, USS Onkahye. f, USS Oneida.
Illustration reduced.

2002, July 18

807 A211 37c Block of 6, #a-f 4.50 4.50

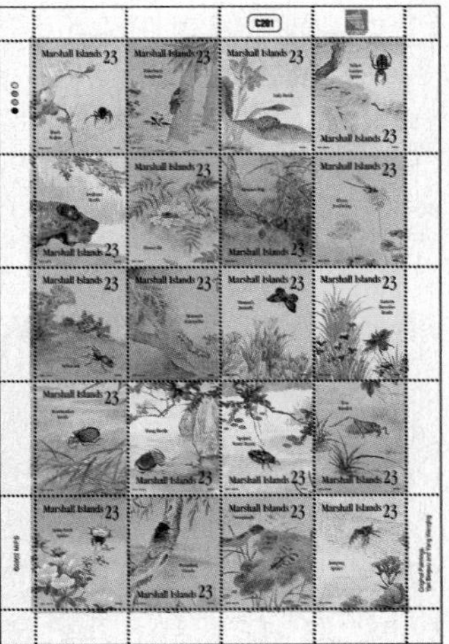

Insects and Spiders — A212

No. 808: a, Black widow spider. b, Elderberry longhorn. c, Ladybug. d, Yellow garden spider. e, Dogbane beetle. f, Flower fly. g, Assassin bug. h, Ebony jewelwing. i, Velvet ant. j, Monarch caterpillar. k, Monarch butterfly. l, Eastern Hercules beetle. m, Bombardier beetle. n, Dung beetle. o, Spotted water beetle. p, True katydid. q, Spiny-back spider. r, Periodical cicada. s, Scorpionfly. t, Jumping spider.

2002, Aug. 2 Litho. *Perf. 13½*

808 A212 23c Sheet of 20, #a-t 9.25 9.25

Classic Cars Type of 2001

No. 809: a, 1934 Hotchkiss. b, 1909 De Dion Bouton. c, 1922 Renault. d, 1927 Amilcar Surbaisse. e, 1943 Austin. f, 1913 Peugeot Bebe. g, 1927 O.M. Type 665 Superba. h, 1922 Elizalde Tipo 20C.

2002, Aug. 15

809 A195 80c Block of 8, #a-h 13.00 13.00

Queen Mother Type of 2000 Redrawn

No. 810: a, As child. b, As young wife. c, As Queen. d, As Queen Mother.

2002, Aug. 30

810 A174 80c Block of 4, #a-d 6.50 6.50

Queen Mother Elizabeth (1900-2002).

Souvenir Sheet

Regal Princess — A213

2002, Sept. 10 *Perf. 13¼x13¾*

811 A213 80c multi 1.60 1.60

World War I Heroes — A214

No. 812: a, Adm. William S. Sims. b, Gen. William E. Mitchell. c, Cpl. Freddie Stowers. d, Maj. Gen. Smedley D. Butler. e, Capt. Edward V. Rickenbacker. f, Sgt. Alvin C. York. g, Maj. Gen. John A. Lejeune. h, Gen. John J. Pershing.
Illustration reduced.

2002, Sept. 23 *Perf. 13½*

812 A214 80c Block of 8, #a-h 13.00 13.00

Christmas — A215

Snowman cookies with denomination in: a, Green. b, Red.
Illustration reduced.

2002, Oct. 26 Litho. *Perf. 13½*

813 A215 37c Horiz. pair, #a-b 1.50 1.50

Souvenir Sheet

New Year 2003 (Year of the Ram) — A216

2003, Jan. 2 Litho. *Perf. 13x13¾*

814 A216 80c multi 1.60 1.60

UN Membership, 12th Anniv. — A217

2003, Jan. 29 *Perf. 11¼x10¼*
815 A217 60c multi 1.25 1.25

Folktales — A218

No. 816: a, Inedel's Magic Kite. b, Lijebake Rescues Her Granddaughter. c, Jebro's Mother Invents the Sail. d, Limajnon Escapes to the Moon.
Illustration reduced.

2003, Jan. 29 *Perf. 13½*
816 A218 50c Block of 4, #a-d, + 4 labels 4.00 4.00

Famous People Type of 2001

Designs: 37c, Oscar deBrum (1929-2002), first Chief Secretary. $3.85, Senator Tipne Philippo (1933-2000). $13.65, Senator Henchi Balos (1946-2000).

Perf. 10¼x11¼
2003, Mar. 25 **Litho.**

817	A184	37c multi	.75	.75
818	A184	$3.85 multi	7.75	7.75
819	A184	$13.65 multi	25.00	25.00
	Nos. 817-819 (3)		33.50	33.50

The denomination of No. 819 was printed in a thermographic ink that changes color when warmed.

Marshallese Culture — A219

No. 820: a, Lagajimi, c. 1870s, by Franz Hernsheim (21x38mm). b, Old-style house with attic-like roof space (46x38mm). c, Tidal lake on Jabwor (46x38mm). d, Kabua, c. 1870s, by Hernsheim (21x38mm). e, Children in mat dresses (21x38mm). f, Jaluit pass, c. 1870s, by Hernsheim (46x38mm). g, Traditional Canoe c. 1870s, by Hernsheim (46x38mm). h, Man in fishing attire (21x38mm).
Illustration reduced.

2003, Mar. 25 *Perf. 13½*
820 A219 37c Block of 8, #a-h 6.00 6.00

Butterflies Type of 2000

No. 821: a, False grayling. b, Green hairstreak. c, Purple-shot copper. d, Black-veined white. e, Arctic grayling. f, Greek clouded yellow. g, American painted lady. h, Wall brown. i, Polar fritillary. j, Mountain clouded yellow. k, Camberwell beauty. l, Large white.

2003, May 2 **Litho.** *Perf. 11¾*
821 A176 80c Sheet of 12, #a-l 20.00 20.00

Powered Flight, Cent. — A220

No. 822: a, 1903 Wright Flyer. b, Curtiss JN-3 "Jenny." c, Douglas World Cruiser. d, "Spirit of St. Louis." e, Lockheed Vega. f, Boeing 314 Clipper. g, Douglas C-47 Skytrain. h, Boeing B-50 Superfortress. i, Antonov An-225 Mriya. j, B-2 Spirit.
Illustration reduced.

2003, June 10 *Perf. 13½*
822 A220 37c Block of 10, #a-j 7.50 7.50

Classic Cars Type of 2001

No. 823: a, 1927 Alfa Romeo RLSS. b, 1912 Austro-Daimler Prince Henry. c, 1923 Mors 14/20 HP Tourer. d, 1926 AC Tourer. e, 1903 Scania, 1897 Vabis. f, 1914 Graf und Stift. g, 1919 Pic-Pic. h, 1911 Hispano-Suiza-Alfonso XIII.

2003, July 10 **Litho.** *Perf. 13½*
823 A195 37c Block of 8, #a-h 6.00 6.00

Marshallese Culture Type of 2003

No. 824: a, Kabua's Daughter on Pandanus, c. 1906, by Augustin Krämer (21x38mm). b, Traditional walap (46x38mm). c, Jabwor, Jaluit Atoll (46x38mm). d, Traditional and Modern Dress, by Augustin Erdland (21x38mm). e, Nemedj, c. 1905, by Krämer (21x38mm). f, Typhoon of 1905, by Josef Schmidlin (46x38mm). g, Marshallese Kor Kor, c. 1905, by Richard Deeken (46x38mm). h, Marshallese Grandfather, by Erdland (21x38mm).

2003, Aug. 7 *Perf. 13½x13¼*
824 A219 37c Block of 8, #a-h 6.00 6.00

Christmas Ornaments — A221

No. 825: a, Snowman. b, Jack-in-the-box. c, Toy soldier. d, Reindeer.
Illustration reduced.

2003, Oct. 24 *Perf. 13½*
825 A221 37c Block of 4, #a-d 3.00 3.00

Souvenir Sheet

New Year 2004 (Year of the Monkey) — A222

2004, Jan. 4 **Litho.** *Perf. 13x13¾*
826 A222 $1 multi 2.00 2.00

Ship Type of 2002

No. 827: a, Bonhomme Richard. b, HMS Resolution, denomination at UR. c, HMS Resolution, denomination at UL.

2004, Feb. 14 *Perf. 13½*
827 A211 37c Horiz. strip of 3, #a-c 2.25 2.25

Classic Cars Type of 2001

No. 828: a, 1906 Wolseley-Siddeley. b, 1901 Mors. c, 1908 Hutton. d, 1907 Metallurgique. e, 1902 Benz. f, 1900 Cudell. g, 1906 Peugeot. h, Mercedes 60.

2004, Mar. 15 *Perf. 13½*
828 A195 37c Block of 8, #a-h 6.00 6.00

Greetings — A223

No. 829: a, Thank you! b, Congratulations. c, Happy birthday. d, Best wishes. e, Get well soon. f, Love you, Dad. g, Love you, Mom. h, Best wishes, Get well soon, Love you, Mom, Congratulations, Love you, Dad, Happy birthday, Thank you.

2004, Apr. 15 **Litho.** *Perf. 13½*
829 A223 37c Sheet of 8, #a-h 6.00 6.00

Marshall Islands Postal Service, 20th Anniv. — A224

Messenger and canoe with background colors of: 37c, Prussian blue. 60c, Brown. $2.30, Purple.

2004, May 2
830-832 A224 Set of 3 6.75 6.75

No. 832 printed in sheets of 8 stamps + 8 adjacent certified mail etiquettes. Value is for set with No. 832 with attached etiquette.

Lewis and Clark Expedition, Bicent. — A225

No. 833 — Inscriptions: a, The saga begins. b, Westward bound. c, Endless bison.

2004, May 14
833 Horiz. strip of 3 2.25 2.25
a.-c. A225 37c Any single .75 .75

See Nos. 840, 845.

D-Day, 60th Anniv. — A226

No. 834: a, Horsa gliders and parachute troops. b, British Typhoon 1B and US P-51B Mustangs. c, German defenses and Pointe du Hoc. d, Allied amphibious landing.
Illustration reduced.

2004, June 6 **Litho.** *Perf. 13½*
834 A226 37c Block of 4, #a-d 3.00 3.00

Marine Life — A227

No. 835: a, Chambered nautilus, map cowrie, fish, coral, trumpet triton (2-1). b, Marlin spike, fish, coral, turban shell, Toulerei's cowrie (2-2).
Illustration reduced.

2004, July 1
835 A227 37c Horiz. pair, #a-b 1.50 1.50

Pres. Ronald Reagan (1911-2004) A228

2004, July 4
836 A228 60c multi 1.25 1.25

First Manned Moon Landing, 35th Anniv. — A229

No. 837: a, Astronaut floating in space (4-1). b, Astronaut in space (4-2). c, Astronaut floating in orbit (4-3). d, Astronaut and Jupiter (4-4).
Illustration reduced.

2004, July 20
837 A229 37c Block of 4, #a-d 3.00 3.00

Festival of Arts — A230

No. 838: a, Woman showing fan making. b, Woman making baskets. c, Men carving. d, Children making canoe models. e, White ginger. f, Vanda. g, Tiare. h, Hibiscus. i, Breadfruit. j, Tattooed warrior. k, Young chiefs. l, Drummers and dancers.

2004, July 22
838 A230 37c Sheet of 12, #a-l 9.00 9.00

Aircraft — A231

No. 839: a, 1903 Wright Flyer. b, Blériot XI. c, Curtiss Golden Flyer. d, Curtiss Flying Boat. e, Deperdussin Racer. f, Sikorsky Il'ya Muromets. g, Fokker E1. h, Junkers J1. i, S.E. 5A. j, Handley Page O/400. k, Fokker D VII. l, Junkers F13. m, Lockheed Vega. n, M-130 Pan Am Clipper. o, Messerschmitt BF 109. p, Spitfire. q, Junkers Ju-88. r, A6M Zero. s, Ilyushin Il-2. t, Heinkel He-178. u, C-47 Skytrain. v, Piper Cub. w, Avro Lancaster. x, B-17F Flying Fortress. y, Messerschmitt Me-262. z, B-29 Superfortress. aa, P-51 Mustang. ab, Yak-9. ac, Bell Model 47 helicopter. ad, Bell X-1. ae, Beechcraft Bonanza. af, AN-225 Mriya. ag, B-47 Stratojet. ah, MiG-15. ai, Saab J35 Draken. aj, B-52 Stratofortress. ak, Boeing 367-80. al, U-2. am, C-130 Hercules. an, F-4 Phantom II. ao, North American X-15. ap, Sikorsky S-61 (HH-3E). aq, Learjet 23. ar, SR-71 Blackbird. as, Boeing 747. at, Concorde. au, Airbus A300. av, MiG-29. aw, F-117A Nighthawk. ax, F/A-22 Raptor.

Perf. 10¼x11¼

2004, Aug. 12 **Litho.**
839 Sheet of 50 23.00 23.00
a.-ax. A231 23c Any single .45 .45

Lewis and Clark Type of 2004

No. 840 — Inscriptions: a, First Fourth of July. b, Death of Sgt. Charles Floyd. c, Setting the prairie on fire.

2004, Aug. 24 ***Perf. 13½***
840 Horiz. strip of 3 2.25 2.25
a.-c. A225 37c Any single .75 .75

John Wayne (1907-79), Actor — A232

2004, Sept. 9 ***Perf. 10¼x11¼***
841 A232 37c multi .75 .75

Miniature Sheet

23rd UPU Congress, Bucharest, Romania — A233

No. 842: a, Great Britain #1. b, Romania #1. c, Marshall Islands #1. d, Marshall Islands #31.

2004, Sept. 15 **Litho.** ***Perf. 13½***
842 A233 $1 Sheet of 4, #a-d 8.00 8.00

Miniature Sheet

Marine Life — A234

No. 843: a, Emperor angelfish. b, Pink anemonefish. c, Humphead wrasse, Moorish idol. d, Black-spotted puffer. e, Snowflake moray eel. f, Lionfish. g, Bumphead parrotfish, threadfin butterflyfish. h, Hawksbill turtle. i, Triton's trumpet. j, Oriental sweetlips.

2004, Oct. 1
843 A234 37c Sheet of 10, #a-j 7.50 7.50

Miniature Sheet

Christmas — A235

No. 844: a, Angel with bells. b, God Almighty. c, Appears the Star of Bethlehem. d, Three Wise Men. e, Procession of the poor people. f, Pastors with sheep. g, Flight to Egypt. h, Holy Family. i, Animals adoring Jesus.

2004, Oct. 27
844 A235 37c Sheet of 9, #a-i 6.75 6.75

Lewis and Clark Type of 2004

No. 845 — Inscriptions: a, The interpreters. b, Sacred bison calling. c, Teton Sioux rob men.

2004, Nov. 22
845 Horiz. strip of 3 2.25 2.25
a.-c. A225 37c Any single .75 .75

Battle of the Bulge, 60th Anniv. — A236

No. 846: a, Infantry. b, Armor. c, Aviation. d, Lt. Col. Creighton Abrams and Brig. Gen. Anthony McAuliffe.
Illustration reduced.

2004, Dec. 1
846 A236 37c Block of 4, #a-d 3.00 3.00

United States Presidents — A237

No. 847: a, 1c, George Washington. b, 2c, John Adams. c, 3c, Thomas Jefferson. d, 4c, James Madison. e, 5c, James Monroe. f, 6c, John Quincy Adams. g, 7c, Andrew Jackson. h, 8c, Martin Van Buren. i, 9c, William Henry Harrison. j, 10c, John Tyler. k, 11c, James K. Polk. l, 12c, Zachary Taylor. m, 13c, Millard Fillmore. n, 14c, Franklin Pierce. o, 15c, James Buchanan. p, 16c, Abraham Lincoln. q, 17c, Andrew Johnson. r, 18c, Ulysses S. Grant. s, 19c, Rutherford B. Hayes. t, 20c, James A. Garfield. u, 21c, Chester A. Arthur. v, 22c, Grover Cleveland. w, 23c, Benjamin Harrison. x, 24c, Grover Cleveland. y, 25c, William McKinley. z, 26c, Theodore Roosevelt. aa, 27c, William Howard Taft. ab, 28c, Woodrow Wilson. ac, 29c, Warren G. Harding. ad, 30c, Calvin Coolidge. ae, 31c, Herbert Hoover. af, 32c, Franklin D. Roosevelt. ag, 33c, Harry S Truman. ah, 34c, Dwight D. Eisenhower. ai, 35c, John F. Kennedy. aj, 36c, Lyndon B. Johnson. ak, 37c, Richard M. Nixon. al, 38c, Gerald R. Ford. am, 39c, Jimmy Carter. an, 40c, Ronald W. Reagan. ao, 41c, George H. W. Bush. ap, 42c, William J. Clinton. aq, 43c, George W. Bush. ar, 60c, White House. as, $1, White House.

2005, Jan. 20 **Litho.** ***Perf. 13½***
847 A237 Sheet of 45, #a-as 31.00 31.00

No. 847 sold for $15.49.

Souvenir Sheet

New Year 2005 (Year of the Rooster) — A238

2005, Feb. 9 **Litho.** ***Perf. 13x13½***
848 A238 $1 multi 2.00 2.00

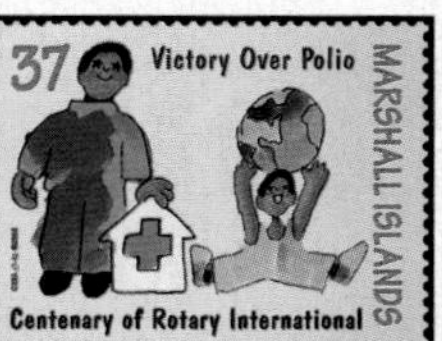

Rotary International, Cent. — A239

2005, Feb. 23 ***Perf. 13½***
849 A239 37c multi .75 .75

Hibiscus Varieties — A240

Designs: 37c, Burgundy Blush. 60c, Fiesta. 80c, June's Joy. $1, Norman Lee.

Perf. 10¼x11¼

2005, Mar. 15 **Litho.**
850 A240 37c multi .75 .75
851 A240 60c multi 1.25 1.25
852 A240 80c multi 1.60 1.60
853 A240 $1 multi 2.00 2.00
Nos. 850-853 (4) 5.60 5.60

See Nos. 860-863.

Hans Christian Andersen (1805-75), Author — A241

No. 854: a, The Princess and the Pea. b, Thumbelina. c, The Little Mermaid. d, The Emperor's New Suit.
Illustration reduced.

2005, Apr. 2 ***Perf. 13½***
854 A241 37c Block of 4, #a-d 3.00 3.00

Lewis and Clark Type of 2004

No. 855 — Inscriptions: a, First grizzly confrontation. b, Lewis reaching the Great Falls. c, Sacajawea and her brother reunite.

2005, Apr. 29
855 Horiz. strip of 3 2.25 2.25
a.-c. A225 37c Any single .75 .75

American First Day Cover Society, 50th Anniv. — A242

No. 856: a, George W. Linn first day cover for US No. 610 (Harding Memorial stamp). b, First day cover for Marshall Islands Nos. 31-34. c, First day cover of US No. C76 with Moon Landing cancel. d, First day cover for Marshall Islands No. 856.
Illustration reduced.

2005, May 2
856 A242 37c Block of 4, #a-d 3.00 3.00

V-E Day, 60th Anniv. — A243

No. 857: a, German surrender, Reims, France. b, Times Square, New York. c, Victory parade, Moscow. d, Royal family and Winston Churchill, Buckingham Palace, London.
Illustration reduced.

2005, May 9
857 A243 37c Block of 4, #a-d 3.00 3.00

Pope John Paul II (1920-2005) — A244

No. 858: a, Wearing red cape, with arm raised. b, Wearing green vestments. c, Close-up. d, Holding crucifix, wearing red vestments. e, Wearing miter.

2005, May 18 Litho. *Perf. 13½*
858 Vert. strip of 5 3.75 3.75
a.-e. A244 37c Any single .75 .75

United Nations, 60th Anniv. — A245

2005, June 26
859 Horiz. pair 2.40 2.40
a. A245 37c Six people .75 .75
b. A245 80c Seven people 1.60 1.60

Hibiscus Varieties Type of 2005

Designs: 1c, Margaret Okano. 24c, Cameo Queen. 39c, Madonna. $4, Estrella Red.

2005, July 13 *Perf. 10¼x11¼*
860 A240 1c multi .20 .20
861 A240 24c multi .50 .50
862 A240 39c multi .80 .80
863 A240 $4 multi 8.00 8.00
Nos. 860-863 (4) 9.50 9.50

Space Shuttles A246

No. 864: a, Columbia. b, Discovery. c, Endeavour. d, Challenger. e, Atlantis.

2005, July 26 *Perf. 13½*
864 Horiz. strip of 5 3.75 3.75
a.-e. A246 37c Any single .75 .75

Classic Cars Type of 2001

No. 865: a, 1925 Excelsior (8-1). b, 1912 Adler K (8-2). c, 1920 Thulin (8-3). d, 1913 Palladium (8-4). e, 1926 Minerva (8-5). f, 1922 Elizalde (8-6). g, 1911 Rolls-Royce Silver Ghost (8-7). h, 1931 Invicta (8-8).

2005, Aug. 4
865 Block of 8 6.00 6.00
a.-h. A195 37c Any single .75 .75

No. 865b is incorrectly inscribed "1926 Minerva."

V-J Day, 60th Anniv. — A247

No. 866: a, Fujiyama and Tokyo Bay. b, USS Missouri. c, US contingent. d, Japanese delegation.

2005, Sept. 2
866 A247 37c Block of 4, #a-d 3.00 3.00

Lewis & Clark Type of 2004

No. 867 — Inscriptions: a, Crossing the Bitterroots. b, Peace agreement. c, Ocean in view.

2005, Sept. 22
867 Horiz. strip of 3 2.25 2.25
a.-c. A225 37c Any single .75 .75

Battle of Trafalgar, Bicent. — A248

No. 868 — Fighting ships: a, Trireme galley. b, Trireme Romano. c, Viking longship. d, Ming treasure ship. e, Mary Rose. f, Nuestra Senora del Rosario. g, Korean turtle ship. h, Brederode. i, Galera Veneziana. j, Santisima Trinidad. k, Ville de Paris. l, HMS Victory. m, Bonhomme Richard. n, USS Constellation. o, USS Hartford. p, Fijian ndrua. q, HMS Dreadnought. r, HMAS Australia. s, HMS Dorsetshire. t, Admiral Graf Spee. u, Yamato. v, USS Tautog. w, Bismarck. x, USS Hornet. y, USS Missouri.
$2, HMS Victory, diff.
Illustration reduced.

2005, Oct. 21 Litho. *Perf. 13½*
868 A248 37c Sheet of 25, #a-y 18.50 18.50

Souvenir Sheet
Imperf

869 A248 $2 multi 4.00 4.00

No. 868 contains twenty-five 40x31mm stamps.

Christmas — A249

No. 870 — Angels with: a, Lute. b, Harp, horn and lute. c, Horn. d, Harp.
Illustration reduced.

2005, Nov. 1 *Perf. 13½*
870 A249 37c Block of 4, #a-d 3.00 3.00

Lewis & Clark Type of 2004

No. 871 — Inscriptions: a, First vote allowed to all. b, Leaving Fort Clatsop. c, At Pompey's Pillar.

2005, Nov. 24
871 Horiz. strip of 3 2.25 2.25
a.-c. A225 37c Any single .75 .75

Marshallese Culture — A250

No. 872 — Photographs: a, First Catholic Church on Jabwor, Jaluit Atoll, by Josef Schmidlin. b, Women on Jaluit Atoll, by Richard Deeken. c, Canoes in Jaluit Harbor, by Deeken. d, Nelu and His Wife Ledagoba, by Augustin Kramer. e, An Old Man from Ebon Atoll, by Augustin Erdland.

2005, Dec. 1
872 Horiz. strip of 5 3.75 3.75
a.-e. A250 37c Any single .75 .75

Miniature Sheet

Benjamin Franklin (1706-90), Statesman — A251

No. 873 — Franklin: a, Painting by J. S. Duplessis. b, Painting by David K. Stone. c, Painting by Mason Chamberlain. d, Painting by John Trumbull. e, Sculpture, by James Earle Fraser. f, Painting by David Martin. g, Painting by Benjamin West. h, Painting by J. B. Greuze. i, Painting by C. N. Cochin.

2006, Jan. 17 *Perf. 13½*
873 A251 48c Sheet of 9, #a-i 8.75 8.75

Souvenir Sheet

New Year 2006 (Year of the Dog) — A252

2006, Jan. 27 *Perf. 13¼x13½*
874 A252 $1 multi 2.00 2.00

Love — A253

2006, Feb. 14 Litho. *Perf. 13½*
875 A253 39c multi .80 .80

Butterflies Type of 2000

No. 876: a, Peacock. b, Southern comma. c, Pale clouded yellow. d, Common blue. e, Wood white. f, Baltic grayling. g, Purple emperor. h, Silky ringlet. i, Peak white. j, Idas blue. k, Cleopatra. l, Chequered skipper.

2006, Mar. 20 *Perf. 11¾*
876 A176 84c Sheet of 12, #a-l 21.00 21.00

First Spaceflight by Yuri Gagarin, 45th Anniv. — A254

2006, Apr. 12 Litho. *Perf. 11¾*
877 A254 39c multi .80 .80

Hibiscus Varieties Type of 2005

Designs: 10c, Butterscotch Sundae. 63c, Magic Moments. 84c, Joanne Boulin. $4.05, Capsicum Red.

2006, May 2 *Perf. 10¼x11¼*
878 A240 10c multi .20 .20
879 A240 63c multi 1.25 1.25
880 A240 84c multi 1.75 1.75
881 A240 $4.05 multi 8.25 8.25
Nos. 878-881 (4) 11.45 11.45

Miniature Sheet

Washington 2006 World Philiatelic Exhibition — A255

No. 882 — Designs of the United States 1922-25 definitive issue inscribed "Marshall Islands Postage": a, ½c, Nathan Hale. b, 1c, Benjamin Franklin. c, 1½c, Warren G. Harding. d, 2c, George Washington. e, 3c, Abraham Lincoln. f, 4c, Martha Washington. g, 5c, Theodore Roosevelt. h, 6c, James A. Garfield. i, 7c, William McKinley. j, 8c, Ulysses S. Grant. k, 9c, Thomas Jefferson. l, 10c, James Monroe. m, 11c, Rutherford B. Hayes. n, 12c, Grover Cleveland. o, 14c, American Indian chief. p, 15c, Statue of Liberty. q, 20c, Golden Gate, horiz. r, 25c, Niagara Falls, horiz. s, 30c, Buffalo, horiz. t, 50c, Arlington Amphitheater, horiz.

2006, May 27 Litho. *Perf. 13½*
882 A255 Sheet of 20, #a-t 4.75 4.75
u. Souvenir sheet, #882o, 882s, imperf. .90 .90

Sharks — A256

No. 883: a, Gray reef shark. b, Silvertip shark. c, Blacktip reef shark. d, Whitetip reef shark.
Illustration reduced.

2006, June 16 *Perf. 13½*
883 A256 39c Block of 4, #a-d 3.25 3.25

Miniature Sheet

Operations Crossroads, 60th Anniv. — A257

No. 884: a, Evacuation of Bikinians. b, Navy preparations. c, "Able" bomb blast. d, "Baker" bomb blast. e, Ghost fleet. f, Effects on the Bikinians.

2006, July 1 **Litho.** ***Perf. 13½***
884 A257 39c Sheet of 6, #a-f, + 6 labels 4.75 4.75

Lewis and Clark Type of 2004

No. 885 — Inscriptions: a, Leaving Sacagawea and Charbonneau. b, Return to St. Louis.

2006, Aug. 24
885 Horiz. pair 1.60 1.60
a.-b. A225 39c Either single .80 .80

Marshallese Culture Type of 2005

No. 886 — Photographs: a, Harbor Front of Jabwor, Jaluit Atoll, by L. Sander. b, Irooj with Family, Jabwor, Jaluit Atoll, by Richard Deeken. c, Traditional Voyaging Canoe at Jaluit Atoll, by Sander. d, Mission Sisters and Girls Doing Laundry, Jaluit, by Hildegard von Bunsen. e, Traditional House on Mile Atoll, by Hans Seidel.

2006, Sept. 22 **Litho.** ***Perf. 13½***
886 Horiz. strip of 5 4.00 4.00
a.-e. A250 39c Any single .80 .80

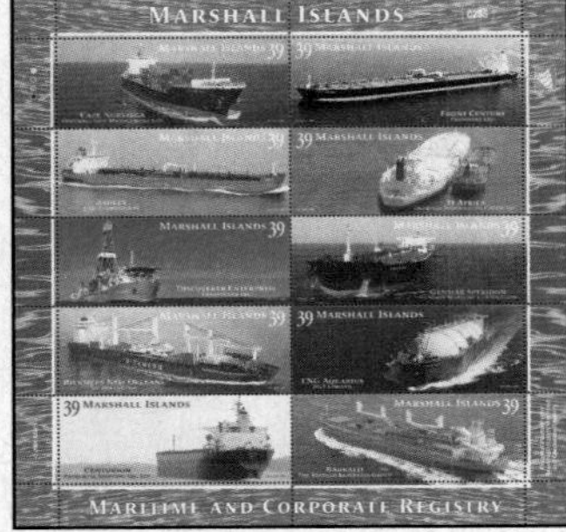

Ships in the Marshallese Maritime and Corporate Registry — A258

No. 887: a, Cape Norviega. b, Front Century. c, Ashley. d, TI Africa. e, Discoverer Enterprise. f, Genmar Spyridon. g, Rickmers New Orleans. h, LNG Aquarius. i, Centurion. j, Barkald.

2006, Oct. 9
887 A258 39c Sheet of 10, #a-j 8.00 8.00

Christmas — A259

2006, Nov. 1
888 A259 39c multi .80 .80

Greetings — A260

No. 889: a, "Happy Birthday." b, "Congratulations." c, "Thank You." d, "Best Wishes."
Illustration reduced.

2007, Jan. 16 ***Perf. 11¾***
889 A260 39c Block of 4, #a-d 3.25 3.25

Souvenir Sheet

New Year 2007 (Year of the Pig) — A261

2007, Feb. 19 **Litho.** ***Perf. 13x13½***
890 A261 $1 multi 2.00 2.00

Trains — A262

No. 891: a, Art Deco train. b, Pennsylvania. c, Santa Fe Chief. d, Hiawatha. e, 20th Century Limited. f, Daylight.
Illustration reduced.

2007, Mar. 26 ***Perf. 13½***
891 A262 39c Block of 6, #a-f 4.75 4.75

Dolphins — A263

No. 892: a, Spotter dolphins. b, Bottlenose dolphins. c, Risso's dolphin. d, Common dolphin.
Illustration reduced.

2007, Apr. 9
892 A263 39c Block of 4, #a-d 3.25 3.25

Fish A264

Designs: 26c, Achilles tang. 41c, Regal angelfish. 52c, Saddled butterflyfish. 61c, Tinker's butterflyfish.

Perf. 10¼x11¼

2007, June 12 **Litho.**
893 A264 26c multi .55 .55
894 A264 41c multi .85 .85
895 A264 52c multi 1.10 1.10
896 A264 61c multi 1.25 1.25
Nos. 893-896 (4) 3.75 3.75

Miniature Sheet

Space Age, 50th Anniv. — A265

No. 897: a, First man in space. b, First man-made satellite. c, First men on the Moon. d, First docking in space. e, First woman in space. f, First manned lunar vehicle. g, First space walk. h, First landing on Mars. i, First probe of Venus. j, First American in orbit.

2007, June 12 ***Perf. 13½***
897 A265 41c Sheet of 10, #a-j 8.25 8.25

Scouting, Cent. — A266

No. 898 — Inscriptions: a, Helping others. b, Physically strong. c, Mentally awake. d, Fun and adventure.
Illustration reduced.

2007, June 25
898 A266 41c Block of 4, #a-d 3.50 3.50

Purple Heart, 225th Anniv. — A267

2007, July 30 **Litho.** ***Perf. 13½***
899 A267 41c multi .85 .85

Miniature Sheet

United States Air Force, 60th Anniv. — A268

No. 900: a, C-54 Skymaster. b, B-36 Peacemaker. c, F-86 Sabre. d, B-47 Stratojet. e, C-124 Globemaster II. f, C-121 Constellation. g, B-52 Stratofortress. h, F-100 Super Sabre. i, F-104 Starfighter. j, C-130 Hercules. k, F-105 Thunderchief. l, KC-135 Stratotanker. m, B-58 Hustler. n, F-4 Phantom II. o, T-38 Talon. p, C-141 Starlifter. q, F-111 Aardvark. r, SR-71 Blackbird. s, C-5 Galaxy. t, A-10 Thunderbolt II. u, F-15 Eagle. v, F-16 Fighting Falcon. w, F-117 Nighthawk. x, B-2 Spirit. y, C-17 Globemaster III.

2007, Aug. 7
900 A268 41c Sheet of 25, #a-y 21.00 21.00

Marshallese Culture Type of 2005

No. 901 — Photographs by J. Debrum: a, Lonkwon Getting Fish from His Trap. b, Alele Style of Fishing at Bilarek. c, Portrait of Lanju and Family. d, Outrigger with Sail. e, Lien and Litublan Collecting Shells.

2007, Sept. 18 **Litho.** ***Perf. 13½***
901 Horiz. strip of 5 4.25 4.25
a.-e. A250 41c Any single .85 .85

Miniature Sheet

Marshall Islands Yacht Registry — A269

No. 902 — Registered yachts: a, Domani. b, Excellence III. c, Aquasition. d, Perfect Symmetry 5. e, Happy Days. f, Mystique. g, Halcyon Days. h, Man of Steel. i, Marathon. j, Sinbad.

2007, Oct. 8
902 A269 41c Sheet of 10, #a-j 8.25 8.25

Christmas — A270

No. 903 — Santa Claus: a, Reading list. b, Standing by fireplace. c, Holding gift. d, Waving from sleigh.

Illustration reduced.

2007, Dec. 12
903 A270 41c Block of 4, #a-d 3.50 3.50

Miniature Sheet

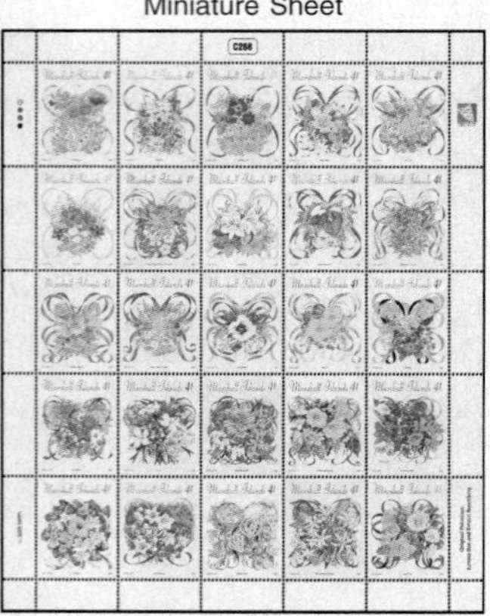

Flower Bouquets — A271

No. 904 — Various bouquets with country name at bottom: a, Scotland. b, Jersey. c, Gibraltar. d, Dominica. e, Canada. f, Cyprus. g, Turks and Caicos Islands. h, Bahamas. i, Montserrat. j, Cayman Islands. k, Bangladesh. l, Falkland Islands. m, Grenada. n, Nevis. o, Jamaica. p, Australia. q, Fiji. r, New Hebrides. s, Pitcairn Islands. t, Cook Islands. u, Tonga. v, Seychelles. w, Zimbabwe. x, Christmas Island. y, Antigua.

2008, Jan. 15 **Litho.** ***Perf. 13½***
904 A271 41c Sheet of 25, #a-y 20.50 20.50

Miniature Sheet

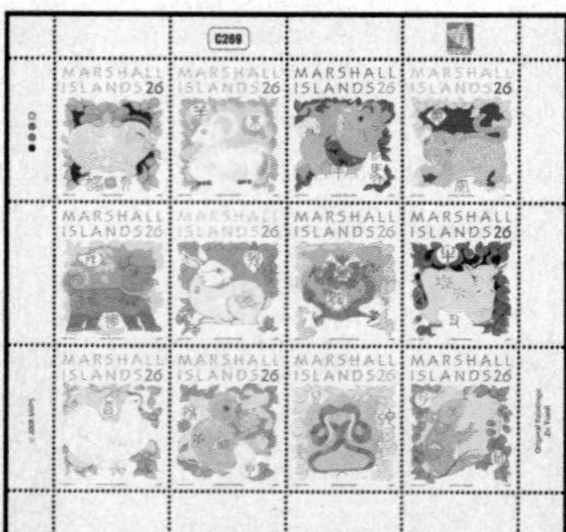

Chinese New Year Animals and Characters — A272

No. 905: a, Pig. b, Ram. c, Horse. d, Tiger. e, Dog. f, Rabbit. g, Dragon. h, Ox. i, Rooster. j, Monkey. k, Snake. l, Rat.

2008, Feb. 7
905 A272 26c Sheet of 12, #a-l 6.25 6.25

United States Lighthouses — A273

No. 906: a, St. Augustine Lighthouse, Florida. b, Old Cape Henry Lighthouse, Virginia. c, Cape Lookout Lighthouse, North Carolina. d, Tybee Island Lighthouse, Georgia. e, Morris Island Lighthouse, South Carolina. f, Hillsboro Inlet Lighthouse, Florida.
Illustration reduced.

2008, Mar. 6 **Litho.** ***Perf. 13½***
906 A273 41c Block of 6, #a-f 5.00 5.00

Miniature Sheet

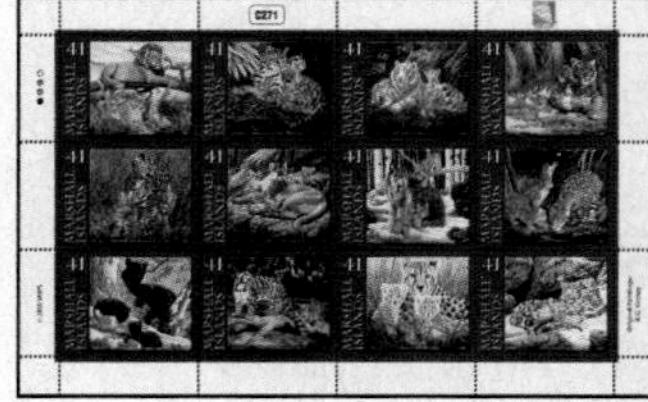

Wild Cats — A274

No. 907: a, Lion family at rest. b, Ocelot mother with cub sitting in grass. c, White Siberian tiger mother with cubs. d, Mother tiger with cubs lying in grass. e, Serval mother with cubs sitting in tall grass. f, North American cougar mother with cubs. g, Lynx mother with cubs. h, Jaguar with cubs at stream. i, Black panther mother with cubs. j, Clouded leopard mother with cubs. k, Cheetah with cubs lying in grass. l, Snow leopard with cubs.

2008, Mar. 26 **Litho.** ***Perf. 13½***
907 A274 41c Sheet of 12, #a-l 10.00 10.00

Miniature Sheet

Sailing Ships — A275

No. 908: a, H.M.S. Victory. b, La Grande Hermine. c, U.S.S. Constitution. d, Fram. e, Tovarisch I. f, Ark and Dove. g, Rainbow. h, Great Republic. i, H.M.S. Resolution. j, La Dauphine. k, Kreuzenshtern. l, Golden Hind.

2008, Apr. 2
908 A275 41c Sheet of 12, #a-l 10.00 10.00

Miniature Sheet

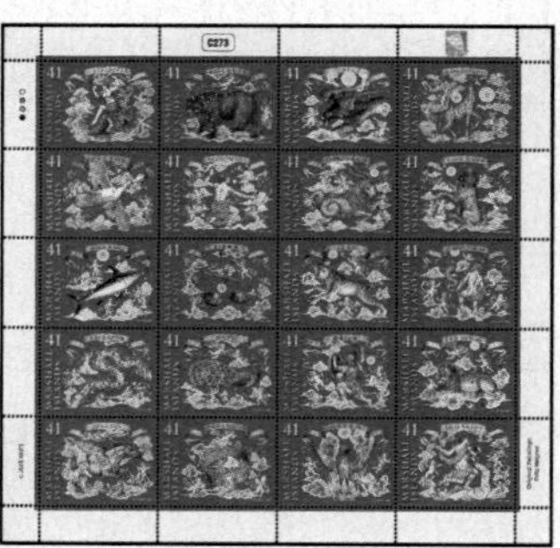

Constellations — A276

No. 909: a, Cassiopeia. b, Ursa Major. c, Corvus. d, Camelopardalis. e, Cygnus. f, Andromeda. g, Capricornus. h, Canis Major. i, Dorado. j, Libra. k, Lynx. l, Serpentarius. m, Eridanus. n, Pavo. o, Orion. p, Leo Minor. q, Pegasus. r, Corona Borealis. s, Phoenix. t, Aquarius.

2008, Apr. 29 **Litho.** ***Perf. 13½***
909 A276 41c Sheet of 20, #a-t 16.50 16.50

Miniature Sheet

US Marine Corps — A277

No. 910: a, US liberates Marshall Islands. b, John Lejeune. c, Holland Smith. d, Smedley D. Butler. e, Daniel J. Daly. f, Lewis "Chesty" Puller. g, John Basilone. h, Alexander Vandegrift. i, Gregory "Pappy" Boyington. j, Marines raising flag on Iwo Jima.

2008, May 12
910 A277 42c Sheet of 10, #a-j 8.50 8.50

Tropical Fish A278

Designs: 1c, Banded butterflyfish. 3c, Damselfish. 5c, Pink skunk clownfish. 27c, Copperband butterflyfish. 42c, Threadfin butterflyfish. 60c, Beau Gregory damselfish. 61c, Porkfish. 63c, Goatfish. 94c, Common longnose butterflyfish. $1, Royal gramma. $4.80, Longfin bannerfish. $5, Blue-striped blenny. $16.50, Emperor butterflyfish.

2008 **Litho.** ***Perf. 11¼x10¼***

911	A278	1c	multi	.20	.20
912	A278	3c	multi	.20	.20
913	A278	5c	multi	.20	.20
914	A278	27c	multi	.55	.55
915	A278	42c	multi	.85	.85
916	A278	60c	multi	1.25	1.25
917	A278	61c	multi	1.25	1.25
918	A278	63c	multi	1.25	1.25
919	A278	94c	multi	1.90	1.90
920	A278	$1	multi	2.00	2.00
921	A278	$4.80	multi	9.75	9.75
922	A278	$5	multi	10.00	10.00
923	A278	$16.50	multi	33.00	33.00
	Nos. 911-923 (13)			62.40	62.40

Issued: Nos. 914, 915, 6/24; Nos. 919, 921, 923, 5/12. Nos. 911-913, 916-918, 920, 922, 9/9.

Miniature Sheet

Birds — A279

No. 924: a, Blue-gray tanager. b, St. Vincent parrot. c, Green-throated carib. d, Yellow oriole. e, Blue-hooded euphonia. f, Crested honeycreeper. g, Purple-capped fruit dove. h, Green magpie. i, Bay-headed tanager. j, Bananaquit. k, Cardinal honeyeater. l, Toco toucan. m, Cattle egret. n, Ringed kingfisher. o, Red-necked parrot. p, Purple gallinule. q, Copper-rumped hummingbird. r, Micronesian pigeon. s, Painted bunting. t, Black-naped oriole. u, Channel-billed toucan. v, Saddle-billed stork. w, Blood pheasant. x, Gray-crowned crane. y, Little blue heron.

2008, June 3 **Litho.** ***Perf. 13½***
924 A279 42c Sheet of 25, #a-y 21.00 21.00

Miniature Sheet

Dinosaurs — A280

No. 925: a, Camarasaurus. b, Allosaurus. c, Parasaurolophus. d, Ornithomimus. e, Goniopholis. f, Camptosaurus. g, Edmontia. h, Ceratosaurus. i, Stegosaurus. j, Einiosaurus. k, Brachiosaurus. l, Corythosaurus.

2008, June 19
925 A280 42c Sheet of 12, #a-l 10.50 10.50

Miniature Sheet

Fishing Flies — A281

No. 926: a, Lefty's Deceiver (25x35mm). b, Apte Tarpon (25x35mm). c, Royal Wulff (50x48mm). d, Muddler Minnow (25x35mm). e, Jock Scott (25x35mm).

2008, July 20
926 A281 42c Sheet of 5, #a-e 4.25 4.25

Miniature Sheet

Personalities of the Wild West — A282

No. 927: a, Wild Bill Hickok. b, Jim Bridger. c, Geronimo. d, Charles Goodnight. e, Chief Joseph. f, Kit Carson. g, Jim Beckwourth. h, Wyatt Earp. i, Bat Masterson. j, Bill Pickett. k, Bill Tilghman. l, Annie Oakley. m, Buffalo Bill Cody. n, Nellie Cashman. o, Sacagawea. p, John Fremont.

2008, Aug. 14
927 A282 42c Sheet of 16, #a-p 13.50 13.50

Endangered Species — A283

No. 928: a, Blue whale. b, Amazonian manatee. c, Hawaiian monk seal. d, Green turtle. e, Giant clam. f, Killer whale.
Illustration reduced.

2008, Aug. 19 Litho. *Perf. 13½*
928 A283 42c Block of 6, #a-f 5.25 5.25

Marshallese Culture Type of 2005

No. 929, vert. — Photographs by J. Debrum: a, Lokeinlik Wearing Traditional Mat for Men. b, Limekto Weaving Hat from Kimej. c, Unfinished Outrigger. d, Young Boys in Mejit. e, Lonkoon with Fish Trap.

2008, Sept. 15 Litho. *Perf. 13½*
929 Horiz. strip of 5 4.25 4.25
a.-e. A250 42c Any single .85 .85

Miniature Sheet

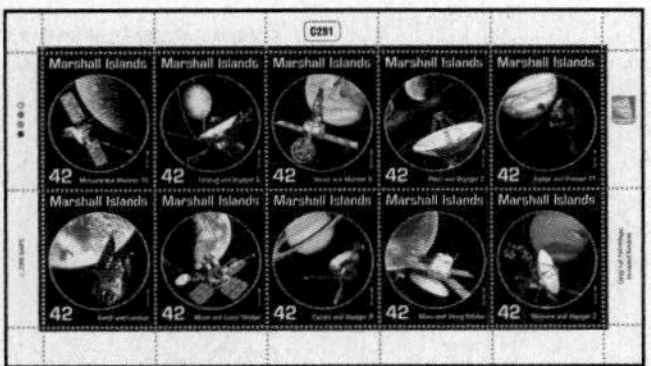

Spacecraft and the Solar System — A284

No. 930: a, Mercury, Mariner 10. b, Uranus, Voyager 2. c, Venus, Mariner 2. d, Pluto, Voyager 2. e, Jupiter, Pioneer 11. f, Earth, Landsat. g, Moon, Lunar Orbiter. h, Saturn, Voyager 2. i, Mars, Viking Orbiter. j, Neptune, Voyager 2.

2008, Oct. 1
930 A284 42c Sheet of 10, #a-j 8.50 8.50

SEMI-POSTAL STAMPS

Operation Crossroads, Nuclear Testing at Bikini Atoll, 50th Anniv. — SP1

Designs: a, Evacuation of Bikinians. b, Navy preparations. c, Able. d, Baker. e, Ghost fleet. f, Effects on Bikinians.

1996, July 1 Litho. *Perf. 13½*
B1 SP1 32c +8c #a.-f. + 6 labels 4.75 4.75

Surtax for the benefit of the people of Bikini.

AIR POST STAMPS

Audubon Type of 1985

1985, Feb. 15 Litho. *Perf. 14*
C1 A11 44c Booby Gannet, vert. .90 .90
C2 A11 44c Esquimaux Curlew, vert. .90 .90
a. Pair, #C1-C2 1.80 1.80

AMERIPEX Type of 1986

Designs: No. C3, Consolidated PBY-5A Catalin Amphibian. No. C4, Grumman SA-16 Albatross. No. C5, McDonnell Douglas DC-6B Super Cloudmaster. No. C6, Boeing &27-100.

1986, May 22 Litho. *Perf. 14*
C3 A20 44c multicolored .85 .85
C4 A20 44c multicolored .85 .85
C5 A20 44c multicolored .85 .85
C6 A20 44c multicolored .85 .85
a. Block of 4, #C3-C6 3.50 3.50

Operation Crossroads Type of 1986
Souvenir Sheet

1986, July 1 Litho. *Perf. 14*
C7 A21 44c USS Saratoga 4.00 4.00

Statue of Liberty Cent., Intl. Peace Year — AP1

1986, Oct. 28 Litho.
C8 AP1 44c multicolored 1.00 .95

Natl. Girl Scout Movement, 20th Anniv. — AP2

1986, Dec. 8 Litho.
C9 AP2 44c Community service .75 .75
C10 AP2 44c Salute .75 .75
C11 AP2 44c Health care .75 .75
C12 AP2 44c Learning skills .75 .75
a. Block of 4, #C9-C12 3.00 3.00

Girl Scout Movement in the US, 75th anniv. (1912-1987).

Marine Birds AP3

1987, Jan. 12 Litho. *Perf. 14*
C13 AP3 44c Wedge-tailed shearwater .75 .75
C14 AP3 44c Red-footed booby .75 .75
C15 AP3 44c Red-tailed tropic-bird .75 .75
C16 AP3 44c Great frigatebird .75 .75
a. Block of 4, #C13-C16 3.00 3.00

CAPEX '87 AP4

Last flight of Amelia Earhart: No. C17, Takeoff at Lae, New Guinea, July 2, 1937. No. C18, USCG Itasca cutter at Howland Is. No. C19, Purported crash landing of the Electra at Mili Atoll. No. C20, Recovery of the Electra by the Koshu, a Japanese survey ship.

1987, June 15 Litho. *Perf. 14*
C17 AP4 44c multicolored .75 .75
C18 AP4 44c multicolored .75 .75
C19 AP4 44c multicolored .75 .75
C20 AP4 44c multicolored .75 .75
a. Block of 4, #C17-C20 3.00 3.00

Space Shuttle Type of 1988

1988, Dec. 23 Litho. *Perf. 14*
C21 A38 45c Astronaut, shuttle over Rongelap .85 .85

Aircraft — AP5

1989, Apr. 24 Litho. *Perf. 14x14½*
C22 AP5 12c Dornier Do228 .25 .25
a. Booklet pane of 10 3.00 —
C23 AP5 36c Boeing 737 .75 .75
a. Booklet pane of 10 8.00 —
C24 AP5 39c Hawker Siddeley 748 .90 .90
a. Booklet pane of 10 9.00 —
C25 AP5 45c Boeing 727 1.00 1.00
a. Booklet pane of 10 10.00 —
b. Bklt. pane, 5 each 36c, 45c 8.75 —
Nos. C22-C25 (4) 2.90 2.90

MARTINIQUE

,mär-tən-ˈēk

LOCATION — Island in the West Indies, southeast of Puerto Rico
GOVT. — French Colony
AREA — 385 sq. mi.
POP. — 261,595 (1946)
CAPITAL — Fort-de-France

Formerly a French colony, Martinique became an integral part of the Republic, acquiring the same status as the departments in metropolitan France, under a law effective Jan. 1, 1947.

100 Centimes = 1 Franc

Catalogue values for unused stamps in this country are for Never Hinged items, beginning with Scott 196 in the regular postage section, Scott C1 in the airpost section, and Scott J37 in the postage due section.

See France Nos. 1278, 1508, French West Africa 70, for stamps inscribed "Martinique."

Stamps of French Colonies 1881-86 Surcharged in Black

Nos. 1, 7

MARTINIQUE
5c
No. 2

MQE
15 c.
No. 3

MQE
15 c.
No. 4

Nos. 5-6, 8

Nos. 9-20

1886-91 Unwmk. *Perf. 14x13½*
1 A9 5 on 20c 45.00 37.50
a. Double surcharge *550.00 550.00*
2 A9 5c on 20c *12,000. 12,000.*
3 A9 15c on 20c ('87) 210.00 175.00
a. Inverted surcharge *1,800. 1,800.*
4 A9 15c on 20c ('87) 80.00 72.50
a. Inverted surcharge *1,100. 1,100.*
5 A9 01 on 20c ('88) 16.00 13.00
a. Inverted surcharge *275.00 260.00*
6 A9 05 on 20c 11.00 8.50
7 A9 15 on 20c ('88) 150.00 140.00
c. Inverted surcharge *600.00 600.00*
8 A9 015 on 20c ('87) 46.50 *46.50*
a. Inverted surcharge *625.00 625.00*
9 A9 01c on 2c ('88) 2.90 2.00
a. Double surcharge *375.00 375.00*

10 A9 01c on 4c ('88) 11.00 3.25
11 A9 05c on 4c ('88) 1,100. 1,100.
12 A9 05c on 10c ('90) 92.50 57.50
a. Slanting "5" *2250.00 175.00*
13 A9 05c on 20c ('88) 22.00 14.50
a. Slanting "5" *110.00 85.00*
b. Inverted surcharge *300.00 275.00*
14 A9 05c on 30c ('91) 26.00 18.00
a. Slanting "5" *110.00 92.50*
15 A9 05c on 35c ('91) 13.50 12.00
a. Slanting "5" *100.00 92.50*
b. Inverted surcharge *225.00 200.00*
16 A9 05c on 40c ('91) 50.00 35.00
a. Slanting "5" *175.00 110.00*
17 A9 15c on 4c ('88) *9,000. 8,250.*
18 A9 15c on 20c ('87) 110.00 82.50
a. Slanting "5" *400.00 300.00*
b. Double surcharge *525.00 525.00*
19 A9 15c on 25c ('90) 25.00 13.50
a. Slanting "5" *110.00 100.00*
b. Inverted surcharge *250.00 225.00*
20 A9 15c on 75c ('91) 140.00 115.00
a. Slanting "5" *425.00 350.00*

French Colonies No. 47 Surcharged

1891
21 A9 01c on 2c brn, *buff* 8.00 8.00

French Colonies Nos. J5-J9 Surcharged

1891-92 Black Surcharge *Imperf.*
22 D1 05c on 5c blk ('92) 12.50 11.50
a. Slanting "5" *52.50 45.00*
23 D1 05c on 15c blk 11.50 11.00
b. Slanting "5" *52.50 45.00*
24 D1 15c on 20c blk 14.50 11.00
a. Inverted surcharge *210.00 210.00*
b. Double surcharge *210.00 210.00*
25 D1 15c on 30c blk 14.50 11.00
a. Inverted surcharge *210.00 210.00*
b. Slanting "5" *57.50 45.00*
Nos. 22-25 (4) 53.00 44.50

Red Surcharge
26 D1 05c on 10c blk 10.00 8.50
a. Inverted surcharge *210.00 210.00*
27 D1 05c on 15c blk 11.00 11.00
28 D1 15c on 20c blk 40.00 29.00
a. Inverted surcharge *300.00 300.00*
Nos. 26-28 (3) 61.00 48.50

French Colonies No. 54 Surcharged in Black

j

k

1892 *Perf. 14x13½*
29 A9 (j) 05c on 25c 50.00 50.00
a. Slanting "5" *210.00 210.00*
30 A9 (j) 15c on 25c 28.00 28.00
a. Slanting "5" *200.00 200.00*
31 A9 (k) 05c on 25c 42.50 40.00
a. "1882" instead of "1892" *500.00 450.00*
b. "95" instead of "05" *600.00 550.00*
c. Slanting "5" *200.00 200.00*
32 A9 (k) 15c on 25c 25.00 24.00
a. "1882" instead of "1892" *450.00 425.00*
b. Slanting "5" *110.00 110.00*
Nos. 29-32 (4) 145.50 142.00

Navigation and Commerce — A15

1892-1906 Typo. *Perf. 14x13½*
"MARTINIQUE" Colony in Carmine or Blue
33 A15 1c blk, *lil bl* 1.25 1.00
a. "MARTINIQUE" in blue 725.00 725.00
34 A15 2c brn, *buff* 1.25 1.10
35 A15 4c claret, *lav* 1.40 1.10

36 A15 5c grn, *grnsh* 1.75 1.10
37 A15 5c yel grn ('99) 2.50 .85
38 A15 10c blk, *lav* 8.50 1.40
39 A15 10c red ('99) 4.00 1.10
40 A15 15c blue, quadrille paper 32.50 6.00
41 A15 15c gray ('99) 11.00 1.60
42 A15 20c red, *grn* 16.00 7.25
43 A15 25c blk, *rose* 18.00 2.50
44 A15 25c blue ('99) 12.00 12.00
45 A15 30c brn, *bis* 24.00 14.00
46 A15 35c blk, *yel* ('06) 12.00 7.25
47 A15 40c red, *straw* 26.50 14.00
48 A15 50c car, *rose* 30.00 18.50
49 A15 50c brn, *az* ('99) 30.00 26.00
50 A15 75c dp vio, *org* 24.00 15.00
51 A15 1fr brnz grn, *straw* 24.00 16.00
52 A15 2fr vio, *rose* ('04) 72.50 62.50
53 A15 5fr lil, *lav* ('03) 82.50 75.00
Nos. 33-53 (21) 435.65 285.25

Perf. 13½x14 stamps are counterfeits.
For surcharges see Nos. 54-61, 101-104.

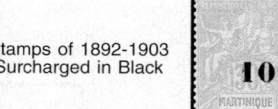

Stamps of 1892-1903 Surcharged in Black

1904

54 A15 10c on 30c brn, *bis* 10.00 10.00
a. Double surcharge 400.00 400.00
55 A15 10c on 5fr lil, *lav* 11.00 11.00

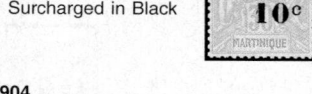

Surcharged

56 A15 10c on 30c brn, *bis* 17.00 17.00
57 A15 10c on 40c red, *straw* 17.00 17.00
a. Double surcharge 325.00 325.00
58 A15 10c on 50c car, *rose* 20.00 20.00
59 A15 10c on 75c dp vio, *org* 14.00 14.00
60 A15 10c on 1fr brnz grn, *straw* 14.00 14.00
a. Double surcharge 210.00 210.00
61 A15 10c on 5fr lil, *lav* 140.00 140.00
Nos. 54-61 (8) 243.00 243.00

Martinique Woman — A16

Girl Bearing Pineapple in Cane Field — A18

View of Fort-de-France — A17

1908-30 **Typo.**

62 A16 1c red brn & brn .20 .20
63 A16 2c ol grn & brn .25 .20
64 A16 4c vio brn & brn .25 .20
65 A16 5c grn & brn .75 .20
66 A16 5c org & brn ('22) .30 .20
67 A16 10c car & brn .90 .40
68 A16 10c bl grn & grn ('22) .40 .20
69 A16 10c brn vio & rose ('25) .40 .20
70 A16 15c brn vio & rose ('17) .45 .20
71 A16 15c bl grn & gray grn ('25) .30 .30
72 A16 15c dp bl & red org ('27) 1.25 1.25
73 A16 20c vio & brn 1.10 .80
74 A17 25c bl & brn 1.60 .80
75 A17 25c org & brn ('22) .65 .40
76 A17 30c brn org & brn 1.60 .80
77 A17 30c dl red & brn ('22) .50 .50
78 A17 30c rose & ver ('24) .45 .45
79 A17 30c ol brn & brn ('25) .45 .45
80 A17 30c sl bl & bl grn ('27) 1.25 1.25
81 A17 35c vio & brn .60 .50
82 A17 40c gray grn & brn .60 .40
83 A17 45c dk brn & brn .60 .40
84 A17 50c rose & brn 1.60 .80
85 A17 50c bl & brn ('22) 1.10 1.10
86 A17 50c org & grn ('25) .60 .20
87 A17 60c dk bl & lil rose ('25) .60 .50
88 A17 65c vio & ol brn ('27) 1.40 1.40
89 A17 75c slate & brn 1.00 .60
90 A17 75c ind & dk bl ('25) .60 .50
91 A17 75c org brn & lt bl ('27) 2.00 2.00
92 A17 90c brn red & brt red ('30) 4.25 4.25
93 A18 1fr dl bl & brn .90 .60
94 A18 1fr dk bl ('25) .75 .60
95 A18 1fr ver & ol grn ('27) 1.60 1.60
96 A18 1.10fr vio & dk brn ('28) 2.50 2.50
97 A18 1.50fr ind & ultra ('30) 4.25 4.25
98 A18 2fr gray & brn 3.25 1.40
99 A18 3fr red vio ('30) 7.25 7.25
100 A18 5fr org red & brn 8.00 6.00
Nos. 62-100 (39) 56.50 45.85

For surcharges see Nos. 105-128, B1.

Nos. 41, 43, 47 and 53 Surcharged in Carmine or Black

1912, Aug.

101 A15 5c on 15c gray (C) .80 .80
102 A15 5c on 25c blk, *rose* (C) 1.25 1.25
103 A15 10c on 40c red, *straw* 1.75 1.75
104 A15 10c on 5fr lil, *lav* 2.25 2.25
Nos. 101-104 (4) 6.05 6.05

Two spacings between the surcharged numerals are found on Nos. 101 to 104. For detailed listings, see the *Scott Classic Specialized Catalogue of Stamps and Covers.*

Nos. 62, 63, 70 Surcharged

1920, June 15

105 A16 5c on 1c 1.60 1.60
a. Double surcharge 32.50 32.50
b. Inverted surcharge 21.00 21.00
106 A16 10c on 2c 1.60 1.60
a. Inverted surcharge 29.00 29.00
107 A16 25c on 15c 1.40 1.40
a. Double surcharge 42.50 42.50
b. Inverted surcharge 42.50 42.50
Nos. 105-107 (3) 4.60 4.60

No. 70 Surcharged in Various Colors

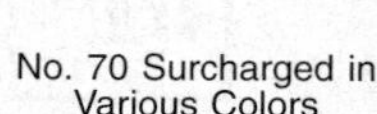

1922, Dec.

108 A16 1c on 15c (Bk) .35 .35
109 A16 2c on 15c (Bl) .35 .35
110 A16 5c on 15c (R) .50 .50
a. Imperf., pair 100.00
Nos. 108-110 (3) 1.20 1.20

Types of 1908-30 Surcharged

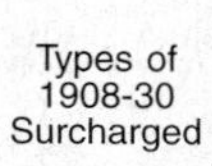

1923-25

111 A17 60c on 75c bl & rose .45 .45
112 A17 65c on 45c ol brn & brn ('25) 1.00 1.00
113 A17 85c on 75c blk & brn (R) ('25) 1.25 1.25
Nos. 111-113 (3) 2.70 2.70

Nos. 63, 73, 76-77, 84-85 Surcharged in Brown

Surcharge is horiz. on #114-115, vert. reading up on #116, 119 and down on #117-118.

1924, Feb. 14

114 A16 1c on 2c 2.10 2.10
a. Double surcharge 260.00 260.00
b. Inverted surcharge 55.00 55.00
115 A16 5c on 20c 3.00 3.00
a. Inverted surcharge 50.00 50.00
116 A17 15c on 30c (#76) 11.50 11.50
a. Surcharge reading down 32.50 32.50
117 A17 15c on 30c (#77) 16.00 16.00
a. Surcharge reading up 50.00 50.00
118 A17 25c on 50c (#84) 210.00 210.00
119 A17 25c on 50c (#85) 7.25 7.25
a. Surcharge reading down 25.00 25.00
Nos. 114-119 (6) 249.85 249.85

Stamps and Types of 1908-30 Surcharged with New Value and Bars

1924-27

120 A16 25c on 15c brn vio & rose ('25) .40 .40
121 A18 25c on 2fr gray & brn .30 .30
122 A18 25c on 5fr org red & brn (Bl) 1.75 1.40
123 A17 90c on 75c brn red & red ('27) 3.00 2.10
124 A18 1.25fr on 1fr dk bl ('26) .85 .70
125 A18 1.50fr on 1fr dk bl & ultra ('27) 1.40 .85
126 A18 3fr on 5fr dl red & grn ('27) 2.10 2.10
127 A18 10fr on 5fr dl grn & dp red ('27) 9.00 9.00
128 A18 20fr on 5fr org brn & red vio ('27) 14.00 13.50
Nos. 120-128 (9) 32.80 30.35

Common Design Types pictured following the introduction.

Colonial Exposition Issue
Common Design Types

1931, Apr. 13 **Engr.** ***Perf. 12½***
Name of Country in Black

129 CD70 40c deep green 4.00 4.00
130 CD71 50c violet 4.00 4.00
131 CD72 90c red orange 4.00 4.00
132 CD73 1.50fr dull blue 4.00 4.00
Nos. 129-132 (4) 16.00 16.00

Village of Basse-Pointe — A19

Government Palace, Fort-de-France — A20

Martinique Women A21

1933-40 **Photo.** ***Perf. 13½***

133 A19 1c red, *pink* .20 .20
134 A20 2c dull blue .20 .20
135 A20 3c sepia ('40) .20 .20
136 A19 4c olive grn .20 .20
137 A20 5c dp rose .25 .25
138 A19 10c blk, *pink* .25 .25
139 A20 15c blk, *org* .25 .25
140 A21 20c org brn .25 .25
141 A19 25c brn vio .25 .25
142 A20 30c green .40 .40
143 A20 30c lt ultra ('40) .25 .25
144 A21 35c dl grn ('38) .65 .60
145 A21 40c olive brn .50 .40
146 A20 45c dk brn 1.60 1.40
147 A20 45c grn ('40) .45 .45
148 A20 50c red .40 .20
149 A19 55c brn red ('38) 1.10 .80
150 A19 60c lt bl ('40) .70 .70
151 A21 65c red, *grn* .40 .40
152 A21 70c brt red vio ('40) .50 .50
153 A19 75c dk brn .85 .65
154 A20 80c vio ('38) .60 .50
155 A19 90c carmine 1.40 1.25
156 A19 90c brt red vio ('39) .70 .70
157 A20 1fr blk, *grn* 1.60 1.00
158 A20 1fr rose red ('38) .60 .50
159 A21 1.25fr dk vio .50 .50
160 A21 1.25fr dp rose ('39) .60 .60
161 A19 1.40fr lt ultra ('40) .60 .60
162 A20 1.50fr dp bl .50 .40
163 A20 1.60fr chnt ('40) .60 .60
164 A21 1.75fr ol grn 6.50 3.50
165 A21 1.75fr dp bl ('38) .50 .50
166 A19 2fr dk bl,*grn* .40 .30
167 A21 2.25fr blue ('39) .60 .60
168 A19 2.50fr sepia ('40) .75 .75
169 A21 3fr brn vio .50 .45
170 A21 5fr red, *pink* .95 .80
171 A19 10fr dk bl, *bl* .75 .60
172 A20 20fr red, *yel* 1.10 .70
Nos. 133-172 (40) 29.60 23.65

For surcharges see Nos. 190-195.

The 3c, 15c, 30c, 50c, and 1.50fr in this series, without the "RF" monogram, were issued in 1942 by the Vichy Government but were never placed on sale in Martinique.

Landing of Bélain d'Esnambuc — A22

Freed Slaves Paying Homage to Victor Schoelcher A23

1935, Oct. 22 **Engr.** ***Perf. 13***

173 A22 40c blk brn 3.25 3.25
174 A22 50c dl red 3.25 3.25
175 A22 1.50fr ultra 12.00 12.00
176 A23 1.75fr lil rose 12.00 12.00
177 A23 5fr brown 12.00 12.00
178 A23 10fr blue grn 9.50 9.50
Nos. 173-178 (6) 52.00 52.00

Tercentenary of French possessions in the West Indies.

Colonial Arts Exhibition Issue
Common Design Type
Souvenir Sheet

1937 ***Imperf.***

179 CD74 3fr brt grn 8.75 *10.50*

Paris International Exposition Issue
Common Design Types

1937, Apr. 15 ***Perf. 13***

180 CD74 20c dp vio 1.25 1.25
181 CD75 30c dk grn 1.40 1.40
182 CD76 40c car rose 1.40 1.40
183 CD77 50c dk brn & blk 1.40 1.40
184 CD78 90c red 1.50 1.50
185 CD79 1.50fr ultra 1.50 1.50
Nos. 180-185 (6) 8.45 8.45

New York World's Fair Issue
Common Design Type

1939, May 10 ***Perf. 12½x12***

186 CD82 1.25fr car lake 1.10 1.10
187 CD82 2.25fr ultra 1.25 1.25

View of Fort-de-France and Marshal Pétain — A23a

1941 Engr. *Perf. 12½x12*

No.	Type	Description	Unused	Used
188	A23a	1fr dull lilac	.50	
189	A23a	2.50fr blue	.50	

Nos. 188-189 were issued by the Vichy government in France, but were not placed on sale in Martinique.

For surcharges, see Nos. B10A-B10B.

Types of 1933-40 without "RF"

1942-44 Photo. *Perf. 13½*

No.	Type	Description	Unused	Used
189A	A20	3c sepia	.40	
189B	A20	15c blk, *org*	.45	
189C	A20	30c yel green	.45	
189D	A20	50c red	1.10	
189E	A20	1.50fr dp bl	.50	
		Nos. 189A-189E (5)	2.90	

Nos. 189A-189E were issued by the Vichy government in France, but were not placed on sale in Martinique.

Nos. 134, 135, 136 and 151 Surcharged with New Values and Bars or Wavy Lines in Red, Black or Blue

1945 *Perf. 13½, 13x13½*

No.	Type	Description	Unused	Used
190	A20	1fr on 2c dl bl (R)	.45	.45
191	A19	2fr on 4c ol grn	.45	.45
192	A20	3fr on 2c dl bl (R)	.60	.60
193	A21	5fr on 65c red, *grn*	1.10	1.10
194	A21	10fr on 65c red, *grn*	1.10	1.10
195	A20	20fr on 3c sepia (Bl)	1.10	1.10
		Nos. 190-195 (6)	4.80	4.80

Catalogue values for unused stamps in this section, from this point to the end of the section, are for Never Hinged items.

Eboue Issue

Common Design Type

1945 Engr. *Perf. 13*

No.	Type	Description	Unused	Used
196	CD91	2fr black	.40	.35
197	CD91	25fr Prussian green	.85	.80

Victor Schoelcher and View of Town of Schoelcher
A24

1945 Unwmk. Litho. *Perf. 11½*

No.	Type	Description	Unused	Used
198	A24	10c dp bl vio & ultra	.20	.20
199	A24	30c dk org brn & lt org brn	.25	.25
200	A24	40c grnsh bl & pale bl	.25	.25
201	A24	50c car brn & rose lil	.30	.30
202	A24	60c org yel & yel	.30	.30
203	A24	70c brn & pale brn	.30	.20
204	A24	80c lt bl grn & pale grn	.30	.20
205	A24	1fr bl & lt bl	.30	.20
206	A24	1.20fr rose vio & rose lil	.30	.20
207	A24	1.50fr red org & org	.30	.20
208	A24	2fr blk & gray	.30	.20
209	A24	2.40fr red & pink	1.00	.85
210	A24	3fr pink & pale pink	.35	.35
211	A24	4fr ultra & lt ultra	.50	.35
212	A24	4.50fr yel grn & lt grn	.75	.35
213	A24	5fr org brn & lt org brn	.55	.35
214	A24	10fr dk vio & lil	.75	.50
215	A24	15fr rose car & lil rose	1.00	.60
216	A24	20fr ol grn & lt ol grn	1.50	.95
		Nos. 198-216 (19)	9.50	6.80

Martinique Girl
A25

Mountains
A30

Cliffs
A26

Gathering Sugar Cane
A27

Mount Pelée
A28

Tropical Fruit — A29

1947, June 2 Engr. *Perf. 13*

No.	Type	Description	Unused	Used
217	A25	10c red brown	.25	.20
218	A25	30c deep blue	.35	.30
219	A25	50c olive brown	.40	.30
220	A26	60c dark green	.40	.35
221	A26	1fr red brown	.50	.35
222	A26	1.50fr purple	.60	.35
223	A27	2fr blue green	1.00	.55
224	A27	2.50fr blk brn	1.10	.50
225	A27	3fr deep blue	1.10	.50
226	A28	4fr dk brown	.95	.50
227	A28	5fr dark green	1.10	.50
228	A28	6fr lilac rose	1.00	.50
229	A29	10fr indigo	1.50	1.00
230	A29	15fr red brown	1.75	1.00
231	A29	20fr blk brown	2.25	1.10
232	A30	25fr violet	2.25	1.25
233	A30	40fr blue grren	2.75	1.60
		Nos. 217-233 (17)	19.25	10.85

SEMI-POSTAL STAMPS

Regular Issue of 1908 Surcharged in Red

Perf. 13½x14

1915, May 15 Unwmk.

No.	Type	Description	Unused	Used
B1	A16	10c + 5c car & brn	1.75	1.25

Curie Issue

Common Design Type

1938, Oct. 24 *Perf. 13*

No.	Type	Description	Unused	Used
B2	CD80	1.75fr + 50c brt ultra	10.00	10.00

French Revolution Issue

Common Design Type

Photo.; Name & Value Typo. in Black

1939, July 5

No.	Type	Description	Unused	Used
B3	CD83	45c + 25c grn	8.00	8.00
B4	CD83	70c + 30c brn	8.00	8.00
B5	CD83	90c + 35c red org	8.00	8.00
B6	CD83	1.25fr + 1fr rose pink	8.00	8.00
B7	CD83	2.25fr + 2fr blue	8.00	8.00
		Nos. B3-B7 (5)	40.00	40.00

Common Design Type and

Colonial Infantry with Machine Gun
SP1

Naval Rifleman
SP2

1941 Photo. *Perf. 13½*

No.	Type	Description	Unused	Used
B8	SP1	1fr + 1fr red	1.00	
B9	CD86	1.50fr + 3fr maroon	1.00	
B10	SP2	2.50fr + 1fr blue	1.00	
		Nos. B8-B10 (3)	3.00	

Nos. B8-B10 were issued by the Vichy government in France, but were not placed on sale in Martinique.

Nos. 188-189 Surcharged in Black or Red

1944 Engr. *Perf. 12½x12*

No.	Description	Unused	Used
B10A	50c + 1.50fr on 2.50fr blue (R)	.60	
B10B	+ 2.50fr on 1fr dull lilac	.60	

Colonial Development Fund.

Nos. B10A-B10B were issued by the Vichy government in France, but were not placed on sale in Martinique.

Red Cross Issue

Common Design Type

1944 *Perf. 14½x14*

No.	Type	Description	Unused	Used
B11	CD90	5fr + 20fr dark purpler	.90	.90

The surtax was for the French Red Cross and national relief.

AIR POST STAMPS

Catalogue values for unused stamps in this section are for Never Hinged items.

Common Design Type

1945 Unwmk. Photo. *Perf. 14½x14*

No.	Type	Description	Unused	Used
C1	CD87	50fr dark green	1.25	.50
C2	CD87	100fr plum	1.75	.55

Two other values, 8.50fr orange and 18fr red brown, were prepared but not issued. Value, $50 each.

Victory Issue

Common Design Type

1946, May 8 Engr. *Perf. 12½*

No.	Type	Description	Unused	Used
C3	CD92	8fr indigo	1.25	.85

European victory of the Allied Nations in WWII.

Chad to Rhine Issue

Common Design Types

1946, June 6

No.	Type	Description	Unused	Used
C4	CD93	5fr orange	.95	.70
C5	CD94	10fr slate grn	1.10	.85
C6	CD95	15fr carmine	1.10	.85
C7	CD96	20fr chocolate	1.10	.85
C8	CD97	25fr deep blue	1.40	.85
C9	CD98	50fr gray blk	1.50	1.00
		Nos. C4-C9 (6)	7.15	5.10

Seaplane and Beach Scene — AP1

Plane over Tropic Shore — AP2

Albatross — AP3

1947, June 2 *Perf. 13*

No.	Type	Description	Unused	Used
C10	AP1	50fr dk brn vio	4.50	2.10
C11	AP2	100fr dk bl grn	6.50	3.00
C12	AP3	200fr violet	32.50	20.00
		Nos. C10-C12 (3)	43.50	25.10

AIR POST SEMI-POSTAL STAMPS

Nurse with Mother & Child — SPAP1

Unwmk.

1942, June 22 Engr. *Perf. 13*

No.	Type	Description	Unused	Used
CB1	SPAP1	1.50fr + 3.50fr green	.60	
CB2	SPAP1	2fr + 6fr brn & red	.60	

Native children's welfare fund.

Nos. CB1-CB2 were issued by the Vichy government in France, but were not placed on sale in Martinique.

Colonial Education Fund

Common Design Type

1942, June 22

No.	Type	Description	Unused	Used
CB3	CD86a	1.20fr + 1.80fr blue & red	.50	

No. CB3 was issued by the Vichy government in France, but was not placed on sale in Martinique.

POSTAGE DUE STAMPS

The set of 14 French Colonies postage due stamps (Nos. J1-J14) overprinted "MARTINIQUE" diagonally in red in 1887 was not an official issue.

Postage Due Stamps of France, 1893-1926 Overprinted

1927, Oct. 10 *Perf. 14x13½*

No.	Type	Description	Unused	Used
J15	D2	5c light blue	1.25	1.25
J16	D2	10c brown	1.40	1.40
J17	D2	20c olive green	1.60	1.60
J18	D2	25c rose	1.90	1.90
J19	D2	30c red	2.25	2.25
J20	D2	45c green	3.75	3.75
J21	D2	50c brn violet	4.75	4.75
J22	D2	60c blue green	4.75	4.75
J23	D2	1fr red brown	6.75	6.75
J24	D2	2fr bright vio	8.25	8.25
J25	D2	3fr magenta	9.50	9.50
		Nos. J15-J25 (11)	46.15	46.15

Tropical Fruit — D3

1933, Feb. 15 Photo. *Perf. 13½*

No.	Type	Description	Unused	Used
J26	D3	5c dk bl, *green*	.35	.35
J27	D3	10c orange brown	.35	.35
J28	D3	20c dk blue	.70	.70

J29 D3 25c red, *pink* .80 .80
J30 D3 30c dk vio .80 .80
J31 D3 45c red, *yel* .60 .60
J32 D3 50c dk brn 1.00 1.00
J33 D3 60c dl grn 1.00 1.00
J34 D3 1fr blk, *org* 1.00 1.00
J35 D3 2fr dp rose 1.00 1.00
J36 D3 3fr dk blue, *bl* 1.00 1.00
Nos. J26-J36 (11) 8.60 8.60

Type of 1933 Without "RF"

1943

J36A D3 10c orange brown .25
J36B D3 20c dk blue .25
J36C D3 25c red, *pink* .35
J36D D3 30c dk vio .35
Nos. J36A-J36D (4) 1.20

Nos. J36A-J36D were issued by the Vichy government in France, but were not placed on sale in Martinique.

Catalogue values for unused stamps in this section, from this point to the end of the section, are for Never Hinged items.

Map — D4

1947, June 2 Engr. *Perf. 14x13*

J37 D4 10c ultra .20 .20
J38 D4 30c brt bl grn .20 .20
J39 D4 50c slate gray .20 .20
J40 D4 1fr org red .20 .20
J41 D4 2fr dk vio brn .60 .55
J42 D4 3fr lilac rose .70 .65
J43 D4 4fr dk brn .90 .80
J44 D4 5fr red .90 .80
J45 D4 10fr black 1.75 1.40
J46 D4 20fr olive grn 1.75 1.40
Nos. J37-J46 (10) 7.40 6.40

PARCEL POST STAMP

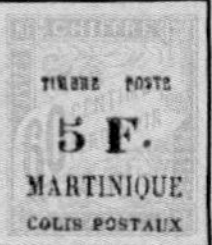

Postage Due Stamp of French Colonies Surcharged in Black

1903, Oct. Unwmk. *Imperf.*

Q1 D1 5fr on 60c brn, *buff* 475.00 *550.00*
a. Inverted surcharge *600.00* *625.00*

MAURITANIA

mor-ə-ta-nē-ə

LOCATION — Northwestern Africa, bordering on the Atlantic Ocean
GOVT. — Republic
AREA — 398,000 sq. mi.
POP. — 2,581,738 (1999 est.)
CAPITAL — Nouakchott

The Islamic Republic of Mauritania was proclaimed Nov. 28, 1958.

Stamps of French West Africa were used in the period between the issues of the colony and the republic.

100 Centimes = 1 Franc
Ouguiya ("um") (1973)

Catalogue values for unused stamps in this country are for Never Hinged items, beginning with Scott 116 in the regular postage section, Scott B16 in the semi-postal section, Scott C14 in the airpost section, Scott J19 in the postage due section, and Scott O1 in the official section.

See French West Africa No. 65 for additional stamp inscribed "Mauritanie" and "Afrique Occidentale Francaise."

General Louis Faidherbe A1

Oil Palms — A2

Dr. Noel Eugène Ballay A3

Perf. 14x13½
1906-07 Typo. Unwmk.
"Mauritanie" in Red or Blue

1 A1 1c slate .60 .60
2 A1 2c chocolate 1.10 .75
3 A1 4c choc, *gray bl* 1.75 1.25
4 A1 5c green .85 .70
5 A1 10c carmine (B) 10.00 4.00
7 A2 20c black, *azure* 18.50 13.00
8 A2 25c blue, *pnksh* 6.25 5.00
9 A2 30c choc, *pnksh* 95.00 50.00
10 A2 35c black, *yellow* 6.75 4.00
11 A2 40c car, *az* (B) 7.25 5.75
12 A2 45c choc, *grnsh* ('07) 8.00 6.00
13 A2 50c deep violet 7.25 5.50
14 A2 75c blue, *org* 6.50 6.00
15 A3 1fr black, *azure* 18.50 18.50
16 A3 2fr blue, *pink* 45.00 45.00
17 A3 5fr car, *straw*(B) 115.00 115.00
Nos. 1-17 (16) 348.30 281.05

Crossing Desert A4

1913-38

18 A4 1c brn vio & brn .25 .20
19 A4 2c black & blue .30 .20
20 A4 4c violet & blk .30 .20
21 A4 5c yel grn & bl grn .85 .50
22 A4 5c brn vio & rose ('22) .20 .20
23 A4 10c rose & red org 1.90 1.25
24 A4 10c yel grn & bl grn ('22) .45 .40
25 A4 10c lil rose, *bluish* ('25) .35 .35
26 A4 15c dk brn & blk ('17) .45 .35
27 A4 20c bis brn & org .45 .35
28 A4 25c blue & vio 1.10 .95
29 A4 25c grn & rose ('22) .20 .20
30 A4 30c bl grn & rose 1.10 1.00
31 A4 30c rose & red org ('22) 1.25 1.25
32 A4 30c black & yel ('26) .20 .20
33 A4 30c bl grn & yel grn ('28) .95 .95
34 A4 35c brown & vio .65 .50
35 A4 35c dp grn & lt grn ('38) 1.00 1.00
36 A4 40c gray & bl grn 2.25 1.75
37 A4 45c org & bis brn 1.25 .95
38 A4 50c brn vio & rose .95 .95
39 A4 50c dk bl & ultra ('22) .40 .40
40 A4 50c gray grn & dp bl ('26) .70 .70
41 A4 60c vio, *pnksh* ('26) .50 .50
42 A4 65c yel brn & lt bl ('26) .70 .70
43 A4 75c ultra & brown .70 .65
44 A4 85c myr grn & lt brn ('26) .80 .80
45 A4 90c brn red & rose ('30) 1.75 1.50
46 A4 1fr rose & black .80 .80
47 A4 1.10fr vio & ver ('28) 9.00 9.00
48 A4 1.25fr dk bl & blk brn ('33) 1.75 1.75
49 A4 1.50fr lt bl & dp bl ('30) 1.00 1.00
50 A4 1.75fr bl grn & brn red ('33) 1.60 1.50
51 A4 1.75fr dk bl & ultra ('38) 1.60 1.10
52 A4 2fr red org & vio 1.60 1.25
53 A4 3fr red violet ('30) 1.60 1.50
54 A4 5fr violet & blue 2.75 2.10
Nos. 18-54 (37) 43.65 38.95

For surcharges see Nos. 55-64, B1-B2.

Stamp and Type of 1913-38 Surcharged

1922-25

55 A4 60c on 75c violet, *pnksh* .70 .70
56 A4 65c on 15c dk brn & blk ('25) 1.40 1.40
57 A4 85c on 75c ultra & brn ('25) 1.40 1.40
Nos. 55-57 (3) 3.50 3.50

Stamp and Type of 1913-38 Surcharged with New Value and Bars

1924-27

58 A4 25c on 2fr red org & vio .80 .80
59 A4 90c on 75c brn red & cer ('27) 1.90 1.90
60 A4 1.25fr on 1fr dk bl & ultra ('26) .45 .45
61 A4 1.50fr on 1fr bl & dp bl ('27) 1.25 1.25
62 A4 3fr on 5fr ol brn & red vio ('27) 5.50 5.50
63 A4 10fr on 5fr mag & bl grn ('27) 5.50 5.50
64 A4 20fr on 5fr bl vio & dp org ('27) 6.50 6.50
Nos. 58-64 (7) 21.90 21.90

Common Design Types pictured following the introduction.

Colonial Exposition Issue

Common Design Types

Engr.; Name of Country Typo. in Black

1931, Apr. 13 *Perf. 12½*

65 CD70 40c deep green 6.00 6.00
66 CD71 50c violet 4.00 4.00
67 CD72 90c red orange 4.00 4.00
68 CD73 1.50fr dull blue 4.00 4.00
Nos. 65-68 (4) 18.00 18.00

Paris International Exposition Issue

Common Design Types

1937, Apr. 15 *Perf. 13*

69 CD74 20c deep violet .95 .95
70 CD75 30c dark green 1.10 1.10
71 CD76 40c carmine rose 1.10 1.10
72 CD77 50c dk brn & blk 1.10 1.10
73 CD78 90c red 1.10 1.10
74 CD79 1.50fr ultra 1.10 1.10
Nos. 69-74 (6) 6.45 6.45

Colonial Arts Exhibition Issue

Common Design Type

Souvenir Sheet

1937 *Imperf.*

75 CD76 3fr dark blue 6.00 *7.50*

Camel Rider — A5

Mauri Couple — A8

Mauris on Camels A6

Family before Tent — A7

1938-40 *Perf. 13*

76 A5 2c violet blk .20 .20
77 A5 3c dp ultra .20 .20
78 A5 4c rose violet .20 .20
79 A5 5c orange red .20 .20
80 A5 10c brown car .30 .30
81 A5 15c dk violet .30 .30
82 A6 20c red .30 .30
83 A6 25c deep ultra .30 .30
84 A6 30c deep brown .20 .20
85 A6 35c Prus green .60 .60
86 A6 40c rose car ('40) .25 .25
87 A6 45c Prus grn ('40) .25 .25
88 A6 50c purple .35 .35
89 A7 55c rose violet .80 .80
90 A7 60c violet ('40) .35 .35
91 A7 65c deep green .80 .80
92 A7 70c red ('40) .60 .60
93 A7 80c deep blue 1.10 1.10
94 A7 90c rose violet ('39) .65 .65
95 A7 1fr red 1.75 1.75
96 A7 1fr dp green ('40) .65 .65
97 A7 1.25fr rose car ('39) 1.25 1.25
98 A7 1.40fr dp blue ('40) .65 .65
99 A7 1.50fr violet .75 .75
99A A7 1.50fr red brn ('40) 82.50 82.50
100 A7 1.60fr black brn ('40) 1.40 1.40
101 A8 1.75fr deep ultra 1.10 1.10
102 A8 2fr rose violet .70 .70
103 A8 2.25fr dull ultra ('39) .60 .60
104 A8 2.50fr black brn ('40) .75 .75
105 A8 3fr deep green .60 .60
106 A8 5fr scarlet .80 .80
107 A8 10fr deep brown 1.40 1.40
108 A8 20fr brown car 1.50 1.50
Nos. 76-108 (34) 104.35 104.35

Nos. 91 and 109 surcharged with new values are listed under French West Africa.

For surcharges see Nos. B9-B12.

Caillie Issue

Common Design Type

1939, Apr. 5 Engr. *Perf. 12½x12*

109 CD81 90c org brn & org .95 .95
110 CD81 2fr brt violet .95 .95
111 CD81 2.25fr ultra & dk bl 1.00 1.00
Nos. 109-111 (3) 2.90 2.90

New York World's Fair Issue

Common Design Type

1939, May 10

112 CD82 1.25fr carmine lake .55 .55
113 CD82 2.25fr ultra .55 .55

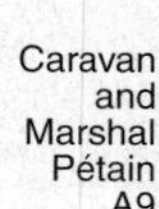

Caravan and Marshal Pétain A9

1941

114 A9 1fr green .50 *1.10*
115 A9 2.50fr deep blue .50 *1.10*

For surcharges, see Nos. B15A-B15B.

Types of 1938-40 Without "RF"

1943-44

115A A5 10c brown car .50
115B A5 15c dk violet .55
115C A6 40c rose car 1.10
115D A6 50c purple 1.10
115E A7 60c violet 1.10
115F A7 1fr dp green 1.10
Nos. 115A-115F (6) 5.45

Nos. 115A-115F were issued by the Vichy government in France, but were not placed on sale in Mauritania.

Catalogue values for unused stamps in this section, from this point to the end of the section, are for Never Hinged items.

Islamic Republic

Camel and Hands Raising Flag — A10

Unwmk.

1960, Jan. 20 Engr. *Perf. 13*
116 A10 25fr multi, *pink* .60 .35

Issued to commemorate the proclamation of the Islamic Republic of Mauritania.

Imperforates
Most Mauritania stamps from 1960 onward exist imperforate in issued and trial colors, and also in small presentation sheets in issued colors.

C.C.T.A. Issue
Common Design Type

1960, May 16
117 CD106 25fr bluish grn & ultra .75 .40

Flag and Map — A11

1960, Dec. 15 Engr. *Perf. 13*
118 A11 25fr org brn, emer & sepia .60 .30

Proclamation of independence, Nov. 28, 1960.

Pastoral Well — A12

Scimitar-horned Oryx — A15

Spotted Hyena A13

Ore Train and Camel Riders A14

Designs: 50c, 1fr, Well. 2fr, Date harvesting. 3fr, Aoudad. 4fr, Fennecs. 5fr, Millet harvesting. 10fr, Shoemaker. 15fr, Fishing boats. 20fr, Nomad school. 25fr, 30fr, Seated dance. No. 130, Religious student. 60fr, Metalworker.

1960-62 Unwmk. *Perf. 13*
119 A12 50c mag, yel & brn ('61) .20 .20
120 A12 1fr brn, yel brn & grn .20 .20
121 A12 2fr dk brn, bl & grn .20 .20
122 A13 3fr bl grn, red brn & gray ('61) .40 .25
123 A13 4fr yel grn & ocher ('61) .40 .25
124 A12 5fr red, dk brn & yel brn .35 .25
125 A14 10fr dk bl & org .40 .25
126 A14 15fr ver, dk brn, grn & bl .70 .25
127 A14 20fr grn, sl grn & red brn .70 .25
128 A12 25fr ultra & gray grn ('61) 1.00 .25
129 A12 30fr lil, bis & indigo 1.00 .25
130 A12 50fr org brn & grn 1.75 .40
131 A14 50fr red brn, bl & ol ('62) 4.75 .80
132 A12 60fr grn, cl & pur 3.00 .40
133 A15 85fr bl, brn & blk ('61) 7.25 1.90
Nos. 119-133 (15) 22.30 6.10

An overprint, "Jeux Olympiques / Rome 1960 / Tokyo 1964," the 5-ring Olympic emblem and a 75fr surcharge were applied to Nos. 126-127 in 1962.

An overprint, "Aide aux Rèfugiès" with uprooted oak emblem, was applied in 1962 to No. 132 and to pink-paper printings of Nos. 129-130.

Other overprints, applied to airmail stamps, are noted after No. C16.

1963, July 6

Designs: 50c, Striped hyena. 1.50fr, Cheetah. 2fr, Guinea baboons. 5fr, Dromedaries. 10fr, Leopard. 15fr, Bongo antelopes. 20fr, Aardvark. 25fr, Patas monkeys. 30fr, Crested porcupine. 50fr, Dorcas gazelle. 60fr, Common chameleon.

134 A15 50c sl grn, blk & org brn .20 .20
135 A13 1fr ultra, blk & yel .20 .20
136 A15 1.50fr ol grn, brn & bis .35 .20
137 A13 2fr dk brn, grn & dp org .30 .25
138 A15 5fr brn, ultra & bis .35 .25
139 A13 10fr blk & bis .75 .25
140 A13 15fr vio bl & red brn .75 .25
141 A13 20fr dk red brn, dk bl & bis .85 .30
142 A15 25fr brt grn, red brn & ol bis 1.25 .30
143 A13 30fr dk brn, dk bl & ol bis 2.40 .30
144 A15 50fr grn, ocher & brn 3.00 .90
145 A13 60fr dk bl, emer & ocher 3.75 1.25
Nos. 134-145 (12) 14.15 4.65

UN Headquarters, New York, and View of Nouakchott — A15a

1962, June 1 Engr. *Perf. 13*
167 A15a 15fr blk, ultra & cop red .30 .30
168 A15a 25fr cop red, sl grn & ultra .45 .35
169 A15a 85fr dk bl, dl pur & cop red 1.25 1.10
Nos. 167-169 (3) 2.00 1.75

Mauritania's admission to the UN.

African-Malagasy Union Issue
Common Design Type

1962, Sept. 8 Photo. *Perf. 12½x12*
170 CD110 30fr multi .75 .50

Organization Emblem and View of Nouakchott — A16

1962, Oct. 15 *Perf. 12½*
171 A16 30fr dk red brn, ultra & brt grn .70 .40

8th Conf. of the Organization to Fight Endemic Diseases, Nouakchott, Oct. 15-18.

Map, Mechanized and Manual Farm Work — A17

1962, Nov. 28 Engr. *Perf. 13*
172 A17 30fr blk, grn & vio brn .75 .35

2nd anniversary of independence.

People in European and Mauritanian Clothes — A18

1962, Dec. 24 Unwmk.
173 A18 25fr multicolored .40 .25

First anniversary of Congress for Unity.

Weather and WMO Symbols — A20

1964, Mar. 23 Unwmk. *Perf. 13*
175 A20 85fr dk brn, dk bl & org 1.50 .75

UN 4th World Meteorological Day, Mar. 23.

IQSY Emblem A21

1964, July 3 Engr.
176 A21 25fr dk bl, red & grn .60 .35

International Quiet Sun Year, 1964-65.

Striped Mullet A22

Designs: 5fr, Mauritanian lobster, vert. 10fr, Royal lobster, vert. 60fr, Maigre fish.

1964, Oct. 5 Engr. *Perf. 13*
177 A22 1fr org brn, dk bl & grn .40 .25
178 A22 5fr org brn, sl grn & choc .50 .25
179 A22 10fr dk bl, bis & sl grn .80 .25
180 A22 60fr dk brn, dp grn & dl bl 5.00 .80
Nos. 177-180 (4) 6.70 1.55

Cooperation Issue
Common Design Type

1964, Nov. 7 Unwmk. *Perf. 13*
181 CD119 25fr mag, sl grn & dk brn .60 .35

Water Lilies A23

Tropical Plants: 10fr, Acacia. 20fr, Adenium obesum. 45fr, Caralluma retrospiciens.

1965, Jan. 11 Engr. *Perf. 13*
182 A23 5fr multi .20 .25
183 A23 10fr multi, vert. .20 .25
184 A23 20fr multi .55 .25
185 A23 45fr multi, vert. 1.10 .50
Nos. 182-185 (4) 2.05 1.25

Hardine A24

Musical Instruments: 8fr, Tobol (drums). 25fr, Tidinit (stringed instruments). 40fr, Musicians.

1965, Mar. 8 *Perf. 13*
186 A24 2fr red brn, brt bl & sep .20 .25
187 A24 8fr red brn, red & brn .40 .25
188 A24 25fr red brn, emer & blk .65 .25
189 A24 40fr vio bl, plum & blk 1.00 .35
Nos. 186-189 (4) 2.25 1.10

Abraham Lincoln (1809-1865) — A25

1965, Apr. 23 Photo. *Perf. 13x12½*
190 A25 50fr lt ultra & multi 1.00 .35

Palms at Adrar A26

Designs: 4fr, Chinguetti mosque, vert. 15fr, Clay pit and donkeys. 60fr, Decorated door, Oualata.

1965, June 14 Engr. *Perf. 13*
191 A26 1fr brn, bl & grn .25 .20
192 A26 4fr dk red, bl & brn .25 .20
193 A26 15fr multi .40 .25
194 A26 60fr grn, dk brn & red brn 1.25 .50
Nos. 191-194 (4) 2.15 1.15

Issued for tourist publicity.

Tea Service in Inlaid Box — A27

7fr, Tobacco pouch and pipe, vert. 25fr, Dagger, vert. 50fr, Mederdra ornamental chest.

1965, Sept. 13 Unwmk. *Perf. 13*
195 A27 3fr gray, choc & ocher .25 .20
196 A27 7fr red lil, Prus bl & org .25 .20
197 A27 25fr blk, org red & brn .55 .25
198 A27 50fr brt grn, brn org & mar 1.10 .35
Nos. 195-198 (4) 2.15 1.00

Choum Railroad Tunnel — A28

10fr, Nouakchott wharf, ships & anchor, horiz. 30fr, as 5fr. 85fr, Nouakchott hospital & caduceus, horiz.

1965, Oct. 18 Engr. *Perf. 13*

199 A28 5fr dk brn & brt grn .20 .20
200 A28 10fr dk vio bl, brn red & Prus bl .25 .20
201 A28 30fr brn red, red & red brn .70 .25
202 A28 85fr dp bl, rose cl & lil 1.10 .55
Nos. 199-202 (4) 2.25 1.20

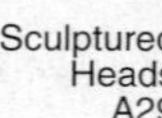

Sculptured Heads A29

Designs: 30fr, "Music and Dance." 60fr, Movie camera and huts.

1966, Apr. Engr. *Perf. 13*

203 A29 10fr brt grn, blk & brn .20 .20
204 A29 30fr brt bl, red lil & blk .50 .25
205 A29 60fr red, org & dk brn 1.00 .45
Nos. 203-205 (3) 1.70 .90

Intl. Negro Arts Festival, Dakar, Senegal, Apr. 1-24.

Mimosa — A30

Myrina Silenus — A31

Flowers: 15fr, Schouwia purpurea. 20fr, Ipomea asarifolia. 25fr, Grewia bicolor. 30fr, Pancratium trianthum. 60fr, Blepharis linariifolia.

1966, Aug. 8 Photo. *Perf. 13x12½*

Flowers in Natural Colors

206 A30 10fr dl bl & dk bl .40 .25
207 A30 15fr dk brn & buff .60 .35
208 A30 20fr grnsh bl & lt bl .70 .40
209 A30 25fr brn & buff 1.00 .50
210 A30 30fr lil & vio 1.50 .75
211 A30 60fr grn & pale grn 2.00 1.25
Nos. 206-211 (6) 6.20 3.50

1966, Oct. 3 Photo. *Perf. 12x12½*

Various Butterflies

212 A31 5fr buff & multi 1.10 .30
213 A31 30fr bl grn & multi 3.50 .45
214 A31 45fr yel grn & multi 4.75 .65
215 A31 60fr dl bl & multi 6.75 1.10
Nos. 212-215 (4) 16.10 2.50

Hunter, Petroglyph from Adrar A32

Designs: 3fr, Two men fighting, petroglyph from Tenses (Adrar). 30fr, Copper jug, Le Mreyer (Adrar). 50fr, Camel caravan.

1966, Oct. 24 Engr. *Perf. 13*

216 A32 2fr dk brn & brn org .30 .20
217 A32 3fr bl & brn org .80 .20
218 A32 30fr sl grn & dk red 1.40 .30
219 A32 50fr mag, sl grn & brn 2.40 .70
Nos. 216-219 (4) 4.90 1.40

Issued for tourist publicity.

UNESCO, 20th Anniv. A33

1966, Dec. 5 Litho. *Perf. 12½x13*

220 A33 30fr multi 1.00 .40

Plaza of Three Cultures, Mexico City — A34

Olympic Village, Grenoble A35

Designs: 40fr, Olympic torch and skating rink. 100fr, Olympic Stadium, Mexico City.

1967, Mar. 11 Engr. *Perf. 13*

221 A34 20fr dl bl, brn & sl grn .50 .25
222 A35 30fr dl bl, brn & grn .60 .35
223 A34 40fr brt bl, dk brn & sep 1.00 .45
224 A35 100fr brn, emer & blk 1.75 .80
Nos. 221-224 (4) 3.85 1.85

#221, 223 for the 19th Olympic Games, Mexico City; #222, 224 the 10th Winter Olympic Games, Grenoble.

Trees — A36

1967 Jamboree Emblem and Campsite — A37

1967, May 15 Engr. *Perf. 13*

225 A36 10fr Prosopis .45 .20
226 A36 15fr Jujube .60 .20
227 A36 20fr Date palm .70 .25
228 A36 25fr Peltophorum .90 .30
229 A36 30fr Baobob 1.25 .35
Nos. 225-229 (5) 3.90 1.30

1967, June 5

Design: 90fr, 1967 Jamboree emblem and Mauritanian Boy Scouts, horiz.

230 A37 60fr brn, ultra & slate grn .95 .30
231 A37 90fr dl red, bl & slate grn 1.40 .45

12th Boy Scout World Jamboree, Farragut State Park, Idaho, Aug. 1-9.

Weavers A38

10fr, Embroiderer, vert. 20fr, Nurse, mother & infant. 30fr, Laundress, vert. 50fr, Seamstresses.

1967, July 3 Engr. *Perf. 13*

232 A38 5fr plum, blk & cl .25 .20
233 A38 10fr plum, brt grn & blk .25 .20
234 A38 20fr brt bl, plum & blk .50 .25
235 A38 30fr dk bl, brn & blk .60 .30
236 A38 50fr plum, sl & blk 1.00 .30
Nos. 232-236 (5) 2.60 1.25

Progress made by working women.

Cattle and Hypodermic Syringe — A39

1967, Aug. 21 Engr. *Perf. 13*

237 A39 30fr sl grn, brt bl & rose cl .80 .35

Campaign against cattle plague.

Monetary Union Issue

Common Design Type

1967, Nov. 4 Engr. *Perf. 13*

238 CD125 30fr gray & orange .45 .25

Fruit — A40

Human Rights Flame — A41

1967, Dec. 4 Engr. *Perf. 13*

239 A40 1fr Doom palm .35 .20
240 A40 2fr Bito, horiz. .40 .20
241 A40 3fr Baobob .50 .20
242 A40 4fr Jujube, horiz. .60 .20
243 A40 5fr Daye .75 .40
Nos. 239-243 (5) 2.60 1.20

For surcharges see Nos. 323-327.

1968, Jan. 8 Photo. *Perf. 13x12½*

244 A41 30fr brt grn, blk & yel .60 .25
245 A41 50fr brn org, blk & yel .75 .35

International Human Rights Year.

Nouakchott Mosque A42

45fr, Amogjar Pass. 90fr, Cavaliers' Towers.

1968, Apr. 1 Photo. *Perf. 12½x13*

246 A42 30fr multi .35 .20
247 A42 45fr multi .50 .20
248 A42 90fr multi .85 .40
Nos. 246-248 (3) 1.70 .80

For surcharges see Nos. 332-333.

UPU Building, Bern, Globe and Map of Africa A43

1968, June 3 Engr. *Perf. 13*

249 A43 30fr ver, ultra & olive .60 .25

Mauritania's admission to the UPU.

Symbolic Water Cycle A44

1968, June 24

250 A44 90fr car, lake, grn & sl grn .75 .35

Hydrological Decade (UNESCO), 1965-74.

Land Yacht Racing — A45

Donkey and Foal — A46

40fr, Three land yachts racing, horiz. 60fr, Crew changing wheel of land yacht.

1968, Oct. 7 Engr. *Perf. 13*

251 A45 30fr ultra, org & ocher .70 .25
252 A45 40fr ultra, dp org & plum .85 .30
253 A45 60fr brt grn, dp org & ocher 1.40 .55
Nos. 251-253 (3) 2.95 1.10

1968, Dec. 16 Photo. *Perf. 13*

Domestic Animals: 10fr, Ewe and lamb. 15fr, Camel and calf. 30fr, Mare and foal. 50fr, Cow and calf. 90fr, Goat and kid.

254 A46 5fr ocher & multi .30 .20
255 A46 10fr multi .40 .25
256 A46 15fr multi .45 .25
257 A46 30fr multi .85 .30
258 A46 50fr pur & multi 1.25 .40
259 A46 90fr multi 2.40 .60
Nos. 254-259 (6) 5.65 2.00

For surcharge see No. 303.

ILO Emblem and Map — A47

Desert Monitor — A48

1969, Apr. 14 Photo. *Perf. 13x12½*

260 A47 50fr dk & lt bl, pur & org .60 .30

ILO, 50th anniversary.

1969, May 5 Photo. *Perf. 13x12½*

Reptiles: 10fr, Horned viper. 30fr, Common spitting cobra. 60fr, Rock python. 85fr, African crocodile.

261 A48 5fr brn, pink & yel .40 .25
262 A48 10fr brn, lt grn & yel .70 .30
263 A48 30fr dk brn, pink & yel 1.75 .40
264 A48 60fr dk brn, lt bl & yel 3.00 1.10
265 A48 85fr dk brn, yel & red 5.50 1.40
Nos. 261-265 (5) 11.35 3.45

Lady Beetle Eating Noxious Insects A49

1969, May 26 Engr. *Perf. 13*

266 A49 30fr indigo, grn & mar 3.00 .70

Natural protection of date palms.

Development Bank Issue

Common Design Type

1969, Sept. 10 Engr. *Perf. 13*

267 CD130 30fr Prus bl, grn & ocher .60 .25

Pendant — A50

Design: 20fr, Rahla headdress, horiz.

1969, Oct. 13 Engr. *Perf. 13*
268 A50 10fr dk brn, lil & brn .25 .20
269 A50 20fr blk, Prus bl & mag .50 .25

For surcharges see Nos. 309-310.

Desalination Plant A51

Designs: 15fr, Fishing harbor, Nouadhibou. 30fr, Meat refrigeration plant, Kaedi.

1969, Dec. 1 Engr. *Perf. 13*
270 A51 10fr brt rose lil, dk bl & red brn .25 .25
271 A51 15fr dk car, blk & dp bl .25 .25
272 A51 30fr blk, dk bl & rose brn .40 .25
Nos. 270-272 (3) .90 .75

Issued to publicize economic progress.

Lenin (1870-1924) A52

Sternocera Interrupta A53

1970, Feb. 16 Photo. *Perf. 12x12½*
273 A52 30fr car, lt bl & blk 1.75 .50

1970, Mar. 16 Engr. *Perf. 13*

Insects: 10fr, Anoplocnemis curvipes. 20fr, Julodis aequinoctialis. 30fr, Thermophilum sexmaculatum marginatum. 40fr, Plocaederus denticornis.

274 A53 5fr red brn, buff & blk .50 .25
275 A53 10fr red brn, yel & brn .85 .25
276 A53 20fr red brn, lil & dk ol 1.25 .25
277 A53 30fr red brn, grn & vio 2.10 .35
278 A53 40fr red brn, lt bl & brn 3.75 .70
Nos. 274-278 (5) 8.45 1.80

For surcharges see Nos. 311-315.

Soccer Players and Hemispheres — A54

Hemispheres & various views of soccer play.

1970, May 11 Engr. *Perf. 13*
279 A54 25fr bl, vio bl & dk brn .45 .20
280 A54 30fr vio bl, brn & ol brn .45 .20
281 A54 70fr brt pink, mar & dk brn .90 .40
282 A54 150fr brn red, grn & dk brn 2.10 .65
Nos. 279-282 (4) 3.90 1.45

9th World Soccer Championships for the Jules Rimet Cup, Mexico City, 5/29-6/21.

UPU Headquarters Issue
Common Design Type

1970, May 20 Engr. *Perf. 13*
283 CD133 30fr grn, dk brn & red brn .50 .25

Woman Wearing "Boubou" — A55

Various Traditional Costumes: 30fr, 70fr, Men. 40fr, 50fr, Women.

1970, Sept. 21 Engr. *Perf. 12½x13*
284 A55 10fr red brn & org .35 .25
285 A55 30fr ol, red brn & ind .55 .25
286 A55 40fr red brn, plum & dk brn .75 .30
287 A55 50fr dk brn & brt bl 1.00 .35
288 A55 70fr bl, brn & dk brn 1.25 .50
Nos. 284-288 (5) 3.90 1.65

People of Various Races — A55a

Design: 40fr, Outstretched hands, vert.

1971, Mar. 22 Engr. *Perf. 13*
288A A55a 30fr brn vio, ol & brt bl .60 .20
288B A55a 40fr brn red, bl & blk .80 .25

Intl. year against racial discrimination.

Gen. Charles de Gaulle (1890-1970), President of France — A56

Design: 100fr, De Gaulle as President.

1971, June 18 Photo. *Perf. 13*
289 A56 40fr gold, blk & grnsh bl 2.00 .65
290 A56 100fr lt bl, gold & blk 4.50 1.25
a. Souvenir sheet of 2, #289-290 6.50 6.50

Iron Ore Freight Train of Miferma Mines — A57

1971, Nov. 8 Photo. *Perf. 12½x12*
291 35fr ore cars 2.00 .65
292 100fr engines 4.50 1.60
a. A57 Pair, #291-292 8.75 8.75

UNICEF Emblem and Child A59

1971, Dec. 11 Litho. *Perf. 13½*
293 A59 35fr lt ultra, blk & brn .60 .25

UNICEF, 25th anniv.

Samuel F. B. Morse and Telegraph — A60

Designs: 40fr, Relay satellite over globes. 75fr, Alexander Graham Bell.

1972, May 17 Engr. *Perf. 13*
294 A60 35fr lilac, indigo & vio .60 .25
295 A60 40fr bl, ocher & choc .65 .25
296 A60 75fr grn, ol grn & Prus bl 1.00 .45
Nos. 294-296 (3) 2.25 .95

4th World Telecommunications Day.
For surcharge see No. 343.

Fossil Spirifer Shell — A61

1972, July 31 Litho. *Perf. 12½*
297 A61 25fr shown 2.50 .70
298 A61 75fr Phacops rana 4.50 1.25

Fossil shells.
For surcharges see Nos. 306, 308.

West African Monetary Union Issue
Common Design Type

1972, Nov. 2 Engr. *Perf. 13*
299 CD136 35fr brn, yel grn & gray .85 .25

Mediterranean Monk Seal and Pup — A63

1973, Feb. 28 Litho. *Perf. 13*
300 A63 40fr multi 2.75 .70

See #C130. For surcharges see #307, C145.

Food Program Symbols and Emblem A64

1973, Apr. 30 Photo. *Perf. 12x12½*
301 A64 35fr gray bl & multi .45 .25

World Food Program, 10th anniversary.

UPU Monument and Globe A65

1973, May 28 Engr. *Perf. 13*
302 A65 100fr grn, ocher & bl 1.60 .65

Universal Postal Union Day.

Currency Change to Ouguiya ("um")
No. 258 Surcharged with New Value, 2 Bars, and Overprinted: "SECHERESSE / SOLIDARITE / AFRICAINE"

1973, Aug. 16 Photo. *Perf. 13*
303 A46 20um on 50fr multi .90 .40

African solidarity in drought emergency.

African Postal Union Issue
Common Design Type

1973, Sept. 12 Engr. *Perf. 13*
304 CD137 20um org, brn & ocher 1.10 .40

INTERPOL Emblem, Detective, Criminal, Fingerprint A66

1973, Sept. 24
305 A66 15um brn, ver & vio 1.00 .40

50th anniv. of Intl. Criminal Police Org.

Nos. 297-298, 300 and 268-269 Surcharged with New Value and Two Bars in Ultramarine, Red or Black

1973-74 Litho. *Perf. 12½*
306 A61 5um on 25fr (U) ('74) 2.00 .80
307 A63 8um on 40fr (R) .95 .40
308 A61 15um on 75fr (U) ('74) 5.25 1.50

Engr.
Perf. 13
309 A50 27um on 10fr (B) ('74) 2.25 .65
310 A50 28um on 20fr (R) ('74) 1.75 .80
Nos. 306-310 (5) 12.20 4.15

Nos. 274-278 Surcharged with New Value and Two bars in Violet Blue or Red

1974, July 29 Engr. *Perf. 13*
311 A53 5um on 5fr 1.25 .45
312 A53 7um on 10fr 1.10 .30
313 A53 8um on 20fr 1.25 .35
314 A53 10um on 30fr (R) 1.75 .40
315 A53 20um on 40fr 3.50 1.00
Nos. 311-315 (5) 8.85 2.50

UPU Emblem and Globes — A67

1974, Aug. 5 Photo. *Perf. 13*
316 A67 30um multi 1.90 .80
317 A67 50um multi 3.25 1.25

Centenary of Universal Postal Union.
For overprints see Nos. 321-322.

5-Ouguiya Coin and Bank Note — A68

Designs: 8um, 10-ouguiya coin. 20um, 20-ouguiya coin. Each design includes picture of different bank note.

1974, Aug. 12 Engr.
318 A68 7um blk, ultra & grn .60 .20
319 A68 8um blk, sl grn & mag .70 .20
320 A68 20um blk, red & bl 1.40 .45
Nos. 318-320 (3) 2.70 .85

First anniversary of currency reform.

Nos. 316-317 Overprinted in Red: "9 OCTOBRE / 100 ANS D'UNION POSTALE / INTERNATIONALE"

1974, Oct. 9 Photo. *Perf. 13*

321 A67 30um multi 2.25 1.00
322 A67 50um multi 4.00 1.40

Centenary of Universal Postal Union.

Nos. 239-243 Surcharged with New Value and Two Bars in Black or Violet Blue

1975, Feb. 14 Engr. *Perf. 13*

323 A40 1um on 5fr multi (B) .30 .20
324 A40 2um on 4fr multi (VB) .30 .20
325 A40 3um on 2fr multi (B) .35 .20
326 A40 10um on 1fr multi (B) .95 .25
327 A40 12um on 3fr multi (VB) 1.10 .30
Nos. 323-327 (5) 3.00 1.15

Hunters, Rock Carvings — A69

White and Black Men, Map of Europe and Africa — A70

Rock Carvings from Zemmour Cave: 5um, Ostrich. 10um, Elephant, horiz.

1975, May 26 Engr. *Perf. 13*

328 A69 4um lt brn & car 1.00 .20
329 A69 5um red lil 1.25 .30
330 A69 10um blue 1.90 .45
Nos. 328-330 (3) 4.15 .95

Europafrica Issue

1975, July 7 Engr. *Perf. 13*

331 A70 40um dk brn & red 2.10 .80

Nos. 247-248 Surcharged in Red or Black

1975, Aug. 25 Photo. *Perf. 12½x13*

332 A42 15um on 45fr (R) 1.25 .50
333 A42 25um on 90fr 2.00 .80

African solidarity in drought emergency.

Map of Africa with Mauritania, Akjoujt Blast Furnace, Camel — A71

Fair Emblem — A72

Design: 12um, Snim emblem, furnace, dump truck, excavator.

1975, Sept. 22 Engr. *Perf. 13*

334 A71 10um brt bl, choc & org .90 .30
335 A71 12um brt bl & multi 1.00 .40

Mining and industry: Somima (Société Minière de Mauritanie) and Snim (Société Nationale Industrielle et Minière).

1975, Oct. 5 Litho. *Perf. 12*

336 A72 10um multi .60 .30

National Nouakchott Fair, Nov. 28-Dec. 7.

Commemorative Medal — A73

Design: 12um, Map of Mauritania, vert.

1975, Nov. 28 Litho. *Perf. 12*

337 A73 10um sil & multi 1.50 .35
338 A73 12um grn, yel & grn 1.50 .35

15th anniversary of independence.

Docked Space Ships and Astronauts — A74

Docked Space Ships and: 10um, Soyuz rocket launch.

1975, Dec. 29 Litho. *Perf. 14*

339 A74 8um multi .70 .25
340 A74 10um multi .85 .25
Nos. 339-340,C156-C158 (5) 7.55 2.65

Apollo Soyuz space test project, Russo-American cooperation, launched July 15, link-up July 17, 1975.

French Legion Infantryman A75

Uniform: 10um, Green Mountain Boy.

1976, Jan. 26 *Perf. 13½x14*

341 A75 8um multi .80 .25
342 A75 10um multi 1.00 .25
Nos. 341-342,C160-C162 (5) 7.30 2.25

American Bicentennial.

No. 296 Surcharged

1976, Mar. 1 Engr. *Perf. 13*

343 A60 12um on 75fr multi .90 .30

Arab Labor Charter, 10th anniversary.

Map of Mauritania with Spanish Sahara Incorporated — A76

1976, Mar. 15 Litho. *Perf. 13x12½*

344 A76 10um grn & multi .80 .30

Reunified Mauritania, Feb. 29, 1976.

LZ-4 over Hangar — A77

75th anniv. of the Zeppelin: 10um, Dr. Hugo Eckener and "Schwaben" (LZ-10). 12um, "Hansa" (LZ-13) over Heligoland. 20um, "Bodensee" (LZ-120) and Dr. Ludwig Dürr.

1976, June 28 Litho. *Perf. 11*

345 A77 5um multi .25 .20
346 A77 10um multi .60 .25
347 A77 12um multi .75 .30
348 A77 20um multi 1.25 .40
Nos. 345-348,C167-C168 (6) 10.10 3.15

Mohenjo-Daro — A78

1976, Sept. 6 Litho. *Perf. 12*

349 A78 15um multi 1.10 .40

UNESCO campaign to save Mohenjo-Daro excavations, Pakistan.

A. G. Bell, Telephone and Satellite — A79

1976, Oct. 11 Engr. *Perf. 13*

350 A79 10um bl, car & red .80 .20

Centenary of first telephone call by Alexander Graham Bell, Mar. 10, 1876.

Mohammed Ali Jinnah (1876-1948), Governor General of Pakistan — A80

1976, Dec. 25 Litho. *Perf. 13*

351 A80 10um multi .60 .30

NASA Control Room, Houston — A81

Design: 12um, Viking components, vert.

1977, Feb. 28 *Perf. 14*

352 A81 10um multi .60 .20
353 A81 12um multi .75 .20
Nos. 352-353,C173-C175 (5) 7.85 1.80

Viking Mars project.

For surcharge and overprints see Nos. 425-426, C192-C195.

Jackals A82

Designs: 5um, Wild rabbits. 12um, Wart-hogs. 14um, Lions. 15um, Elephants.

1977, Mar. 14 Litho. *Perf. 12½*

354 A82 5um multi .40 .20
355 A82 10um multi 1.00 .35
356 A82 12um multi 1.40 .40
357 A82 14um multi 1.50 .50
358 A82 15um multi 3.00 .75
Nos. 354-358 (5) 7.30 2.20

For surcharge see No. 577.

Irene and Frederic Joliot-Curie, Chemistry — A83

Nobel prize winners: 15um, Emil A. von Bering, medicine.

1977, Apr. 29 Litho. *Perf. 14*

359 A83 12um multi 1.10 .20
360 A83 15um multi .90 .20
Nos. 359-360,C177-C179 (5) 10.50 1.80

APU Emblem, Member's Flags — A84

1977, May 30 Photo. *Perf. 13*

361 A84 12um multi .75 .30

Arab Postal Union, 25th anniversary.

Oil Lamp A85

Tegdaoust Pottery: 2um, 4-handled pot. 5um, Large jar. 12um, Jug with filter.

1977, June 13 Engr. *Perf. 13*

362 A85 1um multi .20 .20
363 A85 2um multi .20 .20
364 A85 5um multi .30 .20
365 A85 12um multi .80 .30
Nos. 362-365 (4) 1.50 .90

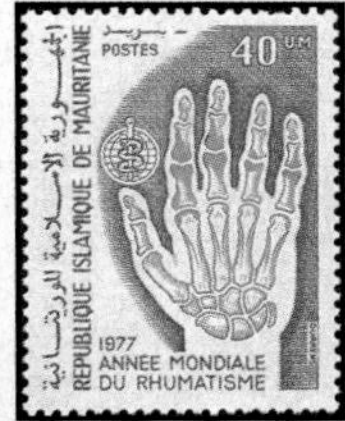

X-ray of Hand — A86

1977, June 27 Engr. *Perf. 12½x13*

366 A86 40um multi 3.00 1.25

World Rheumatism Year.

Charles Lindbergh and "Spirit of St. Louis" — A87

History of aviation: 14um, Clement Ader and "Eole!" 15um, Louis Bleriot over channel. 55um, Italo Balbo and seaplanes. 60um, Concorde. 100um, Charles Lindbergh and "Spirit of St. Louis."

1977, Sept. 19

367 A87 12um multi .65 .20
368 A87 14um multi .70 .20
369 A87 15um multi .85 .30
370 A87 55um multi 3.00 .70
371 A87 60um multi 3.50 .75
Nos. 367-371 (5) 8.70 2.15

Souvenir Sheet

372 A87 100um multi 6.00 1.50

Dome of the Rock, Jerusalem — A88

1977, Oct. 31 Litho. *Perf. 12½*

373 A88 12um multi .60 .25
374 A88 14um multi .75 .40

Palestinian fighters and their families.

Soccer and Emblems — A89

Emblems and: 14um, Alf Ramsey and stadium. 15um, Players and goalkeeper.

1977, Dec. 19 Litho. *Perf. 13½*

375 A89 12um multi .55 .20
376 A89 14um multi .65 .20
377 A89 15um multi .80 .20
Nos. 375-377,C182-C183 (5) 7.50 1.75

Elimination Games for World Cup Soccer Championship, Argentina, 1978.

For overprints see Nos. 399-401, C187-C189.

Helen Fourment and her Children, by Rubens A90

Paintings by Peter Paul Rubens (1577-1640): 14um, Knight in armor. 67um, Three Burghers. 69um, Landscape, horiz. 100um, Rubens with wife and son.

1977, Dec. 26

378 A90 12um multi .75 .20
379 A90 14um multi .90 .35
380 A90 67um multi 4.00 .70
381 A90 69um multi 4.50 .85
Nos. 378-381 (4) 10.15 2.10

Souvenir Sheet

382 A90 100um gold & multi 6.00 1.50

Sable Antelope and Wildlife Fund Emblem — A91

Endangered Animals: 12um, Gazelles, vert. 14um, Manatee. 55um, Aoudad, vert. 60um, Elephant. 100um, Ostrich, vert.

1978, Feb. 28 Litho. *Perf. 13½x14*

383 A91 5um multi *1.10* *.30*
384 A91 12um multi *2.25* *.40*
385 A91 14um multi *2.50* *.70*
386 A91 55um multi *8.50* *.70*
387 A91 60um multi *10.00* *1.25*
388 A91 100um multi *13.00* *2.25*
Nos. 383-388 (6) *37.35* *5.60*

Nouakchott-Nema Road — A91a

1978, June 19 Litho. *Perf. 13*

388A A91a 12um multicolored *12.00* 8.50
388B A91a 14um multicolored *13.50* 9.00

Soccer and Games' Emblem — A92

14um, Rimet Cup. 20um, Soccer ball & F.I.F.A. flag. 50um, Soccer ball & Rimet Cup, horiz.

1978, June 26 Photo. *Perf. 13*

389 A92 12um multi .60 .20
390 A92 14um multi .70 .30
391 A92 20um multi 1.10 .30
Nos. 389-391 (3) 2.40 .80

Souvenir Sheet

392 A92 50um multi 2.50 1.00

11th World Cup Soccer Championship, Argentina, June 1-25.

Raoul Follereau and St. George Slaying Dragon — A93

1978, Sept. 4 Engr. *Perf. 13*

393 A93 12um brn & dp grn 1.50 .60

25th anniversary of the Raoul Follereau Anti-Leprosy Foundation.

Anti-Apartheid Emblem, Fenced-in People — A94

Design: 30um, Anti-Apartheid emblem and free people, vert.

1978, Oct. 9

394 A94 25um bl, red & brn 1.25 .55
395 A94 30um grn, bl & brn 1.75 .75

Anti-Apartheid Year.

Charles de Gaulle A95

14um, King Baudouin. 55um, Queen Elizabeth II.

1978, Oct. 16 Litho. *Perf. 12½x12*

396 A95 12um multi 1.10 .35
397 A95 14um multi 1.10 .35
398 A95 55um multi 2.50 .90
Nos. 396-398 (3) 4.70 1.60

Rulers who helped in de-colonization. No. 398 also commemorates 25th anniversary of coronation of Queen Elizabeth II.

Nos. 375-377 Overprinted in Arabic and French in Silver: "ARGENTINE- / PAYS BAS 3-1"

1978, Dec. 11 Litho. *Perf. 13½*

399 A89 12um multi .70 .20
400 A89 14um multi .75 .30
401 A89 15um multi 1.00 .50
Nos. 399-401,C187-C188 (5) 7.70 3.50

Argentina's victory in World Cup Soccer Championship 1978.

View of Nouakchott — A96

1978, Dec. 18 Litho. *Perf. 12*

402 A96 12um multi .65 .30

20th anniversary of Nouakchott.

Flame Emblem — A97

Leather Key Holder — A98

1978, Dec. 26 *Perf. 12½*

403 A97 55um ultra & red 2.50 1.10

Universal Declaration of Human Rights, 30th anniv.

1979, Feb. 5 Litho. *Perf. 13½x14*

Leather Craft: 7um, Toothbrush case. 10um, Knife holder.

404 A98 5um multi .30 .20
405 A98 7um multi .40 .20
406 A98 10um multi .55 .30
Nos. 404-406 (3) 1.25 .70

Farmers at Market, by Dürer — A99

Engravings by Albrecht Durer (1471-1528): 14um, Young Peasant and Wife. 55um, Mercenary with flag. 60um, St. George Slaying Dragon. 100um, Mercenaries, horiz.

Litho.; Red Foil Embossed

1979, May 3 *Perf. 13½x14*

407 A99 12um blk, *buff* .60 .20
408 A99 14um blk, *buff* 1.00 .20
409 A99 55um blk, *buff* 2.40 .80
410 A99 60um blk, *buff* 3.00 .95
Nos. 407-410 (4) 7.00 2.15

Souvenir Sheet

Perf. 14x13½

411 A99 100um blk, *buff* 5.00 2.00

Buddha, Borobudur Temple and UNESCO Emblem — A100

UNESCO Emblem and: 14um, Hunter on horseback, Carthage. 55um, Caryatid, Acropolis.

1979, May 14 **Photo.** *Perf. 12½*

412 A100 12um multi .70 .30
413 A100 14um multi .90 .35
414 A100 55um multi 2.75 1.10
Nos. 412-414 (3) 4.35 1.75

Preservation of art treasures with help from UNESCO.

Paddle Steamer Sirius, Rowland Hill — A101

Sir Rowland Hill (1795-1879), originator of penny postage, and: 14um, Paddle steamer Great Republic. 55um, S.S. Mauritania. 60um, M.S. Stirling Castle. 100um, Mauritania No. 8.

1979, June 4 **Litho.** *Perf. 13½x14*

415 A101 12um multi .55 .20
416 A101 14um multi .70 .20
417 A101 55um multi 2.40 .55
418 A101 60um multi 2.90 .70
Nos. 415-418 (4) 6.55 1.65

Souvenir Sheet

419 A101 100um multi 5.00 1.25

Embossed Leather Cushion — A102

30um, Satellite, jet, ship, globe & UPU emblem.

1979, June 8 **Litho.** *Perf. 12½*

420 A102 12um multi 1.10 .50

Engr.

Perf. 13

421 A102 30um multi, vert. 3.00 1.40

Philexafrique II, Libreville, Gabon, June 8-17. Nos. 420, 421 each printed in sheets of 10 and 5 labels showing exhibition emblem.

Mother and Children, IYC Emblem — A103

1979, Oct. 2 **Litho.** *Perf. 12½*

422 A103 12um multi .55 .20
423 A103 14um multi .70 .35
424 A103 40um multi 2.00 .90
Nos. 422-424 (3) 3.25 1.45

International Year of the Child

Nos. 352-353 Overprinted in Silver: "ALUNISSAGE / APOLLO XI / JUILLET 1969" and Emblem

1979, Oct. 24 **Litho.** *Perf. 14*

425 A81 10um multi .60 .30
426 A81 12um multi .60 .30
Nos. 425-426,C192-C194 (5) 7.20 3.05

Apollo 11 moon landing, 10th anniversary.

Runner, Moscow '80 Emblem A104

Moscow '80 Emblem and: 14um, 55um, 100um, Running, diff. 60um, Hurdles.

1979, Oct. 26 **Litho.** *Perf. 13½*

427 A104 12um multi .55 .20
428 A104 14um multi .75 .20
429 A104 55um multi 2.10 .50
430 A104 60um multi 2.50 .60
Nos. 427-430 (4) 5.90 1.50

Souvenir Sheet

431 A104 100um multi 4.75 1.25

Pre-Olympic Year.

Scomberesox Saurus Walbaum — A104a

1979, Nov. 12 **Photo.** *Perf. 14*

431A A104a 1um shown .75 .30
431B A104a 5um Trigla lucerna .75 .30

A 20m denomination (Xiphias gladius) also exists. Value $250.

Ice Hockey, Lake Placid '80 Emblem — A105

Various ice hockey plays.

1979, Dec. 6 **Litho.** *Perf. 14½*

432 A105 10um multi .50 .20
433 A105 12um multi .65 .20
434 A105 14um multi .65 .25
435 A105 55um multi 2.40 .50
436 A105 60um multi 2.50 .60
437 A105 100um multi 4.25 1.00
Nos. 432-437 (6) 10.95 2.75

13th Winter Olympic Games. Lake Placid, NY, Feb. 12-24, 1980.

For overprints see Nos. 440-445.

Arab Achievements — A106

1980, Mar. 22 **Litho.** *Perf. 13*

438 A106 12um multi .70 .35
439 A106 15um multi .80 .35

Nos. 432-437 Overprinted:

a. Médaille / de bronze / SUÈDE
b. MÉDAILLE / DE BRONZE / SUÈDE
c. Médaille / d'argent / U.R.S.S.
d. MÉDAILLE / D'ARGENT/ U.R.S.S.
e. MÉDAILLE / D'OR / ÉTATS-UNIS
f. Médaille / d'or / ÉTATS-UNIS

1980, June 14 **Litho.** *Perf. 14½*

440 A105(a) 10um multi .55 .20
441 A105(b) 12um multi .60 .20
442 A105(c) 14um multi .60 .30
443 A105(d) 55um multi 2.10 .75
444 A105(e) 60um multi 3.00 .85
445 A105(f) 100um multi 4.50 1.40
Nos. 440-445 (6) 11.35 3.70

Equestrian, Olympic Rings — A107

Designs: Equestrian scenes. 10um, 20um, 70um, 100um, vert.

1980, June **Litho.** *Perf. 14*

446 A107 10um multi .45 .20
447 A107 20um multi .85 .25
448 A107 50um multi 2.40 .50
449 A107 70um multi 3.25 .70
Nos. 446-449 (4) 6.95 1.65

Souvenir Sheet

450 A107 100um multi 5.50 1.75

22nd Summer Olympic Games, Moscow, July 19-Aug. 3.

For overprints see Nos. 464-468.

Armed Forces Day — A108

1980, July 9 *Perf. 13x12½*

451 A108 12um multi .60 .20
452 A108 14um multi .65 .30

World Red Cross Day — A109

1980, June 14 *Perf. 13*

453 A109 20um multi *12.00* 1.25

Pilgrimage to Mecca — A110

Design: 50um, Mosque, outside view.

1980

454 A110 10um multi 1.00 .35
455 A110 50um multi 3.00 1.25

Man with Turban, by Rembrandt A111

Rembrandt Paintings: 10um, Self-portrait. 20um, His mother. 70um, His son Titus reading. 100um, Polish knight, horiz.

1980, July **Litho.** *Perf. 12½*

456 A111 10um multi .60 .25
457 A111 20um multi 1.00 .30
458 A111 50um multi 2.60 .50
459 A111 70um multi 3.00 .80
Nos. 456-459 (4) 7.20 1.85

Souvenir Sheet

460 A111 100um multi 5.50 1.50

Tea Time A112

1980, Mar. 11 **Litho.** *Perf. 12½*

460A A112 1um multi .40 .20
461 A112 5um multi .60 .20
462 A112 12um multi 1.00 .30
Nos. 460A-462 (3) 2.00 .70

Arbor Day — A113

1980, Aug. 29

463 A113 12um multi 1.10 .40

Nos. 446-450 Overprinted with Winner and Country

1980, Oct. **Litho.** *Perf. 14*

464 A107 10um multi .45 .25
465 A107 20um multi .85 .30
466 A107 50um multi 2.40 .60
467 A107 70um multi 3.00 .80
Nos. 464-467 (4) 6.70 1.95

Souvenir Sheet

468 A107 100um multi 4.50 1.75

Mastodont Locomotive, 1850 — A114

Designs: Various locomotives.

1980, Nov. *Perf. 12½*
469 A114 10um shown .70 .20
470 A114 12um Iron ore train .85 .30
471 A114 14um Chicago-Milwaukee line, 1900 1.10 .40
472 A114 20um Bury, 1837 1.50 .50
473 A114 67um Reseau North line, 1870 5.00 .70
474 A114 100um Potsdam, 1840 7.50 1.10
Nos. 469-474 (6) 16.65 3.20

20th Anniversary of Independence — A115

1980, Nov. 27 *Perf. 13*
475 A115 12um multi .55 .20
476 A115 15um multi .60 .30

El Haram Mosque — A116

1981, Apr. 13 **Litho.** *Perf. 12½*
477 A116 2um shown .20 .20
478 A116 12um Medina Mosque .60 .30
479 A116 14um Chinguetti Mosque .80 .30
Nos. 477-479 (3) 1.60 .80

Hegira, 1500th anniversary.

Prince Charles and Lady Diana, Coach — A117

Designs: Coaches.

1981, July 8 **Litho.** *Perf. 14½*
480 A117 14um multi .60 .20
481 A117 18um multi .75 .20
482 A117 77um multi 2.75 .90
Nos. 480-482 (3) 4.10 1.30

Souvenir Sheet

483 A117 100um multi 4.50 1.10

Royal wedding.
For overprints see Nos. 518-521.

Intl. Year of the Disabled A119

1981, June 29 **Litho.** *Perf. 13x13½*
486 A119 12um multi .80 .40

Battle of Yorktown Bicentenary (American Revolution) — A120

1981, Oct. 5 *Perf. 12½*
487 A120 14um George Washington, vert. .60 .25
488 A120 18um Admiral de Grasse, vert. 1.00 .30
489 A120 63um Surrender of Cornwallis 3.00 1.00
490 A120 81um Battle of Chesapeake Bay 4.00 1.50
Nos. 487-490 (4) 8.60 3.05

475th Death Anniv. of Christopher Columbus (1451-1506) — A121

1981, Oct. 5
491 A121 19um Pinta 1.50 .40
492 A121 55um Santa Maria 4.25 1.10

World Food Day — A122

Kemal Ataturk Birth Cent. — A123

1981, Oct. 16 *Perf. 13*
493 A122 19um multi 1.00 .40

1981, Oct. 29 *Perf. 12½*
494 A123 63um multi 3.00 1.25

Scouting Year — A124

Designs: Boating scenes. 92um vert.

1982, Jan. 20 **Litho.** *Perf. 12½*
495 A124 14um multi .70 .20
496 A124 19um multi 1.00 .20
497 A124 22um multi 1.10 .25
498 A124 92um multi 4.25 .85
Nos. 495-498 (4) 7.05 1.50

Souvenir Sheet
Perf. 13

499 A124 100um Baden-Powell, scout 5.50 1.25

75th Anniv. of Grand Prix — A125

Designs: Winners and their Cars.

1982, Jan. 23 *Perf. 13½*
500 A125 7um Deusenberg, 1921 .60 .20
501 A125 12um Alfa Romeo, 1932 .85 .20
502 A125 14um Juan Fangio, 1949 .95 .20
503 A125 18um Renault, 1979 1.10 .25
504 A125 19um Niki Lauda, 1974 1.25 .30
Nos. 500-504 (5) 4.75 1.15

Souvenir Sheet

505 A125 100um Race 6.00 1.75

Birds of the Arguin Bank A126

1981, Dec. 17 **Photo.** *Perf. 13*
506 A126 2um White pelicans 1.00 .20
507 A126 18um Pink flamingoes 3.75 .75

Battle of Karameh A127

1982, Dec. 19 **Litho.**
508 A127 14um Hand holding tattered flag .80 .35

Deluth Turtle — A128

APU, 30th Anniv. — A129

Designs: Sea turtles.

1981, Dec. 21 **Photo.** *Perf. 14x13½*
509 A128 1um shown 1.50 .25
510 A128 3um Green turtle 2.00 .25
511 A128 4um Shell turtle 2.50 .35
Nos. 509-511 (3) 6.00 .85

1982, May 14 **Litho.** *Perf. 13*
512 A129 14um org & brn .65 .30

A130

A131

1982, May 17 **Photo.** *Perf. 13½x13*
513 A130 21um multi .85 .40

14th World Telecommunications Day.

1982, June 7 **Litho.** *Perf. 12½*
514 A131 14um grnsh bl .65 .30

UN Conf. on Human Environment, 10th anniv.

21st Birthday of Princess Diana of Wales — A132

Portraits.

1982, July *Perf. 14x13½*
515 A132 21um multi .75 .40
516 A132 77um multi 2.50 .85

Souvenir Sheet

517 A132 100um multi 3.75 1.50

Nos. 480-483 Overprinted in Blue: "NAISSANCE ROYALE 1982"

1982, Aug. 2 *Perf. 14½*
518 A117 14um multi .50 .30
519 A117 18um multi .70 .35
520 A117 77um multi 2.50 1.25
Nos. 518-520 (3) 3.70 1.90

Souvenir Sheet

521 A117 100um multi 3.75 1.50

Birth of Prince William of Wales, June 21.

Manned Flight Bicentenary A133

1982, Dec. 29 **Litho.** *Perf. 14*
522 A133 14um Montgolfiere balloon, 1783, vert. .95 .25
523 A133 18um Hydrogen balloon, 1783 .95 .25

524 A133 19um Zeppelin, vert. .95 .35
525 A133 55um Nieuport plane 2.50 .50
526 A133 63um Concorde 2.75 .60
527 A133 77um Apollo II, vert. 3.00 .70
Nos. 522-527 (6) 11.10 2.65

Preservation of Ancient Cities — A134

1983, Feb. 16 Litho. *Perf. 14x14½*
528 A134 14um City Wall, Ouadane .75 .25
529 A134 18um Chinguetti .85 .30
530 A134 24um Staircase, panels, Qualata 1.10 .40
531 A134 30um Ruins, Tichitt 1.75 .60
Nos. 528-531 (4) 4.45 1.55

World Communications Year — A135

1983, June 21 Litho. *Perf. 13*
532 A135 14um multi .70 .30

30th Anniv. of Customs Cooperation Council — A136

1983, June 25
533 A136 14um multi .70 .30

Traditional Houses A137

Ancient Manuscript Page — A138

1983, June 14 Photo. *Perf. 13½*
534 A137 14um Peule *2.50* .30
535 A137 18um Toucouleur *3.25* .45
536 A137 19um Tent *3.50* .50
Nos. 534-536 (3) 9.25 1.25

1983, June 15 Photo. *Perf. 12½x13*
537 A138 2um shown .40 .20
538 A138 5um Ornamental scroll-work .60 .20
539 A138 7um Sheath .75 .20
Nos. 537-539 (3) 1.75 .60

Manned Flight Bicentenary — A139

Early Fliers and their Balloons or Dirigibles. 10um, 14um vert.

1983, Oct. 17 Litho. *Perf. 13½*
540 A139 10um F. Pilatre de Rozier .75 .20
541 A139 14um John Wise .95 .20
542 A139 25um Charles Renard 1.90 .30
543 A139 100um Henri Julliot 5.75 1.10
Nos. 540-543 (4) 9.35 1.80

Souvenir Sheet

544 A139 100um Joseph Montgolfier 6.50 1.25

No. 544 contains one stamp 47x37mm. Nos. 543-544 airmail.

Mortar — A140

Various prehistoric grinding implements.

1983, Dec. 28 Litho. *Perf. 13*
545 A140 10um multi .85 .35
546 A140 14um multi 1.25 .45
547 A140 18um multi 1.75 .75
Nos. 545-547 (3) 3.85 1.55

Pre-Olympics — A141

1983, Dec. 31 Litho. *Perf. 13½*
548 A141 1um Basketball .20 .20
549 A141 20um Wrestling .85 .40
550 A141 50um Equestrian 2.00 .70
551 A141 77um Running 3.50 .95
Nos. 548-551 (4) 6.55 2.25

Souvenir Sheet

552 A141 100um Soccer 4.75 1.25

No. 552 contains one stamp 41x36mm. Nos. 551-552 airmail.

Scouting Year — A142

Artemis, by Rembrandt — A142a

Events & Annivs.: 14um, Johann Wolfgang von Goethe. 25um, Virgin and Child, by Peter Paul Rubens.
No. 553C illustration reduced.

1984, Jan. 24
553 A142 5um Flag, Baden-Powell 1.00 .50
553A A142 14um multicolored 1.00 .50
553B A142 25um multicolored 1.50 .50
Nos. 553-553B (3) 3.50 1.50

Souvenir Sheet

553C A142a 100um multicolored 4.25 1.50

No. 553C is airmail and contains one 42x51mm stamp.

Sand Rose A143

1984, Mar. Litho. *Perf. 14*
554 A143 21um multi *10.00* 1.50

Inscribed 1982.

Anniversaries and Events — A145

1984, Apr. 26
555 A145 10um Albrecht Durer (1471-1528) .80 .20
556 A145 12um Apollo XI, 15th anniv. .95 .25
557 A145 50um Chess 3.00 1.00
Nos. 555-557 (3) 4.75 1.45

1984, Apr. 16 Litho. *Perf. 13½*

Designs: 77um, Prince Charles, Princess Diana. 100um, Prince Charles, Princess Diana, vert.

557A A145 77um multi 3.75 1.60

Miniature Sheet

557B A145 100um multi 5.50 3.00

Nos. 557A-557B airmail.

Fishing Industry A146

1984
558 A146 1um Tuna .40 .20
559 A146 2um Mackerel .40 .20
560 A146 5um Haddock .55 .25
561 A146 14um Black chinchard 1.40 .50
562 A146 18um Boat building 1.75 .60
Nos. 558-562 (5) 4.50 1.75

Nouakchott Olympic Complex A148

1984, Sept. 26 Litho. *Perf. 13½*
569 A148 14um multi 1.00 .40

Infant Survival Campaign A149

1984, Sept. 26 Litho. *Perf. 12½*
570 A149 1um Feeding by glass .40 .20
571 A149 4um Breastfeeding .40 .20
572 A149 10um Vaccinating 1.00 .20
573 A149 14um Weighing 1.25 .30
Nos. 570-573 (4) 3.05 .90

Pilgrimage to Mecca — A150

1984, Oct. 3 Litho. *Perf. 13*
574 A150 14um Tents, mosque .80 .40
575 A150 18um Tents, courtyard 1.25 .60

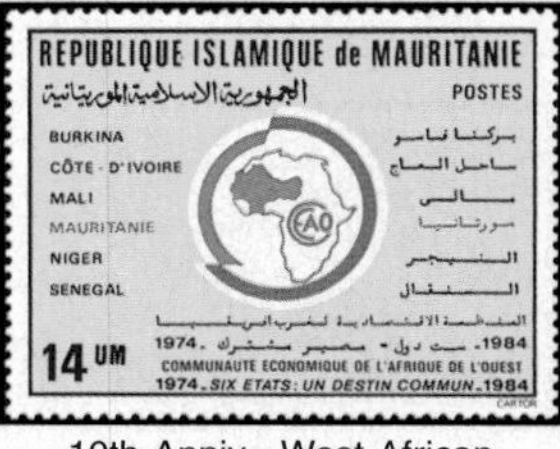

10th Anniv., West African Union — A151

1984, Nov. Litho. *Perf. 13*
576 A151 14um Map of member nations .85 .40

No. 355 Overprinted "Aide au Sahel 84" and Surcharged

1984 Litho. *Perf. 12½*
577 A82 18um on 10um 1.25 .50

Issued to publicize drought relief efforts.

Technical & Cultural Cooperation Agency, 15th Anniv. — A152

1985, Mar. 20 Litho. *Perf. 12½*
578 A152 18um Profiles, emblem 1.00 .45

League of Arab States, 40th Anniv. — A153

1985, May 7 *Perf. 13*
579 A153 14um brt yel grn & blk .75 .40

German Railways 150th Anniv. — A154

Anniversaries and events: 12um, Adler, 1st German locomotive, 1835. 18um, Series 10, 1956, last Fed. German Railways locomotive. 44um, European Music Year, Johann Sebastian Bach, composer, and Angels Making Music, unattributed painting. 77um, George Frideric Handel. 90um, Statue of Liberty, cent., vert. 100um, Queen Mother, 85th birthday, vert.

1985, Sept.

580	A154	12um multi	.65	.25
581	A154	18um multi	1.00	.40
582	A154	44um multi	2.00	1.00
583	A154	77um multi	3.50	1.75
584	A154	90um multi	4.00	2.00
		Nos. 580-584 (5)	11.15	5.40

Souvenir Sheet

585	A154	100um multi	4.75	2.25

World Food Day — A155

1985, Oct. 16 *Perf. 13x12½*

586	A155	18um multi	.70	.40

UN Food and Agriculture Org., 40th anniv.

Fight Against Drought A156

1985 **Litho.** *Perf. 13*

587	A156	14um Antelope	1.00	.30
588	A156	18um Oasis	1.25	.40

Fight Against Desert Encroachment — A157

1985

589	A157	10um Grain harvest, vert.	.55	.30
590	A157	14um Brush fire	2.50	.75
591	A157	18um Planting brush	2.50	.75
		Nos. 589-591 (3)	5.55	1.80

Natl. Independence, 25th Anniv. — A158

1985 *Perf. 15x14½*

592	A158	18um multi	1.00	.40

Intl. Youth Year A159

1986, Feb. 13 **Litho.** *Perf. 13*

593	A159	18um Development	.80	.30
594	A159	22um Participation	1.00	.40
595	A159	25um Peace, vert.	1.40	.50
		Nos. 593-595 (3)	3.20	1.20

Toujounine Satellite Station — A160

1986, May 22 **Litho.** *Perf. 12½*

596	A160	25um multi	1.25	.50

World Wildlife Fund — A161

Monk seal (Monachus monachus).

1986, June 12 *Perf. 13*

597	A161	2um multi	*1.75*	*.35*
598	A161	5um multi	*2.75*	*.60*
599	A161	10um multi	*4.50*	*1.00*
600	A161	18um multi	*8.00*	*2.00*
		Nos. 597-600 (4)	*17.00*	*3.95*

Souvenir Sheet

601	A161	50um multi	*15.00*	*5.00*

Weaving — A162

1986, July 20 **Litho.** *Perf. 12½*

602	A162	18um multi	.80	.40

Sabra and Chatila Massacre, 4th Anniv. — A163

1986, Oct. 18

603	A163	22um multi	.90	.40

A164

Christopher Columbus — A165

Indians, maps on globe and: 2um, Santa Maria. 22um, Nina. 35um, Pinta. 150um, Columbus.

1986, Oct. 14 **Litho.** *Perf. 13½*

604	A164	2um multi	.20	.20
605	A164	22um multi	.80	.35
606	A164	35um multi	1.25	.55
607	A164	150um multi	5.50	2.25
		Nos. 604-607 (4)	7.75	3.35

Souvenir Sheet

608	A165	100um Columbus, Earth	4.50	4.00

Nos. 607-608 are airmail.

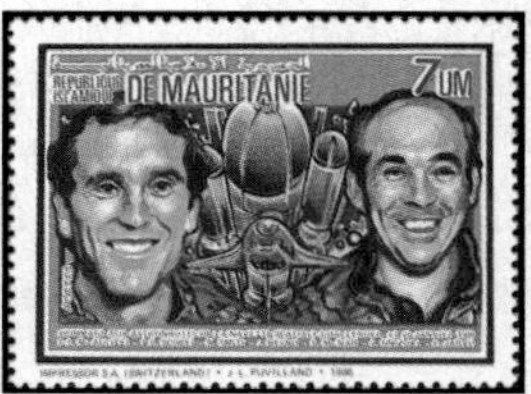

US Space Shuttle Challenger Explosion, Jan. 28, 1986 — A166

Crew members and: 7um, Space shuttle. 22um, Canadarm. 32um, Sky, moon. 43um, Memorial emblem.

1986, Oct. 14

609	A166	7um multi	.25	.20
610	A166	22um multi	.80	.30
611	A166	32um multi	1.25	.50
612	A166	43um multi	1.75	.65
		Nos. 609-612 (4)	4.05	1.65

Souvenir Sheet

613	A166	100um Crew, lift-off	4.00	1.50

Nos. 612-613 are airmail.

Fish A167

1986, Oct. 16 *Perf. 13*

614	A167	4um Dorade	.50	.20
615	A167	98um Truite de mer	7.50	2.25

See Nos. 631-633.

Birds A168

1986, Oct. 16

616	A168	22um Spatule blanche	2.50	.60
617	A168	32um Sterne bridee	3.00	.80

See Nos. 634-635.

World Food Day A169

1986, Nov. 6 *Perf. 12½*

618	A169	22um multi	1.00	.40

A170

Halley's Comet — A171

Space probes and portraits: 5um, J.H. Dort, Giotto probe. 18um, Sir William Huggins (1824-1910), English astronomer, and launch of Giotto on Ariane rocket. 26um, E.J. Opik, Giotto and Vega. 80um, F.L. Whipple, Planet-A. 100um, Edmond Halley, Giotto.

1986, Oct. 14 **Litho.** *Perf. 13½*

619	A170	5um multi	.20	.20
620	A170	18um multi	.60	.25
621	A170	26um multi	1.00	.40
622	A170	80um multi	3.25	1.25
		Nos. 619-622 (4)	5.05	2.10

Souvenir Sheet

623	A171	100um multi	4.00	2.00

Nos. 622-623 are airmail.

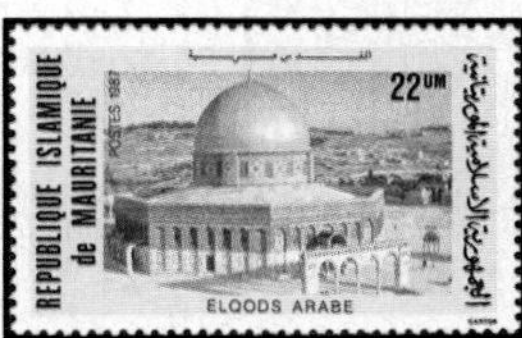

Jerusalem Day — A172

1987, May 21 **Litho.** *Perf. 13½*

624	A172	22um Dome of the Rock	1.00	.40

Cordoue Mosque, 1200th Anniv. A173

1987, Sept. 5 **Litho.** *Perf. 13½*

625	A173	30um multi	1.50	.55

Literacy Campaign A174

1987, Sept. 12

626 A174 18um Classroom .70 .40
627 A174 22um Family reading, vert. .90 .60

World Health Day — A175

1987, Oct. 1 ***Perf. 13***

628 A175 18um multi 1.00 .40

Natl. Population Census A176

1988, Aug. 21 Litho. ***Perf. 13½***

629 A176 20um multi 1.00 .40

WHO, 40th Anniv. — A177

Arab Scouting Movement, 75th Anniv. — A178

1988, Sept. 19 ***Perf. 13***

630 A177 30um multi 1.25 .45

Fish Type of 1986

1988, Sept. 10 Litho. ***Perf. 13***

631 A167 1um Rascasse blanche .60 .25
632 A167 7um Baliste 1.90 .35
633 A167 15um Bonite a ventre raye 2.75 .75
Nos. 631-633 (3) 5.25 1.35

Bird Type of 1986

1988, Sept. 15

634 A168 18um Grand cormorant 2.00 .60
635 A168 80um Royal tern 7.00 2.75

1988, Sept. 29 Litho. ***Perf. 13***

636 A178 35um multi 1.40 .60

1st Municipal Elections — A179

1988, Nov. 22 ***Perf. 13½***

637 A179 20um Men casting ballots .65 .30
638 A179 24um Woman casting ballot 1.00 .40

Organization of African Unity, 25th Anniv. (in 1988) — A180

Intl. Fund for Agricultural Development, 10th Anniv. (in 1988) — A181

1988, Dec. 7 Litho. ***Perf. 13***

639 A180 40um multi 1.25 .65

1988, Dec. 15

640 A181 35um multi 1.75 .70

Autonomy of Nouakchott (Amitie) Port, 1st Anniv. — A182

1988, Dec. 20 Litho. ***Perf. 13***

641 A182 24um multi 1.40 .60

A183

A184

1989, July 7 Litho. ***Perf. 13***

642 A183 35um multi 1.60 .60

French Revolution bicent., PHILEXFRANCE '89.

1989, July 17

643 A184 20um multi 1.00 .40

1990 World Cup Soccer Championships, Italy.

Pilgrimage to Mecca A185

1989, Aug. 26 Litho. ***Perf. 13½***

644 A185 20um Mosque 1.00 .40

African Development Bank, 25th Anniv. — A186

1989, Sept. 2

645 A186 37um lt vio & blk 1.25 .60

Tapestry — A187

1989, Oct. 1 ***Perf. 13***

646 A187 50um multicolored 2.00 .85

Locusts, Moths and Ladybugs A188

1989, Dec. 29

647 A188 2um *Heliothis armigera* .20 .20
648 A188 5um Locust .50 .20
649 A188 6um *Aphis gossypii* .25 .20
650 A188 10um *Agrotis ypsilon* .50 .20
651 A188 20um *Chilo* .95 .35
652 A188 20um Two locusts, egg case 1.00 .35
653 A188 24um Locusts emerging 1.25 .40
654 A188 24um *Plitella xylostella* 1.25 .40
655 A188 30um *Henosepilachna elaterii* 1.60 .50
656 A188 40um Locust flying 2.25 .70
657 A188 42um *Trichoplusia ni* 2.25 .70
658 A188 88um Locust, diff. 5.50 1.40
Nos. 647-658 (12) 17.50 5.60

Revolt — A189

1989, Dec. 8 Litho. ***Perf. 13***

659 A189 35um multicolored 1.60 .60

2nd Anniv. of the Palestinian Uprising and 1st anniv. of the declaration of a Palestinian State.

Maghreb Arab Union, 1st Anniv. — A190

Illustration reduced.

1990, Feb. 17 Litho. ***Perf. 13½***

660 A190 50um multicolored 1.75 .70

Mineral Resources A191

1990, July 27 ***Perf. 11½***

661 A191 60um multicolored 2.75 1.60

Intl. Literacy Year — A192

1990, July 27

662 A192 60um multicolored 2.00 1.00

1992 Summer Olympics, Barcelona A193

Litho. & Typo.

1990, Sept. 2 ***Perf. 13½***

663 A193 5um Equestrian .20 .20
664 A193 50um Archery 1.90 .65
665 A193 60um Hammer throw 2.00 1.00
666 A193 75um Field hockey 2.75 1.00
667 A193 90um Handball 3.50 1.25
668 A193 220um Table tennis 8.50 3.00
Nos. 663-668 (6) 18.85 7.10

Souvenir Sheet

669 A193 150um Runner 6.25 2.00

Nos. 668-669 airmail.

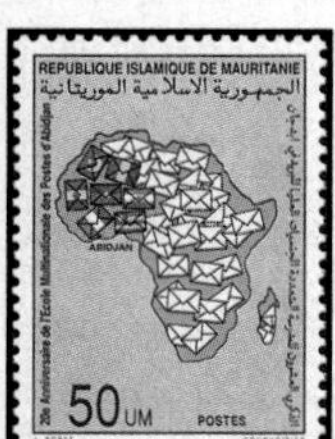

A194

A195

1990, July 27 *Perf. 11½*
670 A194 50um multicolored 2.00 .75

Multinational Postal School, 20th anniv.

1990, Nov. 21 Litho. *Perf. 11½*
671 A195 85um multicolored 3.75 1.60

Declaration of the Palestinian State, 2nd anniv.

1992 Winter Olympics, Albertville
A196

1990, Dec. 10 Litho. *Perf. 13½*
672 A196 60um Downhill skiing 1.75 .75
673 A196 75um Cross-country skiing 2.00 .90
674 A196 90um Ice hockey 2.75 1.10
675 A196 220um Pairs figure skating 6.25 2.75
Nos. 672-675 (4) 12.75 5.50

Souvenir Sheet

676 A196 150um Slalom skiing 5.00 2.50

Nos. 675-676 are airmail.

Release of Nelson Mandela
A197

1990, Dec. 10
677 A197 85um multicolored 5.00 1.75

Return of Senegalese Refugees — A198

1990, Dec. 10
678 A198 50um Cooking at encampment 2.25 1.00
679 A198 75um Women sewing 3.25 1.60
680 A198 85um Drawing water 3.75 1.75
Nos. 678-680 (3) 9.25 4.35

Boy Scouts Observing Nature — A199

Scout: 5um, Picking mushrooms. 50um, Holding mushroom. 60um, Drawing butterfly. 75um, Feeding butterfly. 90um, Photographing butterfly. 220um, Drying mushrooms. No. 687, Using microscope.

1991, Jan. 16 Litho. *Perf. 13½*
681 A199 5um multicolored .40 .20
682 A199 50um multicolored 2.40 .95
683 A199 60um multicolored 2.25 1.10
684 A199 75um multicolored 2.50 1.00
685 A199 90um multicolored 2.50 1.10
686 A199 220um multicolored 5.75 2.75
Nos. 681-686 (6) 15.80 7.10

Souvenir Sheet

687 A199 150um multicolored 6.50 3.00

Nos. 684 and 687 are airmail. Nos. 683-685 exist in souvenir sheets of 1.

Independence, 30th Anniv. — A200

1991, Mar. 5
688 A200 50um Satellite dish antennae 1.90 1.00
689 A200 60um Container ship 2.25 1.40
690 A200 100um Harvesting rice 3.75 1.90
Nos. 688-690 (3) 7.90 4.30

World Meteorology Day — A201

1991, Mar. 23 *Perf. 14x15*
691 A201 100um multicolored 3.75 2.10

World Population Day — A202

1991, July 27 Litho. *Perf. 13½*
692 A202 90um multicolored 3.50 1.75

Domesticated Animals — A203

1991 Litho. *Perf. 13½*
693 A203 50um Cats 3.00 1.00
693A A203 60um Dog 3.50 1.60

Campaign Against Blindness
A204

1991, Nov. 10 Litho. *Perf. 13½*
694 A204 50um multicolored 2.00 1.00

Doctors Without Borders, 20th Anniv.
A205

1991 Litho. *Perf. 13½*
695 A205 60um multicolored 2.50 1.25

Installation of Central Electric Service (in 1989)
A206

1991, Dec. 29 Litho. *Perf. 13½*
696 A206 50um multicolored 2.50 1.00

Mineral Exploration, M'Haoudat
A207

1993 Litho. *Perf. 13½*
697 A207 50um shown 2.10 1.00
698 A207 60um Desert landscape 2.50 1.40

1994 Winter Olympics, Lillehammer
A208

Intifada, 6th Anniv. — A209

1993
699 A208 10um Bobsled .40 .20
700 A208 50um Luge 1.90 .95
701 A208 60um Figure skating 2.25 1.10
702 A208 80um Downhill skiing 3.00 1.50
703 A208 220um Cross-country skiing 8.25 4.00
Nos. 699-703 (5) 15.80 7.75

Souvenir Sheet

704 A208 150um Downhill skiing, diff. 5.75 2.75

No. 704 is airmail.
No. 700 exists dated "1998."

1993

Design: 60um, Palestinian children, horiz.

705 A209 50um multicolored 2.10 1.00
706 A209 60um multicolored 2.50 1.40

First Multiparty Presidential Elections, 1st Anniv.
A209a

Design: 60um, Line at polling place.

1993 Litho. *Perf. 13½*
706B A209a 60um multi — —

An additional stamp was issued in this set. The editors would like to examine any example.

Caravans — A210

1993
707 A210 50um blue & multi 1.90 1.00
708 A210 60um violet & multi 2.25 1.40

Hut
A210a

1994 Litho. *Perf. 13¼x13½*
708A A210a 50um Hut, diff. — —
708B A210a 60um multi — —
708C A210a 80um Hut, diff. —

1994 World Cup Soccer Championships, U.S. — A211

Designs: 10um, Soldier Field. 50um, Foxboro Stadium. 60um, Robert F. Kennedy Stadium. 90um, Stanford Stadium. 220um, Giants Stadium. 150um, Rose Bowl.

1994, Feb. 10 Litho. *Perf. 13*
709 A211 10um multicolored .35 .20
710 A211 50um multicolored 1.90 .95
711 A211 60um multicolored 2.25 1.10
712 A211 90um multicolored 3.25 1.60
713 A211 220um multicolored 8.25 4.00
Nos. 709-713 (5) 16.00 7.85

Souvenir Sheet

714 A211 150um multicolored 5.75 2.75

Birds of Banc d'Arguin National Park — A211a

Various birds.

1994 Litho. *Perf. 13½*
714A A211a 10um lt blue & multi —
714D A211a 50um lt blue & multi — —

Two additional stamps exist in this set. The editors would like to examine any examples.

UN, 50th Anniv. A212

1995 Litho. *Perf. 11½*
715 A212 60um Emblem, #167 1.50 .75

FAO, 50th Anniv. A213

1995

716	A213 50um Working in field	1.25	.60
717	A213 60um With fishing boat	1.50	.75
718	A213 90um Planting garden	2.25	1.10
	Nos. 716-718 (3)	5.00	2.45

Traditional Handicrafts — A214

1995, Aug. 14 Litho. *Perf. 12*
719 A214 50um Weaving rug .50 .25

Perf. 11½x12
720 A214 60um Kettle .60 .30

1996 Summer Olympics, Atlanta — A216

Design: 20um, Sprinters crouching at starting line. 40um, Five Runners. 50um, Runners.

1996, July 19 Litho. *Perf. 11¾*
725 A216 20um pink & multi —
727 A216 40um blue & multi —
728 A216 50um yel & multi —

An additional stamp was issued in this set. The editors would like to examine any example.

Traditional Games A218

Design: 90um, Women and sticks.

1996, Oct. 25 Litho. *Perf. 11¾*
733 A218 90um multi —

Two additional stamps were issued in this set. The editors would like to examine any examples.

French Pres. Jacques Chirac, Mauritanian Pres. Maaouya Ould Sid Ahmed Taya — A219

1997 Litho. *Perf. 13¼x13*
735A A219 60um multi —

State visit of Chirac to Mauritania.

Universal Declaration of Human Rights, 50th Anniv. A220

1998 Litho. *Perf. 13x13¼*
736 A220 60um multi

The editors suspect that other stamps were issued in this set and would like to examine any examples.

No. 649 Surcharged

2000 Method and Perf. As Before
737 A188 50um on 6um #649 —

Independence, 40th Anniv. — A221

2000 Litho. *Perf. 13¼*
738 A221 50um multi 2.00 1.00

Education A222

Designs: 50um, Man with tablet, woman at computer. 60um, Open-air class. 90um, Reading class. 100um, Mathematics class.

2000
739-742 A222 Set of 4 4.00 4.00

Mauritanian postal officials have declared as "illegal" the following items:

Sheets of 9 stamps with 60um denominations depicting Famous actresses (2 different). Classic actresses, Marilyn Monroe, Elvis Presley, The Beatles, Queen, Walt Disney, The Simpsons, Teddy bears.

Sheets of 6 stamps with 80um denominations depicting Birds and Scout emblem (15 different).

Sheets of 6 stamps with 60um denominations depicting Trains (5 different), Penguins and Rotary emblem (2 different), Cats and Rotary emblem (2 different), Elephants and Rotary emblem (2 different), Polar bears and Rotary emblem (2 different), Lighthouses and Rotary emblem (2 different), Firearms and Rotary emblem, Firearms and Scout emblem, Pope John Paul II, Harry Potter, Scooby-Doo.

Sheets of 4 stamps depicting various sports of the Sydney Olympics (2 different).

Souvenir sheet depicting Various sports of the Sydney Olympics.

Se-tenant sets of 4 stamps depicting sports of the Sydney Olympics (2 different).

Flora, Fauna and Mushrooms — A223

No. 743: a, Chelonia mydas. b, Octopus vulgaris. c, Coelacanth.
No. 744: a, Lepiota aspera. b, Lactarius camphoratus. c, Clitocybe gibba.
No. 745: a, Harpa costata. b, Voluta lapponica. c, Tellina variegata.
No. 746: a, Akhal-Teke horse. b, Arabian horse. c, Lipizzaner horse.
No. 747: a, Tibetan dog, Balinese cat. b, Shetland sheepdog, Ragdoll cat. c, Cao de Serra de Aires sheepdog, Abyssinian cat.
No. 748: a, Acraea igati. b, Mylotris humbolti. c, Mylotris ngaziya.
No. 749: a, Zosterops maderaspatana. b, Otus rutilus. c, Nelicurvitus nelicourvi.
No. 750: a, Maxillaria tenuifolia. b, Crotalaria. c, Maxillaria marginata.
No. 751, Russula virescens. No. 752, Black Russian cat.

2000, Nov, 5 Litho. *Perf. 13½*

743	Horiz. strip of 3	1.60	1.60
a.-c.	A223 50um Any single	.50	.50
744	Horiz. strip of 3	1.60	1.60
a.-c.	A223 50um Any single	.50	.50
745	Horiz. strip of 3	1.75	1.75
a.-c.	A223 60um Any single	.55	.55
746	Horiz. strip of 3	2.75	2.75
a.-c.	A223 90um Any single	.90	.90
747	Horiz. strip of 3	3.00	3.00
a.-c.	A223 100um Any single	1.00	1.00
748	Horiz. strip of 3	6.00	6.00
a.-c.	A223 200um Any single	2.00	2.00
749	Horiz. strip of 3	7.00	7.00
a.-c.	A223 220um Any single	2.25	2.25
750	Horiz. strip of 3	2.75	2.75
a.	A223 60um multi	.60	.60
b.	A223 90um multi	.90	.90
c.	A223 100um multi	1.00	1.00
	Nos. 743-750 (8)	26.45	26.45

Souvenir Sheets

751	A223 300um multi	4.75	4.75
752	A223 300um multi	4.75	4.75

Nos. 746-749 exist in souvenir sheets containing one strip of 3 with light blue frames. No. 750 exists imperf.

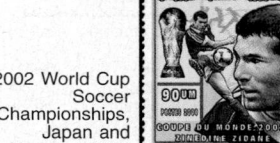

2002 World Cup Soccer Championships, Japan and Korea — A224

No. 753: a, Zinedine Zidane. b, Christian Vieri. c, Alessandro del Piero. d, Lilian Thuram.

No. 754: a, Oliver Bierhoff. b, Jürgen Klinsmann. c, Edgar Davids. d, Dennis Bergkamp.

300um, Jules Rimet Cup, soccer players, horiz.

2000

753	Horiz. strip of 4	4.50	4.50
a.-d.	A224 90um Any single	1.10	1.10
754	Horiz. strip of 4	5.00	5.00
a.-d.	A224 100um Any single	1.25	1.25

Souvenir Sheet
755 A224 300um multi 3.75 3.75

No. 755 contains one 57x51mm stamp. Souvenir sheets of 4 stamps exist with Nos. 753a-753d and 754a-754d with colored stamp frames.

Theodore Monod (1902-2000), Naturalist A225

2003, Jan. 1 *Perf. 13¼x13*
756 A225 370um multi 3.25 3.25

Trains A226

Designs: 100um, Freight train for minerals. 370um, Passenger train. 440um, Desert train.

2003, Jan. 1 *Perf. 13x13¼*
757-759 A226 Set of 3 7.25 7.25

Tourist Attractions A227

Designs: 100um, Sailboats, Banc d'Arguin. 220um, Ben Amera. 370um, Desert warthogs, Diawling Park. 440fr, Palms, Tergit, vert.

2003, Jan. 1 *Perf. 13x13¼, 13¼x13*
760-763 A227 Set of 4 9.00 9.00

Handicrafts A228

Designs: 100um, Wooden chest. 220um, Pipes. 310um, Teapot. 370um, Beads.

2003, Jan. 1 *Perf. 13x13¼*
764-767 A228 Set of 4 8.00 8.00

Historic Towns A229

Designs: 100um, Mosque, Chinguetti. 220um, Mosque, Ouadane. 660um, Wall design, Oualata. 880um, Mosque, Tichitt.

2003, Jan. 1
768-771 A229 Set of 4 15.00 15.00

Promotion of Books and Reading A230

Open book and: 100um, Stack of books, chair. 220um, Camel. 280um, Tower. 370um, Man, construction equipment.

2003, Jan. 1 Litho. *Perf. 13*

772-775	A230	Set of 4	12.50	12.50

Diplomatic Relations Between Mauritania and People's Republic of China, 40th Anniv. A231

Flags and: 100um, Ships and crane. 370um, Ship and crane, vert.

Perf. 13x13¼, 13¼x13

2005, July 19 Litho.

776-777	A231	Set of 2	6.25	6.25

Independence, 45th Anniv. — A232

Denominations: 100um, 370um.

2005, Nov. 16 *Perf. 13*

778-779	A232	Set of 2	6.25	6.25

World Summit on the Information Society, Tunis A233

Denominations: 100um, 370um.

2005, Nov. 16

780-781	A233	Set of 2	6.25	6.25

Musical Instruments — A234

Designs: 100um, Tidinit and gambré. 220um, Ardines, vert. 370um, Tom-toms. 440um, Kora and djembé, vert.

2005, Nov. 28

782-785	A234	Set of 4	13.00	13.00

Flora A235

Designs: 100um, Acacia tree. 220um, Euphorbia, vert. 370um, Jujube tree. 440um, Baobab tree, vert.

2005, Nov. 28

786-789	A235	Set of 4	13.00	13.00

Fauna A236

Designs: 100um, Starred lizard. 220um, Horned viper, vert. 370um, Lizard. 440um, Scorpion, vert.

2005, Nov. 28

790-793	A236	Set of 4	13.00	13.00

Tourism A237

Designs: 100um, People, fish and dolphins in water. 220um, Hodh El Gharbi. 370um, Adrar. 440um, Tiris Zemour.

2005, Nov. 28

794-797	A237	Set of 4	13.00	13.00

Jewelry A238

Designs: 100um, Necklaces. 220um, Khalkhal bracelets. 370um, Strings of beads. 440fr, Bracelets.

2008 Litho. *Perf. 13*

798-801	A238	Set of 4	17.00	17.00

Exploitation of Natural Resources — A239

Designs: 100um, Zouerate iron mine. 280um, Chinguitti oil platform, vert. 310um, Akjoujt copper mine. 370um, Taziast gold mine, vert.

2008

802-805	A239	Set of 4	17.00	17.00

SEMI-POSTAL STAMPS

Nos. 23 and 26 Surcharged in Red

1915-18 Unwmk. *Perf. 14x13½*

B1	A4	10c + 5c rose & red org	1.40	1.40
B2	A4	15c + 5c dk brn & blk ('18)	1.60	1.60

Curie Issue

Common Design Type

1938, Oct. 24 *Perf. 13*

B3	CD80	1.75fr + 50c brt ultra	7.25	7.25

French Revolution Issue

Common Design Type

Photo.; Name and Value Typographed in Black

1939, July 5 Unwmk.

B4	CD83	45c + 25c grn	8.00	8.00
B5	CD83	70c + 30c brn	8.00	8.00
B6	CD83	90c + 35c red org	8.00	8.00
B7	CD83	1.25fr + 1fr rose pink	8.00	8.00
B8	CD83	2.25fr + 2fr bl	8.00	8.00
		Nos. B4-B8 (5)	40.00	40.00

Stamps of 1938 Surcharge in Red or Black

1941

B9	A6	50c + 1fr pur (R)	1.75	1.75
B10	A7	80c + 2fr dp bl (R)	5.75	5.75
B11	A7	1.50fr + 2fr vio (R)	5.75	5.75
B12	A8	2fr + 3fr rose vio (Bk)	5.75	5.75
		Nos. B9-B12 (4)	19.00	19.00

Common Design Type and

Moorish Goumier SP1

White Goumier — SP2

1941 Photo. *Perf. 13½*

B13	SP1	1fr + 1fr red	.70
B14	CD86	1.50fr + 3fr claret	.70
B15	SP2	2.50fr + 1fr blue	.70
		Nos. B13-B15 (3)	2.10

Nos. B13-B15 were issued by the Vichy government in France, but were not placed on sale in Mauritania.

Nos. 114-115 Surcharged in Black or Red

1944 Engr. *Perf. 12½x12*

B15A	50c + 1.50fr on 2.50fr deep blue (R)	.50
B15B	+ 2.50fr on 1fr green	.50

Colonial Development Fund.

Nos. B15A-B15B were issued by the Vichy government in France, but were not placed on sale in Mauritania.

Catalogue values for unused stamps in this section, from this point to the end of the section, are for Never Hinged items.

Islamic Republic

Anti-Malaria Issue

Common Design Type

1962, Apr. 7 Engr. *Perf. 12½x12*

B16	CD108	25fr + 5f light olive grn	.80	.80

Freedom from Hunger Issue

Common Design Type

1963, Mar. 21 Unwmk. *Perf. 13*

B17	CD112	25fr + 5fr multi	.80	.80

Nurse Tending Infant — SP3

1972, May 8 Photo. *Perf. 12½x13*

B18	SP3	35fr + 5fr grn, red & brn	1.50	1.50

Surtax was for Mauritania Red Crescent Society.

AIR POST STAMPS

Common Design Type

Perf. 12½x12

1940, Feb. 8 Engr. Unwmk.

C1	CD85	1.90fr ultra	.45	.45
C2	CD85	2.90fr dk red	.45	.45
C3	CD85	4.50fr dk gray grn	.50	.50
C4	CD85	4.90fr yel bister	.85	.85
C5	CD85	6.90fr deep org	1.00	1.00
		Nos. C1-C5 (5)	3.25	3.25

Common Design Types

1942

C6	CD88	50c car & bl	.20	
C7	CD88	1fr brn & blk	.20	
C8	CD88	2fr dk grn & red brn	.35	
C9	CD88	3fr dk bl & scar	.35	
C10	CD88	5fr vio & brn red	.70	

Frame Engraved, Center Typo.

C11	CD89	10fr ultra, ind & hn	.75	
a.		Center inverted	*750.00*	
C12	CD89	20fr rose car, mag & buff	.75	
C13	CD89	50fr yel grn, dl grn & org	.85	*3.25*
		Nos. C6-C13 (8)	4.15	

There is doubt whether Nos. C6-C12 were officially placed in use.

Catalogue values for unused stamps in this section, from this point to the end of the section, are for Never Hinged items.

Islamic Republic

Flamingoes AP1

Designs: 200fr, African spoonbills. 500fr, Slender-billed gull, horiz.

Unwmk.

1961, June 30 Engr. *Perf. 13*

C14	AP1	100fr red org, brn & ultra	3.75	2.00
C15	AP1	200fr red org, sep & sl grn	6.00	3.25
C16	AP1	500fr red org, gray & bl	20.00	7.25
		Nos. C14-C16 (3)	29.75	12.50

An overprint, "Europa / CECA / MIFERMA," was applied in carmine to No. C16 in 1962. Value $20.

The anti-malaria emblem, including slogan "Le Monde contre le Paludisme," was overprinted on Nos. C14-C15 in 1962.

Air Afrique Issue

Common Design Type

1962, Feb. 17

C17	CD107	100fr sl grn, choc & bis	2.50	1.10

UN Headquarters, New York; View of Nouakchott — AP2

1962, Oct. 27 Engr. *Perf. 13*

C18 AP2 100fr bluish grn, dk bl & org brn 2.50 .85

Mauritania's admission to the UN.

Plane, Nouakchott Airport — AP3

1963, May 3 Unwmk. *Perf. 13*

C19 AP3 500fr dp bl, gldn brn & slate grn 12.50 4.00

Miferma Open-pit Mine at Zouerate — AP4

Design: 200fr, Ore transport at Port Etienne.

1963, June Photo. *Perf. 13x12*

C20 AP4 100fr multi 1.90 .50
C21 AP4 200fr multi 4.75 1.00

African Postal Union Issue
Common Design Type

1963, Sept. 8 Unwmk. *Perf. 12½*

C22 CD114 85fr blk brn, ocher & red 1.75 .60

Globe and Telstar — AP5

Design: 150fr, Relay satellite and stars.

1963, Oct. 7 Engr. *Perf. 13*

C23 AP5 50fr yel grn, pur & red brn .75 .40
C24 AP5 150fr red brn & sl grn 2.75 1.25

Communication through space.

Tiros Satellite and Emblem of WMO — AP6

UN Emblem, Doves and Sun — AP7

1963, Nov. 4

C25 AP6 200fr ultra, brn & grn 4.25 1.50

Space research for meteorology and navigation.

1963 Air Afrique Issue
Common Design Type

1963, Nov. 19 Photo. *Perf. 13x12*

C26 CD115 25fr multi .70 .25

1963, Dec. 10 Engr. *Perf. 13*

C27 AP7 100fr vio, brn, & dk bl 2.00 .75

Universal Declaration of Human Rights, 15th anniv.

Symbols of Agriculture and Industry — AP8

Lichtenstein's Sand Grouse — AP9

Europafrica Issue

1964, Jan. 6 Photo.

C28 AP8 50fr multi 1.40 .75

Signing of economic agreement between the European Economic Community and the African and Malgache Union at Yaoundé, Cameroun, July 20, 1963.

1964, Feb. 3 Engr. *Perf. 13*

Birds: 200fr, Long-tailed cormorant. 500fr, Chanting goshawk.

C29 AP9 100fr ocher, ol & dk brn 3.25 1.00
C30 AP9 200fr blk, dk bl & brn 5.00 1.75
C31 AP9 500fr rose red, grn & sl 15.00 5.25
Nos. C29-C31 (3) 23.25 8.00

Isis, Temple at Philae and Trajan's Kiosk — AP10

1964, Mar. 8 Unwmk. *Perf. 13*

C32 AP10 10fr red brn, Prus bl & blk .60 .20
C33 AP10 25fr red brn, ind & Prus bl .90 .40
C34 AP10 60fr blk brn, Prus bl & red brn 1.90 .60
Nos. C32-C34 (3) 3.40 1.20

UNESCO world campaign to save historic monuments in Nubia.

Syncom Satellite, Globe — AP11

1964, May 4 Engr.

C35 AP11 100fr red, red brn & ultra 1.60 .65

Issued to publicize space communications.

Horse Race on Bowl — AP12

Sport Designs from Ancient Pottery: 50fr, Runner, vert. 85fr, Wrestlers, vert. 100fr, Charioteer.

1964, Sept. 27 Unwmk. *Perf. 13*

C36 AP12 15fr ol bis & choc .60 .30
C37 AP12 50fr bl & org brn 1.25 .50
C38 AP12 85fr crim & brn 2.10 1.00
C39 AP12 100fr emer & dk red brn 2.75 1.25
a. Min. sheet of 4, #C36-C39 8.50 8.50
Nos. C36-C39 (4) 6.70 3.05

18th Olympic Games, Tokyo, Oct. 10-25.

Pres. John F. Kennedy (1917-1963) AP13

1964, Dec. 7 Photo. *Perf. 12½*

C40 AP13 100fr red brn, bl grn & dk brn 2.10 1.00
a. Souv. sheet of 4 7.50 7.50

ITU Emblem, Induction Telegraph and Relay Satellite — AP14

1965, May 17 Engr. *Perf. 13*

C41 AP14 250fr multi 5.50 2.75

ITU, centenary.

Fight Against Cancer — AP15

Winston Churchill — AP16

1965, July 19 Unwmk. *Perf. 13*

C42 AP15 100fr bis, Prus bl & red 1.90 .60

Issued to publicize the fight against cancer.

1965, Dec. 6 Photo. *Perf. 13*

C43 AP16 200fr multi 3.25 1.10

Sir Winston Spencer Churchill (1874-1965), statesman and WWII leader.

Diamant Rocket Ascending AP17

French achievements in space: 60fr, Satellite A-1 and earth, horiz. 90fr, Scout rocket and satellite FR-1, horiz.

1966, Feb. 7 Engr. *Perf. 13*

C44 AP17 30fr dp bl, red & grn .60 .30
C45 AP17 60fr mar, Prus grn & bl 1.25 .50
C46 AP17 90fr dp bl, rose cl & vio 1.90 .75
Nos. C44-C46 (3) 3.75 1.55

Dr. Albert Schweitzer and Clinic — AP18

1966, Feb. 21 Photo. *Perf. 12½*

C47 AP18 50fr multi 1.50 .55

Schweitzer (1875-1965), medical missionary to Gabon, theologian and musician.

Thomas P. Stafford, Walter M. Schirra and Gemini 6 — AP19

Designs: 100fr, Frank A. Borman, James A. Lovell, Jr., and Gemini 7. 200fr, Pavel Belyayev, Alexei Leonov, Voskhod 2.

1966, Mar. 7 Photo. *Perf. 12½*

C48 AP19 50fr multi	.80	.30
C49 AP19 100fr multi	1.75	.45
C50 AP19 200fr multi	3.50	1.00
Nos. C48-C50 (3)	6.05	1.75

Issued to honor achievements in space.

Map of Africa and Dove — AP20

D-1 Satellite over Earth — AP21

1966, May 9 Photo. *Perf. 13*

C51 AP20 100fr red brn, sl & yel grn	1.10	.40

Organization for African Unity.

1966, June 6 Engr.

C52 AP21 100fr bl, dk pur & ocher	1.50	.70

Launching of the D-1 satellite at Hammaguir, Algeria, Feb. 17, 1966.

Bréguet 14 — AP22

Planes: 100fr, Goliath Farman, and camel caravan. 150fr, Couzinet "Arc-en-Ciel." 200fr, Latécoère 28 hydroplane.

1966, July 4 Engr. *Perf. 13*

C53 AP22 50fr sl bl, dl grn & ol bis	1.00	.25
C54 AP22 100fr brt bl, dk grn & dk red brn	2.10	.45
C55 AP22 150fr dl brn, Prus bl & saph	3.25	.70
C56 AP22 200fr dk red brn, bl & ind	4.75	1.10
Nos. C53-C56 (4)	11.10	2.50

Air Afrique Issue, 1966
Common Design Type

1966, Aug. 31 Photo. *Perf. 13*

C57 CD123 30fr red, blk & gray	.80	.30

"The Raft of the Medusa," by Théodore Géricault — AP23

1966, Sept. 5 Photo. *Perf. 12½*

C58 AP23 500fr multi	13.00	6.00

Sinking of the frigate "Medusa" off Mauritania, July 2, 1816.

Symbols of Agriculture and Industry — AP24

1966, Nov. 7 Photo. *Perf. 13x12*

C59 AP24 50fr multi	1.00	.35

Third anniversary, economic agreement between the European Economic Community and the African and Malgache Union.

Crowned Crane — AP25

Eye, Globe and Rockets — AP26

1967, Apr. 3 *Perf. 12½x13*

C60 AP25 100fr shown	2.75	.75
C61 AP25 200fr Common egret	5.25	1.10
C62 AP25 500fr Ostrich	14.00	4.00
Nos. C60-C62 (3)	22.00	5.85

For surcharge see No. C129.

1967, May 2 Engr. *Perf. 13*

C63 AP26 250fr brn, Prus bl & blk	4.25	1.25

EXPO '67 Intl. Exhibition, Montreal, Apr. 28-Oct. 27.

Emblem of Atomic Energy Commission AP27

1967, Aug. 7 Engr. *Perf. 13*

C64 AP27 200fr dk red, brt grn & ultra	3.00	1.10

International Atomic Energy Commission.

African Postal Union Issue, 1967
Common Design Type

1967, Sept. 9 Engr. *Perf. 13*

C65 CD124 100fr brn org, vio brn & brt grn	1.25	.55

Francesca da Rimini, by Ingres AP28

Paintings by and of Ingres: 100fr, Young man's torso. 150fr, "The Iliad" (seated woman). 200fr, Ingres in his Studio, by Alaux. 250fr, "The Odyssey" (seated woman).

1967-68 Photo. *Perf. 12½*

C66 AP28 90fr multi	2.00	.55
C67 AP28 100fr multi ('68)	2.00	.60
C68 AP28 150fr multi ('68)	3.00	.95
C69 AP28 200fr multi	3.50	1.00
C70 AP28 250fr multi ('68)	5.00	1.50
Nos. C66-C70 (5)	15.50	4.60

Jean Dominique Ingres (1780-1867), French painter.

Issued: 90fr, 200fr, 10/2/67; others, 9/2/68.

See No. C79.

Konrad Adenauer AP29

Gymnast AP30

1968, Feb. 5 Photo. *Perf. 12½*

C71 AP29 100fr org brn, lt bl & blk	2.00	.60
a. Souv. sheet of 4	7.50	5.50

Adenauer (1876-1967), chancellor of West Germany (1949-63).

1968, Mar. 4 Engr. *Perf. 13*

Sports: 20fr, Slalom, horiz. 50fr, Ski jump. 100fr, Hurdling, horiz.

C72 AP30 20fr plum, blk & bl	.35	.20
C73 AP30 30fr dl pur, brt grn & brn	.45	.20
C74 AP30 50fr Prus bl, bis & bl grn	.65	.30
C75 AP30 100fr brn, grn & ver	1.40	.45
Nos. C72-C75 (4)	2.85	1.15

1968 Olympic Games.

WHO Emblem, Man and Insects — AP31

1968, May 2 Engr. *Perf. 13*

C76 AP31 150fr red lil, dp bl & org red	2.25	.80

WHO, 20th anniversary.

Martin Luther King — AP32

Design: No. C78, Mahatma Gandhi.

1968, Nov. 4 Photo. *Perf. 12½*

C77 AP32 50fr sl bl, cit & blk	1.00	.30
C78 AP32 50fr sl bl, lt bl & blk	1.00	.30
a. Souv. sheet of 4, 2 each #C77-C78	4.25	4.25

Issued to honor two apostles of peace.

PHILEXAFRIQUE Issue
Painting Type of 1967

Design: 100fr, The Surprise Letter, by Charles Antoine Coypel.

1968, Dec. 9 Photo. *Perf. 12½*

C79 AP28 100fr multi	3.25	1.25

PHILEXAFRIQUE, Phil. Exhib., Abidjan, Feb. 14-23. Printed with alternating brown red label.

2nd PHILEXAFRIQUE Issue
Common Design Type

50fr, Mauritania #89 & family on jungle trail.

1969, Feb. 14 Engr. *Perf. 13*

C80 CD128 50fr sl grn, vio brn & red brn	2.10	.65

Napoleon Installed in Council of State, by Louis Charles Couder AP33

Paintings: 50fr, Napoleon at Council of the 500, by F. Bouchot. 250fr, Farewell at Fontainebleau, by Horace Vernet.

1969, Feb. 24 Photo. *Perf. 12½*

C81 AP33 50fr pur & multi	2.10	.80
C82 AP33 90fr multi	2.75	1.25
C83 AP33 250fr multi	7.25	3.00
Nos. C81-C83 (3)	12.10	5.05

Napoleon Bonaparte (1769-1821).

Camel, Gazelles, and Tourist Year Emblem — AP34

1969, June 9 Engr. *Perf. 13*
C84 AP34 50fr org, dk brn & lt bl 1.40 .40

Year of African Tourism.

Dancers and Temple Ruins, Baalbek — AP35

1969, June 16
C85 AP35 100fr Prus bl, ol brn & rose car 1.40 .45

International Baalbek Festival, Lebanon.

Apollo 8 and Moon Surface — AP36

Embossed on Gold Foil

1969 *Die-cut Perf. 10*
C86 AP36 1000fr gold 22.50 22.50

Man's first flight around the moon, Dec. 21-28, 1968 (US astronauts Col. Frank Borman, Capt. James Lovell and Maj. William Anders).

Mamo Wolde, Ethiopia, Marathon AP37

Designs: 70fr, Bob Beamon, US, broad jump. 150fr, Vera Caslavska, Czechoslovakia, gymnastics.

1969, July 7 Engr. *Perf. 13*
C87 AP37 30fr multi .45 .25
C88 AP37 70fr multi .80 .35
C89 AP37 150fr multi 2.10 .80
Nos. C87-C89 (3) 3.35 1.40

Issued to honor gold medal winners in the 19th Olympic Games, Mexico City.

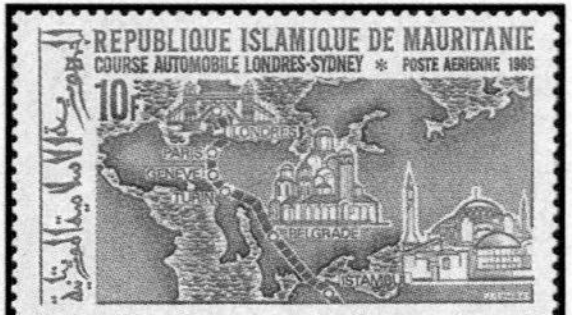
Map of London-Istanbul Route — AP38

London to Sydney automobile rally: 20fr, Map showing Ankara to Teheran route, and compass rose. 50fr, Map showing Kandahar to Bombay route, arms of Afghanistan and elephant. 70fr, Map of Australia with Perth to Sydney route, and kangaroo.

1969, Aug. 14 Engr. *Perf. 13*
C90 AP38 10fr multicolored .25 .20
C91 AP38 20fr multicolored .45 .20
C92 AP38 50fr multicolored .75 .30
C93 AP38 70fr multicolored 1.10 .40
a. Min. sheet of 4, #C90-C93 3.50 3.50
Nos. C90-C93 (4) 2.55 1.10

Palette with World Map, Geisha and EXPO '70 Emblem — AP39

EXPO '70 Emblem and: 75fr, Fan & fireworks. 150fr, Stylized bird, map of Japan & boat.

1970, June 15 Photo. *Perf. 12½*
C94 AP39 50fr multi .80 .20
C95 AP39 75fr multi 1.40 .30
C96 AP39 150fr multi 2.50 .70
Nos. C94-C96 (3) 4.70 1.20

Issued to publicize EXPO '70 International Exhibition, Osaka, Japan, Mar. 15-Sept. 13.

UN Emblem, Balloon, Rocket, Farm Woman, Tractor, Old and New Record Players — AP40

1970, June 22 Engr. *Perf. 13*
C97 AP40 100fr ultra, dk brn & grn 1.40 .55

25th anniversary of the United Nations.

Elliott See (1927-1966), American Astronaut AP41

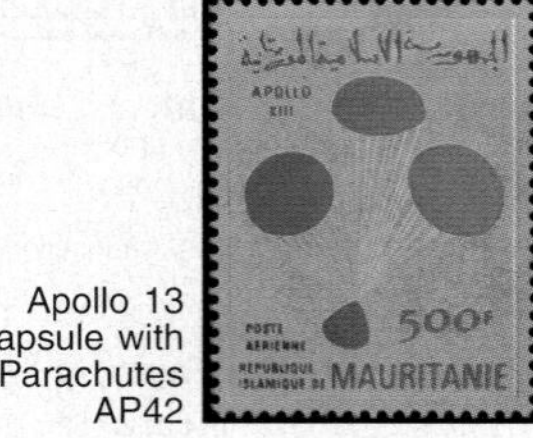
Apollo 13 Capsule with Parachutes AP42

#C99, Vladimir Komarov (1927-67). #C100, Yuri Gagarin (1934-68). #C101, Virgil Grissom (1926-67). #C102, Edward White (1930-67). #C103, Roger Chaffee (1935-67).

1970 Engr. *Perf. 13*

Portrait in Brown

C98 AP41 150fr gray & brt bl 1.50 .70
C99 AP41 150fr gray & org 1.50 .70
C100 AP41 150fr gray & org 1.50 .70
a. Souv. sheet of 3, #C98-C100 5.00 5.00
C101 AP41 150fr ultra & grnsh bl 1.75 .70
C102 AP41 150fr ultra & org 1.75 .70
C103 AP41 150fr ultra & grnsh bl 1.75 .70
a. Souv. sheet of 3, #C101-C103 6.00 6.00
Nos. C98-C103 (6) 9.75 4.20

American and Russian astronauts who died in space explorations.

Gold Embossed

1970, Aug. 17 *Perf. 12½*
C104 AP42 500fr gold, crim & bl 8.00 8.00

Safe return of Apollo 13 crew.

Parliament, Nouakchott, and Coat of Arms — AP43

1970, Nov. 28 Photo. *Perf. 12½*
C105 AP43 100fr multi 1.25 .40

10th anniversary of Independence.

Hercules Wrestling Antaeus — AP44

1971, Mar. 8 Engr. *Perf. 13*
C106 AP44 100fr red lil, brn & ultra 1.90 .75

Pre-Olympic Year. Design from a vase decoration by Euphronius.

Gamal Abdel Nasser (1918-1970), President of U.A.R. — AP46

1971, May 10 Photo. *Perf. 12½*
C109 AP46 100fr gold & multi 1.00 .40

Boy Scout, Emblem and Map of Mauritania AP47

1971, Aug. 16 Photo. *Perf. 12½*
C110 AP47 35fr yel & multi .55 .20
C111 AP47 40fr pink & multi .60 .20
C112 AP47 100fr multi 1.50 .40
Nos. C110-C112 (3) 2.65 .80

13th Boy Scout World Jamboree, Asagiri Plain, Japan, Aug. 2-10.

African Postal Union Issue, 1971

Common Design Type

Design: 100fr, Women musicians and UAMPT building, Brazzaville, Congo.

1971, Nov. 13 Photo. *Perf. 13x13½*
C113 CD135 100fr bl & multi 1.10 .60

Letter and Postal Emblem AP48

1971, Dec. 2 *Perf. 13*
C114 AP48 35fr bis & multi .65 .30

10th anniversary of African Postal Union.

Mosul Monarch, from Book of Songs, c. 1218 AP49

Designs from Mohammedan Miniatures: 40fr, Prince holding audience, Egypt, 1334. 100fr, Pilgrim caravan, from "Maquamat," Baghdad, 1237.

1972, Jan. 10 Photo. *Perf. 13*
C115 AP49 35fr gold & multi .50 .20
C116 AP49 40fr gray & multi .65 .30
C117 AP49 100fr buff & multi 1.75 .60
Nos. C115-C117 (3) 2.90 1.10

For surcharges see Nos. C140, C143-C144.

Grand Canal, by Canaletto — AP50

Designs: 45fr, Venice Harbor, by Carlevaris, vert. 250fr, Santa Maria della Salute, by Canaletto.

1972, Feb. 14
C118 AP50 45fr gold & multi .75 .30
C119 AP50 100fr gold & multi 1.90 .60
C120 AP50 250fr gold & multi 4.25 1.00
Nos. C118-C120 (3) 6.90 1.90

UNESCO campaign to save Venice.

Hurdles and Olympic Rings — AP51

1972, Apr. 27 Engr. *Perf. 13*
C121 AP51 75fr org, vio brn & blk .75 .25
C122 AP51 100fr Prus bl, vio brn & brn 1.10 .40
C123 AP51 200fr lake, vio brn & blk 2.40 .60
a. Min. sheet of 3, #C121-C123 7.00 7.00
Nos. C121-C123 (3) 4.25 1.25

20th Olympic Games, Munich, Aug. 26-Sept. 11.

For overprints see Nos. C126-C128.

Luna 17 on Moon — AP52

75fr, Luna 16 take-off from moon, vert.

1972, Oct. 9

C124 AP52 75fr vio bl, bis & grn .80 .25
C125 AP52 100fr dl pur, sl & ol bis 1.10 .40

Russian moon missions, Luna 16, Sept. 12-14, 1970; and Luna 17, Nov. 10-17, 1970.

Nos. C121-C123 Overprinted in Violet Blue or Red:

a. 110m HAIES / MILBURN MEDAILLE D'OR
b. 400m HAIES / AKII-BUA MEDAILLE D'OR
c. 3.000m STEEPLE / KEINO MEDAILLE D'OR

1972, Oct. 16

C126 AP51(a) 75fr multi (VB) 1.00 .30
C127 AP51(b) 100fr multi (R) 1.25 .45
C128 AP51(c) 200fr multi (VB) 2.75 .90
Nos. C126-C128 (3) 5.00 1.65

Gold medal winners in 20th Olympic Games: Rod Milburn, US, John Akii-Bua, Uganda, and Kipchoge Keino, Kenya.

No. C62 Surcharged with New Value, Two Bars and: "Apollo XVII / December 1972"

1973, Jan. 29 Photo. *Perf. 12½x13*

C129 AP25 250fr on 500fr multi 4.00 1.25

Apollo 17 moon mission, Dec. 7-19, 1972.

Seal Type of Regular Issue

1973, Feb. 28 Litho. *Perf. 13*

C130 A63 135fr Seal's head 4.25 1.75

For surcharge see No. C145.

Lion Eating Caiman, by Delacroix — AP53

Painting: 250fr, Lion Eating Boar, by Delacroix.

1973, Mar. 26 Photo. *Perf. 13x12½*

C131 AP53 100fr blk & multi 2.00 .80
C132 AP53 250fr blk & multi 4.50 2.00

For surcharges see Nos. C148-C149.

Villagers Observing Solar Eclipse — AP54

40fr, Rocket take-off & Concord, vert. 140fr, Scientists with telescopes observing eclipse.

1973, June 20 Engr. *Perf. 13*

C133 AP54 35fr grn & pur .85 .25
C134 AP54 40fr ultra, pur & scar .90 .25
C135 AP54 140fr scar & pur 3.50 .70
a. Souvenir sheet of 3 6.00 6.00
Nos. C133-C135 (3) 5.25 1.20

Solar eclipse, June 30, 1973. No. C135a contains 3 stamps similar to Nos. C133-C135 in changed colors (35fr, 140fr in magenta and violet blue; 40fr in magenta, violet blue and orange).

For surcharges see Nos. C141-C142, C146.

Soccer AP55

1973, Dec. 24 Photo. *Perf. 13*

C136 AP55 7um multi .40 .25
C137 AP55 8um multi .40 .25
C138 AP55 20um multi 1.25 .60
Nos. C136-C138 (3) 2.05 1.10

Souvenir Sheet

C139 AP55 30um multi 1.75 1.75

World Soccer Cup, Munich, 1974.

Nos. C115-C117, C130 and C133-C135 Surcharged with New Value and Two Bars in Red, Black or Ultramarine

1973-74 Photo., Litho. or Engr.

C140 AP49 7um on 35fr (R) ('74) .60 .25
C141 AP54 7um on 35fr (B) .70 .25
C142 AP54 8um on 40fr (B) .70 .25
C143 AP49 8um on 40fr (U) ('74) .60 .25
C144 AP49 20um on 100fr (R) ('74) 2.00 .60
C145 A63 27um on 135fr (R) 3.00 .70
C146 AP54 28um on 140fr (B) 2.25 .70
Nos. C140-C146 (7) 9.85 3.00

Winston Churchill (1874-1965) AP56

Lenin (1870-1924) AP57

1974, June 3 Engr. *Perf. 13*

C147 AP56 40um blk, brn & hn brn 2.00 .90

Nos. C131-C132 Surcharged with New Value and Two Bars in Red

1974, July 15 Photo. *Perf. 13x12½*

C148 AP53 20um on 100fr multi 1.50 .60
C149 AP53 50um on 250fr multi 4.00 1.60

1974, Sept. 16 Engr. *Perf. 13*

C150 AP57 40um slate grn & red 3.75 1.10

Women, IWY Emblem AP58

40um, Woman's head and IWY emblems.

1975, June 16 Engr. *Perf. 13*

C151 AP58 12um multi .60 .25
C152 AP58 40um dk brn, lt brn & bl 2.25 .80

International Women's Year.

Albert Schweitzer and Patients Arriving — AP59

1975, Aug. 4 Engr. *Perf. 13*

C153 AP59 60um multi 3.50 1.50

Schweitzer (1875-1965), medical missionary.

Javelin and Olympic Emblem — AP60

52um, Running and Olympic emblem.

1975, Nov. 17 Engr. *Perf. 13*

C154 AP60 50um sl grn, red & ol 2.50 1.25
C155 AP60 52um car, ocher & ultra 2.50 1.25

Pre-Olympic Year 1975.

Apollo Soyuz Type, 1975

Docked Space Ships and: 20um, Apollo rocket launch. 50um, Handshake in linked-up cabin. 60um, Apollo splash-down. 100um, Astronauts and Cosmonauts.

1975, Dec. 29 Litho. *Perf. 14*

C156 A74 20um multi 1.00 .40
C157 A74 50um multi 2.25 .75
C158 A74 60um multi 2.75 1.00
Nos. C156-C158 (3) 6.00 2.15

Souvenir Sheet

C159 A74 100um multi 4.25 1.25

American Bicentennial Type, 1976

Uniforms: 20um, French Hussar officer. 50um, 3rd Continental Artillery officer. 60um, French infantry regiment grenadier. 100um, American infantryman.

1976, Jan. 26

C160 A75 20um multi .75 .25
C161 A75 50um multi 2.00 .70
C162 A75 60um multi 2.75 .80
Nos. C160-C162 (3) 5.50 1.75

Souvenir Sheet

C163 A75 100um multi 4.50 1.25

Running and Olympic Rings AP61

12um, High jump. 52um, Fencing.

1976, June 14 Engr. *Perf. 13*

C164 AP61 10um pur, grn & brn .80 .25
C165 AP61 12um pur, grn & brn .90 .40
C166 AP61 52um pur, grn & brn 3.00 1.40
Nos. C164-C166 (3) 4.70 2.05

21st Olympic Games, Montreal, Canada, July 17-Aug. 1.

Zeppelin Type, 1976

Designs: 50um, "Graf Zeppelin" (LZ-127) over US Capitol. 60um, "Hindenburg" (LZ-130) over Swiss Alps. 100um, "Führersland" (LZ-129) over 1936 Olympic stadium.

1976, June 28 Litho. *Perf. 11*

C167 A77 50um multi 3.25 .90
C168 A77 60um multi 4.00 1.10

Souvenir Sheet

C169 A77 100um multi 6.75 1.50

Marabou Storks — AP62

African Birds: 50um, Sacred ibis, vert. 200um, Long-crested eagles, vert.

1976, Sept. 20 Litho. *Perf. 13½*

C170 AP62 50um multi 3.50 1.00
C171 AP62 100um multi 6.50 1.75
C172 AP62 200um multi 13.00 3.50
Nos. C170-C172 (3) 23.00 6.25

Viking Type, 1977

Designs: 20um, Viking orbiter in flight to Mars. 50um, Viking "B" in descent to Mars. 60um, Various phases of descent. 100um, Viking lander using probe.

1977, Feb. 28 *Perf. 14*

C173 A81 20um multi 1.00 .25
C174 A81 50um multi 2.50 .50
C175 A81 60um multi 3.00 .65
Nos. C173-C175 (3) 6.50 1.40

Souvenir Sheet

C176 A81 100um multi 5.00 1.50

For surcharge & overprints see #C192-C195.

Nobel Prize Type, 1977

14um, George Bernard Shaw, literature. 55um, Thomas Mann, literature. 60um, Intl. Red Cross Society, peace. 100um, George C. Marshall, peace.

1977, Apr. 29 Litho. *Perf. 14*

C177 A83 14um multi 1.00 .25
C178 A83 55um multi 3.25 .50
C179 A83 60um multi 4.25 .65
Nos. C177-C179 (3) 8.50 1.40

Souvenir Sheet

C180 A83 100um multi 8.00 1.50

Holy Kaaba — AP63

1977, July 25 Litho. *Perf. 12½*

C181 AP63 12um multi 1.75 .40

Pilgrimage to Mecca.

Soccer Type of 1977

50um, Soccer ball. 60um, Eusebio Ferreira. 100um, Players holding pennants.

1977, Dec. 19 Litho. *Perf. 13½*

C182 A89 50um multi 2.50 .50
C183 A89 60um multi 3.00 .65

Souvenir Sheet

C184 A89 100um multi 5.00 1.25

For overprints see Nos. C187-C189.

Franco-African Co-operation — AP63a

1978, June 7 Embossed *Perf. 10½*

C184A	AP63a	250um	silver	12.00	12.00
C184B	AP63a	500um	gold	25.00	25.00

Philexafrique II — Essen Issue
Common Design Types

No. C185, Hyena and Mauritania #C60. No. C186, Wading bird and Hamburg #1.

1978, Nov. 1 Litho. *Perf. 12½*

C185	CD138	20um	multi	1.75	1.00
C186	CD139	20um	multi	1.75	1.00
a.			Pair #C185-C186 + label	5.25	4.00

Nos. C182-C184 Overprinted in Arabic and French in Silver: "ARGENTINE- / PAYS BAS 3-1"

1978, Dec. 11 Litho. *Perf. 13½*

C187	A89	50um	multi	2.25	1.10
C188	A89	60um	multi	3.00	1.40

Souvenir Sheet

C189	A89	100um	multi	5.00	5.00

Argentina's victory in World Cup Soccer Championship 1978.

Flyer A and Prototype Plane — AP64

Design: 40um, Flyer A and supersonic jet.

1979, Jan. 29 Engr. *Perf. 13*

C190	AP64	15um	multi	1.10	.35
C191	AP64	40um	multi	2.50	1.00

75th anniversary of first powered flight.

Nos. C173-C176 Overprinted and Surcharged in Silver: "ALUNISSAGE / APOLLO XI / JUILLET 1969" and Emblem

1979, Oct. 24 Litho. *Perf. 14*

C192	A81	14um on 20um	multi	.75	.30
C193	A81	50um	multi	2.50	.90
C194	A81	60um	multi	2.75	1.25
			Nos. C192-C194 (3)	6.00	2.45

Souvenir Sheet

C195	A81	100um	multi	5.00	5.00

Apollo 11 moon landing, 10th anniversary.

Soccer Players — AP65

Designs: Various soccer scenes.

1980, Sept. 29 Litho. *Perf. 12½*

C196	AP65	10um	multi	.45	.25
C197	AP65	12um	multi	.55	.25
C198	AP65	14um	multi	.55	.25
C199	AP65	20um	multi	1.00	.25
C200	AP65	67um	multi	2.75	.60
			Nos. C196-C200 (5)	5.30	1.60

Souvenir Sheet

C201	AP65	100um	multi	4.75	1.00

World Soccer Cup 1982.
For overprints see Nos. C212-C217.

Flight of Columbia Space Shuttle — AP66

Designs: Views of Columbia space shuttle.

1981, Apr. 27 Litho. *Perf. 12½*

C202	AP66	12um	multi	.60	.25
C203	AP66	20um	multi	1.00	.25
C204	AP66	50um	multi	2.25	.50
C205	AP66	70um	multi	3.25	.70
			Nos. C202-C205 (4)	7.10	1.70

Souvenir Sheet

C206	AP66	100um	multi	5.00	1.25

Dinard Landscape, by Pablo Picasso — AP67

Picasso Birth Centenary: 12um, Harlequin, vert. 20um, Vase of Flowers, vert. 50um, Three Women at the Well. 100um, Picnic.

1981, June 29 Litho. *Perf. 12½*

C207	AP67	12um	multi	.70	.25
C208	AP67	20um	multi	1.10	.30
C209	AP67	50um	multi	2.50	.60
C210	AP67	70um	multi	3.50	.85
C211	AP67	100um	multi	5.00	1.25
			Nos. C207-C211 (5)	12.80	3.25

Nos. C196-C201 Overprinted in Red with Finalists and Score on 1 or 2 Lines

1982, Sept. 18 Litho. *Perf. 12½*

C212	AP65	10um	multi	.45	.25
C213	AP65	12um	multi	.55	.25
C214	AP65	14um	multi	.55	.30
C215	AP65	20um	multi	1.00	.30
C216	AP65	67um	multi	2.75	.75
			Nos. C212-C216 (5)	5.30	1.85

Souvenir Sheet

C217	AP65	100um	multi	4.75	1.25

Italy's victory in 1982 World Cup.

25th Anniv. of Intl. Maritime Org. — AP68

1983, June 18 Litho. *Perf. 12½x13*

C218	AP68	18um	multi	.85	.40

Paul Harris, Rotary Founder AP69

1984, Jan. 20 Litho. *Perf. 13½*

C219	AP69	100um	multi	4.75	1.00

1984 Summer Olympics — AP70

1984, July 15 Litho. *Perf. 14*

C223	AP70	14um	Running, horiz.	.70	.30
C224	AP70	18um	Shot put	.85	.40
C225	AP70	19um	Hurdles	.95	.40
C226	AP70	44um	Javelin	1.90	1.00
C227	AP70	77um	High jump	4.00	1.75
			Nos. C223-C227 (5)	8.40	3.85

Souvenir Sheet

C228	AP70	100um	Steeplechase	6.00	2.00

Olympics Winners — AP71

1984, Dec. 20 Litho. *Perf. 13*

C229	AP71	14um	Van den Berg, sailboard, Netherlands	.85	.30
C230	AP71	18um	Coutts, Finn sailing, N.Z.	1.00	.40
C231	AP71	19um	470 class, Spain	1.10	.45
C232	AP71	44um	Soling, US	2.50	1.00
			Nos. C229-C232 (4)	5.45	2.15

Souvenir Sheet

C233	AP71	100um	Sailing, US	6.00	3.00

PHILEXAFRICA '85, Lome, Togo — AP72

1985, May 23 Litho. *Perf. 13*

C234	AP72	40um	Youths, map, IYY emblem	1.90	.75
C235	AP72	40um	Oil refinery, Nouadhibou	1.90	.75
a.			Pair, #C234-C235 + label	5.00	3.75

Exists with two labels showing map of Africa or Lome '85 emblem.

1985, Nov. 12 *Perf. 13x12½*

C236	AP72	50um	Iron mine, train	2.00	.75
C237	AP72	50um	Boy reading, herding sheep	2.00	.75
a.			Pair, #C236-C237 + label	5.75	5.75

Audubon Birth Bicentenary AP73

1985, Aug. 14

C238	AP73	14um	Passeriformes thraupidae	.80	.25
C239	AP73	18um	Larus philadelphia	1.00	.25
C240	AP73	19um	Cyanocitta cristata	1.25	.35
C241	AP73	44um	Rhyncops nigra	2.75	.70
			Nos. C238-C241 (4)	5.80	1.55

Souvenir Sheet

C242	AP73	100um	Anhinga anhinga	8.00	4.00

1st South Atlantic Crossing, 55th Anniv. — AP74

1986, May 19 Litho. *Perf. 13*

C243	AP74	18um	Comte de Vaux, 1930	.65	.30
C244	AP74	50um	Flight reenactment, 1985	1.75	.90
a.			Pair, #C243-C244 + label	2.75	2.75

1986 World Cup Soccer Championships, Mexico — AP75

Various soccer plays.

1986, June 19 Litho. *Perf. 13*

C245	AP75	8um	No. 279	.30	.20
C246	AP75	18um	No. 280	.75	.30
C247	AP75	22um	No. 281	.95	.35
C248	AP75	25um	No. 282	1.10	.45
C249	AP75	40um	Soccer cup	1.75	.70
			Nos. C245-C249 (5)	4.85	2.00

Souvenir Sheet

C250	AP75	100um	multi	4.75	2.50

Air Africa, 25th Anniv. — AP76

1986, Oct. 6 Litho. *Perf. 13*

C251	AP76	26um	multi	.90	.40

1988 Summer Olympics, Seoul — AP77

1987, Aug. 13 Litho. *Perf. 13*

C252	AP77	30um	Boxing	1.10	.45
C253	AP77	40um	Judo	1.50	.60
C254	AP77	50um	Fencing	1.75	.75
C255	AP77	75um	Wrestling	3.00	1.10
			Nos. C252-C255 (4)	7.35	2.90

Souvenir Sheet

C256	AP77	150um	Judo, diff.	5.75	2.25

1988 Winter Olympics, Calgary — AP78

1987, Sept.
C257 AP78 30um Women's slalom 1.10 .45
C258 AP78 40um Speed skating 1.50 .60
C259 AP78 50um Ice hockey 1.75 .75
C260 AP78 75um Women's downhill skiing 3.00 1.10
Nos. C257-C260 (4) 7.35 2.90

Souvenir Sheet

C261 AP78 150um Men's cross-country skiing 5.75 2.25

For overprints see Nos. C267-C271.

1988 Summer Olympics, Seoul AP79

1988, Sept. 17 Litho. *Perf. 13*
C262 AP79 20um Hammer throw .85 .30
C263 AP79 24um Discus .90 .35
C264 AP79 30um Shot put 1.25 .45
C265 AP79 150um Javelin 5.75 2.00
Nos. C262-C265 (4) 8.75 3.10

Souvenir Sheet

C266 AP79 170um Javelin, diff. 6.50 2.50

Nos. C257-C261 Overprinted "Medaille d'or" in Red or Bright Blue and:
a. "Vreni Schneider (Suisse)"
b. "1500 m / Andre Hoffman (R.D.A.)"
c. "U.R.S.S."
d. "Marina Kiehl (R.F.A.)"
e. "15 km / Mikhail Deviatiarov (U.R.S.S.)"

1988, Sept. 18
C267 AP78(a) 30um multi 1.25 .45
C268 AP78(b) 40um multi (BB) 1.75 .60
C269 AP78(c) 50um multi 2.00 .80
C270 AP78(d) 75um multi 3.50 1.25
Nos. C267-C270 (4) 8.50 3.10

Souvenir Sheet

C271 AP78(e) 150um multi 6.50 3.00

World Cup Soccer Championships, Italy — AP80

Map of Italy and various soccer plays.

1990 Litho. *Perf. 13*
C272 AP80 50um multicolored 2.00 .65
C273 AP80 60um multicolored 2.00 .85
C274 AP80 70um multicolored 2.50 .95
C275 AP80 90um multicolored 3.50 1.25
C276 AP80 150um multicolored 7.50 2.75
Nos. C272-C276 (5) 17.50 6.45

AIR POST SEMI-POSTAL STAMPS

Maternity Hospital, Dakar — SPAP1

Dispensary, Mopti — SPAP2

Nurse Weighing Baby — SPAP3

Unwmk.

1942, June 22 Engr. *Perf. 13*
CB1 SPAP1 1.50fr + 3.50fr green .55
CB2 SPAP2 2fr + 6fr brown .55
CB3 SPAP3 3fr + 9fr carmine .55
Nos. CB1-CB3 (3) 1.65

Native children's welfare fund.

Nos. CB1-CB3 were issued by the Vichy government in France, but were not placed on sale in Mauritania.

Colonial Education Fund

Common Design Type

1942, June 22
CB4 CD86a 1.20fr + 1.80fr bl & red .55

No. CB4 was issued by the Vichy government in France, but was not placed on sale in Mauritania.

POSTAGE DUE STAMPS

D1

D2

Perf. 14x13½

1906-07 Unwmk. Typo.
J1 D1 5c grn, *grnsh* 2.25 2.25
J2 D1 10c red brn 3.50 3.25
J3 D1 15c dk bl 7.25 6.00
J4 D1 20c blk, *yellow* 8.75 7.25
J5 D1 30c red, *straw* 9.50 8.00
J6 D1 50c violet 14.50 14.50
J7 D1 60c blk, *buff* 11.00 9.25
J8 D1 1fr blk, *pinkish* 16.00 14.50
Nos. J1-J8 (8) 72.75 65.00

Issue dates: 20c, 1906; others 1907.

Regular postage stamps canceled "T" in a triangle were used for postage due.

1914
J9 D2 5c green .20 .20
J10 D2 10c rose .20 .20
J11 D2 15c gray .35 .35
J12 D2 20c brown .35 .35
J13 D2 30c blue .65 .65
J14 D2 50c black 1.25 1.25
J15 D2 60c orange 1.00 1.00
J16 D2 1fr violet 1.00 1.00
Nos. J9-J16 (8) 5.00 5.00

Type of 1914 Issue Surcharged

1927, Oct. 10
J17 D2 2fr on 1fr lil rose 2.25 2.25
J18 D2 3fr on 1fr org brn 2.60 2.60

Catalogue values for unused stamps in this section, from this point to the end of the section, are for Never Hinged items.

Islamic Republic

Oualata Motif — D3

Perf. 14x13½

1961, July 1 Typo. Unwmk.

Denominations in Black

J19 D3 1fr plum & org yel .20 .20
J20 D3 2fr red & gray .20 .20
J21 D3 5fr mar & pink .25 .25
J22 D3 10fr dk grn & grn .30 .25
J23 D3 15fr ol & brn org 25
.30 50
J25 D3 25fr grn & vermilion .75 .50
Nos. J19-J25 (6) 2.00 1.65

Vulture (Ruppell's Griffon) — D4

Birds: #J27, Eurasian crane. #J28, Pink-backed pelican. #J29, Garganey teal. #J30, European golden oriole. #J31, Variable sunbird. #J32, Shoveler ducks. #J33, Great snipe. #J34, Vulturine guinea fowl. #J35, Black stork. #J36, Gray heron. #J37, White stork. #J38, Red-legged partridge. #J39, Paradise whydah. #J40, Sandpiper (little stint). #J41, Sudan bustard.

1963, Sept. 7 Engr. *Perf. 11*
J26 D4 50c blk, yel org & red .20 .20
J27 D4 50c blk, yel org & red .20 .20
a. Pair, #J26-J27 .50 .50
J28 D4 1fr blk, red & yel .20 .20
J29 D4 1fr blk, red & yel .20 .20
a. Pair, #J28-J29 .60 .60
J30 D4 2fr blk, bl grn & yel .20 .20
J31 D4 2fr blk, bl grn & yel .20 .20
a. Pair, #J30-J31 .80 .80
J32 D4 5fr blk, grn & red brn .35 .35
J33 D4 5fr blk, grn & red brn .35 .35
a. Pair, #J32-J33 1.25 1.25
J34 D4 10fr blk, red & tan .70 .70
J35 D4 10fr blk, red & tan .70 .70
a. Pair, #J34-J35 2.50 2.50
J36 D4 15fr blk, emer & red .75 .75
J37 D4 15fr blk, emer & red .75 .75
a. Pair, #J36-J37 2.75 2.75
J38 D4 20fr blk, yel grn & red 1.00 1.00
J39 D4 20fr blk, yel grn & red 1.00 1.00
a. Pair, #J38-J39 3.25 3.25
J40 D4 25fr blk, yel grn & brn 1.50 1.50
J41 D4 25fr blk, yel grn & brn 1.50 1.50
a. Pair, #J40-J41 4.50 4.50
Nos. J26-J41 (16) 9.80 9.80

Ornament D5

1976, May 10 Litho. *Perf. 12½x13*
J42 D5 1um buff & multi .20 .20
J43 D5 3um buff & multi .20 .20
J44 D5 10um buff & multi .45 .45
J45 D5 12um buff & multi .55 .55
J46 D5 20um buff & multi .95 .95
Nos. J42-J46 (5) 2.35 2.35

OFFICIAL STAMPS

Catalogue values for unused stamps in this section are for Never Hinged items.

Islamic Republic

Cross of Trarza — O1

Perf. 14x13½

1961, July 1 Typo. Unwmk.
O1 O1 1fr vio & lilac .20 .20
O2 O1 3fr red & slate .20 .20
O3 O1 5fr grn & brown .25 .20
O4 O1 10fr grn & vio bl .25 .20
O5 O1 15fr blue & org .35 .25
O6 O1 20fr sl grn & emer .45 .25
O7 O1 25fr red org & mar .50 .30
O8 O1 30fr maroon & grn .60 .40
O9 O1 50fr dk red & dk brn 1.25 .50
O10 O1 100fr orange & blue 1.90 .90
O11 O1 200fr grn & red org 3.75 1.75
Nos. O1-O11 (11) 9.70 5.15

Ornament O2

1976, May 3 Litho. *Perf. 12½x13*
O12 O2 1um black & multi .20 .20
O13 O2 2um black & multi .20 .20
O14 O2 5um black & multi .25 .20
O15 O2 10um black & multi .50 .25
O16 O2 12um black & multi .70 .30
O17 O2 40um black & multi 2.50 .90
O18 O2 50um black & multi 3.00 1.25
Nos. O12-O18 (7) 7.35 3.30

MAURITIUS

mo-'ri-sh,ē-,əs

LOCATION — Island in the Indian Ocean about 550 miles east of Madagascar
GOVT. — Republic
AREA — 720 sq. mi.
POP. — 1,182,212 (1999 est.)
CAPITAL — Port Louis

12 Pence = 1 Shilling
100 Cents = 1 Rupee (1878)

The British Crown Colony of Mauritius was granted self-government in 1967 and became an independent state on March 12, 1968.

Nos. 1-6, 14-17 unused are valued without gum.

Nos. 3a-8, 14-15 are printed on fragile paper with natural irregularities which might be mistaken for faults.

Very fine examples of Nos. 22-58 will have perforations touching the design on one or more sides. Examples with perfs clear on four sides are scarce and will sell for more. Inferior copies will sell for much reduced prices.

Catalogue values for unused stamps in this country are for Never Hinged items, beginning with Scott 223 in the regular postage section, Scott J1 in the postage due section.

Queen Victoria
A1 A2

1847 Unwmk. Engr. *Imperf.*
1 A1 1p orange *1,250,000.* *900,000.*
2 A1 2p dark blue *1,000,000.*

Nos. 1 and 2 were engraved and printed in Port Louis. There is but one type of each value. The initials "J. B." on the bust are those of the engraver, J. Barnard.

All unused examples of the 2p are in museums. There is one unused example of the 1p in private hands. There are two used examples of the 1p in private hands, both of which have small faults and are valued thus.

1848

Earliest Impressions
Thick Yellowish Paper
3 A2 1p orange *55,000.* *18,500.*
4 A2 2p dark blue *52,500.* *21,000.*
d. "PENOE" *95,000.* *35,000.*

Early Impressions
Yellowish White Paper
3a A2 1p orange *25,000.* *7,250.*
4a A2 2p blue *27,500.* *8,000.*
e. "PENOE" *45,000.* *13,000.*

Bluish Paper
5 A2 1p orange *25,000.* *7,250.*
6 A2 2p blue *27,500.* *8,000.*
c. "PENOE" *45,000.* *13,000.*

Intermediate Impressions
Yellowish White Paper
3b A2 1p red orange *14,500.* 2,750.
4b A2 2p blue *15,000.* 3,750.
f. "PENOE" *24,000.* *6,500.*

Bluish Paper
5a A2 1p red orange *14,500.* 2,750.
6a A2 2p blue *15,000.* 3,750.
d. "PENOE" *24,000.* *6,500.*
f. Double impression —

Worn Impressions
Yellowish White Paper
3c A2 1p orange red 5,500. 750.
d. 1p brownish red 5,500. 750.
4c A2 2p blue 6,250. 1,300.
g. "PENOE" *10,000.* 2,250.

Bluish Paper
5b A2 1p orange red 4,250. 650.
c. 1p brownish red 4,250. 650.
d. Pair, double impression
6b A2 2p blue 6,250. 1,250.
e. "PENOE" 10,000. 2,000.

Latest Impressions
Yellowish or Grayish Paper
3e A2 1p orange red 3,600. 600.
f. 1p brownish red 3,600. 600.
4h A2 2p blue 4,750. 950.
i. "PENOE" *8,000.* 1,600.

Bluish Paper
5e A2 1p orange red 1,800. 600.
f. 1p brownish red 1,800. 600.
6g A2 2p blue 2,500. 950.
h. "PENOE" 4,500. 1,600.

These stamps were printed in sheets of twelve, four rows of three, and each position differs in details. The "PENOE" error is the most pronounced variety on the plates and is from position 7.

The stamps were in use until 1859. Earliest impressions, Nos. 3-4, show the full background of diagonal and vertical lines with the diagonal lines predominant. Early impressions, Nos. 3a-4a, 5-6, show the full background with the vertical lines predominating. As the plate became worn the vertical lines disappeared, giving the intermediate impressions, Nos. 3b-4b, 5a-6a.

Worn impressions, Nos. 3c-4c, 5b-6b, have little background remaining, and latest impressions, Nos. 3e-4h, 5e-6g, have also lost details of the frame and head. The paper of the early impressions is usually rather thick, that of the worn impressions rather thin. Expect natural fibrous inclusions in the paper of all impressions.

"Britannia"
A3 A4

1849-58
7 A3 red brown, *blue* 25.00
8 A3 blue ('58) 7.50

Nos. 7-8 were never placed in use.

1858-59
9 A3 (4p) green, *bluish* 550.00 240.00
10 A3 (6p) red 50.00 *90.00*
11 A3 (9p) mag ('59) 775.00 240.00

No. 11 was re-issued in Nov. 1862, as a 1p stamp. When used as such it is always canceled "B53." Price so used, $200.

1858 Black Surcharge
12 A4 4p green, *bluish* 1,450. 450.00

Queen Victoria — A5

Early Impressions

1859, Mar.
14 A5 2p blue, *grayish* 8,000. 2,400.
a. 2p deep blue, *grayish* 10,000. 2,800.
14B A5 2p blue, *bluish* 8,000. 2,400.
c. Intermediate impression 5,500. 1,100.
d. Worn impression 3,250. 700.00

Type A5 was engraved by Lapirot, in Port Louis, and was printed locally. There were twelve varieties in the sheet.

Early impressions have clear and distinct background lines. In the intermediate impressions, the lines are somewhat blurred, and white patches appear. In the worn impressions, the background lines are discontinuous, with many white patches. Analogous wear is also obvious in the background of the inscriptions on all four sides. Values depend on the state of wear. One should expect natural fibrous inclusions in the paper on all printings.

A6 A7

1859, Oct.
15 A6 2p blue, *bluish* *150,000.* 12,000.

No. 15 was printed from the plate of the 1848 issue after it had been entirely re-engraved by Sherwin. It is commonly known as the "fillet head." The plate of the 1p, 1848, was also re-engraved but was never put in use.

1859, Dec. Litho.

Laid Paper
16 A7 1p vermilion 5,750. 1,200.
a. 1p deep red *9,500.* 2,000.
b. 1p red *7,250.* 1,700.
17 A7 2p pale blue 3,250. 650.
a. 2p slate blue 5,750. 1,100.
b. 2p blue 3,500. 775.

Lithographed locally by Dardenne.

"Britannia" — A8

1859 Wove Paper Engr. *Imperf.*
18 A8 6p blue 750.00 55.00
19 A8 1sh vermilion 3,000. 57.50

1861
20 A8 6p gray violet 32.50 *60.00*
21 A8 1sh green 675.00 150.00

1862 *Perf. 14 to 16*
22 A8 6p slate 30.00 *90.00*
a. Horiz. pair, imperf between *8,000.*
23 A8 1sh deep green 2,750. 400.00

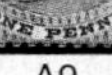

A9 A10

1860-63 Typo. *Perf. 14*
24 A9 1p brown lilac 275.00 30.00
25 A9 2p blue 300.00 55.00
26 A9 4p rose 300.00 35.00
27 A9 6p green ('62) 900.00 160.00
28 A9 6p lilac ('63) 350.00 115.00
29 A9 9p dull lilac 160.00 50.00
30 A9 1sh buff ('62) 350.00 100.00
31 A9 1sh green ('63) 800.00 200.00

For surcharges see Nos. 43-45.

1863-72 Wmk. 1
32 A9 1p lilac brown 85.00 16.00
a. 1p bister brown 160.00 13.00
33 A9 2p blue 100.00 11.50
a. Imperf., pair 1,950. 2,350.
34 A9 3p vermilion 80.00 16.00
35 A9 4p rose 100.00 4.25
36 A9 6p lilac ('64) 325.00 37.50
37 A9 6p blue grn ('65) 190.00 7.25
a. 6p yellow green ('65) 215.00 16.00
38 A9 9p green ('72) 175.00 *275.00*
39 A9 1sh org yel ('64) 275.00 29.00
a. 1sh yellow 240.00 14.50
40 A9 1sh blue ('70) 150.00 27.50
41 A9 5sh red violet 215.00 65.00
a. 5sh bright violet 300.00 65.00
Nos. 32-41 (10) 1,695. 489.00

For surcharges see Nos. 48-49, 51-58, 87.

1872
42 A10 10p claret 325.00 50.00

For surcharges see Nos. 46-47.

No. 29 Surcharged in Black or Red:

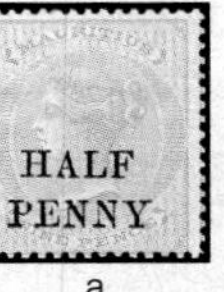

a b

1876 Unwmk.
43 A9(a) ½p on 9p 14.50 *19.00*
a. Inverted surcharge 675.00
b. Double surcharge *2,100.*
44 A9(b) ½p on 9p *4,000.*
45 A9(b) ½p on 9p (R) *2,400.*

Nos. 44 and 45 were never placed in use. No. 45 is valued with perfs cutting into the design.

Stamps of 1863-72 Surcharged in Black:

c d

1876-77 Wmk. 1
46 A10(a) ½p on 10p cl 2.40 *25.00*
47 A10(c) ½p on 10p cl ('77) 7.25 *42.50*
48 A9(d) 1p on 4p rose ('77) 15.50 20.00
49 A9(d) 1sh on 5sh red vio ('77) 300.00 115.00
a. 1sh on 5sh violet ('77) 275.00 140.00
Nos. 46-49 (4) 325.15 *202.50*

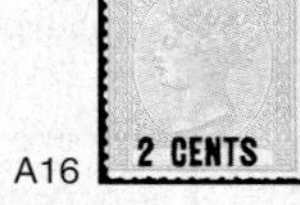

A16

Black Surcharge

1878
50 A16 2c claret 12.00 7.75

Stamps and Type of 1863-72 Surcharged in Black

e

51 A9 4c on 1p bister brn 21.00 7.75
52 A9 8c on 2p blue 90.00 3.25
53 A9 13c on 3p org red 18.00 37.50
54 A9 17c on 4p rose 200.00 4.00
55 A9 25c on 6p sl blue 240.00 7.75
56 A9 38c on 9p violet 32.50 *90.00*
57 A9 50c on 1sh green 110.00 4.25
58 A9 2r50c on 5sh violet 19.00 *22.50*
Nos. 50-58 (9) 742.50 *184.75*

For surcharge see No. 87.

A18

A19

A20 A21

A22 A23

A24

A25

A26

1879-80 **Wmk. 1**
59 A18 2c red brn ('80) 55.00 22.50
60 A19 4c orange 75.00 4.50
61 A20 8c blue ('80) 25.00 4.00
62 A21 13c slate ('80) 150.00 200.00
63 A22 17c rose ('80) 85.00 7.75
64 A23 25c bister 425.00 13.00
65 A24 38c violet ('80) 200.00 300.00
66 A25 50c green ('80) 4.75 4.25
67 A26 2r50c brn vio ('80) 50.00 *72.50*
Nos. 59-67 (9) 1,069. 628.50

Nos. 59-67 are known imperforate.
For surcharges & overprints see #76-78, 83-86, 122-123.

1882-93 **Wmk. 2**
68 A18 1c violet ('93) 2.10 .55
69 A18 2c red brown 37.50 6.00
70 A18 2c green ('85) 3.25 .75
71 A19 4c orange 85.00 4.50
72 A19 4c rose ('85) 3.25 1.25
73 A20 8c blue ('91) 2.75 1.75
74 A23 25c bister ('83) 8.50 3.00
75 A25 50c dp orange ('87) 35.00 14.50
Nos. 68-75 (8) 177.35 32.30

For surcharges and overprint see #88-89, 121.

Nos. 63 and Type of 1882 Surcharged in Black:

f

g

1883 **Wmk. 1**

Surcharge Measures 14x3½mm

76 A22(f) 16c on 17c rose 175.00 65.00
a. Double surcharge 2,500.

Surcharge Measures 15½x3½mm

77 A22(f) 16c on 17c rose 190.00 65.00

Surcharge Measures 15½x2¾mm

78 A22(f) 16c on 17c rose *375.00* *125.00*

Wmk. 2

79 A22(g) 16c on 17c rose 100.00 2.40
Nos. 76-79 (4) *840.00* *257.40*

Queen Victoria — A29

1885-94
80 A29 15c orange brown ('92) 6.00 1.50
81 A29 15c blue ('94) 7.00 1.50
82 A29 16c orange brown 6.00 2.40
Nos. 80-82 (3) 19.00 5.40

For surcharges see Nos. 90, 116.

Various Stamps Surcharged in Black or Red:

h

j

1885-87 **Wmk. 1**
83 A24(h) 2c on 38c violet 140.00 42.50
a. Inverted surcharge 1,000. 975.00
b. Double surcharge 1,100.
c. Without bar 240.00
84 A21(j) 2c on 13c sl (R) ('87) 65.00 *115.00*
a. Inverted surcharge 215.00 *225.00*
b. Double surcharge 975.00 850.00
c. As "b," one on back *975.00*

k

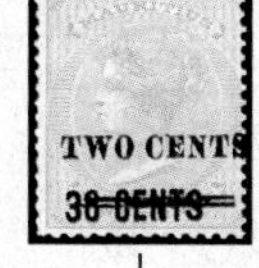

l

1891
85 A22(k) 2c on 17c rose 125.00 *125.00*
a. Inverted surcharge 475.00 —
b. Double surcharge 850.00 850.00
86 A24(k) 2c on 38c vio 6.50 8.50
a. Double surcharge 215.00 225.00
b. Dbl. surch., one invtd. 225.00 240.00
c. Inverted surcharge 1,000. —
87 A9(e+l) 2c on 38c on 9p vio 5.50 5.50
a. Double surcharge 850.00 850.00
b. Inverted surcharge 500.00 —
c. Dbl. surch., one invtd. 190.00 200.00

Wmk. 2

88 A19(k) 2c on 4c rose 1.75 .85
a. Double surcharge 95.00 90.00
b. Inverted surcharge 90.00 —
c. Dbl. surch., one invtd. 95.00 90.00
Nos. 85-88 (4) 138.75 139.85

m

n

1893, Jan.
89 A18(m) 1c on 2c violet 2.40 .90
90 A29(n) 1c on 16c org brown 2.40 *4.00*

Coat of Arms — A38

1895-1904 **Wmk. 2**
91 A38 1c lilac & ultra .90 1.75
92 A38 1c gray blk & black .60 .25
93 A38 2c lilac & orange 5.50 .60
94 A38 2c dull lil & vio 1.25 .25
95 A38 3c lilac .90 .60
96 A38 3c grn & scar, *yel* 4.75 1.50
97 A38 4c lilac & green 4.75 .60
98 A38 4c dull lil & car, *yel* 1.75 .50
99 A38 4c gray green & pur 1.25 *2.40*
100 A38 4c black & car, *blue* 10.00 .75
101 A38 5c lilac & vio, *buff* 8.00 *65.00*
102 A38 5c lilac & blk, *buff* 3.00 3.00
103 A38 6c grn & rose 5.50 5.00
104 A38 6c violet & scar, *red* 2.40 1.00
105 A38 8c gray grn & blk, *buff* 2.75 *10.00*
106 A38 12c black & car rose 2.10 *2.75*
107 A38 15c grn & org 16.00 *8.00*
108 A38 15c blk & ultra, *blue* 65.00 1.50
109 A38 18c gray grn & ultra 15.00 4.25
110 A38 25c grn & car, *grn* 5.00 *20.00*
111 A38 50c green, *yel* 20.00 *60.00*
Nos. 91-111 (21) 176.40 *189.70*

The 25c is on both ordinary and chalky paper. Ornaments in lower panel omitted on #106-111.
Year of issue: #103, 107, 1899; #92, 94, 98, 1900; #96, 99, 101-102, 104-106, 110-111, 1902; #100, 108, 1904; others, 1895.
See #128-135. For surcharges and overprints see #113, 114, 117-120.

Diamond Jubilee Issue

Arms A39

1898, May 23 **Wmk. 46**
112 A39 36c brown org & ultra 14.00 25.00

60th year of Queen Victoria's reign.
For surcharges see Nos. 114 and 127.

No. 109 Surcharged in Red

1899 **Wmk. 2**
113 A38 6c on 18c 2.00 1.25
a. Inverted surcharge 675.00 340.00

No. 112 Surcharged in Blue

Wmk. 46

114 A39 15c on 36c 1.75 *2.10*
a. Without bar 500.00

Admiral Mahe de La Bourdonnais A40

1899, Dec. **Engr.** **Wmk. 1**
115 A40 15c ultra 20.00 5.00

Birth bicent. of Admiral Mahe de La Bourdonnais, governor of Mauritius, 1734-46.

No. 82 Surcharged in Black

1900 **Wmk. 2**
116 A29 4c on 16c orange brown 6.75 19.00

No. 109 Surcharged in Black

r

1902
117 A38 12c on 18c grn & ultra 2.40 *7.25*

Preceding Issues Overprinted in Black

1902
118 A38 4c lilac & car, *yel* 1.50 .35
119 A38 6c green & rose 1.50 *3.25*
120 A38 15c green & orange 4.50 .90
121 A23 25c bister 5.75 3.25

Wmk. 1

122 A25 50c green 9.00 4.75
123 A26 2r50c brown violet 125.00 *190.00*
Nos. 118-123 (6) 147.25 202.50

Coat of Arms — A41

1902 **Wmk. 1**
124 A41 1r blk & car rose 60.00 60.00

Wmk. 2 Sideways

125 A41 2r50c grn & blk, *bl* 29.00 *125.00*
126 A41 5r blk & car, *red* 95.00 *125.00*
Nos. 124-126 (3) 184.00 *310.00*

No. 112 Surcharged type "r" but with longer bar

1902 **Wmk. 46**
127 A39 12c on 36c 1.50 1.75
a. Inverted surcharge 725.00 525.00

Arms Type of 1895-1904

1904-07 **Wmk. 3**

Chalky Paper

128 A38 1c gray blk & black ('07) 10.00 4.25
129 A38 2c dl lil & vio ('05) 24.00 2.10
130 A38 3c grn & scar, *yel* 27.50 11.00
131 A38 4c blk & car, *blue* 18.00 1.75
132 A38 6c vio & scar, *red* ('06) 10.50 .35
133 A38 15c blk & ultra, *bl* 5.00 .40
135 A38 50c green, *yel* 2.25 *2.75*

136 A41 1r black & car rose ('07) 26.00 *55.00*
Nos. 128-136 (8) 123.25 *77.60*

The 2c, 4c, 6c also exist on ordinary paper.
Ornaments in lower panel omitted on 15c and 50c.

Arms — A42

Edward VII — A43

1910 **Wmk. 3**

Ordinary Paper

137 A42 1c black 3.25 .35
138 A42 2c brown 3.25 .20
139 A42 3c green 3.50 .20
140 A42 4c ol grn & rose 4.25 .20
141 A43 5c gray & rose 3.25 *3.50*
142 A42 6c carmine 2.75 .20
143 A42 8c brown orange 3.50 *1.50*
144 A43 12c gray 2.40 *3.25*
145 A42 15c ultramarine 19.00 .20

Chalky Paper

146 A43 25c blk & scar, *yel* 2.50 *15.00*
147 A43 50c dull vio & blk 2.50 *22.50*
148 A43 1r blk, *green* 8.00 *15.00*
149 A43 2r50c blk & car, *bl* 16.00 *87.50*
150 A43 5r grn & car, *yel* 35.00 *125.00*
151 A43 10r grn & car, *grn* 110.00 *225.00*
Nos. 137-151 (15) 219.15 *499.60*

Numerals of 12c, 25c and 10r of type A43 are in color on plain tablet.
See Nos. 161-178.

King George V — A44

Die I

For description of dies I and II see Dies of British Colonial Stamps in the Introduction.
Numeral tablet of 5c, 50c, 1r, 2.50r and 5r of type A44 has lined background with colorless denomination.

1912-22 **Wmk. 3**

Ordinary Paper

152 A44 5c gray & rose 2.10 *4.25*
153 A44 12c gray 5.00 1.10

Chalky Paper

154 A44 25c blk & red, *yel* .50 1.75
a. 25c gray black & red, *yellow*, Die II .90 *17.50*
155 A44 50c dull vio & blk 50.00 *92.50*
156 A44 1r black, *emerald*, die II 2.75 *8.50*
a. 1r black, *emer*, olive back, die I ('21) 9.25 *60.00*
b. blk, *bl grn*, olive back, die I 4.25 *19.00*
157 A44 2r50c blk & red, *bl* 22.50 *62.50*
158 A44 5r grn & red, *yel* 100.00 *150.00*
a. Die II ('22) 55.00 *175.00*
159 A44 10r grn & red, *emer*, die II ('21) 35.00 *125.00*
a. 10r grn & red, *bl grn*, olive back, die I 1,000.
b. 10r green & red, *emer*, die I 50.00 *150.00*
c. 10r grn & red, *emer*, olive back, die I 87.50 *175.00*
d. 10r grn & red, *grn*, die I 75.00 *175.00*

Surface-colored Paper

160 A44 25c blk & red, *yel* ('16) .50 *14.50*
Nos. 152-160 (9) 218.35 *460.10*

1921-26 **Wmk. 4**

Ordinary Paper

161 A42 1c black 1.25 1.25
162 A42 2c brown 1.25 .20
163 A42 2c violet, *yel* ('25) 1.10 .35
164 A42 3c green ('25) 3.25 1.40
165 A42 4c ol grn & rose 1.75 *2.10*
166 A42 4c green 1.25 .20
167 A42 4c brown ('25) 3.25 1.90
168 A42 6c rose red 15.00 8.00
169 A42 6c violet 1.50 .20
170 A42 8c brown org ('25) 2.75 *19.00*
171 A42 10c gray ('22) 2.50 *4.25*
172 A42 10c rose red ('25) 4.75 1.90
173 A42 12c rose red 1.90 .50
174 A42 12c gray ('25) 2.10 *4.25*
175 A42 15c ultramarine 7.00 6.00
176 A42 15c dull blue ('25) 1.75 .25
177 A42 20c ultra ('22) 2.40 .95
178 A42 20c dull vio ('25) 10.50 *12.50*
Nos. 161-178 (18) 65.25 *65.20*

Ornaments in lower panel omitted on #171-178.
For surcharges see Nos. 201-203.

Die II

1922-34

Ordinary Paper

179 A44 1c black .95 *1.50*
180 A44 2c brown .90 .20
181 A44 3c green .90 .50
182 A44 4c olive grn & red ('27) .70 .35
a. Die I ('32) 7.50 *50.00*
183 A44 4c green, die I ('33) 7.00 *.55*
184 A44 5c gray & car 1.10 .20
a. Die I ('32) 7.50 7.50
185 A44 6c olive brn ('28) 1.50 .70
186 A44 8c orange .90 *12.50*
187 A44 10c rose red ('26) 1.50 .20
a. Die I ('32) 7.50 *10.00*
188 A44 12c gray, small "c" ('22) 1.75 *17.00*
189 A44 12c gray, "c" larger & thinner ('34) 6.25 .20
190 A44 12c rose red .35 *4.25*
191 A44 15c dk blue ('28) 1.25 .20
192 A44 20c dull vio .80 .50
193 A44 20c dk blue ('34) 15.00 1.00
a. Die I ('27) 12.00 1.10
194 A44 25c black & red, *yel* .35 .20
a. Die I ('32) 3.25 *40.00*

Chalky Paper

195 A44 50c dull vio & blk 9.25 4.25
196 A44 1r blk, *emerald* 4.50 .60
a. Die I ('32) 20.00 *40.00*
197 A44 2r50c blk & red, *bl* 25.00 7.50
198 A44 5r green & red, *yel* 35.00 *80.00*
199 A44 10r green & red, *emer* ('28) 87.50 *210.00*
Nos. 179-199 (21) 202.45 *342.40*

A45

1924

200 A45 50r lilac & green 850.00 *2,300.*

Nos. 166, 173, 177 Surcharged

1925

201 A42 3c on 4c green 3.50 *4.75*
202 A42 10c on 12c rose red .35 *.60*
203 A42 15c on 20c ultra .65 .60
Nos. 201-203 (3) 4.50 5.95

Common Design Types pictured following the introduction.

Silver Jubilee Issue

Common Design Type

1935, May 6 **Engr.** ***Perf. 13½x14***

204 CD301 5c gray black & ultra .50 .20
205 CD301 12c indigo & green 5.00 .20
206 CD301 20c blue & brown 6.50 .25
207 CD301 1r brt vio & indigo 32.50 *57.50*
Nos. 204-207 (4) 44.50 58.15
Set, never hinged 60.00

Coronation Issue

Common Design Type

1937, May 12 **Wmk. 4** ***Perf. 13½x14***

208 CD302 5c dark purple .20 .20
209 CD302 12c carmine .20 .20
210 CD302 20c bright ultra .25 .25
Nos. 208-210 (3) .65 .65
Set, never hinged 1.60

King George VI — A46

1938-43 **Typo.** ***Perf. 14***

211 A46 2c gray .20 .20
a. Perf. 15x14 ('43) .85 .20
212 A46 3c rose vio & car 1.50 1.40
213 A46 4c green .70 *1.40*
214 A46 5c violet 1.60 .55
a. Perf. 15x14 ('43) 50.00 .20
215 A46 10c carmine 1.60 .20
a. Perf. 15x14 ('43) 30.00 .60
216 A46 12c salmon pink .70 .20
a. Perf. 15x14 ('43) 50.00 .60
217 A46 20c blue .70 .20
218 A46 25c maroon 3.25 .20
219 A46 1r brown black 11.00 *1.40*
220 A46 2.50r pale violet 18.00 8.75
221 A46 5r olive green 19.00 17.00
222 A46 10r rose violet 7.25 *22.50*
Nos. 211-222 (12) 65.50 54.00
Set, never hinged 110.00

Catalogue values for unused stamps in this section, from this point to the end of the section, are for Never Hinged items.

Peace Issue

Common Design Type

Perf. 13½x14

1946, Nov. 20 **Engr.** **Wmk. 4**

223 CD303 5c lilac .20 .20
224 CD303 20c deep blue .20 .20

"Post Office" Stamp of 1847 — A47

1948, Mar. 22 ***Perf. 11½***

225 A47 5c red vio & orange .20 .20
226 A47 12c green & orange .20 .20
227 A47 20c blue & dp blue .20 .20
228 A47 1r lt red brn & dp blue .35 .35
Nos. 225-228 (4) .95 .95

Cent. of the 1st Mauritius postage stamps.

Silver Wedding Issue

Common Design Types

1948, Oct. 25 **Photo.** ***Perf. 14x14½***

229 CD304 5c violet .25 .25

Perf. 11½x11

Engraved; Name Typographed

230 CD305 10r lilac rose 12.00 27.50

UPU Issue

Common Design Types

Engr.; Name Typo. on 20c, 35c

Perf. 13½, 11x11½

1949, Oct. 10 **Wmk. 4**

231 CD306 12c rose carmine .75 .70
232 CD307 20c indigo 1.75 1.50
233 CD308 35c rose violet .75 .70
234 CD309 1r sepia .75 .25
Nos. 231-234 (4) 4.00 3.15

Sugar Factory — A48

Aloe Plant — A49

Designs: 2c, Grand Port. 4c, Tamarind Falls. 5c, Rempart Mountain. 10c, Transporting cane. 12c, Map and dodo. 20c, "Paul et Virginie." 25c, Statue of Mahe La Bourdonnais. 35c, Government House. 50c, Pieter Both Mountain. 1r, Sambar. 2.50r, Port Louis. 5r, Beach scene. 10r, Arms.

Perf. 13½x14½, 14½x13½

1950, July 1 **Photo.**

235 A48 1c red violet .25 .55
236 A48 2c cerise .25 .25
237 A49 3c yel green .70 *2.75*
238 A49 4c green .25 *1.40*
239 A48 5c greenish blue .25 .25
240 A48 10c red .30 *.75*
241 A48 12c olive green 1.50 *2.25*
242 A49 20c brt ultra .70 .25
243 A49 25c vio brown 1.50 .45
244 A48 35c rose violet .30 .25
245 A49 50c emerald 2.25 .55
246 A48 1r sepia 4.75 .25
247 A48 2.50r orange 14.00 6.75
248 A48 5r red brown 17.00 15.00
249 A48 10r gray blue 17.00 *20.00*
Nos. 235-249 (15) 61.00 51.70

Coronation Issue

Common Design Type

1953, June 2 **Engr.** ***Perf. 13½x13***

250 CD312 10c dk green & black 1.00 .25

Sugar Factory — A50

Tamarind Falls — A51

Designs: 2c, Grand Port. 3c, Aloe plant. 5c, Rempart Mountain. 15c, Museum, Mahebourg. 20c, Statue of Mahe La Bourdonnais. 25c, "Paul et Virginie." 35c, Government House. 50c, Pieter Both Mountain. 60c, Map and dodo. 1r, Sambar. 2.50r, Port Louis. 5r, Beach scene. 10r, Arms.

Perf. 13½x14½, 14½x13½

1953-54 **Photo.** **Wmk. 4**

251 A50 2c rose car ('54) .30 .25
252 A51 3c yel green ('54) .35 .25
253 A50 4c red violet .30 *.60*
254 A50 5c grnsh blue ('54) .30 .25
255 A51 10c dk green .30 .25
256 A50 15c scarlet .30 .25
257 A51 20c violet brown .30 .25
a. Imperf., pair
258 A51 25c brt ultra 1.60 .25
259 A50 35c rose vio ('54) .30 .25
260 A51 50c emerald .75 .75
261 A50 60c gray grn ('54) 12.00 .25
262 A50 1r sepia .35 .25
a. Imperf., pair
263 A50 2.50r orange ('54) 16.00 9.25
264 A50 5r red brn ('54) 16.00 9.25
265 A50 10r gray blue ('54) 16.00 1.25
Nos. 251-265 (15) 65.15 23.60

See Nos. 273-275.

King George III and Queen Elizabeth II — A52

Wmk. 314

1961, Jan. 11 **Litho.** ***Perf. 13½***

266 A52 10c dk red & dk brown .20 .20
267 A52 20c lt blue & dk blue .20 .20
268 A52 35c org yel & brown .30 .30
269 A52 1r yel green & dk brn .60 .60
Nos. 266-269 (4) 1.30 1.30

Sesquicentenary of postal service under British administration.

Freedom from Hunger Issue

Common Design Type

1963, June 4 **Photo.** ***Perf. 14x14½***

270 CD314 60c lilac .50 .50

Red Cross Centenary Issue
Common Design Type

1963, Sept. 2 — Litho. — *Perf. 13*

No.	Type	Value	Color	Unused	Used
271	CD315	10c	black & red	.20	.20
272	CD315	60c	ultra & red	.65	.65

Types of 1953-54

Perf. 14½x13½, 13½x14½

1963-64 — Photo. — Wmk. 314

No.	Type	Value	Color	Unused	Used
273	A51	10c	dark green ('64)	.50	.30
274	A50	60c	gray green ('64)	2.75	.30
275	A50	2.50r	orange	9.75	*11.00*
			Nos. 273-275 (3)	13.00	11.60

Gray White-Eye — A53

Birds of Mauritius: 3c, Rodriguez fody. 4c, Olive white-eye. 5c, Mauritius paradise flycatcher. 10c, Mauritius fody. 15c, Rose-ringed parakeet. 20c, Cuckoo shrike. 25c, Mauritian kestrel. 35c, Pink pigeon. 50c, Mauritius olivaceous bulbul. 60c, Mauritius blue pigeon. 1r, Dodo. 2.50r, Rodriguez solitaire. 5r, Van den Broeck's red rail. 10r, Broad-billed Mauritian parrot.

Wmk. 314

1965, Mar. 16 — Photo. — *Perf. 14½*

Birds in Natural Colors

No.	Type	Value	Color	Unused	Used
276	A53	2c	brt yel & brn	.50	.30
a.			Gray (leg, etc.) omitted	210.00	
277	A53	3c	brn & dk brn	1.00	.30
a.			Black (eye, beak) omitted	210.00	
278	A53	4c	dl rose lil & blk	.35	.30
a.			Rose lilac omitted	55.00	
279	A53	5c	gray & ultra	3.25	.30
a.			Wmkd. sideways ('66)	.25	.25
280	A53	10c	dl grn & dk brn	.35	.30
281	A53	15c	lt gray & dk brn	2.10	.30
a.			Carmine (beak) omitted	160.00	
282	A53	20c	pale yel & dk brown	2.10	.30
283	A53	25c	gray & brown	2.10	.30
284	A53	35c	vio bl & blk	2.75	.30
a.			Wmkd. sideways ('67)	.40	.35
285	A53	50c	pale yel & blk	.50	.50
286	A53	60c	pale cit & brn	.60	.30
287	A53	1r	lt yel grn & blk	5.50	.30
a.			Pale gray (ground) omitted	250.00	
b.			Pale orange omitted	175.00	
288	A53	2.50r	pale grn & brn	4.75	6.00
289	A53	5r	pale blue & blk	14.00	9.00
290	A53	10r	pale grn & ultra	26.00	22.50
			Nos. 276-290 (15)	65.85	41.30

On No. 278 the background was printed in two colors. The rose lilac tint is omitted on No. 278a.

See #327-332. For overprints see #306-320.

ITU Issue
Common Design Type

Perf. 11x11½

1965, May 17 — Litho. — Wmk. 314

No.	Type	Value	Color	Unused	Used
291	CD317	10c	dp org & apple grn	.30	.25
292	CD317	60c	yellow & violet	.90	.40

Intl. Cooperation Year Issue
Common Design Type

1965, Oct. 25 — *Perf. 14½*

No.	Type	Value	Color	Unused	Used
293	CD318	10c	lt green & claret	.20	.20
294	CD318	60c	lt violet & green	.45	.45

Churchill Memorial Issue
Common Design Type

1966, Jan. 24 — Photo. — *Perf. 14*

Design in Black, Gold and Carmine Rose

No.	Type	Value	Color	Unused	Used
295	CD319	2c	brt blue	.40	.40
296	CD319	10c	green	.40	.40
297	CD319	60c	brown	1.00	1.00
298	CD319	1r	violet	2.25	2.25
			Nos. 295-298 (4)	4.05	4.05

UNESCO Anniversary Issue
Common Design Type

1966, Dec. 1 — Litho. — *Perf. 14*

No.	Type	Value	Color	Unused	Used
299	CD323	5c	"Education"	.35	.35
300	CD323	10c	"Science"	.35	.35
301	CD323	60c	"Culture"	1.40	.80
			Nos. 299-301 (3)	2.10	1.50

Red-Tailed Tropic Bird — A54

Birds of Mauritius: 10c, Rodriguez bush warbler. 60c, Newton's parakeet. 1r, Mauritius swiftlet.

1967, Sept. 1 — Photo. — *Perf. 14½*

No.	Type	Value	Color	Unused	Used
302	A54	2c	lt ultra & multi	.40	.40
303	A54	10c	emerald & multi	.40	.40
304	A54	60c	salmon & multi	1.25	1.25
305	A54	1r	yellow & multi	2.40	2.40
			Nos. 302-305 (4)	4.45	4.45

Attainment of self-government, Sept. 1, 1967.

Bird Issue of 1965-67 and Type Overprinted: "SELF GOVERNMENT 1967"

1967, Dec. 1 — Photo. — Wmk. 314

No.	Type	Value	Color	Unused	Used
306	A53	2c	multicolored	.25	.25
307	A53	3c	multicolored	.25	.25
308	A53	4c	multicolored	.25	.25
309	A53	5c	multicolored	.25	.25
310	A53	10c	multicolored	.25	.25
311	A53	15c	multicolored	.25	.25
312	A53	20c	multicolored	.25	.25
313	A53	25c	multicolored	.25	.25
314	A53	35c	multicolored	.25	.25
315	A53	50c	multicolored	.40	.25
316	A53	60c	multicolored	.45	.30
317	A53	1r	multicolored	.75	.45
318	A53	2.50r	multicolored	2.10	2.25
319	A53	5r	multicolored	4.25	4.25
320	A53	10r	multicolored	8.00	8.50
			Nos. 306-320 (15)	18.20	18.25

5c, 10c, 35c watermarked sideways.

Independent State

Flag of Mauritius — A55

Designs: 3c, 20c, 1r, Dodo emerging from egg and coat of arms.

Perf. 13½x13

1968, Mar. 12 — Litho. — Unwmk.

No.	Type	Value	Color	Unused	Used
321	A55	2c	brt violet & multi	.20	.20
322	A55	3c	red brown & multi	.20	.20
323	A55	15c	brown & multi	.20	.20
324	A55	20c	multicolored	.50	.20
325	A55	60c	dk green & multi	.65	.40
326	A55	1r	brt violet & multi	1.00	.65
			Nos. 321-326 (6)	2.75	1.85

Independence of Mauritius.

Bird Type of 1965 in Changed Background Colors

Wmk. 314

1968, July 12 — Photo. — *Perf. 14½*

Birds in Natural Colors

No.	Type	Value	Color	Unused	Used
327	A53	2c	lemon & brown	.30	.25
328	A53	3c	ultra & dk brown	.30	.25
329	A53	15c	tan & dk brown	.90	.25
330	A53	20c	dull yel & dk brn	1.40	.25
331	A53	60c	pink & black	3.50	2.50
332	A53	1r	rose lilac & black	5.50	4.50
			Nos. 327-332 (6)	11.90	8.00

Domingue Rescuing Paul and Virginie — A56

Designs: 15c, Paul and Virginie crossing river, vert. 50c, La Bourdonnais visiting Madame de 1a Tour. 60c, Paul and Virginie, vert. 1r, Departure of Virginie for Europe. 2.50r, Bernardin de St. Pierre, vert. The designs are from old prints illustrating "Paul et Virginie."

Perf. 13½

1968, Dec. 2 — Unwmk. — Litho.

No.	Type	Value	Color	Unused	Used
333	A56	2c	multicolored	.25	.25
334	A56	15c	multicolored	.25	.25
335	A56	50c	multicolored	.30	.30
336	A56	60c	multicolored	.40	.40
337	A56	1r	multicolored	.65	.65
338	A56	2.50r	multicolored	1.75	1.75
			Nos. 333-338 (6)	3.60	3.60

Bicent. of the visit of Bernardin de St. Pierre (1737-1814), author of "Paul et Virginie."

Batardé Fish A57

Marine Life: 3c, Red reef crab. 4c, Episcopal miter shell. 5c, Bourse fish. 10c, Starfish. 15c, Sea urchin. 20c, Fiddler crab. 25c, Spiny shrimp. 30c, Single and double harp shells. 35c, Argonaut shell. 40c, Nudibranch (sea-slug). 50c, Violet and orange spider shells. 60c, Blue marlin. 75c, Conus clytospira. 1r, Dorad. 2.50r, Spiny lobster. 5r, Sacré chien rouge fish. 10r, Moonfish.

Wmk. 314 Sideways (#339-344, 351-352), others Upright

1969, Mar. 12 — Photo. — *Perf. 14*

No.	Type	Value	Color	Unused	Used
339	A57	2c	pink & multi	.30	.30
340	A57	3c	yellow & multi	.30	.30
341	A57	4c	multicolored	.30	.30
342	A57	5c	lt blue & multi	.30	.30
343	A57	10c	salmon & multi	.30	.30
344	A57	15c	pale blue & multi	.30	.30
345	A57	20c	pale gray & multi	.30	.30
346	A57	25c	multicolored	.30	.30
347	A57	30c	multicolored	.30	.40
348	A57	35c	multicolored	.30	.40
349	A57	40c	tan & multi	.40	.50
350	A57	50c	lt vio & multi	.50	.60
351	A57	60c	ultra & multi	.70	.75
352	A57	75c	lemon & multi	.85	.85
353	A57	1r	cream & multi	.90	1.10
354	A57	2.50r	lt vio & multi	3.75	4.75
355	A57	5r	multicolored	7.75	10.00
356	A57	10r	multicolored	13.50	17.50
			Nos. 339-356 (18)	31.35	39.25

For overprints see Nos. 368-369.

Wmk. 314 Upright (#339a-344a, 351a-352a), others Sideways

1972-74

No.	Type	Value	Color	Unused	Used
339a	A57	2c	multi ('74)	1.00	1.00
340a	A57	3c	multi ('74)	1.00	1.00
341a	A57	4c	multi ('74)	1.00	1.00
342a	A57	5c	multi ('74)	1.00	1.00
343a	A57	10c	multicolored	1.00	1.00
344a	A57	15c	multi ('74)	1.00	1.00
345a	A57	20c	multicolored	1.00	1.00
346a	A57	25c	multi ('73)	1.00	1.00
347a	A57	30c	multicolored	1.25	1.00
348a	A57	35c	multicolored	1.50	1.25
349a	A57	40c	multicolored	1.50	1.50
350a	A57	50c	multi ('73)	1.50	1.50
351a	A57	60c	multi ('74)	2.00	1.50
352a	A57	75c	multicolored	2.50	2.00
353a	A57	1r	multicolored	3.00	2.50
354a	A57	2.50r	multi ('73)	7.50	7.00
355a	A57	5r	multi ('73)	15.00	12.50
356a	A57	10r	multicolored	29.00	25.00
			Nos. 339a-356a (18)	72.75	63.75

1975-77 — Wmk. 373

No.	Type	Value	Color	Unused	Used
339b	A57	2c	multi ('77)	.75	.75
340b	A57	3c	multi ('77)	.75	.75
341b	A57	4c	multi ('77)	.75	.75
342b	A57	5c	multicolored	.75	.75
344b	A57	15c	multicolored	.75	.75
345b	A57	20c	multi ('76)	.75	.75
346b	A57	25c	multicolored	.95	.75
347b	A57	30c	multicolored	1.10	.95
348b	A57	35c	multi ('76)	1.10	.95
349b	A57	40c	multi ('76)	1.10	1.10
350b	A57	50c	multi ('76)	1.50	1.10
351b	A57	60c	multi ('77)	1.90	1.50
352b	A57	75c	multi ('77)	1.90	1.90
353b	A57	1r	multi ('76)	3.00	2.75
354b	A57	2.50r	multi ('77)	12.50	7.50
355b	A57	5r	multicolored	21.00	16.00
356b	A57	10r	multicolored	50.00	32.50
			Nos. 339b-356b (17)	100.55	71.50

Gandhi as Law Student in London A58

Portraits of Gandhi: 15c, as stretcher bearer during Zulu rebellion. 50c, as member of non-violent movement in South Africa (Satyagrahi). 60c, wearing Indian garment at No. 10 Downing Street, London. 1r, wearing turban in Mauritius, 1901. 2.50r, as old man.

1969, July 1 — Litho. — *Perf. 13½*

No.	Type	Value	Color	Unused	Used
357	A58	2c	dull org & multi	.30	.30
358	A58	15c	brt blue & multi	.30	.30
359	A58	50c	multicolored	.30	.30
360	A58	60c	brick red & multi	.40	.40
361	A58	1r	multicolored	.75	.75
362	A58	2.50r	olive & multi	1.90	1.90
a.			Souvenir sheet of 6, #357-362	7.50	7.50
			Nos. 357-362 (6)	3.95	3.95

Mohandas K. Gandhi (1869-1948), leader in India's struggle for independence.

Vertical Cane Crusher (19th Century) A59

Dr. Charles Telfair (1778-1833) A60

Designs: 15c, The Frangourinier, 18th century cane crusher. 60c, Beau Rivage sugar factory, 1867, painting by Numa Desjardin. 1r, Mon Desert-Alma sugar factory, 1969.

Perf. 11x11½, 11½x11

1969, Dec. 22 — Photo. — Wmk. 314

No.	Type	Value	Color	Unused	Used
363	A59	2c	multicolored	.20	.20
364	A59	15c	multicolored	.20	.20
365	A59	60c	multicolored	.20	.20
366	A59	1r	multicolored	.30	.30
367	A60	2.50r	multicolored	.60	.60
a.			Souvenir sheet of 5	2.75	2.75
			Nos. 363-367 (5)	1.50	1.50

150th anniv. of Telfair's improvements of the sugar industry.

No. 367a contains one each of Nos. 363-367. The 2.50r in the sheet is imperf., the others are perf. 11x11½.

Nos. 351 and 353 Overprinted: "EXPO '70 / OSAKA"

1970, Apr. 7 — *Perf. 14*

No.	Type	Value	Color	Unused	Used
368	A57	60c	ultra & multi	.25	.25
369	A57	1r	cream & multi	.40	.40

EXPO '70 Intl. Exhib., Osaka, Japan, Mar. 15-Sept. 13.

Lufthansa Plane over Mauritius — A61

25c, Brabant Hotel, Morne Beach, horiz.

1970, May 2 Litho. *Perf. 14*

370 A61 25c multicolored .20 .20
371 A61 50c multicolored .40 .40

Lufthansa's inaugural flight from Mauritius to Frankfurt, Germany, May 2, 1970.

Lenin as Student, by V. Tsigal — A62

Design: 75c, Bust of Lenin.

1970, May 15 Photo. *Perf. 12x11½*

372 A62 15c dk slate blue & sil .20 .20
373 A62 75c dk brown & gold .65 .65

Birth cent. of Lenin (1870-1924), Russian communist leader.

UN Emblem and Symbols of UN Activities — A63

1970, Oct. 24 Litho. *Perf. 14*

374 A63 10c blue black & multi .20 .20
375 A63 60c blue black & multi .40 .40

25th anniversary of the United Nations.

Mauritius No. 2, and Post Office before 1870 A64

Designs: 15c, General Post Office Building, 1870-1970. 50c, Mauritius mail coach, 1870. 75c, Port Louis harbor, 1970. 2.50r, Arrival of Pierre André de Suffren de St. Tropez in Port Louis harbor, 1783.

1970, Oct. 15 Litho. *Perf. 14*

376 A64 5c multicolored .20 .20
377 A64 15c multicolored .20 .20
378 A64 50c multicolored .20 .20
379 A64 75c multicolored .30 .30
380 A64 2.50r multicolored 1.00 1.00
a. Souvenir sheet of 5 5.00 5.00
Nos. 376-380 (5) 1.90 1.90

Centenary of the General Post Office and to show the improvements of Port Louis harbor. No. 380a contains one each of Nos. 376-380 and a label showing map of Mauritius.

Waterfall A65

15c, Trois Mamelles Mountains. 60c, Beach scene with sailboats. 2.50r, Marine life.

1971, Apr. 12 Litho. *Perf. 14*

381 A65 10c multicolored .20 .20
382 A65 15c multicolored .20 .20
383 A65 60c multicolored .40 .40
384 A65 2.50r multicolored 1.90 1.90
Nos. 381-384 (4) 2.70 2.70

Tourist publicity. Each stamp has a different 6-line message printed in black on back.

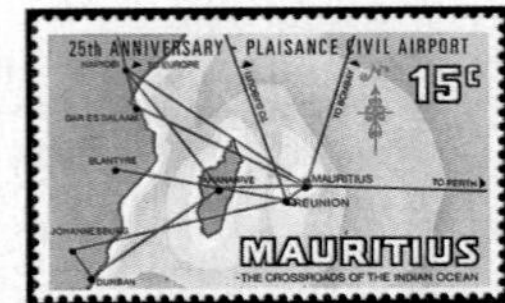

Mauritius at Crossroads of Indian Ocean — A66

60c, Plane at Plaisance Airport. 1r, Stewardesses on plane ramp. 2.50r, Roland Garros' airplane, Choisy Airfield, 1937.

1971, Oct. 23 Wmk. 314 *Perf. 14½*

385 A66 15c multicolored .25 .25
386 A66 60c multicolored .55 .55
387 A66 1r multicolored .65 .65
388 A66 2.50r multicolored 2.75 2.75
Nos. 385-388 (4) 4.20 4.20

25th anniversary of Plaisance Civil Airport.

Princess Margaret Orthopedic Center — A67

75c, Operating room, National Hospital.

1971, Nov. 2 *Perf. 14x14½*

389 A67 10c multicolored .20 .20
390 A67 75c multicolored .30 .30

3rd Commonwealth Medical Conf., Nov. 1971.

Elizabeth II and Prince Philip — A68

Design: 2.50r, Queen Elizabeth II, vert.

1972, Mar. Litho. *Perf. 14½*

391 A68 15c brown & multi .30 .30
392 A68 2.50r ultra & multi 2.75 2.75

Visit of Elizabeth II and Prince Philip.

Port Louis Theater and Masks A69

Design: 1r, Interior view and masks of Comedy and Tragedy.

1972, June 26

393 A69 10c brown & multi .25 .25
394 A69 1r multicolored .45 .45

Sesquicentennial of Port Louis Theater.

Pirate Dhow Entering Tamarind River A70

Perf. 14x14½, 14½x14

1972, Nov. 17 Litho.

395 A70 15c shown .30 .30
396 A70 60c Treasure chest, vert. .85 .85
397 A70 1r Lememe and brig Hirondelle, vert. 2.00 2.00
398 A70 2.50r Robert Surcouf 7.00 7.00
Nos. 395-398 (4) 10.15 10.15

Pirates and privateers.

Mauritius University — A71

60c, Tea development plant. 1r, Bank of Mauritius.

1973, Apr. 10 *Perf. 14½*

399 A71 15c green & multi .20 .20
400 A71 60c yellow & multi .20 .20
401 A71 1r red & multi .30 .30
Nos. 399-401 (3) .70 .70

5th anniversary of independence.

OCAM Emblem A72

Design: 2.50r, Handshake, map of Africa; inscriptions in French, vert.

1973, Apr. 25

402 A72 10c multicolored .20 .20
403 A72 2.50r lt blue & multi .60 .60

Conference of the Organisation Commune Africaine, Malgache et Mauricienne (OCAM), Mauritius, Apr. 25-May 6.

WHO Emblem A73

Perf. 14½x14

1973, Nov. 20 Wmk. 314

404 A73 1r green & multi .40 .40

25th anniv. of WHO.

Meteorological Station, Vacoas — A74

1973, Nov. 27

405 A74 75c multicolored .40 .40

Cent. of intl. meteorological cooperation.

Surcouf and Capture of the "Kent" A75

1974, Mar. 21 Litho. *Perf. 14½x14*

406 A75 60c sepia & multi 1.25 1.25

Bicentenary of the birth of Robert Surcouf (1773-1827), French privateer.

Philibert Commerson and Bougainvillaea A76

1974, Apr. 18 *Perf. 14*

407 A76 2.50r slate grn & multi .70 .70

Philibert Commerson (1727-1773), French physician and naturalist.

FAO Emblem, Woman Milking Cow A77

1974, Oct. 23 *Perf. 14½*

408 A77 60c multicolored .35 .35

8th FAO Regional Conference, Aug. 1-17.

Mail Train and UPU Emblem A78

Design: 1r, New General Post Office Building, Port Louis, and UPU emblem.

1974, Dec. 4 Litho. *Perf. 14½*

409 A78 15c multicolored .30 .30
410 A78 1r multicolored .80 .80

Centenary of Universal Postal Union.

Cottage Life, by F. Leroy A79

Paintings: 60c, Milk Seller, by A. Richard, vert. 1r, Entrance to Port Louis Market, by Thuillier. 2.50r, Washerwomen, by Max Boullé, vert.

1975, Mar. 6 Wmk. 373

411 A79 15c multicolored .25 .25
412 A79 60c multicolored .40 .40
413 A79 1r multicolored .65 .65
414 A79 2.50r multicolored 1.50 1.50
Nos. 411-414 (4) 2.80 2.80

Artistic views of life on Mauritius.

Mace, Map and Arms of Mauritius, Association Emblem — A80

1975, Nov. 21 Litho. Wmk. 373

415 A80 75c multicolored .60 .60

French-speaking Parliamentary Association, conf.

Woman and Aladdin's Lamp A81

1975, Dec. 5 ***Perf. 14½***
416 A81 2.50r multicolored .75 .75

International Women's Year.

Parched Land A82

Drought in Africa: 60c, Map of Africa, carcass and desert, vert.

1976, Feb. 26 **Litho.** **Wmk. 373**
417 A82 50c vermilion & multi .20 .20
418 A82 60c blue & multi .30 .30

Pierre Loti, 1953-1970 — A83

Mail Carriers: 15c, Secunder, 1907. 50c, Hindoostan, 1842. 60c, St. Geran, 1740. 2.50r, Maen, 1638.

1976, July 2 **Litho.** **Wmk. 373**
419 A83 10c multicolored .65 .65
420 A83 15c multicolored .65 .65
421 A83 50c multicolored .95 .95
422 A83 60c multicolored 1.25 1.25
423 A83 2.50r multicolored 5.50 5.50
a. Souvenir sheet of 5, #419-423 13.50 13.50
Nos. 419-423 (5) 9.00 9.00

Flame, and "Hindi Carried Across the Sea" A84

Designs: 75c, like 10c. 1.20r, Flame and tablet with Hindi inscription.

1976, Aug. 28 ***Perf. 14½x14***
424 A84 10c multicolored .20 .20
425 A84 75c lt blue & multi .20 .20
426 A84 1.20r multicolored .35 .35
Nos. 424-426 (3) .75 .75

2nd World Hindi Convention.

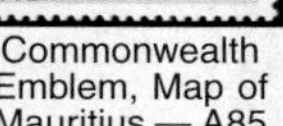

Commonwealth Emblem, Map of Mauritius — A85

King Priest and Steatite Pectoral — A86

2.50r, Commonwealth emblem twice.

1976, Sept. 22 **Litho.** ***Perf. 14x14½***
427 A85 1r multicolored .40 .40
428 A85 2.50r multicolored .90 .90

22nd Commonwealth Parliamentary Association Conference, Mauritius, Sept. 17-30.

1976, Dec. 15 **Wmk. 373** ***Perf. 14***

Designs: 1r, House with well, and goblet. 2.50r, Terracotta goddess and necklace.

429 A86 60c multicolored .35 .35
430 A86 1r multicolored .75 .75
431 A86 2.50r multicolored 1.75 1.75
Nos. 429-431 (3) 2.85 2.85

UNESCO campaign to save Mohenjo-Daro excavations.

Sega Dance A87

1977, Jan. 20 **Litho.** ***Perf. 13***
432 A87 1r multicolored .50 .50

2nd World Black and African Festival, Lagos, Nigeria, Jan. 15-Feb. 12.

Elizabeth II at Mauritius Legislative Assembly — A88

Designs: 75c, Queen holding scepter and orb. 5r, Presentation of scepter and orb.

1977, Feb. 7 ***Perf. 14½x14***
433 A88 50c multicolored .20 .20
434 A88 75c multicolored .20 .20
435 A88 5r multicolored 1.10 1.10
Nos. 433-435 (3) 1.50 1.50

25th anniv. of the reign of Elizabeth II.

Hugonia Tomentosa — A89

Flowers: 1r, Oehna mauritiana, vert. 1.50r, Dombeya acuntangula. 5r, Trochetia blackburniana, vert.

1977, Sept. 22 **Wmk. 373** ***Perf. 14***
436 A89 20c multicolored .20 .20
437 A89 1r multicolored .40 .40
438 A89 1.50r multicolored .60 .60
439 A89 5r multicolored 1.75 1.75
a. Souvenir sheet of 4, #436-439 5.00 5.00
Nos. 436-439 (4) 2.95 2.95

Twin Otter of Air Mauritius — A90

Designs: 50c, Air Mauritius emblem (red-tailed tropic bird) and Twin Otter. 75c, Piper Navajo and Boeing 747. 5r, Air Mauritius Boeing 707 in flight.

1977, Oct. 31 **Litho.** ***Perf. 14½***
440 A90 25c multicolored .60 .60
441 A90 50c multicolored .90 .90
442 A90 75c multicolored 1.00 1.00
443 A90 5r multicolored 5.50 5.50
a. Souvenir sheet of 4, #440-443 12.00 12.00
Nos. 440-443 (4) 8.00 8.00

Air Mauritius International Inaugural Flight.

Mauritius, Portuguese Map, 1519 — A91

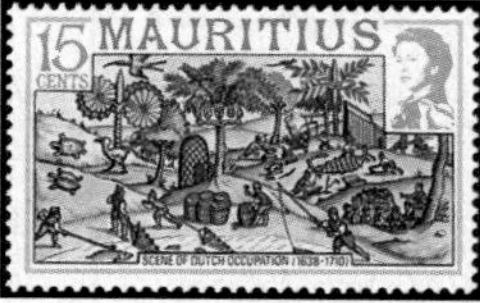

Dutch Occupation, 1638-1710 — A92

Designs: 20c, Mauritius, map by Van Keulen, c. 1700. 25c, 1st settlement of Rodrigues, 1708. 35c, Proclamation, arrival of French settlers, 1715. 50c, Construction of Port Louis, c. 1736. 60c, Pierre Poivre and nutmeg tree. 70c, Map by Belin, 1763. 75c, First coin minted in Mauritius, 1810. 90c, Naval battle of Grand Port, 1810. 1r, Landing of the British, Nov. 1810. 1.20r, Government House, c. 1840. 1.25r, Invitation with No. 1 and ball of Lady Gomm, 1847. 1.50r, Indian immigration in Mauritius, 1835. 2r, Champ de Mars race course, c. 1870. 3r, Place D'Armes, c. 1880. 5r, Postal card commemorating visit of Prince and Princess of Wales, 1901. 10r, Curepipe College, 1914. 15r, Raising flag of Mauritius, 1968. 25r, Raman Osman, first Governor General and Seewoosagur Ramgoolan, first Prime Minister.

1978, Mar. 12 **Wmk. 373** ***Perf. 13½***
444 A91 10c multicolored .25 .25
445 A92 15c multicolored .25 .25
446 A92 20c multicolored .25 .25
447 A91 25c multicolored .25 .25
448 A91 35c multicolored .25 .25
b. Perf. 14½, "1986" .25 .25
449 A92 50c multicolored .25 .25
450 A91 60c multicolored .35 .35
451 A92 70c multicolored .40 .35
452 A91 75c multicolored .45 .40
453 A92 90c multicolored .45 .40
454 A92 1r multicolored .45 .45
455 A92 1.20r multicolored .45 .45
456 A91 1.25r multicolored .45 .45
457 A92 1.50r multicolored .55 .60
458 A92 2r multicolored .75 .80
459 A92 3r multicolored 1.10 1.25
460 A92 5r multicolored 1.90 2.00
461 A92 10r multicolored 3.75 4.00
462 A91 15r multicolored 5.25 6.00
463 A92 25r multicolored 8.75 9.75
Nos. 444-463 (20) 26.55 28.75

Nos. 448, 452, 456, 458 reprinted inscribed 1983; Nos. 444, 447-449, 452, 454, 456, 460 reprinted inscribed 1985.

1985-89 **Wmk. 384** ***Perf. 14½***
446a A92 20c "1987" .20 .20
447a A91 25c "1987" .20 .20
448a A91 35c ('85) .20 .20
449a A92 50c ('85) .20 .20
452a A91 75c ('85) .20 .20
458a A92 2r "1987" .20 .20
459a A92 3r "1989" .40 .40
460a A92 5r "1989" .70 .70
463a A92 25r "1989" 3.45 3.45
Nos. 446a-463a (9) 5.75 5.75

Issued: 20c, 25c, 2r, 1/11/87; 3r-25r, 1/19/89.

Nos. 449a and 458a reprinted inscribed 1989.

Elizabeth II Coronation Anniv. Issue
Common Design Types
Souvenir Sheet

1978, Apr. 21 **Unwmk.** ***Perf. 15***
464 Sheet of 6 2.75 2.75
a. CD326 3r Antelope of Bohun .50 .50
b. CD327 3r Elizabeth II .50 .50
c. CD328 3r Dodo .50 .50

No. 464 contains 2 se-tenant strips of Nos. 464a-464c, separated by horizontal gutter with commemorative and descriptive inscriptions and showing central part of coronation procession with coach.

Dr. Fleming, WWI Casualty, Bacteria — A93

1r, Microscope & 1st mold growth, 1928. 1.50r, Penicillium notatum, close-up. 5r, Alexander Fleming & nurse administering penicillin.

Wmk. 373
1978, Aug. 3 **Litho.** ***Perf. 13½***
465 A93 20c multicolored .80 .80
466 A93 1r multicolored 1.60 1.60
467 A93 1.50r multicolored 2.75 2.75
468 A93 5r multicolored 3.75 3.75
a. Souvenir sheet of 4, #465-468 11.00 11.00
Nos. 465-468 (4) 8.90 8.90

Discovery of penicillin by Dr. Alexander Fleming, 50th anniversary.

Citrus Butterfly — A94

Wildlife Protection (Wildlife Fund Emblem and): 1r, Geckos. 1.50r, Flying foxes. 5r, Mauritius kestrels.

1978, Sept. 21 ***Perf. 13½x14***
469 A94 20c multicolored *4.00* *2.50*
470 A94 1r multicolored *3.50* *2.50*
471 A94 1.50r multicolored *3.50* *2.50*
472 A94 5r multicolored *18.50* *5.00*
a. Souvenir sheet of 4, #469-472 *110.00* *80.00*
Nos. 469-472 (4) *29.50* *12.50*

Le Reduit — A95

15c, Ornate table. 3r, Reduit gardens.

1978, Dec. 21 ***Perf. 14½x14***
473 A95 15c multicolored .20 .20
474 A95 75c multicolored .30 .30
475 A95 3r multicolored 1.00 1.00
Nos. 473-475 (3) 1.50 1.50

Reconstruction of Chateau Le Reduit, 200th anniversary.

Whitcomb, 1949 — A96

Locomotives: 1r, Sir William, 1922. 1.50r, Kitson, 1930. 2r, Garratt, 1927.

1979, Feb. 1 ***Perf. 14½***
476 A96 20c multicolored .25 .25
477 A96 1r multicolored .50 .50
478 A96 1.50r multicolored .95 .95
479 A96 2r multicolored 1.25 1.25
a. Souvenir sheet of 4, #476-479 5.25 5.25
Nos. 476-479 (4) 2.95 2.95

Father Laval and Crucifix — A97

Designs: 1.50r, Jacques Desire Laval. 5r, Father Laval's sarcophagus, horiz.

1979, Apr. 30 Wmk. 373 *Perf. 14*

480 A97 20c multicolored .20 .20
481 A97 1.50r multicolored .30 .30
482 A97 5r multicolored 1.00 1.00
a. Souvenir sheet of 3, #480-482 3.75 3.75
Nos. 480-482 (3) 1.50 1.50

Beatification of Father Laval (1803-1864), physician and missionary.

Souvenir Booklet

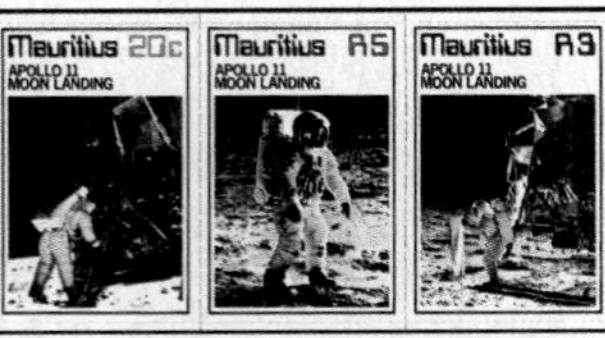

10th Anniv. of Apollo 11 Moon Landing — A98

Imperf. x Roulette 5

1979, July 20 Litho.

Self-adhesive

483 A98 Booklet of 9 8.00
a. 20c Astronaut and Lunar Module .20
b. 3r Neil Armstrong on moon .90
c. 5r Astronaut walking on moon 3.75
d. Bklt. pane of 3 (20c, 5r, 3r) 5.00
e. Bklt. pane of 6 (3 each 20c, 3r) 3.50

No. 483 contains 2 panes printed on peelable paper backing showing map of moon (d) and details of uniform and spacecraft (e).

Rowland Hill and Great Britain No. 23 — A99

1979, Aug. 29 *Perf. 14½*

Rowland Hill and: 2r, Mauritius No. 261. 3r, Mauritius No. 2. 5r, Mauritius No. 1.

484 A99 25c multicolored .20 .20
485 A99 2r multicolored .50 .50
486 A99 5r multicolored 1.25 1.25
Nos. 484-486 (3) 1.95 1.95

Souvenir Sheet

Perf. 14½

487 A99 3r multicolored 1.75 1.75

Sir Rowland Hill (1795-1879), originator of penny postage. No. 487 contains one stamp.

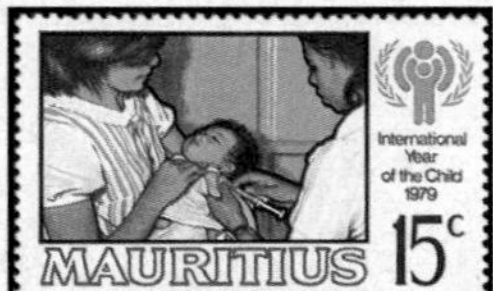

Infant Vaccination — A100

IYC Emblem and: 25c, Children playing. 1r, Coat of arms, vert. 1.50r, Children in laboratory. 3r, Teacher and student working lathe.

Wmk. 373

1979, Oct. 11 Litho. *Perf. 14*

488 A100 15c multicolored .20 .20
489 A100 25c multicolored .20 .20
490 A100 1r multicolored .25 .25
491 A100 1.50r multicolored .35 .35
492 A100 3r multicolored .70 .70
Nos. 488-492 (5) 1.70 1.70

International Year of the Child.

Lienard Obelisk — A101

Designs: 25c, Poivre Avenue, 1r, Pandanus. 2r, Giant water lilies, 5r, Mon Plaisir.

1980, Jan. 24 *Perf. 14x14½*

493 A101 20c multicolored .20 .20
494 A101 25c multicolored .20 .20
495 A101 1r multicolored .20 .20
496 A101 2r multicolored .40 .40
497 A101 5r multicolored 1.00 1.00
a. Souvenir sheet of 5, #493-497 4.25 4.25
Nos. 493-497 (5) 2.00 2.00

Pamplemousses Botanical Gardens.

"Emirne," 19th Century, London 1980 Emblem — A102

1980, May 6 Litho. *Perf. 14½*

498 A102 25c shown .25 .25
499 A102 1r Boissevain, 1930's .50 .50
500 A102 2r La Boudeuse, 18th cent. 1.00 1.00
501 A102 5r Sea Breeze, 19th cent. 2.25 2.25
Nos. 498-501 (4) 4.00 4.00

London 80 Intl. Stamp Exhib., May 6-14.

Helen Keller Reading Braille — A103

1980, June 27 Litho. *Perf. 14½*

502 A103 25c Blind men weaving baskets .25 .25
503 A103 1r Teacher and deaf girl .50 .50
504 A103 2.50r shown 1.25 1.25
505 A103 5r Keller graduating college 2.00 2.00
Nos. 502-505 (4) 4.00 4.00

Helen Keller (1880-1968), blind and deaf writer and lecturer.

Prime Minister Seewoosagur Ramgoolan, 80th Birthday — A104

Litho.; Gold Embossed

1980, Sept. 18 *Perf. 13½*

506 A104 15r multicolored 2.00 2.00

Mauritius Institute, Centenary — A105

1980, Oct. 1 Litho. *Perf. 13*

507 A105 25c shown .25 .25
508 A105 2r Rare Veda copy .50 .50
509 A105 2.50r Rare cone .60 .60
510 A105 5r Landscape, by Henri Harpignies 1.25 1.25
Nos. 507-510 (4) 2.60 2.60

Hibiscus Liliiflorus — A106 Arms of Curepipe — A107

1981, Jan. 15 Litho. *Perf. 14*

511 A106 25c shown .20 .20
512 A106 2r Erythrospermum monticolum .70 .70
513 A106 2.50r Chasalia boryana .90 .90
514 A106 5r Hibiscus columnaris 1.75 1.75
Nos. 511-514 (4) 3.55 3.55

Perf. 13½x13

1981, Apr. 10 Litho. Wmk. 373

Designs: City coats of arms.

515 A107 25c Beau-Bassin / Rose Hill .20 .20
516 A107 1.50r shown .30 .30
517 A107 2r Quatre-Bornes .40 .40
518 A107 2.50r Vacoas/Phoenix .50 .50
519 A107 5r Port Louis 1.00 1.00
a. Souv. sheet of 5, #515-519, perf. 14 3.25 3.25
Nos. 515-519 (5) 2.40 2.40

Royal Wedding Issue

Common Design Type

1981, July 22 Litho. *Perf. 14*

520 CD331 25c Bouquet .20 .20
521 CD331 2.50r Charles .50 .50
522 CD331 10r Couple 2.00 2.00
Nos. 520-522 (3) 2.70 2.70

Emmanuel Anquetil and Guy Rozemont — A108

Famous Men: 25c, Remy Ollier, Sookdeo Bissoondoyal. 1.25r, Maurice Cure, Barthelemy Ohsan. 1.50r, Guy Forget, Renganaden Seeneevassen. 2r, Abdul Razak Mohamed, Jules Koenig. 2.50r, Abdoollatiff Mahomed Osman, Dazzi Rama. 5r, Thomas Lewis.

1981, Aug. 13 *Perf. 14½*

523 A108 20c black & red .25 .25
524 A108 25c black & yellow .25 .25
525 A108 1.25r black & green .35 .35
526 A108 1.50r black & vermilion .40 .40
527 A108 2r black & ultra .55 .55
528 A108 2.50r black & red brn .65 .65
529 A108 5r black & blue grn 1.40 1.40
Nos. 523-529 (7) 3.85 3.85

Chinese Pagoda A109

1981, Sept. 16 *Perf. 13½*

530 A109 20c Tamil Women .25 .25
531 A109 2r Swami Sivananda, vert. .75 .75
532 A109 5r shown 1.90 1.90
Nos. 530-532 (3) 2.90 2.90

World Tamil Culture Conference, 1980 (20c).

A110

A111

1981, Oct. 26 Litho. *Perf. 14*

533 A110 25c Pottery making .20 .20
534 A110 1.25r Dog grooming .20 .20
535 A110 5r Hiking .75 .75
536 A110 10r Duke of Edinburgh 1.50 1.50
Nos. 533-536 (4) 2.65 2.65

Duke of Edinburgh's Awards, 25th anniv.

1981, Nov. 26 Wmk. 373 *Perf. 14½*

537 A111 25c Holy Ka'aba, Mecca .30 .30
538 A111 2r Prophet's Mosque .80 .80
539 A111 5r Holy Ka'aba, Prophet's Mosque 1.90 1.90
Nos. 537-539 (3) 3.00 3.00

Hegira, 1,500th anniv.

Scouting Year — A112

1982, Feb. 25 Litho. *Perf. 14x14½*

540 A112 25c Emblem .25 .25
541 A112 2r Baden-Powell .60 .60
542 A112 5r Grand howl, sign 1.40 1.40
543 A112 10r Scouts, mountain 2.75 2.75
Nos. 540-543 (4) 5.00 5.00

Darwin Death Centenary — A113

1982, Apr. 19 Litho. *Perf. 14*

544 A113 25c Portrait .20 .20
545 A113 2r Telescope .45 .45
546 A113 2.50r Riding elephant .55 .55
547 A113 10r The Beagle 2.25 2.25
Nos. 544-547 (4) 3.45 3.45

Princess Diana Issue

Common Design Type

1982, July 1 Litho. *Perf. 13*

548 CD333 25c Arms .20 .20
549 CD333 2.50r Diana .75 .75
550 CD333 5r Wedding 1.50 1.50
551 CD333 10r Portrait 3.00 3.00
Nos. 548-551 (4) 5.45 5.45

Birth of Prince William of Wales, June 21 — A114

1982, Sept. 22 Litho. *Perf. 14½*

552 A114 2.50r multicolored 1.10 1.10

Issued in sheets of 9.

TB Bacillus Centenary — A115

1982, Dec. 15 *Perf. 14*

553 A115 25c Aphloia theiformis .25 .25
554 A115 1.25r Central Market, Port Louis .55 .55
555 A115 2r Gaertnera psychotrioides .85 .85
556 A115 5r Selaginella deliquescens 1.25 1.25
557 A115 10r Koch 3.75 3.75
Nos. 553-557 (5) 6.65 6.65

A116

1983, Mar. 14 *Perf. 13x13½*

558 A116 25c Flag, arms .20 .20
559 A116 2.50r Satellite view .40 .40
560 A116 5r Sugar cane harvest .85 .85
561 A116 10r Port Louis Harbor 1.75 1.75
Nos. 558-561 (4) 3.20 3.20

Commonwealth Day.

World Communications Year — A117

1983, June 24 **Wmk. 373** *Perf. 14*

562 A117 25c Antique telephone, vert. .20 .20
563 A117 1.25r Early telegraph apparatus .35 .35
564 A117 2r Earth satellite station, vert. .50 .50
565 A117 10r 1st hot air balloon in Mauritius, 1784 2.40 2.40
Nos. 562-565 (4) 3.45 3.45

Namibia Day — A118

1983, Aug. 26

566 A118 25c Map .70 .70
567 A118 2.50r Breaking chains 1.60 1.60
568 A118 5r Family, village 3.25 3.25
569 A118 10r Diamond mining 6.00 6.00
Nos. 566-569 (4) 11.55 11.55

Fishery Resources — A119

1983, Oct. 7

570 A119 25c Fish trap, vert. .25 .25
571 A119 1r Fishermen in boat .40 .40
572 A119 5r Game fishing, vert. 1.75 1.75
573 A119 10r Octopus drying 3.75 3.75
Nos. 570-573 (4) 6.15 6.15

Swami Dayananda, Death Centenary — A120

1983, Nov. 3 **Litho.** **Wmk. 373**

574 A120 25c shown .20 .20
575 A120 35c Last meeting with father .20 .20
576 A120 2r Receiving instruction .30 .30
577 A120 5r Demonstrating strength .80 .80
578 A120 10r Religious gathering 1.75 1.75
Nos. 574-578 (5) 3.25 3.25

Adolf von Plevitz (1837-1893), Social Reformer A121

1983, Dec. 8

579 A121 25c shown .30 .30
580 A121 1.25r Government school .65 .65
581 A121 5r Addressing Commission of Enquiry 1.10 1.10
582 A121 10r Indian field workers 2.50 2.50
Nos. 579-582 (4) 4.55 4.55

Mauritius Kestrels A122

1984, Mar. 26 **Wmk. 373** *Perf. 14*

583 A122 25c Courtship chase .40 .40
584 A122 2r Side view, vert. 2.40 2.40
585 A122 2.50r Fledgling 2.75 2.75
586 A122 10r Bird, diff., vert. 12.00 12.00
Nos. 583-586 (4) 17.55 17.55

Lloyd's List Issue

Common Design Type

1984, May 23 **Litho.** *Perf. 14½x14*

587 CD335 25c Tayeb, Port Lewis .35 .35
588 CD335 1r Taher .70 .70
589 CD335 5r East Indiaman Triton 2.40 2.40
590 CD335 10r Astor 5.50 5.50
Nos. 587-590 (4) 8.95 8.95

Palm Trees — A123

Slave Sale — A124

1984, July 23 **Litho.** *Perf. 14*

591 A123 25c Blue latan .30 .30
592 A123 50c Hyophorbe vaughanii .30 .30
593 A123 2.50r Tectiphiala ferox 1.40 1.40
594 A123 5r Round Isld. bottle-palm 2.75 2.75
595 A123 10r Hyophorbe amaricaulis 5.75 5.75
Nos. 591-595 (5) 10.50 10.50

1984, Aug. *Perf. 14½*

596 A124 25c Woman .30 .30
597 A124 1r shown .95 .95
598 A124 2r Family, horiz. 1.50 1.50
599 A124 10r Immigrant arrival, horiz. 7.50 7.50
Nos. 596-599 (4) 10.25 10.25

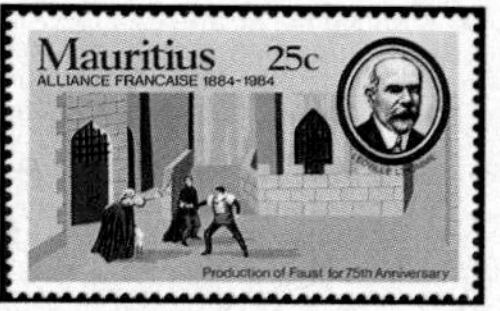

Alliance Francaise Centenary — A125

1984, Sept. 10 *Perf. 14½*

600 A125 25c Production of Faust, 1959 .25 .25
601 A125 1.25r Award ceremony .65 .65
602 A125 5r Headquarters 2.10 2.10
603 A125 10r Lion Mountain 4.50 4.50
Nos. 600-603 (4) 7.50 7.50

Queen Mother 85th Birthday

Common Design Type

Perf. 14½x14

1985, June 7 **Wmk. 384**

604 CD336 25c Portrait, 1926 .25 .25
605 CD336 2r With Princess Margaret .55 .55
606 CD336 5r On Clarence House balcony 1.50 1.50
607 CD336 10r Holding Prince Henry 2.75 2.75
Nos. 604-607 (4) 5.05 5.05

Souvenir Sheet

608 CD336 15r On Royal Barge, reopening Stratford Canal, 1964 6.75 6.75

2nd Annual Indian Ocean Islands Games — A126

Pink Pigeon — A127

1985, Aug. 24 **Wmk. 373** *Perf. 14½*

609 A126 25c High jump .35 .35
610 A126 50c Javelin .75 .75
611 A126 1.25r Cycling 4.75 4.75
612 A126 10r Wind surfing 8.25 8.25
Nos. 609-612 (4) 14.10 14.10

1985, Sept. 2 **Wmk. 384** *Perf. 14*

613 A127 25c Adult and young *6.25* *1.25*
614 A127 2r Nest site display *11.00* *2.75*
615 A127 2.50r Nesting *12.50* *4.25*
616 A127 5r Preening *20.00* *6.00*
Nos. 613-616 (4) *49.75* *14.25*

World Wildlife Fund.

World Tourism Org., 10th Anniv. A128

1985, Sept. 20 *Perf. 14½*

617 A128 25c Patates Caverns .60 .60
618 A128 35c Colored Earth, Chamarel .60 .60
619 A128 5r Serpent Island 2.75 2.75
620 A128 10r Coin de Mire Is. 11.00 11.00
Nos. 617-620 (4) 14.95 14.95

Port Louis, 250th Anniv. A129

1985, Nov. 22 *Perf. 13½*

621 A129 25c Old Town Hall .30 .30
622 A129 1r Al-Aqsa Mosque .90 .90
623 A129 2.50r Tamil-speaking Indians, settlement 1.75 1.75
624 A129 10r Port Louis Harbor 6.50 6.50
Nos. 621-624 (4) 9.45 9.45

Halley's Comet A130

1986, Feb. 21 **Wmk. 384** *Perf. 14*

625 A130 25c Halley, map .55 .55
626 A130 1.25r Newton's telescope, 1682 sighting .75 .75
627 A130 3r Mauritius from space 1.50 1.50
628 A130 10r Giotto space probe 5.00 5.00
Nos. 625-628 (4) 7.80 7.80

Queen Elizabeth II 60th Birthday

Common Design Type

Designs: 25c, In uniform, Grenadier Guards, 1942. 75c, Investiture of the Prince of Wales, 1969. 2r, State visit with Prince Philip. 3r, State visit to Germany, 1978. 15r, Visiting Crown Agents' offices, 1983.

1986, Apr. 21 **Litho.** *Perf. 14½x14*

629 CD337 25c scar, black & sil .20 .20
630 CD337 75c ultra & multi .20 .20
631 CD337 2r green & multi .40 .40
632 CD337 3r violet & multi .55 .55
633 CD337 15r rose vio & multi 2.25 2.25
Nos. 629-633 (5) 3.60 3.60

Intl. Events — A131

Orchids — A132

Designs: 25c, World Food Day. 1r, African Regional Industrial Property Organization, 10th anniv. 1.25r, Intl. Peace Year. 10r, 1986 World Cup Soccer Championships.

1986, July 25 **Litho.** *Perf. 14*

634 A131 25c FAO emblem, corn .30 .30
635 A131 1r ARIPO emblem .65 .65
636 A131 1.25r IPY emblem .95 .95
637 A131 10r Athlete, MFA 7.25 7.25
Nos. 634-637 (4) 9.15 9.15

1986, Oct. 3 **Litho.** *Perf. 14½*

638 A132 25c Cryptopus elatus .65 .65
639 A132 2r Jumellea recta 1.10 1.10
640 A132 2.50r Angraecum mauritianum 1.75 1.75
641 A132 10r Bulbophyllum longiflorum 6.50 6.50
Nos. 638-641 (4) 10.00 10.00

Bridges A133

1987, May 22 **Wmk. 373**

No.	Type	Value	Description	Unused	Used
642	A133	25c	Hesketh Bell	.25	.25
643	A133	50c	Sir Colville Deverell	.60	.60
644	A133	2.50r	Cavendish	1.50	1.50
645	A133	5r	Tamarin	3.00	3.00
646	A133	10r	Grand River North West	6.00	6.00
			Nos. 642-646 (5)	11.35	11.35

The Bar, Bicent. A134

Perf. 14x14½

1987, June 2 **Wmk. 384**

No.	Type	Value	Description	Unused	Used
647	A134	25c	Port Louis Supreme Court	.25	.25
648	A134	1r	Flacq District Court	.50	.50
649	A134	1.25r	Statue of Justice	.55	.55
650	A134	10r	Barristers, 1787-1987	3.25	3.25
			Nos. 647-650 (4)	4.55	4.55

Intl. Festival of the Sea — A135

1987, Sept. 5 **Wmk. 373**

No.	Type	Value	Description	Unused	Used
651	A135	25c	Dodo mascot, vert.	.75	.75
652	A135	1.50r	Sailboats	1.75	1.75
653	A135	3r	Water-skier	2.75	2.75
654	A135	5r	Tall ship Svanen, vert.	4.75	4.75
			Nos. 651-654 (4)	10.00	10.00

Industrialization — A136

1987, Oct. 30 ***Perf. 14***

No.	Type	Value	Description	Unused	Used
655	A136	20c	Toy	.30	.30
656	A136	35c	Spinning	.30	.30
657	A136	50c	Rattan	.30	.30
658	A136	2.50r	Optical	.95	.95
659	A136	10r	Stone carving	3.25	3.25
			Nos. 655-659 (5)	5.10	5.10

Art & Architecture A137

Designs: 25c, Maison Ouvriere, Intl. Year of Shelter for the Homeless emblem. 1r, Paul et Virginie, a lithograph. 1.25r, Chateau Rosney. 2r, Old Farmhouse, Boulle. 5r, Three Peaks, watercolor.

1988, June 29 **Wmk. 384** ***Perf. 14½***

No.	Type	Value	Description	Unused	Used
660	A137	25c	multicolored	.20	.20
661	A137	1r	gray & black	.40	.40
662	A137	1.25r	multicolored	.50	.50
663	A137	2r	multicolored	.60	.60
664	A137	5r	multicolored	1.60	1.60
			Nos. 660-664 (5)	3.30	3.30

Natl. Independence, 20th Anniv. — A138

Designs: 25c, University of Mauritius. 75c, Calisthenics at sunset in stadium. 2.50r, Runners, Sir Maurice Rault Stadium. 5r, Air Mauritius jet at gate, Sir Seewoosagur Ramgoolam Intl. Airport. 10r, Gov.-Gen. Veerasamy Ringadoo and Prime Minister Anerood Jugnauth.

1988, Mar. 11 **Wmk. 373** ***Perf. 14***

No.	Type	Value	Description	Unused	Used
665	A138	25c	multicolored	.25	.25
666	A138	75c	multicolored	.25	.25
667	A138	2.50r	multicolored	.90	.90
668	A138	5r	multicolored	1.60	1.60
669	A138	10r	multicolored	3.25	3.25
			Nos. 665-669 (5)	6.25	6.25

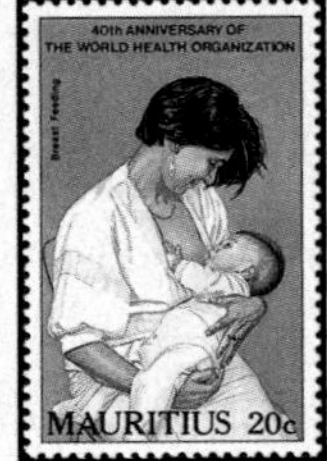

WHO, 40th Anniv. — A139

1988, July 1 **Wmk. 373** ***Perf. 13½***

No.	Type	Value	Description	Unused	Used
670	A139	20c	Breast-feeding	.30	.30
671	A139	2r	Immunization	.90	.90
672	A139	3r	Nutrition	1.75	1.75
673	A139	10r	Emblem	5.00	5.00
			Nos. 670-673 (4)	7.95	7.95

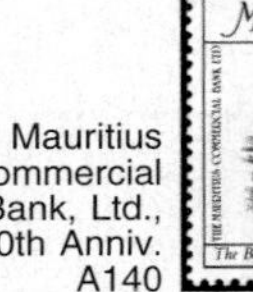

Mauritius Commercial Bank, Ltd., 150th Anniv. A140

1988, Sept. 1 **Wmk. 373** ***Perf. 14***

No.	Type	Value	Description	Unused	Used
674	A140	25c	Bank, 1981, vert.	.30	.30
675	A140	1r	Bank, 1897	.40	.40
676	A140	1.25r	Coat of arms, vert.	.50	.50
677	A140	25r	15-Dollar bank note, 1838	8.00	8.00
			Nos. 674-677 (4)	9.20	9.20

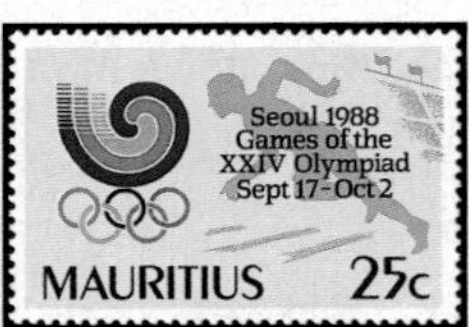

1988 Summer Olympics, Seoul A141

1988, Oct. 1

No.	Type	Value	Description	Unused	Used
678	A141	25c	shown	.25	.25
679	A141	35c	Wrestling	.35	.35
680	A141	1.50r	Running	.65	.65
681	A141	10r	Swimming	4.00	4.00
			Nos. 678-681 (4)	5.25	5.25

Environmental Protection — A142

Wmk. 384 (20c, 40c, 50c, 1r, 10r), 373 (Others)

1989-97 **Litho.** ***Perf. 14***

No.	Type	Value	Description	Unused	Used
682	A142	15c	Tropical reef	.35	.35
683	A142	20c	like #682	.35	.35
684	A142	30c	Greenshank	.40	.40
a.			Wmk. 384	.35	.35
685	A142	40c	shown	.35	.35
a.			Wmk. 373	.35	.35
686	A142	50c	Round Island, vert.	.35	.35
687	A142	60c	like #685	.35	.35
688	A142	75c	Bassin Blanc	.35	.35
689	A142	1r	Mangrove, vert.	.35	.35
690	A142	1.50r	Whimbrel	.40	.40
691	A142	2r	Le Morne	.40	.40
692	A142	3r	Fish	.75	.75
693	A142	4r	Fern tree, vert.	1.00	1.00
694	A142	5r	Riviere du Poste Estuary	1.00	1.00
695	A142	6r	Ecological scenery, vert.	1.50	1.50
696	A142	10r	Phelsuma ornata,vert.	2.40	2.40
a.			Wmk. 373 ('97)	2.40	2.40
697	A142	15r	Benares surf	3.25	3.25
a.			Wmk. 384	3.00	3.00
698	A142	25r	Migratory birds, vert.	5.50	5.50
a.			Wmk. 384 ('96)	5.25	5.25
			Nos. 682-698 (17)	19.05	19.05

Issued: 40c, 3r-10r, 3/11/89; #685a, 2/19/91; 50c, 75c, 2r, 5r, 15r, 10/4/91; 20c, 60c, 3/96; others, 11/22/90.

#682, 685a, 693 exist inscribed "1994," #682-684, 696, "1995," #698, "1996," #685, 687, 696, 698, 698a, "1997." #689, 693-695, 696, 696a, 698, "1998."

For surcharge see No. 781.

A143

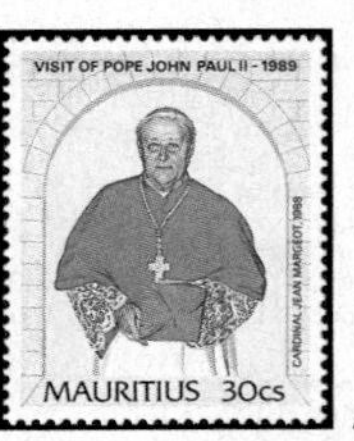

A144

French Revolution, Bicent.: 30c, La Tour Sumeire, Place Du Theatre Municipal. 1r, Salle De Spectacle Du Jardin. 8r, Le Comte De Malartic. 15r, Anniv. emblem.

1989, July 14 **Wmk. 373**

No.	Type	Value	Description	Unused	Used
702	A143	30c	multicolored	.25	.25
703	A143	1r	multicolored	.25	.25
704	A143	8r	multicolored	2.00	2.00
705	A143	15r	multicolored	3.75	3.75
			Nos. 702-705 (4)	6.25	6.25

1989, Oct. 13 ***Perf. 14x13½***

Visit of Pope John Paul II: 30c, Cardinal Jean Margeot. 40c, Pope welcoming Prime Minister Aneerood Jugnauth to the Vatican, 1988. 3r, Mother Mary Magdalene of the Cross (1810-1889) and Filles des Marie Chapel, Port Louis, 1864. 6r, St. Francis of Assisi Church, 1756, Pamplemousses. 10r, Pope John Paul II.

No.	Type	Value	Description	Unused	Used
706	A144	30c	multicolored	.30	.30
707	A144	40c	multicolored	1.00	1.00
708	A144	3r	multicolored	2.00	2.00
709	A144	6r	multicolored	4.25	4.25
710	A144	10r	multicolored	6.75	6.75
			Nos. 706-710 (5)	14.30	14.30

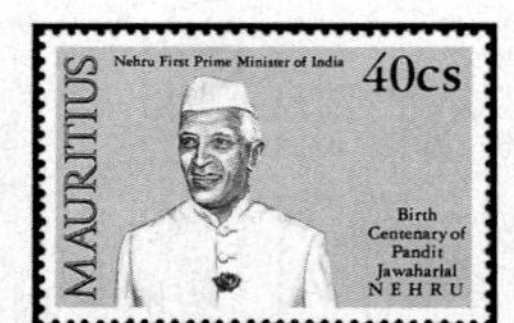

Jawaharlal Nehru, 1st Prime Minister of India — A145

Designs: 1.50r, Nehru and Indira, Rajiv and Sanjay Gandhi. 3r, With Mahatma Gandhi. 4r, With Nasser and Tito. 10r, With children.

1989, Oct. 13 **Wmk. 384** ***Perf. 14***

No.	Type	Value	Description	Unused	Used
711	A145	40c	shown	1.25	1.25
712	A145	1.50r	multicolored	1.50	1.50
713	A145	3r	multicolored	3.00	3.00
714	A145	4r	multicolored	3.75	3.75
715	A145	10r	multicolored	9.00	9.00
			Nos. 711-715 (5)	18.50	18.50

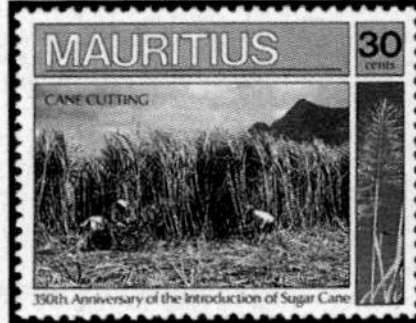

Sugar Cane Industry, 350th Anniv. A146

Perf. 13½x14

1990, Jan. 10 **Litho.** **Wmk. 384**

No.	Type	Value	Description	Unused	Used
716	A146	30c	Cutting cane	.30	.30
717	A146	40c	Refinery, 1867	.30	.30
718	A146	1r	Mechanically loading cane	.75	.75
719	A146	25r	Modern refinery	12.00	12.00
			Nos. 716-719 (4)	13.35	13.35

Prime Minister Jugnauth's 60th Birthday A147

Jugnauth: 35c, And symbols of the industrial estate. 40c, At his desk. 1.50r, And stock exchange emblem. 4r, And Gov.-Gen. Ramgoolam. 10r, And Pope John Paul II, map.

Wmk. 373

1990, Mar. 29 **Litho.** ***Perf. 14***

No.	Type	Value	Description	Unused	Used
720	A147	35c	multicolored	.35	.35
721	A147	40c	multicolored	.35	.35
722	A147	1.50r	multicolored	1.60	1.60
723	A147	4r	multicolored	3.50	3.50
724	A147	10r	multicolored	8.75	8.75
			Nos. 720-724 (5)	14.55	14.55

Mauritian Television, 25th Anniv. A148

Anniversaries and Events: 30c, Death of Desjardins, naturalist, 150th anniversary, vert. 6r, Line barracks, 250th anniversary, vert. 8r, Municipality of Curepipe, centenary.

1990, July 5

No.	Type	Value	Description	Unused	Used
725	A148	30c	lt orange & multi	.50	.50
726	A148	35c	pink & multi	.50	.50
727	A148	6r	lt blue & multi	5.25	5.25
728	A148	8r	lt green & multi	6.50	6.50
			Nos. 725-728 (4)	12.75	12.75

Intl. Literacy Year A149

Wmk. 373

1990, Sept. 28 **Litho.** ***Perf. 14***

No.	Type	Value	Description	Unused	Used
729	A149	30c	shown	.35	.35
730	A149	1r	Blind girl printing braille	1.40	1.40
731	A149	3r	Globe, open book	2.50	2.50
732	A149	10r	Open book, world map	8.75	8.75
			Nos. 729-732 (4)	13.00	13.00

Elizabeth & Philip, Birthdays

Common Design Types

Wmk. 384

1991, June 17 **Litho.** ***Perf. 14½***

No.	Type	Value	Description	Unused	Used
733	CD345	8r	multicolored	1.75	1.75
734	CD346	8r	multicolored	1.75	1.75
a.			Pair, #733-734 + label	3.75	3.75

Port Louis, City Incorporation, 25th Anniv. — A150

Anniversaries and Events: 4r, Col. Draper, 150th death anniv., vert. 6r, Joseph Barnard, engraver of first Mauritius stamps, 175th birth anniv., vert. 10r, Spitfire, Mauritius' contribution to Allied war effort, 1939-1945.

Wmk. 373

1991, Aug. 18 Litho. *Perf. 14*

735 A150 40c multicolored .30 .30
736 A150 4r multicolored 2.10 2.10
737 A150 6r multicolored 3.25 3.25
738 A150 10r multicolored 5.25 5.25
Nos. 735-738 (4) 10.90 10.90

Phila Nippon '91 — A151

Butterflies: 40c, Euploea euphon. 3r, Hypolimnas misippus, female. 8r, Papilio manlius. 10r, Hypolimnas misippus, male.

Perf. 14x14½

1991, Nov. 15 Litho. Wmk. 373

739 A151 40c multicolored .90 .90
740 A151 3r multicolored 2.00 2.00
741 A151 8r multicolored 4.75 4.75
742 A151 10r multicolored 5.50 5.50
Nos. 739-742 (4) 13.15 13.15

Flora and Fauna From Mauritius A152

Designs: 40c, Chelonia mydas, Tromelin. 1r, Ibis, Agalega. 2r, Takamaka flowers, Chagos Archipelago. 15r, Lambis violacea, St. Brandon.

1991, Dec. 13 *Perf. 14*

743 A152 40c multicolored .75 .75
744 A152 1r multicolored 1.25 1.25
745 A152 2r multicolored 1.60 1.60
746 A152 15r multicolored 9.50 9.50
Nos. 743-746 (4) 13.10 13.10

Republic

Proclamation of the Republic of Mauritius — A153

1992, Mar. 12

747 A153 40c President .30 .30
748 A153 4r Prime Minister 1.40 1.40
749 A153 8r Mauritian children 3.00 3.00
750 A153 10r President's flag 3.50 3.50
Nos. 747-750 (4) 8.20 8.20

8th African Track and Field Championships A154

Designs: 40c, Games mascot, Tricolo. 4r, Sir Anerood Jugnauth Stadium, horiz. 5r, High jumper, horiz. 6r, Torch, emblem of games.

1992, June 25 *Perf. 13½*

751 A154 40c multicolored .25 .25
752 A154 4r multicolored .85 .85
753 A154 5r multicolored 1.25 1.25
754 A154 6r multicolored 1.50 1.50
Nos. 751-754 (4) 3.85 3.85

Anniversaries and Events — A155

Designs: 40c, Flower, vert. 1r, Swami Krishnanandji Maharaj, vert. 2r, Boy and dog. 3r, Building, flags. 15r, Radio telescope antennae.

1992, Aug. 13

755 A155 40c multicolored .25 .25
756 A155 1r multicolored .60 .60
757 A155 2r multicolored .95 .95
758 A155 3r multicolored 1.50 1.50
759 A155 15r multicolored 6.50 6.50
Nos. 755-759 (5) 9.80 9.80

Fleurir Maurice, 25th anniv. (#755). 25th anniv. of Swami Maharaj's arrival (#756). Humane education (#757). Indian Ocean Commission, 10th anniv. (#758). Inauguration of radio telescope project (#759).

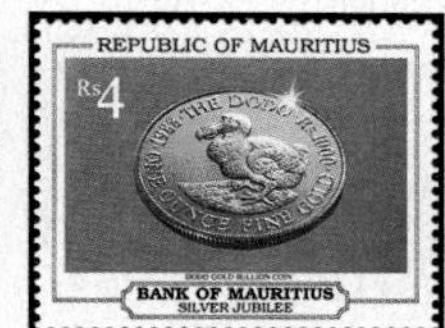

Bank of Mauritius, Silver Jubilee A156

Designs: 40c, Bank of Mauritius building, vert. 4r, Dodo gold bullion coin. 8r, First bank note issues. 15r, Foreign exchange reserves 1967-1992.

Perf. 14½x14, 14x14½

1992, Oct. 29 Litho. Wmk. 373

760 A156 40c multicolored .30 .30
761 A156 4r multicolored 1.60 1.60
762 A156 8r multicolored 3.50 3.50
763 A156 15r multicolored 5.75 5.75
Nos. 760-763 (4) 11.15 11.15

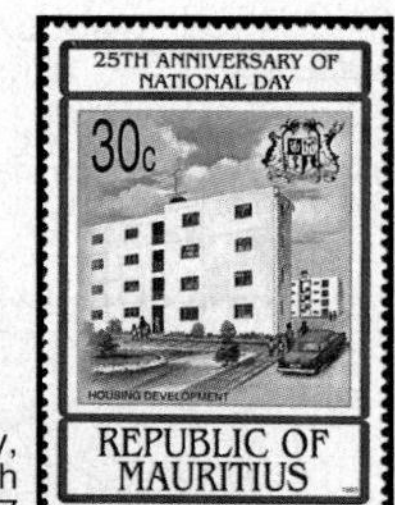

National Day, 25th Anniv. — A157

30c, Housing development. 40c, Computer showing gross domestic product. 3r, Flag in shape of map of Mauritius. 4r, Ballot box. 15r, Medal for Grand Commander of the Order of the Star & Key of the Indian Ocean.

1993, Mar. 12 *Perf. 15x14*

764 A157 30c multicolored .25 .25
765 A157 40c multicolored .25 .25
766 A157 3r multicolored .55 .55
767 A157 4r multicolored .80 .80
768 A157 15r multicolored 2.75 2.75
Nos. 764-768 (5) 4.60 4.60

Air Mauritius Ltd., 25th Anniv. A158

40c, Bell 206B Jet Ranger. 3r, Boeing 747SP. 4r, ATR 42. 10r, Boeing 767-200ER.

1993, June 14 *Perf. 14*

769 A158 40c multicolored .85 .85
770 A158 3r multicolored 1.50 1.50
771 A158 4r multicolored 2.00 2.00
772 A158 10r multicolored 4.75 4.75
a. Souvenir sheet of 4, #769-772 11.50 11.50
Nos. 769-772 (4) 9.10 9.10

5th Francophone Summit — A159

Designs: 1r, 1715 Act of French Seizure of Mauritius, 1810 Act of Surrender. 5r, Signs. 6r, Page from Napoleonic Code. 7r, French publications.

1993, Oct. 16

773 A159 1r multicolored .25 .25
774 A159 5r multicolored 2.50 2.50
775 A159 6r multicolored 3.00 3.00
776 A159 7r multicolored 3.50 3.50
Nos. 773-776 (4) 9.25 9.25

Telecommunications — A160

Designs: 40c, SS Scotia, cable laying. 3r, Morse code, Morse key. 4r, Signal mountain station. 8r, Communications satellite.

1993, Nov. 25 *Perf. 13*

777 A160 40c multicolored .65 .65
778 A160 3r multicolored 1.10 1.10
779 A160 4r multicolored 1.75 1.75
780 A160 8r multicolored 3.50 3.50
Nos. 777-780 (4) 7.00 7.00

No. 686 Surcharged

1993, Sept. 15 Litho. *Perf. 14*

781 A142 40c on 75c multi 2.00 2.00

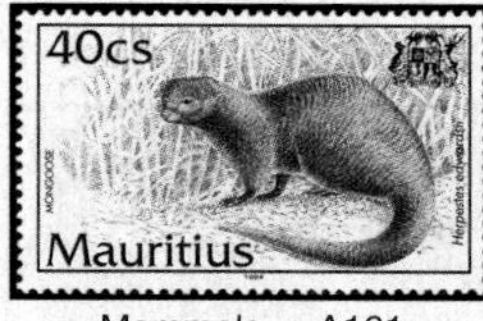

Mammals — A161

Wmk. 384

1994, Mar. 9 Litho. *Perf. 14½*

782 A161 40c Mongoose .30 .30
783 A161 2r Hare 1.25 1.25
784 A161 8r Monkey 4.00 4.00
785 A161 10r Tenrec 4.50 4.50
Nos. 782-785 (4) 10.05 10.05

Anniversaries and Events — A162

40c, Dr. E. Brown-Sequard (1817-94). 4r, Silhouettes of family. 8r, World Cup trophy, US map. 10r, Control Tower, SSR Intl. Airport.

Wmk. 373

1994, June 16 Litho. *Perf. 14*

786 A162 40c multicolored .25 .25
787 A162 4r multicolored .75 .75
788 A162 8r multicolored 1.60 1.60
789 A162 10r multicolored 2.00 2.00
Nos. 786-789 (4) 4.60 4.60

Intl. Year of the Family (#787). 1994 World Cup Soccer Championships, US (#788). ICAO, 50th anniv. (#789).

Wreck of the St. Geran, 250th Anniv. A163

Wmk. 384

1994, Aug. 18 Litho. *Perf. 14*

790 A163 40c Leaving L'Orient .35 .35
791 A163 5r In rough seas 1.50 1.50
792 A163 6r Ship's bell 1.75 1.75
793 A163 10r Relics from ship 3.00 3.00
Nos. 790-793 (4) 6.60 6.60

Souvenir Sheet

794 A163 15r St. Geran, vert. 9.00 9.00

Children's Paintings of Leisure Activities — A164

Designs: 30c, "Ring Around the Rosey." 40c, Playing with balls, jump rope. 8r, Water sports. 10r, "Blindman's Buff."

Wmk. 373

1994, Oct. 25 Litho. *Perf. 13½*

795 A164 30c multicolored .25 .25
796 A164 40c multicolored .25 .25
797 A164 8r multicolored 1.50 1.50
798 A164 10r multicolored 1.90 1.90
Nos. 795-798 (4) 3.90 3.90

Spices — A165

Perf. 13x14

1995, Mar. 10 Litho. Wmk. 373

799 A165 40c Nutmeg .30 .30
800 A165 4r Coriander .85 .85
801 A165 5r Cloves 1.25 1.25
802 A165 10r Cardamon 2.40 2.40
Nos. 799-802 (4) 4.80 4.80

End of World War II

Common Design Type

Designs: No. 803, HMS Mauritius. No. 804, Mauritian servicemen, map of North Africa. No. 805, Catalina, Tombeau Bay.

Wmk. 373

1995, May 8 Litho. *Perf. 14*

Size: 35x28mm

803 CD351 5r multicolored 2.50 2.50
804 CD351 5r multicolored 2.50 2.50
805 CD351 5r multicolored 2.50 2.50
Nos. 803-805 (3) 7.50 7.50

Anniversaries & Events — A166

1995, May 8

806	A166	40c multicolored	.25	.25
807	A166	4r multicolored	1.25	1.25
808	A166	10r multicolored	2.75	2.75
		Nos. 806-808 (3)	4.25	4.25

Construction of Mare Longue Reservoir, 50th anniv. (#806). Construction of Mahebourg-Curepipe Road, bicent. (#807). Great fire of Port Louis, cent. (#808).

A167

A168

Designs: Lighthouses.

Perf. 13x14

1995, Aug. 28 Litho. Wmk. 373

809	A167	30c Ile Plate	1.00	1.00
810	A167	40c Pointe aux Caves	1.00	1.00
811	A167	8r Ile aux Fouquets	4.75	4.75
812	A167	10r Pointe aux Canonniers	6.00	6.00
a.		Souvenir sheet of 4, #809-812	15.00	15.00
		Nos. 809-812 (4)	12.75	12.75

UN, 50th Anniv.

Common Design Type

Designs: 40c, Silhouettes of children under UNICEF umbrella. 4r, ILO contruction site. 8r, WMO satellite view of hurricane. 10r, Bread, grain representing FAO.

Wmk. 373

1995, Oct. 24 Litho. *Perf. 14*

813	CD353	40c multicolored	.25	.25
814	CD353	4r multicolored	.65	.65
815	CD353	8r multicolored	1.40	1.40
816	CD353	10r multicolored	1.60	1.60
		Nos. 813-816 (4)	3.90	3.90

1995, Dec. 8 Litho. *Perf. 13*

817	A168	60c pink & multi	.25	.25
818	A168	4r blue & multi	.55	.55
819	A168	8r yellow & multi	1.25	1.25
820	A168	10r green & multi	1.40	1.40
		Nos. 817-820 (4)	3.45	3.45

Common Market for Eastern and Southern Africa (COMESA).

Snails A169

Designs: 60c, Pachystyla bicolor. 4r, Gonidomus pagodus. 5r, Harmogenanina implicata. 10r, Tropidophora eugeniae.

Wmk. 373

1996, Mar. 11 Litho. *Perf. 13*

821	A169	60c multicolored	.35	.35
822	A169	4r multicolored	1.00	1.00
823	A169	5r multicolored	1.25	1.25
824	A169	10r multicolored	2.50	2.50
		Nos. 821-824 (4)	5.10	5.10

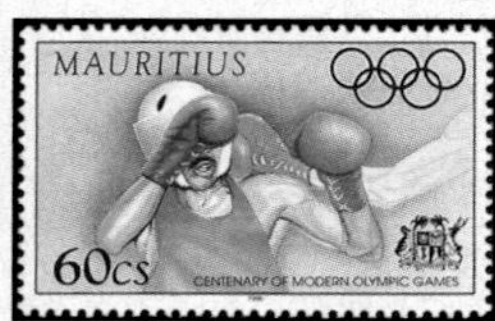
Modern Olympic Games, Cent. A170

Wmk. 384

1996, June 26 Litho. *Perf. 13½*

825	A170	60c Boxing	.30	.30
826	A170	4r Badminton	.75	.75
827	A170	5r Basketball	.95	.95
828	A170	10r Table tennis	2.00	2.00
		Nos. 825-828 (4)	4.00	4.00

Ships A171

Wmk. 373

1996, Sept. 30 Litho. *Perf. 14*

829	A171	60c SS Zambezia	.30	.30
830	A171	4r MV Sir Jules	.80	.80
831	A171	5r MV Mauritius	1.00	1.00
832	A171	10r MS Mauritius Pride	2.10	2.10
a.		Souvenir sheet of 4, #829-832	5.00	5.00
		Nos. 829-832 (4)	4.20	4.20

Post Office Ordinance, 150th Anniv. — A172

Wmk. 384

1996, Dec. 2 Litho. *Perf. 13½*

833	A172	60c Pillar box	.30	.30
834	A172	4r Early handstamp cancel	1.10	1.10
835	A172	5r Mobile post office	1.50	1.50
836	A172	10r Carriole	3.00	3.00
		Nos. 833-836 (4)	5.90	5.90

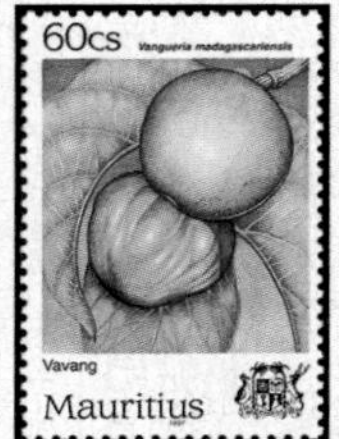
Fruit — A173

Designs: 60c, Vangueria madgascariensis. 4r, Mimusops coriacea. 5r, Syzgium jambos. 10r, Diospyros digyna.

Perf. 14x13½

1997, Mar. 10 Litho. Wmk. 373

837	A173	60c multicolored	.25	.25
838	A173	4r multicolored	.50	.50
839	A173	5r multicolored	.65	.65
840	A173	10r multicolored	1.40	1.40
		Nos. 837-840 (4)	2.80	2.80

Anniversaries and Events — A174

Designs: 60c, Ile de France, Mahé de La Bourdonnais. 1r, Exploration, La Perouse. 4r, Lady Gomm's Ball, Sir William Maynard Gomm. 6r, Skeleton of the Dodo, George Clark. 10r, Professor Brian Abel-Smith.

Wmk. 373

1997, June 9 Litho. *Perf. 13½*

841	A174	60c multicolored	.45	.45
842	A174	1r multicolored	.45	.45
843	A174	4r multicolored	.85	.85
844	A174	6r multicolored	1.25	1.25
845	A174	10r multicolored	2.00	2.00
		Nos. 841-845 (5)	5.00	5.00

First Postage Stamps of Mauritius, 150th Anniv. A175

Stamps: 60c, #1. 4r, #2. 5r, #2, #1, gold background. 10r, #1, #2, silver background. 20r, #2, #1 on "The Bordeaux Cover."

Wmk. 373

1997, Sept. 22 Litho. *Perf. 13½*

846	A175	60c multicolored	.40	.40
847	A175	4r multicolored	1.25	1.25
a.		Sheet of 12, 7 #846, 5 #847	6.75	6.75
848	A175	5r multicolored	1.50	1.50
849	A175	10r multicolored	3.25	3.25
		Nos. 846-849 (4)	6.40	6.40

Souvenir Sheet

850	A175	20r multicolored	5.75	5.75

Booklet Panes and Booklets

846a	Booklet pane of 10	3.50
	Complete booklet, #846a	3.50
847b	Booklet pane of 10	11.00
	Complete booklet, #847b	11.00
848a	Booklet pane of 10	14.50
	Complete booklet, #848a	14.50
849a	Booklet pane of 10	30.00
	Complete booklet, #849a	30.00

Local Occupations — A176

Wmk. 373

1997, Dec. 1 Litho. *Perf. 14½*

851	A176	60c Wheelwright	.40	.40
852	A176	4r Washerman	.70	.70
853	A176	5r Shipwright	.90	.90
854	A176	15r Quarryman	2.75	2.75
		Nos. 851-854 (4)	4.75	4.75

Geckos A177

Designs: 1r, Phelsuma guentheri. 6r, Nactus serpensinsula. 7r, Nactus coindemirensis. 8r, Phelsuma edwardnewtonii.

Wmk. 373

1998, Mar. 11 Litho. *Perf. 13½*

855	A177	1r multicolored	.40	.40
856	A177	6r multicolored	1.25	1.25
857	A177	7r multicolored	1.50	1.50
858	A177	8r multicolored	1.75	1.75
		Nos. 855-858 (4)	4.90	4.90

Inland Transportation — A178

Wmk. 373

1998, June 15 Litho. *Perf. 13½*

859	A178	40c Railroad	.60	.60
860	A178	5r Truck	1.25	1.25
861	A178	6r Bus, bicycles, cars	1.60	1.60
862	A178	10r Boat	2.50	2.50
		Nos. 859-862 (4)	5.95	5.95

Dutch Landing, 400th Anniv. A179

50c, Maurits van Nassau, landing scene. 1r, Otaheite sugar cane, Frederik Hendrik Fort. 7r, Dutch map, 1670. 8r, Landing fleet. 25r, Ships of landing fleet.

Wmk. 373

1998, Sept. 18 Litho. *Perf. 13½*

863	A179	50c multicolored	.35	.35
864	A179	1r multicolored	.35	.35
865	A179	7r multicolored	1.75	1.75
866	A179	8r multicolored	2.25	2.25
		Nos. 863-866 (4)	4.70	4.70

Souvenir Sheet

867	A179	25r multicolored	5.50	5.50

State Visit of South African Pres. Nelson Mandela — A180

1998, Sept. 10 Litho. *Perf. 14*

868	A180	25r multicolored	3.25	3.25

Waterfalls — A181

1r, Balfour Falls. 5r, Rochester Falls. 6r, GRSE Falls, vert. 10r, 500-Foot Falls, vert.

1998 Litho. Wmk. 384 *Perf. 13½*

869	A181	1r multicolored	.50	.50
870	A181	5r multicolored	1.00	1.00
871	A181	6r multicolored	1.40	1.40
872	A181	10r multicolored	2.10	2.10
		Nos. 869-872 (4)	5.00	5.00

Creation of Presidential Residence "Le Réduit," 250th Anniv. — A182

Designs: 1r, Drawing of floor plan, 1823. 4r, Exterior view, by P.A.F. Thuillier, 1814. 5r, "Le Réduit," by Hassen Edun, 1998. 15r, Commemorative monument, 1998.

1998 Litho. Wmk. 373 *Perf. 14½*

873	A182	1r multicolored	.40	.40
874	A182	4r multicolored	.70	.70
875	A182	5r multicolored	.90	.90
876	A182	15r multicolored	2.50	2.50
		Nos. 873-876 (4)	4.50	4.50

Admiral Mahé de la Bourdonnais, 300th Birth Anniv. — A183

Wmk. 373

1999, Feb. 11 Litho. *Perf. 13*

877	A183	7r No. 115	1.75	1.75

Native Flowers A184

Designs: 1r, Clerodendron laciniatum. 2r, Senecio lemarckianus. 5r, Cylindrocline commersonii. 9r, Psiadia pollicina.

1999, Mar. 10 *Perf. 13½*

878	A184	1r multicolored	.40	.40
879	A184	2r multicolored	.40	.40
880	A184	5r multicolored	.70	.70
881	A184	9r multicolored	1.25	1.25
		Nos. 878-881 (4)	2.75	2.75

Paintings — A185

Designs: 1r, "The Washerwomen," by Hervé Masson. 3r, "The Casino," by Gaetan de Rosnay. 4r, "The Four Elements," by Andrée Poilly. 6r, "Coming out of Mass," by Xavier Le Juge de Segrais.

1999, June 18 *Perf. 14x15*

882 A185 1r multicolored .50 .50
883 A185 3r multicolored .60 .60
884 A185 4r multicolored .70 .70
885 A185 6r multicolored 1.10 1.10
Nos. 882-885 (4) 2.90 2.90

Old Sugar Mill Chimneys — A186

Wmk. 384

1999, Sept. 17 Litho. *Perf. 14¼*

886 A186 1r Alma .40 .40
887 A186 2r Antoinette .60 .60
888 A186 5r Belle Mare .90 .90
889 A186 7r Grande Rosalie 1.00 1.00
a. Souvenir sheet of 4, #886-889, Wmk. 373 3.25 3.25
Nos. 886-889 (4) 2.90 2.90

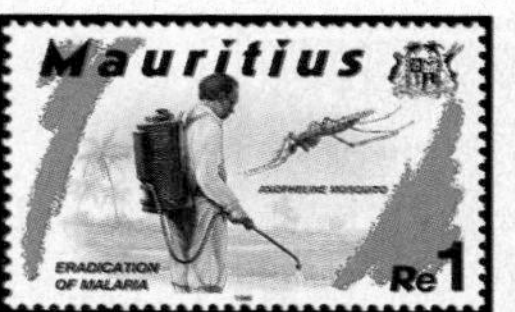

Achievements in the 20th Century — A187

Designs: 1r, Eradication of malaria. 2r, Emancipation of women. 5r, International Conference Center. 9r, Special sugars.

Perf. 13¼x13

1999, Dec. 7 Litho. Wmk. 373

890 A187 1r multi .40 .40
891 A187 2r multi .60 .60
892 A187 5r multi 1.10 1.10
893 A187 9r multi 2.00 2.00
Nos. 890-893 (4) 4.10 4.10

Chamber of Commerce & Industry, 150th Anniv. — A188

1r, Emblem. 2r, Computer chip. 7r, Francis Channell, 1st sec. 15r, Louis Léchelle, 1st pres.

2000, Jan. 25 Litho. *Perf. 13¼*

894 A188 1r multi .40 .40
895 A188 2r multi .60 .60
896 A188 7r multi 1.10 1.10
897 A188 15r multi 2.10 2.10
Nos. 894-897 (4) 4.20 4.20

Insects A189

Designs: 1r, Cratopus striga. 2r, Cratopus armatus. 3r, Cratopus chrysochlorus. 15r, Cratopus nigrogranatus.

Wmk. 373

2000, Mar. 29 Litho. *Perf. 14¼*

898 A189 1r multi .40 .40
899 A189 2r multi .40 .40
900 A189 3r multi .50 .50
901 A189 15r multi 2.40 2.40
a. Souvenir sheet of 4, #898-901 4.00 4.00
Nos. 898-901 (4) 3.70 3.70

2000 Summer Olympics, Sydney — A190

Wmk. 373

2000, June 28 Litho. *Perf. 14½*

902 A190 1r Handball .40 .40
903 A190 2r Archery .60 .60
904 A190 5r Sailing .80 .80
905 A190 15r Judo 2.40 2.40
Nos. 902-905 (4) 4.20 4.20

Sir Seewoosagur Ramgoolam, Birth Cent. — A191

Designs: 1r, Ramgoolam with Mother Teresa. 2r, As elected member of legislative council, vert. 5r, As student, 1926, vert. 15r, As Prime Minister, 1968, vert.

Perf. 13¼x13, 13x13¼

2000, Sept. 18 Litho. Wmk. 373

906-909 A191 Set of 4 4.25 4.25

Fish A192

Designs: 50c, Scarus ghobban. 1r, Cephalopholis sonnerati. 2r, Naso brevirostris. 3r, Lethrinus nebulosus. 4r, Centropyge debelius. 5r, Amphiprion chrysogaster. 6r, Forcipiger flavissimus. 7r, Acanthurus leucosternon. 8r, Pterois volitans. 10r, Siderea grisea. 15r, Carcharhinus wheeleri. 25r, Istiophorus platypterus.

Perf. 14½x14¼

2000, Oct. 9 Litho. Wmk. 373

910 A192 50c multi .40 .40
911 A192 1r multi .40 .40
912 A192 2r multi .40 .40
913 A192 3r multi .40 .40
914 A192 4r multi .50 .50
915 A192 5r multi .60 .60
916 A192 6r multi .75 .75
917 A192 7r multi .80 .80
918 A192 8r multi 1.00 1.00
919 A192 10r multi 1.10 1.10
a. Souvenir sheet, #914, 917-919 3.50 3.50
b. As #919, perf. 13½ ('08) .75 .75
920 A192 15r multi 1.90 1.90
a. Souvenir sheet, #913, 915-916, 920 3.50 3.50
921 A192 25r multi 2.75 2.75
a. Souvenir sheet, #910-912, 921 3.50 3.50
Nos. 910-921 (12) 11.00 11.00

No. 919b issued 5/28/08.

Famous People — A193

Designs: 1r, Affan Tank Wen (1842-1900). 5r, Alphonse Ravaton (1900-92), musician. 7r, Dr. Idrice Goumany (1859-89). 9r, Anjalay Coopen (d. 1943), martyr.

Perf. 14¼x14½

2000, Dec. 13 Wmk. 373

922-925 A193 Set of 4 3.75 3.75

Textile Industry A194

Designs: 1r, Finished sweater. 3r, Computer-aided machinery. 6r, T-shirt folder. 10r, Embroidery machine.

2001, Jan. 10 *Perf. 14½x14¼*

926-929 A194 Set of 4 3.25 3.25

End of Slavery and Indentured Labor, 166th Anniv. — A195

2001, Feb. 1 *Perf. 14x13½*

930 A195 7r multi 2.00 2.00

Trees A196

Designs: 1r, Foetida mauritana. 3r, Diospyros tessellaria. 5r, Sideroxylon puberulum. 15r, Gastonia mauritana.

2001, Mar. 21 Wmk. 373 *Perf. 13½*

931-934 A196 Set of 4 5.00 5.00

Expedition of Nicholas Baudin, Bicent. — A197

Designs: 1r, Ships Géographe and Naturaliste. 4r, Baudin and map of itinerary. 6r, Phedina borbonica. 10r, Napoleon Bonaparte and account of expedition, vert.

Wmk. 373

2001, June 13 Litho. *Perf. 14¼*

935-938 A197 Set of 4 4.00 4.00

20th Century Achievements — A198

Designs: 2r, Hotel School of Mauritius. 3r, Steel bar milling. 6r, Solar energy, Agalega. 10r, Indian Ocean Rim Association for Regional Cooperation.

Wmk. 373

2001, Sept. 12 Litho. *Perf. 13½*

939-942 A198 Set of 4 3.50 3.50

Mahatma Gandhi's Visit to Mauritius, Cent. — A199

2001, Oct. 2 *Perf. 14¾x14*

943 A199 15r No. 361 3.00 3.00

Copra Industry A200

Designs: 1r, Dehusking of coconuts, vert. 5r, Deshelling of coconuts. 6r, Drying copra. 10r, Oil extraction, vert.

2001, Dec. 5 *Perf. 13½*

944-947 A200 Set of 4 4.75 4.75

Republic, 10th Anniv. A201

Designs: 1r, Port development. 4r, Financial services. 5r, Water storage. 9r, Road development.

Perf. 13½x13¾

2002, Mar. 12 Litho. Wmk. 373

948-951 A201 Set of 4 4.00 4.00

Cicadas — A202

Designs: 1r, Abricta brunnea. 6r, Fractuosella darwini. 7r, Distantada thomaseti. 8r, Dinarobia claudeae.

Wmk. 373

2002, June 12 Litho. *Perf. 13½*

952-955 A202 Set of 4 3.50 3.50
a. Souvenir sheet, #952-955 4.00 4.00

Maps of the Southwest Indian Ocean — A203

Maps by: 1r, Alberto Cantino, 1502. 3r, Jorge Reinel, 1520. 4r, Diogo Ribeiro, 1529. 10r, Gerard Mercator, 1569.

2002, Sept. 18
956-959 A203 Set of 4 5.00 5.00

Constellations A204

Designs: 1r, Orion. 7r, Sagittarius. 8r, Scorpius. 9r, Crux.

Perf. 14¼x14½
2002, Dec. 18 Litho. Wmk. 373
960-963 A204 Set of 4 4.00 4.00

2nd U.S. — Sub-Saharan Africa Trade and Economic Forum — A205

Panel color: 1r, Violet blue. 25r, Red.

2003, Jan. *Perf. 14¼*
964-965 A205 Set of 2 3.25 3.25

Worldwide Fund for Nature (WWF) — A206

Echo parakeet: 1r, Chick. 2r, Fledgling. 5r, Female. 15r, Male.

Wmk. 373
2003, Mar. 19 Litho. *Perf. 13½*
966-969 A206 Set of 4 4.00 4.00

Flowers — A207

Designs: 1r, Trochetia boutoniana. 4r, Trochetia uniflora. 7r, Trochetia triflora. 9r, Trochetia parviflora.

Wmk. 373
2003, June 18 Litho. *Perf. 13½*
970-973 A207 Set of 4 3.75 3.75

Anniversaries and Events — A208

Designs: 2r, Sixth Indian Ocean Games, Mauritius. 6r, Mauritius Chamber of Agriculture, 150th anniv. 9r, Visit of Abbé de la Caille, 250th anniv. 10r, Mauritius Sugar Industry Research Institute, 50th anniv.

2003, Aug. 20
974-977 A208 Set of 4 5.75 5.75

Fortresses — A209

Designs: 2r, Batterie de la Pointe du Diable. 5r, Donjon St. Louis. 6r, Martello tower. 12r, Fort Adelaide,

2003, Dec. 10
978-981 A209 Set of 4 4.00 4.00

Indian Ocean Commission, 20th Anniv. — A210

Wmk. 373
2004, Feb. 16 Litho. *Perf. 13½*
982 A210 10r multi 2.25 2.25

Mountains — A211

Designs: 2r, Le Pouce. 7r, Corps de Garde. 8r, Le Chat et La Souris. 25r, Piton du Milieu.

2004, Mar. 11 *Perf. 14½x14¼*
983-986 A211 Set of 4 6.50 6.50

Traditional Trades — A212

Designs: 2r, Tinsmith. 7r, Cobbler. 9r, Blacksmith. 15r, Basket weaver.

Wmk. 373
2004, June 30 Litho. *Perf. 13½*
987-990 A212 Set of 4 5.00 5.00

24th Southern Africa Development Community Summit — A213

Emblem, woman at computer, building and panel in: 2r, Gray. 50r, Red.

Wmk. 373
2004, Aug. 16 Litho. *Perf. 13½*
991-992 A213 Set of 2 7.50 7.50

Rodrigues Regional Assembly — A214

Designs: 2r, Plaine Corail Airport. 7r, Ecotourism. 8r, Agricultural products. 10r, Coat of arms.

Wmk. 373
2004, Oct. 12 Litho. *Perf. 13½*
993-996 A214 Set of 4 5.50 5.50

Anthurium Andreanum Varieties A215

Designs: 2r, Acropolis. 8r, Tropical. 10r, Paradisio. 25r, Fantasia.

2004, Dec. 1 *Perf. 13¼*
997-1000 A215 Set of 4 7.00 7.00

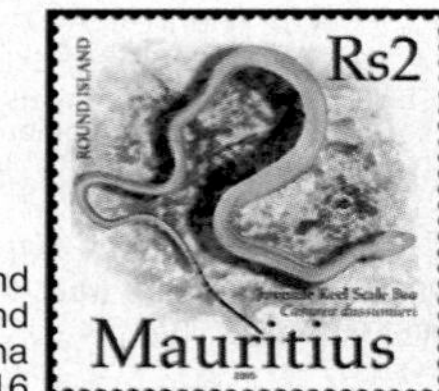

Round Island Flora and Fauna A216

Designs: 2r, Juvenile keel scale boa. 8r, Hurricane palm. 9r, Round Island petrel. 25r, Mazambron.

Wmk. 373
2005, Mar. 18 Litho. *Perf. 13¼*
1001-1004 A216 Set of 4 7.00 7.00

Postal Services A217

Designs: 2r, Counter services. 7r, Mail sorting. 8r, Mail distribution. 10r, Mail transfer.

Wmk. 373
2005, July 14 Litho. *Perf. 13¼*
1005-1008 A217 Set of 4 4.00 4.00

Stone Buildings — A218

Designs: 2r, Vagrant Depot, Grand River North West. 7r, Postal Museum, Port Louis. 16r, Carnegie Library, Curepipe.

Wmk. 373
2005, Oct. 9 Litho. *Perf. 13½*
1009-1011 A218 Set of 3 3.75 3.75

Ship Models — A219

Designs: 7r, 100-gun ship. 8r, Sampan. 9r, Roman galley. 16r, Drakkar.
25r, Drakkar, horiz.

Perf. 13¾x13½
2005, Dec. 20 Litho.
1012-1015 A219 Set of 4 6.00 6.00

Souvenir Sheet
Perf. 13½x13¾
1016 A219 25r multi 4.25 4.25

Mahebourg, Bicent. — A220

Designs: 2r, Market. 7r, Regattas. 8r, Le Lavoir. No. 1020, 16r, Pointe des Régates.
No. 1021, vert.: a, 16r, Mahé de la Bourdonnais. b, 16r, Gen. Charles Decaen.

Wmk. 373
2006, Feb. 4 Litho. *Perf. 13½*
1017-1020 A220 Set of 4 5.00 5.00

Souvenir Sheet
1021 A220 16r Sheet of 2, #a-b 5.25 5.25

Professor Basdeo Bissoondoyal (1906-91), Educator — A221

Wmk. 373
2006, Apr. 15 Litho. *Perf. 13¾*
1022 A221 10r multi 1.10 1.10

Ecological History — A222

Designs: 2r, Biological control of locusts with introduction of mynah birds, 1763. 8r, Fish repopulation with artificial reefs, 1980. 10r, Erosion control with terraces in Rodrigues, 1958. 25r, First captive breeding of giant tortoises, 1881.

2006, June 5 *Perf. 13½*
1023-1026 A222 Set of 4 5.50 5.50

Crabs — A223

Designs: 2r, Tourloulou crab. 7r, Land crab. 8s, Freshwater crab. 25r, Coconut crab.

Wmk. 373
2006, Oct. 9 Litho. *Perf. 13¼*
1027-1030 A223 Set of 4 4.50 4.50

Traditional Children's Activities — A224

Designs: 5r, Sapsiwaye. 10r, Marbles, horiz. 15r, Hop Scotch, horiz. 25r, Kite flying.

Perf. 13¾x13½, 13½x13¾

2006, Dec. 7

1031-1034	A224	Set of 4	3.50	3.50

Corals A225

Designs: 3r, Rodrigues endemic coral. 5r, Soft coral. 10r, Chagos coral. 15r, Head coral. 22r, Table coral. 25r, Tube coral.

Wmk. 373

2007, Apr. 30 Litho. *Perf. 13½*

1035-1040	A225	Set of 6	5.25	5.25

Drawings of Dodo Birds — A226

Drawing: 5r, From Journal of the Gelderland, 1601. 10r, By Adrian van de Venne, 1626. 15r, Published by Harrison, 1798. No. 1044, 25r, By J. W. Frohawk, 1905.

Wmk. 373

2007, June 25 Litho. *Perf. 13½*

1041-1044	A226	Set of 4	3.50	3.50

Dodo Drawings Type of 2007

Souvenir Sheet

Drawing: No. 1045, 25r, By Julian Pender Hume, 2001, vert.

Perf. 13x13¼

2007, June 25 Litho. Wmk. 373

1045	A226	25r multi	1.60	1.60

No. 1045 contains one 28x45mm stamp.

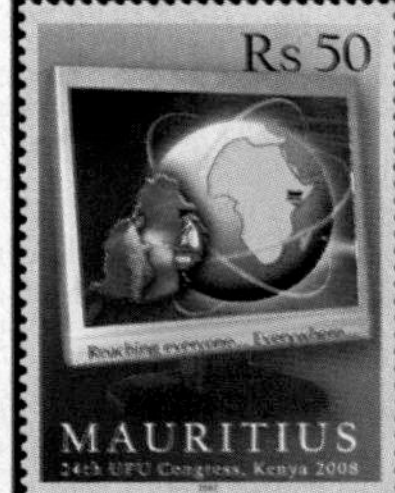

24th UPU Congress, Nairobi A227

Wmk. 373

2007, Oct. 9 Litho. *Perf. 13¼*

1046	A227	50r multi	3.50	3.50

Due to political unrest in Kenya, the UPU Congress was moved to Geneva, Switzerland.

Anniversaries — A228

Designs: 5r, Ministerial System, 50th anniv. 10r, Arrival in Mauritius of Manilall Doctor, cent., vert. 15r, Scouting, cent., vert. 25r, First meteorological observatory in Mauritius, 175th anniv.

2007, Dec. 4 *Perf. 13½*

1047-1050	A228	Set of 4	3.75	3.75

Ministerial System, 50th Anniv. (With Corrected Photograph) — A229

2007, Dec. 4 Litho. *Perf. 13½*

1051	A229	5r multi	.35	.35

The photo in the LR corner on No. 1051 differs from the photo in the LR corner on No. 1047.

Authors Who Mentioned Mauritius — A230

Author and work: 5r, Bernardin de St. Pierre (1737-1814), Paul et Virginie. 10r, Alexandre Dumas (père) (1802-70), Georges. 15r, Charles Baudelaire (1821-67), A une Dame Creole. 22r, Mark Twain (1835-1910), Following the Equator. 25r, Joesph Conrad (1857-1924), A Smile of Fortune.

Wmk. 406

2008, Dec. 8 Litho. *Perf. 13½*

1052-1056	A230	Set of 5	4.75	4.75

SPECIAL DELIVERY STAMPS

SD1

1903 Wmk. 1 *Perf. 14*

Red Surcharge

E1	SD1	15c on 15c ultra	11.00	32.50

SD2

SD3

EXPRESS
DELIVERY
(INLAND)
15 c

New Setting with Smaller "15c" without period — SD3a

1904

E2	SD2	15c on 15c ultra	57.50	77.50
a.		"INLAND" inverted		3,000.
b.		Inverted "A" in "INLAND"	1,575.	1,100.
E3	SD3	15c on 15c ultra	9.50	3.75
a.		Double surcharge, both inverted	1,800.	1,800.
b.		Inverted surcharge	1,000.	*675.00*
c.		Vert. pair, imperf between	*4,800.*	
E3F	SD3a	15c on 15c ultra	800.00	725.00
g.		Inverted surcharge		1,700.
h.		Double surcharge		3,300.
i.		Double surcharge, both inverted	—	5,500.
j.		"c" omitted		2,400.

To make No. E2 the word "INLAND" was printed on No. E1. For Nos. E3 and E3F, new settings of the surcharge were made with different spacing between the words.

SD4

SD5

E4	SD4	15c green & red	7.25	6.00
a.		Double surcharge	675.00	725.00
b.		Inverted surcharge	900.00	800.00
c.		"LNIAND."	—	
d.		As "c," double surcharge	*800.00*	725.00
E5	SD5	18c green & black	3.00	32.50
a.		Exclamation point (!) instead of "I" in "FOREIGN"	675.00	

POSTAGE DUE STAMPS

Catalogue values for unused stamps in this section are for Never Hinged items.

Numeral — D1

Perf. 14½x14

1933-54 Typo. Wmk. 4

J1	D1	2c black	1.50	.60
J2	D1	4c violet	.60	.80
J3	D1	6c red	.70	*.95*
J4	D1	10c green	.85	*1.50*
J5	D1	20c ultramarine	.60	*1.75*
J6	D1	50c dp red lilac ('54)	.65	*19.00*
J7	D1	1r orange ('54)	.85	*19.00*
		Nos. J1-J7 (7)	5.75	*43.60*

1966-68 Wmk. 314 *Perf. 14*

J8	D1	2c black ('67)	2.75	3.25

Perf. 14½14

J9	D1	4c rose violet ('68)	2.00	9.25
J10	D1	6c dp orange ('68)	7.50	22.50
J11	D1	10c yel green ('67)	.35	2.25
J12	D1	20c ultramarine	2.50	5.25
J13	D1	50c dp red lilac ('68)	.85	14.00
		Nos. J8-J13 (6)	15.95	56.50

Nos. 445-446, 450, 455, 457, 462 Surcharged "POSTAGE/ DUE" and New Value

Wmk. 373

1982, Oct. 25 Litho. *Perf. 13½*

J14	A92	10c on 15c multi	.20	.20
J15	A92	20c on 20c multi	.20	.60
J16	A91	50c on 60c multi	.35	.35
J17	A92	1r on 1.20r multi	.45	.35
J18	A92	1.50r on 1.50r multi	.60	.85
J19	A91	5r on 15r multi	1.10	2.50
		Nos. J14-J19 (6)	2.90	4.85

MAYOTTE

mä-ˈyät

LOCATION — One of the Comoro Islands situated in the Mozambique Channel midway between Madagascar and Mozambique (Africa)

GOVT. — French Colony

AREA — 144 sq. mi.

POP. — 149,336 (1999 est.)

CAPITAL — Mamoutzou

See Comoro Islands.

100 Centimes = 1 Franc

100 Cents = 1 Euro (2002)

Stamps of Mayotte were replaced successively by those of Madagascar, Comoro Islands and France. Individual issues were resumed in 1975.

See France No. 2271 for French stamp inscribed "Mayotte."

Catalogue values for unused stamps in this country are for Never Hinged items, beginning with Scott 75 in the regular postage section, and Scott C1 in the airpost section.

Navigation and Commerce — A1

Perf. 14x13½

1892-1907 Typo. Unwmk.

Name of Colony in Blue or Carmine

1	A1	1c blk, *lil bl*	.85	.75
2	A1	2c brn, *buff*	1.25	1.10
a.		Name double	350.00	300.00
3	A1	4c claret, *lav*	1.90	1.10
4	A1	5c grn, *grnsh*	4.00	2.10
5	A1	10c blk, *lavender*	6.50	3.25
6	A1	10c red ('00)	52.50	40.00
7	A1	15c blue, quadrille paper	12.00	7.25
8	A1	15c gray ('00)	95.00	82.50
9	A1	20c red, *grn*	8.00	7.25
10	A1	25c blk, *rose*	10.00	6.00
11	A1	25c blue ('00)	10.00	9.00
12	A1	30c brn, *bis*	15.00	10.00
13	A1	35c blk, *yel*	7.25	5.75
14	A1	40c red, *straw*	15.00	10.00
15	A1	45c blk, *gray grn* ('07)	15.00	14.00
16	A1	50c carmine, *rose*	22.50	16.00
17	A1	50c brn, *az* ('00)	22.50	22.50
18	A1	75c dp vio, *org*	20.00	14.00
19	A1	1fr brnz grn, *straw*	24.00	15.00
20	A1	5fr red lil, *lav* ('99)	100.00	95.00
		Nos. 1-20 (20)	443.25	362.55

Perf. 13½x14 stamps are counterfeits.

Issues of 1892-1907 Surcharged in Black or Carmine

1912

22	A1	5c on 2c brn, *buff*	2.10	2.10
23	A1	5c on 4c cl, *lav* (C)	1.50	1.50
24	A1	5c on 15c bl (C)	1.50	1.50
25	A1	5c on 20c red, *grn*	1.25	1.25
26	A1	5c on 25c blk, *rose* (C)	1.40	1.40
a.		Double surcharge	200.00	
27	A1	5c on 30c brn, *bis* (C)	1.50	1.50
28	A1	10c on 40c red, *straw*	1.50	1.50
a.		Double surcharge	225.00	
29	A1	10c on 45c blk, *gray grn* (C)	1.50	1.50
a.		Double surcharge	200.00	*225.00*
30	A1	10c on 50c car, *rose*	3.25	3.25
31	A1	10c on 75c dp vio, *org*	1.60	1.60
32	A1	10c on 1fr brnz grn, *straw*	2.10	2.10
		Nos. 22-32 (11)	19.20	19.20

Two spacings between the surcharged numerals are found on Nos. 22-32. For detailed listings, see the *Scott Classic Specialized Catalogue of Stamps and Covers.*

Nos. 22-32 were available for use in Madagascar and the entire Comoro archipelago.

Catalogue values for unused stamps in this section, from this point to the end of the section, are for Never Hinged items.

Marianne Type of France Ovtpd. "MAYOTTE"

1997, Jan. 2 Engr. *Perf. 13*

Design A1161

75	10c on #2179	.20	.20
76	20c on #2180	.20	.20
77	50c on #2181	.25	.25
78	1fr on #2182	.55	.55
79	2fr on #2331	1.10	1.10
80	(2.50fr) on #2342	1.25	1.25
81	2.70fr on #2334	1.40	1.40
82	3.80fr on #2337	1.75	1.75
83	5fr on #2194	2.50	2.50
84	10fr on #2195	5.00	5.00
	Nos. 75-84 (10)	14.20	14.20

Ylang Ylang — A5

1997, Jan. 2 Litho. *Perf. 13½x13*

85 A5 2.70fr multicolored 1.50 1.50

Coat of Arms — A6

1997, Jan. 2 *Perf. 13x13½*

86 A6 3fr multicolored 1.25 1.25

a. Sheet of 4 5.00 5.00

#86a issued 6/19/99 for Philex France 99.

Le Banga — A7

1997, May 31 Litho. *Perf. 13*

87 A7 3.80fr multicolored 1.75 1.75

Dzen Dzé Musical Instrument A8

Photo. & Engr.

1997, May 31 *Perf. 12½*

88 A8 5.20fr multicolored 2.50 2.50

Lemur A9

1997, Aug. 30 Engr. *Perf. 12*

89 A9 3fr red & dk brown 1.50 1.50

Face of a Woman A10

1997, Aug. 30 Litho. *Perf. 13*

90 A10 3.50fr multicolored 1.50 1.50

Marine Life — A11

1997, Nov. 29 Litho. *Perf. 13*

91 A11 3fr multicolored 1.50 1.50

Longoni Port — A12

1998, Jan. 31 Litho. *Perf. 13*

92 A12 2.70fr multicolored 1.40 1.40

Chelonia Mydas — A13

1998, Jan. 31

93 A13 3fr multicolored 1.75 1.75

Family Planning — A14

1998, Apr. 1 Litho. *Perf. 13¼x13*

94 A14 1fr multicolored .50 .50

France No. 2604 Ovptd. "MAYOTTE"

Die Cut x Serpentine Die Cut 7

1998, Apr. 15 Engr.

Self-Adhesive

104 A1409 (3fr) red 1.40 1.40

a. Booklet pane of 10 14.00

No. 104a is a complete booklet, the peelable backing serves as a booklet cover.

Children's Carnival A15

1998, May 30 Litho. *Perf. 13*

105 A15 3fr multicolored 1.50 1.50

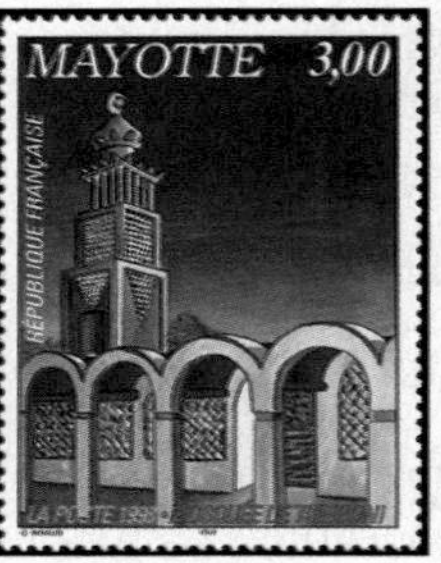

Ferry, "Salama Djema II" — A16

1998, May 30

106 A16 3.80fr multicolored 1.75 1.75

Mosque of Tsingoni A17

1998, Sept. 5 Litho. *Perf. 13*

107 A17 3fr multicolored 1.50 1.50

Mariama Salim — A18

Photo. & Engr.

1998, Oct. 3 *Perf. 13*

108 A18 2.70fr multicolored 1.25 1.25

Traditional Fishing, Djarifa — A19

1998, Nov. 7 Litho. *Perf. 13*

109 A19 2fr multicolored 1.00 1.00

Pomacanthus — A20

1998, Nov. 7

110 A20 3fr multicolored 1.50 1.50

See Nos. 121-124.

Agricultural Tools — A21

1998, Dec. 19 Litho. *Perf. 13*

111 A21 3fr multicolored 1.50 1.50

France Nos. 2589-2593, 2601, 2603 Ovptd. "MAYOTTE"

1999, Jan. 1 Engr. *Perf. 13*

112	A1409	10c brn (#2589)	.20	.20
113	A1409	20c brt bl grn (#2590)	.20	.20
114	A1409	50c purple (#2591)	.20	.20
115	A1409	1fr brt orange (#2592)	.50	.50
116	A1409	2fr brt blue (#2593)	.90	.90
117	A1409	5fr brt grn bl (#2601)	2.00	2.00
118	A1409	10fr violet (#2603)	4.50	4.50
		Nos. 112-118 (7)	8.50	8.50

Map of Mayotte A22

1999, Feb. 6 *Perf. 12x13*

119 A22 3fr multicolored 1.50 1.50

Combani Dam A23

1999, Feb. 6 Litho. *Perf. 13*

120 A23 8fr multicolored 3.50 3.50

Fish Type of 1998

Designs: 2.70fr, Cephalopholis miniatus, vert. 3fr, Pterois volitans. 5.20fr, Pygoplites diacanthus. 10fr, Acanthurus leucosternon.

Perf. 13¼x13, 13x13¼

1999, Apr. 3 Litho.

121	A20	2.70fr multicolored	1.00	1.00
122	A20	3fr multicolored	1.25	1.25
123	A20	5.20fr multicolored	1.75	1.75
124	A20	10fr multicolored	3.50	3.50
		Nos. 121-124 (4)	7.50	7.50

France No. 2691 Ovptd. "MAYOTTE"

1999, May 25 Engr. *Perf. 13*

125 A1470 3fr red & blue 1.25 1.25

Founga — A24

Photo. & Engr.

1999, June 5 *Perf. 13*

126 A24 5.40fr multicolored 2.50 2.50

Baobab Tree — A25

1999, June 5 Litho. ***Perf. 13x13½***
127 A25 8fr multicolored 2.75 2.75

Dzaoudzi Prefecture A26

1999, Sept. 25 Litho. ***Perf. 13x13¼***
128 A26 3fr multicolored 1.40 1.40

Souvenir Sheet

Pirogues — A27

Designs: a, Pirogues on beach, shown. b, Pirogues, vert. c, Pirogues, close-up.

1999, Sept. 25 ***Perf. 13***
129 A27 5fr Sheet of 3, #a.-c. 8.00 8.00

Vanilla A28

1999, Nov. 6 Litho. ***Perf. 13***
130 A28 4.50fr multi 1.75 1.75

Soulou Waterfalls — A29

1999, Dec. 11 ***Perf. 13½x13***
131 A29 10fr multi 4.00 4.00

Year 2000 A30

1999, Dec. 11 ***Perf. 13***
132 A30 3fr multi 1.25 1.25

Indian Ocean Boat — A31

2000, Feb. 5 Litho. ***Perf. 13x13¼***
133 A31 3fr multi 1.25 1.25

Whales A32

2000, Feb. 5 Litho. ***Perf. 13x13¼***
134 A32 5.20fr multi 2.25 2.25

Inner Wheel Rotary District — A33

2000, Mar. 24 ***Perf. 13¼x13***
135 A33 5.20fr multi 2.10 2.10

Lagoon A34

2000, Apr. 29 Litho. ***Perf. 13x13¼***
136 A34 3fr multi 1.25 1.25

Souvenir Sheet

Mahoraise Women — A35

Woman in: a, 3fr, red. b, 5.20fr, white.
Illustration reduced.

2000, Apr. 29 ***Perf. 13¼x13***
137 A35 Sheet of 2, #a-b 3.50 3.50

Tire Race A36

2000, June 24 ***Perf. 13x13¼***
138 A36 3fr multi 1.25 1.25

Tomb of Sultan Andriantsouli — A37

2000, June 24
139 A37 5.40fr multi 2.10 2.10

Souvenir Sheet

Sea Shells — A38

No. 140: a, Cassis cornuta. b, Charonia tritonis. c, Cyraecassis rufa. d, Cyprae mauritania, Cyprae tigris.
Illustration reduced.

2000, Sept. 23 Litho. ***Perf. 13x13½***
140 A38 3fr Sheet of 4, #a-d 5.00 5.00

Zéna M'Déré (1917-99), Politician A39

2000, Oct. 27 ***Perf. 13***
141 A39 3fr multi 1.25 1.25

Ylang Distillery A40

2000, Nov. 25 Litho. ***Perf. 13x13½***
142 A40 2.70fr multi 1.10 1.10

New Hospital — A41

2000, Nov. 25 ***Perf. 13½x13***
143 A41 10fr multi 4.00 4.00

Map of Mayotte — A42

2001, Jan. 1 Litho. ***Perf. 13***
144 A42 2.70fr grn & blk .90 .90
145 A42 (3fr) red & blk 1.00 1.00

Breastfeeding A43

2001, Jan. 27 ***Perf. 13¼x13***
146 A43 3fr multi 1.60 1.60

Return of Pilgrims to Mecca A44

2001, Mar. 10 ***Perf. 13x13¼***
147 A44 2.70fr multi 1.40 1.40

Bush Taxi — A45

2001, Mar. 10 ***Perf. 13***
148 A45 3fr multi 1.40 1.40

Soccer — A46

2001, May 26 Litho. ***Perf. 13¼x13***
149 A46 3fr multi 1.40 1.40

Fish Type of 1998

Design: Pajama fish (gaterin, plectorhinchus orientalis).

2001, May 26 ***Perf. 13x13¼***
150 A20 10fr multi 4.00 4.00

Foreign Legion Detachment in Mayotte, 25th Anniv. — A47

2001, Apr. 30 Litho. ***Perf. 13***
151 A47 5.20fr multi 2.00 2.00

Souvenir Sheet

Flying Foxes — A48

No. 152: a, 3fr, Hanging from branch. b, 5.20fr, In flight.

2001, July 7 Litho. ***Perf. 13x13½***
152 A48 Sheet of 2, #a-b 4.00 4.00

Adapted Military Service Group, 1st Anniv. A49

2001, Sept. 1 Litho. ***Perf. 13x13½***
153 A49 3fr multi 1.00 1.00

Flowers A50

Designs: 3fr, Shown. 5.40fr, Fruits.

2001, Sept. 22 ***Perf. 13***
154-155 A50 Set of 2 3.50 3.50

Lake Dziani Dzaha — A51

2001, Nov. 17
156 A51 5.20fr multi 2.00 2.00

Mayotte Post Office A52

2001, Nov. 17
157 A52 10fr multi 4.00 4.00

100 Cents = 1 Euro (€)

Arms — A53

2002, Jan. 1 Litho. ***Perf. 13x13½***
158 A53 46c multi 1.40 1.40

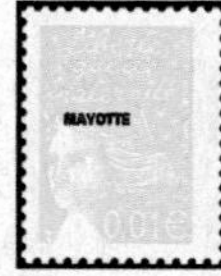

France Nos. 2835, 2849-2863 Overprinted

2002, Jan. 1 Engr. ***Perf. 13***

159	A1583	1c	yellow	.20	.20
160	A1583	2c	brown	.20	.20
161	A1583	5c	brt bl grn	.20	.20
162	A1583	10c	purple	.30	.30
163	A1583	20c	brt org	.60	.60
164	A1583	41c	brt green	1.25	1.25
165	A1409	(46c)	red	1.40	1.40
166	A1583	50c	dk blue	1.50	1.50
167	A1583	53c	apple grn	1.50	1.50
168	A1583	58c	blue	1.75	1.75
169	A1583	64c	dark org	2.00	2.00
170	A1583	67c	brt blue	2.00	2.00
171	A1583	69c	brt pink	2.10	2.10
172	A1583	€1	Prus blue	3.00	3.00
173	A1583	€1.02	dk green	3.00	3.00
174	A1583	€2	violet	6.00	6.00
	Nos. 159-174 (16)			27.00	27.00

Athletics — A54

2002, Mar. 23 Litho. ***Perf. 13***
175 A54 41c multi 1.25 1.25

Kawéni Mangrove Swamp — A55

2002, Mar. 25
176 A55 €1.52 multi 4.50 4.50

Mayotte Communes, 25th Anniv. — A56

2002, June 3 Litho. ***Perf. 13¼x13***
177 A56 46c multi 1.40 1.40

Salt Drying — A57

Illustration reduced.

2002, June 3 ***Perf. 13x13¼***
178 A57 79c multi 2.40 2.40

2002 Census — A58

2002, July 29 Litho. ***Perf. 13¼x13***
179 A58 46c multi 1.40 1.40

Abandoned Sugar Processing Equipment — A59

2002, Sept. 21 Litho. ***Perf. 13***
180 A59 82c multi 2.50 2.50

Miniature Sheet

Birds — A60

No. 181: a, Souimanga. b, Drongo. c, Oiseau-lunette. d, Foudy.

2002, Sept. 21 ***Perf. 13x13¼***
181 A60 46c Sheet of 4, #a-d 5.50 5.50

Mt. Choungui — A61

2002, Nov. 16 Litho. ***Perf. 13¼x13***
182 A61 46c multi 1.40 1.40

Breadfruit — A62

2002, Nov. 16
183 A62 €1.22 multi 3.75 3.75

Vanilla and Ylang Museum A63

2003, Jan. 1 Litho. ***Perf. 13x13½***
184 A63 46c multi 2.00 2.00

Banana Tree — A64

2003, Feb. 1 ***Perf. 13½x13***
185 A64 79c multi 2.40 2.40

Holiday Face Decorations A65

2003, Apr. 5 Litho. ***Perf. 13***
186 A65 46c multi 1.50 1.50

Swordfish — A66

2003, Apr. 5
187 A66 79c multi 2.40 2.40

Gecko — A67

2003, June 14 Litho. ***Perf. 13***
188 A67 50c multi 1.50 1.50

Mraha Game — A68

2003, June 14 **Engr.** ***Perf. 13x12½***
189 A68 €1.52 claret & brown 4.50 4.50

Mtzamboro College A69

2003, Sept. 6 **Litho.** ***Perf. 13x13¼***
190 A69 45c multi 1.40 1.40

Ziyara de Pole — A70

2003, Sept. 6 ***Perf. 13¼x13***
191 A70 82c multi 2.50 2.50

Basketball — A71

2003, Nov. 15 **Litho.** ***Perf. 13¼x13***
192 A71 50c multi 1.50 1.50

Wadaha A72

2004, Jan. 3 ***Perf. 13***
193 A72 50c multi 1.50 1.50

Map Type of 2001 Inscribed "RF" and With Euro Denominations Only

2004

194	A42	1c yel & blk	.20	.20
195	A42	2c gray & blk	.20	.20
196	A42	5c greenish bl & blk	.20	.20
197	A42	10c red vio & blk	.25	.25
198	A42	20c org & blk	.50	.50
199	A42	45c green & black	1.25	1.25
200	A42	50c dk bl & blk	1.25	1.25
201	A42	€1 Prus bl & blk	2.40	2.40
202	A42	€2 violet & blk	5.00	5.00
		Nos. 194-202 (9)	11.25	11.25

Issued: 1c, 2c, 50c, €2, 3/10; 5c, 10c, 20c, €1, 4/17; 45c, 7/17.

Sada Bay — A73

2004, Apr. 3 **Litho.** ***Perf. 13***
203 A73 90c multi 2.40 2.40

Souvenir Sheet

Butterflies — A74

No. 204: a, Junonia rhadama. b, Papilio demodocus. c, Acraea ranavalona. d, Danaus chrysippus.

2004, Apr. 3 ***Perf. 13x13¼***
204 A74 50c Sheet of 4, #a-d 5.50 5.50

Papaya and Papaya Tree A75

2004, June 12 **Litho.** ***Perf. 13x13¼***
205 A75 50c multi 1.25 1.25

Gold Jewelry A76

2004, June 12 **Litho.** ***Perf. 13***
206 A76 €2.40 multi 6.50 6.50

Kwalé River Bridge A77

2004, Sept. 25 **Litho.** ***Perf. 13x13¼***
207 A77 50c multi 1.40 1.40

Maki and Young A78

2004, Sept. 25 ***Perf. 13***
208 A78 75c multi 2.10 2.10

Woman Cooking Food A79

2004, Nov. 13 ***Perf. 13x13¼***
209 A79 45c multi 1.25 1.25

Domino Players — A80

2004, Nov. 13 ***Perf. 13***
210 A80 75c multi 2.25 2.25

Ylang-ylang Trees — A81

2005, Jan. 3 **Litho.** ***Perf. 13***
211 A81 50c multi 1.75 1.75

Traditional Women's Clothing A82

2005, Mar. 14 **Litho.** ***Perf. 13***
212 A82 53c multi 1.40 1.40

Breadfruit and Tree — A83

2005, Mar. 14 ***Perf. 13¼x13***
213 A83 64c multi 1.75 1.75

Rotary International, Cent. — A84

2005, May 13 ***Perf. 13***
214 A84 90c multi 2.25 2.25

Souvenir Sheet

Marine Mammals — A85

No. 215: a, Humpback whale (Baleine à bosse). b, Dolphins. c, Sperm whale (grand cachalot). d, Dugongs.

2005, May 13 ***Perf. 13x13¼***
215 A85 53c Sheet of 4, #a-d 5.75 5.75

Stick Figure Drawings A86

2005, July 4 ***Perf. 13***
216 A86 48c multi 1.25 1.25

Mamoudzou — A87

2005, Sept. 10 **Litho.** ***Perf. 13***
217 A87 48c multi 1.25 1.25

Fisherman in Pirogue A88

2005, Sept. 10
218 A88 75c multi 1.90 1.90

Blacksmith A89

2005, Nov. 12 **Litho.** ***Perf. 13x13¼***
219 A89 53c multi 1.25 1.25

Tam-tam Boeuf Celebration — A90

2005, Nov. 12 ***Perf. 13***
220 A90 53c multi 1.25 1.25

Woman Grating Coconuts A91

2006, Jan. 14 Litho. ***Perf. 13x13¼***
221 A91 53c multi 1.25 1.25

Moya Beach — A92

2006, Mar. 18 Litho. ***Perf. 13***
222 A92 48c multi 1.25 1.25

Souvenir Sheet

"Protection des tortues"

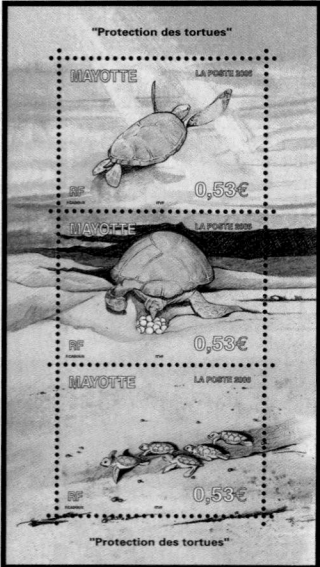

Turtle Protection — A93

No. 223: a, Turtle swimming. b, Turtle laying eggs. c, Hatchlings.

2006, Mar. 18 ***Perf. 13x13¼***
223 A93 53c Sheet of 3, #a-c 4.00 4.00

Farmer's Market — A94

Ferries — A95

2006, May 15 Litho. ***Perf. 13x12¾***
224 A94 53c multi 1.40 1.40
225 A95 €1.07 multi 2.75 2.75

Aloe Mayottensis A96

2006, July 3 Litho. ***Perf. 13¼x13***
226 A96 53c multi 1.40 1.40

Frangipani Shrub and Flowers A97

2006, Sept. 9 ***Perf. 13x13¼***
227 A97 53c multi 1.40 1.40

Moulidi Dance — A98

2006, Sept. 9 ***Perf. 13***
228 A98 75c multi 1.90 1.90

Tropic Birds A99

2006, Nov. 18 Litho. ***Perf. 13***
229 A99 54c multi 1.50 1.50

Resumption of Stamp Issues, 10th Anniv. — A100

2007, Jan. 20 Litho. ***Perf. 13½x13***
230 A100 54c multi 1.40 1.40

Phanelopsis Orchid — A101

2007, Jan. 20 ***Perf. 13x13½***
231 A101 54c multi 1.40 1.40

Audit Office, Bicent. A102

2007, Mar. 19 Engr. ***Perf. 13¼***
232 A102 54c multi 1.50 1.50

Phyllostachys Edulis — A103

2007, Mar. 19 Litho. ***Perf. 13¼x13***
233 A103 €1.01 multi 2.75 2.75

Traditional House A104

2007, May 14 ***Perf. 13x13¼***
234 A104 54c multi 1.50 1.50

General Council, 30th Anniv. — A105

2007, May 12 Litho. ***Perf. 13¼x13***
235 A105 54c multi 1.50 1.50

Souvenir Sheet

Corals — A106

No. 236: a, Corail corne d'elan. b, Gorgone eventail. c, Corail corne de cerf. d, Cerveau de Neptune.

2007, June 16 ***Perf. 13x13¼***
236 A106 54c Sheet of 4, #a-d 6.00 6.00

Mangos and Mango Tree A107

2007, Sept. 17 Litho. ***Perf. 13x13¼***
237 A107 54c multi 1.60 1.60

Chameleon — A108

2007, Sept. 17
238 A108 54c multi 1.60 1.60

Beach Grill and Shelter — A109

2007, Nov. 10 ***Perf. 13***
239 A109 54c multi 1.60 1.60

N'Gouja Beach — A110

Illustration reduced.

2007, Nov. 10 ***Perf. 13x13¼***
240 A110 54c multi 1.60 1.60

Zebu A111

2008, Jan. 28 Litho. ***Perf. 13x13½***
241 A111 54c multi 1.60 1.60

Coconuts and Coconut Palm — A112

2008, Jan. 28 ***Perf. 13x13¼***
242 A112 54c multi 1.60 1.60

Miniature Sheet

Spices — A113

No. 243: a, Cinnamon (cannelle). b, Nutmeg (muscade). c, Turmeric (curcuma). d, Ginger (gingembre).

2008, Mar. 22 Litho. ***Perf. 13x13¼***
243 A113 55c Sheet of 4, #a-d 7.00 7.00

Hibiscus — A114

2008, May 26 ***Perf. 13¼x13***
244 A114 55c multi 1.75 1.75

Wedding Ceremony A115

2008, May 26 ***Perf. 13***
245 A115 55c multi 1.75 1.75

Younoussa Bamana (1935-2007), Politician — A116

2008, June 23 Litho. ***Perf. 13¼x13***
246 A116 55c multi 1.75 1.75

M'Biwi Dance A117

2008, Sept. 22 Litho. ***Perf. 13x13¼***
247 A117 55c multi 1.50 1.50

Embroidery — A118

2008, Nov. 10 Litho. ***Perf. 13x13¼***
248 A118 55c multi 1.40 1.40

Mamoudzou Town Hall — A119

2008, Dec. 8 ***Perf. 13***
249 A119 55c multi 1.50 1.50

Longoni Power Station — A120

2009, Jan. 12
250 A120 55c multi 1.50 1.50

AIR POST STAMPS

Catalogue values for unused stamps in this section are for Never Hinged items.

Opening of New Air Terminal — AP1

1997, Mar. 1 Engr. ***Perf. 13x12½***
C1 AP1 20fmulticolored 10.00 10.00

First Mayotte-Réunion Flight, 20th Anniv. — AP2

Photo. & Engr.
1997, Nov. 29 ***Perf. 13x12½***
C2 AP2 5fr multicolored 2.25 2.25

Pique-boeuf Bird, Zebu — AP3

1998, Apr. 1 Litho. ***Perf. 13***
C3 AP3 30fr multicolored 13.00 13.00

Deba Religious Festival — AP4

1999, Nov. 6 Litho. ***Perf. 13***
C4 AP4 10fr multicolored 3.75 3.75

Dzaoudzi Aero Club — AP5

2001, July 7 Litho. ***Perf. 13***
C5 AP5 20fr multi 8.00 8.00

Dzaoudzi Rock — AP6

2003, Nov. 15 Litho. ***Perf. 13***
C6 AP6 €1.50 multi 4.50 4.50

MEMEL

'mā-məl

LOCATION — In northern Europe, bordering on the Baltic Sea
GOVT. — Special commission (see below)
AREA — 1099 sq. mi.
POP. — 151,960

Following World War I this territory was detached from Germany and by Treaty of Versailles assigned to the government of a commission of the Allied and Associated Powers (not the League of Nations), which administered it until January, 1923, when it was forcibly occupied by Lithuania. In 1924 Memel became incorporated as a semi-autonomous district of Lithuania with the approval of the Allied Powers and the League of Nations.

100 Pfennig = 1 Mark
100 Centu = 1 Litas (1923)

Excellent counterfeits of all Memel stamps exist.

Stamps of Germany, 1905-20, Overprinted

Wmk. Lozenges (125)
1920, Aug. 1 ***Perf. 14, 14½***

1	A16	5pf green	.80	*3.25*
2	A16	10pf car rose	2.25	*9.00*
3	A16	10pf orange	.25	*1.50*
4	A22	15pf violet brown	2.40	*8.00*
5	A16	20pf blue violet	.80	*3.25*
6	A16	30pf org & blk, *buff*	1.75	*4.00*
7	A16	30pf dull blue	.40	*1.60*
8	A16	40pf lake & blk	.25	*1.60*
9	A16	50pf pur & blk, *buff*	.25	*1.60*
10	A16	60pf olive green	1.00	*4.50*
11	A16	75pf grn & blk	2.40	*9.50*
12	A16	80pf blue violet	1.50	*4.75*

Overprinted

13	A17	1m car rose	.40	*1.50*
14	A17	1.25m green	10.50	*47.50*
15	A17	1.50m yel brn	4.00	*15.00*
16	A21	2m blue	2.00	*6.50*
17	A21	2.50m red lilac	12.00	*27.50*
		Nos. 1-17 (17)	42.95	*150.55*

Stamps of France, Surcharged in Black

On A22

On A18

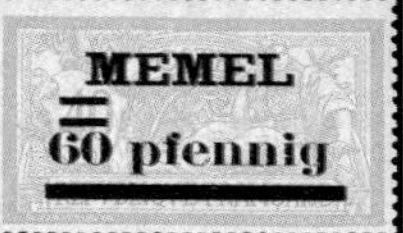

1920 Unwmk. ***Perf. 14x13½***

18	A22	5pf on 5c green	.20	*.55*
19	A22	10pf on 10c red	.20	*1.00*
20	A22	20pf on 25c blue	.20	*.55*
21	A22	30pf on 30c org	.40	*1.00*
22	A22	40pf on 20c red brn	.20	*.55*
23	A22	50pf on 35c vio	.20	*.55*
24	A18	60pf on 40c red & pale bl	.35	*1.00*
25	A18	80pf on 45c grn & bl	.55	*1.60*
26	A18	1m on 50c brn & lav	.20	*1.60*
27	A18	1m 25pf on 60c vio & ultra	1.25	*4.50*
28	A18	2m on 1fr cl & ol grn	.35	*.75*
29	A18	3m on 5fr bl & buff	18.50	*32.50*
		Nos. 18-29 (12)	22.60	*46.15*

For stamps with additional surcharges and overprints see Nos. 43-49, C1-C4.

French Stamps of 1900-20 Surcharged like Nos. 24 to 29 in Red or Black

4
Type I

4
Type II

Four Marks

1920-21 Unwmk. ***Perf. 14x13½***

30	A18	3m on 2fr org & pale bl	14.00	*32.50*
31	A18	4m on 2fr org & pale bl (I) (Bk)	.25	*.65*
a.		Type II	80.00	*125.00*
32	A18	10m on 5fr bl & buff	2.75	*7.25*
33	A18	20m on 5fr bl & buff	35.00	*95.00*
		Nos. 30-33 (4)	52.00	*135.40*

For stamps with additional overprints see Nos. C5, C19.

New Value with Initial Capital

1921

39	A18	60Pf on 40c red & pale bl	4.25	10.50
40	A18	3M on 60c vio & ultra	2.10	*4.00*
41	A18	10M on 5fr bl & buff	1.60	*3.50*
42	A18	20M on 45c grn & bl	6.50	*25.00*
		Nos. 39-42 (4)	14.45	*43.00*

The surcharged value on No. 40 is in italics.
For stamps with additional overprints see Nos. C6-C7, C18.

Stamps of 1920 Surcharged with Large Numerals in Dark Blue or Red

1921-22

43	A22	15pf on 10pf on 10c	.40	*.80*
a.		Inverted surcharge	60.00	*125.00*
44	A22	15pf on 20pf on 25c	.35	*.80*
a.		Inverted surcharge	60.00	*82.50*
45	A22	15pf on 50pf on 35c (R)	.25	*.50*
a.		Inverted surcharge	60.00	*82.50*
46	A22	60pf on 40pf on 20c	.25	*.60*
a.		Inverted surcharge	60.00	*125.00*
47	A18	75pf on 60pf on 40c	.60	*1.00*
48	A18	1.25m on 1m on 50c	.20	*.50*
49	A18	5.00m on 2m on 1fr	.65	*2.00*
a.		Inverted surcharge	300.00	*550.00*
		Nos. 43-49 (7)	2.70	*6.20*

Stamps of France Surcharged in Black or Red

On A20, A22

1922

50 A22 5pf on 5c org .20 .50
51 A22 10pf on 10c red .80 3.50
52 A22 10pf on 10c grn .20 .50
53 A22 15pf on 10c grn .20 .60
54 A22 20pf on 20c red brn 6.50 25.00
55 A22 20pf on 25c bl 7.25 25.00
56 A22 25pf on 5c org .20 .60
57 A22 30pf on 30c red .80 3.25
58 A22 35pf on 35c vio .20 .40
59 A20 50pf on 50c dl bl .20 .50
60 A20 75pf on 15c grn .20 .40
61 A22 75pf on 35c vio .20 .50
62 A22 1m on 25c blue .20 .40
63 A22 1¼m on 30c red .20 .40
64 A22 3m on 5c org .20 2.10
65 A20 6m on 15c grn (R) .35 2.00
66 A22 8m on 30c red .40 6.50

On A18

67 A18 40pf on 40c red & pale bl .20 .50
68 A18 80pf on 45c grn & bl .20 .50
69 A18 1m on 40c red & pale bl .20 .50
70 A18 1.25m on 60c vio & ultra (R) .20 .50
71 A18 1.50m on 45c grn & bl (R) .20 .50
72 A18 2m on 45c grn & bl .50 1.00
73 A18 2m on 1fr cl & ol grn .20 .50
74 A18 2¼m on 40c red & pale bl .20 .35
75 A18 2½m on 60c vio & ultra .35 .75
76 A18 3m on 60c vio & ultra (R) .60 1.60
77 A18 4m on 45c grn & bl .20 .25
78 A18 5m on 1fr cl & ol grn .25 .50
79 A18 6m on 60c vio & ultra .20 .35
80 A18 6m on 2fr org & pale bl .35 .50
81 A18 9m on 1fr cl & ol grn .40 .50
82 A18 9m on 5fr bl & buff (R) .35 1.60
83 A18 10m on 45c grn & bl (R) .40 2.10
84 A18 12m on 40c red & pale bl .20 1.00
85 A18 20m on 40c red & pale bl .40 2.50
86 A18 20m on 2fr org & pale bl .20 1.00
87 A18 30m on 60c vio & ultra .40 2.10
88 A18 30m on 5fr dk bl & buff 4.00 10.00
89 A18 40m on 1fr cl & ol grn .50 2.75
90 A18 50m on 2fr org & pale bl 11.00 25.00
91 A18 80m on 2fr org & pale bl (R) .75 2.75
92 A18 100m on 5fr bl & buff .75 5.50
Nos. 50-92 (43) 41.50 137.25

A 500m on 5fr dark blue and buff was prepared, but not officially issued. Value, $800.

For stamps with additional surcharges and overprints see Nos. 93-99, C8-C17, C20-29C.

Nos. 52, 54, 67, 59 Surcharged "Mark"

1922-23

93 A22 10m on 10pf on 10c .90 4.50
a. Double surcharge 100.00 240.00
94 A22 20m on 20pf on 20c .60 2.00
95 A18 40m on 40pf on 40c ('23) .80 2.50
96 A20 50m on 50pf on 50c 1.90 7.25
Nos. 93-96 (4) 4.20 16.25

Nos. 72, 61, 70 Surcharged with New Values in Red or Black

1922-23

97 A18 10m on 2m on 45c 1.60 7.25
98 A22 25m on 1m on 25c 1.60 7.25
99 A18 80m on 1.25m on 60c (Bk) ('23) 1.25 4.00
Nos. 97-99 (3) 4.45 18.50

For No. 99 with additional surcharges see Nos. N28-N30.

AIR POST STAMPS

Nos. 24-26, 28, 31, 39-40 Overprinted in Dark Blue

1921, July 6 Unwmk. *Perf. 14x13½*

C1 A18 60pf on 40c 40.00 80.00
C2 A18 80pf on 45c 2.75 8.00
C3 A18 1m on 50c 2.75 4.75
C4 A18 2m on 1fr 2.75 7.50
a. "Flugpost" inverted 175.00 325.00
C5 A18 4m on 2fr (I) 4.25 13.00
a. Type II 100.00 225.00

New Value with Initial Capital

C6 A18 60Pf on 40c 4.00 8.00
a. "Flugpost" inverted 175.00 350.00
C7 A18 3M on 60c 3.50 8.00
a. "Flugpost" inverted 175.00 350.00
Nos. C1-C7 (7) 60.00 129.25

The surcharged value on No. C7 is in italics.

Nos. 67-71, 73, 76, 78, 80, 82 Overprinted in Dark Blue

1922, May 12

C8 A18 40pf on 40c .35 2.00
C9 A18 80pf on 45c .35 2.00
C10 A18 1m on 40c .35 2.00
C11 A18 1.25m on 60c .65 2.10
C12 A18 1.50m on 45c .65 2.50
C13 A18 2m on 1fr .65 2.50
C14 A18 3m on 60c .65 2.50
C15 A18 5m on 1fr .80 2.60
C16 A18 6m on 2fr .80 2.60
C17 A18 9m on 5fr .80 2.60

Same Overprint On Nos. 40, 31

C18 A18 3m on 60c 95.00 1,000.
C19 A18 4m on 2fr .65 2.50
Nos. C8-C17,C19 (11) 6.70 25.90

Nos. 67, 69-71, 73, 76, 78, 80, 82 Overprinted in Black or Red

1922, Oct. 17

C20 A18 40pf on 40c 1.20 8.00
C21 A18 1m on 40c 1.20 8.00
C22 A18 1.25m on 60c (R) 1.20 8.00
C23 A18 1.50m on 45c (R) 1.20 8.00
C24 A18 2m on 1fr 1.20 8.00
C25 A18 3m on 60c (R) 1.20 8.00
C26 A18 4m on 2fr 1.20 8.00
C27 A18 5m on 1fr 1.20 8.00
C28 A18 6m on 2fr 1.20 8.00
C29 A18 9m on 5fr (R) 1.20 8.00
Nos. C20-C29 (10) 12.00 80.00

No. C26 is not known without the "FLUGPOST" overprint.

OCCUPATION STAMPS

Issued under Lithuanian Occupation

Surcharged in Various Colors on Unissued Official Stamps of Lithuania Similar to Type O4

On Nos. N1-N6

On Nos. N7-N11

Memel Printing

1923 Unwmk. Litho. *Perf. 11*

N1 O4 10m on 5c bl (Bk) .80 4.75
a. "Memel" and bars omitted 5.75 47.50
N2 O4 25m on 5c bl (R) .80 4.75
N3 O4 50m on 25c red (Bk) .80 5.00
N4 O4 100m on 25c red (G) .80 5.00
N5 O4 400m on 1 l brn (R) 1.25 8.00
N6 O4 500m on 1 l brn (Bl) 1.25 8.00
Nos. N1-N6 (6) 5.70 35.50

Nos. N1 and N3-N6 exist with double surcharge. Value $50 each.

Kaunas Printing

Black Surcharge

N7 O4 10m on 5c blue .50 3.25
N8 O4 25m on 5c blue .50 3.25
N9 O4 50m on 25c red .50 3.25
N10 O4 100m on 25c red .65 3.25
N11 O4 400m on 1 l brn 1.10 6.00
Nos. N7-N11 (5) 3.25 19.00

No. N8 has the value in "Markes," others of the group have it in "Markiu."

For additional surcharge see No. N87.

Surcharged in Various Colors on Unissued Official Stamps of Lithuania Similar to Type O4

1923

N12 O4 10m on 5c bl (R) 1.60 5.75
a. "Markes" instead of "Markiu" 14.50 65.00
N13 O4 20m on 5c bl (R) 1.60 5.75
N14 O4 25m on 25c red (Bl) 1.60 8.00
N15 O4 50m on 25c red (Bl) 3.25 8.00
a. Inverted surcharge 40.00 160.00
N16 O4 100m on 1 l brn (Bk) 3.25 10.50
a. Inverted surcharge 40.00 160.00
N17 O4 200m on 1 l brn (Bk) 4.00 10.50
Nos. N12-N17 (6) 15.30 48.50

No. N14 has the value in "Markes," others of the group have it in "Markiu."

"Vytis"

O4 O5

1923, Mar.

N18 O4 10m lt brown .40 3.50
N19 O4 20m yellow .40 3.50
N20 O4 25m orange .40 3.50
N21 O4 40m violet .40 3.50
N22 O4 50m yellow grn .80 3.50
N23 O5 100m carmine .50 3.50
N24 O5 300m olive grn 4.00 80.00
N25 O5 400m olive brn 1.25 3.75
N26 O5 500m lilac 4.00 80.00
N27 O5 1000m blue 1.10 4.50
Nos. N18-N27 (10) 13.25 189.25

No. N20 has the value in "Markes."

For surcharges see Nos. N44-N69, N88-N114.

No. 99 Surcharged in Green

1923, Apr. 13

N28 A18 100m on No. 99 5.00 21.00
N29 A18 400m on No. 99 5.00 21.00
N30 A18 500m on No. 99 5.00 21.00
Nos. N28-N30 (3) 15.00 63.00

The normal position of the green surcharge is sideways, with the top at the left. It exists reversed on the three stamps.

Ship — O7

Seal — O8

Lighthouse — O9

1923, Apr. 12 Litho.

N31 O7 40m olive grn 3.25 22.50
N32 O7 50m brown 3.25 22.50
N33 O7 80m green 3.25 22.50
N34 O7 100m red 3.25 22.50
N35 O8 200m deep blue 3.25 22.50
N36 O8 300m brown 3.25 22.50
N37 O8 400m lilac 3.25 22.50
N38 O8 500m orange 3.25 22.50
N39 O8 600m olive grn 3.25 22.50
N40 O9 800m deep blue 3.25 22.50
N41 O9 1000m lilac 3.25 22.50
N42 O9 2000m red 3.25 22.50
N43 O9 3000m green 3.25 22.50
Nos. N31-N43 (13) 42.25 292.50

Union of Memel with Lithuania. Forgeries exist.

For surcharges see Nos. N70-N86.

Nos. N20, N24, N26 Surcharged in Various Colors

1923

Thin Figures

N44 O5 2c on 300m (R) 6.50 9.00
N45 O5 3c on 300m (R) 7.00 12.00
N46 O4 10c on 25m (Bk) 7.00 9.00
a. Double surcharge 47.50 190.00
N47 O4 15c on 25m (Bk) 7.00 9.00
N48 O5 20c on 500m (Bl) 9.50 17.50
N49 O5 30c on 500m (Bk) 7.25 9.00
N50 O5 50c on 500m (G) 20.00 22.50
a. Inverted surcharge 65.00 240.00
Nos. N44-N50 (7) 64.25 88.00

Nos. N19, N21-N27 Surcharged:

N51 O4 2c on 20m yellow 3.25 14.00
N52 O4 2c on 50c yel grn 3.25 9.50
N53 O4 3c on 40m violet 4.00 10.50
a. Double surcharge 60.00 175.00
N54 O5 3c on 300m ol grn 2.50 5.00
a. Double surcharge 95.00 325.00
N55 O5 5c on 100m carmine 5.75 5.00
N56 O5 5c on 300m ol grn (R) 3.50 10.00
N57 O5 10c on 400m ol brn 8.00 14.50

N58 O5 30c on 500m lilac 5.50 *17.50*
N59 O5 1 l on 1000m blue 16.00 *45.00*
Nos. N51-N59 (9) 51.75 131.00

There are several types of the numerals in these surcharges. Nos. N56 and N58 have "CENT" in short, thick letters, as on Nos. N44 to N50.

Nos. N18-N23, N25, N27 Surcharged

Thick Figures

N60 O4 2c on 10m lt brn 3.00 *10.00*
N61 O4 2c on 20m yellow 10.00 *110.00*
N62 O4 2c on 50m yel grn 3.00 *11.00*
N63 O4 3c on 10m lt brn 3.00 *11.00*
a. Double surcharge 60.00 200.00
N64 O4 3c on 40m violet 18.00 *125.00*
N65 O5 5c on 100m car 3.00 *12.00*
a. Double surcharge 60.00 200.00
N66 O5 10c on 400m ol brn 90.00 *525.00*
N67 O4 15c on 25m orange 90.00 *525.00*
N68 O5 50c on 1000m blue 5.00 *8.00*
a. Double surcharge 60.00 200.00
N69 O5 1 l on 1000m blue 6.00 *16.00*
a. Double surcharge 90.00 200.00
Nos. N60-N69 (10) 231.00 *1,353.*

No. N69 is surcharged like type "b" in the following group.

Nos. N31-N43 Surcharged:

a

b

N70 O7(a) 15c on 40m ol grn 5.50 *17.50*
N71 O7(a) 30c on 50m brown 5.00 *9.00*
N72 O7(a) 30c on 80m green 5.00 *20.00*
N73 O7(a) 30c on 100m red 5.50 *8.00*
N74 O8(a) 50c on 200m dp blue 6.00 *17.50*
N75 O8(a) 50c on 300m brn 5.00 *8.00*
N76 O8(a) 50c on 400m lilac 5.50 *14.50*
N77 O8(a) 50c on 500m org 5.50 *8.00*
N78 O8(b) 1 l on 600m ol grn 5.50 *22.00*
N79 O9(b) 1 l on 800m dp blue 6.50 *19.00*
N80 O9(b) 1 l on 1000m lil 6.00 *19.00*
N81 O9(b) 1 l on 2000m red 6.00 *20.00*
N82 O9(b) 1 l on 3000m grn 6.50 *20.00*
Nos. N70-N82 (13) 73.50 *202.50*

These stamps are said to have been issued to commemorate the institution of autonomous government.

Double or inverted surcharges exist on Nos. N71, N75-N77. Value, each $60.

Nos. N32, N34, N36, N38 Surcharged in Green

1923

N83 O7 15c on 50m brn 275. *2,000.*
N84 O7 25c on 100m red 150. *1,200.*
N85 O8 30c on 300m brn 250. *1,300.*
N86 O8 60c on 500m org 150. *1,200.*

Surcharges on Nos. N83-N86 are of two types, differing in width of numerals. Values are for stamps with narrow numerals, as illustrated. Stamps with wide numerals sell for two to four times as much.

Nos. N8, N10-N11, N3 Surcharged in Red or Green

N87 O4 10c on 25m on 5c bl (R) 35.00 *47.50*
N88 O4 15c on 100m on 25c red (G) 35.00 *175.00*
a. Inverted surcharge 150.00 350.00
N89 O4 30c on 400m on 1 l brn (R) 17.50 *30.00*
N90 O4 60c on 50m on 25c red (G) 35.00 *190.00*
Nos. N87-N90 (4) 122.50 *442.50*

Nos. N18-N22 Surcharged in Green or Red

N91 O4 15c on 10m 8.00 *24.00*
N92 O4 15c on 20m 3.50 *20.00*
N93 O4 15c on 25m 4.00 *20.00*
N94 O4 15c on 40m 3.50 *20.00*
N95 O4 15c on 50m (R) 3.50 *12.00*
N96 O4 25c on 10m 4.25 *22.50*
N97 O4 25c on 20m 3.50 *17.50*
N98 O4 25c on 25m 4.00 *20.00*
N99 O4 25c on 40m 4.00 *23.00*
N100 O4 25c on 50m (R) 2.60 *12.00*
N101 O4 30c on 10m 6.50 *30.00*
N102 O4 30c on 20m 3.50 *19.00*
N103 O4 30c on 25m 5.00 *22.50*
N104 O4 30c on 40m 3.75 *17.50*
N105 O4 30c on 50m (R) 3.00 *15.00*
Nos. N91-N105 (15) 62.60 *295.00*

Nine stamps between Nos. N95 and N114 exist with inverted surcharge. No. N102 exists with double surcharge.

Nos. N23, N25, N27 Surcharged in Green or Red

N106 O5 15c on 100m 2.50 *12.00*
N107 O5 15c on 400m 2.50 *10.00*
N108 O5 15c on 1000m (R) 60.00 *325.00*
N109 O5 25c on 100m 2.50 *12.00*
N110 O5 25c on 400m 2.50 *9.50*
N111 O5 25c on 1000m (R) 65.00 *350.00*
N112 O5 30c on 100m 3.00 *13.00*
N113 O5 30c on 400m 3.00 *13.00*
N114 O5 30c on 1000m (R) 65.00 *360.00*
Nos. N106-N114 (9) 206.00 *1,104.*

Nos. N96 to N100 and N109 to N111 are surcharged "Centai," the others "Centu."

MESOPOTAMIA

ˌme-s̩ə-pə-ˈtā-mē-ə

LOCATION — In Western Asia, bounded on the north by Syria and Turkey, on the east by Persia, on the south by Saudi Arabia and on the west by Trans-Jordan.
GOVT. — A former Turkish Province
AREA — 143,250 (1918) sq. mi.
POP. — 2,849,282 (1920)
CAPITAL — Baghdad

During World War I this territory was occupied by Great Britain. It was recognized as an independent state and placed under British Mandate but in 1932 the Mandate was terminated and the country admitted to membership in the League of Nations as the Kingdom of Iraq. Postage stamps of Iraq are now in use.

16 Annas = 1 Rupee

Watermark

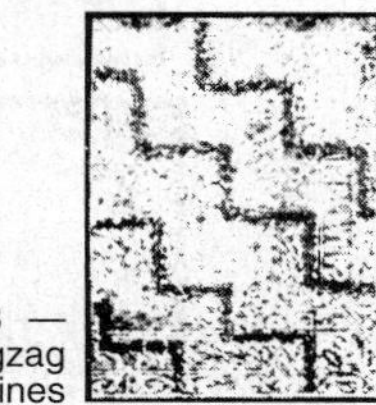

Wmk. 48 — Diagonal Zigzag Lines

Issued under British Occupation

Baghdad Issue

Stamps of Turkey 1901-16 Surcharged

N1

N2

N3

N4

N5

The surcharges were printed from slugs which were arranged to fit the various shapes of the stamps.

1917 Unwmk. *Perf. 12, 13½*

On Turkey Nos. 254, 256, 258-260

N1 ¼a on 2pa red lil 200. 250.
a. "IN BRITISH" omitted *10,000.*
N2 ¼a on 5pa vio brown 150. 160.
a. "¼ An" omitted *9,500.*
N3 ½a on 10pa green 900. *1,150.*
N4 1a on 20pa red 600. *700.*
N5 2a on 1pi blue 225. *275.*
Nos. N1-N5 (5) 2,075. 2,535.

On Turkey No. 249

N6 A22 2a on 1pi ultra 600. *825.*

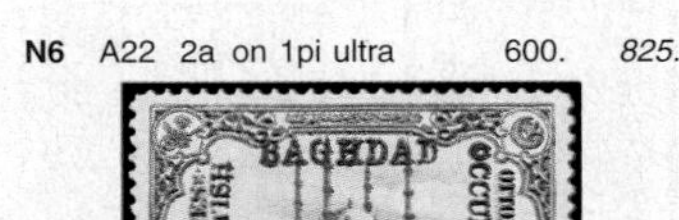

On Turkey No. 251

N7 A23 ½a on 10pa green 1,500. *1,800.*

On Turkey Nos. 272-273

N8 A29 1a on 20pa red 375. *450.*
a. "OCCUPATION" omitted *8,250.*
N9 A30 2a on 1pi blue 4,750. *5,500.*

On Turkey Nos. 346-348

N10 A41 ½a on 10pa car 650. *775.*
N11 A41 1a on 20pa ultra 1,400. 1,800.
a. "1 An" omitted *11,500.*
N12 A41 2a on 1pi vio & black 150. *160.*
a. "BAGHDAD" omitted *8,250.*

On Turkey Nos. 297, 300

N13 A17 ¼a on 5pa purple *9,000.*
N14 A17 2a on 1pi blue 250. 325.

On Turkey No. 306

N15 A18 1a on 20pa car 650.00 *775.00*

On Turkey Nos. 329-331

N16 A22 ½a on 10pa bl grn 150. 160.
N17 A22 1a on 20pa car rose 575. *650.*
a. "1 An" omitted *5,750.* *5,750.*
N18 A22 2a on 1pi ultra 160. 190.

On Turkey No. 337

N19 A22 1a on 20pa car rose *5,500.* *6,500.*

On Turkey No. P125

N20 A17 1a on 20pa car —

On Turkey Nos. B1, B8

Inscription in crescent is obliterated by another crescent handstamped in violet black on Nos. N21-N27.

N21 A18 ½a on 10pa dull grn 175. *200.*
a. "OCCUPATION" omitted *9,000.*
N22 A21 1a on 20pa car rose 600. *700.*

On Semi-Postal Stamps of 1916

On Turkey No. B29

N23 A21 2a on 1pi ultra 2,000. *2,300.*

No. N25

On Turkey Nos. B33-B34

N24 A22 1a on 20pa car rose 175. *200.*
N25 A22 2a on 1pi ultra 250. *325.*
a. "OCCUPATION" omitted *9,500.*
b. "BAGHDAD" omitted *9,500.*

On Turkey No. B42

N26 A41 ½a on 10pa car 225. *275.*
a. "BAGHDAD" double *2,500.*

On Turkey No. B38

N27 A11 1a on 10pa on 20pa vio brn 275. 325.

Iraq Issue

N28

N29

N30

N31

N32

N33

N34

N35

N36

N37

N38

N39

N40

N41

Turkey Nos. 256, 258-269 Surcharged

1918-20 *Perf. 12*

N28 ¼a on 5pa vio brn .25 .60
N29 ½a on 10pa grn .25 .20
N30 1a on 20pa red .25 .20
N31 1½a on 5pa vio brn 3.00 .40
N32 2½a on 1pi blue .95 .20
a. Inverted surcharge *4,000.*
N33 3a on 1½pi car & black .85 .20
a. Double surcharge, red & blk *2,100.*
N34 4a on 1¾pi slate & red brn .85 .20
a. Center inverted *12,000.*
N35 6a on 2pi grn & black 1.60 .90
N36 8a on 2½pi org & ol grn .90 .40
N37 12a on 5pi dl vio 1.75 1.75
N38 1r on 10pi red brown 2.25 1.10
N39 2r on 25pi ol grn 7.75 2.40
N40 5r on 50pi car 20.00 15.00
N41 10r on 100pi dp blue 45.00 12.00
Nos. N28-N41 (14) 85.65 35.55

See #N50-N53. For overprints see #NO1-NO21.

Mosul Issue

A13

A14

A15

A16

A17

A18

A19

1919 **Unwmk.** ***Perf. 11½, 12***

N42 A13 ½a on 1pi grn & brn red 2.40 1.75
N43 A14 1a on 20pa *rose* 1.50 1.75
a. "POSTAGE" omitted
N44 A15 1a on 20pa *rose* 4.50 4.50
a. Double surcharge

Turkish word at right of tughra ("reshad") is large on No. N43, small on No. N44.

Wmk. Turkish Characters
Perf. 12½

N45 A16 2½a on 1pi vio & yel 1.50 1.50
N46 A17 3a on 20pa grn & yel 35.00 *55.00*

Wmk. 48

N47 A17 3a on 20pa green 1.75 *3.50*
N48 A18 4a on 1pi dull vio 3.50 3.50
a. Double surcharge 900.00
b. "4" omitted 1,700.
c. As "b," double surcharge
N49 A19 8a on 10pa claret 3.00 2.40
a. Double surcharge *600.00 725.00*
b. Inverted surcharge *725.00 850.00*
c. 8a on 1pi dull violet *2,875.*
Nos. N42-N49 (8) 53.15 73.90

Value for No. 49c is for copies with the perfs cutting into the design.

Iraq Issue
Types of 1918-20 Issue

1921 **Wmk. 4** ***Perf. 12***

N50 A28 ½a on 10pa green .90 .25
N51 A26 1½a on 5pa dp brn .90 .25
N52 A37 2r on 25pi ol grn 13.00 12.00
Nos. N50-N52 (3) 14.80 12.50

Type of 1918-20 without "Reshad"

1922 **Unwmk.**

N53 A36 1r on 10pi red brn 100.00 20.00

"Reshad" is the small Turkish word at right of the tughra in circle at top center.
For overprint see No. NO22.

OCCUPATIONAL OFFICIAL STAMPS

Nos. N29-N41 Overprinted:

1920 **Unwmk.** ***Perf. 12***

NO1 A28 ½a on 10pa grn 3.00 .60
NO2 A29 1a on 20pa red 1.40 .35
NO3 A26 1½a on 5pa vio brown 7.25 1.50
NO4 A30 2½a on 1pi blue 1.50 1.60
NO5 A31 3a on 1½pi car & black 7.75 .55
NO6 A32 4a on 1¾pi sl & red brn 8.50 1.75
NO7 A33 6a on 2pi grn & black 11.00 3.00
NO8 A34 8a on 2½pi org & ol grn 9.50 1.75
NO9 A35 12a on 5pi dull vio 7.25 3.00
NO10 A36 1r on 10pi red brown 8.50 2.75
NO11 A37 2r on 25pi ol green 16.00 9.50
NO12 A38 5r on 50pi car 30.00 19.00
NO13 A39 10r on 100pi dp blue 50.00 35.00
Nos. NO1-NO13 (13) 161.65 80.35

Same Overprint on Types of Regular Issue of 1918-20

1921-22 **Wmk. 4**

NO14 A28 ½a on 10pa grn .70 .70
NO15 A29 1a on 20pa red 1.60 .70
NO16 A26 1½a on 5pa dp brn 1.60 .50
NO17 A32 4a on 1¾pi gray & red brn 1.60 .90
NO18 A33 6a on 2pi grn & black 9.50 *50.00*
NO19 A34 8a on 2½pi org & yel grn 2.75 1.90
NO20 A35 12a on 5pi dl vio 12.00 *42.50*
NO21 A37 2r on 25pi ol grn 42.50 *55.00*
Nos. NO14-NO21 (8) 72.25 *152.20*

Same Overprint on No. N53

1922 **Unwmk.**

NO22 A36 1r on 10pi red brn 14.00 5.00

MEXICO

'mek-si-ˌkō

LOCATION — Extreme southern part of the North American continent, south of the United States
GOVT. — Republic
AREA — 759,529 sq. mi.
POP. — 100,294,036 (1999 est.)
CAPITAL — Mexico, D.F

8 Reales = 1 Peso
100 Centavos = 1 Peso

Catalogue values for unused stamps in this country are for Never Hinged items, beginning with Scott 792 in the regular postage section, Scott C143 in the airpost section, Scott E8 in the special delivery section, and Scott G4 in the insured letter section.

District Overprints

Nos. 1-149 are overprinted with names of various districts, and sometimes also with district numbers and year dates. Some of the district overprints are rare and command high prices. Values given for Nos. 1-149 are for the more common district overprints.

Watermarks

Wmk. 150 — PAPEL SELLADO in Sheet

Wmk. 151 — R. P. S. in the Sheet (R.P.S. stands for "Renta Papel Sellado")

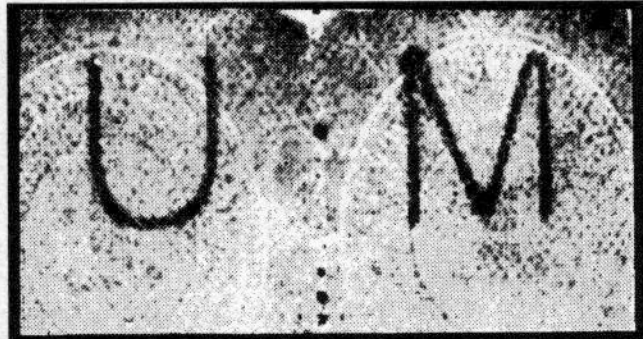

Wmk. 152 — "CORREOS E U M" on Every Horizontal Line of Ten Stamps

Wmk. 153 — "R M" Interlaced

Wmk. 154 — Eagle and R M

Wmk. 155 — SERVICIO POSTAL DE LOS ESTADOS UNIDOS MEXICANOS

Wmk. 156 — CORREOS MEXICO

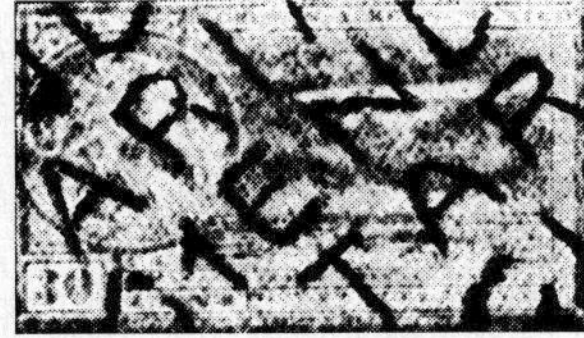

Wmk. 248 — SECRETARIA DE HACIENDA MEXICO

Wmk. 260 — Lines and SECRETARIA DE HACIENDA MEXICO

Wmk. 272 — "S. H. C. P. MEXICO" and Eagle in Circle

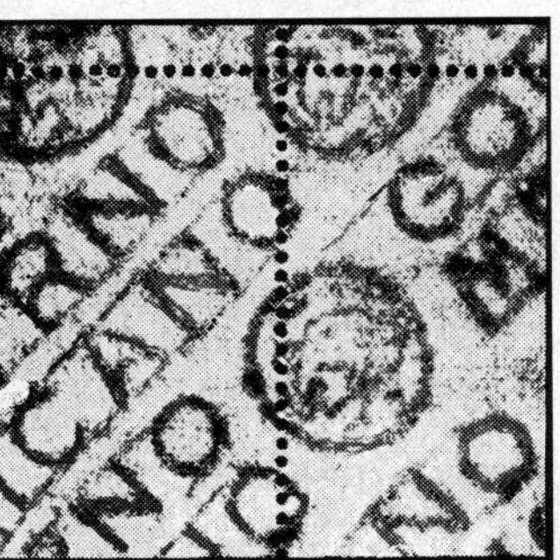

Wmk. 279 — GOBIERNO MEXICANO and Eagle in Circle

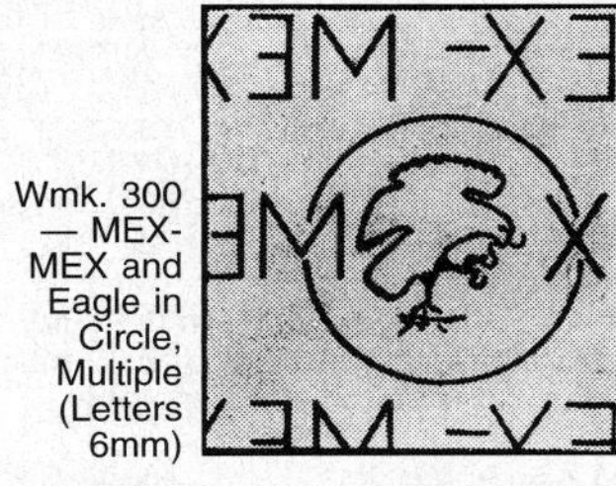

Wmk. 300 — MEX-MEX and Eagle in Circle, Multiple (Letters 6mm)

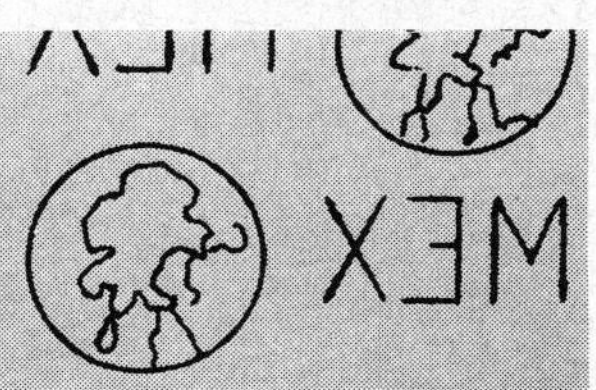

Wmk. 350 — MEX and Eagle in Circle, Multiple. Letters 8-9mm

Miguel Hidalgo y Costilla — A1

Handstamped with District Name

1856	Unwmk.	Engr.	*Imperf.*
1	A1 ½r blue	50.00	40.00
b.	Without overprint	45.00	45.00
2	A1 1r yellow	30.00	5.00
b.	Half used as ½r on cover		*10,000.*
c.	Without overprint	25.00	30.00
d.	1r green (error)		
3	A1 2r yellow grn	27.50	3.50
a.	2r blue green	275.00	40.00
b.	2r emerald	250.00	50.00
c.	Half used as 1r on cover		600.00
d.	Without overprint	40.00	22.50
e.	As "a," without overprint	250.00	45.00
f.	As "b," without overprint		75.00
g.	Printed on both sides (yel green)	300.00	
4	A1 4r red	175.00	110.00
a.	Half used as 2r on cover		250.00
b.	Quarter used as 1r on cover		700.00
c.	Without overprint	140.00	*160.00*
d.	Three quarters used as 3r on cover		*12,000.*
5	A1 8r red lilac	350.00	200.00
a.	8r violet	350.00	200.00
b.	Without overprint	225.00	225.00
c.	Eighth used as 1r on cover		*17,500.*
d.	Quarter used as 2r on cover		225.00
e.	Half used as 4r on cover		900.00
	Nos. 1-5 (5)	632.50	358.50

The 1r and 2r were printed in sheets of 60 with wide spacing between stamps, and in sheets of 190 or 200 with narrow spacing.

No. 3a can be distinguished from the other 2r stamps by the horizontal grain of the paper. The plate for No. 3b has framelines.

All values, except the 1r, have been reprinted, some of them several times. The reprints usually show signs of wear and the impressions are often smudgy. The paper is usually thicker than that of the originals. Reprints are usually on very white paper. Reprints are found with and without overprints and with cancellations made both from the original handstamps and from forged ones.

Counterfeits exist.

See Nos. 6-12. For overprints see Nos. 35-45.

1861			
6	A1 ½r black, *buff*	50.00	45.00
a.	Without overprint	34.00	62.50
7	A1 1r black, *green*	20.00	5.50
a.	Impression of 2r on back		450.00
b.	Without overprint	5.00	22.50
d.	As "b," blk, *pink* (error)	8,000.	*9,000.*
f.	Double impression		150.00
8	A1 2r black, *pink*	15.00	4.50
a.	Impression of 1r on back	2,000.	
b.	Half used as 1r on cover		750.00
c.	Without overprint	3.50	22.50
d.	Printed on both sides		2,250.
e.	Double impression		100.00
f.	As "e," without overprint	—	
9	A1 4r black, *yellow*	200.00	100.00
a.	Half used as 2r on cover		190.00
b.	Without overprint	50.00	100.00
c.	Quarter used as 1r on cover		700.00
d.	Three-quarters used as 3r on cover		*35,000.*
10	A1 4r dull rose, *yel*	200.00	70.00
a.	Half used as 2r on cover		*950.00*
b.	Without overprint	110.00	140.00
c.	Printed on both sides		*9,000.*
d.	Quarter used as 1r on cover		*10,000.*
11	A1 8r black, *red brn*	375.00	250.00
a.	⅛ used as 1r on cover front		11,000.
b.	Quarter used as 2r on cover		250.00
c.	Half used as 4r on cover		750.00
d.	Without overprint	110.00	225.00
e.	Three quarters used as 6r on cover		*45,000.*
12	A1 8r grn, *red brn*	500.00	240.00
a.	Half used as 4r on cover		30,000.
b.	Without overprint	150.00	200.00
c.	Quarter used as 2r on cover		40,000.
d.	Printed on both sides	*12,500.*	*12,500.*
	Nos. 6-12 (7)	1,360.	715.00

Nos. 6, 9, 10, 11 and 12 have been reprinted. Most reprints of the ½r, 4r and 8r are on vertically grained paper. Originals are on horizontally grained paper. The original ½r stamps are much worn but the reprints are unworn. The paper of the 4r is too deep and rich in color and No. 10 is printed in too bright red.

Reprints of the 8r can only be told by experts. All these reprints are found in fancy colors and with overprints and cancellations as in the 1856 issue.

Counterfeits exist.

Hidalgo — A3

Coat of Arms — A4

With District Name

1864			*Perf. 12*
14	A3 1r red	*750.*	*3,000.*
a.	Without District Name	.75	
15	A3 2r blue	*550.*	*1,000.*
a.	Without District Name	.75	

16 A3 4r brown *1,250.* *2,400.*
a. Without District Name 1.25
b. Vert. pair, imperf. between
17 A3 1p black *3,250.* *22,500.*
a. Without District Name 2.00

Nos. 14 to 17 were issued with district overprints of Saltillo or Monterrey on the toned paper of 1864. Overprints on the 1867 white paper are fraudulent. Counterfeits and counterfeit cancellations are plentiful. The 1r red with "½" surcharge is bogus.

Overprint of District Name, etc.

1864-66 ***Imperf.***

Five types of overprints:
I — District name only.
II — District name, consignment number and "1864" in large figures.
III — District name, number and "1864" in small figures.
IV — District name, number and "1865."
V — District name, number and "1866."

18 A4 3c brn (IV, V) 1,300. *2,500.*
a. Without overprint 700.00
b. Laid paper *4,500.* *6,000.*
19 A4 ½r brown (I) 400.00 250.00
a. Type II 2,200. 2,250.
b. Without overprint 200.00 *650.00*
20 A4 ½r lilac (IV) 60.00 55.00
a. Type III 140.00 75.00
b. Type II 200.00 200.00
c. Type V *3,000.*
d. ½r gray (V) 70.00 80.00
e. Without overprint 5.75
f. ½r gray lilac 250.00 100.00
21 A4 1r blue (IV, V) 15.00 9.00
a. Type III 80.00 40.00
b. Without overprint 2.50
c. Half used as ½r on cover *3,000.*
22 A4 1r ultra (I, II) 120.00 30.00
a. Type III 90.00 40.00
b. Without overprint 160.00 150.00
c. Half used as ½r on cover *7,250.*
23 A4 2r org (III, IV, V) 10.00 4.00
a. Type II 20.00 6.00
b. Type I 50.00 7.00
c. 2r dp org, without ovpt., early plate 175.00 65.00
d. Without ovpt., late plate 2.00
e. Half used as 1r on cover *6,000.*
24 A4 4r grn (III, IV, V) 100.00 50.00
a. Types I, II 160.00 77.50
b. 4r dk grn, without ovpt. 4.25 *1,700.*
d. Half used as 2r on cover *700.00*
25 A4 8r red (IV, V) 150.00 90.00
a. Types II, III 175.00 125.00
b. Type I 400.00 175.00
c. 8r dk red, without ovpt. 7.00 *575.00*
f. Quarter used as 2r on cover *15,000.*
g. Three-quarters used as 6r on cover front *50,000.*

The 2r printings from the early plates are 25½mm high; those from the late plate, 24½mm.

Varieties listed as "Without overprint" in unused condition are remainders.

Besides the overprints of district name, number and date, Nos. 18-34 often received, in the district offices, additional overprints of numbers and sometimes year dates. Copies with these "sub-consignment numbers" sell for more than stamps without them.

Genuine copies of No. 20c should bear Mexico district name overprint, together with consignment numbers 1-1866 or 17-1866. Gray lilac copies of other consignments are examples of No. 20f.

Value unused for No. 18 is for an example without gum. Copies with original gum sell for more. Copies of No. 18a on laid paper are forgeries.

No. 25g does not exist on full cover.

Faked quarterlings and bisects of 1856-64 are plentiful.

The 3c has been reprinted from a die on which the words "TRES CENTAVOS," the outlines of the serpent and some of the background lines have been retouched.

Emperor Maximilian — A5

Overprinted with District Name, Number and Date 1866 or 866; also with Number and Date only, or with Name only

1866 **Litho.**

26 A5 7c lilac gray 65.00 125.00
a. 7c deep gray 85.00 140.00
27 A5 13c blue 35.00 35.00
a. Half used as 7c on cover —
b. 13c cobalt blue 25.00 25.00
c. Without overprint 2,500.
28 A5 25c buff 12.50 9.00
a. Half used as 13c on cover —
b. Without overprint 2,500.
29 A5 25c orange 12.00 12.00
a. 25c red orange 20.00 27.50
b. 25c red brown 85.00 47.50
c. 25c brown *110.00* 85.00
30 A5 50c green 25.00 30.00
Nos. 26-30 (5) 149.50 211.00

Litho. printings have round period after value numerals.

Overprinted with District Name, Number and Date 866 or 867; also with Number and Date only

Engr.

31 A5 7c lilac 450.00 *5,500.*
a. Without overprint 3.50
32 A5 13c blue 12.00 12.00
a. Without overprint 1.25
33 A5 25c orange brown 12.00 11.00
a. Without overprint 1.25
34 A5 50c green 700.00 70.00
a. Without overprint 2.50

See "sub-consignment" note after No. 25.

Engraved printings have square period after value numerals.

Varieties listed as "Without overprint" in unused condition are remainders.

Stamps of 1856-61 Overprinted *Mexico*

1867

35 A1 ½r blk, *buff* 2,500. *4,000.*
36 A1 1r blk, *green* 60.00 10.00
37 A1 2r blk, *pink* 22.50 5.00
a. Printed on both sides 140.00
38 A1 4r red, *yel* 625.00 50.00
a. Printed on both sides 175.00
39 A1 4r red *6,000.* *3,250.*
40 A1 8r blk, *red brn* 3,500. 275.00
41 A1 8r grn, *red brn* *4,000.*

Dangerous counterfeits exist of the "Mexico" overprint.

Copies of No. 38 with yellow removed are offered as No. 39.

Same Overprint Thin Gray Blue Paper Wmk. 151

42 A1 ½r gray 275.00 190.00
a. Without overprint 175.00 175.00
43 A1 1r blue 400.00 65.00
b. Without overprint 300.00 125.00
44 A1 2r green 200.00 30.00
a. Printed on both sides 6,000. 3,500.
b. Without overprint 300.00 50.00
45 A1 4r rose 3,000. 75.00
a. Without overprint *5,000.* 225.00

Most copies of Nos. 42-45 do not show the watermark. Values are such copies. Examples showing the watermark sell for more.

Reprints of the ½r and 4r exist on watermarked paper. Reprints of ½r and 8r also exist in gray on thick grayish wove paper, unwatermarked.

Hidalgo — A6

Thin Figures of Value, without Period after Numerals

6 CENT. 12 CENT.
25 CENT. 50 CENT.
100 CENT.

Overprinted with District Name, Number and Abbreviated Date

1868 **Unwmk.** **Litho.** ***Imperf.***

46 A6 6c blk, *buff* 40.00 20.00
47 A6 12c blk, *green* 45.00 20.00
a. Period after "12" 65.00 55.00
48 A6 25c bl, *pink* 75.00 20.00
a. Without overprint 125.00
49 A6 50c blk, *yellow* 600.00 60.00
50 A6 100c blk, *brown* 775.00 140.00
51 A6 100c brn, *brn* 1,750. 500.00

Perf.

52 A6 6c blk, *buff* 35.00 35.00
a. Without overprint 150.00
b. Period after "6" 100.00 75.00
53 A6 12c blk, *green* 35.00 12.00
a. Period after "12" 85.00 30.00
b. Very thick paper 50.00 25.00
c. Without overprint 110.00
54 A6 25c blue, *pink* 55.00 10.00
b. Without overprint 150.00
55 A6 50c blk, *yellow* 325.00 45.00
56 A6 100c blk, *brown* 375.00 110.00
c. Without overprint 350.00
57 A6 100c brn, *brn* 1,000. 375.00
a. Printed on both sides 1,250. 1,000.

Four kinds of perforation are found in the 1868 issue: serrate, square, pin and regular. The narrow spacing between stamps was inadequate for some of these perforation types.

Thick Figures of Value, with Period after Numerals

6.CENT. 12.CENT
25.CENT. 50.CENT.
100.CENT

Overprinted with District Name, Number and Abbreviated Date

Imperf

58 A6 6c blk, *buff* 9.50 4.50
59 A6 12c blk, *green* 4.25 1.25
a. Very thick paper 10.00
c. 12c black, *buff* (error) 575.00 575.00
d. Printed on both sides *3,000.*
e. No period after "12" —
61 A6 25c blue, *pink* 8.00 1.25
a. No period after "25" 90.00
c. Very thick paper 25.00 6.00
d. "85" for "25" 75.00 50.00
e. "35" for "25" 75.00
f. Printed on both sides —
62 A6 50c blk, *yellow* 125.00 15.00
a. No period after "50" 225.00 35.00
b. 50c blue, *lt pink* (error) *3,000.* *2,000.*
c. Half used as 25c on cover 1,000.
d. Very thick paper 50.00
64 A6 100c blk, *brown* 150.00 90.00
a. No period after "100" 175.00 100.00
b. Very thick paper 75.00
c. Quarter used as 25c on cover *2,000.*
Nos. 58-64 (5) 296.75 112.00

Perf.

65 A6 6c blk, *buff* 40.00 20.00
a. Very thick paper 60.00 35.00
66 A6 12c blk, *green* 5.50 5.50
a. Very thick paper 20.00 15.00
b. 12c black, *buff* (error) 575.00 575.00
c. No period after "12" —
68 A6 25c blue, *pink* 20.00 2.50
a. No period after "25" 80.00 80.00
c. Thick paper 30.00 15.00
d. "85" for "25" 80.00 40.00
69 A6 50c blk, *yellow* 200.00 25.00
a. No period after "50" 200.00 30.00
b. 50c blue, *lt pink* (error) *2,500.* *1,500.*
c. Thick paper 60.00
70 A6 100c blk, *brown* 200.00 60.00
a. No period after "100" 200.00 65.00
b. Very thick paper 80.00
Nos. 65-70 (5) 465.50 113.00

Postal forgeries of Nos. 58-70 were printed from original plates with district name overprints forged. These include the pelure paper varieties and some thick paper varieties. The "Anotado" handstamp was applied to some of the confiscated forgeries and they were issued, including Nos. 73a and 78a.

Stamps of 1868 Handstamped

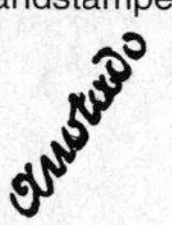

Overprinted with District Name, Number and Abbreviated Date Thick Figures with Period

1872 ***Imperf.***

71 A6 6c blk, *buff* 650.00 675.00
72 A6 12c blk, *green* 85.00 75.00
73 A6 25c bl, *pink* 40.00 45.00
a. Pelure paper 55.00 65.00
b. "85" for "25" 125.00
74 A6 50c blk, *yellow* 850.00 475.00
a. No period after "50" 900.00 475.00
75 A6 100c blk, *brown* 1,250. 1,000.
a. No period after "100" 1,100.

Perf.

76 A6 6c blk, *buff* 750.00
77 A6 12c blk, *green* 90.00 80.00
78 A6 25c blue, *pink* 35.00 42.50
a. Pelure paper 65.00 90.00
79 A6 50c blk, *yellow* 850.00 600.00
a. No period after "50" 550.00
80 A6 100c blk, *brown* 1,200.

Counterfeit "Anotado" overprints abound. Genuine cancellations other than Mexico City or of the Diligencias de Puebla are unknown. It is recommended that these be purchased accompanied by certificates of authenticity from competent experts.

The stamps of the 1872 issue are found perforated with square holes, pin-perf. 13, 14 or 15, and with serrate perforation.

Counterfeits of the 1868 6c, 12c buff, 50c and 100c (both colors) from new plates have clear, sharp impressions and more facial shading lines than the originals. These counterfeits are found perf. and imperf., with thick and thin numerals, and with the "Anotado" overprint.

Hidalgo — A8

Moiré on White Back Overprinted with District Name, Number and Abbreviated Date White Wove Paper

1872 **Litho.** **Wmk. 150** ***Imperf.***

81 A8 6c green 150.00 120.00
82 A8 12c blue 100.00 70.00
a. Laid paper 2,000. 350.00
83 A8 25c red 250.00 50.00
a. Laid paper 2,000. 350.00
84 A8 50c yellow 950.00 500.00
a. 50c blue (error) 3,000.
b. Laid paper 4,000.
c. As "a," without ovpt. 130.00
86 A8 100c gray lilac 700.00 400.00
Nos. 81-86 (5) 2,150. 1,140.

Wmk. "LA + F"

81a A8 6c green 500.00 250.00
82b A8 12c blue 325.00 125.00
83b A8 25c red 425.00 95.00
c. Without overprint 500.00
84d A8 50c yellow 3,000. 1,200.
86a A8 100c gray lilac 1,800. 750.00

1872 **Wmk. 150** ***Pin-perf.***

87 A8 6c green 850.00 850.00
88 A8 12c blue 125.00 100.00
89 A8 25c red 275.00 90.00
b. Laid paper 1,000.
90 A8 50c yellow 1,300. 650.00
a. 50c blue (error) *1,000.* *1,250.*
b. As "a," without overprint 200.00
92 A8 100c gray lilac 750.00 600.00
Nos. 87-92 (5) 3,300. 2,290.

Wmk. "LA + F"

87a A8 6c green 950.00 950.00
88a A8 12c blue 325.00 *350.00*
89a A8 25c red 900.00 225.00
90c A8 50c yellow 2,600. 2,200.
92a A8 100c gray lilac 2,000. 1,350.

The watermark "LA+F" stands for La Croix Frères, the paper manufacturers, and is in double-lined block capitals 13mm high. A single stamp will show only part of this watermark.

Values for Nos. 87-92a are for examples with visible perfs on all sides.

1872 **Unwmk.** ***Imperf.***

93 A8 6c green 12.50 12.50
a. Without moiré on back, without overprint 60.00 65.00
b. Vertically laid paper 3,000. 1,300.
c. Bottom label retouched 100.00 90.00
d. Very thick paper 37.50 37.50
94 A8 12c blue 2.00 1.75
a. Without moiré on back, without overprint 30.00 35.00
b. Vertically laid paper 350.00 210.00
c. Thin gray bl paper of 1867 (Wmk 151) 2,000.
95 A8 25c red 8.50 2.00
a. Without moiré on back, without overprint 30.00 35.00
b. Vertically laid paper 450.00 500.00
c. Thin gray bl paper of 1867 (Wmk 151) 1,500.
96 A8 50c yellow 140.00 35.00
a. 50c orange 140.00 35.00
b. Without moiré on back, without overprint 50.00 70.00
c. Vertically laid paper 2,000.
d. 50c blue (error) 650.00
e. As "d," without overprint 45.00
f. As "e," without moiré on back 65.00
g. Half used as 25c on cover *5,000.*
98 A8 100c gray lilac 90.00 50.00
a. 100c lilac 100.00 42.50
b. Without moiré on back, without overprint 50.00 110.00
c. Vertically laid paper 1,250.
Nos. 93-98 (5) 253.00 101.25

Counterfeits of these stamps are 24½mm high instead of 24mm. The printing is sharper and more uniform than the genuine. Forged district names and consignment numbers exist.

Pin-perf. and Serrate Perf.

99 A8 6c green 90.00 75.00
100 A8 12c blue 3.50 3.00
a. Vertically laid paper 350.00
b. Horiz. pair, imperf. vert. 100.00 100.00
c. Vert. pair, imperf. between 150.00
101 A8 25c red 3.25 1.50
a. Vertically laid paper 500.00
b. Horiz. pair, imperf. vert. 100.00 100.00
102 A8 50c yellow 175.00 50.00
a. 50c orange 160.00 50.00
b. 50c blue (error) 475.00 500.00
c. As "b," without overprint 45.00

104 A8 100c lilac 150.00 80.00
a. 100c gray lilac 125.00 80.00
Nos. 99-104 (5) 421.75 209.50

Values for Nos. 99-104a are for examples with visible perfs on all sides.

Hidalgo
A9 A10

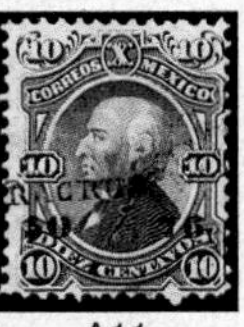

A11 A12

A13 A14

Overprinted with District Name and Number and Date; also with Number and Date only

Thick Wove Paper, Some Showing Vertical Ribbing

1874-80 Unwmk. Engr. *Perf. 12*

105 A9 4c org ('80) 12.50 12.00
a. Vert. pair, imperf. btwn. 60.00
b. Without overprint 6.50 12.50
c. Half used as 2c on cover 1,000.
106 A10 5c brown 4.50 3.00
a. Horizontally laid paper 100.00 55.00
b. Imperf., pair 60.00
c. Horiz. pair, imperf. btwn. 50.00 300.00
d. Vert. pair, imperf. btwn. 110.00 110.00
e. Without overprint 37.50 37.50
f. As "a," wmkd. "LACROIX" 350.00 200.00
107 A11 10c black 2.00 1.25
a. Horizontally laid paper 2.50 2.50
b. Horiz. pair, imperf. btwn. 75.00 75.00
c. Without overprint 35.00 27.50
d. Half used as 5c on cover 2,000.
e. Imperf., pair
f. As "a," wmkd. "LACROIX" 70.00 50.00
108 A11 10c org ('78) 2.00 1.25
a. 10c yellow bister 7.50 4.25
b. Imperf., pair
c. Without overprint 55.00 55.00
d. Half used as 5c on cover 100.00
109 A12 25c blue .85 .70
b. Horizontally laid paper 2.25 1.75
c. Imperf., pair 50.00 25.00
d. Without overprint 35.00 20.00
e. Horiz. pair, imperf. btwn. 125.00
f. As "b," horiz. pair, imperf. vert. 200.00
g. As "b," wmkd. "LACROIX" 60.00 50.00
h. Printed on both sides 1,500.
i. Half used as 10c on cover 2,000.
110 A13 50c green 13.00 13.00
a. Without overprint 50.00
b. Half used as 25c on cover 2,500.
111 A14 100c carmine 18.00 15.00
a. Imperf., pair 200.00 200.00
b. Without overprint 50.00
c. Quarter used as 25c on cover 3,000.
Nos. 105-111 (7) 52.85 46.20

The "LACROIX" watermark is spelled out "LACROIX FRERES" in 2 lines of block capitals without serifs once to a sheet of horiz. laid paper.6-12 stamps may have a portion of the wmk.

1875-77 Wmk. 150

112 A10 5c brown 55.00 35.00
113 A11 10c black 55.00 35.00
114 A12 25c blue 55.00 32.50
115 A13 50c green 325.00 225.00
116 A14 100c carmine 300.00 200.00
Nos. 112-116 (5) 790.00 527.50

1881 Unwmk. Thin Wove Paper

117 A9 4c orange 70.00 70.00
a. Without overprint 20.00 20.00
118 A10 5c brown 10.00 6.50
a. Without overprint .50 20.00
b. As "a," vert. pair, imperf. horiz. 1,000.
119 A11 10c orange 6.00 3.50
a. Imperf., pair
b. Vert. pair, imperf. horiz.
c. Without overprint .75 4.50
d. Vert. pair, imperf. btwn.
e. Half used as 5c on cover 1,500.
120 A12 25c blue 4.00 2.25
a. Imperf., pair 100.00
b. Without overprint .50 8.00
c. Double impression 65.00
d. Printed on both sides *1,500.*
121 A13 50c green 45.00 40.00
a. Without overprint 4.00 30.00
122 A14 100c carmine 50.00 50.00
a. Without overprint 6.00 300.00

The stamps of 1874-81 are found with number and date wide apart, close together or omitted, and in various colors.

The thin paper is fragile and easily damaged. Values for Nos. 117-122 are for undamaged, fine examples.

Benito Juárez — A15

Overprinted with District Name and Number and Date; also with Number and Date only

1879 *Perf. 12*

Thick Wove Paper, Some Showing Vertical Ribbing

123 A15 1c brown 4.00 4.00
a. Without overprint 75.00 140.00
b. 1c gray 20.00 15.00
124 A15 2c dk violet 4.00 4.50
a. Without overprint 75.00 150.00
b. Printed on both sides
c. 2c dark gray 20.00 14.00
125 A15 5c orange 2.25 1.50
a. Without overprint 75.00 90.00
b. Double impression *500.00*
126 A15 10c blue 3.00 2.50
a. Without overprint 75.00 150.00
b. 10c ultra 160.00 160.00
127 A15 25c rose 8.00 30.00
a. Without overprint 1.75 150.00
128 A15 50c green 15.00 50.00
a. Without overprint 1.25 150.00
b. Printed on both sides 165.00
129 A15 85c violet 20.00 250.00
a. Without overprint 2.50
130 A15 100c black 25.00 75.00
a. Without overprint 3.00 150.00
Nos. 123-130 (8) 81.25 417.50

Used values for Nos. 127-130 are for copies with postal cancellations. Pen cancelled copies are worth the same as unused stamps.

Forged cancellations on Nos. 127-130 are plentiful.

1882

Thin Wove Paper

131 A15 1c brown 40.00 37.50
a. Without overprint 125.00
132 A15 2c dk violet 27.50 24.00
a. 2c slate 47.50 50.00
b. Without overprint 110.00
c. Half used as 1c on cover
133 A15 5c orange 9.00 6.00
a. Without overprint 1.25
b. Half used as 2c on cover
c. As "a," vert. pair, imperf. btwn.
134 A15 10c blue 9.00 6.00
a. Without overprint 1.25
b. Half used as 5c on cover
135 A15 10c brown 9.00
a. Imperf., pair 3.00
136 A15 12c brown 7.50 8.00
a. Without overprint 2.50 22.50
b. Imperf., pair 75.00
c. Half used as 6c on cover
137 A15 18c orange brn 9.00 15.00
a. Horiz. pair, imperf. btwn. 100.00
b. Without overprint 2.25 18.00
138 A15 24c violet 9.00 11.00
a. Without overprint 2.25 17.50
139 A15 25c rose 45.00 250.00
a. Without overprint 4.50
140 A15 25c orange brn 5.50
141 A15 50c green 45.00 75.00
a. Without overprint 6.25
142 A15 50c yellow 80.00 350.00
a. Without overprint 150.00
143 A15 85c red violet 55.00
144 A15 100c black 75.00 *250.00*
a. Without overprint 5.00
b. Vert. pair, imperf. btwn. 165.00 165.00
145 A15 100c orange 95.00 400.00
a. Without overprint 175.00
Nos. 131-145 (15) 520.50 1,432.

No. 135, 140 and 143 exist only without overprint. They were never placed in use.

Used values for Nos. 139, 141, 142, 144 and 145 are for postally used copies. Forged cancellations are plentiful. Pen cancelled copies are worth the same as unused stamps.

See note on thin paper after No. 122.

A16

Overprinted with District Name, Number and Abbreviated Date

1882-83

146 A16 2c green 11.00 8.00
a. Without overprint 27.50 20.00
147 A16 3c car lake 11.00 8.00
a. Without overprint 5.25 8.50
148 A16 6c blue ('83) 30.00 40.00
a. Without overprint 30.00 50.00
149 A16 6c ultra 6.00 8.50
a. Without overprint 3.50 6.00
b. As "a," imperf pair 50.00
Nos. 146-149 (4) 58.00 64.50

See note on thin paper after No. 122.

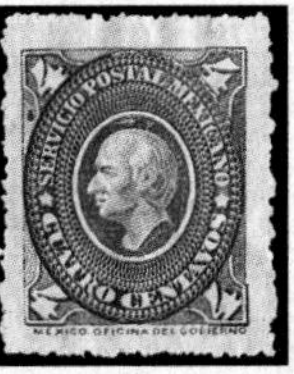

Hidalgo — A17

1884 Wove or Laid Paper *Perf. 12*

150 A17 1c green 4.00 .75
a. Imperf., pair 32.50
b. 1c blue (error) 600.00 475.00
151 A17 2c green 6.75 2.00
a. Imperf., pair 60.00 55.00
b. Half used as 1c on cover
152 A17 3c green 12.50 2.00
a. Imperf., pair 110.00 90.00
b. Horiz. pair, imperf. vert. 125.00 125.00
153 A17 4c green 16.00 2.00
a. Imperf., pair 75.00 65.00
b. Half used as 2c on cover 200.00
154 A17 5c green 17.50 1.50
a. Imperf., pair 110.00 90.00
155 A17 6c green 15.00 1.50
a. Imperf., pair 75.00 65.00
156 A17 10c green 16.00 .75
a. Imperf., pair 75.00 70.00
157 A17 12c green 30.00 3.50
a. Vert. pair, imperf. between 75.00 60.00
b. Half used as 6c on cover 125.00
158 A17 20c green 90.00 2.50
a. Diagonal half used as 10c on cover 200.00
b. Imperf., pair 160.00 125.00
159 A17 25c green 150.00 5.00
a. Imperf., pair 250.00 200.00
160 A17 50c green .60 *5.00*
a. Imperf., pair 25.00 20.00
161 A17 1p blue .60 *11.00*
a. Imperf., pair 60.00 45.00
b. Vert. pair, imperf. between 100.00
162 A17 2p blue .60 *22.50*
a. Imperf., pair 75.00 60.00
163 A17 5p blue 350.00 275.00
164 A17 10p blue 500.00 225.00
Nos. 150-162 (13) 359.55 *60.00*

Imperforate varieties should be purchased in pairs or larger. Single imperforates are usually trimmed perforated stamps.

Beware of copies of No. 150 that have been chemically changed to resemble No. 150b.

Forged cancels on Nos. 161-162 are plentiful.

Some values exist perf. 11.

See Nos. 165-173, 230-231.

1885

165 A17 1c pale green 35.00 7.00
166 A17 2c carmine 25.00 3.50
a. Diagonal half used as 1c on cover 100.00
167 A17 3c orange brn 25.00 6.00
a. Imperf., pair 100.00 100.00
168 A17 4c red orange 42.50 19.00
169 A17 5c ultra 27.50 3.50
170 A17 6c dk brown 32.50 6.00
a. Half used as 3c on cover 210.00
171 A17 10c orange 27.50 1.50
a. 10c yellow 30.00 1.50
b. Horiz. pair, imperf. btwn. 100.00 100.00
172 A17 12c olive brn 57.50 9.00
173 A17 25c grnsh blue 225.00 22.50
Nos. 165-173 (9) 497.50 78.00

Numeral of Value — A18

1886 ***Perf. 12***

174 A18 1c yellow green 2.25 .75
a. 1c blue grn 5.50 4.50
b. Horiz. pair, imperf. btwn. 75.00 60.00
c. Perf. 11 45.00 45.00
175 A18 2c carmine 2.60 .90
a. Horiz. pair, imperf. btwn. 80.00 75.00
b. Vert. pair, imperf. between 75.00 75.00
c. Perf. 11 45.00 45.00
d. Half used as 1c on cover 100.00
176 A18 3c lilac 12.00 7.50
177 A18 4c lilac 18.00 5.25
a. Perf. 11 50.00 *55.00*
178 A18 5c ultra 2.25 1.00
a. 5c blue 2.25 .75
179 A18 6c lilac 30.00 7.50
180 A18 10c lilac 22.50 1.10
a. Perf. 11 125.00
181 A18 12c lilac 25.00 14.00
182 A18 20c lilac 190.00 110.00
183 A18 25c lilac 75.00 19.00
Nos. 174-183 (10) 379.60 167.00

Nos. 175, 191, 194B, 196, 202 exist with blue or black surcharge "Vale 1 Cvo." These were made by the Colima postmaster.

1887

184 A18 3c scarlet 1.90 .60
a. Imperf., pair 75.00
185 A18 4c scarlet 7.50 2.25
186 A18 6c scarlet 12.50 2.25
a. Horiz. pair, imperf. btwn. 75.00
187 A18 10c scarlet 2.75 .60
a. Imperf., pair 75.00
b. Horiz. pair, imperf. btwn. 45.00
188 A18 20c scarlet 18.00 1.50
a. Horiz. pair, imperf. btwn. 75.00
189 A18 25c scarlet 15.00 4.00
Nos. 184-189 (6) 57.65 11.20

Perf. 6

190 A18 1c blue grn 45.00 45.00
191 A18 2c brown car 22.50 42.00
192 A18 5c ultra 15.00 4.50
a. 5c blue 15.00 4.50
193 A18 10c lilac 15.00 4.25
193A A18 10c brown lilac 15.00 3.00
194 A18 10c scarlet 35.00 15.00

Perf. 6x12

194A A18 1c blue grn 62.50 42.50
194B A18 2c brown car 85.00 75.00
194C A18 3c scarlet 300.00 350.00
194D A18 5c ultra 60.00 45.00
194E A18 10c lilac 90.00 75.00
194F A18 10c scarlet 80.00 60.00
194G A18 10c brown lilac 90.00 75.00

Many shades exist.

Paper with colored ruled lines on face or reverse of stamp

1887 ***Perf. 12***

195 A18 1c green 75.00 45.00
196 A18 2c brown car 190.00 47.50
198 A18 5c ultra 110.00 30.00
199 A18 10c scarlet 110.00 25.00

Perf. 6

201 A18 1c green 60.00 20.00
202 A18 2c brown car 60.00 24.00
204 A18 5c ultra 50.00 12.00
205 A18 10c brown lil 42.50 10.00
206 A18 10c scarlet 250.00 40.00
Nos. 201-206 (5) 462.50 106.00

Perf. 6x12

207 A18 1c green 225.00 140.00
208 A18 2c brown car 325.00 140.00
209 A18 5c ultra 225.00 140.00
210 A18 10c brown lil 290.00 135.00
211 A18 10c scarlet 350.00 225.00
Nos. 207-211 (5) 1,415. 780.00

1890-95 Wmk. 152 ***Perf. 11 & 12***
Wove or Laid Paper

212 A18 1c yellow grn .75 .35
a. 1c blue green .75 .35
b. Horiz. pair, imperf. btwn. 35.00 35.00
c. Laid paper 2.50 2.50
d. Horiz. pair, imperf. vert. 35.00 35.00
213 A18 2c carmine 1.50 .75
a. 2c brown car 1.25 1.00
b. Vert. pair, imperf. btwn. 150.00
c. Imperf., pair 200.00
214 A18 3c vermilion 1.00 .60
b. Horiz. pair, imperf. btwn. 80.00
215 A18 4c vermilion 3.25 2.10
a. Horiz. pair, imperf. btwn. 80.00
216 A18 5c ultra .60 .50
a. 5c dull blue 1.00 .50
217 A18 6c vermilion 3.75 2.75
a. Horiz. pair, imperf. btwn. 45.00
218 A18 10c vermilion .50 .35
b. Horiz. or vert. pair, imperf. btwn. 45.00 45.00
c. Vert. pair, imperf. horiz. 45.00
d. Imperf., pair 50.00
219 A18 12c ver ('95) 18.00 18.00
220 A18 20c vermilion 3.50 1.50
220A A18 20c dk violet 160.00 *190.00*
221 A18 25c vermilion 5.00 2.50
Nos. 212-220,221 (10) 37.85 29.40

No. 219 has been reprinted in slightly darker shade than the original.

1892

222 A18 3c orange 4.00 2.00
223 A18 4c orange 4.25 3.00
224 A18 6c orange 5.75 2.00
225 A18 10c orange 27.50 2.00
226 A18 20c orange 50.00 6.00
227 A18 25c orange 16.00 4.50
Nos. 222-227 (6) 107.50 19.50

1892

228 A18 5p carmine 1,250. 900.
229 A18 10p carmine 1,900. 1,250.
230 A17 5p blue green 3,500. 1,200.
231 A17 10p blue green *7,000.* *2,700.*

1894 ***Perf. 5½, 6***

232 A18 1c yellow grn 3.00 3.00
233 A18 3c vermilion 9.00 9.00
234 A18 4c vermilion 40.00 37.50
235 A18 5c ultra 12.50 5.00
236 A18 10c vermilion 7.50 3.00
236A A18 20c vermilion 110.00 110.00
237 A18 25c vermilion 62.50 62.50
Nos. 232-237 (7) 244.50 230.00

Perf. 5½x11, 11x5½, Compound and Irregular

238 A18 1c yellow grn 7.00 7.00
238A A18 2c brown car 16.00 16.00
238B A18 3c vermilion 47.50 32.50
238C A18 4c vermilion 55.00 55.00
239 A18 5c ultra 17.50 12.50
a. 5c blue 12.50 12.50
239C A18 6c vermilion 75.00 75.00
240 A18 10c vermilion 20.00 7.00
240A A18 20c vermilion 200.00 200.00
241 A18 25c vermilion 60.00 55.00
Nos. 238-241 (9) 498.00 460.00

The stamps of the 1890 to 1895 issues are also to be found unwatermarked, as part of the sheet frequently escaped the watermark.

Letter Carrier — A20

Mounted Courier with Pack Mule — A21

Statue of Cuauhtémoc A22

Mail Coach A23

Mail Train — A24

Regular or Pin Perf. 12

1895 **Wmk. 152**
Wove or Laid Paper

242 A20 1c green 3.00 .75
a. Vert. pair, imperf. horiz. 100.00
d. Watermarked sideways ('97) 125.00 15.00
243 A20 2c carmine 3.75 1.00
a. Half used as 1c on cover 50.00
c. Watermarked sideways ('97) 80.00 10.00
244 A20 3c orange brown 3.75 1.00
a. Vert. pair, imperf. horiz. 80.00
d. Watermarked sideways ('97) 125.00 10.00
246 A21 4c orange 12.50 1.50
a. 4c orange red 7.50 1.25
247 A22 5c ultra 7.00 .35
a. Imperf., pair 50.00 50.00
b. Horiz. or vert. pair, imperf. between 65.00 50.00
e. Half used as 2c on cover 60.00
f. Watermarked sideways ('97) 15.00 5.00
248 A23 10c lilac rose 4.50 1.00
a. Horiz. or vert. pair, imperf. between 75.00
b. Half used as 5c on cover 60.00
249 A21 12c olive brown 50.00 12.50
251 A23 15c brt blue 27.50 3.00
b. Watermarked sideways ('97) 100.00
252 A23 20c brown rose 32.50 3.00
b. Half used as 10c on cover 60.00
c. Watermarked sideways ('97) 1,000. 750.00
253 A23 50c purple 70.00 16.00
a. Half used as 25c on cover 100.00
254 A24 1p brown 90.00 35.00
a. Watermarked sideways ('97) 750.00 *900.00*
255 A24 5p scarlet 300.00 190.00
256 A24 10p deep blue 650.00 350.00
Nos. 242-256 (13) 1,254. 615.10

No. 248 exists in perf. 11.

Nos. 242d, 243c, 244d, 247f, 251b, 252c and 254a was a special printing, made in Jan. 1897. The watermark is sideways, the grain of the paper is horizontal (rather than vertical, as appears on Nos. 242-256, and the design is somewhat shorter than the other stamps in this series. The sideways orientation of the watermark is the most easily identifable feature of this printing.

Important: For unwatermarked examples of Nos. 242-256, see the footnote after No. 291.

Perf. 6

242b A20 1c green 60.00 35.00
243b A20 2c carmine 125.00 60.00
244b A20 3c orange brown 90.00 50.00
247c A22 5c ultra 90.00 50.00
248c A23 10c lilac rose 125.00 55.00
249a A21 12c olive brown 100.00 50.00

Perf. 6x12, 12x6 & Compound or Irregular

242c A20 1c green 30.00 20.00
244c A20 3c orange brown 35.00 20.00
246b A21 4c orange 75.00 50.00
247d A22 5c ultra 75.00 50.00
248d A23 10c lilac rose 35.00 20.00
249b A21 12c olive brown 50.00 25.00
251a A23 15c brt blue 60.00 40.00
252a A23 20c brown rose 100.00 70.00
253b A23 50c purple 150.00 100.00

See Nos. 257-291. For overprints see Nos. O10-O48A.

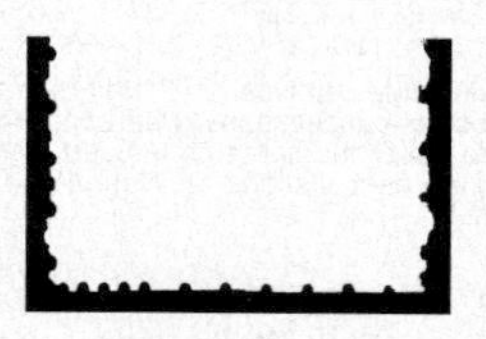

"Irregular" Perfs.

Some copies perf. 6x12, 12x6, 5½x11 and 11x5½ have both perf. 6 and 12 or perf. 5½ and 11 on one or more sides of the stamp. These are known as irregular perfs.

1896-97 Wmk. 153 ***Perf. 12***

257 A20 1c green 14.00 1.25
c. Imperf., pair 250.00
258 A20 2c carmine 17.50 1.50
a. Horiz. pair, imperf. vert.
259 A20 3c orange brn 20.00 1.50
260 A21 4c orange 32.50 1.75
c. 4c deep orange 30.00 6.00
261 A22 5c ultra 9.00 1.25
a. Imperf., pair 60.00
b. Vert. pair, imperf. btwn. 120.00
262 A21 12c olive brn 160.00 80.00
263 A23 15c brt blue 200.00 13.00
264 A23 20c brown rose 750.00 275.00
265 A23 50c purple 175.00 110.00
266 A24 1p brown 300.00 250.00
267 A24 5p scarlet 800.00 600.00
268 A24 10p dp blue 900.00 525.00
Nos. 257-268 (12) 3,378. 1,860.

Perf. 6

257a A20 1c green 35.00 25.00
259a A20 3c orange brown 35.00 20.00
260a A21 4c orange 40.00 25.00
261c A22 5c ultra 110.00 70.00
263a A23 15c bright blue 75.00 35.00

Perf. 6x12, 12x6 and Compound or Irregular

257b A20 1c green 25.00 20.00
258b A20 2c carmine 50.00 25.00
259b A20 3c orange brown 40.00 20.00
260b A21 4c orange 45.00 20.00
261d A22 5c ultra 40.00 20.00
262a A21 12c olive brown 125.00 80.00
263b A23 15c bright blue 250.00 125.00
264a A23 20c brown rose
265a A23 50c purple

1897-98 Wmk. 154 ***Perf. 12***

269 A20 1c green 20.00 3.00
270 A20 2c scarlet 35.00 4.50
271 A21 4c orange 52.50 3.75
a. Horizontal pair, imperf. vertical —
272 A22 5c ultra 50.00 3.75
a. Imperf., pair 85.00
273 A21 12c olive brown 200.00 45.00
275 A23 15c brt blue 275.00 85.00
276 A23 20c brown rose 175.00 15.00
277 A23 50c purple 375.00 75.00
278 A24 1p brown 425.00 200.00
278A A24 5p scarlet — —
Nos. 269-278 (9) 1,607. 435.00

Perf. 6

269a A20 1c green 45.00 25.00
270a A20 2c scarlet 45.00 25.00
272b A22 5c ultra 60.00 25.00
273a A21 12c olive brown 110.00 60.00
276a A23 20c brown rose *650.00*

Perf. 6x12, 12x6 and Compound or Irregular

269b A20 1c green 25.00 15.00
270b A20 2c scarlet 30.00 22.50
271b A21 4c orange 65.00 22.50
272c A22 5c ultra 50.00 15.00
273b A21 12c olive brown 125.00 65.00
275a A23 15c bright blue 125.00 65.00
276b A23 20c brown rose 240.00 30.00
277a A23 50c purple 125.00 50.00

1898 Unwmk. ***Perf. 12***

279 A20 1c green 3.00 .50
a. Horiz. pair, imperf. vert 300.00
b. Imperf., pair 100.00
280 A20 2c scarlet 6.25 .75
a. 2c green (error) *475.00*
281 A20 3c orange brn 6.00 .75
a. Imperf., pair 150.00 150.00
b. Pair, imperf. between 80.00 80.00
282 A21 4c orange 30.00 3.00
b. 4c deep orange 37.50 7.00
283 A22 5c ultra 2.00 .50
a. Imperf., pair 50.00 50.00
b. Pair, imperf. between 125.00
284 A23 10c lilac rose 550.00 175.00
285 A21 12c olive brn 80.00 27.50
a. Imperf., pair 200.00
286 A23 15c brt blue 175.00 8.00
287 A23 20c brown rose 35.00 3.00
a. Imperf., pair 200.00
288 A23 50c purple 150.00 42.50
289 A24 1p brown 175.00 80.00
290 A24 5p carmine rose 550.00 425.00
291 A24 10p deep blue 800.00 575.00
Nos. 279-291 (13) 2,562. 1,341.

Warning: Sheets of Nos. 242-256 (watermarked "CORREOS E U M") have a column of stamps without watermarks, because the watermark did not fit the sheet size. As a result, be careful not to confuse unwatermarked examples of Nos. 242-256 with Nos. 279-291. This is especialy important for No. 284. Nos. 242-256 have a vertical grain or mesh to the paper. Nos. 279-291 have a horizontal grain or mesh to the paper.

Perf. 6

279c A20 1c green 85.00 35.00
280b A20 2c scarlet 75.00 30.00
281c A20 3c orange brown 50.00 35.00
283c A22 5c ultra 65.00 30.00
287b A23 20c brown rose 125.00 75.00
291a A24 10p deep blue

Perf. 6x12, 12x6 and Compound or Irregular

279d A20 1c green 25.00 20.00
280c A20 2c scarlet 25.00 20.00
281d A20 3c orange brown 30.00 20.00
282a A21 4c orange 40.00 25.00
283d A22 5c ultra 20.00 10.00
284a A23 10c lilac rose 125.00 85.00
285b A21 12c olive brown 90.00 60.00
286a A23 15c bright blue 75.00 50.00
287c A23 20c brown rose 100.00 50.00
288a A23 50c purple 575.00 575.00

Forgeries of the 6 and 6x12 perforations of 1895-98 are plentiful.

Coat of Arms
A25 A26

A27

A28

A29

A30

A31

Juanacatlán Falls — A32

View of Mt. Popocatépetl A33

Cathedral, Mexico, D. F. — A34

1899, Nov. 1 Wmk. 155 *Perf. 14, 15*

294	A25	1c green	1.90	.35
295	A26	2c vermilion	4.50	.35
296	A27	3c orange brn	3.00	.35
297	A28	5c dark blue	4.75	.35
298	A29	10c violet & org	6.00	.35
299	A30	15c lav & claret	8.00	.35
300	A31	20c rose & dk bl	9.00	.40
301	A32	50c red lil & blk	35.00	2.25
a.		50c lilac & black	42.50	2.25
302	A33	1p blue & blk	80.00	3.50
303	A34	5p carmine & blk	275.00	12.00
		Nos. 294-303 (10)	427.15	20.25

See Nos. 304-305, 307-309. For overprints see Nos. 420-422, 439-450, 452-454, 482-483, 515-516, 539, 550, O49-O60, O62-O66, O68-O74, O101.

A35

1903

304	A25	1c violet	1.50	.35
305	A26	2c green	2.00	.35
306	A35	4c carmine	5.00	.45
307	A28	5c orange	1.25	.35
308	A29	10c blue & org	5.00	.35
309	A32	50c carmine & blk	75.00	6.50
		Nos. 304-309 (6)	89.75	8.35

For overprints see Nos. 451, O61, O67.

Independence Issue

Josefa Ortiz — A36

Leona Vicario — A37

López Rayón — A38

Juan Aldama — A39

Miguel Hidalgo — A40

Ignacio Allende — A41

Epigmenio González A42

Mariano Abasolo A43

Declaration of Independence A44

Mass on the Mount of Crosses A45

Capture of Granaditas A46

1910 *Perf. 14*

310	A36	1c dull violet	.30	.35
311	A37	2c green	.35	.35
312	A38	3c orange brn	.60	.35
313	A39	4c carmine	2.50	.45
314	A40	5c orange	.35	.35
315	A41	10c blue & org	1.50	.35
316	A42	15c gray bl & cl	8.00	.50
317	A43	20c red & bl	5.00	.40
318	A44	50c red brn & blk	12.00	1.60
319	A45	1p blue & blk	15.00	2.00
320	A46	5p car & blk	57.50	16.50
		Nos. 310-320 (11)	103.10	23.20
		Set, never hinged	135.00	

Independence of Mexico from Spain, cent.

For overprints and surcharges see Nos. 370-380, 423-433, 455-465, 484-494, 517-538, 540-549, 551-558, 577-590, O75-O85, O102-O112, O191-O192, O195, RA13, Merida 1.

CIVIL WAR ISSUES

During the 1913-16 Civil War, provisional issues with various handstamped overprints were circulated in limited areas.

Sonora

A47

Seal

Typeset in a row of five varieties. Two impressions placed tête bêche (foot to foot) constitute a sheet. The settings show various wrong font and defective letters, "!" for "1" in "1913," etc. The paper occasionally has a manufacturer's watermark.

a

b

c

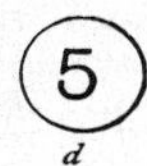

d

Four Types of the Numerals.
a — Wide, heavy-faced numerals.
b — Narrow Roman numerals.
c — Wide Roman numerals.
d — Gothic or sans-serif numerals.

Nos. 321-346 Issued Without Gum
Embossed "CONSTITUCIONAL"

1913 Typeset Unwmk. *Perf. 12*

321	A47 (a)	5c black & red	*4,250.*	800.00
a.		"CENTAVOB"	*4,750.*	*850.00*

Colorless Roulette

322	A47(b)	1c black & red	22.00	25.00
a.		With green seal	*1,500.*	*1,250.*
323	A47(a)	2c black & red	18.00	15.00
a.		With green seal	*2,000.*	*2,000.*
324	A47(c)	2c black & red	87.50	72.50
a.		With green seal	*5,000.*	*5,000.*
325	A47(a)	3c black & red	97.50	77.50
a.		With green seal	*750.00*	*750.00*
326	A47(a)	5c black & red	190.00	77.50
a.		"CENTAVOB"	200.00	50.00
327	A47(d)	5c black & red	1,200.	350.00
a.		With green seal		*1,000.*
328	A47(b)	10c black & red	35.00	*37.50*

Black Roulette

329	A47(d)	5c black & red	300.00	140.00
a.		"MARO"	87.50	52.50

Stamps are known with the embossing double or omitted.

The varieties with green seal are from a few sheets embossed "Constitucional" which were in stock at the time the green seal control was adopted.

Nos. 322-329 are known with "Peerless Mills" papermaker's watermark.

Without Embossing
With Green Seal
Colorless Roulette

336	A47(b)	1c black & red	15.00	10.00
337	A47(a)	3c black & red	14.50	9.00
a.		Imperf.	*350.00*	
338	A47(a)	5c black & red	750.00	250.00
a.		"CENTAVOB"	*800.00*	*275.00*
339	A47(b)	10c black & red	8.00	7.50

Colored Roulette

340	A47(d)	5c brnsh blk & red	25.00	6.00
a.		5c lilac brown & red	75.00	22.50
b.		Double seal	*1,000.*	
c.		Red printing omitted		*1,000.*

1913-14 *Black Roulette*
With Green Seal

341	A47(a)	1c black & red	4.00	4.00
b.		"erano" ('14)	100.00	60.00
342	A47(d)	2c black & red	4.50	4.00
a.		"erano" ('14)	30.00	35.00
343	A47(a)	3c black & red	4.75	4.00
a.		"CENTAVO"	25.00	25.00
b.		"erano" ('14)	35.00	35.00
344	A47(d)	5c black & red	4.75	4.00
b.		Heavy black penetrating roulette	2.75	1.75
c.		As "b," "MARO"	10.50	5.00
d.		Without green seal	*2,250.*	
		Nos. 341-344 (4)	18.00	16.00

Stamps without seal are unfinished remainders.

On Nos. 341-344 the rouletting cuts the paper slightly or not at all. On Nos. 344b-344c the rouletting is heavy, cutting deeply into the paper.

1914

345 A47(a) 5c black & red 5.00 5.00
346 A47(b) 10c black & red 4.25 5.00

Coat of Arms — A49

Revenue Stamps Used for Postage

1913 **Litho.** ***Rouletted 14, 14x7***

347 A49 1c yellow grn 2.00 *2.50*
a. With coupon 7.00 6.00
348 A49 2c violet 3.50 *4.00*
a. With coupon 17.50 14.50
349 A49 5c brown .60 *.75*
a. With coupon 2.00 1.50
350 A49 10c claret 2.50 *3.50*
a. With coupon 15.00 12.00
351 A49 20c gray grn 3.00 *3.50*
a. With coupon 20.00 18.00
352 A49 50c ultra 11.00 *16.00*
a. With coupon 60.00 47.50
353 A49 1p orange 45.00 *55.00*
a. With coupon 175.00 120.00
Nos. 347-353 (7) 67.60 85.25

For a short time these stamps (called "Ejercitos") were used for postage with coupon attached. Later this was required to be removed unless they were to be used for revenue. Stamps overprinted with district names are revenues. Values above 1p were used for revenue. Imperfs exist of all values, but were not issued.

Many examples do not have gum because of a flood.

Use of typeset Sonora revenue stamps for postage was not authorized or allowed.

Coat of Arms
A50 A51

5c (A50): "CINCO CENTAVOS" 14x2mm

1914 ***Rouletted 9½x14***

354 A50 1c deep blue .45 .45
355 A50 2c yellow grn .60 .35
a. 2c green 3.00 1.75
356 A50 4c blue vio 11.00 2.50
a. Horiz. pair, imperf. btwn. 250.00
357 A50 5c gray grn 11.00 3.00
a. Horiz. pair imperf. btwn. 250.00
358 A50 10c red .45 .45
359 A50 20c yellow brn .60 .60
a. 20c deep brown 2.25 2.25
b. Horiz. pair, imperf. btwn. 250.00
360 A50 50c claret 2.50 3.50
a. Horiz. pair, imperf. btwn. 250.00
361 A50 1p brt violet 14.00 16.00
a. Horiz. pair, imperf. btwn. 250.00
Nos. 354-361 (8) 40.60 26.85
Set, never hinged 60.00

Nos. 354-361 (called "Transitorios") exist imperf. but were not regularly issued.

Many copies do not have gum because of a flood.

See Note after No. 465.

See No. 369. For overprints see Nos. 362-368, 559-565.

Overprinted in Black

1914

362 A50 1c deep blue 200.00 175.00
363 A50 2c yellow green 225.00 200.00
364 A50 4c blue violet 250.00 300.00
365 A50 5c gray green 35.00 50.00
a. Horiz. pair, imperf. btwn. 550.00
366 A50 10c red 150.00 150.00
367 A50 20c yellow brn *2,500.* *2,500.*
368 A50 50c claret *3,500.* *3,500.*

Values are for copies with design close to, or just touching, the perfs.

Excellent counterfeits of this overprint exist.

Redrawn
"CINCO CENTAVOS" 16x2½mm

1914 ***Perf. 12***

369 A51 5c gray green 1.00 .35

Imperfs are printers' waste.

Regular Issue of 1910 Overprinted in Violet, Magenta, Black or Green

1914 **Wmk. 155** ***Perf. 14***

370 A36 1c dull violet 1.50 .60
371 A37 2c green 3.00 1.25
372 A38 3c orange brn 3.00 1.25
373 A39 4c carmine 5.00 2.00
374 A40 5c orange 1.00 .35
375 A41 10c blue & org 6.00 2.00
376 A42 15c gray bl & cl 10.00 3.00
377 A43 20c red & blue 20.00 6.00
378 A44 50c red brn & blk 25.00 8.00
379 A45 1p blue & blk 55.00 11.00
380 A46 5p carmine & blk 190.00 160.00
Nos. 370-380 (11) 319.50 195.45
Set, never hinged 375.00

Overprinted On Postage Due Stamps of 1908

381 D1 1c blue 27.50 *30.00*
382 D1 2c blue 27.50 *30.00*
383 D1 4c blue 27.50 *30.00*
384 D1 5c blue 27.50 *30.00*
385 D1 10c blue 27.50 *30.00*
Nos. 381-385 (5) 137.50 150.00
Set, never hinged 200.00

This overprint is found double, inverted, sideways and in pairs with and without the overprint.

There are two or more types of this overprint.

The Postage Due Stamps and similar groups of them which follow were issued and used as regular postage stamps.

Values are for copies where the overprint is clear enough to be expertised.

Counterfeits abound.

A52

A53

1914 **Unwmk.** **Litho.** ***Perf. 12***

386 A52 1c pale blue .35 .50
387 A52 2c light green .35 .45
388 A52 3c orange .50 .50
389 A52 5c deep rose .50 .35
390 A52 10c rose .70 .85
391 A52 15c rose lilac 1.20 1.75
392 A52 50c yellow 2.00 2.50
a. 50c ocher 1.75
393 A52 1p violet 8.50 12.00
Nos. 386-393 (8) 14.10 18.90
Set, never hinged 18.00

Nos. 386-393, are known imperforate.

This set is usually called the Denver Issue because it was printed there.

See Note after No. 465.

For overprints and surcharges see Nos. 566-573, 591-592.

Revenue Stamps Used for Postage

1914, July ***Perf. 12***

393A A53 1c rose 40.00
393B A53 2c lt green 35.00
393C A53 3c lt orange 75.00
393D A53 5c red 15.00
393E A53 10c gray green 70.00
Nos. 393A-393E (5) 235.00

Nos. 393A-393E were used in the northeast. Values are for examples with postal cancellations.

Unused copies are to be considered as revenues.

Pres. Madero

Stamps in this design, featuring Pres. Madero, within a frame very similar to that of the Denver Issue (Nos. 386-393), were ordered in 1915 by Francisco Villa, to be used by the Constitutionalist government. Five values (1c green, 2c brown, 3c carmine, 5c blue, and 10c yellow) were printed by Ellis Brothers & Co., El Paso, Texas. By the time of the stamps' arrival in Mexico City, the Constitutionalist regime had fallen, and the new Conventionist government returned them to the printer, who later sold the unissued stamps within the philatelic market. Value, set $10.

Background as A55 — A54

A55

Nos. 394-410 Issued Without Gum

1915 ***Imperf.***

Values and Inscriptions in Black
Inscribed "SONORA"

394 A54 1c blue & red .35 .35
a. Double seal
b. Without seal 20.00
395 A54 2c green & org .35 .35
a. Without seal 100.00
396 A54 5c yellow & grn .35 .35
a. 5c orange & green 1.50 1.25
b. Without seal *300.00*
397 A54 10c lt bl & red 3.50 1.75
a. 10c blue & red 40.00 15.00
398 A54 20c yellow & grn 1.75 2.00
399 A54 20c orange & bl 15.00 17.50
400 A54 50c green & org 1.25 1.25
Nos. 394-400 (7) 22.55 23.55

Shades. Stamps of type A54 are usually termed the "Coach Seal Issue."

Inscribed "DISTRITO SUR DE LA BAJA CAL"

401 A54 1c yellow & blue 2.00 *30.00*
a. Without seal 50.00
402 A54 2c gray & ol grn 2.50 *25.00*
403 A54 5c olive & rose 2.00 *20.00*
a. Without seal 50.00
404 A54 10c pale red & dl vio 2.00 *20.00*
a. Without seal 50.00
Nos. 401-404 (4) 8.50

Counterfeit cancellations exist.

Inscribed "SONORA"

405 A55 1c blue & red 6.00
a. Without seal 50.00
406 A55 2c green & org .50
407 A55 5c yellow & grn .50 *2.50*
a. Without seal 75.00
408 A55 10c blue & red .50 *2.50*
409 A55 20c yellow & grn 75.00 *15.00*
a. Without seal 95.00
b. Double seal *80.00*
Nos. 405-409 (5) 82.50

With "PLATA" added to the inscription

410 A55 1c blue & red 1.00
a. "PLATA" inverted 60.00
b. Pair, one without "PLATA" 15.00
411 A55 10c blue & red 1.00
412 A55 20c yellow & grn 2.50
a. "PLATA" double 50.00
413 A55 50c gray grn & org 1.75
a. Without seal 1.00
b. As "a," "P" of "PLATA" missing 150.00
Nos. 410-413 (4) 6.25

Stamps of type A55 are termed the "Anvil Seal Issue".

Nos. 394-413 were issued without gum.

Nos. 410-413 were not placed in use.

Oaxaca

Coat of Arms — A56

5c:
Type I — Thick numerals, 2mm wide.
Type II — Thin numerals, 1½mm wide.

Perf. 8½ to 14

1915 **Typo.** **Unwmk.**

414 A56 1c dull violet 2.00 1.25
415 A56 2c emerald 3.00 2.25
a. Inverted numeral 30.00
e. Numeral omitted 35.00
416 A56 3c red brown 4.00 3.50
b. Inverted numeral 30.00
417 A56 5c org (type I) 77.50 77.50
a. Tête bêche pair 175.00 175.00
418 A56 5c org (type II) .50 .75
a. Types I and II in pair 70.00
419 A56 10c blue & car 4.00 4.00
Nos. 414-419 (6) 91.00 89.25
Set, never hinged 120.00

Most used stamps are favor canceled, and used values are for such stamps. Postally used stamps are worth more than these values.

Many printing errors, imperfs and part perfs exist. Mostly these are printers' waste, private reprints or counterfeits.

Nos. 414-419 printed on backs of post office receipt forms.

Regular Issues of 1899-1910 Overprinted in Black

1914 **Wmk. 155** ***Perf. 14***

On Issues of 1899-1903

421 A30 15c lav & claret 250.00 250.00
Never hinged 325.00
422 A31 20c rose & dk bl *1,000.* 500.00

Counterfeits exist.

On Issue of 1910

423 A36 1c dull violet .35 .35
424 A37 2c green .35 .35
425 A38 3c orange brown .40 .40
426 A39 4c carmine .50 .50
427 A40 5c orange .35 .35
428 A41 10c blue & orange .35 .35
429 A42 15c gray bl & claret .70 .60
430 A43 20c red & blue .75 .70

Overprinted

431 A44 50c red brn & blk 1.75 1.50
432 A45 1p blue & blk 8.00 5.50
433 A46 5p carmine & blk 42.50 32.50
Nos. 423-433 (11) 56.00 43.10
Set, never hinged 80.00

In the first setting of the overprint on 1c to 20c, the variety "GONSTITUCIONALISTA" occurs 4 times in each sheet of 100. In the second setting it occurs on the last stamp in each row of 10.

The overprint exists reading downward on Nos. 423-430; inverted on Nos. 431-433; double on Nos. 423-425, 427.

See Note after No. 465.

Postage Due Stamps of 1908 Overprinted

434 D1 1c blue 4.75 5.00
435 D1 2c blue 6.00 5.00
436 D1 4c blue 25.00 26.00
437 D1 5c blue 25.00 26.00
438 D1 10c blue 5.50 5.00
a. Double overprint
Nos. 434-438 (5) 66.25 67.00
Set, never hinged 90.00

Preceding Issues Overprinted

This is usually called the "Villa" monogram. Counterfeits abound.

1915

On Issue of 1899

439 A25 1c green 210.00
440 A26 2c vermilion 210.00
441 A27 3c orange brn 175.00
442 A28 5c dark blue 175.00
443 A29 10c violet & org 175.00
444 A30 15c lav & claret 750.00 750.00
445 A31 20c rose & bl 1,000. —
446 A32 50c red lil & blk 500.00 —
447 A33 1p blue & blk 500.00
448 A34 5p car & blk 750.00 —
Nos. 439-448 (10) 4,445.

On Issue of 1903

449 A25 1c violet 200.00
450 A26 2c green 200.00
451 A35 4c carmine 200.00
452 A28 5c orange 45.00
a. Inverted overprint 75.00
453 A29 10c blue & org 750.00 —
454 A32 50c car & blk — —
Nos. 449-454 (5) 1,395.

In Sept. 1915 Postmaster Hinojosa ordered a special printing of Nos. 439-454 (as valued) for sale to collectors. Earlier a small quantity of Nos. 444-445, 448 and 452-454 was regularly issued. They are hard to distinguish and sell for much more. Counterfeits abound.

On Issue of 1910

455 A36 1c dull violet .85 1.00
456 A37 2c green .40 .60
457 A38 3c orange brown .60 .75
458 A39 4c carmine 4.00 4.50
459 A40 5c orange .35 .35
460 A41 10c blue & orange 7.00 7.50
461 A42 15c gray bl & cl 3.00 4.00
462 A43 20c red & blue 5.50 7.00
463 A44 50c red brn & blk 13.00 14.00
464 A45 1p blue & blk 17.00 20.00
465 A46 5p carmine & blk 150.00
Nos. 455-464 (10) 51.70 59.70

Nos. 455-465 are known with overprint inverted, double and other variations. Most were ordered by Postmaster General Hinojosa for philtelic purposes. They were sold at a premium. This applies to Nos. 354-361, 386-393, 431-433 with this monogram as well.

Overprinted On Postage Due Stamps of 1908

466 D1 1c blue 15.00 20.00
467 D1 2c blue 15.00 20.00
468 D1 4c blue 15.00 20.00
469 D1 5c blue 15.00 20.00
470 D1 10c blue 15.00 20.00
Nos. 466-470 (5) 75.00 100.00
Set, never hinged 90.00

Nos. 466 to 470 are known with inverted overprint. All other values of the 1899 and 1903 issues exist with this overprint. See note after No. 465.

Issues of 1899-1910 Overprinted

This is called the "Carranza" or small monogram. Counterfeits abound.

On Issues of 1899-1903

482 A28 5c orange 40.00 20.00
Never hinged 37.50
483 A30 15c lav & claret 200.00 80.00
Never hinged 190.00

On Issue of 1910

484 A36 1c dull violet .70 .70
485 A37 2c green .70 .60
486 A38 3c orange brn .75 .75
487 A39 4c carmine 2.00 2.00
488 A40 5c orange .35 .35
489 A41 10c blue & org 1.50 1.50
a. Double ovpt., one invtd. 25.00
490 A42 15c gray bl & cl 1.50 1.50
491 A43 20c red & blue 1.50 1.50
492 A44 50c red brn & blk 10.00 10.00
493 A45 1p blue & blk 15.00 15.00
494 A46 5p car & blk 150.00 150.00
Nos. 484-494 (11) 184.00 183.90
Set, never hinged 250.00

All values exist with inverted overprint; all but 5p with double overprint.

Overprinted On Postage Due Stamps of 1908

495 D1 1c blue 22.00 25.00
496 D1 2c blue 22.00 25.00
497 D1 4c blue 22.00 25.00
498 D1 5c blue 22.00 25.00
499 D1 10c blue 22.00 25.00
Nos. 495-499 (5) 110.00 125.00
Set, never hinged 150.00

Nos. 495-499 exist with inverted overprint.

It is stated that, in parts of Mexico occupied by the revolutionary forces, instructions were given to apply a distinguishing overprint to all stamps found in the post offices. This overprint was usually some arrangement or abbreviation of "Gobierno Constitucionalista". Such overprints as were specially authorized or were in general use in large sections of the country are listed. Numerous other handstamped overprints were used in one town or locality. They were essentially military faction control marks necessitated in most instances by the chaotic situation following the split between Villa and Carranza. The fact that some were often struck in a variety of colors and positions suggests the influence of philatelists.

Coat of Arms A57

Statue of Cuauhtémoc A58

Ignacio Zaragoza A59

José María Morelos A60

Francisco Madero — A61

Benito Juárez — A62

1915 Unwmk. Litho. *Rouletted 14*

500 A57 1c violet .20 .20
501 A58 2c green .25 .20
502 A59 3c brown .50 .25
503 A60 4c carmine .50 .25
504 A61 5c orange .75 .25
505 A62 10c ultra .35 .30
Nos. 500-505 (6) 2.55 1.45

Nos. 500-505 exists imperf.; some exist imperf. vertically or horizontally; some with rouletting and perforation combined. These probably were not regularly issued in these forms.

See Nos. 506-511. For overprints see Nos. O86-O97.

Map of Mexico — A63

Veracruz Lighthouse A64

Post Office, Mexico, D.F. — A65

TEN CENTAVOS:
Type I — Size 19½x24mm. Crossed lines on coat.
Type II — Size 19x23½mm. Diagonal lines only on coat.

1915-16 *Perf. 12*

506 A57 1c violet .40 .25
507 A58 2c green .40 .30
508 A59 3c brown .50 .30
509 A60 4c carmine .50 .35
a. "CEATRO" 7.50 7.50
510 A61 5c orange .75 .35
511 A62 10c ultra, type I 1.00 .35
a. 10c ultra, type II .50 .25

Engr.

512 A63 40c slate .75 .35
513 A64 1p brown & blk 1.00 .75
a. Inverted center 200.00
514 A65 5p cl & ultra ('16) 12.00 4.00
a. Inverted center 400.00
Nos. 506-514 (9) 17.30 7.00
Set, never hinged 22.50

Nos. 507-508, 510-514, exist imperf; Nos. 513-514 imperf with inverted center. These varieties were not regularly issued.

See Nos. 626-628, 647. For overprints see Nos. O92-O100, O121-O123, O132-O133, O142-O144, O153-O154, O162-O164, O174, O188, O193, O207, O222.

Issues of 1899-1910 Overprinted in Blue, Red or Black

1916 Wmk. 155 *Perf. 14*

On Issues of 1899-1903

515 A28 5c orange (Bl) 125.00 175.00
Never hinged 225.00
516 A30 15c lav & cl (Bl) 775.00 775.00
Never hinged 675.00

On Issue of 1910

517 A36 1c dull vio (R) 10.00 10.00
518 A37 2c green (R) .50 .35
519 A38 3c orange brn (Bl) .55 .40
a. Double overprint 500.00
520 A39 4c carmine (Bl) 6.00 8.00
521 A40 5c orange (Bl) .25 .25
a. Double overprint 75.00
522 A41 10c blue & org (R) 1.25 1.50
523 A42 15c gray bl & cl (Bk) 1.75 3.00
524 A43 20c red & bl (Bk) 1.75 3.00
525 A44 50c red brn & blk (R) 8.50 5.00
526 A45 1p blue & blk (R) 15.00 6.50
527 A46 5p car & blk (R) 175.00 175.00
Nos. 517-527 (11) 220.55 213.00
Nos. 517-527, never hinged 275.00

Nos. 519-524 exist with this overprint (called the "Corbata") reading downward and Nos. 525-527 with it inverted. Of these varieties only Nos. 519-521 were regularly issued.

On Nos. 423-430

528 A36 1c dull vio (R) 2.50 4.00
529 A37 2c green (R) .75 .60
530 A38 3c orange brn (Bl) .60 .60
531 A39 4c carmine (Bl) .60 .60
532 A40 5c orange (Bl) 1.00 .30
533 A41 10c blue & org (R) .75 .60
534 A42 15c gray bl & cl (Bk) .80 .80
535 A43 20c red & bl (Bk) .80 .80

On Nos. 431-433 in Red

536 A44 50c red brn & blk 7.50 6.00
537 A45 1p blue & blk 16.00 16.00
538 A46 5p carmine & blk 150.00 140.00
a. Tablet inverted 300.00
Nos. 528-538 (11) 181.30 170.30
Nos. Set, never hinged 250.00

Nos. 529 to 535 are known with the overprint reading downward and Nos. 536 to 538 with it inverted.

On No. 482

539 A28 5c orange (Bl) 400.00 400.00

On Nos. 484-494

540 A36 1c dull vio (R) 6.00 6.00
541 A37 2c green (R) .75 .75
a. Monogram inverted 100.00
542 A38 3c orange brn (Bl) .70 .75
543 A39 4c carmine (Bl) 8.50 10.00
544 A40 5c orange (Bl) 1.25 .35
545 A41 10c blue & org (R) 2.00 2.50
546 A42 15c gray bl & cl (Bk) 1.75 .75
a. Tablet double 750.00 750.00
b. Monogram double 750.00
547 A43 20c red & bl (Bk) 1.75 1.50
548 A44 50c red brn & blk (R) 9.00 10.00
a. Monogram inverted 75.00
b. Tablet inverted 85.00
549 A45 1p blue & blk (R) 13.00 14.00
a. Tablet double 200.00
b. Monogram inverted 70.00
Nos. 539-549 (11) 444.70 446.60
Set, never hinged 425.00

Nos. 541-547 exist with overprint reading downward. A few 5p were overprinted for the Post Office collection.

On No. 453

550 A28 5c orange (Bl) 125.00 125.00
Never hinged 275.00

On Nos. 455-462

551 A36 1c dull vio (R) 11.00 15.00
552 A37 2c green (R) 1.50 .90
553 A38 3c org brn (Bl) 3.25 4.50
554 A39 4c carmine (Bl) 13.00 15.00
555 A40 5c orange (Bl) 4.50 6.00
556 A41 10c bl & org (R) 12.00 14.00
a. Monogram inverted 250.00
557 A42 15c gray bl & cl (Bk) 12.00 14.00
a. Monogram inverted 250.00
558 A43 20c red & bl (Bk) 12.00 14.00
a. Monogram inverted 250.00
Nos. 550-558 (9) 194.25 208.40
Set, never hinged 375.00

Stamps of 50c, 1p and 5p were overprinted for the Post Office collection but were not regularly issued.

Issues of 1914 Overprinted

On "Transitorio" Issue

Rouletted 9½x14

Unwmk.

559 A50 1c dp blue (R) 24.00 24.00
Never hinged 50.00
560 A50 2c yellow grn (R) 12.00 18.00
Never hinged 18.00
561 A50 4c blue vio (R) 425.00 375.00
Never hinged 850.00
562 A50 10c red (Bl) 2.00 6.00
Never hinged 2.50
a. Vertical overprint 125.00
563 A50 20c yellow brn (Bl) 3.00 6.00
Never hinged 5.00
564 A50 50c claret (Bl) 15.00 20.00
Never hinged 30.00
565 A50 1p violet (Bl) 24.00 24.00
Never hinged 75.00
a. Horiz. pair, imperf. btwn.
Nos. 559-565 (7) 505.00 473.00

Overprinted in Blue On "Denver" Issue *Perf. 12*

566 A52 1c pale blue 3.75
567 A52 2c lt green 3.75
568 A52 3c orange .45 5.00
569 A52 5c deep rose .45 5.00
570 A52 10c rose .45 5.00
571 A52 15c rose lilac .45 5.00
572 A52 50c yellow 1.10 15.00
573 A52 1p violet 9.50 25.00
Nos. 566-573 (8) 19.90
Set, never hinged 25.00

Many of the foregoing stamps exist with the "G. P. DE M." overprint printed in other colors than those listed. These "trial color" stamps were not regularly on sale at post offices but were available for postage and used copies are known.

There appears to have been speculation in Nos. 516, 517, 520, 528, 539, 540, 543, 566, and 567. A small quantity of each of these stamps was sold at post offices but subsequently they could be obtained only from officials or their agents at advanced prices.

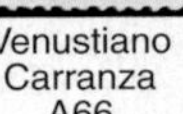

Venustiano Carranza A66

Coat of Arms A67

1916, June 1 Engr. *Perf. 12*

574 A66 10c blue 1.75 1.00
a. Imperf., pair 25.00
575 A66 10c lilac brown 15.00 15.00
a. Imperf., pair 50.00
Nos. 574-575, never hinged 21.00

Entry of Carranza into Mexico, D.F.

Stamps of type A66 with only horizontal lines in the background of the oval are essays.

1916

576 A67 1c lilac .35 .25
Never hinged .45

Issue of 1910 Surcharged in Various Colors

This overprint is called the "Barril."

1916 Wmk. 155 *Perf. 14*

577 A36 5c on 1c dl vio (Br) .50 .50
a. Vertical surcharge 1.25 1.25
b. Double surcharge 150.00
578 A36 10c on 1c dl vio (Bl) .50 .50
a. Double surcharge 100.00
579 A40 20c on 5c org (Br) .50 .50
a. Double surcharge 90.00
580 A40 25c on 5c org (G) .40 .50
581 A37 60c on 2c grn (R) 27.50 20.00
Nos. 577-581 (5) 29.40 22.00
Set, never hinged 32.50

On Nos. 423-424, 427

582 A36 5c on 1c (Br) .50 .50
a. Double tablet, one vertical 100.00
b. Inverted tablet 250.00 250.00
583 A36 10c on 1c (Bl) 1.00 1.00
584 A40 25c on 5c (G) .50 .50
a. Inverted tablet 225.00 225.00
585 A37 60c on 2c (R) 425.00 *425.00*
Never hinged 750.00

No. 585 was not regularly issued.

The variety "GONSTITUCIONALISTA" is found on Nos. 582 to 585.

On No. 459

586 A40 25c on 5c org (G) .25 .25
Never hinged .35

On Nos. 484-485, 488

587 A36 5c on 1c (Br) 15.00 20.00
a. Vertical tablet 100.00 125.00
588 A36 10c on 1c (Bl) 5.00 7.50
589 A40 25c on 5c (G) 1.00 1.50
a. Inverted tablet 225.00
590 A37 60c on 2c (R) 450.00
Never hinged 800.00
Nos. 587-589, never hinged 30.00

No. 590 was not regularly issued.

Surcharged on "Denver" Issue of 1914

1916 Unwmk. *Perf. 12*

591 A52 60c on 1c pale bl (Br) 3.00 6.00
592 A52 60c on 2c lt grn (Br) 3.00 6.00
a. Inverted surcharge *1,250.*
Set, never hinged 10.00

Postage Due Stamps Surcharged Like Nos. 577-581

1916 Wmk. 155 *Perf. 14*

593 D1 5c on 1c blue (Br) 2.50
594 D1 10c on 2c blue (V) 2.50
595 D1 20c on 4c blue (Br) 2.50
596 D1 25c on 5c blue (G) 2.50
597 D1 60c on 10c blue (R) 1.50
598 D1 1p on 1c blue (C) 1.50
599 D1 1p on 2c blue (C) 1.50
600 D1 1p on 4c blue (C) .80 .80
601 D1 1p on 5c blue (C) 2.50
602 D1 1p on 10c blue (C) 2.50
Nos. 593-602 (10) 20.30
Set, never hinged 40.00

There are numerous "trial colors" and "essays" of the overprints and surcharges on Nos. 577 to 602. They were available for postage though not regularly issued.

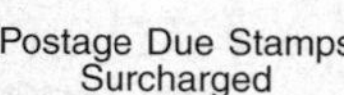

Postage Due Stamps Surcharged

1916

603 D1 2.50p on 1c blue 1.25 1.25
604 D1 2.50p on 2c blue 10.00
605 D1 2.50p on 4c blue 10.00 250.00
606 D1 2.50p on 5c blue 10.00
607 D1 2.50p on 10c blue 10.00
a. Inverted surcharge *1,500.*
Nos. 603-607 (5) 41.25
Set, never hinged 100.00

Regular Issue

Ignacio Zaragoza A68

Ildefonso Vázquez A69

J. M. Pino Suárez A70

Jesús Carranza A71

Maclovio Herrera — A72

F. I. Madero — A73

Belisario Domínguez A74

Aquiles Serdán A75

Rouletted 14½

1917-20 Engr. Unwmk.

Thick Paper

608 A68 1c dull violet 2.00 1.00
Never hinged 2.50
609 A68 1c lilac gray ('20) 5.00 .75
Never hinged 6.75
a. 1c gray ('20) 5.00 5.00
610 A69 2c gray green 1.50 .50
Never hinged 3.00
611 A70 3c bister brn 1.50 1.00
Never hinged 3.00
612 A71 4c carmine 2.50 1.00
Never hinged 7.50
613 A72 5c ultra 2.50 .50
Never hinged 3.25
a. Horiz. pair, imperf. btwn. 75.00
b. Imperf., pair 35.00 75.00
614 A73 10c blue 4.00 .50
Never hinged 5.00
a. Without imprint 7.50 1.00
Never hinged 12.00
615 A74 20c brown rose 40.00 2.00
Never hinged 60.00
a. 20c rose 40.00 2.00
Never hinged 70.00
616 A75 30c gray brown 90.00 3.00
Never hinged 200.00
617 A75 30c gray blk ('20) 100.00 4.00
Never hinged 250.00
Nos. 608-617 (10) 249.00 14.25

Perf. 12

Thick or Medium Paper

618 A68 1c dull violet 35.00 25.00
Never hinged 100.00
619 A69 2c gray green 10.00 6.00
Never hinged 15.00
620 A70 3c bis brn ('17) 200.00 200.00
Never hinged 325.00
622 A72 5c ultra 5.00 .25
Never hinged 8.00
623 A73 10c blue ('17) 5.00 .25
Never hinged 7.00
a. Without imprint ('17) 20.00 15.00
Never hinged 35.00
624 A74 20c rose ('20) 140.00 3.00
Never hinged 350.00
625 A75 30c gray blk ('20) 140.00 2.00
Never hinged 350.00

Thin or Medium Paper

626 A63 40c violet 65.00 1.00
Never hinged 200.00
627 A64 1p blue & blk 50.00 1.50
Never hinged 150.00
a. With center of 5p 800.00
b. 1p bl & dark blue (error) 500.00 20.00
c. Vert. pair, imperf. btwn. 250.00
628 A65 5p green & blk 1.50 *10.00*
Never hinged 1.75
a. With violet or red control number 25.00 10.00
b. With center of 1p 800.00

The 1, 2, 3, 5 and 10c are known on thin paper perforated. It is stated they were printed for Postal Union and "specimen" purposes.

All values exist imperf; these are not known to have been regularly issued. Nos. 627a and 628b were not regularly issued.

All values except 3c have an imprint.

For overprints and surcharges see Nos. B1-B2, O113-O165.

Meeting of Iturbide and Guerrero A77

Entering City of Mexico A78

1921

632 A77 10c blue & brn 25.00 3.00
Never hinged 82.50
a. Center inverted *25,000.*
633 A78 10p black brn & blk 22.50 *37.50*
Never hinged 27.50

Commemorating the meeting of Augustin de Iturbide and Vicente Guerrero and the entry into City of Mexico in 1821.

For overprint see No. O194.

"El Salto de Agua," Public Fountain A79

Pyramid of the Sun at Teotihuacán A80

Chapultepec Castle A81

Columbus Monument A82

Juárez Colonnade, Mexico, D. F. A83

Monument to Josefa Ortiz de Dominguez A84

Cuauhtémoc Monument — A85

1923 Unwmk. *Rouletted 14½*

634 A79 2c scarlet 2.00 .20
635 A80 3c bister brn 2.00 .25
636 A81 4c green 2.50 .75
637 A82 5c orange 5.00 .20
638 A83 10c brown 3.75 .20
639 A85 10c claret 3.50 .20
640 A84 20c dk blue 52.50 1.75
641 A85 30c dk green 52.50 2.00
Nos. 634-641 (8) 123.75 5.55
Set, never hinged 180.00

See Nos. 642-646, 650-657, 688-692, 727A, 735A-736. For overprints see Nos. O166-O173, O178-O181, O183-O187, O196-O197, O199-O206, O210, O212-O214, O217-O222.

Communications Building — A87

Palace of Fine Arts (National Theater) A88

Two types of 1p:
I — Eagle on palace dome.
II — Without eagle.

1923 Wmk. 156 *Perf. 12*

642 A79 2c scarlet 10.00 10.00
643 A81 4c green 1.40 .30
644 A82 5c orange 10.00 7.00
645 A85 10c brown lake 12.50 6.00
646 A83 30c dark green .95 .20
647 A63 40c violet 1.25 .25
648 A87 50c olive brn 1.00 .25
649 A88 1p red brn & bl (I) 1.00 1.00
a. Type II 3.00 *10.00*
Nos. 642-649 (8) 38.10 25.00
Set, never hinged 45.00

Most of Nos. 642-649 are known imperforate or part perforate but probably were not regularly issued.

For overprints see Nos. O175-O176, O189-O190, O208-O209, O223.

1923-34 *Rouletted 14½*

650 A79 2c scarlet .25 .20
651 A80 3c bis brn ('27) .25 .20
652 A81 4c green 47.50 35.00
653 A82 4c green ('27) .25 .20
654 A82 5c orange .25 .20
655 A85 10c lake .25 .20
656 A84 20c deep blue .75 .30
657 A83 30c dk green ('34) .75 .30
Nos. 650-657 (8) 50.25 36.60
Set, never hinged 62.50

Nos. 650 to 657 inclusive exist imperforate.

Medallion A90

Map of Americas A91

Francisco García y Santos — A92

Post Office, Mexico, D. F. — A93

1926 *Perf. 12*

658 A90 2c red 2.50 1.00
659 A91 4c green 2.50 1.00
660 A90 5c orange 2.50 .75
661 A91 10c brown red 4.00 1.00
662 A92 20c dk blue 4.00 1.25
663 A92 30c dk green 7.50 4.00
664 A92 40c violet 13.50 3.00
665 A93 1p brown & blue 27.50 10.00
a. 1p red & blue 37.50 15.00
Nos. 658-665 (8) 64.00 22.00
Set, never hinged 95.00

Pan-American Postal Congress.

Nos. 658-665 were also printed in black, on unwatermarked paper, for presentation to delegates to the Universal Postal Congress at London in 1929. Remainders were overprinted in 1929 for use as airmail official stamps, and are listed as Nos. CO3-CO10.

For overprints see Nos. 667-674, 675A-682, CO3-CO10.

Benito Juárez — A94

1926 ***Rouletted 14½***
666 A94 8c orange .30 .20
Never hinged .40

For overprint see No. O182.

Nos. 658-665 Overprinted

1930 ***Perf. 12***
667 A90 2c red 4.00 2.25
a. Reading down 15.00 15.00
668 A91 4c green 4.00 2.50
a. Reading down 15.00 15.00
669 A90 5c orange 4.00 2.00
a. Reading down 15.00 35.00
b. Double overprint 75.00 *75.00*
670 A91 10c brown red 7.50 2.50
671 A92 20c dk blue 9.50 3.50
672 A92 30c dk green 8.50 4.00
a. Reading down 10.00 12.00
673 A92 40c violet 12.50 8.50
a. Reading down 47.50 50.00
674 A93 1p red brn & bl 11.00 7.00
a. Double overprint 250.00
b. Triple overprint 200.00
Nos. 667-674 (8) 61.00 32.25
Set, never hinged 125.00

Overprint horizontal on 1p.

Arms of Puebla — A95

1931, May 1 **Engr.**
675 A95 10c dk bl & dk brn 3.00 .50
Never hinged 5.00

400th anniversary of Puebla.

Nos. 658-665a Overprinted

1931
676 A91 4c green 70.00 *75.00*
a. Inverted overprint *2,500.*
677 A90 5c orange 13.00 *17.00*
678 A91 10c brown red 13.00 *14.00*
679 A92 20c dk blue 13.00 *18.00*
680 A92 30c dk green 22.50 *25.00*
681 A92 40c violet 32.50 *35.00*
682 A93 1p brown & bl 30.00 *35.00*
a. 1p red & blue 42.50 45.00
Nos. 676-682 (7) 194.00 219.00
Set, never hinged 375.00

Overprint horizontal on 1p.

Nos. 676 and 682 are not known to have been sold to the public through post offices.

Forgeries of overprint exist.

Bartolomé de las Casas A96

Emblem of Mexican Society of Geography and Statistics A97

1933, Mar. 3 **Engr.** ***Rouletted 14½***
683 A96 15c dark blue .30 .20
Never hinged .40

For overprint see No. O215.

1933, Oct. ***Rouletted 14½***
684 A97 2c deep green 1.50 .60
685 A97 5c dark brown 1.75 .50
686 A97 10c dark blue .75 .20
687 A97 1p dark violet 100.00 65.00
Nos. 684-687 (4) 104.00 66.30
Set, never hinged 125.00

XXI Intl. Congress of Statistics and the 1st centenary of the Mexican Society of Geography and Statistics.

Types of 1923 and PT1

1934 ***Perf. 10½, 11 (4c)***
687A PT1 1c brown 1.00 .30
688 A79 2c scarlet .35 .20
689 A82 4c green .35 .20
690 A85 10c brown lake .35 .20
691 A84 20c dark blue .75 .75
692 A83 30c dk blue grn 1.00 1.25
Nos. 687A-692 (6) 3.80 2.90
Set, never hinged 4.50

See 2nd note after Postal Tax stamp No. RA3.

Indian Archer — A99

Indian — A100

Woman Decorating Pottery A101

Peon A102

Potter A103

Sculptor A104

Craftsman A105

Offering to the Gods A106

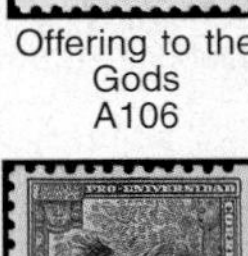

Worshiper — A107

1934, Sept. 1 **Wmk. 156** ***Perf. 10½***
698 A99 5c dk green 4.00 1.00
699 A100 10c brown lake 5.50 1.50
700 A101 20c ultra 13.50 8.00
701 A102 30c black 26.00 20.00
702 A103 40c black brn 37.50 25.00
703 A104 50c dull blue 75.00 75.00
704 A105 1p brn lake & blk 150.00 75.00
705 A106 5p brn blk & red brn 325.00 325.00
706 A107 10p brown & vio 1,100. 1,200.
a. Unwatermarked *3,250.*
Never hinged 5,000.
Nos. 698-706 (9) 1,736. 1,730.
Set, never hinged 2,400.

National University.

The design of the 1p is wider than the rest of the set. Values are for copies with perfs just touching the design.

See Nos. C54-C61, RA13B.

Yalalteca Indian — A108

Tehuana Indian — A109

Arch of the Revolution A110

Tower of Los Remedios A111

Cross of Palenque A112

Independence Monument A113

Independence Monument, Puebla A114

Monument to the Heroic Cadets A115

Stone of Tizoc — A116

Ruins of Mitla — A117

Coat of Arms A118

Charro A119

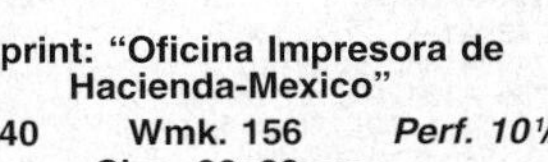

Imprint: "Oficina Impresora de Hacienda-Mexico"

1934-40 **Wmk. 156** ***Perf. 10½***
Size: 20x26mm
707 A108 1c orange .65 .20
708 A109 2c green .65 .20
a. Unwmkd. 3.75 3.75
709 A110 4c carmine .90 .20
710 A111 5c olive brn .65 .20
a. Unwmkd. 400.00 350.00
711 A112 10c dk blue .80 .20
712 A112 10c violet ('35) 1.25 .20
a. Unwmkd. 200.00 40.00
713 A113 15c lt blue 4.00 .30
714 A114 20c gray green 1.90 .20
a. 20c olive green 2.00 .20
715 A114 20c ultra ('35) 1.40 .20
a. Unwmkd. 150.00
716 A115 30c lake .90 .20
a. Unwmkd. 350.00
716B A115 30c lt ultra ('40) 1.00 .20
717 A116 40c red brown 1.00 .20
718 A117 50c grnsh black .90 .20
a. Imperf., pair 110.00
b. Unwmkd. 375.00
719 A118 1p dk brn & org 2.50 .20
a. Imperf., pair 350.00
720 A119 5p org & vio 7.75 .75
Nos. 707-720 (15) 26.25 3.65
Set, never hinged 355.00

No. 718a was not regularly issued.

See Nos. 729-733, 733B, 735, 784-788, 795A-800A, 837-838, 840-841, 844, 846-851. For overprints see Nos. 728, O224-O232.

Tractor — A120

1935, Apr. 1 **Wmk. 156** ***Perf. 10½***
721 A120 10c violet 4.00 .50
Never hinged 5.00

Industrial census of Apr. 10, 1935.

Arms of Chiapas A121

Emiliano Zapata A122

1935, Sept. 14
722 A121 10c dark blue .50 .20
Never hinged .75
a. Unwmkd. 125.00 100.00

The 111th anniversary of the joining of the state of Chiapas with the federal republic of Mexico. See No. 734.

1935, Nov. 20 **Wmk. 156**
723 A122 10c violet .75 .20
Never hinged 1.00

25th anniversary of the Plan of Ayala.

US and Mexico Joined by Highways A123

Matalote Bridge A124

View of Nuevo Laredo Highway — A125

1936 **Wmk. 248** ***Perf. 14***
725 A123 5c blue grn & rose .35 .25
726 A124 10c slate bl & blk .50 .25
727 A125 20c brn & dk grn 1.50 1.00
Nos. 725-727,C77-C79 (6) 3.60 2.40
Set, never hinged 5.00

Opening of the Mexico City — Nuevo Laredo Highway.

Monument Type of 1923

1936 **Wmk. 248** **Engr.** ***Perf. 10½***
727A A85 10c brown lake *2,500.* 650.00

No. 712 Overprinted in Green

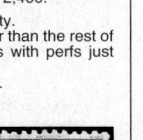

1936, Dec. 15 **Wmk. 156**

728 A112 10c violet .60 .50
Never hinged .90

1st National Congress of Industrial Hygiene and Medicine.

Type of 1934
Redrawn size: 17½x21mm
Imprint: "Talleres de Imp. de Est. y Valores-Mexico"

1937 **Photo.** **Wmk. 156** ***Perf. 14***

729 A108 1c orange .60 .20
a. Imperf., pair 12.50 12.50
Never hinged 25.00
730 A109 2c dull green .60 .20
a. Imperf., pair 12.50 12.50
Never hinged 30.00
731 A110 4c carmine .90 .20
a. Imperf., pair 12.50 12.50
Never hinged 30.00
732 A111 5c olive brn .80 .20
a. Unwmkd. *300.00*
733 A112 10c violet .70 .20
a. Imperf., pair 10.00 12.50
Never hinged 12.00
Nos. 729-733 (5) 3.60 1.00
Set, never hinged 4.25

The imperfs were not regularly issued.

Types of 1934-35

1937 **Wmk. 260**
Size: 17½x21mm

733B A111 5c olive brown *4,000.* 250.00
Never hinged 5,250.

1937 **Engr.** ***Perf. 10½***

734 A121 10c dark blue 35.00 35.00
Never hinged 45.00

1937
Size: 20x26mm

735 A112 10c violet 350.00 55.00

Types of 1923

1934-37 **Wmk. 260** ***Perf. 10½***

735A A79 2c scarlet *6,000.*
735B A85 10c brown lake —

Forged perforations exist.

Rouletted 14½

736 A85 10c claret *5,500.* *175.*

Blacksmith
A126

Revolutionary Soldier
A127

Revolutionary Envoy — A128

Wmk. 156

1938, Mar. 26 **Photo.** ***Perf. 14***

737 A126 5c black & brn .80 .20
738 A127 10c red brown .35 .25
739 A128 20c maroon & org 6.00 1.00
Nos. 737-739,C82-C84 (6) 13.15 4.90
Set, never hinged 20.00

Plan of Guadalupe, 25th anniv.

Arch of the Revolution
A129

Independence Monument
A131

Design: 10c, National Theater.

1938, July 1

740 A129 5c bister brn 4.25 .60
741 A129 5c red brown 25.00 2.25
742 A129 10c orange 15.00 11.00
743 A129 10c chocolate 1.00 .20
744 A131 20c brown lake 6.00 4.00
745 A131 20c black 18.00 15.00
Nos. 740-745 (6) 69.25 33.05
Nos. 740-745,C85-C90 (12) 129.60 63.30
Set, never hinged 190.00

16th Intl. Congress of Planning & Housing.

Arch of the Revolution
A132

1939, May 1

746 A132 10c Prus blue .65 .20
Nos. 746,C91-C93 (4) 4.75 2.95
Set, never hinged 9.75

New York World's Fair.

Indian — A133

1939, May 17

747 A133 10c red orange .45 .20
Nos. 747,C94-C96 (4) 5.55 2.75
Set, never hinged 12.10

Tulsa World Philatelic Convention.

Juan Zumárraga
A134

First Printing Shop in Mexico, 1539
A135

Design: 10c, Antonio de Mendoza.

1939, Sept. 1 **Engr.** ***Perf. 10½***

748 A134 2c brown blk .75 .25
749 A135 5c green .75 .20
750 A134 10c red brown .25 .20
Nos. 748-750,C97-C99 (6) 3.75 1.75
Set, never hinged 4.75

400th anniversary of printing in Mexico.

View of Taxco
A137

Allegory of Agriculture
A138

10c, Two hands holding symbols of commerce.

1939, Oct. 1 **Photo.** ***Perf. 12x13***

751 A137 2c dark carmine 1.25 .20
752 A138 5c sl grn & gray grn .25 .20
753 A138 10c org brn & buff .25 .20
Nos. 751-753,C100-C102 (6) 6.25 1.80
Set, never hinged 8.00

Census Taking.

"Penny Black" of 1840
A140

Roadside Monument
A141

1940, May ***Perf. 14***

754 A140 5c black & lemon .90 .50
755 A140 10c dark violet .25 .20
756 A140 20c lt blue & car .25 .20
757 A140 1p gray & red org 7.00 4.00
758 A140 5p black & Prus bl 50.00 50.00
Nos. 754-758,C103-C107 (10) 141.00 115.90
Set, never hinged 340.00

Postage stamp centenary.

1940 **Wmk. 156**

759 A141 6c deep green .50 .25
Never hinged .70

Opening of the highway between Mexico, D. F., and Guadalajara. See Nos. 789, 842.

Vasco de Quiroga — A142

Melchor Ocampo — A143

College Seal — A144

1940, July 15 **Engr.** ***Perf. 10½***

760 A142 2c violet 1.30 .50
761 A143 5c copper red .80 .20
762 A144 10c olive bister .80 .30
a. Imperf., pair 150.00
Nos. 760-762,C108-C110 (6) 5.10 2.50
Set, never hinged 9.00

Founding of the National College of San Nicolas de Hidalgo, 400th anniv.

Coat of Arms of Campeche
A145

1940, Aug. 7 **Photo.** ***Perf. 12x13***

763 A145 10c bis brn & dk car 5.00 1.25
Never hinged 8.50
Nos. 763,C111-C113 (4) 12.60 6.70
Set, never hinged 30.00

400th anniversary of the founding of Campeche.

Man at Helm
A146

1940, Dec. 1

764 A146 2c red org & blk 1.60 .60
765 A146 5c peacock bl & red brn 8.00 3.50
766 A146 10c slate grn & dk brn 4.00 .85
Nos. 764-766,C114-C116 (6) 21.00 9.45
Set, never hinged 45.00

Inauguration of Pres. Manuel Avila Camacho.

Alternated Perforations
Nos. 763-766, 774-779, 792-795, 801-804, 806-811, 813-818, C100-C102, C111-C116, C123-C128, C143-C162, C430-C431 have alternating small and large perforations.

Javelin Thrower — A147

1941, Nov. 4 ***Perf. 14***

767 A147 10c dull yellow grn 5.00 .50

National Athletic Games of the Revolution, Nov. 4-20, 1941.

Serpent Columns, Chichén Itzá
A148

Mayan Sculpture
A149

Coat of Arms of Merída — A150

1942, June 30

768 A148 2c dk olive bis 1.40 .75
769 A149 5c deep orange 2.25 .60
770 A150 10c dark violet 1.60 .25
Nos. 768-770,C117-C119 (6) 11.50 6.35

400th anniversary of the founding of Merida.

Independence Monument to Hidalgo — A151

Government Palace — A152

View of Guadalajara — A153

1942, Feb. 11 Engr. *Perf. 10x10½*

771 A151 2c bl vio & vio brn .35 .30
772 A152 5c black & cop red 1.25 .50
773 A153 10c red org & ultra 1.25 .40
Nos. 771-773,C120-C122 (6) 7.85 4.20

Founding of Guadalajara, 400th anniv.
No. 773 exists imperf on unwatermarked paper as a color proof.

Black Cloud in Orion A154

Designs: 5c, Total solar eclipse. 10c, Spiral galaxy in the "Hunting Dogs."

1942, Feb. 17 Photo. *Perf. 12x13*

774 A154 2c lt vio & indigo 10.00 3.00
775 A154 5c blue & indigo 15.00 2.00
776 A154 10c red org & indigo 15.00 .75
Nos. 774-776,C123-C125 (6) 100.00 17.25

Astrophysics Congress and the inauguration of an observatory at Tonanzintla, Feb. 17, 1942.

"Mother Earth" A157

Sowing Wheat A158

Western Hemisphere Carrying a Torch — A159

1942, July 1

777 A157 2c chestnut 2.00 .40
778 A158 5c turq blue 3.50 1.10
779 A159 10c red orange 1.50 .55
Nos. 777-779,C126-C128 (6) 12.90 5.50

2nd Inter-American Agricultural Conference.

Fuente Academy A160

1942, Nov. 16 *Perf. 14*

780 A160 10c grnsh black 2.50 .75

75th anniversary of Fuente Academy.

Las Monjas Church — A161

Generalissimo Ignacio José de Allende — A163

Design: 5c, San Miguel Church.

1943, May 11

781 A161 2c intense blue 1.00 .35
782 A161 5c deep brown 1.10 .30
783 A163 10c dull black 3.50 1.00
Nos. 781-783,C129-C131 (6) 10.60 5.35

400th anniv. of the founding of San Miguel de Allende.

Types of 1937

1944 Photo. Wmk. 272

784 A108 1c orange 2.00 .20
785 A109 2c dull green 2.00 .20
786 A110 4c carmine 4.00 .20
787 A111 5c olive brown 4.00 .20
788 A112 10c violet 2.00 .20

Type of 1940

789 A141 6c green 2.00 .20
Nos. 784-789 (6) 16.00 1.20

"Liberty" A164

Juan M. de Castorena A165

1944 Photo.

790 A164 12c violet brown .35 .20

See No. 845.

1944, Oct. 12 Engr. *Perf. 10*

791 A165 12c dark brown .60 .20

Third Book Fair. See No. C142.

Catalogue values for unused stamps in this section, from this point to the end of the section, are for Never Hinged items.

Hands Holding Globe Showing Western Hemisphere A166

1945, Feb. 27 Photo. *Perf. 12x13*

792 A166 12c dark carmine .60 .20
793 A166 1p slate green 1.00 .25
794 A166 5p olive brown 5.75 4.50
795 A166 10p black 17.50 8.00
Nos. 792-795,C143-C147 (9) 54.60 33.70

Inter-American Conf. held at Chapultepec, Feb. 1945.

Types of 1934-40

Wmk. 272

1945-46 Engr. *Perf. 10½*

795A A113 15c lt grnsh bl ('46) 325.00 60.00
796 A114 20c gray grn 2.50 .20
797 A115 30c lt ultra 3.25 .20
798 A116 40c brown 2.50 .20
799 A117 50c grnsh blk 1.60 .20
800 A118 1p dk brn & org 7.00 .20
b. Imperf., pair
800A A119 5p org & vio ('46) 17.00 6.00
Nos. 795A-800A (7) 358.85 67.00

Theater of Peace, San Luis Potosi A167

1945, July 27 Photo. *Perf. 12x13*

801 A167 12c blk & vio brn .45 .20
802 A167 1p blk & bl gray .60 .40
803 A167 5p blk & brn lake 5.50 5.00
804 A167 10p blk & grnsh bl 17.00 12.00
Nos. 801-804,C148-C152 (9) 49.90 35.40

Reconstruction of the Peace Theater (Teatro de la Paz), San Luis Potosi.

Fountain of Diana, the Huntress — A168

1945 *Perf. 14*

805 A168 3c violet blue .55 .20

See No. 839.

Removing Blindfold A169

1945, Nov. 2 *Perf. 12x13*

806 A169 2c bluish grn .40 .20
807 A169 6c orange .40 .20
808 A169 12c ultra .40 .20
809 A169 1p olive .60 .25
810 A169 5p gray & pale rose 3.50 3.00
811 A169 10p bl & yel grn 27.50 20.00
Nos. 806-811 (6) 32.80 23.85
Nos. 806-811,C153-C157 (11) 66.35 55.85

Issued to publicize the national literacy campaign.

M. E. de Almanza — A170

1946 *Perf. 14*

812 A170 8c black 1.25 .25

Martines Enriquez de Almanza, founder of the Mexican posts. See No. 843.

Allegory of World Peace A171

1946, Apr. 10 *Perf. 12x13*

813 A171 2c dk olive bis .35 .20
814 A171 6c red brown .30 .20
815 A171 12c Prus green .25 .20
816 A171 1p lt green .60 .40
817 A171 5p dull red vio 5.50 5.00
818 A171 10p lt ultra 30.00 20.00
Nos. 813-818 (6) 37.00 26.00
Nos. 813-818,C158-C162 (11) 62.15 40.75

United Nations.

Arms of Zacatecas A173

Monument to Gen. Gonzalez Ortega A174

Ramón Lopez Velarde — A175

Francisco Garcia Salinas — A176

Wmk. 279

1946, Sept. 1 Photo. *Perf. 14*

820 A173 2c orange brn .55 .20
821 A173 12c Prus blue .25 .20

Engr.
Perf. 10x10½

822 A174 1p lilac rose .70 .20
823 A175 5p red 5.50 3.00
824 A176 10p dk blue & blk 40.00 10.00
Nos. 820-824 (5) 47.00 13.60
Nos. 820-824,C163-C166 (9) 68.60 32.15

400th anniversary of the founding of the city of Zacatecas.

A177

A178

1947 Photo. *Perf. 14*
825 A177 15c Postman .25 .20
a. Imperf., pair 110.00

1947, May 16

10c, F. D. Roosevelt and Stamp of 1st Mexican Issue. 15c, Arms of Mexico and Stamp of 1st US Issue.

826 A178 10c yellow brown 1.60 1.00
a. 20c green
827 A178 15c green .25 .20
Nos. 826-827,C167-C169 (5) 4.60 2.35

Cent. Intl. Phil. Exhib., NYC, 5/17-25/47.

Justo Sierra — A180

Communications Building — A181

Perf. 10x10½, 10½x10
1947, Engr. Wmk. 279
828 A180 10p brown & dl grn 150.00 40.00
829 A181 20p dk green & lil 1.60 2.00

Cadet Juan Escutia — A182

Gen. Manuel Rincón — A186

Flag of San Blas Battalion — A188

Designs: 2c, Francisco Márquez. 5c, Cadet Fernando Montes de Oca. 10c, Cadet Juan Escutia. 15c, Cadet Agustin Melgar. 1p, Gen. Lucas Balderas.

1947, Sept. 8 Photo. *Perf. 14*
830 A182 2c brown black .45 .20
831 A182 5c red orange .30 .20
832 A182 10c dk brown .25 .20
833 A182 15c dk Prus green .25 .20
834 A186 30c dull olive grn .35 .20

Engr.
Perf. 10x10½
835 A186 1p aqua .45 .45
836 A188 5p dk blue & claret 1.90 1.90
Nos. 830-836 (7) 3.95 3.35
Nos. 830-836,C180-C184 (12) 7.30 6.15

Centenary of the battles of Chapultepec, Churubusco and Molino del Rey.

Types of 1934-46
1947-50 Wmk. 279 Photo. *Perf. 14*
837 A108 1c orange 1.00 .30
a. Imperf., pair 150.00
838 A109 2c dk green .60 .20
839 A168 3c violet blue .60 .20
840 A110 4c dull red 1.90 .20
841 A111 5c olive brown 2.50 .20
842 A141 6c deep green .45 .20
a. Imperf., pair 150.00
843 A170 8c black .35 .20
844 A112 10c violet 1.90 .25
845 A164 12c violet brn 12.00 .75

Types A108 to A112 are in the redrawn size of 1937.

Size: 19x25mm
Engr. *Perf. 10½*
846 A114 20c olive green 1.25 .20
a. 20c green 3.00 .30
847 A115 30c lt ultra 12.00 .40
848 A116 40c red brown 1.40 .25
849 A117 50c green 1.90 .20
a. Imperf., pair 110.00
850 A118 1p dk brn & org 45.00 9.00
851 A119 5p org & vio ('50) 35.00 11.00
Nos. 837-851 (15) 117.85 23.55

Puebla Cathedral — A189

Designs: 3c, Modernistic church, Nuevo Leon. 5c, Modern building, Mexico City. 10c, Convent, Morelos. 15c, Benito Juarez. 30c, Indian dancer, Michoacan. 40c, Stone head, Tabasco. 50c, Carved head, Veracruz. 1p, Convent and carved head, Hidalgo. 5p, Galleon, arms of Campeche. 10p, Francisco I. Madero. 20p, Modern building, Mexico City.

1950-52 Wmk. 279 Photo. *Perf. 14*
856 A189 3c blue vio ('51) .50 .20
857 A189 5c dk red brn .75 .20
858 A189 10c dk green 3.50 .20
859 A189 15c dk green ('51) 1.75 .20
860 A189 20c blue violet 14.00 .20
861 A189 30c red .50 .20
862 A189 40c red orange ('51) 1.00 .20
863 A189 50c blue 1.25 .20

Engr.
864 A189 1p dull brown 4.50 .20
865 A189 5p ultra & bl grn 7.00 4.00
866 A189 10p blk & dp ultra ('52) 7.00 7.00
867 A189 20p pur & grn ('52) 10.00 10.00
Nos. 856-867 (12) 51.75 22.80

See Nos. 875-885, 909, 928-931, 943-952, 1003-1004, 1054-1055, 1072, 1076, 1081, 1090-1091, 1094-1102.

Highway Bridge A190

Symbolical of Construction in 1950 — A191

Railroad Laborer — A192

Perf. 10½x10, 10x10½
1950, May 5 Engr.
868 A190 15c purple .60 .20
869 A191 20c deep blue .40 .20
Nos. 868-869,C199-C200 (4) 4.30 .85

Completion of the International Highway between Ciudad Juarez and the Guatemala border.

Inscribed: "Ferrocarril del Sureste 1950"

Design: 20c, Map and locomotive.

1950, May 24 *Perf. 10x10½*
870 A192 15c chocolate 1.25 .20
871 A192 20c dp carmine .45 .20
Nos. 870-871,C201-C202 (4) 2.55 .90

Opening of the Southeastern Railroad between Veracruz, Coatzocoalcos and Yucatan, 1950.

Postal Service A193

Miguel Hidalgo y Costilla A194

1950, June 25 *Perf. 10x10½*
872 A193 50c purple .40 .20
Nos. 872,C203-C204 (3) 1.25 .70

75th anniv. (in 1949) of the UPU.

Wmk. 300
1953, May 8 Photo. *Perf. 14*
873 A194 20c grnsh bl & dk brn 1.75 .25
Nos. 873,C206-C207 (3) 3.55 .70

Bicentenary of birth of Miguel Hidalgo y Costilla. See Nos. C206-C207.

Type of 1950-52

Designs as before.
Two types of 5p:
Type I — Imprint ½mm high and blurred.
Type II — Imprint ¾mm high and clear.

1954-67 Photo. *Perf. 14*
875 A189 5c red brown .50 .20
876 A189 10c green, redrawn 2.50 .20
a. 10c dark green 2.50 .20
877 A189 15c dk green .40 .20
878 A189 20c bluish blk, white paper, colorless gum ('67) .60 .20
a. 20c dark blue 3.50 .20
879 A189 30c brown red .75 .20
a. 30c redsh brn .75 .20
880 A189 40c red orange 1.50 .20
881 A189 50c lt blue 1.00 .20

Engr.
882 A189 1p olive grn, perf. 11, vert. wmk. ('58) 12.00 .25
a. 1p olive grn, perf. 14 7.00 .20
b. olive brown 12.00 .20
883 A189 5p ultra & bl grn, I 7.00 1.00
a. Type II 500.00 7.00
884 A189 10p sl & dp ultra ('56) 9.00 5.00
a. 10p slate green & ultra 35.00 5.00
885 A189 20p purple & grn 11.00 9.00
a. 20p brn vio & yel grn 75.00 20.00
Nos. 875-885 (11) 46.25 16.65

Nos. 875-881 come only with watermark vertical, and in various shades. Watermark inverted on Nos. 884, 885.

On No. 876, imprint extends full width of stamp.

Vert. pairs, imperf. horiz. of Nos. 878, 880 are noted after No. 1004.

Aztec Messenger of the Sun A195

Symbolizing Adoption of National Anthem A196

1954, Mar. 6
886 A195 20c rose & bl gray 1.10 .20
Nos. 886,C222-C223 (3) 2.85 .80

7th Central American and Caribbean Games.

1954, Sept. 16 Photo.
887 A196 5c rose lil & dk bl .75 .20
888 A196 20c yel brn & brn vio .90 .20
889 A196 1p gray grn & cerise .65 .40
Nos. 887-889,C224-C226 (6) 3.40 1.50

Centenary of the adoption of Mexico's National Anthem.

Torch-Bearer and Stadium — A197

Aztec Designs A198

1955, Mar. 12 Wmk. 300 *Perf. 14*
890 A197 20c dk grn & red brn .85 .20
Nos. 890,C227-C228 (3) 2.35 .80

Second Pan American Games, 1955.

1956, Aug. 1
891 A198 5c "Motion" .50 .20
892 A198 10c Bird .50 .20
893 A198 30c Flowers .40 .20
894 A198 50c Corn .50 .20
895 A198 1p Deer .60 .20
896 A198 5p Man 2.25 2.25
a. Souv. sheet, #891-896, imperf. 75.00 75.00
Nos. 891-896,C229-C234 (12) 7.90 5.55

Centenary of Mexico's 1st postage stamps. No. 896a sold for 15p.

Stamp of 1856 A199

Francisco Zarco — A200

1956, Aug. 1
897 A199 30c brn & intense bl .75 .25

Cent. of 1st Mexican Stamp Intl. Philatelic Exhibition, Mexico City, Aug. 16, 1956.

1956-63

Portraits: 25c, 45c, Guillermo Prieto. 60c, Ponciano Arriaga.

897A A200 25c dk brown ('63) .75 .50
898 A200 45c dk blue green .35 .25
899 A200 60c red lilac .35 .35
900 A200 70c violet blue .40 .20
Nos. 897A-900,C236-C237A (7) 4.45 2.60

Centenary of the constitution (in 1957). See Nos. C289, 1075, 1092-1093.

"Mexico"
A201

Mexican Eagle and Oil Derrick
A202

Design: 1p, National Assembly.

1957, Aug. 31 Photo. *Perf. 14*

901 A201 30c maroon & gold .50 .20
902 A201 1p pale brn & metallic grn .35 .25
Nos. 901-902,C239-C240 (4) 1.70 .90

Constitution, centenary.

1958, Aug. 30 Wmk. 300 *Perf. 14*

Design: 5p, Map of Mexico and refinery.

903 A202 30c lt blue & blk .50 .20
904 A202 5p hn brn & Prus grn 6.00 4.00
Nos. 903-904,C243-C244 (4) 7.15 4.60

20th anniv. of the nationalization of Mexico's oil industry.

UNESCO Building and Eiffel Tower — A203

UN Headquarters, New York — A204

1959, Jan. 20

905 A203 30c dull lilac & blk .50 .20

UNESCO Headquarters opening, Paris, Nov. 9.

1959, Sept. 7 Litho. *Perf. 14*

906 A204 30c org yel & bl .50 .20

Meeting of UNESCO.

Carranza
A205

Humboldt Statue
A206

1960, Jan. 15 Photo. Wmk. 300

907 A205 30c pale grn & plum .35 .20

Birth centenary of Pres. Venustiano Carranza. See No. C246.

1960, Mar. 16 Wmk. 300 *Perf. 14*

908 A206 40c bis brn & grn .35 .20

Cent. of the death (in 1859) of Alexander von Humboldt, German naturalist and geographer.

Type of 1950-52 Inscribed: "HOMENAJE AL COLECCIONISTA DEL TIMBRE DE MEXICO-JUNIO 1960"

1960, June 8 Engr. Wmk. 300

909 A189 10p lil, brn & grn 100.00 75.00

Visit of the Elmhurst (Ill.) Philatelic Society of Mexico Specialists to Mexico, 25th anniv. See No. C249.

Independence Bell & Monument
A207 A208

5p, Bell of Dolores and Miguel Hidalgo.

Wmk. 300

1960, Sept. 15 Photo. *Perf. 14*

910 A207 30c grn & rose red 3.00 .20
911 A208 1p dl grn & dk brn .50 .20
912 A208 5p maroon & dk bl 5.00 5.00
Nos. 910-912,C250-C252 (6) 15.50 8.10

150th anniv. of Mexican independence. See US No. 1157.

Agricultural Reform
A209

Symbols of Health Education — A210

Designs: 20c, Sailor and Soldier, 1960, and Fighter of 1910. 30c, Electrification. 1p, Political development (schools). 5p, Currency stability (Bank and money).

1960-61 Photo. *Perf. 14*

913 A209 10c sl grn, blk & red org .75 .20
914 A210 15c grn & org brn 2.75 .50
915 A210 20c brt bl & lt brn ('61) 1.00 .20
916 A210 30c vio brn & sep .40 .20
917 A210 1p redsh brn & slate .50 .20
918 A210 5p maroon & gray 6.00 3.50
Nos. 913-918,C253-C256 (10) 18.80 8.55

50th anniversary (in 1960) of the Mexican Revolution.

Issued: #913, 11/20/60; #914, 916-918, 12/23/60; #915, 3/14/61.

Tunnel — A211

Microscope, Mosquito and Globe — A212

1961, Dec. 7 Wmk. 300 *Perf. 14*

919 A211 40c blk & brt grn .40 .20
Nos. 919,C258-C259 (3) 1.20 .60

Opening of the railroad from Chihuahua to the Pacific Ocean.

1962, Apr. 7

920 A212 40c dl bl & maroon .40 .20

WHO drive to eradicate malaria.

President Joao Goulart of Brazil — A213

Insurgent at Marker for Battle of Puebla — A214

Wmk. 300

1962, Apr. 11 Photo. *Perf. 14*

921 A213 40c brown olive 1.00 .25

Visit of Joao Goulart, president of Brazil, to Mexico.

1962, May 5

922 A214 40c sepia & dk grn .35 .20

Centenary of the Battle of May 5 at Puebla and the defeat of French forces by Gen. Ignacio Zaragoza. See No. C260.

Draftsman and Surveyor
A215

Plumbline
A216

1962, June 11

923 A215 40c slate grn & dk bl .90 .20

25th anniversary of the National Polytechnic Institute. See No. C261.

1962, June 21

924 A216 20c dp blue & blk 1.40 .20

Issued to publicize the importance of mental health.

"Space Needle" and Gear Wheels
A217

Globe
A218

1962, July 6

925 A217 40c dk grn & gray .35 .20

"Century 21" International Exposition, Seattle, Wash., Apr. 21-Oct. 12.

1962, Oct. 1 *Perf. 14*

926 A218 40c gray & brn .35 .20

1962 meeting of the Inter-American Economic and Social Council. See No. C263.

Pres. Alessandri of Chile
A219

Pres. Betancourt of Venezuela
A220

1962, Dec. 20 Wmk. 300 *Perf. 14*

927 A219 20c olive black .75 .20

Visit of President Jorge Alessandri Rodriguez of Chile to Mexico, Dec. 17-20.

Type of 1950-52

Designs as before.

Wmk. 300, Vertical

1962-74 Photo. *Perf. 14*

928 A189 1p ol gray ('67) 1.25 .20
a. 1p green 4.00 .20
929 A189 5p dl bl & dk grn 3.50 .75
a. 5p bluish gray & dark green, white paper ('67) 3.50 .50
930 A189 10p gray & bl ('63) 8.50 5.00
a. 10p green & deep blue ('74) 8.50 5.50
931 A189 20p lil & blk ('63) 9.00 7.50
a. Redrawn, white paper 10.00 10.00
Nos. 928-931 (4) 22.25 13.45

No. 928 is on thick, luminescent paper. No. 929 is 20½mm high; No. 929a, 20¾mm. Nos. 931a and 1102 (unwmkd.) have more shading in sky and spots on first floor windows.

1963, Feb. 23 Wmk. 300

932 A220 20c slate .70 .20

Visit of President Romulo Betancourt of Venezuela to Mexico.

Congress Emblem
A221

Wheat Emblem
A222

1963, Apr. 22 Wmk. 300 *Perf. 14*

933 A221 40c fawn & blk .60 .20

19th International Chamber of Commerce Congress. See No. C271.

1963, June 23 Wmk. 300 *Perf. 14*

934 A222 40c crim & dk bl .60 .20

FAO "Freedom from Hunger" campaign.

Mercado Mountains and Arms of Durango
A223

Belisario Dominguez
A224

1963, July 13 Photo.

935 A223 20c dk bl & choc .60 .20

400th anniv. of the founding of Durango.

1963, July 13 Photo.

936 A224 20c dk grn & ol gray .60 .20

Centenary of the birth of Belisario Dominguez, revolutionary leader.

Mexico. No. 897, depicting Mexico No. 1 — A225

1963, Oct. 9 Wmk. 350 *Perf. 14*
937 A225 1p int blue & brn 1.25 .75

77th Annual Convention of the American Philatelic Society, Mexico City, Oct. 7-13. See No. C274.

Tree of Life A226

José Morelos A227

1963, Oct. 26 Wmk. 350 *Perf. 14*
938 A226 20c dl bl grn & car .40 .20

Intl. Red Cross, cent. See No. C277.

1963, Nov. 9
939 A227 40c grn & dk sl grn .55 .20

150th anniv. of the 1st congress of Anahuac.

Pres. Victor Paz Estenssoro A228

Arms of Sinaloa University A229

1963, Nov. 9 Wmk. 350 *Perf. 14*
940 A228 40c dk brn & dk red brn .60 .20

Visit of President Victor Paz Estenssoro of Bolivia.

1963 Photo.
941 A229 40c slate grn & ol bister .60 .20

90th anniversary of the founding of the University of Sinaloa.

Diesel Train, Rail Cross Section and Globe A230

1963, Nov. 29 Photo.
942 A230 20c black & dk brn .90 .50

11th Pan-American Railroad Congress. See No. C279.

Type of 1950-52

Designs as before.

1963-66 Wmk. 350 Photo. *Perf. 14*
943 A189 5c red brn ('65) .60 .20
944 A189 10c dk green ('64) .65 .20
945 A189 15c dk green ('66) .60 .20
946 A189 20c dark blue .60 .20
948 A189 40c red orange .70 .20
949 A189 50c blue ('64) 2.00 .20
950 A189 1p olive grn ('64) 4.00 .20
951 A189 5p dl bl & dk grn ('66) 100.00 30.00

952 A189 10p gray & Prus bl ('65) 35.00 25.00
Nos. 943-952 (9) 144.15 56.40

The 20c is redrawn; clouds almost eliminated and other slight variations.

"F.S.T.S.E." Emblem A231

Academy of Medicine Emblem A232

1964, Feb. 15
954 A231 20c red org & dk brn .40 .20

25th anniv. (in 1963) of the Civil Service Statute affecting federal employees.

1964, May 18 Wmk. 350 *Perf. 14*
955 A232 20c gold & blk .40 .20

National Academy of Medicine, cent.

José Rizal A233

View of Zacatecas A234

40c, Miguel Lopez de Legaspi, Spanish navigator.

1964, Nov. 10 Photo. *Perf. 14*
956 A233 20c dk bl & dp grn .50 .20
957 A233 40c dk bl & brt vio .60 .20
Nos. 956-957,C300-C301 (4) 6.10 1.75

Issued to honor 400 years of Mexican-Philippine friendship.

1964, Nov. 10 Wmk. 350
958 A234 40c slate grn & red .55 .20

50th anniv. of the capture of Zacatecas.

Col. Gregorio Mendez A235

Morelos Theater, Aguascalientes A236

1964, Nov. 10
959 A235 40c grysh blk & dk brn .50 .20

Cent. of the Battle of Jahuactal, Tabasco.

1965, Jan. 9 Photo. *Perf. 14*
960 A236 20c dl cl & dk gray .35 .20

50th anniversary of the Aguascalientes Convention, Oct. 1-Nov. 9, 1914.

Andrés Manuel del Río A237

1965, Feb. 18 Wmk. 350 *Perf. 14*
961 A237 30c gray .40 .20

Bicentenary of the birth of Andrés Manuel del Rio, founder of the National School of Mining and discoverer of vanadium.

José Morelos and Constitution A238

Trees A239

1965, Apr. 24 Photo. *Perf. 14*
962 A238 40c brt grn & dk red brn .45 .20

Sesquicentennial (in 1964) of the 1st Mexican constitution.

1965, July 14 Wmk. 350 *Perf. 14*
963 A239 20c blue & green .30 .20

Issued to commemorate Tree Day, July 8.

ICY Emblem A240

1965, Sept. 13 Photo.
964 A240 40c olive gray & slate grn .30 .20

International Cooperation Year, 1965.

Athlete with Sling, Clay Figure A241

Design: 40c, Batter. Clay figures on 20c and 40c found in Colima, period 300-650 A.D.

1965, Dec. 17 Wmk. 350 *Perf. 14*
965 A241 20c olive & vio bl 3.25 .20
966 A241 40c pink & black 1.00 .20
Nos. 965-966,C309-C311 (5) 6.70 1.20

19th Olympic Games, Mexico, 1968.

José Morelos by Diego Rivera — A242

Emiliano Zapata — A243

1965, Dec. 22
967 A242 20c lt vio bl & blk .40 .20

José Maria Morelos y Pavon (1765-1815), priest and patriot in 1810 revolution against Spain.

1966, Jan. 10 Photo.

20c, Corn, cotton, bamboo, wheat and cow.

968 A243 20c carmine rose .35 .20
969 A243 40c black .45 .20

50th anniv. of the Agrarian Reform Law.

Mexican Postal Service Emblem A244

Bartolomé de Las Casas A245

1966, June 24 Wmk. 300 *Perf. 14*
970 A244 40c brt green & blk .40 .20
Nos. 970,C314-C315 (3) 1.00 .60

Congress of the Postal Union of the Americas and Spain, UPAE, Mexico City, June 24-July 23.

1966, Aug. 1 Photo. Wmk. 300
971 A245 20c black & buff .40 .20

400th anniv. of the death of Bartolomé de Las Casas (1474-1566), "Apostle of the Indies."

Mechanical Drawings and Cogwheels A246

1966, Aug. 15 Photo. *Perf. 14*
972 A246 20c gray & grn .30 .20

50th anniversary of the founding of the School of Mechanical and Electrical Engineering (ESIME).

FAO Emblem — A247

1966, Sept. 30 Wmk. 300 *Perf. 14*
973 A247 40c green .30 .20

FAO International Rice Year.

Wrestling, by Diego Rivera A248

1966, Oct. 15
Size: 35x21mm

974 A248 20c Running and Jumping 1.25 .20
975 A248 40c shown 1.00 .20
a. Souvenir sheet 4.00 4.00
Nos. 974-975,C318-C320 (5) 5.70 1.40

Issued to publicize the 19th Olympic Games, Mexico City, D.F., 1968. No. 975a contains 2 imperf. stamps similar to Nos. 974-975 with simulated perforations. Sold for 90c.

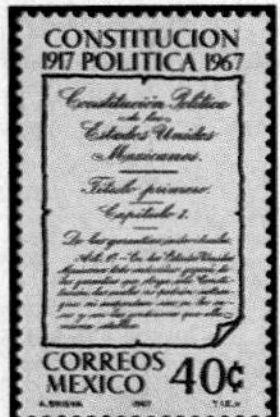

First Page of Constitution
A249

Oil Refinery and Pyramid of the Sun
A250

Wmk. 300
1967, Feb. 5 Photo. *Perf. 14*
976 A249 40c black .50 .20

Constitution, 50th anniv. See #C322.

1967, Apr. 2 Wmk. 300 *Perf. 14*
977 A250 40c lt bl & blk .35 .20

7th Intl. Oil Congress, Mexico City, Sept. 1967.

Nayarit Indian — A251

Wmk. 300
1967, May 1 Photo. *Perf. 14*
978 A251 20c pale grn & blk .30 .20

50th anniversary of Nayarit Statehood.

Degollado Theater, Guadalajara — A252

Wmk. 300
1967, June 12 Photo. *Perf. 14*
979 A252 40c pink & black .35 .20

Centenary of the founding of the Degollado Theater, Guadalajara.

Mexican Eagle over Imperial Crown — A253

Perf. 10x10½
1967, June 19 Litho. Wmk. 350
980 A253 20c black & ocher .30 .20

Centenary of the victory of the Mexican republican forces and of the execution of Emperor Maximilian I.

Canoeing
A254

Designs: 40c, Basketball. 50c, Hockey. 80c, Bicycling. 2p, Fencing.

Wmk. 300
1967, Oct. 12 Photo. *Perf. 14*
981 A254 20c blue & blk .50 .20
982 A254 40c brick red & blk .50 .20
983 A254 50c brt yel grn & blk .50 .20
a. Souvenir sheet of 3, #981-983, imperf. 5.00 3.50
984 A254 80c brt pur & blk 1.25 .25
985 A254 2p orange & blk 2.25 .30
a. Souvenir sheet of 2, #984-985, imperf. 7.00 4.00
Nos. 981-985,C328-C331 (9) 8.75 2.70
Nos. 981-985 (5) 5.00 1.15

Issued to publicize the 19th Olympic Games, Mexico City, Oct. 12-27, 1968.
No. 983a sold for 1.50p; No. 985a sold for 3.50p. Both sheets are watermark 350.
See Nos. 990-995, C335-C338.

Artemio de Valle-Arizpe
A255

Pedro Moreno
A256

1967, Nov. 1 Photo.
986 A255 20c brown & slate .35 .30

Centenary of the Ateneo Fuente, a college at Saltillo, Coahuila.

1967, Nov. 18 Wmk. 300 *Perf. 14*
987 A256 40c blk & lt bl .35 .20

Moreno (1775-1817), revolutionary leader.

Gabino Barreda
A257

Staircase, Palace of Mining
A258

1968, Jan. 27 Photo. *Perf. 14*
988 A257 40c dk bl & rose claret .40 .20
989 A258 40c blk & bl gray .40 .20

Centenary of the founding of the National Preparatory and Engineering Schools.

Type of Olympic Issue, 1967

20c, Wrestling. 40c, Pentathlon. 50c, Water polo. 80c, Gymnastics. 1p, Boxing. 2p, Pistol shoot.

1968, Mar. 21 Wmk. 300 *Perf. 14*
990 A254 20c olive & blk .75 .20
991 A254 40c red lil & blk .75 .20
992 A254 50c brt green & blk .75 .20
a. Souvenir sheet of 3, #990-992, imperf. 7.00 4.00
993 A254 80c brt pink & blk 1.00 .25
994 A254 1p org brn & blk 4.00 3.50
995 A254 2p gray & blk 5.50 3.50
a. Souvenir sheet of 3, #993-995, imperf. 7.50 4.00
Nos. 990-995,C335-C338 (10) 15.45 9.65

19th Olympic Games, Mexico City, Oct. 12-27. No. 992a sold for 1.50p; No. 995a sold for 5p. Both sheets are watermark 350.

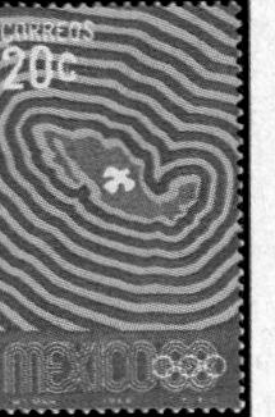

Map of Mexico, Peace Dove
A259

Arms of Veracruz
A261

Symbols of Cultural Events
A260

40c, University City Olympic stadium. 50c, Telecommunications tower. 2p, Sports Palace. 10p, Pyramid of the Sun, Teotihuacan, & Olympic torch.

Wmk. 350
1968, Oct. Photo. *Perf. 14*
996 A259 20c blue, yel & grn .75 .20
997 A259 40c multicolored .75 .20
998 A259 50c multicolored .75 .20
a. Souv. sheet of 3, #996-998, imperf. 20.00 10.00
999 A260 2p multicolored 4.00 .50
1000 A260 5p silver & blk 10.00 1.25
a. Souv. sheet of 2, #999-1000, imperf. 25.00 20.00
1001 A259 10p multicolored 7.50 2.00
Nos. 996-1001,C340-C344 (11) 32.35 8.15

19th Olympic Games, Mexico City, Oct. 12-27 (Nos. 996-1000). Arrival of the Olympic torch in Veracruz (No. 1001).
#998a sold for 1.50p. #1000a sold for 9p.
Issued: #996-1000, 10/12/68; #1001, 10/6/68.

1969, May 20 Wmk. 350 *Perf. 14*
1002 A261 40c multicolored .35 .20

450th anniv. of the founding of Veracruz.

Type of 1950-52
Coil Stamps
Perf. 11 Vert.
1969 Wmk. 300 Photo.
1003 A189 20c dk blue 4.00 2.00
1004 A189 40c red orange 5.00 3.00

Vert. pairs, imperf. horiz. may be from uncut rolls of coils.

Subway Train — A262

1969, Sept. 4 Wmk. 350 *Perf. 14*
1005 A262 40c multicolored .35 .20

Inauguration of Mexico City subway.

Honeycomb, Bee and ILO Emblem
A263

Gen. Allende, by Diego Rivera
A264

1969, Oct. 18 Photo. *Perf. 14*
1006 A263 40c multicolored .30 .20

50th anniversary of the ILO.

1969, Nov. 15 Wmk. 350 *Perf. 14*
1007 A264 40c multicolored .30 .20

Gen. Ignacio Allende Unzaga (1769-1811), hero of Mexican independence.

Tourist Issue

Pyramid of Niches at El Tajin, Veracruz, and Dancers Swinging from Pole
A265

Anthropology Museum, Mexico City — A266

Deer Dance, Sonora — A267

Designs: No. 1010, View of Puerto Vallarta. No. 1011, Puebla Cathedral. No. 1012, Calle Belaunzaran. No. 1014, Ocotlan Cathedral, horiz.

1969-73 Photo. Wmk. 350
1008 A265 40c shown .45 .20
1009 A266 40c shown ('70) .45 .20
1010 A266 40c Jalisco ('70) .45 .20
1011 A266 40c Puebla ('70) .45 .20
1012 A266 40c Guanajuato ('70) .45 .20

Wmk. 300
1013 A267 40c shown ('73) .35 .20
1014 A267 40c Tlaxcala ('73) .35 .20
Nos. 1008-1014,C354-C358 (12) 6.35 2.75
Nos. 1008-1014 (7) 2.95 1.40

No. 1010 is inscribed "1970" below the design. Copies inscribed "1969" are from an earlier, unissued printing. Value $500.
Issued: #1008, 12/13/69; #1009-1012, 1/17/70; #1013-1014, 3/6/73.

Luminescence

Fluorescent stamps include Nos. 1013-1014, 1035, 1038, 1041, 1043-1045, 1047-1050, 1054-1059. (See Luminescence note over No. C527.)

"How Many, Who and What are We?" — A268

40c, "What, How & How Much do we produce?" (horse's head & symbols of agriculture).

1970, Jan. 26 Wmk. 350 *Perf. 14*

1024 A268 20c multicolored .30 .20
1025 A268 40c blue & multi .30 .20

Issued to publicize the 1970 census.

Human Eye and Spectrum A269

1970, Mar. 8 Photo. Wmk. 350

1026 A269 40c multicolored .30 .20

21st International Congress of Ophthalmology, Mexico City, Mar. 8-14.

Helmets of 1920 and 1970 A270

1970, Apr. 11 Wmk. 350 *Perf. 14*

1027 A270 40c dk car rose, blk & lt brn .30 .20

50th anniversary of the Military College.

José Maria Pino Suarez — A271

Coat of Arms of Celaya — A272

1970, Apr. 25 Photo.

1028 A271 40c black & multi .30 .20

Centenary of the birth of José Maria Pino Suarez (1869-1913), lawyer, poet and Vice President of Mexico.

1970, Oct. 12 Photo. *Perf. 14*

1029 A272 40c black & multi .30 .20

City of Celaya, 400th anniversary.

Eclipse of Sun — A273

1970, Nov. 27 Wmk. 350 *Perf. 14*

1030 A273 40c black & gray .30 .20

Total eclipse of the sun, Mar. 7, 1970.

Spheres with Dates 1970-1770 A274

1971, June 26 Photo. *Perf. 14*

1031 A274 40c emerald & blk .30 .20

Bicentenary of National Lottery.

Vasco de Quiroga, Mural by O'Gorman A275

1971, July 10 Photo.

1032 A275 40c multicolored .30 .20

500th anniversary of the birth of Vasco de Quiroga (1470-1565), Archbishop of Michoacan, founder of hospitals and schools.

Amado Nervo (1870-1919), Poet — A276

1971, Aug. 7 Wmk. 350 *Perf. 14*

1033 A276 40c multicolored .30 .20

Waves and Transformer A277

1971, Oct. 8

1034 A277 40c blk, lt bl & lt grn .30 .20

50th anniversary of Mexican radio.

Pres. Lazaro Cardenas (1895-1970) — A278

1971, Oct. 19 Wmk. 300

1035 A278 40c blk & pale lil .30 .20

Keyboard and Lara's Signature A279

1971, Nov. 6 Wmk. 350

1036 A279 40c blk, buff & pale bl .30 .20

Agustin Lara (1900-70), composer.

Arms of Monterrey A280

Cardiology Institute and WHO Emblems A281

1971, Dec. 18

1037 A280 40c black & multi .30 .20

375th anniv. of the founding of Monterrey.

1972, Apr. 8 Wmk. 300

1038 A281 40c multicolored .30 .20

"Your heart is your health," World Health Day 1972. See No. C395.

Gaceta de Mexico, Jan. 1, 1722 A282

1972, June 24 Wmk. 350

1039 A282 40c multicolored .30 .20

250th anniv. of 1st Mexican newspaper.

Lions Intl. Emblem A283

Sailing Ship Zaragoza A284

1972, June 28

1040 A283 40c black & multi .30 .20

55th Lions International Convention.

1972, July 1

1041 A284 40c blue & multi .30 .20

75th anniv. of the Naval School of Veracruz.

Olive Tree and Branch — A285

1972, July 18 Wmk. 350 *Perf. 14*

1042 A285 40c lt grn, ocher & blk .30 .20
a. 40c light green, yellow & black 3.00 3.00

Centenary of Chilpancingo as capital of Guerrero State.

Margarita Maza de Juárez A286

Design: 40c, Benito Juárez, by Diego Rivera.

1972, Sept. 15 Photo. Wmk. 300

1043 A286 20c pink & multi .40 .20
1044 A286 40c dp yellow & multi .40 .20
Nos. 1043-1044,C403-C405 (5) 1.60 1.00

Benito Juárez (1806-1872), revolutionary leader and president of Mexico.

Emperor Justinian I, Mosaic A287

1972, Sept. 30 Wmk. 300

1045 A287 40c multicolored .65 .20

Mexican Bar Association, 50th anniv.

Caravel A288

Library, Book Year Emblem A290

Olympic Emblems A289

1972, Oct. 12 Wmk. 350

1046 A288 80c buff, pur & ocher .40 .20

Stamp Day of The Americas.

1972, Dec. 9 Wmk. 300

1047 A289 40c multicolored 1.00 .20

20th Olympic Games, Munich, Aug. 26-Sept. 11. See Nos. C410-C411.

1972, Dec. 16

1048 A290 40c black & multi .30 .20

International Book Year 1972.

Fish in Clean Water A291

1972, Dec. 16

1049 A291 40c blk & lt bl .40 .20

Anti-pollution campaign. See No. C412.

Metlac Railroad Bridge — A292

1973, Feb. 2 *Perf. 14*

1050 A292 40c multicolored .85 .20

Centenary of Mexican railroads.

Cadet — A293

1973, Oct. 11 Photo. Wmk. 300
1051 A293 40c black & multi .45 .20

Sesquicentennial of Military College.

Madero, by Diego Rivera — A294

Antonio Narro — A295

1973, Nov. 9 Wmk. 350 *Perf. 14*
1052 A294 40c multicolored .30 .20

Pres. Francisco I. Madero (1873-1913).

1973, Nov. 9 Photo.
1053 A295 40c steel gray .35 .20

50th anniversary of the Antonio Narro Agriculture School in Saltillo.

Type of 1950-52

Designs as before.

1973 Unwmk. *Perf. 14*
1054 A189 20c blue violet 5.00 2.00
1055 A189 40c red orange 5.00 2.00

Fluorescent printing on back (or on front of 40c) consisting of network pattern and diagonal inscription.

Unsaturated Hydrocarbon Molecule — A296

Wmk. 300
1973, Dec. 7 Photo. *Perf. 14*
1056 A296 40c blk, dk car & yel .30 .20

Pointing Hand Emblem of Foreign Trade Institute — A297

1974, Jan. 11 Photo. Wmk. 300
1057 A297 40c dk green & blk .30 .20

Export promotion.

A298

1974, Jan. 18 Litho. Wmk. 300
1058 A298 40c black .30 .20

EXMEX 73 Philatelic Exhibition, Cuernavaca, Apr. 7-15. See No. C424.

Manuel M. Ponce at Keyboard A299

1974, Jan. 18 Photo. Wmk. 300
1059 A299 40c gold & multi .30 .20

Manuel M. Ponce (1882-1948), composer.

Silver Statuette of Mexican Woman — A300

1974, Mar. 23 Photo. *Perf. 14*
1060 A300 40c red & multi .30 .20

First World Silver Fair.

Mariano Azuela A301

1974, Apr. 26 Wmk. 300 *Perf. 14*
1061 A301 40c multicolored .30 .20

Mariano Azuela (1873-1952), writer.

Dancing Dogs, Pre-Columbian A302

1974, Apr. 10
1062 A302 40c multicolored .30 .20

6th Traveling Dog Exhibition, Mexico City, Nov. 23-Dec. 1.

Aqueduct, Tepotzotlan — A303

1974, July 1 Photo. Wmk. 300
1063 A303 40c brt blue & blk .45 .20

National Engineers' Day, July 1.

Dr. Rodolfo Robles A304

1974, July 19 *Perf. 14*
1064 A304 40c bister & grn .30 .20

25th anniv. of WHO (in 1973).

EXFILMEX 74 Emblem — A305

1974, July 26 *Perf. 13x12*
1065 A305 40c buff, grn & blk .30 .20

EXFILMEX 74, 5th Inter-American Philatelic Exhibition honoring UPU cent, Mexico City, 10/26-11/3. See #C429.

Demosthenes A306

1974, Aug. 2 Photo. *Perf. 14*
1066 A306 20c green & brn .35 .20

2nd Spanish-American Cong. for Reading and Writing Studies, Mexico City, May 7-14.

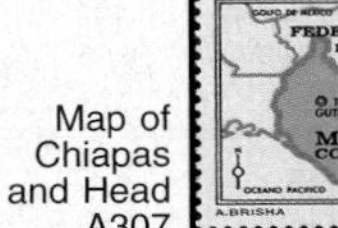

Map of Chiapas and Head A307

1974, Sept. 14 Wmk. 300 *Perf. 14*
1067 A307 20c black & grn .30 .20

Sesquicentenary of Chiapas statehood.

Law of 1824 — A308

Sebastian Lerdo de Tejada — A309

1974, Oct. 11 Wmk. 300
1068 A308 40c gray & grn .30 .20

Sesquicentennial of the establishment of the Federal Republic of Mexico.

1974, Oct. 11 Photo.
1069 A309 40c black & lt bl .30 .20

Centenary of restoration of the Senate.

UPU Monument, Bern A310

1974, Dec. 13 Wmk. 300 *Perf. 14*
1070 A310 40c ultra & org brn .30 .20
Nos. 1070,C437-C438 (3) .80 .60

Cent. of UPU.

Types of 1950-56

Designs (as 1951-56 issues): 2.30p, Guillermo Prieto. 3p, Modernistic church, Nuevo Leon. 50p, Benito Juarez.

1975 Photo. Wmk. 300 *Perf. 14*
1072 A189 80c green .55 .25
1075 A200 2.30p dp violet bl .85 .35
1076 A189 3p brick red .85 .35
1081 A189 50p orange & grn 10.00 7.50
Nos. 1072-1075 (2) 1.40 .60

See No. 1097 for unwmkd. 3p with no shading under "Leon."

Gov. José Maria Mora — A312

1975, Feb. 21 Photo. Wmk. 300
1084 A312 20c yellow & multi .30 .20

Sesquicentennial (in 1974) of establishment of the State of Mexico.

Merchants with Pre-Columbian Goods — A313

1975, Apr. 18 Photo. Unwmk.
1085 A313 80c multicolored .30 .20

Centenary (in 1974) of the National Chamber of Commerce in Mexico City. Design from Florentine Codex.

Juan Aldama, by Diego Rivera
A314

1975, June 6 *Perf. 14*

1086 A314 80c multicolored .30 .20

Juan Aldama (1774-1811), officer and patriot, birth bicentenary.

Indians and Eagle on Cactus Destroying Serpent, from Duran Codex
A315

1975, Aug. 1 **Photo.** **Unwmk.**

1087 A315 80c multicolored .30 .20

650th anniv. of Tenochtitlan (Mexico City).

Julián Carrillo
A316

Academy Emblem
A317

1975, Sept. 12 **Photo.** **Unwmk.**

1088 A316 80c brt grn & red brn .30 .20

Julián Carrillo (1875-1965), violinist and composer, birth centenary.

1975, Sept. 13 *Perf. 14*

1089 A317 80c brown & ocher .30 .20

Cent. of Mexican Academy of Languages.

Types of 1950-56

Designs (as 1950-56 issues): 80c, Indian dancer, Michoacan. 2p, Convent, Morelos.

1975-76 **Photo.** **Unwmk.**

1090 A189 40c orange .35 .20
1091 A189 50c blue .40 .20
1092 A200 60c red lilac .50 .20
1093 A200 70c violet blue .50 .20
1094 A189 80c green .50 .20
1095 A189 1p olive green .50 .20
1096 A189 2p scarlet 1.00 .50
1097 A189 3p brick red 1.00 .50
1099 A189 5p gray bl & grn 2.10 1.00
1101 A189 10p grn & dp ultra ('76) 5.00 2.00
1102 A189 20p lilac & blk ('76) 10.00 4.00
Nos. 1090-1102 (11) 21.85 9.20

University of Guadalajara — A318

1975, Oct. 1 **Photo.** *Perf. 14*

1107 A318 80c multicolored .30 .20

University of Guadalajara, 50th anniversary.

Road Workers — A319

1975, Oct. 17 **Photo.** **Unwmk.**

1108 A319 80c gray grn, grn & blk .30 .20

50 years of road building for progress.

Pistons
A320

Designs: Export Emblem and 5c, 6p, Steel pipes. 20c, Chemistry flasks. 40c, Cup of coffee. 80c, Meat cuts marked on steer. 1p, Electrical conductor. 2p, Abalone. 3p, Men's shoes. 4p, Tiles. 5p, Minerals. 7p, 8p, 9p, Overalls. 10p, Tequila. 15p, Honey. 20p, Wrought iron. 25p, Copper vase. 35p, 40p, No. 1133, 80p, Books. No. 1132, Jewelry. 100p, Strawberry. 200p, Citrus fruit. 300p, Motor vehicles. 400p, Circuit board. 500p, Cotton.

Some stamps have a gray burelage;
Type I — Burelage lines run lower left to upper right with arch towards lower right.
Type II — Burelage lines run lower left to upper right with arch towards upper left.

1975-87 **Photo.** **Unwmk.** *Perf. 14*

1109 A320 5c slate bl ('77) 1.00 .20
1110 A320 20c black ('76) .20 .20
1111 A320 40c dk brn ('76) .90 .20
a. 40c claret brown ('81) 1.00 .25
1112 A320 50c slate, thin paper ('81) .75 .20
a. 50c slate blue ('76) .90 .20
b. 50c black ('83) .60 .20
c. 50c dull blue ('75) .90 .20
1113 A320 80c brt car ('76) 5.50 .20
a. Perf. 11 .40 .20
b. Perf. 11½x11 .75 .20
c. As "a," thin paper ('81) 1.40 .75
d. As "b," thin paper ('81) .75 .75
1114 A320 1p vio bl & org ('78) .90 .20
1115 A320 1p lt vio & org ('83) 1.50 .20
1116 A320 1p black & org ('84) .20 .20
1117 A320 2p grn & brt bl ('81) 1.25 .20
a. 2p bl grn & dk bl ('76) 1.50 .20
1118 A320 3p red brown 2.75 .20
a. 3p brn, perf 11½x11 ('82) 3.00 .20
b. Golden brn, thin paper ('81) .60 .20
1119 A320 4p tan & dk brn ('80) .20 .20
1120 A320 5p gray olive ('78) 2.25 .20
a. Perf 11½x11 ('84) .20 .20
1121 A320 6p brt org ('83) .30 .20
a. Perf 11½x11 ('83) .30 .20
b. Perf 11 ('84) 3.25 .20
1121C A320 6p gray, perf. 11½x11 ('84) .20 .20
1122 A320 7p Prus blue ('84) .20 .20
a. 7p blue gray ('84) 5.00 .20
1123 A320 8p bis brn, perf 11½x11 ('84) .20 .20
a. Perf 11 ('84) 8.00 .20
1124 A320 9p dk bl ('84) .20 .20
1125 A320 10p dk & lt grn ('78) .35 .20
a. Thin paper ('81) .65 .30
b. Dk ol grn & yel grn ('86) 2.00 .20
c. Dk ol grn & brt ol grn ('87) .30 .20
1126 A320 15p yel org & red brn ('84) .30 .20
1127 A320 20p black ('78) 1.25 .20
1128 A320 20p dk gray ('84) .20 .20
1129 A320 25p org brn ('84) .40 .20
1130 A320 35p brt cer & yel ('84) .20 .20
1131 A320 40p org brn & lt yel ('84) .30 .20
1132 A320 50p gray, sil, brt vio & pur ('80) 6.00 .75
1133 A320 50p brt bl & lt yel ('83) 1.50 .20
1133A A320 80p pink & gold ('85) 1.60 .35
1134 A320 100p scar & brt grn, I ('83) 1.50 .80
1135 A320 200p emer & yel grn, I ('83) 4.50 .50
a. Emer & lemon, I ('87) 6.00 1.25
b. Emer & yel grn, II ('83) 5.00 2.00
1136 A320 300p brt bl & red, I ('83) 4.00 2.00
a. Type II ('87) 125.00 20.00
1137 A320 400p lem & red brn, I ('84) 3.00 .75
1138 A320 500p lt ol grn & yel org, I ('84) 4.00 .75
Nos. 1109-1138 (32) 47.60 10.90

No. 1125b is 2mm wider than No. 1125. Size of No. 1125b: 37x21mm.

Nos. 1117, 1119, 1126, 1135 exist with one or more colors missing. These were not regularly issued.

See Nos. 1166-1176, 1465-1470A, 1491-1505, 1583-1603, 1763-1776, C486-C508, C594-C603.

Aguascalientes Cathedral
A323

Jaime Torres Bodet
A324

1975, Nov. 28

1140 A323 50c bl grn & blk .75 .20

400th anniversary of Aguascalientes.

1975, Nov. 28

1141 A324 80c blue & brn .30 .20

Jaime Torres Bodet (1920-1974), writer, director general of UNESCO (1958-1962).

Allegory, by José Clemente Orozco — A325

1975, Dec. 9 *Perf. 14*

1142 A325 80c multicolored .30 .20

Sesquicentennial of Supreme Court.

The Death of Cuauhtemoc, by Chavez Morado — A326

1975, Dec. 12 **Photo.**

1143 A326 80c multicolored .30 .20

450th anniv. of the death of Cuauhtemoc (1495?-1525), last Aztec emperor.

Netzahualcoyotl (Water God) — A327

1976, Jan. 9 **Unwmk.** *Perf. 14*

1144 A327 80c blue & vio bl .30 .20

50th anniv. of Mexican irrigation projects.

Arch, Leon
A328

1976, Jan. 20

1145 A328 80c dk brn & ocher .30 .20

400th anniversary of León, Guanajuato.

Forest Fire
A329

1976, July 8 **Photo.** *Perf. 14*

1146 A329 80c blk, grn & red .30 .20

Prevent fires!

Hat and Scout Emblem
A330

Exhibition Emblem
A331

1976, Aug. 24 **Photo.** **Unwmk.**

1147 A330 80c olive & red brn .30 .20

Mexican Boy Scout Assoc., 50th anniv.

1976, Sept. 2

1148 A331 80c black, red & grn .30 .20

Mexico Today and Tomorrow Exhibition.

New Building, Military College
A332

1976, Sept. 13 *Perf. 14*

1149 A332 50c red brn & ocher .30 .20

Military College, new installations.

Dr. Ricardo Vertiz — A333

1976, Sept. 24 **Photo.** *Perf. 14*

1150 A333 80c blk & redsh brn .30 .20

Our Lady of Light Ophthalmological Hospital, centenary.

National Basilica of Guadeloupe — A334

1976, Oct. 12
1151 A334 50c black & ocher .30 .20

Inauguration of the new National Basilica of Our Lady of Guadeloupe.

"40" and Emblem A335

1976, Oct. 28 Photo. *Perf. 14*
1152 A335 80c blk, lt grn & car .30 .20

Natl. Polytechnic Institute, 40th anniv.

Blast Furnace A336

1976, Nov. 4
1153 A336 50c multicolored .30 .20

Inauguration of the Lazaro Cardenas Steel Mill, Las Truchas.

Saltillo Cathedral A337

Electrification A338

1977, July 25 Photo. *Perf. 14*
1154 A337 80c yel & dk brn .30 .20

400th anniversary of the founding of Saltillo.

1977, Aug. 14 Photo. *Perf. 14*
1155 A338 80c multicolored .30 .20

40 years of Mexican development program.

Flags of Spain and Mexico A339

1977, Oct. 8 Photo. Wmk. 300
1156 A339 50c multicolored .30 .20
1157 A339 80c multicolored .30 .20
Nos. 1156-1157,C537-C539 (5) 1.45 1.00

Resumption of diplomatic relations with Spain.

Aquiles Serdan (1877-1910), Martyr of the Revolution — A340

1977, Nov. 18 Photo. *Perf. 14*
1158 A340 80c lt & dk grn & blk .30 .20

Poinsettia A341

1977, Dec. 2 Wmk. 300 *Perf. 14*
1159 A341 50c multicolored .30 .20

Christmas 1977.

Old and New Telephones — A342

1978, Mar. 15 Photo. *Perf. 14*
1160 A342 80c salmon & maroon .30 .20

Centenary of first telephone in Mexico.

Oil Derrick A343

1978, Mar. 18
1161 A343 80c dp org & mar .30 .20
Nos. 1161,C556-C557 (3) .85 .60

Nationalization of oil industry, 40th anniv.

Institute Emblem A344

1978, July 21 Photo. *Perf. 14*
1162 A344 80c blue & black .30 .20
Nos. 1162,C574-C575 (3) .90 .60

Pan-American Institute for Geography and History, 50th anniv.

Dahlias A345

Decorations and Candles A346

1978, Sept. 29 Photo. Wmk. 300
1163 A345 50c shown .30 .20
1164 A345 80c Frangipani .75 .20

See No. 1196.

1978, Nov. 22 Photo. *Perf. 14*
1165 A346 50c multicolored .30 .20

Christmas 1978.

Export Type of 1975

Designs as before. 50p, Jewelry.

1979-81 Photo. Wmk. 300 *Perf. 14*
1166 A320 20c black ('81) .40 .20
1167 A320 50c slate blue .20 .20
a. 50c bluish black .30 .20
1168 A320 80c brt car, perf 11 1.00 .20
a. Perf. 14 1.00 .20
1169 A320 1p ultra & org .30 .20
1170 A320 2p brt grn & bl .50 .20
1171 A320 3p dk brown .60 .20
1172 A320 4p tan & dk brn ('80) .75 .20
1173 A320 5p gray olive 1.00 .35
1174 A320 10p dk & lt green 2.75 .75
1175 A320 20p black 2.75 .75
1176 A320 50p gray, sil, brt vio & pur 6.75 2.50
Nos. 1166-1176 (11) 17.00 5.75

A347

Soccer Ball — A348

1979, Apr. 26 Wmk. 300 *Perf. 14*
1177 A347 80c multicolored .30 .20

Centenary of Hermosillo, Sonora.

1979, June 15 Photo. Wmk. 300

Designs: 80c, Aztec ball player. 1p, Wall painting showing athletes. 5p, Runners, horiz.

1178 A348 50c blue & blk .30 .20
1179 A348 80c multicolored .30 .20
1180 A348 1p multicolored .30 .20
Nos. 1178-1180,C606-C607 (5) 1.50 1.00

Souvenir Sheet

Imperf

1181 A348 5p multicolored 3.50 3.50

Universiada '79, World Games, Mexico City, 9/79. #1181 has simulated perforations.

Josefa Ortiz de Dominguez, Wife of the Mayor of Queretaro (Miguel Dominguez), 150th Death Anniv. — A349

1979, July 6 *Perf. 14*
1182 A349 80c multicolored .30 .20

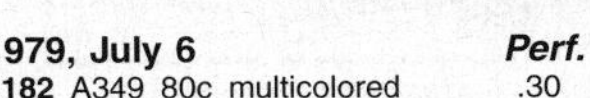

Allegory of National Culture, by Alfaro Siqueiros — A350

3p, Conquest of Energy, by Chavez Morado.

1979, July 10
1183 A350 80c multicolored .30 .20
1184 A350 3p multicolored .30 .20
Nos. 1183-1184,C609-C610 (4) 1.20 .80

National University, 50th anniv. of autonomy.

Emiliano Zapata, by Diego Rivera — A351

1979, Aug. 8 Photo. *Perf. 14*
1185 A351 80c multicolored .30 .20

Emiliano Zapata (1879-1919), revolutionist.

Soccer A352

Designs: 80c, Women's volleyball. 1p, Basketball. 5p, Fencing.

1979, Sept. 2
1186 A352 50c multicolored .30 .20
1187 A352 80c multicolored .30 .20
1188 A352 1p multicolored .30 .20
Nos. 1186-1188,C612-C613 (5) 1.50 1.00

Souvenir Sheet

Imperf

1189 A352 5p multicolored 2.25 2.25

Universiada '79 World University Games, Mexico City. No. 1189 has simulated perforations.

Tepoztlan, Morelos — A353

Tourism: No. 1191, Mexcaltitan, Nayarit.

1979, Sept. 28 Photo. *Perf. 14*
1190 A353 80c multicolored .30 .20
1191 A353 80c multicolored .30 .20
Nos. 1190-1191,C615-C616 (4) 1.10 .80

See #1274-1277, 1318-1321, 1513-1516.

Postmaster Martin de Olivares A354

Shepherd and Sheep A355

1979, Oct. 26 Wmk. 300 *Perf. 14*
1192 A354 80c multicolored .30 .20

Royal proclamation of mail service in the New World (New Spain), 400th anniversary. See Nos. C618-C620.

1979, Nov. 15
1193 A355 50c multicolored .30 .20

Christmas 1979. See No. C623.

Serpent, Mayan Temple
A356

1980, Feb. 16 **Photo.** ***Perf. 14x14½***
1194 A356 80c multicolored .30 .20
Nos. 1194,C625-C626 (3) .90 .60

Pre-Hispanic monuments.

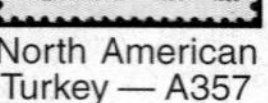

North American Turkey — A357

Tajetes Erecta — A358

Wmk. 300

1980, Mar. 8 **Photo.** ***Perf. 14***
1195 A357 80c multicolored .30 .20
1196 A358 80c multicolored .30 .20
Nos. 1195-1196,C632-C633 (4) 1.05 .80

See Nos. 1163-1164, 1234-1237.

A359

A360

Designs: 50c, China Poblana (woman's costume), Puebla. 80c, Jarocha, Veracruz.

Wmk. 300

1980, Apr. 26 **Photo.** ***Perf. 14***
1197 A359 50c multicolored .30 .20
1198 A359 80c multicolored .30 .20
Nos. 1197-1198,C636 (3) .85 .60

See Nos. 1231-1233.

1980, June 4
1200 A360 3p silver & blk .30 .20

10th national census.

Cuauhtemoc (Last Aztec Emperor), 1520, Matritense Codex — A361

Pre-Hispanic Art (Leaders): 1.60p, Nezahualcoyotl (1402-1472), governor of Tetzcoco, poet, Azcatitlan Codex. 5.50p, Eight Deer Tiger's Claw (1011-1063), 11th king of Mixtec, Nuttall Codex.

1980, June 21
1201 A361 80c multicolored .30 .20
1202 A361 1.60p multicolored .30 .20
1203 A361 5.50p multicolored .45 .20
Nos. 1201-1203 (3) 1.05 .60

See Nos. 1285-1287, 1510-1512.

Xipe (Aztec God of Medicine), Bourbon Codex
A362

1980, June 29
1204 A362 1.60p multicolored .30 .20

22nd Intl. Biennial Cong. of the Intl. College of Surgeons, Mexico City, 6/29-7/4.

Moscow '80 Bronze Medal, Emblem, Misha, Olympic Rings — A363

1980, July 19 **Photo.** ***Perf. 14***
1205 A363 1.60p shown .30 .20
1206 A363 3p Silver medal .30 .20
1207 A363 5.50p Gold medal .40 .25
Nos. 1205-1207 (3) 1.00 .65

22nd Summer Olympic Games, Moscow, July 19-Aug. 3.

Ceremonial Vessel, Tenochtitlan Temple
A364

Wmk. 300

1980, Aug. 23 **Photo.** ***Perf. 14***
1208 A364 80c shown .30 .20
1209 A364 1.60p Caracol .30 .20
1210 A364 5.50p Chacmool .30 .20
Nos. 1208-1210 (3) .90 .60

Pre-Columbian Art.

Sacromonte Sanctuary, Amecameca — A365

Colonial Monuments: No. 1212, St. Catherine's Convent, Patzcuaro. No. 1213, Basilica, Cuilapan, vert. No. 1214, Calvary Hermitage, Cuernavaca.

1980, Sept. 26 **Photo.** ***Perf. 14***
1211 A365 2.50p black .30 .20
1212 A365 2.50p black .30 .20
1213 A365 3p black .30 .20
1214 A365 3p black .30 .20
Nos. 1211-1214 (4) 1.20 .80

See Nos. 1260-1263, 1303-1306, 1338-1341.

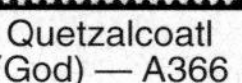

Quetzalcoatl (God) — A366

Sinaloa Coat of Arms — A367

1980, Sept. 27
1215 A366 2.50p multicolored .30 .20

World Tourism Conf., Manila, Sept. 27.

1980, Oct. 13
1216 A367 1.60p multicolored .30 .20

Sinaloa state sesquicentennial.

Straw Angel — A368

Christmas 1980: 1.60p, Poinsettias.

1980 **Photo.** ***Perf. 14***
1217 A368 50c multicolored .30 .20
1218 A368 1.60p multicolored .30 .20

Issued: #1217, 11/15/80; #1218, 10/15/80.

Congress Emblem
A369

1980, Dec. 1
1219 A369 1.60p multicolored .30 .20

4th International Civil Justice Congress.

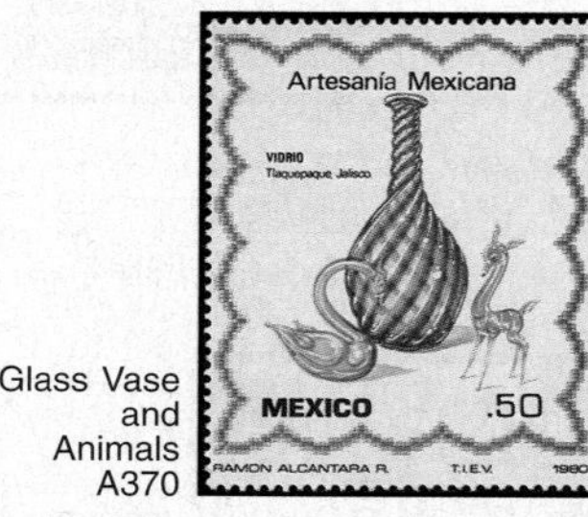

Glass Vase and Animals
A370

1980, Dec. 13 **Wmk. 300**
1220 A370 50c shown .30 .20
1221 A370 1p Poncho .30 .20
1222 A370 3p Wooden mask, 17th century .30 .20
Nos. 1220-1222 (3) .90 .60

See Nos. 1267-1269.

Simon Bolivar, by Paulin Guerin
A371

Vicente Guerrero
A372

1980, Dec. 17
1223 A371 4p multicolored .40 .25

Simon Bolivar death sesquicentennial.

1981, Feb. 14
1224 A372 80c multicolored .30 .20

Vicente Guerrero (1783-1831), statesman.

Valentin Gomez Farias — A373

1981, Feb. 14
1225 A373 80c brt grn & gray .30 .20

First Latin-American Table Tennis Cup — A374

Wmk. 300

1981, Feb. 27 **Photo.** ***Perf. 14***
1226 A374 4p multicolored .40 .25

Jesus Gonzalez Ortega, Politician, Birth Cent.
A375

Gabino Barreda (1818-1881), Physician
A376

Wmk. 300

1981, Feb. 28 **Photo.** ***Perf. 14***
1227 A375 80c brn & yel org .30 .20

1981, Mar. 10
1228 A376 80c multicolored .30 .20

Benito Juarez, 175th Birth Anniv.
A377

1981, Mar. 21
1229 A377 1.60p multicolored .30 .20

450th Anniv. of Puebla City — A378

1981, Apr. 16 **Unwmk.**

1230 A378 80c multicolored .30 .20
a. Wmk. 300 3.00 .20

Costume Type of 1980

1981, Apr. 25 **Unwmk.**

1231 A359 50c Purepecha, Michoacan .30 .20
1232 A359 80c Charra, Jalisco .30 .20
1233 A359 1.60p Mestiza, Yucatan .30 .20
Nos. 1231-1233 (3) .90 .60

Flora and Fauna Types of 1980
Wmk. 300 (#1235), Unwmkd.

1981, May 30

1234 A357 80c Mimus polyglottos .30 .20
1235 A358 80c Persea americana .30 .20
1236 A357 1.60p Trogon mexicanus .30 .20
1237 A358 1.60p Theobromo cacao .30 .20
Nos. 1234-1237 (4) 1.20 .80

Workers' Strike, by David Alfaro Siqueiros — A379

Wmk. 300

1981, June 10 **Photo.** ***Perf. 14***

1238 A379 1.60p multicolored .30 .20

Labor strike martyrs of Cananea, 75th anniv.

Intl. Year of the Disabled A380

1981, July 4 **Unwmk.** ***Perf. 14***

1239 A380 4p multicolored .40 .25

450th Anniv. of Queretaro City — A381

1981, July 25 **Unwmk.**

1240 A381 80c multicolored .30 .20
a. Wmk. 300 3.00 .20

Alexander Fleming (1881-1955), Discoverer of Penicillin — A382

1981, Aug. 6 **Unwmk.**

1241 A382 5p blue & orange .40 .20

No. 1 A383

1981, Aug. 12

1242 A383 4p multicolored .30 .20
a. Wmk. 300 3.00 .20

125th anniv. of Mexican stamps.

St. Francis Xavier Clavijero, 250th Birth Anniv. — A384

1981, Sept. 9 **Unwmk.** ***Perf. 14***

1243 A384 80c multicolored .30 .20

Union Congress Building Opening — A385

1981, Sept. 1

1244 A385 1.60p red & brt grn .30 .20

1300th Anniv. of Bulgarian State A386

1981, Sept. 19 **Photo.** ***Perf. 14***

1245 A386 1.60p Desislava, mural, 1259 .30 .20
1246 A386 4p Thracian gold cup .30 .20
1247 A386 7p Horseman .50 .20
Nos. 1245-1247 (3) 1.10 .60

Pre-Hispanic Art — A387

1981, Sept. 26

1248 A387 80c Squatting diety .30 .20
1249 A387 1.60p Animal head .30 .20
1250 A387 4p Fish .40 .25
Nos. 1248-1250 (3) 1.00 .65

Pablo Picasso (1881-1973) — A388

1981, Oct. 5

1251 A388 5p lt ol grn & grn .40 .25

Christmas 1981 — A389

1981, Oct. 15

1252 A389 50c Shepherd .30 .20
1253 A389 1.60p Girl .30 .20

World Food Day A390

1981, Oct. 16

1254 A390 4p multicolored .30 .20

50th Death Anniv. of Thomas Edison A391

1981, Oct. 18

1255 A391 4p multicolored .30 .20

Intl. Meeting on Cooperation and Development — A392

1981, Oct. 22

1256 A392 4p multicolored .30 .20

Pan-American Railway Congress — A393

1981, Oct. 25 **Unwmk.**

1257 A393 1.60p multicolored .30 .20

50th Anniv. of Mexican Sound Movies A394

1981, Nov. 3 **Photo.** ***Perf. 14***

1258 A394 4p multicolored .30 .20

Inauguration of Zip Codes — A395

1981, Nov. 12

1259 A395 80c multicolored .30 .20

Colonial Monument Type of 1980

#1260, Mascarones House. #1261, La Merced Order Convent. #1262, Third Order Chapel, Texoco. #1263, Friar Tembleque Aqueduct, Otumba.

1981, Nov. 28

1260 A365 4p black .30 .20
1261 A365 4p black .30 .20
1262 A365 5p black .30 .20
1263 A365 5p black .30 .20
Nos. 1260-1263 (4) 1.20 .80

Martyrs of Rio Blanco, 75th Anniv. A396

1982, Jan. 7 **Photo.** ***Perf. 14***

1264 A396 80c multicolored .30 .20

Death Sesquicentennial of Ignacio Lopez Rayon — A397

1982, Feb. 2
1265 A397 1.60p multicolored .30 .20

75th Anniv. of Postal Headquarters — A398

1982, Feb. 17
1266 A398 4p green & ocher .30 .20

Crafts Type of 1980

1982, Mar. 6 **Photo.** ***Perf. 14***
1267 A370 50c Huichole art .30 .20
1268 A370 1p Ceramic snail .30 .20
1269 A370 3p Tiger mask, Madera .30 .20
Nos. 1267-1269 (3) .90 .60

"Use Zip Codes" A399

1982, Mar. 20
1270 A399 80c multicolored .30 .20

TB Bacillus Centenary and World Health Day A400

1982, Apr. 7 **Photo.** ***Perf. 14***
1271 A400 4p multicolored .30 .20

50th Anniv. of Military Academy A401

1982, Apr. 15
1272 A401 80c multicolored .30 .20

Oaxaca City, 450th Anniv. — A402

1982, Apr. 25
1273 A402 1.60p multicolored .30 .20

Tourism Type of 1979

#1274, Basaseachic Cascade, Chihuahua. #1275, Silence Zone, Durango. #1276, Ruins, Maya city of Edzna, Campeche. #1277, Olmec sculpture, Tabasco.

1982, May 29 **Photo.** ***Perf. 14***
1274 A353 80c multicolored .30 .20
1275 A353 80c multicolored .30 .20
1276 A353 1.60p multicolored .30 .20
1277 A353 1.60p multicolored .30 .20
Nos. 1274-1277 (4) 1.20 .80

1982 World Cup A403

Designs: Various soccer players.

1982, June 13
1278 A403 1.60p multicolored 1.00 .20
1279 A403 4p multicolored 1.00 .20
1280 A403 7p multicolored 1.00 .20
Nos. 1278-1280 (3) 3.00 .60

Turtles and Map A404

1982, July 3
1281 A404 1.60p shown 1.00 .20
1282 A404 4p Gray whales 2.00 .20

Gen. Vicente Guerrero (1783-1831) — A405

1982, Aug. 9 **Photo.** ***Perf. 14***
1283 A405 80c multicolored .30 .20

2nd UN Conference on Peaceful Uses of Outer Space, Vienna, Aug. 9-21 A406

1982, Aug. 14
1284 A406 4p multicolored .30 .20

Pre-Hispanic Art Type of 1980

Designs: 80c, Tariacuri, founder of Tarasco Kingdom, Chronicle of Michoacan, 16th cent. 1.60p, Acamapichtli, Aztec emperor, 1376-1396, Azcatitlan Codex. 4p, 10-Deer Tiger's Breastplate, wife of Lord 13-Eagle Tlaloc Copal Ball, 12th cent., Nuttal Mixtec Codex.

1982, Sept. 4
1285 A361 80c multicolored .30 .20
1286 A361 1.60p multicolored .30 .20
1287 A361 4p multicolored .30 .20
Nos. 1285-1287 (3) .90 .60

Papaya A407

1982, Sept. 18 **Unwmk.** ***Perf. 14***
1288 A407 80c shown .30 .20
1289 A407 1.60p Corn .30 .20

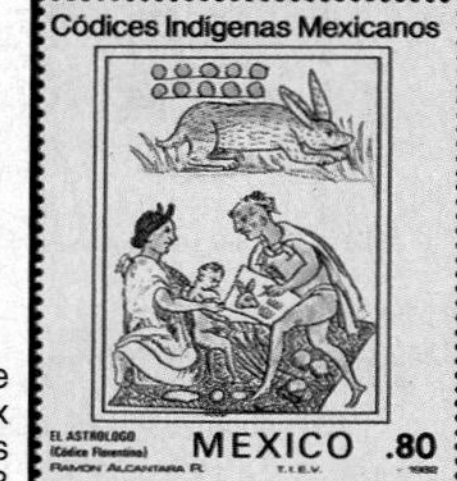

Florentine Codex Illustrations A408

1982, Oct. 2
1290 A408 80c Astrologer .30 .20
1291 A408 1.60p School .30 .20
1292 A408 4p Musicians .30 .20
Nos. 1290-1292 (3) .90 .60

See Nos. 1520-1522.

Manuel Gamio (1883-1960) Anthropologist — A409

Scientists: No. 1294, Isaac Ochoterena (1855-1950), biologist. No. 1295, Angel Maria Garibay K. (1892-1976), philologist. No. 1296, Manuel Sandoval Vallarta (1899-), nuclear physicist. No. 1297, Guillermo Gonzalez Camarena (b. 1917), electronic engineer.

1982, Oct. 16 **Photo.** ***Perf. 14***
1293 A409 1.60p multicolored .30 .20
1294 A409 1.60p multicolored .30 .20
1295 A409 1.60p multicolored .30 .20
1296 A409 1.60p multicolored .30 .20
1297 A409 1.60p multicolored .30 .20
a. Strip of 5, #1293-1297 4.00 4.00

Natl. Archives Opening, Aug. 27 — A410

1982, Oct. 23 ***Perf. 14***
1298 A410 1.60p brt grn & blk .30 .20

Christmas 1982 A411

1982, Oct. 30 ***Perf. 14***
1299 A411 50c Dove .30 .20
1300 A411 1.60p Dove, diff. .30 .20

Mexican Food System A412

1982, Nov. 13 **Photo.** ***Perf. 14***
1301 A412 1.60p multicolored .30 .20

Alfonso Garcia Robles, 1982 Nobel Peace Prize Winner A414

INAUGURACION DEL MUSEO DE LA REVOLUCION CHIHUAHUA, CHIH.
CORREO AEREO-MEXICO
MEXICO 1.60
T.I.E.V. 1982

Opening of Revolutionary Museum, Chihuahua — A413

1982, Nov. 17 ***Perf. 14***
1302 A413 1.60p No. C232 .30 .20

Colonial Monument Type of 1980

Designs: 1.60p, College of Sts. Peter and Paul, Mexico City, 1576. 8p, Convent of Jesus Maria, Mexico City, 1603. 10p, Open Chapel, Tlalmanalco, 1585. 14p, Convent at Actopan, Hidalgo State, 1548.

1982, Nov. 27
1303 A365 1.60p black & gray .30 .20
1304 A365 8p black & gray .30 .20
1305 A365 10p black & gray .30 .20
1306 A365 14p black & gray .40 .20
a. Vert. strip of 4, #1303-1306 + label 15.00 15.00
Nos. 1303-1306 (4) 1.30 .80

1982, Dec. 10 **Unwmk.** ***Perf. 14***
1307 A414 1.60p multicolored .30 .20
1308 A414 14p multicolored .30 .20

Jose Vasconcelos, Philosopher — A415

1982, Dec. 11 ***Perf. 14***
1309 A415 1.60p bl & blk .30 .20

World Communications Year — A416

1983, Feb. 12 Photo. *Perf. 14*
1310 A416 16p multicolored .30 .20

First Philatelic Exposition of the Mexican Revolution A417

1983, Mar. 13 Photo. *Perf. 14*
1311 A417 6p No. 326 .30 .20

25th Anniv. of Intl. Maritime Org. — A418

1983, Mar. 17
1312 A418 16p multicolored .35 .20

Year of Constitutional Right to Health Protection — A419

1983, Apr. 7
1313 A419 6p red & olive .30 .20

Society of Geography and Statistics Sesquicentennial — A420

1983, Apr. 18
1314 A420 6p Founder Gomez Farias .30 .20

2nd World Youth Soccer Championships A421

1983, June 2 Photo. *Perf. 14*
1315 A421 6p green & blk .30 .20
1316 A421 13p red & blk .35 .20
1317 A421 14p blue & blk .35 .20
Nos. 1315-1317 (3) 1.00 .60

Tourism Type of 1979

Designs: No. 1318, Federal Palace Building, Queretaro. No. 1319, Fountain, San Luis Potosi. 13p, Cable car, Zacatecas. 14p, Mayan stone head, Quintana Roo.

1983, June 24 Photo. *Perf. 14*
1318 A353 6p multicolored .25 .20
1319 A353 6p multicolored .25 .20
1320 A353 13p multicolored .35 .20
1321 A353 14p multicolored .35 .20
a. Vert. strip of 4, #1318-1321 + label 2.75 2.75
Nos. 1318-1321 (4) 1.20 .80

Simon Bolivar (1783-1830) — A422

1983, July 24
1322 A422 21p multicolored .40 .20

Angela Peralta, Opera Singer (1845-1883) — A423

1983, Aug. 30 Photo. *Perf. 14*
1323 A423 9p multicolored .30 .20

Mexican Flora A424

1983, Sept. 23 Photo. *Perf. 14*
1324 A424 9p Achras zapota .30 .20
1325 A424 9p Agave atrovirens .30 .20

Mexican Fauna A425

1983, Sept. 23 Photo. *Perf. 14*
1326 A425 9p Boa constrictor imperator 2.00 .20
1327 A425 9p Papilio machaon 2.00 .20

Christmas 1983 — A426

1983, Oct. 15 Photo. *Perf. 14*
1328 A426 9p multicolored .30 .20
1329 A426 20p multicolored .30 .20

Integral Communications and Transportation Systems — A427

1983, Oct. 17 Photo. *Perf. 14*
1330 A427 13p brt blue & blk .30 .20

Carlos Chavez (1899-1978), Musician, Composer — A428

Contemporary Artists: No. 1332, Francisco Goitia (1882-1960), Painter. No. 1333, Salvador Diaz Miron (1853-1927), Lyrical Poet. No. 1334, Carlos Bracho (1899-1966), Sculptor. No. 1335, Fanny Anitua (1887-1968), Singer.

1983, Nov. 7 Photo. *Perf. 14*
1331 A428 9p brown & multi .30 .20
1332 A428 9p brown & multi .30 .20
1333 A428 9p brown & multi .30 .20
1334 A428 9p brown & multi .30 .20
1335 A428 9p brown & multi .30 .20
a. Horiz. strip of 5, #1331-1335 4.00 4.00

Jose Clemente Orozco (1883-1949), Painter — A429

1983, Nov. 23 Photo. *Perf. 14*
1336 A429 9p multicolored .30 .20

35th Anniv. of Human Rights Declaration A430

1983, Dec. 10 *Perf. 14*
1337 A430 20p multicolored .30 .20

Colonial Monument Type of 1980

9p, Convent Garden, Malinalco, 16th cent. 20p, Open Chapel, Cuernavaca Cathedral, Morelos. 21p, Tepeji del Rio Convent, Hidalgo. 24p, Atlatlahuacan Convent, Morelos.

1983, Dec. 16 Photo. *Perf. 14*
1338 A365 9p black & gray .30 .20
1339 A365 20p black & gray .40 .20
1340 A365 21p black & gray .40 .20
1341 A365 24p black & gray .40 .25
a. Vert. strip of 4, #1338-1341 + label 4.00 4.00

Antonio Caso (1883-1946), Philosopher — A431

1983, Dec. 19
Granite Paper
1342 A431 9p multicolored .30 .20

Royal Mining Decree Bicentenary — A432

1983, Dec. 21
1343 A432 9p Joaquin Velazquez Leon, reform author .30 .20

Postal Code Centenary A433

1984, Jan. 2 Photo. *Perf. 14*
1344 A433 12p Envelopes .35 .20

Fight Against Polio A434

1984, Apr. 7 Photo. *Perf. 14*
1345 A434 12p Children dancing .35 .20

Aquatic Birds — A435

1984, May 4 Photo. *Perf. 14*

1346	A435	12p	Muscovy duck	.40	.20
1347	A435	20p	Black-bellied whistling tree duck	.45	.20
a.			Pair, #1346-1347 + label	3.50	3.50

World Dog Exposition, Mexico City A436

1984, May 27

1348	A436	12p	multicolored	1.25	.20

Natl. Bank of Mexico Centenary — A437

1984, June 2

1349	A437	12p	multicolored	.35	.20

Forest Protection and Conservation — A438

1984, July 12 Photo. *Perf. 14*

1350	A438	20p	Hands holding trees	.40	.20

1984 Summer Olympics A439

1984, July 28

1351	A439	14p	Shot put	1.00	.20
1352	A439	20p	Equestrian	1.00	.20
1353	A439	23p	Gymnastics	1.00	.20
1354	A439	24p	Diving	1.00	.20
1355	A439	25p	Boxing	1.00	.20
1356	A439	26p	Fencing	1.00	.20

Size: 56x62mm

Imperf

1357	A439	40p	Rings	3.50	1.50
			Nos. 1351-1357 (7)	9.50	2.70

Mexico-USSR Diplomatic Relations, 60th Anniv. — A440

1984, Aug. 4

1358	A440	23p	Flags	.40	.20

Intl. Population Conference, Aug. 5-14 — A441

1984, Aug. 6

1359	A441	20p	UN emblem, hand	.40	.20

Economic Culture Fund, 50th Anniv. — A442

1984, Sept. 3

1360	A442	14p	multicolored	.35	.20

Gen Francisco J. Mugica A443

1984, Sept. 3

1361	A443	14p	black & brown	.35	.20

Red Cactus, by Sebastian A444

Airline Emblem A445

1984, Sept. 14 Photo. *Perf. 14*

1362	A444	14p	multicolored	.30	.20
1363	A445	20p	blk & org	.30	.20

Aeromexico (airline), 50th anniv.

Palace of Fine Arts, 50th Anniv. A446

1984, Sept. 29

1364	A446	14p	multicolored	.35	.20

275th Anniv. of Chihuahua City A447

1984, Oct. 12

1365	A447	14p	Cathedral exterior detail	.35	.20

Coatzacoalcos Bridge Inauguration — A448

1984, Oct. 17 *Perf. 14*

1366	A448	14p	Aerial view	.35	.20

UN Disarmament Week — A449

1984, Oct. 24 Photo. *Perf. 14*

1367	A449	20p	multicolored	.30	.20

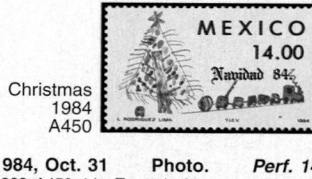

Christmas 1984 A450

1984, Oct. 31 Photo. *Perf. 14*

1368	A450	14p	Toy train & tree	.30	.20
1369	A450	20p	Pinata breaking, vert.	.30	.20

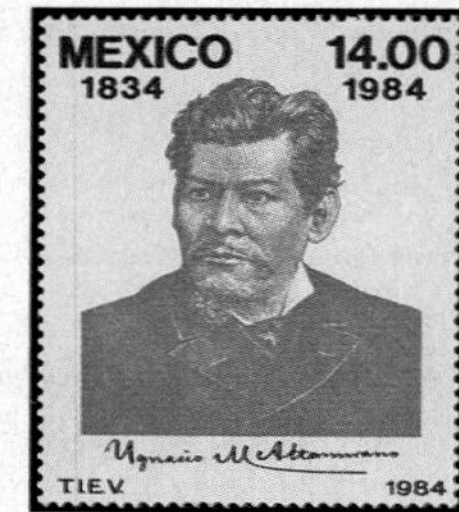

Politician-Journalist Ignacio M. Altamirano (1834-1893) — A451

1984, Nov. 13 Photo. *Perf. 14*

1370	A451	14p	blk & lt red brn	.30	.20

State Audit Office, 160th Anniv. A452

1984, Nov. 16

1371	A452	14p	multicolored	.35	.20

1986 World Cup Soccer Championships, Mexico — A453

1984, Nov. 19

1372	A453	20p	multicolored	*1.75*	*.20*
1373	A453	24p	multicolored	*2.25*	*.20*
a.			Pair, #1372-1373 + label	*5.50*	*5.50*

Romulo Gallegos (1884-1969), Author and Former Pres. of Venezuela — A454

1984, Dec. 6

1374	A454	20p	blue & gray	.30	.20

State Registry Office, 125th Anniv. A455

1984, Dec. 13

1375	A455	24p	slate blue	.30	.20

Natl. Flag, 50th Anniv. A456

1985, Feb. 24

1376	A456	22p	multicolored	.50	.20

Johann Sebastian Bach — A457

Intl. Youth Year — A458

1985, Mar. 21 **Photo.** ***Perf. 14***

1377 A457 35p dl red brn, gold & blk .45 .20

1985, Mar. 28 **Photo.** ***Perf. 14***

1378 A458 35p rose vio, gold & blk .35 .20

Child Survival Campaign A459

1985, Apr. 7 **Photo.** ***Perf. 14***

1379 A459 36p multicolored .45 .20

Mexican Mint, 450th Anniv. A460

1985, May 11 **Photo.** ***Perf. 14***

1380 A460 35p 1st gold & copper coins .45 .20

Victor Hugo A461

1985, May 22 **Photo.** ***Perf. 14***

1381 A461 35p slate .45 .20

MEXFIL '85 — A462

1985, June 9 **Photo.** ***Perf. 14***

1382 A462 22p No. 5 .40 .40
1383 A462 35p No. 574 .40 .40
1384 A462 36p No. 1081 .40 .40
Nos. 1382-1384 (3) 1.20 1.20

Souvenir Sheet

1985, June 27 ***Imperf.***

1385 A462 90p No. 111 on cover 3.50 2.50

Morelos Telecommunications Satellite Launch — A463

1985, June 17 ***Perf. 14***

1386 A463 22p Shuttle launch .25 .20
1387 A463 36p Ground receiver .25 .20
1388 A463 90p Modes of communication .50 .40
a. Strip of 3, #1386-1388 + 2 labels 4.00 4.00
Nos. 1386-1388 (3) 1.00 .80

Souvenir Sheet

Imperf

1389 A463 100p multicolored 3.50 3.00

Nos. 1386-1388 has continuous design. No. 1389 pictures uninscribed continuous design of Nos. 1386-1388.

9th World Forestry Congress, Mexico City, July 1-9 A464

1985, July 1 ***Perf. 14***

1390 A464 22p Conifer .25 .20
1391 A464 35p Silk-cotton tree .25 .20
1392 A464 36p Mahogany .25 .20
a. Strip of 3, #1390-1392 + 2 labels 4.50 4.50
Nos. 1390-1392 (3) .75 .60

Martin Luis Guzman (1887-1977), Journalist, Politician — A465

Contemporary writers: No. 1394, Agustin Yanez (1904-1980), politician. No. 1395, Alfonso Reyes (1889-1959), diplomat. No. 1396, Jose Ruben Romero (1890-1952), diplomat. No. 1397, Artemio de Valle Arizpe (1888-1961), historian.

1985, July 19 ***Perf. 14***

1393 A465 22p multicolored .25 .20
1394 A465 22p multicolored .25 .20
1395 A465 22p multicolored .25 .20
1396 A465 22p multicolored .25 .20
1397 A465 22p multicolored .25 .20
a. Strip of 5, #1393-1397 4.50 4.50
Nos. 1393-1397 (5) 1.25 1.00

Heroes of the Mexican Independence, 1810 — A466

1985, Sept. 15

1398 A466 22p Miguel Hidalgo .25 .20
1399 A466 35p Jose Morelos .25 .20
1400 A466 35p Ignacio Allende .25 .20
1401 A466 36p Leona Vicario .25 .20
1402 A466 110p Vicente Guerrero .75 .75
Nos. 1398-1402 (5) 1.75 1.55

Souvenir Sheet

Imperf

1403 A466 90p Bell, church 3.00 2.50

175th anniv. of independence from Spanish rule. #1403 contains one 56x49mm stamp.

University of Mexico, 75th Anniv. A467

1985, Sept. 22 **Photo.** ***Perf. 14***

1404 A467 26p San Ildefonso, 1910 .25 .20
1405 A467 26p University emblem .25 .20
1406 A467 40p Rectory, 1985 .25 .20
1407 A467 45p 1st Rector Justo Sierra, crest, 1910 .25 .20
1408 A467 90p Crest, 1985 .50 .40
a. Strip of 5, #1404-1408 8.50 8.50
Nos. 1404-1408 (5) 1.50 1.20

Interamerican Development Bank, 25th Anniv. — A468

1985, Oct. 23 **Photo.** ***Perf. 14***

1409 A468 26p multicolored .30 .20

UN Disarmament Week — A469

1985, Oct. 24 ***Perf. 14***

1410 A469 36p Guns, doves .30 .20

UN, 40th Anniv. — A470

1985, Oct. 25 ***Perf. 14***

1411 A470 26p Hand, dove .25 .20

Christmas 1985 A471

Children's drawings.

1985, Nov. 15 **Photo.** ***Perf. 14***

1412 A471 26p multicolored .25 .20
1413 A471 35p multicolored .25 .20

1910 Revolution, 75th Anniv. A472

1985, Nov. 18 ***Perf. 14***

1414 A472 26p Soldadera .25 .20
1415 A472 35p Francisco Villa .25 .20
1416 A472 40p Emiliano Zapata .25 .20
1417 A472 45p Venustiano Carranza .25 .20
1418 A472 110p Francisco Madero .75 .25
Nos. 1414-1418 (5) 1.75 1.05

Souvenir Sheet

Imperf

1419 A472 90p Liberty bell 3.00 2.50

No. 1419 contains one 48x40mm stamp.

Astronaut, by Sebastian A473

The Watchman, by Federico Silva A474

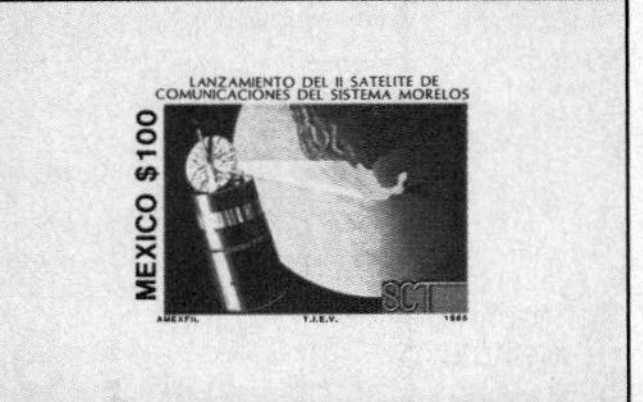

Mexican Astronaut, Rodolfo Neri, by Cauduro — A475

Morelos and Telecommunications Satellite Launch — A476

1985, Nov. 26 ***Perf. 14***

1420 A473 26p multicolored .25 .20
1421 A474 35p multicolored .25 .20
1422 A475 45p multicolored .25 .20
Nos. 1420-1422 (3) .75 .60

Miniature Sheet

Imperf

1423 A476 100p multicolored 3.00 2.50

1986 World Cup Soccer Championships, Mexico — A477

1985, Dec. 15 **Photo.** ***Perf. 14***

1424 A477 26p Olympic Stadium 1.50 .20
1425 A477 45p Aztec Stadium 2.00 .20

1st Free Textbook for Primary Education, 25th Anniv. — A478

1985, Dec. 16

1426 A478 26p Book cover .25 .20

Colonial Monuments A479

Landmarks in Mexico City: 26p, College of the Vizcainas, c. 1735. 35p, Palace of the Counts of Heras and Soto. 40p, Palace of the Counts of Calimaya, 16th cent. 45p, San Carlos Academy, 16th cent.

1985, Dec. 27 ***Perf. 14***

1427 A479 26p grnsh blk & fawn .25 .20
1428 A479 35p grnsh blk & fawn .25 .20
1429 A479 40p grnsh blk & fawn .25 .20
1430 A479 45p grnsh blk & fawn .25 .20
a. Strip of 4, #1427-1430 + label 4.00 4.00
Nos. 1427-1430 (4) 1.00 .80

Natl. Polytechnic Institute, 50th Anniv. A480

1986, Feb. 7 ***Perf. 14***

1431 A480 40p Luis Enrique Erro Planetarium .25 .20
1432 A480 65p School of Arts & Communications .25 .20
1433 A480 75p Emblem, founders .30 .25
a. Strip of 3, #1431-1433 + 2 labels 7.00 7.00
Nos. 1431-1433 (3) .80 .65

Fruit — A481

1986, Feb. 21 ***Perf. 14***

1434 A481 40p Cucurbita pepo .25 .20
1435 A481 65p Nopalea coccinellifera .30 .25

World Health Day A482

1986, Apr. 7 **Photo.** ***Perf. 14***

1436 A482 65p Doll .25 .20

Halley's Comet A483

1986, Apr. 25

1437 A483 90p multicolored .50 .20

Natl. Geology Institute, Cent. A484

1986, May 26

1438 A484 40p multicolored .35 .20

1986 World Cup Soccer Championships — A485

Paintings by Angel Zarraga (1886-1946) and Sergio Guerrero Morales: 30p, Three Soccer Players with Cap. 40p, Portrait of Ramon Novaro. 65p, Dimanche. 70p, Portrait of Ernest Charles Gimpel. 90p, Three Soccer Players. 110p, Poster for 1986 championships, by Morales.

1986, May 31

1439 A485 30p multicolored .50 .20
1440 A485 40p multicolored .50 .20
1441 A485 65p multicolored .50 .20
1442 A485 70p multicolored .50 .20
1443 A485 90p multicolored .50 .30

Size: 120x91mm

Imperf

1444 A485 110p multicolored 6.00 3.00
Nos. 1439-1444 (6) 8.50 4.10

Independence War Heroes — A486

175th Death anniv. of: 40p, Ignacio Allende (1769-1811). 65p, Juan Aldama (1774-1811). 75p, Mariano Jimenez (1781-1811).

1986, June 26 **Photo.** ***Perf. 14***

1445 A486 40p multicolored .35 .20
1446 A486 65p multicolored .35 .20
1447 A486 75p multicolored .35 .20
Nos. 1445-1447 (3) 1.05 .60

Miguel Hidalgo y Costilla (1753-1811), Mural by Jose Clemente Orozco — A487

1986, July 30 **Photo.** ***Perf. 14***

1448 A487 40p multicolored .30 .20

Federal Tax Court, 50th Anniv. — A488

1986, Aug. 27 ***Perf. 14***

1449 A488 40p gray, bl & blk .30 .20

Gen. Nicolas Bravo (1786-1854) — A489

1986, Sept. 10 ***Perf. 14***

1450 A489 40p multicolored .40 .20

Paintings by Diego Rivera — A490

Designs: 50p, Paisaje Zapatista, 1915, vert. 80p, Desnudo con Alcatraces, 1944, vert. 110p, Sueno de una Tarde Dominical en la Alameda Central, 1947-48.

1986, Sept. 26 ***Perf. 14***

1451 A490 50p multicolored .25 .20
1452 A490 80p multicolored .45 .20
1453 A490 110p multicolored .55 .35
Nos. 1451-1453 (3) 1.25 .75

See Nos. 1571-1573.

Guadalupe Victoria (1786-1843), 1st President — A491

1986, Sept. 29 ***Perf. 14***

1454 A491 50p multicolored .30 .20

Natl. Storage Warehouse, 50th Anniv. — A492

1986, Oct. 3

1455 A492 40p multicolored .30 .20

Intl. Post Day A493

1986, Oct. 9 ***Perf. 14***

1456 A493 120p multicolored .50 .20

Natl. Committee Commemorating the 500th Anniv. (1992) of the Meeting of Two Worlds — A494

1986, Oct. 12 ***Perf. 14***

1457 A494 50p black & lake .30 .20

15th Pan American Highways Congress, Mexico City A495

1986, Oct. 17 Photo. *Perf. 14*

1458 A495 80p Palacio de Mineria .40 .20

Franz Liszt, Composer, 175th Birth Anniv. — A496

1986, Oct. 22 *Perf. 14*

1459 A496 100p black & brown .45 .20

Intl. Peace Year A497

1986, Oct. 24

1460 A497 80p blk, bl & dk red .40 .20

Interment of Pino Suarez in the Rotunda of Illustrious Men — A498

1986, Nov. 6

1461 A498 50p multicolored .30 .20

Jose Maria Pino Suarez, vice-president of 1st revolutionary government, 1911.

See Nos. 1472, 1475, 1487, 1563.

Christmas — A499

Clay figurines from Tonala, Jalisco.

1986, Nov. 28

1462 A499 50p King .30 .20
1463 A499 80p Angel .30 .20

Diego Rivera (1886-1957), Painter — A500

1986, Dec. 8 Photo. *Perf. 14*

1464 A500 80p Self-portrait .30 .20

Export Type of 1975

Designs as before and: 60p, Men's shoes. 70p, Copperware. 80p, Denim overalls. 90p, Abalone. 100p, Cup of coffee.

1986-87 Unwmk. *Perf. 11½x11*

1465 A320 20p gray .25 .20

Perf. 14

1466 A320 40p pale grn & gold .35 .20

Perf. 11½x11

1467 A320 60p brown .50 .20
1468 A320 70p orange brn 1.50 .20
a. Perf. 14 1.60 .20

Perf. 14

1469 A320 80p blue .50 .20
1470 A320 90p green & blue .75 .25
1470A A320 100p brown ('88) .50 .20
b. 100p dark brown, perf. 11½x11 ('87) .75 .30
Nos. 1465-1470A (7) 4.35 1.45

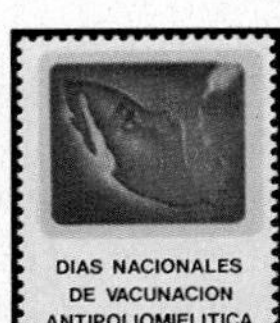

Natl. Polio Vaccination Program, Jan. 24-Mar. 28 — A501

1987, Jan. 20 Photo. *Perf. 14*

1471 A501 50p Oral vaccine .30 .20

Rotunda of Illustrious Men Type of 1986

1987, Feb. 4

1472 A498 100p multicolored .40 .25

Jose Maria Iglesias (1823-1891), president in 1876.

Natl. Teachers' College, 100th Anniv. A503

1987, Feb. 24 *Perf. 14*

1473 A503 100p multicolored .50 .25

Exploration of Pima Indian Territory by Eusebio Francisco Kino, 300th Anniv. — A504

1987, Feb. 27 *Perf. 14*

1474 A504 100p multicolored .50 .25

Rotunda of Illustrious Men Type of 1986

1987, Mar. 20 Photo. *Perf. 14*

1475 A498 100p Pedro Sainz de Baranda .40 .25

World Health Day, UN Child Survival Program A505

1987, Apr. 7

1476 A505 100p blue & slate blue .50 .25

Autonomous University of Puebla, 50th Anniv. — A506

1987, Apr. 23

1477 A506 200p multicolored .75 .50

Battle of Puebla, 125th Anniv. — A507

1987, May 5 Photo. *Perf. 14*

1478 A507 100p multicolored .40 .20

METROPOLIS '87 — A508

1987, May 19

1479 A508 310p gray blk, grn & red 1.25 .75

Cong. of metropolitan areas, Mexico City.

Handicrafts A509

100p, Lacquerware tray, Uruapan, Michoacan. 200p, Blanket, Santa Ana Chiautempan, Tlaxcala. 230p, Lidded jar, Puebla, Pue.

1987, May 29 Photo. *Perf. 14*

1480 A509 100p multicolored .30 .20
1481 A509 200p multicolored .60 .35
1482 A509 230p multicolored 1.00 .50
Nos. 1480-1482 (3) 1.90 1.05

Genaro Estrada, (1887-1937) Political Reformer — A510

1987, June 2

1483 A510 100p pale pink, blk & pale rose .30 .20

See Nos. 1509, 1568-1569.

Native Traders, 1961, Mural by P. O'Higgins — A511

1987, June 8

1484 A511 100p multicolored .30 .20

Nat'l. Bank of Int'l. Commerce, 50th anniv.

Publication of the 1st Shipbuilding Manual in the Americas, by Diego Garcia Palacio, 400th Anniv. — A512

1987, June 15

1485 A512 100p multicolored .30 .20

Nat'l. Food Program, 50th Anniv. A513

1987, June 22

1486 A513 100p multicolored .30 .20

Rotunda of Illustrious Men Type of 1986

1987, June 22
1487 A498 100p multicolored .30 .20

Leandro Valle (1833-1861), jurist.

Paintings by Saturnino Herran (1887-1918) — A514

1917 paintings: No. 1488, Self-portrait with Skull. No. 1489, The Offering. No. 1490, Creole Woman with Mantilla.

1987, July 9
1488 A514 100p black & red brn .35 .20
1489 A514 100p multicolored .35 .20
1490 A514 400p multicolored 1.10 .75
Nos. 1488-1490 (3) 1.80 1.15

Export Type of 1975

Designs: 10p, Meat cuts marked on steer. 20p, Bicycle. 50p, Tomatoes. 300p, Motor vehicle. 500p, Petroleum valves. 600p, Jewelry. 700p, Film. 800p, Construction materials. 900p, Pistons. 1,000p, Agricultural machinery. 2,000p, Wrought iron. 3,000p, Electric wiring. 4,000p, Honey. 5,000p, Cotton.

1987-88 Photo. Unwmk. *Perf. 14*
1491 A320 10p brt carmine .20 .20
1492 A320 20p black & org .20 .20
1493 A320 50p ver & yel grn .45 .20
1494 A320 300p chalky blue & scar, type I .45 .20
1495 A320 300p Prus blue & brt rose .55 .20
a. Thin paper 1.10 .20
b. Brt blue & brt rose .60 .20
1496 A320 500p dark gray & Prus blue .90 .25
1497 A320 600p multicolored 1.75 .30
a. Thin paper 1.50 .20
1498 A320 700p brt yel grn, dark red & blk 1.50 .75
a. Brt yel grn, lilac rose & blk 1.75 .85
1499 A320 800p dark red brn & golden brn 2.50 1.25
1500 A320 900p black 5.00 2.10

Wmk. 300
Granite Paper
Type I Burelage in Gray
1501 A320 1000p dk red & blk 6.00 1.10
1502 A320 2000p black 5.50 1.75
1503 A320 3000p gray blk & org 5.50 1.75
1504 A320 4000p yel org & red brn 5.00 2.50
1505 A320 5000p apple grn & org 6.50 3.25
Nos. 1491-1505 (15) 42.00 16.00

Issue years: 10p-50p, 1987; others, 1988.

A515

10th Pan American Games, Indianapolis — A516

Unwmk.
1987, Aug. 7 Photo. *Perf. 14*
1506 A515 100p multicolored .30 .20
1507 A516 200p blk, brt grn & dk red .30 .20

Federal Power Commission, 50th Anniv. — A517

1987, Aug. 14 Photo. *Perf. 14*
1508 A517 200p multicolored .40 .25

Art and Science Type of 1987

Design: J.E. Hernandez y Davalos (1827-1893), historian.

1987, Aug. 25 *Perf. 14*
1509 A510 100p buff, blk & dull red brn .30 .20

Pre-Hispanic Art Type of 1980

Designs: 100p, Xolotl (d. 1232), king of Amaquemecan. 200p, Nezahualpilli (1460-1516), king of Texcoco, conqueror. 400p, Motecuhzoma Ilhuicamina (Montezuma I d. 1469), emperor of Tenochtitlan (1440-1469).

1987, Aug. 31 *Perf. 14*
1510 A361 100p multicolored .30 .20
1511 A361 200p multicolored .50 .30
1512 A361 400p multicolored .90 .35
Nos. 1510-1512 (3) 1.70 .85

Tourism Type of 1979

Designs: 100p, Central Public Library, Mexico State. No. 1514, Patzcuaro Harbor, Michoacan. No. 1515, Garcia Caverns, Nuevo Leon. No. 1516, Beach resort, Mazatlan, Sinaloa.

1987 *Perf. 14*
1513 A353 100p multicolored .30 .20
1514 A353 150p multicolored .30 .20
1515 A353 150p multicolored .30 .20
1516 A353 150p multicolored .30 .20
Nos. 1513-1516 (4) 1.20 .80

Issue dates: 100p, Sept. 11; others, Oct. 19.

Formula 1 Grand Prix Race, Oct. 18 — A518

1987, Sept. 11
1517 A518 100p multicolored .30 .20

13th Intl. Cartography Conference — A519

1987, Oct. 12
1518 A519 150p Map, 16th cent. .30 .20

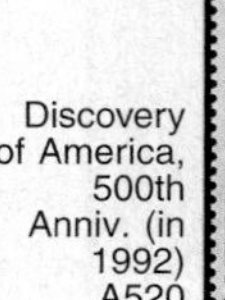

Discovery of America, 500th Anniv. (in 1992) A520

Design: Santa Maria, emblem of the Discovery of America Festival to be held in 1992.

1987, Oct. 12 *Perf. 14*
1519 A520 150p multicolored 3.50 .20

For overprint see No. 1698.

Illuminated Codices Type of 1982

Mendocino Codex (c. 1541): No. 1520, Founding of Tenochtitlan by the Aztecs, 1324. No. 1521, Pre-Hispanic wedding. No. 1522, Montezuma's Council.

1987, Nov. 3
1520 A408 150p multicolored .35 .20
1521 A408 150p multicolored .35 .20
1522 A408 150p multicolored .35 .20
Nos. 1520-1522 (3) 1.05 .60

Christmas 1987 A521

1987, Nov. 6
1523 A521 150p brt pink .30 .20
1524 A521 150p dull blue .30 .20

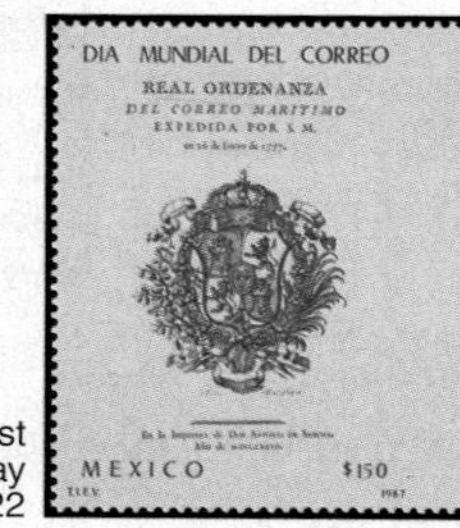

World Post Day A522

Documents: 150p, Ordinance for expediting mail by sea, 1777. 600p, Roster of correspondence transported by coach, 1857.

1987, Nov. 12
1525 A522 150p pale gray & slate gray .30 .20

Size: 129x102mm
Imperf
1526 A522 600p rose lake & yel bis 3.00 1.00

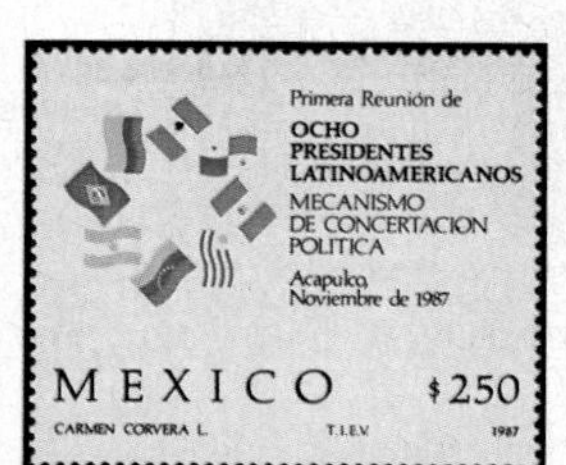

Meeting of Eight Latin American Presidents, 1st Anniv. — A523

1987, Nov. 26 *Perf. 14*
1527 A523 250p shown .40 .20
1528 A523 500p Flags, peace doves .60 .40

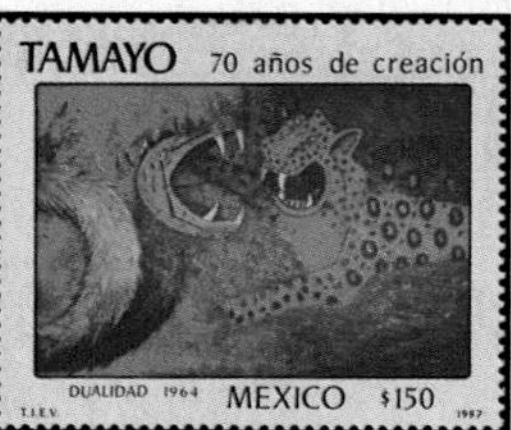

Dualidad 1964, by Rufino Tamayo (b. 1899) — A524

1987, Dec. 9
1529 A524 150p multicolored .35 .20

Nationalization of Mexican Railroads, 50th Anniv. — A525

1987, Dec. 15
1530 A525 150p Metlac Bridge 1.00 .20

Antonio Stradivarius (c. 1644-1737), Italian Violin Maker — A526

1987, Dec. 18 *Perf. 14*
1531 A526 150p bluish lilac .40 .20

Constitutional Tribunal of the Supreme Court, Plenum Hall, Jan. 15 — A527

Design: Statue of Manuel Rejon, author of the Mexican constitution.

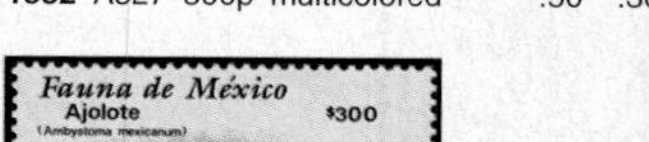

1988, Jan. 15 Photo. *Perf. 14*
1532 A527 300p multicolored .50 .30

Fauna A528

1988, Feb. 29 Photo. *Perf. 14*
1533 A528 300p *Ambystoma mexicanum* 1.00 .40
1534 A528 300p *Trichechus manatus* 1.00 .40

A529

Nationalization of the Petroleum Industry, 50th Anniv. — A530

1988, Mar. 18

1535 A529 300p blue & blk .30 .25
1536 A530 300p PEMEX emblem, vert. .30 .25
1537 A530 500p shown .40 .35
Nos. 1535-1537 (3) 1.00 .85

Vaccination, Detroit, 1932, Mural (detail) by Diego Rivera — A531

1988, Apr. 7

1538 A531 300p olive grn & hen-na brn .35 .25

World Health Day: child immunization.

The People in Pursuit of Health, 1953, by Diego Rivera — A532

1988, Apr. 7

1539 A532 300p multicolored .35 .25

World Health Organization, 40th anniv.

Vallejo in Repose (Large) — A533

Vallejo in Repose (Small) — A534

1988, Apr. 15

1540 A533 300p shown .35 .25
1541 A533 300p Portrait, diff. (large) .35 .25
a. Pair, #1540-1541 + label 3.25 3.25
b. Bklt. pane of 4 (2 each #1540-1541) + label 250.00
1542 A534 300p shown .35 .25
1543 A534 300p As #1541 (small) .35 .25
a. Pair, #1542-1543 + label 3.25 3.25
Nos. 1540-1543 (4) 1.40 1.00

Cesar Vallejo (1892-1938), Peruvian poet. Stamps of the same type printed se-tenant in sheets of 20 stamps containing 10 pairs plus 5 labels between inscribed with various Vallejo quotes or commemorative text.

Issued: #1541b, 11/9/90. Label in No. 1541b is overprinted in red with Mexican Chicagopex '90 souvenir cancel, and had limited distribution.

Sketch of Carlos Pellicer Camara (1897-1977), Poet, by Fontanelly — A535

1988, Apr. 23

1544 A535 300p pale vio, blk & sal .35 .25

MEPSIRREY '88 Philatelic Exhibition, Monterrey, May 27-29 — A536

1988, May 27

1545 A536 300p Youth collectors .35 .25
1546 A536 300p Handstamped cover .35 .25
1547 A536 500p Alfa Planetarium .55 .50
Nos. 1545-1547 (3) 1.25 1.00

Mexico-Elmhurst Philatelic Society Intl. (MEPSI).

1988 Formula I Grand Prix of Mexico — A537

Design: Layout of Hermanos Rodriguez race track, Mexico City, and car.

1988, May 28 Photo. *Perf. 14*

1548 A537 500p multicolored .50 .35

A538

Ramon Lopez Velarde (1888-1921), Poet — A539

1988, June 15

1549 A538 300p multicolored .30 .25
1550 A539 300p multicolored .30 .25
a. Bklt. pane of 4 + label 250.00

Issue date: No. 1550a, Nov. 9, 1990. Label in No. 1550a is overprinted in red with Mexican Chicagopex '90 souvenir cancel, and had limited distribution.

University Military Pentathlon, 50th Anniv. — A540

1988, July 9 Photo. *Perf. 14*

1551 A540 300p multicolored .30 .25

1st Mexico-Japan Friendship, Commerce and Navigation Treaty, Cent. — A541

1988, Aug. 16

1552 A541 500p multicolored .50 .35

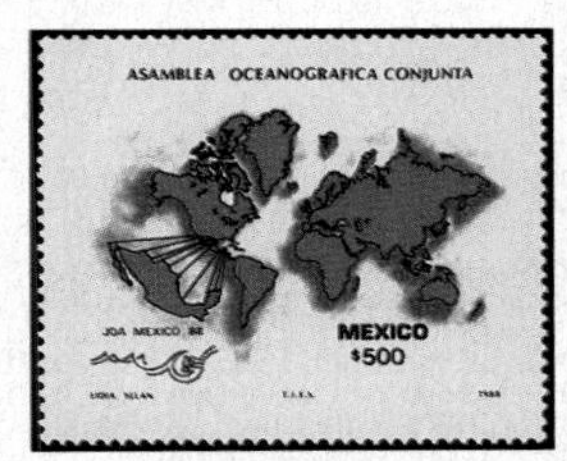

Joint Oceanographic Assembly, Acapulco, Aug. 23-31 — A542

1988, Aug. 23

1553 A542 500p multicolored .50 .35

1988 Summer Olympics, Seoul — A543

1988, Aug. 31 Photo. *Perf. 14*

1554 A543 500p multicolored 1.00 .35

Size: 71x55mm

Imperf

1555 A543 700p Emblems, torch 3.50 .60

World Boxing Council, 25th Anniv. A544

1988, Sept. 9

1556 A544 500p multi .50 .35

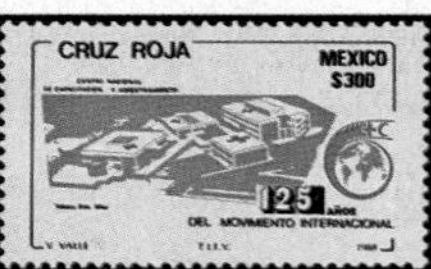

Intl. Red Cross and Red Crescent Organizations, 125th Annivs. — A545

1988, Sept. 23 Photo. *Perf. 14*

1557 A545 300p blk, gray & scar .30 .25

Jose Guadalupe Posada (1852-1913), Painter, Illustrator — A546

1988, Sept. 29

1558 A546 300p sil & blk .30 .25

World Wildlife Fund — A547

Various monarch butterflies, *Danaus plexippus.*

1988, Sept. 30 *Perf. 14*

1559 A547 300p shown 3.00 .65
1560 A547 300p Three adults 3.00 .65
1561 A547 300p Larva, adult, pupa 3.00 .65
1562 A547 300p Five adults 3.00 .65
Nos. 1559-1562 (4) 12.00 2.60

Rotunda of Illustrious Men Type of 1986

Portrait and eternal flame: Manuel Sandoval Vallarta (1899-1977), physicist.

1988, Oct. 5

1563 A498 300p multi .30 .25

World Post Day A548

1988, Oct. 9 *Perf. 14*

1564 A548 500p World map .50 .35

Size: 75x44mm

Imperf

1565 A548 700p Envelope, doves, Earth 3.50 1.00

Discovery of America, 500th Anniv. (in 1992) — A549

Illuminations: Aztec painter Tlacuilo from the Mendocine Codex, 1541, and Dominican scribe from the Yanhuitlan Codex, 1541-50.

1988, Oct. 12 *Perf. 14*
1566 A549 500p multi .50 .35

World Food Day A550

1988, Oct. 16 *Perf. 14*
1567 A550 500p multi .50 .35

Art and Science Type of 1987

#1568, Alfonso Caso (1896-1970), educator, founder of the Natl. Museum of Anthropology. #1569, Vito Alessio Robles (1879-1957), historian.

1988, Oct. 24 *Perf. 14*
1568 A510 300p gray & blk .30 .25
1569 A510 300p pale yel, blk & red brn .30 .25

Act of Independence, 175th Anniv. — A551

1988, Nov. 9
1570 A551 300p claret brn & fawn .30 .25

Art Type of 1986

Paintings by Antonio M. Ruiz (1895-1964): No. 1571, *Parade*, 1936. No. 1572, *La Malinche*, 1939. No. 1573, *Self-portrait*, 1925, vert.

1988, Nov. 21 *Perf. 14*
1571 A490 300p multi .30 .25
1572 A490 300p multi .30 .25
1573 A490 300p multi .30 .25
Nos. 1571-1573 (3) .90 .75

Tempera and Oil Paintings by Jose Reyes (b. 1924) A552

1988, Nov. 25 *Perf. 14*
1574 A552 300p Feast .30 .25
1575 A552 300p Pinata, vert. .30 .25

Christmas.

Municipal Workers' Trade Union, 50th Anniv. A553

1988, Dec. 5 *Perf. 14*
1576 A553 300p pale bister & blk .30 .25

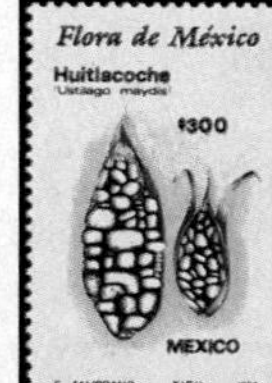

Flora — A554

1988, Dec. 20 *Perf. 14*
1577 A554 300p *Ustilago maydis* .30 .25
1578 A554 300p *Mimosa tenuiflora* .30 .25

Exporta Type of 1975

Designs: 40p, 1400p, Chemistry flasks. 200p, Citrus fruit. 450p, Circuit board. 750p, Film. 950p, Pistons. 1000p, Agricultural machinery. 1100p, Minerals. 1300p, Strawberries. 1500p, Copper vase. 1600p, Steel pipes. 1700p, Tequila. 1900p, Abalone. 2000p, Wrought iron. 2100p, Bicycles. 2500p, Overalls. 5000p, Cotton.

#1588A, 1589, 1592, 1598A, 1599, 1601, 1603 have gray burelage Type I.

1988-92 Photo. Unwmk. *Perf. 14*
Design A320

1583 40p black .20 .20
1584 200p emer & brt yel .50 .20
a. Thin paper 1.10 .40
1585 450p yel bister & lil rose .75 .25
a. Thin paper 1.25 .40
1586 750p brt yel grn, dark red & dark gray 2.00 .40
1587 950p indigo 1.75 .60
a. Thin paper 2.25 .75
1588 1000p dark red & blk 1.10 .25
1588A 1000p dark red & blk, type 1 2.50 .25
1589 1100p dark gray, type I 1.75 .40
1590 1100p dark gray 2.25 .50
1591 1300p red & grn 2.25 .55
1592 1300p red & grn, type I 2.00 .55
a. Thin paper 3.00 .75
1593 1400p black 1.75 .50
1594 1500p tan 1.75 .60
a. 1500p orange brown 1.75 .60
1595 1600p red orange 1.60 .55
1596 1700p dk grn & yel grn 1.60 .60
1597 1900p bl grn & bl 1.75 .65
1598 2000p black 2.75 .75
1598A 2000p black, type 1 2.25 .20
1599 2100p black & orange, type I 4.00 .85
1600 2100p black & ver 7.50 1.00
1601 2500p dark blue, type I 4.00 1.00
1602 2500p slate blue 4.00 .90
1603 5000p apple grn & org, type I 4.50 1.90
Nos. 1583-1603 (23) 54.50 13.65

Issued: 40p, 1/5/88; 200p, 2/27/89; 450p, 2/10/89; #1585a, 950p, #1587a, 1589, 3/30/89; 1,000p, 1989; #1590, 1599, 1601, 1991; #1600, 1602, 5000p, 1992; others, 1990.

Graphic Arts Workshop, 50th Anniv. A555

1989, Feb. 9 Photo. *Perf. 14*
1604 A555 450p yel bis, red & blk .45 .35

Coat of Arms and *E Santo Domingo*, the Natl. Hymn — A556

1989, Feb. 27
1605 A556 450p multicolored .45 .35

Dominican Republic independence, 145th anniv.

Intl. Border and Territorial Waters Commission of Mexico and the US, Cent. — A557

1989, Mar. 1
1606 A557 1100p multi 1.25 .80

10th Intl. Book Fair A558

1989, Mar. 4
1607 A558 450p UNAM School of Engineering .45 .35

Lyricists and Composers Soc., 25th Anniv. A559

1989, Mar. 17
1608 A559 450p multi .45 .35

World Day for the Fight Against AIDS — A560

1989, Apr. 7
1609 A560 450p multi .45 .35

Leona Vicario (1779-1842), Heroine of the Independence Movement A561

Alfonso Reyes (1889-1959), Author, Educator A562

1989, Apr. 20 Photo. *Perf. 14*
1610 A561 450p blk, sepia & golden brn .45 .35

1989, May 17
1611 A562 450p multi .45 .35

Formula 1 Grand Prix of Mexico — A563

1989, May 28 *Perf. 14*
1612 A563 450p multi .45 .35

14th Tourism Congress, Acapulco A564

14th Intl. Gerontology Congress, Mexico A565

1989, June 11 *Perf. 14*
1613 A564 1100p multi 1.10 .80

1989, June 18

Statue: The god Huehueteotl as an old man bearing the weight of the world on his shoulders.

1614 A565 450p multi .45 .35

Battle of Zacatecas, 75th Anniv. — A566

1989, June 23
1615 A566 450p black .45 .35

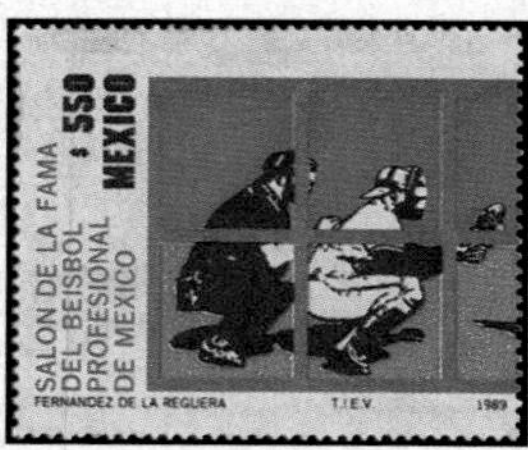

Baseball Hall of Fame of Mexico — A567

1989, June 25
1616 A567 550p Umpire, catcher 3.00 .45
1617 A567 550p Batter 3.00 .45
a. Pair, #1616-1617 + label 15.00 15.00

No. 1617a has continuous design.

35th World Archery Championships, Lausanne, Switzerland, July 4-8 — A568

1989, July 2

1618 A568 650p Bows and arrows 1.50 .50
1619 A568 650p Arrows, target 1.50 .50
a. Pair, #1618-1619 + label 15.00 15.00

No. 1619a has continuous design.

Tijuana, Cent. A569

1989, July 11 **Photo.** ***Perf. 14***

1620 A569 1100p Municipal arms .90 .70

French Revolution, Bicent. A570

1989, July 14

1621 A570 1300p blue, blk & dark red 1.40 .80

Gen. Francisco Xavier Mina (1789-1817), Independence Hero — A571

1989, Sept. 7

1622 A571 450p green, blk & dark red .50 .30

Natl. Museum of Anthropology, Chapultepec, 25th Anniv. — A572

1989, Sept. 17 ***Perf. 14***

1623 A572 450p multicolored .50 .30

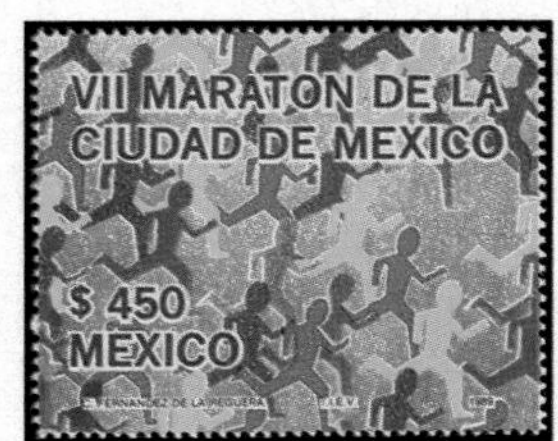

7th Mexico City Marathon — A573

1989, Sept. 24

1624 A573 450p multicolored .50 .30

Printing in America, 450th Anniv. — A574

1989, Sept. 28

1625 A574 450p multicolored .50 .30

World Post Day A575

1989, Oct. 9 **Photo.** ***Perf. 14***

1626 A575 1100p multicolored 1.10 .65

Sovereign Revolutionary Convention of Aguascalientes, 75th Anniv. — A576

1989, Oct. 10

1627 A576 450p multicolored .90 .25

Exploration and Colonization of the Americas by Europeans — A577

1989, Oct. 12

1628 A577 1300p multicolored 2.00 .75

America Issue — A578

UPAE emblem and symbols like those produced on art by pre-Columbian peoples.

1989, Oct. 12

1629 A578 450p shown .50 .25
1630 A578 450p multi, diff., vert. .50 .25

Natl. Tuberculosis Foundation, 50th Anniv. — A579

1989, Nov. 10

1631 A579 450p multicolored .35 .25

Mask of the Bat God, Zapoteca Culture, c. 200-300 A580

1989, Nov. 28

1632 A580 450p multicolored .50 .25

Serfin Commercial Bank of Mexico, 125th Anniv. A581

1989, Nov. 29

1633 A581 450p deep blue, gold & blk .50 .25

Pres. Adolfo Ruiz Cortines (1889-1973) — A582

1989, Dec. 3

1634 A582 450p multicolored .50 .25

Christmas A583

1989, Dec. 11

1635 A583 450p Candlelight vigil .50 .25
1636 A583 450p Man sees star, vert. .50 .25

Natl. Institute of Anthropology and Natural History, 50th Anniv. — A584

1989, Dec. 13

1637 A584 450p dark red, gold & black .60 .25

Nationalization of the Railway System in Mexico, 80th Anniv. — A585

1989

1638 A585 450p multicolored .70 .25

Issue dates for some 1990-1991 issues are based on First Day cancels. Original printings were small. Later printings, made in 1991, were distributed to the stamp trade and seem to be the ones used for "First Day Covers."

Tampico Bridge — A586

1990, Jan. 11 **Photo.** ***Perf. 14***

1639 A586 600p gold, blk & red .80 .30

Eradication of Polio — A587

1990, Feb. 1

1640 A587 700p multicolored .70 .35

Natl. Census A588

1990, Mar. 12

1641 A588 700p lt grn & yel .75 .35

Mexican Philatelic Assoc., 10th Anniv. — A589

1990, Apr. 19
1642 A589 700p multicolored .75 .35

Natl. Archives, Bicentennial — A590

1990, Apr. 24
1643 A590 700p pale violet .75 .35

Intl. Conf. of Advertising Agencies — A591

1990, Apr. 27
1644 A591 700p multicolored .75 .35

Stamp World London '90 — A592

1990, May 3
1645 A592 700p multicolored .80 .35

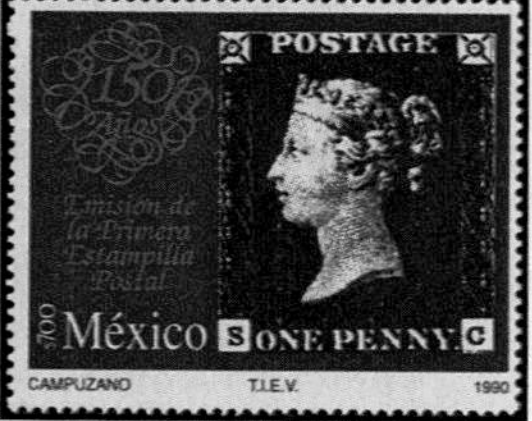

First Postage Stamps, 150th Anniv. — A593

1990, May 6
1646 A593 700p lake, gold & blk .80 .35

15th Tourism Exposition — A594

1990, May 6
1647 A594 700p multicolored .75 .35

Visit of Pope John Paul II A595

1990, May 6
1648 A595 700p multicolored .80 .35

Health of Young Mothers A596

1990, May 10
1649 A596 700p multicolored .75 .35

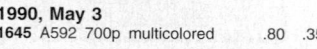

Fight Against Smoking — A597

1990, May 31
1650 A597 700p multicolored .75 .35

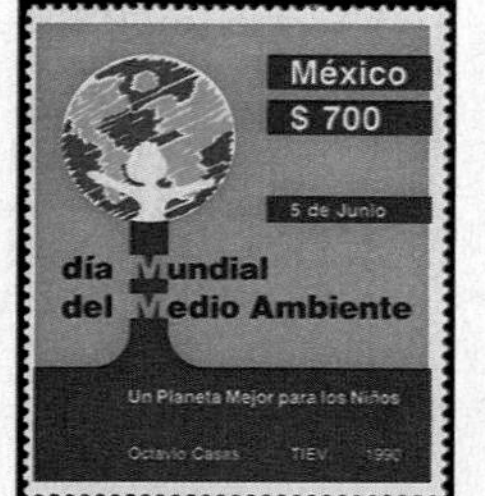

World Environment Day — A598

1990, June 5
1651 A598 700p multicolored .75 .35

Formula 1 Grand Prix of Mexico — A599

1990, June 24
1652 A599 700p grn, red & blk .75 .35

Airport & Auxiliary Services, 25th Anniv. — A600

1990, June 25 Photo. ***Perf. 14***
1653 A600 700p multicolored .70 .35

Fight Against Drugs — A601

1990, June 26
1654 A601 700p multicolored .75 .35

Protection of Rain Forests — A602

1990, July 6
1655 A602 700p multicolored .90 .35

Solidarity with Poor People — A603

1990, Aug. 8
1656 A603 700p multicolored .70 .35

Solidarity is a governmental social program of Pres. Salinas de Gortari. See No. 1704.

Oaxaca Cultural Heritage — A604

1990, Aug. 10
1657 A604 700p multicolored .75 .35

Nature Conservation — A605

1990, Aug. 21
1658 A605 700p blk, gray & org .85 .35

Mexican Institute of Petroleum, 25th Anniv. A606

1990, Aug. 23
1659 A606 700p black & blue .75 .35

8th Mexico City Marathon — A607

1990, Aug. 24
1660 A607 700p blk, red & grn .75 .35

University of Colima, 50th Anniv. A608

1990, Sept. 16
1661 A608 700p gray, bister, red & grn .70 .35

Mexico City Advisory Council, Founded in 1929 — A609

1990, Sept. 17
1662 A609 700p sil, yel, blk & org .70 .35

Nationalization of Electric Industry, 30th Anniv. — A610

1990, Sept. 27
1663 A610 700p gray, grn, red & blk .75 .35

City of Campeche, 450th Anniv. A611

1990, Oct. 4
1664 A611 700p multicolored .70 .35

Silvestre Revueltas (1899-1940), Musician — A612

1990, Oct. 4
1665 A612 700p multicolored .60 .35

Plan of San Luis, 80th Anniv. A613

1990, Oct. 5
1666 A613 700p multicolored .60 .35

14th World Conference of Supreme Counselors — A614

1990, Oct. 8
1667 A614 1500p vio, sil, gold & grn 1.10 .80

Discovery of America, 498th Anniv. — A615

1990, Oct. 12
1668 A615 700p multicolored .50 .35

Mexican Archaeology, Bicentennial — A616

1990, Nov. 18
1669 A616 1500p multicolored 1.50 .80

16th Central American and Caribbean Games — A617

1990, Nov. 20
1670 A617 750p shown .75 .40
1671 A617 750p Mayan ball player .75 .40
1672 A617 750p Mayan ball player, vert. .75 .40
1673 A617 750p Ball court, stone ring, vert. .75 .40
a. Strip of 4, #1670-1673 4.50 4.50
Nos. 1670-1673 (4) 3.00 1.60

Christmas
A618 A619

1990, Dec. 3
1674 A618 700p Poinsettias .70 .35
1675 A619 700p Candles .70 .35

Mexican Canine Federation, 50th Anniv. A620

1990, Dec. 9
1676 A620 700p multicolored .80 .35

World Post Day A621

1990, Oct. 9 **Photo.** ***Perf. 14***
1677 A621 1500p multicolored 1.50 .80

America Issue A622

#1678, Flowers, galleon. #1679, Galleon, parrot.

1990, Oct. 12
1678 A622 700p multicolored .85 .35
1679 A622 700p multicolored .85 .35
a. Pair, #1678-1679 + blank label 2.75 2.75

No. 1679a has continuous design.

Mexican Brewing Industry, Cent. — A623

1990, Nov. 8 ***Perf. 14***
1680 A623 700p multicolored .75 .35

National Chamber of Industrial Development, 50th Anniv. — A624

1990, Dec. 5 ***Perf. 14***
1681 A624 1500p multicolored 1.40 .80

Naval Secretariat, 50th Anniv. A625

1991, Jan. 4 **Photo.** ***Perf. 14***
1682 A625 1000p bl, blk & gold .90 .50

Prevent Transportation Accidents — A626

1991, Jan. 11 **Photo.** ***Perf. 14***
1683 A626 700p multicolored .75 .40

Natl. Consumers Institute, 15th Anniv. — A627

1991, Feb. 11
1684 A627 1000p multicolored .80 .55

Voter Registration A628

1991, Feb. 13 ***Perf. 14***
1685 A628 1000p org, blk & grn .80 .55

Olympic Basketball — A629

1991, Feb. 25 ***Perf. 14***
1686 A629 1000p black & yellow 1.00 .55

Campaign Against Polio — A630

1991, Mar. 8
1687 A630 1000p multicolored 1.25 .55

Nos. 1688-1691, 1697 with "NP" and Post Office eagle head logo or just the logo, are specimens.

Childrens' Day for Peace and Development — A631

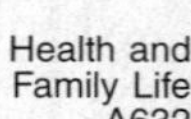

Health and Family Life A632

1991, Apr. 16 ***Perf. 14***

1688 A631 1000p multicolored .95 .55
1689 A632 1000p multicolored .95 .55

Mining in Mexico, 500th Anniv. — A633

1991, Apr. 25 ***Perf. 14***

1690 A633 1000p multicolored .80 .55

Promotion of Breastfeeding — A634

1991, May 10 ***Perf. 14***

1691 A634 1000p multicolored .80 .55

16th Tourism Exposition — A635

1991, May 12 ***Perf. 14***

1692 A635 1000p brt grn & dk grn .85 .60

Rotary Intl. Convention A636

1991, June 2 ***Rouletted 6½***

1693 A636 1000p blue & gold .85 .60

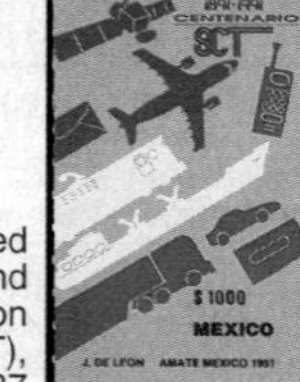

Integrated Communications and Transportation Systems (SCT), Cent. — A637

Designs: No. 1695a, 1000p, Jet landing. b, 1500p, Airport control tower. c, 1000p, FAX machine. d, 1500p, Upper floors, SCT headquarters. e, 1000p, Communications van. f, 1500p, Satellite. g, 1000p, Satellite in orbit, earth. h, 1000p, Boxcars. i, 1500p, Locomotives. j, 1000p, People using telephones. k, 1500p, Lower floors, SCT headquarters. l, 1000p, Hillside road, left section, highway bridge. m, 1500p, Center section, highway bridge. n, 1000p, Right section of bridge. o, 1000p, Cranes loading cargo ship. p, 1500p, Bow of cargo ship. q, 1000p, Television camera. r, 1500p, Bus. s, 1000p, Truck. t, 1500p, Trailers passing through toll plaza. u, 1000p, Bridge construction. Continuous design.

1991, June 11 ***Rouletted 6½***

1694 A637 1000p gray & multi 1.00 .60
1695 A637 Block of 21, #a.-u. 50.00 *55.00*

Jaguar — A638

1991, June 12 ***Perf. 14***

1696 A638 1000p black & orange 2.00 .60

Conservation of the rain forests.

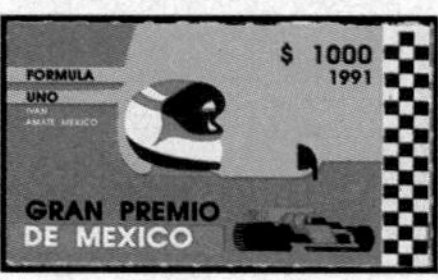

Formula 1 Grand Prix of Mexico A639

1991, June 16 Litho. ***Rouletted 6½***

1697 A639 1000p multicolored .85 .50

No. 1519 Ovptd. in Red

1991, June 14 Photo. ***Perf. 14***

1698 A520 150p multicolored 50.00 *30.00*

No. 1698 was available in strips of 5 only in booklets with limited distribution. Value of booklet, $300.

Total Solar Eclipse — A640

Designs: No. 1699a, 1000p, Denomination at lower right. b, Globe showing Mexico. c, 1000p, Denomination at lower left. Continuous design.

1991, July 5 ***Rouletted 6½***

1699 A640 Strip of 3, #a.-c. 6.50 5.00

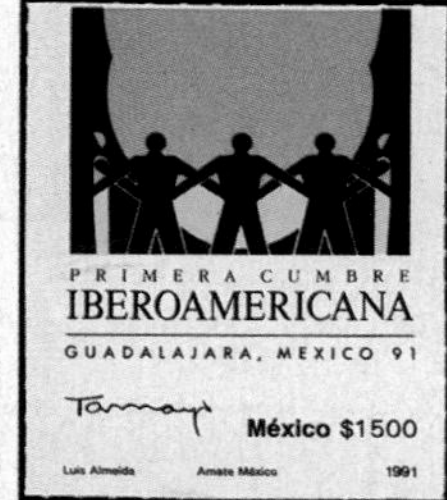

First Latin American Presidential Summit, Guadalajara A641

1991, July 18

1700 A641 1500p blk, org & yel 1.10 .80

Solidarity Bridge — A642

1991, July 31

1701 A642 2000p multicolored 1.75 1.25

A643

A644

1991, Aug. 22

1702 A643 1000p multicolored .85 .60

Ninth Mexico City marathon.

1991, Aug. 27

1703 A644 1000p blue & silver .85 .60

Federal tax court, 55th anniv.

Solidarity Type of 1990 and

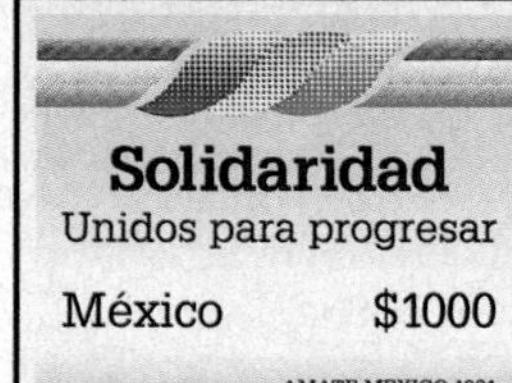

A645

1991 ***Perf. 14***

1704 A603 1000p multicolored .85 .60

Rouletted 6½

1705 A645 1000p multicolored .85 .60

Issued: #1704, Dec. 17; #1705, Sept. 9.

World Post Day — A646

1991, Oct. 9 ***Rouletted 6½***

1706 A646 1000p multicolored .85 .60

Voyages of Discovery A647

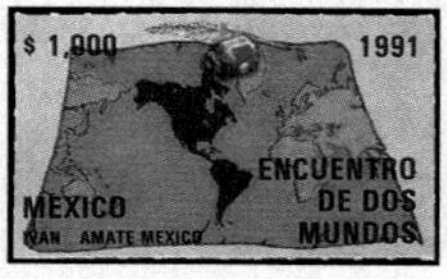

Discovery of America, 500th Anniv. (in 1992) A648

Design: No. 1708, Sailing ship, storm.

1991, Oct. 12

1707 A647 1000p multicolored 1.75 .60
1708 A647 1000p multicolored 1.75 .60
a. Pair, #1707-1708 4.00 1.25
1709 A648 1000p multicolored 2.50 .60
Nos. 1707-1709 (3) 6.00 1.80

No. 1708a has continuous design. Printed in sheets of 20+5 labels.

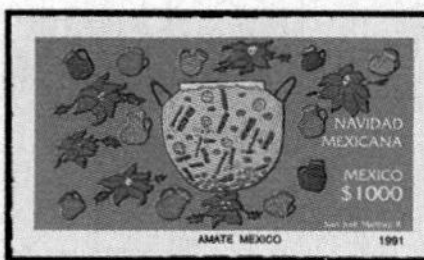

A649

Christmas A650

1991, Nov. 26

1710 A649 1000p multicolored .85 .60
1711 A650 1000p multicolored .85 .60

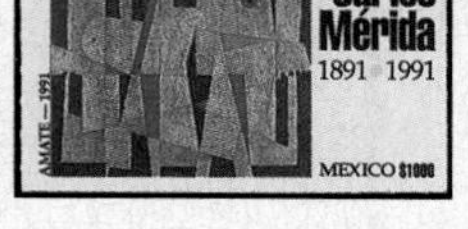

Carlos Merida, Birth Cent. A651

1991, Dec. 2 Photo. ***Rouletted 6½***

1712 A651 1000p multicolored .85 .60

Wolfgang Amadeus Mozart, Death Bicent. A652

1991, Dec. 5

1713 A652 1000p multicolored .85 .60

Self-sufficiency in Corn and Bean Production — A653

1991, Dec. 11 Photo. ***Rouletted 6½***

1714 A653 1000p multicolored .80 .55

City of Morelia, 450th Anniv. A654

1991, Dec. 13

1715 A654 1000p multicolored .80 .55

Merida, 450th Anniv. A655

1992, Jan. 6 Photo. ***Rouletted 6½***

1716 A655 1300p multicolored 1.10 .70

Engineering Education in Mexico, Bicent. A656

1992, Jan. 15

1717 A656 1300p blue & red 1.10 .70

1992 Summer Olympics, Barcelona A657

Design: No. 1719, Stylized Olympic Rings.

1992 Photo. *Rouletted 6½*

1718 A657 2000p multicolored 1.50 1.00
1719 A657 2000p multicolored 1.50 .95

Issued: No. 1718, Feb. 10; No. 1719, Mar. 1.

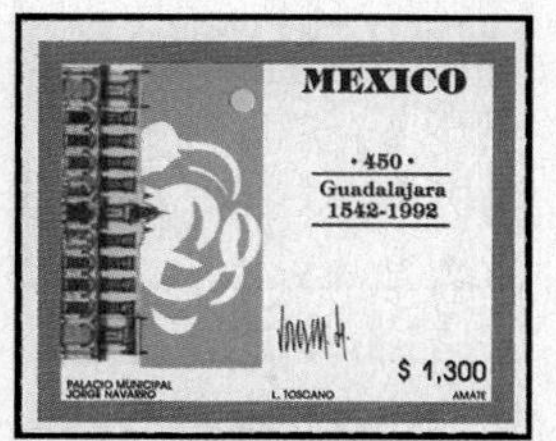

Guadalajara, 450th Anniv. — A658

#1720: a, 1300p, Coat of arms. b, 1300p, Municipal buildings. c, 1300p, Guadalajara Cathedral. d, 1900p, Allegory of the city's founding. e, 1900p, Anniversary emblem.

1992, Feb. 14

1720 A658 Strip of 5, #a.-e. 15.00 15.00

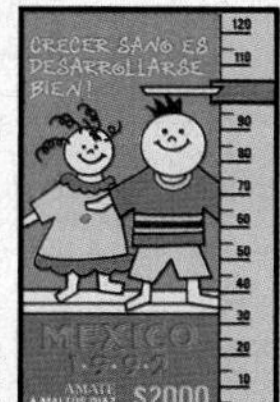

Healthy Child Development — A659

1992, Feb. 26

1721 A659 2000p multicolored 1.50 .95

Formula 1 Grand Prix of Mexico A660

1992, Mar. 22

1722 A660 1300p multicolored 1.00 .65

Introduction of the wheel and domesticated horses to America, 500th anniv.

Telecom '92 — A661

1992, Apr. 6

1723 A661 1300p multicolored 1.00 .65

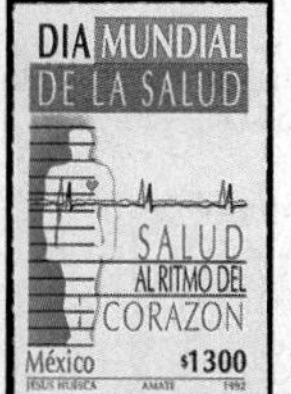

World Health Day — A662

1992, Apr. 7

1724 A662 1300p blk, red & bl 1.00 .65

War College, 60th Anniv. A663

1992, Apr. 15

1725 A663 1300p multicolored 1.00 .65

Discovery of America, 500th Anniv. A664

Paintings: No. 1726, Inspiration of Christopher Columbus, by Jose Maria Obregon. No. 1727, Meeting of the Races, by Jorge Gonzalez Camarena. No. 1728, Spanish, Indian and Mestizo, from the Natl. Historical Museum. No. 1729, Origin of the Sky, from Selden Codex. No. 1730, Quetzalcoatl and Tezcatlipoca, from Borbonico Codex. No. 1731, Human Culture by Camarena.

1992, Apr. 24 Litho. *Perf. 14*

1726 A664 1300p multicolored 2.25 .65
1727 A664 1300p multicolored 2.25 .65
1728 A664 2000p multicolored 3.50 .95
1729 A664 2000p multicolored 3.50 .95
1730 A664 2000p multicolored 3.50 .95
Nos. 1726-1730 (5) 15.00 4.15

Size: 107x84mm

Imperf

1731 A664 7000p multicolored 20.00 4.50

Granada '92. For overprints see Nos. 1752-1757.

Natl. Medical Center in the 21st Cent. — A665

1992, Apr. 27 Photo. *Rouletted 6½*

1732 A665 1300p multicolored 1.00 .65

Rights of the Child A666

1992, Apr. 30

1733 A666 1300p multicolored 1.00 .65

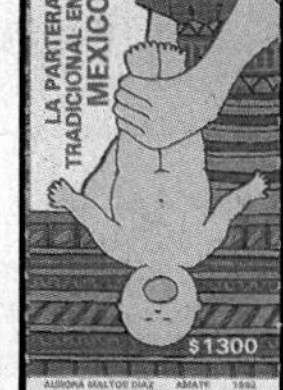

Midwives in Mexico — A667

1992, May 10

1734 A667 1300p multicolored 1.00 .65

Discovery of America, 500th Anniv. — A668

Illustration reduced.

1992, May 22 Litho. *Imperf.*

1735 A668 7000p multicolored 9.00 3.75

World Columbian Stamp Expo, Chicago.

Notary College of Mexico, Mexico City, Bicent. A669

1992, June 18 Litho. *Rouletted 6½*

1736 A669 1300p multicolored 1.00 .70

Arbor Day — A670

1992, July 9 *Rouletted 5*

1737 A670 1300p multicolored 1.00 .70

1992 Summer Olympics, Barcelona A671

1992, July 30 *Perf. 14*

1738 A671 1300p Boxing 1.25 .70
1739 A671 1300p Fencing 1.25 .70
1740 A671 1300p High jump 1.25 .70
1741 A671 1300p Gymnastics 1.25 .70
1742 A671 1300p Shooting 1.25 .70
1743 A671 1900p Swimming 2.50 1.00
1744 A671 1900p Running 2.50 1.00
1745 A671 1900p Rowing 2.50 1.00
1746 A671 1900p Soccer 2.50 1.00
1747 A671 2000p Equestrian 2.50 1.10
Nos. 1738-1747 (10) 18.75 8.60

Souvenir Sheet

Perf. 10

1748 A671 7000p Torch bearer 15.00 8.00

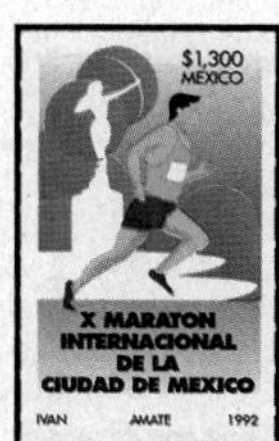

10th Intl. Marathon of Mexico City — A672

1992, Aug. 26 Litho. *Rouletted 5*

1749 A672 1300p multicolored 1.00 .65

Solidarity, United for Progress — A673

1992, Sept. 8 *Perf. 10*

1750 A673 1300p multicolored 1.00 .65

Souvenir Sheet

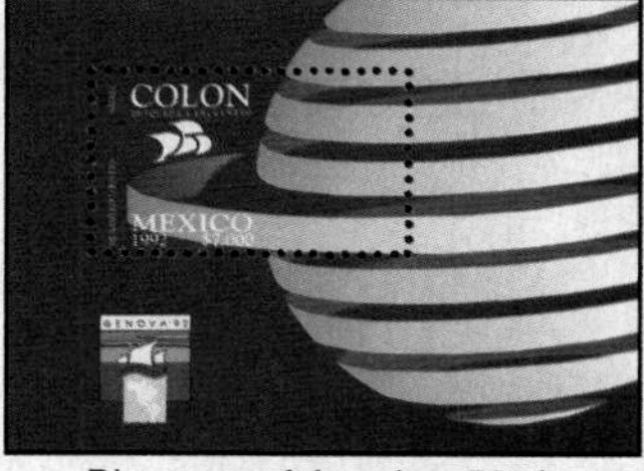

Discovery of America, 500th Anniv. — A674

1992, Sept. 18 *Perf. 10*

1751 A674 7000p multicolored 10.00 3.25

Genoa '92.

Nos. 1726-1731 Ovptd. with emblem of World Columbian Stamp Expo '92, Chicago

1992, Apr. 24 Litho. *Perf. 14*

1752 A664 1300p on #1726 16.00 16.00
1753 A664 1300p on #1727 16.00 16.00
1754 A664 2000p on #1728 16.00 16.00
1755 A664 2000p on #1729 16.00 16.00
1756 A664 2000p on #1730 16.00 16.00
Nos. 1752-1756 (5) 80.00 80.00

Size: 107x84mm

Imperf

1757 A664 7000p on #1731 85.00 85.00

Nos. 1752-1757 were produced in limited quantities and had limited distribution with no advance release information available.

Natl. Council of Radio and Television, 50th Anniv. A675

1992, Oct. 5 Litho. *Perf. 10*

1758 A675 1300p multicolored 1.00 .65

World Post Day A676

1992, Oct. 9 Litho. *Perf. 10*

1759 A676 1300p multicolored 1.00 .65

Communications System of the Americas — A677

1992, Oct. 12

1760 A677 2000p multicolored 2.00 1.00

Discovery of America, 500th Anniv. A678

Designs: No. 1761, Aztec calendar stone. No. 1762, Snake, fish, compass.

1992, Oct. 12

1761 A678 2000p shown 2.00 1.00
1762 A678 2000p multicolored 2.00 1.00
a. Pair, #1761-1762 4.50 2.00

Exporta Type of 1975

Designs: 2200p, Cuts of meat marked on steer. 2800p, Chemistry flasks. 3600p, Pistons. 3900p, Petroleum valves. 4000p, Honey. 4800p, Tomatoes. 6000p, Citrus fruit. 7200p, Film.

1992 Photo. *Perf. 14*

1763 A320 2200p red 1.60 .80
1764 A320 2800p black 2.50 1.00

With Gray Burelage

1765 A320 3600p blk, I 2.75 1.40
1766 A320 3900p gray & bl, II 3.50 1.50
1767 A320 4000p yel org & red brn, I 3.50 1.40
1768 A320 4800p red & grn, I 4.00 1.75
1768A A320 4800p red & green, II 25.00 1.75
1769 A320 6000p yel & grn, I 5.00 2.25
1770 A320 7200p grn, red & blk, I 6.00 2.75
Nos. 1763-1770 (9) 53.85 14.60

San Luis Potosi, 400th Anniv. A679

1992, Nov. 3 Litho. *Perf. 10*

1777 A679 1300p multicolored 1.00 .65

Values are for copies with perfs touching the design.

United for Conservation — A680

1992, Nov. 17

1778 A680 1300p multicolored 2.00 .65

Navy Day A681

1992, Nov. 23

1779 A681 1300p multicolored 1.00 .65

Values are for copies with perfs touching the design.

Christmas A682

1300p, Christmas tree, children, pinata, vert.

1992, Nov. 26

1780 A682 1300p multicolored 1.00 .65
1781 A682 2000p multicolored 2.00 1.00

Tourism in States of Mexico A683

1993-96 Photo. Unwmk. *Perf. 14*

1782 A683 90c Campeche 1.25 .50
1783 A683 1p Guanajuato 1.50 .60
1784 A683 1.10p Guanajuato 1.75 .25
1785 A683 1.30p Colima 1.90 .70
1786 A683 1.80p Coahuila 1.40 .45
1787 A683 1.80p Campeche 1.00 .40
1788 A683 1.80p Colima 1.00 .40
1789 A683 1.80p Chiapas 1.00 .30
1790 A683 1.90p Michoacan, vert. 3.00 1.10
1791 A683 2p Coahuila 2.75 1.10
1792 A683 2p Colima 2.75 .20
1793 A683 2.20p Queretaro 3.25 1.25
1794 A683 2.30p Sinaloa 1.50 .35
1795 A683 2.40p Yucatan 1.75 .40
1796 A683 2.50p Sonora 4.50 1.40
1797 A683 2.70p Mexico 3.00 .60
1798 A683 2.80p Zacatecas, vert. 4.75 1.50
1798A A683 3p Campeche 3.75 .30
1799 A683 3.40p Sinaloa 3.75 .80
1800 A683 3.70p Sinaloa 10.00 1.90
1801 A683 3.80p Yucatan 2.90 .85
1802 A683 4.40p Yucatan 6.75 2.40
1803 A683 4.80p Chiapas 7.75 2.50
1804 A683 6p Mexico 10.00 3.25
1805 A683 6.50p Sonora 5.00 1.50
Nos. 1782-1805 (25) 87.95 25.00

A 2nd printing of #1797 exists. This printing appears crude, with missing and misregistered color dots.

Issued: 90c, 1p, 1.30p, 1.90p, #1791, 2.20p, 2.30p, 2.40p, 2.50p, 2.80p, 3.70p, 4.40p, 4.80p, 6p, 1993; 1.10p, 1.80p, 2.70p, 3.40p, 3.80p, 6.50p, 1995; #1792, 3p, 1996.

See #1960-1980, 2119, 2122-2140.

A685

A686

Designs: No. 1808, Child's drawing, ball, blocks. No. 1809, Hands.

1993, Jan. 19 Litho. *Perf. 10*

1807 A685 1.30p Doctor, child .90 .65
1808 A685 1.30p multicolored 1.00 .75
1809 A685 1.30p multicolored 1.00 .75
1810 A686 1.50p multicolored 1.10 .85
Nos. 1807-1810 (4) 4.00 3.00

Mexican Social Security Institute, 50th anniv. Medical Services (#1807), Day Nursery Social Security Service (#1808), security and solidarity (#1809).

Issued: 1.50p, 1/19; #1807, 5/11; others, 12/7.

Mexican Society of Ophthomolgists, Cent. — A687

1993, Feb. 16 Litho. *Perf. 10*

1811 A687 1.30p multicolored .95 .70

Children's Month — A688

1993, Feb. 23

1812 A688 1.30p multicolored .95 .70

Mexican Geography and Statistics Society, 160th Anniv. A689

1993, Apr. 19 Litho. *Perf. 10*

1813 A689 1.30p blue, blk & red .95 .70

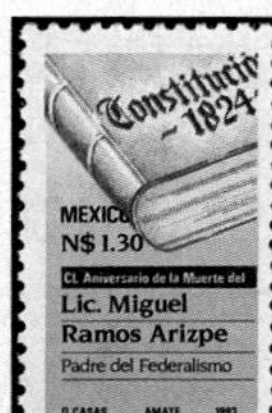

Miguel Ramos Arizpe (1776-1843), Proponent of Mexican Federalism — A690

1993, Apr. 28

1814 A690 1.30p multicolored .95 .70

Federico Gomez Children's Hospital, 50th Anniv. A691

1993, Apr. 29

1815 A691 1.30p multicolored .95 .70

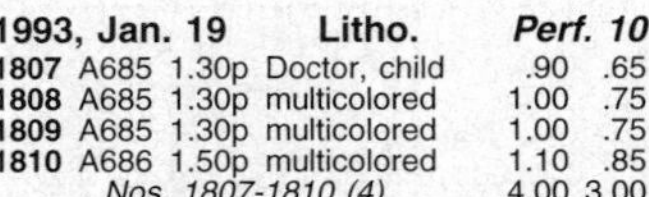

Health Begins at Home A692

1993, May 31

1816 A692 1.30p multicolored .95 .70

Upper Gulf of California, Nature Preserve A693

1993, June 10 Litho. *Perf. 10*

1817 A693 1.30p multicolored .95 .70

Mario Moreno (Cantinflas), Film Actor — A694

1993, June 24 Photo. *Perf. 14*

1818 A694 1.30p black & blue .95 .70

See Nos. 1847-1851.

Secretariat of Health, 50th Anniv. A695

Designs: No. 1819, Dr. Maximiliano Ruiz Castaneda. No. 1820, Dr. Bernardo Sepulveda Gutierrez. No. 1821, Dr. Ignacio Chavez Sanchez. No. 1822, Dr. Mario Salazar Mallen. No. 1823, Dr. Gustavo Baz Prada.

1993 Litho. *Perf. 10*

1819 A695 1.30p multicolored .95 .70
1820 A695 1.30p multicolored .95 .70
1821 A695 1.30p multicolored .95 .70
1822 A695 1.30p multicolored .95 .70
1823 A695 1.30p multicolored .95 .70
Nos. 1819-1823 (5) 4.75 3.50

Issued: #1819, 6/29; #1820, 7/26; #1821, 8/31; #1822, 9/23; #1823, 10/26.

First Postage Stamps of Brazil, 150th Anniv. A696

1993, July 30

1824 A696 2p multicolored 1.50 1.10

A697

1993, Aug. 25

1825 A697 1.30p Runners .95 .70

11th Intl. Marathon of Mexico City.

A698

1993, Sept. 6

1.30p, Open book, lightning bolt. 2p, Buildings.

1826 1.30p multicolored .95 .70

1827 2p multicolored 1.40 1.00

a. A698 Pair, #1826-1827 2.50 2.00

Monterrey Institute of Technology and Higher Studies, 50th anniv.

Solidarity Week A699

1993, Sept. 6

1828 A699 1.30p multicolored .95 .70

Confederation of Mexican Chambers of Industry, 75th Anniv. — A700

1993, Sept. 13 Litho. ***Perf. 10***

1829 A700 1.30p multicolored .95 .70

City of Torreon, Cent. — A701

1993, Sept. 15

1830 A701 1.30p multicolored .95 .70

Europalia '93 — A702

1993, Sept. 22

1831 A702 2p multicolored 1.50 1.10

A703 A704

1993, Oct. 9

1832 A703 2p multicolored 1.50 1.10

World Post Day.

1993, Oct. 10

1833 A704 1.30p multicolored .95 .70

Guadalupe Victoria (1786-1843), first president of Mexico.

Natl. Civil Protection System — A705

1993, Oct. 13

1834 A705 1.30p multicolored .95 .70

Intl. Day for Reduction of Natural Disasters.

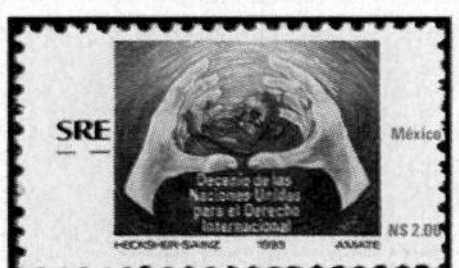

UN Decade for Intl. Law A706

1993, Oct. 19

1835 A706 2p multicolored 1.50 1.10

20th Natl. Wheelchair Games A707

1993, Oct. 21

1836 A707 1.30p multicolored .95 .70

Jose Peon y Contreras, Poet, 150th Anniv. of Birth A708

1993, Oct. 22 Litho. ***Perf. 10***

1837 A708 1.30p purple & black .95 .70

Endangered Species — A709

1993, Oct. 25 Litho. ***Perf. 10***

1838 A709 2p Quetzal 2.50 1.10

1839 A709 2p Pavon, vert. 2.50 1.10

Christmas A710

Designs: No. 1840, Adoration of the Magi. No. 1841, Christmas trees, presents, vert.

1993, Nov. 26 Litho. ***Perf. 10***

1840 A710 1.30p multicolored .95 .70

1841 A710 1.30p multicolored .95 .70

Solidarity A711

1993, Nov. 20

1842 A711 1.30p multicolored 1.00 .75

Natl. Preparatory School, 125th Anniv. — A712

1993, Dec. 2 Litho. ***Perf. 10***

1843 A712 1.30p multicolored 1.00 .75

FSTSE, 55th Anniv. A713

1993, Dec. 6 Photo.

1844 A713 1.30p multicolored 1.00 .75

Mescala Bridge A714

1993, Dec. 7

1845 A714 1.30p multicolored 1.00 .75

Highway of the Sun A715

1993, Dec. 7

1846 A715 1.30p multicolored 1.00 .75

Film Actor Type of 1993

#1847, Pedro Armendariz. #1848, Pedro Infante. #1849, Jorge Negrete. #1850, Maria Felix. #1851, Dolores del Rio.

1993, Dec. 9 ***Perf. 14***

1847 A694 1.30p black & light blue 1.00 .75

1848 A694 1.30p black & green 1.00 .75

1849 A694 1.30p black & purple 1.00 .75

1850 A694 1.30p black & orange 1.00 .75

1851 A694 1.30p black & rose 1.00 .75

Nos. 1847-1851 (5) 5.00 3.75

Secretariat of Education, 72nd Anniv. A716

Famous educators: #1852, Jose Vasconcelos. #1853, Rafael Ramirez Castaneda. #1854, Estefania Castaneda Nunez. #1855, Moises Saenz Garza. #1856, Rosaura Zapata Cano. #1857, Gregorio Torres Quintero. #1858, Lauro Aguirre Espinosa.

1994, Jan. 26 Litho. ***Perf. 10***

1852 A716 1.30p multicolored 1.00 .75

1853 A716 1.30p multicolored 1.00 .75

1854 A716 1.30p multicolored 1.00 .75

1855 A716 1.30p multicolored 1.00 .75

1856 A716 1.30p multicolored 1.00 .75

1857 A716 1.30p multicolored 1.00 .75

1858 A716 1.30p multicolored 1.00 .75

Nos. 1852-1858 (7) 7.00 5.25

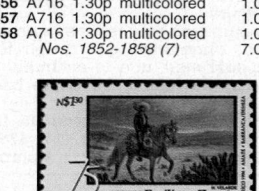

Emiliano Zapata, (1879-1919), Revolutionary — A717

1994, Apr. 10 Litho. ***Perf. 10***

1859 A717 1.30p multicolored .95 .70

ILO, 75th Anniv. — A718

1994, Apr. 18 ***Perf. 14***

1860 A718 2p multicolored 1.40 1.00

School Construction by CAPFCE, 50th Anniv. — A719

1994, Apr. 19

1861 A719 1.30p multicolored .90 .70

Children for Peace A720

1994, Apr. 28

1862 A720 1.30p multicolored .90 .70

Youth Services A721

1994, May 12 ***Rouletted 12***

1863 A721 1.30p green & black .90 .70

United for Conservation — A722

1994, May 6 ***Perf. 10***

1864 A722 1.30p multicolored 2.50 .70

Rouletting on many of the 1994 issues leaves individual stamps with rough, unattractive edges. Some copies are separated by scissors because of the difficulty in separating stamps.

The gum on many issues is poorly applied, often having a rough feel and appearance, due to air bubbles. Gum may not cover the entire back side.

Serial numbers are found on the back of some copies of No. 1896. These may appear on other stamps.

A723

A724

1994, Apr. 26 *Rouletted 12*
1865 A723 1.30p Francisco Zuniga .90 .70

1994, May 16 Litho. *Rouletted 13*
1866 A724 2p multicolored 1.40 1.00

34th World Congress of Publicists, Cancun.

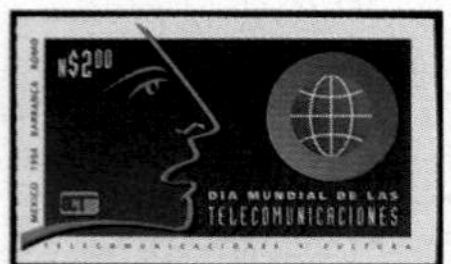

World Telecommunications Day — A725

1994, May 17 Litho. *Rouletted 13*
1867 A725 2p multicolored 1.40 .75

ANIERM (Natl. Assoc. of Importers & Exporters of the Republic of Mexico), 50th Anniv. A726

1994, May 17 *Rouletted 12½*
1868 A726 1.30p multicolored .90 .70

Yumka Natural Wildlife Center A727

1994, May 21 Litho. *Rouletted 13*
1869 A727 1.30p multicolored .90 .70

City of Zacatecas A728

1994, May 26 *Rouletted 12½*
1870 A728 1.30p multicolored .90 .70

Prevention of Mental Retardation — A729

1994, June 1 Litho. *Perf. 14*
1871 A729 1.30p multicolored .90 .70

Month of the Child.

A730

1994, June 1 Litho. *Perf. 14*
1872 A730 1.30p Mother and child .90 .70

Friendship Hospital.

A731

1994, June 7 *Rouletted 13*

Stylized soccer players: a, Kicking ball. b, Behind net.

1873 A731 2p Pair, #a.-b. 3.25 2.25

1994 World Cup Soccer Championships, US.

A732

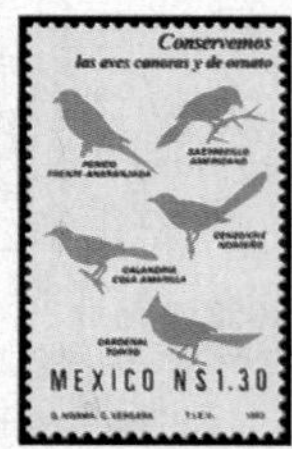

A733

1994, June 8
1874 A732 1.30p multicolored .90 .70

Intl. Fish Fair, Vera Cruz.

1994, June 5 *Perf. 14*

Wildlife conservation: a, Silhouettes of ornamental songbirds (green). b, Silhouettes of cynegetic birds (blue). c, Silhouettes of fierce-looking wildlife (brown). d, Silhouettes of endangered wildlife (red). e, Perico frente-anaranjada. f, Calandria cola amarilla. g, Cardenal torito. h, Sastrecillo americano. i, Cenzontle norteno. j, Guajolote norteno. k, Paloma de ala blanca. l, Pato pijiji de ala blanca. m, Ganso blanco. n, Codorniz de gambel. o, Peregrin falcon. p, Jaguar. q, Jaguarundi. r, Mono saraguato. s, Lobo fino de guadalupe. t, Berrendo peninsular. u, Guacamaya roja. v, Mexican prairie dog. w, Mexican wolf. x, Manati.

1875 A733 1.30p Block of 24 + label 50.00 50.00

Juvenile Integration Centers, 25th Anniv. — A734

Rouletted 12½

1994, June 29 **Litho.**
1876 A734 1.30p multicolored .90 .70

Mexican-Canadian Diplomatic Relations, 50th Anniv. — A735

1994, July 1
1877 A735 2p multicolored 1.40 1.10

Natl. Population Council, 20th Anniv. A736

A737

A738

1994, July 15
1878 A736 1.30p multicolored .90 .70

1994, July 20
1879 A737 2p multicolored 1.40 1.00

Intl. Year of the Family.

Rouletted 12½

1994, Aug. 22 **Photo.**
1880 A738 1.30p Arbor day .90 .70

A739

A740

1994, July 27
1881 A739 1.30p multicolored .90 .70

12th Mexico City Marathon.

1994, Aug. 1
1882 A740 1.30p Giant panda 1.25 .70

Chapultepec Zoo.

A741

A742

1994, Sept. 5 *Perf. 13x13½*
1883 A741 1.30p multicolored .90 .70

Metro System, 25th anniv.

1994, Sept. 5
1884 A742 1.30p multicolored .90 .70

Economic Cultural Foundation, 60th Anniv..

A743

A744

1994, Sept. 22
1885 A743 1.30p multicolored .90 .70

Don Adolfo Lopez Mateos, 25th Death Anniv.

1994, Sept. 22
1886 A744 1.30p multicolored .90 .70

Solidarity Week.

City University, 40th Anniv. A745

1994, Sept. 21 Litho. *Perf. 13½*
1887 A745 1.30p blue & yellow .90 .70

Opening of the Natl. Medical Center A746

1994, Oct. 3
1888 A746 1.30p multicolored .90 .70

Natl. Week of Patriot Symbols A747

1994, Sept. 16
1889 A747 1.30p multicolored .90 .70

Intl. Olympic Committee, Cent. — A748

1994, Sept. 29
1890 A748 2p multicolored 2.50 1.00

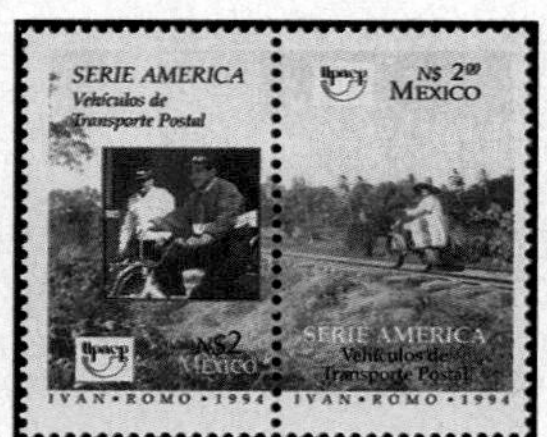
America Issue — A749

1994, Oct. 12

Mail delivery vehicles: a, bicycle. b, Railroad cycle.

1891 A749 2p Pair, #a.-b. 3.75 2.50

City of Salvatierra Guanajuato, 350th Anniv. — A750

1994, Sept. 12

1892 A750 1.30p multicolored .90 .70

Horses — A751

Designs: a, Saddled Aztec racer. b, Light brown quarter horse. c, Black quarter horse. d, Charro on horseback. e, Aztec racer. f, Chinaco riding galloping horse.

1994, Sept. 30 ***Perf. 14***

1893 A751 1.30p Block of 6, #a.-f. 10.00 10.00

Issued in sheets of 3 #1893 + 7 labels.

Grandparents' Day — A752

1994, Oct. 15 ***Perf. 13½***

1894 A752 1.30p multicolored .90 .70

Palace of Fine Arts, Mexico City, 60th Anniv. A753

1994, Sept. 29 **Litho.** ***Perf. 13½***

1895 A753 1.30p multicolored .90 .70

Antoine de Saint-Exupery (1900-44), Writer — A754

1994, Oct. 6 ***Rouletted 13***

1896 A754 2p multicolored 1.40 1.00

World Post Day A755

1994, Oct. 9 ***Perf. 13½***

1897 A755 2p multicolored 1.40 1.00

Natl. Clean Water Program A756

1994, Oct. 17

1898 A756 1.30p multicolored .90 .70

Dr. Jose Luis Mora (1794-1850), Politician — A757

1994, Oct. 27

1899 A757 1.30p multicolored .90 .70

City Theater, Saltillo, 50th Anniv. A758

1994, Nov. 3

1900 A758 1.30p multicolored .90 .70

ICAO, 50th Anniv. A759

1994, Nov. 3

1901 A759 2p multicolored 1.40 1.00

Natl. Museum of Anthropology, 30th Anniv. — A760

Natl. Assoc. of Actors, 60th Anniv. — A761

1994, Nov. 8

1902 A760 1.30p multicolored .90 .70

1994, Nov. 9

1903 A761 1.30p multicolored .90 .70

Ignacio Allende (1769-1811), Independence Hero — A762

1994, Nov. 10

1904 A762 1.30p multicolored .90 .70

Natl. Museum of History, 50th Anniv. — A763

1994, Nov. 22 ***Perf. 14***

1905 A763 1.30p multicolored .90 .70

Coahuila Teachers' College, Cent. — A764

Pumas UNAM Soccer Team, 40th Anniv. — A765

1994, Nov. 23 ***Perf. 13½***

1906 A764 1.30p multicolored .90 .70

1994, Nov. 23

1907 A765 1.30p blue & gold .90 .70

Christmas A766

1994, Nov. 29

1908 A766 2p shown 1.40 1.00
1909 A766 2p Tree, vert. 1.40 1.00

Chalco Valley Solidarity A767

1994, Nov. 30

1910 A767 1.30p multicolored .90 .70

Sr. Juana Ines de la Cruz (1648-95), Writer — A768

1995, Apr. 17 **Litho.** ***Perf. 13½***

1911 A768 1.80p multicolored .75 .60

Wilhelm Roentgen (1845-1923), Discovery of the X-Ray, Cent. — A769

1995, May 8

1912 A769 2p multicolored .85 .65

Teachers' Day A770

1995, May 15

1913 A770 1.80p Ignacio M. Altamirano .75 .60

World Telecommunications Day — A771

1995, May 17 ***Perf. 14x14½***

1914 A771 2.70p multicolored 1.10 .85

A772

A773

1995, May 18 ***Perf. 13½***

1915 A772 1.80p multicolored .75 .60

Natl. Institute of Public Administration, 40th anniv.

1995, May 19 ***Perf. 14x14½***

Jose Marti (1853-95), Cuban patriot.

1916 A773 2.70p multicolored 1.10 .85

A774

A775

1.80p, Venustiano Carranza (1859-1920), politician, President of Mexico, 1917-20.

1995, May 23 ***Perf. 13½***

1917 A774 1.80p multicolored .75 .60

1995, June 11

1918 A775 2.70p multicolored 1.10 .85

Tianquis Turistico, travel trade show, 20th anniv.

A776

A777

a, Face becoming skull with pills, needle. b, Person as puppet. c, Faces behind bars.

1995, June 26
1919 A776 1.80p Strip of 3, #a.-c. 2.25 1.75

Intl. Day Against Illegal Drugs.

1995, June 28
1920 A777 1.80p black .75 .60

Lazaro Cardenas (1895-1970), soldier, politician, President of Mexico, 1934-40.

Natl. School for the Blind, 125th Anniv. A778

1995, July 18 Litho. ***Perf. 13½***
1921 A778 1.30p sepia & black .45 .35

Migratory Wildlife A781

Designs: a, Danaus plexippus. b, Lasiurus cinereus. c, Anas acuta. d, Ceryle alcyon.

1995, Aug. 15 Litho. ***Perf. 13½***
1924 A781 2.70p Block or strip of 4, #a.-d. 8.00 8.00

See Canada Nos. 1563-1567.

13th Mexico City Marathon A782

1995, Aug. 22 Litho. ***Perf. 13½***
1925 A782 2.70p multicolored .95 .70

16th Congress of UPAEP — A783

World Post Day — A785

Louis Pasteur (1822-95) A784

World Food Day A786

1995, Sept. 15
1926 A783 2.70p multicolored .95 .70

1995, Sept. 26 ***Perf. 14***
1927 A784 2.70p multicolored .95 .70

1995, Oct. 9
1928 A785 2.70p multicolored .95 .70

1995, Oct. 16 ***Perf. 14x14½***
1929 A786 1.80p multicolored .85 .50

FAO, 50th Anniv. A787

1995, Oct. 16 ***Perf. 14***
1930 A787 2.70p multicolored .95 .70

Plutarco Elias Calles (1877-1945), President of Mexico 1924-28 — A788

1995, Oct. 19 ***Perf. 13½***
1931 A788 1.80p multicolored .85 .50

Birth of Cuauhtemoc, 500th Anniv. — A789

1995, Oct. 21
1932 A789 1.80p multicolored .85 .50

A790 A791

National Symbols: 1.80p, Natl. flag, Constitution of Apatzingan, words of Natl. Anthem.

1995, Oct. 22
1933 A790 1.80p multicolored .85 .50

1995, Oct. 24 Litho. ***Perf. 14½x14***
1934 A791 2.70p multicolored .95 .70

UN, 50th anniv.

Intl. Year of Travel A792

1995, Nov. 14 Litho. ***Perf. 13½***
1935 A792 2.70p multicolored .85 .65

Viceregal Gallery of Art Painting, The Holy Family, by Andres de Conchas A793

1995, Nov. 16 ***Perf. 14***
1936 A793 1.80p multicolored .75 .40

Famous Generals A794

Designs: No. 1937, Ignacio Zaragoza (1829-62). No. 1938, Sóstenes Rocha (1831-97). No. 1939, Felipe B. Berriozábal (1829-1900). No. 1940, Pedro María Anaya (1795-1854). No. 1941, Leandro Valle (1833-61). No. 1942, Santos Degollado (1811-61).

1995, Nov. 23 ***Perf. 13½***
1937 A794 1.80p yel, blk & bister .75 .40
1938 A794 1.80p yel, blk & bister .75 .40
1939 A794 1.80p yel, blk & bister .75 .40
1940 A794 1.80p yel, blk & bister .75 .40
1941 A794 1.80p yel, blk & bister .75 .40
1942 A794 1.80p yel, blk & bister .75 .40
Nos. 1937-1942 (6) 4.50 2.40

Christmas A795

Children's paintings: 1.80p, Family celebrating Christmas inside house. 2.70p, Adoration of the Magi.

1995, Nov. 27
1943 A795 1.80p multicolored .55 .40
1944 A795 2.70p multicolored .85 .65
a. Pair, Nos. 1943-1944 1.40 1.10

Mexican Health Foundation, 10th Anniv. — A796

1995, Nov. 30 Litho. ***Perf. 14***
1945 A796 1.80p multicolored .80 .45

Wildlife Conservation — A797

1995, Dec. 4 ***Perf. 14***
1946 A797 1.80p Ocelot 2.00 .40

Motion Pictures, Cent. — A798

1995, Dec. 12
1947 A798 1.80p violet & black .75 .40

Natl. Library of Education A799

1995, Dec. 13 ***Perf. 13½***
1948 A799 1.80p bl grn & yel .75 .40

A800

A801

1995, Dec. 15
1949 A800 1.80p multicolored .75 .40

Natl. Arts and Sciences Awards, 50th anniv.

1995, Dec. 19 ***Perf. 14***

Radio personalities: a, Pedro Vargas. b, Agustin Lara. c, Hermanas Aguila. d, Toña "La Negra." e, "Cri-Cri," (F. Gabilondo Soler). f, Emilio Tuero. g, Gonzalo Curiel. h, Lola Beltrán.

1950 A801 1.80p Strip or block of 8, #a.-h. 10.00 10.00

Natl. Council of Science and Technology, 25th Anniv. A802

1995, Dec. 20 ***Perf. 13½***
1951 A802 1.80p multicolored .75 .40

Plaza de Toros, Mexico City, 50th Anniv. A803

Matadors: 1.80p, Silverio Perez, Carlos Arruza, Manolo Martinez. 2.70p, Rodolfo Gaona, Fermin Espinosa "Armillita," Lorenzo Garza.

1996, Feb. 5 Litho. ***Perf. 13½***
1952 A803 1.80p multicolored .55 .40
1953 A803 2.70p multicolored .85 .65
a. Pair, Nos. 1952-1953 1.40 1.10

No. 1953a is a contiunuous design.

Mexican Aviation Day A804

Designs: a, 2.70p, Patrol jet. b, 2.70p, Jet landing, airport terminal. c, 1.80p, Fighter plane, Squadron 201 (1945), map. d, 1.80p, Commercial biplane (1921), commerical jet.

1996, Jan. 20 Litho. ***Perf. 13½***
1954 A804 Strip or block of 4, #a.-d. 7.50 7.50

Dr. Alfonso Caso (1896-1970), Archaeologist — A805

1996, Feb. 1

1955 A805 1.80p multicolored .75 .40

Natl. Consumer Agency, 20th Anniv. A806

1996, Feb. 9 ***Perf. 14***

1956 A806 1.80p multicolored .75 .40

Tourism Type of 1993

Denomination Shown As $

1996-99 Photo. Unwmk. ***Perf. 14***

Design A683

1960	1p	Colima ('97)	1.00	.20
1961	1.80p	Chiapas	1.00	.20
1962	2p	Colima	1.00	.25
1963	2p	Guanajuato ('97)	1.00	.25
1964	2.30p	Chiapas ('97)	1.50	.30
1965	2.50p	Queretaro ('97)	1.50	.40
1966	2.70p	Mexico	2.00	.35
1967	3p	Campeche	2.00	.40
1968	3.10p	Coahuila ('97)	2.00	.35
1969	3.40p	Sinaloa	2.50	.45
a.		Pair, #1799, 1969	*125.00*	*125.00*
1970	3.50p	Mexico ('97)	2.50	.60
1971	3.60p	Sonora ('99)	2.50	.35
1972	3.70p	Campeche ('98)	2.50	.35
1973	4p	Michoacan, vert. ('97)	3.00	.50
1974	4.40p	Yucatan ('97)	3.00	.50
1975	5p	Queretaro	3.00	.65
1976	5p	Colima ('98)	4.00	.50
1977	6p	Zacatecas, vert. ('97)	4.00	.70
1978	6.50p	Sinaloa ('98)	5.00	.65
1979	7p	Sonora ('97)	6.00	.80
1980	8.50p	Mexico ('97)	7.50	1.00
		Nos. 1960-1980 (21)	58.50	9.75

Denomination on #1782-1805 was shown as N$.

Two additional printings of the 3.50p appear crude with missing and mis-registered dots. One of these printings is perf 12.

Two additional printings of No. 1975 exist. These appear crude, with missing and mis-registered color dots. One of the reprints is perf 12.

Orthopedics Society, 50th Anniv. — A807

1996, Apr. 29 Litho. ***Perf. 13½***

1981 A807 1.80p multicolored .75 .40

Juan Rulfo (1917-86), Writer A808

1996, May 3

1982 A808 1.80p multicolored .75 .40

Natl. Polytechnical Institute, 60th Anniv. — A809

1996, May 21

1983 A809 1.80p multicolored .75 .40

A810

A811

Stylized designs: a, 1.80p, Hands reaching toward one another. b, 1.80p, Person helping another out of hole. c, 2.70p, Two people.

1996, June 26 Litho. ***Perf. 13½***

1984 A810 Strip of 3, #a.-c. 3.00 3.00

Decade of United Nations Against Illegal Drug Abuse and Trafficking.

1996, July 19 ***Perf. 14x14½***

1996 Summer Olympic Games, Atlanta: a, Women's gymnastics. b, Soccer. c, Marathon race. d, Hurdles. e, Equestrian show jumping.

1985 A811 Strip of 5, #a.-e. 6.00 6.00

Motion Pictures, Cent. A812

1996, Aug. 6 Litho. ***Perf. 13½***

Color of Film Cells

1986 A812 1.80p grn, ocher & vio .45 .35

1987 A812 1.80p pur, grn & red .45 .35

a. Pair, #1986-1987 2.25 2.25

Justice Dept., 60th Anniv. A813

1996, Aug. 18

1988 A813 1.80p multicolored .75 .35

14th Mexico City Marathon A814

1996, Aug. 20

1989 A814 2.70p multicolored .90 .50

City of Zacatecas, 450th Anniv. A815

1996, Sept. 8

1990 A815 1.80p multicolored .90 .35

Natl. Council to Promote Education, 25th Anniv. A816

1996, Sept. 17

1991 A816 1.80p multicolored .90 .35

Souvenir Sheet

City of Monterrey, 400th Anniv. — A817

Illustration reduced.

1996, Sept. 20

1992 A817 7.40p multicolored 4.50 4.50

Family Planning — A818

1996, Sept. 26

1993 A818 1.80p multicolored .90 .35

Independence, 175th Anniv. — A819

1996, Sept. 27

1994 A819 1.80p multicolored .90 .35

Endangered Species — A820

Designs show a wide variety of species, one from each stamp is: a, Aguila arpia. b, Tortola serrana. c, Monarch butterflies. d, Vernado bura. e, Guacamaya roja. f, Quetzal. g, Venado cola blanca. h, Puma. i, Coyote. j, Jaguar. k, Martucha. l, Woodpecker. m, Cuco canelo. n, Lince. o, Oso hormiguero. p, Ocelote. q, Encino. r, Chachalaca. s, Liebre. t, Tapir. u, Crocodile. v, Armadillo. w, Pecari. x, Cacomixtle.

1996, Oct. 2

Sheet of 24

1995 A820 1.80p #a.-x. + label 24.00 24.00

See US No. 3105.

World Post Day — A821

1996, Oct. 9

1996 A821 2.70p multicolored .90 .50

Salvador Zubirán Natl. Nutrition Institute, 50th Anniv. A822

1996, Oct. 12

1997 A822 1.80p multicolored .90 .35

Radio in Mexico, 75th Anniv. — A823

1996, Oct. 13

1998 A823 1.80p multicolored .90 .35

Paintings in Viceregal Gallery A824

Designs: a, 1.80p, Portrait of a Woman, by Baltasar de Echave Ibia. b, 2.70p, Archangel Michael, by Luis Juarez. c, 1.80p, Portrait of young Joaquín Manuel Fernández of Santa Cruz, by Nicolas Rodriguez Xuarez. d, 2.70p. The Virgin of the Apocalypse, by Miguel Cabrera. e, 1.80p, Portrait of Dona Maria Luisa Gonzaga Foncerrada y Labarrieta, by Jose Maria Vazquez.

1996, Oct. 14 ***Perf. 14***

1999 A824 Strip of 5, #a.-e. 4.75 4.75

World Food Day — A825

1996, Oct. 31 ***Perf. 13½***

2000 A825 2.70p multicolored .90 .50

Mexican Science A826

1996, Sept. 2

2001 A826 1.80p multicolored .90 .35

Intl. Subway Conference A828

1996, Nov. 12 Litho. ***Perf. 13½***

2003 A828 2.70p multicolored .90 .50

Christmas A829

1996, Nov. 14 Litho. *Perf. 13½*

2004 A829 1p Star pinata .35 .20
2005 A829 1.80p Man carrying pinatas .55 .30

Andres Henestrosa, Writer — A830

1996, Nov. 23 Litho. *Perf. 14*

2006 A830 1.80p multicolored .90 .30

Natl. Cancer Institute, 50th Anniv. A831

1996, Nov. 25 Litho. *Perf. 13½*

2007 A831 1.80p multicolored .90 .30

Paisano Program — A832

1996, Nov. 28 Litho. *Perf. 13½*

2008 A832 2.70p multicolored .90 .50

David Alfaro Siqueiros (1896-1974), Painter — A833

1996, Dec. 5 Litho. *Perf. 13½*

2009 A833 1.80p multicolored .90 .30

32nd Natl. Assembly of Surgeons A834

Dr. José Ma. Barceló de Villagrán

1996, Dec. 6 Litho. *Perf. 13½*

2010 A834 1.80p multicolored .90 .30

Wildlife Conservation — A835

1996, Dec. 11 Litho. *Perf. 14*

2011 A835 1.80p Black bear, cubs 2.25 .75

UNICEF, 50th Anniv. A836

1996, Dec. 11 Litho. *Perf. 13½*

2012 A836 1.80p multicolored .90 .30

Palafoxiana Library, Puebla, 350th Anniv. — A837

1996, Dec. 17 Litho. *Perf. 13½*

2013 A837 1.80p multicolored .90 .30

Natl. Institute of Nuclear Research A838

1996, Dec. 19 Litho. *Perf. 13½*

2014 A838 1.80p multicolored .90 .30

A839

A840

1996, Dec. 19 Litho. *Perf. 13½*

2015 A839 1.80p multicolored .90 .30

Intl. Day for Preservation of the Ozone Layer.

1996, Dec. 20 Litho. *Perf. 13½*

2016 A840 1.80p multicolored .90 .30

30 year career of plastic arts sculptor Sebastian.

Mexican Diplomats A841

Design: Isidro Fabela (b. 1882), lawyer, and Genaro Estrada (1887-1977), journalist, politician.

1996, Oct. 24 Litho. *Perf. 13½*

2017 A841 1.80p multicolored .90 .30

Carlos Pellicer (1897-1977), Poet, Museum Founder — A842

1997, Jan. 16

2018 A842 2.30p multicolored 1.00 .40

Andres Eloy Blanco (1896-1955), Poet — A843

1997, Feb. 6 Litho. *Perf. 13½*

2019 A843 3.40p multicolored 1.40 .60

A844

A845

1997, Feb. 10

2020 A844 3.40p multicolored 1.40 .60

UNESCO Intl. Summit on Education, Confederation of American Educators.

1997, Feb. 14

2021 A845 3.40p multicolored 1.40 .60

Treaty of Tlatelolco prohibiting nuclear weapons in Latin America & Caribbean.

Souvenir Sheet

Mexican Central Post Office, 90th Anniv. — A846

Illustration reduced.

1997, Feb. 20

2022 A846 7.40p multicolored 6.00 6.00

A847

A848

Generals: No. 2023, Francisco L. Urquizo. No. 2024, Mariano Escobedo. No. 2025, Jacinto B. Trevino Gonzalez. No. 2026, Felipe Angeles. No. 2027, Candido Aguilar Vargas. No. 2028, Joaquin Amaro Dominguez.

1997, Mar. 5

2023 A847 2.30p multicolored .90 .40
2024 A847 2.30p multicolored .90 .40
2025 A847 2.30p multicolored .90 .40
2026 A847 2.30p multicolored .90 .40
2027 A847 2.30p multicolored .90 .40
2028 A847 2.30p multicolored .90 .40
Nos. 2023-2028 (6) 5.40 2.40

1997, Mar. 8

2029 A848 2.30p multicolored .80 .40

Intl. Women's Day.

1st Intl. Congress for Spanish Language A849

Painting: Allegory, "La Gramatica," by Juan Correa.

1997, Apr. 7 Litho. *Perf. 13½*

2030 A849 3.40p multicolored .90 .40

Dr. Ignacio Chávez, Pres. of Natl. Academy of Medicine, Birth Cent. A850

1997, Apr. 23

2031 A850 2.30p multicolored .80 .40

Mexican Constitution, 80th Anniv. — A851

1997, Apr. 29

2032 A851 2.30p Venustiano Carranza .80 .40

First Edition of "Al Filo Del Agua," by Agustín Yáñez, 50th Anniv. A852

1997, May 9

2033 A852 2.30p multicolored .80 .40

Prof. Rafael Ramírez (1855-1959), Educator — A853

1997, May 15

2034 A853 2.30p green & gray .80 .40

Japanese Emigration to Mexico, Cent. A854

1997, May 12

2035 A854 3.40p multicolored 1.75 .60

See Japan No. 2569.

A855

A856

1997, May 31

2036 A855 2.30p multicolored .80 .40

Autonomous University of Baja California, 40th Anniv.

1997, June 26

Intl. Day to Stop Use of Illegal Drugs: a, 2.30p, Dove, clouds, sunlight. b, 3.40p, Man with one hand on bars, one hand raised toward sky. c, 3.40p, Dove in window behind bars.

2037 A856 Strip of 3, #a.-c. + label 5.50 5.50

Sigmund Freud — A857

Naval Military School, Cent. — A858

1997, June 28

2038 A857 2.30p multicolored .80 .40

1997, July 1

2039 A858 2.30p multicolored .80 .40

Natl. Bank of Foreign Commerce, 60th Anniv. A859

1997, July 4 Litho. *Perf. 13½*

2040 A859 3.40p multicolored 1.25 .60

United for Conservation — A860

1997, July 16

2041 A860 2.30p Vaquita, calf 2.00 .90

Mexican College of Aviation Pilots, 50th Anniv. A861

1997, July 17

2042 A861 2.30p multicolored .90 .40

15th Mexico City Marathon — A862

1997, Aug. 6

2043 A862 3.40p multicolored 1.25 .60

Juarez Hospital of Mexico, 150th Anniv. A863

1997, Aug. 18

2044 A863 2.30p multicolored .90 .40

Battles of 1847 A864

#2045, Battle of Padierna. #2046, Battle of Churubusco. #2047, Battle of Molino del Rey. #2047A, Defense of the Castle of Chapultepec.

1997

2045 A864 2.30p multicolored .90 .40
2046 A864 2.30p multicolored .90 .40
2047 A864 2.30p multicolored .90 .40
2047A A864 2.30p multicolored .90 .40
Nos. 2045-2047A (4) 3.60 1.60

Issued: #2045, 8/19; #2046, 8/20; #2047, 9/8; #2047A, 9/13.

A865

A866

1997, Sept. 3

2048 A865 2.30p multicolored .90 .40

Guillermo Prieto, poet, death cent.

1997, Sept. 12 Litho. *Perf. 13½*

2049 A866 3.40p multicolored 1.25 .60

Battalion of St. Patrick, 150th anniv. See Ireland No. 1085.

A867

A868

1997, Oct. 6

2050 A867 2.30p multicolored .90 .40

Reproductive health for adolescents month.

1997, Oct. 9

2051 A868 3.40p Stamp Day 1.25 .60

Heinrich von Stephan (1831-97) A869

1997, Oct. 9

2052 A869 3.40p multicolored 1.25 .60

Manuel Gómez Morin (1897-1949), Politician — A870

1997, Oct. 14

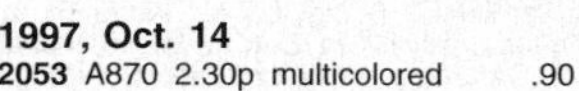

2053 A870 2.30p multicolored .90 .40

Dr. Manuel Gea González General Hospital, 50th Anniv. A871

1997, Oct. 14

2054 A871 2.30p multicolored .90 .40

Mexican Bar Assoc. College of Law, 75th Anniv. — A872

1997, Oct. 30

2055 A872 2.30p multicolored .90 .40

Christmas A873

Children with piñatas: No. 2056, By Ana R. Botello. No. 2057, By Adrián Laris.

1997, Nov. 19

2056 A873 2.30p multicolored .90 .40
2057 A873 2.30p multicolored .90 .40

New Law on Social Security — A874

1997, Dec. 10

2058 A874 2.30p multicolored .90 .40

Central University Hospital, Chihuahua, Cent. — A875

1997, Dec. 5 Litho. *Perf. 13½*

2059 A875 2.30p multicolored .90 .40

Dr. Mario Jose Molina Henriquez, 1995 Nobel Prize Recipient in Chemistry A876

1997, Dec. 8

2060 A876 3.40p multicolored 1.25 .55

Baking Industry Granary, 50th Anniv. A877

Baked goods and: a, Storage shelves. b, Man working at oven. c, Basic ingredients, man working with dough.

1997, Dec. 10

2061 A877 2.30p Vert. strip of 3, #a.-c. + label 4.00 4.00

A878

A879

Modern Mexican art, by Jose Chavez Morado.

1997, Dec. 19

2062 A878 2.30p multicolored .90 .40

Cervantes Festival, Guanajuato, 45th anniv.

1997, Dec. 20

2063 A879 2.30p multicolored .90 .40

City of Loreto, 300th anniv.

Military School of Arms, 50th Anniv. A880

1998, Mar. 1 Litho. *Perf. 13½*

2064 A880 2.30p multicolored .90 .40

Intl. Mother's Day A881

1998, Mar. 8

2065 A881 2.30p multicolored .90 .40

Cinco de Mayo — A882

1998, Apr. 16

2066 A882 3.50p multicolored 1.25 .60

See US No. 3203.

1998 World Cup Soccer Championships, France — A883

Eiffel Tower, national colors of France and Mexico and: No. 2067, Soccer player. No. 2068, Mexican Eagle mascot.

#2069: a, 8.60p, like #2067. b, 6.20p, like #2068.

1998

2067 A883 2.30p multicolored 1.50 1.50
2068 A883 2.30p multicolored 1.50 1.50

Souvenir Sheet

2069 A883 Sheet of 2, #a.-b. 8.00 8.00

Issued: #2067, 4/20; #2068, 5/11; #2069, 5/25. #2069 contains two 24x40mm stamps with a continuous design.

Justo Sierra, Educator, 150th Birth Anniv. — A884

1998, Apr. 23
2070 A884 2.30p multicolored .90 .40

Dr. Salvador Zubiran, Birth Cent. A885

1998, Apr. 24
2071 A885 2.30p multicolored .90 .40

Organization of American States, 50th Anniv. — A886

1998, Apr. 27
2072 A886 3.40p multicolored 1.00 .55

University of Puebla, 25th Anniv. A887

1998, May 6
2073 A887 2.30p multicolored .90 .40

Teacher's Day — A888

1998, May 15
2074 A888 2.30p Soledad Anaya Solorzano .90 .40

State of Tamaulipas (New Santander), 250th Anniv. — A889

1998, May 31
2075 A889 2.30p multicolored .90 .40

Sports Lottery, 20th Anniv. A890

1998, June 2
2076 A890 2.30p multicolored .90 .40

Universal Declaration of Human Rights, 50th Anniv. A891

1998, June 5 **Litho.** ***Perf. 13½***
2077 A891 3.40p multicolored 1.00 .35

Federico García Lorca (1898-1936), Poet — A892

1998, June 5
2078 A892 3.40p multicolored 1.00 .35

Philippine Independence, Cent. — A893

3.40p, Mexican flag, sailing ship. 7.40p, Mexican, Philippine flags, sailing ship.

1998, June 3 **Litho.** ***Perf. 13½***
2079 A893 3.40p multicolored 1.00 .55

Souvenir Sheet

2080 A893 7.40p multicolored 4.75 4.75

See Philippines Nos. 2537-2539, Spain No. 2949.

Intl. Day Against Drugs — A894

1998, June 26
2081 A894 2.30p multicolored .90 .35

Chapultepec Zoological Park, 7th Anniv. — A895

Design: Alfonso L. Herrera, jaguar.

1998, July 6
2082 A895 2.30p multicolored .90 .35

Arbor Day — A896

1998, July 9
2083 A896 2.30p multicolored .90 .35

Opening of the Philatelic Museum, Oaxaca — A897

Designs: No. 2084, Convent of St. Peter and St. Paul, Teposcolula. No. 2085, Burnished vase with carving. No. 2086, San Bartolo Coyotepec, "El Camino," by Francisco Toledo. No. 2087, Golden breast plate from Tomb 7, Monte Alban.

1998, July 9
2084 A897 2.30p multicolored .90 .35
2085 A897 2.30p multicolored .90 .35
2086 A897 3.40p multicolored 1.75 .75
2087 A897 3.40p multicolored 1.75 .75
Nos. 2084-2087 (4) 5.30 2.20

Precinct in Natl. Palace Honoring Benito Juárez (1806-72) A898

1998, July 18 ***Perf. 14***
2088 A898 2.30p multicolored .90 .35

Santo Domingo Cultural Center, Oaxaca — A899

a, Entire complex. b, Portals of museum. c, Francisco da Burgoa Library. d, Ethnobotanical Garden.

1998, July 24 ***Perf. 13½***
2089 A899 2.30p Block of 4, #a.-d. 4.25 4.25

Marine Life A900

a, Frigatebird, gray whale. b, Albatross. c, Whale's tail flukes. d, Dolphins, flamingos. e, Turtles. f, Sea lions. g, Elegant swallows, dolphin. h, Killer whale. i, Flamingos. j, Alligator. k, Sardines. l, Squid, loggerhead turtle. m, Bluefin tuna, jellyfish. n, Barracudas. o, Manatee. p, Garibaldi. q, Hammerhead shark. r, Huachinango, shrimp, ray. s, Octopus, mero. t, Blowfish, turtle. u, Crab, sandollars. v, Seahorse, angelfish. w, Crab, turtle, moray eel. x, Mariposa de cuatro ojos. y, Shark, coral.

1998, Aug. 14

Sheet of 25

2090 A900 2.30p #a.-y. 25.00 25.00

No. 2090 is a continuous design showing many different species of marine life, aquatic birds, and surrounding vegetation. Just a few species from each stamp are described in the above design note.

16th Mexico City Marathon A901

1998, Aug. 19 **Litho.** ***Perf. 13½***
2091 A901 3.40p multicolored 1.00 .55

World Tourism Day A902

1998, Sept. 25
2092 A902 3.40p multicolored 1.00 .55

Natl. Archives, 175th Anniv. A903

1998, Sept. 29 ***Perf. 14***
2093 A903 2.30p multicolored .90 .35

A904 A905

1998, Oct. 1 ***Perf. 13½***
2094 A904 3.40p multicolored 1.00 .55

Interpol, 75th Anniv.

1998, Oct. 5
2095 A905 2.30p multicolored .60 .35

Reproductive Health Month.

Luis Nishizawa (b. 1918), Painter — A906

1998, Oct. 9
2096 A906 2.30p multicolored .60 .35

World Post Day A907

1998, Oct. 9
2097 A907 3.40p multicolored 1.00 .55

Heroic Military College, 175th Anniv. A908

1998, Oct. 11

2098 A908 2.30p multicolored .60 .35

District of Tamaulipas, 250th Anniv. A909

1998, Oct. 12

2099 A909 2.30p multicolored .60 .35

United for Conservation — A910

1998, Oct. 13

2100 A910 2.30p Aguila real .60 .35

World Food Day A911

1998, Oct. 16

2101 A911 3.40p multicolored 1.00 .55

Natl. Mexican Migration Week A912

1998, Oct. 19

2102 A912 2.30p multicolored .60 .35

José Alfredo Jiménez (1926-72), Composer A913

1998, Nov. 11

2103 A913 2.30p multicolored .60 .35

College of Petroleum Engineers, 25th Anniv. — A914

1998, Nov. 11

2104 A914 3.40p multicolored 1.00 .55

Cultural and Economic Cooperation Between Mexico and France — A915

1998, Nov. 12

2105 A915 3.40p multicolored 1.00 .55

City of Colima, 475th Anniv. A916

1998, Nov. 16

2106 A916 2.30p multicolored .60 .35

Christmas A917

Children's drawings: 2.30p, Nativity scene. 3.40p, Pinata, candy, vert.

1998, Nov. 17

Self-Adhesive

2107 A917 2.30p multicolored .60 .35
2108 A917 3.40p multicolored 1.00 .55

Latin American Civil Aviation Commission, 25th Anniv. — A918

1998, Dec. 14 Litho. *Perf. 13½*

2109 A918 3.40p multicolored 1.00 .55

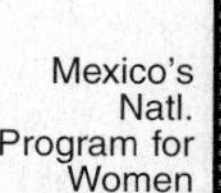

Natl. Institute of Native People, 50th Anniv. A919

1998, Dec. 4

2110 A919 2.30p multicolored .60 .35

Federation of Govt. Workers, 60th Anniv. A920

1998, Dec. 7

2111 A920 2.30p multicolored .60 .35

State University of Sinaloa, 125th Anniv. — A921

1998, Dec. 18

2112 A921 2.30p multicolored .60 .35

Mexico's Natl. Program for Women A922

1999, Mar. 8 Litho. *Perf. 13½*

2113 A922 4.20p multicolored 1.25 .45

A923

1999, Feb. 9

2114 A923 3p multicolored .90 .35

Carnaval '99, Veracruz.

A924

1999, Feb. 27

2115	A924	3p	Hammock	.65	.35
2116	A924	4.20p	Divers	.90	.45
a.			Pair, #2115-2116	4.00	4.00

Acapulco, 200th Anniv.

Launching of SATMEX 5 — A925

1999, Feb. 9

2117 A925 3p multicolored .90 .35

Souvenir Sheet

Visit of Pope John Paul II — A926

Illustration reduced.

1999, Jan. 22

2118 A926 10p multicolored 5.00 5.00

Tourism Type of 1993

Denomination Shown As $

Unwmk.

1999-2001 Photo. *Perf. 14*

2119	A683	50c	Coahuila	.75	.20
2120	A683	70c	Yucatan	.75	.20
2121	A683	1.50p	Chiapas	1.00	.20
2122	A683	2p	Coahuila	1.00	.20
2123	A683	2.50p	Yucatan	1.25	.25
2124	A683	2.60p	Colima	2.00	.30
2125	A683	3p	Michoacan, vert.	1.75	.30
2126	A683	3.60p	Coahuila	1.75	.40
2127	A683	4.20p	Guanajuato	1.75	.45
2128	A683	4.20p	Zacatecas, vert.	3.00	.45
2129	A683	4.50p	Mexico	3.00	.50
2130	A683	4.90p	Sonora	3.00	.50
2131	A683	5.30p	Michoacan, vert.	3.75	.55
2132	A683	5.90p	Queretaro	3.50	.55
2133	A683	6p	Sinaloa	3.50	.70
2134	A683	6p	Michoacan, vert.	4.00	.70
2135	A683	6.50p	Queretaro	4.50	.70
2136	A683	7p	Coahuila	4.50	.75
2137	A683	8p	Zacatecas, vert.	9.00	.85
2138	A683	8p	Sinaloa	4.75	.85
2139	A683	8.50p	Chiapas	4.75	.90
2139A	A683	8.50p	Chiapas, denomination upright	5.50	1.10
2140	A683	8.50p	Zacatecas, vert.	4.75	.95
2141	A683	10p	Campeche	18.00	1.10
2141A	A683	10p	Chiapas	7.50	1.10
2141B	A683	10.50p	Michoacan, vert.	7.00	1.10
2141C	A683	11.50p	Queretaro	8.50	1.25
2141D	A683	30p	Queretaro	19.00	3.25
			Nos. 2119-2141D (28)	133.50	20.35

Issued: #2122, 2124, 2126, 2127, 2130-2133, 2137, 1999; #2120, 2000; #2119, 2121, 2123, 2125, 2128, 2129, 2134-2136, 2138-2141D, 2001.

The denomination of No. 2139 is in italics.

Natl. Commission to Distribute Free Textbooks, 40th Anniv. — A927

1999, Mar. 11 Litho. *Perf. 13½*

2142 A927 3p multicolored 1.00 .35

See Nos. 2155-2156, 2172.

Natl. Population Commission, 25th Anniv. — A928

1999, Mar. 26

2143 A928 3p multicolored 1.00 .35

Souvenir Sheet

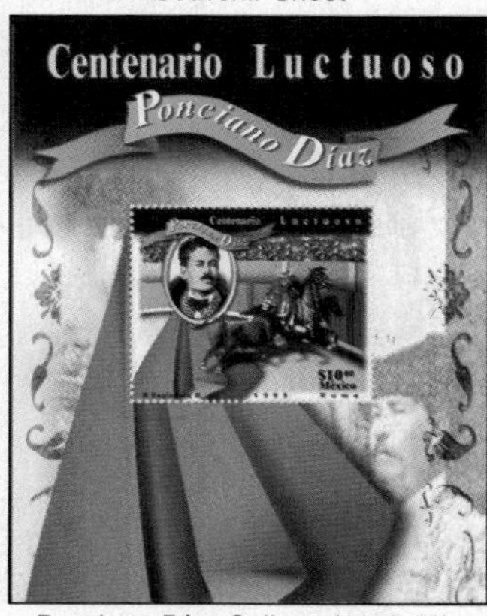

Ponciano Díaz Salinas (1856-99), Bullfighter — A929

Sheet Size: 95x240mm.

Partial illustration reduced.

1999, Apr. 17

2144 A929 10p sheet of 1 5.00 5.00

Ceniceros de Pérez (1908-68), Teacher A930

1999, May 15
2145 A930 3p multicolored .90 .35

Teacher's Day.

AAA Mexican Baseball League, 75th Anniv. A931

Designs: a, Skeleton pitcher, skeleton batter. b, Stylized pitcher. c, Pitcher lifting up large foot, sun. d, Catcher.

1999, May 31
2146 A931 3p Block of 4, #a.-d. 5.00 5.00

Also available in strip of 4 + label.

National Bank of Mexico, 115th Anniv. — A932

Designs: No. 2147, Old, new bank buildings. No. 2148, 10p bill.

1999, June 2
2147 A932 3p multicolored .90 .35
2148 A932 3p multicolored .90 .35

World Dog Show — A933

a, 4.20p, Chihuahua. b, 4.20p, Xoloitzcuintle. c, 3p, German shepherd. d, 3p, Rottweiler.

1999, June 2
2149 A933 Sheet of 4, #a.-d. 7.50 7.50

A934

A935

Perf. 13¼x13½

1999, June 25 **Litho.**
2150 A934 4.20p multicolored 1.25 .45

Intl. Day Against Illegal Drugs.

1999, July 2 **Litho.** ***Perf. 13¼x13½***
2151 A935 3p multicolored .90 .35

National Bank, 65th anniv.

Arbor Day A936

1999, July 26 ***Perf. 13½x13¼***
2152 A936 3p multicolored .90 .35

Civil Register, 140th Anniv. A937

1999, July 27
2153 A937 3p multicolored .90 .35

17th Mexico City Marathon A938

1999, Aug. 11
2154 A938 4.20p multicolored 1.75 .45

Free Textbook Type of 1999

Designs: No. 2155, Children, book, flag, cacti. No. 2156, "Tsuni tsame."

1999 **Litho.** ***Perf. 13¼x13½***
2155 A927 3p green & multi .90 .35
2156 A927 3p orange & multi .90 .35

Issued: #2155, 8/23; #2156, 10/28.

Self-portrait, by Rufino Tamayo (1899-1991) — A939

1999, Aug. 28 ***Perf. 13¼x13½***
2157 A939 3p multicolored .90 .35

City of Toluca, Bicent. A940

1999, Sept. 12 ***Perf. 13½x13¼***
2158 A940 3p copper & brown .90 .35

State of Mexico, 175th Anniv. A941

1999, Sept. 14
2159 A941 3p multicolored 1.00 .35

Union of Latin American Universities, 50th Anniv. — A942

1999, Sept. 22 ***Perf. 13¼x13½***
2160 A942 4.20p multicolored 1.25 .45

Institute of Security & Social Services of State Workers, 40th Anniv. A943

1999, Oct. 1 ***Perf. 13½x13¼***
2161 A943 3p multicolored 1.00 .35

State of Baja California Sur, 25th Anniv. A944

1999, Oct. 4
2162 A944 3p multicolored 1.00 .35

Family Planning, 25th Anniv. A945

1999, Oct. 4
2163 A945 3p multicolored 1.00 .35

Nature Conservation — A946

1999, Oct. 5
2164 A946 3p Harpy eagle 1.00 .35

State of Quintana Roo, 25th Anniv. — A947

1999, Oct. 8 **Litho.** ***Perf. 13¼x13½***
2165 A947 3p multicolored 1.00 .35

UPU, 125th Anniv. — A948

World Post Day — A949

1999, Oct. 9
2166 A948 4.20p multicolored 1.50 .45

1999, Oct. 9
2167 A949 4.20p multicolored 1.50 .45

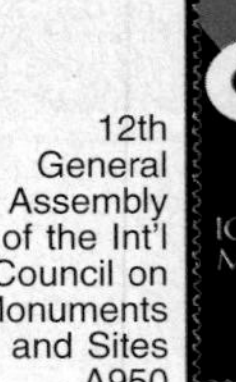
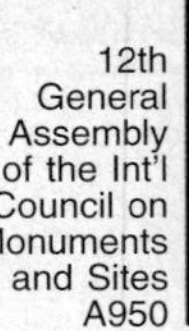

12th General Assembly of the Int'l Council on Monuments and Sites A950

1999, Oct. 17 ***Perf. 13½x13¼***
2168 A950 4.20p multicolored 1.50 .45

Carlos Chavez (1899-1978) & Silvestre Revueltas (1899-1940), Composers — A951

1999, Oct. 21
2169 A951 3p multicolored 1.00 .35

Autonomous Metropolitan University, 25th Anniv. — A952

1999, Oct. 25 ***Perf. 13¼x13½***
2170 A952 3p multicolored 1.00 .35

State of Guerrero, 150th Anniv. A953

1999, Oct. 27 **Litho.** ***Perf. 13½x13¼***
2171 A953 3p multicolored 1.00 .35

Free Textbook Type of 1999

Design: "Ciencias Naturales."

Perf. 13¼x13½

1999, Nov. 12 **Litho.**
2172 A927 3p multi 1.00 .35

Christmas

A954 A955

1999, Nov. 29
2173 A954 3p multi 1.00 .35
2174 A955 4.20p multi 1.75 .45

Natl. Commission of Professional Education, 20th Anniv. — A956

1999, Dec. 1 ***Perf. 13½x 13¼***
2175 A956 3p multi 1.00 .35

Scientific Voyage of Alexander von Humboldt to Americas, Bicent. A957

1999, Dec. 1
2176 A957 3p multi 1.00 .35

The 20th Century A958

Education: a, 3p, Natl. Autonomous University of Mexico. b, 3p, Justo Sierra, José Vasconcelos. c, 3p, Natl. Poytechnic Institute. d, 3p, Free text books. e, 4.20p, Reading programs.

Litho. & Embossed

1999, Dec. 15 ***Perf. 14x14½***
2177 A958 Sheet of 5, #a.-e. 10.00 10.00

Nos. 2177c-2177d are 79x25mm, No. 2177e is oval-shaped and 39x49mm.

See #2180-2181, 2191-2196.

A959

A960

2000, Jan. 24 Litho. ***Perf. 13¼x13½***
2178 A959 3p multi 1.00 .35

2000 census.

2000, Mar. 8 Litho. ***Perf. 13¼x13½***
2179 A960 4.20p multi 1.50 .45

International Women's Day.

The 20th Century Type of 1999

Building Democracy — No. 2180: a, 3p, Mexican presidents from Porfirio Díaz to Lázaro Cárdenas, Mexican Constitution. b, 3p, Pancho Villa, Emiliano Zapata. c, 3p, Mexican presidents from Manuel Avila Camacho to Gustavo Díaz Ordaz. d, 3p, Political figures, protestors, newspaper boy. e, 4.20p, Voter registration card, child at ballot box.

10p, People writing and at computers.

Litho. & Embossed

2000, Mar. 16 ***Perf. 14x14½***
2180 A958 Sheet of 5, #a-e 10.00 10.00

Souvenir Sheet

Litho.

Perf. 13½
2181 A958 10p multi 7.50 7.50

Nos. 2180a and 2180b are 79x25mm, and No. 2180e is oval-shaped and 39x49mm.

Natl. Assoc. of Universities and Institutions of Higher Learning, 50th Anniv. A961

Perf. 13½x13¼

2000, Mar. 24 Litho.
2182 A961 3p multi 1.00 .35

25th Mexican Travel Trade Show, Acapulco A962

2000, Apr. 9
2183 A962 4.20p multi 1.50 .45

Discovery of Brazil, 500th Anniv. A963

2000, Apr. 22
2184 A963 4.20p multi 1.50 .45

Teacher's Day — A964

2000, May 15 ***Perf. 13¼x13½***
2185 A964 3p Luis Alvarez Barret 1.00 .35

Stampin' the Future Children's Stamp Design Contest Winners A965

Art by: 3p, Alejandro Guerra Millán. 4.20p, Carlos Hernández García.

2000, May 17 ***Perf. 13½x13¼***
2186 A965 3p multi 1.00 .35
2187 A965 4.20p multi 1.50 .45

Fourth Meeting of Telecommunications Ministers and Information Industry Leaders — A966

2000, May 24
2188 A966 4.20p multi 1.50 .45

Intl. Day Against Illegal Drugs — A967

Perf. 13¼x13½

2000, June 26 Litho.
2189 A967 4.20p multi 1.50 .45

National Worker's Housing Fund Institute — A968

#2190, Sculptures: a, 3p, Pre-Hispanic building. b, 3p, Pre-Hispanic building with stairway. c, 10p, Pre-Hispanic natives in circle.

2000, June 27 ***Perf. 14¼x13½***
2190 A968 Sheet of 3, #a-c 7.00 7.00

The 20th Century Type of 1999

Cultural Idenity and Diversity — No. 2191: a, Xóchitl Incuícatl. b, Corre y se va. c, Tercera llamada. . . Cácado! d, Al Hablar como al guisar, su granito de sal. e, Children.

Health — No. 2192: a, Six men, certificate, man in tuberculosis prevention truck. b, Children on line. c, Nine men, posters. d, Poster showing tractor, health care. e, Modern medical equipment.

Art — No. 2193: a, El sello de la casa. b, Espíritu del siglo. c, La luz de México. d, Los nostros en que nos reconocemos. e, Building dome, artists and artwork.

Photography — No. 2194: a, Colchón enrollado, by Manuel Alvarez Bravo. b, Roses, by Tina Modotti. c, Four vertical photos, four horizontal photos. d, Two vertical photos, six horizontal photos. e, Three photos.

Commercial Development and Industrialization — No. 2195: a, Tractor. b, Truck cab. c, Store. d, Automobile. e, Globe.

Communications — No. 2196: a, Telephones and telegraph. b, Roads and bridges. c, Postal services. d, Railroads. e, Satellite, satellite dish, train.

Litho. & Embossed

2000 ***Perf. 14x14¼***

2191	Sheet of 5	10.00	10.00
a.-d.	A958 3p Any single	1.00	.30
e.	A958 4.20p multicolored	1.50	.45
2192	Sheet of 5	10.00	10.00
a.-d.	A958 3p Any single	1.00	.30
e.	A958 4.20p multicolored	1.50	.45
2193	Sheet of 5	10.00	10.00
a.-d.	A958 3p Any single	1.00	.30
e.	A958 4.20p multicolored	1.50	.45
2194	Sheet of 5	10.00	10.00
a.-d.	A958 3p Any single	1.00	.30
e.	A958 4.20p multicolored	1.50	.45
2195	Sheet of 5	10.00	10.00
a.-d.	A958 3p Any single	1.00	.30
e.	A958 4.20p multicolored	1.50	.45
2196	Sheet of 5	10.00	10.00
a.-d.	A958 3p Any single	1.00	.30
e.	A958 4.20p multicolored	1.50	.45
	Nos. 2191-2196 (6)	60.00	60.00

Issued: #2191, 7/18; #2192, 10/24; #2193, 11/10; #2194, 12/9; #2195, 12/20; #2196, 12/21.

Nos. 2191c-2196c, 2191d-2196d are 79x25mm and Nos. 2191e-2196e are oval shaped and 39x49mm.

Natl. Program for Development of Handicapped People, 5th Anniv. — A969

2000, Aug. 2 Litho. ***Perf. 13¼x13½***
2197 A969 3p multi 1.00 .35

Latin American Integration Association, 20th Anniv. — A970

2000, Aug. 11 ***Perf. 13½x13¼***
2198 A970 4.20p multi 1.50 .45

Restoration of the Senate, 125th Anniv. — A971

2000, Aug. 17 ***Perf. 13¼x13½***
2199 A971 3p multi 1.00 .35

Souvenir Sheets

Expo 2000, Hanover — A972

a, 1p, Mexican soul. b, 1p, Natl. mosaic. c, 1.80p, Future construction. d, 1.80p, Plaza pyramid. e, 2p, Creation of towns. f, 2p, Millennial construction. g, 3p, Naturea. h, 3p, Humanity. i, 3p, Technology. j, 3.60p, Expo 2000, Hanover. k, 4.20p, Emblem.

Illustration reduced.

Litho. & Embossed

2000, Aug. 20 ***Perf. 14½x14***
2200 A972 Sheet of 11, #a-k 12.50 12.50

No. 2200k is oval shaped and 39x49mm.

Bank of Mexico, 75th Anniv. — A973

Illustration reduced.

2000, Aug. 23 Litho. ***Perf.***
2201 A973 10p multi 5.00 5.00

Stamp is oval-shaped and 49x39mm.

18th Mexico City Marathon A974

2000, Aug. 24 ***Perf. 13½x13¼***
2202 A974 4.20p multi 1.50 .45

2000 Summer Olympics, Sydney A975

2000, Sept. 15
2203 A975 4.20p multi 1.50 .45

Paisano Program A976

2000, Sept. 21
2204 A976 4.20p multi 1.50 .45

2nd Intl. Memory of the World Conference A977

2000, Sept. 12
2205 A977 4.20p multi 1.50 .45

Women's Reproductive Health Month — A978

2000, Oct. 5 ***Perf. 13¼x13½***
2206 A978 3p multi 1.00 .35

Ciudad Victoria, 250th Anniv. A979

2000, Oct. 6 ***Perf. 13½x13¼***
2207 A979 3p multi 1.00 .35

World Post Day — A980

2000, Oct. 9 ***Perf. 13¼x13½***
2208 A980 4.20p multi 1.50 .45

Natl. Human Rights Commission, 10th Anniv. — A981

2000, Oct. 23 ***Perf. 13½x13¼***
2209 A981 3p multi 1.00 .35

World Meteorological Organization, 50th Anniv. — A982

2000, Oct. 27
2210 A982 3p multi 1.00 .35

Intl. Diabetes Federation, 50th Anniv. A983

2000, Nov. 6
2211 A983 4.20p multi 1.50 .45

Telegraphy in Mexico, 150th Anniv. A984

2000, Nov. 11
2212 A984 3p multi 1.00 .35

Luis Buñuel (1900-83), Film Director A985

2000, Nov. 21
2213 A985 3p multi 1.00 .35

Electrical Investigation Institute, 25th Anniv. — A986

2000, Nov. 25
2214 A986 3p multi 1.00 .35

Customs Administration, Cent. — A987

2000, Nov. 28
2215 A987 3p multi 1.00 .35

Christmas A988

2000, Nov. 29
2216 A988 3p shown 1.00 .35
2217 A988 4.20p Poinsettias 1.50 .45

Television in Mexico, 50th Anniv. A989

2000, Nov. 30
2218 A989 3p multi 1.00 .35

Souvenir Sheet

Postal Headquarters — A990

No. 2219: a, 3p, Adamo Boari (1863-1928), architect. b, 3p, Roofline. c, 3p, Gonzalo Garita y Frontera (1867-1922), engineer. d, 10p, Headquarters building.
Illustration reduced.

Litho. & Embossed

2000, Nov. 30 ***Perf. 14¼x13½***
2219 A990 Sheet of 4, #a-d 9.00 9.00

Pre-Hispanic City of El Tajín — A991

Perf. 13½x13¼

2000, Dec. 14 **Litho.**
2220 A991 3p multi 1.00 .35

Nature Conservation — A992

2000, Dec. 15
2221 A992 3p Manatee 1.00 .35

Stamps inscribed 'Aquila Real / Unidos Para Conservacion' with white, yellow or gray backgrounds and 20c denominations have no postal validity.

Francisco Sarabia (1900-39), Aviator — A993

2000, Dec. 20 ***Perf. 13¼x13½***
2222 A993 3p multi 1.00 .35

Law Faculty of National Autonomous University of Mexico, 50th Anniv. A994

2001, Mar. 7 Litho. ***Perf. 13½x13¼***
2223 A994 3p multi 1.00 .30

Intl. Women's Day A995

2001, Mar. 8
2224 A995 4.20p multi 1.50 .45

National Cement Council, 53rd Anniv. A996

2001, Mar. 27
2225 A996 3p multi 1.00 .30

Teacher's Day A997

2001, May 15 ***Perf. 14***
2226 A997 3p José Vasconcelos 1.00 .30

World Refugee Day — A998

Frida Kahlo (1907-54), Painter — A999

2001, June 20
2227 A998 4.20p multi 1.50 .45

2001, June 21
2228 A999 4.20p multi 1.50 .45

Intl. Day Against Illegal Drugs — A1000

2001, June 26
2229 A1000 4.20p multi 1.50 .45

Mario de la Cueva, Educator, Cent. of Birth — A1001

2001, July 11 **Litho.** ***Perf. 14***
2230 A1001 3p multi 1.00 .30

Intl. Volunteers Year A1002

2001, July 25
2231 A1002 4.20p multi 1.50 .45

Souvenir Sheet

Rodolfo Morales (1925-2001), Painter — A1003

2001, Aug. 4 ***Perf. 14¼x13½***
2232 A1003 10p multi 4.50 4.50

Federal Fiscal and Administrative Justice Tribunal, 65th Anniv. — A1004

2001, Aug. 23 ***Perf. 14***
2233 A1004 3p multi 1.00 .30

University of Mexico, 450th Anniv. A1005

2001, Sept. 3
2234 A1005 3p multi 1.00 .30

Adela Formoso de Obregón Santcilia (1907-81), Woman's Rights Activist — A1006

2001, Sept. 6
2235 A1006 3p multi 1.00 .30

Daniel Cosío Villegas (1898-1976), Historian — A1007

2001, Sept. 6
2236 A1007 3p multi 1.00 .30

Mexican Pharmacies A1008

2001, Sept. 27 **Litho.** ***Perf. 14***
2237 A1008 3p multi 1.00 .30

Intl. Day of the Elderly A1009

2001, Oct. 1
2238 A1009 3p multi 1.00 .30

Year of Dialogue Among Civilizations A1010

Women's Health Day A1012

World Post Day — A1011

2001, Oct. 9
2239 A1010 3p multi 1.00 .30

2001, Oct. 9
2240 A1011 3p multi 1.00 .30

2001, Oct. 31
2241 A1012 3p multi 1.00 .30

Ophthalmology Institute, 25th Anniv. — A1013

2001, Nov. 23
2242 A1013 4.20p multi 1.50 .45

United for Conservation — A1014

2001, Nov. 26
2243 A1014 5.30p Chara pinta 2.50 .90

Christmas A1015

2001, Dec. 3
2244 A1015 3p shown 1.00 .30
2245 A1015 4.20p Candles 1.50 .45

Souvenir Sheet

Fund for Indigenous People's Health and Education — A1016

2001, Dec. 4 ***Perf. 13½x14¼***
2246 A1016 3p multi 1.50 1.50

Souvenir Sheet

National Scholarship Fund — A1017

2001, Dec. 4
2247 A1017 3p multi 1.50 1.50

Children's Protection A1018

World Food Day A1019

2001, Dec. 11 ***Perf. 14***
2248 A1018 3p multi 1.00 .30

2001, Dec. 17
2249 A1019 3p multi 1.00 .30

United For Conservation — A1020

2002, Jan. 24 **Litho.** ***Perf. 14***
2250 A1020 6p Borrego cimarrón 2.50 .90

Manuel Alvarez Bravo, Photographer, Cent. of Birth — A1021

2002, Feb. 3
2251 A1021 6p gray & blk 2.25 .70

Mexico — People's Republic of China A1022

Designs: No. 2252, green panel at UL and brown panel at LL. No. 2252A, Like #2252, but with brown panel at UL, green panel at LL.

Diplomatic Relations, 30th Anniv.

2002, Feb. 14 **Litho.** ***Perf. 14***
2252 A1022 6p multi 2.00 .65
2252A A1022 6p multi 2.00 .65
b. Vert. pair, #2252-2252A 5.00 5.00

Conservation — A1023

Designs: 50c, Mangrove swamps. No. 2254, Rivers. No. 2255, Forests. 1.50p, No. 2267, Land mammals. No. 2257, Rain forests. No. 2258, Cacti. 4.50p, Birds. No. 2260, Sea turtles. No. 2261, Reptiles. No. 2262, Butterflies. No. 2263, Eagles. 7p, Reefs. 8.50p, 12p, Tropical forests. No. 2266, Marine mammals. No. 2268, Orchids. No. 2269, Cats. No. 2270, Oceans. No. 2271, Coastal birds. No. 2273, Deserts. No. 2274, Lakes and lagoons.

2002, Feb. 18 **Litho.** ***Perf. 14***
2253 A1023 50c multi .20 .20
2254 A1023 1p multi .20 .20
2255 A1023 1p multi .35 .20
2256 A1023 1.50p multi .50 .20
2257 A1023 2p multi .70 .20
2258 A1023 2p multi .70 .20
2259 A1023 4.50p multi 1.50 .50
2260 A1023 5p multi 1.75 .55
2261 A1023 5p multi 1.75 .55
2262 A1023 6p multi 2.00 .65
2263 A1023 6p multi 2.00 .65
2264 A1023 7p multi 2.40 .75
2265 A1023 8.50p multi 2.75 .95
2266 A1023 10p multi 3.50 1.10
2267 A1023 10p multi 3.50 1.10
2268 A1023 10.50p multi 3.50 1.25
2269 A1023 10.50p multi 3.50 1.25
2270 A1023 11.50p multi 3.75 1.25
2271 A1023 11.50p multi 3.75 1.25
2272 A1023 12p multi 4.00 1.25
2273 A1023 30p multi 10.00 3.25
2274 A1023 30p multi 10.00 3.25
Nos. 2253-2274 (22) 62.30 20.75

2003 ***Perf. 13x13¼***
2253a A1023 50c multi .40 .20
2254a A1023 1p multi 1.10 .20
2255a A1023 1p multi 1.10 .20
2259a A1023 4.50p multi 3.50 .40
2260a A1023 5p multi 1.75 .45
2261a A1023 5p multi 1.75 .45
2262a A1023 6p multi 2.50 .55
2263a A1023 6p multi 2.00 .55
2264a A1023 7p multi 2.50 .65
2265a A1023 8.50p multi 3.75 .75
2266a A1023 10p multi 4.00 .90
2267a A1023 10p multi 4.25 .90
2268a A1023 10.50p multi 5.00 .95
2269a A1023 10.50p multi 4.25 .95
2270a A1023 11.50p multi 6.00 1.00
2271a A1023 11.50p multi 6.00 1.00
Nos. 2253a-2271a (16) 49.85 10.10

See Nos. 2321-2330, 2362-2377, 2394-2436.

2002 Winter Olympics, Salt Lake City A1024

2002, Feb. 20 **Litho.** ***Perf. 14***
2275 A1024 8.50p multi 2.75 .95

Veracruz Port Modernization, Cent. — A1025

2002, Mar. 4
2276 A1025 6p multi 2.25 .70

Mexico — South Korea Diplomatic Relations, 40th Anniv. A1026

2002, Mar. 5
2277 A1026 8.50p multi 2.75 .95

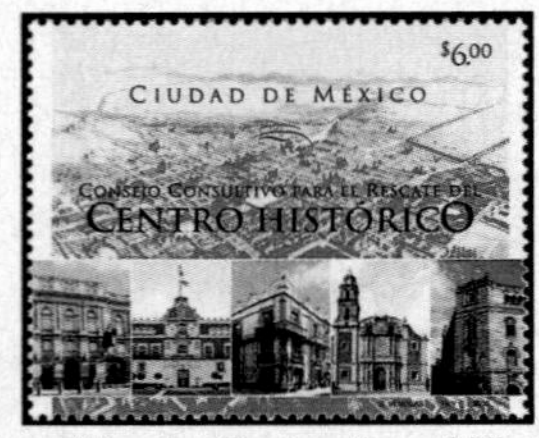

Council for the Restoration of Historic Central Mexico City — A1027

2002, Mar. 7
2278 A1027 6p multi 2.25 .70

Natl. Women's Institute A1028

José Guadalupe Posada (1851-1913), Printmaker A1029

2002, Mar. 8
2279 A1028 8.50p multi 2.75 .95

2002, Mar. 18
2280 A1029 6p gold & black 2.25 .65

Justo Sierra Mendez (1848-1912), Writer — A1030

2002, May 15 **Litho.** ***Perf. 14***
2281 A1030 6p multi 2.25 .65

UN General Assembly Special Session on Children A1031

2002, May 27
2282 A1031 6p multi 2.25 .65

Discovery of the Tomb of Pakal, 50th Anniv. A1032

2002, June 14
2283 A1032 6p multi 2.25 .65

2002 World Cup Soccer Championships, Japan and Korea — A1033

2002, June 15
2284 A1033 8.50p multi 2.75 .85

Intl. Day Against Illegal Drugs — A1034

2002, June 26
2285 A1034 6p multi 2.25 .65

5th Mexico-Central American Summit — A1035

2002, June 27
2286 A1035 6p multi 2.25 .65

Intl. Year of Mountains A1036

2002, July 24 **Litho.** ***Perf. 14***
2287 A1036 6p multi 2.25 .65

Intl. Day of Indigenous People A1037

2002, Aug. 9 ***Perf. 13x13¼***
2288 A1037 6p multi 2.25 .65

Federal Electricity Commission A1038

2002, Aug. 14 ***Perf. 14***
2289 A1038 6p multi 2.25 .65

Natl. Blood Donor Day — A1039

2002, Aug. 23 ***Perf. 13¼x13***
2290 A1039 6p multi 2.25 .65

Campaign Against Corruption A1040

2002, Sept. 12 **Litho.** ***Perf. 13x13¼***
2291 A1040 6p multi 2.25 .60

Code of Ethics for Public Servants — A1041

2002, Sept. 12 ***Perf. 13¼x13***
2292 A1041 6p multi 2.25 .60

World Tourism Day A1042

2002, Sept. 27 ***Perf. 13x13¼***
2293 A1042 8.50p multi 2.75 .85

Natl. Organ Transplant and Donation Week — A1043

2002, Oct. 7 ***Perf. 13¼x13***
2294 A1043 6p multi 2.25 .60

World Post Day A1044

2002, Oct. 9 ***Perf. 13x13¼***
2295 A1044 8.50p multi 2.75 .85

State of Baja California, 50th Anniv. A1045

2002, Nov. 1
2296 A1045 6p multi 2.25 .60

Luis Barragan (1902-88), Architect — A1046

2002, Nov. 7 ***Perf. 13¼x13***
2297 A1046 6p multi 2.25 .60

Renewal of Diplomatic Relations Between Mexico and Spain, 25th Anniv. A1047

2002, Nov. 19 ***Perf. 13x13¼***
2298 A1047 8.50p multi 2.75 .85

Mexico City Intl. Airport, 50th Anniv. — A1048

Details from mural "The Conquest of the Air by Man": a, Indian chief at left, Montgolfier balloon flight at right. b, Charles Lindbergh at left, parachutist at center. c, Wright Brothers at left, Mexico City at center.

Illustration reduced.

2002, Nov. 19 ***Perf. 13¼x13***
2299 Horiz. strip of 3 7.50 7.50
a.-b. A1048 6p Either single 2.25 .60
c. A1048 8.50p multi 2.75 .85

Information Technology Development in Mexico, 75th Anniv. — A1049

2002, Nov. 21
2300 A1049 6p multi 1.75 .60

Anti-Violence Campaign — A1050

2002, Nov. 25 ***Perf. 13x13¼***
2301 A1050 8.50p multi 2.50 .85

Pan-American Health Organization, Cent. — A1051

2002, Dec. 2 ***Perf. 13¼x13***
2302 A1051 8.50p multi 1.75 .85

Acolmiztli Nezahualcóyotl (1402-72), Poet — A1052

2002, Dec. 10
2303 A1052 6p multi 1.75 .60

Christmas A1053

Children's art: 6p, Nativity, by Sara Elisa Miranda Alcaraz. 8.50p, Children with Nativity Scene, by Alejandro Ruíz Sampedro.

2002, Dec. 19 ***Perf. 13x13¼***
2304 A1053 6p multi 1.75 .60
2305 A1053 8.50p multi 2.50 .80

Powered Flight, Cent. A1054

2003, Mar. 6 Litho. ***Perf. 13x13¼***
2306 A1054 8.50p multi 2.50 .80

Iberoamerican University, 60th Anniv. — A1055

2003, Mar. 7 ***Perf. 13¼x13***
2307 A1055 6p multi 1.75 .55

Intl. Women's Day — A1056

2003, Mar. 8
2308 A1056 8.50p multi 2.50 .80

Mexicali, Cent. A1057

2003, Mar. 14 ***Perf. 13x13¼***
2309 A1057 6p multi 1.75 .55

Mexican Chamber of Industry and Construction, 50th Anniv. — A1058

2003, Mar. 26
2310 A1058 6p multi 1.75 .55

Federico Gomez Children's Hospital, 60th Anniv. A1059

2003, Apr. 30 Litho. ***Perf. 13x13¼***
2311 A1059 6p multi 1.75 .60

Miguel Hidalgo y Costilla (1753-1811), Independence Leader — A1060

2003, May 8 ***Perf. 13¼x13***
2312 A1060 6p multi 1.75 .60
a. Perf 14 *350.00 350.00*

Gregorio Torres Quintero (1866-1934), Educator — A1061

2003, May 15
2313 A1061 6p multi 1.75 .55

Natl. Astronomical Observatory, 125th Anniv. — A1062

2003, May 20 ***Perf. 13x13¼***
2314 A1062 6p multi 1.75 .55

World Day Against Tobacco — A1063

2003, May 30 ***Perf. 13¼x13***
2315 A1063 8.50p multi 2.50 .80

Inauguration of Satellite Internet Network — A1064

2003, June 5
2316 A1064 6p multi 1.75 .55

Intl. Day Against Illegal Drugs A1065

2003, June 26 Litho. ***Perf. 13x13¼***
2317 A1065 8.50p multi 2.50 .80

Mexican Baseball Hall of Fame, 30th Anniv. A1066

2003, July 21
2318 A1066 6p multi 1.75 .55

Xavier Villaurrutia (1903-51), Poet A1067

2003, July 24
2319 A1067 6p multi 1.75 .55

Veterinary Medicine Education in Mexico, 150th Anniv. A1068

2003, Aug. 16
2320 A1068 6p multi 1.75 .55

Conservation Type of 2002

Designs: 50c, Oceans. 1p, Reptiles. No. 2323, Land mammals. No. 2324, Rain forests. No. 2325, Coastal birds. 4.50p, Orchids. 6p, Rivers. 8.50p, Cacti. No. 2329, Lakes and lagoons. No. 2330, Sea turtles.

Perf. 13x13¼, 13½ (#2328)

2003-04 **Litho.**

2321	A1023	50c multi ('04)	.50	.20
2322	A1023	1p multi ('04)	.50	.20
2323	A1023	2.50p multi	1.25	.25
2324	A1023	2.50p multi	1.25	.25
2325	A1023	2.50p multi ('04)	1.25	.25
2326	A1023	4.50p multi ('04)	2.00	.40
2327	A1023	6p multi ('04)	2.75	.55
2328	A1023	8.50p multi ('04)	3.50	.75
2329	A1023	10.50pmulti ('04)	4.00	.95
2330	A1023	10.50pmulti ('04)	4.50	.95
		Nos. 2321-2330 (10)	21.50	4.75

This is an expanding set. Numbers may change.

National Pedagogical University, 25th Anniv. — A1069

2003, Aug. 29 Litho. ***Perf. 13¼x13***
2331 A1069 6p multi 1.75 .55

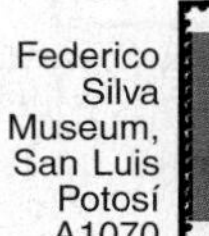

Federico Silva Museum, San Luis Potosí A1070

2003, Sept. 18 ***Perf. 13x13¼***
2332 A1070 6p multi 1.75 .55

National Organ and Tissue Donation Week A1071

2003, Sept. 26
2333 A1071 6p multi 1.75 .55

World Post Day A1072

Woman Suffrage, 50th Anniv. A1073

2003, Oct. 9 ***Perf. 13¼x13***
2334 A1072 8.50p multi 2.25 .75

2003, Oct. 16
2335 A1073 6p multi 1.50 .55

Health Ministry, 60th Anniv. A1074

2003, Oct. 23 ***Perf. 13x13¼***
2336 A1074 6p multi 1.50 .55

Juarez Theater, Cent. A1075

2003, Oct. 27
2337 A1075 6p multi 1.50 .55

Teaching of Law in the Americas, 450th Anniv. — A1076

2003, Nov. 4 ***Perf. 13¼x13***
2338 A1076 8.50p multi 2.25 .80

Central Power and Light, Cent. A1077

2003, Nov. 18 Litho. ***Perf. 13x13¼***
2339 A1077 6p multi 1.50 .55

Christmas A1078

Children's drawings of Nativity by: 6p, Valeria Báez. 8.50p, Octavio Alemán.

2003, Dec. 3
2340 A1078 6p multi 1.50 .55
2341 A1078 8.50p multi 2.25 .75

A1079

A1080

2003, Dec. 5 ***Perf. 13¼x13***
2342 A1079 6p multi 1.50 .55

Children's rights.

2003, Dec. 11
2343 A1080 8.50p multi 2.25 .75

Intl. Year of Fresh Water.

National Technical Education College, 25th Anniv. A1081

2003, Dec. 15 *Perf. 13x13¼*

2344 A1081 6p multi 1.50 .55

First Visit of Pope John Paul II to Mexico, 25th Anniv. A1082

2004, Jan. 28 **Litho.** *Perf. 13x13¼*

2345 A1082 6p multi 1.10 .55

Agustín Yáñez (1904-80), Novelist A1083

2004, May 4

2346 A1083 8.50p multi 1.50 .75

Enrique Aguilar González — A1084

2004, May 15 *Perf. 13¼x13*

2347 A1084 8.50p multi 1.50 .75

Teacher's Day.

Cable Television in Mexico, 50th Anniv. — A1085

2004, May 19

2348 A1085 6p multi 1.10 .55

Mexican Geological Society, Cent. A1086

2004, June 2 *Perf. 13x13¼*

2349 A1086 8.50p multi 1.50 .75

Intl. Day Against Illegal Drugs — A1087

2004, June 25 *Perf. 13¼x13*

2350 A1087 8.50p multi 1.50 .75

Salvador Novo (1904-74), Poet A1088

2004, July 30 *Perf. 13x13¼*

2351 A1088 7p multi 1.25 .60

Gilberto Owen (1905-52), Poet A1089

2004, Aug. 8 **Litho.** *Perf. 13x13¼*

2352 A1089 7p multi 1.25 .60

FIFA (Fédération Internationale de Football Association), Cent. — A1090

2004, Aug. 11

2353 A1090 11.50p multi 2.00 1.00

Mexican Cartooning — A1091

2004, Aug. 13 *Perf. 13¼x13*

2354 A1091 6p multi 1.00 .50

2004 Summer Olympics, Athens — A1092

2004, Aug. 13

2355 A1092 10.50p multi 1.90 .95

Celestino Gorostiza (1904-67), Writer A1093

2004, Aug. 16 **Litho.** *Perf. 13x13¼*

2356 A1093 7p multi 1.25 .60

Fresnillo, 450th Anniv. — A1094

2004, Sept. 2 *Perf. 13¼x13*

2357 A1094 7p multi 1.25 .60

Economic Culture Fund, 70th Anniv. A1095

2004, Sept. 6 *Perf. 13x13¼*

2358 A1095 8.50p multi 1.50 .75

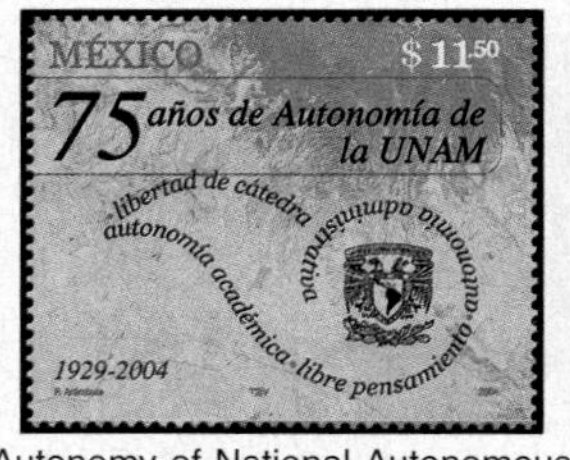

Autonomy of National Autonomous University of Mexico, 75th Anniv. — A1096

2004, Sept. 6 *Perf. 13¼x13*

2359 A1096 11.50p multi 2.00 1.00

Autonomous University of Chihuahua, 50th Anniv. — A1097

2004, Sept. 8 *Perf. 13x13¼*

2360 A1097 7p multi 1.25 .60

Palace of Fine Arts, 70th Anniv. A1098

2004, Sept. 29

2361 A1098 7p multi 1.25 .60

Conservation Type of 2002

Designs: 50c, Cats. No. 2363, Oceans. No. 2364, Rain forests. 2.50p, No. 2374, Reefs. 4.50p, Forests. 5p, No. 2370, Land mammals.

Nos. 2368, 2376, Reptiles. No. 2369, Birds. Nos. 2371, 2375, Deserts. No. 2372, Cacti. No. 2373, Tropical forests. No. 2377, Coastal birds.

2004		**Litho.**		*Perf. 13x13¼*	
2362	A1023	50c	multi	.45	.20
2363	A1023	1p	multi	2.50	.20
2364	A1023	1p	multi	.45	.20
2365	A1023	2.50p	multi	1.25	.20
2366	A1023	4.50p	multi	1.25	.40
2367	A1023	5p	multi	1.90	.45
2368	A1023	6p	multi	1.90	.55
2369	A1023	6p	multi	1.75	.55
2370	A1023	6p	multi	2.00	.55
2371	A1023	7p	multi	2.00	.60
2372	A1023	7p	multi	2.00	.60
2373	A1023	10p	multi	3.50	.90
2374	A1023	10p	multi	3.50	.90
2375	A1023	10.50p	multi	3.50	.95
a.	Microprinting at top in black			4.25	1.00
2376	A1023	30p	multi	8.00	2.25
2377	A1023	30p	multi	8.00	2.25
	Nos. 2362-2377 (16)			43.95	11.75

Microprinting at top on No. 2375 is in gray.

State Workers' Institute of Social Services and Security — A1099

2004, Oct. 1 **Litho.** *Perf. 13¼x13*

2378 A1099 6p multi 1.10 .55

Termination of Walled District of Campeche, 300th Anniv. — A1100

2004, Oct. 6 *Perf. 13x13¼*

2379 A1100 6p multi 1.10 .55

National Anthem, 150th Anniv. A1101

2004, Oct. 8

2380 A1101 6.50p multi 1.25 .60

World Post Day A1102

2004, Oct. 11

2381 A1102 6p bright rose lilac 1.10 .55

Admission to UPU, 125th Anniv. A1103

2004, Oct. 29

2382 A1103 8.50p multi 1.50 .75

Channel 11 Television — A1104

2004, Nov. 10 *Perf. 13¼x13*

2383 A1104 8.50p multi 1.50 .75

Superior Federation Audit, 180th Anniv. — A1105

2004, Nov. 16
2384 A1105 6.50p multi 1.25 .60

Health Secretary's Building, 75th Anniv. A1106

2004, Nov. 22 ***Perf. 13x13¼***
2385 A1106 8.50p multi 1.60 .80

Culture on the Radio — A1107

2004, Nov. 30 ***Perf. 13¼x13***
2386 A1107 6.50p multi 1.25 .60

Natl. Communications and Transportation Department Center, 50th Anniv. — A1108

Illustration reduced.

2004, Nov. 30 ***Perf. 13¼x13***
2387 A1108 6.50p multi 1.25 .60

Souvenir Sheet

Perf. 14¼x14

2388 A1108 7.50p multi 1.40 .70

Town of General Escobedo, 400th Anniv. A1109

2004, Dec. 3 ***Perf. 13x13¼***
2389 A1109 8.50p multi 1.60 .80

Natl. Free Textbook Commission, 45th Anniv. — A1110

2004, Dec. 6
2390 A1110 10.50p multi 1.90 .95

A1111

Christmas — A1112

2004, Dec. 13 ***Perf. 13x13¼***
2391 A1111 7.50p multi 1.40 .70

Perf. 13¼x13

2392 A1112 10.50p multi 1.90 .95

Traffic Accident Prevention — A1113

2004, Dec. 17 Litho. ***Perf. 13¼x13***
2393 A1113 8.50p multi 1.60 .80

Conservation Type of 2002

Designs: Nos. 2394, 2404, Deserts. Nos. 2395, 2406, 2408, 2411, Orchids. Nos. 2396, 2410, 2419, 2435, Sea turtles. Nos. 2397, 2416, Birds. Nos. 2398, 2401, 2421, 2433, Marine mammals. Nos. 2399, 2425, Oceans. Nos. 2400, 2402, 2424, Cats. Nos. 2403, 2430, Rain forests. Nos. 2405, 2412, Eagles. Nos. 2407, 2415, Lakes and lagoons. Nos. 2409, 2436, Butterflies. Nos. 2413, 2423, Tropical forests. Nos. 2414, 2431, Rivers. Nos. 2417, 2429, Reefs. Nos. 2418, 2427, Forests. Nos. 2420, 2434, Coastal birds. No. 2422, Reptiles. Nos. 2426, 2428, Land mammals. No. 2432, Mangrove swamps.

2004-05 Litho. ***Perf. 13½x13¼***

Inscribed "ROMO" at Lower Right

No.	Type	Denom.	Color	Unused	Used
2394	A1023	50c	multi	.20	.20
2395	A1023	1p	multi	.20	.20
2396	A1023	2.50p	multi	.50	.25
2397	A1023	6.50p	multi	1.25	.60
2398	A1023	6.50p	multi	150.00	.60
2399	A1023	7p	multi	1.40	.70
2400	A1023	7.50p	multi	1.40	.70
2401	A1023	8.50p	multi	1.50	.75
	Complete booklet, 6 #2401			9.00	
2402	A1023	10.50p	multi	1.90	.95
	Complete booklet, 6 #2402			11.50	
2403	A1023	13p	multi	2.50	1.25

Inscribed "TIEV" at Lower Right

Perf. 13x13¼

No.	Type	Denom.	Color	Unused	Used
2404	A1023	50c	multi	.20	.20
2405	A1023	50c	multi	.20	.20
2406	A1023	50p	multi	.20	.20
2407	A1023	1p	multi	.20	.20
2408	A1023	1p	multi	.20	.20
a.	Perf. 14			.20	.20
2409	A1023	2p	multi	.20	.20
2410	A1023	2.50p	multi	.50	.25
2411	A1023	2.50p	multi	.50	.25
2412	A1023	2.50p	multi	.50	.25
2413	A1023	5p	multi	.95	.45
2414	A1023	5p	multi	.95	.45
2415	A1023	5p	multi	.95	.45
2416	A1023	6.50p	multi	1.25	.60
2417	A1023	6.50p	multi	1.25	.60
2418	A1023	6.50p	multi	1.25	.60
2419	A1023	6.50p	multi	1.25	.60
2420	A1023	6.50p	multi	1.25	.60
2421	A1023	6.50p	multi	1.25	.60
2422	A1023	6.50p	multi	1.25	.60
2423	A1023	7p	multi	1.40	.70
2424	A1023	7.50p	multi	1.40	.70
2425	A1023	7.50p	multi	1.40	.70
2426	A1023	7.50p	multi, denomination in black	1.40	.70
a.	Denomination in gray			1.40	.70
2427	A1023	8.50p	multi	1.60	.80
2428	A1023	10.50p	multi	2.00	1.00
2429	A1023	10.50p	multi	2.00	1.00
2430	A1023	13p	multi	2.50	1.25
2431	A1023	13p	multi	2.50	1.25
2432	A1023	13p	multi	2.50	1.25
2433	A1023	14.50p	multi	2.75	1.40
2434	A1023	14.50p	multi	2.75	1.40
2435	A1023	30.50p	multi	5.75	2.75
2436	A1023	30.50p	multi	5.75	2.75
	Nos. 2394-2436 (43)			210.85	31.35

Issued: Nos. 2401, 2402, 2004. Others, 2005. Colors are duller on stamps inscribed "TIEV" than those on similar stamps inscribed "ROMO."

Mexico General Hospital, Cent. — A1114

2005, Feb. 4 Litho. ***Perf. 13¼x13***
2437 A1114 6.50p multi 1.25 .60

Intl. Women's Day A1115

2005, Mar. 8 ***Perf. 13x13¼***
2438 A1115 6.50p multi 1.25 .60

Publication of Pedro Paramo by Juan Rulfo, 50th Anniv. A1116

2005, Mar. 13
2439 A1116 6.50p multi 1.25 .60

Natl. University Games A1117

World Without Polio A1118

2005, Apr. 18 ***Perf. 13¼x13***
2440 A1117 7.50p multi 1.40 .70

2005, Apr. 29
2441 A1118 10.50p multi 1.90 .95

Eulalia Guzmán A1119

2005, May 15 ***Perf. 13x13¼***
2442 A1119 6.50p multi 1.25 .60

Teacher's Day.

Souvenir Sheet

Publication of Don Quixote, 400th Anniv. — A1120

No. 2443: a, 6.50p, Silhouette of Don Quixote. b, 10.50p, Crowd, horse and rider. c, 10.50p, Don Quixote.

2005, May 23 ***Perf. 13¼x13***
2443 A1120 Sheet of 3, #a-c 5.25 5.25

Intl. Year of Physics — A1121

2005, May 26
2444 A1121 7.50p multi 1.40 .70

Natl. Human Rights Commission — A1122

2005, June 5 ***Perf. 13x13¼***
2445 A1122 6.50p multi 1.25 .60

Society of Mexican Architects, Cent. — A1123

2005, June 8 ***Perf. 13¼x13***
2446 A1123 6.50p multi 1.25 .60

Intl. Day Against Illegal Drugs — A1124

2005, June 24

2447	A1124	10.50p multi	2.00	1.00

Baseball — A1125

2005, June 27

2448	A1125	7.50p multi	1.40	.70

Information Access and Transparency — A1126

Illustration reduced.

2005, June 27

2449	A1126	6.50p multi	1.25	.60

Memin Pinguin, by Yolanda Vargas Dulche — A1127

Memin Pinguin: a, And comic book page. b, Holding flower. c, Holding open comic book. d, Wearing tuxedo. e, Holding closed book.

2005, June 28 *Perf. 13*

2450		Horiz. strip of 5	*9.50*	*9.50*
a.-e.	A1127	6.50p Any single	*1.90*	*.95*

Multiple Self-portrait, by Juan O'Gorman (1905-82) — A1128

2005, June 29 *Perf. 13¼x13*

2451	A1128	7.50p multi	1.40	.70

Conservation Type of 2002

Designs: No. 2452, Butterflies. Nos. 2453, 2473, Sea turtles. No. 2454, Coastal birds. Nos. 2456, 2463, Marine mammals. Nos. 2457, 2459, Rivers. Nos. 2458, 2462, 2466, Oceans. No. 2460, Lakes and lagoons. Nos. 2461, 2469, Cats. No. 2464, Reptiles. No. 2465, Mangrove swamps. No. 2467, Birds. No. 2468, Cacti. No. 2470, Reefs. No. 2471, Eagles. No. 2472, Tropical forests.

2005 Litho. *Perf. 13x13¼*

Inscribed "TIEV" at Lower Right

2452	A1023	50c multi	.20	.20
2453	A1023	50c multi	.20	.20
2454	A1023	1p multi	.20	.20
2456	A1023	1p multi	.20	.20
2457	A1023	2.50p multi	.50	.25
2458	A1023	5p multi	.95	.50
2459	A1023	6.50p multi	1.25	.60
2460	A1023	6.50p multi	1.25	.60
2461	A1023	6.50p multi	1.25	.60
2462	A1023	7p multi	1.40	.70
2463	A1023	7p multi	1.40	.70
2464	A1023	7.50p multi	1.40	.70
2465	A1023	7.50p multi	1.40	.70
2466	A1023	10.50p multi	2.00	1.00
2467	A1023	10.50p multi	2.00	1.00
2468	A1023	13p multi	2.50	1.25
2469	A1023	13p multi	2.50	1.25
2470	A1023	13p multi	2.50	1.25
2471	A1023	14.50p multi	2.75	1.40
2472	A1023	30.50p multi	5.75	2.75

Inscribed "ROMO" at Lower Right

Booklet Stamp

2473	A1023	(15.75p) multi	3.00	1.50
a.		Booklet pane of 4	12.00	—
		Complete booklet, 4 #2473	12.00	
		Nos. 2452-2473 (21)	34.60	17.55

See No. 2399 for 7p Oceans stamp with "ROMO" inscription. No. 2473 is inscribed "Porte mundial" at lower left.

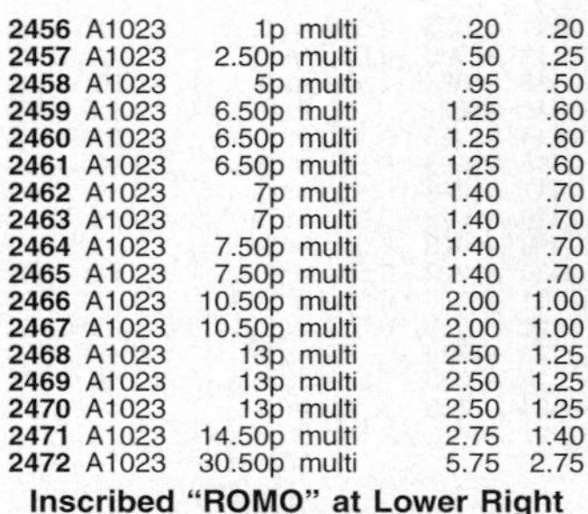

Minerals — A1129

No. 2474: a, Silver. b, Argentite. c, Marcasite, quartz and galena. d, Allende meteorite. e, Gold. f, Galena. g, Pyrargyrite. h, Gypsum. i, Manganocalcite. j, Barite. k, Stephanite. l, Red calcite. m, Calcite. n, Asbestos. o, Valencianite. p, Livingstoneite. q, Beryl. r, Smithsonite. s, Fluorite. t, Amethyst quartz. u, Azurite. v, Hemimorphite. w, Apatite. x, Pyromorphite. y, Actinolite with talc.

2005, Aug. 3 *Perf. 13¼x13*

2474		Sheet of 25	32.50	32.50
a.-y.	A1129	6.50p Any single	1.25	.60

Ignacio L. Vallarta (1830-94), Chief Justice A1130

2005, Aug. 23 *Perf. 13x13¼*

2475	A1130	7.50p multi	1.40	.70

Judicial Anniversaries — A1131

Designs: No. 2476, Federal Justice Council, 10th anniv. No. 2477, Supreme Court, 180th anniv. 10.50p, Supreme Justice Tribunal, 190th anniv.

2005, Aug. 23

2476	A1131	6.50p multi	1.25	.60
2477	A1131	6.50p multi	1.25	.60
2478	A1131	10.50p multi	2.00	1.00
a.		Souvenir sheet, #2476-2478	4.50	4.50

Expo 2005, Aichi, Japan — A1132

2005, Sept. 15 *Perf. 13¼x13*

2479	A1132	13p multi	2.40	1.25

Federal District Superior Court, 150th Anniv. — A1133

No. 2480 — Buildings from: a, 1855. b, 2005. c, 1964.

Illustration reduced.

2005, Oct. 6

2480		Horiz. strip of 3	4.00	4.00
a.-b.	A1133	6.50p Either single	1.25	.60
c.	A1133	7.50p multi	1.40	.70

World Post Day — A1134

2005, Oct. 10

2481	A1134	10.50p multi	2.00	1.00

United Nations Day A1135

2005, Oct. 24 *Perf. 13x13¼*

2482	A1135	10.50p multi	2.00	1.00

Jalisco Philatelic Organization, Cent. — A1136

2005, Oct. 27

2483	A1136	6.50p multi	1.25	.60

Lebanese in Mexico, 125th Anniv. — A1137

2005, Nov. 11 *Perf. 13¼x13*

2484	A1137	10.50p multi	2.00	1.00

Rodolfo Usigli (1905-79), Playwright — A1138

2005, Nov. 15

2485	A1138	7.50p multi	1.50	.75

San Juan de Ulua, Last Spanish Redoubt — A1139

2005, Nov. 23

2486	A1139	7.50p multi	1.50	.75

Gómez Palacio, Cent. — A1140

2005, Nov. 24

2487	A1140	6.50p multi	1.25	.60

Folk Art — A1141

Designs: 50c, Legged earthen pot. 1p, Lacquered wooden chest. 1.50p, Horn comb. 2p, Black clay jug. 2.50p, Paper bull. 5p, Silk shawl. No. 2494, Model. No. 2495, Glazed basin. No. 2496, Vase. No. 2497, Wooden mask. No. 2498, Tin rooster. 7p, Doll. 7.50p, Copper jar. 9p, Embroidered tablecloth. 10.50p, Woven basket. 13p, Silver pear. 14.50p, Amber marimba. 30.50p, Obsidian and opal turtle.

2005, Nov. 30 Litho. *Perf. 13¼x13*

2488	A1141	50c multi	.20	.20
2489	A1141	1p multi	.20	.20
2490	A1141	1.50p multi	.30	.20
2491	A1141	2p multi	.40	.20
2492	A1141	2.50p multi	.50	.25
2493	A1141	5p multi	.95	.50
2494	A1141	6.50p multi	1.25	.60
2495	A1141	6.50p multi	1.25	.60
2496	A1141	6.50p multi	1.25	.60
2497	A1141	6.50p multi	1.25	.60
2498	A1141	6.50p multi	1.25	.60
a.		Horiz. or vert. strip of 5, #2494-2498	6.25	3.00
2499	A1141	7p multi	1.40	.70
2500	A1141	7.50p multi	1.50	.75
2501	A1141	9p multi	1.75	.85
2502	A1141	10.50p multi	2.00	1.00
2503	A1141	13p multi	2.50	1.25
2504	A1141	14.50p multi	2.75	1.40
2505	A1141	30.50p multi	6.00	3.00
		Nos. 2488-2505 (18)	26.70	13.50

Nos. 2488-2500, 2502-2505 exist dated "2006," "2007," and "2008."

Christian Brothers in Mexico, Cent. — A1142

2005, Dec. 2 ***Perf. 13¼x13***
2506 A1142 6.50p multi 1.25 .60

Jews in Mexico, Cent. — A1143

2005, Dec. 6
2507 A1143 7.50p multi 1.40 .70

Indigenous Popular Culture A1144

2005, Dec. 16 ***Perf. 13x13¼***
2508 A1144 6.50p multi 1.25 .60

A1145

Christmas A1146

2005, Dec. 20
2509 A1145 6.50p multi 1.25 .60
2510 A1146 7.50p multi 1.40 .70

Souvenir Sheet

National Polytechnic Institute, 70th Anniv. — A1147

2006, Feb. 27 **Litho.** ***Perf. 13¼x13***
2511 A1147 10.50p multi 2.00 1.00

Wolfgang Amadeus Mozart (1756-91), Composer — A1148

2006, Mar. 31
2512 A1148 7.50p multi 1.40 .70

Central Library of National Autonomous University of Mexico, 50th Anniv. — A1149

2006, Apr. 5
2513 A1149 6.50p multi 1.25 .60

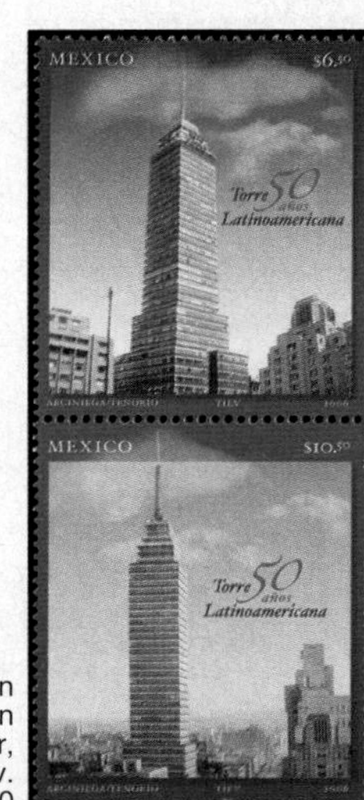

Latin American Tower, 50th Anniv. A1150

2006, Apr. 26 ***Perf. 13x13¼***
2514 6.50p multi 1.25 .60
2515 10.50p multi 2.00 1.00
a. A1150 Vert. pair, #2514-2515 3.25 1.60

Isidro Castillo Pérez, Educator — A1151

2006, May 15 ***Perf. 13¼x13***
2516 A1151 6.50p multi 1.25 .60

Vasconcelos Library — A1152

2006, May 16
2517 A1152 6.50p multi 1.25 .60

Intl. Women's Day A1153

2006, May 31 ***Perf. 13x13¼***
2518 A1153 6.50p multi 1.25 .60

2006 World Cup Soccer Championships, Germany — A1154

Illustration reduced.

2006, June 9 ***Perf. 13¼x13***
2519 A1154 13p multi 2.40 1.25

Souvenir Sheet

President Benito Juarez (1806-72) — A1155

2006, June 22 ***Perf. 13x13¼***
2520 A1155 13p multi 2.40 1.25

Navy Qualification Center, 50th Anniv. — A1156

2006, Aug. 11 **Litho.**
2521 A1156 6.50p multi 1.25 .60

Popular Television Characters — A1157

No. 2522: a, El Chayo del Ocho and barrel. b, El Chapulín Colorado with arms crossed. c, El Chayo del Ocho, door and window d, El Chapulín Colorado with arms spread. e, El Chayo del Ocho holding suspenders.

2006, Aug. 21 ***Perf. 13¼x13***
2522 Horiz. strip of 5 9.75 4.75
a. A1157 6.50p multi 1.25 .60
b. A1157 7.50p multi 1.40 .70
c. A1157 10.50p multi 1.90 .95
d. A1157 13p multi 2.40 1.25
e. A1157 14.50p multi 2.60 1.25

Intl. Year of Deserts and Desertification — A1158

2006, Sept. 20
2523 A1158 6.50p multi 1.25 .60

Souvenir Sheet

Dinosaurs — A1159

No. 2524: a, 6.50p, Muzzy (40x24mm). b, 7.50p, Sabinosaurus (40x48mm). c, 10.50p, Aramberri Monster (40x48mm).

2006, Sept. 29 ***Perf. 13x13¼***
2524 A1159 Sheet of 3, #a-c 4.50 2.25

Engineering Institute of National Autonomous University of Mexico, 50th Anniv. — A1160

2006, Oct. 5 ***Perf. 13¼x13***

2525 A1160 6.50p multi 1.25 .60

Miniature Sheet

First Mexican Stamps, 150th Anniv. — A1161

No. 2526 — Miguel Hidalgo y Costilla and inscription: a, Aguascalientes. b, Colima. c, Edo. de México. d, Michoacán. e, Nayarit. f, Quintana Roo. g, Tamaulipas. h, Baja California. i, Chiapas. j, Guanajuato. k, Morelos. l, Nuevo León. m, San Luis Potosí. n, Tlaxcala.

o, Baja California Sur. p, Chihuahua. q, Guerrero. r, Oaxaca. s, Sinaloa. t, Veracruz. u, Campeche. v, Distrito Federal. w, Hidalgo. x, Puebla. y, Sonora. z, Yucatán. aa, Coahuila. ab, Durango. ac, Jalisco. ad, Querétaro. ae, Tabasco. af, Zacatecas. ag, Estados Unidos Mexicanos (70x22mm).

Litho., Litho. & Embossed (50p)

2006, Oct. 9

2526	A1161	Sheet of 33	65.00	65.00
a.-g.		6.50p Any single	1.25	.60
h.-n.		7.50p Any single	1.40	.70
o.-t.		9p Any single	1.75	.85
u.-z.		10.50p Any single	1.90	.95
aa.-af.		13p Any single	2.40	1.25
ag.		50p multi	9.25	4.75

World Post Day — A1162

2006, Oct. 9 **Litho.**

2527 A1162 13p multi 2.40 1.25

Popular Television Characters — A1163

Xavier López "Chabelo": 6.50p, Boy with ice cream cone. 10.50p, Man seated.

2006, Oct. 30

2528	6.50p multi	1.25	.60
2529	10.50p multi	2.00	1.00
a.	A1163 Horiz. pair, #2528-2529	3.25	1.60

Letter Carrier's Day — A1164

Illustration reduced.

2006, Nov. 10

2530 A1164 6.50p multi 1.25 .60

Transformation of the Autonomous Scientific and Literary Institute, Autonomous University of the State of Mexico, 50th Anniv. — A1165

2006, Nov. 17 ***Perf. 13x13¼***

2531 A1165 10.50p multi 1.90 .95

"Children, The Future of Mexico" A1166

2006, Nov. 22

2532 A1166 10.50p multi + label 1.90 .95

Andrés Henestrosa, Writer, Cent. of Birth — A1167

2006, Nov. 23 ***Perf. 13¼x13***

2533 A1167 9p multi 1.75 .85

Edmundo O'Gorman (1906-95), Historian A1168

2006, Nov. 28 ***Perf. 13x13¼***

2534 A1168 10.50p multi 1.90 .95

Mexico in Intl. Telecommunications Union, Cent. — A1169

2006, Nov. 30 ***Perf. 13¼x13***

2535 A1169 7p multi 1.40 .70

Christmas A1170

Children's art by: 7.50p, Ricardo Salas Pineda. 10.50p, Maria José Goytia.

2006, Dec. 6 **Litho.** ***Perf. 13x13¼***

2536	7.50p multi	1.40	.70
2537	10.50p multi	2.00	1.00
a.	A1170 Pair, #2536-2537	3.40	1.70

El Universal Newspaper, 90th Anniv. — A1171

2006, Dec. 22 ***Perf. 13¼x13***

2538 A1171 10.50p multi + label 2.00 1.00

Teacher's Day — A1172

2007, May 15

2539 A1172 7.50p multi 1.40 .70

Frida Kahlo (1907-54), Painter A1173

2007, June 13 ***Perf. 13x13¼***

2540 A1173 13p multi 2.40 1.25

Scouting, Cent. — A1174

Designs: 6.50p, Dove and compass. 10.50p, Centenary emblem, compass.

2007, June 30 ***Perf. 13¼x13***

2541	6.50p multi	1.25	.60
2542	10.50p multi	2.00	1.00
a.	A1174 Pair, #2541-2542	3.25	1.60

Miniature Sheet

Chichén Itzá — A1175

No. 2543: a, Pelota ring, Jaguar Temple, serpent head. b, Colonnade. c, Observatory. d, Castillo, jaguar head. e, Chac Mool.

2007, July 13

2543	A1175	Sheet of 5 + label	9.25	4.75
a.-b.		6.50p Either single	1.25	.60
c.		10.50p multi	1.90	.95
d.-e.		13p Either single	2.40	1.25

State of Colima, 150th Anniv. — A1176

2007, July 19

2544 A1176 10.50p multi 1.90 .95

Miniature Sheet

Postal Headquarters Building, Cent. — A1177

No. 2545: a, Nude boy writing (40x23mm). b, Nude boy touching item on pedestal (40x23mm). c, Two nude boys, chalice (40x23mm). d, Two nude boys, press (40x23mm). e, Boy, gear (40x23mm). f, Clock and machinery (40x23mm). g, Sculpture of UPU emblem, photographs (80x23mm). h, Mercury and caduceus (40x23mm). i, Two nude boys (40x23mm). j, Two nude boys, diff. (40x23mm). k, Seated nude boy with arms extended, holding bird (40x23mm). l, Seated nude boy holding bird (40x23mm). m, Stairway (40x48mm). n, Glass ceiling (40x48). o, Stairways (80x48mm). p, Building exterior (80x48mm).

2007, Aug. 1 *Perf. 13x13¼*

2545	A1177	Sheet of 16	35.00	35.00
a.-b.		5.50p Either single	1.00	.50
c.-g.		6.50p Any single	1.25	.60
h.-i.		9p Either single	1.75	.85
j.		10.50p multi	1.90	.95
k.-l.		13p Either single	2.40	1.25
m.-n.		14.50p Either single	2.75	1.40
o.		15.50p multi	3.00	1.50
p.		39.50p multi	7.25	3.50

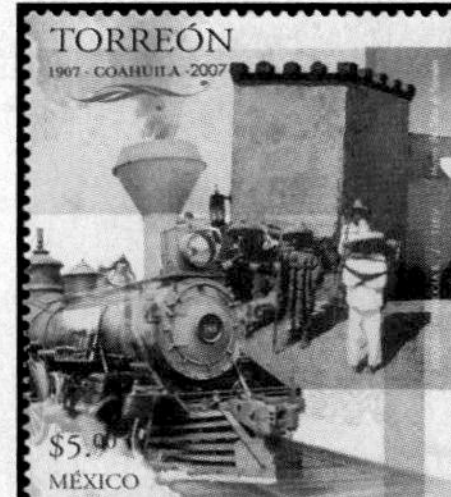

Torreón, Cent. A1178

No. 2546: a, Locomotive, Torreón Station Museum. b, Bridge, church spires. c, Isauro Martínez Theater. d, Statue of Jesus Christ. e, Bilbao Dunes, Tower.

2007, Sept. 5

2546	Horiz. strip of 5	8.75	4.50
a.	A1178 5p multi	.90	.45
b.-c.	A1178 6.50p Either single	1.25	.60
d.-e.	A1178 14.50p Either single	2.60	1.25

Cultural Forum, Monterrey A1179

No. 2547: a, Dove and hand. b, Child and books. c, Children, windmill, hand picking orange. d, Woman and artist. e, Sculpture and figurines.

2007, Aug. 20 Litho. *Perf. 13x13¼*

2547	Horiz. strip of 5	9.00	4.50
a.	A1179 7p multi	1.25	.60
b.-c.	A1179 7.50p Either single	1.40	.70
d.-e.	A1179 13p Either single	2.40	1.25

Central University City Campus of National Autonomous University of Mexico World Heritage Site — A1180

No. 2548: a, Olympic Stadium and artwork. b, University building, University Library. c, Rectory Building.

2007, Sept. 21

2548	Horiz. strip of 3	5.25	2.75
a.	A1180 6.50p multi	1.25	.60
b.	A1180 9p multi	1.60	.80
c.	A1180 13p multi	2.40	1.25

University of Baja California, 50th Anniv. A1181

2007, Oct. 1

2549	A1181 7.50p multi	1.40	.70

Ozone Layer Protection A1182

No. 2550: a, Doves, tree, leaves. b, Doves, Earth in hands.

2007, Oct. 1

2550	A1182 Vert. pair	4.00	2.00
a.	7p multi	1.25	.60
b.	14.50p multi	2.75	1.40

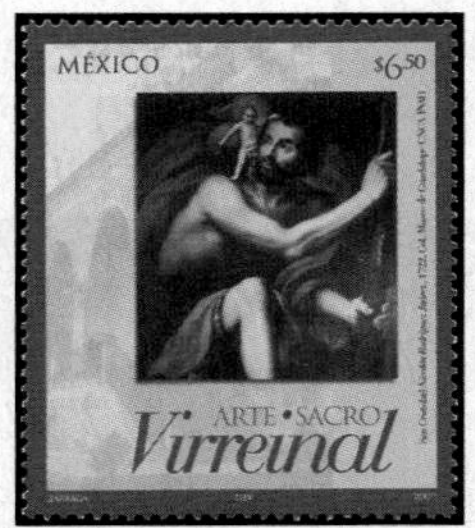

St. Christopher, by Nicolás Rodríguez Juárez — A1183

2007, Oct. 3

2551	A1183 6.50p multi	1.25	.60

Autonomous University of Coahuila, 50th Anniv. — A1184

2007, Oct. 4 *Perf. 13¼x13*

2552	A1184 7.50p multi	1.40	.70

World Post Day A1185

No. 2553 — Envelope with denomination in: a, Yellow. b, Black.

2007, Oct. 9 *Perf. 13x13¼*

2553	A1185 Vert. pair	3.25	1.60
a.	7p multi	1.25	.60
b.	10.50p multi	2.00	1.00

Rights of People With Disabilities A1186

2007, Oct. 11

2554	A1186 6.50p multi	1.25	.60

Miniature Sheet

Francisco Gabilondo Soler (1907-90), Composer of Children's Songs — A1187

No. 2555: a, Turtle, giraffe, peacock (Caminito de la Escuela). b, Dog, camel, mouse (Caminito de la Escuela). c, Duck and ducklings (La Patita). d, Girl and mouse (La Muñeca Fea). e, Cat with guitar (Gato de Barrio). f, King and cakes (Bombón I). g, Three pigs and cakes (Cochinitos Dormilones). h, Three pigs in bed (Cochinitos Dormilones). i, Old woman and cat (Di Por Que). j, Mouse in cowboy's clothes (El Ratón Vaquero). k, Boy eating watermelon (Negrito Sandía). l, Cricket holding stick (Cri-Cri). m, Soler. n, Cricket at music stand (Cri-Cri). o, Ant and fountain (El Chorrito).

2007, Oct. 11 *Perf. 13¼x13*

2555	A1187 Sheet of 15	18.50	18.50
a.-b.	5p Either single	.90	.45
c.-k.	6.50p Any single	1.25	.60
l.-n.	7p Any single	1.25	.60
o.	7.50p multi	1.40	.70

Degrees in Administration, 50th Anniv. — A1188

2007, Oct. 19 *Perf. 13x13¼*

2556	A1188 7.50p multi	1.40	.70

Cuauhtemoc Sailing School — A1189

2007, Nov. 4 *Perf. 13¼x13*

2557	A1189 7.50p multi	1.40	.70

A1190

A1191

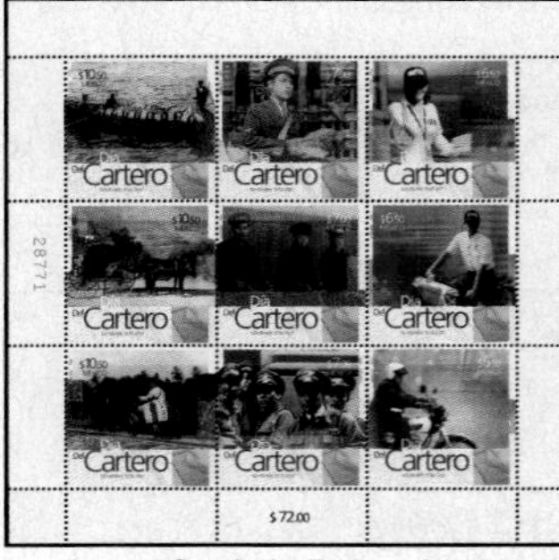

Letter Carrier's Day — A1192

No. 2559: a, Girl writing letter, letter carrier on bicycle. b, Girl mailing letter in mailbox. c, Letter carrier on bicycle. d, Letter carrier delivering letter.

No. 2560: a, Female letter carrier. b, Letter carrier on bicycle. c, Letter carrier on motorcycle. d, Letter carrier with mail bag. e, Three letter carriers. f, Five letter carriers. g, Letter carriers on rowboat. h, Horse-drawn carriage. i, Letter carrier and mail bag on railway hand car.

Illustrations A1191, A1192 reduced.

2007, Nov. 12 *Perf. 13*

2558	A1190	10.50p multi	2.00	1.00
2559	A1191	Block of 4	5.00	2.50
a.-d.		6.50p Any single	1.25	.60
2560	A1192	Sheet of 9	13.50	13.50
a.-c.		6.50p Any single	1.25	.60
d.-f.		7p Any single	1.25	.60
g.-i.		10.50p Any single	2.00	1.00

Mountains — A1193

Designs: No. 2561, Mt. Minya Konka, People's Republic of China. No. 2562, Popocatépetl, Mexico.

2007, Nov. 22 Litho. *Perf. 13¼x13*

2561	A1193 6.50p multi	1.25	.60
2562	A1193 6.50p multi	1.25	.60

See People's Republic of China Nos. 3635-3636.

Intl. Day Against Violence Towards Women — A1194

2007, Nov. 26

2563	A1194 7p multi	1.40	.70

Mariano Otero (1817-50), Judicial and Constitutional Reformer — A1195

2007, Nov. 27 *Perf. 13x13¼*

2564	A1195 10.50p multi	2.00	1.00

Trials of Amparo, legal protection of individual constitutional guarantees in federal courts.

Miniature Sheet

Monte Albán Archaeological Site — A1196

No. 2565: a, Scribe of Cuilapan. b, Head with jaguar helmet. c, Building II, Cocijo urn. d, Building I, Central Plaza, Cocijo urn. e, Observatory, Southern Platform, Central Plaza.

2007, Dec. 11 *Perf. 13¼x13*

2565	A1196 Sheet of 5 + label	9.50	4.75
a.-b.	6.50p Either single	1.25	.60
c.	10.50p multi	2.00	1.00
d.-e.	13p Either single	2.40	1.25

Christmas A1197

2007, Dec. 12 *Perf. 13*

2566	Horiz. strip of 5	10.00	5.00
a.	A1197 6.50p Candle	1.25	.60
b.	A1197 7p Bell	1.40	.70
c.	A1197 10.50p Angel	2.00	1.00
d.	A1197 13.50p Magi	2.50	1.25
e.	A1197 14.50p Holy Family	2.75	1.40

Miniature Sheet

Dogs — A1198

No. 2567: a, Two English bulldogs. b, Two rottweilers. c, Two boxers. d, Two beagles. e, Head of English Bulldog. f, Head of Rottweiler. g, Head of boxer. h, Head of beagle. i, English bulldog. j, Rottweiler. k, Boxer. l, Beagle.

2007, Dec. 14

2567	A1198 Sheet of 12	19.00	9.50
a.-d.	6.50p Any single	1.25	.60
e.-h.	7p Any single	1.40	.70
i.-l.	10.50p Any single	2.00	1.00

Jesús García Corona (1883-1907), Heroic Railroad Engineer — A1199

Illustration reduced.

2007, Dec. 17 *Perf. 13¼x13*

2568	A1199 10.50p multi	2.00	1.00

Satélite Towers, Naucalpan, 50th Anniv. A1200

2007, Dec. 19 *Perf. 13x13¼*

2569	A1200 6.50p multi	1.25	.60

El Cajón Dam — A1201

Aerial view of: 7p, Open spillway. 13p, Dam. Illustration reduced.

2007, Dec. 28 *Perf. 13¼x13*

2570	A1201 7p multi	1.40	.70
2571	A1201 13p multi	2.40	1.25

Letter and Heart A1202

2008, Jan. 29 Litho. *Perf. 13½x13¼*

2572	A1202 6.50p multi	1.25	.60

Mother's Day A1203

2008, May 2 *Perf. 13x13¼*

2573	A1203 6.50p multi	1.25	.60

Pres. Miguel Alemán Valdés (1900-83) A1204

2008, May 14 *Perf. 13x13¼*

2574	A1204 6.50p multi	1.25	.60

The Fruits, by Diego Rivera A1205

2008, May 15

2575	A1205 6.50p multi	1.25	.60

Teacher's Day.

Miniature Sheet

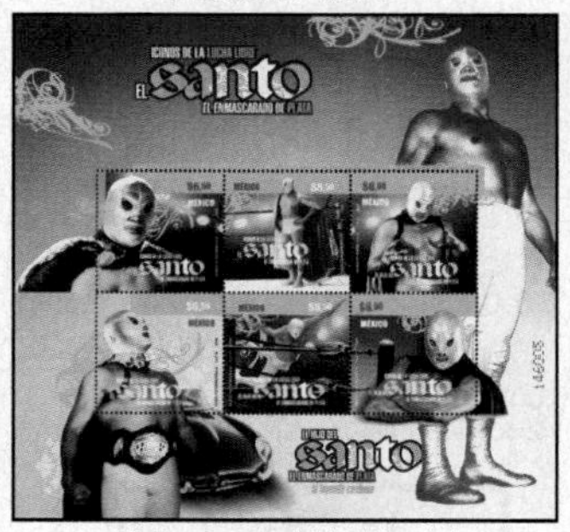

El Santo and El Hijo del Santo — A1206

No. 2576: a, El Santo wearing silver mask and robe. b, El Santo in ring. c, El Hijo del Santo with hands outstretched. d, El Santo with automobile. e, El Hijo del Santo in ring. f, El Hijo del Santo with arms crossed.

2008, June 17 *Perf. 13*

2576	A1206 Sheet of 6	7.50	3.75
a.-f.	6.50p Any single	1.25	.60

El Santo (Rodolfo Guzmán Huerta, 1917-84), El Hijo del Santo (Jorge Guzmán), wrestling legends and film stars.

2008 Summer Olympics, Beijing A1207

Designs: No. 2577, Rowing. No. 2578, Weight lifting. No. 2579, Rhythmic gymnastics.

2008, Aug. 8 *Perf. 13*

2577	A1207 6.50p multi	1.25	.60
2578	A1207 6.50p multi	1.25	.60
2579	A1207 6.50p multi	1.25	.60
	Nos. 2577-2579 (3)	3.75	1.80

Electoral Justice — A1208

2008, Aug. 19 Litho. *Perf. 13¼x13*

2580	A1208 6.50p multi	1.25	.60

Mexico Post Emblem — A1209

2008, Sept. 8

2581	A1209 6.50p multi	1.25	.60

Fight for Mexican Independence, Bicent. — A1210

Designs: No. 2582, Ignacio Allende (1769-1811), revolutionary leader. No. 2583, Josefa Ortíz de Dominguez (1768-1829), revolutionary leader. No. 2584, José María Morelos y Pavón (1765-1815), revolutionary leader. No. 2585, Battle of Monte de las Cruces, 1810, horiz. No. 2586, Battle of Alhóndiga de Granditas, 1810, horiz. No. 2587, Meeting of Miguel Hidalgo and Morelos, horiz. No. 2588, Querétaro Conspiracy, horiz. No. 2589, Francisco Primo de Verdad y Ramos (1760-1808), promoter of Mexican independence, horiz. No. 2590, Miguel Hidalgo and Cry of Independence. No. 2591, Crowd on Mexico City Alameda.

2008, Sept. 15 *Perf. 13x13¼*

2582	A1210 6.50p multi	1.25	.60
2583	A1210 6.50p multi	1.25	.60
2584	A1210 6.50p multi	1.25	.60
	Perf. 13¼x13		
2585	A1210 6.50p multi	1.25	.60
	Size: 71x30mm		
2586	A1210 6.50p multi	1.25	.60
2587	A1210 6.50p multi	1.25	.60
2588	A1210 6.50p multi	1.25	.60
2589	A1210 6.50p multi	1.25	.60
	Nos. 2582-2589 (8)	10.00	4.80
	Imperf		
	Size:80x80mm		
2590	A1210 10.50p multi	1.90	.95
2591	A1210 10.50p multi	1.90	.95

Miniature Sheet

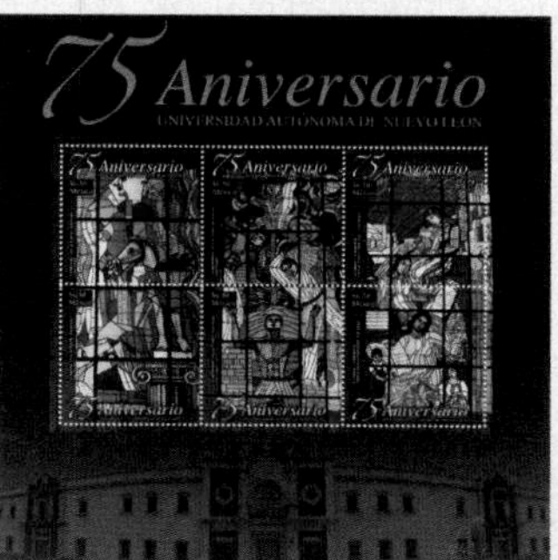

Autonomous University of Nuevo León, 75th Anniv. — A1211

No. 2592 — Stained-glass windows by Roberto Montenegro: a, Top of "La Historia." b, Top of "La Agricultura." c, Top of "La Ciencia y la Sabiduría." d, Bottom of "La Historia." e, Bottom of "La Agricultura." f, Bottom of "La Ciencia y la Sabiduría."

2008, Sept. 25 *Perf. 13*

2592 A1211 Sheet of 6 7.50 7.50
a.-f. 6.50p Any single 1.25 .60

World Post Day A1212

2008, Oct. 9 *Perf. 13x13¼*

2593 A1212 10.50p multi 1.60 .80

Flowers — A1213

No. 2594: a, Hylocereus undulatus. b, Curcubita pepo.
Illustration reduced.

2008, Oct. 10 *Perf. 13*

2594 A1213 Horiz. pair 2.00 1.00
a.-b. 6.50p Either single 1.00 .50

Juarez Autonomous University of Tabasco, 50th Anniv. — A1214

2008, Nov. 3 **Litho.** *Perf. 13x13¼*

2595 A1214 6.50p multi 1.00 .50

Miniature Sheet

Letter Carrier's Day — A1215

No. 2596: a, Letter carrier with large shoulder pouch. b, Letter carrier on bicycle. c, Letter carrier on motorcycle with sidecar. d, Letter carrier on motor scooter. e, Postal service automobile. f, Postal truck. g, Letter carriers, bicycles and truck. h, Postal van, letter carrier on bicycle.

2008, Nov. 12 *Perf. 13*

2596 A1215 Sheet of 8 7.75 7.75
a.-h. 6.50p Any single .95 .50

National Employment Service — A1216

2008, Nov. 19 *Perf. 13¼x13½*

2597 A1216 6.50p multi .95 .50

Mexican Revolution, Cent. (in 2011) A1217

Designs: No. 2598, José María Pino Suárez (1869-1913), politician. No. 2599, Aquiles Serdán (1876-1910), politician. No. 2600, Ricardo Flores Magón (1874-1922), anarchist, and Regeneración Newspaper. No. 2601, Mexican Liberal Party. No. 2602, Cananea Strike. No. 2603, Railway system. No. 2604, Rio Blanco Strike. No. 2605, Revolutionary Junta of Puebla.

No. 2606, Triumphal Entry of Francisco I. Madero. No. 2607, Tienda de raya (company store).

2008, Nov. 20 *Perf. 13x13¼*

2598 A1217 6.50p multi .95 .50
2599 A1217 6.50p multi .95 .50
2600 A1217 6.50p multi .95 .50

Size: 71x30mm

Perf. 13¼x13

2601 A1217 6.50p multi .95 .50
2602 A1217 6.50p multi .95 .50
2603 A1217 6.50p multi .95 .50
2604 A1217 6.50p multi .95 .50
2605 A1217 6.50p multi .95 .50
Nos. 2598-2605 (8) 7.60 4.00

Imperf

Size: 80x80mm

2606 A1217 10.50p multi 1.60 .80
2607 A1217 10.50p multi 1.60 .80

Parque La Venta Archaeological Museum, La Venta — A1218

2008, Dec. 4 *Perf. 13*

2608 A1218 6.50p multi .95 .50

Christmas A1219

Designs: 6.50p, Adoration of the Shepherds, by Cristóbal de Villalpando. 10.50p, Adoration of the Magi, by unknown artist.

2008, Dec. 10 *Perf. 13x13¼*

2609 A1219 6.50p multi 1.00 .50
2610 A1219 10.50p multi 1.60 .80
a. Horiz. pair, #2609-2610 2.60 1.30

Dr. Gonzalo Aguirre Beltrán (1908-96), Anthropologist — A1220

2008, Dec. 16 *Perf. 13¼x13*

2611 A1220 6.50p multi .95 .50

Miniature Sheet

Palenque Archaeological Site — A1221

No. 2612: a, Mayan hieroglyphic cartouches, tomb, seated figure. b, Jade mask, skull mask, tablet. c, Palace and tower. d, Temple of the Sun, Temples 14 and 15. e, Temple of Inscriptions, incense holder.

2008, Dec. 19 **Litho.**

2612 A1221 Sheet of 5 + label 7.25 7.25
a.-b. 6.50p Either single .95 .50
c. 10.50p multi 1.50 .75
d.-e. 13p Either single 1.90 .95

Mexican Academy of Film Ariel Awards, 50th Anniv. — A1222

2008, Dec. 24 *Perf. 13¼x13*

2613 A1222 6.50p multi .95 .50

SEMI-POSTAL STAMPS

Nos. 622, 614 Surcharged in Red

1918, Dec. 25 **Unwmk.** *Perf. 12*

B1 A72 5c + 3c ultra 20.00 25.00

Rouletted 14½

B2 A73 10c + 5c blue 25.00 25.00
Set, never hinged 57.50

AIR POST STAMPS

Eagle AP1

Unwmk.

1922, Apr. 2 **Engr.** *Perf. 12*

C1 AP1 50c blue & red brn 67.50 50.00
Never hinged 85.00
a. 50c dark blue & claret ('29) 90.00 90.00
Never hinged 125.00

See #C2-C3. For overprints and surcharges see #C47-C48, CO1-CO2B, CO18-CO19, CO29.

1927, Oct. 13 Wmk. 156

C2	AP1 50c dk bl & red brn	.75	.25
	Never hinged	1.00	
a.	50c dark blue & claret ('29)	.75	.25
	Never hinged	1.25	
b.	Vert. strip of 3, imperf. btwn.	*7,500.*	

The vignettes of Nos. C1a and C2a fluoresce a bright rose red under UV light.

1928

C3	AP1 25c brn car & gray brn	.45	.20
C4	AP1 25c dk grn & gray brn	.45	.20
	Set, never hinged	1.25	

On May 3, 1929, certain proofs or essays were sold at the post office in Mexico, D. F. They were printed in different colors from those of the regularly issued stamps. There were 7 varieties perf. and 2 imperf. and a total of 225 copies. They were sold with the understanding that they were for collections but the majority of them were used on air mail sent out that day.

Capt. Emilio Carranza and his Airplane "México Excelsior"
AP2

1929, June 19

C5	AP2 5c ol grn & sepia	1.10	.65
C6	AP2 10c sep & brn red	1.25	.70
C7	AP2 15c vio & dk grn	3.00	1.25
C8	AP2 20c brown & blk	1.25	.75
C9	AP2 50c brn red & blk	7.50	5.00
C10	AP2 1p black & dk brn	15.00	10.00
	Nos. C5-C10 (6)	29.10	18.35
	Set, never hinged	57.50	

1st anniv. of death of Carranza (1905-28).
For overprints see Nos. C29-C36, C40-C44.

Coat of Arms and Airplane
AP3

1929-34 *Perf. 11½, 12*

C11	AP3 10c violet	.35	.20
C12	AP3 15c carmine	1.35	.20
C13	AP3 20c brown olive	37.50	1.25
C14	AP3 30c gray black	.20	.20
C15	AP3 35c blue green	.35	.25
a.	Imperf., pair	1,200.	
C16	AP3 50c red brn ('34)	1.25	.65
C17	AP3 1p blk & dk bl	1.25	.65
C18	AP3 5p claret & dp bl	4.00	3.50
C19	AP3 10p vio & ol brn	6.00	7.00
	Nos. C11-C19 (9)	52.25	13.90
	Set, never hinged	75.00	

1930-32 *Rouletted 13, 13½*

C20	AP3 5c lt blue ('32)	.35	.20
C21	AP3 10c violet	.35	.20
C22	AP3 15c carmine	.35	.20
a.	15c rose carmine	.40	.20
C23	AP3 20c brown olive	1.50	.20
a.	20c brown	.50	.20
b.	20c yellow brown	.50	.20
c.	Horiz. pair, imperf. btwn.		
C24	AP3 25c violet	.95	.80
C25	AP3 50c red brown	.90	.75
	Nos. C20-C25 (6)	4.40	2.35
	Set, never hinged	5.50	

Trial impressions of No. C20 were printed in orange but were never sold at post offices.
See Nos. C62-C64, C75. For overprints and surcharges see Nos. C28, C38-C39, C46, C49-C50, CO17, CO20-CO28, CO30.

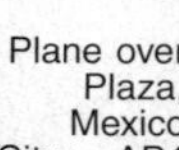

Plane over Plaza, Mexico City — AP4

1929, Dec. 10 Wmk. 156 *Perf. 12*

C26	AP4 20c black violet	1.25	1.00
C27	AP4 40c slate green	85.00	75.00
	Set, never hinged	125.00	

Aviation Week, Dec. 10-16.
For overprint see No. CO11.

No. C21 Overprinted in Red

1930, Apr. 20 *Rouletted 13, 13½*

C28	AP3 10c violet	2.00	1.25
	Never hinged	2.25	

National Tourism Congress at Mexico, D. F., Apr. 20-27, 1930.

Nos. C5 and C7 Overprinted

1930, Sept. 1 *Perf. 12*

C29	AP2 5c ol grn & sepia	5.50	4.50
a.	Double overprint	225.00	*250.00*
C30	AP2 15c violet & dk grn	9.00	7.75
	Set, never hinged	45.00	

Nos. C5-C10 Overprinted

1930, Dec. 18

C31	AP2 5c ol grn & sepia	7.00	6.50
C32	AP2 10c sep & brn red	3.50	4.00
a.	Double overprint	50.00	50.00
C33	AP2 15c vio & dk grn	7.50	7.00
C34	AP2 20c brown & blk	7.00	5.50
C35	AP2 50c brn red & blk	14.00	10.00
C36	AP2 1p black & brn	4.00	2.75
	Nos. C31-C36 (6)	43.00	35.75
	Set, never hinged	130.00	

Plane over Flying Field
AP5

1931, May 15 Engr. *Perf. 12*

C37	AP5 25c lake	4.00	4.50
	Never hinged	4.50	
a.	Imperf., pair	80.00	72.50
	Never hinged	100.00	

Aeronautic Exhibition of the Aero Club of Mexico. Of the 25c, 15c paid air mail postage and 10c went to a fund to improve the Mexico City airport.
For surcharge see No. C45.

Nos. C13 and C23 Surcharged in Red

1931

C38	AP3 15c on 20c brn ol	32.50	35.00
	Never hinged	40.00	

Rouletted 13, 13½

C39	AP3 15c on 20c brn ol	.30	.20
	Never hinged	.35	
a.	Inverted surcharge	150.00	
b.	Double surcharge	150.00	
c.	Pair, one without surcharge	350.00	

Nos. C5 to C9 Overprinted

1932, July 13 *Perf. 12*

C40	AP2 5c ol grn & sep	6.00	5.00
a.	Imperf., pair	50.00	50.00
C41	AP2 10c sep & brn red	5.00	3.00
a.	Imperf., pair	50.00	50.00
C42	AP2 15c vio & bk grn	6.00	4.00
a.	Imperf., pair	50.00	50.00
C43	AP2 20c brn & blk	5.00	2.75
a.	Imperf., pair	50.00	50.00
C44	AP2 50c brn red & blk	35.00	35.00
a.	Imperf., pair	50.00	50.00
	Nos. C40-C44 (5)	57.00	49.75
	Set, never hinged	160.00	
	Set, C40a-C44a never hinged	300.00	

Death of Capt. Emilio Carranza, 4th anniv.

No. C37 Surcharged

1932

C45	AP5 20c on 25c lake	.70	.30
	Never hinged	2.00	
a.	Imperf., pair	72.50	72.50
	Never hinged	90.00	

No. C13 Surcharged

C46	AP3 30c on 20c brn ol	30.00	30.00
	Never hinged	40.00	

Similar Surcharge on Nos. C3 and C4

C47	AP1 40c on 25c (#C3)	.90	.90
	Never hinged	1.25	
a.	Inverted surcharge	*11,000.*	
C48	AP1 40c on 25c (#C4)	50.00	50.00
	Never hinged	60.00	

Surcharged on Nos. C23 and C24
Rouletted 13, 13½

C49	AP3 30c on 20c brn ol	.35	.20
	Never hinged	.50	
a.	Inverted surcharge		*2,750.*
C50	AP3 80c on 25c dl vio	1.75	1.25
	Never hinged	2.50	
	Nos. C45-C50 (6)	83.70	82.65

Palace of Fine Arts — AP6

1933, Oct. 1 Engr. *Perf. 12*

C51	AP6 20c dk red & dl vio	3.50	1.40
C52	AP6 30c dk brn & dl vio	6.75	6.00
C53	AP6 1p grnsh blk & dl vio	67.50	70.00
	Nos. C51-C53 (3)	77.75	77.40
	Set, never hinged	180.00	

21st Intl. Cong. of Statistics and the cent. of the Mexican Soc. of Geography and Statistics.

National University Issue

Nevado de Toluca
AP7

Pyramids of the Sun and Moon
AP8

View of Ajusco
AP9

Volcanoes Popocatepetl and Iztaccíhuatl — AP10

Bridge over Tepecayo
AP11

Chapultepec Fortress — AP12

Orizaba Volcano (Citlaltépetl) — AP13

Mexican Girl and Aztec Calendar Stone
AP14

1934, Sept. 1 Wmk. 156 *Perf. 10½*

C54	AP7 20c orange	5.00	5.00
C55	AP8 30c red lilac & vio	9.00	9.00
C56	AP9 50c ol grn & bis brn	11.00	*12.00*
C57	AP10 75c blk & yel grn	12.00	*15.00*
C58	AP11 1p blk & pck bl	15.00	15.00
C59	AP12 5p bis brn & dk bl	75.00	*95.00*
C60	AP13 10p indigo & mar	240.00	175.00
C61	AP14 20p brn & brn lake	1,250.	*1,300.*
	Nos. C54-C61 (8)	1,617.	1,626.
	Set, never hinged	2,600.	

Type of 1929-34

1934-35 *Perf. 10½, 10½x10*

C62	AP3 20c olive green	.35	.20
a.	20c slate	500.00	500.00
	Never hinged	600.00	
C63	AP3 30c slate	.40	.40
C64	AP3 50c red brn ('35)	2.00	2.00
	Nos. C62-C64 (3)	2.75	2.60
	Set, never hinged	3.50	

Symbols of Air Service
AP15

Tláloc, God of Water (Quetzalcóatl Temple) — AP16

Orizaba Volcano (Citlaltépetl) AP17

"Eagle Man" AP18

Symbolical of Flight AP19

Aztec Bird-Man — AP20

Allegory of Flight and Pyramid of the Sun AP21

"Eagle Man" and Airplanes AP22

Natives Looking at Airplane and Orizaba Volcano — AP23

Imprint: "Oficina Impresora de Hacienda-Mexico"

Perf. 10½x10, 10x10½

1934-35 Wmk. 156

C65 AP15 5c black .45 .20
a. Imperf., pair
C66 AP16 10c red brown .90 .20
C67 AP17 15c gray green 1.25 .20
a. Imperf., pair *400.00*
C68 AP18 20c brown car 3.00 .20
a. 20c lake 4.00 .20
b. Imperf., pair
C69 AP19 30c brown olive .70 .20
C70 AP20 40c blue ('35) 1.25 .20
C71 AP21 50c green 2.50 .20
a. Imperf., pair 275.00
C72 AP22 1p gray grn & red brn 3.50 .20
C73 AP23 5p dk car & blk 7.25 .70
Nos. C65-C73 (9) 20.80 2.30
Set, never hinged 30.00

See Nos. C76A, C80, C81, C132-C140, C170-C177A. For overprint see No. C74.

No. C68 Overprinted in Violet

1935, Apr. 16

C74 AP18 20c lake *3,250. 4,000.*
Never hinged *5,000.*

Amelia Earhart's goodwill flight to Mexico.

Arms-Plane Type of 1929-34

1935 Wmk. 248 *Perf. 10½x10*

C75 AP3 30c slate 3.00 5.00
Never hinged 3.50

Francisco I. Madero AP24

1935, Nov. 20 Wmk. 156

C76 AP24 20c scarlet .30 .25
Never hinged .45

Plan of San Luis, 25th anniv. See No. C76B.

Eagle Man Type of 1934-35

1936 Wmk. 260

C76A AP18 20c lake *4,500.* 60.00
Never hinged 6,000.

Madero Type of 1935

C76B AP24 20c scarlet *12,500.*

Tasquillo Bridge AP25

Corona River Bridge AP26

Bridge on Nuevo Laredo Highway AP27

Wmk. 248

1936, July 1 Photo. *Perf. 14*

C77 AP25 10c slate bl & lt bl .35 .20
C78 AP26 20c dl vio & org .35 .20
C79 AP27 40c dk bl & dk grn .55 .50
Nos. C77-C79 (3) 1.25 .90
Set, never hinged 2.25

Opening of Nuevo Laredo Highway.

Eagle Man Type of 1934-35

Perf. 10½x10

1936, June 18 Engr. Unwmk.

C80 AP18 20c brown carmine 10.00 7.00
Never hinged 22.50

Imprint: "Talleres de Imp. de Est. y Valores-Mexico"

1937 Wmk. 156 Photo. *Perf. 14*

C81 AP18 20c rose red 1.25 .20
Never hinged 1.50
a. 20c brown carmine 1.50 .20
Never hinged 2.00
b. 20c dark carmine 2.00 .20
Never hinged 4.50
c. Imperf., pair 37.50 50.00
Never hinged 60.00

There are two sizes of watermark 156. No. C81c was not regularly issued.

Cavalryman AP28

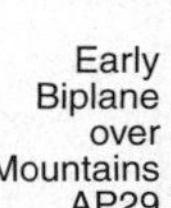

Early Biplane over Mountains AP29

Venustiano Carranza on Horseback AP30

1938, Mar. 26

C82 AP28 20c org red & bl .50 .20
C83 AP29 40c bl & org red .75 *1.00*
C84 AP30 1p bl & bis brn 4.75 2.25
Nos. C82-C84 (3) 6.00 3.45
Set, never hinged 18.00

Plan of Guadalupe, 25th anniversary.

Reconstructed edifices of Chichén Itzá — AP31

Designs: Nos. C85, C86, The Zócalo and Cathedral, Mexico City. Nos. C89, C90, View of Acapulco.

1938, July 1

C85 AP31 20c carmine rose .35 .25
C86 AP31 20c purple 20.00 10.00
C87 AP31 40c brt green 10.00 5.00
C88 AP31 40c dark green 10.00 5.00
C89 AP31 1p light blue 10.00 5.00
C90 AP31 1p slate blue 10.00 5.00
Nos. C85-C90 (6) 60.35 30.25
Set, never hinged 175.00

16th Intl. Cong. of Planning & Housing.

Statue of José María Morelos — AP34

1939 Engr. *Perf. 10½*

C91 AP34 20c green .70 .50
Never hinged 1.00
C92 AP34 40c red violet 2.00 1.25
Never hinged 5.00
C93 AP34 1p vio brn & car 1.40 1.00
Never hinged 1.75
Nos. C91-C93 (3) 4.10 2.75
Set, never hinged 7.75

New York World's Fair. Released in New York May 2, in Mexico May 24.

Type of 1939 Overprinted in Cerise

1939, May 23

C93A AP34 20c blue & red 425.00 425.00
Never hinged 450.00

Issued for the flight of Francisco Sarabia from Mexico City to New York on May 25.

Statue of Pioneer Woman, Ponca City, OK — AP35

1939, May 17

C94 AP35 20c gray brown 1.00 .40
Never hinged 1.50
C95 AP35 40c slate green 2.50 1.25
Never hinged 8.00
C96 AP35 1p violet 1.60 .90
Never hinged 2.00
Nos. C94-C96 (3) 5.10 2.55
Set, never hinged 11.50

Tulsa World Philatelic Convention.

First Engraving Made in Mexico, 1544 — AP36

First Work of Legislation Printed in America, 1563 — AP37

Designs: 1p, Reproduction of oldest preserved Mexican printing.

1939, Sept. 7 Wmk. 156

C97 AP36 20c slate blue .25 .20
a. Unwmkd. 50.00
C98 AP37 40c slate green .65 .20
a. Imperf., pair *700.00*
C99 AP37 1p dk brn & car 1.10 .70
Nos. C97-C99 (3) 2.00 1.10
Set, never hinged 2.50

400th anniversary of printing in Mexico.

Alternated Perforations

Nos. 763-766, 774-779, 792-795, 801-804, 806-811, 813-818, C100-C102, C111-C116, C123-C128, C143-C162, C430-C431 have alternating small and large perforations.

Transportation — AP39

Designs: 40c, Finger counting and factory. 1p, "Seven Censuses."

Perf. 12x13, 13x12

1939, Oct. 2 Photo.

C100 AP39 20c dk bl & bl 1.00 .20
C101 AP39 40c red org & org .75 .25
C102 AP39 1p ind & vio bl 2.75 .75
Nos. C100-C102 (3) 4.50 1.20
Set, never hinged 6.00

National Census of 1939-40.

Penny Black Type of Regular Issue, 1940

1940, May *Perf. 14*

C103 A140 5c blk & dk grn .65 .55
C104 A140 10c bis brn & dp bl .55 .25
C105 A140 20c car & bl vio .40 .20
C106 A140 1p car & choc 6.00 5.00

C107 A140 5p gray grn & red brn 75.00 55.00
Nos. C103-C107 (5) 82.60 61.00
Set, never hinged 200.00

Issue dates: 5c-1p, May 2; 5p, May 15.

Part of Original College at Pátzcuaro AP43

College at Morelia (18th Century) — AP44

College at Morelia (1940) AP45

1940, July 15 Engr. *Perf. 10½*

C108	AP43	20c brt green	.45	.20
C109	AP44	40c orange	.50	.30
C110	AP45	1p dp pur, red brn & org	1.25	1.00
		Nos. C108-C110 (3)	2.20	1.50
		Set, never hinged	5.00	

400th anniv. of the founding of the National College of San Nicolas de Hidalgo.

Pirate Ship AP46

Designs: 40c, Castle of San Miguel. 1p, Temple of San Francisco.

Perf. 12x13, 13x12

1940, Aug. 7 Photo.

C111	AP46	20c red brn & bis brn	1.10	.70
C112	AP46	40c blk & sl grn	1.50	.75
C113	AP46	1p vio bl & blk	5.00	4.00
		Nos. C111-C113 (3)	7.60	5.45
		Set, never hinged	21.00	

400th anniversary of Campeche.

Inauguration Type of Regular Issue, 1940

1940, Dec. 1 *Perf. 12x13*

C114	A146	20c gray blk & red org	1.90	1.00
C115	A146	40c chnt brn & dk sl	2.00	1.50
C116	A146	1p brt vio bl & rose	3.50	2.00
		Nos. C114-C116 (3)	7.40	4.50
		Set, never hinged	20.00	

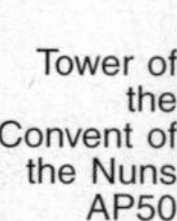

Tower of the Convent of the Nuns AP50

Casa de Montejo — AP51

1p, Campanile of Cathedral at Merída.

1942, Jan. 2 *Perf. 14*

C117	AP50	20c Prus blue	1.50	.75
C118	AP51	40c grnsh blk (C)	2.25	2.00
a.		Without overprint	7.50	7.50
C119	AP50	1p carmine	2.50	2.00
		Nos. C117-C119 (3)	6.25	4.75

400th anniversary of Merída.

No. C118 bears the overprint "Servicio Aereo" in carmine.

Church of Zapopan AP53

Our Lady of Guadalupe Church AP54

Guadalajara Arms — AP55

1942, Feb. 11 Engr. *Perf. 10½x10*

C120	AP53	20c green & blk	1.60	.75
C121	AP54	40c ol & yel grn	1.75	1.00
C122	AP55	1p purple & sepia	1.65	1.25
		Nos. C120-C122 (3)	5.00	3.00

400th anniversary of Guadalajara.

Astrophysics Type of Regular Issue

Designs: 20c, Spiral Galaxy NGC 4594. 40c, Planetary Nebula in Lyra. 1p, Russell Diagrams.

1942, Feb. 17 Photo. *Perf. 12x13*

C123	A154	20c dk grn & ind	20.00	3.00
C124	A154	40c car lake & ind	15.00	4.00
C125	A154	1p orange & blk	25.00	4.50
		Nos. C123-C125 (3)	60.00	11.50

Corn AP59

1942, July 1

C126	AP59	20c shown	1.90	.70
C127	AP59	40c Coffee	1.50	.75
C128	AP59	1p Bananas	2.50	2.00
		Nos. C126-C128 (3)	5.90	3.45

2nd Inter-American Agricultural Conf.

View of San Miguel de Allende AP62

Designs: 40c, Birthplace of Allende. 1p, Church of Our Lady of Health.

1943, May 18 *Perf. 14*

C129	AP62	20c dk slate grn	1.00	.60
C130	AP62	40c purple	1.25	.60
C131	AP62	1p dp carmine	2.75	2.50
		Nos. C129-C131 (3)	5.00	3.70

400th anniversary of the founding of San Miguel de Allende.

Types of 1934-35

1944 Photo. Wmk. 272

C132	AP18	20c brown carmine	.75	.20

Perf. 10½x10

1944-46 Engr. Wmk. 272

C133	AP15	5c black	.50	.20
C134	AP16	10c red brn ('45)	1.25	.20
C135	AP17	15c gray grn ('45)	.85	.20
C136	AP19	30c brown ol ('45)	12.50	.75
C137	AP20	40c gray bl ('45)	1.10	.20
C138	AP21	50c green	.85	.20
C139	AP22	1p gray grn & red brn ('45)	6.00	1.50
C140	AP23	5p dk car & blk ('46)	4.75	2.00
		Nos. C133-C140 (8)	27.80	5.25

Symbol of Flight AP65

Microphone, Book and Camera AP66

1944 Photo. *Perf. 14*

C141	AP65	25c chestnut brown	.35	.20

See No. C185.

1944, Nov. 8 Wmk. 272

C142	AP66	25c dull slate grn	.65	.20

Issued to commemorate the third Book Fair.

Catalogue values for unused stamps in this section, from this point to the end of the section, are for Never Hinged items.

Globe-in-Hands Type

1945, Feb. 27 *Perf. 12x13*

C143	A166	25c red orange	.35	.20
C144	A166	1p brt green	.40	.30
C145	A166	5p indigo	2.50	2.00
C146	A166	10p brt rose	6.50	5.25
C147	A166	20p brt vio bl	20.00	13.00
		Nos. C143-C147 (5)	29.75	20.75

Theater Type

1945, July 27

C148	A167	30c slate & ol	.25	.20
C149	A167	1p slate & lil	.35	.35
C150	A167	5p slate & blk	2.75	2.50
C151	A167	10p sl & lt ultra	5.00	4.25
C152	A167	20p blk & gray grn	18.00	10.50
		Nos. C148-C152 (5)	26.35	17.80

Blindfold Type

1945, Nov. 21

C153	A169	30c slate green	.20	.20
C154	A169	1p brown red	.35	.30
C155	A169	5p red brn & pale bl	3.00	2.50
C156	A169	10p sl blk & pale lil	5.00	5.00
C157	A169	20p grn & lt brn	25.00	24.00
		Nos. C153-C157 (5)	33.55	32.00

Torch, Laurel and Flag-decorated ONU — AP70

1946, Apr. 10

C158	AP70	30c chocolate	.20	.20
C159	AP70	1p slate grn	.35	.30
C160	AP70	5p chnt & dk grn	1.60	1.25
C161	AP70	10p dk brn & chnt	5.00	4.00
C162	AP70	20p sl grn & org red	18.00	9.00
		Nos. C158-C162 (5)	25.15	14.75

Issued to honor the United Nations.

Father Margil de Jesus and Plane over Zacatecas AP71

Zacatecas scene and: 1p, Genaro Codina. 5p, Gen. Enrique Estrada. 10p, Fernando Villalpando.

Perf. 10½x10

1946, Sept. 13 Engr. Wmk. 279

C163	AP71	30c gray	.20	.20
C164	AP71	1p brn & Prus grn	.40	.35
C165	AP71	5p red & olive	3.00	3.00
C166	AP71	10p Prus grn & dk brn	18.00	15.00
		Nos. C163-C166 (4)	21.60	18.55

400th anniversary of Zacatecas.

Franklin D. Roosevelt and Stamp of 1st Mexican Issue AP72

30c, Arms of Mexico & Stamp of 1st US Issue.

1947, May 16 Photo. *Perf. 14*

C167	AP72	25c lt violet bl	.90	.50
C168	AP72	30c gray black	.60	.25
a.		Imperf., pair	325.00	
C169	AP72	1p blue & carmine	1.25	.40
		Nos. C167-C169 (3)	2.75	1.15

Centenary International Philatelic Exhibition, New York, May 17-25, 1947.

Type of 1934-35

Perf. 10½x10, 10x10½

1947 Engr. Wmk. 279

C170	AP15	5c black	1.50	.20
C171	AP16	10c red brown	3.00	.30
C172	AP17	15c olive grn	3.00	.30
C173	AP19	30c brown ol	2.00	.20
C174	AP20	40c blue gray	2.00	.20
C175	AP21	50c green	12.50	.30
a.		Imperf., pair	450.00	
C176	AP22	1p gray grn & red brn	3.50	.25
a.		Imperf., pair	500.00	
C177	AP23	5p red & blk	9.00	1.25
c.		5p dark car & black	200.00	3.00

Perf. 14

C177A	AP18	20c brown car	2.75	.50
b.		Imperf., pair	250.00	
		Nos. C170-C177A (9)	39.25	3.50

Emilio Carranza AP74

Douglas DC-4 AP75

1947, June 25 Engr. *Perf. 10½x10*

C178	AP74	10p red & dk brn	1.75	1.50
a.		10p dark carmine & brown		8.00
C179	AP75	20p bl & red brn	2.75	2.75

Cadet Vincente Suárez AP76

Chapultepec Castle — AP78

30c, Lieut. Juan de la Barrera. 1p, Gen. Pedro M. Anaya. 5p, Gen. Antonio de Leon.

1947, Sept. 8 Photo. *Perf. 14*
C180 AP76 25c dull violet .25 .20
C181 AP76 30c blue .25 .20

Engr.
Perf. 10x10½
C182 AP78 50c deep green .35 .20
C183 AP78 1p violet .50 .20
C184 AP78 5p aqua & brn 2.00 2.00
a. Imperf. pair 600.00
Nos. C180-C184 (5) 3.35 2.80

Centenary of the battles of Chapultepec, Churubusco and Molino del Rey.

Flight Symbol Type of 1944

1947 Wmk. 279 Photo. *Perf. 14*
C185 AP65 25c chestnut brown .40 .20
a. Imperf., pair 250.00

Puebla, Dance of the Half Moon AP81

Designs: 5c, Guerrero, Acapulco waterfront. 10c, Oaxaca, dance. 20c, Chiapas, musicians (Mayan). 25c, Michoacan, masks. 30c, Cuauhtemoc. 35c, Guerrero, view of Taxco. 40c, San Luis Potosi, head. 50c, Chiapas, bas-relief profile, Mayan culture. 80c, Mexico City University Stadium. 5p, Queretaro, architecture. 10p, Miguel Hidalgo. 20p, Modern building.

Two types of 20p:
Type I — Blue gray part 21¼mm wide. Child's figure touching left edge.
Type II — Blue gray part 21¾mm wide; "LQ" at lower left corner. Child's figure 1mm from left edge.

Imprint: "Talleres de Impresion de Estampillas y Valores-Mexico"

Perf. 10½x10

1950-52 Wmk. 279 Engr.
C186 AP81 5c aqua ('51) .50 .20
C187 AP81 10c brn org ('51) 2.75 .50
C188 AP81 20c carmine 1.25 .20
C189 AP81 25c redsh brown 1.25 .20
C190 AP81 30c olive bister .50 .20
C191 AP81 35c violet 2.75 .20
a. Retouched die 19.00 .30
b. As "a," imperf., pair 300.00
C192 AP81 40c dk gray bl ('51) 2.25 .20
a. Imperf., pair 300.00
C193 AP81 50c green 3.75 .20
C194 AP81 80c claret ('52) 2.25 .50
a. Imperf., pair 300.00
C195 AP81 1p blue gray 1.40 .20
C196 AP81 5p dk brn & org ('51) 5.00 1.00
a. Imperf., pair *1,800.*
C197 AP81 10p blk & aqua ('52) 95.00 20.00
C198 AP81 20p car & bl gray, I ('52) 8.50 9.00
a. Type II 400.00 100.00
Nos. C186-C198 (13) 127.15 32.60

No. C191a: A patch of heavy shading has been added at right of "MEXICO;" lines in sky increased and strengthened. On Nos. C191, C191a, the top of the highest tower is even with the top of the "o" in "Guerrero," and has no frame line at right. No. C220C has frame line at right and tower top is even with "Arquitectura."
Many shades exist of Nos. C186-C198.
See Nos. C208-C221, C249, C265-C268, C285-C288, C290-C298, C347-C349, C422, C444, C446-C450, C471-C480.

Pres. Aleman and Highway Bridging Map of Mexico AP82

Design: 35c, Pres. Juarez and map.

1950, May 21 Engr.
C199 AP82 25c lilac rose 3.00 .25
C200 AP82 35c deep green .30 .20

Completion of the Intl. Highway between Ciudad Juarez and the Guatemala border.

Trains Crossing Isthmus of Tehuantepec — AP83

Design: 35c, Pres. Aleman and bridge.

1950, May 24
C201 AP83 25c green .50 .25
C202 AP83 35c ultra .35 .25

Opening of the Southeastern Railroad between Veracruz, Coatzocoalcos and Yucatan, 1950.

Aztec Courier, Plane, Train AP84

80c, Symbols of universal postal service.

1950, June 15
C203 AP84 25c red orange .35 .20
C204 AP84 80c blue .50 .30

75th anniv. (in 1949) of the UPU.

Miguel Hidalgo AP86

Design: 35c, Hidalgo and Mexican Flag.

Wmk. 300

1953, May 8 Photo. *Perf. 14*
C206 AP86 25c gray bl & dk red brn .90 .20
C207 AP86 35c slate green .90 .25
a. Wmk. 279 —

Bicentenary of birth of Miguel Hidalgo y Costilla (1753-1811), priest and revolutionist.

Type of 1950-52

Designs as before.

Imprint: "Talleres de Impresion de Estampillas y Valores-Mexico"

Wmk. 300, Horizontal

1953-56 Engr. *Perf. 10½x10*
C208 AP81 5c aqua .50 .20
C209 AP81 10c orange brn 5.50 3.50
a. 10c orange 11.50 2.50
C210 AP81 30c gray olive 18.00 10.00
C211 AP81 40c gray bl ('56) 18.00 1.50
C212 AP81 50c green 350.00 250.00
C213 AP81 80c claret 100.00 10.00
C214 AP81 1p blue gray 3.00 .30
C215 AP81 5p dk brn & org 2.75 .60
C216 AP81 10p black & aqua 6.25 1.25
C217 AP81 20p car & bl gray (II) ('56) 75.00 8.00
Nos. C208-C211,C213-C217 (9) 229.00 35.35

Printed in sheets of 30.

Type of 1950-52

Designs as in 1950-52. 2p, Guerrero, view of Taxco. 2.25p, Michoacan, masks.

Two types of 2p:
I — No dots after "Colonial". Frame line at right broken near top.
II — Three dots in a line after "Colonial". Right frame line unbroken.

Wmk. 300, Vertical

1955-65 *Perf. 11½x11*

Design AP81
C218 5c bluish grn ('56) .20 .20

Perf. 11
C219 10c orange brn ('60) .35 .20
a. Perf. 11½x11 1.10 .40
C220 20c carmine ('60) .35 .20
k. Perf. 11½x11 ('57) 1.60 .20
C220A 25c vio brn, perf. 11½x11 1.75 .20
C220B 30c olive gray ('60) .35 .20
l. Perf. 11½x11 .90 .20
C220C 35c dk vio, perf. 11½x11 .90 .20
C220D 40c slate bl ('60) .35 .20
m. Perf. 11½x11 10.00 .20
C220E 50c green, perf. 11½x11 .90 .20
n. Perf. 11 ('60) 1.10 .20
q. 50c yellow green 1.10 .20
C220F 80c claret ('60) 5.00 .70
o. Perf. 11½x11 5.00 .60
C220G 1p grn gray ('60) 1.10 .30
p. Perf. 11½x11 12.50 .30
C220H 2p dk org brn, II ('63) 1.10 .60
i. 2p lt org brn, perf. 11½x11 ('65) 150.00 40.00
j. 2p org brn, I, perf. 11 8.50 1.25
C221 2.25p maroon ('63) .65 .70
Nos. C218-C221 (12) 13.00 3.90

Printed in sheets of 45 and 50. Nos. C218-C221 have been re-engraved.
No. C218 has been redrawn and there are many differences. "CTS" measures 7mm; it is 5½mm on No. C208.
Nos. C208-C221 exist in various shades.
For No. C220C, see note after No. C198.
No. C220n was privately overprinted in red: "25vo Aniversario / Primer Cohete Internacional / Reynosa, Mexico-McAllen, U.S.A. / 1936-1961."

Mayan Ball Court and Player AP87

Design: 35c, Modern Stadium, Mexico.

1954, Mar. 6 Photo. *Perf. 14*
C222 AP87 25c brn & dk bl grn 1.00 .35
C223 AP87 35c dl sl grn & lil rose .75 .25

7th Central American & Caribbean Games.

Allegory AP88

1954, Sept. 15
C224 AP88 25c red brn & dp bl .50 .25
C225 AP88 35c dk bl & vio brn .30 .20
C226 AP88 80c blk & bl grn .30 .25
Nos. C224-C226 (3) 1.10 .70

Centenary of national anthem.

Aztec God Tezcatlipoca and Map — AP89

Design: 35c, Stadium and map.

1955, Mar. 12
C227 AP89 25c dk Prus grn & red brn .75 .30
C228 AP89 35c carmine & brn .75 .30

2nd Pan American Games, 1955.

Ornaments and Mask, Archeological Era — AP90

Designs: 10c, Virrey Enriquez de Almanza, bell tower and coach, colonial era. 50c, Jose Maria Morelos and cannon, heroic Mexico. 1p, Woman and child and horse back rider, revolutionary Mexico. 1.20p, Sombrero and Spurs, popular Mexico. 5p, Pointing hand and school, modern Mexico.

Perf. 11½x11

1956, Aug. 1 Engr. Wmk. 300
C229 AP90 5c black .40 .20
C230 AP90 10c lt blue .40 .20
C231 AP90 50c violet brn .30 .20
C232 AP90 1p blue gray .40 .20
C233 AP90 1.20p magenta .40 .25
C234 AP90 5p blue grn 1.25 1.25
a. Souv. sheet of 6, #C229-C234, perf. 10½x10 60.00 60.00
Nos. C229-C234 (6) 3.15 2.30

Centenary of Mexico's 1st postage stamps. No. C234a sold for 15 pesos.

Paricutín Volcano AP91

1956, Sept. 5 Photo. *Perf. 14*
C235 AP91 50c dk violet bl .50 .20

20th Intl. Geological Cong., Mexico City.

Valentin Gomez Farias and Melchor Ocampo AP92

1.20p, Leon Guzman and Ignacio Ramirez.

1956-63 Wmk. 300 *Perf. 14*
C236 AP92 15c intense blue .50 .20
C237 AP92 1.20p dk grn & pur .85 .35
b. Dark green omitted 110.00
c. Purple omitted 125.00
C237A AP92 2.75p purple ('63) 1.25 .75
Nos. C236-C237A (3) 2.60 1.30

Centenary of the constitution (in 1957). See Nos. C289, C445, C451, C471A.

Map AP93

1956, Dec. 1
C238 AP93 25c gray & dk bl .35 .20

4th Inter-American Regional Tourism Congress of the Gulf of Mexico and the Caribbean (in 1955).

Eagle Holding Scales AP94

1p, Allegorical figure writing the law.

1957, Aug. 31 Photo. *Perf. 14*
C239 AP94 50c metallic red brn & green .35 .20
C240 AP94 1p metallic lilac & ultra .50 .25

Centenary of 1857 Constitution.

Globe, Weights and Measure
AP95

1957, Sept. 21

C241 AP95 50c metallic bl & blk .40 .20

Centenary of the adoption of the metric system in Mexico.

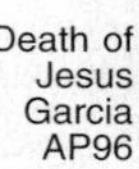

Death of Jesus Garcia
AP96

1957, Nov. 7 Wmk. 300 *Perf. 14*

C242 AP96 50c car rose & dk vio .35 .20

50th anniversary of the death of Jesus Garcia, hero of Nacozari.

Oil Industry Symbols
AP97

Design: 1p, Derricks at night.

1958, Aug. 30

C243 AP97 50c emerald & blk .25 .20
C244 AP97 1p car & bluish blk .40 .20

Nationalization of Mexico's oil industry, 20th anniv.

Independence Monument Figure — AP98

1958, Dec. 15 Engr. *Perf. 11*

C245 AP98 50c gray blue .35 .20

10th anniversary of the signing of the Universal Declaration of Human Rights.

Pres. Venustiano Carranza
AP99

1960, Jan. 15 Photo. *Perf. 14*

C246 AP99 50c salmon & dk bl .35 .20

Centenary of the birth of President Venustiano Carranza.

Alberto Braniff's 1910 Plane, Douglas DC-7 and Mexican Airlines Map
AP100

1960, May 15 Wmk. 300 *Perf. 14*

C247 AP100 50c lt brn & vio .50 .20
C248 AP100 1p lt brn & bl grn .40 .20

50th anniversary of Mexican aviation.

Type of 1950-52 inscribed: "HOMENAJE AL COLECCIONISTA DEL TIMBRE DE MEXICO-JUNIO 1960"

1960, June 8 Engr. *Perf. 10½x10*

C249 AP81 20p lil, brn & lt grn 100.00 100.00

See note below No. 909.

Flag
AP101

Designs: 1.20p, Bell of Dolores and eagle. 5p, Dolores Church.

Wmk. 300

1960, Sept. 16 Photo. *Perf. 14*

C250 AP101 50c dp grn & brt red .40 .20
C251 AP101 1.20p grnsh bl & dk brn .60 .25
C252 AP101 5p sepia & green 6.00 2.25
Nos. C250-C252 (3) 7.00 2.70

150th anniversary of independence.

Aviation (Douglas DC-8 Airliner)
AP102

Designs: 1p, Oil industry. 1.20p, Road development. 5p, Water power (dam).

1960, Nov. 20 Photo. *Perf. 14*

C253 AP102 50c gray bl & blk .40 .20
C254 AP102 1p dk grn & rose car .50 .25
C255 AP102 1.20p dk grn & sep .50 .30
C256 AP102 5p blue & lilac 6.00 3.00
Nos. C253-C256 (4) 7.40 3.75

50th anniversary of Mexican Revolution.

Count de Revillaggigedo
AP103

1960, Dec. 23

C257 AP103 60c dk car & blk .60 .20

80th census and to honor Juan Vicente Güémez Pacheco de Padilla Horcasitas, Count de Revillagigedo, who conducted the 1st census in America, 1793.

Railroad Tracks and Map
AP104

Design: 70c, Railroad bridge.

1961, Nov. Wmk. 300 *Perf. 14*

C258 AP104 60c chlky bl & dk grn .40 .20
C259 AP104 70c dk blue & gray .40 .20

Opening of the railroad from Chihuahua to the Pacific Ocean.

Gen. Ignacio Zaragoza and View of Puebla
AP105

1962, May 5

C260 AP105 1p gray grn & slate grn .60 .20

Centenary of the Battle of May 5 at Puebla and the defeat of French forces by Gen. Ignacio Zaragoza.

Laboratory
AP106

1962, June 11

C261 AP106 1p olive & vio bl .60 .20

National Polytechnic Institute, 25th anniv.

Pres. John F. Kennedy
AP107

1962, June 29

C262 AP107 80c brt blue & car 1.75 .40

Commemorates visit of President John F. Kennedy to Mexico, June 29-30.

Globe
AP108

1962, Oct. 20

C263 AP108 1.20p violet & dk brn .60 .25

Inter-American Economic and Social Council meeting.

Balloon over Mexico City, 1862 — AP109

1962, Dec. 21 Wmk. 300 *Perf. 14*

C264 AP109 80c lt blue & blk 1.60 .60

Cent. of the 1st Mexican balloon ascension by Joaquin de la Cantolla y Rico.

Type of 1950-52
Imprint: "Talleres de Imp. de Est. y Valores-Mexico"

Designs as before.

Two sizes of 80c:
I — 35½x20mm.
II — 37x20½mm.

Wmk. 300, Vertical

1962-72 Photo. *Perf. 14*

C265 AP81 80c cl, I ('63) 1.40 .30
a. Perf. 11½x11, size II ('63) 4.00 .35
b. Perf. 11, size II ('63) 3.50 .30
c. Perf. 11, size I ('72) 2.50 .20
C266 AP81 5p dk brn & yel org 4.00 1.00
C267 AP81 10p blk & lt grn ('63) 7.00 3.75
C268 AP81 20p car & bl gray 15.00 3.50
a. 20p carmine & aqua 17.00 4.75
Nos. C265-C268 (4) 27.40 8.55

Vert. pairs, imperf. horiz. of No. C265, perf. 11, may be from uncut rolls of No. C348.

ALALC Emblem
AP110

1963, Feb. 15 Wmk. 300

C269 AP110 80c orange & dl pur 1.10 .30

2nd general session of the Latin American Free Trade Assoc. (ALALC), held in 1962.

Mexican Eagle and Refinery
AP111

1963, Mar. 23

C270 AP111 80c red org & slate .60 .20

Nationalization of the oil industry, 25th anniv.

Polyconic Map
AP112

1963, Apr. 22 Photo. *Perf. 14*

C271 AP112 80c blue & blk .85 .30

19th Intl. Chamber of Commerce Congress.

EXMEX Emblem and Postmark
AP113

1963, Oct. 9 Wmk. 350 *Perf. 14*

C274 AP113 5p rose red 2.75 1.75

77th Annual Convention of the American Philatelic Society, Mexico City, Oct. 7-13.

Marshal Tito
AP114

1963, Oct. 15 Wmk. 350 *Perf. 14*

C275 AP114 2p dk grn & vio 2.00 .70

Visit of Marshal Tito of Yugoslavia.

Modern Architecture — AP115

1963, Oct. 19

C276 AP115 80c dk blue & gray .70 .25

Intl. Architects' Convention, Mexico City.

Dove
AP116

1963, Oct. 26

C277 AP116 80c dl bl grn & car 1.25 .35

Centenary of the International Red Cross.

Don Quixote by José Guadalupe Posada
AP117

1963, Nov. 9 Engr. *Perf. 10½x10*

C278 AP117 1.20p black 1.75 .50

50th anniversary of the death of José Guadalupe Posada, satirical artist.

Horse-drawn Rail Coach, Old and New Trains — AP118

Wmk. 350

1963, Nov. 29 Photo. *Perf. 14*

C279 AP118 1.20p violet bl & bl .90 .35

11th Pan-American Railroad Congress.

Eleanor Roosevelt, Flame and UN Emblem AP119

1964, Feb. 22 Wmk. 350 *Perf. 14*

C280 AP119 80c lt ultra & red .85 .25

15th anniversary (in 1963) of the Universal Declaration of Human Rights and to honor Eleanor Roosevelt.

Gen. Charles de Gaulle AP120

1964, Mar. 16 Photo.

C281 AP120 2p dl vio bl & brn 2.50 .80

Visit of President Charles de Gaulle of France to Mexico, Mar. 16-18.

Pres. John F. Kennedy and Pres. Adolfo López Mateos and Map AP121

1964, Apr. 11 Photo.

C282 AP121 80c vio bl & gray .85 .25

Ratification of the Chamizal Treaty, returning the Chamizal area of El Paso, Texas, to Mexico, July 18, 1963.

Queen Juliana AP122

1964, May 8 Wmk. 350 *Perf. 14*

C283 AP122 80c bister & vio bl 1.25 .25

Visit of Queen Juliana of the Netherlands.

Lt. José Azueta and Cadet Virgilio Uribe AP123

1964, June 18 Wmk. 350 *Perf. 14*

C284 AP123 40c dk brn & blk .55 .20

50th anniversary of the defense of Veracruz (against US Navy).

Types of 1950-62

Designs as before.

Engraved; Photogravure (C296-C298)

Perf. 11 (20c, 40c, 50c, 80c, 2p); 14

1964-73 Wmk. 350

C285 AP81 20c carmine ('71) .75 1.25

C286 AP81 40c gray bl ('71) 125.00 *100.00*

C287 AP81 50c green ('71) .50 .50

C288 AP81 80c claret, I ('73) .50 .50

C289 AP92 1.20p dk grn & pur 6.50 2.50

C290 AP81 2p red brn, II ('71) 1.75 1.40

C296 AP81 5p brn & org ('66) 11.00 9.00

C297 AP81 10p black & aqua 35.00 17.50

C298 AP81 20p car & bl gray 55.00 40.00

Nos. C285-C290,C296-C298 (9) 236.00 *172.65*

National Emblem, Cahill's Butterfly World Map, Sword and Scales of Justice AP124

1964, July 29 Photo.

C299 AP124 40c sepia & dp bl .60 .20

10th conference of the International Bar Association, Mexico City, July 27-31.

Galleon AP125

Map Showing 16th Century Voyages Between Mexico and Philippines — AP126

1964, Nov. 10 Wmk. 350 *Perf. 14*

C300 AP125 80c ultra & indigo 2.25 .35

C301 AP126 2.75p brt yel & blk 2.75 1.00

400 years of Mexican-Philippine friendship.

Netzahualcoyotl Dam, Grijalva River — AP127

1965, Feb. 19 Photo. *Perf. 14*

C302 AP127 80c vio gray & dk brn .50 .20

Radio-electric Unit of San Benito, Chiapas — AP128

80c, Microwave tower, Villahermosa, Tabasco.

1965, June 19 Wmk. 350 *Perf. 14*

C303 AP128 80c lt bl & dk bl .65 .30

C304 AP128 1.20p dk grn & blk .70 .30

Centenary of the ITU.

Campfire, Tent and Scout Emblem AP129

1965, Sept. 27 Photo. *Perf. 14*

C305 AP129 80c lt ultra & vio bl .65 .30

20th World Scout Conference, Mexico City, Sept. 27-Oct. 3.

King Baudouin, Queen Fabiola and Arms of Belgium AP130

1965, Oct. 18 Wmk. 350 *Perf. 14*

C306 AP130 2p slate grn & dl bl 1.00 .40

Visit of the King and Queen of Belgium.

Mayan Antiquities and Unisphere AP131

1965, Nov. 9 Photo.

C307 AP131 80c lemon & emerald .50 .20

Issued for the NY World's Fair, 1964-65.

Dante by Raphael — AP132

Perf. 10x10½

1965, Nov. 23 Wmk. 350 Engr.

C308 AP132 2p henna brown 1.25 .65

700th anniv. of the birth of Dante Alighieri.

Runner in Starting Position, Terra Cotta Found in Colima, 300-650 A.D. AP133

Designs: 1.20p, Chin cultic disk, ball game scoring stone with ball player in center, Mayan culture, c. 500 A.D., found in Chiapas. 2p, Clay sculpture of ball court, players, spectators and temple. Pieces on 80c and 2p from 300-650 A.D.

1965, Dec. 17 Photo. *Perf. 14*

Size: 35x21mm

C309 AP133 80c orange & sl .80 .25

C310 AP133 1.20p bl & vio bl .90 .30

a. Souv. sheet of 4, #965-966, C309-C310, imperf. 3.50 3.50

Size: 43x36mm

C311 AP133 2p brt bl & dk brn .75 .25

a. Souv. sheet, imperf. 3.50 3.50

Nos. C309-C311 (3) 2.45 .80

19th Olympic Games, Mexico, 1968. No. C310a sold for 3.90p. No. C311a sold for 3p.

Nos. C310a and C311a have large watermark of national arms (diameter 54mm) and "SECRETARIA DE HACIENDA Y CREDITO PUBLICO." Issued without gum.

Ruben Dario — AP134

1966, Mar. 17 Wmk. 350 *Perf. 14*

C312 AP134 1.20p sepia .60 .35

Ruben Dario (pen name of Felix Ruben Garcia Sarmiento, 1867-1916), Nicaraguan poet, newspaper correspondent and diplomat.

Father Andres de Urdaneta and Compass Rose AP135

Perf. 10½x10

1966, June 4 Engr. Wmk. 350

C313 AP135 2.75p bluish blk 1.25 .60

4th centenary of Father Urdaneta's return trip from the Philippines.

UPAE Type of Regular Issue

Designs: 80c, Pennant and post horn. 1.20p, Pennant and UPAE emblem, horiz.

Wmk. 300

1966, June 24 Photo. *Perf. 14*

C314 A244 80c magenta & blk .25 .20

C315 A244 1.20p lt ultra & blk .35 .20

U Thant and UN Emblem AP136

1966, Aug. 24 Photo. Wmk. 300

C316 AP136 80c black & ultra .75 .20

Visit of U Thant, Secretary General of the UN.

AP137

1966, Aug. 26 *Perf. 14*

C317 AP137 80c green & red .25 .20

Issued to publicize the year of friendship between Mexico and Central America.

Olympic Type of Regular Issue

Designs by Diego Rivera: 80c, Obstacle race. 2.25p, Football. 2.75p, Lighting Olympic torch.

1966, Oct. 15 Wmk. 300 *Perf. 14*

Size: 57x21mm

C318 A248 80c org brn & blk .55 .20

C319 A248 2.25p green & blk .90 .35

C320 A248 2.75p dp pur & blk 2.00 .45

a. Souvenir sheet of 3 3.00 3.00

Nos. C318-C320 (3) 3.45 1.00

Issued to publicize the 19th Olympic Games, Mexico City, D.F., 1968. No. C320a contains 3 imperf. stamps similar to Nos. C318-C320 with simulated perforations. Sold for 8.70p.

UNESCO Emblem AP138

Litho. & Engr.

1966, Nov. 4 ***Perf. 11***

C321 AP138 80c blk, car, brt grn & org .50 .20
a. Perf. 10½ 5.00 2.00
b. Perf. 10½x11 25.00
c. Perf. 11x10½ 12.50 5.00

UNESCO 20th anniv. The 4th color varies from yellow to orange. A number of perforation varieties exist on the perf 11 stamps.

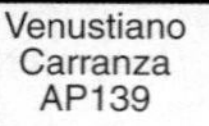

Venustiano Carranza AP139

Tiros Satellite over Earth AP140

1967, Feb. 5 **Photo.** ***Perf. 14***

C322 AP139 80c dk red brn & ocher .35 .20

Constitution, 50th anniv. Venustiano Carranza (1859-1920), was president of Mexico 1917-20.

1967, Mar. 23 **Photo.** **Wmk. 300**

C323 AP140 80c blk & dk bl .50 .20

World Meteorological Day, Mar. 23.

Medical School Emblem AP141

Captain Horacio Ruiz Gaviño AP142

1967, July 10 **Wmk. 300** ***Perf. 14***

C324 AP141 80c black & ocher .35 .20

Mexican Military Medical School, 50th anniv.

1967, July 17 **Photo.**

Design: 2p, Biplane, horiz.

C325 AP142 80c black & brown .25 .20
C326 AP142 2p black & brown .45 .25

50th anniv. of the 1st Mexican airmail flight, from Pachuca to Mexico City, July 6, 1917.

Marco Polo and ITY Emblem — AP143

1967, Sept. 9 **Wmk. 300** ***Perf. 14***

C327 AP143 80c rose cl & blk .25 .20

Issued for International Tourist Year, 1967.

Olympic Games Type of Regular Issue, 1967

Designs: 80c, Diving. 1.20p, Runners. 2p, Weight lifters. 5p, Soccer.

1967, Oct. 12 **Photo.** ***Perf. 14***

C328 A254 80c dp lil rose & blk .45 .20
C329 A254 1.20p brt grn & blk .45 .20
a. Souv. sheet of 2, #C328-C329, imperf. 5.50 3.75
C330 A254 2p yellow & blk 1.25 .40
C331 A254 5p olive & blk 1.60 .75
a. Souv. sheet of 2, #C330-C331, imperf. 7.50 4.00
Nos. C328-C331 (4) 3.75 1.55

No. C329a sold for 2.50p; No. C331a sold for 9p. Both sheets are watermark 350.

Heinrich Hertz and James Clerk Maxwell AP144

1967, Nov. 15 **Photo.** **Wmk. 300**

C332 AP144 80c brt grn & blk .30 .20

2nd Intl. Telecommunications Plan Conf., Mexico City, Oct. 30-Nov. 15.

EFIMEX Emblem, Showing Official Stamp of 1884 — AP145

1968, Feb. 24 **Wmk. 300** ***Perf. 14***

C333 AP145 80c black & grn .45 .25
C334 AP145 2p black & ver .45 .25

EFIMEX '68, International Philatelic Exhibition, Mexico City, Nov. 1-9, 1968.

Olympic Games Type of Regular Issue, 1967

Designs: 80c, Sailing. 1p, Rowing. 2p, Volleyball. 5p, Equestrian.

1968, Mar. 21 **Photo.** ***Perf. 14***

C335 A254 80c ultra & blk .25 .20
C336 A254 1p brt bl grn & blk .35 .20
a. Souv. sheet of 2, #C335-C336, imperf. 3.50 2.75
C337 A254 2p yellow & blk .70 .30
C338 A254 5p red brn & blk 1.40 1.10
a. Souv. sheet of 2, #C337-C338, imperf. 7.50 4.50
Nos. C335-C338 (4) 2.70 1.80

No. C336a sold for 2.40p; No. C338a sold for 9p. Both sheets are watermark 350.

Martin Luther King, Jr. — AP146

1968, June 8 **Photo.** **Wmk. 300**

C339 AP146 80c black & gray .35 .20

Rev. Dr. Martin Luther King, Jr. (1929-1968), American civil rights leader.

Olympic Types of Regular Issue, 1968

Designs: 80c, Peace dove and Olympic rings. 1p, Discobolus. 2p, Olympic medals. 5p, Symbols of Olympic sports events. 10p, Symbolic design for Mexican Olympic Games.

1968, Oct. 12 **Wmk. 350** ***Perf. 14***

C340 A259 80c green, lil & org .35 .20
C341 A259 1p green, bl & blk .45 .20
C342 A259 2p multicolored .90 .50
a. Souvenir sheet of 3, #C340-C342, imperf. 20.00 17.50
C343 A260 5p multicolored 4.00 1.40
C344 A260 10p black & multi 2.90 1.50
a. Souvenir sheet of 2, #C343-C344, imperf. 20.00 17.50
Nos. C340-C344 (5) 8.60 3.80

19th Olympic Games, Mexico City, Oct. 12-27. No. C342a sold for 5p. No. C344a sold for 20p.

Souvenir Sheet

EFIMEX Emblem — AP147

1968, Nov. 1 **Photo.** ***Imperf.***

C345 AP147 5p black & ultra 3.50 2.50

EFIMEX '68 International philatelic exhibition, Mexico City, Nov. 1-9. No. C345 contains one stamp with simulated perforations.

Father Francisco Palóu (See footnote) AP148

1969, July 16 **Wmk. 350** ***Perf. 14***

C346 AP148 80c multicolored .40 .20

Issued to honor Father Junipero Serra (1713-1784), Franciscan missionary, founder of San Diego, Calif. The portrait was intended to be that of Father Serra. By error the head of Father Palóu, his coworker, was taken from a painting (c. 1785) by Mariano Guerrero which also contains a Serra portrait.

Type of 1950-52 Redrawn Coil Stamps

Wmk. 300 Vert.

1969 **Photo.** ***Perf. 11 Vert.***

Imprint: "T.I.E.V."

C347 AP81 20c carmine 2.75 2.00

Imprint: "Talleres de Imp de Est y Valores-Mexico"

C348 AP81 80c claret 4.00 2.00

Imprint: "T.I.E.V."

C349 AP81 1p gray grn 4.00 2.25
Nos. C347-C349 (3) 10.75 6.25

Soccer Ball AP149

Design: 2p, Foot and soccer ball.

1969, Aug. 16 **Wmk. 350** ***Perf. 14***

C350 AP149 80c red & multi 1.25 .20
C351 AP149 2p green & multi 1.25 .20

9th World Soccer Championships for the Jules Rimet Cup, Mexico City, May 30-June 21, 1970.

Mahatma Gandhi AP150

Astronaut's Footprint AP151

1969, Sept. 27 **Photo.** ***Perf. 14***

C352 AP150 80c multicolored .30 .20

Mohandas K. Gandhi (1869-1948), leader in India's fight for independence.

1969, Sept. 29 **Photo.**

C353 AP151 2p black .50 .25

Man's 1st landing on the moon, July 20, 1969. See note after US No. C76.

Tourist Issue

Type of Regular Issue, 1969-73 and

"Sound and Light" at Pyramid, Teotihuacan — AP152

Designs: No. C355, Acapulco Bay. No. C356, El Caracol Observatory, Yucatan. No. C357, Dancer with fruit basket, Oaxaca. No. C358, Sports fishing, Lower California, horiz.

1969-73 **Wmk. 350** ***Perf. 14***

C354 AP152 80c shown .90 .30
C355 AP152 80c multicolored .90 .30
C356 AP152 80c multicolored .90 .30

Wmk. 300

C357 A267 80c multicolored .35 .25
C358 A267 80c multicolored .35 .20
Nos. C354-C358 (5) 3.40 1.35

Issue dates: Nos. C354-C356, Nov. 1, 1969. Nos. C357-C358, Mar. 16, 1973.

Red Crosses AP154

1969, Nov. 8 **Photo.** **Wmk. 350**

C370 AP154 80c black & multi .35 .20
a. Red omitted 150.00

50th anniv. of the League of Red Cross Societies.

AP155

AP156

1969, Dec. 6 **Wmk. 350** ***Perf. 14***

C371 AP155 80c multicolored .35 .20

Installation of the ground station for communications by satellite at Tulancingo, Hidalgo.

1970, May 31 **Wmk. 350** ***Perf. 14***

Design: 80c, Soccer Ball, and Mexican Masks. 2p, Pre-Columbian sculptured heads and soccer ball.

C372 AP156 80c blue & multi 1.25 .20
C373 AP156 2p multicolored 1.25 .20

World Soccer Championships for the Jules Rimet Cup, Mexico City, May 30-June 21, 1970. The design of Nos. C372-C373 is continuous.

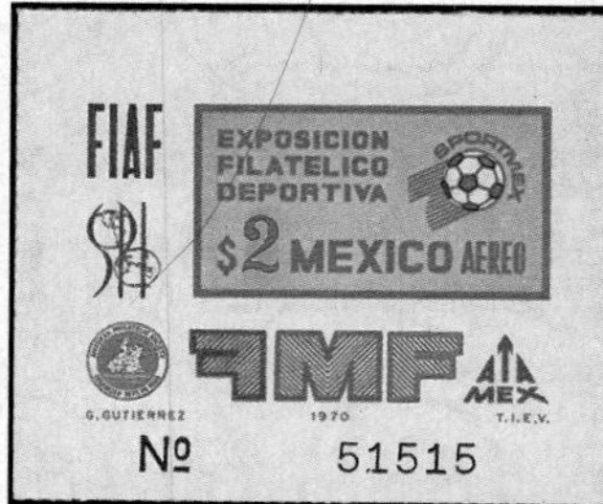

SPORTMEX '70 Emblem — AP157

1970, June 19 ***Rouletted 13***

C374 AP157 2p gray & car 5.00 3.00

SPORTMEX '70 philatelic exposition devoted to sports, especially soccer, on stamps. Mexico City, June 19-28. The 2p stamp of No. C374 is imperf.

Ode to Joy and Beethoven's Signature AP158

1970, Sept. 26 **Wmk. 350** ***Perf. 14***

C375 AP158 2p multicolored .50 .25

200th anniversary of the birth of Ludwig van Beethoven (1770-1827), composer.

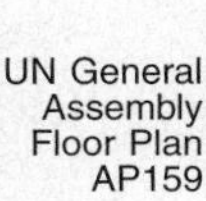

UN General Assembly Floor Plan AP159

1970, Oct. 24 **Photo.** ***Perf. 14***

C376 AP159 80c multicolored .30 .20

25th anniversary of United Nations.

Isaac Newton AP160

1971, Feb. 27 **Wmk. 350** ***Perf. 14***

C377 AP160 2p shown .45 .20

C378 AP160 2p Galileo .45 .20

C379 AP160 2p Johannes Kepler .45 .20

Nos. C377-C379 (3) 1.35 .60

Mayan Warriors, Dresden Codex AP161

Designs: No. C381, Sister Juana, by Miguel Cabrera (1695-1768). No. C382, José Maria Velasco (1840-1912), self-portrait. No. C383, El Paricutin (volcano), by Gerardo Murillo ("Dr. Atl," 1875-1964). No. C384, Detail of mural, Man in Flames, by José Clemente Orozco (1883-1949).

Imprint includes "1971"

1971, Apr. 24 **Photo.** **Wmk. 350**

C380 AP161 80c multicolored .30 .20

C381 AP161 80c multicolored .30 .20

C382 AP161 80c multicolored .30 .20

C383 AP161 80c multicolored .30 .20

C384 AP161 80c multicolored .30 .20

Nos. C380-C384 (5) 1.50 1.00

Mexican art and science through the centuries. See Nos. C396-C400, C417-C421, C439-C443, C513-C517, C527-C531.

Stamps of Venezuela, Mexico and Colombia AP162

1971, May 22 **Photo.** **Wmk. 350**

C385 AP162 80c multicolored .35 .20

EXFILCA 70, 2nd Interamerican Philatelic Exhibition, Caracas, Venezuela, Nov. 27-Dec. 6, 1970.

Francisco Javier Clavijero AP163

1971, July 10 **Wmk. 350** ***Perf. 14***

C386 AP163 2p lt ol bis & dk brn .50 .25

Francisco Javier Clavijero (1731-1786), Jesuit and historian, whose remains were returned from Italy to Mexico in 1970.

Waves AP164

Mariano Matamoros, by Diego Rivera AP165

1971, Aug. 7 **Wmk. 350** ***Perf. 14***

C387 AP164 80c multicolored .25 .20

3rd World Telecommunications Day, May 17.

1971, Aug. 28 **Photo.**

C388 AP165 2p multicolored .45 .20

Bicentenary of the birth of Mariano Matamoros (1770-1814), priest and patriot.

Vicente Guerrero AP166

Circles AP167

1971, Sept. 27

C389 AP166 2p multicolored .40 .20

Vicente Guerrero (1783-1831), independence leader, president of Mexico. Painting by Juan O'Gorman.

1971, Nov. 4 **Wmk. 300**

C390 AP167 80c grnsh bl, dk bl & blk .30 .20

25th anniv. of UNESCO.

Stamps of Venezuela, Mexico, Colombia and Peru AP168

1971, Nov. 4

C391 AP168 80c multicolored .45 .20

EXFILIMA '71, 3rd Interamerican Philatelic Exhibition, Lima, Peru, Nov. 6-14.

Faces and Hand AP169

1971, Nov. 29

C392 AP169 2p blk, dk bl & pink .45 .20

5th Congress of Psychiatry, Mexico City, Nov. 28-Dec. 4.

Ex Libris by Albrecht Dürer AP170

1971, Dec. 18

C393 AP170 2p blk & buff .65 .20

Albrecht Dürer (1471-1528), German painter and engraver.

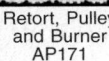

Retort, Pulley and Burner AP171

Scientists and WHO Emblem AP172

1972, Feb. 26 **Wmk. 300** ***Perf. 14***

C394 AP171 2p lilac, blk & yel .35 .20

Anniversary of the National Council on Science and Technology.

1972, Apr. 8

C395 AP172 80c multicolored .25 .20

World Health Day 1972. Stamp shows Willem Einthoven and Frank Wilson.

Art and Science Type of 1971

Designs: No. C396, King Netzahuacoyotl (1402-1472) of Texcoco, art patron. No. C397, Juan Ruiz de Alarcon (c. 1580-1639), lawyer. No. C398, José Joaquin Fernandez de Lizardi (1776-1827), author. No. C399, Ramon Lopez Velarde (1888-1921), writer. No. C400, Enrique Gonzalez Martinez (1871-1952), poet.

Imprint includes "1972"

1972, Apr. 15 **Wmk. 350**

Black Inscriptions

C396 AP161 80c ocher 1.25 .25

C397 AP161 80c green 1.25 .25

C398 AP161 80c brown 1.25 .25

C399 AP161 80c carmine 1.25 .25

C400 AP161 80c gray blue 1.25 .25

Nos. C396-C400 (5) 6.25 1.25

Mexican art and science through the centuries.

Rotary Emblem AP173

1972, Apr. 15

C401 AP173 80c multicolored .30 .20

Rotary Intl. in Mexico, 50th anniv.

Tire Treads AP174

1972, May 11 **Wmk. 300**

C402 AP174 80c gray & blk .30 .20

74th Assembly of the International Tourism Alliance, Mexico City, May 8-11.

Benito Juárez AP175

Designs: 80c, Page of Civil Register. 1.20p, Juárez, by Pelegrin Clavé.

1972 **Photo.** ***Perf. 14***

C403 AP175 80c gray bl & blk .20 .20

C404 AP175 1.20p multi .25 .20

C405 AP175 2p yellow & multi .35 .20

Nos. C403-C405 (3) .80 .60

Benito Juárez (1806-1872), revolutionary leader and president of Mexico.

Issue dates: 80c, 2p, July 18; 1.20p, Sept. 15.

Atom Symbol, Olive Branch — AP176

1972, Oct. 3 **Photo.** **Wmk. 300**

C406 AP176 2p gray, bl & blk .40 .20

16th Conference of the Atomic Energy Commission, Mexico City, Sept. 26.

"Over the Waves," by Juventino Rosas AP177

1972, Oct. 16 ***Perf. 14***

C407 AP177 80c olive bister .25 .20

28th Intl. Cong. of the Societies of Authors and Composers, Mexico City, Oct. 16-21.

Child with Doll, by Guerrero Galvan, UNICEF Emblem — AP178

1972, Nov. 4

C408 AP178 80c multicolored .75 .20

25th anniv. (in 1971) of UNICEF.

Pedro de Gante, by Rodriguez y Arangorti AP179

Map of Americas with Tourists' Footprints AP180

1972, Nov. 22 *Perf. 14*
C409 AP179 2p multicolored .35 .20

Brother Pedro de Gante (Pedro Moor or van der Moere; 1480?-1572), Franciscan brother who founded first school in Mexico, and writer.

Olympic Games Type of Regular Issue, 1972

Designs: 80c, Olympic emblems and stylized soccer game. 2p, Olympic emblems, vert.

1972, Dec. 9 Photo. Wmk. 300
C410 A289 80c green & multi .35 .20
C411 A289 2p yel grn, blk & bl .65 .20

20th Olympic Games, Munich, Aug. 26-Sept. 11.

Anti-pollution Type of Regular Issue

80c, Bird sitting on ornamental capital, vert.

1972, Dec. 16
C412 A291 80c lt blue & blk .25 .20

Anti-pollution campaign.

1972, Dec. 23
C413 AP180 80c black, yel & grn .25 .20

Tourism Year of the Americas.

Mexico #O1, Brazil #992, Colombia #130, Venezuela #22, Peru #C320 AP181

1973, Jan. 19 *Perf. 14*
C414 AP181 80c multicolored .25 .20

4th Interamerican Philatelic Exhibition, EXFILBRA 72, Rio de Janeiro, Brazil, Aug. 26-Sept. 2, 1972.

Aeolus, God of Winds — AP182

1973, Sept. 14 Photo. Wmk. 300
C415 AP182 80c brt pink, blk & bl .60 .20

Cent. of intl. meteorological cooperation.

Nicolaus Copernicus AP183

San Martin Monument AP184

Wmk. 300
1973, Oct. 10 Photo. *Perf. 14*
C416 AP183 80c slate green .30 .20

500th anniversary of the birth of Nicolaus Copernicus (1473-1543), Polish astronomer.

Art and Science Type of 1971

Designs: No. C417, Aztec calendar stone. No. C418, Carlos de Sigüenza y Gongora (1645-1700), mathematician, astronomer. No. C419, Francisco Diaz Covarrubias (1833-1889), topographer. No. C420, Joaquin Gallo (1882-1965), geographer, astronomer. No. C421, Luis Enrique Erro (1897-1955), founder of Tonanzintla Observatory.

Imprint includes "1973"

1973, Nov. 21 Wmk. 350
C417 AP161 80c car & sl grn .20 .20
C418 AP161 80c multicolored .20 .20
C419 AP161 80c multicolored .20 .20
C420 AP161 80c multicolored .20 .20
C421 AP161 80c multicolored .20 .20
Nos. C417-C421 (5) 1.00 1.00

Type of 1950-52

Design: Mexico City University Stadium.

Imprint: "Talleres de. Imp. de Est. y Vallores-Mexico"

1973 Unwmk. *Perf. 11*
C422 AP81 80c claret, I 3.00 .95

Fluorescent printing on front or back of stamps consisting of beehive pattern and diagonal inscription.

Wmk. 350
1973, Dec. 14 Photo. *Perf. 14*
C423 AP184 80c orange, indigo & yel .25 .20

Erection of a monument to San Martin in Mexico City, a gift of Argentina.

Palace of Cortes, Cuernavaca — AP185

Wmk. 300
1974, Feb. 22 Litho. *Perf. 14*
C424 AP185 80c black & multi .25 .20

EXMEX 73 Philatelic Exhibition, Cuernavaca, Apr. 7-15.

Gold Brooch, Mochica Culture AP186

1974, Mar. 6 Photo. Wmk. 300
C425 AP186 80c gold & multi .25 .20

Exhibition of Peruvian gold treasures, Mexico City, 1973-74.

Luggage — AP187

1974, Mar. 22 *Perf. 14*
C426 AP187 80c multicolored .25 .20

16th Convention of the Federation of Latin American Tourist Organizations (COTAL), Acapulco, May 1974.

CEPAL Emblem AP188

1974, Mar. 22
C427 AP188 80c black & multi .25 .20
a. Red omitted 100.00

25th anniversary (in 1973) of the Economic Commission for Latin America (CEPAL).

"The Enameled Casserole," by Picasso — AP189

1974, Mar. 29 Wmk. 300
C428 AP189 80c multicolored .35 .20

Pablo Ruiz Picasso (1881-1973), painter and sculptor.

EXFILMEX Type of 1974

1974, July 26 *Perf. 13x12*
C429 A305 80c buff, red brn & blk .25 .20

See note after No. 1065.

Biplane — AP190

Perf. 13x12
1974, Aug. 20 Photo. Wmk. 300
C430 AP190 80c shown .25 .20
C431 AP190 2p Jet plane .25 .20

50th anniversary of Mexican Airlines (MEXICANA).

Transmitter and Waves Circling Globe — AP191

1974, Oct. 4 Wmk. 300 *Perf. 14*
C432 AP191 2p multicolored .25 .20

First International Congress of Electric and Electronic Communications, Sept. 17-21.

Volleyball AP192

1974, Oct. 12 *Perf. 13x12*
C433 AP192 2p orange, bis & blk .25 .20

8th World Volleyball Championship. Perforation holes are of two sizes.

Souvenir Sheet

Mexico #O1, Colombia #130, Venezuela #22, Peru #C320, Brazil #992, Mexico #123 — AP193

Wmk. 300
1974, Oct. 26 Photo. *Imperf.*
C434 AP193 10p multicolored 3.50 1.50

EXFILMEX 74, 5th Inter-American Philatelic Exhibition, Mexico City, Oct. 26-Nov. 3. Exists with red omitted.

Felipe Carrillo Puerto AP194

1974, Nov. 8 *Perf. 14*
C435 AP194 80c grn & gldn brn .25 .20

Birth centenary of Felipe Carrillo Puerto (1874-1924), politician and journalist.

Mask, Bat and Catcher's Mitt — AP195

1974, Nov. 29 Wmk. 350 *Perf. 14*
C436 AP195 80c multi .25 .20

Mexican Baseball League, 50th anniversary.

Man's Face, Mailbox, Colonial Period
AP196

Design: 2p, Heinrich von Stephan, contemporary engraving.

1974, Dec. 13 Photo. Wmk. 300

C437	AP196	80c multicolored	.25	.20
C438	AP196	2p green & ocher	.25	.20

Centenary of Universal Postal Union.

Art and Science Type of 1971

Designs: No. C439, Mayan mural (8th century), Bonampak, Chiapas. No. C440, First musical score printed in Mexico, 1556. No. C441, Miguel Lerdo de Tejada (1869-1941), composer. No. C442, Silvestre Revueltas (1899-1940), composer (bronze bust). No. C443, Angela Peralta (1845-1883), singer.

Imprint includes "1974"

1974, Dec. 20 Wmk. 300

C439	AP161	80c multi	.25	.20
C440	AP161	80c multi	.25	.20
C441	AP161	80c multi	.25	.20
C442	AP161	80c multi	.25	.20
C443	AP161	80c multi	.25	.20
		Nos. C439-C443 (5)	1.25	1.00

Types of 1950-56

Designs (as 1950-56 issues): 40c, San Luis Potosi, head. 60c, Leon Guzman and Ignacio Ramirez. 1.60p, Chiapas, Mayan bas-relief. 1.90p, Guerrero, Acapulco waterfront. 4.30p, Oaxaca, dance. 5.20p, Guerrero, view of Taxco. 5.60p, Michoacan, masks. 50p, Valentin Gomez Farias and Melchor Ocampo.

Engraved (40c), Photogravure
Perf. 11 (40c, 1.60p), 14

1975 Wmk. 300

C444	AP81	40c bluish gray	.35	.20
C445	AP92	60c yellow grn	.90	.30
C446	AP81	1.60p red	3.00	.35
C447	AP81	1.90p rose red	3.00	.35
C448	AP81	4.30p ultra	1.00	.25
C449	AP81	5.20p purple	1.75	.40
C450	AP81	5.60p blue grn	2.25	.50
C451	AP92	50p dk bl & brick red	15.00	3.50
		Nos. C444-C451 (8)	27.25	5.85

Women's Year Emblem — AP199

1975, Jan. 3 Wmk. 300 *Perf. 14*

C456	AP199	1.60p brt pink & blk	.25	.20

International Women's Year 1975.

Declaration, UN Emblem, Mexican Flag
AP200

1975, Feb. 7 Photo. Wmk. 300

C457	AP200	1.60p multi	.25	.20

Declaration of Economic Rights and Duties of Nations.

Balsa Raft "Acali" — AP201

1975, Mar. 7 Wmk. 300 *Perf. 14*

C458	AP201	80c multicolored	.25	.20

Trans-Atlantic voyage of the "Acali" from Canary Islands to Yucatan, May-Aug. 1973.

Dr. Miguel Jimenez, by I. Ramirez
AP202

Miguel de Cervantes
AP203

1975, Mar. 24 Unwmk. *Perf. 14*

C459	AP202	2p multicolored	.25	.20

Fifth World Gastroenterology Congress.

1975, Apr. 26 Photo. Unwmk.

C460	AP203	1.60p bl blk & dk car	.25	.20

Third International Cervantes Festival, Guanajuato, Apr. 26-May 11.

Four-reales Coin, 1535 — AP204

1975, May 2

C461	AP204	1.60p bl, gold & blk	.25	.20

Intl. Numismatic Convention, Mexico City, Mar. 28-30, 1974.

Salvador Novo, by Roberto Montenegro — AP205

1975, May 9

C462	AP205	1.60p multi	.25	.20

Salvador Novo (1904-1974), author.

Mural, Siqueiros — AP206

1975, May 16

C463	AP206	1.60p multi	.25	.20

David Alfaro Siqueiros (1896-1974), painter.

UN and IWY Emblems
AP207

1975, June 19

C464	AP207	1.60p ultra & pink	.25	.20

International Women's Year World Conference, Mexico City, June 19-July 2.

Mexico City Coat of Arms
AP208

Unwmk.
1975, Aug. 1 Photo. *Perf. 14*

C465	AP208	1.60p multi	.25	.20

650th anniv. of Tenochtitlan (Mexico City).

Domingo F. Sarmiento
AP209

Teachers' Monument
AP210

Unwmk.
1975, Aug. 9 Photo. *Perf. 14*

C466	AP209	1.60p brown & sl grn	.25	.20

1st International Congress of Third World Educators, Acapulco, Aug. 5-9. Domingo Faustino Sarmiento (1811-1888), Argentinian statesman, writer and educator.

1975, Aug. 9

C467	AP210	4.30p green & ocher	.35	.20

Mexican-Lebanese friendship. The monument in Mexico City, by I Naffa al Rozzi, shows Cadmus, a mythical Phoenician, teaching the alphabet.

7th Pan American Games' Emblem
AP211

1975, Aug. 29

C468	AP211	1.60p multi	.25	.20

Pan American Games, Mexico City, Oct. 13-26.

Dr. Atl, Self-portrait
AP212

Unwmk.
1975, Oct. 3 Photo. *Perf. 14*

C469	AP212	4.30p multi	.35	.20

Geraldo Murillo ("Dr. Atl," 1875-1924), painter and writer, birth centenary.

Globe and Traffic Circle — AP213

1975, Oct. 17

C470	AP213	1.60p bl, blk & gray	.25	.20

15th World Road Congress, Mexico City, Oct. 12-26.

Type of 1950-52

Designs: 40c, San Luis Potosi, head. 60c, Leon Guzman & Ignacio Ramirez. 80c, Mexico City University stadium. 1p, Puebla, Half Moon dance. 1.60p, Chiapas, Mayan bas-relief. 5p, Queretaro, architecture. 5.60p, Michoacan, masks. 10p, Miguel Hidalgo. 20p, Modern building.

Engraved (40c, 1p), Photogravure
Perf. 11 (40c, 80c, 1p, 1.60p), 14

1975-76 Unwmk.

C471	AP81	40c bluish gray	.35	.35
C471A	AP92	60c yel grn	*1,200.*	
C472	AP81	80c claret, II	.60	.50
C473	AP81	1p grysh grn	1.00	.80
C474	AP81	1.60p red	1.75	1.00
C476	AP81	5p dk brn & org ('76)	1.50	1.00
a.		5p dark brown & red orange	2.00	2.00
C477	AP81	5.60p bluish grn ('76)	4.75	3.25
C479	AP81	10p blk & grn	4.00	2.50
C480	AP81	20p red & dl grn ('76)	7.50	4.00
		Nos. C471,C472-C480 (8)	21.45	13.40

Bicycle and Export Emblem
AP214

Designs: Export Emblem and 30c, Copper vase. 80c, Overalls. 1.90p, Oil valves. 2p, Books. 4p, Honey. 4.30p, Strawberry. 5p, Motor vehicles. 5.20p, Farm machinery. 5.60p, Cotton. 20p, Film. 50p, Cotton thread.

1975-82 Unwmk. Photo. *Perf. 14*

C486	AP214	30c copper ('76)	.20	.20
C489	AP214	80c dull blue ('76)	.25	.20
C491	AP214	1.60p black & org	.35	.20
a.		Thin paper ('81)	1.00	.20
C492	AP214	1.90p ver & dk grn	.35	.20
C493	AP214	2p ultra & gold ('76)	.65	.20
C495	AP214	4p yel bis & brn ('82)	1.25	.20
C496	AP214	4.30p brt pink & ol	.50	.20
C497	AP214	5p dk bl & ocher ('76)	1.50	.20
C498	AP214	5.20p red & blk ('76)	.75	.40
C499	AP214	5.60p yel grn & org ('76)	.35	.20

C503 AP214 20p multi, thin paper ('81) 1.00 .20
C508 AP214 50p multi ('82) 4.00 2.00
Nos. C486-C508 (12) 11.15 4.40

See Nos. C594-C603.

Art and Science Type of 1971

Designs: No. C513, Title page of "Medical History of New Spain," by Francisco Hernandez, 1628. No. C514, Alfonso L. Herrera (1868-1942), biologist. No. C515, Title page, Aztec Herbal, 1552. No. C516, Arturo S. Rosenblueth (1900-1970). No. C517, Alfredo Augusto Duges (1826-1910) French-born naturalist.

Imprint includes "1975"

1975, Nov. 21 Unwmk. *Perf. 14*

C513 AP161 1.60p buff, red & blk .25 .20
C514 AP161 1.60p vio bl & multi .25 .20
C515 AP161 1.60p black & multi .25 .20
C516 AP161 1.60p gray & multi .25 .20
C517 AP161 1.60p green & multi .25 .20
a. Thin paper 400.00
Nos. C513-C517 (5) 1.25 1.00

Telephone AP216

60-peso Gold Coin, Oaxaca, 1917 AP217

1976, Mar. 10 Photo.

C518 AP216 1.60p gray & blk .25 .20

Centenary of first telephone call by Alexander Graham Bell, Mar. 10, 1876.

1976, Mar. 25 Photo. Unwmk.

C519 AP217 1.60p black, ocher & yel .25 .20

4th International Numismatic Convention, Mexico City, March 1976.

Rain God Tlaloc and Calles Dam AP218

1976, Mar. 29 *Perf. 14*

C520 AP218 1.60p vio brn & dk grn .25 .20

12th International Great Dams Congress, Mar. 29-Apr. 2.

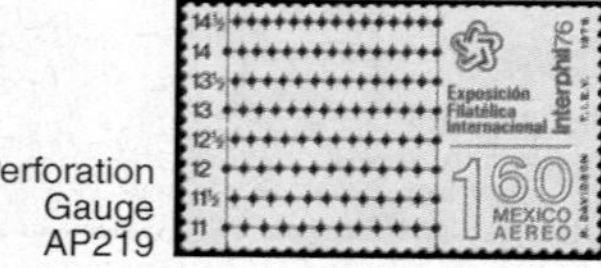

Perforation Gauge AP219

1976, May 7 Photo. Unwmk.

C521 AP219 1.60p blk, red & bl .25 .20

Interphil 76 International Philatelic Exhibition, Philadelphia, Pa., May 29-June 6.

Rainbow over City — AP220

1976, May 31 Unwmk. *Perf. 14*

C522 AP220 1.60p black & multi .25 .20

Habitat, UN Conf. on Human Settlements, Vancouver, Canada, May 31-June 11.

Liberty Bell AP221

"Peace" AP222

1976, July 4 Photo. *Perf. 14*

C523 AP221 1.60p ultra & red .25 .20

American Bicentennial.

1976, Aug. 3 Photo. *Perf. 14*

Design: "Peace" written in Chinese, Japanese, Hebrew, Hindi and Arabic.

C524 AP222 1.60p multi .25 .20

30th Intl. Cong. of Science and Humanities of Asia and North Africa, Mexico, Aug. 3-8.

Television Screen AP223

1976, Aug. 24 Photo. Unwmk.

C525 AP223 1.60p multi .25 .20

1st Latin-American Forum on Children's Television.

Luminescence

Fluorescent airmail stamps include Nos. C265, C265c, C288, C357-C358, C390-C415, C422-C423.

Airmail stamps issued on both ordinary and fluorescent paper include Nos. C220, C220D-C220E, C220G-C220H, C265b, C266-C268, C286.

Sky, Sun, Water and Earth AP224

1976, Nov. 8 Photo. *Perf. 14*

C526 AP224 1.60p multi .25 .20

World Conservation Day.

Art and Science Type of 1971

Designs: No. C527, Coatlicue, Mother of Earth, Aztec sculpture. No. C528, El Caballito, statue of Charles IV of Spain, by Manuel Tolsá. No. C529, Chief Tlahuicole, bronze statue by Manuel Vilar. No. C530, Today's God, Money, seated ceramic figure, by L. Ortiz Monasterio. No. C531, Signal, abstract sculpture by Angela Gurria.

Imprint includes "1976"

1976, Dec. 10 Photo. *Perf. 14*

C527 AP161 1.60p black & yel .25 .20
C528 AP161 1.60p blk & red brn .25 .20
C529 AP161 1.60p black & multi .25 .20
C530 AP161 1.60p car & multi .25 .20
C531 AP161 1.60p carmine & blk .25 .20
Nos. C527-C531 (5) 1.25 1.00

Score for El Pesebre by Casals AP225

1976, Dec. 29

C532 AP225 4.30p lt bl, blk & brn .35 .20

Pablo Casals (1876-1973), cellist and composer, birth centenary.

Mankind Destroyed by Nuclear Power AP226

1977, Feb. 14 Photo. *Perf. 14*

C533 AP226 1.60p multi .25 .20
a. Wmk. 300 50.00 40.00

10th anniv. of the Agreement of Tlatelolco, banning nuclear arms in Latin America.

Soccer AP227

Anniversary Emblem — AP228

1977, Aug. 23 Wmk. 300 *Perf. 14*

C534 AP227 1.60p multicolored .25 .20
C535 AP228 4.30p black, bl & yel .35 .20

Mexican Soccer Fed., 50th anniv.

Hands and Scales AP229

1977, Sept. 23 Photo. *Perf. 14*

C536 AP229 1.60p org, brn & blk .25 .20

Federal Council of Reconciliation and Arbitration, 50th anniversary.

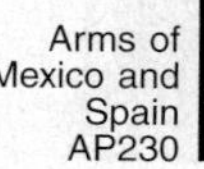

Arms of Mexico and Spain AP230

1.90p, Maps of Mexico & Spain. 4.30p, Pres. José Lopez Portillo & King Juan Carlos.

1977, Oct. 8 *Perf. 14*

C537 AP230 1.60p dull bl & blk .25 .20
C538 AP230 1.90p lt grn & maroon .25 .20
C539 AP230 4.30p tan, grn & brn .35 .20
Nos. C537-C539 (3) .85 .60

Resumption of diplomatic relations with Spain.

Tlaloc, the Rain God AP231

Ludwig van Beethoven AP232

Wmk. 300

1977, Nov. 4 Photo. *Perf. 14*

C540 AP231 1.60p multi .25 .20

National Central Observatory, centenary.

1977, Nov. 10 Photo.

C541 AP232 1.60p brt grn & brn .25 .20
C542 AP232 4.30p lilac rose & bl .30 .20

Tractor and Dam AP233

1977, Nov. 25 Photo. *Perf. 14*

C543 AP233 1.60p multi .25 .20

United Nations Desertification Conference.

Mexico City-Cuernavaca Highway — AP234

1977, Nov. 30

C544 AP234 1.60p multi .25 .20

25th anniversary of first national highway.

Arms of Campeche — AP235

1977, Dec. 3

C545 AP235 1.60p multi .25 .20

200th anniv. of the naming of Campeche.

Congress Emblem AP236

1977, Dec. 9

C546 AP236 1.60p multi .25 .20

20th World Congress for Education, Hygiene and Recreation, July 18-24, 1977.

Freighter Navimex AP237

1977, Dec. 16
C547 AP237 1.60p multi .25 .20

60th anniv. of National Merchant Marine.

Mayan Dancer, Jaina — AP238

Pre-Columbian Sculptures: No. C549, Aztec dance god. No. C550, Snake dancer, bas-relief. No. C551, Monte Alban, bas-relief. No. C552, Totonaca figurine.

1977, Dec. 26 ***Perf. 14***
C548 AP238 1.60p sal, blk & car .25 .20
C549 AP238 1.60p lt & dk bl & blk .25 .20
C550 AP238 1.60p yel, blk & gray .25 .20
C551 AP238 1.60p bl grn, blk & grn .25 .20
C552 AP238 1.60p gray, blk & red brn .25 .20
Nos. C548-C552 (5) 1.25 1.00

Mexican art.

Tumor Clinic, by David A. Siqueiros — AP239

4.30p, La Raza Medical Center, by Diego Rivera.

1978, Jan. 19 **Photo.** **Wmk. 300**
C553 AP239 1.60p multi .25 .20
C554 AP239 4.30p multi .30 .20

Mexican Social Security Institute, 35th anniv.

Moorish Fountain — AP240

1978, Mar. 1 **Photo.** ***Perf. 14***
C555 AP240 1.60p multi .25 .20

Founding of Chiapa de Corzo, Chiapas, 450th anniv.

Oil Industry Type of 1978

Designs: 1.60p, Gen. Lazaro Cardenas. 4.30p, Offshore oil rig.

Wmk. 300

1978, Mar. 18 **Photo.** ***Perf. 14***
C556 A343 1.60p brt bl & lil rose .25 .20
C557 A343 4.30p bl, brt bl & blk .30 .20

Oil industry nationalization, 40th anniv.

Arms of Diego de Mazariegos AP241

Wmk. 300

1978, Apr. 3 **Photo.** ***Perf. 14***
C558 AP241 1.60p pink, blk & pur .25 .20

400th anniversary of the founding of San Cristobal de las Casas, Chiapas, by Diego de Mazariegos.

Blood Pressure Gauge, Map of Mexico AP242

Globe, Snake, Hand Holding Stethoscope AP243

1978, Apr. 7
C559 AP242 1.60p dk bl & car .25 .20
C560 AP243 4.30p org & dk bl .30 .20

Drive against hypertension and World Health Day.

X-ABC1 Plane AP244

1978, Apr. 15
C561 AP244 1.60p ultra & multi .25 .20
C562 AP244 4.30p ultra & multi .30 .20

1st Mexican airmail route, 50th anniv.

Globe, Cogwheel, UN Emblem — AP245

4.30p, Globe, flags, cogwheel, UN emblem.

1978, Apr. 21
C563 AP245 1.60p multi .25 .20
C564 AP245 4.30p multi .30 .20

World Conference on Technical Cooperation of Underdeveloped Countries.

Soccer — AP246

Designs: 1.90p, Goalkeeper catching ball. 4.30p, Soccer player.

Wmk. 300

1978, June 1 **Photo.** ***Perf. 14***
C565 AP246 1.60p multi .25 .20
C566 AP246 1.90p multi .25 .20
C567 AP246 4.30p multi .35 .20
Nos. C565-C567 (3) .85 .60

11th World Cup Soccer Championship, Argentina, June 1-25.

Francisco (Pancho) Villa AP247

1978, June 5
C568 AP247 1.60p multi .25 .20

Pancho Villa (1878-1923), revolutionary leader.

Mexico No. C6, Independence Monument, Washington Monument — AP248

1978, June 11
C569 AP248 1.60p ol gray & red .25 .20

50th anniversary of flight Mexico to Washington by Emilio Carranza (1905-1928).

Woman and Calendar Stone — AP249

Wmk. 300

1978, July 15 **Photo.** ***Perf. 14***
C570 AP249 1.60p rose, blk & brn .25 .20
C571 AP249 1.90p brt grn, blk & brn .25 .20
C572 AP249 4.30p org, blk & brn .35 .20
Nos. C570-C572 (3) .85 .60

Miss Universe contest, Acapulco, July 1978.

Alvaro Obregón AP250

1978, July 17
C573 AP250 1.60p multi .25 .20

Obregón (1880-1928), president of Mexico.

Geographical Institute Type of 1978

Institute emblem in different arrangements.

1978, July 21 **Photo.** **Wmk. 300**
C574 A344 1.60p emerald & blk .25 .20
C575 A344 4.30p ocher & blk .35 .20

Pan-American Institute for Geography and History, 50th anniversary.

Sun Rising over Ciudad Obregón AP251

1978, Aug. 4 ***Perf. 14***
C576 AP251 1.60p multi .25 .20

Founding of the city of Obregón, 50th anniv.

Mayan Figure, Castle and Pawn AP252

Aristotle (384-322 B.C.), Philosopher AP253

1978, Aug. 19 **Photo.** ***Perf. 14***
C577 AP252 1.60p multi .25 .20
C578 AP252 4.30p multi .35 .20

World Youth Team Chess Championship, Ajedrez, Aug. 19-Sept. 7.

1978, Aug. 25

Design: 4.30p, Statue of Aristotle.

C579 AP253 1.60p multi .25 .20
C580 AP253 4.30p multi .35 .20

Mule Deer AP254

Man's Head, Dove, UN Emblem AP255

1978, Sept. 8 **Photo.** **Wmk. 300**
C581 AP254 1.60p shown .25 .20
C582 AP254 1.60p Ocelot .35 .20

Protected animals.

1978, Sept. 22 ***Perf. 14***

4.30p, Woman's head, dove, UN emblem.

C583 AP255 1.60p ver, gray & blk .25 .20
C584 AP255 4.30p lil, gray & blk .35 .20

Anti-Apartheid Year.

Emblem — AP256

Wmk. 300

1978, Oct. 23 **Photo.** ***Perf. 14***
C585 AP256 1.60p multi .25 .20

13th Congress of International Union of Architects, Mexico City, Oct. 23-27.

Dr. Rafael Lucio (1819-1886) AP257

Franz Schubert, "Death and the Maiden" AP258

1978, Nov. 13 **Wmk. 350**

C586 AP257 1.60p yellow grn .25 .20

11th International Anti-Leprosy Congress.

1978, Nov. 19 **Photo.** ***Perf. 14***

C587 AP258 4.30p brn, grn & blk .35 .20

Schubert (1797-1828), Austrian composer.

Children, Christmas Decorations AP259

Antonio Vivaldi AP260

Wmk. 350

1978, Nov. 22 **Photo.** ***Perf. 14***

C588 AP259 1.60p multi .25 .20

Christmas 1978.

1978, Dec. 1

C589 AP260 4.30p multi .35 .20

Antonio Vivaldi (1675-1741), Italian violinist and composer.

Wright Brothers' Flyer AP261

Design: 4.30p, Flyer, different view.

1978, Dec. 17

C590 AP261 1.60p multi .25 .20
C591 AP261 4.30p multi .35 .20

75th anniversary of 1st powered flight.

Einstein and his Equation AP262

Wmk. 300

1979, Apr. 20 **Photo.** ***Perf. 14***

C592 AP262 1.60p multi .25 .20

Albert Einstein (1879-1955), theoretical physicist.

Rowland Hill — AP263

1979, Apr. 27

C593 AP263 1.60p multi .25 .20

Sir Rowland Hill (1795-1879), originator of penny postage.

Export Type of 1975

Designs: Export Emblem and 50c, Circuit board. 1.60p, Bicycle. 1.90p, Oil valves. 2.50p, Tomato. 4p, Honey. 5p, Motor vehicles. 10p, Citrus fruit. 50p, Cotton thread.

1979-81 **Photo.** **Wmk. 300**

C594 AP214 50c ocher & red brn .35 .20
C596 AP214 1.60p black & org .35 .20
C597 AP214 1.90p ver & dk grn ('81) .50 .40
C599 AP214 2.50p ver & grn .35 .20
C600 AP214 4p yel bis & brn ('81) .35 .25
C601 AP214 5p dk bl & dl org 4.50 .50
C602 AP214 10p grn & yel grn ('81) .90 .75
C603 AP214 50p multicolored 6.00 1.50
Nos. C594-C603 (8) 13.30 4.00

No. C600 exists with brown omitted.

Children, Child's Drawing — AP264

1979, May 16

C604 AP264 1.60p multi .25 .20

International Year of the Child.

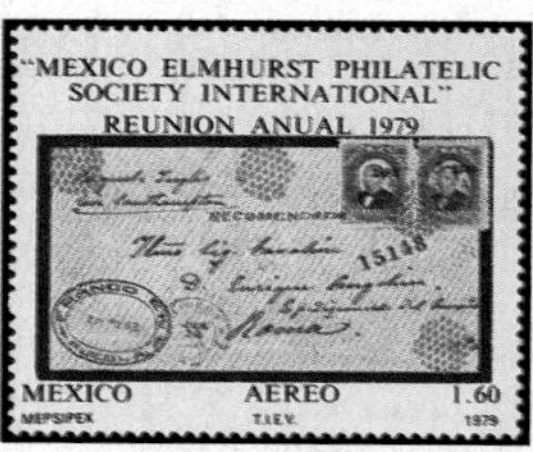

Registered Letter from Mexico to Rome, 1880 — AP265

Wmk. 300

1979, June 7 **Photo.** ***Perf. 14***

C605 AP265 1.60p multi .25 .20

MEPSIPEX '79, 3rd Intl. Exhibition of Elmhurst Philatelic Society, Mexico City, 6/7-10.

Sports Type of 1979

Designs: 1.60p, Games emblem. 4.30p, Symbolic flame and birds. 10p, Women gymnasts, horiz.

1979, June 15

C606 A348 1.60p multi .25 .20
C607 A348 4.30p multi .35 .20

Souvenir Sheet

Imperf

C608 A348 10p multi 2.00 2.00

No. C608 has simulated perforations.

University Type of 1979

Paintings: 1.60p, The Return of Quetzalcoatl, by Chavez Morado. 4.30p, Students Reaching for Culture, by Alfaro Siqueiros.

1979, July 10 ***Perf. 14***

C609 A350 1.60p multi .25 .20
C610 A350 4.30p multi .35 .20

Messenger and UPU Emblem AP266

1979, July 27 **Photo.** **Wmk. 300**

C611 AP266 1.60p multi .25 .20

Cent. of Mexico's membership in UPU.

Sports Type of 1979

1979, Sept. 2 **Wmk. 300** ***Perf. 14***

C612 A352 1.60p Tennis .25 .20
C613 A352 5.50p Swimming .35 .20

Souvenir Sheet

Imperf

C614 A352 10p Various sports 1.75 1.75

Tourism Type of 1979

#C615, Agua Azul Waterfall, Chiapas. #C616, King Coliman statue, Colima.

Wmk. 300

1979, Sept. 28 **Photo.** ***Perf. 14***

C615 A353 1.60p multi .25 .20
C616 A353 1.60p multi .25 .20

Graphic Design AP267

1979, Oct. 14 **Photo.** **Wmk. 300**

C617 AP267 1.60p multi .25 .20

ICSID, 11th Congress and Assembly of the Intl. Industrial Design Council, Oct. 1979.

Mail Service Type of 1979

Designs: 1.60p, Martin Enriquez de Almanza, Viceroy of New Spain. 5.50p, King Philip II of Spain. 10p, Sailing ship, horiz.

1979, Oct. 26

C618 A354 1.60p multi .25 .20
C619 A354 5.50p multi .35 .20

Souvenir Sheet

Imperf

C620 A354 10p multi 4.50 1.50

#C620 contains stamp with simulated perfs.

Early Lamp — AP268

1979, Oct. 21 **Wmk. 300**

C621 AP268 1.60p multi .25 .20

Centenary of invention of electric light.

Union Emblem AP269

Wmk. 300

1979, Nov. 12 **Photo.** ***Perf. 14***

C622 AP269 1.60p multi .25 .20

Latin American Universities Union, 8th general assembly.

Christmas Type of 1979

Design: 1.60p, Girl and Christmas tree.

1979, Nov. 15

C623 A355 1.60p multi .25 .20

Moon Symbol from Mexican Codex AP270

1979, Nov. 30

C624 AP270 2.50p multi .25 .20

Apollo 11 moon landing, 10th anniversary.

Monument Type of 1980

Stone Sculptures: 1.60p, Tlaloc, water god. 5.50p, Coyolxauqui, goddess.

1980, Feb. 16 **Photo.** ***Perf. 14***

C625 A356 1.60p multi .25 .20
C626 A356 5.50p multi .35 .20

16th Century Church, Acolman AP271

16th Century Churches in: No. C628, Actopan Convent. No. C629, Tlayacapan. No. C630, Yanhuitlan. No. C631, Yuriria. No. C628 actually shows Tlayacapan; No. C629, Actopan convent (inscriptions reversed).

1980, Feb. 1

C627 AP271 1.60p multi .25 .20
C628 AP271 1.60p multi .25 .20
C629 AP271 1.60p multi .25 .20
C630 AP271 1.60p multi .25 .20
C631 AP271 1.60p multi .25 .20
Nos. C627-C631 (5) 1.25 1.00

Flora and Fauna Types of 1980

1980, Mar. 8 ***Perf. 14***

C632 A357 1.60p Flamingo .25 .20
C633 A358 1.60p Vanilla plant .20 .20

Jules Verne AP272

Wmk. 300

1980, Mar. 24 **Photo.** ***Perf. 14***

C634 AP272 5.50p blk & red brn .35 .20

Jules Verne (1828-1905) French science fiction writer.

Skeleton Smoking Cigar, UN Emblem AP273

1980, Apr. 7 ***Perf. 14***
C635 AP273 1.60p multi .25 .20

World Health Day/Fight against cigarette smoking.

Costume Type

1980, Apr. 26 ***Perf. 14***
C636 A359 1.60p Chiapaneca, Chiapas .25 .20

Items inscribed "MEXICO" and "correo aereo" picturing Emiliano Zapata are not postage stamps.

AIR POST OFFICIAL STAMPS

Nos. C4 and C3 Overprinted in Black or Red

1929 **Wmk. 156** ***Perf. 12***
CO1 AP1 25c dk grn & gray brn 4.50 3.25
a. Without period 20.00 20.00
CO2 AP1 25c dk grn & gray brn (R) 4.00 *5.00*
a. Without period 21.00 21.00
CO2B AP1 25c brn car & gray brn 10.00 *12.50*
c. Without period 25.00 25.00
Nos. CO1-CO2B (3) 18.50 20.75
Set, never hinged 27.50

Types of Regular Issue of 1926 Overprinted in Red

1929, Oct. 15 **Unwmk.**
CO3 A90 2c black 75.00 *90.00*
CO4 A91 4c black 75.00 *90.00*
CO5 A90 5c black 75.00 *90.00*
CO6 A91 10c black 75.00 *90.00*
CO7 A92 20c black 75.00 *90.00*
CO8 A92 30c black 75.00 *90.00*
CO9 A92 40c black 75.00 *90.00*
Nos. CO3-CO9 (7) 525.00 630.00
Set, never hinged 675.00

Horizontal Overprint

CO10 A93 1p black *2,250.* *2,250.*
Never hinged 3,000.

#CO3-CO9 also exist with overprint reading up.

No. C26 Overprinted in Black

1930 **Wmk. 156**
CO11 AP4 20c black violet 1.10 *1.75*
Never hinged 1.30
a. Without period 20.00 *20.00*
b. Inverted overprint 18.00 *18.00*
c. As "a," inverted overprint 210.00 210.00

No. CO11 with red overprint is believed not to have been issued for postal purposes.

Plane over Mexico City OA1

1930 **Engr.**
CO12 OA1 20c gray black 6.00 6.00
CO13 OA1 35c lt violet 1.10 *1.90*
CO14 OA1 40c ol brn & dp bl 1.25 *1.75*
CO15 OA1 70c vio & ol gray 1.25 *1.75*
Nos. CO12-CO15 (4) 9.60 *11.40*
Set, never hinged 17.50

No. CO12 Surcharged in Red

1931
CO16 OA1 15c on 20c .85 *1.40*
Never hinged 1.20
a. Inverted surcharge 140.00
b. Double surcharge 140.00

No. C20 Overprinted

1932 ***Rouletted 13, 13½***
CO17 AP3 5c light blue .80 *.90*
Never hinged 1.10

Air Post Stamps of 1927-32 Overprinted

On No. C1a

1932 **Unwmk.** ***Perf. 12***
CO18 AP1 50c dk bl & cl 1,000. 1,000.
Never hinged 1,600.

On Nos. C2, C2a
Wmk. 156

CO19 AP1 50c dk bl & red brn 1.25 *1.50*
Never hinged 1.60
a. 50c dark blue & claret 1.40 *1.60*

See note after No. C2.

On Nos. C11 and C12

1932 ***Perf. 12***
CO20 AP3 10c violet 22.50 *25.00*
Never hinged 26.00
CO21 AP3 15c carmine 350.00 *375.00*
Never hinged 400.00

On Nos. C21 to C23
Rouletted 13, 13½

CO22 AP3 10c violet .35 *.55*
CO23 AP3 15c carmine 1.40 *2.00*
CO24 AP3 20c brn olive 1.40 *2.00*

Nos. C20, C21 C23 and C25 Overprinted

1933-34 ***Rouletted 13½***
CO25 AP3 5c light blue .30 *.55*
CO26 AP3 10c violet ('34) .30 *.90*
CO27 AP3 20c brown olive .75 *1.25*
CO28 AP3 50c red brn ('34) 1.25 *1.90*

On No. C2
Perf. 12

CO29 AP1 50c dk bl & red brn 1.10 *2.00*
a. 50c dark blue & claret 1.60 *2.50*

On No. C11
Perf. 12

CO30 AP3 10c violet ('34) 140.00 *175.00*
a. Double overprint *325.00*

Forgeries exist.

SPECIAL DELIVERY STAMPS

Motorcycle Postman SD1

1919 **Unwmk.** **Engr.** ***Perf. 12***
E1 SD1 20c red & black 70.00 2.75

1923 **Wmk. 156**
E2 SD1 20c blk car & blk .30 .25

For overprint see No. E7

Messenger with Quipu — SD2

1934
E3 SD2 10c brn red & blue .30 .50

Indian Archer — SD3

Imprint: "Oficina Impresora de Hacienda Mexico."

1934 ***Perf. 10x10½***
E4 SD3 10c black violet 1.50 .50

See Nos. E5-E6, E8-E9.

Redrawn

Imprint: "Talleres de Imp. de Est. y Valores-Mexico."

1938-41 **Photo.** ***Perf. 14***
E5 SD3 10c slate violet .75 .25
a. Unwatermarked 50.00
E6 SD3 20c orange red ('41) .50 .20

Imperforate copies of No. E6 were not regularly issued.

No. E2 Overprinted "1940" in Violet

1940 **Engr.** ***Perf. 12***
E7 SD1 20c red & black .40 .20

Catalogue values for unused stamps in this section, from this point to the end of the section, are for Never Hinged items.

Redrawn Archer Type of 1941

1944-47 **Wmk. 272** **Photo.** ***Perf. 14***
E8 SD3 20c orange red 1.40 .25

Wmk. 279

E9 SD3 20c orange red ('47) 1.75 .25

Special Delivery Messenger SD4

Messengers' Hands Transferring Letter — SD5

1950-51 **Photo.** **Wmk. 279**
E10 SD4 25c bright red .35 .20
E11 SD5 60c dk bl grn ('51) 2.00 .95

Redrawn

1951
E12 SD4 25c bright red 40.00 5.00

Sharper Impression, heavier shading; motorcycle sidecar ½mm from "s" of "centavos;" imprint wider, beginning under "n" of "inmediata."

Second Redrawing

1952
E13 SD4 25c bright red 15.00 2.00

Design 35½mm wide (33mm on Nos. E10 and E12); finer lettering at left, and height of letters in imprint reduced 50 per cent; three distinct lines in tires.

Redrawn Type of 1951

1954 **Wmk. 300**
E14 SD4 25c red orange .45 .20

Type of 1951

1954
E15 SD5 60c dk blue grn .55 *1.10*

Hands and Pigeon SD6

Plane Circling Globe SD7

1956 **Wmk. 300** **Photo.** ***Perf. 14***
E16 SD6 35c red lilac .25 .20
E17 SD7 80c henna brown .35 *1.40*

1962
E18 SD6 50c green .80 .20
E19 SD7 1.20p dark purple 1.25 *1.40*

1964 **Wmk. 350**
E20 SD6 50c green .65 .20
E21 SD7 1.20p dk purple 1.40 1.00

1973 **Unwmk.**
E22 SD6 50c green 3.50 3.25

Fluorescent printing on front or back consists of beehive pattern and diagonal inscription.

1975 **Wmk. 300**
E23 SD6 2p orange .20 *1.00*
E24 SD7 5p vio bl 1.25 .90

1976 **Unwmk.**
E25 SD6 2p red org .25 .40
E26 SD7 5p dk vio bl .35 1.00

Watch SD8

1976 **Unwmk.** **Photo.** ***Perf. 14***
E27 SD8 2p org & blk .25 *1.00*

INSURED LETTER STAMPS

Insured Letters — IL1

Registered Mailbag — IL2

Safe — IL3

1935 Engr. Wmk. 156 *Perf. 10½*

No.	Type	Description	Unused	Used
G1	IL1	10c vermilion	1.75	.75
a.		Perf. 10x10½		
G2	IL2	50c dk bl	10.00	.60
G3	IL3	1p turq grn	1.25	.85
		Nos. G1-G3 (3)	13.00	2.20

Nos. G1 and G4 were issued both with and without imprint.

Catalogue values for unused stamps in this section, from this point to the end of the section, are for Never Hinged items.

1944-45 Wmk. 272 *Perf. 10x10½*

No.	Type	Description	Unused	Used
G4	IL1	10c ver ('45)	12.50	1.50
G5	IL2	50c dk bl	2.00	.50
G6	IL3	1p turq grn	3.50	.65
		Nos. G4-G6 (3)	18.00	2.65

1947 Wmk. 279 *Perf. 10x10½*

No.	Type	Description	Unused	Used
G7	IL1	10c vermilion	9.50	.85
G8	IL2	50c dark blue	12.00	1.50
G9	IL3	1p turq grn	4.00	1.00
		Nos. G7-G9 (3)	25.50	3.35

Vault — IL4

1950-51 Photo. *Perf. 14*

No.	Type	Description	Unused	Used
G10	IL4	20c blue	3.75	.45
G11	IL4	40c purple	.40	.20
G12	IL4	1p yel grn ('51)	1.75	.50
G13	IL4	5p dk bl & gray grn ('51)	1.40	1.00
G14	IL4	10p car & ultra ('51)	4.00	4.00
		Nos. G10-G14 (5)	11.30	6.15

1954-71 Wmk. 300

No.	Type	Description	Unused	Used
G15	IL4	20c blue ('56)	.25	.20
G16	IL4	40c lt pur ('56)	.25	.20
G17	IL4	1p yel grn	.40	.20
a.		Size: 37x20¼mm ('71)	2.00	1.10
G18	IL4	5p bl & grn ('59)	1.25	1.00
G19	IL4	10p car & ultra ('63)	4.75	2.50
		Nos. G15-G19 (5)	6.90	4.10

No. G17 measures 35x19½mm. Vertical measurement excludes imprint.

1967 Wmk. 350 *Perf. 14*

No.	Type	Description	Unused	Used
G21	IL4	40c light purple	2.00	1.50
G22	IL4	1p yellow green	2.00	1.50

1975 Photo. Wmk. 300

No.	Type	Description	Unused	Used
G23	IL4	2p lilac rose	.40	.30
G24	IL4	20p orange & gray	3.25	3.00

Padlock — IL5

1976-81 Unwmk. Photo. *Perf. 14*

No.	Type	Description	Unused	Used
G25	IL5	40c black & blue	.30	.30
G26	IL5	1p black & blue	.30	.30
G26A	IL5	2p blk & bl ('81)	.35	.30
G27	IL5	5p black & blue	1.50	.50
G28	IL5	10p black & blue	1.50	.50
G28A	IL5	20p black & blue	2.25	.55
		Nos. G25-G28A (6)	6.20	2.45

1979 Photo. Wmk. 300

No.	Type	Description	Unused	Used
G29	IL5	40c black & blue	.90	.40
G30	IL5	1p black & blue	.90	.30
G31	IL5	5p black & blue	1.50	.45
G32	IL5	10p black & blue	4.00	.40
G33	IL5	20p black & blue	4.00	.75
		Nos. G29-G33 (5)	11.30	2.30

Perf. 14½x14

1983-86 Photo. Unwmk.

Size of Lock: 20x31mm

No.	Type	Description	Unused	Used
G36	IL5	5p black & blue	1.25	.40
G37	IL5	10p black & blue	1.00	.40
G38	IL5	20p black & blue	1.00	.40
G39	IL5	50p black & blue	2.50	.45
G40	IL5	100p blk & bl ('86)	5.00	3.00
		Nos. G36-G40 (5)	10.75	4.65

This is an expanding set. Numbers will change if necessary.

POSTAGE DUE STAMPS

D1

1908 Engr. Wmk. 155 *Perf. 14*

No.	Type	Description	Unused	Used
J1	D1	1c blue	1.00	*3.00*
J2	D1	2c blue	1.00	*3.00*
J3	D1	4c blue	1.00	*3.00*
J4	D1	5c blue	1.00	*3.00*
J5	D1	10c blue	1.00	*3.00*
		Nos. J1-J5 (5)	5.00	*15.00*

For overprints and surcharges see Nos. 381-385, 434-438, 466-470, 495-499, 593-607.

PORTE DE MAR STAMPS

These stamps were used to indicate the amount of cash to be paid to the captains of the mail steamers taking outgoing foreign mail.

PM2

PM3

1875 Unwmk. Litho. *Imperf.*

No.	Type	Description	Unused	Used
JX9	PM2	2c black	.60	*50.00*
a.		"5" added to make 25c	12.00	*100.00*
JX10	PM2	10c black	.80	*30.00*
JX11	PM2	12c black	.80	*50.00*
JX12	PM2	20c black	1.00	*50.00*
JX13	PM2	25c black	3.25	*50.00*
JX14	PM2	35c black	3.25	*60.00*
JX15	PM2	50c black	3.00	*60.00*
JX16	PM2	60c black	3.00	*75.00*
JX17	PM2	75c black	3.50	*75.00*
JX18	PM2	85c black	3.25	*100.00*
JX19	PM2	100c black	4.00	*100.00*
		Nos. JX9-JX19 (11)	26.45	700.00

Same, Numerals Larger

No.	Type	Description	Unused	Used
JX20	PM2	5c black	1.00	*50.00*
JX21	PM2	25c black	1.65	*50.00*
JX22	PM2	35c black	250.00	
JX23	PM2	50c black	1.00	*50.00*
JX24	PM2	60c black	125.00	
JX25	PM2	100c black	.60	*100.00*
		Nos. JX20-JX25 (6)	379.25	*250.00*

In Nos. JX9-JX19 the figures of value are 7mm high and "CENTAVOS" is 7½mm long. On Nos. JX20-JX25 the figures of value are 8mm high and "CENTAVOS" is 9½mm long.

Nos. JX9-JX25 exist with overprints of district names.

Counterfeits exist of Nos. JX9-JX31.

1879

No.	Type	Description	Unused
JX26	PM3	2c brown	.50
JX27	PM3	5c yellow	.50
JX28	PM3	10c red	.50
JX29	PM3	25c blue	.50
JX30	PM3	50c green	.50
JX31	PM3	100c violet	.50
		Nos. JX26-JX31 (6)	3.00

Nos. JX26-JX31 were never put in use.

Nos. JX26-JX31 were printed on paper watermarked "ADMINISTRACION GENERAL DE CORREOS MEXICO." Aprroximately ¾ of the stamps do not show any of the watermark.

Stamps of this design were never issued. Copies appeared on the market in 1884. Value, set, $22.

All were printed in same sheet of 49 (7x7). Sheet consists of 14 of 10c; 7 each of 25c, 35c, 50c; 4 each of 60c, 85c; 3 each of 75c, 100c. There are four varieties of 10c, two of 25c, 35c and 50c.

OFFICIAL STAMPS

Hidalgo — O1

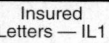

Wove or Laid Paper

1884-93 Unwmk. Engr. *Perf. 12*

No.	Type	Description	Unused	Used
O1	O1	red	1.40	1.00
a.		Vert. pair, imperf. betwn.	120.00	
O1B	O1	scarlet ('85)	1.40	1.00
O2	O1	olive brn ('87)	.90	.70
a.		Horiz. pair, imperf. betwn.	—	
b.		Blue ruled lines on paper		
O3	O1	orange ('88)	2.50	.90
a.		Vert. pair, imperf. betwn.	110.00	
b.		Perf. 11	15.00	12.00
O4	O1	blue grn ('93)	1.40	.80
a.		Imperf., pair	15.00	12.00
b.		Perf. 11	15.00	12.00
		Nos. O1-O4 (5)	7.60	4.40

Pin-perf. 6

No.	Type	Description	Unused	Used
O5	O1	olive brown ('87)	100.00	50.00

Wmk. "Correos E U M" on every Vertical Line of Ten Stamps (152)

1894 *Perf. 5½*

No.	Type	Description	Unused	Used
O6	O1	ultra	3.00	2.75
a.		Vert. pair, imperf. horiz.	35.00	
b.		Imperf., pair	45.00	

Perf. 11, 12

No.	Type	Description	Unused	Used
O7	O1	ultra	1.75	1.60

Perf. 5½x11, 11x5½

No.	Type	Description	Unused	Used
O9	O1	ultra	12.00	8.00
		Nos. O6-O9 (3)	16.75	12.35

Regular Issues with Handstamped Overprint in Black

1895 *Perf. 12*

No.	Type	Description	Unused	Used
O10	A20	1c green	17.50	6.00
O11	A20	2c carmine	20.00	6.00
O12	A20	3c orange brn	17.50	6.00
O13	A21	4c red orange	26.00	12.00
a.		4c orange	42.50	14.00
O14	A22	5c ultra	35.00	12.00
O15	A23	10c lilac rose	32.50	3.00
O16	A21	12c olive brn	70.00	30.00
O17	A23	15c brt blue	42.50	18.00
O18	A23	20c brown rose	42.50	18.00
O19	A23	50c purple	90.00	42.50
O20	A24	1p brown	200.00	90.00
O21	A24	5p scarlet	475.00	250.00
O22	A24	10p deep blue	750.00	500.00
		Nos. O10-O22 (13)	1,818.	993.50

Similar stamps with red overprint were not officially placed in use.

Black Overprint

1896-97 Wmk. 153

No.	Type	Description	Unused	Used
O23	A20	1c green	60.00	10.00
O24	A20	2c carmine	60.00	12.00
O25	A20	3c orange brn	60.00	12.00
O26	A21	4c red orange	60.00	12.00
a.		4c orange	75.00	22.50
O27	A22	5c ultra	60.00	12.00
O28	A21	12c olive brn	80.00	30.00
O29	A23	15c brt blue	100.00	30.00
O29A	A23	50c purple	650.00	650.00
		Nos. O23-O29A (8)	1,130.	768.00

Black Overprint

1897 Wmk. 154

No.	Type	Description	Unused	Used
O30	A20	1c green	100.00	30.00
O31	A20	2c scarlet	90.00	35.00
O33	A21	4c orange	125.00	60.00
O34	A22	5c ultra	100.00	35.00
O35	A21	12c olive brn	125.00	42.50
O36	A23	15c brt blue	160.00	42.50
O37	A23	20c brown rose	110.00	18.00
O38	A23	50c purple	150.00	30.00
O39	A24	1p brown	375.00	125.00
		Nos. O30-O39 (9)	1,335.	418.00

Black Overprint

1898 Unwmk.

No.	Type	Description	Unused	Used
O40	A20	1c green	35.00	9.50
O41	A20	2c scarlet	35.00	9.50
O42	A20	3c orange brn	35.00	9.50
O43	A21	4c orange	60.00	12.00
O44	A22	5c ultra	60.00	20.00
O45	A23	10c lilac rose	650.00	500.00
O46	A21	12c olive brn	125.00	30.00
O47	A23	15c brt blue	125.00	30.00
O48	A23	20c brown rose	225.00	75.00
O48A	A23	50c purple	375.00	150.00
O48B	A24	10p deep blue		—
		Nos. O40-O48A (10)	1,725.	845.50

Black Overprint

1900 Wmk. 155 *Perf. 14, 15*

No.	Type	Description	Unused	Used
O49	A25	1c green	37.50	2.50
O50	A26	2c vermilion	50.00	4.00
O51	A27	3c yellow brn	50.00	2.50
O52	A28	5c dark blue	50.00	4.50
O53	A29	10c violet & org	65.00	5.50
O54	A30	15c lavender & cl	65.00	5.50
O55	A31	20c rose & dk bl	75.00	2.50
O56	A32	50c red lil & blk	150.00	25.00
O57	A33	1p blue & blk	300.00	25.00
O58	A34	5p carmine & blk	575.00	75.00
		Nos. O49-O58 (10)	1,417.	152.00

Black Overprint

1903

No.	Type	Description	Unused	Used
O59	A25	1c violet	35.00	4.00
O60	A26	2c green	35.00	4.00
O61	A35	4c carmine	65.00	2.50
O62	A28	5c orange	65.00	13.00
O63	A29	10c blue & org	70.00	4.00
O64	A32	50c carmine & blk	200.00	25.00
		Nos. O59-O64 (6)	470.00	52.50

Regular Issues Overprinted

On Issues of 1899-1903

1910

O65 A26 2c green 175.00 6.50
O66 A27 3c orange brn 175.00 4.00
O67 A35 4c carmine 200.00 10.00
O68 A28 5c orange 225.00 50.00
O69 A29 10c blue & org 200.00 4.00
O70 A30 15c lav & claret 225.00 6.50
O71 A31 20c rose & dk bl 275.00 3.00
O72 A32 50c carmine & blk 375.00 35.00
O73 A33 1p blue & blk 575.00 125.00
O74 A34 5p carmine & blk 200.00 125.00
Nos. O65-O74 (10) 2,625. 369.00

On Issue of 1910

1911

O75 A36 1c violet 5.00 5.00
O76 A37 2c green 3.75 2.25
O77 A38 3c orange brn 5.00 2.50
O78 A39 4c carmine 5.50 2.25
O79 A40 5c orange 12.50 7.00
O80 A41 10c blue & org 5.50 2.50
O81 A42 15c gray bl & cl 13.00 8.50
O82 A43 20c red & blue 10.00 2.50
O83 A44 50c red brn & blk 35.00 15.00
O84 A45 1p blue & blk 60.00 25.00
O85 A46 5p carmine & blk 300.00 125.00
Nos. O75-O85 (11) 455.25 197.50

Nos. 500 to 505 Overprinted

1915 **Unwmk.** ***Rouletted 14½***

O86 A57 1c violet 1.00 *2.00*
O87 A58 2c green 1.00 *2.00*
O88 A59 3c brown 1.25 *2.00*
O89 A60 4c carmine 1.00 *2.00*
O90 A61 5c orange 1.00 *2.00*
O91 A62 10c ultra 1.25 *2.00*
Nos. O86-O91 (6) 6.50 12.00

All values are known with inverted overprint. All values exist imperforate and part perforate but were not regularly issued in these forms.

On Nos. 506 to 514

1915-16 ***Perf. 12***

O92 A57 1c violet 1.50 *2.00*
O93 A58 2c green 1.50 *2.00*
O94 A59 3c brown 1.50 *2.00*
O95 A60 4c carmine 1.50 *2.00*
a. "CEATRO" 21.00 *30.00*
O96 A61 5c orange 1.50 *2.00*
O97 A62 10c ultra, type II 1.50 *2.00*
a. Double overprint *475.00*
O98 A63 40c slate 8.00 *14.50*
a. Inverted overprint 24.00 *25.00*
b. Double overprint 40.00
O99 A64 1p brown & blk 10.00 *14.50*
a. Inverted overprint 27.50 *27.50*
O100 A65 5p claret & ultra 60.00 *60.00*
a. Inverted overprint 80.00
Nos. O92-O100 (9) 87.00 101.00

Nos. O98 and O99 exist imperforate but probably were not issued in that form.

Preceding Issues Overprinted in Red, Blue or Black

On No. O74

1916 **Wmk. 155**

O101 A34 5p carmine & blk 900.00

On Nos. O75 to O85

O102 A36 1c violet 6.50
O103 A37 2c green 1.25
O104 A38 3c orange brn (Bl) 1.75
O105 A39 4c carmine (Bl) 7.00
O106 A40 5c orange (Bl) 1.75
O107 A41 10c blue & org 1.75
O108 A42 15c gray bl & cl (Bk) 1.75
O109 A43 20c red & bl (Bk) 1.90
O110 A44 50c red brn & blk 200.00
O111 A45 1p blue & blk 11.00
O112 A46 5p carmine & blk *3,250.*
Nos. O102-O111 (10) 234.65

No. O102 with blue overprint is a trial color. Counterfeits exist of Nos. O110, O112.

Nos. 608, 610 to 612, 615 and 616 Overprinted Vertically in Red or Black

Thick Paper

1918 **Unwmk.** ***Rouletted 14½***

O113 A68 1c violet (R) 60.00 35.00
O114 A69 2c gray grn (R) 65.00 35.00
O115 A70 3c bis brn (R) 60.00 35.00
O116 A71 4c carmine (Bk) 60.00 35.00
O117 A74 20c rose (Bk) 125.00 90.00
O118 A75 30c gray brn (R) 190.00 175.00

On Nos. 622-623
Medium Paper
Perf. 12

O119 A72 5c ultra (R) 40.00 40.00
O120 A73 10c blue (R) 35.00 25.00
a. Double overprint 400.00 *400.00*
Nos. O113-O120 (8) 635.00 470.00

Overprinted Horizontally in Red

On Nos. 626-628
Thin Paper

O121 A63 40c violet (R) 35.00 27.50
O122 A64 1p bl & blk (R) 85.00 70.00
O123 A65 5p grn & blk (R) *575.00* *600.00*
Nos. O121-O123 (3) *695.00* *697.50*

Nos. 608 and 610 to 615 Overprinted Vertically Up in Red or Black

Thick Paper

1919 ***Rouletted 14½***

O124 A68 1c dull vio (R) 6.00 6.00
a. "OFICIAN" 70.00 *80.00*
O125 A69 2c gray grn (R) 9.50 3.50
a. "OFICIAN" 70.00 *80.00*
O126 A70 3c bis brn (R) 14.00 6.00
a. "OFICIAN" 95.00 *100.00*
O127 A71 4c car (Bk) 29.00 13.00
c. "OFICIAN" —
O127A A72 5c ultra 200.00 125.00
b. "OFICIAN" *500.00*
O128 A73 10c blue (R) 9.50 2.50
a. "OFICIAN" 85.00 60.00
O129 A74 20c rose (Bk) 60.00 47.50
a. "OFICIAN" 140.00

On Nos. 618, 622
Perf. 12

O130 A68 1c dull violet (R) 47.50 47.50
a. "OFICIAN" 140.00 100.00
O131 A72 5c ultra (R) 47.50 22.50
a. "OFICIAN" 140.00 100.00

Overprinted Horizontally
On Nos. 626-627
Thin Paper

O132 A63 40c violet (R) 47.50 35.00
O133 A64 1p bl & blk (R) 60.00 50.00
Nos. O124-O133 (11) 530.50 358.50

Nos. 608 to 615 and 617 Overprinted Vertically down in Black, Red or Blue

Size: 17½x3mm

1921 ***Rouletted 14½***

O134 A68 1c gray (Bk) 30.00 12.00
a. 1c dull violet (Bk) 17.00 7.00
O135 A69 2c gray grn (R) 5.00 3.00
O136 A70 3c bis brn (R) 8.50 4.50
O137 A71 4c carmine (Bk) 27.50 21.00
O138 A72 5c ultra (R) 25.00 12.00
O139 A73 10c bl, reading down (R) 32.50 12.00
a. Overprint reading up 60.00 60.00
O140 A74 20c rose (Bl) 47.50 27.50
O141 A75 30c gray blk (R) 25.00 25.00

Overprinted Horizontally
On Nos. 626-628
Perf. 12

O142 A63 40c violet (R) 32.50 32.50
O143 A64 1p bl & blk (R) 25.00 25.00
O144 A65 5p grn & blk (Bk) *600.00* *600.00*
Nos. O134-O144 (11) *858.50* *774.50*

Nos. 609 to 615 Overprinted Vertically Down in Black

1921-30 ***Rouletted 14½***

O145 A68 1c gray 5.00 2.50
a. 1c lilac gray 1.00 .70
O146 A69 2c gray green 1.75 .70
O147 A70 3c bister brn .80 .70
a. "OFICAL" 47.50 25.00
b. "OIFCIAL" 47.50 25.00
c. Double overprint 140.00
O148 A71 4c carmine 22.50 2.50
O149 A72 5c ultra 1.00 .70
O150 A73 10c blue 1.00 .70
a. "OIFCIAL" 50.00
O151 A74 20c brown rose 9.00 9.50
a. 20c rose 5.00 2.50

On No. 625, Overprint Reading Up
Perf. 12

O152 A75 30c gray black 7.25 2.50

Overprinted Horizontally
On Nos. 626, 628

O153 A63 40c violet 7.00 5.00
a. "OFICAL" 60.00 60.00
b. "OICIFAL" 60.00 60.00
c. Inverted overprint 90.00 *125.00*
O154 A65 5p grn & blk ('30) 375.00 *375.00*
Nos. O145-O154 (10) 430.30 *399.80*

Overprinted Vertically Down in Red On Nos. 609, 610, 611, 613 and 614

1921-24 ***Rouletted 14½***

O155 A68 1c lilac 1.60 1.00
O156 A69 2c gray green 1.50 .90
O157 A70 3c bister brown 4.00 1.00
O158 A72 5c ultra 1.60 .80
O159 A73 10c blue 35.00 3.50
a. Double overprint

On Nos. 624-625
Perf. 12

O160 A74 20c rose 7.25 1.60
O161 A75 30c gray black 19.00 5.00

Overprinted Horizontally
On Nos. 626-628

O162 A63 40c violet 14.00 7.50
a. Vert. pair, imperf. btwn.
O163 A64 1p blue & blk 35.00 25.00
O164 A65 5p green & blk 300.00 *300.00*

Overprinted Vertically Down in Blue on No. 612
Rouletted 14½

O165 A71 4c carmine 7.00 3.50
Nos. O155-O165 (11) 425.95 *349.80*

Same Overprint Vertically Down in Red on Nos. 635 and 637

1926-27 ***Rouletted 14½***

O166 A80 3c bis brn, ovpt. horiz. 12.00 12.00
a. Period omitted 30.00 30.00
O167 A82 5c orange 27.50 *30.00*

Same Overprint Vertically Down in Blue or Red On Nos. 650, 651, 655 and 656
Wmk. 156

O168 A79 2c scarlet (Bl) 20.00 20.00
a. Overprint reading up 30.00 30.00
O169 A80 3c bis brn, ovpt. horiz. (R) 5.00 5.00
a. Inverted overprint 60.00
O170 A85 10c claret (Bl) 35.00 16.00
O171 A84 20c deep blue (R) 14.00 12.00
a. Overprint reading up 14.00 12.00

Overprinted Horizontally in Red On Nos. 643, 646-649
Perf. 12

O172 A81 4c green 6.00 6.00
O173 A83 30c dk grn 6.00 6.00
O174 A63 40c violet 16.00 16.00
a. Inverted overprint 80.00
O175 A87 50c olive brn 1.50 1.50
a. 50c yellow brown 18.00 18.00
O176 A88 1p red brn & bl 15.00 15.00
Nos. O168-O176 (9) 118.50 97.50

Same Overprint Horizontally on No. 651, Vertically Up on Nos. 650, 653-656, 666, RA1

1927-31 ***Rouletted 14½***

O177 PT1 1c brown ('31) .70 *1.00*
O178 A79 2c scarlet .70 *1.00*
a. "OFICAIL" 30.00 30.00
b. Overprint reading down 1.50 *2.00*
O179 A80 3c bis brn 2.00 1.50
a. "OFICAIL" 40.00 30.00
O180 A82 4c green 1.50 1.00
a. "OFICAIL" 40.00 40.00
b. Overprint reading down 10.00 2.00
O181 A82 5c orange 4.00 3.00
a. Overprint reading down 4.00 2.50
O182 A94 8c orange 12.00 8.00
a. Overprint reading down 7.00 6.00
O183 A85 10c lake 2.00 2.00
a. Overprint reading down 2.00 2.00
O184 A84 20c dark blue 10.00 4.00
a. "OFICAIL" 40.00 40.00
b. Overprint reading down 20.00 20.00
Nos. O177-O184 (8) 32.90 21.50

Overprinted Vertically Up on #O186, Horizontally
On Nos. 643 and 645 to 649

1927-33 ***Perf. 12***

O185 A81 4c green 6.00 5.00
a. Inverted overprint 30.00 30.00
O186 A85 10c brown lake 55.00 45.00
O187 A83 30c dark green 1.40 1.00
a. Inverted overprint 30.00 30.00
b. Pair, tête bêche overprints 35.00 35.00
c. "OFICAIL" 35.00 35.00
O188 A63 40c violet 12.00 8.00
O189 A87 50c olive brn ('33) 3.25 *4.00*
O190 A88 1p red brn & bl 24.00 20.00
Nos. O185-O190 (6) 101.65 83.00

The overprint on No. O186 is vertical.

Nos. 320, 628, 633 Overprinted Horizontally

On Stamp No. 320

1927-28 **Wmk. 155** ***Perf. 14, 15***

O191 A46 5p car & blk (R) 175.00 *250.00*
O192 A46 5p car & blk (Bl) 175.00 *250.00*

Unwmk. ***Perf. 12***

O193 A65 5p grn & blk (Bk) 375.00 *500.00*
a. Inverted overprint — —
O194 A78 10p blk brn & blk (Bl) 200.00 *300.00*

No. 320 Overprinted Horizontally

Wmk. 155 ***Perf. 14***

O195 A46 5p carmine & blk 300.00

Nos. 650 and 655 Overprinted Horizontally

1928-29 **Wmk. 156** ***Rouletted 14½***

Size: 16x2½mm

O196 A79 2c dull red 18.00 12.00
O197 A85 10c rose lake 27.50 12.00

Nos. RA1, 650-651, 653-656 Overprinted

1932-33

O198 PT1 1c brown .70 *1.00*
O199 A79 2c dull red .80 *1.00*
O200 A80 3c bister brn 3.00 3.00
O201 A82 4c green 10.00 8.00
O202 A82 5c orange 12.00 8.00
O203 A85 10c rose lake 3.25 3.00
O204 A84 20c dark blue 15.00 10.00
a. Double overprint *200.00* *90.00*
Nos. O198-O204 (7) 44.75 34.00

Nos. 651, 646-649 Overprinted Horizontally

1933 ***Rouletted 14½***

O205 A80 3c bister brn 3.00 3.00

Perf. 12

O206 A83 30c dk green 8.00 3.00
O207 A63 40c violet 15.00 6.00
O208 A87 50c olive brn 2.50 3.00
a. "OFICIAL OFICIAL" 50.00 50.00
O209 A88 1p red brn & bl, type I 3.00 3.00
a. Type II 2.75 3.50

Overprinted Vertically On No. 656
Rouletted 14½

O210 A84 20c dark blue 18.00 10.00
Nos. O205-O210 (6) 49.50 28.00

Nos. RA1, 651, 653, 654, 683 Overprinted Horizontally

1934-37 ***Rouletted 14½***
Size: 13x2mm

O211 PT1 1c brown 5.00 *6.00*
O212 A80 3c bister brn .70 .70
O213 A82 4c green 12.00 10.00
O214 A82 5c orange .70 .70
O215 A96 15c dk blue ('37) 1.00 1.00
Nos. O211-O215 (5) 19.40 18.40

See No. O217a.

Same Overprint on Nos. 687A-692

1934-37 ***Perf. 10½***

O216 PT1 1c brown ('37) 1.00 *1.25*
O217 A79 2c scarlet 1.00 *1.50*
a. On No. 650 (error) 350.00
b. Double overprint 275.00
O218 A82 4c green ('35) 1.40 1.60
O219 A85 10c brown lake 1.00 1.00
O220 A84 20c dk blue ('37) 1.25 1.25
O221 A83 30c dk bl grn ('37) 2.00 2.00

On Nos. 647 and 649
Perf. 12, 11½x12

O222 A63 40c violet 3.00 3.50
O223 A88 1p red brn & bl (I) 5.00 *6.00*
a. Type II 4.00 4.00
Nos. O216-O223 (8) 15.65 18.10

On Nos. 707 to 709, 712, 715, 716, 717, 718 and 719

O224 A108 1c orange 2.00 *4.00*
O225 A109 2c green 1.25 *2.00*
O226 A110 4c carmine 1.25 *1.40*
O227 A112 10c violet 1.25 *2.50*
O228 A114 20c ultra 1.60 *2.50*
O229 A115 30c lake 2.00 *4.00*
O230 A116 40c red brown 2.50 *4.00*
O231 A117 50c black 2.75 *2.75*
O232 A118 1p dk brn & org 8.00 *12.00*
Nos. O224-O232 (9) 22.60 *35.15*

PARCEL POST STAMPS

Railroad Train PP1

1941 **Photo.** **Wmk. 156** ***Perf. 14***

Q1 PP1 10c brt rose 2.75 .35
Q2 PP1 20c dk vio bl 1.75 .35

1944-46 **Wmk. 272**

Q3 PP1 10c brt rose 1.75 1.00
Q4 PP1 20c dk vio bl ('46) 5.00 2.50

1947-49 **Wmk. 279**

Q5 PP1 10c brt rose 1.25 .60
Q6 PP1 20c dk vio bl ('49) 1.60 .60

Streamlined Locomotive PP2

1951

Q7 PP2 10c rose pink 5.00 .40
Q8 PP2 20c blue violet 4.00 .70

1954 **Wmk. 300**

Q9 PP2 10c rose pink 4.25 .60
Q10 PP2 20c blue violet 4.25 1.50

POSTAL TAX STAMPS

Morelos Monument — PT1

Rouletted 14½

1925 **Engr.** **Wmk. 156**

RA1 PT1 1c brown .35 .20
a. Imperf. 30.00

1926 ***Perf. 12***

RA2 PT1 1c brown .75 *5.00*
a. Booklet pane of 2 12.00

1925 **Unwmk.** ***Rouletted 14½***

RA3 PT1 1c brown 75.00 19.00

It was obligatory to add a stamp of type PT1 to the regular postage on every article of domestic mail matter. The money obtained from this source formed a fund to combat a plague of locusts.

In 1931, 1c stamps of type PT1 were discontinued as Postal Tax stamps. It was subsequently used for the payment of postage on drop letters (announcement cards and unsealed circulars) to be delivered in the city of cancellation. See No. 687A.

For overprints see Nos. O177, O198, O211, O216, RA4.

Red Overprint

1929 **Wmk. 156**

RA4 PT1 1c brown .35 .20
a. Overprint reading down 75.00 75.00

There were two settings of this overprint. They may be distinguished by the two lines being spaced 4mm or 6mm apart.

The money from sales of this stamp was devoted to child welfare work.

Mother and Child — PT3

1929 **Litho.** ***Rouletted 13, 13½***

RA5 PT3 1c violet .35 .20

PT4

PT5

1929 **Unwmk.**
Size: 18x24½mm

RA6 PT4 2c deep green .40 .20
RA7 PT4 5c brown .40 .20
a. Imperf., pair 60.00 60.00

For surcharges see Nos. RA10-RA11.

1929 **Size: 19x25¼mm**

Two types of 1c:

Type I — Background lines continue through lettering of top inscription. Denomination circle hangs below second background line. Paper and gum white.

Type II — Background lines cut away behind some letters. Circle rests on second background line. Paper and gum yellowish.

RA8 PT5 1c violet, type I .35 .20
a. Booklet pane of 4 10.00
b. Booklet pane of 2 18.00
c. Type II .40 .20
d. Imperf., pair 50.00 50.00
RA9 PT5 2c deep green .65 .20
a. Imperf., pair 12.00

The use of these stamps, in addition to the regular postage, was compulsory. The money obtained from their sale was used for child welfare work.

For surcharge see No. RA12.

Nos. RA6, RA7, RA9 Surcharged

1930

RA10 PT4 1c on 2c dp grn .75 .40
RA11 PT4 1c on 5c brown 1.00 .60
RA12 PT5 1c on 2c dp grn 2.00 1.00
Nos. RA10-RA12 (3) 3.75 2.00

Used stamps exist with surcharge double or reading down.

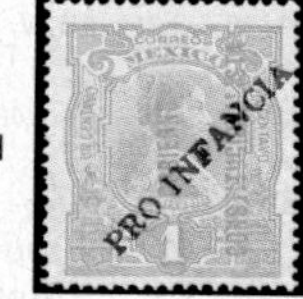

No. 423 Overprinted

1931, Jan. 30 **Wmk. 155** ***Perf. 14***

RA13 A36 1c dull violet .40 .40
a. "PRO INFANCIA" double 50.00

Indian Mother and Child — PT6

Mosquito Attacking Man — PT7

Wmk. 156

1934, Sept. 1 **Engr.** ***Perf. 10½***

RA13B PT6 1c dull orange .30 .20

1939 **Photo.** **Wmk. 156** ***Perf. 14***

RA14 PT7 1c Prus blue 1.50 .20
a. Imperf. 3.00 3.00

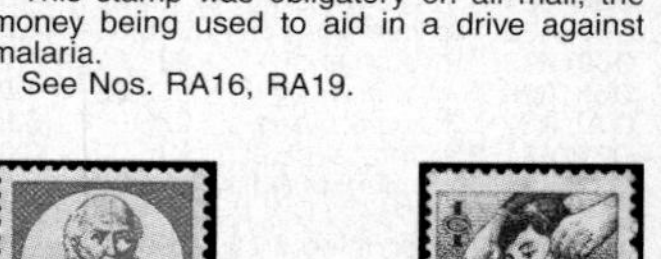

This stamp was obligatory on all mail, the money being used to aid in a drive against malaria.

See Nos. RA16, RA19.

Miguel Hidalgo y Costilla PT8

Learning Vowels PT9

1941

RA15 PT8 1c brt carmine .45 .20

Type of 1939

1944 **Wmk. 272** ***Perf. 14***

RA16 PT7 1c Prus blue 1.00 .20

1946 **Photo.** **Wmk. 279**

RA17 PT9 1c black brown .45 .20
a. 1c green black 1.00 1.00

1947 **Wmk. 272**

RA18 PT9 1c black brown 65.00 5.00

Type of 1939
Wmk. 279

RA19 PT7 1c Prus blue 3.50 .30

PROVISIONAL ISSUES

During the struggle led by Juarez to expel the Emperor Maximilian, installed June, 1864 by Napoleon III and French troops, a number of towns when free of Imperial forces issued provisional postage stamps. Maximilian was captured and executed June 19, 1867, but provisional issues continued current for a time pending re-establishment of Republican Government.

Campeche

A southern state in Mexico, comprising the western part of the Yucatan peninsula.

A1

White Paper
Numerals in Black

1876 **Handstamped** ***Imperf.***

1 A1 5c gray blue & blue *2,000.*
2 A1 25c gray blue & blue *1,100.*
3 A1 50c gray blue & blue *4,500.*

The stamps printed in blue-black and blue on yellowish paper, formerly listed as issued in 1867, are now known to be an unofficial production of later years. They are reprints, but produced without official sanction.

Chiapas

A southern state in Mexico, bordering on Guatemala and the Pacific Ocean.

A1

1866 **Typeset**

1	A1 ½r blk, *gray bl*	2,000.	1,300.
2	A1 1r blk, *lt grn*		850.
3	A1 2r blk, *rose*		900.
4	A1 4r blk, *lt buff*		2,000.
a.	Vertical half used as 2r on cover		3,000.
5	A1 8r blk, *rose*		15,000.
a.	Quarter used as 2r on cover		4,000.
b.	Half used as 4r on cover		5,000.

Chihuahua

A city of northern Mexico and capital of the State of Chihuahua.

A1

1872 **Handstamped**

1	A1 12(c) black	1,200.
2	A1 25(c) black	1,000.

Specialists question the authenticity of these stamps. The Catalogue Editors would appreciate any information on this issue.

Cuautla

A town in the state of Morelos.

A1

1867 **Handstamped**

1	A1 (2r) black	7,000.

All known examples on cover are uncanceled. Examples are known without the "73" inside the oval.

Cuernavaca

A city of Mexico, just south of the capital, and the capital of the State of Morelos.

A1

1867 **Handstamped**

1	A1 (1r) black	1,750.
2	A1 (2r) black	40,000.

No. 1 was canceled at Cuernavaca with the district name overprint. Supplies of overprinted stamps were sent to the Tetecala and Yquala sub-offices, where they were canceled with the usual local postmarks.

No. 2 was created by doubling the impression of the basic stamp and applying the district name overprint twice.

Unused examples of Nos. 1 and 2 do not exist.

Counterfeits exist.

Guadalajara

A city of Mexico and capital of the State of Jalisco.

A1

Dated "1867"
1st Printing
Medium Wove Paper

1867 **Handstamped** ***Imperf.***

1	A1 Medio r blk, *white*	350.00	250.00
2	A1 un r blk, *gray bl*		200.00
a.	Overprinted "Cd. Guzman"		1,000.
3	A1 un r blk, *dk bl*		450.00
4	A1 un r blk, *white*		150.00
a.	Overprinted "Cd. Guzman"		750.00
5	A1 2r blk, *dk grn*	80.00	21.00
a.	Overprinted "Cd. Guzman"		500.00
6	A1 2r blk, *white*		125.00
a.	Overprinted "Cd. Guzman"		400.00
7	A1 4r blk, *rose*	250.00	300.00
a.	Half used as 2r on cover		500.00
b.	Overprinted "Cd. Guzman"		900.00
8	A1 4r blk, *white*		500.00
9	A1 un p blk, *lilac*	250.00	300.00

Serrate Perf.

10	A1 un r blk, *gray bl*		400.00
11	A1 2r blk, *dk grn*		250.00
12	A1 4r blk, *rose*		350.00
12A	A1 4r blk, *lilac*		1,750.

2nd Printing
No Period after "2" or "4"
Thin Quadrille Paper
Imperf

13	A1 2r blk, *green*	30.00	20.00
a.	Half used as 1r on cover		400.00

Serrate Perf.

14	A1 2r blk, *green*		225.00

Thin Laid Batonné Paper
Imperf

15	A1 2r blk, *green*	45.00	24.00

Serrate Perf.

16	A1 2r blk, *green*		225.00

3rd Printing
Capital "U" in "Un" on 1r, 1p
Period after "2" and "4"
Thin Wove Paper
Imperf

16A	A1 Un r blk, *white*		125.00
17	A1 Un r blk, *blue*		90.00
17A	A1 Un r blk, *lilac*	100.00	
18	A1 2r blk, *rose*		50.00
18A	A1 4r blk, *blue*	500.00	1,000.

Serrate Perf.

19	A1 Un r blk, *blue*		300.00
19A	A1 Un r blk, *rose*		750.00

Thin Quadrille Paper
Imperf

20	A1 2r blk, *rose*	42.50	42.50
21	A1 4r blk, *blue*	15.00	30.00
22	A1 4r blk, *white*	90.00	
23	A1 Un p blk, *lilac*	15.00	60.00
24	A1 Un p blk, *rose*	65.00	

Serrate Perf.

25	A1 Un p blk, *lilac*	750.00	750.00
25A	A1 Un p blk, *rose*		300.00

Thin Laid Batonné Paper
Imperf

26	A1 Un r blk, *green*	22.50	17.50
27	A1 2r blk, *rose*	27.50	22.50
27A	A1 2r blk, *green*		47.50
28	A1 4r blk, *blue*	17.50	42.50
29	A1 4r blk, *white*	100.00	
30	A1 Un p blk, *lilac*	30.00	52.50
31	A1 Un p blk, *rose*	65.00	

Serrate Perf.

32	A1 Un r blk, *green*	65.00	
33	A1 2r blk, *rose*	70.00	200.00
34	A1 4r blk, *blue*		250.00
34A	A1 4r blk, *white*		1,750.

Thin Oblong Quadrille Paper
Imperf

35	A1 Un r blk, *blue*	250.00	22.50
36	A1 4r blk, *blue*		600.00

Serrate Perf.

37	A1 Un r blk, *blue*		300.00

4th Printing
Dated "1868"
Wove Paper

1868 ***Imperf.***

38	A1 2r blk, *lilac*	30.00	14.00
a.	Half used as 1r on cover		500.00
39	A1 2r blk, *rose*	52.50	65.00

Serrate Perf.

40	A1 2r blk, *lilac*		52.50
41	A1 2r blk, *rose*		95.00

Laid Batonné Paper
Imperf

42	A1 un r blk, *green*	12.50	12.50
a.	"nu" instead of "un"		300.00
43	A1 2r blk, *lilac*	12.50	12.50

Serrate Perf.

44	A1 un r blk, *green*	250.00	200.00

Quadrille Paper.
Imperf

45	A1 2r blk, *lilac*	25.00	14.00

Serrate Perf.

46	A1 2r blk, *lilac*	300.00	300.00

Laid Paper
Imperf

47	A1 un r blk, *green*	13.00	17.00
a.	Watermarked "LA + F"	750.00	1,000.
48	A1 2r blk, *lilac*	32.50	32.50
49	A1 2r blk, *rose*	37.50	37.50

Serrate Perf.

50	A1 un r blk, *green*		55.00
51	A1 2r blk, *rose*	110.00	

Counterfeits of Nos. 1-51 abound.

Merida

A city of southeastern Mexico, capital of the State of Yucatan.

Mexico No. 521 Surcharged **25**

1916 **Wmk. 155** ***Perf. 14***

1	A40 25(c) on 5c org, on cover	500.00

The G.P.D.E.M. overprint reads down.

Authorities consider the Monterrey, Morelia and Patzcuaro stamps to be bogus.

Tlacotalpan

A village in the state of Veracruz.

A1

Handstamped Monogram, Value in Manuscript

1856, Oct.

1	A1 ½(r) black	30,000.

REVOLUTIONARY ISSUES

SINALOA

A northern state in Mexico, bordering on the Pacific Ocean. Stamps were issued by a provisional government.

Coat of Arms — A1

1929 **Unwmk.** **Litho.** ***Perf. 12***

1	A1 10c blk, red & bl	5.00
a.	Tête bêche pair	35.00
2	A1 20c blk, red & gray	5.00

Just as Nos. 1 and 2 were ready to be placed on sale the state was occupied by the Federal forces and the stamps could not be used. At a later date a few copies were canceled by favor.

A recent find included a number of errors or printer's waste.

YUCATAN

A southeastern state of Mexico.

Chalchiuitlicue, Nahuatl Water Goddess — A1

"Casa de Monjas" — A2

Temple of the Tigers — A3

Without Gum

1924 **Unwmk.** **Litho.** ***Imperf.***

1	A1 5c violet	10.00	15.00
2	A2 10c carmine	40.00	50.00
3	A3 50c olive green	175.00	

Perf. 12

4	A1 5c violet	50.00	60.00
5	A2 10c carmine	50.00	75.00
6	A3 50c olive green	200.00	

Nos. 3 and 6 were not regularly issued.

MICRONESIA, FEDERATED STATES OF

ˌmī-krə-ˈnē-zhə

LOCATION — A group of over 600 islands in the West Pacific Ocean, north of the Equator.
GOVT. — Republic
AREA — 271 sq. miles
POP. — 131,500 (1999 est.)
CAPITAL — Palikir

These islands, also known as the Caroline Islands, were bought by Germany from Spain in 1899. Caroline Islands stamps issued as a German territory are listed in Vol. 2 of this Catalogue. Seized by Japan in 1914, they were taken by the US in WWII and became part of the US Trust Territory of the Pacific in 1947. By agreement with the USPS, the islands began issuing their own stamps in 1984, with the USPS continuing to carry the mail to and from the islands.

On Nov. 3, 1986 Micronesia became a Federation as a Sovereign State in Compact of Free Association with the US.

100 Cents = 1 Dollar

Catalogue values for all unused stamps in this country are for Never Hinged items.

Postal Service Inauguration — A1

1984, July 12 Litho. Perf. 14

1 A1 20c Yap .45 .45
2 A1 20c Truk .45 .45
3 A1 20c Pohnpei .45 .45
4 A1 20c Kosrae .45 .45
a. Block of 4, #1-4 1.90 1.90

For surcharges see Nos. 48-51.

Fernandez de Quiros — A2

Men's House, Yap — A3

Designs: 1c, 19c, Pedro Fernandez de Quiros, Spanish explorer, first discovered Pohnpei, 1595. 2c, 20c, Louis Duperrey, French explorer. 3c, 30c, Fyedor Lutke, Russian explorer. 4c, 37c, Dumont d'Urville. 10c, Sleeping Lady, Kosrae. 13c, Liduduhriap Waterfall, Pohnpei. 17c, Tonachau Peak, Truk. 50c, Devil mask, Truk. $1, Sokeh's Rock, Pohnpei. $2, Canoes, Kosrae. $5, Stone money, Yap.

1984, July 12 Perf. 13½x13

5 A2 1c Prussian blue .20 .20
6 A2 2c deep claret .20 .20
7 A2 3c dark blue .20 .20
8 A2 4c green .20 .20
9 A3 5c yellow brown .20 .20
10 A3 10c dark violet .20 .20
11 A3 13c dark blue .20 .20
12 A3 17c brown lake .25 .25
13 A2 19c dark violet .30 .30
14 A2 20c olive green .30 .30
15 A2 30c rose lake .45 .45
16 A2 37c deep violet .55 .55
17 A3 50c brown .75 .75
18 A3 $1 olive 1.50 1.50
19 A3 $2 Prussian blue 3.00 3.00
20 A3 $5 brown lake 7.50 7.50
Nos. 5-20 (16) 16.00 16.00

See Nos. 33, 36, 38.

Ausipex '84 A4

1984, Sept. 21 Litho. Perf. 13½

21 A4 20c Truk Post Office .40 .40
Nos. 21,C4-C6 (4) 3.00 3.00

Christmas A5

Child's drawing.

1984, Dec. 20

22 A5 20c Child in manger .90 .90
Nos. 22,C7-C9 (4) 3.55 3.55

Ships — A6

1985, Aug. 19

23 A6 22c U.S.S. Jamestown .55 .55
Nos. 23,C10-C12 (4) 3.00 3.00

Christmas A7

1985, Oct. 15 Litho. Perf. 13½

24 A7 22c Lelu Protestant Church, Kosrae .75 .60
Nos. 24,C13-C14 (3) 2.90 2.75

Audubon Birth Bicentenary — A8

1985, Oct. 30 Perf. 14½

25 A8 22c Noddy tern .60 .60
26 A8 22c Turnstone .60 .60
27 A8 22c Golden plover .60 .60
28 A8 22c Black-bellied plover .60 .60
a. Block of 4, #25-28 2.60 2.60
Nos. 25-28,C15 (5) 3.40 3.40

Types of 1984 and

Birds — A9

Tall Ship Senyavin A10

Natl. Seal A11

Perf. 13½ (A8a), 13½x13

1985-88 Litho.

31 A9 3c Long-billed white-eye .20 .20
32 A9 14c Truk monarch .30 .30
33 A3 15c Liduduhriap Waterfall, Pohnpei .30 .30
a. Booklet pane of 10 6.00 —
34 A10 22c bright blue green .35 .35
35 A9 22c Pohnpei mountain starling .45 .45
36 A3 25c Tonachau Peak, Truk .50 .50
a. Booklet pane of 10 6.50 —
b. Booklet pane, 5 15c + 5 25c 7.50 —
37 A10 36c ultramarine .70 .70
38 A3 45c Sleeping Lady, Kosrae .90 .90
39 A11 $10 bright ultra 15.00 15.00
Nos. 31-39,C34-C36 (12) 21.70 21.70

Issued: $10, 10/15; #34, 4/14/86; 3c, 14c, #35, 8/1/88; 15c, 25c, 36c, 45c, 9/1/88.

Nan Madol Ruins, Pohnpei A16

1985, Dec. Litho. Perf. 13½

45 A16 22c Land of the Sacred Masonry .60 .60
Nos. 45,C16-C18 (4) 3.00 3.00

Intl. Peace Year — A17

1986, May 16

46 A17 22c multicolored .65 .60

Nos. 1-4 Surcharged

1986, May 19 Litho. Perf. 14

48 A1 22c on 20c No. 1 .40 .40
49 A1 22c on 20c No. 2 .40 .40
50 A1 22c on 20c No. 3 .40 .40
51 A1 22c on 20c No. 4 .40 .40
a. Block of 4, #48-51 1.75 1.75

AMERIPEX '86 A18

Bully Hayes (1829-1877), Buccaneer.

1986, May 22 Perf. 13½

52 A18 22c At ship's helm .50 .50
Nos. 52,C21-C24 (5) 4.00 4.00

First Passport A19

1986, Nov. 4 Litho. Perf. 13½

53 A19 22c multicolored .60 .60

Christmas A20

Virgin and child paintings: 5c, Italy, 18th cent. 22c, Germany, 19th cent.

1986, Oct. 15 Litho. Perf. 14½

54 A20 5c multicolored .20 .20
55 A20 22c multicolored .75 .75
Nos. 54-55,C26-C27 (4) 3.35 3.35

Anniversaries and Events — A21

1987, June 13 Litho. Perf. 14½

56 A21 22c Intl. Year of Shelter for the Homeless .50 .50
Nos. 56,C28-C30 (4) 3.20 3.20

Souvenir Sheet

57 A21 $1 CAPEX '87 3.25 3.25

Christmas A22

22c, Archangel Gabriel appearing before Mary.

1987, Nov. 16 Litho. Perf. 14½

58 A22 22c multicolored .60 .60
Nos. 58,C31-C33 (4) 3.30 3.30

Colonial Eras — A23

1988, July 20 Litho. Perf. 13x13½

59 A23 22c German .60 .60
60 A23 22c Spanish .60 .60
61 A23 22c Japanese .60 .60
62 A23 22c US Trust Territory .60 .60
a. Block of 4, #59-62 2.40 2.40
Nos. 59-62,C37-C38 (6) 4.30 4.30

Printed se-tenant in sheets of 28 plus 4 center labels picturing flags of Spain (UL), Germany (UR), Japan (LL) and the US (LR).

1988 Summer Olympics, Seoul — A24

1988, Sept. 1 Litho. Perf. 14

63 A24 25c Running .50 .50
64 A24 25c Women's hurdles .50 .50
a. Pair, #63-64 1.00 1.00
65 A24 45c Basketball .80 .80
66 A24 45c Women's volleyball .80 .80
a. Pair, #65-66 1.65 1.65
Nos. 63-66 (4) 2.60 2.60

Christmas — A25

Children decorating tree: No. 67, Two girls, UL of tree. No. 68, Boy, girl, dove, UR of tree. No. 69, Boy, girl, LL of tree. No. 70, Boy, girl, LR of tree. Se-tenant in a continuous design.

1988, Oct. 28 Litho. Perf. 14

67 A25 25c multicolored .45 .45
68 A25 25c multicolored .45 .45
69 A25 25c multicolored .45 .45
70 A25 25c multicolored .45 .45
a. Block of 4, #67-70 1.90 1.90

Miniature Sheet

Truk Lagoon State Monument — A26

a, Sun and stars angelfish. b, School of fish. c, 3 divers. d, Goldenjack. e, Blacktip reef shark. f, 2 schools of fish. g, Squirrelfish. h, Batfish. i, Moorish idols. j, Barracudas. k, Spot banded butterflyfish. l, Three-spotted dam-selfish. m, Foxface. n, Lionfish. o, Diver. p, Coral. q, Butterflyfish. r, Bivalve, fish, coral.

1988, Dec. 19 Litho. *Perf. 14*

71 Sheet of 18 9.50 9.50
a.-r. A26 25c any single .50 .50

Mwarmwarms — A27

1989, Mar. 31 Litho. *Perf. 14*

72 A27 45c Plumeria .65 .65
73 A27 45c Hibiscus .65 .65
74 A27 45c Jasmine .65 .65
75 A27 45c Bougainvillea .65 .65
a. Block of 4, #72-75 2.75 2.75

Souvenir Sheet

Pheasant and Chrysanthemum, 1830s, by Hiroshige (1797-1858) — A28

1989, May 15 Litho. *Perf. 14½*

76 A28 $1 multicolored 1.60 1.60

Hirohito (1901-1989), emperor of Japan.

Sharks A29

1989, July 7

77 A29 25c Whale .40 .40
78 A29 25c Hammerhead .40 .40
a. Pair, #77-78 .80 .80
79 A29 45c Tiger, vert. .75 .75
80 A29 45c Great white, vert. .75 .75
a. Pair, #79-80 1.50 1.50
Nos. 77-80 (4) 2.30 2.30

Miniature Sheet

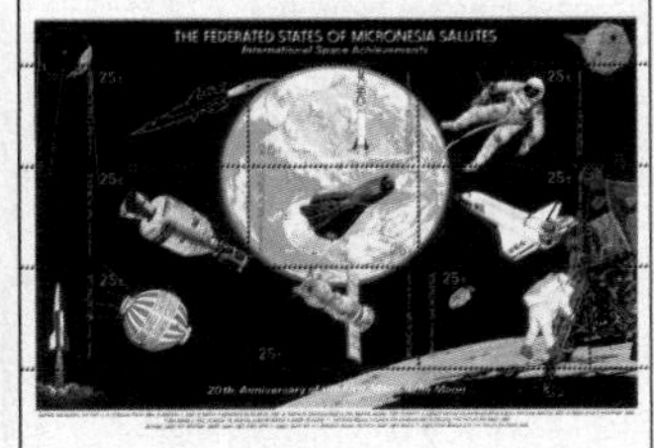

First Moon Landing, 20th Anniv. — A30

Space achievements: a, X-15 rocket plane, 1959. b, *Explorer 1* launched into orbit, 1958. c, Ed White, 1st American to walk in space, Gemini 4 mission, 1965. d, Apollo 18 command module, 1975. e. Gemini 4 capsule. f, Space shuttle *Challenger*, 1983-86. g, *San Marco 2*, satellite engineered by Italy. h, Soyuz 19 spacecraft, 1975. i, *Columbia* command module and Neil Armstrong taking man's first step onto the Moon during the Apollo 11 mission, 1969.

1989, July 20 Litho. *Perf. 14*

81 A30 Sheet of 9 5.25 4.50
a.-i. 25c any single .50 .45

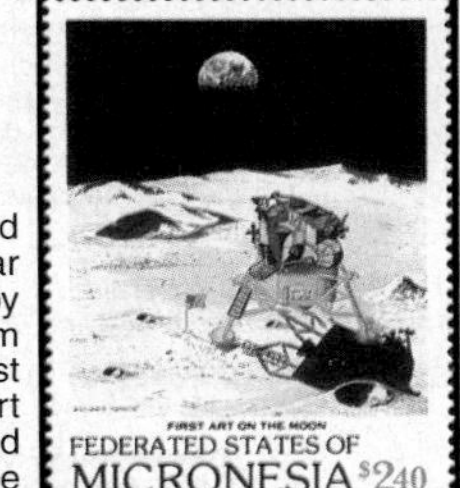

Earth and Lunar Module, by William Hanson, 1st Art Transported to the Moon — A31

1989, July 20 *Perf. 13½x14*

82 A31 $2.40 multicolored 4.50 4.00

First Moon landing, 20th anniv.

Seashells — A32

1989, Sept. 26 *Perf. 14*

83 A32 1c Horse's hoof .20 .20
84 A32 3c Rare spotted cowrie .20 .20
85 A32 15c Commercial trochus .20 .20
a. Booklet pane of 10 5.00 —
87 A32 20c General cone .30 .30
88 A32 25c Triton's trumpet .40 .40
a. Booklet pane of 10 7.50 —
b. Booklet pane, 5 each 15c, 25c 7.50 —
90 A32 30c Laciniated conch .45 .45
91 A32 36c Red-mouthed olive .55 .55
93 A32 45c Map cowrie .70 .70
95 A32 50c Textile cone .75 .75
100 A32 $1 Orange spider conch 1.75 1.75
101 A32 $2 Golden cowrie 3.50 3.50
102 A32 $5 Episcopal miter 8.50 8.50
Nos. 83-102 (12) 17.50 17.50

Booklet panes issued Sept. 14, 1990.
This is an expanding set. Numbers will change if necessary.

Miniature Sheet

Fruits and Flowers Endemic to Kosrae A33

Designs: a, Orange. b, Lime. c, Tangerine. d, Mango. e, Coconut. f, Breadfruit. g, Sugar cane. h, Thatched dwelling. i, Banana. j, Girl, boy. k, Pineapple picker. l, Taro. m, Hibiscus. n, Ylang ylang. o, White ginger. p, Plumeria. q, Royal poinciana. r, Yellow allamanda.

1989, Nov. 18 Litho. *Perf. 14*

103 Sheet of 18 9.00 9.00
a.-r. A33 25c any single .45 .45

Margin inscribed for World Stamp Expo '89.

Christmas — A34

1989, Dec. 14 Litho. *Perf. 14½*

104 A34 25c Heralding angel .50 .50
105 A34 45c Three wise men .90 .90

World Wildlife Fund A35

Micronesian kingfishers and pigeons.

1990, Feb. 19 Litho. *Perf. 14*

106 A35 10c Kingfisher (juvenile) *.55 .55*
107 A35 15c Kingfisher (adult) *1.25 1.25*
108 A35 20c Pigeon *1.75 1.75*
109 A35 25c Pigeon, diff. *2.50 2.50*
Nos. 106-109 (4) 6.05 6.05

Stamp World London '90 — A36

Exhibition emblem, artifacts and whaling vessels: No. 110, Wooden whale stamp, *Lyra,* 1826. No. 111, Harpoons, *Prudent,* 1827. No. 112, Scrimshaw (whale), *Rhone,* 1851. No. 113, Scrimshaw on whale tooth, *Sussex,* 1843. $1, Whalers at kill.

1990, May 3 Litho. *Perf. 14*

110 A36 45c multicolored .80 .80
111 A36 45c multicolored .80 .80
112 A36 45c multicolored .80 .80
113 A36 45c multicolored .80 .80
a. Block of 4, #110-113 3.25 3.25

Souvenir Sheet

114 A36 $1 multicolored 2.00 2.00

Souvenir Sheet

Penny Black, 150th Anniv. — A37

1990, May 6 *Perf. 14*

115 A37 $1 Great Britain No. 1 2.00 2.00

Main Building — A38

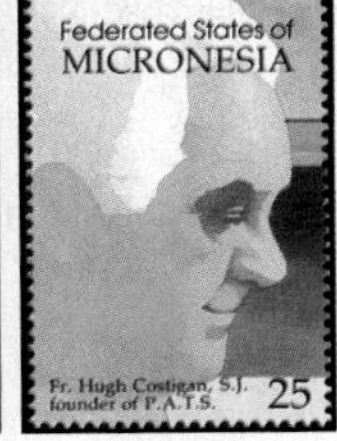

Fr. Hugh Costigan, School Founder — A39

Designs: No. 117, Fr. Costigan, students. No. 119, Fr. Costigan, Isaphu Samuel Hadley. No. 120, New York City Police Badge.

1990, July 31 Litho. *Perf. 14*

116 A38 25c multicolored .50 .50
117 A38 25c multicolored .50 .50
118 A39 25c multicolored .50 .50
119 A38 25c multicolored .50 .50
120 A38 25c multicolored .50 .50
a. Strip of 5, #116-120 2.50 2.50

Pohnpei Agriculture and Trade School, 25th anniversary. Printed in sheets of 15.

Souvenir Sheet

Expo '90, Intl. Garden and Greenery Exposition, Osaka, Japan — A40

1990, July 31 Litho. *Perf. 14*

121 A40 $1 multicolored 1.75 1.75

Loading Mail, Pohnpei Airport, 1990 A41

Pacifica Emblem and: 45c, Japanese mail boat, Truk Lagoon, 1940.

1990, Aug. 24

122 A41 25c multicolored .50 .50
123 A41 45c multicolored 1.25 1.25

Canoe, Flag of Federated States of Micronesia A42

Designs: No. 124, Stick chart, canoe, flag of Marshall Islands. No. 125, Frigate bird, eagle, USS Constitution, flag of US.

1990, Sept. 28 *Perf. 13½*

124 A42 25c multicolored .55 .55
125 A42 25c multicolored .55 .55
126 A42 25c multicolored .55 .55
a. Strip of 3, #124-126 1.75 1.75

Compact of Free Association with the US. Printed in sheets of 15. See #253, US #2506, Marshall Islands #381.

Moths A43

1990, Nov. 10 Litho. *Perf. 14*

127 A43 45c Gracillariidae .80 .80
128 A43 45c Yponomeatidae .80 .80
129 A43 45c shown .80 .80
130 A43 45c Cosmopterigidae, diff. .80 .80
a. Block of 4, #127-130 3.25 3.25

Miniature Sheet

Christmas A44

Designs: a, Cherub. b, Star of Bethlehem. c, Cherub blowing horn. d, Goats. e, Nativity scene. f, Children, outrigger canoe. g, Messenger blowing a conch shell. h, Family walking. i, People carrying bundles.

1990, Nov. 19 Litho. *Perf. 14*

131 Sheet of 9 4.50 4.50
a.-i. A44 25c any single .50 .50

Souvenir Sheets

New Capital of Micronesia — A45

1991, Jan. 15 Litho. *Perf. 14x13½*

132 Sheet of 2 1.40 1.40
a. A45 25c Executive Branch .50 .50
b. A45 45c Legislative, Judicial Branches .90 .90
133 A45 $1 New Capitol 2.00 2.00

Turtles — A46

1991, Mar. 14 Litho. *Perf. 14*

134 A46 29c Hawksbill on beach 1.10 1.10
135 A46 29c Green 1.10 1.10
a. Pair, #134-135 2.25 2.25
136 A46 50c Hawksbill 1.40 1.40
137 A46 50c Leatherback 1.40 1.40
a. Pair, #136-137 2.75 2.75
Nos. 134-137 (4) 5.00 5.00

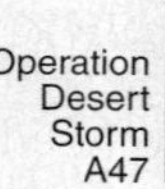

Operation Desert Storm A47

1991, July 30 Litho. *Perf. 14*

138 A47 29c Battleship Missouri .60 .60
139 A47 29c Multiple launch rocket system .60 .60
140 A47 29c F-14 Tomcat .60 .60
141 A47 29c E-3 Sentry (AWACS) .60 .60
a. Block or strip of 4, #138-141 2.40 2.40

Size: 51x38mm

142 A47 $2.90 Frigatebird, flag 5.00 5.00
a. Souvenir sheet of 1 5.50 5.50
Nos. 138-142 (5) 7.40 7.40

Miniature Sheets

Phila Nippon '91 — A48

Ukiyo-e prints by Paul Jacoulet (1902-1960) — #143: a, Evening Flowers, Toloas, Truk, 1941. b, The Chief's Daughter, Mogomog, 1953. c, Yagourouh and Mio, Yap, 1938. No. 144a, Yap Beauty and Orchids, 1934. b, The Yellow-eyed Boys, Ohlol, 1940. c, Violet Flowers, Tomil, 1937. $1, First Love, Yap, 1937, horiz.

1991, Sept. Litho. *Perf. 14*

143 Sheet of 3 2.25 2.25
a.-c. A48 29c any single .75 .75
144 Sheet of 3 3.50 3.50
a.-c. A48 50c any single 1.25 1.25

Souvenir Sheet

145 A48 $1 multicolored 2.40 2.40

Christmas — A49

Handicraft scenes: 29c, Nativity. 40c, Adoration of the Magi. 50c, Adoration of the Shepherds.

1991, Oct. 30 *Perf. 14x13½*

146 A49 29c multicolored .50 .50
147 A49 40c multicolored .75 .75
148 A49 50c multicolored 1.00 1.00
Nos. 146-148 (3) 2.25 2.25

Pohnpei Rain Forest A50

Designs: a, Pohnpei fruit bat. b, Purple capped fruit-dove. c, Micronesian kingfisher. d, Birdnest fern. e, Island swiftlet. f, Long-billed white-eye. g, Brown noddy. h, Pohnpei lory. i, Pohnpei flycatcher. j, Caroline ground-dove. k, White-tailed tropicbird. l, Micronesian honeyeater. m, Ixora. n, Pohnpei fantail. o, Gray white-eye. p, Blue-faced parrotfinch. q, Cicadabird. r, Green skink.

1991, Nov. 18

149 Sheet of 18 13.00 13.00
a.-r. A50 29c any single .65 .65

Peace Corps — A51

Designs: a, Learning crop planting techniques. b, Education. c, John F. Kennedy. d, Public health nurses. e, Recreation.

1992, Apr. 10 Litho. *Perf. 14*

150 A51 29c Strip of 5, #a.-e. 2.50 2.50

Printed in sheets of 15.

Discovery of America, 500th Anniv. — A52

Designs: a, Queen Isabella I. b, Santa Maria. c, Columbus.

1992, May 23 Litho. *Perf. 13½*

151 A52 29c Strip of 3, #a.-c. 5.00 5.00

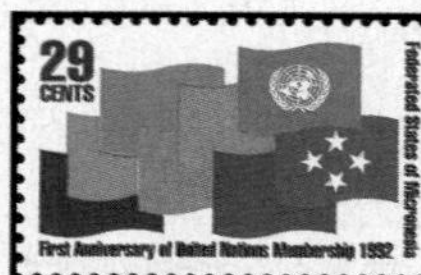

Admission to the UN, First Anniv. A53

1992, Sept. 24 *Perf. 11x10½*

152 A53 29c multicolored 1.50 1.50
153 A53 50c multicolored 2.25 2.25
a. Souvenir sheet of 2, #152-153 3.50 3.50

Christmas A54

1992, Dec. 4 *Perf. 13½*

154 A54 29c multicolored 1.90 1.90

Pioneers of Flight A55

a, Andrei N. Tupolev. b, John A. Macready. c, Edward V. Rickenbacker. d, Manfred von Richtofen. e, Hugh M. Trenchard. f, Glenn H. Curtiss. g, Charles E. Kingsford-Smith. h, Igor I. Sikorsky.

1993, Apr. 12

155 A55 29c Block of 8, #a.-h. 4.75 4.75

See Nos. 178, 191, 200, 210, 233, 238, 249.

Fish — A56

Designs: 10c, Bigscale soldierfish. 19c, Bennett's butterflyfish. 20c, Peacock grouper. 22c, Great barracuda. 25c, Coral grouper. 29c, Regal angelfish. 30c, Bleeker's parrotfish. 35c, Picassofish. 40c, Mandarinfish. 45c, Bluebanded surgeonfish. 50c, Orange-striped triggerfish. 52c, Palette surgeonfish. 75c, Oriental sweetlips. $1, Zebra moray. $2, Foxface rabbitfish. $2.90, Orangespine unicornfish.

1993-94 Litho. *Perf. 13½*

156	A56	10c multicolored	.20	.20
157	A56	19c multicolored	.35	.35
158	A56	20c multicolored	.35	.35
159	A56	22c multicolored	.40	.40
160	A56	25c multicolored	.45	.45
161	A56	29c multicolored	.55	.55
162	A56	30c multicolored	.55	.55
162A	A56	35c multicolored	.65	.65
163	A56	40c multicolored	.70	.70
163A	A56	45c multicolored	.75	.75
164	A56	50c multicolored	.90	.90
164A	A56	52c multicolored	1.00	1.00
164B	A56	75c multicolored	1.40	1.40
165	A56	$1 multicolored	1.75	1.75
166	A56	$2 multicolored	3.50	3.50
167	A56	$2.90 multicolored	5.50	5.50
		Nos. 156-167 (16)	19.00	19.00

Issued: 19c, 29c, 50c, $1, 5/14/93; 22c, 30c, 40c, 45c, 8/26/93; 10c, 20c, 35c, $2.90, 5/20/94; 25c, 52c, 75c, $2, 8/5/94.

See Nos. 213-227, 250.

A57

A59

Sailing Ships: a, Great Republic. b, Benjamin F. Packard. c, Stag Hound. d, Herald of the Morning. e, Rainbow. f, Flying Cloud. g, Lightning. h, Sea Witch. i, Columbia. j, New World. k, Young America. l, Courier.

1993, May 21 Litho. *Perf. 13½*

168 A57 29c Sheet of 12, #a.-l. 15.00 15.00

1993, July 4 Litho. *Perf. 13½*

172 A59 29c multicolored .80 .80

Thomas Jefferson, 250th anniv. of birth.

Pacific Canoes — A60

1993, July 21 Litho. *Perf. 13½*

173 A60 29c Yap .80 .80
174 A60 29c Kosrae .80 .80
175 A60 29c Pohnpei .80 .80
176 A60 29c Chuuk .80 .80
a. Block of 4, #173-176 3.25 3.25

Local Leaders — A61

Designs: a, Ambilos Iehsi, (1935-81), educator. b, Andrew Roboman (1905-92), Yap chief. c, Joab N. Sigrah (1932-88), first vice-speaker of Congress. d, Petrus Mailo (1902-71), Chuuk leader.

1993, Sept. 16 Litho. *Perf. 13½*

177 A61 29c Strip of 4, #a.-d. 2.50 2.50

See Nos. 204-207.

Pioneers of Flight Type of 1993

Designs: a, Hugh L. Dryden. b, Theodore von Karman. c, Otto Lilienthal. d, Thomas O.M. Sopwith. e, Lawrence B. Sperry. f, Alberto Santos-Dumont. g, Orville Wright. h, Wilbur Wright.

1993, Sept. 25 Litho. *Perf. 13½*

178 A55 50c Block of 8, #a.-h. 6.75 6.75

Tourist Attractions, Pohnpei — A62

1993, Oct. 5

179 A62 29c Kepirohi Falls .75 .75
180 A62 50c Spanish Wall 1.50 1.50

Souvenir Sheet

181 A62 $1 Sokehs Rock 2.00 2.00

No. 181 contains one 80x50mm stamp.

See Nos. 187-189.

Butterflies — A63

Christmas — A64

#182a, Great eggfly female (typical). #182b, Great eggfly female (local variant). #183a, Monarch. #183b, Great eggfly male.

1993, Oct. 20 **Litho.** ***Perf. 13½***
182 A63 29c Pair, #a.-b. 1.40 1.40
183 A63 50c Pair, #a.-b. 2.00 2.00

See No. 190.

1993, Nov. 11
184 A64 29c We Three Kings .75 .75
185 A64 50c Silent Night, Holy Night 1.25 1.25

Miniature Sheet

Yap Culture A65

Designs: a, Baby basket. b, Bamboo raft. c, Baskets, handbag. d, Fruit bat. e, Forest. f, Outrigger canoe. g, Dioscorea yams. h, Mangroves. i, Manta ray. j, Cyrtosperma taro. k, Fish weir. l, Seagrass, fish. m, Taro bowl. n, Thatched house. o, Coral reef. p, Lavalava. q, Dance. r, Stone money.

1993, Dec. 15 **Litho.** ***Perf. 13½x14***
186 A65 29c Sheet of 18, #a.-r. 12.50 12.50

Tourist Attractions Type of 1993

Sites on Kosrae: 29c, Sleeping Lady Mountain. 40c, Walung. 50c, Lelu Ruins.

1994, Feb. 11 **Litho.** ***Perf. 13½***
187 A62 29c multicolored .55 .55
188 A62 40c multicolored .75 .75
189 A62 50c multicolored .95 .95
Nos. 187-189 (3) 2.25 2.25

Butterfly Type of 1993 with Added Inscription
Souvenir Sheet

a, 29c, like No. 182a. b, 29c, like No. 182b. c, 50c, like No. 183a. d, 50c, like No. 183b.

1994, Feb. 18
190 A63 Sheet of 4, #a.-d. 4.25 4.25

Inscription reads "Hong Kong '94 Stamp Exhibition" in Chinese on Nos. 190a, 190d, and in English on Nos. 190b-190c.
Inscriptions on Nos. 190a-190d are in black.

Pioneers of Flight Type of 1993

Designs: a, Edwin E. Aldrin, Jr. b, Neil A. Armstrong. c, Michael Collins. d, Wernher von Braun. e, Octave Chanute. f, T. Claude Ryan. g, Frank Whittle. h, Waldo D. Waterman.

1994, Mar. 4 **Litho.** ***Perf. 13½***
191 A55 29c Block of 8, #a.-h. 5.75 5.75

1994 Micronesian Games — A66

Designs: a, Spearfishing. b, Basketball. c, Coconut husking. d, Tree climbing.

1994, Mar. 26 ***Perf. 13½x14***
192 A66 29c Block of 4, #a.-d. 2.75 2.75

Native Costumes — A67

a, Pohnpei. b, Kosrae. c, Chuuk. d, Yap.

1994, Mar. 31 ***Perf. 13½***
193 A67 29c Block of 4, #a.-d. 2.75 2.75

Constitution, 15th Anniv. — A68

1994, May 10 **Litho.** ***Perf. 11x10½***
194 A68 29c multicolored 1.50 1.50

Flowers — A69

Designs: a, Fagraea berteriana. b, Pangium edule. c, Pittosporum ferrugineum. d, Sonneratia caseolaris.

1994, June 6 **Litho.** ***Perf. 13½***
195 A69 29c Strip of 4, #a.-d. 2.75 2.75

1994 World Cup Soccer Championships, US — A70

Design: No. 197, Soccer players, diff.

1994, June 17 **Litho.** ***Perf. 13½***
196 A70 50c red & multi 2.25 2.25
197 A70 50c blue & multi 2.25 2.25
a. Pair, #196-197 4.50 4.50

No. 197a has a continuous design.

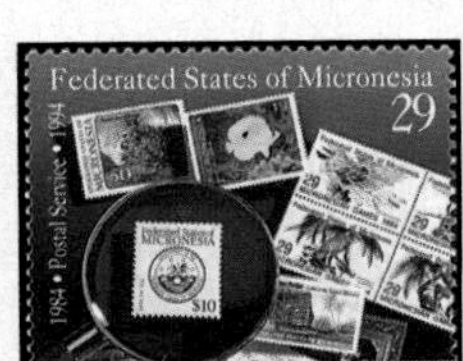

Micronesian Postal Service, 10th Anniv. — A71

Stamps: a, #39, 45, 54 (c), 159, 189, 192 (b). b, #58 (d), 151, 161 (d), 176a, 183a (d). c, #4a, 137a, 184 (a), C12 (d), C39, C41. d, #161 (b), 183a (b), 183b, 193, C12, C40, C42.

1994, July 12 **Litho.** ***Perf. 13½***
198 A71 29c Block of 4, #a.-d. 5.00 5.00

No. 198 is a continuous design.

Souvenir Sheet

PHILAKOREA '94 — A72

Dinosaurs: a, 29c, Iguanodons (b). b, 52c, Coelurosaurs (c). c, $1, Camarasaurus.

1994, Aug. 16 **Litho.** ***Perf. 13½***
199 A72 Sheet of 3, #a.-c. 5.25 5.25

Pioneers of Flight Type of 1993

a, William A. Bishop. b, Karel J. Bossart. c, Marcel Dassault. d, Geoffrey de Havilland. e, Yuri A. Gagarin. f, Alan B. Shepard, Jr. g, John H. Towers. h, Hermann J. Oberth.

1994, Sept. 20 **Litho.** ***Perf. 13½***
200 A55 50c Block of 8, #a.-h. 6.75 6.75

Migratory Birds — A73

Designs: a, Oriental cuckoo. b, Long-tailed cuckoo. c, Short-eared owl. d, Dollarbird.

1994, Oct. 20 **Litho.** ***Perf. 13½***
201 A73 29c Block of 4, #a.-d. 2.50 2.50

Christmas A74

1994, Nov. 2
202 A74 29c Doves .60 .60
203 A74 50c Angels 1.00 1.00

Local Leaders Type of 1993

Pioneers of island unification: No. 204, Johnny Moses (1900-91), Pohnpei. No. 205, Belarmino Hatheylul (1907-93), Yap. No. 206, Anton Ring Buas (1907-79), Chuuk. No. 207, Paliknoa Sigrah (King John) (1875-1957), Kosrae.

1994, Dec. 15 **Litho.** ***Perf. 13½***
204 A61 32c multicolored .65 .65
205 A61 32c multicolored .65 .65
206 A61 32c multicolored .65 .65
207 A61 32c multicolored .65 .65
Nos. 204-207 (4) 2.60 2.60

Souvenir Sheet

New Year 1995 (Year of the Boar) — A75

Illustration reduced.

1995, Jan. 2
208 A75 50c multicolored 1.00 1.00

Chuuk Lagoon A76

Underwater scenes: a, Photographer with light. b, Various species of fish, coral. c, Diver. d, Two gold fish.

1995, Feb. 6
209 A76 32c Block of 4, #a.-d. 2.50 2.50

Pioneers of Flight Type of 1993

Designs: a, Robert H. Goddard. b, Leroy R. Grumman. c, Hugo Junkers. d, James A. Lovell, Jr. e, Louis-Charles Breguet. f, Juan de la Cierva. g, Donald W. Douglas. h, Reginald J. Mitchell.

1995, Mar. 4 **Litho.** ***Perf. 13½***
210 A55 32c Block of 8, #a.-h. 5.25 5.25

Dogs A77

a, West Highland white terrier. b, Welsh springer spaniel. c, Irish setter. d, Old English sheepdog.

1995, Apr. 5 **Litho.** ***Perf. 13½***
211 A77 32c Block of 4, #a.-d. 2.50 2.50

Fish Type of 1993

Designs: 23c, Yellow-fin tuna. 32c, Saddled butterflyfish. 46c, Achilles tang. 55c, Moorish idol. 60c, Skipjack tuna. 78c, Square-spot fairy basslet. 95c, Bluelined snapper. $3, Flame angelfish. $5, Cave grouper.

#227: a, like #157. b, like #161. c, like #164. d, like #165. e, like #159. f, like #162. g, like #163. h, like #163A. i, like #156. j, like #158. k, like #162A. l, like #167. m, like #217. n, like #160. o, like #164A. p, like #164B. q, like #166. r, like #214. s, like #218. t, like #222. u, like #225. v, like #213. w, like #219. x, like #223. y, like #226.

1996 **Litho.** ***Perf. 13½***
213 A56 23c multicolored .45 .45
214 A56 32c multicolored .65 .65
217 A56 46c multicolored .95 .95
218 A56 55c multicolored 1.10 1.10
219 A56 60c multicolored 1.25 1.25
222 A56 78c multicolored 1.50 1.50
223 A56 95c multicolored 1.90 1.90
225 A56 $3 multicolored 6.00 6.00
226 A56 $5 multicolored 10.00 10.00
Nos. 213-226 (9) 23.80 23.80

Miniature Sheet

227 A56 32c Sheet of 25, #a.-y. 16.00 16.00

Issued: 32c, 55c, 78c, $3, 5/15/95. 23c, 60c, 95c, $5, 8/4/95; 46c, 4/10/96.
This is an expanding set. Numbers may change.

Hibiscus — A78

a, Tiliaceus. b, Huegelii. c, Trionum. d, Splendens.

1995, June 1 **Litho.** ***Perf. 13½***
228 A78 32c Strip of 4, #a.-d. 2.50 2.50

No. 228 is a continuous design.

Souvenir Sheet

UN, 50th Anniv. — A79

Illustration reduced.

1995, June 26 Litho. *Perf. 13½*
229 A79 $1 multicolored 2.00 2.00

Miniature Sheet

Singapore '95 — A80

Orchids: a, Paphiopedilum henrietta fujiwara. b, Thunia alba. c, Lycaste virginalis. d, Laeliocattleya prism palette.

1995, Sept. 1 Litho. *Perf. 13½*
230 A80 32c Sheet of 4, #a.-d. 2.60 2.60

End of World War II, 50th Anniv. — A81

US warships: a, USS Portland. b, USS Tillman. c, USS Soley. d, USS Hyman.

1995, Sept. 2
231 A81 60c Block of 4, #a.-d. 5.00 5.00

Souvenir Sheet

Intl. Stamp & Coin Expo, Beijing '95 — A82

Illustration reduced.

1995, Sept. 14
232 A82 50c Temple of Heaven 1.00 1.00

Pioneers of Flight Type of 1993

Designs: a, Hugh C.T. Dowding. b, William Mitchell. c, John K. Northrop. d, Frederick Handley Page. e, Frederick H. Rohr. f, Juan T. Trippe. g, Konstantin E. Tsiolkovsky. h. Ferdinand Graf von Zeppelin.

1995, Sept. 21 Litho. *Perf. 13½*
233 A55 60c Block of 8, #a.-h. 9.50 9.50

Christmas Poinsettias A83

1995, Oct. 30 Litho. *Perf. 13½*
234 A83 32c gray & multi .65 .65
235 A83 60c bister & multi 1.25 1.25

Yitzhak Rabin (1922-95), Israeli Prime Minister — A84

1995, Nov. 30 Litho. *Perf. 13½*
236 A84 32c multicolored .65 .65

No. 236 was issued in sheets of 8.

Souvenir Sheet

New Year 1996 (Year of the Rat) — A85

Illustration reduced.

1996, Jan. 5 Litho. *Perf. 13½*
237 A85 50c multicolored 1.00 1.00

Pioneers of Flight Type of 1993

Designs: a, James H. Doolittle. b, Claude Dornier. c, Ira C. Eaker. d, Jacob C.H. Ellehammer. e, Henry H. Arnold. f, Louis Blériot. g, William E. Boeing. h, Sydney Camm.

1996, Feb. 21 Litho. *Perf. 13½*
238 A55 32c Block of 8, #a.-h. 5.25 5.25

Tourism in Yap — A86

a, Meeting house. b, Stone money. c, Churu dancing. d, Traditional canoe.

1996, Mar. 13 Litho. *Perf. 13½*
239 A86 32c Block of 4, #a.-d. 2.50 2.50

Sea Stars A87

Designs: a, Rhinoceros. b, Necklace c, Thick-skinned. d, Blue.

1996, Apr. 26 Litho. *Perf. 12*
240 A87 55c Block of 4, #a.-d. 4.50 4.50

Olympic Games, Cent. — A88

First Olympic stamps, Greece: a, #120. b, #122. c, #121. d, #128.

1996, Apr. 27
241 A88 60c Block of 4, #a.-d. 4.75 4.75

Souvenir Sheet

China '96, 9th Asian Intl. Philatelic Exhibition — A89

Design: The Tarrying Garden, Suzhou. Illustration reduced.

1996, May 15 *Perf. 13x13½*
242 A89 50c multicolored 1.00 1.00

Patrol Boats — A90

1996, May 3 Litho. *Perf. 13½*
243 A90 32c FSS Palikir .65 .65
244 A90 32c FSS Micronesia .65 .65
a. Pair, #243-244 1.30 1.30

No. 244a is a continuous design.

First Ford Automobile, Cent. — A91

a, 1896 Quadricycle. b, 1917 Model T truck. c, 1928 Model A Tudor Sedan. d, 1932 V-8 Sport Roadster. e, 1941 Lincoln Continental. f, 1953 F-100 Truck. g, 1958 Thunderbird convertible. h, 1996 Mercury Sable.

1996, June 4 *Perf. 13½*
245 A91 55c Sheet of 8, #a.-h. 8.75 8.75

Officer Reza, Member of Natl. Police Drug Enforcement Unit — A93

1996, July 31 Litho. *Perf. 13½*
247 A93 32c multicolored .65 .65

Citrus Fruit — A94

a, Orange. b, Lime. c, Lemon. d, Tangerine.

1996, Aug. 24 Litho. *Perf. 13½*
248 A94 50c Strip of 4, #a.-d. 4.00 4.00

Pioneers of Flight Type of 1993

Designs: a, Gianni Caproni. b, Henri Farman. c, Curtis E. LeMay. d, Grover Loening. e, Sergey P. Korolyov. f, Isaac M. Laddon. g, Glenn L. Martin. h, Alliott Verdon Roe.

1996, Sept. 18
249 A55 60c Block of 8, #a.-h. 12.50 12.50

Fish Type of 1993

Designs: a, like #157. b, like #165. c, like #162A. d, like #218.

1996, Oct. 21 Litho. *Perf. 13½*
250 A56 32c Block of 4, #a.-d. 2.50 2.50

Taipei '96, 10th Asian Intl. Philatelic Exhibition. Nos. 250a, 250d have English inscriptions. Nos. 250b-250c have Chinese inscriptions.

Magi Following Star to Bethlehem A95

1996, Oct. 30 Litho. *Perf. 13½*
251 A95 32c dark blue & multi .65 .65
252 A95 60c blue & multi 1.25 1.25

Christmas.

Canoe, Flag of Federated States of Micronesia Type of 1990

1996, Nov. 3 *Perf. 11x10½*
253 A42 $3 like #124 6.00 6.00

No. 253 inscribed "Free Association United States of America."

Deng Xiaoping (1904-97) — A96

Portraits: a, Wearing white-collared shirt. b, Looking left. c, Looking right. d, Wearing hat. $3, Looking left, diff.

1997 Litho. *Perf. 14*
254 A96 60c Sheet of 4, #a.-d. 4.75 4.75

Souvenir Sheet

255 A96 $3 multicolored 6.00 6.00

Souvenir Sheet

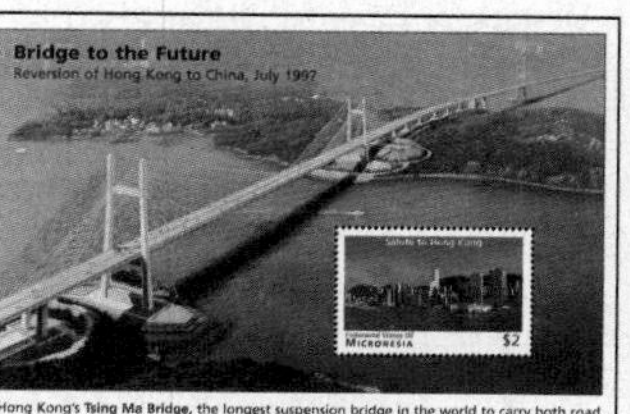

Hong Kong — A97

Illustration reduced.

1997
256 A97 $2 multicolored 4.00 4.00

New Year 1997 (Year of the Ox) — A98

1997 Litho. *Perf. 14*
257 A98 32c multicolored .65 .65

Souvenir Sheet

258 A98 $2 like #257 4.00 4.00

Return of Hong Kong to China A99

Flowers, Victoria Harbor: a, Melia azedarach. b, Sail from ship, Victoria Peak. c, Sail from ship, dendrobium chrysotoxum. d, Bauhinia blakeana. e, Cassia surattensis, Chinese junk. f, Junk, nelumbo nucifera.
$3, Strongylodon macrobatrys, pagoda.

1997, July 1
259 A99 60c Sheet of 6, #a.-f. 7.25 7.25

Souvenir Sheet

260 A99 $3 multicolored 6.00 6.00

Sea Goddesses of the Pacific — A100

a, Giant serpent, woman holding child, Walutahanga of Melanesia. b, Sailing ship in storm, woman holding lantern, Tien-Hou of China. c, Woman swimming to bottom of sea gathering fish into basket, Lorop of Micronesia. d, Woman swimming to man in canoe, Oto-Hime of Japan. e, Woman holding seashell, Nomoi of Micronesia. f, Three women in canoe, Junkgowa sisters of Australia.

1997, May 29 Litho. *Perf. 14*
261 A100 32c Sheet of 6, #a.-f. 3.75 3.75

PACIFIC 97.

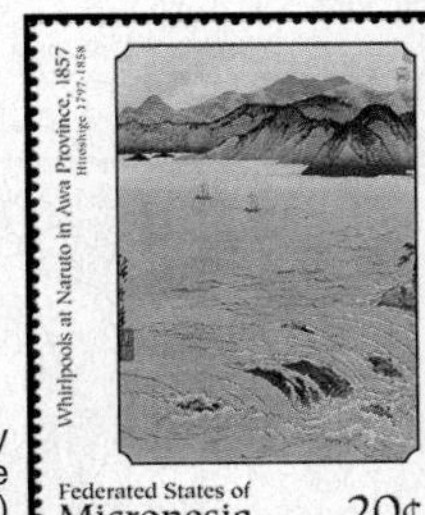

Paintings by Hiroshige (1797-1858) A101

Whirlpools at Naruto in Awa Province, 1857: No. 262: a, Sailboats in distance. b, Island of trees at left. c, Island of trees at right.
Tale of Genji: Viewing the Plum Blossoms, 1852: No. 263: a, Small evergreen trees in front of woman. b, Woman. c, Trees, house in distance with woman.
Snow on the Sumida River, 1847: No. 264: a, House, river. b, Two women under umbrella. c, Woman with folded umbrella.
Each $2: No. 265, Rapids in Bitchu Province, 1854. No. 266, Fuji from Satta Point, 1858.

1997, July 25 *Perf. 13½x14*
262 A101 20c Sheet of 3, #a.-c. 1.25 1.25
263 A101 50c Sheet of 3, #a.-c. 3.00 3.00
264 A101 60c Sheet of 3, #a.-c. 3.50 3.50

Souvenir Sheets

265-266 A101 Set of 2 8.00 8.00

Second Federated States of Micronesia Games — A102

a, Tennis. b, Discus. c, Swimming. d, Canoeing.

1997, Aug. 15 Litho. *Perf. 14*
267 A102 32c Block of 4, #a.-d. 2.50 2.50

No. 267 was issued in sheets of 16 stamps.

Elvis Presley (1935-77) A103

Various portraits.

1997, Aug. 16
268 A103 50c Sheet of 6, #a.-f. 6.00 6.00

Ocean Exploration A104

#269: a, Simon Lake, Argonaut, 1897. b, William Beebe, Bathysphere, 1934. c, Auguste Piccard, Bathyscaphe, 1954. d, Harold Edgerton, deep-sea camera, 1954. e, Jacques Piccard, Trieste, 1960. f, Edwin Link, Man-in-Sea Project, 1962. g, Melvin Fisher, search for treasure, 1971. h, Robert Ballard, Alvin, 1978. i, Sylvia Earle, Deep Rover, 1979.
Each $2: No. 270, C. Wyville Thomson, deep-sea dredge, vert. No. 271, Shinkai 6500 exploring bottom of sea, vert. No. 272, Jacques-Yves Cousteau, vert.

1997, Oct. 6 Litho. *Perf. 14*
269 A104 32c Sheet of 9, #a.-i. 4.25 4.25

Souvenir Sheets

270-272 A104 Set of 3 30.00 30.00

Diana, Princess of Wales (1961-97) A105

1997, Nov. 26 Litho. *Perf. 14*
273 A105 60c multicolored 1.25 1.25

No. 273 was issued in sheets of 6.

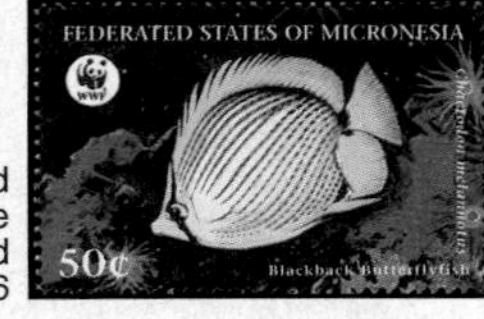

World Wildlife Fund A106

Butterfly fish: a, Blackback. b, Saddled. c, Threadfin. d, Bennett's.

1997, Nov. 24 Litho. *Perf. 14*
274 A106 50c Block of 4, #a.-d. 6.75 6.75

No. 274 was issued in sheets of 16 stamps.

Christmas Paintings A107

Christ Glorified in the Court of Heaven, by Fra Angelico: No. 275, Angels playing musical instruments. No. 276, Choir of Angels.
A Choir of Angels, by Simon Marmion: No. 277, Two angels blowing long horns. No. 278, One angel blowing horn.

1997, Nov. 25
275 A107 32c multicolored .65 .65
276 A107 32c multicolored .65 .65
a. Horiz. pair, Nos. 275-276 1.30 1.30
277 A107 60c multicolored 1.25 1.25
278 A107 60c multicolored 1.25 1.25
a. Vert. pair, Nos. 277-278 2.50 2.50

Nos. 276a, 278a were each issued in sheets of 8 pairs.

Souvenir Sheets

New Year 1998 (Year of the Tiger) — A108

Illustration reduced.

1998, Jan. 2 Litho. *Perf. 14*
279 A108 50c shown 1.00 1.00
280 A108 50c Chinese toy (face) 1.00 1.00

Souvenir Sheet

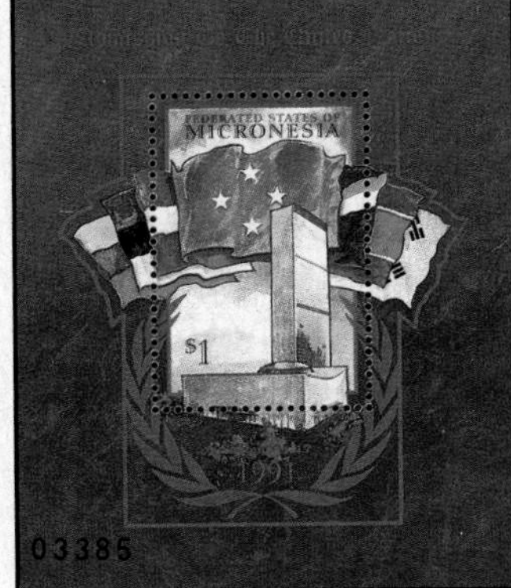

Micronesia's Admission to United Nations, 7th Anniv. — A109

Illustration reduced.

1998, Feb. 13 *Perf. 13½*
281 A109 $1 multicolored 2.00 2.00

Winnie the Pooh — A110

No. 282: a, Rabbit. b, Owl. c, Eeyore. d, Kanga and Roo. e, Piglet. f, Tigger. g, Pooh. h, Christopher Robin.
Each $2: No. 283, Piglet, Pooh, and Tigger. No. 284, Rabbit and Pooh.

1998, Feb. 16 *Perf. 14x14½*
282 A110 32c Sheet of 8, #a.-h. 5.25 5.25

Souvenir Sheets

283-284 A110 Set of 2 8.00 8.00

1998 World Cup Soccer Championships, France — A111

Various soccer plays, color of foreground player's shirt & shorts — #285: a, White & black. b, Green & white. c, Yellow & blue, socks with colored stripes. d, Green & black. e, Yellow & black. f, Red & blue. g, Yellow & blue, plain socks. h, Red & white.
Each $2: No. 286, Red & blue. No. 287, Green, black & white.

1998, Mar. 20 Litho. *Perf. 13½*
285 A111 32c Sheet of 8, #a.-h. 5.00 5.00

Souvenir Sheets

286-287 A111 Set of 2 8.00 8.00

Souvenir Sheet

Micronesia's Recognition by Intl. Olympic Committee — A112

Illustration reduced.

1998, Mar. 20
288 A112 $3 multicolored 6.00 6.00

Old Testament Bible Stories — A113

Adam and Eve — #289: a, Land of plenty. b, Adam, Eve before the fall. c, Serpent of temptation.

Joseph and his brethren — #290: a, Brothers plan to sell Joseph. b, Joseph in his many-colored coat. c, Ishmaelites take Joseph.

Rebekah — #291: a, Rebekah at the well. b, Abraham's servant Eliezer. c, Angel sent to prosper Eliezer's way.

Each $2: No. 292, Adam and Eve sent forth from Eden. No. 293, Joseph forgives his brothers. No. 294, Isaac takes Rebekah to wife.

1998, May 13 Litho. *Perf. 13½x14*

289 A113 32c Sheet of 3, #a.-c. 1.90 1.90
290 A113 40c Sheet of 3, #a.-c. 2.50 2.50
291 A113 60c Sheet of 3, #a.-c. 3.50 3.50

Souvenir Sheets

292-294 A113 Set of 3 12.00 12.00

Israel '98.

Intl. Year of the Ocean A114

Deep sea research — #295: a, Marine observation satellite. b, Support vessel, Natsushima. c, Research vessel, Kaiyo. d, Deep sea anemone. e, Shinkai 2000. f, Deep tow. g, Tripod fish. h, Towed deep survey system. i, Black smokers.

Each $2: No. 296, Communications satellite. No. 297, Ocean observation buoy, vert. No. 298, Weather satellite.

1998, June 2 Litho. *Perf. 13*

295 A114 32c Sheet of 9, #a.-i. 5.75 5.75

Souvenir Sheets

296-298 A114 Set of 3 12.00 12.00

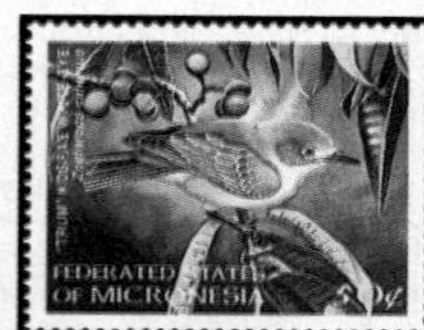

Native Birds A115

No. 299: a, Kosrae white-eye. b, Chuuk monarch. c, Yap monarch. d, Pohnpei lory.

$3, Pohnpei mountain starling.

1998, June 30 *Perf. 14x14½*

299 A115 50c Block or strip of 4, #a.-d. 4.00 4.00

Souvenir Sheet

300 A115 $3 multicolored 6.00 6.00

No. 299 was issued in sheets of 16 stamps.

Fish — A116

Designs: 1c, White-tipped soldierfish. 2c, Red-breasted wrasse. 3c, Bicolor angelfish. 4c, Falco hawkfish. 5c, Convict tang. 10c, Square-spot fairy basslet. 13c, Orangeband surgeonfish. 15c, Multibarred goatfish. 17c, Masked rabbitfish. 20c, White-spotted surgeonfish. 22c, Blue-girdled angelfish. 32c, Wedge picassofish. 39c, Red parrotfish. 40c, Lemonpeel angelfish. 60c, Humphead wrasse. 78c, Sapphire damselfish. $1, Bluefin travally. $3, Whitespot hawkfish. $5, Spotted trunkfish. $10.75, Pinktail triggerfish.

1998 Litho. *Perf. 14½*

301	A116	1c multi	.20	.20
302	A116	2c multi	.20	.20
303	A116	3c multi	.20	.20
304	A116	4c multi	.20	.20
305	A116	5c multi	.20	.20
306	A116	10c multi	.20	.20
307	A116	13c multi	.25	.25
308	A116	15c multi	.30	.30
309	A116	17c multi	.35	.35
310	A116	20c multi	.40	.40
311	A116	22c multi	.45	.45
312	A116	32c multi	.65	.65
313	A116	39c multi	.75	.75
314	A116	40c multi	.80	.80
315	A116	60c multi	1.25	1.25
316	A116	78c multi	1.50	1.50
317	A116	$1 multi	1.90	1.90
318	A116	$3 multi	5.75	5.75
319	A116	$5 multi	10.00	10.00
319A	A116	$10.75 multi	21.00	21.00
	Nos. 301-319A (20)		46.55	46.55

Issued: $10.75, 9/8; others, 7/20.

See Nos. 328-333.

Fala, Franklin D. Roosevelt's Scottish Terrier — A117

Designs: a, Roosevelt's hand petting dog. b, Radio at right. c, Radio at left. d, In car with FDR. e, Presidential seal. f, Closeup of Fala looking left.

1998, Aug. 27 Litho. *Perf. 13½*

320 A117 32c Sheet of 6, #a.-f. 3.75 3.75

Christmas A118

Twentieth cent. art — #321: a, Eskimo Madonna, by Claire Fejes. b, Madonna, by Man Ray. c, Peasant Mother, by David Siquerios.

No. 322: a, Mother and Child, by Pablo Picasso. b, Gypsy Woman with Baby, by Amedeo Modigliani. c, Mother and Child, by José Orozco.

$2, Detail from The Family, by Marisol, horiz.

1998, Sept. 15 Litho. *Perf. 13½x14*

321 A118 32c Sheet of 3, #a.-c. 1.90 1.90
322 A118 60c Sheet of 3, #a.-c. 3.75 3.75

Souvenir Sheet

Perf. 14x13½

323 A118 $2 multicolored 4.00 4.00

John Glenn's Return to Space — A119

Each 60c: No. 324: Various photos of Friendship 7 mission, 1962.

Each 60c: No. 325: Various photos of Discovery space shuttle mission, 1998.

Each $2: No. 326, Launch of Friendship 7. No. 327, Portrait of Glenn, 1998.

1998, Oct. 29 Litho. *Perf. 14*

Sheets of 8, #a-h

324-325 A119 Set of 2 19.00 19.00

Souvenir Sheets

326-327 A119 Set of 2 8.00 8.00

Fish Type of 1998

Designs: 33c, Black jack. 50c, Whitecheek surgeonfish. 55c, Long-jawed squirrelfish. 77c, Onespot snapper. $3.20, Tan-faced parrotfish. $11.75, Yellow-faced angelfish.

1999 Litho. *Perf. 14½*

328 A116 33c multicolored .65 .65
329 A116 50c multicolored 1.00 1.00
330 A116 55c multicolored 1.10 1.10
331 A116 77c multicolored 1.50 1.50
332 A116 $3.20 multicolored 6.50 6.50

Perf. 14

Size: 45x21mm

333 A116 $11.75 multicolored 22.50 22.50
Nos. 328-333 (6) 33.25 33.25

Issued: $11.75, 3/31; others, 2/22.

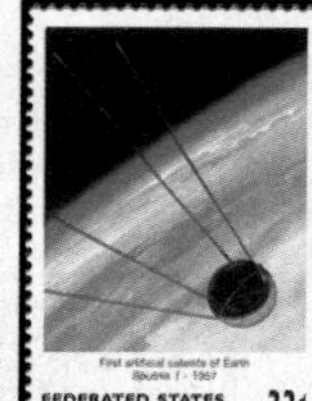

Russian Space Exploration A120

No. 334: a, Sputnik 1, 1957. b, Leika in Sputnik 2, 1957. c, Luna 1, 1959. d, Luna 3, 1959. e, Yuri Gagarin in Vostok 1, 1961. f, Venera 1, 1961. g, Mars 1, 1962. h, Valentina Tereshkova in Vostok 6, 1963. i, Voskhod 1, 1964. j, Aleksei Leonov in Voskhod 2, 1965. k, Venera 3, 1966. l, Luna 10. m, Luna 9. n, Luna 16, 1970. o, Luna 17, 1970. p, Mars 3, 1971. q, Leonid Popov, Valeri Ryumin, Soyuz 35, 1980. r, Vega 1, 1985. s, Vega 1, Halley's Comet, 1986. t, Mir, 1986-98.

Each $2: No. 335, Russian Space Station, Mir, 1998. No. 336, Docking of USSR Soyuz 19 and Apollo 18, horiz.

1999, Mar. 15 *Perf. 14*

334 A120 33c Sheet of 20, #a.-t. 13.50 13.50

Souvenir Sheets

335-336 A120 Set of 2 8.00 8.00

See Nos. 344-346.

"Romance of the Three Kingdoms," by Lo Kuan-Chung A121

No. 337: a, Men, women conferring. b, Four men, one grabbing on clothes of another. c, Two men jousting. d, Four men looking down at one man. e, Man kneeling before another man in wheelchair.

No. 338: a, Mounted warriors approaching drawbridge. b, Warriors fighting in front of fire, banners. c, Warrior fighting off others, smoke. d, Man, woman kneeling before old man. e, Two men looking up at smoke coming from boiling pot.

No. 339, Three men in boat, raging fire.

1999, Mar. 19 Litho. *Perf. 13½*

Sheets of 5

337 A121 33c #a.-e. 3.25 3.25
338 A121 50c #a.-e. 5.00 5.00

Souvenir Sheet

339 A121 $2 multicolored 4.00 4.00

No. 339 contains one 52x79mm stamp.

IBRA '99, World Stamp Exhibition, Nuremberg, Germany — A122

Designs: No. 340, The Leipzig-Dresden Railway, Caroline Islands #4. No. 341, Gölsdorf 4-4-0, Caroline Islands #16.

$2, Exhibition emblem, Caroline Islands #6, vert.

Illustration reduced.

1999, Apr. 27 *Perf. 14x14½*

340 A122 55c multicolored 1.10 1.10
341 A122 55c multicolored 1.10 1.10

Souvenir Sheet

342 A122 $2 multicolored 4.00 4.00

Voyages of the Pacific A123

Designs: a, Map of Pacific Ocean. b, Parrot. c, Bird in flight, leaves. d, Map, ship's stern. e, Part of ship, various blocks. f, Flower. g, Sailing ship, side view. h, Three flowers, compass rose. i, Fish over ship's drawing. j, Map, flag LL. k, Map, flag UR. l, Map, flag LR. m, Three sections of coconut. n, Three flowers, plant. o, Fish. p, Flag, UL, "Equator." q, Sextant. r, Bottom of plant. s, Fish, compass rose. t, Sailing ship, bow on.

1999, Mar. 19 Litho. *Perf. 13½*

343 A123 33c Sheet of 20, #a.-t. 13.50 13.50

Space Achievements Type of 1999

US space achievements — #344: a, Explorer 1, 1958. b, OSO 1, 1962. c, Mariner 2 to Venus, 1962. d, Mariner 2, 1962. e, Apollo 8, 1968. f, First step onto moon, Apollo 11, 1969. g, First samples from moon, Apollo 11, 1969. h, Apollo 15, 1971. i, Mariner 9, 1971. j, Pioneer 10, 1973. k, Mariner 10, 1974. l, Viking 1, 1976. m, Pioneer 11, 1979. n, STS 1, 1981. o, Pioneer 10, 1983. p, Solar Maximum Mission, 1984. q, Cometary Explorer, 1985. r, Voyager 2, 1989. s, Gallileo to Gaspra, 1992. t, Sojourner, 1997.

Each $2: No. 345, International space station. No. 346, Shuttle mission to repair Hubble Telescope, 1993.

1999, Mar. 15 Litho. *Perf. 14*

344 A120 33c Sheet of 20, #a.-t. 13.50 13.50

Souvenir Sheets

345-346 A120 Set of 2 8.00 8.00

Illustrations on Nos. 344p and 344q are incorrect.

Earth Day — A124

Endangered, extinct, and prehistoric species — #347: a, Black rhinoceros. b, Cheetah. c, Jackass penguin. d, Blue whale. e, Red-headed woodpecker. f, African elephant. g, Aurochs. h, Dodo bird. i, Tasmanian wolf. j, Giant lemur. k, Quagga. l, Steller's sea cow. m, Pteranodon. n, Shonisaurus. o, Stegosaurus. p, Galliminus. q, Tyrannosaurus. r, Archelon. s, Brachiosaurus. t, Triceratops.

Each $2: No. 348, Moa. No. 349, Suchominus tenerensis, horiz.

1999

347 A124 33c Sheet of 20, #a.-t. 13.50 13.50

Souvenir Sheets

348-349 A124 Set of 2 8.00 8.00

Nos. 348-349 contain one 50x38mm and one 38x50mm stamp, respectively.

Paintings by Hokusai (1760-1849) A125

Details or entire paintings — #305, each 33c: a, Ghost of O-Iwa. b, Horse Drawings (head down). c, Abe Nakamaro. d, Ghost of Kasane. e, Horse Drawings (head up). f, The Ghost of Kiku and the Priest Mitazuki.

No. 306, each 33c: a, Belly Band Float. b, Drawing of Women (facing left). c, Swimmers.

d, Eel Climb. e, Drawings of Women (facing right). f, Kimo Ga Imo Ni Naru.

Each $2: No. 352, Whaling off Goto. No. 353, Fishing by Torchlight.

1999, July 20 Litho. *Perf. 13¾x14*

Sheets of 6, #a-f

350-351 A125 Set of 2 8.00 8.00

Souvenir Sheets

352-353 A125 Set of 2 8.00 8.00

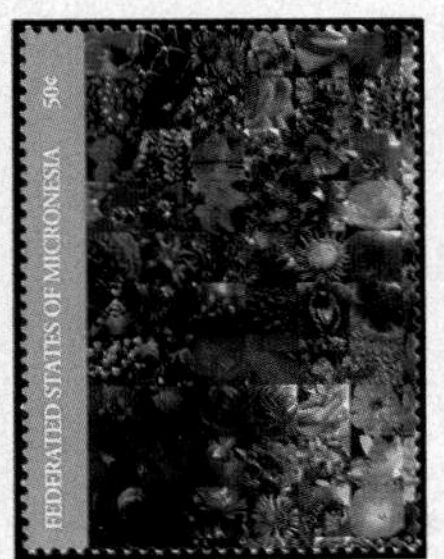

Flowers A126

Various flowers making up a photomosaic of Princess Diana.

1999 Litho. *Perf. 13¼*

354 A126 50c Sheet of 8, #a.-h. 8.00 8.00

See No. 393, 403.

Millennium A127

No. 355 — Highlights of the 12th Century: a, Death of Emperor Henry IV. b, Taira and Minamoto clans. c, Order of the Knights of the Hospital of St. John founded. d, Nautical compass invented. e, "White Ship" disaster. f, Pope Calixtus and Henry V end dispute. g, Death of Omar Khyyam. h, Death of Duke William IX. i, Roger II crowned King of Sicily. j, Stephen of Blois, Matilda. k, Birth of Maimonides. l, Church condemns Peter Abelard. m, Crusaders defeated at Damascus. n, Fall of city of Tula. o, Completion of Angkor Wat. p, Chimu culture flourishes (60x40mm). q, Honen becomes hermit.

No. 356 — Science and Technology of Ancient China: a, Well drilling. b, Chain pump. c, Magic lantern. d, Seismograph. e, Dial and pointer devices. f, Refined value of pi. g, Porcelain. h, Water mill. i, Stirrup. j, Tea. k, Umbrella. l, Brandy and whiskey. m, Printing. n, Paper money. o, Gunpowder. p, Arch bridge (60x40mm). q, Mercator map projection.

1999, Oct. 4 *Perf. 12¾x12½*

Sheets of 17

355 A127 20c #a.-q. + label 7.00 7.00

356 A127 33c #a.-q. + label 11.50 11.50

Inscriptions on Nos. 355g, 355o, and perhaps others, are incorrect or misspelled.

See No. 377.

Costumes A128

Designs: a, French princess gown (head at R). b, As "a," (head at B). c, As "a," (bust). d, As "a," (umbrella). e, Scissors. f, Tools for fabric making. g, Micronesian wedding costume (head at R). h, As "g," (midriff). i, As "g," (feet). j, Japanese fabrics. k, Masai warrior costume (head at L). l, As "k," (head at R). m, African fabric details. n, Kabuki theater costume (head). o, As "n," (midriff). p, French Renaissance costume (head at B). q, Textile patterns. r, As "p," (head at R). s, Rulers. t, Iron.

1999, Nov. 22 *Perf. 14¾*

357 A128 33c Sheet of 20, #a.-t. 13.50 13.50

Vertical strips of 2, 3 or 5 have continuous designs.

Christmas A129

Paintings by Anthony Van Dyck: 33c, Holy Family with St. John. 60c, Madonna with Child. No. 360, The Virgin and Child with Two Donors (detail).

No. 361, The Adoration of the Shepherds.

1999, Dec. 1 Litho. *Perf. 13¾*

358 A129 33c multi .65 .65

359 A129 60c multi 1.25 1.25

360 A129 $2 multi 4.00 4.00

Nos. 358-360 (3) 5.90 5.90

Souvenir Sheet

361 A129 $2 multi 4.00 4.00

Millennium — A130

Airplanes — No. 362: a, Wright Flyer I. b, Blériot XI. c, Fokker D VII. d, Dornier Komet I. e, Ryan NYP. f, Mitsubishi A6M. g, Boeing B-29. h, Messerschmitt 262A. i, Bell X-1. j, MiG-19. k, Lockheed U-2. l, Boeing 707. m, Concorde. n, McDonnell Douglas DC-10. o, B-2.

No. 363, P38. No. 364, Dornier Do X.

1999, Dec. 9 *Perf. 14*

362 A130 33c Sheet of 15, #a.-o. 10.00 10.00

Souvenir Sheets

Perf. 13¾

363 A130 $2 multi 4.00 4.00

364 A130 $2 multi 4.00 4.00

No. 363 contains one 32x48mm stamp. No. 364 contains one 48x32mm stamp.

Orchids — A131

No. 365: a, Baptistonia echinata. b, Bulbophyllum lobbii. c, Cattleya bicolor. d, Cischweinfia dasyandra. e, Cochleanthes discolor. f, Dendrobium bellatulum.

No. 366: a, Esmeralda clarkei. b, Gomesa crispa. c, Masdevallia elephanticeps. d, Maxillaria variabilis. e, Mitoniopsis roezlii. f, Oncidium cavendishianum.

No. 367: a, Oncidium obryzatum. b, Oncidium phalaenopsis. c, Oncidium pulvinatum. d, Paphiopedilum armeniacum. e, Paphiopedilum dayanum. f, Paphiopedilum druryi.

No. 368, Paphiopedilum hirutissimum. No. 369, Licoglossum oerstedii.

2000, Jan. 5 *Perf. 14¼x14*

Sheets of 6

365 A131 33c #a.-f. 4.00 4.00

366 A131 33c #a.-f. 4.00 4.00

367 A131 33c #a.-f. 4.00 4.00

Souvenir Sheets

Perf. 14x14¼

368 A131 $1 multi 2.00 2.00

369 A131 $1 multi 2.00 2.00

Nos. 368-369 each contain one 31x53mm stamp.

Leaders of the 20th Century A132

Designs: a, Martin Luther King, Jr. b, Albert Schweitzer. c, Pope John Paul II. d, Sarvepalli Radhakrishnan. e, Toyohiko Kagawa. f, Mahatma Gandhi. g, Mother Teresa. h, Khyentse Rinpoche. i, Desmond Tutu. j, Chiara Lubich. k, 14th Dalai Lama. l, Abraham Heschel.

2000, Jan. 18 Litho. *Perf. 14¼*

370 A132 33c Sheet of 12, #a.-l. 8.00 8.00

Souvenir Sheet

New Year 2000 (Year of the Dragon) — A133

Illustration reduced.

2000, Feb. 5 *Perf. 13¾*

371 A133 $2 multi 4.00 4.00

Butterflies A134

No. 372: a, Salamis parhassus. b, Morpho rhetenor. c, Danaus plexippus. d, Phyciodes actinote. e, Idea leucone. f, Actinote negra.

No. 373: a, Graphium sarpedon. b, Papilio machaon. c, Ornithoptera priamus. d, Ornithoptera chimaerea. e, Graphium antiphates. f, Pachliopta aristochiae.

Each $2: No. 374, Hamadryas amphinome, vert. No. 375, Colias croceus, vert. No. 376, Butterfly collector, vert.

2000, Feb. 28 Litho. *Perf. 14*

Sheets of 6

372 A134 20c #a.-f. 2.40 2.40

373 A134 55c #a.-f. 6.75 6.75

Souvenir Sheets

374-376 A134 Set of 3 12.00 12.00

Millennium Type of 1999

Highlights of the 1920s: a, Mahatma Gandhi leads non-violent reform in India. b, International Dada Fair in Berlin. c, American women win right to vote. d, Sacco and Vanzetti case. e, Hermann Rorshach develops inkblot test. f, Thomas J. Watson incorporates IBM. g, First successful commercial 35mm camera. h, Scopes "Monkey Trial." i, Charles Lindbergh makes first solo transatlantic flight. j, George Lemaitre develops "Big Bang" theory of cosmology. k, Chiang Kai-shek becomes generalissimo of China. l, Werner Heisenberg states "uncertainty principle" of physics. m, Alexander Fleming isolates Penicillium mold. n, Hirohito enthroned as Japanese emperor. o, Stock market crash starts Great Depression. p, First round-the-world flight (60x40mm). q, "All Quiet on the Western Front" published.

2000, Mar. 13 *Perf. 12¾x12½*

Sheet of 17

377 A127 20c #a.-q. + label 7.00 7.00

Inscriptions are incorrect or misspelled on Nos. 377a, 377f and 377m.

Millennium Type of 1999 with "Millennium 2000" Inscription

Perf. 13¼x13½

2000, Mar. 13 Litho.

378 A127 33c Like #356o .65 .65

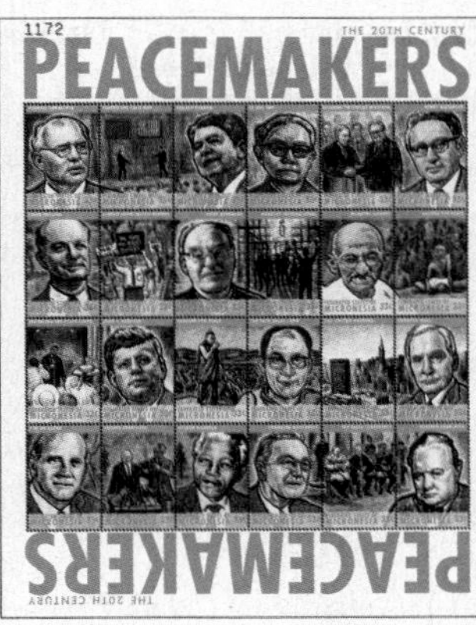

Peacemakers — A135

a, Mikhail Gorbachev. b, Ending the Cold War. c, Ronald Reagan. d, Le Duc Tho. e, Resolving the conflict in Viet Nam. f, Henry Kissinger. g, Linus Pauling. h, Protest against nuclear weapons. i, Peter Benenson. j, Amnesty Intl. k, Mahatma Gandhi. l, Fasting for peace. m, Initiating the Peace Corps. n, John F. Kennedy. o, Praying for peace. p, The 14th Dalai Lama. q, The UN. r, Cordell Hull. s, F. W. De Klerk. t, Ending apartheid. u, Nelson Mandela. v, Franklin Roosevelt. w, Yalta Conference. x, Winston Churchill.

Illustration reduced.

2000, Mar. 28 *Perf. 14*

379 A135 33c Sheet of 24, #a-x 16.00 16.00

Mushrooms — A137

No. 381, each 33c: a, Fairies' bonnets. b, Black bulgar. c, Amethyst deceiver. d, Common morel. e, Bird's nest fungus. f, Trumpet clitocybe.

No. 382, each 33c: a, Bonnet mycena. b, Horse mushroom. c, Velvet boletus. d, Oyster. d, Aztec mandala. e, Fly agaric.

Each $2: No. 383, Magpie ink cap. No, 384, Brown birch bolete.

Illustration reduced.

Philanthropists — A136

a, Andrew Carnegie. b, John D. Rockefeller. c, Henry Ford. d, Madam C. J. Walker. e, James B. Duke. f, Andrew Mellon. g, Charles F. Kettering. h, Robert W. Woodruff. i, Brooke Astor. j, Howard Hughes. k, Jesse H. Jones. l, Paul Mellon. m, J. Paul Getty. n, George Soros. o, Phyllis Wattis. p, Ted Turner.

Illustration reduced.

2000, May 1 *Perf. 14¼x14½*

380 A136 33c Sheet of 16, #a-p 11.00 11.00

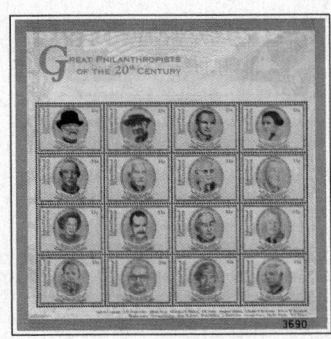

2000, May 15 ***Perf. 13¾x14¼***

Sheets of 6, #a-f

381-382 A137 Set of 2 8.00 8.00

Souvenir Sheets

383-384 A137 Set of 2 8.00 8.00

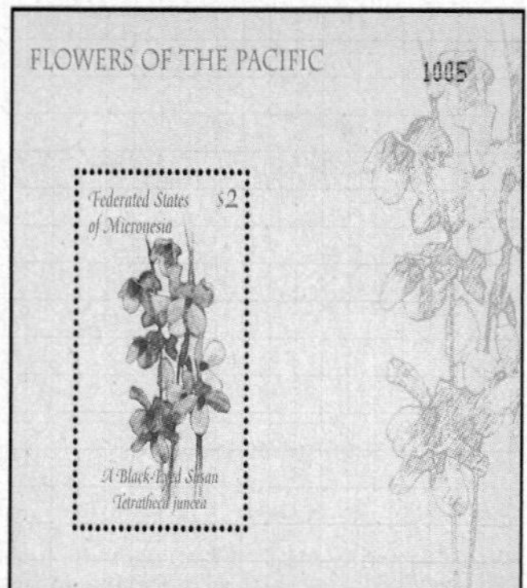

Flowers of the Pacific — A138

Wildflowers — A139

No. 385: a, Freycinetia arborea. b, Mount Cook lily. c, Sun orchid. d, Bossiaea ensata. e, Swamp hibiscus. f, Gardenia brighamii.

No. 386: a, Eleagant brodiaea. b, Skyrocket. c, Hedge bindweed. d, Woods' rose. e, Swamp rose. f, Wake robin.

No. 387, Black-eyed Susan. No. 388, Yellow meadow lily.

Illustrations reduced.

2000, May 29 ***Perf. 14x13¾***

385 A138 33c Sheet of 6, #a-f 4.00 4.00
386 A139 33c Sheet of 6, #a-f 4.00 4.00

Souvenir Sheets

387 A138 $2 multi 4.00 4.00
388 A139 $2 multi 4.00 4.00

Souvenir Sheet

2000 Summer Olympics, Sydney — A140

No. 389: a, Henry Taylor. b, Cycling. c, Olympic Stadium, Munich and German flag. d, Ancient Greek wrestling.

Illustration reduced.

2000, July 10 **Litho.** ***Perf. 14***

389 A140 33c Sheet of 4, #a-d 2.75 2.75

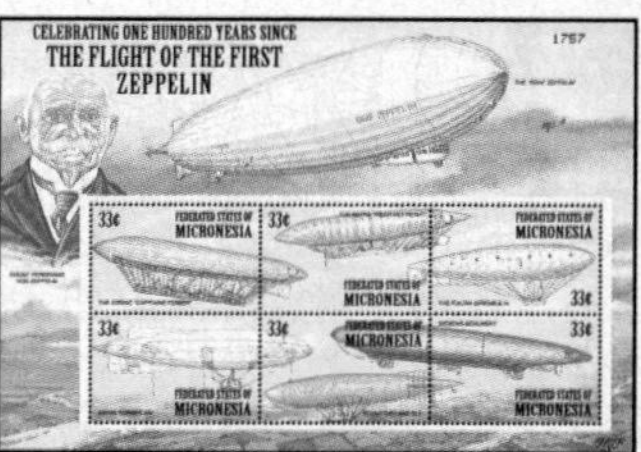

Zeppelins and Airships — A141

No. 390: a, Zodiac Capitaine Ferber. b, Astra Adjutant Reau. c, Italian dirigible IA. d, Astra-Torres XIV. e, Schuttle-Lanz SL3. f, Siemens-Schukert.

Each $2: No. 391, Graf Zeppelin. No. 392, Dupuy de Lome airship.

Illustration reduced.

2000, Aug. 7 **Litho.** ***Perf. 14***

390 A141 33c Sheet of 6, #a-f 4.00 4.00

Souvenir Sheets

391-392 A141 Set of 2 8.00 8.00

First Zeppelin flight, cent. (#390, 391).

Flower Photomosaic Type of 1999

Various flowers making up a photomosaic of the Queen Mother.

2000, Sept. 5 **Litho.** ***Perf. 13¾***

393 A126 33c Sheet of 8, #a-h 5.25 5.25

Souvenir Sheet

2000 Summer Olympics, Sydney — A142

No. 394: a, 33c, Weight lifting. b, 33c, Basketball. c, $1, Weight lifting.

Illustration reduced.

2000, Sept. 11 ***Perf. 14***

394 A142 Sheet of 3, #a-c 3.50 3.50

Olymphilex 2000, Sydney.

Fish A143

Designs: No. 395, Rock beauty. No. 396, Bluestreak cleaner wrasse. No. 397, Chevroned butterflyfish (with frame). No. 398, Longfin bannerfish (with frame).

No. 399: a, Mandarinfish. b, Emperor snapper. c, Copper-banded butterflyfish. d, Chevroned butterflyfish (no frame). e, Lemonpeel angelfish. f, Harlequin tuskfish. g, Clown triggerfish. h, Coral hind. i, Longfin bannerfish (no frame).

No. 400: a, Six-spot grouper. b, Common jellyfish. c, Palette surgeonfish. d, Bicolor angelfish. e, Threadfin butterflyfish. f, Clown anemonefish. g, Three-banded demoiselle. h, Reef shark. i, Starfish.

No. 401, Long-nosed butterflyfish. No. 402, Emperor angelfish.

2000, Nov. 1

395-398 A143 33c Set of 4 2.60 2.60

Sheets of 9, #a-i

399-400 A143 33c Set of 2 12.00 12.00

Souvenir Sheets

401-402 A143 $2 Set of 2 8.00 8.00

Flower Photomosaic Type of 1999

Various photos with religious themes making up a photomosaic of Pope John Paul II.

2000, Nov. 1 **Litho.** ***Perf. 13¾x14***

403 A126 50c Sheet of 8, #a-h 8.00 8.00

Christmas A144

Designs: 20c, The Holy Trinity, by Titian. 33c, The Adoration of the Magi, by Diego Velazquez. 60c, The Holy Nereus, by Peter Paul Rubens. $3.20, St. Gregory With Saints Around Him, by Rubens.

2000, Dec. 1 ***Perf. 14¼***

404-407 A144 Set of 4 8.75 8.75

Dogs and Cats — A145

No. 408, 33c: a, Afghan hound. b, Yellow Labrador retriever. c, Greyhound. d, German shepherd. e, King Charles spaniel. f, Jack Russell terrier.

No. 409, 33c: a, Siamese. b, Mackerel tabby. c, British shorthair. d, Persian. e, Turkish angora. f, Calico.

No. 410, $2, Dog in field. No. 411, $2, Cat stalking bird.

2000, June 26 **Litho.** ***Perf. 14***

Sheets of 6, #a-f

408-409 A145 Set of 2 8.00 8.00

Souvenir Sheets

410-411 A145 Set of 2 8.00 8.00

Souvenir Sheets

New Year 2001 (Year of the Snake) — A146

Designs: No. 412, 60c, Snake on ground. No. 413, 60c, Snake in bamboo, vert.

2001, Jan. 2

412-413 A146 Set of 2 2.40 2.40

Pokémon — A147

No. 414: a, Weepinbell. b, Snorlax. c, Seel. d, Hitmonchan. e, Jynx. f, Ponyta.

2001, Feb. 13 ***Perf. 13¾***

414 A147 50c Sheet of 6, #a-f 6.00 6.00

Souvenir Sheet

415 A147 $2 Farfetch'd 4.00 4.00

Whales — A148

No. 416, 50c: a, Fin. b, Right. c, Pygmy right. d, Humpback. e, Blue. f, Bowhead.

No. 417, 60c: a, True's beaked. b, Cuvier's beaked. c, Shepherd's beaked. d, Baird's beaked. e, Northern bottlenose. f, Pygmy sperm.

No. 418, $2, Killer. No. 419, $2, Sperm.

2001, Feb. 27 ***Perf. 13¼x13¾***

Sheets of 6, #a-f

416-417 A148 Set of 2 13.50 13.50

Souvenir Sheets

418-419 A148 Set of 2 8.00 8.00

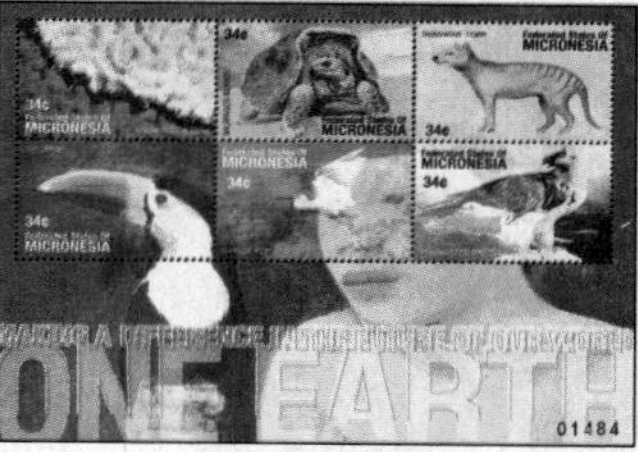

Ecology — A149

No. 420: a, Coral reef in peril. b, Galapagos Islands tortoise. c, Tasmanian tiger. d, Yanomani. e, Bird from Florida Keys. f, Eagle, Endangered species act.

No. 421: a, Pollution. b, Deforestation. c, Acid rain. d, Greenhouse effect.

No. 422, $2, Bird in flight. No. 423, Chimpanzee, vert.

Perf. 13¼x13¾, 13¾x13¼

2001, Feb. 27 **Litho.**

420 A149 34c Sheet of 6, #a-f 4.25 4.25
421 A149 60c Sheet of 4, #a-d 5.00 5.00

Souvenir Sheets

422-423 A149 $2 Set of 2 8.00 8.00

Fish Type of 1998

Designs: 11c, Yellow damselfish. 34c, Rainbow runner. 70c, Whitelined grouper. 80c, Purple queen anthias. $3.50, Eibl's angelfish. $12.25, Blue-spotted boxfish.

2001, Mar. 28 ***Perf. 14½x14¾***

424 A116	11c multi	.25	.25
425 A116	34c multi	.70	.70
426 A116	70c multi	1.40	1.40
427 A116	80c multi	1.60	1.60
428 A116	$3.50 multi	7.00	7.00
429 A116	$12.25 multi	25.00	25.00
	Nos. 424-429 (6)	35.95	35.95

Japanese Art — A150

Designs: No. 430, 34c, Parody of the Allegory of the Sage Chin Kao Riding a Carp, by Suzuki Harunobu. No. 431, 34c, The Courtesan Hinazuru of the Choji-Ya, by Chokosai Eisho. No. 432, 34c, Girl Tying Her Hair Ribbon, by Tori Kiyomine. No. 433, 34c, The Iris Garden, by Kiyonaga Torii. No. 434, 34c, The Courtesan Mayuzumi of the Daimonji-Ya, by Shunsho Katsukawa. No. 435, 34c, Bath House Scene, by Toyokuni Utagawa.

No. 436 — Paintings by Utamaro: a, Dance of a Kamisha. b, The Courtesan Hinazura at the Keizetsuro. c, Toilet Scene. d, Applying Lip Rouge. e, Beauty Reading a Letter. f, The Geisha Kamekichi.

No. 437, $2, Allegory of Ariwara No Narihira, by Kikugawa Eizan, horiz. No. 438, $2, Girl Seated by a Brook, by Harunobu, horiz.

2001, Apr. 20 ***Perf. 14***

430-435 A150 Set of 6 4.25 4.25
436 A150 34c Sheet of 6, #a-f 4.25 4.25

Imperf

Size: 118x88mm

437-438 A150 Set of 2 8.00 8.00

Phila Nippon '01, Japan (Nos. 436-438).

Toulouse-Lautrec Paintings — A151

No. 439: a, Oscar Wilde. b, Doctor Tapie in a Theater Corridor. c, Monsieur Delaporte.
$2, The Clowness Cha-U-Kao.

2001, May 15 ***Perf. 13¾***

439 A151 60c Sheet of 3, #a-c 3.75 3.75

Souvenir Sheet

440 A151 $2 multi 4.00 4.00

Queen Victoria (1819-1901) — A152

Various portraits.

2001, May 15 ***Perf. 14***

441 A152 60c Sheet of 6, #a-f 7.25 7.25

Souvenir Sheet

Perf. 13¾

442 A152 $2 shown 4.00 4.00

No. 441 contains six 28x42mm stamps.

Queen Elizabeth II, 75th Birthday — A153

No. 443: a, With necklace and brooch. b, Color photograph. c, As girl. d, As child. e, With dog. f, Facing left.
$2, Portrait in color.

2001, May 15 ***Perf. 14***

443 A153 60c Sheet of 6, #a-f 7.25 7.25

Souvenir Sheet

444 A153 $2 multi 4.00 4.00

Marine Life — A154

No. 445, 60c, horiz.: a, Striped dolphin. b, Olive Ridley turtle. c, Goldrim tang. d, Blue shark. e, Picasso triggerfish. f, Polkadot grouper.

No. 446, 60c, horiz.: a, Loggerhead turtle. b, Striped marlin. c, Bicolor cherub. d, Clown wrasse. e, Clown triggerfish. f, Japanese tang.

No. 447, $2, Adult and juvenile emperor angelfish. No. 448, $2, Harlequin tuskfish, horiz.

2001, July 16 ***Perf. 14***

Sheets of 6, #a-f

445-446 A154 Set of 2 14.50 14.50

Souvenir Sheets

Perf. 13¾

447-448 A154 Set of 2 8.00 8.00

Nos. 445-446 each contain six 42x28mm stamps.

Prehistoric Animals — A155

Designs: No. 449, 60c, Allosaurus (with frame). No. 450, 60c, Psittacosaurus. No. 451, 60c, Triceratops. No. 452, 60c, Archaeopteryx (with frame).

No. 453, 60c: a, Tyrannosaurus. b, Pteranodon. c, Brachiosaurus. d, Spinosaurus. e, Deinonychus. f, Teratosaurus.

No. 454, 60c: a, Parasaurolophus. b, Plateosaurus. c, Archaeopteryx (no frame). d, Allosaurus (no frame). e, Torosaurus. f, Euoplocephalus.

No. 455, $2, Tyrannosaurus. No. 456, $2, Parasaurolophus, horiz.

2001, Aug. 12 **Litho.** ***Perf. 14***

449-452 A155 Set of 4 4.75 4.75

Sheets of 6, #a-f

453-454 A155 Set of 2 14.50 14.50

Souvenir Sheets

455-456 A155 Set of 2 8.00 8.00

Shells — A156

No. 457, 50c: a, Bat volute. b, Horned helmet. c, Troschel's murex. d, Lotorium triton. e, Orange-mouthed olive. f, Phos whelk.

No. 458, 50c, vert.: a, Oblique nutmeg. b, Imperial volute. c, Pontifical miter. d, Eburneus cone. e, Variegated sundial. f, Heart cockle.

No. 459, $2, Eyed auger. No. 460, $2, Geography cone.

2001, Oct. 15 **Litho.** ***Perf. 14***

Sheets of 6, #a-f

457-458 A156 Set of 2 12.00 12.00

Souvenir Sheets

459-460 A156 Set of 2 8.00 8.00

On Nos. 485a-458f, the descriptions of the shells are transposed. Our descriptions are those of the stamps as they are printed.

Birds A157

Designs: 5c, Malleefowl. 22c, Corncrake. 23c, Hooded merganser. $2.10, Purple gallinule.

No. 465, 60c: a, Fairy wren. b, Golden-crowned kinglet warbler. c, Flame-tempered babbler. d, Golden-headed cisticola. e, White-browed babbler. f, White-breasted dipper.

No. 466, 60c: a, Logrunner. b, Eurasian treecreeper. c, Goldfinch. d, Rufous fantail. e, Orange-billed flowerpecker. f, American goldfinch.

No. 467, $2, Emperor bird of paradise. No. 468, $2, Yellow-eyed cuckooshrike, vert.

2001, Oct. 29 **Litho.** ***Perf. 14***

461-464 A157 Set of 4 5.25 5.25

Sheets of 6, #a-f

465-466 A157 Set of 2 14.50 14.50

Souvenir Sheets

467-468 A157 Set of 2 8.00 8.00

Nobel Prizes, Cent. — A158

No. 469, 60c — Physiology or Medicine laureates: a, Alexis Carrel, 1912. b, Max Theiler, 1951. c, Niels Finsen, 1903. d, Philip S. Hench, 1950. e, Sune Bergström, 1982. f, John R. Vane, 1982.

No. 470, 60c — Laureates: a, Bengt Samuelsson, Physiology or Medicine, 1982. b, Johannes Fibiger, Physiology or Medicine, 1926. c, Theodore Richards, Chemistry, 1914. d, Tadeus Reichstein, Physiology or Medicine, 1950. e, Frederick Soddy, Chemistry, 1921. f, Albert Szent-Györgyi, 1937.

No. 471, $2, Irving Langmuir, Chemistry, 1932. No. 472, $2, Artturi Illmari Virtanen, Chemistry, 1945.

2001, Nov. 12

Sheets of 6, #a-f

469-470 A158 Set of 2 14.50 14.50

Souvenir Sheets

471-472 A158 Set of 2 8.00 8.00

Christmas A159

Santa Claus: 22c, On cat. 34c, Between Christmas trees. 60c, In sleigh. $1, On dog.
$2, Entering chimney, vert.

2001, Dec. 5

473-476 A159 Set of 4 4.50 4.50

Souvenir Sheet

477 A159 $2 multi 4.00 4.00

Attack on Pearl Harbor, 60th Anniv. — A160

No. 478, 60c: a, Rollover of USS Oklahoma. b, Japanese attack Wheeler Air Field. c, Japanese sailors loading bombs onto planes. d, Destroyer USS Ward sinks a Japanese submarine. e, USS Arizona sunk by Japanese bombs. f, Ewa Marine Base attacked by Japanese.

No. 479, 60c: a, Memorial poster showing attack. b, Japanese Prime Minister Hideki Tojo. c, Rescue at Bellows Field. d, Rescue of USS Arizona crew. e, Admiral Isoroku Yamamoto. f, Memorial poster showing soldier and flag.

No. 480, $2, USS Arizona Memorial. No. 481, $2, Pres. Franklin D. Roosevelt.

2001, Dec. 7

Sheets of 6, #a-f

478-479 A160 Set of 2 14.50 14.50

Souvenir Sheets

480-481 A160 Set of 2 8.00 8.00

Souvenir Sheet

New Year 2002 (Year of the Horse) — A161

Various horses.

2002, Jan. 24 ***Perf. 13¾x13¼***

482 A161 60c Sheet of 5, #a-e 6.00 6.00

Reign of Queen Elizabeth II, 50th Anniv. — A162

No. 483: a, Queen wearing flowered dress. b, Prince Philip. c, Queen waving, holding flowers. d, Queen with children.

$2, Queen wearing scarf.

2002, Feb. 6 ***Perf. 14¼***

483 A162 80c Sheet of 4, #a-d 6.50 6.50

Souvenir Sheet

484 A162 $2 multi 4.00 4.00

United We Stand — A163

2002, Feb. 20 ***Perf. 13¾x13¼***

485 A163 $1 multi 2.00 2.00

Issued in sheets of 4.

2002 Winter Olympics, Salt Lake City — A164

Designs: No. 486, $1, Luge. No. 487, $1, Ice hockey.

2002, Mar. 18 ***Perf. 14***

486-487 A164 Set of 2 4.00 4.00

a. Souvenir sheet, #486-487 4.00 4.00

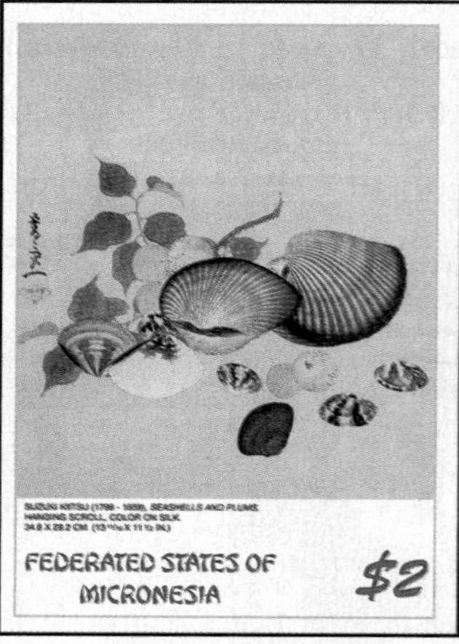

Japanese Art — A165

Birds and Flowers of the Twelve Months, by Hoitsu Sakai — No. 488, 60c: a, January. b, February. c, March. d, April. e, May. f, June.

No. 489, 60c: a, July. b, August. c, September. d, October. e, November. f, December.

No. 490, $2, Seashells and Plums by Kiitsu Suzuki. No. 491, Peacock and Peonies, by Rosetsu Nagasawa.

2002, Mar. 25 Litho. ***Perf. 14x14¾***

Sheets of 6, #a-f

488-489 A165 Set of 2 14.50 14.50

Imperf

490-491 A165 Set of 2 8.00 8.00

Nos. 488-489 each contain six 77x26mm stamps.

Intl. Year of Mountains — A166

No. 492: a, Matterhorn, Switzerland. b, Maroonbells, U.S. c, Wetterhorn, Switzerland. d, Mt. Tsaranora, Africa.

$2, Cerro Fitzroy, South America.

2002, Mar. 30 ***Perf. 14***

492 A166 80c Sheet of 4, #a-d 6.50 6.50

Souvenir Sheet

493 A166 $2 multi 4.00 4.00

Pres. John F. Kennedy (1917-63) — A167

No. 494: a, Dark blue background. b, Lilac background, name at left. c, Tan background, name at right. d, Light blue background.

$2, Purple background.

2002, Mar. 30

494 A167 60c Sheet of 4, #a-d 5.00 5.00

Souvenir Sheet

495 A167 $2 multi 4.00 4.00

Princess Diana (1961-97) — A168

No. 496: a, Wearing wedding veil. b, Wearing tiara and necklace. c, Wearing brimless hat. d, Wearing scarf. e, Hatless. f, Wearing tiara and large collar.

$2, Wearing hat with brim.

2002, Mar. 30

496 A168 60c Sheet of 6, #a-f 7.25 7.25

Souvenir Sheet

497 A168 $2 multi 4.00 4.00

Intl. Year of Ecotourism — A169

No. 498: a, Lizard. b, Canoes. c, Micronesian house. d, Three children in costume. e, Woman. f, Two dancers, house.

$2, Fishermen.

Perf. 13¼x13½

2002, June 17 Litho.

498 A169 80c Sheet of 6, #a-f 9.75 9.75

Souvenir Sheet

499 A169 $2 multi 4.00 4.00

20th World Scout Jamboree, Thailand — A170

No. 500: a, Thai temple. b, American scout insignia. c, Scout cap.

$2, Merit badges.

2002, June 17 ***Perf. 13½x13¼***

500 A170 $1 Sheet of 3, #a-c 6.00 6.00

Souvenir Sheet

501 A170 $2 multi 4.00 4.00

Winter Olympics Type of 2002 Redrawn With White Panel Behind Olympic Rings

Designs: No. 502, $1, Luge. No. 503, $1, Ice hockey.

2002, July 15

502-503 A164 Set of 2 4.00 4.00

a. Souvenir sheet, #502-503 4.00 4.00

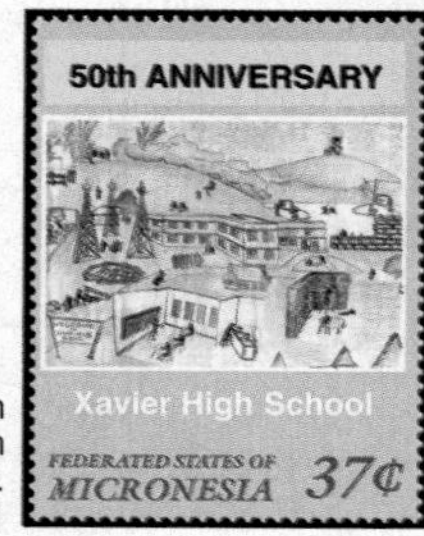

Xavier High School, 50th Anniv. A171

2002, July 31 ***Perf. 13½x13¾***

504 A171 37c multi .75 .75

Queen Mother Elizabeth (1900-2002) — A172

No. 505, horiz.: a, At age 7. b, At wedding. c, At birth of Princess Elizabeth. d, At coronation of King George VI, 1937.

$2, As elderly lady.

2002, Aug. 12 ***Perf. 14***

505 A172 80c Sheet of 4, #a-d 6.50 6.50

Souvenir Sheet

506 A172 $2 multi 4.00 4.00

Teddy Bears, Cent. — A173

No. 507: a, Burglar bear. b, White bear with heart. c, Blue bear with flowers. d, Brown bear with heart.

2002, Sept. 23 Litho. ***Perf. 14***

507 A173 80c Sheet of 4, #a-d 6.50 6.50

Elvis Presley (1935-77) — A174

Presley with: a, Hand below guitar. b, Head on guitar. c, Hat. d, Checked shirt, no hat. e, Arms raised. f, Microphone.

2002, Oct. 7 *Perf. 13¾*

508 A174 37c Sheet of 6, #a-f 4.50 4.50

Christmas A175

Paintings: 21c, Madonna and Child, by Filippino Lippi, vert. 37c, Madonna and Child, by Giovanni Bellini, vert. 70c, Madonna and Child Between St. Stephen and St. Ladislaus, by Simone Martini. 80c, Holy Family, by Bronzino, vert. No. 513, $2, Holy Family, by Martini, vert.

No. 514, Sacred Conversation, by Bellini, vert.

2002, Nov. 4 *Perf. 14*

509-513 A175 Set of 5 8.25 8.25

Souvenir Sheet

Perf. 14x14¼

514 A175 $2 multi 4.00 4.00

Flora, Fauna and Mushrooms — A176

No. 515, 37c — Moths: a, White-lined sphinx. b, Tropical fruit-piercer. c, Coppery dysphania. d, Large agarista. e, Indian moon moth. f, Croker's frother.

No. 516, 55c — Mushrooms: a, Phellinus robustus. b, Purple coincap. c, Shaggy parasol. d, King bolete. e, Boletus crocipodius. f, Sharp-scaled parasol.

No. 517, 60c — Orchids: a, Eria javanica. b, Cymbidium finlaysonianum. c, Coelogyne asperata. d, Spathoglottis affinis. e, Vanda tricolor. f, Calanthe rosea.

No. 518, 60c — Butterflies: a, Meadow argus. b, Cairns birdwing. c, Large green-banded blue. d, Beak butterfly. e, Palmfly. f, Broad-bordered grass yellow.

No. 519, 80c — Insects and spiders: a, Stag beetle. b, Honeybee. c, Black widow spider. d, Mosquito. e, Black ant. f, Cicada.

No. 520, $2, Zodiac moth. No. 521, $2, Lepiota acutesquamosa mushroom. No. 522, $2, Dendrobium phalaenopsis orchid. No. 523, $2, Yamfly butterfly. No. 524, $2, Dragonfly, horiz.

2002, Dec. 16 *Perf. 14*

Sheets of 6, #a-f

515-519 A176 Set of 5 35.00 35.00

Souvenir Sheets

520-524 A176 Set of 5 20.00 20.00

Birds — A177

Designs: 3c, Greater flame-backed woodpecker. 5c, Red-tailed tropicbird. 21c, Hair-crested drongo. 22c, Pale white-eye. 23c, White-backed munia. 37c, Yap monarch. 60c, Eclectus parrot. 70c, Sulphur-crested cockatoo. 80c, Giant white-eye. $2, Green magpie. $3.85, Dollarbird.

2002, Dec. 30 *Perf. 14¼x14*

525	A177	3c multi	.20	.20
526	A177	5c multi	.20	.20
527	A177	21c multi	.40	.40
528	A177	22c multi	.45	.45
529	A177	23c multi	.45	.45
530	A177	37c multi	.75	.75
531	A177	60c multi	1.25	1.25
532	A177	70c multi	1.40	1.40
533	A177	80c multi	1.60	1.60
534	A177	$2 multi	4.00	4.00

Perf. 13¾

535	A177	$3.85 multi	7.75	7.75
536	A177	$5 multi	10.00	10.00
537	A177	$13.65multi	27.50	27.50
		Nos. 525-537 (13)	55.95	55.95

First Non-stop Solo Transatlantic Flight, 75th Anniv. (in 2002) — A178

No. 538: a, Charles Lindbergh, Donald Hall, Spirit of St. Louis. b, Spirit of St. Louis, Apr. 28, 1927. c, Towing of Spirit of St. Louis, May 20. d, Lindbergh taking off from Roosevelt Field, May 20. e, Lindbergh's arrival in Paris, May 21. f, Lindbergh in ticker tape parade, New York.

2003, Jan. 13 **Litho.** *Perf. 14*

538 A178 60c Sheet of 6, #a-f 7.25 7.25

New Year 2003 (Year of the Ram) — A179

No. 539: a, Black ram facing left, country name at left. b, Black ram facing left, country name at right. c, White ram facing right, country name at left. d, White ram facing forward, country name at right.

2003, Feb. 1 **Litho.** *Perf. 14¼x14*

539 A179 37c Sheet of 6, #a-b, 2 each #c-d 4.50 4.50

Astronauts Killed in Space Shuttle Columbia Accident — A180

No. 540: a, Mission Specialist 1 David M. Brown. b, Commander Rick D. Husband. c, Mission Specialist 4 Laurel Blair Salton Clark. d, Mission Specialist 4 Kalpana Chawla. e, Payload Commander Michael P. Anderson. f, Pilot William C. McCool. g, Payload Specialist Ilan Ramon.

2003, Apr. 7 *Perf. 13½x13¼*

540 A180 37c Sheet of 7, #a-g 5.25 5.25

Coronation of Queen Elizabeth II, 50th Anniv. — A181

No. 541: a, Wearing pearl necklace. b, Wearing sash and tiara. c, Wearing robe.

$2, Wearing crown.

2003, May 13 *Perf. 14x14¼*

541 A181 $1 Sheet of 3, #a-c 6.00 6.00

Souvenir Sheet

542 A181 $2 multi 4.00 4.00

Prince William, 21st Birthday — A182

No. 543: a, Wearing checked shirt and striped sweater. b, Facing right, wearing sweater, shirt and tie. c, Wearing suit and tie.

$2, Wearing raincoat.

2003, May 14

543 A182 $1 Sheet of 3, #a-c 6.00 6.00

Souvenir Sheet

544 A182 $2 multi 4.00 4.00

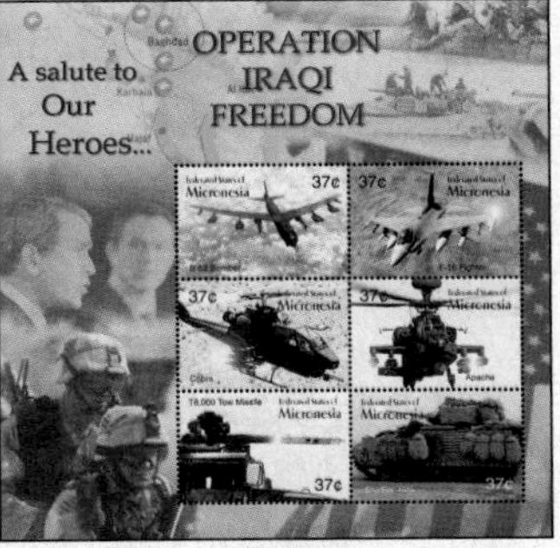

Operation Iraqi Freedom — A183

No. 545, 37c: a, B-52 Bomber. b, F-16 Fighter. c, Cobra Helicopter. d, Apache Helicopter. e, T8000 Tow Missile. f, Bradley Tank.

No. 546, 37c: a, Stealth Fighter. b, AC-130 Cargo plane. c, MH-53j Pave Low II Helicopter. d, Predator. e, Challenger Two Tank. f, Aegis Cruiser.

2003, May 14 *Perf. 14*

Sheets of 6, #a-f

545-546 A183 Set of 2 9.00 9.00

Tour de France Bicycle Race, Cent. — A184

No. 547: a, Greg LeMond, 1990. b, Miguel Indurain, 1991. c, Indurain, 1992. d, Indurain, 1993.

$2, Marco Pantani, 1998.

2003, July 1 *Perf. 13½*

547 A184 60c Sheet of 4, #a-d 5.00 5.00

Souvenir Sheet

548 A184 $2 multi 4.00 4.00

Intl. Year of Fresh Water — A185

No. 549: a, Kosrae mangroves. b, Chuuk Lagoon. c, Pohnpei's waterfalls.

$2, Pohnpei Lagoon.

2003, July 21 *Perf. 13½*

549 A185 $1 Sheet of 3, #a-c 6.00 6.00

Souvenir Sheet

550 A185 $2 multi 4.00 4.00

Powered Flight, Cent. — A186

No. 551: a, Concorde. b, Boeing 757. c, Junkers F13a. d, Martin M-130 China Clipper. e, Handley Page H.P.42W. f, Wright Flyer II.

$2, Boeing 747.

2003, Aug. 7 *Perf. 14*

551 A186 55c Sheet of 6, #a-f 6.75 6.75

Souvenir Sheet

552 A186 $2 multi 4.00 4.00

2003 APS Stampshow, Columbus, Ohio (#551).

Circus Performers — A187

No. 553, 80c: a, Glen Little. b, Joseph Grimaldi. c, Beverly Reno Bergerson. d, Coco Michael Polakov.

No. 554, 80c: a, Jana Mandana. b, Maxim Papazov. c, Harry Keaton. d, Giraffe.

2003, Aug. 25 ***Perf. 14***

Sheets of 4, #a-d

553-554 A187 Set of 2 13.00 13.00

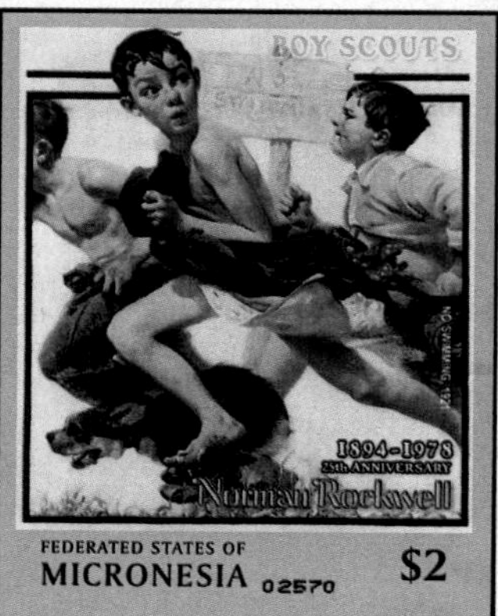

Paintings of Boy Scouts by Norman Rockwell (1894-1978) — A188

No. 555: a, Scout with plaid neckerchief, from 1963 Boy Scout Calendar. b, A Scout is Helpful. c, The Scoutmaster. d, Scout with red neckerchief, from 1963 Boy Scout Calendar.

$2, No Swimming.

2003, Sept. 8 ***Perf. 14***

555 A188 80c Sheet of 4, #a-d 6.50 6.50

Imperf

556 A188 $2 multi 4.00 4.00

No. 555 contains four 28x42mm stamps.

Paintings by Paul Gauguin (1848-1903) — A189

No. 557: a, Vahine No Te Tiare. b, Les Amants. c, Trois Tahitiens Conversation. d, Arearea.

$2, Ta Matete.

2003, Sept. 8 ***Perf. 13¾***

557 A189 80c Sheet of 4, #a-d 6.50 6.50

Imperf

558 A189 $2 multi 4.00 4.00

No. 557 contains four 51x38mm stamps.

Paintings of James McNeill Whistler (1834-1903) — A190

Designs: 37c, Blue and Silver Blue: Wave, Biarritz. 55c, Brown and Silver: Old Battersea Bridge. 60c, Nocturne in Blue and Silver: The Lagoon, Venice. 80c, Crepuscule in Flesh Color and Green: Valparaiso.

No. 563: a, Symphony in White No. 2: The Little White Girl, vert. b, At the Piano (75x50mm). c, Symphony in White No. 1: The White Girl, vert.

$2, Portrait of Thomas Carlyle: Arrangement in Gray and Black No. 2, vert.

2003, Oct. 6 ***Perf. 14¼***

559-562 A190 Set of 4 4.75 4.75

563 A190 $1 Sheet of 3, #a-c 6.00 6.00

Size: 83x104mm

Imperf

564 A190 $2 multi 4.00 4.00

Christmas A191

Designs: 37c, Madonna of the Carnation, by Leonardo da Vinci. 60c, Madonna with Yarn Winder, by da Vinci. 80c, Litta Madonna, by da Vinci. $1, Madonna of the Grand Duke, by Raphael.

$2, The Adoration of the Magi, by Giambattista Tiepolo.

2003, Nov. 5 ***Perf. 14¼***

565-568 A191 Set of 4 5.75 5.75

Souvenir Sheet

569 A191 $2 multi 4.00 4.00

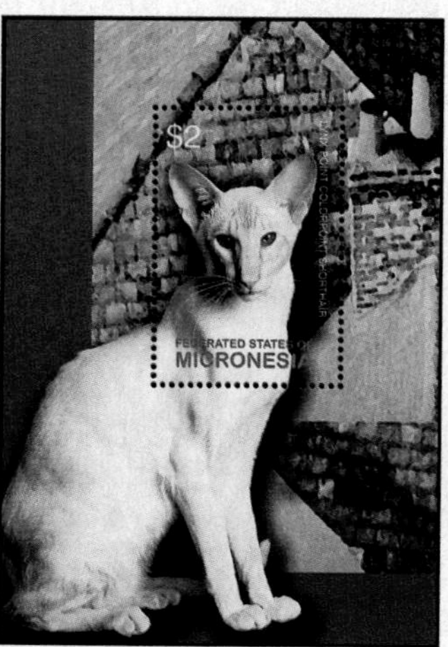

Cats, Dogs, Birds, Reptiles & Amphibians — A192

No. 570, 80c — Cats: a, Ragdoll. b, Calico Shorthaired Japanese Bobtail. c, Blue Mackerel Taffy Exotic Shorthair. d, Dilute Calico.

No. 571, 80c — Dogs: a, Australian shepherd. b, Greyhound. c, English bulldog. d, Schnauzer.

No. 572, 80c, horiz. — Birds: a, Green-winged macaw. b, American flamingo. c, Blue and gold macaw. d, Abyssinian ground hornbill.

No. 573, 80c, horiz. — Reptiles and amphibians: a, Leopard gecko. b, Red-eyed tree frog. c, Panther chameleon. d, Green and black poison frog.

No. 574, $2, Lynx Point Colorpoint Shorthair. No. 575, $2, Toy poodle. No. 576, $2, American flamingo. No. 577, $2, Madagascan chameleon, horiz.

2003, Dec. 22 ***Perf. 14***

Sheets of 4, #a-d

570-573 A192 Set of 4 26.00 26.00

Souvenir Sheets

574-577 A192 Set of 4 16.00 16.00

Pres. Bailey Olter (1932-99) — A193

2004, Feb. 16 **Litho.** ***Perf. 14***

578 A193 37c multi .75 .75

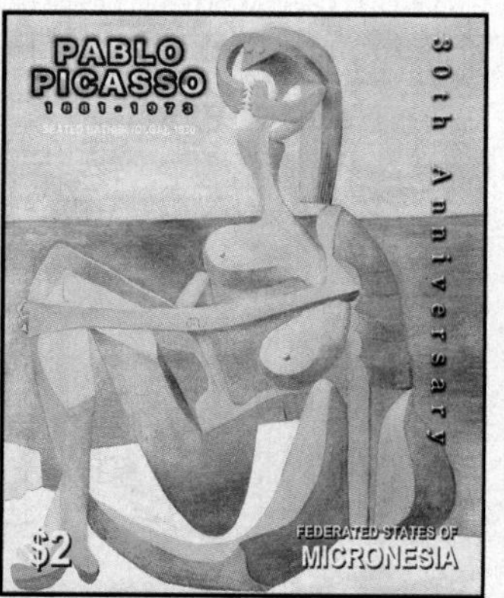

Paintings by Pablo Picasso (1881-1973) — A194

No. 579: a, Marie-Thérèse Leaning on One Elbow. b, Portrait of Jaime Sabartés. c, Portrait of Emilie Marguerite Walter (Mémé). d, Bust of a Woman Leaning on One Elbow.

$2, Seated Bather (Olga).

Illustration reduced.

2004, Mar. 8 ***Perf. 14¼***

579 A194 80c Sheet of 4, #a-d 6.50 6.50

Imperf

580 A194 $2 multi 4.00 4.00

No. 579 contains four 37x50mm stamps.

Paintings in the Hermitage, St. Petersburg, Russia A195

Designs: 22c, A Young Lady in a Theatrical Costume, by Alexis Grimou. 37c, Portrait of Mrs. Harriet Greer, by George Romney. 80c, Portrait of Prince Nikolai Yusupov, by Friedrich Heinrich Füger. $1, Portrait of Richard Brinsley Sheridan, by John Hoppner.

$2, Spanish Concert (Conversation Espagnole), by Carle Vanloo.

2004, Mar. 8 ***Perf. 14¼***

581-584 A195 Set of 4 5.00 5.00

Imperf

Size: 64x81mm

585 A195 $2 multi 4.00 4.00

New Year 2004 (Year of the Monkey) — A196

Designs: 50c, Moon-struck Gibbon, by Gao Qi-feng. $1, Detail from Moon-struck Gibbon.

2004, Mar. 9 ***Perf. 13¼***

586 A196 50c multi 1.00 1.00

Souvenir Sheet

Perf. 13¼x13

587 A196 $1 multi 2.00 2.00

No. 587 contains one 30x40mm stamp. No. 586 printed in sheets of four.

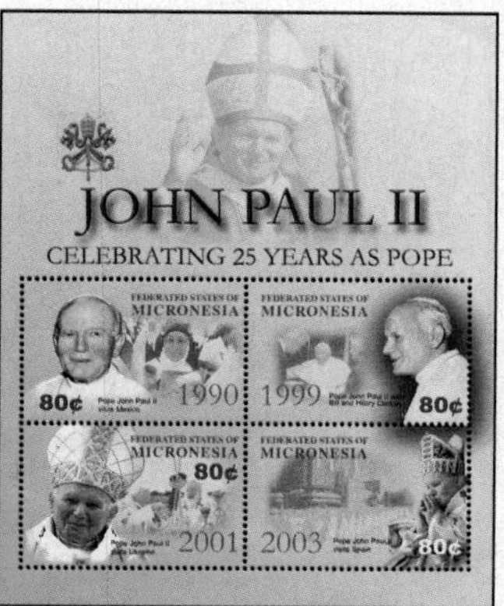

Election of Pope John Paul II, 25th Anniv. (in 2003) — A197

No. 588 — Pope John Paul II: a, Visiting Monaco, 1990. b, With Bill and Hillary Clinton, 1999. c, Visiting Ukraine, 2001. d, Visiting Spain, 2003.

2004, Sept. 1 ***Perf. 14¼x14***

588 A197 80c Sheet of 4, #a-d 6.50 6.50

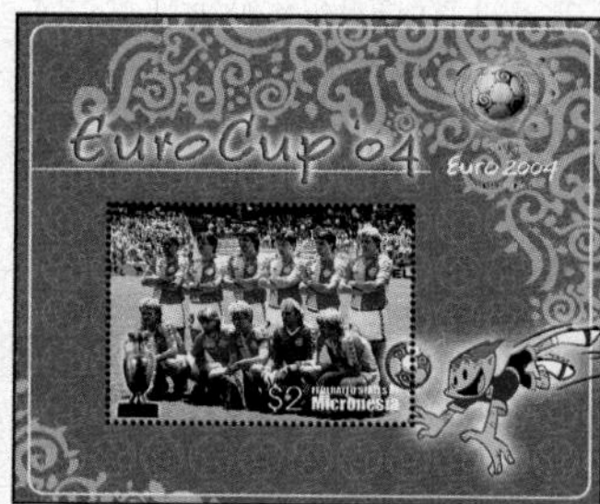

2004 European Soccer Championships, Portugal — A198

No. 589: a, Lars Olsen. b, Juergen Klinsmann. c, Peter Schmeichel. d, Nya Ullevi Stadium.

$2, 1992 Denmark team, horiz.

2004, Sept. 1 ***Perf. 14***

589 A198 80c Sheet of 4, #a-d 6.50 6.50

Souvenir Sheet

Perf. 14¼

590 A198 $2 multi 4.00 4.00

No. 589 contains four 28x42mm stamps.

D-Day, 60th Anniv. — A199

No. 591: a, Landing craft vehicle personnel. b, Destroyer Thompson. c, LST-391. d, Rhino Ferry 2, Rhino Tug 3. e, HMS Mauritius. f, Battleship Arkansas.
$2, LCI 1539.

2004, Sept. 1 ***Perf. 14***
591 A199 50c Sheet of 6, #a-f 6.00 6.00

Souvenir Sheet

592 A199 $2 multi 4.00 4.00

Souvenir Sheet

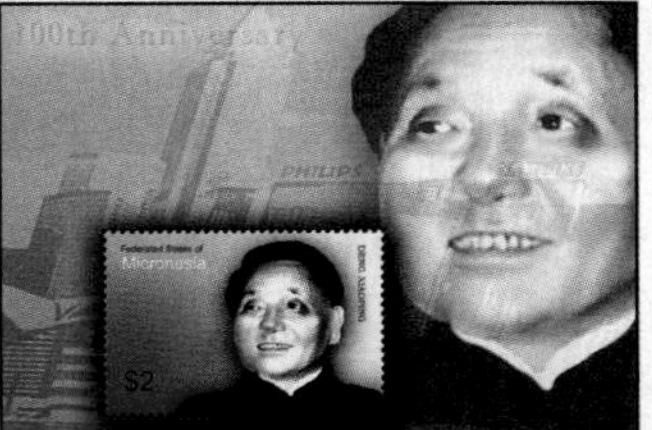

Deng Xiaoping (1904-97), Chinese Leader — A200

2004, Sept. 1 **Litho.** ***Perf. 14***
593 A200 $2 multi 4.00 4.00

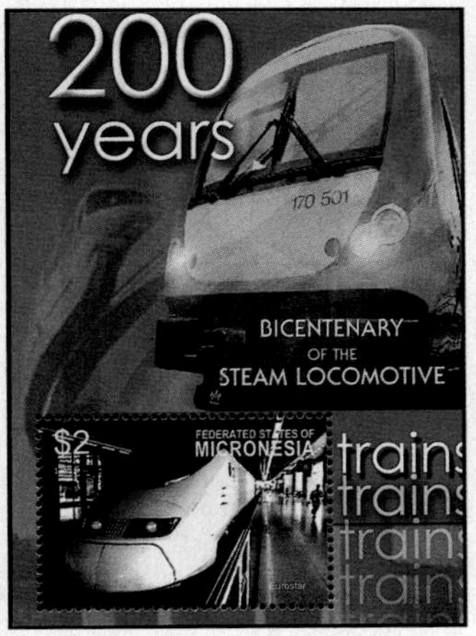

Locomotives, Bicent. — A201

No. 594, 80c: a, CFL N5520. b, Inter-region trains. c, SW-600. d, WSOR 3801.
No. 595, 80c: a, Baldwin 2-8-0. b, F-10 #1114 Diesel. c, BNSF locomotive (incorrectly inscribed "Okinawa Hitachi trains". d, Shinkansen.
No. 596, 80c: a, RS-1 #22. b, Diesel class 630. c, Okinawa Hitachi train. d, Eurostar.
No. 597, $2, Eurostar, diff. No. 598, $2, Locomotive 231-065. No. 599, $2, Michigan Central locomotive.

2004, Sept. 1 **Sheets of 4, #a-d**
594-596 A201 Set of 3 19.50 19.50

Souvenir Sheets

597-599 A201 Set of 3 12.00 12.00

Birds Type of 2002

Designs: 2c, Blue-gray gnatcatcher. 10c, Clapper rail.

2004, Nov. 1 ***Perf. 13¼***
600 A177 2c multi .20 .20
601 A177 10c multi .20 .20

Miniature Sheet

Intl. Year of Peace — A202

No. 602: a, Nelson Mandela. b, Dalai Lama. c, Pope John Paul II.

2004, Nov. 1 ***Perf. 14***
602 A202 80c Sheet of 3, #a-c 5.00 5.00

2004 Summer Olympics, Athens — A203

Designs: 37c, Ancient bronze sculpture of horse and rider. 55c, Pin from 1912 Stockholm Olympics, vert. 80c, Baron Pierre de Coubertin, Intl. Olympic Committee President, vert. $1, Poster from 1968 Mexico City Olympics, vert.

2004, Nov. 1 ***Perf. 14¼***
603-606 A203 Set of 4 5.50 5.50

Miniature Sheets

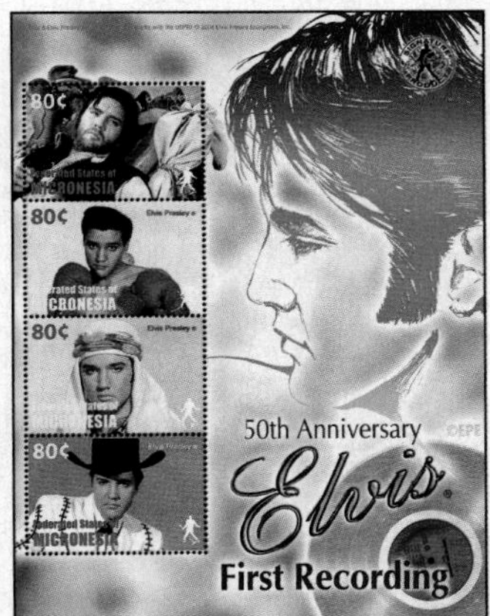

Elvis Presley's First Recording, 50th Anniv. — A204

No. 607, 80c — Presley with: a, Beard. b, Boxing gloves. c, Kaffiyeh. d, Cowboy hat.
No. 608, 80c, vert. — Presley with denomination in: a, Red. b, Purple. c, Blue. d, Orange yellow.

2004, Nov. 1 ***Perf. 14***

Sheets of 4, #a-d

607-608 A204 Set of 2 13.00 13.00

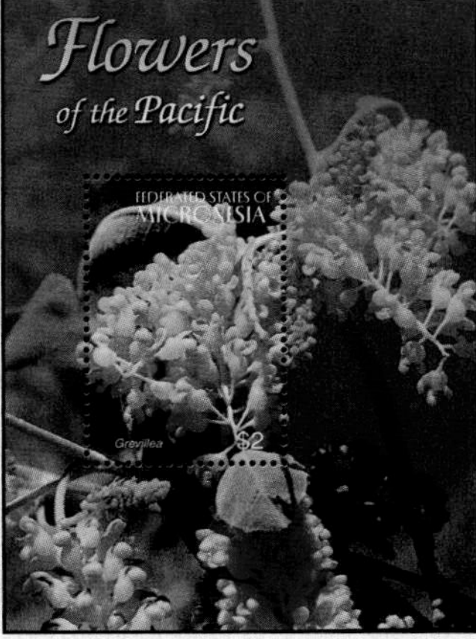

Flowers — A205

No. 609, horiz.: a, Epiphytic aeschynanthus. b, Darwinia collina. c, Rhododendron. d, Rhododendron retusum. e, Eucryphia lucida. f, Microporus xanthopus.
$2, Grevillea.

2004, Nov. 1 ***Perf. 13¼x13½***
609 A205 55c Sheet of 6, #a-f 6.75 6.75

Souvenir Sheet

Perf. 13½x13¼

610 A205 $2 multi 4.00 4.00

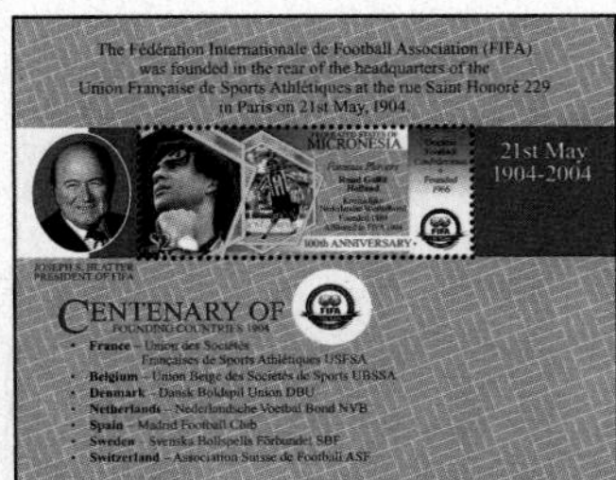

FIFA (Fédération Internationale de Football Association), Cent. — A206

No. 611: a, Herman Crespo. b, Peter Shilton. c, Klaus Augenthaler. d, Bryan Robson.
$2, Ruud Gullit.

2004, Nov. 1 ***Perf. 12¾x12½***
611 A206 80c Sheet of 4, #a-d 6.50 6.50

Souvenir Sheet

612 A206 $2 multi 4.00 4.00

National Basketball Association Players — A207

Designs: No. 613, 20c, Dirk Nowitzki, Dallas Mavericks. No. 614, 20c, Vince Carter, Toronto Raptors.

2004 ***Perf. 14***
613-614 A207 Set of 2 .80 .80

Issued: No. 613, 11/2; No. 614, 11/3. Each stamp issued in sheets of 12.

Prehistoric Animals — A208

No. 615, 80c: a, Indricotheres. b, Hyaenodons. c, Deinotherium. d, Chalicotheres.
No. 616, 80c: a, Apatosaurus. b, Pachyrhinosaurus. c, Kentrosaurus. d, Saltasaurus.
No. 617, 80c, vert.: a, Allosaurus. b, Tyrannosaurus. c, Troodon. d, Carnotaurus.
No. 618, $2, Moeritherium. No. 619, $2, Coelophysis. No. 620, $2, Deinonychus.

Perf. 14½x14, 14x14½

2004, Dec. 13 **Litho.**

Sheets of 4, #a-d

615-617 A208 Set of 3 19.50 19.50

Souvenir Sheets

618-620 A208 Set of 3 12.00 12.00

Fish and Coral — A209

No. 621: a, Clown triggerfish. b, Striped-face unicornfish. c, Firefish. d, Longnose hawkfish. e, Annella mollis. f, Dendronephthya.
$2, Great barracuda.

2004, Nov. 1 **Litho.** ***Perf. 13½***
621 A209 55c Sheet of 6, #a-f 6.75 6.75

Souvenir Sheet

622 A209 $2 multi 4.00 4.00

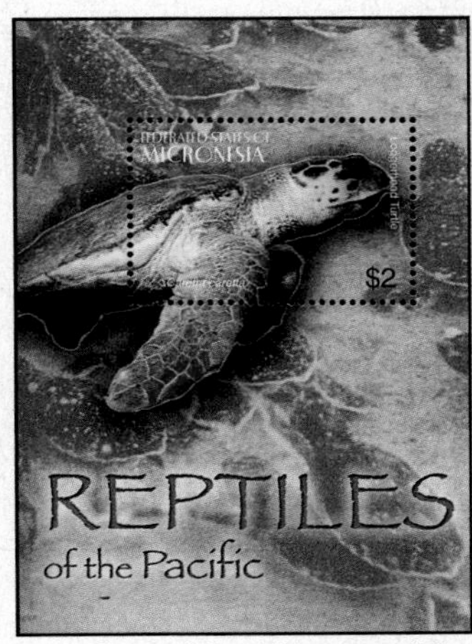

Reptiles and Amphibians — A210

No. 623: a, Blue coral snake. b, Solomon Islands horned frog. c, Levuka wrinkled ground frog. d, Flying lizard. e, Platymantis vitensis. f, Pacific ground boa.
$2, Loggerhead turtle.

2004, Nov. 1
623 A210 55c Sheet of 6, #a-f 6.75 6.75

Souvenir Sheet

624 A210 $2 multi 4.00 4.00

No. 623c has incorrect inscription as stamp depicts a lizard.

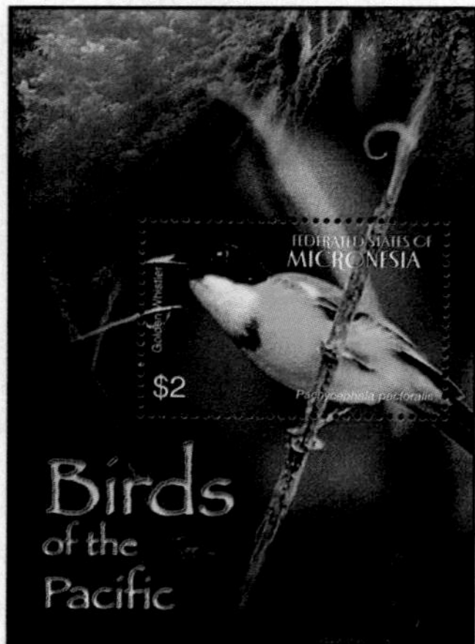

Birds — A211

No. 625, vert.: a, Black-faced woodswallows. b, Brown boobies. c, Rainbow lorikeets. d, Wandering albatross. e, Kagu. f, Great frigatebird.
$2, Golden whistler.

2004, Nov. 1
625 A211 55c Sheet of 6, #a-f 6.75 6.75

Souvenir Sheet

626 A211 $2 multi 4.00 4.00

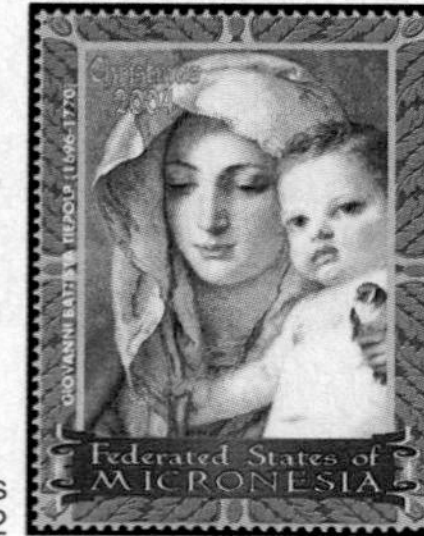

Christmas A212

Madonna and Child paintings by: 37c, Giovanni Battista Tiepolo. 60c, Raphael. 80c, Jan Gossaert (Mabuse). $1, Fra Filippo Lippi.
$2, Unknown artist.

2004, Dec. 27 ***Perf. 14¼***
627-630 A212 Set of 4 5.75 5.75

Souvenir Sheet

631 A212 $2 multi 4.00 4.00

New Year 2005 (Year of the Rooster) — A213

2005, Jan. 17 ***Perf. 12¾***
632 A213 50c multi 1.00 1.00

Printed in sheets of 4.

Basketball Players Type of 2004

Design: Luke Walton, Los Angeles Lakers.

2005, Feb. 24 ***Perf. 14***
633 A207 20c multi .40 .40

Pres. Ronald Reagan (1911-2004) — A214

No. 634: a, With British Prime Minister Margaret Thatcher. b, With Israeli Prime Minister Yitzhak Shamir.
Illustration reduced.

2005, Mar. 21 ***Perf. 13¼x13½***
634 A214 55c Horiz. pair, #a-b 2.25 2.25

Printed in sheets containing 3 each Nos. 634a and 634b.

Elvis Presley (1935-2005) — A215

No. 635, 60c — Photos from: a, 1955. b, 1956. c, 1960 (with arm outstretched). d, 1968. e, 1970. f, 1973.
No. 636, 60c — Photos from: a, 1957. b, 1960 (in army uniform). c, 1963. d, 1965. e, 1967. f, 1969.

2005, Mar. 21 ***Perf. 13½x13¼***

Sheets of 6, #a-f

635-636 A215 Set of 2 14.50 14.50

End of World War II, 60th Anniv. — A216

No. 637, 60c: a, U.S. soldiers marching in Ireland. b, British troops cross Volturno River, Italy. c, Hawker Typhoon attacks enemy on the Rhine River. d, Damaged Remagen Bridge. e, Meeting of Russian and American armies near Torgau, Germany.
No. 638, 60c: a, Poster remembering Pearl Harbor. b, Chula Beach, Tinian Island. c, Paul Tibbets and the Enola Gay. d, Hiroshima atomic bomb mushroom cloud. e, Newspaper announcing Japanese surrender.

2005, Mar. 31 ***Perf. 14***

Sheets of 5, #a-e

637-638 A216 Set of 2 12.00 12.00

Friedrich von Schiller (1759-1805), Writer — A217

No. 639: a, Wearing red cape. b, Statue. c, With head on hand.

2005, Mar. 31
639 A217 $1 Sheet of 3, #a-c 6.00 6.00

Souvenir Sheet

640 A217 $2 shown 4.00 4.00

Battle of Trafalgar, Bicent. — A218

Various depictions of ships in battle: 37c, 55c, 80c, $1.
$2, Death of Admiral Horatio Nelson.

2005, Mar. 31 ***Perf. 14¼***
641-644 A218 Set of 4 5.50 5.50

Souvenir Sheet

645 A218 $2 multi 4.00 4.00

Pope John Paul II (1920-2005) A219

2005, June 27 ***Perf. 13½x13¼***
646 A219 $1 multi 2.00 2.00

Printed in sheets of 6.

Rotary International, Cent. — A220

No. 647, vert.: a, Child. b, Emblem. c, 2004-05 Rotary International President Glenn E. Estess, Sr.
$2, 2002-03 Rotary International President Bhichai Rattakul.

2005, July 12 ***Perf. 12¾***
647 A220 $1 Sheet of 3, #a-c 6.00 6.00

Souvenir Sheet

648 A220 $2 multi 4.00 4.00

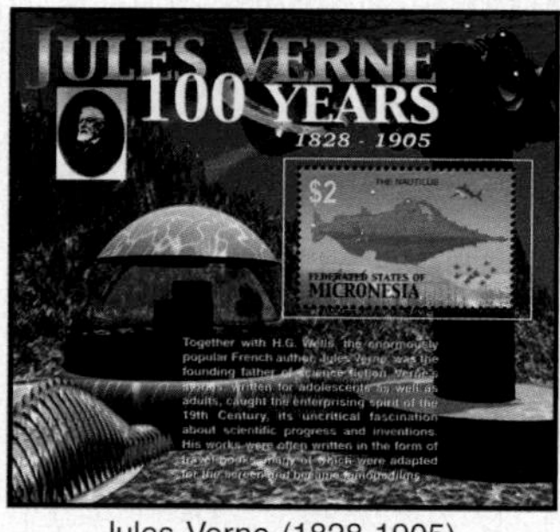

Jules Verne (1828-1905), Writer — A221

No. 649, vert.: a, Around the World in 80 Days. b, Phineas Fogg in India. c, Phineas Fogg, explorer and adventurer.
$2, Nautilus.

2005, June 7 **Litho.** ***Perf. 12¾***
649 A221 $1 Sheet of 3, #a-c 6.00 6.00

Souvenir Sheet

650 A221 $2 multi 4.00 4.00

Souvenir Sheet

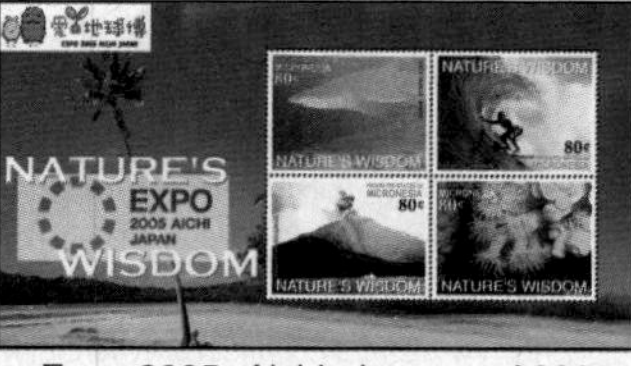

Expo 2005, Aichi, Japan — A222

No. 651: a, Gray nurse shark. b, Surfer. c, Krakatoa Volcano. d, Yellow coral.

2005, June 27 ***Perf. 12x12¼***
651 A222 80c Sheet of 4, #a-d 6.50 6.50

Boats — A223

No. 652: a, 37c, Papyrus boat. b, 55c, Outrigger canoe. c, 80c, Papyrus sailboat. d, $1, Arab dhow.
$2, Lateen-rigged Nile riverboat.

2005, June 27 ***Perf. 12¾***
652 A223 Sheet of 4, #a-d 5.50 5.50

Souvenir Sheet

653 A223 $2 multi 4.00 4.00

Kosrae Government Building Complex — A224

Views of various buildings with frame colors of: 4c, Light yellow. 10c, Light blue. 22c, Pink. 37c, Light green.

2005, July 8 ***Perf. 14***
654-657 A224 Set of 4 1.50 1.50

Vatican City No. 67 — A225

2005, Aug. 9 ***Perf. 13x13¼***
658 A225 37c multi .75 .75

Pope John Paul II (1920-2005). Printed in sheets of 12.

Worldwide Fund for Nature (WWF) — A226

No. 659: a, Stephanometra echinus. b, Oxycomanthus bennetti. c, Alloeocomatella polycaldia. d, Dichrometra flagellata.
Illustration reduced.

2005, Aug. 31 ***Perf. 14***

659 A226 50c Block or vert. strip of 4, #a-d 4.00 4.00
e. Souvenir sheet, 2 each #659a-659d 8.00 8.00

Souvenir Sheet

Albert Einstein (1879-1955), Physicist — A227

No. 660 — Various portraits with "Albert Einstein (1879-1955)" in: a, Orange. b, Blue. c, Red. d, Black.

2005, Sept. 20 ***Perf. 12¾***

660 A227 $1 Sheet of 4, #a-d 8.00 8.00

Bananas A228

Designs: 4c, Mother feeding banana to child. 10c, Four bananas. 22c, Bunch of bananas. 37c, Banana plant.

2005, Oct. 14 ***Perf. 14***

661-664 A228 Set of 4 1.50 1.50

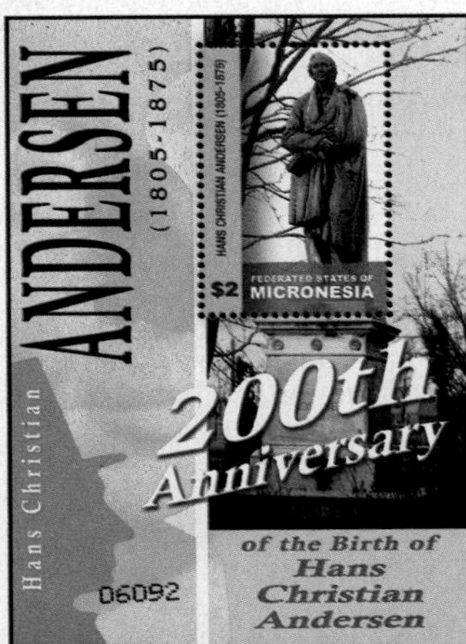

Hans Christian Andersen (1805-75), Author — A229

No. 665: a, Bust of Andersen. b, Statue of seated Andersen. c, Bust of Andersen on pedestal.
$2, Statue of standing Andersen.

2005, Nov. 15 ***Perf. 12¾***

665 A229 80c Sheet of 3, #a-c 5.00 5.00

Souvenir Sheet

666 A229 $2 multi 4.00 4.00

Pope Benedict XVI — A230

2005, Nov. 21 **Litho.** ***Perf. 13½***

667 A230 80c multi 1.60 1.60

Printed in sheets of 4.

Christmas — A231

Painting details: 37c, Kanigani Madonna, by Raphael. 60c, Madonna with the Fish, by Raphael. 80c, The Holy Family, by Bartolomé Esteban Murillo. $1, Madonna with the Book, by Raphael.
$2, The Holy Family, by Murillo, diff.

2005, Dec. 1 **Litho.** ***Perf. 14***

668-671 A231 Set of 4 5.75 5.75

Souvenir Sheet

672 A231 $2 multi 4.00 4.00

Flowers — A232

Designs: 4c, Tecoma stans. 10c, Ipomoea fistulosa. 22c, Hibiscus rosa-sinensis. 37c, Gerbera jamesonii. No. 677, 80c, Helianthus annuus. $1, Ixora casei.
No. 679, 80c: a, Tapeinochilos ananassae. b, Bauhnia monandra. c, Galphimia gracilis. d, Hibiscus rosa-sinensis, diff.
No. 680, $2, Helianthus annuus, diff. No. 681, $2, Phinia variegata.

2005, Nov. 15 **Litho.** ***Perf. 12***

673-678 A232 Set of 6 5.25 5.25
679 A232 80c Sheet of 4, #a-d 6.50 6.50

Souvenir Sheets

680-681 A232 Set of 2 8.00 8.00

New Year 2006 (Year of the Dog) — A233

Paintings by Liu Jiyou: 50c, Wolf Dog. $1, Wolf Dog, horiz.

2006, Jan. 3 ***Perf. 13¼***

682 A233 50c multi 1.00 1.00

Souvenir Sheet

683 A233 $1 multi 2.00 2.00

No. 683 contains one 48x35mm stamp.
No. 682 was issued in sheets of 4.

Birds — A234

Designs: No. 684, Glaucous-winged gull. No. 685, Slaty-headed parakeet. No. 686, Harlequin duck. No. 687, Purple sunbird. 75c, Plum-headed parakeet. 84c, Yellow-wattled lapwing. $4.05, Eurasian collared dove, horiz.

2006 ***Perf. 12***

684 A234 24c multi .50 .50
685 A234 24c multi .50 .50
686 A234 39c multi .80 .80
687 A234 39c multi .80 .80
688 A234 75c multi 1.50 1.50
689 A234 84c multi 1.75 1.75
690 A234 $4.05 multi 8.25 8.25
Nos. 684-690 (7) 14.10 14.10

Issued: Nos. 684, 686, 2/21; others, 4/20.

Vice-President Petrus Tun (1936-99) — A235

2006, Mar. 19 ***Perf. 12¾***

691 A235 39c multi .80 .80

Printed in sheets of 4.

Rembrandt (1606-69), Painter — A236

No. 692: a, Saskia as Flora. b, Young Girl at a Window. c, Girl with a Broom. d, Prodigal Son in the Tavern.
$2, Man in Oriental Costume.

2006, June 22 ***Perf. 13¼***

692 A236 $1 Sheet of 4, #a-d 8.00 8.00

Imperf

693 A236 $2 multi 4.00 4.00

No. 692 contains four 38x50mm stamps.

Queen Elizabeth II, 80th Birthday — A237

No. 694 — Dogs and Queen in: a, Red violet dress. b, Beige dress. c, Purple dress. d, Light blue dress.
$2, Green dress.

2006, June 22 ***Perf. 14¼***

694 A237 84c Sheet of 4, #a-d 6.75 6.75

Souvenir Sheet

695 A237 $2 multi 4.00 4.00

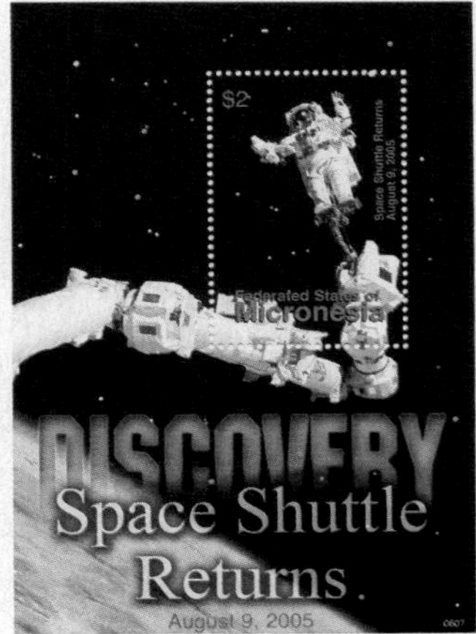

Space Achievements — A238

No. 696 — Various views of Venus Express: a, Text in black. b, Country name in black, denomination in white. c, Country name in white, denomination in black. d, Country name and denomination in white. e, Country name and denomination in red, "Venus Express" at left. f, Country name and denomination in red, "Venus Express" at right.
No. 697, $1, horiz. — Return to space of Space Shuttle Discovery: a, Denomination in white. b, Shuttle arm. c, Shuttle with cargo bay open. d, Shuttle tail.
No. 698, $1, horiz. — Spacecraft for future trips to: a, Moon, black denomination. b, Moon, blue denomination. c, Mars, red denomination. d, Mars, white denomination.
No. 699, $2, Space Shuttle Discovery astronaut space-walking. No. 700, $2, Mars Reconnaissance Orbiter. No. 701, $2, Stardust probe, horiz.

2006, July 11 ***Perf. 14¼***

696 A238 75c Sheet of 6, #a-f 9.00 9.00

Sheets of 4, #a-d

697-698 A238 Set of 2 16.00 16.00

Souvenir Sheets

699-701 A238 Set of 3 12.00 12.00

Butterflies A239

Designs: 1c, Papilio euchenor. 2c, Golden birdwing. 4c, Delias henningia. 5c, Bassarona duda. 10c, Common bluebottle. 19c, Arhopala cleander. 20c, Arhopala argentea. 22c, Danaus aspasia. 75c, Arhopala aurea. 84c, Caleta mindaurus. $1, Black and white tit. $4.05, Grand imperial. $5, Jamides abdul. $10, Paralaxita lacoon.

2006, Nov. 15 *Perf. 12*

702	A239	1c multi	.20	.20
703	A239	2c multi	.20	.20
704	A239	4c multi	.20	.20
705	A239	5c multi	.20	.20
706	A239	10c multi	.20	.20
707	A239	19c multi	.40	.40
708	A239	20c multi	.40	.40
709	A239	22c multi	.45	.45
710	A239	75c multi	1.50	1.50
711	A239	84c multi	1.75	1.75
712	A239	$1 multi	2.00	2.00
713	A239	$4.05 multi	8.25	8.25
714	A239	$5 multi	10.00	10.00
715	A239	$10 multi	20.00	20.00
		Nos. 702-715 (14)	45.75	45.75

Christmas — A240

Designs: 22c, Christmas tree. 24c, Stocking. 39c, Snowman. 75c, Candle. 84c, Ornament.

2006, Dec. 4 *Perf. 13½*
716-720 A240 Set of 5 5.00 5.00

Concorde — A241

No. 721, 75c — Concorde's Jubilee Flypast: a, With statue. b, Without statue.

No. 722, 75c — Concorde 001: a, In flight. b, On ground.

Illustration reduced.

Perf. 13¼x13½

2006, Dec. 20 **Litho.**

Pairs, #a-b

721-722 A241 Set of 2 6.00 6.00

New Year 2007 (Year of the Pig) — A242

2007, Jan. 3 *Perf. 13¼*
723 A242 75c multi 1.50 1.50

Printed in sheets of 4.

Souvenir Sheet

Wolfgang Amadeus Mozart (1756-91), Composer — A243

2007, Jan. 11
724 A243 $2 multi 4.00 4.00

Souvenir Sheet

Ludwig Durr (1878-1956), Engineer — A244

No. 725 — Durr and: a, Walrus Hula airship. b, Walrus heavy transport blimp. c, Hindenburg.

2007, Jan. 11
725 A244 $1 Sheet of 3, #a-c 6.00 6.00

Souvenir Sheet

Marilyn Monroe (1926-62), Actress — A245

No. 726: a, Looking right. b, With puckered lips. c, Wearing beret. d, With eyes closed, facing left.

2007, Jan. 11
726 A245 $1 Sheet of 4, #a-d 8.00 8.00

Scouting, Cent. — A246

2007, Jan. 11
727 A246 $1 shown 2.00 2.00

Souvenir Sheet

728 A246 $2 Scouts, flag 4.00 4.00

No. 727 was printed in sheets of 3. No. 728 contains one 37x50mm stamp.

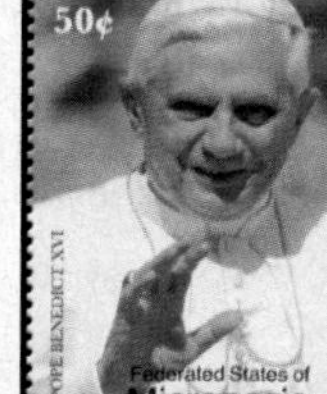

Pope Benedict XVI, 80th Birthday — A247

2007, May 25
729 A247 50c multi 1.00 1.00

Printed in sheets of 8.

Miniature Sheet

Wedding of Queen Elizabeth II and Prince Philip, 60th Anniv. — A248

No. 730 — Queen and Prince: a, Standing, red frame. b, Seated, red frame. c, Seated, white frame. d, Standing, white frame. e, Standing, blue frame. f, Seated, blue frame.

2007, May 25
730 A248 60c Sheet of 6, #a-f 7.25 7.25

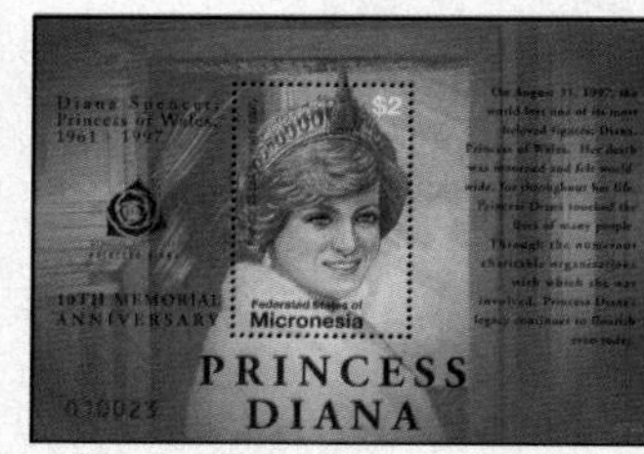

Princess Diana (1961-97) — A249

No. 731 — Various portraits with background color of: a, Pink. b, Lilac. c, Bister. d, Light green.

$2, Diana wearing tiara.

2007, May 25
731 A249 90c Sheet of 4, #a-d 7.25 7.25

Souvenir Sheet

732 A249 $2 multi 4.00 4.00

Bananas — A250

Inscriptions: 22c, Utim was. 26c, Utin lap. 41c, Mangat. 58c, Ipali. 80c, Daiwang. 90c, Akadahn Weitahta, horiz. $1.14, Peleu. $4.60, Utin Kerenis.

Perf. 14x14¾, 14¾x14

2007, June 12

733	A250	22c multi	.45	.45
734	A250	26c multi	.55	.55
735	A250	41c multi	.85	.85
736	A250	58c multi	1.25	1.25
737	A250	80c multi	1.60	1.60
738	A250	90c multi	1.90	1.90
739	A250	$1.14 multi	2.40	2.40
740	A250	$4.60 multi	9.25	9.25
		Nos. 733-740 (8)	18.25	18.25

Miniature Sheet

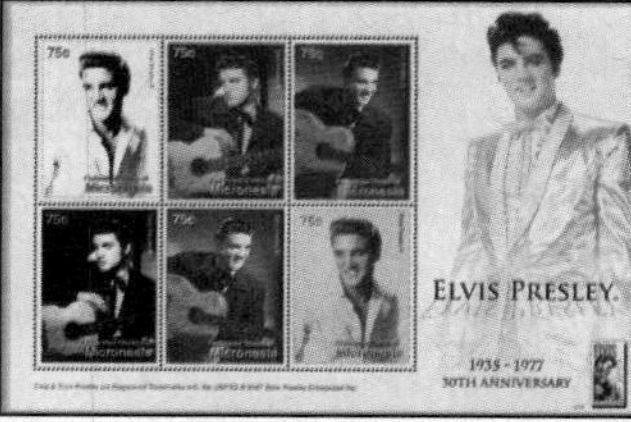

Elvis Presley (1935-77) — A251

No. 741 — Various portraits with denomination color of: a, Blue (country name in gray). b, Pink. c, Blue (country name in blue). d, Green. e, Buff. f, Lilac.

2007, June 20 *Perf. 14¼*
741 A251 75c Sheet of 6, #a-f 9.00 9.00

Fish — A252

No. 742: a, Longnose hawkfish. b, Fingerprint sharpnose puffer. c, Ornate butterflyfish. d, Longnose filefish.

$2, Multi-barred goatfish.

2007, June 21 *Perf. 13¼*
742 A252 90c Sheet of 4, #a-d 7.25 7.25

Souvenir Sheet

743 A252 $2 multi 4.00 4.00

Flowers — A253

No. 744: a, White plumeria. b, Yellow plumeria. c, White lily. d, Yellow ginger lily.

$2, Bougainvillea glabra.

2007, June 21
744 A253 90c Sheet of 4, #a-d 7.25 7.25

Souvenir Sheet

745 A253 $2 multi 4.00 4.00

Souvenir Sheet

Peace Corps in Micronesia, 40th Anniv. (in 2006) — A254

No. 746 — Inscriptions: a, Yap State. b, Kosrae State. c, Pohnpei State. d, Chuuk State.

2007, June 22

746 A254 90c Sheet of 4, #a-d 7.25 7.25

Miniature Sheet

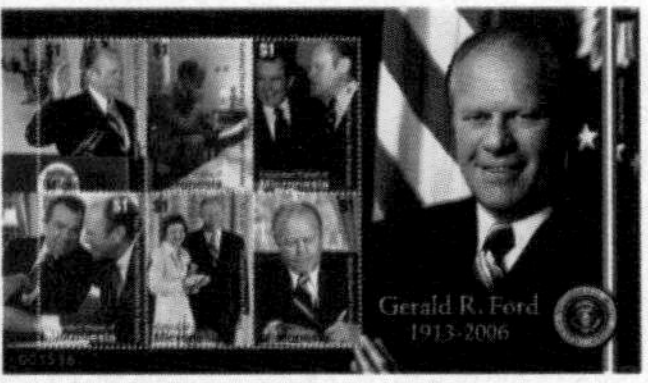

Pres. Gerald R. Ford (1913-2006) — A255

No. 747 — Ford: a, With hand raised. b, Seated, reading documents. c, With Pres. Richard Nixon, denomination at UL. d, With Nixon, denomination at UR. e, With wife, Betty. f, Signing Nixon's pardon.

2007, Aug. 7

747 A255 $1 Sheet of 6, #a-f 12.00 12.00

Intl. Polar Year — A256

No. 748: a, African penguins. b, Emperor penguins. c, Galapagos penguin. d, Humboldt penguin. e, Magellanic penguin. f, Rockhopper penguin.

$3.50, Gentoo penguins.

2007, Aug. 7

748 A256 75c Sheet of 6, #a-f 9.00 9.00

Souvenir Sheet

749 A256 $3.50 multi 7.00 7.00

Souvenir Sheet

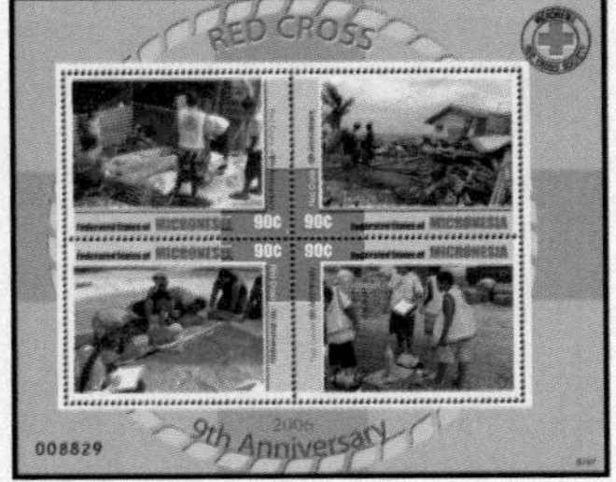

Micronesian Red Cross, 9th Anniv. — A257

No. 750 — Various pictures of relief efforts with denomination at: a, LR. b, LL. c, UR. d, UL.

2007, Aug. 20

750 A257 90c Sheet of 4, #a-d 7.25 7.25

Cats — A258

Designs: 22c, Scottish Fold. 26c, Munchkin. 41c, Abyssinian. 90c, Somali, horiz.

$2, Blue Silver Shaded Tiffanie.

Perf. 13½x13, 13x13½

2007, Sept. 24 **Litho.**

751-754 A258 Set of 4 3.75 3.75

Souvenir Sheet

Perf. 12½x12¾

755 A258 $2 multi 4.00 4.00

No. 755 contains one 29x42mm stamp.

Christmas A259

Churches: 22c, Mother Church, United Church of Christ, Pohnpei. 26c, St. Mary's Church, Yap, horiz. 41c, Sapore Bethesca Church, Fefan, Chuuk, horiz. 90c, Lelu Congregational Church, Kosrae, horiz.

Perf. 14¼x14¾, 14¾x14¼

2007, Nov. 12

756-759 A259 Set of 4 3.75 3.75

America's Cup Yachting Races, Valencia, Spain — A260

Sails of various sailboats.

2007, Dec. 12 ***Perf. 13¼***

760 Strip of 4 8.50 8.50

- *a.* A260 26c aquamarine & multi .50 .50
- *b.* A260 80c red & multi 1.60 1.60
- *c.* A260 $1.14 yellow & multi 2.40 2.40
- *d.* A260 $2 orange & multi 4.00 4.00

First Helicopter Flight, Cent. — A261

No. 761: a, AH-1 Huey Cobra. b, 206 Jet Ranger. c, H-43 Huskie. d, AS-350 Ecureuil.

$2.50, Fa 223 Drache.

2007, Dec. 12 ***Perf. 13¼***

761 A261 $1 Sheet of 4, #a-d 8.00 8.00

Souvenir Sheet

762 A261 $2.50 multi 5.00 5.00

Princess Diana (1961-97) — A262

Illustration reduced.

Serpentine Die Cut 7¾

2007, Dec. 12 **Litho. & Embossed**

Without Gum

763 A262 $8 multi 16.00 16.00

Miniature Sheet

Pres. John F. Kennedy (1917-63) — A263

No. 764 — Kennedy: a, With curtain at left. b, Color portrait. c, With Presidential Seal. d, At microphones.

2008, Jan. 2 **Litho.** ***Perf. 14***

764 A263 90c Sheet of 4, #a-d 7.25 7.25

New Year 2008 (Year of the Rat) — A264

2008, Jan. 2 **Litho.** ***Perf. 12***

765 A264 90c multi 1.90 1.90

Printed in sheets of 4.

Miniature Sheet

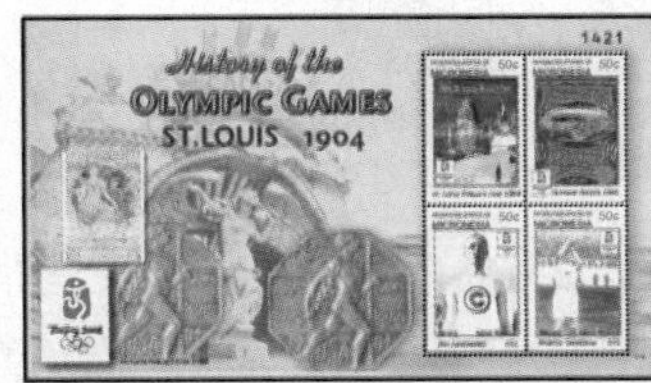

2008 Olympic Games, Beijing — A265

No. 766: a, Cover of book with music from 1904 World's Fair. b, Poster for 1904 Olympic Games and World's Fair. c, Jim Lightbody. d, Martin Sheridan.

2008, Jan. 8 ***Perf. 14***

766 A265 50c Sheet of 4, #a-d 4.00 4.00

Souvenir Sheet

Breast Cancer Awareness — A266

2008, Mar. 12

767 A266 $2 multi 4.00 4.00

Hummer Vehicles — A267

No. 768: a, Front bumper of Hummer H3x, denomination at UR. b, Side view of Hummer H3x, denomination at LR. c, Front view of Hummer H3x, denomination at LR. d, Rear view of Hummer H3x, denomination at UR.

$2, Hummer H3.

2008, May 6 ***Perf. 13¼***

768 A267 90c Sheet of 4, #a-d 7.25 7.25

Souvenir Sheet

769 A267 $2 multi 4.00 4.00

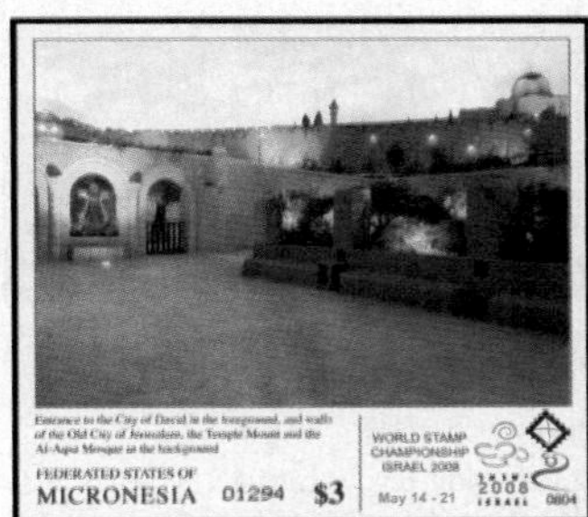

Jerusalem — A268

Illustration reduced.

2008, May 14 ***Imperf.***

770 A268 $3 multi 6.00 6.00

World Stamp Championship, Israel, 2008.

Miniature Sheet

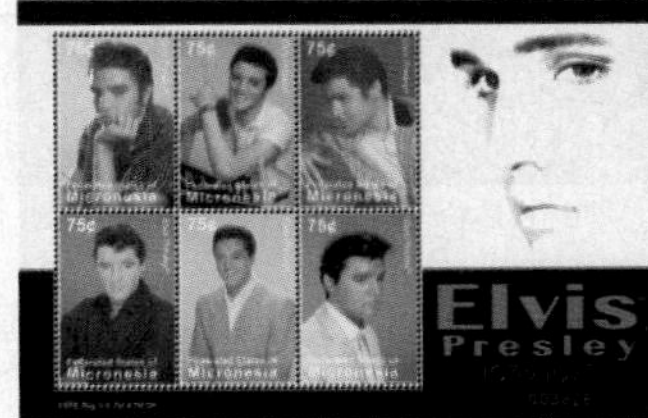

Elvis Presley (1935-77) — A269

No. 771 — Presley: a, With head on hand, buff background. b, Sitting in director's chair, gray background. c, Wearing striped jacket, brown background. d, Wearing brown shirt, red brown background. e, Wearing gray suit, yellow orange background. f, Wearing gray suit, blue gray background.

2008, June 12 ***Perf. 13¼***

771 A269 75c Sheet of 6, #a-f 9.00 9.00

Miniature Sheet

Members of Phoenix Suns Basketball Team — A270

No. 772 — Emblem of National Basketball Association and: a, Amare Stodemire. b, Boris Diaw. c, Brian Skinner. d, D. J. Strawberry. e, Shaquille O'Neal. f, Grant Hill. g, Leandro Barbosa. h, Raja Bell. i, Steve Nash.

2008, June 19
772 A270 42c Sheet of 9, #a-i 7.75 7.75

Miniature Sheet

Royal Air Force, 90th Anniv. — A271

No. 773 — Aircraft: a, Tornado. b, Harrier. c, Typhoon. d, Hawk.

2008, May 6 Litho. *Perf. 13¼*
773 A271 90c Sheet of 4, #a-d 7.25 7.25

Miniature Sheet

Visit of Pope Benedict XVI to United States — A272

No. 774 — Pope Benedict XVI and one quarter of Papal arms at: a, LR. b, LL. c, UR. d, UL.

2008, Sept. 9 *Perf. 13¼*
774 A272 94c Sheet of 4, #a-d 7.75 7.75

Miniature Sheets

A273

Muhammad Ali, Boxer — A274

No. 775 — Ali: a, Wearing protective headgear. b, Receiving adjustment of headgear. c, Looking right. d, In boxing ring, looking right. e, In boxing ring, looking left. f, With trainer, looking at hands.

No. 776 — Ali fighting: a, Throwing left jab. b, Ready to deliver punch. c, With hands in front of his chest. d, With opponent's punch missing.

2008, Sept. 9 *Perf. 11½x11¼*
775 A273 75c Sheet of 6, #a-f 9.00 9.00

Perf. 13¼
776 A274 94c Sheet of 4, #a-d 7.75 7.75

Star Trek — A275

No. 777: a, U.S.S. Enterprise. b, Mr. Spock and woman. c, Captain Kirk. d, Uhura and Chekov. e, Starbase 11. f, Dr. McCoy and Mr. Spock.

No. 778: a, Scotty. b, Captain Kirk. c, Dr. McCoy and Uhura. d, Chekov.

2008, Sept. 9 *Perf. 12x11½*
777 A275 75c Sheet of 6, #a-f 9.00 9.00

Perf. 13¼
778 A275 94c Sheet of 4, #a-d 7.75 7.75

No. 778 contains four 38x60mm stamps.

Christmas A276

Ornaments: 22c, Angel. 27c, Snowflake. 42c, Cross. 94c, Angel, diff.

2008, Sept. 9 *Perf. 14x14¾*
779-782 A276 Set of 4 3.75 3.75

Famous Men — A277

No. 783: a, Ioanis Artui, Palikiri chief. b, Dr. Eluel K. Pretrick, Human Resources Secretary.

2008, Oct. 17 *Perf. 13¼*
783 A277 94c Pair, #a-b 3.75 3.75

AIR POST STAMPS

Boeing 727, 1968 AP1

1984, July 12 Litho. *Perf. 13½*
C1 AP1 28c shown .60 .60
C2 AP1 35c SA-16 Albatross, 1960 .80 .80
C3 AP1 40c PBY-5A Catalina, 1951 1.00 1.00
Nos. C1-C3 (3) 2.40 2.40

Ausipex Type of 1984

Ausipex '84 emblem and: 28c, Caroline Islands No. 4. 35c, No. 7. 40c, No. 19.

1984, Sept. 21 Litho. *Perf. 13½*
C4 A4 28c multicolored .65 .65
C5 A4 35c multicolored .85 .85
C6 A4 40c multicolored 1.10 1.10
Nos. C4-C6 (3) 2.60 2.60

Christmas Type

Children's drawings.

1984, Dec. 20
C7 A5 28c Illustrated Christmas text .65 .65
C8 A5 35c Decorated palm tree .90 .90
C9 A5 40c Feast preparation 1.10 1.10
Nos. C7-C9 (3) 2.65 2.65

Ships Type

1985, Aug. 19
C10 A6 33c L'Astrolabe .65 .65
C11 A6 39c La Coquille .80 .80
C12 A6 44c Shenandoah 1.00 1.00
Nos. C10-C12 (3) 2.45 2.45

Christmas Type

1985, Oct. 15 Litho. *Perf. 13½*
C13 A7 33c Dublon Protestant Church .90 .90
C14 A7 44c Pohnpei Catholic Church 1.25 1.25

Audubon Type

1985, Oct. 31 *Perf. 14½*
C15 A8 44c Sooty tern 1.00 1.00

Ruins Type

1985, Dec. Litho. *Perf. 13½*
C16 A16 33c Nan Tauas inner courtyard .70 .70
C17 A16 39c Outer wall .80 .80
C18 A16 44c Tomb .90 .90
Nos. C16-C18 (3) 2.40 2.40

Halley's Comet AP2

1986, May 16
C19 AP2 44c dk bl, bl & blk 1.40 1.25

Return of Nauruans from Truk, 40th Anniv. AP3

1986, May 16
C20 AP3 44c Ship in port 1.40 1.25

AMERIPEX '86 Type

Bully Hayes (1829-1877), buccaneer.

1986, May 22
C21 A18 33c Forging Hawaiian stamp .55 .55
C22 A18 39c Sinking of the Leonora, Kosrae .70 .70
C23 A18 44c Hayes escapes capture .75 .75
C24 A18 75c Biography, by Louis Becke 1.50 1.50
Nos. C21-C24 (4) 3.50 3.50

Souvenir Sheet

C25 A18 $1 Hayes ransoming chief 3.25 3.25

Christmas Type

Virgin and child paintings: 33c, Austria, 19th cent. 44c, Italy, 18th cent., diff.

1986, Oct. 15 Litho. *Perf. 14½*
C26 A20 33c multicolored 1.00 1.00
C27 A20 44c multicolored 1.40 1.40

Anniversaries and Events Type

1987, June 13 Litho. *Perf. 14½*
C28 A21 33c US currency, bicent. .60 .60
C29 A21 39c 1st American in orbit, 25th anniv. 1.00 1.00
C30 A21 44c US Constitution, bicent. 1.10 1.10
Nos. C28-C30 (3) 2.70 2.70

Christmas Type

1987, Nov. 16 Litho. *Perf. 14½*
C31 A22 33c Holy Family .80 .80
C32 A22 39c Shepherds .90 .90
C33 A22 44c Three Wise Men 1.00 1.00
Nos. C31-C33 (3) 2.70 2.70

Bird Type

1988, Aug. 1 Litho. *Perf. 13½*
C34 A9 33c Great truk white-eye .55 .55
C35 A9 44c Blue-faced parrotfinch .70 .70
C36 A9 $1 Yap monarch 1.75 1.75
Nos. C34-C36 (3) 3.00 3.00

Colonial Era Type

1988, July 20 *Perf. 13x13½*
C37 A23 44c Traditional skills (boat-building) .95 .95
C38 A23 44c Modern Micronesia (tourism) .95 .95
a. Pair, #C37-C38 1.90 1.90

Printed se-tenant in sheets of 28 plus 4 center labels picturing flags of Kosrae (UL), Truk (UR), Pohnpei (LL) and Yap ((LR).

Flags of the Federated States of Micronesia AP4

1989, Jan. 19 Litho. *Perf. 13x13½*
C39 AP4 45c Pohnpei .70 .70
C40 AP4 45c Truk .70 .70
C41 AP4 45c Kosrae .70 .70
C42 AP4 45c Yap .70 .70
a. Block of 4, #C39-C42 2.80 2.80

This issue exists with 44c denominations but was not issued.

Aircraft Serving Micronesia AP5

1990, July 16 Litho. *Perf. 14*
C43 AP5 22c shown .40 .40
C44 AP5 36c multi, diff. .65 .65
C45 AP5 39c multi, diff. .75 .75
C46 AP5 45c multi, diff. .85 .85

1992, Mar. 27
C47 AP5 40c Propeller plane, outrigger canoe .70 .70
C48 AP5 50c Passenger jet, sailboat .85 .85
Nos. C43-C48 (6) 4.20 4.20

Souvenir Sheet

First Manned Moon Landing, 25th Anniv. — AP6

Illustration reduced.

1994, July 20 Litho. *Perf. 13½*

C49	AP6 $2.90 US #C76	4.25	4.25

MIDDLE CONGO

'mi-dəl 'käŋ-gō

LOCATION — Western Africa at the Equator, bordering on the Atlantic Ocean
GOVT. — Former French Colony
AREA — 166,069
POP. — 746,805 (1936)
CAPITAL — Brazzaville

In 1910 Middle Congo, formerly a part of French Congo, was declared a separate colony. It was grouped with Gabon and the Ubangi-Shari and Chad Territories and officially designated French Equatorial Africa. This group became a single administrative unit in 1934. See Gabon.

See Congo People's Republic for issues of 1959 onward.

100 Centimes = 1 Franc

See French Equatorial Africa No. 191 for additional stamp inscribed "Moyen Congo" and "Afrique Equatoriale Francaise."

Leopard A1

Bakalois Woman — A2

Coconut Grove — A3

Perf. 14x13½

1907-22 Typo. Unwmk.

1	A1	1c ol gray & brn	.35	.30
2	A1	2c vio & brn	.35	.30
3	A1	4c blue & brn	.75	.60
4	A1	5c dk grn & bl	.75	.35
5	A1	5c yel & bl ('22)	.85	.35
6	A1	10c car & bl	.75	.60
7	A1	10c dp grn & bl grn ('22)	3.25	2.75
8	A1	15c brn vio & rose	2.00	.65
9	A1	20c brown & bl	2.50	2.10
10	A2	25c blue & grn	1.25	.80
11	A2	25c bl grn & gray ('22)	1.00	.80
12	A2	30c scar & grn	2.00	1.25
13	A2	30c dp rose & rose ('22)	1.75	1.40
14	A2	35c vio brn & bl	1.90	1.00
15	A2	40c dl grn & brn	1.90	1.00
16	A2	45c violet & red	5.25	3.00
17	A2	50c bl grn & red	2.25	1.50
18	A2	50c bl & grn ('22)	1.90	1.50
19	A2	75c brown & bl	6.50	4.00
20	A3	1fr dp grn & vio	10.00	6.50
21	A3	2fr vio & gray grn	11.00	5.75
22	A3	5fr blue & rose	30.00	21.00
		Nos. 1-22 (22)	88.25	57.50

For stamps of types A1-A3 in changed colors, see Chad and Ubangi-Shari. French Congo A4-A6 are similar but inscribed "Congo Francais."

For overprints and surcharges see Nos. 23-60, B1-B2.

Stamps and Types of 1907-22 Overprinted in Black, Blue or Red

1924-30

23	A1	1c ol gray & brn	.25	.20
24	A1	2c violet & brn	.25	.20
25	A1	4c blue & brn	.25	.20
26	A1	5c yellow & bl	.35	.20
27	A1	10c grn & bl grn (R)	.80	.20
28	A1	10c car & gray ('25)	.30	.30
29	A1	15c brn vio & rose (Bl)	.60	.35
a.		Double surcharge	85.00	
30	A1	20c brown & blue	.50	.45
31	A1	20c bl grn & yel grn ('26)	.30	.30
32	A1	20c dp brn & rose lil ('27)	1.10	.40

Overprinted

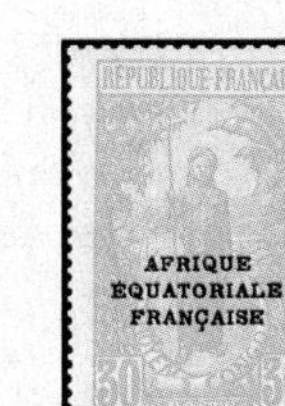

33	A2	25c bl grn & gray	.75	.35
34	A2	30c rose & pale rose (Bl)	1.10	.40
35	A2	30c gray & bl vio (R) ('25)	.60	.50
36	A2	30c dk grn & grn ('27)	1.25	.95
37	A2	35c choc & bl	.50	.50
38	A2	40c ol grn & brn	1.25	.80
39	A2	45c vio & pale red (Bl)	1.25	.80
a.		Inverted overprint	100.00	100.00
40	A2	50c blue & grn (R)	1.10	.60
41	A2	50c org & blk ('25)	.65	.50
a.		Without overprint	125.00	
42	A2	65c org brn & bl ('27)	2.25	1.40
43	A2	75c brown & blue	1.25	.80
44	A2	90c brn red & pink ('30)	4.00	2.75
45	A3	1fr green & vio	1.50	1.00
a.		Double overprint	175.00	140.00
46	A3	1.10fr vio & brn ('28)	3.75	2.50
47	A3	1.50fr ultra & bl ('30)	5.50	3.50
48	A3	2fr vio & gray grn	1.50	1.00
49	A3	3fr red violet ('30)	6.25	4.25
50	A3	5fr blue & rose	4.25	2.50
		Nos. 23-50 (28)	43.40	27.90

Nos. 48 and 50 Surcharged with New Values

1924

51	A3 25c on 2fr vio & gray grn	.85	.85
52	A3 25c on 5fr bl & rose (Bl)	.85	.85

Types of 1924-27 Surcharged with New Values in Black or Red

1925-27

53	A3	65c on 1fr red org & ol brn	.80	.80
54	A3	85c on 1fr red org & ol brn	.80	.80
55	A2	90c on 75c brn red & rose red ('27)	1.40	1.25
56	A3	1.25fr on 1fr dl bl & ultra (R)	.60	.60
57	A3	1.50fr on 1fr ultra & bl ('27)	1.40	1.25
a.		New value omitted	100.00	
58	A3	3fr on 5fr org brn & dl red ('27)	3.00	2.00
a.		New value omitted	225.00	
59	A3	10fr on 5fr ver & bl grn ('27)	9.50	8.00
60	A3	20fr on 5fr org brn & vio ('27)	10.00	8.00
		Nos. 53-60 (8)	27.50	22.70

Bars cover old values on Nos. 56-60.

Common Design Types pictured following the introduction.

Colonial Exposition Issue
Common Design Types

1931 Engr. *Perf. 12½*
Name of Country in Black

61	CD70	40c deep green	3.25	2.75
62	CD71	50c violet	2.50	2.00
63	CD72	90c red orange	2.50	2.50
64	CD73	1.50fr dull blue	4.00	3.25
		Nos. 61-64 (4)	12.25	10.50

Viaduct at Mindouli A4

Pasteur Institute at Brazzaville A5

Government Building, Brazzaville — A6

1933 Photo. *Perf. 13½*

65	A4	1c lt brown	.20	.20
66	A4	2c dull blue	.20	.20
67	A4	4c olive grn	.25	.20
68	A4	5c red violet	.45	.20
69	A4	10c slate	.45	.20
70	A4	15c dk violet	.95	.50
71	A4	20c red, *pink*	7.25	4.25
72	A4	25c orange	.95	.70
73	A4	30c yellow grn	1.75	1.10
74	A5	40c orange brn	2.00	.95
75	A5	45c blk, *green*	1.10	.95
76	A5	50c black violet	.75	.60
77	A5	65c brn red, *grn*	1.25	.60
78	A5	75c black, *pink*	11.00	5.75
79	A5	90c carmine	1.40	.70
80	A5	1fr dark red	.95	.55
81	A5	1.25fr Prus blue	1.75	.75
82	A5	1.50fr dk blue	8.00	2.75
83	A6	1.75fr dk violet	1.90	.80
84	A6	2fr grnsh blk	1.90	.90
85	A6	3fr orange	4.00	2.75
86	A6	5fr slate blue	13.50	10.00
87	A6	10fr black	45.00	23.50
88	A6	20fr dark brown	26.00	19.00
		Nos. 65-88 (24)	132.95	78.10

SEMI-POSTAL STAMPS

No. 6 Surcharged in Black

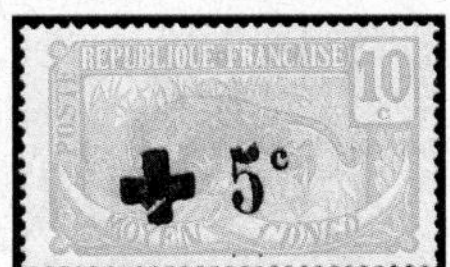

1916 Unwmk. *Perf. 14x13½*

B1	A1 10c + 5c car & blue	1.10	1.00
a.	Double surcharge	95.00	95.00
b.	Inverted surcharge	85.00	85.00

A printing with the surcharge placed lower and more to the left was made and used in Ubangi.

No. 6 Surcharged in Red

B2	A1 10c + 5c car & blue	1.00	1.00

POSTAGE DUE STAMPS

Postage Due Stamps of France Overprinted

1928 Unwmk. *Perf. 14x13½*

J1	D2	5c light blue	.35	.35
J2	D2	10c gray brn	.60	.60
J3	D2	20c olive grn	.80	.80
J4	D2	25c brt rose	1.00	1.00
J5	D2	30c lt red	1.10	1.10
J6	D2	45c blue grn	1.10	1.10
J7	D2	50c brown vio	1.25	1.25
J8	D2	60c yellow brn	2.00	2.00
J9	D2	1fr red brn	2.00	2.00
J10	D2	2fr orange red	2.75	2.75
J11	D2	3fr brt violet	4.50	4.50
		Nos. J1-J11 (11)	17.45	17.45

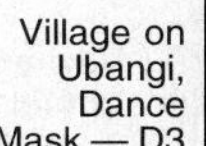

Village on Ubangi, Dance Mask — D3

Steamer on Ubangi River — D4

1930 Typo.

J12	D3	5c dp bl & ol	.60	.60
J13	D3	10c dp red & brn	.90	.90
J14	D3	20c green & brn	2.10	2.10
J15	D3	25c lt bl & brn	3.00	3.00
J16	D3	30c bis brn & Prus bl	4.00	4.00
J17	D3	45c Prus bl & ol	4.75	4.75
J18	D3	50c red vio & brn	4.75	4.75
J19	D3	60c gray lil & bl blk	5.25	5.25
J20	D4	1fr bis brn & bl blk	9.00	9.00
J21	D4	2fr violet & brn	9.75	9.75
J22	D4	3fr dk red & brn	9.75	9.75
		Nos. J12-J22 (11)	53.85	53.85

Rubber Trees and Djoué River — D5

1933 Photo. *Perf. 13½*

J23	D5	5c apple green	.60	.60
J24	D5	10c dk bl, *bl*	.60	.60
J25	D5	20c red, *yel*	1.10	1.10
J26	D5	25c chocolate	1.10	1.10
J27	D5	30c orange red	1.60	1.60
J28	D5	45c dk violet	1.60	1.60
J29	D5	50c gray black	2.10	2.10
J30	D5	60c blk, *orange*	3.25	3.25
J31	D5	1fr brown rose	4.75	4.75
J32	D5	2fr orange yel	5.75	5.75
J33	D5	3fr Prus blue	9.25	9.25
		Nos. J23-J33 (11)	31.70	31.70

MOHELI

mo-'ā-lē

LOCATION — One of the Comoro Islands, situated in the Mozambique Channel midway between Madagascar and Mozambique (Africa)
GOVT. — French Colony
AREA — 89 sq. mi.
POP. — 4,000
CAPITAL — Fomboni
See Comoro Islands

100 Centimes = 1 Franc

Navigation and Commerce — A1

Perf. 14x13½
1906-07 Typo. Unwmk.
Name of Colony in Blue or Carmine

1 A1 1c blk, *lil bl* 3.75 1.50
2 A1 2c brn, *buff* 1.25 1.00
3 A1 4c claret, *lav* 4.00 1.75
4 A1 5c yellow grn 4.00 1.75
5 A1 10c carmine 5.00 1.75
6 A1 20c red, *green* 11.00 5.25
7 A1 25c blue 11.00 4.25
8 A1 30c brn, *bister* 13.00 10.00
9 A1 35c blk, *yellow* 7.50 3.25
10 A1 40c red, *straw* 13.00 9.25
11 A1 45c blk, *gray grn* ('07) 57.50 42.50
12 A1 50c brn, *az* 18.00 11.00
13 A1 75c dp vio, *org* 20.00 18.00
14 A1 1fr brnz grn, *straw* 18.00 12.00
15 A1 2fr vio, *rose* 26.50 26.50
16 A1 5fr lil, *lavender* 110.00 100.00
Nos. 1-16 (16) 323.50 249.75

Perf. 13½x14 stamps are counterfeits.
No. 12, affixed to pressboard with animals printed on the back, was used as emergency currency in the Comoro Islands in 1920.

Issue of 1906-07 Surcharged in Carmine or Black

1912

17 A1 5c on 4c cl, *lav* (C) 1.50 1.50
18 A1 5c on 20c red, *grn* 2.75 2.75
19 A1 5c on 30c brn, *bis* (C) 1.60 1.60
20 A1 10c on 40c red, *straw* 1.60 1.60
21 A1 10c on 45c blk, *gray grn* (C) 1.50 1.50
a. "Moheli" double 350.00
b. "Moheli" triple 350.00
22 A1 10c on 50c brn, *az* (C) 2.75 2.75
Nos. 17-22 (6) 11.70 11.70

Two spacings between the surcharged numerals are found on Nos. 17 to 22. For detailed listings, see the *Scott Classic Specialized Catalogue of Stamps and Covers.*

The stamps of Mohéli were supposed to have been superseded by those of Madagascar, January, 1908. However, Nos. 17-22 were surcharged in 1912 to use up remainders. These were available for use in Madagascar and the entire Comoro archipelago. In 1950 stamps of Comoro Islands came into use.

MOLDOVA

mäl-'dō-və

(Moldavia)

LOCATION — Southeastern Europe, bounded by Romania and the Ukraine
GOVT. — Independent republic, member of the Commonwealth of Independent States
AREA — 13,012 sq. mi.
POP. — 4,460,838 (1999 est.)
CAPITAL — Chisinau

With the breakup of the Soviet Union on Dec. 26, 1991, Moldova and ten former Soviet republics established the Commonwealth of Independent States.

100 Kopecks = 1 Ruble
100 Bani = 1 Leu (1993)

Catalogue values for all unused stamps in this country are for Never Hinged items.

Coat of Arms — A1

Flag — A2

1991, June 23 Litho. *Imperf.*
Without Gum

1 A1 7k grn & multi .20 .20
2 A1 13k blue & multi .30 .50
3 A2 30k multi .50 .50
Nos. 1-3 (3) 1.00 1.20

Codrii Nature Preserve A6

1992, Feb. 8 Litho. *Perf. 12*
25 A6 25k multicolored .30 .30

Natl. Arms — A7

1992, May 24 Photo. *Perf. 13½*
26 A7 35k green .20 .20
27 A7 50k red .20 .20
28 A7 65k brown .20 .20
29 A7 1r purple .20 .20
30 A7 1.50r blue .20 .20
Nos. 26-30 (5) 1.00 1.00

Birds — A8

Designs: 50k, Merops apiaster. 65k, Oriolus oriolus. 2.50r, Picus viridis. 6r, Coracias garrulus. 7.50r, Upupa epops. 15r, Cuculus canorus.

1992, Aug. 5 Litho. *Perf. 13½x14*
31 A8 50k multicolored .30 .30
32 A8 65k multicolored .30 .30
33 A8 2.50r multicolored .45 .45
34 A8 6r multicolored .75 .75
35 A8 7.50r multicolored .95 .95
36 A8 15r multicolored 2.00 2.00
Nos. 31-36 (6) 4.75 4.75

No. 31 incorrectly inscribed "ariaster."
See Nos. 75-81.

Church of St. Panteleimon, Cent. — A9

1992, Aug. 10 Photo. *Perf. 11½*
37 A9 1.50r multicolored .35 .35

She-Wolf Suckling Romulus and Remus — A10

1992, Aug. 10 *Perf. 12x11½*
38 A10 5r multicolored .50 .50

Russia Nos. 4598-4599, 5839 Surcharged "MOLDOVA" and New Value in Black or Red

1992, Aug. 31 Litho. *Perf. 12x12½*
39 A2138 2.50r on 4k #4599 .40 .40
40 A2139 6r on 3k #4598 .45 .45
41 A2138 8.50r on 4k #4599 .60 .60
42 A2765 10r on 3k #5839 (R) .70 .70
a. Black surcharge .70 .70
b. Brown red surcharge .70 .70
Nos. 39-42 (4) 2.15 2.15

Sheets of #39, 41 had row 5 inverted. On #40 only the 1st 5 stamps of row 5 were inverted. Counterfeit inverts were made using the original plates but with all 100 surcharges inverted. All inverts on #42 are fakes.

Russia Nos. 4596-4598 Surcharged in Black, Green or Red

1992, Oct. 20 Litho. *Perf. 12x12½*
43 A2138 45k on 2k #4597 (G) .40 .40
44 A2138 46k on 2k #4597 .40 .40
45 A2138 63k on 1k #4596 (R) .40 .40
46 A2138 63k on 3k #4598 .70 .70
47 A2138 70k on 1k #4596 (R) .40 .40
50 A2138 4r on 1k #4596 .70 .70
a. Red surcharge .70 .70
Nos. 43-50 (6) 3.00 3.00

Nos. 45-46 exist with overprint inverted (6th row of sheet).

1992 Summer Olympics, Barcelona — A11

1992, Oct. 24 Litho. *Perf. 13*
53 A11 35k High jump .30 .30
54 A11 65k Wrestling .35 .35
55 A11 1r Archery .35 .35
56 A11 2.50r Swimming .75 .75
57 A11 10r Equestrian 2.50 2.50
a. Souvenir sheet, #53-57 + label 4.50 4.50
Nos. 53-57 (5) 4.25 4.25

Nos. 55-56 Ovptd. with Name of Medalist, Medal and Olympic Rings in Bronze or Silver

1992, Oct. 24
58 A11 1r "NATALIA VALEEV / bronz" (BR) .55 .55
59 A11 2.50r "IURIE BASCATOV / argint" 1.00 1.00

Souvenir Sheet

Tudor Casapu, 1992 Weight Lifting Gold Medalist — A12

1992, Oct. 24 *Perf. 14½*
60 A12 25r multicolored 5.00 5.00

Admission of Moldova to UN — A13

Designs: 12r, UN Headquarters at left, Statue of Liberty, UN emblem, Moldovan flag.

1992, Oct. 24 *Perf. 13*
61 A13 1.30r multicolored .45 .45
62 A13 12r multicolored .80 .80

Moldovan Participation in Conference on European Security and Cooperation — A14

1992, Oct. 24
63 A14 2.50r Flag, Prague Castle .40 .40
64 A14 25r Helsinki Cathedral, flag 1.25 1.25

Traditional Folk Art — A15

1992, Nov. 21 *Perf. 12x11½*
65 A15 7.50r Rug, pottery .45 .45

Admission of Moldova to UPU A16

1992, Dec. 26 *Perf. 12*
66 A16 5r Train, flag, emblem .40 .40
67 A16 10r Plane, flag, emblem .80 .80

Discovery of America, 500th Anniv. — A17

1992, Dec. 26 Litho. Perf. 12

68 A17 1r Galleon .20 .20
69 A17 6r Carrack .75 .75
70 A17 6r Caravel .75 .75
a. Pair, #69-70 3.25 3.25
Nos. 68-70 (3) 1.70 1.70

Souvenir Sheet

71 A17 25r Columbus 5.00 5.00

Elaphe Longissima A18

Denominations at: a, UL. b, UR. c, LL. d, LR.

1993, July 3 Litho. Perf. 13½

72 A18 3r Block of 4, #a.-d. 2.50 2.50
73 A18 15r Natrix natrix 1.00 1.00
74 A18 25r Vipera berus 1.40 1.40
Nos. 72-74 (3) 4.90 4.90

Bird Type of 1992

1993, July 24 Litho. Perf. 13x13½

75 A8 2r like #31 .30 .30
76 A8 3r like #32 .30 .30
77 A8 5r like #33 .30 .30
78 A8 10r like #34 .30 .30
79 A8 15r like #35 .35 .35
80 A8 50r like #36 .90 .90
81 A8 100r Hirundo rustica 2.00 2.00
Nos. 75-81 (7) 4.45 4.45

Natl. Arms — A19

1993, Aug. 7 Photo. Perf. 12x12½

82 A19 2k blue .20 .20
83 A19 3k purple .20 .20
84 A19 6k green .20 .20
85 A19 10k olive & purple .20 .20
86 A19 15k olive & purple .20 .20
87 A19 20k gray & purple .20 .20
88 A19 30k yellow & purple .20 .20
89 A19 50k pink & purple .20 .20

Size: 21x32½mm

Perf. 12½x12

90 A19 100k multicolored .50 .50
91 A19 250k multicolored 1.25 1.25
Nos. 82-91 (10) 3.35 3.35

Butterflies — A20 Flowers — A21

1993, Dec. 22 Litho. Perf. 13

94 A20 6b Pyrameis atalanta .20 .20
95 A20 10b Papilio machaon .20 .20
96 A20 50b Vanessa jo .60 .60
97 A20 250b Saturnia pavonia 2.75 2.75
Nos. 94-97 (4) 3.75 3.75

1993, Dec. 25 Litho. Perf. 13½

Designs: 6b, Tulipa bibersteiniana. 15b, Convallaria majalis. 25b, Galanthus nivalis. 30b, Paeonia peregrina. 50b, Galanthus plicatus. 90b, Pulsatilla grandis. 250b, Cypripedium calceolus.

98 A21 6b multicolored .20 .20
99 A21 15b multicolored .20 .20
100 A21 25b multicolored .35 .35
101 A21 30b multicolored .40 .40
102 A21 50b multicolored .65 .65
103 A21 90b multicolored 1.10 1.10
Nos. 98-103 (6) 2.90 2.90

Souvenir Sheet

104 A21 250b multicolored 3.00 3.00

No. 104 contains one 30x45mm stamp.

A22

A23

Famous Men: 6b, Dragos Voda. 25b, Bogdan Voda I. 50b, Latcu Voda. 100b, Petru I Musat. 150b, Roman Voda Musat. 200b, Stefan I.

1993, Dec. 29 Litho. Perf. 13

105 A22 6b multicolored .20 .20
106 A22 25b multicolored .20 .20
107 A22 50b multicolored .25 .25
108 A22 100b multicolored .45 .45
109 A22 150b multicolored .65 .65
110 A22 200b multicolored 1.10 1.10
Nos. 105-110 (6) 2.85 2.85

1993, Dec. 29 Litho. Perf. 13

Europa (Contemporary art): 3b, History of Man, by M. Grecu. 150b, Springtime, by I. Vieru.

111 A23 3b multicolored .75 .75
112 A23 150b multicolored 5.75 5.75

1994 Winter Olympics, Lillehammer A24

1994, Feb. 12 Litho. Perf. 13½

113 A24 3b Biathlete, skiiers .35 .35
114 A24 150b Biathlete, diff. 1.50 1.50

Russia No. 4596 Surcharged in Dark Blue

1994, Apr. 11 Litho. Perf. 12x12½

114A A2138 3b on 1k olive grn .20 .20
114B A2138 25b on 1k olive grn .20 .20
114C A2138 50b on 1k olive grn .35 .35
Nos. 114A-114C (3) .75 .75

First Manned Moon Landing, 25th anniv. — A25

1994, June 18 Litho. Perf. 14

Europa: 1b, Gemini space mission, Titan II rocket. 45b, Ed White, Gemini IV. 2.50 l, Lunar landing module.

115 A25 1b multicolored .50 .50
116 A25 45b multicolored 2.50 2.50
117 A25 2.50 l multicolored 5.50 5.50
Nos. 115-117 (3) 8.50 8.50

Natl. Arms — A26

1994 Perf. 13½x14

118 A26 1b multicolored .25 .25
119 A26 10b multicolored .25 .25
120 A26 30b multicolored .25 .25
121 A26 38b multicolored .25 .25
122 A26 45b multicolored .50 .50
123 A26 75b multicolored .60 .60
125 A26 1.50 l multicolored 1.10 1.10
126 A26 1.80 l multicolored 1.10 1.10
127 A26 2.50 l multi, size: 23½x29mm 1.75 1.75
128 A26 4.50 l multicolored 3.50 3.50
128A A26 5.40 l multicolored 3.75 3.75
128B A26 6.90 l multicolored 4.50 4.50

Size: 23½x29mm

128C A26 7.20 l multicolored 4.50 4.50
129 A26 13 l multicolored 8.50 8.50
130 A26 24 l multicolored 16.00 16.00
Nos. 118-130 (15) 46.80 46.80

Issued: 1b, 45b, 1.50 l, 4.50 l, 6/11/94; 10b, 20b, 5.40 l, 6.90 l, 13 l, 7/16/94; 38b, 75b, 1.80 l, 2.50 l, 7.20 l, 8/13/94.

This is a expanding set. Numbers may change.

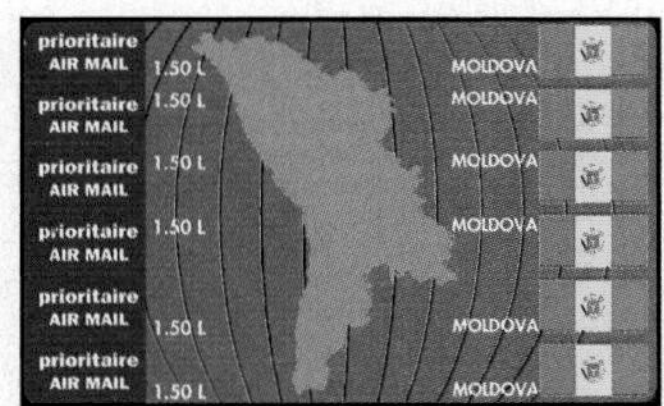

Stamp Card — A27

Designs: 1.50 l, 4.50 l, Map of Moldova.

Rouletted 26 on 2 or 3 Sides

1994, Dec. 22 Litho.

Self-Adhesive

Cards of 6 + 6 labels

131 A27 1.50 l #a.-f., lt vio & multi 5.00
132 A27 4.50 l #a.-f., dp red vio & multi 15.00

Individual stamps measure 70x9mm and have a card backing. Se-tenant labels inscribed "AIR MAIL."

Famous People A28

Designs: 3b, Maria Cibotari (1910-49), singer. 90b, Dumitru Caraciobanu (1937-80), actor. 150b, Eugeniu Coca (1893-1954), composer. 250b, Igor Vieru (1923-83), actor.

1994, June 30 Litho. Perf. 13½

133 A28 3b multicolored .30 .30
134 A28 90b multicolored .40 .40
135 A28 150b multicolored .80 .80
136 A28 250b multicolored 1.40 1.40
Nos. 133-136 (4) 2.90 2.90

Stamp Day A29

Designs: 10b, Designing stamp. 45b, Printing stamps. 2 l, Inspecting finished sheets.

1994, July 22 Litho. Perf. 14

137 A29 10b multicolored .35 .35
138 A29 45b multicolored .70 .70
139 A29 2 l multicolored 2.25 2.25
Nos. 137-139 (3) 3.30 3.30

Intl. Olympic Committee, Cent. — A30

1994, Aug. 29 Litho. Perf. 13½x14

140 A30 60b Pierre de Coubertin .60 .60
141 A30 1.50 l Olympic rings, symbol 1.40 1.40

Moldova's Entrance into NATO — A31

Intl. Year of the Family — A32

Designs: 60b, Moldova Pres. Mircea Snegur, NATO Secretary General Manfred Worner signing documents. 2.50 l, World map centered on Europe.

1994, Nov. 8 Litho. Perf. 13½

142 A31 60b multicolored 1.00 1.00
143 A31 2.50 l multicolored 4.00 4.00

1994, Nov. 26 Perf. 14

144 A32 30b Family .60 .60
145 A32 60b Mother breast-feeding 1.25 1.25
146 A32 1.50 l Child painting 2.40 2.40
Nos. 144-146 (3) 4.25 4.25

1996 European Soccer Championships, England — A33

Designs: 10b, Handshaking. 40b, Players legs, soccer ball. 1.20 l, Goalie.

No. 150: a, 1.10 l, Soccer federation, German flags. b, 2.20 l, Soccer ball, German, Moldovan flags. c, 2.40 l, Players.

1994, Dec. 10

147 A33 10b multicolored .40 .40
148 A33 40b multicolored .70 .70
149 A33 2.40 l multicolored 3.00 3.00
Nos. 147-149 (3) 4.10 4.10

Souvenir Sheet

150 A33 Sheet of 3, #a.-c. 5.25 5.25

Christmas
A34

Mushrooms — A35

Paintings of Birth of Christ by: 20b, unknown artist, 18th cent. 3.60 l, Gherasim, 1808.

1994, Dec. 29

151 A34 20b multicolored .50 .50
152 A34 3.60 l multicolored 4.50 4.50

1995, Feb. 8

153 A35 4b Russula virescens .50 .50
154 A35 10b Boletus luridus .80 .80
155 A35 20b Cantherellus cibarius 1.60 1.60
156 A35 90b Leccinum aurantiacum 4.75 4.75
157 A35 1.80 l Leccinum duriusculum 9.00 9.00
Nos. 153-157 (5) 16.65 16.65

European Nature Conservation Year — A36

Designs: 4b, Hieraaetus pennatus. 45b, Capreolus capreolus. 90b, Sus scrofa.

1995, Mar. 18 **Litho.** ***Perf. 14***

158 A36 4b multicolored .95 .95
159 A36 45b multicolored 4.50 4.50
160 A36 90b multicolored 9.25 9.25
Nos. 158-160 (3) 14.70 14.70

Museum of Natural Sciences — A37

Designs: 4b, Jars. 10b+2b, Dinotherium gigantissimum. 1.80 l+30b, Silver coin, 3rd-2nd cent. BC.

1995 **Litho.** ***Perf. 14***

161 A37 4b multicolored .55 .55
162 A37 10b +2b multi 1.10 1.10
163 A37 1.80 l +30b multi 7.75 7.75
Nos. 161-163 (3) 9.40 9.40

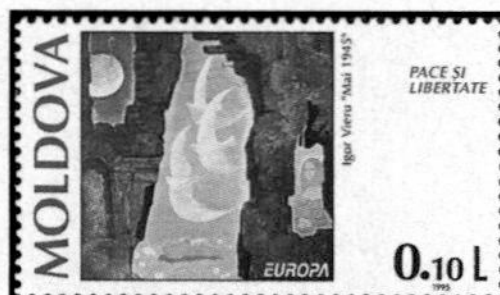

Peace & Freedom — A38

Paintings: 10b, May 1945, by Igor Vieru. 40b, Linistea, by Sergiu Cuciuc. 2.20 l, Primavara 1944, by Cuciuc.

1995, May 9 **Litho.** ***Perf. 14***

164 A38 10b multicolored .45 .45
165 A38 40b multicolored 2.75 2.75
166 A38 2.20 l multicolored 5.25 5.25
Nos. 164-166 (3) 8.45 8.45

Europa.

A39

A40

Famous People: 90b, Constantin Stere (1865-1936), writer. 10b, Tamara Ceban (1914-90), musician. 40b, Alexandru Plamadeala (1888-1940), artist. 1.80 l, Lucian Blaga (1895-1961), writer.

1995, June 17 **Litho.** ***Perf. 14***

167 A39 9b dp cl & gray .30 .30
168 A39 10b brt mag & gray .30 .30
169 A39 40b violet & gray .95 .95
170 A39 1.80 l dk grn & gray 4.75 4.75
Nos. 167-170 (4) 6.30 6.30

1995, July 2 **Litho.** ***Perf. 14***

Kings of Moldova, reign: No. 171, Alexandru Cel Bun, 1400-32. No. 172, Petru Aron, 1451-52, 1454-57. No. 173, Stefan Cel Mare, 1457-1504. 45 l, Petru Rares, 1527-38, 1541-46. 90 l, Alexandru Lapusneanu, 1552-61, 1564-68. 1.80 l, Ion Voda Cel Cumplit, 1572-74. 5 l, Stefan Cel Mare, 1457-1504.

171 A40 10 b multicolored .45 .45
172 A40 10 b multicolored .45 .45
173 A40 10 b multicolored .45 .45
174 A40 45 b multicolored 1.90 1.90
175 A40 90 b multicolored 3.50 3.50
176 A40 1.80 l multicolored 7.75 7.75
Nos. 171-176 (6) 14.50 14.50

Souvenir Sheet

177 A40 5 l multicolored 3.50 3.50

No. 177 contains one 24x29mm stamp.

Citadels of Moldova A41

1995, July 29

178 A41 10 b Soroca .35 .35
179 A41 20 b Tighina .65 .65
180 A41 60 b Alba 1.40 1.40
181 A41 1.30 l Hotin 3.75 3.75
Nos. 178-181 (4) 6.15 6.15

A42

UN, 50th Anniv. — A43

Designs inside of stylized eye: No. 182, Devastation of war. No. 183, Fighter plane. No. 184, Prisoner of war.

Nos. 185-186: a, 1. b, 2. c, 3. d, 4. e, 5. f, 6. g, 7. h, 8. i, 9. j, 10.

1995, Oct. 24 **Litho.** ***Perf. 14***

182 A42 10b yellow & multi .50 .50
183 A42 10b blue & multi .50 .50
184 A42 1.50 l green & multi 6.50 6.50
Nos. 182-184 (3) 7.50 7.50

Stamp Cards

Rouletted 15 on 2 or 3 Sides

Self-Adhesive

Cards of 10

185 A43 90b #a.-j. 11.00 11.00
186 A43 1.50 l #a.-j. 19.00 19.00

Background color of stamps gradually shifts from light blue (#1) to dark blue (#10). Each stamp is individually numbered.

Motion Pictures, Cent. — A44

Films: 10b, Last Moon of Autumn. 40b, Lautarii. 2.40 l, Dimitrie Cantemir.

1995, Dec. 28 **Litho.** ***Perf. 14***

187 A44 10b red brn & blk .65 .65
188 A44 40b olive & black 2.00 2.00
189 A44 2.40 l ultra & black 6.50 6.50
Nos. 187-189 (3) 9.15 9.15

Mushrooms A45

1996 Summer Olympic Games, Atlanta A46

No. 190, Amanita muscaria. No. 191, Boletus satanas. 65b, Amanita phalloides. 1.30 l, Hypholoma fasciculare. 2.40 l, Amanita virosa.

1996, Mar. 23 **Litho.** ***Perf. 14***

190 A45 10b multicolored .70 .70
191 A45 10b multicolored .70 .70
192 A45 65b multicolored 1.10 1.10
193 A45 1.30 l multicolored 1.75 1.75
194 A45 2.40 l multicolored 4.75 4.75
Nos. 190-194 (5) 9.00 9.00

1996, Mar. 30

195 A46 10b Weight lifting .45 .45
196 A46 20b +5b Judo .45 .45
197 A46 45b +10b Running .85 .85
198 A46 2.40 l +30b Canoeing 4.75 4.75
Nos. 195-198 (4) 6.50 6.50

Souvenir Sheet

199 A46 2.20 l Archery 2.50 2.50
a. With added inscription in sheet margin 3.50 3.50

No. 199 contains one 34x29mm stamp.

No. 199a inscribed "Nicolae JURAVSCHI Victor RENEISCHI / -canoe, argint- / Serghei MUREICO/ -lupte greco-romane,bronz-".

Monasteries A47

1996, Apr. 26

200 A47 10b Rudi, 18th cent. .45 .45
201 A47 90b Japca, 17th cent. .80 .80
202 A47 1.30 l Curchi, 18th cent. 1.40 1.40
203 A47 2.80 l Saharna, 18th cent. 3.00 3.00
204 A47 4.40 l Capriana, 16th cent. 4.75 4.75
Nos. 200-204 (5) 10.40 10.40

Birds — A48

Designs: 9b, Gallinula chloropus. 10b, Anser anser. No. 207, Streptopelia turtur. 4.40 l, Anas platyrhynchos.

No. 209, Phasianus colchicus.

1996, May 17

205 A48 9b multicolored .35 .35
206 A48 10b multicolored .35 .35
207 A48 2.20 l multicolored 2.50 2.50
208 A48 4.40 l multicolored 4.25 4.25
Nos. 205-208 (4) 7.45 7.45

Souvenir Sheet

209 A48 2.20 l multicolored 2.50 2.50

Europa

A49

A50

Famous Women: 10b, Elena Alistar (1873-1955), president of women's league. 3.70 l, Marie Curie (1867-1934), chemist, physicist. 2.20 l, Julia Hasdeu (1869-1888), writer.

1996, June 21 **Litho.** ***Perf. 14***

210 A49 10b multicolored .50 .50
211 A49 3.70 l multicolored 5.25 5.25

Souvenir Sheet

212 A49 2.20 l multicolored 4.25 4.25

1996, July 30 **Litho.** ***Perf. 14***

Famous Men: #213, Gavriil Banulescu-Bodoni (1746-1821). #214, Mihail Eminescu (1850-69), poet. 2.20 l, Ion Creanga (1837-89). 3.30 l, Vasile Alecsandri (1821-90). 5.40 l, Petru Movila (1596-1646), theologian.

1.80 l, Eminescu, diff., vert.

213	A50	10b gray vio & brn	.25	.25
214	A50	10b lt brn & dk brn	.25	.25
215	A50	2.20 l gray & brn	1.75	1.75
216	A50	3.30 l ol & brn	2.25	2.25
217	A50	5.40 l red brn & brn	3.75	3.75
		Nos. 213-217 (5)	8.25	8.25

Souvenir Sheet

218	A50	1.80 l brn	1.50	1.50

City of Chisinau, 560th Anniv. — A51

Building, year erected: 10b, City Hall, 1902. 1.30 l, Palace of Culture, 1911. 2.40 l, Mazarache Church, 1752.

1996, Oct. 6 Litho. *Perf. 14*

219	A51	10b multicolored	.75	.75
220	A51	1.30 l multicolored	2.50	2.50
221	A51	2.40 l multicolored	5.75	5.75
		Nos. 219-221 (3)	9.00	9.00

A52

A53

Christmas: 10b, Children carrying star. 2.20 l+30b, Mother and child in center of star. 2.80 l+50b, Children decorating Christmas tree.

1996, Dec. 12 Litho. *Perf. 14*

222	A52	10b multicolored	.30	.30
223	A52	2.20 l +30b multicolored	2.40	2.40
224	A52	2.80 l +50b multicolored	2.75	2.75
		Nos. 222-224 (3)	5.45	5.45

1997, Jan. 17 Litho. *Perf. 14*

Wines of Moldova.

225	A53	10b Feteasca	.45	.45
226	A53	45b Cabernet-Sauvignon	.55	.55
227	A53	65b Sauvignon	.90	.90
228	A53	3.70 l Rara neagra	4.75	4.75
		Nos. 225-228 (4)	6.65	6.65

Easter — A54

Designs: 3.30b, Colored eggs, grass on plate. 5 l, Basket of eggs, food.

1997, Apr. 25 Litho. *Perf. 13½*

229	A54	10b multicolored	.40	.40
230	A54	3.30 l multicolored	3.00	3.00

Souvenir Sheet

231	A54	5 l multicolored	5.50	5.50

Composers — A55

Designs: No. 232, Franz Schubert (1797-1828). No. 233, Gavriil Musicescu (1847-1903). 45b, Sergei Rachmaninoff (1873-1943). 4.40 l, Georges Enesco (1881-1955).

1997, Feb. 22 Litho. *Perf. 14*

232	A55	10b slate & bl grn	.40	.40
233	A55	10b slate & bl grn	.40	.40
234	A55	45b slate & bl grn	.70	.70
235	A55	4.40 l slate & bl grn	5.50	5.50
		Nos. 232-235 (4)	7.00	7.00

Stories and Legends A56

Europa: 10b, Man holding up arms, goose flying, arrows from fortress. 2.80 l, Man upside down, church, sun in sky with stars and eye. 5 l, Angel touching flowers during winter.

1997, June 20 Litho. *Perf. 13½*

236	A56	10b multicolored	1.00	1.00
237	A56	2.80 l multicolored	6.50	6.50

Souvenir Sheet

238	A56	5 l multicolored	8.50	8.50

Red Book Insects — A57

Insects on plants, flowers: 25b, Mantis religiosa. 80b, Ascalphus macaronius scop. 1 l, Calosoma sycophanta. 2.20 l, Liometopum microcephalum.

5 l, Scolia maculata drury.

1997, July 26 Litho. *Perf. 14*

239	A57	25b multicolored	.30	.30
240	A57	80b multicolored	.85	.85
241	A57	1 l multicolored	1.00	1.00
242	A57	2.20 l multicolored	2.40	2.40
		Nos. 239-242 (4)	4.55	4.55

Souvenir Sheet

243	A57	5 l multicolored	5.50	5.50

World Post Day — A58

Designs: 10b, Chisinau post office building, 1997. 2.20 l, Mail coach, Chisinaupost office building. 3.30 l, Heinrich von Stephan (1831-97), vert.

1997, Oct. 18 Litho. *Perf. 14*

244	A58	10b multicolored	.40	.40
245	A58	2.20 l multicolored	1.90	1.90
246	A58	3.30 l multicolored	4.00	4.00
		Nos. 244-246 (3)	6.30	6.30

Christmas A59

Designs: 10b, Noul Neamt Monastery. 45b, "Adoration of the Shepherds," Noul Neamt Monastery. 5 l, "Nativity," Natl. Museum of Plastic Arts.

1997, Dec. 17 Litho. *Perf. 13½*

247	A59	10b multicolored	.20	.20
248	A59	45b multicolored	.30	.30
249	A59	5 l multicolored	3.50	3.50
		Nos. 247-249 (3)	4.00	4.00

A60

A61

UNESCO World Heritage Sites: 7b, Nicolai Zelinski High School, Tiraspol. No. 251, Railway station, Tighina. No. 252, Cathedral, Balti. 90b, Church, Causeni. 1.30 l, Cathedral, Kagul. 3.30 l, Art Institute, Chisinau.

1997, Dec. 16 Litho. *Perf. 14*

250	A60	7b black & lilac	.40	.40
251	A60	10b black & red violet	.40	.40
252	A60	10b black & grn blue	.40	.40
253	A60	90b black & yel org	.90	.90
254	A60	1.30 l black & blue	1.25	1.25
255	A60	3.30 l black & gray	3.00	3.00
		Nos. 250-255 (6)	6.35	6.35

1997, Dec. 17

Princes of Moldova, reign: No. 256, Petru Schiopul (1574-77, 78-79, 82-91). No. 257, Ieremia Movila (1595-1606). 45b, Stefan Tomsa (1611-15, 1621-23). 1.80 l, Radu Mihnea (1616-19, 1623-26). 2.20 l, Miron Barnovschi Movila (1626-29, 1633). 2.80 l, Bogdan Orbul (1504-17).

5 l, Mihai Viteazul, 1600.

256	A61	10b multicolored	.30	.30
257	A61	10b multicolored	.30	.30
258	A61	45b multicolored	.50	.50
259	A61	1.80 l multicolored	2.00	2.00
260	A61	2.20 l multicolored	2.25	2.25
261	A61	2.80 l multicolored	3.00	3.00
		Nos. 256-261 (6)	8.35	8.35

Souvenir Sheet

262	A61	5 l multicolored	5.50	5.50

No. 262 contains one 23x29mm stamp.

1998 Winter Olympic Games, Nagano A62

1998, Feb. 28

263	A62	10b Slalom skiing	.25	.25
264	A62	45b Figure skating	.50	.50
265	A62	2.20 l Biathlon	2.25	2.25
		Nos. 263-265 (3)	3.00	3.00

A63

A64

Famous People: 10b, Alexei Mateevici (1888-1917). 40b, Pantelimon Halippa (1883-1979). 60b, Stefan Ciobanu (1883-1950). 2 l, Constantin Stamati-Ciurea (1828-98).

5 l, Nicolae Milescu-Spatarul (1636-1708).

1998, May 9 Litho. *Perf. 14*

266	A63	10b multicolored	.25	.25
267	A63	40b multicolored	.40	.40
268	A63	60b multicolored	.55	.55
269	A63	2 l multicolored	1.75	1.75
		Nos. 266-269 (4)	2.95	2.95

Souvenir Sheet

270	A63	5 l multicolored	4.75	4.75

1998, May 13 *Perf. 14½x14*

Monuments and Works of Art: 10b, Monument to Stefan cel Mare, by Alexandru Plamadeala. 60b, The Resurrected Christ, by 19th cent. artist. 1 l, Steel column, by Constantin Brancusi. 2.60 l, Trajan's Column, by Apollodorus of Damascus, Rome.

271	A64	10b multicolored	.30	.30
272	A64	60b multicolored	.70	.70
273	A64	1 l multicolored	1.00	1.00
274	A64	2.60 l multicolored	2.75	2.75
		Nos. 271-274 (4)	4.75	4.75

Natl. Holidays and Festivals A65

Europa: 10b, Eugène Ionesco biennial Theater Festival. 2.20 l, Lurceni ceramics, Nisporeni.

5 l, Music Festival, Martisor.

1998, July 18 Litho. *Perf. 14*

275	A65	10b multicolored	.65	.65
276	A65	2.20 l multicolored	4.00	4.00

Souvenir Sheet

277	A65	5 l multicolored	7.50	7.50

Fruit — A66

1998, Aug. 15

278	A66	7b Cerasus avium	.35	.35
279	A66	10b Prunus domestica	.35	.35
280	A66	1 l Malus domestica	.95	.95
281	A66	2 l Cydonia oblonga	1.90	1.90
		Nos. 278-281 (4)	3.55	3.55

Diana, Princess of Wales (1961-97) A67

Various portraits: a, 10b. b, 90b. c, 1.80 l. d, 2.20 l. e, 1.80 l.

1998, Aug. 31 Litho. *Perf. 14*

282	A67	Sheet of 5, #a.-e. + label	8.00	8.00

First Stamps Used in Moldova, 140th Anniv. A68

Stamps on stamps: 10b, Romania #1-2, Type A2. 90b, Romania #2, #329, Type A177. 2.20 l, Romania #4, Russia #4132, #5916. 2.40 l, Moldova #122, #214, Romania #3.

Photo. & Engr.

1998, Oct. 9 *Perf. 14*
283 A68 10b multicolored .20 .20
284 A68 90b multicolored .50 .50
285 A68 2.20 l multicolored 2.00 2.00
286 A68 2.40 l multicolored 2.40 2.40
Nos. 283-286 (4) 5.10 5.10

Medieval Fortresses — A69

1998, Sept. 26 Litho. *Perf. 14*
287 A69 10b Chilia .40 .40
288 A69 60b Orhei .70 .70
289 A69 1 l Suceava 1.10 1.10
290 A69 2 l Ismail 2.40 2.40
Nos. 287-290 (4) 4.60 4.60

Birds A70

25b, Bubo bubo, vert. 2 l, Anthropoides virgo.

1998, Oct. 31
291 A70 25b multicolored .40 .40
292 A70 2 l multicolored 2.40 2.40

Regional Costumes A71

1998, Nov. 28 Litho. *Perf. 14*
293 A71 25b Vara .40 .40
294 A71 90b Vara, diff. .95 .95
295 A71 1.80 l Iarna 1.90 1.90
296 A71 2 l Iarna, diff. 2.10 2.10
Nos. 293-296 (4) 5.35 5.35

Annexation of Bessarabia to Romania, 80th Anniv. — A72

1998, Dec. 10
297 A72 90b multicolored .95 .95

Universal Declaration of Human Rights, 50th Anniv. — A73

1998, Dec. 10
298 A73 2.40 l multicolored 2.50 2.50

UPU, 125th Anniv. A74

1999, Apr. 9 Litho. *Perf. 14*
299 A74 25b multicolored .50 .50

Council of Europe, 50th Anniv. A75

1999, Apr. 9
300 A75 2.20 l multicolored 2.50 2.50

Nature Reserves — A76

Europa: 25b, Prutul de Jos. 2.40 l, Padurea Domneasca. 5 l, Codru.

1999, May 5 Litho. *Perf. 14*
301 A76 25b multicolored .60 .60
302 A76 2.40 l multicolored 3.25 3.25

Souvenir Sheet

303 A76 5 l multicolored 7.00 7.00

Honoré de Balzac (1799-1850), Writer — A77

Aleksandr Pushkin (1788-1837), Poet — A78

1999, May 20
304 A77 90b multicolored 1.00 1.00

1999, June 6
305 A78 65b brown & black .75 .75

National Sports — A79

1999, June 26 Litho. *Perf. 13¾*
306 A79 25b Wrestling .35 .35
307 A79 1.80 l Oina 2.00 2.00

First Manned Moon Landing, 30th Anniv. A80

1999, July 20 Litho. *Perf. 14*
308 A80 25b Michael Collins .35 .35
309 A80 25b Neil Armstrong .35 .35
310 A80 5 l Edwin Aldrin 5.00 5.00
Nos. 308-310 (3) 5.70 5.70

Medals — A81 Crafts — A82

1999, July 31 Litho. *Perf. 14*
311 A81 25b Meritul Militar .35 .35
312 A81 25b Pentru Vitejie .35 .35
313 A81 25b Meritul Civic .35 .35
314 A81 90b Mihai Eminescu .35 .35
315 A81 1.10 l Gloria Muncii 1.25 1.25
316 A81 2.40 l Stefan cel Mare 3.00 3.00
Nos. 311-316 (6) 5.65 5.65

Souvenir Sheet

317 A81 5 l Ordinul Republicii 5.25 5.25

1999, Aug. 7
318 A82 5b Wood carving .20 .20
319 A82 25b Embroidery .30 .30
320 A82 95b Pottery .65 .65
321 A82 1.80 l Wicker furniture 1.90 1.90
Nos. 318-321 (4) 3.05 3.05

Johann Wolfgang von Goethe (1749-1832), German Poet — A83

1999, Aug. 20
322 A83 1.10 l multicolored 1.75 1.75

Return to Use of Latin Letters for Moldavian Language, 10th Anniv. — A84

1999, Aug. 31 *Perf. 13¾*
323 A84 25b multicolored .40 .40

A85

A86

Metropolitans: 25b, Varlaam (1590-1657). 2.40 l, Gurie Grosu (1877-1943).

1999, Sept. 12 Litho. *Perf. 14*
324 A85 25b multicolored .25 .25
325 A85 2.40 l multicolored 2.25 2.25

1999, Oct. 16 Litho. *Perf. 14¼x14*

Moldavian Rulers, dates ruled: No. 326, Bogdan II (1449-51). No. 327, Bogdan IV (1568-72). No. 328, Constantin Cantemir (1685-93). 1.50 l, Simion Movila (1606-07). 3 l, Duke Gheorghe III (1665-66, 1668-72, 1678-84). 3.90 l, Ilias Alexandru (1666-68). 5 l, Vasile Lupu (1634-53).

326 A86 25b multi .25 .25
327 A86 25b multi .25 .25
328 A86 25b multi .25 .25
329 A86 1.50 l multi 1.00 1.00
330 A86 3 l multi 2.00 2.00
331 A86 3.90 l multi 3.25 3.25
Nos. 326-331 (6) 7.00 7.00

Souvenir Sheet

Perf. 13¾x14

332 A86 5 l multi 4.50 4.50

No. 332 contains one 24x30mm stamp. Compare with Type A110.

Fauna A87

Designs: 25b, Lutra lutra. 1.80 l, Huso huso. 3.60 l, Rhinolophus ferrumequinum.

1999, Nov. 20 *Perf. 14x14¼*
333 A87 25b multi .25 .25
334 A87 1.80 l multi 1.25 1.25
335 A87 3.60 l multi 2.50 2.50
Nos. 333-335 (3) 4.00 4.00

1999 Women's Chess Championships, Chisinau — A88

1999, Nov. 27 *Perf. 13¾*
336 A88 25b Woman .25 .25
337 A88 2.20 l Building 2.75 2.75

A89

A90

Items From National History Museum: 25b, Helmet, candleholder. 1.80 l, Ceramic jug. 3.60 l, Bible.

Perf. 14¼x13¾

1999, Dec. 11 Litho.
338 A89 25b multi .25 .25
339 A89 1.80 l multi 1.25 1.25
340 A89 3.60 l multi 3.25 3.25
Nos. 338-340 (3) 4.75 4.75

2000, Jan. 15 Litho. *Perf. 13¾x14*

a, 20b, Raluca Eminovici. b, 5 l, Mihail Eminescu (1850-89), Poet. c, 25b, Gheorghe Eminovici. d, 3 l, Veronica Micle. e, 1.50 l, Iosif Vulcan.

341 A90 Sheet of 5, #a.-e., + label 7.00 7.00

Fairy Tales A91

Designs: 25b, Ileana Cosinzeana. 1.50 l, Fat Frumos. 1.80 l, Harap Alb.

2000, Feb. 15 Litho. *Perf. 14*
342 A91 25b multi *.25 .25*
343 A91 1.50 l multi *1.50 1.50*
344 A91 1.80 l multi *1.90 1.90*
Nos. 342-344 (3) *3.65 3.65*

Famous People — A92

Designs: No. 345, Henri Coanda (1886-1972), physicist. No. 346, Toma Ciorba (1864-1936), doctor. 2 l, Guglielmo Marconi (1874-1937), physicist. 3.60 l, Norbert Wiener (1894-1964), mathematician.

2000, Feb. 26 ***Perf. 13¾x14***

345 A92 25b multi .25 .25
346 A92 25b multi .25 .25
347 A92 2 l multi 2.00 2.00
348 A92 3.60 l multi 3.75 3.75
Nos. 345-348 (4) 6.25 6.25

Events of the 20th Century A93

Designs: 25b, Moon landing, vert. 1.50 l, Nuclear fission, vert. 3 l, Global computerization, vert. 3.90 l, Reconciliation between Partiarch Teoctist and Pope John Paul II.

2000, Apr. 12 ***Perf. 14***

349 A93 25b multi .25 .25
350 A93 1.50 l multi 1.40 1.40
351 A93 3 l multi 2.75 2.75
352 A93 3.90 l multi 3.75 3.75
Nos. 349-352 (4) 8.15 8.15

Easter — A94

Religious artwork from: 25b, 1841. 3 l, 19th cent.

2000, Apr. 30 ***Perf. 14x13¾***

353 A94 25b multi .25 .25
354 A94 3 l multi 2.75 2.75

Europa, 2000

Common Design Type

2000, May 9 Litho. ***Perf. 14¼x14***

355 CD17 3 l multi 3.50 3.50
Booklet, 6 #355 19.00

Exhibitions A95

Designs: 25b, Faces, Expo 2000 emblem. 3.60 l+25b, WIPA 2000 Emblem, No. 118.

2000, May 30 Litho. ***Perf. 14x13¾***

356 A95 25b multi .25 .25
357 A95 3.60 l +25b multi 1.50 1.50

Churches and Monasteries — A96

Designs: 25b, Monastery, Tipova, 16th-17th Cent. 1.50 l, Church, Heciul Vechi, 1791. 1.80 l, Church, Palanca, 18th-19th Cent. 3 l, Monastery, Butuceni, 15th-16th Cent.

2000, Aug. 12 Litho. ***Perf. 14***

358-361 A96 Set of 4 4.75 4.75

2000 Summer Olympics, Sydney — A97

Olympic flag and: 25b, Judo. 1.80 l, Wrestling. 5 l, Weight lifting.

2000, Sept. 15 Litho. ***Perf. 14x13¾***

362-364 A97 Set of 3 5.75 5.75

Teacher's Day A98

25b, Child, teacher, class. 3.60 l, Teacher.

2000, Oct. 5 ***Perf. 14x14¼***

365-366 A98 Set of 2 3.00 3.00

Christmas A99

Icons: 25b, Adoration of the Shepherds. 1.50 l, Nativity.

2000, Nov. 11 Litho. ***Perf. 13¾***

367-368 A99 Set of 2 1.75 1.75

Souvenir Sheet

Perf. 13¾x14

369 A99 5 l Madonna and Child 4.75 4.75

No. 369 contains one 27x33mm stamp.

UN High Commissioner for Refugees, 50th Anniv. — A99a

2001, Jan. 19 ***Perf. 14***

369A A99a 3 l multi 2.75 2.75

Worldwide Fund for Nature (WWF) — A100

Crex crex: a, On rock. b, With mouth open. c, With eggs. d, With chicks.
Illustration reduced.

2001, Mar. 31 Litho. ***Perf. 14x14¼***

370 A100 3 l Block of 4, #a-d 6.00 6.00

First Manned Spaceflight, 40th Anniv. — A101

2001, Apr. 12 ***Perf. 14***

371 A101 1.80 l Yuri Gagarin 1.75 1.75

See No. 377.

Famous Women A102

Designs: 25b, Maria Dragan (1947-86), singer. 1 l, Marlene Dietrich (1901-92), actress. 2 l, Ruxandra Lupu (1630?-87). 3 l, Lidia Lipkovski (1884-1958).

2001, Apr. 28 ***Perf. 14x14¼***

372-375 A102 Set of 4 5.75 5.75

Europa — A103

2001, May 5 ***Perf. 14***

376 A103 3 l multi 2.75 2.75
Booklet, 6 #376 16.50

Space Anniversary Type of 2001

Design: Dumitru Prunariu, first Romanian cosmonaut.

2001, May 14

377 A101 1.80 l multi 1.75 1.75

Prunariu's flight, 20th anniv.

Children's Art — A104

Art by: No. 378, 25b, Cristina Mereacre. No. 379, 25b, Ion Sestacovschi. No. 380, 25b, Aliona-Valeria Samburic. 1.80 l, Andrei Sestacovschi.

2001, June 1

378-381 A104 Set of 4 2.75 2.75

Souvenir Sheet

Moldovan Stamps, 10th Anniv. — A105

Pre-independence era stamps: a, 40b, 7c Arms stamp (27x32mm). b, 2 l, 13c Arms stamp (27x32mm). c, 3 l, 30c Flag stamp (42x25mm).

2001, June 23 ***Perf. 13¾x14, 14 (3 l)***

382 A105 Sheet of 3, #a-c 5.00 5.00

Animals in Chisinau Zoo — A106

Designs: 40b, Panthera tigris tigris. 1 l Equus quagga. 1.50 l, Ursus arctos. 3 l+30b, Boselaphus tragocamelus.
5 l, Panthera leo.

2001, July 14 ***Perf. 13¾***

383-386 A106 Set of 4 5.75 5.75

Souvenir Sheet

387 A106 5 l multi 4.50 4.50

Declaration of Independence, 10th Anniv. — A107

2001, Aug. 27 Litho. ***Perf. 14x13¾***

388 A107 1 l multi .95 .95

Musical Instruments A108

Year of Dialogue Among Civilizations A109

Designs: 40b, Cimpol. 1 l, Fluier. 1.80 l, Nai. 3 l, Taragot.

2001, Oct. 6 ***Perf. 14x13¾***

389-392 A108 Set of 4 5.75 5.75

2001, Oct. 9 ***Perf. 14x14¼, 14¼x14***

Designs: 40b, Heads, spacecraft, horiz. 3.60b, Emblem.

393-394 A109 Set of 2 3.75 3.75

A110

Moldavian Rulers — A111

Ruler, dates ruled: No. 395, 40b, Mihai Racovita (1703-05, 1707-09, 1716-26). No. 396, 40b, Nicolae Mavrocordat (1709-10, 1711-15). No. 397, 40b, Constantin Mavrocordat (1733-35, 1741-43, 1748-49, 1769). No. 398, 40b, Grigore Callimachi (1761-64, 1767-69). 1 l, Grigore Alexandru Ghica (1764-67, 1774-77). 3 l, Antion Cantemir (1695-1700, 1705-07).
5 l, Dimitrie Cantemir (1710-11).

2001, Oct. 27 ***Perf. 14¼x14***
395-400 A110 Set of 6 *5.25 5.25*

Souvenir Sheet
Perf. 14x14¼

401 A111 5 l multi *4.75 4.75*

Compare with type A86.

Christmas — A112

Designs: 40b, Church, 1821. 1 l, Church, 1841. 3 l, Church, 1636. 3.90 l, Cathedral, 1836.

2001, Nov. 10 ***Perf. 13¾x14***
402-405 A112 Set of 4 *8.75 8.75*

Commonwealth of Independent States, 10th Anniv. — A113

2001, Dec. 14 ***Perf. 14¼x14***
406 A113 1.50 l multi *1.60 1.60*

2002 Winter Olympics, Salt Lake City — A114

Designs: 40b, Cross-country skiing. 5 l, Biathlon.

2002, Feb. 8 **Litho.** ***Perf. 13¾x14***
407-408 A114 Set of 2 *3.75 3.75*

Dances A115

Designs: 40b, Hora. 1.50 l, Sirba.

2002, Mar. 16 ***Perf. 14x14¼***
409-410 A115 Set of 2 *2.00 2.00*

Paintings A116

Designs: No. 411, 40b, Fetele din Ceadir-lunga, by Mihai Grecu. No. 412, 40b, Meleag Natal, by Eleonora Romanescu. 1.50 l, Fata la Fereastra, by Valentina Rusu-Ciobanu. 3 l, In Doi, by Igor Vieru.

2002, Apr. 20 **Litho.** ***Perf. 13¾***
411-414 A116 Set of 4 *5.00 5.00*

Europa — A117

2002, May 9 ***Perf. 14***
415 A117 3 l multi *3.00 3.00*
Booklet, 6 #415 *18.00*

Souvenir Sheet

Botanical Gardens, Chisinau — A118

No. 416: a, 40b, Rose. b, 40b, Peony. c, 1.50 l, Aster. d, 3 l, Iris.

2002, June 14 ***Perf. 13¾x14***
416 A118 Sheet of 4, #a-d *4.50 4.50*

Souvenir Sheet

Leonardo da Vinci (1452-1519) — A119

No. 417: a, 40b, Lady with an Ermine. b, 1.50 l, Virgin and Child with St. Anne. c, 3 l, Mona Lisa.

2002, July 25
417 A119 Sheet of 3, #a-c *4.00 4.00*

Famous Men — A120

Designs: No. 418, 40b, Grigore Ureche (1590-1647), chronicler. No. 419, 40b, Nicolae Costin (1660-1712). No. 420, 40b, Ion Neculce (1672-1745), chronicler. No. 421, 40b, Nicolae Testemiteanu (1927-86). 1.50 l, Sergiu Radautan (1926-98), scientist. 3.90 l, Alexandre Dumas (father) (1802-70), novelist.

2002, Aug. 24
418-423 A120 Set of 6 *6.50 6.50*

Horses A121

Designs: 40b, Vladimir. 1.50 l, Orlov. 3 l, Arabian.

2002, Sept. 20 ***Perf. 14***
424-426 A121 Set of 3 *5.25 5.25*

The Post in Children's Art — A122

Art by: 40b, Alexandry Catranji. 1.50 l, Natalia Corcodel. 2 l, Dana Lungu.

2002, Oct. 3 **Litho.** ***Perf. 14***
427-429 A122 Set of 3 *4.25 4.25*

Commonwealth of Independent States Summit — A123

CIS emblem and: 1.50 l, National leaders and flags. 3.60 l, Handshake.

2002, Oct. 6 **Litho.** ***Perf. 13½***
430-431 A123 Set of 2 *4.75 4.75*

Cricova Wine Industry, 50th Anniv. A124

Designs: No. 432, 40b, Truck in warehouse. No. 433, 40b, Entrance to underground warehouse. 1.50 l, Wine glasses on table, vert. 2 l, Dusty wine bottles, wine cellar, statue. 3.60 l, Wine glasses and bottles, vert.

2002, Oct. 11 ***Perf. 13¼x13, 13x13¼***
432-436 A124 Set of 5 *7.00 7.00*

Dirigibles — A125

Designs: 40b, Tissandier dirigible, France, 1883. 2 l, Ucebnii dirigible, Russia, 1908. 5 l, Graf Zeppelin, Germany, 1928.

2003, Apr. 22 **Litho.** ***Perf. 13¼***
437-439 A125 Set of 3 *5.50 5.50*

Butterflies — A126

Designs: 40b, Iphiclides podalirius. 2 l, Callimorpha quadripunctaria. 3 l, Marumba quercus. 5 l, Polyommatus daphnis.

2003, Apr. 30 ***Perf. 13¼x13***
440-443 A126 Set of 4 *8.50 8.50*
443a Souvenir sheet, #440-443 *8.50 8.50*
443b Booklet pane, #441-442, 2 each #440, 443 *13.00* —
Complete booklet, #443b *13.00*

Europa — A127

Poster art: 3 l, Popular Dance Ensemble poster. 5 l, Eminescu Exhibition poster.

2003, June 12 ***Perf. 13¼***
444-445 A127 Set of 2 *8.25 8.25*
445a Booklet pane, 3 each #444-445 *25.00* —
Complete booklet, #445a *25.00*

Souvenir Sheet

Moldovan Europa Stamps, 10th Anniv. — A128

No. 446: a, 1.50 l, Rural landscape. b, 5 l, Chisinau.

2003, June 12 ***Perf. 13½***
446 A128 Sheet of 2, #a-b + label *6.00 6.00*

Red Cross A129

Emblem and: 40b, Flag. 5 l, Red Cross workers at disaster site.

2003, July 4 ***Perf. 13¼x13***
447-448 A129 Set of 2 *4.50 4.50*

Youth Olympics, Paris — A130

Designs: 40b, Runner. 3 l, Cyclists. 5 l, Gymnast.

2003, July 25 ***Perf. 13½***
449-451 A130 Set of 3 *7.00 7.00*

Battle Against Terrorism A131

Art: 40b, Luminari, by A. Ahlupin, vert. 3.90 l, Pax Cultura, by N. Roerich.

2003, Oct. 21
452-453 A131 Set of 2 *4.00 4.00*

Dimitrie Cantemir (1673-1723), Historian A132

2003, Oct. 24 *Perf. 13*
454 A132 3.60 l multi *2.75 2.75*

Visit of Pres. Vladimir Voronin to European Union — A133

2003, Nov. 5 *Perf. 13½*
455 A133 3 l multi *2.75 2.75*

Famous Men — A134

Designs: 40b, Nicolae Donici (1874-1956), astronomer. 1.50 l, Nicolae Dimo (1873-1959), agronomist. 2 l, Nicolai Costenco (1913-93), writer. 3.90 l, Lewis Milestone (1895-1980), film director. 5 l, Vincent van Gogh (1853-90), painter.

2003, Nov. 14
456-460 A134 Set of 5 *10.00 10.00*

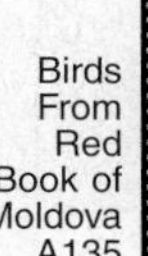

Birds From Red Book of Moldova A135

Designs: 40b, Cygnus olor. 2 l, Egretta alba. 3 l, Aquila rapax, vert. 5 l, Tetrax tetrax, vert.

2003, Dec. 18 **Litho.** *Perf. 13¾*
461-464 A135 Set of 4 *7.00 7.00*
464a Souvenir sheet, #461-464, perf. 13 *7.00 7.00*

Famous People — A136

Designs: 40b, Natalia Gheorghiu (1914-2001), surgeon. 1.50 l, Metropolitan Dosoftei (1624-93).

2004, Apr. 30 **Litho.** *Perf. 14x14½*
465-466 A136 Set of 2 *1.75 1.75*

Europa A137

Designs: 40b, Archaeological dig. 4.40 l, Tourists at winery.

2004, June 25 **Litho.** *Perf. 14x14½*
467-468 A137 Set of 2 *4.50 4.50*
468a Booklet pane, 2 each #467-468 *9.00* —
Complete booklet, #468a *9.00*

Stephen the Great (1437-1504), Prince of Moldavia — A138

Stephen the Great and: 40b, Soroca Fortress. 2 l, Capriana Monastery.
4.40 l, Map of Moldova.

2004, July 2 *Perf. 14½x14*
469-470 A138 Set of 2 *1.75 1.75*

Souvenir Sheet

471 A138 4.40 l multi + 2 labels *3.00 3.00*

FIFA (Fédération Internationale de Football Association), Cent. — A139

No. 472: a, 2 l, Goalie catching ball. b, 4.40 l, Player dribbling ball.
Illustration reduced.

2004, Aug. 14
472 A139 Horiz. pair, #a-b, + central label *5.00 5.00*

Souvenir Sheet

Iasi-Chisinau Operation Memorial — A140

2004, Aug. 22
473 A140 2 l multi + label *1.50 1.50*
Iasi-Chisinau Operation, 60th anniv.

2004 Summer Olympics, Athens — A141

Designs: 40b, Boxing. 4.40 l, Weight lifting.

2004, Dec. 28 *Perf. 14x14½*
474-475 A141 Set of 2 *3.25 3.25*

Ancient Jewelry A142

Designs: 40b, Earrings, 4th cent. B.C. 1 l, Necklace, 4th-3rd cent. B.C. 1.50 l, Silver temple earring, 14th-15th cent. 2 l, Bronze bracelet, 4th cent. B.C.

2004, Dec. 28
476-479 A142 Set of 4 *3.25 3.25*

Flowering Bushes — A143

Designs: 40b, Ephedra distachya. 1.50 l, Pyrus elaeagrifolia. No. 482, 2 l, Padus avium. No. 483, 2 l, Crataegus pentagyna.

2004, Dec. 29 *Perf. 14½x14*
480-483 A143 Set of 4 *4.00 4.00*

Locomotives — A144

Designs: 60b, ER. 1 l, ChME3. 1.50 l, D 777-3. 4.40 l, 3TE10M.

2005, Apr. 2 **Litho.** *Perf. 14x14½*
484-487 A144 Set of 4 *5.00 5.00*

St. George's Church, Capriana Monastery — A145

2005, May 6 *Perf. 14½x14*
488 A145 40b multi *.40 .40*

End of World War II, 60th Anniv. — A146

2005, May 9
489 A146 1.50 l multi *.90 .90*

Europa A147

Designs: 1.50 l, Cheese, corn meal mush, pitcher and cup. 4.40 l, Pies, stein and bottle of wine.

2005, May 20 *Perf. 14x14½*
490-491 A147 Set of 2 *4.75 4.75*
491a Miniature sheet, 3 each #490-491 *14.50* —

No. 491a was sold with, but not attached to, a booklet cover.

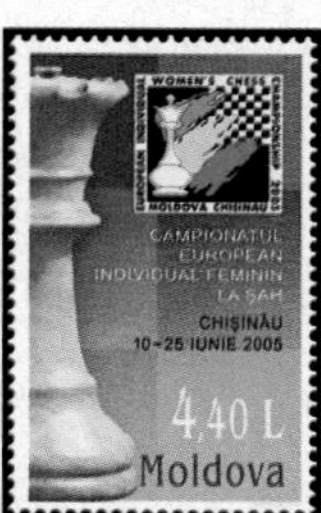

European Women's Chess Championships, Chisinau — A148

2005, June 10 *Perf. 14½x14*
492 A148 4.40 l multi *3.00 3.00*

Composers — A149

Designs: 40b, Serghei Lunchevici (1934-95). 1 l, Valeriu Cupcea (1929-89). 2 l, Anton Rubinstein (1829-94).

2005, July 1 *Perf. 14x14½*
493-495 A149 Set of 3 *2.50 2.50*

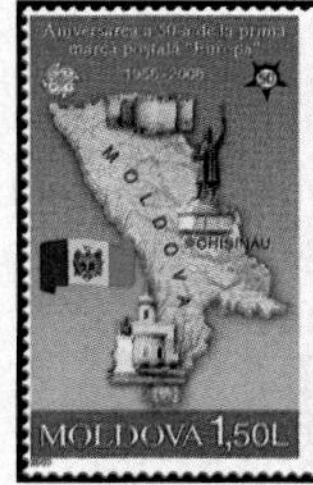

First Europa Stamps, 50th Anniv. (in 1996) — A150

Designs: No. 496, 1.50 l, Moldovan landmarks, flag and map. 15 l, Vignette of 1956 Europa stamps.
No. 498a, Moldoveanca, by Anatol Silitkii.

2005, July 20 **Litho.** *Perf. 14½x14*
496-497 A150 Set of 2 *5.00 5.00*

Souvenir Sheet

498 Sheet, #497, 498a *5.00 5.00*
a. A150 1.50 l multi *.55 .55*

World Summit on the Information Society, Tunis — A151

2005, Sept. 14
499 A151 4.40 l multi *2.50 2.50*

Souvenir Sheet

Moldovan Passports, 10th Anniv. — A152

No. 500: a, 40b, Three passport pages with pictures. b, 1.50 l, Two closed passports. c, 4.40 l, Two passport pages with pictures.

2005, Sept. 16
500 A152 Sheet of 3, #a-c *4.25 4.25*

Endangered Reptiles and Amphibians — A153

Designs: Nos. 501, 505a, 40b, Emys orbicularis. Nos. 502, 505b, 1 l, Eremias arguta. Nos. 503, 505c, 1.50 l, Pelobates fuscus. Nos. 504, 505d, 2 l, Vipera ursini.

2005, Sept. 29 ***Perf. 14x14½***

With White Frames

501-504 A153 Set of 4 *3.75 3.75*

Souvenir Sheet

Without White Frames

505 A153 Sheet of 4, #a-d, + 2 labels *3.75 3.75*

St. Nicholas Church — A154

2005, Oct. 30 ***Perf. 14½x14***

506 A154 40b multi *.35 .35*

Christmas — A155

Designs: 40b, St. Ierarh Nicolae Church, Falesti. 6 l, Varzaresti Monastery.

2005, Dec. 19 **Litho.** ***Perf. 14x14½***

507-508 A155 Set of 2 3.75 3.75

Makler Newspaper, 15th Anniv. — A156

2006, Jan. 20

509 A156 60b multi .30 .30

2006 Winter Olympics, Turin — A157

Designs: 60b, Luge. 6.20 l, Skiing.

2006, Feb. 10

510-511 A157 Set of 2 3.00 3.00

Buildings — A158

Designs: 22b, Post Office No. 21, Balti. 40b, Saint Gates, Chisinau. 53b, Museum of History, Cahul. 57b, Old Post and Telegraph Office, Soroca. 60b, Adormirea Maicii Domnului Church, Copceac. 3.50 l, National Museum of Fine Arts, Chisinau.

2006, Mar. 23 ***Perf. 14½x14***

512 A158 22b dark blue .50 .50
513 A158 40b brown .50 .50
514 A158 53b dark blue .50 .50
515 A158 57b green .50 .50
516 A158 60b olive green .50 .50
517 A158 3.50 l red brown 1.60 1.60
Nos. 512-517 (6) 4.10 4.10

Textile Arts and Native Costumes — A159

Designs: 40b, Crocheting. 60b, Moldavian woman, 19th cent., vert. 3 l, Moldavian man, 19th cent., vert. 4.50 l, Embroidery.

2006, Apr. 14 ***Perf. 14x14½, 14½x14***

518-521 A159 Set of 4 3.25 3.25

Gheorghe Mustea, Conductor — A160

2006, Apr. 28 ***Perf. 14x14½***

522 A160 60b multi .30 .30

Europa A161

Designs: 60b, Children and town on globe. 4.50 l, Artist and musicians, vert.

2006, May 6 ***Perf. 14x14½, 14½x14***

523-524 A161 Set of 2 2.75 2.75
524a Miniature sheet, 3 each #523-524 8.25 8.25

No. 524a was sold with, but not attached to, a booklet cover.

37th Chess Olympiad, Turin — A162

2006, May 24 ***Perf. 14x14½***

525 A162 4.50 l multi 1.75 1.75

2006 World Cup Soccer Championships, Germany — A163

World Cup, emblem and: 2 l, Players. 3 l, Mascot. 4.50 l, Players, diff.

2006, June 28

526-528 A163 Set of 3 4.00 4.00

Famous People — A164

Designs: 40b, Ion Halippa (1871-1941), archaeologist. 1 l, Eufrosinia Cuza (1856-1910), singer. 2 l, Petre Stefanuca (1906-42), folklorist. 4.50 l, Wolfgang Amadeus Mozart (1756-91), composer.

2006, Aug. 11 ***Perf. 14½x14***

529-532 A164 Set of 4 5.00 5.00

Endangered Animals — A165

Designs: 60b, Martes martes. 1 l, Mustela erminea. 2 l, Mustela lutreola. 3 l, Mustela eversmanni.
6.20 l, Felis silvestris, vert.

2006, Aug. 16 ***Perf. 14x14½***

533-536 A165 Set of 4 3.00 3.00

Souvenir Sheet

Perf. 14½x14

537 A165 6.20 l multi + label 2.75 2.75

Independence, 15th Anniv. — A166

2006, Aug. 27 ***Perf. 14½x14***

538 A166 2.60 l multi 1.25 1.25

Dogs A167

Designs: 40b, German shepherd. 60b, Collie. 2 l, Standard poodle. 6.20 l, Hungarian greyhound.

2006, Sept. 8 ***Perf. 14x14½***

539-542 A167 Set of 4 3.75 3.75
542a Sheet, 2 each #539-542 7.50 7.50

National Wine Day — A168

2006, Oct. 7

543 A168 60b multi .35 .35

Christmas — A169

Paintings by: 40b, Valerii, Metleaev, 1988. 3 l, Mihail Statnii, 1986, vert. 6.20 l, Elena Bontea, 1973.

Perf. 14x14½, 14½x14

2006, Dec. 12 **Litho.**

544 A169 40b multi .30 .30
545 A169 3 l multi .80 .80
546 A169 6.20 l multi 1.90 1.90
a. Strip of 3, #544-546 3.00 3.00

Nos. 544 and 545 were each printed in sheets of 10 and in sheets of 9 containing 3 each of Nos. 544-546.

No. 25 Surcharged

Methods and Perfs As Before

2007, Jan. 11

547 A6 85b on 25k #547 .65 .65

Portraits in Natl. Art Museum — A170

Designs: 65b, Petrarch, by Raphael. 85b, Napoleon Bonaparte, by unknown artist. 2 l, Freidrich von Schiller, by Johann Gotthard Muller. 4.50 l, Johann Wolfgang von Goethe by James Hopwood.

2007, Feb. 28 **Litho.** ***Perf. 14½x14***

548-551 A170 Set of 4 2.50 2.50

Mushrooms — A171

Designs: 65b, Morchella steppicola. 85b, Phylloporus rhodoxantus. 2 l, Amanita solitaria. 6.20 l, Boletus aereus.

2007, Apr. 23 **Litho.** ***Perf. 14x14½***

552-555 A171 Set of 4 2.75 2.75

Europa A172

Designs: 2.85 l, Scouts with pencil and paint brush. 4.50 l, Scouts examining butterfly.

2007, May 8

556-557 A172 Set of 2 2.25 2.25

Scouting, cent.

No. 83 Surcharged in Blue or Black

Methods and Perfs As Before

2007, June 7

558 A19 25b on 3k #83 (Bl) .30 .30
559 A19 85b on 3k #83 (Bk) .30 .30

Cats
A173

Designs: 65b, Mixed breed. 1 l, Siamese, vert. 1.50 l, Birman, vert. 6.20 l, Persian.

Perf. 14x14½, 14½x14

2007, June 20 **Litho.**
560-563 A173 Set of 4 3.00 3.00

Birds
A174

Designs: 75b, Otis tarda. 1 l, Neophron percnopterus. 2.50 l, Lyrurus tetrix. 5 l, Gyps fulvus.
6.20 l, Tetrao urogallus.

2007, Aug. 14 **Litho.** ***Perf. 14x14½***
564-567 A174 Set of 4 3.00 3.00

Souvenir Sheet

568 A174 6.20 l multi + label 2.00 2.00

Dniester River Fish
Preservation — A175

No. 569: a, Acipenser gueldenstaedtii. b, Zingel zingel.

2007, Sept. 6
569 Horiz. pair + central label 1.25 1.25
a. A175 1 l multi .30 .30
b. A175 3 l multi .95 .95

See Ukraine No. 694.

Famous People — A176

Designs: 75b, Ion Luca Caragiale (1852-1912), writer. 1 l, Anastasia Dicescu (1887-1945), opera singer. 3 l, Mircea Eliade (1907-86), historian.
6.20 l, Maria Biesu, opera singer, vert.

2007, Sept. 15 ***Perf. 14x14½***
570-572 A176 Set of 3 1.50 1.50

Souvenir Sheet

Perf. 14½x14

573 A176 6.20 l multi + label 2.00 2.00

World Chess Championships,
Mexico — A177

2007, Sept. 29 ***Perf. 14x14½***
574 A177 6.20 l multi 1.90 1.90

A178

Christmas — A179

2007, Dec. 1 **Litho.** ***Perf. 14x14½***
575 A178 1 l multi .25 .25
576 A179 4.50 l multi 1.00 1.00
a. Miniature sheet, 6 #575, 3 #576 4.00 4.00

Covered
Wells — A180

Well in: 10b, Peresecina. 75b, Duruitoarea. 1 l, Ciripcau, vert. 3 l, Ocnita, vert.

2008, Feb. 19 ***Perf. 14½x14, 14x14½***
577-580 A180 Set of 4 1.10 1.10

2008 Summer Olympics,
Beijing — A181

Designs: 1 l, Cycling. 6.20 l, Boxing. 15 l, Weight lifting.

2008, Mar. 5 ***Perf. 14x14½***
581-583 A181 Set of 3 5.25 5.25

Europa
A182

Designs: 3.50 l, Post rider, scroll, castle. 4.50 l, Letters, computer screen.

2008, Apr. 30 **Litho.** ***Perf. 14x14½***
584-585 A182 Set of 2 2.00 2.00
585a Sheet, 2 each #584-585 4.00 4.00

No. 585a was sold with, but not attached to, a booklet cover.

First Postage Stamps of Moldavia,
150th Anniv. — A183

Designs: 1 l, Romania #1-2. 3 l, Romania #3-4.

2008, May 23
586-587 A183 Set of 2 1.00 1.00
587a Booklet pane of 4, 2 each #586-587 2.00 2.00
Complete booklet, #587a 2.00

UEFA Euro 2008 Soccer
Championships, Austria and
Switzerland — A184

2008, June 28
588 A184 4.50 l multi 1.25 1.25

Flowers — A185

Designs: 1 l, Maianthemum bifolium. 3 l, Hepatica nobilis. 5 l, Nymphaea alba.

2008, Aug. 19 **Litho.** ***Perf. 14x14½***
589-591 A185 Set of 3 2.40 2.40
591a Souvenir sheet of 3, #589-591, + 3 labels 2.40 2.40

Famous
People
A186

Designs: 1.20 l, Onisifor Ghibu (1883-1972), teacher. 1.50 l, Ciprian Porumbescu (1853-83), composer. 3 l, Leo Tolstoy (1828-1910), author. 4.50 l, Maria Tanase (1913-63), singer.

2008, Sept. 5
592-595 A186 Set of 4 2.75 2.75

Deer — A187

No. 596: a, Cervus nippon. b, Cervus elaphus sibiricus.
Illustration reduced.

2008, Sept. 18
596 A187 3 l Horiz. pair, #a-b 1.50 1.50

See Kazakhstan No. 577.

Souvenir Sheet

Bender (Tighina), 600th
Anniv. — A188

2008, Oct. 8
597 A188 4.20 l brn & buff + 3 labels 1.00 1.00

Princes — A189

Designs: 1.20 l, Prince Antiokh Cantemir (1708-44). 3 l, Prince Dimitrie Cantemir (1673-1723).

2008, Oct. 27 ***Perf. 14½x14***
598 A189 1.20 l brown .30 .30

Souvenir Sheet

599 A189 3 l brown + label .70 .70

Princes — A190

Designs: 85b, Prince Mihail Grigore Sutu (1784-1864). 1.20 l, Prince Grigore Alexandru Ghica (1807-57). 1.50 l, Prince Mihail Sturza (1795-1884). 2 l, Prince Alexandru Ipsilanti (1726-1807). 3 l, Prince Ioan Sandu Sturza (1761-1842). 4.50 l, Prince Scarlat Callimachi (1773-1821).
6.20 l, Prince Alexandru Ioan Cuza (1820-73).

2008, Nov. 14
600-605 A190 Set of 6 3.25 3.25

Souvenir Sheet

606 A190 6.20 l multi + 5 labels 1.50 1.50

No. 582 Overprinted in Bronze

2008, Nov. 21 ***Perf. 14x14½***
607 A161 6.20 l multi 1.50 1.50

Souvenir Sheet

Moldovan Presidency of the Central
European Initiative — A191

No. 608 — CEI emblems and map of: a, 1.20 l, Western Europe. b, 4.50 l, Eastern Europe.

2008, Nov. 27 ***Perf. 14½x14***
608 A191 Sheet of 2, #a-b 1.40 1.40

AIR POST STAMPS

TU-144 — AP1

1992-93 Litho. *Perf. 12*

No.	Type	Denomination	Unused	Used
C1	AP1	1.75r maroon	.25	.25
C2	AP1	2.50r red vio	.30	.30
C3	AP1	7.75r blue	1.00	1.00
C4	AP1	8.50r blue green	1.25	1.25
C5	AP1	25r red brown	.35	.35
C6	AP1	45r brown	.60	.60
C7	AP1	50r olive green	.75	.75
C8	AP1	90r blue	1.50	1.50
		Nos. C1-C8 (8)	6.00	6.00

Issued: #C1-C4, 7/20/92; #C5-C8, 7/24/93.

POSTAGE DUE STAMPS

Dove, Envelope — D1

1994, Nov. 12 Litho. *Perf. 14*

No.	Type	Denomination	Unused	Used
J1	D1	30b lt olive & brown	.55	.55
J2	D1	40b pale vio & slate	.65	.65

In use, Nos. J1-J2 were torn apart, one half being affixed to the postage due item and the other half being pasted into the postman's record book. Values are for unused and canceled-to-order pairs.

MONACO

ˈmä-nə-ˌkō

LOCATION — Southern coast of France, bordering on the Mediterranean Sea
GOVT. — Principality
AREA — 481 acres
POP. — 31,842 (2001 est.)
CAPITAL — Monaco

100 Centimes = 1 Franc
100 Cents = 1 Euro (2002)

Catalogue values for unused stamps in this country are for Never Hinged items, beginning with Scott 182 in the regular postage section, Scott B51 in the semi-postal section, Scott C2 in the airpost section, Scott CB1 in the airpost semi-postal section, and Scott J28 in the postage due section.

Values for unused stamps are for examples with original gum as defined in the catalogue introduction. Very fine examples of Nos. 1-181, B1-B50, C1 and J1-J27 will have perforations clear of the design and/or frameline. Very well centered are worth more than the values quoted.

Prince Charles III — A1

Prince Albert I — A2

1885 Unwmk. Typo. *Perf. 14x13½*

No.	Type	Denomination	Unused	Used
1	A1	1c olive green	25.00	17.50
2	A1	2c dull lilac	57.50	27.50
3	A1	5c blue	70.00	35.00
4	A1	10c brown, *straw*	85.00	40.00
5	A1	15c rose	350.00	18.00
6	A1	25c green	700.00	75.00
7	A1	40c slate, *rose*	85.00	45.00
8	A1	75c black, *rose*	275.00	125.00
9	A1	1fr black, *yellow*	1,750.	500.00
10	A1	5fr rose, *green*	3,000.	2,000.

1891-1921

No.	Type	Denomination	Unused	Used
11	A2	1c olive green	.70	.70
12	A2	2c dull violet	.80	.80
13	A2	5c blue	50.00	6.00
14	A2	5c yellow grn ('01)	.40	.35
15	A2	10c brown, *straw*	100.00	16.00
16	A2	10c carmine ('01)	3.25	.70
17	A2	15c rose	175.00	10.00
a.		Double impression	*1,400.*	
18	A2	15c vio brn, *straw* ('01)	3.00	1.00
19	A2	15c gray green ('21)	2.00	*2.50*
20	A2	25c green	275.00	32.50
21	A2	25c deep blue ('01)	15.00	5.00
22	A2	40c slate, *rose* ('94)	3.50	2.40
23	A2	50c violet, *org*	7.00	4.75
24	A2	75c vio brn, *buff* ('94)	27.50	18.00
25	A2	75c ol brn, *buff* ('21)	20.00	*24.00*
26	A2	1fr black, *yellow*	19.00	11.00
27	A2	5fr rose, *grn*	100.00	87.50
28	A2	5fr dull violet ('21)	200.00	*250.00*
29	A2	5fr dark green ('21)	22.50	27.50
		Nos. 11-29 (19)	1,024.	*500.70*

The handstamp "OL" in a circle of dots is a cancellation, not an overprint.

For shades, see the *Scott Classic Specialized Catalogue.*

See No. 1782. For overprints and surcharges see Nos. 30-35, 57-59, B1.

Stamps of 1901-21 Overprinted or Surcharged:

1921, Mar. 5

No.	Type	Denomination	Unused	Used
30	A2	5c lt green	.70	.70
31	A2	75c brown, *buff*	5.25	*6.25*
32	A2	2fr on 5fr dull vio	32.50	*52.50*
		Nos. 30-32 (3)	38.45	*59.45*

Issued to commemorate the birth of Princess Antoinette, daughter of Princess Charlotte and Prince Pierre, Comte de Polignac.

Stamps and Type of 1891-1921 Surcharged

1922

No.	Type	Denomination	Unused	Used
33	A2	20c on 15c gray green	1.10	*1.40*
34	A2	25c on 10c rose	.70	.90
35	A2	50c on 1fr black, *yel*	6.00	*6.50*
		Nos. 33-35 (3)	7.80	*8.80*

Prince Albert I — A5

Oceanographic Museum — A6

"The Rock" of Monaco — A7

Royal Palace — A8

1922-24 Engr. *Perf. 11*

No.	Type	Denomination	Unused	Used
40	A5	25c deep brn	4.00	*4.75*
41	A6	30c dark green	.90	.90
42	A6	30c scarlet ('23)	.50	.45
43	A6	50c ultra	4.25	4.25
44	A7	60c black brn	.35	.35
45	A7	1fr black, *yellow*	.25	.25
46	A7	2fr scarlet	.50	.45
47	A8	5fr red brown	32.50	*37.50*
48	A8	5fr dk green, *lil* ('24)	10.50	10.50
49	A8	10fr carmine	14.00	18.00
		Nos. 40-49 (10)	67.75	*77.40*

Nos. 40-49 exist imperf.

For shades, see the *Scott Classic Specialized Catalogue.*

Prince Louis II
A9 A10

St. Dévote Viaduct ("Bridge of Suicides") A11

1923-24 Engr.

No.	Type	Denomination	Unused	Used
50	A9	10c deep green	.35	*.55*
51	A9	15c car rose ('24)	.45	*.70*
52	A9	20c red brown	.35	*.55*
53	A9	25c violet	.25	*.45*
a.		Without engraver's name	25.00	25.00
54	A11	40c orange brn ('24)	.65	.55
55	A10	50c ultra	.35	*.45*
		Nos. 50-55 (6)	2.40	*3.25*

The 25c comes in 2 types, one with larger "5" and "c" touching frame of numeral tablet.

Stamps of the 1922-24 issues sometimes show parts of the letters of a papermaker's watermark.

The engraved stamps of type A11 measure 31x21½mm. The typographed stamps of that design measure 36x21½mm.

See #86-88. For surcharges see #95-96.

Stamps and Type of 1891-1921 Surcharged

1924, Aug. 5 *Perf. 14x13½*

No.	Type	Denomination	Unused	Used
57	A2	45c on 50c brn ol, *buff*	.50	*.70*
a.		Double surcharge	775.00	775.00
58	A2	75c on 1fr blk, *yel*	.50	*.70*
a.		Double surcharge	*550.00*	*550.00*
59	A2	85c on 5fr dk green	.50	*.70*
a.		Double surcharge	650.00	650.00
		Nos. 57-59 (3)	1.50	2.10

Grimaldi Family Coat of Arms — A12

Prince Louis II — A13

Louis II — A14

View of Monaco A15

1924-33 Typo.

No.	Type	Denomination	Unused	Used
60	A12	1c gray black	.20	.20
61	A12	2c red brown	.20	.20
62	A12	3c brt violet ('33)	2.75	1.90
63	A12	5c orange ('26)	.35	.30
64	A12	10c blue	.20	.20
65	A13	15c apple green	.20	.20
66	A13	15c dull vio ('29)	2.75	1.90
67	A13	20c violet	.20	.20
68	A13	20c rose	.35	.25
69	A13	25c rose	.20	.20
70	A13	25c red,*yel*	.20	*.25*
71	A13	30c orange	.20	.20
72	A13	40c black brown	.25	.20
73	A13	40c lt bl, *bluish*	.35	.35
74	A13	45c gray black ('26)	.90	.70
75	A14	50c myrtle grn ('25)	.20	*.25*
76	A13	50c brown, *org*	.20	.20
77	A14	60c yellow brn ('25)	.20	.25
78	A13	60c ol grn, *grnsh*	.20	*.25*
79	A13	75c ol grn, *grnsh* ('26)	.70	.35
80	A13	75c car, *straw* ('26)	.35	.20
81	A13	75c slate	.90	.55
82	A13	80c red, *yel* ('26)	.40	.30
83	A13	90c rose, *straw* ('27)	2.00	1.60
84	A13	1.25fr bl, *bluish* ('26)	.20	.20
85	A13	1.50fr bl, *bluish* ('27)	3.75	1.90
		Size: 36x21½mm		
86	A11	1fr blk, *orange*	.20	*.25*
87	A11	1.05fr red violet ('26)	.20	*.25*
88	A11	1.10fr blue grn ('27)	8.00	6.00
89	A15	2fr vio & ol brn ('25)	2.75	1.00
90	A15	3fr rose & ultra, *yel* ('27)	25.00	12.00
91	A15	5fr green & rose ('25)	8.50	6.00
92	A15	10fr yel brn & bl ('25)	25.00	17.50
		Nos. 60-92 (33)	88.05	56.30
		Set, never hinged	175.00	

Nos. 60 to 74 and 76 exist imperforate.

For surcharges see Nos. 93-94, 97-99, C1.

Type of 1924-33 Surcharged with New Value and Bars

1926-31

No.	Type	Denomination	Unused	Used
93	A13	30c on 25c rose	.30	.25
94	A13	50c on 60c ol grn, *grnsh* ('28)	1.50	.35
95	A11	50c on 1.05fr red vio ('28)	1.10	.70
a.		Double surcharge	65.00	
96	A11	50c on 1.10fr bl grn ('31)	14.00	8.75
97	A13	50c on 1.25fr bl, *bluish* (R) ('28)	1.60	.65
98	A13	1.25fr on 1fr bl, *bluish*	.80	.50
99	A15	1.50fr on 2fr vio & ol brn ('28)	7.00	5.25
		Nos. 93-99 (7)	26.30	16.45
		Set, never hinged	40.00	

Princes Charles III, Louis II and Albert I A17

1928, Feb. 18 Engr. *Perf. 11*

No.	Type	Denomination	Unused	Used
100	A17	50c dull carmine	2.50	*4.75*
101	A17	1.50fr dark blue	2.50	*4.75*
102	A17	3fr dark violet	2.50	*4.75*
		Nos. 100-102 (3)	7.50	14.25
		Set, never hinged	18.00	

Nos. 100-102 were sold exclusively at the Intl. Phil. Exhib. at Monte Carlo, Feb., 1928. One set was sold to each purchaser of a ticket of admission to the exhibition which cost 5fr.

Exist imperf. Value, set $27.50

Old Watchtower A20

Royal Palace A21

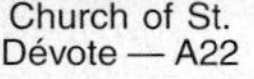
Church of St. Dévote — A22

Prince Louis II — A23

"The Rock" of Monaco A24

Gardens of Monaco A25

Fortifications and Harbor — A26

1932-37 ***Perf. 13, 14x13½***

No.	Type	Denomination	Color	Unused	Used
110	A20	15c	lilac rose	.80	.25
111	A20	20c	orange brn	.80	.25
112	A21	25c	olive blk	1.10	.35
113	A22	30c	yellow grn	1.40	.35
114	A23	40c	dark brown	3.25	1.40
115	A24	45c	brown red	3.50	1.10
a.		45c	red	425.00	425.00
116	A23	50c	purple	3.25	.85
117	A25	65c	blue green	3.50	1.10
118	A26	75c	deep blue	4.00	1.75
119	A23	90c	red	9.50	3.25
120	A22	1fr	red brown ('33)	27.50	7.75
121	A26	1.25fr	rose lilac	6.75	4.50
122	A23	1.50fr	ultra	40.00	10.50
123	A21	1.75fr	rose lilac	35.00	9.50
124	A21	1.75fr	car rose ('37)	24.00	13.00
125	A24	2fr	dark blue	13.50	4.75
126	A20	3fr	purple	20.00	9.00
127	A21	3.50fr	orange ('35)	47.50	32.50
128	A22	5fr	violet	27.50	20.00
129	A21	10fr	deep blue	125.00	70.00
130	A25	20fr	black	175.00	140.00
		Nos. 110-130 (21)		572.85	332.15
		Set, never hinged		1,150.	

Postage Due Stamps of 1925-32 Surcharged or Overprinted in Black:

1937-38 ***Perf. 14x13***

No.	Type	Denomination	Description	Unused	Used
131	D3	5c	on 10c violet	1.00	1.00
132	D3	10c	violet	1.00	1.00
133	D3	15c	on 30c bister	1.00	1.00
134	D3	20c	on 30c bister	1.00	1.00
135	D3	25c	on 60c red	1.50	1.50
136	D3	30c	bister	2.40	2.40
137	D3	40c	on 60c red	2.40	2.40
138	D3	50c	on 60c red	2.40	2.40
139	D3	65c	on 1fr lt bl	2.25	2.00
140	D3	85c	on 1fr lt bl	5.00	4.50
141	D3	1fr	light blue	7.75	7.75
142	D3	2.15fr	on 2fr dl red	7.75	7.75
143	D3	2.25fr	on 2fr dl red ('38)	19.00	19.00
144	D3	2.50fr	on 2fr dl red ('38)	29.00	29.00
		Nos. 131-144 (14)		83.45	82.70
		Set, never hinged		175.00	

Grimaldi Arms — A27

Prince Louis II — A28

1937-43 **Engr.**

No.	Type	Denomination	Color	Unused	Used
145	A27	1c	dk vio brn ('38)	.20	.20
146	A27	2c	emerald	.20	.20
147	A27	3c	brt red violet	.20	.20
148	A27	5c	red	.20	.20
149	A27	10c	ultra	.20	.20
149A	A27	10c	black ('43)	.20	.20
150	A27	15c	violet ('39)	1.75	1.50
150A	A27	30c	dull grn ('43)	.20	.20
150B	A27	40c	rose car ('43)	.20	.20
150C	A27	50c	brt violet ('43)	.20	.20
151	A28	55c	red brown ('38)	5.75	2.25
151A	A27	60c	Prus blue ('43)	.20	.20
152	A28	65c	violet ('38)	26.00	12.50
153	A28	70c	red brn ('39)	.35	.35
153A	A27	70c	red brn ('43)	.20	.20
154	A28	90c	violet ('39)	.35	.30
155	A28	1fr	rose red ('38)	16.00	9.50
156	A28	1.25fr	rose red ('39)	.35	.35
157	A28	1.75fr	ultra ('38)	16.00	9.50
158	A28	2.25fr	ultra ('39)	.35	.25
		Nos. 145-158 (20)		69.10	38.70
		Set, never hinged		150.00	

#151, 152, 155, 157 exist imperforate.

Souvenir Sheet

Prince Louis II — A29

1938, Jan. 17 **Unwmk.** ***Imperf.***

No.	Type	Denomination	Color	Unused	Used
159	A29	10fr	magenta	65.00	65.00
		Never hinged		175.00	

"Fête Nationale" Jan. 17, 1938. Size: 99x120mm.

Cathedral of Monaco — A30

St. Nicholas Square — A31

Palace Gate — A32

Palace of Monaco — A34

Panorama of Monaco A33

Harbor of Monte Carlo A35

1939-46 ***Perf. 13***

No.	Type	Denomination	Color	Unused	Used
160	A30	20c	rose lilac	.25	.25
161	A31	25c	gldn brown	.45	.30
162	A32	30c	dk blue grn	.35	.30
162A	A32	30c	brown red ('40)	.35	.25
163	A31	40c	henna brn	.70	.50
164	A33	45c	brt red vio	.50	.50
165	A34	50c	dk blue grn	.35	.25
166	A32	60c	rose carmine	.40	.35
166A	A32	60c	dk green ('40)	.90	.70
166B	A35	70c	brt red vio ('41)	.40	.25
167	A35	75c	dark green	.40	.25
167A	A30	80c	dull green ('43)	.20	*.25*
168	A34	1fr	brown black	.40	.20
168A	A33	1fr	claret ('43)	.20	.20
168B	A35	1.20fr	ultra ('46)	.25	*.35*
168C	A34	1.30fr	brn blk ('41)	.40	.35
168D	A31	1.50fr	ultra ('46)	.40	.40
169	A31	2fr	rose violet	.40	.30
169A	A35	2fr	lt ultra ('43)	.20	.20
169B	A34	2fr	green ('46)	.35	.25
170	A33	2.50fr	red	25.00	17.50
171	A33	2.50fr	dp blue ('40)	1.75	1.75
172	A35	3fr	brown red	.45	.35
172A	A31	3fr	black ('43)	.20	.20
172B	A30	4fr	rose lil ('46)	1.25	.55
172C	A34	4.50fr	brt violet ('43)	.20	.20
173	A30	5fr	Prus blue	5.25	4.00
173A	A32	5fr	dp grn ('43)	.20	.20
173B	A34	6fr	lt violet ('46)	.70	.55
174	A33	10fr	green	1.40	*1.60*
174A	A30	10fr	dp bl ('43)	.20	*.25*
174B	A35	15fr	rose pink ('43)	.40	*.25*
175	A32	20fr	brt ultra	1.60	1.25
175A	A33	20fr	sepia ('43)	.40	.25
175B	A35	25fr	bl grn ('46)	1.40	1.25
		Nos. 160-175B (35)		48.25	36.55
		Set, never hinged		100.00	

See Nos. 214-221, 228-232, 274-275, 319-320, 407-408, 423, 426, 428-429, B36-B50.

Louis II Stadium A36

1939, Apr. 23 **Engr.**

No.	Type	Denomination	Color	Unused	Used
176	A36	10fr	dark green	100.00	*110.00*
		Never hinged		175.00	

Inauguration of Louis II Stadium.

Louis II Stadium A37

1939, Aug. 15

No.	Type	Denomination	Color	Unused	Used
177	A37	40c	dull green	1.25	1.25
178	A37	70c	brown black	1.60	1.60
179	A37	90c	dark violet	2.25	2.25
180	A37	1.25fr	copper red	3.00	3.00
181	A37	2.25fr	dark blue	4.25	4.25
		Nos. 177-181 (5)		12.35	12.35
		Set, never hinged		22.50	

8th International University Games.

Imperforates

Nearly all Monaco stamps from 1940 onward exist imperforate. Officially 20 sheets, ranging from 25 to 100 subjects, were left imperforate.

Catalogue values for unused stamps in this section, from this point to the end of the section, are for Never Hinged items.

Prince Louis II — A38

1941-46 ***Perf. 14x13***

No.	Type	Denomination	Color	Unused	Used
182	A38	40c	brown carmine	.65	.50
183	A38	80c	deep green	.65	.50
184	A38	1fr	rose violet	.25	.20
185	A38	1.20fr	green ('42)	.25	.20
186	A38	1.50fr	rose	.25	.20
187	A38	1.50fr	violet ('42)	.25	.20
187A	A38	2fr	lt green ('46)	.65	.35
188	A38	2.40fr	red ('42)	.25	.20
189	A38	2.50fr	deep ultra	1.10	*1.25*
190	A38	4fr	blue ('42)	.20	.20
		Nos. 182-190 (10)		4.50	3.80

Prince Louis II — A39

1943 ***Perf. 13***
191 A39 50fr purple 2.00 1.10

A40

Prince Louis II — A41

1946 **Unwmk.** **Engr.** ***Perf. 14x13***
192 A40 2.50fr dk blue green .70 .25
193 A40 3fr brt red violet .70 .25
194 A40 6fr brt red .70 .35
195 A40 10fr brt ultra .70 .35

Perf. 13
196 A41 50fr dp Prus green 4.00 2.10
197 A41 100fr red 5.25 2.75
Nos. 192-197 (6) 12.05 6.05

Nos. 196-197 exist imperforate.
See Nos. 222-227, 233-236. For overprints see Nos. C8-C9.

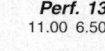

Franklin D. Roosevelt — A42

Harbor of Monte Carlo A43

Palace of Monaco A44

Map of Monaco — A45

Prince Louis II — A46

1946, Dec. 13 **Unwmk.** ***Perf. 13***
198 A42 10c red violet .50 .45
199 A43 30c deep blue .50 .45
200 A44 60c blue black .50 .45
201 A45 1fr sepia 1.50 1.25
202 A45 3fr lt violet 2.25 1.75
Nos. 198-202,B93,C14-C15,CB6 (9) 10.35 8.65

Issued in tribute to the memory of Franklin D. Roosevelt.

1947, May 15
203 A46 10fr dark blue green 4.50 4.50

25th anniv. of the reign of Prince Louis II. See Nos. B94, C20a.

Hurdler A47

Runner — A48

Designs: 2fr, Discus thrower. 2.50fr, Basketball. 4fr, Swimmer.

1948, July 1 ***Perf. 13***
204 A47 50c blue green .25 .25
205 A48 1fr rose brown .25 .25
206 A48 2fr grnsh blue 1.25 .85
207 A48 2.50fr vermilion 3.50 2.50
208 A48 4fr slate gray 4.00 3.25
Nos. 204-208,CB7-CB10 (9) 91.25 89.10

Issued to publicize Monaco's participation in the 1948 Olympic Games held at Wembley, England, during July and August.

Nymph Salmacis A49

Hercules — A50

Aristaeus — A51

Hyacinthus A52

François J. Bosio and Louis XIV Statue — A53

1948, July 12
209 A49 50c dark green .55 .35
210 A50 1fr red .55 .35
211 A51 2fr deep ultra 1.90 .75
212 A52 2.50fr deep violet 4.75 2.25
213 A53 4fr purple 4.75 2.50
Nos. 209-213,CB11-CB14 (9) 94.50 88.20

Issued to honor François J. Bosio (1768-1845), sculptor. No. 213 inscribed "J F Bosio."

Scenic Types of 1939

1948 **Engr.**
214 A30 50c sepia .35 .25
215 A31 60c rose pink .35 .25
216 A32 3fr violet rose 1.10 .35
217 A31 4fr emerald 1.10 .35
218 A34 8fr red brown 4.25 2.00
219 A34 10fr brown red 4.50 1.75
220 A33 20fr carmine rose 1.50 .65
221 A35 25fr gray black 32.50 16.00
Nos. 214-221 (8) 45.65 21.60

Louis II Type of 1946

1948, July ***Perf. 14x13***
222 A40 30c black .30 .20
223 A40 5fr orange brown .45 .30
224 A40 6fr purple 5.00 1.75
225 A40 10fr orange .45 .30
226 A40 12fr deep carmine 6.00 2.50
227 A40 18fr dark blue 9.50 6.00
Nos. 222-227 (6) 21.70 11.05

Scenic Types of 1939

1949 ***Perf. 13***
228 A33 5fr blue green .85 .35
229 A35 10fr orange 1.75 .65
230 A32 25fr blue 52.50 16.00
231 A30 40fr brown red 9.25 4.75
232 A30 50fr purple 5.75 1.00
Nos. 228-232 (5) 70.10 22.75

Louis II Type of 1946

1949, Mar. 10 ***Perf. 14x13***
233 A40 50c olive .35 .20
234 A40 1fr dk violet bl .25 .25
235 A40 12fr dk slate grn 8.50 6.00
236 A40 15fr brown carmine 8.50 3.50
Nos. 233-236 (4) 17.60 9.95

Hirondelle I A54

Cactus Plants — A55

Designs: 4fr, Oceanographic Museum. 5fr, Princess Alice II at Spitzbergen. 6fr, Albert I Monument. 10fr, Hirondelle II. 12fr, Albert I whaling. 18fr, Bison.

1949, Mar. 5 ***Perf. 13***
237 A54 2fr brt blue .25 .25
238 A55 3fr dark green .25 .25
239 A54 4fr blk brn & bl .25 .25
240 A54 5fr crimson 1.10 1.10
241 A55 6fr dark violet 1.00 1.00
242 A54 10fr black brown 1.25 1.25
243 A54 12fr brt red violet 2.75 2.75
244 A54 18fr dk brn & org brn 4.00 4.00
Nos. 237-244 (8) 10.85 10.85

See Nos. C21-C26.

Palace, Globe and Pigeon A56

1949-50 **Engr.** **Unwmk.**
245 A56 5fr blue green .60 .60
245A A56 10fr orange 7.00 7.00
246 A56 15fr carmine .60 .60
Nos. 245-246,C30-C33 (7) 21.35 21.35

75th anniversary of the UPU.
Nos. 245, 245A and 246 exist imperf.
Issued: 5fr, 15fr, 12/27; 10fr, 9/12/50.

Prince Rainier III
A57 A58

1950, Apr. 11
247 A57 10c red & blk brn .20 .20
248 A57 50c dp yel & dk brn .20 .20
249 A57 1fr purple .45 .35
250 A57 5fr dark green 3.50 1.90
251 A57 15fr carmine 5.25 5.25
252 A57 25fr ultra, ol grn & ind 5.25 5.25
Nos. 247-252,C34-C35 (8) 33.60 30.15

Enthronement of Prince Rainier III.

1950, Apr. **Engr.** ***Perf. 14x13***
253 A58 50c purple .35 .20
254 A58 1fr orange brown .35 .30
255 A58 8fr blue green 9.00 2.40
256 A58 12fr blue 2.25 .50
257 A58 15fr crimson 4.25 .70
Nos. 253-257 (5) 16.20 4.10

1951, Apr. 31 **Typo.**
258 A58 5fr emerald 12.00 4.75
259 A58 10fr orange 20.00 7.75

See Nos. 276-279.

Statue of Prince Albert I — A59

1951, Apr. 11 **Engr.** ***Perf. 13***
260 A59 15fr deep blue 11.00 6.50

Edmond and Jules de Goncourt A60

1951, Apr. 11
261 A60 15fr violet brown 11.00 6.50

50th anniversary of the foundation of Goncourt Academy.

St. Vincent de Paul — A61

Judgment of St. Dévote — A62

Symbolizing Monaco's Adoption of Catholicism — A63

Mosaic of the Immaculate Conception A64

Blessed Rainier of Westphalia A65

Holy Year, 1951: 50c, Pope Pius XII. 12fr, Prince Rainier III at Prayer. 15fr, St. Nicholas de Patare. 20fr, St. Roman. 25fr, St. Charles Borromée. 40fr, Cross, arms and Roman Coliseum. 50fr, Chapel of St. Dévote.

Inscribed: "Anno Santo"

1951, June 4 Unwmk. *Perf. 13*

No.	Type	Description	Unused	Used
262	A61	10c ultra & red	.25	.25
263	A61	50c dk rose lake & pur	.25	.25
264	A62	1fr brown & dk grn	.30	.30
265	A63	2fr vio brn & ver	.35	.35
266	A64	5fr blue green	.45	.45
267	A63	12fr rose violet	.70	.70
268	A63	15fr vermilion	4.50	4.50
269	A63	20fr red brown	6.50	6.50
270	A63	25fr ultra	9.00	9.00
271	A63	40fr dk car rose & pur	10.50	10.50
272	A63	50fr ol grn & dk vio brn	14.00	14.00
273	A65	100fr dk violet brn	27.50	27.50
		Nos. 262-273 (12)	74.30	74.30

Scenic Types of 1939-46

1951, Dec. 22 *Perf. 13*

No.	Type	Description	Unused	Used
274	A31	3fr deep turq green	2.75	.90
275	A32	30fr slate black	8.50	3.50

Rainier Type of 1950

1951, Dec. 22 *Perf. 14x13*

No.	Type	Description	Unused	Used
276	A58	6fr blue green	1.75	.75
277	A58	8fr orange	1.75	.75
278	A58	15fr indigo	2.50	.45
279	A58	18fr crimson	6.25	1.50
		Nos. 276-279 (4)	12.25	3.45

Radio Monte Carlo — A66

Knight in Armor — A67

1951, Dec. 22 *Perf. 13*

No.	Type	Description	Unused	Used
280	A66	1fr blue, car & org	1.10	.35
281	A66	15fr pur, car & rose vio	4.25	1.25
282	A66	30fr indigo & red brn	21.00	6.50
		Nos. 280-282 (3)	26.35	8.10

1951, Dec. 22

No.	Type	Description	Unused	Used
283	A67	1fr purple	1.25	.55
284	A67	5fr gray black	3.75	2.25
285	A67	8fr deep carmine	7.75	3.75
286	A67	15fr emerald	12.50	7.50
287	A67	30fr slate black	21.00	15.00
		Nos. 283-287 (5)	46.25	29.05

See Nos. 328-332, 2025-2026.

Nos. B96-B99a Surcharged with New Values and Bars in Black

1951, Dec. *Perf. 13½x13, Imperf.*

No.	Type	Description	Unused	Used
288	SP51	1fr on 10fr + 5fr	12.50	12.50
289	SP52	3fr on 15fr + 5fr	12.50	12.50
290	SP52	5fr on 25fr + 5fr	13.00	12.50
291	SP51	6fr on 40fr + 5fr	13.00	12.50
b.		Block of 4, #288-291	51.00	50.00

Gallery of Hercules, Royal Palace A68

1952, Apr. 26 Engr. *Perf. 13*

No.	Type	Description	Unused	Used
292	A68	5fr red brn & brn	2.25	.55
293	A68	15fr purple & lil rose	2.75	.75
294	A68	30fr indigo & ultra	3.25	.90
		Nos. 292-294 (3)	8.25	2.20

Opening of a philatelic museum at the royal palace, Apr. 26, 1952.

Basketball — A69

2fr, Soccer. 3fr, Sailing. 5fr, Cyclist. 8fr, Gymnastics. 15fr, Louis II Stadium.

1953, Feb. 23 Unwmk. *Perf. 11*

No.	Type	Description	Unused	Used
295	A69	1fr dk purple & mag	.25	.25
296	A69	2fr dk grn & sl bl	.25	.25
297	A69	3fr blue & lt blue	.25	.25
298	A69	5fr dk brn & grnsh blk	.90	.45
299	A69	8fr brown lake & red	2.25	1.00
300	A69	15fr bl, brn blk & dk grn	1.25	.90
		Nos. 295-300,C36-C39 (10)	78.15	53.10

Issued to publicize Monaco's participation in the Helsinki Olympic Games.

Books, Pens and Proof Pages A70

1953, June 29 *Perf. 13*

No.	Type	Description	Unused	Used
301	A70	5fr dark green	.55	.45
302	A70	15fr red brown	3.75	.70

Publication of a first edition of the unexpurgated diary of Edmond and Jules Goncourt.

Physalia and Laboratory Ship Hirondelle II — A71

1953, June 29

No.	Type	Description	Unused	Used
303	A71	2fr Prus green, pur & choc	.25	.20
304	A71	5fr dp mag, red & Prus grn	.90	.40
305	A71	15fr ultra, vio brn & Prus grn	3.25	1.75
		Nos. 303-305 (3)	4.40	2.35

50th anniversary of the discovery of anaphylaxis by Charles Richet and Paul Portier.

Frederic Ozanam — A72

Nun — A73

1954, Apr. 12 Engr. *Perf. 13*

No.	Type	Description	Unused	Used
306	A72	1fr bright red	.25	.25
307	A73	5fr dark blue	.50	.50
308	A72	15fr black	2.10	1.90
		Nos. 306-308 (3)	2.85	2.65

Centenary of the death of Frederic Ozanam, founder of the Society of Saint Vincent de Paul.

Jean Baptiste de la Salle
A74 A75

1954, Apr. 12

No.	Type	Description	Unused	Used
309	A74	1fr dark carmine	.25	.25
310	A75	5fr black brown	.50	.50
311	A74	15fr bright ultra	2.10	1.90
		Nos. 309-311 (3)	2.85	2.65

Jean Baptiste de la Salle, founder of the Christian Brothers Institute and saint.

A76

A77

Grimaldi Arms — A78

Knight in Armor — A79

Perf. 13½x14, 14x13½

1954, Apr. 12 Typo.

Various Forms of Grimaldi Arms in Black and Red or Black, Red and Deep Plum (5fr)

No.	Type	Description	Unused	Used
312	A76	50c black & mag	.20	.20
313	A77	70c black & aqua	.20	.20
314	A76	80c black, red & dk grn	.20	.20
315	A77	1fr violet blue	.20	.20
316	A77	2fr black & dp org	.25	.25
317	A77	3fr black & green	.25	.25
318	A78	5fr black & lt grn	.25	.25
		Nos. 312-318 (7)	1.55	1.55

Scenic Types of 1939-46

1954, Apr. 12 Engr. *Perf. 13*

No.	Type	Description	Unused	Used
319	A34	25fr bright red	3.75	.75
320	A31	75fr dark green	25.00	8.50

1954, Apr. 12 Unwmk. *Perf. 13*

No.	Type	Description	Unused	Used
321	A79	4fr dark red	1.50	.40
322	A79	8fr dark green	1.50	.80
323	A79	12fr dark purple	6.00	1.75
324	A79	24fr dark maroon	11.00	4.75
		Nos. 321-324 (4)	20.00	7.70

Nos. 321-324 were issued precanceled only. Values for precanceled stamps in first column are for those which have not been through the post and have original gum. Values in the second column are for postally used, gumless stamps.

See Nos. 400-404, 430-433, 466-469.

Lambarene Landing, Gabon — A80

Dr. Albert Schweitzer — A81

Design: 15fr, Lambarene hospital.

1955, Jan. 14 *Perf. 11x11½*

No.	Type	Description	Unused	Used
325	A80	2fr ol grn, bl grn & ind	.30	.25
326	A81	5fr dk grnsh bl & grn	1.40	1.40
327	A81	15fr dk bl grn, dp cl & brn blk	3.75	3.00
		Nos. 325-327 (3)	5.45	4.65

Issued to honor Dr. Albert Schweitzer, medical missionary. See No. C40.

Knight Type of 1951

1955, Jan. 14 *Perf. 13*

328	A67	5fr purple	3.50	1.10
329	A67	6fr red	6.25	2.25
330	A67	8fr red brown	6.25	3.25
331	A67	15fr ultra	15.00	5.00
332	A67	30fr dark green	25.00	15.00
		Nos. 328-332 (5)	56.00	26.60

Automobile and Representation of Eight European Cities — A82

Prince Rainier III — A83

1955, Jan. 14 **Unwmk.**

333	A82	100fr dk brown & red	90.00	65.00

25th Monte Carlo Automobile Rally.

1955, June 7 **Engr.** *Perf. 13*

334	A83	6fr green & vio brn	.70	.40
335	A83	8fr red & violet	.70	.40
336	A83	12fr carmine & green	.70	.40
337	A83	15fr purple & blue	1.40	.40
338	A83	18fr orange & blue	4.50	.40
339	A83	30fr ultra & gray	14.00	7.75
		Nos. 334-339 (6)	22.00	9.75

See Nos. 405-406, 424-425, 427, 462-465, 586, 603-604A, 725-728, 730, 789, 791.

"Five Weeks in a Balloon" — A84

"A Floating City" and Jules Verne — A85

"Michael Strogoff" — A86

"Around the World in 80 Days" — A87

USS Nautilus and Verne — A88

Designs (Scenes from Jules Verne's Books): 3fr, The House of Vapors. 6fr, The 500 Millions of the Begum. 8fr, The Magnificent Orinoco. 10fr, A Journey to the Center of the Earth. 25fr, Twenty Thousand Leagues under the Sea.

1955, June 7

340	A84	1fr red brn & bl gray	.20	.20
341	A85	2fr blue, ind & brn	.20	.20
342	A85	3fr red brn, gray & sl	.20	.20
343	A86	5fr car & blk brn	.25	.25
344	A84	6fr blk brn & bluish gray	.45	.45
345	A86	8fr ol grn & aqua	.35	.35
346	A85	10fr indigo, turq & brn	1.25	1.00
347	A87	15fr rose brn & ver	1.00	.70
348	A85	25fr bl grn, grn & gray	2.50	1.75
349	A88	30fr violet, turq & blk	6.25	5.25
		Nos. 340-349,C45 (11)	40.15	35.35

50th anniv. of the death of Jules Verne.

Virgin by Francois Brea — A89

Blessed Rainier — A90

Marian Year: 10fr, Pieta by Louis Brea.

1955, June 7

350	A89	5fr vio brn, gray & dk grn	.25	.25
351	A89	10fr vio brn, gray & dk grn	.40	.35
352	A90	15fr black brn & org brn	.60	.55
		Nos. 350-352 (3)	1.25	1.15

Rotary Emblem, World Map — A91

1955, June 7

353	A91	30fr blue & orange	1.10	1.10

50th anniv. of the founding of Rotary Intl.

George Washington — A92

Franklin D. Roosevelt — A93

Dwight D. Eisenhower — A94

Palace of Monaco, c. 1790 — A95

Palace of Monaco, c. 1750 — A96

Designs: 3fr, Abraham Lincoln. 30fr, Columbus landing in America. 40fr, Prince Rainier III. 100fr, Early Louisiana scene.

1956, Apr. 3 **Engr.** *Perf. 13*

354	A92	1fr dark purple	.20	.20
355	A93	2fr claret & dk pur	.30	.30
356	A93	3fr vio & dp ultra	.30	.30
357	A94	5fr brown lake	.40	.40
358	A95	15fr brn blk & vio brn	1.00	1.00
359	A95	30fr ind, blk & ultra	3.75	2.00
360	A94	40fr dk brn & vio brn	6.00	2.50
361	A96	50fr vermilion	6.00	2.50
362	A96	100fr Prus green	6.00	3.50
a.		Strip of 3, #360-362	19.00	19.00
		Nos. 354-362 (9)	23.95	12.70

5th Intl. Phil. Exhib. (FIPEX), NYC, Apr. 28-May 6, 1956.

Ski Jump, Cortina d'Ampezzo — A97

Design: 30fr, Olympic Scenes.

1956, Apr. 3

363	A97	15fr brn vio, brn & dk grn	1.10	.55
364	A97	30fr red orange	2.25	1.60

Issued to publicize Monaco's participation in the 1956 Olympic Games.

"Glasgow to Monte Carlo" — A98

1956, Apr. 3 **Unwmk.**

365	A98	100fr red brn & red	25.00	25.00

The 26th Monte Carlo Automobile Rally.

See Nos. 411, 437, 460, 483, 500, 539, 549, 600, 629.

Princess Grace and Prince Rainier III — A99

1956, Apr. 19 **Engr.** *Perf. 13*

Portraits in Black

366	A99	1fr dark green	.20	.20
367	A99	2fr dark carmine	.35	.25
368	A99	3fr ultra	.45	.35
369	A99	5fr brt yellow grn	1.00	.55
370	A99	15fr redsh brown	1.40	.65
		Nos. 366-370,C46-C48 (8)	10.00	8.60

Wedding of Prince Rainier III to Grace Kelly, Apr. 19, 1956.

Nos. J41-J47, J50-J56 Overprinted with Bars and Surcharged in Indigo, Red or Black

Unwmk.

1956, Apr. 3 **Engr.** *Perf. 11*

Designs: Early Transportation.

371	D6	2fr on 4fr (I)	.50	.45
a.		Pair, #371, 381	1.00	1.00
372	D6	3fr (R)	.50	.45
a.		Pair, #372, 382	1.00	1.00
373	D6	5fr on 4fr	.70	.70
a.		Pair, #373, 383	1.40	1.40
374	D6	10fr on 4fr (R)	1.40	1.10
a.		Pair, #374, 384	2.75	2.75
375	D6	15fr on 5fr (I)	1.75	1.75
a.		Pair, #375, 385	3.50	3.50
376	D6	20fr (R)	2.75	2.75
a.		Pair, #376, 386	5.50	5.50
377	D6	25fr on 20fr	5.00	5.00
a.		Pair, #377, 387	10.00	10.00
378	D6	30fr on 10fr (I)	9.50	9.50
a.		Pair, #378, 388	19.00	19.00
379	D6	40fr on 50fr (R)	13.50	13.50
a.		Pair, #379, 389	27.00	27.00
380	D6	50fr on 100fr	16.00	16.00
a.		Pair, #380, 390	32.00	32.00

Designs: Modern Transportation.

381	D7	2fr on 4fr (I)	.50	.50
382	D7	3fr (R)	.50	.45
383	D7	5fr on 4fr	.70	.70
384	D7	10fr on 4fr (R)	1.40	1.10
385	D7	15fr on 5fr (I)	1.75	1.75
386	D7	20fr (R)	2.75	2.75
387	D7	25fr on 20fr	5.00	5.00
388	D7	30fr on 10fr (I)	9.50	9.50
389	D7	40fr on 50fr (R)	13.50	13.50
390	D7	50fr on 100fr	16.00	16.00
		Nos. 371-390,C49-C50 (22)	124.20	123.45

Pairs se-tenant at the base.

Princess Grace — A100

1957, May 11 Engr. *Perf. 13*

No.	Type	Description	Unused	Used
391	A100	1fr blue violet	.20	.20
392	A100	2fr lt olive grn	.20	.20
393	A100	3fr yellow brown	.25	.20
394	A100	5fr magenta	.35	.25
395	A100	15fr pink	.35	.25
396	A100	25fr Prus blue	1.10	.65
397	A100	30fr purple	1.10	.90
398	A100	50fr scarlet	1.75	.90
399	A100	75fr orange	3.00	2.50
		Nos. 391-399 (9)	8.30	6.05

Birth of Princess Caroline of Monaco.

Knight Type of 1954

1957 Unwmk. *Perf. 13*

No.	Type	Description	Unused	Used
400	A79	5fr dark blue	.40	.25
401	A79	10fr yellow green	.30	.20
402	A79	15fr brt orange	1.40	.90
403	A79	30fr brt blue	2.00	.90
404	A79	45fr crimson	3.25	1.75
		Nos. 400-404 (5)	7.35	4.00

Nos. 400-404 were issued precanceled only. See note after No. 324.

Types of 1955 and 1939-46

1957

No.	Type	Description	Unused	Used
405	A83	20fr greenish blue	2.00	.50
406	A83	35fr red brown	4.00	1.60
407	A33	65fr brt violet	10.00	6.50
408	A30	70fr orange yellow	9.50	6.00
		Nos. 405-408 (4)	25.50	14.60

Princesses Grace and Caroline A101

1958, May 15 Engr. *Perf. 13*

409 A101 100fr bluish black 8.50 6.00

Birth of Prince Albert Alexander Louis, Mar. 14.

Order of St. Charles — A102

1958, May 15

410 A102 100fr carmine, grn & bis 2.25 2.00

Cent. of the Natl. Order of St. Charles.

Rally Type of 1956

Design: 100fr, "Munich to Monte Carlo."

1958, May 15

411 A98 100fr red, grn & sepia 8.00 7.00

27th Monte Carlo Automobile Rally.

Virgin Mary, Popes Pius IX and XII — A103

Bernadette Soubirous A104

Tomb of Bernadette, Nevers A105

Designs: 3fr, Shepherdess Bernadette at Bartres. 5fr, Bouriette kneeling (first miracle). 8fr, Stained glass window showing apparition. 10fr, Empty grotto at Lourdes. 12fr, Grotto with statue and altar. 20fr, Bernadette praying. 35fr, High Altar at St. Peter's during canonization of Bernadette. 50fr, Bernadette, Pope Pius XI, Mgr. Laurence and Abbe Peyramale.

1958, May 15 Unwmk.

No.	Type	Description	Unused	Used
412	A103	1fr lilac gray & vio brn	.20	.20
413	A104	2fr blue & violet	.20	.20
414	A104	3fr green & sepia	.20	.20
415	A104	5fr gray brn & vio bl	.20	.20
416	A104	8fr blk, ol bis & ind	.35	.25
417	A105	10fr multicolored	.35	.35
418	A105	12fr ind, ol bis & ol grn	.45	.25
a.		Strip of 3, #416-418	3.50	3.50
419	A104	20fr dk sl grn & rose	.45	.35
420	A104	35fr ol, gray ol & dk sl grn	.55	.45
421	A103	50fr lake, ol grn & ind	.90	.55
422	A105	65fr indigo & grnsh bl	1.25	.85
		Nos. 412-422,C51-C52 (13)	9.35	7.75

Centenary of the apparition of the Virgin Mary at Lourdes.

Sizes: Nos. 413-415, 419-420 26x36mm. No. 416 22x36mm. Nos. 417-418 48x36mm. No. 422 36x26mm.

Types of 1939-46 and 1955

1959 Engr. *Perf. 13*

No.	Type	Description	Unused	Used
423	A32	5fr copper red	1.10	.55
424	A83	25fr orange & blk	1.10	.55
425	A83	30fr dark violet	4.25	2.10
426	A34	35fr dark blue	8.50	3.25
427	A83	50fr bl grn & rose cl	5.50	2.10
428	A31	85fr dk carmine rose	12.50	6.50
429	A33	100fr brt grnsh blue	12.50	6.50
		Nos. 423-429 (7)	45.45	21.55

Knight Type of 1954

1959

No.	Type	Description	Unused	Used
430	A79	8fr deep magenta	.75	.35
431	A79	20fr bright green	1.40	1.25
432	A79	40fr chocolate	2.75	1.10
433	A79	55fr ultra	4.50	2.75
		Nos. 430-433 (4)	9.40	5.45

Nos. 430-433 were issued precanceled only. See note after No. 324.

Princess Grace Polyclinic — A106

1959, May 16

434 A106 100fr gray, brn & grn 3.75 2.25

Opening of Princess Grace Hospital.

UNESCO Building, Paris, and Cultural Emblems — A107

50fr, UNESCO Building, children of various races.

1959, May 16

No.	Type	Description	Unused	Used
435	A107	25fr multicolored	.30	.30
436	A107	50fr ol, bl grn & blk brn	.40	.40

Opening of UNESCO Headquarters in Paris, Nov. 3, 1958.

Rally Type of 1956

Design: 100fr, "Athens to Monaco."

1959, May 16

437 A98 100fr vio bl, red & sl grn, *bl* 6.50 5.50

28th Monte Carlo Automobile Rally.

Carnations — A108

Bougainvillea — A109

Flowers: 10fr on 3fr, Princess Grace Carnations. 15fr on 1fr, Mimosa, vert. 25fr on 6fr, Geranium, vert. 35fr, Oleander. 50fr, Jasmine. 85fr on 65fr, Lavender. 100fr, Grace de Monaco Rose.

1959, May 16

No.	Type	Description	Unused	Used
438	A108	5fr brn, Prus grn & rose car	.25	.20
439	A108	10fr on 3fr brn, grn & rose	.35	.25
440	A109	15fr on 1fr dk grn & cit	.35	.25
441	A109	20fr ol grn & mag	.90	.55
442	A109	25fr on 6fr yel grn & red	1.25	.75
443	A109	35fr dk grn & pink	2.50	1.75
444	A109	50fr dk brn & dk grn	3.00	2.10
445	A109	85fr on 65fr ol grn & gray vio	3.50	3.00
446	A108	100fr green & pink	4.75	4.25
		Nos. 438-446 (9)	16.85	13.10

Nos. 439-440, 442 and 445 were not issued without surcharge.

View of Monaco and Uprooted Oak Emblem — A110

1960, June 1 Unwmk. *Perf. 13*

447 A110 25c bl, olive grn & sepia .35 .25

World Refugee Year, 7/1/59-6/30/60.

Entrance to Oceanographic Museum — A111

Museum and Aquarium — A112

Designs: 15c, Museum conference room. 20c, Arrival of equipment, designed by Prince Albert I. 25c, Research on electrical qualities of cephalopodes. 50c, Albert I and vessels Hirondelle I and Princesse Alice.

1960, June 1 Engr. *Perf. 13*

No.	Type	Description	Unused	Used
448	A111	5c blue, sepia & cl	.55	.25
449	A112	10c multicolored	.70	.35
450	A112	15c sep, ultra & bis	.70	.35
451	A112	20c rose lil, blk & bl	1.10	.55
452	A112	25c grnsh blue	2.25	1.60
453	A112	50c lt ultra & brown	2.50	1.75
		Nos. 448-453 (6)	7.80	4.85

Inauguration of the Oceanographic Museum of Monaco, 50th anniv. See #475.

Horse Jumping — A113

Sports: 10c, Women swimmers. 15c, Broad jumper. 20c, Javelin thrower. 25c, Girl figure skater. 50c, Skier.

1960, June 1

No.	Type	Description	Unused	Used
454	A113	5c dk brn, car & emer	.25	.25
455	A113	10c red brn, bl & grn	.25	.25
456	A113	15c dl red brn, ol & mag	.35	.35
457	A113	20c black, bl & grn	2.75	2.75
458	A113	25c dk grn & dull pur	.90	.90
459	A113	50c dk bl, grnsh bl & dl pur	1.10	1.10
		Nos. 454-459 (6)	5.60	5.60

Nos. 454-457 for the 17th Olympic Games, Rome, Aug. 25-Sept. 11; Nos. 458-459 for the 8th Winter Olympic Games, Squaw Valley, Feb. 18-29.

Rally Type of 1956

Design: 25c, "Lisbon to Monte Carlo."

1960, June 1

460 A98 25c bl, brn & car, *bluish* 2.25 2.00

29th Monte Carlo Automobile Rally.

Stamps of Sardinia and France, 1860, and Stamp of Monaco, 1885
A114

1960, June 1 Engr. & Embossed

461 A114 25c violet, blue & ol .80 .70

75th anniv. of postage stamps of Monaco.

Prince Rainier Type of 1955

1960 Engr. *Perf. 13*

462 A83 25c orange & blk .55 .20
463 A83 30c dark violet .55 .20
464 A83 50c bl grn & rose lil 2.25 .35
465 A83 65c yel brn & slate 14.00 4.25
Nos. 462-465 (4) 17.35 5.00

Knight Type of 1954

1960

466 A79 8c deep magenta 1.60 .55
467 A79 20c brt green 2.75 .55
468 A79 40c chocolate 4.50 1.10
469 A79 55c ultra 6.75 1.60
Nos. 466-469 (4) 15.60 3.80

Nos. 466-469 were issued precanceled only. See note after No. 324.

Sea Horse — A115

#471 Cactus (Cereanee). #472, Cactus (Nopalea dejecta). #473, Scorpion fish, horiz.

1960, June 1

470 A115 15c org brn & sl grn .80 .25
471 A115 15c ol grn, yel & brn .95 .20
472 A115 20c maroon & ol grn .95 .25
473 A115 20c brn, red brn, red & ol .80 .35
Nos. 470-473 (4) 3.50 1.05

See Nos. 581-584.

Type of 1960 and

Palace of Monaco
A116

Designs: 10c, Type A111 without inscription. 45c, Aerial view of Palace. 85c, Honor court. 1fr, Palace at night.

1960, June 1 Engr.

474 A116 5c green & sepia .20 .20
475 A111 10c dk bl & vio brn .55 .35
476 A116 45c dk bl, sep & grn 6.75 .70
477 A116 85c slate, gray & bis 8.75 2.10
478 A116 1fr dk bl, red brn & sl grn 1.10 .40
Nos. 474-478 (5) 17.35 3.75

See #585, 602, 729, 731, 731A, 790, 792.

Sphinx of Wadi-es-Sebua — A117

1961, June 3 Unwmk. *Perf. 13*

479 A117 50c choc, dk bl & ocher 1.25 .80

Issued as publicity to save historic monuments in Nubia.

Murena, Starfish, Sea Urchin, Sea Cucumber and Coral — A118

1961, June 3

480 A118 25c vio buff & dk red .25 .25

Issued to commemorate the World Congress of Aquariology, Monaco, Nov. 1960.

Medieval Town and Leper — A119

1961, June 3

481 A119 25c ol gray, ocher & car .25 .25

Issued to honor the Sovereign Order of the Knights of Malta.

Hand and Ant
A120

1961, June 3

482 A120 25c magenta & dp car .40 .40

Issued to publicize "Respect for Life."

Rally Type of 1956

Design: 1fr, "Stockholm to Monte Carlo."

1961, June 3

483 A98 1fr multicolored 1.50 1.50

30th Monte Carlo Automobile Rally.

Turcat-Mery, 1911 Winner, and 1961 Car — A121

1961, June 3

484 A121 1fr org brn, vio & rose red 1.60 1.60

50th anniv. of the founding of the Monte Carlo Automobile Rally.

Chevrolet, 1912
A122

Automobiles (pre-1912): 2c, Peugeot. 3c, Fiat. 4c, Mercedes. 5c, Rolls Royce. 10c, Panhard-Levassor. 15c, Renault. 20c, Ford. 25c, Rochet-Schneider. 30c, FN-Herstal. 45c, De Dion Bouton. 50c, Buick. 65c, Delahaye. 1fr, Cadillac.

1961, June 13 Engr.

485 A122 1c org brn, dk brn & grn .20 .20
486 A122 2c org red, dk bl & brn .20 .20
487 A122 3c multicolored .20 .20
488 A122 4c multicolored .20 .20
489 A122 5c ol bis, sl grn & car .20 .20
490 A122 10c brn, sl & red .25 .25
491 A122 15c grnsh bl & dk sl grn .25 .25
492 A122 20c pur, blk & red .25 .25
493 A122 25c dk brn lil & red .45 .45
494 A122 30c ol grn & dl pur 1.10 1.10
495 A122 45c multicolored 2.10 2.10
496 A122 50c brn blk, red & ultra 2.10 2.10
497 A122 65c multicolored 3.25 3.25
498 A122 1fr brt pur, ind & red 3.75 3.75
Nos. 485-498 (14) 14.50 14.50

See Nos. 648-661.

Bugatti, First Winner, and Course — A123

1962, June 6 Unwmk. *Perf. 13*

499 A123 1fr lilac rose 1.50 1.50

20th Automobile Grand Prix of Monaco.

Rally Type of 1956

Design: 1fr, "Oslo to Monte Carlo."

1962, June 6

500 A98 1fr multicolored 1.50 1.50

31st Monte Carlo Automobile Rally.

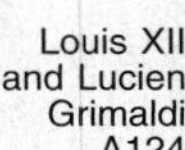

Louis XII and Lucien Grimaldi
A124

50c, Document granting sovereignty. 1fr, Seals of Louis XII & Lucien Grimaldi.

1962, June 6 Engr.

501 A124 25c ver, blk & vio bl .30 .30
502 A124 50c dk bl, brn & mag .45 .45
503 A124 1fr dk brn, grn & car .70 .70
Nos. 501-503 (3) 1.45 1.45

450th anniversary of Monaco's reception of sovereignty from Louis XII.

Mosquito and Swamp
A125

1962, June 6

504 A125 1fr brn ol & lt grn .60 .60

WHO drive to eradicate malaria.

Aquatic Stadium at Night
A126

1962, June 6

505 A126 10c dk bl, ind & grn .25 .20

Sun, Flowers and Hope Chest
A127

1962, June 6

506 A127 20c multicolored .25 .25

Issued to publicize the National Multiple Sclerosis Society of New York.

Wheat Harvest
A128

1962, June 6

507 A128 25c dk bl, red brn & brn *.50* *.30*
508 A128 50c ind, ol bis & dk bl grn *.50* *.35*
509 A128 1fr red lil & olive bister *1.00* *.65*
Nos. 507-509,C61 (4) 4.00 2.30

Europa. See No. C61.

Blood Donor's Arm and Globe
A129

1962, Nov. 15 Engr. *Perf. 13*

510 A129 1fr dk red, blk & orange .90 .90

3rd International Blood Donors' Congress, Nov. 15-18 at Monaco.

Yellow Wagtails — A130

Birds: 10c, European robins. 15c, European goldfinches. 20c, Blackcaps. 25c, Great spotted woodpeckers. 30c, Nightingale. 45c, Barn owls. 50c, Common starlings. 85c, Red crossbills. 1fr, White storks.

1962, Dec. 12 **Unwmk.**

511 A130 5c green, sep & yel .25 .25
512 A130 10c bis, dk pur & red .25 .25
513 A130 15c multicolored .35 .35
514 A130 20c mag, grn & blk .45 .35
515 A130 25c multicolored .55 .45
516 A130 30c brn, sl grn & bl .85 .65
517 A130 45c vio & gldn brn 1.40 1.25
518 A130 50c bl grn, blk & yel 2.25 1.40
519 A130 85c multicolored 2.75 2.00
520 A130 1fr blk, grn & red 3.25 2.25
Nos. 511-520 (10) 12.35 9.20

Protection of useful birds.

Divers A131

10c, Galeazzi's turret, vert. 25c, Williamson's photosphere, 1914 & bathyscape "Trieste," 1962. 45c, Diving suits. 50c, Diving chamber. 85c, Fulton's "Nautilus," 1800 and modern submarine. 1fr, Alexander the Great's underwater chamber and bathysphere of the N. Y. Zoological Society.

1962, Dec. 12

521 A131 5c bluish grn, vio & blk .20 .20
522 A131 10c multicolored .25 .25
523 A131 25c bis, bluish grn & sl grn .25 .25
524 A131 45c green, ind & blk .45 .45
525 A131 50c cit & dk bl .70 .70
526 A131 85c Prus grn & dk vio bl 1.25 1.25
527 A131 1fr dk bl, dk brn & dk grn 2.00 2.00
Nos. 521-527 (7) 5.10 5.10

Issued in connection with an exhibition at the Oceanographic Museum "Man Under Water," showing ancient and modern methods of under-water exploration.

Dancing Children and UN Emblem — A132

Children on Scales A133

Designs: 10c, Bird feeding nestlings, vert. 20c, Sun shining on children of different races, vert. 25c, Mother and child, vert. 50c, House and child. 95c, African mother and child, vert. 1fr, Prince Albert and Princess Caroline.

1963, May 3 **Unwmk.** ***Perf. 13***

528 A132 5c ocher, dk red & ultra .20 .20
529 A133 10c vio bl, emer & ol gray .25 .20
530 A133 15c ultra, red & grn .25 .25
531 A133 20c multicolored .25 .25
532 A133 25c blue, brn & pink .25 .25
533 A133 50c multicolored .70 .45
534 A133 95c multicolored 1.25 .70
535 A132 1fr multicolored 2.00 1.25
Nos. 528-535 (8) 5.15 3.55

Publicizing the UN Children's Charter.

Figurehead with Red Cross, Red Crescent and Red Lion and Sun — A134

1fr, Centenary emblem, Gustave Moynier, Henri Dunant and Gen. Henri Dufour, horiz.

1963, May 3 **Engr.**

536 A134 50c bluish grn, red & red brn .50 .50
537 A134 1fr blue, sl grn & red .75 .75

Centenary of International Red Cross.

Racing Cars on Monte Carlo Course and Map of Europe A135

1963, May 3

538 A135 50c multicolored .70 .45

European Automobile Grand Prix.

Rally Type of 1956

Design: 1fr, "Warsaw to Monte Carlo."

1963, May 3

539 A98 1fr multicolored 1.50 1.50

32nd Monte Carlo Auto Race.

Lions International Emblem — A136

1963, May 3

540 A136 50c bis, lt vio & bl .75 .60

Issued to commemorate the founding of the Lions Club of Monaco, Mar. 24, 1962.

Hôtel des Postes, Paris, and UPU Allegory — A137

1963, May 3

541 A137 50c multicolored .60 .40

1st Intl. Postal Conference, Paris, 1863.

Globe and Telstar A138

1963, May 3

542 A138 50c grn, dk pur & maroon .75 .50

1st television connection of the US and Europe through the Telstar satellite, July 11-12, 1962.

Holy Spirit over St. Peter's and World A139

1963, May 3

543 A139 1fr grn, red brn & bl .75 .60

Vatican II, the 21st Ecumenical Council of the Roman Catholic Church.

Wheat Emblem and Dove Feeding Nestlings A140

1963, May 3 **Engr.**

544 A140 1fr multicolored .80 .80

FAO "Freedom from Hunger" campaign.

Henry Ford and 1903 Model A — A141

1963, Dec. 12 **Unwmk.** ***Perf. 13***

545 A141 20c slate grn & lil rose .75 .50

Centenary of the birth of Henry Ford, American automobile manufacturer.

Bicyle Racer in Town A142

Design: 50c, Bicyclist on country road.

1963, Dec. 12

546 A142 25c bl, sl grn & red brn .50 .50
547 A142 50c bl, gray grn, & blk brn .50 .50

50th anniv. of the Bicycle Tour de France.

Pierre de Coubertin and Myron's Discobolus A143

1963, Dec. 12

548 A143 1fr dp cl, car & ocher .75 .75

Baron Pierre de Coubertin, organizer of the modern Olympic Games, birth cent.

Rally Type of 1956

Design: 1fr, "Paris to Monte Carlo."

1963, Dec. 12

549 A98 1fr multicolored 1.10 1.10

33rd Monte Carlo Automobile Rally.

Children with Stamp Album and UNESCO Emblem A144

1963, Dec. 12

550 A144 50c dp ultra, red & vio .45 .45

International Philatelic and Educational Exposition, Monaco, Nov.-Dec., 1963.

Europa Issue, 1963

Woman, Dove and Lyre — A145

1963, Dec. 12

551 A145 25c brn, grn & car *1.50* *.35*
552 A145 50c dk brn, bl & car *2.00* *.60*

Wembley Stadium and British Football Association Emblem — A146

Overhead Kick A147

Soccer Game, Florence, 16th Century A148

Tackle A149

Designs: 3c, Goalkeeper. 4c, Louis II Stadium and emblem of Sports Association of Monaco, with black overprint: "Championnat /1962-1963/Coupe de France." 15c, Soule Game, Brittany, 19th century. 20c, Soccer, England, 1827. 25c, Soccer, England, 1890. 50c, Clearing goal area. 95c, Heading the ball. 1fr, Kicking the ball.

1963, Dec. 12

553 A146 1c grn, vio & dk red .20 .20
554 A147 2c black, red & grn .20 .20
555 A147 3c gray ol, org & red .20 .20
556 A146 4c bl, red, grn, pur & blk .20 .20
557 A148 10c dk bl, car & sep .20 .20
558 A148 15c sepia & car .20 .20

559 A148 20c sepia & dk bl .25 .25
560 A148 25c sepia & lilac .25 .25
a. Block of 4 1.00 1.00
561 A149 30c green, sep & red .45 .45
562 A149 50c sepia, grn & red .70 .70
563 A149 95c sepia, grn & red 1.00 1.00
564 A149 1fr sepia, grn & red 1.25 1.25
a. Block of 4 4.00 4.00
Nos. 553-564 (12) 5.10 5.10

Cent. of British Football Assoc. (organized soccer). No. 556 also for the successes of the soccer team of Monaco, 1962-63 (overprint typographed). No. 556 was not regularly issued without overprint. Value $750.

The 4 stamps of No. 560a are connected by an 1863 soccer ball in red brown; the stamps of No. 564a by a modern soccer ball.

Design from 1914 Rally Post Card — A150

Farman Biplane over Monaco — A151

Designs: 3c, Nieuport monoplane. 4c, Breguet biplane. 5c, Morane-Saulnier monoplane. 10c, Albatros biplane. 15c, Deperdussin monoplane. 20c, Vickers-Vimy biplane and map (Ross Smith's flight London-Port Darwin, 1919). 25c, Douglas Liberty biplane (first American around-the-world flight. 4 planes, 1924). 30c, Savoia S-16 hydroplane (De Pinedo's Rome-Australia-Japan-Rome flight, 1925). 45c, Trimotor Fokker F-7 monoplane (first aerial survey of North Pole, Richard E. Byrd and James Gordon Bennett, 1925). 50c, Spirit of St. Louis (first crossing of Atlantic, New York-Paris, Charles Lindbergh, 1927). 65c, Breguet 19 (Paris-New York, Coste and Bellonte, 1930). 95c, Laté 28 hydroplane (first South Atlantic airmail route, Dakar-Natal, 1930). 1fr, Dornier DO-X, (Germany-Rio de Janeiro, 1930).

1964, May 22 Engr. *Perf. 13*

565 A150 1c green, bl & ol .20 .20
566 A151 2c bl, bis & red brn .20 .20
567 A151 3c olive, grn & bl .20 .20
568 A151 4c red brn, bl & Prus grn .20 .20
569 A151 5c gray ol, vio & mag .20 .20
570 A151 10c violet, bl & ol .25 .20
571 A151 15c blue, org & brn .25 .20
572 A151 20c brt grn, blk & bl .35 .25
573 A151 25c red, bl & ol .35 .35
574 A151 30c bl, sl grn & dp cl .45 .45
575 A151 45c red brn, grnsh bl & blk .75 .55
576 A151 50c purple, ol & bis .90 .75
577 A151 65c steel bl, blk & red 1.20 1.00
578 A151 95c ocher, sl grn & red 1.60 1.25
579 A151 1fr sl grn, bl & vio brn 2.25 1.60
Nos. 565-579,C64 (16) 12.10 10.35

50th anniv. of the 1st airplane rally of Monte Carlo. Nos. 565-571 show planes which took part in the 1914 rally, Nos. 572-579 and C64 show important flights from 1919 to 1961.

Ancient Egyptian Message Transmitters and Rocket — A152

1964, May 22 Unwmk.

580 A152 1fr dk bl, indigo & org brn .70 .70

Issued to publicize "PHILATEC", International Philatelic and Postal Techniques Exhibition, Paris, June 5-21, 1964.

Types of 1955-60

1c, Crab (Macrocheira Kampferi), horiz. 2c, Flowering cactus (Selenicereus Gr.). 12c, Shell (Fasciolaria trapezium). 18c, Aloe ciliaris. 70c, Honor court of palace (like #477). 95c, Prince Rainier III.

1964, May 19 *Perf. 13*

581 A115 1c bl grn & dk red .20 .20
582 A115 2c dk grn & multi .20 .20
583 A115 12c vio & brn red .50 .20
584 A115 18c grn, yel & car .55 .20
585 A116 70c lt grn, choc & red org .70 .40
586 A83 95c ultra 1.50 .50
Nos. 581-586 (6) 3.65 1.70

Rainier III Aquatic Stadium A153

1964-67 Engr. *Perf. 13*

587 A153 10c dk car, rose, bl & blk 1.75 .25
587A A153 15c dk car, rose, brt bl & blk ('67) 1.00 .25
588 A153 25c dl grn, dk bl & blk 1.00 .25
589 A153 50c lil, bl grn & blk 1.75 1.00
Nos. 587-589 (4) 5.50 1.75

Nos. 587-589 were issued precanceled only. See note after No. 324. The "1962" date has been obliterated with 2 bars. See Nos. 732-734, 793-796, 976-979.

Common Design Types pictured following the introduction.

Europa Issue, 1964

Common Design Type

1964, Sept. 12

Size: 22x34½mm

590 CD7 25c brt red, brt grn & dk grn *1.00* .20
591 CD7 50c ultra, ol bis & dk red brn *1.50* .45

Weight Lifter — A154

1964, Dec. 3 Unwmk. *Perf. 13*

592 A154 1c shown .20 .20
593 A154 2c Judo .20 .20
594 A154 3c Pole vault .20 .20
595 A154 4c Archery .20 .20
Nos. 592-595 (4) .80 .80

18th Olympic Games, Tokyo, 10/10-25. See #C65.

Pres. John F. Kennedy and Mercury Capsule — A155

1964, Dec. 3

596 A155 50c brt bl & indigo .60 .60

Pres. John F. Kennedy (1917-63).

Television Set and View of Monte Carlo A156

1964, Dec. 3

597 A156 50c dk car rose, dk bl & brn .50 .50

Fifth International Television Festival.

Frédéric Mistral, (1830-1914), Provençal Poet — A157

1964, Dec. 3 Engr.

598 A157 1fr gray olive & brn red .55 .55

Scales of Justice and Code A158

1964, Dec. 3

599 A158 1fr gldn brn & slate grn .60 .60

Universal Declaration of Human Rights.

Rally Type of 1956

Design: 1fr, "Minsk to Monte Carlo."

1964, Dec. 3

600 A98 1fr bl grn, ocher & brn 1.00 1.00

34th Monte Carlo Automobile Rally.

International Football Association Emblem — A159

1964, Dec. 3

601 A159 1fr red, bl & ol bister .85 .85

60th anniv. of FIFA, the Federation Internationale de Football (soccer).

Types of 1955 and 1960

Designs: 40c, Aerial view of palace. 60c, 1.30fr, 2.30fr, Prince Rainier III.

1965-66 Engr. *Perf. 13*

602 A116 40c sl grn, dl cl & brt grn .75 .25
603 A83 60c sl grn & blk 1.10 .35
604 A83 1.30fr dk red & blk 3.25 .75
604A A83 2.30fr org & rose lil ('66) 2.75 .75
Nos. 602-604A (4) 7.85 2.10

Telstar and Pleumeur-Bodou Relay Station — A160

Alexander Graham Bell and Telephone A161

Designs (ITU Emblem and): 5c, Syncom II and Earth. 10c, Echo II and Earth. 12c, Relay satellite and Earth, vert. 18c, Lunik III and Moon. 50c, Samuel Morse and telegraph. 60c, Edouard Belin, belinograph and newspaper. 70c, Roman signal towers and Chappe telegraph. 95c, Cable laying ships; "The Great Eastern" (British, 1858) and "Alsace" (French, modern). 1fr, Edouard Branly, Guglielmo Marconi and map of English Channel.

1965, May 17

605 A161 5c vio bl & slate grn .20 .20
606 A161 10c dk bl & sepia .20 .20
607 A161 12c gray, brn & dk car .25 .25
608 A161 18c ind, dk car & plum .25 .25
609 A160 25c vio, ol & rose brn .25 .25
610 A161 30c dk brn, ol & bis brn .35 .35
611 A161 50c green & indigo .35 .35
612 A161 60c dl red brn & brt bl .70 .70
613 A160 70c brn blk, org & dk bl .85 .85
614 A160 95c indigo, blk & bl 1.00 1.00
615 A160 1fr brn, blk & ultra 1.40 1.40
Nos. 605-615,C66 (12) 10.55 10.55

International Telecommunication Union, cent.

Europa Issue, 1965

Common Design Type

1965, Sept. 25 Engr. *Perf. 13*

Size: 36x22mm

616 CD8 30c red brn & grn *1.25* *.65*
617 CD8 60c violet & dk car *2.00* *1.00*

Palace of Monaco, 18th Century A162

Views of Palace: 12c, From the Bay, 17th century. 18c, Bay with sailboats, 18th century. 30c, From distance, 19th century. 60c, Close-up, 19th century. 1.30fr, Aerial view, 20th century.

1966, Feb. 1 Engr. *Perf. 13*

618 A162 10c vio, dl grn & ind .20 .20
619 A162 12c bl, bis brn & dk brn .20 .20
620 A162 18c blk, grn & bl .25 .25
621 A162 30c vio bl, sep & red brn .35 .35
622 A162 60c bl, grn & brn .70 .70
623 A162 1.30fr dk grn & red brn 1.25 1.25
Nos. 618-623 (6) 2.95 2.95

750th anniversary of Palace of Monaco.

Dante Alighieri — A163

Designs: 60c, Dante facing Panther of Envy. 70c, Dante and Virgil boating across muddy swamp of 5th Circle. 95c, Dante watching the arrogant and Cross of Salvation. 1fr, Invocation of St. Bernard; Dante and Beatrice.

1966, Feb. 1

624 A163 30c crimson & dp grn .40 .40
625 A163 60c dl grn, Prus bl & ind .75 .75
626 A163 70c black, sep & car .90 .90
627 A163 95c red lilac & blue 1.40 1.40
628 A163 1fr ultra & bluish grn 1.50 1.50
Nos. 624-628 (5) 4.95 4.95

700th anniv. (in 1965) of the birth of Dante (1265-1321), poet.

Rally Type of 1956

Design: 1fr, "London to Monte Carlo."

1966, Feb. 1

629 A98 1fr purple, red & indigo .95 .75

The 35th Monte Carlo Automobile Rally.

Nativity by Gerard van Honthorst A164

1966, Feb. 1

630 A164 30c brown .25 .25

Issued to honor the World Association for the Protection of Children.

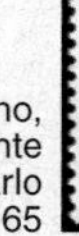

Casino, Monte Carlo A165

View of La Condamine, 1860, and Francois Blanc — A166

Designs: 12c, Prince Charles III, vert. 40c, Charles III monument, Bowling Green Gardens. 60c, Seaside Promenade and Rainier III. 70c, René Blum, Sergei Diaghilev and "Petroushka." 95c, Jules Massenet and Camille Saint-Saens. 1.30fr, Gabriel Fauré and Maurice Ravel.

1966, June 1 Engr. *Perf. 13*

631 A165 12c dp blue, blk & mag .20 .20
632 A165 25c multicolored .25 .25
633 A166 30c bl, plum, grn & org .25 .25
634 A165 40c multicolored .25 .25
635 A166 60c multicolored .45 .45
636 A166 70c rose cl & ind .45 .45
637 A165 95c purple & blk .75 .75
638 A165 1.30fr brn org, ol bis & brn 1.10 1.10
Nos. 631-638,C68 (9) 6.45 6.45

Centenary of founding of Monte Carlo.

Europa Issue, 1966

Common Design Type

1966, Sept. 26 Engr. *Perf. 13*

Size: 21½x35½mm

639 CD9 30c orange *.75* *.25*
640 CD9 60c light green *1.25* *.40*

Prince Albert I, Yachts Hirondelle I and Princesse Alice — A167

1966, Dec. 12 Engr. *Perf. 13*

641 A167 1fr ultra & dk vio brn .85 .85

1st Intl. Congress of the History of Oceanography, Monaco, Dec. 12-17. Issued in sheets of 10.

Red Chalk Drawing by Domenico Zampieri — A168

1966, Dec. 12

642 A168 30c brt rose & dk brn .25 .25
643 A168 60c brt bl & yel brn .35 .35

20th anniv. of UNESCO.

Television Screen and Cross over Monaco — A169

1966, Dec. 12

644 A169 60c dk car rose, lil & red .35 .25

10th meeting of "UNDA," the International Catholic Association for Radio and Television.

Precontinent III and Divers on Ocean Floor — A170

1966, Dec. 12

645 A170 1fr Prus bl, yel & dk brn .60 .35

First anniversary of the submarine research station Precontinent III.

WHO Headquarters, Geneva — A171

1966, Dec. 12

646 A171 30c dp bl, ol brn & dp bl grn .25 .20
647 A171 60c dk grn, crim & dk brn .35 .35

Opening of WHO Headquarters, Geneva.

Automobile Type of 1961

Automobiles (Previous Winners): 1c, Bugatti, 1931. 2c, Alfa Romeo, 1932. 5c, Mercedes, 1936. 10c, Maserati, 1948. 18c, Ferrari, 1955. 20c, Alfa Romeo, 1950. 25c, Maserati, 1957. 30c, Cooper-Climax, 1958. 40c, Lotus-Climax, 1960. 50c, Lotus-Climax, 1961. 60c, Cooper-Climax, 1962. 70c, B.R.M., 1963-66. 1fr, Walter Christie, 1907. 2.30fr, Peugeot, 1910.

1967, Apr. 28 Engr. *Perf. 13x12½*

648 A122 1c ind, red & brt bl .20 .20
649 A122 2c green, red & blk .20 .20
650 A122 5c red, ind & gray .20 .20
651 A122 10c violet, red & ind .25 .20
652 A122 18c indigo & red .45 .25
653 A122 20c dk grn, red & ind .25 .25
654 A122 25c ultra, red & ind .35 .25
655 A122 30c brown, ind & grn .45 .35
656 A122 40c car rose, ind & grn .55 .45
657 A122 50c lilac, ind & grn .75 .45
658 A122 60c carmine, ind & grn 1.00 .55
659 A122 70c dl yel, bl grn & ind 1.25 1.00
660 A122 1fr brn red, blk & gray 1.50 1.10
661 A122 2.30fr multicolored 2.75 2.25
Nos. 648-661,C73 (15) 12.55 10.10

25th Grand Prix of Monaco, May 7.

Dog, Egyptian Statue — A172

1967, Apr. 28 *Perf. 12½x13*

662 A172 30c dk grn, brn & blk .50 .40

Congress of the International Dog Fanciers Federation, Monaco, Apr. 5-9.

View of Monte Carlo — A173

1967, Apr. 28 *Perf. 13*

663 A173 30c slate grn, brt bl & brn .40 .40

International Tourist Year, 1967.

Chessboard and Monte Carlo Harbor — A174

1967, Apr. 28

664 A174 60c brt bl, dk pur & blk .85 .85

International Chess Championships, Monaco, Mar. 19-Apr. 1.

Melvin Jones, View of Monte Carlo and Lions Emblem — A175

1967, Apr. 28

665 A175 60c ultra, slate bl & choc .60 .40

50th anniversary of Lions International.

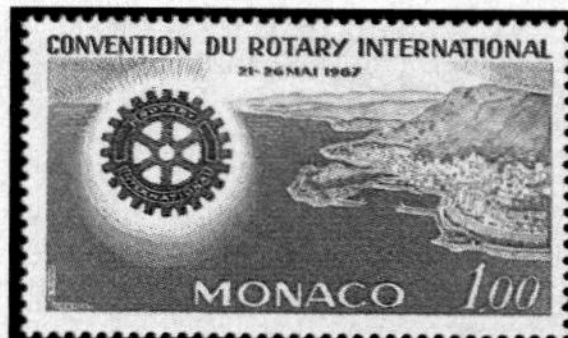

Rotary Emblem and View of Monte Carlo — A176

1967, Apr. 28

666 A176 1fr brt bl & lt ol grn .60 .50

Issued to publicize the Rotary International Convention, Monaco, May 21-26.

EXPO '67 Monaco Pavilion — A177

1967, Apr. 28

667 A177 1fr multicolored .55 .45

EXPO '67, International Exhibition, Montreal, Apr. 28-Oct. 27, 1967.

Map of Europe A178

1967, Apr. 28

668 A178 1fr choc, lemon & Prus bl .55 .45

Issued to publicize the International Committee for European Migration, CIME.

Europa Issue, 1967

Common Design Type

1967, Apr. 28 *Perf. 12½x13*

669 CD10 30c brt car, rose lil & brt vio *1.00* *.30*
670 CD10 60c grn ol & bl grn *1.75* *.40*

Skier and Olympic Emblem — A179

1967, Dec. 7 Engr. *Perf. 13*

671 A179 2.30fr red brn, gray & brt bl 1.50 1.10

10th Winter Olympic Games, Grenoble, France, Feb. 6-18, 1968.

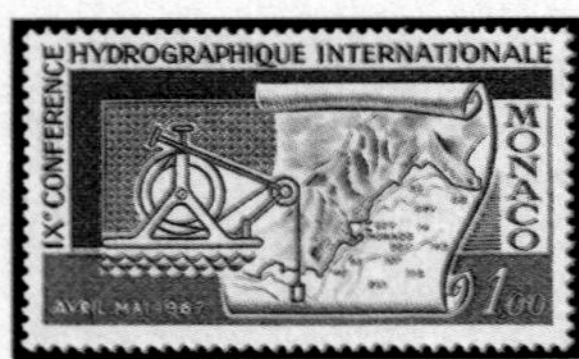

Sounding Line and Map — A180

1967, Dec. 7
672 A180 1fr dk bl, grn & ol .55 .45

9th International Hydrographic Conference, Monte Carlo, April-May, 1967.

Marie Curie, Chemical Apparatus and Atom Symbol — A181

1967, Dec. 7
673 A181 1fr brn, ultra & ol .70 .50

Marie Curie (1867-1934), discoverer of radium and polonium.

Princes of Monaco Issue

Rainier I, by Eugene Charpentier — A182

#675, Lucien Grimaldi, by Ambrogio di Predis.

1967, Dec. 7 ***Perf. 12x13***
674 A182 1fr multicolored .90 .90
675 A182 1fr multicolored .90 .90

See Nos. 710-711, 735-736, 774-775, 813-814, 860-861, 892-893, 991-992, 1035-1036, 1093, 1135-1136, 1187-1188, 1246-1247, 1302-1303.

Shot Put — A183

Sport: 30c, High jump. 60c, Gymnast on rings. 70c, Water polo. 1fr, Wrestling. 2.30fr, Gymnast.

1968, Apr. 29 **Engr.** ***Perf. 13***
676 A183 20c brt bl, grn & brn .25 .25
677 A183 30c vio bl, sep & brn vio .25 .25
678 A183 60c car, brt rose lil & dp bl .35 .35
679 A183 70c ocher, brn org & Prus bl .35 .35
680 A183 1fr brn org, brn & ind .55 .55
681 A183 2.30fr dk car, vio bl & ol 1.10 1.10
Nos. 676-681,C74 (7) 4.60 4.60

19th Olympic Games, Mexico City, 10/12-27.

St. Martin and the Beggar A184

1968, Apr. 29
682 A184 2.30fr brn red, Prus bl & blk brn 1.25 1.00

Red Cross of Monaco, 20th anniversary.

Anemones, by Raoul Dufy — A185

1968, Apr. 29 **Photo.** ***Perf. 12x13***
683 A185 1fr lt blue & multi .75 .60

International Flower Show in Monte Carlo. See Nos. 766, 776, 815-816, 829, 865.

Arms of Pope Pius IX and Prince Charles III — A186

St. Nicholas — A187

Designs: 30c, St. Benedict. 60c, Benedictine Monastery, Subiaco (Italy). 1fr, Church of St. Nicholas, Monaco, 13th century, horiz.

Perf. 12½x13, 13x12½

1968, Apr. 29 **Engr.**
684 A186 10c red & brown .25 .20
685 A187 20c sl grn, ocher & car .25 .20
686 A187 30c ultra & ol grn .35 .25
687 A187 60c lt bl, brn & dk grn .35 .35
688 A187 1fr ind, bl & ol bis .55 .45
Nos. 684-688 (5) 1.75 1.45

Centenary of the elevation of St. Nicholas Church to an Abbey *Nullius,* directly subject to the Holy See.

Europa Issue, 1968

Common Design Type

1968, Apr. 29 ***Perf. 13***

Size: 36x22mm

689 CD11 30c dp orange & car *.90* .20
690 CD11 60c carmine & ultra *2.25* .30
691 CD11 1fr green & red brn *2.25* .40
Nos. 689-691 (3) 5.40 .90

Locomotive 030, 1868 — A188

Locomotives and Views: 30c, Type "C"-220, 1898. 60c, Type 230-"C", 1910. 70c, Type 231-"F," 1925. 1fr, Type 241-"A," 1932. 2.30fr, Type "BB," 1968.

1968, Dec. 12 **Engr.** ***Perf. 13***
692 A188 20c vio bl, brn & blk .70 .35
693 A188 30c dk ol grn, bl & blk .70 .55
694 A188 60c bl, bis & blk 1.10 1.00
695 A188 70c vio, red brn & blk 2.10 1.40
696 A188 1fr bl, brn red & blk 3.25 2.40
697 A188 2.30fr sal pink, brt bl & blk 5.00 3.50
Nos. 692-697 (6) 12.85 9.20

Centenary of the Nice-Monaco Railroad.

Chateaubriand and Combourg Castle — A189

Scenes from Chateaubriand Novels: 20c, The Genius of Christianity. 25c, René. 30c, The Last Abencerage. 60c, The Martyrs. 2.30fr, Atala.

1968, Dec. 12
698 A189 10c dk grn, grn & pur .20 .20
699 A189 20c brt bl, vio & mag .25 .20
700 A189 25c slate, pur & brn .25 .20
701 A189 30c dp brn, brn & pur .25 .25
702 A189 60c brn red, bl grn & dk brn .35 .35
703 A189 2.30fr dk bl, ol & mag 1.10 1.10
Nos. 698-703 (6) 2.40 2.30

Vicomte François René de Chateaubriand (1768-1848), novelist and statesman.

"France" and "Fidelity" by Bosio — A190

François Joseph Bosio (1768-1845), Sculptor — A191

25c, Henri IV as a boy. 60c, Louis XIV on horseback, Place des Victoires. 2.30fr, Busts of Louis XVIII, Napoleon I and Charles X.

1968, Dec. 12
704 A190 20c brown .25 .20
705 A191 25c sal pink & dk brn .25 .20
706 A191 30c slate & vio bl .25 .25
707 A191 60c dk ol grn & gray grn .55 .35
708 A190 2.30fr black & slate 1.00 .90
Nos. 704-708 (5) 2.30 1.90

WHO Emblem — A192

1968, Dec. 12 **Photo.**
709 A192 60c multicolored .35 .25

World Health Organization, 20th anniv.

Princes of Monaco Type of 1967

Designs: 1fr, Charles II (1581-89). 2.30fr, Jeanne Grimaldi (1596-1620).

1968, Dec. 12 **Engr.** ***Perf. 12x13***
710 A182 1fr multicolored .70 .70
711 A182 2.30fr multicolored 1.10 1.10

Faust and Mephistopheles — A193

Scenes from "Damnation of Faust" by Berlioz: 10c, Rakoczy March. 25c, Auerbach's Cellar. 30c, Dance of the Sylphs. 40c, Dance of the Sprites. 50c, Faust and Marguerite. 70c, Woods and Meadows. 1fr, The Ride to the Abyss. 1.15fr, Heaven.

1969, Apr. 26 **Engr.** ***Perf. 13***
712 A193 10c bl grn, pur & org brn .20 .20
713 A193 20c mag, dk ol & lt brn .20 .20
714 A193 25c ind, brn & mag .25 .20
715 A193 30c yel grn, sl & blk .25 .25
716 A193 40c org red, sl & blk .25 .25
717 A193 50c ol, plum & sl .35 .25
718 A193 70c dp grn, sl & lt brn .45 .35
719 A193 1fr mag, blk & ol bis .45 .45
720 A193 1.15fr Prus bl, blk & ultra .70 .70
Nos. 712-720,C75 (10) 4.35 4.10

Hector Berlioz (1803-69), French composer.

St. Elizabeth and Husband, Louis IV, Landgrave of Thuringia A194

1969, Apr. 26
721 A194 3fr dk red, slate & gray 1.60 1.40

Issued for the Red Cross.

See Nos. 767, 812, 830, 905, 963, 1037, 1094, 1189.

Europa Issue, 1969

Common Design Type

1969, Apr. 26

Size: 36x26mm

722 CD12 40c scarlet & purple *2.00* .30
723 CD12 70c brt blue & blk *4.25* .85
724 CD12 1fr yel bis, brn & bl *4.25* .85
Nos. 722-724 (3) *10.50* 2.00

Prince Rainier Type of 1955 and Palace Type of 1960

Designs: 80c, Aerial view of Palace. 1.15fr, 1.30fr, Honor Court.

1969-70 Engr. *Perf. 13*

725	A83	40c olive & rose red	.70	.20
726	A83	45c slate & ocher	.70	.25
727	A83	50c ocher & mar	.70	.35
728	A83	70c dk pur & brt vio bl	1.40	.70
729	A116	80c bl, red brn & grn	1.90	.70
730	A83	85c dk vio & brt grn	1.90	1.25
731	A116	1.15fr blk, bl & mar	2.75	1.60
731A	A116	1.30fr ol brn, lt bl & dl grn ('70)	1.50	1.50
		Nos. 725-731A (8)	11.55	6.55

Aquatic Stadium Type of 1964-67, "1962" Omitted

1969 Engr. *Perf. 13*

732	A153	22c choc, brt bl & blk	.50	.20
733	A153	35c Prus bl, brt bl & blk	.50	.25
734	A153	70c black & vio bl	.80	.35
		Nos. 732-734 (3)	1.80	.80

Nos. 732-734 were issued precanceled only. See note after No. 324.

Princes of Monaco Type of 1967

Designs: 1fr, Honoré II (1604-1662), by Philippe de Champaigne. 3fr, Louise-Hippolyte (1697-1731), by Pierre Gobert.

1969, Nov. 25 Engr. *Perf. 12x13*

735	A182	1fr multicolored	.60	.60
736	A182	3fr multicolored	1.25	1.25

Woman's Head, by Leonardo da Vinci — A195

Drawings by Leonardo da Vinci: 40c, Self-portrait. 70c, Head of old man. 80c, Study for head of St. Magdalene. 1.15fr, Man's head. 3fr, Professional soldier.

1969, Nov. 25 *Perf. 13*

737	A195	30c dull brown	.25	.25
738	A195	40c brn & rose red	.35	.25
739	A195	70c gray green	.35	.25
740	A195	80c dk brown	.45	.35
741	A195	1.15fr orange brn	.75	.55
742	A195	3fr olive brown	1.75	1.20
		Nos. 737-742 (6)	3.90	2.85

Leonardo da Vinci (1452-1519), Florentine painter, sculptor and scientist.

Alphonse Daudet and Scenes from "Letters from My Windmill" — A196

Various Scenes from "Letters from My Windmill" (Lettres de Mon Moulin).

1969, Nov. 25

743	A196	30c blue grn & multi	.25	.25
744	A196	40c brn, vio bl & ol	.35	.35
745	A196	70c pur, brn & ol gray	.45	.35
746	A196	80c sl grn, vio bl & mar	.55	.45
747	A196	1.15fr ocher, sep & blk	.70	.70
		Nos. 743-747 (5)	2.30	2.10

Centenary of publication of "Letters from My Windmill," by Alphonse Daudet (1840-1897).

ILO Emblem A197

1969, Nov. 25 *Perf. 13x12½*

748	A197	40c dk blue & dk pur	.35	.30

50th anniv. of the ILO.

World Map and JCI Emblem A198

1969, Nov. 25

749	A198	40c olive, dk bl & bl	.35	.25

25th anniversary of the Junior Chamber of Commerce in Monaco.

Television Camera and View of Monte Carlo A199

1969, Nov. 25

750	A199	40c red brn, lil & bl	.35	.25

10th International Television Festival in 1970.

King Alfonso XIII, Prince Albert I and Underwater Scene — A200

1969, Nov. 25 *Perf. 12½x13*

751	A200	40c dk brn, blk & grnsh bl	.45	.45

50th anniv. of the International Commission for the Scientific Exploration of the Mediterranean.

Congress Building, Princes Albert I and Rainier III — A201

1970, Feb. 21 Engr. *Perf. 13*

752	A201	40c gray & carmine	.35	.25

Meeting of the Interparliamentary Union, Monaco, Mar. 30-Apr. 5.

EXPO '70 Emblem, Japanese Scroll — A202

Designs (EXPO '70 Emblem and): 30c, Ibis. 40c, Torii. 70c, Cherry blossoms, horiz. 1.15fr, Palace and arms of Monaco, Osaka Castle and arms, horiz.

1970, Mar. 16

753	A202	20c brn, yel grn & car	.25	.25
754	A202	30c brn, yel grn & buff	.25	.25
755	A202	40c olive bis & pur	.35	.35
756	A202	70c lt gray & red	.70	.70
757	A202	1.15fr red & multi	.75	.75
		Nos. 753-757 (5)	2.30	2.30

Issued to publicize EXPO '70 International Exposition, Osaka, Japan, Mar. 15-Sept. 13.

Harbor Seal Pup A203

1970, Mar. 16

758	A203	40c red lil, bl & gray	.75	.55

Protection of seal pups.

Doberman Pinscher A204

1970, Apr. 25

759	A204	40c ocher & black	1.65	.75

International Dog Show, Monte Carlo, Apr. 25. See No. 996.

Basque Ponies A205

Designs: 30c, Parnassius Apollo butterfly. 50c, Harbor seal in Somme Bay. 80c, Pyrenean chamois, vert. 1fr, Whitetailed sea eagles, vert. 1.15fr, European otter, vert.

1970, May 4

760	A205	30c Prus bl & multi	.40	.25
761	A205	40c blue & multi	.65	.35
762	A205	50c grnsh bl, bis & brn	.90	.50
763	A205	80c gray grn, sl bl & brn	1.90	1.00
764	A205	1fr gray, brown & bis	2.50	2.00
765	A205	1.15fr dk brn, lt bl & yel grn	3.25	2.25
		Nos. 760-765 (6)	9.60	6.35

20th anniversary of the International Federation of Animal Protection.

Flower Type of 1968

Roses and Anemones, by Vincent van Gogh.

1970, May 4 Photo. *Perf. 12x13*

766	A185	3fr black & multi	2.00	1.75

International Flower Show, Monte Carlo.

Red Cross Type of 1969

3fr, St. Louis giving alms to the poor.

1970, May 4 Engr. *Perf. 13*

767	A194	3fr dk gray, ol gray & slate grn	1.50	1.50

Issued for the Red Cross.

Europa Issue, 1970
Common Design Type

1970, May 4

Size: 26x36mm

768	CD13	40c deep rose lilac	*.85*	*.30*
769	CD13	80c bright green	*2.75*	*.90*
770	CD13	1fr deep blue	*2.75*	*.90*
		Nos. 768-770 (3)	6.35	2.10

UPU Headquarters and Monument, Bern — A206

1970, May 4

771	A206	40c brn ol, gray & bl grn	.25	.25

New UPU Headquarters in Bern opening.

Plaque and Flag on the Moon, Presidents Kennedy and Nixon — A207

Design: 80c, Astronauts and landing module on moon, and Apollo 11 emblem.

1970, May 4 Photo.

772	A207	40c multicolored	.60	.50
773	A207	80c multicolored	.80	.70

Man's first landing on moon, July 20, 1969. US astronauts Neil A. Armstrong and Col. Edwin E. Aldrin, Jr., with Lt. Col. Michael Collins piloting Apollo 11.

Princes of Monaco Type of 1967

Designs: 1fr, Louis I (1662-1701), by Jean Francois de Troy. 3fr, Charlotte de Gramont (1639-1678), by Sebastian Bourdon.

1970, Dec. 15 Engr. *Perf. 12x13*

774	A182	1fr multicolored	.55	.55
775	A182	3fr multicolored	1.25	1.25

Painting Type of 1968

Design: 3fr, Portrait of Dédie, by Amedeo Modigliani (1884-1920).

1970, Dec. 15

776	A185	3fr multicolored	2.75	2.00

Beethoven and "Ode to Joy" A208

1970, Dec. 15

777	A208	1.30fr brown & maroon	2.25	1.10

Ludwig van Beethoven (1770-1827), composer.

Dumas and Scene from "Three Musketeers" — A209

Designs: 40c, Henri Rougier and biplane over Monaco. 80c, Alphonse de Lamartine and scenes from his works.

1970, Dec. 15
778 A209 30c blue, brown & gray .35 .25
779 A209 40c blue, sepia & gray .35 .25
780 A209 80c multicolored .45 .35
Nos. 778-780 (3) 1.15 .85

Alexandre Dumas, père (1802-70), novelist; 1st flight over the Mediterranean by Henri Rougier, 60th anniv.; publication of "Méditations Poétiques" by Alphonse de Lamartine (1790-1869), poet, 150th anniv.

Camargue Horse A210

Horses: 20c, Anglo-Arabian thoroughbred. 30c, French saddle horse. 40c, Lippizaner. 50c, Trotter. 70c, English thoroughbred. 85c, Arabian. 1.15fr, Barbary.

1970, Dec. 15 Engr. *Perf. 13*
781 A210 10c bl, ol bis & dk bl .35 .20
782 A210 20c vio bl, brn & ol .35 .25
783 A210 30c blue, brn & grn .70 .45
784 A210 40c gray, ind & ol bis 1.40 .70
785 A210 50c blue, dk brn & ol 1.75 1.00
786 A210 70c dk grn, ol brn & red brn 3.25 2.00
787 A210 85c dk grn, ol & sl 3.25 2.25
788 A210 1.15fr blue, emer & blk 3.25 2.25
Nos. 781-788,C77 (9) 16.30 11.10

Prince Rainier Type of 1955 and Palace Type of 1960

90c, Honor Court. 1.40fr, Aerial view of Palace.

1971 Engr. *Perf. 13*
789 A83 60c plum & blk 2.75 .70
790 A116 90c dk car, ultra & blk 2.75 .75
791 A83 1.10fr gray & ultra 3.25 1.60
792 A116 1.40fr pur, org & grn 3.25 2.40
Nos. 789-792 (4) 12.00 5.45

Aquatic Stadium Type of 1964-67, "1962" Omitted

1971
793 A153 26c pur, ultra & blk .45 .20
794 A153 30c cop red, bl, lil & blk .55 .20
795 A153 45c sl grn, vio bl & blk .90 .35
796 A153 90c ol, Prus bl & blk 1.40 .55
Nos. 793-796 (4) 3.30 1.30

Nos. 793-796 were issued precanceled only. See note after No. 324.

Europa Issue, 1971

Common Design Type

1971, Sept. 6
797 CD14 50c carmine rose *2.50* .50
798 CD14 80c brt blue *6.25* .80
799 CD14 1.30fr slate green *6.25* *1.50*
Nos. 797-799 (3) *15.00* 2.80

Old Bridge at Sospel — A211

80c, Roquebrune Castle. 1.30fr, Grimaldi Castle. 3fr, Roman Monument, La Turbie, vert. All views in Alpes-Maritimes Department, France.

1971, Sept. 6
800 A211 50c sl grn, bl & ol brn .25 .25
801 A211 80c sl grn, sl & brn .45 .25
802 A211 1.30fr brn, sl grn & red .55 .45
803 A211 3fr brt bl, sl & olive 1.50 1.10
Nos. 800-803 (4) 2.75 2.05

Protection of historic monuments.

Theodolite, Underwater Scene and Coast Line — A212

1971, Sept. 6
804 A212 80c blue grn & multi .55 .45

International Hydrographical Bureau, 50th anniv.

Sea Bird Covered with Oil — A213

1971, Sept. 6
805 A213 50c dp blue & indigo .55 .45

Against pollution of the seas.

"Arts" (Organ Pipes and Michelangelo's Creation of Adam) — A214

"Science" (Alchemist, Radar and Rocket) — A215

Prince Pierre of Monaco — A216

Design: 80c, "Culture" (medieval scholar, book, film and television).

1971, Sept. 6 Engr. *Perf. 13*
806 A214 30c brt bl, pur & brn .25 .20
807 A215 50c slate & brn org .35 .25
808 A214 80c emerald & brn .35 .35

Photo. *Perf. 12½x13*
809 A216 1.30fr gray green .70 .45
Nos. 806-809 (4) 1.65 1.25

25th anniv. of UNESCO.

Cocker Spaniel A217

1971, Sept. 6 *Perf. 13x12½*
810 A217 50c multicolored 2.50 1.60

Intl. Dog Show. See Nos. 826, 879, 910.

Hand Holding Blood Donor Emblem A218

1971, Sept. 6 Engr. *Perf. 13*
811 A218 80c red, violet & gray .45 .45

7th International Blood Donors Congress, Monaco, Oct. 21-24.

Red Cross Type of 1969

3fr, St. Vincent de Paul appearing to prisoners.

1971, Sept. 6
812 A194 3fr bl grn, ol grn & dp grn 1.40 1.25

Princes of Monaco Type of 1967

Designs: 1fr, Antoine I (1701-1731), by Hyacinthe Rigaud. 3fr, Marie de Lorraine (1674-1724), French School.

1972, Jan. 18 *Perf. 12x13*
813 A182 1fr multicolored .70 .70
814 A182 3fr multicolored 1.40 1.40

Painting Type of 1968

Designs: 2fr, The Cradle, by Berthe Morisot. 3fr, Clown, by Jean Antoine Watteau.

1972, Jan. 18
815 A185 2fr green & multi 1.60 1.00
816 A185 3fr multicolored 2.25 1.60

No. 815 issued for 25th anniv. (in 1971) of UNICEF.

Christ Before Pilate, by Dürer A219

1972, Jan. 18 *Perf. 13*
817 A219 2fr lt brown & blk 1.40 1.10

500th anniv. of the birth of Albrecht Dürer (1471-1528), German painter and engraver.

La Fontaine and Animals — A220

Saint-Saens and "Samson et Dalila" — A221

1.30fr, Charles Baudelaire, nudes and cats.

1972, Jan. 18
818 A220 50c brn, grn & sl grn .65 .35
819 A221 90c dk brn & yel brn .60 .45
820 A220 1.30fr blk, red & vio brn .95 .70
Nos. 818-820 (3) 2.20 1.50

350th anniv. of the birth of Jean de La Fontaine (1621-1695), fabulist; 50th anniv. of the death of Camille Saint-Saens (1835-1921), composer; 150th anniv. of the birth of Charles Baudelaire (1821-1867), poet.

Father Christmas A222

1972, Jan. 18
821 A222 30c bis, slate bl & red .25 .20
822 A222 50c vio brn, grn & red .25 .25
823 A222 90c ocher, indigo & red .55 .35
Nos. 821-823 (3) 1.05 .80

Christmas 1971.

Battle of Lepanto — A223

1972, Jan. 18
824 A223 1fr dull bl, red & brn .65 .45

400th anniversary of the Battle of Lepanto against the Turks.

Steam and Diesel Locomotives, UIC Emblem — A224

1972, Apr. 27 Engr. *Perf. 13*
825 A224 50c dk car, lilac & choc 1.00 .75

50th anniversary of the founding of the International Railroad Union (UIC).

Dog Type of 1971

1972, Apr. 27 Photo. *Perf. 13x12½*
826 A217 60c Great Dane 2.50 1.60

International Dog Show.

Serene Landscape, Pollution, Destruction — A225

1972, Apr. 27 **Engr.** ***Perf. 13***
827 A225 90c grn, brn & blk .70 .45

Anti-pollution fight.

Ski Jump, Sapporo '72 Emblem — A226

1972, Apr. 27
828 A226 90c bl grn, dk red & blk .70 .55

11th Winter Olympic Games, Sapporo, Japan, Feb. 3-13.

Flower Type of 1968

3fr, Flowers in Vase, by Paul Cezanne.

1972, Apr. 27 **Photo.** ***Perf. 12x13***
829 A185 3fr multicolored 3.25 2.75

International Flower Show, Monte Carlo.

Red Cross Type of 1969

3fr, St. Francis of Assisi comforting poor man.

1972, Apr. 27 **Engr.** ***Perf. 13***
830 A194 3fr dk purple & brn 1.75 1.40

For the Red Cross.

Europa Issue 1972
Common Design Type

1972, Apr. 27 ***Perf. 12½x13***
Size: 26x36mm
831 CD15 50c vio blue & org *1.75* .60
832 CD15 90c vio blue & emer *3.25* .80

Church of Sts. John and Paul (detail), by Canaletto A227

Designs: 60c, Church of St. Peter of Castello, by Francesco Guardi. 2fr, St. Mark's Square, by Bernardo Bellotto.

1972, Apr. 27 ***Perf. 13***
Sizes: 36x48mm (30c, 2fr); 26½x48mm (60c)
833 A227 30c rose red .40 .25
834 A227 60c brt purple .50 .35
835 A227 2fr Prus blue 1.90 1.25
Nos. 833-835 (3) 2.80 1.85

UNESCO campaign to save Venice.

Dressage A228

Equestrian Events: 90c, Jump over fences. 1.10fr, Jump over wall. 1.40fr, Jump over gates.

1972, Apr. 27
836 A228 60c rose car, vio bl & brn .85 .85
837 A228 90c vio bl, rose car & brn 1.10 1.10
838 A228 1.10fr brn, rose car & vio bl 1.75 1.75
839 A228 1.40fr vio bl, rose car & brn 2.75 2.75
a. Block of 4 + 2 labels 11.00 11.00

20th Olympic Games, Munich, Aug. 26-Sept. 10. Nos. 836-839 printed se-tenant in sheets of 24 stamps and 6 labels.

Auguste Escoffier and his Birthplace A229

1972, May 6 **Engr.** ***Perf. 13***
840 A229 45c black & olive .50 .25

125th anniversary of the birth of Georges Auguste Escoffier (1846-1935), French chef.

Young Drug Addict — A230

1972, July 3
841 A230 50c carmine, sep & org .50 .25
842 A230 90c slate grn, sep & ind .75 .45

Fight against drug abuse.

Congress Emblem, Birds and Animals — A231

1972, Sept. 25

Designs: 50c, Congress emblem, Neptune, sea, earth and land creatures, horiz. 90c, Globe, land, sea and air creatures.

843 A231 30c ol, brt grn & car .25 .25
844 A231 50c ocher, brn & org brn .35 .25
845 A231 90c org brn, bl & ol .55 .45
Nos. 843-845 (3) 1.15 .95

17th Intl. Zoology Cong., Monaco, 9/24-30.

Arrangement of Lilies and Palm — A232

Designs: Floral arrangements.

1972, Nov. 13 **Photo.** ***Perf. 13***
846 A232 30c orange red & multi .65 .40
847 A232 50c multicolored 1.00 .60
848 A232 90c black & multi 1.50 1.00
Nos. 846-848 (3) 3.15 2.00

International Flower Show, Monte Carlo, May, 1973. See Nos. 894-896.

Child and Adoration of the Kings A233

1972, Nov. 13 **Engr.**
849 A233 30c gray, vio bl & brt pink .25 .20
850 A233 50c dp car, lil & brn .25 .25
851 A233 90c violet bl & pur .45 .35
Nos. 849-851 (3) .95 .80

Christmas 1972.

Louis Bleriot and his Monoplane — A234

50c, Roald Amundsen & Antarctic landscape. 90c, Louis Pasteur & laboratory.

1972, Dec. 4
852 A234 30c choc & brt blue .25 .25
853 A234 50c Prus blue & ind .35 .30
854 A234 90c choc & ocher .70 .55
Nos. 852-854 (3) 1.30 1.10

Louis Bleriot (1872-1936), French aviation pioneer (30c); Roald Amundsen (1872-1928), Norwegian polar explorer (50c); Louis Pasteur (1822-1895), French chemist and bacteriologist (90c).

Gethsemane, by Giovanni Canavesio — A235

Frescoes by Canavesio, 15th century, Chapel of Our Lady of Fountains at La Brique: 50c, Christ Stripped of His Garments. 90c, Christ Carrying the Cross. 1.40fr, Resurrection. 2fr, Crucifixion.

1972, Dec. 4
855 A235 30c bright rose .25 .25
856 A235 50c indigo .35 .25
857 A235 90c slate green .50 .50
858 A235 1.40fr bright red .70 .70
859 A235 2fr purple 1.10 .70
Nos. 855-859 (5) 2.90 2.40

Protection of historic monuments.

Princes of Monaco Type of 1967

1fr, Jacques I, by Nicolas de Largillière. 3fr, Louise Hippolyte (1697-1731), by Jean Baptiste Vanloo.

1972, Dec. 4 ***Perf. 12x13***
860 A182 1fr multicolored .75 .55
861 A182 3fr multicolored 1.50 1.25

Girl, Syringe, Addicts A236

1973, Jan. 5 **Engr.** ***Perf. 13***
862 A236 50c brt bl, claret & sl grn .35 .25
863 A236 90c orange, lil & emer .55 .45

Fight against drug abuse.

Souvenir Sheet

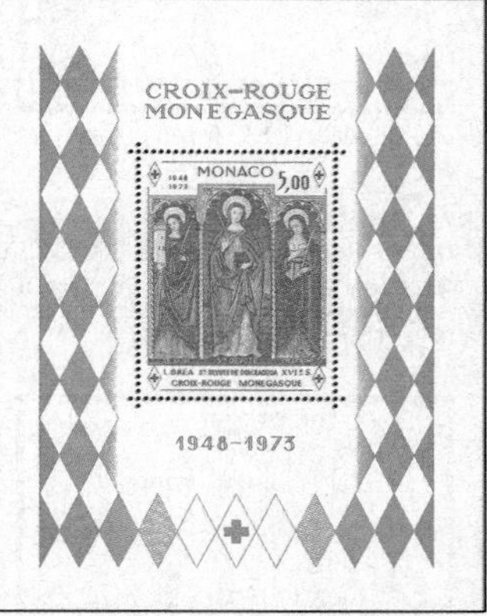

Sts. Barbara, Dévote and Agatha, by Louis Brea — A237

1973, Apr. 30
864 A237 5fr dull red 14.00 14.00

Red Cross of Monaco, 25th anniv.

Flower Type of 1968

Flowers in Vase, by Ambrosius Bosschaert.

1973, Apr. 30 **Photo.** ***Perf. 12x13***
865 A185 3.50fr multicolored 4.75 3.25

International Flower Show, Monte Carlo.

Europa Issue 1973
Common Design Type

1973, Apr. 30 **Engr.** ***Perf. 13***
Size: 36x26mm
866 CD16 50c orange *6.00* .90
867 CD16 90c blue green *9.00* *1.50*

Molière, Scene from "Le Malade Imaginaire" A238

1973, Apr. 30
868 A238 20c red, vio bl & brn .45 .35

Tricentenary of the death of Molière (1622-1673), French actor and writer.

Costumed Players and Mask — A239

1973, Apr. 30

869 A239 60c red, lilac & blue .50 .35

5th International Amateur Theater Festival.

Virgin Mary, St. Teresa, Lisieux Basilica — A240

1973, Apr. 30

870 A240 1.40fr indigo, ultra & brn .80 .55

Centenary of the birth of St. Teresa of Lisieux (Thérèse Martin, 1873-1897), Carmelite nun.

Charles Peguy and Cathedral of Chartres — A241

1973, Apr. 30

871 A241 50c dp claret, ol brn & sl .40 .35

Centenary of the birth of Charles Pierre Peguy (1873-1914), French writer.

Colette, Books and Cat A242

Designs: No. 873, Eugene Ducretet and transmission from Eiffel Tower to Pantheon. 45c, Jean Henri Fabre and insects. 50c, Blaise Pascal, vert. 60c, Radar installation and telegraph wire insulators. No. 877, William Webb Ellis and rugby. No. 878, Sir George Cayley and early model plane.

1973, Apr. 30

872 A242 30c dp org, bl & dk bl 1.10 .45
873 A242 30c brown & multi .35 .25
874 A242 45c dp blue & multi 2.50 1.25
875 A242 50c vio bl, lil & dk pur .35 .35
876 A242 60c brn, bl blk & brt bl .45 .35
877 A242 90c brown & car rose .80 .45
878 A242 90c red & multi .70 .50
Nos. 872-878 (7) 6.25 3.60

Anniversaries: Colette (1873-1954), French writer (#872); 75th anniv. of 1st Hertzian wave transmission (#873); Fabre (1823-1915), entomologist (45c); Pascal (1623-1662), scientist and philosopher (50c); 5th Intl. Telecommunications Day (60c); Sesquicentennial of the invention of rugby (#877); Cayley (1821-95), aviation pioneer (#878).

Dog Type of 1971

1973, Apr. 30 Photo. ***Perf. 13x12½***

879 A217 45c German shepherd 10.50 5.75

International Dog Show.

The First Crèche, by Giotto — A243

Paintings of the Nativity by: 45c, School of Filippo Lippi. 50c, Giotto. 1fr, 15th century miniature, vert. 2fr, Fra Angelico, vert.

Perf. 13x12, 12x13

1973, Nov. 12 **Engr.**

880 A243 30c purple .45 .35
881 A243 45c rose magenta 1.10 .70
882 A243 50c brown orange 1.00 .75
883 A243 1fr slate green 1.90 1.25
884 A243 2fr olive green 3.50 3.00
Nos. 880-884,C78 (6) 10.20 7.80

750th anniversary of the first crèche assembled by St. Francis of Assisi.

Picnic and View of Monte Carlo — A244

Designs: 20c, Dance around maypole, vert. 30c, "U Brandi" folk dance. 45c, Dance around St. John's fire. 50c, Blessing of the Christmas bread. 60c, Blessing of the sea. 1fr, Good Friday procession.

1973, Nov. 12 ***Perf. 13***

885 A244 10c sl grn, dk bl & sep .20 .20
886 A244 20c blue, ol & lil .25 .25
887 A244 30c lt grn, bl & brn .25 .25
888 A244 45c dk brn, vio & red brn .55 .55
889 A244 50c black, brn & ver .70 .70
890 A244 60c blue, mag & vio bl .75 .75
891 A244 1fr ind, vio & ol bis 1.25 1.25
Nos. 885-891 (7) 3.95 3.95

Monegasque customs.

Princes of Monaco Type of 1967

Paintings of Charlotte Grimaldi, by Pierre Gobert, 1733: No. 892, in court dress, No. 893, in nun's habit.

1973, Nov. 12 ***Perf. 12x13***

892 A182 2fr multicolored 1.75 1.50
893 A182 2fr multicolored 1.75 1.50

Flower Type of 1972

Designs: Floral arrangements.

1973, Nov. 12 Photo. ***Perf. 13***

894 A232 45c vio blue & multi 1.25 .80
895 A232 60c dk brown & multi 2.00 1.10
896 A232 1fr brown org & multi 3.50 2.00
Nos. 894-896 (3) 6.75 3.90

Intl. Flower Show, Monte Carlo, May 1974.

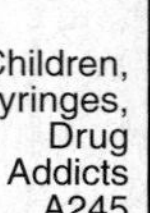

Children, Syringes, Drug Addicts A245

1973, Nov. 12 **Engr.**

897 A245 50c blue, grn & brn .35 .25
898 A245 90c red, brn & indigo .70 .45

Fight against drug abuse.

Souvenir Sheet

Prince Rainier III — A246

1974, May 8 **Engr.** ***Imperf.***

899 A246 10fr black 6.50 6.50

25th anniv. of the accession of Prince Rainier III.

Art from Around the World — A247

70c, Hands holding letters. 1.10fr, Famous buildings, Statue of Liberty and Sphinx.

1974, May 8 ***Perf. 13***

900 A247 50c choc & org brn .35 .25
901 A247 70c aqua & multi .45 .45
902 A247 1.10fr indigo & multi .90 .70
Nos. 900-902 (3) 1.70 1.40

Centenary of the Universal Postal Union.

King of Rome (Napoleon's Son), by Bosio — A248

Europa: 1.10fr, Madame Elisabeth (sister of Louis XVI), by Francois Josef Bosio.

1974, May 8

903 A248 45c slate grn & sep *1.50 .50*
904 A248 1.10fr brn & ol brn *3.00 .85*
a. Souv. sheet, 5 #903, 5 #904 *45.00 25.00*

Red Cross Type of 1969

Design: St. Bernard of Menthon rescuing mountain traveler.

1974, May 8

905 A194 3fr Prus bl & vio brn 1.60 1.25

For the Red Cross.

Henri Farman and Farman Planes A249

Designs: 40c, Guglielmo Marconi, circuit diagram and ships which conducted first tests. 45c, Ernest Duchesne and penicillin. 50c, Fernand Forest and 4-cylinder motor.

1974, May 8

906 A249 30c multicolored .25 .25
907 A249 40c multicolored .45 .25
908 A249 45c multicolored .45 .25
909 A249 50c multicolored .45 .25
Nos. 906-909 (4) 1.60 1.00

Farman (1874-1934), French aviation pioneer; Marconi (1874-1937), Italian inventor; Duchesne (1874-1912), French biologist; Forest (1851-1914), inventor.

Dog Type of 1971

1974, May 8 Photo. ***Perf. 13x12½***

910 A217 60c Schnauzer 5.00 3.25

Intl. Dog Show, Monte Carlo, Apr. 6-7.

Ronsard and Scenes from his Sonnet à Hélène — A250

1974, May 8 **Engr.** ***Perf. 13***

911 A250 70c choc & dk car .55 .35

450th anniversary of the birth of Pierre de Ronsard (1524-1585), French poet.

Winston Churchill — A251

1974, May 8

912 A251 1fr gray & brn .65 .45

Centenary of the birth of Sir Winston Churchill (1874-1965), statesman.

Palaces of Monaco and Vienna — A252

1974, May 8

913 A252 2fr multicolored 1.40 1.00

60th anniversary of the first International Police Congress, Monaco, Apr. 1914.

The Box, by Auguste Renoir A253

Rising Sun, by Claude Monet — A254

Impressionist Paintings: No. 915, Dancing Class, by Edgar Degas. No. 917, Entrance to Voisins Village, by Camille Pissarro. No. 918, House of the Hanged Man, by Paul Cezanne. No. 919, The Flooding of Port Marly, by Alfred Sisley.

Perf. 12x13, 13x12

1974, Nov. 12 **Engr.**

914	A253 1fr multicolored		1.75	1.60
915	A253 1fr multicolored		1.75	1.60
916	A254 2fr multicolored		4.00	4.00
917	A254 2fr multicolored		4.00	3.25
918	A254 2fr multicolored		4.00	3.25
919	A254 2fr multicolored		4.00	3.25
	Nos. 914-919 (6)		19.50	16.95

Trainer and Tigers A255

Prancing Horses — A256

Perf. 13x12½, 12½x13

1974, Nov. 12

920	A255	2c shown	.20	.20
921	A256	3c shown	.20	.20
922	A255	5c Elephants	.20	.20
923	A256	45c Equestrian act	.55	.35
924	A255	70c Clowns	.75	.70
925	A256	1.10fr Jugglers	1.10	.90
926	A256	5fr Trapeze act	5.00	3.75
		Nos. 920-926 (7)	8.00	6.30

International Circus Festival.

Honoré II Coin A257

1974, Nov. 12 ***Perf. 13***

927	A257 60c rose red & blk	.50	.35

350th anniversary of coins of Monaco.

Underwater Fauna and Flora — A258

Designs: 45c, Fish, and marine life. 1.10fr, Coral.

1974, Nov. 12 **Photo.** ***Perf. 13x12½***

Size: 35x25mm

928	A258 45c multicolored	1.10	.65

Size: 48x27mm

Perf. 13

929	A258 70c multicolored	1.60	1.10
930	A258 1.10fr multicolored	2.25	2.00
	Nos. 928-930 (3)	4.95	3.75

Congress of the International Commission for the Scientific Exploration of the Mediterranean, Monaco, Dec. 6-14.

A259

Floral Arrangements A260

1974, Nov. 12 ***Perf. 13x12½***

931	A259 70c multicolored	1.00	.70
932	A260 1.10fr multicolored	1.60	1.10

International Flower Show, Monte Carlo, May 1975. See Nos. 1003-1004, 1084-1085.

Prince Rainier III — A261

1974-78 **Engr.** ***Perf. 13***

933	A261	60c slate green	1.25	.35
934	A261	80c red	1.25	.45
935	A261	80c brt green	.55	.25
936	A261	1fr brown	3.25	1.10
937	A261	1fr scarlet	.75	.25
938	A261	1fr slate green	.60	.20
939	A261	1.20fr violet bl	7.75	2.50
940	A261	1.20fr red	.70	.20
941	A261	1.25fr blue	1.40	1.00
942	A261	1.50fr black	.90	.70
943	A261	1.70fr dp blue	1.00	.70
944	A261	2fr dk purple	2.75	1.60
945	A261	2.10fr olive bister	1.40	.75
946	A261	2.50fr indigo	2.25	1.60
947	A261	9fr brt violet	5.50	3.50
		Nos. 933-947 (15)	31.30	15.15

Issued: 60c, #934, 936, 939, 2fr, Dec. 23; #935, 937, 1.25fr, 2.50fr, Jan. 10, 1977; #938, 940, 1.50fr, 1.70fr, 2.10fr, 9fr, Aug. 18, 1978.

See Nos. 1200-1204, 1255-1256.

Monte Carlo Beach A262

Prince Albert I Statue and Museum — A264

1974-77

948	A262	25c shown	2.50	.55
949	A264	50c Clock tower	2.50	.55
950	A262	1.10fr Like #948 ('77)	2.10	1.10
951	A264	1.40fr shown	3.25	1.00
952	A262	1.70fr All Saints' Tower	4.50	2.40
953	A264	3fr Fort Antoine	6.50	2.50
954	A262	5.50fr La Condamine (view)	9.25	5.00
		Nos. 948-954 (7)	30.60	13.10

Issue: 1.10fr, Jan. 10; others, Dec. 23.

See Nos. 1005-1008, 1030-1033, 1069-1072, 1095-1098, 1138-1152.

Haageocereus A265

1974, Dec. 23 **Photo.** ***Perf. 12½x13***

955	A265	10c *shown*	.25	.25
956	A265	20c *Matucana*	.35	.25
957	A265	30c *Parodia*	.55	.35
958	A265	85c *Mediolobivia*	2.25	1.10
959	A265	1.90fr *Matucana*	3.75	2.50
960	A265	4fr *Echinocereus*	6.00	4.25
		Nos. 955-960 (6)	13.15	8.70

Plants from Monaco Botanical Gardens.

Europa Issue 1975

Sailor, by Philibert Florence — A266

St. Dévote, by Ludovic Brea — A267

1975, May 13 **Engr.** ***Perf. 13***

961	A266	80c brt red lilac	*1.75*	*.50*
962	A267	1.20fr brt blue	*2.25*	*.85*
a.		Souv. sheet, 5 ea #961-962	*40.00*	*20.00*

Red Cross Type of 1969

Design: St. Bernardino of Siena (1380-1444) burying the dead.

1975, May 13

963	A194 4fr pur & Prus bl	2.75	1.75

For the Red Cross.

Carmen, at the Tavern A268

Scenes from Carmen: 30c, Prologue, vert. 80c, The smugglers' hide-out. 1.40fr, Entrance to bull ring.

1975, May 13

964	A268 30c multicolored	.20	.20
965	A268 60c multicolored	.40	.25
966	A268 80c multicolored	.85	.45
967	A268 1.40fr multicolored	1.25	.90
	Nos. 964-967 (4)	2.70	1.80

Centenary of first performance of opera Carmen by George Bizet (1838-1875).

Louis de Saint-Simon A269

Albert Schweitzer A270

1975, May 13

968	A269 40c bluish black	.40	.30
969	A270 60c black & dull red	.85	.40

300th birth anniversary of Louis de Saint-Simon (1675-1755), statesman and writer, and birth centenary of Albert Schweitzer (1875-1965), medical missionary.

ARPHILA 75 Emblem, G Clef — A271

1975, May 13

970	A271 80c sepia & org brn	.70	.45

ARPHILA 75 International Philatelic Exhibition, Paris, June 6-16.

Seagull and Rising Sun A272

1975, May 13 **Photo.**

971	A272 85c multicolored	.85	.65

Oceanexpo 75, International Exhibition, Okinawa, July 20, 1975-Jan. 1976.

Charity Label and "1f" Destroying Cancer A273

1975, May 13 **Engr.**

972	A273 1fr multicolored	.85	.60

Fight against cancer.

Jesus with Crown of Thorns, Holy Year Emblem — A274

1975, May 13

973	A274 1.15fr lilac, bis & ind	1.00	.70

Holy Year 1975.

Villa Sauber, by Charles Garnier A275

1975, May 13

974	A275 1.20fr multicolored	1.10	.70

European Architectural Heritage Year 1975.

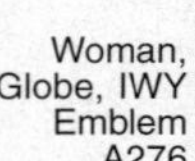

Woman, Globe, IWY Emblem A276

1975, May 13
975 A276 1.20fr multicolored 1.10 .70

International Women's Year.

Nos. 793-796 Surcharged

1975, Apr. 1 Engr. *Perf. 13*
976 A153 42c on 26c multi 2.50 1.10
977 A153 48c on 30c multi 3.25 1.75
978 A153 70c on 45c multi 3.75 2.25
979 A153 1.35fr on 90c multi 5.75 3.00
Nos. 976-979 (4) 15.25 8.10

Nos. 976-979 were issued precanceled only. See note after No. 324.

Rolls Royce "Silver Ghost" 1907 — A277

1975, Nov. Engr. *Perf. 13*
980 A277 5c shown .20 .20
981 A277 10c Hispano Suiza, 1926 .20 .20
982 A277 20c Isotta Fraschini, 1928 .25 .20
983 A277 30c Cord L. 29 .35 .25
984 A277 50c Voisin, 1930 .90 .70
985 A277 60c Duesenberg, 1933 1.00 .75
986 A277 80c Bugatti, 1938 1.75 1.25
987 A277 85c Delahaye, 1940 2.25 2.00
988 A277 1.20fr Cisitalia, 1946 3.25 2.75
989 A277 1.40fr Mercedes Benz, 1955 4.25 3.00
990 A277 5.50fr Lamborghini, 1974 13.00 9.50
Nos. 980-990 (11) 27.40 20.80

Development of the automobile.

Princes of Monaco Type of 1967

Paintings (Unknown Artists): 2fr, Prince Honoré III (1733-1795). 4fr, Princess Catherine de Brignole (1759-1813).

1975, Nov.
991 A182 2fr multicolored 1.90 1.10
992 A182 4fr multicolored 3.75 3.00

Caged Dog A278

Designs: 80c, Cat chased up a tree, vert. 1.20fr, Horses pulling heavy load.

1975, Nov.
993 A278 60c black & brown 1.10 .70
994 A278 80c blk, gray & brn 1.60 1.00
995 A278 1.20fr mag & sl grn 2.10 1.60
Nos. 993-995 (3) 4.80 3.30

125th anniv. of the Grammont (J. P. Delmas Grammont) Law against cruelty to animals.

Dog Type of 1970

1975, Nov.
996 A204 60c Poodle 4.50 3.25

International Dog Show, Monte Carlo.

Maurice Ravel — A279

1.20fr, Johann Strauss and dancers.

1975, Nov.
997 A279 60c maroon & sepia 1.00 .60
998 A279 1.20fr maroon & indigo 2.10 1.40

Maurice Ravel (1875-1937), birth centenary, and Johann Strauss (1804-1849), sesquicentennial of birth, composers.

Clown — A280

1975, Nov. Photo. *Perf. 12½x13*
999 A280 80c multicolored 1.25 .55

2nd Intl. Circus Festival, Monte Carlo, Dec. 1975.

Honoré II Florin, 1640 — A281

1975, Nov. Engr. *Perf. 13*
1000 A281 80c slate & gray .75 .55

See Nos. 1040, 1088, 1234.

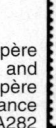

Ampère and Ampère Balance A282

1975, Nov.
1001 A282 85c ultra & indigo .75 .60

André Marie Ampère (1775-1836), physicist, birth bicentennial.

Lamentation for the Dead Christ, by Michelangelo — A283

1975, Nov.
1002 A283 1.40fr black & ol gray 1.25 .80

Michelangelo Buonarroti (1475-1564), Italian sculptor, painter and architect.

Flower Types of 1974

Designs: Floral arrangements.

1975, Nov. Photo. *Perf. 13x12½*
1003 A259 60c multicolored 1.10 .60
1004 A260 80c multicolored 1.60 .85

Intl. Flower Show, Monte Carlo, May 1976.

Clock Tower Type, 1974

1976, Jan. 26 Engr. *Perf. 13*
1005 A263 50c brown lake .65 .35
1006 A263 60c olive green .75 .50
1007 A263 90c purple 1.10 .75
1008 A263 1.60fr brt blue 1.60 1.40
Nos. 1005-1008 (4) 4.10 3.00

Nos. 1005-1008 were issued precanceled only. See note after No. 324.

Prince Pierre — A284

André Maurois and Colette — A285

Portraits: 25c, Jean and Jerome Tharaud. 30c, Emile Henriot, Marcel Pagnol, Georges Duhamel. 50c, Philippe Heriat, Jules Supervielle, L. Pierard. 60c, Roland Dorgeles, M. Achard, G. Bauer. 80c, Franz Hellens, A. Billy, Msgr. Grente. 1.20fr, Jean Giono, L. Pasteur-Vallery-Radot, M. Garcon.

1976, May 3 Engr. *Perf. 13*
1009 A284 10c black .25 .25
1010 A285 20c red & slate .35 .25
1011 A285 25c red, dk bl & blk .35 .25
1012 A285 30c brown .55 .45
1013 A285 50c brn, red & vio bl .55 .45
1014 A285 60c grn, brn & lt brn .70 .45
1015 A285 80c black & magenta 1.10 .90
1016 A285 1.20fr blk, vio & cl 1.75 1.50
Nos. 1009-1016 (8) 5.60 4.50

Literary Council of Monaco, 25th anniv.

Dachshunds — A286

1976, May 3 Photo.
1017 A286 60c multicolored 8.00 4.25

International Dog Show, Monte Carlo.

Bridge Table, Coast A287

1976, May 3 Engr.
1018 A287 60c multicolored .70 .45

Fifth Bridge Olympiade, Monte Carlo.

A. G. Bell, Telephone, 1876, Satellite Dish A288

1976, May 3
1019 A288 80c multicolored .55 .35

Centenary of first telephone call by Alexander Graham Bell, Mar. 10, 1976.

Federation Emblem — A289

1976, May 3
1020 A289 1.20fr multicolored .85 .55

International Federation of Philately (F.I.P.), 50th anniversary.

US Liberty Bell Type of 1926 — A290

1976, May 3
1021 A290 1.70fr carmine & blk 1.40 .95

American Bicentennial.

Fritillaria, by Vincent van Gogh A291

1976, May 3 Photo. *Perf. 12x13*
1022 A291 3fr multicolored 9.00 5.50

Intl. Flower Show, Monte Carlo, May 1976.

Plate with Lemon Branch — A292

Europa: 1.20fr, The Peddler, 19th century figurine, and CEPT emblem.

1976, May 3 *Perf. 12½x13*
1023 A292 80c salmon & multi *1.25* .35
1024 A292 1.20fr ultra & multi *1.75* .50
a. Souv. sheet of 10, 5 each #1023-1024 *32.50* *25.00*

21st Summer Olympic Games, Montreal, Canada — A293

60c, Diving. 80c, Athlete on parallel bars. 85c, Hammer throw. 1.20fr, Rowing, horiz. 1.70fr, Boxing, horiz.

1976, May 3 Engr. *Perf. 13*
1025 A293 60c multicolored .35 .35
1026 A293 80c multicolored .45 .35
1027 A293 85c multicolored .55 .45
1028 A293 1.20fr multicolored .80 .60
1029 A293 1.70fr multicolored 1.40 1.10
a. Souv. sheet of 5, #1025-1029, perf. 14 4.25 4.25
Nos. 1025-1029 (5) 3.55 2.85

Clock Tower Type, 1974

1976, Sept. 1 Engr. *Perf. 13*
1030 A263 52c bister .45 .25
1031 A263 62c red lilac .55 .45
1032 A263 95c scarlet 1.10 .55
1033 A263 1.70fr blue green 1.75 1.00
Nos. 1030-1033 (4) 3.85 2.25

Nos. 1030-1033 were issued precanceled only. See note after No. 324.

Princes of Monaco Type of 1967

Paintings: 2fr, Honoré IV (1815-1819), by Francois Lemoyne. 4fr, Louise d'Aumont-Mazarin (1750-1826), by Marie Verroust.

1976, Nov. 9 *Perf. 12½x13*
1035 A182 2fr violet brown 2.25 1.60
1036 A182 4fr multicolored 3.25 2.25

Red Cross Type of 1969

Design: St. Louise de Marillac and children.

1976, Nov. 9 *Perf. 13*
1037 A194 4fr grn, gray & plum 2.50 2.00

St. Vincent de Paul, View of Monaco A294

1976, Nov. 9
1038 A294 60c multicolored .55 .45

St. Vincent de Paul Conference, Monaco, July 31, 1876, centenary.

Marquise de Sevigné — A295

1976, Nov. 9
1039 A295 80c multicolored .55 .35

Marie de Rabutin-Chantal, Marquise de Sevigné (1626-1696), writer.

Coin Type of 1975

Design: 80c, Honoré II 2-gros coin.

1976, Nov. 9
1040 A281 80c grn & steel bl .75 .45

Richard E. Byrd, Roald Amundsen, North Pole — A296

1976, Nov. 9
1041 A296 85c olive, blk & bl 1.75 1.25

1st flights over the North Pole, 50th anniv.

Gulliver Holding King, Queen and Enemy Fleet — A297

1976, Nov. 9
1042 A297 1.20fr indigo, bl & brn .80 .55

250th anniversary of the publication of Gulliver's Travels, by Jonathan Swift.

Child and Christmas Decorations A298

1976, Nov. 9 *Perf. 13x12½*
1043 A298 60c multicolored .40 .25
1044 A298 1.20fr multicolored .85 .50

Christmas 1976.

"Trapped by Drugs" A299

1976, Nov. 9
1045 A299 80c grn, ultra & org .60 .35
1046 A299 1.20fr red brn, vio & car .85 .50

Fight against drug abuse.

Floral Arrangement A300

Design: 1fr, Floral arrangement. Designs by Princess Grace.

1976, Nov. 9 Photo. *Perf. 13½x13*
1047 A300 80c yellow grn & multi 1.50 .90
1048 A300 1fr lt blue & multi 2.25 1.50

International Flower Show, Monte Carlo, May 1977. See Nos. 1124-1125, 1191.

Clown and Circus Acts — A301

1976, Nov. 9
1049 A301 1fr multi 1.90 1.10

3rd Intl. Circus Festival, Dec. 26-30.

L'Hirondelle I — A302

Prince Albert I — A303

Designs (Gouaches by Louis Tinayre): 30c, Crew of L'Hirondelle. 80c, L'Hirondelle in Storm. 1fr, The Helmsman, vert. 1.25fr, L'Hirondelle in Storm. 1.40fr, Shrimp Fishermen in Boat. 1.90fr, Hauling in the Net, vert. 2.50fr, Catching Opah Fish.

1977, May 3 Engr. *Perf. 13*
1050 A302 10c multicolored .20 .20
1051 A303 20c multicolored .25 .20
1052 A302 30c multicolored .30 .25
1053 A302 80c multicolored .45 .45
1054 A302 1fr multicolored .75 .55
1055 A302 1.25fr multicolored 1.10 .90
1056 A302 1.40fr multicolored 1.60 .25
1057 A302 1.90fr multicolored 2.75 2.25
1058 A302 2.50fr multicolored 2.25 1.50
Nos. 1050-1058 (9) 9.65 6.55

75th anniversary of publication of "The Career of a Sailor," by Prince Albert I.
See Nos. 1073-1081.

Pyreneean Mountain Dogs — A304

1977, May 3 Photo.
1059 A304 80c multicolored 6.25 3.75

International Dog Show, Monte Carlo.
See No. 1199.

Motherhood, by Mary Cassatt — A305

1977, May 3 Engr.
1060 A305 80c multicolored 1.10 .90

World Association of the Friends of Children.

Archers, Target and Monte Carlo — A306

1977, May 3
1061 A306 1.10fr multicolored .80 .55

10th Intl. Rainier III Archery Championships.

Spirit of St. Louis and Lindbergh — A307

1977, May 3
1062 A307 1.90fr multicolored 1.75 1.25

50th anniversary of first transatlantic flight by Charles Lindbergh.

The Dock at Deauville, by Dufy — A308

1977, May 3 Photo.
1063 A308 2fr multicolored 4.50 3.00

Raoul Dufy (1877-1953), painter, birth centenary.

Young Girl, by Rubens — A309

Rubens Paintings: 1fr, Duke of Buckingham. 1.40fr, Rubens' son Nicolas, 2 years old.

1977, May 3 Engr.
1064 A309 80c multicolored .75 .55
1065 A309 1fr multicolored 1.10 .70
1066 A309 1.40fr multicolored 2.00 1.25
Nos. 1064-1066 (3) 3.85 2.50

Peter Paul Rubens (1577-1640).

Helmet Tower, Monaco — A310

Europa: 1.40fr, St. Michael's Church, Menton.

1977, May 3
1067 A310 1fr multicolored *1.25* .50
1068 A310 1.40fr multicolored *3.00* .80
a. Souv. sheet, 5 each #1067-1068 *35.00* *25.00*

Clock Tower Type of 1974

1977, Apr. 1 Engr. *Perf. 13*
1069 A263 54c brt green .45 .35
1070 A263 68c orange .55 .45
1071 A263 1.05fr olive 1.10 .55
1072 A263 1.85fr brown 1.75 1.00
Nos. 1069-1072 (4) 3.85 2.35

Nos. 1069-1072 were issued precanceled only. See note after No. 324.

Career of a Sailor Types of 1977

Designs (Gouaches by Louis Tinayre): 10c, Yacht Princess Alice II, Kiel harbor. 20c, Laboratory on board ship. 30c, Yacht amidst ice floes. 80c, Crew in arctic outfits. 1fr, Yacht in polar region. 1.25fr, Yacht in snow storm. 1.40fr, Building camp on ice. 1.90fr, Yacht under steam amidst ice floes. 3fr, Yacht passing iceberg.

1977, Nov. Engr. *Perf. 13*
1073 A302 10c blk & brt bl .20 .20
1074 A302 20c Prus blue .25 .20
1075 A302 30c blk & brt bl .25 .25
1076 A303 80c multicolored .55 .45
1077 A302 1fr brt grn & blk .70 .55
1078 A302 1.25fr vio, sep & blk 1.00 .75
1079 A302 1.40fr ol, bl & pur 1.60 1.25
1080 A302 1.90fr blk & brt bl 2.75 2.25
1081 A302 3fr dk grn, ol & brt bl 4.00 3.00
Nos. 1073-1081 (9) 11.30 8.90

75th anniversary of publication of "The Career of a Sailor," by Prince Albert I.

Santa Claus A311

1977, Nov.
1082 A311 80c multicolored .60 .25
1083 A311 1.40fr multicolored .80 .40

Christmas 1977.

Flowers Types of 1974

Designs: 80c, Snapdragons and bellflowers. 1fr, Ikebana arrangement.

1977, Nov. Photo. *Perf. 13½x13*
1084 A259 80c multicolored 1.25 .70
1085 A260 1fr multicolored 1.75 1.10

Intl. Flower Show, Monte Carlo, May 1978.

Face (Van Gogh), Syringe, Hallucination Pattern — A312

1977, Nov. Engr. *Perf. 13*
1086 A312 1fr multicolored .75 .45

Fight against drug abuse.

Clown, Flags of Participants A313

1977, Nov. Photo. *Perf. 13½x13*
1087 A313 1fr multicolored 1.75 1.25

Fourth International Circus Festival. Monte Carlo, December 1977.

Coin Type of 1975

Design: 80c, Doubloon of Honoré II, 1648.

1977, Nov. Engr. *Perf. 13*
1088 A281 80c lil & brn .70 .45

Mediterranean Landscape and Industrial Pollution — A314

1977, Nov.
1089 A314 1fr multicolored .85 .50

Protection of the Mediterranean. Meeting of the UN Mediterranean Environmental Protection Group, Monte Carlo, Nov. 28-Dec. 6.

Men Spreading Tar, Dr. Guglielminetti, 1903 Car — A315

1977, Nov.
1090 A315 1.10fr multicolored .80 .45

75th anniversary of first tarred roads, invented by Swiss Dr. Guglielminetti.

View of Monaco and Tennis Emblem — A316

First Match at Wimbledon and Stadium — A317

1977, Nov.
1091 A316 1fr multicolored 1.40 .70
1092 A317 1.40fr multicolored 1.50 1.00

Lawn Tennis Federation of Monaco, 50th anniv. and cent. of 1st intl. tennis match at Wimbledon.

Prince of Monaco Type of 1967

Honoré V (1819-1841), by Marie Verroust.

1977, Nov. *Perf. 12½x13*
1093 A182 6fr multicolored 4.50 3.25

Red Cross Type of 1969

Design: 4fr, St. John Bosco and boys.

1977, Nov. *Perf. 13*
1094 A194 4fr multicolored 2.50 2.00

Nos. 1069-1072 Surcharged

1978, Jan. 17
1095 A263 58c on 54c brt grn .55 .40
1096 A263 73c on 68c orange .90 .55
1097 A263 1.15fr on 1.05fr olive 1.25 .90
1098 A263 2fr on 1.85fr brn 2.10 1.40
Nos. 1095-1098 (4) 4.80 3.25

See note after No. 324.

Illustrations, Novels by Jules Verne — A318

5c, Shipwreck. 25c, The Abandoned Ship, from "Mysterious Island". 30c, Secret of the Island. 80c, Robur, the Conqueror. 1fr, Master Zacharius. 1.40fr, The Castle in the Carpathians. 1.70fr, The Children of Capt. Grant. 5.50fr, Jules Verne and allegories.

1978, May 2 Engr. *Perf. 13*
1099 A318 5c multicolored .20 .20
1100 A318 25c multicolored .30 .20
1101 A318 30c multicolored .30 .25
1102 A318 80c multicolored .55 .50
1103 A318 1fr multicolored 1.00 .60
1104 A318 1.40fr multicolored 1.20 .85
1105 A318 1.70fr multicolored 1.75 1.40
1106 A318 5.50fr multicolored 4.25 3.25
Nos. 1099-1106 (8) 9.55 7.25

Jules Verne (1828-1905), science fiction writer, birth sesquicentennial.

Congress Center and Monte Carlo A319

1.40fr, Congress Center, view from the sea.

1978, May 2
1107 A319 1fr multicolored .60 .50
1108 A319 1.40fr multicolored .80 .50

Inauguration of Monaco Congress Center.

Soccer Players and Globe — A320

1978, May 2
1109 A320 1fr multicolored .75 .75

11th World Soccer Cup Championship, Argentina, June 1-25.

Vivaldi and St. Mark's Place, Venice — A321

1978, May 2
1110 A321 1fr dk brown & red .90 .80

Antonio Vivaldi (1675?-1741), Italian violinist and composer.

Control Ship and Grimaldi Palace — A322

1fr, Map of coastal area and city emblems.

1978, May 2
Size: 26x36mm
1111 A322 80c multi .60 .50
Size: 48x27mm
1112 A322 1fr multi, horiz. .60 .50

Protection of the environment, signing of "Ra Mo Ge" agreement for the protection of the Mediterranean Coast between Saint-Raphael, France, and Genoa, Italy (including Monaco).

Monaco Cathedral A323

Europa: 1.40fr, View of Principality from East.

1978, May 2 *Perf. 12½x13*
1113 A323 1fr multicolored *1.75 .40*
1114 A323 1.40fr multicolored *3.25 .70*
a. Souv. sheet, 5 each #1113-1114 *40.00 25.00*

Cinderella — A324

Mother Goose Tales: 25c, Puss in Boots. 30c, Sleeping Beauty. 80c, Fairy tale princess. 1fr, Little Red Riding Hood. 1.40fr, Bluebeard. 1.70fr, Tom Thumb. 1.90fr, Riquet with the Tuft of Hair. 2.50fr, The Fairies.

1978, Nov. 8 Engr. *Perf. 13*
1115 A324 5c multicolored .20 .20
1116 A324 25c multicolored .25 .20
1117 A324 30c multicolored .25 .25
1118 A324 80c multicolored .60 .50
1119 A324 1fr multicolored .80 .60
1120 A324 1.40fr multicolored 1.00 .85
1121 A324 1.70fr multicolored 1.25 1.10
1122 A324 1.90fr multicolored 1.75 1.25
1123 A324 2.50fr multicolored 2.40 1.75
Nos. 1115-1123 (9) 8.50 6.70

Charles Perrault (1628-1703), compiler of Mother Goose Tales.

Flower Type of 1976

Van Gogh Paintings: 1fr, Sunflowers. 1.70fr, Iris.

1978, Nov. 8 Photo. *Perf. 12½x13*
1124 A300 1fr multicolored 2.75 2.25
1125 A300 1.70fr multicolored 3.75 2.25

Intl. Flower show, Monte Carlo, May 1979, and 125th birth anniv. of Vincent van Gogh (1853-1890), Dutch painter.

Afghan Hound A325

Design: 1.20fr, Russian wolfhound.

1978, Nov. 8 *Perf. 13x12½*
1126 A325 1fr multicolored 3.00 2.40
1127 A325 1.20fr multicolored 4.50 3.00

International Dog Show, Monte Carlo.

Child Holding Gift of Shoes — A326

1978, Nov. 8 Engr. *Perf. 12½x13*
1128 A326 1fr multicolored .80 .50

Christmas 1978.

Catherine and William Booth, Salvation Army Band — A327

1978, Nov. 8 Engr. *Perf. 13*
1129 A327 1.70fr multicolored 1.20 1.00

Centenary of founding of Salvation Army.

Trained Seals A328

1fr, Lions, vert. 1.40fr, Equestrian act. 1.90fr, Monkey music band. 2.40fr, Trapeze act.

1978, Nov. 8 *Perf. 13x12½*
1130 A328 80c multicolored .70 .50
1131 A328 1fr multicolored 1.00 .80
1132 A328 1.40fr multicolored 1.40 1.00
1133 A328 1.90fr multicolored 2.40 2.00
1134 A328 2.40fr multicolored 3.50 2.40
Nos. 1130-1134 (5) 9.00 6.70

5th Intl. Circus Festival, Monte Carlo.

Princes of Monaco Type of 1967

Paintings: 2fr, Florestan I (1841-1856), by G. Dauphin. 4fr, Caroline Gilbert de Lametz (1793-1879), by Marie Verroust.

1978, Nov. 8 Engr. *Perf. 12½x13*
1135 A182 2fr multicolored 2.00 1.40
1136 A182 4fr multicolored 3.50 3.00

Souvenir Sheet

Henri Dunant and Battle Scene — A329

1978, Nov. 8 Engr. *Perf. 13*
1137 A329 5fr multicolored 4.25 4.25

Henri Dunant (1828-1910), founder of Red Cross.

View Types of 1974

1978-80
1138 A262 25c All Saints' Tower .35 .35
1139 A262 65c Monte Carlo Beach .35 .35
1140 A263 70c Exotic Garden, cacti ('80) .70 .55
1142 A262 1.10fr Palais de Justice ('80) .75 .55
1144 A263 1.30fr Cathedral .75 .45
1145 A264 1.50fr Prince Albert Statue and Museum ('80) 1.25 1.10
1146 A262 1.80fr La Condamine 1.25 1.00
1148 A262 2.30fr Palace ('80) 2.25 1.60
1152 A262 6.50fr Monte Carlo Auditorium 3.75 2.75
Nos. 1138-1152 (9) 11.40 8.70

Convention Center, Monte Carlo A330

1978-79
1154 A330 61c vermilion .40 .20
1155 A330 64c green .40 .20
1156 A330 68c brt blue .40 .20
1157 A330 78c dp rose lilac .55 .20
1158 A330 83c violet blue .45 .20
1159 A330 88c orange .45 .20
1160 A330 1.25fr brown .90 .45
1161 A330 1.30fr purple .75 .45
1162 A330 1.40fr brt yel grn .70 .40
1163 A330 2.10fr violet blue 1.10 .80
1164 A330 2.25fr brown org 1.25 .75
1165 A330 2.35fr lilac rose 1.40 .75
Nos. 1154-1165 (12) 8.75 4.80

Issued precanceled only. See note after No. 324.

Issue dates: 61c, 78c, 1.25fr, 2.10fr, July 10, 1978. Others, 1979.

Souvenir Sheet

Prince Albert — A331

1979, Apr. 30 Engr. *Perf. 12½x13*
1166 A331 10fr multicolored 8.25 8.25

21st birthday of Hereditary Prince Albert.

The Juggler of Notre Dame, by Jules Massenet A332

1.20fr, Hans, the Flute Player, by Gaston L. Ganne. 1.50fr, Don Quichotte, by Massenet. 1.70fr, L'Aiglon, by Jacques Ibert & Arthur Honegger, vert. 2.10fr, The Child & the Sorcerer, by Maurice Ravel. 3fr, Monte Carlo Opera & Charles Garnier, architect.

1979, Apr. 30 *Perf. 13*
1167 A332 1fr multicolored .55 .45
1168 A332 1.20fr multicolored .75 .55
1169 A332 1.50fr multicolored 1.10 .90
1170 A332 1.70fr multicolored 1.40 1.25
1171 A332 2.10fr multicolored 2.25 2.00
1172 A332 3fr multicolored 3.25 3.00
Nos. 1167-1172 (6) 9.30 8.15

Centenary of the Salle Garnier, Monte Carlo Opera.

Flower, Bird, Butterfly, IYC Emblem A333

Children's Drawings (IYC Emblem and): 1fr, Horse and child. 1.20fr, Children shaking hands, and heart. 1.50fr, Children of the world for peace. 1.70fr, Children against pollution.

1979, Apr. 30
1173 A333 50c multicolored .25 .25
1174 A333 1fr multicolored .65 .50
1175 A333 1.20fr multicolored .85 .80
1176 A333 1.50fr multicolored 1.50 1.25
1177 A333 1.70fr multicolored 1.75 1.60
Nos. 1173-1177 (5) 5.00 4.40

International Year of the Child.

Armed Messenger, 15th-16th Centuries A334

Europa (designs similar to 1960 postage dues); 1.50fr, Felucca, 18th cent. 1.70fr, Arrival of 1st train, Dec. 12, 1868.

1979, Apr. 30
1178 A334 1.20fr multicolored *1.25* .40
1179 A334 1.50fr multicolored 5.00 *.60*
1180 A334 1.70fr multicolored 5.00 *.85*
a. Souv. sheet of 6, 2 each #1178-1180, perf. 13x12½ *27.50 18.00*
Nos. 1178-1180 (3) 11.25 1.85

Les Biches, by Francis Poulenc A335

Ballets: 1.20fr, Les Matelots, by George Auric. 1.50fr, Le Spectre de 1a Rose, by Carl Maria Weber, vert. 1.70fr, Gaieté Parisienne, by Jacques Offenbach. 2.10fr, Dance of Salomé, by Richard Strauss, vert. 3fr, Instrumental Music, ceiling decoration of Salle Garnier.

1979, Nov. 12
Size: 26x36mm, 36x26mm
1181 A335 1fr multicolored .70 .50
1182 A335 1.20fr multicolored .85 .65
1183 A335 1.50fr multicolored 1.25 1.00
1184 A335 1.70fr multicolored 1.60 1.40
1185 A335 2.10fr multicolored 2.75 2.25
Size: 48x27mm
1186 A335 3fr multicolored 4.00 3.25
Nos. 1181-1186 (6) 11.15 9.05

Salle Garnier, Monte Carlo Opera, cent.

Princes of Monaco Type of 1967

Paintings: 3fr, Charles III (1856-1889). 4fr, Antoinette de Merode (1828-1864).

1979, Nov. 12 *Perf. 12½x13*
1187 A182 3fr multicolored 2.25 1.75
1188 A182 4fr multicolored 3.25 2.40

Red Cross Type of 1969

5fr, St. Peter Claver preaching to slaves.

1979, Nov. 12 *Perf. 13*
1189 A194 5fr multicolored 3.25 2.40

Princess Grace Orchid — A336

1979, Nov. 12 Photo.
1190 A336 1fr multicolored 2.75 1.75

Intl. Orchid Exhibition, Monte Carlo, Apr. 1980.

Flower Type of 1976

Design: 1.20fr, Princess Grace rose.

1979, Nov. 12
1191 A300 1.20fr multicolored 2.75 1.75

Intl. Flower Show, Monte Carlo, May 1980.

Clown Balancing on Globe — A337

1979, Nov. 12
1192 A337 1.20fr multicolored 2.00 1.25

6th International Circus Festival, Monte Carlo, Dec. 6-10.

Rowland Hill, Penny Black — A338

1979, Nov. 12 Engr. *Perf. 13*
1193 A338 1.70fr multicolored 1.00 .65

Sir Rowland Hill (1795-1879), originator of penny postage.

Albert Einstein, Equations A339

1979, Nov. 12
1194 A339 1.70fr multicolored 1.40 .80

Albert Einstein (1879-1955), theoretical physicist.

St. Patrick's Cathedral, New York City, Cent. — A340

1979, Nov. 12
1195 A340 2.10fr multicolored 1.25 .75

Nativity
A341

1979, Nov. 12

1196	A341	1.20fr multicolored	.80	.65

Christmas 1979.

Bugatti, Monte Carlo, 1929 Winner
A342

1979, Nov. 12

1197	A342	1fr multicolored	1.10	.70

50th anniv. of Grand Prix auto race, Monte Carlo.

Arms of Charles V and Monaco, View of Monaco — A343

1979, Nov. 12

1198	A343	1.50fr multicolored	.90	.65

Emperor Charles V visit to Monaco, 450th anniversary.

Dog Type of 1977

Design: 1.20fr, Setter and pointer.

1979, Nov. 12 **Photo.**

1199	A304	1.20fr multicolored	5.00	3.50

International Dog Show, Monte Carlo.

Prince Rainier Type of 1974

1980, Jan. 17 **Engr.** ***Perf. 13***

1200	A261	1.10fr emerald	.70	.25
1201	A261	1.30fr rose red	.70	.25
1202	A261	1.60fr dk blue gray	1.25	.55
1203	A261	1.80fr grnsh blue	2.00	1.90
1204	A261	2.30fr red lilac	2.50	1.40
		Nos. 1200-1204 (5)	7.15	4.35

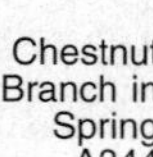

Chestnut Branch in Spring
A344

Designs of 1980, 1981 stamps show chestnut branch. 1982 stamps show peach branch. 1983 stamps show apple branch.

1980-83 **Engr.** ***Perf. 13x12½***

1205	A344	76c shown	.50	.40
1206	A344	88c Spring ('81)	.50	.40
1207	A344	97c Spring ('82)	.50	.40
1208	A344	99c Summer	.80	.60
1209	A344	1.05fr Spring ('83)	.80	.60
1210	A344	1.14fr Summer ('81)	.80	.60
1211	A344	1.25fr Summer ('82)	.80	.60
1212	A344	1.35fr Summer ('83)	.85	.60
1213	A344	1.60fr Autumn	1.25	.85
1214	A344	1.84fr Autumn ('81)	1.25	.85
1215	A344	2.03fr Autumn ('82)	1.25	.85
1216	A344	2.19fr Autumn ('83)	1.40	1.00
1217	A344	2.65fr Winter	1.75	1.20
1218	A344	3.05fr Winter ('81)	1.60	1.25
1219	A344	3.36fr Winter ('82)	1.75	1.25
1220	A344	3.63fr Winter ('83)	1.60	1.60
		Nos. 1205-1220 (16)	17.40	13.05

Issued precanceled only. See note after No. 324. See Nos. 1406-1409, 1457-1460.

Gymnast — A345

1980, Apr. 28

1221	A345	1.10fr shown	.40	.25
1222	A345	1.30fr Handball	.50	.35
1223	A345	1.60fr Shooting	.65	.45
1224	A345	1.80fr Volleyball	.85	.60
1225	A345	2.30fr Ice hockey	1.00	.85
1226	A345	4fr Slalom	1.60	1.25
		Nos. 1221-1226 (6)	5.00	3.75

22nd Summer Olympic Games, Moscow, July 19-Aug. 3; 13th Winter Olympic Games, Lake Placid, NY, Feb. 12-24.

Colette, Novelist — A346

Europa: 1.80fr, Marcel Pagnol (1895-1974), French playwright.

1980, Apr. 28 ***Perf. 12½x13***

1227	A346	1.30fr multicolored	1.00	*.35*
1228	A346	1.80fr multicolored	1.50	*.35*
a.		Souv. sheet, 5 each #1227-1228	*15.00*	*10.00*

The Source, by Ingres
A347

1980, Apr. 28

1229	A347	4fr multicolored	8.00	5.50

Jean Auguste Dominique Ingres (1780-1867).

Michel Eyquem de Montaigne
A348

1980, Apr. 28 ***Perf. 13***

1230	A348	1.30fr multicolored	.70	.45

Essays of Montaigne (1533-1592), 400th anniversary of publication.

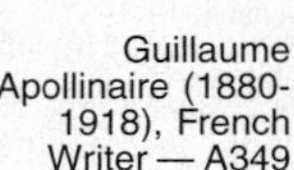

Guillaume Apollinaire (1880-1918), French Writer — A349

1980, Apr. 28

1231	A349	1.10fr multicolored	.70	.45

Paul P. Harris, Chicago Skyline, Rotary Emblem — A350

1980, Apr. 28

1232	A350	1.80fr multicolored	.75	.55

Rotary International, 75th anniversary.

Convention Center, Map of Europe, Kiwanis Emblem — A351

1980, Apr. 28

1233	A351	1.30fr multicolored	.70	.50

Kiwanis International, European Convention, Monte Carlo, June.

Coin Type of 1975

Design: 1.50fr, Honoré II silver ecu, 1649.

1980, Apr. 28

1234	A281	1.50fr multicolored	.75	.55

Lhasa Apso and Shih-Tzu — A352

1980, Apr. 28 **Photo.**

1235	A352	1.30fr multicolored	5.00	3.25

International Dog Show, Monte Carlo.

The Princess and the Pea — A353

Hans Christian Andersen (1805-1875) Fairy Tales: 1.30fr, The Little Mermaid. 1.50fr, The Chimneysweep and the Shepherdess. 1.60fr, The Brave Little Tin Soldier. 1.80fr, The Little Match Girl. 2.30fr, The Nightingale.

1980, Nov. 6 **Engr.** ***Perf. 13***

1236	A353	70c multicolored	.50	.25
1237	A353	1.30fr multicolored	.70	.60
1238	A353	1.50fr multicolored	1.00	.85
1239	A353	1.60fr multicolored	1.40	.85
1240	A353	1.80fr multicolored	1.40	1.10
1241	A353	2.30fr multicolored	2.00	1.20
		Nos. 1236-1241 (6)	7.00	4.85

Women on Balcony, by Van Dongen — A354

Paintings from 1905 Paris Fall Salon: 2fr, The Road, by de Vlaminck. 4fr, Woman Reading, by Matisse. 5fr, Three Women in a Meadow, by Andrè Derain.

1980, Nov. 6 ***Perf. 13x12***

1242	A354	2fr multicolored	2.50	1.75
1243	A354	3fr multicolored	3.75	2.50
1244	A354	4fr multicolored	5.00	4.25
1245	A354	5fr multicolored	6.00	5.00
		Nos. 1242-1245 (4)	17.25	13.50

Princes of Monaco Type of 1967

Paintings: No. 1246, Prince Albert I (1848-1922), by Leon Bonnat. No. 1247, Princess Alice (1857-1925), by L. Maeterlinck.

1980, Nov. 6 ***Perf. 12½x13***

1246	A182	4fr multicolored	3.00	2.40
1247	A182	4fr multicolored	3.00	2.40

Sun and Birds, by Perrette Lambert — A355

1980, Nov. 6 ***Perf. 13***

1248	A355	6fr multicolored	4.00	3.25

Red Cross.

7th International Circus Festival — A356

1980, Nov. 6 ***Perf. 13x12½***

1249	A356	1.30fr multicolored	2.00	1.25

Christmas 1980
A357

1980, Nov. 6

1250	A357	1.10fr multicolored	.55	.35
1251	A357	2.30fr multicolored	1.20	.75

Princess Stephanie of Monaco Rose — A358

1980, Nov. 6 Photo. *Perf. 12½x13*

1252 A358 1.30fr shown 1.40 .65
1253 A358 1.80fr Ikebana 2.25 1.40

International Flower Show, Monte Carlo, May 1981.

Prince Rainier Type of 1974

1980 Engr. *Perf. 13*

1255 A261 1.20fr bright green 1.10 .25
1256 A261 1.40fr red 1.25 .20

Issue dates: 1.20fr, Aug. 19; 1.40fr, Aug. 11.

Paramuricea Clavata — A359

5c-20c, 40c, 50c, vert.

1980, Nov. 6 *Perf. 13x12½*

1259 A359 5c Spirographis spallanzanii .20 .20
1260 A359 10c Anemonia sulcata .20 .20
1261 A359 15c Leptosammia pruvoti .20 .20
1262 A359 20c Pteroides .25 .20
1263 A359 30c shown .25 .25
1264 A359 40c Alcyonium .35 .25
1265 A359 50c Corallium rubrum .55 .45
1266 A359 60c Caliactis parisitica 1.00 .65
1267 A359 70c Cerianthus membranaceus 1.25 .90
1268 A359 1fr Actinia equina 1.25 .90
1269 A359 2fr Protula 2.50 1.10
Nos. 1259-1269 (11) 8.00 5.30

See Nos. 1316-1321, 1380.

25th Wedding Anniversary of Prince Rainier and Princess Grace — A360

1981, May 4 *Perf. 13*

1270 A360 1.20fr green & blk 1.50 1.00
1271 A360 1.40fr carmine & blk 2.00 1.50
1272 A360 1.70fr olive grn & blk 2.50 1.90
1273 A360 1.80fr brown & blk 2.75 2.25
1274 A360 2fr brt blue & blk 3.75 2.75
Nos. 1270-1274 (5) 12.50 9.40

Mozart with his Father and Sister, by Carmontelle — A361

Wolfgang Amadeus Mozart (1756-1791), 225th Birth Anniversary (Paintings): 2fr, Portrait, by Lorenz Vogel (26x36mm). 3.50fr, Conducting his Requiem Two Days Before his Death, by F.C. Baude.

1981, May 4 Engr. *Perf. 13½x13*

1275 A361 2fr multicolored 1.65 1.50
1276 A361 2.50fr multicolored 2.40 2.00
1277 A361 3.50fr multicolored 3.25 2.50
a. Strip of 3, #1275-1277 8.50 8.50

Cross of Palms — A362

Europa (Palm Sunday Traditions): 2fr, Children with palms at benediction.

1981, May 4 *Perf. 12½x13*

1278 A362 1.40fr multicolored .75 *.35*
1279 A362 2fr multicolored 1.25 *.55*
a. Souv. sheet, 5 ea #1278-1279 *18.00 9.00*

European Soccer Cup, 25th Anniversary A363

1981, May 4 *Perf. 13*

1280 A363 2fr black & blue 1.25 .85

International Year of the Disabled — A364

1981, May 4

1281 A364 1.40fr brt grn & bl 1.00 .60

Monegasque National Pavilion Centenary — A365

1981, May 4

1282 A365 2fr multicolored 1.25 .85

Oceanographic Institute, Monaco and Museum, Paris — A366

1981, May 4

1283 A366 1.20fr multicolored .95 .80

75th anniversary of the Oceanographic Institute (Monaco-France).

50th Anniversary of the International Hydrographic Bureau — A367

1981, May 4

1284 A367 2.50fr multicolored 1.75 1.25

Rough Collies and Shetland Sheepdogs — A368

1981, May 4 Photo.

1285 A368 1.40fr multicolored 5.50 4.00

International Dog Show, Monte Carlo.

Marine Life Preservation A369

1981, Mar. 21 Photo.

1286 A369 1.20fr multicolored 1.00 .70

Prince Rainier III and Hereditary Prince Albert — A370

1981-84 Engr. *Perf. 13*

1287 A370 1.40fr dark green 1.00 .25
1288 A370 1.60fr carmine 1.40 .25
1289 A370 1.60fr olive grn ('82) .75 .25
1290 A370 1.70fr bluish grn ('84) 1.00 .25
1291 A370 1.80fr magenta ('82) .95 .20
1292 A370 2fr red ('83) 1.10 .20
1293 A370 2.10fr red ('84) 1.10 .20
1294 A370 2.30fr blue 3.50 2.75
1295 A370 2.60fr violet bl ('82) 2.25 1.90
1296 A370 2.80fr steel bl ('83) 2.25 1.60
1297 A370 3fr sky blue ('84) 2.25 1.60
1298 A370 4fr brown 1.75 .75
1299 A370 5.50fr black 2.10 1.50
Nos. 1287-1299 (13) 21.40 11.70

See Nos. 1505-1515.

Hauling Ice Floes, 17th Cent. Map Arctic A371

1981, Oct. 5

1301 A371 1.50fr multicolored 1.60 1.25

First Intl. Arctic Committee Congress, Rome, Oct. 5-9.

Princes of Monaco Type of 1967

Paintings by P.A. de Laszlo, 1929: 3fr, Prince Louis II. 5fr, Princess Charlotte.

1981, Nov. 5 Engr. *Perf. 12½x13*

1302 A182 3fr multicolored 2.50 1.25
1303 A182 5fr multicolored 3.50 2.40

Ettore Bugatti, Auto Designer and Racer, Birth Centenary A372

1981, Nov. 5 *Perf. 13*

1304 A372 1fr multicolored 1.25 .85

George Bernard Shaw (1856-1950) A373

1981, Nov. 5

2.50fr, Fernand Leger, painter, birth cent.

1305 A373 2fr multicolored 1.25 1.00
1306 A373 2.50fr multicolored 1.25 1.00

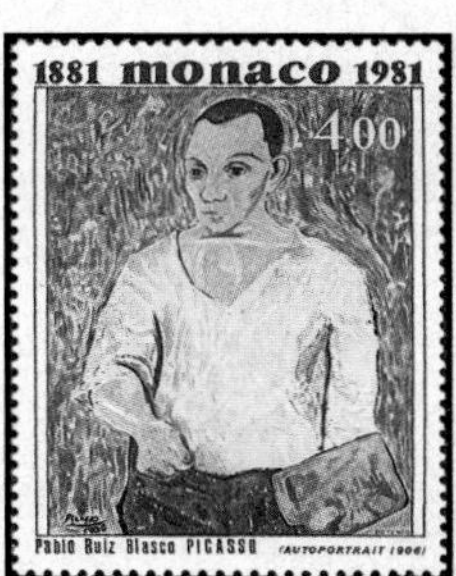

Self-portrait, by Pablo Picasso (1881-1973) — A374

#1308, Self-portrait, by Rembrandt (1606-69).

1981, Nov. 5 *Perf. 12½x13*

1307 A374 4fr multicolored 4.50 3.25
1308 A374 4fr multicolored 4.50 3.25

Ikebana, Painting by Ikenobo, 1673 — A375

Intl. Flower Show, Monte Carlo, 1982: 1.40fr, Elegantines, morning glories.

1981, Nov. 5 Photo. *Perf. 12½*

1309 A375 1.40fr multicolored 1.40 1.00
1310 A375 2fr multicolored 2.25 1.75

Catherine Deneuve Rose A376

1981, Nov. 5 *Perf. 13x12½*

1311 A376 1.80fr multicolored 4.00 2.50

First Intl. Rose Competition, Monte Carlo, June 12-14.

8th Intl. Circus Festival, Monte Carlo, Dec. 10-14 — A377

1981, Nov. 5 **Engr.** ***Perf. 13***
1312 A377 1.40fr multicolored 2.50 1.40

Christmas 1981 A378

1981, Nov. 5
1313 A378 1.20fr multicolored .75 .60

50th Monte Carlo Auto Race — A379

1981, Nov. 5
1314 A379 1fr Lancia-Stratos 1.50 1.10

Souvenir Sheet

Persimmon Branch in Spring A380

1981, Nov. 5 ***Perf. 13x12½***
1315 Sheet of 4 8.50 8.50
a. A380 1fr shown .80 .80
b. A380 2fr Summer 1.50 1.50
c. A380 3fr Autumn 2.50 2.50
d. A380 4fr Winter 3.00 3.00

Coral Type of 1980

Exotic Plants. 1.40fr, 1.60fr, 2.30fr vert.

Perf. 12½x13, 13x12½

1981-82 **Photo.**
1316 A359 1.40fr Hoya bella 3.25 1.60
1317 A359 1.60fr Bolivicereus samaipatanus 2.75 1.10
1317A A359 1.80fr Trichocereus grandiflorus 2.25 1.10
1318 A359 2.30fr Euphorbia milii 2.75 1.10
1319 A359 2.60fr Echinocereus fitchii 2.75 1.10
1320 A359 2.90fr Rebutia heliosa 2.75 1.10
1321 A359 4.10fr Echinopsis multiplex 3.25 2.75
Nos. 1316-1321 (7) 19.75 9.85

Issued: 1.80fr, June 7; others Dec. 10.

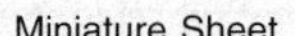

Miniature Sheet

1982 World Cup A381

Designs: Various soccer players.

1982, May 3 ***Perf. 13***
1322 Sheet of 4 8.00 8.00
a. A381 1fr multicolored .75 .75
b. A381 2fr multicolored 1.50 1.50
c. A381 3fr multicolored 2.25 2.25
d. A381 4fr multicolored 2.75 2.75

Mercantour Natl. Park Birds — A382

1982, May 3 ***Perf. 12½x13, 13x12½***
1323 A382 60c Nutcracker 1.00 .85
1324 A382 70c Black grouse 1.20 1.10
1325 A382 80c Rock partridge 1.20 1.10
1326 A382 90c Wall creeper, horiz. 2.25 1.75
1327 A382 1.40fr Ptarmigan, horiz. 3.00 2.40
1328 A382 1.60fr Golden eagle 3.75 2.40
Nos. 1323-1328 (6) 12.40 9.60

Europa — A383

1982, May 3 ***Perf. 12½x13***
1329 A383 1.60fr Guelph attacking Fortress of Monaco, 1297 *1.50* .40
1330 A383 2.30fr Treaty of Peronne, 1641 *1.50* .50
a. Souv. sheet, 5 ea #1329-1330 *18.00* *9.00*

Fontvielle Landfill Project A384

1982, May 3 ***Perf. 13x12½***
1331 A384 1.40fr Old coastline 1.00 .50
1332 A384 1.60fr Landfill site 1.00 .60
1333 A384 2.30fr Completed site 1.50 1.00
Nos. 1331-1333 (3) 3.50 2.10

Fontvielle Stadium — A385

1982, May 3 ***Perf. 13***
1334 A385 2.30fr multicolored 1.25 1.00

PHILEXFRANCE '82 Stamp Exhibition,Paris, June 11-21 — A386

1982, May 3
1335 A386 1.40fr multicolored 1.00 .80

Intl. Dog Show, Monte Carlo A387

1982, May 3 **Photo.** ***Perf. 13x12½***
1336 A387 60c Old English sheepdog 3.25 1.75
1337 A387 1fr Briard terrier 3.25 1.75

See Nos. 1366, 1431, 1479, 1539, 1676, 1704, 1756, 1806, 1855, 1900, 1940, 1990, 2035, 2069A, 2108.

Monaco Cathedral, Arms of Pope John Paul II and Monaco A388

1982, May 3 **Engr.**
1338 A388 1.60fr multicolored .85 .80

Creation of archbishopric of Monaco, July 25, 1981.

800th Birth Anniv. of St. Francis of Assisi — A389

1982, May 3 ***Perf. 12½x13***
1339 A389 1.40fr multicolored 1.00 .80

TB Bacillus Cent. — A390

1982, May 3
1340 A390 1.40fr multicolored 1.00 .85

Scouting Year — A391

1982, May 3
1341 A391 1.60fr dk brown & blk 1.60 1.00

Intl. Hunting Council, 29th Meeting — A392

1982, June 11 **Photo.** ***Perf. 12½***
1342 A392 1.60fr St. Hubert 1.20 1.00

Intl. Bibliophile Assoc. General Assembly — A393

1982, Sept. 30 **Engr.** ***Perf. 13***
1343 A393 1.60fr multicolored .80 .60

Monte Carlo and Monaco During the Belle Epoch (1870-1925), by Hubert Clerissi — A394

Photogravure and Engraved

1982, Nov. 8 ***Perf. 13x12½***
1344 A394 3fr Casino, 1870 1.75 1.25
1345 A394 5fr Palace, 1893 3.75 2.00

See Nos. 1385-1386, 1436-1437, 1488-1489, 1546-1547, 1605-1606, 1638-1639, 1695-1696.

Nicolo Paganini (1782-1840), Composer and Violinist — A395

1.80fr, Anna Pavlova (1881-1931), ballerina. 2.60fr, Igor Stravinsky (1882-1971), composer.

1982, Nov. 8 **Engr.** ***Perf. 12½x13***
1346 A395 1.60fr multicolored 1.25 1.00
1347 A395 1.80fr multicolored 1.75 1.20
1348 A395 2.60fr multicolored 2.00 1.40
Nos. 1346-1348 (3) 5.00 3.60

In a Boat, by Manet (1832-1883) — A396

Design: No. 1350, Les Poissons Noir, by Georges Braque (1882-1963).

Photogravure and Engraved

1982, Nov. 8 ***Perf. 13x12½***
1349 A396 4fr multicolored 4.00 3.00
1350 A396 4fr multicolored 4.00 3.00

Intl. Flower Show, Monte Carlo — A397

Designs: Various floral arrangements.

1982, Nov. 8 Photo. *Perf. 12½x13*
1351 A397 1.60fr multicolored 2.10 1.25
1352 A397 2.60fr multicolored 2.10 1.25

Bouquet — A398

1982 *Perf. 13*
1353 A398 1.60fr multicolored 2.50 1.75

Christmas 1982 — A399

1982, Nov. 8 Engr. *Perf. 12½x13*
1354 A399 1.60fr Three Kings .60 .35
1355 A399 1.80fr Holy Family .75 .35
1356 A399 2.60fr Shepherds 1.10 .50
a. Souv. sheet of 3, #1354-1356 3.25 3.25
Nos. 1354-1356 (3) 2.45 1.20

Intl. Polar Year Centenary — A400

1982, Nov. 8 Engr. *Perf. 13*
1358 A400 1.60fr Prince Louis, Discovery 2.25 1.60

Discovery of Greenland Millenium — A401

1982, Nov. 8
1359 A401 1.60fr Erik the Red's longship 2.25 1.60

Death Bimillenium of Virgil — A402

1982, Nov. 8
1360 A402 1.80fr Scene from Aeneid, Book 6 2.25 1.60

50th Anniv. of Botanical Garden A403

1983, Feb. 11 Photo. *Perf. 12½x13*
1361 A403 1.80fr Cacti, vert. 1.50 1.10
1362 A403 2fr Exotic plants, vert. 1.75 1.20
1363 A403 2.30fr Intl. exhibits, vert. 2.00 1.75
1364 A403 2.60fr Cave 2.50 1.75
1365 A403 3.30fr Prehistoric Anthropology Museum 3.50 2.75
Nos. 1361-1365 (5) 11.25 8.55

Monte Carlo Dog Show Type

1983, Apr. 13 *Perf. 13x12½*
1366 A387 1.80fr Alaskan malamute 7.25 4.75

Souvenir Sheet

EN HOMMAGE A

LA PRINCESSE GRACE

1929-1982

Princess Grace (1929-1982) — A405

1983, Apr. 19 Engr. *Perf. 13*
1367 A405 10fr black 8.25 8.25

Europa — A406

1983, Apr. 27 *Perf. 12½x13*
1368 A406 1.80fr Montgolfiere balloon flight, 1783 1.75 *.35*
1369 A406 2.60fr Columbia space shuttle 1.75 *.50*
a. Souv. sheet, 5 ea #1368-1369 20.00 *8.00*

St. Charles' Church, Monte Carlo, Cent. — A407

1983, Apr. 27 Engr.
1370 A407 2.60fr St. Charles Borromeo 1.00 .90

Franciscan College Centenary A408

1983, Apr. 27 *Perf. 13x12½*
1371 A408 2fr Church, medallion .90 .70

Fontvielle Stadium Interior — A409

1983, Apr. 28 *Perf. 13*
1372 A409 2fr multicolored .90 .70

Automobile Centenary — A410

1983, Apr. 27
1373 A410 2.90fr Benz, 1883, Formula One racer 3.25 1.90

Save the Whales Campaign — A411

1983, Apr. 27
1374 A411 3.30fr Blue whale 3.75 3.00

World Communications Year — A412

1983, Apr. 27
1375 A412 4fr lil rose & brn vio 1.60 1.20

Souvenir Sheet

Fig Branch in Spring A413

1983, Nov. 9 Engr. *Perf. 13x12½*
1376 Sheet of 4 8.00 8.00
a. A413 1fr shown .75 .75
b. A413 2fr Summer 1.40 1.40
c. A413 3fr Autumn 2.25 2.25
d. A413 4fr Winter 2.75 2.75

Exotic Plant Type of 1980

1983, Nov. 9 Photo. *Perf. 13*
1380 A359 2fr Argyroderma roseum 1.75 .65

Belle Epoch Type of 1982

Paintings by Hubert Clerissi: 3fr, Thermes Valentia from the Beach, 1902. 5fr, Cafe de Paris and Place du Casino, 1905.

Photogravure and Engraved

1983, Nov. 9 *Perf. 13x12½*
1385 A394 3fr multicolored 3.00 2.40
1386 A394 5fr multicolored 4.25 3.50

Portrait of a Young Man, by Raphael (1483-1520) — A414

Passage Cottin, by Maurice Utrillo (1883-1955) — A415

Photogravure and Engraved

1983, Nov. 9 *Perf. 13*
1387 A414 4fr multicolored 3.25 2.40
1388 A415 4fr multicolored 3.25 2.40

Johannes Brahms (1833-1897), Composer — A416

#1390, Giacomo Puccini (1858-1924), composer, scene from Madame Butterfly.

1983, Nov. 9 Engr. *Perf. 13½x13*
1389 A416 3fr multicolored 1.40 1.20
1390 A416 3fr multicolored 1.60 1.20

9th Intl. Circus Festival, Monte Carlo, Dec. 8-12 — A417

1983, Nov. 9 *Perf. 13*
1391 A417 2fr multicolored 1.75 1.40

Intl. Flower Show, Monte Carlo — A418

1983, Nov. 9 Photo.
1392 A418 1.60fr Pansies, convolvulus, carnations 1.50 1.00
1393 A418 2.60fr Oriental poppies 2.25 1.50

Christmas 1983 — A419

1983, Nov. 9 **Photo.**
1394 A419 2fr Provencal creche figures 1.60 1.10

Alfred Nobel (1833-1896), Literature Medal — A420

1983, Nov. 9 **Engr.**
1395 A420 2fr multicolored 1.00 .80

Sesquicentenary of Society of St. Vincent de Paul — A421

1983, Nov. 9 **Engr.**
1396 A421 1.80fr F. Ozanam, founder, Paris headquarters 1.00 .60

A422

1983, Nov. 9
1397 A422 5fr Offshore petroleum plant 2.25 1.25

19th Cent. Figurines, Galea Toy Collection A423

1983, Nov. 9 **Photo.** ***Perf. 12½x13***
1398 A423 50c Water pipe smoker .25 .25
1399 A423 60c Clown with yo-yo .40 .25
1400 A423 70c Smoking monkey .40 .25
1401 A423 80c Farmer and pig .50 .50
1402 A423 90c Buffalo Bill .60 .60
1403 A423 1fr Snake charmer .60 .60
1404 A423 1.50fr Piano and harp player 1.00 .80
1405 A423 2fr Girl powdering her face 1.75 1.00
Nos. 1398-1405 (8) 5.50 4.25

Quince Branch in Spring A424

1984, May 10 **Photo.** ***Perf. 13x12½***
1406 A424 1.14fr shown .80 .50
1407 A424 1.47fr Summer .85 .60
1408 A424 2.38fr Autumn 1.50 1.00
1409 A424 3.95fr Winter 1.90 1.50
Nos. 1406-1409 (4) 5.05 3.60

Issued precanceled only. See note after No. 324.

Place de la Visitation, by Hubert Clerissi — A425

Drawings by Hubert Clerissi: 10c, Town Hall. 15c, Rue Basse. 20c, Place Saint-Nicolas. 30c, Quai du Commerce. 40c, Rue des Iris. 3fr, Bandstand. 6fr, Opera House.

1984, May 10 **Engr.** ***Perf. 12½x13***
1410 A425 5c brown .20 .20
1411 A425 10c claret .20 .20
1412 A425 15c violet .20 .20
1413 A425 20c dark blue .25 .20
1414 A425 30c deep blue .25 .20
1415 A425 40c dark green .70 .25
1416 A425 3fr red brown 2.25 .90
1417 A425 6fr yellow green 1.25 1.10
Nos. 1410-1417 (8) 5.30 3.25

See #1516-1524, 1750-1755, 1821-1825.

Souvenir Sheet

1984 Los Angeles Olympics A426

Rhythmic Gymnastics.

1984, May 10 ***Perf. 13***
1418 Sheet of 4 7.50 7.50
a. A426 2fr Ball .95 .95
b. A426 3fr Clubs 1.40 1.40
c. A426 4fr Ribbon 1.75 1.75
d. A426 5fr Hoop 2.40 2.40

1984 Winter Olympics — A427

1984, May 10
1422 A427 2fr Rink, speed skater .90 .55
1423 A427 4fr Skater, snowflake 1.60 1.10

Europa (1959-84) A428

1984, May 10 ***Perf. 13x12½***
1424 A428 2fr blue 1.50 *.40*
1425 A428 3fr yel grn 2.50 *.85*
a. Souv. sheet, 4 ea #1424-1425 *20.00* 8.50

Butterflies and Rare Flowers, Mercantour Natl. Park A429

1.60fr, Boloria graeca tendensis, ranunculus montanus. 2fr, Zygaena vesubiana, saxifraga aizoides. 2.80fr, Erebia aethiopella, myosotis alpestris. 3fr, Parnassius phoebus gazeli, rhododendron ferrugineum. 3.60fr, Papilio alexanor, myrrhis odorata. Nos. 1426-1428 vert.

Perf. 12½x13, 13x12½
1984, May 10 **Photo.**
1426 A429 1.60fr multicolored 1.50 1.25
1427 A429 2fr multicolored 2.40 1.40
1428 A429 2.80fr multicolored 2.25 1.75
1429 A429 3fr multicolored 3.00 2.25
1430 A429 3.60fr multicolored 4.00 2.50
Nos. 1426-1430 (5) 13.15 9.15

Monte Carlo Dog Show Type

1984, May 10 ***Perf. 13x12½***
1431 A387 1.60fr Auvergne pointer 4.00 2.50

Sanctuary of Our Lady of Laghet — A431

1984, May 10 **Engr.** ***Perf. 12½x13***
1432 A431 2fr Statue, rosary, pilgrimage sanctuary .90 .45

Auguste Piccard, Birth Cent. — A432

1984, May 10
1433 A432 2.80fr Stratosphere balloon 1.10 .60
1434 A432 4fr Bathyscaphe 1.50 .85

25th Anniv. of Princely Palace Concerts A433

1984, May 10 ***Perf. 13x12½***
1435 A433 3.60fr Orchestra 1.60 .90

Belle Epoch Type of 1982

Paintings by Hubert Clerissi: 4fr, Rue Grimaldi, 1908. 5fr, Train Entering Monte Carlo Station, 1910.

Photo. & Engr.
1984, Nov. 8 ***Perf. 12½x13***
1436 A394 4fr multicolored 3.50 2.40
1437 A394 5fr multicolored 5.50 3.75

25th Intl. Television Festival, Monte Carlo, Feb. 1985 — A434

1984, Nov. 8 **Engr.** ***Perf. 13***
1438 A434 2.10fr Lights 1.00 .60
1439 A434 3fr Golden nymph (prize) 1.40 .85

Intl. Flower Show, Monte Carlo — A435

1984, Nov. 8 **Photo.** ***Perf. 12½x13***
1440 A435 2.10fr Mixed bouquet 1.60 1.00
1441 A435 3fr Ikebana 2.40 1.25

See Nos. 1491-1492, 1552-1553.

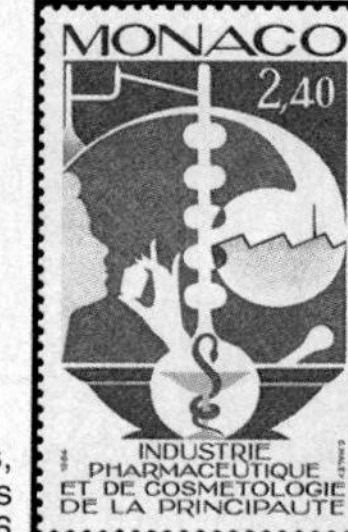

Pharmaceuticals, Cosmetics Industry — A436

1984, Nov. 8 **Engr.** ***Perf. 13***
1442 A436 2.40fr multicolored 1.10 .85

Illustration from Gargantua, by Rabelais — A437

Francois Rabelais (1490-1553), 17th Cent. Drawing — A438

1984, Nov. 8 ***Perf. 13x12½, 12½x13***
1443 A437 2fr With animals 1.10 .60
1444 A437 2fr With sheep of Panurge 1.10 .60
1445 A438 4fr multicolored 2.50 1.25
Nos. 1443-1445 (3) 4.70 2.45

Souvenir Sheet

10th Intl. Circus Festival, Dec. 6-10 — A439

1984, Nov. 8 Photo. *Perf. 13*
1446 A439 5fr Poster 4.00 4.00

La Femme a la Potiche, by Degas A440

1984, Nov. 8 Engr. *Perf. 12x13*
1447 A440 6fr multicolored 5.00 2.75

Christmas 1984 — A441

Figurines from Provence.

1984, Nov. 8 *Perf. 12½x13*
1448 A441 70c Shepherd .45 .40
1449 A441 1fr Blind man .55 .50
1450 A441 1.70fr Happy man 1.20 1.00
1451 A441 2fr Woman spinning 1.25 1.10
1452 A441 2.10fr Angel 1.40 1.20
1453 A441 2.40fr Garlic seller 1.60 1.40
1454 A441 3fr Drummer 1.90 1.60
1455 A441 3.70fr Knife grinder 2.40 2.00
1456 A441 4fr Elderly couple 2.75 2.40
Nos. 1448-1456 (9) 13.50 11.60

See Nos. 1737-1739, 1766-1768, 1838-1840, 1883-1885, 1919-1921, 1976-1978.

Cherry Tree A442

1985, Mar. 1 Engr. *Perf. 13*
1457 A442 1.22fr Spring .80 .50
1458 A442 1.57fr Summer 1.00 .60
1459 A442 2.55fr Fall 1.60 1.10
1460 A442 4.23fr Winter 2.10 1.75
Nos. 1457-1460 (4) 5.50 3.95

Issued precanceled only. See note after No. 324.

No. 1 in Green A443

1985, Mar. 25
1461 A443 1.70fr shown .85 .50
1462 A443 2.10fr #1 in scarlet 1.00 .25
1463 A443 3fr #1 in lt peacock bl 1.20 .85
Nos. 1461-1463 (3) 3.05 1.60

Stamp centenary, Natl. Stamp Exhibition, Dec. 5-8, Monte Carlo.

Europa 1985 — A444

Portraits: 2.10fr Prince Antoine I (1661-1731), Founder of Monaco Palace, music library. 3fr, Jean-Baptiste Lully (1632-1687), composer, violinist, superintendent of music to King Louis XIV.

1985, May 23 *Perf. 12½x13*
1464 A444 2.10fr brt blue 1.75 *.50*
1465 A444 3fr dark carmine 3.00 *.75*
a. Souv. sheet, 5 #1464, 5 #1465 *25.00 15.00*

Flowers in Mercantour Park A444a

Perf. 13x12½, 12½x13
1985, May 23 Photo.
1466 A444a 1.70fr Berardia subacaulis .85 .80
1467 A444a 2.10fr Saxifraga florulenta, vert. 1.00 .85
1468 A444a 2.40fr Fritillaria moggridgei, vert. 1.20 1.00
1469 A444a 3fr Sempervivum allionii, vert. 1.75 1.20
1470 A444a 3.60fr Silene cordifolia, vert. 2.40 1.60
1471 A444a 4fr Primula allionii 3.00 2.00
Nos. 1466-1471 (6) 10.20 7.45

Japanese Medlar A445

1985, May 23 Engr. *Perf. 13x12½*
1472 Sheet of 4 6.50 6.50
a. A445 1fr Spring .55 .55
b. A445 2fr Summer 1.25 1.25
c. A445 3fr Autumn 1.90 1.90
d. A445 4fr Winter 2.40 2.40

Nadia Boulanger (1887-1979), Musician, Composer, Conductor A446

Portraits, manuscripts and music: 2.10fr, Georges Auric (1899-1983), composer of film, ballet music, Music Foundation council president.

1985, May 23 *Perf. 13*
1473 A446 1.70fr brown 1.00 .60
1474 A446 2.10fr brt ultra 1.25 .90

Prince Pierre de Monaco Music Foundation composition prize, 25th anniv.

Natl. Oceanographic Museum, 75th Anniv. — A447

1985, May 23
1475 A447 2.10fr brt bl, grn & blk 1.00 .80

Graphs, Fish, Molecular Structures, Lab Apparatus — A448

1985, May 23
1476 A448 3fr dk bl grn, blk & dk rose lil 1.25 .70

Prince Rainier III Scientific Research Center, 25th anniv.

Intl. Athletic Championships, May 25-26 — A449

1985, May 23
1477 A449 1.70fr Running .70 .55
1478 A449 2.10fr Swimming 1.00 .55

Opening of Louis II Stadium, May 25.

Monte Carlo Dog Show Type

1985, May 3 Photo. *Perf. 13x12½*
1479 A387 2.10fr Boxer 3.25 2.00

Intl. Youth Year A450

1985, May 23 Engr. *Perf. 13*
1480 A450 3fr fawn, sepia & dp grn 1.25 .75

Fish, Natl. Oceanographic Museum Aquarium A451

1985, Aug. 13 Photo. *Perf. 12½x13*
1481 A451 1.80fr Pygoplites diacanthus 1.40 1.10
1482 A451 2.20fr Acanthurus leucosternon 1.40 1.10
1483 A451 3.20fr Chaetodon collare 2.25 1.60
1484 A451 3.90fr Balistoides conspicillum 2.75 2.25

Size: 40x52mm

Perf. 13
1485 A451 7fr Aquarium 4.75 3.50
Nos. 1481-1485 (5) 12.55 9.55

See Nos. 1560-1561, 1610-1615.

Souvenir Sheet

Transatlantic Yachting Race, Oct. 13 — A452

Yacht classes: a, Catamaran. b, Monocoque. c, Trimaran.

1985, Oct. Engr. *Perf. 13*
1486 Sheet of 3 6.00 6.00
a.-c. A452 4fr, any single 1.75 1.75

Monaco-New York competition.

ITALIA '85, Rome, Oct. 25-Nov. 3 — A453

Design: Exhibition emblem, St. Peter's Cathedral and Temple of Castor ruins.

1985, Oct. 25 *Perf. 13½x13*
1487 A453 4fr int blk, brt grn & red rose 1.75 1.00

Belle Epoch Type of 1982

Illustrations by Hubert Clerissi.

Photo. & Engr.

1985, Nov. 7 *Perf. 13x12½*
1488 A394 4fr Port of Monaco, 1912 3.00 1.75
1489 A394 6fr La Gare Vers Avenue, 1920 3.50 3.00

11th Intl. Circus Festival, Dec. 5-9 — A454

1985, Nov. 7 Photo. *Perf. 13*
1490 A454 1.80fr multi 1.50 1.10

Intl. Flower Show Type of 1984

1985, Nov. 7

1491 A435 2.20fr Roses, tulips, jonquils 1.40 1.00
1492 A435 3.20fr Ikebana of chrysanthemums, bryony 2.10 1.90

Dated 1986.

Factory, Ship, Fish, Crustaceans A455

1985, Nov. 7 Engr. *Perf. 13x13½*

1493 A455 2.20fr brt bl, dp brn & dk grnsh bl 1.00 .60

Monagasque fishing industry, Fontvieille District. See No. 1555.

Christmas 1985 — A456

1985, Nov. 7 Photo. *Perf. 12½x13*

1494 A456 2.20fr multi 1.25 .50

EUTELSAT Orbiting Earth — A457

1985, Nov. 7 Engr. *Perf. 13*

1495 A457 3fr int blk, dp rose lil & dk bl 1.40 1.00

European Telecommunications Satellite Org.

Sacha Guitry (1885-1957), Actor, Dramatist — A458

Authors, composers: 4fr, Brothers Grimm. 5fr, Frederic Chopin and Robert Schumann, composers. 6fr, Johann Sebastian Bach and George Frideric Handel, composers.

1985, Nov. 7

1496 A458 3fr brn blk & gldn brn 1.50 1.20
1497 A458 4fr dp rose lil, sep & turq bl 2.00 1.20
1498 A458 5fr stl bl, dp bl & grnsh bl 2.50 1.90
1499 A458 6fr blk, brn & stl bl 3.00 2.40
Nos. 1496-1499 (4) 9.00 6.70

Souvenir Sheet

Natl. Postage Stamp Cent. — A459

Altered designs: a, Type A1. b, Type A2. c, Type A13. d, Type A83.

1985, Dec. 5

1500 Sheet of 4 8.00 8.00
a.-d. A459 5fr, any single 2.00 2.00

Rainier and Albert Type of 1981-84

1985-88 Engr. *Perf. 13*

1505 A370 1.80fr brt grn 1.10 .25
1506 A370 1.90fr ol grn ('86) 1.90 .55
1507 A370 2fr emer grn ('87) 1.25 .25
1508 A370 2.20fr red rose 1.25 .20
1509 A370 2.50fr dk brn 1.50 .75
1510 A370 3.20fr brt bl 2.75 2.25
1511 A370 3.40fr ind ('86) 4.25 2.25
1512 A370 3.60fr dp ultra ('87) 2.75 1.25
1513 A370 10fr claret ('86) 4.75 1.10
1514 A370 15fr dk bl grn ('86) 9.25 2.25
1515 A370 20fr brt blue ('88) 11.00 2.75
Nos. 1505-1515 (11) 41.75 13.85

Views of Old Monaco Type of 1984

Illustrations by Hubert Clerissi: 50c, Port of Monaco. 60c, St. Charles Church. 70c, Promenade. 80c, Harbor, olive trees. 90c, Quay. 1fr, Palace Square. 2fr, Ships, harbor mouth. 4fr, Monaco Tram Station. 5fr, Mail coach.

1986, Jan. 23

1516 A425 50c red .25 .20
1517 A425 60c Prus blue .25 .20
1518 A425 70c orange .55 .35
1519 A425 80c brt yel grn .35 .25
1520 A425 90c rose violet .35 .25
1521 A425 1fr brt blue .45 .20
1522 A425 2fr black .95 .45
1523 A425 4fr ultramarine 1.90 .75
1524 A425 5fr olive green 2.40 .75
Nos. 1516-1524 (9) 7.45 3.40

Hazel Nut Tree A460

1986, Feb. 24 Engr. *Perf. 13x12½*

1525 A460 1.28fr Spring .70 .45
1526 A460 1.65fr Summer .90 .55
1527 A460 2.67fr Fall 1.40 1.00
1528 A460 4.44fr Winter 2.00 1.60
Nos. 1525-1528 (4) 5.00 3.60

Nos. 1525-1528 known only precanceled. See note after No. 324.

See Nos. 1580-1583, 1616-1619, 1685-1688, 1719-1722, 1809-1812.

Port of Monaco, 18th Cent. A461

1986, Feb. 24

1529 A461 2.20fr ultra, gray & brown 1.10 .45

Publication of Annales Monegasques, 10th anniv.

Europa 1986 — A462

1986, May 22 Engr. *Perf. 12½x13*

1530 A462 2.20fr Ramoge Nature Protection Treaty 1.75 *.40*
1531 A462 3.20fr Natl. marine reserve 2.25 *.75*
a. Souv. sheet, 5 each #1530-1531 25.00 *14.00*

Souvenir Sheet

1986 World Cup Soccer Championships, Mexico — A463

1986, May 22

1532 Sheet of 2 6.50 6.50
a. A463 5fr Player 2.50 2.50
b. A463 7fr Goalie 3.50 3.50

Ovis Musimon A464

1986, May 22 *Perf. 13x12½*

1533 A464 2.20fr shown 1.25 .60
1534 A464 2.50fr Capra ibex 1.25 1.00
1535 A464 3.20fr Rupicapra rupicapra 1.75 1.60
1536 A464 3.90fr Marmota marmota 2.50 2.00
1537 A464 5fr Lepus timidus varronis 3.00 2.75
1538 A464 7.20fr Mustela erminea 3.75 3.25
Nos. 1533-1538 (6) 13.50 11.20

Nos. 1536-1538 vert.

Monte Carlo Dog Show Type

1986, May 22 Photo. *Perf. 13x12½*

1539 A387 1.80fr Terriers 5.00 3.25

Prince Albert I, Parliament — A465

1986, May 22 *Perf. 13*

1540 A465 2.50fr brn & ol grn 1.10 .75

First Constitution, 75th anniv.

Serge Diaghilev, Founder — A466

1986, May 22 *Perf. 13*

1541 A466 3.20fr brn blk, carm rose & blk 1.90 1.60

Diaghilev's first permanent ballet company, 75th anniv., and creation of Monte Carlo Ballet Company, 1986.

1st Monte Carlo Auto Rally, 75 Anniv. — A467

Winner Henri Rougier and Turcat-Mery, 1911.

1986, May 22

1542 A467 3.90fr rose mag & car 2.50 2.00

Statue of Liberty, Cent. — A468

1986, May 22

1543 A468 5fr multi 2.00 1.40

Halley's Comet — A469

1986, May 22

1544 A469 10fr Sightings, 1986, 1352 4.25 3.00

AMERIPEX '86, Chicago, May 22-June 1 — A470

1986, May 22

1545 A470 5fr US flag, skyline 2.00 1.20

Belle Epoch Type of 1982

Illustrations by Hubert Clerissi.

Photo. & Engr.

1986, Oct. 28 *Perf. 12½x13*

1546 A394 6fr Pavilion, 1920, vert. 4.00 2.40
1547 A394 7fr Beau Rivage Avenue, 1925, vert. 5.75 3.00

Premiere of El Cid, by Pierre Corneille, 350th Anniv. — A471

1986, Oct. 28 Engr. *Perf. 13*

1548 A471 4fr Scenes 1.75 1.20

Franz Liszt, Composer — A472

1986, Oct. 28

1549 A472 5fr dk red brn & brt ultra 2.00 1.40

The Olympic Swimmer, 1961, by Emma de Sigaldi A473

1986, Oct. 28 ***Perf. 12½x13***
1550 A473 6fr multi 2.50 1.60

Intl. Insurers Congress, Monte Carlo, Sept. 30 — A474

1986, Oct. 28 ***Perf. 13½x13***
1551 A474 3.20fr brn, dp grn & brt bl 1.50 1.00

Intl. Flower Show Type of 1984

2.20fr, Bouquet of roses, acidenthera. 3.90fr, Ikebana of lilies, beech branches.

1986, Oct. 28 Photo. ***Perf. 12½x13***
1552 A435 2.20fr multi 1.90 .80
1553 A435 3.90fr multi 2.75 1.75

Dated 1987.

12th Intl. Circus Festival, Dec. 4-8 — A475

1986, Oct. 28 ***Perf. 13***
1554 A475 2.20fr multi 1.75 1.00

Industries Type of 1985

Design: 3.90fr, Plastics industry.

1986, Oct. 28 **Engr.**
1555 A455 3.90fr dk red, dk gray & bl grn 1.75 1.20

Christmas A476

1986, Oct. 28 Photo. ***Perf. 12½x13***
1556 A476 1.80fr Holly .85 .30
1557 A476 2.50fr Poinsettia 1.25 .50

Ascent of Mt. Blanc by J. Balmat and M.G. Paccard, Bicent. — A477

1986, Oct. 28 Engr. ***Perf. 13***
1558 A477 5.80fr red, brt bl & slate bl 2.50 1.75

Miniature Sheet

Arbutus Tree A478

1986, Oct. 28 ***Perf. 13x12½***
1559 Sheet of 4 9.50 9.50
a. A478 3fr Spring 1.25 1.25
b. A478 4fr Summer 1.90 1.90
c. A478 5fr Fall 2.75 2.75
d. A478 6fr Winter 2.50 2.50

See Nos. 1645, 1680, 1736, 1775, 1804, 1852, 1934, 1943.

Aquarium Type of 1985

1986, Sept. 25 Photo. ***Perf. 12½x13***
1560 A451 1.90fr like No. 1481 2.25 1.00
1561 A451 3.40fr like No. 1483 4.00 2.50

Prince Rainier III — A479

Villa Miraflores, Seat of the Philatelic Bureau — A480

#1562b, Prince Louis II, founder of the bureau.

1987, Apr. 23 Engr. ***Perf. 12½x13***
1562 Strip of 3 8.50 8.50
a. A479 4fr bright blue 1.90 1.90
b. A479 4fr dark red 1.90 1.90
c. A480 8fr multi 3.75 3.75

Philatelic Bureau, 50th anniv.
See No. 1607.

Louis II Stadium A481

1987, Apr. 23 ***Perf. 13x12½***
1563 A481 2.20fr Exterior 1.75 *.40*
1564 A481 3.40fr Interior 2.00 *.75*
a. Min. sheet, 5 each #1563-1564 25.00 *13.00*

Europa 1987.

Insects — A482

1987, Apr. 23 **Photo.**
1565 A482 1fr Carabe de solier .55 .55
1566 A482 1.90fr Guepe dorec 1.00 .90
1567 A482 2fr Cicindele 1.25 1.00
1568 A482 2.20fr Grande aeschne 1.50 1.00
1569 A482 3fr Chrysomele 2.40 1.75
1570 A482 3.40fr Grande sauterelle verte 3.25 2.50
Nos. 1565-1570 (6) 9.95 7.70

Nos. 1565, 1567 and 1569 horiz.

St. Devote Parish, Cent. — A483

1987, Apr. 23 Engr. ***Perf. 12½x13***
1571 A483 1.90fr black .90 .45

Monaco Diocese, Cent. — A484

1987, Apr. 23
1572 A484 2.50fr dk yellow grn 1.00 .55

50th Intl. Dog Show, Monte Carlo A485

1987, Apr. 23 ***Perf. 13x12½***
1573 A485 1.90fr Dog breeds 2.00 1.25
1574 A485 2.70fr Poodle 3.50 1.90

Stamp Day — A486

1987, Apr. 23 ***Perf. 13***
1575 A486 2.20fr multi 1.00 .45

Red Curley Tail, Mobile by Alexander Calder (1898-1976), Sculptor — A487

1987, Apr. 23 **Photo.**
1576 A487 3.70fr multi 1.60 1.00

Sculpture Exhibition, Monte Carlo.

2nd Small European Countries Games, May 14-17 — A488

1987, Apr. 23 **Engr.**
1577 A488 3fr Tennis 2.00 1.60
1578 A488 5fr Windsurfing 2.50 1.75

Miniature Sheet

Grape Vines A489

1987, Apr. 23 ***Perf. 13x12½***
1579 Sheet of 4 12.00 12.00
a. A489 3fr Spring 1.60 1.60
b. A489 4fr Summer 2.25 2.25
c. A489 5fr Autumn 3.25 3.25
d. A489 6fr Winter 3.75 3.75

Four Seasons Type of 1986

Life cycle of the chestnut tree.

1987, Mar. 17 Engr. ***Perf. 13x12½***
1580 A460 1.31fr Spring .70 .45
1581 A460 1.69fr Summer .90 .70
1582 A460 2.74fr Fall 1.40 1.10
1583 A460 4.56fr Winter 2.00 1.60
Nos. 1580-1583 (4) 5.00 3.85

Nos. 1580-1583 known only precanceled. See note after No. 324.

The Life of St. Devote, Patron Saint of Monaco A490

Text: 4fr, Born in 283, in Quercio, Devote was martyred in Mariana, Corsica. 5fr, Devote's nurse teaches the saint about Christianity.

1987, Nov. 13 Photo. ***Perf. 13x12½***
1584 A490 4fr multi 1.90 .85
1585 A490 5fr multi 2.40 1.40

Red Cross of Monaco.
See Nos. 1643-1644, 1692-1693, 1714-1715, 1776-1777, 1836-1837.

Philately A491

Butterflies and butterflies on simulated stamps.

1987, July 28 **Engr.**
1586 A491 1.90fr brt grn & dk gray .90 .40
1587 A491 2.20fr rose red & rose lake .95 .50
1588 A491 2.50fr red lil & vio 1.25 .80
1589 A491 3.40fr brt bl & bluish blk 1.90 .85
Nos. 1586-1589 (4) 5.00 2.55

13th Int'l. Circus Festival, Monte Carlo, Jan. 28-Feb. 1 — A492

1987, Nov. 13 Photo. ***Perf. 12½x13***
1590 A492 2.20fr multi 2.10 1.00

1988 Int'l Flower Show — A493

1987, Nov. 13

1591	A493 2.20fr Ikebanas	1.25	.60
1592	A493 3.40fr multi, horiz.	2.10	1.20

Dated 1988. See Nos. 1651, 1749.

Christmas A494

1987, Nov. 13 Engr. *Perf. 13x12½*

1593 A494 2.20fr crimson 1.00 .50

5-Franc Prince Honoré V Coin A495

1987, Nov. 13 *Perf. 13*

1594 A495 2.50fr scar & dk gray 1.10 .45

Recapture of the Mint, 150th anniv.

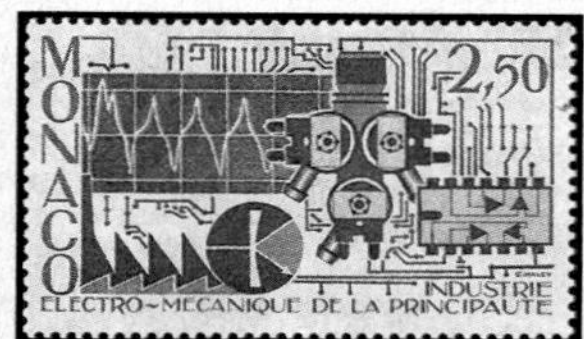

Electronics Industry — A496

1987, Nov. 13

1595 A496 2.50fr henna brn, vio bl & grn 1.10 .80

Int'l. Marine Radioactivity Laboratory, 25th Anniv. — A497

Design: Monaco Oceanographic Museum and Int'l. Agency of Atomic Energy, Vienna.

1987, Nov. 13

1596 A497 5fr brt bl, red brn & blk 2.25 1.40

Louis Jouvet (b.1887), French Actor A498

1987, Nov. 16 *Perf. 13x12½*

1597 A498 3fr black 1.25 1.10

A499

1987, Nov. 16

1598 A499 3fr The River Crossing 1.25 1.10

Paul and Virginia, by Bernardin de Saint-Pierre, first edition bcent. (in 1988).

Marc Chagall (1887-1985), Painter — A500

1987, Nov. 16 *Perf. 13*

1599 A500 4fr terra cotta & bl gray 2.25 1.25

Jean Jenneret (Le Corbusier, 1887-1965), French Architect — A501

1987, Nov. 16

1600 A501 4fr Architect, Ronchamp Chapel 1.90 1.20

Newton's Theory of Gravity, 300th Anniv. — A502

Invention of the Telegraph by Samuel Morse, 150th Anniv. — A503

1987, Nov. 16

1601	A502 4fr magenta & dk bl	2.10	1.10
1602	A503 4fr brt vio, turq bl & brn	2.10	1.10

Don Juan, Opera by Mozart, Bicent. — A504

Mass of the Dead, by Berlioz — A505

1987, Nov. 16

1603	A504 5fr ind, vio brn & sage grn	2.50	1.50
1604	A505 5fr sl grn, vio brn & bl	2.50	1.50

Belle Epoch Type of 1982

Illustrations by Hubert Clerissi. 6fr, 7fr vert.

Photo. & Engr.

1987, Nov. 16 *Perf. 12½x13*

1605	A394 6fr Rampe Major	3.75	2.50
1606	A394 7fr Old Monte Carlo Station	5.00	3.75

Philatelic Bureau Type of 1987

1987, Nov. 13 Engr. *Perf. 12½x13*

1607	Sheet of 3	8.00	8.00
a.	A479 4fr blk vio, like #1562a	1.90	1.90
b.	A479 4fr blk vio, like #1562b	1.90	1.90
c.	A480 8fr blk vio, like #1562c	3.75	3.75

Postage Due Arms Type of 1985 Booklet Stamps

1987-88 Photo. *Perf. 13 on 3 Sides*

Size: 17x23mm

1608	D10 2fr multi ('88)	1.00	.40
a.	Bklt. pane of 10	11.00	
1609	D10 2.20fr multi	1.00	.60
a.	Bklt. pane of 10	11.00	

Issued: 2fr, Jan. 15; 2.20fr, Nov. 13.

Aquarium Type of 1985

Perf. 13x12½, 12½x13

1988, Jan. 15 Photo.

1610	A451 2fr Bodianus rufus	1.25	.80
1611	A451 2.20fr Chelmon rostratus	1.75	.50
1612	A451 2.50fr Oxymonacanthus longirostris	2.00	1.10
1613	A451 3fr Ostracion lentiginosum	1.50	.80
1614	A451 3.70fr Pterois volitans	2.50	2.10
1615	A451 7fr Thalassoma lunare, horiz.	3.50	2.25
	Nos. 1610-1615 (6)	12.50	7.55

Four Seasons Type of 1986

Life cycle of the pear tree.

1988, Feb. 15 *Perf. 13x12½*

1616	A460 1.36fr Spring	.70	.45
1617	A460 1.75fr Summer	.90	.70
1618	A460 2.83fr Fall	1.40	1.10
1619	A460 4.72fr Winter	2.00	1.60
	Nos. 1616-1619 (4)	5.00	3.85

Nos. 1616-1619 known only precanceled. See note after No. 324.

Souvenir Sheet

Biathlon, 1988 Winter Olympics, Calgary — A506

Litho. & Engr.

1988, Feb. 15 *Perf. 13*

1620	Sheet of 2	13.50	13.50
a.	A506 4fr Skiing	5.75	5.75
b.	A506 6fr Shooting	6.75	6.75

51st Intl. Dog Show, Monte Carlo — A507

1988, Mar. 30 Photo. *Perf. 12½x13*

1621 A507 3fr Dachshunds 3.00 2.00

World Assoc. of the Friends of Children (AMADE), 25th Anniv. A508

1988, Mar. 30 Engr. *Perf. 13*

1622 A508 5fr dark vio blue, dark brn & brt olive grn 2.50 1.75

Europa 1988 — A509

Transport and communication: 2.20fr, Globe picturing hemispheres, man, brain, telecommunications satellite. 3.60fr, Plane propeller and high-speed locomotive.

1988, Apr. 21 *Perf. 12½x13*

1623	A509 2.20fr multi	*1.50*	*.50*
1624	A509 3.60fr multi	*2.75*	*1.00*
a.	Souv. sheet, 5 each #1623-1624	*27.50*	*12.50*

Mushrooms of Mercantour Natl. Park A510

Perf. 13x12½, 12½x13

1988, May 26 Photo.

1625	A510 2fr Leccinum rotundifoliae	1.25	.90
1626	A510 2.20fr Hygrocybe punicea	1.50	.85
1627	A510 2.50fr Pholiota flammans	1.60	1.50
1628	A510 2.70fr Lactarius lignyotus	2.10	1.75
1629	A510 3fr Cortinarius traganus	2.50	2.25
1630	A510 7fr Russula olivacea	4.50	4.25
	Nos. 1625-1630 (6)	13.45	11.50

Nos. 1629-1630 vert.

Nautical Soc., Cent. — A511

1988, May 26 Engr. *Perf. 13*

1631 A511 2fr dk red, lt blue & dk grn 1.10 .70

5th Year of Restoration of Our Lady of Laghet Sanctuary
A512

1988, May 26 ***Perf. 12½***
1632 A512 5fr multicolored 2.50 1.40

World Health Organization, 40th Anniv. — A513

1988, May 26 ***Perf. 13***
1633 A513 6fr brt blue & lake 2.75 1.75

Intl. Red Cross and Red Crescent Organizations, 125th Annivs. — A514

1988, May 26 **Photo.** ***Perf. 13x12½***
1634 A514 6fr dull red, blk & gray 2.75 1.75

Jean Monnet (1888-1979), Nobel Peace Prize Winner in 1922 — A515

Maurice Chevalier (1888-1972), Actor — A516

1988, May 26 **Engr.** ***Perf. 12½x13***
1635 A515 2fr brt blue, dark olive bister & blk 3.50 1.75
1636 A516 2fr blk & dark blue 3.75 1.75

1st Crossing of Greenland by Fridtjof Nansen (1861-1930), Cent. — A517

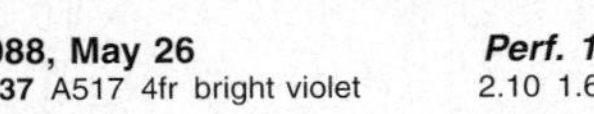

1988, May 26 ***Perf. 13***
1637 A517 4fr bright violet 2.10 1.60

Belle Epoch Type of 1982

Illustrations by Hubert Clerissi.

Photo. & Engr.

1988, Sept. 8 ***Perf. 13x12½***
1638 A394 6fr Packet in Monte Carlo Harbor, 1910 4.00 2.50
1639 A394 7fr Monte Carlo Station, c. 1910 4.50 3.25

Souvenir Sheet

1988 Summer Olympics, Seoul
A518

Woman wearing Korean regional costume, Games emblem and event: 2fr, Women's tennis. 3fr, Women's table tennis. 5fr, Women's yachting. 7fr, Women's cycling.

1988, Sept. 8 **Engr.**
1640 Sheet of 4 9.50 9.50
a. A518 2fr blk, light ultra & brown 1.10 1.10
b. A518 3fr blk, light ultra & brown 1.40 1.40
c. A518 5fr blk, light ultra & brown 2.40 2.40
d. A518 7fr blk, light ultra & brown 3.25 3.25

Monte Carlo Congress Center, 10th Anniv. — A519

1988, Sept. 8 ***Perf. 13***
1641 2fr dark blue grn 1.00 1.00
1642 3fr henna brn 1.25 1.25
a. A519 Pair, #1641-1642 2.50 2.50

Monegasque Red Cross Type of 1987

The Life of St. Devote, patron saint of Monaco: 4fr, Devote witnessing the arrival of the governor of Rome. 5fr, Devote and the governor.

1988, Oct. 20 **Photo.** ***Perf. 13x12½***
1643 A490 4fr multicolored 2.00 1.00
1644 A490 5fr multicolored 2.50 1.50

Tree Type of 1986

Life cycle of the olive tree.

1988, Oct. 20 **Engr.** ***Perf. 13x12½***
1645 Sheet of 4 12.50 12.50
a. A478 3fr Spring 2.25 2.25
b. A478 4fr Summer 2.75 2.75
c. A478 5fr Fall 3.25 3.25
d. A478 6fr Winter 3.75 3.75

Le Nain and Brothers, Detail of a Painting in the Louvre, by Antoine Le Nain (c. 1588-1648)
A521

1988, Oct. 20 ***Perf. 12½x13***
1646 A521 5fr ol brn, dull brn & car rose 3.25 1.90

Les Grands Archeologues, Bronze Sculpture by Giorgio De Chirico (1888-1978), Italian Painter and Sculptor — A522

1988, Oct. 20 ***Perf. 13***
1647 A522 5fr ol bis, blk brn & dark bl 3.25 1.90

Pierre Carlet de Chamblain de Marivaux (1688-1763), French Playwright, Novelist — A523

1988, Oct. 20
1648 A523 3fr dull ol & ultra 1.75 1.00

Lord Byron (1788-1824), English Poet — A524

1988, Oct. 20
1649 A524 3fr grnsh bl, brn & blk 1.75 .85

14th Intl. Circus Festival, Monte Carlo, Feb. 2-6, 1989 — A525

1988, Oct. 20 **Photo.** ***Perf. 12½x13***
1650 A525 2fr multi 1.50 1.00

Intl. Flower Show Type of 1987

1988, Oct. 20
1651 A493 3fr Ikebana 2.10 1.25

22nd Intl. Flower Show and Flower Arranging Contest, Monte Carlo.

Textile Industry (Ready-to-Wear Clothes by Bettina and Le Squadra)
A526

1988, Oct. 20 **Engr.** ***Perf. 13***
1652 A526 3fr blk, yel org & dk ol grn 1.40 1.00

Christmas
A527

1988, Oct. 20 **Litho.** ***Perf. 12½x13***
1653 A527 2fr black & lemon 1.25 .70

Petroglyphs, Mercantour Natl. Park — A528

Perf. 13x12½, 12½x13

1989, Feb. 8 **Litho.**
1654 A528 2fr multi 1.00 .80
1655 A528 2.20fr multi, diff. 1.00 .80
1656 A528 3fr multi, diff. 1.40 1.20
1657 A528 3.60fr multi, diff. 2.00 1.50
1658 A528 4fr multi, diff., vert. 2.25 1.75
1659 A528 5fr multi, diff., vert. 2.75 2.00
Nos. 1654-1659 (6) 10.40 8.05

St. Nicolas Place — A528a

1989, Feb. 8 **Litho.** ***Perf. 13½x13***

Booklet Stamps

1660 A528a 2fr Rue des Spelugues 1.00 .50
b. Booklet pane of 10 12.00
1660A A528a 2.20fr shown 1.25 .60
c. Booklet pane of 10 14.00

See Nos. 1702-1703, 1826-1827.

Prince Rainier III — A529

1989-91 **Photo. & Engr.** ***Perf. 13***
1661 A529 2fr pale blue grn & Prus grn 1.00 .35
1662 A529 2.10fr lt blue & Prus blue 1.00 .25
1663 A529 2.20fr pink & rose brn 1.10 .20
1664 A529 2.20fr pale greenish bl & greenish bl 1.00 .35
1665 A529 2.30fr pale pink & car lake 1.10 .20
1666 A529 2.50fr pale rose & rose lake 1.25 .20
1667 A529 3.20fr pale blue & brt blue 1.50 .90
1668 A529 3.40fr lt bl & dk bl 1.75 1.00
1669 A529 3.60fr lt blue & sapphire 2.00 1.25
1670 A529 3.80fr pale pink & dk lil rose 1.75 .55
1671 A529 4fr pale vio & rose vio 1.90 1.25
1672 A529 5fr buff & dark vio brn 2.40 .55
1673 A529 15fr pale vio & indigo 7.00 1.75
1673A A529 20fr pink & rose car 9.50 2.75

1674 A529 25fr pale gray & blk 11.50 2.00
Nos. 1661-1674 (15) 45.75 13.55

Issued: 2fr, #1663, 3.60fr, 5fr, 15fr, 3/14; 2.10fr, 2.30fr, 25fr, 1/11/90; 3.20fr, 3.80fr, 3/15/90; 20fr, 4/26/91; #1664, 2.50fr, 3.40fr, 4fr, 9/24/91.

See Nos. 1790-1799.

5th Magic Grand Prix, Monte Carlo, Mar. 17-19
A530

1989, Mar. 14 Engr. *Perf. 13x12½*
1675 A530 2.20fr multi 1.40 .80

Dog Show Type of 1982

1989, Mar. 14 Photo.
1676 A387 2.20fr Yorkshire terrier 2.00 1.10

Our Lady of Mercy Soc., 350th Anniv.
A531

1989, Mar. 14 Engr. *Perf. 13*
1677 A531 3fr choc, dark red & blk 1.25 .75

Theater & Film — A532

Designs: 3fr, Jean Cocteau (1889-1963), French writer, artist. 4fr, Charlie Chaplin (1889-1977), English actor, film producer.

1989, Mar. 14
1678 A532 3fr Prus grn, olive grn & dp rose lil 1.40 1.10
1679 A532 4fr dk grn, dk vio & dk red 2.75 1.60

Tree Type of 1986

Life cycle of the pomegranate tree.

1989, Mar. 14 *Perf. 13x12½*

Miniature Sheet

1680 Sheet of 4 10.00 10.00
a. A478 3fr Spring 1.40 1.40
b. A478 4fr Summer 2.00 2.00
c. A478 5fr Fall 2.75 2.75
d. A478 6fr Winter 3.00 3.00

Souvenir Sheet

Reign of Prince Rainier III, 40th Anniv. — A533

1989, May 9 Engr. *Perf. 13*
1681 A533 20fr rose vio 11.00 11.00

See No. 2128.

Europa 1989 — A534

Children's games.

1989, May 9 *Perf. 12½x13*
1682 A534 2.20fr Marbles 1.50 *.40*
1683 A534 3.60fr Jumping rope 2.75 *.70*
a. Souv. sheet, 5 each #1682-1683 27.50 *14.00*

Souvenir Sheet

French Revolution, Bicent., PHILEXFRANCE '89 — A535

a, Liberty. b, Equality. c, Fraternity.

1989, July 7 Engr. *Perf. 12½x13*
1684 A535 Sheet of 3 7.50 7.50
a. 5fr sapphire 2.40 2.40
b. 5fr black 2.40 2.40
c. 5fr dark red 2.40 2.40

Four Seasons Type of 1986

Life cycle of the pear tree.

1989, July 27 Photo. *Perf. 13x12½*
1685 A460 1.39fr like No. 1616 .80 .50
1686 A460 1.79fr like No. 1617 1.00 .80
1687 A460 2.90fr like No. 1618 1.60 1.25
1688 A460 4.84fr like No. 1619 2.00 1.75
Nos. 1685-1688 (4) 5.40 4.30

Nos. 1685-1688 known only precanceled. See note after No. 324.

Portrait of the Artist's Mother, by Philibert Florence
A536

Regatta at Molesey, by Alfred Sisley (1839-1899) — A537

Paintings: 8fr, *Enclosed Courtyard, Auvers,* by Paul Cezanne (1839-1906), vert.

Perf. 13, 13x12½ (6fr), 12½x13 (8fr)

1989, Sept. 7 Engr.
1689 A536 4fr olive black 2.50 1.75
1690 A537 6fr multi 3.25 2.00
1691 A537 8fr multi 4.25 3.00
Nos. 1689-1691 (3) 10.00 6.75

Birth sesquicentennials of painters.

Monegasque Red Cross Type of 1987

The life of St. Devote, patron saint of Monaco: 4fr, Eutychius refuses to betray Devote to Barbarus and is poisoned. 5fr, Devote is condemned to torture by Barbarus when she refuses to make sacrifices to the Gods.

1989, Sept. 7 Photo. *Perf. 13x12½*
1692 A490 4fr multi 1.75 1.20
1693 A490 5fr multi 2.50 1.40

Interparliamentary Union, Cent. — A538

1989, Oct. 26 Engr. *Perf. 13*
1694 A538 4fr multi 2.00 1.00

Belle Epoch Type of 1982

Illustrations by Hubert Clerissi.

1989, Oct. 26 *Perf. 12½x13*
1695 A394 7fr Ship in Monaco Port 3.75 2.50
1696 A394 8fr Gaming hall, Monte Carlo Casino 4.25 3.00

Souvenir Sheet

Princess Grace Foundation, 25th Anniv. — A539

a, Princess Grace. b, Princess Caroline.

1989, Oct. 26
1697 Sheet of 2 9.25 9.25
a.-b. A539 5fr any single 3.50 3.50

20th UPU Congress — A540

Design: Views of the Prince of Monaco's palace and the White House.

1989, Oct. 26 *Perf. 13*
1698 A540 6fr multicolored 2.75 1.75

Christmas
A541

1989, Oct. 26 Litho. *Perf. 12½x13*
1699 A541 2fr Poinsettia 2.25 .80

15th Intl. Circus Festival, Monte Carlo, Feb. 1-5, 1990 — A542

1989, Dec. 7 Photo. *Perf. 12½x13*
1700 A542 2.20fr multicolored 3.50 1.00

Monaco Aid and Presence, 10th Anniv.
A543

1989, Dec. 7 Engr. *Perf. 13x12½*
1701 A543 2.20fr brown & red 2.25 1.00

Avenues Type of 1989

1990, Feb. 8 Litho. *Perf. 13½x13*
1702 A528a 2.10fr The Great Stairs 1.00 .50
a. Bklt. pane of 10 + 2 labels 10.50
1703 A528a 2.30fr Mayoral Court of Honor 1.25 .50
a. Bklt. pane of 10 + 2 labels 12.50

Dog Show Type of 1982

1990, Mar. 15 *Perf. 13x12½*
1704 A387 2.30fr Bearded collie 2.25 1.25

Sir Rowland Hill, Great Britain No. 1 — A544

1990, Mar. 15 Engr. *Perf. 13*
1705 A544 5fr royal bl & blk 2.75 2.00

Penny Black, 150th anniv.

Flowers Named for Members of the Royal Family — A545

1990, Mar. 15 Litho. *Perf. 12½x13*

1706 A545 2fr Princess Grace .95 .55
1707 A545 3fr Prince Rainier III 1.40 .70
1708 A545 3fr Grace Patricia 1.40 .90
1709 A545 4fr Principessa Grace 1.90 1.10
1710 A545 5fr Caroline of Monaco 3.25 1.75
Nos. 1706-1710 (5) 8.90 5.00

Intl. Telecommunications Union, 125th Anniv. — A546

1990, Mar. 15 Engr. *Perf. 13*

1711 A546 4fr pink, deep vio & dull blue grn 2.00 1.50

Antony Noghes (1890-1978), Creator of the Monaco Grand Prix and Monte Carlo Rally — A547

1990, Mar. 15

1712 A547 3fr deep vio, blk & dark red 1.50 1.00

Automobile Club, Cent. — A548

1990, Mar. 15

1713 A548 4fr brt pur, sepia & brt blue 2.10 1.40

Monegasque Red Cross Type of 1987

The life of St. Devote, patron saint of Monaco: 4fr, Devote tortured to death (whipped). 5fr, Body layed out in a small boat.

1990, Mar. 15 Litho. *Perf. 13x12½*

1714 A490 4fr multicolored 1.90 1.25
1715 A490 5fr multicolored 2.50 1.75

Europa — A549

1990, May 3 Engr. *Perf. 12½x12*

1716 A549 2.30fr multicolored 1.50 *.35*
1717 A549 3.70fr multicolored 2.25 *.55*
a. Souv. sheet, 4 each, perf. 12½x13 27.50 *13.00*

Souvenir Sheet

World Cup Soccer Championships, Italy — A550

1990, May 3 *Perf. 13x12½*

1718 A550 Sheet of 4 13.00 13.00
a. 5fr Players, trophy 3.25 3.25
b. 5fr Player dribbling ball 3.25 3.25
c. 5fr Ball 3.25 3.25
d. 5fr Players, stadium 3.25 3.25

Four Seasons Type of 1986

Life cycle of the plum tree.

1990, Sept. 17 *Perf. 13*

1719 A460 1.46fr Spring .80 .50
1720 A460 1.89fr Summer 1.00 .80
1721 A460 3.06fr Fall 1.60 1.25
1722 A460 5.10fr Winter 2.25 1.75
Nos. 1719-1722 (4) 5.65 4.30

Nos. 1719-1722 known only precanceled. See note after No. 324.

Minerals, Mercantour Natl. Park A551

Perf. 13x12½, 12½x13

1990, Sept. 4 Litho.

1723 A551 2.10fr Anatase 1.00 .50
1724 A551 2.30fr Albite 1.00 .50
1725 A551 3.20fr Rutile 1.50 1.10
1726 A551 3.80fr Chlorite 2.00 1.25
1727 A551 4fr Brookite 2.50 1.75
1728 A551 6fr Quartz 3.25 2.75
Nos. 1723-1728 (6) 11.25 7.85

Nos. 1727-1728 vert.

Pierrot Ecrivain — A552

1990, Sept. 4 Engr. *Perf. 12½x13*

1729 A552 3fr dark blue 1.50 .80

Helicopter, Monaco Heliport A553

5fr, Helicopters, Monte Carlo skyline.

1990, Sept. 4 *Perf. 13*

1730 A553 3fr red, brn & blk 1.25 .60
1731 A553 5fr blk, gray bl & brn 2.50 1.40

30th World Congress of Civilian Airports, Monte Carlo.

C. Samuel Hahnemann (1755-1843), Physician — A554

1990, Sept. 4

1732 A554 3fr multicolored 1.40 .85

Homeopathic medicine, bicentennial.

Jean-Francois Champollion (1790-1832), Egyptologist — A555

1990, Sept. 4

1733 A555 5fr blue & brown 2.40 1.25

Offshore Power Boating World Championships A556

6fr, Petanque World Championships.

1990, Sept. 4

1734 A556 2.30fr brt ultra, brn & red 1.10 .70
1735 A556 6fr brn org, brn & bl 2.75 1.60

Tree Type of 1986

Miniature Sheet

Life cycle of the lemon tree.

1990, Oct. 17 Litho. *Perf. 13x12½*

1736 Sheet of 4 9.50 9.50
a. A478 3fr Spring 1.25 1.25
b. A478 4fr Summer 1.75 1.75
c. A478 5fr Fall 2.40 2.40
e. A478 6fr Winter 2.75 2.75

Type of 1984

1990, Oct. 17 Litho. *Perf. 12½x13*

1737 A441 2.30fr Miller riding donkey 1.25 .45
1738 A441 3.20fr Woman carrying firewood 1.60 .80
1739 A441 3.80fr Baker 2.10 1.25
Nos. 1737-1739 (3) 4.95 2.50

The Cathedral, by Auguste Rodin (1840-1917) A558

1990, Oct. 17 Engr. *Perf. 12½*

1740 A558 5fr bl & cream 2.25 1.25

La Pie by Claude Monet (1840-1926) — A559

1990, Oct. 17 *Perf. 13x12*

1741 A559 7fr multicolored 5.00 4.00

Peter Ilich Tchaikovsky (1840-1893), Composer A560

1990, Oct. 17 *Perf. 12½x13*

1742 A560 5fr dark grn & bl 2.25 1.25

16th Intl. Circus Festival, Monte Carlo — A561

1991, Jan. 2 Photo. *Perf. 13*

1743 A561 2.30fr multicolored 1.50 .85

See No. 1801.

Intl. Symposium on Migratory Birds — A562

Migratory birds and their continents: 2fr, Ciconia abdimii, Africa. 3fr, Selasphorus platycercus, America. 4fr, Anas querquedula, Asia. 5fr, Eurystomus orientalis, Australia. 6fr, Merops apiaster, Europe.

1991, Feb. 22 Litho. *Perf. 12½x13*

1744 A562 2fr multicolored 1.00 .60
1745 A562 3fr multicolored 1.25 1.00
1746 A562 4fr multicolored 2.00 1.25
1747 A562 5fr multicolored 2.50 2.00
1748 A562 6fr multicolored 3.25 2.50
Nos. 1744-1748 (5) 10.00 7.35

Intl. Flower Show Type of 1987

1991, Feb. 22

1749 A493 3fr Cyclamen 2.00 .85

Views of Old Monaco Type of 1984

Designs: 20c, Cliffs of Monaco, Port de Fontvieille. 40c, Place du Casino. 50c, Place de la Cremaillere. 70c, Prince's Palace. 80c, Avenue du Beau Rivage. 1fr, Place d'Armes.

1991, Feb. 22 Engr.

1750 A425 20c rose violet .25 .20
1751 A425 40c dk green .25 .20
1752 A425 50c claret .25 .20
1753 A425 70c ol green .25 .20
1754 A425 80c ultramarine .30 .25
1755 A425 1fr dk blue .40 .25
Nos. 1750-1755 (6) 1.70 1.30

Dog Show Type of 1982

1991, Feb. 22 Litho. *Perf. 12*

1756 A387 2.50fr Schnauzer 2.25 1.40

Oceanographic Museum — A563

1991, Feb. 22
1757 A563 2.10fr Phytoplankton 1.25 .80

1992 Olympics A564

Design: No. 1758b, Cross country skiiers, diff. No. 1759a, Relay runner receiving baton. No. 1759b, Runner passing baton.

1991, Apr. 26 Engr. *Perf. 13x12½*
1758 Pair 3.50 3.50
a. A564 3fr dark green, blue & olive 1.40 1.25
b. A564 4fr dark green, blue & olive 2.00 1.60
1759 Pair 4.00 4.00
a. A564 3fr brown & Prussian blue 1.40 1.25
b. A564 5fr brown & Prussian blue 2.50 2.00

Nos. 1758 and 1759 have continuous designs.

Europa A565

1991, Apr. 26
1760 A565 2.30fr Eutelsat 1.75 *.45*
1761 A565 3.20fr Inmarsat 3.00 *.60*
a. Min. sheet, 5 ea. #1760-1761 30.00 *13.00*

25th Intl. Contemporary Art Competition A566

1991, Apr. 26 Engr. *Perf. 12½x13*
1762 A566 4fr multicolored 2.00 1.25

Prince Pierre Foundation, 25th Anniv. — A567

1991, Apr. 26
1763 A567 5fr multicolored 2.25 1.25

Coral — A568

1991, Apr. 26 Photo. *Perf. 12*
1764 A568 2.20fr shown 1.25 .80
1765 A568 2.40fr Coral necklace 1.25 .85

Christmas Type of 1984

1991, Nov. 7 Litho. *Perf. 12*
1766 A441 2.50fr Consul 1.25 .50
1767 A441 3.50fr Woman from Arles 2.00 1.10
1768 A441 4fr Mayor 2.50 1.40
Nos. 1766-1768 (3) 5.75 3.00

Conifers, Mercantour Natl. Park A569

1991, Nov. 7
1769 A569 2.50fr Epicea .95 .35
1770 A569 3.50fr Sapin 1.40 .70
1771 A569 4fr Pin a crochets 1.50 .90
1772 A569 5fr Pin sylvestre, vert. 1.90 1.10
1773 A569 6fr Pin cembro 2.25 1.50
1774 A569 7fr Meleze, vert. 2.75 1.75
Nos. 1769-1774 (6) 10.75 6.30

Tree Type of 1986
Miniature Sheet

Life cycle of an orange tree.

1991, Nov. 7 Engr. *Perf. 13x12½*
1775 Sheet of 4 9.50 9.50
a. A478 3fr Spring 1.25 1.25
b. A478 4fr Summer 1.75 1.75
c. A478 5fr Fall 2.50 2.50
d. A478 6fr Winter 2.75 2.75

Monagasque Red Cross Type of 1987

Life of St. Devote, Monaco's Patron Saint: 4.50fr, The Storm is Rising. 5.50fr, Arrival of the Rock of Monaco.

1991, Nov. 7 Photo.
1776 A490 4.50fr multicolored 2.00 .90
1777 A490 5.50fr multicolored 2.50 1.25

Testudo Hermanni A570

1991, Nov. 7 Litho. *Perf. 12*
1778 A570 1.25fr Two crawling right 1.40 .80
1779 A570 1.25fr Peering from shell 1.40 .80
1780 A570 1.25fr Walking in grass 1.40 .80
1781 A570 1.25fr Walking amid plants 1.40 .80
a. Block or strip of 4, #1778-1781 7.00 7.00

Prince Albert I Type of 1891
Miniature Sheet

1991, Nov. 7 Engr. *Perf. 13*
Stamp size: 22½x28mm
1782 Sheet of 3 13.00 13.00
a. A2 10fr dark red 4.25 4.25
b. A2 10fr dark blue green 4.25 4.25
c. A2 10fr deep violet 4.25 4.25

Portrait of Claude Monet by Auguste Renoir A571

1991, Nov. 7 Engr. *Perf. 12½x13*
1783 A571 5fr multicolored 2.40 1.75

Treaty of Peronne, 350th Anniv. A572

Portraits by Philippe de Champaigne (1602-1674): 6fr, Honore II (1604-1662), Monaco. 7fr, Louis XIII (1610-1643), France.

1991, Nov. 7
1784 A572 6fr multicolored 3.00 2.50
1785 A572 7fr multicolored 3.75 2.50

Princess Grace Theatre, 10th Anniv. A573

1991, Nov. 7 Litho.
1786 A573 8fr Princess Grace 5.00 3.75

Prince Rainier III Type of 1989

1991-96 Photo. & Engr. *Perf. 13*
1790 A529 2.40fr pale greenish bl & dk Prus bl 1.10 .50
1791 A529 2.70fr pale bl grn, dk bl grn 1.60 .80
1791A A529 (2.70fr) pale & Prus grn 1.25 .50
b. With strengthened lines in military ribbon at LR 1.25 .50
1792 A529 2.80fr pale rose & rose lake 1.25 .60
1793 A529 3fr pale red, red brn 1.75 .90
1793A A529 (3fr) pink & red 1.40 .55
1794 A529 3.70fr pale bl & dk bl 1.75 .80
1795 A529 3.80fr pale bl & dk bl 2.25 1.10
1796 A529 (3.80fr) pale & dk bl 1.75 .70
1797 A529 10fr lt bl grn & dp bl grn 4.75 1.90
1799 A529 40fr pale brn & dk brn 18.00 8.25
Nos. 1790-1799 (11) 36.85 16.60

Nos. 1791A, 1793A, 1796 are dated "1999."

Issued: 10fr, 11/7/91; 2.40fr, 2.80fr, 3.70fr, 40fr, 7/28/93; 2.70fr, 3/18/96; 3fr, 3.80fr, 7/8/96; #1791A, 1793A, 1796, 11/28/98. No. 1791Ab, Apr. 2003.

No. 1791Ab sold for 41c on day of issue and has other strengthened lines other than those in the military ribbon.

See No. 1863b.

This is an expanding set. Numbers will change if necessary.

16th Intl. Circus Festival Type

1992, Jan. 6 Photo. *Perf. 12½x13*
1801 A561 2.50fr multicolored 1.60 1.00

1992 Winter and Summer Olympics, Albertville and Barcelona A574

Designs: 7fr, Two-man bobsled. 8fr, Soccer.

1992, Feb. 7 Engr. *Perf. 13*
1802 A574 7fr multicolored 3.25 1.50
1803 A574 8fr multicolored 3.75 2.00

Tree Type of 1986
Miniature Sheet

Life cycle of a cactus plant.

1992, Apr. 24 Photo. *Perf. 13x12½*
1804 Sheet of 4 10.00 10.00
a. A478 3fr Spring 1.25 1.25
b. A478 4fr Summer 1.75 1.75
c. A478 5fr Fall 2.50 2.50
d. A478 6fr Winter 3.50 3.50

60th Monte Carlo Rally A575

1992, Mar. 13 Engr. *Perf. 13x12½*
1805 A575 4fr dk bl grn, blk & red 2.00 1.25

Intl. Dog Show Type of 1982

1992, Mar. 13 Litho. *Perf. 13x12½*
1806 A387 2.20fr Labrador retriever 1.90 1.00

50th Grand Prix of Monaco A576

1992, Mar. 13 Engr.
1807 A576 2.50fr vio brn, blk & brt bl 1.50 .80

25th Intl. Flower Show, Monte Carlo — A577

1992, Mar. 13 Photo. *Perf. 12½x13*
1808 A577 3.40fr multicolored 1.90 1.25

See No. 1848.

Four Seasons Type of 1986

Life cycle of a walnut tree.

1992, Mar. 13 Photo.
1809 A460 1.60fr Spring .85 .50
1810 A460 2.08fr Summer 1.00 .80
1811 A460 2.98fr Fall 1.50 1.25
1812 A460 5.28fr Winter 2.25 1.75
Nos. 1809-1812 (4) 5.60 4.30

Nos. 1809-1812 known only precanceled. See the note after No. 324.

Souvenir Sheet

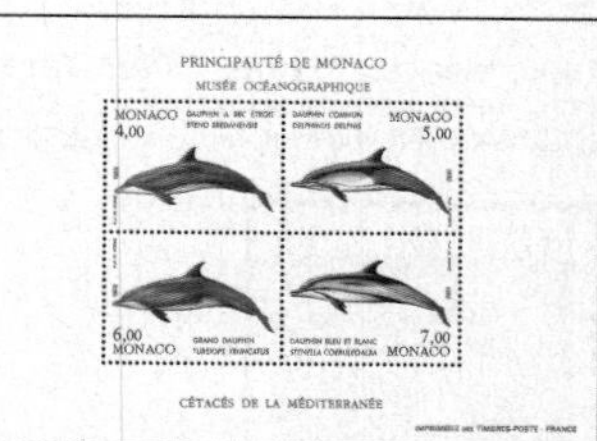

Dolphins — A578

1992, Mar. 13
1813 A578 Sheet of 4 11.50 11.50
a. 4fr Steno bredanensis 1.90 1.90
b. 5fr Delphinus delphis 2.40 2.40
c. 6fr Tursiops truncatus 3.00 3.00
d. 7fr Stenella coeruleoalba 3.50 3.50

See Nos. 1853, 1898.

Discovery of America, 500th Anniv. A579

1992, Apr. 24
1814 A579 2.50fr Pinta 1.50 *.45*
1815 A579 3.40fr Santa Maria 2.75 *.80*
1816 A579 4fr Nina 4.00 *1.25*
a. Sheet, 2 each #1814-1816 30.00 *13.50*
Nos. 1814-1816 (3) 8.25 2.50

Europa.

Ameriflora Intl. Flower Show, Columbus, Ohio A580

1992, Apr. 24 Litho. *Perf. 12½x13*
1817 A580 4fr Fruits & vegetables 1.90 1.10
1818 A580 5fr Vase of flowers 2.40 1.75

Columbus Exposition, Genoa '92 — A581

1992, Apr. 24 Engr. *Perf. 13*
1819 A581 6fr multicolored 3.00 1.75

Expo '92, Seville — A582

1992, Apr. 24
1820 A582 7fr multicolored 3.00 2.00

Views of Old Monaco Type of 1984

Illustrations by Hubert Clerissi: 60c, National Council. 90c, Port of Fontvieille. 2fr, Condamine Market. 3fr, Sailing ship. 7fr, Oceanographic Museum.

1992, May 25 Engr. *Perf. 12½x13*
1821 A425 60c dark blue .25 .20
1822 A425 90c violet brown .35 .25
1823 A425 2fr vermilion .95 .40
1824 A425 3fr black 1.40 .60
1825 A425 7fr gray blue & blk 3.25 1.40
Nos. 1821-1825 (5) 6.20 2.85

Avenues Type of 1989

1992, May 25 Litho. *Perf. 13x13½*
Booklet Stamps
1826 A528a 2.20fr Porte Nueve, horiz. 1.10 .40
a. Bklt. pane of 10 + 2 labels 11.00
1827 A528a 2.50fr Placette Bosio, horiz. 1.10 .45
a. Bklt. pane of 10 + 2 labels 11.00

Genoa '92 — A583

Roses: 3fr, Christopher Columbus. 4fr, Prince of Monaco.

1992, Sept. 18 Litho. *Perf. 12*
1828 A583 3fr multicolored 1.75 1.10
1829 A583 4fr multicolored 1.75 1.10

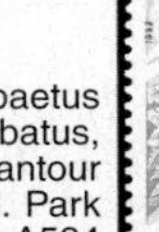

Gypaetus Barbatus, Mercantour Natl. Park A584

1992, Oct. 20 Engr. *Perf. 13x12½*
1830 A584 2.20fr grn, org & blk 1.25 1.00

Seabus A585

1992, Oct. 20
1831 A585 4fr multicolored 1.75 1.40

Phytoplankton A586

Designs: 2.20fr, Ceratium ranipes. 2.50fr, Ceratium hexacanthum.

1992, Oct. 20 Litho. *Perf. 12*
1832 A586 2.20fr multicolored 1.25 .80
1833 A586 2.50fr multicolored 1.25 .40

Baron de Coubertin's Call for Modern Olympics, Cent. — A587

1992, Oct. 20 Engr. *Perf. 13*
1834 A587 10fr blue 4.75 2.50

Chapel of St. Catherine — A588

Prince of Monaco, the Marquisat of Baux-de-Provence.

1992, Oct. 20 Litho. & Engr.
1835 A588 15fr multicolored 6.50 3.50

Monagasque Red Cross Type of 1987

The life of St. Devote, patron saint of Monaco: 6fr, Fire aboard ship. 8fr, Procession of the reliquary.

1992, Oct. 20 Engr.
Size: 48x36mm
1836 A490 6fr multicolored 2.75 1.75
1837 A490 8fr multicolored 3.50 2.50

Christmas Type of 1984

1992, Oct. 20 Litho. *Perf. 12*
1838 A441 2.50fr Basket maker 1.25 .50
1839 A441 3.40fr Fishmonger 1.90 .85
1840 A441 5fr Drummer 2.50 1.50
Nos. 1838-1840 (3) 5.65 2.85

Miniature Sheet

Postal Museum — A589

Litho. & Engr.
1992, Oct. 20 *Perf. 13*
1841 A589 Sheet of 2 10.50 10.50
a. 10fr Sardinia Type A4 4.75 4.75
b. 10fr France Type A3 4.75 4.75

17th Intl. Circus Festival, Monte Carlo — A590

1993, Jan. 5 Litho. *Perf. 13½x13*
1842 A590 2.50fr multicolored 1.40 .60

Birds, Mercantour Natl. Park — A591

Perf. 13x12½, 12½x13
1993, Feb. 15 Engr.

Designs: 2fr, Circaetus gallicus, horiz. 3fr, Falco peregrinus, horiz. 4fr, Bubo bubo. 5fr, Pernis apivorus. 6fr, Aegolius funereus.

1843 A591 2fr multicolored .95 .55
1844 A591 3fr multicolored 1.40 .70
1845 A591 4fr multicolored 1.90 1.10
1846 A591 5fr multicolored 2.40 1.50
1847 A591 6fr multicolored 2.75 1.75
Nos. 1843-1847 (5) 9.40 5.60

Intl. Flower Show Type of 1992

1993, Mar. 1 Photo. *Perf. 12½x13*
1848 A577 3.40fr multicolored 1.75 .85

10th World Amateur Theater Festival — A592

1993, Mar. 1 Litho. *Perf. 13*
1849 A592 4.20fr multicolored 2.00 .85

Intl. Civil Protection Day — A593

1993, Mar. 1 Engr. *Perf. 12½x13*
1850 A593 6fr multicolored 3.00 1.75

A594

1993, Mar. 24 Engr. *Perf. 13*
1851 A594 5fr Princess Grace 2.40 1.40

See US No. 2749.

Tree Type of 1986

Miniature Sheet

Life cycle of an almond tree: a, Spring. b, Summer. c, Autumn. d, Winter.

1993, Mar. 24 Photo. *Perf. 13x12½*
1852 Sheet of 4 10.50 10.50
a.-d. A478 5fr any single 2.40 2.40

Marine Mammals Type of 1992

Miniature Sheet

1993, Mar. 24
1853 Sheet of 4 11.50 11.50
a. A578 4fr Balaenoptera physalus 1.90 1.90
b. A578 5fr Balaenoptera acutorostrata 2.40 2.40
c. A578 6fr Physeter catodon 3.00 3.00
d. A578 7fr Ziphius cavirostris 3.25 3.25

10th Monte Carlo Open Golf Tournament A595

1993, Mar. 24 Photo. *Perf. 12*
1854 A595 2.20fr multicolored 1.00 .70

Dog Show Type of 1982

1993, Mar. 24 Litho. *Perf. 13x13½*
1855 A387 2.20fr Newfoundland 1.75 1.10

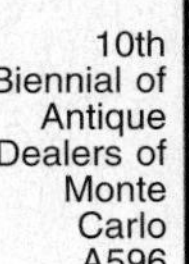

10th Biennial of Antique Dealers of Monte Carlo A596

1993, Mar. 24 *Perf. 12*
1856 A596 7fr multicolored 3.25 1.60

Flowering Cacti — A597

1993, May 4 Engr. *Perf. 13x13½*

Booklet Stamps

1857 A597 2.50fr Echinopsis multiplex 1.10 .70
1858 A597 2.50fr Zygocactus truncatus 1.10 .70
1859 A597 2.50fr Echinocereas procumbens 1.10 .70
1860 A597 2.50fr Euphorbia virosa 1.10 .70
a. Booklet pane, 2 each #1857-1860 9.25
Nos. 1857-1860 (4) 4.40 2.80

See Nos. 1889-1892, 1914-1918, 2007-2009, 2086-2089.

Europa A598

1993, May 4 *Perf. 12½x12*
1861 A598 2.50fr Monte Carlo Ballet .90 *.40*
1862 A598 4.20fr Sigaldi sculpture 1.25 *.70*
a. Souvenir sheet, 3 each, #1861-1862, perf. 13x12½ 7.50 *7.50*

Souvenir Sheet

Admission to the UN — A599

1993, July 28 Engr. *Perf. 13*
1863 A599 Sheet of 3 12.50 12.50
a. 10fr light blue 4.00 4.00
b. 10fr brn vio (Design A529) 4.00 4.00
c. 10fr brown violet & red 4.00 4.00

Intl. Olympic Committee, 101st Session A600

Litho. & Engr.

1993, Sept. 20 *Perf. 13½x13*

Booklet Stamps

1864 A600 2.80fr Coat of arms 1.25 1.25
1865 A600 2.80fr Bobsledding 1.25 1.25
1866 A600 2.80fr Skiing 1.25 1.25
1867 A600 2.80fr Sailing 1.25 1.25
1868 A600 2.80fr Rowing 1.25 1.25
1869 A600 2.80fr Swimming 1.25 1.25
1870 A600 2.80fr Cycling 1.25 1.25
1871 A600 2.80fr shown 1.25 1.25
a. Bklt. pane of 8, #1864-1871 10.00
1872 A600 4.50fr like #1864 2.00 2.00
1873 A600 4.50fr Gymnastics 2.00 2.00
1874 A600 4.50fr Judo 2.00 2.00
1875 A600 4.50fr Fencing 2.00 2.00
1876 A600 4.50fr Hurdles 2.00 2.00
1877 A600 4.50fr Archery 2.00 2.00
1878 A600 4.50fr Weight lifting 2.00 2.00
1879 A600 4.50fr like #1871 2.00 2.00
a. Bklt. pane of 8, #1872-1879 16.00

See No. 1899.

Red Cross of Monaco — A601

Design: 6fr, Red, white crosses.

1993, Nov. 10 Litho. *Perf. 13½x13*
1880 A601 5fr red, black & yellow 2.10 1.25
1881 A601 6fr red & black 2.50 2.00

Monaco Philatelic Union, Cent. A602

1993, Nov. 10 *Perf. 13x13½*
1882 A602 2.40fr multicolored 1.10 .45

Christmas Type of 1984

1993, Nov. 10 *Perf. 13½x13*
1883 A441 2.80fr Donkey 1.25 .50
1884 A441 3.70fr Shepherd 1.75 .85
1885 A441 4.40fr Cow 2.10 1.25
Nos. 1883-1885 (3) 5.10 2.60

Edvard Grieg (1843-1907), Composer — A603

Joan Miro (1893-1943), Artist — A604

Georges de La Tour (1593-1652), Painter — A605

Litho. (#1887), Engr.

1993, Dec. 10 *Perf. 13*
1886 A603 4fr blue 2.50 1.25
1887 A604 5fr multicolored 2.50 1.60

Perf. 12x13
1888 A605 6fr multicolored 2.75 1.75

Flowering Cacti Type of 1993

1994, Jan. 7 Engr. *Perf. 13*
1889 A597 20c like #1857 .20 .20
1890 A597 30c like #1858 .20 .20
1891 A597 40c like #1860 .20 .20
1892 A597 4fr like #1859 1.50 .70
Nos. 1889-1892 (4) 2.10 1.30

18th Intl. Circus Festival, Monte Carlo — A606

1994, Jan. 7 Litho. *Perf. 13½x13*
1893 A606 2.80fr multicolored 1.25 .60

Figurines, Natl. Museum — A607

Designs: No. 1894, Poet. No. 1895, Japanese geisha. No. 1896, Shepherdess with lamb. No. 1897, Parisian woman.

1994, Jan. 7 Engr. *Perf. 12½x13*
1894 A607 2.80fr blue 1.25 .60
1895 A607 2.80fr magenta 1.25 .60
1896 A607 2.80fr purple 1.25 .60
1897 A607 2.80fr blue green 1.25 .60
Nos. 1894-1897 (4) 5.00 2.40

Marine Mammals Type of 1992

Miniature Sheet

1994, Feb. 11 Photo. *Perf. 13x12½*
1898 Sheet of 4 12.00 12.00
a. A578 4fr Orcinus orca 2.10 2.10
b. A578 5fr Grampus griseus 2.50 2.50
c. A578 6fr Pseudorca crassidens 2.90 2.90
d. A578 7fr Globicephala melas 3.50 3.50

Intl. Olympic Committee Type of 1993

Souvenir Sheet

1994, Feb. 11 Engr. *Perf. 13*
1899 Sheet of 2 10.00 10.00
a. A600 10fr like #1866 4.50 4.50
b. A600 10fr like #1865 4.50 4.50

1994 Winter Olympics, Lillehammer.

Intl. Dog Show Type of 1982

1994, Mar. 14 Litho. *Perf. 13x13½*
1900 A387 2.40fr King Charles spaniel 3.50 .80

27th Intl. Flower Show — A608

1994, Mar. 14 *Perf. 13½x13*
1901 A608 4.40fr Iris 2.50 1.25

See Nos. 1941, 1989, 2028.

10th Grand Prix of Magic, Monte Carlo A609

1994, Mar. 14 Engr. *Perf. 13x12½*
1902 A609 5fr lake, black & blue 2.50 1.50

25th Conference of the Grand Cordon of French Cuisine A610

1994, Mar. 14 *Perf. 12½*
1903 A610 6fr multicolored 2.75 1.75

Prince Albert I, Research Ship Princess Alice II — A611

Europa: 4.50fr, Opisthoproctus Grimaldii, Eryoneicus Alberti, Oceanographic Museum, Monaco.

1994, May 5 Engr. *Perf. 13x12½*
1904 A611 2.80fr multicolored 1.25 *.75*
1905 A611 4.50fr multicolored 2.10 *1.10*
a. Min. sheet, 3 each #1904-1905 12.00 *9.00*

Intl. Olympic Committee, Cent. — A612

1994, May 17 Engr. *Perf. 12½x12*
1906 A612 3fr multicolored 1.40 .75

Institute for Preservation of the Sea — A613

1994, May 17 Litho. *Perf. 13*
1907 A613 6fr multicolored 2.75 1.75

Intl. Year of the Family — A614

1994, May 17 Engr. *Perf. 13*
1908 A614 7fr multicolored 3.25 2.00

1994 World Cup Soccer Championships, US — A615

1994, May 17 *Perf. 12½x13*
1909 A615 8fr red & black 3.50 2.25

Intl. Amateur Athletic Federation — A616

1994, June 10 *Perf. 13*
1910 A616 8fr multicolored 3.50 2.25

1903 De Dion Bouton A617

1994, Aug. 22 Engr. *Perf. 13x12½*
1911 A617 2.80fr lil, blk & brn 1.25 .85

Intl. Assoc. of Philatelic Catalogue Editors (ASCAT) — A618

1994, Aug. 22 Litho. *Perf. 13*
1912 A618 3fr blk, lil rose & grn 1.40 .75

21st UPU Congress, Seoul, Korea — A619

1994, Aug. 22
1913 A619 4.40fr bl, red & blk 2.75 1.25

Flowering Cacti Type of 1993

1994, Oct. 17 Engr. *Perf. 13*
1914 A597 50c Selenicereus grandiflorus .20 .20
1915 A597 60c Opuntia basilaris .30 .20
1916 A597 70c Aloe plicatilis .35 .20
1917 A597 80c Opuntia hybride .35 .20
1918 A597 2fr Aporocactus flagelliformis .95 .40
Nos. 1914-1918 (5) 2.15 1.20

Christmas Type of 1984

1994, Oct. 17 Litho. *Perf. 13*
1919 A441 2.80fr Mary 1.25 .55
1920 A441 4.50fr Christ child 2.10 .90
1921 A441 6fr Joseph 2.75 1.10
Nos. 1919-1921 (3) 6.10 2.55

Currency Museum — A620

1994, Oct. 17 Engr. *Perf. 12½*
1922 A620 3fr Prince Albert 1.40 .85
1923 A620 4fr Arms of Grimaldi 2.00 1.25
1924 A620 7fr Prince Rainier III 3.25 2.00
Nos. 1922-1924 (3) 6.65 4.10

Souvenir Sheet

Perf. 12½x13

1925 Sheet of 3 14.00 14.00
a. A620 10fr like #1922 4.50 4.50
b. A620 10fr like #1923 4.50 4.50
c. A620 10fr like #1924 4.50 4.50

Red Cross Campaigns — A621

Designs: 6fr, Fight against cancer. 8fr, Fight against AIDS.

1994, Oct. 17 Litho. *Perf. 13*
1926 A621 6fr lake, blue & black 2.75 1.90
1927 A621 8fr lake, grn & blk 3.75 2.50

See Nos. 1983-1984.

ICAO, 50th Anniv. A622

Helicopters and: 5fr, Monaco Heliport. 7fr, Monaco skyline.

1994, Oct. 17 Engr. *Perf. 13*
1928 A622 5fr multicolored 2.40 1.50
1929 A622 7fr multicolored 3.25 2.00

Voltaire (1694-1778), Writer — A623

Sarah Bernhardt (1844-1923), Actress — A624

Publication of Robinson Crusoe, by Daniel Defoe, 275th Anniv. — A625

The Snake Charmer, by Henri Rousseau (1844-1910) — A626

1994, Oct. 17 Engr. *Perf. 13*
1930 A623 5fr olive green 2.40 1.25
1931 A624 6fr multicolored 2.75 1.50

Litho.

1932 A625 7fr multicolored 3.25 1.90
1933 A626 9fr multicolored 4.25 2.25
Nos. 1930-1933 (4) 12.65 6.90

Tree Type of 1986

Miniature Sheet

Life cycle of an apricot tree.

1994, Oct. 17 Photo. *Perf. 13x12½*
1934 Sheet of 4 14.00 14.00
a. A478 6fr Spring 2.75 2.75
b. A478 7fr Summer 3.25 3.25
c. A478 8fr Autumn 3.75 3.75
d. A478 9fr Winter 4.25 4.25

19th Intl. Circus Festival, Monte Carlo — A627

1995, Jan. 3 Litho. *Perf. 13½x13*
1935 A627 2.80fr multicolored 1.25 .60

Monte Carlo Television, 35th Festival — A628

1995, Feb. 13 Engr. *Perf. 12½x13*
1936 A628 8fr Prince Albert 3.50 1.75

European Nature Conservation Year — A629

1995, Apr. 3 Litho. *Perf. 13x13½*
1937 A629 2.40fr multicolored 1.10 .55

Intl. Special Olympics A630

1995, Apr. 3
1938 A630 3fr multicolored 1.40 .80

Rotary Intl. Convention, Nice A631

1995, Apr. 3 Engr. *Perf. 13x12½*
1939 A631 4fr blue 2.00 1.00

Intl. Dog Show Type of 1982

1995, Apr. 3 Litho. *Perf. 13x13½*
1940 A387 4fr American cocker spaniel 2.75 1.25

Intl. Flower Show Type of 1993

1995, Apr. 3 *Perf. 13½x13*
1941 A608 5fr Perroquet tulips 2.40 1.25

European Bonsai Congress A632

1995, Apr. 3 *Perf. 12*
1942 A632 6fr Acer palmatum 2.75 1.40

Tree Type of 1986

Miniature Sheet

Life cycle of a jujube tree.

1995, Apr. 3 Photo. *Perf. 12x12½*
1943 Sheet of 4 10.50 10.50
a. A478 4fr Spring 1.90 1.90
b. A478 5fr Summer 2.40 2.40
c. A478 6fr Fall 2.75 2.75
d. A478 7fr Winter 3.25 3.25

Peace & Liberty A633

Europa: 2.80fr, Dove with olive branch, Alfred Nobel. 5fr, Chain broken over concentration camp, flowers.

Photo. & Engr.

1995, May 8 *Perf. 12x12½*
1944 A633 2.80fr multicolored 1.25 .80
1945 A633 5fr multicolored 2.40 1.25

50th anniversaries: End of World War II (#1944), liberation of the concentration camps (#1945).

A634

Designs: 5fr, Jean Giono (1895-1970), writer. 6fr, Marcel Pagnol (1895-1974), film producer, writer.

1995, May 8 Engr. *Perf. 12½x13*
1946 A634 5fr multicolored 2.40 1.00
1947 A634 6fr multicolored 2.75 1.40

Princess Caroline, Pres. of World Assoc. of Friends of Children — A635

1995, May 8 Photo. *Perf. 13½x13*
1948 A635 7fr blue 3.25 2.00

Intl. Council of Wildlife Conservation — A636

1995, May 8 Engr. *Perf. 13*
1949 A636 6fr St. Hubert, stag 2.75 1.25

IAAF Track & Field Championships, Louis II Stadium — A637

1995, May 8
1950 A637 7fr multicolored 3.25 1.60

Alps Monument A638

1995, May 8
1951 A638 8fr multicolored 3.75 2.00

Prince Pierre of Monaco (1895-1964) A639

1995, May 8
1952 A639 10fr lake 4.50 2.40

Souvenir Sheet

Stamp & Coin Museum — A640

a, #927. b, Museum entrance. c, #294. Illustration reduced.

1995, May 8
1953 A640 Sheet of 3, #a.-c. 13.50 13.50
a.-c. 10fr any single 4.50 4.50

St. Anthony of Padua (1195-1231) A641

1995, Sept. 25 Litho. *Perf. 13½*
1954 A641 2.80fr multicolored 1.25 .60

UN, 50th Anniv. A642

Designs: #1955, 1963a, Soldiers, UN Charter. #1956, 1963b, Grain, child. #1957, 1963c, Childrens' faces. #1958, 1963d, Musical notes, temple of Abu Simbel. #1959, 1963e, UN Security Council. #1960, 1963f, Hand holding grain, field. #1961, 1963g, Letters from various languages. #1962, 1963h, UNESCO Headquarters.

1995, Oct. 24 Engr. *Perf. 13*
1955 A642 2.50fr multicolored 1.10 .50
1956 A642 2.50fr multicolored 1.10 .50
1957 A642 2.50fr multicolored 1.10 .50
1958 A642 2.50fr multicolored 1.10 .50
1959 A642 3fr multicolored 1.40 .70
1960 A642 3fr multicolored 1.40 .70
1961 A642 3fr multicolored 1.40 .70
1962 A642 3fr multicolored 1.40 .70
Nos. 1955-1962 (8) 10.00 4.80

Miniature Sheet

1963 Sheet of 8 16.00 16.00
a.-d. A642 3fr any single 1.40 1.40
e.-h. A642 4.50fr any single 2.10 2.10

A643

Flowers: No. 1964, Rose *Grace of Monaco.* No. 1965, Fuschia *Lakeland Princess.* No. 1966, Carnation *Century of Monte Carlo.* No. 1967, Fuschia *Grace.* No. 1968, Rose *Princess of Monaco.* No. 1969, Alstroemeria *Gracia.* No. 1970, Lily *Princess Grace.* No. 1971, Carnation *Princess Caroline.* No. 1972, Rose *Stephanie of Monaco.* No. 1973, Carnation *Prince Albert.* No. 1974, Sweet pea *Grace of Monaco.* No. 1975, Gerbera *Gracia.*

1995, Oct. 24 Litho. *Perf. 13½*

Booklet Stamps

1964 A643 3fr multicolored 1.40 .80
1965 A643 3fr multicolored 1.40 .80
1966 A643 3fr multicolored 1.40 .80
1967 A643 3fr multicolored 1.40 .80
1968 A643 3fr multicolored 1.40 .80
1969 A643 3fr multicolored 1.40 .80
1970 A643 3fr multicolored 1.40 .80
1971 A643 3fr multicolored 1.40 .80
1972 A643 3fr multicolored 1.40 .80
1973 A643 3fr multicolored 1.40 .80
1974 A643 3fr multicolored 1.40 .80
1975 A643 3fr multicolored 1.40 .80
a. Bklt. pane, #1964-1975 + 2 labels 17.00
Complete booklet, #1975a 18.00

Christmas Type of 1984

1995, Oct. 24 Litho. *Perf. 13½x13*
1976 A441 3fr Balthazar 1.40 .65
1977 A441 5fr Gaspard 2.40 1.10
1978 A441 6fr Melchior 2.75 1.25
Nos. 1976-1978 (3) 6.55 3.00

Monagasque Assoc. for Protection of Nature, 20th Anniv. — A644

1995, Oct. 24 Engr. *Perf. 13*
1980 A644 4fr green, black & red 1.90 .85

Wilhelm Röntgen (1845-1923), Discovery of X-Rays, Cent. — A645

1995, Oct. 24
1981 A645 6fr multicolored 2.75 1.25

Motion Pictures, Cent. — A646

1995, Oct. 24
1982 A646 7fr dark blue 3.25 1.75

Red Cross Campaigns Type of 1994

Designs: 7fr, World fight against leprosy. 8fr, Drs. Prakash and Mandakini Amte, Indian campaign against leprosy.

1995, Oct. 24 Litho.
1983 A621 7fr multicolored 3.25 1.50
1984 A621 8fr multicolored 3.75 1.75

Pneumatic Automobile Tires, Cent. — A647

1995, Oct. 24 Engr.
1985 A647 8fr claret & dk purple 3.75 1.75

Springtime, by Sandro Botticelli (1445-1510) — A648

1995, Oct. 24
1986 A648 15fr blue 9.25 5.25
a. Souvenir sheet of 1 9.25 5.25

No. 1986 printed in sheets of 10 + 5 labels.
No. 1986a inscribed in sheet margin as a winner of the 4th World Cup of Stamps, portrait of Botticelli. Issued 11/6/97.

20th Intl. Circus Festival, Monte Carlo — A649

1996, Jan. 10 Litho. *Perf. 13*
1987 A649 2.40fr multicolored 1.10 .50

Magic Festival, Monte Carlo A650

1996, Jan. 10 Engr.
1988 A650 2.80fr black & gray 1.25 .55

Intl. Flower Show Type of 1994

1996, Jan. 26 Litho.
1989 A608 3fr Rhododendron 1.40 .65

Intl. Dog Show Type of 1982

1996, Jan. 26
1990 A387 4fr Fox terrier 2.00 1.00

Opening of Chapel of Notre Dame of Miséricorde, 350th Anniv. — A651

1996, Jan. 26 Engr. *Perf. 12x13*
1991 A651 6fr multicolored 2.75 2.00

Oceanographic Voyages of Prince Albert I of Monaco and King Charles I of Portugal, Cent. — A652

3fr, Fish in sea, net, Prince Albert I holding binoculars, ship. 4.50fr, Ship, King Charles I holding sextant, microscope, sea life.
Illustration reduced.

1996, Feb. 1 Litho. *Perf. 12*

1992	A652	3fr multicolored	1.40	.70
1993	A652	4.50fr multicolored	2.10	1.25

See Portugal Nos. 2084-2085.

Prince Rainer III Type of 1974 Inscribed "MUSEE DES TIMBRES ET DES MONNAIES"

1996, Mar. 11 Engr. *Perf. 13*

1994	AP37	10fr purple	4.50	2.25
1995	AP37	15fr henna brown	7.00	3.50
1996	AP37	20fr ultra	9.50	4.75
		Nos. 1994-1996 (3)	21.00	10.50

Stamp and Currency Museum.

Princess Grace — A653

1996, Apr. 29

1997	A653	3fr red & brown	1.40	.70

Europa.

RAMOGE Agreement Between France, Italy, Monaco, 20th Anniv. A654

Photo. & Engr.

1996, May 14 *Perf. 13*

1998	A654	3fr multicolored	1.40	.65

See France #2524, Italy #2077.

Annales Monegasques, 20th Anniv. — A655

Famous people: a, Saint Nicolas of Myra, by Louis Brea. b, Guillaume Apollinaire (1880-1918), poet. c, Jean-Baptiste Francois Bosio (1764-1827), painter. d, Francois-Joseph Bosio (1768-1845), sculptor. e, Hector Berlioz (1803-69), composer. f, Niccolo Machiavelli (1469-1527), writer. g, Sidonie-Gabrielle Colette (1873-1954), writer. h, Michael Montaigne (1533-92), essayist.

1996, May 14 Engr. *Perf. 12½x13*

1999		Sheet of 8	21.00	21.00
a., e.	A655	3fr any single	1.60	1.60
b., f.	A655	4fr any single	2.00	2.00
c., g.	A655	5fr any single	2.50	2.50
d., h.	A655	6fr any single	3.00	3.00

Souvenir Sheet

CHINA '96, 9th Asian Intl. Philatelic Exhibition — A656

Designs: a, Chinese acrobats in Monaco. b, Fuling Tomb, Shenyang.

1996, May 14 Litho. *Perf. 13*

2000	A656	Sheet of 2	5.00	5.00
a.-b.		5fr any single	2.50	2.50

Introduction of Telephone Area Code 377 for Monaco — A657

1996, June 21 Engr. *Perf. 13*

2001	A657	3fr dark blue	1.75	.90
2002	A657	3.80fr vermilion	2.25	1.10

1996 Summer Olympic Games, Atlanta — A658

1996, July 19 Litho. *Perf. 13½x13*

2003	A658	3fr Javelin, 1896	1.75	.90
2004	A658	3fr Women's softball, 1996	1.75	.90
2005	A658	4.50fr Runners, 1896	2.75	1.40
2006	A658	4.50fr Cycling, 1996	2.75	1.40
		Nos. 2003-2006 (4)	9.00	4.60

Flowering Cacti Type of 1993

Designs: 10c, Bromelia brevifolia. 1fr, Stapelia flavirostris. 5fr, Cereus peruvianus.

1996, Sept. 16 Engr. *Perf. 13*

2007	A597	10c multicolored	.20	.20
2008	A597	1fr multicolored	.40	.20
2009	A597	5fr multicolored	2.40	1.00
		Nos. 2007-2009 (3)	3.00	1.40

Tree Type of 1986

Life cycle of thorn (ronce) tree.

1996, Oct. 14 Photo. *Perf. 13*

2010		Sheet of 4	11.00	11.00
a.	A478	4fr Spring	1.75	1.75
b.	A478	5fr Summer	2.25	2.25
c.	A478	6fr Fall	2.75	2.75
d.	A478	7fr Winter	3.25	3.25

Red Cross Campaigns Type of 1994

Designs: 7fr, Fight against tuberculosis. 8fr, Camille Guérin, Albert-Leon C. Calmette, developers of BCG vaccine against tuberculosis.

1996, Oct. 14

2011	A621	7fr multicolored	3.25	1.50
2012	A621	8fr multicolored	3.75	2.00

UNICEF, 50th Anniv. — A658a

1996, Oct. 14 Engr. *Perf. 12½x13*

2013	A658a	3fr multicolored	1.40	.70

Discovery of the Planet, Neptune, 150th Anniv. — A659

Photo. & Engr.

1996, Oct. 14 *Perf. 13x12½*

2014	A659	4fr multicolored	1.75	.80

René Descartes (1596-1650), Philosopher, Mathematician — A660

1996, Oct. 14 Engr. *Perf. 13*

2015	A660	5fr blue & carmine	2.50	1.25

Christmas A661

1996, Oct. 14 Litho. *Perf. 13*

2016	A661	3fr Angel	1.40	.65
2017	A661	6fr Angels	2.75	1.25

Self-Portrait, by Corot (1796-1875) — A662

7fr, Self-portrait (detail), by Goya (1746-1828).

Photo. & Engr.

1996, Oct. 14 *Perf. 12x13*

2018	A662	6fr multicolored	2.75	1.50
2019	A662	7fr multicolored	3.25	1.75

Stamp and Coin Museum — A663

Designs: No. 2020, Printing and engraving stamps. No. 2021, Coins, screw press. 10fr, Front entrance to museum.

1996, Oct. 14 Engr. *Perf. 13*

2020	A663	5fr dk olive & violet	2.50	2.50
2021	A663	5fr dk ol & dk bl	2.50	2.50
2022	A663	10fr dk ol & dk bl	4.75	4.75
a.		Souvenir sheet, #2020-2022	9.75	9.75
		Nos. 2020-2022 (3)	9.75	9.75

No. 2022 is 48x36mm.

Grimaldi Dynasty, 700th Anniv. A664

No. 2023: a, Francois Grimaldi, 1297. b, Rainier I, d. 1314. c, Charles I, d. 1357. d, Rainier II, 1350-1407. e, Jean I, 1382-1454. f, Catalan, d. 1457. g, Lambert, d. 1494. h, Jean II, 1468-1505. i, Lucien, 1481-1523. j, Augustin, d. 1532. k, Honoré I, 1522-1581. l, Charles II, 1555-1589. m, Hercule I, 1562-1604.

No. 2024: a, Honoré II (1597-1662). b, Louis I (1642-1701). c, Antoine (1661-1731). d, Louise-Hippolyte (1697-1731). e, Jacques I (1689-1751). f, Honoré III (1720-95). g, Honoré IV (1758-1819). h, Honoré V (1778-1841). i, Florestan I (1785-1856). j, Charles III (1818-89). k, Albert I (1848-1922). l, Louis II (1870-1949). m, Rainier III.

1997 Litho. *Perf. 13*

2023		Sheet of 13 + 2 labels	35.00	35.00
a.	A664	7fr multicolored	3.25	3.25
b.-d.	A664	1fr multi, each	.45	.45
e, g.	A664	2fr multi, each	.95	.95
f.	A664	9fr multicolored	4.25	4.25
h.-j	A664	9fr multi, each	4.25	4.25
k.-m.	A664	7fr multi, each	3.25	3.25
2024		Sheet of 13 + 2 labels	35.00	35.00
a.-c.	A664	1fr multi, each	.45	.45
d.	A664	9fr multicolored	4.25	4.25
e.	A664	2fr multicolored	.95	.95
f.-i.	A664	9fr multi, each	4.25	4.25
j.-m.	A664	7fr multi, each	3.25	3.25

Portions of the designs on Nos. 2023-2024 were applied by a thermographic process producing a shiny, raised effect.

Issued: #2023, 1/8; #2024, 7/3.

Knight in Armor Type of 1951 Inscribed "1297-1997"

1996-97 Engr. *Perf. 13*

2025	A67	2.70fr bl, brn & red	1.25	.60

Sheet of 8

2026		2 ea #a.-c., 2025	11.00	11.00
a.	A67	2.70fr red	1.50	1.50
b.	A67	2.70fr brown	1.50	1.50
c.	A67	2.70fr blue	1.50	1.50

Issued: #2025, 12/19/96; #2026, 1/8/97.

Yacht Club of Monaco — A665

1996, Dec. 12 Litho. *Perf. 13*

2027	A665	3fr multicolored	1.40	.70

Intl. Flower Show Type of 1993

1996, Dec. 19 *Perf. 13½x13*

2028	A608	3.80fr Camellia	1.75	.75

Tennis Tournaments in Monaco, Cent. — A666

1997, Feb. 1 Litho. *Perf. 13*

2029 A666 4.60fr multicolored 2.10 1.00

Portions of the design on No. 2029 were applied by a thermographic process producing a shiny, raised effect.

For overprint see No. 2049.

37th Festival of Television in Monte Carlo — A667

1996, Dec. 19 *Perf. 13½x13*

2030 A667 4.90fr multicolored 2.25 1.00

Campanule "Medium" — A668

1996, Dec. 19 Litho. *Perf. 13*

2031 A668 5fr multicolored 2.40 1.10

Auto Sports in Monaco — A669

1996, Dec. 19 Litho. *Perf. 13*

2032 A669 3fr multicolored 1.40 .65

Philatelic Events A670

Stamp & Coin Museum and: No. 2033, Pictures, engraving tools, picture on stamps. No. 2034, Stamp, magnifying glass, envelopes.

1996, Dec. 19 Engr. *Perf. 13*

2033 A670 3fr multicolored 1.40 .60

2034 A670 3fr multicolored 1.40 .60

a. Pair, #2033-2034 3.00 3.00

Monaco Philatelic Office, 60th anniv. (#2033). Monaco Intl. Philatelic Exhibition (#2034).

Dog Show Type of 1982

1996, Dec. 19 Litho. *Perf. 13x13½*

2035 A387 4.40fr Afghan hound 2.25 1.00

21st Intl. Circus Festival, Monte Carlo — A671

1996, Dec. 19 Litho. *Perf. 13½x13*

2036 A671 3fr multicolored 1.40 .60

Intl. Grand Prix of Philately — A672

1997, Apr. 5 Litho. *Perf. 13*

2041 A672 4.60fr multicolored 2.10 1.25

Red Cross Campaign Against Drug Abuse — A673

1997, May 5 *Perf. 13½x13*

2042 A673 7fr multicolored 3.25 1.60

Europa (Stories and Legends) A674

No. 2043, Legend of St. Devote. No. 2044, Port Hercules named for mythological Hercules.

1997, May 5 Engr. *Perf. 12½x13*

2043 A674 3fr multicolored 1.50 .65

2044 A674 3fr multicolored 1.50 .65

a. Pair, #2043-2044 3.00 3.00

PACIFIC 97 Intl. Philatelic Exhibition A675

Design: US types A2 & A1, Monaco #1995.

1997, May 29 *Perf. 13x12½*

2045 A675 4.90fr multicolored 2.25 1.25

Uniforms of the Carabiniers (Palace Guards) A676

Years uniforms used: 3fr, 1997. 3.50fr, 1750-1853. 5.20fr, 1865-1935.

1997, May 31 Litho. *Perf. 13x13½*

2046 A676 3fr multicolored 1.40 .50

2047 A676 3.50fr multicolored 1.60 .60

2048 A676 5.20fr multicolored 2.50 .90

Nos. 2046-2048 (3) 5.50 2.00

No. 2029 Ovptd. "M. RIOS"

1997 *Perf. 13*

2049 A666 4.60fr multicolored 2.10 1.40

13th Grand Prix of Magic, Monte Carlo — A677

1997 Litho. *Perf. 13½x13*

2050 A677 4.40fr multicolored 2.10 1.25

Monaco Soccer Assoc., 1996 French Division 1 Champions — A678

1997 *Perf. 13*

2051 A678 3fr multicolored 1.40 .80

Francois Grimaldi, by Ernando Venanzi A679

9fr, Saint Peter and Saint Paul, by Rubens.

1997, Sept. 8 Engr. *Perf. 13½x13*

2052 A679 8fr multicolored 3.75 2.00

2053 A679 9fr multicolored 4.25 2.50

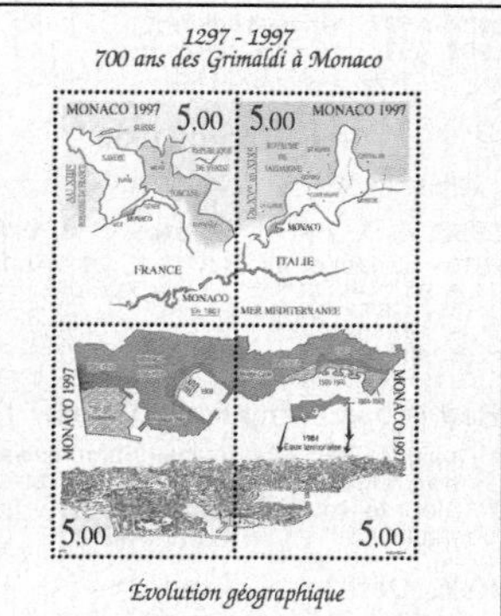

Evolution of the Geographic Territory of Monaco — A680

Designs: a, 13th century. b, 15th-19th century. c, Map of western half of Monaco, panoramic view. d, Map of eastern half of Monaco, panoramic view.

1997, Oct. 6 Litho. & Engr. *Perf. 13*

2054 A680 5fr Sheet of 4, #a.-d. 9.50 9.50

Grimaldi Dynasty, 700th anniv.

49th Session of Intl. Whaling Commission — A681

1997, Oct. 20 Photo. *Perf. 13x13½*

2055 A681 6.70fr multicolored 3.00 1.75

22nd Intl. Circus Festival, Monte Carlo — A682

1997, Nov. 30 Litho. *Perf. 13½x13*

2057 A682 3fr multicolored 1.40 .70

Princess Charlotte (1898-1977) — A683

1997, Nov. 28 Engr. *Perf. 13x12½*

2058 A683 3.80fr brown 1.75 .90

A684

Designs by Monagasque Students — A685

Perf. 13½x13, 13x13½

1997, Nov. 29 Litho.

2059 A684 4fr Under 13 group 1.90 .90

2060 A685 4.50fr Over 13 group 2.10 .90

31st Intl. Flower Show — A686

1997, Nov. 30 *Perf. 13½x13*

2061 A686 4.40fr multicolored 2.10 1.25

1998 Winter Olympic Games, Nagano A687

Designs: No. 2062, 4-Man bobsled, speed skating, ice hockey, figure skating. No. 2063, Downhill skiing, biathlon, luge, ski jumping, slalom skiing.

1997, Nov. 28 Photo. *Perf. 12½*
2062 A687 4.90fr multicolored 2.25 1.25
2063 A687 4.90fr multicolored 2.25 1.25
a. Pair, #2062-2063 4.50 4.50

Moscow '97 — A688

Ballet Russes de Monte Carlo.

1997, Nov. 28 Photo. *Perf. 13½x13*
2064 A688 5fr multicolored 2.40 1.25

J.L. David (1748-1825), Painter — A689

1997, Nov. 30 Engr. *Perf. 12½x13*
2065 A689 5.20fr red brn & dk grn 2.40 1.10

Papal Bull for the Parish of Monaco, 750th Anniv. A690

1997, Nov. 30 *Perf. 12½x13*
2066 A690 7.50fr Pope Innocent IV 3.50 1.90

Prince Albert I (1848-1922) — A691

Illustration reduced.

1997, Nov. 29 Photo. *Perf. 13x12½*
2067 A691 8fr multicolored 3.75 2.40

38th Television Festival — A692

1998, Feb. 4 Litho. *Perf. 13½x13*
2068 A692 4.50fr multicolored 2.10 1.00

Marcel Kroenlein Arboretum, 10th Anniv. — A693

1997, Nov. 28 Photo. *Perf. 13*
2069 A693 9fr multicolored 4.25 2.50

No. 2069 was issued in sheets of 2.

Dog Show Type of 1987

1998, Mar. 19 Litho. *Perf. 13x13½*
2069A A387 2.70fr Boxer, Doberman 1.50 .80

Intl. Academy of Peace A694

1998, Mar. 19 Litho. *Perf. 13*
2070 A694 3fr green & blue 1.40 .70

Portions of the design of No. 2070 were applied by a thermographic process producing a shiny, raised effect.

15th Spring Arts Festival A695

1998, Mar. 19 Litho. *Perf. 13x13½*
2071 A695 4fr multicolored 1.75 .90

Pierre and Marie Curie, Discovery of Radium, Cent. A696

1998, Mar. 19 Engr. *Perf. 13x12½*
2072 A696 6fr lilac & green blue 2.75 1.40

Monegasque Red Cross, 50th Anniv. — A697

Prince Albert, Prince Louis II, Princess Grace, Prince Rainier III.

1998, Mar. 3 Litho. *Perf. 13*
2073 A697 5fr sepia, red & dk brown 2.40 1.25

Prince Albert I (1848-1922) — A698

Illustration reduced.

1998, May 6 Engr.
2074 A698 7fr dark brown 3.25 1.50

Charles Garnier (1825-98), Architect, Designer of Casino of Monte Carlo — A699

1998, May 6 Litho.
2075 A699 10fr multicolored 4.75 2.25

Festival of St. Dévote — A700

Illustration reduced.

1998, May 6 Litho. *Perf. 13x13½*
2076 A700 3fr multicolored 1.40 .65

Europa.
Portions of the design on No. 2076 were applied by a thermographic process producing a shiny, raised effect.

Joseph Kessel (1898-1979), Writer and Journalist A701

1998, May 6 Engr. *Perf. 13½*
2077 A701 3.90fr multicolored 1.75 .90

Expo '98, Lisbon A702

1998, May 6 Litho. *Perf. 13x13½*
2078 A702 2.70fr multicolored 1.25 .60

1st Formula 3000 Grand Prix in Monaco A703

1998, May 20 Engr. *Perf. 12*
2079 A703 3fr red & black 1.40 .70

European Conference of the Youth Chamber of Economics A705

1998, May 6 Litho. *Perf. 13½x13*
2081 A705 3fr multicolored 1.40 .70

World Music Awards — A706

1998, May 6
2082 A706 10fr multicolored 4.25 2.75

Porcelain — A707

1998, June 24 *Perf. 13*
2083 A707 8fr multicolored 3.75 1.75

Publication of Monaco's Works of Art — A708

1998, June 24
2084 A708 9fr multicolored 4.25 2.00

National Festival — A709

Europa: Prince Albert, Prince Rainier III, national palace. Illustration reduced.

1998, May 31 Litho. *Perf. 13*
2085 A709 3fr multicolored 1.40 .70

Portions of the design on No. 2085 were applied by a thermographic process producing a shiny, raised, effect.

Flowering Cacti Type of 1993

2.70fr, Opuntia dejecta. 4fr, Echinocereus blanckii. 6fr, Euphorbia milii. 7fr, Stapelia variegata.

1998, Aug. 3 Engr. *Perf. 13*
2086 A597 2.70fr multicolored 1.25 .50
2087 A597 4fr multicolored 1.75 .75
2088 A597 6fr multicolored 2.75 1.10
2089 A597 7fr multicolored 3.25 1.25
Nos. 2086-2089 (4) 9.00 3.60

1998 World Cup Soccer Championships, France — A710

1998, Aug. 3
2090 A710 15fr multicolored 7.00 3.50

No. 2090 contains hexagonal perforated label in center.

Enzo Ferrari (1898-1988), Automobile Manufacturer — A711

1998, Aug. 14 Litho.
2091 A711 7fr multicolored 3.25 1.75

George Gershwin (1898-1937), Composer — A712

1998, Aug. 14 Engr. *Perf. 13x12½*
2092 A712 7.50fr bl, bl grn & blk 3.50 1.75

Intl. College for Study of Marine Pollution, Marine Environment Laboratory — A713

1998, Sept. 4 Litho. *Perf. 13x13½*
2093 A713 4.50fr multicolored 2.10 .90

Plenary Assembly of the European Post, Monte Carlo A714

1998, Sept. 4
2094 A714 5fr multicolored 2.40 .90

Expo '98, World Philatelic Exhibition, Lisbon A715

1998, Sept. 4 Litho. & Engr.
2095 A715 6.70fr multicolored 3.00 1.50

Intl. Assoc. Against Violence in Sports, 30th Anniv. A716

Photo. & Engr.
1998, Sept. 14 *Perf. 13x13½*
2096 A716 4.20fr multicolored 2.00 1.00

Magic Stars Magic Festival, Monte Carlo — A717

1998, Sept. 26 Litho. *Perf. 13½x13*
2097 A717 3.50fr red & bister 1.60 .80

See No. 2140.

Giovanni Lorenzo Bernini (1598-1680), Architect, Sculptor — A718

1998, Sept. 26 Engr. *Perf. 13x12½*
2098 A718 11.50fr blue & brown 5.50 3.25

Italia '98, Intl. Philatelic Exhibition, Milan — A719

1998, Oct. 23 *Perf. 12½x13*
2099 A719 4.90fr Milan Cathedral 2.25 1.10

Christmas A720

3fr, Ornament. 6.70fr, Nativity scene, horiz. 15fr, Icon of Madonna and Child, 18th cent.

Perf. 13½x13, 13x13½
1998, Oct. 26 Litho.
2100 A720 3fr multicolored 1.40 .50
2101 A720 6.70fr multicolored 3.00 1.25

Souvenir Sheet
Engr.
Perf. 13
2102 A720 15fr multicolored 5.75 5.75

No. 2102 contains one 36x49mm stamp.

23rd Intl. Circus Festival, Monte Carlo — A721

1998, Nov. 20 Litho. *Perf. 13½x13*
2103 A721 2.70fr multicolored 1.25 .50

Grimaldi Seamounts A722

1998, Nov. 20 *Perf. 13*
2104 A722 10fr multicolored 4.25 2.00

Souvenir Sheet

Reign of Prince Rainier III, 50th Anniv. — A723

Illustration reduced.

1998, Nov. 20 Engr.
2105 A723 25fr red & yel bister 12.00 12.00

Congress Center Auditorium of Monaco, 20th Anniv. A724

1999, Feb. 12 Litho. *Perf. 13x13½*
2106 A724 2.70fr multicolored 1.25 .50

39th Intl. Television Festival, Monte Carlo — A725

1999, Jan. 18 Litho. *Perf. 13½x13*
2107 A725 3.80fr multicolored 1.75 .80

Dog Show Type of 1982

Cocker spaniel and American cocker spaniel.

1999, Jan. 18 Litho. *Perf. 13x13½*
2108 A387 4fr multicolored 2.10 1.10

Geneva Conventions, 50th Anniv. — A726

1999, Jan. 18 Engr. *Perf. 13½x13*
2109 A726 4.40fr black & red 2.10 .80

32nd Intl. Flower Show, Monte Carlo — A727

1999, Jan. 18 Litho. *Perf. 13½x13*
2110 A727 4.50fr multicolored 2.10 1.10

Monaco '99, Intl. Philatelic Exhibition — A728

Photo. & Engr.

1999, Jan. 18 *Perf. 13x12*
2111 A728 3fr multicolored 1.40 .50

Beginning with No. 2112, denominations are indicated on the stamps in both Francs and Euros. The listing value is shown in Francs.

10th Piano Masters Competition, Monte Carlo — A729

1999, Feb. 12 *Perf. 13x13½*
2112 A729 4.60fr multicolored 2.10 .80

Flowers — A730

Designs: 4.90fr, Prince of Monaco Jubilee Rose. 6fr, Paphiopedilum Prince Rainier III, Prince of Monaco and Grimaldi Roses.

1999 **Litho.** *Perf. 13½x13*
2113 A730 4.90fr multicolored 2.25 1.25
2114 A730 6fr multicolored 2.75 1.40

Issued: 4.90fr, 2/14; 6fr, 2/13.

Monaco Charity Assoc., 20th Anniv. A731

1999, Jan. 28 **Litho.** *Perf. 13*
2115 A731 6.70fr multicolored 3.00 1.50

Formula 1 Grand Prix of Monaco, 70th Anniv. — A732

1999, Apr. 16 **Photo.** *Perf. 12¼*
2116 A732 3fr multicolored 1.40 .80

Intl. Grand Prix of Philately, Monaco — A733

1999, Apr. 16 *Perf. 13¼*
2117 A733 4.40fr multicolored 2.00 1.10

Fifth Intl. Show Jumping Championships, Monte Carlo — A734

Illustration reduced.

1999, Apr. 16 **Engr.** *Perf. 13x12½*
2118 A734 5.20fr blk, dk grn & red 2.40 1.50

ASM Sports Club, 75th Anniv. — A735

Cutouts of soccer players over: No. 2119, Palace. No. 2120, Aerial view of city.
Illustration reduced.

1999, Apr. 16 **Litho.** *Perf. 13x12¾*
2119 A735 7fr multicolored 3.25 1.90
2120 A735 7fr multicolored 3.25 1.90
a. Pair, #2119-2120 6.50 6.50

Grimaldi Forum A736

1999, Apr. 25 **Photo.** *Perf. 13¼*
2121 A736 3fr multicolored 1.40 .50

Oceanography Museum, Cent. — A737

1999, Apr. 25 **Engr.** *Perf. 13¼x13*
2122 A737 5fr multicolored 2.40 1.25

Philexfrance '99, Intl Philatelic Exhibition A738

France #1, Eiffel Tower, map of France, exhibition emblem, arms of Monaco.

1999, May 5 **Engr.** *Perf. 13¼*
2123 A738 2.70fr multicolored 1.25 .60

See No. 2133.

A739

1999, May 5 **Photo.** *Perf. 13*
2124 A739 3fr Casino, Cliffs 1.50 .65

Size: 51x28mm

2125 A739 3fr Park in Fontvieille 1.50 .65
a. Pair, #2124-2125 3.25 3.25

Europa.

Monegasque Economic Growth — A740

Chart and: No. 2126, Fontveille and underground train station. No. 2127, Larvotto and Grimaldi Forum.
Illustration reduced.

1999, May 5 **Photo.** *Perf. 13x13¼*
2126 A740 5fr multi 2.40 .95
2127 A740 5fr multi 2.40 .95
a. Pair, #2126-2127 5.00 5.00

Souvenir Sheet

Reign of Prince Rainier III, 50th Anniv. — A741

Illustration reduced.

1999, May 9 **Engr.** *Perf. 13*
2128 A741 20fr blue & gold 9.50 9.50

See No. 1681.

Honoré de Balzac (1799-1850), Writer — A742

Design: 5.20fr, Countess of Ségur (1799-1874), children's storyteller.

1999 *Perf. 12¾x13*
2129 A742 4.50fr red & blue 2.10 1.10
2130 A742 5.20fr multicolored 2.40 1.25

Reign of Prince Rainier III, 50th Anniv. — A743

Design: #256, 337, 427, 937, 1287, 1669.
Illustration reduced.

1999 **Engr.** *Perf. 12¾x13*
2131 A743 30fr multicolored 14.00 14.00

UNESCO, 50th Anniv. A744

1999, July 2 **Engr.** *Perf. 13x12½*
2132 A744 4.20fr multicolored 2.00 .80

PhilexFrance Type of 1999

1999, July 2 **Engr.** *Perf. 13¼*
2133 A738 7fr France #4, 92, Monaco #3 3.25 1.50

Sportel, 10th Anniv. A745

1999, July 2 Litho. *Perf. 12¼*
2134 A745 10fr multicolored 4.75 2.40

Sovereign Military Order of Malta, 900th Anniv. A746

1999, July 2 Engr. *Perf. 11*
2135 A746 11.50fr multicolored 5.50 2.75

UPU, 125th Anniv. — A747

1999, July 2 Engr. *Perf. 13¼*
2136 A747 3fr multicolored 1.40 .70

Rose, Iris Named After Prince Rainier III — A748

1999, July 2 Litho. *Perf. 13¼x13*
2137 A748 4fr multicolored 1.90 .90

Stamp, Coin and Postcard Show, Fontvieille A749

3fr, Aerial photograph, coin obverse, No. 1793A. 6.50fr, Aerial photograph, 100fr coin, #257.

1999 Photo. *Perf. 13¼*
2138 A749 3fr multicolored 1.40 .50

Perf. 13¼x13½
2139 A749 6.50fr multicolored 3.00 1.75

Jubilee Bourse (#2139).
Issued: 3fr, 7/3; 6.50fr, 9/26.

Magic Stars Type of 1998
Inscribed "99"
Litho. & Typo.

1999, Sept. 6 *Perf. 13¼x13*
2140 A717 4.50fr red & gold 2.10 1.00

Development Projects — A750

Designs: a, Fontveille 1 & 2. b, La Digue (with jetty). c, Grimaldi Forum. d, La Gare.

1999, Sept. 26 Photo. *Perf. 13*
2141 Sheet of 4 + label 20.00 20.00
a. A750 4fr multicolored 1.90 1.90
b.-c. A750 9fr Any single 4.25 4.25
d. A750 19fr multicolored 9.00 9.00

No. 2141d is 80x40mm.

24th Intl. Circus Festival, Monte Carlo — A751

1999, Dec. 13 Litho. *Perf. 13¼x13*
2142 A751 2.70fr multi 1.25 .55

A752

1999, Dec. 13 Engr. *Perf. 13¼*
2143 A752 3fr Christmas 1.40 .60

Holy Year 2000 A753

1999, Dec. 13 Litho. *Perf. 13x13¼*
2144 A753 3.50fr multi 1.60 .95

33rd Intl. Flower Show — A754

1999, Dec. 13 *Perf. 13¼x13*
2145 A754 4.50fr multi 2.10 1.00

Monaco 2000 Intl. Philatelic Exposition A755

1999, Dec. 23 Engr. *Perf. 13¼x13*
2146 A755 3fr multi 1.40 .55

Bust of Napoleon, by Antonio Canova — A756

Litho. & Embossed

2000, Jan. 17 *Perf. 13¼*
2147 A756 4.20fr multi 2.00 .90

40th Intl. Television Festival, Monte Carlo — A757

2000, Jan. 17 Litho. *Perf. 13¼x13*
2148 A757 4.90fr multi 2.25 .95

The Twelve Apostles — A758

Saints: 4fr, Peter and James the Great. 5fr, John and Andrew. 6fr, Philip and Bartholomew. 7fr, Matthew and Thomas. 8fr, James the Less and Judas. 9fr, Simon and Matthias.

Engr. with Foil Application

2000, Apr. 3 *Perf. 13¼*
2149 A758 4fr multi 1.90 .80
2150 A758 5fr multi 2.40 .95
2151 A758 6fr multi 2.75 1.25
2152 A758 7fr multi 3.25 1.50
2153 A758 8fr multi 3.75 2.00
2154 A758 9fr multi 4.25 2.40
Nos. 2149-2154 (6) 18.30 8.90

Labrador Retriever and Golden Retriever A759

2000, Apr. 3 Engr. *Perf. 13¼*
2155 A759 6.50fr multi 3.00 1.50

Intl. Dog Show, Monte Carlo.

1993 Intl. Olympic Committee Meeting Awarding 2000 Games to Sydney A760

2000, Apr. 25 Photo.
2156 A760 7fr multi 3.25 1.50

Souvenir Sheet

Art Depicting Monaco and the Sea A761

Artwork by: a, Adami. b, Arman. c, Cane. d, Folon. e, Fuchs. f, E. De Sigaldi. g, Sosno. h, Verkade.

2000, Apr. 25 *Perf. 13x12½*
2157 Sheet of 8 + label 25.00 25.00
a.-h. A761 6.55fr Any single 3.00 1.50

2nd Historic Automobile Grand Prix — A762

2000, May 9 Litho. *Perf. 13½x13*
2158 A762 4.40fr multi 2.10 1.00

Monaco Pavilion, Expo 2000, Hanover A763

2000, May 9 *Perf. 13x13¼*
2159 A763 5fr multi 2.40 1.25

Saints Mark, Matthew, John and Luke — A764

2000, May 9 Engr. *Perf. 12¾x13*
2160 A764 20fr multi 9.50 6.00

Europa, 2000
Common Design Type and

Flags and Map of Europe — A765

2000, May 9 Litho. *Perf. 13¼x13*
2161 CD17 3fr multi 1.40 .70
2162 A765 3fr multi 1.40 .70
a. Pair, #2161-2162 3.00 3.00

WIPA 2000 Philatelic Exhibition, Vienna — A766

2000, May 30 Engr. *Perf. 13¼*
2163 A766 4.50fr multi 2.10 1.00

Professional-Celebrity Golf Tournament, Monte Carlo — A767

2000, June 19 Photo. *Perf. 13¼*
2164 A767 4.40fr multi 2.10 1.00

Club de Monte Carlo Exhibition of Rare Philatelic Material — A768

2000, June 23
2165 A768 3.50fr multi 1.60 .75

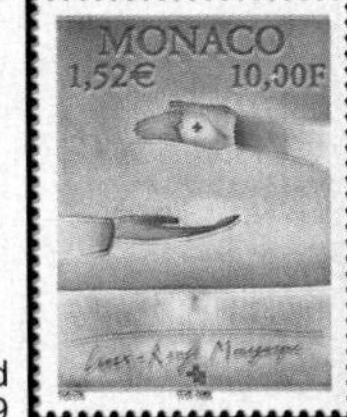

Red Cross — A769

2000, June 23
2166 A769 10fr multi 4.75 2.00

2000 Summer Olympics, Sydney A770

Olympic rings and: 2.70fr, Fencing, emblem of Monegasque Fencing Federation. 4.50fr, Rowers, flag of Monegasque Nautical Society.

2000, June 23 Engr. & Embossed
2167-2168 A770 Set of 2 3.50 1.75

Automobiles in Prince Rainier III Collection — A771

Woman and: 3fr, 1911 Humber Type Beeston. 6.70fr, 1947 Jaguar 4 cylinder. 10fr, 1956 Rolls-Royce Silver Cloud. 15fr, 1986 Lamborghini Countach.

2000, June 23 Engr. *Perf. 13x13¼*
2169-2172 A771 Set of 4 16.00 10.50

See Nos. 2186-2188.

World Stamp Expo 2000, Anaheim — A772

2000, July 7 Litho. *Perf. 13¼x13*
2173 A772 4.40fr multi 2.10 .90

Magic Stars Magic Festival, Monte Carlo — A773

2000, Sept. 4 Photo. *Perf. 13¼*
2174 A773 4.60fr multi 2.10 1.25

Intl. Mathematics Year — A774

2000, Sept. 4 Engr.
2175 A774 6.50fr brown 3.00 1.50

Souvenir Sheet

Retable of St. Nicholas, by Ludovic Bréa, Monaco Cathedral — A775

Illustration reduced.

2000, Sept. 4 Photo.
2176 A775 Sheet of 2 14.00 14.00
a. 10fr Two figures, 31x52mm 4.50 1.75
b. 20fr Three figures, 53x52mm 9.50 4.50

New Aquarium, Oceanographic Museum — A776

2000, Oct. 2 Engr.
2177 A776 3fr multi 1.40 .70

España 2000 Intl. Philatelic Exhibition A777

2000, Oct. 2
2178 A777 3.80fr multi 1.75 .80

Observatory Grotto, 50th Anniv. and Anthropological Museum, 40th Anniv. — A778

2000, Oct. 2
2179 A778 5.20fr multi 2.40 .80

Fish A779

5fr, Fish, coral. 9fr, Fish, starfish, seaweed.

2000, Oct. 2 Photo.
2180-2181 A779 Set of 2 6.50 3.00

Fifth Congress of Aquariums (No. 2180), Monegasque Nature Protection Association, 25th anniv. (No. 2181).

Fifth Congress of Aquariums — A780

Illustration reduced.

2000, Nov. 25 Photo. *Perf. 13x12¾*
2182 A780 7fr multi 3.25 1.75

Christmas A781

2000, Dec. 1 Photo. *Perf. 13¼*
2183 A781 3fr multi 1.40 .50

Princess Stephanie, President of AMAPEI — A782

2000, Dec. 1 Engr.
2184 A782 11.50fr red & slate 5.50 3.00

Souvenir Sheet

Monaco 2000 Intl. Philatelic Exhibition — A783

2001, Dec. 1 Photo. *Imperf.*
2185 A783 Sheet of 2 #2185a 19.00 19.00
a. 20fr multi 9.50 9.50

Prince's Automobiles Type of 2000

Woman and: 5fr, 1989 Ferrari F1. 6fr, 1955 Fiat 600 Type Jolly. 8fr, 1929 Citroen C4F Autochenille.

2000, Dec. 1 Engr. *Perf. 13x13¼*
2186-2188 A771 Set of 3 9.00 4.50

Exhibit of Chinese Terra-cotta Figures, Grimaldi Forum — A784

2000, Dec. 2 Photo. *Perf. 13¼*
2189 A784 2.70fr multi 1.25 .40

Postal Museum, 50th Anniv. — A785

2000, Dec. 2
2190 A785 3fr multi 1.40 .50

Coat of Arms — A786

Serpentine Die Cut 11
2000, Dec. 4 Photo.
Booklet Stamp
Self-Adhesive

2191 A786 (3fr) red & black 1.40 .30
a. Booklet of 10 14.00

Princess Caroline of Monaco Iris — A787

2000, Dec. 2 Photo. *Perf. 13¼*
2192 A787 3.80fr multi 1.75 .70

34th Intl. Flower Show.

Sardinian Postage Stamps, 150th Anniv. (in 2001) A788

2000, Dec. 2 Engr. *Perf. 13x12½*
2193 A788 6.50fr Sardinia #1-3 3.00 1.75

RAMOGE Agreement, 25th Anniv. A789

2000, Dec. 2
2194 A789 6.70fr multi 3.00 1.75

Awarding of ASCAT Grand Prize to Bertrand Piccard — A790

2000, Dec. 2 Photo. *Perf. 13¼*
2195 A790 9fr Balloon, #1433 4.25 2.00

Monaco Team, 2000 French Soccer Champions A791

2000, Dec. 3
2196 A791 4.50fr multi 2.10 .90

French, Italian and Monegasque Marine Mammal Sanctuary — A792

2000, Dec. 3
2197 A792 5.20fr multi 2.40 1.25

Neapolitan Creche, Natl. Museum — A793

Illustration reduced.

2000, Dec. 3 *Perf. 13x12½*
2198 A793 10fr multi 4.75 3.00

25th Intl. Circus Festival, Monte Carlo — A794

No. 2200: a, Clown with guitar. b, Clown. c, Tiger and tent top. d, Acrobats, tiger, lion, horses, clowns. e, Chimpanzee and high-wire acrobat.

2000, Dec. 3 *Perf. 13¼*
2199 A794 2.70fr shown 1.25 .60
2200 A794 6fr Sheet of 5, #a-e + label 14.00 14.00

41st Intl. Television Festival, Monte Carlo — A795

2001, Feb. 5 Photo. *Perf. 13½x13*
2201 A795 3.50fr multi 1.60 .90

Leonberger and Newfoundland — A796

2001, Apr. 14 Litho. *Perf. 13x13¼*
2202 A796 6.50fr multi 3.00 1.25

Euroflora Flower Show — A797

2001, Apr. 21 Photo. *Perf. 13¼*
2203 A797 6.70fr multi 3.00 1.25

Europa — A798

Designs: No. 2204, 3fr, Palace of Monaco, water droplets. No. 2205, 3fr, Wash house.

2001, May 7 Litho. *Perf. 13½x13*
2204-2205 A798 Set of 2 2.75 1.10

Prince Rainier III Literary Prize, 50th Anniv. — A799

2001, May 14 Engr. *Perf. 13¼*
2206 A799 2.70fr multi 1.25 .45

André Malraux (1901-76), Novelist — A800

2001, May 14 Litho. *Perf. 13¼x13*
2207 A800 10fr black & red 4.75 1.75

Belgica 2001 Intl. Stamp Exhibition, Brussels — A801

2001, June 9 Engr. *Perf. 13¼*
2208 A801 4fr brt blue & red 1.90 .70

2001 Philatelic and Numismatic Bourse — A802

2001, July 2 Photo. *Perf. 13¼*
2209 A802 2.70fr multi 1.25 .45

Princess Grace Dance Academy, 25th Anniv. — A803

2001 July 2 Photo. *Perf. 13¼*
2210 A803 4.40fr multi 2.10 .90

Naval Museum A804

2001, July 2 Photo. *Perf. 13¼*
2211 A804 4.50fr multi 2.10 .90

37th Petanque World Championships — A805

2001, July 2 *Perf. 13x13¼*
2212 A805 5fr multi 2.40 .80

Emilie Littré, Denis Diderot, and Reference Books A806

2001, Aug. 1 Engr. *Perf. 13¼*
2213 A806 4.20fr multi 2.00 .95

Prince Albert I Oceanography Prize, 30th Anniv. — A807

2001, Aug. 1 Engr. *Perf. 13¼*
2214 A807 9fr bright blue 4.25 1.50

David, by Michelangelo, 500th Anniv. — A808

2001, Aug. 1 Engr. *Perf. 13*
2215 A808 20fr multi 9.50 6.00

Palace of Monaco — A809

Designs: 3fr, Fireplace, Throne Hall. 4.50fr, Blue Hall. 6.70fr, York Chamber. 15fr, Fresco, ceiling of Throne Hall.

2001, Aug. 1 Photo. *Perf. 13x13¼*
2216-2219 A809 Set of 4 13.50 6.50

A810

Nobel Prizes, Cent. — A811

Designs: 5fr, Alfred Nobel. 8fr, Jean-Henri Dunant, 1901 Peace laureate. 11.50fr, Enrico Fermi, 1938 Physics laureate.

2001, Sept. 3 Engr. *Perf. 13¼*

2220	A810	5fr multi	2.40	.95
2221	A810	8fr multi	3.75	1.50
2222	A811	11.50fr multi	5.50	3.25
		Nos. 2220-2222 (3)	11.65	5.70

36th Meeting of Intl. Commission for Scientific Exploration of the Mediterranean — A812

2001, Oct. 1 Photo. *Perf. 13x13¼*
2223 A812 3fr multi 1.40 .50

Christmas — A813

2001, Oct. 1 *Perf. 13¼*
2224 A813 3fr multi 1.40 .50

100 Cents = 1 Euro (€)

Flora & Fauna A814

Designs: 1c, Arctia caja, vert. 2c, Luria lurida. 5c, Thunbergia grandiflora, vert. 10c, Parus major. 20c, Anthias anthias. 50c, Charaxes jasius, vert. €1, Mitra zonata. €2, Datura sanguinea, vert. €5, Parus cristatus, vert. €10, Macroamphosus scolopax.

2002, Jan. 1 Engr. *Perf. 13¼*

2225	A814	1c multi	.20	.20
2226	A814	2c multi	.20	.20
2227	A814	5c multi	.20	.20
2228	A814	10c multi	.30	.20
2229	A814	20c multi	.60	.20
2230	A814	50c multi	1.50	.75
2231	A814	€1 multi	3.00	1.50
2232	A814	€2 multi	6.00	3.00
2233	A814	€5 multi	15.00	7.50
2234	A814	€10 multi	30.00	15.00
		Nos. 2225-2234 (10)	57.00	28.75

See No. 2275.

Palace of Monaco A815

Designs: 41c, Gallery of Mirrors, vert. 46c, Throne room. 58c, Painting in Gallery of Mirrors.

2002, Jan. 1 Photo.
2235-2237 A815 Set of 3 4.25 2.00

26th Intl. Circus Festival — A816

2002, Jan. 1
2238 A816 41c multi 1.25 .60

35th Intl. Flower Show A817

2002, Jan. 1
2239 A817 53c multi 1.50 .75

Souvenir Sheet

Automobile Club of Monaco, Cent. — A818

No. 2240: a, Old and new cars, emblem of 70th Monte Carlo Rally. b, Racing cars in 3rd Historic Grand Prix and 60th Grand Prix races.

2002, Jan. 16 *Perf. 13¼x13*

2240	A818	Sheet of 2	6.75	6.75
a.		€1.07 multi	3.00	1.50
b.		€1.22 multi	3.50	1.75

Prehistoric Anthropology Museum, Cent. — A819

2002, Feb. 8 *Perf. 13¼*
2241 A819 64c multi 1.90 .95

La Carrière d'un Navigateur, by Prince Albert I, Cent. A820

2002, Feb. 8
2242 A820 67c multi 2.00 1.00

2002 Winter Olympics, Salt Lake City — A821

No. 2243: a, Denomination at UL. b, Denomination at UR.
Illustration reduced.

2002, Feb. 8 *Perf. 12¼*

2243	A821	Horiz. pair	1.75	1.75
a.-b.		23c Either single	.85	.40

Jules Cardinal Mazarin (1602-61) A822

2002, Feb. 18
2244 A822 69c multi 2.00 1.00

Legion of Honor, Bicent. — A823

2002, Feb. 18 *Perf. 13¼*
2245 A823 70c multi 2.10 1.00

Cetacean Conservation Accord — A824

2002, Feb. 18 Engr.
2246 A824 75c multi 2.25 1.10

Leonardo da Vinci (1452-1519) — A825

2002, Mar. 21 Photo.
2247 A825 76c multi 2.25 1.10

St. Bernard and Swiss Bouvier A826

2002, Mar. 21 Engr.
2248 A826 99c multi 3.00 1.50

Intl. Dog Show.

Police, Cent. — A827

2002, Apr. 23 Photo.
2249 A827 53c multi 1.60 .70

European Academy of Philately, 25th Anniv. A828

2002, Apr. 27 Engr.
2250 A828 58c multi 1.75 .85

20th Intl. Swimming Meet — A829

2002, May 3 Photo. *Perf. 13¼*
2251 A829 64c multi 1.90 .95

Europa — A830

Designs: No. 2252, 46c, Clown on globe, juggler, elephant, tent tops. No. 2253, 46c, "Jours de Cirque," circus acts.

2002, May 3
2252-2253 A830 Set of 2 *2.75 1.25*

First Experiment with Tar Roads, Cent. A831

2002, May 31 Engr.
2254 A831 41c multi 1.25 .60

MonacoPhil 2002 Intl. Philatelic Exhibition — A832

2002, May 31
2255 A832 46c multi 1.40 .65

42nd Intl. Television Festival, Monte Carlo — A833

2002, May 31 Photo. ***Perf. 13¼x13***
2256 A833 70c multi 2.10 1.00

2002 World Cup Soccer Championships, Japan and Korea — A834

2002, May 31 Engr. ***Perf. 13¼***
2257 A834 75c multi 2.25 1.10

"Pelléas et Mélisande," Opera by Claude Debussy, Cent. of Debut — A835

2002, June 21
2258 A835 69c multi 2.10 1.00

Saint Dévote, Dove and Boat A836

2002, June 21
2259 A836 €1.02 multi 3.00 1.50
Red Cross.

Intl. Year of Mountains A837

2002, June 21 Litho. ***Perf. 13x13¼***
2260 A837 €1.37 multi 4.00 2.00

Euro Coinage — A838

No. 2261: a, Obverse of 1c, 2c, and 5c coins and reverse. b, Obverse of 10c, 20c, and 50c coins and reverse.
No. 2262: a, Obverse and reverse of €1 coin. b, Obverse and reverse of €2 coin.

Litho. & Embossed

2002, June 21 ***Perf. 13¼***
2261 A838 Horiz. pair 3.00 3.00
a.-b. 46c Either single 1.40 .70
2262 A838 Horiz. pair 9.25 9.25
a.-b. €1.50 Either single 4.50 4.50

Victor Hugo (1802-85), Writer — A839

No. 2263: a, Hugo and illustration from *Notre-Dame de Paris.* b, Hugo and illustration from *La Légende de Siécles.*

2002, July 1 Engr. ***Perf. 13¼***
2263 A839 Horiz. pair 3.25 3.25
a. 50c multi 1.50 .75
b. 57c multi 1.75 .85

Alexandre Dumas (Father) (1802-70), Writer — A840

No. 2264: a, Dumas. b, Characters, manuscript.

2002, July 1 **Photo.**
2264 A840 Horiz. pair 3.50 3.50
a.-b. 61c Either single 1.75 .85

26th Publication of "Annales Monegasques" A841

2002, July 15
2265 A841 €1.75 multi 5.25 2.50

Christmas — A842

2002, Sept. 2
2266 A842 50c multi 1.50 .75

Debut of Movie "Le Voyage dans le Lune," by Georges Méliès, Cent. — A843

2002, Sept. 2 ***Perf. 13¼***
2267 A843 76c multi 2.25 1.10

17th Magic Stars Magic Festival, Monte Carlo — A844

2002, Sept. 2
2268 A844 €1.52 multi 4.50 2.25

Awarding of ASCAT Grand Prize to Luis Figo — A845

2002, Nov. 29 **Engr.**
2269 A845 91c multi 2.75 1.25

Automobiles in Prince Rainier III Collection A846

Designs: 46c, 1949 Mercedes 220A Cabriolet. 69c, 1956 Rolls-Royce Silver Cloud I. €1.40, 1974 Citroen DS 21.

2002, Nov. 29 **Photo.**
2270-2272 A846 Set of 3 7.50 3.75

Souvenir Sheet

The Four Seasons, Frescos in Prince's Palace — A847

2002, Nov. 29 ***Perf. 13x13¼***
2273 A847 Sheet of 4 15.00 15.00
a. 50c Spring 1.50 .75
b. €1 Summer 3.00 1.50
c. €1.50 Autumn 4.50 2.25
d. €2 Winter 6.00 3.00

Souvenir Sheet

MonacoPhil 2002 Intl. Philatelic Exhibition — A848

No. 2274: a, Monaco attractions. b, Emblem of Club de Monte Carlo.

2002, Nov. 29 ***Imperf.***
2274 A848 Sheet of 2 18.00 18.00
a.-b. €3 Either single 9.00 4.50

Flora & Fauna Type of 2002

2002, Nov. 30 Engr. ***Perf. 13¼***
2275 A814 41c Helix aspersa, vert. 1.25 .60

36th Intl. Flower Show — A849

2002, Nov. 30 **Photo.**
2276 A849 67c multi 2.00 1.00

World Association of Friends of Children, 40th Anniv. (in 2003) A850

2002, Nov. 30
2277 A850 €1.25 multi 3.75 1.75

Martyrdom of St. George, 1700th Anniv. — A851

2002, Dec. 1
2278 A851 53c multi 1.60 .70

Saint Cyr Military School, Bicent. — A852

2002, Dec. 1
2279 A852 61c multi 1.75 .85

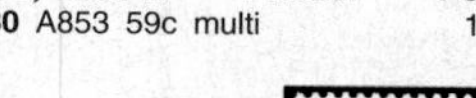

27th Intl. Circus Festival — A853

2003, Jan. 2 Photo. ***Perf. 13¼***
2280 A853 59c multi 1.75 .70

15th New Circus Artists' Festival — A854

2003, Feb. 1
2281 A854 €2.82 multi 8.50 4.00

10th World Bobsled Push Championships, Ilsenberg, Germany — A855

2003, Feb. 3
2282 A855 80c multi 2.40 .95

Monaco Yacht Club, 50th Anniv. — A856

2003, Feb. 5
2283 A856 46c multi 1.40 .60

Intl. Institute for Peace, Cent. — A857

2003, Mar. 3
2284 A857 €1.19 multi 3.50 1.75

Tennis Tournament at Monte Carlo Country Club, 75th Anniv. — A858

2003, Mar. 3
2285 A858 €1.30 multi 4.00 2.00

Dog Show Type of 2002

2003, Mar. 24 Litho. ***Perf. 13x13½***
2286 A826 79c Rough collie 2.50 1.25

Junior Economic Chamber of Monaco, 40th Anniv. A859

2003, Apr. 5 Photo. ***Perf. 13¼***
2287 A859 41c multi 1.25 .60

Monte Carlo Country Club, 75th Anniv. A860

2003, Apr. 12
2288 A860 46c multi 1.40 .70

General Bathymetric Charts of the Oceans, Cent. — A861

No. 2289: a, Prince Albert I, map of Arctic region, chart of Northern hemisphere. b, Oceanographic museum, map of Antarctica, chart of Southern hemisphere.
Illustration reduced.

2003, Apr. 14 ***Perf. 13x12½***
2289 A861 €1.25 Vert. pair, #a-b 7.50 7.50

Poster by Alfons Mucha — A862

Poster by Jean-Gabriel Domergue — A863

2003, May 5 ***Perf. 13¼***
2290 A862 50c multi 1.50 .75
2291 A863 50c multi 1.50 .75

Europa.

Grand Bourse 2003 — A864

2003, June 2
2292 A864 45c multi 1.40 .70

43rd Intl. Television Festival, Monte Carlo — A865

2003, June 2 ***Perf. 13¼x13***
2293 A865 90c multi 2.75 1.25

15th Antiques Biennale — A866

2003, June 2 ***Perf. 13¼***
2294 A866 €1.80 multi 5.50 2.75

Navigation of Northwest Passage by Roald Amundsen, Cent. A867

2003, June 30
2295 A867 90c multi 2.75 1.40

Powered Flight, Cent. A868

2003, June 30
2296 A868 €1.80 multi 5.50 2.75

Hector Berlioz (1803-69), Composer A869

2003, July 21 **Engr.**
2297 A869 75c red & black 2.25 1.10

Aram Khatchaturian (1903-78), Composer — A870

2003, July 21
2298 A870 €1.60 multi 4.75 2.40

Portrait of a Woman, by François Boucher (1703-70) A871

Self-portrait, by Vincent van Gogh (1853-90) — A872

Self-portrait, by Francesco Mazzola, "Il Parmigianino" (1503-40) — A873

2003, Aug. 6 ***Perf. 13¼x13***
2299 A871 €1.30 multi 4.00 1.90
2300 A872 €3 black & pink 9.00 4.25
2301 A873 €3.60 black & tan 10.50 5.00
Nos. 2299-2301 (3) 23.50 11.15

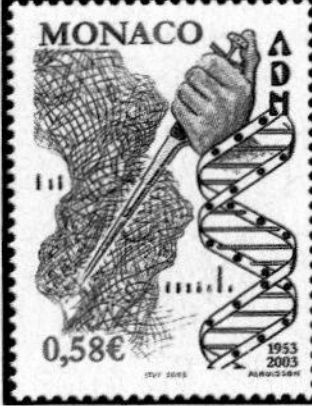

Discovery of Structure of DNA Molecule, 50th Anniv. — A874

2003, Sept. 1 ***Perf. 13¼***
2302 A874 58c multi 1.75 .85

Nostradamus (1503-66), Astrologer — A875

2003, Sept. 1 **Photo.**
2303 A875 70c multi 2.00 1.00

2003 Magic Stars Festival, Monte Carlo — A876

2003, Sept. 1 Litho. ***Perf. 13½x13***
2304 A876 75c multi 2.25 1.10

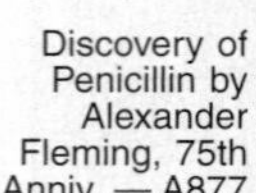

Discovery of Penicillin by Alexander Fleming, 75th Anniv. — A877

2003, Sept. 1 **Engr.** ***Perf. 13¼***
2305 A877 €1.11 multi 3.25 1.60

Awarding of Nobel Physics Prize to Pierre and Marie Curie, Cent. A878

2003, Sept. 1 **Photo.**
2306 A878 €1.20 multi 3.50 1.75

Conquest of Mt. Everest, by Sir Edmund Hillary, 50th Anniv. A879

2003, Sept. 29 **Engr.** ***Perf. 13¼***
2307 A879 €1 multi 3.00 1.50

Saint Dévote — A880

No. 2308: a, Kneeling before cross. b, Standing before soldiers. c, Boat and dove. d, Standing in front of church.

2003, Sept. 29
2308 A880 45c Block of 4, #a-d 5.50 5.50

Christmas — A881

2003, Oct. 13 **Photo.**
2309 A881 50c multi 1.50 .75

MonacoPhil 2004 Intl. Philatelic Exhibition — A882

2003, Dec. 15
2310 A882 50c multi 1.50 .75

28th Intl. Circus Festival, Monte Carlo — A883

2003, Dec. 15
2311 A883 70c multi 2.10 1.00

Beausoleil, France, Cent. A884

2004, Jan. 5 **Photo.** ***Perf. 13¼***
2312 A884 75c multi 2.25 1.10

Saint Dévote A885

Designs: 50c, Arrest of St. Dévote, vert. 75c, Proceedings against St. Dévote. 90c, Stoning of St. Dévote. €1, St. Dévote in boat, vert. €4, Protection of St. Dévote.

2004, Jan. 5 **Engr.**
2313 A885 50c red brn & red 1.50 .75
2314 A885 75c brn & orange 2.25 1.10
2315 A885 90c dk brn & brn 2.75 1.50
2316 A885 €1 dk brn & yel brn 3.00 1.50
2317 A885 €4 dk brn & red brn 12.00 6.00
Nos. 2313-2317 (5) 21.50 10.85

6th Monegasque Biennale of Cancerology — A886

2004, Jan. 29 **Photo.** ***Perf. 13¼***
2318 A886 €1.11 multi 3.25 1.50

Princess Grace Foundation, 40th Anniv. — A887

Princess Grace Irish Library, 20th Anniv. A888

Statue of Princess Grace, by Daphné du Barry — A889

Princess Grace Rose Garden, 20th Anniv. — A890

Photo., Litho. (#2320-2321)

2004, Jan. 29
2319 A887 50c multi 1.50 .75
2320 A888 €1.11 grn & brown 3.25 1.50
2321 A889 €1.45 multi 4.25 2.00
2322 A890 €1.90 multi 5.50 2.75
Nos. 2319-2322 (4) 14.50 7.00

Flora & Fauna Type of 2002

Designs: 75c, Hyla meridionalis, vert. €4.50, Lacerta viridis, vert.

2004, Mar. 8 **Engr.** ***Perf. 13¼***
2323 A814 75c multi 2.25 1.10
2324 A814 €4.50 multi 13.50 6.75

20th Spring of Arts A891

2004, Apr. 2
2325 A891 €1 multi 3.00 1.50

Cathedral Choir School, Cent. — A892

2004, Apr. 5 **Photo.**
2326 A892 45c multi 1.40 .70

37th Intl. Flower Show — A893

2004, Apr. 5
2327 A893 58c multi 1.75 .85

Dog Show Type of 2002

2004, Apr. 9 **Litho.** ***Perf. 13x13¼***
2328 A826 90c Cavalier King Charles Spaniel 2.75 1.40

Monaco Grand Prix, 75th Anniv. A894

2004, Apr. 14 **Photo.** ***Perf. 13¼***
2329 A894 €1.20 multi 3.50 1.75

International School of Monaco, 10th Anniv. — A895

2004, Apr. 26 **Litho.** ***Perf. 13x13¼***
2330 A895 50c multi 1.50 .75

Europa — A896

Travel posters: No. 2331, 50c, Shown. No. 2332, 50c, Women in bathing suits at beach.

2004, May 3 **Photo.** ***Perf. 13¼***
2331-2332 A896 Set of 2 3.00 1.50

Order of Grimaldi, 50th Anniv. — A897

Litho. & Embossed

2004, May 3 ***Perf. 13¼x13***
2333 A897 90c multi 2.75 1.40

2004 Summer Olympics, Athens — A898

No. 2334: a, Stadium, modern runners. b, Stadium, ancient runners.
Illustration reduced.

2004, May 3 ***Perf. 13x13¼***
2334 A898 45c Vert. pair, #a-b 2.75 1.40

Napoleon I and Monegasque Princes in Imperial Army — A899

Stéphanie de Beauharnais, by Baron Gérard — A900

Designs: 75c, Imperial symbols of Napoleon I, horiz. €2.40, Napoleon I, by Gérard.

Perf. 12¼x13, 13x13¼ (75c)

2004, May 28 **Photo.**

2335	A899	58c multi	1.75	.85
2336	A899	75c multi	2.25	1.10
2337	A900	€1.90 multi	5.75	2.75
2338	A900	€2.40 multi	7.25	3.50
	Nos. 2335-2338 (4)		17.00	8.20

Sergey Diaghilev (1872-1929), George Balanchine (1904-83) and Dancers of Ballet Russes de Monte Carlo — A901

2004, June 14 **Engr.** ***Perf. 13¼***
2339 A901 €1.60 multi 4.75 2.40

44th Television Festival, Monte Carlo — A902

2004, June 14 **Litho.** ***Perf. 13¼x13***
2340 A902 €1.80 multi 5.50 2.75

Frédéric Mistral (1830-1914), 1904 Nobel Laureate in Literature — A903

2004, June 26 **Engr.** ***Perf. 13¼***
2341 A903 45c multi 1.40 .70

23rd UPU Congress, Bucharest, Romania A904

2004, June 26
2342 A904 50c multi 1.50 .75

Marco Polo (1254-1324), Explorer — A905

2004, June 26
2343 A905 50c multi 1.50 .75

Salon du Timbre, Paris A906

2004, June 26
2344 A906 75c multi 2.25 1.10

Translation into French of *A Thousand and One Nights*, 300th Anniv. — A907

Litho. & Silk Screened

2004, June 26 ***Perf. 13x13¼***
2345 A907 €1 deep blue & gray 3.00 1.50

Monte Carlo Beach Hotel, 75th Anniv. A908

2004, July 5 **Photo.** ***Perf. 13¼***
2346 A908 45c multi 1.40 .70

FIFA (Fédération Internationale de Football Association), Cent. — A909

2004, Aug. 2
2347 A909 €1.60 multi 4.75 2.40

Magic Stars Magic Festival, Monte Carlo A910

2004, Sept. 6 **Litho.** ***Perf. 13x13¼***
2348 A910 45c multi 1.40 .70

Souvenir Sheet

Princess Grace (1929-82) — A911

Portraits of Princess Grace engraved by: a, 75c, Pierre Albuisson. b, €1.75, Czeslaw Slania. c, €3.50, Martin Mörck.

2004, Oct. 4 **Engr.** ***Perf. 13¼x13***

2349	A911	Sheet of 3 + label	18.00	18.00
a.		75c green & blue	2.25	1.10
b.		€1.75 green & blue	5.25	2.50
c.		€3.50 green & blue	10.50	5.25

Christmas A912

2004, Oct. 4 **Photo.** ***Perf. 13¼***
2350 A912 50c multi 1.50 .75

Admission to Council of Europe A913

2004, Oct. 5 **Engr.** ***Perf. 13x12½***
2351 A913 50c red & blue 1.50 .75

29th Intl. Circus Festival, Monte Carlo — A914

2004, Dec. 3 **Photo.** ***Perf. 13¼***
2352 A914 45c multi 1.40 .70

Louis II Stadium, 20th Anniv. — A915

2004, Dec. 3 **Engr.** ***Perf. 12½x13***
2353 A915 50c multi 1.50 .75

University of Paris Student Hostel, 70th Anniv. — A916

2004, Dec. 3 ***Perf. 13¼***
2354 A916 58c multi 1.75 .85

Palace of Justice, 75th Anniv. — A917

2004, Dec. 3 **Photo.**
2355 A917 75c multi 2.25 1.10

French Alliance of Monaco, 25th Anniv. — A918

2004, Dec. 3
2356 A918 75c multi 2.25 1.10

38th Intl. Flower Show — A919

2004, Dec. 3 **Photo.** ***Perf. 13¼***
2357 A919 90c multi 2.75 1.40

Luigi Valentino Brugnatelli (1761-1818), Inventor of Electroplating — A920

Litho. & Engr.

2004, Dec. 3 ***Perf. 13¼***
2358 A920 €1 blk & brn 3.00 1.50

Jean-Paul Sartre (1905-80), Author A921

2004, Dec. 3 **Photo.**
2359 A921 €1.11 multi 3.25 1.60

Invention of Safety Matches by Johan Edvard Lundstrom, 150th Anniv. A922

2004, Dec. 3
2360 A922 €1.20 multi 3.50 1.75

Publication of Don Quixote, by Miguel de Cervantes, 400th Anniv. — A923

2004, Dec. 3 **Engr.**
2361 A923 €1.20 multi 3.50 1.75

Léo Ferré (1916-93), Singer A924

2004, Dec. 3 **Photo.**
2362 A924 €1.40 multi 4.25 2.10

Invention of Hypodermic Syringe by Alexander Wood, 150th Anniv. — A925

2004, Dec. 3 **Engr.**
2363 A925 €1.60 multi 4.75 2.40

Development of Carbon 14 Dating by Willard F. Libby, 50th Anniv. — A926

2004, Dec. 3 ***Perf. 12½x13***
2364 A926 €1.80 multi 5.50 2.75

Princes and Palace of Monaco — A927

No. 2365: a, Prince Rainier III (30x31mm). b, Palace of Monaco (60x31mm). c, Hereditary Prince Albert (30x31mm).
Illustration reduced.

2004, Dec. 3 ***Perf. 13¼***
2365 A927 50c Horiz. strip of 3, #a-c 4.50 2.25

First World Cup Soccer Championships, 75th Anniv. — A928

No. 2366: a, World Cup, goalie catching soccer ball. b, Flag of Uruguay, player dribbling ball.

2004, Dec. 3 **Photo.** ***Perf. 13¼***
2366 A928 €1 Horiz. pair, #a-b 6.00 3.00

Princess Grace Type of 2004 in Changed Colors with "MonacoPhil 2004" Added in Sheet Margin
Souvenir Sheet

Designs like No. 2349.

2004, Dec. 3 **Engr.** ***Imperf.***
2367 A911 Sheet of 3 18.00 18.00
a. 75c blue & emerald 2.25 2.25
b. €1.75 blue & emerald 5.25 5.25
c. €3.50 blue & emerald 10.50 10.50

Rotary International, Cent. — A929

Designs: 55c, Rotary emblem, founder, president, treasurer and secretary of original club. 70c, Rotary emblem, vert.

Litho. & Engr., Litho. (70c)
Perf. 13¼, 13¼x13 (70c)
2005, Feb. 23
2368-2369 A929 Set of 2 3.75 1.90

UNESCO Fine Arts Committee, 50th Anniv. — A930

2005, Mar. 1 **Photo.** ***Perf. 13¼***
2370 A930 48c multi 1.40 .70

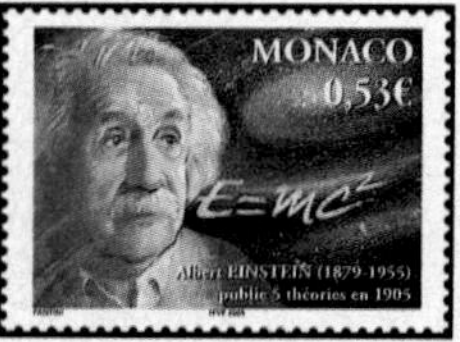

Publication of Albert Einstein's Theory of Relativity, Cent. — A931

2005, Mar. 1
2371 A931 53c multi 1.60 .80

First Awarding of Diplomas From School of Fine Arts — A932

2005, Mar. 1 **Litho.** ***Perf. 13¼x13***
2372 A932 64c black & red 1.90 .95

Dog Show Type of 2002

2005, Mar. 1 **Photo.** ***Perf. 13¼***
2373 A826 82c Dachshund (teckel) 2.50 1.25

Intl. Automobile Federation, Cent. — A933

2005, Apr. 1 **Photo.** ***Perf. 13¼***
2374 A933 55c multi 1.60 1.60

21st World Exhibition of Hybrid and Electric Vehicles A934

Designs, 75c, Fetish, first electric sports car. €1.30, Stylized automobile with electric plug.

2005, Apr. 1
2375-2376 A934 Set of 2 6.00 6.00

Tenth Horse Jumping International, Monte Carlo — A935

2005, Apr. 1 **Engr.** ***Perf. 13¼***
2377 A935 90c multi 2.75 1.40

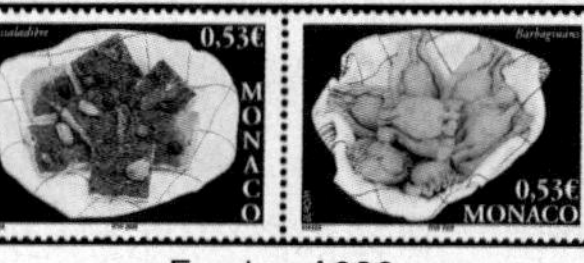

Food — A936

No. 2378, 53c: a, Pissaladière. b, Barbaguians.
No. 2379, 55c: a, Tourte de blettes. b, Desserts.
Illustration reduced.

2005, May 3 **Photo.**
Horiz. Pairs, #a-b
2378-2379 A936 Set of 2 *6.50 3.25*

Europa (#2378).

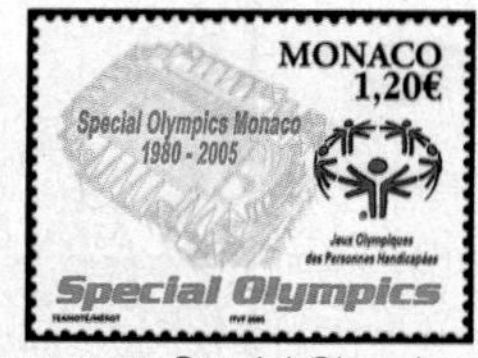

Monegasque Special Olympics, 25th Anniv. — A937

2005, June 3 **Litho.** ***Perf. 13x13¼***
2380 A937 €1.20 multi 3.50 1.75

Early 20th Century Advertising Art A938

Advertisements for: 77c, Bains de Mer de Monaco. €2.50, English Sanitary Co. €3.10, Scapini Biscuits.

2005, June 3 **Photo.** ***Perf. 12¼x13***
2381-2383 A938 Set of 3 19.00 9.50

Monaco Yacht Show — A939

2005, July 4 ***Perf. 13¼***
2384 A939 82c multi 2.40 1.25

Admission to UPU, 50th Anniv. — A940

2005, July 4 **Engr.**
2385 A940 €3.03 multi 9.00 4.50

Astronomers A941

Designs: €1.22, Edmond Halley (1656-1742). €1.98, Gerard P. Kuiper (1905-73). €3.80, Clyde Tombaugh (1906-97).

2005, July 4 ***Perf. 12½x13***
2386-2388 A941 Set of 3 21.00 10.50

Coat of Arms Type of 2000 Inscribed "20g Ecopli" at Top
Serpentine Die Cut 11
2005, July 12 **Photo.**
Booklet Stamp
Self-Adhesive
2389 A786 (48c) grn, blk & red 1.40 1.40
a. Booklet pane of 10 14.00

10th European Patrimony Day — A942

2005, Sept. 5 **Engr.** ***Perf. 13¼***
2390 A942 48c multi 1.40 1.40

20th Magic Stars Festival, Monte Carlo A943

2005, Sept. 5 Litho. ***Perf. 13x13¼***
2391 A943 €1.45 red, gold & blk 4.25 4.25

Christmas A944

2005, Oct. 3 Engr. ***Perf. 13¼***
2392 A944 53c blk & red 1.60 1.60

Monte Carlo Bay Hotel and Resort A945

2005, Oct. 7 **Photo.**
2393 A945 55c multi 1.60 1.60

Nadia Boulanger (1887-1979), Conductor, and Lili Boulanger (1893-1918), Composer — A946

2005, Oct. 21 **Engr.**
2394 A946 90c multi 2.75 2.75

Miniature Sheet

Restoration of Garnier Hall, Monte Carlo Opera — A947

No. 2395: a, "Song." b, Garnier Hall. c, "Comedy." d, "Dance." e, Charles Garnier (1825-98), architect. f, "Music."

2005, Nov. 16
2395 A947 82c Sheet of 6, #a-f 14.50 14.50

Souvenir Sheet

Prince Rainier III (1923-2005) — A948

2005, Nov. 19 ***Perf. 13***
2396 A948 €4 black 12.00 12.00

Prince Albert II — A949

2005, Nov. 19 ***Perf. 13x13¼***
2397 A949 (48c) green 1.40 1.40
2398 A949 (53c) red 1.60 1.60
2399 A949 (75c) blue 2.25 2.25
Nos. 2397-2399 (3) 5.25 5.25

National Day — A950

No. 2400: a, Fontveille (26x27mm, country name at UL). b, Palace (56x27mm). c, La Condamine and Monte Carlo (26x27mm, country name at UR).

2005, Nov. 19 Photo. ***Perf. 13¼***
2400 A950 €1.01 Horiz. strip of 3, #a-c 9.00 9.00

MonacoPhil 2006 Philatelic Exhibition A951

2005, Dec. 12
2401 A951 55c multi 1.60 1.60

30th Intl. Circus Festival, Monte Carlo

A952

A952a

No. 2403: a, Charles Rivel, 1974 Golden Clown. b, Fredy Knie, 1977 Golden Clown. c, Alexis Gruss, Sr., 1975 Golden Clown. d, Golden Clown award. e, Georges Carl, 1979 Golden Clown.

2005, Dec. 14
2402 A952 64c shown 1.90 1.90
2403 A952a 75c Sheet of 5, #a-e, + label 11.00 11.00

The label on No. 2403 has the same vignette as No. 2402, lacking country name and denomination, but with a gray background.

A953

2006 Winter Olympics, Turin A954

No. 2404: a, Red mascot. b, Blue mascot.

2006, Jan. 9 Photo. ***Perf. 13¼***
2404 A953 55c Horiz. pair, #a-b 3.25 3.25
2405 A954 82c multi 2.40 2.40

Museum of Postage Stamps and Money, 10th Anniv. A955

2006, Jan. 30 **Engr.**
2406 A955 53c multi 1.60 1.60

5th Intl. Film and Literature Forum — A956

2006, Feb. 6 Photo. ***Perf. 13¼***
2407 A956 82c multi 2.40 2.40

Léopold Sédar Senghor (1906-2001), First President of Senegal — A957

Litho. & Engr.

2006, Mar. 6 ***Perf. 13x13¼***
2408 A957 €1.45 multi 4.25 4.25

100th Monte Carlo Tennis Tournament A958

2006, Mar. 8 Photo. ***Perf. 13¼***
2409 A958 55c multi 1.60 1.60

Coat of Arms Type of 2000 Inscribed "20g Zone A" at Top

Serpentine Die Cut 11

2006, Apr. 6 **Photo.**

Self-Adhesive Booklet Stamp

2410 A786 (55c) red & black 1.60 1.60
a. Booklet pane of 10 16.00

Monte Carlo Philharmonic Orchestra, 150th Anniv. — A959

2006, Apr. 6 ***Perf. 13¼***
2411 A959 64c multi 1.90 1.90

Arctic Oceanographic Expeditions of Prince Albert I, Cent. — A960

Litho. & Engr.

2006, Apr. 10 ***Perf. 13x13¼***
2412 A960 €1.60 multi 4.75 4.75

Dog Show Type of 2002

2006, Apr. 14 Photo. ***Perf. 13¼***
2413 A826 64c Special schnauzer 1.90 1.90

39th Intl. Flower Show — A961

2006, Apr. 18
2414 A961 77c multi 2.25 2.25

2006 World Cup Soccer Championships, Germany — A962

No. 2415: a, World Cup, stadium. b, Stadium and 2006 World Cup emblem.

2006, Apr. 18
2415 A962 90c Horiz. pair, #a-b 5.25 5.25

A963

Europa A964

2006, May 5 Photo. *Perf. 13¼*
2416 A963 53c multi 1.60 1.60
2417 A964 55c multi 1.60 1.60

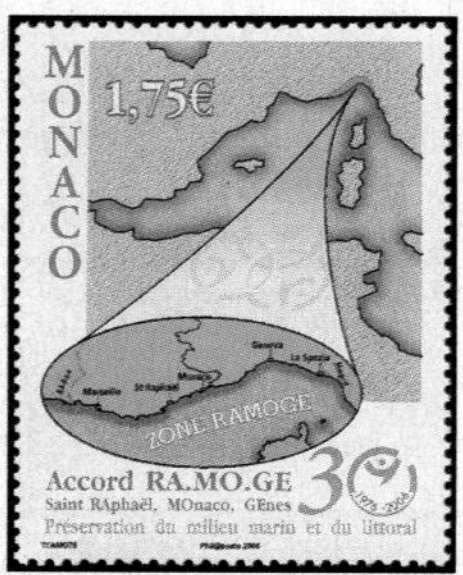
RAMOGE Agreement, 30th Anniv. — A965

2006, May 9 *Perf. 12¼x13*
2418 A965 €1.75 multi 5.25 5.25

Washington 2006 World Philatelic Exhibition A966

2006, May 27 Engr. *Perf. 13¼*
2419 A966 90c blue & red 2.75 2.75

John Huston (1906-87), Film Director — A967

2006, May 27 *Perf. 13x12¼*
2420 A967 €1.80 black & henna brn 5.25 5.25

Prince Albert Challenge Sabre Tournament — A968

2006, June 6 Photo. *Perf. 13¼*
2421 A968 48c multi 1.40 1.40

Pierre Corneille (1606-84), Dramatist A969

2006, June 17
2422 A969 53c multi 1.60 1.60

46th Intl. Television Festival, Monte Carlo — A970

2006, June 17
2423 A970 82c multi 2.40 2.40

Wolfgang Amadeus Mozart (1756-91), Composer — A971

2006, June 17 Engr. *Perf. 13x12¼*
2424 A971 €1.22 org red & blue 3.50 3.50

Prince Pierre Foundation, 40th Anniv. — A972

2006, June 20 *Perf. 12½x13*
2425 A972 €2.50 multi 7.50 7.50

Dino Buzzati (1906-72), Writer A973

2006, July 17 Photo. *Perf. 13¼*
2426 A973 55c multi 1.60 1.60

Cetacean Conservation Accord, 10th Anniv. — A974

2006, July 17 *Perf. 13x12¼*
2427 A974 90c multi 2.75 2.75

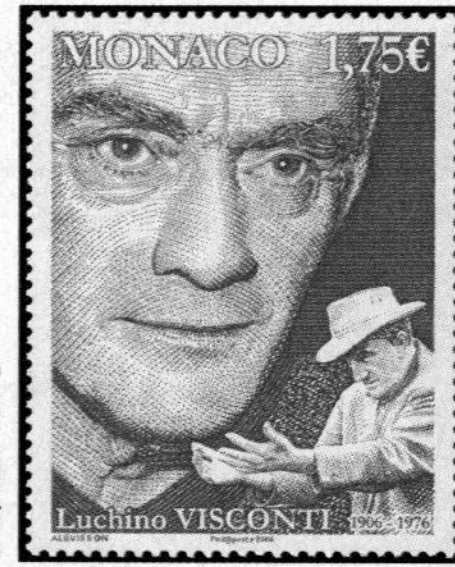
Luchino Visconti (1906-76), Film Director A975

2006, July 17 Engr. *Perf. 12¼x13*
2428 A975 €1.75 henna brn 5.25 5.25

Rolls-Royce Automobiles, Cent. — A976

2006, Sept. 4 Engr. *Perf. 13¼*
2429 A976 64c multi 1.90 1.90

2006 Magic Stars Festival, Monte Carlo — A977

2006, Sept. 4 Photo.
2430 A977 77c multi 2.25 2.25

Monaco Red Cross — A978

2006, Oct. 2
2431 A978 48c multi 1.40 1.40

Christmas A979

Perf. 13½x13¼
2006, Oct. 2 Litho. & Engr.
2432 A979 53c multi 1.60 1.60

Prince Albert II — A980

2006, Dec. 1 Engr. *Perf. 13x13¼*
2433 A980 (49c) green 1.40 1.40
2434 A980 (54c) red 1.50 1.50
2435 A980 (60c) blue 1.60 1.60
Nos. 2433-2435 (3) 4.50 4.50

Dated 2007.

Prince Albert II and Coat of Arms A981

2006, Dec. 1 Photo. *Perf. 13¼x13*
2436 A981 60c multi 1.60 1.60

Souvenir Sheet
Perf. 13x13¼
2437 A981 €6 multi 16.00 16.00

MonacoPhil 2006 Intl. Philatelic Exhibition. Dated 2007.

World AIDS Day A982

2006, Dec. 1 Litho. *Perf. 13x13¼*
2438 A982 49c multi 1.40 1.40

Dated 2007.

Josephine Baker (1906-75), Singer and Dancer — A983

2006, Dec. 1 *Perf. 13¼x13*
2439 A983 49c multi 1.40 1.40

Princess Grace Theater, 25th anniv. Dated 2007.

Philatelic Anniversaries A984

2006, Dec. 1 Photo. *Perf. 13¼*
2440 A984 54c multi 1.50 1.50

Creation of Philatelic Bureau, 70th anniv. (in 2007), Consultative Commission of the

Prince's Philatelic Collection, 20th anniv. (in 2007). Dated 2007.

Les Enfants de Frankie Children's Charity, 10th Anniv. (in 2007) — A985

2006, Dec. 1
2441 A985 70c multi 1.90 1.90

Dated 2007.

Albert Camus (1913-60), 1957 Nobel Literature Laureate — A986

2006, Dec. 1 **Engr.**
2442 A986 84c multi 2.25 2.25

Dated 2007.

Auguste Escoffier (1846-1935), Chef — A987

2006, Dec. 1
2443 A987 85c multi 2.25 2.25

Dated 2007.

Daniel Bovet (1907-92), 1957 Nobel Medicine Laureate A988

2006, Dec. 1
2444 A988 86c dk blue & red 2.40 2.40

Dated 2007.

Cardiothoracic Center, 20th Anniv. (in 2007) — A989

2006, Dec. 1
2445 A989 €1.15 multi 3.25 3.25

Dated 2007.

Rudyard Kipling (1865-1936), 1907 Nobel Literature Laureate — A990

2006, Dec. 1
2446 A990 €1.57 multi 4.25 4.25

Dated 2007.

Opening of Institute of Sports Medicine and Surgery A991

2006, Dec. 1
2447 A991 €1.70 multi 4.75 4.75

Dated 2007.

Meeting of Prince Albert II and Pope Benedict XVI, 1st Anniv. — A992

2006, Dec. 1 **Photo.** ***Perf. 13x13¼***
2448 A992 €1.70 multi 4.75 4.75

Dated 2007.

Paul-Emile Victor (1907-95), Explorer — A993

2006, Dec. 1 **Engr.** ***Perf. 13x12¼***
2449 A993 €2.11 multi 5.75 5.75

Dated 2007.

European Philatelic Academy, 30th Anniv. (in 2007) — A994

2006, Dec. 1 **Photo.** ***Perf. 13x13¼***
2450 A994 €2.30 multi 6.25 6.25

Dated 2007.

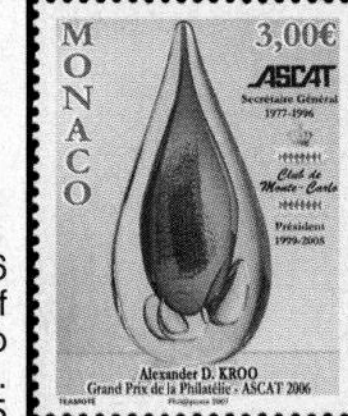

Awarding of 2006 Grand Prix of Philately to Alexander D. Kroo — A995

2006, Dec. 1 **Litho.** ***Perf. 13¼x13***
2451 A995 €3 multi 8.00 8.00

Dated 2007.

Auto Racing — A996

No. 2452: a, 65th Monaco Grand Prix. b, 75th Monte Carlo Rally.

2006, Dec. 1
2452 A996 60c Horiz. pair, #a-b 3.25 3.25

Dated 2007.

Art in Grimaldi Forum by Nall — A997

No. 2453: a, Purple Flower. b, Yellow Flower

2006, Dec. 1 **Photo.** ***Perf. 13¼***
2453 A997 €1.70 Pair, #a-b 9.25 9.25

Printed in panes of 2 pairs. Dated 2007.

A998

31st Intl. Circus Festival, Monte Carlo — A999

2006, Dec. 1 **Photo.** ***Perf. 13¼***
2454 A998 60c multi 1.60 1.60

Litho.
Perf. 13¼x13
2455 A999 84c multi 2.25 2.25

Dated 2007.

Souvenir Sheet

40th Intl. Flower Show — A1000

No. 2456: a, Classic composition. b, Modern composition. c, Contemporary composition. d, Japanese composition.

2006, Dec. 1 **Photo.** ***Perf. 13¼***
2456 A1000 €1.30 Sheet of 4, #a-d 14.00 14.00

Dated 2007.

Stenella Coeruleoalba — A1001

2007, Jan. 2 **Litho.** ***Perf. 13x13¼***
2457 A1001 (36c) multi .95 .95

Issued precanceled only. See note after No. 324.

Giuseppe Garibaldi (1807-82), Italian Nationalist Leader A1002

2007, Mar. 16 **Engr.** ***Perf. 13¼***
2458 A1002 €1.40 ol brn & red 3.75 3.75

Carlo Goldoni (1707-93), Playwright A1003

Litho. & Silk-screened
2007, Mar. 16 ***Perf. 13x13¼***
2459 A1003 €4.54 multi 12.50 12.50

Monaco Olympic Committee, Cent. — A1004

2007, Apr. 2 **Photo.** ***Perf. 13¼***
2460 A1004 60c multi 1.60 1.60

Dalmatian
A1005

2007, Apr. 2 ***Perf. 13x13¼***
2461 A1005 70c multi 1.90 1.90

Intl. Dog Show.

12th Games of Small European States
A1006

2007, Apr. 2 ***Perf. 13¼***
2462 A1006 86c multi 2.40 2.40

Princess Grace Exposition, Grimaldi Forum
A1007

2007, May 4 **Litho.** ***Perf. 13***
2463 A1007 85c multi 2.40 2.40

First Flight of Helicopter Designed by Maurice Leger, Cent. — A1008

2007, May 4 **Engr.** ***Perf. 12½x13***
2464 A1008 €1.15 multi 3.25 3.25

47th Television Festival, Monte Carlo — A1009

2007, May 4 **Litho.** ***Perf. 13¼x13***
2465 A1009 €2.90 multi 8.00 8.00

Scouting, Cent. — A1010

No. 2466: a, Scouts and campfire. b, Lord Robert Baden-Powell.
Illustration reduced.

2007, May 4 **Photo.** ***Perf. 13¼***
2466 A1010 60c Horiz. pair, #a-b 3.25 3.25

Cartophily, Numismatics and Philately Grand Bourse — A1011

Litho. & Silk-Screened
2007, June 25 ***Perf. 13¼x13***
2467 A1011 49c multi 1.40 1.40

22nd Magic Stars Festival, Monte Carlo — A1012

2007, June 25 **Litho.**
2468 A1012 €1.30 red & black 3.50 3.50

Monaco Harbor — A1013

2007, Oct. 1 **Engr.** ***Perf. 13x12½***
2469 A1013 85c multi 2.40 2.40

Christmas
A1014

Litho. & Silk-screened
2007, Oct. 1 ***Perf. 13¼x13***
2470 A1014 54c multi 1.60 1.60

32nd Intl. Circus Festival, Monte Carlo — A1015

2007, Oct. 15 **Photo.** ***Perf. 13¼***
2471 A1015 60c multi 1.75 1.75

Giacomo Puccini (1858-1924), Composer
A1016

2007, Dec. 7 **Engr.** ***Perf. 13¼***
2472 A1016 €1.40 blue & red 4.25 4.25

41st Intl. Flower Show — A1017

2008, Jan. 3 **Photo.**
2473 A1017 49c multi 1.50 1.50

Reformed Church of Monaco, 50th Anniv. — A1018

2008, Jan. 3 **Engr.** ***Perf. 13¼***
2474 A1018 49c blue & brown 1.50 1.50

Consecration of St. Charles Church, 125th Anniv. — A1019

2008, Mar. 3
2475 A1019 54c gray blue & red 1.60 1.60

Arc de Triomphe du Carrousel Quadriga, Paris, by François Joseph Bosio
A1020

2008, Jan. 3
2476 A1020 54c multi 1.60 1.60

Andrea Palladio (1508-80), Architect
A1021

2008, Jan. 3 **Photo.** ***Perf. 13¼***
2477 A1021 60c multi 1.75 1.75

10th Special Session of United Nations Environment Program, Monaco
A1022

2008, Jan. 3 **Photo.** ***Perf. 13¼***
2478 A1022 85c multi 2.50 2.50

Johannes Brahms (1833-97), Composer
A1023

2008, Jan. 3 **Engr.** ***Perf. 13¼***
2479 A1023 €1.15 Prus grn & red 3.50 3.50

Return of Comet Predicted by Edmond Halley, 250th Anniv.
A1024

2008, Jan. 3 **Photo.** ***Perf. 13¼***
2480 A1024 €1.57 multi 4.75 4.75

Marcel Kroenlein Arboretum, Roure, France, 20th Anniv. — A1025

2008, Jan. 3 **Engr.** ***Perf. 13¼***
2481 A1025 €2.11 multi 6.25 6.25

Poster for Monte Carlo Country Club, by Raymond Gid
A1026

Poster for Monte Carlo Beach Hotel, by Raymond Gid
A1027

2008, Jan. 3 **Photo.** ***Perf. 12¼x13***
2482 A1026 70c multi 2.10 2.10

Litho.
Perf. 13
2483 A1027 85c multi 2.50 2.50

Poster for Monte Carlo Golf Club, by Raymond Gid
A1028

Monte Carlo Tourism Poster, by Louis Rué A1029

2008, Jan. 3 Photo. *Perf. 12¼x13*

2484 A1028 €1.15 multi 3.50 3.50
2485 A1029 €2.90 multi 8.50 8.50

Gen. André Massena (1758-1817) A1030

2008, Jan. 21 Engr. *Perf. 13¼*

2486 A1030 86c grn & yel brown 2.60 2.60

Apparition at Lourdes, France, 150th Anniv. A1031

2008, Feb. 11 Engr. *Perf. 13x12¾*

2487 A1031 €1.30 dark blue & blue 4.00 4.00

Introduction of the Ford Model T, Cent. — A1032

2008, Mar. 10 *Perf. 13¼*

2488 A1032 €1.70 multi 5.50 5.50

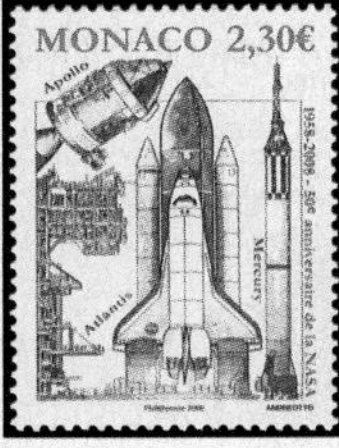

National Aeronautics and Space Administration, 50th Anniv. — A1033

2008, Mar. 10

2489 A1033 €2.30 multi 7.25 7.25

Alfred Nobel (1833-1906), Inventor and Philantropist A1034

2008, Mar. 10

2490 A1034 €4 blk & claret 12.50 12.50

Dog Show Type of 2002

2008, Mar. 17 Photo. *Perf. 13¼*

2491 A826 88c Greyhound, vert. 2.75 2.75

Expo Zaragoza 2008 A1035

2008, Mar. 18 Litho. *Perf. 13x13¼*

2492 A1035 65c multi 2.10 2.10

Mother's Day — A1036

2008, Apr. 8 *Perf. 13¼x13*

2493 A1036 55c multi 1.75 1.75

Stendhal (Marie-Henri Beyle) (1783-1842), Writer — A1037

2008, Apr. 8 Engr. *Perf. 13¼*

2494 A1037 €1.33 multi 4.25 4.25

Boris Pasternak (1890-1960), Writer — A1038

2008, Apr. 8

2495 A1038 €2.18 multi 7.00 7.00

2008 Summer Olympics, Beijing — A1039

No. 2496 — Olympic rings and: a, Pagoda, basketball, tennis, javelin. b, Beijing Olympics emblem, baseball, fencing, shooting.

Illustration reduced.

2008, Apr. 8 *Perf. 13x12½*

2496 A1039 Horiz. pair 4.50 4.50
a. 55c red & black 1.75 1.75
b. 85c red & black 2.75 2.75

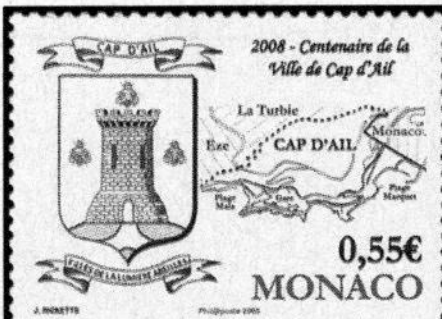

Cap d'Ail, France, Cent. A1040

2008, Apr. 21 Litho. *Perf. 13x13¼*

2497 A1040 55c multi 1.75 1.75

Exotic Garden, 75th Anniv. A1041

2008, May 2 Engr. *Perf. 13¼*

2498 A1041 50c multi 1.60 1.60

2008 Magic Stars Festival, Monte Carlo — A1042

2008, May 5 Photo.

2499 A1042 72c multi 2.25 2.25

Europa A1043

Designs: 55c, Letters encircling globe. 65c, Postmen, letter, means of postal communication.

2008, May 5 Engr.

2500-2501 A1043 Set of 2 3.75 3.75

Intl. Skating Union, 52nd Congress A1044

2008, May 16 Litho. *Perf. 13¼x13*

2502 A1044 50c multi 1.60 1.60

Prince Albert II of Monaco Foundation A1045

Litho. & Engr.

2008, May 16 *Perf. 13x13¼*

2503 A1045 88c multi 2.75 2.75

48th Intl. Television Festival, Monte Carlo — A1046

2008, June 2 Photo. *Perf. 13¼*

2504 A1046 €2.80 multi 9.00 9.00

Monegasque International Cooperation — A1047

Designs: 65c, Education. €1, Health. €1.25, Campaign against poverty. €1.70, Campaign against desertification.

2008, June 5 Engr.

2505-2508 A1047 Set of 4 14.50 14.50

Monaco 2008 Intl. Numismatic Exhibition A1048

Litho. & Embossed With Foil Application

2008, June 16 *Perf. 13½x13*

2509 A1048 65c multi 2.10 2.10

Schönbrunn Palace, Vienna — A1049

2008, Sept. 18 Engr. *Perf. 13¼*

2510 A1049 65c multi 1.90 1.90

WIPA 2008 Intl. Philatelic Exhibition, Vienna.

Order of Saint Charles, 150th Anniv. A1050

Photo. & Embossed With Foil Application

2008, Sept. 18 *Perf. 13x13¼*

2511 A1050 €1.50 multi 4.25 4.25

Coins of Monaco A1051

Obverse and reverse of: 50c, 1837 Franc. 55c, 1943 Franc. 72c, 1950 Franc. €1.25, 1960 Franc. €1.64, Euro coinage of 2002. €1.70, Euro coinage of 2006.

Litho. & Embossed With Foil Application

2008, Sept. 18

2512-2517 A1051 Set of 6 17.50 17.50

Christmas A1052

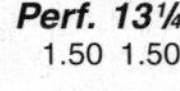

2008, Sept. 19 Photo. *Perf. 13¼*

2518 A1052 55c multi 1.50 1.50

33rd Intl. Circus Festival, Monte Carlo — A1053

2008, Dec. 19 Photo. *Perf. 13¼*

2519 A1053 85c multi 2.40 2.40

Prince Albert I — A1054

Flag of Monaco and Intl. Polar Year Emblem A1055

Prince Albert II — A1056

2008, Dec. 19 *Perf. 13x12¼*

2520	Horiz. strip of 3	7.25 7.25
a.	A1054 85c multi	2.40 2.40
b.	A1055 85c multi	2.40 2.40
c.	A1056 85c multi	2.40 2.40

Admiral Robert E. Peary (1856-1920), Arctic Explorer, and Dog Sleds — A1057

Peary, Flag of US and Map of Arctic Area A1058

Matthew Henson (1866-1955), Arctic Explorer and Ship — A1059

Litho. & Engr.

2008, Dec. 19 *Perf. 13¼*

2521	Horiz. strip of 3	7.25 7.25
a.	A1057 87c multi	2.40 2.40
b.	A1058 87c multi	2.40 2.40
c.	A1059 87c multi	2.40 2.40

Monaco Firefighting Corps, Cent. A1060

Designs: 50c, Railway and road emergency vehicle. 72c, Ladder truck, 1909. 87c, Fireman, ladder truck.

2009, Jan. 5 Photo. *Perf. 13¼*

2522-2524 A1060 Set of 3 5.75 5.75

Princess Grace Rose Garden, 25th Anniv. — A1061

2009, Jan. 5 *Perf. 13¼x13*

2525 A1061 €1.25 multi 3.50 3.50

Spring Arts Festival, 25th Anniv. — A1062

2009, Jan. 5

2526 A1062 €1.33 multi 3.75 3.75

First Flight Across English Channel by Louis Blériot, Cent. A1063

Litho. & Engr.

2009, Jan. 29 *Perf. 13x12½*

2527 A1063 87c multi 2.25 2.25

Felix Mendelssohn Bartholdy (1809-47), Composer A1064

2009, Jan. 29 Engr. *Perf. 13¼*

2528 A1064 €1.50 olive grn & blue 4.00 4.00

Beatification of Joan of Arc, Cent. — A1065

2009, Jan. 29

2529 A1065 €2.22 multi 5.75 5.75

Chihuahua and Cavalier King Charles Spaniel A1067

2009, Feb. 7 Photo. *Perf. 13¼*

2531 A1067 72c multi 1.90 1.90

Intl. Dog Show.

Association of Members of the Order of Academic Palms World Conference — A1069

2009, Feb. 7 Engr. *Perf. 13x12½*

2533 A1069 88c multi 2.25 2.25

Barbie Doll, 50th Anniv. — A1070

2009, Feb. 7 Photo. *Perf. 13¼*

2534 A1070 88c multi 2.25 2.25

SEMI-POSTAL STAMPS

No. 16 Surcharged in Red

1914, Oct. Unwmk. *Perf. 14x13½*

B1 A2 10c + 5c carmine 8.00 8.00

View of Monaco — SP2

1919, Sept. 20 Typo.

B2	SP2	2c + 3c lilac	32.50	*35.00*
B3	SP2	5c + 5c green	21.00	*20.00*
B4	SP2	15c + 10c rose	21.00	*20.00*
B5	SP2	25c + 15c blue	39.00	40.00
B6	SP2	50c + 50c brn, *buff*	190.00	*175.00*
B7	SP2	1fr + 1fr blk, *yel*	300.00	*375.00*
B8	SP2	5fr + 5fr dull red	1,000.	*1,200.*
		Nos. B2-B8 (7)	1,603.	*1,865.*

Nos. B4-B8 Surcharged

1920, Mar. 20

B9	SP2	2c + 3c on #B4	40.00	*45.00*
a.		"c" of "3c" inverted	*1,500.*	*1,750.*
B10	SP2	2c + 3c on #B5	40.00	*45.00*
a.		"c" of "3c" inverted	*1,500.*	*1,750.*
B11	SP2	2c + 3c on #B6	40.00	*45.00*
a.		"c" of "3c" inverted	*1,500.*	*1,750.*
B12	SP2	5c + 5c on #B7	40.00	*45.00*
B13	SP2	5c + 5c on #B8	40.00	*45.00*

Overprinted

B14	SP2	15c + 10c rose	25.00	25.00
B15	SP2	25c + 15c blue	16.00	16.00
B16	SP2	50c + 50c brown, *buff*	55.00	55.00
B17	SP2	1fr + 1fr black, *yel*	75.00	75.00
B18	SP2	5fr + 5fr red	*6,500.*	*6,500.*
		Nos. B9-B17 (9)	371.00	396.00

Marriage of Princess Charlotte to Prince Pierre, Comte de Polignac.

Palace Gardens SP3

"The Rock" of Monaco SP4

Bay of Monaco SP5

Prince Louis II — SP6

1937, Apr. **Engr.** ***Perf. 13***

No.	Type	Description	Unused	Used
B19	SP3	50c + 50c green	3.00	3.00
B20	SP4	90c + 90c carmine	3.00	3.00
B21	SP5	1.50fr + 1.50fr blue	6.00	6.00
B22	SP6	2fr + 2fr violet	11.50	11.50
B23	SP6	5fr + 5fr brn red	100.00	100.00
		Nos. B19-B23 (5)	123.50	123.50
		Set, never hinged	250.00	

The surtax was used for welfare work.

Pierre and Marie Curie — SP7

Monaco Hospital, Date Palms SP8

1938, Nov. 15 ***Perf. 13***

No.	Type	Description	Unused	Used
B24	SP7	65c + 25c dp bl grn	11.00	11.00
B25	SP8	1.75fr + 50c dp ultra	11.00	11.00
		Set, never hinged	40.00	

B24 and B25 exist imperforate.

The surtax was for the International Union for the Control of Cancer.

Lucien — SP9

Honoré II — SP10

Louis I — SP11

Charlotte de Gramont — SP12

Antoine I — SP13

Marie de Lorraine — SP14

Jacques I SP15

Louise-Hippolyte SP16

Honoré III — SP17

"The Rock," 18th Century SP18

1939, June 26

No.	Type	Description	Unused	Used
B26	SP9	5c + 5c brown blk	1.90	1.10
B27	SP10	10c + 10c rose vio	1.90	1.10
B28	SP11	45c + 15c brt green	6.75	5.00
B29	SP12	70c + 30c brt red vio	10.00	10.00
B30	SP13	90c + 35c violet	10.00	0.00
B31	SP14	1fr + 1fr ultra	25.00	24.00
B32	SP15	2fr + 2fr brn org	25.00	24.00
B33	SP16	2.25fr + 1.25fr Prus bl	30.00	30.00
B34	SP17	3fr + 3fr dp rose	40.00	42.50
B35	SP18	5fr + 5fr red	75.00	77.50
		Nos. B26-B35 (10)	225.55	215.20
		Set, never hinged	450.00	

Types of Regular Issue, 1939 Surcharged in Red

1940, Feb. 10 **Engr.** ***Perf. 13***

No.	Type	Description	Unused	Used
B36	A30	20c + 1fr violet	2.75	2.75
B37	A31	25c + 1fr dk green	2.75	2.75
B38	A32	30c + 1fr brn red	2.75	2.75
B39	A31	40c + 1fr dk blue	2.75	2.75
B40	A33	45c + 1fr rose car	2.75	2.75
B41	A34	50c + 1fr brown	2.75	2.75
B42	A32	60c + 1fr dk green	3.50	3.50
B43	A35	75c + 1fr brown blk	3.50	3.50
B44	A34	1fr + 1fr scarlet	4.50	4.50
B45	A31	2fr + 1fr indigo	4.50	4.50
B46	A33	2.50fr + 1fr dk green	11.00	11.00
B47	A35	3fr + 1fr dk blue	11.00	11.00
B48	A30	5fr + 1fr brn blk	15.00	15.00
B49	A33	10fr + 5fr lt blue	28.00	28.00
B50	A32	20fr + 5fr brn vio	29.00	29.00
		Nos. B36-B50 (15)	126.50	126.50
		Set, never hinged	300.00	

The surtax was used to purchase ambulances for the French government.

Catalogue values for unused stamps in this section, from this point to the end of the section, are for Never Hinged items.

Symbol of Charity and View of Monaco SP19

Symbol of Charity and View of Monaco — SP20

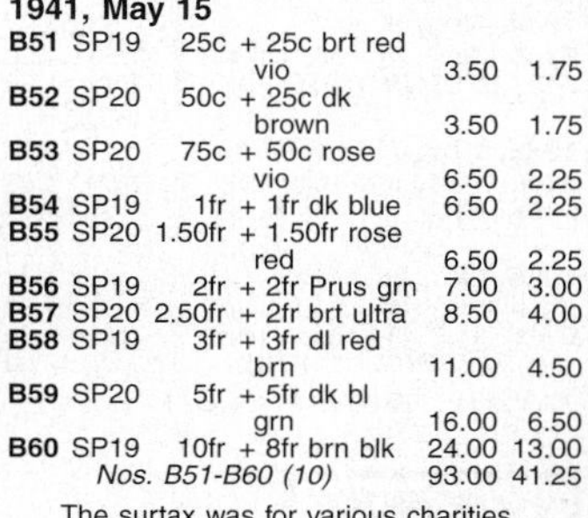

1941, May 15

No.	Type	Description	Unused	Used
B51	SP19	25c + 25c brt red vio	3.50	1.75
B52	SP20	50c + 25c dk brown	3.50	1.75
B53	SP20	75c + 50c rose vio	6.50	2.25
B54	SP19	1fr + 1fr dk blue	6.50	2.25
B55	SP20	1.50fr + 1.50fr rose red	6.50	2.25
B56	SP19	2fr + 2fr Prus grn	7.00	3.00
B57	SP20	2.50fr + 2fr brt ultra	8.50	4.00
B58	SP19	3fr + 3fr dl red brn	11.00	4.50
B59	SP20	5fr + 5fr dk bl grn	16.00	6.50
B60	SP19	10fr + 8fr brn blk	24.00	13.00
		Nos. B51-B60 (10)	93.00	41.25

The surtax was for various charities.

Rainier Grimaldi — SP21

Designs: 5c, Charles II. 10c, Jeanne Grimaldi. 20c, Charles-August Goyon de Matignon. 30c, Jacques I. 40c, Louise-Hippolyte. 50c, Charlotte Grimaldi. 75c, Marie-Charles Grimaldi. 1fr, Honore III. 1.50fr, Honore IV. 2.50fr, Honore V. 3fr, Florestan I. 5fr, Charles III. 10fr, Albert I. 20fr, Marie-Victoire. Frames differ.

1942, Dec. 10

No.	Type	Description	Unused	Used
B61	SP21	2c + 3c ultra	.50	.50
B62	SP21	5c + 5c org ver	.50	.50
B63	SP21	10c + 5c blk	.50	.50
B64	SP21	20c + 10c brt grn	.50	.50
B65	SP21	30c + 30c brn vio	.50	.50
B66	SP21	40c + 40c rose red	.50	.50
B67	SP21	50c + 50c vio	.50	.50
B68	SP21	75c + 75c brt red vio	.50	.50
B69	SP21	1fr + 1fr dk grn	.50	.50
B70	SP21	1.50fr + 1fr car brn	.50	.50
B71	SP21	2.50fr + 2.50fr pur	5.50	4.75
B72	SP21	3fr + 3fr turq bl	6.00	4.75
B73	SP21	5fr + 5fr sepia	6.75	6.00
B74	SP21	10fr + 5fr rose lil	7.25	6.75
B75	SP21	20fr + 5fr ultra	8.75	7.75
		Nos. B61-B75 (15)	39.25	35.00

Saint Dévote SP36

Procession SP37

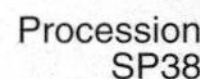

Procession SP38

Church of St. Dévote — SP39

Burning of Symbolic Boat — SP40

Blessing of the Sea SP41

Church of St. Dévote SP42

Trial of St. Barbara — SP43

Arrival of St. Dévote at Monaco — SP44

1944, Jan. 27 **Unwmk.** ***Perf. 13***

No.	Type	Description	Unused	Used
B76	SP36	50c + 50c sepia	.25	.25
B77	SP37	70c + 80c dp ultra	.25	.25
B78	SP38	80c + 70c green	.25	.25
B79	SP39	1fr + 1fr rose vio	.25	.25
B80	SP40	1.50fr + 1.50fr red	.45	.45
B81	SP41	2fr + 2fr brn vio	.85	.85
B82	SP42	5fr + 2fr violet	.85	.85
B83	SP43	10fr + 40fr royal bl	.85	.85
B84	SP44	20fr + 60fr chlky bl	6.00	6.00
		Nos. B76-B84 (9)	10.00	10.00

Issued in honor of St. Dévote.

Type SP43 is inscribed "Jugement de Sainte Dévote," but actually shows the trial of St. Barbara in 235 A.D.

Needy Child — SP45

Nurse and Child — SP46

1946, Feb. 18 **Engr.**

No.	Type	Description	Unused	Used
B85	SP45	1fr + 3fr dp bl grn	.35	.35
B86	SP45	2fr + 4fr rose pink	.35	.35
B87	SP45	4fr + 6fr dk bl	.35	.35
B88	SP45	5fr + 40fr dk vio	1.10	.90

B89	SP45	10fr + 60fr brn red	1.10	.90
B90	SP45	15fr + 100fr indigo	1.60	1.40
		Nos. B85-B90 (6)	4.85	4.25

The surtax was for child welfare.

1946, Feb. 18

B91	SP46	2fr + 8fr brt blue	.75	.70

The surtax was used for prevention of tuberculosis.

19th Century Steamer and Map SP47

1946

B92	SP47	3fr + 2fr deep blue	.50	.50

Stamp Day, June 23, 1946.

Harbor of Monte Carlo SP48

1946, Dec. 13

B93	SP48	2fr + 3fr dk bluish grn	1.40	1.40

Issued in tribute to the memory of Franklin D. Roosevelt. The surtax was for a fund to erect a monument in his honor.

Prince Louis II Type
Souvenir Sheet
Unwmk.

1947, May 15 Engr. *Imperf.*

B94	A46	200fr + 300fr dk red & choc	42.50	24.00

Prince Charles III — SP50

1948, Mar. 6 *Perf. 14x13*

B95	SP50	6fr + 4fr dk bl grn, *lt bl*	.55	.55

Issued for Stamp Day, Mar. 6.

Princess Charlotte SP51

Prince Rainier III SP52

Perf. 13½x13, Imperf.

1949, Dec. 27 Engr.

Cross Typo. in Red

B96	SP51	10fr + 5fr red brown	12.00	12.00
B97	SP52	15fr + 5fr brt red	12.00	12.00
B98	SP52	25fr + 5fr dk vio bl	12.00	12.00
B99	SP51	40fr + 5fr dull green	12.00	12.00
a.		Block of 4, #B96-B99	50.00	50.00

Printed in sheets measuring 151x173mm, perf. and imperf., containing 4 of No. B99a.
The surtax was for the Red Cross.
For surcharges see Nos. 288-291.

Hercules Strangling the Lion of Nemea — SP53

Twelve Labors of Hercules: No. B101, Killing the Hydra of Lerna. No. B102, Capturing the Erymanthean boar. No. B103, Killing Stymphalian birds. No. B104, Hercules and the Ceryneian Hind. No. B105, The Augean Stables. No. B106, Hercules and the Cretan Bull. No. B107, Wild horses of Diomedes. No. B108, Hercules and the Oxen of Geryon. No. B109, Hercules and the Belt of Hippolytus. No. B110, Winning the golden apple of Hesperides. No. B111, Battling Cerberus.

1981, Nov. 5 Engr. *Perf. 13*

B100	SP53	2.50fr + 50c multi	1.60	1.60
B101	SP53	3.50fr + 50c multi	1.60	1.60

1982, Nov. 8

B102	SP53	2.50fr + 50c multi	1.60	1.60
B103	SP53	3.50fr + 50c multi	1.60	1.60

1983, Nov. 9

B104	SP53	2.50fr + 50c multi	1.60	1.60
B105	SP53	3.50fr + 50c multi	1.60	1.60

1984, Nov. 8

B106	SP53	3fr + 50c multi	1.50	1.50
B107	SP53	4fr + 50c multi	1.90	1.90

1985, Nov. 7

B108	SP53	3fr + 70c multi	1.50	1.50
B109	SP53	4fr + 80c multi	1.90	1.90

1986, Oct. 28

B110	SP53	3fr + 70c multi	1.50	1.50
B111	SP53	4fr + 80c multi	1.90	1.90
		Nos. B100-B111 (12)	19.80	19.80

Surtax on #B100-B111 for the Red Cross.

Monegasque Committee to Fight Tuberculosis and Respiratory Diseases — SP54

1994, Mar. 14 Litho. *Perf. 13½x13*

B112	SP54	2.40fr +60c multi	1.25	1.25

AIR POST STAMPS

No. 91 Surcharged in Black

Perf. 14x13½

1933, Aug. 22 Unwmk.

C1	A15	1.50fr on 5fr	25.00	25.00
a.		Imperf., pair	375.00	

Catalogue values for unused stamps in this section, from this point to the end of the section, are for Never Hinged items.

Plane over Monaco — AP1

Plane Propeller and Buildings — AP2

Pegasus — AP3

Sea Gull — AP4

Plane, Globe and Arms of Monaco AP5

1942, Apr. 15 Engr. *Perf. 13*

C2	AP1	5fr blue green	.35	.35
C3	AP1	10fr ultra	.35	.35
C4	AP2	15fr sepia	.70	.70
C5	AP3	20fr henna brown	1.00	1.00
C6	AP4	50fr red violet	5.00	4.00
C7	AP5	100fr red & vio brn	5.00	4.00
		Nos. C2-C7 (6)	12.40	10.40

For surcharges see Nos. CB1-CB5.

Nos. 196-197 Overprinted in Blue

1946, May 20

C8	A41	50fr dp Prus green	4.75	4.25
C9	A41	100fr red	4.75	4.25
a.		Inverted overprint	*37,500.*	
b.		Double overprint	*22,500.*	

Douglas DC-3 and Arms AP6

1946, May 20

C10	AP6	40fr red	1.25	.60
C11	AP6	50fr red brown	2.00	.85
C12	AP6	100fr dp blue grn	3.00	1.60
C13	AP6	200fr violet	3.25	2.40
		Nos. C10-C13 (4)	9.50	5.45

Exist imperforate. See Nos. C27-C29.

Harbor of Monte Carlo AP7

Map of Monaco — AP8

1946, Dec. 13

C14	AP7	5fr carmine rose	.65	.65
C15	AP8	10fr violet black	.65	.65

Issued in tribute to the memory of Franklin D. Roosevelt.

Franklin D. Roosevelt Examining his Stamp Collection AP9

Main Post Office, New York City AP10

Oceanographic Museum, Monaco — AP11

Harbor of Monte Carlo — AP12

Statue of Liberty and New York City Skyline — AP13

1947, May 15 Unwmk.

C16	AP9	50c violet	1.25	1.25
C17	AP10	1.50fr rose violet	.55	.55
C18	AP11	3fr henna brown	.55	.55
C19	AP12	10fr deep blue	4.00	4.00
C20	AP13	15fr rose carmine	7.50	7.50
a.		Strip of 3, #C20, 203, C19	16.00	16.00
		Nos. C16-C20 (5)	13.85	13.85

Monaco's participation in the Centenary Intl. Philatelic Exhibition, NYC, May, 1947.

Crowd Acclaiming Constitution of 1911 AP14

Anthropological Museum — AP15

Designs: 25fr, Institute of Human Paleontology, Paris. 50fr, Albert I. 100fr, Oceanographic Institute, Paris. 200fr, Albert I medal.

1949, Mar. 5 **Engr.** ***Perf. 13***

C21 AP14 20fr brown red .75 .75
C22 AP14 25fr indigo .75 .75
C23 AP15 40fr blue green 2.00 2.00
C24 AP15 50fr blk, brn & grn 2.75 2.75
C25 AP15 100fr cerise 9.25 9.25
C26 AP14 200fr deep orange 15.00 15.00
Nos. C21-C26 (6) 30.50 30.50

Plane-Arms Type of 1946

1949, Mar. 10

C27 AP6 300fr dp ultra & ind 70.00 70.00
C28 AP6 500fr grnsh blk & bl grn 45.00 45.00
C29 AP6 1000fr black & red vio 75.00 70.00
Nos. C27-C29 (3) 190.00 185.00

UPU Type of Regular Issue

1949-50

C30 A56 25fr deep blue .65 .65
C31 A56 40fr red brown & sep 2.50 2.50
C32 A56 50fr dk green & ultra 4.00 4.00
C33 A56 100fr dk car & dk grn 6.00 6.00
Nos. C30-C33 (4) 13.15 13.15

75th anniv. of the UPU.

Nos. C30-C33 exist imperforate, also No. C30 in deep plum and violet, imperforate.

Issued: 25fr, 12/27; others, 9/12/50.

Rainier Type of Regular Issue

1950, Apr. 11 **Unwmk.**

C34 A57 50fr black & red brn 7.75 6.50
C35 A57 100fr red brn, sep & ind 11.00 10.50

Enthronement of Prince Rainier III.

Runner — AP18

Designs: 50fr, Fencing. 100fr, Target Shooting. 200fr, Olympic Torch.

1953, Feb. 23 ***Perf. 11***

C36 AP18 40fr black 12.00 9.00
C37 AP18 50fr brt purple 15.00 10.00
C38 AP18 100fr dk slate grn 20.00 15.00
C39 AP18 200fr deep carmine 26.00 16.00
Nos. C36-C39 (4) 73.00 50.00

Issued to publicize Monaco's participation in the Helsinki Olympic Games.

Dr. Albert Schweitzer and Ogowe River Scene, Gabon — AP19

1955, Jan. 14 ***Perf. 13***

C40 AP19 200fr multicolored 42.50 35.00

Dr. Albert Schweitzer, medical missionary.

Mediterranean Sea Swallows — AP20

Birds: 200fr, Sea gulls. 500fr, Albatross. 1000fr, Great cormorants.

1955-57 ***Perf. 11***

C41 AP20 100fr dp blue & indigo 30.00 13.50
a. Perf. 13 32.50 20.00
C42 AP20 200fr bl & blk 32.50 14.50
a. Perf. 13 350.00 175.00
C43 AP20 500fr gray & dk grn 47.50 32.50

Perf. 13

C44 AP20 1000fr dk bl grn & blk brn 100.00 67.50
a. Perf. 11 325.00 225.00
Nos. C41-C44 (4) 210.00 128.00

Issued: Perf. 11, 1/14/55; Perf. 13, 1957.

"From the Earth to the Moon" and Jules Verne — AP21

1955, June 7 **Unwmk.**

C45 AP21 200fr dp blue & slate 27.50 25.00

50th anniv. of the death of Jules Verne.

Wedding Type of Regular Issue

1956, Apr. 19 **Engr.**

Portraits in Brown

C46 A99 100fr purple 1.25 1.25
C47 A99 200fr carmine 1.60 1.60
C48 A99 500fr gray violet 3.75 3.75
Nos. C46-C48 (3) 6.60 6.60

Wedding of Prince Rainier III to Grace Kelly, Apr. 19, 1956.

Nos. J45 and J54 Surcharged and Overprinted "Poste Aerienne" and bars

1956, Apr. ***Perf. 11***

C49 D6 100fr on 20fr 10.50 10.50
a. Double surcharge *475.00*
C50 D7 100fr on 20fr 10.50 10.50
a. Double surcharge *475.00*
b. Pair, #C49, C50 22.50 22.50

See footnote after No. 390.

Basilica of Lourdes — AP23

200fr, Pope Pius X, underground basilica.

1958, May 15 **Unwmk.** ***Perf. 13***

C51 AP23 100fr dk bl, grn & gray 1.75 1.40
C52 AP23 200fr red brn & sepia 2.50 2.50

Centenary of the apparition of the Virgin Mary at Lourdes.

Prince Rainier III and Princess Grace — AP24

1959, May 16

C53 AP24 300fr dark purple 14.00 9.25
C54 AP24 500fr blue 20.00 16.00

St. Dévote AP25

1960, June 1 **Engr.** ***Perf. 13***

C55 AP25 2fr green, bl & vio 1.10 .75
C56 AP24 3fr dark purple 39.00 19.00
C57 AP24 5fr blue 39.00 27.50
C58 AP25 10fr green & brown 6.50 4.00
Nos. C55-C58 (4) 85.60 51.25

1961, June 3

C59 AP25 3fr ultra, grn & gray ol 2.10 1.10
C60 AP25 5fr rose carmine 4.50 2.10

Europa Issue, 1962

Mercury over Map of Europe AP26

1962, June 6 **Unwmk.** ***Perf. 13***

C61 AP26 2fr dk grn, sl grn & brn *2.00 1.00*

Oceanographic Museum, Atom Symbol and Princes Albert I and Rainier III — AP27

1962, June 6

C62 AP27 10fr violet, bl & bis 6.00 6.50

Establishment of a scientific research center by agreement with the Intl. Atomic Energy Commission.

Roland Garros AP28

1963, Dec. 12 **Engr.** ***Perf. 13***

C63 AP28 2fr dk blue & dk brn 1.25 1.25

50th anniversary of the first airplane crossing of the Mediterranean by Roland Garros (1888-1918).

Type of Regular Issue, 1964

Design: 5fr, Convair B-58 Hustler (New York-Paris in 3 hours, 19 minutes, 41 seconds, Maj. William R. Payne, USAF, 1961).

1964, May 22 **Unwmk.** ***Perf. 13***

C64 A151 5fr brown, blk & bl 2.75 2.75

1st airplane rally of Monte Carlo, 50th anniv.

Bobsledding — AP29

1964, Dec. 3 **Engr.** ***Perf. 13***

C65 AP29 5fr multicolored 2.75 2.75

9th Winter Olympic Games, Innsbruck, Austria, Jan. 29-Feb. 9, 1964.

ITU Type of Regular Issue

Design: 10fr, ITU Emblem and Monte Carlo television station on Mount Agel, vert.

1965, May 17 **Engr.** ***Perf. 13***

C66 A161 10fr bis brn, sl grn & bl 4.75 4.75

Princess Grace with Albert Alexander Louis, Caroline and Stephanie — AP30

1966, Feb. 1 **Engr.** ***Perf. 13***

C67 AP30 3fr pur, red brn & Prus bl 2.25 1.50

Birth of Princess Stephanie, Feb. 1, 1965.

Opera House Interior AP31

1966, June 1 **Engr.** ***Perf. 13***

C68 AP31 5fr Prus bl, bis & dk car rose 2.75 2.75

Centenary of founding of Monte Carlo.

Prince Rainier III and Princess Grace — AP32

1966-71 **Engr.** ***Perf. 13***

C69 AP32 2fr pink & slate 1.10 .40
C70 AP32 3fr emerald & slate 2.10 .80
C71 AP32 5fr lt blue & slate 2.75 1.10
C72 AP32 10fr lemon & sl ('67) 5.00 3.50
C72A AP32 20fr orange & brn ('71) 42.50 35.00
Nos. C69-C72A (5) 53.45 40.80

Issue dates: 10fr, Dec. 7, 1967; 20fr, Sept. 6, 1971. Others, Dec. 12, 1966.

Panhard-Phenix, 1895 — AP33

1967, Apr. 28 Engr. *Perf. 13*
C73 AP33 3fr Prus blue & blk 2.40 2.40

25th Grand Prix of Monaco.

Olympic Games Type of Regular Issue

1968, Apr. 29 Engr. *Perf. 13*
C74 A183 3fr Field hockey 1.75 1.75

Berlioz Monument, Monte Carlo — AP34

1969, Apr. 26 Engr. *Perf. 13*
C75 AP34 2fr green, blk & ultra 1.25 1.25

Hector Berlioz (1803-69), French composer.

Napoleon, by Paul Delaroche AP35

1969, Apr. 26 Photo. *Perf. 12x13*
C76 AP35 3fr multicolored 1.60 1.60

Bicentenary of birth of Napoleon I.

Horses, Prehistoric Drawing from Lascaux Cave — AP36

1970, Dec. 15 Engr. *Perf. 13*
C77 AP36 3fr multicolored 2.00 2.00

Nativity Type of Regular Issue

Design: 3fr, Nativity, Flemish School, 15th century, vert.

1973, Nov. 12 Engr. *Perf. 12x13*
C78 A243 3fr Prus green 2.25 1.75

Prince Rainier III — AP37

1974, Dec. 23 Engr. *Perf. 12½x13*
C81 AP37 10fr dark purple 6.75 3.00
C82 AP37 15fr henna brown 9.25 6.25
C83 AP37 20fr ultra 15.00 8.50
Nos. C81-C83 (3) 31.00 17.75

See Nos. 1994-1996.

Prince Rainier and Hereditary Prince Albert AP38

1982-84 Engr. *Perf. 13x13½*
C84 AP38 5fr deep violet 1.60 .60
C85 AP38 10fr red 5.00 1.10
C86 AP38 15fr dk blue grn 6.00 1.75
C87 AP38 20fr brt blue 7.00 2.25
C88 AP38 30fr brown ('84) 11.00 4.50
Nos. C84-C88 (5) 30.60 10.20

AIR POST SEMI-POSTAL STAMPS

Catalogue values for unused stamps in this section are for Never Hinged items.

Types of 1942 Air Post Stamps Surcharged with New Values and Bars

Unwmk.

1945, Mar. 27 Engr. *Perf. 13*
CB1 AP1 1fr + 4fr on 10fr rose red .60 .60
CB2 AP2 1fr + 4fr on 15fr red brown .60 .60
CB3 AP3 1fr + 4fr on 20fr sepia .60 .60
CB4 AP4 1fr + 4fr on 50fr ultra .60 .60
CB5 AP5 1fr + 4fr on 100fr bright red violet .60 .60
Nos. CB1-CB5 (5) 3.00 3.00

Surtax for the benefit of prisoners of war.

Franklin D. Roosevelt Type

1946, Dec. 13
CB6 A42 15fr + 10fr red 2.40 1.60

The surtax was for a fund to erect a monument in his honor.

1948 Olympic Type

1948, July
CB7 A48 5fr +5fr Rowing 11.00 11.00
CB8 A48 6fr +9fr Skiing 16.00 16.00
CB9 A48 10fr +15fr Tennis 22.50 22.50
CB10 A47 15fr +25fr Sailing 32.50 32.50
Nos. CB7-CB10 (4) 82.00 82.00

Salmacis Nymph SPAP4

Designs similar to regular issue.

1948, July
CB11 A50 5fr + 5fr blk bl 19.00 19.00
CB12 A51 6fr + 9fr dk grn 19.00 19.00
CB13 A52 10fr + 15fr crim 20.00 20.00
CB14 SPAP4 15fr + 25fr red brown 24.00 24.00
Nos. CB11-CB14 (4) 82.00 82.00

François J. Bosio (1769-1845), sculptor.

POSTAGE DUE STAMPS

D1

Prince Albert I — D2

Perf. 14x13½

1905-43 Unwmk. Typo.
J1 D1 1c olive green .45 .55
J2 D1 5c green .45 .55
J3 D1 10c rose .45 .55
J4 D1 10c brn ('09) 350.00 125.00
J5 D1 15c vio brn, *straw* 3.50 1.75
J6 D1 20c bis brn, *buff* ('26) .35 .35
J7 D1 30c blue .45 .55
J8 D1 40c red vio ('26) .35 .35
J9 D1 50c brn, *org* 4.50 4.00
J10 D1 50c blue grn ('27) .35 .35
J11 D1 60c gray blk ('26) .35 .65
J12 D1 60c brt vio ('34) 21.00 27.50
J13 D1 1fr red brn, *straw* ('26) .35 .25
J14 D1 2fr red org ('27) 1.00 1.50
J15 D1 3fr mag ('27) 1.00 1.50
J15A D1 5fr ultra ('43) .80 1.00
Nos. J1-J15A (16) 385.35 166.40

For surcharge see No. J27.

1910
J16 D2 1c olive green .25 .45
J17 D2 10c light violet .45 .60
J18 D2 30c bister 190.00 160.00

In January, 1917, regular postage stamps overprinted "T" in a triangle were used as postage due stamps.

Nos. J17 and J18 Surcharged

1918
J19 D2 20c on 10c lt vio 4.00 7.50
a. Double surcharge *1,000.*
J20 D2 40c on 30c bister 4.50 8.50

D3

1925-32
J21 D3 1c gray green .40 .50
J22 D3 10c violet .40 .55
J23 D3 30c bister .50 .75
J24 D3 60c red .70 .75
J25 D3 1fr lt bl ('32) 80.00 80.00
J26 D3 2fr dull red ('32) 80.00 80.00
Nos. J21-J26 (6) 162.00 162.55

Nos. J25 and J26 have the numerals of value double-lined.

"Recouvrements" stamps were used to recover charges due on undelivered or refused mail which was returned to the sender.

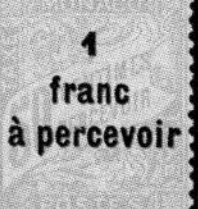

No. J9 Surcharged

1925
J27 D1 1fr on 50c brn, *org* .80 .55
a. Double surcharge *750.00*

Catalogue values for unused stamps in this section, from this point to the end of the section, are for Never Hinged items.

D4

D5

1946-57 Engr. *Perf. 14x13, 13*
J28 D4 10c sepia .20 .20
J29 D4 30c dark violet .20 .20
J30 D4 50c deep blue .20 .20
J31 D4 1fr dark green .20 .20
J32 D4 2fr yellow brn .20 .20
J33 D4 3fr brt red vio .30 .30
J34 D4 4fr carmine .45 .45
J35 D5 5fr chocolate .35 .35
J36 D5 10fr deep ultra .65 .65
J37 D5 20fr grnsh blue .70 .70
J38 D5 50fr red vio & red ('50) 55.00 55.00
J38A D5 100fr dk grn & red ('57) 12.00 12.00
Nos. J28-J38A (12) 70.45 70.45

Sailing Vessel — D6

S. S. United States — D7

Early Postal Transport (D6): 1fr, Carrier pigeons. 3fr, Old railroad engine. 4fr, Old monoplane. 5fr, Steam automobile. 10fr, daVinci's flying machine. 20fr, Balloon. 50fr, Post rider. 100fr, Old mail coach.

Modern Postal Transport (D7): 1fr, Sikorsky S-51 helicopter. 3fr, Modern locomotive. 4fr, Comet airliner. 5fr, Sabre sports car. 10fr, Rocket. 20fr, Graf Zeppelin. 50fr, Motorcyclist. 100fr, Railroad mail car.

1953-54 *Perf. 11*
J39 D6 1fr dk grn & brt red ('54) .20 .20
a. Pair, Nos. J39, J48 .20 .20
J40 D6 2fr dp ultra & bl grn .20 .20
a. Pair, Nos. J40, J49 .40 .40
J41 D6 3fr Prus grn & brn lake .20 .20
a. Pair, Nos. J41, J50 .40 .40
J42 D6 4fr dk brn & Prus grn .35 .35
a. Pair, Nos. J42, J51 .70 .70
J43 D6 5fr ultra & pur .85 .85
a. Pair, Nos. J43, J52 1.75 1.75
J44 D6 10fr dp ultra & dk bl 9.00 9.00
a. Pair, Nos. J44, J53 18.00 18.00
J45 D6 20fr indigo & pur 6.00 6.00
a. Pair, Nos. J45, J54 12.00 12.00
J46 D6 50fr red & dk brn 12.00 12.00
a. Pair, Nos. J46, J55 24.00 24.00
J47 D6 100fr vio brn & dp grn 20.00 20.00
a. Pair, Nos. J47, J56 40.00 40.00
J48 D7 1fr brt red & dk grn ('54) .20 .20
J49 D7 2fr bl grn & dp ultra .20 .20
J50 D7 3fr brn lake & Prus grn .20 .20
J51 D7 4fr Prus grn & dk brn .35 .35
J52 D7 5fr purple & ultra .85 .85

J53 D7 10fr dk bl & dp ultra 9.00 9.00
J54 D7 20fr purple & indigo 6.00 6.00
J55 D7 50fr dk brn & red 12.00 12.00
J56 D7 100fr dp grn & vio brn 20.00 20.00
Nos. J39-J56 (18) 97.60 97.60

Pairs se-tenant at the base.
For overprints see Nos. 371-390.

Felucca, 18th Century D8

2c, Paddle steamer La Palmaria, 19th cent. 5c, Arrival of 1st train. 10c, Armed messenger, 15th-16th cent. 20c, Monaco-Nice courier, 18th cent. 30c, "Charles III," 1866. 50c, Courier on horseback, 17th cent. 1fr, Diligence, 19th cent.

1960-69	**Engr.**	***Perf. 13***	
J57 D8	1c bl grn, bis brn & bl	.20	.20
J58 D8	2c sl grn, sep & ultra	.20	.20
J59 D8	5c grnsh bl, gray & red brn	.20	.20
J60 D8	10c vio bl, blk & grn	.20	.20
J61 D8	20c blue, brn & grn	.90	.90
J62 D8	30c brn, brt grn & brt bl ('69)	1.40	1.40
J63 D8	50c dk bl, brn & sl grn	1.90	1.90
J64 D8	1fr sl grn, bl & brn	2.50	2.50
	Nos. J57-J64 (8)	7.50	7.50

Knight in Armor D9

1980-83	**Engr.**	***Perf. 13***	
J65 D9	5c red & gray	.20	.20
J66 D9	10c salmon & red	.20	.20
J67 D9	15c violet & red	.20	.20
J68 D9	20c lt green & red	.20	.20
J69 D9	30c blue & red	.20	.20
J70 D9	40c lt brown & red	.35	.35
J71 D9	50c lilac & red	.45	.45
J72 D9	1fr black & blue	.70	.70
J73 D9	2fr dk brn & org ('82)	1.10	1.10
J74 D9	3fr sl bl & rose car ('83)	1.60	1.60
J75 D9	4fr red & dk grn ('82)	2.25	2.25
J76 D9	5fr magenta & brn ('83)	2.75	2.75
	Nos. J65-J76 (12)	10.20	10.20

Nos. J65-J76 printed in horizontal rows with princely coat of arms between stamps. Sold in strips of 3 only.

Issued: #J65-J72, 2/8; #J73, J75, 2/15; 3J74, J76, 1/3.

Natl. Coat of Arms — D10

1985-86	**Photo.**	***Perf. 13x12½***	
J77 D10	5c multicolored	.20	.20
J78 D10	10c multicolored	.20	.20
J79 D10	15c multicolored	.20	.20
J80 D10	20c multicolored	.20	.20
J81 D10	30c multicolored	.20	.20
J82 D10	40c multicolored	.20	.20
J83 D10	50c multicolored ('86)	.20	.20
J84 D10	1fr multicolored ('86)	.45	.45
J85 D10	2fr multicolored ('86)	.75	.75
J86 D10	3fr multicolored	1.25	1.25
J87 D10	4fr multicolored ('86)	1.60	1.60
J88 D10	5fr multicolored	2.25	2.25
	Nos. J77-J88 (12)	7.70	7.70

See Nos. 1608-1609.

MONGOLIA

män-ˈgōl-yə

(Mongolian People's Republic)

(Outer Mongolia)

LOCATION — Central Asia, bounded on the north by Siberia, on the west by Sinkiang, on the south and east by China proper and Manchuria
GOVT. — Republic
AREA — 604,250 sq. mi.
POP. — 2,617,379 (1999 est.)
CAPITAL — Ulan Bator

Outer Mongolia, which had long been under Russian influence although nominally a dependency of China, voted at a plebescite on October 20, 1945, to sever all ties with China and become an independent nation. See Tannu Tuva.

100 Cents = 1 Dollar
100 Mung = 1 Tugrik (1926)

Catalogue values for unused stamps in this country are for Never Hinged items, beginning with Scott 149 in the regular postage section, Scott B1 in the semi-postal section, Scott C1 in the airpost section, and Scott CB1 in the airpost semi-postal section.

Watermark

Wmk. 170 — Greek Border and Rosettes

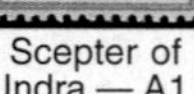

Scepter of Indra — A1

A2

1924 Litho. Unwmk. *Perf. 10, 13½*

Surface Tinted Paper

No.	Type	Denom.	Description	Unused	Used
1	A1	1c	multi, *bister*	4.50	4.50
2	A1	2c	multi, *brnsh*	5.50	3.75
a.			Perf. 13½	37.50	32.50
3	A1	5c	multi	27.50	22.50
a.			Perf. 10	37.50	32.50
4	A1	10c	multi, *gray bl*	10.00	7.75
a.			Perf. 10	20.00	13.00
5	A1	20c	multi, *gray*	20.00	11.00
6	A1	50c	multi, *salmon*	32.50	20.00
7	A1	$1	multi, *yellow*	50.00	30.00
b.			Perf. 10	650.00	190.00
			Nos. 1-7 (7)	150.00	99.50

These stamps vary in size from 19x25mm (1c) to 30x39mm ($1). They also differ in details of the design.

Errors of perforating and printing exist.

Some quantities of Nos. 1-2, 4-7 were defaced with horizontal perforation across the center.

The 5c exists perf 11½. Value, $325 unused, hinged, $190 used.

Revenue Stamps Handstamp Overprinted "POSTAGE" in Violet

Sizes: 1c to 20c: 22x36mm
50c, $1: 26x43½mm
$5: 30x45½mm

1926 ***Perf. 11***

No.	Type	Denom.	Description	Unused	Used
16	A2	1c	blue	11.00	11.00
17	A2	2c	orange	11.00	11.00
18	A2	5c	plum	15.00	13.00
19	A2	10c	green	20.00	17.00
20	A2	20c	yel brn	22.50	19.00
21	A2	50c	brn & ol grn	*190.00*	*175.00*
22	A2	$1	brn & salmon	*550.00*	*475.00*
23	A2	$5	red, yel & gray	*650.00*	—
			Nos. 16-23 (8)	*1,469.*	*721.00*

Black Overprint

No.	Type	Denom.	Description	Unused	Used
16a	A2	1c	blue	20.00	13.00
17a	A2	2c	orange	24.00	15.00
18a	A2	5c	plum	27.50	17.50
19a	A2	10c	green	37.50	20.00
20a	A2	20c	yellow brown	50.00	45.00
21a	A2	50c	brown & olive grn	*500.00*	*140.00*
22a	A2	$1	brown & salmon	*450.00*	*350.00*
23a	A2	$5	red, yellow & gray		
			Nos. 16a-22a (7)	*1,109.*	*600.50*

Red Overprint

No.	Type	Denom.	Description
16b	A2	1c	blue
17b	A2	2c	orange
18b	A2	5c	plum
19b	A2	10c	green
20b	A2	20c	yellow brown

The preceding handstamped overprints may be found inverted, double, etc. Counterfeits abound.

For overprints and surcharges see #48-61.

Yin Yang and other Symbols
A3 A4

TYPE I — The pearl above the crescent is solid. The devices in the middle of the stamp are not outlined.

TYPE II — The pearl is open. The devices and panels are all outlined in black.

1926-29 ***Perf. 11***

Type I

Size: 22x28mm

No.	Type	Denom.	Description	Unused	Used
32	A3	5m	lilac & blk	5.00	5.00
33	A3	20m	blue & blk	4.50	4.50

Type II

Size: 22x29mm

No.	Type	Denom.	Description	Unused	Used
34	A3	1m	yellow & blk	1.50	.90
35	A3	2m	brn org & blk	1.75	1.00
36	A3	5m	lilac & blk	2.75	1.50
37	A3	10m	lt blue & blk	1.75	1.25
a.			Imperf, pair		
39	A3	25m	yel grn & blk	4.50	1.90
a.			Imperf, pair	125.00	110.00

Size: 26x34mm

No.	Type	Denom.	Description	Unused	Used
40	A3	40m	lemon & blk	6.25	2.25
41	A3	50m	buff & blk	7.75	3.50

Size: 28x37mm

No.	Type	Denom.	Description	Unused	Used
42	A4	1t	brown, grn & blk	20.00	8.50
43	A4	3t	red, yel & blk	42.50	32.50
44	A4	5t	brn vio, rose & blk	65.00	52.50
			Nos. 32-44 (12)	163.25	115.30

In 1929 a change was made in the perforating machine. Every fourth pin was removed, which left the perforation holes in groups of three with blank spaces between the groups. Nos. 44A-44D have only this interrupted perforation. Nos. 37 and 39 are found with both perforations.

For overprints and surcharges see #45-47.

Yin Yang and other Symbols — A5

1929, July ***Interrupted Perf 11***

No.	Type	Denom.	Description	Unused	Used
44A	A5	5m	lilac & black	25.00	20.00
44B	A5	10m	lt grnish blue & black	100.00	65.00
a.			imperf, pair	—	
44C	A5	20m	blue & black	35.00	25.00
a.			imperf, pair	—	
b.			Horiz. pair, imperf btwn.		—
44D	A5	25m	yel grn & black	27.50	22.50
a.			imperf, pair	—	

See note after No. 44.

Nos. 34, 35, 40 Handstamped With New Values in Black

1930

No.	Type	Denom.	Description	Unused	Used
45	A3	10m	on 1m	32.50	30.00
46	A3	20m	on 2m	45.00	40.00
47	A3	25m	on 40m	50.00	45.00
			Nos. 45-47 (3)	127.50	115.00

Symbols of Government
A6 A7

Violet Overprint, Handstamped

1931

No.	Type	Denom.	Description	Unused	Used
48	A6	1c	blue	19.00	9.00
a.			Blue overprint	87.50	37.50
49	A6	2c	orange	20.00	6.50
50	A6	5c	brown vio	27.50	6.50
a.			Blue overprint	65.00	22.50
51	A6	10c	green	22.50	6.50
a.			Blue overprint	65.00	37.50
52	A6	20c	bister brn	35.00	9.25
53	A6	50c	brown & ol yel	—	—
54	A6	$1	brown & salmon	—	—
			Nos. 48-54 (5)	124.00	37.75

Revenue Stamps Surcharged in Black, Red or Blue

1931

No.	Type	Denom.	Description	Unused	Used
59	A7	5m	on 5c brn vio (Bk)	32.50	12.50
a.			Inverted surcharge		35.00
b.			Imperf., pair	225.00	225.00
60	A7	10m	on 10c green (R)	47.50	27.50
a.			Inverted surcharge	90.00	50.00
b.			Imperf., pair	225.00	225.00
61	A7	20m	on 20c bis brn (Bl)	60.00	35.00
a.			Inverted surcharge		55.00
b.			Imperf., pair	225.00	225.00
			Nos. 59-61 (3)	140.00	75.00

On Nos. 59-61, "Postage" is always diagonal, and may read up or down.

Weaver at Loom — A8

Telegrapher A9

Sukhe Bator A10

Lake and Mountains — A11

Designs: 5m, Mongol at lathe. 10m, Government building, Ulan Bator. 15m, Young Mongolian revolutionary. 20m, Studying Latin alphabet. 25m, Mongolian soldier. 50m, Monument to Sukhe Bator. 3t, Sheep shearing. 5t, Camel caravan. 10t, Chasing wild horses.

Perf. 12½x12

1932 Photo. Wmk. 170

No.	Type	Denom.	Description	Unused	Used
62	A8	1m	brown	2.00	1.25
63	A9	2m	red violet	2.00	1.25
64	A8	5m	indigo	1.00	.50
65	A8	10m	dull green	1.00	.50
66	A9	15m	dp brown	1.00	.50
67	A9	20m	rose red	1.50	.50
68	A9	25m	dull violet	1.50	.50
69	A10	40m	gray black	1.50	.50
70	A10	50m	dull blue	1.50	.50

Perf. 11x12

No.	Type	Denom.	Description	Unused	Used
71	A11	1t	dull green	1.50	.75
72	A11	3t	dull violet	4.50	1.50
73	A11	5t	brown	17.50	10.00
74	A11	10t	ultra	25.00	15.00
			Nos. 62-74 (13)	61.50	33.25

Used values are for c-t-o's.

Nos. 70-74 Handstamped With New Values in Black or Violet

1941

Black handstamp

No.	Type	Denom.	Description	Unused	Used
74A	A11	5m	on 5t	—	—
74B	A10	10m	on 50m	—	—
74C	A11	10m	on 10t	—	—
74D	A11	15m	on 5t	—	—
74E	A11	20m	on 1t	—	—
74F	A11	30m	on 3t	—	—

Violet handstamp

No.	Type	Denom.	Description	Unused	Used
74G	A11	5m	on 5t	—	—
74H	A11	15m	on 5t	—	—
74I	A11	20m	on 1t	—	—
74J	A11	30m	on 3t	—	—

Mongolian Man — A12

Mongolian Woman — A13

Soldier — A14

Camel Caravan A15

Modern School A16

Arms of the Republic — A17

Sukhe Bator — A18

Pasture Scene — A19

Paper with network as in italics

1943	**Typo.**	**Perf. 12½**	
75	A12 5m green, *green*	12.00	10.00
76	A13 10m dp blue, *lt bl*	20.00	11.00
77	A14 15m rose, *lt rose*	22.50	15.00
78	A15 20m org brn, *org*	32.50	27.50
79	A16 25m red brn, *buff*	32.50	32.50
80	A17 30m carmine, *red*	37.50	37.50
81	A18 45m purple, *mauve*	50.00	50.00
82	A19 60m dp green, *grn*	90.00	90.00
	Nos. 75-82 (8)	297.00	273.50

Marshal Kharloin Choibalsan — A21

1945	**Unwmk.**	**Perf. 12½**	
83	A21 1t black brown	60.00	30.00

Choibalsan A22

Victory Medal A24

Sukhe Bator and Choibalsan A23

Designs: #86, Choibalsan as young man. #87, Choibalsan University, Ulan Bator. 1t, Anniversary medal. 2t, Sukhe Bator.

1946, July	**Photo.**	**Perf. 12½**	
84	A22 30m olive bister	6.50	6.50
85	A23 50m dull purple	7.75	7.75
86	A24 60m black	8.00	8.00
87	A23 60m orange brown	14.00	14.00
88	A24 80m dk orange brn	12.50	12.50
89	A24 1t indigo	16.00	16.00
90	A24 2t deep brown	22.50	22.50
	Nos. 84-90 (7)	87.25	87.25

25th anniversary of independence.

New Housing A25

School Children — A26

Mongolian Arms and Flag — A27

Sukhe Bator — A28

Flags of Communist Countries — A29

Lenin — A30

Designs: 15m, Altai Hotel. No. 94, State Store. No. 95, Like 30m. 25m, University. 40m, National Theater. 50m, Pedagogical Institute. 60m, Sukhe Bator monument. Sizes of type A25: Nos. 91, 93-94, 98-99, 32½x22mm. 25m, 55x26mm.

1951, July			
91	A25 5m brn, *pink*	6.75	6.75
92	A26 10m dp bl, *pink*	8.25	8.25
93	A25 15m grn, *grnsh*	10.00	10.00
94	A25 20m red org	10.00	10.00
95	A27 20m dk bl & multi	10.00	10.00
96	A25 25m bl, *bluish*	10.00	10.00
97	A27 30m red & multi	10.00	10.00
98	A25 40m pur, *pink*	10.00	10.00
99	A25 50m brn, *grysh*	20.00	20.00
100	A28 60m brn blk	20.00	20.00
101	A29 1t multi	20.00	20.00
102	A28 2t dk brn & org brn	25.00	25.00
103	A30 3t multi	25.00	25.00
	Nos. 91-103 (13)	185.00	185.00

30th anniversary of independence.

Choibalsan — A31

Choibalsan and Farmer — A32

Choibalsan in uniform — A32a

Choibalsan and Sukhe Bator — A33

Designs: No. 108, 30m, Choibalsan and factory worker (47x33mm). 50m, Choibalsan and Young Pioneer. No. 112, 2t, Choibalsan in uniform.

1953, Dec.	**Photo.**	**Perf. 12½**	
104	A31 15m dull blue	5.00	5.00
105	A32 15m dull green	5.00	5.00
106	A31 20m dull green	10.00	10.00
107	A32 20m sepia	10.00	10.00
108	A32 20m violet blue	10.00	10.00
109	A32 30m dark brown	10.00	10.00
110	A33 50m orange brn	10.00	10.00
111	A33 1t carmine rose	10.00	10.00
112	A32a 1t sepia	15.00	15.00
113	A32a 2t red	15.00	15.00
114	A33 3t sepia	20.00	20.00
115	A33 5t red	40.00	40.00
	Nos. 104-115 (12)	160.00	160.00

First anniversary of death of Marshal Karloin Choibalsan (1895-1952).

Arms of Mongolia — A34

1954, Mar.	**Litho.**	**Perf. 12½**	
116	A34 10m carmine	12.00	7.00
117	A34 20m carmine	60.00	50.00
118	A34 30m carmine	12.00	8.00
119	A34 40m carmine	40.00	40.00
120	A34 60m carmine	12.00	10.00
	Nos. 116-120 (5)	136.00	115.00

Sukhe Bator and Choibalsan — A35

Lake Hubsugul A36

Guard with Dog — A37

#122, Lenin Statue, Ulan Bator. 50m, Choibalsan University. 1t, Arms and flag of Mongolia.

1955, June	**Photo.**	**Perf. 12½**	
121	A35 30m green	1.25	1.00
122	A35 30m orange ver	2.50	1.00
123	A36 30m brt blue	2.25	1.25
124	A37 40m dp red lilac	5.00	1.75
125	A36 50m ocher	5.00	2.25
126	A37 1t red & multi	9.00	7.00
	Nos. 121-126 (6)	25.00	14.25

35th anniversary of independence.

1955

Design: 2t, Lenin.

127	A35 2t bright blue	10.00	5.00

85th anniversary of birth of Lenin.

Flags of Communist Countries A38

Arms of Mongolia A39

1955

128	A38 60m blue & multi	5.00	4.00

Fight for peace.

1956	**Photo.**	**Perf. 12½**	
129	A39 20m dark brown	3.00	2.00
130	A39 30m dark olive	4.00	3.00
131	A39 40m bright blue	5.00	4.00
132	A39 60m blue green	6.00	4.50
133	A39 1t deep carmine	10.00	8.00
	Nos. 129-133 (5)	28.00	21.50

Kremlin, Moscow, Train and Sukhe Bator Monument A40

Design: 2t, Flags of Mongolia and USSR.

1956

134	A40 1t dk blue & multi	25.00	15.00
135	A40 2t red & multi	10.00	8.00

Establishment of railroad connection between Moscow and Ulan Bator.

Mongolian Arms and Flag — A41

Hunter with Golden Eagle — A42

Wrestlers A43

Designs: No. 138, 3 children (33x26½mm).

1956, July Typo. *Perf. 9*

136	A41	30m blue	10.00	5.00
137	A42	30m pale brown	50.00	50.00
138	A42	60m orange	20.00	20.00
139	A43	60m yellow green	20.00	20.00
		Nos. 136-139 (4)	100.00	95.00

35th anniversary of independence.

Types A41 and A43 without "XXXV"

1958

140	A41	20m red	5.00	3.00
141	A43	50m brown, *pink*	12.50	3.00

Nos. 140-143 were issued both with and without gum.

Poster — A44

Globe and Dove — A45

1958, Mar. Litho. *Perf. 9*

142	A44	30m maroon & salmon	5.00	4.00

13th Congress of Mongolian People's Party.

1958, May

143	A45	60m deep blue	5.00	4.00

4th Congress of International Democratic Women's Federation, Vienna, June, 1958. Nos. 142-143 exist imperf.

Yak — A46

No. 144, Pelicans, vert. No. 145, Siberian ibex, vert. No. 147, Yak. No. 148, Camels.

1958, July Typo. *Perf. 9*

144	A46	30m lt blue	25.00	5.00
145	A46	30m brt green	5.00	4.00
146	A46	60m orange	5.00	4.00
147	A46	1t blue	6.00	5.00
148	A46	1t rose	6.00	5.00
		Nos. 144-148 (5)	47.00	23.00

Shades exist.

Canceled to Order

Some quantity of all issues not printed by the State Printing Works, Ulan Bator, except Nos. 296-303, were canceled to order.

Used values are for c-t-o. Postally used specimens sell for considerably more.

Catalogue values for unused stamps in this section, from this point to the end of the section, are for Never Hinged items.

Stallion A47

Holy Flame (Tulaga) — A48

Designs: 5m, 40m, Goat. 10m, 30m, Ram. 15m, 60m, Stallion. 20m, 50m, Bull. 25m, 1t, Bactrian camel.

Perf. 10½x11½

1958, Nov. 11 Litho.

149	A47	5m yellow & brn	.25	.20
150	A47	10m lt grn & brn	.25	.20
151	A47	15m lilac & brn	.40	.20
152	A47	20m lt bl & brn	.40	.20
153	A47	25m rose & brn	.55	.20
154	A47	30m lilac & pur	.65	.20
155	A47	40m lt & dk green	.65	.20
156	A47	50m salmon & brn	.75	.25
157	A47	60m lt blue & ind	1.25	.35
158	A47	1t yellow & brn	3.00	1.00
		Nos. 149-158 (10)	8.15	3.00

1959, May 1 Litho. *Perf. 9*

159	A48	1t multi	5.00	2.00

See No. C36.

Archer — A49

Mongol Sports: 5m, Taming wild horse. 10m, Wrestlers. 15m, Horseback riding. 25m, Horse race. 30m, Archers. 70m, Hunting wild horse. 80m, Proclaiming a champion.

1959, June 6 Photo. *Perf. 11*

160	A49	5m multi	.25	.20
161	A49	10m multi	.25	.20
162	A49	15m multi	.25	.20
163	A49	20m multi	.40	.20
164	A49	25m multi	.50	.20
165	A49	30m multi	.50	.20
166	A49	70m multi	.75	.35
167	A49	80m multi	1.50	.75
		Nos. 160-167 (8)	4.40	2.30

Young Wrestlers A50

Youth Festival Emblem — A51

Designs: 5m, Young musician, horiz. 20m, Boy on horseback. 25m, Two opera singers. 40m, Young Pioneers with flags, horiz.

Photo.; Litho. (30m)

1959, July *Perf. 12, 11 (30m)*

168	A50	5m vio bl & rose car	.20	.20
169	A50	10m bl grn & brn	.30	.20
170	A50	20m claret & grn	.30	.20
171	A50	25m green & vio bl	.30	.20
172	A51	30m lil & lt bl	.50	.25
173	A50	40m green & pur	2.00	1.00
		Nos. 168-173 (6)	3.60	2.05

Mongolian Youth Festival.

The 30m was printed by State Printing Works, Ulan Bator.

Issue dates: 30m, July 11; others July 10.

"Mongol" in Stylized Uighur Script — A52

"Mongol" in Various Scripts: 40m, Soyombo. 50m, Kalmuck. 60m, Square (Pagspa). 1t, Cyrillic.

Printed by State Printing Works, Ulan Bator.

1959, Sept. 1 Litho. *Perf. 11*

Size: 29x42½mm

174	A52	30m black & multi	6.50	6.50
175	A52	40m black & multi	6.50	6.50
a.		Horiz. pair, imperf between and at right	*150.00*	
176	A52	50m black & multi	8.50	8.50
177	A52	60m black & multi	14.00	14.00

Size: 21x31mm

Perf. 9

178	A52	1t black & multi	17.50	17.50
		Nos. 174-178 (5)	53.00	53.00

1st Intl. Mongolian Language Congress.

Battle Emblem A53

Battle Monument A54

1959, Sept. 15 Photo. *Perf. 12½x12*

179	A53	40m yellow, brn & car	1.00	.50
180	A54	50m multicolored	1.00	.50

Ha-lo-hsin (Khalka) River Battle, 20th anniv.

Congress Emblem A55

Printed by State Printing Works, Ulan Bator.

1959, Dec. Litho. *Perf. 11*

181	A55	30m green	4.50	4.50

2nd meeting of rural economy cooperatives of Mongolia.

Sable — A56

Pheasants — A57

Perf. 15, 11x13

1959, Dec. 21 Photo.

182	A56	5m shown	.25	.20
183	A57	10m shown	.25	.20
184	A56	15m Muskrat	.25	.20
185	A57	20m Otter	.55	.20
186	A56	30m Argali	.55	.25
187	A57	50m Saigas	1.00	.35
188	A57	1t Musk deer	2.00	.75
		Nos. 182-188 (7)	4.85	2.15

Lunik 3 — A58

50m, Lunik 3 with path around moon, horiz.

1959, Dec. 30 Photo. *Perf. 12*

189	A58	30m violet & yel grn	1.00	.40
190	A58	50m red, dk bl & grn	1.50	.40

Lunik 3 Russian moon mission, Oct. 7, 1959.

Motherhood Badge — A59

Flower Emblem — A60

1960, Mar. 8 *Perf. 11, 12½x11½*

191	A59	40m blue & bister	1.00	.30
192	A60	50m blue, grn & yel	1.50	.50

International Women's Day.

Lenin — A61

Jacob's-ladder — A62

1960, Apr. 22 Photo. ***Perf. 11½x12***

193 A61 40m dk rose car 1.00 .30
194 A61 50m rose violet 1.25 .50

90th anniversary, birth of Lenin.

1960, May 31 ***Perf. 11½x12***

195 A62 5m Larkspur .25 .20
196 A62 10m Tulips .25 .20
197 A62 15m shown .25 .20
198 A62 20m Globeflowers .25 .20
199 A62 30m Bellflowers .35 .20
200 A62 40m Parnassia .75 .25
201 A62 50m Geranium 1.00 .50
202 A62 1t Begonia 1.50 1.00
Nos. 195-202 (8) 4.60 2.75

For overprints see Nos. 296-303.

Equestrian — A63

Running — A64

1960, Aug. 1 ***Perf. 15, 11***

203 A63 5m shown .20 .20
204 A64 10m shown .25 .20
205 A63 15m Diving .25 .20
206 A64 20m Wrestling .30 .20
207 A63 30m Hurdling .50 .20
208 A64 50m Gymnastics, women's .65 .30
209 A63 70m High jump 1.00 .50
210 A64 1t Discus, women's 1.25 .70
Nos. 203-210 (8) 4.40 2.50

17th Olympic Games, Rome, 8/25-9/11.

Red Cross A65

1960, Aug. 29 ***Perf. 11***

211 A65 20m blue, red & yel 1.00 .50

Newspaper "Unen" (Truth) — A66

1960, Dec. 19 ***Perf. 12x11½***

212 A66 20m red, yel & sl grn .75 .50
213 A66 30m grn, yel & red .75 .50

40th anniversary of Mongolian press.

Golden Orioles — A67

Songbirds: 5m, Rose-colored starling. 10m, Hoopoe. 20m, Black-billed capercaillie. 50m, Oriental broad-billed roller. 70m, Tibetan sandgrouse. 1t, Mandarin duck.
Triangle points down on 5m, 50m, 70m, 1t.

1961, Jan. 3 ***Perf. 11***

214 A67 5m multi .60 .20
215 A67 10m multi .85 .20
216 A67 15m multi 1.00 .20
217 A67 20m multi 1.40 .25
218 A67 50m multi 1.60 .50
219 A67 70m multi 2.00 .70
220 A67 1t multi 2.50 1.00
Nos. 214-220 (7) 9.95 3.05

Federation Emblem — A68

Design: 30m, Worker and emblem, vert.

Perf. 11½x12, 12x11½

1961, Jan. 29 **Photo.**

221 A68 30m dk gray & rose .50 .20
222 A68 50m ultra & red .75 .30

World Federation of Trade Unions, 15th anniv.

Patrice Lumumba (1925-1961), Premier of Congo — A69

1961, Apr. 8 ***Perf. 11½x12***

223 A69 30m brown 1.00 .50
224 A69 50m violet gray 2.00 .50

Bridge A70

Designs: 10m, Shoemaker. 15m, Department Store, Ulan Bator. 20m, Government building. 30m, State Theater, Ulan Bator. 50m, Machinist. 1t, Modern and old buildings.

1961, Apr. 30 ***Perf. 11½x12, 15***

Sizes: 31½x21mm, 59x20mm (20m)

225 A70 5m emerald .20 .20
226 A70 10m blue .20 .20
227 A70 15m rose red .25 .20
228 A70 20m brown .25 .20
229 A70 30m blue .35 .20
230 A70 50m olive green .50 .25
231 A70 1t violet 1.00 .35
Nos. 225-231 (7) 2.75 1.60

40th anniversary of independence; modernization of Mongolia.

Yuri Gagarin and Globe — A71

Designs: 20m, Gagarin with rocket, vert. 50m, Gagarin making parachute descent, vert. 1t, Gagarin wearing helmet, globe.

1961, May 31 ***Perf. 15***

232 A71 20m multi .60 .25
233 A71 30m multi .90 .40
234 A71 50m multi 1.00 .60
235 A71 1t multi 1.75 .80
Nos. 232-235 (4) 4.25 2.05

Yuri A. Gagarin, 1st man in space, 4/12/61.

Postman on Reindeer A72

15m, #241a, Postman on camel. 10m, 20m, Postman with yaks. 25m, #241c, Postman with ship. 30m, 50m, Diesel train.

1961, June 5 ***Perf. 15***

236 A72 5m multi .20 .20
237 A72 15m multi .25 .20
238 A72 20m multi .25 .20
239 A72 25m multi .25 .20
240 A72 30m multi 4.00 2.00
Nos. 236-240,C1-C3 (8) 6.95 3.60

Souvenir Sheet

Perf. 11

241 Sheet of 4 6.00 6.00
a. A72 5m light blue & brown 1.50 1.00
b. A72 10m green, brown & blue 1.50 1.00
c. A72 15m green, violet & brown 1.50 1.00
d. A72 50m violet, green & black 1.50 1.00

40th anniv. of independence; postal modernization. See No. C4b for 25m, perf. 11.

Souvenir Sheet

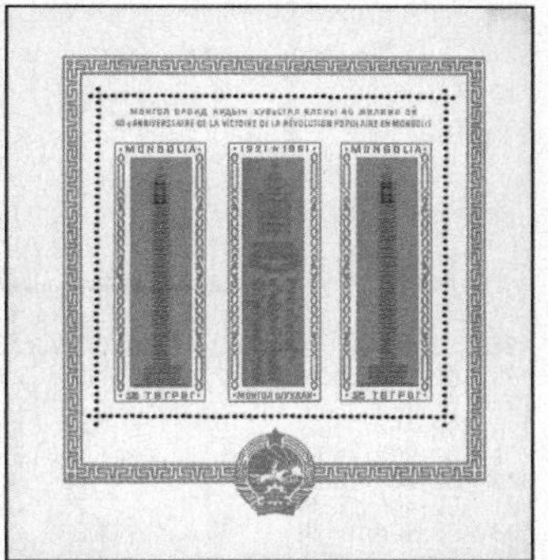

Ornamental Column — A73

1961, June 20 ***Perf. 12***

242 A73 Sheet of 2 + label 6.00 6.00
a. 2t blue, red & gold 2.75 2.00

40th anniversary of the Mongolian People's Revolution. No. 242 contains two No. 242a and label, imperf. between.

Herdsman and Oxen — A74

Designs: Herdsmen and domestic animals (except 1t and No. 252a).

1961, July 10 ***Perf. 13***

243 A74 5m Rams .20 .20
244 A74 10m shown .20 .20
245 A74 15m Camels .25 .20
246 A74 20m Pigs and geese .25 .20
247 A74 25m Angora goats .30 .25
248 A74 30m Horses .40 .25
249 A74 40m Sheep .50 .25
250 A74 50m Cows .75 .30
251 A74 1t Combine harvester 1.10 .75
Nos. 243-251 (9) 3.95 2.60

Souvenir Sheets

Perf. 12

252 Sheet of 3 2.50 2.50
a. A74 5m Combine harvester .75 .50
b. A74 15m Angora goats .75 .50
c. A74 40m Oxen .75 .50
253 Sheet of 3 2.50 2.50
a. A74 10m Pigs and geese .75 .50
b. A74 20m Horses .75 .50
c. A74 30m Cows .75 .50
254 Sheet of 3 3.00 3.00
a. A74 25m Camels .90 .75
b. A74 50m Rams .90 .75
c. A74 1t Sheep .90 .75

40th anniversary of independence. Nos. 252-254 each contain 3 stamps imperf. between.

Horseback Riders — A75

5m, Young wrestlers & instructor. 15m, Camel & pony riders. 20m, Falconers. 30m, Skier. 50m, Archers. 1t, Male dancers.

1961, Aug. 10 ***Perf. 11***

255 A75 5m multi .25 .20
256 A75 10m multi .25 .20
257 A75 15m multi .25 .20
258 A75 20m multi 1.10 .35
259 A75 30m multi .55 .45
260 A75 50m multi .65 .50
261 A75 1t multi 1.10 .70
Nos. 255-261 (7) 4.15 2.60

Independence, 4th anniv.; Mongolian youth sports.

Statue of Sukhe Bator — A76

Arms of Mongolia — A77

Designs: 5m, Mongol youth. 10m, Mongol chieftain. 20m, Singer. 30m, Dancer. 50m, Dombra player. 70m, Musicians. 1t, Gymnast. 5m, 10m, 70m, 1t, horiz.

Perf. 12x11½, 11½x12

1961, Sept. 16

262 A76 5m brt grn & red lil .20 .20
263 A76 10m red & dk bl .20 .20
264 A76 15m bl & lt brn .25 .20
265 A76 20m pur & brt grn .25 .20
266 A76 30m vio bl & car .35 .25
267 A76 50m ol & vio .65 .35
268 A76 70m brt lil rose & ol .80 .45
269 A76 1t dk bl & ver 1.50 .75
Nos. 262-269 (8) 4.20 2.60

40th anniv. of independence; Mongolian culture.

1961, Nov. 17 ***Perf. 11½x12***

270 A77 5m multi .40 .40
271 A77 10m multi .40 .40
272 A77 15m multi .40 .40
273 A77 20m multi .40 .40
274 A77 30m multi .50 .50
275 A77 50m multi 1.00 1.00

276	A77	70m multi	1.50	1.50
277	A77	1t multi	2.00	2.00
		Nos. 270-277 (8)	6.60	6.60

For surcharges see Nos. 2144A, 2302D.

Congress Emblem A78

1961, Dec. 4 Litho. *Perf. 11½*

278	A78	30m vio bl, yel & red	.40	.30
279	A78	50m brn, yel & red	.60	.50

5th World Congress of Trade Unions, Moscow, Dec. 4-16.

UN Emblem and Arms of Mongolia — A79

10m, Globe, map of Mongolia, dove. 50m, Flags of UN & Mongolia. 60m, UN Headquarters, New York. Parliament, Ulan Bator. 70m, UN assembly, UN & Mongolian flags.

1962, Mar. 15 Photo. *Perf. 11*

280	A79	10m gold & multi	.20	.20
281	A79	30m gold & multi	.30	.25
282	A79	50m gold & multi	.60	.45
283	A79	60m gold & multi	.75	.50
284	A79	70m gold & multi	.80	.60
		Nos. 280-284 (5)	2.65	2.00

Mongolia's admission to UN.

Soccer — A80

Designs: 10m, Soccer ball, globe and flags. 50m, Soccer players, globe and ball. 60m, Goalkeeper. 70m, Stadium.

1962, May 15 Litho. *Perf. 10½*

285	A80	10m multi	.70	.20
286	A80	30m multi	.70	.30
287	A80	50m multi	.70	.45
288	A80	60m multi	1.00	.50
289	A80	70m multi	1.40	.50
		Nos. 285-289 (5)	4.50	1.95

World Soccer Championship, Chile, 5/30-6/17.

D. Natsagdorji A81

Solidarity Emblem A82

1962, May 15 Photo. *Perf. 15x14½*

290	A81	30m brown	.40	.25
291	A81	50m bluish grn	.75	.50

Mongolian writers' congress.
For overprints see Nos. 430-431.

1962, May 22 Litho. *Perf. 11½x10½*

292	A82	20m yel grn & multi	.35	.20
293	A82	30m bl & multi	.60	.40

Afro-Asian Peoples' solidarity.

Flags of USSR and Mongolia — A83

Perf. 11½x10½

1962, June 25 Litho.

294	A83	30m brn & multi	.40	.20
295	A83	50m vio bl & multi	.75	.40

Mongol-Soviet friendship.

Nos. 195-202 Overprinted

1962, July 20 Photo. *Perf. 11½x12*

296	A62	5m multi	.35	.25
297	A62	10m multi	.35	.25
298	A62	15m multi	.45	.25
299	A62	20m multi	.45	.25
300	A62	30m multi	.60	.40
301	A62	40m multi	.75	.60
302	A62	50m multi	1.25	.90
303	A62	1t multi	2.00	1.25
		Nos. 296-303 (8)	6.20	4.15

WHO drive to eradicate malaria.

Military Field Emblem — A84

Designs: 30m, Tablets with inscriptions. 50m, Stone column. 60m, Genghis Khan.

1962, July 20 *Perf. 11½x12*

304	A84	20m blue & multi	7.50	7.50
305	A84	30m red & multi	7.50	7.50
306	A84	50m pink, brn & blk	15.00	15.00
307	A84	60m blue & multi	15.00	15.00
		Nos. 304-307 (4)	45.00	45.00

Genghis Khan (1162-1227), Mongol conqueror.

For overprints see Nos. 1846-1849. For surcharge, see No. 2378A.

River Perch — A85

1962, Dec. 28 *Perf. 11*

308	A85	5m shown	.20	.20
309	A85	10m Burbot	.20	.20
310	A85	15m Arctic grayling	.30	.20
311	A85	20m Shorthorn sculpin	.45	.25
312	A85	30m Marine zander	.65	.30
313	A85	50m Siberian sturgeon	.90	.45
314	A85	70m Waleck's chub minnow	1.25	.85
315	A85	1.50t Cottocomephorid	2.00	1.25
		Nos. 308-315 (8)	5.95	3.70

Sukhe Bator (1893-1923), National Hero — A86

1963, Feb. 2 Photo. *Perf. 11½x12*

316	A86	30m blue	.25	.20
317	A86	60m rose car	.60	.50

Laika and Rocket — A87

Designs: 15m, Rocket launching, vert. 25m, Lunik 2, vert. 70m, Andrian G. Nikolayev and Pavel R. Popovich. 1t, Mars rocket.

1963, Apr. 1 Litho. *Perf. 12½x12*

Size: 46x32mm

318	A87	5m multicolored	.20	.20

Size: 20x68mm

319	A87	15m multicolored	.25	.20
320	A87	25m multicolored	.40	.35

Size: 46x32mm

321	A87	70m multicolored	1.25	.80
322	A87	1t multicolored	1.60	1.10
		Nos. 318-322 (5)	3.70	2.65

Soviet space explorations.

Blood Transfusion — A88

1963, Aug. 15 *Perf. 10½*

323	A88	20m Packing Red Cross parcels	.30	.20
324	A88	30m shown	.50	.25
325	A88	50m Vaccination	.75	.40
326	A88	60m Ambulance service	1.00	.60
327	A88	1.30t Centenary emblem	1.50	.80
		Nos. 323-327 (5)	4.05	2.25

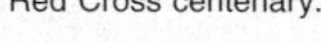

Red Cross centenary.

Karl Marx — A89

Mongolian Woman — A90

1963, Sept. 16 Photo. *Perf. 11½x12*

328	A89	30m blue	.35	.20
329	A89	60m dk car rose	.70	.50

145th anniversary of birth of Karl Marx.

1963, Sept. 26

330	A90	30m blue & multi	.50	.35

5th Intl. Women's Cong., Moscow, 6/24-29.

Inachis A91

Designs: Mongolian butterflies.

1963, Nov. 7 Litho. *Perf. 11½*

331	A91	5m shown	.50	.25
332	A91	10m Gonepteryxrhamni	.75	.40
333	A91	15m Aglais urticae	1.00	.50
334	A91	20m Parnassius apollo	1.25	.65
335	A91	30m Papilio machaon	1.75	.90
336	A91	60m Agrodiaetus damon	2.25	1.10
337	A91	1t Limenitis populi	3.00	1.50
		Nos. 331-337 (7)	10.50	5.30

UNESCO Emblem, Globe and Scales — A92

1963, Dec. 10 Photo. *Perf. 12*

338	A92	30m multicolored	.40	.20
339	A92	60m multicolored	.60	.40

Universal Declaration of Human Rights, 15th anniversary.

Coprinus Comatus — A93

Designs: Mushrooms.

1964, Jan. 1 Litho. *Perf. 10½*

340 A93 5m shown .50 .25
341 A93 10m Lactarius torminosus .75 .40
342 A93 15m Psalliota campestris .95 .50
343 A93 20m Russula delica 1.10 .55
344 A93 30m Ixocomus granulatus 1.25 .60
345 A93 50m Lactarius scrobiculatus 1.50 .75
346 A93 70m Lactarius deliciosus 1.75 .90
347 A93 1t Ixocomus variegatus 2.25 2.10
Nos. 340-347 (8) 10.05 6.05

Souvenir Sheet

Skier — A94

1964, Feb. 12 Photo. *Perf. 12x11½*

348 A94 4t gray 4.50 4.50

9th Winter Olympic Games, Innsbruck, Jan. 29-Feb. 9.

Lenin — A95

1964 Photo. *Perf. 11½x12*

349 A95 30m salmon & multi .75 .40
350 A95 50m blue & multi 1.00 .50

60th anniversary of Communist Party. Nos. 349-350 printed with alternating label showing Lenin quotation.

Javelin — A96

1964, Apr. 30 Litho. *Perf. 10½*

351 A96 5m Gymnastics, women's .20 .20
352 A96 10m shown .25 .20
353 A96 15m Wrestling .30 .20
354 A96 20m Running, women's .35 .25
355 A96 30m Equestrian .40 .30
356 A96 50m Diving, women's .75 .40
357 A96 60m Bicycling 1.00 .50
358 A96 1t Olympic Games emblem 1.25 .75
Nos. 351-358 (8) 4.50 2.80

Souvenir Sheet

Perf. 12x11½

359 A96 4t Wrestling 4.50 4.50

18th Olympic Games, Toyko, Oct. 10-25. No. 359 contains one horizontal stamp, 37x27½mm. Issued Sept. 1.

Congress Emblem — A97

1964, Sept. 30 Photo. *Perf. 11*

360 A97 30m multicolored .40 .30

4th Mongolian Women's Congress.

Lunik 1 — A98

Space Research: 10m, Vostok 1 and 2. 15m, Tiros weather satellite, vert. 20m, Cosmos circling earth, vert. 30m, Mars probe, vert. 60m, Luna 4, vert. 80m, Echo 2. 1t, Radar and rockets.

1964, Oct. 30

361 A98 5m multicolored .20 .20
362 A98 10m multicolored .20 .20
363 A98 15m multicolored .25 .20
364 A98 20m multicolored .35 .25
365 A98 30m multicolored .50 .35
366 A98 60m multicolored .65 .40
367 A98 80m multicolored .95 .45
368 A98 1t multicolored 1.25 .55
Nos. 361-368 (8) 4.35 2.60

Rider Carrying Flag — A99

1964, Nov. 26 Photo. *Perf. 11½x12*

369 A99 25m multicolored .40 .20
370 A99 50m multicolored .50 .40

40th anniversary of Mongolian constitution.

Weather Balloon A100

Designs: 5m, Oceanographic exploration. 60m, Northern lights and polar bears. 80m, Geomagnetism. 1t, I.Q.S.Y. emblem and Mercator map.

1965, May 15 Photo. *Perf. 13½*

371 A100 5m gray & multi .20 .20
372 A100 10m grn & multi .25 .30
373 A100 60m blue, blk & pink .85 .50
374 A100 80m citron & multi 1.00 .60
375 A100 1t brt green & multi 1.50 .90
Nos. 371-375,C6-C8 (8) 7.70 3.55

International Quiet Sun Year.

Horses — A101

Designs: Mares and Foals.

1965, Aug. 25 *Perf. 11*

376 A101 5m shown .20 .20
377 A101 10m Falconers .20 .20
378 A101 15m Taming wild horse .25 .20
379 A101 20m Horse race .35 .25
380 A101 30m Hurdles .50 .35
381 A101 60m Wolf hunt .65 .40
382 A101 80m Milking a mare .95 .45
383 A101 1t Mare and foal 1.25 .55
Nos. 376-383 (8) 4.35 2.60

Girl Holding Lambs — A102

1965, Oct. 10 Photo. *Perf. 11*

384 A102 5m shown .20 .20
385 A102 10m Boy and girl drummers .30 .20
386 A102 20m Camp fire .60 .20
387 A102 30m Wrestlers .90 .35
388 A102 50m Emblem 1.50 .90
Nos. 384-388 (5) 3.50 1.85

40th anniv. of Mongolian Youth Org.

Chinese Perch — A103

1965, Nov. 25

389 A103 5m shown .30 .20
390 A103 10m Lenok trout .35 .25
391 A103 15m Siberian sturgeon .40 .35
392 A103 20m Amur salmon .45 .40
393 A103 30m Bagrid catfish .55 .45
394 A103 60m Siluri catfish 1.00 .50
395 A103 80m Northern pike 1.40 .60
396 A103 1t River perch 2.00 .75
Nos. 389-396 (8) 6.45 3.50

Marx and Lenin — A104

1965, Dec. 15 *Perf. 11½x12*

397 A104 10m red & blk .35 .25

6th Conference of Postal Ministers of Communist Countries, Peking, June 21-July 15.

Sable — A105

1966, Feb. 15 Photo. *Perf. 12½*

398 A105 5m shown .40 .20
399 A105 10m Fox .40 .20
400 A105 15m Otter, vert. .40 .20
401 A105 20m Cheetah, vert. .40 .25
402 A105 30m Pallas's cat .40 .25
403 A105 60m Stone marten .75 .30
404 A105 80m Ermine, vert. 1.00 .40
405 A105 1t Woman in mink coat, vert. 1.25 .75
Nos. 398-405 (8) 5.00 2.55

Opening of WHO Headquarters, Geneva — A106

1966, May 3 Photo. *Perf. 12x11½*

406 A106 30m bl grn, bl & gold .40 .20
407 A106 50m red, bl & gold .60 .40

For overprints see Nos. 483-484.

Soccer — A107

Designs: 30m, 60m, 80m, Various soccer plays. 1t, British flag and World Soccer Cup emblem. 4t, Wembley Stadium, horiz.

1966, May 31 Photo. *Perf. 11*

408 A107 10m multicolored .20 .20
409 A107 30m multicolored .30 .25
410 A107 60m multicolored .40 .30
411 A107 80m multicolored .50 .40
412 A107 1t multicolored 1.10 .60
Nos. 408-412 (5) 2.50 1.75

Souvenir Sheet

Perf. 12½, Imperf.

413 A107 4t gray & brown 2.75 2.00

World Soccer Championship for Jules Rimet Cup, Wembley, England, July 11-30. No. 413 contains one stamp 61x83mm.

Sukhe Bator, Parliament Building, Ulan Bator — A108

1966, June 7 Litho. *Perf. 12x12½*

414 A108 30m red, bl & brn .40 .20

15th Congress of Mongolian Communist Party.

Wrestling A109

Designs: Various wrestling holds.

1966, June 15 Photo. *Perf. 11½x12*

No.	Type	Description	Unused	Used
415	A109	10m multicolored	.20	.20
416	A109	30m multicolored	.20	.20
417	A109	60m multicolored	.25	.20
418	A109	80m multicolored	.30	.20
419	A109	1t multicolored	.35	.20
		Nos. 415-419 (5)	1.30	1.00

World Wrestling Championship, Toledo, Spain.

Emblem and Map of Mongolia A110

Sukhe Bator, Grain and Factories A111

Perf. 11½x12, 12x11½

1966, July 11 Litho.

No.	Type	Description	Unused	Used
420	A110	30m red & multi	1.10	.80
421	A111	50m red & multi	2.75	1.00

45th anniversary of independence.
For overprints see Nos. 552-553.

Lilium Tenuifolium — A112

1966, Oct. 15 Photo. *Perf. 12x11½*

No.	Type	Description	Unused	Used
422	A112	5m Physochlaena physaloides	.20	.20
423	A112	10m Allium polyrrchizum	.30	.20
424	A112	15m shown	.40	.20
425	A112	20m Thermopsis lanceolata	.50	.20
426	A112	30m Amygdalus mongolica	.60	.30
427	A112	60m Caryopteris mongolica	.85	.40
428	A112	80m Piptanthus mongolicus	1.00	.55
429	A112	1t Iris bungei	1.25	.75
		Nos. 422-429 (8)	5.10	2.80

Nos. 290-291 Overprinted: "1906/1966"

1966, Oct. 26 Photo. *Perf. 15x14½*

No.	Type	Description	Unused	Used
430	A81	30m brown	10.00	10.00
431	A81	50m bluish grn	14.00	14.00

60th anniv. of birth of D. Natsagdorji, writer.
50m exists double, one inverted.

Child with Dove — A113

1966, Dec. 2 *Perf. 11½x12, 12x11½*

No.	Type	Description	Unused	Used
432	A113	10m shown	.25	.20
433	A113	15m Children with reindeer	.35	.20
434	A113	20m Boys wrestling, vert.	.40	.20
435	A113	30m Horseback riding	.45	.25
436	A113	60m Children riding camel, vert.	.70	.40
437	A113	80m Child with sheep	.95	.50
438	A113	1t Boy archer, vert.	1.25	.75
		Nos. 432-438 (7)	4.35	2.50

Children's Day.

Proton 1 — A114

Perf. 11½x12½, 12½x11½

1966, Dec. 28 Photo.

No.	Type	Description	Unused	Used
439	A114	5m Vostok 2, vert.	.20	.20
440	A114	10m shown	.20	.20
441	A114	15m Telstar 1, vert.	.25	.20
442	A114	20m Molnija 1, vert.	.40	.25
443	A114	30m Syncom 3, vert.	.50	.35
444	A114	60m Luna 9	.70	.20
445	A114	80m Luna 12, vert.	1.00	.40
446	A114	1t Mariner 4	1.25	.70
		Nos. 439-446 (8)	4.50	2.50

Space exploration.

Tarbosaurus — A115

1967, Mar. 31 *Perf. 12x11½*

No.	Type	Description	Unused	Used
447	A115	5m shown	.50	.25
448	A115	10m Talarurus	.55	.30
449	A115	15m Proceratops	.60	.35
450	A115	20m Indricotherium	.70	.40
451	A115	30m Saurolophus	1.00	.50
452	A115	60m Mastodon	2.00	.90
453	A115	80m Mongolotherium	2.25	1.00
454	A115	1t Mammoth	2.50	1.25
		Nos. 447-454 (8)	10.10	4.95

Prehistoric animals.

A116

A117

Congress emblem.

1967, June 9 Litho. *Perf. 12*

No.	Type	Description	Unused	Used
455	A116	30m lt blue & multi	.40	.20
456	A116	50m pink & multi	.60	.40

9th Youth Festival for Peace and Friendship, Sofia.

1967, Oct. 25 Litho. *Perf. 11½x12*

Design: 40m, Sukhe Bator and soldiers. 60m, Lenin and soldiers.

No.	Type	Description	Unused	Used
457	A117	40m red & multi	.50	.20
458	A117	60m red & multi	.80	.50

Russian October Revolution, 50th anniv.

Ice Hockey and Olympic Rings A118

1967, Dec. 29 *Perf. 12x12½*

No.	Type	Description	Unused	Used
459	A118	5m Figure skating	.20	.20
460	A118	10m Speed skating	.25	.20
461	A118	15m shown	.35	.20
462	A118	20m Ski jump	.45	.25
463	A118	30m Bobsledding	.75	.35
464	A118	60m Figure skating, pair	1.00	.50
465	A118	80m Slalom	1.50	.80
		Nos. 459-465 (7)	4.50	2.50

Souvenir Sheet

Perf. 12

No.	Type	Description	Unused	Used
466	A118	4t Women's figure skating	4.00	4.00

10th Winter Olympic Games, Grenoble, France, Feb. 6-18.

Bactrian Camels A119

1968, Jan. 15 Photo. *Perf. 12*

No.	Type	Description	Unused	Used
467	A119	5m shown	.20	.20
468	A119	10m Yak	.20	.20
469	A119	15m Lamb	.25	.20
470	A119	20m Foal	.40	.20
471	A119	30m Calf	.50	.25
472	A119	60m Bison	.65	.35
473	A119	80m Roe deer	.90	.40
474	A119	1t Reindeer	1.40	.70
		Nos. 467-474 (8)	4.50	2.50

Young animals.

Black Currants — A120

Berries: 5m, Rosa acicularis. 15m, Gooseberries. 20m, Malus. 30m, Strawberries. 60m, Ribes altissimum. 80m, Blueberries. 1t, Hippophae rhamnoides.

Lithographed & Engraved

1968, Feb. 15

No.	Type	Description	Unused	Used
475	A120	5m blue & ultra	.20	.20
476	A120	10m buff & brn	.20	.20
477	A120	15m lt grn & grn	.25	.20
478	A120	20m yel & red	.40	.20
479	A120	30m pink & car	.50	.25
480	A120	60m sal & org brn	.80	.35
481	A120	80m pale & dl bl	1.10	.40
482	A120	1t lt yel & red	1.20	.75
		Nos. 475-482 (8)	4.65	2.55

Nos. 406-407 Overprinted

1968, Apr. 16 Photo. *Perf. 12x11½*

No.	Type	Description	Unused	Used
483	A106	30m bl grn, bl & gold	6.50	6.50
484	A106	50m red, blue & gold	6.50	6.50

WHO, 20th anniversary.

Human Rights Flame — A121

1968, June 20 Litho. *Perf. 12*

No.	Type	Description	Unused	Used
485	A121	30m turq & vio bl	.50	.25

International Human Rights Year.

"Das Kapital," by Karl Marx A122

Design: 50m, Karl Marx.

1968, July 1 Litho. *Perf. 12*

No.	Type	Description	Unused	Used
486	A122	30m blue & multi	.40	.20
487	A122	50m red & multi	.60	.40

Karl Marx (1818-1883).

Artist, by A. Sangatzohyo — A123

Paintings: 10m, On Remote Roads, by Sangatzohyo. 15m, Camel calf, by B. Avarzad. 20m, Milk, by Avarzad. 30m, The Bowman, by B. Gombosuren. 80m, Girl Sitting on Yak, by Sangatzohyo. 1.40t, Cagan Dara Eke, by Janaivajara. 4t, Meeting, by Sangatzohyo, horiz.

1968, July 11 Litho. *Perf. 12*

No.	Type	Description	Unused	Used
488	A123	5m brown & multi	.25	.20
489	A123	10m brown & multi	.30	.20
490	A123	15m brown & multi	.35	.20
491	A123	20m brown & multi	.45	.40
492	A123	30m brown & multi	.65	.50
493	A123	80m brown & multi	1.25	.75
494	A123	1.40t brown & multi	2.25	1.40
		Nos. 488-494 (7)	5.50	3.65

Miniature Sheets

Perf. 11½, Imperf.

No.	Type	Description	Unused	Used
495	A123	4t brown & multi	5.50	5.50

Paintings from national museum, Ulan Bator. #495 contains one 54x84mm stamp.

Volleyball — A124

Olympic Rings and: 10m, Wrestling. 15m, Bicycling. 20m, Javelin, women's. 30m, Soccer. 60m, Running. 80m, Gymnastics, women's. 1t, Weight lifting. 4t, Equestrian.

1968, Sept. 1 Litho. *Perf. 12*

No.	Type	Description	Unused	Used
496	A124	5m multicolored	.20	.20
497	A124	10m multicolored	.20	.20
498	A124	15m multicolored	.20	.20

499 A124 20m multicolored .25 .20
500 A124 30m multicolored .40 .25
501 A124 60m multicolored .75 .35
502 A124 80m multicolored 1.00 .45
503 A124 1t multicolored 1.50 .65
Nos. 496-503 (8) 4.50 2.50

Souvenir Sheets

Perf. 11½, Imperf.

504 A124 4t orange & multi 4.00 4.00

19th Olympic Games, Mexico City, Oct. 12-27. #504 contains one 52x44mm stamp.

A125

A126

Hammer, spade & cogwheel.

1968, Sept. 17 Litho. *Perf. 11½*
505 A125 50m blue & vermilion .40 .20

Industrial development in town of Darhan.

1968, Nov. 6 Litho. *Perf. 12*
506 A126 60m turquoise & sepia .40 .25

Maxim Gorki (1868-1936), Russian writer.

Madonna and Child, by Boltraffio
A127

Paintings: 10m, St. Roch Healed by an Angel, by Brescia. 15m, Madonna and Child with St. Anne, by Macchietti. 20m, St. John on Patmos, by Cano. 30m, Lady with Viola da Gamba, by Kupetzky. 80m, Boy, by Amerling. 1.40t, Death of Adonis, by Furini. 4t, Portrait of a Lady, by Renoir.

1968, Nov. 20 Litho. *Perf. 12*
507 A127 5m gray & multi .25 .20
508 A127 10m gray & multi .30 .20
509 A127 15m gray & multi .40 .25
510 A127 20m gray & multi .50 .25
511 A127 30m gray & multi .60 .30
512 A127 80m gray & multi 1.00 .40
513 A127 1.40t gray & multi 1.50 .90
Nos. 507-513 (7) 4.55 2.50

Miniature Sheet

514 A127 4t gray & multi 4.50 4.50

UNESCO, 22nd anniv.

Jesse Owens, US — A128

Olympic Gold Medal Winners: 5m, Paavo Nurmi, Finland. 15m, Fanny Blankers-Koen, Netherlands. 20m, Laszlo Papp, Hungary. 30m, Wilma Rudolph, US. 60m, Boris Sahlin, USSR. 80m, Donald Schollander, US. 1t Akinori Nakayama, Japan. 4t, Jigjidin Munhbat, Mongolia.

1969, Mar. 25 Litho. *Perf. 12*
515 A128 5m multicolored .20 .20
516 A128 10m multicolored .20 .20
517 A128 15m multicolored .20 .20
518 A128 20m multicolored .25 .20
519 A128 30m multicolored .40 .25
520 A128 60m multicolored .75 .35
521 A128 80m multicolored 1.00 .45
522 A128 1t multicolored 1.50 .65
Nos. 515-522 (8) 4.50 2.50

Souvenir Sheet

523 A128 4t green & multi 4.50 4.50

Bayit Woman
A129

Regional Costumes: 10m, Torgut man. 15m, Dzakhachin woman. 20m, Khalkha woman. 30m, Dariganga woman. 60m, Mingat woman. 80m, Khalkha man. 1t, Bargut woman.

1969, Apr. 20 Litho. *Perf. 12*
524 A129 5m multicolored .25 .20
525 A129 10m multicolored .25 .20
526 A129 15m multicolored .30 .20
527 A129 20m multicolored .50 .20
528 A129 30m multicolored .60 .25
529 A129 60m multicolored .70 .25
530 A129 80m multicolored .90 .40
531 A129 1t multicolored 1.25 .75
Nos. 524-531 (8) 4.75 2.45

Red Cross Emblem and Helicopter — A130

50m, Emblem, Red Cross car, shepherd.

1969, May 15 Litho. *Perf. 12*
532 A130 30m multicolored 1.25 .30
533 A130 50m multicolored 1.25 .40

30th anniversary of Mongolian Red Cross.

Landscape and Edelweiss — A131

Mongolian landscapes and flowers.

1969, May 20
534 A131 5m shown .25 .20
535 A131 10m Pinks .25 .20
536 A131 15m Dianthus superbus .30 .20
537 A131 20m Geranium .50 .20
538 A131 30m Dianthus ramosissimus .60 .25
539 A131 60m Globeflowers .70 .25
540 A131 80m Delphinium .80 .40
541 A131 1t Haloxylon 1.25 .80
Nos. 534-541 (8) 4.65 2.50

See No. 1105.

Bull Fight, by Tsewegdjaw — A132

Paintings from National Museum: 10m, Fighting Colts, by O. Tsewegdjaw. 15m, Horseman and Herd, by A. Sangatzohyo. 20m, Camel Caravan, by D. Damdinsuren. 30m, On the Steppe, by N. Tsultem. 60m, Milking Mares, by Tsewegdjaw. 80m, Going to School, by B. Avarzad. 1t, After Work, by G. Odon. 4t, Horses, by Damdinsuren.

1969, July 11 Litho. *Perf. 12*
542 A132 5m multicolored .20 .20
543 A132 10m multicolored .20 .20
544 A132 15m multicolored .20 .20
545 A132 20m multicolored .50 .20
546 A132 30m multicolored .60 .25
547 A132 60m multicolored .75 .25
548 A132 80m multicolored .90 .40
549 A132 1t multicolored 1.25 .75
Nos. 542-549 (8) 4.60 2.45

Souvenir Sheet

550 A132 4t multicolored 4.50 4.50

10th anniversary of cooperative movement. No. 550 contains one stamp 65x42mm.

Mongolian Flag and Emblem
A133

1969, Sept. 20 Litho. *Perf. 11½*
551 A133 50m multicolored .50 .30

Battle of Ha-lo-hsin (Khalka) River, 30th anniversary.

For surcharge, see No. 2384A.

Nos. 420-421 Overprinted

Perf. 11½x12, 12x11½

1969, Nov. 26 Photo.
552 A110 30m red & multi *8.00 8.00*
553 A111 50m red & multi *10.00 10.00*

45th anniv. of Mongolian People's Republic.

Mercury 7 — A134

Designs: 5m, Sputnik 3. 10m, Vostok 1. 20m, Voskhod 2. 30m, Apollo 8. 60m, Soyuz 5. 80m, Apollo 12.

1969, Dec. 6 Photo. *Perf. 12x11½*
554 A134 5m multicolored .20 .20
555 A134 10m multicolored .20 .20
556 A134 15m multicolored .20 .20
557 A134 20m multicolored .20 .20
558 A134 30m multicolored .25 .20
559 A134 60m multicolored .40 .20
560 A134 80m multicolored .55 .20
Nos. 554-560 (7) 2.00 1.40

Souvenir Sheet

561 A134 4t multicolored 4.50 4.50

Space achievements of US and USSR.

Wolf — A135

Designs: 10m, Brown bear. 15m, Lynx. 20m, Wild boar. 30m, Moose. 60m, Bobac marmot. 80m, Argali. 1t, Old wall carpet showing hunter and dog.

1970, Mar. 25 Photo. *Perf. 12*
562 A135 5m multicolored .25 .20
563 A135 10m multicolored .25 .20
564 A135 15m multicolored .35 .20
565 A135 20m multicolored .40 .20
566 A135 30m multicolored .45 .25
567 A135 60m multicolored .75 .40
568 A135 80m multicolored 1.00 .60
569 A135 1t multicolored 1.25 .80
Nos. 562-569 (8) 4.70 2.85

Lenin and Mongolian Delegation, by Sangatzohyo — A136

Designs: 20m, Lenin, embroidered panel, by Cerenhuu, vert. 1t, Lenin, by Mazhig, vert.

1970, Apr. 22 Photo. & Litho.
570 A136 20m multicolored .40 .20
571 A136 50m multicolored .75 .25
572 A136 1t lt bl, blk & red 1.25 .50
Nos. 570-572 (3) 2.40 .95

Centenary of the birth of Lenin.

Souvenir Sheet

EXPO '70 Pavilion of Matsushita Electric Co. and Time Capsule — A137

1970, May 26 Photo. *Perf. 12½*
573 A137 4t gold & multi 4.50 4.50

EXPO '70 International Exposition, Osaka, Japan, Mar. 15-Sept. 13.

Sumitomo Fairy Tale Pavilion — A138

1970, June 5 Photo. *Perf. 12x11½*

574	A138	1.50t multi + label	1.00	1.00

EXPO '70 International Exposition, Osaka. No. 574 printed in sheets of 20 (5x4) with alternating horizontal rows of tabs showing various fairy tales and EXPO '70 emblem.

Soccer, Rimet Cup — A139

Soccer players of various teams in action.

1970, June 20 *Perf. 12½x11½*

575	A139	10m multi	.25	.20
576	A139	20m multi	.30	.20
577	A139	30m multi	.40	.25
578	A139	50m multi	.50	.25
579	A139	60m multi	.60	.30
580	A139	1t multi	1.00	.40
581	A139	1.30t multi	1.50	.90
		Nos. 575-581 (7)	4.55	2.50

Souvenir Sheet

Perf. 12½

582	A139	4t multi	3.50	3.50

World Soccer Championship for Jules Rimet Cup, Mexico City, May 30-June 21. No. 582 contains one stamp 51x37mm.

Old World Buzzard A140

Birds of Prey: 20m, Tawny owls. 30m, Northern goshawk. 50m, White-tailed sea eagle. 60m, Peregrine falcon. 1t, Old world kestrel. 1.30t, Black kite.

1970, June 30 Litho. *Perf. 12*

583	A140	10m bl & multi	.75	.25
584	A140	20m pink & multi	1.00	.30
585	A140	30m yel grn & multi	1.25	.50
586	A140	50m bl & multi	1.50	.75
587	A140	60m yel & multi	1.75	1.00
588	A140	1t grn & multi	2.25	1.25
589	A140	1.30t bl & multi	2.50	1.50
		Nos. 583-589 (7)	11.00	5.55

Russian War Memorial, Berlin — A141

1970, July 11 Litho. *Perf. 12*

590	A141	60m blue & multi	.75	.40

25th anniversary of end of World War II.

Bogdo-Gegen Palace — A142

Designs: 10m, Archer. 30m, Horseman. 40m, "White Mother" Goddess. 50m, Girl in national costume. 60m, Lion statue. 70m, Dancer's mask. 80m, Detail from Bogdo-Gegen Palace, Ulan Bator.

1970, Sept. 20 Litho. *Perf. 12*

591	A142	10m multi	.35	.25
592	A142	20m multi	.35	.25
593	A142	30m multi	.35	.25
594	A142	40m multi	.35	.30
595	A142	50m multi	.75	.65
596	A142	60m multi	.90	.75
597	A142	70m multi	1.00	.85
598	A142	80m multi	1.25	1.10
a.		Block of 4, #595-598		
		Nos. 591-598 (8)	5.30	4.40

Souvenir Sheet

Recovery of Apollo 13 Capsule — A143

1970, Nov. 1 Litho. *Perf. 12*

599	A143	4t blue & multi	4.50	4.50

Space missions of Apollo 13, Apr. 11-17, and Soyuz 9, June 1-10, 1970.

Mongolian Flag, UN and Education Year Emblems — A144

1970, Nov. 7

600	A144	60m multi	.80	.40

International Education Year.

Mounted Herald A145

1970, Nov. 7 Litho. *Perf. 12*

601	A145	30m gold & multi	.75	.40

50th anniv. of newspaper Unen (Truth).

Apollo 11 Lunar Landing Module — A146

Designs: 10m, Vostok 2 & 3. 20m, Voskhod 2, space walk. 30m, Gemini 6 & 7 capsules. 50m, Soyuz 4 & 5 docking in space. 60m, Soyuz 6, 7 & 8 group flight. 1t, Apollo 13 with damaged capsule. 1.30t, Luna 16 unmanned moon landing. 4t, Radar ground tracking station.

1971, Feb. 25 Litho. *Perf. 12*

602	A146	10m multi	.20	.20
603	A146	20m multi	.20	.20
604	A146	30m multi	.20	.20
605	A146	50m multi	.50	.20
606	A146	60m multi	.60	.25
607	A146	80m multi	.75	.25
608	A146	1t multi	.90	.40
609	A146	1.30t multi	1.25	.75
		Nos. 602-609 (8)	4.60	2.45

Souvenir Sheet

610	A146	4t vio bl & multi	4.00	4.00

US and USSR space explorations.

Rider with Mongolian Flag — A147

Designs: 30m, Party meeting. 90m, Lenin with Mongolian leader. 1.20t, Marchers, pictures of Lenin and Marx.

1971, Mar. 1 Photo. *Perf. 12½*

611	A147	30m gold & multi	.30	.20
612	A147	60m gold & multi	.40	.30
613	A147	90m gold & multi	.50	.40
614	A147	1.20t gold & multi	.60	.50
		Nos. 611-614 (4)	1.80	1.40

Mongolian Revolutionary Party, 50th anniv.

Souvenir Sheet

Lunokhod 1 on Moon — A148

Design: No. 615b, Apollo 14 on moon.

1971, Apr. 15 Photo. *Perf. 14*

615	A148	Sheet of 2	4.00	4.00
a.-b.		2t any single	1.75	1.75

Luna 17 unmanned automated moon mission, Nov. 10-17, 1970, and Apollo 14 moon landing, Jan. 31-Feb. 9, 1971.

Dancer's Mask A149

Designs: Various masks for dancers.

1971, Apr. 25 Litho. *Perf. 12*

616	A149	10m gold & multi	.20	.20
617	A149	20m gold & multi	.30	.20
618	A149	30m gold & multi	.50	.20
619	A149	50m gold & multi	.55	.25
620	A149	60m gold & multi	.60	.30
621	A149	1t gold & multi	1.10	.70
622	A149	1.30t gold & multi	1.40	1.00
		Nos. 616-622 (7)	4.65	2.85

Red Flag and Emblems A150

1971, May 31 Photo. *Perf. 12x11½*

623	A150	60m bl, red & gold	.40	.25

16th Congress of Mongolian Revolutionary Party.

Steam Locomotive — A151

1971, July 11 Litho. *Perf. 12*

624	A151	20m shown	.50	.20
625	A151	30m Diesel locomotive	.50	.20
626	A151	40m Truck	.65	.20
627	A151	50m Automobile	.75	.25
628	A151	60m Biplane PO-2	1.00	.35
629	A151	80m AN-24 plane	1.25	.60
630	A151	1t Fishing boat	1.75	1.00
		Nos. 624-630 (7)	6.40	2.80

50th anniversary of modern transportation. For overprints see Nos. 850A-850G.

Arms of Mongolia and Soldier — A152

Design: 1.50t, Arms, policeman and child.

1971, July 11 Litho. *Perf. 12*

631	A152	60m multi	.50	.20
632	A152	1.50t multi	.75	.40

50th anniversary of the people's army and police.

Mongolian Flag and Emblem — A153

1971, Aug. 25 Photo. ***Perf. 12x11½***
633 A153 60m lt bl & multi .40 .25

International Year Against Racial discrimination.

Flag of Youth Organization — A154

1971, Aug. 25 Litho. ***Perf. 12***
634 A154 60m org & multi .60 .30

50th anniversary of Mongolian revolutionary youth organization.

The Woodsman and the Tiger
A155

Designs: Various Mongolian fairy tales.

1971, Sept. 15 Litho. ***Perf. 12***
635 A155 10m gold & multi .20 .20
636 A155 20m gold & multi .20 .20
637 A155 30m gold & multi .30 .20
638 A155 50m gold & multi .40 .25
639 A155 60m gold & multi .60 .25
640 A155 80m gold & multi .80 .30
641 A155 1t gold & multi 1.00 .40
642 A155 1.30t gold & multi 1.25 .65
Nos. 635-642 (8) 4.75 2.45

Bactrian Camel — A156

1971, Nov. 1 Litho. ***Perf. 12½***
643 A156 20m Yaks .25 .20
644 A156 30m shown .25 .20
645 A156 40m Sheep .35 .25
646 A156 50m Goats .50 .25
647 A156 60m Cattle .75 .40
648 A156 80m Horses .85 .40
649 A156 1t White horse 1.40 .75
Nos. 643-649 (7) 4.35 2.45

Mongolian livestock breeding.

Cross-country Skiing — A157

Designs (Sapporo Olympic Emblem and): 20m, Bobsledding. 30m, Women's figure skating. 50m, Slalom. 60m, Speed skating. 80m, Downhill skiing. 1t, Ice hockey. 1.30t, Figure skating, pairs. 4t, Ski jump.

Perf. 12½x11½
1972, Jan. 20 Photo.
650 A157 10m multi .25 .20
651 A157 20m ol & multi .25 .20
652 A157 30m ultra & multi .35 .20
653 A157 50m brt bl & multi .45 .25
654 A157 60m multi .55 .25
655 A157 80m grn & multi .65 .25
656 A157 1t bl & multi .85 .35
657 A157 1.30t vio & multi 1.10 .60
Nos. 650-657 (8) 4.45 2.30

Souvenir Sheet
Perf. 12½
658 A157 4t lt bl & multi 4.00 4.00

11th Winter Olympic Games, Sapporo, Japan, Feb. 3-13.

Taming Wild Horse
A158

Paintings: 20m, Mythological animal in winter. 30m, Lancer on horseback. 50m, Athletes. 60m, Waterfall and horses. 80m, The Wise Musician, by Sarav. 1t, Young musician. 1.30t, Old sage with animals.

1972, Apr. 15 Litho. ***Perf. 12***
659 A158 10m multi .20 .20
660 A158 20m multi .20 .20
661 A158 30m multi .30 .20
662 A158 50m multi .40 .25
663 A158 60m multi .50 .25
664 A158 80m multi .80 .45
665 A158 1t multi .90 .45
666 A158 1.30t multi 1.25 .55
Nos. 659-666 (8) 4.55 2.55

Paintings by contemporary artists in Ulan Bator Museum.

Calosoma Fischeri
A159

Designs: Various insects.

1972, Apr. 30 Litho. ***Perf. 12***
667 A159 10m multi .20 .20
668 A159 20m multi .30 .20
669 A159 30m multi .40 .20
670 A159 50m multi .50 .25
671 A159 60m multi .70 .25
672 A159 80m multi 1.00 .50
673 A159 1t multi 1.25 .75
674 A159 1.30t multi 1.75 .95
Nos. 667-674 (8) 6.10 3.30

UN Emblem
A160

1972, Aug. 30 Photo. ***Perf. 12***
675 A160 60m multi .60 .40

ECAFE (UN Economic Commission for Asia and the Far East), 25th anniv.

Slow Lizard — A161

Designs: 15m, Radd's toad. 20m, Pallas's viper. 25m, Toad-headed agamid. 30m, Siberian wood frog. 60m, Przewalski's lizard. 80m, Taphrometopon lineolatum (snake). 1t, Stoliczka's agamid.

1972, Sept. 5 Litho. ***Perf. 12***
676 A161 10m multi .25 .20
677 A161 15m multi .30 .20
678 A161 20m multi .35 .20
679 A161 25m multi .50 .20
680 A161 30m multi .60 .25
681 A161 60m multi .75 .50
682 A161 80m multi 1.25 .75
683 A161 1t multi 1.50 1.10
Nos. 676-683 (8) 5.50 3.40

Symbols of Technical Knowledge — A162

Design: 60m, University of Mongolia.

1972, Sept. 25
684 A162 50m org & multi .55 .20
685 A162 60m lil & multi .75 .30

30th anniversary of Mongolian State University.

Virgin and Child with St. John, by Bellini — A163

Paintings by Venetian Masters: 20m, Transfiguration, by Bellini, vert. 30m, Virgin and Child, by Bellini, vert. 50m, Presentation in the Temple, by Bellini. 60m, St. George, by Mantegna, vert. 80m, Departure of St. Ursula, by Carpaccio, vert. 1t, Departure of St. Ursula, by Carpaccio.

1972, Oct. 1
686 A163 10m multi .25 .20
687 A163 20m multi .25 .20
688 A163 30m multi .45 .25
689 A163 50m multi .60 .25
690 A163 60m multi .90 .40
691 A163 80m multi 1.25 .80
692 A163 1t multi 1.40 1.00
Nos. 686-692 (7) 5.10 3.10

Save Venice campaign. See No. B3.

Manlay Bator Damdinsuren — A164

Designs: 20m, Ard Ayus, horiz. 50m, Hatan Bator Magsarzhav. 60m, Has Bator, horiz. 1t, Sukhe Bator.

1972, Oct. 20 Litho. ***Perf. 12***
693 A164 10m gold & multi .20 .20
694 A164 20m gold & multi .35 .30
695 A164 50m gold & multi .55 .40
696 A164 60m gold & multi .75 .50
697 A164 1t gold & multi 1.25 .60
Nos. 693-697 (5) 3.10 2.00

Paintings of national heroes.

Spasski Tower, Moscow — A165

1972, Nov. 7 Photo. ***Perf. 11***
698 A165 60m multi + label .75 .40

50th anniversary of USSR.

Mark Spitz, US, Gold Medal — A166

Designs (Medal and): 10m, Ulrike Meyfarth, Germany. 20m, Sawao Kato, Japan. 30m, András Balczó, Hungary. 60m, Lasse Viren, Finland. 80m, Shane Gould, Australia. 1t, Anatoli Bondarchuk, USSR. 4t, Khorloo Baianmunk, Mongolia.

1972, Dec. 15 Photo. ***Perf. 12½***
699 A166 5m grn & multi .20 .20
700 A166 10m ver & multi .25 .20
701 A166 20m bl & multi .40 .20
702 A166 30m multi .60 .25
703 A166 60m lt vio & multi 1.00 .25
704 A166 80m ol & multi 1.10 .40
705 A166 1t lem & multi 1.25 .60
Nos. 699-705 (7) 4.80 2.10

Souvenir Sheet
706 A166 4t red & multi 2.00 2.00

Winners in 20th Olympic Games, Munich.

Chimpanzee on Bicycle — A167

Circus Scenes: 10m, Seal playing ball. 15m, Bear riding wheel. 20m, Woman acrobat on camel. 30m, Woman equestrian. 50m, Clown playing flute. 60m, Woman gymnast. 1t, Circus building, Ulan Bator, horiz.

1973, Jan. 29 Litho. *Perf. 12*

707 A167 5m multi .20 .20
708 A167 10m multi .25 .20
709 A167 15m multi .35 .20
710 A167 20m multi .45 .20
711 A167 30m multi .55 .25
712 A167 50m multi .70 .35
713 A167 60m multi .90 .45
714 A167 1t multi 1.25 .75
Nos. 707-714 (8) 4.65 2.60

Postrider A168

Designs: 60m, Diesel locomotive. 1t, Truck.

1973, Jan. 31 Photo. *Perf. 12x11½*

715 A168 50m brown 1.00 .20
716 A168 60m green 3.50 .40
717 A168 1t rose claret 1.75 .60
Nos. 715-717,C34 (4) 7.05 1.40

For surcharges, see Nos. 2405-2407.

Sukhe Bator and Merchants A169

Paintings of Sukhe Bator: 20m, With elders. 50m, Leading partisans. 60m, With revolutionary council. 1t, Receiving deputation, horiz.

1973, Feb. 2 Photo. *Perf. 11½x12*

718 A169 10m gold & multi .20 .20
719 A169 20m gold & multi .30 .20
720 A169 50m gold & multi .70 .30
721 A169 60m gold & multi 1.00 .40
722 A169 1t gold & multi 1.50 .60
Nos. 718-722 (5) 3.70 1.70

Sukhe Bator (1893-1923).

Nicolaus Copernicus A170

Marx and Lenin — A171

Designs: 60m, 2t, Copernicus in laboratory, by Jan Matejko, horiz., 55x35mm. Nos. 725, 726b, Portrait. No. 726a, like 50m.

1973, Mar. Litho. *Perf. 12*

723 A170 50m gold & multi .50 .25
724 A170 60m gold & multi .70 .40
725 A170 1t gold & multi 1.25 .60
Nos. 723-725 (3) 2.45 1.25

Souvenir Sheet

726 Sheet of 3 4.00 3.00
a. A170 1t multi .60 .60
b. A170 1t multi .60 .60
c. A170 2t multi 1.50 1.50

500th anniversary of the birth of Nicolaus Copernicus (1473-1543), Polish astronomer.

1973, July 15 Photo. *Perf. 11½x12*

727 A171 60m gold, car & ultra .75 .40

9th meeting of postal administrations of socialist countries, Ulan Bator.

Common Shelducks — A172

Designs: Aquatic birds.

1973, Aug. 10 Litho. *Perf. 12x11*

728 A172 5m shown .40 .25
729 A172 10m Arctic loons .75 .25
730 A172 15m Bar-headed geese 1.25 .25
731 A172 30m Great crested grebe 1.50 .40
732 A172 50m Mallards 2.00 .60
733 A172 60m Mute swans 2.50 .80
734 A172 1t Greater scaups 2.75 1.25
Nos. 728-734 (7) 11.15 3.80

1973, Aug. 25 Litho. *Perf. 12x11*

Designs: Fur-bearing animals.

735 A172 5m Siberian weasel .25 .20
736 A172 10m Siberian chipmunk .25 .20
737 A172 15m Flying squirrel .30 .20
738 A172 20m Eurasian badger .40 .20
739 A172 30m Eurasian red squirrel .60 .25
740 A172 60m Wolverine 1.00 .50
741 A172 80m Mink 1.25 .70
742 A172 1t White hare 1.60 .90
Nos. 735-742 (8) 5.65 3.15

1973, Dec. 15 Litho. *Perf. 12x11*

Designs: Flowers.

743 A172 5m Alpine aster .25 .20
744 A172 10m Mongolian silene .25 .20
745 A172 15m Rosa davurica .30 .20
746 A172 20m Mongolian dandelion .40 .20
747 A172 30m Rhododendron dahuricum .60 .25
748 A172 50m Clematis tangutica 1.00 .50
749 A172 60m Siberian primula 1.25 .70
750 A172 1t Pasqueflower 1.60 .90
Nos. 743-750 (8) 5.65 3.15

Globe and Red Flag Emblem — A173

1973, Dec. 10 Photo. *Perf. 12x12½*

751 A173 60m gold, red & blue .60 .30

15th anniversary of the review "Problems of Peace and Socialism," published in Prague.

Limenitis Populi A174

Butterflies: 10m, Arctia hebe. 15m, Rhyparia purpurata. 20m, Catocala pacta. 30m, Isoceras kaszabi. 50m, Celerio costata. 60m, Arctia caja. 1t, Diacrisia sannio.

1974, Jan. 15 Litho. *Perf. 11*

752 A174 5m lil & multi .50 .25
753 A174 10m brn & multi .60 .25
754 A174 15m bl & multi .75 .25
755 A174 20m brn org & multi .90 .25
756 A174 30m lt vio & multi 1.10 .30
757 A174 50m dl red & multi 1.50 .60
758 A174 60m yel grn & multi 1.75 .90
759 A174 1t ultra & multi 2.50 1.25
Nos. 752-759 (8) 9.60 4.05

"Hehe Namshil" by L. Merdorsh A175

Designs (Various Scenes from): 20m, "Sive Hiagt," by D. Luvsansharav. 25m, 80m, 1t, "Edre," by D. Namdag. 30m, "The 3 Khans of Sara-Gol" (legend). 60m, "Amarsana," by B. Damdinsuren. 20m and 30m horizontal.

1974, Feb. 20 Litho. *Perf. 12*

760 A175 15m sil & multi .25 .20
761 A175 20m sil & multi .35 .25
762 A175 25m sil & multi .50 .25
763 A175 30m sil & multi .60 .30
764 A175 60m sil & multi .70 .30
765 A175 80m sil & multi .95 .40
766 A175 1t sil & multi 1.25 .80
Nos. 760-766 (7) 4.60 2.50

Mongolian operas and dramas.

Government Building and Sukhe Bator — A176

1974, Mar. 1 Photo. *Perf. 11*

767 A176 60m gold & multi .75 .40

50th anniv. of renaming capital Ulan Bator.

Juggler A177

10m, Circus horses, horiz. 30m, Trained elephant. 40m, Yak pushing ball, horiz. 60m, Acrobats with ring. 80m, Woman acrobat on unicycle.

1974, May 4 Litho. *Perf. 12*

768 A177 10m multi .25 .20
769 A177 20m multi .40 .20
770 A177 30m multi .50 .30
771 A177 40m multi .80 .40
772 A177 60m multi 1.00 .50
773 A177 80m multi 1.60 .75
Nos. 768-773,C65 (7) 5.55 2.85

Mongolian Circus. No. 773 has se-tenant label, with similar design.

Girl on Bronco — A178

Children's Activities: 20m, Boy roping calf. 30m, 40m, Boy taming horse (different designs). 60m, Girl with doves. 80m, Wrestling. 1t, Dancing.

1974, June 2 Litho. *Perf. 12*

774 A178 10m dl yel & multi .20 .20
775 A178 20m lt bl & multi .25 .20
776 A178 30m grn & multi .35 .20
777 A178 40m yel & multi .50 .30
778 A178 60m pink & multi .75 .30
779 A178 80m bl & multi .95 .50
780 A178 1t dl bl & multi 1.50 .75
Nos. 774-780 (7) 4.50 2.45

Children's Day.

Archer — A179

National Sports: 20m, Two horsemen fighting for goatskin. 30m, Archer on horseback. 40m, Horse race. 60m, Riding wild horse. 80m, Rider chasing riderless horse. 1t, Boys wrestling.

1974, July 11 Photo. *Perf. 11*

781 A179 10m vio bl & multi .20 .20
782 A179 20m yel & multi .25 .20
783 A179 30m lil & multi .35 .20
784 A179 40m multi .50 .30
785 A179 60m multi .75 .30
786 A179 80m multi .95 .50
787 A179 1t multi 1.50 .75
Nos. 781-787 (7) 4.50 2.45

Nadom, Mongolian national festival.

Grizzly Bear A180

1974, July Litho. *Perf. 12*

788 A180 10m shown .25 .25
789 A180 20m Common panda .30 .25
790 A180 30m Giant panda .35 .25
791 A180 40m Two brown bears .50 .35
792 A180 60m Sloth bear .75 .35
793 A180 80m Asiatic black bears 1.00 .50
794 A180 1t Giant brown bear 1.50 .75
Nos. 788-794 (7) 4.65 2.70

Stag in Zuun Araat Wildlife Preserve — A181

1974, Sept. Litho. *Perf. 12*

795 A181 10m shown .25 .25
796 A181 20m Beaver .30 .25
797 A181 30m Leopard .35 .25
798 A181 40m Great black-backed gull .50 .35
799 A181 60m Deer .75 .35
800 A181 80m Mouflon 1.00 .50
801 A181 1t Deer and entrance to Bogd-uul Preserve 1.50 .75
Nos. 795-801 (7) 4.65 2.70

Protected fauna in Mongolian wildlife preserves.

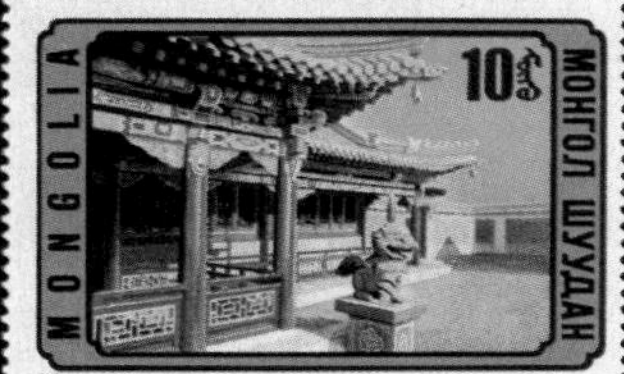

Buddhist Temple, Bogdo Gegen Palace — A182

Mongolian Architecture: 15m, Buddhist Temple, now Museum. 30m, Entrance to Charity Temple, Ulan Bator. 50m, Mongolian yurta. 80m, Gazebo in convent yard.

1974, Oct. 15 Litho. *Perf. 12*

802 A182 10m bl & multi .30 .20
803 A182 15m multi .35 .20
804 A182 30m grn & multi .45 .30
805 A182 50m multi .60 .40
806 A182 80m yel & multi 1.00 .50
Nos. 802-806 (5) 2.70 1.60

Spasski Tower, Sukhe Bator Statue A183

1974, Nov. 26 Photo. *Perf. 11½x12*

807 A183 60m multi .75 .40

Visit of General Secretary Brezhnev and a delegation from the USSR to participate in celebration of 50th anniversary of People's Republic of Mongolia.

Sukhe Bator Proclaiming Republic A184

Designs: No. 808, "First Constitution," symbolic embroidery. No. 809, Flag over landscape, plane and communications tower.

1974, Nov. 28 Litho.

808 A184 60m multi .75 .40
809 A184 60m multi .75 .40
810 A184 60m multi .75 .40
Nos. 808-810 (3) 2.25 1.20

50th anniv. of People's Republic of Mongolia.

Decanter A185

Designs: 20m, Silver jar. 30m, Night lamp. 40m, Tea jug. 60m, Candelabra. 80m, Teapot. 1t, Silver bowl on 3-legged stand.

1974, Dec. 1 Photo.

811 A185 10m blue & multi .25 .25
812 A185 20m claret & multi .30 .25
813 A185 30m multi .35 .25
814 A185 40m dp bl & multi .50 .35
815 A185 60m multi .75 .35
816 A185 80m grn & multi 1.00 .50
817 A185 1t lilac & multi 1.50 .75
Nos. 811-817 (7) 4.65 2.70

Mongolian 19th century goldsmiths' work.

Lapwing (plover) — A186

1974, Dec. Litho. *Perf. 11*

818 A186 10m shown .60 .25
819 A186 20m Fish .70 .25
820 A186 30m Marsh marigolds .90 .30
821 A186 40m White pelican 1.00 .30
822 A186 60m Perch 1.10 .50
823 A186 80m Mink 1.25 .75
Nos. 818-823,C66 (7) 6.55 2.85

Water and nature protection.

American Mail Coach, UPU Emblem — A187

Designs (UPU Emblem and): 20m, French two-wheeled coach. 30m, Changing horses, Russian coach. 40m, Swedish caterpillar mail truck. 50m, First Hungarian mail truck. 60m, German Daimler-Benz mail truck. 1t, Mongolian dispatch rider.

1974, Dec. Litho. *Perf. 12*

824 A187 10m multi .25 .20
825 A187 20m multi .30 .20
826 A187 30m multi .35 .25
827 A187 40m multi .50 .35
828 A187 50m multi .75 .45
829 A187 60m multi 1.00 .60
830 A187 1t multi 1.50 .80
Nos. 824-830 (7) 4.65 2.85

Cent. of the UPU and Stockholmia 74.

Soviet Flag, Broken Swastika A188

1975, May 9 Photo. *Perf. 11½x12*

832 A188 60m multi .75 .40

30th anniversary of the end of World War II and victory over fascism.

Mongolian Woman A189

1975, May

833 A189 60m multi .75 .45

International Women's Year 1975.

Zygophyllum Xanthoxylon — A190

Medicinal Plants: 20m, Ingarvillea potaninii. 30m, Lancea tibetica. 40m, Jurinea mongolica. 50m, Saussurea involucrata. 60m, Allium mongolicum. 1t, Adonis mongolica.

1975, May 24 Photo. *Perf. 11x11½*

834 A190 10m dp org & multi .25 .20
835 A190 20m grn & multi .40 .20
836 A190 30m yel & multi .60 .25
837 A190 40m vio & multi .75 .35
838 A190 50m brn & multi .85 .60
839 A190 60m bl & multi 1.10 .90
840 A190 1t multi 1.75 1.25
Nos. 834-840 (7) 5.70 3.75

12th International Botanists' Conference.

Shepherd — A191

Puppet Theater: 20m, Boy on horseback. 30m, Boy and disobedient bull calf. 40m, Little orphan camel's tale. 50m, Boy and obedient little yak. 60m, Boy riding swan. 1t, Children's choir.

1975, June 30 Litho. *Perf. 12*

841 A191 10m multi .25 .20
842 A191 20m multi .30 .20
843 A191 30m multi .35 .30
844 A191 40m multi .50 .30
845 A191 50m multi .75 .40
846 A191 60m multi 1.00 .50
847 A191 1t multi 1.50 .75
Nos. 841-847 (7) 4.65 2.65

Pioneers Tending Fruit Tree — A192

60m, Pioneers studying, and flying model plane. 1t, New emblem of Mongolian Pioneers.

1975, July 15 *Perf. 12x11½*

848 A192 50m multi .60 .30
849 A192 60m multi .85 .30
850 A192 1t multi 1.00 .60
Nos. 848-850 (3) 2.45 1.20

Mongolian Pioneers, 50th anniversary.

Nos. 624-630 Overprinted

1975, July 15 Litho. *Perf. 12*

850A	A151 20m multi		5.00	5.00
850B	A151 30m multi		5.00	5.00
850C	A151 40m multi		4.00	4.00
850D	A151 50m multi		4.00	4.00
850E	A151 60m multi		5.00	5.00
850F	A151 80m multi		5.00	5.00
850G	A151 1t multi		6.00	6.00
	Nos. 850A-850G (7)		34.00	34.00

Fifty years of communication.

Golden Eagle Hunting Fox — A193

Hunting Scenes: 20m, Dogs treeing lynx, vert. 30m, Hunter stalking marmots. 40m, Hunter riding reindeer, vert. 50m, Boar hunt. 60m, Trapped wolf, vert. 1t, Bear hunt.

1975, Aug. 25 Litho. *Perf. 12*

851	A193 10m multi	.50	.20
852	A193 20m multi	.60	.25
853	A193 30m multi	.70	.30
854	A193 40m multi	.80	.40
855	A193 50m multi	.90	.50
856	A193 60m multi	1.00	.70
857	A193 1t multi	1.10	.90
	Nos. 851-857 (7)	5.60	3.25

Hunting in Mongolia.

Mesocottus Haitej — A194

Various Fish: 20m, Pseudaspius lepto cephalus. 30m, Oreoleuciscus potanini. 40m, Tinca tinca. 50m, Coregonus lavaretus pidschian. 60m, Erythroculter mongolicus. 1t, Carassius auratus.

1975, Sept. 15 Photo. *Perf. 11*

858	A194 10m multi	.25	.20
859	A194 20m multi	.35	.20
860	A194 30m multi	.50	.30
861	A194 40m bl & multi	.75	.30
862	A194 50m grn & multi	.90	.40
863	A194 60m lil & multi	1.00	.70
864	A194 1t vio bl & multi	1.75	.90
	Nos. 858-864 (7)	5.50	3.00

Neck and Bow of Musical Instrument (Morin Hur) — A195

National Handicraft: 20m, Saddle. 30m, Silver headgear. 40m, Boots. 50m, Tasseled Woman's cap. 60m, Pipe and tobacco pouch. 1t, Sable cap.

1975, Oct. 10 Litho. *Perf. 11½x12½*

865	A195 10m multi	.20	.20
866	A195 20m multi	.25	.20
867	A195 30m multi	.50	.30
868	A195 40m multi	.65	.30
869	A195 50m multi	.85	.40
870	A195 60m multi	.95	.45
871	A195 1t multi	1.10	.65
	Nos. 865-871 (7)	4.50	2.50

Revolutionists with Flags — A196

1975, Nov. 15 Litho. *Perf. 11½x12*

872	A196 60m multi	.75	.40

70th anniversary of Russian Revolution.

Ski Jump, Olympic Games Emblem A197

Winter Olympic Games Emblem and: 20m, Ice hockey. 30m, Skiing. 40m, Bobsled. 50m, Biathlon. 60m, Speed skating. 1t, Figure skating, women's. 4t, Skier carrying torch.

Perf. 11½x12½

1975, Dec. 20 Litho.

873	A197 10m multi	.20	.20
874	A197 20m multi	.25	.20
875	A197 30m brn & multi	.50	.30
876	A197 40m grn & multi	.65	.30
877	A197 50m multi	.85	.40
878	A197 60m ol & multi	.95	.45
879	A197 1t multi	1.10	.65
	Nos. 873-879 (7)	4.50	2.50

Souvenir Sheet

880	A197 4t multi	4.00	4.00

12th Winter Olympic Games, Innsbruck, Austria, Feb. 4-15, 1976.

Taming Wild Horse A198

Mongolian Paintings: 20m, Camel caravan, horiz. 30m, Man playing lute. 40m, Woman adjusting headdress, horiz. 50m, Woman wearing ceremonial costume. 60m, Women fetching water. 1t, Woman musician. 4t, Warrior on horseback.

1975, Nov. 30 *Perf. 12*

881	A198 10m brown & multi	.20	.20
882	A198 20m blue & multi	.25	.20
883	A198 30m olive & multi	.50	.30
884	A198 40m lilac & multi	.65	.30
885	A198 50m blue & multi	.85	.40
886	A198 60m lilac & multi	.95	.45
887	A198 1t silver & multi	1.25	.65
	Nos. 881-887 (7)	4.65	2.50

Souvenir Sheet

888	A198 4t bl & multi	4.50	4.00

House of Young Technicians A199

Designs: 60m, Hotel Ulan Bator. 1t, Museum of the Revolution.

1975, Dec. 30 Photo. *Perf. 12x11½*

893	A199 20m ultra	.65	.20
894	A199 60m bl grn	.75	.30
895	A199 1t brick red	1.10	.60
	Nos. 893-895 (3)	2.50	1.10

Camels in Gobi Desert — A200

20m, Horse taming. 30m, Herding. 40m, Pioneers' camp. 60m, Young musician. 80m, Children's festival. 1t, Mongolian wrestling.

1976, June 1 Litho. *Perf. 12*

896	A200 10m multi	.25	.20
897	A200 20m multi	.30	.20
898	A200 30m multi	.35	.20
899	A200 40m multi	.50	.30
900	A200 60m multi	.75	.30
901	A200 80m multi	1.00	.50
902	A200 1t multi	1.50	.75
	Nos. 896-902 (7)	4.65	2.45

International Children's Day.

Red Star — A201

1976, May 1 Photo. *Perf. 11x12½*

903	A201 60m red, maroon & silver	.75	.40

17th Congress of the Mongolian People's Revolutionary Party, June 14.

Archery, Montreal Games' Emblem, Canadian Flag — A202

20m, Judo. 30m, Boxing. 40m, Vaulting. 60m, Weight lifting. 80m, High Jump. 1t, Target shooting.

1976, May 20 Litho. *Perf. 12½x11½*

904	A202 10m yel & multi	.20	.20
905	A202 20m yel & multi	.25	.20
906	A202 30m yel & multi	.50	.20
907	A202 40m yel & multi	.65	.30
908	A202 60m yel & multi	.85	.30
909	A202 80m yel & multi	.95	.50
910	A202 1t yel & multi	1.10	.75
	Nos. 904-910 (7)	4.50	2.45

21st Olympic Games, Montreal, Canada, July 17-Aug. 1. See No. C81.

Partisans A203

Fighter and Sojombo Independence Symbol — A204

Perf. 12x11½, 11½x12

1976, June 15 Litho.

911	A203 60m multi	1.00	.50
912	A204 60m multi	1.00	.50

55th anniversary of Mongolia's independence. See No. C82.

Souvenir Sheet

Sukhe Bator Medal — A205

1976, July 11 *Perf. 11½*

913	A205 4t multi	4.00	4.00

Mongolian honors medals.

Osprey — A206

Protected Birds: 20m, Griffon vulture. 30m, Bearded lammergeier. 40m, Marsh harrier. 60m, Black vulture. 80m, Golden eagle. 1t, Tawny eagle.

1976, Aug. 16 Litho. *Perf. 12*

914	A206	10m multi	.75	.25
915	A206	20m multi	1.00	.25
916	A206	30m multi	1.25	.35
917	A206	40m multi	1.50	.55
918	A206	60m multi	1.75	.75
919	A206	80m multi	2.00	.95
920	A206	1t multi	2.50	1.10
		Nos. 914-920 (7)	10.75	4.20

"Nadom" Military Game — A207

Paintings by O. Cevegshava: 10m, Taming Wild Horse, vert. 30m, Hubsugul Lake Harbor. 40m, The Steppe Awakening. 80m, Wrestlers. 1.60t, Yak Descending in Snow, vert.

1976, Sept. Litho. *Perf. 12*

921	A207	10m multi	.25	.20
922	A207	20m multi	.40	.20
923	A207	30m multi	.50	.20
924	A207	40m multi	.60	.30
925	A207	80m multi	1.00	.60
926	A207	1.60t multi	1.75	1.00
		Nos. 921-926 (6)	4.50	2.50

Interlocking Circles, Industry and Transport — A208

1976, Oct. 15 Photo. *Perf. 12x11½*

927	A208	60m brn, bl & red	1.25	.75

Soviet-Mongolian friendship.

John Naber, US Flag, Gold Medals A209

Designs: 20m, Nadia Comaneci, Romanian flag. 30m, Kornelia Ender, East German flag. 40m, Mitsuo Tsukahara, Japanese flag. 60m, Gregor Braun, German flag. 80m, Lasse Viren, Finnish flag. 1t, Nikolai Andrianov, Russian flag.

1976, Nov. 30 Litho. *Perf. 12*

928	A209	10m multi	.20	.20
929	A209	20m multi	.25	.20
930	A209	30m multi	.50	.20
931	A209	40m multi	.65	.30
932	A209	60m multi	.85	.30
933	A209	80m multi	.85	.50
934	A209	1t multi	1.10	.75
		Nos. 928-934 (7)	4.40	2.45

Gold medal winners, 21st Olympic Games, Montreal. See No. C83.

Stone Tablet on Tortoise A210

Carved Tablet, 6th-8th Centuries A211

1976, Dec. 15 Litho. *Perf. 11½x12*

935	A210	50m brn & lt bl	1.00	.35
936	A211	60m gray & brt grn	1.50	.40

Intl. Archaeological Conference, Ulan Bator.

R-1 Plane — A212

Designs: Various Mongolian planes.

1976, Dec. 22 *Perf. 12*

937	A212	10m multi	.25	.20
938	A212	20m multi	.35	.20
939	A212	30m multi	.45	.20
940	A212	40m multi	.55	.25
941	A212	60m multi	.75	.35
942	A212	80m multi	.95	.55
943	A212	1t multi	1.25	.75
		Nos. 937-943 (7)	4.55	2.50

Dancers — A213

Folk Dances: 20m, 13th century costumes. 30m, West Mongolian dance. 40m, "Ekachi," or horse-dance. 60m, "Bielge," West Mongolian trunk dance. 80m, "Hodak," or friendship dance. 1t, "Dojarka."

1977, Mar. 20 Litho. *Perf. 12½*

944	A213	10m multi	.25	.20
945	A213	20m multi	.35	.20
946	A213	30m multi	.45	.30
947	A213	40m multi	.55	.30
948	A213	60m multi	.75	.40
949	A213	80m multi	1.00	.50
950	A213	1t multi	1.25	.75
		Nos. 944-950 (7)	4.60	2.65

Miniature Sheet

Path of Pioneer from Earth to Jupiter, deflected by Mars — A214

Isaac Newton — A215

1977, Mar. 31 Litho. *Perf. 11½x12*

951	Sheet of 9	4.50	2.50
a.	A214 60m shown	.40	.25
b.	A215 60m Apple tree	.40	.25
c.	A214 60m Sextant and planets	.40	.25
d.	A214 60m Astronauts in space	.40	.25
e.	A215 60m shown	.40	.25
f.	A214 60m Prism and spectrum	.40	.25
g.	A214 60m Rain falling on earth	.40	.25
h.	A215 60m Motion of celestial bodies	.40	.25
i.	A214 60m Pioneer 10 over Jupiter	.40	.25

Sir Isaac Newton (1642-1727), English natural philosopher and mathematician.

Nos. 951a-951i arranged in 3 rows of 3. Nos. 951d and 951i inscribed AIR MAIL.

D. Natsagdorji, Writer, and Quotation — A216

Design: No. 953, Grazing horses, landscape, ornament and quotation.

1977 *Perf. 11½x12*

952	A216	60m multi	1.00	.50
953	A216	60m multi	1.00	.50

D. Natsagdorji, founder of modern Mongolian literature. Label and vignette separated by simulated perforations.

Primitive Tortoises — A217

Prehistoric Animals: 20m, Ungulate (titanothere). 30m, Beaked dinosaurs. 40m, Entelodon (swine). 60m, Antelope. 80m, Hipparion. 1t, Aurochs.

1977, May 7 Photo. *Perf. 12½*

954	A217	10m multi	.35	.20
955	A217	20m multi	.50	.20
956	A217	30m multi	.55	.25
957	A217	40m multi	.75	.30
958	A217	60m multi	1.25	.30
959	A217	80m multi	1.50	.60
960	A217	1t multi	1.75	.90
		Nos. 954-960 (7)	6.65	2.75

Souvenir Sheet

Mongolia, Type A2 and Netherlands No. 1 — A218

1977, May 20

961	A218	4t multi	4.50	3.50

AMPHILEX '77 International Philatelic Exhibition, Amsterdam, May 27-June 5. No. 961 contains one 37x52mm stamp.

Boys on Horseback — A219

20m, Girl on horseback. 30m, Hunter on horseback. 40m, Grazing horses. 60m, Mare & foal. 80m, Grazing horse & student. 1t, White stallion.

1977, June 15 Litho. *Perf. 12*

962	A219	10m multi	.25	.20
963	A219	20m multi	.35	.20
964	A219	30m multi	.45	.20
965	A219	40m multi	.55	.25
966	A219	60m multi	.75	.35
967	A219	80m multi	.95	.55
968	A219	1t multi	1.25	.75
		Nos. 962-968 (7)	4.55	2.50

Copper and Molybdenum Plant, Vehicles A220

1977, June 15 Litho. *Perf. 12*

969	A220	60m multi	1.50	.50

Erdenet, a new industrial town.

Bucket Brigade Fighting Fire — A221

Fire Fighting: 20m, Horse-drawn fire pump. 30m, Horse-drawn steam pump. 40m, Men in protective suits fighting forest fire. 60m, Modern foam extinguisher. 80m, Truck and ladder. 1t, Helicopter fighting fire on steppe.

1977, Aug. Litho. *Perf. 12*

970	A221	10m multi	.25	.20
971	A221	20m multi	.40	.20
972	A221	30m multi	.55	.30
973	A221	40m multi	.75	.30
974	A221	60m multi	.90	.40
975	A221	80m multi	1.10	.50
976	A221	1t multi	1.25	.60
		Nos. 970-976 (7)	5.20	2.50

Radar and Molnya Satellite on TV Screen — A222

1977, Sept. 12 Photo. *Perf. 12x11½*

977	A222	60m gray, bl & blk	.80	.50

40th anniversary of Technical Institute.

Lenin Museum, Ulan Bator — A223

1977, Oct. 1 Litho. *Perf. 12*

978	A223	60m multi	1.00	.40

Inauguration of Lenin Museum in connection with the 60th anniversary of the Russian October Revolution.

Dove, Globe, Decree of Peace A224

Designs: 50m, Cruiser Aurora and Russian flag, vert. 1.50t, Globe and "Freedom."

Perf. 11½x12, 12x11½

1977, Oct. 1 **Photo.**

979	A224	50m gold & multi	.85	.30
980	A224	60m gold & multi	.75	.30
981	A224	1.50t gold & multi	1.40	.90
		Nos. 979-981 (3)	3.00	1.50

60th anniversary of the Russian Revolution.

Aporia Crataegi — A225

Moths: 20m, Gastropacha quercifolia. 30m, Colias chrysoteme. 40m, Dasychira fascelina. 60m, Malocosoma neustria. 80m, Diacrisia sanno. 1t, Heodes virgaureae.

1977, Sept. 25 **Photo.** ***Perf. 12½***

982	A225	10m multi	.30	.20
983	A225	20m multi	.50	.25
984	A225	30m multi	.75	.30
985	A225	40m multi	1.10	.35
986	A225	60m multi	1.50	.40
987	A225	80m multi	1.75	.60
988	A225	1t multi	2.25	1.00
		Nos. 982-988 (7)	8.15	3.10

Giant Pandas — A226

Pandas: 10m, Eating bamboo, vert. 30m, Female and cub in washtub, vert. 40m, Male and cub playing with bamboo. 60m, Female and cub, vert. 80m, Family. 1t, Male, vert.

1977, Nov. 25 **Litho.** ***Perf. 12***

989	A226	10m multi	.25	.20
990	A226	20m multi	.40	.20
991	A226	30m multi	.55	.25
992	A226	40m multi	.75	.35
993	A226	60m multi	1.00	.50
994	A226	80m multi	1.75	.75
995	A226	1t multi	2.00	1.00
		Nos. 989-995 (7)	6.70	3.25

Souvenir Sheet

Helen Fourment and her Children, by Rubens — A227

1977, Dec. 5 ***Perf. 11½x10½***

996	A227	4t multi	4.50	4.50

Peter Paul Rubens (1577-1640).

Ferrari Racing Car — A228

Experimental Racing Cars: 30m, Ford McLaren. 40m, Madi, USSR. 50m, Mazda. 60m, Porsche. 80m, Russian model car. 1.20t, The Blue Flame, US speed car.

1978, Jan. 28 **Litho.** ***Perf. 12***

997	A228	20m multi	.35	.20
998	A228	30m multi	.45	.25
999	A228	40m multi	.60	.25
1000	A228	50m multi	.80	.35
1001	A228	60m multi	1.00	.35
1002	A228	80m multi	1.25	.50
1003	A228	1.20t multi	1.50	.60
		Nos. 997-1003 (7)	5.95	2.50

Boletus Variegatus — A229

Mushrooms: 30m, Russula cyanoxantha. 40m, Boletus aurantiacus. 50m, Boletus scaber. 60m, Russula flava. 80m, Lactarius resimus. 1.20t, Flammula spumosa.

1978, Feb. 28 **Photo.** ***Perf. 11x11½***

1004	A229	20m yel & multi	.50	.20
1005	A229	30m yel & multi	.75	.25
1006	A229	40m yel & multi	1.00	.35
1007	A229	50m yel & multi	1.25	.45
1008	A229	60m yel & multi	1.50	.55
1009	A229	80m yel & multi	1.75	.65
1010	A229	1.20t yel & multi	2.50	1.00
		Nos. 1004-1010 (7)	9.25	3.45

Young Couple with Youth Flag — A230

1978, Apr. **Litho.** ***Perf. 11½x12***

1011	A230	60m multi	1.00	.40

17th Congress of Mongolian Youth Organization, Ulan Bator, Apr. 1978.

Soccer, Sugar Loaf Mountain, Rio de Janeiro, Brazil 1950 Emblem — A231

Designs (Various Soccer Scenes and): 30m, Old Town Tower, Bern, Switzerland, 1954. 40m, Town Hall, Stockholm, Sweden, 1958. 50m, University of Chile, Chile, 1962. 60m, Parliament and Big Ben, London, 1966. 80m, Degolladeo Theater, Guadalajara, Mexico, 1970. 1.20t, Town Hall and TV Tower, Munich, Germany.

1978, Apr. 15 ***Perf. 12***

1012	A231	20m multi	.25	.20
1013	A231	30m multi	.35	.25
1014	A231	40m multi	.45	.25
1015	A231	50m multi	.55	.35
1016	A231	60m multi	.65	.35
1017	A231	80m multi	.90	.40
1018	A231	1.20t multi	1.40	.60
		Nos. 1012-1018 (7)	4.55	2.40

11th World Cup Soccer Championship, Argentina, June 1-25. See No. C109.

Capex Emblem, Eurasian Beaver and Canada #336 — A232

30m, Tibetan sand grouse & Canada #478. 40m, Red-throated loon & Canada #369. 50m, Argali & Canada #324. 60m, Eurasian brown bear & Canada #322. 80m, Moose & Canada #323. 1.20t, Great black-backed gull & Canada #343.

1978, June **Litho.** ***Perf. 12***

1019	A232	20m multi	.30	.20
1020	A232	30m multi	.50	.25
1021	A232	40m multi	.65	.30
1022	A232	50m multi	.90	.40
1023	A232	60m multi	1.00	.50
1024	A232	80m multi	1.10	.60
1025	A232	1.20t multi	1.50	.80
		Nos. 1019-1025 (7)	5.95	3.05

CAPEX '78 International Philatelic Exhibition, Toronto, June 9-18. See No. C110.

Marx, Engels and Lenin A233

1978, July 11 **Photo.** ***Perf. 12x11½***

1026	A233	60m gold, blk & red	1.00	.50

50th anniversary of publication in Prague of "Problems of Peace and Socialism."

Souvenir Sheet

Outdoor Rest, by Amgalan — A234

Paintings by D. Amgalan: No. 1027b, Winter Night (dromedary and people in snow). No. 1027c, Saddling up.

1978, Aug. 10 **Litho.** ***Perf. 12***

1027		Sheet of 3	4.50	4.50
a.-c.	A234	1.50t any single	1.25	

Philatelic cooperation between Hungary and Mongolia, 20th anniversary. No. 1027 contains 3 stamps and 3 labels.

Papillon — A235

Dogs: 20m, Black Mongolian sheepdog. 30m, Puli. 40m, St. Bernard. 50m, German shepherd. 60m, Mongolian watchdog. 70m, Samoyed. 80m, Laika (1st dog in space) and rocket. 1.20t, Cocker spaniel and poodles.

1978, Sept. 25 **Litho.** ***Perf. 12***

1028	A235	10m multi	.35	.20
1029	A235	20m multi	.35	.20
1030	A235	30m multi	.55	.25
1031	A235	40m multi	.65	.35
1032	A235	50m multi	.85	.35
1033	A235	60m multi	1.00	.35
1034	A235	70m multi	1.10	.60
1035	A235	80m multi	1.25	.75
1036	A235	1.20t multi	2.00	.90
		Nos. 1028-1036 (9)	8.10	3.95

Open Book and Pen — A236

1978, Oct. 20 **Photo.** ***Perf. 12x11½***

1037	A236	60m car & ultra	.75	.45

Mongolian Writers' Association, 50th anniversary.

Souvenir Sheets

Clothed Maya, by Goya — A237

Melancholy, by Dürer — A238

Paintings: No. 1038b, "Ta Matete," by Gauguin. No. 1038c, Bridge at Arles, by Van Gogh.

1978, Oct. 30 **Litho.** ***Perf. 12***

1038		Sheet of 3 + 3 labels	4.50	4.50
a.-c.	A237	1.50t any single + label	1.25	1.25

Perf. 11½

1039	A238	4t black	4.50	4.50

Anniversaries of European painters: Francisco Goya; Paul Gauguin; Vincent van Gogh; Albrecht Dürer.

Camel and Calf — A239

Bactrian Camels: 30m, Young camel. 40m, Two camels. 50m, Woman leading pack camel. 60m, Old camel. 80m, Camel pulling cart. 1.20t, Race.

1978, Nov. 30 **Litho.** ***Perf. 12***

1040	A239	20m multi	.30	.25
1041	A239	30m multi	.40	.25
1042	A239	40m multi	.55	.35
1043	A239	50m multi	.75	.35
1044	A239	60m multi	.90	.50
1045	A239	80m multi	1.00	.75
1046	A239	1.20t multi	1.60	.90
		Nos. 1040-1046 (7)	5.50	3.35

Flags of Comecon Members, Globe — A240

1979, Jan. 2 Litho. *Perf. 12*
1047 A240 60m multi + label .75 .40

30th anniversary of the Council of Mutual Assistance (Comecon).
Label and vignette separated by simulated perforations.

Silver Tabby — A241

Domestic Cats: 30m, White Persian. 50m, Red Persian. 60m, Cream Persian. 70m, Siamese. 80m, Smoky Persian. 1t, Burmese.

1979, Feb. 10
1048 A241 10m multi .30 .20
1049 A241 30m multi .50 .25
1050 A241 50m multi .65 .25
1051 A241 60m multi .90 .35
1052 A241 70m multi 1.10 .45
1053 A241 80m multi 1.25 .60
1054 A241 1t multi 1.40 .80
Nos. 1048-1054 (7) 6.10 2.90

Potaninia Mongolica — A242

Flowers: 30m, Sophora alopecuroides. 50m, Halimodendron halodendron. 60m, Forget-me-nots. 70m, Pincushion flower. 80m, Leucanthemum Sibiricum. 1t, Edelweiss.

1979, Mar. 10 Litho. *Perf. 12*
1055 A242 10m multi .40 .20
1056 A242 30m multi .75 .20
1057 A242 50m multi .90 .25
1058 A242 60m multi 1.00 .35
1059 A242 70m multi 1.25 .45
1060 A242 80m multi 1.50 .55
1061 A242 1t multi 1.75 .75
Nos. 1055-1061 (7) 7.55 2.75

Finland-Czechoslovakia, Finnish Flag — A243

Ice Hockey Games and 1980 Olympic Emblems: 30m, German Fed. Rep.-Sweden, German flag. 50m, US-Canada, US flag. 60m, USSR-Sweden, Russian flag. 70m, Canada-USSR, Canadian flag. 80m, Swedish goalie and flag. 1t, Czechoslovakia-USSR, Czechoslovak flag.

1979, Apr. 10 Litho. *Perf. 12*
1062 A243 10m multi .20 .20
1063 A243 30m multi .25 .20
1064 A243 50m multi .35 .25
1065 A243 60m multi .50 .35
1066 A243 70m multi .60 .45
1067 A243 80m multi 1.00 .55
1068 A243 1t multi 1.60 .75
Nos. 1062-1068 (7) 4.50 2.75

Ice Hockey World Championship, Moscow, Apr. 14-27.

Lambs — A244

Paintings: 30m, Milking, camels. 50m, Plane bringing supplies in winter. 60m, Herdsmen and horses. 70m, Milkmaids, vert. 80m, Summer Evening (camels). 1t, Landscape with herd. 4t, After the Storm.

Perf. 12x11½, 11½x12
1979, May 3 Litho.
1069 A244 10m multi .20 .20
1070 A244 30m multi .25 .20
1071 A244 50m multi .45 .25
1072 A244 60m multi .55 .35
1073 A244 70m multi .65 .45
1074 A244 80m multi .95 .50
1075 A244 1t multi 1.10 .55
Nos. 1069-1075 (7) 4.15 2.50

Souvenir Sheet
1076 A244 4t multi 4.00 4.00

20th anniv. of 1st agricultural cooperative.

Souvenir Sheet

Mongolia No. 4, Bulgaria No. 1, Philaserdica Emblem — A245

Designs (Rowland Hill and): No. 1077b, American mail coach. No. 1077c, Mail car, London-Birmingham railroad, 1838. 1077d, Packet leaving Southampton, Sept. 24, 1842, opening Indian mail service.

1979, May 15 Litho. *Perf. 12*
1077 Sheet of 4, multi 6.00 6.00
a.-d. A245 1t any single 1.50 1.50

Philaserdica '79, Sofia, May 18-27, and Rowland Hill (1795-1879), originator of penny postage.

Rocket, Manchester, 1829 — A246

Locomotives: 20m, "Adler" Nuremberg-Furth, 1835. 30m, American engine, 1860. 40m, Ulan Bator-Nalajh run, 1931. 50m, Moscow-Ulan Bator run, 1936. 60m, Moscow-Ulan Bator, 1970. 70m, Tokyo-Osaka run, 1963. 80m, Orleans Aerotrain, 1967. 1.20t, Soviet Rapidity, experimental train.

1979, June 8 Litho. *Perf. 12*
1078 A246 10m multi .25 .20
1079 A246 20m multi .35 .20
1080 A246 30m multi .55 .20
1081 A246 40m multi .65 .25
1082 A246 50m multi .75 .30
1083 A246 60m multi .85 .40
1084 A246 70m multi 1.00 .40
1085 A246 80m multi 1.10 .55
1086 A246 1.20t multi 1.25 .75
Nos. 1078-1086 (9) 6.75 3.25

Intl. Transportation Exhibition, Hamburg.

For surcharge see No. 2144B.

Mongolian and Russian Flags — A247

Battle Scene and Emblem A248

1979, Aug. 10 Photo. *Perf. 11½x12*
1087 A247 60m multi 1.00 .50
1088 A248 60m multi 1.00 .50

Battle of Ha-lo-hsin River, 40th anniversary.

Manuls A249

Wild Cats: 30m, Lynx. 50m, Tigers. 60m, Snow leopards. 70m, Black panthers. 80m, Cheetahs. 1t, Lions.

1979, Sept. 10 Litho. *Perf. 12*
1089 A249 10m multi .25 .20
1090 A249 30m multi .45 .25
1091 A249 50m multi .75 .30
1092 A249 60m multi .85 .30
1093 A249 70m multi .95 .40
1094 A249 80m multi 1.10 .50
1095 A249 1t multi 1.25 .60
Nos. 1089-1095 (7) 5.60 2.55

Souvenir Sheet

Brazil No. 1582 — A250

b, Brazil #1144 (Pele). c, Mongolia #C1.

1979, Sept. 15 Litho. *Perf. 11*
1096 Sheet of 3 + 3 labels 7.50 7.50
a.-c. A250 1.50t any single + label 2.50 2.50

Brasiliana '79, 3rd World Thematic Stamp Exhibition, Rio de Janeiro, Sept. 15-23.

Cross-Country Skiing, Lake Placid '80 Emblem — A251

30m, Biathlon. 40m, Ice hockey. 50m, Ski jump. 60m, Downhill skiing. 80m, Speed skating. 1.20t, Bobsledding. 4t, Figure skating.

1980, Jan. 20 Litho. *Perf. 11½x12½*
1097 A251 20m multi .20 .20
1098 A251 30m multi .25 .20
1099 A251 40m multi .35 .25
1100 A251 50m multi .50 .35
1101 A251 60m multi .75 .40
1102 A251 80m multi .95 .45
1103 A251 1.20t multi 1.50 .70
Nos. 1097-1103 (7) 4.50 2.55

Souvenir Sheet
1104 A251 4t multi 2.75 2.75

13th Winter Olympic Games, Lake Placid, NY, Feb. 12-24.

Flower Type of 1969
Souvenir Sheet

Design: Landscape and edelweiss.

1980, May 5 Litho. *Perf. 11*
1105 A131 4t multi 4.50 4.50

London 1980 Intl. Stamp Exhib., May 6-14. No. 1105 contains one stamp 43x26mm.

Weightlifting, Moscow '80 Emblem — A252

1980, June 2 Litho. *Perf. 12*
1106 A252 20m shown .20 .20
1107 A252 30m Archery .25 .20
1108 A252 40m Gymnast .40 .25
1109 A252 50m Running .50 .25
1110 A252 60m Boxing .60 .35
1111 A252 80m Judo .75 .35
1112 A252 1.20t Bicycling 1.00 .70
Nos. 1106-1112 (7) 3.70 2.30

Souvenir Sheet
1113 A252 4t Wrestling 4.50 4.50

22nd Summer Olympic Games, Moscow, July 19-Aug. 3.

Gold Medal, Swimmer, Moscow '80 Emblem — A253

Gold Medal, Moscow '80 Emblem and Number of Medals won by Top Countries: 30m, Fencing. 50m, Judo. 60m, Track. 80m, Boxing. 1t, Weight lifting. 1.20t, Kayak.

1980, Sept. 15 Litho. *Perf. 12½*
1114 A253 20m multi .20 .20
1115 A253 30m multi .25 .20
1116 A253 50m multi .35 .30
1117 A253 60m multi .55 .30
1118 A253 80m multi .75 .40
1119 A253 1t multi 1.00 .50
1120 A253 1.20t multi 1.25 .60
Nos. 1114-1120 (7) 4.35 2.50

See No. C144.

A254

A255

1980, Sept. 17 ***Perf. 11½x12***

1121 A254 60m Jumdshaigiin Zedenbal .75 .50
1122 A254 60m Zedenbal, 1941, grn .75 .50
1123 A254 60m Zedenbal, 1979, gray grn .75 .50
1124 A254 60m with Brezhnev, horiz. .75 .50
1125 A254 60m with children .75 .50
1126 A254 60m Sukhe Bator, dk brn .75 .50
1127 A254 60m Choibalsan, ultra .75 .50
Nos. 1121-1127 (7) 5.25 3.50

Miniature Sheet

Cosmonauts from various Intercosmos flights: a, A. Gubarjev. b, Czechoslovakia #2222. c, P. Klimuk. d, Poland #2270. e, V. Bykovsky. f, DDR #1947. g, N. Rukavishnikov. h, Bulgaria #2576. i, V. Kubasov. j, Hungary #C417.

1980, Oct. 10 **Litho.** ***Perf. 12***

1128 Sheet of 10 4.50 4.50
a.-j. A255 40m any single .40 .40

Intercosmos cooperative space program. See No. 1232.

Benz, Germany, 1885 — A256

Antique Cars: 30m, President, Austria-Hungary, 1897. 40m, Armstrong Siddley, 1904. 50m, Russo-Balt, 1909. 60m, Packard, United States, 1909. 80m, Lancia, Italy, 1911. 1.60t, Marne taxi, France, 1914. 4t, Nami-1, Russia, 1927.

1980, Nov. 20 **Litho.** ***Perf. 12½***

1129 A256 20m multi .25 .20
1130 A256 30m multi .25 .20
1131 A256 40m multi .45 .25
1132 A256 50m multi .50 .35
1133 A256 60m multi .60 .40
1134 A256 80m multi .80 .50
1135 A256 1.60t multi 1.75 .75
Nos. 1129-1135 (7) 4.60 2.65

Souvenir Sheet

1136 A256 4t multi 4.50 4.50

Penguins A257

1980, Dec. 1 ***Perf. 12***

1137 A257 20m shown .90 .25
1138 A257 30m Giant blue whale 1.25 .40
1139 A257 40m Albatross 1.50 .50
1140 A257 50m Weddell seals 1.75 .60
1141 A257 60m Emperor penguins 2.00 .70
1142 A257 70m Skua 2.25 .80
1143 A257 80m Grampus 2.75 1.00
1144 A257 1.20t Penguins, Soviet plane 3.25 1.25
Nos. 1137-1144 (8) 15.65 5.50

Souvenir Sheet

1145 A257 4t World map showing continental drift 7.50 7.50

Antarctic animals and exploration. No. 1145 contains one 44mm circular stamp.

Souvenir Sheet

A258

1980, Dec. 20 **Litho.** ***Perf. 11***

1146 Sheet of 2 4.00 2.50
a. A258 2t shown 1.75 1.00
b. A258 2t Old Marketplace 1.75 1.00

The Shepherd Speaking the Truth, IYC Emblem A259

IYC Emblem and Nursery Tales: 30m, Above Them the Sky is Always Clear. 40m, Winter's Joys. 50m, Little Musicians. 60m, Happy Birthday. 80m, The First Day of School. 1.20t, May Day. 4t, The Wonder-working Squirrels.

1980, Dec. 29 ***Perf. 12***

1147 A259 20m multi .20 .20
1148 A259 30m multi .25 .20
1149 A259 40m multi .45 .25
1150 A259 50m multi .60 .25
1151 A259 60m multi .90 .40
1152 A259 80m multi 1.10 .60
1153 A259 1.20t multi 1.25 .80
Nos. 1147-1153 (7) 4.75 2.70

Souvenir Sheet

1154 A259 4t multi 4.50 3.50

Intl. Year of the Child (1979).

60th Anniversary of People's Army — A260

1981, Jan. 31 **Litho.** ***Perf. 12***

1155 A260 60m multi 1.00 .40

60th Anniversary of People's Revolutionary Party — A261

1981, Feb. 2

1156 A261 60m multi 1.00 .40

Ice Racing — A262

Designs: Various racing motorcycles.

1981, Feb. 28 ***Perf. 12½***

1157 A262 10m multi .20 .20
1158 A262 20m multi .25 .20
1159 A262 30m multi .30 .25
1160 A262 40m multi .40 .25
1161 A262 50m multi .50 .25
1162 A262 60m multi .60 .30
1163 A262 70m multi .70 .30
1164 A262 80m multi .80 .30
1165 A262 1.20t multi .90 .45
Nos. 1157-1165 (9) 4.65 2.50

Cosmonauts Boarding Soyuz 39 — A263

Designs: 30m, Rocket designer Koroljov. 40m, Vostok I, Yuri Gagarin. 50m, Salyut space station. 60m, Satellite photographing earth. 80m, Light crystallization from Salyut spacecraft. 1.20t, Salyut, Kremlin, Sukhe Bator statue. 4t, Soviet and Mongolian cosmonauts.

1981, Mar. 22 **Litho.** ***Perf. 12***

1166 A263 20m multi .25 .20
1167 A263 30m multi .35 .20
1168 A263 40m multi .40 .25
1169 A263 50m multi .50 .35
1170 A263 60m multi .75 .45
1171 A263 80m multi 1.00 .50
1172 A263 1.20t multi 1.25 .60
Nos. 1166-1172 (7) 4.50 2.55

Souvenir Sheet

Perf. 11½

1173 A263 4t multi 4.50 3.50

Intercosmos cooperative space program (Mongolia-USSR). No. 1173 contains one 29x39mm stamp.

A264

1981, Apr. 28 **Litho.** ***Perf. 12***

1174 Sheet of 4 + 4 labels 6.00 6.00
a. A264 1t No. 240, Ulan Bator + label 1.40 1.25
b. A264 1t Germany #8N4, 8N34 + label 1.40 1.25
c. A264 1t Austria #B110 + label 1.40 1.25
d. A264 1t Japan #827 + label 1.40 1.25

1981 Stamp Exhibitions: Mongolian Natl., Ulan Bator; Naposta, Stuttgart; WIPA, Vienna; Japex, Tokyo.

Star Shining on Factories and Sheep A265

1981, May 5

1175 A265 60m multi .75 .40

18th Congress of Revolutionary People's Party, May.

Souvenir Sheet

Statue of Sukhe Bator, Mongolian Flag — A266

1981, May 20 ***Perf. 12½***

1176 A266 4t multi 3.50 3.50

Mongolian Revolutionary People's Party, 60th anniv.

Sheep Farming (Economic Development) — A267

1981, June 1 ***Perf. 12½x11½***

1177 A267 20m shown .25 .20
1178 A267 30m Transportation .35 .20
1179 A267 40m Telecommunications .40 .25
1180 A267 50m Public health service .50 .35
1181 A267 60m Agriculture .75 .45
1182 A267 80m Power plant 1.00 .50
1183 A267 1.20t Public housing 1.25 .60
Nos. 1177-1183 (7) 4.50 2.55

A268

Souvenir Sheet

1981, July 11 Litho. ***Perf. 12½x11½***
1184 A268 4t multi 4.50 3.50

20th anniv. of UN membership.

A269

1981, Aug. 1 ***Perf. 12***

Designs: Sailing ships. 10m, 20m, horiz.

1185 A269 10m Egyptian, 15th cent. BC .25 .20
1186 A269 20m Mediterranean, 9th cent. .30 .25
1187 A269 40m Hansa Cog, 12th cent. .40 .30
1188 A269 50m Venitian, 13th cent. .60 .30
1189 A269 60m Santa Maria .70 .40
1190 A269 80m Endeavor .80 .40
1191 A269 1t Poltava, 18th cent. .90 .45
1192 A269 1.20t US schooner, 19th cent. 1.00 .50
Nos. 1185-1192 (8) 4.95 2.80

Mongolian-USSR Friendship Pact — A270

1981, Sept. 1 ***Perf. 11½x12***
1193 A270 60m multi 1.00 .50

Flora, by Rembrandt A271

1981, Sept. 1 ***Perf. 11½x12½***
1194 A271 20m shown .25 .20
1195 A271 30m Hendrickje in the Bed .35 .25
1196 A271 40m Young Woman with Earrings .40 .25
1197 A271 50m Young Girl in the Window .50 .30
1198 A271 60m Hendrickje like Flora .75 .30
1199 A271 80m Saskia with Red Flower 1.00 .50
1200 A271 1.20t Holy Family with Drape 1.25 .60
Nos. 1194-1200 (7) 4.50 2.40

Souvenir Sheet

1201 A271 4t Self-portrait with Saskia 4.50 4.50

375th birth anniv. of Rembrandt.

Goat (Pawn) — A272

Designs: Wood chess pieces.

1981, Sept. 30 Litho. ***Perf. 12½***
1202 A272 20m shown .30 .20
1203 A272 40m Cart (castle) .50 .25
1204 A272 50m Camel (bishop) .60 .35
1205 A272 60m Horse (knight) .70 .45
1206 A272 80m Lion (queen) 1.00 .55
1207 A272 1.20t Man and dog (king) 1.25 .75
Nos. 1202-1207 (6) 4.35 2.55

Souvenir Sheet

1208 A272 4t Men playing 4.50 4.50

Camel and Circus Tent A273

1981, Oct. 30 Litho. ***Perf. 12***
1209 A273 10m shown .20 .20
1210 A273 20m Horsemen .25 .25
1211 A273 40m Wrestlers .35 .25
1212 A273 50m Archers .45 .30
1213 A273 60m Folksinger .55 .30
1214 A273 80m Girl playing jat-ga .75 .35
1215 A273 1t Ballet dancers 1.00 .40
1216 A273 1.20t Statue 1.10 .50
Nos. 1209-1216 (8) 4.65 2.55

Wolfgang Amadeus Mozart and Scene from his Magic Flute — A274

Composers and Scenes from their Works.

1981, Nov. 16
1217 A274 20m shown .30 .20
1218 A274 30m Beethoven, Fidelio .45 .25
1219 A274 40m Bartok, Miraculous Mandarin .45 .25
1220 A274 50m Verdi, Aida .55 .35
1221 A274 60m Tchaikovsky, Sleeping Beauty .65 .35
1222 A274 80m Dvorak, New World Symphony score .85 .45
1223 A274 1.20t Chopin, piano 1.25 .50
Nos. 1217-1223 (7) 4.50 2.35

Ribbon Weaver A275

Designs: Mongolian women.

Perf. 11½x12½

1981, Dec. 10 Litho.
1224 A275 20m multi .35 .20
1225 A275 30m multi .45 .25
1226 A275 40m multi .55 .25
1227 A275 50m multi .65 .25
1228 A275 60m multi .75 .30
1229 A275 80m multi 1.00 .40
1230 A275 1.20t multi 1.10 .50
Nos. 1224-1230 (7) 4.85 2.15

Souvenir Sheet

1231 A275 4t multi 4.50 4.50

Intercosmos Type of 1980

Designs: a, V. Gorbatko. b, Y. Romanenko. c, V. Dzhanibekov. d, L. Popov. e, Vietnamese stamp. f, Cuban stamp. g, No. 1173. h, Romania No. C241.

1981, Dec. 28 ***Perf. 12***
1232 Sheet of 8, multi 4.50 4.50
a.-h. A255 50m, any single .50 .35

Historic Bicycles A276

1982, Mar. 25 Litho. ***Perf. 11***
1233 A276 10m Germany, 1816 .20 .20
1234 A276 20m Scotland, 1838 .25 .20
1235 A276 40m US, 1866 .35 .25
1236 A276 50m France, 1863 .45 .25
1237 A276 60m "Kangaroo", 1877 .55 .30
1238 A276 80m England, 1870 .75 .30
1239 A276 1t 1878 .90 .40
1240 A276 1.20t Modern bike 1.10 .50
Nos. 1233-1240 (8) 4.55 2.40

Souvenir Sheet

Perf. 12½

1241 A276 4t Racing 4.50 4.50

No. 1241 contains one stamp 47x47mm.

1982 World Cup A277

1982, Apr. 20 ***Perf. 12***
1242 A277 10m Brazil, 1950 .20 .20
1243 A277 20m Switzerland, 1954 .25 .20
1244 A277 40m Sweden, 1958 .35 .25
1245 A277 50m Chile, 1962 .45 .25
1246 A277 60m England, 1966 .55 .30
1247 A277 80m Mexico, 1970 .75 .30
1248 A277 1t Germany, 1974 .90 .40
1249 A277 1.20t Argentina, 1978 1.00 .50
Nos. 1242-1249 (8) 4.45 2.40

Souvenir Sheet

Perf. 11

1250 A277 4t Spain, 1982 4.50 3.50

No. 1250 contains one stamp 48x48mm.

12th Trade Union Congress, Ulan Bator A278

1982, May 20 Litho. ***Perf. 11½x12½***
1251 A278 60m multi 1.00 .50

Souvenir Sheet

PHILEXFRANCE Intl. Stamp Exhibition, Paris, June 11-21 — A279

1982, June 11 ***Imperf.***
1252 A279 4t No. B13 design 4.00 3.00

George Dimitrov (1882-1949), First Prime Minister of Bulgaria — A280

1982, June 18 ***Perf. 12***
1253 A280 60m gold & blk 1.00 .40

Chicks — A281

1982, June 25 ***Perf. 11***
1254 A281 10m shown .25 .20
1255 A281 20m Colt .30 .20
1256 A281 30m Lamb .45 .25
1257 A281 40m Fawn .55 .25
1258 A281 50m Camel calf .65 .25
1259 A281 60m Kid .75 .30
1260 A281 70m Calf .85 .45
1261 A281 1.20t Young boar 1.00 .55
Nos. 1254-1261 (8) 4.80 2.45

Coal Mining Industry — A282

1982, July 5 ***Perf. 12***
1262 A282 60m Mine, truck 1.00 .50

18th Mongolian Youth Org. Congress A283

1982, Aug. 14 ***Perf. 11½x12***
1263 A283 60m multi 1.00 .50

Siberian Pine A284

1982, Aug. 16

1264	A284	20m	shown	.25	.20
1265	A284	30m	Abies sibirica	.35	.20
1266	A284	40m	Populus diversifolia	.45	.25
1267	A284	50m	Larix sibirica	.60	.25
1268	A284	60m	Pinus silvestris	.75	.25
1269	A284	80m	Betula platyphylla	.90	.35
1270	A284	1.20t	Picea obovata	1.00	.45
			Nos. 1264-1270 (7)	4.30	1.95

60th Anniv. of Mongolian Youth Org. — A285

1982, Aug. 30

1271 A285 60m multi 1.00 .40

Iseki-6500 Tractor, Japan — A286

1982, Oct. 1 Litho. *Perf. 12½*

1272	A286	10m	shown	.20	.20
1273	A286	20m	Deutz-DX-230, Germany	.25	.20
1274	A286	40m	Bonser, Gt. Britain	.35	.25
1275	A286	50m	Intl.-884, US	.45	.25
1276	A286	60m	Renault TX-145-14, France	.60	.35
1277	A286	80m	Belarus-611, USSR	.75	.35
1278	A286	1t	K-7100, USSR	.90	.45
1279	A286	1.20t	DT-75, USSR	1.00	.50
			Nos. 1272-1279 (8)	4.50	2.55

Scenes from The Foal and The Hare Folktale A287

1983, Jan. 1 Litho. *Perf. 14*

1280	A287	10m	multi	.20	.20
1281	A287	20m	multi	.25	.20
1282	A287	30m	multi	.30	.25
1283	A287	40m	multi	.35	.30
1284	A287	50m	multi	.45	.30
1285	A287	60m	multi	.55	.40
1286	A287	70m	multi	.75	.40
1287	A287	80m	multi	.95	.40
1288	A287	1.20t	multi	1.10	.50
			Nos. 1280-1288 (9)	4.90	2.95

Souvenir Sheet

Imperf

1289 A287 7t multi 4.50 4.50

No. 1289 contains one stamp 58x58mm.

Scenes from Walt Disney's The Sorcerer's Apprentice — A288

1983, Jan. 1

1290	A288	25m	multi	.25	.20
1291	A288	35m	multi	.30	.20
1292	A288	45m	multi	.35	.25
1293	A288	55m	multi	.45	.30
1294	A288	65m	multi	.55	.30
1295	A288	75m	multi	.65	.30
1296	A288	85m	multi	.85	.30
1297	A288	1.40t	multi	1.00	.40
1298	A288	2t	multi	1.10	.45
			Nos. 1290-1298 (9)	5.50	2.70

Souvenir Sheet

1299 A288 7t multi 4.50 4.50

Fish, Lake Hevsgel — A289

1982, Nov. 30 *Perf. 12*

1300	A289	20m	shown	.25	.20
1301	A289	30m	Sheep, Zavhan Highlands	.25	.25
1302	A289	40m	Beaver, Lake Hovd	.30	.25
1303	A289	50m	Horses, Lake Uvs	.40	.35
1304	A289	60m	Chamois, Bajanhongor Steppe	.50	.45
1305	A289	80m	Mounted hunter, eagle, Bajan-Elgij Highlands	1.40	.45
1306	A289	1.20t	Camels, Gobi Desert	1.40	.50
			Nos. 1300-1306 (7)	4.50	2.45

Mongolian Skin Tent (Yurt) — A290

1983, Mar. 30 Litho. *Perf. 14*

1307	A290	20m	Antonov AN-24B plane	.30	.20
1308	A290	30m	shown	.40	.25
1309	A290	40m	Deer	.50	.25
1310	A290	50m	Bighorn sheep	.60	.30
1311	A290	60m	Eagle	.75	.50
1312	A290	80m	Museum of the Khans, Ulan Bator	.90	.55
1313	A290	1.20t	Sukhe Bator monument, Ulan Bator	1.10	.60
			Nos. 1307-1313 (7)	4.55	2.65

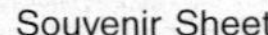
Souvenir Sheet

90th Birth Anniv. of Sukhe Bator — A291

1983 *Perf. 13x14*

1314 A291 4t multi 4.50 4.50

Local Flowers — A292

1983, Feb. 4 Photo. *Perf. 13*

1315	A292	20m	Rose	.25	.20
1316	A292	30m	Dahlias	.35	.20
1317	A292	40m	Tagetes faula	.45	.20
1318	A292	50m	Narcissus	.55	.20
1319	A292	60m	Violets	.75	.30
1320	A292	80m	Tulips	.90	.30
1321	A292	1.20t	Heliopsis helianthoides	1.10	.40
			Nos. 1315-1321 (7)	4.35	1.80

50th Anniv. of Border Forces — A293

1983, Feb. 9 Litho. *Perf. 14*

1322 A293 60m multi 1.00 .40

Souvenir Sheet

BRASILIANA, Philatelic Exhibition — A294

1983, July 10 Litho. *Perf. 14*

1323 A294 4t multi 4.00 3.00

Karl Marx — A295

1983, Oct. 1 Litho. *Perf. 14*

1324 A295 60m gold, dp car & bl 1.00 .40

18th Party Congress, Ulan Bator — A296

1983, Nov. 1 Litho. *Perf. 14*

1325	A296	10m	Cattle	.25	.20
1326	A296	20m	Coal	.25	.20
1327	A296	30m	Garment	.30	.20
1328	A296	40m	Agricultural	.40	.30
1329	A296	60m	Communications	.60	.30
1330	A296	80m	Transportation	1.50	.60
1331	A296	1t	Educational System	1.00	.60
			Nos. 1325-1331 (7)	4.30	2.40

Souvenir Sheet

Sistine Madonna, by Raphael (1483-1520) — A297

1983, Dec. 15 Litho. *Perf. 14x13½*

1332 A297 4t multi 4.50 4.50

A298

Children in Various Activities.

1984, Jan. 1 Photo. *Perf. 13*

1333	A298	10m	multi	.25	.20
1334	A298	20m	multi	.25	.20
1335	A298	30m	multi	.30	.20
1336	A298	40m	multi	.45	.25
1337	A298	50m	multi	.75	.35
1338	A298	70m	multi	1.10	.50
1339	A298	1.20t	multi	1.50	.75
			Nos. 1333-1339 (7)	4.60	2.45

Rodents — A299

Various rodents.

1984, Jan. 15 Litho. *Perf. 13½x13*

1340 A299 20m multi .30 .20
1341 A299 30m multi .50 .25
1342 A299 40m multi .60 .30
1343 A299 50m multi .70 .40
1344 A299 60m multi .80 .50
1345 A299 80m multi 1.00 .75
1346 A299 1.20t multi 1.25 1.00
Nos. 1340-1346 (7) 5.15 3.40

1984 Winter Olympics — A300

1984, Feb. 15 Litho. *Perf. 14*

1347 A300 20m Bobsledding .25 .20
1348 A300 30m Cross-country skiing .30 .20
1349 A300 40m Hockey .45 .20
1350 A300 50m Speed skating .55 .20
1351 A300 60m Downhill skiing .75 .25
1352 A300 80m Figure skating 1.00 .25
1353 A300 1.20t Biathlon 1.25 .40
Nos. 1347-1353 (7) 4.55 1.70

Souvenir Sheet

1354 A300 4t Ski jumping 4.00 3.00

Size of No. 1354: 134x106mm. Nos. 1347-1352 vert.

Children Feeding Lambs — A301

1984, Mar. 1 Litho. *Perf. 12*

1355 A301 20m Ice skating .25 .20
1356 A301 30m shown .30 .20
1357 A301 40m Planting tree .45 .20
1358 A301 50m Playing on beach .55 .20
1359 A301 60m Carrying pail .75 .25
1360 A301 80m Dancing 1.00 .25
1361 A301 1.20t Dancing, diff. 1.25 .35
Nos. 1355-1361 (7) 4.55 1.65

Souvenir Sheet

1362 A301 4t Boy, girl 4.50 3.50

No. 1362 contains one stamp 48x46mm.

Mail Car, Communications Emblems — A302

1984, Apr. 15 *Perf. 13½x14*

1363 A302 10m shown .25 .20
1364 A302 20m Earth satellite receiving station .30 .20
1365 A302 40m Airplane .40 .25
1366 A302 50m Central PO .50 .35
1367 A302 1t Radar station .90 .40
1368 A302 1.20t Train 2.00 1.00
Nos. 1363-1368 (6) 4.35 2.40

Souvenir Sheet

Imperf

1369 A302 4t Dish antenna 4.50 3.50

1984 Summer Olympics — A303

1984, June 1 Photo. *Perf. 14*

1370 A303 20m Gymnastics .25 .20
1371 A303 30m Bicycling .30 .20
1372 A303 40m Weight lifting .45 .20
1373 A303 50m Judo .55 .20
1374 A303 60m Archery .75 .25
1375 A303 80m Boxing 1.00 .25
1376 A303 1.20t High jump 1.25 .35
Nos. 1370-1376 (7) 4.55 1.65

Souvenir Sheet

1377 A303 4t Wrestling 4.50 3.50

Souvenir Sheet

AUSIPEX '84 and ESPANA '84 — A304

1984, May Litho. *Perf. 14*

1378 A304 4t Jet 4.50 4.50

Cuban Revolution, 25th Anniv. — A304a

1984, June 2 Litho. *Perf. 14*

1378A A304a 60m multi 1.00 .50

State Bank, 60th Anniv. A304b

1984, Sept. 25 *Perf. 13½x13*

1378B A304b 60m Commemorative coins, 1981 .75 .40

Radio Broadcasting in Mongolia, 50th Anniv. — A304c

1984, Sept. 1 Litho. *Perf. 13x13½*

1378C A304c 60m multicolored 1.00 .50

Scenes from Walt Disney's Mickey and the Beanstalk — A305

1984, Dec. 20 Litho. *Perf. 11*

1379 A305 25m multi .30 .20
1380 A305 35m multi .40 .20
1381 A305 45m multi .55 .25
1382 A305 55m multi .65 .25
1383 A305 65m multi .75 .30
1384 A305 75m multi .85 .40
1385 A305 85m multi .95 .50
1386 A305 1.40t multi 1.10 .65
1387 A305 2t multi 1.40 .80
Nos. 1379-1387 (9) 6.95 3.55

Miniature Sheet

Perf. 14

1388 A305 7t multi 6.00 6.00

Fairy Tales — A306

1984, Dec. 20 Litho. *Perf. 13½*

1389 A306 10m multi .25 .20
1390 A306 20m multi .30 .20
1391 A306 30m multi .35 .20
1392 A306 40m multi .40 .20
1393 A306 50m multi .45 .25
1394 A306 60m multi .50 .25
1395 A306 70m multi .60 .35
1396 A306 80m multi .75 .40
1397 A306 1.20t multi .90 .55
Nos. 1389-1397 (9) 4.50 2.60

Miniature Sheet

1398 A306 4t multi 4.50 4.50

Souvenir Sheet

60th Anniv. of Mongolian Stamps — A308

1984, Dec. 20 Litho. *Perf. 14*

1400 A308 4t No. 1 4.50 3.50

Ulan Bator, 60th Anniv. — A309

Mongolian People's Republic, 60th Anniv. — A310

1984, Nov. 26 Litho. *Perf. 13x13½*

1401 A309 60m multicolored 1.00 .50

Perf. 14

1402 A310 60m multicolored .90 .45

Mongolian People's Party, 60th Anniv. — A311

1984, Nov. 26 Litho. *Perf. 14*

1403 A311 60m multi .90 .45

Native Masks — A312

1984, Dec. 31 Litho. *Perf. 14*

1404 A312 20m multi .25 .20
1405 A312 30m multi .30 .20
1406 A312 40m multi .45 .25
1407 A312 50m multi .55 .25
1408 A312 60m multi .75 .30
1409 A312 80m multi 1.00 .30
1410 A312 1.20t multi 1.25 .50
Nos. 1404-1410 (7) 4.55 2.00

Souvenir Sheet

1411 A312 4t multi 4.50 4.50

Dogs A313

1984, Dec. 31 Litho. *Perf. 13*

1412 A313 20m Collie .25 .20
1413 A313 30m German Sheep-dog .30 .20
1414 A313 40m Papillon .45 .25

1415 A313 50m Cocker Spaniel .55 .25
1416 A313 60m Puppy .75 .30
1417 A313 80m Dalmatians 1.00 .30
1418 A313 1.20t Mongolian Sheepdog 1.25 .50
Nos. 1412-1418 (7) 4.55 2.00

Cattle — A314

1985, Jan. ***Perf. 14***
1419 A314 20m Shar tarlan .25 .20
1420 A314 30m Bor khaliun .30 .20
1421 A314 40m Sarlag .45 .20
1422 A314 50m Dornod taliin bukh .55 .25
1423 A314 60m Char tarlan .75 .25
1424 A314 80m Nutgiin uulderiin unee 1.00 .35
1425 A314 1.20t Tsagaan tolgoit 1.25 .35
Nos. 1419-1425 (7) 4.55 1.80

1984 Olympic Winners — A315

Gold medalists: 20m, Gaetan Boucher, Canada, 1500-meter speed skating. 30m, Eirik Kvalfoss, Norway, 10-kilometer biathlon. 40m, Marja-Lissa Haemaelainen, Finland, 5-kilometer Nordic skiing. 50m, Max Julen, Switzerland, men's giant slalom. 60m, Jens Weissflag, German Democratic Republic, 70-meter ski jump. 80m, W. Hoppe and D. Schauerhammer, German Democratic Republic, 2-man bobsled. 1.20t, Elena Valova and Oleg Vassiliev, USSR, pairs figure skating. 4t, USSR, ice hockey. Nos. 1430-1432 vert.

1985, Apr. 25
1426 A315 20m multi .25 .20
1427 A315 30m multi .30 .20
1428 A315 40m multi .45 .25
1429 A315 50m multi .50 .30
1430 A315 60m multi .70 .30
1431 A315 80m multi .95 .40
1432 A315 1.20t multi 1.10 .50
Nos. 1426-1432 (7) 4.25 2.15

Souvenir Sheet

1433 A315 4t multi 4.00 3.00

Souvenir Sheet

Girl, Fawn — A316

1985, Apr. 25
1434 A316 4m multi 4.50 4.50

Birds — A317

World Youth Festival, Moscow A318

1985, May 1 ***Perf. 12½x13***
1435 A317 20m Ciconia nigra .25 .20
1436 A317 30m Haliaetus albicilla .35 .20
1437 A317 40m Grus leucogeranus .50 .25
1438 A317 50m Paradoxornis heudei .60 .25
1439 A317 60m Grus monahas .80 .30
1440 A317 80m Grus vipio 1.00 .40
1441 A317 1.20t Buteo lagopus 1.25 .50
Nos. 1435-1441 (7) 4.75 2.10

National Wildlife Preservation Association.

1985, June ***Perf. 14***
1442 A318 60m Girls in folk costumes .80 .40

Camelus Bactrianus — A319

Panthera Unicias — A320

Cervus Elaphus — A321

Camels, leopards and deer.

1985
1443 A319 50m Adults, young 2.00 1.00
1444 A319 50m Facing right 2.00 1.00
1445 A319 50m Facing left 2.00 1.00
1446 A319 50m Trotting 2.00 1.00
1447 A320 50m Hunting 1.00 .40
1448 A320 50m Standing in snow 1.00 .40
1449 A320 50m Female, young 1.00 .40
1450 A320 50m Adults 1.00 .40
1451 A321 50m Fawn 1.00 .40
1452 A321 50m Doe in woods 1.00 .40
1453 A321 50m Adult male 1.00 .40
1454 A321 50m Adults, fawn 1.00 .40
Nos. 1443-1454 (12) 16.00 7.20

#1443-1446 show the World Wildlife Fund emblem, #1447-1454 the Natl. Wildlife Preservation emblem. Issue dates: #1443-1446, July 1; #1447-1454, Aug. 1.

UN, 40th Anniv. A322

1985, Aug. 1 ***Perf. 13½x13***
1455 A322 60m Flags, UN building .75 .40

Indigenous Flowering Plants — A323

1985, Aug. 1 ***Perf. 14***
1456 A323 20m Rosa davurica .25 .20
1457 A323 30m Matricaria chamomilla .35 .20
1458 A323 40m Taraxacum officinale .55 .20
1459 A323 50m Saxzifraga hirculus .65 .25
1460 A323 60m Vaccinium vitis idaea .75 .25
1461 A323 80m Sanguisorba officinalis .85 .30
1462 A323 1.20t Plantago major .95 .40
Nos. 1456-1462 (7) 4.35 1.80

Souvenir Sheet

1463 A323 4t Hippophae rhamnoides 4.50 4.50

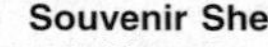

A324

A325

1985, Sept. 15 ***Perf. 13x13½***
1464 A324 60m Monument .30 .25

Defeat of Nazi Germany, 40th anniv.

1985, Oct. 1 ***Perf. 14***

Various soccer plays. No. 1472 horiz.

1465 A325 20m multi .25 .20
1466 A325 30m multi .30 .20
1467 A325 40m multi .40 .20
1468 A325 50m multi .60 .20
1469 A325 60m multi .80 .20
1470 A325 80m multi .90 .25
1471 A325 1.20t multi 1.00 .25
Nos. 1465-1471 (7) 4.25 1.50

Souvenir Sheet

1472 A325 4t multi 4.00 3.00

1985 Junior World Soccer Championships, Moscow.

Souvenir Sheet

ITALIA '85 — A326

1985, Oct. 1
1473 A326 4t Horseman 4.00 3.00

Conquest of Space — A327

Russian spacecraft.

1985, Nov. 1
1474 A327 20m Soyuz .30 .20
1475 A327 30m Cosmos .40 .20
1476 A327 40m Venera 9 .50 .20
1477 A327 50m Salyut .60 .20
1478 A327 60m Luna 9 .70 .25
1479 A327 80m Train .90 .55
1480 A327 1.20t Dish receiver 1.10 .25
Nos. 1474-1480 (7) 4.50 1.85

Souvenir Sheet

1985, Dec. 15
1481 A327 4t Cosmonaut on space walk 4.50 3.50

Mushrooms — A328

1985, Dec. 1 ***Perf. 13½***
1482 A328 20m Tricholoma mongolica .45 .20
1483 A328 30m Cantharellus cibarius .55 .20
1484 A328 40m Armillariella mellea .65 .20
1485 A328 50m Amanita caesarea .75 .25
1486 A328 70m Xerocomus badius .85 .30
1487 A328 80m Agaricus silvaticus .95 .30
1488 A328 1.20t Boletus edulis 2.00 .40
Nos. 1482-1488 (7) 6.20 1.85

Souvenir Sheet

Phalacrocorax Penicillatus — A329

1986, Jan. 15 *Perf. 12½x13*
1489 A329 4t multi 4.50 4.50

No. 1489 contains one stamp plus 2 labels picturing various bird species.

Young Pioneers A330

Victory Monument A331

1985, Dec. 31 Litho. *Perf. 13x13½*
1490 A330 60m multi .70 .30

1985, Dec. 31 *Perf. 12½x13*
1491 A331 60m multi .70 .30

Victory over Japan ending WWII, 40th anniv.

Natl. Costumes A332

1986, Mar. 1 Litho. *Perf. 14*

Background Color

1492 A332 60m yel grn, shown .60 .30
1493 A332 60m red .60 .30
1494 A332 60m pale yel grn .60 .30
1495 A332 60m violet .60 .30
1496 A332 60m ultra .60 .30
1497 A332 60m bluish grn .60 .30
1498 A332 60m pale org brn .60 .30
Nos. 1492-1498 (7) 4.20 2.10

Ernst Thalmann (1886-1944) A333

1986, May 15 Litho. *Perf. 14*
1499 A333 60m gold, redsh brn & dk brn .75 .30

Natl. Revolution, 65th Anniv. — A334

1986, May 15
1500 A334 60m Statue of Sukhe Bator .70 .30

19th Socialist Party Congress A335

1986, May 15
1501 A335 60m multi .70 .30

1986 World Cup Soccer Championships, Mexico — A336

FIFA emblem and various soccer plays. Nos. 1502-1503, 1505-1508 vert.

1986, May 31
1502 A336 20m multi .20 .20
1503 A336 30m multi .25 .20
1504 A336 40m multi .35 .20
1505 A336 50m multi .45 .20
1506 A336 60m multi .55 .25
1507 A336 80m multi .65 .25
1508 A336 1.20t multi .80 .30
Nos. 1502-1508 (7) 3.25 1.60

Souvenir Sheet

1509 A336 4t multi 1.90

Mink, Wildlife Conservation — A337

1986, June 15
1510 A337 60m Spring .75 .40
1511 A337 60m Summer .75 .40
1512 A337 60m Autumn .75 .40
1513 A337 60m Winter .75 .40
Nos. 1510-1513 (4) 3.00 1.60

Flowers — A338

Butterflies — A339

1986, June 1 Litho. *Perf. 14*
1514 A338 20m Valeriana officinalis .25 .20
1515 A338 30m Hyoscymus niger .30 .20
1516 A338 40m Ephedra sinica .35 .20
1517 A338 50m Thymus gobica .40 .20
1518 A338 60m Paeonia anomala .50 .25
1519 A338 80m Achilea millefolium .75 .30
1520 A338 1.20t Rhododendron adamsii 1.00 .40
Nos. 1514-1520 (7) 3.55 1.75

1986, Aug. 1 *Perf. 13½*
1521 A339 20m Neptis coenobita .25 .20
1522 A339 30m Colias tycha .30 .20
1523 A339 40m Leptidea amurensis .35 .20
1524 A339 50m Oeneis tarpenledevi .40 .25
1525 A339 60m Mesoacidalia charlotta .50 .25
1526 A339 80m Smerinthus ocellatus .75 .30
1527 A339 1.20t Pericalia matronula 1.00 .40
Nos. 1521-1527 (7) 3.55 1.80

Circus — A340

Animal trainers & acrobats. #1531-1534 vert.

1986, Aug. 1 *Perf. 14*
1528 A340 20m multi .25 .20
1529 A340 30m multi .30 .20
1530 A340 40m multi .35 .20
1531 A340 50m multi .40 .20
1532 A340 60m multi .50 .25
1533 A340 80m multi .75 .25
1534 A340 1.20t multi 1.00 .30
Nos. 1528-1534 (7) 3.55 1.60

Przewalski's Horses — A341

1986, Aug. 1 Litho. *Perf. 14*
1535 A341 50m Two horses, foal .75 .40
1536 A341 50m One facing left, two facing right .75 .40
1537 A341 50m Three facing right .75 .40
1538 A341 50m Four in storm .75 .40
Nos. 1535-1538 (4) 3.00 1.60

Pelicans *(Pelecanus)* — A341a

1986, Sept. 1 Litho. *Perf. 14*
1538A A341a 60m *crispus* feeding .80 .50
1538B A341a 60m *crispus* wading .80 .50
1538C A341a 60m *onocrotalus* flying .80 .50
1538D A341a 60m *onocrotalus* on land .80 .50
Nos. 1538A-1538D (4) 3.20 2.00

Saiga tatarica mongolica — A341b

1986, Sept. 15
1538E A341b 60m Spring (doe, fawn) .75 .40
1538F A341b 60m Summer (buck, doe) .75 .40
1538G A341b 60m Fall (buck) .75 .40
1538H A341b 60m Winter (buck, doe) .75 .40
Nos. 1538E-1538H (4) 3.00 1.60

Musical Instruments — A342

1986, Sept. 4
1539 A342 20m Morin khuur .25 .20
1540 A342 30m Bishguur .30 .20
1541 A342 40m Ever buree .35 .20
1542 A342 50m Shudarga .40 .25
1543 A342 60m Khiil .50 .25
1544 A342 80m Janchir .75 .30
1545 A342 1.20t Jatga 1.00 .30
Nos. 1539-1545 (7) 3.55 1.70

Souvenir Sheet

1546 A342 4t like 20m, vert. 3.50 3.50

STOCKHOLMIA '86. Nos. 1539-1543 vert.

Intl. Peace Year — A342a

1986, Sept. 20 Litho. *Perf. 13x13½*
1546A A342a 10m multicolored .75 .30

North American Bird Species — A343

1986, Oct. 1
1547 A343 60m Anthus spinoletta .80 .50
1548 A343 60m Aythya americana .80 .50

1549 A343 60m Bonasa umbellus .80 .50
1550 A343 60m Olor columbianus .80 .50
Nos. 1547-1550 (4) 3.20 2.00

Eastern Architecture — A343a

Various two-story buildings.

1986, Oct. 1

Color of Border

1551 A343a 60m dark grn & blk .80 .45
1552 A343a 60m beige & blk .80 .45
1553 A343a 60m apple grn & blk .80 .45
1554 A343a 60m red brn & blk .80 .45
Nos. 1551-1554 (4) 3.20 1.80

Classic Automobiles — A344

1986, Oct. 1 **Litho.** ***Perf. 14***

1554A A344 20m 1922 Alfa Romeo RL Sport, Italy .25 .20
1554B A344 30m 1912 Stutz Bearcat, US .30 .20
1554C A344 40m 1902 Mercedes Simplex, Germany .35 .20
1554D A344 50m 1923 Tatra 11, Czechoslovakia .40 .20
1554E A344 60m 1908 Ford Model T, US .50 .25
1554F A344 80m 1905 Vauxhall, England .75 .30
1554G A344 1.20t 1913 Russo-Baltik, Russia 1.00 .40
Nos. 1554A-1554G (7) 3.55 1.75

Souvenir Sheet

1554H A344 4t like 1.20t 3.50 3.50

Woodpeckers A344a

1986, Nov. 1

1555 A344a 20m Picus canus .25 .20
1556 A344a 30m Jynx torquilla .30 .20
1557 A344a 40m Dryobates major .35 .20
1558 A344a 50m Dryobates leucotos .40 .20
1559 A344a 60m Dryobates minor .50 .25
1560 A344a 80m Dryocopus martius .75 .30
1561 A344a 1.20t Picoides tridactylus 1.00 .40
Nos. 1555-1561 (7) 3.55 1.75

Souvenir Sheet

1562 A344a 4t Saphopipo noguchi 4.50 4.50

Chess Champions — A345

Portraits and chessmen on boards in match-winning configurations. No. 1562H, Chess champions Gary Kasparov, Jose R. Capablanca, Max Euwe, Vassily Smyslow, Mikhail Tal, Tigran Petrosian, Boris Spasski and Bobby Fischer; W. Menchik, L. Rudenko, E. Bykowa and O. Rubzowa.

1986, Nov. 1 ***Perf. 14***

1562A A345 20m Steinitz, Austria .25 .20
1562B A345 30m Lasker, Germany .30 .20
1562C A345 40m Alekhine, France .35 .20
1562D A345 50m Botvinnik, USSR .40 .20
1562E A345 60m Karpov, USSR .50 .25
1562F A345 80m N. Gaprindashvili .75 .25
1562G A345 1.20t M. Chiburdanidze 1.00 .30

Size: 110x100mm

Imperf

1562H A345 4t multi 4.50 4.50
Nos. 1562A-1562H (8) 8.05 6.10

Souvenir Sheet

Halley's Comet — A346

1986, Nov. 30 **Litho.** ***Perf. 14***

1563 A346 4t multicolored 4.50 4.00

Ovis Ammon Ammon — A347

1987, Jan. 1

1564 A347 60m shown .75 .40
1565 A347 60m In the mountains .75 .40
1566 A347 60m Close-up of head .75 .40
1567 A347 60m Male, female, lamb .75 .40
Nos. 1564-1567 (4) 3.00 1.60

Children's Activities A348

1987, Feb. 1

1568 A348 20m Backpacking, hunting butterflies .25 .20
1569 A348 30m Playing with calves .30 .20
1570 A348 40m Chalk-writing on cement .35 .20
1571 A348 50m Playing soccer .40 .20
1572 A348 60m Go-cart, model rocket, boat .45 .25
1573 A348 80m Agriculture .55 .25
1574 A348 1.20t Playing the morin khuur, dancing .80 .30
Nos. 1568-1574 (7) 3.10 1.60

Int'l. Peace Year (40m); Child Survival Campaign (50m).

13th Trade Unions Congress — A349

1987, Feb. 15 ***Perf. 13½x13***

1575 A349 60m multi 1.50 1.00

Equestrian Sports — A350

1987, Mar. 1

1576 A350 20m Lassoer .30 .20
1577 A350 30m Breaking horse .35 .20
1578 A350 40m Shooting bow .40 .20
1579 A350 50m Race .45 .20
1580 A350 60m Retrieving flags .50 .25
1581 A350 80m Tug-of-war .60 .25
1582 A350 1.20t Racing wolf .90 .30
Nos. 1576-1582 (7) 3.50 1.60

Admission into Comecon, 25th Anniv. — A351

1987, Apr. 15 ***Perf. 13x13½***

1583 A351 60m multi .75 .40

Fruit — A352

A353

1987, June 1 ***Perf. 13½***

1584 A352 20m Hippophae rhamnoides .30 .20
1585 A352 30m Ribes nigrum .35 .20
1586 A352 40m Ribes rubrus .40 .20
1587 A352 50m Ribes altissimum .50 .20
1588 A352 60m Rubus sachalinensis .55 .25
1589 A352 80m Padus asiatica .60 .25
1590 A352 1.20t Fragaria orientalis .90 .25
Nos. 1584-1590 (7) 3.60 1.55

Souvenir Sheet

Perf. 14

1591 A353 4t Malus domestica 3.50 3.50

Soviet-Mongolian Diplomatic Relations, 50th Anniv. — A354

Russian Revolution, 70th Anniv. — A355

1987, July 1 ***Perf. 13x13½***

1592 A354 60m multi .75 .45

1987, July 1

1593 A355 60m multi .75 .45

Folk Dances — A356

1987, Aug. 1 ***Perf. 14***

1594 A356 20m multi .20 .20
1595 A356 30m multi, diff. .25 .20
1596 A356 40m multi, diff. .35 .20
1597 A356 50m multi, diff. .55 .20
1598 A356 60m multi, diff. .65 .25
1599 A356 80m multi, diff. .75 .25
1600 A356 1.20t multi, diff. 1.00 .30
Nos. 1594-1600 (7) 3.75 1.60

Antiques A357

Full costume and accessories.

1987, Aug. 10

1601 A357 20m Folk costumes .20 .20
1602 A357 30m Gilded nunchaku .25 .20
1603 A357 40m Brooches .35 .20
1604 A357 50m Draw-string pouch, rice bowl .55 .20

1605 A357 60m Headdress .65 .25
1606 A357 80m Pouches, bottle, pipe .75 .25
1607 A357 1.20t Sash, brooch 1.00 .30
Nos. 1601-1607 (7) 3.75 1.60

Souvenir Sheet

HAFNIA '87 — A358

1987, Aug. 10
1608 A358 4t multi 4.00 3.00

Swans — A359

1987, Aug. 15
1609 A359 60m Cygnus olor on land .80 .50
1610 A359 60m Cygnus olor in water .80 .50
1611 A359 60m Cygnus beruickii .80 .50
1612 A359 60m Cygnus beruickii, gunus and olor .80 .50
Nos. 1609-1612 (4) 3.20 2.00

Domestic and Wild Cats — A360

1987, Oct. 1 Litho. *Perf. 14*
1613 A360 20m multi, vert. .30 .20
1614 A360 30m multi, vert. .35 .20
1615 A360 40m multi, vert. .40 .20
1616 A360 50m shown .50 .25
1617 A360 60m multi .60 .25
1618 A360 80m multi .75 .30
1619 A360 1.20t multi 1.10 .30
Nos. 1613-1619 (7) 4.00 1.70

Miniature Sheet

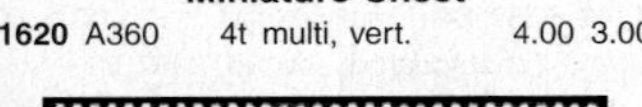

1620 A360 4t multi, vert. 4.00 3.00

Helicopter — A361

1987, Oct. 3 *Perf. 12½x11½*
1621 A361 20m B-12 .20 .20
1622 A361 30m Westland-WG-30 .25 .20
1623 A361 40m Bell-S-206L .45 .20
1624 A361 50m Kawasaki-369HS .50 .20
1625 A361 60m KA-32 .65 .25
1626 A361 80m MI-17 .80 .25
1627 A361 1.20t MI-10K 1.10 .30
Nos. 1621-1627 (7) 3.95 1.60

Disney Cartoons — A362

The Brave Little Tailor (25m-55m, 2t, No. 1637), and The Celebrated Jumping Frog of Calaveras County (65m-1.40t, No. 1638).

1987, Nov. 23 *Perf. 14*
1628 A362 25m multi .20 .20
1629 A362 35m multi .40 .20
1630 A362 45m multi .50 .20
1631 A362 55m multi .55 .20
1632 A362 65m multi .65 .25
1633 A362 75m multi .75 .25
1634 A362 85m multi 1.00 .30
1635 A362 1.40t multi 1.25 .50
1636 A362 2t multi 2.00 .75
Nos. 1628-1636 (9) 7.30 2.85

Souvenir Sheets

1637 A362 7t multi 5.50 5.50
1638 A362 7t multi 5.50 5.50

A363

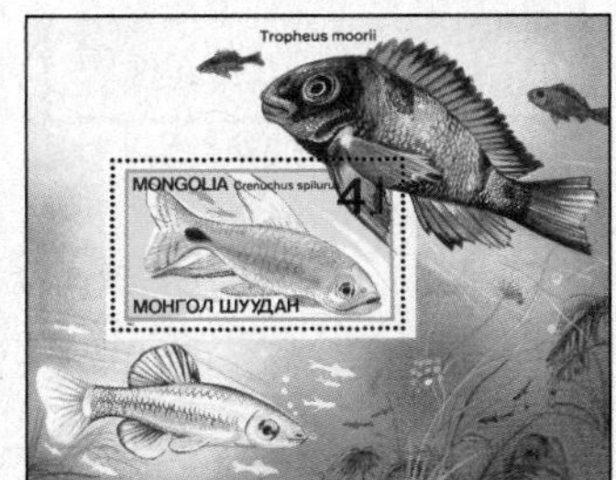

Tropical Fish — A364

1987, Oct. *Perf. 13x12½, 12½x13*
1639 A363 20m Betta splendens .30 .20
1640 A363 30m Carassius auratus .35 .20
1641 A363 40m Rasbora hengeli .40 .20
1642 A363 50m Aequidens .50 .20
1643 A363 60m Xiphophorus macalatus .65 .25
1644 A363 80m Xiphophorus helleri .90 .25
1645 A363 1.20t Pterophyllum scalare, vert. 1.25 .30
Nos. 1639-1645 (7) 4.35 1.60

Miniature Sheet
Perf. 14

1646 A364 4t Crenuchus spilurus 4.50 4.50

19th Communist Party Congress A365

1987, Dec. *Perf. 14*
1647 A365 60m Family .50 .20
1648 A365 60m Construction .50 .20
1649 A365 60m Jet, harvesting, produce .50 .20
1650 A365 60m Education .50 .20
1651 A365 60m Transportation .50 .20
1652 A365 60m Heavy industry .50 .20
1653 A365 60m Science and technology .50 .20
Nos. 1647-1653 (7) 3.50 1.40

Vulpes Vulpes (Fox) — A366

1987, Dec.
1654 A366 60m Adult in snow .75 .45
1655 A366 60m Adult, young .75 .45
1656 A366 60m Adult in field .75 .45
1657 A366 60m Close-up of head .75 .45
Nos. 1654-1657 (4) 3.00 1.80

Souvenir Sheet

INTERCOSMOS — A367

1987, Dec. 15 Litho. *Perf. 14*
1658 A367 4t multi 3.50 3.00

Souvenir Sheet

PRAGA '88 — A368

1988, Jan. 30
1659 A368 4t 1923 Tatra 11 3.50 3.00

Sukhe Bator — A369

1988, Feb. 2 *Perf. 13x13½*
1660 A369 60m multi .80 .50

Roses — A370

19th Communist Youth Congress — A371

1988, Feb. 20 *Perf. 14*
1661 A370 20m Invitation .30 .20
1662 A370 30m Meilland .55 .20
1663 A370 40m Pascali .40 .20
1664 A370 50m Tropicana .50 .20
1665 A370 60m Wendy Cussons .55 .25
1666 A370 80m Blue moon .60 .25
1667 A370 1.20t Diorama .90 .30
Nos. 1661-1667 (7) 3.80 1.60

Souvenir Sheet

1668 A370 4t shown 3.50 3.00

1988, Apr. 15 *Perf. 12½x13*
1669 A371 60m multicolored .80 .50

Puppets — A372

Folk tales.

1988, Apr. 1 Litho. *Perf. 14*
1670 A372 20m Ukhaant Ekhner .20 .20
1671 A372 30m Altan Everte Mungun Turuut .30 .20
1672 A372 40m Aduuchyn Khuu .40 .20
1673 A372 50m Suulenkhuu .45 .20
1674 A372 60m Khonchyn Khuu .60 .25
1675 A372 80m Argat Byatskhan Baatar .80 .25
1676 A372 1.20t Botgochyn Khuu 1.25 .30
Nos. 1670-1676 (7) 4.00 1.60

1988 Summer Olympics, Seoul — A373

Soviet Space Achievements
A374

1988, Feb. 15

1677 A373 20m Judo .20 .20
1678 A373 30m Women's archery .25 .20
1679 A373 40m Weight lifting .40 .20
1680 A373 50m Women's gymnastics .45 .20
1681 A373 60m Cycling .50 .25
1682 A373 80m Running .60 .25
1683 A373 1.20t Wrestling 1.00 .30
Nos. 1677-1683 (7) 3.40 1.60

Souvenir Sheet

1684 A373 4t Boxing 3.50 3.00

1988, May 15

1685 A374 20m Cosmos .20 .20
1686 A374 30m Meteor .25 .20
1687 A374 40m Salyut-Soyuz .40 .20
1688 A374 50m Prognoz-6 .45 .20
1689 A374 60m Molniya-1 .50 .20
1690 A374 80m Soyuz .60 .20
1691 A374 1.20t Vostok 1.00 .25
Nos. 1685-1691 (7) 3.40 1.45

Effigies of Buddhist Deities — A375

Various statues.

1988, June 15 **Litho.** ***Perf. 14***

1692 A375 20m multi .20 .20
1693 A375 30m multi, diff. .25 .20
1694 A375 40m multi, diff. .35 .20
1695 A375 50m multi, diff. .50 .20
1696 A375 60m multi, diff. .65 .25
1697 A375 70m multi, diff. .85 .25
1698 A375 80m multi, diff. 1.00 .30
1699 A375 1.20t multi, diff. 1.50 .30
Nos. 1692-1699 (8) 5.30 1.90

Wildlife Conservation — A376

Eagles, Haliaeetus albicilla. Nos. 1700-1702 vert.

1988, Aug. 1 **Litho.** ***Perf. 14***

1700 A376 60m Eagle facing left, diff. .80 .50
1701 A376 60m Landing on branch .80 .50
1702 A376 60m Facing right .80 .50
1703 A376 60m shown .80 .50
Nos. 1700-1703 (4) 3.20 2.00

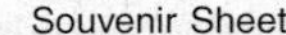
Souvenir Sheet

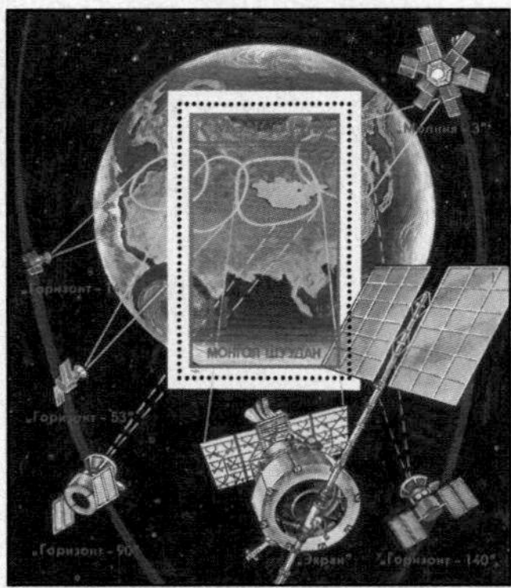

Cosmos — A377

1988, Sept. 15 **Litho.** ***Perf. 14***

1704 A377 4t Satellite links 4.00 4.00

Opera — A378

1988, Oct. 1 **Litho.** ***Perf. 13x12½***

1705 A378 60m multi + label 1.50 .75

Equus hemionus — A380

1988, May 3

1713 A380 60m Mare, foal .80 .50
1714 A380 60m Ass's head .80 .50
1715 A380 60m Ass galloping .80 .50
1716 A380 60m Ass cantering .80 .50
Nos. 1713-1716 (4) 3.20 2.00

Winners of the 1988 Winter Olympics, Calgary — A381

1988, July 1

1717 A381 1.50t Matti Nykaenen, Finland 1.00 .45
1718 A381 1.50t Bonnie Blair, US 1.00 .45
1719 A381 1.50t Alberto Tomba, Italy 1.00 .45
1720 A381 1.50t USSR hockey team 1.00 .45
Nos. 1717-1720 (4) 4.00 1.80

Souvenir Sheet

1721 A381 4t Katarina Witt, DDR 4.00 4.00

Nos. 1718-1720 vert.

A382

A383

1988, Sept. 1

1722 A382 10m shown .20 .20
1723 A382 20m Horsemanship .25 .20
1724 A382 30m Archery .35 .20
1725 A382 40m Wrestling .45 .20
1726 A382 50m Archery, diff. .55 .25
1727 A382 70m Horsemanship, diff. .80 .25
1728 A382 1.20t Horsemanship, wrestling, archery 1.50 .30
Nos. 1722-1728 (7) 4.10 1.60

1988, Dec. 1 ***Perf. 13x13½***

1729 A383 60m multicolored 1.00 .50

Socialism and Peace.

Goats — A384

Various species.

1989, Jan. 15 ***Perf. 14***

1730 A384 20m multi .20 .20
1731 A384 30m multi .35 .20
1732 A384 40m multi .50 .20
1733 A384 50m multi .60 .20
1734 A384 60m multi .75 .25
1735 A384 80m multi .85 .25
1736 A384 1.20t multi 1.25 .30
Nos. 1730-1736 (7) 4.50 1.60

Souvenir Sheet

1737 A384 4t multi, vert. 4.00 4.00

Souvenir Sheet

Child Survival — A385

1989, Jan. 28 **Litho.** ***Perf. 14***

1738 A385 4t Drawing by H. Jargalsuren 4.00 4.00

Karl Marx — A386

1989, Feb. 25 **Litho.** ***Perf. 13x13½***

1739 A386 60m multicolored .80 .30

Miniature Sheet

Statue of Sukhe Bator — A387

Mongolian Airline Jet — A388

1989, July 1 ***Perf. 14***

1740 Sheet of 3 8.00 8.00
a. A387 20m Concorde jet .75 .50
b. A387 60m TGV high-speed train 2.00 1.75
c. A387 1.20t shown 4.50 4.00

Souvenir Sheet

1741 A388 4t shown 4.50 4.50

PHILEXFRANCE '89, BULGARIA '89.
For overprint see No. 1756.

World War II Memorial
A389

1989, Sept. 2

1742 A389 60m multicolored 1.00 .50

For surcharge, see No. 2384B.

Cacti — A390

1989, Sept. 7

1743 A390 20m *O. microdasys* .20 .20
1744 A390 30m *E. multipiex* .25 .20
1745 A390 40m *R. tephracanthus* .45 .20
1746 A390 50m *B. haselbergii* .60 .20
1747 A390 60m *G. mihanovichii* .70 .25
1748 A390 80m *C. strausii* .85 .25
1749 A390 1.20t *Horridocactus tuberisvicatus* 1.10 .30
Nos. 1743-1749 (7) 4.15 1.60

Souvenir Sheet

1750 A390 4t *Astrophytum ornatum* 4.00 4.00

A391

A392

Winners at the 1988 Summer Olympics, Seoul.

1989, Oct. 1

1751 A391 60m Kristin Otto, East Germany .80 .45
1752 A391 60m Florence Griffith-Joyner, US .80 .45
1753 A391 60m Gintaoutas Umaras, USSR .80 .45
1754 A391 60m Stefano Cerioni, Italy .80 .45
Nos. 1751-1754 (4) 3.20 1.80

Souvenir Sheet

1755 A391 4t N. Enkhbat, Mongolia 4.00 4.00

No. 1740 Overprinted for WORLD STAMP EXPO '89

1989, Nov. 17 **Miniature Sheet**

1756 Sheet of 3 8.00 8.00
a. A387 20m multicolored .75 .50
b. A387 60m multicolored 2.00 1.50
c. A387 1.20t multicolored 4.50 4.00

1989, Dec. 1

1757 A392 60m Books, fountain pen .75 .45

Beavers *(Castor fiber birulai)* — A393

1989, Dec. 10

1758 A393 60m Cutting down saplings .80 .50
1759 A393 60m Rolling wood across ground .80 .50
1760 A393 60m Beaver on land, in water .80 .50
1761 A393 60m Beaver and young .80 .50
Nos. 1758-1761 (4) 3.20 2.00

Medals and Military Decorations — A394

1989, Dec. 31 ***Perf. 13x13½***

1762 A394 60m pink & multi 1.25 .75
1763 A394 60m lt blue grn & multi 1.25 .75
1764 A394 60m vio & multi 1.25 .75
1765 A394 60m org & multi 1.25 .75
1766 A394 60m brt blue & multi 1.25 .75
1767 A394 60m ver & multi 1.25 .75
1768 A394 60m vio blue & multi 1.25 .75
Nos. 1762-1768 (7) 8.75 5.25

Bears and Giant Pandas — A395

1990, Jan. 1 ***Perf. 14***

1769 A395 20m *Ursus pruinosis* .20 .20
1770 A395 30m *Ursus arctos syriacus* .30 .20
1771 A395 40m *Ursus thibetanus* .40 .25
1772 A395 50m *Ursus maritimus* .55 .30
1773 A395 60m *Ursus arctos bruinosus* .65 .40
1774 A395 80m *Ailuropus melanoleucus* .85 .50
1775 A395 1.20t *Ursus arctos isabellinus* 1.25 1.00
Nos. 1769-1775 (7) 4.20 2.85

Souvenir Sheet

1776 A395 4t *Ailuropus melanoleucus,* diff. 6.00 4.00

Winter Sports — A396

1990, Jan. 6

1777 A396 20m 4-man bobsled .20 .20
1778 A396 30m Luge .30 .20
1779 A396 40m Women's figure skating .40 .20
1780 A396 50m 1-man bobsled .50 .20
1781 A396 60m Pairs figure skating .60 .25
1782 A396 80m Speed skating .75 .25
1783 A396 1.20t Ice speedway 1.25 .30
Nos. 1777-1783 (7) 4.00 1.60

Souvenir Sheet

1784 A396 4t Ice hockey 4.25 4.25

Space Exploration — A397

Rockets and spacecraft: 20m, Soyuz, USSR. 30m, Apollo-Soyuz, US-USSR. 40m, *Columbia* space shuttle, US, vert. 50m, *Hermes,* France. 60m, *Nippon,* Japan, vert. 80m, *Enerqy,* USSR, vert. 1.20t, *Buran,* USSR, vert. 4t, *Sanger,* West Germany.

1990, Jan. 30

1785 A397 20m shown .20 .20
1786 A397 30m multicolored .30 .20
1787 A397 40m multicolored .40 .25
1788 A397 50m multicolored .50 .25
1789 A397 60m multicolored .60 .30
1790 A397 80m multicolored .75 .30
1791 A397 1.20t multicolored 1.25 .40
Nos. 1785-1791 (7) 4.00 1.90

Souvenir Sheet

1792 A397 4t multicolored 4.25 4.25

Jawaharlal Nehru, 1st Prime Minister of Independent India — A398

1990, Feb. 10

1793 A398 10m gold, blk & dark red brn 1.50 .75

Statue of Sukhe Bator — A399

1990, Feb. 27

1794 A399 10m multicolored 1.50 .75

Mongolian Ballet — A400

Dancers in scenes from various ballets. 40m, 80m, 1.20t vert.

1990, Feb. 28

1795 A400 20m shown .20 .20
1796 A400 30m multi .30 .20
1797 A400 40m multi .45 .20
1798 A400 50m multi .55 .20
1799 A400 60m multi .65 .25
1800 A400 80m multi .75 .25
1801 A400 1.20t multi 1.10 .30
Nos. 1795-1801 (7) 4.00 1.60

Automobiles — A401

1990, Mar. 26

1802 A401 20m Citroen, France .20 .20
1803 A401 30m Volvo 760 GLF, Sweden .30 .20
1804 A401 40m Honda, Japan .40 .20
1805 A401 50m Volga, USSR .50 .20
1806 A401 60m Ford Granada, US .60 .25
1807 A401 80m BAZ 21099, USSR .75 .25
1808 A401 1.20t Mercedes Class 190, West Germany 1.25 .30
Nos. 1802-1808 (7) 4.00 1.60

Souvenir Sheet

1809 A401 4t like 50m 4.50 4.50

Lenin — A402

1990, Mar. 27 ***Perf. 13x13½***

1810 A402 60m gold, black & ver 1.00 .50

Unen Newspaper, 70th Anniv. — A403

1990, Apr. 1 ***Perf. 14***

1811 A403 60m multicolored 1.00 .50

End of World War II, 45th Anniv. — A404

1990, Apr. 1

1812 A404 60m multicolored 1.25 .60

Buddhist Deities (18th-20th Cent. Paintings)
A405

1990, Apr. 1

1813 A405 20m Damdin Sandub .25 .20
1814 A405 30m Pagwa Lama .40 .20
1815 A405 40m Chu Lha .50 .25
1816 A405 50m Agwanglobsan .60 .30
1817 A405 60m Dorje Dags Dan .75 .30
1818 A405 80m Wangchikdorje .85 .40
1819 A405 1.20t Buddha 1.10 .50
Nos. 1813-1819 (7) 4.45 2.15

Souvenir Sheet

1820 A405 4t Migjed Jang-Rasek 6.50 6.50

A406

Aspects of a Cooperative Settlement — A407

Paintings: 20m, Animals on plain, rainbow. 30m, Workers, reindeer, dog, vert. 40m, Two men, mountains, Bactrian camels. 50m, Man, Bactrian camels. 60m, Huts, animal shelter, corral. 80m, Breaking horses, vert. 1.20t, Sheep, shepherd girl on horse. 4t, Wrestling match.

Illustration A407 reduced.

1990, Apr. 1

1821 A406 20m shown .40 .20
1822 A406 30m multicolored .50 .20
1823 A406 40m multicolored .60 .25
1824 A406 50m multicolored .70 .30
1825 A406 60m multicolored .90 .40
1826 A406 80m multicolored 1.25 .50
1827 A406 1.20t multicolored 1.75 .55
Nos. 1821-1827 (7) 6.10 2.40

Souvenir Sheet

1828 A407 4t shown 7.00 7.00

Scenes from Various Mongolian-made Films — A408

1990, Apr. 1

1829 A408 20m shown .30 .20
1830 A408 30m multi, diff. .40 .25
1831 A408 40m multi, diff. .60 .30
1832 A408 50m multi, diff. .80 .40
1833 A408 60m multi, diff. 1.10 .50
1834 A408 80m multi, diff. 1.25 .65
1835 A408 1.20t multi, diff. 1.75 1.00
Nos. 1829-1835 (7) 6.20 3.30

Souvenir Sheet

1836 A408 4t multi, diff., vert. 7.00 7.00

Souvenir Sheet

Stamp World London '90 — A409

1990, Apr. 1

1837 A409 4t multicolored 5.50 5.50

1990 World Cup Soccer Championships, Italy — A410

Trophy and various athletes.

1990, Apr. 30

1838 A410 20m multicolored .20 .20
1839 A410 30m multicolored .30 .20
1840 A410 40m multicolored .40 .20
1841 A410 50m multicolored .50 .20
1842 A410 60m multicolored .60 .20
1843 A410 80m multicolored .75 .25
1844 A410 1.20t multicolored 1.25 .25
Nos. 1838-1844 (7) 4.00 1.50

Souvenir Sheet

1845 A410 4t Trophy, vert. 4.50 4.50

Nos. 304-307 Ovptd.

CHINGGIS KHAN CROWNATION 1189

1990, May 1 Photo. *Perf. 11½x12*

1846 A84 20m multicolored *10.00*
1847 A84 30m multicolored *12.50*
1848 A84 50m multicolored *12.50*
1849 A84 60m multicolored *15.00*
Nos. 1846-1849 (4) *50.00*

Coronation of Genghis Khan, 800th anniv. (in 1989).

Souvenir Sheet

Genghis Khan — A411

1990, May 8 Litho. *Perf. 13½*

1850 A411 7t multicolored 7.50 7.50

Stamp World London '90. Exists imperf. Exists without "Stamp World London '90" and Great Britain No. 1.

Cranes *(Grus vipio pallas)* — A412

1990, May 23 *Perf. 14*

1851 A412 60m brt blue & multi .90 .60
1852 A412 60m brt rose lil & multi .90 .60
1853 A412 60m red lil & multi .90 .60
1854 A412 60m car rose & multi .90 .60
Nos. 1851-1854 (4) 3.60 2.40

Nos. 1853-1854 are vert.

Marine Mammals — A413

1990, June 20 Litho. *Perf. 14*

1855 A413 20m Balaenoptera physalus .30 .20
1856 A413 30m Megaptera novaeangliae .40 .20
1857 A413 40m Monodon monoceros .45 .25
1858 A413 50m Grampus griseus .55 .30
1859 A413 60m Tursiops truncatus .70 .40
1860 A413 80m Lagenorhynchus acutius .95 .50
1861 A413 1.20t Balaena mysticetus 1.40 .55
Nos. 1855-1861 (7) 4.75 2.40

Souvenir Sheet

1861A A413 4t Killer whale 4.50 4.50

A414

Cultural Heritage — A415

1990, Aug. 13 *Perf. 13x12½*

1862 A414 10m shown .25 .20
1863 A414 10m Like No. 1862, arrows at left .25 .20
1864 A415 40m Fire ring .60 .20
1865 A415 60m Genghis Khan .80 .25
1866 A414 60m Tent .80 .25
1867 A414 60m Horses .80 .25
1868 A414 80m Royal family (green panel) 1.25 .40
1869 A414 80m Royal court (dk bl panel) 1.25 .40
a. Souv. sheet, #1862-1869 + label 8.00 8.00
Nos. 1862-1869 (8) 6.00 2.15

20th Party Congress
A416

1990, Mar. 1 Litho. *Perf. 14*

1870 A416 60m multicolored 1.00 .50

Dinosaurs — A417

1990, Aug. 25

1871 A417 20m shown .40 .20
1872 A417 30m multi, diff. .50 .20
1873 A417 40m multi, diff. .65 .25
1874 A417 50m multi, diff .75 .30
1875 A417 60m multi, vert. 1.00 .40
1876 A417 80m multi, diff. 1.25 .50

Size: 60x21mm

Perf. 13

1877 A417 1.20t multi, diff. 1.75 .55
Nos. 1871-1877 (7) 6.30 2.40

Souvenir Sheet

1878 A417 4t multi, diff. 6.00 6.00

Giant Pandas — A418

1990, Aug. 15 Litho. *Perf. 14*

1879 A418 10m Adult on rock, vert. .25 .20
1880 A418 20m Adult, eating, vert. .30 .20
1881 A418 30m Adult and cub, vert. .45 .25
1882 A418 40m shown .60 .30
1883 A418 50m Adult and cub, resting .70 .40
1884 A418 60m Adult, mountains .90 .50
1885 A418 80m Adult and cub, playing 1.25 .65
1886 A418 1.20t Adult, in winter 1.75 1.00
Nos. 1879-1886 (8) 6.20 3.50

Souvenir Sheet

1887 A418 4t Family 6.00 6.00

Pyramids of Egypt — A419

Seven wonders of the ancient world: 20m, Lighthouse of Alexander, vert. 40m, Statue of Zeus, vert. 50m, Colossus of Rhodes, vert. 60m, Mausoleum of Halicarnassus, vert. 80m, Temple of Artemis. 1.20t, Hanging gardens of Babylon, vert. 4t, Pyramids of Egypt, vert.

1990, Sept. 25

1888 A419 20m multicolored .35 .20
1889 A419 30m shown .45 .20
1890 A419 40m multicolored .65 .25
1891 A419 50m multicolored .75 .25
1892 A419 60m multicolored 1.00 .25
1893 A419 80m multicolored 1.25 .40
1894 A419 1.20t multicolored 1.75 .65
Nos. 1888-1894 (7) 6.20 2.20

Souvenir Sheet

1895 A419 4t multicolored 6.00 6.00

Moschus Moschiferus — A419a

1990, Sept. 26 **Litho.** ***Perf. 14***

1895A A419a 60m shown .90 .60
1895B A419a 60m In snow .90 .60
1895C A419a 60m Facing left .90 .60
1895D A419a 60m Two, one on ground .90 .60
Nos. 1895A-1895D (4) 3.60 2.40

Parrots — A420

1990, Oct. 25 **Litho.** ***Perf. 14***

1896 A420 20m shown .30 .20
1897 A420 30m multi, diff. .40 .20
1898 A420 40m multi, diff. .60 .25
1899 A420 50m multi, diff. .70 .30
1900 A420 60m multi, diff. .90 .40
1901 A420 80m multi, diff. 1.25 .50
1902 A420 1.20t multi, diff. 1.50 .55
Nos. 1896-1902 (7) 5.65 2.40

Souvenir Sheet

1903 A420 4t multi, diff. 5.50 5.50

Butterflies — A421

Designs: 20m, Purpurbar. 30m, Grosses nachtpfauenauge. 40m, Grosser C-Falter. 50m, Stachelbeerspanner. 60m, Damenbrett. 80m, Schwalbenschwanz. 1.20t, Aurorafalter. 4t, Linienschwarmer, vert.

1990, Nov. 25 **Litho.** ***Perf. 14***

1904 A421 20m multicolored .30 .20
1905 A421 30m multicolored .40 .20
1906 A421 40m multicolored .60 .25
1907 A421 50m multicolored .80 .30
1908 A421 60m multicolored .90 .40
1909 A421 80m multicolored 1.10 .50
1910 A421 1.20t multicolored 1.60 .55
Nos. 1904-1910 (7) 5.70 2.40

Souvenir Sheet

1911 A421 4t multicolored 5.50 5.50

Flintstones Visit Mongolia — A422

Designs: 25m, Dino, Bamm-Bamm. 35m, Dino, Bamm-Bamm, diff., vert. 45m, Betty, Wilma, Bamm-Bamm, Pebbles. 55m, Fred, Barney, Dino. 65m, Flintstones & Rubbles. 75m, Bamm-Bamm riding Dino. 85m, Fred, Barney, Bamm-Bamm. 1.40t, Flintstones, Rubbles in car. 2t, Fred, Barney. No. 1921, Wilma, Betty & Bamm-Bamm. No. 1922, Bamm-Bamm, Pebbles riding Dino.

1991, Feb. 10 **Litho.** ***Perf. 14***

1912 A422 25m multicolored .30 .20
1913 A422 35m multicolored .40 .20
1914 A422 45m multicolored .55 .25
1915 A422 55m multicolored .65 .25
1916 A422 65m multicolored .80 .25
1917 A422 75m multicolored .90 .30
1918 A422 85m multicolored 1.00 .30
1919 A422 1.40t multicolored 1.70 .40
1920 A422 2t multicolored 2.40 .40
Nos. 1912-1920 (9) 8.70 2.55

Souvenir Sheets

1921 A422 7t multicolored 5.50 5.50
1922 A422 7t multicolored 5.50 5.50

The Jetsons A423

Designs: 20m, Jetsons blasting off in spaceship. 25m, Jetsons on planet, horiz. 30m, George, Jane, Elroy & Astro. 40m, George, Judy, Elroy & Astro. 50m, Jetsons in spaceship, horiz. 60m, George, Jane, Elroy & Mr. Spacely, horiz. 70m, George, Elroy wearing jet packs. 80m, Elroy. 1.20t, Elroy, Judy & Astro. No. 1932, Elroy, red flowers. No. 1933, Elroy, blue flowers.

1991, Feb. 10

1923 A423 20m multicolored .25 .20
1924 A423 25m multicolored .30 .20
1925 A423 30m multicolored .35 .25
1926 A423 40m multicolored .50 .25
1927 A423 50m multicolored .60 .30
1928 A423 60m multicolored .70 .30
1929 A423 70m multicolored .85 .30
1930 A423 80m multicolored 1.00 .40
1931 A423 1.20t multicolored 1.50 .40
Nos. 1923-1931 (9) 6.05 2.60

Souvenir Sheets

1932 A423 7t multicolored 5.50 5.50
1933 A423 7t multicolored 5.50 5.50

Mongolian People's Revolutionary Party, 70th Anniv. — A423a

1991, Mar. 1 **Litho.** ***Perf. 14***

1933A A423a 60m multicolored .90 .40

A424

Stamp World London '90 — A425

Various birds.

1991, Mar. 3 **Litho.** ***Perf. 14½***

1934 A424 25m multicolored .25 .20
1935 A424 35m multicolored .35 .20
1936 A424 45m multicolored .50 .20
1937 A424 55m multicolored .60 .20
1938 A424 65m multicolored .75 .25
1939 A424 75m multi, horiz. .80 .30
1940 A424 85m multicolored 1.00 .40
1941 A424 1.40t multicolored 1.50 .50
1942 A424 2t multicolored 2.25 .55
Nos. 1934-1942 (9) 8.00 2.80

Souvenir Sheets

1943 A424 7t multicolored 7.00 7.00
1944 A425 7t multicolored 7.00 7.00

Butterflies and Flowers of Mongolia — A426

Designs: 20m, 30m-60m, various butterflies. Others, various flowers.

1991, Mar. 3 **Litho.** ***Perf. 14½***

1945 A426 20m multicolored .45 .20
1946 A426 25m multicolored .50 .20
1947 A426 30m multicolored .65 .20
1948 A426 40m multicolored .85 .20
1949 A426 50m multicolored 1.00 .25
1950 A426 60m multicolored 1.25 .25
1951 A426 70m multicolored 1.50 .30
1952 A426 80m multicolored 1.75 .30
1953 A426 1.20t multicolored 2.25 .40
Nos. 1945-1953 (9) 10.20 2.30

Nos. 1945-1953 and Types Overprinted

1991, Mar. 3

1954 A426 20m multicolored .45 .20
1955 A426 25m multicolored .50 .20
1956 A426 30m multicolored .65 .20
1957 A426 40m multicolored .85 .20
1958 A426 50m multicolored 1.00 .25
1959 A426 60m multicolored 1.25 .25
1960 A426 70m multicolored 1.50 .30
1961 A426 80m multicolored 1.75 .30
1962 A426 1.20t multicolored 2.25 .40
Nos. 1954-1962 (9) 10.20 2.30

Souvenir Sheets

1963 A426 7t Butterfly 10.00 10.00
1964 A426 7t Flower 10.00 10.00

Nos. 1963-1964 were not issued without overprint which appears in sheet margin only.

Mongolian People's Army, 70th Anniv. — A426a

1991, Mar. 18 **Litho.** ***Perf. 14***

1964A A426a 60m multicolored .80 .50

Birds — A427

1991, Apr. 1 ***Perf. 14***

1965 A427 20m Lururus tetrix .30 .20
1966 A427 30m Tadorna tadorna .50 .20
1967 A427 40m Phasianus colchicus .60 .25
1968 A427 50m Clangula byemalis .80 .30
1969 A427 60m Tetrastes bonasia 1.00 .40
1970 A427 80m Mergus serrator 1.25 .50
1971 A427 1.20t Bucephala clangula 1.75 .75
Nos. 1965-1971 (7) 6.20 2.60

Souvenir Sheet

1972 A427 4t Anas crecca, vert. 6.00 6.00

Flowers — A428

1991, Apr. 15

1973 A428 20m Dianthus superbus .25 .20
1974 A428 30m Gentiana puenmonanthe .40 .20
1975 A428 40m Taraxacum officinale .60 .25
1976 A428 50m Iris sibrica .70 .30
1977 A428 60m Lilium martagon .80 .40
1978 A428 80m Aster amellus 1.10 .50
1979 A428 1.20t Cizsium rivulare 1.60 .55
Nos. 1973-1979 (7) 5.45 2.40

Souvenir Sheet

1980 A428 4t Campanula persicifolia 5.50 5.50

Buddhist Effigies — A429

1991, May 1

1981 A429 20m Defend .35 .20
1982 A429 30m Badmasanhava .40 .20
1983 A429 40m Avalokitecvara .55 .25
1984 A429 50m Buddha .75 .30
1985 A429 60m Mintugwa .80 .40

1986	A429	80m	Shyamatara	1.10	.50
1987	A429	1.20t	Samvara	1.50	.55
			Nos. 1981-1987 (7)	5.45	2.40

Souvenir Sheet

1988	A429	4t	Lamidhatara	5.50	5.50

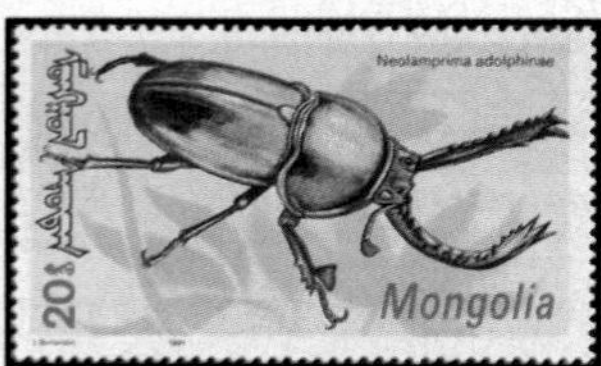

Insects — A430

1991, May 22

1989	A430	20m	Neolamprima adolphinae	.35	.20
1990	A430	30m	Chelorrhina polyphemus	.40	.20
1991	A430	40m	Coptolabrus coelestis	.55	.25
1992	A430	50m	Epepeotes togatus	.75	.30
1993	A430	60m	Cicindela chinensis	.80	.40
1994	A430	80m	Macrodontia cervicornis	1.25	.50
1995	A430	1.20t	Dynastes hercules	1.50	.55
			Nos. 1989-1995 (7)	5.60	2.40

Souvenir Sheet

1991, May 22 Litho. *Perf. 14*

1995A	A430	4t	Cercopis sanguinolenta, vert.	5.50	5.50

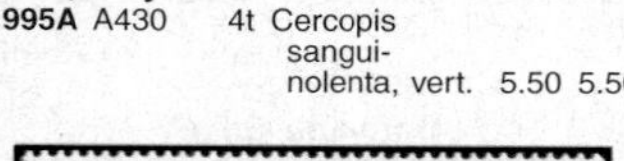

African Animals — A431

1991, May 23

1996	A431	20m	Zebras	.30	.20
1997	A431	30m	Cheetah	.40	.20
1998	A431	40m	Black rhinos	.60	.25
1999	A431	50m	Giraffe, vert.	.80	.30
2000	A431	60m	Gorilla	.90	.40
2001	A431	80m	Elephants	1.10	.50
2002	A431	1.20t	Lion, vert.	1.50	.55
			Nos. 1996-2002 (7)	5.60	2.40

Souvenir Sheet

2003	A431	4t	Gazelle	5.50	5.50

No. 1997 is incorrectly spelled "Cheetan."

Exhibition of Meiso Mizuhara's Mongolian Stamp Collection — A432

1991, June Litho. *Perf. 13½*

2004	A432	1.20t	multicolored	3.00	1.25

Lizards — A433

1991, Oct. 29 *Perf. 14*

2005	A433	20m	Iguana iguana	.30	.20
2006	A433	30m	Ptychozoon kihli	.40	.20
2007	A433	40m	Chlamydosaurus kingii	.65	.25
2008	A433	50m	Cordylus cordylus	.75	.30
2009	A433	60m	Basiliscus basilisus	.80	.40
2010	A433	80m	Tupinambis teguixin	1.10	.50
2011	A433	1.20t	Amblyrhynchus cristatus	1.75	.55
			Nos. 2005-2011 (7)	5.75	2.40

Souvenir Sheet

2012	A433	4t	Varanus bengalensis, vert.	5.50	5.50

Masks and Costumes A434

Various masks and costumes.

1991, Oct. 1

2013	A434	35m	multicolored	.40	.20
2014	A434	45m	multicolored	.50	.25
2015	A434	55m	multicolored	.65	.25
2016	A434	65m	multicolored	.75	.30
2017	A434	85m	multicolored	1.00	.50
2018	A434	1.40t	multicolored	1.65	.80
2019	A434	2t	multicolored	2.35	1.00
			Nos. 2013-2019 (7)	7.30	3.30

Souvenir Sheet

2020	A434	4t	multicolored	5.50	5.50

Phila Nippon '91 — A435

1991, Oct. 29

2021	A435	1t	Pagoda	.55	.50
2022	A435	2t	Japanese beauty	1.00	.75
2023	A435	3t	Mongolian woman	1.75	1.00
2024	A435	4t	Mongolian building	2.75	1.25
			Nos. 2021-2024 (4)	6.05	3.50

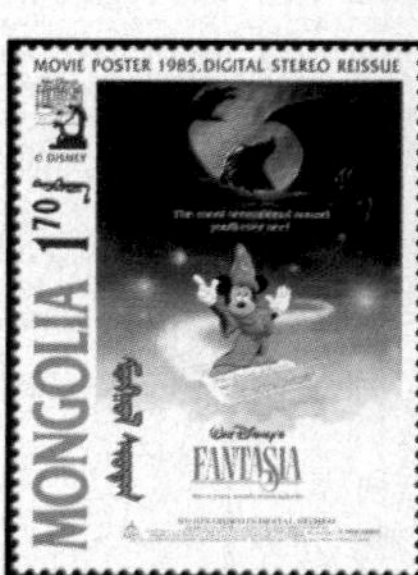

Fantasia, 50th Anniv. A436

Designs: 1.70t, Poster, 1985. 2t, Poster, 1940. 2.30t, Poster, 1982. 2.60t, Poster, 1981. 4.20t, Poster, 1969. 10t, Poster, 1941. 15t, Drawing of Mlle. Upanova, 1940. 16t, Sketch of Mickey as Sorcerer's Apprentice.

No. 2033, Mickey as Sorcerer's Apprentice. No. 2034, Dinosaurs from "The Rite of Spring," horiz. No. 2035, Thistles and orchids from "Russian Dance," horiz. No. 2036, Dancing mushrooms from "Chinese Dance," horiz.

1991, Dec. 31 *Perf. 13½x14, 14x13½*

2025	A436	1.70t	multicolored	.40	.20
2026	A436	2t	multicolored	.60	.20
2027	A436	2.30t	multicolored	.75	.25
2028	A436	2.60t	multicolored	1.00	.25
2029	A436	4.20t	multicolored	1.25	.40
2030	A436	10t	multicolored	1.75	.50
2031	A436	15t	multicolored	2.75	1.20
2032	A436	16t	multicolored	3.00	1.20
			Nos. 2025-2032 (8)	11.50	4.20

Souvenir Sheets

2033	A436	30t	multicolored	7.50	7.50
2034	A436	30t	multicolored	7.50	7.50
2035	A436	30t	multicolored	7.50	7.50
2036	A436	30t	multicolored	7.50	7.50

1992 Winter Olympics, Albertville — A437

1992, Feb. 1 *Perf. 14*

2037	A437	60m	Speed skating, vert.	.40	.20
2038	A437	80m	Ski jumping, vert.	.50	.20
2039	A437	1t	Hockey, vert.	.60	.20
2040	A437	1.20t	Figure skating, vert.	.70	.20
2041	A437	1.50t	Biathlon	.80	.20
2042	A437	2t	Downhill skiing	.90	.20
2043	A437	2.40t	Two-man bobsled	1.00	.25
			Nos. 2037-2043 (7)	4.90	1.45

Souvenir Sheet

2044	A437	8t	Four-man bobsled, vert.	5.00	5.00

Dogs — A438

Various breeds of dogs.

1991, Dec. 1 Litho. *Perf. 14*

2045	A438	20m	multi	.25	.20
2046	A438	30m	multi, vert.	.40	.20
2047	A438	40m	multi, vert.	.55	.25
2048	A438	50m	multi	.75	.30
2049	A438	60m	multi	1.00	.40
2050	A438	80m	multi	1.25	.50
2051	A438	1.20t	multi	1.50	.70
			Nos. 2045-2051 (7)	5.70	2.55

Souvenir Sheet

2052	A438	4t	multi	5.50	5.50

Cats — A439

Various breeds of cats.

1991, Dec. 27

2053	A439	20m	multi	.25	.20
2054	A439	30m	multi, vert.	.40	.20
2055	A439	40m	multi	.55	.25
2056	A439	50m	multi, vert.	.75	.30
2057	A439	60m	multi, vert.	1.00	.40
2058	A439	80m	multi, vert.	1.25	.50
2059	A439	1.20t	multi, vert.	1.50	.70
			Nos. 2053-2059 (7)	5.70	2.55

Souvenir Sheet

2060	A439	4t	multi	5.50	5.50

Alces Alces — A440

1992, May 1 Litho. *Perf. 14*

2061	A440	3t	Male	1.00	.65
2062	A440	3t	Two females	1.00	.65
2063	A440	3t	One female, vert.	1.00	.65
2064	A440	3t	Male's head, vert.	1.00	.65
			Nos. 2061-2064 (4)	4.00	2.60

Souvenir Sheet

Ferdinand von Zeppelin (1838-1917), Airship Designer — A441

1992, May 1

2065	A441	16t	multicolored	4.00	4.00

Souvenir Sheets

People and Events — A442

#2066, Pres. Punsalmaagiyn Orchirbat visiting Pres. George Bush at White House. #2067, Mother Teresa helping poor in Calcutta. #2068, Pope John Paul II at mass. #2069-2070, Boy Scout blowing bugle.

1992, May 22 *Perf. 14x13½*

2066	A442	30t	silver & multi	5.50	5.50

Perf. 14

2067	A442	30t	silver & multi	5.50	5.50
2068	A442	30t	silver & multi	5.50	5.50
2069	A442	30t	silver & multi	5.50	5.50
2070	A442	30t	silver & multi	5.50	5.50
			Nos. 2066-2070 (5)	27.50	27.50

Nos. 2067-2070 each contain one 43x28mm stamp. Nos. 2069-2070 exist with gold inscription and border. No. 2069, 17th World Boy Scout Jamboree, Korea. No. 2070, 18th World Boy Scout Jamboree, Netherlands, 1995.

Souvenir Sheet

Discovery of America, 500th Anniv. — A443

Designs: a, Columbus. b, Sailing ship.

1992, May 22

2071	A443	30t	Sheet of 2, #a.-b.	9.25	9.25

World Columbian Stamp Expo '92, Chicago, Genoa '92.

Miniature Sheets

Railways of the World — A444

Designs: No. 2072a, 3t, Tank locomotive, Darjeeling-Himalaya Railway, India. b, 3t, Royal Scot, Great Britain. c, 6t, Bridge on the River Kwai, Burma-Siam Railway. d, 6t, Baltic tank engine, Burma. e, 8t, Baldwin locomotive, Thailand. f, 8t, Western Railway locomotive, Pakistan. g, 16t, P.36 class locomotive, USSR. h, 16t, Shanghai-Beijing Express, China.

Orient Express: No. 2073a, 3t, 1931 Advertising poster. b, 3t, 1928 poster. c, 6t, Dawn departure. d, 6t, Golden Arrow departing Victoria Station. e, 8t, Waiting at station in Yugoslavia. f, 8t, Turn of the century picture of train. g, 16t, Fleche d'Or locomotive approaching Etaples, France. h, 16t, Arrival in Istanbul, Turkey.

No. 2074, New Tokaido line, Japan. No. 2076a, Emblem of Pullman Car Company. b, Emblem of Intl. Wagons-lits Company. No. 2075, TGV, France. No. 2077, Passengers waiting to board Orient Express.

1992, May 24

2072 A444 Sheet of 8, #a.-h. 15.00 11.00
2073 A444 Sheet of 8, #a.-h. 15.00 11.00

Souvenir Sheets

2074 A444 30t multicolored 6.00 5.00
2075 A444 30t multicolored 6.00 5.00
2076 A444 30t Sheet of 2, #a.-b. 12.00 11.00
2077 A444 30t black & gold 6.00 5.00

Nos. 2074-2075 contain one 58x42mm stamp.

Miniature Sheet

Birds — A445

Various birds: a, 3t. b, 3t, Owl. c, 6t, Gull, horiz. d, 6t, horiz. e, 8t. f, 8t, horiz. g, 16t. h, 16t, horiz.

1992, May 24

2078 A445 Sheet of 8, #a.-h. 15.00 10.00

Souvenir Sheet

Perf. 14x13½

2079 A445 30t Ducks, 30t in UR 6.00 6.00
2080 A445 30t Duck, 30t in LR 6.00 6.00

Nos. 2079-2080 contain one 50x38mm stamp.

Miniature Sheet

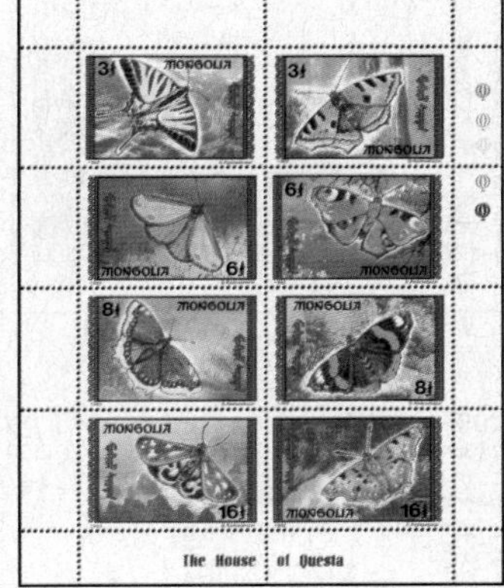

Butterflies and Moths — A446

Various butterflies or moths and: a, 3t, Mountains. b, 3t, Desert. c, 6t, Grass. d, 6t, Lake. e, 8t, Mountain, diff. f, 8t, Flowers. g, 16t, Rocks. h, 16t, Lake, diff.

1992, May 24 ***Perf. 14***

2081 A446 Sheet of 8, #a.-h. 15.00 10.00

Souvenir Sheet

Perf. 14x13½

2082 A446 30t pink & multi 6.00 5.00
2083 A446 30t blue & multi 6.00 5.00

Nos. 2082-2083 contain one 50x38mm stamp.

1992 Summer Olympics, Barcelona — A447

Designs: a, Gold medal. b, Torch.

1992, Jan. 22 **Litho.** ***Perf. 14***

2084 A447 30t Sheet of 2, #a.-b. 9.50 9.50

Souvenir Sheet

Genghis Khan — A448

1992, June 15 **Litho.** ***Perf. 14***

2085 A448 16t multicolored *20.00 20.00*

Mushrooms — A449

Designs: 20m, Marasmius oreades. 30m, Boletus luridus. 40m, Hygrophorus marzuelus. 50m, Cantharellus cibarius. 60m, Agaricus campester. 80m, Boletus aereus. 1.20t, Amanita caesarea. 2t, Tricholoma terreum. 4t, Mitrophora hybrida.

1991, June 18 **Litho.** ***Perf. 13***

2086 A449 20m multicolored .30 .20
2087 A449 30m multicolored .40 .20
2088 A449 40m multicolored .60 .25
2089 A449 50m multicolored .70 .25
2090 A449 60m multicolored .80 .30
2091 A449 80m multicolored 1.00 .40
2092 A449 1.20t multicolored 1.25 .55
2093 A449 2t multicolored 2.00 .80
Nos. 2086-2093 (8) 7.05 2.95

Souvenir Sheet

2094 A449 4t multicolored 6.50 6.50

Dated 1990. No. 2094 contains one 32x40mm stamp.

Discovery of America, 500th Anniv. — A450

Columbus and: 3t, Two sailing ships. 7t, Natives approaching Santa Maria. 10t, Pinta. 16t, Santa Maria, vert. 30t, Santa Maria, diff. 40t, Santa Maria, dolphins. 50t, Nina.

#2102, Ship, vert. #2103, Portrait, vert.

1992, Aug. **Litho.** ***Perf. 14***

2095 A450 3t multicolored .25 .20
2096 A450 7t multicolored .50 .20
2097 A450 10t multicolored .75 .25
2098 A450 16t multicolored 1.00 .30
2099 A450 30t multicolored 1.75 .80
2100 A450 40t multicolored 2.25 1.40
2101 A450 50t multicolored 3.50 1.75
Nos. 2095-2101 (7) 10.00 4.90

Souvenir Sheets

Perf. 13½x14

2102 A450 80t multicolored 5.50 5.50
2103 A450 80t multicolored 5.50 5.50

Nos. 2102-2103 each contain one 38x52mm stamp.

Miniature Sheet

Butterflies A451

#2104: a, 3t, Anthocharis cardamines. b, 8t, Inachis io. c, 10t, Fabriciana adippe. d, 16t, Limenitis reducta. e, 30t, Agrumaenia carniolica. f, 40t, Polyommatus icarus. g, 50t, Parnassius apollo. h, 60t, Saturnia pyri.

No. 2105, Limenitis populi. No. 2106, Heodes virgaureae.

1992, Dec. **Litho.** ***Perf. 14***

2104 A451 Sheet of 8, #a.-h. 12.00 11.00

Souvenir Sheets

Perf. 14x13½

2105 A451 80t multicolored 5.50 4.50
2106 A451 80t multicolored 5.50 4.50

Nos. 2105-2106 each contain one 51x38mm stamp.

1992 Summer Olympics, Barcelona — A452

1993, Jan. **Litho.** ***Perf. 13½***

2107 A452 3t Long jump .20 .20
2108 A452 6t Pommel horse .20 .20
2109 A452 8t Boxing .25 .20
2110 A452 16t Wrestling .60 .20
2111 A452 20t Archery, vert. .70 .25
2112 A452 30t Cycling .80 .25
2113 A452 40t Equestrian .90 .30
2114 A452 50t High jump 1.00 .30
2115 A452 60t Weight lifting 1.25 .40
Nos. 2107-2115 (9) 5.90 2.30

Souvenir Sheet

Perf. 15x14

2116 A452 80t Judo 5.00 4.00
2117 A452 80t Javelin 5.00 4.00

Nos. 2116-2117 contain one 40x30mm stamp.

Miniature Sheet

Birds A453

Designs: No. 2118a, 3t, Tetrae tetrix. b, 8t, Gallinula chloropus. c, 10t, Regulus satrapa. d, 16t, Alcede atthis. e, 30t, Gavia stellata. f, 40t, Ardes cinerea. g, 50t, Upupa epops. h, 60t, Niltava rubeculoides. No. 2119, Gyps fulvus. No. 2120, Podiceps cristatus.

1993, Feb. **Litho.** ***Perf. 14***

2118 A453 Sheet of 8, #a.-h. 12.00 11.00

Souvenir Sheets

Perf. 14x13½

2119 A453 80t multicolored 5.00 4.00
2120 A453 80t multicolored 5.00 4.00

Nos. 2119-2120 each contain one 51x38mm stamp.

Souvenir Sheets

Polska '93 — A454

#2121a, 2122, Copernicus. #2121b, Chopin. #2121c, 2123, Pope John Paul II.

1993, May 1 **Litho.** ***Perf. 13½x14***

2121 A454 30t Sheet of 3, #a.-c. 10.00 8.00
2122 A454 80t multicolored 8.00 7.00
2123 A454 80t multicolored 8.00 7.00
Nos. 2121-2123 (3) 26.00 22.00

Animals, Sports, & Transportation — A455

Designs in gold: No. 2124, Cats, dogs. No. 2125, Turtle, bee, wildcat, butterfly. No. 2126, Owl, butterfly, mushroom, dinosaur. Nos. 2127, Chessmen, archer, baseball player, wrestlers, horse and rider. Nos. 2128, Modern transportation.

No. 2129, Dinosaur, whales, butterflies. No. 2130, Mushroom, turtle, flowers.

1993, Jan. 5 **Embossed** ***Perf. 9***

2124-2128 A455 200t Set of 5

Nos. 2124-2128 exist in silver and in either gold or silver imperf. souvenir sheets of 1.

Embossed

1993, June 1 ***Perf. 8½x9***

Size: 79x53mm

2129 A455 200t silver

Souvenir Sheet

Imperf

Litho. & Embossed

2130 A455 200t gold

No. 2130, Topex '93, Madison, WI. No. 2129 exists in imperf. souvenir sheet of 1. No. 2130 exists in silver.

Souvenir Sheets

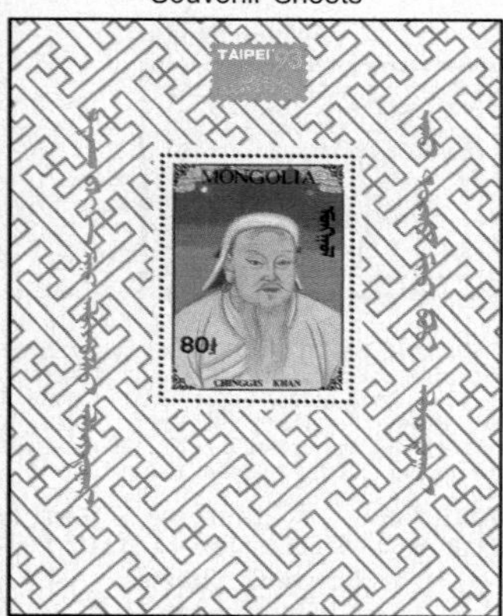

Taipei '93 — A456

1993, Aug. 14 Litho. ***Perf. 13½x14***

2137 A456 80t Genghis Khan *15.00*
2138 A456 80t Sun Yat-Sen *20.00*

Dirigible Flight Over Ulan Bator — A457

1993, Aug. 27 Litho. ***Perf. 14***

2139 A457 80t multicolored 3.00 3.00

No. 2139 has a holographic image. Soaking in water may affect the hologram.
Issued in sheets of 4

Buddhist Deities A458

Various statues and paintings.

1993, Oct. 3 ***Perf. 13½x14***

2140 A458 50t multicolored .35 .25
2141 A458 100t multicolored .70 .30
2142 A458 150t multicolored 1.00 .50
2143 A458 200t multicolored 1.40 .65
a. Miniature sheet of 4 5.25 5.25
Nos. 2140-2143 (4) 3.45 1.70

Souvenir Sheet

2144 A458 300t multicolored 2.00 2.00

Bangkok '93.

Nos. 276 & 1084 Surcharged

1993 ***Perfs., Etc. as Before***

2144A A77 8t on 70m #276 *7.50*
2144B A246 15t on 70m #1084 *15.00*

No. 2144A exists with double surcharge. The surcharge on No. 2144B exists with four different type fonts.

New Year 1994 (Year of the Dog) — A459

No. 2146, Stylized dog running, vert.

1994, Jan. 10 ***Perf. 14x13½, 13½x14***

2145 A459 60t multicolored 3.00 .75
2146 A459 60t multicolored 3.00 .75

1994 World Cup Soccer Championships, U.S. — A460

Championship teams: #2147, Uruguay, 1930, 1950. #2148, Italy, 1954. #2149, Brazil, 1959. #2150, West Germany, 1954. #2151, Argentina, 1978, 1986. #2152, Italy, 1938. #2153, Brazil, 1962. #2154, West Germany, 1974. #2155, Brazil, 1970. #2156, Italy, 1982. #2157, West Germany, 1990.

1994, Jan. 15 ***Perf. 14x13½***

2147 A460 150t multicolored 1.00 .25
2148 A460 150t multicolored 1.00 .25
2149 A460 150t multicolored 1.00 .25
2150 A460 150t multicolored 1.00 .25
2151 A460 150t multicolored 1.00 .25
a. Souv. sheet of 2, #2147, 2151 2.00 2.00
2152 A460 200t multicolored 1.40 .40
2153 A460 200t multicolored 1.40 .40
2154 A460 200t multicolored 1.40 .40
2155 A460 250t multicolored 1.75 .55
a. Souvenir sheet of 3, #2149, 2153, 2155 4.25 4.25
2156 A460 250t multicolored 1.75 .55
a. Souvenir sheet of 3, #2148, 2152, 2156 4.25 4.25
2157 A460 250t multicolored 1.75 .55
a. Souvenir sheet of 3, #2150, 2154, 2157 4.25 4.25
b. Miniature sheet of 4, #2151, 2155-2157 6.25 6.25
Nos. 2147-2157 (11) 14.45 4.10

Souvenir Sheet

Punsalmaagiin Ochirbat, First President of Mongolia — A461

1994, Apr. 1 ***Perf. 14***

2158 A461 150t multicolored 2.00 2.00

1994 Winter Olympics, Lillehammer A462

1994, Apr. 10 Litho. ***Perf. 13½***

2159 A462 50t Biathlon .40 .20
2160 A462 60t Two-man bob-sled .50 .25
2161 A462 80t Slalom skiing .60 .40
2162 A462 100t Ski jumping .75 .50
2163 A462 120t Pairs figure skating .95 .55
2164 A462 200t Speed skating 1.40 .90
Nos. 2159-2164 (6) 4.60 2.80

Souvenir Sheet

2165 A462 400t Ice hockey 5.00 5.00

Souvenir Sheet

Dalai Lama, 1989 Nobel Peace Prize Winner — A463

1994, June 27 Litho. ***Perf. 13½***

2166 A463 400t multicolored *30.00*

A464

People's Army — A465

1994 Litho. ***Perf. 14***

2167 A464 60m multicolored .90 .90

Souvenir Sheet

2168 A465 4t multicolored 3.50 3.50

Miniature Sheet of 18

Wildlife A466

Designs: a, Brown raptor. b, Woodpecker. c, Cranes in flight. d, White raptor. e, Yellow bird on tree branch (i). f, Two birds flying left. g, Raptor perched on rock. h, Two birds flying right. i, Squirrel. j, Dragonfly (f). k, Water bird standing near pond (o). l, Duck in flight over pond. m, Brown bird. n, Ground hog. o, Ladybug on flower. p, Bird's eggs. q, Grasshopper (m). r, Butterfly.

1994, July 15

2169 A466 60t #a.-r. + 2 labels 12.00 10.00

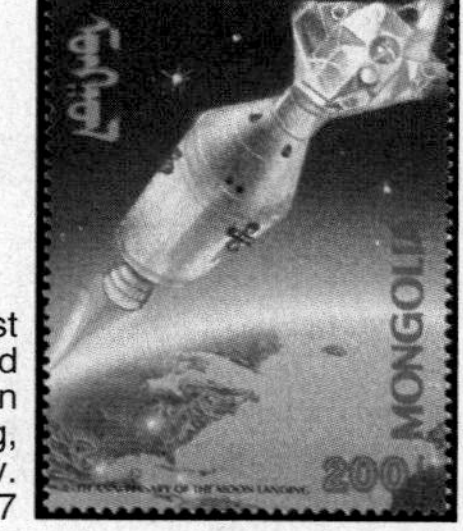

First Manned Moon Landing, 25th Anniv. A467

1994, July 20 Litho. ***Perf. 13½***

2170 A467 200t Trans-lunar injection 1.00 .60
2171 A467 200t Astronaut on moon 1.00 .60
2172 A467 200t Space shuttle, earth 1.00 .60
2173 A467 200t Astronaut, shuttle 1.00 .60
a. Miniature sheet of 4, #2170-2173 5.00 4.00
Nos. 2170-2173 (4) 4.00 2.40

Singpex '94 — A468

1994, Aug. 31

2174 A468 300t Butterfly 1.50 1.00

Souvenir Sheet

2175 A468 400t Dog *6.00 5.00*

New Year 1994 (Year of the Dog).

A469

PHILAKOREA '94 — A470

1994 Litho. *Perf. 14*

2176	A469 600t Korea #1749	2.75	1.00
2177	A469 600t #433	2.75	1.00
2178	A470 600t #1	2.75	1.00
2179	A470 600t Korea #1	2.75	1.00
	Nos. 2176-2179 (4)	11.00	4.00

Souvenir Sheets

Perf. 13½x14

2180	A470 400t #5	4.00	4.00

Perf. 14

2181	A469 600t Yong Sik Hong	5.00	5.00

First Mongolian Stamp, 70th anniv. (#2180). No. 2180 contains one 34x46mm stamp.
Issued: No. 2180, 11/23, others, 8/16.
For surcharges see #2247C-2247G.

Dinosaurs — A471

1994, Nov. 30 *Perf. 14*

2182	A471 60t Mammuthus, vert.	.40	.25
2183	A471 80t Stegosaurus, vert.	.50	.30
2184	A471 100t Talararus	.60	.40
2185	A471 120t Gorythosaurus	.75	.55
2186	A471 200t Tyrannosaurus	1.25	.90
	Nos. 2182-2186 (5)	3.50	2.40

Souvenir Sheet

2187	A471 400t Triceratops	*3.50*	*3.50*

Nos. 2182-2187 exist in imperf. sheets of 1.
No. 2182 is misspelled.

Mongolian-Japanese Friendship — A472

1994, Dec. 15 *Perf. 14x13½*

2188	A472 20t multicolored	*1.00*	.30

New Year 1995 (Year of the Boar) — A474

1995, Jan. 1 *Perf. 14x13½, 13½x14*

2190	A474 200t shown	1.00	.30
2191	A474 200t Boar, diff, vert.	1.00	.30

A475

Litho. & Typo.

1994, July 25 *Perf. 15x14*

Denomination in Black

2192	A475 10t Flower	—	—
2192A	A475 10t Flower, red denomination	—	—
2193	A475 18t Ram	—	—
2194	A475 22t Airplane	—	—
2195	A475 22t Airplane, red denomination	—	—
2196	A475 44t like #2193	—	—
2197	A475 44t Ram, blue denomination	—	—

Dated 1993.
No. 2192A issued 1994(?).
This is an expanding set. Numbers may change.

Religious Masked Dancing — A476

Various masked dancers in traditional costumes.

1995, Feb. 25 Litho. *Perf. 14*

2201	A476 20t multicolored	.20	.20
2202	A476 50t multicolored	.30	.20
2203	A476 60t multicolored	.35	.25
2204	A476 100t multicolored	.60	.30
2205	A476 120t multicolored	.70	.30
2206	A476 150t multicolored	.85	.40
2207	A476 200t multicolored	1.10	.50
	Nos. 2201-2207 (7)	4.10	2.15

Souvenir Sheet

2208	A476 400t multicolored	4.00	4.00

Saiga Tatarica A477

1995, Mar. 30 Litho. *Perf. 14*

2209	A477 40t shown	.40	.20
2210	A477 55t Two adults	.50	.25
2211	A477 70t One running left	.60	.30
2212	A477 200t One up close	1.60	.80
a.	Block of 4, #2209-2212	3.50	3.50

World Wildlife Fund.

Souvenir Sheet

First Philately & Collections Fair, Hong Kong '95 — A478

Designs: a, Butterfly. b, Flowers.

1995, June 6 Litho. *Perf. 14*

2213	A478 200t Sheet of 2, #a.-b. + 2 labels	4.25	4.25

Goldfish — A479

Designs: 20t, Yellow oranda. 50t, Red and white wen-yu. 60t, Brown oranda with red head. 100t, Calico pearl-scale with phoenix tail. 120t, Red lion-head. 150t, Brown oranda. 200t, Red and white oranda with narial.
400t, White and gold unidentified fish.

1995, Sept. 1 Litho. *Perf. 14*

2214-2220	A479 Set of 7	5.50	4.00

Souvenir Sheet

2221	A479 400t multicolored	5.50	4.00

No. 2221 contains one 50x38mm stamp.

Miniature Sheet

Motion Pictures, Cent. A480

Various portraits of Marilyn Monroe (1926-62): No. 2222a, 60t. b, 80t. c, 100t. d, 120t. e, 150t. f, 200t. g, 250t. h, 300t. i, 350t.
No. 2223, In white-collared blouse. No. 2224, With lion. No. 2225, In black lace dress. No. 2226, In scene from movie, Niagara.

1995, Oct. 20

2222	A480 Sheet of 9, #a.-i.	9.00	8.00

Souvenir Sheets

2223	A480 200t multi	5.50	5.50
2224-2226	A480 300t each	5.50	5.50

Miniature Sheet

UN, 50th Anniv. — A481

Exterior views of UN complexes, Secretaries General: a, Trygve Lie. b, Dag Hammarskjold. c, U Thant. d, Kurt Waldheim. e, Jose Perez de Cuellar. f, Boutros Boutros-Ghali.

1995, Oct. 15

2227	A481 60t Sheet of 6, #a.-f.	10.00	9.00

Miniature Sheet

Elvis Presley (1935-77) A482

Various portraits: No. 2228a, 60t. b, 80t. c, 100t. d, 120t. e, 150t. f, 200t. g, 250t. h, 300t. i, 350t.
No. 2229, Wearing yellow sweater. No. 2230, With dancing girl. No. 2231, With guitar. No. 2232, In army uniform, wife Priscilla.

1995, Oct. 20

2228	A482 Sheet of 9, #a.-i.	9.00	8.00

Souvenir Sheets

2229	A482 200t multi	5.00	5.00
2230	A482 300t multi	5.00	5.00
2231-2232	A482 400t each	6.50	5.00

Miniature Sheet

X-Men Comic Characters A483

Designs: No. 2233a, 30t, Bishop. b, 50t, Beast. c, 60t, Rogue. d, 70t, Gambit. e, 80t, Cyclops. f, 100t, Storm. g, 200t, Professor X. h, 250t, Wolverine.
No. 2234: a, Wolverine, horiz. b, Magneto, horiz.

1995, Sept. 15

2233	A483 Sheet of 8, #a.-h.	4.25	4.00

Souvenir Sheet of 2

2234	A483 250t #a.-b.	4.25	4.10

New Year 1996 (Year of the Rat) A484

1996, Jan. 1 Litho. *Perf. 14*

2235	A484 150t Rat, diff., vert.	1.00	.60
2236	A484 200t shown	1.50	.85

CHINA '96 — A485

Designs: a, Monument of Sukhe Bator. b, Temple of Heaven, Beijing. c, Migjed Jang-Rasek. d, Great Wall.

1996, Apr. 25 Litho. *Perf. 13½x14*

2237	A485 65t Sheet of 4, #a.-d.	10.00	10.00

1996 Summer Olympic Games, Atlanta A486

30t, Cycling. 60t, Women's shooting. 80t, Weight lifting. 100t, Boxing. 120t, Women's archery, vert. 150t, Rhythmic gymnastics, vert. 200t, Hurdles, vert. 350t, Equestrian. 400t, Wrestling.
500t, Basketball. 600t, Judo.

1996 Litho. *Perf. 14*

2238	A486 30t multicolored	.20	.20
2239	A486 60t multicolored	.20	.20
2240	A486 80t multicolored	.30	.20
2241	A486 100t multicolored	.30	.20
2242	A486 120t multicolored	.30	.20
2243	A486 150t multicolored	.40	.25
2244	A486 200t multicolored	.50	.30
2245	A486 350t multicolored	1.00	.70
2246	A486 400t multicolored	1.10	.80
	Nos. 2238-2246 (9)	4.30	3.05

Souvenir Sheets

2246A A486 500t multicolored 4.00 3.00
2246B A486 600t multicolored 4.00 4.00

No. 2246A contains one 37x53mm stamp, No. 2246B one 52x39mm stamp.
Olymphilex '96 (#2246A-2246B).

Mongolian postal authorities have declared as "unauthorized" two sheets of nine 350t Train stamps similar to Nos. 2442-2443, two souvenir sheets of one 2000t Train stamps similar to Nos. 2444-2445, and one sheet of six 300t Ferrari stamps similar to No. 2446.

Genghis Khan — A486a

Die Cut Perf. 7½
1996, Aug. 28 **Embossed**
Self-Adhesive

2246C A486a 10,000t gold *60.00 60.00*

CAPEX '96 — A487

Designs: a, 350t, #2. b, 400t, Canada #1.

1996 **Litho.** ***Perf. 12½***
2247 A487 Sheet of 2, #a.-b. 8.00 8.00

No. 2247b is 40x30mm. No. 2247 exists with blue at upper right margin corner and different colored margin picture of CN Tower.

Nos. 2176-2179, 2181 Overprinted

1996, Sept. 8 **Litho.** ***Perf. 14***
2247C A469 600t On #2176 2.50 2.50
2247D A469 600t On #2177 2.50 2.50
2247E A470 600t On #2178 2.50 2.50
2247F A470 600t On #2179 2.50 2.50
Nos. 2247C-2247F (4) 10.00 10.00

Souvenir Sheet

2247G A469 600t On No. 2181 4.00 4.00

Mongolian National Democratic and Social Democratic Parties A487a

1996, Sept. 25 **Litho.** ***Perf. 13¾***
2247H A487a 100t multicolored .60 .50

Souvenir Sheet

Taipei '96 — A487b

1996, Oct. 21 **Litho.** ***Perf. 12¾***
2247I A487b 750t multicolored 5.00 5.00
r. Overprinted "Taipei 2005" in margin in silver 5.00 5.00

No. 2247Ir issued 8/19/2005.

Children & Scouting Emblem — A487c

1996, Dec. 16 **Litho.** ***Perf. 14***
Country Flags

2247J A487c 250t Mongolia 1.75 1.75
2247K A487c 250t US 1.75 1.75
2247L A487c 250t Germany 1.75 1.75
2247M A487c 250t Russia 1.75 1.75
2247N A487c 250t Japan 1.75 1.75
2247O A487c 250t PRC 1.75 1.75
q. Souvenir sheet, #2247J-2247O 15.00 15.00
Nos. 2247J-2247O (6) 10.50 10.50

Souvenir Sheet
Perf. 12¾x12¾

2247P A487c 700t No flag 5.00 5.00

UNICEF (#2247P).

New Year 1997 (Year of the Ox) A488

1997 **Litho.** ***Perf. 14***
2248 A488 300t Ox, vert. 1.25 1.00
2249 A488 350t shown 1.50 1.25

Souvenir Sheet

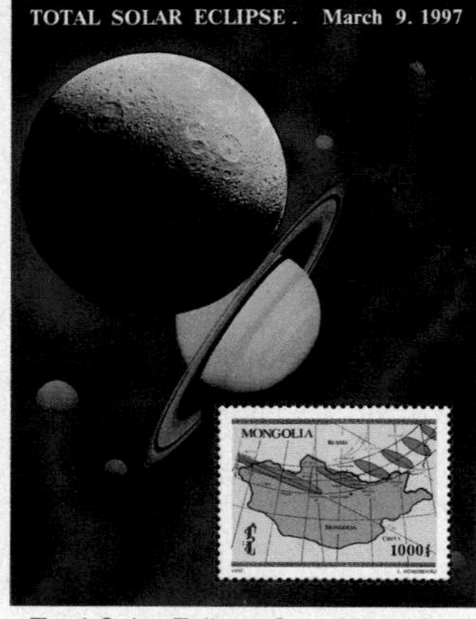

Total Solar Eclipse Over Mongolia, Mar. 9, 1997 — A489

Illustration reduced.

1997 **Litho.** ***Perf. 12½***
2250 A489 1000t Map of Mongolia 5.00 4.75

Return of Hong Kong to China A490

Designs: 200t, Former Chinese Pres. Deng Xioaping, Queen Elizabeth II. 250t, Chinese Pres. Jiang Zemin and Chief Executive of the Special Administrative Region of Hong Kong, Tung Chee-hwa.

1997 **Litho.** ***Perf. 13½***
2251 A490 200t multicolored 1.00 1.00
2252 A490 250t multicolored 1.50 1.50
a. Pair, #2251-2252 2.50 2.50

Seven Joys — A491

Designs: a, Wheel. b, Gem. c, Minister. d, Queen. e, Elephant. f, Horse. g, General.

1997 **Litho.** ***Perf. 11***
2253 A491 200t Sheet of 7, #a.-g., + 2 labels 6.00 6.00

Souvenir Sheet

Moscow '97 — A492

Illustration reduced.

1997 ***Perf. 12½x11½***
2254 A492 1000t No. 264 5.00 5.00
a. With Irkutsk 2007 emblem and inscirption added in sheet margin ('07) 1.75 1.75

No. 2254a issued 6/8/2007.

Monument to the Politically Repressed A493

1997 ***Perf. 13x13½***
2255 A493 150t black & gray .95 .60

Trains A493a

Designs: 20t, VL-80 electric locomotive. 40t, Japanese high speed electric train. 120t, BL-80 Diesel locomotive. 200t, German steam locomotive. 300t, Lass "FDp" steam locomotive. 350t, 0-6-0 tank locomotive. 400t, Diesel locomotive. 500t, T6-106 Diesel locomotive. 600t, Magnetic train.
No. 2255K, "Rocket." No. 2255L, London-Paris train.

1997, Dec. 5 **Litho.** ***Perf. 14x14¼***
2255A A493a 20t multi .20 .20
2255B A493a 40t multi .20 .20
2255C A493a 120t multi .50 .50
2255D A493a 200t multi .85 .85
2255E A493a 300t multi 1.25 1.25
2255F A493a 350t multi 1.50 1.50
2255G A493a 400t multi 1.75 1.75
2255H A493a 500t multi 2.10 2.10
2255I A493a 600t multi 2.50 2.50
Nos. 2255A-2255I (9) 10.85 10.85

Souvenir Sheets
Perf. 11¼

2255K A493a 800t multi 4.50 4.50
2255L A493a 800t multi 4.50 4.50

Nos. 2255K, 2255L each contain one 59x43mm stamp.

Emperors of Mongolia A494

a, Genghis Khan. b, Ogadai Khan. c, Guyuk Khan. d, Mangu Khan. e, Kublai Khan.

Perf. 11½x12½
1997, Dec. 25 **Litho.**
2256 A494 1000t Strip of 5, #a.-e. 20.00 20.00

Nos. 2256a-2256e exist in souvenir sheets containing 1 or 2 21x33mm stamps.

New Year 1998 (Year of the Tiger) A495

Various stylized tigers.

1998, Feb. 1 *Perf. 12*

2257 A495 150t multicolored 1.00 1.00
2258 A495 200t multicolored 1.50 1.50
2259 A495 300t multicolored 2.00 2.00
Nos. 2257-2259 (3) 4.50 4.50

Design on No. 2259 is oriented point down.

Mongolian Yaks A496

Various yaks: 20t, Three. 30t, One white. 50t, With carts. 100t, One male. 150t, Female with calf. 200t, Three, campsite. 300t, One with horns, flowing hair. 400t, Brown yak looking back.
800t, Carrying children and supplies.

1998, Mar. 15 **Litho.** *Perf. 12*

2260 A496 20t multicolored .20 .20
2261 A496 30t multicolored .20 .20
2262 A496 50t multicolored .25 .25
2263 A496 100t multicolored .35 .35
2264 A496 150t multicolored .55 .55
2265 A496 200t multicolored .75 .75

Size: 50x36mm

2266 A496 300t multicolored 1.10 1.10
2267 A496 400t multicolored 1.50 1.50
Nos. 2260-2267 (8) 4.90 4.90

Souvenir Sheet
Perf. 11

2268 A496 800t multicolored 5.50 5.50

No. 2268 contains one 60x47mm stamp.

Butterflies and Orchids — A497

Designs: 100t, Adonis blue, dendrobium cunninghamii. 150t, Brown hairstreak, oncidium ampliatum. 200t, Large skipper, maxillaria triloris. 250t, Orange tip, calypso bulbosa. 300t, Painted lady, catasetum pileatum. 350t, Purple hairstreak, epidedrum fimbratum. 400t, Red admiral, cleistes rosea. 450t, Small copper, ponthieva maculata. 500t, Small tortoiseshell, cypripeium calceolus.
Each 800t: No. 2278, Red admiral, c. macranthum. No. 2279, Adonis blue, c. guttatum.

1997, Dec. 5 **Litho.** *Perf. 14*

2269-2277 A497 Set of 9 6.00 6.00

Souvenir Sheets

2278-2279 A497 Set of 2 9.00 9.00

Souvenir Sheet

1998 World Cup Soccer Championships, France — A498

Illustration reduced.

1998, June 1 *Perf. 13*

2280 A498 1000t multicolored 5.50 5.50

Souvenir Sheet

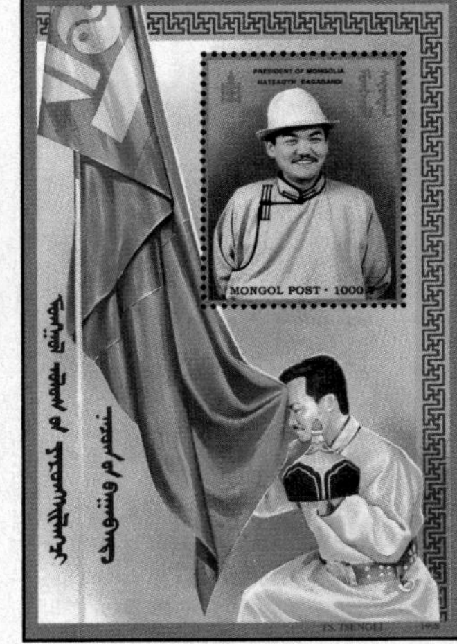

Pres. Natsagyn Bagabandi — A499

1998, July 15 **Litho.** *Perf. 12½*

2281 A499 1000t multicolored 4.50 4.50

Greenpeace, 26th Anniv. — A500

Designs: 200t, Penguin in snow. 400t, Six penguins, water, mountain. 500t, Two penguins at water's edge. 800t, Large group of penguins.
No. 2286: a, like #2282. b. like #2283. c, like #2284. d, like #2285. e, like #2287.
1000t, Greenpeace ship.

1997, Sept. 15 **Litho.** *Perf. 13½*

2282-2285 A500 Set of 4 6.00 6.00
2286 A500 Sheet of 5, #a.-e. 6.00 6.00

Souvenir Sheet

2287 A500 1000t multicolored 6.00 6.00

Country name, denominations, "Greenpeace" in red on No. 2286. Nos. 2282-2287 exist imperf.

Diana, Princess of Wales (1961-97) A501

Various portraits with bister background — #2288: a, 50t. b, 100t. c, 150t, d, 200t. e, 250t. f, 300t. g, 350t. h, 400t. i, 450t.
Various portraits with pale brown background — #2289a, 50t. b. 100t. c, 150t. d, 200t. e, 250t. f, 300t. g, 350t. h, 400t. i, 450t.
Each 1000t: No. 2290, Diana holding infant son. No. 2291, Diana wearing tiara. No. 2292, Diana in pink dress. No. 2293, Diana in white (Mother Teresa in margin).

1997, Dec. 15

Sheets of 9, #a-i

2288-2289 A501 Set of 2 12.00 12.00

Souvenir Sheets

2290-2293 A501 Set of 4 16.00 16.00

Nos. 2288-2289 exist imperf.

Genghis Khan's Soldiers A502

Various soldiers in traditional attire, background color: 100t, tan. 150t, pale violet. 200t, green blue. 250t, green. 300t, gray. 350t, pink. 400t, blue. 600t, pale brown.
Army on the march — #2302: a, 600t, One standing, others on horses. b, 1000t, Leaders riding decorated horses. c, 600t, Two standing, leopards, others on horses.

1997, Dec. 20 *Perf. 12*

2294-2301 A502 Set of 8 8.50 8.50

Souvenir Sheet

2302 A502 Sheet of 3, #a.-c. 8.50 8.50

No. 2302b is 65x56mm.

No. 276 Surcharged

1996, Dec. 25 **Photo.** *Perf. 11½x12*

2302D A77 200t on 70m multicolored *10.00 5.00*

National Symbols — A503

1998, Jan. 1

2303 A503 300t Natl. flag, horiz. 1.00 .75
2304 A503 300t shown 1.00 .75

Ursus Arctos Gobiensis A504

100t, Adult looking forward. 150t, Adult walking left. 200t, Two bears. 250t, Mother, cubs.

1998, July 20

2305-2308 A504 Set of 4 7.00 7.00
2307a Sheet of 2, #2305, 2307 3.00 3.00
2308a Sheet of 2, #2306, 2308 4.00 4.00

Fish A505

Designs: 20t, Lebistes reticulatus. 30t, Goldfish. 50t, Balistes conspicillum. 100t, Goldfish, diff. 150t, Synchirops splendidus. 200t, Auratus. 300t, Xiphophorus helleri. 400t, Pygoplites diacanthus. 600t, Chaetodon auriga.
Various fish, denomination (800t): No. 2318, At top. No. 2319, At bottom.

1998, July 20 *Perf. 12½*

2309-2317 A505 Set of 9 6.00 6.00

Souvenir Sheets
Perf. 11

2318-2319 A505 Set of 2 12.00 12.00

Nos. 2318-2319 each contain one 95x49mm stamp.

Domestic Cats A506

Designs: 50t, Red Persian. 100t, Manx cat. 150t, Smoke Persian. 200t, Long-haired white Persian. 250t, Silver tabby. 300t, Siamese.
1000t, Kittens, basket.

1998, Sept. 1 *Perf. 12*

2320-2325 A506 Set of 6 5.00 5.00

Souvenir Sheet

2326 A506 1000t multicolored 5.00 5.00

Jerry Garcia (1942-95) and The Grateful Dead A507

Nos. 2327-2328, Various portraits of Jerry Garcia.
No. 2328A — Black and white photos: f, 100t. g, 150t. h, 50t.
No. 2328B — Blue guitar: i, 150t. j, 200t. k, 100t.
No. 2328C — Red guitar: l, 200t. m, 250t. n, 150t.
No. 2328D — White guitar: o, 200t. p, 250t. q, 150t.
No. 2328E — Dark background: r, 300t. s, 350t. t, 250t.
No. 2329: Various portraits of Garcia: a, 50t. b, 100t. c, 150t. d, 200t. e, 250t. f, 300t. g, 350t. h, 400t. i, 450t.
No. 2330: Various pictures of bears (Grateful Dead emblem) in sports activities: a, 50t, Dirt biking. b, 100t, Soccer. c, 150t, Basketball. d, 200t, Golf. e, 250t, Baseball. f, 300t, Roller blading. g, 350t, Ice hockey. h, 400t, Football. i, 450t, Skiing.
Each 1000t: No. 2331, Garcia holding guitar. No. 2331A, Garcia with left hand on guitar, right hand in air.

1998-99 *Perf. 12½*

2327 A507 100t multicolored .25 .25
2328 A507 200t multicolored .50 .50

Strips of 3

2328A-2328E A507 Set of 5 9.00 9.00

Sheets of 9, #a-i

2329-2330M A507 Set of 2 11.50 11.50

Souvenir Sheets

2331-2331A A507 Set of 2 5.00 5.00

Nos. 2327-2328 were each issued in sheets of 9. Nos. 2331-2331A contain one 51x76mm.
Dot of "I" in Garcia is a diamond on Nos. 2327-2329, 2331-2331A. "Jerry Garcia" is in pink letters with rose shadowing on Nos. 2328A-2328E.
Issued: No. 2331A, 1/1/99; #2328A-2328E, 1999; others 10/15/98.
See Nos. 2385-2389.

Bob Marley (1947-81) A508

Portraits: 200t, Up close. 1000t, At microphone.

1998, Oct. 15
2332 A508 200t multicolored .50 .50

Souvenir Sheet

2333 A508 1000t multicolored 2.50 2.50

No. 2332 was issued in sheets of 9. No. 2333 contains one 51x76mm stamp.

Carlos Santana A509

1998, Oct. 15
2334 A509 200t multicolored .50 .50

No. 2334 was issued in sheets of 9.

The Three Stooges — A510

Scenes from "The Three Stooges" motion pictures — #2335: a, 50t, Guns, cigars. b, 100t, Road signs. c, 150t, Dynamite. d, 200t, Golf clubs. e, 240t, Medals on uniform. f, 300t, Dove. g, 350t, Flower bouquets. h, 400t, Bright green cap. i. 450t, Whisk broom, cigar.

No. 2336: a, 50t, Doctor's equipment. b, 100t, Musical instruments. c, 150t, Clothes press. d, 200t, Long cord. e, 250t, Vise. f, 300t, Brick wall. g, 350t, Pliers. h, 400t, Turkey. i, 450t, Door.

No. 2337: a, 50t, Union soldiers. b, 100t, French Foreign Legion. c, 150t, Confederate soldiers, women. d, 200t, Horse. e, 250t, Army uniform, grenade. f, 300t, Cannon. g, 350t, Confederate soldiers, whiskey flask. 400t, Army uniforms, officer. 450t, Scarecrow.

Each 800t: No. 2338, like #2335b. No. 2339, like #2336c, vert. No. 2340, With football.

1998, Nov. 25 Litho. *Perf. 13½*

Sheets of 9, #a-i.

2335-2337 A510 Set of 3 22.50 22.50

Souvenir Sheets

2338-2340 A510 Set of 3 9.00 9.00

Nos. 2335-2340 exist imperf. Nos. 2338-2340 each contain one 51x41mm stamp.

Eight Offerings of Buddha — A511

#2341, The White Sign of Luck. #2342, The Auspicious Wheel. #2343, The Auspicious Cup. #2344, The White Couch. #2345, The White Umbrella. #2346, The Duaz of Victory. #2347, The White Lotus. #2348, The Auspicious Fish.

1998, Dec. 10 Litho. *Perf. 12*
2341-2348 A511 200t Set of 8 5.00 5.00

Howdy Doody Television Show — A512

No. 2349: a, 50t, Chief Thunderthud. b, 100t, Princess Summerfall Winterspring. c, 150t, Howdy in Mexican outfit. d, 150t, Buffalo Bob in gray shirt, Howdy. e, 200t, Buffalo Bob in red and white shirt, Howdy. f, 250t, Howdy, Buffalo Bob rubbing noses. g, 450t, Howdy in military uniform. h, 250t, Clarabell the Clown. i, 450t, Howdy lying down.

Each 800t: No. 2350, Howdy. No. 2351, Buffalo Bob, Howdy, horiz. No. 2352, Howdy, Buffalo Bob.

Perf. 13½x14, 14x13½x14

1999, Apr. 1
2349 A512 Sheet of 9, #a.-i. 7.00 7.00

Souvenir Sheets

Perf. 14 (#2352)

2350-2352 A512 Set of 3 9.00 9.00

No. 2352 contains one 48x61mm stamp.

Prime Ministers of Mongolia — A513

a, T. Namnansuren. b, Badamdorj. c, D. Chagdarjav. d, D. Bodoo. e, S. Damdinbazar. f, B. Tserendorj. g, A. Amar. h, Ts. Jigjidjav. i, P. Genden. j, Kh. Ghoibalsan. k, Yu. Tsedenbal. l, J. Batmunkh. m, D. Sodnom. n, Sh. Gungaadorj. o, D. Byambasuren. p, P. Jasrai. q, M. Enkhsaikhan. r, Ts. Elbegdorj.

1998, Dec. 1 *Perf. 12*
2353 A513 200t Sheet of 18, #a.-r. 18.00 18.00

Natl. Wrestling Champions A514

Designs: a, D. Damdin. b, S. Batsuury. c, J. Munkhbat. d, H. Bayanmunkh. e, B. Tubdendorj. f, D. Tserentogtokh. g, B. Baterdne.

1998, Dec. 26 *Perf. 12½*
2354 A514 200t Sheet of 7, #a.-g. 7.00 7.00

John Glenn's Return to Space A515

Mercury Friendship 7 — #2355: a, 50t, Mercury capsule in outer space. b, 100t, NASA emblem. c, 150t, Friendship 7 mission patch. d, 150t, Launch of Friendship 7. e, 200t, Glenn, 1962. f, 250th, Recovery of capsule. g, 450t, Moon. h, 250t, Capsule re-entering atmosphere. i, 450t, Stars.

Shuttle Discovery mission — #2356: a, 50t, NASA emblem. b, 100t, Glenn in red launch suit. c, 150t, Discovery mission patch. d, 150t, Launch of Discovery. e, 200t, Glenn, 1998. f, 250t, Discovery landing. g, 450t, Sun. h, 250t, Discovery in outer space. i, 450t, NASA "40" emblem.

1998, Dec. 31 *Perf. 14*

Sheets of 9

2355-2356 A515 #a.-i., each 9.00 9.00

Postal Delivery — A516

Post office: a, 100t, Brown. b, 200t, Blue. c, 200t, Blue green. d, 400t, Red lilac. e, 400t, Violet.

Electronic services: f, 100t, Blue. g, 200t, Blue green. h, 200t, Red lilac. i, 400t, Violet. j, 400t, Brown.

EMS delivery: k, 100t, Blue green. l, 200t, Red lilac. m, 200t, Violet. n, 400t, Brown. o, 400t, Blue.

Mail train: p, 100t, Red lilac. q, 200t, Violet. r, 200t, Brown. s, 400t, Blue. t, 400t, Blue green.

Jet plane: u, 100t, Violet. v, 200t, Brown. w, 200t, Blue. x, 400t, Blue green. y, 400t, Red lilac.

1998, Nov. 15 *Perf. 12*
2357 A516 Sheet of 25, #a.-y. 25.00 25.00

Universal Declaration of Human Rights, 50th Anniv. — A517

1998, Dec. 25 Litho. *Perf. 12*
2358 A517 450t multi + label 3.50 3.50

New Year 1999 (Year of the Rabbit) A518

1999, Feb. 17
2359 A518 250t Rabbit, vert. 2.00 2.00
2360 A518 300t shown 2.00 2.00

Buddha Migjed Jankraisig, Ulan Bator A519

Designs: 200t, Temple.

Each 1000t: No. 2363, Statue. No. 2364, Statue, drawing of Temple.

1999, Apr. 15
2361 A519 200t multicolored 1.00 1.00
2362 A519 400t multicolored 2.00 2.00

Souvenir Sheets

Perf. 11

2363-2364 A519 Set of 2 8.00 8.00

Nos. 2363-2364 each contain one 49x106mm stamp.

Falcons — A520

Falcon: a, 300t, Subbuteo. b, 250t, Naumanni. c, 200t, Tinnunculus. d, 170t, Peregrinus. e, 800t, Rusticolus by nest. f, 600t, Rusticolus in flight. g, 400t, Pelegrinoides over kill. h, 350t, Pelegrinoides on branch. i, 150t, Columbarius. j, 100t, Vespertinus. k, 50t, Cherrug. l, 30t, Amurensis.

1999, Mar. 20 *Perf. 12*
2365 A520 Sheet of 12, #a.-l. 12.00 12.00

"I Love Lucy" Television Show — A521

Various scenes — #2366: a, 50t. b, 100t. c, 150t. d, 150t. e, 200t. f, 250t. g, 450t. h, 250t. i, 450t.

Each 800t: No. 2367, Lucy talking with woman. No. 2368, Ethel looking at Lucy locked in cold storage locker.

1999, July 15 Litho. *Perf. 13½x14*
2366 A521 250t Sheet of 9, #a.-i. 7.00 7.00

Souvenir Sheets

2367-2368 A521 Set of 2 6.00 6.00

Nos. 2367-2368 each contain one 38x51mm stamp.

Betty Boop Cartoon Character A522

Various pictures of Betty Boop — #2369: a, 50t. b, 100t. c, 150t. d, 150t. e, 200t. f, 250t. g, 450t. h, 250t. i, 450t.
Each 800t: No. 2370, Betty in dog's eyes, horiz. No. 2371, Up close, horiz.

1999, July 15
2369 A522 Sheet of 9, #a.-i. 7.00 7.00

Souvenir Sheets
Perf. 14x13½
2370-2371 A522 Set of 2 6.00 6.00

Nos. 2370-2371 each contain one 51x38mm stamp.

Folk Tales A523

Designs: 50t, Man, yurt, two demons. 150t, Chess players. 200t, Lion carrying logs. 250t, Flying horse. 300t, Archer, bird, sun. 450t, Horses, cranes.
1000t, Birds, camel in flight.

1999, June 15 Litho. *Perf. 13x13¼*
2372-2377 A523 Set of 6 7.50 7.50

Souvenir Sheet
Perf. 12½
2378 A523 1000t multicolored 7.50 7.50

No. 2378 contains one 41x32mm stamp.

No. 307 Surcharged

Methods and Perfs as Before
1999, June 15
2378A A84 810t on 60m bl & multi *20.00 20.00*

Miniature Sheet

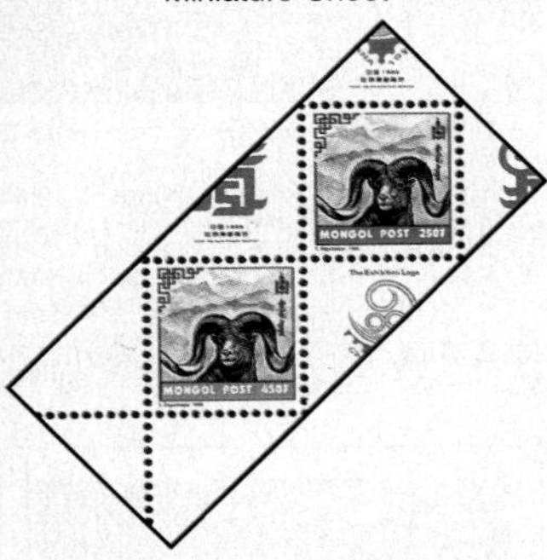

Ram — A524

Panel color: a, 250t, Blue. b, 450t, Red.

1999, Aug. 21 Litho. *Perf. 12½*
2379 A524 Miniature sheet of 2, #a.-b. 2.00 2.00

China 1999 World Philatelic Exhibition. No. 2379 is cut from a larger sheet of alternating stamps and labels. The cutting is through the labels along the diagonal axes.

UPU, 125th Anniv. — A525

Designs: No. 2380, Rider, two horses. No. 2381, Rider, one horse. No. 2382, Train and truck. No. 2382, Airplane and computer.
800t, Ogodei Khan (1186-1241).

1999, Oct. 9
2380-2383 A525 250t Set of 4 4.00 4.00

Souvenir Sheet
2384 A525 800t multi 4.50 4.50

No. 2384 contains one 31x41mm stamp.

Nos. 551, 1742 Surcharged

Methods and Perfs. as Before
1999, Aug. 25
2384A A133 250t on 50m multi 10.00 10.00
2384B A389 250t on 60m multi 10.00 10.00

Victory in Khalkh-gol War, 60th anniv.

Genghis Khan A525a

Die Cut Perf. 11½
1999, Sept. 27 Embossed
Self-Adhesive
2384C A525a 15,000t gold & sil 60.00 —

Jerry Garcia Type of 1998

No. 2385 — Rose and blue speckled background: a, 50t. b, 100t. c, 150t.
No. 2386 — Pink-toned vignette extension backgrounds: a, 100t. b, 150t. c, 200t.
No. 2387 — Pink, blue and purple curved line backgrounds: a, 150t. b, 200t. c, 250t.
No. 2388 — Dark blue and purple straight line backgrounds: a, 150t. b, 200t. c, 250t.
No. 2389 — Blue green and green backgrounds: a, 250t. b, 300t. c, 350t.

1999 Litho. *Perf. 12½*
"Jerry Garcia" In Black-Shadowed Letters
2385-2389 A507 Set of 5 strips of 3 9.00 9.00

Stone Carvings A526

Designs: 50t, Stele with Uigur inscriptions, vert. 150t, Turtle, 13th cent. 200t, Kul Tegin burial site, 7th-8th cent., vert. 250t, Kul Tegin, 8th cent., vert. 300t, Dragon, 8th-9th cent. 450t, Man, 5th-7th cent., vert.

2000, Jan. 17 Litho. *Perf. 12*
2390-2395 A526 Set of 6 5.00 5.00

A527

World Teachers' Day — A528

Academicians: #2396, 2398, Dr. Tsendiin Damdinsuren (1908-86). #2397, 2399, Dr. B. Rinchin (1905-77).

1999, Dec. 5

2396	A527 250t blue & blk	.50	.50
2397	A527 250t grn & blk	.50	.50
2398	A527 450t pur & blk	.85	.85
2399	A527 450t brn & blk	.85	.85
2400	A528 600t multi	1.10	1.10
	Nos. 2396-2400 (5)	3.80	3.80

Souvenir Sheet

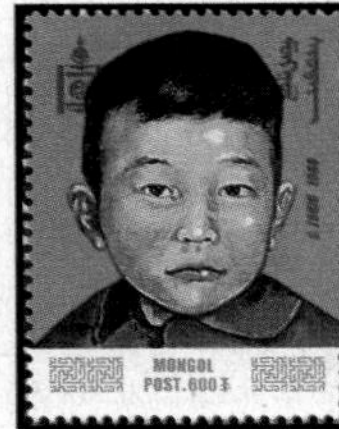

Sanjaasuregin Zorig (1962-98), Politician — A529

Designs: a, 600t, Zorig in 1968. b, 1000t, Three people, flag. c, 600t, Zorig in 1998.

1999, Oct. 1 *Perf. 13¼x13*
2401 A529 Sheet of 3, #a.-c. 6.00 6.00

Size of No. 2401b: 59x39mm.

World Intellectual Property Organization, 20th Anniv. — A529a

No. 2401D: e, 250t, Satellite, airplane. f, 450t, Statue, television. g, 250t, Cauldron, toy. h, 250t, Copier, stamps. i, 450t, Camera, yurt, Mongolian couple. j, 250t, Red automobile. k, 250t, Grille of antique auto, bottles, cellular phones, wristwatch. l, 450t, Perfume bottles. m, 250t, Pack of cigarettes, soccer ball, volley ball, basketball, bottle of motor oil, boom box.

1999, Dec. 24 Litho. *Perf. 12*
2401D A529a Sheet of 9, #e-m 8.00 8.00

Souvenir Sheet

Japan-Mongolia Friendship — A530

a, Sumo wrestler. b, Symbols of countries.

1999, Dec. 28 *Perf. 13½*
2402 A530 450t Sheet of 2, #a.-b. 4.50 4.50

New Year 2000 (Year of the Dragon) — A531

Background color: 250t, Red. 450t, Blue, vert.

2000, Jan. 10 Litho. *Perf. 12*
2403-2404 A531 Set of 2 4.00 4.00

Nos. 715-717, C34 Surcharged

Methods and Perfs as Before
2000, Jan. 19

2405	A168	1000t on 50m brn	7.00	7.00
2406	A168	2000t on 60m grn	8.00	8.00
2407	A168	5000t on 1t rose claret	15.00	15.00
2408	AP12	10,000t on 1.50t bl	30.00	30.00
		Nos. 2405-2408 (4)	60.00	60.00

Wolves — A532

Designs: 150t, Pair, one with snout up. 250t, Eating deer. 300t, Nursing young. 450t, Snarling.

2000, Jan. 17 Litho. *Perf. 12*
2409-2412 A532 Set of 4 4.00 4.00

Souvenir Sheet
2413 A532 800t Pair baying 4.00 4.00

No. 2413 contains one 50x30mm stamp.

Sheep — A533

Breeds: 50t, Sumber. 100t, Orkhon. 150t, Baidrag. 250t, Barga. 400t, Uzemchin. 450t, Bayad.

2000, Jan. 20

2414-2419 A533 Set of 6 4.00 4.00

Souvenir Sheet

2420 A533 800t Govi-Altai 4.00 4.00

One Day of Mongolia, by Balduugiin Sharav — A534

Various parts of painting: a, 50t. b, 100t, c, 150t. d, 200t. e, 250t. f, 300t. g, 350t. h, 450t. i, 600t.

2000, Jan. 24

2421 A534 Sheet of 9, #a-i 9.00 9.00

Huts and Yurts A535

Designs: 50t, Hunters returning to hut. 100t, Mother, daughter, animals near hut. 150t, Yurt near hill. 250t, Two yurts, motorcycle, and satellite dish. 450t, Yurt construction.

No. 2427, 800t, Yurt's furnishings. No. 2428, 800t, Yurt and wagon.

2000, Jan. 25

2422-2426 A535 Set of 5 4.00 4.00

Souvenir Sheets

2427-2428 A535 Set of 2 8.00 8.00

Union of Mongolian Production and Service Cooperatives, 10th Anniv. — A536

Panel colors: 300t, Blue. 450t, Green.

2000, Mar. 27 ***Perf. 12***

2429-2430 A536 Set of 2 4.00 4.00

A537

A538

A539

A540

A541

A542

A543

Costumes of Mongolian Lords — A544

2000, May 11 ***Perf. 13¼***

2431 A537 550t multi 1.50 1.00
2432 A538 550t multi 1.50 1.00
2433 A539 550t multi 1.50 1.00
2434 A540 550t multi 1.50 1.00
2435 A541 550t multi 1.50 1.00
2436 A542 550t multi 1.50 1.00
2437 A543 550t multi 1.50 1.00
2438 A544 550t multi 1.50 1.00
Nos. 2431-2438 (8) 12.00 8.00

Buddhas A545

No. 2439: a, Jigjid. b, Gombo. c, Tsamba. d, Jamsran. e, Baldanlkham. f, Ochirvani. g, Namsrai. h, Gongor. i, Damdinchoijoo. j, Shalshi.

2000, July 1 ***Perf. 13x13½***

2439 Block of 10 15.00 11.00
a.-j. A545 550t Any single 1.50 1.10

Worldwide Fund for Nature (WWF) — A546

Two Przewalski's horses: No. 2440a, 300t, No. 2441a, 100t, Standing apart. No. 2440b, 150t, No. 2441b, 250t, Galloping. No. 2440c, 100t, No. 2441d, 200t, Grazing. No. 2440d, 200t, No. 2441c, 50t, Standing together.

2000, July 5 **Litho.** ***Perf. 13½***

2440 A546 Block or strip of 4, #a-d 4.50 4.50

Litho. & Holography

Size: 50x35mm

2441 A546 Block of 4, #a-d 5.50 5.50

Illustrations on No. 2441 are mirror images of those on No. 2440.

Trains — A547

No. 2442: a, 200t, Guaari-Current electric locomotive, France. b, 400t, 2-10-0 Austerity, Great Britain. c, 300t, ALG Bo-Bo electric locomotive, Great Britain. d, 400t, Diesel-electric locomotive, Australia. e, 300t, E-10 Bo-Bo electric locomotive, Germany. f, 200t, C38 Class Pacific, US. g, 300t, 46 Class electric locomotive, US. h, 200t, Bo-Bo electric locomotive, New Zealand. i, 400t, Bo-Bo electric locomotive, Netherlands.

No. 2443: a, 300t, Italian second-clas carriage. b, 400t, Bodmin & Wadebridge Railway composite carriage. c, 200t, Stephenson 2-2-2, Russia. d, 200t, 2-2-2 Walt, US. e, 300t, The General, US. f, 400t, 4-4-0 Washington, US. g, 400t, Braithwaite 0-4-0, Great Britain. h, 200t, Ross Winans Muddigger locomotive, US. i, 300t, 4-4-0 Ramapo, US.

No. 2444, 800t, The Ringmaster, US. No. 2445, 800t, Deltic electric locomotive, Great Britain.

2000, July 7 **Litho.** ***Perf. 14***

Sheets of 9, #a-i

2442-2443 A547 Set of 2 14.00 14.00

Souvenir Sheets

2444-2445 A547 Set of 2 8.00 8.00

Ferrari Race Cars — A548

No. 2446: a, 1975 312 T. b, 1961 156 F1. c, 1979 312 T4. d, 1964 158 F1. e, 1981 126 CK. f, 1974 312 B3.

2000, July 15

2446 A548 350t Sheet of 6, #a-f 18.00 18.00

2000 Summer Olympics, Sydney A549

Designs: 100t, Boxing. 200t, Wrestling. 300t, Judo. 400t, Shooting.

2000, July 21 ***Perf. 13x13¼***

2447-2450 A549 Set of 4 4.00 4.00

Albert Einstein (1879-1955) — A550

Einstein: a, 100t, At blackboard. b, 300t, Wearing hat. c, 200t, Wearing green sweater. d, 200t, With violin. e, 550t, Close-up. f, 100t, At lectern. g, 100t, Holding pipe. h, 400t, Receiving award. i, 300t, Holding clock.

2000, Aug. 10 ***Perf. 12½***

2451 A550 Sheet of 9, #a-i 7.50 7.50

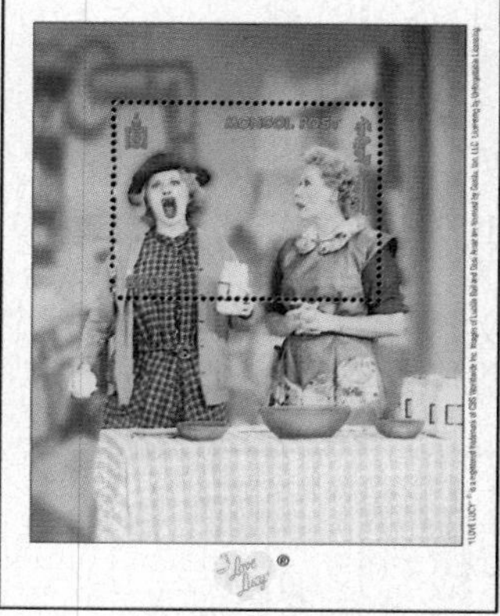

I Love Lucy — A551

No. 2452, vert.: a, 100t, Lucy, wiping hands, and Ethel. b, 400t, Lucy, reading letter, and Ethel. c, 200t, Lucy, setting table, and Fred. d, 200t, Lucy on telephone. e, 300t, Lucy with chin on fist. f, 100t, Lucy with head on hands. g, 100t, Lucy and Ethel waving. h, 550t, Lucy, holding bowl, and Ethel. i, 300t, Lucy, wearing brown sweater and holding jar, and Ethel.

No. 2453, 800t, Lucy, with mouth open, holding jar, and Ethel. No. 2454, 800t, Lucy, wearing stole, and Ethel.

2000, Aug. 15 Litho. *Perf. 12½*
2452 A551 Sheet of 9, #a-i 7.00 7.00

Souvenir Sheets

2453-2454 A551 Set of 2 3.00 3.00

The Three Stooges — A552

No. 2455, horiz.: a, 100t, Moe, Larry and woman. b, 400t, Moe, Shemp and Larry attempting jail escape. c, 300t, Moe, with blow torch, Shemp and Larry. d, 200t, Moe, Larry and Joe Besser with musical instruments. e, 300t, Man knocking together heads of Shemp, Larry and Moe. f, 100t, Man with hammer, Moe, Larry and Shemp. g, 100t, Larry, Joe Besser and Moe in kitchen. h, 550t, Moe, Shemp and Larry with large wrench. i, 200t, Larry, Moe and Shemp in kitchen.

No. 2456, 800t, Moe, with fingers in ears, and Shemp. No. 2457, 800t, Shemp and Larry in army uniforms.

2000, Aug. 17
2455 A552 Sheet of 9, #a-i 7.00 7.30

Souvenir Sheets

2456-2457 A552 Set of 2 3.00 3.00

20th Century Events in Mongolia — A553

No. 2458: a, Independence, 1911. b, National revolution, 1921. c, Declaration of Mongolian People's Republic, 1924. d, Political repression, 1937. e, War years, 1939-45. f, Voting for independence, 1945. g, Agricultural reform, 1959. h, Member of UN, 1961. i, Space flight, 1981. j, Democratic revolution, 1990.

2000, Sept. 13 Litho. *Perf. 13½x13*
2458 A553 300t Sheet of 10, #a-j + 2 labels 8.00 8.00

See No. 2482.

Marmota Sidisica — A554

Number of marmots: 100t, One. 200t, Three. 300t, Two. 400t, Three, diff.

2000, Sept. 15 *Perf. 13¼x13*
2459-2462 A554 Set of 4 6.00 6.00

Souvenir Sheet

Perf. 13x13¼

2463 A554 800t One marmot, horiz. 5.50 5.50

Traditional Patterns A555

Various designs: 50t, 200t, 250t, 300t, 400t, 550t.

50t, 250t, 550t are horiz.

Perf. 13¼x13, 13x13¼

2000, Sept. 20
2464-2469 A555 Set of 6 10.00 10.00

John F. Kennedy, Jr. (1960-99) — A556

2000, Sept. 25 *Perf. 14*
2470 A556 300t multi 1.50 1.50

Printed in sheets of 6.

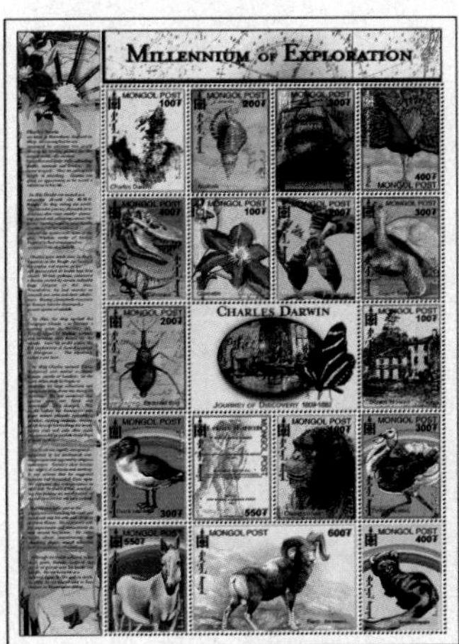

Millennium — A557

Exploration: a, 100t, Charles Darwin. b, 200t, Mollusk. c, 300t, HMS Beagle. d, 400t, Peacock. e, 400t, Dinosaur. f, 100t, Clematis. g, 200t, Orchid. h, 300t, Giant tortoise. i, 200t, Reduviid bug. j, 100t, Down House. k, 300t, Duck. l, 550t, The Origin of Species. m, 100t, Chimpanzee. n, 300t, Turkey. o, 550t, Horse. p, 600t, Ram (60x40mm). q, Vormela peregugna.

2000, Oct. 5 *Perf. 12¾x12½*
2471 A557 Sheet of 17, #a-q + label 18.00 18.00

State Symbols — A558

No. 2472: a, Headdress on spike. b, Horn. c, Bow, arrows and quiver. d, Robe. e, Crossed swords. f, Saddle. g, Belt. h, Seated man. i, Throne.

2000, Oct. 25 Litho. *Perf. 12*
2472 A558 300t Sheet of 9, #a-i 15.00 15.00

Queens — A559

No. 2473: a, Oulen. b, Borteujin. c, Turakana. d, Caymish. e, Chinbay.

2000, Oct. 30
2473 Horiz. strip of 5 7.50 7.50
a.-e. A559 300t Any single 1.50 1.50

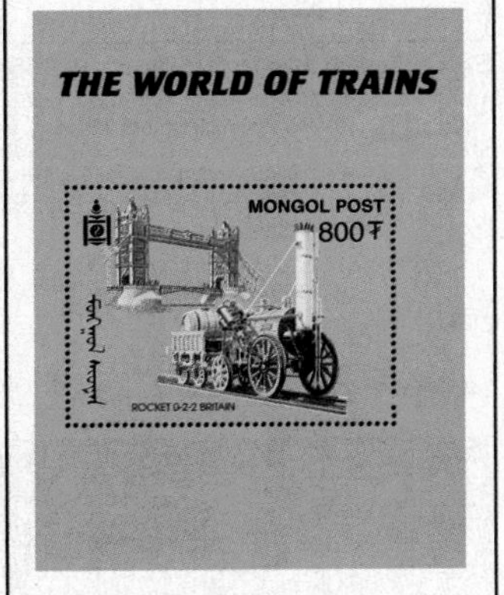

Trains — A560

No. 2474: a, 200t, TGV, France. b, 100t, X200, Sweden. c, 300t, Regio Runner, Netherlands. d, 100t, Deltic, Great Britain. e, 300t, Type M1200, Burma. f, 200t, ICE, Germany. g, 300t, G Class, Australia. h, 200t, Class E444, Italy. i, 100t, GM F7 Warbonnet, US.

No. 2475: a, 200t, Class 18 4-6-2, Germany. b, 100t, Class GS-4 4-8-4, US. c, 300t, Class 25 4-8-4, South Africa. d, 100t, Class 685 2-6-2, Italy. e, 300t, Class HP, India. f, 200t, Class SY 2-8-2, China. g, 300t, Liner A3 Pacific, Great Britain. h, 200t, Class 231C 4-6-2, France. i, 100t, Class 3700, Netherlands.

No. 2476, 800t, Rocket 0-2-2, Great Britain. No. 2477, 800t, Eurostar, France and Great Britain, vert.

2000, Nov. 25 *Perf. 14*

Sheets of 9, #a-i

2474-2475 A560 Set of 2 13.50 13.50

Souvenir Sheets

2476-2477 A560 Set of 2 9.00 9.00

Nos. 2474-2475 each contain nine 42x28mm stamps.

Endangered Animals of Gobi Desert — A561

No. 2478: a, 100t, Scarabaeus typhon (40x30mm). b, 400t, Ursus arctos gobiensis (40x40mm). c, 300t, Camelus bactrianus ferus (40x40mm). d, 300t, Saiga tatarica mongolica (40x40mm). e, 550t, Ovis ammon (40x40mm). f, 550t, Uncia uncia (40x40mm). g, 100t, Phrynosephalus helioscopus(40x30mm). h, 200t, Coliber spinalus (40x30mm). i, 200t, Euchoreutes paso (40x30mm). j, 300t, Chlamydotis undulata (40x40mm).

2000, Dec. 25 *Perf. 12½*
2478 A561 Sheet of 10, #a-j 15.00 15.00

Souvenir Sheet

Advent of New Millennium — A562

Litho. & Embossed with Foil Application

2001, Jan. 1 *Perf. 13½*
2479 A562 5000t multi 15.00 15.00

New Year 2001 (Year of the Snake) — A563

Color behind snake: 300t, Pink. 400t, green, vert.

2001, Jan. 15 Litho. *Perf. 13¼*
2480-2481 A563 Set of 2 4.00 4.00

20th Century Events Type of 2000

World events: a, First World War, 1914. b, October Revolution, 1917. c, Power seized by Fascists, 1933. d, Second World War, 1939. e, Nuclear weapons, 1945. f, Establishment of the United Nations, 1945. g, End of colonialism, 1940. h, Space travel, 1961. i, Downfall of socialism, 1989. j, Establishment of Mongolia, 1911.

2001, Mar. 15 *Perf. 13½x13*
2482 A553 300t Sheet of 10, #a-j, + 2 labels 8.00 8.00

Armed Forces, 80th Anniv. — A564

Designs: No. 2483, 300t, Marshal G. Demid (blue green). No. 2484, 300t, Marshal J.

Lhagvasuren (dark green). No. 2485, 300t, L. Dandar (olive green).

2001, Mar. 18 ***Perf. 13¾x13¼***
2483-2485 A564 Set of 3 3.00 3.00

Souvenir Sheet

Mountaineers — A565

No. 2486: a, Mountaineer waving. b, Mountaineers starting climb.

2001, Apr. 1 ***Perf. 13¼x13***
2486 A565 400t Sheet of 2, #a-b 4.00 4.00

I Love Lucy — A566

No. 2487, horiz.: a, 100t, Lucy drinking from cup, Ricky reading newspaper. b, 400t, Ricky and Fred. c, 300t, Lucy, Ethel and two candy factory workers. d, 200t, Lucy with arms outstretched, candy factory worker. e, 300t, Lucy looking at candy factory worker. f, 100t, Lucy smearing chocolate on worker's face. g, 100t, Worker smearing Lucy's face with chocolate. h, 550t, Ricky holding stocking, Fred. i, 200t, Ethel and Lucy.

No. 2488, 800t, Lucy wrapping chocolates. No. 2489, 800t, Fred and Ricky preparing dinner.

2001, Apr. 15 ***Perf. 12½***
2487 A566 Sheet of 9, #a-i 7.00 7.00

Souvenir Sheets

2488-2489 A566 Set of 2 3.00 3.00

The Three Stooges — A567

No. 2490: a, 100t, Larry. b, 400t, Larry and Shemp inserting instrument into man's mouth. c, 300t, Moe and Shemp. d, 200t, Moe, Larry and Shemp on telephones. e, 300t, Moe with chef's toque, Shemp, Larry. f, 100t, Moe looking in tube. g, 100t, Moe hitting Larry, Shemp. h, 550t, Shemp, Larry, Moe and woman. i, 200t, Moe with gavel, Curly on telephone.

No. 2491, 800t, Shemp and Larry as shown on #2490e. No. 2492, 800t, Shemp as angel, vert.

2001, Apr. 15
2490 A567 Sheet of 9, #a-i 7.00 7.00

Souvenir Sheets

2491-2492 A567 Set of 2 3.00 3.00

Philatelic Exhibitions — A568

Nomading, by T.S. Minjuur and exhibition emblem of: a, Hong Kong 2001. b, Hafnia 01. c, Phila Nippon '01. d, Belgica 2001.

2001, May 15 ***Perf. 13½***
2493 A568 400t Sheet of 4, #a-d 6.00 6.00

Souvenir Sheet

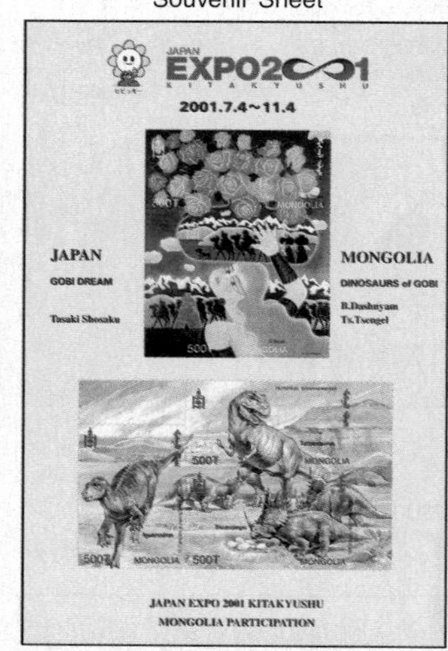

Expo 2001, Kitakyushu, Japan — A569

No. 2494: a, Roses from Gobi Dream, by Shosaku Tasaki (52x24mm). b, Dreamer from Gobi Dream, vert. (32x42mm). c, Tarbosaurus (48x25mm). d, Iguanodon, vert. (30x41mm). e, Triceratops (48x25mm).

Serpentine Die Cut 10¾, 12¼ (#2494c-2494e)

2001, July 1

Self-Adhesive

2494 A569 500t Sheet of 5, #a-e 9.00 9.00

Children and Sports — A570

No. 2495: a, Chess. b, Bicycling. c, Baseball.

No. 2496: a, 200t, Mongolian children on horses. b, 350t, Ice hockey. c, 500t, Flag, Mongolian boy on horse. d, 150t, Children playing soccer. e, 300t, Mongolian girl on horse. f, 450t, Boy playing soccer. g, 100t, Mongolian children on horses. h, 250t, Golf. i, 400t, Mongolian children on horses.

Illustration reduced.

2001, Sept. 1 ***Perf. 12½***
2495 A570 500t Horiz. strip of 3, #a-c 4.00 4.00
2496 A570 Sheet of 9, #a-i 12.00 12.00

Scouting and Nature — A571

No. 2497: a, 100t, Salpingotus. b, 200t, Uncia uncia. c, 300t, Haliaeetus albicilla. d, 400t, Pandion haliatus. e, 450t, Panciawus colchicus.

No. 2498: a, 50t, Butterfly. b, 100t, Bat. c, 200t, Butterfly, diff. d, 300t, Mushrooms. e, 400t, Dinosaur. f, 450t, Puffin.

No. 2499, vert.: a, 150t, Sea shell. b, 300t, Owl. c, 450t, Sea turtle. d, 100t, Frog. e, 250t, Butterfly. f, 400t, Orchid. g, 50t, Penguins. h, 200t, Elephant. i, 350t, Whale.

2001, Sept. 1
2497 A571 Sheet of 5, #a-e, + label 5.00 5.00
2498 A571 Sheet of 6, #a-f 5.00 5.00
2499 A571 Sheet of 9, #a-i 7.50 7.50

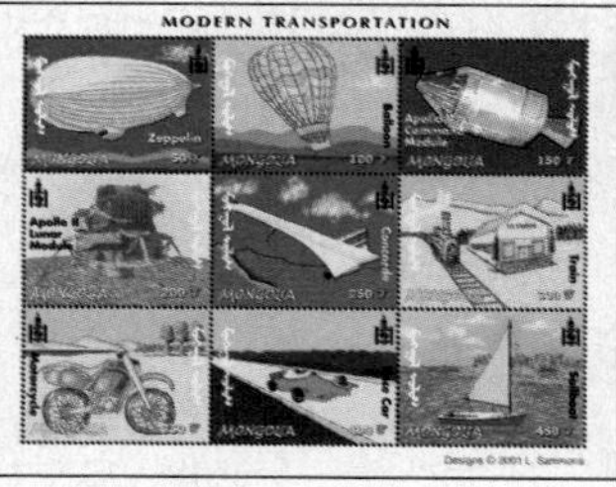

Modern Transportation — A572

No. 2500: a, 50t, Zeppelin. b, 100t, Balloon. c, 150t, Apollo 11 command module. d, 200t, Apollo Lunar Module. e, 250t, Concorde. f, 300t, Train. g, 350t, Motorcycle. h, 400t, Race car. i, 450t, Sailboat.

2001, Sept. 15
2500 A572 Sheet of 9, #a-i 7.50 7.50

Admission to United Nations, 40th Anniv. — A573

No. 2501: a, Dove, map. b, UN and Mongolian flags.

2001, Oct. 27 ***Perf. 13***
2501 A573 400t Horiz. pair, #a-b 3.00 3.00

Year of Dialogue Among Civilizations A574

2001, Dec. 20 ***Perf. 13¼x13***
2502 A574 300t multi 2.50 2.50

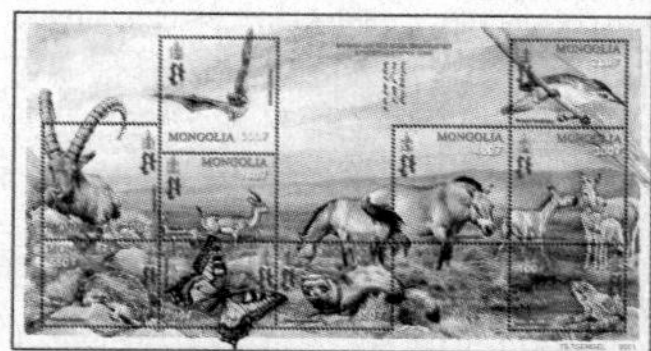

Endangered Species in Steppe Zone — A575

No. 2503: a, 300t, Vespertilio superans (40x40mm). b, 200t, Podoces hendersoni (40x30mm). c, 300t, Capra sibirica (40x40mm). d, 100t, Gazella subgutturosa (40x30mm). e, 400t, Equus przewalskii (40x40mm). f, 300t, Equus hemionus hemionus (40x40mm). g, 550t, Erinaceus dauricus (40x30mm). h, 200t, Papilio machaon (40x30mm). i, 550t, Vormela peregusna (40x30mm). j, 100t, Rana chensinensis (40x30mm).

2001, Dec. 30 ***Perf. 13½x13¼***
2503 A575 Sheet of 10, #a-j 10.00 10.00

History of Humanity — A576

Prominent features of stamps: a, Leaning Tower of Pisa, Romulus and Remus suckling she-wolf. b, Eagle, warrior with shield. c, Great Wall of China. d, Mosque, warrior on horseback. e, Celtic cross, castle, warrior with shield. f, Mona Lisa, by Leonardo da Vinci, David, by Michelangelo, other sculptures and religious paintings. g, Mask, Easter Island statues, boomerang, native, hut. h, Sir Isaac Newton, telescope, planets, Nicolaus Copernicus. i, Eiffel tower, Napoleon bonaparte on horseback, French flag, Arc de Triomphe. j, Astronaut, Earth, DNA molecule, computer. k, Greek soldier and amphora. l, Taj Mahal, Asoka pillar. m, Statue of Buddha. n, Genghis Khan. o, Yurt, Buddhist statue. p, Jesus Christ, Madonna and Child. q, Globe, ship, Christopher Columbus. r, Statue of Liberty, U.S. Capitol, Indian chief, U.S. flag, George Washington, city skyline. s, Printing press, man on horseback, letters of alphabet. t, Tower Bridge, British flag, Penny Black.

2001, Dec. 30 ***Perf. 13¼***
2504 Sheet of 20 20.00 20.00
a.-j. A576 200t Any single 1.00 1.00
k.-t. A576 300t Any single 1.00 1.00

New Year 2002 (Year of the Horse) A577

Mane color: 300t, Gray, vert. 400t, Yellow brown.

2002, Feb. 13 ***Perf. 13¼x13, 13x13¼***
2505-2506 A577 Set of 2 4.00 4.00

Birds of Prey — A578

Designs: 100t, Gyps himalayensis. 150t, Gyps fulvus. 300t, Neophron percnopterus. 400t, Aegypius monachus. 550t, Gypaetus barbatus.

2002, Apr. 1 ***Perf. 12½***
2507-2511 A578 Set of 5 5.00 5.00

Souvenir Sheets

Mongolia - Japan Diplomatic Relations, 30th Anniv. — A579

No. 2512, 550t: a, Camel. b, Przewalski's horse.

No. 2513, 550t, vert. (38x50mm): a, Rider on horseback. b, Face of cartoon character.

2002, Apr. 27 ***Perf. 12***
2512-2513 A579 Set of 2 8.00 8.00

Dogs A580

Dogs with: 100t, Sheep. 200t, Cattle. 300t, Camel and yurt. 400t, Camels.
800t, Dog.

2002, May 1 *Perf. 13¼x13*
2514-2517 A580 Set of 4 4.00 4.00

Souvenir Sheet

2518 A580 800t multi 3.50 3.50

2002 World Cup Soccer Championships, Japan and Korea — A581

No. 2519: a, 300t, Stadium, Seoul. b, 400t, 1998 French team and flag, World Cup trophy. c, 400t, 1966 English team and flag, Jules Rimet Cup. d, 300t, Stadium, Yokohama.

2002, May 31 *Perf. 12*
2519 A581 Sheet of 4, #a-d 4.50 4.50

Flowers — A582

Designs: 100t, Thermopsis. No. 2521, 150t, Chelidonium. No. 2522, 150t, Hypencum. 200t, Plantago. 250t, Saussurea. 300t, Rosa acicularis. 450t, Lilium.

2002, June 15 **Litho.** *Perf. 12*
2520-2526 A582 Set of 7 7.00 7.00

Rock Paintings — A583

Various paintings with background colors of: 50t, Pink. 100t, Beige. 150t, Greenish blue. 200t, Green. 300t, Blue. 400t, Blue.
800t, Dark blue.

2002, July 1
2527-2532 A583 Set of 6 6.00 6.00

Souvenir Sheet

2533 A583 800t multi 3.50 3.50

New Year 2003 (Year of the Sheep) — A584

Sheep with background colors of: 300t, Yellow. 400t, Green, horiz.

2003, Jan. 1
2534-2535 A584 Set of 2 4.00 4.00

Mushrooms and Birds A585

Designs: 50t, Russula aeruginosa, Coccothraustes coccothraustes. 100t, Boletus edulis, Loxia curvirostra. 150t, Boletus badius, Carpodacus erythrinus. 200t, Agaricus campester, Garrulus glandarius. 250t, Marasmius onreades, Luscinia megarhynchos. 300t, Cantharellus cibarius, Locustella certhiola. 400t, Amanita phalloides, Ardea cinerea. 550t, Suillus granulatus, Accipter gentilis.
No. 2544, 800t, Lactarius tormmosus, Aeqithalos caudatus. No. 2545, 800t, Tricholoma pertentosum, Lanius collurio.

2003, Feb. 1 *Perf. 13¼x13*
2536-2543 A585 Set of 8 12.00 12.00

Souvenir Sheets

2544-2545 A585 Set of 2 12.00 12.00

Nos. 2544-2545 each contain one 60x40mm stamp.

Visit Mongolia — A586

No. 2546: a, 100t, Statue of Sukhe Bator. b, 200t, City buildings. c, 300t, Rock formation. d, 400t, Yurts.
No. 2547: a, 100t, Camels. b, 200t, Yaks. c, 300t, Hunter with eagle. d, 400t, Snow leopard.

2003, July 11 *Perf. 12*

Sheets of 4, #a-d

2546-2547 A586 Set of 2 8.00 8.00

Endangered Species in Khangai Zone — A587

No. 2548: a, 300t, Pandion haliaetus (40x30mm). b, 200t, Dryomys nitedula (40x30mm) c, 300t, Rangifer tarandus (40x40mm). d, 100t, Moschus moschiferus (40x40mm). e, 550t, Alces alces pfizenmayeri (40x40mm). f, 400t, Alces alces cameloides (40x40mm). g, 300t, Sus scrofa nigripes (40x40mm). h, 550t, Phasianus colchicus (40x30mm). i, 200t, Lutra lutra (40x30mm). j, 100t, Castor fiber birulai (40x30mm).

2003, Aug. 15 *Perf. 13½*
2548 A587 Sheet of 10, #a-j 10.00 10.00

Birds, Butterflies, Orchids and Mushrooms — A588

No. 2549, 800t — Birds: a, Common bush tanager. b, Black-headed hemispingus. c, Scarlet-rumped tanager. d, Band-tailed seedeater.
No. 2550, 800t — Butterflies: a, Thecla teresina. b, Theritas cypria. c, Theritas coronata. d, Thecla phaleros.
No. 2551, 800t — Orchids: a, Vanda rothschildiana. b, Paphiopedium parishii. c, Dendrobium nobile. d, Cattleya loddigesii.
No. 2552, 800t — Mushrooms: a, Hypholoma fasciculare. b, Marasmiellus ramealis. c, Collybia fusipes. d, Kuehneromyces mutabilis.
No. 2553, 2500t, Andean hillstar. No. 2554, 2500t, Thecla pedusa. No. 2555, 2500t, Barkeria skinnerii. No. 2556, 2500t, Psathyrella multipedata, vert.

Perf. 13¼x13½, 13½x13¼

2003, Dec. 10

Sheets of 4, #a-d

2549-2552 A588 Set of 4 20.00 20.00

Souvenir Sheets

2553-2556 A588 Set of 4 16.00 16.00

Souvenir Sheet

Yang Liwei, First Chinese Astronaut — A589

2003, Dec. 25 **Litho.** *Perf. 12*
2557 A589 800t multi 4.00 4.00

New Year 2004 (Year of the Monkey) — A590

Monkey and background in: 300t, Blue. 400t, Red.

2004, Feb. 21
2558-2559 A590 Set of 2 4.00 4.00

Peace Mandala — A591

No. 2560: a, 50t, Tushita Heaven. b, 100t, Elephant and Lady Maya. c, 150t, Birth of Buddha. d, 200t, Buddha as prince of Shakya clan. e, 250t, Prince shaving off hair. f, 300t, Buddha beating the devil. g, 400t, Buddha preaching for first time. h, 550t, Great Nirvana Sutra. i, 5000t, Various scenes in Buddha's life.
No. 2561, Central details of No. 2560i.
Size of Nos. 2560a-2560h, 41x38mm; No. 2560i, 132x182mm.

Serpentine Die Cut 10, 6¾ (#2560i, 2561)

2004, June 3 **Litho.**

Self-Adhesive

2560 A591 Sheet of 9, #a-i 18.00 18.00

Souvenir Sheet

Litho. With Foil Application

2561 A591 5000t gold & brn 20.00 20.00

Mammals — A592

Designs: (100t), Equus przewalskii. (300t), Camelus bactrianus ferus. (400t), Ovis ammon. (550t), Capra sibirica.

2004, July 1 **Litho.** *Perf. 13¼x13*
2562 A592 (100t) multi .50 .50
2563 A592 (300t) multi .75 .75
2564 A592 (400t) multi 1.25 1.25
2565 A592 (550t) multi 1.50 1.50
Nos. 2562-2565 (4) 4.00 4.00

Genghis Khan (c. 1162-1227) — A593

Various depictions of Genghis Khan: 200t, 300t, 350t, 550t. 300t is horiz.

2004, July 11 *Perf. 13*
2566-2569 A593 Set of 4 4.00 4.00

Unification of Mongolia, 800th anniv. (in 2006).

2004 Summer Olympics, Athens — A594

Designs: 100t, Judo. 200t, Wrestling, horiz. 300t, Boxing. 400t, Pistol shooting, horiz.

2004, Aug. 13 ***Perf. 12***
2570-2573 A594 Set of 4 4.00 4.00

UPU, 130th Anniv. — A595

2004, Sept. 15 ***Perf. 12¾***
2574 A595 300t multi 1.50 1.50

Nos. 776, 778, 841, 842 Surcharged

Methods and Perfs as Before
2004, Oct. 5

2575	A191 550t on 10m #841	—	—
2576	A191 550t on 20m #842	—	—
2577	A178 550t on 30m #776	—	—
2578	A178 550t on 60m #778	—	—

A596

A597

A598

Soccer A599

Designs: No. 2581, Goalie making save. No. 2582, Player kicking ball. No. 2583, Three players. No. 2584, Player and goalie.

2004, Oct. 15 **Litho.** ***Perf. 12¾x13***

2579	A596 50t multi	.25	.25
2580	A597 50t multi	.25	.25
2581	A597 100t multi	.40	.40
2582	A597 100t multi	.40	.40
2583	A597 150t multi	.55	.55
2584	A597 150t multi	.55	.55
2585	A598 200t multi	.80	.80
2586	A599 200t multi	.80	.80
	Nos. 2579-2586 (8)	4.00	4.00

Souvenir Sheet

First Mongolian Stamp, 80th Anniv. — A600

2004, Dec. 4 ***Perf. 13¼x13***
2587 A600 800t multi 3.50 3.50

Miniature Sheets

Insects and Flowers — A601

No. 2588: a, 100t, Mantis religiosa. b, 100t, Aster alpina. c, 200t, Echinops humilis. d, 200t, Apis mellifera. e, 300t, Angaraeris barabensis. f, 300t, Nymphaea candida.

No. 2589: a, 100t, Lytta caraganae. b, 100t, Rosa acicularis. c, 200t, Aguilegia sibirica. d, 200t, Tabanus bovinus. e, 300t, Corizus hyoscyami. f, 300t, Lilium pumilum.

2004, Dec. 25 ***Perf. 13***
Sheets of 6, #a-f
2588-2589 A601 Set of 2 10.00 10.00

Women's Headdresses — A602

No. 2590: a, Kazakh headdress, denomination at left. b, Mongol headdress, denomination at right.

Illustration reduced.

2004, Dec. 31 ***Perf. 11½x11¾***
2590 A602 550t Horiz. pair, #a-b 5.00 5.00

See Kazakhstan No. 472.

New Year 2005 (Year of the Rooster) A603

Roosters with frame color of: 300t, Red violet. 400t, Blue, vert.

2005, Jan. 1 ***Perf. 12***
2591-2592 A603 Set of 2 4.00 4.00

Souvenir Sheet

Expo 2005, Aichi, Japan — A604

No. 2593: a, 100t, Butterfly on flower. b, 150t, Flower. c, 200t, Puppy. d, 550t, Kitten.

2005, Mar. 25
2593 A604 Sheet of 4, #a-d 4.50 4.50

World Vision A605

2005, Apr. 1
2594 A605 550t multi 1.50 1.00

Native Costumes — A606

No. 2595, 200t — Blue frame: a, Man with white and blue costume. b, Woman with green and white costume.

No. 2596, 200t — Green frame: a, Man with stringed instrument. b, Woman with red costume.

No. 2597, 200t — Rose pink frame: a, Man with white and blue costume. b, Woman with green costume.

2005, June 20 ***Perf. 13½x13***
Horiz. pairs, #a-b
2595-2597 A606 Set of 3 5.00 5.00

Maharanza A607

No. 2595 — Color of face: a, White. b, Blue. c, Red. d, Yellow brown.

2005, July 8 ***Perf. 13x12¾***
2598 Horiz. strip of 4 4.00 4.00
a.-d. A607 400t Any single 1.00 1.00

Souvenir Sheet

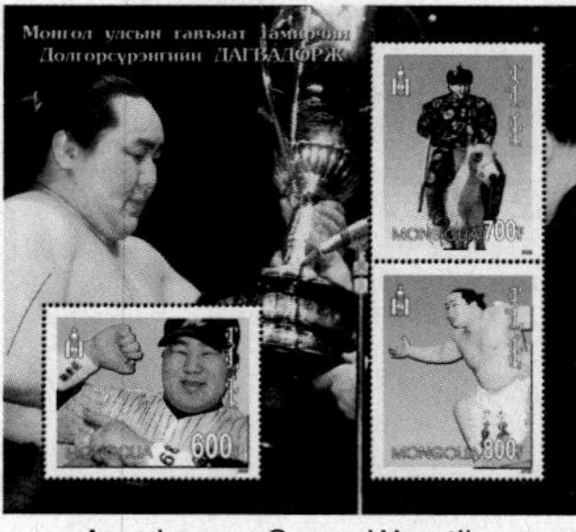
Asashorou, Sumo Wrestling Champion — A608

No. 2599 — Asashorou: a, 600t, Wearing baseball cap. b, 700t, On horse, vert. c, 800t, In wrestling loincloth, vert.

2005, July 18 ***Perf. 13***
2599 A608 Sheet of 3, #a-c 5.00 5.00

World Vision A609

2005, Sept. 20 ***Perf. 12***
2600 A609 550t multi 1.50 1.00

Headdresses A610

People wearing various headdresses: 50t, 100t, 150t, 200t, 250t, 300t.
800t, National headdress.

2005, Oct. 3 ***Perf. 12¾x13***
2601-2606 A610 Set of 6 4.00 4.00

Souvenir Sheet
Perf. 12
2607 A610 800t multi 3.50 3.50

No. 2607 contains one 37x56mm stamp.

Souvenir Sheets

Shenzhou IV Space Flight — A611

No. 2608, 800t, Astronauts waving. No. 2609, 800t, Astronauts in spacecraft.

2005, Dec. 9 ***Perf. 12***
2608-2609 A611 Set of 2 8.00 8.00

Souvenir Sheet

Coins of the Mongolian Empire — A612

No. 2610 — Various coins with background color of: a, Blue. b, Grayish lilac. c, Deep bister.

2006, Jan. 11 ***Perf. 13x12¾***
2610 A612 550t Sheet of 3, #a-c 5.00 5.00

New Year 2006 (Year of the Dog) A613

Mongolian emblem and "Year of the Dog" at: 300t, Right. 400t, Left.

2006, Jan. 27 ***Perf. 13x13¼***
2611-2612 A613 Set of 2 3.50 3.50

Miniature Sheet

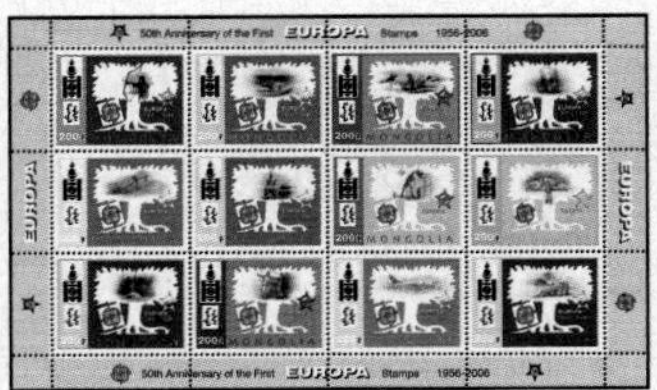

Europa Stamps, 50th Anniv. — A614

No. 2613: a, Archer. b, Camels. c, Boys herding livestock. d, Goat. e, Rocks. f, Building spire. g, Dinosaur skeleton. h, Circus performers. i, Yurt. j, Two men in native costumes. k, Airplane. l, Ox.

2006, Feb. 1 ***Perf. 12½x13***
2613 A614 200t Sheet of 12, #a-l 8.00 8.00
m. Souvenir sheet, #2613a-2613b, perf. 13 1.50 1.50
n. Souvenir sheet, #2613c-2613d, perf. 13 1.50 1.50
o. Souvenir sheet, #2613e-2613f, perf. 13 1.50 1.50
p. Souvenir sheet, #2613g-2613h, perf. 13 1.50 1.50
q. Souvenir sheet, #2613i-2613j, perf. 13 1.50 1.50
r. Souvenir sheet, #2613k-2613l, perf. 13 1.50 1.50

World Vision — A615

No. 2614: a, Children riding ox. b, Child riding horse.
Illustration reduced.

2006, May 5 **Litho.** ***Perf. 12***
2614 A615 550t Horiz. pair, #a-b 3.50 3.50

Souvenir Sheet

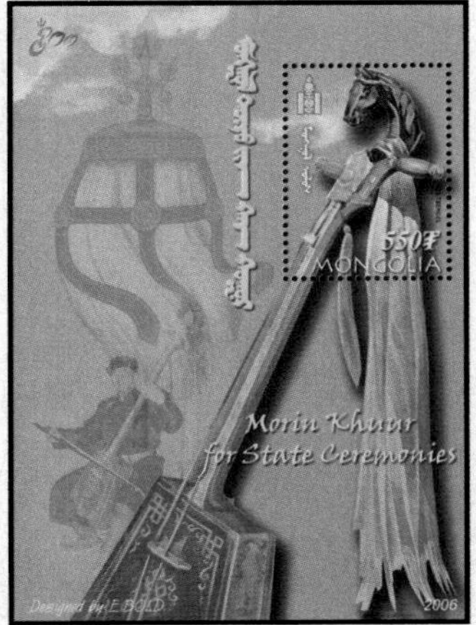

Morin Khuur — A616

2006, June 16
2615 A616 550t multi 2.00 2.00

Souvenir Sheet

Pres. Nambaryn Enkhbayar — A617

2006, June 21
2616 A617 800t multi 3.50 3.50

Souvenir Sheet

2006 World Cup Soccer Championships, Germany — A618

No. 2617 — Various stylized players: a, 200t. b, 250t. c, 300t. d, 400t.

2006, June 23
2617 A618 Sheet of 4, #a-d 5.00 5.00

Souvenir Sheet

State Visit of US Pres. George W. Bush — A619

2006, June 30 ***Perf. 13x13¼***
2618 A619 600t multi 3.00 3.00

Souvenir Sheets

A620

Famous Mongols — A621

No. 2619 — Various unnamed Mongols: a, 50t (23x33mm). b, 100t (23x33mm). c, 300t (23x33mm). d, 400t (23x33mm). e, 500t (80x56mm).

2006 ***Perf. 13, 11½ (#2619e)***
2619 A620 Sheet of 5, #a-e 6.00 6.00
Perf. 11½x11¾
2620 A621 3800t shown 12.00 12.00

Issued: No. 2619, 7/8; No. 2620, 9/19. Mongolian State, 800th anniv.

Souvenir Sheet

Horse Sculptures — A622

No. 2621: a, 300t, Horse and rider. b, 400t, Horse only.

2006, Sept. 28 ***Perf. 12***
2621 A622 Sheet of 2, #a-b 3.50 3.50

See India No. 2167.

Miniature Sheet

Friendly Exchange Philatelic Exhibition — A623

No. 2622: a, 150t, Olympic Stadium, Beijing. b, 200t, Waterfalls. c, 250t, City street at night.

2006, Oct. 25 **Litho.** ***Perf. 12***
2622 A623 Sheet of 3, #a-c 1.10 1.10

Hucho Taimen Fish — A624

No. 2623 — Various depictions of fish: a, 100t. b, 200t. c, 300t. d, 400t.
Illustration reduced.

2006, Dec. 17
2623 A624 Block of 4, #a-d 1.75 1.75

New Year 2007 (Year of the Pig) — A625

Designs: 300t, Two pigs. 400t, Two pigs, diff.

2006, Dec. 17
2624-2625 A625 Set of 2 1.25 1.25

Souvenir Sheet

Diplomatic Relations Between Mongolia and the United States, 20th Anniv. — A626

No. 2626: a, 400t, Statue of Genghis Khan, Ulan Bator. b, 550t, Statue of Abraham Lincoln, Washington, DC.

2007, Jan. 29 **Litho.** ***Perf. 12***
2626 A626 Sheet of 2, #a-b 1.75 1.75

Lama Tsonghapa (1357-1419), Buddhist Teacher — A627

2007, Jan. 30 ***Perf. 12¾***
2627 A627 100t multi .20 .20

Souvenir Sheet

Diplomatic Relations Between Mongolia and Japan, 35th Anniv. — A628

No. 2628: a, 550t, Mt. Fuji, Japan. 700t, Mt. Otgontenger, Mongolia.

2007, Feb. 23 ***Perf. 12***
2628 A628 Sheet of 2, #a-b 2.25 2.25

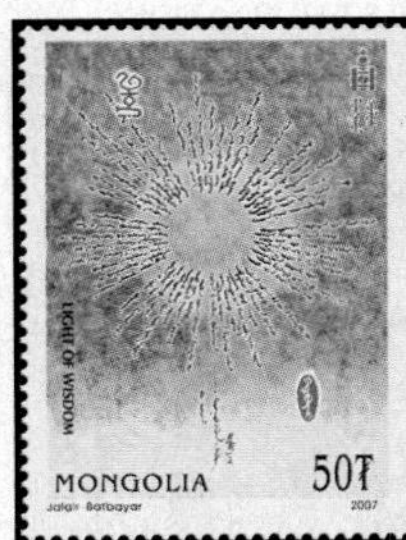

Calligraphy A629

Designs: 50t, Light of wisdom. 100t, Butterfly. 150t, Flower. 200t, Horse. 250t, Spring. 300t, Leaves. 400t, Wow. 550t, Wild camel. 800t, Sky.

2007, Aug. 2 ***Perf. 13x12¾***

2629-2636 A629 Set of 8 3.50 3.50

Souvenir Sheet

Perf. 12¾

2637 A629 800t multi 1.40 1.40

No. 2637 contains one 43x57mm stamp.

Souvenir Sheets

Modern Art — A630

Art by: No. 2638, 400t, Ts. Tsegmid. No. 2639, 400t, S. Sarantsatsralt. No. 2640, 400t, Ts. Enkhjin. No. 2641, 400t, Do. Bold, horiz. No. 2642, 400t, Sh. Chimeddorj, horiz.

2007, Aug. 21 ***Perf. 13***

2638-2642 A630 Set of 5 3.50 3.50

Miniature Sheet

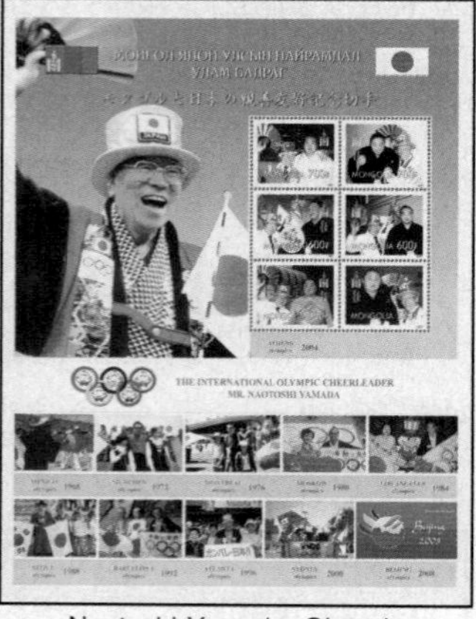

Naotoshi Yamada, Olympic Cheerleader, and Mongolian Sumo Wrestlers — A631

No. 2643 — Yamada and various wrestlers with Mongolian emblem and inscriptions at: a, 500t, Right. b, 500t, Left. c, 600t, Right. d, 600t, Left. e, 700t, Right. f, 700t, Left.

2007, Oct. 3 ***Die Cut***

Self-Adhesive

2643 A631 Sheet of 6, #a-f, + 10 labels 6.25 6.25

SEMI-POSTAL STAMPS

Catalogue values for unused stamps in this section are for Never Hinged items.

Vietnamese Mother and Child — SP1

1967, Dec. 22 **Photo.** ***Perf. 12x11½***

B1 SP1 30m + 20m multi .60 .30
B2 SP1 50m + 30m multi .60 .30

Solidarity with Vietnam.

Save Venice Type of Regular Issue
Souvenir Sheet

Departure of St. Ursula, by Carpaccio.

1972, Oct. 1 **Litho.** ***Perf. 12***

B3 A163 3t + 1t multi 4.00 4.00

Save Venice Campaign. No. B3 contains one horizontal stamp.

Girl Feeding Lambs SP2

UNICEF Emblem and: 20m+5m, Boy playing flute and dancing girl. 30m+5m, Girl chasing butterflies. 40m+5m, Girl with ribbon. 60m+5m, Girl with flowers. 80m+5m, Girl carrying bucket. 1t+5m, Boy going to school.

1977, June 1 **Litho.** ***Perf. 12***

B4 SP2 10m + 5m multi .25 .20
B5 SP2 20m + 5m multi .25 .20
B6 SP2 30m + 5m multi .35 .20
B7 SP2 40m + 5m multi .50 .30
B8 SP2 60m + 5m multi .75 .35
B9 SP2 80m + 5m multi .85 .55
B10 SP2 1t + 5m multi 1.10 .70
Nos. B4-B10 (7) 4.05 2.50

Surtax was for Mongolian Children's Village. See No. CB1.

Boys on Horseback — SP3

Children and IYC Emblem: 30m+5m, Raising chickens. 50m+5m, With deer. 60m+5m, With flowers. 70m+5m, Planting tree. 80m+5m, Studying space project. 1t+5m, Dancing. 4t+50m, Girl on horseback.

1979, Jan. 10

B11 SP3 10m + 5m multi .30 .20
B12 SP3 30m + 5m multi .30 .20
B13 SP3 50m + 5m multi .45 .20
B14 SP3 60m + 5m multi .50 .25
B15 SP3 70m + 5m multi .65 .35
B16 SP3 80m + 5m multi .80 .40
B17 SP3 1t + 5m multi 1.10 .65
Nos. B11-B17 (7) 4.10 2.25

Souvenir Sheet

B18 SP3 4t + 50m multi 4.00 4.00

International Year of the Child.

1998 Winter Olympic Games, Nagano — SP4

1998 **Litho.** ***Perf. 12***

B19 SP4 150t +15t Speed skating .60 .60
B20 SP4 200t +20t Ski jumping .90 .90
B21 SP4 300t +30t Snowboarding 1.30 1.30
B22 SP4 600t +60t Freestyle skiing 2.75 2.75
Nos. B19-B22 (4) 5.55 5.55

Ulan Bator, 360th Anniv. — SP5

Designs, 300t +30t each: No. B23, Flags and arms. No. B24, Seated man. No. B25, Arms.

No. B26, Various views of Ulan Bator.

1999 **Litho.** ***Perf. 12½***

B23-B25 SP5 Set of 3 3.00 3.00

Sheet of 9

Perf. 12½x12¼

B26 SP5 200t +20t #a.-i. 8.00 8.00

No. B26 contains nine 45x27mm stamps.

Unity Against Terrorism — SP6

World Trade Center, Statue of Liberty, American flag and country name in: 300t+50t, Red. 400t+50t, Blue.

Perf. 13½x13¼

2001, Nov. 11 **Litho.**

B27-B28 SP6 Set of 2 3.00 3.00

AIR POST STAMPS

Catalogue values for unused stamps in this section are for Never Hinged items.

Postal Modernization Type of Regular Issue

Designs: 10m, 20m, Postman with horses. 25m, Postman with reindeer. 30m, 50m, Plane over map of Mongolia. 1t, Post horn and flag of Mongolia.

1961, June 5 **Photo.** ***Perf. 15***

C1 A72 10m multicolored .30 .20
C2 A72 50m multicolored .60 .20
C3 A72 1t multicolored 1.10 .40
Nos. C1-C3 (3) 2.00 .80

Souvenir Sheet

Perf. 11

C4 Sheet of 4 4.00 4.00
a. A72 20m lt blue grn & multi 1.00 1.00
b. A72 25m light blue & multi 1.00 1.00
c. A72 30m light green & multi 1.00 1.00
d. A72 1t rose carmine & multi 1.00 1.00

40th anniversary of independence; postal modernization. No. C4b is not inscribed Airmail.

Souvenir Sheet

Austria Type SP55, Austrian and Mongolian Stamps Circling Globe — AP1

1965, May 1 **Engr.** ***Perf. 11½***

C5 AP1 4t brown carmine 4.50 3.50

Vienna Intl. Philatelic Exhibition, WIPA, June 4-13. #C5 contains one 61x38mm stamp.

Weather Satellite AP2

Designs: 20m, Antarctic exploration. 30m, Space exploration.

1965, May 15 **Photo.** ***Perf. 13½***

C6 AP2 15m lilac, gold & blk .50 .20
C7 AP2 20m blue & multi 2.75 .60
C8 AP2 30m rose & multi .65 .25
Nos. C6-C8 (3) 3.90 1.05

International Quiet Sun Year, 1964-65.

ITU Emblem — AP3

Design: 4t, Communications satellite.

1965, Dec. 20 ***Perf. 11½x12***

C9 AP3 30m blue & bister 1.00 .50
C10 AP3 50m red & bister 1.00 .50

Souvenir Sheet

Perf. 11, Imperf.

C11 AP3 4t gold, bl & blk 4.50 3.50

ITU, centenary. No. C11 contains one stamp, 38x51mm. Exists imperf. Values: unused $5.50; used $4.50.

Souvenir Sheet

Luna 10, Moon and Earth — AP4

1966, July 10 Photo. *Imperf.*

C12 AP4 4t multicolored 4.50 3.50

Luna 10 Russian moon mission, Apr. 3, 1966.

Souvenir Sheet

Astronaut and Landing Module — AP5

1969, Aug. 20 Litho. *Perf. 11½*

C13 AP5 4t ultra & multi 4.50 3.50

Apollo 11 US moon mission, first man landing on moon.

Souvenir Sheet

Apollo 16 — AP6

Perf. 12½x11½

1972, Apr. 16 Photo.

C14 AP6 4t multicolored 4.00 3.00

Apollo 16 moon mission, Apr. 15-27.

Souvenir Sheet

Mongolian Horse — AP7

1972, May 10 Photo. *Perf. 12½*

C15 AP7 4t multicolored 4.00 3.00

Centenary of the discovery of the Przewalski wild horse, bred in captivity in Berlin Zoo.

Telecommunication — AP8

Designs: 30m, Horse breeding. 40m, Train and plane. 50m, Corn and farm machinery. 60m, Red Cross ambulance and hospital. 80m, Actors. 1t, Factories.

1972, July 11 Litho. *Perf. 12*

C16 AP8 20m olive & multi .40 .35
C17 AP8 30m violet & multi .40 .35
C18 AP8 40m rose & multi .40 .35
C19 AP8 50m red & multi .40 .35
C20 AP8 60m multicolored .70 .35
C21 AP8 80m lt blue & multi .70 .35
C22 AP8 1t green & multi 1.00 .90
Nos. C16-C22 (7) 4.00 3.00

Mongolian Achievements.

Mongolian Flag, Globe and Radar — AP9

Perf. 12½x11½

1972, July 20 Photo.

C23 AP9 60m olive & multi 1.00 .50

Intl. Telecommunications Day, May 17, 1972.

Running and Olympic Rings — AP10

Olympic Rings and: 15m, Boxing. 20m, Judo. 25m, High jump. 30m, Rifle shooting. 60m, Wrestling. 80m, Weight lifting. 1t, Mongolian flag and sport emblem. 4t, Woman archer, vert.

Perf. 12½x11½

1972, July 30 Photo.

C24 AP10 10m multicolored .30 .30
C25 AP10 15m multicolored .30 .30
C26 AP10 20m multicolored .30 .30
C27 AP10 25m multicolored .30 .30
C28 AP10 30m multicolored .30 .30
C29 AP10 60m multicolored .65 .30
C30 AP10 80m multicolored .85 .50
C31 AP10 1t multicolored 1.00 .70
Nos. C24-C31 (8) 4.00 3.00

Souvenir Sheet

Perf. 11½x12½

C32 AP10 4t orange & multi 4.00 3.00

20th Olympic Games, Munich, 8/26-9/11.

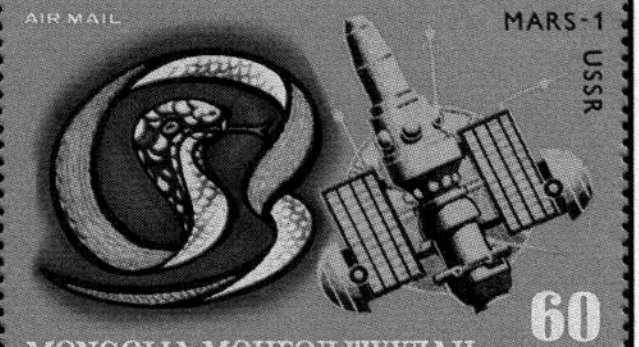

U.S./U.S.S.R. Space Achievements — AP11

Astrological Signs of the Eastern Calendar and Space Project: a, Snake, Mars 1. b, Dragon and Mariner 2. c, Hare, Soyuz 5. d, Monkey, Explorer 6. e, Cock, Venus 1. f, Rat, Apollo 15. g, Horse, Apollo 8. h, Boar, Cosmos 110. i, Tiger, Gemini 7. j, Sheep, Electron 2. k, Dog, Ariel 2. l, Ram, Venus 4.

1972, Dec. 4 Photo. *Perf. 12*

C33 Sheet of 12 6.00 5.00
a.-f. AP11 60m any single, size: 55x35mm .50 .40
g.-l. AP11 60m any single, size: 35x35mm .50 .40

Airliner — AP12

1973, Jan. Photo. *Perf. 12*

C34 AP12 1.50t blue .80 .20

For surcharge, see No. 2408.

Weather Satellite, Earth Station, WMO Emblem — AP13

1973, Feb. Photo. *Perf. 12x11½*

C35 AP13 60m multicolored 1.00 .50

Intl. meteorological cooperation, cent.

Holy Flame Type of 1959

Souvenir Sheet

1973, Apr. 15 Photo. *Perf. 12½*

C36 A48 4t gold & multi 4.00 3.00

IBRA München 1973 Intl. Stamp Exhibition, Munich, May 11-20. No. C36 contains one 40x63mm stamp in redrawn design of A48 with simulated perforations and wide gold margin.

Mongolia #236 — AP14

Designs: Stamps (with mail-connected designs) of participating countries.

1973, July 31 Litho. *Perf. 12½*

C37 AP14 30m Russia No. 3100 .65 .30
C38 AP14 30m shown .65 .30
C39 AP14 30m Bulgaria #1047 .65 .30
C40 AP14 30m Hungary #B202 .65 .30
C41 AP14 30m Czechoslavia #C72 .65 .30
C42 AP14 30m German Dem. Rep. #369 .65 .30
C43 AP14 30m Cuba #C31 .65 .30
C44 AP14 30m Romania #2280 .65 .30
C45 AP14 30m Poland #802 .65 .30
Nos. C37-C45 (9) 5.85 2.70

Conference of Permanent Committee for Posts and Telecommunications of Council for Economic Aid (COMECON), Ulan Bator, Aug. 1973.

Launching of Soyuz Spacecraft — AP15

1973, Oct. 26 Litho. *Perf. 12½*

C46 AP15 5m shown .30 .20
C47 AP15 10m Apollo 8 .30 .20
C48 AP15 15m Soyuz 4 & 5 docking .30 .20
C49 AP15 20m Apollo 11 lunar module .30 .20
C50 AP15 30m Apollo 14 splashdown .50 .20
C51 AP15 50m Soyuz 6, 7 & 8 .75 .25
C52 AP15 60m Apollo 16 moon rover .80 .50
C53 AP15 1t Lunokhod 1 on moon 1.25 .75
Nos. C46-C53 (8) 4.50 2.50

Souvenir Sheet

C54 AP15 4t Soyuz and Apollo 4.50 3.50

US and Russian achievements in space.

Comecon Building, Moscow — AP16

1974, Feb. 28 Photo. *Perf. 11½x12*

C55 AP16 60m blue & multi 1.00 .50

25th anniversary of the Council of Mutual Economic Assistance.

Souvenir Sheet

Mongolia No. 4 — AP17

1974, Mar. 15 Photo. *Perf. 12½*

C56 AP17 4t multicolored 4.00 3.00

50th anniv. of 1st stamps of Mongolia.

Postrider and UPU Emblem — AP18

UPU emblem & means of transportation.

1974, Apr. Litho. *Perf. 12*

C57 AP18 50m shown .65 .35
C58 AP18 50m Reindeer post .65 .35
C59 AP18 50m Mail coach .65 .35
C60 AP18 50m Balloon post .65 .35
C61 AP18 50m Steamship and AN-2 plane .65 .35
C62 AP18 50m Train, truck and city .65 .35
C63 AP18 50m Rocket over North Pole .65 .35
Nos. C57-C63 (7) 4.55 2.45

Souvenir Sheet

C64 AP18 4t Globe and post horn, vert. 4.50 3.50

Centenary of Universal Postal Union.

Circus Type of 1974

Design: 1t, Two women contortionists.

1974, May 4 Litho. *Perf. 12*

C65 A177 1t multicolored 1.00 .50

No. C65 has se-tenant label, with similar design.

Nature Type of Regular Issue

1t, Scientist checking water, globe. 4t, Wild rose.

1974, Dec. Litho. *Perf. 11*

C66 A186 1t multicolored 1.00 .50

Souvenir Sheet

Perf. 12½

C67 A186 4t multicolored 4.50 3.50

UPU Type of 1974

Souvenir Sheet

Design: UPU Emblem, vert.

1974, Dec. *Perf. 11½x12*

C68 A187 4t multicolored 5.00 4.00

Soyuz on Launching Pad, Project Emblem — AP19

Project Emblem and: 20m, Radar and Apollo. 30m, Apollo, Soyuz and earth. 40m, Spacecraft before docking. 50m, Spacecraft after docking. 60m, Soyuz circling earth. 1t, Spacecraft, space station and earth. 4t, Russian and American astronauts.

1975, June 14 Litho. *Perf. 12*

C69 AP19 10m blue & multi .25 .20
C70 AP19 20m multicolored .25 .20
C71 AP19 30m sepia & multi .35 .20
C72 AP19 40m silver & multi .50 .30
C73 AP19 50m multicolored .75 .40
C74 AP19 60m multicolored 1.00 .40
C75 AP19 1t multicolored 1.40 .80
Nos. C69-C75 (7) 4.50 2.50

Souvenir Sheet

C76 AP19 4t black & multi 3.00 3.00

Apollo Soyuz space test project (Russo-American space cooperation), launching July 15; link-up July 17.

Mongolian Mountain Sheep — AP20

1975, Aug. 4 Litho. *Perf. 12*

C77 AP20 1.50t multi + label 2.00 1.00

South Asia Tourism Year.

Satellite over Weather Map of Mongolia AP21

1976, Mar. 20 *Perf. 12x11½*

C78 AP21 60m blue & yellow 1.50 .75

40th anniversary of meteorological service.

Souvenir Sheet

Girl with Books and Flowers — AP22

1976, Mar. 30 *Perf. 12*

C79 AP22 4t multicolored 4.00 3.00

30th anniversary of UNESCO.

Souvenir Sheet

The Wise Musician, by Sarav — AP23

1976, May 3 Litho. *Perf. 11½x12½*

C80 AP23 4t multicolored 4.00 3.00

Interphil 76 Phil. Exhib., Philadelphia, Pa., May 29-June 6.

Olympic Games Type of 1976

Souvenir Sheet

1976, May 20 *Perf. 12½x11½*

C81 A202 4t Wrestling 4.50 3.50

Independence Type of 1976

60m, Progress in agriculture and industry.

1976, June 20 Litho. *Perf. 12x11½*

C82 A203 60m multicolored 1.00 .50

Olympic Medalists Type, 1976

Souvenir Sheet

Design: 4t, Oidov Zeveg, Mongolian flag.

1976, Nov. 30 Litho. *Perf. 11x11½*

C83 A209 4t multicolored 4.50 3.50

Mounting Carrier Rocket with Bell-shaped Gear — AP24

Designs: 20m, Launching of Intercosmos 3. 30m, Marine Observatory Gagarin (ship). 40m, Satellite observation of lunar eclipse. 60m, Observatory with multiple antenna system. 80m, Examination of Van Allen Zone, magnetosphere. 1t, Meteorological earth satellite. 4t, Intercosmos satellite with lines showing participating countries on globe.

1977, June 20 Litho. *Perf. 12*

C84 AP24 10m multicolored .20 .20
C85 AP24 20m multicolored .25 .20
C86 AP24 30m multicolored .35 .20
C87 AP24 40m multicolored .55 .20
C88 AP24 60m multicolored .80 .45
C89 AP24 80m multicolored 1.00 .55
C90 AP24 1t multicolored 1.25 .65
Nos. C84-C90 (7) 4.40 2.45

Souvenir Sheet

Perf. 12½

C91 AP24 4t multicolored 4.50 3.50

11th anniv. of Intercosmos program, cooperation of 9 socialist countries for space research. No. C91 contains one stamp 58x37mm.

Trade Union Emblem, Factory and Sheep AP25

1977, June *Perf. 12x11½*

C92 AP25 60m multicolored 1.25 .75

11th Cong. of Mongolian Trade Unions, May 12.

Montgolfier's Balloon — AP26

Dirigibles: 30m, Zeppelin over North Pole, 1931. 40m, Osoaviahim, Russian Arctic cargo. 50m, North, Russian heavy duty cargo. 60m, Aeron-340, Russian planned. 80m, Machinery transport, Russian planned. 1.20t, Flying crane, French planned. 4t, Russia No. C26 (stamp) and Sukhe Bator statue.

1977, Dec. Litho. *Perf. 12*

C93 AP26 20m multicolored .25 .20
C94 AP26 30m multicolored .25 .20
C95 AP26 40m multicolored .35 .20
C96 AP26 50m multicolored .50 .35
C97 AP26 60m multicolored .75 .35
C98 AP26 80m multicolored 1.00 .50
C99 AP26 1.20t multicolored 1.50 .65
Nos. C93-C99 (7) 4.60 2.45

Souvenir Sheet

Perf. 12½x11½

C100 AP26 4t multicolored 4.00 3.00

History of airships.

A. F. Mozhaiski and his Plane, 1884 — AP27

Designs: 30m, Henry Farman and his plane, 1909. 40m, Geoffrey de Havilland and D. H. 66 Hercules, 1920's. 50m, Charles A. Lindbergh, Spirit of St. Louis and route New York to Paris, 1927. 60m, Mongolian pilots Shagdarsuren and Demberel and plane over Altai Mountains, 1935. 80m, Soviet aviators Chkalov, Baidukov, Beliakov, plane and route Moscow to Vancouver, 1937. 1.20t, A. N. Tupolev, supersonic plane TU 154, route Moscow to Alma-Ata, 1968. 4t, Wilbur and Orville Wright and their plane.

1978, Mar. 25 Litho. *Perf. 12½x11*

C101 AP27 20m multi .25 .20
C102 AP27 30m multi .30 .20
C103 AP27 40m multi .40 .25
C104 AP27 50m multi .50 .35
C105 AP27 60m multi .60 .35
C106 AP27 80m multi .85 .50
C107 AP27 1.20t multi 1.25 .75
Nos. C101-C107 (7) 4.15 2.60

Souvenir Sheet

C108 AP27 4t multi 4.00 4.00

75th anniversary of first powered flight, Wright brothers, 1903.

Soccer Type of 1978

Souvenir Sheet

Design: 4t, Two soccer players.

1978, Apr. 15 *Perf. 11½*

C109 A231 4t multi 4.25 4.25

World Soccer Championships, Argentina 78, June 1-25. #C109 contains 1 45x38mm stamp.

Souvenir Sheet

Canada No. 553 and Mongolia No. 549 — AP28

1978, June Litho. *Perf. 12½*

C110 AP28 4t multi 4.50 4.50

CAPEX '78, Intl. Phil. Exhibition, Toronto, June 9-18.

Map of Cuba, Ship, Plane and Festival Emblem — AP29

1978, July 28 Litho. *Perf. 12*

C111 AP29 1t multicolored 2.00 .75

11th World Youth Festival, Havana, 7/28-8/5.

Souvenir Sheet

Aleksei Gubarev and Vladimir Remek, PRAGA '78 Emblem — AP30

1978, Sept. 5 Litho. *Perf. 12*

C112 AP30 4t multicolored 4.00 4.00

PRAGA '78 Intl. Phil. Exhib., Prague, Sept. 8-17, and Russian-Czechoslovak space cooperation, Intercosmos.

DDR Flag, TV Tower, Berlin, Satellite AP31

1979, Oct. 9 Litho. *Perf. 11½x12*

C113 AP31 60m multicolored .75 .40

German Democratic Republic, 30th anniv.

Demoiselle Crane AP32

Protected Birds: 30m, Hawk warbler. 50m, Ruddy shelduck. 60m, Blue magpie. 70m, Goldfinch. 80m, Titmouse. 1t, Golden oriole.

1979, Oct. 25

C114	AP32	10m	multi	.40	.20
C115	AP32	30m	multi	.60	.20
C116	AP32	50m	multi	.75	.25
C117	AP32	60m	multi	1.00	.25
C118	AP32	70m	multi	1.10	.30
C119	AP32	80m	multi	1.25	.30
C120	AP32	1t	multi	1.50	.35
			Nos. C114-C120 (7)	6.60	1.85

Venera 5 and 6 — AP33

American and Russian Space Missions: 30m, Mariner 5. 50m, Mars 3. 60m, Viking 1 and 2. 70m, Luna 1, 2 and 3. 80m, Lunokhod 2. 1t, Apollo 15. 4t, Apollo 11, astronauts on moon.

Perf. 12½x11½

1979, Nov. 24 **Litho.**

C121	AP33	10m	multi	.20	.20
C122	AP33	30m	multi	.25	.20
C123	AP33	50m	multi	.40	.20
C124	AP33	60m	multi	.55	.25
C125	AP33	70m	multi	.70	.35
C126	AP33	80m	multi	.85	.45
C127	AP33	1t	multi	1.00	.50
			Nos. C121-C127 (7)	3.95	2.15

Souvenir Sheet

C128	AP33	4t	multi	4.00	4.00

Apollo 11 moon landing, 10th anniversary.

Andrena Scita — AP34

Insects: 30m, Paravespula germanica. 40m, Perilampus ruficornis. 50m, Bumblebee. 60m, Honey bee. 80m, Stilbum cyanurum. 1.20t, Ruby tail.

1980, Feb. 25 **Litho.** ***Perf. 11x12***

C129	AP34	20m	multi	.20	.20
C130	AP34	30m	multi	.30	.20
C131	AP34	40m	multi	.45	.30
C132	AP34	50m	multi	.55	.30
C133	AP34	60m	multi	.65	.40
C134	AP34	80m	multi	.85	.50
C135	AP34	1.20t	multi	1.25	.60
			Nos. C129-C135 (7)	4.25	2.50

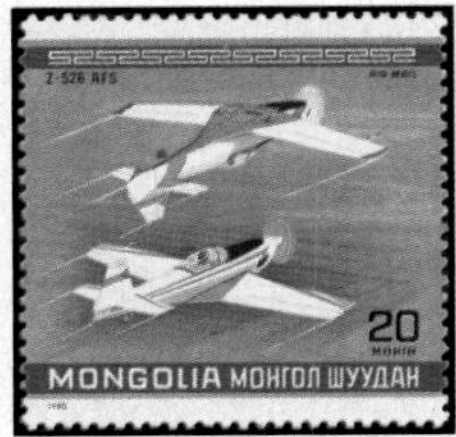

Z-526 AFS Stunt Planes, Czechoslovakia — AP35

1980, Aug. 4 **Litho.** ***Perf. 12***

C136	AP35	20m	shown	.20	.20
C137	AP35	30m	RS-180 "Sportsman," Germany	.30	.20
C138	AP35	40m	Yanki-Anu, US	.45	.30
C139	AP35	50m	MJ-2 "Tempete," France	.60	.30
C140	AP35	60m	"Pits," Canada	.75	.45
C141	AP35	80m	"Acrostar," Switzerland	.90	.60
C142	AP35	1.20t	JAK-50, USSR	1.30	.75
			Nos. C136-C142 (7)	4.50	2.80

Souvenir Sheet

C143	AP35	4t	JAK-52, USSR	4.00	4.00

10th World Aerobatic Championship, Oshkosh, Wisconsin, Aug. 17-30. No. C143 contains one 50x43mm stamp.

Olympic Type of 1980
Souvenir Sheet

1980, Sept. 15 **Litho.** ***Perf. 12½***

C144	A253	4t	Wrestlers	4.00	4.00

J. Davaajav, Mongolian silver medalist, 22nd Summer Olympic Games, Moscow. Inscribed "Los Angeles '84".

Souvenir Sheet

AP36

1980, Dec. 10 **Litho.** ***Perf. 11½x11***

C145	AP36	4t	multi	4.00	4.00

Johannes Kepler (1571-1630), German astronomer.

AP37

1981, Oct. 5 **Litho.** ***Perf. 12x11½***

Graf Zeppelin and: 20m, Germany #C40, sea eagle. 30m, Germany #C41, polar fox. 40m, Germany #C42, walrus. 50m, Russia #C26, polar bear. 60m, Russia #C27, snowy owl. 80m, Russia #C28, puffin. 1.20t, Russia #C29, seal. 4t, Icebreaker Maligin.

C146	AP37	20m	multi	.50	.20
C147	AP37	30m	multi	.50	.25
C148	AP37	40m	multi	.75	.40
C149	AP37	50m	multi	1.00	.35
C150	AP37	60m	multi	1.50	.45
C151	AP37	80m	multi	1.75	.70
C152	AP37	1.20t	multi	2.00	.85
			Nos. C146-C152 (7)	8.00	3.20

Souvenir Sheet

C153	AP37	4t	multi	5.50	5.50

Graf Zeppelin polar flight, 50th anniv. No. C153 contains one stamp 36x51mm.

ITU Plenipotentiaries Conference, Nairobi, Sept. — AP38

1982, Sept. 27 **Litho.** ***Perf. 12***

C154	AP38	60m	Map	1.00	.60

2nd UN Conference on Peaceful Uses of Outer Space, Vienna, Aug. 9-21 — AP39

1982, Dec. 15 **Litho.** ***Perf. 12***

C155	AP39	60m	Sputnik 1	.55	.30
C156	AP39	60m	Sputnik 2	.55	.30
C157	AP39	60m	Vostok 1	.55	.30
C158	AP39	60m	Venera 8	.55	.30
C159	AP39	60m	Vostok 6	.55	.30
C160	AP39	60m	Voskhod 2	.55	.30
C161	AP39	60m	Apollo II	.55	.30
C162	AP39	60m	Soyuz 6	.55	.30
			Nos. C155-C162 (8)	4.40	2.40

Souvenir Sheet

Perf. 12½x12

C163	AP39	4t	Soyuz 39, Salyut 6	4.00	4.00

Balloon Flight Bicentenary AP40

1982, Dec. 31 ***Perf. 11½x12½***

C164	AP40	20m	Montgolfiere, 1783	.20	.20
C165	AP40	30m	Blanchard, 1785	.30	.20
C166	AP40	40m	Royal-Vauzhall, 1836	.45	.30
C167	AP40	50m	Oernen, 1897	.60	.30
C168	AP40	60m	Gordon Bennett Race, 1906	.75	.30
C169	AP40	80m	Paris, 1931	.90	.45
C170	AP40	1.20t	USSR-VR-62, 1933	1.50	.60
			Nos. C164-C170 (7)	4.70	2.35

Souvenir Sheet

C171	AP40	4t	Mongolia, 1977	4.00	4.00

Souvenir Sheet

Revolutionary Mongolia Monument — AP41

1983 **Litho.** ***Imperf.***

C172	AP41	4t	multi	4.50	4.50

Concorde — AP42

1984, Aug. 15 **Litho.** ***Perf. 14***

C173	AP42	20m	DC-10, vert.	.25	.20
C174	AP42	30m	Airbus A-300 B-2	.35	.25
C175	AP42	40m	shown	.55	.35
C176	AP42	50m	Boeing 747	.60	.45
C177	AP42	60m	IL-62	.70	.45
C178	AP42	80m	TU-154	1.00	.70
C179	AP42	1.20t	IL-86	1.50	.70
			Nos. C173-C179 (7)	4.95	3.10

Souvenir Sheet

C180	AP42	4t	Yak-42	4.75	4.75

1988 Winter Olympics, Calgary AP43

1988, Jan. 20 **Litho.** ***Perf. 14***

C181	AP43	20m	Bobsled	.20	.20
C182	AP43	30m	Ski jumping	.30	.20
C183	AP43	40m	Downhill skiing	.45	.30
C184	AP43	50m	Biathlon	.60	.30
C185	AP43	60m	Speed skating	.75	.45
C186	AP43	80m	Women's figure skating	.90	.45
C187	AP43	1.20t	Ice hockey	1.00	.60
			Nos. C181-C187 (7)	4.20	2.50

Souvenir sheet

C188	AP43	4t	Cross-country skiing	4.25	4.25

Souvenir Sheet

Hong Kong '94 — AP44

1994, Feb. 18 **Litho.** ***Perf. 14½x15***

C189	AP44	600t	multicolored	4.25	4.25
a.			With Hong Kong '97 emblem in sheet margin	4.25	4.25

Issued: #C189a, 1/12/97.

Souvenir Sheet
No. C163 Surcharged in Red

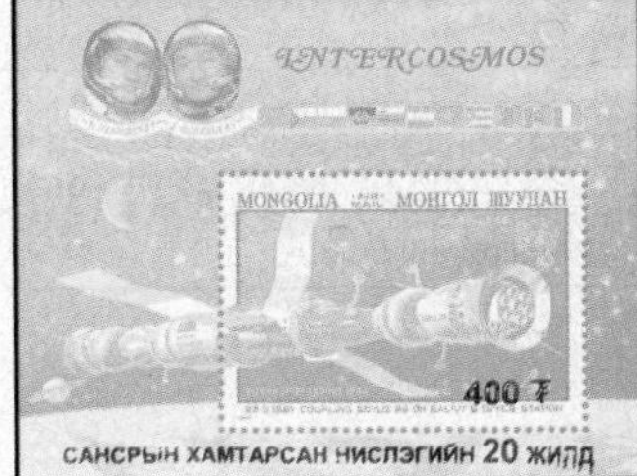

Illustration reduced.

2001, Mar. 22	**Litho.**		***Perf. 12½x12***		
C190	AP39	400t on 4t multi		*25.00*	*25.00*

Joint Soviet-Mongolian space flight, 20th anniv.

AIR POST SEMI-POSTAL STAMP

Catalogue values for unused stamps in this section are for Never Hinged items.

UNICEF Type of 1977
Souvenir Sheet

Design: 4t+50m, Balloon with Mongolian flag, children and UNICEF emblem.

1977, June 1	**Litho.**		***Perf. 12***		
CB1	SP2	4t + 50m multi		4.25	4.25

First balloon flight in Mongolia. Surtax was for Children's Village.

MONTENEGRO

ˌmän-tə-ˈnē-ˌgrō

LOCATION — Southern Europe, bordering on the Adriatic Sea
GOVT. — Republic in southern Europe.
AREA — 5,415 sq. mi.
POP. — 620,145 (2003)
CAPITAL — Cetinje

Montenegro maintained a precarious independence from the Ottoman Turks during the 16th-19th centuries as a theocracy, under a succession of bishop princes. In 1852 it became an independent principality. On December 1, 1918, Montenegro, along with Bosnia and Herzegovina, Croatia, Dalmatia and Slovenia, was absorbed by Serbia to form the Kingdom of the Serbs, Croats and Slovenes, which became the Kingdom of Yugoslavia in 1929.

During World War II, an Italian satellite regime was established in an enlarged Montenegrin state, but after the war, Montenegro became one of the constituent republics of the Socialist Federal Republic of Yugoslavia.

In 1992, with the dissolution of the greater Yugoslav republic, only Montenegro remained associated with Serbia, first in the Federal Republic of Yugoslavia and, after 2002, in the looser federation of Serbia & Montenegro.

On May 21, 2006, Montenegrins endorsed independence and complete separation from Serbia in a national referendum, and the Republic of Montenegro declared independence on June 3. On June 7, Serbia officially recognized Montenegro's independence.

100 Novcic = 1 Florin
100 Helera = 1 Kruna (1902)
100 Para = 1 Kruna (1907)
100 Para = 1 Perper (1910)
100 cents = 1 euro (2003)

Canceled to Order
Used values for Nos. 1-110, H1-H5, J1-J26, are for canceled to order stamps. Postally used specimens sell for considerably more.

Watermark

Wmk. 91 — "BRIEF-MARKEN" (#1-14) or "ZEITUNGS-MARKEN" (#15-21) in Double-lined Capitals once across sheet

Wmk. 140 — Crown

Prince Nicholas I — A1

1874 Typo. Wmk. 91

Early Printings

Perf. 10½ Large Holes, pointed teeth

Narrow Spacing (2-2½mm)

No.	Type	Denom.	Color	Unused	Used
1	A1	2n	yellow	30.00	30.00
2	A1	3n	green	40.00	30.00
3	A1	5n	rose red	37.50	27.50
4	A1	7n	lt lilac	37.50	25.00
5	A1	10n	blue	100.00	65.00
6	A1	15n	yel bister	125.00	97.50
7	A1	25n	lilac gray	225.00	150.00
			Nos. 1-7 (7)	595.00	425.00

Middle Printings (1879)

Perf. 12, 12½, 13 and Compound

Narrow spacing

No.	Type	Denom.	Color	Unused	Used
8	A1	2n	yellow	10.00	7.00
a.			Perf. 12-13x10½	65.00	65.00
9	A1	3n	green	7.50	5.50
10	A1	5n	red	7.50	5.50
11	A1	7n	rose lilac	7.50	5.50
a.			7n lilac	19.00	14.00
12	A1	10n	blue	13.00	11.00
a.			Perf. 12-13x10½	65.00	52.50
13	A1	15n	bister brn	19.00	11.00
14	A1	25n	gray lilac	25.00	16.00
			Nos. 8-14 (7)	89.50	61.50

Late Printings (1893?)

Perf. 10½, 11½ Small holes, broad teeth
(Perf. 11½ also with pointed teeth)

Narrow and wide spacing
(2¾-3½mm)

No.	Type	Denom.	Color	Unused	Used
15	A1	2n	yellow	3.00	1.60
a.			Perf. 11 ('94)	27.50	17.50
16	A1	3n	green	3.00	2.00
17	A1	5n	red	3.25	1.50
18	A1	7n	rose	2.50	1.25
a.			Perf. 11 ('94)	12.00	9.00
19	A1	10n	blue	3.00	2.10
20	A1	15n	brown	3.00	2.40
21	A1	25n	brown violet	3.25	2.50
			Nos. 15-21 (7)	21.00	13.35

Dates of issue of the late printings are still being researched.

Types of 1874-93 Overprinted in Black or Red

1893 ***Perf. 10½, 11½***

No.	Type	Denom.	Color	Unused	Used
22	A1	2n	yellow	35.00	6.50
a.			Perf. 11	*35.00*	*35.00*
23	A1	3n	green	2.40	1.40
24	A1	5n	red	1.60	.85
25	A1	7n	rose	4.00	2.50
a.			Perf. 12	60.00	50.00
b.			7n rose lilac	5.00	3.00
c.			7n lilac, perf. 12	*125.00*	
d.			Perf. 11	*40.00*	*30.00*
26	A1	10n	blue	2.50	2.00
27	A1	10n	blue (R)	4.00	3.25
28	A1	15n	brown	3.00	1.60
a.			Perf. 12	50.00	42.50
29	A1	15n	brown (R)	*1,250.*	*1,100.*
30	A1	25n	brown violet	2.75	2.00
31	A1	25n	brn vio (R)	4.00	3.00
a.			Perf. 12½		*225.00*
			Nos. 22-28,30-31 (9)	59.25	23.10

Introduction of printing to Montenegro, 400th anniversary.

This overprint had many settings. Several values exist with "1494" or "1495" instead of "1493", or with missing letters or numerals due to wearing of the clichés. Double and inverted overprints exist. Some printings were made after 1893 to supply a philatelic demand, but were available for postage.

The 7n with red overprint was not issued.

1894-98 Wmk. 91 ***Perf. 10½, 11½***

No.	Type	Denom.	Color	Unused	Used
32	A1	1n	gray blue	.20	.20
33	A1	2n	emerald ('98)	.20	.20
34	A1	3n	carmine rose ('98)	.20	.20
35	A1	5n	orange ('98)	1.50	.40
36	A1	7n	gray lilac ('98)	.30	.30
37	A1	10n	magenta ('98)	.30	.30
38	A1	15n	red brown ('98)	.25	.25
39	A1	20n	brown orange	.25	.20
40	A1	25n	dull blue ('98)	.25	.25
41	A1	30n	maroon	.25	.20
42	A1	50n	ultra	.30	.25
43	A1	1fl	deep green	.50	.50
44	A1	2fl	red brown	.75	.75
			Nos. 32-44 (13)	5.25	4.00

Monastery at Cetinje (Royal Mausoleum) A3

Perf. 10½, 11½

1896, Sept. 1 Litho. Unwmk.

No.	Type	Denom.	Color	Unused	Used
45	A3	1n	dk blue & bis	.20	.20
46	A3	2n	magenta & yel	.25	.25
47	A3	3n	org brn & yel grn	.25	.25
48	A3	5n	bl grn & bis	.25	.25
49	A3	10n	yellow & ultra	.25	.25
50	A3	15n	dk blue & grn	.25	.25
a.			Perf. 11½	30.00	30.00
51	A3	20n	bl grn & ultra	.25	.25
a.			Perf. 11½	27.50	27.50
52	A3	25n	dk blue & yel	.25	.25
53	A3	30n	magenta & bis	.25	.25
54	A3	50n	red brn & gray bl	.25	.25
55	A3	1fl	rose & gray bl	.40	.40
56	A3	2fl	brown & black	.40	.40
			Nos. 45-56 (12)	3.25	3.25

Bicentenary of the ruling dynasty, founded by the Vladika, Danilo Petrovich of Nyegosh.

Inverted centers and other errors exist, but experts believe these to be printer's waste.

Perf. 11½ counterfeits are common.

Prince Nicholas I
A4 A5

Perf. 13x13½, 13x12½ (2h, 5h, 50h, 2k, 5k), 12½ (1h, 25h)

1902, July 12

No.	Type	Denom.	Color	Unused	Used
57	A4	1h	ultra	.20	.20
58	A4	2h	rose lilac	.20	.20
59	A4	5h	green	.20	.20
60	A4	10h	rose	.20	.20
61	A4	25h	dull blue	.25	.25
62	A4	50h	gray green	.40	.40
63	A4	1k	chocolate	.35	.35
64	A4	2k	pale brown	.45	.45
65	A4	5k	buff	.60	.60
			Nos. 57-65 (9)	2.85	2.85

The 2h black brown and 25h indigo were not issued. The 25h, perf. 12½, probably was never issued.

Constitution Issue

Same Overprinted in Red or Black "Constitution" 15mm

1905, Dec. 5

No.	Type	Denom.	Color	Unused	Used
66	A4	1h	ultra (R)	.20	.20
67	A4	2h	rose lilac	.20	.20
68	A4	5h	green (R)	.20	.20
69	A4	10h	rose	.20	.20
70	A4	25h	dull blue (R)	.20	.20
71	A4	50h	gray green (R)	.20	.20
72	A4	1k	chocolate (R)	.25	.25
73	A4	2k	pale brown (R)	.40	.40
74	A4	5k	buff	.50	.50
			Nos. 66-74 (9)	2.35	2.35

Overprints in other colors are proofs.

1906

"Constitution" 16½mm

No.	Type	Denom.	Color	Unused	Used
66a	A4	1h	ultra (R)	.20	.20
67a	A4	2h	rose lilac	.20	.20
68a	A4	5h	green (R)	.20	.20
69a	A4	10h	rose	.20	.20
70a	A4	25h	dull blue (R)	.20	.20
71a	A4	50h	gray green (R)	.20	.20
72a	A4	1k	chocolate (R)	.20	.20
73a	A4	2k	pale brown (R)	.25	.25
74a	A4	5k	buff	.50	.50
			Nos. 66a-74a (9)	2.15	2.15

Three settings of Nos. 66a-74a containing four types of "YCTAB": I, 9¾mm, II, 11¼mm, III, 10¼mm, IV, 8½mm. Type IV occurs only in one setting, at two positions. Nos. 67a, 69a-74a, H3a exist in type IV.

Two errors occur: "Constitutton" and "Coustitution." Many other varieties including reversed color overprints exist.

Values are for types I and II.

1907, June 1 Engr. ***Perf. 12½***

No.	Type	Denom.	Color	Unused	Used
75	A5	1pa	ocher	.20	.20
76	A5	2pa	black	.20	.20
77	A5	5pa	yellow green	.25	.20
78	A5	10pa	rose red	.25	.20
79	A5	15pa	ultra	.20	.20
80	A5	20pa	red orange	.20	.20
81	A5	25pa	indigo	.20	.20
82	A5	35pa	bister brown	.20	.20
83	A5	50pa	dull violet	.30	.20
84	A5	1kr	carmine rose	.30	.25
85	A5	2kr	green	.30	.30
86	A5	5kr	red brown	.40	.35
			Nos. 75-86 (12)	3.00	2.70

Many Montenegro stamps exist imperforate or part perforate. Experts believe these to be printer's waste.

King Nicholas I as a Youth — A6

King Nicholas I and Queen Milena — A7

King Nicholas I — A11

Prince Nicholas — A12

5pa, 10pa, 25pa, 35pa, Nicholas in 1910. 15pa, Nicholas in 1878. 20pa, King and Queen, diff.

1910, Aug. 28 Engr.

No.	Type	Denom.	Color	Unused	Used
87	A6	1pa	black	.20	.20
88	A7	2pa	purple brown	.20	.20
89	A6	5pa	dark green	.20	.20
90	A6	10pa	carmine	.20	.20
91	A6	15pa	slate blue	.20	.20
92	A7	20pa	olive green	.20	.20
93	A6	25pa	deep blue	.20	.20
94	A6	35pa	chestnut	.20	.20
95	A11	50pa	violet	.25	.20
96	A11	1per	lake	.25	.20
97	A11	2per	yellow green	.50	.30
98	A12	5per	pale blue	.65	.40
			Nos. 87-98 (12)	3.25	2.70

Proclamation of Montenegro as a kingdom, the 50th anniv. of the reign of King Nicholas and the golden wedding celebration of the King and Queen.

King Nicholas I — A13

1913, Apr. 1 **Typo.**

99 A13 1pa orange .20 .20
100 A13 2pa plum .20 .20
101 A13 5pa deep green .20 .20
102 A13 10pa deep rose .20 .20
103 A13 15pa blue gray .20 .20
104 A13 20pa dark brown .20 .20
105 A13 25pa deep blue .20 .20
106 A13 35pa vermilion .25 .25
107 A13 50pa pale blue .20 .20
108 A13 1per yellow brown .20 .20
109 A13 2per gray violet .20 .20
110 A13 5per yellow green .20 .20
Nos. 99-110 (12) 2.45 2.45

SERBIA & MONTENEGRO

100 Cents=1 Euro

Yugoslavia became Serbia & Montenegro Feb. 4, 2003, with each section of the country maintaining and operating their own postal service, and each having their own currency. After a referendum on independence on May 21, 2006, Montenegro seceded from Serbia and Montenegro, declaring independence on June 3. Serbia formally recognized Montenegro's independence on June 7.

The stamps below are inscribed only with euro denominations, used solely within Montenegro. Stamps inscribed with dinar denominations, issued for use in Serbia, and those denominated in both dinar and euro currencies, for use in either region, are found under the Serbia listings.

Budva A20

Durmitor A21

2003, Sept. 15 **Litho.** ***Perf. 12½***

120 A20 25c multi 1.25 1.25
121 A21 40c multi 2.25 2.25

Christmas — A22

2003, Nov. 21 ***Perf. 13¼***

122 A22 25c multi 1.75 1.75
Complete booklet, 10 #122 17.50

National Symbols A23

Small coat of arms, outline map of Europe and: 25c, Map of Montenegro. 40c, Parliament Building and map of Montenegro. 50c, Large coat of arms and map of Montenegro. 60c, Flag and map of Montenegro.

2005, Dec. 15 **Litho.** ***Perf. 13***

123-126 A23 Set of 4 8.00 8.00

See Nos. 140-142.

Europa A24

Designs: 25c, Fish, shrimp, and mussels. 50c, Meat, olives, cheese and fruit.

No. 128C: d, 25c, Bee, honeycomb and honey. e, 50c, Grapes, grapevine, wine.

2005, Dec. 30 ***Perf. 13½x13¾***

127 A24 25c multicolored *4.75 4.75*
a. As #127, perf. 13½x 13¾x 13½x imperf. *9.25 9.25*
128 A24 50c multicolored 9.25 9.25
a. As #128, perf. 13½x imperf. x 13½x 13¾ *18.00 18.00*
b. Souvenir sheet, #127a, 128a *27.50 27.50*

Souvenir Sheet

Perf. 13½x13¾

128C A24 Sheet of 2, #d-e *27.50 27.50*

A25

Europa Stamps, 50th Anniv. — A26

No. 129: a, Montenegro #100, common vignette of 1960 Europa stamps. b, Montenegro #101, common vignette of 1961-62 Europa stamps. c, Montenegro #102, bee and honeycomb. d, Montenegro #105, common vignette of 1956 Europa stamps.

No. 129E: f, Like #129a. g, Like #129b. h, Like #129c. i, Like #129d.

2006, Jan. 3 **Litho.** ***Perf. 13½x13¾***

Stamps with Frames

129 Horiz. strip of 4 18.00 18.00
a. A25 50c multi 1.60 1.60
b. A25 €1 multi 3.25 3.25
c.-d. A25 €2 Either single 6.25 6.25

Souvenir Sheet

Stamps Without Frames

129E A25 Sheet of 4, #f-i 21.00 21.00

Litho. with Foil Application

Imperf

Size: 103x76mm

130 A26 €5.50 multi 15.00 15.00

2006 Winter Olympics, Turin A27

Designs: 60c, Figure skating. 90c, Ski jumping.

2006, Feb. 7 **Litho.** ***Perf. 13½x13¾***

131-132 A27 Set of 2 5.25 5.25

Flowers A28

Designs: 25c, Petteria ramentacea. 50c, Viola nikolai.

2006, Mar. 15

133-134 A28 Set of 2 2.75 2.75

Introduction of Perper Currency, Cent. — A29

Central Bank of Montenegro and: 40c, 1906 1-para coin. 50c, 1906 20-para coin.

2006, Apr. 27 **Litho.** ***Perf. 13½x13¾***

135-136 A29 Set of 2 3.25 3.25

2006 World Cup Soccer Championships, Germany — A30

Designs: No. 137, 60c, Players in match. No. 138, 90c, Players in match, diff.

No. 139: a, 60c, Players, empty stadium in background. b, 90c, Players, empty stadium in background, diff.

2006, May 30 ***Perf. 13¾x13½***

137-138 A30 Set of 2 5.25 5.25

Souvenir Sheet

139 A30 Sheet of 2, #a-b 5.25 5.25

National Symbols Type of 2005 Redrawn With "Posta Crne Gore" Under Postal Emblem

Designs as before.

2006, June **Litho.** ***Perf. 13¾***

140 A23 25c multi .90 .90
'a. Perf. 13 .90 .90
141 A23 40c multi 1.40 1.40
'a. Perf. 13 1.40 1.40
142 A23 60c multi 2.25 2.25
Nos. 140-142 (3) 4.55 4.55

Nos. 140a and 141a are dated "2005," while Nos. 140-142 are dated "2006."

Tourism A31

Designs: 25c, Durmitor. 50c, Sveti Stefan.

2006, July 5 ***Perf. 13½x13¾***

143-144 A31 Set of 2 2.75 2.75

Independence Referendum of May 21 — A32

2006, July 13

145 A32 50c multi 1.75 1.75

Europa — A33

Designs: No. 146, 60c, Women linking chain. No. 147, 90c, People and sun, horiz.

No. 148: a, 60c, Man with suitcase. b, 90c, People of different races.

2006, Aug. 30 ***Perf. 13¾***

146-147 A33 Set of 2 5.25 5.25

Souvenir Sheet

148 A33 Sheet of 2, #a-b 5.25 5.25

Capt. Ivo Visin (1806-68), Circumnavigator, and Ship, Splendido — A34

2006, Sept. 5 ***Perf. 13½x13¾***

149 A34 40c multi 1.50 1.50

Stamp Day — A35

2006, Oct. 2 ***Perf. 13¾***

150 A35 25c multi .85 .85

Mona Lisa, by Leonardo da Vinci, 500th Anniv. — A36

2006, Oct. 18 ***Perf. 13¾x13½***

151 A36 50c multi 1.75 1.75

Cultural Heritage A37

Designs: No. 152, 25c, Ruins, Dukla Archaeological Site. No. 153, 25c, Glassware.

2006, Nov. 3 ***Perf. 13¾x13½***
152-153 A37 Set of 2 1.75 1.75

Tara River A38

Perf. 13½x13¾

2006, Nov. 15 **Litho.**
154 A38 40c multi 1.50 1.50

Gregorian Calendar, 425th Anniv. A39

2007, Jan. 4 ***Perf. 13¾x13***
155 A39 50c multi 1.75 1.75
Printed in sheets of 8 + label.

Wildlife Protection A40

2007, Feb. 7
156 A40 50c multi 1.75 1.75
Printed in sheets of 8 + label.

Europa — A41

Map of Montengro and: Nos. 157, 159a, 60c, Montengro Scouting emblem. Nos. 158, 159b, 90c, Tent and campfire.

2007, Apr. 20 **Litho.** ***Perf. 13¾***
157 A41 60c multi 2.00 2.00
158 A41 90c multi 2.75 2.75
a. Souvenir sheet, #157-158 5.25 5.25

Perf. 13¾ (Imperf. Between Stamps)

159 Sheet of 2 5.25 5.25
a. A41 60c multi, 42x28mm 2.00 2.00
b. A41 90c multi, 42x28mm 2.75 2.75

Nos. 157 and 158 were each printed in sheets of 8 + label. No. 159 was sold with but not attached to a booklet cover.

Birds — A42

No. 160: a, 25c, Gull. b, 50c, Eagle.

2007, May 11 **Litho.** ***Perf. 13¾***
160 A42 Pair, #a-b 2.75 2.75

Migration of Montenegrins to Istria, 350th Anniv. — A43

2007, June 21 ***Perf. 13¾***
161 A43 60c multi 2.10 2.10
Printed in sheets of 8 + label.

Postal History A44

Glagolithic Text — A45

Mountains A46

Stylized Butterfly A47

2007, July 3
162 A44 25c multi .90 .90
163 A45 40c multi 1.40 1.40
164 A46 50c multi 1.75 1.75
165 A47 60c multi 2.25 2.25
Nos. 162-165 (4) 6.30 6.30

Petar Lubarda (1907-74), Painter A48

2007, July 27 ***Perf. 13¾***
166 A48 40c multi 1.40 1.40

Ship — A49

2007, Aug. 1
167 A49 60c multi 2.10 2.10
Printed in sheets of 8 + label.

Joy of Europe — A50

2007, Oct. 2
168 A50 50c multi 1.75 1.75

Regional Telephone Service, Cent. — A51

Designs: 25c, Telephone dial. 50c, Telephone dial and red dots.

2007, Nov. 9 **Litho.** ***Perf. 13¾***
169-170 A51 Set of 2 2.25 2.25

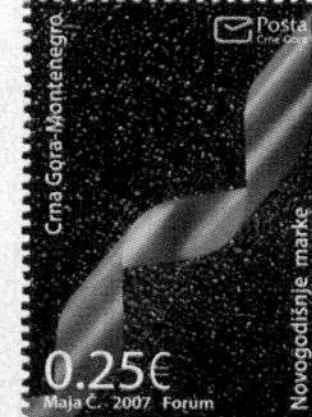

New Year's Day — A52

Designs: No. 171, 25c, Twisted ribbon. No. 172, 25c, Christmas ornament on tree branch. 50c, Wreath and bells. €1, Lit candle.

2007, Dec. 5 ***Perf. 14x13¾***
171-174 A52 Set of 4 6.00 6.00

Stabilization and Association Agreement Between Montenegro and the European Union — A53

Jigsaw puzzle pieces with: 60c, Montenegro coat of arms and European Union ring of stars.

No. 176: a, 40c, Montenegro coat of arms. b, 50c, European Union ring of stars.

2008, Feb. 1 **Litho.** ***Perf. 13¾***
175 A53 60c multi 1.75 1.75

Souvenir Sheet

176 A53 Sheet of 2, #a-b 2.75 2.75

Flowers — A54

Designs: 25c, Draba bertiscea. 40c, Edraianthus wettsteinii. 50c, Protoedriantus tarae. 60c, Dianthus nitidus.

2008, Feb. 20
177-180 A54 Set of 4 5.50 5.50

Nos. 177-180 each were printed in sheets of 5 + label.

2008 Summer Olympics, Beijing A55

Stylized athletes, Beijing Olympics emblem and: 60c, Map of Montenegro. 90c, Montenegro coat of arms.

2008, Mar. 26
181-182 A55 Set of 2 4.75 4.75

Europa — A56

Designs: No. 183, 60c, Boy, envelope with stamp. No. 184, 90c, Girl, letter.

No. 185: a, 60c, Boy, right half of envelope. b, 90c, Girl, left half of envelope.

2008, Apr. 2
183-184 A56 Set of 2 4.75 4.75

Souvenir Sheet

185 A56 Sheet of 2, #a-b 4.75 4.75

Nos. 183-184 each were printed in sheets of 8 + label.

Marka Miljanova (1833-1901), Writer — A57

2008, Apr. 24
186 A57 60c multi 1.90 1.90

Battle of Grahovac, 150th Anniv. — A58

2008, Apr. 29
187 A58 25c multi .80 .80

Tourism A59

Designs: 25c, Hillside hut. 40c, Fortress. 50c, Pier and boats. 60c, Boat on lake.

2008, May 21
188-191 A59 Set of 4 5.50 5.50

ACKNOWLEDGMENT OF RECEIPT STAMPS

Prince Nicholas I
AR1 AR2

Perf. 10½, 11½

1895 Litho. Wmk. 91
H1 AR1 10n ultra & rose .50 .50

1902 Unwmk. *Perf. 12½*
H2 AR2 25h orange & carmine .50 .50

Constitution Issue

#H2 Overprinted in Black Like #66-74

1905
H3 AR2 25h orange & carmine .50 .50
a. "Constitution" 16½mm ('06) .50 .50

See note after 74a.

AR3

Nicholas I — AR4

1907 Engr.
H4 AR3 25pa olive .25 .25

1913 Typo.
H5 AR4 25pa olive green .25 .25

POSTAGE DUE STAMPS

D1

D2

Perf. 10½, 11, 11½

1894 Litho. Wmk. 91
J1 D1 1n red 1.50 1.00
J2 D1 2n yellow green .50 .30
J3 D1 3n orange .40 .30
J4 D1 5n olive green .25 .20
J5 D1 10n violet .25 .20
J6 D1 20n ultra .25 .20
J7 D1 30n emerald .25 .20
J8 D1 50n pale gray grn .25 .20
Nos. J1-J8 (8) 3.65 2.60

1902 Unwmk. *Perf. 12½*
J9 D2 5h orange .20 .20
J10 D2 10h olive green .20 .20
J11 D2 25h dull lilac .20 .20
J12 D2 50h emerald .20 .20
J13 D2 1k pale gray green .20 .20
Nos. J9-J13 (5) 1.00 1.00

Constitution Issue

Postage Due Stamps of 1902 Overprinted in Black or Red Like Nos. 66-74

1905
J14 D2 5h orange .20 .20
J15 D2 10h olive green (R) .20 .20
J16 D2 25h dull lilac .20 .20
J17 D2 50h emerald .20 .20
J18 D2 1k pale gray green .20 .20
Nos. J14-J18 (5) 1.00 1.00

The 10h with "Constitution" 16½mm is not known used. It is an unissued stamp.

D3

D4

1907 Typo. *Perf. 13x13½*
J19 D3 5pa red brown .20 .20
J20 D3 10pa violet .20 .20
J21 D3 25pa rose .20 .20
J22 D3 50pa green .20 .20
Nos. J19-J22 (4) .80 .80

1913 *Perf. 12½*
J23 D4 5pa gray .20 .20
J24 D4 10pa violet .20 .20
J25 D4 25pa blue gray .20 .20
J26 D4 50pa lilac rose .20 .20
Nos. J23-J26 (4) .80 .80

ISSUED UNDER AUSTRIAN OCCUPATION

Austrian Military Stamps of 1917 Overprinted

1917 Unwmk. *Perf. 12½*
1N1 M1 10h blue 13.50 11.00
1N2 M1 15h car rose 13.50 11.00

Austrian Military Stamps of 1917 Overprinted in Black

1918
1N3 M1 10h blue 37.50
1N4 M1 15h car rose 1.90

Nos. 1N3-1N4 were never placed in use.

This overprint exists on other stamps of Austria and Bosnia and Herzegovina, and in blue or red.

ISSUED UNDER ITALIAN OCCUPATION

Yugoslavia Nos. 142, 144-154 Overprinted

1941 Unwmk. Typo. *Perf. 12½*
2N1 A16 25p black .40 *1.25*
2N2 A16 1d yel grn .40 *1.25*
2N3 A16 1.50d red .40 *1.25*
2N4 A16 2d dp mag .40 *1.25*
2N5 A16 3d dull red brn .40 *1.25*
2N6 A16 4d ultra .40 *1.25*
2N7 A16 5d dark blue 1.10 *3.00*
2N8 A16 5.50d dk vio brn 1.10 *3.00*
2N9 A16 6d slate blue 1.10 *3.00*
2N10 A16 8d sepia 1.10 *3.00*
2N11 A16 12d brt violet 1.10 *3.00*
2N12 A16 16d dull violet 1.10 *3.00*
2N13 A16 20d blue 95.00 *190.00*
2N14 A16 30d brt pink 32.50 *90.00*
Nos. 2N1-2N14 (14) 136.50 *305.50*
Set, never hinged 335.00

The 25p, 1d, 3d, 6d and 8d exist with inverted overprint.

Stamps of Italy, 1929, Overprinted in Red or Black

1941 Wmk. 140 *Perf. 14*
2N15 A90 5c ol brn (R) .30 *.90*
2N16 A92 10c dark brn .30 *.90*
2N17 A93 15c sl grn (R) .30 *.90*
2N18 A91 20c rose red .30 *.90*
2N19 A94 25c deep grn .30 *.90*
2N20 A95 30c ol brn (R) .30 *.90*
2N21 A95 50c pur (R) .30 *.90*
2N22 A94 75c rose red .30 *.90*
2N23 A94 1.25 l dp bl (R) .30 *.90*
Nos. 2N15-2N23 (9) 2.70 *8.10*
Set, never hinged 8.00

Yugoslavia Nos. 144-145, 147-148, 148B, 149-152 Overprinted in Black

1942 Unwmk. Typo. *Perf. 12½*
2N24 A16 1d yel grn 1.00 1.90
2N25 A16 1.50d red 42.50 60.00
2N26 A16 3d dull red brn 1.00 1.90
2N27 A16 4d ultra 1.00 1.90
2N28 A16 5.50d dk vio brn 1.00 1.90
2N29 A16 6d slate blue 1.00 1.90
2N30 A16 8d sepia 1.00 1.90
2N31 A16 12d brt violet 1.00 1.90
2N32 A16 16d dull violet 1.00 1.90
Nos. 2N24-2N32 (9) 50.50 75.20
Set, never hinged 110.00

Yugoslavia Nos. 142 and 146 with this overprint in red were not officially issued.

Red Overprint

2N24a A16 1d 1.10 *2.50*
2N25a A16 1.50d 60.00 *190.00*
2N26a A16 3d 1.10 *2.50*
2N27a A16 4d 1.10 *2.50*
2N28a A16 5.50d 1.10 *2.50*
2N29a A16 6d 1.10 *2.50*
2N30a A16 8d 1.10 *2.50*
2N31a A16 12d 1.10 *2.50*
2N32a A16 16d 1.10 *2.50*
Nos. 2N24a-2N32a (9) 68.80 *210.00*
Set, never hinged 150.00

Peter Nyegosh and Mt. Lovchen View OS1

Mt. Lovchen Scene OS2

Peter Petrovich Nyegosh — OS3

Designs: 15c, Mountain Church, Eve of Trinity Feast. 20c, Chiefs at Cetinje Monastery. 25c, Folk Dancing at Cetinje Monastery. 50c, Eagle dance. 1.25 l, Chiefs taking loyalty oath. 2 l, Moslem wedding procession. 5 l, Group sitting up with injured standard bearer.

Perf. 14.

1943, May 9 Unwmk. Photo.
2N33 OS1 5c deep violet 1.00 *3.75*
2N34 OS2 10c dull olive grn 1.00 *3.75*
2N35 OS1 15c brown 1.00 *3.75*
2N36 OS1 20c dull orange 1.00 *3.75*
2N37 OS1 25c dull green 1.00 *3.75*
2N38 OS1 50c rose pink 1.00 *3.75*
2N39 OS1 1.25 l sapphire 1.00 *3.75*
2N40 OS1 2 l blue green 1.50 *5.50*
2N41 OS2 5 l dark red, *sal* 2.50 *9.75*
2N42 OS3 20 l dark vio, *gray* 6.50 *19.00*
Nos. 2N33-2N42 (10) 17.50 *60.50*
Set, never hinged 45.00

Quotations from national poem on backs of stamps.

For overprints and surcharges see Nos. 3N10-3N14, 3NB3-3NB8.

OCCUPATION AIR POST STAMPS

Yugoslavia Nos. C7-C14 Overprinted Like Nos. 2N1-2N14

Perf. 12½, 11½x12½, 12½x11½

1941 Photo. Unwmk.
2NC1 AP6 50p brown 3.00 7.50
2NC2 AP7 1d yel grn 2.25 7.50
2NC3 AP8 2d blue gray 2.25 7.50
2NC4 AP9 2.50d rose red 3.00 7.50
2NC5 AP6 5d brn vio 18.00 55.00
2NC6 AP7 10d brn lake 18.00 55.00
2NC7 AP8 20d dark grn 37.50 92.50
2NC8 AP9 30d ultra 21.00 55.00
Nos. 2NC1-2NC8 (8) 105.00 287.50
Set, never hinged 260.00

Italy No. C13 Overprinted in Red Like Nos. 2N15-2N23

1941 Wmk. 140 *Perf. 14*
2NC9 AP3 50c olive brn .40 .90
Never hinged .75

Yugoslavia Nos. C7-C14 Overprinted in Black

a

Governatorato del Montenegro Valore in Lire

b

Perf. 12½, 11½x12½, 12½x11½

1942, Jan. 9 Unwmk.
2NC10 AP6(a) 50p brown 2.50 *5.50*
2NC11 AP7(a) 1d yel grn 2.50 *5.50*
2NC12 AP8(b) 2d blue gray 2.50 *5.50*
2NC13 AP9(b) 2.50d rose red 2.50 *5.50*
2NC14 AP6(a) 5d brn vio 2.50 *5.50*
2NC15 AP7(a) 10d brn lake 2.50 *5.50*

2NC16 AP8(b) 20d dk grn 100.00 190.00
2NC17 AP9(b) 30d ultra 16.50 40.00
Nos. 2NC10-2NC17 (8) 131.50 263.00
Set, never hinged 335.00

Nos. 2NC10-2NC17 exist with red overprints. Value, each $80 unused, $150 used.

Governatorato del Montenegro
c

Overprints *a, b* or *c* were applied in 1941-42 to the following Yugoslavia stamps under Italian occupation:
a. or *b.* Nos. B120-B123 (4 values) in black and in red.
c. Nos. B116-B119 (4 values) in black and in red.

Cetinje AP1

Mt. Durmitor — AP6

Designs: 1 l, Seacoast. 2 l, Budus. 5 l, Mt. Lovchen. 10 l, Rieka River.

1943 Unwmk. Photo. *Perf. 14*
2NC18 AP1 50c brown .45 *2.40*
2NC19 AP1 1 l ultra .45 *2.40*
2NC20 AP1 2 l rose pink .60 *2.40*
2NC21 AP1 5 l green .75 *2.50*
2NC22 AP1 10 l lake, *rose buff* 3.75 *13.00*
2NC23 AP6 20 l indigo, *rose* 9.00 *27.50*
Nos. 2NC18-2NC23 (6) 15.00 *50.20*
Set, never hinged 37.50

For overprints and surcharges see Nos. 3NC1-3NC5, 3NCB1-3NCB6.

OCCUPATION POSTAGE DUE STAMPS

Yugoslavia Nos. J28-J32 Overprinted Like Nos. 2N1-2N14

1941 Unwmk. Typo. *Perf. 12½*
2NJ1 D4 50p violet .50 *1.90*
2NJ2 D4 1d deep magenta .50 *1.90*
2NJ3 D4 2d deep blue .50 *1.90*
2NJ4 D4 5d orange 40.00 *90.00*
2NJ5 D4 10d chocolate 3.25 *9.75*
Nos. 2NJ1-2NJ5 (5) 44.75 *105.45*
Set, never hinged 120.00

Postage Due Stamps of Italy, 1934, Overprinted in Black Like Nos. 2N15-2N23

1942 Wmk. 140 *Perf. 14*
2NJ6 D6 10c blue .60 *2.25*
2NJ7 D6 20c rose red .60 *2.25*
2NJ8 D6 30c red orange .60 *2.25*
2NJ9 D6 50c violet .60 *2.25*
2NJ10 D7 1 l red orange .60 *2.25*
Nos. 2NJ6-2NJ10 (5) 3.00 *11.25*
Set, never hinged 7.50

ISSUED UNDER GERMAN OCCUPATION

Yugoslavia Nos. 147-148 Surcharged

1943 Unwmk. Typo. *Perf. 12½*
3N1 A16 50c on 3d 3.00 *26.00*
3N2 A16 1 l on 3d 3.00 *26.00*
3N3 A16 1.50 l on 3d 3.00 *26.00*
3N4 A16 2 l on 3d 4.25 *52.50*
3N5 A16 4 l on 3d 4.25 *52.50*
3N6 A16 5 l on 4d 4.50 *52.50*
3N7 A16 8 l on 4d 10.50 *100.00*
3N8 A16 10 l on 4d 15.00 *160.00*
3N9 A16 20 l on 4d 30.00 *375.00*
Nos. 3N1-3N9 (9) 77.50 *870.50*
Set, never hinged 190.00

Montenegro Nos. 2N37-2N41 Ovptd.

1943 Photo. *Perf. 14*
3N10 OS1 25c dull green 7.50 *175.00*
3N11 OS1 50c rose pink 7.50 *175.00*
3N12 OS1 1.25 l sapphire 7.50 *175.00*
3N13 OS1 2 l blue green 7.50 *175.00*
3N14 OS2 5 l dk red, *sal* 160.00 *2,250.*
Nos. 3N10-3N14 (5) 190.00 *2,950.*
Set, never hinged 450.00

Counterfeits exist.

SEMI-POSTAL STAMPS

Yugoslavia Nos. 147-148 Surcharged

1944 Unwmk. Typo. *Perf. 12½*
3NB1 A16 15pf + 85pf on 3d 7.25 *160.00*
3NB2 A16 15pf + 85pf on 4d 7.25 *160.00*

Montenegro Nos. 2N37-2N40 Surcharged

d

1944 Photo. *Perf. 14*
3NB3 OS1 15pf +85pf on 25c 7.25 *160.00*
3NB4 OS1 15pf +1.35m on 50c 7.25 *160.00*
3NB5 OS1 25pf +1.75m on 1.25 l 7.25 *160.00*
3NB6 OS1 25pf +1.75m on 2 l 7.25 *160.00*
Nos. 3NB1-3NB6 (6) 43.50 *960.00*
Set, never hinged 110.00

Surtax on Nos. 3NB1-3NB6 aided refugees.

Montenegro Nos. 2N37-2N38 and Yugoslavia Nos. 147-148 Surcharged

e

f

1944
3NB7 OS1 15pf + 85pf on 25c (e) 5.50 *160.00*
3NB8 OS1 15pf + 1.35m on 50c (e) 5.50 *160.00*
3NB9 A16 50pf + 2.50m on 3d (f) 5.50 *160.00*
3NB10 A16 50pf + 2.50m on 4d (f) 5.50 *160.00*
Nos. 3NB7-3NB10 (4) 22.00 *640.00*
Set, never hinged 55.00

The surtax on Nos. 3NB7-3NB10 aided the Montenegro Red Cross.

AIR POST STAMPS

Montenegro Nos. 2NC18-2NC22 Overprinted Like Nos. 3N10-3N14

1943 Unwmk. Photo. *Perf. 14*
3NC1 AP1 50c brown 10.50 *175.00*
3NC2 AP1 1 l ultra 10.50 *175.00*
3NC3 AP1 2 l rose pink 10.50 *175.00*
3NC4 AP1 5 l green 10.50 *175.00*
3NC5 AP1 10 l lake, *rose buff* 1,900. *18,000.*
Nos. 3NC1-3NC5 (5) 1,942. *18,700.*
Set, never hinged 3,350.

Counterfeits exist.

AIR POST SEMI-POSTAL STAMPS

Montenegro Nos. 2NC18-2NC20 Surcharged Type "d"

1944 Unwmk. Photo. *Perf. 14*
3NCB1 AP1 15pf +85pf on 50c 7.25 *175.00*
3NCB2 AP1 25pf +1.25m on 1 l 7.25 *175.00*
3NCB3 AP1 50pf +1.50m on 2 l 7.25 *175.00*
Nos. 3NCB1-3NCB3 (3) 21.75 *525.00*
Set, never hinged 55.00

The surtax aided refugees.

Same Surcharged Type "e"

1944
3NCB4 AP1 25pf +1.75m on 50c 5.50 *160.00*
3NCB5 AP1 25pf +2.75m on 1 l 5.50 *160.00*
3NCB6 AP1 50pf +2m on 2 l 5.50 *160.00*
Nos. 3NCB4-3NCB6 (3) 16.50 *480.00*
Set, never hinged 40.00

The surtax aided the Montenegro Red Cross.

MONTSERRAT

ˌmänt-sə-ˈrat

LOCATION — West Indies southeast of Puerto Rico
GOVT. — British Crown Colony
AREA — 39 sq. mi.
POP. — 12,853 (1999 est.)

Montserrat was one of the four presidencies of the former Leeward Islands colony until it became a colony itself in 1956.

Montserrat stamps were discontinued in 1890 and resumed in 1903. In the interim, stamps of Leeward Islands were used. In 1903-56, stamps of Montserrat and Leeward Islands were used concurrently.

12 Pence = 1 Shilling
20 Shillings = 1 Pound
100 Cents = 1 Dollar (1951)

Catalogue values for unused stamps in this country are for Never Hinged items, beginning with Scott 104 in the regular postage section, Scott B1 in the semi-postal section, Scott O45 in the officials section.

Watermark

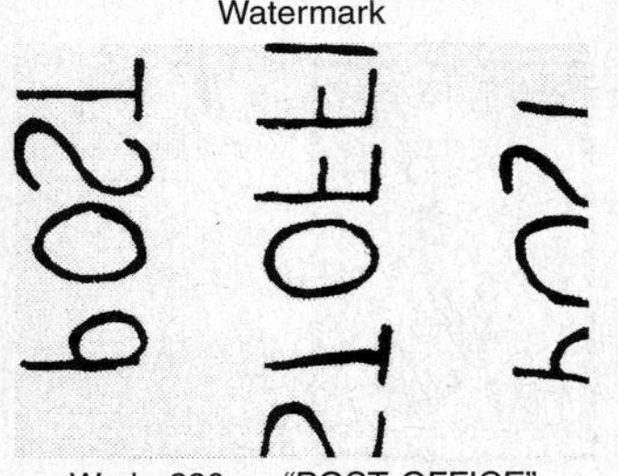

Wmk. 380 — "POST OFFICE"

Values for unused stamps are for examples with original gum as defined in the catalogue introduction. Very fine examples of Nos. 1-2, 6 and 11 will have perforations touching the design on at least one side due to the narrow spacing of the stamps on the plates. Stamps with perfs clear of the framelines on all four sides are scarce and will command higher prices.

Stamps of Antigua Overprinted in Black

1876 Engr. Wmk. 1 *Perf. 14*
1 A1 1p red 27.50 19.00
a. Vert. or diag. half used as ½p on cover 1,650.
c. "S" inverted 1,250. 875.00
2 A1 6p green 75.00 50.00
a. Vertical half used as 3p on cover —
b. Vertical third used as 2p on cover *6,000.*
c. "S" inverted 1,750. 1,350.
d. 6p blue green 1,350.
e. As "d," "S" inverted *12,750.*

Some experts consider Nos. 2d, 2e to be from a trial printing.

Queen Victoria — A2

1880 Typo.
3 A2 2½p red brown 300.00 225.00
4 A2 4p blue 160.00 47.50

See Nos. 5, 7-10.

1884 Wmk. 2
5 A2 ½p green 1.25 *8.75*

Antigua No. 18 Overprinted type "a"

1884 Engr.
6 A1 1p rose red 19.00 20.00
a. Vert. half used as ½p on cover 1,550.
b. "S" inverted 1,100. 1,100.

Type of 1880

1884-85 Typo.
7 A2 2½p red brown 275.00 77.50
8 A2 2½p ultra ('85) 25.00 22.50
9 A2 4p blue 2,100. 300.00
10 A2 4p red lilac ('85) 6.00 3.50

Antigua No. 20 Overprinted type "a"

1884 Engr. *Perf. 12*
11 A1 1p red 82.50 65.00
a. "S" inverted 2,350. 1,550.
b. Vert. half used as ½p on cover 1,900.

Symbol of the Colony — A3
King Edward VII — A4

1903 Wmk. 2 Typo. *Perf. 14*
12 A3 ½p gray green .90 17.00
13 A3 1p car & black .90 .50
14 A3 2p brown & black 6.50 35.00
15 A3 2½p ultra & black 1.75 2.10
16 A3 3p dk vio & brn orange 5.00 35.00
17 A3 6p ol grn & vio 5.75 57.50
18 A3 1sh vio & gray grn 12.00 20.00
19 A3 2sh brn org & gray green 30.00 20.00
20 A3 2sh6p blk & gray grn 22.50 *45.00*

Wmk. 1
21 A4 5sh car & black 125.00 *175.00*
Nos. 12-21 (10) 210.30 *407.10*

1904-08 Wmk. 3
Chalky Paper
22 A3 ½p grn & gray grn 5.50 2.25
23 A3 1p car & blk ('08) 17.00 *30.00*
24 A3 2p brown & black 2.50 1.40
25 A3 2½p ultra & blk ('06) 3.00 *7.75*
26 A3 3p dk vio & brn orange 11.00 2.75
27 A3 6p ol grn & vio 11.00 *6.50*
28 A3 1sh violet & gray grn ('08) 11.50 8.50
29 A3 2sh brn org & gray grn ('08) 35.00 *52.50*
30 A3 2sh6p blk & gray grn ('08) 50.00 *57.50*
31 A4 5sh car & blk ('07) 110.00 *125.00*
Nos. 22-31 (10) 256.50 *294.15*

The ½, 2, 3 and 6p are also on ordinary paper.

1908-13
Ordinary Paper
31A A3 ½p deep green 8.25 1.10
32 A3 1p carmine 1.75 .35
33 A3 2p gray 2.00 *18.00*
34 A3 2½p ultramarine 2.50 4.25

Chalky Paper
35 A3 3p vio, *yellow* 1.10 *22.50*
36 A3 6p red vio & gray vio 7.75 *60.00*
37 A3 1sh blk, *green* 10.00 *55.00*
38 A3 2sh bl & vio, *bl* 35.00 *67.50*
39 A3 2sh 6p car & blk, *blue* 35.00 *87.50*
40 A4 5sh grn & scar, *yel* 60.00 92.50

Surface-colored Paper
41 A3 3p vio, *yel* ('13) 4.50 35.00
Nos. 31A-41 (11) 167.85 *443.70*

King George V
A5 A6

1913
Chalky Paper
42 A5 5sh green & scar, *yel* 80.00 110.00

1916-22 Wmk. 3 *Perf. 14*
Ordinary Paper
43 A6 ½p green .65 2.75
44 A6 1p scarlet 1.10 .90
45 A6 2p gray 2.25 *5.00*
46 A6 2½p ultramarine 3.50 *21.00*

Chalky Paper
47 A6 3p violet, *yel* 1.40 *9.75*
48 A6 4p blk & red, *yel* ('22) 6.50 *42.50*
49 A6 6p dl vio & red violet 3.50 *24.00*
50 A6 1sh blk, *bl grn,* ol back 3.50 *26.00*
51 A6 2sh vio & ultra, *bl* 17.00 *35.00*
52 A6 2sh 6p blk & red, *bl* 26.00 *60.00*
53 A6 5sh grn & red, *yel* 45.00 *60.00*
Nos. 43-53 (11) 110.40 *286.90*

For overprints see Nos. MR1-MR3.

1922-29 Wmk. 4
Ordinary Paper
54 A6 ¼p brown .35 6.25
55 A6 ½p green ('23) .20 .25
56 A6 1p dp violet ('23) .80 .70
57 A6 1p carmine ('29) 1.10 1.75
58 A6 1½p orange 3.50 *11.00*
59 A6 1½p rose red ('23) .60 *4.25*
60 A6 1½p fawn ('29) 2.00 .55
61 A6 2p gray .80 *2.25*
62 A6 2½p ultramarine 9.25 18.00
63 A6 2½p orange ('23) 2.75 *21.00*
64 A6 3p ultra ('23) .80 *18.00*

Chalky Paper
65 A6 3p vio, *yel* ('26) 2.00 *5.50*
66 A6 4p black & red, *yel* ('23) 1.75 *14.00*
67 A6 5p dull vio & ol grn 4.50 *11.00*
68 A6 6p dull vio & red vio ('23) 3.50 *8.50*
69 A6 1sh blk, *emer* ('23) 3.50 *8.00*
70 A6 2sh vio & ultra, *bl* 8.00 *16.00*
71 A6 2sh 6p blk & red, *bl* ('23) 14.00 *57.50*
72 A6 3sh green & vio 14.00 *21.00*
73 A6 4sh black & scar 17.50 *42.50*
74 A6 5sh grn & red, *yel* ('23) 30.00 *47.50*
Nos. 54-74 (21) 120.90 *315.50*

Tercentenary Issue

New Plymouth and Harbor A7

1932, Apr. 18 Engr.
75 A7 ½p green .85 *7.75*
76 A7 1p red .85 *6.50*
77 A7 1½p orange brown 1.40 *2.75*
78 A7 2p gray 1.90 *19.00*
79 A7 2½p ultra 1.40 *18.00*
80 A7 3p orange 1.90 *19.00*
81 A7 6p violet 2.50 *32.50*
82 A7 1sh olive green 14.50 *42.50*
83 A7 2sh6p lilac rose 52.50 *87.50*
84 A7 5sh dark brown 115.00 *200.00*
Nos. 75-84 (10) 192.80 *435.50*
Set, never hinged 400.00

300th anniv. of the colonization of Montserrat.

Common Design Types pictured following the introduction.

Silver Jubilee Issue
Common Design Type

1935, May 6 *Perf. 11x12*
85 CD301 1p car & dk blue 1.25 4.25
86 CD301 1½p gray blk & ultra 1.90 *3.75*
87 CD301 2½p ultra & brn 2.75 *4.25*
88 CD301 1sh brn vio & ind 4.25 *18.00*
Nos. 85-88 (4) 10.15 *30.25*
Set, never hinged 19.00

Coronation Issue
Common Design Type

1937, May 12 *Perf. 13½x14*
89 CD302 1p carmine .20 .35
90 CD302 1½p brown .25 .25
91 CD302 2½p bright ultra .25 .70
Nos. 89-91 (3) .70 1.30
Set, never hinged 1.10

Carr's Bay — A8

Sea Island Cotton — A9

Botanic Station A10

1941-48 *Perf. 14*
92 A8 ½p dk grn ('42) .20 .20
93 A9 1p car ('42) .40 .35
94 A9 1½p rose vio ('42) .40 *.55*
95 A10 2p red orange 1.20 .80
96 A9 2½p brt ultra ('43) .40 .35
97 A8 3p brown ('42) 1.50 .45
98 A10 6p dull vio ('42) 2.00 .70
99 A8 1sh brn lake ('42) 1.75 .35
100 A10 2sh6p slate bl ('43) 13.50 3.00
101 A8 5sh car rose ('42) 16.00 3.50

Perf. 12
102 A10 10sh blue ('48) 10.00 *30.00*
103 A8 £1 black ('48) 10.00 *30.00*
Nos. 92-103 (12) 57.35 70.25
Set, never hinged 85.00

1938, Aug. 2 *Perf. 13*
92a A8 ½p 2.50 *4.25*
93a A8 1p 2.50 *4.25*
94a A9 1½p 10.00 *16.00*
95a A10 2p 10.00 *16.00*
96a A9 2½p .85 *1.50*
97a A8 3p 2.00 *3.25*
98a A10 6p 10.00 *16.00*
99a A8 1sh 10.00 *16.00*
100a A10 2sh6p 17.50 *27.50*
101a A8 5sh 21.00 *35.00*
Nos. 92a-101a (10) 86.35 *139.75*
Set, never hinged 140.00

Catalogue values for unused stamps in this section, from this point to the end of the section, are for Never Hinged items.

Peace Issue
Common Design Type

1946, Nov. 1 Engr. *Perf. 13½x14*
104 CD303 1½p deep magenta .20 .20
105 CD303 3p brown .20 .20

Silver Wedding Issue
Common Design Types

1949, Jan. 3 Photo. *Perf. 14x14½*
106 CD304 2½p brt ultra .20 .20

Engraved; Name Typographed
Perf. 11½x11
107 CD305 5sh rose carmine 7.75 *11.50*

UPU Issue
Common Design Types
Engr.; Name Typo. on 3p and 6p
Perf. 13½, 11x11½

1949, Oct. 10 Wmk. 4
108 CD306 2½p ultramarine .45 .45
109 CD307 3p chocolate .65 .65
110 CD308 6p lilac .75 .75
111 CD309 1sh rose violet 1.10 1.10
Nos. 108-111 (4) 2.95 2.95

University Issue
Common Design Types

1951, Feb. 16 Engr. *Perf. 14x14½*
112 CD310 3c rose lil & gray blk .25 .25
113 CD311 12c violet & black .80 .80

Government House
A11

Designs (portrait at right on 12c, 24c and $2.40): 2c, $1.20, Cotton field. 3c, Map of Presidency. 4c, 24c, Picking tomatoes. 5c, 12c, St. Anthony's Church. 6c, $4.80, Badge of Presidency. 8c, 60c, Cotton ginning.

Perf. 11½x11
1951, Sept. 17 Engr. Wmk. 4
114 A11 1c gray .20 .20
115 A11 2c green .20 .20
116 A11 3c orange brown .20 .20
117 A11 4c rose carmine .20 .20
118 A11 5c red violet .20 .20
119 A11 6c dark brown .30 .30
120 A11 8c dark blue .45 .45
121 A11 12c red brn & blue .90 .90
122 A11 24c emer & rose carmine 1.25 1.25
123 A11 60c rose car & gray black 2.50 2.50
124 A11 $1.20 dp bl & emer 8.25 8.25
125 A11 $2.40 dp grn & gray black 10.00 *12.00*
126 A11 $4.80 pur & gray blk 20.00 *26.00*
Nos. 114-126 (13) 44.65 *52.65*

Coronation Issue
Common Design Type

1953, June 2 *Perf. 13½x13*
127 CD312 2c dark green & black .50 .50

Type of 1951 with Portrait of Queen Elizabeth II

½c, 3c, "Map of Presidency." 48c, Cotton field.

1953-57 *Perf. 11½x11*
128 A11 ½c violet ('56) .20 .20
129 A11 1c gray black .20 .20
130 A11 2c green .20 .20
131 A11 3c orange brown .65 .65
132 A11 4c rose car ('55) .20 .20
133 A11 5c red vio ('55) .20 .20
134 A11 6c dk brown ('55) .70 .70
135 A11 8c dp ultra ('55) .20 .20
136 A11 12c red brn & blue ('55) .20 .20
137 A11 24c emer & rose car ('55) .80 .80
138 A11 48c rose violet & olive ('57) 1.60 1.60
139 A11 60c rose car & blk ('55) 2.00 2.00
140 A11 $1.20 bl & emer ('55) 4.00 4.00
141 A11 $2.40 dp green & blk ('55) 8.00 8.00
142 A11 $4.80 pur & gray black ('55) 35.00 35.00
Nos. 128-142 (15) 54.15 54.15

See Nos. 146-149, 156.

West Indies Federation
Common Design Type
Perf. 11½x11

1958, Apr. 22 Engr. Wmk. 314
143 CD313 3c green .45 .20
144 CD313 6c blue .65 .45
145 CD313 12c carmine rose 1.25 .65
Nos. 143-145 (3) 2.35 1.30

Type of 1953-57

As before, but inscribed: "Map of the Colony" (½c, 3c) "Badge of the Colony" (6c, $4.80).

1958 Wmk. 4 *Perf. 11½x11*
146 A11 ½c violet .50 .20
147 A11 3c orange brown .50 .75
148 A11 6c dark brown .25 .20
149 A11 $4.80 pur & gray blk 11.00 *9.00*
Nos. 146-149 (4) 12.25 *10.15*

Freedom from Hunger Issue
Common Design Type
Perf. 14x14½

1963, June 4 Photo. Wmk. 314
150 CD314 12c lilac .75 .65

Red Cross Centenary Issue
Common Design Type

1963, Sept. 2 Litho. *Perf. 13*
151 CD315 4c black & red .20 .20
152 CD315 12c ultra & red .75 .55

Shakespeare Issue
Common Design Type

1964, Apr. 23 Photo. *Perf. 14x14½*
153 CD316 12c slate blue .35 .25

Type of 1953-57
Perf. 11½x11

1964, Oct. 30 Engr. Wmk. 314
156 A11 2c green 1.00 .20

ITU Issue
Common Design Type
Perf. 11x11½

1965, May 17 Litho. Wmk. 314
157 CD317 4c ver & lilac .20 .20
158 CD317 48c emer & rose red 1.00 .90

Pineapple — A12

Wmk. 314 Upright
1965, Aug. 16 Photo. *Perf. 15x14*
159 A12 1c shown .20 .20
160 A12 2c Avacado .20 .20
161 A12 3c Soursop .20 .20
162 A12 4c Peppers .20 .20
163 A12 5c Mango .20 .20
164 A12 6c Tomatoes .20 .20
165 A12 8c Guava .20 .20
166 A12 10c Okra .20 .20
167 A12 12c Limes .25 .20
168 A12 20c Oranges .35 .20
169 A12 24c Bananas .55 .25
170 A12 42c Onion 1.10 .80
171 A12 48c Cabbage 1.40 .90
172 A12 60c Papayas 1.50 1.10
173 A12 $1.20 Pumpkin 1.75 1.50
174 A12 $2.40 Sweet potato 4.50 3.50
175 A12 $4.80 Eggplant 9.00 7.25
Nos. 159-175 (17) 22.00 17.30

For surcharges see Nos. 193-198.

1969 Wmk. 314 Sideways
159a A12 1c .20 .20
160a A12 2c .45 *.50*
161a A12 3c .50 .40
162a A12 4c .75 .40
163a A12 5c .90 *1.00*
166a A12 10c 1.75 *2.00*
168a A12 20c 2.10 *2.40*
Nos. 159a-168a (7) 6.45 6.90

Intl. Cooperation Year Issue
Common Design Type

1965, Oct. 25 Litho. *Perf. 14½*
176 CD318 2c lt green & claret .20 .20
177 CD318 12c lt violet & green .40 .40

Churchill Memorial Issue
Common Design Type

1966, Jan. 24 Photo. *Perf. 14*
Design in Black, Gold and Carmine Rose
178 CD319 1c bright blue .20 .20
179 CD319 2c green .20 .20
180 CD319 24c brown .35 .30
181 CD319 42c violet .75 .75
Nos. 178-181 (4) 1.50 1.45

Royal Visit Issue
Common Design Type
Perf. 11x12

1966, Feb. 4 Litho. Wmk. 314
182 CD320 14c violet blue .50 .20
183 CD320 24c dk carmine rose .95 .95

WHO Headquarters Issue
Common Design Type

1966, Sept. 20 Litho. *Perf. 14*
184 CD322 12c multicolored .20 .20
185 CD322 60c multicolored .75 .75

UNESCO Anniversary Issue
Common Design Type

1966, Dec. 1 Litho. *Perf. 14*
186 CD323 4c "Education" .20 .20
a. Orange omitted 50.00
187 CD323 60c "Science" .40 .40
188 CD323 $1.80 "Culture" 1.75 1.75
Nos. 186-188 (3) 2.35 2.35

On No. 186a, the squares of the lowercase letters appear in yellow.

Sailing and ITY Emblem
A13

ITY Emblem and: 15c, Waterfall, Chance Mountain, vert. 16c, Beach scene. 24c, Golfers.

1967, Dec. 29 Photo. Wmk. 314
189 A13 5c multicolored .35 .35
190 A13 15c multicolored .35 .35
191 A13 16c multicolored .45 .45
192 A13 24c multicolored .95 .95
Nos. 189-192 (4) 2.10 2.10

Issued for International Tourist Year.

Nos. 167, 169, 171, 173-175 and Type Surcharged

1968, May 6 *Perf. 15x14*
193 A12 15c on 12c multi .25 .25
a. Wmkd. sideways ('69) 1.50 *1.75*
194 A12 25c on 24c multi .40 .40
a. Wmkd. sideways ('69) 2.50 *3.00*
195 A12 50c on 48c multi .85 .85
a. Wmkd. sideways ('69) 5.25 *6.00*
196 A12 $1 on $1.20 multi 1.25 1.25
197 A12 $2.50 on $2.40 multi 2.75 2.75
198 A12 $5 on $4.80 multi 5.50 5.50
Nos. 193-198 (6) 11.00 11.00

The surcharge bars are slightly thinner on the "Wmkd. sideways" varieties.

Woman Runner
A14

Designs: 25c, Weight lifter. 50c, Athlete on rings. $1, Runner and Toltec sculptures, vert.

Perf. 14½x14, 14x14½
1968, July 31 Photo. Wmk. 314
199 A14 15c gold, brt grn & rose claret .20 .20
200 A14 25c gold, org & blue .20 .20
201 A14 50c gold, ver & green .25 .25
202 A14 $1 multicolored .55 .55
Nos. 199-202 (4) 1.20 1.20

19th Olympic Games, Mexico City, 10/12-27.

Albert T. Marryshow — A15

Portraits and Human Rights Flame: 5c, Alexander Hamilton. 25c, William Wilberforce. 50c, Dag Hammarskjold. $1, Rev. Martin Luther King, Jr.

1968, Dec. 2 Photo. *Perf. 14x14½*
203 A15 5c multicolored .20 .20
204 A15 15c multicolored .20 .20
205 A15 25c multicolored .20 .20
206 A15 50c multicolored .20 .20
207 A15 $1 multicolored .50 .50
Nos. 203-207 (5) 1.30 1.30

International Human Rights Year.

The Two Trinities, by Murillo
A16

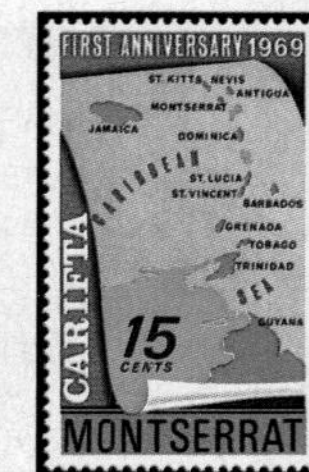

Map of Caribbean
A17

Christmas: 15c, 50c, The Adoration of the Magi, by Botticelli.

1968, Dec. 16 *Perf. 14½x14*
208 A16 5c red & multi .20 .20
209 A16 15c dk green & multi .20 .20
210 A16 25c purple & multi .20 .20
211 A16 50c brown & multi .40 .40
Nos. 208-211 (4) 1.00 1.00

1969, May 27 Photo. *Perf. 14*

Design: 35c, 50c, "Strength in Unity," horiz.

212 A17 15c green & multi .20 .20
213 A17 20c brown & multi .20 .20
214 A17 35c dp carmine & multi .25 .25
215 A17 50c multicolored .35 .35
Nos. 212-215 (4) 1.00 1.00

First anniversary of CARIFTA (Caribbean Free Trade Area).

Telephone and Map — A18

Development Projects (Map and): 25c, Book and "New Schools." 50c, Planes (air transport service). $1, Pylon and power lines.

Wmk. 314
1969, July 29 Litho. *Perf. 13½*
216 A18 15c multicolored .20 .20
217 A18 25c multicolored .20 .20
218 A18 50c multicolored .30 .30
219 A18 $1 multicolored .60 .60
Nos. 216-219 (4) 1.30 1.30

Dolphin
A19

Fish: 15c, Atlantic sailfish. 25c, Blackfin tuna and fishing boat. 40c, Spanish mackerel.

1969, Nov. 1 Photo. *Perf. 13x14*
220 A19 5c multicolored .20 .20
221 A19 15c multicolored .35 .35
222 A19 25c multicolored .70 .70
223 A19 40c multicolored 1.25 1.25
Nos. 220-223 (4) 2.50 2.50

King Caspar, Virgin and Child (Stained-glass Window) — A20

Christmas: 50c, Nativity, by Leonard Limosin, horiz.

Perf. 12½x13, 13x12½

1969, Dec. 10 Litho. Wmk. 314

224	A20	15c violet & multi	.20	.20
225	A20	25c red & multi	.25	.25
226	A20	50c orange & multi	.45	.45
		Nos. 224-226 (3)	.90	.90

Red Cross and Distribution of Hearing Aids — A21

Red Cross and: 3c, Fund raising sale and invalid. 15c, Car bringing handicapped to work. 20c, Instruction for blind worker.

1970, Apr. 13 Litho. *Perf. 14½*

227	A21	3c multicolored	.20	.20
228	A21	4c multicolored	.20	.20
229	A21	15c multicolored	.25	.25
230	A21	20c multicolored	.35	.35
		Nos. 227-230 (4)	1.00	1.00

Centenary of British Red Cross Society.

Red-footed Booby A22

Birds: 2c, Killy hawk, vert. 3c, Frigate bird, vert. 4c, White egret, vert. 5c, Brown pelican, vert. 10c, Bananaquit, vert. 15c, Common ani. 20c, Tropic bird. 25c, Montserrat oriole. 50c, Greenthroated carib, vert. $1, Antillean crested hummingbird. $2.50, Little blue heron, vert. $5, Purple-throated carib. $10, Forest thrush.

Wmk. 314 Upright on Horiz. Stamps, Sideways on Vert. Stamps

Perf. 14x14½, 14½x14

1970-74 Photo.

231	A22	1c	yel org & multi	.20	.20
232	A22	2c	lt vio & multi	.20	.20
233	A22	3c	multicolored	.20	.20
234	A22	4c	lt grn & multi	.20	.20
235	A22	5c	bister & multi	.20	.20
236	A22	10c	gray & multi	.20	.20
237	A22	15c	multicolored	.50	.40
238	A22	20c	rose brn & multi	.65	.55
239	A22	25c	brown & multi	.85	.70
240	A22	50c	lt vio & multi	1.75	1.40
241	A22	$1	multicolored	3.00	2.40
242	A22	$2.50	dl bl & multi	6.75	5.50
243	A22	$5	multicolored	13.50	11.00
243A	A22	$10	blue & multi	26.00	22.50
			Nos. 231-243A (14)	54.20	45.65

Issued: $10, 10/30/74; others 7/2/70.

For surcharges and overprints see Nos. 314, 317, 337-339, O1-O4.

Wmk. Sideways on Horiz. Stamps, Upright on Vert. Stamps

1972-74

231a	A22	1c multicolored	.75	*1.25*
232a	A22	2c multicolored	.95	*1.25*
233a	A22	3c multicolored	.95	*1.25*
234a	A22	4c multicolored	1.40	*1.60*
235a	A22	5c multicolored	1.75	*2.00*
237a	A22	15c multicolored	4.75	*4.75*
238a	A22	20c multicolored	6.75	*7.75*
239a	A22	25c multicolored	9.50	*9.75*
		Nos. 231a-239a (8)	26.80	*29.60*

Issued: 1c, 2c, 3c, 7/21/72; 5c, 15c, 3/8/73; 20c, 10/2/73; 4c, 2/4/74; 25c, 5/17/74.

"Madonna and Child with Animals," after Dürer — A23

Christmas: 15c, $1, Adoration of the Shepherds, by Domenichino (Domenico Zampieri).

1970, Sept. 21 Litho. *Perf. 14*

244	A23	5c lt blue & multi	.20	.20
245	A23	15c red orange & multi	.20	.20
246	A23	20c ol green & multi	.25	.25
247	A23	$1 multicolored	1.00	1.00
		Nos. 244-247 (4)	1.65	1.65

War Memorial, Plymouth — A24

Tourist Publicity: 15c, Fort St. George and view of Plymouth. 25c, Beach at Carrs Bay. 50c, Golf Course.

1970, Nov. 30 Litho. *Perf. 14*

248	A24	5c multicolored	.20	.20
249	A24	15c multicolored	.40	.40
250	A24	25c multicolored	.70	.70
251	A24	50c multicolored	1.50	1.50
a.		Souvenir sheet of 4, #248-251	7.50	7.50
		Nos. 248-251 (4)	2.80	2.80

Girl Guide — A25

"Noli me Tangere," by Orcagna (Andrea di Cione) — A26

Girl Guides' 60th Anniv.: 15c, 25c, Brownie.

1970, Dec. 31

252	A25	10c orange & multi	.20	.20
253	A25	15c lt blue & multi	.20	.20
254	A25	25c lilac & multi	.30	.30
255	A25	40c multicolored	.50	.50
		Nos. 252-255 (4)	1.20	1.20

Perf. 13½x13

1971, Mar. 22 Photo. Wmk. 314

Easter: 5c, 20c, Descent from the Cross, by Jan van Hemessen.

256	A26	5c orange brn & multi	.20	.20
257	A26	15c multicolored	.20	.20
258	A26	20c green & multi	.25	.25
259	A26	40c blue green & multi	.50	.50
		Nos. 256-259 (4)	1.15	1.15

Distinguished Flying Cross and Medal — A27

"Nativity with Saints" (detail), by Romanino A28

Highest Awards for Military Personnel: 20c, Military Cross and Medal. 40c, Distinguished Service Cross and Medal. $1, Victoria Cross.

Perf. 14½x14

1971, July 8 Litho. Wmk. 314

260	A27	10c gray, vio & silver	.20	.20
261	A27	20c green & multi	.25	.25
262	A27	40c lt bl, dk bl & sil	.45	.45
263	A27	$1 red, dk brn & gold	1.25	1.25
		Nos. 260-263 (4)	2.15	2.15

50th anniversary of the British Commonwealth Ex-services League.

1971, Sept. 16 *Perf. 14x13½*

Christmas (Paintings): 15c, $1, Angels' Choir, by Simon Marmion.

264	A28	5c brown & multi	.20	.20
265	A28	15c emerald & multi	.20	.20
266	A28	20c ultra & multi	.20	.20
267	A28	$1 red & multi	1.10	1.10
		Nos. 264-267 (4)	1.70	1.70

Piper Apache, First Landing at Olveston Airfield — A29

Designs: 10c, Beech Twin Bonanza. 15c, De Havilland Heron. 20c, Britten Norman Islander. 40c, De Havilland Twin Otter. 75c, Hawker Siddeley 748 and stewardesses.

1971, Dec. 16 *Perf. 13½x14*

268	A29	5c multicolored	.20	.20
269	A29	10c multicolored	.30	.30
270	A29	15c multicolored	.45	.45
271	A29	20c multicolored	.65	.65
272	A29	40c multicolored	1.25	1.25
273	A29	75c multicolored	2.00	2.00
a.		Souvenir sheet of 6, #268-273	19.00	19.00
		Nos. 268-273 (6)	4.85	4.85

14th anniversary of Leeward Islands Air Transport (LIAT).

Chapel of Christ in Gethsemane, Coventry Cathedral — A30

Easter: 10c, 75c, The Agony in the Garden, by Giovanni Bellini.

1972, Mar. 9 Litho. *Perf. 13½x13*

274	A30	5c red & multi	.20	.20
275	A30	10c blue & multi	.20	.20
276	A30	20c emerald & multi	.25	.25
277	A30	75c lilac & multi	1.25	1.25
		Nos. 274-277 (4)	1.90	1.90

Iguana A31

Designs: 15c, Spotted ameiva (lizard), vert. 20c, Frog ("mountain chicken"), vert. $1, Redfoot tortoises.

1972, June 8 Litho. *Perf. 14½*

278	A31	15c lilac rose & multi	.50	.50
279	A31	20c black & multi	.60	.60
280	A31	40c blue & multi	1.25	1.25
281	A31	$1 green & multi	2.50	2.50
		Nos. 278-281 (4)	4.85	4.85

Madonna of the Chair, by Raphael A32

Christmas (Paintings): 35c, Virgin and Child with Cherubs, by Bernardino Fungai. 50c, Magnificat Madonna, by Botticelli. $1, Virgin and Child with St. John and Angel, by Botticelli.

1972, Oct. 18 *Perf. 13½*

282	A32	10c violet & multi	.20	.20
283	A32	35c brt red & multi	.40	.40
284	A32	50c red brown & multi	.70	.70
285	A32	$1 olive & multi	1.50	1.50
		Nos. 282-285 (4)	2.80	2.80

Silver Wedding Issue, 1972

Common Design Type

Design: Queen Elizabeth II, Prince Philip, tomatoes, papayas, limes.

Perf. 14x14½

1972, Nov. 20 Photo. Wmk. 314

286	CD324	35c car rose & multi	.20	.20
287	CD324	$1 ultra & multi	.60	.60

Passionflower A33

Designs: 35c, Passiflora vitifolia. 75c, Passiflora amabilis. $1, Passiflora alata caerulea.

1973, Apr. 9 Litho. *Perf. 14x13½*

288	A33	20c purple & multi	.50	.50
289	A33	35c multicolored	.85	.85
290	A33	75c brt blue & multi	1.25	1.25
291	A33	$1 multicolored	2.25	2.25
		Nos. 288-291 (4)	4.85	4.85

Easter. Black backprinting gives story of passionflower.

Montserrat Monastery, Spain — A34

35c, Columbus aboard ship sighting Montserrat. 60c, Columbus' ship off Montserrat. $1, Arms and map of Montserrat & neighboring islands.

1973, July 16 Litho. *Perf. 13½x14*

292	A34	10c multicolored	.45	.45
293	A34	35c multicolored	1.00	1.00
294	A34	60c multicolored	1.60	1.60
295	A34	$1 multicolored	2.50	2.50
a.		Souvenir sheet of 4, #292-295	25.00	25.00
		Nos. 292-295 (4)	5.55	5.55

480th anniversary of the discovery of Montserrat by Columbus.

Virgin and Child, Studio of David — A35

Masqueraders A36

Christmas (Paintings): 35c, Holy Family with St. John, by Jacob Jordaens. 50c, Virgin and Child, by Bellini. 90c, Virgin and Child by Carlo Dolci.

1973, Oct. 15 Litho. *Perf. 14x13½*

296 A35 20c blue & multi .25 .25
297 A35 35c ol bister & multi .40 .40
298 A35 50c brt green & multi .95 .95
299 A35 90c brt rose & multi 1.90 1.90
Nos. 296-299 (4) 3.50 3.50

Princess Anne's Wedding Issue
Common Design Type

1973, Nov. 14 *Perf. 14*

300 CD325 35c brt green & multi .20 .20
301 CD325 $1 multicolored .65 .65

1974, Apr. 8

302 A36 20c Steel band, horiz. .25 .25
303 A36 35c shown .60 .60
304 A36 60c Girl weaving .90 .90
305 A36 $1 University Center, horiz. 1.40 1.40
a. Souvenir sheet of 4, #302-305 11.00 11.00
Nos. 302-305 (4) 3.15 3.15

University of the West Indies, 25th anniv.
For surcharge see No. 316.

Hands Holding Letters, UPU Emblem A37

Designs: 2c, 5c, $1, Hands and figures from UPU Monument, Bern; UPU emblem. 3c, 50c, like 1c.

1974, July 3 Litho. *Perf. 14*

306 A37 1c violet & multi .20 .20
307 A37 2c red & black .20 .20
308 A37 3c olive & multi .20 .20
309 A37 5c orange & black .20 .20
310 A37 50c brown & multi .35 .35
311 A37 $1 grnsh blue & black .85 .85
Nos. 306-311 (6) 2.00 2.00

Centenary of Universal Postal Union.
For surcharges see Nos. 315-318.

Churchill, Parliament, Big Ben — A38

Churchill and Blenheim Palace — A39

Perf. 13x13½

1974, Nov. 30 Unwmk.

312 A38 35c ocher & multi .20 .20
313 A39 70c brt green & multi .60 .60
a. Souvenir sheet of 2, #312-313 1.10 1.10

Sir Winston Churchill (1874-1965).

Nos. 241, 304, 310-311 Surcharged with New Value and Two Bars

Perf. 14x14½, 14
Photo., Litho.

1974, Oct. 2 Wmk. 314

314 A22 2c on $1 multi .20 .20
315 A37 5c on 50c multi 1.10 1.10
316 A36 10c on 60c multi 3.00 3.00
317 A22 20c on $1 multi 1.00 1.00
a. One bar in surcharge 2.25 2.25
318 A37 35c on $1 multi 2.25 2.25
Nos. 314-318 (5) 7.55 7.55

Carib Carbet (House) A40

Carib Artifacts: 20c, Necklace (caracoli). 35c, Club. 70c, Canoe.

Wmk. 314

1975, Mar. 3 Litho. *Perf. 14*

319 A40 5c dk red, ocher & blk .20 .20
320 A40 20c blk, och & dk red .20 .20
321 A40 35c blk, dk red & och .30 .30
322 A40 70c ocher, dk red & blk .55 .55
a. Souvenir booklet 3.00
Nos. 319-322 (4) 1.25 1.25

No. 322a contains 2 self-adhesive panes printed on peelable paper backing with bicolored advertising on back. One pane of 6 contains 3 each similar to Nos. 320-321; the other pane of 4 contains one each similar to Nos. 319-322. Stamps are imperf. x roulette. Panes have commemorative marginal inscription.

One Bitt A41

Old Local Coinage (1785-1801): 10c, Eighth of a dollar. 35c, Quarter dollars. $2, One dollar.

1975, Sept. 1 Litho. *Perf. 14*

323 A41 5c ultra, silver & blk .20 .20
324 A41 10c brown org, sil & blk .20 .20
325 A41 35c green, silver & blk .35 .35
326 A41 $2 brt rose, sil & blk 1.75 1.75
a. Souvenir sheet of 4, #323-326 3.00 3.00
Nos. 323-326 (4) 2.50 2.50

Explanation and description of coinage printed in black on back of souvenir sheet.

Montserrat Nos. 1 and 2 — A42

10c, Post Office, Montserrat & #1a with AO8 cancel. 40c, Cover with #1a, 1b. 55c, #A4 (G.B. #27 with AO8 cancel) & #2. 70c, 2 #1, 1 #1a with AO8 cancels. $1.10, Packet "Antelope" & #2.

1976, Jan. 5 *Perf. 13½*

327 A42 5c multicolored .20 .20
328 A42 10c multicolored .20 .20
329 A42 40c multicolored .50 .50
330 A42 55c multicolored .65 .65
331 A42 70c multicolored .85 .85
332 A42 $1.10 multicolored 1.25 1.25
a. Souvenir sheet of 6, #327-332 4.50 4.50
Nos. 327-332 (6) 3.65 3.65

Centenary of Montserrat's postage stamps.

Trinity, by Orcagna — A43

Paintings by Orcagna (Andrea di Cione): 40c, Resurrection. 55c, Ascension. $1.10, Pentecost.

Perf. 14x13½

1976, Apr. 5 Litho. Wmk. 373

333 A43 15c multicolored .20 .20
334 A43 40c multicolored .25 .25
335 A43 55c multicolored .25 .25
336 A43 $1.10 multicolored .60 .60
a. Souvenir sheet of 4 1.90 1.90
Nos. 333-336 (4) 1.30 1.30

Easter 1976. Nos. 333-336 were prepared, but not issued in 1975. Stamps are surcharged with new values; date "1975" obliterated with heavy bar. No. 336a contains one each of Nos. 333-336; "1975" in margin obliterated with heavy bar.

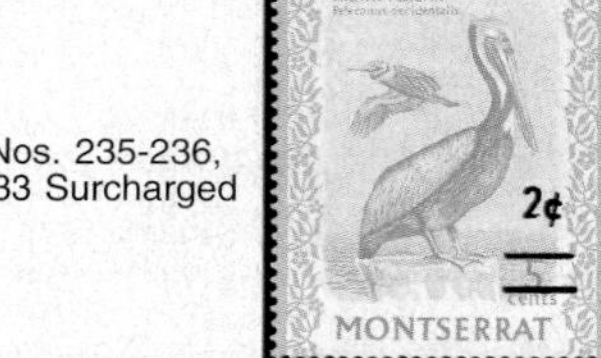

Nos. 235-236, 233 Surcharged

Perf. 14½x14

1976, Apr. 12 Photo. Wmk. 314

337 A22 2c on 5c multi .20 .20
338 A22 30c on 10c multi .50 .50
339 A22 45c on 3c multi .85 .85
Nos. 337-339 (3) 1.55 1.55

For overprints see Nos. O3-O4.

White Frangipani — A44

Designs: Flowering trees of Montserrat.

Perf. 13½x14

1976, July 5 Litho. Wmk. 373

340 A44 1c shown .20 .20
341 A44 2c Cannonball tree .20 .20
342 A44 3c Lignum vitae .20 .20
343 A44 5c Malay apple .20 .20
344 A44 10c Jacaranda .20 .20
345 A44 15c Orchid tree .20 .20
346 A44 20c Manjak .20 .20
347 A44 25c Tamarind .20 .20
348 A44 40c Flame of the Forest .20 .20
349 A44 55c Pink cassia .30 .30
350 A44 70c Long John .35 .35
351 A44 $1 Saman .50 .50
352 A44 $2.50 Immortelle 1.25 1.25
353 A44 $5 Yellow poui 2.50 2.50
354 A44 $10 Flamboyant 5.00 5.00
Nos. 340-354 (15) 11.70 11.70

For surcharges and overprints see Nos. 374-376, 420, 435-440, O10-O44.

Mary and Joseph on Road to Bethlehem — A45

Christmas (Map of Montserrat and): 20c, Shepherds. 55c, Virgin and Child. $1.10, Three Kings.

1976, Oct. 4 *Perf. 14½*

355 A45 15c vio blue & multi .20 .20
356 A45 20c green & multi .20 .20
357 A45 55c lilac & multi .40 .40
358 A45 $1.10 multicolored .90 .90
a. Souvenir sheet of 4, #355-358 2.50 2.50
Nos. 355-358 (4) 1.70 1.70

Hudson River Review of Opsail 76 — A46

Designs: 40c, Raleigh. 75c, HMS Druid (Raleigh attacking Druid, 1776).

1976, Dec. 13 Litho. *Perf. 13*

359 15c multicolored .20 .20
a. A46 Pair, #359, 362 1.75 1.75
360 40c multicolored .50 .50
361 75c multicolored 1.00 1.00
a. A46 Pair, #360-361 1.50 1.50
362 $1.25 multicolored 1.50 1.50
a. A46 Souvenir sheet of 4, #359-362, perf. 14x13½ 3.50 3.50
Nos. 359-362 (4) 3.20 3.20

American Bicentennial.

Queen Arriving for 1966 Visit, Yacht Britannia — A48

Designs: 45c, Firing of cannons at Tower of London. $1, The crowning.

1977, Feb. 7

363 A48 30c multicolored .25 .25
364 A48 45c multicolored .35 .35
365 A48 $1 multicolored .90 .90
Nos. 363-365 (3) 1.50 1.50

25th anniv. of the reign of Elizabeth II.
#363-365 were issued also in booklet panes of 4.

Epiphyllum Hookeri — A49

Flowers of the Night: 15c, Ipomoea alba, vert. 55c, Cereus hexagonus. $1.50, Cestrum nocturnum, vert.

1977, June 1 Litho. *Perf. 14*

366 A49 15c multicolored .20 .20
367 A49 40c multicolored .40 .40
368 A49 55c multicolored .50 .50
369 A49 $1.50 multicolored 1.50 1.50
a. Souvenir sheet of 4, #366-369 3.50 3.50
Nos. 366-369 (4) 2.60 2.60

Princess Anne at Ground-breaking Ceremony, Glendon Hospital — A50

Designs: 40c, New deep-water jetty, Plymouth. 55c, Glendon Hospital. $1.50, Freighter unloading at new jetty.

1977, Oct. 3 Wmk. 373 *Perf. 14½*

370 A50 20c multicolored .20 .20
371 A50 40c multicolored .20 .20
372 A50 55c multicolored .30 .30
373 A50 $1.50 multicolored .80 .80
a. Souvenir sheet of 4, #370-373 2.50 2.50
Nos. 370-373 (4) 1.50 1.50

Development.

Nos. 349-350, 352 Surcharged with New Value and Bars and Overprinted: "SILVER JUBILEE 1977 / ROYAL VISIT / TO THE CARIBBEAN"

1977, Oct. Litho. *Perf. 13½x14*

374 A44 $1 on 55c multi .60 .60
375 A44 $1 on 70c multi .60 .60
376 A44 $1 on $2.50 multi .60 .60
Nos. 374-376 (3) 1.80 1.80

Caribbean visit of Queen Elizabeth II. Surcharge has bars of differing thickness and length. No. 374 has two settings.

"Silent Night, Holy Night" — A51

Christmas Carols and Map of Montserrat: 40c, "We Three Kings of Orient Are." 55c, "I Saw Three Ships Come Sailing In." $2, "Hark the Herald Angels Sing."

1977, Nov. 14 Litho. *Perf. 14½*

377 A51 5c blue & multi .20 .20
378 A51 40c bister & multi .20 .20
379 A51 55c lt blue & multi .20 .20
380 A51 $2 rose & multi .85 .85
a. Souvenir sheet of 4, #377-380 1.50 1.50
Nos. 377-380 (4) 1.45 1.45

Four-eye Butterflyfish — A52

Fish: 40c, French angelfish. 55c, Blue tang. $1.50, Queen triggerfish.

1978, Feb. 27 Wmk. 373 *Perf. 14*

381 A52 30c multicolored .30 .30
382 A52 40c multicolored .40 .40
383 A52 55c multicolored .55 .55
384 A52 $1.50 multicolored 1.50 1.50
a. Souvenir sheet of 4, #381-384 5.25 5.25
Nos. 381-384 (4) 2.75 2.75

Elizabeth II and St. Paul's, London — A53

Designs: 55c, Chichester Cathedral. $1, Lincoln Cathedral. $2.50, Llandaff Cathedral, Cardiff.

1978, June 2 *Perf. 13½*

385 A53 40c multicolored .20 .20
386 A53 55c multicolored .20 .20
387 A53 $1 multicolored .30 .30
388 A53 $2.50 multicolored .70 .70
a. Souvenir sheet of 4, #385-388 1.40 1.40
Nos. 385-388 (4) 1.40 1.40

25th anniversary of coronation of Elizabeth II, Defender of the Faith. Nos. 385-388 printed in sheets of 10 stamps and 2 labels. #385-388 also issued in bklt. panes of 2.

Alpinia — A54 Private, 1796 — A55

Flowering Plants: 55c, Allamanda cathartica. $1, Blue tree petrea. $2, Amaryllis.

1978, Sept. 18 Litho. *Perf. 13½x13*

389 A54 40c multicolored .20 .20
390 A54 55c multicolored .35 .35
391 A54 $1 multicolored .65 .65
392 A54 $2 multicolored 1.25 1.25
Nos. 389-392 (4) 2.45 2.45

1978, Nov. 20 Litho. *Perf. 14½*

Uniforms: 40c, Corporal, 1831. 55c, Sergeant, 1837. $1.50, Officer, 1784.

393 A55 30c multicolored .20 .20
394 A55 40c multicolored .20 .20
395 A55 55c multicolored .35 .35
396 A55 $1.50 multicolored 1.00 1.00
a. Souvenir sheet of 4, #393-396 2.00 2.00
Nos. 393-396 (4) 1.75 1.75

See Nos. 401-404.

Cub Scouts A56

Boy Scouts: 55c, Signaling. $1.25, Cooking, vert. $2, Flag folding ceremony, vert.

1979, Apr. 2 Litho. *Perf. 14*

397 A56 40c multicolored .25 .25
398 A56 55c multicolored .35 .35
399 A56 $1.25 multicolored .80 .80
400 A56 $2 multicolored 1.25 1.25
a. Souvenir sheet of 4, #397-400 3.00 3.00
Nos. 397-400 (4) 2.65 2.65

50th anniversary of Scouting in Montserrat.

Uniform Type of 1978

30c, Private, 1783. 40c, Private, 1819. 55c, Officer, 1819. $2.50, Highlander officer, 1830.

1979, July 4 Wmk. 373 *Perf. 14*

401 A55 30c multicolored .20 .20
402 A55 40c multicolored .25 .25
403 A55 55c multicolored .30 .30
404 A55 $2.50 multicolored 1.50 1.50
a. Souvenir sheet of 4, #401-404 2.50 2.50
Nos. 401-404 (4) 2.25 2.25

IYC Emblem, Learning to Walk — A56a

1979, Sept. 17 Litho. *Perf. 13½x14*

405 A56a $2 brown org & black .85 .85
a. Souvenir sheet 2.00 2.00

International Year of the Child.

Hill, Penny Black, Montserrat No. 1 — A57

Designs: 55c, UPU Emblem, charter. $1, UPU Emblem, cover. $2, Hill, Post Office regulations.

1979, Oct. 1 *Perf. 14*

406 A57 40c multicolored .20 .20
407 A57 55c multicolored .20 .20
408 A57 $1 multicolored .40 .40
409 A57 $2 multicolored .80 .80
a. Souvenir sheet of 4, #406-409 3.50 3.50
Nos. 406-409 (4) 1.60 1.60

Sir Rowland Hill (1795-1879), originator of penny postage; UPU membership, centenary.

Tree Lizard A58

1980, Feb. 4 Litho. *Perf. 14*

410 A58 40c Tree frog .20 .20
411 A58 55c shown .35 .35
412 A58 $1 Crapaud .65 .65
413 A58 $2 Wood slave 1.25 1.25
Nos. 410-413 (4) 2.45 2.45

Marquis of Salisbury, 1817; Postmarks, 1838, London 1980 Emblem — A59

Ships or Planes, Stamps of Montserrat: 55c, H.S. 748, #349. #416, La Plata, 1901, type A4. #417, Lady Hawkins, 1929, #84. #418, Avon, 1843, Gt Britain #3. #419, Aeronca, #140.

1980, Apr. 14 Litho. *Perf. 14½*

414 A59 40c multicolored .20 .20
415 A59 55c multicolored .30 .30
416 A59 $1.20 multicolored .55 .60
417 A59 $1.20 multicolored .55 .60
418 A59 $1.20 multicolored .55 .60
419 A59 $1.20 multicolored .55 .60
a. Souvenir sheet of 6, #414-419 2.75 2.75
Nos. 414-419 (6) 2.70 2.90

London 1980 Intl. Stamp Exhib., May 6-14.
For surcharges see Nos. 736-740.

No. 352 Overprinted: 75th Anniversary of / Rotary International

1980, July 7 Litho. *Perf. 13½x14*

420 A44 $2.50 multicolored .90 .90

Discus Thrower, Stadium, Olympic Rings — A60

Flags of Host Countries: 40c, Greece, 1896; France, 1900; U.S., 1904. 55c, Great Britain, 1908; Sweden, 1912; Belgium, 1920. 70c, France, 1924; Netherlands, 1928; US, 1932. $1, Germany, 1936; Great Britain, 1948; Finland, 1952. $1.50, Australia, 1956; Italy, 1960; Japan, 1964. $2, Mexico, 1968,; Fed. Rep. of Germany, 1972; Canada, 1976.

1980, July 7 Litho. *Perf. 14*

421 A60 40c multicolored .20 .20
422 A60 55c multicolored .20 .20
423 A60 70c multicolored .30 .30
424 A60 $1 multicolored .40 .40
425 A60 $1.50 multicolored .50 .50
426 A60 $2 multicolored .70 .70
427 A60 $2.50 multicolored .90 .90
a. Souv. sheet of 7, #421-427 + 2 labels 3.50 3.50
Nos. 421-427 (7) 3.20 3.20

22nd Summer Olympic Games, Moscow, July 19-Aug. 3.

Lady Nelson, 1928 A61

1980 Litho. *Perf. 14*

428 A61 40c shown .20 .20
429 A61 55c Chignecto, 1913 .40 .40
430 A61 $1 Solent, 1878 .75 .75
431 A61 $2 Dee, 1841 1.40 1.40
Nos. 428-431 (4) 2.75 2.75

Plume Worm — A62

1980 Litho. *Perf. 14*

432 A62 40c shown .40 .40
433 A62 55c Sea fans .55 .55
434 A62 $2 Coral, sponges 1.40 1.40
Nos. 432-434 (3) 2.35 2.35

Nos. 340, 342, 345, 348 Surcharged

1980, Sept. 30 Litho. *Perf. 14*

435 A44 5c on 3c (#342) .20 .20
436 A44 35c on 1c (#340) .20 .20
437 A44 35c on 3c (#342) .20 .20
438 A44 35c on 15c (#345) .20 .20
439 A44 55c on 40c (#348) .20 .20
440 A44 $5 on 40c (#348) 1.25 1.40
Nos. 435-440 (6) 2.25 2.40

Zebra Butterfly — A63

Spadefish — A64

1981, Feb. 2 **Wmk. 373**

441 A63 50c shown .75 .50
442 A63 65c Tropical checkered skipper .90 .55
443 A63 $1.50 Large orange sulphur 1.10 1.00
444 A63 $2.50 Monarch 1.60 1.40
Nos. 441-444 (4) 4.35 3.45

Wmk. 373

1981, Mar. 20 **Litho.** ***Perf. 13½***

445 A64 5c shown .20 .25
446 A64 10c Hogfish .20 .25
447 A64 15c Creole wrasse .20 .25
448 A64 20c Yellow damselfish .20 .25
449 A64 25c Sergeant major .20 .25
450 A64 35c Clown wrasse .20 .25
451 A64 45c Schoolmaster .40 .40
452 A64 55c Striped parrotfish 1.25 1.25
453 A64 65c Bigeye .55 .55
454 A64 75c French grunt .60 .60
455 A64 $1 Rock beauty .85 .85
456 A64 $2 Blue chromis 1.75 1.75
457 A64 $3 Fairy basslet, blueheads 2.75 2.75
458 A64 $5 Cherubfish 4.25 4.25
459 A64 $7.50 Longspine squirrelfish 4.75 4.75
460 A64 $10 Longsnout butterflyfish 7.25 7.25
Nos. 445-460 (16) 25.60 25.90

For surcharges and overprints see Nos. 507-508, 511-512, 515, O45-O55, O95-O97.

Inscribed 1983

1983 **Wmk. 380**

445a A64 5c .30 .20
446a A64 10c .35 .20
449a A64 25c .40 .20
450a A64 35c .45 .30
454a A64 75c .65 .55
455a A64 $1 .85 .70
458a A64 $5 3.75 3.75
460a A64 $10 6.75 6.75
Nos. 445a-460a (8) 13.50 12.65

Fort St. George (National Trust) — A65

1981, May 18 **Wmk. 373** ***Perf. 13½***

461 A65 50c shown .20 .20
462 A65 65c Bird Sanctuary, Fox's Bay .25 .25
463 A65 $1.50 The Museum .55 .65
464 A65 $2.50 Bransby Point Battery 1.00 1.10
Nos. 461-464 (4) 2.00 2.20

Prince Charles, Lady Diana, Royal Yacht Charlotte A66

Prince Charles and Lady Diana — A67

Illustration A67 is reduced.

Wmk. 380

1981, July 13 **Litho.** ***Perf. 14***

465 A66 90c shown .40 .40
a. Booklet pane of 4, perf. 12 2.00
466 A67 90c shown 1.40 1.40
467 A66 $3 Portsmouth .95 .95
468 A67 $3 like #466 2.40 2.40
a. Booklet pane of 2, perf. 12 4.00
469 A66 $4 Britannia 1.25 1.25
470 A67 $4 like #466 2.75 2.75
Nos. 465-470 (6) 9.15 9.15

Royal wedding. Each denomination issued in sheets of 7 (6 type A66, 1 type A67).

For surcharges and overprints see Nos. 509-510, 513-514, 578-579, O56-O61.

Souvenir Sheet

1981, Dec. ***Perf. 12***

471 A67 $5 multicolored 2.50 2.50

50th Anniv. of Airmail Service A68

1981, Aug. 31 **Wmk. 373** ***Perf. 14***

472 A68 50c Seaplane, Dorsetshire .40 .40
473 A68 65c Beechcraft Twin Bonanza .50 .50
474 A68 $1.50 DeHaviland Dragon Rapide 1.00 1.00
475 A68 $2.50 Hawker Siddeley Avro 748 1.60 1.60
Nos. 472-475 (4) 3.50 3.50

Methodist Church, Bethel — A69

Christmas (Churches): 65c, St. George's Anglican, Harris. $1.50, St. Peter's Anglican, St. Peter's. $2.50, St. Patrick's Roman Catholic, Plymouth.

1981, Nov. 16 **Litho.** ***Perf. 14***

476 A69 50c multicolored .25 .25
477 A69 65c multicolored .35 .35
478 A69 $1.50 multicolored .55 .55
479 A69 $2.50 multicolored 1.00 1.00
a. Souvenir sheet of 4, #476-479 3.00 3.00
Nos. 476-479 (4) 2.15 2.15

Wild Flowers First Discovered on Montserrat — A70

1982, Jan. 18 **Litho.** ***Perf. 14½***

480 A70 50c Rondeletia buxifolia, vert. .20 .20
481 A70 65c Heliotropium ternatum .25 .25
482 A70 $1.50 Picramnia pentandra, vert. .55 .55
483 A70 $2.50 Diospyros revoluta 1.50 1.50
Nos. 480-483 (4) 2.50 2.50

350th Anniv. of Settlement of Montserrat by Sir Thomas Warner — A70a

Jubilee Type of 1932.

Wmk. 373

1982, Apr. 17 **Litho.** ***Perf. 14½***

483A A70a 40c green .20 .20
483B A70a 55c red .30 .30
483C A70a 65c brown .35 .35
483D A70a 75c gray .40 .40
483E A70a 85c ultra .50 .50
483F A70a 95c orange .55 .55
483G A70a $1 purple .60 .60
483H A70a $1.50 olive .85 .85
483I A70a $2 car rose 1.10 1.10
483J A70a $2.50 sepia 1.50 1.50
Nos. 483A-483J (10) 6.35 6.35

A70b

A71

1982, June **Wmk. 380** ***Perf. 14***

484 A70b 75c Catherine of Aragon, 1501 .30 .30
485 A70b $1 Aragon arms .30 .30
486 A70b $5 Diana 1.75 1.75
Nos. 484-486 (3) 2.35 2.35

21st birthday of Princess Diana, July 1.

For surcharges and overprints see Nos. 574, O62-O64.

1982, Sept. 13 **Litho.** ***Perf. 14***

487 A71 $1.50 Scout .85 .85
488 A71 $2.50 Baden-Powell 1.40 1.40

Scouting Year.

Christmas A72

1982, Nov. 18 **Wmk. 373** ***Perf. 14***

489 A72 35c Annunciation .20 .20
490 A72 75c Shepherds' vision .40 .40
491 A72 $1.50 Virgin and Child .70 .70
492 A72 $2.50 Flight into Egypt 1.25 1.25
Nos. 489-492 (4) 2.55 2.55

Dragonflies — A73

1983, Jan. 19 **Litho.** ***Perf. 13½x14***

493 A73 50c Lepthemis vesiculosa .50 .50
494 A73 65c Orthemis ferruginea .65 .65
495 A73 $1.50 Triacanthagyna trifida 1.40 1.40
496 A73 $2.50 Erythrodiplax umbrata 1.90 1.90
Nos. 493-496 (4) 4.45 4.45

Blue-headed Hummingbird A74

1983, May 24 **Wmk. 373** ***Perf. 14***

497 A74 35c shown .90 .90
498 A74 75c Green-throated carib 1.25 1.25
499 A74 $2 Antillean crested hummingbird 3.25 3.25
500 A74 $3 Purple-throated carib 4.50 4.50
Nos. 497-500 (4) 9.90 9.90

Arms — A75

1983, July 25 **Litho.** ***Perf. 14½***

501 A75 $12 red & black 5.00 *7.50*
502 A75 $30 blue & red 15.00 *20.00*

Manned Flight Bicentenary — A76

Designs: 35c, Montgolfiere, 1783, vert. 75c, De Havilland Twin Otter 310, 1981. $1.50, Lockheed Vega's around the world flight, 1933. $2, British R34 airship transatlantic flight, 1919.

1983, Sept. 19 **Litho.** ***Perf. 14***

503 A76 35c multicolored .25 .25
504 A76 75c multicolored .35 .35
505 A76 $1.50 multicolored .55 .55
506 A76 $2 multicolored .85 .85
a. Souvenir sheet of 4, #503-506 3.00 3.00
Nos. 503-506 (4) 2.00 2.00

For surcharges see Nos. 573, 577.

Nos. 449, 446, 467-468, 453-454, 469-470, 456 Surcharged

Wmk. 373 (A64), 380

1983, Aug. 15 **Litho.** ***Perf. 13½x14***

507 A64 40c on 25c multi .50 .50
508 A64 70c on 10c multi .80 .80
509 A66 70c on $3 multi .70 .70
510 A67 70c on $3 multi 1.60 1.60
511 A64 90c on 65c multi .90 .90
512 A64 $1.15 on 75c multi 1.10 1.10
513 A66 $1.15 on $4 multi .90 .90
514 A67 $1.15 on $4 multi 2.10 2.10
515 A64 $1.50 on $2 multi 1.40 1.40
Nos. 507-515 (9) 10.00 10.00

Christmas Carnival 1983 A77

1983, Nov. 18 **Wmk. 380** ***Perf. 14***

516 A77 55c Clowns .20 .20
517 A77 90c Star Bursts .25 .25
518 A77 $1.15 Flower Girls .40 .40
519 A77 $2 Masqueraders .65 .65
Nos. 516-519 (4) 1.50 1.50

See Nos. 547-550.

Nos. 503-506 were overprinted "INAUGURAL FLIGHT Montserrat — Nevis — St. Kitts." These exist on souvenir covers with first day cancel of Dec. 15, 1983. No announcement of this set was made nor were mint stamps generally available.

1984 Summer Olympics — A78

1984, Mar. 6 Litho. *Perf. 14*

520 A78 90c Discobolus .40 .40
521 A78 $1 Torch .50 .50
522 A78 $1.15 Stadium .55 .55
523 A78 $2.50 Flags .90 .90
a. Souvenir sheet of 4, #520-523 2.75 2.75
Nos. 520-523 (4) 2.35 2.35

Cattle Egret A79

1984, May 11

524 A79 5c shown .45 .35
525 A79 10c Carib grackles .45 .35
526 A79 15c Common gallinule .45 .35
527 A79 20c Brown boobys .60 .35
528 A79 25c Black-whiskered vireos .60 .50
529 A79 40c Scaly-breasted thrashers .90 .55
530 A79 55c Laughing gulls 1.10 .35
531 A79 70c Glossy ibis 1.40 .50
532 A79 90c Green heron 1.50 .70
533 A79 $1 Belted kingfisher 1.90 .90
534 A79 $1.15 Bananaquits 2.40 1.60
535 A79 $3 Sparrow hawks 5.00 *6.00*
536 A79 $5 Forest thrush 7.00 *8.00*
537 A79 $7.50 Black-crowned night heron 9.00 *14.50*
538 A79 $10 Bridled quail doves 10.50 *15.00*
Nos. 524-538 (15) 43.25 50.00

For surcharges see Nos. 651-655, 663-666.
For overprints see Nos. O65-O78.

Packet Boats A80

1984, July 9 Wmk. 380 *Perf. 14*

539 A80 55c Tagus, 1907 .30 .30
540 A80 90c Cobequid, 1913 .45 .45
541 A80 $1.15 Lady Drake, 1942 .55 .55
542 A80 $2 Factor, 1948 .90 .90
a. Souvenir sheet of 4, #539-542 4.00 4.00
Nos. 539-542 (4) 2.20 2.20

Marine Life A81

1984, Sept. Wmk. 380 *Perf. 14*

543 A81 90c Top shell & hermit crab 1.60 1.60
544 A81 $1.15 Rough file shell 2.00 2.00
545 A81 $1.50 True tulip snail 3.00 3.00
546 A81 $2.50 West Indian fighting conch 4.00 4.00
Nos. 543-546 (4) 10.60 10.60

Christmas Carnival Type of 1983

1984, Nov. 12

547 A77 55c Bull Man .65 .65
548 A77 $1.15 Masquerader Captain 1.60 1.60
549 A77 $1.50 Carnival Queen contestant 1.75 1.75
550 A77 $2.30 Contestant, diff. 2.75 2.75
Nos. 547-550 (4) 6.75 6.75

National Emblems — A82

Indigenous Orchids — A83

1985, Feb. 8 Litho. *Perf. 14*

551 A82 $1.15 Mango .30 *.60*
552 A82 $1.50 Lobster Claw .40 *.80*
553 A82 $3 Montserrat Oriole .60 *1.25*
Nos. 551-553 (3) 1.30 2.65

1985, May 9 Wmk. 380 *Perf. 14*

554 A83 90c Oncidium urophyllum .45 *.55*
555 A83 $1.15 Epidendrum difforme .45 *.60*
556 A83 $1.50 Epidendrum ciliare .50 *.65*
557 A83 $2.50 Brassavola cucullata .60 *.75*
a. Souvenir sheet of 4, #554-557 5.00 5.00
Nos. 554-557 (4) 2.00 2.55

Queen Mother, 85th Birthday — A84

#558a, 564a, Facing right. #558b, 564b, Facing forward. #559a, Facing right. #559b, Facing left. #560a, Facing right. #560b, Glancing right. #561a, 563a, Facing right. #561b, 563b, Facing left. #562a, Facing right. #562b, Facing forward.

1985-86 Unwmk. *Perf. 12½*

558 A84 55c Pair, #a.-b. .40 .40
559 A84 90c Pair, #a.-b. .70 .70
560 A84 $1.15 Pair, #a.-b. .80 .80
561 A84 $1.50 Pair, #a.-b. 1.10 1.10
Nos. 558-561 (4) 3.00 3.00

Souvenir Sheets of 2

562 A84 $2 #a.-b. 1.75 1.75
563 A84 $3.50 #a.-b. 3.50 3.50
564 A84 $6 #a.-b. 5.50 5.50

Issued: #563-564, 1/10/86; others, 8/7/85.
For surcharges see No. 575.

Cotton Industry A85

1985, Sept. 23 Unwmk. *Perf. 15*

569 A85 90c Cotton plants .20 *.30*
570 A85 $1 Carding .25 *.35*
571 A85 $1.15 Automated loom .25 *.35*
572 A85 $2.50 Hand loom .40 *.50*
a. Souvenir sheet of 4, #569-572 4.25 4.25
Nos. 569-572 (4) 1.10 1.50

Nos. 504, 485, 560, 505, 469-470 Ovptd. or Surcharged "CARIBBEAN ROYAL VISIT 1985" in 2 or 3 Lines

Perf. 14, 12½ ($1.15)
Wmk. as Before

1985, Nov. 14 Litho.

573 A76 75c multi 4.75 4.75
574 A70b $1 multi 6.75 6.75
575 A84 $1.15 Pair, #a.-b. 14.50 14.50
577 A76 $1.50 multi 9.25 9.25
578 A66 $1.60 on $4 multi 4.75 4.75
579 A67 $1.60 on $4 multi 16.00 16.00
Nos. 573-579 (6) 56.00 56.00

No. 579 surcharged but not overprinted.

Audubon Birth Bicentenary — A86

Illustrations of North American bird species by John J. Audubon: #580a, Black-throated blue warbler. #580b, Palm warbler. #581a, Bobolink. #581b, Lark sparrow. #582a, Chipping sparrow. #582b, Northern oriole. #583a, American goldfinch. #583b, Blue grosbeak.

1985, Nov. 29 Unwmk. *Perf. 12½*

580 A86 15c Pair, #a.-b. .20 .20
581 A86 30c Pair, #a.-b. .25 .25
582 A86 55c Pair, #a.-b. .40 .40
583 A86 $2.50 Pair, #a.-b. 1.40 1.40
Nos. 580-583 (4) 2.25 2.25

Christmas A87

1985, Dec. 2 Wmk. 380 *Perf. 15*

588 A87 70c Angel of the Lord .20 .20
589 A87 $1.15 Three wise men .35 .35
590 A87 $1.50 Caroling, Plymouth War Memorial .40 .40
591 A87 $2.30 Our Lady of Montserrat .70 .70
Nos. 588-591 (4) 1.65 1.65

A set of 8 stamps for the 1986 World Cup was printed but not issued. Stamps became available with the liquidation of the printer.

Girl Guides, 50th Anniv. — A88

#592a, Lord Baden-Powell. #592b, Guide giving oath. #593a, Lady Baden-Powell. #593b, Guide cutting hair. #594a, Lord and Lady Baden-Powell. #594b, Guides in public service. #595a, Troop inspection, 1936. #595b, Guides saluting.

1986, Apr. 11

592 A88 20c Pair, #a.-b. .20 .20
593 A88 75c Pair, #a.-b. .75 .75
594 A88 90c Pair, #a.-b. .85 .85
595 A88 $1.15 Pair, #a.-b. 1.10 1.10
Nos. 592-595 (4) 2.90 2.90

For overprints see Nos. 966-967.

Queen Elizabeth II, 60th Birthday — A89

Various portraits.

1986, Apr. 11 Unwmk. *Perf. 12½*

600 A89 10c multicolored .20 .20
601 A89 $1.50 multicolored .35 *.35*
602 A89 $3 multicolored .55 *.55*
603 A89 $6 multi, vert. .85 *.85*
Nos. 600-603 (4) 1.95 1.95

Souvenir Sheet

604 A89 $8 multicolored 5.00 5.00

Halley's Comet — A90

Designs: 35c, 40c, #613a, Bayeux Tapestry (detail), 1066 sighting. 50c, $1.75, #613b, Adoration of the Magi, by Giotto. 70c, $2, #613c, Edmond Halley, trajectory diagram, 1531 sighting. $1, $3, #613d, Sightings, 1066 and 1910. $1.15, 55c, #614a, Sighting, 1910. $1.50, 60c, #614b, Giotto space probe, comet, diagram. $2.30, 80c, #614c, U.S. Space Telescope, comet. $4, $5, #614d, Computer picture of photograph, 1910.

1986 *Perf. 14*

605-612 A90 Set of 8 4.50 4.50

Souvenir Sheets

613 A90 Sheet of 4, #a.-d. 3.00 3.00
614 A90 Sheet of 4, #a.-d. 3.00 3.00

Issued: #613-614, 10/10; others, 5/9.
For overprints see Nos. 656-657.

A91

Wedding of Prince Andrew and Sarah Ferguson — A92

No. 615: a, Andrew, vert. b, Sarah, vert.
No. 616: a, Andrew wearing cowboy hat. b, Sarah wearing fur hat.

1986 Litho. *Perf. 12½x13, 13x12½*

615 A91 70c Pair, #a.-b. .70 .70
616 A91 $2 Pair, #a.-b 1.00 1.00
c. Souvenir booklet 5.00

Souvenir Sheet

617 A92 $10 multicolored 5.00 5.00

#616c contains 2 imperf panes. One pane contains 2 #615; the other 2 #616.
Issued: #617, 10/15; others, 7/23.
For overprints see Nos. 628-629.

Clipper Ships A93

1986, Aug. 29 *Perf. 14*

618 A93 90c Antelope, 1793 1.90 1.25
619 A93 $1.15 Montagu, 1840 3.00 3.00
620 A93 $1.50 Little Catherine, 1813 3.25 3.25
621 A93 $2.30 Hinchingbrook, 1813 4.25 4.75
a. Souvenir sheet of 4, #618-621 12.00 12.00
Nos. 618-621 (4) 12.40 12.25

Communications — A94

Designs: 70c, Radio Montserrat, near Dagenham. $1.15, Radio Gem ZGM-FM 94, Plymouth. $1.50, Radio Antilles, O'Garro's, $2.30, Cable & Wireless telegraph office, Plymouth.

1986, Sept. 29 Wmk. 380 *Perf. 14*

622 A94 70c multicolored 1.10 .65
623 A94 $1.15 multicolored 1.60 1.25
624 A94 $1.50 multicolored 1.90 1.90
625 A94 $2.30 multicolored 2.40 *3.00*
Nos. 622-625 (4) 7.00 6.80

Nos. 615-616 Ovptd. in Silver "Congratulations to T.R.H. The Duke & Duchess of York"

Perf. 12½x13, 13x12½

1986, Nov. 14 Litho.

628 A91 70c Pair, #a.-b. 1.75 1.75
629 A91 $2 Pair, #a.-b. 4.00 4.00

Christmas — A95

1986, Dec. 12 Unwmk. *Perf. 14*

632 A95 70c Christmas rose .85 .85
633 A95 $1.15 Candle flower 1.40 1.40
634 A95 $1.50 Christmas tree kalanchoe 2.00 2.00
635 A95 $2.30 Snow on the mountain 3.00 *3.50*
a. Souvenir sheet of 4, #632-635, perf. 12x12½ 11.00 11.00
Nos. 632-635 (4) 7.25 7.75

Souvenir Sheets

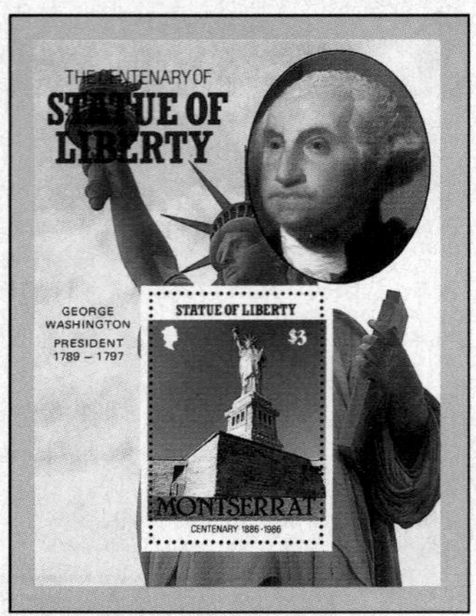

Statue of Liberty, Cent. — A96

1986, Nov. 18 Litho. *Perf. 14*

636 A96 $3 Statue, pedestal 2.00 2.00
637 A96 $4.50 Head 2.75 2.75
638 A96 $5 Statue, NYC 3.25 3.25
Nos. 636-638 (3) 8.00 8.00

Sailing A97

1986, Dec. 10 *Perf. 15*

639 A97 70c shown .50 .50
640 A97 $1.15 Golf .75 *1.00*
641 A97 $1.50 Plymouth Public Market .75 *1.00*
642 A97 $2.30 Air Studios 1.50 *2.00*
Nos. 639-642 (4) 3.50 4.50

For surcharge see No. B3.

Sharks A98

1987, Feb. 2 Wmk. 380 *Perf. 14*

643 A98 40c Tiger 1.75 .50
644 A98 90c Lemon 3.00 1.25
645 A98 $1.15 White 3.50 2.00
646 A98 $3.50 Whale 7.00 *8.50*
a. Souvenir sheet of 4, #643-646, perf. 12½x12 16.00 16.00
Nos. 643-646 (4) 15.25 12.25

Butterflies A99

1987, Aug. 10 Wmk. 380 *Perf. 14*

647 A99 90c Straight-line sulpher 2.25 2.25
648 A99 $1.15 Red rim 3.00 3.00
649 A99 $1.50 Hammock skipper 3.75 3.75
650 A99 $2.50 Mimic 6.00 6.00
Nos. 647-650 (4) 15.00 15.00

Nos. 531, 527, 525, 532 and 535 Surcharged

1987, Apr. 6

651 A79 5c on 70c multi .65 .95
652 A79 $1 on 20c multi 2.10 .95
653 A79 $1.15 on 10c multi 2.50 1.60
654 A79 $1.50 on 90c multi 3.00 2.25
655 A79 $2.30 on $3 multi 4.25 *5.25*
Nos. 651-655 (5) 12.50 11.00

Nos. 613-614 Ovptd. for CAPEX '87 in Red and Black
Souvenir Sheets of 4

1987, June 13 Unwmk.

656 A90 #a.-d. 3.25 3.25
657 A90 #a.-d. 3.25 3.25

Orchids — A100

1987, Nov. 13 Unwmk. *Perf. 14*

658 A100 90c Oncidium variegatum, vert. .90 .90
659 A100 $1.15 Vanilla planifolia 1.10 1.10
660 A100 $1.50 Gongora quinquenervis, vert. 1.50 1.50
661 A100 $3.50 Brassavola nodosa 3.75 3.75
Nos. 658-661 (4) 7.25 7.25

Souvenir Sheet

662 A100 $5 Oncidium lanceanum 15.00 15.00

Christmas.

Nos. 525, 528-529 and 532 Surcharged "40th Wedding Anniversary / HM Queen Elizabeth II / HRH Duke of Edinburgh / November 1987." and New Value

Wmk. 380

1987, Nov. 20 Litho. *Perf. 14*

663 A79 5c on 90c No. 532 .55 .55
664 A79 $1.15 on 10c No. 525 .70 .70
665 A79 $2.30 on 25c No. 528 1.60 1.60
666 A79 $5 on 40c No. 529 3.25 3.25
Nos. 663-666 (4) 6.10 6.10

Exists spelled "Edingburgh." Value, set $35.

Tropical Bats — A101

Marine Birds — A102

1988, Feb. 8 Wmk. 380 *Perf. 14*

667 A101 55c Free-tailed bat 1.00 1.00
668 A101 90c Fruit bat 1.75 1.75
669 A101 $1.15 Fisherman bat 2.25 2.25
670 A101 $2.30 Fruit bat, diff. 4.50 4.50
Nos. 667-670 (4) 9.50 9.50

Souvenir Sheet

671 A101 $2.50 Funnel-eared bat 10.00 10.00

1988, Apr. 2 Unwmk.

672 A102 90c Magnificent frigatebird 1.00 1.00
673 A102 $1.15 Caribbean elaenia 1.25 1.25
674 A102 $1.50 Glossy ibis 1.50 1.50
675 A102 $3.50 Purple-throated carib 3.25 3.25
Nos. 672-675 (4) 7.00 7.00

Souvenir Sheet

676 A102 $5 Brown pelican 5.50 5.50

Easter.

1988 Summer Olympics, Seoul — A103

Eastern architecture and events: 90c, Women's discus. $1.15, High jump. $3.50, Women's 200-meter and Seoul university building. $5, Single scull rowing, pagoda.

Unwmk.

1988, July 29 Litho. *Perf. 14*

677 A103 90c multicolored .95 .95
678 A103 $1.15 multicolored 1.00 1.00
679 A103 $3.50 multicolored 3.25 3.25
Nos. 677-679 (3) 5.20 5.20

Souvenir Sheet

680 A103 $5 multicolored 5.25 5.25

Sea Shells A104

1988, Aug. 30

681 A104 5c Golden tulip .20 .25
682 A104 10c Little knobby scallop .20 .25
683 A104 15c Sozoni's cone .20 .25
684 A104 20c Globular coral shell .20 .25
685 A104 25c Sundial .20 .25
686 A104 40c King helmet .40 .45
687 A104 55c Channeled turban .50 .60
688 A104 70c True tulip shell .65 .75
689 A104 90c Music volute .85 1.00
690 A104 $1 Flame auger .90 1.10
691 A104 $1.15 Rooster-tail conch 1.10 1.40
692 A104 $1.50 Queen conch 1.40 1.75
693 A104 $3 Teramachi's slit shell 3.25 3.50
694 A104 $5 Florida crown conch 4.50 5.50
695 A104 $7.50 Beau's murex 7.00 8.50
696 A104 $10 Triton's trumpet 9.75 11.50
Nos. 681-696 (16) 31.30 37.30

For surcharges see Nos. 698-701, 767-770. For overprints see Nos. O79-O94.

University of the West Indies, 40th Anniv. — A105

1988, Oct. 4 Litho. *Perf. 14*

697 A105 $5 multicolored 4.00 4.00

Nos. 687, 690, 693 and 694 Surcharged

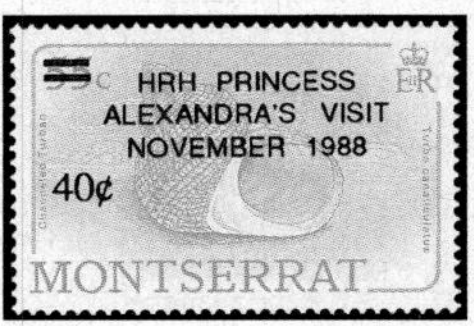

Unwmk.

1988, Nov. 4 Litho. *Perf. 14*

698 A104 40c on 55c No. 687 .40 .40
699 A104 90c on $1 No. 690 1.00 1.00
700 A104 $1.15 on $3 No. 693 1.25 1.25
701 A104 $1.50 on $5 No. 694 1.75 1.75
Nos. 698-701 (4) 4.40 4.40

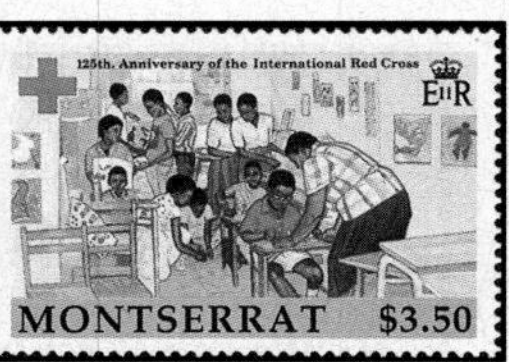

Intl. Red Cross, 125th Anniv. A106

1988, Dec. 16

702 A106 $3.50 multicolored 2.00 2.00

Christmas — A107

Birds.

1988, Nov. 28 *Perf. 14x13½*

703 A107 90c Spotted sandpiper .90 .90
704 A107 $1.15 Ruddy turnstone 1.10 1.10
705 A107 $3.50 Red-footed booby 3.50 3.50
Nos. 703-705 (3) 5.50 5.50

Souvenir Sheet

Perf. 13½x14

706 A107 $5 Aububon's shearwater 5.75 5.75

Uniforms A108

1989, Feb. 24 Litho. *Perf. 14*

707 A108 90c Drum major 1.10 1.10
708 A108 $1.15 Fatigue clothing 1.25 1.25
709 A108 $1.50 Khaki uniform 1.60 1.60
710 A108 $3.50 Dress uniform 4.25 4.25
Nos. 707-710 (4) 8.20 8.20

Souvenir Sheet

711 A108 $5 Cadet (girl), woman 6.25 6.25

Defense Force, 75th anniv.

Easter Lilies A109

1989, Mar. 21 **Litho.** ***Perf. 14***

712 A109 90c Amazon .75 .75
713 A109 $1.15 Salmon blood, vert. .90 .90
714 A109 $1.50 Amaryllis, vert. 1.10 1.10
715 A109 $3.50 Amaryllis, diff., vert. 3.00 3.00
Nos. 712-715 (4) 5.75 5.75

Souvenir Sheet

716 A109 $5 Resurrection, vert. 7.25 7.25

Ships Built in Montserrat — A110

Designs: 90c, Schooner Morning Prince, 1942-1948. $1.15, Cargo boat Western Sun. $1.50, Cargo boat Kim G under construction. $3.50, Cargo and passenger boat MV Romaris.

1989, June 30 **Litho.** ***Perf. 13½x14***

717 A110 90c multicolored 1.40 1.40
718 A110 $1.15 multicolored 1.60 1.60
719 A110 $1.50 multicolored 2.10 2.10
720 A110 $3.50 multicolored 5.00 5.00
Nos. 717-720 (4) 10.10 10.10

For surcharges see Nos. B1-B2.

Making of the Film *The Wizard of Oz*, 50th Anniv. — A111

1989, Sept. 22 **Litho.** ***Perf. 14***

721 A111 90c Scarecrow .70 .70
722 A111 $1.15 Cowardly Lion .80 .80
723 A111 $1.50 Tin Man 1.10 1.10
724 A111 $3.50 Dorothy 2.50 2.50
Nos. 721-724 (4) 5.10 5.10

Souvenir Sheet

725 A111 $5 shown 5.00 5.00

Nos. 721-724 vert.

1st Moon Landing, 20th Anniv. — A112

Designs: $1.15, Armstrong on ladder, descending from lunar module. $1.50, Eagle, astronaut on lunar surface. $3.50, Recovery of command module after splashdown. $5, Astronaut on the Moon, vert.

Perf. 13½x14, 14x13½

1989, Dec. 19 **Litho.**

726 A112 90c shown .60 .60
727 A112 $1.15 multicolored .75 .75
728 A112 $1.50 multicolored 1.00 1.00
729 A112 $3.50 multicolored 2.10 2.10
Nos. 726-729 (4) 4.45 4.45

Souvenir Sheet

730 A112 $5 multicolored 7.25 7.25

For overprints see Nos. 847-850.

World War II Battle Ships A113

1990, Feb. 12 **Litho.** ***Perf. 14***

731 A113 70c I.J.N. Yamato 2.25 2.25
732 A113 $1.15 USS Arizona 4.25 4.25
733 A113 $1.50 K.M. Bismarck on fire 5.50 5.50
734 A113 $3.50 HMS Hood 12.50 12.50
Nos. 731-734 (4) 24.50 24.50

Souvenir Sheet

735 A113 $5 K.M. Bismarck, map 20.00 20.00

Nos. 414-418 Surcharged in Bright Rose Lilac

1990, May 3 ***Perf. 14½***

736 A59 70c on 40c #414 1.10 1.10
737 A59 90c on 55c #415 1.40 1.40
738 A59 $1 on $1.20 #416 1.50 1.50
739 A59 $1.15 on $1.20 #417 1.75 1.75
740 A59 $1.50 on $1.20 #418 2.25 2.25
Nos. 736-740 (5) 8.00 8.00

Stamp World London '90.

Penny Black, 150th Anniv. A114

Designs: 90c, Montserrat #5, General P.O. $1.15, Montserrat #1, postal workers sorting mail, vert. $1.50, Great Britain #1, man and woman mailing letters, vert. $3.50, Great Britain #2, mailman delivering to residence. $5, Chateau Barrack cover of 1836, Great Britain #1, landscape.

1990, June 1 ***Perf. 13½x14, 14x13½***

741 A114 90c shown 1.25 1.25
742 A114 $1.15 multicolored 1.60 1.60
743 A114 $1.50 multicolored 1.90 1.90
744 A114 $3.50 multicolored 4.50 4.50
Nos. 741-744 (4) 9.25 9.25

Souvenir Sheet

745 A114 $5 multicolored 10.00 10.00

Stained-glass Windows — A115

1990, Apr. 12 **Litho.** ***Perf. 14x15***

746 A115 Strip of 3 7.00 7.00
a. $1.15 The Empty Tomb 1.25 1.25
b. $1.50 The Ascension 1.75 1.75
c. $3.50 Risen Christ with Disciples 3.75 3.75

Souvenir Sheet

747 A115 $5 The Crucifixion 7.50 7.50

World Cup Soccer Championships, Italy — A116

Designs: 90c, Montserrat vs. Antigua. $1.15, U.S. vs. Trinidad. $1.50, Montserrat team. $3.50, West Germany vs. Wales. $5, World Cup trophy.

1990, July 8 **Litho.** ***Perf. 14***

748 A116 90c multicolored .90 .90
749 A116 $1.15 multicolored 1.25 1.25
750 A116 $1.50 multicolored 1.60 1.60
751 A116 $3.50 multicolored 3.75 3.75
Nos. 748-751 (4) 7.50 7.50

Souvenir Sheet

752 A116 $5 multicolored 8.50 8.50

Spinner Dolphin A117

1990, Sept. 25 **Litho.** ***Perf. 14***

753 A117 90c shown 2.10 1.10
754 A117 $1.15 Common dolphin 2.50 1.60
755 A117 $1.50 Striped dolphin 3.50 3.25
756 A117 $3.50 Atlantic spotted dolphin 5.75 6.25
Nos. 753-756 (4) 13.85 12.20

Souvenir Sheet

757 A117 $5 Atlantic white-sided dolphin 15.00 12.00

Fish A118

1991, Feb. 7 **Litho.** ***Perf. 14***

758 A118 90c Spotted goatfish 1.75 1.75
759 A118 $1.15 Cushion star-fish 2.25 2.25
760 A118 $1.50 Rock beuaty 3.00 3.00
761 A118 $3.50 French grunt 6.50 6.50
Nos. 758-761 (4) 13.50 13.50

Souvenir Sheet

762 A118 $5 Trunkfish 14.00 14.00

For surcharges and overprints see Nos. O98-O99, O104, O107.

Birds A119

1991, Apr. 17 **Litho.** ***Perf. 14***

763 A119 90c Duck .95 .95
764 A119 $1.15 Hen, chicks 1.25 1.25
765 A119 $1.50 Rooster 1.50 1.50
766 A119 $3.50 Helmeted guinea fowl 3.50 3.50
Nos. 763-766 (4) 7.20 7.20

For surcharges and overprints see Nos. O100, O102, O105, O108.

Nos. 684-685, 692, 695 Surcharged

1991 **Litho.** ***Perf. 14***

767 A104 5c on 20c #684 .35 .35
768 A104 5c on 25c #685 .35 .35
769 A104 $1.15 on $1.50 #692 4.25 4.25
770 A104 $1.15 on $7.50 #695 4.25 4.25
Nos. 767-770 (4) 9.20 9.20

Mushrooms A120

Lilies — A121

1991, June 13 **Litho.** ***Perf. 14***

771 A120 90c Panaeolus antillarum 1.50 1.50
772 A120 $1.15 Cantharellus cinnabarinus 1.90 1.90
773 A120 $1.50 Gymnopilus chrysopellus 2.50 2.50
774 A120 $2 Psilocybe cubensis 3.50 3.50
775 A120 $3.50 Leptonia caeruleo-capitata 5.75 5.75
Nos. 771-775 (5) 15.15 15.15

1991, Aug. 8

776 A121 90c Red water lily .90 .90
777 A121 $1.15 Shell ginger 1.10 1.10
778 A121 $1.50 Early day lily 1.40 1.40
779 A121 $3.50 Anthurium 3.50 3.50
Nos. 776-779 (4) 6.90 6.90

For surcharges and overprints see Nos. O101, O103, O106, O109.

Frogs and Toads — A122

1991, Oct. 9 **Litho.** ***Perf. 14***

780 A122 $1.15 Tree frog 2.75 2.75
781 A122 $2 Crapaud toad 5.00 5.00
782 A122 $3.50 Mountain chicken 8.00 8.00
Nos. 780-782 (3) 15.75 15.75

Souvenir Sheet

Perf. 14½x14

783 A122 $5 Sheet of 1 12.00 12.00

No. 783 contains one 81x48mm stamp that incorporates designs of Nos. 780-782.

Cats A123

1991, Dec. 5

784 A123 90c Black British shorthair 1.50 1.50
785 A123 $1.15 Seal point siamese 1.90 1.90
786 A123 $1.50 Silver tabby persian 2.50 2.50
787 A123 $2.50 Birman temple cat 4.00 4.00
788 A123 $3.50 Egyptian mau 5.50 5.50
Nos. 784-788 (5) 15.40 15.40

Discovery of America, 500th Anniv. A124

No. 789: a, $1.50, Navigating instruments. b, $1.50, Coat of arms, Columbus. c, $1.50, Columbus, Bahamian natives. d, $1.50, Queen Isabella, Columbus with petition. e, $1.50, Exotic birds. f, $1.50, Exotic plants. g, $3.00, Santa Maria, Nina & Pinta.

1992, Jan. 16 Litho. *Perf. 14*

789 A124 Sheet of 7, #a.-g. 17.50 17.50

No. 789g is 85x28mm. See No. 829.

Dinosaurs A125

1992, Aug. 1 Litho. *Perf. 14*

790 A125 $1 Tyrannosaurus 2.10 2.10
791 A125 $1.15 Diplodocus 2.40 2.40
792 A125 $1.50 Apatosaurus 3.00 3.00
793 A125 $3.45 Dimetrodon 7.00 7.00
Nos. 790-793 (4) 14.50 14.50

Souvenir Sheet

794 A125 $4.60 Owen with bone, vert. 12.50 12.50

Sir Richard Owen, cent. of death.

1992 Summer Olympics, Barcelona A126

1992, Apr. 10

795 A126 $1 Torch bearer 1.25 1.25
796 A126 $1.15 Flags 1.50 1.50
797 A126 $2.30 Olympic flame, map 2.75 2.75
798 A126 $3.60 Various events 4.50 4.50
Nos. 795-798 (4) 10.00 10.00

Montserrat Oriole — A127

1992, June 30 Litho. *Perf. 13½x14*

799 A127 $1 Male 1.50 1.50
800 A127 $1.15 Male, female 1.75 1.75
801 A127 $1.50 Female feeding chicks 2.25 2.25
802 A127 $3.60 Map, male 5.50 5.50
Nos. 799-802 (4) 11.00 11.00

Insects A128

1992, Aug. 20 Litho. *Perf. 15x14*

803 A128 5c Grasshopper .20 .20
804 A128 10c Field cricket .20 .20
805 A128 15c Dragonfly .20 .20
806 A128 20c Red skimmer .20 .20
807 A128 25c Pond skater .20 .20
808 A128 40c Leaf weevil .35 .40
809 A128 55c Leaf cutter ants .45 .50
810 A128 70c Paper wasp .60 .65
811 A128 90c Bee fly .80 .90
812 A128 $1 Lacewing .95 1.00
813 A128 $1.15 Orange-barred sulphur 1.00 1.10
814 A128 $1.50 Painted lady 1.25 1.40
815 A128 $3 Bella moth 2.50 3.00
816 A128 $5 Plume moth 4.25 4.75
817 A128 $7.50 White peacock 6.50 7.25
818 A128 $10 Postman 8.75 9.75
Nos. 803-818 (16) 28.40 31.70

For overprints see #871-872, O110-O125.

A used example of No. 806 with a 10c surcharge was shown to the editors, but Montserrat Postal officials were unable to provide any information about it stating "this was prior to the appointment of the present manager." The editors would like to receive information from any knowledgeable source about this stamp and the possible existence of other similar surcharges.

Christmas — A129

Designs: $1.15, Adoration of the Magi. $4.60, Angel appearing before shepherds.

1992, Nov. 26 Litho. *Perf. 13½x14*

819 A129 $1.15 multicolored 1.75 1.75
820 A129 $4.60 multicolored 7.00 7.00

Coins and Bank Notes — A130

Designs: $1, One-dollar coin, twenty-dollar notes. $1.15, Ten-cent, twenty-five cent coins, ten-dollar notes. $1.50, Five-cent coin, five-dollar notes. $3.60, One-cent, two-cent coins, one-dollar notes.

1993, Feb. 10 *Perf. 14x13½*

821 A130 $1 multicolored 1.50 1.50
822 A130 $1.15 multicolored 1.60 1.60
823 A130 $1.50 multicolored 2.10 2.10
824 A130 $3.60 multicolored 5.25 5.25
Nos. 821-824 (4) 10.45 10.45

Discovery of America, 500th Anniv. (in 1992) — A131

1993, Mar. 10 Litho. *Perf. 14*

825 A131 $1 Coming ashore 2.25 2.25
826 A131 $2 Natives, ships 4.25 4.25

Organization of East Caribbean States.

Coronation of Queen Elizabeth II, 40th Anniv. — A132

Designs: $1.15, Queen, M.H. Bramble. $4.60, Queen riding in Gold State Coach.

1993, June 2 *Perf. 13½x14*

827 A132 $1.15 multicolored 1.50 1.50
828 A132 $4.60 multicolored 5.50 5.50

Columbus Type of 1992 with Added Text

No. 829: a, $1.15, like #789a. b, $1.15, like #789b. c, $1.15, like #789c. d, $1.50, like #789d. e, $1.50, like #789e. f, $1.50, like #789f. g, $3.45, like #789g.

1993, Sept. 7 Litho. *Perf. 14*

829 A124 Sheet of 7, #a.-g. 25.00 25.00

Nos. 829a-829g each have different added text.

Royal Air Force, 75th Anniv.
Common Design Type

Designs: 15c, Boeing Sentry, 1993. 55c, Vickers Valiant, 1962. $1.15, Handley Page Hastings, 1958. $3, 1943 Lockheed Ventura, 1943.

No. 834: a, Felixstowe F5, 1921. b, Armstrong Whitworth Atlas, 1934. c, Fairey Gordon, 1935. d, Boulton Paul Overstrand, 1936.

Wmk. 373

1993, Nov. 17 Litho. *Perf. 14*

830 CD350 15c multicolored .20 .20
831 CD350 55c multicolored .70 .70
832 CD350 $1.15 multicolored 1.60 1.60
833 CD350 $3 multicolored 4.25 4.25
Nos. 830-833 (4) 6.75 6.75

Souvenir Sheet

834 CD350 $1.50 Sheet of 4, #a.-d. 7.25 7.25

Beetles A133

Perf. 15x14

1994, Jan. 21 Litho. Unwmk.

835 A133 $1 Ground beetle 1.25 1.25
836 A133 $1.15 Click beetle 1.60 1.60
837 A133 $1.50 Harlequin beetle 1.90 1.90
838 A133 $3.45 Leaf beetle 4.50 4.50
Nos. 835-838 (4) 9.25 9.25

Souvenir Sheet

839 A133 $4.50 Scarab beetle 5.75 5.75

Hibiscus Flowers and Fruits — A134

Designs: 90c, Cotton. $1.15, Sorrel. $1.50, Okra. $3.50, Hibiscus rosa sinensis.

1994, Mar. 22 Litho. *Perf. 14x13½*

840 A134 90c multicolored 1.25 1.25
841 A134 $1.15 multicolored 1.60 1.60
842 A134 $1.50 multicolored 2.00 2.00
843 A134 $3.50 multicolored 5.00 5.00
Nos. 840-843 (4) 9.85 9.85

Aquatic Dinosaurs A135

No. 844: a, $1, Elasmosaurus. b, $1.15, Plesiosaurus. c, $1.50, Nothosaurus. d, $3.45, Mosasaurus.

1994, May 6 Litho. *Perf. 15x14*

844 A135 Strip of 4, #a.-d. 12.50 12.50

1994 World Cup Soccer Championships, U.S. — A136

No. 845: a, 90c, Montserrat youth soccer. b, $1, 1990 World Cup, US vs. England. c, $1.15, Rose Bowl Stadium, Pasadena, Calif., US. d, $3.45, German team, 1990 World Cup Winners.

No. 846: a, Jules Rimet. b, Bobby Moore, England Team Captain, 1966. c, Lew Jaschin. d, Sepp Herberger, German trainer.

1994, May 20 *Perf. 14*

845 A136 Vert. strip of 4, #a.-d. 10.00 10.00

Souvenir Sheet
Perf. 14x14½

846 A136 $2 Sheet of 4, #a.-d. 11.00 11.00

No. 845 printed in sheets of 2 strips + 4 labels.

Nos. 726-729 Ovptd. in Red or Surcharged in Red and Black

Inscribed "Space Anniversaries" and: 40c, "Yuri Gagarin / First man in space / April 12, 1961." $1.15, "First Joint US / Soviet Mission / July 15, 1975." $1.50, "25th Anniversary / First Moon Landing / Apollo XI-July 20, 1994." $2.30, "Columbia / First Space Shuttle / April 12, 1981."

1994, July 20 *Perf. 13½x14*

847 A112 40c on 90c multi .75 .75
848 A112 $1.15 multi 3.00 3.00
849 A112 $1.50 multi 3.50 3.50
850 A112 $2.30 on $3.50 multi 5.75 5.75
Nos. 847-850 (4) 13.00 13.00

Obliterator on Nos. 847, 850 is black.

Woodstock Festival, 25th Anniv. A137

1994, Oct. 20 *Perf. 12½*

851 A137 $1.15 1969 Poster 1.60 1.60
852 A137 $1.50 1994 Poster 1.75 1.75

Souvenir Sheets

853 A137 $4.50 like #851 6.00 6.00
854 A137 $4.50 like #852 6.00 6.00

Sea Vegetation A138

1995, Feb. 14 *Perf. 14x15*

855 A138 $1 Sea fan .85 .85
856 A138 $1.15 Sea lily 1.00 1.00
857 A138 $1.50 Sea pen 1.40 1.40
858 A138 $3.45 Sea fern 3.25 3.25
Nos. 855-858 (4) 6.50 6.50

Souvenir Sheet

859 A138 $4.50 Sea rose 4.50 4.50

Motion Pictures, Cent. A139

No. 860: a.-i., Various portraits of Marilyn Monroe.
$6, Marilyn Monroe & Elvis Presley.

1995, June 13 Litho. *Perf. 12½*

860	A139	$1.15	Sheet of 9, #a-i	12.00	12.00

Souvenir Sheet

861	A139	$6	multicolored	7.50	7.50

No. 861 contains one 51x57mm stamp.

1995 IAAF World Track & Field Championships, Gothenburg, Sweden — A140

No. 862: a, Jesse Owens, U.S. b, Eric Lemming, Sweden. c, Rudolf Harbig, Germany. d, Montserrat youth.

1995, Aug. 3 *Perf. 14*

862	A140	$1.50	Sheet of 4, #a-d	7.50	7.50

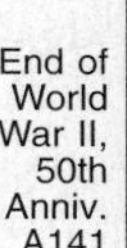

End of World War II, 50th Anniv. A141

No. 863: a, Atmospheric sounding experiments using V-2 rockets. b, Space Shuttle Challenger.
No. 864: a, 1st successful nuclear reactor. b, Calder Hall Atomic Power Station, England.
No. 865: a, Ju88G-7a nightfighter equipped with SN2 radar. b, NATO Boeing E6 AWACS.
No. 866: a, Gloster Meteor III jet aircraft. b, British Airways Concorde.

1995, Aug. 15

863	A141	$1.15	Pair, #a.-b.	3.00	3.00
864	A141	$1.15	Pair, #a.-b.	3.00	3.00
865	A141	$1.50	Pair, #a.-b.	4.25	4.25
866	A141	$1.50	Pair, #a.-b.	4.25	4.25
			Nos. 863-866 (4)	14.50	14.50

Nos. 812, 818 Ovptd.

1995 Litho. *Perf. 15x14*

871	A128	$1	multicolored	1.00	1.00
872	A128	$10	multicolored	10.50	10.50

UN, 50th Anniv. — A142

1995, Sept. 4 Litho. *Perf. 14*

873	A142	$1.15	Food	1.25	1.25
874	A142	$1.50	Education	1.50	1.50
875	A142	$2.30	Health	2.50	2.50
876	A142	$3	Peace	3.25	3.25
			Nos. 873-876 (4)	8.50	8.50

Souvenir Sheet

877	A142	$6	Justice	7.00	7.00

Natl. Trust, 25th Anniv. A143

Designs: $1.15, Headquarters building. $1.50, 17th cent. cannon, Bransby Point. $2.30, Painting of original Galways sugar mill, vert. $3, Great Alps Falls, vert.

1995, Nov. 15 Litho. *Perf. 14*

878-881	A143		Set of 4	12.50	12.50

Scavengers of the Sea — A144

1996, Feb. 14 Litho. *Perf. 15x14*

882	A144	$1	Bull shark	1.10	1.10
883	A144	$1.15	Sea mouse	1.25	1.25
884	A144	$1.50	Bristleworm	1.60	1.60
885	A144	$3.45	Prawn xiphocaris	3.75	3.75
			Nos. 882-885 (4)	7.70	7.70

Souvenir Sheet

886	A144	$4.50	Man o'war	6.00	6.00

Radio, Cent. (in 1995) A145

Designs: $1.15, Guglielmo Marconi, transmitting equipment, 1901. $1.50, Wireless laboratory, Marconi's yacht, Elettra. $2.30, First transatlantic radio message, Newfoundland, 1901. $3, First air/ground radio station, Croydon, 1920.
$4.50, First radio telescope, Jodrell Bank, Cheshire, England.

1996, Mar. 19 Litho. *Perf. 14*

887-890	A145		Set of 4	8.50	8.50

Souvenir Sheet

891	A145	$4.50	multi	5.25	5.25

1996 Summer Olympic Games, Atlanta A146

1896 Medalists: $1.15, Paul Masson, cycling. $1.50, Robert Garrett, discus. $2.30, Spiridon Louis, marathon. $3, John Boland, tennis.

1996, June 24 Litho. *Perf. 14*

892-895	A146		Set of 4	7.50	7.50

Mythical Creatures — A147

1996, Aug. 15 Litho. *Perf. 14*

896	A147	5c	Leprechaun	.20	.20
897	A147	10c	Pegasus	.20	.20
898	A147	15c	Griffin	.20	.20
899	A147	20c	Unicorn	.20	.20
900	A147	25c	Gnome	.20	.20
901	A147	40c	Mermaid	.30	.30
902	A147	55c	Cockatrice	.40	.40
903	A147	70c	Fairy	.55	.55
904	A147	90c	Goblin	.70	.70
905	A147	$1	Faun	.75	.75
906	A147	$1.15	Dragon	.90	.90
907	A147	$1.50	Giant	1.10	1.10
908	A147	$3	Elf	2.25	2.25
909	A147	$5	Centaur	3.75	3.75
910	A147	$7.50	Phoenix	5.75	5.75
911	A147	$10	Erin	7.50	7.50
			Nos. 896-911 (16)	24.95	24.95

For overprints see Nos. O126-O140.

James Dean (1931-55), Actor — A148

Various portraits.

1996, June 28 Litho. *Perf. 12½*

912	A148	$1.15	Sheet of 9, #a.-i.	11.50	11.50

Souvenir Sheet

913	A148	$6	multicolored	7.50	7.50

No. 913 contains one 51x57mm stamp.
For overprint see No. 921.

Dancing Bears, Emblem of "The Grateful Dead" — A149

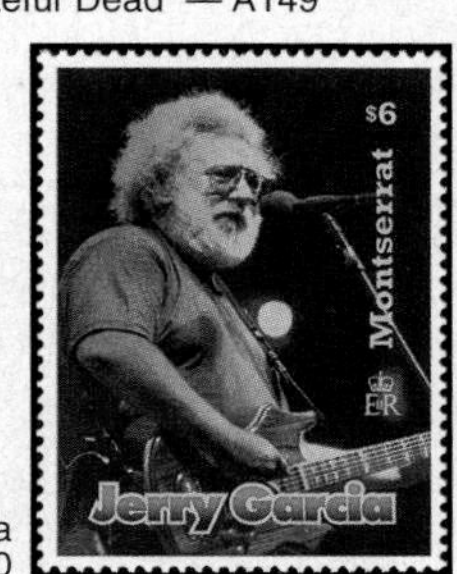

Jerry Garcia A150

No. 914 - Color of bears: a, blue violet, green. b, yellow. c, orange, pink.

1996, Oct. 21 Litho. *Perf. 12½*

914	A149	$1.15	Strip of 3, #a.-c.	3.50	3.50
915	A150	$6	multicolored	6.25	6.25

For overprint and surcharge see #920A, 928. Compare with #955-956 and #970-83.

Scavenger Birds A151

1997, Jan. 28 Litho. *Perf. 14½x14*

916	A151	$1	Turkey vulture	1.00	1.00
917	A151	$1.15	American crow	1.25	1.25
918	A151	$1.50	Great skua	1.50	1.50
919	A151	$3.45	Kittiwake	3.50	3.50
			Nos. 916-919 (4)	7.25	7.25

Souvenir Sheet

920	A151	$4.50	King vulture	5.00	5.00

No. 914 Overprinted "Hong Kong '97" Across Strip in Dark Blue

Methods and Perfs as before

1997, Mar. 26

920A	A149	$1.15	Strip of 3, #b-d	3.00	3.00

No. 912 Overprinted

1997, June 2 Litho. *Perf. 12½*

921	A148	$1.15	Sheet of 9, #a.-i.	12.50	12.50

Overprints are placed over vertical perfs separating each column of stamps. Each stamp in the left and right columns has only half the overprint. The stamps in the center column contains two incomplete halves of the overprint. The overprints also appear twice in sheet margin.

Eruption of Mt. Soufriere, Endangered Species — A152

No. 922: a, Heavy ash eruption, Plymouth, 1995. b, First pyroclastic flow entering sea. c, Double venting at Castle Peak. d, Mangrove cuckoo. e, Nocturnal lava flow, Soufriere Hills, 1996. f, Antillean crested hummingbird. g, Ash cloud engulfing Plymouth. h, Lava spine extruded, Soufriere Hills, 1996. i, New land created from pyroclastic flows.

1997, June 23 ***Perf. 14***

922 A152 $1.50 Sheet of 9, #a.-i. 10.50 10.50

j. Additional inscription in sheet margin 10.50 10.50

No. 922j is inscribed in sheet margin: "MUSIC FOR" and "IN AID OF THE VICTIMS OF SOUFRIERE HILLS VOLCANO," "ROYAL ALBERT HALL LONDON" and "15th SEPTEMBER 1997."

Elvis Presley (1935-77) A153

American rock stars: No. 924, Jimi Hendrix (1942-70). No. 925, Jerry Garcia (1942-95). No. 926, Janis Joplin (1943-70).

1997, Aug. 29 **Litho.** ***Perf. 12½***

923 A153 $1.15 multicolored 1.50 1.50
924 A153 $1.15 multicolored 1.50 1.50
925 A153 $1.15 multicolored 1.50 1.50
926 A153 $1.15 multicolored 1.50 1.50
Nos. 923-926 (4) 6.00 6.00

Abstract Art — A154

1997, Aug. 29 **Litho.** ***Perf. 12½***

927 A154 $1.50 multicolored 2.50 2.50

No. 915 Surcharged in Gold and Black

$1 50

1997 **Litho.** ***Perf. 12½***

928 A150 $1.50 on $6 multi 2.50 2.50

Medicinal Plants — A155

A156

1998, Mar. 30 **Litho.** ***Perf. 15***

929 A155 $1 Prickly pear .70 .70
930 A155 $1.15 Pomme coolie .80 .80
931 A155 $1.50 Aloe 1.00 1.00
932 A155 $3.45 Bird pepper 2.50 2.50
Nos. 929-932 (4) 5.00 5.00

1998, May 18 **Litho.** ***Perf. 12½***

Famous People of the 20th Cent.: No. 933, Jean-Henri Dunant. No. 934, Mohandas Gandhi. No. 935, Pablo Picasso. No. 936, David Ben-Gurion. No. 937, Dwight D. Eisenhower. No. 938, Wernher von Braun. No. 939, Eva & Juan Perón. No. 940, Konrad Adenauer. No. 941, Mao Tse-tung. No. 942, Lord Mountbatten. No. 943, Charles Lindbergh. No. 944, Anne Frank. $3, John F. Kennedy.

933 A156 $1.15 multicolored 1.50 1.50
934 A156 $1.15 multicolored 1.50 1.50
935 A156 $1.15 multicolored 1.50 1.50
936 A156 $1.15 multicolored 1.50 1.50
937 A156 $1.15 multicolored 1.50 1.50
938 A156 $1.15 multicolored 1.50 1.50
939 A156 $1.15 multicolored 1.50 1.50
940 A156 $1.50 multicolored 2.10 2.10
941 A156 $1.50 multicolored 2.10 2.10
942 A156 $1.50 multicolored 2.10 2.10
943 A156 $1.50 multicolored 2.10 2.10
944 A156 $1.50 multicolored 2.10 2.10
Nos. 933-944 (12) 21.00 21.00

Souvenir Sheet

945 A156 $3 multicolored 3.50 3.50

No. 945 contains one 51x38mm stamp.

Issued in sheets of 4 with illustrated right margin.

1998, May 18 **Litho.** ***Perf. 12½***

Royalty of the 20th cent.: No. 946, Grand Duchess Charlotte (1896-1985) & Felix, Luxembourg. No. 947, Leopold III (1901-83) & Astrid, Belgium. No. 948, Wilhelmina (1880-1962), Netherlands. No. 949, Gustav V (1858-1950), Sweden. No. 950, Alfonso XIII (1886-1931), Spain. No. 951, Christian X (1870-1947), Denmark. No. 952, Haakon VII (1872-1957) & Olav, Denmark. No. 953, George VI (1895-1952), Great Britain.

946 A156 $1.15 multicolored 1.10 1.10
947 A156 $1.15 multicolored 1.10 1.10
948 A156 $1.50 multicolored 1.25 1.25
949 A156 $1.50 multicolored 1.25 1.25
950 A156 $1.50 multicolored 1.25 1.25
951 A156 $1.50 multicolored 1.25 1.25
952 A156 $1.50 multicolored 1.25 1.25
953 A156 $1.50 multicolored 1.25 1.25
Nos. 946-953 (8) 9.70 9.70

Issued in sheets of 4 with illustrated right margin.

Bob Marley (1947-81) A157

Various portraits.

1998, Aug. 6

954 A157 $1.15 Sheet of 8, #a.-h. + label 10.00 10.00

Jerry Garcia (1947-95) A158

Various portraits.

1998, Aug. 6

955 A158 $1.15 Sheet of 9, #a.-i. 10.00 10.00

Souvenir Sheet

956 A158 $5 multicolored 6.50 6.50

No. 956 contains one 51x76mm stamp. Compare with #914-915 and #970-983.

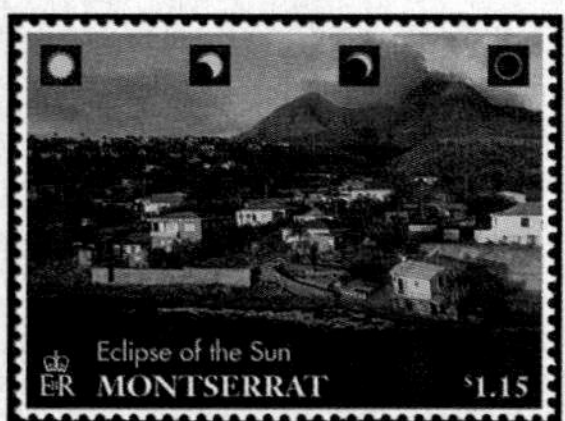

Eclipse of the Sun, Feb. 26, 1998 — A159

Views of Mt. Soufriere volcano: No. 957, Homes near water. No. 958, Looking across mountain tops. No. 959, Ash on mountainside, home. No. 960, Ash, steam rising in air.

$6, View of eclipse, vert.

1998 **Litho.** ***Perf. 12½***

957 A159 $1.15 multicolored 1.75 1.75
958 A159 $1.15 multicolored 1.75 1.75
959 A159 $1.15 multicolored 1.75 1.75
960 A159 $1.15 multicolored 1.75 1.75
Nos. 957-960 (4) 7.00 7.00

Souvenir Sheet

961 A159 $6 multicolored 7.25 7.25

Diana, Princess of Wales (1961-97) A160

1998 **Litho.** ***Perf. 12½***

962 A160 $1.15 As bride 1.25 1.25
963 A160 $1.50 Princess of charities 1.50 1.50
964 A160 $3 At Royal Ascot 3.00 3.00
Nos. 962-964 (3) 5.75 5.75

Souvenir Sheet

965 A160 $6 Rose, Diana 5.75 5.75

No. 965 contains one 51x38mm stamp.

Nos. 592-593 Ovptd. in Red with emblem and "13th WORLD JAMBOREE MONDIALE CHILE 1999"

Wmk. 380

1998, Dec. 29 **Litho.** ***Perf. 15***

966 20c Pair, #a.-b. .50 .50
967 75c Pair, #a.-b. 2.00 2.00

Nos. 873-874 Overprinted

Unwmk.

1999, Apr. 27 **Litho.** ***Perf. 14***

968 A142 $1.15 on #873 2.40 2.40
969 A142 $1.50 on #874 2.75 2.75

Jerry Garcia (1947-95) — A161

Garcia: No. 970, $1.15, Wearing purple shirt, microphone at right, light blue background. No. 971, $1.15, In red light, dark blue background. No. 972, $1.15, Wearing purple shirt, microphone at left. No. 973, $1.15, Like #971, blue green background. No. 974, $1.15, Wearing black shirt, playing guitar. No. 975, $1.15, Wearing red shirt. No. 976, $1.15, Wearing blue shirt, microphone at right, vert. No. 977, $1.15, Wearing blue shirt, microphone to left of face, vert. No. 978, $1.15, Wearing blue shirt, microphone partially covering face, vert. No. 979, $1.15, Wearing black shirt, orange rectangular frame, vert. No. 980, $1.15, Wearing blue shirt, orange and blue frame, vert. No. 981, $1.15, Wearing black shirt, orange and blue frame, vert.

No. 982, $6, Vignette of #980. No. 983, $6, Wearing black shirt, vert.

1999 **Litho.** **Unwmk.** ***Perf. 12½***

970-981 A161 Set of 12 20.00 20.00

Souvenir Sheets

982-983 A161 Set of 2 40.00 40.00

Issued in sheets of 9 containing 3 each of Nos. 970-972, 973-975, 976-978, 979-981 respectively. Nos. 982-983 contain one 76x51mm or 51x76mm stamp, respectively. Compare with #914-915 and #955-956.

Fruit A162

1999 **Litho.** **Wmk. 380** ***Perf. 12½***

984 A162 $1.15 Mango 1.10 1.10
985 A162 $1.50 Breadfruit 1.50 1.50
986 A162 $2.30 Papaya 2.40 2.40
987 A162 $3 Lime 3.00 3.00
988 A162 $6 Akee 6.25 6.25
a. Sheet of 5, #984-988 +label 15.00 15.00
Nos. 984-988 (5) 14.25 14.25

Dogs A163

1999

989 A163 70c Yorkshire terrier 1.00 1.00
990 A163 $1 Welsh corgi 1.40 1.40
991 A163 $1.15 King Charles spaniel 1.50 1.50
992 A163 $1.50 Poodle 2.10 2.10
993 A163 $3 Beagle 4.00 4.00
a. Sheet of 5, #989-993 + label 10.00 10.00
Nos. 989-993 (5) 10.00 10.00

World Teachers' Day — A164

World map and: $1, Ruler, scissors, compass, pencil, paint brush. $1.15, Teacher lecturing, $1.50, Compass, flag, camera, globe, plumb bob, theodolite. $5, Pen, flask, funnel, thermometer, calipers, microscope.

1999 **Litho.** ***Perf. 12½***

994-997 A164 Set of 4 12.50 12.50

Worldwide Fund for Nature A165

No. 998 - Great hammerhead shark: a, Pair swimming. b, Pair near ocean floor. c, Trio swimming. d, One swimming.

Perf. 13¼

1999, Nov. 29 **Litho.** **Unwmk.**

998 Horiz. strip of 4 3.50 3.50
a.-d. A165 50c Any single .70 .70

Millennium — A166

2000, Jan. 1 **Unwmk.**

999 A166 $1.50 multi 2.25 2.25

100th Test Cricket Match at Lord's Ground — A167

Designs: $1, Alfred Valentine. $5, George Headley.
$6, Lord's Ground, horiz.

2000, May 5 Litho. *Perf. 13½x13¼*
1000-1001 A167 Set of 2 5.75 5.75

Souvenir Sheet
Perf. 13¼x13½
1002 A167 $6 multi 7.00 7.00

The Stamp Show 2000, London A168

Battle of Britain, 60th anniv.: 70c, Scramble. $1.15, Hurricane Mk.1 overhaul. $1.50, Hurricane Mk. 1 and enemy plane. $5, Spitfire Mk. 1a of Flight Lt. Frank Howell.
$6, Plane in air.

Wmk. 373
2000, May 22 Litho. *Perf. 14*
1003 A168 70c multi .70 .70
1004 A168 $1.15 multi 1.10 1.10
1005 A168 $1.50 multi 1.50 1.50
1006 A168 $5 multi 5.00 5.00
Nos. 1003-1006 (4) 8.30 8.30

Souvenir Sheet
1007 A168 $6 multi 6.75 6.75

Millennium — A169

People of Montserrat and: 90c, Statue of Liberty. $1.15, Great Wall of China. $1.50, Eiffel Tower. $3.50, Millennium Dome, Great Britain.

Perf. 13½
2000, July 3 Litho. Unwmk.
1008-1011 A169 Set of 4 7.25 7.25

Queen Mother, 100th Birthday A170

Queen Mother and various buildings. Panel color under country name in: 70c, Yellow. $1.15, Purple. $3, Green. $6, Orange.

2000, Aug. 4 *Perf. 13½x13*
1012-1015 A170 Set of 4 11.50 11.50
1015a Souvenir sheet, #1012-1015 12.00 12.00

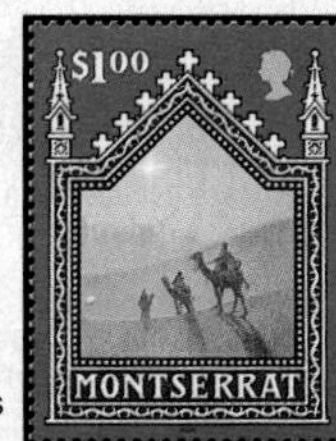

Christmas A171

Designs: $1, The three Magi. $1.15, Cavalla Hill Methodist Church. $1.50, Shepherds. $3, $6, Mary and Joseph arriving in Bethlehem.

Perf. 14x14¾
2000, Nov. 29 Wmk. 373
1016-1019 A171 Set of 4 7.25 7.25

Souvenir Sheet
1020 A171 $6 multi 4.25 4.25

Birds A172

Designs: $1, Golden swallow, vert. $1.15, Crested quail dove. $1.50, Red-legged thrush. $5, Fernandina's flicker, vert.
$8, St. Vincent parrot.

2001, Mar. 26 Litho. *Perf. 13¼*
1021-1024 A172 Set of 4 7.25 7.25

Souvenir Sheet
1025 A172 $8 St. Vincent parrot 5.75 5.75

Philatelic Personalities — A173

Designs: $1, Edward Stanley Gibbons, Charles J. Phillips. $1.15, John Lister. $1.50, Theodore Champion and 19th cent. French postilion. $3, Thomas de la Rue.
$8, Sir Rowland Hill, Bruce Castle.

2001, Apr. 30 *Perf. 13¼*
1026-1029 A173 Set of 4 7.25 7.25

Souvenir Sheet
1030 A173 $8 multi 8.00 8.00

Queen Elizabeth II, 75th Birthday — A174

Dress color: 90c, Black. $1.15, Yellow. $1.50, Pink. $5, Green.
$6, Lilac.

2001, June 22 *Perf. 13¼*
1031-1034 A174 Set of 4 10.00 10.00

Souvenir Sheet
1035 A174 $6 multi 7.25 7.25

Buildings — A175

Designs: 70c, Lookout community. $1, St. John's Hospital. $1.15, Tropical Mansion Suites. $1.50, Montserrat Secondary School. $3, Golden Years Home.

2001, Aug. 15 Litho. *Perf. 13½*
1036-1040 A175 Set of 5 8.00 8.00

Fruit A176

Designs: 5c, West Indian cherries. 10c Mammee apples. 15c, Limes. 20c, Grapefruits. 25c, Orange. 40c, Passion fruits. 55c, Bananas. 70c, Papayas. 90c, Pomegranates. $1, Guavas. $1.15, Mangos. $1.50, Sugar apple. $3, Cashews. $5, Soursops. $7.50, Watermelon. $10, Pineapple.

2001, Oct. 10 Litho. *Perf. 13½x13¼*
1041 A176 5c multi .20 .20
1042 A176 10c multi .20 .20
1043 A176 15c multi .20 .20
1044 A176 20c multi .20 .20
1045 A176 25c multi .20 .20
1046 A176 40c multi .40 .40
1047 A176 55c multi .50 .50
1048 A176 70c multi .65 .65
1049 A176 90c multi .85 .85
1050 A176 $1 multi 1.00 1.00
1051 A176 $1.15 multi 1.10 1.10
1052 A176 $1.50 multi 1.40 1.40
1053 A176 $3 multi 3.00 3.00
1054 A176 $5 multi 4.75 4.75
1055 A176 $7.50 multi 7.50 7.50
1056 A176 $10 multi 9.75 9.75
Nos. 1041-1056 (16) 31.90 31.90

Butterflies — A177

Designs: $1, Common long-tail skipper. $1.15, Straight-line skipper. $1.50, Giant hairstreak. $3, Monarch.
$10, Painted lady.

2001, Dec. 20 Litho. *Perf. 13¼*
1057-1060 A177 Set of 4 8.00 8.00

Souvenir Sheet
1061 A177 $10 multi 10.50 10.50

2002 Winter Olympics, Salt Lake City — A178

No. 1062: a, $3, Downhill skiing. b, $5, Bobsled.
Illustration reduced.

2002, Mar. 12 Litho. *Perf. 13¼*
1062 A178 Horiz. pair, #a-b 8.75 8.75

Fish A179

Designs: $1, Sergeant major. $1.15, Mutton snapper. $1.50, Lantern bass. $5, Shy hamlet.
$8, Queen angelfish.

Perf. 13¼
2002, July 29 Litho. Unwmk.
1063-1066 A179 Set of 4 10.00 10.00

Souvenir Sheet
1067 A179 $8 multi 10.00 10.00

Nos. 1012-1015 Overprinted

2002, Sept. 23 Litho. *Perf. 13½x13*
1068 A170 70c on #1012 .75 .75
1069 A170 $1.15 on #1013 1.25 1.25
1070 A170 $3 on #1014 3.25 3.25
1071 A170 $6 on #1015 6.75 6.75
Nos. 1068-1071 (4) 12.00 12.00

Wild Flowers — A180

Designs: 70c, Allamanda cathartica. $1.15, Lantana camara. $1.50, Leonotis nepetifolia. $5, Plumeria rubra.
$8, Alpinia purpurata.

Perf. 13¼
2002, Nov. 29 Litho. Unwmk.
1072-1075 A180 Set of 4 9.00 9.00

Souvenir Sheet
1076 A180 $8 multi 9.00 9.00

Coronation of Queen Elizabeth II, 50th Anniv. — A181

No. 1077: a, Queen wearing crown. b, Crown on pillow. c, Queen wearing tiara and purple sash.
$6, Queen wearing crown, diff.

2003, Apr. 30 *Perf. 14*
1077 A181 $3 Sheet of 3, #a-c 6.75 6.75

Souvenir Sheet
1078 A181 $6 multi 5.25 5.25

Powered Flight, Cent. — A182

No. 1079: a, Wright Flyer II in blue. b, Wright Flyer II in brown. c, Wright Brothers. d, Wright Flyer I.
$6, Wright Flyer II.

2003, June 30 Litho. *Perf. 14*
1079 A182 $2 Sheet of 4, #a-d 6.75 6.75

Souvenir Sheet
1080 A182 $6 multi 5.25 5.25

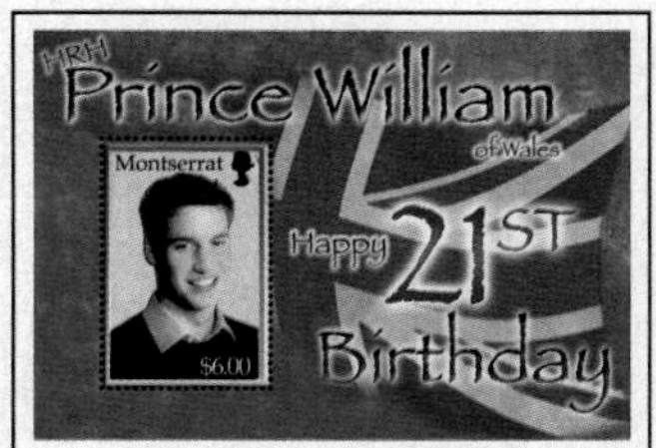

Prince William, 21st Birthday — A183

No. 1081 — Prince William in suit and tie with: a, Frame obscured at LL and LR by portrait. b, Frame obscured at LL by portrait. c, Frame not obscured.
$6, Wearing sweater and shirt with open collar.

2003, Aug. 20

1081	A183	$3 Sheet of 3, #a-c	6.75	6.75

Souvenir Sheet

1082	A183	$6 multi	7.00	7.00

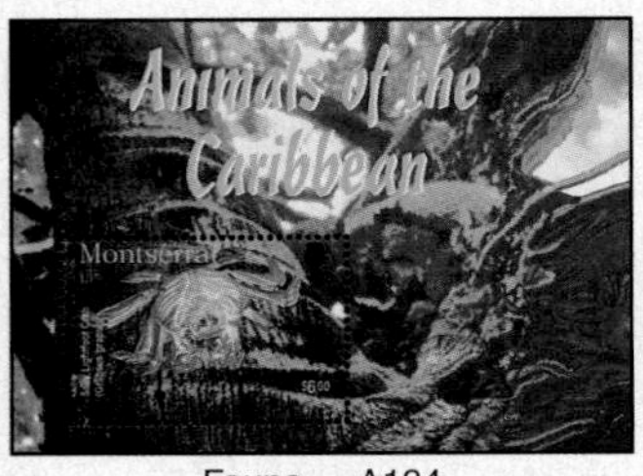

Fauna — A184

No. 1083: a, Piping frog. b, Land hermit crab. c, Spix's pinche. d, Dwarf gecko. e, Green sea turtle. f, Indian mongoose.
$6, Sally Lightfoot crab.

2003, Nov. 28

1083	A184	$1.50 Sheet of 6, #a-f	7.50	7.50

Souvenir Sheet

1084	A184	$6 multi	6.00	6.00

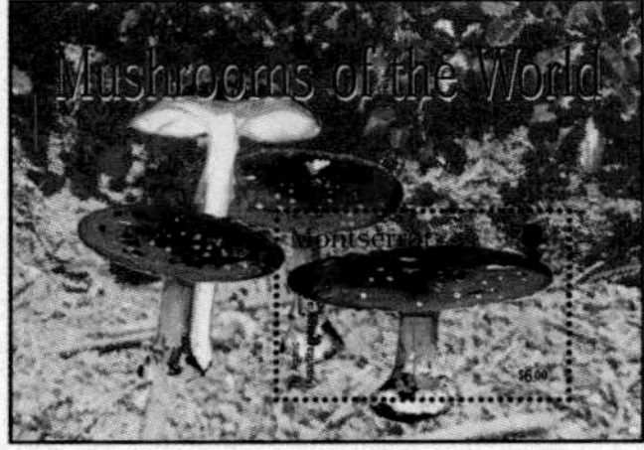

Mushrooms — A185

No. 1085: a, Slimy lead milk cap. b, Rosy spike cap. c, Stump puffball. d, Parasol. e, Crab russula. f, Scaly vase chanterelle.
$6, Fly agaric.

2003, Nov. 28

1085	A185	$1.50 Sheet of 6, #a-f	6.75	6.75

Souvenir Sheet

1086	A185	$6 multi	5.25	5.25

Birds A186

Designs: 90c, Belted kingfisher. $1.15, Yellow warbler. No. 1089, $1.50, Hooded warbler. $5, Cedar waxwing.
No. 1091: a, Roseate spoonbill. b, Laughing gull. c, White-tailed tropicbird. d, Bare-eyed thrush. e, Glittering-throated emerald. f, Lesser Antillean grackle.
$6, Bananaquit.

2003, Nov. 28

1087-1090	A186	Set of 4	6.50	6.50
1091	A186	$1.50 Sheet of 6, #a-f	6.75	6.75

Souvenir Sheet

1092	A186	$6 multi	6.00	6.00

2004 Summer Olympics, Greece A187

Designs: 90c, 1932 Los Angeles Olympics poster. $1.15, 1972 Munich Olympics pin. $1.50, 1976 Montreal Olympics poster. $5, Pankration, horiz.

2004, June 30 Litho. *Perf. 13¼*

1093-1096	A187	Set of 4	6.50	6.50

Butterflies — A188

No. 1097: a, Lacewing. b, Swallowtail. c, Shoemaker. d, White peacock.
$6, Flashing astraptes.

2004, July 6 Litho. *Perf. 14*

1097	A188	$2.30 Sheet of 4, #a-d	7.00	7.00

Souvenir Sheet

1098	A188	$6 multi	4.50	4.50

Cats — A189

Designs: $1.15, Singapura. $1.50, Burmese. $2, Abyssinian. $5, Norwegian.
$6, Russian Blue.

2004, Aug. 23

1099-1102	A189	Set of 4	7.25	7.25

Souvenir Sheet

1103	A189	$6 multi	4.50	4.50

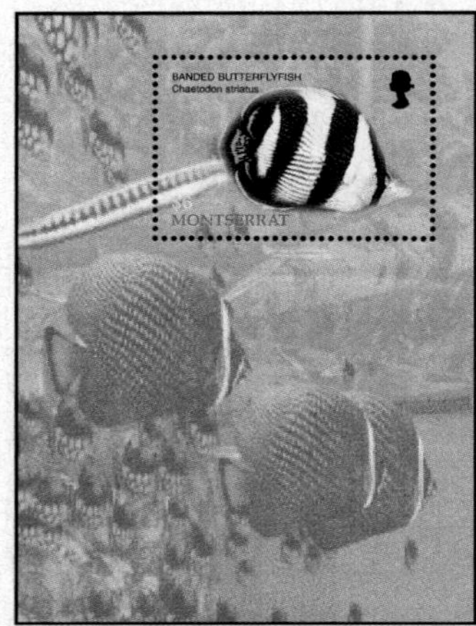

Fish — A190

No. 1104: a, Blue-girdled angelfish. b, Regal angelfish. c, Emperor angelfish. d, Blotch-eyed soldierfish.
$6, Banded butterflyfish.

2004, Sept. 30

1104	A190	$2.30 Sheet of 4, #a-d	7.00	7.00

Souvenir Sheet

1105	A190	$6 multi	4.50	4.50

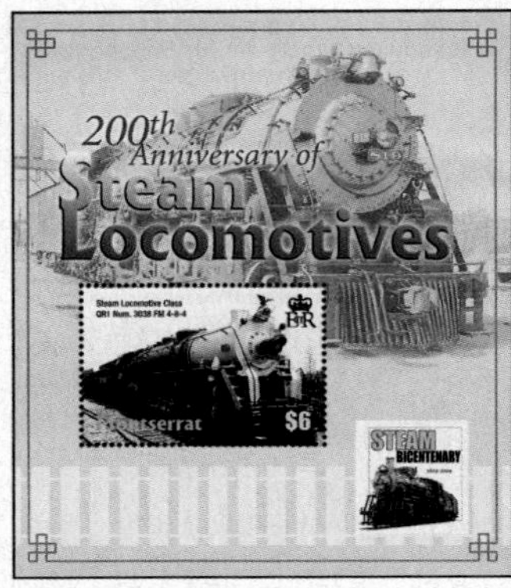

Locomotives, 200th Anniv. — A191

No. 1106: a, Austerity. b, Deli Vasut. c, Class 424 No. 424.247/287. d, L-1646. e, Steam locomotive 324.1564. f, Class Ia.
No. 1107: a, Old Class TV. b, Class Va 7111. c, Class 424 No. 424.009. d, Class III.
$6, Class QR1.

2004, Oct. 29 *Perf. 14½x14*

1106	A191	$1.50 Sheet of 6, #a-f	6.75	6.75
1107	A191	$2 Sheet of 4, #a-d	6.00	6.00

Souvenir Sheet

1108	A191	$6 multi	4.50	4.50

World AIDS Day — A192

2004, Dec. 1 *Perf. 13½*

1109	A192	$3 multi	2.25	2.25

Printed in sheets of 4.

D-Day, 60th Anniv. A193

Designs: $1.15, Air assault begins. $1.50, Troops assault beaches of Normandy. $2, Field Marshal Montgomery. $5, HMS Belfast.

2004, Dec. 24 *Perf. 14*

1110-1113	A193	Set of 4	7.25	7.25

National Soccer Team — A194

2004, Dec. 24 Litho. *Perf. 12*

1114	A194	$6 multi	4.50	4.50

Nos. 1036-1040 Overprinted

2005, Feb. 21 Litho. *Perf. 13½*

1115	A175	70c multi	.55	.55
1116	A175	$1 multi	.75	.75
1117	A175	$1.15 multi	.85	.85
1118	A175	$1.50 multi	1.10	1.10
1119	A175	$3 multi	2.25	2.25
		Nos. 1115-1119 (5)	5.50	5.50

Birds — A195

No. 1120: a, Brown pelican. b, Red-billed tropicbird. c, Galapagos Island cormorant. d, Waved albatross.
$6, Common tern.

2005, Apr. 25 Litho. *Perf. 13¼x13½*

1120	A195	$2.30 Sheet of 4, #a-d	7.00	7.00

Souvenir Sheet

1121	A195	$6 multi	4.50	4.50

Orchids — A196

No. 1122: a, Cattleya lueddemanniana. b, Cattleya luteola. c, Cattleya trianaei. d, Cattleya mossiae.
$6, Cattleya mendelii.

2005, Apr. 25

1122	A196	$2.30 Sheet of 4, #a-d	7.00	7.00

Souvenir Sheet

1123	A196	$6 multi	4.50	4.50

Molluscs and Shells A197

Designs: $1.15, Liguus virgineus. $1.50, Liguus fasciatus testudineus. $2, Liguus fasciatus. $5, Cerion striatella.
$6, Liguus fasciatus, vert.

2005, June 1 *Perf. 13¼x13½*

1124-1127	A197	Set of 4	7.25	7.25

Souvenir Sheet

Perf. 13½x13¼

1128	A197	$6 multi	4.50	4.50

Miniature Sheet

Soufriere Hills Volcanic Eruption, 10th Anniv. — A198

No. 1129: a, Dome glow. b, Explosion. c, Tar River Delta. d, Belham River. e, MVO Building. f, Pyroclastic flow entering the sea. g,

Blackburne Airport, destroyed in 1997. h, Helicopter maintenance and monitoring. i, Instruments used for monitoring.

2005, July 18 Litho. *Perf. 14*
1129 A198 $2 Sheet of 9, #a-i 13.50 13.50

Rotary International, Cent. — A199

Emblem and: $1, Shamrock. $1.15, Heliconia flower. $1.50, Lady and the Harp. $5, Map of Montserrat.
$6, Medical care for children, horiz.

2005, Sept. 12 *Perf. 12¾*
1130-1133 A199 Set of 4 6.50 6.50

Souvenir Sheet

1134 A199 $6 multi 4.50 4.50

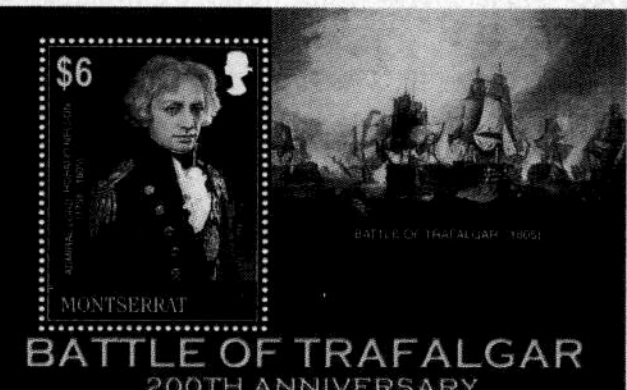

Battle of Trafalgar, Bicent. — A200

No. 1135: a, Napoleon Bonaparte. b, Admiral Horatio Nelson. c, Battle of the Nile. d, Battle of Trafalgar.
$6, Nelson, diff.

2005, Nov. 4 Litho. *Perf. 12*
1135 A200 $2 Sheet of 4, #a-d 6.00 6.00

Souvenir Sheet

1136 A200 $6 multi 4.50 4.50

Hans Christian Andersen (1805-75), Author — A201

No. 1137: a, Thumbelina. b, The Flying Trunk. c, The Buckwheat.
$6, The Little Mermaid.

2005, Dec. 23 *Perf. 12¾*
1137 A201 $3 Sheet of 3, #a-c 6.75 6.75

Souvenir Sheet

Perf. 12

1138 A201 $6 multi 4.50 4.50

No. 1137 contains three 39x25mm stamps.

Famous People A202

Designs: No. 1139, $1.15, William Henry Bramble (1901-88), first chief minister. No. 1140, $1.15, Michael Simmons Osborne (1902-67), merchant and parliamentarian. No. 1141, $1.15, Robert William Griffith (1904-96), union leader. No. 1142, $1.15, Patricia Griffin (1907-86), social worker. No. 1143, $1.15, Lilian Cadogan (1907-92), nurse. No. 1144, $1.15, Samuel Aymer (1911-79), folk musician.

2005, Dec. 5 Litho. *Perf. 12¾*
1139-1144 A202 Set of 6 5.25 5.25
1140a Inscribed "Symmons" instead of "Simmons" .85 .85
1144a Souvenir sheet, #1139, 1140a, 1141-1144 5.25 5.25

Nos. 1022, 1058-1059, 1072 and 1075 Overprinted

Methods and Perfs As Before

2006, Apr. 1
1145 A180 70c on #1072 .55 .55
1146 A172 $1 on #1022 .75 .75
1147 A177 $1.15 on #1058 .90 .90
1148 A177 $1.50 on #1059 1.10 1.10
1149 A180 $5 on #1075 3.75 3.75
Nos. 1145-1149 (5) 7.05 7.05

Overprint is on four lines on No. 1146.

Marine Life — A203

No. 1150: a, Giant Caribbean anemone. b, Beadlet anemone. c, Golden crinoid. d, Oval cup coral.
$6, Tube-dwelling anemone.

2006, May 2 Litho. *Perf. 12*
1150 A203 $2.30 Sheet of 4, #a-d 7.00 7.00

Souvenir Sheet

1151 A203 $6 multi 4.50 4.50

Moths — A204

No. 1152: a, Cecropia moth. b, Madagascan sunset moth. c, Great peacock moth. d, Zodiac moth.
$6, White-lined sphinx moth.

2006, May 2
1152 A204 $2.30 Sheet of 4, #a-d 7.00 7.00

Souvenir Sheet

1153 A204 $6 multi 4.50 4.50

Dogs — A205

Designs: $1.15, Rottweiler. $1.50, Boxer. $2, Corgi. $5, Great Dane.
$6, St. Bernard.

2006, Aug. 16
1154-1157 A205 Set of 4 7.25 7.25

Souvenir Sheet

1158 A205 $6 multi 4.50 4.50

Worldwide Fund for Nature (WWF) — A206

No. 1159 — Various depictions of Mountain chicken frog: a, 70c. b, $1. c, $1.15. d, $1.50.
Illustration reduced.

2006, Aug. 16 *Perf. 13¼*
1159 A206 Block of 4, #a-d 3.25 3.25
e. Miniature sheet, 2 #1159 6.50 6.50

Souvenir Sheet

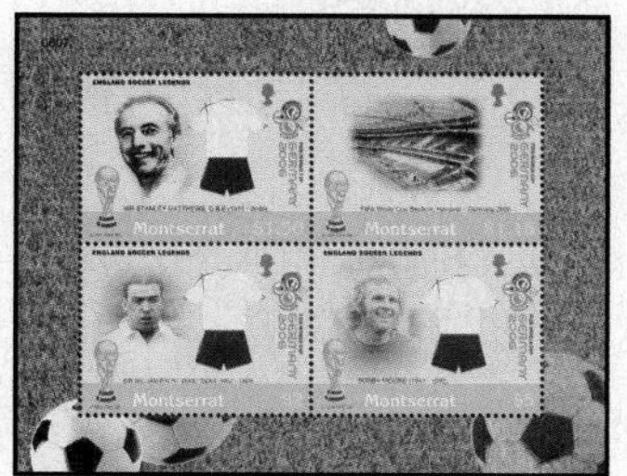
2006 World Cup Soccer Championships, Germany — A207

No. 1160 — World Cup, emblem and: a, $1.15, FIFA World Cup Stadium, Hanover. b, $1.50, Sir Stanley Matthews, England team uniform. c, $2, Sir Ralph "Dixie" Dean, England team uniform. d, $5, Bobby Moore, England team uniform.

2006, Aug. 31 *Perf. 12*
1160 A207 Sheet of 4, #a-d 7.25 7.25

Christopher Columbus (1451-1506), Explorer — A208

Designs: $1.15, Map of North and South America, Columbus's vessels. $1.50, Columbus and map of voyage. $2, Ship, Earth, Columbus. $5, Columbus, vert.
$6, Earth, Columbus and crew with flag, vert.

2006, Oct. 27 *Perf. 12¾*
1161-1164 A208 Set of 4 7.25 7.25

Souvenir Sheet

1165 A208 $6 multi 4.50 4.50

A209

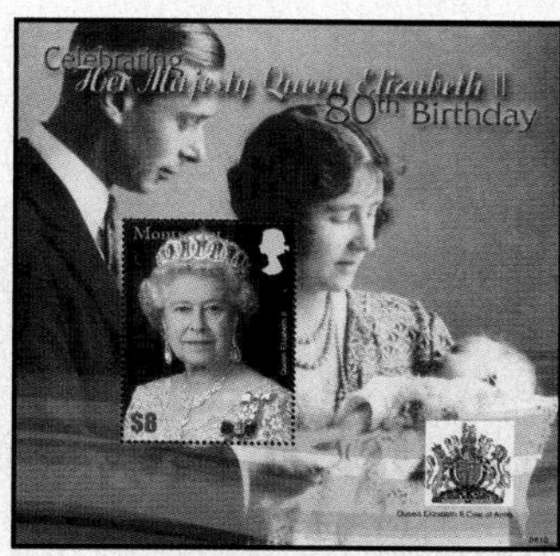

Queen Elizabeth II, 80th Birthday — A210

No. 1166: a, Queen wearing crown, country name in black. b, Queen wearing crown, country name in white, c, Queen wearing tiara. d, Queen wearing tiara and sash.

2006, Oct. 27 *Perf. 13¼*
1166 A209 $2.30 Sheet of 4, #a-d 7.00 7.00

Souvenir Sheet

1167 A210 $8 shown 6.00 6.00

2007 Cricket World Cup, West Indies — A211

Designs: $3, 2007 Cricket World Cup emblem, map and flag of Montserrat. $5, Cricket team, horiz.
$8, 2007 Cricket World Cup emblem.

2007, Mar. 9 Litho. *Perf. 13¼*
1168-1169 A211 Set of 2 6.00 6.00

Souvenir Sheet

1170 A211 $8 multi 6.00 6.00

Scouting, Cent. — A212

No. 1171, horiz. — Scouts: a, Looking at flower. b, Working at construction site. c, In sailboat. d, Feeding goat. e, Making campfire. f, Installing birdhouse.
$6, Lord Robert Baden-Powell.

2007, Mar. 9
1171 A212 $2 Sheet of 6, #a-f 9.00 9.00

Souvenir Sheet

1172 A212 $6 multi 4.50 4.50

Flowers — A213

Designs: 10c, Poinsettia. 30c, Periwinkle. 35c, Bougainvillea. 50c, Ixora. 70c, Heliconia. 80c, Morning glory. 90c, Poinciana. $1, Cup of gold. $1.10, Chenille plant. $1.50, Oleander. $2.25, Hibiscus. $2.50, Frangipani. $2.75, Bird of paradise. $5, Madagascar jasmine. $10, Yellow poui. $20, Rose.

2007, May 14 Litho. *Perf. 12½*

1173	A213	10c multi	.20	.20
1174	A213	30c multi	.25	.25
1175	A213	35c multi	.25	.25
1176	A213	50c multi	.40	.40
1177	A213	70c multi	.55	.55
1178	A213	80c multi	.60	.60
1179	A213	90c multi	.70	.70
1180	A213	$1 multi	.75	.75
1181	A213	$1.10 multi	.85	.85
1182	A213	$1.50 multi	1.10	1.10
1183	A213	$2.25 multi	1.75	1.75
1184	A213	$2.50 multi	1.90	1.90
1185	A213	$2.75 multi	2.10	2.10
1186	A213	$5 multi	3.75	3.75
1187	A213	$10 multi	7.50	7.50
1188	A213	$20 multi	15.00	15.00
	Nos. 1173-1188 (16)		37.65	37.65

Princess Diana (1961-97) — A214

No. 1189 — Diana wearing tiara and: a, Blue dress. b, Black dress. c, White dress. d, White dress with high neck.
$7, Diana without tiara.

2007, Aug. 8 Litho. *Perf. 13¼*
1189 A214 $3.40 Sheet of 4, #a-d 10.50 10.50

Souvenir Sheet

1190 A214 $7 multi 5.25 5.25

Turtles — A215

No. 1191: a, Hawksbill turtle. b, Green turtle. c, Leatherback turtle. d, Loggerhead turtle.
$7, Kemp's Ridley sea turtle.

2007, Aug. 8 *Perf. 13¼x13½*
1191 A215 $3.40 Sheet of 4, #a-d 10.50 10.50

Souvenir Sheet

1192 A215 $7 multi 5.25 5.25

Parrots — A216

No. 1193: a, Green-winged macaw. b, Mitred conure. c, Sun conure. d, Blue-and-yellow macaw.
$7, Hyacinth macaw.

2007, Oct. 11 Litho. *Perf. 13½x13¼*
1193 A216 $3.40 Sheet of 4, #a-d 10.50 10.50

Souvenir Sheet

1194 A216 $7 multi 5.25 5.25

Lilies — A217

No. 1195, horiz.: a, Hippeastrum puniceum. b, Hymenocallis caribaea. c, Zephyranthes puertoricensis. d, Belamcanda chinensis.
$7, Crinum erubescens.

2007, Oct. 11 *Perf. 13¼x13½*
1195 A217 $3.40 Sheet of 4, #a-d 10.50 10.50

Souvenir Sheet
Perf. 13½x13¼

1196 A217 $7 multi 5.25 5.25

Miniature Sheet

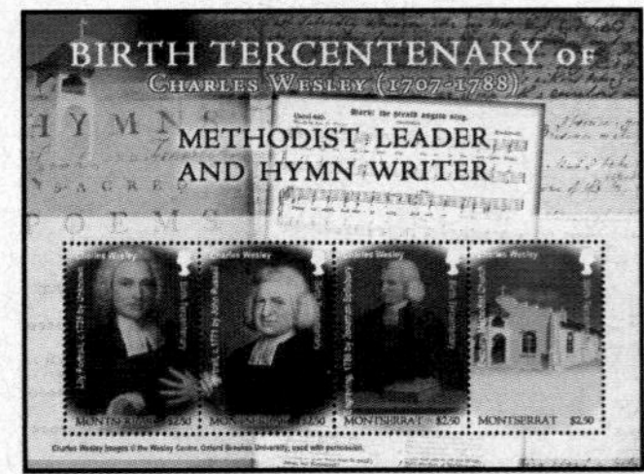

Charles Wesley (1707-88), Hymn Writer — A218

No. 1197: a, Portrait of Wesley by unknown artist. b, Portrait of Wesley by John Russell. c, Engraving of Wesley by Jonathan Spilsbury. d, Bethany Methodist Church.

2007, Dec. 18 Litho. *Perf. 13¼*
1197 A218 $2.50 Sheet of 4, #a-d 7.50 7.50

Whales — A219

No. 1198: a, Sperm whale. b, Minke whale. c, Cuvier's beaked whale. d, Humpback whale.
$7, Blue whale.

2008, May 2 *Perf. 12¾*
1198 A219 $3.55 Sheet of 4, #a-d 11.00 11.00

Souvenir Sheet

1199 A219 $7 multi 5.25 5.25

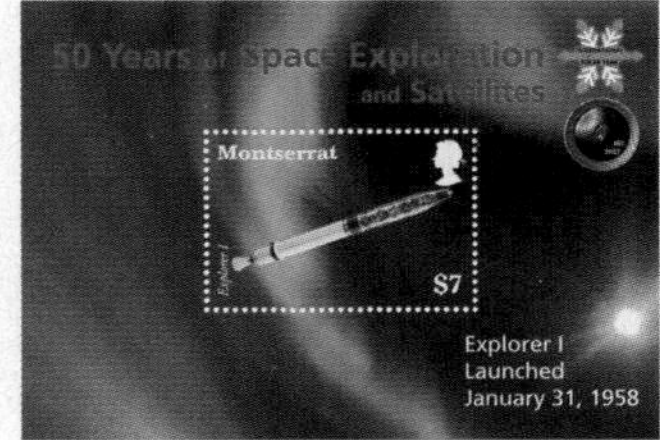

Space Exploration, 50th Anniv. — A220

No. 1200, vert.: a, Explorer I on Juno I launch rocket. b, Dr. James Van Allen, Explorer I. c, Explorer I. d, Drs. William Pickering, James Van Allen and Wernher von Braun with Explorer I model.
$7, Explorer I, diff.

2008, May 29 *Perf. 13¼*
1200 A220 $3.55 Sheet of 4, #a-d 11.00 11.00

Souvenir Sheet

1201 A220 $7 multi 5.25 5.25

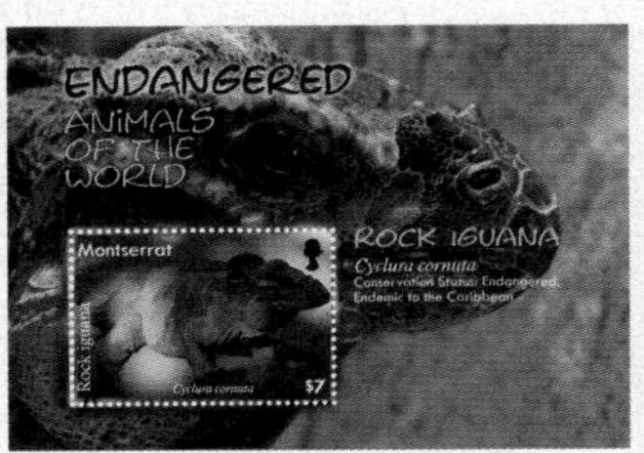

Endangered Animals — A221

No. 1202, vert.: a, African elephant. b, Bald eagle. c, Sumatran tiger. d, Hawksbill turtle. e, Indian rhinoceros. f, Western gorilla.
$7, Rock iguana.

2008, July 3
1202 A221 $2.25 Sheet of 6, #a-f 10.00 10.00

Souvenir Sheet

1203 A221 $7 multi 5.25 5.25

Miniature Sheet

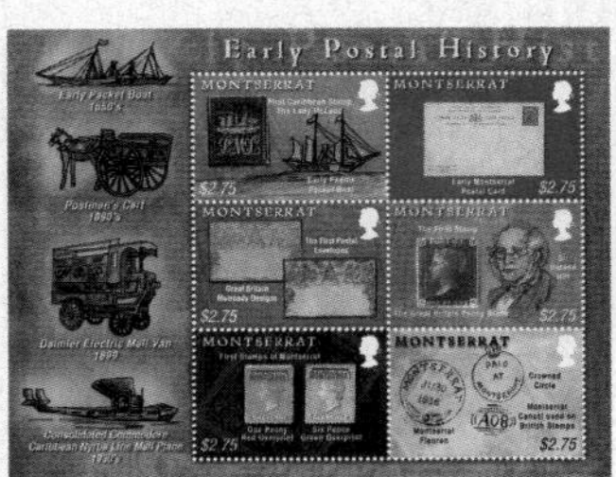

Early Postal History — A222

No. 1204: a, "Lady McLeod" stamp, early paddle packet boat. b, Early Montserrat postal card. c, Great Britain #U1-U2. d, Great Britain #1, Sir Rowland Hill. e, Montserrat #1-2. f, Montserrat cancels.

2008, July 31 Litho. *Perf. 13½*
1204 A222 $2.75 Sheet of 6, #a-f 12.50 12.50

Miniature Sheets

Royal Air Force, 90th Anniv. — A223

No. 1205, $3.55: a, English Electric Lightning P3. b, Hurricane IIC. c, Jet Provost T3A. d, Jaguar GR3A.
No. 1206, $3.55: a, Westland Sea King HAR3 helicopter. b, Gloster Javelin FAW9. c, P-66 Pembroke C1. d, Chinook HC2 helicopter.

2008, Sept. 5 Litho. *Perf. 13¼*
Sheets of 4, #a-d

1205-1206 A223 Set of 2 22.00 22.00

University of the West Indies, 60th Anniv. — A224

Designs: $2, Building on Montserrat campus. $5, University arms, diploma.

2008, Sept. 30
1207-1208 A224 Set of 2 5.50 5.50

Miniature Sheets

Orchids — A225

No. 1209, $2.75: a, Cattleya labiata. b, Phalaenopsis cultivar with pink spots. c, Cymbidium annabelle. d, Phalaenopsis taisuco.
No. 1210, $2.75: a, Phalaenopsis amabilis. b, Cattleya aurantiaca. c, Phalaenopsis cultivar with pink lines. d, Dendrobium nobile.

2008, Nov. 27 *Perf. 13¼*
Sheets of 4, #a-d

1209-1210 A225 Set of 2 17.00 17.00

Dolphins — A226

No. 1211: a, Common dolphin. b, Bottlenose dolphin. c, Pantropical spotted dolphin. d, Long-snouted spinner dolphin.
$7, Risso's dolphin.

2008, Nov. 27 *Perf. 12¾*
1211 A226 $3.55 Sheet of 4, #a-d 11.00 11.00

Souvenir Sheet

1212 A226 $7 multi 5.50 5.50

SEMI-POSTAL STAMPS

Catalogue values for unused stamps in this section, from this point to the end of the section, are for Never Hinged items.

Nos. 719-720 Surcharged

1989, Oct. 20 Litho. *Perf. 13½x14*

B1	A110	$1.50 +$2.50 multi	2.75	2.75
B2	A110	$3.50 +$2.50 multi	4.25	4.25

Surcharge for hurricane relief.

No. 642 Surcharged

1995, Dec. 29 Litho. *Perf. 15*

B3	A97	$2.30 +$5 multi	7.00	7.00

Surcharge for volcano relief.

WAR TAX STAMPS

No. 43 Overprinted in Red or Black

1917-18 Wmk. 3 *Perf. 14*

MR1	A6	½p green (R)	.20	*1.75*
MR2	A6	½p green ('18)	.20	*2.25*

Type of Regular Issue of 1919 Overprinted

1918

MR3	A6	1½p orange & black	.30	*.35*

Denomination on No. MR3 in black on white ground. Two dots under "d."

OFFICIAL STAMPS

Nos. O1-O44 used on Post Office and Philatelic Bureau mail. Not sold to public, used or unused.

Nos. 235-236, 338-339 Overprinted O.H.M.S.

Perf. 12½x14

1976, Apr. 12 Photo. Wmk. 314

O1	A22	5c multicolored	1.90
O2	A22	10c multicolored	2.50
O3	A22	30c on 10c multi	5.00
O4	A22	45c on 3c multi	6.00
		Nos. O1-O4 (4)	15.40

Nos. 243-243A also received this overprint.

Nos. 343-347, 349-351, 353 Overprinted

Perf. 13½x14

1976, Oct. 1 Litho. Wmk. 373

O10	A44	5c multicolored	.20
O11	A44	10c multicolored	.20
O12	A44	15c multicolored	.20
O13	A44	20c multicolored	.20
O14	A44	25c multicolored	.20
O15	A44	55c multicolored	.40
O16	A44	70c multicolored	.50
O17	A44	$1 multicolored	.70
O18	A44	$5 multicolored	3.50
O19	A44	$10 multicolored	7.00
		Nos. O10-O19 (10)	13.10

Nos. 343-347, 349-351, 353-354 Overprinted

1980, Sept. 30 *Perf. 14*

O20	A44	5c multicolored	.20
O21	A44	10c multicolored	.20
O22	A44	15c multicolored	.20
O23	A44	20c multicolored	.20
O24	A44	25c multicolored	.20
O25	A44	55c multicolored	.35
O26	A44	70c multicolored	.45
O27	A44	$1 multicolored	.65
O28	A44	$5 multicolored	3.25
O29	A44	$10 multicolored	6.50
		Nos. O20-O29 (10)	12.20

Nos. 341-351, 353-354 Overprinted or Surcharged

1980, Sept. 30 Litho. *Perf. 14*

O30	A44	5c multicolored	.20
O31	A44	5c on 3c multi	.20
O32	A44	10c multicolored	.20
O33	A44	15c multicolored	.20
O34	A44	20c multicolored	.20
O35	A44	25c multicolored	.20
O36	A44	30c on 15c multi	.25
O37	A44	35c on 2c multi	.40
O38	A44	40c multicolored	.30
O39	A44	55c multicolored	.45
O40	A44	70c multicolored	.60
O41	A44	$1 multicolored	.80
O42	A44	$2.50 on 40c multi	2.00
O43	A44	$5 multicolored	4.00
O44	A44	$10 multicolored	8.00
		Nos. O30-O44 (15)	18.00

Catalogue values for unused stamps in this section, from this point to the end of the section, are for Never Hinged items.

Fish Issue of 1981 Nos. 445-449, 451, 453, 455, 457-458, 460 Overprinted

1981, Mar. 20 Litho. *Perf. 13½*

O45	A64	5c multicolored	.20	.20
O46	A64	10c multicolored	.20	.20
O47	A64	15c multicolored	.20	.20
O48	A64	20c multicolored	.20	.20
O49	A64	25c multicolored	.20	.20
O50	A64	45c multicolored	.35	.35
O51	A64	65c multicolored	.50	.50
O52	A64	$1 multicolored	.75	.75
O53	A64	$3 multicolored	2.25	2.25
O54	A64	$5 multicolored	3.75	3.75
O55	A64	$10 multicolored	7.50	7.50
		Nos. O45-O55 (11)	16.10	16.10

Nos. 465-470 Surcharged

1982, Nov. 17 Litho. *Perf. 14*

O56	A66	45c on 90c (#465)	.40	.40
O57	A67	45c on 90c (#466)	.40	.40
O58	A66	75c on $3 (#467)	.70	.70
O59	A67	75c on $3 (#468)	.70	.70
O60	A66	$1 on $4 (#469)	.90	.90
O61	A67	$1 on $4 (#470)	.90	.90
		Nos. O56-O61 (6)	4.00	4.00

Princess Diana Issue, Nos. 484-486 Overprinted or Surcharged

1983, Oct. 19 Litho. *Perf. 14*

O62	A64	70c on 75c (#484)	1.00	1.00
O63	A64	$1 (#485)	1.40	1.40
O64	A64	$1.50 on $5 (#486)	2.00	2.00
		Nos. O62-O64 (3)	4.40	4.40

Nos. 524-536, 538 Overprinted

1985, Apr. 12 Wmk. 380 *Perf. 14*

O65	A79	5c multicolored	.50	.20
O66	A79	10c multicolored	.50	.20
O67	A79	15c multicolored	.50	.20
O68	A79	20c multicolored	.50	.20
O69	A79	25c multicolored	.50	.20
O70	A79	40c multicolored	.80	.40
O71	A79	55c multicolored	.90	.45
O72	A79	70c multicolored	1.25	.65
O73	A79	90c multicolored	1.60	.80
O74	A79	$1 multicolored	1.90	.90
O75	A79	$1.15 multicolored	2.00	1.00
O76	A79	$3 multicolored	5.25	2.50
O77	A79	$5 multicolored	9.25	4.75
O78	A79	$10 multicolored	17.50	9.00
		Nos. O65-O78 (14)	42.95	21.45

Nos. 681-694 and 696 Overprinted

Unwmk.

1989, May 9 Litho. *Perf. 14*

O79	A104	5c multicolored	.20	.20
O80	A104	10c multicolored	.20	.20
O81	A104	15c multicolored	.20	.20
O82	A104	20c multicolored	.20	.20
O83	A104	25c multicolored	.20	.20
O84	A104	40c multicolored	.40	.40
O85	A104	55c multicolored	.60	.55
O86	A104	70c multicolored	.75	.70
O87	A104	90c multicolored	.95	.90
O88	A104	$1 multicolored	1.00	.95
O89	A104	$1.15 multicolored	1.25	1.25
O90	A104	$1.50 multicolored	1.60	1.40
O91	A104	$3 multicolored	3.00	2.75
O92	A104	$5 multicolored	5.25	4.75
O94	A104	$10 multicolored	10.50	9.50
		Nos. O79-O94 (15)	26.30	24.15

Nos. 446, 454a and 456 Surcharged

1989 Wmk. 373 *Perf. 13½*

O95	A64	70c on 10c multi	1.75	1.75
O96	A64	$1.15 on 75c multi	3.25	3.25
O97	A64	$1.50 on $2 multi	4.00	4.00
		Nos. O95-O97 (3)	9.00	9.00

Nos. 758-761, 763-766, 776-779 Surcharged or Overprinted "OHMS"

1992 Litho. *Perf. 14*

O98	A118	70c on 90c #758	1.50	1.50
O99	A118	70c on $3.50 #761	1.50	1.50
O100	A119	70c on 90c #763	1.50	1.50
O101	A121	70c on 90c #776	1.50	1.50
O102	A119	$1 on $3.50 #766	2.00	2.00
O103	A121	$1 on $3.50 #779	2.00	2.00
O104	A118	$1.15 on #759	2.25	2.25
O105	A119	$1.15 on #764	2.25	2.25
O106	A121	$1.15 on #777	2.25	2.25
O107	A118	$1.50 on #760	3.00	3.00
O108	A119	$1.50 on #765	3.00	3.00
O109	A121	$1.50 on #778	3.00	3.00
		Nos. O98-O109 (12)	25.75	25.75

Nos. 803-816, 818 Ovptd. "OHMS" in Red

1993, Apr. 14 Litho. *Perf. 15x14*

O110	A128	5c multicolored	.20	.20
O111	A128	10c multicolored	.20	.20
O112	A128	15c multicolored	.20	.20
O113	A128	20c multicolored	.20	.20
O114	A128	25c multicolored	.20	.20
O115	A128	40c multicolored	.40	.40
O116	A128	55c multicolored	.60	.60
O117	A128	70c multicolored	.70	.70
O118	A128	90c multicolored	.85	.85
O119	A128	$1 multicolored	.95	.95
O120	A128	$1.15 multicolored	1.10	1.10
O121	A128	$1.50 multicolored	1.40	1.40
O122	A128	$3 multicolored	3.00	3.00
O123	A128	$5 multicolored	4.75	4.75
O125	A128	$10 multicolored	9.75	9.75
		Nos. O110-O125 (15)	24.50	24.50

A number has been reserved for an additional value in this set.

Nos. 896-909, 911 Ovptd. "O.H.M.S." In Red

1997 Litho. *Perf. 14*

O126	A147	5c multicolored	.20	.20
O127	A147	10c multicolored	.20	.20
O128	A147	15c multicolored	.20	.20
O129	A147	20c multicolored	.20	.20
O130	A147	25c multicolored	.20	.20
O131	A147	40c multicolored	.40	.40
O132	A147	55c multicolored	.50	.50
O133	A147	70c multicolored	.70	.70
O134	A147	90c multicolored	.90	.90
O135	A147	$1 multicolored	.95	.95
O136	A147	$1.15 multicolored	1.10	1.10
O137	A147	$1.50 multicolored	1.40	1.40
O138	A147	$3 multicolored	3.00	3.00
O139	A147	$5 multicolored	4.75	4.75
O140	A147	$10 multicolored	9.75	9.75
		Nos. O126-O140 (15)	24.45	24.45

Nos. 1041-1054, 1056 Overprinted

Perf. 13½x13¼

2002, June 14 Litho.

O141	A176	5c multi	.20	.20
O142	A176	10c multi	.20	.20
O143	A176	15c multi	.20	.20
O144	A176	20c multi	.20	.20
O145	A176	25c multi	.20	.20
O146	A176	40c multi	.30	.30
O147	A176	55c multi	.40	.40
O148	A176	70c multi	.80	.80
O149	A176	90c multi	1.10	1.10
O150	A176	$1 multi	1.25	1.25
O151	A176	$1.15 multi	1.50	1.50
O152	A176	$1.50 multi	1.90	1.90
O153	A176	$3 multi	4.00	4.00
O154	A176	$5 multi	6.50	6.50
O155	A176	$10 multi	13.00	13.00
		Nos. O141-O155 (15)	31.75	31.75

Nos. 1173-1186, 1188 Overprinted

2007, May 14 Litho. *Perf. 12½*

O156	A213	10c multi	.20	.20
O157	A213	30c multi	.25	.25
O158	A213	35c multi	.25	.25

O159 A213 50c multi .40 .40
O160 A213 70c multi .55 .55
O161 A213 80c multi .60 .60
O162 A213 90c multi .70 .70
O163 A213 $1 multi .75 .75
O164 A213 $1.10 multi .85 .85
O165 A213 $1.50 multi 1.10 1.10
O166 A213 $2.25 multi 1.75 1.75
O167 A213 $2.50 multi 1.90 1.90
O168 A213 $2.75 multi 2.10 2.10
O169 A213 $5 multi 3.75 3.75
O170 A213 $20 multi 15.00 15.00
Nos. O156-O170 (15) 30.15 30.15

Size and location of overprint varies.

MOROCCO

mə-ˈrä-ˌkō

LOCATION — Northwest coast of Africa
GOVT. — Kingdom
AREA — 171,953 sq. mi.
POP. — 29,661,636 (1999 est.)
CAPITAL — Rabat

A powerful kingdom from the 8th century, during the Middle Ages, Morocco ruled large areas of northwest Africa and Spain. By the turn of the 20th century, it had contracted to roughly its present borders and was the focus of an intense rivalry between France and Germany, who actively competed for control of the country. In 1912 most of Morocco became a French protectorate, with Spain acting as protector of zones in the extreme northern and southern parts of the country. Tangier was designated an international zone, administered by France, Spain, Britain and, later, Italy.

In 1956 the three zones of Morocco, French, Spanish and Tangier, were united to form an independent nation. Nos. 1-24 and C1-C3 were intended for use only in the southern (French currency) zone. Issues of the northern zone (Spanish currency) are listed after Postage Due stamps.

For earlier issues see French Morocco and Spanish Morocco.

400 Moussonats = 1 Rial (1912)
100 Centimes = 1 Franc (1956)
100 Centimes = 1 Dirham (1962)

Catalogue values for all unused stamps in this country are for Never Hinged items, except for Nos. A1-A14.

In 1892 the Sultan of Morocco established a postal service for most of the country's chief towns and cities. This service, utilizing handstuck franks, carried official correspondence, as well as some private correspondence. With French guidance, it was reorganized as the *Administration Cherifienne des Postes, Telegraphes et Telephones* in Sept. 1911. In 1912 Morocco became a French protectorate, and on Oct. 1, 1913, the Cherifian PTT was merged with the French *Administration des Postes et Telegraphes.*

Stamps were issued by the Moroccan post office in 1912, and these remained in use throughout the country until 1915 and in Tangier until 1919.

Aissaouas Mosque, Tangier — A1a

On White Paper

1912, May 25 Litho. *Perf. 11*

Narrow Margins

A1 A1a 1m light gray 9.25 8.50
A2 A1a 2m lilac 10.00 9.25
A3 A1a 5m blue green 12.50 8.50
A4 A1a 10m vermilion 19.00 8.50
A5 A1a 25m blue 29.00 24.00
A6 A1a 50m violet 42.50 37.50
Nos. A1-A6 (6) 122.25 96.25

On Nos. A1-A12, the 5m and 10m values always have the name of the engraver beneath the design, while the 1m, 25m and 50m always lack name, and the 2m value exists both with and without name.

Aissaouas Mosque, Tangier — A1b

On Lightly Tinted Paper

1913, Feb.

Wide Margins

A7 A1b 1m gray 1.25 1.25
A8 A1b 2m brown lilac 1.25 1.25
A9 A1b 5m blue green 1.75 1.75
A10 A1b 10m vermilion 1.75 1.75
A11 A1b 25m blue 3.75 3.75
A12 A1b 50m gray violet 4.50 4.50
Nos. A7-A12 (6) 14.25 14.25

No. A6 Surcharged with New Values

1913, Nov.

A13 A1a .05 on 50c violet 1,750. *2,000.*
A14 A1a .10 on 50c violet 1,750. *2,000.*

Sultan Mohammed V — A1

Men Reading — A2

1956-57 Unwmk. Engr. *Perf. 13*

1 A1 5fr brt bl & indigo .20 .20
2 A1 10fr bis brn & choc .20 .20
3 A1 15fr dp grn & magenta .20 .20
4 A1 25fr purple ('57) .85 .20
5 A1 30fr green ('57) 1.60 .20
6 A1 50fr rose red ('57) 2.00 .20
7 A1 70fr dk brn & brn red ('57) 3.00 .55
Nos. 1-7 (7) 8.05 1.75

For surcharges see Nos. B1-B5, B8-B9.

1956, Nov. 5

Campaign against illiteracy: 15fr, Girls reading. 20fr, Instructor and pupils. 30fr, Old man and child reading. 50fr, Girl pointing out poster.

8 A2 10fr pur & vio 1.25 .90
9 A2 15fr car & rose lake 2.00 1.25
10 A2 20fr bl grn & grn 2.25 1.90
11 A2 30fr rose lake & brt red 4.00 2.25
12 A2 50fr dp bl & bl 5.25 4.00
Nos. 8-12 (5) 14.75 10.30

Sultan Mohammed V — A3

Prince Moulay el Hassan — A4

1957, Mar. 2 Photo. *Perf. 13½x13*

13 A3 15fr blue green 1.10 .80
14 A3 25fr gray olive 1.50 .80
15 A3 30fr deep rose 2.75 1.25
Nos. 13-15 (3) 5.35 2.85

Anniversary of independence.

1957, July 9 *Perf. 13*

16 A4 15fr blue .85 .60
17 A4 25fr green 1.10 .85
18 A4 30fr car rose 1.75 1.25
Nos. 16-18 (3) 3.70 2.70

Designation of Prince Moulay el Hassan as heir to the throne.

King Mohammed V — A5

1957, Nov. *Perf. 12½*

19 A5 15fr blk & brt grn .50 .45
20 A5 25fr blk & rose red .95 .60
21 A5 30fr blk & vio 1.10 .80
Nos. 19-21 (3) 2.55 1.85

Enthronement of Mohammed V, 30th anniv.

Morocco Pavilion, Brussels World's Fair — A6

1958, Apr. 20 Engr. *Perf. 13*

22 A6 15fr brt grnsh bl .30 .25
23 A6 25fr carmine .30 .30
24 A6 30fr indigo .45 .35
Nos. 22-24 (3) 1.05 .90

World's Fair, Brussels.

UNESCO Building, Paris, and Mohammed V — A7

1958, Nov. 23

25 A7 15fr green .25 .20
26 A7 25fr lake .25 .25
27 A7 30fr blue .50 .30
Nos. 25-27 (3) 1.00 .75

UNESCO Headquarters opening, Paris, Nov. 3.

Ben Smin Sanatorium A8

1959, Jan. 18 Unwmk. *Perf. 13*

28 A8 50fr dk brn, car & slate grn .50 .30

Red Cross-Red Crescent Society.

Mohammed V — A9

Princess Lalla Amina — A10

1959, Aug. 18 Engr. *Perf. 13*

29 A9 15fr dk car rose .45 .30
30 A9 25fr brt bl .60 .40
31 A9 45fr dk grn .80 .45
Nos. 29-31 (3) 1.85 1.15

50th birthday of King Mohammed V.

1959, Nov. 17

32 A10 15fr blue .30 .20
33 A10 25fr green .35 .20
34 A10 45fr rose lil .45 .30
Nos. 32-34 (3) 1.10 .70

Issued for International Children's Week.

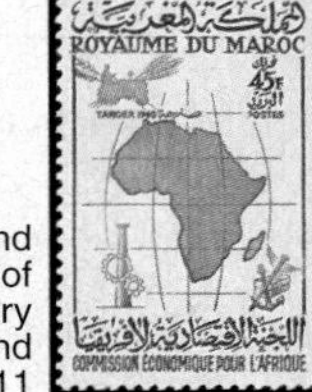

Map of Africa and Symbols of Agriculture, Industry and Commerce — A11

1960, Jan. 31 *Perf. 13*

35 A11 45fr vio, ocher & emer .65 .45

Issued to publicize the meeting of the Economic Commission for Africa, Tangier.

Refugees and Uprooted Oak Emblem A12

45fr, Refugee family and uprooted oak emblem.

1960, Apr. 7 Unwmk. *Perf. 13*

36 A12 15fr ocher, blk & grn .20 .20
37 A12 45fr blk & grn .35 .30

World Refugee Year, July 1, 1959-June 30, 1960.

Marrakesh A13

1960, Apr. 25 Engr. *Perf. 13*

38 A13 100fr grn, bl & red brn .90 .60

900th anniversary of Marrakesh.

Lamp — A14

Wrestlers — A16

Arab League Center, Cairo and Mohammed V — A15

Designs: 25fr, Fountain and arched door. 30fr, Minaret. 35fr, Ornamented wall. 45fr, Moorish architecture.

1960, May 12 *Perf. 13½*

39 A14 15fr rose lil .55 .50
40 A14 25fr dk bl .65 .55
41 A14 30fr org red 1.25 .65

42 A14 35fr black 1.50 1.10
43 A14 45fr yel grn 2.25 1.50
Nos. 39-43 (5) 6.20 4.30

1,100th anniv. of Karaouiyne University, Fez.

1960, June 28 Photo. *Perf. 12½*

44 A15 15fr grn & blk .25 .20

Opening of the Arab League Center and the Arab Postal Museum, Cairo.

1960, Sept. 26 Engr. *Perf. 13*

Sports: 10fr, Gymnast. 15fr, Bicyclist. 20fr, Weight lifter. 30fr, Runner. 40fr, Boxers. 45fr, Sailboat. 70fr, Fencers.

45 A16 5fr ol, vio bl & plum .20 .20
46 A16 10fr org brn, bl & brn .20 .20
47 A16 15fr emer, bl & org brn .30 .20
48 A16 20fr ultra, ol & brn .35 .20
49 A16 30fr vio bl, mar & sep .40 .20
50 A16 40fr grnsh bl, dk pur & red brn .65 .25
51 A16 45fr grn, plum & ultra .80 .30
52 A16 70fr dk brn, bl & gray 1.10 .40
Nos. 45-52 (8) 4.00 1.95

17th Olympic Games, Rome, 8/25-9/11.

Runner A17

1961, Aug. 30 Unwmk. *Perf. 13*

53 A17 20fr dk grn .20 .20
54 A17 30fr dk car rose .35 .25
55 A17 50fr brt bl .45 .40
Nos. 53-55 (3) 1.00 .85

3rd Pan-Arabic Games, Casablanca.

Post Office, Tangier — A18

View of Tangier and Gibraltar A19

Design: 30fr, Telephone operator.

1961, Dec. 8 Litho. *Perf. 12½*

56 A18 20fr red vio .30 .20
57 A18 30fr green .40 .25
57A A19 90fr lt bl & vio bl .70 .50
Nos. 56-57A (3) 1.40 .95

Conference of the African Postal and Telecommunications Union, Tangier.

Mohammed V and Map of Africa — A20

Patrice Lumumba and Map of Congo — A21

1962, Jan. 4 Unwmk. *Perf. 11½*

58 A20 20c buff & vio brn .25 .20
59 A20 30c lt & dk bl .30 .20

1st anniv. of the conference of African heads of state at Casablanca.

1962, Feb. 12 *Perf. 12½*

60 A21 20c bis & blk .25 .20
61 A21 30c dl red brn & blk .30 .25

1st death anniv. of Patrice Lumumba, Premier of Congo Democratic Republic.

Moroccan Students — A22

Arab League Building, Cairo — A23

1962, Mar. 5 Engr.

62 A22 20fr multi .35 .20
63 A22 30fr multi .35 .25
64 A22 90fr gray grn, indigo & brn .60 .45
Nos. 62-64 (3) 1.30 .90

Issued to honor the nation's students.

1962, Mar. 22 Photo. *Perf. 13½x13*

65 A23 20c red brn .35 .20

Arab Propaganda Week, 3/22-28. See #146.

Malaria Eradication Emblem and Swamp A24

50c, Dagger stabbing mosquito, vert.

1962, Sept. 3 Engr. *Perf. 13*

66 A24 20c dk grn & grnsh blk .20 .20
67 A24 50c dk grn & mag .40 .30

WHO drive to eradicate malaria.

Fish and Aquarium — A25

1962, Nov. 5 Unwmk. *Perf. 13*

68 A25 20c shown .45 .20
69 A25 30c Moray eel .55 .20

Casablanca Aquarium.

Courier and Sherifian Stamp of 1912 A26

Designs: 30c, Courier on foot and round Sherifian cancellation. 50c, Sultan Hassan I and octagonal cancellation.

1962, Dec. 15 Unwmk.

70 A26 20c Prus grn & redsh brn .65 .20
71 A26 30c dk car rose & blk .65 .35
72 A26 50c bl & bister .95 .45
Nos. 70-72 (3) 2.25 1.00

Stamp Day; 1st National Stamp Exhibition, Dec. 15-23; 75th anniv. of the Sherifian Post and the 50th anniv. of its reorganization.

Boy Scout — A27

King Hassan II — A28

1962, Aug. 8 Litho. *Perf. 11½*

73 A27 20c vio brn & lt bl .20 .20

5th Arab Boy Scout Jamboree, Rabat.

1962 Engr. *Perf. 13½x13*

75 A28 1c gray olive .20 .20
76 A28 2c violet .20 .20
77 A28 5c black .20 .20
78 A28 10c brn org .20 .20
79 A28 15c Prus grn .20 .20
80 A28 20c purple .25 .20
81 A28 30c dp yel grn .30 .20
82 A28 50c vio brn .60 .20
83 A28 70c deep blue .90 .20
84 A28 80c magenta 1.50 .25
Nos. 75-84 (10) 4.55 2.05

"Mazelin" (designer-engraver) reads down on Nos. 75-84. See Nos. 110-114.

King Moulay Ismail — A29

Al Idrissi, Geographer — A30

1963, Mar. 3 *Perf. 12½*

85 A29 20c sepia .40 .25

Tercentenary of Meknes as Ismaili capital.

1963-66 Engr.

#87, 88A, Ibn Batota, explorer. #88, Ibn Khaldoun, historian and sociologist.

86 A30 20c dk sl grn .40 .30
87 A30 20c dk car rose .40 .30
88 A30 20c black .40 .30
88A A30 40c dk vio bl ('66) .45 .30
Nos. 86-88A (4) 1.65 1.20

Famous medieval men of Morocco (Maghreb). No. 88A also marks the inauguration of the ferryboat "Ibn Batota" connecting Tangier and Malaga.

Issued: #86-88, 5/7/63; #88A, 7/15/66.

Sugar Beet and Sugar Refinery, Sidi Slimane A31

1963, June 10 Unwmk. *Perf. 13*

89 A31 20c shown .35 .20
90 A31 50c Tuna fisherman, vert. .50 .35

FAO "Freedom from Hunger" campaign.

Heads of Ramses II, Abu Simbel A32

Designs: 30c, Isis, Kalabsha Temple, vert. 50c, Temple of Philae.

1963, July 15 Engr. *Perf. 11½*

91 A32 20c black .20 .20
92 A32 30c vio, *grysh* .35 .20
93 A32 50c maroon, *buff* .50 .25
Nos. 91-93 (3) 1.05 .65

Campaign to save historic monuments in Nubia.

Agadir Before Earthquake A33

30c, Like 20c, with "29 Février 1960" and crossed bars added. 50c, Agadir rebuilt.

Engr.; Engr. & Photo. (No. 95)

1963, Oct. 10 *Perf. 13½x13*

94 A33 20c bl & brn red .35 .25
95 A33 30c bl, brn red & red .40 .30
96 A33 50c bl & brn red .80 .45
Nos. 94-96 (3) 1.55 1.00

Issued to publicize the rebuilding of Agadir.

Centenary Emblem and Plan of Agadir Hospital A34

1963, Oct. 28 Photo. *Perf. 12½x13*

97 A34 30c blk, dp car & sil .35 .20

Centenary of the International Red Cross.

Arms of Morocco and Rabat — A35

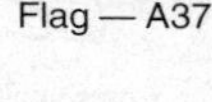

Flag — A37

Hands Breaking Chain A36

1963, Nov. 18 *Perf. 13x12½*

98 A35 20c gold, red, blk & emer .30 .20

Installation of Parliament.

1963, Dec. 10 Engr. *Perf. 13*

99 A36 20c dk brn, grn & org .35 .20

15th anniversary of the Universal Declaration of Human Rights.

1963, Dec. 25 Photo. *Perf. 13x12½*

100 A37 20c blk, dp car & grn .40 .20

Evacuation of all foreign military forces from Moroccan territory.

Moulay Abd-er-Rahman, by Delacroix — A38

1964, Mar. 3 Engr. *Perf. 12x13*

101 A38 1d multi 2.00 1.40

Coronation of King Hassan II, 3rd anniv.

Weather Map of Africa and UN Emblem — A39

Children on Vacation A40

30c, World map and barometer trace, horiz.

1964, Mar. 23 Photo. *Perf. 11½*
Granite Paper

102 A39 20c multi .30 .20
103 A39 30c multi .40 .30

UN 4th World Meteorological Day. See No. C10.

1964, July 6 Litho. *Perf. 12½*

30c, Heads of boy and girl, buildings.

104 A40 20c multi .25 .20
105 A40 30c multi .35 .25

Issued for vacation camps for children of P.T.T. employees.

Olympic Torch A41

Cape Spartel Lighthouse, Sultan Mohammed ben Abd-er-Rahman A42

1964, Sept. 22 Engr. *Perf. 13*

106 A41 20c car lake, dk pur & grn .30 .20
107 A41 30c bl, dk grn & red brn .45 .30
108 A41 50c grn, red & brn .60 .50
Nos. 106-108 (3) 1.35 1.00

18th Olympic Games, Tokyo, Oct. 10-25.

Perf. 12½x11½
1964, Oct. 15 Photo.

109 A42 25c multi .35 .20

Centenary of the Cape Spartel lighthouse.

King Type of 1962

1964-65 Engr. *Perf. 12½x13*
Size: 17x23mm

110 A28 20c purple (redrawn) 2.00 .30

Perf. 13½x13
Size: 18x22mm

111 A28 25c rose red ('65) .35 .20
112 A28 35c slate ('65) .55 .20
113 A28 40c ultra ('65) .55 .20
114 A28 60c red lilac ('65) .85 .20
Nos. 110-114 (5) 4.30 1.10

The Arabic inscription touches the frame on No. 110. "Mazelin" (designer-engraver) reads up on No. 110, down on Nos. 111-114. No. 110 is a coil stamp with red control numbers on the back of some copies.

Iris — A43

Mohammed V Arriving by Plane — A44

1965 Photo. *Perf. 11½*
Granite Paper

115 A43 25c shown .75 .50
116 A43 40c Gladiolus segetum 1.00 .60
117 A43 60c Capparis spinosa, horiz. 1.60 1.10
Nos. 115-117 (3) 3.35 2.20

Printed in sheets of 10. Five tête-bêche pairs in every sheet; vertical stamps arranged 5x2, horizontal stamps 2x5.
See Nos. 129-131.

1965, Mar. 15 Litho. *Perf. 12½*

118 A44 25c lt bl & dk grn .25 .20

10th anniv. of the return of King Mohammed V from exile and the restoration of the monarchy.

ITU Emblem, Punched-Tape Writer and Telegraph Wires — A45

Design: 40c, ITU emblem, Syncom satellite, radio waves and "ITU" in Morse code.

Perf. 13x14
1965, May 17 Unwmk. Typo.

119 A45 25c multi .25 .20
120 A45 40c lt bl, dp bl & bis .35 .25

ITU, centenary.

ICY Emblem A46

1965, June 14 Engr. *Perf. 13*

121 A46 25c slate grn .25 .20
122 A46 60c dk car rose .35 .25

International Cooperation Year.

Royal Prawn A47

#123, Triton shell. #124, Varnish shell (pitaria chione). #125, Great voluted shell (cymbium neptuni). #126, Helmet crab, vert. 40c, Mantis shrimp, vert.

1965 Photo. *Perf. 11½*
Granite Paper

123 A47 25c vio & multi 1.00 .40
124 A47 25c lt bl & multi 1.00 .40
125 A47 25c org & multi 1.00 .40
126 A47 25c lt grn & multi 1.00 .40
127 A47 40c bl & multi 1.75 .60
128 A47 1d yel & multi 2.50 1.25
Nos. 123-128 (6) 8.25 3.45

Printed in sheets of 10. Nos. 126-127 (5x2); others (2x5). Five tête bêche pairs in every sheet.

Flower Type of 1965

Orchids: 25c, Ophrys speculum. 40c, Ophrys fusca. 60c, Ophrys tenthredinifera (front and side view), horiz.

1965, Dec. 13 Photo. *Perf. 11½*
Granite Paper

129 A43 25c yel & multi .50 .30
130 A43 40c dl rose & multi .60 .30
131 A43 60c lt bl & multi 1.10 .90
Nos. 129-131 (3) 2.20 1.50

Note on tête bêche pairs after No. 117 also applies to Nos. 129-131.

Grain — A48

40c, Various citrus fruit. 60c, Olives, horiz.

1966 Photo. *Perf. 11½*
Granite Paper

133 A48 25c blk & bisTER .30 .20
136 A48 40c multi .50 .25
137 A48 60c gray & multi .55 .25
Nos. 133-137 (3) 1.35 .70

For surcharge see No. 231.

Flag, Map and Dove A49

1966, Mar. 2 Typo. *Perf. 14x13*

139 A49 25c brt grn & red .20 .20

Tenth anniversary of Independence.

King Hassan II — A50

1966, Mar. 2 Engr. *Perf. 13*

140 A50 25c red, brt grn & indigo .20 .20

Coronation of King Hassan II, 5th anniv.

Cross-country Runner — A51

1966, Mar. 20 Engr. *Perf. 13*

141 A51 25c blue green .30 .20

53rd International Cross-country Race.

WHO Headquarters from West — A52

40c, WHO Headquarters from the East.

1966, May 3 Engr. *Perf. 13*

142 A52 25c rose lil & blk .25 .20
143 A52 40c dp bl & blk .35 .25

Inauguration of the WHO Headquarters, Geneva.

Crown Prince Hassan Kissing Hand of King Mohammed V — A53

25c, King Hassan II and parachutist.

Perf. 12½x12
1966, May 14 Photo. Unwmk.

144 A53 25c gold & blk .30 .25
145 A53 40c gold & blk .35 .30
a. Strip of 2, #144-145 + label .70 .55

10th anniv. of the Royal Armed Forces.

Type of 1962 Inscribed: "SEMAINE DE LA PALESTINE"

1966, May 16 *Perf. 11x11½*

146 A23 25c slate blue .20 .20

Issued for Palestine Week.

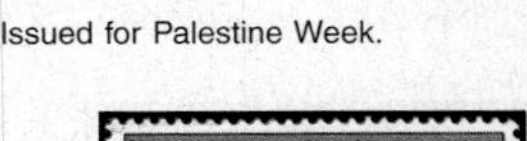

Train — A54

1966, Dec. 19 Photo. *Perf. 13½*

147 A54 25c shown .80 .25
148 A54 40c Ship .75 .30
149 A54 1d Autobus 1.00 .45
Nos. 147-149 (3) 2.55 1.00

Twaite Shad A55

Fish: 40c, Plain bonito. 1d, Bluefish, vert.

1967, Feb. 1 Photo. *Perf. 11½*
Granite Paper

150 A55 25c yel & multi .75 .30
151 A55 40c yel & multi .85 .30
152 A55 1d lt grn & multi 1.90 .90
Nos. 150-152 (3) 3.50 1.50

Printed tête bêche in sheets of 10. Nos. 150-151 (2x5); No. 152 (5x2).

Ait Aadel Dam — A56

1967, Mar. 3 Engr. *Perf. 13*

153 A56 25c sl grn, Prus bl & gray .35 .25
154 A56 40c Prus bl & lt brn .50 .25

Inauguration of Ait Aadel Dam.

Rabat Hilton Hotel, Map of Morocco and Roman Arch — A57

1967, Mar. 3

155 A57 25c brt bl & blk .30 .25
156 A57 1d brt bl & pur .60 .25

Opening of the Rabat Hilton Hotel.

Torch, Globe, Town and Lions Emblem — A58

1967, Apr. 22 Photo. *Perf. 12½*

157 A58 40c gold & saph bl .40 .25
158 A58 1d gold & slate grn .65 .25

Lions International, 50th anniversary.

Three Hands Holding Pickax — A59

1967, July 9 Engr. *Perf. 13*

159 A59 25c slate green .25 .20

Community Development Campaign.

Intl. Tourism Year Emblem A60

1967, Aug. 9 Photo. *Perf. 12½*

160 A60 1d lt ultra & dk bl .60 .35

Arrow and Map of Mediterranean A61

1967, Sept. 8 *Perf. 13x12*

161 A61 25c dk bl, ultra, red & tan .30 .20
162 A61 40c blk, bl grn, red & tan .35 .20

Mediterranean Games, Tunis, Sept. 8-17.

Steeplechase — A62

1967, Oct. 14 Photo. *Perf. 12½*

163 A62 40c yel grn, blk & brt rose lilac .35 .25
164 A62 1d lt ultra, blk & brt rose lilac .55 .35

International Horseshow.

Cotton — A63

Human Rights Flame — A64

1967, Nov. 15 Photo. *Perf. 12½*

165 A63 40c lt bl, grn & yel .50 .25

1968, Jan. 10 Engr. *Perf. 13*

166 A64 25c gray .30 .20
167 A64 1d rose claret .35 .25

International Human Rights Year.

King Hassan II — A65

1968-74 Litho. *Perf. 13*

Portrait in Magenta, Brown and Black

Size: 23x30mm

169 A65 1c cream & blk .20 .20
170 A65 2c lt grnsh bl & blk .20 .20
171 A65 5c lt ol grn & blk .20 .20
172 A65 10c pale rose & blk .20 .20
173 A65 15c gray bl & blk .20 .20
174 A65 20c pink & blk .25 .20
175 A65 25c white & blk .25 .20
176 A65 30c pale rose & blk .30 .20
177 A65 35c bl & blk .50 .30
178 A65 40c gray & blk .50 .20
179 A65 50c lt bl & blk .60 .20
180 A65 60c salmon & blk .85 .20
181 A65 70c gray & blk 3.50 .90
182 A65 75c pale yel ('74) 1.00 .30
183 A65 80c ocher & blk 1.00 .30

Perf. 13½x14

Size: 26x40mm

184 A65 90c lt bl grn & blk 1.40 .45
185 A65 1d tan & blk 1.75 .30
186 A65 2d lt ultra & blk 2.50 .60
187 A65 3d bluish lil & blk 5.25 1.10
188 A65 5d apple grn & blk 8.50 3.25
Nos. 169-188 (20) 29.15 9.70

For overprints & surcharges see #224, B17-B18.

Nurse and Child — A66

Pendant — A67

1968, Apr. 8 Engr. *Perf. 13*

189 A66 25c ultra, red & olive .25 .20
190 A66 40c slate, red & olive .35 .20

WHO, 20th anniv.

1968, May 15 Photo. *Perf. 11½*

191 A67 25c shown .65 .25
192 A67 40c Bracelet .75 .30
a. Pair, #191-192, vertically tête-bêche 1.50 1.25

Moroccan Red Crescent Society. See Nos. 373-374.

Map of Morocco and Rotary Emblem — A68

1968, May 23 *Perf. 13*

193 A68 40c multi .45 .20
194 A68 1d ultra & multi .70 .30

Rotary Intl. District Conference, Casablanca, May 24-25.

Ornamental Design A69

Designs: Various patterns used for sashes.

1968, July 12 Photo. *Perf. 11½*

195 A69 25c multi 1.75 .75
196 A69 40c multi 2.25 1.00
197 A69 60c multi 3.25 1.75
198 A69 1d multi 5.75 2.75
Nos. 195-198 (4) 13.00 6.25

Berber (Riff), North Morocco — A70

Princess Lalla Meryem — A71

Regional Costumes: 10c, Man from Ait Moussa ou Ali. 15c, Woman from Ait Mouhad. No. 200, Bargeman from Rabat Salé. No. 201, Citadin man. 40c, Citadin woman. 60c, Royal Mokhazni. No. 204, Zemmours man. No. 204A, Man from Meknassa. No. 206, Msouffa woman, Sahara.

1968-74 Litho. *Perf. 13x12½*

198A A70 10c multi ('69) .45 .30
199 A70 15c yel & multi ('69) .75 .40
200 A70 25c bis & multi .75 .45
201 A70 25c tan & multi ('69) .85 .45
202 A70 40c lt bl & multi .90 .65
203 A70 60c emer & multi 1.25 .85
204 A70 1d lt bl & multi 1.60 1.10
204A A70 1d gray & multi ('69) 1.50 .75

Perf. 15

205 A70 1d bis & multi 1.40 .90
206 A70 1d grn & multi 1.40 .90
a. Souvenir sheet of 10, #198A-206, perf. 13 15.00 13.00
b. As "a," with red overprint & surcharge 18.00 16.00
Nos. 198A-206 (10) 10.85 6.75

No. 206a issued June 30, 1970, for the opening of the National P.T.T. Museum, Rabat. Sold for 10d.

No. 206b issued Nov. 22, 1974, for the 8th Cong. of the Intl. Fed. of Blood Donors. Each stamp overprinted vertically "8eme Congres de la F.I.O.D.S." and blood container emblem. Black marginal inscription partially obliterated with lines, new Arabic inscription and price added. Sold for 20d.

1968, Oct. 7 Litho. *Perf. 13½*

Children's Week: 40c, Princess Lalla Asmaa. 1d, Crown Prince Sidi Mohammed.

207 A71 25c red & multi .40 .20
208 A71 40c yel & multi .50 .30
209 A71 1d lt bl & multi .60 .50
Nos. 207-209 (3) 1.50 1.00

Wrestling, Aztec Calendar Stone and Olympic Rings — A72

1968, Oct. 25 Photo. *Perf. 12x11½*

210 A72 15c shown .25 .20
211 A72 20c Basketball .25 .20
212 A72 25c Cycling .40 .30
213 A72 40c Boxing .45 .30
214 A72 60c Running .55 .30
215 A72 1d Soccer .75 .50
Nos. 210-215 (6) 2.65 1.80

19th Olympic Games, Mexico City, 10/12-27.

10 Dirham Coin of Tetuan, 1780 — A73

Women from Zagora A74

Coins: 25c, Dirham, Agmat, c. 1138 A.D. 40c, Dirham, El Alya (Fes), c. 840 A.D. 60c, Dirham, Marrakesh, c. 1248 A.D.

1968, Dec. 17 Photo. *Perf. 11½*

Granite Paper

216 A73 20c dp plum, sil & blk .40 .25
217 A73 25c dk rose brn, gold & blk .50 .35
218 A73 40c dk grn, sil & blk 1.00 .45
219 A73 60c dk red, gold & blk 1.25 .65
Nos. 216-219,C16-C17 (6) 14.40 7.70

Issued with tabs.

1969, Jan. 21 Litho. *Perf. 12*

Design: 25c, Women from Ait Adidou.

220 A74 15c multi .90 .50
221 A74 25c multi 1.10 .70
Nos. 220-221,C15 (3) 4.00 2.05

Painting by Belkahya — A75

King Hassan II — A76

1969, Mar. 27 Litho. ***Perf. 11½x12***
222 A75 1d lt grnsh bl, blk & brn .45 .25

International Day of the Theater.

1969, July 9 Photo. ***Perf. 11½***
223 A76 1d gold & multi .80 .40

40th birthday of King Hassan II. A souvenir sheet contains one No. 223. Size: 75x105mm. Sold for 2.50d.

No. 185 Overprinted

1969, Sept. 22 Litho. ***Perf. 13***
224 A65 1d tan & multi 4.50 2.75

First Arab Summit Conference, Rabat.

Mahatma Gandhi — A77

1969, Oct. 16 Photo. ***Perf. 11½***
225 A77 40c pale vio, blk & gray .75 .40

Mohandas K. Gandhi (1869-1948), leader in India's struggle for independence.

ILO Emblem A78

1969, Oct. 29
226 A78 50c multi .40 .25

ILO, 50th anniv.

King Hassan II on Way to Prayer — A79

1969, Nov. 20 Photo. ***Perf. 11½***
227 A79 1d multi .75 .40

1st Arab Summit Conference, Rabat, Sept. 1969. For overprint see No. 311.

Spahi Horsemen, by Haram al Glaoui A80

1970, Jan. 23 Engr. ***Perf. 12x13***
228 A80 1d multi .75 .40

Main Sewer, Fez — A81

Guedra Dance, by P. C. Beaubrun A82

1970, Mar. 23 Litho. ***Perf. 12***
229 A81 60c multi .30 .20

50th Congress of Municipal Engineers, Rabat, Mar. 1970.

1970, Apr. 15
230 A82 40c multi .55 .25

Folklore Festival, Marrakesh, May 1970.

No. 137 Overprinted "1970", "Census" in Arabic in Red and Surcharged in Black

1970, July 9 Photo. ***Perf. 11½***
231 A48 25c on 60c multi .45 .25

Issued to publicize the 1970 census.

Radar Station at Souk El Arba des Sehoul, and Satellite — A83

Ruddy Shelduck — A84

1970, Aug. 20
232 A83 1d lt ultra & multi .50 .30

Revolution of King and People, 17th anniv.

1970, Sept. 25 Photo. ***Perf. 11½***
233 A84 25c shown .75 .40
234 A84 40c Houbara bustard .90 .45

Campaign to save Moroccan wildlife.

Man Reading Book, Intl. Education Year Emblem — A85

1970, Oct. 20 Litho. ***Perf. 12x11½***
235 A85 60c dl yel & multi .45 .25

Symbols of Peace, Justice and Progress A86

1970, Oct. 27 ***Perf. 13½***
236 A86 50c multi .40 .25

United Nations, 25th anniversary.

Arab League Countries and Emblem A87

1970, Nov. 13 Photo. ***Perf. 11½***
237 A87 50c multi .40 .25

Arab League, 25th anniversary.

Olive Grove, Tree and Branch A88

1970, Dec. 3 Litho. ***Perf. 12***
238 A88 50c red brn & grn .55 .30

International Olive Year.

Es Sounna Mosque, Rabat A89

1971, Jan. 5 Engr. ***Perf. 13***
239 A89 60c ol bis, bl & sl grn .40 .25

Restoration of Es Sounna Mosque, Rabat, built in 1785.

Heart and Horse — A90

1971, Feb. 23 Photo. ***Perf. 12x12½***
240 A90 50c blk & multi .40 .20

European heart research week, Feb. 21-28.

Dam and Hassan II — A91

1971, Mar. 3 ***Perf. 11½***
241 A91 25c multi .35 .20
a. Souv. sheet of 4 2.50 2.00

Accession of King Hassan II, 10th anniv. No. 241a issued Mar. 24. Sold for 2.50d.

Black and White Hands with Dove and Emblem A92

1971, June 16 Photo. ***Perf. 13***
242 A92 50c brn & multi .30 .20

Intl. Year against Racial Discrimination.

Children Around the World — A93

Shah Mohammed Riza Pahlavi of Iran — A94

1971, Oct. 4 Litho. ***Perf. 13x14***
243 A93 40c emer & multi .25 .20

International Children's Day.

1971, Oct. 11 Photo. ***Perf. 11½***
244 A94 1d bl & multi .50 .35

2500th anniv. of the founding of the Persian empire by Cyrus the Great.

Mausoleum of Mohammed V — A95

50c, Mausoleum, close-up view, and Mohammed V. 1d, Decorated interior wall.

1971, Nov. 10 Litho. ***Perf. 14***
245 A95 25c multi .35 .20
246 A95 50c multi .45 .20
247 A95 1d multi, vert. .75 .25
Nos. 245-247 (3) 1.55 .65

Soccer Ball and Games Emblem A96

1971, Nov. 30 Photo. ***Perf. 13x13½***
248 A96 40c shown .45 .25
249 A96 60c Runner .55 .25

Mediterranean Games, Izmir, Turkey, Oct. 6-17.

Arab Postal Union Emblem A97

1971, Dec. 23 Litho. *Perf. 13x12½*

250	A97 25c dk & lt bl & org	.20	.20

25th anniv. of the Conference of Sofar, Lebanon, establishing APU.

Sun over Cultivated Sand Dunes — A98

Torch and Book Year Emblem — A99

1971, Dec. 30 Photo. *Perf. 12½*

251	A98 70c blk, bl & yel	.35	.20

Sherifian Phosphate Office (fertilizer production and export), 50th anniversary.

1972, Jan. 12 *Perf. 11½*

252	A99 1d silver & multi	.40	.20

International Book Year.

National Lottery — A100

Bridge of Sighs — A101

1972, Feb. 7 Photo. *Perf. 13*

253	A100 25c tan, blk & gold	.20	.20

Creation of a national lottery.

1972, Feb. 25

Designs: 50c, St. Mark's Basilica and waves, horiz. 1d, Lion of St. Mark.

254	A101 25c multi	.20	.20
255	A101 50c red, blk & buff	.30	.20
256	A101 1d lt bl & multi	.50	.35
	Nos. 254-256 (3)	1.00	.75

UNESCO campaign to save Venice.

Bridge, Road, Map of Africa — A102

1972, Apr. 21 *Perf. 13*

257	A102 75c blue & multi	.40	.25

2nd African Road Conf., Rabat, Apr. 17-22.

Morocco No. 223 — A103

1972, Apr. 27 *Perf. 11½*

258	A103 1d lt ultra & multi	.45	.25

Stamp Day.

The Engagement of Imilchil, by Tayeb Lahlou A104

1972, May 26 Litho. *Perf. 13x13½*

259	A104 60c blk & multi	.60	.35

Folklore Festival, Marrakesh, May 26-June 4.

Map of Africa, Dove and OAU Emblem — A105

1972, June 12 Photo. *Perf. 11½*

260	A105 25c multi	.25	.20

9th Summit Conference of Organization for African Unity, Rabat, June 12-15.

Landscape, Environment Emblem — A106

1972, July 20 Photo. *Perf. 12½x12*

261	A106 50c bl & multi	.30	.20

UN Conference on Human Environment, Stockholm, June 5-16

Olympic Emblems, Running A107

1972, Aug. 29 Photo. *Perf. 13x13½*

262	A107 25c shown	.20	.20
263	A107 50c Wrestling	.25	.20
264	A107 75c Soccer	.45	.25
265	A107 1d Cycling	.55	.35
	Nos. 262-265 (4)	1.45	1.00

20th Olympic Games, Munich, 8/26-9/11.

Sow Thistle — A108

Mountain Gazelle — A109

1972, Sept. 15 Litho. *Perf. 14*

266	A108 25c shown	.35	.20
267	A108 40c Amberboa crupinoides	.45	.25

See No. 305-306.

1972, Sept. 29 Photo. *Perf. 11½*

268	A109 25c shown	.60	.35
269	A109 40c Barbary sheep	.90	.40

Nos. 266-269 issued for nature protection.

Rabat Rug — A110

Child and UNICEF Emblem — A111

25c, High Atlas rug. 70c, Tazenakht rug. 75c, Rabat rug, different pattern.

Perf. 13½ (25fr, 70fr), 11½

1972-73 Photo.

270	A110 25c multi	.70	.25
270A	A110 50c multi	.90	.20
271	A110 70c multi	1.25	.50
271A	A110 75c multi	1.40	.50
	Nos. 270-271A (4)	4.25	1.45

Issued: 50c, 75c, 10/27; 25c, 70c, 12/28/73.
See Nos. 326-327.

1972, Dec. 20 Photo. *Perf. 13½x13*

272	A111 75c brt grn & bl	.25	.20

International Children's Day.

Symbolic Letter Carrier and Stamp A112

1973, Jan. 30 Photo. *Perf. 13x13½*

273	A112 25c brn & multi	.20	.20

Stamp Day.

Weather Map, Northern Hemisphere A113

1973, Feb. 23 Photo. *Perf. 13*

274	A113 70c silver & multi	.40	.25

Intl. meteorological cooperation, cent.

King Hassan II, Coat of Arms — A114

1973-76 Photo. *Perf. 14*

275	A114	1c pale yel & multi	.20	.20
276	A114	2c pale bl & multi	.20	.20
277	A114	5c pale ol & multi	.20	.20
278	A114	10c brn org & multi	.20	.20
279	A114	15c vio gray & multi	.20	.20
280	A114	20c pink & multi	.25	.20
281	A114	25c pale bl & multi	.20	.20
282	A114	30c rose & multi	.25	.20
283	A114	35c org yel & multi	.35	.20
284	A114	40c lt gray & multi	4.00	.35
285	A114	50c ultra & multi	.50	.20
286	A114	60c sal & multi	.60	.20
287	A114	70c yel grn & multi	.50	.20
288	A114	75c lem & multi	.45	.20
289	A114	80c multi	.50	.30
290	A114	90c brt grn & multi	.55	.20
291	A114	1d beige & multi	1.75	.20
292	A114	2d gray & multi	3.50	.50
293	A114	3d lt lil & multi	4.50	.75
294	A114	5d lt brn & multi ('75)	3.50	1.00
294A	A114	5d pink & multi ('76)	3.50	1.00
		Nos. 275-294A (21)	25.90	6.90

Nos. B26-B27 Surcharged to Obliterate Surtax

1973, Mar. 13 *Perf. 11½*

295	SP1 25c multi	1.75	1.75
296	SP1 70c multi	2.00	2.00
a.	Pair, #295-296, vert. tête-bêche	5.00	5.00

Tourism Conference 1973. Arabic overprint and date on one line on No. 296.
See Nos. 351-352.

Holy Ka'aba, Mecca, Mosque and Minaret, Rabat A115

1973, May 3 Photo. *Perf. 13½x14*

297	A115 25c lt bl & multi	.20	.20

Mohammed's 1,403rd birthday.

Roses and M'Gouna
A116

1973, May 14 *Perf. 13*
298 A116 25c bl & multi .20 .20

Rose Festival of M'Gouna.

Hands, Torch, OAU Emblem — A117

1973, May 25 Photo. *Perf. 14x13*
299 A117 70c deep claret & multi .30 .20

OAU, 10th anniversary.

Dancers with Tambourines — A118

Design: 1d, Dancer with handbells, Marrakesh Minaret, Atlas Mountain.

1973, May 30 *Perf. 12½x13*
300 A118 50c multi .40 .20
301 A118 1d multi .50 .30

Folklore Festival, Marrakesh.

Copernicus
A119

1973, June 29 *Perf. 13x13½*
302 A119 70c Heliocentric system .45 .25

Microscope, WHO Emblem, World Map — A120

1973, July 16 Photo. *Perf. 13x12½*
303 A120 70c multi .40 .20

WHO, 25th anniversary.

INTERPOL Emblem, Fingerprint
A121

1973, Sept. 12 Photo. *Perf. 13x13½*
304 A121 70c brn, sil & bl .30 .20

50th anniv. of Intl. Criminal Police Org.

Flower Type of 1972

1973, Oct. 12 Litho. *Perf. 14*
305 A108 25c Daisies, horiz. .55 .20
306 A108 1d Thistle .95 .35

Nature protection.

Berber Hyena
A122

Design: 50c, Eleonora's falcon, vert.

1973, Nov. 23 Photo. *Perf. 14*
307 A122 25c multi .70 .25
308 A122 50c multi 1.40 .40

Nature protection.

Map and Colors of Morocco, Algeria and Tunisia
A123

1973, Dec. 7 *Perf. 13x13½*
309 A123 25c gold & multi .25 .20

Maghreb Committee for Coordination of Posts and Telecommunications.

Fairway and Drive over Water Hazard — A124

1974, Feb. 8 Photo. *Perf. 14x13*
310 A124 70c multi 1.25 .25

International Golf Grand Prix for the Hassan II Morocco trophy.

No. 227 Overprinted in Red

1974, Feb. 25 *Perf. 11½*
311 A79 1d multi 2.00 1.25

Islamic Conference, Lahore, India, 1974.

Map of Africa, Scales, Human Rights Flame — A125

1974, Mar. 15 Photo. *Perf. 14x13½*
312 A125 70c gold & multi .40 .20

25th anniversary of the Universal Declaration of Human Rights.

Vanadinite
A126

1974-75 Photo. *Perf. 13*

313	A126	25c	shown	1.50	.40
313A	A126	50c	Aragonite	1.40	.25
314	A126	70c	Erythrine	2.75	.50
314A	A126	1d	Agate	2.75	.40
			Nos. 313-314A (4)	8.40	1.55

Issued: 25c, 70c, 4/30/74; 50c, 1d, 2/14/75.

Minaret, Marrakesh Mosque, Rotary Emblem — A127

1974, May 11 Photo. *Perf. 14*
315 A127 70c multi .40 .20

District 173 Rotary International annual meeting, Marrakesh, May 10-12.

UPU Emblem, Congress Dates — A128

1d, Scroll with UPU emblem, Lausanne coat of arms & 17th UPU Congress emblem, horiz.

1974, May 30 Photo.
316 A128 25c lt grn, org & blk .25 .20
317 A128 1d dk grn & multi .50 .25

Centenary of Universal Postal Union.

Drummer and Dancers — A129

1974, June 7 Photo. *Perf. 14*

Design: 70c, Knife juggler and women.

318 A129 25c multi .35 .20
319 A129 70c multi .90 .35

National folklore festival, Marrakesh.

Environment Emblem, Polution, Clean Water and Air — A130

1974, June 25 *Perf. 13*
320 A130 25c multi .25 .20

World Environment Day.

Simulated Stamps, Cancel and Magnifier
A131

1974, Aug. 2 Photo. *Perf. 13*
321 A131 70c sil & multi .25 .20

Stamp Day.

No. J5 Surcharged

1974, Sept. 25 Photo. *Perf. 14*
322 D2 1d on 5c multi 1.40 .90

Agricultural census.

World Soccer Cup — A132

Double-spurred Francolin — A133

1974, Oct. 11
323 A132 1d brt bl & multi .70 .45

World Cup Soccer Championship, Munich, June 13-July 7.

A stamp similar to No. 323, also issued Oct. 11, has gold inscription: "CHAMPION: R.F.A." in French and Arabic, honoring the German Federal Republic as championship winner. Value $32.50.

Perf. 14x13½, 13½x14

1974, Dec. 5 Photo.
324 A133 25c green & multi .60 .25
325 A133 70c Leopard, horiz. 1.25 .35

Nature protection.

Zemmour Rug
A134

Columbine
A135

Design: 1d, Beni Mguilo rug.

1974, Dec 20 *Perf. 13*
326 A134 25c multi .50 .20
327 A134 1d multi 1.00 .30

See Nos. 349-350, 398-400.

1975 Photo. *Perf. 13½*

328	A135	10c	Daisies	.20	.20
329	A135	25c	Columbine	.35	.20
330	A135	35c	Orange lilies	.40	.20
331	A135	50c	Anemones	.45	.20
332	A135	60c	White starflower	.55	.35
333	A135	70c	Poppies	.60	.35
334	A135	90c	Carnations	.90	.50
335	A135	1d	Pansies	.80	.60
			Nos. 328-335 (8)	4.25	2.60

Issued: 25c, 35c, 70c, 90c, 1/10; others, 4/29.

Water Carrier, by Feu Tayeb Lahlou A136

1975, Apr. 3 *Perf. 13*
338 A136 1d multicolored .80 .35

Stamp Collector, Carrier Pigeon, Globe — A137

Musicians and Dancers — A138

1975, May 21 Photo. *Perf. 13*
339 A137 40c gold & multi .30 .20

Stamp Day.

1975, June 12 Photo. *Perf. 14x13½*
340 A138 1d multicolored .70 .30

16th Folklore Festival, Marrakesh, 5/30-6/15.

Guitar and Association for the Blind Emblem A139

1975, July 8 *Perf. 13x13½*
341 A139 1d purple & multi .75 .35

Week of the Blind.

Animals in Forest — A140

1975, July 25 Photo. *Perf. 13x13½*
342 A140 25c multicolored .25 .20

Children's Week.

Games' Emblem, Runner, Weight Lifter — A141

1975, Sept. 4 Photo. *Perf. 13*
343 A141 40c gold, maroon & buff .30 .20

7th Mediterranean Games, Algiers, 8/23-9/6.

Bald Ibis A142

1975, Oct. 21 Photo. *Perf. 13*
344 A142 40c shown .90 .30
345 A142 1d Persian lynx, vert. 1.10 .55

Nature protection.

King Mohammed V Greeting Crowd, Prince Moulay Hassan at Left — A143

King Hassan II A144

#348, King Mohammed V wearing fez.

1975, Nov. 21 Photo. *Perf. 13½*
346 A143 40c blk, sil & dk bl .40 .20
347 A144 1d blk, gold & dk bl .55 .35
348 A144 1d blk, gold & dk bl .55 .35
a. Sheet of 3, #346-348 12.50 12.50

20th anniversary of independence.

Rug Type of 1974

25c, Ouled Besseba. 1d, Ait Ouaouzguid.

1975, Dec. 11
349 A134 25c red & multi .65 .35
350 A134 1d orange & multi .95 .40

A number of issues have been printed se-tenant in sheets of 10 (5x2) arranged vertically tête bêche.

Nos. B29-B30 Surcharged in Green to Obliterate Surtax

1975 *Perf. 11½*
351 SP1 25c blue & multi 1.75 1.75
352 SP1 70c orange & multi 1.90 1.90
a. Pair, #351-352, vertically tête-bêche 5.00 5.00

March of Moroccan people into Spanish Sahara, Dec. 1975.

"Green March of the People" — A145

1975, Dec. 30 Photo. *Perf. 13½x13*
353 A145 40c multicolored .25 .20

March of Moroccan people into Spanish Sahara, Dec. 1975.

Copper Coin, Fez, 1883-84 — A146

1976 Photo. *Perf. 14x13½*

Coins: 15c, 50c, silver coin, Rabat, 1774-75. 35c, 65c, Gold coin, Sabta, 13th-14th centuries. 1d, Square coin, Sabta, 12th-13th centuries.

354 A146 5c dull rose & multi .20 .20
355 A146 15c brown & multi .20 .20
356 A146 35c gray & multi .50 .20
357 A146 40c ocher & multi .40 .20
358 A146 50c ultra & blk .50 .20
359 A146 65c yellow & multi .55 .30
360 A146 1d multicolored .90 .45
Nos. 354-360 (7) 3.25 1.75

Issued: #354-356, 4/26; #357-360, 1/20.

1976, Sept. 9

Designs: Various Moroccan coins.

361 A146 5c green & multi .20 .20
362 A146 15c dp rose & multi .20 .20
363 A146 20c lt bl & multi .25 .20
364 A146 30c lil rose & multi .25 .20
365 A146 35c green & multi .45 .20
366 A146 70c orange & multi .60 .20
Nos. 361-366 (6) 1.95 1.20

See Nos. 403-406A, 524B-524C.

Family — A147

1976, Feb. 12 *Perf. 14x13½*
367 A147 40c multicolored .30 .20

Family planning.

Arch, Ibn Zaidoun Mosque — A148

Perf. 13½x14, 14x13½
1976, Feb. 12 Photo.

40c, Hall, Ibn Zaidoun Mosque, horiz.

368 A148 40c multicolored .25 .20
369 A148 65c multicolored .40 .25

Ibn Zaidoun Mosque, millennium.

Medersa bou Anania, Fez A149

1976, Feb. 26 *Perf. 13x14½*
370 A149 1d multicolored .45 .25

Borobudur Temple — A150

Design: 40c, Bas-relief, Borobudur.

1976, Mar. 11 Photo. *Perf. 13*
371 A150 40c multicolored .20 .20
372 A150 1d multicolored .50 .20

UNESCO campaign to save Borobudur Temple, Java.

Islamic Conference, 6th Anniv. — A151

1976 Litho. *Perf. 13½x13*
372A A151 1d Dome of the Rock 1.50 .25

Jewelry Type of 1968

Designs: 40c, Pendant. 1d, Breastplate.

1976, June 29 Photo. *Perf. 14x13½*
373 A67 40c blue & multi .35 .20
374 A67 1d olive & multi .70 .30
a. Pair, #373-374, vertically tête-bêche 1.25 .40

Moroccan Red Crescent Society.

Bicentennial Emblem, Flags and Map of US and Morocco — A152

Design: 1d, George Washington, King Hassan, Statue of Liberty and Royal Palace, Rabat, vert.

1976, July 27 Photo. *Perf. 14*
375 A152 40c multicolored .40 .20
376 A152 1d multicolored .65 .35

American Bicentennial.

Wrestling A153

1976, Aug. 11 *Perf. 13x13½*

377 A153 35c shown .20 .20
378 A153 40c Cycling .25 .20
379 A153 50c Boxing .35 .30
380 A153 1d Running .70 .45
Nos. 377-380 (4) 1.50 1.15

21st Olympic Games, Montreal, Canada, July 17-Aug. 1.

Old and New Telephones, Radar — A154

1976, Sept. 29 **Photo.** *Perf. 14*

381 A154 1d gold & multi .45 .20

Centenary of first telephone call by Alexander Graham Bell, Mar. 10, 1876.

Blind Person's Identification A155

1976, Oct. 12 **Photo.** *Perf. 13½x14*

382 A155 50c multicolored .30 .20

Week of the Blind.

Chanting Goshawk A156

1976, Oct. 29 *Perf. 13x13½*

383 A156 40c shown 1.00 .40
384 A156 1d Purple gallinule 1.50 .70

Nature protection.

King Hassan, Star, Torch, Map of Morocco — A157

Africa Cup — A159

Globe and Dove A158

1976, Nov. 19 **Photo.** *Perf. 12½x13*

385 A157 40c multicolored .35 .20

Green March into Spanish Sahara, 1st anniv.

Nos. B34-B35 Overprinted with 2 Bars over Surcharge and 4-line Arabic Inscription

1976, Nov. 29 **Photo.** *Perf. 13½*

386 SP1 25c ultra, blk & org 1.40 1.40
387 SP1 70c red, blk & org 1.60 1.60
a. Pair, #386-387, vert. tête-bêche 4.00 4.00

5th African Tuberculosis Conference, Rabat.

1976, Dec. 16 *Perf. 13*

388 A158 1d blue, blk & red .35 .20

5th Summit Meeting of Non-aligned Countries, Colombo, Aug. 9-19, and 25th anniv. of Org. of Non-aligned Countries.

1976, Dec. 29 **Photo.** *Perf. 14*

389 A159 1d multicolored .40 .20

African Soccer Cup.

Letters Circling Globe, Postmark A160

1977, Jan. 24 **Photo.** *Perf. 13½*

390 A160 40c multicolored .30 .20

Stamp Day.

Aeonium Arboreum A161

Malope Trifida — A162

1d, Hesperolaburnum platyclarpum.

Perf. 13x13½, 14 (A162)

1977, Feb. 22

391 A161 40c multicolored .40 .30
392 A162 50c multicolored .75 .35
393 A161 1d multicolored .85 .45
Nos. 391-393 (3) 2.00 1.10

Ornamental Lamps, View of Salé — A163

1977, Mar. 24 **Photo.** *Perf. 14*

394 A163 40c multicolored .30 .20

Candle procession of Salé.

No. J6 Surcharged in Orange

1977, May 11 **Photo.** *Perf. 14*

395 D2 40c on 10c multi .55 .30

Cherry Festival.

Map of Arab Countries, Emblem A164

1977, June 2 **Photo.** *Perf. 14*

396 A164 50c multicolored .25 .20

5th Congress of Organization of Arab Cities.

APU Emblem, Members' Flags A165

1977, June 20

397 A165 1d multicolored .35 .20

Arab Postal Union, 25th anniversary.

Rug Type of 1974

Designs: 35c, No. 399A, Marmoucha rug, diff. No. 399, Ait Haddou rug. 1d, Salé rug.

Perf. 11½x12, 13½ (#399A)

1977-79 **Photo.**

398 A134 35c multicolored .45 .20
399 A134 40c multicolored .60 .20
399A A134 40c multicolored ('79) .85 .25
400 A134 1d multicolored 1.00 .40
Nos. 398-400 (4) 2.90 1.05

Issued: #399A, 3/8/79; others, 7/21/77.

Cithara — A166

Ali Jinnah and Map of Pakistan — A167

1977, Aug. 18 **Photo.** *Perf. 14*

401 A166 1d multi .55 .25

Week of the Blind.

1977, Oct. 10 **Photo.** *Perf. 13½x13*

402 A167 70c multi .25 .20

Mohammed Ali Jinnah (1876-1948), first Governor General of Pakistan.

Coin Type of 1976

Designs: Various Moroccan coins.

1977-81 *Perf. 14x13½*

403 A146 10c gray & multi .20 .20
403A A146 25c ap grn & multi ('81) 1.10 .35
404 A146 60c dk red & multi ('78) .35 .20
405 A146 75c citron & multi .30 .20
405A A146 80c pale vio & mult ('81) 2.50 .50
406 A146 2d yel grn & multi 1.00 .35
406A A146 3d beige & multi ('81) 5.00 1.75
Nos. 403-406A (7) 10.45 3.55

Marcher with Flag, Map of Morocco and Spanish Sahara — A168

1977, Nov. 6 **Photo.** *Perf. 14*

407 A168 1d multi .45 .20

Green March into Spanish Sahara, 2nd anniv.

Chamber of Representatives — A169

1977, Nov. 6 *Perf. 13½*

408 A169 1d multi .45 .20
a. Souvenir sheet 2.00 2.00

Opening of Chamber of Representatives. No. 408a sold for 3d.

Enameled Silver Brooch — A170

Copper Vessel — A171

1977, Dec. 14 **Photo.** *Perf. 11½*

409 A170 1d multi .80 .20

Moroccan Red Crescent Society.

1978, Jan. 5 **Photo.** *Perf. 13*

1d, Standing filigree copper bowl with cover.

410 A171 40c gold & multi .30 .20
411 A171 1d gold & multi .60 .25
a. Pair, #410-411, vert. tête-bêche 1.30 1.30

Map of Sahara, Cogwheel Emblem — A172

1d, Map of North Africa, fish in net, camels.

1978, Feb. 27 Photo. *Perf. 14*

412 A172 40c multi .25 .20
413 A172 1d multi, horiz .40 .25

Promotion of the Sahara. See Nos. 441-442 for similar stamps overprinted.

Covered Jar — A173

1978, Mar. 27 *Perf. 13½x13*

414 A173 1d shown .50 .25
415 A173 1d Vase .50 .25

Week of the Blind.

Red Crescent, Red Cross, Arab Countries A174

1978, Apr. 14 *Perf. 13x13½*

416 A174 1d multi .45 .25

10th Conference of Arab Red Crescent and Red Cross Societies, Apr. 10-15.

View of Fez, Rotary Emblem — A175

1978, Apr. 22 Photo. *Perf. 14*

417 A175 1d multi .45 .25

Rotary Intl. Meeting, Fez, District 173.

Dome of the Rock, Jerusalem — A176

1978, May 29 *Perf. 14½*

418 A176 5c multi .20 .20
419 A176 10c multi .20 .20

Palestinian fighters and their families. For overprints see Nos. 502-502A.

Folk Dancers and Flutist — A177

1978, June 15 *Perf. 13½x13*

420 A177 1d multi .55 .25

National Folklore Festival, Marrakesh.

Sugar Cane Field, and Conveyor Belt A178

1978, July 24 Photo. *Perf. 13*

421 A178 40c multi .25 .20

Sugar industry.

Games Emblem — A179

Bird, Tree, Tent, Scout Emblem — A180

1978, Aug. 25

422 A179 1d multi .60 .25

World sailing championships.

1978, Sept. 26 Photo. *Perf. 13*

423 A180 40c multi 2.00 .50

Pan-Arab Scout Jamboree, Rabat.

View of Fez A181

1978, Oct. 10

424 A181 40c multi .25 .20

Moulay Idriss the Great, Festival, Fez.

Flame Emblem — A182

Houses, Agadir — A183

1978, Dec. 21 Photo. *Perf. 14*

425 A182 1d multi .45 .20

30th anniversary of Universal Declaration of Human Rights.

1979, Jan. 25 Photo. *Perf. 12*

426 A183 40c shown .30 .20
427 A183 1d Old Fort, Marrakesh .55 .25

Soccer and Cup A184

1979, Mar. 2 *Perf. 13*

428 A184 40c multi .25 .20

Mohammed V Soccer Cup.

Vase — A185

Procession A186

1979, Mar. 29 Photo. *Perf. 14*

429 A185 1d multi .45 .25

Week of the Blind.

1979, Apr. 18 *Perf. 13x13½, 13½x13*

1d, Festival, by Mohamed Ben Ali Rbati, horiz.

430 A186 40c multi .45 .20
431 A186 1d multi .55 .25

Brass Containers, Red Crescent A187

Perf. 13x13½, 13½x13

1979, May 16 Photo.

432 A187 40c shown .30 .20
433 A187 1d Heated coffee urn, vert. .60 .30

Red Crescent Society.

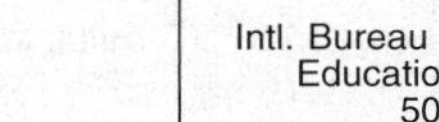

Dancers — A188

Silver Dagger — A189

1979, June 1 Photo. *Perf. 13*

434 A188 40c multi .25 .20

National Festival of Marrakech.

1979, June 20 *Perf. 14*

435 A189 1d multi .40 .20

King Hassan II, 50th Birthday — A190

1979, July 9 Photo. *Perf. 14*

436 A190 1d multi .45 .20

4th Arab Youth Festival, Rabat A191

1979, July 30 Photo. *Perf. 13½x14*

437 A191 1d multi .45 .20

King Hassan II and Crowd — A192

1979, Aug. 20 *Perf. 14x13½*

438 A192 1d multi .35 .20

Revolution of the King and the People, 25th anniv.

Intl. Bureau of Education, 50th Anniv. — A193

1979, Sept. 28 Photo. *Perf. 13x13½*

439 A193 1d multi .45 .20

Pilgrimage to Mecca, Mt. Arafat, Holy Ka'aba
A194

1979, Oct. 25 *Perf. 13½*
440 A194 1d multi .45 .20

No. 413 Redrawn in Smaller Size and Overprinted in Red

1979, Nov. 7 **Litho.** *Perf. 14*
Size: 33x23mm
441 A172 40c multi .30 .20
442 A172 1d multi .55 .30

Return of Oued Eddahab province, Aug. 14.

Leucanthemum Catanance — A195

Children, Globe, IYC Emblem — A196

1979, Nov. 21 **Photo.** *Perf. 14½*
443 A195 40c Centaurium .25 .20
444 A195 1d shown .55 .20

1979, Dec. 3 *Perf. 14*
445 A196 40c multi .70 .25

International Year of the Child.

Otter — A197

Traffic Signs and Road — A198

1979, Dec. 18 *Perf. 13½x13*
446 A197 40c shown .40 .20
447 A197 1d Redstart .80 .25

1980, Jan. 3 **Photo.** *Perf. 14*
448 A198 40c shown .20 .20
449 A198 1d Children at curb .45 .20

Fortress A199

1980, Jan. 29 *Perf. 13x13½*
450 A199 1d multi .40 .20

Copper Bowl and Lid, Red Crescent — A200

Week of the Blind — A201

Red Crescent Soc.: 70c, Copper kettle, brazier.

1980, Feb. 28 **Photo.** *Perf. 14*
451 A200 50c multi .40 .20
452 A200 70c multi .50 .20
a. Pair, #451-452, vert. tête-bêche 1.10 1.10

1980, Mar. 19 **Photo.** *Perf. 14*
453 A201 40c multi .25 .20

Rabat Mechanical Sorting Office — A202

1980, Apr. 17
454 A202 40c multi .25 .20

Stamp Day.

Rotary Intl., 75th Anniv. — A203

Cloth and Leather Goods — A204

1980, May 14 **Photo.** *Perf. 14*
455 A203 1d multi .35 .20

1980, May 31 **Photo.** *Perf. 13½x13*
456 A204 1d multi .40 .20

4th Textile and Leather Exhibition, Casablanca, May 2-9.

Gypsum — A205

Falcon — A206

1980, June 19 **Photo.** *Perf. 13½x13*
457 A205 40c multi .70 .20

See Nos. 477-478.

1980, July 26 *Perf. 11½*
458 A206 40c multi .60 .30

Hunting with falcons.

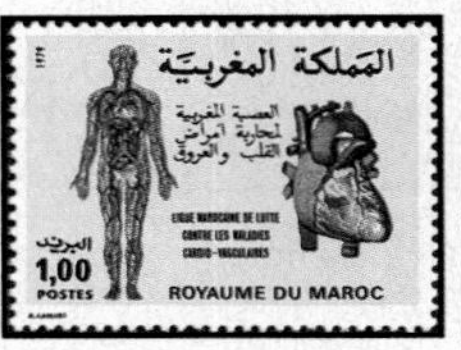

Fight against Heart Disease A207

1980, Aug. 7 **Photo.** *Perf. 13x13½*
459 A207 1d multi .45 .20

A208

A210

Ornamental Saddle and Harness A209

1980, Aug. 18 *Perf. 14*
460 A208 40c shown .20 .20
461 A208 1d Emblems, diff. .40 .20

United Nations Decade for Women.

1980, Sept. 3 *Perf. 14½*
462 A209 40c Saddle, harness, diff. .30 .20
463 A209 1d shown .55 .25

1980, Sept. 18
464 A210 40c multi .20 .20

World Meteorological Day.

Hand Holding Dry Gas Pump A211

1980, Oct. 6 **Photo.** *Perf. 14*
465 A211 40c Light bulb, gas can .20 .20
466 A211 1d shown .40 .20

Energy conservation.

World Tourism Conference, Manila, Sept. 27 — A212

1980, Oct. 22 *Perf. 11½x12*
467 A212 40c multi .20 .20

Symbolic Tree Rooted in Europe and Africa A213

1980, Oct. 30 *Perf. 14*
468 A213 1d multi .55 .25

Straits of Gibraltar linking Europe and Africa.

5th Anniversary of the Green March — A214

1980, Nov. 6
469 A214 1d multi .40 .20

Holy Ka'aba — A215

Senecio Antheuphorbium A216

1980, Nov. 9
470 A215 40c shown .20 .20
471 A215 1d Mecca Mosque .50 .20
a. Souv. sheet of 2, #470-471 1.40 1.40

No. 471a sold for 3d.

1980, Dec. 4 *Perf. 13*
472 A216 50c shown .40 .20
473 A216 1d Periploca laevigata .70 .40

Leaves, by Mahjoubi Aherdan — A217

Nejjarine Fountain, Fes — A218

Design: 40c. Untitled painting by Mahjoubi Aherdan (23x38mm).

1980, Dec. 18 *Perf. 12*
474 A217 40c multi .20 .20
475 A217 1d multi .55 .20

1981, Jan. 22 *Perf. 14x13½*
476 A218 40c multi .25 .20

Mineral Type of 1980

1981, Feb. 19 Photo. *Perf. 13½x13*
477 A205 40c Onyx .70 .20
478 A205 1d Malachite-azurite 1.40 .30

Inscribed 1980.

King Hassan II — A219

1981, Mar. 2 *Perf. 14*
479 A219 60c shown .25 .20
480 A219 60c Map of Morocco .25 .20
481 A219 60c King Mohammed V .25 .20
a. Strip of 3, #479-481 .75 .30

25th anniv. of independence.

25th Anniv. of King Hassan II Coronation — A220

1981, Mar. 3
482 A220 1.30d multi .45 .25

The Source, by Jillali Gharbaoui — A221

1981, Apr. 8 *Perf. 13x12½*
483 A221 1.30d multi 1.00 .35

Anagalis Monelli — A222

Army Badge — A223

1981, Apr. 23 *Perf. 13*
484 A222 40c shown .20 .20
485 A222 70c Bubonium intricatum .35 .20

1981, May 14 Photo. *Perf. 14x13½*

Moroccan Armed Forces, 25th Anniv: Nos. 486, 488, King Hassan as army major general.

486 A223 60c Facing right .25 .20
487 A223 60c multi .25 .20
488 A223 60c Facing left .25 .20
a. Strip of 3, #486-488 .75 .30

13th World Telecommunications Day — A224

1981, May 18 *Perf. 14x13*
489 A224 1.30d multi .40 .25

Hand-painted Plate — A225

22nd Marrakesh Arts Festival — A226

1981, June 5 *Perf. 14*
490 A225 50c shown .20 .20
491 A225 1.30d Plate, diff. .40 .20

Week of the Blind.

1981, June 18 *Perf. 13½x13*
492 A226 1.30d multi .30 .20

For overprint see No. 579.

Seboula Dagger, Oujda — A227

Copper Mortar and Pestle, Red Crescent — A228

1981, Sept. 7 Photo. *Perf. 13½*
493 A227 1.30d multi .45 .20

1981, Sept. 24 *Perf. 14*
494 A228 60c shown .25 .20
495 A228 1.30d Tripod .55 .25

Intl. Year of the Disabled — A229

Iphiclides Feisthamelii A230

1981, Oct. 15 *Perf. 13½*
496 A229 60c multi .25 .20

1981, Oct. 29 *Perf. 13½x13*
497 A230 60c shown 1.75 .45
498 A230 1.30d Zerynthia rumina 3.25 .90

See Nos. 528-529.

6th Anniv. of Green March — A231

Intl. Palestinian Solidarity Day — A232

1981, Nov. 6 *Perf. 13x13½*
499 A231 1.30d multi .50 .25

1981, Nov. 22 *Perf. 13½x13*
500 A232 60c multi .40 .25

Congress Emblem — A233

1981, Nov. 22 *Perf. 13½*
501 A233 1.30d multi .40 .25

World Federation of Twin Cities, 10th Congress, Casablanca, Nov. 15-18.

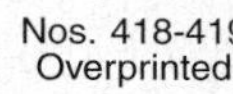

Nos. 418-419 Overprinted

1981, Nov. 25 Photo. *Perf. 14½*
502 A176 40c on 5c multi 6.00 3.00
502A A176 40c on 10c multi 5.00 2.25

First Anniv. of Mohammed V Airport — A234

King Hassan II — A236

Al Massirah Dam Opening A235

1981, Dec. 8 Photo. *Perf. 14x13*
503 A234 1.30d multi .45 .25

1981, Dec. 17 *Perf. 11½*
504 A235 60c multi .30 .20

1981, Dec. 28 *Perf. 13x12½*
505 A236 5c multi .20 .20
506 A236 10c multi .20 .20
507 A236 15c multi .20 .20
508 A236 20c multi .20 .20
509 A236 25c multi .20 .20
510 A236 30c multi .20 .20
511 A236 35c multi .20 .20
512 A236 40c multi .40 .20
513 A236 50c multi .20 .20
514 A236 60c multi .20 .20
515 A236 65c multi .20 .20
516 A236 70c multi .20 .20
a. Perf 12x11¾, granite paper .20 .20
517 A236 75c multi .20 .20
518 A236 80c multi .30 .20
519 A236 90c multi .50 .20

No. 516a is dated 1999 and has the denomination and "Postes" closer to the shoulder than to the chin.

1983, Mar. 1 Photo. *Perf. 14½*

Size: 25x32mm

520 A236 1d multi .30 .20
521 A236 1.40d multi .40 .20
522 A236 2d multi .45 .20
523 A236 3d multi .75 .20
524 A236 5d multi 1.10 .45
524A A236 10d multi 2.25 .80
e. Perf 11½, granite paper 2.00 1.00
Nos. 505-524A (21) 8.85 5.05

No. 524Ae is dated 1999 and has the denomination and "Postes" closer to the shoulder than to the chin.

See Nos. 566-575, 715-724.

Type of 1976

1979-81 Photo. ***Perf. 12½***

Size: 18x23mm

524B A146 40c ocher & multi .20 .20
d. Bklt. pane of 10 1.25
524C A146 50c brt bl, blk & dk brn ('81) .20 .20

Equestrian Sports A237

1981, Dec. 29 ***Perf. 13x13½***
525 A237 1.30d multi .90 .25

Traditional Carpet Design — A238

1982, Jan. 21
526 A238 50c Glaoua pattern .20 .20
527 A238 1.30d Ouled Besseba pattern .45 .25

Butterfly Type of 1981

1982, Feb. 25 ***Perf. 13½x13***
528 A230 60c Celerio oken lineata 1.25 .35
529 A230 1.30d Mesoacidalia aglaja lyauteyi 2.75 .55

World Forest Day — A240

Blind Week — A241

1982, Apr. 8 ***Perf. 14***
531 A240 40c multi .20 .20

1982, May 10
532 A241 1d Jug .25 .20

Folk Dancers, Rabat — A242

Copper Candlestick, Red Crescent — A243

1982, June 3
533 A242 1.40d multi .45 .25

1982, July 1
534 A243 1.40d multi .45 .25

Women in Traditional Clothing, by M. Mezian — A244

ITU Conf., Nairobi, Sept. — A246

Natl. Census A245

1982, Aug. 16 Photo. ***Perf. 14***
535 A244 1.40d multi .45 .25

1982, Sept. 6 Photo. ***Perf. 11½***
536 A245 60c multi .20 .20

1982 ***Perf. 13½x13***
537 A246 1.40d multi .40 .25

TB Bacillus Centenary A247

World Food Day — A248

1982, Sept. 30
538 A247 1.40d multi .50 .25

1982, Oct. 16 ***Perf. 14***
539 A248 60c multi .20 .20

Unity Railroad A249

1982, Nov. 6 ***Perf. 13x13½***
540 A249 1.40d multi 1.00 .35

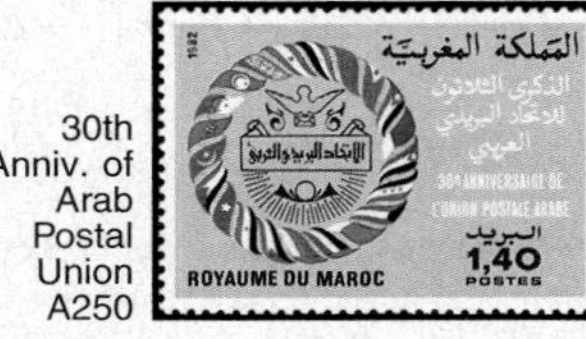

30th Anniv. of Arab Postal Union A250

1982, Nov. 17 ***Perf. 14***
541 A250 1.40d multi .40 .20

Intl. Palestinian Solidarity Day — A251

Red Coral, Al-Hoceima A252

1982, Nov. 29 ***Perf. 14***
542 A251 1.40d sil & multi .40 .20

1982, Dec. 20 ***Perf. 13½***
543 A252 1.40d multi .70 .30

Stamp Day — A253

Week of the Blind — A254

1983, Jan. 26 ***Perf. 13½x13***
544 A253 1.40d Nos. 3, 178 .40 .20

1983, Apr. 20 Photo. ***Perf. 14***
545 A254 1.40d multi .40 .20

Popular Arts A255

1983, June 27 Photo. ***Perf. 14***
546 A255 1.40d multi .55 .20

Wrought-Iron Lectern — A256

Moroccan Flora — A258

Economic Commission for Africa, 25th Anniv. — A257

1983, July 7 Litho. ***Perf. 13½***
547 A256 1.40d multi .40 .20

1983, July 18 Photo. ***Perf. 14***
548 A257 1.40d multi .40 .20

1983, Aug. 1 Litho. ***Perf. 14***
549 A258 60c Tecoma .35 .20
550 A258 1.40d Strelitzia .65 .30

Kings Mohammed V and Hassan II — A259

1983, Aug. 20 Litho. ***Perf. 14***
551 A259 80c multi 1.75 1.75
a. Souvenir sheet of 1 .90 .90

King and People's Revolution, 30th Anniv. No. 551a sold for 5 dinars.

Mediterranean Games — A260

Palestinian Solidarity — A262

Touiza A261

1983, Sept. 3 Photo. *Perf. 14*
552 A260 80c Stylized sportsmen .40 .25
553 A260 1d Emblem .55 .30
554 A260 2d Stylized runner, horiz. 1.60 .45
a. Souv. sheet of 3, #552-554, imperf. 3.00 3.00
Nos. 552-554 (3) 2.55 1.00

No. 554a sold for 5d.

1983, Sept. 30 Photo. *Perf. 13*
555 A261 80c Tractors .20 .20

1983, Nov. 10 Photo. *Perf. 13½x13*
556 A262 80c multi .25 .20

8th Anniv. of the Green March into Spanish Sahara A263

1983, Nov. 17 *Perf. 13x13½*
557 A263 80c multi .20 .20

Ouzoud Waterfall — A264

1983, Nov. 28 *Perf. 14*
558 A264 80c multi .20 .20

Children's Day — A265

Zemmouri Carpet — A266

1983, Dec. 5 Photo. *Perf. 13½x13*
559 A265 2d multi .45 .20

1983, Dec. 15 *Perf. 13½*
Various carpets.
560 A266 60c multi .20 .20
561 A266 1.40d multi .40 .20

World Communications Year — A267

1983, Dec. 20 *Perf. 14*
562 A267 2d multi .70 .25

Twin Cities, Jerusalem and Fez A268

1984, Jan. 16 Photo. *Perf. 13x13½*
563 A268 2d multi .70 .25

Desert Fox — A269

1984, Feb. 13 *Perf. 11½x12, 12x11½*
564 A269 80c shown .70 .30
565 A269 2d Jumping mouse, vert. 1.60 .55

King Hassan II Type of 1981

1984-88 Photo. *Perf. 14½*
Size: 25x32mm

566	A236	1.20d multi ('88)	.30	.20
567	A236	1.25d multi	.25	.20
568	A236	1.60d multi ('87)	.35	.25
569	A236	2.50d multi ('87)	.50	.35
570	A236	3.60d multi ('88)	1.00	.40
571	A236	4d multi	.80	.50
572	A236	5.20d multi ('88)	1.40	.60
573	A236	6.50d multi ('87)	1.40	.90
574	A236	7d multi ('87)	1.50	1.00
575	A236	8.50d multi ('87)	1.75	1.25
		Nos. 566-575 (10)	9.25	5.65

Dated 1986: 1.60d, 2.50d, 6.50d, 7d, 8.50d. Issued: 1.20d, 3.60d, 5.20d, Dec. 26, 1988.

39th Anniv. of Arab League A270

1984, May 24 *Perf. 14½x14*
578 A270 2d Emblem .45 .20

No. 492 Overprinted

1984, June 12 *Perf. 13½x13*
579 A226 1.30d multi .60 .25

25th Anniv. of Marrakesh Arts Festival.

Local Plants — A271

Red Crescent — A273

Week of the Blind A272

1984, June 13 *Perf. 14*
580 A271 80c Mentha viridis .25 .20
581 A271 2d Aloe .60 .40

See Nos. 602-603.

1984, July 10 *Perf. 13x13½*
582 A272 80c Painted bowl .25 .20

1984, July 16 *Perf. 14*
583 A273 2d Octagonal brass container .60 .35

1984 Summer Olympics — A274

Intl. Child Victims' Day — A275

1984, Aug. 8 *Perf. 13½x13*
584 A274 2d Sports .60 .35

1984, Aug. 22 *Perf. 14*
585 A275 2d Children held by dove .60 .35

UPU Day — A276

World Food Day — A277

1984, Oct. 9 Photo. *Perf. 13½*
586 A276 2d multi .50 .25

1984, Oct. 16 *Perf. 14*
587 A277 80c multi .20 .20

Intl. Civil Aviation Org., 40th Anniv. — A278

Green March, 9th Anniv. — A279

1984, Oct. 20 *Perf. 13½*
588 A278 2d multi .90 .50

1984, Nov. 6 *Perf. 14*
589 A279 80c Scroll, text .40 .20

Palestinian Solidarity — A281

UN Human Rights Declaration, 36th Anniv. — A282

1984, Nov. 29 *Perf. 13½*
591 A281 2d Arab Revolt flag, 1918-19 1.00 .50

1984, Dec. 10 *Perf. 14*
592 A282 2d multi .65 .35

Native Dogs — A283

UN Child Survival Campaign A284

1984, Dec. 21 Photo. *Perf. 14*
593 A283 80c Aidi .35 .20
594 A283 2d Sloughi .75 .40

1985, Mar. 5 Photo. *Perf. 14*
595 A284 80c Growth monitoring .30 .20

1st SOS Children's Village in Morocco A285

1985, Mar. 11 *Perf. 13x13½*
596 A285 2d multi .50 .25

Sherifian Hand Stamp, 1892 — A287

World Environment Day — A288

1985, Mar. 25 Photo. *Perf. 14*
597 A287 2d dl pink, blk & gray .50 .25

Souvenir Sheet

Perf. 13½

598 Sheet of 6 3.00 3.00
a. A287 80c green, black & gray .40 .30
b. A287 80c yellow, black & gray .40 .30
c. A287 80c blue, black & gray .40 .30
d. A287 80c red, black & gray .40 .30
e. A287 80c purple, black & gray .40 .30
f. A287 80c brown, black & gray .40 .30

Stamp Day. #598 sold for 5d.

See #615-616, 633-634, 668-669, 684-685, 701-702, 733-734, 756-757, 790-791, 806-807, 821-822, 835-836.

1985, June 5 *Perf. 13*
599 A288 80c Emblem, ecosystem .30 .20

Susi Dancers from Marrakesh and Kutabia, Minaret A289

1985, June 7 *Perf. 13x13½*
600 A289 2d multi .65 .40

Folk Arts Festival.

Week of the Blind — A290

Berber Woman — A291

1985, June 24 *Perf. 14*
601 A290 80c Ceramic bowl .25 .20

See type A316.

Flower Type of 1984

1985, July 1
602 A271 80c Bougainvillea .50 .30
603 A271 2d Red hibiscus 1.10 .50

1985, July 15 *Perf. 14*
604 A291 2d multi 1.00 .35

Red Crescent Society.

6th Pan-Arab Games — A292

UN, 40th Anniv. — A293

1985 *Perf. 14½x13½*
605 A292 2d Torch, emblem, map .60 .35

1985, Oct. 7 *Perf. 13*
606 A293 2d multi .50 .35

Intl. Youth Year — A294

Green March, 10th Anniv. — A295

1985, Oct. 21
607 A294 2d multi .50 .25

1985, Nov. 6 *Perf. 14½x13½*
608 A295 2d Commemorative medal .50 .25

Palestinian Solidarity A296

Butterflies A297

1985, Nov. 29 *Perf. 13½*
609 A296 2d multi .50 .25

1985, Dec. 16 Photo. *Perf. 14*
610 A297 80c Euphydryas desfontainii 1.50 .45
611 A297 2d Colotis evagore 3.25 1.10

Accession of King Hassan II, 25th Anniv. — A298

Perf. 13x13½, 13½x13

1986, Mar. 3 Litho.
612 A298 80c Natl. arms, vert. .25 .20
613 A298 2d shown .65 .40
a. Souv. sheet of 2, #612-613, imperf. 1.00 1.00

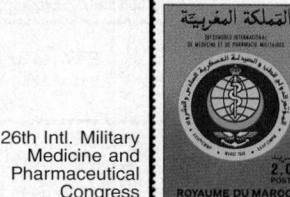

26th Intl. Military Medicine and Pharmaceutical Congress A299

1986, Mar. 24 Photo. *Perf. 14*
614 A299 2d multi .40 .45

Hand Stamp Type of 1985

Sherifian postal seals of Maghzen-Safi, 1892.

1986, Apr. 7
615 A287 80c orange & blk .20 .20
616 A287 2d green & blk .45 .25

Week of the Blind — A300

1986 World Cup Soccer Championships, Mexico — A301

1986, Apr. 21
617 A300 1d multi .25 .20

1986, May 31 *Perf. 13½*
618 A301 1d Emblems, horiz. .40 .20
619 A301 2d Soccer cup, emblems .70 .35

Red Crescent Soc. — A302

Flowers — A304

Popular Arts A303

1986, June *Perf. 14*
620 A302 2d multi .90 .35

1986, June
621 A303 2d Folk band, dancers .65 .30

1986, July 21 Photo. *Perf. 14*
622 A304 1d Warionia saharae .55 .20
623 A304 2d Mandragora autumnalis .90 .40

Intl. Peace Year — A305

18th Skydiving Championships A306

1986, Aug. 4 ***Perf. 13***
624 A305 2d multi .45 .30

1986, Aug. 18 ***Perf. 13½x13***
625 A306 2d multi .55 .30

Horse Week A307

1986, Oct. 10 ***Perf. 13***
626 A307 1d multicolored .40 .20

Green March, 11th Anniv. — A308

World Food Day — A309

1986, Nov. 6 **Photo.** ***Perf. 14***
627 A308 1d multicolored .25 .20

1986, Nov. 12
628 A309 2d multicolored .45 .25

Aga Khan Architecture Prize A310

1986, Nov. 24 **Litho.** ***Perf. 13***
629 A310 2d multicolored .45 .25

Operation Grain: One Million Hectares — A311

Butterflies A312

1986, Dec. 8
630 A311 1d multicolored .25 .20

1986, Dec. 22 ***Perf. 14***
631 A312 1d Elphinstonia charlonia 1.00 .40
632 A312 2d Anthocharis belia 2.50 1.00

Hand Stamp Type of 1985

Stamp Day: Sherifian postal seals of Maghzen-Tetouan, 1892.

1987, Jan. 26 **Photo.**
633 A287 1d blue & blk .25 .20
634 A287 2d red & black .45 .30

King Mohammed V, Flag, 1947 — A313

1987, Apr. 9 **Photo.** ***Perf. 13½x13***
635 A313 1d shown .30 .20
636 A313 1d King Hassan II, 1987 .30 .20
a. Souvenir sheet of 2, Nos. 635-636 1.00 1.00

Tangiers Conf., 40th anniv. #636a sold for 3d.

Red Crescent Society — A314

UN Child Survival Campaign A315

1987, May 1 **Photo.** ***Perf. 14***
637 A314 2d Brass lamp .50 .35

1987, May 25 ***Perf. 12½x13***
638 A315 1d Oral rehydration .25 .20

See Nos. 647, 687.

Week of the Blind — A316

1987, June 8 ***Perf. 14***
639 A316 1d Porcelain cup .25 .20

Flowering Plants — A317

US-Morocco Diplomatic Relations, 200th Anniv. — A318

1987, July 6 **Photo.**
640 A317 1d Zygophyllum fontanesii .25 .20
641 A317 2d Otanthus maritimus .50 .35

See Nos. 661-662.

1987, July **Litho & Engr.**
642 A318 1d lt bl, blk & scar .25 .20

See United States No. 2349.

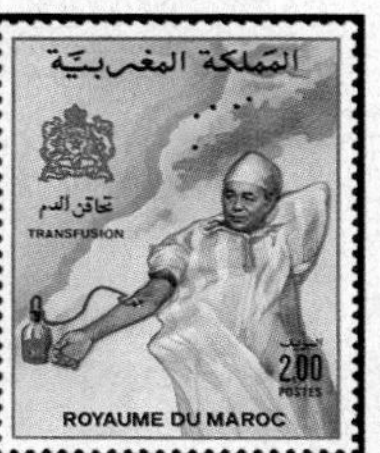

Give Blood — A319

1987, Aug. 20 **Photo.** ***Perf. 13x13½***
643 A319 2d King Hassan II, map .60 .45

Desert Costumes, the Sahara — A320

13th Intl. Cong. on Irrigation and Drainage — A321

1987, Sept. 14 ***Perf. 13***
644 A320 1d Woman from Melhfa .30 .25
645 A320 2d Man from Derraa .65 .50

See Nos. 711-712, 740-741.

1987, Sept. 21
646 A321 1d multi .35 .30

UN Child Survival Type of 1987

1987, Sept. 28
647 A315 1d Universal immunization .35 .30

Congress on Mineral Industries, Marrakesh A322

Green March, 12th Anniv. — A323

1987, Oct.
648 A322 1d Azurite .40 .25
649 A322 2d Wulfenite .75 .50

See No. 769.

1987, Nov. 6 **Photo.** ***Perf. 14***
650 A323 1d multicolored .30 .25

See Nos. 667, 683, 695, 727, 750, 802, 820, 834, 848.

Royal Armed Forces Social Services Month A324

1987, Nov. 13 ***Perf. 13x12½***
651 A324 1d multicolored .30 .25

Birds — A325

1987, Dec. 1 **Litho.** ***Perf. 14***
652 A325 1d Passer simplex saharae .50 .25
653 A325 2d Alectoris barbara 1.10 .45

Natl. Postage Stamp 75th Anniv. — A326

Design: Postmark and Sherifian postage stamp (French Morocco) of 1912.

1987, Dec. 31 **Photo.** ***Perf. 14x13½***
654 A326 3d pale lil rose, blk & blue grn .90 .70

Cetiosaurus Mogrebiensis — A327

1988, Jan. 18 Photo. *Perf. 13½*
655 A327 2d multicolored 2.75 .75

A328

A329

1988, Feb. 16 Litho. *Perf. 14*
656 A328 2d multicolored .60 .45

Intl. Symposium on Mohammed V, Aug. 16-Nov. 20, 1987.

Perf. 14½x13½
1988, Mar. 13 Photo.
657 A329 3d multi .85 .75

16th Africa Cup Soccer Championships.

Horse Week A330

1988, Mar. 20 Litho. *Perf. 14*
658 A330 3d multi 1.00 .75

Intl. Red Cross and Red Crescent Orgs., 125th Annivs. — A331

1988, Apr. 30 Photo. *Perf. 12½x13*
659 A331 3d pink, blk & dark red .85 .65

Week of the Blind — A332

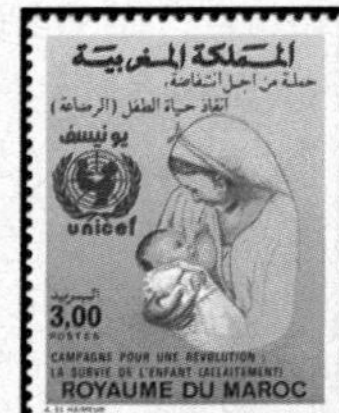

UN Child Survival Campaign A333

1988, May 25 Litho. *Perf. 14*
660 A332 3d Pottery bottle .85 .65

Flower Type of 1987

1988, June 27 Litho. *Perf. 14*
661 A317 3.60d Citrullus colocynthis 1.00 .75
662 A317 3.60d Calotropis procera 1.00 .75

1988, July 18 Litho. *Perf. 12½x13*
663 A333 3d multi .80 .60

1988 Summer Olympics, Seoul — A334

Birds — A335

Perf. 14½x13½
1988, Sept. 19 Litho.
664 A334 2d multi .60 .50

1988, Oct. 26 Litho. *Perf. 14*
665 A335 3.60d Grande outarde 1.25 .75
666 A335 3.60d Flamant rose 1.25 .75

Green March Anniv. Type of 1987

1988, Nov. 6
667 A323 2d multi .55 .40

Green March, 13th anniv.

Hand Stamp Type of 1985

Sherifian postal seals of Maghzen-El Jadida, 1892: No. 668, Octagonal. No. 669, Circular.

1988, Nov. 22 Photo. *Perf. 14*
668 A287 3d olive bister & blk .90 .60
669 A287 3d violet & blk .90 .60

Stamp Day.

Housing of the Ksours and Casbahs A336

1989, Jan. 23 *Perf. 13x13½*
670 A336 2d multi .55 .40

Royal Chess Federation, 25th Anniv. — A337

1989, Apr. 17 Litho. *Perf. 14*
671 A337 2d multi .50 .40

Red Crescent Society — A338

Week of the Blind — A339

1989, May 29 Litho. *Perf. 14x13½*
672 A338 2d multi .55 .40

1989, June 12 *Perf. 14*
673 A339 2d multi .55 .40

A340

A341

1989, July 9 Litho. *Perf. 13x13½*
674 A340 2d multi .50 .40
675 A340 2d King Hassan II, diff. .50 .40
a. Souvenir sheet of 2, #674-675, imperf. & embossed 1.25 1.25

King Hassan II, 60th birthday. No. 675a sold for 5d.

1989, Sept. 11 Litho. *Perf. 14*

Flowering plants.

676 A341 2d *Narcissus papyraceus* .60 .45
677 A341 2d *Cerinthe major* .60 .45

See Nos. 709-710, 742-743.

World Telecommunications Day — A342

1989, Sept. 25 *Perf. 13x12½*
678 A342 2d multicolored .60 .45

13th World Congress on Fertility and Sterility — A343

1989, Oct. 6 *Perf. 14*
679 A343 2d multicolored .60 .45

Birds A344

1989, Oct. 16 *Perf. 14*
680 A344 2d Desert beater .70 .45
681 A344 3d Gorget lark 1.00 .70

Interparliamentary Union, Cent. — A345

1989, Oct. 27
682 A345 2d multicolored .60 .45

Green March Anniv. Type of 1987

1989, Nov. 6
683 A323 3d multicolored .90 .70

Green March, 14th anniv.

Hand Stamp Type of 1985

Sherifian postal seals of Maghzen-Casablanca, 1892: 2d, Circular. 3d, Octagonal.

1990, Jan. 15 Photo. *Perf. 14*
684 A287 2d orange & blk .65 .45
685 A287 3d green & blk 1.00 .70

Maghreb Union, 1st Anniv. A346

1990, Feb. 17 *Perf. 13½x14*
686 A346 2d multicolored .60 .45
a. Souv. sheet of one, perf. 13½ .95 .95

No. 686a sold for 3d.

Child Survival Type of 1987

1990 *Perf. 12½x13*
687 A315 3d Breast feeding .95 .70

3rd World Olive Day A347

1990, May 14 Litho. *Perf. 14*

688 A347 2d Olive press .50 .35

689 A347 3d King Hassan II .75 .55

Week of the Blind A348

1990, May 28 Litho. *Perf. 14*

690 A348 2d multicolored .70 .50

Red Crescent Society A349

1990, June 11

691 A349 2d multicolored .55 .35

A350

A353

Birds A351

1990, Sept. 17 Litho. *Perf. 14*

692 A350 3d blk, yel grn & grn 1.10 .80

Intl. Literacy Year

1990, Oct. 26

693 A351 2d Tourterelle, vert. .85 .50

694 A351 3d Huppe fasciee 1.25 .80

Green March Type of 1987

1990, Nov. 5

695 A323 3d multicolored 1.10 .80

Green March, 15th anniv.

1990, Nov. 18

696 A353 3d multicolored 1.10 .80

Independence, 35th anniv.

Dam A354

1990, Nov. 26

697 A354 3d multicolored 1.10 .80

A355

A357

A356

1990, Dec. 28 Litho. *Perf. 14*

698 A355 3d multicolored 1.00 .75

Royal Academy of Morocco, 10th anniv.

1990, Dec. 31 Litho. *Perf. 13½x13*

Opening of Postal Museum, 20th Anniv.: No. 699, Telegraph machine. No. 700, Horse-drawn mail carriage fording river.

699 A356 2d multicolored .65 .50

700 A356 3d multicolored 1.00 .75

a. Souv. sheet of 2, #699-700, imperf. 2.10 2.10

No. 700a sold for 6d, has simulated perforations.

Hand Stamp Type of 1985

Sherifian postal seals of Maghzen-Rabat, 1892: 2d, Circular. 3d, Octagonal.

1991, Jan. 25 *Perf. 14*

701 A287 2d ver & blk .65 .50

702 A287 3d blue & blk 1.00 .75

1991, Feb. 18

703 A357 3d multicolored 1.00 .75

UN Development Program, 40th anniv.

A358

A359

1991, Mar. 3 Litho. *Perf. 14½x13*

704 A358 3d shown 1.00 .75

705 A358 3d Wearing business suit 1.00 .75

a. Souv. sheet of 2, #704-705, imperf. 3.00 2.35

Coronation of King Hassan II, 30th anniv. Nos. 704-705 exist tete beche. No. 705a has simulated perforations and sold for 10d.

1991, Mar. 28 Litho. *Perf. 14*

706 A359 3d multicolored 1.00 .75

Phosphate Mining, 70th anniv.

Week of the Blind — A360

Red Crescent Society — A361

1991, May 15 Photo. *Perf. 14*

707 A360 3d multicolored 1.00 .75

1991, May 27 Litho. *Perf. 14*

708 A361 3d multicolored .95 .70

Flowering Plants Type of 1989

1991, June 27 Litho. *Perf. 14*

709 A341 3d Pyrus mamorensis 1.00 .70

710 A341 3d Cynara humilis 1.00 .70

Desert Costumes Type of 1987

Costumes of Ouarzazate.

1991, July 31 Photo.

711 A320 3d Woman 1.00 .70

712 A320 3d Man 1.00 .70

King Hassan II Type of 1981

1991-98 Photo. *Perf. 14½*

Size: 25x32mm

715 A236 1.35d multicolored .45 .20

717 A236 1.70d multicolored .40 .20

719 A236 2.30d multicolored .50 .25

a. Perf 11½, granite paper .50 .25

722 A236 5.50d multicolored 1.25 1.00

a. Perf 11½, granite paper 2.00 1.00

723 A236 6d multicolored 1.25 .95

724 A236 20d multicolored 5.00 3.50

Nos. 715-724 (6) 8.85 6.10

Issued: 1.35d, Sept. 2; 1.70d, 1994; 2.30d, 6d, 1998.

This is an expanding set. Numbers will change if necessary.

Nos. 719a and 722a are dated 1999, and have the denomination and "Postes" closer to the shoulder than to the chin.

A362

A363

1991, Sept. 23 Litho. *Perf. 14*

725 A362 3d multicolored .95 .70

19th World Congress on Roads, Marrakesh.

1991, Oct. 30 Litho.

726 A363 3d multicolored .95 .70

4th Session of the Council of Presidents of the Maghreb Arab Union.

Green March Anniv. Type of 1987

1991, Nov. 6 Photo. *Perf. 14*

727 A323 3d multicolored .95 .70

Green March, 16th anniv.

Birds — A364

Fight Against AIDS — A365

1991, Nov. 20 Litho. *Perf. 14*

728 A364 3d Merops apiaster 1.00 .80

729 A364 3d Ciconia ciconia 1.00 .80

See Nos. 748-749.

1991, Dec. 16

730 A365 3d multicolored 1.00 .80

Organization of the Islamic Conference, 20th Anniv. — A366

1991, Dec. 16

731 A366 3d multicolored 1.00 .80

A367

A368

1991 **Litho.** ***Perf. 14***
732 A367 3d multicolored 1.00 .80

African Tourism Year.

Handstamp Type of 1985

Sherifian postal seals of Maghzen-Essaouira, 1892: No. 733, Circular. No. 734, Octagonal.

1992, Jan. 13
733 A287 3d olive & blk 1.00 .80
734 A287 3d purple & blk 1.00 .80

1992, Feb. 17
735 A368 3d multicolored 1.00 .80

Intl. Space Year.

Week of the Blind — A369

Red Crescent Society — A370

1992, Mar. 19 **Photo.** ***Perf. 14***
736 A369 3d multicolored 1.00 .80

1992, Mar. 30
737 A370 3d multicolored 1.00 .80

Minerals — A371

A372

1992, May 11 **Litho.** ***Perf. 14***
738 A371 1.35d Quartz .50 .40
739 A371 3.40d Calcite 1.25 1.00

Desert Costumes Type of 1987

Costumes of Tata.

1992, May 25 **Photo.** ***Perf. 14***
740 A320 1.35d Woman .50 .40
741 A320 3.40d Man 1.25 1.00

Flowering Plants Type of 1989

1992, July 13
742 A341 1.35d Campanula afra .50 .40
743 A341 3.40d Thymus broussonetii 1.25 1.00

1992, July 24
744 A372 3.40d multicolored 1.25 1.00

1992 Summer Olympics, Barcelona.

Modes of Transportation and Communications, Map of Africa — A373

1992, Sept. 14 **Litho.** ***Perf. 14***
745 A373 3.40d multicolored .95 .75

Expo '92, Seville — A374

1992, Oct. 12
746 A374 3.40d multicolored .95 .75

Discovery of America, 500th Anniv. A375

1992, Oct. 12
747 A375 3.40d multicolored .95 .75

Bird Type of 1991

1992, Oct. 26 **Litho.** ***Perf. 14***
748 A364 3d Gyps fulvus .80 .65
749 A364 3d Ganga cata, horiz. .80 .65

Green March Anniv. Type of 1987

1992, Nov. 6 **Litho.** ***Perf. 14***
750 A323 3.40d multicolored .95 .75

Green March, 17th anniv.

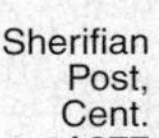

Sherifian Post, Cent. A377

Designs: 3.40d, Octagonal Sherifian postal seal, scroll, Sultan Moulay Hassan I. 5d, Scroll, various circular and octagonal Sherifian postal seals, Sultan.

1992, Nov. 22 **Litho.** ***Perf. 14***
751 A377 1.35d multicolored .40 .25
752 A377 3.40d multicolored .95 .75

Size: 165x115mm

Imperf

753 A377 5d multicolored 1.40 1.00
Nos. 751-753 (3) 2.75 2.00

Intl. Conference on Nutrition, Rome — A378

1992, Dec. 7 **Litho.** ***Perf. 14***
754 A378 3.40d multicolored .95 .75

Al Massira Airport, Agadir — A379

1992, Dec. 21 **Litho.** ***Perf. 14***
755 A379 3.40d multicolored 1.00 .80

Hand Stamp Type of 1985

Sherifian postal seals of Maghzen-Tanger, 1892: 1.70, Circular. 3.80d, Octagonal.

1993, Jan. 29 **Litho.** ***Perf. 14***
756 A287 1.70d green & black .45 .35
757 A287 3.80d orange & black 1.00 .80

Stamp Day.

Week of the Blind A380

1993, Mar. 15 **Litho.** ***Perf. 14***
758 A380 4.40d multicolored 1.25 1.00

World Meteorology Day — A381

1993, Mar. 23
759 A381 4.40d multicolored 1.25 1.00

A382

A383

1993, Apr. 26 **Litho.** ***Perf. 14***
760 A382 4.40d multicolored 1.25 1.00

Red Crescent Society.

1993, June 14
761 A383 4.40d multicolored 1.25 1.00

World Telecommunications Day.

A384

A385

Argania spinosa.

1993, July 26 **Litho.** ***Perf. 14***
762 A384 1.70d Extracting oil .45 .35
763 A384 4.80d Tree branch 1.25 1.00

1993, Aug. 21
764 A385 4.80d multicolored 1.25 1.00

Prince Sidi Mohammed, 30th birthday.

Inauguration of the Hassan II Mosque A386

1993, Aug. 30 ***Perf. 13***
765 A386 4.80d multicolored 1.25 1.00

A387

A388

1993, Sept. 30 Litho. *Perf. 14*
766 A387 4.80d multicolored 1.25 1.00

King and People's Revolution, 40th Anniv.

1993, Oct. 15
767 A388 4.80d multicolored 1.25 1.00

World Post Day.

New Islamic University — A389

1993, Nov. 1 Litho. *Perf. 14*
768 A389 4.80d multicolored 1.25 1.00

Green March Anniv. Type of 1987

1993, Nov. 6
769 A323 4.80d multicolored 1.25 1.00

Green March, 18th anniv.

Water Birds A390

1993, Dec. 13 Litho. *Perf. 14*
770 A390 1.70d Sarcelle marbree .40 .30
771 A390 4.80d Foulque a crete 1.10 .85

Manifest of Independence, 50th Anniv. — A391

1994, Mar. 31 Litho. *Perf. 14*
772 A391 4.80d multicolored 1.10 .85

A392

General Agreement on Tariffs and Trade (GATT), 1994 Summit, Marrakech A393

No. 774Ab, 1.70d, like #773. c, 4.80d, like #774. Illustration reduced.

1994, Apr. 29 Litho. *Perf. 14*
773 A392 1.70d multicolored .40 .30
774 A393 4.80d multicolored 1.10 .80

Sheet of 2
Rouletted

774A A393 #b.-c. 3.50 3.00

Buildings and background are all in shades of claret on Nos. 774b-774c. No. 773 has building and background in shades of green. No. 774 has black building with claret background. No. 774A sold for 10d.

Week of the Blind — A394

Red Crescent Society — A395

1994, May 9
775 A394 4.80d multicolored 1.10 .85

1994, May 18
776 A395 4.80d multicolored 1.10 .85

Natl. Conference on Children's Rights — A396

1994, May 25
777 A396 1.70d shown .40 .30
778 A396 4.80d Boy, girl under sun 1.10 .85

1994 World Cup Soccer Championships, US — A397

1994, June 17 *Perf. 13*
779 A397 4.80d multicolored 1.10 .85

King Hassan II, 65th Birthday A398

Designs: 1.70d, Wearing business suit. 4.80d, Wearing traditional costume, vert.

1994 *Perf. 13x12½, 12½x13*
780 A398 1.70d multicolored .40 .30
781 A398 4.80d multicolored 1.10 .45

A399

A400

1994 *Perf. 12½x13*
782 A399 4.80d multicolored 1.10 .45

Intl. Olympic Committee, Cent.

1994
783 A400 4.80d multicolored 1.10 .45

Death of Antoine de Saint-Exupery, 50th anniv.

Flowers A401

1994 *Perf. 13x12½, 12½x13*
784 A401 1.70d Chamaelon gummifer .40 .30
785 A401 4.80d Pancratium maritimum, vert. 1.10 .45

Water Birds A402

1994, Oct. 24 Photo. *Perf. 13x13½*
786 A402 1.70d Courlis a bec grele .40 .30
787 A402 4.80d Goeland d'audouin 1.10 .80

A403

A404

Green March, 19th Anniv.: 4.80d, Marchers, map, inscription.

1994, Nov. 6 Litho. *Perf. 12½*
788 A403 1.70d multicolored .40 .30
789 A403 4.80d multicolored 1.10 .80

Hand Stamp Type of 1985

Sherifan postal seals of Maghzen-Marrakesh: 1.70d, Circular. 4.80d, Octagonal.

1994, Nov. 22 *Perf. 12½*
790 A287 1.70d blue & black .40 .30
791 A287 4.80d vermilion & black 1.10 .80

Stamp Day.

1995, Feb. 27 Litho. *Perf. 13½*
792 A404 4.80d multicolored 1.10 .80

Week of the Blind.

A405

A406

1995, Mar. 22 Litho. *Perf. 13½*
793 A405 4.80d multicolored 1.10 .80

Arab League, 50th anniv.

1995, Apr. 24 Litho. *Perf. 13½x13*
794 A406 4.80d multicolored 1.10 .80

Red Crescent Society.

Flowers — A407

Birds — A408

1995, May 29 Litho. *Perf. 13½x13*
795 A407 2d Malva hispanica .50 .35
796 A407 4.80d Phlomis crinita 1.10 .85

1995, Sept. 18 Litho. *Perf. 13½x13*
797 A408 1.70d Coracias garrulus .40 .30
798 A408 4.80d Carduelis carduelis 1.10 .85

See Nos. 818-819, 832-833, 846-847.

FAO, 50th Anniv. A409

1995, Oct. 16 Photo. *Perf. 13½*
799 A409 4.80d multicolored 1.10 .85

UN, 50th Anniv. A410

1.70d, "50," Moroccan, UN flags. 4.80d, Moroccan flag, UN emblem, map of Africa.

1995, Oct. 24 *Perf. 12½*
800 A410 1.70d multicolored .40 .30
801 A410 4.80d multicolored 1.10 .85

Green March Anniv. Type of 1987 and

Green March, 20th Anniv. — A411

1995, Nov. 6 Photo. *Perf. 12½*
802 A323 1.70d multicolored .40 .30
803 A411 4.80d multicolored 1.10 .85

A412

A413

Independence, 40th anniv.: 4.80d, Crown, national flag. 10d, King Mohammed V, crown over flag, King Hassan II.

1995, Nov. 18 Litho. *Perf. 12½*
804 A412 4.80d multicolored 1.10 .85

Size: 112x83mm
Imperf
805 A412 10d multicolored 2.75 2.00

Hand Stamp Type of 1985

Sherifan postal seals of Maghzen-Meknes, 1892: 1.70d, Circular. 4.80d, Octagonal.

1995, Nov. 22 Photo. *Perf. 12½*
806 A287 1.70d olive & black .40 .30
807 A287 4.80d violet & black 1.10 .85

Stamp Day.

1996, Mar. 3 Litho. *Perf. 13½*
808 A413 2d Natl. arms .45 .35
809 A413 5.50d King Hassan II 1.25 .95

Size: 134x86mm
Imperf
810 A413 10d Crown, King 2.50 1.75

Accession of King Hassan II, 35th anniv.

Traditional Crafts — A414

Flowers — A415

1996, Mar. 25 Photo. *Perf. 13½x13*
811 A414 5.50d Pottery 1.25 1.00
812 A414 5.50d Copper 1.25 1.00

1996, Apr. 25
813 A415 2d Cleonia lusitanica .50 .40
814 A415 5.50d Tulipa sylvestris 1.25 1.00

A416

A417

King Hassan II: 2d, In uniform. 5.50d, Wearing traditional headpiece.

1996, May 14 Photo. *Perf. 13x13½*
815 A416 2d multicolored .50 .40
816 A416 5.50d multicolored 1.25 1.00

Royal Armed Forces, 40th anniv.

1996, July 19 Photo. *Perf. 13½x13*
817 A417 5.50d multicolored 1.25 1.00

1996 Summer Olympics, Atlanta.

Bird Type of 1995

1996, Oct. 21 Photo. *Perf. 13½x13*
818 A408 2d Pandion haliaetus .50 .40
819 A408 5.50d Egretta garzetta 1.25 1.00

Green March Anniv. Type of 1987

1996, Nov. 6 Litho. *Perf. 13½*
820 A323 5.50d multicolored 1.25 1.00

Green March, 21st anniv.

Hand Stamp Type of 1985

Sherifan postal seals of Maghzen-Fes, 1892: 2d, Circular. 5.50d, Octagonal.

1996, Nov. 22 Photo. *Perf. 13½*
821 A287 2d orange & black .45 .35
822 A287 5.50d green & black 1.25 1.00

Stamp Day.

UNICEF, 50th Anniv. A418

1996, Dec. 11 *Perf. 13x13½*
823 A418 5.50d multicolored 1.25 1.00

Moroccan Pottery A419

1997, Feb. 24 Photo. *Perf. 13x13½*
824 A419 5.50d multicolored 1.10 .90

Flowers — A420

A421

1997, Mar. 24 Photo. *Perf. 13½x13*
825 A420 2d Lupinus luteus .50 .20
826 A420 5.50d Silybum marianum 1.25 .60

1997, Apr. 9 Litho. *Perf. 13½x13*

Speakers, 1947: No. 827, Crown Prince Hassan. No. 828, Sultan Mohammed V.

827 A421 2d multicolored .50 .20
828 A421 2d multicolored .50 .20

Speech in Tangier by King Hassan II, 50th anniv.

World Reading and Copyright Day — A422

1997, Apr. 23
829 A422 5.50d multicolored 1.25 .60

Intl. Meeting on Ibn Battuta (1304-77?), Traveler and Writer — A423

1997, May 9 *Perf. 13x13½*
830 A423 5.50d multicolored 1.25 .60

Moroccan Copper — A424

1997, July 21 Photo. *Perf. 13½*
831 A424 5.50d multicolored 1.10 .55

Bird Type of 1995

Designs: 2d, Anthropoides virgo. 5.50d, Parus caeruleus ultramarinus.

1997, Oct. 20 Photo. *Perf. 13½x13*
832 A408 2d multicolored .50 .20
833 A408 5.50d multicolored 1.10 .60

Green March Anniv. Type of 1987

1997, Nov. 6 *Perf. 13½*
834 A323 5.50d multicolored 1.10 .60

Green March, 22nd anniversary.

Hand Stamp Type of 1985

Sherifan postal seals of Maghzen-Larache, 1892: 2d, Circular. 5.50d, Octagonal.

1997 Photo. *Perf. 13½*
835 A287 2d blue & black .50 .20
836 A287 5.50d vermilion & black 1.10 .60

Flowers — A425

A426

1998 Photo. *Perf. 13½x13*

837 A425 2.30d Rhus pentaphylla .65 .30
838 A425 6d Orchis papilionacea 1.60 .80

1998

839 A426 6d multicolored 1.60 .80

25th Intl. Road Transportation Congress.

A427

A428

1998

840 A427 6d Copper ornament 1.60 .80

1998

841 A428 6d multicolored 1.60 .80

1998 World Cup Soccer Championships, France.

Pottery A429

1998 *Perf. 13x13½*

842 A429 6d multicolored 1.60 .80

Intl. Year of the Ocean A430

1998

843 A430 6d multicolored 1.60 .80

King & People's Revolution, 45th Anniv. A431

1998

844 A431 6d multicolored 1.60 .80

World Stamp Day — A432

1998 Photo. *Perf. 13½x13*

845 A432 6d multicolored 1.60 .80

Bird Type of 1995

Designs: 2.30d, Luscinia megarhynchos. 6d, Struthio camelus.

1998 Photo.

846 A408 2.30d multicolored .65 .30
847 A408 6d multicolored 1.60 .80

Green March Anniv. Type

1998, Nov. 6 *Perf. 13½*

848 A323 6d multicolored 1.60 .80

Green March, 23rd anniv.

A433

A434

1998 Litho. *Perf. 13½x13*

849 A433 6d multicolored 1.60 .80

Public Liberties, 40th anniv.

1998 Photo.

850 A434 6d multicolored 1.60 .80

Universal Declaration of Human Rights, 50th anniv.

A435

A436

1999 Litho. *Perf. 13¼*

851 A435 6d multi 1.50 .75

World Theater Day.

1999

Flora: 2.30d, Eryngium triquetrum. 6d, Viscum cruciatum.

852 A436 2.30d multi .60 .30
853 A436 6d multi 1.50 .75

Bab Mansour Laalej — A437

1999 *Perf. 13x13¼*

854 A437 6d multi 1.50 .75

Jewelry A438

1999 *Perf. 13¼*

855 A438 6d multi 1.50 .75

A439

A440

1999

856 A439 2.30d On throne .60 .30
857 A439 6d In robes 1.50 .75
a. Souvenir sheet, #856-857, imperf, without gum 2.25 1.10

King Hassan II, 70th birthday.

1999

858 A440 6d multi 1.50 .75

World Environment Day.

UPU, 125th Anniv. — A441

1999, Oct. 9 Photo. *Perf. 13¼*

859 A441 6d multi 1.25 .60

FAO Medal Awarded by King Hassan II — A442

1999, Oct. 16

860 A442 6d multi 1.25 .60

Anti-poverty Week — A443

1999, Nov. 11 Photo. *Perf. 11¾*
Granite Paper

861 A443 6d multi

Compare with type A461.

Green March Anniv. Type of 1987

1999, Nov. 6 Photo. *Perf. 13¼*

862 A323 6d multi 1.25 .60

Green March, 24th anniv.

Fish A444

Designs: 2.30d, Diplodus cervinus. 6d, Lampris guttatus.

1999, Nov. 29 Photo. *Perf. 13¼*

863 A444 2.30d multi .55 .25
864 A444 6d multi 1.50 .75

Miniature Sheet

Morocco Year in France A445

No. 865: a, Stork on nest. b, People in robes. c, Mandolin, pillars. d, Boat at dock.

1999, Dec. 13 *Perf. 13¼x13*

865 Sheet of 4 6.25 3.00
a.-d. A445 6d Any single 1.50 .75

African Cup Soccer Tournament — A446

2000, Jan. 25 *Perf. 11¾x11½*
Granite Paper

866 A446 6d multi 1.50 .75

Year 2000
A447

2000, Jan. 31
Granite Paper

867 A447 6d multi 1.50 .75

Reconstruction of Agadir, 40th Anniv. — A448

2000, Feb. 29 Photo. *Perf. 11¾*
Granite Paper

868 A448 6.50d multi 1.60 .80

Islamic Development Bank — A449

2000, Mar. 6 Photo. *Perf. 11¾x11½*
Granite Paper

869 A449 6.50d multi 1.60 .80

Natl. Day of the Handicapped — A450

2000, Mar. 30
Granite Paper

870 A450 6.50d multi 1.60 .80

Flora
A451

Designs: 2.50d, Jasione montana. 6.50d, Pistorica breviflora.

2000, Apr. 27 Photo. *Perf. 11¾*
Granite Paper

871-872 A451 Set of 2 2.50 1.10

World Meteorological Organization, 50th Anniv. — A452

2000, May 15 Granite Paper

873 A452 6.50d multi 1.60 .80

Marrakesh Arts Festival
A453

2000, June 5 Photo. *Perf. 11¾*
Granite Paper

874 A453 6.50d multi 1.60 .80

Intl. Peace Year
A454

2000 Photo. *Perf. 11¾*
Granite Paper

875 A454 6.50d multi 1.60 .80

Enthronement of King Mohammed VI, 1st Anniv. — A455

King in: 2.50d, Business suit. 6.50d, Robe.

2000, July 30 Photo. *Perf. 11¾*
Granite Paper

877-878 A455 Set of 2 2.10 1.00
878a Souvenir sheet of 2, #877-878, imperf. 2.50 1.25

No. 878a sold for 10d.

Intl. Festival, Volubilis
A456

2000, Sept. 8 *Perf. 11¾*
Granite Paper

879 A456 6.50d multi 1.60 .80

2000 Summer Olympics, Sydney — A457

2000, Sept. 15 Granite Paper

880 A457 6.50d multi 1.60 .80

SOS Children's Villages — A458

2000, Oct. 12 Granite Paper

881 A458 6.50d multi 1.60 .80

World Teacher's Day — A459

2000, Oct. 25 Photo. *Perf. 11¾*
Granite Paper

882 A459 6.50d multi 1.60 .80

Anti-poverty Week — A461

2000, Nov. 1 Photo. *Perf. 11¾*
Granite Paper

884 A461 6.50d multi 1.60 .80

Compare with type A443. Value is for stamp with surrounding selvage.

Green March Anniv. Type of 1987 and

Map and Inscription
A462

2000, Nov. 6 Photo. *Perf. 11¾*
Granite Paper

885 A323 2.50d multi .60 .25
886 A462 6.50d multi 1.60 .80

Green March, 25th anniv.

Antoine de Saint-Exupéry (1900-44), Aviator, Writer — A463

2000, Nov. 13 Photo. *Perf. 11¾*
Granite Paper

887 A463 6.50d multi 1.60 .80

Independence, 45th Anniv. — A464

2000, Nov. 18 Granite Paper

888 A464 6.50d multi 1.60 .80

Fish
A465

Designs: 2.50d, Apogon imberbis. 6.50d, Scorpaena loppei.

2000, Dec. 25 Granite Paper

889-890 A465 Set of 2 2.00 1.00

El Gharbi Gate
A466

2001, Mar. 22 Photo. *Perf. 11¾*
Granite Paper

891 A466 6.50d multi 1.60 .70

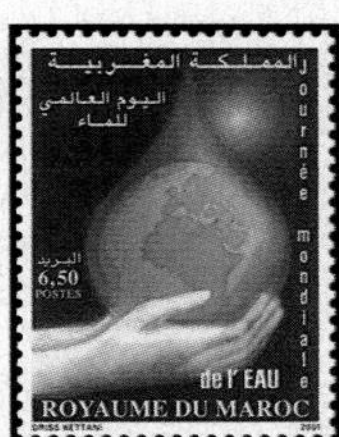
World Water Day — A467

2001, Mar. 30 **Granite Paper**
892 A467 6.50d multi 1.60 .70

Armed Forces, 45th Anniv. — A468

Designs: 2.50d, Soldier and insignia. 6.50d, Soldier in frame.

2001, May 16 Litho. *Perf. 14¼x13¾*
893-894 A468 Set of 2 2.25 .95

Flora — A469

Designs: 2.50d, Euphorbia rigida. 6.50d, Glaucium flavum.

2001, June 7 Photo. *Perf. 11¾*
Granite Paper
895-896 A469 Set of 2 2.25 .95

Houses of Worship — A470

Designs: 2.50d, Koekelberg Basilica, Belgium. 6.50d, Hassan II Mosque, Casablanca.

2001, June 10 **Granite Paper**
897-898 A470 Set of 2 1.90 .95

See Belgium Nos. 1855-1856.

Natl. Diplomacy Day — A471

Perf. 14¼x13¾
2001, June 29 **Litho.**
899 A471 6.50d multi 1.40 .70

A472

A473

A474

King Mohammed VI A475

Perf. 12¾x13¼, 13¼x12¾
2001, July 31 **Litho.**
Size: 24x33mm
900 A472 2.50d multi .55 .25
901 A473 6d multi 1.40 .55
902 A474 6.50d multi 1.50 .60
32x24mm
Arms 9mm Tall
903 A475 10d multi 2.40 .85
Nos. 900-903 (4) 5.85 2.25

See Nos. 934A-934B.

Marine Life — A476

Designs: 2.50d, Lophius budegassa. 6.50d, Monachus monachus, horiz.

2001, Sept. 28 Litho. *Perf. 11¾*
Granite Paper
904-905 A476 Set of 2 2.25 .95

Hand Stamp Type of 1985

Hand stamps of Ksar el Kebir, 1892: 2.50d, Round. 6.50d, Octagonal.

2001, Oct. 9 Litho. *Perf. 14¼x13¾*
906 A287 2.50d olive & black .60 .25
907 A287 6.50d violet & black 1.60 .70

World Day to Combat Desertification A477

2001, Oct. 29 Litho. *Perf. 13¼*
908 A477 6.50d multi 1.25 .60

7th UN Climate Change Conference A478

2001, Oct. 29
909 A478 6.50d multi 1.25 .60

Green March, 26th Anniv. A479

2001, Nov. 7 Photo. *Perf. 13x13¼*
910 A479 6.50d multi 1.25 .60

Anti-Poverty Week Type of 2000 and

Anti-Poverty Week A480

2001, Nov. 8 ***Perf. 12½***
911 A461 6.50d multi 1.25 .60
Perf. 13x13¼
912 A480 6.50d multi 1.25 .60

Value of No. 911 is for stamp with surrounding selvage.

Year of Dialogue Among Civilizations A481

2001, Dec. 14 ***Perf. 13¼x13***
913 A481 6.50d multi 1.25 .60

Fountains — A482

Designs: 2.50d, Wallace Fountain, Paris. 6.50d, Nejjarine Fountain, Fez.

2001, Dec. 14 ***Perf. 13¼***
914-915 A482 Set of 2 2.25 .85

See France Nos. 2847-2848.

Chellah Gate A483

2002, Feb. 28 ***Perf. 13x13¼***
916 A483 6.50d multi 1.25 .60

Intl. Women's Day — A484

2002, Mar. 8 ***Perf. 13¼x13***
917 A484 6.50d multi 1.25 .60

Cedar Tree — A485

2002, Mar. 29
918 A485 6.50d multi 1.25 .60

2nd World Assembly on the Elderly A486

2002, Apr. 30 ***Perf. 13x13¼***
919 A486 6.50d multi 1.25 .60

Special Session of UN General Assembly on Children — A487

2002, May 8 ***Perf. 13¼x13***
920 A487 6.50d multi 1.25 .60

Dated 2001.

Flora — A488

Designs: 2.50d, Linaria bipartita. 6.50d, Verbascum pseudocreticum.

2002, June 5 Photo. *Perf. 13¼x13*
921-922 A488 Set of 2 2.25 .80

Intl. Telecommunications Union Plenipotentiary Conference, Marrakesh — A489

2002, Sept. 23 Photo. *Perf. 13¼*
923 A489 6.50d multi 1.25 .60

Size: 120x90mm
Imperf
Without Gum

924 A489 10d multi 2.40 1.00

Palestinian Intifada A490

2002, Sept. 28 ***Perf. 13¼***
925 A490 6.50d multi 1.40 .70

Intl. Year of Ecotourism A491

2002, Sept. 30
926 A491 6.50d multi 1.40 .70

Green March, 27th Anniv. — A492

2002, Nov. 7
927 A492 6.50d multi 1.40 .70

Anti-Poverty Week Type of 2000 and

Anti-Poverty Week — A493

2002, Nov. 8 ***Perf. 12½***
928 A461 6.50d multi 1.40 .70
Perf. 13¼
929 A493 6.50d multi 1.40 .70

Value of No. 928 is for stamp with surrounding selvage.

Maghzen Post, 110th Anniv. A494

Sultan Moulay Hassan I and: 2.50d, Circular postal seal. 6.50d, Octagonal postal seal.

2002, Nov. 22 ***Perf. 12½, 13 (6.50d)***
930-931 A494 Set of 2 2.25 .95

Value of Nos. 930-931 are for stamps with surrounding selvage. No. 931 is ocatagonally shaped.

UN Year for Cultural Heritage A495

2002, Dec. 18 ***Perf. 13¼x13***
932 A495 6.50d multi 1.40 .70

Fish A496

Designs: 2.50d, Alosa alosa. 6.50d, Epinephelus marginatus.

2002, Dec. 30 ***Perf. 13¼***
933-934 A496 Set of 2 2.50 .95

King Mohammed VI Type of 2001
2002 **Litho.** ***Perf. 11½***
Granite Paper
Size: 24x30mm

934A A472 2.50d multi .50 .25
934B A473 6d multi 1.25 .60

Bab el Okla, Tetuan A497

2003, Feb. 28 **Photo.** ***Perf. 13¼***
935 A497 6.50d multi 1.40 .70

Fir Trees A498

2003, Mar. 28
936 A498 6.50d multi 1.40 .70

Intl. Year of Fresh Water — A499

2003, Apr. 28 ***Perf. 13¼x13***
937 A499 6.50d multi 1.40 .70

Flora — A500

Designs: 2.50d, Limonium sincatum. 6.50d, Echinops spinosus.

2003, May 30 ***Perf. 13¼***
938-939 A500 Set of 2 2.00 1.00

King Mohammed VI Type of 2001
2003 **Litho.** ***Perf. 13¼x12¾***

940 A475 70c lt bl & multi .20 .20
941 A475 80c pur & multi .20 .20
942 A475 5d yel & multi 1.00 .50
943 A475 20d lil & multi 4.75 2.10
Nos. 940-943 (4) 6.15 3.00

Salé Grand Mosque, 1000th Anniv. — A501

2003, July 11 **Photo.** ***Perf. 13x12¼***
944 A501 6.50d multi 1.40 .70

World Youth Congress A502

2003, Aug. 12 ***Perf. 13¼***
945 A502 6.50d multi 1.40 .70

Revolution of the King and People, 50th Anniv. A503

2003, Aug. 20
946 A503 6.50d multi 1.40 .70

King Mohammed VI, 40th Birthday — A504

Designs: Nos. 947, 949a, 2.50d, King in suit and tie. Nos. 948, 949b, 6.50d, King in robe.

2003, Aug. 21
947-948 A504 Set of 2 2.00 .95

Souvenir Sheet
Stamps With Pink Frames

949 A504 Sheet of 2, #a-b 2.50 1.25

No. 949 sold for 10d. Compare with type A545.

Fish A505

Designs: 2.50d, Sparisoma cretense. 6.50d, Anthias anthias.

2003, Sept. 30 **Photo.** ***Perf. 13¼***
950-951 A505 Set of 2 2.25 1.00

World Post Day — A506

2003, Oct. 9
952 A506 6.50d multi 1.40 .70

Anti-Poverty Week Type of 2000 and

King Mohammed VI Visiting Sick Child — A507

2003, Oct. 31 **Photo.** ***Perf. 12¾***
953 A461 6.50d multi 1.40 .70
954 A507 6.50d multi 1.40 .70

Green March, 28th Anniv. — A508

2003, Nov. 5 **Photo.** ***Perf. 13¼***
955 A508 6.50d multi 1.40 .70

Rabat, 2003 Arab Culture Capital — A509

2003, Dec. 19 **Litho.** ***Perf. 13x13¼***
956 A509 6.50d multi 1.50 .75

Philately at School A510

2003, Dec. 29 ***Perf. 13¼***
957 A510 6.50d multi 1.50 .75

UN Literacy Decade — A511

2003, Dec. 29 ***Perf. 13x13¼***
958 A511 6.50d multi 1.50 .75

Morocco - People's Republic of China Diplomatic Relations, 45th Anniv. — A512

2003, Dec. 31 ***Perf. 12***
959 A512 6.50d multi 1.50 .75

Types of 2001 Redrawn With Added Frame Lines

2002-3 Litho. ***Perf. 11½***

Size: 24x30mm

960 A474 6.50d multi — —

Size: 32x23mm

Arms 7mm Tall

961 A475 10d multi 2.40 1.00

Booklet Stamps

Self-Adhesive

Serpentine Die Cut 11

Size: 20x23mm

962 A472 2.50d multi ('03) .60 .25
a. Booklet pane of 10 6.00
963 A482 6.50d Like #915 ('03) 1.60 .70
a. Booklet pane of 10 16.00

Issued: 6.50d, 10d, 2002. 2.50d, 6.50d, 9/3/03.

On No. 903, arms are 9mm tall.

FAO Medal Type of 1999

2003, July Photo. ***Perf. 13x13¼***

Size: 48x38mm

964 A442 6d multi 1.60 .80

Ibn Battutah (1304-68), Traveler and Author — A513

2004, Feb. 24 Photo. ***Perf. 13x12¼***
965 A513 6.50d multi 1.50 .75

Bab Agnaou, Marrakesh A514

2004, Mar. 18 ***Perf. 13¼***
966 A514 6.50d multi 1.50 .75

Flowers — A515

Designs: 2.50d, Linaria gharbensis. 6.50d, Nigella damascena.

2004, Mar. 29
967-968 A515 Set of 2 2.25 1.00

16th World Military Equestrian Championships, Témara — A516

2004, Apr. 18
969 A516 6.50d multi 1.40 .70

Hassan II Tennis Grand Prix, 20th Anniv. — A517

2004, May 14
970 A517 6.50d multi 1.40 .70

10th World Sacred Music Festival, Fez A518

2004, May 28 ***Perf. 12¼x13***
971 A518 6.50d multi 1.40 .70

Caftan — A519

2004, June 18 ***Perf. 13¼***
972 A519 6.50d multi 1.40 .70

Dinosaur Fossils Found in Tazouda A520

2004, July 12
973 A520 6.50d multi 1.75 .75

30th Intl. Military History Congress A521

2004, July 29
974 A521 6.50d multi 1.40 .70

Enthronement of King Mohammed VI, 5th Anniv. — A522

Designs: Nos. 975, 977a, 2.50d, King in suit. Nos. 976, 977b, 6d, King in robe.

2004, July 30
975-976 A522 Set of 2 1.90 .95

Souvenir Sheet

Stamps With Yellow Frames

977 A522 Sheet of 2, #a-b 2.50 1.25

No. 977 sold for 10d.

Intl. Peace Day — A523

2004, Sept. 21 Photo. ***Perf. 13¼***
978 A523 6d multi 1.40 .70

Anti-Poverty Week Type of 2000 and

Anti-Poverty Week — A524

2004, Oct. 22 ***Perf. 12¾***
979 A461 6.50d multi 1.50 .75

Perf. 13¼

980 A524 6.50d multi 1.50 .75

Value for No. 979 is for stamp with surrounding selvage.

Green March, 29th Anniv. — A525

2004, Nov. 6 Photo. ***Perf. 13¼***
981 A525 6d multi 1.40 .70

Marine Life A526

Designs: 2.50d, Xiphias gladius. 6.50d, Octopus vulgaris.

2004, Nov. 16 Photo. ***Perf. 13¼***
982-983 A526 Set of 2 2.50 1.10

World Children's Day — A527

2004, Nov. 24
984 A527 6.50d multi 1.60 .80

Rotary International, Cent. — A528

2005, Feb. 23 ***Perf. 13x13¼***
985 A528 6.50d multi 1.60 .80

Arab League, 60th Anniv. — A529

2005, Mar. 22 ***Perf. 13¼x13***
986 A529 6.50d multi 1.60 .80

Bab Boujloud, Fez A530

2005, Mar. 30 ***Perf. 13¼***
987 A530 6.50d multi 1.60 .80

Amnesty International A531

2005, May 6 Photo. ***Perf. 13¼***
988 A531 6.50d multi 1.50 .75

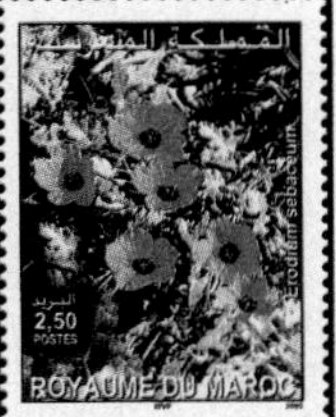

Flora — A532

Designs: 2.50d, Erodium sebaceum. 6.50d, Linaria ventricosa.

2005, May 26 Photo. ***Perf. 13¼***
989-990 A532 Set of 2 2.25 1.00

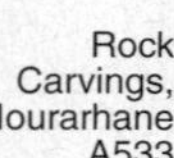

Rock Carvings, Iourarhane A533

2005, May 31
991 A533 6.50d multi 1.50 .75

13th World Neurosurgery Congress, Marrakesh A534

2005, June 19
992 A534 6.50d multi 1.50 .75

Phosphates Office, 80th Anniv. — A535

2005, Aug. 31 Photo. *Perf. 13¼*
993 A535 6.50d multi 1.50 .75

United Nations, 60th Anniv. — A536

2005, Oct. 24
994 A536 6.50d multi 1.50 .75

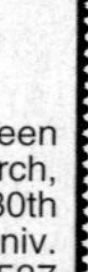

Green March, 30th Anniv. A537

Marchers and "30" in: 2.50d, Light blue. 6d, Green.

2005, Nov. 6
995-996 A537 Set of 2 1.90 .95

Anti-Poverty Week Type of 2000 and

Anti-Poverty Week — A538

2005, Nov. 7 *Perf. 12¾*
997 A461 6.50d multi 1.40 .70

Perf. 13¼
998 A538 6.50d multi 1.40 .70

Values for No. 997 are for stamps with surrounding selvage.

Friendship of Morocco and the Netherlands, 400th Anniv. — A539

Designs: No. 999, 6.50d, Five tourist attractions. No. 1000, 6.50d, Arch and waterway, vert.

2005, Nov. 14 *Perf. 13¼*
999-1000 A539 Set of 2 3.00 1.40

World Summit on the Information Society, Tunis A540

2005, Nov. 16
1001 A540 6d multi 1.40 .70

Return from Exile of King Mohammed V, 50th Anniv. — A541

Country name in: No. 1002, Red. No. 1003a, Green.

2005, Nov. 16 *Perf. 13¼x13*
1002 A541 6.50d multi 1.60 .70

Souvenir Sheet

1003 Sheet, #1002, 1003a 3.75 2.00
a. A541 6.50d multi 1.60 .70

Souvenir Sheet

Children's Art — A542

No. 1004: a, Children and flower, by Kaoutar Azizi Alaoui. b, Children and dove, by Sara Bourquiba. c, House and trees, by Mohcine Kahyouchat. d, Sun on horizon, by Anise Anico.

2005, Nov. 21 *Perf. 13x13¼*
1004 A542 2.50d Sheet of 4, #a-d 2.75 2.00

Intl. Year of Microcredit A543

2005, Nov. 30 *Perf. 13¼*
1005 A543 6.50d multi 1.40 .70

Marine Life A544

Designs: 2.50d, Sparus aurata. 6d, Sepia officinalis.

2005, Dec. 22
1006-1007 A544 Set of 2 2.50 .95

King Mohammed VI — A545

Designs: No. 1008, King in suit and tie. No. 1009, King in robe.

2005 Litho. *Serpentine Die Cut 11*
Booklet Stamps
Self-Adhesive

1008 A545 2.50d multi .55 .25
1009 A545 2.50d multi .55 .25
a. Booklet pane, 5 each #1008-1009 5.50

Compare type A545 with A504.

Bustard A546

Melierax Metabates A547

Egretta Garzetta A548

Pandion Haliaetus A549

Alectoris Barbara A550

Porphyrio Porphyrio A551

Carduelis Carduelis A552

Bird A553

Duck A554

Falcon A555

2005 *Serpentine Die Cut 11*
Self-Adhesive

1010 Booklet pane of 10 6.00
a. A546 2.50d multi .60 .25
b. A547 2.50d multi .60 .25
c. A548 2.50d multi .60 .25
d. A549 2.50d multi .60 .25
e. A550 2.50d multi .60 .25
f. A551 2.50d multi .60 .25
g. A552 2.50d multi .60 .25
h. A553 2.50d multi .60 .25
i. A554 2.50d multi .60 .25
j. A555 2.50d multi .60 .25

Two Women A556

Ait Mouhad A557

Saharaoui Derraa A558

Two Women A559

Citadin A560

Saharaoui Melhfa A561

Tata Woman A562

Tata Man A563

Meknassa A564

Mokhazni du Roi A565

2005 *Serpentine Die Cut 11*
Self-Adhesive

1011 Booklet pane of 10 14.00
a. A556 6d multi 1.40 .65
b. A557 6d multi 1.40 .65
c. A558 6d multi 1.40 .65
d. A559 6d multi 1.40 .65
e. A560 6d multi 1.40 .65
f. A561 6d multi 1.40 .65
g. A562 6d multi 1.40 .65
h. A563 6d multi 1.40 .65
i. A564 6d multi 1.40 .65
j. A565 6d multi 1.40 .65

Traffic Safety Day — A566

2006, Feb. 18 Photo. *Perf. 13½x13*
1012 A566 6.50d multi 1.40 .70

OPEC Intl. Development Fund, 30th Anniv. — A567

2006, Feb. 28 *Perf. 13¼*
1013 A567 6.50d multi 1.40 .70

Bab Marshan, Tangiers A568

2006, Mar. 30

1014	A568	6.50d multi	1.50	.75

Foreign Affairs Ministry, 50th Anniv. A569

2006, Apr. 26

1015	A569	6d multi	1.40	.70

Flowers — A570

Designs: 2.50d, Narcissus cantabricus. 6.50d, Paeonia mascula.

2006, Apr. 28

1016-1017	A570	Set of 2	2.10	1.10

Royal Armed Forces, 50th Anniv. A571

Kings Mohammed VI, Hassan II, and Mohammed V, anniversary emblem, airplanes and: 2.50d, Tank . 6.50d, Ships.

2006, May 14

1018-1019	A571	Set of 2	2.10	1.10
a.		Souvenir sheet, #1018-1019	2.40	2.40

No. 1019a sold for 10d.

Type of 2001 and

A572

King Mohammed VI — A573

2006, July 1 **Litho.** ***Perf. 11½***

Granite Paper

1020	A472	3.25d blue & multi	.75	.40
1021	A572	7.80d lt grn & multi	1.90	.95
1022	A573	13d lilac & multi	3.00	1.50
		Nos. 1020-1022 (3)	5.65	2.85

Compare types A572 and A573 with types A473 and A475.

Barbary Ape — A574

Atlas Lion — A575

2006, July 31 ***Perf. 13¼x13***

1023	A574	3.25d multi	.75	.40
1024	A575	7.80d multi	1.90	.95

Green March, 31st Anniv. A576

Designs: No. 1025, 7.80d, King Mohammed VI waving to crowd. No. 1026, 7.80d, Mohammed VI Mosque, Boujdour.

2006, Nov. 7 **Photo.** ***Perf. 13¼***

1025-1026	A576	Set of 2	3.75	1.90

Anti-Poverty Week Type of 2000

2006, Nov. 10

1027	A461	7.80d multi	1.90	.95

Values are for stamps with surrounding selvage.

Stamp Day — A577

2006, Nov. 22

1028	A577	7.80d multi	1.90	.95

Values are for stamps with surrounding selvage.

Admission to the United Nations, 50th Anniv. — A578

2006, Nov. 24

1029	A578	7.80d multi	1.90	.95

World AIDS Day A579

2006, Dec. 1 **Litho.** ***Perf. 13¼***

1030	A579	7.80d multi	1.90	.95

Diplomatic Relations Between Morocco and Japan, 50th Anniv. A580

Designs: 3.25d, Dove, maps and flags. 7.80d, Flags, arches, pottery.

2006, Dec. 20 **Photo.** ***Perf. 13¼***

1031-1032	A580	Set of 2	2.60	1.25

Fish A581

Designs: 3.25d, Thunnus thynnus. 7.80d, Sardina pilchardus.

2006, Dec. 25

1033-1034	A581	Set of 2	2.60	1.25

African Soccer Confederation, 50th Anniv. — A582

2007, Feb. 26 **Litho.** ***Perf. 13¼***

1035	A582	7.80d multi	1.90	.95

Values are for stamps with surrounding selvage.

Mohammed V University, 50th Anniv. — A583

2007, Mar. 15

1036	A583	3.25d multi	.80	.40

Ibn Khaldun (1332-1406), Philosopher — A584

2007, Mar. 28

1037	A584	7.80d multi	1.90	.95

Souvenir Sheet

Intl. Agricultural Exhibition, Meknès — A585

No. 1038: a, Palm trees. b, Argans. c, Cattle, horiz. d, Olives, horiz.

Perf. 12¾x13¼, 13¼x12¾ (horiz. stamps)

2007, Apr. 19

1038	A585	Sheet of 4	6.00	6.00
a.-b.		3.25d Either single	.90	.45
c.-d.		7.80d Either single	2.10	1.10

No. 1038 sold for 24d.

Couscous A586

2007, June 1 ***Perf. 13¼x13***

1039	A586	7.80d multi	1.90	.95

Andalusian Music — A587

2007, June 8 ***Perf. 13x13¼***

1040	A587	7.80d multi	1.90	.95

Souvenir Sheet

Paintings — A588

No. 1041: a, Fulgurance, by M. Qotbi, vert. b, Horses and Riders, by, H. Glaoui. c, Symphonie d'Eté, by Qotbi. d, Horses, by Glaoui.

2007, June 21 ***Perf. 13***

1041	A588	3.25d Sheet of 4, #a-d	3.25	3.25

Scouting, Cent. — A589

2007, Aug. 7 Litho. *Perf. 13¼*
1042 A589 7.80d multi 1.90 .95

Buildings — A590

Designs: 3.25d, Silves Castle, Portugal. 7.80d, Tower, Arzila, Morocco.

2007, Sept. 26
1043-1044 A590 Set of 2 2.75 1.40

See Portugal Nos. 2955-2956.

World Post Day A591

2007, Oct. 9
1045 A591 3.25d multi .85 .40

Fez, 2007 Islamic Cultural Capital A592

2007, Oct. 30
1046 A592 7.80d multi 2.00 1.00

Compare with Type A618.

Green March, 32nd Anniv. A593

2007, Nov. 6
1047 A593 7.80d multi 2.00 1.00

Anti-Poverty Week Type of 2000

2007, Nov. 8
1048 A461 7.80d multi 2.00 1.00

Values are for stamps with surrounding selvage.

National Quality Week — A594

2007, Nov. 12
1049 A594 7.80d multi 2.00 1.00

World Children's Day — A595

2007, Nov. 20
1050 A595 7.80d multi 2.00 1.00

Supreme Court, 50th Anniv. — A596

2007, Nov. 21
1051 A596 3.25d multi .85 .40

Bab Lamrissa — A597

2007, Dec. 7 Litho. *Perf. 13¼*
1052 A597 7.80d multi 2.00 1.00

Royal Air Morocco, 50th Anniv. A598

2007, Dec. 19
1053 A598 7.80d multi 2.00 1.00

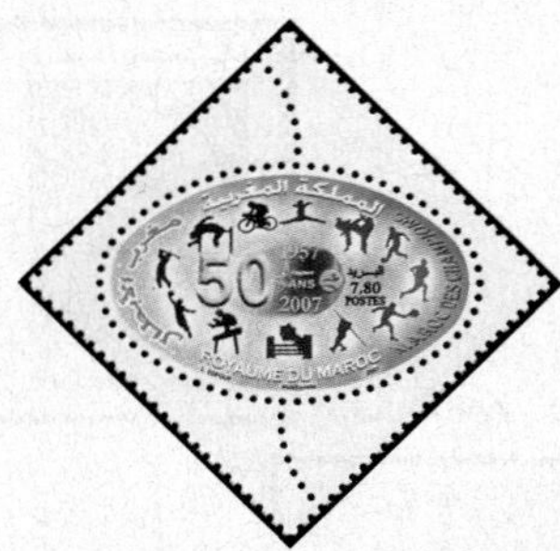
"Morocco of Champions" — A599

2007, Dec. 28
1054 A599 7.80d multi 2.00 1.00

Values are for stamps with surrounding selvage.

Moroccan Travel Market A600

2008, Jan. 17
1055 A600 7.80d multi 2.00 1.00

Africa Cup of Nations Soccer Championships — A601

2008, Jan. 31
1056 A601 7.80d multi 2.10 1.10

Export Trophy — A602

2008, Apr. 4 Litho. *Perf. 13¼*
1057 A602 3.25d multi .90 .45

Fez, 1200th Anniv. — A603

2008, Apr. 5
1058 A603 3.25d multi .90 .45

Buildings in Morocco and Iran — A605

No. 1061: a, 3.25d, Flags of Morocco and Iran, Kasbah, Oudayas, Morocco, and Falak-Ol-Aflak Castle, Iran. b, 3,25d, Scroll and Falak-Ol-Aflak Castle. c, 7.80d, Scroll and Kasbah, Oudayas, Morocco.
Illustration reduced.

2008, May 12 Litho. *Perf. 13¼*
1061 A605 Horiz. strip of 3, #a-c 4.00 2.00

See Iran No. 2955.

Children's Art — A606

No. 1062: a, Earth, by Narjiss Lasfar. b, House and trees, by Chaimae Abbaich. c, Polluted sphere, by Ahmed Anas Bennis, vert. d, House and sun, by Wassim Chakou, vert.

2008, May 26
1062 Horiz. strip of 4 3.75 1.90
a.-d. A606 3.25d Any single .90 .45

World Environment Day — A607

2008, June 5
1063 A607 7.80d multi 2.25 1.10

Rug From Salé A608

Rug From Marmoucha A609

Rug From Ouled Besseba A610

Rug From Haut Atlas A611

Rug From Ait Haddou A612

Rug From Tazenakht A613

Rug From Marmoucha A614

Rug From Rabat A615

Rug From Ait Ouaouzguid
A616

Rug From Rabat
A617

2008 *Serpentine Die Cut 11*
Self-Adhesive

1064	Booklet pane of 10	22.50	
a.	A608 7.80d multi	2.25	1.10
b.	A609 7.80d multi	2.25	1.10
c.	A610 7.80d multi	2.25	1.10
d.	A611 7.80d multi	2.25	1.10
e.	A612 7.80d multi	2.25	1.10
f.	A613 7.80d multi	2.25	1.10
g.	A614 7.80d multi	2.25	1.10
h.	A615 7.80d multi	2.25	1.10
i.	A616 7.80d multi	2.25	1.10
j.	A617 7.80d multi	2.25	1.10

Fez, 1200th Anniv.
A618

2008, June 23 *Perf. 13¼*
1065 A618 7.80d multi 2.25 1.10

Compare with Type A592.

Bouregreg Valley Light Rail Line — A619

No. 1066: a, 3.25d, Train, bridge. b, 7.80d, Train, fortress.
Illustration reduced.

2008, July 21
1066 A619 Horiz. pair, #a-b 3.00 1.50

2008 Summer Olympics, Beijing — A620

No. 1067 — Olympic rings and: a, Four runners. b, Three hurdlers. c, Boxers. d, Runner.

2008, Aug. 8 Photo. *Perf. 13¼*
1067 Horiz. strip of 4 3.50 1.75
a.-d. A620 3.25d Any single .85 .40

Arab Post Day — A621

No. 1068 — Emblem and: a, World map, pigeon. b, Camel caravan.
Illustration reduced.

2008, Aug. 28 Litho. *Perf. 12¾*
1068 Sheet of 2 4.00 2.00
a.-b. A621 7.80d Either single 2.00 1.00

Marine Life
A622

Designs: 3.25d, Isurus oxyrinchus. 7.80d, Haliotis tuberculata.

2008, Sept. 18 *Perf. 13¼*
1069-1070 A622 Set of 2 2.75 1.40

Miniature Sheet

Art and Culture — A623

No. 1071: a, Musicians. b, Ezzellij tiles. c, Haik (white garment). d, Koran school.

2008, Oct. 10 Photo. *Perf. 13¼x13*
1071 A623 3.25d Sheet of 4, #a-d 3.25 1.60

SEMI-POSTAL STAMPS

Nos. 1-5 Surcharged

1960, Mar. Unwmk. Engr. *Perf. 13*

B1	A1	5fr + 10fr brt bl & ind	.30	.25
B2	A1	10fr + 10fr bis brn & choc	.35	.35
B3	A1	15fr + 10fr dp grn & mag	.80	.70
B4	A1	25fr + 15fr purple	.90	.75
B5	A1	30fr + 20fr green	1.50	1.50
		Nos. B1-B5 (5)	3.85	3.55

The surtax aided families whose members consumed adulterated cooking oil with crippling or fatal results.

French Morocco Nos. 321 and 322 Surcharged

1960, Sept. 12

B6	A71	15fr + 3fr on 18fr dk grn	.55	.55
B7	A71	20fr + 5fr brown lake	.80	.80

Nos. 1 and 6 Surcharged in Red or Black

1963, Jan. 28 Engr. *Perf. 13*

B8	A1	20c + 5c on 5fr brt bl & ind (R)	.50	.50
B9	A1	30c + 10c on 50fr rose red	.60	.55

The surtax was for flood victims.

Moroccan Brooch — SP1

Design: 40c+10c, Brooch with pendants.

1966, May 23 Photo. *Perf. 11½*
Granite Paper

B10	SP1	25c + 5c ultra, sil, blk & red	.60	.40
B11	SP1	40c + 10c mag, sil, blk, ultra & bl	.90	.50
a.		Pair, #B10-B11, vertically tête-bêche	2.25	2.25

Meeting in Morocco of the Middle East and North African Red Cross-Red Crescent Seminar. The surtax was for the Moroccan Red Crescent Society.

See Nos. B12-B13, B15-B16, B19-B22, B26-B27, B29-B30, B34-B35.

1967, May 15 **Granite Paper**

Designs: 60c+5c, Two brooches, by silver drapery. 1d+10c, Two bracelets.

B12	SP1	60c + 5c yel bis & multi	.70	.70
a.		Pair, vertically tête-bêche	2.25	2.25
B13	SP1	1d + 10c emer & multi	1.40	1.40
a.		Pair, vertically tête-bêche	3.50	3.50

Surtax for the Moroccan Red Crescent Society.

Hands Reading Braille and Map of Morocco — SP2

1969, Mar. 21 Photo. *Perf. 12½*
B14 SP2 25c + 10c multi .35 .20

Week of the Blind, Mar. 21-29.

Jewelry Type of 1966

Designs: 25c+5c, Silver earrings. 40c+10c, Gold ear pendant.

1969, May 9 Photo. *Perf. 11½*
Granite Paper

B15	SP1	25c + 5c gray grn & multi	.60	.45
B16	SP1	40c + 10c tan & multi	.90	.55
a.		Pair, #B15-B16, vert. tête-bêche	2.25	2.25

50th anniv. of the League of Red Cross Societies. Surtax was for Moroccan Red Crescent Society.

Nos. 173-174 Surcharged

1970, Feb. 26 Litho. *Perf. 13*

B17	A65	10c + 25c multi	2.50	2.50
B18	A65	15c + 25c multi	2.50	2.50

The surtax was for flood victims.

Jewelry Type of 1966

Designs: 25c+5c, Necklace with pendants. 50c+10c, Earring with 5 pendants.

1970, May 25 Photo. *Perf. 11½*
Granite Paper

B19	SP1	25c + 5c gray & multi	.75	.65
B20	SP1	50c + 10c brt vio & multi	1.10	.95
a.		Pair, #B19-B20, vert. tête-bêche	2.50	2.50

Surtax for Moroccan Red Crescent Society.

1971, May 10

25c+5c, Brooch. 40c+10c, Stomacher.

Granite Paper

B21	SP1	25c + 5c gray & multi	.55	.45
B22	SP1	40c + 10c yel & multi	.80	.70
a.		Pair, #B21-B22, vertically tête-bêche	1.75	1.75

Globe and Map of Palestine
SP3

1971, Apr. 30 *Perf. 13*
B23 SP3 25c + 10c multi .60 .30

Palestine Week, May 3-8.

String Instrument and Bow — SP4

1971, June 28 Photo. *Perf. 12*
B24 SP4 40c + 10c multi .40 .25

Week of the Blind.

Mizmar (Double Flute) — SP5

1972, Mar. 31 Photo. *Perf. 13x13½*
B25 SP5 25c + 10c multi .45 .45

Week of the Blind.

Jewelry Type of 1966

Designs: 25c+5c, Jeweled bracelets. 70c+10c, Rectangular pendant with ball drop.

1972, May 8 Photo. *Perf. 11½*
Granite Paper

B26	SP1	25c + 5c brn & multi	.55	.55
B27	SP1	70c + 10c dp grn & multi	.80	.80
a.		Pair, #B26-B27, vert. tête-bêche	1.75	1.75

For overprints see Nos. 295-296.

Drums
SP6

1973, Mar. 30 Photo. *Perf. 13x14*
B28 SP6 70c + 10c multi .45 .35

Week of the Blind.

Jewelry Type of 1966

25c+5c, Silver box pendant. 70c+10c, Bracelet.

1973, June 15 Photo. *Perf. 11½*

B29	SP1	25c + 5c bl & multi	.75	.45
B30	SP1	70c + 10c org & multi	.90	.70
a.		Pair, #B29-B30, vert. tête-bêche	2.25	2.25

Moroccan Red Crescent Society. For overprints see Nos. 351-352.

Pistol — SP7

Erbab (Fiddle) — SP8

70c+10c, Decorated antique powder box.

1974, July 8 Photo. *Perf. 14x13½*

B31 SP7 25c + 5c multi .55 .55
B32 SP7 70c + 10c multi .80 .80
a. Pair, #B31-B32, vert. tête-bêche 1.75 1.75

Moroccan Red Crescent Society.

1975, Jan. 10 Photo. *Perf. 13*

B33 SP8 70c + 10c multi .55 .35

Week of the Blind.

Jewelry Type of 1966

25c+5c, Silver pendant. 70c+10c, Earring.

1975, Mar. 13 Photo. *Perf. 13½*

B34 SP1 25c + 5c multi .55 .55
B35 SP1 70c + 10c multi .80 .70
a. Pair, #B34-B35, vert. tête-bêche 1.75 1.75

Moroccan Red Crescent Society. For overprints see #386-387.

AIR POST STAMPS

Sultan's Star over Casablanca
AP1

King Hassan II
AP2

Unwmk.

1957, May 4 Engr. *Perf. 13*

C1 AP1 15fr car & brt grn .90 .75
C2 AP1 25fr brt grnsh bl 1.40 .90
C3 AP1 30fr red brn 2.00 1.25
Nos. C1-C3 (3) 4.30 2.90

Intl. Fair, Casablanca, May 4-19.

1962

C5 AP2 90c black .55 .20
C6 AP2 1d rose red .80 .20
C7 AP2 2d deep blue .90 .45
C8 AP2 3d dl bl grn 1.75 .80
C9 AP2 5d purple 3.50 1.25
Nos. C5-C9 (5) 7.50 2.90

Meteorological Day Type of Regular Issue

1964, Mar. 23 Photo. *Perf. 11½*
Granite Paper

C10 A39 90c Anemometer & globe .90 .50

Intl. Fair, Casablanca, 20th Anniv. — AP3

1964, Apr. 30 Photo. *Perf. 12½*

C11 AP3 1d bl, bis & org .55 .50

Moroccan Pavilion and Unisphere
AP4

1964, May 25 Unwmk. *Perf. 12½*

C12 AP4 1d dk grn, red & bl .75 .55

New York World's Fair, 1964-65.

Ramses II and UNESCO Emblem — AP5

Litho. & Engr.

1966, Oct. 3 *Perf. 12x11½*

C13 AP5 1d magenta, *yel* 1.00 .55

UNESCO, 20th anniv.

Jet Plane — AP6

Perf. 12½x13½

1966, Dec. 19 Photo.

C14 AP6 3d multi 3.00 1.50

Costume Type of Regular Issue

Design: 1d, Women from Ait Ouaouzguit.

1969, Jan. 21 Litho. *Perf. 12*

C15 A74 1d multi 2.00 .85

Coin Type of Regular Issue, 1968

Coins: 1d, King Mohammed V, 1960. 5d, King Hassan II, 1965.

1969, Mar. 3 Photo. *Perf. 11½*
Granite Paper

C16 A73 1d brt bl, sil & blk 3.75 1.50
C17 A73 5d vio blk, sil & blk 7.50 4.50

King Hassan II — AP7

1983, Mar. 1 Photo. *Perf. 12*
Granite Paper

C18 AP7 1.40d multi .45 .20
C19 AP7 2d multi .50 .20
C20 AP7 3d multi .70 .25
C21 AP7 5d multi 1.10 .40
C22 AP7 10d multi 2.25 .75
Nos. C18-C22 (5) 5.00 1.80

No. C19 Overprinted

1987, Mar. 23 Photo. *Perf. 12*
Granite Paper

C23 AP7 2d multi .60 .45

1st World Congress of Friday Preachers, Al Joumouaa.

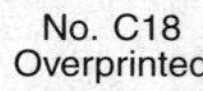

No. C18 Overprinted

1989, Mar. 27 Photo. *Perf. 12*
Granite Paper

C24 AP7 1.40d multi .40 .30

Maghreb Union, agreement between Morocco, Algeria and Tunisia.

No. C18 Surcharged

2000, July 6 Photo. *Perf. 12*
Granite Paper

C25 AP7 6.50d on 1.40d multi 1.25 .60

Intl. Colloquium on King Hassan II.

POSTAGE DUE STAMPS

D1

Oranges — D2

1965 Unwmk. Typo. *Perf. 14x13½*

J1 D1 5c green 9.00 .75
J2 D1 10c bister brown .45 .25
J3 D1 20c red .45 .25
J4 D1 30c brown black 1.00 .45
Nos. J1-J4 (4) 10.90 1.70

See French Morocco Nos. J27-J34, J46-J56.

1974-96 Photo. *Perf. 14*

J5 D2 5c shown .20 .20
J6 D2 10c Cherries .30 .20
J7 D2 20c Grapes .40 .20
J8 D2 30c Peaches, horiz. .55 .20
J9 D2 40c Grapes ('78) .35 .20
J10 D2 60c Peaches, horiz. ('78) .50 .20
J11 D2 80c Oranges ('78) .70 .20
J12 D2 1d Apples ('86) .40 .20
J13 D2 1.20d Cherries ('84) .70 .20
J14 D2 1.60d Peaches ('85) .70 .25
J15 D2 2d Strawberries ('86) .75 .35

Litho.

J16 D2 5d like #J12 ('96) 1.25 1.00
Nos. J5-J16 (12) 6.80 3.40

For surcharges see Nos. 322, 395.

Strawberries — D3

Strawberries — D3a

Grapes
D4

Apples
D5

Cherries — D6

2003 Photo. *Perf. 13x13½*

J17 D3 1.50d multi .30 .20
J17A D3a 1.50d multi .35 .20
J18 D4 2d multi .40 .20
J19 D5 5d multi 1.10 .55
J20 D6 2d multi .45 .20
Nos. J17-J20 (5) 2.60 1.35

Fruit Type of 1974-96

2005 ? Litho. *Perf. 14*

J21 D2 60c Peaches .20 .20

No. J21 has a background of solid color. No. J10 has a background of dots. The text is thicker and heavier on No. J10 than on No. J21.

NORTHERN ZONE

100 Centimos = 1 Peseta

All Northern Zone issues except Nos. 21-22 were also sold imperforate in limited quantities.

Sultan Mohammed V — A1

Villa Sanjurjo Harbor
A2

Designs: 25c, Polytechnic school. 50c, 10p, Institute of Culture, Tetuan.

Perf. 13x12½, 12½x13

1956, Aug. 23 Photo. Unwmk.

1 A1 10c deep rose .20 .20
2 A2 15c yellow brn .20 .20
3 A2 25c dk bl gray .20 .20
4 A1 50c dark olive .20 .20
5 A1 80c brt green .20 .20
6 A2 2p brt red lil 2.00 1.25
7 A2 3p brt blue 5.00 2.25
8 A1 10p green 17.50 9.00
Nos. 1-8 (8) 25.50 13.50

A3

Sultan Mohammed V — A4

1957, Mar. 2 *Perf. 13½x13*

9	A3	80c blue green	.50	.35
10	A3	1.50p gray olive	2.00	.90
11	A3	3p deep rose	5.50	3.25
		Nos. 9-11 (3)	8.00	4.50

1st anniv. of independence. See Morocco #13-15.

1957 **Engr.** *Perf. 13*

12	A4	30c brt bl & indigo	.25	.20
13	A4	70c bis, brn & choc	.25	.20
14	A4	80c brt violet	.90	.20
15	A4	1.50p dp grn & mag	.25	.20
16	A4	3p green	.35	.25
17	A4	7p rose red	1.50	.40
		Nos. 12-17 (6)	3.50	1.45

Prince Moulay el Hassan — A5

King Mohammed V — A6

1957, July 15 **Photo.** *Perf. 13*

18	A5	80c blue	.30	.30
19	A5	1.50p green	2.00	.90
20	A5	3p carmine rose	6.50	3.75
		Nos. 18-20 (3)	8.80	4.95

Exist imperf. Value, set $250.

Nos. 13 and 15 Surcharged in Carmine or Black

1957 **Engr.**

21	A4	15c on 70c (C)	.30	.25
22	A4	1.20p on 1.50p (Bk)	.75	.25

1957, Nov. **Photo.** *Perf. 12½*

23	A6	1.20p blk & brt grn	.60	.25
24	A6	1.80p blk & rose red	.60	.35
25	A6	3p black & violet	1.75	.55
		Nos. 23-25 (3)	2.95	1.15

Enthronement of Mohammed V, 30th anniv.

NORTHERN ZONE AIR POST STAMPS

Plane over Lau Dam AP1

1.40p, 4.80p, Plane over Nekor bridge.

Perf. 12½x13

1956, Dec. 17 **Photo.** **Unwmk.**

C1	AP1	25c rose violet	.25	.20
C2	AP1	1.40p lilac rose	.25	.20
C3	AP1	3.40p org vermilion	1.25	.75
C4	AP1	4.80p dull violet	1.75	1.10
		Nos. C1-C4 (4)	3.50	2.25

MOZAMBIQUE

mō-zəm-'bēk

LOCATION — Southeastern Africa, bordering on the Mozambique Channel

GOVT. — Republic

AREA — 308,642 sq. mi.

POP. — 16,542,800 (1997)

CAPITAL — Maputo

Formerly a Portuguese colony, Mozambique, or Portuguese East Africa, was divided into eight districts: Lourenco Marques, Inhambane, Quelimane, Tete, Mozambique, Zambezia, Nyassa and the Manica and Sofala region formerly administered by the Mozambique Company. At various times the districts issued their own stamps which were eventually replaced by those inscribed "Mocambique."

Mozambique achieved independence June 25, 1975, taking the name People's Republic of Mozambique.

1000 Reis = 1 Milreis
100 Centavos = 1 Escudo (1913)
100 Centavos = 1 Metical (1980)

Catalogue values for unused stamps in this country are for Never Hinged items, beginning with Scott 330 in the regular postage section, Scott C29 in the airpost section, Scott J51 in the postage due section, and Scott RA55 in the postal tax section.

Portuguese Crown — A1

King Luiz — A2

Perf. 12½, 13½

1877-85 **Typo.** **Unwmk.**

1	A1	5r black	2.00	1.00
a.		Perf. 13½	3.00	1.60
2	A1	10r yellow	15.00	4.50
3	A1	10r green ('81)	1.50	.60
4	A1	20r bister	1.50	.75
a.		Perf. 13½	3.00	2.00
5	A1	20r rose ('85)	350.00	150.00
6	A1	25r rose	1.00	.35
a.		Perf. 13½	6.75	1.60
7	A1	25r violet ('85)	3.00	2.00
8	A1	40r blue	25.00	15.00
9	A1	40r yel buff ('81)	2.00	1.60
a.		Perf. 12½	3.50	3.00
10	A1	50r green	70.00	25.00
a.		Perf. 13½	125.00	60.00
11	A1	50r blue ('81)	.75	.40
12	A1	100r lilac	1.00	.50
13	A1	200r orange	2.00	1.40
a.		Perf. 12½	5.25	4.50
14	A1	300r chocolate	2.25	2.00
		Nos. 1-4,6-14 (13)	127.00	55.10

The reprints of the 1877-85 issues are printed on a smooth white chalky paper, ungummed, with rough perforation 13½, also on thin white paper, with shiny white gum and clean-cut perforation 13½.

Typographed and Embossed

1886 *Perf. 12½*

15	A2	5r black	1.50	.60
16	A2	10r green	1.50	.70
17	A2	20r rose	2.00	1.50
18	A2	25r dull lilac	9.00	1.40
19	A2	40r chocolate	1.75	.85
20	A2	50r blue	2.25	.50
21	A2	100r yellow brn	2.50	.50
22	A2	200r gray violet	4.25	1.75
23	A2	300r orange	4.50	2.00
		Nos. 15-23 (9)	29.25	9.80

Perf. 13½

15a	A2	5r	4.00	2.75
16a	A2	10r	4.25	2.75
17a	A2	20r	13.00	6.00
18a	A2	25r	13.00	6.00
19a	A2	40r	15.00	9.50
20a	A2	50r	16.00	4.50
22a	A2	200r	15.00	12.50
		Nos. 15a-22a (7)	80.25	44.00

Nos. 15, 18, 19, 20, 21 and 23 have been reprinted. The reprints have shiny white gum and clean-cut perforation 13½. Many of the colors are paler than those of the originals.

For surcharges and overprints see Nos. 23A, 36-44, 46-48, 72-80, 192, P1-P5.

No. 19 Surcharged in Black

PROVISORIO

5 5

1893, Jan. *Perf. 12½*

Without Gum

23A	A2	5r on 40r choc	125.00	50.00

There are three varieties of No. 23A:

I — "PROVISORIO" 19mm long, numerals 4½mm high.

II — "PROVISORIO" 19½mm long, numerals 5mm high.

III — "PROVISORIO" 19½mm long, numerals of both sizes.

King Carlos I — A3

1894 **Typo.** *Perf. 11½, 12½*

24	A3	5r yellow	.50	.45
25	A3	10r red lilac	.50	.35
26	A3	15r red brown	1.25	.75
27	A3	20r gray lilac	1.25	.50
28	A3	25r blue green	1.25	.20
29	A3	50r lt blue	5.00	1.50
a.		Perf. 12½	7.50	2.00
30	A3	75r rose	1.75	1.25
31	A3	80r yellow grn	2.00	1.00
32	A3	100r brown, *buff*	1.75	1.25
33	A3	150r car, *rose*	8.00	4.00
a.		Perf. 11½		
34	A3	200r dk blue, *blue*	5.00	3.00
35	A3	300r dk blue, *salmon*	7.00	3.00
		Nos. 24-35 (12)	35.25	17.25

Nos. 28 and 31-33 have been reprinted with shiny white gum and clean-cut perf. 13½.

For surcharges and overprints see Nos. 45, 81-92, 193-198, 201-205, 226-228, 238-239.

Stamps of 1886 Overprinted in Red or Black

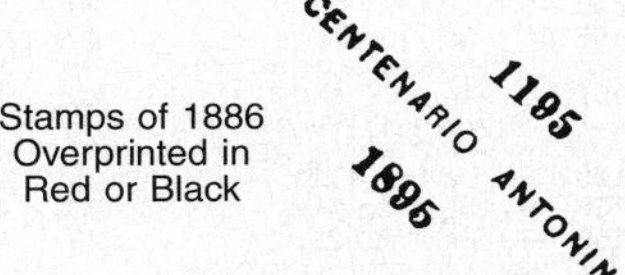

1895, July 1 *Perf. 12½*

Without Gum

36	A2	5r black (R)	11.00	5.50
37	A2	10r green	12.50	6.50
38	A2	20r rose	14.00	6.00
39	A2	25r violet	16.00	6.50
a.		Double overprint		
40	A2	40r chocolate	17.50	7.50
41	A2	50r blue	17.50	7.50
a.		Perf. 13½	80.00	55.00
42	A2	100r yellow brown	17.50	8.25
43	A2	200r gray violet	27.50	13.00
a.		Perf. 13½	100.00	65.00
44	A2	300r orange	37.50	17.50
		Nos. 36-44 (9)	171.00	78.25

Birth of Saint Anthony of Padua, 7th cent.

No. 35 Surcharged in Black

50

réis

1897, Jan. 2 *Perf. 12½*

Without Gum

45	A3	50r on 300r dk bl, *sal*	150.00	40.00

Nos. 17, 19 Surcharged

a

MOCAMBIQUE
2 ½
REIS

b

MOCAMBIQUE
2½
RÉIS

c

1898

Without Gum

46	A2 (a)	2½r on 20r rose	42.50	11.00
47	A2 (b)	2½r on 20r rose	27.50	10.00
a.		Inverted surcharge	55.00	45.00
48	A2 (c)	5r on 40r choc	35.00	10.00
a.		Inverted surcharge	90.00	45.00
		Nos. 46-48 (3)	105.00	31.00

King Carlos I — A4

1898-1903 **Typo.** *Perf. 11½*

Name and Value in Black except 500r

49	A4	2½r gray	.20	.20
50	A4	5r orange	.20	.20
51	A4	10r lt green	.25	.20
52	A4	15r brown	3.00	1.50
53	A4	15r gray grn ('03)	.70	.55
54	A4	20r gray violet	.85	.40
55	A4	25r sea green	.85	.40
56	A4	25r carmine ('03)	.70	.30
57	A4	50r dark blue	1.50	.50
58	A4	50r brown ('03)	2.00	1.50
59	A4	65r dull blue ('03)	15.00	12.00
60	A4	75r rose	7.00	2.75
61	A4	75r red lilac ('03)	3.00	1.75
62	A4	80r violet	6.00	3.25
63	A4	100r dk blue, *bl*	2.00	1.00
64	A4	115r org brn, *pink* ('03)	10.00	5.00
65	A4	130r brown, *straw* ('03)	10.00	5.00
66	A4	150r brown, *straw*	10.00	2.75
67	A4	200r red lilac, *pnksh*	2.00	1.40
68	A4	300r dk blue, *rose*	8.00	3.25
69	A4	400r dl bl, *straw* ('03)	13.00	7.50
70	A4	500r blk & red, *bl* ('01)	20.00	8.00
71	A4	700r vio, *yelsh* ('01)	25.00	9.00
		Nos. 49-71 (23)	141.25	68.40

For overprints and surcharges see Nos. 94-113, 200, 207-220.

Stamps of 1886-94 Surcharged

1902 *Perf. 12½, 13½*

On Stamps of 1886

Red Surcharge

72	A2	115r on 5r blk	5.00	2.00

Black Surcharge

73	A2	65r on 20r rose	5.00	2.50
a.		Double surcharge	50.00	50.00
74	A2	65r on 40r choc	6.00	4.00
75	A2	65r on 200r violet	5.00	1.75
76	A2	115r on 50r blue	2.00	1.00
77	A2	130r on 25r red vio	3.00	.90
78	A2	130r on 300r orange	3.00	.90
79	A2	400r on 10r green	7.50	3.25
80	A2	400r on 100r yel brn	40.00	25.00
		Nos. 72-80 (9)	76.50	41.30

The reprints of Nos. 74, 75, 76, 77, 79 and 80 have shiny white gum and clean-cut perforation 13½.

On Stamps of 1894

Perf. 11½

81	A3	65r on 10r red lil	3.50	2.00
82	A3	65r on 15r red brn	3.50	2.00
a.		Pair, one without surcharge		
83	A3	65r on 20r gray lil	3.75	2.00
84	A3	115r on 5r yel	4.00	2.00
a.		Inverted surcharge		

85 A3 115r on 25r bl grn 3.50 2.00
86 A3 130r on 75r rose 4.00 2.25
87 A3 130r on 100r brn, *buff* 6.00 5.00
88 A3 130r on 150r car, *rose* 4.00 2.00
89 A3 130r on 200r bl, *bl* 5.00 3.50
90 A3 400r on 50r lt bl 1.00 1.40
91 A3 400r on 80r yel grn 1.00 1.40
92 A3 400r on 300r bl, *sal* 1.00 1.40

On Newspaper Stamp of 1893

Perf. 13½

93 N3 115r on 2½r brn 2.00 2.25
Nos. 81-93 (13) 42.25 29.20

Reprints of No. 87 have shiny white gum and clean-cut perforation 13½.

Overprinted in Black

On Stamps of 1898

Perf. 11½

94 A4 15r brown 2.00 .85
95 A4 25r sea green 2.50 .85
96 A4 50r blue 3.00 1.75
97 A4 75r rose 5.00 2.00
Nos. 94-97 (4) 12.50 5.45

No. 59 Surcharged in Black

1905

98 A4 50r on 65r dull blue 3.00 2.00

Stamps of 1898-1903 Overprinted in Carmine or Green

1911

99 A4 2½r gray .30 .20
a. Inverted overprint 15.00 15.00
100 A4 5r orange .30 .20
101 A4 10r lt green 2.00 .50
102 A4 15r gray grn .30 .20
103 A4 20r gray vio 2.00 .40
104 A4 25r carmine (G) .30 .20
a. 25r gray violet (error)
105 A4 50r brown .50 .20
106 A4 75r red lilac 1.00 .50
107 A4 100r dk blue, *bl* 1.00 .50
108 A4 115r org brn, *pink* 1.50 .85
109 A4 130r brown, *straw* 1.50 .85
a. Double overprint
110 A4 200r red lil, *pnksh* 3.00 .70
111 A4 400r dull bl, *straw* 3.50 .85
112 A4 500r blk & red, *bl* 4.00 .85
113 A4 700r vio, *straw* 4.50 .85
Nos. 99-113 (15) 25.70 7.85

King Manoel — A5

Overprinted in Carmine or Green

1912 ***Perf. 11½x12***

114 A5 2½r violet .20 .20
115 A5 5r black .20 .20
116 A5 10r gray grn .20 .20
117 A5 20r carmine (G) .55 .40
118 A5 25r vio brn .20 .20
119 A5 50r dp blue .50 .35
120 A5 75r bis brn .50 .35
121 A5 100r brn, *lt grn* .50 .35
122 A5 200r dk grn, *salmon* 1.00 .70
123 A5 300r black, *azure* 1.00 .70

Perf. 14x15

124 A5 500r ol grn & vio brn 2.00 1.25
Nos. 114-124 (11) 6.85 4.90

Vasco da Gama Issue of Various Portuguese Colonies Common Design Types Surcharged

1913

On Stamps of Macao

125 CD20 ¼c on ½a bl grn 1.50 1.50
126 CD21 ½c on 1a red 1.50 1.50
127 CD22 1c on 2a red vio 1.50 1.50
128 CD23 2½c on 4a yel grn 1.50 1.50
a. Double surcharge 50.00 50.00
129 CD24 5c on 8a dk bl 2.50 2.50
130 CD25 7½c on 12a vio brn 2.00 2.00
131 CD26 10c on 16a bis brn 1.75 1.75
132 CD27 15c on 24a bis 1.50 1.00
Nos. 125-132 (8) 13.75 13.25

On Stamps of Portuguese Africa

133 CD20 ¼c on 2½r bl grn 1.25 1.25
134 CD21 ½c on 5r red 1.25 1.25
135 CD22 1c on 10r red vio 1.25 1.25
a. Inverted surcharge 45.00 45.00
136 CD23 2½c on 25r yel grn 1.25 1.25
137 CD24 5c on 50r dk bl 1.25 1.25
138 CD25 7½c on 75r vio brn 1.75 1.75
139 CD26 10c on 100r bis brn 1.50 1.50
140 CD27 15c on 150r bis 1.50 1.50
Nos. 133-140 (8) 11.00 11.00

On Stamps of Timor

141 CD20 ¼c on ½a bl grn 1.50 1.50
142 CD21 ½c on 1a red 1.50 1.50
143 CD22 1c on 2a red vio 1.50 1.50
144 CD23 2½c on 4a yel grn 1.50 1.50
145 CD24 5c on 8a dk bl 1.50 1.50
146 CD25 7½c on 12a vio brn 3.00 3.00
147 CD26 10c on 16a bis brn 1.50 1.50
148 CD27 15c on 24a bis 2.00 2.00
Nos. 141-148 (8) 14.00 14.00
Nos. 125-148 (24) 38.75 38.25

Ceres — A6

1914-26 Typo. ***Perf. 15x14, 12x11½***

Name and Value in Black

149 A6 ¼c olive brown .20 .20
a. Name and value printed twice 12.00
b. Name and value printed triple —
150 A6 ½c black .20 .20
151 A6 1c blue green .20 .20
a. Name and value printed twice 16.00
152 A6 1½c lilac brown .20 .20
153 A6 2c carmine .20 .20
154 A6 2c gray ('26) .20 .20
155 A6 2½c lt vio .20 .20
156 A6 3c org ('21) .20 .20
a. Name and value printed twice —
157 A6 4c pale rose ('21) .20 .20
a. Name and value printed twice 16.00
b. Value omitted 15.00
158 A6 4½c gray ('21) .20 .20
159 A6 5c deep blue .20 .20
160 A6 6c lilac ('21) .20 .20
a. Name and value printed twice
161 A6 7c ultra ('21) .20 .20
162 A6 7½c yel brn .20 .20
163 A6 8c slate .20 .20
164 A6 10c org brn .20 .20
165 A6 12c gray brn ('21) .25 .20
166 A6 12c blue grn ('22) .20 .20
167 A6 15c plum 1.40 1.00
a. Perf. 12x11½ ('30) .65 .35
168 A6 15c brn rose ('22) .20 .20
169 A6 20c yel grn .20 .20
170 A6 24c ultra ('26) 4.50 2.00
171 A6 25c choc ('26) 1.50 1.25
172 A6 30c brown, *grn* 1.50 1.10
173 A6 30c deep green ('21) 1.00 .20
174 A6 30c gray bl, *pink* ('21) 1.50 1.25
175 A6 40c brn, *pink* 1.25 .85
176 A6 40c turq blue ('22) 1.00 .30
177 A6 50c org, *salmon* 2.75 3.00
178 A6 50c lt violet ('26) .50 .20
179 A6 60c red brn, *pink* ('21) 1.00 .85
180 A6 60c dk blue ('22) 1.00 .30
181 A6 60c rose ('26) 1.10 .25
182 A6 80c dk brn, *bl* ('21) 1.10 .85
183 A6 80c brt rose ('22) 1.00 .25
184 A6 1e grn, *bl*, perf. 12x11½ ('21) 1.40 .60
a. Perf. 15x14 6.00 2.00
185 A6 1e rose ('21) 1.60 .50
186 A6 1e blue ('26) 1.60 .65
187 A6 2e brt vio, *pink* ('21) 1.40 .60
188 A6 2e dk violet ('22) 1.00 .35
189 A6 5e buff ('26) 7.25 2.50
190 A6 10e pink ('26) 15.00 5.00
191 A6 20e pale turq ('26) 40.00 17.50
Nos. 149-191 (43) 95.40 45.35

For surcharges see Nos. 232-234, 236-237, 249-250, J46-50.

Stamps of 1902 Overprinted Locally in Carmine

1915

On Provisional Stamps of 1902

192 A2 115r on 5r black 150.00 100.00
193 A3 115r on 5r yellow 1.25 .75
194 A3 115r on 25r bl grn 1.25 .75
195 A3 130r on 75r rose 1.25 .75
196 A3 130r on 100r brn, *buff* 1.25 .75
197 A3 130r on 150r car, *rose* 1.25 .75
198 A3 130r on 200r bl, *bl* 1.25 .75
199 N3 115r on 2½r brn .80 .40

On No. 97

200 A4 75r rose 1.50 1.10
Nos. 192-200 (9) 159.80 106.00

Stamps of 1902-05 Overprinted in Carmine

1915

On Provisional Stamps of 1902

201 A3 115r on 5r yellow .80 .50
202 A3 115r on 25r bl grn .80 .55
203 A3 130r on 75r rose .80 .55
204 A3 130r on 150r car, *rose* 1.00 .50
205 A3 130r on 200r bl, *bl* 1.00 .50
206 N3 115r on 2½r brn 1.00 .50

On No. 96

207 A4 50r blue 1.00 .50

On No. 98

208 A4 50r on 65r dull blue 1.00 .50
Nos. 201-208 (8) 7.40 4.10

Stamps of 1898-1903 Overprinted Locally in Carmine Like Nos. 192-200

1917

209 A4 2½r gray 20.00 17.50
210 A4 15r gray grn 15.00 12.50
211 A4 20r gray vio 15.00 12.50
212 A4 50r brown 14.00 11.00
213 A4 75r red lilac 32.50 25.00
214 A4 100r blue, *bl* 6.00 2.50
215 A4 115r org brn, *pink* 8.00 3.00
216 A4 130r brown, *straw* 7.50 3.00
217 A4 200r red lil, *pnksh* 7.50 2.50
218 A4 400r dull bl, *straw* 7.50 3.00
219 A4 500r blk & red, *bl* 7.00 2.50
220 A4 700r vio, *yelsh* 15.00 6.00
Nos. 209-220 (12) 155.00 101.00

War Tax Stamps of 1916-18 Surcharged

1918 ***Rouletted 7***

221 WT2 2½c on 5c rose 2.50 1.50

Perf. 11, 12

222 WT2 2½c on 5c red 1.10 .70
a. "PETRIA" 2.00 2.00
b. "PEPUBLICA" 2.00 2.00
c. "1910" for "1916" 9.00 4.00

War Tax Stamps of 1916-18 Surcharged

1919 ***Perf. 11***

224 WT1 1c on 1c gray grn .75 .40
a. "PEPUBLICA" 4.75 4.00
b. Rouletted 7 300.00 100.00

Perf. 12

225 WT2 1½c on 5c red .40 .35
a. "PETRIA" 3.00 2.00
b. "PEPUBLICA" 3.00 2.50
c. "1910" for "1916" 7.50 3.75

Stamps of 1902 Overprinted Locally in Carmine Like Nos. 192-200

1920

226 A3 400r on 50r lt blue 1.25 1.25
227 A3 400r on 80r yel grn 1.25 1.25
228 A3 400r on 300r bl, *sal* 1.25 1.25
Nos. 226-228 (3) 3.75 3.75

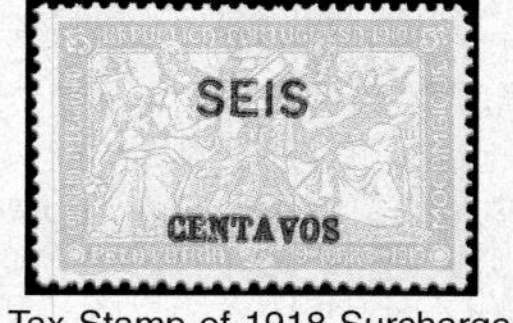

War Tax Stamp of 1918 Surcharged in Green

1920 ***Perf. 12***

229 WT2 6c on 5c red .60 .48
a. "1910" for "1916" 8.00 5.00
b. "PETRIA" 2.50 2.00
c. "PEPUBLICA" 2.50 2.00

Lourenco Marques Nos. 117, 119 Surcharged in Red or Bue

1921 ***Perf. 15x14***

230 A4 10c on ½c blk (R) .75 .40
231 A4 30c on 1½c brn (Bl) 1.25 .70

Same Surcharge on Mozambique Nos. 150, 152, 155 in Red, Blue or Green

232 A6 10c on ½c blk (R) 1.00 .85
233 A6 30c on 1½c brn (Bl) 1.10 .70
234 A6 60c on 2½c vio (G) 1.50 .80
Nos. 230-234 (5) 5.60 3.45

War Tax Stamp of 1918 Surcharged in Green

1921 ***Perf. 12***

235 WT2 2e on 5c red 1.00 .50
a. "PETRIA" 2.50 2.25
b. "PEPUBLICA" 4.25 2.50
c. "1910" for "1916" 8.00 6.50

No. 157 Surcharged

1923 ***Perf. 12x11½***

236 A6 50c on 4c pale rose 1.00 .55

No. 183 Overprinted in Green

1924

237 A6 80c bright rose 1.00 .60

4th centenary of the death of Vasco da Gama.

Nos. 90 and 91 Surcharged

1925 *Perf. 11½*

238 A3 40c on 400r on 50r .70 .70
239 A3 40c on 400r on 80r .60 .50
a. "a" omitted 42.50 42.50

Postage Due Stamp of 1917 Overprinted in Black and Bars in Red

1929, Jan. *Perf. 12*

247 D1 50c gray .85 .55

No. 188 Surcharged

1931 *Perf. 11½*

249 A6 70c on 2e dk vio 1.00 .50
250 A6 1.40e on 2e dk vio 1.50 .50

"Portugal" Holding Volume of the "Lusiads" — A7

Wmk. Maltese Cross (232)

1933, July 13 Typo. *Perf. 14*

Value in Red or Black

251 A7 1c bister brn (R) .20 .20
252 A7 5c black brn .20 .20
253 A7 10c dp violet .20 .20
254 A7 15c black (R) .20 .20
255 A7 20c light gray .20 .20
256 A7 30c blue green .20 .20
257 A7 40c orange red .20 .20
258 A7 45c brt blue .40 .20
259 A7 50c dk brown .30 .20
260 A7 60c olive grn .25 .20
261 A7 70c orange brn .20 .20
262 A7 80c emerald .20 .20
263 A7 85c deep rose 1.00 .50
264 A7 1e red brown .75 .25
265 A7 1.40e dk blue (R) 7.00 1.10
266 A7 2e dk violet 2.00 .35
267 A7 5e apple green 3.00 .50
268 A7 10e olive bister 7.00 1.00
269 A7 20e orange 22.50 2.00
Nos. 251-269 (19) 46.00 8.10

See Nos. 298-299.

Common Design Types pictured following the introduction.

Common Design Types

Perf. 13½x13

1938, Aug. Engr. Unwmk.

Name and Value in Black

270 CD34 1c gray green .20 .20
271 CD34 5c orange brn .20 .20
272 CD34 10c dk carmine .20 .20
273 CD34 15c dk vio brn .20 .20
274 CD34 20c slate .20 .20
275 CD35 30c rose vio .20 .20
276 CD35 35c brt green .30 .20
277 CD35 40c brown .40 .20
278 CD35 50c brt red vio .40 .20
279 CD36 60c gray black .50 .20
280 CD36 70c brown vio .50 .20
281 CD36 80c orange .75 .20
282 CD36 1e red .70 .20
283 CD37 1.75e blue 1.75 .30
284 CD37 2e brown car 1.50 .30
285 CD37 5e olive green 3.50 .50
286 CD38 10e blue vio 9.00 1.00
287 CD38 20e red brown 22.50 1.40
Nos. 270-287 (18) 43.00 6.10

For surcharges see Nos. 297, 301.

No. 258 Surcharged in Black

1938, Jan. 16 Wmk. 232 *Perf. 14*

288 A7 40c on 45c brt blue 2.50 1.40

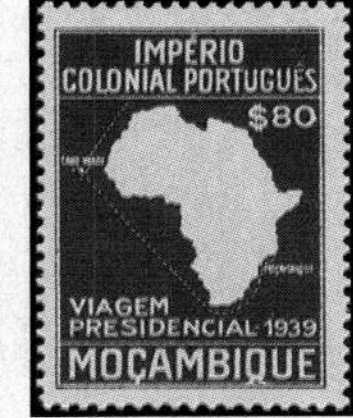

Map of Africa — A7a

Perf. 11½x12

1939, July 17 Litho. Unwmk.

289 A7a 80c vio, *pale rose* 1.50 1.25
290 A7a 1.75e bl, *pale bl* 4.00 2.75
291 A7a 3e grn, *yel grn* 6.00 4.00
292 A7a 20e brn, *buff* 30.00 50.00
Nos. 289-292 (4) 41.50 58.00

Presidential visit.

New Cathedral, Lourenço Marques — A8

Railroad Station A9

Municipal Hall — A10

1944, Dec. Litho. *Perf. 11½*

293 A8 50c dk brown .70 .40
294 A8 50c dk green .70 .40
295 A9 1.75e ultra 4.00 .85
296 A10 20e dk gray 8.50 .85
Nos. 293-296 (4) 13.90 2.50

4th cent. of the founding of Lourenço Marques. See No. 302. For surcharge see No. 300.

No. 283 Surcharged in Carmine

1946 Engr. *Perf. 13½x13*

297 CD37 60c on 1.75e blue 1.00 .40

Lusiads Type of 1933

1947 Wmk. 232 Typo. *Perf. 14*

Value in Black

298 A7 35c yellow grn 4.00 2.00
299 A7 1.75e deep blue 4.50 2.00

No. 296 Surcharged in Pink

1946 Unwmk. *Perf. 11½*

300 A10 2e on 20e dk gray 1.40 .40

No. 273 Surcharged with New Value and Wavy Lines

Perf. 13½x13

301 CD34 10c on 15c dk vio brn .70 .40
a. Inverted surcharge 30.00

Cathedral Type of 1944 Commemorative Inscription Omitted

1948 Litho. *Perf. 11½*

302 A8 4.50e brt vermilion 1.75 .40

Antonio Enes — A11

1948, Oct. 4 *Perf. 14*

303 A11 50c black & cream 1.00 .35
304 A11 5e vio brn & cream 3.00 .85

Birth centenary of Antonio Enes.

Gogogo Peak — A12

Zambezi River Bridge — A13

Zumbo River A14

Waterfall at Nhanhangare A15

Lourenço Marques A16

Plantation, Baixa — A17

Pungwe River at Beira — A18

Lourenço Marques A19

Polana Beach — A20

Malema River — A21

Perf. 13½x13, 13x13½

1948-49 Typo. Unwmk.

305 A12 5c orange brn .25 .50
306 A13 10c violet brn .25 .20
307 A14 20c dk brown .25 .20
308 A12 30c plum .25 .20
309 A14 40c dull green .25 .20
310 A16 50c slate .25 .20
311 A15 60c brown car .25 .20
312 A16 80c violet blk .25 .20
313 A17 1e carmine .35 .20
314 A13 1.20e slate gray .35 .20
315 A18 1.50e dk purple .50 .20
316 A20 1.75e dk blue ('49) .75 .25
317 A18 2e brown .50 .20
318 A19 2.50e dk slate ('49) 1.50 .20
319 A20 3e gray ol ('49) 1.00 .20
320 A15 3.50e olive gray 1.10 .20
321 A17 5e blue grn 1.10 .20
322 A19 10e choc ('49) 2.50 .35
323 A21 15e dp carmine ('49) 7.25 1.75
324 A21 20e orange ('49) 12.00 1.75
Nos. 305-324 (20) 30.90 7.60

On No. 320 the "$" is reversed.

Lady of Fatima Issue

Common Design Type

1948, Oct. Litho. *Perf. 14½*

325 CD40 50c blue 1.00 .50
326 CD40 1.20e red violet 3.00 1.00
327 CD40 4.50e emerald 6.00 1.50
328 CD40 20e chocolate 10.00 1.50
Nos. 325-328 (4) 20.00 4.50

Symbols of the UPU — A21a

1949, Apr. 11 *Perf. 14*

329 A21a 4.50e ultra & pale gray 1.00 .50

75th anniversary of UPU.

Catalogue values for unused stamps in this section, from this point to the end of the section, are for Never Hinged items.

Holy Year Issue

Common Design Types

1950, May *Perf. 13x13½*

330 CD41 1.50e red orange .70 .25
331 CD42 3e brt blue .75 .30

Spotted Triggerfish
A22

Pennant Coral Fish — A22a

Fish: 10c, Golden butterflyfish. 15c, Orange butterflyfish. 20c, Lionfish. 30c, Sharpnose puffer. 40c, Porky filefish. 50c, Dark brown surgeonfish. 1.50e Rainbow wrasse. 2e, Orange-spotted gray-skin. 2.50e, Kasmir snapper. 3e, Convict fish. 3.50e, Stellar triggerfish. 4e, Cornetfish. 4.50e, Vagabond butterflyfish. 5e, Mail-cheeked fish. 6e, Pinnate batfish. 8e, Moorish idol. 9e, Triangulate boxfish. 10e, Flying gurnard. 15e, Redtooth triggerfish. 20e, Striped triggerfish. 30e, Horned cowfish. 50e, Spotted cowfish.

Photogravure and Lithographed
1951 Unwmk. *Perf. 14x14½*
Fish in Natural Colors

332 A22 5c dp yellow .30 *.75*
333 A22 10c lt blue .20 *.50*
334 A22 15c yellow .80 *1.00*
335 A22 20c pale olive .40 .20
336 A22 30c gray .40 .20
337 A22 40c pale green .30 .20
338 A22 50c pale buff .30 .20
339 A22a 1e aqua .30 .20
340 A22 1.50e olive .25 .20
341 A22 2e blue .30 .20
342 A22 2.50e brnsh lilac .60 .20
343 A22 3e aqua .60 .20
344 A22 3.50e olive grn .60 .20
345 A22 4e blue gray 1.40 1.00
346 A22 4.50e green .90 2.00
347 A22 5e buff .90 .20
348 A22a 6e salmon pink .90 .20
349 A22a 8e gray blue .90 .25
350 A22 9e lilac rose 3.50 .30
351 A22 10e gray lilac 12.00 2.00
352 A22 15e gray 25.00 5.50
353 A22 20e lemon 20.00 3.50
354 A22 30e yellow grn 20.00 4.00
355 A22 50e gray vio 30.00 6.50
Nos. 332-355 (24) 120.85 29.70

Holy Year Extension Issue
Common Design Type

1951, Oct. Litho. *Perf. 14*
356 CD43 5e carmine & rose + label 1.75 1.00

No. 356 without label attached sells for less.

Victor Cordon — A23

Plane and Ship — A24

1951, Oct. *Perf. 11½*
357 A23 1e dk brown 1.00 .35
358 A23 5e black & slate 2.00 1.00

Centenary of the birth of Victor Cordon, explorer.

Medical Congress Issue
Common Design Type

Design: Miguel Bombarda Hospital.

1952, June 19 Litho. *Perf. 13½*
359 CD44 3e dk bl & brn buff .85 .35

1952, Sept. 15 Unwmk.
360 A24 1.50e multi .50 .35

4th African Tourism Congress.

Missionary
A25

Papilio Demodocus
A26

1953
361 A25 10c red brn & pale vio .20 .20
362 A25 1e red brn & pale yel grn .50 .20
363 A25 5e blk & lt bl 1.40 .35
Nos. 361-363 (3) 2.10 .75

Exhibition of Sacred Missionary Art, held at Lisbon in 1951.

Canceled to Order
Certain issues, including Nos. 364-383, were canceled to order under Republican administration.

Photogravure and Lithographed
1953, May 28 *Perf. 13x14*
Various Butterflies and Moths in Natural Colors

364 A26 10c lt blue .20 .20
365 A26 15c cream .20 .20
366 A26 20c yellow grn .20 .20
367 A26 30c lt violet .20 .20
368 A26 40c brown .20 .20
369 A26 50c bluish gray .20 .20
370 A26 80c brt blue .20 .20
371 A26 1e gray bl .20 .20
372 A26 1.50e ocher .25 .20
373 A26 2e orange brn 3.50 .50
374 A26 2.30e blue 3.50 .35
375 A26 2.50e citron 5.25 .35
376 A26 3e lilac rose 1.90 .20
377 A26 4e light blue .35 .20
378 A26 4.50e orange .35 .20
379 A26 5e green .35 .20
380 A26 6e pale vio .50 .20
381 A26 7.50e buff 4.00 .30
382 A26 10e pink 6.25 .75
383 A26 20e grnsh gray 8.00 .70
Nos. 364-383 (20) 35.80 5.75

Value of set canceled-to-order, 50 cents.
For overprints see Nos. 517, 527.

Stamps of Portugal and Mozambique
A27

Stamp of Portugal and Arms of Colonies
A27a

1953, July 23 Litho. *Perf. 14*
384 A27 1e multicolored .55 .40
385 A27 3e multicolored 1.90 .70

Issued in connection with the Lourenço Marques philatelic exhibition, July 1953.

Stamp Centenary Issue
1953 Photo. *Perf. 13*
386 A27a 50c multicolored .55 .40

Map — A28

1954, Oct. 15 Litho.
Color of Colony

387 A28 10c pale rose lilac .20 .20
388 A28 20c pale yellow .20 .20
389 A28 50c lilac .20 .20
390 A28 1e orange yel .20 .20
391 A28 2.30e white .45 .20
392 A28 4e pale salmon .60 .20
393 A28 10e lt green 1.90 .20
394 A28 20e brown buff 2.50 .35
Nos. 387-394 (8) 6.25 1.75

For overprints see Nos. 516, 530.

Sao Paulo Issue
Common Design Type

1954, July 2
395 CD46 3.50e dk gray, cream & ol .35 .30

Arms of Beira
A29

Mousinho de Albuquerque
A30

Paper with network as in parenthesis

1954, Dec. 1 *Perf. 13x13½*
Arms in Silver, Gold, Red and Pale Green

396 A29 1.50e dk bl *(bl)* .35 .30
397 A29 3.50e brn *(buff)* .75 .35

Issued to publicize the first philatelic exhibition of Manica and Sofala.

1955, Feb. 1 Litho. *Perf. 11½x12*

2.50e, Statue of Mousinho de Albuquerque.

398 A30 1e gray, blk & buff .60 .35
399 A30 2.50e ol bis, blk & bl .85 .50

100th anniversary of the birth of Mousinho de Albuquerque, statesman.

A31

A32

Eight Races Holding Arms of Portugal

1956, Aug. 4 Unwmk. *Perf. 14½*
Central Design in Multicolored

400 A31 1e pale yellow & multi .30 .20
401 A31 2.50e lt blue & multi .70 .30

Issued to commemorate the visit of President Antonio Oscar de Fragoso Carmona.

1957, Aug. 15 Litho.
402 A32 2.50e View of Beira .50 .30

50th anniversary of the city of Beira.

Brussels Fair Issue

Exhibition Emblems and View — A32a

1958, Oct. 8 Unwmk. *Perf. 14½*
403 A32a 3.50c blk, grn, yel, red & bl .25 .20

Tropical Medicine Congress Issue
Common Design Type

Design: Strophanthus grandiflorus.

1958, Sept. 14 *Perf. 13½*
404 CD47 1.50e sal brn, grn & red 1.25 .50

Caravel — A33

Technical Instruction
A34

1960, June 25 Litho. *Perf. 13½*
405 A33 5e multicolored .30 .20

500th anniversary of the death of Prince Henry the Navigator.

1960, Nov. 21 Unwmk. *Perf. 14½*
406 A34 3e multicolored .30 .20

Commission for Technical Co-operation in Africa South of the Sahara (C.C.T.A.), 10th anniv.

Arms of Lourenço Marques — A35

Arms of various cities of Mozambique.

1961, Jan. 30 Litho. *Perf. 13½*
Arms in Original Colors; Black, Ultramarine and Red Inscriptions

407 A35 5c salmon .20 .20
408 A35 15c pale green .20 .20
409 A35 20c lt vio gray .20 .20
410 A35 30c buff .20 .20
411 A35 50c bluish gray .20 .20
412 A35 1e pale ol .20 .20
413 A35 1.50e lt blue .20 .20
414 A35 2e pale pink .20 .20
415 A35 2.50e lt bl grn .70 .20
416 A35 3e beige .25 .20
417 A35 4e yellow .25 .20
418 A35 4.50e pale gray .25 .20
419 A35 5e pale bluish grn .25 .20
420 A35 7.50e rose .55 .25
a. "CORREIOS 7$50" omitted
421 A35 10e lt yel grn .90 .25
422 A35 20e beige 1.90 .35
423 A35 50e gray 4.00 .75
Nos. 407-423 (17) 10.65 4.20

Sports Issue
Common Design Type

50c, Water skiing. 1e, Wrestling. 1.50e, Woman gymnast. 2.50e, Field hockey. 4.50e, Women's basketball. 15e, Speedboat racing.

1962, Feb. 10 Unwmk. *Perf. 13½*
Multicolored Designs

424 CD48 50c gray green .25 .20
425 CD48 1e dk gray .60 .20
426 CD48 1.50e pink .30 .20
427 CD48 2.50e buff .50 .20
428 CD48 4.50e gray .75 .35
429 CD48 15e gray green 1.25 .75
Nos. 424-429 (6) 3.65 1.90

For overprints see Nos. 522, 526, 529.

Anti-Malaria Issue
Common Design Type

Design: Anopheles funestus.

1962, Apr. 5 *Perf. 13½*
430 CD49 2.50e multicolored .85 .20

Planes over Mozambique A36

Lourenço Marques 1887 and 1962 A37

1962, Oct. 15 **Litho.** ***Perf. 14½***
431 A36 3e multicolored .35 .20

25th anniversary of DETA airlines.

1962, Nov. 1 ***Perf. 13***
432 A37 1e multicolored .25 .20

75th anniversary of Lourenço Marques.

Vasco da Gama Statue and Arms — A38

1963, Apr. 25 **Unwmk.** ***Perf. 14½***
433 A38 3e multicolored .20 .20

Founding of Mozambique City, 200th anniv.

Airline Anniversary Issue

Common Design Type

1963, Oct. 21 **Litho.** ***Perf. 14½***
434 CD50 2.50e brt pink & multi .20 .20

Barque, 1430 — A39

Caravel, 1436 — A40

Development of Sailing Ships: 30c, Lateen-rigged caravel, 1460. 50c, "Sao Gabriel," 1497. 1e, Dom Manuel's ship, 1498. 1.50e, Warship, 1500. 2e, "Flor de la Mar," 1511. 2.50e, Redonda caravel, 1519. 3.50e, 800-ton ship, 1520. 4e, Portuguese India galley, 1521. 4.50e, "Santa Tereza," 1639. 5e, "Nostra Senhora da Conceiçao," 1716. 6e, "Nostra Senhora do Bom Sucesso," 1764. 7.50e, Launch with mortar, 1788. 8e, Brigantine, 1793. 10e, Corvette, 1799. 12.50e, Schooner "Maria Teresa," 1820. 15e, "Vasco da Gama," 1841. 20e, Frigate "Dom Fernando II," 1843. 30e, Training Ship "Sagres," 1924.

1963, Dec. 1 **Litho.** ***Perf. 14½***

435	A39	10c	multicolored	.20	.20
436	A40	20c	multicolored	.20	.20
437	A40	30c	multicolored	.20	.20
438	A40	50c	multicolored	.20	.20
439	A40	1e	multicolored	.35	.20
440	A40	1.50e	multicolored	.20	.20
441	A40	2e	multicolored	.30	.20
442	A39	2.50e	multicolored	.50	.20
443	A40	3.50e	multicolored	.45	.30
444	A39	4e	multicolored	.60	.20
445	A40	4.50e	multicolored	1.10	.25
446	A40	5e	multicolored	3.00	.20
447	A39	6e	multicolored	1.00	.25
448	A39	7.50e	multicolored	1.10	.30
449	A39	8e	multicolored	1.10	.30
450	A39	10e	multicolored	1.25	.60
451	A39	12.50e	multicolored	1.40	.75
452	A39	15e	multicolored	1.40	.60
453	A40	20e	multicolored	2.00	.70
454	A40	30e	multicolored	2.75	1.25
			Nos. 435-454 (20)	19.30	7.30

National Overseas Bank Issue

Modern Bank Building, Luanda A40a

1964, May 16 ***Perf. 13½***
455 A40a 1.50e bl, yel gray & grn .20 .20

National Overseas Bank of Portugal, cent.

Pres. Americo Rodrigues Thomaz — A41

1964, July 23 **Litho.** ***Perf. 13½x12½***
456 A41 2.50e multicolored .20 .20

Visit of Pres. Americo Rodrigues Thomaz of Portugal to Mozambique, in July.

Royal Barge of King John V, 1728 A42

Designs: 35c, Barge of Dom Jose I, 1753. 1e, Customs barge, 1768. 1.50e, Sailor, 1780, vert. 2.50e, Royal barge, 1780. 5e, Barge of Dona Carlota Joaquina, 1790. 9e, Barge of Dom Miguel, 1831.

1964, Dec. 18 **Litho.** ***Perf. 14½***

457	A42	15c	multicolored	.20	.20
458	A42	35c	lt bl & multi	.20	.20
459	A42	1e	gray & multi	.50	.20
460	A42	1.50e	gray & multi	.30	.20
461	A42	2.50e	multicolored	.25	.20
462	A42	5e	multicolored	.30	.20
463	A42	9e	multicolored	.50	.40
			Nos. 457-463 (7)	2.25	1.60

ITU Issue

Common Design Type

1965, May 17 **Unwmk.** ***Perf. 14½***
464 CD52 1e yellow & multi .30 .20

National Revolution Issue

Common Design Type

Design: 1e, Beira Railroad Station, and Antonio Enes School.

1966, May 28 **Litho.** ***Perf. 11½***
465 CD53 1e multicolored .20 .20

Harquebusier, 1560 — A42a

30c, Harquebusier, 1640. 40c, Infantry soldier, 1777. 50c, Infantry officer, 1777. 80c, Drummer, 1777. 1e, Infantry sergeant, 1777. 2e, Infantry major, 1784. 2.50e, Colonial officer, 1788. 3e, Infantry soldier, 1789. 5e, Colonial bugler, 1801. 10e, Colonial officer, 1807. 15e, Colonial infantry soldier, 1817.

1967, Jan. 12 **Photo.** ***Perf. 14***

466	A42a	20c	multicolored	.20	.20
467	A42a	30c	multicolored	.20	.20
468	A42a	40c	multicolored	.20	.20
469	A42a	50c	multicolored	.20	.20
470	A42a	80c	multicolored	.20	.20
471	A42a	1e	multicolored	.20	.20
472	A42a	2e	multicolored	.20	.20
473	A42a	2.50e	multicolored	.25	.20
474	A42a	3e	multicolored	.25	.25
475	A42a	5e	multicolored	.35	.25
476	A42a	10e	multicolored	.45	.25
477	A42a	15e	multicolored	.65	.35
			Nos. 466-477 (12)	3.35	2.70

Navy Club Issue

Common Design Type

Designs: 3e, Capt. Azevedo Coutinho and gunboat (stern-wheeler) Tete. 10e, Capt. Joao Roby and gunboat (paddle steamer) Granada.

1967, Jan. 31 **Litho.** ***Perf. 13***
478 CD54 3e multicolored .20 .20
479 CD54 10e multicolored .45 .25

Virgin's Crown, Presented by Portuguese Women — A43

1967, May 13 **Litho.** ***Perf. 12½x13***
480 A43 50c multicolored .20 .20

50th anniversary of the appearance of the Virgin Mary to 3 shepherd children at Fatima.

Cabral Issue

Raising the Cross at Porto Seguro — A44

Designs: 1.50e, First mission to Brazil. 3e, Grace Church, Santarem, vert.

1968, Apr. 22 **Litho.** ***Perf. 14***

481	A44	1e	multicolored	.20	.20
482	A44	1.50e	multicolored	.20	.20
483	A44	3e	multicolored	.30	.20
			Nos. 481-483 (3)	.70	.60

500th birth anniv. of Pedro Alvares Cabral, navigator who took possession of Brazil for Portugal.

Admiral Coutinho Issue

Common Design Type

Design: 70c, Adm. Coutinho and Adm. Gago Coutinho Airport.

1969, Feb. 17 **Litho.** ***Perf. 14***
484 CD55 70c multicolored .20 .20

Luiz Vaz de Camoens — A45

Sailing Ship, 1553 — A46

Designs: 1.50e, Map of Mozambique, 1554. 2.50e, Chapel of Our Lady of Baluarte, 1552. 5e, Excerpt from Lusiads about Mozambique (1st Song, 14th Stanza).

Perf. 12½x13, 13x12½

1969, June 10 **Litho.**

485	A45	15c	multicolored	.20	.20
486	A46	50c	multicolored	.20	.20
487	A45	1.50e	multicolored	.20	.20
488	A46	2.50e	multicolored	.20	.20
489	A45	5e	multicolored	.30	.20
			Nos. 485-489 (5)	1.10	1.00

Visit to Mozambique of Luiz Vaz de Camoens (1524-80), poet, 400th anniv.

Vasco da Gama Issue

Map Showing Voyage to Mozambique and India — A47

1969, Aug. 29 **Litho.** ***Perf. 14***
490 A47 1e multicolored .20 .20

Vasco da Gama (1469-1524), navigator.

Administration Reform Issue

Common Design Type

1969, Sept. 25 **Litho.** ***Perf. 14***
491 CD56 1.50e multicolored .20 .20

King Manuel I Issue

Illuminated Miniature of King's Arms — A48

1969, Dec. 1 **Litho.** ***Perf. 14***
492 A48 80c multicolored .20 .20

500th anniversary of the birth of King Manuel I.

Marshal Carmona Issue

Common Design Type

5e, Antonio Oscar Carmona in marshal's uniform.

1970, Nov. 15 **Litho.** ***Perf. 14***
493 CD57 5e multicolored .20 .20

Fossil Fern A49

Fossils and Minerals: 50c, Fossil snail. 1e, Stibnite. 1.50e, Pink beryl. 2e, Dinosaur. 3e, Tantalocolumbite. 3.50e, Verdelite. 4e, Zircon. 10e, Petrified wood.

1971, Jan. 15 **Litho.** ***Perf. 13***

494	A49	15c	gray & multi	.20	.20
495	A49	50c	lt ultra & multi	.20	.20
496	A49	1e	green & multi	.30	.20
497	A49	1.50e	multicolored	.40	.20
498	A49	2e	multicolored	.75	.20
499	A49	3e	lt bl & multi	1.50	.20
500	A49	3.50e	lilac & multi	2.00	.20
501	A49	4e	multicolored	3.00	.20
502	A49	10e	dl red & multi	4.00	.40
			Nos. 494-502 (9)	12.35	2.00

For overprints see Nos. 525, 528.

Mozambique Island — A49a

1972, May 25 **Litho.** ***Perf. 13***
503 A49a 4e ultra & multi .30 .20

4th centenary of publication of The Lusiads by Luiz Camoens.

Olympic Games Issue
Common Design Type

3e, Hurdles and swimming, Olympic emblem.

1972, June 20 *Perf. 14x13½*
504 CD59 3e multi .20 .20

For overprint see No. 523.

Lisbon-Rio de Janeiro Flight Issue
Common Design Type

1e, "Santa Cruz" over Recife harbor.

1972, Sept. 20 Litho. *Perf. 13½*
505 CD60 1e multi .20 .20

Sailboats A50

Designs: Various sailboats.

1973, Aug. 21 Litho. *Perf. 12x11½*
506 A50 1e multi .20 .20
507 A50 1.50e multi .20 .20
508 A50 3e multi .30 .20
Nos. 506-508 (3) .70 .60

World Sailing Championships, Vauriens Class, Lourenço Marques, Aug. 21-30.
For overprints see Nos. 519-520, 524.

WMO Centenary Issue
Common Design Type

1973, Dec. 15 Litho. *Perf. 13*
509 CD61 2e rose red & multi .20 .20

For overprint see No. 521.

Radar Station A51

1974, June 25 Litho. *Perf. 13*
510 A51 50c multi .20 .20

Establishment of satellite communications network via Intelsat among Portugal, Angola and Mozambique.
For overprint see No. 518.

"Bird" Made of Flags of Portugal and Mozambique — A52

1975, Jan. Litho. *Perf. 14½*
511 A52 1e pink & multi .20 .20
512 A52 1.50e yel & multi .20 .20
513 A52 2e gray & multi .20 .20
514 A52 3.50e lem & multi .30 .20
515 A52 6e lt bl & multi .75 .30
a. Souv. sheet of 5, #511-515 + label 2.00
Nos. 511-515 (5) 1.65 1.10

Lusaka Agreement, Sept. 7, 1974, which gave Mozambique independence from Portugal, effective June 25, 1975.
No. 515a sold for 25e.
For overprints see Nos. 543-545.

Republic
Issues of 1953-74 Overprinted in Red or Black:

a

b

1975, June 25
516 A28 (a) 10c (R; #387) .20 .20
517 A26 (a) 40c (R; #368) .20 .20
518 A51 (b) 50c (B; #510) .20 .20
519 A50 (b) 1e (B; #506) .20 .20
520 A50 (b) 1.50e (B; #507) .20 .20
521 CD61 (a) 2e (B; #509) .20 .20
522 CD48 (b) 2.50e (B; #427) .40 .20
523 CD59 (a) 3e (R; #504) .40 .20
524 A50 (b) 3e (B; #508) .40 .40
525 A49 (b) 3.50e (B; #500) .40 .40
526 CD48 (b) 4.50e (B; #428) 2.50 1.75
527 A26 (a) 7.50e (R; #381) .85 .40
528 A49 (b) 10e (B; #502) 1.75 .60
529 CD48 (b) 15e (B; #429) 1.75 .85
530 A28 (a) 20e (R; #394) 1.00 .60
Nos. 516-530,C35-C38 (19) 13.80 7.60

Workers, Farmers and Children A53

Designs: 30c, 50c, 2.50e, like 20c. 4.50e, 5e, 10e, 50e, Dancers, workers, armed family.

1975 Litho. *Perf. 12x11½*
531 A53 20c pink & multi .20 .20
532 A53 30c bis & multi .20 .20
533 A53 50c bl & multi .20 .20
534 A53 2.50e grn & multi .20 .20
535 A53 4.50e brn & multi .20 .20
536 A53 5e bis & multi .20 .20
537 A53 10e bl & multi .35 .20
538 A53 50e yel & multi 1.60 .80
a. Souvenir sheet of 8 3.25 3.25
Nos. 531-538 (8) 3.15 2.20

No. 538a contains 8 stamps similar to Nos. 531-538 with simulated perforation. Sold for 75e.
For overprint see No. 554.

Farm Woman — A54

1976, Apr. 7 Litho. *Perf. 14½*
539 A54 1e shown .20 .20
540 A54 1.50e Teacher .20 .20
541 A54 2.50e Nurse .25 .25
542 A54 10e Mother .50 .35
Nos. 539-542 (4) 1.15 1.00

Day of the Mozambique Woman, Apr. 7.

Nos. 513-515 Overprinted in Red:
"PRESIDENTE KENNETH KAUNDA / PRIMEIRA VISITA 20/4/1976"

1976, Apr. 20 Litho. *Perf. 14½*
543 A52 2e gray & multi .20 .20
544 A52 3.50e lem & multi .30 .30
545 A52 6e lt bl & multi .50 .50
Nos. 543-545 (3) 1.00 1.00

Visit of President Kaunda of Zambia.

Pres. Machel's Arrival at Maputo — A55

Mozambique No. 1 — A56

Designs: 1e, Independence proclamation ceremony. 2.50e, Pres. Samora Moises Machel taking office. 7.50e, Military parade. 20e, Flame of Unity and festival.

1976, June 25
546 A55 50c multi .20 .20
547 A55 1e multi .20 .20
548 A55 2.50e multi .20 .20
549 A55 7.50e multi .40 .25
550 A55 20e multi 1.00 .50
Nos. 546-550 (5) 2.00 1.35

First anniversary of independence.

1976, July *Perf. 11½x12*
551 A56 1.50e ocher & multi .20 .20
552 A56 6e red & multi .35 .30

Centenary of Mozambique postage stamps.

Flag and Weapons A57

1976, Sept. 25 Litho. *Perf. 14½*
553 A57 3e multi .25 .20

Army Day 1976.

No. 534 Overprinted in Silver:
"FACIM"

1976 Litho. *Perf. 12x11½*
554 A53 2.50e multi .30 .20

FACIM, Industrial Fair.

Bush Baby — A58

Animals: 1e, Honey badger. 1.50e, Pangolin. 2e, Steinbok. 2.50e, Guenon (monkey). 3e, Cape hunting dog. 4e, Cheetah. 5e, Spotted hyena. 7.50e, Wart hog. 8e, Hippopotamus. 10e, Rhinoceros. 15e, Sable antelope. 1e, 2e, 3e, 4e, 7.50e, 8e, 10e horiz.

1977, Jan. Litho. *Perf. 14½*
555 A58 50c multi .20 .20
556 A58 1e multi .20 .20
557 A58 1.50e multi .20 .20
558 A58 2e multi .20 .20
559 A58 2.50e multi .20 .20
560 A58 3e multi .20 .20
561 A58 4e multi .30 .20
562 A58 5e multi .35 .20
563 A58 7.50e multi .50 .20
564 A58 8e multi .55 .30
565 A58 10e multi .70 .30
566 A58 15e multi 1.00 .40
Nos. 555-566 (12) 4.60 2.80

Congress Emblem — A59

Monument in Maputo — A60

Design: 3.50e, Monument in Macheje, site of 2nd Frelimo Congress, horiz.

1977, Feb. 7 *Perf. 14½*
567 A59 3e multi .20 .20

Perf. 12x11½, 11½x12
568 A60 3.50e multi .30 .30
569 A60 20e multi 1.00 .35
Nos. 567-569 (3) 1.50 .85

3rd FRELIMO Party Congress, Maputo, Feb. 3-7.

Women, Child's Design — A61

Worker and Farmer — A62

1977, Apr. 7 Litho. *Perf. 14½*
570 A61 5e dp org & multi .30 .20
571 A61 15e lt grn & multi .70 .20

Mozambique Women's Day 1977.

1977, May 1 Litho. *Perf. 14½*
572 A62 5e red, blk & yel .40 .30

Labor Day.

People, Flags and Rising Sun — A63

1977, June 25 Litho. *Perf. 11½x12*
573 A63 50c multi .20 .20
574 A63 1.50e multi .20 .20
575 A63 3e multi .20 .20
576 A63 15e multi .70 .20
Nos. 573-576 (4) 1.30 .80

2nd anniversary of independence.

Bread Palm A64

1977, Dec. 21 Litho. *Perf. 12x11½*
577 A64 1e shown .20 .20
578 A64 10e Nyala .50 .25

Nature protection and Stamp Day.

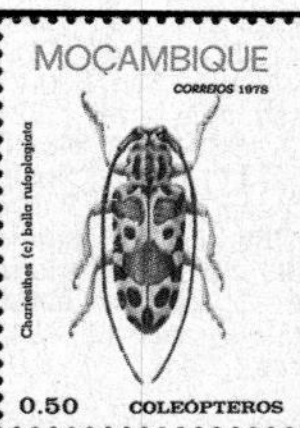

Chariesthes Bella Rufoplagiata A65

Violet-crested Touraco — A66

Beetles: 1e, Tragocephalus variegata. 1.50e, Monochamus leuconotus. 3e, Prosopocera lactator meridionalis. 5e, Dinocephalus ornatus. 10e, Tragiscoschema nigroscriptum maculata.

1978, Jan. 20 Litho. *Perf. 11½x12*

579	A65	50c multi	.20	.20
580	A65	1e multi	.20	.20
581	A65	1.50e multi	.25	.20
582	A65	3e multi	.30	.20
583	A65	5e multi	.40	.35
584	A65	10e multi	.65	.35
		Nos. 579-584 (6)	2.00	1.50

1978, Mar. 20 Litho. *Perf. 11½*

Birds of Mozambique: 1e, Lilac-breasted roller. 1.50e, Weaver. 2.50e, Violet-backed starling. 3e, Peter's twinspot. 15e, European bee-eater.

585	A66	50c multi	.20	.20
586	A66	1e multi	.20	.20
587	A66	1.50e multi	.25	.20
588	A66	2.50e multi	.30	.20
589	A66	3e multi	.35	.20
590	A66	15e multi	.70	.35
		Nos. 585-590 (6)	2.00	1.35

Mother and Child, WHO Emblem A67

1978, Apr. 17 *Perf. 12*

591 A67 15e multi .50 .30

Smallpox eradication campaign.

Crinum Delagoense A68

No. 1, Canada No. 1 — A69

Flowers of Mozambique: 1e, Gloriosa superba. 1.50e, Eulophia speciosa. 3e, Erithrina humeana. 5e, Astripomoea malvacea. 10e, Kigelia africana.

1978, May 16 *Perf. 11½x12*

592	A68	50c multi	.20	.20
593	A68	1e multi	.20	.20
594	A68	1.50e multi	.20	.20
595	A68	3e multi	.20	.20
596	A68	5e multi	.25	.25
597	A68	10e multi	.50	.30
		Nos. 592-597 (6)	1.55	1.35

1978, June 9

598 A69 15e multi .50 .30

CAPEX Canadian International Philatelic Exhibition, Toronto, Ont., June 9-18.

National Flag — A70

Soldiers, Festival Emblem — A71

1.50e, Coat of arms. 7.50e, Page of Constitution people. 10e, Music band & natl. anthem.

1978, June 25 *Perf. 11½x12*

599	A70	1e multi	.20	.20
600	A70	1.50e multi	.20	.20
601	A70	7.50e multi	.30	.20
602	A70	10e multi	.50	.25
a.		Souvenir sheet of 4	1.75	1.75
		Nos. 599-602 (4)	1.20	.85

3rd anniversary of proclamation of independence. No. 602a contains 4 stamps similar to Nos. 599-602 with simulated perforations. Sold for 30e.

1978, July 28

2.50e, Student. 7.50e, Farmworkers.

603	A71	2.50e multi	.20	.20
604	A71	3e multi	.20	.20
605	A71	7.50e multi	.25	.20
		Nos. 603-605 (3)	.65	.60

11th World Youth Festival, Havana, 7/28-8/5.

Czechoslovakia No. B126 and PRAGA '78 Emblem — A72

1978, Sept. 8 Litho. *Perf. 12x11½*

606	A72	15e multi	.50	.25
a.		Souvenir sheet	2.50	2.50

PRAGA '78 International Philatelic Exhibition, Prague, Sept. 8-17.

No. 606a contains one stamp with simulated perforations. Sold for 30e.

Soccer A73

Stamp Day: 1.50e, Shotput. 3e, Hurdling. 7.50e, Fieldball. 12.50e, Swimming. 25e, Roller skate hockey.

1978, Dec. 21 Litho. *Perf. 12x11½*

607	A73	50c multi	.20	.20
608	A73	1.50e multi	.20	.20
609	A73	3e multi	.20	.20
610	A73	7.50e multi	.30	.20
611	A73	12.50e multi	.35	.20
612	A73	25e multi	.75	.35
		Nos. 607-612 (6)	2.00	1.35

Carrier Pigeon, UPU Emblem A74

1979, Jan. 1 Litho. *Perf. 11x11½*

613 A74 20e multi .55 .40

Membership in Universal Postal Union.

Soldier Giving Gourd to Woman — A75

Edward Chivambo Mondlane A76

Designs: 3e, Frelimo soldiers. 7.50e, Mozambique children in school.

1979, Feb. 3 *Perf. 11½x11, 11x11½*

614	A75	1e multi	.20	.20
615	A75	3e multi	.20	.20
616	A75	7.50e multi	.30	.20
617	A76	12.50e multi	.55	.20
		Nos. 614-617 (4)	1.25	.80

Dr. Edward Chivambo Mondlane (1920-1969), educator, founder of Frelimo Party.

Shaded Silver Cat — A77

Cats: 1.50e, Manx. 2.50e, English blue. 3e, Turkish. 12.50e, Long-haired Mid-East tabby. 20e, African wild cat.

1979, Mar. 27 Litho. *Perf. 11*

618	A77	50c multi	.20	.20
619	A77	1.50e multi	.25	.20
620	A77	2.50e multi	.25	.20
621	A77	3e multi	.30	.20
622	A77	12.50e multi	.65	.20
623	A77	20e multi	1.00	.30
		Nos. 618-623 (6)	2.65	1.30

Wrestling and Moscow '80 Emblem — A78

Sport and Moscow '80 Emblem: 2e, Running. 3e, Equestrian. 5e, Canoeing. 10e, High jump. 15e, Archery.

1979, Apr. 24 Litho. *Perf. 11*

624	A78	1e gray grn & blk	.20	.20
625	A78	2e brt bl & blk	.20	.20
626	A78	3e lt brn & blk	.25	.20
627	A78	5e multi	.30	.20
628	A78	10e grn & blk	.35	.20
629	A78	15e lil rose & blk	.70	.20
		Nos. 624-629 (6)	2.00	1.20

Souvenir Sheet

Imperf

630 A78 30e rose & dk brn 2.50 2.50

22nd Olympic Games, Moscow, July 10-Aug. 3, 1980. No. 630 contains one 47x37mm stamp.

Garden and IYC Emblem A79

Children's Drawings and IYC Emblem: 1.50e, Dancers. 3e, City. 5e, Farmers. 7.50e, Village. 12.50e, Automobiles, train and flowers.

1979, June 1 Litho. *Perf. 11*

631	A79	50c multi	.20	.20
632	A79	1.50e multi	.20	.20
633	A79	3e multi	.25	.20
634	A79	5e multi	.30	.20
635	A79	7.50e multi	.40	.20
636	A79	12.50e multi	.65	.20
		Nos. 631-636 (6)	2.00	1.20

International Year of the Child.

Flight from Colonialism — A80

Designs: 2e, Founding of FRELIMO and Pres. Eduardo Chivambo Mondlane. 3e, Advance of armed strruggle and death of Mondlane. 7.50e, Final fight for liberation. 15e, Proclamation of victory, Pres. Samora Moises Machel, flag and torch. Designs after mural in Heroes' Square, Maputo. 30e, Building up the country.

1979, June 25

637	A80	50c multi	.20	.20
638	A80	2e multi	.20	.20
639	A80	3e multi	.20	.20
640	A80	7.50e multi	.20	.20
641	A80	15e multi	.50	.20
b.		Strip of 5, #537-641	1.25	1.00

Souvenir Sheet

Imperf

641A A80 30e multi 3.25 3.25

4th anniversary of independence. No. 641A contains one stamp with simulated perforations. No. 641b has continuous design.

Scorpion Fish A81

Tropical Fish: 1.50e, King fish. 2.50e, Gobius inhaca. 3e, Acanthurus lineatus. 10e, Gobuchthys lemayi. 12.50e, Variola louti.

1979, Aug. 7 Litho. *Perf. 11*

642	A81	50c multi	.20	.20
643	A81	1.50e multi	.20	.20
644	A81	2.50e multi	.20	.20
645	A81	3e multi	.20	.20
646	A81	10e multi	.50	.20
647	A81	12.50e multi	.60	.20
		Nos. 642-647 (6)	1.90	1.20

For surcharge see No. 1254.

Quartz A82

Mozambique Minerals.

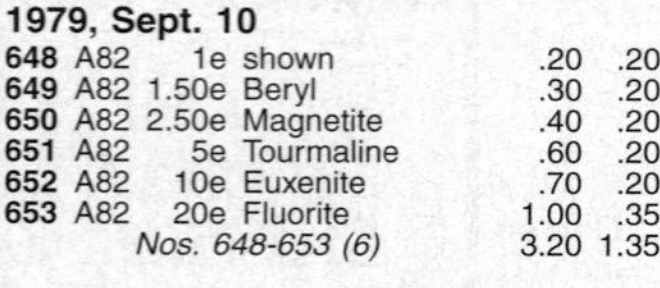

1979, Sept. 10

648 A82 1e shown .20 .20
649 A82 1.50e Beryl .30 .20
650 A82 2.50e Magnetite .40 .20
651 A82 5e Tourmaline .60 .20
652 A82 10e Euxenite .70 .20
653 A82 20e Fluorite 1.00 .35
Nos. 648-653 (6) 3.20 1.35

Citizens Gathering Arms — A83

1979, Sept. 25

654 A83 5e multi .30 .20

15th anniversary of independence.

Locomotive — A85

Designs: Historic Locomotives.

1979, Nov. 11 Litho. *Perf. 11*

656 A85 50c multi .20 .20
657 A85 1.50e multi .25 .20
658 A85 3e multi .30 .20
659 A85 7.50e multi .40 .20
660 A85 12.50e multi .50 .20
661 A85 15e multi .75 .20
Nos. 656-661 (6) 2.40 1.20

For surcharge see No. 1298.

Dalmatian — A86

Perf. 11½x11, 11x11½

1979, Dec. 17 Litho.

662 A86 50c Basenji, vert. .20 .20
663 A86 1.50e shown .20 .20
664 A86 3e Boxer .25 .20
665 A86 7.50e Blue gasconha braco .40 .20
666 A86 12.50e Cocker spaniel .50 .20
667 A86 15e Pointer .75 .20
Nos. 662-667 (6) 2.30 1.20

For surcharge see No. 1299.

Nireus Lyaeus — A87

Butterflies: 1.50e, Amauris ochlea. 2.50e, Pinacopterix eriphia. 5e, Junonia hierta cebrene. 10e, Nephronia argia. 20e, Catacroptera cloanthe.

1979, Dec. 21

668 A87 1e multi .20 .20
669 A87 1.50e multi .25 .20
670 A87 2.50e multi .30 .20
671 A87 5e multi .40 .20

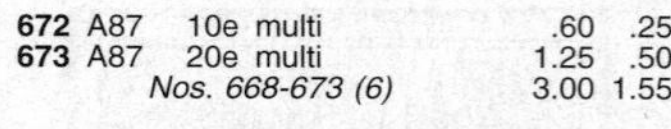

672 A87 10e multi .60 .25
673 A87 20e multi 1.25 .50
Nos. 668-673 (6) 3.00 1.55

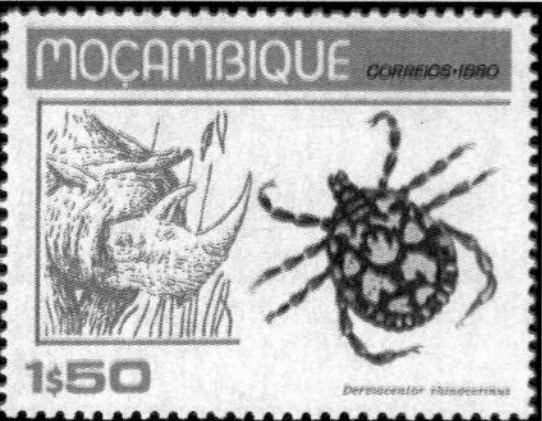

Dermacentor Rhinocerinus, Rhinoceros — A88

Ticks and Animals: 50c, Dermacentor circumguttatus cunhasilvai, elephant. 2.50e, Green tick, giraffe. 3e, Red tick, antelope. 5e, Ambloymma theilerae, cattle. 7.50e, Buffalo tick, buffalo.

1980, Jan. 29 Litho. *Perf. 11½x11*

674 A88 50c multi .20 .20
675 A88 1.50e multi .20 .20
676 A88 2.50e multi .25 .20
677 A88 3e multi .35 .20
678 A88 5e multi .40 .20
679 A88 7.50e multi .50 .20
Nos. 674-679 (6) 1.90 1.20

Ford Hercules, 1950 — A89

Public Transportation: 1.50e, Scania Marcopolo, 1978. 3e, Bussing Nag, 1936. 5e, Articulated Ikarus, 1978. 7.50e, Ford taxi, 1929. 12.50e, Fiat 131 taxi, 1978.

1980, Feb. 29 Litho. *Perf. 11*

680 A89 50c multi .20 .20
681 A89 1.50e multi .20 .20
682 A89 3e multi .20 .20
683 A89 5e multi .20 .20
684 A89 7.50e multi .35 .20
685 A89 12.50e multi .50 .20
Nos. 680-685 (6) 1.65 1.20

Marx, Engels, and Lenin A90

1980, May 1 Litho. *Perf. 11*

686 A90 10e multi .30 .20

Workers' Day.

"Heads," by Malangatana, London 1980 Emblem — A91

Paintings by Mozambique Artists: 1.50e, Crowded Market, by Moises Simbine. 3e, Heads with Helmets, by Malangatana. 5e, Women with Goods, by Machiana. 7.50e, Crowd with Masks, by Malangatana. 12.50e, Man and Woman with Spear, by Mankeu.

1980, May 6

687 A91 50c multi .20 .20
688 A91 1.50e multi .20 .20
689 A91 3e multi .20 .20
690 A91 5e multi .20 .20
691 A91 7.50e multi .30 .20
692 A91 12.50e multi .50 .20
Nos. 687-692 (6) 1.60 1.20

London 1980 Intl. Stamp Exhibition, 5/6-14.

World Telecommunications Day — A92

1980, May 17 Litho. *Perf. 12*

693 A92 15e multi .50 .30

Mueda Massacre, 20th Anniv. — A93

People with Weapons and Flag — A94

1980, June 16 Litho. *Perf. 11*

694 A93 15e multi .50 .30

1980, June 25

695 A94 1e Development projects, 1975 .20 .20
696 A94 2e shown .20 .20
697 A94 3e Arms, flags, 1977 .20 .20
698 A94 4e Raised fists, 1978 .20 .20
699 A94 5e Hand holding grain, flags, 1979 .25 .20
700 A94 10e Year banners, 1980 .40 .20
Nos. 695-700 (6) 1.45 1.20

Souvenir Sheet

Litho. *Imperf.*

700A A94 30e Soldiers 3.00

5th anniv. of independence. No. 700A contains one stamp with simulated perforations.

Gymnast, Moscow '80 Emblem — A95

1980, July 19

701 A95 50c shown .20 .20
702 A95 1.50e Soccer .20 .20
703 A95 2.50e Running .20 .20
704 A95 3e Volleyball .20 .20
705 A95 10e Bicycling .40 .20
706 A95 12.50e Boxing .50 .30
Nos. 701-706 (6) 1.70 1.30

22nd Summer Olympic Games, Moscow, July 19-Aug. 3.

Soldier, Map of Southern Africa Showing Zimbabwe — A96

1980, Apr. 18

707 A96 10e multi .30 .20

Establishment of independent Zimbabwe, Apr. 18.

Narina Trogon — A97

1980, July 30 Litho. *Perf. 11*

708 A97 1m shown .20 .20
709 A97 1.50m Crowned crane .25 .20
710 A97 2.50m Red-necked francolin .30 .20
711 A97 5m Ostrich .40 .20
712 A97 7.50m Spur-winged goose .50 .20
713 A97 12.50m Fish eagle .60 .25
Nos. 708-713 (6) 2.25 1.25

For surcharges see Nos. 1253A, 1255.

First Census, Aug. 1-15 A98

1980, Aug. 12 *Perf. 11*

714 A98 3.5m multi .20 .20

Brush Fire Control Campaign — A99

1980, Sept. 7

715 A99 3.5m multi .20 .20

Harpa Major A100

1980, Dec. 12 Litho. *Perf. 11*

716 A100 1m shown .20 .20
717 A100 1.50m Lambis chiragra .25 .20
718 A100 2.50m Murex pecten .30 .20
719 A100 5m Architectonia perspectiva .35 .20
720 A100 7.50m Murex ramosus .40 .20
721 A100 12.50m Strombus aurisdinae .75 .25
Nos. 716-721 (6) 2.25 1.25

Pres. Machel and Symbols of Industry and Transportation — A101

Decade of Development, 1981-1990 (Pres. Machel and): 7.50m, Soldiers. 12.50m, Symbols of education.

1981, Jan. 1 Litho. *Perf. 11x11½*

722 A101 3.50m red & bl .20 .20
723 A101 7.50m grn & red brn .30 .20
724 A101 12.50m dk bl & lil rose .50 .20
Nos. 722-724 (3) 1.00 .60

Bilbao Soccer Stadium, Soccer Player — A102

Soccer players and various stadiums.

1981, Jan. 30 Litho. *Perf. 11*

725 A102 1m multi .20 .20
726 A102 1.50m multi .20 .20
727 A102 2.50m multi .20 .20
728 A102 5m multi .20 .20
729 A102 7.50m multi .30 .20
730 A102 12.50m multi .50 .20
c. Souvenir sheet of 6 1.25 1.25
Nos. 725-730 (6) 1.60 1.20

Souvenir Sheets

Imperf

730A A102 20m multi .85 .85
730B A102 20m multi .85 .85

ESPANA '82 World Cup Soccer Championship. No. 730c contains Nos. 725-730 with simulated perforations. Sizes: No. 730A, 105x85mm; 730B, 141x111mm.

For surcharge see No. 1303.

Giraffe — A103

1981, Mar. 3 *Perf. 11*

731 A103 50c shown .20 .20
732 A103 1.50m Tsessebe .25 .20
733 A103 2.50m Aardvark .30 .20
734 A103 3m African python .35 .20
735 A103 5m Loggerhead turtle .40 .20
736 A103 10m Marabou .50 .20
737 A103 12.50m Saddlebill stork .65 .20
738 A103 15m Kori bustard .75 .30
Nos. 731-738 (8) 3.40 1.70

Pankwe A104

1981, Apr. 8 Litho. *Perf. 11*

739 A104 50c Chitende, vert. .20 .20
740 A104 2m shown .20 .20
741 A104 2.50m Kanyembe, vert. .20 .20
742 A104 7m Nyanga .30 .30
743 A104 10m Likuti and m'petheni .40 .40
Nos. 739-743 (5) 1.30 1.30

International Year of the Disabled — A105

1981, Apr. 18

744 A105 5m multi .20 .20

African Buffalo and Helicopter, Exhibition Emblem — A106

1981, June 14 *Perf. 11*

745 A106 2m shown .20 .20
746 A106 5m Hunters, blue kids .25 .20
747 A106 6m Hunter, impala .30 .20
748 A106 7.50m Hunters shooting .40 .20
749 A106 12.50m Elephants .50 .20
750 A106 20m Trap 1.00 .30
a. Souv. sheet of 6, #745-750, imperf. 3.00 2.50
Nos. 745-750 (6) 2.65 1.30

World Hunting Exhibition, Plovdiv, Bulgaria. No. 750a sold for 60m.

For surcharge see No. 1258.

50-centavo Coin, Obverse and Reverse A107

First Anniversary of New Currency (Coins on stamps of matching denomination).

1981, June 16

751 A107 50c multi .20 .20
752 A107 1m multi .25 .20
753 A107 2.50m multi .35 .20
754 A107 5m multi .40 .20
755 A107 10m multi .60 .20
756 A107 20m multi .90 .30
a. Souv. sheet of 6, #751-756, imperf. 2.50 1.75
Nos. 751-756 (6) 2.70 1.30

No. 756a sold for 40m.

Sunflower — A108

1981, July 24 Litho. *Perf. 14½*

757 A108 50c shown .20 .20
758 A108 1m Cotton .20 .20
759 A108 1.50m Sisal .20 .20
760 A108 2.50m Cashews .20 .20
761 A108 3.50m Tea leaves .20 .20
762 A108 4.50m Sugar cane .20 .20
763 A108 10m Castor-oil plant .40 .20
764 A108 12.50m Coconut .50 .20
765 A108 15m Tobacco leaves .60 .20
766 A108 25m Rice 1.00 .40
767 A108 40m Corn 1.60 .60
768 A108 60m Peanut 2.50 .85
Nos. 757-768 (12) 7.80 3.65

For surcharges see Nos. 1034A, 1185, 1216, 1218, 1252, 1300, 1399, 1420.

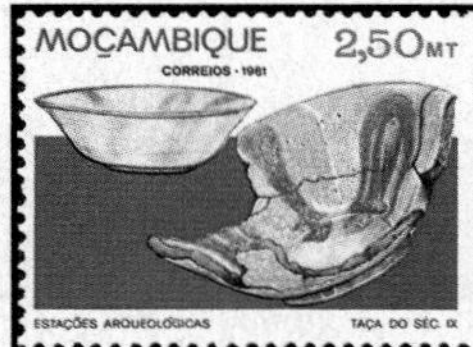

9th Cent. Persian Bowl, Chibuene Excavation Site — A109

1981, Aug. 30 *Perf. 11*

769 A109 1m Manyikeni Museum .20 .20
770 A109 1.50m Hand ax, Massingir Dam .20 .20
771 A109 2.50m shown .20 .20
772 A109 7.50m Pot, Chibuene, 9th cent. .30 .20
773 A109 12.50m Gold beads, Manyikeni .50 .20
774 A109 20m Iron, Manyikeni, 15th cent. .80 .30
Nos. 769-774 (6) 2.20 1.30

For surcharge see No. 1213.

Sculptures A110

1981, Sept. 25 Litho. *Perf. 11*

775 A110 50c Mapiko mask .20 .20
776 A110 1m Suffering woman .20 .20
777 A110 2.50m Mother and child .20 .20
778 A110 3.50m Man making fire .20 .20
779 A110 5m Chietane .50 .30
780 A110 12.50m Chietane, diff. .50 .50
Nos. 775-780 (6) 1.80 1.60

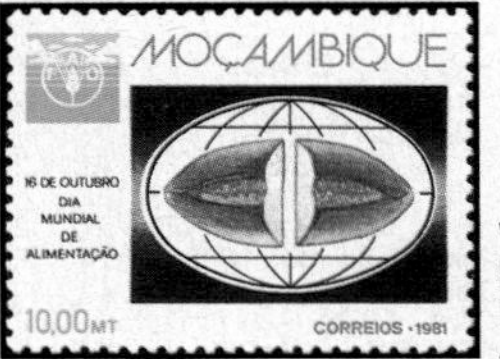

World Food Day A111

1981, Oct. 16 Litho. *Perf. 11*

781 A111 10m multi .40 .20

Ocean Tanker Matchedje — A112

1981, Nov. 22 Litho. *Perf. 11*

782 A112 50c shown .20 .20
783 A112 1.50m Tugboat Macuti .20 .20
784 A112 3m Prawn trawler Vega 7 .20 .20
785 A112 5m Freighter Linde .20 .20
786 A112 7.50m Ocean freighter Pemba .30 .20
787 A112 12.50m Dredger Rovuma .50 .25
Nos. 782-787 (6) 1.60 1.25

Chinaman Crab — A113

1981, Dec. 6

788 A113 50c Portunus Pelagieus .20 .20
789 A113 1.50m Scylla serrata .20 .20
790 A113 3m Penaeus indicus .20 .20
791 A113 7.50m Palinurus delagoae .30 .20
792 A113 12.50m Lusiosquilla maculata .50 .20
793 A113 15m Panulirus ornatus .60 .30
Nos. 788-793 (6) 2.00 1.30

For surcharges see Nos. 1214, 1219, 1253, 1392.

Hypoxis Multiceps A114

1981, Dec. 21 Litho. *Perf. 11*

794 A114 1m shown .20 .20
795 A114 1.50m Pelargonium luridum .20 .20
796 A114 2.50m Caralluma melananthera .20 .20
797 A114 7.50m Ansellia gigantea .30 .20
798 A114 12.50m Stapelia leendertsiae .50 .20
799 A114 25m Adenium multiflorium 1.00 .30
Nos. 794-799 (6) 2.40 1.30

For surcharges see Nos. 1215, 1217, 1251, 1301.

First Anniv. of Posts and Telecommunications Dept. — A115

1982, Jan. 1 Litho. *Perf. 11*

800 A115 6m Phone, globe .25 .20
801 A115 15m Envelope .60 .20

Gasoline Conservation — A116

1982, Jan. 25

802 A116 5m Piston .20 .20
803 A116 7.50m Car .30 .20
804 A116 10m Truck .40 .20
Nos. 802-804 (3) .90 .60

Sea Snake A117

1982, Feb. 27 **Litho.** ***Perf. 11***

805 A117 50c shown .20 .20
806 A117 1.50m Mozambique spitting cobra .20 .20
807 A117 3m Savanna vine snake .20 .20
808 A117 6m Black mamba .25 .20
809 A117 15m Boomslang .60 .20
810 A117 20m Bitis arietans .80 .30
Nos. 805-810 (6) 2.25 1.30

TB Bacillus Centenary — A118

1982, Mar. 15 **Litho.** ***Perf. 11***

811 A118 20m multi .80 .30

ITU Plenipotentiary Conference, Nairobi, Sept. 28-Nov. 5 — A119

1982, Mar. 31 ***Perf. 13½***

812 A119 20m multi .80 .35

1982 World Cup — A120

Designs: Various soccer players.

1982, Apr. 19 **Litho.** ***Perf. 13½***

813 A120 1.5m multi .20 .20
814 A120 3.5m multi .20 .20
815 A120 7m multi .30 .20
816 A120 10m multi .40 .20
817 A120 20m multi .80 .30
Nos. 813-817 (5) 1.90 1.10

Souvenir Sheet

Imperf

818 A120 50m multi 2.00 2.00

Souvenir Sheet

Two Tahitian Women, by Gauguin — A121

1982, June 11 **Litho.** ***Imperf.***

819 A121 35m multi 4.00 2.50

PHILEXFRANCE '82 Intl. Stamp Exhibition, Paris, June 11-21.

Natl. Liberation Front, 20th Anniv. — A122

Vangueria Infausta A123

1982, June 25 ***Perf. 13***

820 A122 4m Pres. Mondland addressing crowd .20 .20
821 A122 8m Guarded fields .30 .20
822 A122 12m Procession .50 .20
Nos. 820-822 (3) 1.00 .60

1982, Sept. 13 ***Perf. 11***

Designs: Fruits.

823 A123 1m shown .20 .20
824 A123 2m Mimusops caffra .20 .20
825 A123 4m Sclerocarya caffra .20 .20
826 A123 8m Strychnos spinosa .35 .20
827 A123 12m Salacia kraussi .50 .20
828 A123 32m Trichilia emetica 1.40 .40
Nos. 823-828 (6) 2.85 1.40

25th Anniv. of Sputnik 1 Flight A124

1982, Oct. 4 **Litho.** ***Perf. 11***

829 A124 1m Sputnik, 1957 .20 .20
830 A124 2m Yuri Gagarin's flight, 1961 .20 .20
831 A124 4m A. Leonov's spacewalk, 1965 .20 .20
832 A124 8m Apollo 11, 1969 .35 .20
833 A124 16m Apollo-Soyuz, 1975 .70 .25
834 A124 20m Salyut-6, 1978 .85 .30
a. Min. sheet of 6, #829-834 2.50 2.50
Nos. 829-834 (6) 2.50 1.35

People's Vigilance Day — A125

Caique — A126

1982, Oct. 11 ***Perf. 13½***

835 A125 4m multi .20 .20

1982, Nov. 29

Traditional boats. 4m, 8m, 12m, 16m horiz.

836 A126 1m shown .20 .20
837 A126 2m Machua .20 .20
838 A126 4m Calaua .20 .20
839 A126 8m Chitatarro .35 .20
840 A126 12m Cangaia .50 .20
841 A126 16m Chata (flatboat) .70 .25
Nos. 836-841 (6) 2.15 1.25

Marine Life — A127

1982, Dec. 21 **Litho.** ***Perf. 11***

842 A127 1m Ophiomastix venosa .20 .20
843 A127 2m Protoreaster lincki .20 .20
844 A127 4m Tropiometra carinata .20 .20
845 A127 8m Holothuria scabra .35 .20
846 A127 12m Prionocidaris baculosa .50 .20
847 A127 16m Colobocentrotus atnatus .70 .25
Nos. 842-847 (6) 2.15 1.25

Frelimo Party 4th Congress — A128

1983, Jan. 17

848 A128 4m Map, soldier .20 .20
849 A128 8m Voters .35 .20
850 A128 16m Farm workers .70 .20
Nos. 848-850 (3) 1.25 .60

Seaweed A129

1983, Feb. 28 **Litho.** ***Perf. 11***

851 A129 1m Codium duthierae .20 .20
852 A129 2m Halimeda cuncata .20 .20
853 A129 4m Dictyota liturata .20 .20
854 A129 8m Encorachne bing hamiae .35 .20
855 A129 12m Laurencia flexuosa .50 .20
856 A129 20m Acrosorium sp. .85 .35
Nos. 851-856 (6) 2.30 1.35

1984 Olympic Games, Los Angeles A130

1983, Mar. 31 **Litho.** ***Perf. 11***

857 A130 1m Diving .20 .20
858 A130 2m Boxing .20 .20
859 A130 4m Basketball .20 .20
860 A130 8m Handball .35 .20
861 A130 12m Volleyball .50 .20
862 A130 16m Running .70 .25
863 A130 20m Sailing .85 .35
Nos. 857-863 (7) 3.00 1.60

Souvenir Sheet

Imperf

864 A130 50m Discus 2.00 2.00

For surcharge see No. 1257.

Steam Locomotives — A131

1983, Apr. 29 **Litho.** ***Perf. 11***

865 A131 1m 1912 .20 .20
866 A131 2m 1947 .20 .20
867 A131 4m 1923 .20 .20
868 A131 8m 1924 .30 .20
869 A131 16m 1924, diff. .70 .30
870 A131 32m 1950 1.40 .40
Nos. 865-870 (6) 3.00 1.50

20th Anniv. of Org. of African Unity A132

1983, May 25 **Litho.** ***Perf. 11***

871 A132 4m multi .20 .20

Mammals A133

1983, May 30

872 A133 1m Petrodromus tetradactylus .20 .20
873 A133 2m Rhabdomys pumilio .20 .20
874 A133 4m Paraxerus vincenti .20 .20
875 A133 8m Cryptomys hottentotus .35 .20
876 A133 12m Pronolagus crassicaudatus .50 .20
877 A133 16m Eidolon helvum .70 .30
Nos. 872-877 (6) 2.15 1.30

Souvenir Sheet

Marimba Players — A134

1983, July 29 **Litho.** ***Perf. 11***

878 A134 30m multi 1.50 1.50

BRASILIANA '83 Intl. Stamp Show, Rio de Janeiro, July 29-Aug. 7.

World Communications Year — A135

1983, Aug. 26 **Litho.** ***Perf. 11***

879 A135 8m multi .35 .20

Fishing Techniques — A136

1983, Oct. 29 Litho. *Perf. 11*

880 A136 50c Line fishing .20 .20
881 A136 2m Chifonho .20 .20
882 A136 4m Momba .20 .20
883 A136 8m Gamboa .30 .20
884 A136 16m Mono .55 .20
885 A136 20m Lema .70 .30
Nos. 880-885 (6) 2.15 1.30

World Communications Year, Stamp Day — A137

1983, Dec. 21 Litho.

886 A137 50c Horn .20 .20
887 A137 1m Drum .20 .20
888 A137 4m Native mail carriers .20 .20
889 A137 8m Boat .30 .20
890 A137 16m Truck .55 .20
891 A137 20m Train .70 .30
Nos. 886-891 (6) 2.15 1.30

2nd Anniv. of Mozambique Red Cross (July 10) — A138

1983, Oct. 29 Litho. *Perf. 11*

892 A138 4m Flood relief .20 .20
893 A138 8m Rescue truck .30 .20
894 A138 16m First aid .55 .20
895 A138 32m Field first aid 1.10 .40
Nos. 892-895 (4) 2.15 1.00

Olympic Games 1984, Los Angeles A139

1984, Jan. 2 Litho. *Perf. 11*

896 A139 50c Swimming .20 .20
897 A139 4m Soccer .20 .20
898 A139 8m Hurdles .30 .20
899 A139 16m Basketball .55 .25
900 A139 32m Handball 1.10 .30
901 A139 60m Boxing 2.00 .50
Nos. 896-901 (6) 4.35 1.65

Indigenous Trees — A140

1984, Mar. 30 Litho. *Perf. 11*

902 A140 50c Trichilia emetica .20 .20
903 A140 2m Brachystegia spiciformis .20 .20
904 A140 4m Androstachys johnsonii .20 .20
905 A140 8m Pterocarpus angolensis .20 .20
906 A140 16m Milletia stuhlmannii .30 .20
907 A140 50m Dalbergia melanoxylon 1.00 .40
Nos. 902-907 (6) 2.10 1.40

Nkomati Accord, Mar. 16 — A141

1984, Mar. 16

908 A141 4m Dove .20 .20

Natl. Arms A142

1984, May 1

909 A142 4m shown .20 .20
910 A142 8m Natl. flag .20 .20

Traditional Dances A143

1984, May 9

911 A143 4m Makway .20 .20
912 A143 8m Mapiko .20 .20
913 A143 16m Wadjaba .30 .20
Nos. 911-913 (3) .70 .60

LUBRAPEX '84, May 9-17.

Museums and Artifacts — A144

Designs: 50c, Nampula Museum, African carrying water jar, wooden statue. 4m, Museum of Natural History, preserved bird. 8m, Revolution Museum, guerrilla fighter statue. 16m, Colonial Occupation Museum, fort and cannon. 20m, Numismatic Museum, coins. 30m, Palace of St. Paul, char, 19th cent.

1984, June 25

914 A144 50c multi .20 .20
915 A144 4m multi .20 .20
916 A144 8m multi .20 .20
917 A144 16m multi .30 .20
918 A144 20m multi .40 .25
919 A144 30m multi .60 .30
Nos. 914-919 (6) 1.90 1.35

Freshwater Fish — A145

1984, Aug. 24

920 A145 50c Alestes imberi .20 .20
921 A145 4m Labeo congoro .20 .20
922 A145 12m Syndontis zambezensis .40 .20
923 A145 16m Notobranchius zachovii .55 .30
924 A145 40m Barbus paludinosus 1.40 .40
925 A145 60m Barilius zambezensis 2.00 .60
Nos. 920-925 (6) 4.75 1.90

For surcharge see No. 1311.

Intl. Fair, Maputo — A145a

1984, Aug. 24 Litho. *Perf. 11*

925A A145a 16m multicolored 1.25 .40

Traditional Weapons A146

1984, Sept. 25

926 A146 50c Knife, cudgel *.45 .20*
927 A146 4m Axes *.60 .20*
928 A146 8m Shield, assagai *1.25 .20*
929 A146 16m Bow and arrow *2.40 .30*
930 A146 32m Muzzleloader *3.00 .40*
931 A146 50m Assagai, arrow *5.00 .50*
Nos. 926-931 (6) *12.70 1.80*

Natl. Revolution, 20th anniv.
For surcharge see No. 1256.

Natl. Trade Unions, 1st Anniv. — A147

1984, Oct. 13 *Perf. 13½*

932 A147 4m Workers, emblem .20 .20

Stamp Day — A149

Cancellations on altered stamps and stationery: 4m, Barue cancel on 1885 20r postal card. 8m, Zumbo cancel on design similar to No. 52. 12m, Mozambique Co. cancel on design similar to Mozambique Company Type API. 16m, Macequece cancel on design similar to Mozambique Company No. 190.

1984, Dec. 21 *Perf. 11½x11*

936 A149 4m multi .20 .20
937 A149 8m multi .30 .20
938 A149 12m multi .40 .20
939 A149 16m multi .55 .25
Nos. 936-939 (4) 1.45 .85

African Development Bank, 20th Anniv. — A150

1984, Sept. 16 Photo. *Perf. 11½x11*

940 A150 4m multi .20 .20

Apiculture A151

1985, Feb. 3

941 A151 4m Beekeeper .20 .20
942 A151 8m Bee gathering pollen .20 .20
943 A151 16m Entering nest .20 .20
944 A151 20m Building honeycomb .30 .20
Nos. 941-944 (4) .90 .80

OLYMPHILEX '85, Lausanne A152

1985, Mar. 18 *Perf. 11*

945 A152 16m Shot putter .25 .20

World Meteorology Day — A153

1985, Mar. 23 Litho. *Perf. 11*

946 A153 4m multi .20 .20

Southern African Development Coordination Conference, 5th Anniv. — A154

1985, Apr. 1

947 A154 4m Map .20 .20
948 A154 8m Map, transmission tower .20 .20
949 A154 16m Industry .25 .20
950 A154 32m Flags .45 .20
Nos. 947-950 (4) 1.10 .80

Independence, 10th Anniv. — A155

Colonial resistance battles: 1m, Mujenga, 1896. 4m, Mungari, 1917. 8m, Massangano, 1868. 16m, Marracuene, 1895, and Gungunhana (c. 1840-1906), resistance leader.

1985, June 25 Litho. *Perf. 11*

951 A155 1m multi .20 .20
952 A155 4m multi .20 .20
953 A155 8m multi .20 .20
954 A155 16m multi .25 .20
Nos. 951-954 (4) .85 .80

UN, 40th Anniv. — A156

1985, June 26

955 A156 16m multi *9.00 9.00*

Traditional Games — A157

1985, Aug. 28 Litho. *Perf. 11*

956 A157 50c Mathacuzana .20 .20
957 A157 4m Mudzobo .20 .20
958 A157 8m Muravarava .35 .35
959 A157 16m N'Tshuwa .70 .70
Nos. 956-959 (4) 1.45 1.45

Frogs and Toads A158

1985, Oct. 25 Litho. *Perf. 11*

960 A158 50c Rana angolensis .20 .20
961 A158 1m Hyperolius pictus .20 .20
962 A158 4m Ptychadena porosissima .20 .20
963 A158 8m Afrixalus formasinii .20 .20
964 A158 16m Bufo regularis .25 .20
965 A158 32m Hyperolius marmoratus .45 .25
Nos. 960-965 (6) 1.50 1.25

Medicinal Plants — A159

1985, Nov. 28 Litho. *Perf. 11*

966 A159 50c Aloe ferox .20 .20
967 A159 1m Boophone disticha .20 .20
968 A159 3.50m Gloriosa superba .20 .20
969 A159 4m Cotyledon orbiculata .20 .20
970 A159 8m Homeria breyniana .20 .20
970A A159 50m Haemanthus coccineus .70 .25
Nos. 966-970A (6) 1.70 1.25

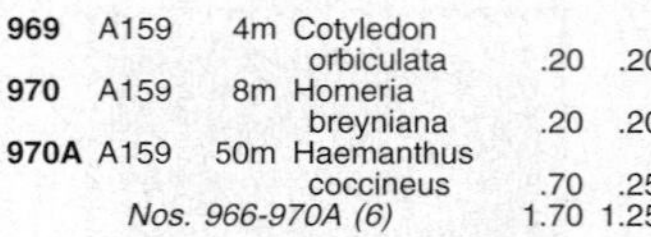

Stamp Day A160

Stamps: 1m, Mozambique Company No. 126. 4m, Nyassa Type A6. 8m, Mozambique Company No. 110. 16m, Nyassa No. J2.

1985, Dec. 21

971 A160 1m multi .20 .20
972 A160 4m multi .20 .20
973 A160 8m multi .20 .20
974 A160 16m multi .25 .20
Nos. 971-974 (4) .85 .80

Halley's Comet — A161

Comet and: 4m, Space probe. 8m, Trajectory diagram. 16m, Newton's telescope, observatory, probe. 30m, Earth.

1986, Jan. 2

975 A161 4m multi .20 .20
976 A161 8m multi .20 .20
977 A161 16m multi .25 .20
978 A161 30m multi .45 .25
Nos. 975-978 (4) 1.10 .85

1986 World Cup Soccer Championships, Mexico — A162

Players.

1986, Feb. 28 Litho. *Perf. 11½x11*

979 A162 3m Vicente .20 .20
980 A162 4m Coluna .20 .20
981 A162 8m Costa Pereira .20 .20
982 A162 12m Hilario .20 .20
983 A162 16m Matateu .25 .20
984 A162 50m Eusebio .70 .40
Nos. 979-984 (6) 1.75 1.40

Intl. Peace Year — A163

1986, Mar. 18 *Perf. 11*

985 A163 16m multi .25 .20

Mushrooms A164

1986, Apr. 8

986 A164 4m Amanita muscaria .20 .20
987 A164 8m Lactarius deliciosus .20 .20
988 A164 16m Amanita phaloides .25 .20
989 A164 30m Tricholoma nudum .35 .20
Nos. 986-989 (4) 1.00 .80

Souvenir Sheet

Statue of Liberty, Cent. — A165

1986, May 22 *Imperf.*

990 A165 100m multi 2.00 2.00

AMERIPEX '86. #990 has simulated perfs.

Traditional Women's Hair Styles — A166

1986, June Litho. *Perf. 11½x11*

991 A166 1m Tanzanian .20 .20
992 A166 4m Miriam .20 .20
993 A166 8m Estrelinhas .20 .20
994 A166 16m Toto .25 .20
Nos. 991-994 (4) .85 .80

Marine Mammals — A167

1986, Aug. *Perf. 11*

995 A167 1m Dugongo dugon .20 .20
996 A167 8m Delphinus delphis .25 .20
997 A167 16m Neobalena marginata .35 .20
998 A167 50m Balaenoptera physalus 1.00 .25
Nos. 995-998 (4) 1.80 .85

Continuing Youth Education Organization, 1st Anniv. — A168

1986, Sept. 16 Litho. *Perf. 11½x11*

999 A168 4m multi .20 .20

Natl. Savings Campaign — A169

Bank notes, front and back.

1986, Oct. 22 Litho. *Perf. 11½x11*

1000 A169 4m 50m note .20 .20
1001 A169 8m 100m note .30 .20
1002 A169 16m 500m note .40 .20
1003 A169 30m 1000m note 1.00 .20
Nos. 1000-1003 (4) 1.90 .80

For surcharge see No. 1302.

Stamp Day A170

Post offices.

1986, Dec. 21 Litho. *Perf. 11*

1004 A170 3m Quelimane .20 .20
1005 A170 4m Maputo .25 .20
1006 A170 8m Beira .30 .20
1007 A170 16m Nampula .50 .20
Nos. 1004-1007 (4) 1.25 .80

Minerals A171

1987, Jan. 2 *Perf. 11x11½*

1008 A171 4m Pyrite .25 .20
1009 A171 8m Emerald .30 .20
1010 A171 12m Agate .40 .20
1011 A171 16m Malachite .50 .20
1012 A171 30m Garnet .75 .25
1013 A171 50m Amethyst 1.00 .40
Nos. 1008-1013 (6) 3.20 1.45

For surcharges see #1304-1305.

Frelimo Party, 10th Anniv. — A172

1987, Feb. 3 *Perf. 11*

1014 A172 4m multi .20 .20

Pequenos Libombos Dam — A173

1987, Feb. 17 ***Perf. 11½x11***
1015 A173 16m multi .25 .20

World Health Day A174

1987, Apr. 7 **Litho.** ***Perf. 11x11½***
1016 A174 50m multi .70 .25

Birds — A175

1987, Apr. 27 **Litho.** ***Perf. 11½x11***
1017 A175 3m Granatina granatina .20 .20
1018 A175 4m Halcyon senegalensis .20 .20
1019 A175 8m Mellittophagus bullockoides .20 .20
1020 A175 12m Perinestes minor .20 .20
1021 A175 16m Coracias naevia mosambica .25 .25
1022 A175 30m Cimmyris neergardi .40 .30
Nos. 1017-1022 (6) 1.45 1.35

Souvenir Sheet

CAPEX '87, Toronto, June 13-21 — A176

1987, June ***Imperf.***
1023 A176 200m multi 2.00 2.00

No. 1023 contains one stamp having simulated perforations.

1988 Summer Olympics, Seoul — A177

1987, May **Litho.** ***Perf. 11½x11***
1024 A177 12.50m Soccer players and ball .20 .20
1025 A177 25m Runner's legs .25 .20
1026 A177 50m Volleyball .50 .30
1027 A177 75m Chess .75 .40
1028 A177 100m Basketball 1.00 .50
1029 A177 200m Swimming 2.00 .75
Nos. 1024-1029 (6) 4.70 2.35

Tapestries — A178

1987, Aug. ***Perf. 11***
1030 A178 20m Incomplete pattern on loom .20 .20
1031 A178 40m Diamond-shaped pattern .20 .20
1032 A178 80m Landscape pattern .30 .25
1033 A178 200m Oriental pattern .80 .35
Nos. 1030-1033 (4) 1.50 1.00

Maputo City A179

Early Portuguese map of Lourenco Marques.

1987, Nov. 10 **Litho.** ***Perf. 11***
1034 A179 20m multi .20 .20

No. 762 Surcharged in Silver and Dark Red

1987 **Litho.** ***Perf. 14½***
1034A A108 4m on 4.50m multi *5.00 5.00*

1988 Summer Olympics, Seoul — A180

1988, Feb. 10 **Litho.** ***Perf. 11***
1035 A180 10m Javelin .20 .20
1036 A180 20m Baseball .30 .20
1037 A180 40m Boxing .60 .25
1038 A180 80m Field hockey 1.10 .40
1039 A180 100m Gymnastic rings 1.40 .50
1040 A180 400m Cycling 5.75 1.90
Nos. 1035-1040 (6) 9.35 3.45

Nos. 1036-1040 horiz.

Flowering Plants — A181

1988, Mar. 18 ***Perf. 11½x11***
1041 A181 10m Heamanthus nelsonii .20 .20
1042 A181 20m Crinum polyphyllum .30 .20
1043 A181 40m Boophane disticha .60 .25
1044 A181 80m Cyrtanthus contractus 1.10 .40
1045 A181 100m Nerine angustifolia 1.40 .50
1046 A181 400m Cyrtanthus galpinnii 5.75 1.90
Nos. 1041-1046 (6) 9.35 3.45

World Health Organization, 40th Anniv. — A182

1988, Apr. 7
1047 A182 20m multi .30 .30

Anti-smoking campaign.

Wickerwork — A183

1988, June 16 **Litho.** ***Perf. 11***
1048 A183 20m Mat .20 .20
1049 A183 25m Lidded container .20 .20
1050 A183 80m Market basket .60 .20
1051 A183 100m Fan .75 .25
1052 A183 400m Flat basket 2.00 1.00
1053 A183 500m Funnel basket 3.00 1.25
Nos. 1048-1053 (6) 6.75 3.10

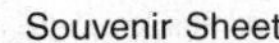
Souvenir Sheet

FINLANDIA '88 — A184

1988, June 12 **Litho.** ***Imperf.***
1054 A184 500m multi 3.00 1.00

Stamp in No. 1054 has simulated perfs.

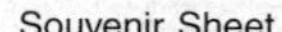
Souvenir Sheet

State Visit of Pope John Paul II, Sept. 16-19 — A185

1988 **Litho.** ***Perf. 13½***
1055 A185 500m multi 3.00 1.50

Horses A186

1988, Sept. 20 **Litho.** ***Perf. 11***
1056 A186 20m Percheron .25 .20
1057 A186 40m Arab .50 .20
1058 A186 80m Thoroughbred 1.00 .25
1059 A186 100m Pony 1.50 .35
Nos. 1056-1059 (4) 3.25 1.00

Pres. Samora Machel (1933-1986) A187

1988, Oct. 19 **Litho.** ***Perf. 11***
1060 A187 20m multi .20 .20

Stamp Day A188

1988, Dec. 21 ***Perf. 11x11½, 11½x11***
1061 A188 20m P.O. trailer .20 .20
1062 A188 40m Mailbox, vert. .20 .20

Ports A189

1988, Nov. 30 ***Perf. 11***
1063 A189 25m Inhambane .20 .20
1064 A189 50m Quelimane, vert. .20 .20
1065 A189 75m Pemba .30 .20
1066 A189 100m Beira .40 .20
1067 A189 250m Nacala, vert. 1.00 .25
1068 A189 500m Maputo 2.10 .50
Nos. 1063-1068 (6) 4.20 1.55

5th Frelimo Party Congress A190

1989, Jan. 19

1069 Strip of 5 2.60 1.25
a. A190 25m Corn .20 .20
b. A190 50m Axe .25 .20
c. A190 75m Abstract shapes .35 .20
d. A190 100m 2½ Gearwheels .50 .25
e. A190 250m ½ Gearwheel 1.25 .60

Printed se-tenant in a continuous design.

French Revolution Bicent. — A191

Designs: 100m, *Storming of the Bastille,* by Thevenin. 250m, *Liberty Guiding the People,* by Delacroix. 500m, *Declaration of the Rights of Man and the Citizen,* a print by Blanchard.

1989, Feb. 16 ***Perf. 11***

1070 A191 100m multi .30 .20
1071 A191 250m multi .75 .25

Souvenir Sheet

1072 A191 500m multi 1.50 .75

No. 1072 is a continuous design.

Eduardo Chivambo Mondlane (1920-1969), Frelimo Party Founder, 20th Death Anniv. — A192

1989, Feb. 3 **Litho.** ***Perf. 11***

1073 A192 25m blk, gold & dark red .20 .20

Venomous Species — A193

1989, Mar. 23

1074 A193 25m Pandinus .20 .20
1075 A193 50m Naja haje .20 .20
1076 A193 75m Bombus .30 .20
1077 A193 100m Paraphysa .40 .20
1078 A193 250m Conus marmoreus 1.00 .25
1079 A193 500m Pterois volitans 2.10 .50
Nos. 1074-1079 (6) 4.20 1.55

Coral A194

1989, May 2 **Litho.** ***Perf. 11***

1080 A194 25m Acropora pulchra .20 .20
1081 A194 50m Eunicella papilosa .20 .20
1082 A194 100m Dendrophyla migrantus .30 .20
1083 A194 250m Favia fragum .70 .25
Nos. 1080-1083 (4) 1.40 .85

1990 World Cup Soccer Championships, Italy — A195

Athletes executing various plays.

1989, June 22 **Litho.** ***Perf. 11½x11***

1084 A195 30m multi .20 .20
1085 A195 60m multi .20 .20
1086 A195 125m multi .30 .20
1087 A195 200m multi .55 .20
1088 A195 250m multi .70 .25
1089 A195 500m multi 1.40 .45
Nos. 1084-1089 (6) 3.35 1.50

Lighthouses A196

1989, July 24 **Litho.** ***Perf. 11***

1090 A196 30m Macuti .20 .20
1091 A196 60m Pinda .20 .20
1092 A196 125m Cape Delgado .35 .20
1093 A196 200m Isle of Goa .55 .20
1094 A196 250m Caldeira Point .70 .25
1095 A196 500m Vilhena 1.40 .45
Nos. 1090-1095 (6) 3.40 1.50

Filigree Workmanship in Silver — A197

1989, Aug. 30 **Litho.** ***Perf. 11x11½***

1096 A197 30m shown .20 .20
1097 A197 60m Flower on band .20 .20
1098 A197 125m Necklace .30 .20
1099 A197 200m Decorative box .50 .20
1100 A197 250m Utensils .60 .25
1101 A197 500m Butterfly 1.25 .45
Nos. 1096-1101 (6) 3.05 1.50

Natl. Liberation War, 25th Anniv. A198

1989, Sept. 25

1102 A198 30m multicolored .20 .20

Meteorological Instruments A199

Designs: 30m, Rain gauge. 60m, Weather system on radar. 125m, Instrument shelter. 200m, Computer monitor and keyboard.

1989, Oct. 12 ***Perf. 11½x11***

1103 A199 30m multicolored .20 .20
1104 A199 60m multicolored .25 .20
1105 A199 125m multicolored .40 .20
1106 A199 200m multicolored .75 .25
Nos. 1103-1106 (4) 1.60 .85

Souvenir Sheet

World Stamp Expo '89, Washington, DC — A200

1989, Nov. 17 ***Perf. 13½***

1107 A200 500m Washington Monument 2.50 1.50

Stamp Day — A201

1989, Dec. 21 **Litho.** ***Perf. 11½x11***

1108 A201 30m UPU emblem .20 .20
1109 A201 60m P.O. emblem .20 .20

Southern African Development Coordination Conf. (SADCC), 10th Anniv. — A201a

1990, Jan. 31 ***Perf. 11½x11***

1109A A201a 35m multicolored .20 .20

Textile Designs A202

1990, Feb. 28 **Litho.** ***Perf. 11x11½***

1110 A202 42m multi, diff. .20 .20
1111 A202 90m multi, diff. .30 .20
1112 A202 150m multi, diff. .45 .25
1113 A202 200m multi, diff. .60 .30
1114 A202 400m multi, diff. 1.25 .60
1115 A202 500m multi, diff. 1.50 .75
Nos. 1110-1115 (6) 4.30 2.30

Forts A203

1990, Mar. 20 ***Perf. 11x11½***

1116 A203 45m Sena .20 .20
1117 A203 90m Santo Antonio .30 .20
1118 A203 150m Santo Sebastiao .45 .25
1119 A203 200m Santo Caetano .60 .30
1120 A203 400m Our Lady of Conceicao 1.25 .60
1121 A203 500m Santo Luis 1.50 .75
Nos. 1116-1121 (6) 4.30 2.30

Souvenir Sheet

Penny Black, Mozambique No. 1 — A204

1990, May 3 **Litho.** ***Perf. 11½x11***

1122 A204 1000m red, blk & bl 4.00 3.00

Penny Black, 150th anniversary. Stamp World London '90.

Bank of Mozambique, 15th Anniv. — A205

1990, May 17 **Litho.** ***Perf. 11x11½***

1123 A205 100m multicolored .30 .20

Natl. Independence, 15th Anniv. — A206

1990, June 25 ***Perf. 11***

1124 A206 42.50m Eduardo Mondlane .20 .20
1125 A206 150m Samora Machel .45 .25

Endangered Species — A207

1990, Aug. 20 Litho. *Perf. 11x11½*

1126 A207 42.50m Ceratotherium simum .20 .20
1127 A207 100m Dugong dugong .30 .20
1128 A207 150m Loxodonta africana .45 .25
1129 A207 200m Acinonix jubatus .60 .30
1130 A207 400m Lutra maculicollis 1.25 .60
1131 A207 500m Eretmochelys imbricata 1.50 .70
Nos. 1126-1131 (6) 4.30 2.25

Trees and Plants — A208

1990, Oct. 15 Litho. *Perf. 11½x11*

1132 A208 42.50m Dichrostachys cinerea .20 .20
1133 A208 100m Queimadas .30 .20
1134 A208 150m Casuariana equisetifolia .45 .25
1135 A208 200m Rhizophora muronata .60 .30
1136 A208 400m Estrato herbaceo 1.25 .60
1137 A208 500m Atzelia cuanzensis 1.50 .70
Nos. 1132-1137 (6) 4.30 2.25

Stamp Day — A209

No. 1138: a, Pick-up at letter box. b, Canceling letters. c, Letter carrier. d, Delivery to recipient.

1990, Dec. 21 Litho. *Perf. 11½x11*

1138 Strip of 4 .60 .40
a.-d. A209 42.50m any single .20 .20

Governmental Departments A210

Designs: No. 1139, Post Office Dept., 10th anniv. No. 1140, Telecommunications Dept.

1991, Jan. 2

1139 A210 50m dk bl, red & blk .20 .20
1140 A210 50m grn, blk & brn .20 .20

Flowers — A211

1991, Feb. 25 Litho. *Perf. 11½x11*

1141 A211 50m Strilitzia reginae .20 .20
1142 A211 125m Anthurium andraeanum .55 .25
1143 A211 250m Zantedeschia pentlandii 1.00 .50
1144 A211 300m Canna indica 1.25 .60
Nos. 1141-1144 (4) 3.00 1.55

Alcelaphus Lichtensteini A212

1991, Mar. 27 *Perf. 14*

1145 Strip of 4 12.50 7.50
a. A212 50m Two adults .50 .30
b. A212 100m Adult 1.25 .30
c. A212 250m Adult grazing 3.00 .75
d. A212 500m Nursing calf 6.00 2.00

Fountains of Maputo — A213

Designs: 50m, Mpompine. 125m, Chinhambanine. 250m, Sao Pedro-Zaza. 300m, Xipamanine.

1991, Apr. 15 Litho. *Perf. 11½x11*

1146 A213 50m multicolored .20 .20
1147 A213 125m multicolored .30 .20
1148 A213 250m multicolored .55 .30
1149 A213 300m multicolored .65 .30
Nos. 1146-1149 (4) 1.70 1.00

Paintings by Mozambican Artists — A214

1991, May 18 Litho. *Perf. 11½x11*

1150 A214 180m Samale .40 .20
1151 A214 250m Malangatana .55 .30
1152 A214 560m Malangatana, diff. 1.25 .60
Nos. 1150-1152 (3) 2.20 1.10

1992 Summer Olympics, Barcelona A215

1991, June 25 Litho. *Perf. 11½x11*

1153 A215 10m Swimming .20 .20
1154 A215 50m Roller hockey .20 .20
1155 A215 100m Tennis .25 .20
1156 A215 200m Table tennis .45 .25
1157 A215 500m Running 1.10 .55
1158 A215 1000m Badminton 2.25 1.10
Nos. 1153-1158 (6) 4.45 2.50

For surcharges, see Nos. 1393A, 1396.

British-Portuguese Agreement on Mozambique Borders, Cent. — A216

1991, Oct. 9 Litho. *Perf. 11½x11*

1159 A216 600m Map of 1890 .85 .40
1160 A216 800m Map of 1891 1.10 .60

Souvenir Sheet

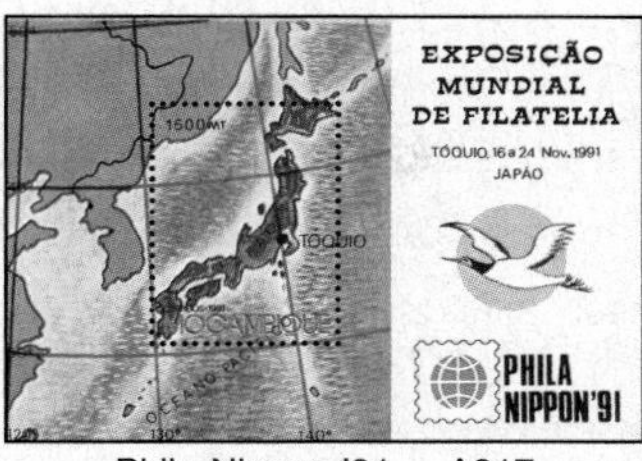

Phila Nippon '91 — A217

1991, Nov. 15 Litho. *Perf. 11½x11*

1161 A217 1500m Map of Japan 1.75 1.75

Children's Games — A218

1991, Dec. 21

1162 A218 40m Jumping rope .20 .20
1163 A218 150m Spinning top .20 .20
1164 A218 400m Marbles .35 .20
1165 A218 900m Hopscotch .80 .40
Nos. 1162-1165 (4) 1.55 1.00

Stained Glass Windows — A219

No. 1166 — Various designs: a, 40m. b, 150m. c, 400m. d, 900m.

1992, Jan. 22

1166 A219 Block of 4, #a.-d. 1.40 .70

Plants — A220

1992, Mar. 23 Litho. *Perf. 11½x11*

1167 A220 300m Rhisophora mucronata .50 .30
1168 A220 600m Cymodocea ciliata 1.10 .50
1169 A220 1000m Sophora inhambanensis 1.75 .90
Nos. 1167-1169 (3) 3.35 1.70

Traditional Tools — A221

1992, May 9

1170 A221 100m Spear, spear-thrower .20 .20
1171 A221 300m Pitch forks .50 .25
1172 A221 500m Hatchet .90 .45
1173 A221 1000m Dagger 1.75 .90
Nos. 1170-1173 (4) 3.35 1.80

Lubrapex '92, Lisbon.

A222

Birds: 150m, Chalcomitra amethystina. 200m, Ceropis senegalensis. 300m, Cossypha natalensis. 400m, Lamprocolius chloropterus. 500m, Malaconotus poliocephalus. 800m, Oriolus auratus.

1992, July 24 Litho. *Perf. 11½x11*

1174 A222 150m multicolored .30 .20
1175 A222 200m multicolored .35 .20
1176 A222 300m multicolored .50 .25
1177 A222 400m multicolored .70 .35
1178 A222 500m multicolored .85 .40
1179 A222 800m multicolored 1.40 .70
Nos. 1174-1179 (6) 4.10 2.10

Eduardo Mondlane University, 30th Anniv. — A223

1992, Aug. 21

1180 A223 150m grn, brn & blk .30 .20

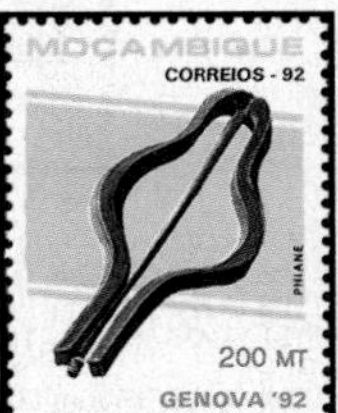

Traditional Musical Instruments A224

1992, Sept. 18

1181 A224 200m Phiane .35 .20
1182 A224 300m Xirupe .50 .25
1183 A224 500m Ngulula .85 .40
1184 A224 1500m Malimba 2.50 1.25
a. Souvenir sheet of 4, #1181-1184, imperf. 4.25 2.10
Nos. 1181-1184 (4) 4.20 2.10

Genoa '92. #1184a has simulated perfs.

No. 757 Surcharged

1992, Oct. Litho. *Perf. 14½*

1185 A108 50m on 50c #757 .80 .40

Intl. Conference on Nutrition — A225

1992, Oct. 16 ***Perf. 11½x11***

1186 A225 450m multicolored .75 .40

Parachuting A226

Various parchutists descending from sky.

1992, Nov. 10 Litho. ***Perf. 11½x11***

1187 A226 50m multicolored .20 .20
1188 A226 400m multicolored .60 .30
1189 A226 500m multicolored .80 .40
1190 A226 1500m multicolored 2.40 1.10
Nos. 1187-1190 (4) 4.00 2.00

Medals — A227

1993, Feb. 3 Litho. ***Perf. 11½x11***

1191 A227 400m Order of Peace & Amity .30 .20
1192 A227 800m Baga moyo .55 .30
1193 A227 1000m Order of Eduardo Mondlane .70 .35
1194 A227 1500m War veterans 1.00 .50
Nos. 1191-1194 (4) 2.55 1.35

Pollution A228

1993, Apr. 8 ***Perf. 11x11½***

1195 A228 200m Deforestation .20 .20
1196 A228 750m Factory smoke .50 .25
1197 A228 1000m Oil spill from ship .70 .35
1198 A228 1500m Automobile exhaust 1.00 .50
Nos. 1195-1198 (4) 2.40 1.30

Natl. Parks A229

Park, animal, map: 200m, Gorongosa, lion. 800m, Banhine, giraffes. 1000m, Bazaruto, manatees. 1500m, Zinave, ostriches.

1993, May 25 Litho. ***Perf. 11x11½***

1199 A229 200m multicolored .20 .20
1200 A229 800m multicolored .60 .30
1201 A229 1000m multicolored .70 .35
1202 A229 1500m multicolored 1.00 .50
Nos. 1199-1202 (4) 2.50 1.35

Natl. Conference on Culture — A230

1993, Sept. 27 Litho. ***Perf. 11½x11***

1203 A230 200m multicolored .20 .20

Union of Portuguese Speaking Capitals A231

1993, July 30 Litho. ***Perf. 11x11½***

1204 A231 1500m multicolored 1.75 .85

Brasilana '93.

Forest Plants — A232

Designs: 200m, Cycas cercinalis. 250m, Cycas revoluta. 900m, Encephalartos ferox. 2000m, Equisetum ramosissimum.

1993, Dec. 29 Litho. ***Perf. 11½x11***

1205 A232 200m multicolored .20 .20
1206 A232 250m multicolored .20 .20
1207 A232 900m multicolored .55 .30
1208 A232 2000m multicolored 1.25 .60
Nos. 1205-1208 (4) 2.20 1.30

Medicinal Plants — A233

1994 Litho. ***Perf. 11½x11***

1209 A233 200m Anacardium occidentale .20 .20
1210 A233 250m Sclerocarya caffra .20 .20
1211 A233 900m Annona senegalensis .55 .30
1212 A233 2000m Crinum delagoense 1.25 .65
Nos. 1209-1212 (4) 2.20 1.35

Nos. 763-764, 772, 791-792, 797-798 Surcharged

1994

Perfs. and Printing Methods as Before

1213 A109 50m on 7.50m #772 .20 .20
1214 A113 50m on 7.50m #791 .20 .20
1215 A114 50m on 7.50m #797 .20 .20
1216 A108 100m on 10m #763 .20 .20
1217 A114 100m on 12.50m #798 .20 .20
1218 A108 200m on 12.50m #764 .20 .20
1219 A113 250m on 12.50m #792 .20 .20
Nos. 1213-1219 (7) 1.40 1.40

Size and location of surcharge varies. Surcharge on Nos. 1214-1215, 1219 does not contain an obliterator.

For additional surcharge, see No. 1391.

PHILAKOREA '94 — A234

Reptiles: 300m, Ichnotropis squamulosa. 500m, Lepidachelys olivacea. 2000m, Prosyma frontalis. 3500m, Rampholeon marshalli. 4000m, Snake eating a lizard.

1994, Aug. 16 Litho. ***Perf. 11½x11***

1220 A234 300m multicolored .20 .20
1221 A234 500m multicolored .20 .20
1222 A234 2000m multicolored .85 .40
1223 A234 3500m multicolored 1.40 .70
Nos. 1220-1223 (4) 2.65 1.50

Souvenir Sheet

1224 A234 4000m multicolored 1.75 .90

ICAO, 50th Anniv. A235

Designs: 300d, Crop dusting. 500m, Airport terminal. 2000m, Passenger jet in flight. 3500m, Maintenance man inspecting jet engine.

1994, Oct. 12 Litho. ***Perf. 11x11½***

1225 A235 300m multicolored .20 .20
1226 A235 500m multicolored .30 .20
1227 A235 2000m multicolored 1.25 .60
1228 A235 3500m multicolored 2.00 1.00
Nos. 1225-1228 (4) 3.75 2.00

World Food Day — A236

1994, Oct. 24 ***Perf. 11½x11***

1229 A236 2000m multicolored 1.25 .60

Lubrapex '94.

National Elections — A237

1994, Oct. 26

1230 A237 900m multicolored .70 .35

Fight Against Illegal Drugs — A238

Designs: 500m, Couple using drugs. 1000m, Hypodermic needle, couple tied in rope, skeleton. 2000m, Man with drug dependency. 5000m, Dog apprehending man with contraband.

1994, Dec. 7

1231 A238 500m multicolored .30 .20
1232 A238 1000m multicolored .60 .30
1233 A238 2000m multicolored 1.25 .60
1234 A238 5000m multicolored 3.00 1.50
Nos. 1231-1234 (4) 5.15 2.60

Lusaka Accord, 20th Anniv. — A239

1994, Nov. 9

1235 A239 1500m multicolored .90 .45

Basketry — A240

1995, Apr. 15 Litho. ***Perf. 11½x11***

1236 A240 250m shown .20 .20
1237 A240 300m Two-handled basket .20 .20
1238 A240 1200m Round purse .55 .35
1239 A240 5000m Purse, diff. 2.25 1.25
Nos. 1236-1239 (4) 3.20 2.00

Clothing — A241

Various styles of women's traditional clothing.

1995, May 25

1240 A241 250m blue & multi .20 .20
1241 A241 300m pink & multi .20 .20
1242 A241 1200m blue & multi .55 .35
1243 A241 5000m red & multi 2.25 1.25
Nos. 1240-1243 (4) 3.20 2.00

Inauguration of Pres. Joaquim A. Chissano, Dec. 9, 1994 — A242

No. 1244: a, 900m, Natl. arms. b, 5000m, Pres. Chissano. c, 2500m, Natl. flag.

1995, June 25 Litho. ***Perf. 11½x11***
1244 A242 Strip of 3, #a.-c. 2.25 1.25

No. 1244 has a common inscription across the bottom.

Wild Animals — A243

Designs: 500m, Crassicadautus lombergi. 2000m, Tragelaphus strepsceros, horiz. 3000m, Potamochoerus porcus nyasae, horiz. 5000m, Tragelaphus scriptus.

Perf. 11½x11, 11x11½
1995, Aug. 29 Litho.
1245 A243 500m multicolored .20 .20
1246 A243 2000m multicolored .45 .25
1247 A243 3000m multicolored .65 .35
1248 A243 5000m multicolored 1.10 .55
Nos. 1245-1248 (4) 2.40 1.35

FAO, 50th Anniv. — A244

1995, Oct. 16 ***Perf. 11½x11***
1249 A244 5000m multicolored 1.10 .55

UN, 50th Anniv. — A245

1995, Oct. 24
1250 A245 5000m blue & black 1.10 .55

Nos. 647, 711, 713, 749, 763, 792, 798, 862, 929 Surcharged

Perfs. and Printing Methods as Before

1995, Oct. 4
1251 A114 250m on 12.50m #798 .20 .20
1252 A108 300m on 10m #763 .20 .20
1253 A113 500m on 12.50m #792 .20 .20
1253A A97 600m on 5m #711 — —
1254 A81 900m on 12.50m #647 .20 .20
1255 A97 1000m on 12.50m #713 .25 .20
1256 A146 1500m on 16m #929 .35 .20
1257 A130 2000m on 16m #862 .45 .25
1258 A106 2500m on 12.50m #749 .55 .30
Nos. 1251-1258 (8) 2.40 1.75

UNICEF, 20th Anniv. — A246

1995, Nov. 22 Litho. ***Perf. 11½***
1259 A246 5000m multicolored 1.10 .55

Mozambique-South Africa Soccer Match — A247

Various soccer plays.

1996, Apr. 5 Litho. ***Perf. 11x11½***
1260 A247 1000m multicolored .20 .20
1261 A247 2000m multicolored .40 .20
1262 A247 4000m multicolored .80 .40
1263 A247 6000m multicolored 1.25 .60
Nos. 1260-1263 (4) 2.65 1.40

Masks — A248

Various masks.

1996, July 2 Litho. ***Perf. 11½x11***
1264 A248 1000m multicolored .20 .20
1265 A248 2000m multicolored .40 .20
1266 A248 4000m multicolored .80 .40
1267 A248 6000m multicolored 1.25 .60
Nos. 1264-1267 (4) 2.65 1.40

Red Cross of Mozambique, 15th Anniv. — A249

1996, July 10
1268 A249 5000m multicolored .90 .45

Endangered Wildlife — A250

1996, Sept. 3 Litho. ***Perf. 11½x11***
1269 A250 1000m Loxodona africana .20 .20
1270 A250 2000m Ceratotherum simum .40 .20
1271 A250 4000m Panthera pardus .80 .40
1272 A250 6000m Scotopelia peli 1.25 .60
Nos. 1269-1272 (4) 2.65 1.40

Removal of Land Mines — A251

Designs: 2000m, Mine, tripwire across path. 6000m, Warning sign posted. 8000m, Using mine detector. 10,000m, Removing mine.

1996, Nov. 9 Litho. ***Perf. 11½x11***
1273 A251 2000m multicolored .35 .20
1274 A251 6000m multicolored 1.10 .55
1275 A251 8000m multicolored 1.40 .70
1276 A251 10,000m multicolored 1.75 .90
Nos. 1273-1276 (4) 4.60 2.35

Keep The City Clean Campaign A252

1996, Dec. 16 Litho. ***Perf. 11½x11***
1277 A252 2000m multicolored .40 .20

Mozambique Postage Stamps, 120th Anniv. — A253

1996, Dec. 16 Litho. ***Perf. 11½x11***
1278 A253 2000m No. 1 .35 .20

Mozambique Boats — A254

1997, Apr. 10 Litho. ***Perf. 11x11½***
1279 A254 2000m Mitumbui .35 .20
1280 A254 6000m Muterere 1.10 .55
1281 A254 8000m Lancha 1.40 .70
1282 A254 10,000m Dau 1.75 .90
Nos. 1279-1282 (4) 4.60 2.35

Children's Day A255

1997, June 1 Litho. ***Perf. 11x11½***
1283 A255 2000m multicolored .35 .20

Aquatic Birds A256

Designs: 2000m, Mycteria ibis. 4000m, Himantopus himantopus. 8000m, Calidris subminuta. 10,000m, Pelecanus onocrotalus.

Perf. 11½x11, 11x11½
1997, June 10
1284 A256 2000m multi, vert. .35 .20
1285 A256 4000m multi, vert. .65 .30
1286 A256 8000m multi 1.40 .65
1287 A256 10,000m multi, vert. 1.75 .85
Nos. 1284-1287 (4) 4.15 2.00

Independence of India, 50th Anniv. — A258a

1997 Litho. ***Perf. 11x11½***
1287A A258a 2000m multi .95 .45

Insects A257

Designs: 2000m, Enaretta conifera. 6000m, Zographus heiroglyphicus. 8000m, Tragiscoschema bertolonii. 10,000m, Tragocephala ducalis.

1997, July 5 Litho. ***Perf. 11x11½***
1288 A257 2000m multicolored .35 .20
1289 A257 6000m multicolored 1.00 .50
1290 A257 8000m multicolored 1.40 .70
1291 A257 10,000m multicolored 1.70 .85
a. Souvenir sheet, #1288-1291 4.50 2.25
Nos. 1288-1291 (4) 4.45 2.25

Labrapex '97 (#1291a).

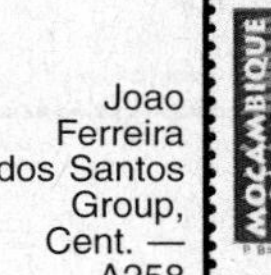

Joao Ferreira dos Santos Group, Cent. — A258

1997, Sept. 5 Litho. ***Perf. 11x11½***
1292 A258 2000m multi .40 .20

Protection of the Ozone Layer — A259

1997, Sept. 16 Litho. ***Perf. 11½x11***
1293 A259 2000m multicolored .40 .20

Peace Accord, 5th Anniv. — A260

1997, Oct. 4 Litho. ***Perf. 11½x11***
1294 A260 2000m multi .45 .25

Souvenir Sheet

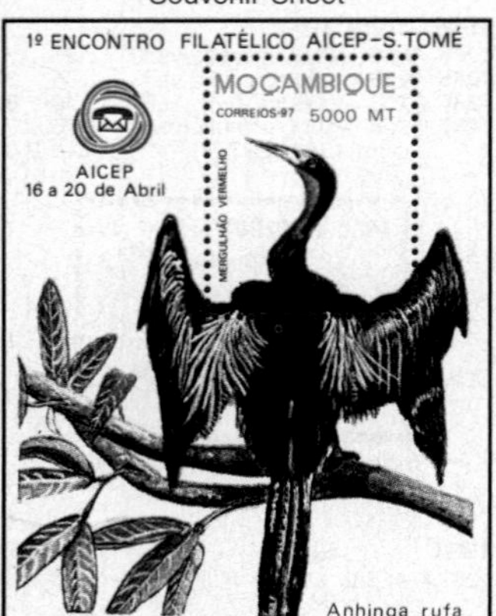

Anhinga — A261

1997 Litho. *Perf. 11½x11*
1295 A261 5000m multi 3.00 .75

Food Products A262

1998, June 1 Litho. *Perf. 11x11½*
1296 A262 2000m multicolored .35 .20

Expo '98, Lisbon A263

1998, May 22
1297 A263 2000m Coelacanth .35 .20

Nos. 660, 666, 730, 764, 797, 1002, 1009, 1011 Surcharged

Printing Methods and Perfs as before

1998 (?)
1298 A85 2000m on 12.50e #660 1.25 1.25
1299 A86 2000m on 12.50e #666 1.25 1.25
1300 A108 4000m on 12.50m #764 1.00 1.00
1301 A114 6000m on 7.50m #797 2.00 2.00
1302 A169 7500m on 16m #1002 2.75 2.50
1303 A102 10,000m on 12.50m #730 2.00 1.00
1304 A171 12,500m on 8m #1009 3.00 3.00
1305 A171 12,500m on 16m #1011 2.25 2.25
Nos. 1298-1305 (8) 15.50 14.25

For surcharges, see Nos. 1400-1400A.

Diana, Princess of Wales (1961-97) A264

Nos. 1306-1308: Various portraits.
No. 1309, 30,000m, Wearing Red Cross vest. No. 1310, 30,000m, Wearing purple dress.

1998 Litho. *Perf. 13½*
1306 A264 2000m Sheet of 9, #a.-i. 2.00 1.00
1307 A264 5000m Sheet of 9, #a.-i. 4.00 2.00
1308 A264 8000m Sheet of 9, #a.-i. 5.00 3.00

Souvenir Sheets

1309-1310 A264 Set of 2 7.50 4.00

Nos. 1309-1310 each contain one 42x60mm stamp.

No. 923 Surcharged in Silver

1998 Litho. *Perf. 14*
1311 A145 500m on 16m multi

Promotion of Breast Feeding — A265

1998 Litho. *Perf. 11½x11*
1312 A265 2000m multi .45 .25

Mother Teresa (1910-97) A266

1998 *Perf. 11x11½*
1313 A266 2000m multi .45 .25

UPAP, 18th Anniv. A267

1998, Oct. 9 *Perf. 11½x11*
1314 A267 2000m multi .45 .25

Mother's Day — A268

Designs: 2000m, Breast feeding. 4000m, Teacher. 8000m, Using computer. 10,000m, Woman in field.

1998, June 25 *Perf. 11½x11*
1315-1318 A268 Set of 4 *5.25 5.25*

For surcharge, see No. 1417.

Plants — A269

Designs: 2000m Garcinia livingstonei. 7500m, Tabernaemontana elegans. 12,500m, Ximenia caffra. 25,000m, Syzygium guineense.
50,000m, Uapaca kirkiana.

1998, Oct. 9 *Perf. 11¾x12*
1319-1322 A269 Set of 4 *6.50 6.50*

Souvenir Sheet

1323 A269 50,000m multi *7.50 7.50*

For surcharges, see Nos. 1418-1419.

Dwellings A270

Various dwellings: 2000m, 4000m, 6000m, 8000m, 10,000m, 15,000m, 20,000m, 30,000m, 50,000m, 100,000m.

1998 Litho. *Perf. 11x11¼*
1324-1333 A270 Set of 10 *25.00 25.00*

For surcharge, see No. 1399A.

Souvenir Sheets

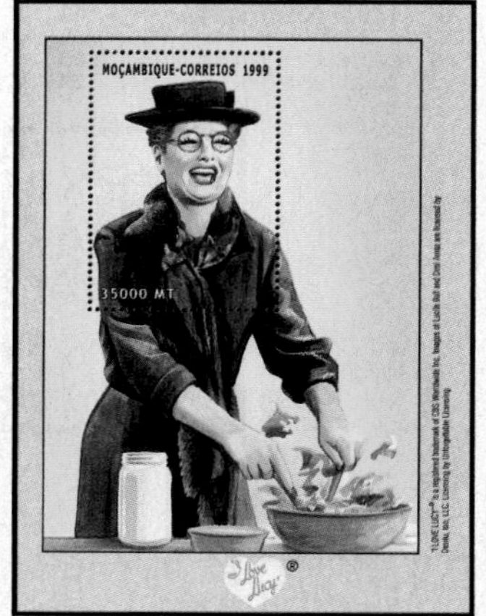

I Love Lucy — A270a

Designs: No. 1333A, 35,000m, Lucy wearing hat. No. 1333B, 35,000m, Lucy as ballet dancer.

1999 Litho. *Perf. 13½*
1333A-1333B A270a Set of 2 *6.50 3.00*

A271

Diana, Princess of Wales (1961-97) — A272

No. 1334: a, purple, shown. b, Dull brown, looking left. c, Orange brown, wearing pearls. d, Olive green. e, Purple, wearing feathers & hat, looking right. f, Red brown, wearing round earring.

No. 1335 — Diana with: a, Large white collar, earring (purple vignette). b, Hat, looking left (red violet vignette). c, White dress (red brown vignette). d, Dangling earrings (brown vignette). e, Patterned dress (blue violet vignette). f, Flower bouquet (olive green vignette).

1999 *Perf. 14*
1334 A271 6500m Sheet of 6, #a.-f. *5.00 2.00*
1335 A271 6500m Sheet of 6, #a.-f. *5.00 2.00*

Litho. & Embossed
Die Cut Perf. 7

1336 A272 25,000m gold & multi

Issued: #1336, 6/30.

The Three Stooges — A272a

No. 1336A: b, Joe Besser, Larry, Moe, frying pan. c, Shemp wearing hat. d, Moe and Larry putting pan on Joe Besser's head. e, Moe with pipe. f, Larry and Moe pouring liquids on Curly's head. g, Larry wearing hat. h, Joe Besser and Larry, pulling Moe's tooth. i, Curly. j, Shemp, Larry and Moe.

No. 1336K, 35,000m, Larry in pink shirt. No. 1336L, 35,000m, Larry holding shovel.

1999 Litho. *Perf. 13½*
1336A A272a 5000m Sheet of 9, #b-j *4.50 2.00*

Souvenir Sheets

1336K-1336L A272a Set of 2 *7.50 3.00*

Trains — A273

2000m, DE-AC Blue Tiger, Germany. #1338, 2500m, DB 218 (red & black), Germany. #1339, 3000m, Mt. Pilatus inclined railroad car, Switzerland. 3500m, Berlin subway train, Germany.

No. 1341: a, DB V200, Germany. b, Union Pacific, US. c, Class 613, Germany. d, Canadian Pacific 4242, Canada. e, Duchess of Hamilton, Great Britain. f, Pacific Delhi, India. g, ISA, South Africa. h, DR VT 18-16-07, Germany. i, DB-DE, Australia.

No. 1342: a, DB 218 (green & yellow), Germany. b, QJ Class 2-10-2, China. c, 232

232.9, Germany. d, Flying Scotsman, Scotland. e, WR 360 CH, Germany. f, Henschel 2-8-2. g, Santa Fe 39C, US. h, Balkan Express, Greece. i, DB 218 (red & white), Germany.
No. 1343, 25,000m, Steam 2-8-2, Germany. No. 1344, 25,000m, DMU, Germany.

1999, Oct. 12 Litho. *Perf. 14*

1337-1340 A273	Set of 4	1.90	1.90
1341 A273 2500m	Sheet of 9, #a.-i.	4.00	4.00
1342 A273 3000m	Sheet of 9, #a.-i.	4.75	4.75

Souvenir Sheets

1343-1344 A273	Set of 2	9.00	9.00

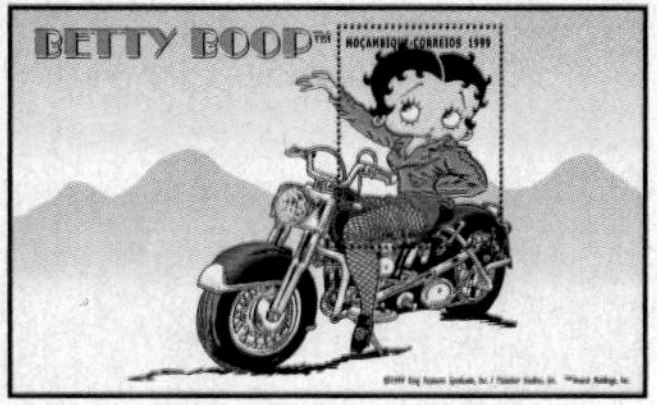

Betty Boop — A273a

No. 1344A: b, Seated on motorcycle, winking, wearing cap. c, Seated on motocycle, winking, without cap. d, Wearing cap. e, Seated on motorcycle, wearing cap, not winking. f, Hands folded across handlebars. g, Riding motorcycle. h, Hitchhiking. i, Seated on motorcycle, wearing bandana. j, Seated on motorcyle, hand raised.
No. 1344K, 35,000m, Seated on motorcycle, hand raised. No. 1344L, 35,000m, Seated next to motorcycle.

1999 Litho. *Perf. 13½*

1344A A273a 3500m	Sheet of 9, #b-j	*5.50*	*2.75*

Souvenir Sheets

1344K-1344L A273a	Set of 2	*8.00*	*3.50*

Cats — A274

No. 1345, 4000m, : a, Chartreux. b, Australian Mist. c, Egyptian Mau. d, Scottish Fold. e, Cornish Rex. f, Abyssinian.
No. 1346, 4000m: a, Himalayan. b, Balinese. c, Persian. d, Turkish Van. e, Norwegian Forest Cat. f, Maine Coon Cat.
No. 1347, 25,000m, Ragdoll. No. 1348, 25,000m, Siamese.

2000, Mar. 29 Litho. *Perf. 14*

Sheets of 6, #a-f

1345-1346 A274	Set of 2	6.50	6.50

Souvenir Sheets

1347-1348 A274	Set of 2	6.50	6.50

Dated 1999.

Dogs — A275

No. 1349, 4500m, vert.: a, Shetland sheepdog. b, Basenji. c, Poodle. d, St. Bernard. e, Shar Pei. f, Spinone Italiano.
No. 1350, 4500m, vert.: a, Jack Russell terrier. b, Schweizer Laufhund. c, Japanese Spitz. d, Australian Shepherd. e, Saluki. f, Siberian Husky.
No. 1351, 25,000m, Border Collie. No. 1352, 25,000m, Eurasier.

2000, Mar. 29 Litho. *Perf. 14*

Sheets of 6, #a-f

1349-1350 A275	Set of 2	7.00	7.00

Souvenir Sheets

1351-1352 A275	Set of 2	6.50	6.50

Dated 1999.

Dinosaurs — A276

No. 1353, 3000m: a, Pteranodon. b, Bothriospondylus. c, Iguanodon. d, Stegosaurus. e, Nodosaurus. f, Elaphrosaurus. g, "Petrolaccisaurus." h, Procompsognathus. i, Dimetrodon.
No. 1354, 3000m, : a, Plesiosaur. b, "Ceresiosaurus." c, Cryptoclidus. d, Placochelys. e, Plotosaurus. f, Ichthyosaurus. g, Platecarpus. h, Archelon. i, Mosasaur.
No. 1355, 20,000m, Tyrannosaurus Rex. No. 1356, 20,000m, "Honodus."

2000, Apr. 28

Sheets of 9, #a-i

1353-1354 A276	Set of 2	7.00	7.00

Souvenir Sheets

1355-1356 A276	Set of 2	5.25	5.25

Dated 1999.

A277

Butterflies — A278

Designs: 2000m, Palla ussheri. 2500m, Euschemon rafflesia. No. 1359, 3000m, Buttus philenor. No. 1360, 3000m, Hypolimnas bolina. 3500m, Lycorea cleobaea. 4000m, Dynastor napoleon. No. 1363, 4500m, Callimorpha dominula. 5000m, Pereute leucodrosime.
No. 1365, 4500m: a, Tisiphone abeone. b, Pseudacraea boisduvali. c, Mylothris chloris. d, Papilio glaucus. e, Mimacraea marshalli. f, Gonepteryx cleopatra.
No. 1366, 4500m: a, Palla ussheri, diff. b, Hypolimnas salmacis. c, Pereute leucodrosime, diff. d, Anteos clorinde. e, Colias eurytheme. f, Hebomoia glaucippe.
No. 1367, 4500m, horiz.: a, Thauria aliris. b, Catocala ilia. c, Colotis danae. d, Agrias claudia. e, Euploe core. f, Scoptes alphaeus.
No. 1368, 4500m, horiz.: a, Phoebis philea. b, Anteos clorinde, diff. c, Arhopala amantes. d, Mesene phareus. e, Euploea mulciber. f, Heliconius ricini.
No. 1369, 4500m, vert.: a, Euphaedra neophorn. b, Catopsilia florella. c, Charaxes bohemani. d, Junonia orithya. e, Colotis danae, diff. f, Eurytela dryope.
No. 1370, 4500m, vert.: a, Papilio demodocus. b, Kallimoides rumia. c, Danaus chrysippus. d, Palla ussheri, diff. e, Hypolimnas salmacis, diff. f, Zinina otis.
No. 1371, 20,000m, Papilio glaucus, diff. No. 1372, 20,000m, Delias mysis, horiz. No. 1373, 20,000m, Mylothris chloris, horiz. No. 1374, 20,000m, Loxura atymnus, horiz. No. 1375, 20,000m, Hemiolaus coeculus. No. 1376, 20,000m, Euxanthe wakefieldii.

2000, Apr. 28

1357-1364 A277	Set of 8	3.50	3.50

Sheets of 6, #a-f

1365-1368 A277	Set of 4	14.00	14.00
1369-1370 A278	Set of 2	7.00	7.00

Souvenir Sheets

1371-1374 A277	Set of 4	10.50	10.50
1375-1376 A278	Set of 2	5.25	5.25

Dated 1999.

Worldwide Fund for Nature — A279

No. 1377: a, Two adult gnus. b, Adult and juvenile gnus. c, Lion catching gnu. d, Adult gnu.
Illustration reduced.

2000, Apr. 28

1377 A279 6500m	Block of 4, #a-d	8.00	8.00

Dated 1999.

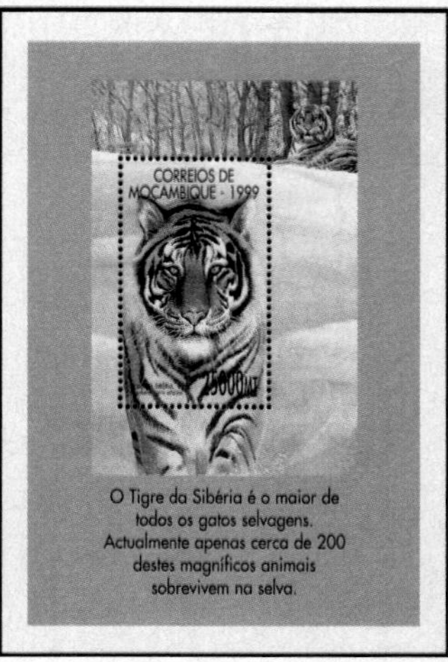

Wild Cats — A280

No. 1378, 3000m: a, Leptailurus several. b, Panthera onca. c, Panthera tigris corbetti. d, Puma concolor. e, Panthera leo persica. f, Felis pardina. g, Lepardus pardalia. h, Acinonyx jubatus. i, Felis wrangeli.
No. 1379, 3000m: a, Felis silvestris grampia. b, Felis ourata. c, Panthera tigris tigris. d, Panthera uncia. e, Felis caracal. f, Panthera pardus. g, Panthera tigris amoyensis. h, Panthera onca (spotted). i, Neofelis nabuloso.
No. 1380, 25,000m, Panthera tigris altaica. No. 1381, 25,000m, Panthera tigris, horiz.

2000, Apr. 28

Sheets of 9, #a-i

1378-1379 A280	Set of 2	7.00	7.00

Souvenir Sheets

1380-1381 A280	Set of 2	6.50	6.50

Dated 1999.

Flowers — A281

No. 1382, 3000m: a, Laetiocattleya. b, Papaver oriental. c, Anemone blanda. d, Ipoema alba. e, Phalaenopsis luma. f, Iris ensata. g, Coenagrion puella. h, Rosa raubritter. i, Iris x daylilies hybridizers.
No. 1383, 3000m: a, Lilium auratum. b, Oncidium macianthum. c, Dendrobium. d, Cobaea scandens. e, Paphiopedilum gilda. f, Papaver nudicaule. g, Colocasia esculenta. h, Carinatum tricolor. i, Phalaenopsis.
No. 1384, vert.: a, Euanthe sanderiana. b, Torenia fourleri. c, "Amor Perfeito." d, Borboleto matizada. e, Dendrobium primulinum. f, "Lasurstern" Clematite. g, Helianthus annuus. h, Jacinto grana.
No. 1385, 20,000m, Viola x wittrockiana. No. 1386, 20,000m, Nelimbo nucifera. No. 1387, 20,000m, Gerbera jamesonii. No. 1388, 20,000m, Narcissuses and anemones.
Illustration reduced.

2000, Apr. 28

Sheets of 9, #a-i

1382-1383 A281	Set of 2	7.00	7.00
1384 A281 3500m	Sheet of 8, #a-h	3.75	3.75

Souvenir Sheets

1385-1388 A281	Set of 4	10.50	10.50

Dated 1999.

Nos. 792, 797, 1147, 1153, 1154, 1156, 1214 Surcharged

2000 Methods & Perfs. As Before

1390 A114 10,000m on 7.50m #797 — —
1391 A113 10,000m on 50m on 7.50m #1214 — —
1392 A113 10,000m on 12.50m #792 —
1393 A215 17,000m on 10m #1153 — —
1393A A215 17,000m on 50m #1154 — —
1394 A213 17,000m on 125m #1147 — —
1395 A215 17,000m on 200m #1156 — —
1396 A215 17,000m on 1000m #1158 — —

No. 1393A and 1396 lack "2000" date in surcharge. No. 1391 contains "Correios — 2000) in surcharge.

The editors suspect that other surcharges may exist and would like to examine any examples.

No. 764 Surcharged in Black and Brown

2000 Litho. *Perf. 14½*

1399 A108 2000m on 12.50m #764 — —

No. 1325 Overprinted

2000 Method and Perf. as Before

1399A A270 4000m on #1325 — —

Nos. 1300, 1301 Ovptd. in Brown or Black

2000 Litho. *Perf. 14½*

1400 A108 4000m on 12.50m #1300 (BR) — —
1400A A114 6000m on 7.50m #1301 — —

Sports and Chess — A282

No. 1401, 6500m: a, Cycling. b, Volleyball. c, Boxing. d, Weight lifting. e, Fencing. f, Judo.

No. 1402, 9000m — Chess pieces: a, Six pieces, red queen at left. b, Six pieces, gray bishop fifth from left. c, Five knights. d, Six rooks, elephant rook at left. e, Six pawns. f, Six pawns, spearholder pawn at right.

No. 1403, 9500m — Chess champions: a, Paul Morphy. b, Mikhail Botvinnik. c, Emanuel Lasker. d, Wilhelm Steinitz. e, José Raul Capablanca. f, Howard Staunton.

No. 1404, 12,500m: a, Cricket batsmen and bowler. b, Three cricket batsman, one fielder. c, Polo, rider with red shirt at left. d, Polo, player wearing #1 at right. e, Golf, flag stick at right. f, Golf, woman golfer at right.

No. 1405, 14,000m: a, Tennis, woman with headband at right. b, Table tennis, players with blue shirts. c, Table tennis, player with pink shirt in center. d, Tennis, two men at left. e, Tennis, man with cap at left. f, Table tennis, player with red shirt at left.

No. 1406, 35,000m, Table tennis. No. 1407, 35,000m, Chess player Garry Kasparov.

2000 Litho. *Perf. 13¼*

Sheets of 6, #a-f

1401-1405 A282 Set of 5 45.00 22.50

Souvenir Sheets

1406-1407 A282 Set of 2 10.50 5.25

Nos. 1401-1405 each contain six 59x29mm stamps.

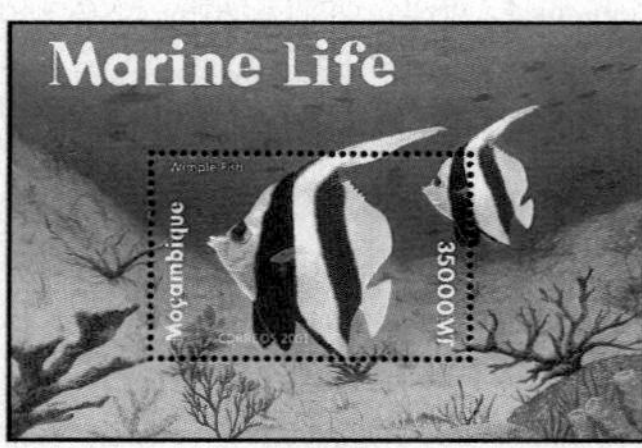

A283

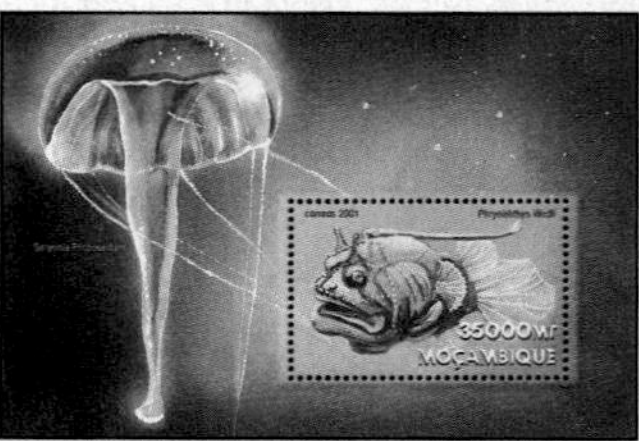

Marine Life — A284

No. 1408: a, Threadfin butterflyfish. b, Common clownfish. c, Regal tang. d, Regal angelfish. e, Copperbanded butterflyfish. f, Blue-girdled angelfish. g, Sharpnosed pufferfish. h, Humbug damselfish. i, Tailbar lionfish. j, Forcepsfish. k, Powder blue surgeon. l, Moorish idol.

No. 1409, 9500m: a, Oceanic whitetip shark. b, Gray reef shark. c, Tiger shark. d, Silky shark. e, Basking shark. f, Epaulette shark.

No. 1410, 9500m: a, Sperm whale. b, Giant squid. c, Killer whale. d, Great white shark. e, Manta ray. f, Octopus.

No. 1411, 9500m: a, Blue whale. b, Dolphinfish. c, Hammerhead shark. d, Whale shark. e, Leatherback turtle. f, Porkfish.

No. 1412, 35,000m, Wimple fish. No. 1413, 35,000m, Queen angelfish.

No. 1414, 35,000m, Phryniethys wedli. No. 1415, 35,000m, Bull shark. No. 1416, 35,000m, Spotted trunkfish.

2001, Aug. 8 *Perf. 14*

1408 A283 4550m Sheet of 12, #a-l *5.25 2.60*

Sheets of 6, #a-f

1409-1411 A284 Set of 3 *16.00 8.00*

Souvenir Sheets

1412-1413 A283 Set of 2 *6.50 3.25*
1414-1416 A284 Set of 3 *9.75 4.75*

Nos. 763, 1317, 1329 and 1330 Surcharged

Methods and Perfs As Before

2001 ?

1417 A268 3000m on 8000m #1317 — —
1418 A270 3000m on 15,000m #1329 — —
1419 A270 3000m on 20,000m #1330 — —
1420 A108 5000m on 10m #763 — —

2000 European Soccer Championships — A285

No. 1421, 10,000m: a, Luis Figo dribbling ball. b, Fernando Couto. c, Figo diving. d, Sergio Conceicao. e, Nuno Gomes. f, Rui Costa.

No. 1422, 17,000m: a, Nicolas Anelka. b, Didier Deschamps. c, Emmanuel Petit. d, Thierry Henry. e, Marcel Desailly. f, Zinedine Zidane.

No. 1422G, 75,000m, Zinedine Zidane. No. 1422H, 75,000m, Rivaldo.

2001 Litho. *Perf. 13¼x12¾*

Sheets of 6, #a-f

1421-1422 A285 Set of 2 14.00 14.00

Souvenir Sheets

1422G-1422H A285 Set of 2 13.00 13.00

2000 Summer Olympics Medalists — A286

No. 1423, 8500m: a, Domenico Fivaranti. b, Stacy Dragila. c, Pieter van den Hoogenband. d, David O'Connor. e, Venus Williams. f, Maurice Greene. g, Joy Fawcett. h, Marion Jones. i, Patricio Ormazabal and Jeff Agoos.

No. 1424, 10,000m: a, Agnes Kovacs. b, Youila Raksina. c, Kong Linghui and Liu Guoliang. d, Nicolas Gill. e, Anky van Grunsven. f, Brian Olson. g, Wang Nan. h, Megan Quann. i, Venus Williams.

No. 1425, 17,000m: a, Vince Carter. b, Blaine Wilson. c, Steve Keir. d, Wen Xiao Wang and Chris Xu. e, Venus and Serena Williams. f, Gu Jun and Ge Fei.

No. 1426, 20,000m: a, Clara Hughes. b, Martina Hingis. c, Otilla Badescu. d, Isabel Fernandez. e, Coralie Simmons. f, Mia Hamm.

No. 1427, 28,000m: a, Patrick Rafter. b, Tadahiro Nomura. c, Seiko Iseki. d, Michael Dodge. e, Ann Dow. f, David Beckham.

No. 1428, 50,000m, Andre Agassi. No. 1429, 50,000m, Chang Jun Gao and Michelle Do. No. 1430, 50,000m, Kong Linghui. No. 1431, 100,000m, Michelle Do. No. 1432, 100,000m, Serena Williams. No. 1433, Christophe Legout.

2001 Litho.

Sheets of 9, #a-i

1423-1424 A286 Set of 2 10.00 10.00

Sheets of 6, #a-f

1425-1427 A286 Set of 3 15.00 15.00

Souvenir Sheets

1428-1433 A286 Set of 6 20.00 20.00

Chess Champions — A287

No. 1434, 10,000m: a, Mikhail Botvinnik. b, Garry Kasparov. c, Wilhelm Steinitz. d, Emanuel Lasker. e, Paul Morphy. f, Anatoly Karpov. g, Tigran Petrossian. h, Mikhail Tal. i, José Raul Capablanca.

No. 1435, 10,000m: a, Judith Polgar (wearing brown sweater). b, Xie Jun. c, Zsuza Polgar. d, Nana Ioseliani. e, Alisa Galliamova. f, Judith Polgar (head in hands). g, Judith Polgar (wearing blouse). h, Monica Calzetta. i, Anjelina Belakovskaia.

No. 1436, 100,000m, Kasparov. No. 1437, 100,000m, Judith Polgar.

2001 *Perf. 13¼x12¾*

Sheets of 9, #a-i

1434-1435 A287 Set of 2 8.00 8.00

Souvenir Sheets

1436-1437 A287 Set of 2 10.00 10.00

2002 Winter Olympics, Salt Lake City — A288

No. 1438, 17,000m: a, Martin Brodeur. b, Svetlana Vysokova. c, Ray Bourque and Patrik Elias. d, Rachel Belliveau. e, Scott Gomez and Janne Laukkanen. f, Sonja Nef.

No. 1439, 20,000m: a, Rusty Smith. b, Sandra Schmirler. c, Totmianina and Marinin. d, Brigitte Obermoser. e, Roman Turek. f, Jennifer Heil.

No. 1440, 28,000m: a, Kovarikova and Novotny. b, Li Song. c, Armin Zoeggeler. d, Michael von Gruenigen. e, Tami Bradley. f, Chris Drury, Turner Stevenson and Greg de Vries.

No. 1441, 50,000m, Armin Zoeggeler. No. 1442, 75,000m, Tommy Salo. No. 1443, 100,000m, Jayne Torvill and Christopher Dean.

2001 Litho.

Sheets of 6, #a-f

1438-1440 A288 Set of 3 15.00 15.00

Souvenir Sheets

1441-1443 A288 Set of 3 12.00 12.00

On illustrated sheets lacking design information the lettering of minors starts with the upper left stamp, goes right and down and ends with the lower right stamp.

2002 World Cup Soccer Championships, Japan and Korea — A289

No. 1444: a, Filippo Inzaghi. b, Georghe Hagi. c, Gabriel Batistuta pointing. d, Mateja Kezman. e, Ivan Zamorano. f, Michael Owen wearing blue uniform.

No. 1445: a, Marcio Amoroso. b, Alessandro Nesta. c, Robbie Keane. d, Michel Owen kicking ball. e, Stefan Effenberg. f, Oliver Kahn.

No. 1446: a, Zinedine Zidane without ball. b, Zoran Mirkovic. c, Robbie Fowler with fist raised. d, Romario wearing red jersey. e, Francesco Totti. f, Ryan Giggs.

No. 1447: a, Javier Saviola. b, Alan Smith. c, Raul Gonzalez. d, Dwight Yorke. e, Joe Cole. f, David Beckham wearing red jersey.

No. 1448: a, Angelo Peruzzi. b, Jaap Stam. c, Jamie Redknapp. d, Rivaldo with ball at feet. e, Alan Shearer. f, Boudewijn Zenden.

No. 1449: a, Hernan Jorge Crespo. b, Gianluigi Buffon. c, Arnold Bruggink. d, Antonio Cassano. e, Mohamed Kallon. f, Jonathan Bachini.

No. 1450: a, Didier Deschamps. b, Cafu wearing green jersey. c, Dennis Bergkamp. d, Lilian Thuram. e, David Beckham wearing red jersey, diff. f, Francesco Totti, diff. g, Carsten Jancker. h, Martin Palermo. i, Andy Cole running left.

No. 1451: a, David Beckham sitting on ball. b, Edgar Davids wearing orange shirt. c, Michael Owen with hands on ball. d, Andy Cole with one leg raised. e, Ronaldo sitting. f, Emmanuel Petit with ball. g, Rivaldo with ball at chest. h, Robbie Fowler looking at ball. i, Romario wearing blue jacket.

No. 1453: a, Shinji Ono. b, Rigobert Song. c, Matias Jesus Almeyda. d, Ronaldinho. e, Gabriel Batistuta wearing striped jersey. f, Rivaldo sitting on ground. g, Thierry Henry. h, Zinedine Zidane kicking ball. i, Ronaldo with ball.

No. 1454: a, Florain Maurice. b, Nicolas Anelka. c, Zinedine Zidane without ball, wearing striped jersey. d, Kazuyoshi Miura. e, Patrick Vieira. f, Gianfranco Zola. g, Emmanuel Petit without ball. h, Roberto Carlos. i, Teddy Sheringham.

No. 1455, 75,000m, Fabien Barthez. No. 1456, 75,000m, Edgar Davids wearing striped shirt. No. 1457, 75,000m, Cafu wearing red shirt.

No. 1458, 100,000m, Ronaldo wearing striped uniform. No. 1459, 100,000m, Romario wearing yellow shirt. No. 1460, 100,000m, Rivaldo dribbling ball. No. 1461, 100,000m, Nwankwo Kanu. No. 1462, 100,000m, Michael Owen wearing yellow shirt. No. 1463, 100,000m, Franz Beckenbauer. No. 1464, 100,000m, Pelé. No. 1465, 100,000m, Diego Maradona.

2001 **Litho.** ***Perf. 13¼x12¾***

1444	A289	5000m	Sheet of 6, #a-f	2.60	2.60
1445	A289	10,000m	Sheet of 6, #a-f	5.25	5.25
1446	A289	12,000m	Sheet of 6, #a-f	6.25	6.25
1447	A289	15,000m	Sheet of 6, #a-f	8.00	8.00
1448	A289	17,000m	Sheet of 6, #a-f	9.00	9.00
1449	A289	20,000m	Sheet of 6, #a-f	10.50	10.50
	Nos. 1444-1449 (6)			41.60	41.60
1450	A289	5000m	Sheet of 9, #a-i	4.00	4.00
1451	A289	5000m	Sheet of 9, #a-i	4.00	4.00
1453	A289	8500m	Sheet of 9, #a-i	6.75	6.75
1454	A289	8500m	Sheet of 9, #a-i	6.75	6.75
	Nos. 1450-1454 (4)			21.50	21.50

Souvenir Sheets

1455-1457	A289	Set of 3	2.00	2.00
1458-1465	A289	Set of 8	70.00	70.00

On illustrated sheets lacking design information, the lettering of minors starts with the upper left stamp, continues right and down and ends with the lower right stamp.

Paintings

Madonna Paintings — A290

Alfred Sisley — A291

Hieronymus Bosch — A292

Pieter Brueghel — A293

Paul Cézanne — A294

Salvador Dali — A295

Henri Matisse — A296

Michelangelo — A297

Vincent van Gogh — A298

Johannes Vermeer — A299

Michelangelo — A300

Amadeo Modigliani — A301

Gustav Klimt — A303

Perf. 13¼x12¾

2001, Dec. 28 **Litho.**

1466	A290	5000m	Sheet of 6 #a-f	2.60	2.60
1467	A291	10,000m	Sheet of 6, #a-f	5.25	5.25
1468	A292	12,000m	Sheet of 6, #a-f	6.25	6.25
1469	A293	12,000m	Sheet of 6, #a-f	6.25	6.25
1470	A294	12,000m	Sheet of 6, #a-f	6.25	6.25
1471	A295	12,000m	Sheet of 6, #a-f	6.25	6.25
1472	A296	12,000m	Sheet of 6, #a-f	6.25	6.25
1473	A297	12,000m	Sheet of 6, #a-f	6.25	6.25
1474	A298	12,000m	Sheet of 6, #a-f	6.25	6.25
1475	A299	12,000m	Sheet of 6, #a-f	6.25	6.25
1476	A300	15,000m	Sheet of 6, #a-f	8.00	8.00
1477	A301	15,000m	Sheet of 6, #a-f	8.00	8.00
1479	A303	28,000m	Sheet of 6, #a-f	15.00	15.00
	Nos. 1466-1479 (13)			88.85	88.85

Paintings

Marc Chagall — A304

Salvador Dali — A305

Edgar Degas — A306

Paul Delvaux — A307

Paul Gauguin — A308

Pablo Picasso — A309

Pierre Auguste Renoir — A310

Henri de Toulouse-Lautrec — A311

Vincent van Gogh — A312

Pablo Picasso — A313

Individual stamps depicting various works of art lack titles. On Nos. 1489-1512 artist name is in margin.

No. 1489, Pieter Breughel. No. 1490, Lucas Cranach. No. 1491, Paul Delvaux. No. 1492, El Greco. No. 1493, Wassily Kandinsky. No. 1494, Gustav Klimt. No. 1495, Johannes Vermeer. No. 1496, Paul Cézanne. No. 1497, Marc Chagall. No. 1498, Albrecht Dürer. No. 1499, Thomas Gainsborough. No. 1500, Francisco de Goya. No. 1501, Edouard Manet. No. 1502, Claude Monet. No. 1503, Henri Matisse. No. 1504, Camille Pissarro. No. 1505, Vincent van Gogh. No. 1506, Salvador Dali. No. 1507, Paul Gauguin. No. 1508, Joan Miró. No. 1509, Amadeo Modigliani. No. 1511, Picasso, diff. No. 1512, Henri de Toulouse-Lautrec. No. 1513, Religious icon.

Perf. 13¾x12¾

2001, Dec. 28 **Litho.**

1480 A304 10,000m Sheet of 9, #a-i 6.75 6.75
1481 A305 10,000m Sheet of 9, #a-i 6.75 6.75
1482 A306 10,000m Sheet of 9, #a-i 6.75 6.75
1483 A307 10,000m Sheet of 9, #a-i 6.75 6.75
1484 A308 10,000m Sheet of 9, #a-i 6.75 6.75
1485 A309 10,000m Sheet of 9, #a-i 6.75 6.75
1486 A310 10,000m Sheet of 9, #a-i 6.75 6.75
1487 A311 10,000m Sheet of 9, #a-i 6.75 6.75
1488 A312 10,000m Sheet of 9, #a-i 6.75 6.75
Nos. 1480-1488 (9) 60.75 60.75

Souvenir Sheets

1489 A313 50,000m multi 3.75 3.75
1490 A313 50,000m multi 3.75 3.75
1491 A313 50,000m multi 3.75 3.75
1492 A313 50,000m multi 3.75 3.75
1493 A313 50,000m multi 3.75 3.75
1494 A313 50,000m multi 3.75 3.75
1495 A313 50,000m multi 3.75 3.75
1496 A313 75,000m multi 5.75 5.75
1497 A313 75,000m multi 5.75 5.75
1498 A313 75,000m multi 5.75 5.75
1499 A313 75,000m multi 5.75 5.75
1500 A313 75,000m multi 5.75 5.75
1501 A313 75,000m multi 5.75 5.75
1502 A313 75,000m multi 5.75 5.75
1503 A313 75,000m multi 5.75 5.75
1504 A313 75,000m multi 5.75 5.75
1505 A313 75,000m multi 5.75 5.75
1506 A313 100,000m multi 7.50 7.50
1507 A313 100,000m multi 7.50 7.50
1508 A313 100,000m multi 7.50 7.50
1509 A313 100,000m multi 7.50 7.50
1510 A313 100,000m shown 7.50 7.50
1511 A313 100,000m multi 7.50 7.50
1512 A313 100,000m multi 7.50 7.50
1513 A313 100,000m multi 7.50 7.50
Nos. 1489-1513 (25) 143.75 143.75

Souvenir Sheet

Lance Armstrong, Cyclist — A314

2001 **Litho.** ***Perf. 13¼x12¾***
1514 A314 100,000m multi 8.75 8.75

2004 Olympic Games, Athens.

New Year 2002 (Year of the Horse) — A315

No. 1515 — Chinese characters in: a, Yellow. b, Purple. c, Pink. d, Brown.
22,000m, Maroon, vert.

2002, May 6 **Litho.** ***Perf. 13¼***
1515 A315 11,000m Sheet of 4, #a-d 3.75 3.75

Souvenir Sheet

Perf. 13½x13¼

1516 A315 22,000m multi 1.90 1.90

No. 1516 contains one 28x42mm stamp.

2002 Winter Olympics, Salt Lake City A316

Designs: 10,000m, Freestyle skiing. 17,000m, Freestyle skiing, vert.

Perf. 13¼x13½, 13½x13¼

2002, May 6

1517-1518 A316 Set of 2 2.40 2.40

Intl. Year of Mountains A317

Designs: No. 1519, 17,000m, Mt. Namuli. No. 1520, 17,000m, Mt. Binga.

No. 1521: a, Mt. Kenya, Kenya. b, Mt. Cook, New Zealand. c, Mt. Ararat, Turkey. d, Mt. Paine, Chile. e, Mt. Everest, Nepal. f, Mt. Kilimanjaro, Tanzania.
50,000m, Zugspitze, Germany.

2002, May 6 ***Perf. 13¼x13½***
1519-1520 A317 Set of 2 3.00 3.00
1521 A317 17,000m Sheet of 6, #a-f 8.75 8.75

Souvenir Sheet

1522 A317 50,000m multi 4.25 4.25

20th World Scout Jamboree, Thailand — A318

No. 1523, horiz.: a, 1933 Jamboree patch. b, 19th World Jamboree patch. c, Patch and mascot. d, Jamboree emblem, scout.
No. 1524, Scout.

2002, May 6 ***Perf. 13¼x13½***
1523 A318 28,000m Sheet of 4, #a-d 9.50 9.50

Souvenir Sheet

Perf. 13½x13¼

1524 A318 28,000m multi 2.40 2.40

Amerigo Vespucci (1452-1512), Explorer — A319

No. 1525, horiz.: a, Vespucci observing stars. b, Brotogeris chiriri, ship. c, Huts, ship.
50,000m, Map of voyages to South America.

2002, May 6 ***Perf. 13¼x13½***
1525 A319 30,000m Sheet of 3, #a-c 7.75 7.75

Souvenir Sheet

Perf. 13½x13¼

1526 A319 50,000m multi 4.25 4.25

Ships — A320

No. 1527, 13,500m: a-f, Various unnamed ships (shown).
No. 1528, 13,500m: a, Viking ship. b, Kayak. c, Gondola, bridge. d, Fishing boat. e, Light ship. f, Tugboat.
No. 1529, 40,000m, Aircraft carrier. No. 1530, 40,000m, Ship's figurehead, vert.

Perf. 13¼x13½, 13½x13¼

2002, May 6

Sheets of 6, #a-f

1527-1528 A320 Set of 2 14.00 14.00

Souvenir Sheets

1529-1530 A320 Set of 2 6.75 6.75

2002 World Cup Soccer Championships, Japan and Korea — A321

No. 1531, 28,000m: a, Zico. b, 1958 World Cup poster. c, Flag, player from Nigeria. d, Flag, player from Morocco. e, Gwangju Stadium, Korea, horiz. (56x42mm).

No. 1532, 28,000m: a, 1966 World Cup poster. b, Paolo Rossi. c, Flag, player from Denmark. d, Flag, player from Colombia. e, Inchon Munhak Stadium, Korea, horiz. (56x42mm)

No. 1533, 50,000m, Pele. No. 1534, 50,000m, Morlock, horiz.

Perf. 13½x13¼, 13¼x13½

2002, May 6

Sheets of 5, #a-e

1532-1533	A321	Set of 2	*12.00*	*12.00*

Souvenir Sheets

1534-1535	A321	Set of 2	*6.00*	*6.00*

A322

A323

Princess Diana (1961-97) — A324

No. 1538, 50,000m, Brown background. No. 1539, 50,000m, Purple background. No. 1540, 50,000m, Pink lilac background.

2002, May 6 ***Perf. 13½x13¼***

1535 A322 28,000m Sheet of 4, #a-d		5.00	5.00
1536 A323 28,000m Sheet of 4, #a-d		5.00	5.00
1537 A324 28,000m Sheet of 4, #a-d		5.00	5.00
Nos. 1535-1537 (3)		15.00	15.00

Souvenir Sheets

1538-1540 A324	Set of 3	10.00	10.00

Butterflies — A325

Designs: 5000m, Papilio demoleus. No, 1542, 10,000m, Euschemom rafflesia. 17,000m, Liphyra brassolis. 28,000m, Mimacraea marshalli.

No. 1545, 10,000m: a, Eurema brigitta. b, Loxura atymunus. c, Arhopala amantes. d, Junonia coenia. e, Eurides isabella. f, Hiliconius ricini. g, Zipaetis scylax. h, Cepheuptychia cephus. i, Philaethria dido.

No. 1546, 10,000m: a, Parides coon. b, Delias mysis. c, Troides brookiana. d, Syrmatia dorilas. e, Danis danis. f, Lycaena dispar. g, Mesene phareus. h, Kallima inachus. i, Morpho rhetenor.

No. 1547, 50,000m, Papilio cresphontes. No. 1548, 50,000m, Ornithoptera alexandrae caterpillar.

2002, June 17 ***Perf. 14***

1541-1544 A325	Set of 4	5.25	5.25

Sheets of 9, #a-i

1545-1546 A325	Set of 2	16.00	16.00

Souvenir Sheets

1547-1548 A325	Set of 2	8.50	8.50

Fauna, Flora and Mushrooms — A326

No. 1549, 10,000m: a, Pandion haliaetus. b, Flying squirrel. c, Fox squirrel. d, Agelaius phoeniceus. e, Papilio polyxenes. f, Didelphus virginiana. g, Hyla crucifer. h, Odocoileus virginianus, standing. i, Procyon lotor.

No. 1550, 10,000m: a, Heraclides cresphontes. b, Tyto alba. c, Drocopus pileatus. d, Cypripedium parviflorum, Archilochus colobris. e, Vulpes vulpes. f, Odocoileus virginianus. g, Enallagma sp. h, Amanita muscaria. i, Tamiasciurus hudsonicus.

2002, June 17 ***Perf. 14***

Sheets of 9, #a-i

1549-1550 A326	Set of 2	8.00	8.00

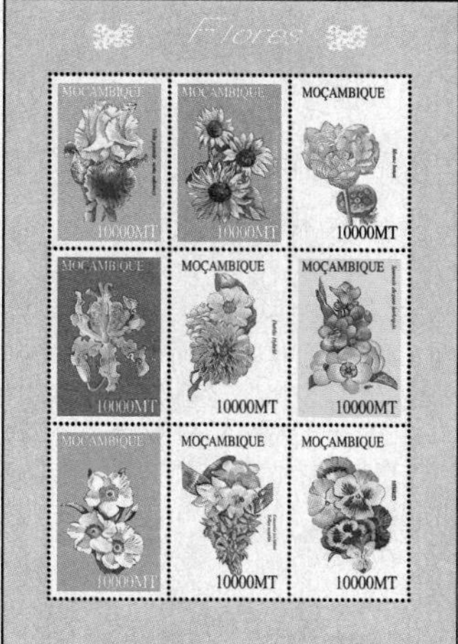

Flowers — A327

No. 1551, 10,000m: a, Viola jeannie, Viola cultivar. b, Sunflower Moonshadow. c, Momo botan. d, Schomburgkia orchid. e, Dahlia hybrid. f, Sparaxis elegans harlequin. g, Dianhus. h, Camassia leichtlinii, Tulipa saxatilis. i, Pansy hybrid.

No. 1552, 10,000m, horiz.: a, Hemerocallis. b, Narcissus (Nazcissys). c, Hybrid tea rose. d, Rainbow Promised Cayenne Capers and flying insect. e, Anemone cordnazia. f, Hymenocallis narcissiflora. g, Hymenocallis. h, Tulipa. i, Lachenalia aloides, Meconopsis poppies.

No. 1553, 10,000m, horiz.: a, Narcissus. b, L. bulbiferun var. Croceum. c, Iris purpureobractea. d, Neomarica caerulea. e, Peonia lactiflora, Primula chungensis, Viola cornuta. f, Rainbow Promised Cayenne Capers and beetle. g, Iris purpureobractea (puzpuzeobractea). h, Tuberous begonia cultivar. i, Oriental hybrid lily.

2002, June 17 ***Perf. 14***

Sheets of 9, #a-i

1551-1553 A327	Set of 3	10.00	10.00

Dogs, Cats and Horses — A328

No. 1554, 17,000m — Dogs: a, Labrador retriever. b, Bulldog. c, Cocker spaniel. d, Golden retriever. e, Boxer. f, Bloodhound.

No. 1555, 17,000m — Cats: a, Maine Coon. b, Cornish Rex. c, La Perm. d, Sphynx. e, Siamese. f, Persian.

No. 1556, 17,000m — Horses: a, Hanoverian. b, Haflinger. c, Nonius. d, Belgian heavy drafts. e, Australian-bred Arab. f, Thoroughbred.

No. 1557, 40,000m, Basset hound. No. 1558, 50,000m, Chestnut Oriental Longhair cat. No. 1559, 50,000m, Don horses.

2002, June 17 ***Perf. 13¼***

Sheets of 6, #a-f

1554-1556 A328	Set of 3	10.00	10.00

Souvenir Sheets

1557-1559 A328	Set of 3	6.00	6.00

Dinosaurs A329

Designs: 5000m, Protosaurus. No. 1561, 10,000m, Psittacosaurus. 17,000m, Torosaurus. 28,000m, Triceratops.

No. 1564, 10,000m: a, Diplodocus head. b, Pterosaurs. c, Diplodocuses. d, Afrovenator. e, Parasaurolophus. f, Ramphorhynchus. g, Lambeosaur. h, Euoplocephalus. i, Cynodont.

No. 1565, 10,000m: a, Brachiosaur. b, Monoclonius. c, Homalocephalus. d, Pterodactyl. e, Deinonychus. f, Archaeopteryx. g, Cretaceous landscape. h, Hypsilophodon. i, Lystrosaur.

No. 1566, 50,000m, Baryonyx. No. 1567, 50,000m, Styracosaurus, vert.

2002, June 17 ***Perf. 14***

1560-1563 A329	Set of 4	5.25	5.25

Sheets of 9, #a-i, + 3 labels

1564-1565 A329	Set of 2	10.00	10.00

Souvenir Sheets

1566-1567 A329	Set of 2	6.00	6.00

A330 Birds — A331

Designs: No. 1568, 5000m, Tachymarptis melba. No. 1569, 5000m, Falco tinnunculus. No. 1570, 10,000m, Pitta angolensis. No. 1571, 10,000m, Ardea cinerea. No. 1572, 17,000m, Corythaeola cristata. No. 1573, 28,000m, Butastur rufipennis.

No. 1574, 5000m, Creagrus furcatus. No. 1575, 10,000m, Larosterna inca. No. 1576, 17,000m, Pelecanus crispus. No. 1577, 28,000m, Morus bassanus.

No. 1578, 10,000m: a, Phaeton aethereus. b, Catharacta maccormicki. c, Diomedea bulleri. d, Puffinus iherminieri. e, Oceanites oceanicus. f, Pterodroma hasitata. g, Fregata magnificens. h, Sula nebouxii. i, Uria aagle.

No. 1579, 17,000m: a, Psittacus erithacus. b, Ficedula hypleuca. c, Tchagra senegala. d, Oriolus oriolus. e, Luscinia megarhynchos. f, Halcyon malimbica.

No. 1580, 17,000m: a, Coracias garrulus. b, Estrilda astrild. c, Upupa epops. d, Merops apiaster. e, Ploceus cucullatus. f, Clamator glandarius.

No. 1581, 50,000m, Falco subbuteo. No. 1582, 50,000m, Strix varia. No. 1583, 50,000m, Butorides striatus. No. 1584, 50,000m, Actophilornis africanus, horiz.

No. 1585, 50,000m, Spheniscus demersus. No. 1586, 50,000m, Rhynchops niger, horiz.

2002, June 17

1568-1573 A330	Set of 6	6.50	6.50
1574-1577 A331	Set of 4	5.25	5.25
1578 A331 10,000m Sheet of 9, #a-i		7.75	7.75

Sheets of 6, #a-f

1579-1580 A330	Set of 2	17.50	17.50

Souvenir Sheets

1581-1584 A330	Set of 4	17.00	17.00
1585-1586 A331	Set of 2	8.50	8.50

Worldwide Fund for Nature (WWF) A332

African savannah elephant: Nos. 1587a, 1588a, Herd. Nos. 1587b, 1588b, And birds. Nos. 1587c, 1588c, With juvenile. Nos. 1587d, 1588d, With rainbow.

2002, Sept. 20 ***Perf. 13¼x13½***

Size: 40x26½mm

Large Year

1587	Strip of 4	7.50	7.50
a.-d.	A332 19,000m Any single	1.75	1.75

Size: 39x25mm

Small Year

1588	Miniature sheet of 4 + 4 labels	9.50	9.50
a.-d.	A332 19,000m Any single	2.25	2.25

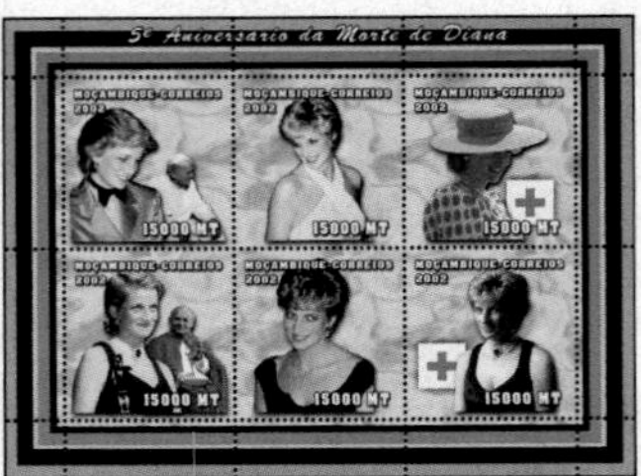

Princess Diana — A333

Pope John Paul II — A334

Elvis Presley — A335

Marilyn Monroe — A336

Marilyn Monroe — A337

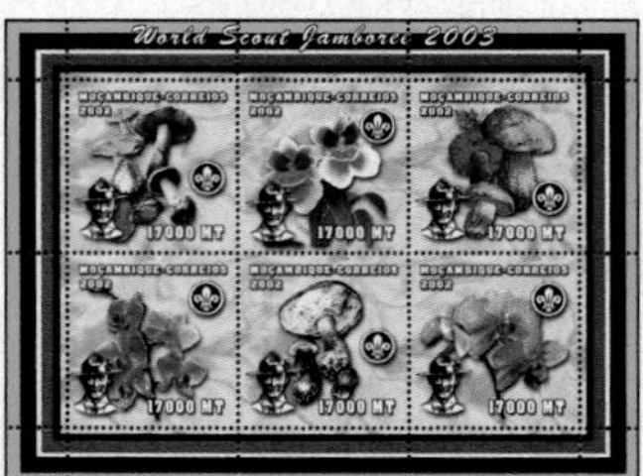

Lord Robert Baden-Powell, Scout Emblem, Mushrooms and Flowers — A338

Astronauts and the Concorde — A339

Composers — A340

Louis Pasteur and Dogs — A341

Robert Stephenson and Locomotives — A342

Pope John Paul II — A343

Pope John Paul II, Madonna and Child — A344

Pope John Paul II, Madonna and Child — A345

Robert Stephenson — A346

Robert Stephenson — A347

No. 1593 — Famous men: a, Henri Dunant. b, Theodore Roosevelt. c, Albert Einstein. d, Ernest Hemingway. e, Thomas Nast. f, Albert Camus.

No. 1594 — Egyptian rulers: a, Seti I. b, Djedefre. c, Smekhkare. d, Seti II. e, Senusret III. f, Tutankhamun.

No. 1597: a, Michael Collins. b, Concorde. c, John Glenn. d, Concorde, diff. e, Neil Armstrong. f, Concorde, diff.

No. 1598 — Chess players and pieces: a, Tigran Petrosian, Lions emblem. b, Robert Fischer, Rotary emblem. c, Boris Spassky, Lions emblem. d, Raul Capablanca, Rotary emblem. e, Max Euwe, Lions emblem. f, Emanuel Lasker, Rotary emblem.

No. 1599 — Nobel Prize winners: a, Albert Einstein. b, Dalai Lama. c, Winston Churchill. d, Hideki Yukawa. e, Albert Schweitzer. f, Linus Pauling.

No. 1600 — Scout emblem and: a, Lord Robert Baden-Powell. b, Morpho aega, Baden-Powell. c, Prepona meander, Baden-Powell. d, Charaxes bernardus, Baden-Powell. e, Hypolimnas salmacis, Baden-Powell. f, Morpho rhetenor, Baden-Powell.

No. 1601 — Egyptian rulers: a, Netjenkhet Djoser. b, Tutankhamun. c, Neferefre. d, Amenhotep III. e, Pepi I. f, Amenmesses.

No. 1602 — Composers: a, Antonio Vivaldi. b, Franz Liszt. c, Ludwig van Beethoven. d, Wolfgang Mozart.

No. 1603 — Famous Men: a, Che Guevara. b, Pope John Paul II (blue gray background). c, Dr. Martin Luther King, Jr. d, Mao Zedong.

No. 1604 — Princess Diana and Pope John Paul II: a, Princess Diana in deep blue dress. b, Diana holding flowers. c, Pope John Paul II, hand showing. d, Pope John Paul II.

No. 1605 — Nelson Mandela and: a, Heulandite. b, Adamite. c, Wulfenite. d, Hemimorphite.

No. 1606 — Auto racing: a, Ayrton Senna. b, Modern race car. c, Old race car. d, Juan Manuel Fangio.

No. 1607 — Egyptian queens (tan background): a, Nefertiti facing right. b, Cleopatra VII. c, Nefertiti facing left. d, Nefertiti facing forward.

No. 1608 — Egyptian rulers (gray background): a, Nefertari. b, Tutankhamun. c, Tuthmosis. d, Nefertiti.

No. 1609 — Egyptian rulers (green background): a, Amenhotemp II. b, Merenptah. c, Amenophis IV. d, Tuthmosis.

No. 1610 — Famous people: a, Dalai Lama. b, Mother Teresa. c, Pope John Paul II. d, Mahatma Gandhi.

No. 1611 — Explorers: a, Vasco da Gama. b, Ferdinand Magellan. c, Christopher Columbus. d, Amerigo Vespucci.

No. 1612 — Aviation: a, Antoine de Saint-Exupéry. b, Charles Lindbergh standing. c, Lindbergh seated. d, Concorde.

No. 1613 — Lions and Rotary Founders: a, Paul Harris (color picture), Rotary emblem. b, Melvin Jones (sepia picture), Lions emblem. c, Harris (sepia picture), Rotary emblem. d, Jones (color picture), Lions emblem.

No. 1614 — Film personalities: a, Charlie Chaplin. b, Frank Sinatra. c, Alfred Hitchcock. d, Walt Disney.

No. 1615: a, Scipionyx. b, Beipiaosaurus. c, Haroun Tazieff and vanadinite. d, Tazieff and adamite.

No. 1616 — Famous men: a, Winston Churchill. b, John F. Kennedy. c, Konrad Adenauer. d, Charles de Gaulle.

No. 1619 — Scientists: a, Charles Darwin, Byronosaurus. b, Alexander Fleming, Tricholoma terreum. c, Fleming, Boletus edulis. d, Darwin, Irratator.

No. 1620 — Famous men: a, Albert Schweitzer. b, Claude Bernard. c, Henri Dunant. d, Raoul Follerau.

No. 1621: a, John J. Audubon. b, Audubon, Aix sponsa. c, Audubon, Toxastoma montanum, Ixoreus naevius. d, Audubon, Loxia leucoptera.

No. 1625, John Glenn. No. 1626, Lord Robert Baden-Powell. No. 1627, Victor Hugo. No. 1628, John F. Kennedy. No. 1629, Princess Diana. No. 1630, Wolfgang Mozart. No. 1631, Alexander Fleming. No. 1632, Garry Kasparov. Nos. 1633, 1634, Marilyn Monroe. No. 1635, Mother Teresa. No. 1636, Henri Dunant. No. 1637, Nelson Mandela. No. 1638, Elvis Presley. No. 1639, Vasco da Gama. No. 1640, Paul Emile Victor. No. 1641, Tutankhamun. No. 1642, Nefertiti. No. 1643, John J. Audubon, Patagioenas leucophal. No. 1644, Audubon, Quiscalus quiscula.

2002, Sept. 30 ***Perf. 13¼x12¾***

1589	A333 15,000m Sheet of 6, #a-f	7.75	7.75
1590	A334 15,000m Sheet of 6, #a-f	7.75	7.75
1591	A335 15,000m Sheet of 6, #a-f	7.75	7.75
1592	A336 15,000m Sheet of 6, #a-f	7.75	7.75
1593	A336 15,000m Sheet of 6, #a-f	7.75	7.75
1594	A336 15,000m Sheet of 6, #a-f	7.75	7.75
1595	A337 17,000m Sheet of 6, #a-f	8.75	8.75
1596	A338 17,000m Sheet of 6, #a-f	8.75	8.75
1597	A339 17,000m Sheet of 6, #a-f	8.75	8.75
1598	A339 17,000m Sheet of 6, #a-f	8.75	8.75
1599	A339 17,000m Sheet of 6, #a-f	8.75	8.75
1600	A339 17,000m Sheet of 6, #a-f	8.75	8.75
1601	A339 17,000m Sheet of 6, #a-f	8.75	8.75

1602	A340	5000m	Sheet of 4, #a-d	1.75	1.75
1603	A340	20,000m	Sheet of 4, #a-d	6.75	6.75
1604	A340	20,000m	Sheet of 4, #a-d	6.75	6.75
1605	A340	20,000m	Sheet of 4, #a-d	6.75	6.75
1606	A340	20,000m	Sheet of 4, #a-d	6.75	6.75
1607	A340	20,000m	Sheet of 4, #a-d	6.75	6.75
1608	A340	20,000m	Sheet of 4, #a-d	6.75	6.75
1609	A340	20,000m	Sheet of 4, #a-d	6.75	6.75
1610	A340	22,000m	Sheet of 4, #a-d	7.50	7.50
1611	A340	22,000m	Sheet of 4, #a-d	7.50	7.50
1612	A340	22,000m	Sheet of 4, #a-d	7.50	7.50
1613	A340	25,000m	Sheet of 4, #a-d	8.50	8.50
1614	A340	25,000m	Sheet of 4, #a-d	8.50	8.50
1615	A340	25,000m	Sheet of 4, #a-d	8.50	8.50
1616	A340	25,000m	Sheet of 4, #a-d	8.50	8.50
1617	A341	25,000m	Sheet of 4, #a-d	8.50	8.50
1618	A342	25,000m	Sheet of 4, #a-d	8.50	8.50
1619	A342	33,000m	Sheet of 4, #a-d	11.50	11.50
1620	A342	33,000m	Sheet of 4, #a-d	11.50	11.50
1621	A342	33,000m	Sheet of 4, #a-d	11.50	11.50
	Nos. 1589-1621 (33)			264.75	264.75

Souvenir Sheets

1622	A343	88,000m	shown	7.50	7.50
1623	A344	88,000m	shown	7.50	7.50
1624	A345	88,000m	shown	7.50	7.50
1625	A345	88,000m	multi	7.50	7.50
1626	A345	88,000m	multi	7.50	7.50
1627	A345	88,000m	multi	7.50	7.50
1628	A345	88,000m	multi	7.50	7.50
1629	A345	88,000m	multi	7.50	7.50
1630	A345	88,000m	multi	7.50	7.50
1631	A345	88,000m	multi	7.50	7.50
1632	A345	88,000m	multi	7.50	7.50
1633	A345	88,000m	multi	7.50	7.50
1634	A345	110,000m	multi	9.50	9.50
1635	A345	110,000m	multi	9.50	9.50
1636	A345	110,000m	multi	9.50	9.50
1637	A345	110,000m	multi	9.50	9.50
1638	A345	110,000m	multi	9.50	9.50
1639	A345	110,000m	multi	9.50	9.50
1640	A345	110,000m	multi	9.50	9.50
1641	A345	110,000m	multi	9.50	9.50
1642	A345	110,000m	multi	9.50	9.50
1643	A345	110,000m	multi	9.50	9.50
1644	A345	110,000m	multi	9.50	9.50
1645	A346	110,000m	shown	9.50	9.50
1646	A347	110,000m	shown	9.50	9.50
	Nos. 1622-1646 (25)			213.50	213.50

World of the Sea

Ships — A348

Aircraft — A349

Sea Lions — A350

Polar Bears — A351

Killer Whales — A352

Whales — A353

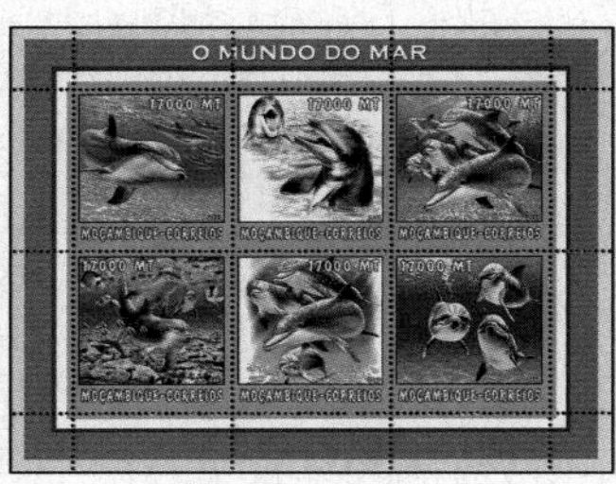

Dolphins — A354

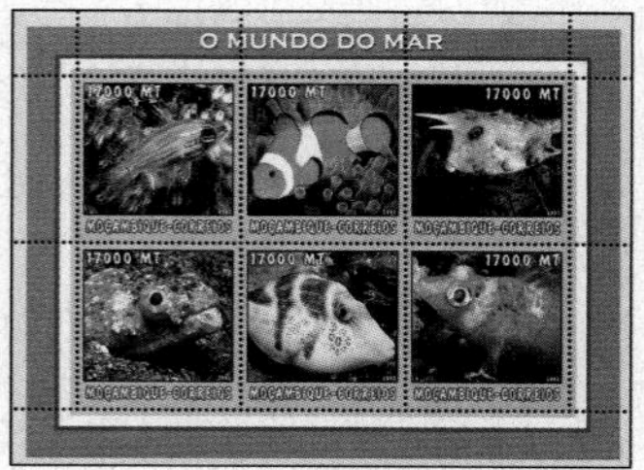

Fish — A355

Fish — A356

Fish — A357

Fish — A358

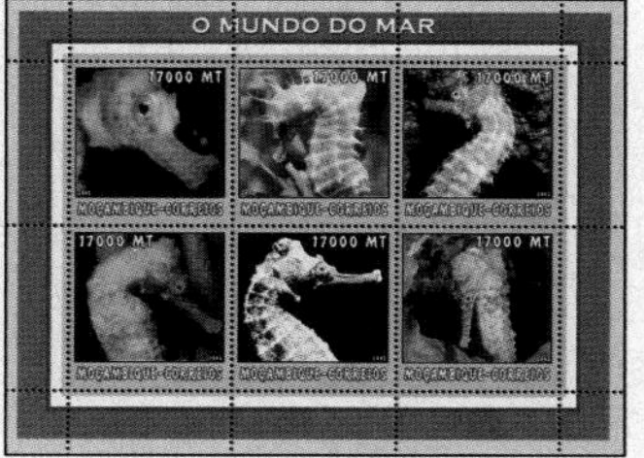

Sea Horses — A359

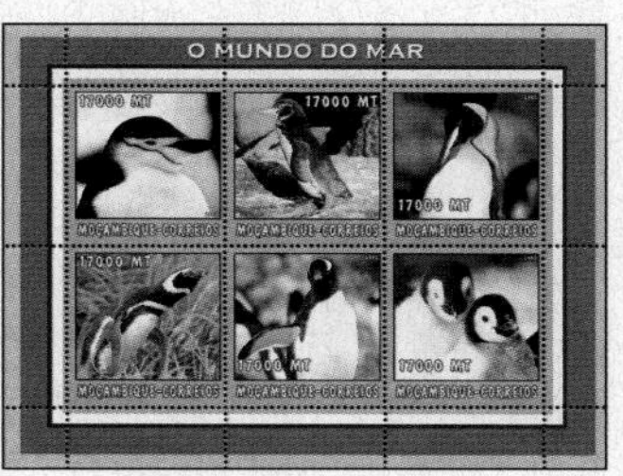

Penguins — A360

Penguins — A361

Sea Birds — A362

Sea Birds — A363

Sea Birds — A364

Crustaceans — A365

Snails — A366

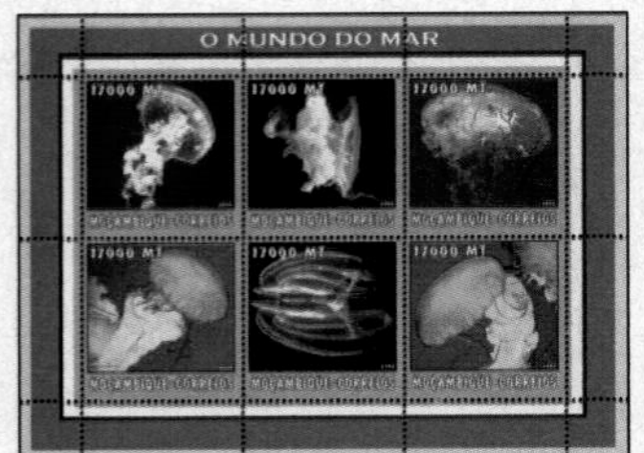

Jellyfish — A367

Coral — A368

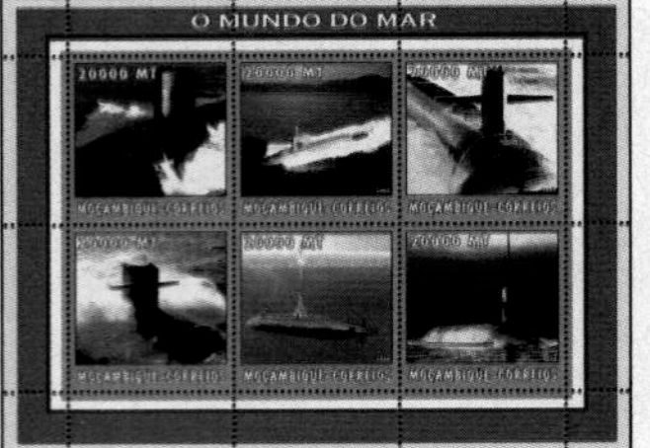

Submarines — A369

Lighthouses — A370

Ship — A371

Ship — A372

Fish — A373

Fish — A374

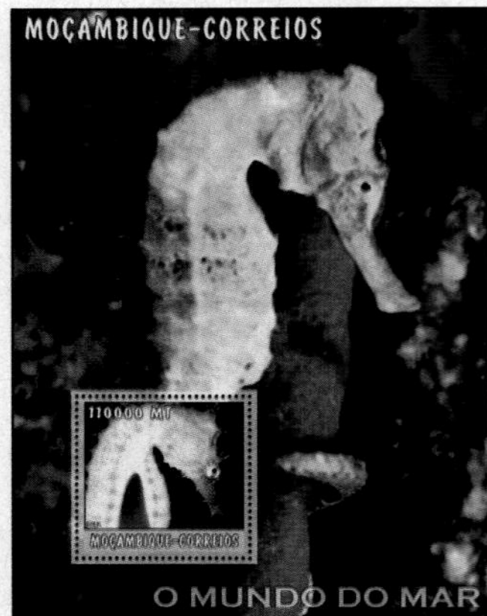

Sea Horse — A375

Sea Horse — A376

Penguin — A377

Penguin — A378

Sea Bird — A379

Sea Bird — A380

Sea Bird — A381

No. 1668 — Marine invertebrates: a, Phyllidia elegans. b, Phyllidia coelestis. c, Hypselodoris bullocki. d, Glossodoris hikuerensis. e, Glossodoris cruentus. f, Chromodoris leopardus.

No. 1669 — Shells: a, Murex brassica (showing shell opening). b, Cassis cornuta. c, Strombus gigas. d, Rapana rapiformis (showing shell opening). e, Chicoreus ramosus. f, Bursa bubo.

No. 1670 — Shells: a, Chicoreus virgineus. b, Tonna galea. c, Murex erythrostomus. d, Strombus gigas. e, Murex brassica (showing front of shell). f, Rapana rapiformis (showing front of shell).

No. 1671 — Tubeworms and seaweed: a, Kallymenia cribosa. b, Ulva lactuca. c, Chondrus crispus. d, Gigartina disticha. e, Palmaria palmata. f, Filogranella elatensis.

No. 1685, Seal flensing. No. 1686, Polar bear. No. 1687, Killer whale breaching surface. No. 1688, Whales underwater. No. 1689, Dolphins with open mouths. No. 1690, Lobster. No. 1691, Jellyfish. No. 1692 Coral and fish. No. 1693, Filogranella elatensis. No. 1694, Chromodoris leopardus. No. 1695, Tonna galea. No. 1696, Turbo marmoratus. No. 1697, Submarine. No. 1698, Christopher Columbus.

Perf. 12¾x13¼, 13¼x12¾

2002, Nov. 1

1647	A348	5000m	Sheet of 6, #a-f	2.60	2.60
1648	A349	17,000m	Sheet of 6, #a-f	8.75	8.75
1649	A350	17,000m	Sheet of 6, #a-f	8.75	8.75
1650	A351	17,000m	Sheet of 6, #a-f	8.75	8.75
1651	A352	17,000m	Sheet of 6, #a-f	8.75	8.75
1652	A353	17,000m	Sheet of 6, #a-f	8.75	8.75
1653	A354	17,000m	Sheet of 6, #a-f	8.75	8.75
1654	A355	17,000m	Sheet of 6, #a-f	8.75	8.75
1655	A356	17,000m	Sheet of 6, #a-f	8.75	8.75
1656	A357	17,000m	Sheet of 6, #a-f	8.75	8.75
1657	A358	17,000m	Sheet of 6, #a-f	8.75	8.75
1658	A359	17,000m	Sheet of 6, #a-f	8.75	8.75
1659	A360	17,000m	Sheet of 6, #a-f	8.75	8.75
1660	A361	17,000m	Sheet of 6, #a-f	8.75	8.75
1661	A362	17,000m	Sheet of 6, #a-f	8.75	8.75
1662	A363	17,000m	Sheet of 6, #a-f	8.75	8.75
1663	A364	17,000m	Sheet of 6, #a-f	8.75	8.75
1664	A365	17,000m	Sheet of 6, #a-f	8.75	8.75
1665	A366	17,000m	Sheet of 6, #a-f	8.75	8.75
1666	A367	17,000m	Sheet of 6, #a-f	8.75	8.75
1667	A368	17,000m	Sheet of 6, #a-f	8.75	8.75
1668	A368	17,000m	Sheet of 6, #a-f	8.75	8.75
1669	A368	17,000m	Sheet of 6, #a-f	8.75	8.75
1670	A368	17,000m	Sheet of 6, #a-f	8.75	8.75
1671	A368	17,000m	Sheet of 6, #a-f	8.75	8.75
1672	A369	20,000m	Sheet of 6, #a-f	10.50	10.50
1673	A370	33,000m	Sheet of 6, #a-f	17.00	17.00
	Nos. 1647-1673 (27)			240.10	240.10

Souvenir Sheets

1674	A371	110,000m	shown	9.50	9.50
1675	A372	110,000m	shown	9.50	9.50
1676	A373	110,000m	shown	9.50	9.50
1677	A374	110,000m	shown	9.50	9.50
1678	A375	110,000m	shown	9.50	9.50
1679	A376	110,000m	shown	9.50	9.50
1680	A377	110,000m	shown	9.50	9.50
1681	A378	110,000m	shown	9.50	9.50
1682	A379	110,000m	shown	9.50	9.50
1683	A380	110,000m	shown	9.50	9.50
1684	A381	110,000m	shown	9.50	9.50
1685	A350	110,000m	multi	9.50	9.50
1686	A351	110,000m	multi	9.50	9.50
1687	A352	110,000m	multi	9.50	9.50
1688	A353	110,000m	multi	9.50	9.50
1689	A354	110,000m	multi	9.50	9.50
1690	A365	110,000m	multi	9.50	9.50
1691	A367	110,000m	multi	9.50	9.50
1692	A368	110,000m	multi	9.50	9.50
1693	A368	110,000m	multi	9.50	9.50
1694	A368	110,000m	multi	9.50	9.50
1695	A368	110,000m	multi	9.50	9.50
1696	A368	110,000m	multi	9.50	9.50
1697	A369	110,000m	multi	9.50	9.50
1698	A369	110,000m	multi	9.50	9.50
	Nos. 1674-1698 (25)			237.50	237.50

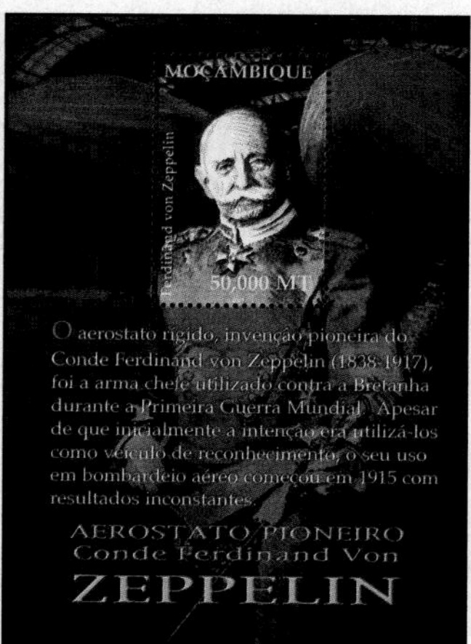

Zeppelins — A382

No. 1699, 28,000m, horiz.: a, Ferdinand von Zeppelin, brown and yellow background. b, LZ-2 in flight. c, LZ-10 in flight. d, LZ-1, purple background.

No. 1700, 28,000m, horiz.: a, LZ-1, blue and yellow background. b, LZ-2 tethered. c, LZ-10 above sheep. d, Ferdinand von Zeppelin with binoculars.

No. 1701, 50,000m, Ferdinand von Zeppelin, in military uniform. No. 1702, 50,000m, Ferdinand von Zeppelin, in suit.

2002, Nov. 18 ***Perf. 13¼x13½***

Sheets of 4, #a-d

1699-1700 A382 Set of 2 12.00 12.00

Souvenir Sheets

Perf. 13½x13¼

1701-1702 A382 Set of 2 6.00 6.00

Locomotives — A383

No. 1703, 17,000m, horiz.: a, London, Midland and Scottish Railway, England. b, Great Northern Railway, Ireland. c, Southern Railway, England. d, Great Northern Railway, US. e, Chicago, Milwaukee, St. Paul and Pacific Railroad, US. f, London and Northeastern Railway, England.

No. 1704, 17,000m, horiz.: a, Great Southern Railway, Spain. b, Shantung Railway, China. c, Shanghai-Nanking Railway, China. d, Austrian State Railway. e, Victorian Government Railways, Australia. f, London and Northwester Railways, England.

No. 1705, 17,000m, horiz.: a, Western Railways, France. b, Netherlands State Railway (green locomotive on bridge). c, Great Indian Peninsula Railway. d, Paris-Orleans Railway, France. e, Madras and Southern Mahratta Railway, India. f, Netherlands State Railway (green locomotive).

No. 1706, 50,000m, London, Brighton and South Coast Railway, England. No. 1707, 50,000m, New York Central, US.

2002, Nov. 18 ***Perf. 13¼x13½***

Sheets of 6, #a-f

1703-1705 A383 Set of 3 12.00 12.00

Souvenir Sheets

1706-1707 A383 Set of 2 6.00 6.00

A384

Automobiles — A385

No. 1708, 13,000m: a, 1912 Bentley. b, 1914 Delage Grand Prix. c, 1949, Healey Silverstone. d, 1922 Duesenberg. e, Delage 1500cc Grand Prix. f, 1961 Ferrari 375/F1.

No. 1709, 13,000m: a, 1906 Mercedes. b, 1951 Morgan. c, 1912 Sunbeam. d, 1922 Sunbeam. e, 1925 Sunbeam Tiger. f, 1908 Austin 100hp.

No. 1710, 17,000m: a, 1937, Bugatti Type 57 Alalante coupe. b, 1948 Tucker Torpedo. c, 1966 Honda S 800m. d, 1946 Cisitalia 202 GT. e, 1958 Chevrolet Impala. f, 1934 Cadillac LaSalle convertible.

No. 1711, 17,000m: a, 1908 Austin. b, 1937 Studebaker coupe. c, 1930 Bugatti Type 40GP. d, 1931 Ford Model A roadster. e, 1937 Alfa Romeo 2900B. f, 1937 Cord 812.

No. 1712, 40,000m, 1931 Alfa Romeo. No. 1713, 40,000m, 1911 Marmon Wasp.

No. 1714, 50,000m, 1957 Plymouth Fury. No. 1715, 50,000m, 1928 Mercedes-Benz SSK.

Perf. 13¼x13½, 13½x13¼

2002, Nov. 18

Sheets of 6, #a-f

1708-1709 A384 Set of 2 9.00 9.00
1710-1711 A385 Set of 2 10.00 10.00

Souvenir Sheets

1712-1713 A384 Set of 2 5.00 5.00
1714-1715 A385 Set of 2 6.00 6.00

Pottery — A386

Designs: 1000m, Pote. 2000m, Chaleira. 4000m, Taças. 5000m, Cantaro. 17,000m, Panela. 28,000m, Alguidar. 50,000m, Jarra. 100,000m, Bilhas.

2002, Dec. 2 ***Perf. 12¾***

1716-1723 A386 Set of 8 8.00 8.00

Dated 2001.

Justino Chemane, Composer of National Anthem — A387

2003, July 11

1724 A387 6000m multi .55 .55

Minerals — A388

Designs: 5000m, Bauxite. 14,000m, Marble. 19,000m, shown. 33,000m, Gold.

2004, Apr. 30

1725-1728 A388 Set of 4 6.00 6.00

Dated 2003.

Paintings by Jean-Auguste Ingres — A389

Paintings by James Tissot — A390

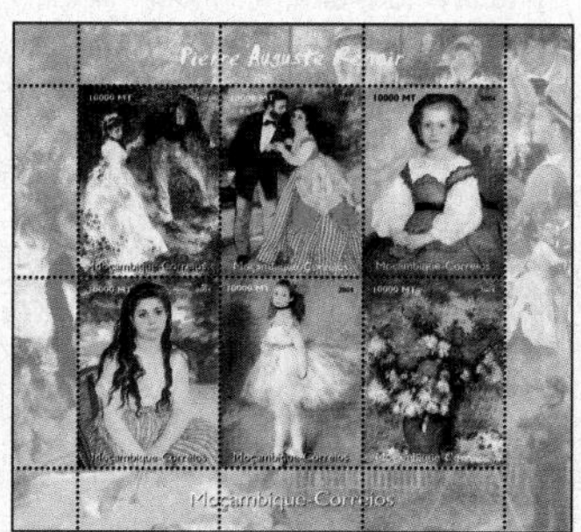

Paintings by Pierre-Auguste Renoir — A391

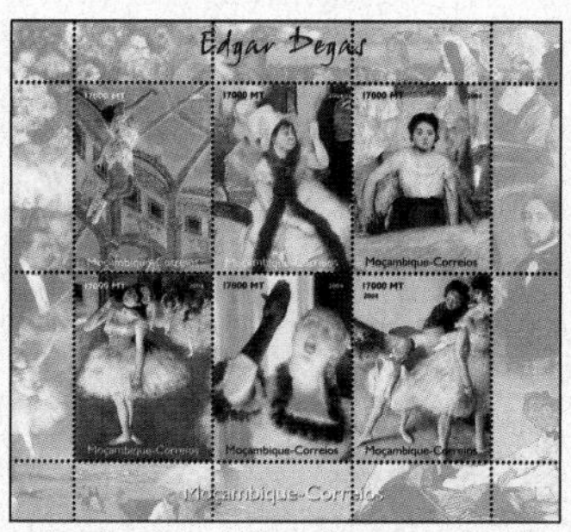

Paintings by Edgar Degas — A392

Various unnamed paintings.

2004, June 17 Litho. ***Perf. 13½x13***

1729 A389 6500m Sheet of 6, #a-f 3.50 3.50
1730 A390 6500m Sheet of 6, #a-f 3.50 3.50
g. Souvenir sheet, #1730e .60 .60
1731 A391 10,000m Sheet of 6, #a-f 5.50 5.50
1732 A392 17,000m Sheet of 6, #a-f 9.25 9.25
Nos. 1729-1732 (4) 21.75 21.75

Diplomatic Relations Between Mozambique and People's Republic of China, 30th Anniv. — A395

No. 1735: a, Flags, buildings and animals. b, Arms, Admiral Zheng He, building, vase, sculpture.

Illustration reduced.

2005, June 25 Litho. ***Perf. 13¼***

1735 A395 33,000m Pair, #a-b 5.50 5.50

Exists imperf.

Southern African Development Community, 25th Anniv. — A396

2005, Aug. 11 ***Perf. 11¼x11***

1736 A396 8000m multi .65 .65

Traditional African Medicine Day A397

2005, Aug. 31 ***Perf. 11x11¼***

1737 A397 8000m multi .65 .65

World Summit on the Information Society, Tunis — A398

2005, Oct. 9 ***Perf. 11¼x11***

1738 A398 8000m multi .65 .65

Nos. 1320, 1576, 1717 Surcharged Like No. 1417 and

No. 1321 Surcharged in Black and Silver

Methods and Perfs as Before

2005 ?

1739 A386 6000m on 2000m #1717 .50 .50
1740 A331 8000m on 17,000m #1576 .70 .70
1741 A269 33,000m on 7500m #1320 2.75 2.75
1742 A269 33,000m on 12,500m #1321 (B&S) 2.75 2.75
Nos. 1739-1742 (4) 6.70 6.70

Mozambique Telecommunications Company, 25th Anniv. — A399

2006, June 10 Litho. *Perf. 11½x11*

1743 A399 8000m multi .65 .65

No. 1743 also has denomination expressed in revalued meticals, which were put into service on July 1.

For surcharge, see No. 1747.

Presidential Initiative Against AIDS — A400

Pres. Armando Guebuza: 8m, Holding gavel. 16m, Behind microphones. 33m, With arm raised.

2006, Oct. 9 *Perf. 11x11½*

1744-1746 A400 Set of 3 4.50 4.50

No. 1743 Surcharged

2006 Litho. *Perf. 11½x11*

1747 A399 33m on 8000m #1743 —

The following items inscribed "Moçambique Correios" have been declared "illegal" by Mozambique postal officials:

Sheet of nine stamps of various denominations depicting Princess Diana;

Sheet of six 5000m stamps depicting the art of Paul Delvaux;

Sheet of six 17,000m stamps depicting the art of Edgar Degas;

Stamps depicting the art of Lucas Cranach;

Six different 15,000m souvenir sheets of one depicting Pope John Paul II;

Souvenir sheet of one 30,000m stamp depicting French Pres. Nicolas Sarkozy.

A set of 12 stamps with denominations of 5,000m, 19,000m, and 33,000m depicting Europa stamps, 50th anniv.

Stamps depicting Wolfgang Amadeus Mozart; Pierre Auguste Renoir; Jean Auguste Ingres Bessieres; Marilyn Monroe; Rotary International; Lions International; Formula 1 Racing; Astronauts; 2007 Rugby World Cup.

No. 1575 Surcharged

Methods and Perfs As Before

2006 ?

1748 A331 33m on 10,000m #1575 *6.75 6.75*

Cahora Bassa Dam A401

Designs: 8m, Dam and reservoir. 20m, Dignitaries shaking hands. 33m, Dam and flag of Mozambique.

2007, Nov. 26 Litho. *Perf. 11x11¼*

1749-1751 A401 Set of 3 4.75 4.75

Reign of Aga Khan, 50th Anniv. — A402

Designs: 8m, Building. No. 1753, 20m, People on beach. No. 1754, 20m, People under shelter. No. 1755, 33m, Polana Serena Hotel. No. 1756, 33m, Students in classroom, vert. (30x40mm).

Perf. 12¾, 11¼x11 (#1756)

2007, Nov.

1752-1756 A402 Set of 5 9.00 9.00

Fauna, Flora and Minerals — A403

No. 1757 — Map of Africa and wild cats: a, 8m, Acionyx jubatus. b, 8m, Panthera leo with closed mouth. c, 8m, Panthera leo with open mouth. d, 33m, Male Panthera leo. e, 33m, Female Panthera leo, diff. f, 33m, Panthera pardus.

No. 1758 — Map of Africa and elephants: a, 8m, Loxodonta cyclotis facing right. b, 8m, Loxodonta africana. c, 8m, Loxodonta cyclotis facing left. d, 33m, Loxodonta africana facing right. e, 33m, Loxodonta cyclotis, diff. f, 33m, Loxodonta africana facing left.

No. 1759 — Lighthouses and marine mammals: a, 8m, Sousa teuszii. b, 8m, Stenella frontalis. c, 8m, Stenella clymene. d, 33m, Sotalia fluviatilis. e, 33m, Stenella longirostris. f, 33m, Tursiops truncatus.

No. 1760 — Map of Africa and birds of prey: a, 8m, Haliaeetus leucocephalus. b, 8m, Terathopius ecaudatus. c, 8m, Accipiter gentilis. d, 33m, Buteo lagopus. e, 33m, Head of Aquila verreauxii. f, 33m, Aquila verreauxi on branch.

No. 1761 — Hummingbirds and orchids: a, 8m, Tachybaptus, Malaxis uniflora. b, 8m, Fregata magnificus, Coryanthes speciosa. c, 8m, Gallinula, Calochilus robertsonii. d, 33m, Veniliornis, Stanhopea. e, 33m, Basilinna leucotis, Habaneria saccata. f, 33m, Actitis macularia, Diuris filifolia.

No. 1762 — Map of Africa and bees: a, 8m, Polubia. b, 8m, Apis mellifera scutellata. c, 8m, Pompilus. d, 33m, Tiphiidae. e, 33m, Vespula vulgaris. f, 33m, Scoliidae.

No. 1763 — Map of Africa and butterflies: a, 8m, Danaus chrysippus. b, 8m, Libytheana carineta. c, 8m, Papilio morondavana. d, 33m, Danaus gilippus. e, 33m, Amblypodia tyrannus. f, 33m, Lycaena cupreus.

No. 1764 — Map of Africa and crocodiles: a, 8m, Crocodylus porosus. b, 8m, Crocodylus novaeguineae. c, 8m, Crocodylus rhombifer. d, 33m, Crocodylus niloticus. e, 33m, Osteolaemus tetraspis. f, 33m, Crocodylus siamensis.

No. 1765 — Map of Africa and frogs: a, 8m, Gastrotheca. b, 8m, Mantella. c, 8m, Rana esculenta. d, 33m, Litoria rubella. e, 33m, Dendrobatidae. f, 33m, Pyxicephalus.

No. 1766 — Dinosaurs: a, 8m, Aublysodon. b, 8m, Ornithomimus. c, 8m, Coelurus. d, 33m, Velociraptor. e, 33m, Abelisaurus. f, 33m, Saurornithoides.

No. 1767 — Map of Africa and cacti: a, 8m, Hoodia gordonii. b, 8m, Hoodia officinalis. c, 8m, Hoodia ruschii. d, 33m, Hoodia flava. e, 33m, Hoodia officinalis, diff. f, 33m, Hoodia currorii.

No. 1768 — Fruit: a, 8m, Citrus vulgaris. b, 8m, Cola acuminata. c, 8m, Cocos nucifera. d, 33m, Citrus limonum. e, 33m, Cocos nucifera, diff. f, 33m, Citrus bergamia.

No. 1769 — Map of Africa, diamonds and minerals: a, 8m, Fluorite, quartz. b, 8m, Elbaite tourmaline, quartz. c, 8m, Staurolite. d, 33m, Fluorite, pyrite. e, 33m, Benitoite, neptunite. f, 33m, Celestine.

No. 1770, 20m — Map of Africa and primates: a, Cebidae. b, Nomascus leucogenys. c, Borneo proboscis monkey. d, Symphalangus syndactylus. e, Pan troglodytes. f, Cercopithecidae.

No. 1771, 20m — Lighthouses and whales: a, Balaenoptera borealis. b, Orcinus orca. c, Eschrichtius robustus. d, Balaenoptera physalus. e, Three Orcinus orca. f, Megaptera novaeangliae.

No. 1772, 20m — Map of Africa and owls: a, Strix woodfordii. b, Tyto capensis. c, Phodilus badius on thin branch. d, Phodilus badius on thick branch. e, Tytonidae. f, Otus senegalensis.

No. 1773, 20m — Map of Africa and parrots: a, Psittacopes. b, Serudaptus. c, Pseudasturidae. d, Quercypsittidae. e, Xenopsitta. f, Palaeopsittacus.

No. 1774, 20m — Butterflies or moths and unnamed flowers: a, Inachis io. b, Saturnia pavonia. c, Papilio xuthus. d, Prepona praeneste. e, Speyeria cybele. f, Nymphalidae.

No. 1775, 20m — Map of Africa and fish: a, Scorpaenidae. b, Balistodae. c, Antennarius. d, Triglidae. e, Hydrocynus. f, Lophius.

No. 1776, 20m — Map of Africa and marine life: a, Birgus latro. b, Panulirus. c, Gecarcoidea natalis. d, Loligo opalescens. e, Genus ocypode. f, Hapalochlaena.

No. 1777, 20m — Map of Africa and reptiles: a, Vaanus niloticus. b, Chamaeleo jacksonii. c, Veranus exanthematicus. d, Scincus. e, Brookesia. f, Furcifer pardalis.

No. 1778, 20m — Map of Africa and turtles: a, Natator depressus. b, Eretmochelys imbricata. c, Lepidochelys olivacea with dark neck. d, Lepidochelys olivacea with light neck. e, Caretta caretta. f, Chelonia mydas.

No. 1779, 20m — Map of Africa and snakes: a, Bitis nasicornis. b, Bitis gabonica. c, Ophiophagus hannah. d, Thelolornis kirtlandii. e, Dendroaspis angusticeps. f, Atheris.

No. 1780, 20m — Dinosaurs: a, Therizinosaurus. b, Heterdontosaurus. c, Prosaurolophus. d, Melanorosaurus. e, Megalosaurus. f, Proceratosaurus.

No. 1781, 20m — Trees: a, Punica granatum, fruit split, and on branch. b, Elaeis guineensis. c, Cola acuminata. d, Areca catechu. e, Hevea brasiliensis. f, Punica granatum, flowers on branches and split.

No. 1782, 20m — Map of Africa and orchids: a, Purple Cattleya lueddemanniana. b, Paphiopedilum delenatii. c, Vanda coerulea. d, Pink Cattleya lueddmanniana. e, Paphiopedilum. f, Spathoglottis.

No. 1783, 20m — Map of Africa and minerals: a, Carrollite. b, Ettringite. c, Cerrusite, barite. d, Malachite. e, Carrolite, calcite. f, Dioptase.

No. 1784, 132m, Map of Africa and Nomascus nasutus. No. 1785, 132m, Map of Africa and Panthera leo. No. 1786, 132m, Loxodonta africana. No. 1787, 132m, Stenella logirostris, diff. No. 1788, 132m, Orcinus orca and lighthouse, diff. No. 1789, 132m, Lepidocolaptes, Spathoglottis plicata. No. 1790, 132m, Pulchrapollia. No. 1791, 132m, Accipiter nisus. No. 1792, 132m, Map of Africa and Polubia. No. 1793, 132m, Arctia hebe. No. 1794, 132m, Papilio homerus, Caladeria reptans. No. 1795, 132m, Map of Africa and Thassophryninae. No. 1796, 132m, Map of Africa and Chauliodus. No. 1797, 132m, Map of Africa and Dendroaspis polylepis. No. 1798, 132m, Map of Africa and Pogona vitticeps. No. 1799, 132m, Map of Africa and Crocodylus niloticus, diff. No. 1800, 132m, Map of Africa and Eretmochelys imbircata, diff. No. 1801, 132m, Map of Africa and Pychicephalus adspersus. No. 1802, 132m, Hadrosaurus. No. 1803, 132m, Adansonia tree. No. 1804, 132m, Map of Africa and Euphorbia enopla. No. 1805, 132m, Map of Africa, Diuris filifolia, Malaxis uniflora. No. 1806, 132m, Cirtus vulgaris, diff. No. 1807, 132m, Vanadinite, poldervaartite. No. 1808, 132m, Malachite, barite and malachite.

Perf. 12¾x13¼

2007, Dec. 10 Litho.

Sheets of 6, #a-f

1757-1769 A403 Set of 13 125.00 125.00
1770-1783 A403 Set of 14 130.00 130.00

Souvenir Sheets

Perf. 13¼ Syncopated

1784-1808 A403 Set of 25 260.00 260.00

Minerva Central Publishers, Cent. A404

Background color: 8m, Red. 20m, Olive green. 33m, Purple.

2008, Apr. 10 Litho. *Perf. 11x11¼*

1809-1811 A404 Set of 3 4.75 4.75

Second Frelimo Party Congress, 40th Anniv. — A405

2008, July 25 *Perf. 11¼x11*

1812 A405 8m multi .65 .65

Miniature Sheets

2008 Summer Olympics, Beijing — A406

No. 1813 Surcharged

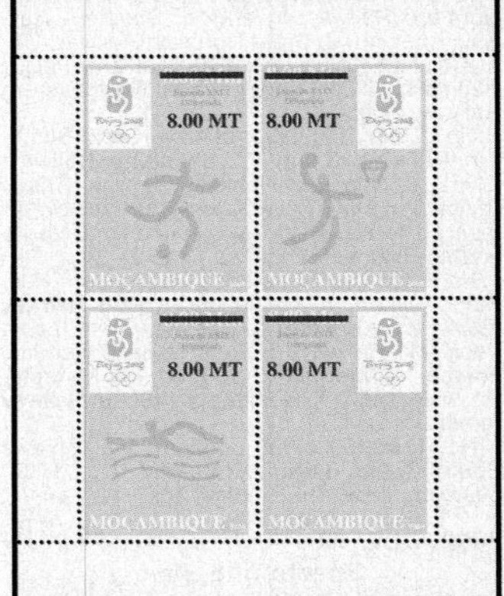

Nos. 1813 and 1814: a, Soccer. b, Basketball. c, Swimming. d, Running.

2008 *Perf. 13¼x12¾*

1813 A406 8m Sheet of 4, #a-d *5.00 5.00*
1814 A406 8m on 8m Sheet of 4, #a-d 2.50 2.50

No. 1813 shows an incorrect abbreviation for the currency, which was corrected by the surcharge.

Food — A407

Designs: 8m, Bolo de milho (corn cake). 20m, Mathapa com caranguejo (cassava with crab). 33m, Quiabo com camarao (Okra and shrimp).

2008, Oct. 9 *Perf. 11¼x11*

1815-1817	A407	Set of 3	4.75	4.75

Maria de Lurdes Mutola, 800-Meter Gold Medalist in 2000 Summer Olympics
A408

2009, Jan. 21 *Perf. 11x11¼*

1818	A408	8m multi	.65	.65

SEMI-POSTAL STAMPS

"History" Pointing out to "the Republic" Need for Charity
SP1

Nurse Leading Wounded Soldiers
SP2

Veteran Relating Experiences — SP3

Perf. 11½

1920, Dec. 1 **Litho.** **Unwmk.**

B1	SP1	¼c olive	3.50	3.50
B2	SP1	½c olive blk	3.50	3.50
B3	SP1	1c dp bister	3.50	3.50
B4	SP1	2c lilac brn	3.50	3.50
B5	SP1	3c lilac	3.50	3.50
B6	SP1	4c green	3.50	3.50
B7	SP2	5c grnsh blue	3.50	3.50
B8	SP2	6c light blue	3.50	3.50
B9	SP2	7½c red brown	3.50	3.50
B10	SP2	8c lemon	3.50	3.50
B11	SP2	10c gray lilac	3.50	3.50
B12	SP2	12c pink	3.50	3.50
B13	SP3	18c rose	3.50	3.50
B14	SP3	24c vio brn	3.50	3.50
B15	SP3	30c pale ol grn	3.50	3.50
B16	SP3	40c dull red	3.50	3.50
B17	SP3	50c yellow	3.50	3.50
B18	SP3	1e ultra	3.50	3.50
		Nos. B1-B18 (18)	63.00	63.00

Nos. B1-B18 were used Dec. 1, 1920, in place of ordinary stamps. The proceeds were for war victims.

AIR POST STAMPS

Common Design Type
Perf. 13½x13

1938, Aug. **Engr.** **Unwmk.**
Name and Value in Black

C1	CD39	10c red orange	.30	.20
C2	CD39	20c purple	.30	.20
C3	CD39	50c orange	.30	.20
C4	CD39	1e ultra	.40	.30
C5	CD39	2e lilac brn	1.00	.30
C6	CD39	3e dk green	1.75	.40
C7	CD39	5e red brown	2.00	.70
C8	CD39	9e rose car	4.25	.75
C9	CD39	10e magenta	5.50	1.10
		Nos. C1-C9 (9)	15.80	4.15

No. C7 exists with overprint "Exposicao Internacional de Nova York, 1939-1940" and Trylon and Perisphere.

No. C7 Surcharged in Black

1946, Nov. 2 *Perf. 13½x13*

C10	CD39	3e on 5e red brn	6.00	1.75
a.		Inverted surcharge		

Plane — AP1

1946, Nov. 2 **Typo.** *Perf. 11½*
Denomination in Black

C11	AP1	1.20e carmine	1.10	.85
C12	AP1	1.60e blue	1.40	.90
C13	AP1	1.70e plum	3.50	1.40
C14	AP1	2.90e brown	3.50	1.90
C15	AP1	3e green	3.00	1.75
		Nos. C11-C15 (5)	12.50	6.80

Inscribed "Taxe perçue" and Denomination in Brown Carmine or Black

1947, May 20

C16	AP1	50c blk (BrC)	.50	.25
C17	AP1	1e pink	.50	.25
C18	AP1	3e green	1.00	.40
C19	AP1	4.50e yel grn	2.50	.75
C20	AP1	5e red brown	2.50	.90
C21	AP1	10e ultra	6.00	1.25
C22	AP1	20e violet	11.00	4.00
C23	AP1	50e orange	15.00	6.00
		Nos. C16-C23 (8)	39.00	13.80

Dangerous counterfeits exist.

Planes Circling Globe — AP2

Oil Refinery, Sonarep
AP3

1949, Mar.

C24	AP2	50c sepia	.30	.20
C25	AP2	1.20e violet	.50	.30
C26	AP2	4.50e dull blue	1.25	.50
C27	AP2	5e blue green	1.75	.50
C28	AP2	20e chocolate	4.00	.85
		Nos. C24-C28 (5)	7.80	2.35

Catalogue values for unused stamps in this section, from this point to the end of the section, are for Never Hinged items.

1963, Mar. 5 **Litho.** *Perf. 13*

Designs: 2e, Salazar High School, Lourenço Marques. 3.50e, Lourenço Marques harbor. 4.50e, Salazar dam. 5e, Trigo de Morais bridge. 20e, Marcelo Caetano bridge.

C29	AP3	1.50e multi	.60	.20
C30	AP3	2e multi	.30	.20
C31	AP3	3.50e multi	.60	.20
C32	AP3	4.50e multi	.40	.20
C33	AP3	5e multi	.50	.20
C34	AP3	20e multi	1.10	.50
		Nos. C29-C34 (6)	3.50	1.50

Republic

Nos. C31-C34 Overprinted in Red

1975, June 25 **Litho.** *Perf. 13*

C35	AP3	3.50e multi	.20	.20
C36	AP3	4.50e multi	.35	.20
C37	AP3	5e multi	.85	.20
C38	AP3	20e multi	1.75	.40
		Nos. C35-C38 (4)	3.15	1.00

DeHavilland Dragonfly, 1937 — AP4

Designs: 1.50m, Junker JU-52-3M, 1938. 3m, Lockheed Lodestar L-18-08, 1940. 7.50m, DeHavilland Dove DH-104, 1948. 10m, Douglas Dakota DC-3, 1956. 12.5m, Fokker Friendship F-27, 1962.

1981, May 14 **Litho.** *Perf. 11*

C39	AP4	50c multi	.90	.20
C40	AP4	1.50m multi	1.10	.20
C41	AP4	3m multi	1.75	.20
C42	AP4	7.50m multi	2.50	.20
C43	AP4	10m multi	3.00	.35
C44	AP4	12.5m multi	4.50	.50
		Nos. C39-C44 (6)	13.75	1.65

Piper Navajo Over Hydroelectric Dam — AP5

Designs: 40m, De Havilland Hornet trainer, 1936. 80m, Boeing 737, Maputo Airport, 1973. 120m, Beechcraft King-Air. 160m, Piper Aztec. 320m, Douglas DC-10, 1982.

1987, Oct. 28 **Litho.** *Perf. 11*

C45	AP5	20m multi	.20	.20
C46	AP5	40m multi	.20	.20
C47	AP5	80m multi	.30	.20
C48	AP5	120m multi	.50	.25
C49	AP5	160m multi	.65	.35
C50	AP5	320m multi	1.25	.40
		Nos. C45-C50 (6)	3.10	1.60

POSTAGE DUE STAMPS

D1

1904 **Unwmk.** **Typo.** *Perf. 11½x12*
Name and Value in Black

J1	D1	5r yellow grn	.40	.20
J2	D1	10r slate	.40	.20
J3	D1	20r yellow brn	.40	.25
J4	D1	30r orange	.75	.60
J5	D1	50r gray brn	.70	.40
J6	D1	60r red brown	3.25	1.60
J7	D1	100r red lilac	2.75	1.60
J8	D1	130r dull blue	1.25	.85
J9	D1	200r carmine	1.75	1.00
J10	D1	500r violet	2.25	1.00
		Nos. J1-J10 (10)	13.90	7.70

See J34-J43. For overprints see Nos. 247, J11-J30.

Same Overprinted in Carmine or Green

1911

J11	D1	5r yellow green	.20	.20
J12	D1	10r slate	.20	.20
J13	D1	20r yellow brn	.30	.20
J14	D1	30r orange	.30	.20
J15	D1	50r gray brown	.40	.30
J16	D1	60r red brown	.50	.35
J17	D1	100r red lilac	.55	.45
J18	D1	130r dull blue	1.10	.80
J19	D1	200r carmine (G)	1.10	.90
J20	D1	500r violet	1.25	.85
		Nos. J11-J20 (10)	5.90	4.45

Nos. J1-J10 Overprinted Locally in Carmine

1916

J21	D1	5r yellow grn	3.75	3.00
J22	D1	10r slate	5.00	1.75
J23	D1	20r yellow brn	75.00	52.50
J24	D1	30r orange	20.00	11.00
J25	D1	50r gray brown	75.00	52.50
J26	D1	60r red brown	60.00	40.00
J27	D1	100r red lilac	75.00	50.00
J28	D1	130r dull blue	2.25	2.00
J29	D1	200r carmine	2.50	2.75
J30	D1	500r violet	5.25	4.50
		Nos. J21-J30 (10)	323.75	220.00

War Tax Stamps of 1916 Overprinted Diagonally

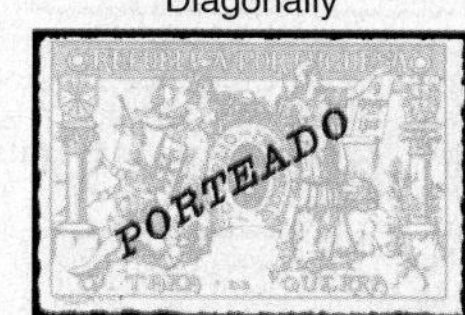

1918 *Rouletted 7*

J31	WT1	1c gray green	.85	.70
J32	WT2	5c rose	.85	.70
a.		Inverted overprint	8.25	7.50

Perf. 11

J33	WT1	1c gray green	.85	.70
a.		"PEPUBLICA"	50.00	40.00
		Nos. J31-J33 (3)	2.55	2.10

Type of 1904 Issue With Value in Centavos

1917 *Perf. 12*

J34	D1	½c yellow green	.20	.20
J35	D1	1c slate	.20	.20
J36	D1	2c orange brown	.20	.20
J37	D1	3c orange	.20	.20
J38	D1	5c gray brown	.20	.20
J39	D1	6c pale brn	.20	.20
J40	D1	10c red violet	.20	.20
J41	D1	13c deep blue	.20	.20
J42	D1	20c rose	.20	.20
J43	D1	50c gray	.20	.20
		Nos. J34-J43 (10)	2.00	2.00

Lourenco Marques Nos. 117, 119 Surcharged in Red

1921

J44	A4	5c on ½c blk	1.50	.70
J45	A4	10c on 1½c brn	1.50	.70

Same Surcharge on Mozambique Nos. 151, 155, 157 in Red or Green

J46	A6	6c on 1c bl grn (R)	1.50	.85
J47	A6	20c on 2½c vio (R)	1.00	.70
J48	A6	50c on 4c rose (G)	1.00	.70
		Nos. J44-J48 (5)	6.50	3.65

Regular Issues of 1921-22 Surcharged in Black or Red

1924 ***Perf. 12x11½***

J49	A6	20c on 30c ol grn (Bk)	1.00	.40
a.		Perf. 15x14	19.00	4.50
J50	A6	50c on 60c dk bl (R)	1.00	.55

Catalogue values for unused stamps in this section, from this point to the end of the section, are for Never Hinged items.

Common Design Type
Photo. and Typo.

1952 **Unwmk.** ***Perf. 14***

Numeral in Red Orange or Red; Frame Multicolored

J51	CD45	10c carmine (RO)	.20	.20
J52	CD45	30c black brn	.20	.20
J53	CD45	50c black	.20	.20
J54	CD45	1e violet blue	.20	.20
J55	CD45	2e olive green	.20	.20
J56	CD45	5e orange brown	.50	.30
		Nos. J51-J56 (6)	1.50	1.30

WAR TAX STAMPS

Coats of Arms of Portugal and Mozambique on Columns, Allegorical Figures of History of Portugal and the Republic Holding Scroll with Date of Declaration of War — WT1

Prow of Galley of Discoveries. Left, "Republic" Teaching History of Portugal; Right "History" with Laurels (Victory) and Sword (Symbolical of Declaration of War) — WT2

1916 **Unwmk.** **Litho.** ***Rouletted 7***

MR1	WT1	1c gray green	2.00	.50
a.		Imperf., pair	15.00	
MR2	WT2	5c rose	2.00	.50
a.		Imperf., pair	15.00	

1918 ***Perf. 11, 12***

MR3	WT1	1c gray green	.50	.50
a.		"PEPUBLICA"	8.50	4.75
MR4	WT2	5c red	.70	.60
a.		"PETRIA"	2.25	2.25
b.		"PEPUBLICA"	2.50	2.25
c.		"1910" for "1916"	10.00	5.00
d.		Imperf., pair		
		Nos. MR1-MR4 (4)	5.20	2.10

For surcharges and overprints see Nos. 221-225, 229, 235, J31-J33.

NEWSPAPER STAMPS

No. 19 Surcharged in Black, Red or Blue:

JORNAES JORNAES

2 ½ REIS 2½ 2½
a b

1893 **Unwmk.** ***Perf. 11½, 12½, 13½***

P1	A2 (a)	2½r on 40r		200.00	90.00
P2	A2 (a)	5r on 40r		175.00	90.00
P3	A2 (a)	5r on 40r (R)		150.00	75.00
P4	A2 (a)	5r on 40r (Bl)		180.00	75.00
P5	A2 (b)	2½r on 40r		22.50	16.00
		Nos. P1-P5 (5)		727.50	346.00

Nos. P1-P5 exist with double surcharge, Nos. P2-P4 with inverted surcharge.

N3

1893 **Typo.** ***Perf. 11½, 13½***

P6	N3	2½r brown	.35	.30

For surcharge and overprint see Nos. 93, 199, 206.

No. P6 has been reprinted on chalk-surfaced paper with clean-cut perforation 13½. Value, 50 cents.

POSTAL TAX STAMPS

Pombal Commemorative Issue
Common Design Types

1925 **Engr.** ***Perf. 12½***

RA1	CD28	15c brown & black	.30	.25
RA2	CD29	15c brown & black	.30	.25
RA3	CD30	15c brown & black	.30	.25
		Nos. RA1-RA3 (3)	.90	.75

Seal of Local Red Cross Society
PT7 PT8
Surcharged in Various Colors

1925 **Typo.** ***Perf. 11½***

RA4	PT7	50c slate & yel (Bk)	1.40	1.40

1926

RA5	PT8	40c slate & yel (Bk)	3.00	3.00
RA6	PT8	50c slate & yel (R)	3.00	3.00
RA7	PT8	60c slate & yel (V)	3.00	3.00
RA8	PT8	80c slate & yel (Br)	3.00	3.00
RA9	PT8	1e slate & yel (Bl)	3.00	3.00
RA10	PT8	2e slate & yel (G)	3.00	3.00
		Nos. RA5-RA10 (6)	18.00	18.00

Obligatory on mail certain days of the year. The tax benefited the Cross of the Orient Society.

Type of 1926 Issue

1927

Black Surcharge

RA11	PT8	5c red & yel	3.00	3.00
RA12	PT8	10c green & yel	3.00	3.00
RA13	PT8	20c gray & yel	3.00	3.00
RA14	PT8	30c lt bl & yel	3.00	3.00
RA15	PT8	40c vio & yel	3.00	3.00
RA16	PT8	50c car & yel	3.00	3.00
RA17	PT8	60c brown & yel	3.00	3.00
RA18	PT8	80c blue & yel	3.00	3.00
RA19	PT8	1e olive & yel	3.00	3.00
RA20	PT8	2e yel brn & yel	3.00	3.00
		Nos. RA11-RA20 (10)	30.00	30.00

See note after No. RA10.

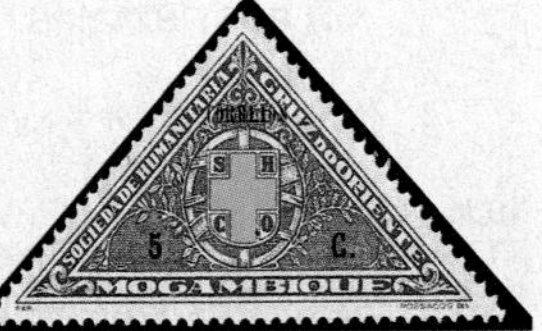

PT9

1928 **Litho.**

RA21	PT9	5c grn, yel & blk	4.00	4.00
RA22	PT9	10c sl bl, yel & blk	4.00	4.00
RA23	PT9	20c gray blk, yel & blk	4.00	4.00
RA24	PT9	30c brn rose, yel & blk	4.00	4.00
RA25	PT9	40c cl brn, yel & blk	4.00	4.00
RA26	PT9	50c red org, yel & blk	4.00	4.00
RA27	PT9	60c brn, yel & blk	4.00	4.00
RA28	PT9	80c dk brn, yel & blk	4.00	4.00
RA29	PT9	1e gray, yel & blk	4.00	4.00
RA30	PT9	2e red, yel & blk	4.00	4.00
		Nos. RA21-RA30 (10)	40.00	40.00

See note after RA10.

Mother and Children PT10 — Mousinho de Albuquerque PT11

1929 **Photo.** ***Perf. 14***

RA31	PT10	40c ultra, cl & blk	2.50	2.50

The use of this stamp was compulsory on all correspondence to Portugal and Portuguese Colonies for eight days beginning July 24, 1929.

See Nos.RA39-RA47.

1930-31 ***Perf. 14½x14***

		Inscribed: "MACONTENE"		
RA32	PT11	50c lake, red & gray	3.50	4.00
		Inscribed: "COOLELA"		
RA33	PT11	50c red vio, red brn & gray	3.50	4.00
		Inscribed: "MUJENGA"		
RA34	PT11	50c org red, red & gray	3.50	4.00
		Inscribed: "CHAIMITE"		
RA35	PT11	50c dp grn, bl grn & gray	3.50	4.00
		Inscribed: "IBRAHIMO"		
RA36	PT11	50c dk bl, blk & gray	3.50	4.00
		Inscribed: "MUCUTO-MUNO"		
RA37	PT11	50c ultra, blk & gray	3.50	4.00
		Inscribed: "NAGUEMA"		
RA38	PT11	50c dk vio, lt vio & gray	3.50	4.00
		Nos. RA32-RA38 (7)	24.50	28.00

The portrait is that of Mousinho de Albuquerque, the celebrated Portuguese warrior, and the names of seven battles in which he took part appear at the foot of the stamps. The stamps were issued for the memorial fund bearing his name and their use was obligatory on all correspondence posted on eight specific days in the year.

Type of 1929 Issue
Denominations in Black
No. RA42 Without Denomination

1931-40 ***Perf. 14***

RA39	PT10	40c rose & vio	4.00	3.25
RA40	PT10	40c ol grn & vio ('32)	5.00	4.00
RA41	PT10	40c bis brn & rose ('33)	5.00	4.00
RA42	PT10	bl grn & rose ('34)	3.50	2.75
RA43	PT10	40c org & ultra ('36)	5.00	4.00
RA44	PT10	40c choc & ultra ('37)	5.00	4.00
RA45	PT10	40c grn & brn car ('38)	7.00	5.00
RA46	PT10	40c yel & blk ('39)	7.00	5.00
RA47	PT10	40c gray brn ('40)	7.00	5.00
		Nos. RA39-RA47 (9)	48.50	37.00

Allegory of Charity PT12

White Pelican — PT13

1942 **Unwmk.** **Litho.** ***Perf. 11½***

Denomination in Black

RA48	PT12	50c rose carmine	8.25	1.40

1943-51 ***Perf. 11½, 14***

Denomination in Black

RA49	PT13	50c rose carmine	17.00	1.25
RA50	PT13	50c emerald	10.00	1.25
RA51	PT13	50c purple	15.00	1.25
RA52	PT13	50c blue	12.00	1.25
RA53	PT13	50c red brown	50.00	1.25
RA54	PT13	50c olive bister	18.00	1.25
		Nos. RA49-RA54 (6)	122.00	7.50

There are two sizes of the numeral on No. RA49.

Catalogue values for unused stamps in this section, from this point to the end of the section, are for Never Hinged items.

Inscribed: "Provincia de Mocambique"

1954-56 ***Perf. 14½x14***

RA55	PT13	50c orange	1.40	.30
RA56	PT13	50c olive grn ('56)	1.40	.30
RA57	PT13	50c brown ('56)	1.40	.30
		Nos. RA55-RA57 (3)	4.20	.90

No. RA57 Surcharged with New Value and Wavy Lines

1956

RA58	PT13	30c on 50c brown	.85	.35

Pelican Type of 1954-56

1958 **Litho.** ***Perf. 14***

Denomination in Black

RA59	PT13	30c yellow	.70	.35
RA60	PT13	50c salmon	.70	.35

Imprint: "Imprensa Nacional de Mocambique"

1963-64

Denomination Typographed in Black

RA61	PT13	30c yellow ('64)	.50	.20
RA62	PT13	50c salmon	.35	.20

Women and Children PT14 — Lineman on Pole and Map of Mozambique PT15

1963-65 **Litho.** ***Perf. 14***

RA63	PT14	50c blk, bis & red	.30	.25
RA64	PT14	50c blk, pink & red ('65)	.30	.25

See Nos. RA68-RA76.

1965, Apr. 1 **Unwmk.** ***Perf. 14***

30c, Telegraph poles and map of Mozambique.

Size: 23x30mm

RA65 PT15 30c blk, salmon & lil .20 .20

Size: 19x36mm

RA66 PT15 50c blk, bl & sepia .20 .20
RA67 PT15 1e blk, yel & org .20 .20

The tax was for improvement of the telecommunications system. Obligatory on inland mail. A 2.50e in the design of the 30c was issued for use on telegrams.

Type of 1963

1967-70 Litho. ***Perf. 14***

RA68 PT14 50c blk, lt yel grn & red .40 .25
RA69 PT14 50c blk, lt bl & red ('69) .40 .20
RA70 PT14 50c blk, buff & brt red ('70) .40 .20
Nos. RA68-RA70 (3) 1.20 .65

1972-73

RA71 PT14 30c blk, lt grn & red .20 .20
RA72 PT14 50c blk, gray & red ('73) 1.00 .20
RA73 PT14 1e blk, bis & red ('73) .20 .20
Nos. RA71-RA73 (3) 1.40 .60

1974-75

RA74 PT14 50c blue, yel & red .20 .20
RA75 PT14 1e blk, gray & ver .85 .20
RA76 PT14 1e blk, lil rose & red ('75) .40 .20
Nos. RA74-RA76 (3) 1.45 .60

Intl. Year of the Child — PT16

1979 Litho. ***Perf. 14¼***

RA77 PT16 50e red 1.50 1.50

POSTAL TAX DUE STAMPS

Pombal Commemorative Issue
Common Design Types

1925 Unwmk. ***Perf. 12½***

RAJ1 CD28 30c brown & black .50 .60
RAJ2 CD29 30c brown & black .50 .60
RAJ3 CD30 30c brown & black .50 .60
Nos. RAJ1-RAJ3 (3) 1.50 1.80

MOZAMBIQUE COMPANY

mō-zəm-'bēk 'kəmp-nē

LOCATION — Comprises the territory of Manica and Sofala of the Mozambique Colony in southeastern Africa
GOVT. — A part of the Portuguese Colony of Mozambique
AREA — 51,881 sq. mi.
POP. — 368,447 (1939)
CAPITAL — Beira

The Mozambique Company was chartered by Portugal in 1891 for 50 years. The territory was under direct administration of the Company until July 18, 1941.

1000 Reis = 1 Milreis
100 Centavos = 1 Escudo (1916)

Mozambique Nos. 15-23 Overprinted in Carmine or Black

1892 Unwmk. ***Perf. 12½, 13½***

1 A2 5r black (C) 1.25 .25
a. Pair, one without overprint 50.00 22.50
2 A2 10r green 1.25 .25
3 A2 20r rose 1.25 .25
a. Perf. 13½ 45.00 30.00
4 A2 25r violet 1.50 .35
a. Double overprint 27.50
5 A2 40r chocolate 1.25 .30
a. Double overprint 20.00
6 A2 50r blue 1.50 .25
7 A2 100r yellow brown 1.25 .35
8 A2 200r gray violet 2.50 .45
9 A2 300r orange 3.50 .70
Nos. 1-9 (9) 15.25 3.15

Nos. 1 to 6, 8-9 were reprinted in 1905. These reprints have white gum and clean-cut perf. 13½ and the colors are usually paler than those of the originals.

Company Coat of Arms — A2

Perf. 11½, 12½, 13½

1895-1907 **Typo.**

Black or Red Numerals

10 A2 2½r olive yellow .25 .25
11 A2 2½r gray ('07) 1.50 1.50
12 A2 5r orange .25 .20
a. Value omitted 15.00
b. Perf. 13½ 2.00 1.10
13 A2 10r red lilac .40 .30
14 A2 10r yel grn ('07) 2.50 .40
a. Value inverted at top of stamp 20.00 20.00
15 A2 15r red brown 1.00 .30
16 A2 15r dk green ('07) 2.50 .40
17 A2 20r gray lilac 1.50 .30
18 A2 25r green .75 .30
a. Perf. 13½ 1.90 1.25
19 A2 25r carmine ('07) 2.50 .60
a. Value omitted 15.00 10.00
20 A2 50r blue .90 .30
21 A2 50r brown ('07) 2.50 .60
a. Value omitted 15.00
22 A2 65r slate blue ('02) .75 .35
23 A2 75r rose .55 .30
24 A2 75r red lilac ('07) 5.00 1.00
25 A2 80r yellow green .35 .30
26 A2 100r brown, *buff* .40 .30
27 A2 100r dk bl, *bl* ('07) 4.00 1.00
28 A2 115r car, *pink* ('04) 1.00 .70
29 A2 115r org brn, *pink* ('07) 6.00 1.40
30 A2 130r grn, *pink* ('04) 1.50 .70
31 A2 130r brn, *yel* ('07) 6.00 1.40
32 A2 150r org brn, *pink* .35 .35
33 A2 200r dk blue, *bl* .35 .35
a. Perf. 13½ 2.00 1.60
34 A2 200r red lil, *pink* ('07) 7.00 1.40
35 A2 300r dk bl, *salmon* .50 .30
a. Perf. 13½ 2.50 1.40
36 A2 400r brn, *bl* ('04) 2.50 .70
37 A2 400r dl bl, *yel* ('07) 8.00 1.90
38 A2 500r blk & red .55 .40
39 A2 500r blk & red, *bl* ('07) 8.00 1.90
a. 500r pur & red, *yel* (error)
40 A2 700r slate, *buff* ('04) 8.50 2.00
41 A2 700r pur, *yel* ('07) 5.00 2.00
42 A2 1000r violet & red .90 .40
Nos. 10-42 (33) 83.75 24.60

#12b, 18a, 33a, 35a were issued without gum.

For overprints & surcharges see #43-107, B1-B7.

Nos. 25 and 6 Surcharged or Overprinted in Red:

PROVISORIO

25

b

PROVISORIO

c

1895 ***Perf. 12½, 13½***

43 A2(b) 25r on 80r yel grn 22.50 15.00
44 A2(c) 50r blue 9.00 4.00

Overprint "c" on No. 44 also exists reading from upper left to lower right.

Stamps of 1895 Overprinted in Bister, Orange, Violet, Green, Black or Brown

1898 ***Perf. 12½, 13½***

Without Gum

45 A2 2½r olive yel (Bi) 5.00 1.50
a. Double overprint 40.00 25.00
b. Red overprint 60.00 50.00
46 A2 5r orange (O) 7.00 1.50
47 A2 10r red lilac (V) 7.00 1.50
48 A2 15r red brown (V) 10.00 3.00
a. Red overprint
49 A2 20r gray lilac (V) 10.00 3.00
50 A2 25r green (G) 12.00 3.00
a. Inverted overprint 65.00 40.00
51 A2 50r blue (Bk) 12.00 4.00
a. Inverted overprint 60.00 40.00
52 A2 75r rose (V) 12.50 5.00
a. Inverted overprint 75.00 40.00
b. Red overprint
53 A2 80r yellow grn (G) 17.50 5.00
a. Inverted overprint
54 A2 100r brn, *buff* (Br) 17.50 5.00
55 A2 150r org brn, *pink* (O) 17.50 5.00
a. Inverted overprint 75.00 30.00
b. Double overprint
56 A2 200r dk blue, *bl* (Bk) 16.00 7.50
57 A2 300r dk blue, *sal* (Bk) 20.00 10.00
a. Inverted overprint 60.00 50.00
b. Green overprint
Nos. 45-57 (13) 164.00 55.00

Vasco da Gama's discovery of route to India, 400th anniversary.
No. 57b was prepared but not issued.
Nos. 45 and 49 were also issued with gum.
The "Centenario" overprint on stamps perf. 11½ is forged.

Nos. 23, 12, 17 Surcharged in Black, Carmine or Violet

25

PROVISORIO

e

25

Réis

f

RÉIS

g

1899 ***Perf. 12½***

59 A2(e) 25r on 75r rose (Bk) 4.00 2.00

1900 ***Perf. 12½, 12½x11½***

60 A2(f) 25r on 5r org (C) 1.75 1.25
61 A2(g) 50r on half of 20r gray lil (V) 2.00 1.00
b. Entire stamp 15.00 9.00

No. 61b is perf. 11½ vertically through center.

Stamps of 1895-1907 Overprinted Locally in Carmine or Green

1911 ***Perf. 11½, 13½***

61A A2 2½r gray (C) 7.00 3.00
62 A2 5r orange (G) 6.00 3.00
63 A2 10r yellow grn (C) .70 .50
64 A2 15r dk green (C) .90 .50
a. Double overprint 40.00 20.00
65 A2 20r gray lilac (G) 1.25 .50
a. Perf. 13½ 1.40 .80
66 A2 25r carmine (G) 1.25 .60
67 A2 50r brown (G) .70 .45
68 A2 75r red lilac (G) 1.10 .45
69 A2 100r dk bl, *bl* (C) 1.25 .50
70 A2 115r org brn, *pink* (G) 2.00 .60
71 A2 130r brn, *yel* (G) 3.00 .60
72 A2 200r red lil, *pink* (G) 3.00 .60
73 A2 400r dull bl, *yel* (C) 3.00 .60
74 A2 500r blk & red, *bl* (C) 4.00 .95
75 A2 700r pur, *yel* (G) 4.00 .95
Nos. 61A-75 (15) 39.15 13.80

Nos. 63, 67 and 71 exist with inverted overprint; Nos. 63, 72 and 75 with double overprint.

Overprinted in Lisbon in Carmine or Green

1911 ***Perf. 11½, 12½***

75B A2 2½r gray .30 .20
76 A2 5r orange .30 .20
77 A2 10r yellow grn .25 .20
78 A2 15r dark green .35 .20
79 A2 20r gray lilac .40 .20
80 A2 25r carmine (G) .35 .20
a. Value inverted at top of stamp 18.00
81 A2 50r brown .70 .20
82 A2 75r red lilac .70 .20
a. Value omitted 15.00
83 A2 100r dk blue, *bl* 1.00 .20
84 A2 115r org brn, *pink* 2.50 .30
85 A2 130r brown, *yel* 3.00 .35
a. Double overprint 30.00
86 A2 200r red lil, *pink* 3.00 .25
87 A2 400r dull bl, *yel* 5.00 .30
88 A2 500r blk & red, *bl* 7.50 .30
89 A2 700r pur, *yel* 5.00 .50
Nos. 75B-89 (15) 30.35 3.80

Nos. 75B-89 Surcharged

1916 ***Perf. 11½***

90 A2 ¼c on 2½r gray .20 .20
91 A2 ½c on 5r org .20 .20
a. "½c" double 20.00
92 A2 1c on 10r yel grn .40 .20
93 A2 1½c on 15r dk grn .40 .20
a. Imperf., pair 35.00
94 A2 2c on 20r gray lil .50 .20
95 A2 2½c on 25r car 1.00 .25
96 A2 5c on 50r brn .40 .20
a. Imperf., pair 40.00
97 A2 7½c on 75r red lil .65 .20
98 A2 10c on 100r dk bl, *bl* 1.25 .30
a. Inverted surcharge 40.00 40.00
99 A2 11½c on 115r org brn, *pink* 3.50 .35
a. Inverted surcharge 50.00 50.00
100 A2 13c on 130r brn, *yel* 6.50 .30
101 A2 20c on 200r red lil, *pink* 5.50 .30
102 A2 40c on 400r dl bl, *yel* 6.50 .35
103 A2 50c on 500r blk & red, *bl* (R) 8.00 .70
104 A2 70c on 700r pur, *yel* 8.00 .75
Nos. 90-104 (15) 43.00 4.70

Nos. 87 to 89 Surcharged

1918 ***Perf. 11½***

105 A2 ½c on 700r pur, *yel* 2.50 .95
106 A2 2½c on 500r blk & red, *bl* (Bl) 3.50 .95
107 A2 5c on 400r dl bl, *yel* 4.50 .95
Nos. 105-107 (3) 10.50 2.85

Native and Village — A9

Man and Ivory Tusks — A10

Corn — A11

Tapping Rubber Tree — A12

Sugar Refinery — A13

Buzi River Scene — A14

Tobacco Field — A15

View of Beira — A16

Coffee Plantation A17

Orange Tree A18

Cotton Field A19

Sisal Plantation A20

Scene on Beira R. R. — A21

Court House at Beira — A22

Coconut Palm A23

Mangroves A24

Cattle — A25

Company Arms — A26

1918-31 Engr. *Perf. 14, 15, 12½*

No.	Type	Description	Unused	Used
108	A9	¼c brn & yel grn	.25	.20
109	A9	¼c ol grn & blk ('25)	.20	.20
110	A10	½c black	.25	.20
111	A11	1c green & blk	.25	.20
112	A12	1½c black & grn	.25	.25
113	A13	2c carmine & blk	.25	.20
114	A13	2c ol blk & blk ('25)	.25	.25
115	A14	2½c lilac & blk	.20	.20
116	A11	3c ocher & blk ('23)	.25	.20
117	A15	4c grn & brn ('21)	.25	.20
118	A15	4c red & blk ('25)	.20	.20
119	A9	4½c gray & blk ('23)	.20	.20
120	A16	5c blue & blk	.20	.20
121	A17	6c claret & bl ('21)	.80	.30
122	A17	6c lilac & blk ('25)	.20	.20
123	A21	7c ultra & blk ('23)	1.00	.50
124	A18	7½c orange & grn	.75	.30
125	A19	8c violet & blk	.20	.20
126	A20	10c red org & blk	.20	.20
128	A19	12c brn & blk ('23)	1.00	.35
129	A19	12c bl grn & blk ('25)	2.00	.35
130	A21	15c carmine & blk	.40	.30
131	A22	20c dp green & blk	.35	.20
132	A23	30c red brn & blk	3.50	.70
133	A23	30c gray grn & blk ('25)	2.00	.25
134	A23	30c bl grn & blk ('31)	3.50	.40
135	A24	40c yel grn & blk	.85	.45
136	A24	40c grnsh bl & blk ('25)	.70	.30
137	A25	50c orange & blk	2.25	.75
138	A25	50c lt vio & blk ('25)	2.25	.45
139	A25	60c rose & brn ('23)	1.50	.50
140	A20	80c ultra & brn ('23)	4.00	.70
141	A20	80c car & blk ('25)	1.00	.35
142	A26	1e dk green & blk	2.25	.45
143	A26	1e blue & blk ('25)	2.25	.35
144	A16	2e rose & vio ('23)	5.00	.70
145	A16	2e lilac & blk ('25)	4.00	.45
		Nos. 108-145 (37)	45.00	12.40

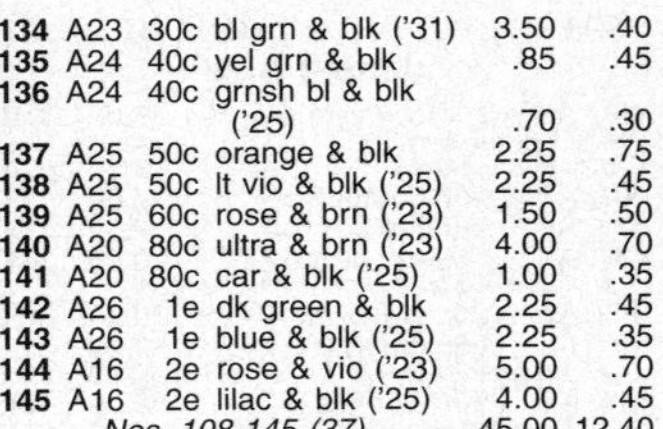

Shades exist of several denominations.

For surcharges see Nos. 146-154, RA1.

Nos. 132, 142, 115, 120, 131, 135, 125, 137 Surcharged with New Values in Red, Blue, Violet or Black:

h

i

j

1920 *Perf. 14, 15*

No.	Type	Description	Unused	Used
146	A23(h)	½c on 30c (Bk)	6.00	4.50
147	A26(h)	½c on 1e (R)	6.00	4.50
148	A14(h)	1½c on 2½c (Bl)	4.00	2.25
149	A16(h)	1½c on 5c (V)	4.00	3.50
150	A14(h)	2c on 2½c (R)	1.75	1.75
151	A22(i)	4c on 20c (V)	7.50	4.50
152	A24(i)	4c on 40c (V)	8.50	5.00
153	A19(j)	6c on 8c (R)	8.00	5.50
154	A25(j)	6c on 50c (Bk)	9.00	5.50
		Nos. 146-154 (9)	54.75	37.00

The surcharge on No. 148 is placed vertically between two bars. On No. 154 the two words of the surcharge are 13mm apart.

Native — A27

View of Beira — A28

Tapping Rubber Tree — A29

Picking Tea — A30

Zambezi River — A31

1925-31 Engr. *Perf. 12*

No.	Type	Description	Unused	Used
155	A27	24c ultra & blk	1.00	.50
156	A28	25c choc & ultra	1.00	.50
157	A27	85c brn red & blk ('31)	.85	.45
158	A28	1.40e dl bl & blk ('31)	.85	.45
159	A29	5e yel brn & ultra	1.25	.30
160	A30	10e rose & blk	1.75	.75
161	A31	20e green & blk	1.75	.75
		Nos. 155-161 (7)	8.45	3.70

Ivory Tusks — A32

Panning Gold — A33

1931 Litho. *Perf. 14*

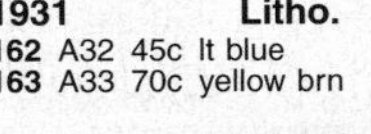

No.	Type	Description	Unused	Used
162	A32	45c lt blue	2.00	.85
163	A33	70c yellow brn	1.40	.35

Zambezi Railroad Bridge A34

1935 Engr. *Perf. 12½*

No.	Type	Description	Unused	Used
164	A34	1e dk blue & blk	2.00	1.40

Opening of a new bridge over the Zambezi River.

Airplane over Beira — A35

1935

No.	Type	Description	Unused	Used
165	A35	5c blue & blk	.45	.35
166	A35	10c red org & blk	.45	.35
a.		Square pair, imperf. between	50.00	
167	A35	15c red & blk	.45	.35
a.		Square pair, imperf. between	50.00	
168	A35	20c yel grn & blk	.45	.35
169	A35	30c green & blk	.45	.35
170	A35	40c gray bl & blk	.45	.35
171	A35	45c blue & blk	.45	.35
172	A35	50c violet & blk	.45	.35
a.		Square pair, imperf. btwn.	60.00	
173	A35	60c carmine & brn	.60	.35
174	A35	80c carmine & blk	.60	.35
		Nos. 165-174 (10)	4.80	3.50

Issued to commemorate the opening of the Blantyre-Beira Salisbury air service.

Giraffe — A36

Thatched Huts — A37

Rock Python — A41

Coconut Palms A50

Zambezi Railroad Bridge A52

Sena Gate — A53

Company Arms — A54

Designs: 10c, Dhow. 15c, St. Caetano Fortress, Sofala. 20c, Zebra. 40c, Black rhinoceros. 45c, Lion. 50c, Crocodile. 60c, Leopard. 70c, Mozambique woman. 80c, Hippopotami. 85c, Vasco da Gama's flagship. 1e, Man in canoe. 2e, Greater kudu.

1937, May 16 *Perf. 12½*

No.	Type	Description	Unused	Used
175	A36	1c yel grn & vio	.20	.20
176	A37	5c blue & yel grn	.20	.20
177	A36	10c ver & ultra	.20	.20
178	A37	15c carmine & blk	.20	.20
179	A36	20c green & ultra	.20	.20
180	A41	30c dk grn & ind	.20	.30
181	A41	40c gray bl & blk	.20	.30
182	A41	45c blue & brn	.20	.30
183	A41	50c dk vio & emer	.20	.30
184	A37	60c carmine & bl	.20	.20
185	A36	70c yel brn & pale grn	.20	.20
186	A37	80c car & pale grn	.40	.30
187	A41	85c org red & blk	.40	.40
188	A41	1e dp bl & blk	.30	.20
189	A50	1.40e dk bl & pale grn	.30	.20
190	A41	2e pale lilac & brn	.70	.20
191	A52	5e yel brn & bl	1.00	.70
192	A53	10e carmine & blk	2.00	1.40
193	A54	20e grn & brn vio	2.50	2.75
		Nos. 175-193 (19)	9.80	8.75

Stamps of 1937 Overprinted in Red or Black

1939, Aug. 28

No.	Type	Description	Unused	Used
194	A41	30c dk grn & ind (R)	1.50	.85
195	A41	40c gray bl & blk (R)	1.50	.85
196	A41	45c blue & brn (Bk)	1.50	.85
197	A41	50c dk vio & emer (R)	2.00	1.00
198	A41	85c org red & blk (Bk)	2.00	1.00
199	A41	1e dp bl & blk (R)	1.75	1.25
200	A41	2e pale lil & brn (Bk)	2.50	1.60
		Nos. 194-200 (7)	12.75	7.40

Visit of the President of Portugal to Beira in 1939.

King Alfonso Henriques A55

King John IV A56

1940, Feb. 16 Typo. *Perf. 11½x12*

No.	Type	Description	Unused	Used
201	A55	1.75e blue & lt blue	.70	.70

800th anniv. of Portuguese independence.

1941 Engr. *Perf. 12½*

No.	Type	Description	Unused	Used
202	A56	40c gray grn & blk	.30	.20
203	A56	50c dk vio & brt grn	.30	.20
204	A56	60c brt car & dp bl	.30	.20
205	A56	70c brn org & dk grn	.30	.20
206	A56	80c car & dp grn	.30	.20
207	A56	1e dk bl & blk	.30	.20
		Nos. 202-207 (6)	1.80	1.20

300th anniv. of the restoration of the Portuguese Monarchy.

Mozambique Company's charter terminated July 18th, 1941 after which date its stamps were superseded by those of the territory of Mozambique.

SEMI-POSTAL STAMPS

Lisbon Issue of 1911 Overprinted in Red

1917 **Unwmk.** ***Perf. 11½***

B1 A2 2½r gray 7.50 *10.50*
a. Double overprint 75.00 *75.00*
B2 A2 10r yellow grn 8.75 *15.00*
B3 A2 20r gray lilac 12.00 *20.00*
B4 A2 50r brown 20.00 *25.00*
B5 A2 75r red lilac 65.00 *70.00*
B6 A2 100r dk blue, *bl* 65.00 *70.00*
B7 A2 700r purple, *yel* 160.00 *225.00*
Nos. B1-B7 (7) 338.25 *435.50*

Nos. B1-B7 were used on July 31, 1917, in place of ordinary stamps. The proceeds were given to the Red Cross.

AIR POST STAMPS

Airplane over Beira — AP1

1935 **Unwmk.** **Engr.** ***Perf. 12½***

C1 AP1 5c blue & blk .20 .20
C2 AP1 10c org red & blk .20 .20
C3 AP1 15c red & blk .20 .20
C4 AP1 20c yel grn & blk .20 .20
C5 AP1 30c green & blk .20 .20
C6 AP1 40c gray bl & blk .20 .20
C7 AP1 45c blue & blk .20 .20
C8 AP1 50c dk vio & blk .40 .20
C9 AP1 60c car & brn .40 .20
C10 AP1 80c car & blk .50 .20
C11 AP1 1e blue & blk .50 .20
C12 AP1 2e mauve & blk 1.25 .25
C13 AP1 5e bis brn & bl 1.25 .40
C14 AP1 10e car & blk 1.40 .60
C15 AP1 20e bl grn & blk 2.75 .85
Nos. C1-C15 (15) 9.85 4.30

POSTAGE DUE STAMPS

D1

1906 **Unwmk.** **Typo.** ***Perf. 11½x12***
Denominations in Black

J1 D1 5r yellow grn .70 .30
J2 D1 10r slate .70 .30
J3 D1 20r yellow brn 1.25 .30
J4 D1 30r orange 1.50 1.00
J5 D1 50r gray brown 1.50 1.00
J6 D1 60r red brown 22.50 9.00
J7 D1 100r red lilac 4.00 2.50
J8 D1 130r dull blue 32.50 12.00
J9 D1 200r carmine 13.00 4.00
J10 D1 500r violet 18.00 5.00
Nos. J1-J10 (10) 95.65 35.40

Nos. J1-J10 Overprinted in Carmine or Green

1911

J11 D1 5r yellow grn .20 .20
J12 D1 10r slate .20 .20
J13 D1 20r yellow brn .20 .20
J14 D1 30r orange .20 .20
J15 D1 50r gray brown .30 .20
J16 D1 60r red brown .40 .30
J17 D1 100r red lilac .40 .30
J18 D1 130r dull blue 2.00 1.00
J19 D1 200r carmine (G) 1.25 .85
J20 D1 500r violet 2.50 1.00
Nos. J11-J20 (10) 7.65 4.45

D2

Company Arms — D3

1916 **Typo.**
With Value in Centavos in Black

J21 D2 ½c yellow grn .30 .20
J22 D2 1c slate .30 .20
J23 D2 2c orange brn .30 .20
J24 D2 3c orange .60 .25
J25 D2 5c gray brown .60 .25
J26 D2 6c pale brown .60 .25
J27 D2 10c red lilac .60 .30
J28 D2 13c gray blue .90 .55
J29 D2 20c rose 1.25 .65
J30 D2 50c gray 3.00 .85
Nos. J21-J30 (10) 8.45 3.70

1919 **Engr.** ***Perf. 12½, 13½, 14, 15***

J31 D3 ½c green .20 .20
J32 D3 1c slate .20 .20
J33 D3 2c red brown .20 .20
J34 D3 3c orange .20 .20
J35 D3 5c gray brown .20 .20
J36 D3 6c lt brown .45 .45
J37 D3 10c lilac rose .45 .45
J38 D3 13c dull blue .45 .45
J39 D3 20c rose .45 .45
J40 D3 50c gray .45 .45
Nos. J31-J40 (10) 3.25 3.25

NEWSPAPER STAMP

Newspaper Stamp of Mozambique Overprinted Like Nos. 1-9

1894 **Unwmk.** ***Perf. 11½***

P1 N3 2½r brown .50 .40
a. Inverted overprint 30.00 30.00
b. Perf. 12½ .85 .50

Reprints are on stout white paper with clean-cut perf. 13½. Value $1.

POSTAL TAX STAMPS

No. 116 Surcharged in Black

1932 ***Perf. 12½***

RA1 A11 2c on 3c org & blk 1.40 *2.00*

Charity — PT2

1933 **Litho.** ***Perf. 11***

RA2 PT2 2c magenta & blk 1.00 *2.00*

PT3

PT4

1940 **Unwmk.** ***Perf. 10½***

RA3 PT3 2c black & ultra 15.00 *16.00*

1941

RA4 PT4 2c black & brt red 15.00 *16.00*

NAMIBIA

nə-ˈmi-bē-ə

LOCATION — In southwestern Africa between Angola and South Africa, bordering on the Atlantic Ocean
GOVT. — Republic
AREA — 318,261 sq. mi.
POP. — 1,648,270 (1999 est.)
CAPITAL — Windhoek

Formerly South West Africa.

100 Cents = 1 Rand
100 Cents = 1 Dollar (1993)

Catalogue values for unused stamps in this country are for Never Hinged items.

Pres. Sam Nujoma, Map and Natl. Flag — A137

Perf. 14½x14, 14x14½

1990, Mar. 21 **Litho.** **Unwmk.**

659 A137 18c shown .40 .30
660 A137 45c Dove, map, hands unchained, vert. 1.10 1.00
661 A137 60c Flag, map 1.75 1.50
Nos. 659-661 (3) 3.25 2.80

Independence from South Africa.

Sights of Namibia A138

1990, Apr. 26 ***Perf. 14½x14***

662 A138 18c Fish River Canyon .55 .40
663 A138 35c Quiver-tree Forest .80 .60
664 A138 45c Tsaris Mountains 1.00 .80
665 A138 60c Dolerite Hills 1.40 1.10
a. Souvenir sheet of 1 4.75 4.75
Nos. 662-665 (4) 3.75 2.90

No. 665a publicizes the 150th anniv. of the Penny Black. Sold for 1.50r.

Architectural Development of Windhoek A139

Designs: 18c, Early central business area. 35c, Modern central business area. 45c, First municipal building. 60c, Current municipal building.

1990, July 26 ***Perf. 14½x14***

666 A139 18c multicolored .40 .40
667 A139 35c multicolored .65 .65
668 A139 45c multicolored .85 .85
669 A139 60c multicolored 1.10 1.10
Nos. 666-669 (4) 3.00 3.00

Farming and Ranching A140

1990, Oct. 11 ***Perf. 14½x14***

670 A140 20c Cornfields .40 .30
671 A140 35c Sanga cattle .65 .55
672 A140 50c Damara sheep .95 .75
673 A140 65c Irrigation 1.25 1.00
Nos. 670-673 (4) 3.25 2.60

Gypsum — A141

Oranjemund Alluvial Diamond Mine A142

1991, Jan. 2 ***Perf. 14½x14***

674 A141 1c shown .20 .20
675 A141 2c Fluorite .20 .20
676 A141 5c Mimetite .25 .20
677 A141 10c Azurite .35 .20
679 A141 20c Dioptase .40 .25
680 A142 25c shown .40 .30
681 A142 30c Tsumeb mine .50 .40
682 A142 35c Rosh Pinah mine .60 .40
683 A141 40c Diamond .75 .50
684 A142 50c Uis mine .75 .50
685 A141 65c Boltwoodite .85 .70
686 A142 1r Rossing mine 1.25 1.00
687 A141 1.50r Wulfenite 2.00 1.40
688 A141 2r Gold 2.50 2.25
689 A141 5r Willemite 6.25 5.50
Nos. 674-689 (15) 17.25 14.00

Nos. 676, 677 were reprinted in 1992 on phosphorescent paper.

Namibian Weather Service, Cent. A143

1991, Feb. 2 ***Perf. 14½x14***

690 A143 20c Weather balloon .30 .20
691 A143 35c Sunshine recorder .50 .45
692 A143 50c Measuring equipment .70 .60
693 A143 65c Gobabeb weather station .80 .75
Nos. 690-693 (4) 2.30 2.00

Mountain Zebra A144

1991, Apr. 18 ***Perf. 14½x14***

694 A144 20c Four zebras *2.50 .65*
695 A144 25c Mother suckling foal *3.25 .75*
696 A144 45c Three zebras *4.00 1.75*
697 A144 60c Two zebras *4.75 3.00*
Nos. 694-697 (4) *14.50 6.15*

A souvenir sheet of 1 #696 was sold for 1.50r by the Philatelic Foundation of South Africa. Value $10.

Mountains A145

1991, July 18 ***Perf. 14½x14***

698 A145 20c Karas .40 .40
699 A145 25c Gamsberg .50 .50
700 A145 45c Brukkaros .70 .70
701 A145 60c Erongo .85 .85
Nos. 698-701 (4) 2.45 2.45

Tourist Camps A146

Designs: 20c, Bernabe De la Bat Tourist Camp, Waterberg. 25c, Von Bach Recreation Resort. 45c, Gross Barmen Hot Springs. 60c, Namutoni Rest Camp.

1991, Oct. 24 *Perf. 14½x14*

702 A146 20c multicolored	.40	.30
703 A146 25c multicolored	.50	.40
704 A146 45c multicolored	.75	.65
705 A146 60c multicolored	1.00	.85
Nos. 702-705 (4)	2.65	2.20

Windhoek Conservatoir, 21st Anniv. — A147

Designs: 20c, Artist's palette, brushes. 25c, French horn, neck of violin. 45c, Pan pipes, masks of Comedy and Tragedy, lyre. 60c, Ballet pas de deux.

1992, Jan. 30 *Perf. 14x14½*

706 A147 20c multicolored	.25	.20
707 A147 25c multicolored	.35	.20
708 A147 45c multicolored	.60	.50
709 A147 60c multicolored	.80	.80
Nos. 706-709 (4)	2.00	1.70

Freshwater Fish — A148

1992, Apr. 16 *Perf. 14½x14*

710 A148 20c Blue kurper	.40	.30
711 A148 25c Yellow fish	.45	.35
712 A148 45c Carp	.85	.65
713 A148 60c Catfish	.95	.95
Nos. 710-713 (4)	2.65	2.25

A souvenir sheet of 1 #712 was sold by the Philatelic Foundation of South Africa. Value, $4.

Views of Swakopmund — A149

1992, July 2 *Perf. 14½x14*

714 A149 20c Jetty	.50	.30
715 A149 25c Swimming pool	.60	.40
716 A149 45c State House, lighthouse	.85	.60
717 A149 60c Palm beach	1.10	.85
a. Souvenir sheet of 4, #714-717	3.75	3.75
Nos. 714-717 (4)	3.05	2.15

1992 Summer Olympics, Barcelona A150

1992, July 24 *Perf. 14½x14*

718 A150 20c Runners	.30	.25
719 A150 25c Flag, emblem	.40	.35
720 A150 45c Swimmers	.80	.60
721 A150 60c Olympic stadium	1.00	.80
a. Souvenir sheet of 4, #718-721	3.00	3.00
Nos. 718-721 (4)	2.50	2.00

No. 721a sold for 2r.

Disabled Workers — A151

Designs: 20c, Wrapping cucumbers. 25c, Finishing a woven mat. 45c, At a spinning wheel. 60c, Cleaning potted plants.

1992, Sept. 10 *Perf. 14x14½*

722 A151 20c multicolored	.30	.20
723 A151 25c multicolored	.40	.30
724 A151 45c multicolored	.70	.50
725 A151 60c multicolored	.90	.75
Nos. 722-725 (4)	2.30	1.75

Endangered Animals A152

1993, Feb. 25 *Perf. 14½x14*

726 A152 20c Loxodonta africana	.55	.40
727 A152 25c Tragelaphus spekei	.65	.50
728 A152 45c Diceros bicornis	1.00	.80
729 A152 60c Lycaon pictus	1.10	.95
a. Souvenir sheet of 4, #726-729	4.75	4.75
Nos. 726-729 (4)	3.30	2.65

Namibia Nature Foundation. No. 729a sold for 2.10r.

Arrival of Simmentaler Cattle in Namibia, Cent. A153

1993, Apr. 16 *Perf. 14½x14*

730 A153 20c Cows and calves	.35	.20
731 A153 25c Cow and calf	.40	.30
732 A153 45c Head of stud bull	.60	.50
733 A153 60c Arrival on boat, 1893	.85	.75
Nos. 730-733 (4)	2.20	1.75

A souvenir sheet of one No. 732 has inscription for National Philatelic Exhibition. Sold for 3r. Value, $3.50.

Namib Desert A154

1993, June 4 *Perf. 14½x14*

734 A154 30c Sossusvlei	.40	.40
735 A154 40c Blutkuppe	.50	.50
736 A154 65c Homeb	.75	.75
737 A154 85c Moon landscape	.95	.95
Nos. 734-737 (4)	2.60	2.60

SOS Children's Village A155

1993, Aug. 6 **Litho.** *Perf. 14*

738 A155 30c Happiness	.40	.25
739 A155 40c A loving family	.55	.35
740 A155 65c Home sweet home	.80	.60
741 A155 85c My village	1.00	.80
Nos. 738-741 (4)	2.75	2.00

A156

Butterflies: 5c, Charaxes jasius saturnus. 10c, Acraea anemosa. 20c, Papilio nireus lyaeus. 30c, Junonia octavia sesamus. (35c), Graphium antheus. 40c, Hypolimnas misippus. 50c, Physcaeneura panda. 65c, Charaxes candiope. 85c, Junonia hierta cebrene. 90c, Colotis celimene pholoe. $1, Cacyreus dicksoni. $2, Charaxes bohemani. $2.50, Stugeta bowkeri tearei. $5, Byblia anvatara acheloia.

1993-94 *Perf. 14x14½*

742 A156 5c multicolored	.20	.20
743 A156 10c multicolored	.20	.20
744 A156 20c multicolored	.20	.20
745 A156 30c multicolored	.20	.20
745A A156 (35c) multicolored	.35	.35
746 A156 40c multicolored	.25	.25
747 A156 50c multicolored	.30	.30
748 A156 65c multicolored	.40	.40
749 A156 85c multicolored	.50	.50
750 A156 90c multicolored	.55	.55
751 A156 $1 multicolored	.60	.60
752 A156 $2 multicolored	1.25	1.25
753 A156 $2.50 multicolored	1.50	1.50
754 A156 $5 multicolored	3.25	3.25
Nos. 742-754 (14)	9.75	9.75

No. 745A is inscribed "STANDARDISED MAIL" and sold for 35c when issued.

Issued: No. 745A, 4/8/94; others, 10/1/93.

Perf. 14½x15 Syncopated Type A

1997

742a A156 5c multicolored	.65	.65
747a A156 50c multicolored	1.25	1.25

Issued: Nos. 742a, 747a, 3/3/97.

Coastal Angling A157

1994, Feb. 4 **Litho.** *Perf. 14*

755 A157 30c Blacktail	.25	.25
756 A157 40c Kob	.35	.30
757 A157 65c Steenbras	.60	.55
758 A157 85c Galjoen	.80	.75
a. Souvenir sheet of 4, #755-758	2.75	2.75
Nos. 755-758 (4)	2.00	1.85

Incorporation of Walvis Bay into Namibia A158

1994, Mar. 1

759 A158 30c Quay	.40	.25
760 A158 65c Aerial view	.70	.45
761 A158 85c Map of Namibia	.90	.70
Nos. 759-761 (3)	2.00	1.40

A159

A160

Flowers: 35c, Adenolobus pechuelii. 40c, Hibiscus elliottiae. 65c, Pelargonium cortusifolium. 85c, Hoodia macrantha.

1994, Apr. 8 **Litho.** *Perf. 14*

762 A159 35c multicolored	.30	.25
763 A159 40c multicolored	.35	.30
764 A159 65c multicolored	.60	.50
765 A159 85c multicolored	.75	.65
Nos. 762-765 (4)	2.00	1.70

1994, June 3 **Litho.** *Perf. 14*

Storks of Etosha.

766 A160 35c Yellowbilled	.35	.25
767 A160 40c Abdim's	.45	.30
768 A160 80c Openbilled	.70	.60
769 A160 $1.10 White	.95	.85
Nos. 766-769 (4)	2.45	2.00

Trains A161

1994, Aug. 5 **Litho.** *Perf. 13½x14*

770 A161 35c Steam railcar	.40	.30
771 A161 70c Class Krauss	.75	.55
772 A161 80c Class 24	.85	.75
773 A161 $1.10 Class 7C	1.25	1.00
Nos. 770-773 (4)	3.25	2.60

A souvenir sheet of 1 #772 was sold for 3r by the Philatelic Foundation of South Africa. Value $2.75.

Railways in Namibia, Cent. A162

Locomotives: 35c, Prince Edward, 1st in service. 70c, Ex-German SWA 2-8-0 tank. 80c, Class 8. $1.10, Class 33 400 diesel electric.

1995, Mar. 8 **Litho.** *Perf. 14*

774 A162 35c multicolored	.30	.25
775 A162 70c multicolored	.50	.35
776 A162 80c multicolored	.75	.60
777 A162 $1.10 multicolored	1.75	.80
a. Souvenir sheet of 4, #774-777	2.50	2.50
Nos. 774-777 (4)	3.30	2.00

No. 777a sold for $3.50.

No. 777a exists inscribed "Reprint November 1996." Value $4.75.

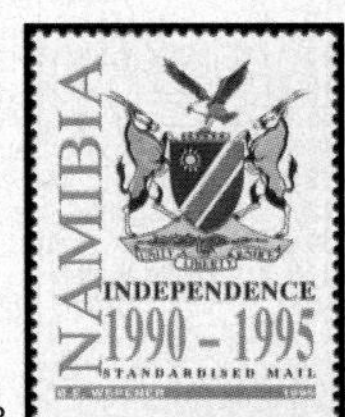

A163

A164

1995, Mar. 21 Litho. *Perf. 14*
778 A163 (35c) multicolored .50 .50

Independence, 5th anniv. No. 778 is inscribed "STANDARDISED MAIL" and sold for 35c on day of issue.

1995, May 24 Litho. *Perf. 14*

Fossils: 40c, Geochelone stromeri. 80c, Diamantornis wardi. 90c, Prohyrax hendeyi. $1.20, Crocodylus lloydi.

779 A164 40c multicolored .25 .20
780 A164 80c multicolored .55 .40
781 A164 90c multicolored .60 .45
782 A164 $1.20 multicolored .75 .55
Nos. 779-782 (4) 2.15 1.60

A souvenir sheet of 1 #780 was sold for 3r by the Philatelic Foundation of South Africa. Value $3.

Finnish Mission, 125th Anniv. A165

Designs: 40c, Mission church, Martti Rautanen (1845-1926). 80c, Albin Savola (1867-1934), Oniipa printing press. 90c, Oxwagon, Karl Emanuel August Weikkolin (1842-91). $1.20, Dr. Selma Raino (1873-1939), Onandjokwe Hospital.

1995, July 10 Litho. *Perf. 14*
783 A165 40c multicolored .45 .25
784 A165 80c multicolored .70 .50
785 A165 90c multicolored .75 .55
786 A165 $1.20 multicolored .90 .70
Nos. 783-786 (4) 2.80 2.00

Traditional Adornments — A166

1995, Aug. 16 Litho. *Perf. 14½x14*
787 A166 40c Ivory buttons .35 .20
788 A166 80c Conus shell .60 .45
789 A166 90c Cowrie shells .65 .50
790 A166 $1.20 Shell button .80 .65
Nos. 787-790 (4) 2.40 1.80

Souvenir Sheet

Singapore '95 — A167

Illustration reduced.

1995, Sept. 10 Litho. *Perf. 14*
791 A167 $1.20 Phacochoerus aethiopicus 1.50 1.50

UN, 50th Anniv. A168

1995, Oct. 24
792 A168 40c blue & black .40 .40

Tourism A169

1996, Apr. 1 Litho. *Perf. 15x14*
793 A169 (45c) Bogenfels Arch .25 .20
794 A169 90c Ruacana Falls .45 .35
795 A169 $1 Epupa Falls .50 .50
796 A169 $1.30 Wild horses .65 .60
Nos. 793-796 (4) 1.85 1.65

No. 793 is inscribed "Standardised Mail" and sold for 45c on day of issue.

Catholic Missions in Namibia A170

50c, Döbra Education and Training Centre. 95c, Heirachabis. $1, Windhoek St. Mary's Cathedral. $1.30, Ovamboland Old Church & School.

1996, May 27 Litho. *Perf. 15x14*
797 A170 50c multicolored .25 .25
798 A170 95c multicolored .45 .45
799 A170 $1 multicolored .45 .45
800 A170 $1.30 multicolored .60 .60
Nos. 797-800 (4) 1.75 1.75

Souvenir Sheet

CAPEX 96 — A171

Illustration reduced.

1996, June 8 Litho. *Perf. 14½x14*
801 A171 $1.30 African lynx 1.00 1.00

UNICEF, 50th Anniv. A172

Designs: (45c), Children have rights. $1.30, Educate the girl.

1996, June 14 Litho. *Perf. 15x14*
802 A172 (45c) multicolored .25 .20
803 A172 $1.30 multicolored .70 .60

No. 802 is inscribed "Standard Postage" and sold for 45c on day of issue.

1996 Summer Olympic Games, Atlanta A173

1996, June 27
804 A173 (45c) Boxing .20 .20
805 A173 90c Cycling .45 .45
806 A173 $1 Swimming .50 .50
807 A173 $1.30 Running .60 .60
Nos. 804-807 (4) 1.75 1.75

No. 804 is inscribed "Standard Postage" and sold for 45c on day of issue.

Constellations — A174

Designs: (45c), Scorpio. 90c, Sagittarius. $1, Southern Cross. $1.30, Orion.

1996, Sept. 12 Litho. *Perf. 15x14*
808 A174 (45c) multicolored .25 .25
809 A174 90c multicolored .55 .55
810 A174 $1 multicolored .60 .60
a. Souvenir sheet of 1 2.25 2.25
811 A174 $1.30 multicolored .70 .70
Nos. 808-811 (4) 2.10 2.10

No. 808 is inscribed "Standard Postage" and sold for 45c on day of issue.

No. 810a sold for $3.50. No. 810a exists inscribed "Reprint February 17, 1997. Sold in aid of organized philately N$3.50."

Early Pastoral Pottery — A175

Designs: (45c), Urn-shaped storage vessel. 90c, Bag-shaped cooking vessel. $1, Reconstructed pot. $1.30, Large storage vessel.

1996, Oct. 17 *Perf. 14x15*
812 A175 (45c) multicolored .20 .20
813 A175 90c multicolored .45 .45
814 A175 $1 multicolored .50 .50
815 A175 $1.30 multicolored .60 .60
Nos. 812-815 (4) 1.75 1.75

No. 812 is inscribed "Standard Postage" and sold for 45c on day of issue.

Ancient //Khauxa!nas Ruins, near Karasburg — A176

Various views of stone wall.

1997, Feb. 6 Litho. *Perf. 15x14*
816 A176 (45c) multicolored .30 .30
817 A176 $1 multicolored .55 .55
818 A176 $1.10 multicolored .55 .55
819 A176 $1.50 multicolored .75 .75
Nos. 816-819 (4) 2.15 2.15

No. 816 is inscribed "Standard Postage" and sold for 45c on day of issue.

Souvenir Sheet

Hong Kong '97, Intl. Stamp Exhibition — A176a

1997, Feb. 12 Litho. *Perf. 14½x14*
819A A176a $1.30 Sanga bull *2.50 2.50*

No. 819A sold for $3.50. An inscription, "REPRINT 1 APRIL 1997," was added to a later printing of this sheet. Value $3.50.

A177

A178

1997, Apr. 8 Litho. *Perf. 14x14½*
820 A177 $2 multicolored 1.00 1.00

Heinrich von Stephan (1831-97), founder of UPU.

1997, May 15 Litho. *Perf. 14x14½*

Jackass Penguins.

821 A178 (45c) shown .40 .40
822 A178 $1 Nesting .70 .70
823 A178 $1.10 With young .90 .90
824 A178 $1.50 Swimming 1.10 1.10
Nos. 821-824 (4) 3.10 3.10

Sheet of 4

824A A178 #b.-e. 3.50 3.50

World Wildlife Fund. No. 821 is inscribed "Standard Postage" and sold for 45c on day of issue.

Nos. 824Ab-824Ae are like Nos. 821-824 but do not have the WWF emblem. No. 824A sold for $5.

Wild Cats A179

1997, June 12 Litho. *Perf. 14½x14*
825 A179 (45c) Felis caracal .20 .20
826 A179 $1 Felis lybica .45 .45
827 A179 $1.10 Felis serval .55 .55
828 A179 $1.50 Felis nigripes .70 .70
Nos. 825-828 (4) 1.90 1.90

No. 825 is inscribed "Standard Postage" and sold for 45c on day of issue. A souvenir sheet containing a $5 stamp like #828 exists. Value $2.50.

Helmeted Guineafowl A180

1997, June 5 ***Perf. 14½x14***

829 A180 $1.20 multicolored .75 .75

A181 A182

Baskets: 50c, Collecting bag. 90c, Powder basket. $1.20, Fruit basket. $2, Grain basket.

1997, July 8 **Litho.** ***Perf. 14x14½***

830 A181 50c multicolored .25 .20
831 A181 90c multicolored .40 .30
832 A181 $1.20 multicolored .55 .40
833 A181 $2 multicolored .90 .70
Nos. 830-833 (4) 2.10 1.60

Perf. 14x14½ Syncopated Type A

1997, May 5

Cinderella Waxbill.

Booklet Stamps

834 A182 50c shown .25 .25
835 A182 60c Blackchecked waxbill .30 .30
a. Booklet pane, 5 each #834-835 3.00
Complete booklet, #835a 3.00

A183

Greetings Stamps A184

Flowers: No. 836, Catophractes alexandri. No. 837, Crinun paludosum. No. 838, Gloriosa superba. No. 839, Tribulus zeyheri. No. 840, Aptosimum pubescens.

Helmeted guineafowl: No. 841, In bed. No. 842, Holding flowers. No. 843, As music conductor. No. 844, Prepared to travel. No. 845, Wearing heart necklace.

1997, July 11 **Litho.** ***Perf. 14x13½***

Booklet Stamps

836 A183 (45c) multicolored .45 .45
837 A183 (45c) multicolored .45 .45
838 A183 (45c) multicolored .45 .45
839 A183 (45c) multicolored .45 .45
840 A183 (45c) multicolored .45 .45
a. Booklet pane, 2 each #836-840 + 10 labels 4.50
Complete booklet, #840a 4.50
841 A184 50c multicolored .40 .40
842 A184 50c multicolored .40 .40
843 A184 50c multicolored .40 .40
844 A184 $1 multicolored .80 .80
845 A184 $1 multicolored .80 .80
a. Booklet pane, 2 each #841-845 + 10 labels 5.50
Complete booklet, #845a 5.50

Nos. 836-840 are inscribed "Standard Postage" and sold for 45c on day of issued.

Namibian Veterinary Assoc., 50th Anniv. — A185

1997, Sept. 12 ***Perf. 14***

846 A185 $1.50 multicolored .70 .70

Souvenir Sheet

Triceratops — A186

Illustration reduced.

1997, Sept. 27 **Litho.** ***Perf. 13***

847 A186 $5 multicolored 2.25 2.25

World Post Day — A187

Trees — A188

1997, Oct. 9 **Litho.** ***Perf. 14x15***

848 A187 (45c) multicolored .60 .40

No. 848 is inscribed "Standard Postage" and sold for 45c on day of issue.

1997, Oct. 10

849 A188 (45c) False mopane .25 .20
850 A188 $1 Ana tree .45 .40
851 A188 $1.10 Shepherd's tree .55 .50
852 A188 $1.50 Kiaat .75 .65
Nos. 849-852 (4) 2.00 1.75

No. 849 is inscribed "Standard Postage" and sold for 45c on day of issue.

Fauna and Flora — A189

1997, Nov. 3 **Litho.** ***Perf. 13½***

853 A189 5c Flame lily .20 .20
854 A189 10c Bushman poison .20 .20
855 A189 20c Camel's foot .20 .20
856 A189 30c Western rhigozum .20 .20
857 A189 40c Bluecheeked bee-eater .20 .20
858 A189 (50c) Rosyfaced lovebird .25 .25
a. Booklet pane of 10, perf 14x13½ 2.50
Complete booklet, #858a 2.50
859 A189 50c Laughing dove .25 .25
860 A189 60c Lappetfaced vulture .30 .25
861 A189 90c Yellowbilled hornbill .40 .35
862 A189 $1 Lilac-breasted roller .45 .40
863 A189 $1.10 Hippopotamus .50 .40
864 A189 ($1.20) Leopard .55 .45
a. Booklet pane of 10, perf 14x13½ 5.50
Complete booklet, #864a 5.50
865 A189 $1.20 Giraffe .45 .40
866 A189 $1.50 Elephant .60 .50
867 A189 $2 Lion .75 .65
868 A189 $4 Buffalo 1.50 1.50
869 A189 $5 Black rhinoceros 1.75 1.60
870 A189 $10 Cheetah 3.50 3.00
a. Bklt. pane, 1 ea #853-870, perf 14x13½ 12.25
Complete booklet, #870a 12.25
Nos. 853-870 (18) 12.25 11.00

Self-Adhesive

Die Cut Perf. 12x12½

870B A189 (45c) like #858 .25 .25
870C A189 $1 like #862 .45 .45
870D A189 ($1.20) like #864 .60 .60
Nos. 870B-870D (3) 1.30 1.30

No. 858 is inscribed "Standard Postage" and sold for 50c on day issue. No. 864 is inscribed "Postcard Rate" and sold for $1.20 on day of issue.

For surcharges see #959-962.

Christmas A190

Various pictures of a helmeted guineafowl.

1997, Nov. 3 ***Perf. 13x12½***

871 A190 (50c) multicolored .25 .20
872 A190 $1 multicolored .45 .40
873 A190 $1.10 multicolored .50 .45
874 A190 $1.50 multicolored .60 .55
Nos. 871-874 (4) 1.80 1.60

Souvenir Sheet

875 A190 $5 multi, vert. 2.50 2.50

No. 871 is inscribed "Standard Postage" and sold for 50c on day of issue.

A191

A192

1997, Nov. 27 ***Perf. 14x15***

876 A191 (50c) multicolored .50 .50

John Muafangejo (1943-87), artist. No. 876 is inscribed "Standard Postage" and sold for 50c on day of issue.

1998, Jan. 15

877 A192 (50c) brown & gray .35 .35

Gabriel B. Taapopi (1911-85). No. 877 is inscribed "Standard Postage" and sold for 50c on day of issue.

Wild Cats Type of 1997

Designs: $1.20, Panthera pardus. $1.90, Panthera leo, female carrying young. $2, Panthera leo, male. $2.50, Acinonyx jubatus.

1998, Jan. 26 ***Perf. 13x12½***

878 A179 $1.20 multicolored .60 .60
879 A179 $1.90 multicolored .95 .95
880 A179 $2 multicolored 1.00 1.00
881 A179 $2.50 multicolored 1.25 1.25
a. Souvenir sheet, #878-881 4.25 4.25
Nos. 878-881 (4) 3.80 3.80

Narra Plant — A194

Water Awareness A195

1998, Feb. 9 ***Perf. 12½x13***

882 A194 $2.40 multicolored 1.25 1.25

1998, Mar. 23 **Litho.** ***Perf. 14x15***

883 A195 (50c) multicolored .35 .35

No. 883 is inscribed "Standard Postage" and sold for 50c on date of issue.

Nos. 885-895 were initially not available in Namibia. They were issued Nov. 23, 1997, at a Shanghai, China, stamp exhibition by a Chinese stamp dealer acting for the Namibia Post Office. There is some question whether they were sold in Namibia, but if they were, it was not until early 1998.

A197

Lunar New Year — A198

Chinese inscriptions, wood cut images of a tiger, stylized drawings of tiger in — #885: a, orange. b, light green. c, yellow. d, blue. e, dark green. f, lilac.

No. 886: Various tiger figures, Chinese inscriptions.

No. 887, Chinese inscriptions, stylized tigers.

Illustration A197 reduced.

Perf. 13½x12½

1997, Nov. 23 **Litho.**

885 A197 $2.50 Sheet of 6, #a.-f. 7.00 7.00

Perf. 14x13½

886 A198 $2.50 Sheet of 6, #a.-f. 7.00 7.00

Souvenir Sheets

Perf. 12½

887 A197 $6 multicolored 2.75 2.75
888 A198 $6 multicolored 2.75 2.75

Nos. 887-888 each contain one 69x38mm stamp.

Macau Returns to China in 1999 A199

Designs: No. 890, Flag, building. No. 892, Flag, Deng Xiaoping, building.

1997, Nov. 23 ***Perf. 13½***

889 A199 $4.50 multicolored 2.25 2.25

Size: 59x27mm

Perf. 13½x13

890 A199 $4.50 multicolored 3.00 3.00

Souvenir Sheets

Perf. 13½x12½

891 A199 $6 multicolored 3.00 3.00

Perf. 12½

892 A199 $6 multicolored 3.00 3.00

Nos. 889-890 issued in sheets of 3. No. 891 contains one 62x33mm stamp, No. 892 one 69x33mm stamp.

Return of Hong Kong to China — A200

Chinese landmarks — #892A: b, Beijing, Natl. Capital of China. c, Return of Hong Kong, 1997. d, Return of Macao, 1999. e, The Taiwan Region.

Illustration reduced.

1997, Nov. 17 **Litho.** ***Perf. 14x13½***

892A A200 $3.50 Sheet of 4, #b.-e. 6.25 6.25

Souvenir Sheet

Perf. 12½

893 A200 $6 Chinese landmarks 2.50 2.50

No. 893 contains one 72x41mm stamp.

Shanghai Communique, 25th Anniv. — A201

No. 894: a, Pres. Nixon, Mao Zedong, 1972. b, Pres. Carter, Deng Xiaoping, 1979. c, Pres. Reagan, Deng Xiaoping, 1984. d, Pres. Bush, Deng Xiaoping, 1989.

$6, Nixon, Zhou Enlai, 1972.

Illustration reduced.

1997, Nov. 17 ***Perf. 13½x12½***

894 A201 $3.50 Sheet of 4, #a.-d. 5.50 5.50

Souvenir Sheet

Perf. 14x13½

895 A201 $6 multicolored 2.50 2.50

No. 895 contains one 67x33mm stamp.

Owls — A204

1998, Apr. 1 **Litho.** ***Perf. 13½x13***

Booklet Stamps

898 A204 55c Rat (prey) .30 .30

Size: 38x23mm

899 A204 $1.50 Whitefaced owl .65 .65
900 A204 $1.50 Barred owl .65 .65
901 A204 $1.90 Spotted eagle owl .75 .75

Size: 61x21mm

902 A204 $1.90 Barn owl .75 .75
a. Booklet pane, #898-902 3.50
Complete booklet, #902a 3.50

See No. 950.

Shells A205

Designs: (50c), Patella granatina. $1.10, Cymatium cutaceum africanum. $1.50, Conus mozambicus. $6, Venus verrucosa.

1998, May 14 **Litho.** ***Perf. 12½***

903 A205 (50c) multicolored .20 .20
904 A205 $1.10 multicolored .45 .45
905 A205 $1.50 multicolored .60 .60
906 A205 $6 multicolored 2.40 2.40
a. Souvenir sheet, #903-906 3.75 3.75
Nos. 903-906 (4) 3.65 3.65

No. 903 inscribed "Standard Postage."

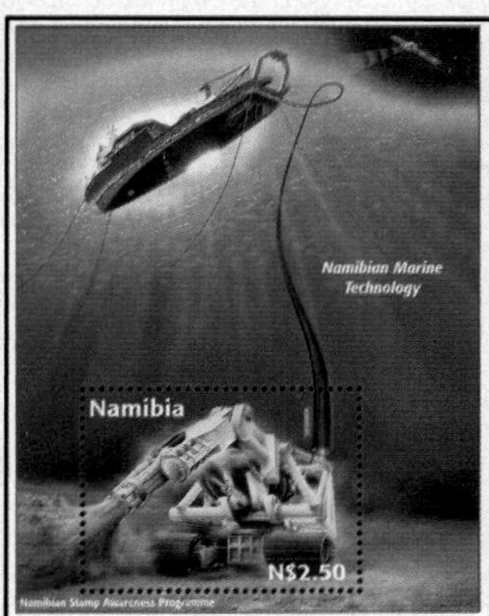

Namibian Marine Technology — A206

Illustration reduced.

1998, May 18 **Litho.** ***Perf. 14½x14***

908 A206 $2.50 multicolored 1.75 1.75

Diana, Princess of Wales (1961-97)

Common Design Type

Working for removal of land mines: a, Wearing face shield. b, Wearing Red Cross shirt. c, In white blouse. d, With child.

1998, May 18 **Litho.** ***Perf. 14½x14***

909 CD355 $1 Sheet of 4, #a.-d. 1.90 1.90

World Environment Day — A207

1998, June 5 **Litho.** ***Perf. 13x13½***

910 A207 (55c) Namibian coast .30 .30
911 A207 $1.10 Okavango sunset .50 .50
912 A207 $1.50 Sossusvlei .65 .65
913 A207 $1.90 African moringo .80 .80
Nos. 910-913 (4) 2.25 2.25

No. 913 is inscribed "Standard Postage."

Souvenir Sheet

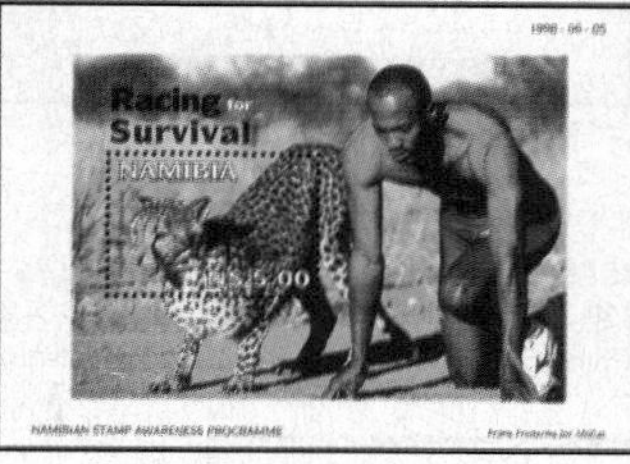

Racing for Survival — A208

Illustration reduced.

1998, June 5 ***Perf. 13***

914 A208 $5 Acinonyx jubatus 2.10 2.10

Animals and Their Young — A209

a, Chacma baboon. b, Blue wildebeest. c, Suricate. d, Elephant. e, Burchell's zebra.

1998, June 18 ***Perf. 13½x13***

915 A209 $1.50 Sheet of 5, #a.-e. 3.00 3.00

Souvenir Sheet

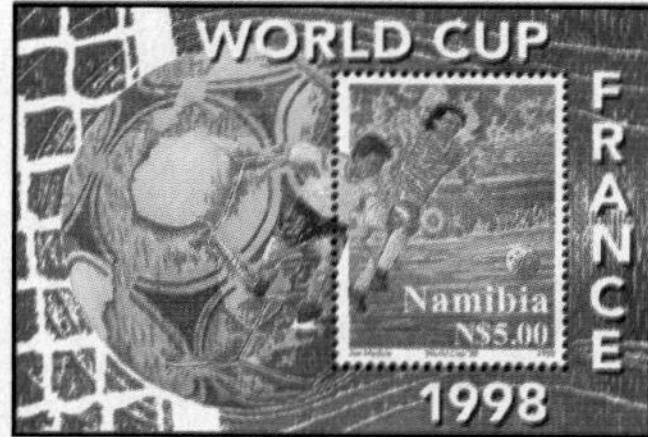

1998 World Cup Soccer Championships, France — A210

1998, July 1 **Litho.** ***Perf. 14***

916 A210 $5 multicolored 2.00 2.00

Flora and Fauna of the Caprivi Strip A211

Designs: a, Carmine bee-eater. b, Sable antelope. c, Lechwe. d, Woodland waterberry. e, Nile monitor. f, African jacana. g, African fish eagle. h, Woodland kingfisher. i, Nile crocodile. j, Black mamba.

1998, Sept. 26 **Litho.** ***Perf. 12½***

917 A211 60c Sheet of 10, #a.-j. 12.50 12.50

#917b-917c, 917e are 40x40mm, #917i is 54x30mm, #917j is 32x30mm.

Souvenir Sheet

Black Rhinoceros — A212

Illustration reduced.

1998, Oct. 20 **Litho.** ***Perf. 13***

918 A212 $5 multicolored 2.25 2.25

Ilsapex '98, Intl. Philatelic Exhibition, Johannesburg.

Souvenir Sheet

Whales — A213

Illustration reduced.

1998, Oct. 9 **Litho.** ***Perf. 13½x14***

919 A213 $5 multicolored 2.25 2.25

See Norfolk Island No. 665, South Africa No. 1095.

Animals
A214 A215

1999, Jan. 18 **Litho.** ***Perf. 13½***

920 A214 $1.80 Damara dik dik 2.50 2.50
921 A215 $2.65 Striped tree squirrel 4.25 4.25

"Yoka" the Snake — A216

"Yoka" the Snake A217

Cartoon pictures of Yoka: No. 922, Turning head. No. 923, Wrapped around tree branch. No. 924, Tail wrapped around branch and female snake. No. 925, With female snake and mouse. No. 926, In love. No. 927, Yoka tied up in knots. No. 928, Smashed with footprint. No. 929, Female snake's tail, Yoka's head. No. 930, Female snake singing to dazed Yoka. No. 931, Lying with tail over nose.

Serpentine Die Cut

1999, Feb. 1 **Litho.**

Booklet Stamps

Self-Adhesive

922 A216 $1.60 multicolored .60 .60
923 A217 $1.60 multicolored .60 .60
924 A216 $1.60 multicolored .60 .60
925 A217 $1.60 multicolored .60 .60

926	A216	$1.60 multicolored	.60	.60
927	A217	$1.60 multicolored	.60	.60
928	A216	$1.60 multicolored	.60	.60
929	A216	$1.60 multicolored	.60	.60
930	A216	$1.60 multicolored	.60	.60
931	A217	$1.60 multicolored	.60	.60
a.		Bklt. pane of 10, #922-931	6.00	

The peelable paper backing serves as a booklet cover.

Souvenir Sheet

Passenger Liner "Windhuk" — A218

Illustration reduced.

1999, Mar. 18 *Perf. 14*
932 A218 $5.50 multicolored 2.25 2.25

Gliders A219

1999, Apr. 13 **Litho.** *Perf. 13*
933 A219 $1.60 Zögling, 1928 .90 .90
934 A219 $1.80 Schleicher, 1998 1.40 1.40

Souvenir Sheet

IBRA '99, Nuremberg, Germany — A220

Illustration reduced.

1999, Apr. 27 **Litho.** *Perf. 14x14¼*
935 A220 $5.50 multi 2.00 2.00

Falcons — A221

60c, Greater kestrel. $1.60, Rock kestrel. $1.80, Red-necked falcon. $2.65, Lanner falcon.
Illustration reduced.

1999, May 18 **Litho.** *Perf. 13¼x13½*

936	A221	60c multicolored	.35	.35
937	A221	$1.60 multicolored	.85	.85
938	A221	$1.80 multicolored	1.00	1.00
939	A221	$2.65 multicolored	1.50	1.50
		Nos. 936-939 (4)	3.70	3.70

Souvenir Sheet

Termitomyces Schimperi — A222

Illustration reduced.

1999, June 19 **Litho.** *Perf. 13¾*
940 A222 $5.50 multicolored 2.00 2.00

PhilexFrance '99 World Philatelic Exhibition.

Wetland Birds A223

Designs: $1.60, Wattled crane. $1.80, Burchell's sand grouse. $1.90, Rock pratincole. $2.65, Eastern white pelican.

1999, June 28 *Perf. 12¾*

941	A223	$1.60 multicolored	.80	.80
942	A223	$1.80 multicolored	.95	.95
943	A223	$1.90 multicolored	.95	.95
944	A223	$2.65 multicolored	1.40	1.40
		Nos. 941-944 (4)	4.10	4.10

Orchids A224

Designs: $1.60, Eulophia hereroensis. $1.80, Ansellia africana. $2.65, Eulophia leachii. $3.90, Eulophia speciosa. $5.50, Eulophia walleri.

Litho. & Embossed

1999, Aug. 21 *Perf. 12¾*

945	A224	$1.60 multicolored	.85	.85
946	A224	$1.80 multicolored	1.00	1.00
947	A224	$2.65 multicolored	1.40	1.40
948	A224	$3.90 multicolored	2.10	2.10
		Nos. 945-948 (4)	5.35	5.35

Souvenir Sheet

949 A224 $5.50 multicolored 3.00 3.00

Embossing is found only on the margin of No. 949. China 1999 World Philatelic Exhibition (No. 949).

Owl Type of 1998
Souvenir Sheet

Perf. 13½x12¾

1999, Sept. 30 **Litho.**
950 A204 $11 Like #902 5.75 5.75

Selection of stamp design as "most beautiful," 5th Stamp World Cup.

Urieta Kazahendike (Johanna Gertze) (1836-1935) A225

1999, Oct. 1 **Litho.** *Perf. 12¾*
951 A225 $20 multicolored 7.25 7.25

Souvenir Sheet

Turn of the Millennium — A226

Illustration reduced.

Perf. 13¾x13¼

1999, Dec. 31 **Litho.**
952 A226 $9 multi 4.00 4.00

No. 952 has a holographic image. Soaking in water may affect the hologram.

Sunset Over Namibia — A227

Illustration reduced.

1999-2000 *Perf. 13¼x13¾*
953 A227 $2.20 shown 1.25 1.25
954 A227 $2.40 Sunrise 1.40 1.40

Issued: $2.20, 12/31; $2.40, 1/1/00.

Ducks A228

Designs: $2, South African shelduck. $2.40, Whitefaced duck. $3, Knobbilled duck. $7, Cape shoveller.

2000, Feb. 18 **Litho.** *Perf. 13*

955	A228	$2 multi	.75	.75
956	A228	$2.40 multi	.90	.90
957	A228	$3 multi	1.10	1.10
958	A228	$7 multi	2.75	2.75
		Nos. 955-958 (4)	5.50	5.50

Nos. 853-856 Surcharged

2000, Mar. 1 **Litho.** *Perf. 13½*

959	A189	(65c) on 5c multi	.30	.30
960	A189	$1.80 on 30c multi	.85	.85
961	A189	$3 on 10c multi	1.40	1.40
962	A189	$6 on 20c multi	2.75	2.75
		Nos. 959-962 (4)	5.30	5.30

See No. 1000.

Independence, 10th Anniv. — A229

2000, Mar. 21 *Perf. 13¼x13¾*
963 A229 65c Children .30 .30
964 A229 $3 Flag 1.40 1.40

Passion Play — A230

Designs: $2.10, Jesus with crown of thorns. $2.40, Carrying cross.

2000, Apr. 1 *Perf. 13¾*
965 A230 $2.10 multi .80 .80
966 A230 $2.40 multi .95 .95

Fauna of the Namib Desert — A231

Designs: a, $2, Tenebrionid beetle. b, $2 Brown hyena. c, $2, Namib golden mole. d, $2, Shovel-snouted lizard. e, $2, Dune lark. f, $6, Namib side-winding adder.
Illustration reduced.

2000, May 22 *Perf. 14½*
967 A231 Sheet of 6, #a-f 7.00 7.00

The Stamp Show 2000, London.
Sizes of stamps: Nos. 967a-967c, 30x25mm; No. 967d, 30x50mm; Nos. 967e-967f, 26x37mm. Portions of the design were applied by a thermographic process, producing a shiny raised effect.

Welwitschia Mirabilis — A232

Various views of Welwitschia plants. Denominations: (65c), $2.20, $3, $4.

2000, June 21 **Litho.** *Perf. 13¾*
968-971 A232 Set of 4 3.50 3.50

No. 968 is inscribed "Standard inland mail."

Souvenir Sheet

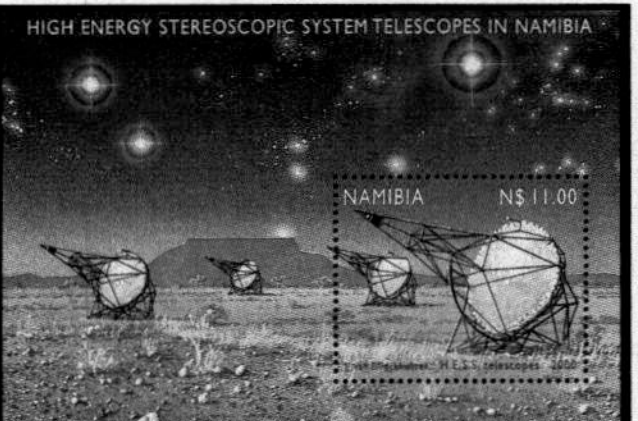

High Energy Stereoscopic Sytem Telescopes — A233

Illustration reduced.

2000, July 7 *Perf. 13¼x13¾*
972 A233 $11 multi 6.00 6.00

Fruit Trees — A234

Designs: (70c), Jackalberry. $2, Sycamore fig. $2.20, Bird plum. $7, Marula.
Illustration reduced.

2000, Aug. 16 **Litho.** *Perf. 13¼x14*
973-976 A234 Set of 4 4.00 4.00

No. 973 is inscribed "Standard inland mail" and sold for 65c on day of issue.

Souvenir Sheet

Yoka in Etosha — A235

Illustration reduced.

2000, Sept. 1 *Perf. 13¼x13*
977 A235 $11 multi 5.00 5.00

Coelenterates
A236

Designs: (70c), Anthothoe stimpsoni. $2.45, Bundosoma capensis. $3.50, Anthopleura stephensoni. $6.60, Pseudactinia flagellifera.

2001, Apr. 18 **Litho.** *Perf. 13¾*
978-981 A236 Set of 4 4.50 4.50

No. 978 is inscribed "Standard inland mail."

Civil
Aviation
A237

Designs: (70c), Cessna 210 Turbo. $2.20, Douglas DC-6B. $2.50, Pitts 52A. $13.20, Bell 407 helicopter.

2001, May 9 *Perf. 13¼x13¾*
982-985 A237 Set of 4 6.50 6.50

No. 982 is inscribed "Standard inland mail."

Renewable Energy
Resources
A238

No. 986: a, Wood efficient stove. b, Biogas digester. c, Solar cooker. d, Repair, reuse, recycle. e, Solar water pump. f, Solar home system. g, Solar street light. h, Solar water heater. i, Solar telecommunication. j, Wind water pump.

2001, Aug. 15 *Perf. 13½x14*
986 Sheet of 10 7.75 7.75
a.-e. A238 ($1) Any single .30 .30
f.-j. A238 $3.50 Any single 1.25 1.25

Nos. 986a-986e are inscribed "Standard Mail."

Central Highlands Flora and Fauna — A239

No. 987: a, ($1.00), Ruppell's parrot (31x29mm). b, $3.50, Camel thorn (54x29mm). c, ($1.00), Flap-necked chameleon (39x29mm). d, ($1.00), Klipspringer (39x29mm). e, $3.50, Berg aloe (39x29mm). f, $3.50, Kudu (39x39mm). g, ($1.00), Rockrunner (39x29mm). h, $3.50, Namibian rock agama (39x39mm). i, ($1.00), Pangolin (39x39mm). j, $3.50, Armored ground cricket (39x29mm).

2001, Sept. 5 *Perf. 12½x12¾*
987 A239 Sheet of 10, #a-j 7.50 7.50

Nos. 987a, 987c, 987d, 987g, 987i are inscribed "Standard Mail."

Tribal Women — A240

No. 988, ($1.30): a, Mbalantu. b, Damara. c, Herero (leather headdress). d, San. e, Mafue. f, Baster.

No. 989, ($1.30): a, Mbukushu. b, Herero (flowered headdress). c, Himba. d, Kwanyama. e, Nama. f, Ngandjera/Kwaluudhi.

2002, Apr. 20 **Litho.** *Perf. 13¼x13*
Sheets of 6, #a-f
988-989 A240 Set of 2 6.50 6.50
988g Sheet of 6 with incorrect back inscriptions 7.50 7.50
989g Sheet of 6 with incorrect back inscriptions 7.50 7.50

Stamps are inscribed "Standard Mail."

The back inscriptions on Nos. 988g and 989g are placed incorrectly so that the inscriptions for the stamps on the left side of the sheet have the back inscriptions of the stamps on the right side of the sheet, and vice versa.

The Mbukushu stamp on No. 989g reads "Standard Maiil."

Birds — A241

Designs: ($1.30), African hoopoe. $2.20, Paradise flycatchers. $2.60, Swallowtailed bee-eaters. $2.80, Malachite kingfisher.

2002, May 15 *Perf. 13¾x13¼*
990-993 A241 Set of 4 3.50 3.50

No. 990 is inscribed "Standard Mail."

Ephemeral
Rivers
A242

Designs: ($1.30), Kuiseb River floods halting movement of sand dunes, vert. (36x48mm). $2.20, Bird flying over lake of Tsauchab River flood water. $2.60, Elephants in dry bed of Hoarusib River (86x22mm). $2.80, Birds near Nossob River flood water. $3.50, Birds near Fish River, vert. (55x21mm).

2002, July 1 *Perf. 13x13¼,13¼x13*
994-998 A242 Set of 5 5.00 5.00

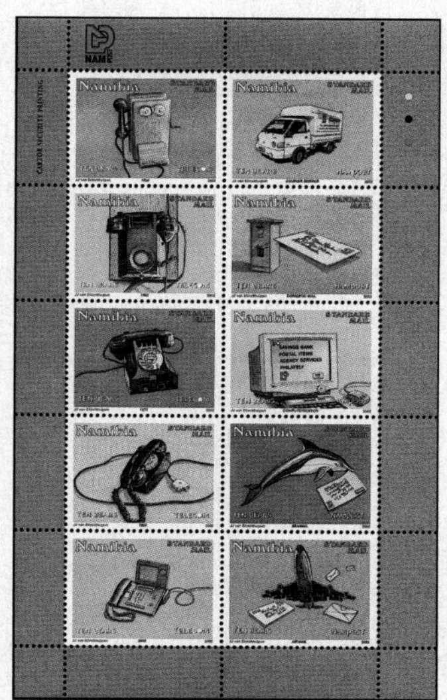

Namibia Post and Telecommunications, 10th Anniv. — A243

No. 999: a, Telephone, blue background. b, Telephone, yellow background. c, Telephone, green background. d, Telephone, lilac background. e, Picturephone, brown background. f, Mail van. g, Pillar box and letter. h, Computer. i, Dolphin with letter. j, Airplane and letters.

2002, Aug. 1 **Litho.** *Perf. 13¼x13*
999 A243 ($1.30) Sheet of 10, #a-j 5.00 5.00
k. Sheet of 10, 2 each #a-e 5.00 5.00
l. Sheet of 10, 2 each #f-j 5.00 5.00

Stamps are inscribed "Standard Mail."

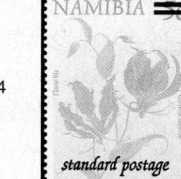

Nos. 853-854
Surcharged

2002, Oct. 21 **Litho.** *Perf. 13½*
1000 A189 ($1.45) on 5c #853 .45 .45
1001 A189 ($1.45) on 10c #854 .45 .45

Surcharge on No. 1000 has letters that lean more to the right than those on No. 959. The two "d's" have tops that curve to the right on No. 1000, but have serifs that point left on No. 959. The cross line of the "t's" are lower on No. 1000 than on No. 959.

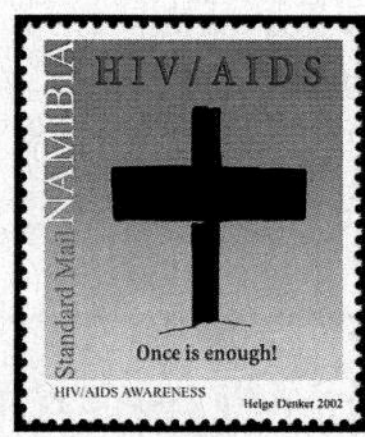

Prevention of
AIDS — A244

Designs: ($1.45), Cross. $2.45, Condom. $2.85, Man and hand. $11.50, Test tubes.

2002, Dec. 1 *Perf. 13½x13*
1002-1005 A244 Set of 4 5.25 5.25

No. 1002 is inscribed "Standard Mail."

Recent Biological
Discoveries
A245

Designs: $1.10, Sulphur bacteria. $2.45, Whiteheadia etesionamibensis. $2.85, Cunene flathead (catfish), horiz. $3.85, Zebra racer, horiz. $20, Gladiator (insect).

Perf. 13¾x13¼, 13¼x13¾
2003, Feb. 24
1006-1010 A245 Set of 5 8.50 8.50

Rural Development — A246

Designs: $1.45, Water and electricity supply. ($2.75), Conservancy formation and land use diversification. $4.40, Education and health services. ($11.50), Communication and road infrastructure.

Illustration reduced.

2003, Apr. 17 **Litho.** *Perf. 13¼x13¾*
1011-1014 A246 Set of 4 6.25 6.25

No. 1012 is inscribed "Postcard Rate" and No. 1014 is inscribed "Registered Mail."

Wetlands — A247

Designs: $1.10, Women and cattle near oshana. $2.85, Birds at Omadhiya Lakes. ($3.85), Cuvelai Drainage.

Illustration reduced.

2003, June 6
1015-1017 A247 Set of 3 4.75 4.75

No. 1017 is inscribed "Non-Standard Mail."

Heroes Acre Monuments — A248

Various monuments with inscriprions: ($1.45), Standard Mail. ($2.75), Postcard Rate. ($3.85), Non-Standard Mail.

2003, Aug. 27 *Perf. 13¼*
1018-1020 A248 Set of 3 3.50 3.50

Souvenir Sheet

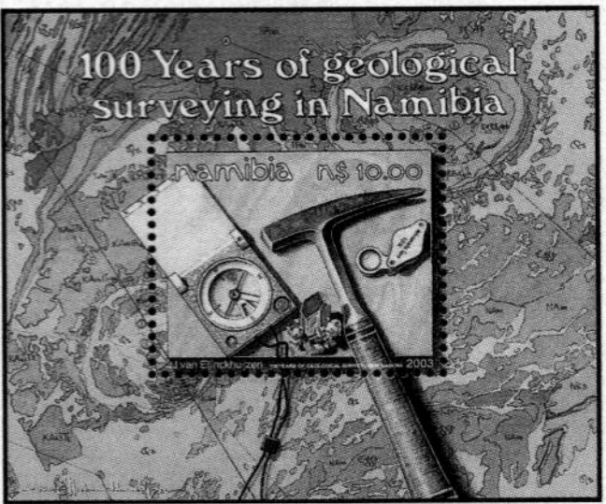

Geological Surveying in Namibia, Cent. — A249

2003, Sept. 10 *Perf. 13¼x13¾*
1021 A249 $10 multi 5.00 5.00

Souvenir Sheet

Windhoek Philatelic Society, 25th Anniv. — A250

2003, Sept. 10
1022 A250 $10 multi 4.50 4.50

Ephemeral Rivers Type of 2002
Souvenir Sheet

2003, Dec. 8 *Perf. 13¼x13*
1023 A242 $3.15 Like #996 2.50 2.50

Design voted "most beautiful stamp" at 8th Stamp World Cup, Paris.

Vervet Monkeys — A251

Designs: $1.60, Adult holding fruit. $3.15, Two monkeys on tree branches. $3.40, Adult and young. ($14.25), Adult chewing on twig. $4.85, Like #1024.

2004, Jan. 30 *Perf. 13*
1024-1027 A251 Set of 4 7.50 7.50

Souvenir Sheet

1028 A251 $4.85 multi 2.25 2.25

No. 1027 is inscribed "Inland Registered Mail Paid." 2004 Hong Kong Stamp Expo (#1028).

Honeybees on Flowers A252

Honeybees on: ($1.60), Sickle bush. $2.70, Daisy. ($3.05), Aloe. $3.15, Cat's claw. ($14.25), Edging senecio. $4.85, Pretty lady.

2004, Feb. 2 *Perf. 13x13¼*
1029-1033 A252 Set of 5 8.50 8.50

Souvenir Sheet

1034 A252 $4.85 multi 2.25 2.25

No. 1029 is inscribed "Standard mail;" No. 1031, "Post card rate;" No. 1033, "Inland registered mail paid."

Anti-Colonial Resistance, Cent. — A253

2004, Mar. 23 Litho. *Perf. 13¼*
1035 A253 ($1.60) multi 1.00 1.00

Souvenir Sheet

1036 A253 $5 multi 2.00 2.00

No. 1035 is inscribed "Standard Mail."

Education in Namibia — A254

Designs: $1.60, Pre-school education enhances individual development potential. $2.75, Primary and secondary school education for all lays the foundation for equal opportunity. $4.40, Advanced learning and vocational training provide career options. ($12.65), Lifelong learning encourages personal growth and the capacity for leadership.

2004, Apr. 19 *Perf. 13¼x13¾*
1037-1040 A254 Set of 4 7.00 7.00

No. 1040 is inscribed "Registered Mail."

Fishing Industry — A255

Fish and: $1.60, Ship and dockworkers. $2.75, Ship. $4.85, Workers at processing plant.

Illustration reduced.

Perf. 13¼x13¾

2004, June 22 Litho.
1041-1043 A255 Set of 3 3.75 3.75

Historic Buildings in Bethanie A256

Designs: ($1.60), Joseph Ferdericks House. ($3.05), Schmelen House. ($4.40), Rhenish Mission Church. ($12.65), Stone Church.

2004, July 7 *Perf. 14x13½*
1044-1047 A256 Set of 4 8.00 8.00

No. 1044 is inscribed "Standard Mail;" No. 1045, "Postcard rate;" No. 1046, "Non-Standard Mail," No. 1047, "Registered Mail."

2004 Summer Olympics, Athens A257

Designs: ($1.60), Wrestling. $2.90, Boxing, vert. $3.40, Pistol shooting. $3.70, Mountain biking, vert.

Perf. 14x13¼, 13¼x14

2004, Aug. 3 Litho.
1048-1051 A257 Set of 4 4.25 4.25
a. Inscribed "XXVIII Olympiad" *6.00 6.00*

No. 1048 is inscribed "Standard Mail."
No. 1051 has incorrect inscription "XVIII Olympiad."
No. 1051a issued 9/14.

Miniature Sheet

Birds — A258

No. 1052: a, African fish eagles, national bird of Namibia. b, African fish eagles, national bird of Zimbabwe. c, Peregrine falcons, national bird of Angola. d, Cattle egrets, national bird of Botswana. e, Purple-crested louries, national bird of Swaziland. f, Blue cranes, national bird of South Africa. g, Bat-tailed trogons. h, African fish eagles, national bird of Zambia.

2004, Oct. 11 Litho. *Perf. 14*
1052 A258 $3.40 Sheet of 8, #a-h 10.00 10.00

See Angola No., Botswana Nos. 792-793, Malawi No., South Africa No. 1342, Swaziland Nos. 727-735, Zambia No., and Zimbabwe No. 975.

Rotary International, Cent. — A259

2005, Feb. 23 Litho. *Perf. 13x13¼*
1053 A259 $3.70 multi 1.75 1.75

Pres. Hifikepunye Pohamba A260

2005, Mar. 21 *Perf. 13¼x14*
1054 A260 ($1.70) multi .80 .80

Inscribed "Standard Mail."

Sunbirds A261

Designs: $2.90, Marico sunbird. $3.40, Dusky sunbird. ($4.80), White-bellied sunbird. ($15.40), Scarlet-chested sunbird. $10, Amethyst sunbird, horiz.

2005, Apr. 14 Litho. *Perf. 13¼x14*
1055-1058 A261 Set of 4 10.00 10.00

Souvenir Sheet

Perf. 14x13¼

1059 A261 $10 multi 4.00 4.00

No. 1057 is inscribed "Non-Standard Mail"; No. 1058, "Registered Inland Postage Paid."

Nos. 855, 859, 861 and 868 Surcharged

a

b

c

2005, June 7 Litho. *Perf. 13½*
1060 A189(a) ($1.70) on 50c #859 .75 .75
1061 A189(b) $2.90 on 20c #855 1.25 1.25
1062 A189(c) ($4.80) on $4 #868 1.75 1.75
1063 A189(b) $5.20 on 90c #861 2.00 2.00
Nos. 1060-1063 (4) 5.75 5.75

Medicinal Plants A262

Designs: ($1.70), Nara. $2.90, Devil's claw. ($3.10), Hoodia. ($4.80), Tsamma.

2005, July 22 *Perf. 14x13¼*
1064-1067 A262 Set of 4 4.50 4.50

No. 1064 is inscribed "Standard Mail;" No. 1066, "Postcard Rate;" No. 1067, "Non-Standard Mail."

Crops — A263

Designs: $2.90, Vegetables. $3.40, Pearl millet. ($13.70), Corn.

2005, Aug. 2 *Perf. 13¼x13¾*
1068-1070 A263 Set of 3 6.75 6.75

No. 1070 is inscribed "Registered Mail."

Nos. 855, 861, 862, 866, 868-870 Surcharged Type "b" and

d

e

NAMIBIA Registered Standard Mail

f

g

2005, Aug. 10 Litho. *Perf. 13½*

1071	A189(d)	($1.70) on 20c #855		.75	.75
1072	A189(d)	($1.70) on 90c #861		.75	.75
1073	A189(d)	($1.70) on $1 #862		.75	.75
1074	A189(b)	$2.90 on 90c #861		1.25	1.25
1075	A189(e)	($4.80) on $1.50 #866		2.00	2.00
1076	A189(b)	$5.20 on 20c #855		2.25	2.25
1077	A189(f)	($15.40) on $4 #868		6.00	6.00
1078	A189(g)	($18.50) on $10 #870		7.50	7.50
1079	A189(b)	$25 on $5 #869		10.00	10.00
1080	A189(b)	$50 on $10 #870		20.00	20.00
	Nos. 1071-1080 (10)			51.25	51.25

Gulls
A264

Designs: $3.10, Cape gulls. $4, Hartlaub's gulls. $5.50, Sabine's gull. ($16.20), Gray-headed gulls.

2006, Feb. 28 Litho. *Perf. 14x13¼*

1081-1084 A264 Set of 4 11.00 11.00

No. 1084 is inscribed "Inland Registered Mail Paid."

Nos. 1003, 1030, 1042 Surcharged

Methods and Perfs As Before

2006, Apr. 13

1085	A244	$3.10 on $2.45 #1003		1.50	1.10
1086	A252	$3.10 on $2.70 #1030		1.50	1.50
1087	A255	$3.10 on $2.75 #1042		1.50	1.50
	Nos. 1085-1087 (3)			4.50	4.10

Size, location and fonts of surcharges differ.

Dolphins
A265

Designs: ($1.80), Risso's dolphin. $3.10, Southern right-whale dolphins, vert. $3.70, Benguela dolphin. $4, Common dolphins. $5.50, Bottlenose dolphins, vert.

Perf. 13x13¼, 13¼x13

2006, Apr. 26 Litho.

1088-1092 A265 Set of 5 7.50 7.50

No. 1088 is inscribed "Standard Mail."

Miniature Sheets

Traditional Roles of Men — A266

No. 1093, ($1.80): a, Father. b, Musician. c, Carver. d, Shaman. e, Planter. f, Hunter.

No. 1094, ($1.80): a, Leader. b, Blacksmith. c, Protector. d, Pastoralist. e, Trader. f, Storyteller.

2006, May 24 *Perf. 13x13¼*

Sheets of 6, #a-f

1093-1094 A266 Set of 2 7.50 7.50

Nos. 862, 865 Surcharged

2006, June 20 Litho. *Perf. 13½*

1095	A189	($3.30) on $1 #862	1.50	1.50
1096	A189	($3.30) on $1.20 #865	1.50	1.50

Nos. 1095-1096 are inscribed "Postcard Rate." Location of surcharges differs.

Perennial
Rivers
A267

Designs: $3.10, Orange River. $5.50, Kumene River, vert. (21x55mm). ($19.90), Zambezi River (87x22mm).

Perf. 14x13¼, 13½ ($5.50)

2006, July 24

1097-1099 A267 Set of 3 10.00 10.00

No. 1099 is inscribed "Registered Non Standard Mail."

Otavi Mines and Railway Company (OMEG) Rail Line, Cent
A268

Designs: $3.10, Construction of the rail line. $3.70, Henschel Class NG15 locomotive No. 41. $5.50, Narrow gauge Class Jung tank locomotive No. 9.

2006, Aug. 9 *Perf. 14¾x14*

1100-1102 A268 Set of 3 4.50 4.50

Otjiwarongo, Cent. — A269

2006, Nov. 17 *Perf. 14*

1103 A269 $1.90 multi .75 .75

Printed in sheets of 10.

Flora and
Fauna
A270

Named species: 5c, Bullfrog. 10c, Mesemb. 30c, Solifuge. 40c, Jewel beetle. 60c, Compass jellyfish. ($1.90), Web-footed gecko. $2, Otjikoto tilapia. No. 1111, $6, Milkbush. No. 1112, ($6), African hawk eagle. $10, Black-faced impala. $25, Lichens. $50, Baobab tree.

2007, Feb. 15 Litho. *Perf. 14x13¼*

1104	A270	5c	multi	.20	.20
1105	A270	10c	multi	.20	.20
1106	A270	30c	multi	.20	.20
1107	A270	40c	multi	.20	.20
1108	A270	60c	multi	.20	.20
1109	A270	($1.90)	multi	.50	.50
1110	A270	$2	multi	.55	.55
1111	A270	$6	multi	1.60	1.60
1112	A270	($6)	multi	1.60	1.60
1113	A270	$10	multi	2.75	2.75
1114	A270	$25	multi	7.00	7.00
1115	A270	$50	multi	14.00	14.00
	Nos. 1104-1115 (12)			29.00	29.00

No. 1109 is inscribed "Standard Mail." No. 1112 is inscribed "Non-standard Mail."

A271

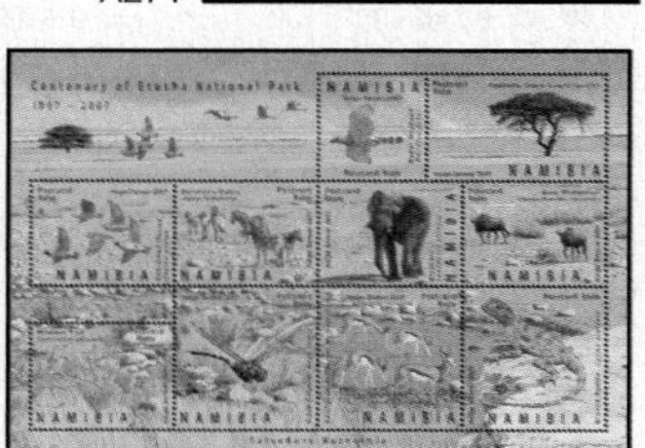

Etosha National Park, Cent. — A272

Designs: ($1.90), Otjovasandu Wilderness Area. $3.40, Okaukuejo Waterhole. ($17.20), Scientist conducting anthrax research.

No. 1119: a, Gabar goshawk (30x30mm). b, Umbrella thorn tree (50x30mm). c, Red-billed queleas (40x30mm). d, Burchell's zebras (40x30mm). e, Elephant (40x30mm). f, Blue wildebeest (40x30mm). g, Mustard tree (40x30mm). h, Black emperor dragonfly (40x40mm). i, Springbok (40x40mm). j, Ground agama (40x40mm).

Litho. With Foil Application

2007, Mar. 22 *Perf. 14x13¼*

1116-1118 A271 Set of 3 7.25 7.25

Miniature Sheet

Litho.

1119 A272 ($2.25) Sheet of 10, #a-j 7.25 7.25

No. 1116 is inscribed "Standard Mail;" No. 1118, "Inland Registered Mail Paid;" Nos. 1119a-1119j, "Postcard Rate."

Dragonflies — A273

Designs: ($1.90), Blue emperor dragonfly. $3.90, Rock dropwing dragonfly. $4.40, Red-veined dropwing dragonfly. ($6), Jaunty dropwing dragonfly.

$6, Blue basker dragonfly.

2007, Apr. 16 Litho. *Perf. 12¾x14*

1120-1123 A273 Set of 4 6.00 6.00

Souvenir Sheet

Perf. 14x13¼

1124 A273 $6 multi 2.75 2.75

No. 1120 is inscribed "Standard Mail;" No. 1123, "Non Standard Mail Paid."

Trees
A274

Designs: ($1.90), Commiphora kraeuseliana. $3.40, Commiphora wildii. $3.90, Commiphora glaucescens. ($6), Commiphora dinteri.

2007, July 20 Litho. *Perf. 13¼x13¾*

1125-1128 A274 Set of 4 5.00 5.00

No. 1125 is inscribed "Standard Mail;" No. 1128, "Non-standard Mail."

Flowers — A275

Designs: ($1.90), Cheiridopsis carolischmidtii. ($6), Namibia ponderosa. ($17.20), Fenestraria rhopalophylla.

2007, Aug. 31

1129-1131 A275 Set of 3 7.00 7.00

No. 1129 is inscribed "Standard Mail;" No. 1130, "Non-standard Mail;" No. 1131, "Inland Registered Mail Paid."

Nos. 1129-1131 were each printed in sheets of 10 + 5 labels.

Nos. 861, 865, 866 and 868 Surcharged

h

i

j

k

2007, Oct. 1 Litho. *Perf. 13½*

1132 A189(h) ($2) on 90c #861 .65 .65
1133 A189(h) ($2) on $1.20 #865 .65 .65
1134 A189(h) ($2) on $1.50 #866 .65 .65
1135 A189(h) ($2) on $4 #868 .65 .65
1136 A189(i) $3.70 on $1.20 #865 1.25 1.25
1137 A189(i) $4.20 on $1.20 #865 1.40 1.40
1138 A189(i) $4.85 on $1.20 #865 1.50 1.50
1139 A189(j) ($6.50) on $1.20 #865 2.10 2.10
1140 A189(k) ($16.45) on $1.20 #865 5.00 5.00
Nos. 1132-1140 (9) 13.85 13.85

Location of surcharge varies.

Miniature Sheets

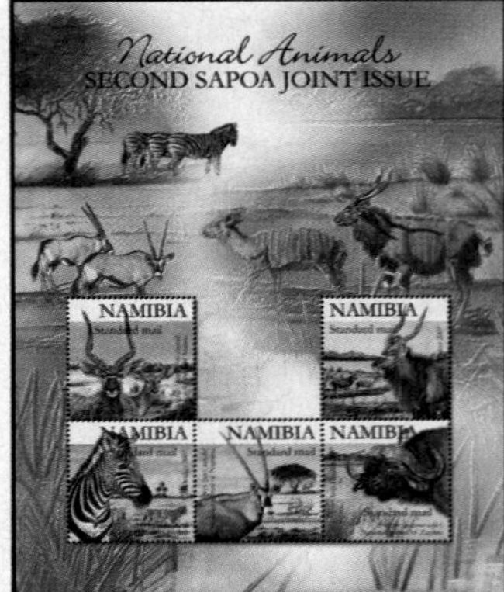

National Animals — A276

Nos. 1141 and 1142: a, Nyala (Malawi). b, Nyala (Zimbabwe). c, Bruschell's zebra (Botswana). d, Oryx (Namibia). e, Buffalo (Zambia).

2007, Oct. 9 Litho. *Perf. 13¾*

Granite Paper (#1141)

Country Name in Black

1141 A276 ($2) Sheet of 5, #a-e 4.50 4.50

Litho. With Foil Application

Country Name in Silver

1142 A276 ($2) Sheet of 5, #a-e 4.50 4.50

Nos. 1141a-1141e, 1142a-1142e are inscribed "Standard mail."

See Botswana No. 838, Malawi Nos., Zambia Nos. 1097-1101, Zimbabwe Nos. 1064-1068.

Weaver Birds — A277

Designs: ($2), Southern masked weaver. $3.70, Red-headed weaver. ($3.90), White-browed sparrow weaver. $4.20, Sociable weaver. ($18.45), Thick-billed weaver.

2008, Feb. 28 Litho. *Perf. 13½x14*

1143-1147 A277 Set of 5 8.50 8.50

No. 1143 is inscribed "Standard Mail;" No. 1145, "Postcard Rate;" No. 1147, "Inland Registered Mail Paid."

Euphorbia Flowers — A278

Designs: ($3.90), Euphorbia virosa. $6.45, Euphorbia dregeana. ($22.95), Euphorbia damarana.

$6.45 — Type I: "E" over "I" in Latin inscription. Type II: Corrected version, no "I".

2008

1148 A278 ($3.90) multi 1.00 1.00
1149 A278 $6.45 multi, Type I 1.60 1.60
a. Type II 1.75 1.75
1150 A278 ($22.95) multi 5.75 5.75
Nos. 1148-1150 (3) 8.35 8.35

Issued: Nos. 1148-1150, 3/3; No. 1149a, 5/27. No. 1148 inscribed "Postcard Rate;" No. 1150, "Registered Non-Standard Mail."

Miniature Sheet

Discovery of Diamonds in Namibia, Cent. — A279

No. 1151: a, Uncut diamonds. b, Land mining. c, Marine mining. d, Diamond jewelry.

Litho. With Foil Application

2008, Apr. 15 *Perf. 14x13½*

1151 A279 $2 Sheet of 4, #a-d 2.10 2.10

Miniature Sheet

Traditional Houses — A280

No. 1152: a, Herero. b, Kavango. c, Owambo. d, Nama. e, Caprivi. f, San.

2008, May 27 Litho.

1152 A280 ($2.20) Sheet of 6, #a-f 3.50 3.50

Nos. 1152a-1152f are each inscribed "Standard Mail."

Twyfelfontein UNESCO World Heritage Site — A281

Rock drawings: No. 1153, ($7.20), No. 1156a ($2.20), Lion man. No. 1154, ($7.20), No. 1156b ($2.20), Giraffe, Dancing kudu. No. 1155, ($7.20), No. 1156c ($2.20), Elephant.

2008, June 27 *Perf. 13½x13¾*

1153-1155 A281 Set of 3 5.50 5.50

Souvenir Sheet

1156 A281 ($2.20) Sheet of 3, #a-c 1.75 1.75

Nos. 1153-1155 are each inscribed "Non-Standard Mail;" Nos. 1156a-1156c, "Standard Mail."

Ediacaran Fossils — A282

Designs: ($2), Rangea. ($3.90), Swartpuntia. ($18.45), Pteridinium. ($22.95), Ernietta.

Litho. & Embossed

2008, Aug. 8 *Perf. 13¼x14*

1157-1160 A282 Set of 4 12.50 12.50

No. 1157 is inscribed "Standard Mail;" No. 1158, "Postcard Rate;" No. 1159, "Registered Non-standard Mail;" No. 1160, "Registered Inland Mail Paid."

2008 Summer Olympics, Beijing — A283

Designs: $2, Female runner, sun and Earth. $3.70, Athlete with arms raised. $3.90, Athlete at finish line. $4.20, Female runner with arms extended.

2008, Aug. 15 Litho. *Perf. 13¼x13*

1161-1164 A283 Set of 4 3.75 3.75

Flora and Fauna Type of 2007

Designs: $4.10, Thimble grass. $4.60, Bronze whaler shark. $5.30, Deep sea red crab. ($18.20), False ink cap mushroom.

2008, Oct. 1 Litho. *Perf. 14x13¼*

1165 A270 $4.10 multi 1.00 1.00
1166 A270 $4.60 multi 1.10 1.10
1167 A270 $5.30 multi 1.25 1.25
1168 A270 ($18.20) multi 4.50 4.50
Nos. 1165-1168 (4) 7.85 7.85

No. 1168 is inscribed "Registered Mail."

NATAL

nə-'tal

LOCATION — Southern coast of Africa, bordering on the Indian Ocean
GOVT. — British Crown Colony
AREA — 35,284 sq. mi.
POP. — 1,206,386 (1908)
CAPITAL — Pietermaritzburg

Natal united with Cape of Good Hope, Orange Free State and the Transvaal in 1910 to form the Union of South Africa.

12 Pence = 1 Shilling
20 Shillings = 1 Pound

Values for Nos. 1-7 are for examples with complete margins and free from damage. Unused values for No. 8 on are for stamps with original gum as defined in the catalogue introduction. Very fine examples of Nos. 8-49, 61-63 and 79 will have perforations touching the design on one or more sides due to the narrow spacing of the stamps on the plates. Stamps with perfs clear of the design on all four sides are scarce and will command higher prices.

Watermark

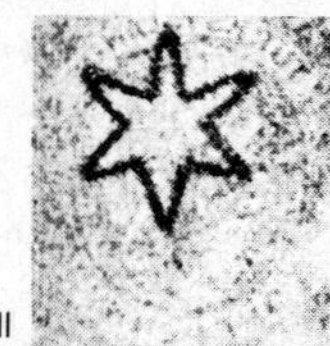

Wmk. 5 — Small Star

Crown and V R (Victoria Regina)
A1 A2

Crown and Laurel — A3

A4 A5

Colorless Embossing

1857 Unwmk. *Imperf.*
1 A1 3p *rose* 550.
a. Tete beche pair *45,000.*
2 A2 6p *green* 1,400.
a. Diagonal half used as 3p on cover *11,000.*
3 A3 9p *blue* — *9,000.*
4 A4 1sh *buff* *7,500.*

1858
5 A5 1p *blue* 1,400.
6 A5 1p *rose* 2,200.
a. No. 1 embossed over No. 6 —
7 A5 1p *buff* 1,275.

Reprints: The paper is slightly glazed, the embossing sharper and the colors as follows: 1p pale blue, deep blue, carmine rose or yellow; 3p pale rose or carmine rose; 6p bright green or yellow green; 1sh pale buff or pale yellow. Bogus cancellations are found on the reprints.

The stamps printed on surface-colored paper are revenue stamps with trimmed perforations.

Listings of shades will be found in the *Scott Classic Specialized Catalogue.*

Queen Victoria
A6 A7

1860 Engr. *Perf. 14*
8 A6 1p rose 160.00 90.00
9 A6 3p blue 200.00 55.00

1863 *Perf. 13*
10 A6 1p red 110.00 35.00

1861 *Clean-cut Perf. 14 to 16*
11 A6 3p blue 275.00 80.00

1862 *Rough Perf. 14 to 16*
12 A6 3p blue 140.00 40.00
a. Imperf., pair *4,500.*
b. Imperf. horiz. or vert., pair *4,750.*
13 A6 6p gray 250.00 65.00

1862 Wmk. 5
14 A6 1p rose 175.00 82.50

Imperforate copies of the 1p and 3p on paper watermarked small star are proofs.

1864 Wmk. 1 *Perf. 12½*
15 A6 1p carmine red 110.00 50.00
16 A6 6p violet 70.00 35.00

No. 15 imperf is a proof.

1867 Typo. *Perf. 14*
17 A7 1sh green 200.00 40.00

For types A6 and A7 overprinted or surcharged see Nos. 18-50, 61-63, 76, 79.

Stamps of 1860-67 Overprinted: **Postage.**

1869

Overprint 12¾mm
18 A6 1p rose red (#15) 375.00 82.50
b. Double overprint — *1,700.*
19 A6 3p blue (#12) 575.00 100.00
19A A6 3p blue (#9) — 400.00
19B A6 3p blue (#11) 700.00 260.00
20 A6 6p violet (#16) 525.00 95.00
21 A7 1sh green (#17) *6,750.* 1,175.

Same Overprint 13¾mm
22 A6 1p rose (#15) 950.00 225.00
23 A6 3p blue (#12) 1,900. 450.00
a. Inverted overprint
23B A6 3p blue (#9) — —
23C A6 3p blue (#11) — 900.00
24 A6 6p violet (#16) 1,900. 175.00
25 A7 1sh green (#17) *11,500.* *2,300.*

Same Overprint 14½ to 15½mm
26 A6 1p rose (#15) 750.00 190.00
27 A6 3p blue (#12) — 350.00
27A A6 3p blue (#11) — 575.00
27B A6 3p blue (#9) — —
28 A6 6p violet (#16) 1,500. 115.00
29 A7 1sh green (#17) *16,750.* *2,100.*

Overprinted

30 A6 1p rose red (#15) 125.00 55.00
b. Inverted overprint
31 A6 3p blue (#12) 225.00 55.00
a. Double overprint 1,275.
31B A6 3p blue (#11) 200.00 62.50
31C A6 3p blue (#9) 375.00 95.00
32 A6 6p violet (#16) 175.00 65.00
33 A7 1sh green (#17) 250.00 82.50

Overprinted

34 A6 1p rose (#15) 475.00 100.00
35 A6 3p blue (#12) 650.00 115.00
35A A6 3p blue (#11) 825.00 325.00
35B A6 3p blue (#9) *2,600.* *775.00*
36 A6 6p violet (#16) 600.00 100.00
b. Inverted overprint
37 A7 1sh green (#17) *9,250.* *1,550.*

Overprinted in Black or Red

1870-73 Wmk. 1 *Perf. 12½*
38 A6 1p red 100.00 16.00
39 A6 3p ultra (R) ('72) 110.00 16.00
40 A6 6p lilac ('73) 200.00 32.50
Nos. 38-40 (3) 410.00 64.50

Overprinted in Red, Black or Green

g

1870 *Perf. 14*
41 A7 1sh green (R) — *4,500.*
42 A7 1sh green (Bk) *3,250.* *1,550.*
a. Double overprint *3,250.*
43 A7 1sh green (G) 110.00 12.50

See No. 76.

Type of 1867 Overprinted

1873
44 A7 1sh brown lilac 250.00 27.50

No. 44 without overprint is a revenue.

Type of 1864 Overprinted

1874 *Perf. 12½*
45 A6 1p rose red 325.00 95.00
a. Double overprint

Overprinted

1875
46 A6 1p rose red 140.00 82.50
b. Double overprint 625.00 500.00

Overprinted

Overprint 14½mm

1875 *Perf. 12½*
47 A6 1p yellow 90.00 90.00
48 A6 1p rose red 115.00 82.50
a. Inverted overprint 1,275. 575.00
49 A6 6p violet 77.50 10.00
a. Inverted overprint 900.00 190.00
b. Double overprint 775.00

Perf. 14
50 A7 1sh green 115.00 9.00
a. Double overprint 425.00
Nos. 47-50 (4) 397.50 191.50

The 1p yellow without overprint is a revenue.

A8 A9

A10 A11

Queen Victoria — A12

1874-78 Typo. Wmk. 1 *Perf. 14*
51 A8 1p rose 32.50 4.25
52 A9 3p ultramarine 140.00 27.50
a. Perf. 14x12½ 2,000. 1,100.
53 A10 4p brown ('78) 150.00 14.00
54 A11 6p violet 70.00 9.00

Perf. 15½x15
55 A12 5sh claret 450.00 115.00

Perf. 14
56 A12 5sh claret ('78) 225.00 62.50
57 A12 5sh carmine ('78) 95.00 37.50

Perf. 12½
58 A10 4p brown ('78) 425.00 82.50

See Nos. 65-71. For types A8-A10 surcharged see Nos. 59-60, 72-73, 77, 80.

Surcharged in Black:

n

No. 60

o

1877 *Perf. 14*
59 A8(n) ½p on 1p rose 37.50 *82.50*
a. Double surcharge "1/2"
60 A8(n) ½p on 1p rose 60.00 *100.00*

The "1/2" only of No. 60 is illustrated. Surcharge "n" exists in 3 or more types each of the large "1/2" (No. 59) and the small "1/2" (No. 60).

"HALF" and "½" were overprinted separately; "½" may be above, below or overlapping.

Perf. 12½
61 A6(o) ½p on 1p yel 110.00 12.50
a. Double surcharge 325.00 225.00
b. Inverted surcharge 350.00 240.00
c. Pair, one without surcharge 2,750. 1,650.
d. "POTAGE" 300.00 250.00
e. "POSAGE" 325.00 325.00
f. "POSTAGE" omitted 2,000. —
62 A6(o) 1p on 6p vio 65.00 12.50
a. "POSTAGE" omitted
b. "POTAGE" 475.00 190.00
63 A6(o) 1p on 6p rose 125.00 57.50
a. Inverted surcharge 700.00 375.00
b. Double surcharge — 325.00

c.	Dbl. surch., one inverted	325.00	250.00
d.	Triple surch., one invtd.		
e.	Quadruple surcharge	475.00	250.00
f.	"POTAGE"	650.00	375.00
	Nos. 61-63 (3)	300.00	82.50

No. 63 without overprint is a revenue.

A14

1880 Typo. *Perf. 14*

64	A14	½p blue green	17.50	25.00
a.		Vertical pair, imperf. between		

1882-89 Wmk. Crown and CA (2)

65	A14	½p blue green ('84)	115.00	20.00
66	A14	½p gray green ('84)	4.00	1.25
67	A8	1p rose ('84)	4.00	.25
68	A9	3p ultra ('84)	125.00	21.00
69	A9	3p gray ('89)	5.75	2.50
70	A10	4p brown	7.50	1.60
71	A11	6p violet	7.00	1.90
		Nos. 65-71 (7)	268.25	48.50

Surcharged in Black:

p

q

1885-86

72	A8(p)	½p on 1p rose	20.00	14.00
73	A9(q)	2p on 3p gray ('86)	24.00	7.00

A17

A20

1887

74	A17	2p olive green, die B	4.00	1.75
a.		Die A	45.00	2.75

For explanation of dies A and B see "Dies of British Colonial Stamps" in the catalogue introduction.

No. 76

Type of 1867 Overprinted Type "g" in Red

1888

76	A7	1sh orange	6.00	1.90
a.		Double overprint		*1,900.*

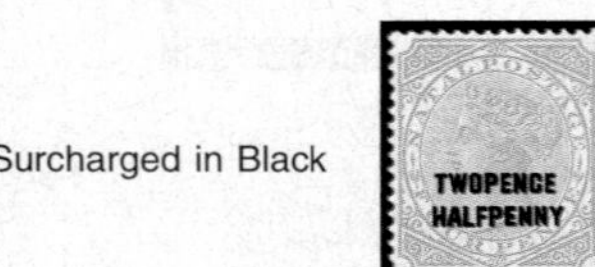
Surcharged in Black

1891

77	A10	2½p on 4p brown	12.50	16.00
a.		"PENGE"	62.50	*82.50*
b.		"PENN"	325.00	250.00
c.		Double surcharge	350.00	250.00
d.		Inverted surcharge	475.00	375.00

1891, June

78	A20	2½p ultramarine	7.50	1.60

Surcharged in Red or Black:

No. 79

No. 80

1895, Mar. Wmk. 1 *Perf. 12½*

79	A6	½p on 6p vio (R)	2.50	*5.25*
a.		"Ealf"	25.00	*40.00*
b.		"Penny"	22.50	*40.00*
c.		Double surcharge, one vert.	325.00	
d.		Double surcharge	325.00	

Stamps with fancy "P," "T" or "A" in surcharge sell for twice as much.

Wmk. 2 *Perf. 14*

80	A8	½p on 1p rose (Bk)	3.50	2.50
a.		Double surcharge	450.00	450.00
b.		Pair, one without surcharge and the other with double surcharge		—

A23 King Edward VII — A24

1902-03 Typo. Wmk. 2 *Perf. 14*

81	A23	½p blue green	3.75	.35
82	A23	1p rose	10.00	.20
83	A23	1½p blk & blue grn	4.25	3.25
84	A23	2p ol grn & scar	3.25	.30
85	A23	2½p ultramarine	1.90	4.00
86	A23	3p gray & red vio	1.60	1.90
87	A23	4p brown & scar	5.75	22.50
88	A23	5p org & black	2.75	3.50
89	A23	6p mar & bl grn	2.75	3.50
90	A23	1sh pale bl & dp rose	3.75	4.00
91	A23	2sh vio & bl grn	62.50	11.50
92	A23	2sh6p red violet	50.00	15.00
93	A23	4sh yel & dp rose	90.00	95.00

Wmk. 1

94	A24	5sh car lake & dk blue	37.50	14.00
95	A24	10sh brn & dp rose	90.00	32.50
96	A24	£1 ultra & blk	225.00	70.00
97	A24	£1 10sh vio & bl green	500.00	125.00
		Revenue cancel		6.25
98	A24	£5 black & vio	*3,500.*	*825.00*
		Revenue cancel		14.00
99	A24	£10 org & green	*9,500.*	*4,000.*
		Revenue cancel		110.00
100	A24	£20 green & car	*20,000.*	*10,000.*
		Revenue cancel		175.00
		Nos. 81-96 (16)	594.75	281.50

1904-08 Wmk. 3

101	A23	½p blue green	7.50	.20
102	A23	1p rose	7.75	.20
a.		Booklet pane of 6		
b.		Booklet pane of 5 + 1 label	350.00	
103	A23	2p ol green & scar	11.50	4.00
104	A23	4p brn & scar	3.50	1.60
105	A23	5p org & blk ('08)	5.50	6.00
106	A23	1sh pale bl & dp rose	100.00	9.00
107	A23	2sh vio & bl grn	70.00	47.50
108	A23	2sh6p red violet	65.00	47.50
109	A24	£1 10sh vio & org brn, chalky paper	1,525.	1,550.
		Revenue cancel		
		Nos. 101-108 (8)	270.75	116.00

A25

A26

1908-09

110	A25	6p red violet	5.75	3.50
111	A25	1sh black, *green*	7.75	3.25
112	A25	2sh bl & vio, *bl*	19.00	3.75
113	A25	2sh6p red & blk, *bl*	32.50	3.75
114	A26	5sh red & grn, *yellow*	27.50	32.50
115	A26	10sh red & grn, *green*	95.00	100.00
116	A26	£1 blk & vio, *red*	350.00	315.00
		Nos. 110-116 (7)	537.50	461.75

OFFICIAL STAMPS

Nos. 101-103, 106 and Type A23 Overprinted

1904 Wmk. 3 *Perf. 14*

O1	A23	½p blue green	3.75	.45
O2	A23	1p rose	5.75	.90
O3	A23	2p ol grn & scar	30.00	15.00
O4	A23	3p gray & red vio	17.50	*5.00*
O5	A23	6p mar & bl grn	60.00	82.50
O6	A23	1sh pale bl & dp rose	190.00	*250.00*
		Nos. O1-O6 (6)	307.00	*353.85*

Stamps of Natal were replaced by those of the Union of South Africa.

NAURU

nä-'ü-ˌrü

LOCATION — An island on the Equator in the west central Pacific Ocean, midway between the Marshall and Solomon Islands.
GOVT. — Republic
AREA — 8½ sq. mi.
POP. — 10,605 (1999 est.)
CAPITAL — None. Parliament House is in Yaren District.

The island, a German possession, was captured by Australian forces in 1914 and, following World War I, was mandated to the British Empire. It was administered jointly by Great Britain, Australia and New Zealand.

In 1947 Nauru was placed under United Nations trusteeship, administered by Australia. On January 31, 1968, Nauru became a republic.

See North West Pacific Islands.

12 Pence = 1 Shilling
100 Cents = 1 Dollar (1966)

Catalogue values for unused stamps in this country are for Never Hinged items, beginning with Scott 39.

Watermarks

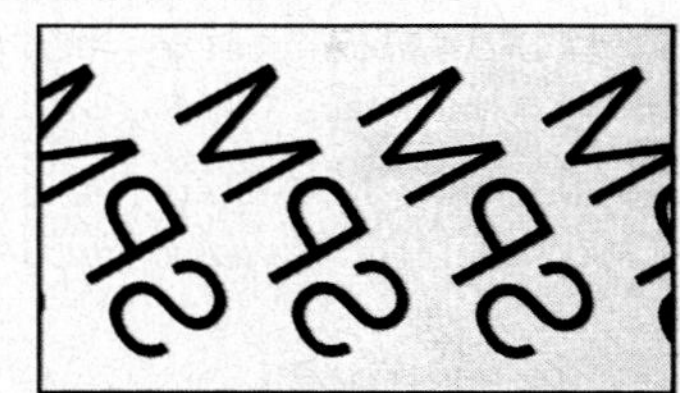
Wmk. 388 — Multiple "SPM"

Great Britain Stamps of 1912-13 Overprinted at Bottom of Stamp

1916-23 Wmk. 33 *Perf. 14½x14*

1	A82	½p green	3.50	*10.00*
2	A83	1p scarlet	2.25	*8.75*
3	A84	1½p red brn ('23)	57.50	*85.00*
4	A85	2p org (die I)	3.00	*15.00*
c.		2p deep orange (die II) ('23)	75.00	*110.00*
6	A86	2½p ultra	5.00	*12.00*
7	A87	3p violet	3.00	*11.00*
8	A88	4p slate green	3.00	*14.50*
a.		Double overprint	240.00	
9	A89	5p yel brown	4.50	*15.00*
10	A89	6p dull violet	10.00	*17.00*
11	A90	9p black brown	14.00	*24.00*
12	A90	1sh bister	13.00	*22.50*
		Nos. 1-12 (11)	118.75	*234.75*

Overprinted

Wmk. 34 *Perf. 11x12*

13	A91	2sh6p light brown	90.00	*125.00*
a.		2sh6p black brown	625.00	*725.00*
14	A91	5sh carmine	150.00	200.00
a.		5sh rose carmine	3,000.	2,750.
15	A91	10sh lt blue (R)	375.00	*400.00*
a.		10sh indigo blue	*12,500.*	*6,000.*

Same Ovpt. on Great Britain No. 179

1920

16	A91	2sh6p gray brown	92.50	*150.00*
		Nos. 13-16 (4)	707.50	*875.00*
		Nos. 1-16 (15)	826.25	*1,109.*

Double and triple overprints, with one overprint albino, exist for most of the 1-16 overprints. Additional color shades exist for No. 13-16, and values given are for the most common varieties. For detailed listings, see *Scott Classic Specialized Catalogue.*

Overprint Centered

1923

1b	A82	½p	8.00	*55.00*
2c	A83	1p	22.50	*40.00*
3a	A84	1½p	35.00	*57.50*
4d	A85	2p As No. 4a	40.00	*75.00*
		Nos. 1b-4d (4)	105.50	*227.50*

On Nos. 1-12 "NAURU" is usually 12¾mm wide and at the foot of the stamp. In 1923 four values were overprinted with the word 13½mm wide and across the middle of the stamp.

Forged overprints exist.

Freighter — A1

George VI — A2

1924-47 Unwmk. Engr. *Perf. 11*

17	A1	½p orange brown	2.00	*3.00*
b.		Perf. 14 ('47)	1.25	*10.00*
18a	A1	1p green	1.90	*4.00*
19a	A1	1½p red	1.10	*2.00*
20a	A1	2p orange	1.90	*8.00*
21a	A1	2½p blue ('48)	2.25	*4.00*
c.		Horiz. pair, imperf between	*12,500.*	*18,000.*
d.		Vert. pair, imperf between	*12,500.*	*18,000.*
22a	A1	3p grnsh gray ('47)	3.00	*14.00*
23a	A1	4p olive green	3.75	*15.00*
24a	A1	5p dk brown	5.25	*5.00*
25a	A1	6p dark violet	5.25	*6.00*
26a	A1	9p brown olive	9.00	*20.00*
27a	A1	1sh brown red	6.00	4.50
28a	A1	2sh6p slate green	25.00	*40.00*

No.	Type	Value	Description	Unused	Used
29a	A1	5sh	claret	35.00	*60.00*
30a	A1	10sh	yellow	60.00	*125.00*
			Nos. 17-30a (14)	161.40	*310.50*

Two printings were made of Nos. 17-30, the first (1924-34) on unsurfaced, grayish paper (Nos. 17-30), the second (1937-48) on glazed surfaced white paper (Nos. 17a-30a). Values are for the most common type. For detailed listings, see *Scott Classic Specialized Catalogue.*

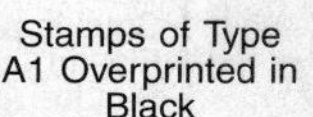

Stamps of Type A1 Overprinted in Black

1935, July 12 — ***Perf. 11***

Glazed Paper

No.	Type	Value	Description	Unused	Used
31	A1	1½p	red	1.00	*1.25*
32	A1	2p	orange	2.00	*6.50*
33	A1	2½p	blue	2.00	2.00
34	A1	1sh	brown red	6.00	*5.50*
			Nos. 31-34 (4)	11.00	*15.25*
			Set, never hinged	21.00	

25th anniv. of the reign of George V.

1937, May 10 — **Engr.**

No.	Type	Value	Description	Unused	Used
35	A2	1½p	salmon rose	.25	.50
36	A2	2p	dull orange	.25	1.00
37	A2	2½p	blue	.25	.50
38	A2	1sh	brown violet	.50	.50
			Nos. 35-38 (4)	1.25	2.50
			Set, never hinged	2.75	

Coronation of George VI & Elizabeth.

Catalogue values for unused stamps in this section, from this point to the end of the section, are for Never Hinged items.

Casting Throw-net — A3

Anibare Bay — A4

3½p, Loading phosphate. 4p, Frigate bird. 6p, Nauruan canoe. 9p, Meeting house (domaneab). 1sh, Palms. 2sh6p, Buada lagoon. 5sh, Map.

1954, Feb. 6 — ***Perf. 14½x14, 14x14½***

No.	Type	Value	Description	Unused	Used
39	A3	½p	purple	.20	.20
40	A4	1p	green	.20	.20
41	A3	3½p	red	.75	.75
42	A3	4p	deep blue	1.00	1.00
43	A3	6p	orange	.45	.30
44	A3	9p	brown lake	.75	.45
45	A4	1sh	dk rose violet	.85	.60
46	A3	2sh6p	dk gray green	4.00	2.25
47	A4	5sh	lilac rose	9.25	4.00
			Nos. 39-47 (9)	17.45	9.75

See Nos. 58-71.

Balsam — A5 Black Lizard — A6

Capparis — A7 Coral Pinnacles — A8

White Tern — A9

2p, Micronesian pigeon, vert. 3p, Poison nut flower. 3sh3p, Nightingale reed warbler.

Perf. 13½, Perf. 14½x13½ (10p), Perf. 14½ (2sh3p)

Photo.; Engraved (10p, 2sh3p)

1963-65 — **Unwmk.**

No.	Type	Value	Description	Unused	Used
49	A9	2p	multi ('65)	.20	.90
50	A6	3p	red org, sl grn & yel ('64)	.30	.25
51	A5	5p	gray, bl grn & yellow	.75	.50
52	A6	8p	green & black	1.50	.65
53	A7	10p	black ('64)	2.00	1.10
54	A9	1sh3p	ap grn, blk & Prus bl ('65)	3.00	2.75
55	A8	2sh3p	vio blue ('64)	3.75	2.50
56	A6	3sh3p	lt yel, bl, brn & blk ('65)	7.50	5.00
			Nos. 49-56 (8)	19.00	13.65

Issue dates: 5p, Apr. 22. 8p, July 1. 3p, 10p, 2sh3p, Apr. 16. 2p, 1sh3p, 3sh3p, May 3.

"Simpson and His Donkey" by Wallace Anderson — A9a

Perf. 13½x13

1965, Apr. 14 — **Photo.** — **Unwmk.**

No.	Type	Value	Description	Unused	Used
57	A9a	5p	brt green, sepia & blk	.65	.60

See note after Australia No. 387.

Types of 1954-65
Values in Cents and Dollars

Designs: 1c, Anibare Bay. 2c, Casting throw-net. 3c, Loading phosphate. 4c, Balsam. 5c, Palms. 7c, Black lizard. 8c, Capparis. 10c, Frigate bird. 15c, White tern. 25c, Coral pinnacles. 30c, Poison nut flower. 35c, Reed warbler. 50c, Micronesian pigeon, vert. $1, Map.

Engr.; Photo. (4c, 7c, 15c, 30c-50c)

1966 — ***Perf. 14½x14, 14x14½***

No.	Type	Value	Description	Unused	Used
58	A4	1c	dark blue	.20	.20
59	A3	2c	claret	.20	.35
60	A3	3c	green	.30	.80
61	A5	4c	lilac, grn & yel	.20	.20
62	A4	5c	violet blue	.20	.20
63	A6	7c	fawn & black	.20	.20
64	A7	8c	olive green	.25	.20
65	A3	10c	dark red	.30	.20
66	A9	15c	ap grn, blk & Prus blue	.60	.90
67	A3	25c	sepia	.55	.75
68	A6	30c	brick red, sl grn, & yellow	.75	.85
69	A6	35c	lt yel, bl, brn & black	1.10	1.00
70	A9	50c	yel, bluish blk & brown	1.25	1.25
71	A4	$1	claret	2.75	1.75
			Nos. 58-71 (14)	8.85	8.85

The engraved stamps are luminescent.

Issued: 2c, 3c, 5c, 15c, 25c, 35c, 5/25; others, 2/14.

Republic

Nos. 58-71 Overprinted in Red, Black or Orange
"REPUBLIC / OF / NAURU"

1968

No.	Type	Value	Description	Unused	Used
72	A4	1c	dark blue (R)	.20	.35
73	A3	2c	claret	.20	.25
74	A3	3c	green	.20	.25
75	A5	4c	lilac, grn & yel	.20	.25
76	A4	5c	violet blue (O)	.20	.25
77	A6	7c	fawn & blk (R)	.20	.25
78	A7	8c	olive green (R)	.20	.25
79	A3	10c	dark red	.20	.30
80	A9	15c	ap grn, blk & Prus blue	1.75	*3.50*
81	A3	25c	sepia (R)	.50	.30
82	A6	30c	brick red, sl grn & yellow	.85	.30
83	A6	35c	multicolored	1.10	.50
84	A9	50c	yel, bluish blk & brown	1.25	.60
85	A4	$1	claret	2.50	.80
			Nos. 72-85 (14)	9.55	8.15

Issued: 4c, 7c, 30c, 35c, 5/15; others, 1/31.

Nauru Woman Watching Rising Sun — A10

Planting Seedling and Map of Nauru — A11

Perf. 13x13½

1968, Sept. 11 — **Photo.** — **Unwmk.**

No.	Type	Value	Description	Unused	Used
86	A10	5c	multicolored	.20	.20
87	A11	10c	brt blue, blk & green	.25	.20

Independence of Nauru.

Flag of Nauru — A12

1969, Jan. 31 — **Litho.** — ***Perf. 13½***

No.	Type	Value	Description	Unused	Used
88	A12	15c	dk vio blue, yel & org	.55	.55

For overprint see No. 90.

Commission Emblem and Nauru — A13

1972, Feb. 7 — **Litho.** — ***Perf. 14½x14***

No.	Type	Value	Description	Unused	Used
89	A13	25c	blue, yellow & black	.55	.55

South Pacific Commission, 25th anniv.

No. 88 Overprinted in Gold:

1973, Jan. 31 — ***Perf. 13½***

No.	Type	Value	Description	Unused	Used
90	A12	15c	multicolored	.35	.35

Fifth anniversary of independence.

Lotus (Ekwenababae) A14

Map of Nauru, Artifacts A15

Catching Flyingfish A16

Designs: 2c, Kauwe iud. 3c, Rimone. 4c, Denea. 5c, Beach morning-glory. 7c, Golden butterflyfish. 10c, Nauruan ball game (itsibweb). 15c, Nauruan wrestling. 20c, Snaring frigate birds. 25c, Nauruan girl with flower garland. 30c, Men catching noddies. 50c, Frigate birds.

1973 — **Litho.** — ***Perf. 13½x14***

No.	Type	Value	Description	Unused	Used
91	A14	1c	pale yellow & multi	.20	.20
92	A14	2c	pale ocher & multi	.20	.20
93	A14	3c	pale violet & multi	.20	.20
94	A14	4c	pale green & multi	.20	.20
95	A14	5c	pale blue & multi	.20	.20
			Perf. 14½x14, 14x14½		
96	A16	7c	blue & multi	.20	.20
97	A16	8c	black & multi	.25	.25
98	A16	10c	multicolored	.30	.30
99	A15	15c	green & multi	.35	.35
100	A15	20c	blue & multi	.40	.40
101	A15	25c	yellow & multi	.45	.45
102	A16	30c	multicolored	.65	.65
103	A16	50c	multicolored	1.25	1.25
104	A15	$1	blue & multi	2.40	2.40
			Nos. 91-104 (14)	7.25	7.25

Issue dates: Nos. 97-100, May 23; Nos. 96, 101-103, July 25; others Mar. 28, 1973.

Cooperative Store — A17 Eigigu, the Girl in the Moon — A18

Design: 25c, Timothy Detudamo and cooperative store emblem.

1973, Dec. 20 — **Litho.** — ***Perf. 14½x14***

No.	Type	Value	Description	Unused	Used
105	A17	5c	multicolored	.80	.80
106	A17	25c	multicolored	.80	.80
107	A18	50c	multicolored	1.50	1.50
			Nos. 105-107 (3)	3.10	3.10

50th anniversary of Nauru Cooperative Society, founded by Timothy Detudamo.

"Eigamoiya" — A19

10c, Phosphate mining. 15c, "Nauru Chief" plane over Nauru. 25c, Nauru chieftain with frigate-bird headdress. 35c, Capt. J. Fearn, sailing ship "Hunter" & map of Nauru. 50c, "Hunter" off Nauru.

Perf. 13x13½, 13½x13

1974, May 21 — **Litho.**

Sizes: 70x22mm (7c, 35c, 50c); 33x20mm (10c, 15c, 25c)

No.	Type	Value	Description	Unused	Used
108	A19	7c	multicolored	.20	.20
109	A19	10c	multicolored	.25	.25
110	A19	15c	multicolored	.45	.45
111	A19	25c	multicolored	1.10	1.10
112	A19	35c	multicolored	4.50	4.50
113	A19	50c	multicolored	4.00	4.00
			Nos. 108-113 (6)	10.50	10.50

175th anniversary of Nauru's first contact with the outside world.

Map of Nauru A20 Post Office A21

UPU Emblem and: 20c, Mailman on motorcycle. $1, Flag of Nauru and UPU Building, Bern, vert.

1974, July 23 Litho. *Perf. 14*

No.	Type	Description	Unused	Used
114	A20	5c multicolored	.20	.20

Perf. 13½x13, 13x13½

No.	Type	Description	Unused	Used
115	A21	8c multicolored	.20	.20
116	A21	20c multicolored	.40	.30
117	A21	$1 multicolored	2.25	2.25
a.		Souv. sheet of 4, #114-117, imperf.	5.50	5.50
		Nos. 114-117 (4)	3.05	2.95

Cent. of the UPU.

Rev. P. A. Delaporte — A22

1974, Dec. 10 Litho. *Perf. 14½*

No.	Type	Description	Unused	Used
118	A22	15c brt pink & multi	.35	.35
119	A22	20c blue & multi	.80	.80

Christmas 1974. Delaporte, a German-born American missionary, took Christianity to Nauru and translated the New Testament into Nauruan.

Nauru, Grain, Albert Ellis, Phosphate Rock — A23

Designs: 7c, Phosphate mining and coolie carrying load. 15c, Electric freight train, tugs and ship. 25c, Excavator, cantilever and truck.

1975, July 23 Litho. *Perf. 14½x14*

No.	Type	Description	Unused	Used
120	A23	5c multicolored	.20	.20
121	A23	7c multicolored	.20	.20
122	A23	15c multicolored	.95	.95
123	A23	25c multicolored	1.25	1.25
		Nos. 120-123 (4)	2.60	2.60

75th anniv. of discovery of phosphate (5c); 70th anniv. of Pacific Phosphate Co. Mining Agreement (7c); 50th anniv. of British Phosphate Commissioners (15c); 5th anniv. of Nauru Phosphate Corp. (25c).

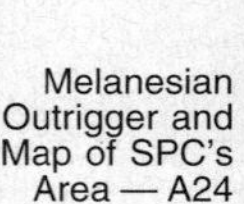

Melanesian Outrigger and Map of SPC's Area — A24

1975, Sept. 1 Litho. *Perf. 14x14½*

No.	Type	Description	Unused	Used
124	A24	20c Micronesian outrigger	.60	.50
125	A24	20c Polynesian double hull	.60	.50
126	A24	20c shown	.60	.50
127	A24	20c Polynesian outrigger	.60	.50
a.		Block of 4, #124-127	3.00	3.00
		Nos. 124-127 (4)	2.40	2.00

South Pacific Commission Conference, Nauru, Sept. 29-Oct. 10.

New Civic Center A25

Design: 50c, "Domaneab" (meeting house) and flags of participating nations.

1975, Sept. 29 Litho. *Perf. 14½*

No.	Type	Description	Unused	Used
128	A25	30c multicolored	.40	.40
129	A25	50c multicolored	.75	.75

South Pacific Commission Conference, Nauru, Sept. 29-Oct. 10.

Virgin Mary, Stained-glass Window — A26

Christmas: 7c, 15c, "Suffer little children to come unto me," stained-glass window, Orro Protestant Church. 25c, like 5c, Yaren Catholic Church.

1975, Nov. 7 Litho. *Perf. 14½*

No.	Type	Description	Unused	Used
130	A26	5c gray blue & multi	.20	.20
131	A26	7c green & multi	.20	.20
132	A26	15c brown & multi	.25	.40
133	A26	25c lilac & multi	.50	.65
		Nos. 130-133 (4)	1.15	1.45

Frangipani Forming Lei Around Nauru A27

14c, Hand crowning Nauru with lei. 25c, Reed warbler, birds flying from Truk to Nauru. 40c, Reunion of islanders in Boar Harbor.

1976, Jan. 31 Litho. *Perf. 14½*

No.	Type	Description	Unused	Used
134	A27	10c green & multi	.20	.20
135	A27	14c violet & multi	.20	.20
136	A27	25c red & multi	.30	.30
137	A27	40c blue & multi	.55	.55
		Nos. 134-137 (4)	1.25	1.25

30th anniversary of the return of the islanders from Japanese internment on Truk.

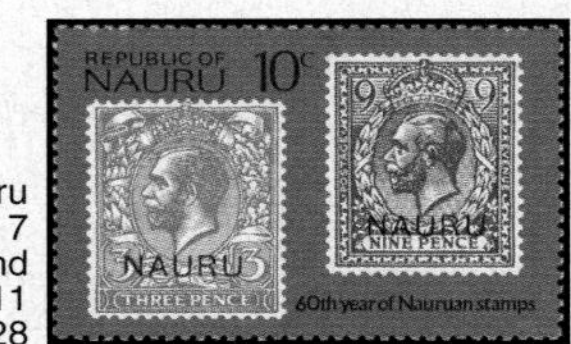

Nauru Nos. 7 and 11 A28

15c, Nauru Nos. 10, 12. 25c, Nauru No. 13. 50c, Nauru No. 14, "Specimen."

1976, May 6 Litho. *Perf. 13½x14*

No.	Type	Description	Unused	Used
138	A28	10c multicolored	.20	.20
139	A28	15c multicolored	.20	.20
140	A28	25c multicolored	.30	.30
141	A28	50c multicolored	.55	.55
		Nos. 138-141 (4)	1.25	1.25

60th anniv. of Nauru's 1st postage stamps.

Nauru Shipping and Pandanus — A29

Designs: 20c, Air Nauru Boeing 737 and Fokker F28, and tournefortia argentea. 30c, Earth satellite station and thespesia populnea. 40c, Area produce and cordia subcordata.

1976, July 26 Litho. *Perf. 13½x14*

No.	Type	Description	Unused	Used
142	A29	10c multicolored	.20	.20
143	A29	20c multicolored	.25	.25
144	A29	30c multicolored	.30	.30
145	A29	40c multicolored	.55	.55
		Nos. 142-145 (4)	1.30	1.30

7th South Pacific Forum, Nauru, July 1976.

Nauruan Children's Choir — A30

20c, Angels. #146, 148, denominations at lower right. #147, 149, denominations at lower left.

1976, Nov. Litho. *Perf. 14x13½*

No.	Type	Description	Unused	Used
146		15c multicolored	.25	.25
147		15c multicolored	.25	.25
a.	A30	Pair, #146-147	.55	.55
148		20c multicolored	.35	.35
149		20c multicolored	.35	.35
a.	A30	Pair, #148-149	.75	.75
		Nos. 146-149 (4)	1.20	1.20

Christmas.

Nauru House, Melbourne, and Coral Pinnacles — A32

Cable-laying Ship Anglia, 1902 — A33

30c, Nauru House and Melbourne skyline.

1977, Apr. 14 Photo. *Perf. 14½*

No.	Type	Description	Unused	Used
150	A32	15c multicolored	.30	.30
151	A32	30c multicolored	.60	.60

Opening of Nauru House in Melbourne, Australia.

For surcharges see Nos. 161-164.

1977, Sept. 7 Photo. *Perf. 14½*

Designs: 15c, Nauru radar station. 20c, Stern of Anglia. 25c, Radar antenna.

No.	Type	Description	Unused	Used
152	A33	7c multicolored	.20	.20
153	A33	15c multicolored	.25	.25
154	A33	20c multicolored	.30	.30
155	A33	25c multicolored	.40	.40
		Nos. 152-155 (4)	1.15	1.15

1st transpacific cable, 75th anniv., and 1st artificial earth satellite, 20th anniv.

Catholic Church, Yaren, and Father Kayser — A34

Coat of Arms of Nauru — A35

Designs: 25c, Congregational Church, Orro. 30c, Catholic Church, Arubo.

1977, Oct. Photo. *Perf. 14½*

No.	Type	Description	Unused	Used
156	A34	15c multicolored	.20	.20
157	A34	25c multicolored	.25	.25
158	A34	30c multicolored	.30	.30
		Nos. 156-158 (3)	.75	.75

Christmas, and 55th anniversary of first Roman Catholic Church on Nauru.

1978, Jan. 31 Litho. *Perf. 14½*

No.	Type	Description	Unused	Used
159	A35	15c blue & multi	.20	.20
160	A35	60c emerald & multi	.60	.60

10th anniversary of independence.

Nos. 150-151 Surcharged with New Value and Two Bars

1978, Apr. Photo. *Perf. 14½*

No.	Type	Description	Unused	Used
161	A32	4c on 15c multi	2.25	2.75
162	A32	5c on 15c multi	2.25	2.75
163	A32	8c on 30c multi	2.25	2.75
164	A32	10c on 30c multi	2.25	2.75
		Nos. 161-164 (4)	9.00	11.00

Girls Catching Fish in Buada Lagoon A36

Designs: 1c, Fisherman and family collecting shellfish. 2c, Pigs foraging near coral reef. 3c, Gnarled tree and birds. 4c, Girl catching fish with hands. 5c, Bird catching fish. 10c, Ijuw Lagoon. 15c, Young girl and coral formation. 20c, Reef pinnacles, Anibare Bay. 25c, Pinnacles, Meneng shore. 30c, Frigate bird. 32c, Coconut palm and noddies. 40c, Iwiyi, wading bird. 50c, Frigate birds. $1, Pinnacles, Topside. $2, Newly uncovered pinnacles, Topside. $5, Old pinnacles, Topside.

1978-79 Photo. *Perf. 14½*

No.	Type	Description	Unused	Used
165	A36	1c multicolored	.20	.20
166	A36	2c multicolored	.20	.20
167	A36	3c multicolored	.20	.20
168	A36	4c multicolored	.20	.20
169	A36	5c multicolored	.20	.20
170	A36	7c multicolored	.20	.20
171	A36	10c multicolored	.20	.20
172	A36	15c multicolored	.20	.25
173	A36	20c multicolored	.30	.30
174	A36	25c multicolored	.35	.35
175	A36	30c multicolored	.45	.45
176	A36	32c multicolored	.50	.50
177	A36	40c multicolored	.60	.55
178	A36	50c multicolored	.75	.70
179	A36	$1 multicolored	1.50	1.00
180	A36	$2 multicolored	3.00	2.00
181	A36	$5 multicolored	7.50	7.00
		Nos. 165-181 (17)	16.55	14.50

Issued: #166-169, 6/6/79; others, 5/1978.

"APU" — A37

Mother and Child — A38

1978, Aug. 28 Litho. *Perf. 13½*

No.	Type	Description	Unused	Used
182	A37	15c multicolored	.50	.90
183	A37	20c gold, blk & dk blue	.75	1.10

14th General Assembly of Asian Parliamentary Union, Nauru, Aug. 28-Sept. 1. On sale during conference only.

1978, Nov. 1 Litho. *Perf. 14*

Christmas: 15c, 20c, Angel over the Pacific, horiz. 30c, like 7c.

No.	Type	Description	Unused	Used
184	A38	7c multicolored	.20	.20
185	A38	15c multicolored	.20	.20
186	A38	20c multicolored	.20	.20
187	A38	30c multicolored	.30	.30
		Nos. 184-187 (4)	.90	.90

Lord Baden-Powell and Cub Scout — A39

30c, Boy Scout. 50c, Explorer.

1978, Dec. 1 Litho. *Perf. 14*

No.	Type	Description	Unused	Used
188	A39	20c multicolored	.20	.20
189	A39	30c multicolored	.35	.35
190	A39	50c multicolored	.55	.55
		Nos. 188-190 (3)	1.10	1.10

70th anniversary of 1st Scout Troop.

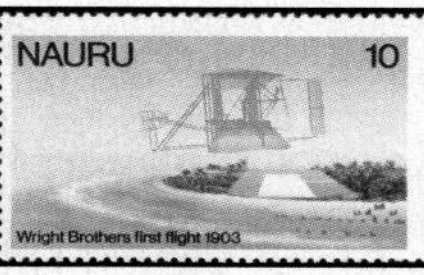

Flyer A over Nauru Airfield A40

Designs: No. 192, "Southern Cross" and Boeing 727. No. 193, "Southern Cross" and Boeing 737. 30c, Wright Flyer over Nauru.

1979, Jan. *Perf. 14½*

191 A40 10c multicolored .20 .20
192 A40 15c multicolored .20 .20
193 A40 15c multicolored .30 .30
a. Pair, #192-193 .50 .50
194 A40 30c multicolored .45 .40
Nos. 191-194 (4) 1.15 1.10

1st powered flight, 75th anniv. and Kingsford Smith's US-Australia and Australia-New Zealand flights, 50th anniv.

Nos. 192-193 printed checkerwise.

Rowland Hill, Marshall Islands No. 15 with Nauru Cancel A41

1979, Feb. 27 **Litho.** *Perf. 14½*

195 A41 5c shown .20 .20
196 A41 15c Nauru No. 15 .20 .20
197 A41 60c Nauru No. 160 .80 .60
a. Souvenir sheet of 3, #195-197 1.25 1.25
Nos. 195-197 (3) 1.20 1.00

Sir Rowland Hill (1795-1879), originator of penny postage.

Dish Antenna, Earth Station, ITU Emblem — A42

ITU Emblem and: 32c, Woman operating Telex machine. 40c, Radio beacon operator.

1979, Aug. **Litho.** *Perf. 14½*

198 A42 7c multicolored .20 .20
199 A42 32c multicolored .40 .35
200 A42 40c multicolored .55 .45
Nos. 198-200 (3) 1.15 1.00

Intl. Radio Consultative Committee (CCIR) of the ITU, 50th anniv.

Nauruan Girl — A43

IYC Emblem, Nauruan Children: 15c, Boy. 25c, 32c, 50c, Girls, diff.

1979, Oct. 3 **Litho.** *Perf. 14½*

201 A43 8c multicolored .20 .20
202 A43 15c multicolored .20 .20
203 A43 25c multicolored .30 .20
204 A43 32c multicolored .40 .25
205 A43 50c multicolored .65 .35
a. Strip of 5, #201-205 1.75 1.75

International Year of the Child.

Star, Scroll, Ekwenababa Flower — A44

Star and Flowers: 15c, Milos. 20c, Denea. 30c, Morning glories.

1979, Nov. 14 **Litho.** *Perf. 14½*

206 A44 7c multicolored .20 .20
207 A44 15c multicolored .20 .20
208 A44 20c multicolored .25 .25
209 A44 30c multicolored .25 .25
Nos. 206-209 (4) .90 .90

Christmas.

Nauruan Plane over Melbourne — A45

Air Nauru, 10th Anniversary (Plane Over): 20c, Tarawa. 25c, Hong Kong. 30c, Auckland.

1980, Feb. 28 **Litho.** *Perf. 14½*

210 A45 15c multicolored .25 .25
211 A45 20c multicolored .25 .25
212 A45 25c multicolored .35 .30
213 A45 30c multicolored .45 .40
Nos. 210-213 (4) 1.30 1.20

Early Steam Locomotive A46

1980, May 6 **Litho.** *Perf. 15*

214 A46 8c shown .20 .20
215 A46 32c Electric locomotive .45 .40
216 A46 60c Clyde diesel-hydraulic locomotive .85 .75
a. Souvenir sheet of 3, #214-216 1.75 2.00
Nos. 214-216 (3) 1.50 1.35

Nauru Phosphate Corp., 10th anniv. No. 216a also for London 1980 Intl. Stamp Exhibition, May 6-14; Penny Black, 140th anniv.

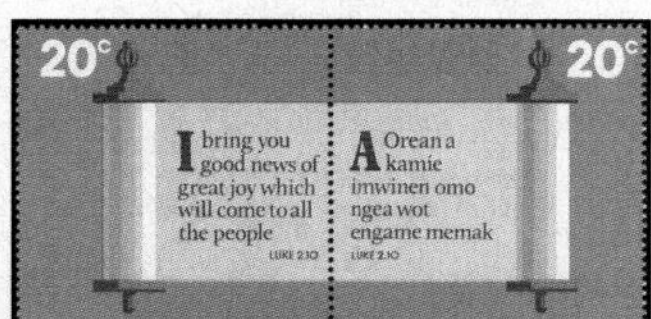

Christmas 1980 — A47

Designs: 30c, "Glory to God in the Highest . . ." in English and Nauruan.

1980, Sept. 24 **Litho.** *Perf. 15*

217 20c English .30 .25
218 20c Nauruese .30 .25
a. A47 Pair, #217-218 .60 .60
219 30c English .30 .25
220 30c Nauruese .30 .25
a. A47 Pair, #219-220 .60 .60
Nos. 217-220 (4) 1.20 1.00

See Nos. 236-239.

Flags of Nauru, Australia, Gt. Britain and New Zealand, UN Emblem — A49

1980, Dec. 20 **Litho.** *Perf. 14½*

221 A49 25c shown .35 .30

Size: 72x22mm

Perf. 14

222 A49 30c UN Trusteeship Council .40 .35
223 A49 50c 1968 independence ceremony .65 .55
Nos. 221-223 (3) 1.40 1.20

UN de-colonization declaration, 20th anniv.

No. 222 printed se-tenant with label showing flags of UN and Nauru, issued Feb. 11, 1981.

Timothy Detudamo (Former Head Chief), Domaneab (Meeting House) — A50

1981, Feb. **Litho.** *Perf. 14½*

224 A50 20c shown .30 .25
225 A50 30c Raymond Gadabu .40 .30
226 A50 50c Hammer DeRoburt .65 .55
Nos. 224-226 (3) 1.35 1.10

Legislative Council, 30th anniversary.

Casting Net by Hand A51

1981 **Litho.** *Perf. 12*

227 A51 8c shown .20 .20
228 A51 20c Ancient canoe .30 .25
229 A51 32c Powered boat .40 .40
230 A51 40c Fishing vessel .50 .50
a. Souvenir sheet of 4, #230 2.00 2.00
Nos. 227-230 (4) 1.40 1.35

Bank of Nauru, 5th Anniv. A52

1981, July 21 **Litho.** *Perf. 14x14½*

231 A52 $1 multicolored 1.25 1.25

ESCAP Secy. Maramis Delivering Inaugural Speech — A53

1981, Oct. 24 **Litho.** *Perf. 14½*

232 A53 15c shown .20 .20
233 A53 20c Maramis, Pres. de Robert .25 .25
234 A53 25c Plaque .30 .30
235 A53 30c Raising UN flag .35 .35
Nos. 232-235 (4) 1.10 1.10

UN Day and first anniv. of Economic and Social Commission for Asia and Pacific (ESCAP) liaison office in Nauru.

Christmas Type of 1980

Christmas (Biblical Scriptures in English and Nauruan): 20c, "His Name Shall Be Called Emmanuel." 30c, "To You is Born This Day . . ."

1981, Nov. 14 **Litho.** *Perf. 14½*

236 A47 20c multicolored .30 .25
237 A48 20c multicolored .30 .25
a. Pair, #236-237 .60 .60
238 A47 30c multicolored .30 .25
239 A48 30c multicolored .30 .25
a. Pair, #238-239 .60 .60
Nos. 236-239 (4) 1.20 1.00

10th Anniv. of South Pacific Forum A54

1981, Dec. 9 **Litho.** *Perf. 13½x14*

240 A54 10c Globe, dish antenna .20 .20
241 A54 20c Ship .25 .25
242 A54 30c Jet .40 .40
243 A54 40c Produce .50 .50
Nos. 240-243 (4) 1.35 1.35

Scouting Year — A55

1982, Feb. 23 **Litho.** *Perf. 14*

244 A55 7c Carrying packages .20 .20
245 A55 8c Scouts, life preserver, vert. .20 .20
246 A55 15c Pottery making, vert. .20 .20
247 A55 20c Inspection .25 .25
248 A55 25c Scout, cub .35 .35
249 A55 40c Troop .50 .50
a. Souv. sheet of 6, #244-249, imperf. 1.75 1.75
Nos. 244-249 (6) 1.70 1.70

A56

Ocean Thermal Energy Conversion — A57

Designs: No. 250, Plant under construction. No. 251, Completed plant.

1982, June 10 **Litho.** *Perf. 13½*

250 Pair + 2 labels .90 .90
a.-b. A56 25c any single .45 .45
251 Pair + 2 labels 1.40 1.40
a.-b. A57 40c any single .70 .70

75th Anniv. of Phosphate Industry A58

1982, Oct. 11 **Litho.** *Perf. 14*

252 A58 5c Freighter Fido, 1907 .25 .20
253 A58 10c Locomotive Nellie, 1907 .40 .30
254 A58 30c Modern Clyde diesel train, 1982 .80 .80
255 A58 60c Flagship Eigamoiya, 1969 1.40 1.40
Nos. 252-255 (4) 2.85 2.70

Souvenir Sheet

256 A58 $1 Freighters 1.75 1.75

ANPEX '82 Natl. Stamp Exhibition, Brisbane, Australia, Nos. 252-255 se-tenant with labels describing stamp. No. 256 contains one 68x27mm stamp.

Visit of Queen Elizabeth II and Prince Philip A59

1982, Oct. 21 *Perf. 14½*

257 A59 20c Elizabeth, vert. .30 .25
258 A59 50c Philip, vert. .70 .60
259 A59 $1 Couple 1.25 1.10
Nos. 257-259 (3) 2.25 1.95

Christmas A60

Clergymen: 20c, Father Bernard Lahn, Catholic Mission Church. 30c, Rev. Itubwa Amram, Orro Central Church. 40c, Pastor James Aingimea, Tsiminita Memorial Church, Denigomodu. 50c, Bishop Paul Mea, Diocese of Tarawa-Nauru-Tuvalu.

1982, Nov. 17

260 A60 20c multicolored .25 .25
261 A60 30c multicolored .40 .35
262 A60 40c multicolored .55 .50
263 A60 50c multicolored .70 .65
Nos. 260-263 (4) 1.90 1.75

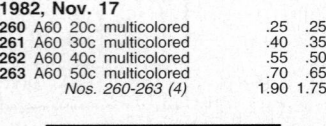

15th Anniv. of Independence — A61

1983, Mar. 23 Wmk. 373 ***Perf. 14½***

264 A61 15c Speaker of Parliament, vert. .25 .25
265 A61 20c People's Court, vert. .30 .30
266 A61 30c Law Courts .35 .35
267 A61 50c Parliament .65 .65
Nos. 264-267 (4) 1.55 1.55

World Communications Year — A62

1983, May. 11 Litho. ***Perf. 14***

268 A62 5c Earth Satellite Staion NZ .20 .20
269 A62 10c Omni-directional Range Installation .20 .20
270 A62 20c Fixed-station ambulance driver .30 .30
271 A62 25c Radio Nauru broadcaster .40 .40
272 A62 40c Air mail service .60 .60
Nos. 268-272 (5) 1.70 1.70

Angam Day (Homecoming) — A63

Perf. 14x13½

1983, Sept. 14 Litho. Wmk. 373

273 A63 15c MV Trinza arriving .20 .20

Size: 25x40mm

Perf. 14

274 A63 20c Elsie Agio in exile .30 .30
275 A63 30c Baby on scale .40 .40
276 A63 40c Children .55 .55
Nos. 273-276 (4) 1.45 1.45

Christmas A64

Designs: 5c, The Holy Virgin, the Holy Child and St. John, School of Raphael. 15c, The Mystical Betrothal of St. Catherine with Jesus, School of Paolo Veronese. 50c, Madonna on the Throne Surrounded by Angels, School of Seville.

Perf. 14½x14, 14x14½

1983, Nov. 16 Litho. Wmk. 373

277 A64 5c multi, vert. .20 .20
278 A64 15c multi, vert. .20 .20
279 A64 50c multicolored .65 .50
Nos. 277-279 (3) 1.05 .90

Common Design Types pictured following the introduction.

Lloyd's List Issue

Common Design Type

1984, May 23 Litho. ***Perf. 14½x14***

280 CD335 20c Ocean Queen .40 .35
281 CD335 25c Enna G. .50 .50
282 CD335 30c Baron Minto loading phosphate .75 .75
283 CD335 40c Triadic, 1940 1.25 1.25
Nos. 280-283 (4) 2.90 2.85

1984 UPU Congress — A65

1984, June 4 Wmk. 373 ***Perf. 14***

284 A65 $1 No. 117 1.50 1.40

Coastal Scene A66

Perf. 13½x14, 14x13½

1984, Sept. 21

285 A66 1c shown .20 .20
286 A66 3c Woman, vert. .25 .20
287 A66 5c Fishing vessel .30 .25
288 A66 10c Golfer .85 .50
289 A66 15c Phosphate excavation, vert. .90 .50
290 A66 20c Surveyor, vert. .55 .45
291 A66 25c Air Nauru jet .75 .50
292 A66 30c Elderly man, vert. .60 .60
293 A66 40c Social service 1.00 .95
294 A66 50c Fishing, vert. 1.10 1.00
295 A66 $1 Tennis, vert. 2.75 2.25
296 A66 $2 Lagoon Anabar 4.25 4.25
Nos. 285-296 (12) 13.50 11.65

For surcharges see Nos. 425-427.

Local Butterflies A67

1984, July 24 ***Perf. 14***

297 A67 25c Common eggfly (female) .50 .50
298 A67 30c Common eggfly (male) .60 .60
299 A67 50c Wanderer (female) 1.00 1.00
Nos. 297-299 (3) 2.10 2.10

Christmas A68

1984, Nov. 14

300 A68 30c Buada Chapel, vert. .55 .55
301 A68 40c Detudamo Memorial Church, vert. .70 .70
302 A68 50c Candle-light service .90 .90
Nos. 300-302 (3) 2.15 2.15

Air Nauru, 15th Anniv. A69

1985, Feb. 26 Wmk. 373 ***Perf. 14***

303 A69 20c Jet .50 .40
304 A69 30c Crew, vert. .75 .60
305 A69 40c Fokker F28 over Nauru 1.00 1.00
306 A69 50c Cargo handling, vert. 1.50 1.50
Nos. 303-306 (4) 3.75 3.50

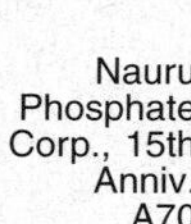

Nauru Phosphate Corp., 15th Anniv. A70

1985, July 31

307 A70 20c Open-cut mining .90 .60
308 A70 25c Rail transport 1.75 .90
309 A70 30c Phosphate drying plant 1.75 .90
310 A70 50c Early steam engine 3.00 1.50
Nos. 307-310 (4) 7.40 3.90

Christmas — A71

1985, Oct.

311 50c Canoe 1.25 1.25
312 50c Mother and child 1.25 1.25
a. A71 Pair, #311-312 2.50 2.50

No. 312a has a continuous design.

Audubon Birth Bicentenary A72

Illustrations of the brown noddy by John J. Audubon.

1985, Dec. 31

313 A72 10c Adult and young .35 .35
314 A72 20c Flying .65 .65
315 A72 30c Two adults .80 .80
316 A72 50c Adult 1.40 1.40
Nos. 313-316 (4) 3.20 3.20

Early Transportation — A73

1986, Mar. 5 Wmk. 384

317 A73 15c Douglas motorcycle .90 .70
318 A73 20c Truck 1.00 .80
319 A73 30c German steam locomotive, 1910 1.60 1.25
320 A73 40c Baby Austin 2.00 2.00
Nos. 317-320 (4) 5.50 4.75

Bank of Nauru, 10th Anniv. A74

Winning drawings of children's competition.

1986, July 21 Litho. ***Perf. 14***

321 A74 20c multicolored .30 .30
322 A74 25c multicolored .40 .40
323 A74 30c multicolored .50 .50
324 A74 40c multicolored .70 .70
Nos. 321-324 (4) 1.90 1.90

Flowers A75

1986, Sept. 30 Wmk. 384

325 A75 20c Plumeria rubra .50 .40
326 A75 25c Tristellateia australis .75 .60
327 A75 30c Bougainvillea cultivar .85 .75
328 A75 40c Delonix regia 1.25 1.25
Nos. 325-328 (4) 3.35 3.00

Christmas A76

1986, Dec. 8 Wmk. 373

329 A76 20c Men caroling .60 .50
330 A76 $1 Carolers, invalid 2.50 2.00

Tribal Dances — A77

1987, Jan. 31

331 A77 20c Girls .70 .70
332 A77 30c Men and women .90 .90
333 A77 50c Boy, vert. 1.90 1.90
Nos. 331-333 (3) 3.50 3.50

Artifacts A78

1987, July 30 ***Perf. 14***

334 A78 25c Hibiscus-fiber skirt .65 .65
335 A78 30c Headband, necklaces .75 .75
336 A78 45c Necklaces 1.25 1.25
337 A78 60c Pandanus-leaf fan 1.50 1.50
Nos. 334-337 (4) 4.15 4.15

World Post Day — A79

Perf. 14½x14

1987, Oct. 9 Litho. Wmk. 384

338 A79 40c UPU emblem, air-mail label 1.50 1.50

Souvenir Sheet

1987, Oct. 20 ***Imperf.***

339 A79 $1 Emblem, vert. 3.50 3.50

Nauru Congregational Church, Cent. — A80

Perf. 13x13½

1987, Nov. 5 Wmk. 373

340 A80 40c multicolored 1.00 1.00

Island Christmas Celebration — A81

1987, Nov. 27 Wmk. 384 ***Perf. 14***

341 A81 20c shown .60 .50
342 A81 $1 Sign on building 3.25 3.00

A82

Natl. Independence, 20th Anniv. — A83

Heraldic elements independent of or as part of the natl. arms: 25c, Phosphate mining and shipping. 40c, Tomano flower, vert. 55c, Frigate bird, vert. $1, Natl. arms.

Perf. 13½x14, 14x13½

1988, May 16 **Unwmk.**
343 A82 25c multicolored .45 .45
344 A82 40c multicolored .75 .75
345 A82 55c multicolored 1.00 1.00

Perf. 13

346 A83 $1 multicolored 7.00 7.00
Nos. 343-346 (4) 9.20 9.20

Nauru Post Office, 80th Anniv. A84

30c, Nauru highlighted on German map of the Marshall Islands, & canceled Marshall Islands #25. 50c, Letter mailed from Nauru to Dresden & post office, 1908. 70c, Post office, 1988, & Nauru #348 canceled on airmail cover.

1988, July 14 **Wmk. 384** ***Perf. 14***
347 A84 30c multicolored .75 .50
348 A84 50c multicolored 1.25 1.00
349 A84 70c multicolored 2.00 2.00
Nos. 347-349 (3) 4.00 3.50

String Games A85

1988, Aug. 1 **Unwmk.** ***Perf. 13½x14***
350 A85 25c Mat .35 .35
351 A85 40c The Pursuer .55 .55
352 A85 55c Holding Up the Sky .85 .85
353 A85 80c Manujie's Sword 1.25 1.25
Nos. 350-353 (4) 3.00 3.00

UPU, Cent. — A86

1988, Oct. 1 ***Perf. 13½x14***
354 A86 $1 multicolored 1.50 1.50

Hark! The Herald Angels Sing, by Charles Wesley (1703-91) A87

1988, Nov. 28 ***Perf. 13½***
355 A87 20c "Hark..." .35 .35
356 A87 60c "Glory to..." 1.00 1.00
357 A87 $1 "Peace on Earth" 1.75 1.75
Nos. 355-357 (3) 3.10 3.10

A88

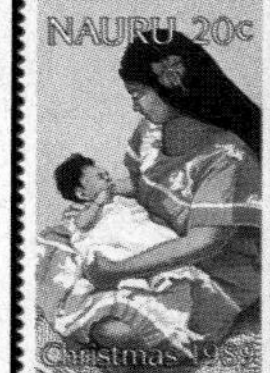

Christmas — A89

1989, Nov. 19 ***Perf. 14x15***
358 A88 15c NIC emblem .35 .35
359 A88 50c APT, ITU emblems .90 .90
360 A88 $1 Mounted photograph 1.75 1.75
361 A88 $2 UPU emblem, US Capitol 3.75 3.75
Nos. 358-361 (4) 6.75 6.75

Annivs. and events: Nauru Insurance Corp., 15th Anniv. (15c). World Telecommunications Day and 10th anniv of the Asia-Pacific Telecommunity (50c); Photography 150th anniv. ($1); and 20th UPU Congress, Washington, DC ($2).

1989, Dec. 15 **Litho.** ***Perf. 14x15***
362 A89 20c shown .65 .65
363 A89 $1 Children opening gifts 2.50 2.50

A90

A91

Legend of Eigigu, The Girl in the Moon: 25c, Eigigu works while sisters play, rocket lift-off. 30c, Eigigu climbing tree, capsule in lunar orbit. 50c, Eigigu stealing from blind woman, lunar module on moon. $1, Eigigu with husband, Maramen (the moon), astronaut stepping on moon.

1989, Dec. 22 **Litho.** ***Perf. 14x15***
364 A90 25c multicolored *3.75 3.00*
365 A90 30c multicolored *4.00 3.25*
366 A90 50c multicolored *7.50 6.50*
367 A90 $1 multicolored *13.00 10.00*
Nos. 364-367 (4) *28.25 22.75*

Limited supplies of Nos. 364-367 were available through agent.

1990, July 3 **Litho.** ***Perf. 14x15***
368 A91 50c Mining by hand 1.10 1.10
369 A91 $1 Mechanized extraction 1.90 1.90

Nauru Phosphate Corp., 20th anniv.

Christmas — A92

1990, Nov. 26 **Litho.** ***Perf. 14***
370 25c Children 1.40 1.40
371 25c Telling Christmas story 1.40 1.40
a. A92 Pair, #370-371 3.00 3.00

Legend of Eoiyepiang, Daughter of Thunder and Lightning — A93

1990, Dec. 24 **Litho.** ***Perf. 14x15***
372 A93 25c Woman with baby .60 .60
373 A93 30c Weaving flowers .90 .90
374 A93 50c Listening to storm 1.50 1.50
375 A93 $1 Couple 3.00 3.00
Nos. 372-375 (4) 6.00 6.00

Flowers A94

1991, July 15 **Litho.** ***Perf. 14½***
380 A94 15c Oleander .25 .25
381 A94 20c Lily .30 .30
382 A94 25c Passion Flower .40 .40
383 A94 30c Lily, diff. .45 .45
384 A94 35c Caesalpinia .55 .55
385 A94 40c Clerodendron .60 .60
387 A94 45c Bauhina pinnata .65 .65
388 A94 50c Hibiscus, vert. .70 .70
389 A94 75c Apocynaceae 1.10 1.10
390 A94 $1 Bindweed, vert. 1.25 1.25
391 A94 $2 Tristellateia, vert. 2.90 2.90
392 A94 $3 Impala lily, vert. 4.50 4.50
Nos. 380-392 (12) 13.65 13.65

This is an expanding set. Numbers will change if necessary.

Souvenir Sheet

Christmas — A95

1991, Dec. 12 **Litho.** ***Perf. 14***
395 A95 $2 Stained glass window 5.00 5.00

Asian Development Bank, 25th Meeting A96

1992, May 4 **Litho.** ***Perf. 14x14½***
396 A96 $1.50 multicolored 2.25 2.25

Christmas A97

Children's drawings: 45c, Christmas trees, flags and balloons. 60c, Santa in sleigh, reindeer on flag.

1992, Nov. 23 **Litho.** ***Perf. 14½x14***
397 A97 45c multicolored 1.25 1.25
398 A97 60c multicolored 1.50 1.50

Hammer DeRoburt (1922-1992) A98

1993, Jan. 31 **Litho.** ***Perf. 14x14½***
399 A98 $1 multicolored 2.50 2.50

Independence, 25th anniv.

Constitution Day, 15th Anniv. — A99

1993, May 17 **Litho.** ***Perf. 14x14½***
400 A99 70c Runners 1.40 1.40
401 A99 80c Declaration of Republic 1.60 1.60

24th South Pacific Forum — A100

1993, Aug. 9 **Litho.** ***Perf. 14½x14***
402 A100 60c Seabirds 1.50 1.50
403 A100 60c Birds, dolphin 1.50 1.50
404 A100 60c Coral, fish 1.50 1.50
405 A100 60c Fish, coral, diff. 1.50 1.50
a. Block of 4, #402-405 7.25 7.25
b. Souvenir sheet of 4, #402-405 9.50 9.50

No. 405a is a continuous design.

No. 405b exists with SINGPEX '93 overprint, sold at the exhibition. Value, unused or used, $7.75.

Christmas — A101

Designs: 55c, "Peace on earth..." 65c, "Hark the Herald Angels Sing."

1993, Nov. 29 **Litho.** ***Perf. 14½x14***
406 A101 55c multicolored 1.10 1.10
407 A101 65c multicolored 1.25 1.25

Child's Best Friend — A102

Illustration reduced.

1994, Feb. 10 Litho. *Perf. 14*

408 $1 Girls, dogs 2.00 2.00
409 $1 Boys, dogs 2.00 2.00
a. A102 Pair, #408-409 4.25 4.25
b. Souvenir sheet of 2, #408-409 4.25 4.25
c. As "b," ovptd. in sheet margin 5.00 5.00
d. As "b," ovptd. in sheet margin 5.50 5.50

No. 409c ovptd. with Hong Kong '94 emblem. No. 409d ovptd. with SINGPEX '94 emblem in gold.

Issued: #409c, 2/18/94; #409d, 8/31/94.

15th Commonwealth Games, Victoria — A103

1994, Sept. 8 Litho. *Perf. 14x14½*

410 A103 $1.50 Weight lifting 2.25 2.25

ICAO, 50th Anniv. A104

55c, Emblems. 65c, Nauru Intl. Airport. 80c, DVOR navigational aid. $1, Airport fire engines.

1994, Dec. 14

411 A104 55c multicolored .80 .70
412 A104 65c multicolored .95 .80
413 A104 80c multicolored 1.10 1.10
414 A104 $1 multicolored 1.50 1.25
a. Souvenir sheet of 4, #411-414 5.50 5.50
Nos. 411-414 (4) 4.35 3.85

United Nations, 50th Anniv. A105

1995, Jan. 1 *Perf. 14x14½*

415 A105 75c Natl. flag 1.40 1.40
416 A105 75c Natl. coat of arms 1.40 1.40
417 A105 75c Canoe, UN emblem 1.40 1.40
418 A105 75c Jet, ship, UN emblem 1.40 1.40
a. Block of 4, #415-418 5.75 5.75
b. Souvenir sheet of 4, #415-418 6.25 6.25

Nos. 417-418 are a continuous design.

Christmas — A106

1994, Nov. 20 Litho. *Perf. 14½x14*

419 A106 65c shown 1.00 1.00
420 A106 75c Star over Bethlehem 1.10 1.10

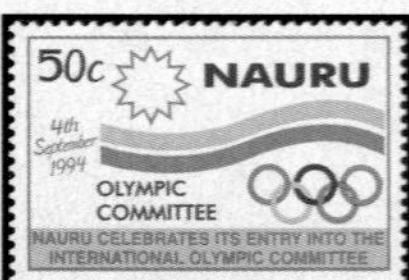

Membership in Intl. Olympic Committee A107

1994, Dec. 27 *Perf. 14x14½*

421 A107 50c multicolored .75 .75

Nauru Phosphate Corporation, 25th Anniv. A108

Designs: No. 422, Signing of Phosphate Agreement, June 15, 1967. No. 423, Nauru Pres. Bernard Dowiyogo, Australian Prime Minister Paul Keating at signing Nauru-Australia Compact of Settlement. $2, Mining phosphate.

1995, July 1 Litho. *Perf. 14x15*

422 A108 60c multicolored 1.50 1.50
423 A108 60c multicolored 1.50 1.50
a. Pair, #422-423 4.00 4.00

Souvenir Sheet

424 A108 $2 multicolored 4.00 4.00

No. 291 Surcharged

1995, Aug. 19 Litho. *Perf. 13½x14*
Overprinted:

425 A66 50c on 25c "at Beijing" .95 .95
426 A66 $1 on 25c "at Singapore" 1.90 1.90
427 A66 $1 on 25c "at Jakarta" 1.90 1.90
a. Strip of 3, #425-427 5.00 5.00

UN, 50th Anniv. A109

Designs: 75c, Nauru coastline. $1.50, UN headquarters, US, aerial view of Nauru.

1995, Oct. 24 Litho. *Perf. 14*

428 A109 75c multicolored 1.50 1.50
429 A109 $1.50 multicolored 2.50 2.50

Christmas — A110

1995, Dec. 7 Litho. *Perf. 14*

430 60c Seeking the Way .95 .95
431 70c Finding the Way 1.10 1.10
a. A110 Pair, #430-431 2.40 2.40

Return From Truk, 50th Anniv. A111

1996, Jan. 31 *Perf. 12*

432 A111 75c multicolored 1.40 1.40
433 A111 $1.25 multicolored 2.25 2.25
a. Souvenir sheet of 2, #432-433 4.00 4.00

Souvenir Sheet

Nanjing Stone Carving, Keeping off the Evils — A112

Illustration reduced.

1996, Mar. 20 Litho. *Perf. 12*

434 A112 45c multicolored 1.25 1.25

CHINA '96, 9th Asian Intl. Philatelic Exhibition.

End of World War II, 50th Anniv. — A113

Designs: 75c, Children playing on old cannon. $1.50, Girls making flower leis in front of pillbox.

1996, Sept. 13 Litho. *Perf. 14x13½*

435 A113 75c multicolored 2.25 2.25
436 A113 $1.50 multicolored 4.75 4.75
a. Pair, Nos. 435-436 + label 7.00 7.00
b. Ovptd. in gold on label 10.00 10.00
c. Ovptd. in gold on label 10.00 10.00

Gold overprint on labels are Hongpex '96 Exhibition emblem (#436b) and silhouette of a rat (#436c).

Issued: #436b, 436c, 1996.

1996 Summer Olympic Games, Atlanta A114

Discobolus and: 40c, Running pictograph, vert. 50c, Weight lifting pictograph, vert. 60c, Weight lifter. $1, Runner.

Perf. 13½x14, 14x13½

1996, July 21 Litho.

437 A114 40c multicolored .80 .65
438 A114 50c multicolored 1.00 .80
439 A114 60c multicolored 1.25 1.00
440 A114 $1 multicolored 2.00 1.90
Nos. 437-440 (4) 5.05 4.35

Christmas A115

Designs: 50c, Candles, angel with trumpet, nativity. 70c, Angel, candles, map, fauna.

1996, Dec. 16 Litho. *Perf. 14*

441 A115 50c multicolored 1.00 .80
442 A115 70c multicolored 1.25 1.25

World Wildlife Fund A116

Fish: a, 20c, Dolphinfish. b, 30c, Wahoo. c, 40c, Pacific sailfish. d, 50c, Yellowfin tuna.

1997, Feb. 12 Litho. *Perf. 11½*

443 A116 Strip of 4, #a.-d. 4.25 4.25

A117

A118

Giant Buddha (various statues): a, 1c. b, 2c. c, 5c. d, 10c. e, 12c. f, 15c. g, 25c.

1997, Feb. 12 *Perf. 14*

444 A117 Sheet of 7, #a.-g. 2.50 2.50

Hong Kong '97, Hong Kong's return to China. No. 444g is 60x80mm.

1997, July 15 Litho. *Perf. 13½*

Designs: 80c, Engagement portrait. $1.20, 50th Wedding anniversary portrait.

445 A118 80c multicolored 1.50 1.50
446 A118 $1.20 multicolored 2.00 2.00
a. Souvenir sheet, #445-446 5.00 5.00

Queen Elizabeth II and Prince Philip, 50th wedding anniv.

Christmas A119

1997, Nov. 5 Litho. *Perf. 13½*

447 A119 60c Monument .90 .75
448 A119 80c Church 1.10 1.10

Nauru Congregational Church, 110th anniv.

Souvenir Sheet

Commonwealth, Oceania and South Pacific Weight Lifting Championships A120

Various contestants lifting weights: a, 40c. b, 60c. c, 80c. d, $1.20.

1998, Mar. 25 Litho. *Perf. 14*

449 A120 Sheet of 4, #a.-d. 4.25 4.25

Visit of Juan Antonio Samaranch, Pres. of Intl. Olympic Committee — A121

1998, May 4 *Perf. 13½*

450 A121 $2 multicolored 3.00 3.00

Souvenir Sheet

28th Parliamentary Conference — A122

Illustration reduced.

1997, July 24 Litho. *Perf. 14*
451 A122 $2 multicolored 3.00 3.00

A123 A125

Diana, Princess of Wales (1961-97): a, In yellow. b, White blouse. c, Wearing tiara. d, White & black outfit. e, Pink hat. f, White dress.

1998, Aug. 31
452 A123 70c Sheet of 6, #a.-f. 6.00 6.00

1998, Sept. 11 Litho. *Perf. 13½x14*

1998 Commonwealth Games, Kuala Lumpur: 40c, Gymnast on pommel horse. 60c, Throwing discus. 70c, Runner. 80c, Weight lifter.

454 A125 40c multicolored .60 .60
455 A125 60c multicolored .90 .90
456 A125 70c multicolored 1.00 1.00
457 A125 80c multicolored 1.10 1.10
a. Souvenir sheet, #454-457 3.50 3.50
Nos. 454-457 (4) 3.60 3.60

Independence, 30th Anniv. — A126

Squadron Leader L.H. Hicks and: $1, Band. $2, National anthem.

1998, Oct. 26 Litho. *Perf. 14*
458 A126 $1 multicolored 1.50 1.50
459 A126 $2 multicolored 3.00 3.00
a. Souvenir sheet, #458-459 4.50 4.50

Christmas — A127

Star, island scene and: 85c, Fish, candle, flowers. 95c, Flowers, fruits, Christmas present.

1998 *Perf. 13½x12½*
460 A127 85c multicolored 1.25 1.25
461 A127 95c multicolored 1.40 1.40

First Contact with Island, Bicent. — A128

Designs: No. 462, Sailing ship Snow Hunter. No. 463, Capt. John Fearn.

1998, Dec. 1 *Perf. 12*
462 A128 $1.50 multicolored 2.25 2.25
463 A128 $1.50 multicolored 2.25 2.25
a. Pair, #462-463 4.50 4.50
b. Souvenir sheet, #463a 5.00 5.00

Ships A129

Designs: a, 70c, HMAS Melbourne. b, 80c, HMAS D'Amantina. c, $1.10, Traditional Nauruan canoe. d, 90c, Alcyone. e, $1, MV Rosie D.

1999, Mar. 19 Litho. *Perf. 12*
464 A129 Sheet of 5, #a.-e. 6.50 6.50

Australia '99, World Stamp Expo. No. 464c is 80x30mm.

1st Manned Moon Landing, 30th Anniv.

Common Design Type

Designs: 70c, Neil Armstrong. 80c, Service module and lunar module fire towards moon. 90c, Aldrin deploying EASEP. $1, Command module enters earth atmosphere.
$2, Earth as seen from moon.

Perf. 14x13¾
1999, July 20 Litho. Wmk. 384
465 CD357 70c multicolored 1.00 .90
466 CD357 80c multicolored 1.10 1.10
467 CD357 90c multicolored 1.25 1.25
468 CD357 $1 multicolored 1.50 1.50
Nos. 465-468 (4) 4.85 4.75

Souvenir Sheet
Perf. 14
469 CD357 $2 multicolored 3.00 3.00

No. 469 contains one circular stamp 40mm in diameter.

China 1999 World Philatelic Exhibition — A130

a, Tursiops truncatus. b, Xiphias gladius.

Perf. 12¾x12½
1999, Aug. 21 Litho. Unwmk.
470 A130 50c Sheet of 2, #a.-b. 1.50 1.50

UPU, 125th Anniv. A131

1999, Aug. 23 Litho. *Perf. 11¾*
471 A131 $1 multicolored 1.50 1.50

Christmas — A132

Designs: 65c, Native woman. 70c, Christmas tree and candle.

Perf. 13½x13¾
1999, Nov. 10 Litho. Wmk. 388
472 A132 65c multi .95 .85
473 A132 70c multi 1.00 1.00

Millennium A133

70c, Woman in native costume, fishermen on beach. $1.10, Satellite dish, runner, cross, airplane, crane, jeep and boat. $1.20, Man on computer, woman holding globe.

Perf. 11¾x12
2000, Jan. 1 Litho. Wmk. 388
474 A133 70c multi 1.00 .85
475 A133 $1.10 multi 1.60 1.60
476 A133 $1.20 multi 1.75 1.75
a. Souvenir sheet of 3, #474-476 4.50 4.50
Nos. 474-476 (3) 4.35 4.20

Nauru Phosphate Corp. 30th Anniv. A134

Designs: $1.20, Power plant. $1.80, Phosphate train. $2, Albert Ellis.

2000, May 27 Litho. *Perf. 12½x12¾*
477-479 A134 Set of 3 7.25 7.25
a. Souv. sheet, #477-479, perf 12 7.25 7.25

No. 479a exists imperf.

Queen Mother, 100th Birthday A135

Designs: $1, Dark blue hat. $1.10, Lilac hat. $1.20, Waving, light blue hat. $1.40, Blue hat.

2000, Aug. 4 *Perf. 14¼*
480-483 A135 Set of 4 7.00 7.00
a. Souvenir sheet, #480-483, perf. 13¾x13½ 7.00 7.00

2000 Summer Olympics, Sydney — A136

Olympic rings, map of Australia, Sydney Opera House and: 90c, Running. $1, Basketball. $1.10, Weight lifting. $1.20, Olympic torch and runner.

2000 Photo. *Perf. 11¾*
484-487 A136 Set of 4 6.00 6.00

Christmas A137

Designs: 65c, Flower, girl decorating Christmas tree, star, decorated Christmas tree. 75c, Ornament, child on toy train, palm tree, gift.

2000 Litho. *Perf. 13¾x13½*
488-489 A137 Set of 2 2.50 2.50
a. Souvenir sheet, #488-489 2.75 2.75

Stamps from No. 489a are perf. 14¼x14¼x13¾x14¼.

32nd Pacific Islands Forum — A138

No. 490 — Island and: a, 90c, Yellow flowers, bird flying to right. b, $1, Red flowers, bird flying to left. c, $1.10, Yellow flowers, birds facing right. d, $2, Red flowers, bird facing left. Illustration reduced.

Perf. 14½x14
2001, Aug. 14 Litho. Unwmk.
490 A138 Block of 4, #a-d 11.00 11.00
e. Souvenir sheet, #490 11.00 11.00

Reign Of Queen Elizabeth II, 50th Anniv. Issue

Common Design Type

Designs: Nos. 491, 495a, 70c, Princess Elizabeth in uniform, 1946. Nos. 492, 495b, 80c, Wearing patterned hat. Nos. 493, 495c, 90c, Wearing hat, 1951. Nos. 494, 495d, $1, In 1997. No. 495e, $4, 1955 portrait by Annigoni (38x50mm).

Perf. 14¼x14½, 13¾ (#495e)
2002, Feb. 6 Litho. Wmk. 373

With Gold Frames
491-494 CD360 Set of 4 6.50 6.50

Souvenir Sheet
Without Gold Frames
495 CD360 Sheet of 5, #a-e 11.00 11.00

Miniature Sheet

In Remembrance of Sept. 11, 2001 Terrorist Attacks — A139

No. 496: a, 90c. b, $1. c, $1.10. d, $2.

Wmk. 373
2002, May 17 Litho. *Perf. 13¾*
496 A139 Sheet of 4, #a-d 9.00 9.00

Butterflies — A140

No. 497: a, Parthenos sylvia. b, Delias madetes. c, Danaus philene. d, Arhopala hercules. e, Papilio canopus. f, Danaus schenkii.

g, Parthenos figrina. h, Mycalesis phidon. i, Vindula sapor.
$2, Graphium agamemnon.

2002, June 28 ***Perf. 13¾x14¼***
497 A140 50c Sheet of 9, #a-i 12.00 12.00

Souvenir Sheet

498 A140 $2 multi 4.50 4.50

Queen Mother Elizabeth (1900-2002)
Common Design Type

Designs: Nos. 499, 501a, $1.50, Wearing hat (black and white photograph). Nos. 500, 501b, $1.50, Wearing blue hat.

Perf. 13¾x4¼
2002, Aug. 5 Litho. Wmk. 373
With Purple Frames
499-500 CD361 Set of 2 6.75 6.75

Souvenir Sheet
Without Purple Frames
Perf. 14½x14¼
501 CD361 Sheet of 2, #a-b 7.00 7.00

Fire Fighting A141

Designs: 20c, Building fire. 50c, Blaze at sea. 90c, Forest fire. $1, New and old fire helmets. $1.10, Modern ladder truck, old pump engine. $2, Modern and late 19th cent. firefighters.
$5, Modern fire engine and rescue vehicle.

Perf. 14x14¼
2002, Aug. 31 Litho. Wmk. 373
502-507 A141 Set of 6 9.50 9.50

Souvenir Sheet

508 A141 $5 multi 11.00 11.00

Roman Catholic Church in Nauru, Cent. — A142

No. 509: a, First church building, Arubo. b, Father Friedrich Gründl, first missionary. c, Sister Stanisla, first sister. d, Second church building, Ibwenape. e, Brother Kalixtus Bader, first lay brother. f, Father Alois Kayser, missionary.

Wmk. 373
2002, Dec. 8 Litho. ***Perf. 13¾***
509 A142 $1.50 Sheet of 6, #a-f 13.00 13.00

Christmas — A143

Designs: 15c, The Holy Family with Dancing Angels, by Sir Anthony Van Dyck. $1, The Holy Virgin with the Child, by Luca Cangiasus. $1.20, The Holy Family with the Cat, by Rembrandt. $3, The Holy Family with St. John, by Raphael.

2002, Dec. 8
510-513 A143 Set of 4 8.00 8.00

Worldwide Fund For Nature (WWF) A144

Designs: 15c, Red-and-black anemone fish, Bubble tentacle sea anemone. $1, Orange-fin anemone fish, Leathery sea anemone. $1.20, Pink anemone fish, Magnificent sea anemone. $3, Clark's anemone fish, Merten's sea anemone.

Wmk. 373
2003, Apr. 29 Litho. ***Perf. 14***
514-517 A144 Set of 4 10.00 10.00
517a Miniature sheet, 4 each #514-517 37.50 37.50

Powered Flight, Cent. — A145

No. 518: a, Santos-Dumont wins the Deutsch Prize, Oct. 1901. b, USS Shenandoah at Lakehurst, NJ. c, R101 at Cardington Mast, U.K., Oct. 1929. d, R34 crossing Atlantic, July 1919. e, Zeppelin No. 1, 1900. f, USS Los Angeles moored to the USS Patoka. g, Goodyear C-71 airship. h, LZ-130 Graf Zeppelin II at Friedrichshafen, Germany. i, Zeppelin NT.
No. 519 — LZ-127 Graf Zeppelin: a, Over Mt. Fuji. b, Over San Francisco. c, Exchanging mail with Russian ice breaker, Franz Josef Land.

2003, Oct. 26
518 A145 50c Sheet of 9, #a-i 10.00 10.00
519 A145 $2 Sheet of 3, #a-c 13.00 13.00

Bird Life International A146

Nauru reed warbler: No. 520, Bird on reed. No. 521, Bird on branch with insect in beak, vert. No. 522a, Close-up of head. No. 522b, Bird with open beak, vert. No. 522c, Nest with chicks.

2003, Nov. 10 ***Perf. 14¼x13¾***
520 A146 $1.50 multi 4.00 4.00
a. Perf. 14¼x14½ 4.00 4.00

Perf. 13¾x14¼
521 A146 $1.50 multi 4.00 4.00
a. Perf. 14½x14¼ 4.00 4.00

Souvenir Sheet
Perf. 14¼x14½, 14½x14¼ (#522b)
522 Sheet, #520a, 521a, 522a-522c 15.00 15.00
a.-c. A146 $1.50 Any single 4.00 4.00

Battle of Trafalgar, Bicent. — A147

Designs: 25c, Aigle in action against HMS Defiance. 50c, French "Eprouvette." 75c, Santissima Trinidad in action against HMS Africa. $1, Emperor Napoleon Bonaparte, vert. $1.50, HMS Victory. No. 528, $2.50, Vice-Admiral Sir Horatio Nelson, vert.
No. 529, $2.50, vert.: a, Admiral Pierre Villeneuve. b, Formidable.

2005, Mar. 29 Litho. ***Perf. 13¼***
523-528 A147 Set of 6 12.00 12.00

Souvenir Sheet

529 A147 $2.50 Sheet of 2, #a-b 9.50 9.50

No. 527 has particles of wood from the HMS Victory embedded in the areas covered by a thermographic process that produces a shiny, raised effect.

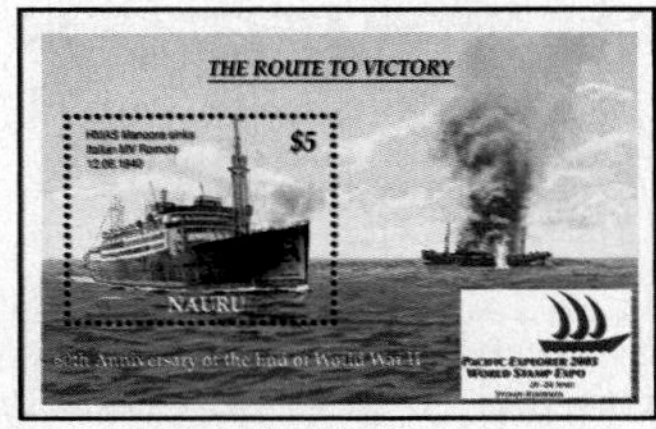

End of World War II, 60th Anniv. — A148

No. 530: a, German raider Komet shells Nauru, 1940. b, French warship Le Triomphant assists in evacuation of civilians, 1942. c, Japanese forces occupy Nauru, 1942. d, US Air Force B-24 Liberator aircraft bombing missions, 1943. e, USS Paddle stationed off Nauru, 1943. f, B-25G Mitchell "Coral Princess" shot down over Nauru, 1944. g, Spitfires, Battle of Britain, 1940. h, HMAS Diamantine arrives at Nauru, 1945. i, D-Day landings, 1944. j, Union Jack is hoisted again, 1945.
$5, HMAS Manoora sinks Italian MV Romolo, 1940.

2005, Apr. 21 ***Perf. 13¾***
530 A148 75c Sheet of 10, #a-j 13.50 13.50

Souvenir Sheet

531 A148 $5 multi 8.75 8.75

Pacific Explorer 2005 World Stamp Expo, Sydney (No. 531).

Pope John Paul II (1920-2005) A149

2005, Aug. 18 Litho. ***Perf. 14x14¼***
532 A149 $1 multi 1.75 1.75

Rotary International, Cent. — A150

2005, Sept. 12 ***Perf. 14½x14¼***
533 A150 $2.50 multi 4.25 4.25

BirdLife International — A151

No. 534, 25c: a, Rota bridled white-eye. b, Faichuk white-eye. c, Samoan white-eye. d, Bridled white-eye. e, Long-billed white-eye. f, Golden white-eye.
No. 535, 50c: a, Kuhl's lorikeet. b, Masked shining parrot. c, Crimson shining parrot. d, Blue lorikeet. e, Henderson lorikeet. f, Ultramarine lorikeet.
No. 536, $1: a, Atoll fruit dove. b, Henderson fruit dove. c, Cook Islands fruit dove. d, Rapa fruit dove. e, Whistling dove. f, Mariana fruit dove.

Perf. 14¼x14½
2005, Sept. 12 Litho.
Sheets of 6, #a-f
534-536 A151 Set of 3 24.00 24.00

Christmas — A152

Stories by Hans Christian Andersen (1805-75): 25c, The Little Fir Tree. 50c, The Wild Swans. 75c, The Farmyard Cock and the Weather Cock. $1, The Storks. $2.50, The Toad. $5, The Ice Maiden.

2005, Oct. 10 ***Perf. 14***
537-542 A152 Set of 6 15.00 15.00

Battle of Trafalgar, Bicent. — A153

Designs: 50c, HMS Victory. $1, Ships in battle, horiz. $5, Admiral Horatio Nelson.

2005, Oct. 18 ***Perf. 13½***
543-545 A153 Set of 3 12.00 12.00

Anniversaries — A154

No. 546, 25c: a, Wolfgang Amadeus Mozart. b, Piano and violin.
No. 547, 50c: a, Isambard Kingdom Brunel. b, Chain and pulley.
No. 548, 75c: a, Edmond Halley. b, Halley's quadrant.
No. 549, $1: a, Charles Darwin. b, Early microscope.
No. 550, $1.25: a, Thomas Alva Edison. b, Light bulb.
No. 551, $1.50: a, Christopher Columbus. b, Astrolabe.

2006, May 27 Litho. ***Perf. 13¼x12½***
Horiz. Pairs, #a-b
546-551 A154 Set of 6 16.00 16.00

Birth of Mozart, 250th anniv., Birth of Brunel, bicent., Birth of Halley, 350th anniv., Darwin's voyage on the Beagle, 175th anniv., Death of Edison, 75th anniv., Death of Columbus, 500th anniv.

2006 World Cup Soccer Championships, Germany — A155

Scenes from championship matches won by: $1, Uruguay, 1950. $1.50, Argentina, 1978. $2, Italy, 1982. $3, Brazil, 2002.

2006, June 9 ***Perf. 14***
552-555 A155 Set of 4 11.50 11.50

Dinosaurs A156

Designs: 10c, Parasaurolophus. 25c, Quetzalcoatlus. 50c, Spinosaurus. 75c, Triceratops. $1, Tyrannosaurus rex. $1.50, Euoplocephalus. $2, Velociraptor. $2.50, Protoceratops.

2006, Aug. 14 ***Perf. 13¼x13½***
556-563 A156 Set of 8 13.00 13.00

Miniature Sheet

Victoria Cross, 150th Anniv. — A157

No. 564: a, Lt. Gerald Graham carrying wounded man. b, Pvt. Mac Gregor shooting rifle. c, Pvt. Alexander Wright repelling a sortie. d, Cpl. John Ross viewing evacuation of the Redan. e, Sgt. McWheeney digging with bayonet. f, Brevet Maj. G. L. Goodlake surprising enemy. Descriptions of vignettes are on labels below each stamp.

2006, Sept. 12 ***Perf. 13¼x12½***
564 A157 $1.50 Sheet of 6, #a-f, + 6 labels 13.50 13.50

Miniature Sheet

Inaugural Flight of the Concorde, 30th Anniv. — A158

No. 565: a, British Airways Concorde G-BOAF on ground. b, First flight of Concorde 002, 1969. c, Concorde landing. d, Queen's Golden Jubilee flypast, 2002. e, 50th anniv. of Battle of Britain, 1990. f, Concorde at 60,000 feet. g, Extreme condition testing. h, Concorde on runway. i, First commercial flight, 1976. j, Concorde above Earth. k, British Airways Concorde G-BOAF in flight. l, Two Concordes on ground.

2006, Oct. 10 ***Perf. 14¼x13¾***
565 A158 $1 Sheet of 12, #a-l, + 3 labels 18.00 18.00

Miniature Sheet

Year of Three Kings, 70th Anniv. — A159

No. 566: a, Queen Elizabeth II. b, King George V and Princess Elizabeth. c, King Edward VIII and Princess Elizabeth. d, King George VI and Princess Elizabeth.

2006, Oct. 17
566 A159 $1.50 Sheet of 4, #a-d 9.00 9.00

Wedding of Queen Elizabeth II and Prince Philip, 60th Anniv. — A160

Designs: $1, Couple. $1.50, Couple in coach. $2, At wedding ceremony. $3, Couple walking.
$5, Queen Elizabeth II in bridal gown.

2007, Jan. 31 **Litho.** ***Perf. 13¾***
567-570 A160 Set of 4 12.00 12.00

Souvenir Sheet

Perf. 14¼

571 A160 $5 multi 7.75 7.75

No. 571 contains one 43x57mm stamp.

A161

Royal Air Force, 90th Anniv. — A162

Aviation pioneers: No. 572, 70c, Sir Douglas Bader (1910-82), World War II fighter ace. No. 573, 70c, R. J. Mitchell (1895-1937), designer of Spitfire airplane. No. 574, 70c, Sir Frank Whittle (1907-96), inventor of jet engine. No. 575, 70c, Sir Sydney Camm (1893-1966), designer of Hawker Hurricane airplane. No. 576, 70c, Air Vice Marshal James E. "Johnnie" Johnson (1915-2001), World War II fighter ace.
$3, Avro Vulcan.

Wmk. 373

2008, May 19 **Litho.** ***Perf. 14***
572-576 A161 Set of 5 6.75 6.75

Souvenir Sheet

577 A162 $3 multi 5.75 5.75

Nos. 572-576 were each printed in sheets of 8 + central label.

2008 Summer Olympics, Beijing A163

Designs: 15c, Bamboo, badminton. 25c, Dragon, archery. 75c, Lanterns, weight lifting. $1, Fish, diving.

Perf. 13¼

2008, Aug. 8 **Litho.** **Unwmk.**
578-581 A163 Set of 4 4.00 4.00

A164

End of World War I, 90th Anniv. — A165

World War I recruitment posters inscribed: No. 582, $1, "A Happy New Year to our Gallant Soldiers." No. 583, $1, "The Empire Needs Men." No. 584, $1, "South Australians." No. 585, $1, "Your King and Country Need You." No. 586, $1, "Britons." No. 587, $1, "An Appeal to You."
$2, Queen's Wreath of Remembrance.

Wmk. 406

2008, Sept. 16 **Litho.** ***Perf. 14***
582-587 A164 Set of 6 9.50 9.50

Souvenir Sheet

588 A165 $2 multi 3.25 3.25

Worldwide Fund for Nature (WWF) A166

Greater frigate bird: 25c, Adult and chick. 75c, Two in flight. $1, Landing. $2, One in flight.

Perf. 13¼x13

2008, Oct. 14 **Unwmk.**
589-592 A166 Set of 4 5.50 5.50
592a Sheet, 4 each #589-592, perf. 13 22.00 22.00

SEMI-POSTAL STAMP

Miniature Sheet of 4

1996 Summer Olympics, Atlanta — SP1

Designs: a, Birds, denomination UR. b, Birds, denomination UL. c, 4 dolphins. d, 2 dolphins.

1995, Sept. 1 **Litho.** ***Perf. 12***
B1 SP1 60c +15c, #a.-d. 5.50 5.50

Surcharge for sports development in Nauru.

NEPAL

nə-'pol

LOCATION — In the Himalaya Mountains between India and Tibet
GOVT. — Kingdom
AREA — 56,136 sq. mi.
POP. — 24,302,653 (1999 est.)
CAPITAL — Kathmandu

Nepal stamps were valid only in Nepal and India until April 1959, when they became valid to all parts of the world.

4 Pice = 1 Anna
64 Pice = 16 Annas = 1 Rupee
100 Paisa = 1 Rupee (1958)

Catalogue values for unused stamps in this country are for Never Hinged items, beginning with Scott 103 in the regular postage section, Scott C1 in the air post section and Scott O1 in the officials section.

Nos. 1-24, 29A were issued without gum.

Sripech and Crossed Khukris — A1

Siva's Bow and Two Khukris — A2

1881 **Typo.** **Unwmk.** ***Pin-perf.***

European Wove Paper

1 A1 1a ultramarine 200.00 *450.00*
2 A1 2a purple 300.00 200.00
a. Tete beche pair
3 A1 4a green 450.00 *550.00*

Imperf

4 A1 1a blue 110.00 90.00
5 A1 2a purple 150.00 *200.00*
a. Tete beche pair
6 A1 4a green 200.00 *450.00*

1886 **Native Wove Paper** ***Imperf.***
7 A1 1a ultramarine 20.00 8.00
a. Tete beche pair *150.00* *175.00*
8 A1 2a violet 25.00 10.00
a. Tete beche pair *200.00* *200.00*
9 A1 4a green 55.00 12.00
a. Tete beche pair *300.00* *250.00*
Nos. 7-9 (3) 100.00 30.00

Used values for Nos. 9-49 are for telegraph cancels.

1899-1917 ***Imperf.***

Native Wove Paper

10 A2 ½a black 7.00 .50
a. Tete beche pair *100.00* 1.75
11 A2 ½a red orange ('17) *1,750.* 350.00
a. Tete beche pair

Pin-perf.

12 A2 ½a black 7.00
a. Tete beche pair *50.00*

No. 11 is known postally used on six covers.

Type of 1881

1898-1917 ***Imperf.***
13 A1 1a pale blue 12.50 6.00
a. 1a bluish green 50.00 50.00
b. Tete beche pair *150.00* *150.00*
14 A1 2a gray violet 25.00 10.00
a. Tete beche pair *100.00* *100.00*
15 A1 2a claret ('17) 30.00 12.00
a. Tete beche pair *100.00* *100.00*
16 A1 2a brown ('17) 10.00
a. Tete beche pair 25.00
17 A1 4a dull green 10.00 15.00
a. Tete beche pair 70.00 *350.00*
b. Cliche of 1a in plate of 4a ('04) *350.00* 350.00
Nos. 13-17 (5) 87.50 43.00

#17b has the recut frame of the 1904 issue. #17b probably was used only on telegraph/telephone forms.

Pin-perf.

18 A1 1a pale blue 17.50 10.00
a. Tete beche pair *75.00* *50.00*
19 A1 2a gray violet 25.00 12.00
a. Tete beche pair *75.00* *75.00*
20 A1 2a claret ('17) 8.75 6.00
a. Tete beche pair 30.00 30.00

21 A1 2a brown ('17) 7.50
a. Tete beche pair 30.00 30.00
22 A1 4a dull green 50.00 18.00
a. Tete beche pair *100.00 100.00*

Frame Recut on All Cliches, Fewer Lines

1903-04 Native Wove Paper *Imperf.*

23 A1 1a bright blue 10.00
a. Tete beche pair 50.00

Pin-perf.

24 A1 1a bright blue 15.00
a. Tete beche pair *100.00*

European Wove Paper

23b A1 1a blue *750.00* 300.00
23c Tete beche pair *1,750.*

Pin-perf.

24b A1 1a blue 900.00
24c Tete beche pair *2,750.*

Siva Mahadeva — A3

A4

1907 Engr. *Perf. 13½*

European Wove Paper

26 A3 2p brown 4.00 .50
27 A3 4p green 6.00 .50
28 A3 8p carmine 14.00 .50
29 A3 16p violet 27.50 1.50
Nos. 26-29 (4) 51.50 3.00

Type A3 has five characters in bottom panel, reading "Gurkha Sirkar." Date divided in lower corners is "1964." Outer side panels carry denomination (also on A5).

1917-18 *Imperf.*

29A A4 1a bright blue 9.00 3.00
b. 1a indigo 10.00 4.00
c. Pin-perf. 13.00 11.00

No. 29A may not have been used postally.

In 1917 a telegraph system was started and remainder stocks and further printings of designs A1 and A2 were used to pay telegrams fees. Design A4 was designed for telegraph use but was valid for postal use. After 1929 design A3 was used for telegrams. The usual telegraph cancellation is crescent-shaped.

Type of 1907 Redrawn

A5

Nine characters in bottom panel reading "Nepal Sirkar"

1929 *Perf. 14, 14½*

Size: 24¾x18¾mm

30 A5 2p dark brown 5.00 .30
31 A5 4p green 5.00 .50
32 A5 8p deep red 17.50 1.25
33 A5 16p dark red vio 12.50 1.00
34 A5 24p orange yellow 10.00 2.00
35 A5 32p dark ultra 12.50 2.00

Size: 26x19½mm

36 A5 1r orange red 15.00 4.00

Size: 28x21mm

37 A5 5r brown & black 30.00 *25.00*
Nos. 30-37 (8) 107.50 *36.05*

On Nos. 30-37 the date divided in lower corners is "1986."

Type of 1929 Redrawn

Date characters in Lower Corners read "1992"

1935 Unwmk. Engr. *Perf. 14*

38 A5 2p dark brown 2.75 .45
39 A5 4p green 3.00 .75
40 A5 8p bright red 150.00 8.00
41 A5 16p dk red violet 4.75 1.25
42 A5 24p orange yellow 4.75 2.00
43 A5 32p dark ultra 10.00 3.25
Nos. 38-43 (6) 175.25 15.70

Redrawn Type of 1935

Perf. 11, 11x11½, 12x11½

1941-46 Typo.

44 A5 2p black brown 1.25 .40
a. 2p green (error) 4.00
45 A5 4p bright green 2.50 .50
46 A5 8p rose red 3.75 .20
47 A5 16p chocolate ('42) 22.50 2.25
48 A5 24p orange ('46) 6.25 2.75
49 A5 32p deep blue ('46) 6.25 6.25

Size: 29x19½mm

50 A5 1r henna brown ('46) 45.00 15.00
Nos. 44-50 (7) 87.50 27.35

Exist imperf. vert. or horiz.

Swayambhunath Stupa — A6

Temple of Krishna — A7

View of Kathmandu A8

Pashupati (Siva Mahadeva) A9

Designs: 4p, Temple of Pashupati. 6p, Tri-Chundra College. 8p, Mahabuddha Temple. 24p, Guheswori Temple, Patan. 32p, The 22 Fountains, Balaju.

Perf. 13½x14, 13½, 14

1949, Oct. 1 Litho. Unwmk.

51 A6 2p brown 1.25 .50
52 A6 4p green 1.25 .50
53 A6 6p rose pink 2.25 .50
54 A6 8p vermilion 2.25 .75
55 A7 16p rose lake 2.25 .75
56 A8 20p blue 5.25 1.25
57 A8 24p carmine 4.50 .75
58 A8 32p ultramarine 10.00 1.25
59 A9 1r red orange 45.00 12.50
Nos. 51-59 (9) 74.00 18.75

King Tribhuvana Bir Bikram — A10

1954, Apr. 15 Unwmk. *Perf. 14*

Size: 18x22mm

60 A10 2p chocolate 1.00 .30
61 A10 4p green 4.00 .80
62 A10 6p rose .75 .30
63 A10 8p violet .60 .30
64 A10 12p red orange 7.00 1.40

Size: 25½x29½mm

65 A10 16p red brown .75 .30
66 A10 20p car rose 2.00 .80
67 A10 24p rose lake 1.25 .80
68 A10 32p ultramarine 1.50 .80
69 A10 50p rose pink 18.00 *4.00*
70 A10 1r vermilion 22.50 *6.00*
71 A10 2r orange 20.00 *5.00*
Nos. 60-71 (12) 79.35 *20.80*

Map of Nepal A11

1954, Apr. 15

Size: 29½x17½mm

72 A11 2p chocolate 1.25 .40
73 A11 4p green 2.50 .60
74 A11 6p rose 19.00 1.00
75 A11 8p violet .75 .40
76 A11 12p red orange 19.00 1.00

Size: 38x21½mm

77 A11 16p red brown 1.00 .45
78 A11 20p car rose 1.50 .45
79 A11 24p rose lake 1.50 .45
80 A11 32p ultramarine 2.00 .80
81 A11 50p rose pink 20.00 3.00
82 A11 1r vermilion 25.00 3.50
83 A11 2r orange 17.50 3.50
Nos. 72-83 (12) 111.00 15.55

Planting Rice — A12

Throne — A13

Hanuman Gate — A14

King Mahendra Bir Bikram and Queen Ratna — A15

Design: 8p, Ceremonial arch and elephant.

Perf. 13½x14, 11½, 13½, 14

Litho., Photo. (6p)

1956 Granite Paper Unwmk.

84 A12 4p green 3.50 *5.25*
85 A13 6p crimson & org 2.00 *2.75*
86 A12 8p light violet 2.00 *1.25*
87 A14 24p carmine rose 3.50 *5.25*
88 A15 1r brown red 100.00 85.00
Nos. 84-88 (5) 111.00 *99.50*

Coronation of King Mahendra Bir Bikram and Queen Ratna Rajya Lakshmi.

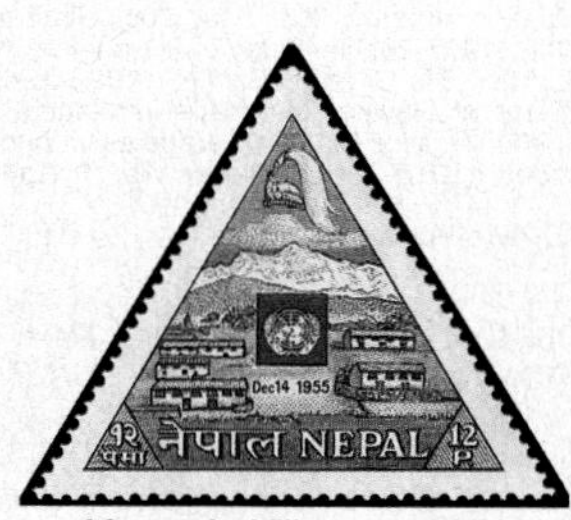

Mountain Village and UN Emblem — A16

1956, Dec. 14 Litho. *Perf. 13½*

89 A16 12p ultra & orange 4.00 5.00

1st anniv. of Nepal's admission to the UN.

Crown of Nepal — A17

Lumbini Temple — A18

Perf. 13½x14

1957, June 22 Unwmk.

Size: 18x22mm

90 A17 2p dull red brown .20 *.50*
91 A17 4p light green .20 *.50*
92 A17 6p pink .20 *.50*
93 A17 8p light violet .20 *.90*
94 A17 12p orange vermilion 2.00 *.80*

Size: 25½x30mm

95 A17 16p red brown 3.00 1.00
96 A17 20p deep pink 12.00 1.40
97 A17 24p brt car rose 2.25 1.40
98 A17 32p ultramarine 2.00 1.40
99 A17 50p rose red 12.00 3.00
100 A17 1r brown orange 15.00 5.75
101 A17 2r orange 5.00 *7.00*
Nos. 90-101 (12) 54.05 *24.15*

1958, Dec. 10 Typo. *Perf. 11*

Without Gum

102 A18 6p yellow 1.75 1.25

10th anniversary of Universal Declaration of Human Rights. Exists imperf.

Catalogue values for unused stamps in this section, from this point to the end of the section, are for Never Hinged items.

Map and Flag — A19

1959, Feb. 18 Engr. *Perf. 14½*

103 A19 6p carmine & light green .50 .30

First general elections in Nepal.

Statue of Vishnu, Changu Narayan A20

Krishna Conquering Black Serpent A21

Designs: 4p, Nepalese glacier. 6p, Golden Gate, Bhaktapur. 8p, Nepalese musk deer. 12p, Rhinoceros. 16p, 20p, 24p, 32p, 50p, Nyatapola Temple, Bhatgaon. 1r, 2r, Himalayan impeyan pheasant. 5r, Satyr tragopan.

Perf. 13½x14, 14x13½

1959-60 Litho. Unwmk.

Size: 18x22mm

104 A20 1p chocolate .20 .20
105 A21 2p gray violet .20 .20
106 A20 4p light ultra .20 .30
107 A20 6p vermilion .20 .20
108 A21 8p sepia .20 .20
109 A21 12p greenish gray .20 .20

Size: 25½x30mm

110 A20 16p brown & lt vio .20 .20
111 A20 20p blue & dull rose .35 .20
112 A20 24p green & pink .20 .20
113 A20 32p brt vio & ultra .35 .50
114 A20 50p rose red & grn .55 .50
115 A20 1r redsh brn & bl 15.00 2.75
116 A20 2r rose lil & ultra 12.00 4.50
117 A20 5r vio & rose red ('60) 100.00 52.50
Nos. 104-117 (14) 129.85 62.65

Nepal's admission to the UPU.

Spinning Wheel
A22

King
Mahendra
A23

1959, Apr. 10 Typo. *Perf. 11*
118 A22 2p dark red brown .55 .30

Issued to promote development of cottage industries.
Exists imperf. Value $26.

1959, Apr. 14
119 A23 12p bluish black .55 .35

Nepal's admission to UPU. Exists imperf. and ungummed.

King Mahendra Opening
Parliament — A24

1959, July 1 Unwmk. *Perf. 10½*
120 A24 6p deep carmine 1.00 1.00

First session of Parliament. Exists imperf.

Sri Pashupati
Nath — A25

King
Mahendra — A26

1959, Nov. 19 *Perf. 11*
Size: 18x24½mm
121 A25 4p dp yellow green .50 .20
Size: 20½x28mm
122 A25 8p carmine 1.25 .35
Size: 24½x33mm
123 A25 1r light blue 11.00 .75
Nos. 121-123 (3) 12.75 1.30

Renovation of Sri Pashupati Temple. Nos. 121-123 exist imperf. between.

1960, June 11 Photo. *Perf. 14*
Size: 25x30mm
124 A26 1r red lilac 2.40 .40

King Mahendra's 40th birthday. See Nos. 147-151A. For overprint see No. O15.

Children, Temple
and Mt.
Everest — A27

Mount
Everest — A28

1960 Typo. *Perf. 11*
125 A27 6p dark blue 25.00 10.00

1st Children's Day, Mar. 1, 1960. Printed in sheets of four. Exists imperf.; value $45 unused.

1960-61 Photo. *Perf. 14*

Himalaya mountain peaks: 5p, Machha Puchhre. 40p, Mansalu.

126 A28 5p claret & brown ('61) .50 .20
127 A28 10p ultra & rose lilac .70 .20
128 A28 40p violet & red brn ('61) 1.00 .20
Nos. 126-128 (3) 2.20 .60

King Tribhuvana
A29

King Mahendra
A30

1961, Feb. 18 *Perf. 13x13½*
129 A29 10p red brown & orange .25 .20

Tenth Democracy Day.

1961, June 11 *Perf. 14x14½*
130 A30 6p emerald .20 .20
131 A30 12p ultramarine .30 .30
132 A30 50p carmine rose .50 .50
133 A30 1r brown 1.25 1.25
Nos. 130-133 (4) 2.25 2.25

King Mahendra's 41st birthday.

Prince Gyanendra
Canceling
Stamps — A31

Malaria
Eradication
Emblem and
Temple — A32

1961 Typo. *Perf. 11*
134 A31 12p orange 40.00 35.00

Children's Day, Mar. 1, 1961. Exists imperf. Value, $75.

1962, Apr. 7 Litho. *Perf. 13x13½*

Design: 1r, Emblem and Nepalese flag.

135 A32 12p blue & lt blue .20 .20
136 A32 1r magenta & orange .90 .35

WHO drive to eradicate malaria.

King
Mahendra
A33

1962, June 11 Unwmk. *Perf. 13*
137 A33 10p slate blue .20 .20
138 A33 15p brown .25 .25
139 A33 45p dull red brown .45 .45
140 A33 1r olive gray 1.00 1.00
Nos. 137-140 (4) 1.90 1.90

King Mahendra's 42nd birthday.

Bhanu Bhakta
Acharya
A34

King
Mahendra
A35

10p, Moti Ram Bhatta. 40p, Shambu Prasad.

1962 Photo. *Perf. 14x14*
141 A34 5p orange brown .45 .25
142 A34 10p deep aqua .45 .25
143 A34 40p olive bister .65 .50
Nos. 141-143 (3) 1.55 1.00

Issued to honor Nepalese poets.

Mahendra Type of 1960 and Type A35

1962-66 *Perf. 14½x14*
144 A35 1p car rose .20 .20
145 A35 2p brt blue .20 .20
145A A35 3p gray ('66) .20 .20
146 A35 5p golden brown .20 .20

Perf. 14x14½
Size: 21½x38mm
147 A26 10p rose claret .20 .20
148 A26 40p brown .20 .20
149 A26 75p blue green 10.00 10.00

Perf. 14
Size: 25x30mm
150 A26 2r red orange 1.40 .45
151 A26 5r gray green 4.00 1.00
151A A26 10r violet ('66) 10.00 8.00
Nos. 144-151A (10) 26.60 20.65

See No. 199. For overprints see Nos. O12-O14.

Blackboard, Book and UN
Emblem — A36

1963, Jan. 6 *Perf. 14½x14*
152 A36 10p dark gray .40 .20
153 A36 15p brown .60 .25
154 A36 50p violet blue 1.50 .75
Nos. 152-154 (3) 2.50 1.20

UNESCO "Education for All" campaign.

Five-pointed Star
and Hands
Holding
Lamps — A37

Man, Tractor
and
Wheat — A38

Unwmk.
1963, Feb. 19 Photo. *Perf. 13*
155 A37 5p blue .45 .20
156 A37 10p reddish brown .50 .20
157 A37 50p rose lilac 1.00 .20
158 A37 1r blue green 1.75 .20
Nos. 155-158 (4) 3.70 .80

Panchayat System and National Day.

1963, Mar. 21 *Perf. 14x14½*
159 A38 10p orange .50 .20
160 A38 15p dark ultra 1.00 .30
161 A38 50p green 1.75 .60
162 A38 1r brown 4.00 .80
Nos. 159-162 (4) 7.25 1.90

FAO "Freedom from Hunger" campaign.

Map of
Nepal and
Hand
A39

1963, Apr. 14 Unwmk. *Perf. 13*
163 A39 10p green .50 .20
164 A39 15p claret 1.00 .30
165 A39 50p slate 1.75 .40
166 A39 1r violet blue 4.00 .50
Nos. 163-166 (4) 7.25 1.40

Rastriya Panchayat system.

King
Mahendra — A40

1963, June 11 *Perf. 13*
167 A40 5p violet .30 .20
168 A40 10p brown orange .40 .20
169 A40 15p dull green .65 .20
Nos. 167-169 (3) 1.35 .60

King Mahendra's 43rd birthday.

East-West
Highway on
Map of
Nepal and
King
Mahendra
A41

1964, Feb. 19 Photo. *Perf. 13*
170 A41 10p blue & dp orange .40 .20
171 A41 15p dk blue & dp org .60 .20
172 A41 50p dk grn & redsh brn 1.25 .20
Nos. 170-172 (3) 2.25 .60

Issued to publicize the East-West Highway as "The Prosperity of the Country."

King Mahendra Speaking Before Microphone — A42

Crown Prince Birendra — A43

1964, June 11 ***Perf. 14***

173 A42 1p brown olive .40 .20
174 A42 2p gray .40 .20
175 A42 2r golden brown 2.00 .60
Nos. 173-175 (3) 2.80 1.00

King Mahendra's 44th birthday.

Perf. 14x14½

1964, Dec. 28 **Photo.** **Unwmk.**

176 A43 10p dark green 1.40 .50
177 A43 15p brown 1.40 .50

19th birthday (coming of age) of Crown Prince Birendra Bir Bikram Shah Deva.

Nepalese Flag and Swords, Olympic Emblem A44

1964, Dec. 31 **Litho.** ***Perf. 13x13½***

178 A44 10p red & ultra 1.75 .80

18th Olympic Games, Tokyo, Oct. 10-25.

Farmer Plowing — A45

Family — A46

Designs: 5p, Grain. 10p, Chemical plant.

1965 **Photo.** ***Perf. 13½***

179 A45 2p brt green & black .30 .30
180 A45 5p pale yel green & brn .30 .30
181 A45 10p gray & purple .30 .30
182 A46 15p yellow & brown .60 .60
Nos. 179-182 (4) 1.50 1.50

Issued to publicize land reform.

The 2p also exists on light green paper.

Issue dates: 15p, Feb. 10; others, Dec. 16.

Mail Circling Globe A47

1965, Apr. 13 ***Perf. 14½x14***

183 A47 15p rose lilac .40 .40

Issued for Nepalese New Year.

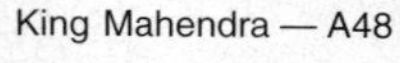

King Mahendra — A48

Perf. 14x14½

1965, June 11 **Photo.** **Unwmk.**

184 A48 50p rose violet .90 .70

King Mahendra's 45th birthday.

Victims of Revolution, 1939-40 — A49

1965, June 11 ***Perf. 13***

185 A49 15p bright green .40 .20

The men executed by the Rana Government 1939-40 were: Shukra Raj Shastri, Dasharath Chand, Dharma Bhakta and Ganga Lal Shresta.

ITU Emblem A50

Devkota A51

1965, Sept. 15 **Photo.** ***Perf. 13***

186 A50 15p deep plum & black .40 .20

Cent. of the ITU.

1965, Oct. 14 ***Perf. 14x14½***

187 A51 15p red brown .40 .20

Lakshmi Prasad Devkota (1908-1959), poet.

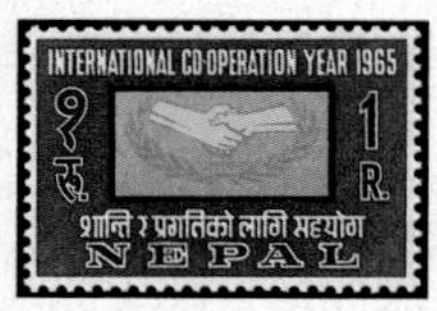

ICY Emblem A52

Engr. and Litho.

1965, Oct. 24 ***Perf. 11½x12***

188 A52 1r multicolored 1.00 .80

International Cooperation Year.

Nepalese Flag and King A53

1966, Feb. 18 **Photo.** ***Perf. 14½x14***

189 A53 15p deep blue & red .70 .50

Issued for Democracy Day.

Siva, Parvati and Pashupati Temple — A54

1966, Feb. 18 ***Perf. 14***

190 A54 15p violet .40 .20

Hindu festival Maha Sivaratri.

Emblem — A55

Perf. 14½x14

1966, June 10 **Photo.** **Unwmk.**

191 A55 15p dk green & orange .50 .20

National Philatelic Exhib., June 10-16.

King Mahendra A56

Kanti Rajya Lakshmi A57

1966, June 11 ***Perf. 13x13½***

192 A56 15p yellow & vio brown .40 .20

Issued for King Mahendra's 46th birthday.

1966, July 5 **Photo.** ***Perf. 14x14½***

193 A57 15p golden brown .40 .20

60th birthday of Queen Mother Kanti Rajya Lakshmi.

Queen Ratna Rajya Lakshmi Devi Shah — A58

1966, Aug. 19 **Photo.** ***Perf. 13***

194 A58 15p yellow & brown .40 .20

Issued for Children's Day.

Krishna with Consort Radha and Flute — A59

1966, Sept. 7

195 A59 15p dk purple & yellow .50 .20

Krishnastami 2023, the birthday of Krishna.

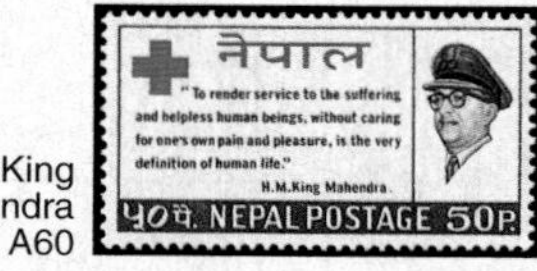

King Mahendra A60

1966, Oct. 1 **Photo.** ***Perf. 14½x14***

196 A60 50p slate grn & dp car 4.00 1.00

Issued to commemorate the official recognition of the Nepalese Red Cross.

Opening of WHO Headquarters Building, Geneva — A61

Lekhnath Paudyal — A62

1966, Nov. 11 **Photo.** ***Perf. 14***

197 A61 1r purple 2.00 1.20

1966, Dec. 29 **Photo.** ***Perf. 14***

198 A62 15p dull violet blue .40 .20

Lekhnath Paudyal (1884-1966), poet.

King Type of 1962

1967, Feb. 10 **Photo.** ***Perf. 14½x14***

199 A35 75p blue green 1.25 .50

Rama and Sita — A63

Buddha — A64

1967, Apr. 18 **Litho.** ***Perf. 14***

200 A63 15p brown & yellow .40 .20

Rama Navami 2024, the birthday of Rama.

1967, May 23 **Photo.** ***Perf. 13½x13***

201 A64 75p orange & purple 1.00 1.00

2,511th birthday of Buddha.

King Mahendra Addressing Crowd and Himalayas — A65

1967, June 11 ***Perf. 13***

202 A65 15p dk brown & lt blue .40 .20

King Mahendra's 47th birthday.

Queen Ratna among Children A66

1967, Aug. 20 **Photo.** ***Perf. 13***

203 A66 15p pale yel & dp brown .40 .20

Issued for Children's Day on the birthday of Queen Ratna Rajya Lakshmi Devi Shah.

Durbar Square, Bhaktapur A67

5p, Ama Dablam Mountain, ITY emblem.

1967, Oct. 24 ***Perf. 13½x14***

Size: 29½x21mm

204 A67 5p violet .40 .40

Perf. 14½x14

Size: 37½x19½mm

205 A67 65p brown .60 .60

Intl. Tourist Year, 1967. See No. C2.

Official Reading Proclamation — A68

1967, Dec. 16 Litho. *Perf. 13*
206 A68 15p multicolored .40 .20

"Back to the Villages" campaign.

Crown Prince Birendra, Boy Scouts and Scout Emblem A69

1967, Dec. 29 Photo. *Perf. 14½x14*
207 A69 15p ultramarine 1.00 .50

60th anniv. of Boy Scouts.

Prithvi Narayan — A70

Arms of Nepal — A71

1968, Jan. 11 *Perf. 14x14½*
208 A70 15p blue & rose .80 .50

Rajah Prithvi Narayan (1779-1839), founder of modern Nepal.

1968, Feb. 19 Photo. *Perf. 14x14½*
209 A71 15p crimson & dk blue .80 .50

Issued for National Day.

WHO Emblem and Flag of Nepal A72

1968, Apr. 7 *Perf. 13*
210 A72 1.20r dull yel, red & ultra 3.00 2.00

World Health Day (UN WHO).

Goddess Sita and Shrine A73

1968, May 6 Photo. *Perf. 14½x14*
211 A73 15p violet & org brown .50 .20

King Mahendra, Pheasant and Himalayas A74

1968, June 11 Photo. *Perf. 13½*
212 A74 15p multicolored .60 .20

King Mahendra's 48th birthday.

Flag, Children and Queen Ratna — A75

1968, Aug. 19 Litho. *Perf. 13x13½*
213 A75 5p blue grn, yel & ver .40 .20

Fourth National Children's Day.

Buddha and Human Rights Flame A76

1968, Dec. 10 Photo. *Perf. 14½x14*
214 A76 1r dk green & red 3.00 2.00

International Human Rights Year.

Young People Dancing Around Flag A77

1968, Dec. 28 Photo. *Perf. 14½x14*
215 A77 25p violet blue .80 .20

23rd birthday of Crown Prince Birendra, which is celebrated as Youth Festival.

UN Building, Nepalese and UN Flags — A78

Amsu Varma — A79

1969, Jan. 1 *Perf. 13½x13*
216 A78 1r multicolored 1.25 .80

Issued to commemorate Nepal's admission to the UN Security Council for 1969-1970.

1969, Apr. 13 Photo. *Perf. 14x14½*

Portraits: 25p, Ram Shah. 50p, Bhimsen Thapa.

217 A79 15p green & purple .30 .30
218 A79 25p blue green .70 .70
219 A79 50p orange brown 1.00 1.00
Nos. 217-219 (3) 2.00 2.00

Amsu Varma, 7th cent. ruler and reformer; Ram Shah, 17th cent. ruler and reformer, and Bhimsen Thapa, 18-19th cent. administrator and reformer.

ILO Emblem A80

1969, May 1 Photo. *Perf. 14½x14*
220 A80 1r car rose, blk & lt brown 5.50 3.00

50th anniv. of the ILO.

King Mahendra — A81

1969, June 20 *Perf. 13½x13*
221 A81 25p gold & multi .40 .20

King Mahendra's 49th birthday (50th by Oriental count). Issuance delayed from June 11 to 20.

King Tribhuvana and Wives A82

1969, July 1 *Perf. 14½x14*
222 A82 25p yellow & ol gray .40 .20

64th anniv. of the birth of King Tribhuvana.

Queen Ratna & Child Playing A83

Rhododendron & Himalayas A84

1969, Aug. 20 Photo. *Perf. 14x14½*
223 A83 25p gray & rose car .40 .20

5th Natl. Children's Day and to for the 41st birthday of Queen Ratna Rajya Lakshmi Devi Shah.

1969, Sept. 17 Photo. *Perf. 13½*

Flowers: No. 225, Narcissus. No. 226, Marigold. No. 227, Poinsettia.

224 A84 25p lt blue & multi .75 .25
225 A84 25p brown red & multi .75 .25
226 A84 25p black & multi .75 .25
227 A84 25p multicolored .75 .25
a. Block of 4, #224-227 3.00 3.00

Durga, Goddess of Victory — A85

Crown Prince Birendra and Princess Aishwarya A86

1969, Oct. 17 Photo. *Perf. 14x14½*
228 A85 15p black & orange .40 .35
229 A85 50p black, bis brn & vio .80 .65

Issued to celebrate the Dasain Festival.

1970, Feb. 27 Photo. *Perf. 13½*
230 A86 25p multicolored .40 .20

Wedding of Crown Prince Birendra Bir Bikram Shah Deva and Crown Princess Aishwarya Rajya Lakshmi Devi Rana, Feb. 27-28.

Agricultural Products, Cow, Fish — A87

1970, Mar. 21 Litho. *Perf. 12½*
231 A87 25p multicolored .40 .20

Issued to publicize the Agricultural Year.

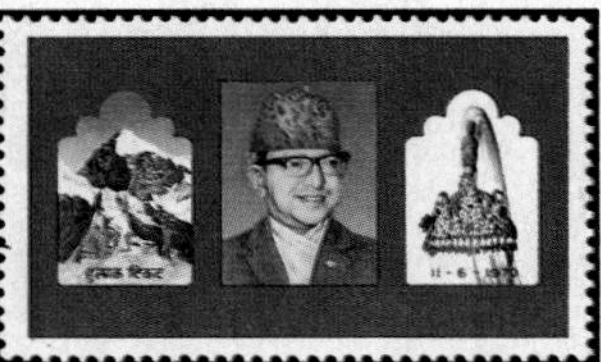

Bal Bhadra Kunwar A88

1970, Apr. 13 Photo. *Perf. 14½x14*
232 A88 1r ol bister & red lilac 1.20 .80

Bal Bhadra Kunwar, leader in the 1814 battle of Kalanga against British forces.

King Mahendra, Mountain Peak and Crown — A89

1970, June 11 Litho. *Perf. 11½*
233 A89 50p gold & multi .75 .20

King Mahendra's 50th birthday.

Gosainkund A90

Lakes: 25p, Phewa Tal. 1r, Rara Daha.

1970, June 11 Photo. *Perf. 13½*
234 A90 5p dull yellow & multi .25 .25
235 A90 25p gray & multi .50 .35
236 A90 1r pink & multi .90 .90
Nos. 234-236 (3) 1.65 1.50

A.P.Y. Emblem A91

1970, July 1 *Perf. 14½x14*
237 A91 1r dark blue & blue .75 .25

Asian Productivity Year 1970.

Bal Mandir Building and Queen Ratna A92

1970, Aug. 20 Photo. *Perf. 14½x14*
238 A92 25p gray & bister brn .40 .20

Issued for Children's Day. The Bal Mandir Building in Taulihawa is the headquarters of the National Children's Organization.

New UPU Headquarters, Bern — A93

1970, Oct. 9 Photo. *Perf. 14½x14*

239	A93	2.50r ocher & sepia	1.80	1.50

UN Flag A94

1970, Oct. 24 Photo. *Perf. 14½x14*

240	A94	25p blue & brown	.40	.20

25th anniversary of the United Nations.

Royal Palace and Square, Patan A95

25p, Bodhnath stupa, near Kathmandu, vert. 1r, Gauri Shankar, holy mountain.

Perf. 11x11½, 11½x11

1970, Dec. 28 Litho.

241	A95	15p multicolored	.30	.20
242	A95	25p multicolored	.50	.20
243	A95	1r multicolored	.70	.30
		Nos. 241-243 (3)	1.50	.70

Crown Prince Birendra's 25th birthday.

Statue of Harihar (Vishnu-Siva) — A96

1971, Jan. 26 Photo. *Perf. 14x14½*

244	A96	25p bister brn & black	.40	.20

Torch and Target A97

1971, Mar. 21 Photo. *Perf. 13½x13*

245	A97	1r bluish gray & dp org	1.00	.80

Intl. year against racial discrimination.

King Mahendra and Subjects A98

1971, June 11 Photo. *Perf. 14½x14*

246	A98	25p dull purple & blue	.40	.20

King Mahendra's 51st birthday.

Sweta Bhairab (Siva) — A99

Sculptures of Siva: 25p, Manhankal Bhairab. 50p, Kal Bhairab.

1971, July 11 *Perf. 13x13½*

247	A99	15p orange brown & black	.40	.30
248	A99	25p lt green & black	.40	.30
249	A99	50p blue & black	.70	.60
		Nos. 247-249 (3)	1.50	1.20

Queen Ratna Receiving Garland A100

1971, Aug. 20 Photo. *Perf. 11½*

Granite Paper

250	A100	25p gray & multi	.40	.20

Children's Day, Queen Ratna's birthday.

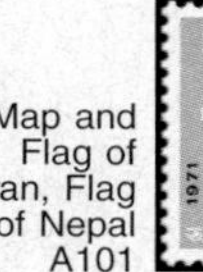

Map and Flag of Iran, Flag of Nepal A101

1971, Oct. 14

Granite Paper

251	A101	1r pink & multi	1.00	.80

2500th anniversary of the founding of the Persian empire by Cyrus the Great.

UNICEF Emblem, Mother and Child A102

1971, Dec. 11 *Perf. 14½x14*

252	A102	1r gray blue	1.20	.80

25th anniversary of UNICEF.

Everest A103

Himalayan Peaks: 1r, Kangchenjunga. 1.80r, Annapurna I.

1971, Dec. 28 *Perf. 13½x13*

253	A103	25p blue & brown	.40	.30
254	A103	1r dp blue & brown	.60	.45
255	A103	1.80r blue & yel brown	1.25	.75
		Nos. 253-255 (3)	2.25	1.50

"Visit Nepal."

Royal Standard — A104

1972, Feb. 19 Photo. *Perf. 13*

256	A104	25p dark red & black	.40	.20

National Day.

Araniko and White Dagoba, Peking — A105

1972, Apr. 13 Litho. *Perf. 13*

257	A105	15p lt blue & ol gray	.20	.20

Araniko, a 14th century Nepalese architect, who built the White Dagoba at the Miaoying Monastery, Peking, 1348.

Book Year Emblem, Ancient Book A106

1972, Sept. 8 Photo. *Perf. 14½x14*

258	A106	2p ocher & brown	.20	.20
259	A106	5p tan & black	.20	.20
260	A106	1r blue & black	.50	.25
		Nos. 258-260 (3)	.90	.65

International Book Year.

Heart and WHO Emblem — A107

1972, Nov. 6 Photo. *Perf. 13x13½*

261	A107	25p dull grn & claret	.50	.20

"Your heart is your health," World Health Month.

King Mahendra (1920-1972) A108

1972, Dec. 15 Photo. *Perf. 13½x13*

262	A108	25p brown & black	.40	.20

King Birendra — A109

1972, Dec. 28 Photo. *Perf. 13x13½*

263	A109	50p ocher & purple	.45	.20

King Birendra's 27th birthday.

Northern Border Costume A110

1973, Feb. 18 Photo. *Perf. 13*

Nepalese Costumes: 50p, Hill dwellers. 75p, Kathmandu Valley couple. 1r, Inner Terai couple.

264	A110	25p dull lilac & multi	.20	.20
265	A110	50p lemon & multi	.40	.40
266	A110	75p multicolored	.60	.60
267	A110	1r multicolored	.80	.80
a.		Block of 4, #264-267	2.00	2.00

National Day.

Babu Ram Acharya (1888-1972), Historian — A111

1973, Mar. 12 Photo. *Perf. 13*

268	A111	25p olive gray & car	.35	.20

Nepalese Family and Home A112

1973, Apr. 7 Photo. *Perf. 14½x14*

269	A112	1r Prus blue & ocher	.75	.30

25th anniv. of the WHO.

Lumbini Garden, Birthplace of Buddha — A113

1973, May 17 Photo. *Perf. 13x13½*

270	A113	25p shown	.30	.20
271	A113	75p Mt. Makalu	.50	.20
272	A113	1r Gorkha Village	.70	.20
		Nos. 270-272 (3)	1.50	.60

FAO Emblem, Women Farmers A114

1973, June 29 Photo. *Perf. 14½x14*

273	A114	10p dark gray & violet	.20	.20

World food program, 10th anniversary.

INTERPOL Headquarters and Emblem — A115

1973, Sept. 3

274	A115	25p bister & blue	.35	.20

50th anniversary of the International Criminal Police Organization (INTERPOL).

Shom Nath Sigdyal (1884-1972), Scholar — A116

1973, Oct. 5 Photo. *Perf. 13x13½*

275	A116	1.25r violet blue	.75	.25

Cow
A117

1973, Oct. 25 Photo. *Perf. 13½x13*
276 A117 2p shown .20 .20
277 A117 3.25r Yak 1.50 .75

Festival of Lights (Tihar).

King Birendra — A118

Perf. 13, 13½x14, 15x14½
1973-74 Photo.
278 A118 5p dark brown .20 .20
279 A118 15p ol brn & dk brn ('74) .20 .20
280 A118 1r reddish brn & dk brn ('74) .60 .35
Nos. 278-280 (3) 1.00 .75

King Birendra's 28th birthday.

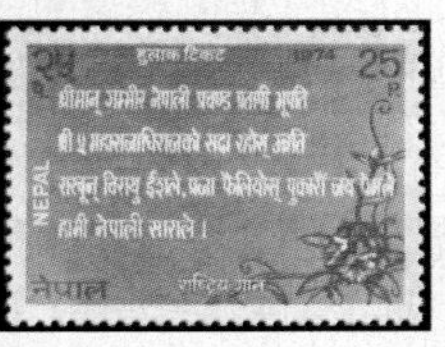

National Anthem
A119

Natl. Day: 1r, Score of national anthem.

1974, Feb. 18 Photo. *Perf. 13½x13*
281 A119 25p rose carmine .40 .20
282 A119 1r deep green .60 .25

King Janak on Throne — A120

1974, Apr. 14 Litho. *Perf. 13½*
283 A120 2.50r multicolored 1.50 1.00

Children's Village and SOS Emblem — A121

1974, May 20 Litho. *Perf. 13½x13*
284 A121 25p ultra & red .35 .20

25th anniv. of SOS Children's Village Intl.

Baghchal
A122

1974, July 1 Litho. *Perf. 13*
285 A122 2p Soccer .20 .20
286 A122 2.75r shown 1.00 .60

Popular Nepalese games.

WPY Emblem — A123
UPU Monument, Bern — A124

1974, Aug. 19 Litho. *Perf. 13*
287 A123 5p ocher & blue .25 .20

World Population Year.

1974, Oct. 9 Litho. *Perf. 13*
288 A124 1r olive & black .75 .35

Centenary of Universal Postal Union.

Butterfly
A125

Designs: Nepalese butterflies.

1974, Oct. 16
289 A125 10p lt brown & multi .25 .20
290 A125 15p lt blue & multi .40 .30
291 A125 1.25r multicolored 1.25 .90
292 A125 1.75r buff & multi 1.75 1.00
Nos. 289-292 (4) 3.65 2.40

King Birendra
A126
Muktinath
A127

Peacock Window
A128

1974, Dec. 28 Litho. *Perf. 13½x13*
293 A126 25p gray green & black .25 .20

King Birendra's 29th birthday.

1974, Dec. 31 *Perf. 13x13½, 13½x13*
294 A127 25p multicolored .35 .20
295 A128 1r multicolored .65 .20

Tourist publicity.

Guheswari Temple — A129

Pashupati Temple — A131

Rara
A130

King Birendra and Queen Aishwarya — A132

Designs: 1r, Throne. 1.25r, Royal Palace.

1975, Feb. 24 Litho. *Perf. 13x13½*
296 A129 25p multicolored .30 .20

Photo.
Perf. 14½x14
297 A130 50p multicolored .30 .20

Granite Paper
Perf. 11½, 11 (A131)
298 A132 1r olive & multi .45 .20
299 A132 1.25r multicolored 1.00 .25
300 A131 1.75r multicolored .75 .50
301 A132 2.75r gold & multi 1.25 .50
  a. Souvenir sheet of 3 4.00 4.00
Nos. 296-301 (6) 4.05 1.85

Coronation of King Birendra, Feb. 24, 1975. No. 301a contains 3 imperf. stamps similar to Nos. 298-299, 301 and label with inscription.

Tourist Year Emblem
A133

Swayambhunath Stupa, Kathmandu — A134

Perf. 12½x13½, 13½x12½
1975, May 25 Litho.
302 A133 2p yellow & multi .20 .20
303 A134 25p violet & black .35 .25

South Asia Tourism Year.

Tiger
A135

1975, July 17 Litho. *Perf. 13*
304 A135 2p shown .35 .35
305 A135 5p Deer, vert. .40 .40
306 A135 1r Panda .75 .75
Nos. 304-306 (3) 1.50 1.50

Wildlife conservation.

Queen Aishwarya and IWY Emblem — A136

1975, Nov. 8 Litho. *Perf. 13*
307 A136 1r lt blue & multi .40 .25

International Women's Year.

Ganesh Peak — A137

Rupse Falls — A138
Kumari, Living Goddess of Nepal — A139

1975, Dec. 16 Litho. *Perf. 13½*
308 A137 2p multicolored .20 .20
309 A138 25p multicolored .20 .20
310 A139 50p multicolored .45 .25
Nos. 308-310 (3) .85 .65

Tourist publicity.

King Birendra — A140

1975, Dec. 28 Photo. *Perf. 13*
311 A140 25p rose lil & red lil .25 .20

King Birendra's 30th birthday.

Flag and Map of Nepal
A141

1976, Feb. 19 Litho. *Perf. 13*
312 A141 2.50r dark blue & red 1.00 .45

National or Democracy Day.

Rice Cultivation — A142

1976, Apr. 11 Litho. *Perf. 13*
313 A142 25p multicolored .25 .20

Agricultural development.

Flags of Nepal and Colombo Plan — A143

Runner — A144

1976, July 1 Photo. ***Perf. 13x13½***

314 A143 1r multicolored .55 .30

Colombo Plan, 25th anniversary.

1976, July 31 Photo. ***Perf. 13x13½***

315 A144 3.25r black & ultra 1.60 .75

21st Olympic Games, Montreal, Canada, July 17-Aug. 1.

Dove and Map of South East Asia — A145

1976, Aug. 17 Litho. ***Perf. 13½***

316 A145 5r bister, black & ultra 1.75 .85

5th Summit Conference of Non-aligned Countries, Colombo, Sri Lanka, Aug. 9-19.

Folk Dances A146

1976, Sept. 27 Litho. ***Perf. 13½x13***

317 A146 10p Lakha mask .20 .20
318 A146 15p Maruni .20 .20
319 A146 30p Jhangad .35 .20
320 A146 1r Sebru .50 .25
Nos. 317-320 (4) 1.25 .85

Nepalese Lily A147

King Birendra A148

Flowers: No. 322, Meconopsis grandis. No. 323, Cardiocrinum giganteum, horiz. No. 324, Megacodon stylophorus, horiz.

1976-77 Litho. ***Perf. 13***

321 A147 30p lt ultra & multi .55 .20
322 A147 30p brown & multi .55 .20
323 A147 30p violet & multi .55 .20
324 A147 30p violet & multi .55 .20
Nos. 321-324 (4) 2.20 .80

Issue dates: Nov. 7, 1976, Jan. 24, 1977.

1976, Dec. 28 Photo. ***Perf. 14***

325 A148 5p green .20 .20
326 A148 30p multicolored .35 .20

King Birendra's 31st birthday.

Bell and American Bicentennial Emblem — A149

1976, Dec. 31 Litho. ***Perf. 13½***

327 A149 10r multicolored 3.00 1.75

American Bicentennial.

Warrior Kazi Amar Singh Thapa, Natl. Hero A150

1977, Feb. 18 Photo. ***Perf. 13x13½***

328 A150 10p multicolored .20 .20

Terracotta Figurine, Kapilavastu Excavations — A151

Asoka Pillar, Lumbini A152

1977, May 3 Photo. ***Perf. 14½x14***

329 A151 30p dark violet .20 .20
330 A152 5r green & brown 1.90 .90

Tourist publicity.

Cheer Pheasant A153

Birds of Nepal: 5p, Great pied hornbill, vert. 1r, Green magpie. 2.30r, Nepalese laughing thrush, vert.

1977, Sept. 17 Photo. ***Perf. 13***

331 A153 5p multicolored .45 .20
332 A153 15p multicolored .80 .20
333 A153 1r multicolored 1.40 .35
334 A153 2.30r multicolored 2.75 .50
Nos. 331-334 (4) 5.40 1.25

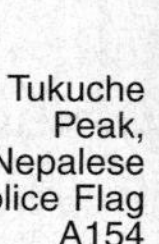

Tukuche Peak, Nepalese Police Flag A154

1977, Oct. 2

335 A154 1.25r multicolored .55 .25

Ascent of Tukuche, Himalaya Mountains, by Nepalese police team, first anniversary.

Scout Emblem, Map of Nepal — A155

1977, Nov. 7 Litho. ***Perf. 13½***

336 A155 3.50r multicolored 1.10 .65

Boy Scouts of Nepal, 25th anniversary.

Dhanwantari, Health Goddess — A156

1977, Nov. 9 Photo. ***Perf. 13***

337 A156 30p bluish green .25 .20

Health Day.

Flags, Map of Nepal — A157

King Birendra — A158

1977, Dec. 5 Photo. ***Perf. 13½***

338 A157 1r multicolored .35 .20

Colombo Plan, 26th Consultative Meeting, Kathmandu, Nov. 29-Dec. 7.

1977, Dec. 28

339 A158 5p olive .20 .20
340 A158 1r red brown .35 .35

King Birendra's 32nd birthday.

Post Office Seal, New Post Office A159

75p, Post Office date stamp & new Post Office.

1978, Apr. 14 Photo. ***Perf. 14½x14***

341 A159 25p org brn & blk .20 .20
342 A159 75p bister & black .35 .25

Centenary of Nepalese postal service.

Mt. Everest A160

Design: 4r, Mt. Everest, different view.

1978, May 29 Photo. ***Perf. 13½x13***

343 A160 2.30r red brn & slate .90 .40
344 A160 4r grn & vio blue 1.40 .75

1st ascent of Mt. Everest, 25th anniv.

Mountains, Trees, Environmental Emblem — A161

1978, June 5

345 A161 1r blue green & orange .35 .20

World Environment Day, June 5.

Queen Mother Ratna — A162

1978, Aug. 20 Photo. ***Perf. 14***

346 A162 2.30r olive gray .75 .40

Queen Mother Ratna, 50th birthday.

Trisula River Rapids A163

Tourist Publicity: 50p, Nepalese window. 1r, Dancer, Mahakali dance, vert.

1978, Sept. 15 Litho. ***Perf. 14***

347 A163 10p multicolored .20 .20
348 A163 50p multicolored .20 .20
349 A163 1r multicolored .40 .25
Nos. 347-349 (3) .80 .65

Human Rights Emblem — A164

1978, Oct. 10 Litho. ***Perf. 13½***

350 A164 25p red brown & red .20 .20
351 A164 1r dark blue & red .35 .20

Universal Declaration of Human Rights, 30th anniversary.

Choerospondias Axillaris — A165

Designs: 1r, Castanopsis indica, vert. 1.25r, Elaeocarpus sphaericus.

1978, Oct. 31 Photo. ***Perf. 13***

352 A165 5p multicolored .20 .20
353 A165 1r multicolored .40 .25
354 A165 1.25r multicolored .75 .30
Nos. 352-354 (3) 1.35 .75

King Birendra — A166

1978, Dec. 17 *Perf. 13½x14*
355 A166 30p brown & indigo .20 .20
356 A166 2r violet & black .60 .35

King Birendra's 33rd birthday.

Kamroop and Patan Temples and Deity A167

Red Machhindra Chariot — A168

Perf. 14½x14, 13½
1979 **Photo., Litho.**
357 A167 75p claret & olive .25 .20
358 A168 1.25r multicolored .40 .25

Red Machhindra Nath Festival, Lalitpur (Patan).
Issue dates: 75p, Apr. 27; 1.25r, July 25.

Bas-relief — A169

Tree Planting — A170

1979, May 12 **Photo.** *Perf. 13*
359 A169 1r yellow & brown .35 .20

Lumbini Year.

1979, June 29 **Photo.** *Perf. 13x13½*
360 A170 2.30r multicolored .90 .50

Afforestation campaign.

Children with Flag, IYC Emblem — A172

1979, Aug. 20 *Perf. 13½*
362 A172 1r light brown .40 .25

Intl. Year of the Child; Natl. Children's Day.

Mount Pabil A173

Tourism: 50p, Swargadwari Temple. 1.25r, Altar with statues of Shiva and Parbati.

1979, Sept. 26 **Photo.** *Perf. 13½x13*
363 A173 30p dk blue green .20 .20
364 A173 50p multicolored .20 .20
365 A173 1.25r multicolored .35 .35
Nos. 363-365 (3) .75 .75

Northern Shrike — A174

Coin, Lichhavi Period, Obverse — A175

Malla Period, Obverse A175a

Shaw Period, Obverse A175b

Perf. 14½x13½
1979, Nov. 22 **Photo.**
366 A174 10p shown .25 .20
367 A174 10r Aethopyga ignicauda 5.50 2.25

Intl. World Pheasant Assoc. Symposium, Kathmandu, Nov. 21-23. See No. C7.

1979, Dec. 16 **Photo.** *Perf. 15*

Ancient Coins: No. 369, Lichhavi Period, reverse. No. 371, Malla Period, reverse. No. 373, Shah Period, reverse.

368 A175 5p brn & brn org .20 .20
369 A175 5p brn & brn org .20 .20
a. Pair, #368-369 .30 .30
370 A175a 15p dark blue .20 .20
371 A175a 15p dark blue .20 .20
a. Pair, #370-371 .30 .30
372 A175b 1r slate blue .40 .40
373 A175b 1r slate blue .40 .40
a. Pair, #372-373 .90 .90
Nos. 368-373 (6) 1.60 1.60

King Birendra — A176

Ban-Ganga Dam — A177

1979, Dec. 28 **Litho.** *Perf. 14*
374 A176 25p multicolored .20 .20
375 A177 2.30r multicolored .90 .45

King Birendra's 34th birthday.

Samyak Pooja Festival A178

1980, Jan. 15 *Perf. 13½*
376 A178 30p vio brn & gray .40 .20

Holy Basil — A179

1980, Mar. 24 **Photo.** *Perf. 14x14½*
377 A179 5p shown .25 .20
378 A179 30p Himalayan valerian .30 .20
379 A179 1r Nepalese pepper .50 .25
380 A179 2.30r Himalayan rhubarb 1.00 .50
Nos. 377-380 (4) 2.05 1.15

Gyandil Das A180

Nepalese Writers: 30p, Shddhi Das Amatya. 1r, Pahal Man Singh Snwar. 2.30r, Jay Prithibi Bahadur Singh.

1980, Apr. 13 *Perf. 13½x13*
381 A180 5p bister & rose lilac .20 .20
382 A180 30p vio brn & lt red brn .20 .20
383 A180 1r blue & olive gray .30 .20
384 A180 2.30r ol grn & dk blue .55 .40
Nos. 381-384 (4) 1.25 1.00

Jwalaji Dailekh (Temple), Holy Flame — A181

Temple Statue — A182

1980, Sept. 14 **Litho.** *Perf. 14½*
385 A181 10p shown .20 .20
386 A181 1r Godavari Pond .35 .20
387 A181 5r Mt. Dhaulagiri 1.25 .90
Nos. 385-387 (3) 1.80 1.30

1980, Oct. 29 *Perf. 14x13½*
388 A182 25r multicolored 5.00 4.50

World Tourism Conf., Manila, Sept. 27.

King Birendra's 35th Birthday — A183

1980, Dec. 28 **Litho.** *Perf. 14*
389 A183 1r multicolored .40 .20

International Year of the Disabled A184

1981, Jan. 1
390 A184 5r multicolored 1.40 .75

Nepal Rastra Bank, 25th Anniv. A185

1981, Apr. 26 **Litho.** *Perf. 14*
391 A185 1.75r multicolored .50 .35

A186

A187

1981, July 16
392 A186 10p No. 1 .20 .20
393 A186 40p No. 2 .20 .20
394 A186 3.40r No. 3 1.25 .60
a. Souvenir sheet of 3, #392-394 2.50 2.50
Nos. 392-394 (3) 1.65 1.00

Nepalese stamp cent.

1981, Oct. 30 **Litho.** *Perf. 14*
395 A187 1.75r multicolored .40 .35

Intl. Hotel Assoc., 70th council meeting, Kathmandu.

Stamp Centenary A188

King Birendra's 36th Birthday A189

1981, Dec. 27 **Litho.** *Perf. 14*
396 A188 40p multicolored .20 .20

Nepal '81 Stamp Exhibition, Kathmandu, Dec. 27-31.

1981, Dec. 28
397 A189 1r multicolored .35 .20

Hrishikesh, Buddhist Stone Carving, Ridi — A190

1981, Dec. 30
398 A190 5p shown .20 .20
399 A190 25p Tripurasundari Pavilion, Baitadi .20 .20
400 A190 2r Mt. Langtang Lirung .35 .35
Nos. 398-400 (3) .75 .75

Royal Nepal Academy, 25th Anniv. A191

Balakrishna Sama — A192

1982, June 23 Litho. *Perf. 14*

401 A191 40p multicolored .20 .20

1982, July 21 *Perf. 13½*

402 A192 1r multicolored .25 .20

Dish Antenna, Satellite — A193

Mt. Nuptse — A194

1982, Nov. 7 Litho. *Perf. 14*

403 A193 5r multicolored 1.40 .90

1982, Nov. 18 *Perf. 13½*

Intl. Union of Alpinists Assoc., 50th Anniv. (Himalaya Peaks): b, Mt. Lhotse (31x31mm). c, Mt. Everest (40x31mm). Continuous design.

404 Strip of 3 2.50 2.50
- ***a.*** A194 25p multicolored .20 .20
- ***b.*** A194 2r multicolored .60 .40
- ***c.*** A194 3r multicolored 1.40 .60

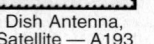

9th Asian Games — A195

1982, Nov. 19 *Perf. 14*

405 A195 3.40r multicolored .90 .65

Kulekhani Hydro-electric Plant — A196

1982, Dec. 2 *Perf. 13½*

406 A196 2r Lake, dam .55 .35

A197

A198

1982, Dec. 28 *Perf. 12½*

407 A197 5p multicolored .20 .20

King Birendra's 37th birthday.

1983, June 15 Litho. *Perf. 14*

408 A198 50p multicolored .20 .20

25th anniv. of Nepal Industrial Development Co.

25th Anniv. of Royal Nepal Airlines A199

1983, Aug. 1 *Perf. 13½*

409 A199 1r multicolored .45 .20

World Communications Year — A200

1983, Oct. 30 Litho. *Perf. 12*

410 A200 10p multicolored .20 .20

A201

A202

Musical instruments.

1983, Nov. 3

411	A201	5p Sarangi	.25	.20
412	A201	10p Kwota	.25	.20
413	A201	50p Narashinga	.25	.20
414	A201	1r Murchunga	.25	.25
		Nos. 411-414 (4)	1.00	.85

1983, Dec. 20

415 A202 4.50r multicolored 1.10 .55

Chakrapani Chalise (1883-1957), national anthem composer and poet.

King Birendra's 38th Birthday A203

1983, Dec. 28 *Perf. 14*

416 A203 5r multicolored 1.25 .50

Temple, Barahkshetra A204

1983, Dec. 30 *Perf. 14*

417	A204	1r shown	.25	.20
418	A204	2.20r Triveni pilgrimage site	.40	.25
419	A204	6r Mt. Cho-oyu	1.25	.65
		Nos. 417-419 (3)	1.90	1.10

Auditor General, 25th Anniv. A204a

1984, June 28 Litho. *Perf. 14*

419A A204a 25p Open ledger .20 .20

A205

A206

1984, July 1 Litho. *Perf. 14*

420 A205 5r Transmission tower 1.25 .75

Asia-Pacific Broadcasting Union, 20th anniv.

1984, July 8

421 A206 50p University emblem .25 .20

Tribhuvan University, 25th anniv.

A207

A208

1984, Aug. 5

422 A207 10r Boxing 2.25 1.00

1984 Summer Olympic Games, Los Angeles.

1984, Sept. 18

423 A208 1r multicolored .25 .20

Family Planning Assoc., 25th anniv.

Social Services Day — A209

1984, Sept. 24

424 A209 5p multicolored .20 .20

Wildlife A210

1984, Nov. 30

425	A210	10p Gavialis gangeticus	.20	.20
426	A210	25p Panthera uncia	.30	.20
427	A210	50p Antilope cervicapra	.50	.25
		Nos. 425-427 (3)	1.00	.65

Chhinna Masta Bhagvati Temple and Goddess Sakhandeshwari Devi, Statue — A211

Designs: 10p, Lord Vishu the Giant, Yajna Ceremony on Bali, bas-relief, A. D. 467, vert. 5r, Mt. Api, Himalayas, vert.

1984, Dec. 21

428	A211	10p multicolored	.20	.20
429	A211	1r multicolored	.25	.20
430	A211	5r multicolored	1.40	.55
		Nos. 428-430 (3)	1.85	.95

King Birendra, 39th Birthday A212

1984, Dec. 28

431 A212 1r multicolored .25 .20

Sagarmatha Natl. Park — A213

1985, May 6

432 A213 10r Mt. Everest, wildlife 2.50 1.00

King Mahendra Trust Congress for Nature Conservation, May 6-11.

Illustration from Shiva Dharma Purana, 13th Cent. Book — A214

Design: Maheshware, Lord Shiva, with brahma and vishnu. #433b, left person sitting on wall. #433d, left person on throne.

1985, May 30

433 Strip of 5 1.25 1.25
- ***a.-e.*** A214 50p any single .20 .20
- ***f.*** Strip of 5, imperf within 1.25

#433 has a continuous design. Sizes: #433a, 433e, 26x22mm; #433b, 433d, 24x22mm; #433c, 17x22mm.

UN, 40th Anniv. — A215

1985, Oct. 24 Litho. *Perf. 13½x14*

434 A215 5r multicolored 1.10 .50

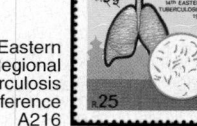

14th Eastern Regional Tuberculosis Conference A216

1985, Nov. 25

435 A216 25r multicolored 5.00 3.00

First South Asian Regional Cooperation Summit — A217

1985, Dec. 8 *Perf. 14*

436 A217 5r Flags 1.10 .50

Temple of Jaleshwar, Mohottary Underwater Project — A218

1985, Dec. 15 Litho. *Perf. 14x13½*

437 A218 10p shown .20 .20
438 A218 1r Temple of Shaileshwari, Doti .25 .20
439 A218 2r Lake Phoksundo, Dolpa .40 .20
Nos. 437-439 (3) .85 .60

Intl. Youth Year — A219

Devi Ghat Hydro-electric Dam Project A220

1985, Dec. 21 *Perf. 14*

440 A219 1r multicolored .25 .20

1985, Dec. 28 Litho. *Perf. 14*

441 A220 2r multicolored .55 .25

King Birendra, 40th Birthday — A221

Panchayat System, 25th Anniv. — A222

1985, Dec. 28

442 A221 50p Portrait .20 .20

1986, Apr. 10 *Perf. 13½*

443 A222 4r multicolored .90 .50

Pharping Hydroelectric Station, 75th Anniv. — A223

1986, Oct. 9 Litho. *Perf. 14x13½*

444 A223 15p multicolored .20 .20

Architecture, Artifacts — A224

1986, Oct. 9 Photo. *Perf. 13x13½*

445 A224 5p Pashupati Temple .20 .20
446 A224 10p Lumbini Fort .20 .20
446A A224 50p like 5p ('87) .20 .20
447 A224 1r Crown of Nepal .20 .20
Nos. 445-447 (4) .80 .80

No. 446A issued Apr. 14.

Asian Productivity Org., 25th Anniv. A225

1986, Oct. 26 Litho. *Perf. 13½x14*

448 A225 1r multicolored .25 .20

Reclining Buddha, Kathmandu Valley — A226

Mt. Pumori, Khumbu Range A227

Perf. 14, 13½x13

1986, Oct. 26 Litho.

449 A226 60p multicolored .20 .20
450 A227 8r multicolored 1.50 .75

King Birendra, 41st Birthday — A228

Intl. Peace Year — A229

1986, Dec. 28 Litho. *Perf. 13x13½*

451 A228 1r multicolored .25 .20

1986, Dec. 28 *Perf. 14*

452 A229 10r multicolored 1.60 .85

Social Service Natl. Coordination Council, 10th Anniv. — A230

1987, Sept. 22 Litho. *Perf. 13½*

453 A230 1r Natl. flag, emblem .25 .20

Birth of Buddha A231

Design: Asoka Pillar, enlargement of commemorative text and bas-relief of birth.

1987, Oct. 28 *Perf. 14*

454 A231 4r multicolored .75 .45

First Natl. Boy Scout Jamboree, Kathmandu — A232

1987, Oct. 28 Litho. *Perf. 14*

455 A232 1r multicolored .45 .20

A233

A234

1987, Nov. 2

456 A233 60p gold & lake .20 .20

3rd SAARC (Southeast Asian Assoc. for Regional Cooperation) Summit Conference, Kathmandu.

1987, Nov. 10

457 A234 4r multicolored .75 .45

Rastriya Samachar Samiti nNatl. news agency), 25th anniv.

Intl. Year of Shelter for the Homeless A235

1987, Dec. 21 Litho. *Perf. 14*

458 A235 5r multicolored .85 .85

Kashthamandap Temple, Kathmandu A236

Surya Bikram Gyawali (b. 1898), Historian — A237

1987, Dec. 21 Photo. *Perf. 13½x13*

459 A236 25p multicolored .20 .20

1987, Dec. 21 *Perf. 13x13½*

460 A237 60p multicolored .20 .20

King Birendra, 42nd Birthday — A238

Perf. 14½x13½

1987, Dec. 28 Litho.

461 A238 25p multicolored .20 .20

Mount Kanjiroba A239

1987, Dec. 30 *Perf. 14*

462 A239 10r multicolored 1.70 1.00

Crown Prince Dipendra's 18th Birthday — A240

Nepal Bank, Ltd., 50th Anniv. — A241

1988, Mar. 28 Litho. *Perf. 14*

463 A240 1r multicolored .25 .20

1988, Apr. 8

464 A241 2r multicolored .40 .25

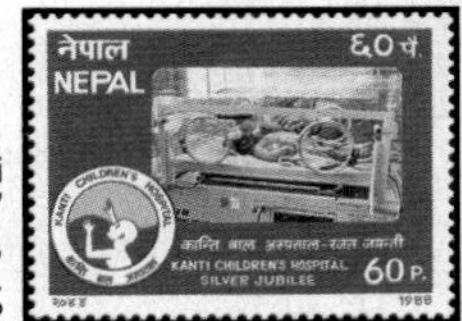

Kanti Childrens' Hospital, 25th Anniv. A242

1988, Apr. 8

465 A242 60p multicolored .20 .20

Royal Shuklaphanta Wildlife Reserve A243

1988, Apr. 8

466 A243 60p Swamp deer .35 .20

A244

A245

1988, Aug. 20 Litho. ***Perf. 14x13½***
467 A244 5r multicolored .95 .75

Queen Mother Ratna Rajya Laxmi Devi Shah, 60th birthday.

1988, Sept. 12 Litho. ***Perf. 14x13½***
468 A245 1r dull fawn & dark red .25 .20

Nepal Red Cross, 25th anniv.

Bindhyabasini, Pokhara — A246

1988, Oct. 16 Litho. ***Perf. 14½***
469 A246 15p multicolored .20 .20

A247

A248

1988, Dec. 28 Litho. ***Perf. 14***
470 A247 4r multicolored .70 .45

King Birendra, 43rd birthday.

1989, Mar. 3 Litho. ***Perf. 13½x14***
471 A248 1r Temple .25 .20

Pashupati Area Development Trust.

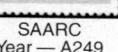

SAARC Year — A249

A250

1989, Dec. 8 ***Perf. 13x13½***
472 A249 60p multicolored .20 .20

Combating Drug Abuse & Trafficking.

1989, Oct. 5 ***Perf. 14***
473 A250 4r vio, brt grn & blk .50 .30

Asia-Pacific Telecommunity, 10th anniv.

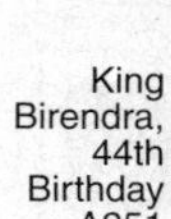

King Birendra, 44th Birthday A251

Perf. 13½x14½
1989, Dec. 28 Litho.
474 A251 2r multicolored .35 .20

Child Survival — A252

Design: Oral rehydration therapy, immunization, breast-feeding and growth monitoring.

1989, Dec. 31 ***Perf. 13½***
475 A252 1r multicolored .20 .20

Rara Natl. Park — A253

1989, Dec. 31 ***Perf. 14½x15***
476 A253 4r multicolored .50 .30

Mt. Ama Dablam A254

1989, Dec. 31 ***Perf. 14***
477 A254 5r multicolored .75 .30

A255

A257

Temple of the Goddess Manakamana, Gorkha — A256

1990, Jan. 3
478 A255 1r multicolored .20 .20

Crown Prince Dipendra investiture, Jan. 3.

1990, Apr. 12 Litho. ***Perf. 14½***
479 A256 60p deep blue & black .20 .20

1990, Aug. 20 Litho. ***Perf. 14***
480 A257 1r multicolored .20 .20

Nepal Children's Organization, 25th anniv.

A258

A259

1990, Sept. 13 Litho. ***Perf. 14x13½***
481 A258 60p orange, blue & red .20 .20

Bir Hospital, cent.

1990, Oct. 9 ***Perf. 14½***
482 A259 4r multicolored .55 .30

Asian-Pacific Postal Training Center, 20th anniv.

SAARC Year of the Girl Child A260

1990, Dec. 24 Litho. ***Perf. 14½***
483 A260 4.60r multicolored .65 .30

Bageshwori Temple, Nepalganj A261

Mt. Saipal A262

1990, Dec. 24 ***Perf. 13½***
484 A261 1r multicolored .20 .20
485 A262 5r multicolored .70 .30

B.P. Koirala (1914-82) — A263

King Birendra, 45th Birthday A264

1990, Dec. 31 ***Perf. 14***
486 A263 60p red, org brn & blk .25 .20

1990, Dec. 28
487 A264 2r multicolored .20 .20

Royal Chitwan Natl. Park A265

1991, Feb. 10 Litho. ***Perf. 14½***
488 A265 4r multicolored .75 .30

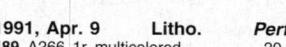

Restoration of Multiparty Democracy, 1st Anniv. — A266

Natl. Census — A267

1991, Apr. 9 Litho. ***Perf. 14***
489 A266 1r multicolored .20 .20

1991, May 3 ***Perf. 14x13½***
490 A267 60p multicolored .20 .20

A268

A269

1991, Aug. 15 ***Perf. 14½x13½***
491 A268 3r multicolored .35 .25

Federation of Nepalese Chambers of Commerce and Industry, 25th anniv.

1991, Sept. 4 Litho. ***Perf. 14***
492 A269 60p gray & red .20 .20

Nepal Junior Red Cross, 25th anniv.

Re-establishment of Parliament, 1st Session — A270

1991, Sept. 10 ***Perf. 14½***
493 A270 1r multicolored .20 .20

Constitution Day — A271

1991, Nov. 9 Litho. ***Perf. 15x14***
494 A271 50p multicolored .20 .20

Mt. Kumbhakarna — A272

1991, Oct. Litho. ***Perf. 13½x14***
495 A272 4.60r multicolored .55 .30

Vivaha Mandap — A274

SAARC Year of Shelter — A275

1991, Dec. 11 *Perf. 11½*

497 A274 1r multicolored .20 .20

1991, Dec. 28 *Perf. 13½x14*

498 A275 9r multicolored .95 .50

King Birendra, 46th Birthday — A276

1991, Dec. 28 *Perf. 14x13½*

499 A276 8r multicolored .90 .40

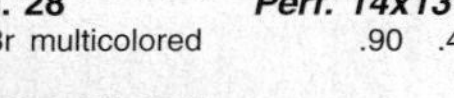

Nepal Philatelic Society, 25th Anniv. — A277

1992, July 11 **Litho.** *Perf. 13*

500 A277 4r multicolored .45 .25

Protect the Environment A278

1992, Oct. 24 **Litho.** *Perf. 12½x13*

501 A278 60p multicolored .20 .20

Rights of the Child A279

1992, Oct. 24 *Perf. 13½x13*

502 A279 1r multicolored .20 .20

A280

A281

Temples: 75p, Thakurdwara. 1r, Namo Buddha. 2r, Narijhowa. 11r, Dantakali.

1992, Nov. 10 *Perf. 14*

503 A280 75p multicolored .20 .20
504 A280 1r multicolored .20 .20
505 A280 2r multicolored .20 .20
506 A280 11r multicolored 1.50 .50
Nos. 503-506 (4) 2.10 1.10

No. 506 is airmail.

1992, Dec. 20 **Photo.** *Perf. 13x13½*

507 A281 40p brown & green .20 .20

Agricultural Development Bank, 25th anniv.

Birds — A282

1r, Pin-tailed green pigeon. 3r, Bohemian waxwing. 25r, Rufous-tailed finch lark.

1992, Dec. 20 **Litho.** *Perf. 11½*

508 A282 1r multicolored .20 .20
509 A282 3r multicolored .40 .20
510 A282 25r multicolored 2.75 1.25
Nos. 508-510 (3) 3.35 1.65

King Birendra, 47th Birthday A283

1992, Dec. 28 *Perf. 12½x13*

511 A283 7r multicolored .80 .40

Poets A284

1992 Summer Olympics, Barcelona A285

Designs: No. 512, Pandit Kulchandra Gautam. No. 513, Chittadhar Hridaya. No. 514, Vidyapati. No. 515, Teongsi Sirijunga.

1992, Dec. 31 *Perf. 11½*

512 A284 1r blue & multi .20 .20
513 A284 1r brown & multi .20 .20
514 A284 1r tan & multi .20 .20
515 A284 1r gray & multi .20 .20
Nos. 512-515 (4) .80 .80

1992, Dec. 31

516 A285 25r multicolored 3.00 1.50

Fish — A286

Designs: 25p, Tor putitora. 1r, Schizothorax plagiostomus. 5r, Anguilla bengalensis, temple of Chhabdi Barahi. 10r, Psilorhynchus pseudecheneis.

1993, Aug. 6 **Litho.** *Perf. 11½*

Granite Paper

517 A286 25p multicolored .20 .20
518 A286 1r multicolored .20 .20
519 A286 5r multicolored .35 .35
520 A286 10r multicolored .75 .75
a. Souvenir sheet of 4, #517-520 1.75 1.75
Nos. 517-520 (4) 1.50 1.50

World AIDS Day — A287

1993, Dec. 1 **Litho.** *Perf. 13½x14½*

521 A287 1r multicolored .20 .20

Tanka Prasad Acharga — A288

1993, Dec. 2 *Perf. 13½*

522 A288 25p shown .20 .20
523 A288 1r Sungdare Sherpa .20 .20
524 A288 7r Siddhi Charan Shrestha .50 .30
525 A288 15r Falgunand 1.10 .65
Nos. 522-525 (4) 2.00 1.35

Holy Places A289

1.50r, Halesi Mahadev, Khotang. 5r, Devghat, Tanahun. 8r, Bagh Bhairab, Kirtipur.

Perf. 13½x14½

1993, Dec. 28 **Litho.**

526 A289 1.50r multicolored .20 .20
527 A289 5r multicolored .35 .35
528 A289 8r multicolored .60 .60
Nos. 526-528 (3) 1.15 1.15

Tourism A290

Designs: 5r, Tushahiti Sundari Chowk, Patan. 8r, White water rafting.

1993, Dec. 28

529 A290 5r multicolored .35 .35
530 A290 8r multicolored .60 .60

King Birendra, 48th Birthday — A291

1993, Dec. 28 *Perf. 14*

531 A291 10r multicolored .75 .40

Large Building, Courtyard A293

Pagoda, Courtyard A293a

Monument A294

Arms A295

Fort — A296

Mt. Everest — A299

Pagoda (Nyata Pola) — A300

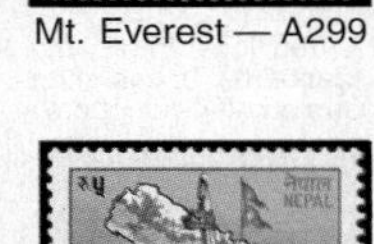

Map of Nepal — A301

Design: 50p, Pagoda, vert.

Perf. 14½, 12, (#533A, 538, 540)

Photo., Litho. (#533A, 538, 540)

1994-96

533 A293 10p green .20 .20
533A A293a 10p claret & black .20 .20
534 A294 20p violet brown .20 .20
535 A295 25p carmine .20 .20
536 A296 30p slate .20 .20
537 A293 50p dark blue .20 .20
538 A293a 50p black & claret .20 .20
539 A299 1r multicolored .20 .20
539A A300 1r blue & claret .20 .20

Perf. 14½x13½

540 A301 5r multicolored .35 .35
Nos. 533-540 (10) 2.15 2.15

Issued: 20p, 25p, 30p, 5/17/94; #539, 7/6/94; 5r, 9/22/94; #533, 537, 1995; #533A, 538, 539A, 10/9/96. This is an expanding set. Numbers may change.

Pasang Lhamu Sherpa (1960-1993) A304

1994, Sept 2 **Litho.** *Perf. 14*

544 A304 10r multicolored .75 .40

Stop Smoking Campaign A305

1994, Sept. 26 *Perf. 13½x14*

545 A305 1r multicolored .20 .20

A306

A307

Methods of transporting mail.

1994, Oct. 9 *Perf. 13x13½*
546 A306 1.50r multicolored .20 .20

1994, Oct. 9 *Perf. 14*

Traditional Weapons: No. 547: a, Daggers, scabbards. b, Yataghans. c, Sabers, shield. d, Carved stone daggers.

547 A307 5r Block of 4, #a.-d. 1.50 1.50

ILO, 75th Anniv. A308

1994, Oct. 9 *Perf. 13*
548 A308 15r blue & bister 1.10 .75

World Food Day — A309

1994, Oct. 23 *Perf. 14*
549 A309 25r multicolored 1.90 1.00

A310 A311

Orchids: a, Dendrobium densiflorum. b, Coelogyne flaccida. c, Cymbidium devonianum. d, Coelogyne corymbosa.

1994, Nov. 7 *Perf. 14x13½*
550 A310 10r Block of 4, #a.-d. 4.00 4.00

1994, Dec. 5 *Perf. 12½x13*
551 A311 9r green & red .75 .70

Intl. Year of the Family.

A312

A313

1994, Dec. 7
552 A312 11r blue & bister .80 .80

ICAO, 50th anniv.

1994, Dec. 20 *Perf. 14*

Mushrooms.

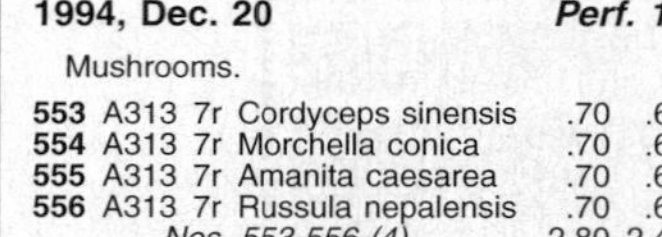

553 A313 7r Cordyceps sinensis .70 .60
554 A313 7r Morchella conica .70 .60
555 A313 7r Amanita caesarea .70 .60
556 A313 7r Russula nepalensis .70 .60
Nos. 553-556 (4) 2.80 2.40

Famous Men — A314

Designs: 1r, Dharanidhar Koirala, poet. 2r, Narayan Gopal Guruwacharya, singer. 6r, Bahadur Shah, military leader, vert. 7r, Balaguru Shadananda, religious leader.

1994, Dec. 23 *Perf. 13½x14, 14x13½*
557 A314 1r multicolored .20 .20
558 A314 2r multicolored .20 .20
559 A314 6r multicolored .45 .45
560 A314 7r multicolored .50 .50
Nos. 557-560 (4) 1.35 1.35

King Birendra, 49th Birthday A315

1994, Dec. 28 *Perf. 14*
561 A315 9r multicolored .70 .70

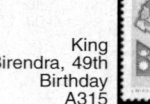

Tilicho Lake, Manang A316

11r, Taleju Temple, Katmandou, vert.

1994, Dec. 28 *Perf. 13½x14, 14x13½*
562 A316 9r multicolored .70 .70
563 A316 11r multicolored .80 .80

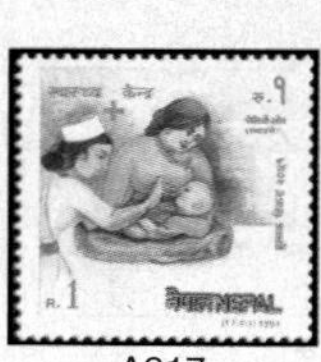
A317

A318

Care of Children: #564: a, Vaccination. b, Education. c, Playground activities. d, Stamp collecting.

1994, Dec. 30 *Perf. 14*
564 A317 1r Block of 4, #a.-d. .45 .45

1995, June 23 **Litho.** *Perf. 14x13½*
565 A318 2r red & black .20 .20

Fight against cancer.

A319

A320

Famous People: a, Bhim Nidhi Tiwari, writer. b, Yuddha Prasad Mishra, writer. c, Chandra Man Singh Maskey, artist. d, Parijat, writer.

1995, July 11 *Perf. 14*
566 A319 3r Block of 4, #a.-d. 1.00 1.00

1995, Sept. 1 **Litho.** *Perf. 14x13½*

Famous Men: 15p, Bhakti Thapa, warrior. 1r, Madan Bhandari, politician. 4r, Prakash Raj Kaphley, human rights activist.

567 A320 15p multicolored .20 .20
568 A320 1r multicolored .20 .20
569 A320 4r multicolored .30 .30
Nos. 567-569 (3) .70 .70

Animals A321

Designs: a, Bos gaurus. b, Felis lynx. c, Macaca assamensis. d, Hyaena hyaena.

1995, Sept. 1 **Litho.** *Perf. 12*
570 A321 10p Block of 4, #a.-d. 3.00 3.00

Tourism A322

1r, Bhimeshwor Temple, Dolakha, vert. 5r, Ugra Tara Temple, Dadeldhura. 7r, Mt. Nampa. 18r, Thanka art, Nrity Aswora, vert.

Perf. 14x13½, 13½x14

1995, Nov. 8 **Litho.**
574 A322 1r multicolored .20 .20
575 A322 5r multicolored .40 .35
576 A322 7r multicolored .55 .50

Size: 26x39mm

577 A322 18r multicolored 1.40 1.25
Nos. 574-577 (4) 2.55 2.30

FAO, 50th Anniv. A323

1995, Oct. 16 **Litho.** *Perf. 13½x14*
578 A323 7r multicolored .60 .45

UN, 50th Anniv. A324

1995, Oct. 22 **Litho.** *Perf. 11½*

Granite Paper

579 A324 50r multicolored 3.75 3.25

Lumbini, Birth Place of Gautama Buddha — A325

1995, Dec. 23 **Litho.** *Perf. 14*
580 A325 20r multicolored 1.60 1.40

King Birendra, 50th Birthday
A326 A327

1995, Dec. 28 *Perf. 12*

Granite Paper (No. 581)

581 A326 1r multicolored .20 .20

Perf. 13x13½

582 A327 12r multicolored 1.00 .85

SAARC, 10th Anniv. A328

1995, Dec. 28 *Perf. 13½*
583 A328 10r multicolored .80 .70

Karnali Bridge — A329

1996, May 13 **Litho.** *Perf. 14*
584 A329 7r multicolored .60 .50

1996 Summer Olympic Games, Atlanta — A330

1996, Oct. 9 **Photo.** *Perf. 12*

Granite Paper

585 A330 7r multicolored .60 .45

Kaji Kalu Pande A331

Hem Raj Sharma, Grammarian A332

#587, Pushpa Lal Shrestha. #589, Padma Prasad Bhattarai, scholar, philosopher. #590, Suvarna Shamsher Rana. #591, Bhawani Bhikshu, novelist, writer.

Perf. 13½x14, 14x13½

1996, Aug. 6 **Litho.**
586 A331 75p multicolored .20 .20
587 A331 1r multicolored .20 .20
588 A332 1r multicolored .20 .20
589 A332 3r multicolored .25 .20
590 A331 5r multicolored .40 .30
591 A332 5r multicolored .40 .30
Nos. 586-591 (6) 1.65 1.40

See Nos. 614-615.

Asoka Pillar, Lumbini — A333

1996, Dec. 1 Litho. *Perf. 11½*
592 A333 12r multicolored 1.60 .85

Tourism A334

Designs: 1r, Arjun Dhara, Jhapa. 2r, Palace of Nuwakot. 8r, Traditional Gaijatra, Bhaktapur. 10r, Begnash Lake, Kaski.

1996, Nov. 20 Litho. *Perf. 14*
593 A334 1r multicolored .20 .20
594 A334 2r multicolored .20 .20
595 A334 8r multicolored .70 .50
596 A334 10r multicolored .90 .65
Nos. 593-596 (4) 2.00 1.55

Butterflies and Birds — A335

Designs: a, Krishna pea-cock butterfly. b, Great Himalayan barbet. c, Sarus crane. d, Northern junglequeen butterfly.

1996, Nov. 20 Litho. *Perf. 14*
597 A335 5r Block of 4, #a.-d. 2.50 2.50

Annapurna Mountain Range — A336

Designs: a, Annapurna South, Annapurna I. b, Machhapuchhre, Annapurna III. c, Annapurna IV, Annapurna II.

1996, Dec. 28 Litho. *Perf. 14*
601 A336 18r Strip of 3, #a.-c. 3.75 3.75

King Birendra, 51st Birthday — A337

1996, Dec. 28 Photo. *Perf. 12*
Granite Paper
602 A337 10r multicolored .65 .65

Accession of King Birendra to Throne, 25th Anniv. A338

1997, Feb. 1 Litho. *Perf. 14*
603 A338 2r multicolored .20 .20

Nepal Postal Service — A339

1997, Apr. 12 Litho. *Perf. 14*
604 A339 2r brown & red .20 .20

Nepalese-Japanese Diplomatic Relations, 40th Anniv. — A340

1997, Apr. 6 Photo. *Perf. 12*
605 A340 18r multicolored 1.50 1.10

Visit Nepal '98 — A341

2r, Emblem. 10r, Upper Mustang. 18r, Rafting Sunkoshi. 20r, Changunarayan (Bhaktapur), vert.

1997, July 6 Litho. *Perf. 14*
606 A341 2r multicolored .20 .20
607 A341 10r multicolored 1.00 .70
608 A341 18r multicolored 1.75 1.10
609 A341 20r multicolored 2.00 1.25
Nos. 606-608 (3) 2.95 2.00

A342

A343

Traditional costumes.

1997, Sept. 30 Litho. *Perf. 14*
610 A342 5r Rana Tharu .45 .30
611 A342 5r Gurung .45 .30
612 A342 5r Chepang .45 .30
Nos. 610-612 (3) 1.35 .90

1997, Sept. 30 *Perf. 11½*
613 A343 20r multicolored 1.60 1.25

Diplomatic relations between Nepal and US, 50th anniv.

Personality Type of 1996

Designs: No. 614, Riddhi Bahadur Malla, writer. No. 615, Dr. K.I. Singh, political leader.

1997, Nov. 6 Litho. *Perf. 11½*
614 A332 2r multicolored .20 .20
615 A332 2r multicolored .20 .20

A344

Traditional Technology A345

#616, Janto (grinder), horiz. #617, Dhiki, horiz. #618, Okhal. #619, Kol (oil mill).

1997, Dec. 29 Litho. *Perf. 14*
616 A344 5r multicolored .40 .30
617 A344 5r multicolored .40 .30
618 A344 5r multicolored .40 .30
619 A345 5r multicolored .40 .30
Nos. 616-619 (4) 1.60 1.20

Flowers A346

40p, Jasminum gracile. 1r, Callistephus chinensis. 2r, Manglietia insignis. 15r, Luculia gratissima.

1997, Dec. 11
620 A346 40p multicolored .20 .20
621 A346 1r multicolored .20 .20
622 A346 2r multicolored .20 .20
623 A346 15r multicolored 1.25 .85
Nos. 620-623 (4) 1.85 1.45

King Birendra, 52nd Birthday — A347

1997, Dec. 29 Photo. *Perf. 11½*
624 A347 10r multicolored .75 .60

Visit Nepal '98 — A348

Designs: 2r, Sunrise, Shree Antudanda, Ilam. 10r, Maitidevi Temple, Kathmandu. 18r, Great Reunification Gate, Kapilavastu. 20r, Mt. Cholatse, Solukhumbu, vert.

1998, May 8 Photo. *Perf. 11½*
625 A348 2r multicolored .20 .20
626 A348 10r multicolored .75 .30
627 A348 18r multicolored 1.25 .60
628 A348 20r multicolored 1.50 .65
Nos. 625-628 (4) 3.70 1.75

Famous People — A349

Designs: 75p, Ram Prasad Rai, freedom fighter. 1r, Imansingh Chemjong, philologist. No. 631, Tulsi Meher Shrestha, social worker. No. 632, Dadhi Ram Marasini, Sanskrit expert. 5.40r, Mahananda Sapkota, linguist.

1998, June 26 Litho. *Perf. 14x13½*
629 A349 75p brown & black .20 .20
630 A349 1r rose lilac & black .20 .20
631 A349 2r blue & black .25 .20
632 A349 2r olive & black .25 .20
633 A349 5.40r red & black .40 .20
Nos. 629-633 (5) 1.30 1.00

1998 World Cup Soccer Championships, France — A350

1998, June 26 *Perf. 14*
634 A350 12r multicolored .90 .60

Ganesh Man Singh (1915-97), Senior Democratic Leader A351

1998, Sept. 18 Photo. *Perf. 11½*
635 A351 5r multicolored .35 .25

Peace Keeping Mission of the Royal Nepalese Army, 40th Anniv. A352

1998, Oct. 9 Litho. *Perf. 13½x13*
636 A352 10r multicolored .75 .30

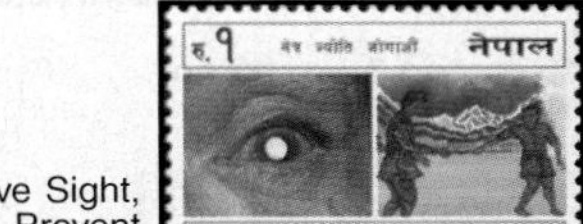
Save Sight, Prevent Blindness A353

1998, Nov. 29 Photo. *Perf. 12*
Granite Paper
637 A353 1r multicolored .20 .20

Snakes A354

1.70r, King cobra. 2r, Golden tree snake. 5r, Asiatic rock python. 10r, Karan's pit viper.

1998, Nov. 29 Litho. *Perf. 14*

638 A354 1.70r multicolored .20 .20
639 A354 2r multicolored .30 .20
640 A354 5r multicolored .40 .20
641 A354 10r multicolored .75 .30
Nos. 638-641 (4) 1.65 .90

Universal Declaration of Human Rights, 50th Anniv. A355

1998, Dec. 10 Litho. *Perf. 14*

642 A355 10r multicolored .75 .30

A356

A357

1998, Dec. 27 *Perf. 14x13½*

643 A356 10r multicolored .75 .30

Asian and Pacific Decade of Disabled Persons, 1993-2002.

1998, Dec. 29 *Perf. 13x13½*

644 A357 2r multicolored .20 .20

King Birendra, 53rd birthday.

Marsyangdi Dam and Hydro-Electric Power Station — A358

1998, Dec. 29 *Perf. 11½*
Granite Paper

645 A358 12r multicolored .90 .45

Nepal Eye Hospital, 25th Anniv. A359

1999, Apr. 8 Litho. *Perf. 14*

646 A359 2r multicolored .20 .20

Tourism A360

Designs: No. 647, Kalika Bhagawati Temple, Baglung. No. 648, Chandan Nath Temple, vert. 12r, Bajra Yogini Temple, Sankhu, vert. No. 650, Mt. Everest. No. 651, Lumbini Pillar Script translated into English.

1999, June 7 *Perf. 13½x13, 13x13½*

647 A360 2r multicolored .20 .20
648 A360 2r multicolored .20 .20
649 A360 12r multicolored 1.25 .50
650 A360 15r multicolored 1.40 .65
651 A360 15r multicolored 1.40 .65
Nos. 647-651 (5) 4.45 2.20

Tetracerus Quadricornis A361

1999, June 7 Photo. *Perf. 11¾*
Granite Paper

652 A361 10r shown .85 .40
653 A361 10r Ovis ammon hodgsonii .85 .40

8th SAF Games, Kathmandu A362

Perf. 13½x14¼
1999, Sept. 30 Litho.

654 A362 10r multicolored .90 .40

UPU, 125th Anniv. — A363

1999, Oct. 9 *Perf. 13½*

655 A363 15r multicolored 1.25 .60

Famous People A364

Designs: No. 656, Ram Narayan Mishra (1922-67), freedom fighter. No. 657, Bhupi Sherchan (1935-89), poet. No. 658, Master Mitrasen (1895-1946), writer. No. 659, Rudra Raj Pandey (1901-87), writer. No. 660, Gopal Prasad Rimal (1917-73), writer. No. 661, Mangaladevi Singh (1924-96), politician.

1999, Nov. 20 Litho. *Perf. 13¾*

656 A364 1r multicolored .20 .20
657 A364 1r multicolored .20 .20
658 A364 1r multicolored .20 .20
659 A364 2r multicolored .20 .20
660 A364 2r multicolored .20 .20
661 A364 2r multicolored .20 .20
Nos. 656-661 (6) 1.20 1.20

Dances A365

1999, Dec. 26 Litho. *Perf. 11¾x12*

662 A365 5r Sorathi .45 .20
663 A365 5r Bhairav .45 .20
664 A365 5r Jhijhiya .45 .20
Nos. 662-664 (3) 1.35 .60

Intl. Labor Organization's Campaign Against Child Labor — A366

1999, Dec. 29 *Perf. 13½x14¼*

665 A366 12r multi 1.10 .50

A367

A368

1999, Dec. 29 *Perf. 14¼x13½*

666 A367 5r multi .45 .20

King Birendra's 54th birthday.

2000, Apr. 2 Photo. *Perf. 12x11¾*
Granite Paper

667 A368 15r multi 1.25 .45

Queen Aishwarya Rajya Laxmi Devi Shah, 50th birthday (in 1999).

Radio Nepal, 50th Anniv. A369

2000, Apr. 2 Litho. *Perf. 13½x14¼*

668 A369 2r multi .20 .20

Gorkhapatra Newspaper, Cent. — A370

2000, May 5 *Perf. 14*

669 A370 10r multi .75 .30

Tourism A371

Designs: 12r, Tchorolpa Glacial Lake, Dolakha. 15r, Dakshinkali Temple, Kathmandu. 18r, Annapurna.

2000, June 30 Litho. *Perf. 13¾x14*

670-672 A371 Set of 3 3.50 1.25

First ascent of Annapurna, 50th anniv. (No. 672).

Rani Pokhari and Temple, Kathmandu A372

Frame color: 50p, Orange. 1r, Blue. 2r, Brown.

2000, July 7 Photo. *Perf. 11½*

673-675 A372 Set of 3 .30 .20

Geneva Conventions, 50th Anniv. A373

2000, Sept. 7 Litho. *Perf. 13½x14¼*

676 A373 5r multi .45 .20

2000 Summer Olympics, Sydney A374

2000, Sept. 7 Photo. *Perf. 11¾x12*
Granite Paper

677 A374 25r multi 2.25 .70

Famous People — A375

Designs: No. 678, 2r, Hridayachandra Singh Pradhan, writer (olive green frame). No. 679, 2r, Thir Bam Malla, revolutionary (brown frame). No. 680, 5r, Krishna Prasad Koirala, social reformer (indigo frame). No. 681, 5r, Manamohan Adhikari, politician (red frame).

2000, Sept. 7 Litho. *Perf. 14*

678-681 A375 Set of 4 1.10 .40

Worldwide Fund for Nature (WWF) A376

#682, Bengal florican. #683, Lesser adjutant stork. #684, Female greater one-horned rhinoceros and calf. #685, Male greater one-horned rhinoceros.

2000, Nov. 14 Photo. *Perf. 11¾*
Granite Paper

682-685 A376 10r Set of 4 5.00 3.00

King Birendra's 55th Birthday — A377

2000, Dec. 28 Photo. *Perf. 12x11¾*
Granite Paper

686 A377 5r multi .45 .20

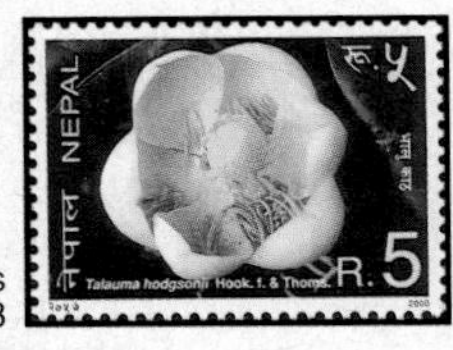

Flowers
A378

Designs: No. 687, Talauma hodgsonii. No. 688, Mahonia napaulensis. No. 689, Dactylorhiza hatagirea, vert.

2000, Dec. 28 ***Perf. 11¾x12, 12x11¾***
Granite Paper

687-689 A378 5r Set of 3 1.25 .45

Establishment of Democracy, 50th Anniv.
A379

Perf. 11¾x11½

2001, Feb. 16 **Photo.**
Granite Paper

690 A379 5r King Tribhuvan .45 .20

2001 Census
A380

2001, Apr. 17 **Photo.** ***Perf. 11¾***
Granite Paper

691 A380 2r multi .20 .20

Famous Nepalese — A381

Designs: No. 692, 2r, Khaptad Baba (bright pink background, white Nepalese numeral at UR), ascetic. No. 693, 2r, Bhikkhu Pragyananada Mahathera (red violet background), religious teacher. No. 694, 2r, Guru Prasad Mainali (pink background, red Nepalese numeral at UR), writer. No. 695, 2r, Tulsi Lal Amatya (brown violet background), politician. No. 696, 2r, Madan Lal Agrawal (light blue background), industrialist.

Perf. 14¼x13½

2001, June 29 **Litho.**

692-696 A381 Set of 5 .75 .75

Ficus Religiosa — A382

2001, Nov. 2 **Litho.** ***Perf. 14¼x13½***

697 A382 10r multi .90 .45

UN High Commissioner for Refugees, 50th Anniv. — A383

2001, Nov. 2 ***Perf. 14***

698 A383 20r multi 1.50 .75

Herbs — A384

Designs: 5r, Water pennywort. 15r, Rockfoil. 30r, Himalayan yew.

2001, Nov. 2 ***Perf. 13¾***

699-701 A384 Set of 3 4.00 2.00

Nepalese Flag — A385

2001, Nov. 28 ***Perf. 14***

702 A385 10r multi .30 .30

King Birendra (1945-2001)
A386

2001, Dec. 28 ***Perf. 14¼x13½***

703 A386 15r multi 1.25 .40

Year of Dialogue Among Civilizations
A387

2001, Dec. 28 ***Perf. 14***

704 A387 30r multi 2.50 .80

Tourism
A388

Designs: 2r, Amargadi Fort. 5r, Hiranyavarna Mahavihar, vert. 15r, Jugal Mountain Range.

Perf. 13½x14¼, 14¼x13½

2001, Dec. 28

705-707 A388 Set of 3 2.00 1.00

Nepal Scouts, 50th Anniv. — A389

2002, Apr. 9 **Litho.** ***Perf. 14¼x13½***

708 A389 2r red brn & olive .25 .20

2002 World Cup Soccer Championships, Japan and Korea — A390

2002, May 31 **Litho.** ***Perf. 13½x12¾***

709 A390 15r multi 1.25 .40

King Gyanendra's Accession to Throne, 1st Anniv. — A391

2002, June 5 ***Perf. 13¾***

710 A391 5r multi .45 .20

King Birendra (1945-2001) and Queen Aishwarya (1949-2001)
A392

2002, June 5 ***Perf. 14***

711 A392 10r multi .45 .25

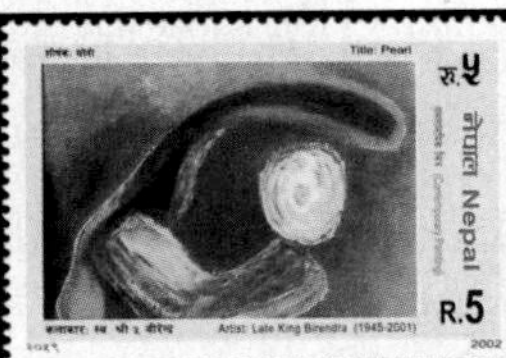

Paintings — A393

Designs: No. 712, 5r, Pearl, by King Birendra. No. 713, 5r, Aryabalokiteshwor, by Siddhimuni Shakya, vert.

Perf. 13½x13¾, 13¾x13½

2002, July 29

712-713 A393 Set of 2 .90 .60

Insects — A394

Designs: 3r, Leaf beetle. 5r, Locust.

2002, Sept. 6 ***Perf. 14***

714-715 A394 Set of 2 .90 .40

Societal Messages
A395

Designs: 1r, Untouchable family behind barbed wire (untouchables should not be discriminated against). 2r, Children and parents waving (female children should not be discriminated against).

2002, Sept. 6 ***Perf. 14¼x14***

716-717 A395 Set of 2 .20 .20

Intl. Year of Mountains — A396

2002, Oct. 9 **Litho.** ***Perf. 14***

718 A396 5r multi .45 .25

Tourism
A397

Designs: No. 719, 5r, Mt. Nilgiri, Mustang. No. 720, 5r, Pathibhara Devisthan, Taplejung. No. 721, 5r, Ramgram Stupa, Hawalparasi. No. 722, 5r, Galeshwor Mahadevsthan, Myagdi.

2002, Oct. 9

719-722 A397 Set of 4 1.75 1.00

South Asian Association for Regional Cooperation Charter Day — A398

2002, Dec. 8 ***Perf. 13½x12¾***

723 A398 15r multi 1.25 .40

Famous Men — A399

Designs: 2r, Dava Bir Singh Kansakar, social worker. 25r, Rev. Ekai Kawaguchi (1866-1945), Buddhist scholar.

2002, Dec. 8 ***Perf. 13x13½***

724-725 A399 Set of 2 2.00 1.00

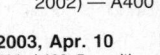

Nepal Chamber of Commerce, 50th Anniv. (in 2002) — A400

2003, Apr. 10 **Litho.** ***Perf. 14***

726 A400 5r multi .35 .20

Industry and Commerce Day — A401

2003, Apr. 11 *Perf. 13½x12¾*

727 A401 5r multi .35 .20

First Ascent of Mt. Everest, 50th Anniv. A402

2003, May 29 Litho. *Perf. 13½x14¼*

728 A402 25r multi 1.25 .70

Babu Chiri Sherpa (1965-2001), Mountaineer — A403

2003, June 27 *Perf. 14*

729 A403 5r multi .45 .20

King Gyanendra, 56th Birthday A404

2003, July 7 *Perf. 13½x14¼*

730 A404 5r multi .45 .20

Tea Garden, Eastern Nepal A405

2003, July 7 *Perf. 14*

731 A405 25r multi 1.25 .70

Dr. Dilli Raman Regmi (1913-2001), Politician and Historian — A406

2003, Aug. 31

732 A406 5r brown & blk .35 .20

Gopal Das Shrestha (1930-98), Journalist A407

2003, Sept. 23 Litho. *Perf. 14*

733 A407 5r multi .35 .20

Export Year 2003 — A408

2003, Oct. 9 *Perf. 13½x14*

734 A408 25r multi 1.25 .70

Sankhadhar Sakhwaa, Initiator of Nepalese Calendar A409

2003, Oct. 26 *Perf. 13½x12¾*

735 A409 5r multi .35 .20

Flowers — A410

No. 736: a, Lotus. b, Picrorhiza. c, Himalayan rhubarb. d, Night jasmine.

Perf. 14¼x13½

2003, Dec. 23 Litho.

736 A410 10r Block of 4, #a-d 1.50 1.50

Tourism A411

Designs: No. 737, 5r, Kali Gandaki "A" hydroelectric dam site. No. 738, 5r, Ganesh idol, Kageshwar, vert. 30r, Buddha icon, Swayambhunath.

2003, Dec. 23 *Perf. 14*

737-739 A411 Set of 3 1.75 1.10

Social Services of United Mission to Nepal, 50th Anniv. — A412

2004, Mar. 5 Litho. *Perf. 14*

740 A412 5r multi .20 .20

National Society of Comprehensive Eye Care, 25th Anniv. — A413

2004, Mar. 25

741 A413 5r multi .20 .20

Marwadi Sewa Samiti, 50th Anniv. A414

2004, Apr. 9

742 A414 5r multi .20 .20

King Gyanendra, 57th Birthday — A415

2004, July 7 Litho. *Perf. 14*

743 A415 5r multi .20 .20

Management Education, 50th Anniv. — A416

2004, Sept. 24 Litho. *Perf. 14*

744 A416 5r multi .20 .20

Asia-Pacific Telecommunity, 25th Anniv. — A417

2004, Sept. 24

745 A417 5r multi .20 .20

FIFA (Fédération Internationale de Football Association), Cent. — A418

2004, Sept. 24

746 A418 20r multi .55 .55

Mountains A419

No. 747: a, Mt. Everest. b, Mt. Kanchenjunga Main. c, Mt. Lhotse. d, Mt. Makalu I. e, Mt. Cho Oyu. f, Mt. Dhaulagiri. g, Mt. Manasalu. h, Mt. Annapurna I.

2004, Oct. 19 Litho. *Perf. 14*

747 Block of 8 2.40 2.40

a.-h. A419 10r Any single .30 .30

Famous Men — A420

Designs: No. 748, 5r, Nayaraj Panta (1913-2002), historian. No. 749, 5r, Narahari Nath (1914-2003), yogi.

2004, Nov. 3

748-749 A420 Set of 2 .30 .30

Flora and Fauna — A421

No. 750: a, Rufous piculet woodpecker. b, Giant atlas moth. c, Serma guru. d, High altitude rice.

Illustration reduced.

2004, Nov. 3

750 A421 10r Block of 4, #a-d 1.25 1.25

Mayadevi Temple, Lumbini A422

Gadhimai Temples, Bara A423

2004, Nov. 30 *Perf. 13½x13*

751 A422 10r multi .30 .30

752 A423 10r multi .30 .30

Madan Puraskar Trust, 50th Anniv. — A424

2004, Dec. 13 *Perf. 14*

753 A424 5r multi .20 .20

Sculptures — A425

No. 754: a, Jayavarma. b, Umamaheshwar. c, Vishwarupa. d, Banshagopal.
Illustration reduced.

2004, Dec. 27 ***Perf. 13½***
754 A425 10r Block of 4, #a-d 1.25 1.25

Nepal Rastra Bank, 50th Anniv. (in 2006) A426

2005, Apr. 27 **Litho.** ***Perf. 14***
755 A426 2r multi .20 .20

First Ascent of Mt. Makalu, 50th Anniv. — A427

2005, May 15
756 A427 10r multi .30 .30

First Ascent of Mt. Kanchanjunga, 50th Anniv. — A428

2005, May 25
757 A428 12r multi .35 .35

King Gyanendra, 58th Birthday — A429

2005, July 7 **Litho.** ***Perf. 14***
758 A429 5r multi .20 .20

Life of Buddha A430

No. 759: a, Birth at Lumbini. b, Enlightenment at Bodhagaya. c, First Sermon at Sarnath. d, Mahaparinirvana at Kushinagar.

2005, July 21
759 Horiz. strip of 4, any background color 1.25 1.25
a.-d. A430 10r Any single, any background color .30 .30
Sheet of 4 horiz. strips 5.00 —

The sheet has four horizontal strips with background colors of yellow, green, red and purple.

Queen Mother Ratna Rajya Laxmi Devi Shah A431

2005, Aug. 20
760 A431 20r multi .60 .60

Fruits and Nuts — A432

No. 761: a, Indian gooseberry. b, Walnut. c, Wood apple. d, Golden evergreen raspberry.
Illustration reduced.

2005, Aug. 20
761 A432 10r Block of 4, #a-d 1.25 1.25

Mammals A433

No. 762: a, Gangetic dolphin. b, Indian pangolin. c, Asiatic wild elephant. d, Clouded leopard.

2005, Aug. 31 **Litho.** ***Perf. 14***
762 Horiz. strip of 4, any background color 1.25 1.25
a.-d. A433 10r Any single, any background color .30 .30
Sheet of 4 horiz. strips 5.00 —

The sheet has four horizontal strips with background colors of yellow, green, red and purple.

Late Bhupalmansingh Karki, Social Worker — A434

2005, Sept. 24
763 A434 2r multi .20 .20

Tourism — A435

No. 764: a, Ghodaghodi Lake, Kailali. b, Budhasubba, Sunasari. c, Kalinchok Bhagawati, Dolakha. d, Panauti City, Kabhrepalanchok.
Illustration reduced.

2005, Oct. 9
764 A435 5r Block of 4, #a-d .60 .60

Diplomatic Relations Between Nepal and People's Republic of China, 50th Anniv. — A436

2005, Dec. 26
765 A436 30r multi .85 .85

Admission to United Nations, 50th Anniv. A437

2005, Dec. 26
766 A437 50r multi 1.40 1.40

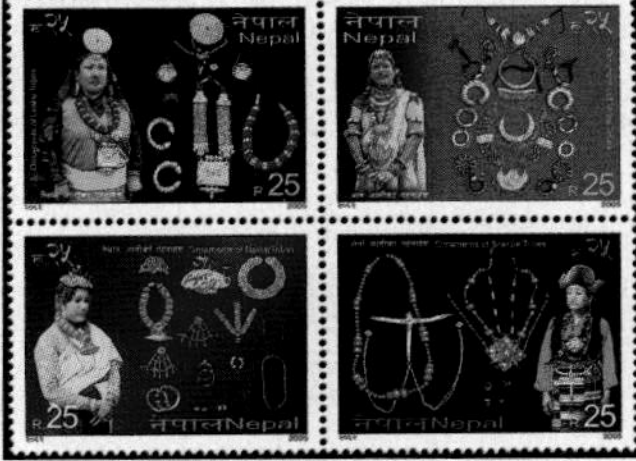

Tribal Ornaments — A438

No. 767 — Ornaments of: a, Limbu tribes. b, Tharu tribes. c, Newar tribes. d, Sherpa tribes.
Illustration reduced.

2005, Dec. 26
767 A438 25r Block of 4, #a-d 2.75 2.75

King Tribhuvan (1906-55) A439

2006, Feb. 17 **Litho.** ***Perf. 13¼x13***
768 A439 5r multi .20 .20

Democracy Day.

Queen Komal Rayja Laxmi Devi Shah — A440

2006, Mar. 8
769 A440 5r multi .20 .20

Intl. Women's Day.

World Hindu Federation, 25th Anniv. — A441

2006, Apr. 6 ***Perf. 12¾***
770 A441 2r multi .20 .20

First Ascent of Mt. Lhotse, 50th Anniv. A442

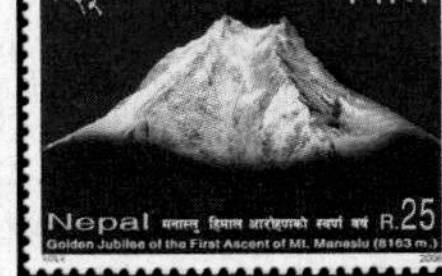

First Ascent of Mt. Manaslu, 50th Anniv. A443

2006, May 9 ***Perf. 13x13¼***
771 A442 25r multi .70 .70
772 A443 25r multi .70 .70

Supreme Court, 50th Anniv. A444

2006, May 21
773 A444 5r multi .20 .20

Fauna, Flora and Mushrooms A445

Designs: No. 774, Imperial butterfly. No. 774A, Nepalese primrose. No., 774B, Chaffer beetle. No. 774C, Beautiful stream frog. No. 774D, White pine mushroom.

2006, June 12 ***Perf. 12¾***
774-774D Set of 5 1.40 1.40

Nos. 774-774D were printed se-tenant, with Nos. 774-774C existing in a horizontal strip, with other strip combinations possibly existing, but stamps appearing in the marketplace are singles.

Diplomatic Relations Between Nepal and Russia, 50th Anniv. — A446

2006, Aug. 22 *Perf. 13¼x13*
775 A446 30r multi .85 .85

Diplomatic Relations Between Nepal and Japan, 50th Anniv. A447

2006, Sept. 1 *Perf. 13x13¼*
776 A447 30r multi .85 .85

Mt. Everest — A448

Stag Beetle — A449

2006, Sept. 19 *Perf. 14¼x14*
777 A448 1r blk & bl grn .20 .20
778 A449 2r black .20 .20

Perf. 14x13¾
Size: 29x25mm

779 A448 5r blk, pink & blue .20 .20
Nos. 777-779 (3) .60 .60

Membership in UPU, 50th Anniv. — A450

2006, Oct. 9 *Perf. 13x13¼*
780 A450 15r multi .45 .45

Nepalese Postage Stamps, 125th Anniv. — A451

Designs: 5r, #1. 20r, #2. 100r, #3. 125r, #1-3.

2006, Oct. 9 *Perf. 13¼*
781-783 A451 Set of 3 3.50 3.50

Size: 91x75mm
Imperf

784 A451 125r multi 3.50 3.50

No. 784 contains a perforated label that is not valid for postage showing Nepal #1-3.

Birth of Buddha, 2550th Anniv. — A452

2006, Dec. 20 *Perf. 13¼x13*
785 A452 30r multi .85 .85

Chhatrapati Free Clinic, 50th Anniv. — A453

2007, Feb. 6 **Litho.** *Perf. 13x13¼*
786 A453 2r multi .20 .20

Mt. Everest A454

2007, Mar. 14
787 A454 5r multi .20 .20

Miniature Sheet

Orchids — A455

No. 788: a, Satyrium nepalense. b, Dendrobium heterocarpum. c, Pelantheria insectifera. d, Coelogyne ovalis. e, Coelogyne cristata. f, Dendrobium chrysanthum. g, Phalaenopsis mannii. h, Dendrobium densiflorum. i, Esmeralda clarkei. j, Acampe rigida. k, Bulbophyllum leopardinum. l, Dendrobium fimbriatum. m, Arundina graminifolia. n, Dendrobium moschatum. o, Rhynchostylis retusa. p, Cymbidium devonianum.

2007, Apr. 12
788 A455 10r Sheet of 16, #a-p 5.00 5.00

Sports A456

Designs: No. 789, 5r, Taekwondo. No. 790, 5r, Cricket.

2007 *Perf. 13x13¼*
789-790 A456 Set of 2 .35 .35

Issued: No. 789, 4/25; No. 790, 4/28.

Miniature Sheet

Martyrs of the Democratic Movement — A457

No. 791: a, Setu B. K. b, Tulasi Chhetri. c, Anil Lama. d, Umesh Chandra Thapa. e, Chakraraj Joshi. f, Chandra Bayalkoti. g, Devilal Poudel. h, Govindanath Sharma. i, Prof. Hari Raj Adhikari. j, Horilal Rana Tharu. k, Lal Bahadur Bista. l, Mohamad Jahangir. m, Pradhumna Khadka. n, Rajan Giri. o, Suraj Bishwas. p, Sagun Tamrakar. q, Bhimsen Dahal. r, Shivahari Kunwar. s, Basudev Ghimire. t, Bishnu Prasad Panday. u, Yamlal Lamichhane. v, Deepak Kami. w, Darshanial Yadab. x, Tahir Hussain Ansari. y, Hiralal Gautam.

2007, June 4 *Perf. 12½*
791 A457 2r Sheet of 25, #a-y 1.60 1.60

Diplomatic Relations Between Nepal and Sri Lanka, 50th Anniv. A458

2007, July 1 *Perf. 13x13¼*
792 A458 5r multi .20 .20

Diplomatic Relations Between Nepal and Egypt, 50th Anniv. A459

2007, July 24
793 A459 5r multi .20 .20

Scouting, Cent. A460

2007, Sept. 4
794 A460 2r multi .20 .20

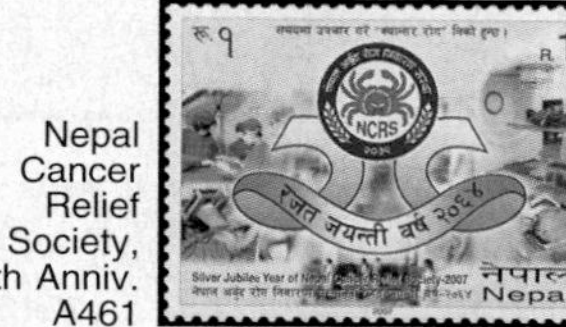

Nepal Cancer Relief Society, 25th Anniv. A461

2007, Sept. 17
795 A461 1r multi .20 .20

Nepalese Parliament Building and Documents — A462

No. 796, 1r : a, Reinstatement of the House of Representatives. b, Proclamation of the House of Representatives.
No. 797, 1r: a, Constitution of Legislature-Parliament. b, Interim Constitution of Nepal.
Illustration reduced.

2007, Dec. 28 **Litho.** *Perf. 13x13¼*
Horiz. Pairs, #a-b
796-797 A462 Set of 2 .20 .20

Chhaya Devi Parajuli (1918-2006), Politician — A463

2007, Dec. 30
798 A463 2r multi .20 .20

Famous People — A464

No. 799, 5r: a, Shivapuri Baba (1862-1963), religious leader. b, Mahesh Chandra Regmi (1929-2003), writer.
No. 800, 5r: a, Princess Bhrikuti (617-49). b, Pundit Udayananda Arjyal, writer.
No. 801, 5r: a, Ganesh Lal Shrestha, musician. b, Tara Devi (1945-2006), singer.
Illustration reduced.

2007, Dec. 30 **Litho.**
Horiz. Pairs, #a-b
799-801 A464 Set of 3 .95 .95

Tourism A465

No. 802: a, Mt. Abi. b, Shree Bhageshwor Temple, Dadeldhura. c, Shree Shaillya Malikarjun Temple, Darchula. d, Shiddakali Temple, Bhojpur. e, Buddha's Victory over the Mara.

2007, Dec. 30
802 Vert. strip of 5 .80 .80
a.-e. A465 5r Any single .20 .20

Diplomatic Relations Between Nepal and Germany, 50th Anniv. A466

2008, Apr. 2 **Litho.** *Perf. 13x13¼*
803 A466 25r multi .80 .80

Nativity of Buddha — A467

2008, July 18 *Perf. 13¼x13*
804 A467 2r multi .20 .20

Nepal Coat of Arms — A468

2008, Aug. 21

805	A468	1r multi	.20	.20

2008 Summer Olympics, Beijing — A469

2008, Aug. 21 *Perf. 12¾*

806	A469	15r multi	.45	.45

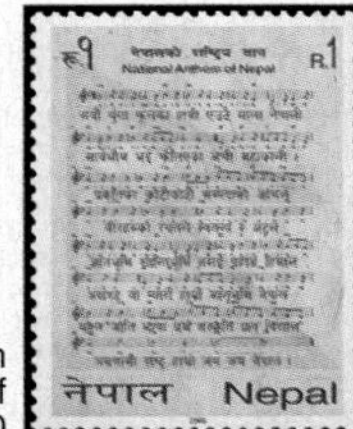

National Anthem and Flag of Nepal — A470

2008, Nov. 13 Litho. *Perf. 13¼x13*

807	A470	1r multi	.20	.20

Kaiser Library, Cent. A471

2008, Nov. 13 *Perf. 13x13¼*

808	A471	5r multi	.20	.20

Dr. Harka Gurung (1935-2006), Minister of Tourism, and Dr. Harka Gurung Peak — A472

2008, Dec. 24 **Litho.**

Granite Paper

809	A472	5r multi	.20	.20

Flora, Fauna and Mushrooms — A473

No. 810: a, Serpentine. b, Long-horned beetle. c, Russula chloroides. d, Golden monitor lizard.

Illustration reduced.

2008, Dec. 24 *Perf. 13x13¼*

Granite Paper

810	A473	5r Block of 4, #a-d	.50	.50

Tourism A474

No. 811: a, Mustang village, Mustang District. b, Syarpu Lake, Rukum District. c, Jaljala Hill, Rolpa District. d, Pindeswor Babadham, Dharan. e, Shree Kumair Chariot Festival, Kathmandu.

2008, Dec. 24 **Litho.**

Granite Paper

811		Vert. strip of 5	.65	.65
a.-e.		A474 5r Any single	.20	.20

AIR POST STAMPS

Catalogue values for unused stamps in this section are for Never Hinged items.

Bird over Kathmandu AP1

Rough Perf 11½

1958, Oct. 16 Typo. Unwmk.

Without Gum

C1	AP1	10p dark blue	1.50	1.50

Plane over Kathmandu AP2

1967, Oct. 24 Photo. *Perf. 13½x13*

C2	AP2	1.80r multicolored	1.50	1.00

International Tourist Year.

God Akash Bhairab and Nepal Airlines Emblem AP3

Map of Nepal with Airlines Network AP4

Design: 2.50r, Plane over Himalayas.

Perf. 14½x14, 13 (65p)

1968, July 1 **Photo.**

C3	AP3	15p blue & bis brn	.45	.25
C4	AP4	65p violet blue	.80	.50
C5	AP3	2.50r dp blue & scar	2.25	1.75
		Nos. C3-C5 (3)	3.50	2.50

10th anniv. of the Royal Nepal Airlines Corp.

Flyer and Jet — AP5

1978, Dec. 12 Photo. *Perf. 13*

C6	AP5	2.30r blue & ocher	.75	.45

75th anniversary of 1st powered flight.

Pheasant Type of 1979

1979, Nov. 22 Photo. *Perf. 14½x14*

C7	A174	3.50r Impeyan pheasant, horiz.	2.25	1.25

OFFICIAL STAMPS

Catalogue values for unused stamps in this section are for Never Hinged items.

Soldiers and Arms of Nepal — O1

Perf. 13½

1959, Nov. 1 Litho. Unwmk.

Size: 29x17½mm

O1	O1	2p reddish brown	.20	.20
O2	O1	4p yel green	.20	.20
O3	O1	6p salmon pink	.20	.20
O4	O1	8p brt violet	.20	.20
O5	O1	12p red orange	.20	.20

Size: 37½x21½mm

O6	O1	16p red brown	.25	.20
O7	O1	24p carmine	.30	.20
O8	O1	32p rose car	.45	.20
O9	O1	50p ultramarine	.60	.20
O10	O1	1r rose red	1.25	.20
O11	O1	2r orange	2.75	.30
		Nos. O1-O11 (11)	6.60	2.30

Nos. 144-146 and 124 Overprinted in Black

1960-62 Photo. *Perf. 14½x14*

Overprint 12½mm Long

O12	A35	1p carmine rose ('62)	.20	.20
O13	A35	2p bright blue ('62)	.20	.20
O14	A35	5p golden brown ('62)	.20	.20
		Nos. O12-O14 (3)	.60	.60

Perf. 14

Overprint 14½mm Long

O15	A26	1r red lilac	.20	

The overprint, "Kaj Sarkari" in Devanagari characters means "Service." Five other denominations, 10p, 40p, 75p, 2r and 5r, were similarly overprinted but not issued. A few exist on 1960 first day covers.

In 1983 substantial quantities of the set of nine values were sold as remainders by the Post Office at face value (under $1 for the set).

The existence of covers from 1985-86 indicate that some of these may have been used as regular postage stamps.

NETHERLANDS

'ne-t͟hər-lən͵d͵z

(Holland)

LOCATION — Northwestern Europe, bordering on the North Sea

GOVT. — Kingdom

AREA — 16,029 sq. mi.

POP. — 15,807,641 (1999 est.)

CAPITAL — Amsterdam

100 Cents = 1 Gulden (Guilder or Florin)

100 Cents = 1 Euro (2002)

Catalogue values for unused stamps in this country are for Never Hinged items, beginning with Scott 216 in the regular postage section, Scott B123 in the semi-postal section, Scott C13 in the airpost section, Scott J80 in the postage due section, and Scott O44 in the official section.

Values for unused stamps are for examples with original gum as defined in the catalogue introduction. Very fine examples of Nos. 4-12 will have perforations touching the frameline on one or more sides due to the narrow spacing of the stamps on the plates. Stamps with perfs clear on all four sides are very scarce and command higher prices.

Watermarks

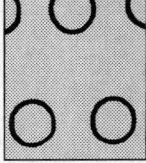

Wmk. 158

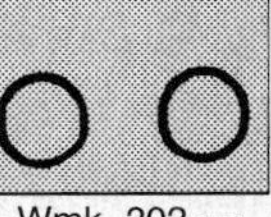
Wmk. 202 — Circles

Syncopated Perforations

Type A

Type C

Type B

These special "syncopated" or "interrupted" perforations, devised for coil stamps, are found on Nos. 142-156, 158-160, 164-166, 168-185, 187-193 and certain semipostals of 1925-33, between Nos. B9 and B69. There are four types:

A (1st stamp is #142a). On two shorter sides, groups of four holes separated by blank spaces equal in width to two or three holes.

B (1st stamp is #164a). As "A," but on all four sides.

C (1st stamp is #164b). On two shorter sides, end holes are omitted.

D (1st stamp is #174c). Four-hole sequence on horiz. sides, three-hole on vert. sides.

King William III

A1 A2

Wmk. 158

1852, Jan. 1 Engr. *Imperf.*

1	A1	5c blue	400.00	32.50
a.		5c light blue	450.00	40.00
b.		5c steel blue	750.00	90.00
c.		5c dark blue	450.00	32.50
2	A1	10c lake	450.00	24.00
3	A1	15c orange	650.00	125.00

In 1895 the 10c was privately reprinted in several colors on unwatermarked paper by Joh. A. Moesman, whose name appears on the back.

1864 Unwmk. *Perf. 12½x12*

No.	Type	Description	Unused	Used
4	A2	5c blue	300.00	16.00
5	A2	10c lake	425.00	8.00
6	A2	15c orange	1,050.	100.00
a.		15c yellow	1,350.	115.00

The paper varies considerably in thickness. It is sometimes slightly bluish, also vertically ribbed.

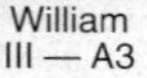
William III — A3

Coat of Arms — A4

Perf. 12½x12, 13, 13½, 14 and Compound

1867

No.	Type	Description	Unused	Used
7	A3	5c ultra	97.50	2.50
8	A3	10c lake	200.00	4.75
9	A3	15c orange brn	650.00	35.00
10	A3	20c dk green	550.00	24.00
11	A3	25c dk violet	2,100.	110.00
12	A3	50c gold	2,350.	160.00

The paper of Nos. 7-22 sometimes has an accidental bluish tinge of varying strength. During its manufacture a chemical whitener (bluing agent) was added in varying quantities. No particular printing was made on bluish paper.

Two varieties of numerals in each value, differing chiefly in the thickness.

Oxidized copies of the 50c are worth much less.

Imperforate varieties of Nos. 7-12 are proofs.

See the *Scott Classic Specialized Catalogue* for listings by perforations.

1869 *Perf. 10½x10*

No.	Type	Description	Unused	Used
7c	A3	5c ultra	140.00	9.00
8c	A3	10c lake	220.00	4.00
9c	A3	15c orange brown	*2,650.*	1,050.
10c	A3	20c dark green	*1,400.*	135.00

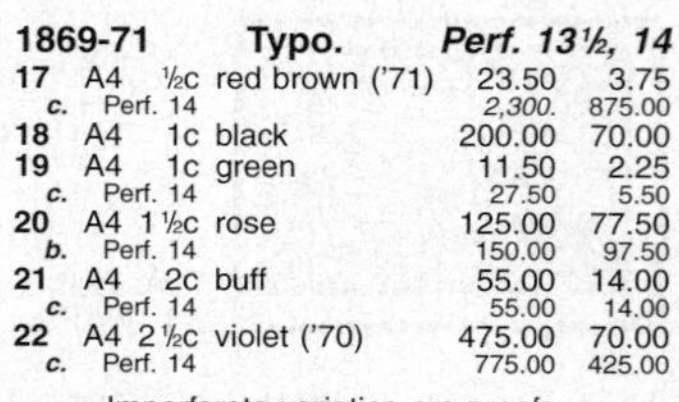

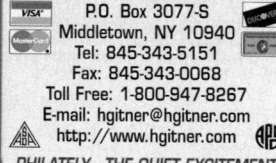

1869-71 Typo. *Perf. 13½, 14*

No.	Type	Description	Unused	Used
17	A4	½c red brown ('71)	23.50	3.75
c.		Perf. 14	*2,300.*	875.00
18	A4	1c black	200.00	70.00
19	A4	1c green	11.50	2.25
c.		Perf. 14	27.50	5.50
20	A4	1½c rose	125.00	77.50
b.		Perf. 14	150.00	97.50
21	A4	2c buff	55.00	14.00
c.		Perf. 14	55.00	14.00
22	A4	2½c violet ('70)	475.00	70.00
c.		Perf. 14	775.00	425.00

Imperforate varieties are proofs.

A5

A6

Perf. 12½, 13, 13½, 13x14, 14, 12½x12 and 11½x12

1872-88

No.	Type	Description	Unused	Used
23	A5	5c blue	11.50	.30
a.		5c ultra	14.00	1.25
24	A5	7½c red brn ('88)	35.00	18.00
25	A5	10c rose	57.50	1.60
26	A5	12½c gray ('75)	62.50	2.40
27	A5	15c brn org	350.00	5.25
28	A5	20c green	425.00	5.00
29	A5	22½c dk grn ('88)	77.50	42.50
30	A5	25c dull vio	525.00	4.00
31	A5	50c bister	650.00	11.00
32	A5	1g gray vio ('88)	475.00	40.00
33	A6	2g50c rose & ultra	900.00	105.00

Imperforate varieties are proofs.

Numeral of Value — A7

HALF CENT:

Type I — Fraction bar 8 to 8½mm long.

Type II — Fraction bar 9mm long and thinner.

Perf. 12½, 13½, 14, 12½x12, 11½x12

1876-94

No.	Type	Description	Unused	Used
34	A7	½c rose, II	11.50	.25
a.		½c rose, I	14.50	.50
c.		Laid paper		60.00
d.		Perf. 14, I	1,950.	575.00
35	A7	1c emer grn ('94)	2.75	.20
b.		As "c," laid paper	70.00	5.50
c.		1c green	8.00	.20
36	A7	2c olive yel ('94)	32.50	2.75
a.		2c yellow	65.00	3.50
37	A7	2½c violet ('94)	14.00	.25
b.		2½c dark violet ('94)	17.50	.45
c.		2½c lilac	100.00	.80
d.		Laid paper	—	—
		Nos. 34-37 (4)	60.75	3.45

Imperforate varieties are proofs.

Princess Wilhelmina
A8 A9

1891-94 *Perf. 12½*

No.	Type	Description	Unused	Used
40	A8	3c orange ('94)	8.00	2.30
a.		3c orange yellow ('92)	11.50	2.75
41	A8	5c lt ultra ('94)	4.00	.25
a.		5c dull blue	5.00	.25
42	A8	7½c brown ('94)	17.00	6.25
a.		7½c red brown	27.50	6.25
43	A8	10c brt rose ('94)	23.50	1.50
a.		10c brick red	45.00	2.30
44	A8	12½c bluish gray ('94)	23.50	1.50
a.		12½c gray	40.00	1.75
45	A8	15c yel brn ('94)	55.00	5.00
a.		15c orange brown	80.00	5.50
46	A8	20c green ('94)	62.50	3.00
a.		20c yellow green	80.00	3.00
47	A8	22½c dk grn ('94)	31.00	13.50
a.		22½c deep blue green	55.00	13.50
48	A8	25c dl vio ('94)	110.00	6.00
a.		25c dark violet	110.00	6.00
49	A8	50c yel brn ('94)	550.00	20.00
a.		50c bister	575.00	27.50
50	A8	1g gray vio	625.00	77.50

The paper used in 1891-93 was white, rough and somewhat opaque. In 1894, a thinner, smooth and sometimes transparent paper was introduced.

The 5c orange was privately produced.

1893-96 *Perf. 11½x11*

No.	Type	Description	Unused	Used
51	A9	50c emer & yel brn ('96)	70.00	8.50
a.		Perf. 11	*2,500.*	200.00
52	A9	1g brn & ol grn ('96)	200.00	20.00
a.		Perf. 11	225.00	60.00
53	A9	2g 50c brt rose & ultra	400.00	125.00
a.		2g 50c lil rose & ultra, perf. 11	475.00	125.00
b.		Perf. 11½	500.00	140.00

Perf. 11

No.	Type	Description	Unused	Used
54	A9	5g brnz grn & red brn ('96)	675.00	350.00

A10

Queen Wilhelmina — A11

Perf. 12½, 11½, 11½x11, 11x11½

1898-1924

No.	Type	Description	Unused	Used
55	A10	½c violet	.45	.20
56	A10	1c red	.90	.20
b.		Imperf., pair	*2,000.*	
57	A10	1½c ultra ('08)	6.00	.85
58	A10	1½c dp blue ('13)	3.00	.35
59	A10	2c yellow brn	3.75	.20
60	A10	2½c deep green	3.25	.20
b.		Imperf., pair	*6,000.*	
61	A11	3c orange	16.25	3.25
62	A11	3c pale ol grn ('01)	1.10	.20
63	A11	4c claret ('21)	1.60	.90
64	A11	4½c violet ('19)	3.75	3.75
65	A11	5c car rose	1.60	.20
66	A11	7½c brown	.60	.20
a.		Tête bêche pair ('24)	80.00	70.00
67	A11	10c gray lilac	6.25	.20
68	A11	12½c blue	3.25	.25
69	A11	15c yellow brn	80.00	3.25
70	A11	15c bl & car ('08)	6.25	.20
71	A11	17½c vio ('06)	50.00	11.50
73	A11	17½c ultra & brn ('10)	15.00	.80
74	A11	20c yellow green	100.00	.65
75	A11	20c ol grn & gray ('08)	10.00	.45
76	A11	22½c brn & ol grn	9.25	.50
77	A11	25c carmine & blue	9.00	.35
78	A11	30c lil & vio brn ('17)	24.00	.40
79	A11	40c grn & org ('20)	34.00	.80
80	A11	50c brnz grn & red brn	92.50	.90
81	A11	50c gray & vio ('14)	70.00	.80
a.		Perf. 11½x11	70.00	16.00
82	A11	60c ol grn & grn ('20)	34.00	1.10
a.		Perf. 11½	200.00	20.00
		Nos. 55-82 (27)	585.75	32.65
		Set, never hinged	2,100.	

See Nos. 107-112. For overprints and surcharges see Nos. 102-103, 106, 117-123, 135-136, O1-O8.

A12

Type I Type II

Type I — The figure "1" is 3¾mm high and 2¾mm wide.

Type II — The figure "1" is 3½mm high and 2½mm wide, it is also thinner than in type I.

Perf. 11, 11x11½, 11½, 11½x11

1898-1905 Engr.

No.	Type	Description	Unused	Used
83	A12	1g dk grn, II ('99)	52.50	.40
a.		1g dark green, I ('98)	160.00	90.00
84	A12	2½g brn lil ('99)	100.00	3.25
85	A12	5g claret ('99)	225.00	5.00
86	A12	10g orange ('05)	725.00	625.00
		Set, Nos. 83-86, never hinged	2,450.	

For surcharge see No. 104.

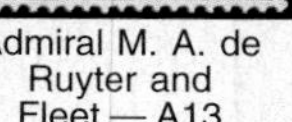
Admiral M. A. de Ruyter and Fleet — A13

King William I — A14

1907, Mar. 23 Typo. *Perf. 12x12½*

No.	Type	Description	Unused	Used
87	A13	½c blue	1.60	1.10
88	A13	1c claret	3.25	2.25
89	A13	2½c vermilion	5.75	2.10
		Nos. 87-89 (3)	10.60	5.45
		Set, never hinged	27.00	

De Ruyter (1607-1676), naval hero.

For surcharges see Nos. J29-J41.

Perf. 11½, 11½x11

1913, Nov. 29 Engr.

Designs: 2½c, 12½c, 1g, King William I. 3c, 20c, 2½g, King William II. 5c, 25c, 5g, King William III. 10c, 50c, 10g, Queen Wilhelmina.

No.	Type	Description	Unused	Used
90	A14	2½c green, *grn*	.80	.80
91	A14	3c buff, *straw*	1.10	1.10
92	A14	5c rose red, *sal*	1.10	.80
93	A14	10c gray blk	3.75	2.25
94	A14	12½c dp blue, *bl*	3.00	1.90
95	A14	20c orange brn	11.50	9.50
96	A14	25c pale blue	13.50	7.75
97	A14	50c yellow grn	30.00	25.00
98	A14	1g claret	42.50	17.50
a.		Perf. 11½	60.00	17.50
99	A14	2½g dull violet	100.00	42.50
100	A14	5g yel, *straw*	225.00	37.50
101	A14	10g red, *straw*	675.00	650.00
		Nos. 90-101 (12)	1,107.	796.60
		Set, never hinged	2,560.	

Centenary of Dutch independence.

For surcharge see No. 105.

No. 78 Surcharged in Red or Black

a

b

1919, Dec. 1 *Perf. 12½*

No.	Type	Description	Unused	Used
102	A11 (a)	40c on 30c (R)	22.50	3.25
103	A11 (b)	60c on 30c (Bk)	22.50	3.25
		Set, never hinged	140.00	

Nos. 86 and 101 Surcharged in Black

1920, Aug. 17 *Perf. 11, 11½*

No.	Type	Description	Unused	Used
104	A12	2.50g on 10g	140.00	100.00
		Never hinged	300.00	
105	A14	2.50g on 10g	140.00	85.00
		Never hinged	300.00	

No. 64 Surcharged in Red

1921, Mar. 1 Typo. *Perf. 12½*

No.	Type	Description	Unused	Used
106	A11	4c on 4½c vio	4.00	1.60
		Never hinged	8.00	

A17

1921-22 Typo. *Perf. 12½*

107 A17 5c green ('22) 8.25 .20
108 A17 12½c vermilion ('22) 18.00 1.75
109 A17 20c blue 27.50 .25
Nos. 107-109 (3) 53.75 2.20
Set, never hinged 170.00

Queen Type of 1898-99, 10c Redrawn

1922 *Perf. 12½*

110 A11 10c gray 29.00 .25
Never hinged 75.00

Imperf

111 A11 5c car rose 6.50 6.50
Never hinged 13.50
112 A11 10c gray 7.25 7.25
Never hinged 14.00
Nos. 110-112 (3) 42.75 14.00

In redrawn 10c the horizontal lines behind the Queen's head are wider apart.

Orange Tree and Lion of Brabant A18

Post Horn and Lion A19

Numeral of Value — A20

1923, Mar. 9 *Perf. 12½*

113 A18 1c dark violet .55 .60
114 A18 2c orange 6.00 .25
115 A19 2½c bluish green 1.75 .65
116 A20 4c deep blue 1.25 .60
Nos. 113-116 (4) 9.55 2.10
Set, never hinged 16.00

Nos. 56, 58, 62, 65, 68, 73, 76 Surcharged in Various Colors

c

d

1923, July *Perf. 12½*

117 A10(c) 2c on 1c (Bl) .45 .20
118 A10(c) 2c on 1½c (Bk) .45 .25
119 A11(d) 10c on 3c (Br) 4.25 .20
120 A11(d) 10c on 5c (Bk) 8.00 .55
121 A11(d) 10c on 12½c (R) 7.25 .90

Perf. 11½x11

122 A11(d) 10c on 17½c (R) 2.75 3.50
a. Perf. 11½ *1,600.* *800.00*
b. Perf. 12½ 4.25 4.25
Never hinged 8.00
123 A11(d) 10c on 22½c (R) 2.75 3.50
a. Perf. 11½ 3.00 3.50
b. Perf. 12½ 4.25 4.25
Never hinged 8.00
Nos. 117-123 (7) 25.90 9.10
Set, never hinged 57.50

Queen Wilhelmina
A21 A22

Perf. 11½x12½, 11½x12 (5c)

1923, Oct. Engr.

124 A22 2c myrtle green .25 .20
a. Vert. pair, imperf. between *2,000.*
125 A21 5c green .35 .20
a. Vert. pair, imperf. between *1,800.*
126 A22 7½c carmine .40 .20
127 A22 10c vermilion .40 .20
a. Vert. pair, imperf. between *550.00* *575.00*
128 A22 20c ultra 3.50 .50
129 A22 25c yellow 5.00 .75

Perf. 11½

130 A22 35c orange 5.00 2.00
131 A22 50c black 17.00 .50
132 A21 1g red 27.50 6.50
133 A21 2½g black 200.00 175.00
134 A21 5g dark blue 175.00 150.00
Nos. 124-134 (11) 434.40 336.05
Set, never hinged 900.00

25th anniv. of the assumption as monarch of the Netherlands by Queen Wilhelmina at the age of 18.

Nos. 119, 73 Overprinted in Red "DIENSTZEGEL PORTEN AANTEEKENRECHT; No. 73 with New Value in Blue

1923 Typo. *Perf. 12½*

135 A11 10c on 3c 1.10 1.00
Never hinged 8.00
136 A11 1g on 17½c 62.50 15.00
Never hinged 150.00
a. Perf. 11½ 85.00 32.50
b. Perf. 11½x11 72.50 25.00

Stamps with red surcharge were prepared for use as Officials but were not issued.

Queen Wilhelmina — A23

1924, Sept. 6 Photo. *Perf. 12½*

137 A23 10c slate green 30.00 30.00
Never hinged 52.50
138 A23 15c gray black 40.00 40.00
Never hinged 65.00
139 A23 35c brown orange 30.00 30.00
Never hinged 52.50
Nos. 137-139 (3) 100.00 100.00

These stamps were available solely to visitors to the International Philatelic Exhibition at The Hague and were not obtainable at regular post offices.

See Nos. 147-160, 172-193. For overprints and surcharge see Nos. 194, O11, O13-O15.

Ship in Distress — A23a

Lifeboat — A23b

1924, Sept. 15 Litho. *Perf. 11½*

140 A23a 2c black brn 3.25 2.50
Never hinged 6.50
141 A23b 10c orange brn 6.00 2.00
Never hinged 12.00

Centenary of Royal Dutch Lifeboat Society.

Type A23 and

Gull — A24

1924-26 *Perf. 12½*

142 A24 1c deep red .50 .60
143 A24 2c red orange 2.25 .20
144 A24 2½c deep green 2.60 .80
145 A24 3c yel grn ('25) 12.50 1.00
146 A24 4c dp ultra 2.75 .70

Photo.

147 A23 5c dull green 3.25 .65
148 A23 6c org brn ('25) .65 .50
149 A23 7½c orange ('25) .35 .20
150 A23 9c org red & blk ('26) 1.50 1.25
151 A23 10c red, *shades* 1.25 .20
152 A23 12½c deep rose 1.60 .35
153 A23 15c ultra 6.00 .40
154 A23 20c dp blue ('25) 10.00 .60
155 A23 25c olive bis ('25) 22.50 .85
156 A23 30c violet 13.00 .65
157 A23 35c olive brn ('25) 30.00 6.00
158 A23 40c dp brown 30.00 .65
159 A23 50c blue grn ('25) 60.00 .60
160 A23 60c dk violet ('25) 27.50 .80
Nos. 142-160 (19) 228.20 17.00
Set, never hinged 725.00

See Nos. 164-171, 243A-243Q. For overprints and surcharges see Nos. 226-243, O9-O10.

Syncopated, Type A (2 Sides)

1925-26

142a A24 1c deep red .80 .80
143a A24 2c red orange 2.75 1.90
144a A24 2½c deep green 2.75 1.25
145a A24 3c yellow green 18.00 20.00
146a A24 4c deep ultra 2.75 1.90
147a A23 5c dull green 5.50 2.50
148a A23 6c orange brown 110.00 100.00
149a A23 7½c orange 1.10 1.00
150a A23 9c org red & blk 1.75 1.25
151a A23 10c red 11.00 2.75
152a A23 12½c deep rose 1.75 1.50
153a A23 15c ultra 67.50 5.50
154a A23 20c deep blue 10.00 4.00
155a A23 25c olive bister 42.50 45.00
156a A23 30c violet 14.50 10.50
158a A23 40c deep brown 45.00 36.00
159a A23 50c blue green 55.00 20.00
160a A23 60c dark violet 27.50 11.00
Nos. 142a-160a (18) 420.15 266.85
Set, never hinged 950.00

A25

1925-30 Engr. *Perf. 11½, 12½*

161 A25 1g ultra 8.00 .30
Never hinged 25.00
162 A25 2½g car ('27) 80.00 3.00
Never hinged 175.00
163 A25 5g gray blk 160.00 1.75
Never hinged 275.00
Nos. 161-163 (3) 248.00 5.05

Types of 1924-26 Issue

Perf. 12½, 13½x12½, 12½x13½

1926-39 Wmk. 202 Litho.

164 A24 ½c gray ('28) .90 1.00
165 A24 1c dp red ('27) .20 .20
166 A24 1½c red vio ('28) 1.10 .20
c. "CEN" for "CENT" 160.00 275.00
d. "GENT" for "CENT" 125.00 110.00
167 A24 1½c gray ('35) .20 .20
a. 1½c dark gray .20 .20
168 A24 2c dp org .20 .20
a. 2c red orange .20 .20
169 A24 2½c green ('27) 2.75 .25
170 A24 3c yel grn ('27) .20 .20
171 A24 4c dp ultra ('27) .20 .20

Photo.

172 A23 5c dp green .20 .20
173 A23 6c org brn ('27) .20 .20
174 A23 7½c dk vio ('27) 3.25 .20
175 A23 7½c red ('28) .20 .20
176 A23 9c org red & blk ('28) 11.00 12.00
b. Value omitted *14,500.*
177 A23 10c red 1.25 .20
178 A23 10c dl vio ('29) 2.50 .20
179 A23 12½c dp rose ('27) 42.50 4.50
180 A23 12½c ultra ('28) .40 .20
181 A23 15c ultra 7.25 .20
182 A23 15c orange ('29) 1.25 .20
183 A23 20c dp blue ('28) 7.25 .20
184 A23 21c ol brn ('31) 25.00 .90
185 A23 22½c ol brn ('27) 7.25 3.00
186 A23 22½c dp org ('39) 15.00 16.00
187 A23 25c ol bis ('27) 4.50 .20
188 A23 27½c gray ('28) 4.50 .75
189 A23 30c violet 5.25 .20
190 A23 35c olive brn 62.50 12.50
191 A23 40c dp brown 10.00 .20
192 A23 50c blue grn 5.25 .20
193 A23 60c black ('29) 27.50 .90
Nos. 164-193 (30) 249.75 55.80
Set, never hinged 558.05

Syncopated, Type A (2 Sides), 12½

1926-27

168b A24 2c deep orange .40 .40
170a A24 3c yellow green .60 .60
171a A24 4c deep ultra .60 .60
172a A23 5c deep green .70 .60
173a A23 6c orange brown .40 .45
174a A23 7½c dark violet 4.50 2.00
177a A23 10c red 1.00 .85
181a A23 15c ultra 7.00 3.00
185a A23 22½c olive brown 7.00 2.50
187a A23 25c olive bister 20.00 18.00
189a A23 30c violet 19.00 12.00
190a A23 35c olive brown 77.50 22.50
191a A23 40c deep brown 50.00 40.00
Nos. 168b-191a (13) 188.70 103.50
Set, never hinged 360.00

1928 *Syncopated, Type B (4 Sides)*

164a A24 ½c gray .80 .65
165a A24 1c deep red .30 .30
166a A24 1½c red violet .80 .25
168c A24 2c deep orange 1.00 .60
169a A24 2½c green 2.75 .20
170b A24 3c yellow green .75 .75
171b A24 4c deep ultra .75 .65
172b A23 5c deep green 1.00 .75
173b A23 6c orange brown .75 .50
174b A23 7½c dark violet 4.25 2.00
175a A23 7½c red .25 .25
176a A23 9c org red & blk 10.00 12.50
178a A23 10c dull violet 5.25 5.00
179a A23 12½c deep rose 80.00 80.00
180a A23 12½c ultra 1.40 .40
181b A23 15c ultra 9.00 2.00
182a A23 15c orange .75 .30
183a A23 20c deep blue 7.00 3.00
187b A23 25c olive bister 17.00 10.00
188a A23 27½c gray 4.50 2.00
189b A23 30c violet 15.00 8.00
191b A23 40c deep brown 35.00 22.50
192a A23 50c blue green 55.00 45.00
193a A23 60c black 45.00 22.50
Nos. 164a-193a (24) 298.30 220.10
Set, never hinged 600.00

Syncopated, Type C (2 Sides, Corners Only)

1930

164b A24 ½c gray 1.00 .70
165b A24 1c deep red 1.00 .40
166b A24 1½c red violet .90 .25
168d A24 2c deep orange .80 .70
169b A24 2½c green 2.75 .25
170c A24 3c yellow green 1.10 .50
171c A24 4c deep ultra .50 .25
172c A23 5c deep green .70 .70
173c A23 6c orange brown .70 .70
178b A23 10c dull violet 8.00 7.00
183b A23 20c deep blue 7.75 3.75
184a A23 21c olive brown 25.00 9.00
189c A23 30c violet 12.00 7.00
192b A23 50c blue green 45.00 45.00
Nos. 164b-192b (14) 107.20 76.20
Set, never hinged 225.00

1927

Syncopated, Type D (3 Holes Vert., 4 Holes Horiz.)

174c A23 7½c dark violet *2,750.* *2,100.*
Never hinged *3,750.*

No. 185 Surcharged in Red

1929, Nov. 11 *Perf. 12½*

No.	Type	Description	Unused	Used
194	A23	21c on 22½c ol brn	20.00	1.00
		Never hinged	40.00	

Queen Wilhelmina — A26

1931, Oct. Photo. *Perf. 12½*

No.	Type	Description	Unused	Used
195	A26	70c dk bl & red	27.50	.40
		Never hinged	100.00	
a.		Perf. 14½x13½ ('39)	32.50	7.50
		Never hinged	125.00	

See No. 201.

Arms of the House of Orange — A27

William I — A28

Designs: 5c, William I, Portrait by Goltzius. 6c, Portrait of William I by Van Key. 12½c, Portrait attributed to Moro.

1933, Apr. 1 Unwmk. Engr.

No.	Type	Description	Unused	Used
196	A27	1½c black	.50	.20
197	A28	5c dark green	1.60	.35
198	A28	6c dull violet	2.50	.20
199	A28	12½c deep blue	15.00	2.50
		Nos. 196-199 (4)	19.60	3.25
		Set, never hinged	47.50	

400th anniv. of the birth of William I, Count of Nassau and Prince of Orange, frequently referred to as William the Silent.

Star, Dove and Sword — A31

1933, May 18 Photo. Wmk. 202

No.	Type	Description	Unused	Used
200	A31	12½c dp ultra	8.00	.30
		Never hinged	24.00	

For overprint see No. O12.

Queen Wilhelmina Design of 1931

Queen Wilhelmina and ships.

Perf. 14½x13½

1933, July 26 Wmk. 202

No.	Type	Description	Unused	Used
201	A26	80c Prus bl & red	100.00	2.50
		Never hinged	325.00	

Willemstad Harbor — A33

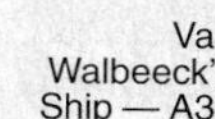

Van Walbeeck's Ship — A34

Perf. 14x12½

1934, July 2 Engr. Unwmk.

No.	Type	Description	Unused	Used
202	A33	6c violet blk	3.00	.20
203	A34	12½c dull blue	19.00	2.00
		Set, never hinged	62.50	

Tercentenary of Curacao.

Minerva — A35

Design: 12½c, Gisbertus Voetius.

Wmk. 202

1936, May 15 Photo. *Perf. 12½*

No.	Type	Description	Unused	Used
204	A35	6c brown lake	2.50	.20
205	A35	12½c indigo	3.75	3.25
		Set, never hinged	12.50	

300th anniversary of the founding of the University at Utrecht.

A37

A38

A39

1937, Apr. 1 *Perf. 14½x13½*

No.	Type	Description	Unused	Used
206	A37	1½c Boy Scout Emblem	.35	.20
207	A38	6c "Assembly"	1.25	.20
208	A39	12½c Mercury	3.00	1.00
		Nos. 206-208 (3)	4.60	1.40
		Set, never hinged	10.00	

Fifth Boy Scout World Jamboree, Vogelenzang, Netherlands, 7/31-8/13/37.

Wilhelmina A40

St. Willibrord A41

1938, Aug. 27 *Perf. 12½x12*

No.	Type	Description	Unused	Used
209	A40	1½c black	.20	.20
210	A40	5c red orange	.20	.20
211	A40	12½c royal blue	3.25	1.00
		Nos. 209-211 (3)	3.65	1.40
		Set, never hinged	11.00	

Reign of Queen Wilhelmina, 40th anniv.

Perf. 12½x14

1939, June 15 Engr. Unwmk.

Design: 12½c, St. Willibrord as older man.

No.	Type	Description	Unused	Used
212	A41	5c dk slate grn	.75	.20
213	A41	12½c slate blue	4.00	2.00
		Set, never hinged	11.00	

12th centenary of the death of St. Willibrord.

Woodburning Engine A43

Queen Wilhelmina A45

Design: 12½c, Streamlined electric car.

Perf. 14½x13½

1939, Sept. 1 Photo. Wmk. 202

No.	Type	Description	Unused	Used
214	A43	5c dk slate grn	.75	.20
215	A43	12½c dark blue	8.00	2.75
		Set, never hinged	22.50	

Centenary of Dutch Railroads.

Catalogue values for unused stamps in this section, from this point to the end of the section, are for Never Hinged items.

1940-47 *Perf. 13½x12½*

No.	Type	Description	Unused	Used
216	A45	5c dk green	.20	.20
216B	A45	6c hn brn ('47)	.55	.20
217	A45	7½c brt red	.20	.20
218	A45	10c brt red vio	.20	.20
219	A45	12½c sapphire	.20	.20
220	A45	15c light blue	.20	.20
220B	A45	17½c slate bl ('46)	1.25	.70
221	A45	20c purple	.35	.20
222	A45	22½c olive grn	1.25	.85
223	A45	25c rose brn	.35	.20
224	A45	30c bister	.80	.35
225	A45	40c brt green	1.25	.60
225A	A45	50c orange ('46)	9.50	.60
225B	A45	60c pur brn ('46)	8.50	2.00
		Nos. 216-225B (14)	24.80	6.70

Imperf. copies of Nos. 216, 218-220 were released through philatelic channels during the German occupation, but were never issued at any post office. Value, set, $1.

For overprints see Nos. O16-O24.

Type of 1924-26 Surcharged in Black or Blue

Perf. 12½x13½

1940, Oct. Photo. Wmk. 202

No.	Type	Description	Unused	Used
226	A24	2½c on 3c ver	2.00	.20
227	A24	5c on 3c lt grn	.20	.20
228	A24	7½c on 3c ver	.20	.20
a.		Pair, #226, 228	4.00	1.50
229	A24	10c on 3c lt grn	.20	.20
230	A24	12½c on 3c lt bl (Bl)	.30	.20
231	A24	17½c on 3c lt grn	.60	.65
232	A24	20c on 3c lt grn	.40	.20
233	A24	22½c on 3c lt grn	.80	.85
234	A24	25c on 3c lt grn	.50	.20
235	A24	30c on 3c lt grn	.65	.30
236	A24	40c on 3c lt grn	.80	.60
237	A24	50c on 3c lt grn	.70	.40
238	A24	60c on 3c lt grn	1.60	.85
239	A24	70c on 3c lt grn	3.75	1.75
240	A24	80c on 3c lt grn	5.50	4.00
241	A24	1g on 3c lt grn	35.00	32.50
242	A24	2.50g on 3c lt grn	40.00	37.50
243	A24	5g on 3c lt grn	37.50	35.00
		Nos. 226-243 (18)	130.70	115.80
		Set, hinged	70.00	

No. 228a is from coils.

Gull Type of 1924-26

1941

No.	Type	Description	Unused	Used
243A	A24	2½c dk green	1.25	.35
b.		Booklet pane of 6	10.00	
243C	A24	5c brt green	.20	.20
243E	A24	7½c henna	.20	.20
r.		Pair, #243A, 243E	1.00	1.00
243G	A24	10c brt violet	.20	.20
243H	A24	12½c ultra	.20	.20
243J	A24	15c lt blue	.20	.20
243K	A24	17½c red org	.20	.20
243L	A24	20c lt violet	.20	.20
243M	A24	22½c dk ol grn	.20	.20
243N	A24	25c lake	.20	.20
243O	A24	30c olive	3.50	.20
243P	A24	40c emerald	.20	.20
243Q	A24	50c orange brn	.20	.20
		Nos. 243A-243Q (13)	6.95	2.75

No. 243r is from coils.

Post Horn and Lion — A46

Gold Surcharge

1943, Jan. 15 Photo. *Perf. 12½x12*

No.	Type	Description	Unused	Used
244	A46	10c on 2½c yel	.20	.20
a.		Surcharge omitted	*6,000.*	*6,500.*

Founding of the European Union of Posts and Telegraphs at Vienna, Oct. 19, 1942. Surcharge reads: "Europeesche P T T Vereeniging 19 October 1942 10 Cent."

Sea Horse — A47

Triple-crown Tree — A48

Admiral M. A. de Ruyter — A54

Designs: 2c, Swans. 2½c, Tree of Life. 3c, Tree with snake roots. 4c, Man on horseback. 5c, Rearing white horses. 10c, Johan Evertsen. 12½c, Martin Tromp. 15c, Piet Hein. 17½c, Willem van Ghent. 20c, Witte de With. 22½c, Cornelis Evertsen. 25c, Tjerk de Vries. 30c, Cornelis Tromp. 40c, Cornelis Evertsen De Jongste.

Perf. 12x12½, 12½x12

1943-44 Photo. Wmk. 202

No.	Type	Description	Unused	Used
245	A47	1c black	.20	.20
246	A48	1½c rose lake	.20	.20
247	A47	2c dk blue	.20	.20
248	A48	2½c dk blue grn	.20	.20
249	A47	3c copper red	.20	.20
250	A48	4c black brown	.20	.20
251	A47	5c dull yel grn	.20	.20
		Unwmk.		
252	A54	7½c henna brn	.20	.20
a.		Thinner numerals and letters ('44)	.20	.20
253	A54	10c dk green	.20	.20
254	A54	12½c blue	.20	.20
255	A54	15c dull lilac	.20	.20
256	A54	17½c slate ('44)	.20	.20
257	A54	20c dull brown	.20	.20
258	A54	22½c org red	.20	.25
259	A54	25c vio rose ('44)	.35	.55
260	A54	30c cobalt bl ('44)	.20	.20
		Engr.		
261	A54	40c bluish blk	.20	.20
		Nos. 245-261 (17)	3.55	3.80

In 1944, 200,000 copies of No. 247 were privately punched with a cross and printed on the back with a number and the words "Prijs 15 Cent toeslag ten bate Ned. Roode Kruis." These were sold at an exhibition, the surtax going to the Red Cross. The Dutch post office tolerated these stamps.

Soldier — A64

S. S. "Nieuw Amsterdam" — A65

Pilot — A66

Cruiser "De Ruyter" — A67

Queen Wilhelmina — A68

Perf. 12, 12½

1944-46 Unwmk. Engr.

No.	Type	Description	Unused	Used
262	A64	1½c black	.20	.20
263	A65	2½c yellow grn	.20	.20
264	A66	3c dull red brn	.20	.20
265	A67	5c dk blue	.20	.20
266	A68	7½c vermilion	.20	.20
267	A68	10c yellow org	.20	.20
268	A68	12½c ultra	.20	.20
269	A68	15c dl red brn ('46)	1.40	1.00
270	A68	17½c gray grn ('46)	1.00	1.00
271	A68	20c violet	.35	.25
272	A68	22½c rose red ('46)	.55	.80
273	A68	25c brn org ('46)	2.00	1.40
274	A68	30c blue grn	.20	.20
275	A68	40c dk vio brn ('46)	2.00	1.90
276	A68	50c red vio ('46)	1.10	1.00
		Nos. 262-276 (15)	10.00	8.95

These stamps were used on board Dutch war and merchant ships until Netherlands' liberation.

Lion and Dragon — A69

Queen Wilhelmina — A70

1945, July 14 *Perf. 12½x14*

No.	Type	Description	Unused	Used
277	A69	7½c red orange	.20	.20

Netherlands' liberation or "rising again."

1946 Engr. *Perf. 13½x14*

No.	Type	Description	Unused	Used
278	A70	1g dark blue	1.00	.40
279	A70	2½g brick red	125.00	7.00
280	A70	5g dk olive grn	125.00	21.00
281	A70	10g dk purple	125.00	21.00
		Nos. 278-281 (4)	376.00	49.40
		Set, hinged	200.00	

A71

Perf. 12½x13½

1946-47 Wmk. 202 Photo.

No.	Type	Description	Unused	Used
282	A71	1c dark red	.20	.20
283	A71	2c ultra	.20	.20
284	A71	2½c dp orange ('47)	7.00	1.40
285	A71	4c olive green	.35	.20
		Nos. 282-285 (4)	7.75	2.00

The 1c was reissued in 1969 on phosphorescent paper in booklet pane No. 345b. The 4c was reissued on fluorescent paper in 1962.

The 2c was issued in coils in 1972. Every fifth stamp has black control number on back.

See Nos. 340-343A, 404-406.

Queen Wilhelmina
A72 A73

1947-48 *Perf. 13½x12½*

No.	Type	Description	Unused	Used
286	A72	5c olive grn ('48)	.90	.20
287	A72	6c brown black	.30	.20
288	A72	7½c dp red brn ('48)	.30	.20
289	A72	10c brt red vio	.55	.20
290	A72	12½c scarlet ('48)	.55	.30
291	A72	15c purple	6.50	.20
292	A72	20c deep blue	7.00	.20
293	A72	22½c ol brn ('48)	.55	.55
294	A72	25c ultra	13.00	.20
295	A72	30c dp orange	13.00	.25
296	A72	35c dk blue grn	13.00	.50
297	A72	40c henna brown	16.00	.50
		Engr.		
298	A73	45c dp bl ('48)	17.50	10.00
299	A73	50c brown ('48)	11.50	.25
300	A73	60c red ('48)	14.50	1.75
		Nos. 286-300 (15)	115.15	15.50
		Set, hinged	60.00	

For surcharge see No. 330.

Type of 1947

1948 Photo.

No.	Type	Description	Unused	Used
301	A72	6c gray blue	.45	.20

Queen Wilhelmina A74

Queen Juliana A75

Perf. 12½x14

1948, Aug. 30 Engr. Unwmk.

No.	Type	Description	Unused	Used
302	A74	10c vermilion	.20	.20
303	A74	20c deep blue	1.50	1.40

Reign of Queen Wilhelmina, 50th anniv.

Perf. 14x13

1948, Sept. 7 Photo. Wmk. 202

No.	Type	Description	Unused	Used
304	A75	10c dark brown	1.10	.20
305	A75	20c ultra	1.40	.45

Investiture of Queen Juliana, Sept. 6, 1948.

Queen Juliana
A76 A77

1949 *Perf. 13½x12½*

No.	Type	Description	Unused	Used
306	A76	5c olive green	.55	.20
307	A76	6c gray blue	.30	.20
308	A76	10c deep orange	.30	.20
309	A76	12c orange red	1.50	1.50
310	A76	15c olive brown	3.25	.20
311	A76	20c brt blue	3.00	.20
312	A76	25c orange brn	9.50	.20
313	A76	30c violet	7.50	.20
314	A76	35c gray	13.00	.20
315	A76	40c red violet	27.50	.20
316	A76	45c red orange	1.40	.80
317	A76	50c blue green	7.50	.20
318	A76	60c red brown	11.00	.20
		Nos. 306-318 (13)	86.30	4.50

See No. 325-327. For surcharge see No. B248.

1949 Unwmk. Engr. *Perf. 12½x12*

No.	Type	Description	Unused	Used
319	A77	1g rose red	3.50	.20
320	A77	2½g black brn	240.00	1.00
321	A77	5g orange brn	375.00	2.50
322	A77	10g dk vio brn	275.00	12.00
		Nos. 319-322 (4)	893.50	15.70
		Set, hinged	400.00	

Two types exist of No. 321.

Post Horns Entwined — A78

Janus Dousa — A79

Perf. 11½x12½

1949, Oct. 1 Photo. Wmk. 202

No.	Type	Description	Unused	Used
323	A78	10c brown red	.75	.20
324	A78	20c dull blue	6.75	2.00

75th anniversary of the UPU.

Juliana Type of 1949

1950-51 *Perf. 13½x12½*

No.	Type	Description	Unused	Used
325	A76	12c scarlet ('51)	6.00	.60
326	A76	45c violet brn	42.50	.30
327	A76	75c car rose ('51)	85.00	1.25
		Nos. 325-327 (3)	133.50	2.15

1950, Oct. 3 *Perf. 11½x13*

Design: 20c, Jan van Hout.

No.	Type	Description	Unused	Used
328	A79	10c olive brown	3.75	.20
329	A79	20c deep blue	4.25	1.60

375th anniversary of the founding of the University of Leyden.

No. 288 Surcharged with New Value

1950, May *Perf. 13½x12½*

No.	Type	Description	Unused	Used
330	A72	6c on 7½c dp red brn	2.00	.20

Miner — A80

Perf. 12x12½

1952, Apr. 16 Engr. Unwmk.

No.	Type	Description	Unused	Used
331	A80	10c dark blue	2.50	.20

50th anniversary of the founding of Netherlands' mining and chemical industry.

Telegraph Poles and Train of 1852 — A81

Designs: 6c, Radio towers. 10c, Mail Delivery 1852. 20c, Modern postman.

1952, June 28 *Perf. 13x14*

No.	Type	Description	Unused	Used
332	A81	2c gray violet	.45	.20
333	A81	6c vermilion	.45	.20
334	A81	10c green	.45	.20
335	A81	20c gray blue	8.25	2.00
		Nos. 332-335 (4)	9.60	2.60

Centenary of Dutch postage stamps and of the telegraph service.

1952, June 28

No.	Type	Description	Unused	Used
336	A81	2c chocolate	22.50	15.00
337	A81	6c dk bluish grn	22.50	15.00
338	A81	10c brown carmine	22.50	15.00
339	A81	20c violet blue	22.50	15.00
		Nos. 336-339 (4)	90.00	60.00

Nos. 336 to 339 sold for 1.38g, which included the price of admission to the International Postage Stamp Centenary Exhibition, Utrecht.

Numeral Type of 1946-47

Perf. 12½x13½

1953-57 Wmk. 202 Photo.

No.	Type	Description	Unused	Used
340	A71	3c dp org brn	.20	.20
341	A71	5c orange	.20	.20
342	A71	6c gray ('54)	.20	.20
343	A71	7c red org	.20	.20
343A	A71	8c brt lilac ('57)	.20	.20
		Nos. 340-343A (5)	1.00	1.00

The 5c and 7c perf. on 3 sides, and with watermark vertical, are from booklet panes Nos. 346a-346b. The 5c perf. on 3 sides, with wmk. horiz., is from No. 349a.

In 1972 the 5c was printed on phosphorescent paper.

A82

Queen Juliana — A83

1953-71 Wmk. 202 *Perf. 13½x12½*

No.	Type	Description	Unused	Used
344	A82	10c dk red brn	.20	.20
a.		Bklt. pane of 6 (1 #344 + 5 #346C)('65)	5.00	
345	A82	12c dk Prus grn ('54)	.20	.20
a.		Bklt. pane of 7 + label (5 #345 + 2 #347)('67)	5.50	
b.		Bklt. pane, 4 #282 + 8 #345 ('69)	12.50	
346	A82	15c dp carmine	.20	.20
a.		Bklt. pane of 8 (2 #341 in vert. pair + 6 #346)('64)	17.00	
b.		Bklt. pane of 12 (10 #343 + 2 #346)('64)	12.50	
e.		Bklt. pane of 8 (2 #341 in horiz. pair + 6 #346)('70)	9.00	
346C	A82	18c dull bl ('65)	.30	.20
d.		Bklt. pane of 10 (8 #343A + 2 #346C)('65)	4.50	
347	A82	20c dk gray	.20	.20
b.		Bklt. pane of 5 + label ('66)	4.00	
347A	A82	24c olive ('63)	.30	.20
348	A82	25c deep blue	.20	.20
349	A82	30c deep orange	.40	.20
a.		Bklt. pane of 5 + label (2 #341 + 3 #349)('71)	22.50	
350	A82	35c dk ol brn ('54)	.95	.20
351	A82	37c aqua ('58)	.55	.20
352	A82	40c dk slate	.25	.20
353	A82	45c scarlet	.40	.20
354	A82	50c dk bl grn	.30	.20
355	A82	60c brown bister	.30	.20
356	A82	62c dl red lil ('58)	4.50	4.00
357	A82	70c blue ('57)	.45	.20
358	A82	75c deep plum	.45	.20
359	A82	80c brt vio ('58)	.50	.20
360	A82	85c brt bl grn ('56)	.70	.20
360A	A82	95c org brn ('67)	1.40	.25
		Nos. 344-360A (20)	12.75	7.85

Coils of the 12, 15, 20, 25, 30, 40, 45, 50, 60, 70, 75 and 80c were issued in 1972. Black control number on back of every fifth stamp.

Watermark is vertical on some stamps from booklet panes.

Some booklet panes, Nos. 344a, 347b, 349a, etc., have a large selvage the size of four or six stamps, with printed inscription and sometimes illustration.

Phosphorescent paper was introduced in 1967 for the 12, 15, 20 and 45c; in 1969 for the 25c, and in 1971 for the 30, 40, 50, 60, 70, 75 and 80c.

Of the booklet panes, Nos. 345a, 345b, 346d, 346e and 347b were issued on both ordinary and phosphorescent paper, and No. 349a only on phosphorescent paper.

See No. 407. For surcharge see No. 374.

Perf. 12½x12

1954-57 Unwmk. Engr.

No.	Type	Description	Unused	Used
361	A83	1g vermilion	2.75	.20
362	A83	2½g dk green ('55)	9.00	.20
363	A83	5g black ('55)	3.00	.25
364	A83	10g vio bl ('57)	16.00	1.50
		Nos. 361-364 (4)	30.75	2.15

St. Boniface — A84

Queen Juliana — A84a

1954, June 16

No.	Type	Description	Unused	Used
365	A84	10c blue	2.40	.20

1200th anniv. of the death of St. Boniface.

Wmk. 202

1954, Dec. 15 Photo. *Perf. 13½*

No.	Type	Description	Unused	Used
366	A84a	10c scarlet	.80	.20

Issued to publicize the Charter of the Kingdom, adopted December 15, 1954.

Flaming Sword — A85

"Rebuilding Europe" — A86

1955, May 4 ***Perf. 12½x12***
367 A85 10c crimson 1.50 .20

10th anniv. of Netherlands' liberation.

1956, Sept. 15 Unwmk. ***Perf. 13x14***
368 A86 10c rose brn & blk *2.50* .20
369 A86 25c brt bl & blk *70.00 1.50*

Europa. Issued to symbolize the cooperation among the six countries comprising the Coal and Steel Community.

Admiral M. A. de Ruyter — A87

"United Europe" — A88

30c, Flagship "De Zeven Provincien."

1957, July 2 Engr. ***Perf. 12½x12***
370 A87 10c orange .75 .20
371 A87 30c dk blue 4.00 1.75

Adm. M. A. de Ruyter (1607-1676).

1957, Sept. 16 Photo. ***Perf. 13x14***
372 A88 10c blk, gray & ultra *1.00* .20
373 A88 30c dull grn & ultra *9.50 1.25*

United Europe for peace and prosperity.

No. 344 Surcharged in Silver with New Value and Bars

Perf. 13½x12½

1958, May 16 Photo. Wmk. 202
374 A82 12c on 10c 1.10 .20
a. Double surcharge 400.00 400.00
b. Inverted surcharge 400.00 400.00

Common Design Types pictured following the introduction.

Europa Issue, 1958
Common Design Type
Perf. 13x14
1958, Sept. 13 Litho. Unwmk.
Size: 22x33mm
375 CD1 12c org ver & blue *.50* .20
376 CD1 30c blue & red *2.00 .50*

NATO Emblem — A89

1959, Apr. 3 ***Perf. 12½x12***
377 A89 12c yel org & blue .20 .20
378 A89 30c red & blue 1.00 .45

10th anniversary of NATO.

Europa Issue, 1959.
Common Design Type
1959, Sept. 19 ***Perf. 13x14***
Size: 22x33mm
379 CD2 12c crimson *.90* .20
380 CD2 30c yellow grn *9.00 1.00*

Douglas DC-8 and World Map — A90

J. C. Schroeder van der Kolk — A91

Design: 30c, Douglas DC-8 in flight.

1959, Oct. 5 Engr. ***Perf. 14x13***
381 A90 12c carmine & ultra .20 .20
382 A90 30c dp blue & dp grn 1.50 .90

40th anniversary of the founding of KLM, Royal Dutch Airlines.

Perf. 12½x12
1960, July 18 Unwmk.

Design: 30c, Johannes Wier.

383 A91 12c red .70 .20
384 A91 30c dark blue 5.50 1.50

Issued to publicize Mental Health Year and to honor Schroeder van der Kolk and Johannes Wier, pioneers of mental health.

Europa Issue, 1960
Common Design Type
1960, Sept. 19 Photo. ***Perf. 12x12½***
Size: 27x21mm
385 CD3 12c car rose & org *.40* .20
386 CD3 30c dk blue & yel *3.25 1.25*

1st anniv. of CEPT. Spokes symbolize 19 founding members of Conference.

Europa Issue, 1961
Common Design Type
1961, Sept. 18 ***Perf. 14x13***
Size: 32½x21½mm
387 CD4 12c golden brown .20 .20
388 CD4 30c Prus blue *.30 .25*

Queen Juliana and Prince Bernhard A92

Telephone Dial — A93

Perf. 14x13
1962, Jan. 5 Unwmk. Photo.
389 A92 12c dk red .20 .20
390 A92 30c dk green 1.25 1.00

Silver wedding anniversary of Queen Juliana and Prince Bernhard.

1962, May 22 ***Perf. 13x14, 14x13***

Designs: 12c, Map showing telephone network. 30c, Arch and dial, horiz.

391 A93 4c brown red & blk .20 .20
392 A93 12c brown ol & blk .60 .20
393 A93 30c black, bis & Prus bl 1.90 1.25
Nos. 391-393 (3) 2.70 1.65

Completion of the automation of the Netherlands telephone network.

Europa Issue, 1962
Common Design Type
1962, Sept. 17 ***Perf. 14x13***
Size: 33x22mm
394 CD5 12c lemon, yel & blk *.30* .20
395 CD5 30c blue, yel & blk *1.10 .50*

Polder with Canals and Windmills — A94

Design: 4c, Cooling towers, Limburg State Coal Mines. 10c, Dredging in Delta.

Perf. 12½x13½
1962-66 Wmk. 202 Photo.
399 A94 4c dk blue ('63) .20 .20
401 A94 6c grn & dk grn .70 .20
403 A94 10c dp claret ('63) .20 .20
a. Booklet pane of 10 ('66) 4.00
Nos. 399-403 (3) 1.10 .60

The 10c was issued in coils in 1972. Every fifth stamp has black control number on back. See No. 461b.

Types of 1946 and 1953

1962-73 Unwmk.
Phosphorescent Paper
404 A71 4c olive green .60 .20
405 A71 5c orange ('73) .40 .20
406 A71 8c bright lilac 13.00 12.00
407 A82 12c dk Prus green .75 .40
Nos. 404-407 (4) 14.75 12.80

The 5c is from booklets and has the phosphor on the front only.
Issue dates: 5c, Jan. 12; others Aug. 27.
See Nos. 460d, 461c, 461d and 463a.

Wheat Emblem and Globe — A95

Inscription in Circle — A96

1963, Mar. 21 Photo. ***Perf. 14x13***
413 A95 12c dl bl, dk bl & yel .20 .20
414 A95 30c dl car, rose & yel 1.10 .95

FAO "Freedom from Hunger" campaign.

Perf. 13x14
1963, May 7 Unwmk. Litho.
415 A96 30c brt blue, blk & grn 1.40 1.00

1st Intl. Postal Conf., Paris, cent.

Europa Issue, 1963
Common Design Type
1963, Sept. 16 Photo. ***Perf. 14x13***
Size: 33x22mm
416 CD6 12c red brown & yel *.50* .20
417 CD6 30c Prus green & yel *1.75 .75*

Prince William of Orange Landing at Scheveningen A97

Designs: 12c, G. K. van Hogendorp, A. F. J. A. Graaf van der Duyn van Maasdam and L. Graaf van Limburg Stirum, Dutch leaders, 1813. 30c, Prince William taking oath of allegiance.

1963, Nov. 18 Photo. ***Perf. 12x12½***
Size: 27½x27½mm
418 A97 4c dull bl, blk & brn .20 .20
419 A97 5c dk grn, blk & red .20 .20
420 A97 12c olive & blk .20 .20
421 A97 30c maroon & blk .50 .50
Nos. 418-421 (4) 1.10 1.10

150th anniversary of the founding of the Kingdom of the Netherlands.

Knights' Hall, The Hague — A98

Arms of Groningen University — A99

1964, Jan. 9 ***Perf. 14x13***
422 A98 12c olive & blk .20 .20

500th anniversary of the meeting of the States-General (Parliament).

1964, June 16 Engr. ***Perf. 12½x12***

Design: 30c, Initials "AG" and crown.

423 A99 12c slate .20 .20
424 A99 30c yellow brown .20 .20

350th anniv. of the University of Groningen.

Railroad Light Signal A100

Design: 40c, Electric locomotive.

1964, July 28 Photo. ***Perf. 14x13***
425 A100 15c black & brt grn .20 .20
426 A100 40c black & yellow .80 .55

125th anniv. of the Netherlands railroads.

Bible, Chrismon and Dove — A101

1964, Aug. 25 Unwmk.
427 A101 15c brown red .20 .20

150th anniversary of the founding of the Netherlands Bible Society.

Europa Issue, 1964
Common Design Type
1964, Sept. 14 Photo. ***Perf. 13x14***
Size: 22x33mm
428 CD7 15c dp olive grn *.40* .20
429 CD7 20c yellow brown *1.40 .35*

Benelux Issue

King Baudouin, Queen Juliana and Grand Duchess Charlotte A101a

1964, Oct. 12 ***Perf. 14x13***
Size: 33x22mm
430 A101a 15c purple & buff .20 .20

20th anniversary of the signing of the customs union of Belgium, Netherlands and Luxembourg.

Queen Juliana — A102

"Killed in Action" and "Destroyed Town" — A103

1964, Dec. 15 Photo. *Perf. 13x14*
431 A102 15c green .25 .20

10th anniversary of the Charter of the Kingdom of the Netherlands.

1965, Apr. 6 Photo. *Perf. 12x12½*

Statues: 15c, "Docker" Amsterdam, and "Killed in Action" Waalwijk. 40c, "Destroyed Town" Rotterdam, and "Docker" Amsterdam.

432 A103 7c black & dk red .20 .20
433 A103 15c black & dk olive .20 .20
434 A103 40c black & dk red .75 .60
Nos. 432-434 (3) 1.15 1.00

Resistance movement of World War II.

Knight Class IV, Order of William — A104

ITU Emblem A105

1965, Apr. 29 *Perf. 13x14*
435 A104 1g gray .90 .75

150th anniversary of the establishment of the Military Order of William.

1965, May 17 Litho. *Perf. 14x13*
436 A105 20c dull bl & tan .20 .20
437 A105 40c tan & dull bl .40 .30

Centenary of the International Telecommunication Union.

Europa Issue, 1965
Common Design Type

1965, Sept. 27 Photo.
Size: 33x22mm
438 CD8 18c org brn, dk red & blk *.25 .20*
439 CD8 20c sapphire, brn & blk *.50 .30*

Marines of 1665 and 1965 — A106

1965, Dec. 10 Engr. *Perf. 13x14*
440 A106 18c dk vio bl & car .20 .20

Netherlands Marine Corps, 300th anniv.

Europa Issue, 1966
Common Design Type

1966, Sept. 26 Photo. *Perf. 13x14*
Size: 22x33mm
441 CD9 20c citron *.50 .20*
442 CD9 40c dull blue *1.00 .40*

Assembly Hall, Delft University A107

1967, Jan. 5 Litho. *Perf. 14x13*
443 A107 20c lemon & sepia .20 .20

125th anniversary of the founding of the Delft University of Technology.

Europa Issue, 1967
Common Design Type
Perf. 13x14
1967, May 2 Unwmk. Photo.
Ordinary Paper
Size: 22x32½mm
444 CD10 20c dull blue *.75 .20*
445 CD10 45c dull vio brn *1.75 .60*

Wmk. 202
446 CD10 20c dull blue *.75 .40*
447 CD10 45c dull vio brn *1.75 .60*
Nos. 444-447 (4) 5.00 1.80

Nos. 446-447 are on phosphorescent paper.

Stamp of 1852, #1 — A108

1967, May 8 Engr. Unwmk.
448 A108 20c shown 3.25 2.25
449 A108 25c No. 5 3.25 2.25
450 A108 75c No. 10 3.25 2.25
Nos. 448-450 (3) 9.75 6.75

AMPHILEX 67, Amsterdam, May 11-21. Sold only in complete sets together with a 2.50g admission ticket to Amsterdam Philatelic Exhibition. Issued in sheets of 10 (5x2).

Coins and Punched Card — A109

1968, Jan. 16 Photo. *Perf. 14x13*
451 A109 20c ver, blk & dl yel .20 .20

50th anniversary of the postal checking service.

Luminescence

All commemorative issues from No. 451 to No. 511 are printed on phosphorescent paper except No. 478 which is printed with phosphorescent ink, and Nos. 490-492. Some later issues are tagged.

Europa Issue, 1968
Common Design Type

1968, Apr. 29 Photo. *Perf. 14x13*
Size: 32½x22mm
452 CD11 20c deep blue .50 .20
453 CD11 45c crimson 1.60 *.45*

National Anthem — A110

Fokker F.2, 1919, and Friendship F.29 — A111

1968, Aug. 27 Litho. *Perf. 13x14*
454 A110 20c gray, org, car & dk bl .25 .20

400th anniversary of the national anthem "Wilhelmus van Nassouwe."

1968, Oct. 1 Photo. *Perf. 14x13*

Planes: 12c, Wright A, 1909, and Cessna sports plane. 45c, De Havilland DH-9, 1919, and Douglas DC-9.

455 A111 12c crim, pink & blk .20 .20
456 A111 20c brt grn, bl grn & blk .20 .20
457 A111 45c brt bl, lt grn & blk 1.40 1.10
Nos. 455-457 (3) 1.80 1.50

50th anniv. of the founding in 1919 of Royal Dutch Airlines and the Royal Netherlands Aircraft Factories Fokker, and the 60th anniv. in 1967 of the Royal Netherlands Aeronautical Assoc.

"iao" — A112

Design is made up of 28 minute lines, each reading "1919 internationale arbeids-organisatie 1969".

1969, Feb. 25 Engr. *Perf. 14x13*
458 A112 25c brick red & blk .45 .20
459 A112 45c ultra & blue 1.00 .65

International Labor Organization, 50th anniv.

A113

Queen Juliana — A114

Perf. 13½ horiz. x 12½ on one vert. side

1969-75 Photo.
460 A113 25c orange ver .95 .20
a. Bklt. pane of 4 + 2 labels 12.50
460B A113 25c dull red ('73) .45 .20
c. Booklet pane of 6 (#460B + 5 #461A) 27.50
d. Booklet pane of 12 (5 #405 + 7 #460B) 16.00

Perf. 13x12½
461 A113 30c choc ('72) .20 .20
d. Bklt. pane of 10 (4 #405 + 6 #461 + 2 labels)('74) 6.50
461A A113 35c grnsh bl ('72) .20 .20
b. Bklt. pane of 5 (3 #403, 2 #461A + label)('72) 25.00
c. Bklt. pane of 10 (5 #405 + 5 #461A + 2 labels)('75) 4.50
462 A113 40c car rose ('72) .20 .20
a. Bklt. pane of 5 + label ('73) 7.50
463 A113 45c ultra ('72) .25 .20
a. Bklt. pane of 8 (4 #405 + 4 #463) ('74) 4.00
464 A113 50c lilac ('72) .25 .20
a. Bklt. pane of 4 + 2 labels ('75) 3.00
465 A113 60c slate bl ('72) .30 .20
a. Bklt. pane of 5 + label ('80) 3.00
466 A113 70c bister ('72) .35 .20
467 A113 75c green ('72) .35 .20
468 A113 80c red org ('72) .40 .20
468A A113 90c gray ('75) .50 .20

Perf. 13x14
469 A114 1g yel green .45 .20
470 A114 1.25g maroon .60 .20
471 A114 1.50g yel bis ('71) .75 .20
471A A114 2g dp rose lil ('72) .95 .20
472 A114 2.50g grnsh bl 1.25 .20
473 A114 5g gray ('70) 2.40 .20
474 A114 10g vio bl ('70) 4.75 .85
Nos. 460-474 (19) 15.55 4.45

Both 25c stamps issued only in booklets.

Printings were both ordinary and phosphorescent paper for Nos. 460, 460a, 469, 471-474.

Coil printings were issued later for Nos. 461, 462-472. Black control number on back of every fifth stamp.

Booklet panes have a large selvage the size of 4 or 6 stamps, with printed inscription.

See No. 542.

Europa Issue, 1969
Common Design Type

1969, Apr. 28 Photo. *Perf. 14x13*
Size: 33½x22mm
475 CD12 25c dark blue *.60 .20*
476 CD12 45c red *2.00 .90*

A114a

A115

Möbius strip in Benelux colors.

1969, Sept. 8 Photo. *Perf. 13x14*
477 A114a 25c multicolored .25 .20

25th anniversary of the signing of the customs union of Belgium, Netherlands and Luxembourg.

Photo. & Engr.
1969, Sept. 30 *Perf. 13x14*
478 A115 25c yellow grn & maroon .25 .20

Desiderius Erasmus (1469-1536), scholar.

Queen Juliana and Rising Sun — A116

1969, Dec. 15 Photo. *Perf. 14x13*
479 A116 25c blue & multi .25 .20

15th anniversary of the Charter of the Kingdom of the Netherlands.

Prof. E. M. Meijers A117

1970, Jan. 13 Photo. *Perf. 14x13*
480 A117 25c blue, vio bl & grn .25 .20

Issued to publicize the new Civil Code and to honor Prof. Meijers, who prepared it.

Dutch Pavilion, EXPO '70 — A118

1970, Mar. 10 Photo. *Perf. 14x13*
481 A118 25c multicolored .25 .20

EXPO '70 International Exposition, Osaka, Japan, Mar. 15-Sept. 13.

"V" for Victory — A119

1970, Apr. 21 Photo. *Perf. 13x14*
482 A119 12c red, ultra, brn ol & lt bl .25 .20

25th anniv. of liberation from the Germans.

Europa Issue, 1970
Common Design Type

1970, May 4 Photo. ***Perf. 14x13***
Size: 32½x21½mm

483 CD13 25c carmine *.50* *.20*
484 CD13 45c dk blue *2.00* *.90*

Panels — A120 Globe — A121

1970, June 23 Photo. ***Perf. 13x14***
485 A120 25c gray, blk & brt yel grn .30 .20
486 A121 45c ultra, blk & pur .60 .50

#485 publicizes the meeting of the interparliamentary Union; #486 the UN 25th anniv.

Punch Cards — A122

1971, Feb. 16 Photo. ***Perf. 14x13***
487 A122 15c dp rose lilac .20 .20

14th national census, 1971.

Europa Issue, 1971
Common Design Type

1971, May 3 Photo. ***Perf. 14x13***
Size: 33x22mm

488 CD14 25c lil rose, yel & blk *.50* *.20*
489 CD14 45c ultra, yel & blk *2.00* *.90*

No. 488 was issued in coils and sheets. In the coils every fifth stamp has a black control number on the back.

Prince Bernhard, Fokker F27, Boeing 747 B — A123

Designs: 15c, Stylized carnation (Prince Bernhard Fund). 20c, Giant Panda (World Wildlife Fund). 15c, 20c horiz.

Photo., Litho. (20c)

1971, June 29 ***Perf. 13x14***
490 A123 15c black & yellow .20 .20
491 A123 20c multicolored 4.00 2.50
492 A123 25c multicolored .30 .20
Nos. 490-492,B475 (4) 6.75 5.15

60th birthday of Prince Bernhard. See No. B475.

Map of Delta — A124

1972, Feb. 15 Photo. ***Perf. 14x13***
493 A124 20c bl, grn, blk & red .25 .20

Publicity for the Delta plan, a project to shorten the coastline and to build roads.

Europa Issue 1972
Common Design Type

1972, May 5 Photo. ***Perf. 13x14***
Size: 22x33mm

494 CD15 30c blue & bis *1.25* .20
495 CD15 45c orange & bis *2.00* *.90*

No. 494 was issued in coils and sheets. In the coils every fifth stamp has a black control number on the back.

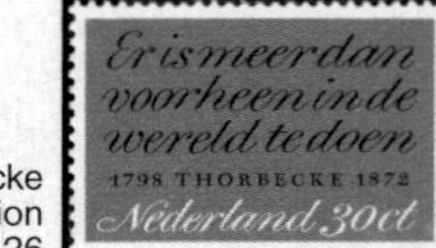

Thorbecke Quotation A126

1972, June 2 Photo. ***Perf. 14x13***
496 A126 30c lt ultra & blk .20 .20

Jan Rudolf Thorbecke (1798-1872), statesman, who said: "There is more to be done in the world than ever before."

Dutch Flag — A127

1972 ***Perf. 13x14***
497 A127 20c blue & multi .30 .20
498 A127 25c blue & multi .70 .20

400th anniversary of the Dutch flag. Issue dates: 20c, July 4; 25c, Nov. 1.

Woman Hurdler A128

30c, Woman swimmer. 45c, Bicycling.

1972, July 11 ***Perf. 14x13***
499 A128 20c multicolored .20 .20
500 A128 30c crimson & multi .35 .20
501 A128 45c violet & multi .60 .60
Nos. 499-501 (3) 1.15 1.00

20th Olympic Games, Munich, 8/26-9/11.

Red Cross — A129

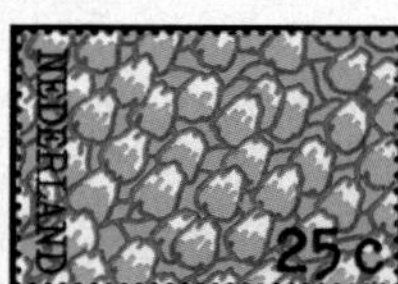

Tulips — A130

1972, Aug. 15 Photo. ***Perf. 13x14***
502 A129 5c red .20 .20
Nos. 502,B485-B488 (5) 2.95 2.50

Netherlands Red Cross.

1973, Mar. 20 Photo. ***Perf. 14x13***
503 A130 25c rose, brt grn & blk .40 .20

Dutch flower and bulb exports.

Europa Issue 1973
Common Design Type

1973, May 1 Photo. ***Perf. 14x13***
Size: 32½x22mm

504 CD16 35c bright blue *1.10* .20
505 CD16 50c purple *1.75* *.85*

Hockey A132

Woman Gymnast A133

Antenna, Burum A134

Rainbow, Measures A135

Photo. (25c, 35c); Litho. (30c, 50c)

1973, July 31 ***Perf. 13x14, 14x13***
506 A132 25c black & green .30 .20
507 A133 30c gray & multi 1.10 .35
508 A134 35c blue & multi .40 .20
509 A135 50c blue & multi .55 .45
Nos. 506-509 (4) 2.35 1.20

Netherlands Hockey Assoc., 75th anniv. (25c); Rhythmical Gymnastics World Championship, Rotterdam (30c); inauguration of satellite ground station at Burum (35c); cent. of intl. meteorological cooperation (50c).

Queen Juliana, Dutch and House of Orange Colors A136

Engr. & Photo.

1973, Sept. 4 ***Perf. 13x12***
510 A136 40c silver & multi .45 .20

25th anniversary of reign of Queen Juliana.

Chain with Open Link — A137

1973, Oct. 16 Photo. ***Perf. 13x14***
511 A137 40c grn, blk, gold & sil .75 .20

Development Corporation.

Nature and Environment — A138

1974, Feb. 19 Photo. ***Perf. 13x14***
512 A138 Strip of 3 2.10 1.75
a. 25c Bird of prey .70 .35
b. 25c Tree .70 .35
c. 25c Fisherman in boat and frog .70 .35

75th anniv. of the Netherlands Assoc. for the Protection of Birds and of the State Forestry Service.

Soccer Ball — A139

Tennis Ball — A140

Perf. 14x13, 13x14

1974, June 5 **Photo.**
513 A139 25c multicolored .30 .20
514 A140 40c multicolored .45 .20

World Cup Soccer Championship, Munich, June 13-July 7 (25c) and 75th anniversary of the Royal Dutch Lawn Tennis Association (40c).

Cattle — A141

Pierced Crab under Lens — A142

Shipwreck Seen Through Binoculars — A143

1974, July 30 ***Perf. 13x14***
515 A141 25c multicolored 5.50 1.40
516 A142 25c salmon pink & multi .50 .20
517 A143 40c dk violet & multi .45 .20
Nos. 515-517 (3) 6.45 1.80

Cent. of the Netherlands Cattle Herdbook Soc. (#515); 25th anniv. of Queen Wilhelmina Fund (for cancer research) (#516); sesquicentennial of Royal Dutch Lifeboat Soc. (#517).

BENELUX Issue

"BENELUX" A143a

1974, Sept. 10 Photo. ***Perf. 14x13***
518 A143a 30c bl grn, dk grn & lt bl .35 .20

30th anniv. of the signing of the customs union of Belgium, Netherlands and Luxembourg.

Council of Europe Emblem A144

NATO Emblem and Sea Gull A145

1974, Sept. 10 ***Perf. 13x14***

519 A144 45c black, bl & yel .50 .20
520 A145 45c dk blue & silver .50 .20

25th anniv. of Council of Europe (No. 519) and of North Atlantic Treaty Organization (No. 520).

Letters and Hands, Papier-maché Sculpture — A146

1974, Oct. 9

521 A146 60c purple & multi .35 .25

Centenary of Universal Postal Union.

People and Map of Dam Square A147

Brain with Window Symbolizing Free Thought A148

Design: No. 523, Portuguese Synagogue and map of Mr. Visser Square. 35c, No. 526, like No. 522.

1975 **Photo.** ***Perf. 13x14***

522 A147 30c multicolored .35 .20
523 A147 30c multicolored .35 .20
524 A147 35c multicolored .40 .20
525 A148 45c dp blue & multi .50 .20
Nos. 522-525 (4) 1.60 .80

Coil Stamps

Perf. 13 Horiz.

526 A147 30c multicolored .35 .20
527 A147 35c multicolored .40 .20

700th anniv. of Amsterdam (No. 522); 300th anniv. of the Portuguese Synagogue in Amsterdam (No. 523) and 400th anniv. of the founding of the University of Leyden and the beginning of higher education in the Netherlands (No. 525).

Issue dates: Nos. 522-523, 525-526, Feb. 26; Nos. 524, 527, Apr. 1.

Eye Looking over Barbed Wire — A149

1975, Apr. 29 **Photo.** ***Perf. 13x14***

528 A149 35c black & carmine .40 .20

Liberation of the Netherlands from Nazi occupation, 30th anniversary.

Company Emblem and "Stad Middelburg" A150

1975, May 21 **Photo.** ***Perf. 14x13***

529 A150 35c multicolored .40 .20

Zeeland Steamship Company, centenary.

Albert Schweitzer in Boat — A151

1975, May 21

530 A151 50c multicolored .55 .20

Albert Schweitzer (1875-1965), medical missionary.

Symbolic Metric Scale — A152

1975, July 29 **Litho.** ***Perf. 14x13***

531 A152 50c multicolored .55 .20

Cent. of Intl. Meter Convention, Paris, 1875.

Playing Card with Woman, Man, Pigeons, Pens — A153

Fingers Reading Braille — A154

1975, July 29 ***Perf. 13x14***

532 A153 35c multicolored .40 .20

International Women's Year 1975.

1975, Oct. 7 **Photo.** ***Perf. 13x14***

533 A154 35c multicolored .40 .20

Sesquicentennial of the invention of Braille system of writing for the blind by Louis Braille (1809-1852).

Rubbings of 25¢ Coins A155

1975, Oct. 7 ***Perf. 14x13***

534 A155 50c green, blk & bl .55 .20

To publicize the importance of saving.

Lottery Ticket, 18th Century A156

1976, Feb. 3 **Photo.** ***Perf. 14x13***

535 A156 35c multicolored .40 .20

250th anniversary of National Lottery.

Queen Type of 1969 and

A157

1976-86 **Photo.** ***Perf. 12½x13½***

536 A157 5c gray .20 .20

Booklet Panes

a. (3 #536, 2 #537, 3 #542) 3.00
b. (4 #536, 2 #537, 4 #539 + 2 labels) 3.25
c. (#536, 2 #537, 5 #542) 3.00
d. (4 #536, 7 #539 + label) 3.00
e. (2 #536, 2 #540, 4 #541) 3.00
f. (5 #536, 2 #537, 2 #540, 3 #542) + 2 labels 4.00
g. (1 #536, 2 #537, 5 #543) ('86) 3.00

537 A157 10c ultra .20 .20
538 A157 25c violet .30 .20
539 A157 40c sepia .45 .20
540 A157 45c brt blue .50 .20
541 A157 50c lil rose ('80) .55 .20
a. Bklt. pane, 5 each #537, 541 + 2 labels 2.75
542 A113 55c carmine .60 .20
543 A157 55c brt grn ('81) .60 .20
544 A157 60c apple grn ('81) .65 .20
545 A157 65c dk red brn ('86) .70 .20
Nos. 536-545 (10) 4.75 2.00

Compare No. 544 with No. 791. No. 542 also issued in coils with control number on the back of every 5th stamp.

Coil Stamps

1976-86 ***Perf. 13½ Vert.***

546 A157 5c slate gray .20 .20
547 A157 10c ultra .20 .20
548 A157 25c violet .30 .20
549 A157 40c sepia ('77) .45 .20
550 A157 45c brt blue .50 .20
551 A157 50c brt rose ('79) .55 .20
552 A157 55c brt grn ('81) .60 .20
553 A157 60c apple grn ('81) .65 .20
554 A157 65c dk red brn ('86) .70 .20
Nos. 546-554 (9) 4.15 1.80

See Nos. 772, 774, 786, 788, 791.

De Ruyter Statue, Flushing A158

1976, Apr. 22 **Photo.** ***Perf. 14x13***

555 A158 55c multicolored .60 .20

Adm. Michiel Adriaenszon de Ruyter (1607-1676), Dutch naval hero, 300th death anniversary.

Van Prinsterer and Page — A159

1976, May 19 **Photo.** ***Perf. 14x13***

556 A159 55c multicolored .60 .20

Guillaume Groen van Prinsterer (1801-1876), statesman and historian.

Women Waving American Flags — A160

Design is from a 220-year old permanent wooden calendar from Ameland Island.

1976, May 25 **Litho.**

557 A160 75c multicolored .80 .25

American Bicentennial.

Marchers A161

1976, June 15 **Photo.** ***Perf. 14x13***

558 A161 40c multicolored .45 .20

Nijmegen 4-day march, 60th anniversary.

A number of stamps issued from 1970 on appear to have parts of the designs misregistered, blurry, or look off-center. These stamps are deliberately designed that way. Most prominent examples are Nos. 559, 582, 602, 656, 711-712, 721, B638-B640, B662-B667.

Runners A162

1976, June 15 **Litho.**

Tagged

559 A162 55c multicolored .60 .20

Royal Dutch Athletic Soc., 75th anniv.

Printing: One Communicating with Many — A163

1976, Sept. 2 **Photo.** ***Perf. 13x14***

560 A163 45c blue & red .50 .20

Netherlands Printers Organization, 75th anniv.

Sailing Ship and City — A164

Design: 75c, Sea gull over coast.

1976, Sept. 2 **Litho.** ***Perf. 14x13***

Tagged

561 A164 40c bister, red & bl .45 .20
562 A164 75c ultra, yel & red .80 .30

Zuider Zee Project, the conversion of water areas into land.

Radiation of Heat and Light — A165

Ballot and Pencil A166

Perf. 13x14, 14x13

1977, Jan. 25 **Photo.**

563 A165 40c multicolored .45 .20
564 A166 45c black, red & ocher .50 .20

Coil Stamps

Perf. 13 Horiz.

565 A165 40c multicolored .45 .20

Perf. 13 Vert.

566 A166 45c multicolored .50 .20

Publicity for wise use of energy (40c) and forthcoming elections (45c). Nos. 565-566 have black control number on back of every 5th stamp.

For overprint see No. 569.

Spinoza — A167

1977, Feb. 21 Photo. *Perf. 13x14*
567 A167 75c multicolored .80 .25

Baruch Spinoza (1632-1677), philosopher, 300th death anniversary.

Delft Bible Text, Old Type, Electronic "a" — A168

1977, Mar. 8 *Perf. 14x13*
568 A168 55c ocher & black .60 .25

Delft Bible (Old Testament), oldest book printed in Dutch, 500th anniversary. Printed in sheets of 50 se-tenant with label inscribed with description of stamp design and purpose.

No. 564 Overprinted in Blue

1977, Apr. 15 Photo. *Perf. 14x13*
569 A166 45c multicolored .50 .20

Elections of May 25.

Kaleidoscope of Activities — A169

1977, June 9 Litho. *Perf. 13x14*
570 A169 55c multicolored .60 .20

Netherlands Society for Industry and Commerce, bicentenary.

Man in Wheelchair Looking at Obstacles A170

Engineer's Diagram of Water Currents A171

Teeth, Dentist's Mirror — A172

1977, Sept. 6 Photo. *Perf. 14x13*
571 A170 40c multicolored .45 .20

Litho.

572 A171 45c multicolored .50 .20

Perf. 13x14

573 A172 55c multicolored .60 .20
Nos. 571-573 (3) 1.55 .60

50th anniversaries of AVO (Actio vincit omnia), an organization to help the handicapped (40c), and of Delft Hydraulic Laboratory (45c); centenary of Dentists' Training in the Netherlands (55c).

"Postcode" A173

1978, Mar. 14 Photo. *Perf. 14x13*
574 A173 40c dk blue & red .45 .20
575 A173 45c red, dk & lt bl .50 .20

Introduction of new postal code.

European Human Rights Treaty — A174

Haarlem City Hall — A175

1978, May 2 Photo. *Perf. 13x14*
576 A174 45c gray, blue & blk .50 .20

European Treaty of Human Rights, 25th anniv.

Europa Issue

1978, May 2
577 A175 55c multicolored *1.00* .20

Chess Board and Move Diagram A176

Korfball A177

1978, June 1 Photo. *Perf. 13x14*
578 A176 40c multicolored .45 .20

Litho.

579 A177 45c red & vio bl .50 .20

18th IBM Chess Tournament, Amsterdam, July 12, and 75th anniversary of korfball in the Netherlands.

Man Pointing to his Kidney — A178

Heart, Torch, Gauge and Clouds — A179

1978, Aug. 22 Photo. *Perf. 13x13½*
580 A178 40c multicolored .45 .20

Perf. 13x14

581 A179 45c multicolored .50 .20

Importance of kidney transplants and drive against hypertension.

Epaulettes, Military Academy — A180

1978, Sept. 12 Photo. *Perf. 13x14*
582 A180 55c multicolored .60 .20

Royal Military Academy, sesquicentennial. Printed in continuous design in sheets of 100 (10x10).

Verkade as Hamlet A181

1978, Oct. 17 Photo. *Perf. 14x13*
583 A181 45c multicolored .50 .20

Eduard Rutger Verkade (1878-1961), actor and producer.

Clasped Hands and Arrows — A182

1979, Jan. 23 Engr. *Perf. 13x14*
584 A182 55c blue .60 .20

Union of Utrecht, 400th anniversary.

European Parliament A183

1979, Feb. 20 Litho. *Perf. 13½x13*
585 A183 45c blue, blk & red .50 .20

European Parliament, first direct elections, June 7-10.

Queen Juliana A184

1979, Mar. 13 Photo. *Perf. 13½x14*
586 A184 55c multicolored .60 .20

70th birthday of Queen Juliana.

A185

A186

Europa: 55c, Dutch Stamps and magnifying glass. 75c, Hand on Morse key, and ship at sea.

1979, May 2 Litho. *Perf. 13x13½*
587 A185 55c multicolored *.50* .20
588 A185 75c multicolored *1.25* .30

1979, June 5 Litho. *Perf. 13x14*

Map of Netherlands with chamber locations.

589 A186 45c multicolored .50 .20

Netherlands Chambers of Commerce and 175th anniversary of Maastricht Chamber.

Soccer A187

1979, Aug. 28 Litho. *Perf. 14x13*
590 A187 45c multicolored .50 .20

Centenary of soccer in the Netherlands.

Suffragettes — A188

1979, Aug. 28 Photo. *Perf. 13x14*
591 A188 55c multicolored .60 .20

Voting right for women, 60th anniversary.

Inscribed Tympanum and Architrave A189

1979, Oct. 2 Photo. *Perf. 14x13*
592 A189 40c multicolored .45 .20

Joost van den Vondel (1587-1679), Dutch poet and dramatist.

"Gay Company," Tile Floor — A190

1979, Oct. 2
593 A190 45c multicolored .50 .20

Jan Steen (1626-1679), Dutch painter.

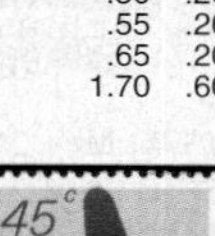
Alexander de Savornin Lohman (1837-1924) — A191

Politicians: 50c, Pieter Jelles Troelstra (1860-1930), Social Democratic Workmen's Party leader. 60c, Pieter Jacobus Oud (1886-1968), mayor of Rotterdam.

1980, Mar. 4 Photo. *Perf. 13x13½*
594 A191 45c multicolored .50 .20
595 A191 50c multicolored .55 .20
596 A191 60c multicolored .65 .20
Nos. 594-596 (3) 1.70 .60

British Bomber Dropping Food, Dutch Flag — A192

Anne Frank — A193

Perf. 13x14, 14x13

1980, Apr. 25 **Photo.**

597 A192 45c multicolored .50 .20
598 A193 60c multicolored .65 .20

35th anniv. of liberation from the Germans.

Queen Beatrix, Palace — A194

1980, Apr. 30 ***Perf. 13x14, 13x13½***

599 A194 60c multicolored .65 .20

Installation of Queen Beatrix.
See No. 608.

Boy and Girl Inspecting Stamp — A195

1980, May 1 ***Perf. 14x13***

600 A195 50c multicolored .55 .20

Youth philately; NVPH Stamp Show, s'Gravenhagen, May 1-3 and JUPOSTEX Stamp Exhibition, Eindhoven, May 23-27. No. 600 printed se-tenant with label.

Bridge Players, "Netherlands" Hand — A196

1980, June 3 **Litho.** ***Perf. 13x14***

601 A196 50c multicolored .55 .20

6th Bridge Olympiad, Valkenburg, 9/27-10/11.

Truck Transport A197

1980, Aug. 26 **Photo.** ***Perf. 13½x13***

602 A197 50c shown .55 .20
603 A197 60c Two-axle railway hopper truck .65 .20
604 A197 80c Inland navigation barge .90 .20
Nos. 602-604 (3) 2.10 .60

Queen Wilhelmina, Excerpt from Speech, Netherlands Flag — A198

1980, Sept. 23 **Litho.** ***Perf. 13½x13***

605 A198 60c shown *.50* .20
606 A198 80c Winston Churchill, British flag *1.00* *.30*

Europa.

Abraham Kuyper, University Emblem, "100" — A199

1980, Oct. 14 **Litho.** ***Perf. 13½x13***

607 A199 50c multicolored .55 .20

Free University centennial (founded by Kuyper).

Queen Beatrix Type of 1980

Perf. 13x13½, 13x14

1981, Jan. 6 **Photo.**

608 A194 65c multicolored .70 .20

Parcel A200

Designs: 55c, Dish antenna and telephone. 65c, Bank books.

1981, May 19 **Litho.** ***Perf. 13½x13***

609 A200 45c multicolored .50 .20
610 A200 55c multicolored .60 .20
611 A200 65c multicolored .70 .20
a. Souvenir sheet of 3, #609-611 2.75 2.75

Centenaries: Parcel Post Service (45c); Public telephone service (55c); National Savings Bank (65c).

Huis ten Bosch (Royal Palace), The Hague A201

1981, June 16 **Litho.** ***Perf. 13½x13***

612 A201 55c multicolored .60 .20

Europa Issue 1981

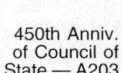

Carillon A202

1981, Sept. 1 **Litho.** ***Perf. 13½x13***

613 A202 45c shown *.50* .20
614 A202 65c Barrel organ *.65* *.25*

450th Anniv. of Council of State — A203

1981, Oct. 1 **Photo.** ***Perf. 13½x13***

615 A203 65c multi .70 .20

Excavator and Ship's Screw (Exports) A204

1981, Oct. 20 **Photo.** ***Perf. 13½x13***

616 A204 45c shown .50 .20
617 A204 55c Cast iron component, scale .60 .20
618 A204 60c Tomato, lettuce .65 .25
619 A204 65c Egg, cheese .70 .20
Nos. 616-619 (4) 2.45 .85

Queen Beatrix — A205

Black Vignette

1981-86 **Photo.** ***Perf. 13½x12½***

620 A205 65c tan .70 .20
621 A205 70c lt vio ('82) .75 .20
a. Bklt. pane, 4 #536, 4 #621 4.00
622 A205 75c pale pink ('82) .85 .20
a. Bklt. pane of 4 ('86) 3.25
623 A205 90c lt grn('82) 1.00 .20
624 A205 1g lt vio('82) 1.10 .20
625 A205 1.40g pale grn('82) 1.50 .20
626 A205 2g lem ('82) 2.25 .20
627 A205 3g pale vio ('82) 3.25 .20
628 A205 4g brt yel grn ('82) 4.50 .20
629 A205 5g lt grnsh bl ('82) 5.50 .20
630 A205 6.50g lt lil rose ('82) 7.25 .20
631 A205 7g pale bl ('86) 7.75 .25
Nos. 620-631 (12) 36.40 2.45

Coil Stamps

Perf. 13½ Horiz.

632 A205 70c lt vio ('82) 1.10 .20
633 A205 75c pale pink ('86) .80 .20
634 A205 1g lt vio ('82) 1.10 .20
635 A205 2g lem ('82) 2.25 .20
636 A205 6.50g lt lil rose ('82) 7.25 .20
637 A205 7g pale bl ('86) 7.75 .25
Nos. 632-637 (6) 20.25 1.25

See Nos. 685-699.

University of Amsterdam, 350th Anniv. A206

1982, Jan. 14 **Litho.** ***Perf. 13½x13***

638 A206 65c multi .70 .20

Royal Dutch Skating Assoc. Centenary — A207

1982, Feb. 26 **Litho.** ***Perf. 13x13½***

639 A207 45c multi .50 .20

Bicentenary of US-Netherlands Diplomatic Relations — A208

1982, Apr. 20 **Photo.** ***Perf. 13½x13***

640 A208 50c multi .55 .20
641 A208 65c multi .70 .20

See US No. 2003.

Sandwich Tern and Eider Duck, Waddenzee A209

1982, June 8 **Litho.** ***Perf. 13½x13***

642 A209 50c shown .55 .20
643 A209 70c Barnacle geese .75 .20

Dutch Road Safety Assoc, 50th Anniv. — A210

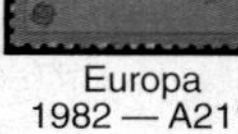

Europa 1982 — A211

1982, Aug. 24 **Photo.** ***Perf. 13x14***

644 A210 60c multi .65 .20

1982, Sept. 16 **Litho.** ***Perf. 13x13½***

Fortification Layouts.

645 A211 50c Enkhuizen, 1590 *.60* .20
646 A211 70c Coevorden, 1680 *.75* *.25*

Royal Palace, Dam Square, Amsterdam — A212

1982, Oct. 5 **Litho.** ***Perf. 13x13½***

647 A212 50c Facade, cross-section .55 .20
648 A212 60c Aerial view .65 .20

Royal Dutch Touring Club Centenary A213

1983, Mar. 1 **Litho.** ***Perf. 13½x13***

649 A213 70c multi .75 .20

A214

A215

Europa: 50c, Netherlands Newspaper Publishers Assoc., 75th anniv. 70c, Launching of European Telecommunication Satellite Org. ECS F-1 rocket, June 3.

1983, May 17 **Litho.** ***Perf. 13x13½***

650 A214 50c multi *.85* .20
651 A214 70c multi *1.00* *.25*

1983, June 21 **Litho.** ***Perf. 13x13½***

De Stijl ("The Style") Modern Art Movement, 1917-31: 50c, Composition 1922, by P. Mondriaan. 65c, Maison Particuliere contra Construction, by C. van Eesteren and T. van Doesburg.

652 A215 50c multi .55 .20
653 A215 65c multi .70 .20

Symbolic Separation of Church — A216

1983, Oct. 11 **Litho.** ***Perf. 13x13½***

654 A216 70c multi .75 .20

Martin Luther (1483-1546).

2nd European Parliament Election, June 14 — A217

1984, Mar. 13 Litho. ***Perf. 13½x13***

655 A217 70c multicolored .75 .20

St. Servatius (d. 384) — A218

1984, May 8 Photo. ***Perf. 13x14***

656 A218 60c Statue, 1732 .65 .20

Europa (1959-84) A219

1984, May 22 ***Perf. 13½x13***

657 A219 50c blue *.85 .25*
a. Perf. 14x13 *3.00 2.50*
658 A219 70c yellow green *1.50 .30*
a. Perf. 14x13 *3.00 2.50*

Perf. 14x13 stamps are coils. Every fifth stamp has a control number on the back.

William of Orange (1533-84) A220

1984, July 10 Photo. ***Perf. 14x13***

659 A220 70c multicolored .75 .20

World Wildlife Fund — A221

1984, Sept. 18 Litho. ***Perf. 14x13***

660 A221 70c Pandas, globe 2.75 .40

11th Intl. Small Business Congress, Amsterdam, Oct. 24-26 — A222

1984, Oct. 23 Litho. ***Perf. 13x13½***

661 A222 60c Graph, leaf .65 .20

Guide Dog Fund — A223

Photogravure and Engraved

1985, Jan. 22 ***Perf. 14x13***

662 A223 60c Sunny, first guide dog .65 .20

A224

Tourism A224a

1985, Feb. 26 **Photo.**

663 A224 50c multicolored .55 .20
664 A224a 70c multicolored .75 .20

Cent. of the Tourist office "Geuldal," and 50th anniv. of the Natl. Park "De Hoge Veluwe."

Liberation from German Forces, 40th Anniv. A225

Designs: 50c, Jewish star, mastheads of underground newspapers, resistance fighter. 60c, Allied supply air drop, masthead of The Flying Dutchman, Polish soldier at Arnhem. 65c, Liberation Day in Amsterdam, masthead, first edition of Het Parool (underground newspaper), American cemetery at Margraten. 70c, Dutch women in Japanese prison camp, Japanese occupation currency, building of the Burma Railway.

1985, May 5 Photo. ***Perf. 14x13***

665 A225 50c blk, buff & red .55 .20
666 A225 60c blk, buff & brt bl .65 .20
667 A225 65c blk, buff & org .70 .30
668 A225 70c blk, buff & brt grn .75 .20
Nos. 665-668 (4) 2.65 .90

WWII resistance effort (1940-1945) and liberation of Europe, 1945.

Europa '85 — A226

1985, June 4 Litho. ***Perf. 13x13½***

669 A226 50c Piano keyboard *1.00 .25*
670 A226 70c Stylized organ pipes *1.25 .30*

Natl. Museum of Fine Arts, Amsterdam, Cent. — A227

Anniversaries and events: 60c, Nautical College, Amsterdam, bicent. 70c, SAIL-85, Amsterdam.

1985, July 2 Photo. ***Perf. 13½x13***

671 A227 50c Museum in 1885, 1985 .55 .20
672 A227 60c Students training .65 .20

Perf. 14x13

673 A227 70c Sailboat rigging .75 .20
Nos. 671-673 (3) 1.95 .60

Wildlife Conservation A228

Designs: 50c, Porpoise, statistical graph. 70c, Seal, molecular structure models.

1985, Sept. 10 Litho. ***Perf. 13½x13***

674 A228 50c multicolored .55 .20
675 A228 70c multicolored .75 .20

Penal Code, Cent. — A229

Amsterdam Datum Ordinance, 300th Anniv. A230

Lithographed, Photogravure (60c)

1986, Jan. 21 ***Perf. 14x13***

676 A229 50c Text .55 .25
677 A230 60c Elevation gauge .65 .25

Sexbierum Windmill Test Station Inauguration A231

1986, Mar. 4 Litho. ***Perf. 14x13***

678 A231 70c multicolored .75 .20

Het Loo Palace Gardens, Apeldorn — A232

1986, May 13 Litho. ***Perf. 13x14***

679 A232 50c shown *.75 .25*

Photo.

680 A232 70c Air and soil pollution *1.00 .30*

Europa 1986.

Utrecht Cathedral A233

Willem Drees (1886-1988), Statesman A234

1986, June 10 Photo. ***Perf. 13x14***

681 A233 50c shown .55 .20
682 A233 60c German House, c.1350 .65 .20

Perf. 14x13

683 A233 70c Utrecht University charter, horiz. .75 .20
Nos. 681-683 (3) 1.95 .60

Cathedral restoration, 1986. Heemschut Conservation. Soc., 75th anniv. Utrecht University, 350th anniv.

1986, July 1 Litho. ***Perf. 13x13½***

684 A234 55c multicolored .60 .20

Queen Type of 1981

1986-90 Photo. ***Perf. 13½x12½***

685 A205 1.20g citron & blk 1.40 .20
686 A205 1.50g lt rose vio & blk 1.60 .20
688 A205 2.50g tan & blk 2.75 .20
694 A205 7.50g lt grn & blk 8.25 1.00
Nos. 685-694 (4) 14.00 1.60

Coil Stamps

Perf. 13½ Horiz.

697 A205 1.50g lt rose vio & blk 1.60 .20
699 A205 2.50g tan & blk 2.75 .20

Issue dates: Nos. 685, 688, 699, Sept. 23. Nos. 686, 697, Aug. 19. 7.50g, May 29, 1990.

This is an expanding set. Numbers will change if necessary.

Billiards A235

Perf. 14x13, 13x14

1986, Sept. 9 **Photo.**

705 A235 75c shown .80 .35
706 A235 75c Checkers, vert. .80 .35

Royal Dutch Billiards Assoc., Checkers Association, 75th annivs.

Delta Project Completion A236

1986, Oct. 7 Photo. ***Perf. 14x13***

708 A236 65c Storm-surge barrier .70 .20
709 A236 75c Barrier withstanding flood .80 .20

Princess Juliana and Prince Bernhard, 50th Wedding Anniv. — A237

1987, Jan. 6 Photo. ***Perf. 13x14***

710 A237 75c multicolored .80 .20

Intl. Year of Shelter for the Homeless A238

Designs: 75c, Salvation Army, cent.

1987, Feb. 10 Photo. ***Perf. 14x13***

711 A238 65c multicolored .70 .20
712 A238 75c multicolored .80 .20

Dutch Literature A239

Authors: 55c, Eduard Douwes Dekker (1820-1887) and De Harmonie Club, Batavia. 75c, Constantijn Huygens (1596-1687) and Scheveningseweg, The Hague.

1987, Mar. 10 Litho. ***Perf. 13½x13***

713 A239 55c multicolored .60 .20
714 A239 75c multicolored .80 .20

Europa 1987 — A240

Modern architecture: 55c, Scheveningen Dance Theater, designed by Rem Koolhaas. 75c, Montessori School, Amsterdam, designed by Herman Hertzberger.

1987, May 12 Litho. *Perf. 14x13*
715 A240 55c multicolored 1.00 .30
716 A240 75c multicolored 1.25 .35

Produce Auction at Broeck op Langedijk, 1887 — A241

Designs: 65c, Field in Groningen Province, signatures of society founders. 75c, Auction, bidding, price indicator, 1987.

1987, June 16 Photo. *Perf. 14x13*
717 A241 55c shown .60 .20
718 A241 65c multicolored .70 .20
719 A241 75c multicolored .80 .20
Nos. 717-719 (3) 2.10 .60

Sale of produce by auction in the Netherlands, cent., and Groningen Agricultural Society, 150th anniv. (No. 718).

Union of the Netherlands Municipalities, 75th Anniv. — A242

1987, Oct. 6 Litho. *Perf. 13x14*
720 A242 75c multicolored .80 .20

Noordeinde Palace, The Hague A243

1987, Oct. 27 Photo. *Perf. 14x13*
721 A243 65c multicolored .70 .20

A244

Booklet Stamps
Perf. 13½x13 on 3 Sides
1987, Dec. 1 Photo.
722 A244 50c dk ultra, emer & dk red .55 .20
723 A244 50c dk red, dk ultra & yel .45 .20
724 A244 50c dk ultra, yel & dk red .45 .20
725 A244 50c dk red, emer & yel .45 .20
726 A244 50c emer, dk red & dk ultra .45 .20
a. Bklt. pane, 4 each #722-726 12.00
Nos. 722-726 (5) 2.35 1.00

Netherlands Cancer Institute, 75th Anniv. A246

1988, Apr. 19 Litho. *Perf. 13½x13*
728 A246 75c multicolored .80 .20

Europa 1988 — A247

Modern transportation meeting ecological requirements: 55c, Cyclist, rural scenery, chemical formulas, vert. 75c, Cyclists seen through car-door mirror.

1988, May 17 Litho. *Perf. 13x13½*
729 A247 55c multicolored 1.25 .20
Perf. 13½x13
730 A247 75c multicolored 1.50 .25

Coronation of William III and Mary Stuart, King and Queen of England, 300th Anniv. (in 1989) — A248

Designs: 65c, Prism splitting light as discovered by Sir Isaac Newton, planet Saturn as observed by Christian Huygens, and pendulum clock, c. 1688. 75c, William of Orange (1650-1702) and Mary II (1662-1694).

1988, June 14 *Perf. 14x13*
731 A248 65c multicolored .70 .20
732 A248 75c multicolored .80 .20

Arrival of Dutch William in England, 300th anniv.

Modern Art — A249

Paintings by artists belonging to Cobra: 55c, *Cobra Cat,* 1950, by Appel. 65c, *Stag Beetle,* 1948, by Corneille. 75c, *Fallen Horse,* 1950, by Constant.

1988, July 5 Litho. *Perf. 13½x13*
733 A249 55c multicolored .60 .35
734 A249 65c multicolored .70 .35
735 A249 75c multicolored .80 .20
Nos. 733-735 (3) 2.10 .90

Each stamp printed se-tenant with label picturing the featured artist's signature.

Cobra, an intl. organization established in 1948 by expressionist artists from Copenhagen, Brussels and Amsterdam.

Australia Bicentennial — A250

1988, Aug. 30 Photo. *Perf. 13x14*
736 A250 75c multicolored .80 .20

A251

A252

1988, Sept. 27 Litho. *Perf. 13x13½*
737 A251 75c dk green & green .80 .20
738 A252 75c bright violet .80 .20

Erasmus University, Rotterdam, 75th anniv. (#737), Amsterdam Concertgebouw & Orchestra, cent. (#738).

Holiday Greetings — A253

1988, Dec. 1 Photo. *Perf. 13½x12½*
739 A253 50c multicolored .55 .20

"Holland," etc.

Stamps inscribed "Holland," "Stadspost," etc., are private issues. In some cases overprints or surcharges on Netherlands stamps may be created.

Privatization of the Netherlands Postal Service — A254

Mailbox, sorting machine, mailbag, mailman, telephone key pad, fiber optics cable, microwave transmitter & telephone handset.

Litho. & Engr.
1989, Jan. 3 *Perf. 13x13½*
740 A254 75c multicolored .80 .20

Dutch Trade Unions — A255

1989, Feb. 7 Litho. *Perf. 13x13½*
741 A255 55c shown .60 .20
Photo.
Perf. 13x14
742 A255 75c Hands, mouths .80 .20

NATO, 40th Anniv. A256

1989, Mar. 14 Litho. *Perf. 14x13*
743 A256 75c multicolored .80 .20

Europa 1989 — A257

Children's games (string telephone): 55c, Boy. 75c Girl.

1989, May 9 Litho. *Perf. 13½x13*
744 A257 55c multicolored 1.00 .25
745 A257 75c multicolored 1.25 .30

Dutch Railways, 150th Anniv. A258

1989, June 20 Litho. *Perf. 13½x13*
746 A258 55c Rails .60 .20
747 A258 65c Trains .70 .20
Perf. 14x13
748 A258 75c Passengers .80 .20
Nos. 746-748 (3) 2.10 .60

Royal Dutch Soccer Assoc., Cent. — A259

Treaty of London, 150th Anniv. — A260

1989, Sept. 5 Photo. *Perf. 13x14*
749 A259 75c multicolored .80 .20

1989, Oct. 2 Litho. *Perf. 13x14*
750 A260 75c Map of Limburg Provinces .80 .20

See Belgium No. 1327.

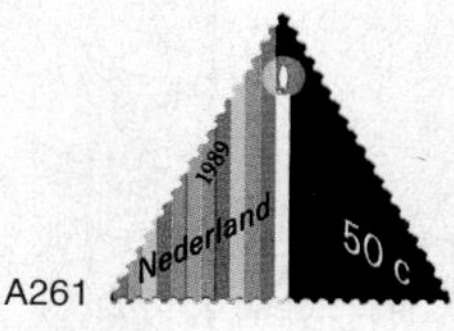

A261

Perf. 13x13x13½
1989, Nov. 30 Photo.
751 A261 50c multicolored .55 .20

Sold only in sheets of 20.

Anniversaries A262

Vincent van Gogh (1853-1890) A263

Designs: 65c, Leiden coat of arms (tulip), and layout of the Hortus Botanicus in 1601. 75c, Assessing work conditions (clock, sky, wooden floor), horiz.

1990, Feb. 6 Litho. *Perf. 13x13½*
752 A262 65c multicolored .70 .20
Perf. 13½x13
753 A262 75c multicolored .80 .20

Hortus Botanicus, Leiden, 400th anniv. (65c); Labor Inspectorate, cent. (75c).

1990, Mar. 6 *Perf. 13x13½*

Details of works by van Gogh: 55c, *Self-portrait,* pencil sketch, 1886-87. 75c, *The Green Vineyard,* painting, 1888.

754 A263 55c multicolored .60 .20
755 A263 75c multicolored .80 .20

Rotterdam Reconstruction — A264

1990, May 8 Litho. *Perf. 13½x13*
756 A264 55c shown .60 .20
757 A264 65c Diagram .70 .20
758 A264 75c Modern bldgs. .80 .20
Nos. 756-758 (3) 2.10 .60

Europa A264a

Post offices.

1990, June 12

759 A264a 55c Veere *1.25 .30*
760 A264a 75c Groningen *1.40 .35*

Dutch East India Co. Ships — A265

Sail '90 — A266

1990, July 3 ***Perf. 13x13½***

761 A265 65c multicolored .70 .20
762 A266 75c multicolored .80 .20

Queens of the House of Orange A267

1990, Sept. 5 **Litho.** ***Perf. 13½***

763 A267 150c multicolored 1.60 .50

Century of rule by Queens Emma, Wilhelmina, Juliana and Beatrix.

A268

A269

1990, Oct. 9 **Photo.** ***Perf. 13x14***

764 A268 65c multicolored .70 .20

Natl. emergency phone number.

1990, Nov. 29 **Photo.** ***Perf. 14***

765 A269 50c multicolored .55 .20
a. Tete-beche pair 1.10 .40

All pairs in sheet are tete-beche.

Threats to the Environment A270

1991, Jan. 30 **Litho.** ***Perf. 13½x13***

766 A270 55c Air pollution .60 .20
767 A270 65c Water pollution .70 .20
768 A270 75c Soil pollution .80 .20
Nos. 766-768 (3) 2.10 .60

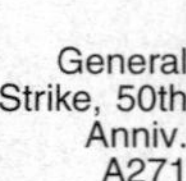
General Strike, 50th Anniv. A271

1991, Feb. 25 **Photo.** ***Perf. 14x13***

769 A271 75c multicolored .80 .20

Queen Beatrix and Prince Claus, 25th Wedding Anniv. A272

1991, Mar. 11 **Litho.** ***Perf. 13½x13***

770 A272 75c shown .80 .20
771 A272 75c Riding horses .80 .20
a. Pair, #770-771 1.60 1.60

Numeral Type of 1976 and

Queen Beatrix — A273

Perf. 12½x13½, 13½x12½

1991-94 **Photo.**

772 A157 70c gray violet .75 .20
a. Booklet pane, 5 each #537, 772 5.00
773 A273 75c green .80 .25
a. Bklt. pane of 4 + 2 labels 3.50
774 A157 80c red lilac .90 .20
774A A273 80c red brown .90 .20
b. Booklet pane of 5 + label 4.75
Complete booklet, #774Ab 4.75
775 A273 90c blue 1.00 .20
776 A273 1g purple 1.10 .20
777 A273 1.30g gray blue 1.40 .30
778 A273 1.40g gray olive 1.50 .30
779 A273 1.60g magenta 1.75 .30
780 A273 2g yel brown 2.75 .35
781 A273 2.50g red lilac 3.25 .60
782 A273 3g blue 5.50 .40
783 A273 5g brown red 4.00 .75

Perf. 14x13, Syncopated

784 A273 7.50g purple 8.25 2.00
785 A273 10g green 11.00 1.25
Nos. 772-785 (15) 44.85 7.50

Coil Stamps

Perf. 13½ Vert. (A157), Horiz. (A273)

786 A157 70c gray violet .75 .20
787 A273 75c green .80 .80
788 A157 80c red lilac .90 .20
789 A273 80c red brown .90 .20
790 A273 1.60g magenta 1.75 .30
Nos. 786-790 (5) 5.10 1.70

Booklet Stamp

Perf. 12½x13½

791 A157 60c lemon .65 .20
a. Bklt. pane, 2 #791, 4 #772 4.50

Issued: 75c, 3/14/91; 60c, 70c, #774, 1.60g, 6/25/91; #774A, 789, 1.30g, 1.40g, 9/3/91; 1g, 2g, 3g, 5g, 11/11/92; 90c, 2/2/93; 2.50g, 9/7/93; 10g, 11/29/93; 7.50g, 11/28/94.
See #902, 906-913.

A274

A276

A275

Designs: 55c, Gerard Philips, carbon filament experiments, 1890. 65c, Electrical wiring. 75c, Laser video disk experiment.

Perf. 13x14, 14x13

1991, May 15 **Photo.**

792 A274 55c multicolored .60 .25
793 A275 65c multicolored .70 .20
794 A274 75c multicolored .80 .20
Nos. 792-794 (3) 2.10 .65

Philips Electronics, cent. (Nos. 792, 794). Netherlands Normalization Institute, 75th anniv. (No. 793).

1991, June 11 **Litho.** ***Perf. 13x13½***

Europa: 75c, Ladders to another world.

795 A276 55c multicolored *1.00 .30*
796 A276 75c multicolored *1.25 .35*

Nijmegen Four Days Marches, 75th Anniv. A277

1991, July 9 **Photo.** ***Perf. 14x13***

797 A277 80c multicolored .90 .20

Dutch Nobel Prize Winners A278

Designs: 60c, Jacobus H. Van't Hoff, chemistry, 1901. 70c, Pieter Zeeman, physics, 1902. 80c, Tobias M. C. Asser, peace, 1911.

1991, Sept. 3 ***Perf. 14x13***

798 A278 60c multicolored .65 .25
799 A278 70c multicolored .75 .20
800 A278 80c multicolored .90 .20
Nos. 798-800 (3) 2.30 .65

Public Libraries, Cent. — A279

1991, Oct. 1 **Litho.** ***Perf. 13½x13***

801 A279 70c Children reading .75 .25
802 A279 80c Books .90 .20

A280

1991, Nov. 28 **Photo.** ***Perf. 14***

803 A280 55c multicolored .60 .20

Delft University of Technology, Sesquicent. A281

New Civil Code — A282

1992, Jan. 7 **Litho.** ***Perf. 13½x13***

804 A281 60c multicolored .65 .20
805 A282 80c multicolored .90 .25

A283

A284

1992 Olympics, Albertville and Barcelona: No. 806a, Volleyball, rowing. b, Shotput, rowing. c, Speedskating, rowing. d, Field hockey.

1992, Feb. 4 **Litho.** ***Perf. 13x14***

Souvenir Sheet

806 A283 80c Sheet of 4, #a.-d. 3.75 3.75

1992, Feb. 25 **Litho.** ***Perf. 13x12½***

807 A284 70c Tulips .75 .25

Photo.

Perf. 13x14

808 A284 80c Map .90 .25

Expo '92, Seville.

Discovery of New Zealand and Tasmania by Abel Tasman, 350th Anniv. A285

1992, Mar. 12 **Photo.** ***Perf. 14x13***

809 A285 70c multicolored .75 .25

A286

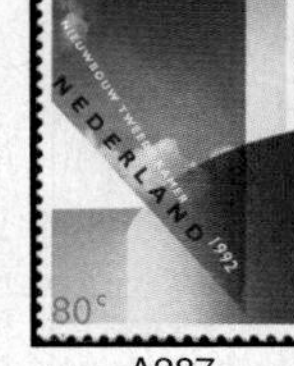

A287

1992, Apr. 28 **Litho.** ***Perf. 13x13½***

810 A286 60c multicolored .65 .20
811 A287 80c multicolored .90 .25

Royal Assoc. of Netherlands Architects, 150th Anniv. (#810). Opening of Building for Lower House of States General (#811).

Discovery of America, 500th Anniv. A288

Perf. 13½x13, 13x13½

1992, May 12 **Litho.**

812 A288 60c Globe, Columbus *1.25 .35*
813 A288 80c Sailing ship, vert. *1.75 .35*

Europa. On normally centered stamps the white border appears at the left side of No. 813.

Royal Netherlands Numismatics Society, Cent. — A289

1992, May 19 **Photo.** ***Perf. 13x14***

814 A289 70c multicolored .75 .25

Netherlands Pediatrics Society, Cent. — A290

1992, June 16 **Litho.** ***Perf. 13½x13***

815 A290 80c multicolored .90 .25

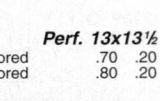

First Deportation Train from Westerbork Concentration Camp, 50th Anniv. — A291

1992, Aug. 25 *Perf. 13x13½*
816 A291 70c multicolored .75 .25

Single European Market A292

1992, Oct. 6 *Perf. 13½x13*
817 A292 80c multicolored .90 .25

Queen Beatrix, 12½Years Since Investiture — A293

1992, Oct. 30 *Perf. 13x13½*
818 A293 80c multicolored 1.00 .25

Christmas Rose — A294

1992, Nov. 30 **Photo.** *Perf. 14*
819 55c Red flower .60 .20
820 55c Silver flower .60 .20
a. A294 Pair, #819-820 1.25 .25

Netherlands Cycle and Motor Industry Assoc. (RAI), Cent. — A295

Designs: 70c, Couple riding bicycle. 80c, Early automobile.

1993, Jan. 5 **Litho.** *Perf. 13½x13*
821 A295 70c multicolored .80 .20
822 A295 80c black & yellow .90 .20

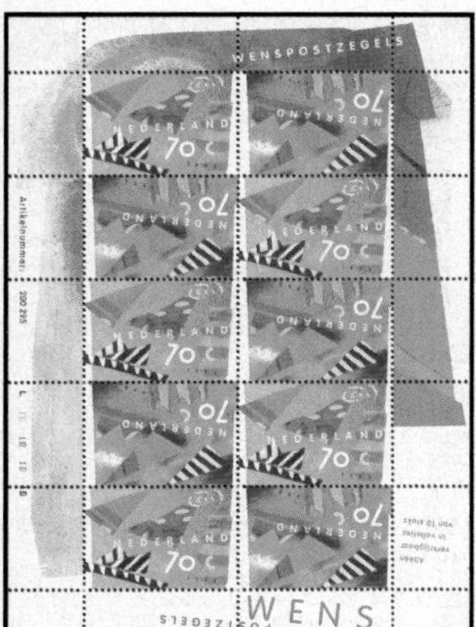
Greetings Stamps — A296

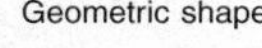
Geometric shapes.

1993, Feb. 2 **Photo.** *Perf. 14x13½*
823 A296 70c multi .80 .20
824 A296 70c multi, diff. .80 .20
a. Tete-beche pair, #823-824 1.60 .25

Mouth-to-mouth Resuscitation A297

Royal Horse Artillery Lead Driver, Horses A298

Leaf, Insect Pests — A299

1993, Feb. 16 **Litho.** *Perf. 13x13½*
825 A297 70c multicolored .80 .20
826 A298 80c multicolored .90 .20
827 A299 80c multicolored .90 .20
Nos. 825-827 (3) 2.60 .60

Royal Netherlands First Aid Assoc., cent. (#825). Royal Horse Artillery, bicent. (#826). University of Agriculture, 75th anniv. (#827).

On No. 826, normally centered stamps show design extending to top and right sides only.

Royal Dutch Notaries' Assoc., 150th Anniv. — A300

Litho. & Engr.

1993, Mar. 2 *Perf. 14x13*
828 80c Top half of emblem .90 .20
829 80c Bottom half of emblem .90 .20
a. A300 Pair, #828-829 1.80 .35

No. 829a has continuous design.

Butterflies A301

Designs: 70c, Pearl-bordered fritillary (Zilvervlek). 80c, Large tortoiseshell (Grote vos). 90c, Large white (Koolwitje). 160c, Polyommatus icarus.

1993, Mar. 23 **Photo.**
830 A301 70c black & multi .80 .20
831 A301 80c yellow & multi .90 .20
832 A301 90c green & multi 1.00 .20
Nos. 830-832 (3) 2.70 .60

Souvenir Sheet

833 A301 160c red & multi 1.75 1.75

On normally centered stamps the white border appears at the right side.

Radio Orange — A302

Designs: No. 834, Woman broadcasting. No. 835, Man listening.

1993, May 5 **Photo.** *Perf. 14x13*
834 80c orange red & purple .95 .20
835 80c purple & orange red .95 .20
a. A302 Pair, #834-835 1.90 .40

European Youth Olympic Days — A303

Symbols of Olympic sports.

1993, June 1 *Perf. 13x14*
836 A303 70c blue & multi .85 .20
837 A303 80c yellow & multi .95 .20

Europa A304

Contemporary sculpture by: 70c, Wessel Couzijn. 80c, Per Kirkeby. 160c, Naum Gabo, vert.

Perf. 13½x13, 13x13½

1993, July 6 **Litho.**
838 A304 70c blk, blue & grn 1.00 *.50*
839 A304 80c black, red & yel 1.25 *.30*
840 A304 160c black, blue & pur 1.40 *.90*
Nos. 838-840 (3) 3.65 1.70

Dutch Nobel Prize Winners — A305

Designs: 70c, J.D. van der Waals, physics, 1910. 80c, Willem Einthoven, medicine, 1924. 90c, Christiaan Eijkman, medicine, 1929.

1993, Sept. 7 **Litho.** *Perf. 13x13½*
841 A305 70c multicolored .85 .20
842 A305 80c multicolored .95 .20
843 A305 90c multicolored 1.10 .25
Nos. 841-843 (3) 2.90 .65

Letter Writing Day — A306

1993, Sept. 14 **Photo.** *Perf. 14x13*
844 80c Pencils, pen .95 .25
845 80c Envelope, contents .95 .25
a. A306 Pair, #844-845 1.90 .50

Stamp Day — A307

1993, Oct. 8 **Litho.** *Perf. 13½x13*
846 A307 70c shown .80 .20
847 A307 80c Dove with envelope .95 .25

December Stamps — A308

Clock hand pointing to "12:" and: No. 848, Star, candle, Christmas tree. No. 849, Fireworks.

1993, Nov. 29 **Photo.** *Perf. 12*
848 A308 55c blue & multi .60 .20
849 A308 55c red & multi .60 .20
a. Pair, #848-849 1.25 .20

Issued in sheets of 20, 10 each #848-849 + label. Each stamp contains perforations placed within the design to resemble snowflakes.

Piet Mondrian (1872-1944), Painter A309

Details from paintings: 70c, The Red Mill. 80c, Rhomboid with Yellow Lines. 90c, Broadway Boogie Woogie.

1994, Feb. 1 **Litho.** *Perf. 13½x13*
850 A309 70c multicolored .80 .20
851 A309 80c multicolored .95 .25
852 A309 90c multicolored 1.10 .25
Nos. 850-852 (3) 2.85 .70

Wild Flowers A310

1994, Mar. 15 **Photo.** *Perf. 14]x13*
853 A310 70c Downy rose .80 .20
854 A310 80c Daisy .95 .25
855 A310 90c Woods forget-me-not 1.10 .25
Nos. 853-855 (3) 2.85 .70

Souvenir Sheet

856 A310 160c Fire lily croceum 3.00 2.25

Dutch Aviation, 75th Anniv. A311

1994, Apr. 6 **Litho.** *Perf. 13½x13*
857 A311 80c KLM .95 .25
858 A311 80c Fokker .95 .25
859 A311 80c NLR .95 .25
Nos. 857-859 (3) 2.85 .75

Planetarium, Designed by Eise Eisinga — A312

Design: 90c, Television image of moon landing, footprint on moon.

1994, May 5 **Photo.** *Perf. 13x14*
860 A312 80c multicolored .90 .20
861 A312 90c multicolored 1.00 .25

First manned moon landing, 25th anniv. (#861).

1994 World Cup Soccer Championships, U.S. — A313

1994, June 1
862 A313 80c multicolored .90 .20

No. 862 printed with se-tenant label.

Stock Exchange Floor, Initials KPN A314

1994, June 13 Litho. ***Perf. 13½***

863	A314 80c multicolored	.90	.20

Offering of shares in Royal PTT Netherlands NV (KPN).

Bicycle, Car, Road Sign — A315

80c, Silhouettes of horses, riders, carriage.

1994, June 14 Photo. ***Perf. 14x13***

864	A315 70c multicolored	.85	.20

Litho.

Perf. 13½x13

865	A315 80c multicolored	.90	.20

First road signs placed by Dutch motoring assoc. (ANWB), cent. (#864). World Equestrian Games, The Hague (#865).

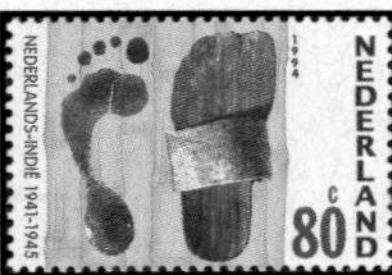

War in Dutch East Indies (1941-45) A316

Operation Market Garden (1944) — A316a

Perf. 14x13, 13x14

1994, Aug. 15 Photo.

866	A316 80c multicolored	1.00	.25
867	A316a 90c multicolored	1.10	.30

Lighthouses A317

Designs: 70c, Brandaris, Terschelling Island. 80c, Ameland Island, vert. 90c, Vlieland Island, vert.

Perf. 13½x13, 13x13½

1994, Sept. 13 Litho.

868	A317 70c multicolored	.90	.25
869	A317 80c multicolored	1.00	.25
870	A317 90c multicolored	1.10	.30
	Nos. 868-870 (3)	3.00	.80

December Stamps — A318

1994, Nov. 28 Photo. ***Perf. 13½***

871	A318 55c Snowflake, tree	.65	.20
872	A318 55c Candle, star	.65	.20
a.	Pair, #871-872	1.30	.30
b.	Min. sheet, 10 #872a + label	13.00	

One stamp in #872a is rotated 90 degrees to the other stamp.

Cow, Dutch Products A319

1995, Jan 2 Photo. ***Perf. 14x13½***

873	A319 100c multicolored	1.25	.30

Hendrik Nicolaas Werkman (1882-1945), Printer — A320

Mesdag Museum Restoration A321

Mauritius No. 2 — A322

1995, Jan. 17 Litho. ***Perf. 14x13½***

874	A320 80c multicolored	1.00	.25
875	A321 80c multicolored	1.00	.25

Litho. & Engr.

Perf. 13½x14

876	A322 80c multicolored	1.00	.25
	Nos. 874-876 (3)	3.00	.75

Acquisition of Mauritius No. 2 by Netherlands PTT Museum (#876).

Motion Pictures, Cent. — A323

70c, Joris Iven, documentary film maker. 80c, Scene from film, "Turkish Delight," 1972.

1995, Feb. 28 Photo. ***Perf. 14x13***

877	A323 70c multicolored	.90	.25
878	A323 80c multicolored	1.00	.25

Mahler Festival A324

Design: 80c, Gustav Mahler, (1860-1911), composer, 7th Symphony score.

1995, Mar. 21 Litho. ***Perf. 13½x13***

879	A324 80c blue & black	1.00	.25

Institute of Registered Accountants, Cent. — A325

Assoc. of Building Contractors, Cent. — A326

1995, Mar. 28

880	A325 80c multicolored	1.00	.20
881	A326 80c multicolored	1.00	.20

50th Anniversaries A327

Designs: No. 882, End of World War II, "45, 95" No. 883, Liberation of the Netherlands, "40, 45." No. 884, Founding of the UN, "50."

1995, May 3 Litho. ***Perf. 13x13½***

882	A327 80c multicolored	1.00	.20
883	A327 80c multicolored	1.00	.20
884	A327 80c multicolored	1.00	.20
	Nos. 882-884 (3)	3.00	.60

Signs of the Zodiac, Birthday Cake — A328

1995, May 22 Photo. ***Perf. 14x13½***

885	A328 70c multicolored	1.10	.20

18th World Boy Scout Jamboree — A329

Sail Amsterdam '95 — A330

Perf. 13x13½, 13½x13

1995, June 6 Litho.

886	A329 70c multicolored	.90	.20
887	A330 80c multicolored	1.00	.20

Birds of Prey A330a

Perf. 13x14, 14x13

1995, Sept. 5 Photo.

888	A330a 70c Kestrel, vert.	.90	.20
889	A330a 80c Hen harrier	1.00	.20
890	A330a 100c Red kite	1.25	.25
	Nos. 888-890 (3)	3.15	.65

Souvenir Sheet

891	A330a 160c Honey buzzard	2.00	2.00

Nobel Prize Winners A331

No. 892, F. Zernike, physics, 1953. No. 893, P.J.W. Debye, chemistry, 1936. No. 894, J. Tinbergen, economics, 1969.

1995, Sept. 26 Litho. ***Perf. 13½x13***

892	A331 80c green & multi	1.00	.20
893	A331 80c blue & multi	1.00	.20
894	A331 80c red & multi	1.00	.20
	Nos. 892-894 (3)	3.00	.60

Dutch Cabaret, Cent. A332

Designs: 70c, Eduard Jacobs (1868-1914), Jean-Louis Pisuisse (1880-1927). 80c, Wim Kan (1911-83), Freek de Jonge (b. 1944).

1995, Oct. 17 Litho. ***Perf. 13½x14***

895	A332 70c multicolored	.90	.20
896	A332 80c multicolored	1.00	.20

Queen Beatrix Type of 1991

1995-98 Photo. ***Perf. 13½x12½***

902	A273 1.50g green	1.50	.40

Numeral Type of 1976 and Queen Type of 1991

2001 Photo. ***Die Cut Perf. 14¼***

Self-Adhesive

Booklet Stamps

903	A157 5c gray	.20	.20
a.	Double-sided pane of 10	.45	
904	A157 10c ultramarine	.20	.20
a.	Double-sided pane of 10	.85	
905	A157 25c violet	.30	.20
a.	Double sided pane of 10	3.00	
906	A273 85c blue green	.95	.20
a.	Booklet pane of 5	5.00	
907	A273 1g purple	1.10	.20
a.	Booklet pane of 5	5.50	
908	A273 1.10g blue	1.25	.25
a.	Booklet pane of 5	6.25	
909	A273 1.45g green	1.60	.30
a.	Booklet pane of 5	8.00	
910	A273 2.50g red lilac	2.75	.55
a.	Booklet pane of 5	14.00	
911	A273 5g brown red	5.50	1.10
a.	Booklet pane of 5	27.50	
	Nos. 903-911 (9)	13.85	3.20

Issued: 5c, 10c, 25c, 6/18; 85c, 1.45g, 7/2; 1g, 1.10g, 2.50g, 5g, 9/3. 85c has added euro denomination.

Coil Stamp

Perf. 13½ Horiz.

912	A273 1g gray violet	1.10	.25
913	A273 1.10g blue	1.25	.25

Issued: 1g, 10/5/95; 1.50g, 3/17/98, 1.10g, 8/1/00.

December Stamps — A333

Serpentine Die Cut 12½x13

1995, Nov. 27

Self-Adhesive

916	A333 55c Children, star	.70	.20
917	A333 55c Children, stars	.70	.20
a.	Pair, Nos. 916-917	1.40	

Issued in sheets of 20, checkerboard style.

Paintings by Johannes Vermeer (1632-75) — A334

Entire paintings or details: 70c, A Lady Writing a Letter, with Her Maid. 80c, The Love Letter. 100c, A Woman in Blue Reading a Letter.

1996, Feb. 27 Litho. ***Perf. 13x13½***

918	A334 70c multicolored	.80	.20
919	A334 80c multicolored	.95	.20
920	A334 100c multicolored	1.25	.25
a.	Souvenir sheet, Nos. 918-920	3.00	.60
	Nos. 918-920 (3)	3.00	.65

Spring Flowers A335

Designs: 70c, Daffodil bulb, garden tools. 80c, Closeup of woman, tulip. 100c, Snake's head (fritillaria). 160c, Crocuses.

1996, Mar. 21 Litho. *Perf. 13½x13*

921 A335 70c multicolored .80 .20
922 A335 80c multicolored .95 .20
923 A335 100c multicolored 1.25 .25
Nos. 921-923 (3) 3.00 .65

Souvenir Sheet

924 A335 160c multicolored 1.90 .40

A336

A337

1996, Apr. 1 *Perf. 13x13½*

925 A336 70c Moving stamp .85 .20

No. 925 was sold in sheets of 20. See #951.

1996, May 14 Litho. *Perf. 13½x13*

Mr. Olivier B. Bommel, by Marten Toonder: a, O.B. Bommel preparing for holiday. b, O.B. Bommel receives letter.

926 Sheet of 2 + 2 labels 1.75 1.75
a. A337 70c multicolored .80 .80
b. A337 80c multicolored .95 .95

Comic strips, cent.

Vacations A338

Scene, flower: No. 927, Beach, sunflower. No. 928, Cyclists, gerbera. 80c, Gables in Amsterdam, cornflower. 100c, Windmills at "Zaanse Schans'" open air museum, anemone.

1996, May 31

927 A338 70c multicolored .85 .20
928 A338 70c multicolored .85 .20
929 A338 80c multicolored .95 .20
930 A338 100c multicolored 1.25 .25
Nos. 927-930 (4) 3.90 .85

Province of North Brabant, Bicent. A339

1996, June 13 Litho. *Perf. 13½x13*

931 A339 80c multicolored .90 .20

Sporting Events A340

Designs: 70c, Lighting the Olympic Torch, 1996 Summer Olympic Games, Atlanta. 80c, Tour de France cycling race. 100c, Euro '96 Soccer Championships, Wembley Stadium, England. 160c, Olympic rings, track sports, Atlanta stadium.

1996, June 25

932 A340 70c multicolored .80 .20
933 A340 80c multicolored .90 .25
934 A340 100c multicolored 1.10 .30
935 A340 160c multicolored 1.75 .45
Nos. 932-935 (4) 4.55 1.20

Erasmus Bridge, Rotterdam A341

UNICEF, 50th Anniv. A342

Designs: No. 936, Martinus Nijhoff Bridge over Waal River, horiz. No. 938, Wijker Tunnel under North Sea Canal, horiz.

1996, Aug. 6 *Perf. 13½x13, 13x13½*

936 A341 80c multicolored .90 .25
937 A341 80c shown .90 .25
938 A341 80c multicolored .90 .25
Nos. 936-938 (3) 2.70 .75

1996, Sept. 3 *Perf. 13x13½*

Designs: 70c, School children from Ghana. 80c, Girl from Ghana with tray on head.

939 A342 70c multicolored .80 .20
940 A342 80c multicolored .90 .25

Sesame Street in Netherlands, 20th Anniv. A343

70c, Bert & Ernie. 80c, Pino, Ieiemienie & Tommie.

1996, Sept. 3 *Perf. 13½x13*

941 A343 70c multicolored .80 .20
942 A343 80c multicolored .90 .25

Voyages of Discovery A344

Voyages of: 70c, Petrus Plancius (1552-1622), cartographer. #944, Willem Barents (d. 1597). #945, Cornelis de Houtman (1540-99). 100c, Mahu en De Cordes (1598-1600).

1996, Oct. 1

943 A344 70c multicolored .80 .20
944 A344 80c multicolored .90 .25
945 A344 80c multicolored .90 .25
946 A344 100c multicolored 1.10 .30
Nos. 943-946 (4) 3.70 1.00

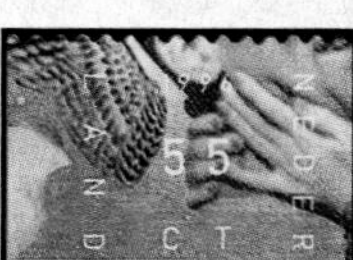

December Stamps — A345

Collage of faces, hands: No. 947, Wing, ear, hands. No. 948, Mouth, two faces. No. 949, Woman with eyes closed, hand. No. 950, Eyes, face with mouth open.

Serpentine Die Cut 9 Horiz.

1996, Nov. 26

Self-Adhesive

947 A345 55c multicolored .65 .20
948 A345 55c multicolored .65 .20
949 A345 55c red violet & multi .65 .20
950 A345 55c blue & multi .65 .20
a. Block or strip of 4, #947-950 2.60

Issued in sheets of 20.

Moving Stamp Type of 1996

Die Cut Perf. 13

1997, Jan. 2 Photo.

Self-Adhesive

951 A336 80c like No. 925 .90 .25

No. 951 sold in panes of 20.

Business Stamps A346

Geometric designs.

Sawtooth Die Cut 13½, Syncopated (on 1 Side)

1997, Jan. 2

Self-Adhesive

Coil Stamps

952 A346 80c pink & multi .90 .25
953 A346 160c green & multi 1.75 .50

Cross-Country Skating Championships — A347

1997, Jan. 4 Photo. *Perf. 14x13*

954 A347 80c multicolored .90 .25

Surprise Stamps A348

Inscriptions beneath scratch-off heart-shaped panels: b, Schrijf me. c, Groetjes. d, Ik hou van je. e, Tot gauw. f, Ik denk aan je. g, XXX-jes. h, Ik mis je. i, Geintje. j, Zomaar. k, Wanneer?

1997, Jan. 21 *Perf. 14x13½*

955 Sheet of 10 9.00 2.50
a. A348 80c Any single, unscratched heart .90 .25
b.-k. A348 80c Any single, scratched heart .25

Unused value for #955a is with attached selvage. Inscriptions are shown in selvage beside each stamp.

Nature and Environment A349

1997, Feb. 25 Litho. *Perf. 13½x13*

956 A349 80c Pony .90 .25
957 A349 100c Sheep 1.10 .30

Souvenir Sheet

958 A349 160c Sheep, diff. 1.75 1.00

Suske & Wiske Comic Strip Characters A350

#959, Suske, Wiske, Tante Sidonia, & Lambik. #960a, Jerome making exclamation.

Perf. 13½x12½

1997, Mar. 18 Litho.

959 A350 80c multicolored .90 .20

Souvenir Sheet

960 Sheet of 2, #959, 960a 1.90 1.00
a. A350 80c violet & red .90 .20

A351

Greetings Stamps A352

#961, Birthday cake. #962, Amaryllis surrounded by cup of coffee, two glasses of wine, hand writing card, candlelight.

1997, May 6 Photo. *Perf. 14x13½*

961 A351 80c multicolored .90 .20
962 A352 80c multicolored .90 .20

See No. 1035.

Marshall Plan, 50th Anniv. — A353

Designs: No. 963, Map of Europe. No. 964, Flag, quotation from George C. Marshall.

1997, May 27 Litho. *Perf. 13½x13*

963 80c multicolored .90 .20
964 80c multicolored .90 .20
a. A353 Pair, #963-964 1.90 1.90

Court of Audit, 550th Anniv. A354

1997, May 27 *Perf. 13½x13*

965 A354 80c multicolored .90 .20

European Council of Ministers Meeting, Amsterdam A355

1997, June 17 Litho. *Perf. 13½*

966 A355 100c multicolored 1.25 .30

Water Recreation A356

1997, July 1 *Perf. 13½x13*

967 A356 80c Swimming, row boat 1.00 .25
968 A356 1g Sailboats 1.25 .30

Royal Institute of Engineers, 150th Anniv. A357

1997, Aug. 5

969 A357 80c multicolored 1.00 .25

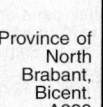

Netherlands Asthma Center, Cent. — A358

1997, Aug. 5
970 A358 80c multicolored 1.00 .25

Horticultural Education at Florens College, Aalsmeer, Cent. — A359

1997, Aug. 5
971 A359 80c multicolored 1.00 .25

Franz Schubert (1797-1828), Composer A360

1997, Aug. 5
972 A360 80c multicolored 1.00 .25

A361

Youth Stamps A362

1997, Sept. 2
973 A361 80c multicolored 1.00 .25
a. Bklt. pane of 5 + 2 labels 5.00
Complete booklet, #973a 5.00
974 A362 80c multicolored 1.00 .25

Issued: No. 973a, 7/6/99.

Birth Announcement Stamp — A363

Die Cut Perf. 13½x13
1997, Oct. 7 **Photo.**
Self-Adhesive
975 A363 80c multicolored .90 .25

See No. 1033.

A364

A365

December Stamps: Stylized people head to head showing either a star or heart in the center.

Serpentine Die Cut
1997, Nov. 25 **Photo.**
Self-Adhesive
Background Colors
976 A364 55c yellow .60 .20
977 A364 55c blue .60 .20
978 A364 55c orange .60 .20
979 A364 55c red .60 .20
980 A364 55c yellow green .60 .20
981 A364 55c green .60 .20
a. Sheet, 3 ea #976, 978-979, 981, 4 ea #977, 980 12.50 12.50

1998, Jan. 2 **Litho.** ***Perf. 13½***
982 A365 80c gray blue .90 .25

Death announcement stamp.

Delftware A366

100c, Cow, tiles with pictures of sailing ships. 160c, Tiles, one picturing boy standing on head.

1998, Jan. 2 **Photo.** ***Die Cut***
Self-Adhesive
983 A366 100c multicolored 1.10 .30
984 A366 160c multicolored 1.75 .45

Issued in both coil strips and sheets with priority labels.

A368

A369

Growing Fruit in the Four Seasons: No. 986, Orchard in bloom, spring. No. 987, Strawberries, summer. No. 988, Harvesting, autumn. No. 989, Pruning, winter.

1998, Feb. 17 **Litho.** ***Perf. 13x13½***
Booklet Stamps
986 A368 80c multicolored .90 .20
987 A368 80c multicolored .90 .20
988 A368 80c multicolored .90 .20
989 A368 80c multicolored .90 .20
a. Booklet pane, #986-989 3.75
Complete booklet, #989a 3.75

Die Cut Perf. 13½
1998, Mar. 17 **Photo.**
Self-Adhesive
990 A369 80c multicolored .90 .20

Marriage and wedding anniversaries. No. 990 was issued in sheets of 10.

See No. 1034.

Anniversaries A370

#991, Men shaking hands, Treaty of Munster, 350th anniv. #992, Statue of John Rudolf Thorbecke, Dutch constitution, 150th anniv. #993, Child on swing, Universal Declaration of Human Rights, 50th anniv.

1998, Mar. 17 **Litho.** ***Perf. 13½x13***
991 A370 80c multicolored .90 .20
992 A370 80c multicolored .90 .20
993 A370 80c multicolored .90 .20
a. Strip of 3, #991-993 2.75 2.75

Letter Writing Day A371

1998, May 8 **Litho.** ***Perf. 13½***
994 A371 80c multicolored .90 .20

1998 World Cup Soccer Championships, France — A372

1998, May 19 **Litho.** ***Perf. 13½***
995 A372 80c multicolored .90 .25

Rabo Bank, Cent. — A373

1998, May 19 ***Perf. 13½x13***
996 A373 80c multicolored .90 .25

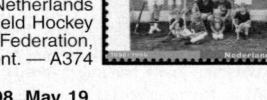

Royal Netherlands Field Hockey Federation, Cent. — A374

1998, May 19
997 A374 80c multicolored .90 .25

Central Administration in Friesland, 500th Anniv. A375

1998, June 9 **Litho.** ***Perf. 13½x13***
998 A375 80c multicolored .90 .20

Water Management A375a

1998, June 9
999 A375a 80c shown .90 .20
1000 A375a 1g Aerial view 1.10 .30

Split of Royal Netherlands PTT — A376

#1001, TNT Post Groep. #1002, KPN NV.

1998, June 29
1001 80c red, black & blue .90 .20
1002 80c blue, blk & grn .90 .20
a. Vert. pair, #1001-1002 1.90 1.90

No. 1002a is a continuous design.

Natl. Library of the Netherlands, Bicent. A377

1998, July 7
1003 A377 80c multicolored .90 .20

A378

A379

No. 1004, Maurits Cornelis Escher (1898-1972), Graphic Artist. No. 1005, Simon Vestdijk (1898-1971), writer.

1998, July 7 ***Perf. 13x13½***
1004 A378 80c multicolored .90 .20
1005 A378 80c multicolored .90 .20
a. Pair, #1004-1005 1.90 1.90

Souvenir Sheet

1998, Sept. 1 **Litho.** ***Perf. 13x13½***

Inauguration of Queen Wilhelmina, Cent.: a, Queen Wilhelmina. b, Gilded Coach.

1006 A379 80c Sheet of 2, #a.-b. 1.90 1.90

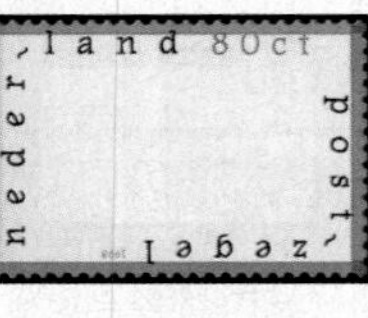

Greetings Stamps A380

Colors of stamp edges, clockwise from side adjacent to "Neder:" No. 1007: a, yellow, orange, red, red. b, red, orange, pink, yellow orange. c, red, orange, rose, orange. d, orange, red, light orange, yellow orange. e, yellow, orange, pink, red.

Serpentine Die Cut Perf. 13½x13
1998, Sept. 1 **Litho.**
Self-Adhesive
1007 A380 80c Sheet of 10, 2 each #a.-e. 9.00
a.-e. any single .90 .20

Each side of No. 1007 contains a pane of 1 each #1007a-1007e and 10 different self-adhesive labels.

Nos. 1008-1011 are unassigned.

Pets — A381

1998, Sept. 22 ***Perf. 13½x13***
1012 A381 80c Dog .90 .20
a. Bklt. pane of 5 + 2 labels 4.75
Complete booklet, #1012a 4.75
1013 A381 80c Kittens .90 .20
1014 A381 80c Rabbits .90 .20
Nos. 1012-1014 (3) 2.70 .60

Issued: No. 1012a, 7/6/99.

Jan, Jans en de Kinderen Comic Strip, by Jan Kruis — A382

Characters: No. 1015, Writing letters. No. 1016, In automobile, mailing letter.

1998, Oct. 6 **Litho.** ***Perf. 13½x13***
1015 A382 80c multicolored .90 .20
a. Booklet pane, 10 #1015 + 20 labels 9.00
Complete booklet, #1015a 9.00
1016 A382 80c multicolored .90 .20
a. Sheet of 2, #1015-1016 + 3 labels 1.90 .40

December Stamps — A383

25c, Stylized tree, house on top of earth. No. 1018:
Silhouetted against moon: a, Rabbit. b, House. c, Bird. d, Tree. e, Deer.
Silhouetted against horizon: f, Rabbit. g, House. h, Bird. i, Tree. j, Deer.
House with: k, Rabbit. l, Heart. m. Bird. n, Tree. o, Deer.
Tree with: p, Rabbit. q, House. r, Bird. s, Heart. t, Deer.

1998-99 Litho. *Perf. 13*
1017 A383 25c multicolored .30 .20

Self-Adhesive
Die Cut Perf. 9

1018 A383 55c Sheet of 20, #a.-t. 12.50 3.25

Issued: #1018, 11/24; #1017, 1/5/99.

Introduction of the Euro — A384

1999, Jan. 5 Litho. *Perf. 13x12½*
1019 A384 80c multicolored .90 .25

Netherlands Postal Services, Bicent. — A385

1999, Jan. 15 Litho. *Perf. 13½x14*
1020 A385 80c multi + label .90 .25

See No. 1039

A386

A387

1999, Feb. 2 Litho. *Perf. 12¾x13¼*
1021 A386 80c Spoonbill .90 .25
1022 A386 80c Globe, tern .90 .25

Protection of birds and migrating waterfowl. Netherlands Society for Protection of Birds, cent (#1021). African-Eurasian Waterbird Agreement (#1022).

1999, Feb. 2 *Perf. 12¾x13¼*
Booklet Stamp

1023 A387 80c multicolored .90 .25
a. Booklet pane of 4 3.75
Complete booklet, #1023a 3.75

Royal Dutch Lawn Tennis Assoc., cent.

Views During the Four Seasons A388

Designs: a, Haarlemmerhout in fall. b, Sonsbeek in winter. c, Weerribben in spring. d, Keukenhof in summer.

1999, Mar. 2 Litho. *Perf. 13¼x12¾*
1024 Booklet pane of 4, #a.-d. 3.75 3.75
a.-d. A388 80c Any single .90 .25
Complete booklet, #1024 3.75

I Love Stamps A389

1999, May 6 Litho. *Perf. 13¼x12¾*
1025 A389 80c I Love Stamps .90 .75
1026 A389 80c Stamps Love Me .90 .75
a. Booklet pane, 3 #1025, 2 #1026 + 2 labels 4.50
Complete booklet, #1026a 4.50

Nos. 1025-1026 each contain a hologram. Soaking may affect the hologram.

Maritime Anniversaries A390

1999, May 6 Litho. *Perf. 12¾x13¼*
1027 A390 80c Freighters .90 .25
1028 A390 80c Lifeboats .90 .25

Schuttevaer Ship Masters Assoc., 150th anniv. (#1027). Netherlands Lifeboat Assoc., 175th anniv. (#1028).

Paintings A391

No. 1029: a, The Goldfinch, by Carel Fabritius. b, Self-portrait, by Rembrandt. c, Self-portrait, by Judith Leyster. d, St. Sebastian, by Hendrick Ter Brugghen. e, Beware of Luxury, by Jan Steen. f, The Sick Child, by Gabriel Metsu. g, Gooseberries, by Adriaen Coorte. h, View of Haarlem, by Jacob van Ruisdael. i, Mariaplaats Utrecht, by Pieter Saenredam. j, Danae, by Rembrandt.
1g, The Jewish Bride, by Rembrandt.

1999, June 8 Litho. *Perf. 13¼x13¾*
1029 Sheet of 10, #a.-j. 9.00 9.00
a.-j. A391 80c any single .90 .25

Self-Adhesive
Die Cut Syncopated

1030 A391 1g multicolored 1.10 .30

No. 1030 issued in sheets of 5 stamps and blue priority mail etiquettes.

A392

1999, July 6 Litho. *Perf. 13¼x12¾*
1031 A392 80c multicolored .90 .25

Self-Adhesive
Die Cut 13½ Syncopated

1032 A392 80c multicolored .90 .25

Birth Announcement Type of 1997 and Marriage Type of 1998

1999, July 6 Litho. *Perf. 13¼x12¾*
Booklet Stamps

1033 A363 80c multicolored .90 .25
a. Booklet pane of 5 + 2 labels 4.50
Complete booklet, #1033a 4.50

Perf. 13¼

1034 A369 80c multicolored .90 .25
a. Booklet pane of 5 + 2 labels 4.50
Complete booklet, #1034a 4.50

Greetings Type of 1997
Die Cut 13½ Syncopated

1999, July 6 Litho.
Self-Adhesive

1035 A352 80c multicolored .90 .25

VNO-NCW Employer Organization, Cent. A392a

1999, Sept. 7 Litho. *Perf. 13¼x12¾*
1036 A392a 80c multicolored .90 .25

Tintin — A393

#1037, Tintin, Snowy in space suits. #1038a, Tintin, Snowy, Capt. Haddock in spacecraft.

1999, Oct. 8 *Perf. 13¼x13¾*
1037 A393 80c multicolored .90 .25
a. Booklet pane of 5 + 2 labels 4.50
Complete booklet, #1037a 4.50

Souvenir Sheet

1038 Sheet of 2, #1037, 1038a 1.90 1.90
a. A393 80c multicolored .90 .25

Postal Service Bicentennial Type
Souvenir Sheet

1999, Oct. 15 Litho. *Perf. 13¼x13¾*
1039 A385 5g multicolored 5.50 5.50

The numeral in the denomination is made up of perforations.

Millennium A394

Highlights of the 20th Century: a, Construction of barrier dam, 1932. b, Satellite. c, Amsterdam Bourse, 1903, designed by H. P. Berlage. d, Empty highway, 1973-74 oil crisis. e, Prime Minister Willem Drees's social welfare programs, 1947. f, Flood control projects 1953-97. g, European soccer champions, 1988. h, Liberation, 1945. i, Woman suffrage. j, Eleven-city skating race.

1999, Oct. 25 Litho. *Perf. 13¼x12¾*
1040 Sheet of 10 9.00 9.00
a.-j. A394 80c any single .90 .25

December Stamps — A395

Designs: a, Santa's head. b, Angel, musical notes, vert. c, Ornaments in box. d, Crescent-shaped Santa's head, vert. e, Santa, four trees. f, Clock, vert. g, Skater. h, Tree of people holding candles, vert. i, Man and woman. j, Woman, tree, star, vert. k, Angel, musical score. l, Hand, vert. m, Tree. n, Cat with crown, vert. o, Bird, house. p, Baby as angel, vert. q, Dog with cap. r, Angel with halo, vert. s, Family in house. t, Tree with presents, vert.
Illustration reduced.

Serpentine Die Cut 7

1999, Nov. 30 Photo.
Self-Adhesive

1041 A395 Sheet of 20, #a-t 12.00
a.-t. 55c any single .60 .20

A396

2000, Jan. 4 Litho. *Perf. 13x12¾*
1042 A396 25c multi .30 .20

Souvenir Sheet

Holy Roman Emperor Charles V (1500-58) — A397

Designs: a, Gulden coin, Charles' aunt and guardian, Margaret of Austria, Charles V on Horseback in Bologna, by Juan de la Corte. b, Map of the Netherlands, Charles V on Horseback at the Battle of Mühlberg, by Titian, Charles' daughter, Margaret of Parma.

2000, Jan. 4 *Perf. 13¼*
1043 A397 Sheet of 2 + label 1.90 1.90
a.-b. 80c Any single .90 .20

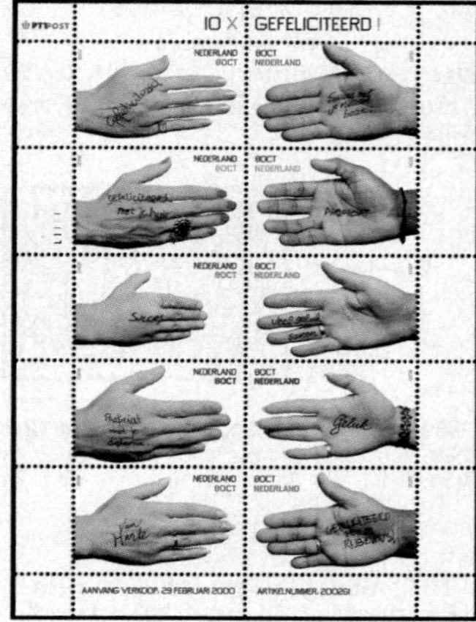

Greetings — A398

Color of denomination or country name and hands (back or palm) with written messages: a, Pink, back. b, Pink, palm. c, Orange, back. d, Orange, palm. e, Green, back. f, Green, palm. g, Blue, back. h, Blue, palm. i, Red, back. j, Red, palm.
Illustration reduced.

Perf. 13¼x13¾

2000, Feb. 29 Litho.
1044 A398 Sheet of 10, #a-j 9.00 9.00
a.-j. 80c any single .90 .25

European Soccer Championships, Netherlands and Belgium — A399

2000, Mar. 25 *Perf. 12¾x13¼*
Booklet Stamps

1045 A399 80c Crowd, players .90 .25
1046 A399 80c Crowd, ball .90 .25
a. Booklet pane, 3 #1045, 2 #1046 + 2 labels 4.50
Booklet, #1046a 4.50

See Belgium No. 1796.

Items in Rijksmuseum — A400

a, Feigned Sorrow (woman wiping eye), by Cornelis Troost. b, Harlequin and Colombine, Meissen porcelain piece, by J. J. Kändler. c, Kabuki Actor Ebizo Ichikawa IV, by Sharaku. d, Apsara from India. e, Carved head of St. Vitus. f, Woman in Turkish Costume, by Jean Etienne Liotard. g, J. van Speyk (man with epaulet), by J. Schoemaker Doyer. h, Engraving of King Saul, by Lucas van Leyden. i, Statue, L'Amour Menacant, by E. M. Falconet. j, Photograph of two men, by C. Ariens.

100c, The Night Watch, by Rembrandt.

Illustration reduced.

2000, Apr. 14 ***Perf. 13¼x13¾***

1047 A400 Sheet of 10, #a-j 9.00 9.00
a.-j. 80c any single .90 .25

Die Cut Syncopated

Self-Adhesive

1048 A400 100c multi 1.10 .30

#1048 issued in sheets of 5 + 5 priority mail etiquettes.

Doe Maar, Popular Musical Group A401

2000, May 2 Litho. ***Perf. 13¼x12¾***

1049 A401 80c Song titles .90 .25
1050 A401 80c Album cover .90 .25
a. Booklet pane, 2 #1049, 3 #1050, + 2 labels 4.50
Booklet, #1050a 4.50

Rijksmuseum Type of 2000 with Priority Mail Emblem Added and

Dutch Landscape, by Jeroen Krabbé — A402

Designs: Nos. 1051, 1053, The Night Watch, by Rembrandt.

Die cut perf. 4 on right side and right parts of top and bottom sides.

Die Cut Similar to Sync.

2000, Aug. 1 **Litho.**

Self-Adhesive

1051 A400 110c pur & multi 1.20 .30

Die Cut Sync.

1052 A402 110c multi 1.20 .30

Coil Stamp

Die Cut Similar to Sync.

1053 A400 110c blue & multi 1.20 .30
Nos. 1051-1053 (3) 3.60 .90

Nos. 1051-1052 issued in sheets of 5. No. 1051 lacks die cut "holes" on left side and at upper left. No. 1053 lacks die cut "holes" on left side, but has only two at upper left.

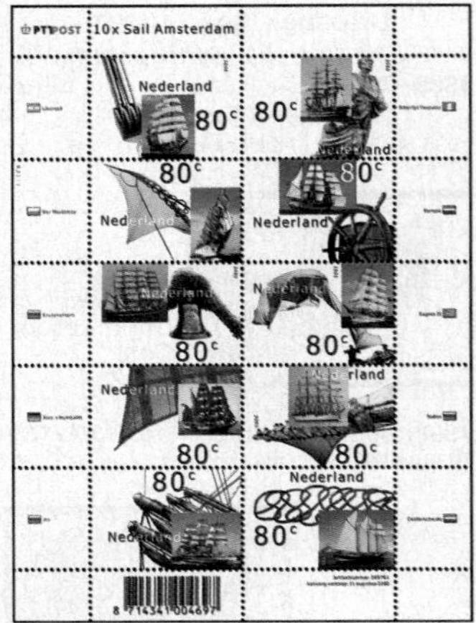

Sail 2000, Amsterdam Harbor — A403

No. 1054: a, Block and Libertad, Argentina. b, Figurehead and Amerigo Vespucci, Italy. c, Unfurled white sail, Dar Mlodziezy, Poland. d, Ship's wheel, Europa, Netherlands. e, Bell, Kruzenshtern, Russia. f, Deckhand adjusting sail, Sagres II, Portugal. g, Green sail, Alexander von Humboldt, Germany. h, Crewmen on bowsprit, Sedov, Russia. i. Spreaders, furled sails and ropes, Mir, Russia. j, Rope, Oosterschelde, Netherlands.

Perf. 13¼x12¾

2000, Aug. 21 **Litho.**

1054 A403 Sheet of 10 9.00 9.00
a.-j. 80c Any single .90 .25

Sjors and Sjimmie A404

Comic strip characters: No. 1055, Rollerblading. No. 1056, In go-kart. No. 1057, Wearing headphones. No. 1058, Hanging on rope.

2000, Sept. 23

1055 A404 80c multi .90 .25
1056 A404 80c multi .90 .25
a. Pair, #1055-1056 1.90 1.90
1057 A404 80c multi .90 .25
a. Souvenir sheet, #1056-1057 1.90 1.90

Booklet Stamp

1058 A404 80c multi .90 .25
a. Booklet pane, 3 #1057, 2 #1058 + 2 labels 4.50
Booklet, #1058a 4.50
Nos. 1055-1058 (4) 3.60 1.00

Death Announcement Type of 1998

Die Cut Perf. 13¼

2000, Oct. 10 **Photo.**

1059 A365 80c gray blue .90 .25

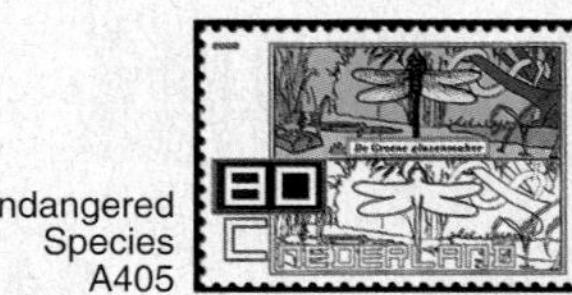

Endangered Species A405

Designs: No. 1060, Aeshna viridis (Groene glazenmaker). No. 1061, Misgurnus fossilis (Grote modderkruiper).

2000, Oct. 10 Litho. ***Perf. 13¼x12¾***

Booklet Stamps

1060 A405 80c multi .90 .25
1061 A405 80c multi .90 .25
a. Booklet pane, 3 #1060, 2 #1061 + 2 labels 4.50
Booklet, #1061a 4.50

Souvenir Sheet

Amphilex 2002 Intl. Stamp Show, Amsterdam — A406

No. 1062: a, Boat. b, Carriage.

2000, Oct. 10

1062 A406 Sheet of 2 1.90 1.90
a.-b. 80c Any single .90 .25

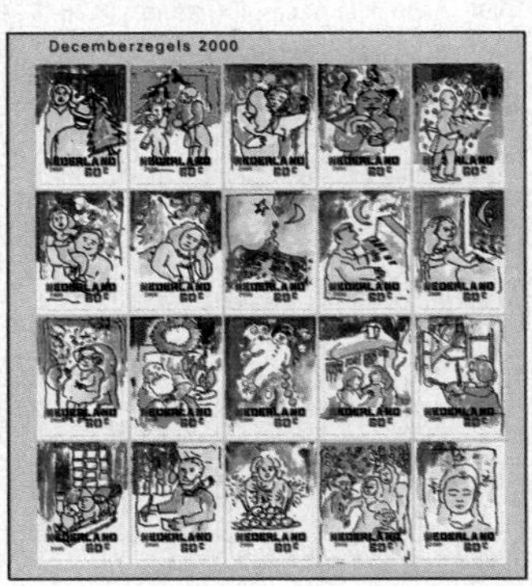

Christmas — A407

No. 1063: a, Woman, man with tree on shoulder. b, Woman, child decorating tree. c, Couple dancing. d, Tuba player. e, Man carrying hat and tree. f, Man with child on shoulder. g, Woman reading. h, Couple kissing. i, Piano player. j, Woman at window. k, Woman in chair. l, Santa by fire. m, Snowman. n, Couple in front of house. o, Violin player. p, Children on sled. q, Man writing letter. r, Woman with food tray. s, Four people. t, Woman asleep.

Serpentine Die Cut 14½x15

2000, Nov. 28 **Photo.**

Self-Adhesive

1063 A407 Sheet of 20 13.00
a.-t. 60c Any single .65 .20

A408

2001, Jan. 2 Litho. ***Perf. 12¾x13¼***

1064 A408 20c multi .20 .20

Royal Dutch Nature Society, Cent. — A409

No. 1065: a, Whinchat thrush. b, People in rowboat. c, Fox. d, People with binoculars. e, Scotch rose and June beetles.

2001, Jan. 26 Litho. ***Perf. 13½x12¾***

1065 Booklet pane of 5, #a-e, +2 labels 4.50 —
a.-e. A409 80c Any single .90 .25
Booklet, #1065 4.50

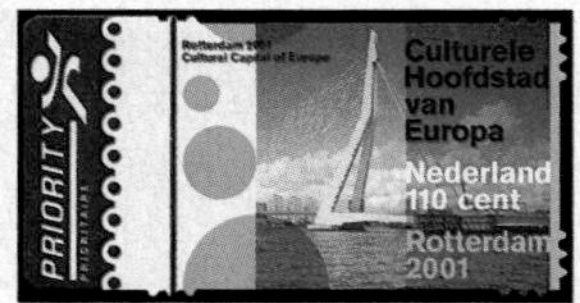

Rotterdam, 2001 European Cultural Capital — A410

Die Cut Similar to Sync.

2001, Mar. 14 **Litho.**

Self- Adhesive

1066 A410 110c multi 1.25 .30

Printed in sheets of 5. Die cutting has no "holes" at left, but has "holes" at top and bottom at the thin vertical line.

Book Week — A411

No. 1067: a, Quote by Edgar du Perron. b, Photograph by Ulay. c, Quote by Hafid Bouazza. d, Photograph by Ed van der Elsken. e, Quote by Adriaan van Dis. f, Photograph by Anton Corbijn. g, Quote by Kader Abdolah. h, Photographs by Celine van Balen. i, Quote by Ellen Ombre. j, Photograph by Cas Oorthuys.

2001, Mar. 14 ***Perf. 13¼x13¾***

1067 A411 Sheet of 10 9.00 9.00
a.-j. 80c Any single .90 .25

Souvenir Sheet

Max Euwe (1901-81), Chess Champion — A412

No. 1068: a, Chessboard. b, Euwe, chess pieces.

2001, Apr. 3 ***Perf. 13¼x12¾***

1068 A412 Sheet of 2 1.90 1.90
a.-b. 80c Any single .90 .25

Souvenir Sheet

Intl. Volunteers Year — A413

No. 1069: a, Rescue workers. b, People with animal cages.

2001, Apr. 3

1069 A413 Sheet of 2 1.90 1.90
a.-b. 80c Any single .90 .25

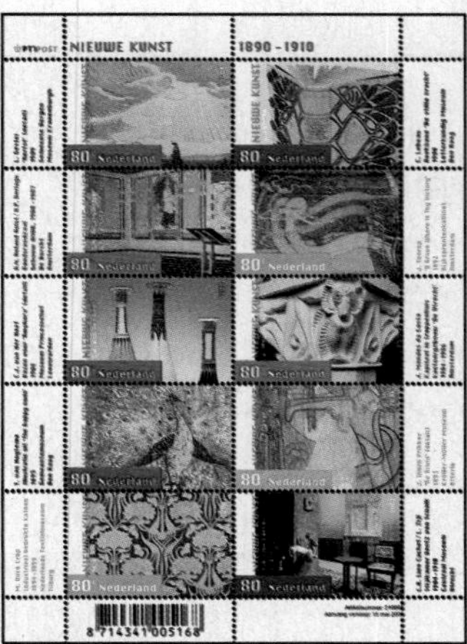

Art of 1892-1910 — A414

Art: a, "Autumn," L. Gestel. b, Book cover for "De Stille Kracht," C. Lebeau. c, Burcht Federal Council Hall, R. N. Roland Holst and H. P. Berlage. d, "O grave, where is thy victory?," J. Toorop. e, Vases from "Amphoras," C. J. van der Hoef. f, De Utrecht office building capital, J. Mendes da Costa. g, Illustration from "The Happy Owls," T. van Hoytema. h, "The Bride," J. Thorn Prikker. i, Printed fabric, M. Duco Crop. j, Dentz van Schaik period room, Central Museum, Utrecht, C. A. Lion Cachet and L. Zijl.

2001, May 15 ***Perf. 14¾***
1070 A414 Sheet of 10 9.00 9.00
a.-j. 80c Any single .90 .25

Birth Announcement Type of 1997 with Added Euro Denomination

Die Cut Perf. 13¼x12¾

2001, July 2 **Litho.**

Booklet Stamp

Self-Adhesive

1071 A363 85c multi .95 .20
a. Booklet pane of 5 4.75

Death Announcement Type of 1998 with Added Euro Denomination

Die Cut Perf. 13¼

2001, July 2 **Litho.**

Self-Adhesive

1072 A365 85c gray blue .95 .20

Wedding Stamp — A415

Die Cut Perf. 13¼x12¾

2001, July 2 **Photo.**

Booklet Stamp

Self-Adhesive

1073 A415 85c multi .95 .20
a. Booklet pane of 5 4.75

A416

2001, July 2 **Booklet Stamp**

Self-Adhesive

1074 A416 85c multi .95 .20
a. Booklet pane of 10 9.50

Arrows A417

Serpentine Die Cut 14x13½

2001, July 2 **Photo.**

Coil Stamp

Self-Adhesive

1075 A417 85c pur & silver .95 .20

See Nos. 1106-1107.

Change of Address Stamp — A418

Die Cut Perf. 14½x14

2001, July 2 **Photo.**

Self-Adhesive

1076 A418 85c orange & blk .95 .20

Polder — A419

Coast at Zandvoort — A420

Design: 1.65g, Cyclists on Java Island, Amsterdam.

2001, July 2 ***Die Cut Perf. 13¼x12¾***

Booklet Stamps

Self-Adhesive

1077 A419 85c multi .95 .20
a. Booklet pane of 5 4.75

Serpentine Die Cut 12¾ Syncopated

1078 A420 1.20g multi 1.25 .25
a. Booklet pane of 5 6.25
1079 A420 1.65g multi 1.75 .35
a. Booklet pane of 5 8.75

Nos. 1078 and 1079 have rouletting between stamp and etiquette.

Cartoon Network Cartoons A421

No. 1080: a, Tom and Jerry. b, The Flintstones. c, Johnny Bravo. d, Dexter's Laboratory. e, The Powerpuff Girls.

Perf. 13½x12¾

2001, Aug. 28 **Litho.**
1080 Booklet pane of 5, #a-e, + 2 labels 4.75 —
a.-e. A421 85c Any single .95 .25
Booklet, #1080 4.75

Greetings — A422

No. 1081: a, Veel Geluk (9 times). b, Gefeliciteerd! (11 times). c, Veel Geluk (4 times), horiz. d, Gefeliciteerd! (5 times), horiz. e, Proficiat (7 times). f, Succes! (7 times). g, Van Harte. . . (9 times). h, Proficiat (3 times), horiz. i, Succes! (3 times), horiz. j, Van Harte. . . (4 times), horiz.

Die Cut Perf. 13x13¼, 13¼x13

2001, Sept. 3 **Photo.**

Self-Adhesive

1081 Booklet of 10 9.50
a.-j. A422 85c Any single .95 .25

Change From Guilder to Euro Currency — A423

Etched on Silver Foil

2001, Sept. 25 ***Die Cut Perf. 12¾***

Self-Adhesive

1082 A423 12.75g Guilder coins 12.50 —

Cancels can be easily removed from these stamps.

Souvenir Sheet

Royal Dutch Association of Printers, Cent. — A424

No. 1083 - Magnifying glass and: a, Color dots. b, Spectrum.

Photo. & Embossed

2001, Oct. 12 ***Perf. 14x13½***
1083 A424 Sheet of 2 1.90 1.90
a.-b. 85c Any single .95 .20

Souvenir Sheet

Dutch Stamps, 150th Anniv. (in 2002) — A425

No. 1084 : a, Waigaat Canal and ramparts, Williamstad, Curacao. b, Pangka sugar refinery, Java Island, Netherlands Indies.

2001, Oct. 12 **Photo.** ***Perf. 14x13½***
1084 A425 Sheet of 2 1.90 1.90
a.-b. 85c Any single .95 .20

Amphilex 2002 Intl. Stamp Show, Amsterdam.

December Stamps — A426

No. 1085: a, Clock, grapes. b, Grapes, stars, doughnut balls. c, Doughnut balls, spire of church tower. d, Cherub. e, Champagne bottle. f, Wreath, roof. g, Windows of church tower. h, Ornament on Christmas tree. i, Christmas tree on sign. j, Cake in window. k, Christmas tree with ornaments, church tower. l, Santa Claus. m, Mug of hot chocolate on sign, snowman's head. n, Candles in window. o, Church tower, decorated market stalls. p, Reindeer. q, Snowman. r, Wrapped gift. s, Bonfire. t, Children on sled.

Serpentine Die Cut 13¼x13

2001, Nov. 27 **Photo.**

Self-Adhesive

1085 Sheet of 20 13.00
a.-t. A426 60c Any single .65 .20

100 Cents = 1 Euro (€)

Queen Type of 1991, Arrows Type of 2001 With Euro Denominations Only and

A427

Die Cut Perf. 14¼, Serpentine Die Cut 14 (#1086, 12c), Serpentine Die Cut 14¼ (55c, 57c 70c, 72c), Perf 14¼x13½ (#1087, 5c, 10c)

Photo, Litho (5c, 12c)

2002, Jan. 2

Self-Adhesive

1086 A427 2c red .20 .20
a. Booklet pane of 5 .20

Water-Activated Gum

1087 A427 2c red .20 .20
1088 A427 5c red violet .20 .20
1089 A427 10c blue .25 .20

Self-Adhesive Booklet Stamps

1090 A427 12c green .30 .20
a. Booklet pane of 5 1.50
1091 A273 25c brn & dk grn .60 .20
a. Booklet pane of 5 3.00
1092 A273 39c bl grn & red .95 .20
a. Booklet pane of 5 4.75
b. Booklet pane of 10 9.50
1093 A273 40c bl & brn .95 .20
a. Booklet pane of 5 4.75
1094 A273 50c fawn & emer 1.25 .25
a. Booklet pane of 5 6.25
1095 A273 55c lilac & brown 1.40 .25
a. Booklet pane of 5 7.00
1096 A273 57c brn & blue grn 1.50 .30
a. Booklet pane of 5 7.50
1097 A273 61c pur & red brn 1.60 .30
a. Booklet pane of 5 8.00
1098 A273 65c grn & pur 1.60 .30
a. Booklet pane of 5 8.00
1099 A273 70c ol grn & bl grn 1.75 .30
a. Booklet pane of 5 8.75
1100 A273 72c blue & brt vio 1.90 .30
a. Booklet pane of 5 9.50
1101 A273 76c olive & grn 2.00 .30
a. Booklet pane of 5 10.00
1102 A273 78c bl & ol brn 1.90 .30
a. Booklet pane of 5 9.50
1103 A273 €1 grn & blue 2.40 .40
a. Booklet pane of 5 12.00
1104 A273 €3 red vio & grn 7.25 1.25
a. Booklet pane of 5 37.50
Nos. 1086-1104 (19) 28.20 5.85

Coil Stamps

Self-Adhesive

Serpentine Die Cut Perf. 14x13½

1105 A417 39c pur & silver .95 .20
1106 A417 78c blue & gold 1.90 .30

Issued: 12c, 25c, 39c, 40c, 50c, 65c, 78c, €1, €3, 1/2/02; 2c (#1086), 1/28/02; 2c (#1087), 9/2/02; 10c, 11/26/02; 5c, 55c, 70c, 1/2/03; 57c, 72c, 1/2/04; 61c, 76c, 1/3/05.

Souvenir Sheet

Wedding of Prince Willem-Alexander and Máxima Zorreguieta — A428

No. 1108: a, Portraits. b, Names.

2002, Jan. 10 **Photo.** ***Perf. 14***
1108 A428 Sheet of 2 1.90 1.90
a.-b. 39c Either single .95 .20

Types of 1998-2001 With Euro Denominations Only

Die Cut Perf. 13¼x12¾

Photo., Litho. (#1110)

2002, Jan. 28

Self-Adhesive

1109 A363 39c multi .95 .20
a. Booklet pane of 5 4.75

Die Cut Perf. 13¼

1110 A365 39c gray blue .95 .20

Die Cut Perf. 13¼x12¾

1111 A415 39c multi .95 .20
a. Booklet pane of 5 4.75
1112 A416 39c multi .95 .20
a. Booklet pane of 10 9.50

Die Cut Perf. 14½x14

1113 A418 39c orange & blk .95 .20

Die Cut Perf. 13¼x12¾

1114 A419 39c multi .95 .20
a. Booklet pane of 5 4.75

Serpentine Die Cut 12¾ Syncopated

1115 A420 54c Like #1078 1.25 .25
a. Booklet pane of 5 6.25
1116 A420 75c Like #1079 1.75 .35
a. Booklet pane of 5 8.75
Nos. 1109-1116 (8) 8.70 1.80

Nos. 1115-1116 have rouletting between stamp and etiquette.

Greetings Type of 2001 with Euro Denominations Only

No. 1117: a, Veel Geluk (9 times). b, Gefeliciteerd! (11 times). c, Veel Geluk (4 times), horiz. d, Gefeliciteerd! (5 times), horiz. e, Proficiat (7 times). f, Succes! (7 times). g, Van Harte. . . (9 times). h, Proficiat (3 times), horiz. i, Succes! (3 times), horiz. j, Van Harte. . . (4 times), horiz.

Die Cut Perf. 13x13¼, 13¼x13

2002, Jan. 28 **Photo.**

Self-Adhesive

1117 Booklet of 10 9.50
a.-j. A422 39c Any single .95 .25

Provinces A429

2002 **Litho.** ***Perf. 14½x14¾***
1118 A429 39c Friesland .95 .25
1119 A429 39c Drenthe .95 .25
1120 A429 39c Noord-Holland .95 .25
1121 A429 39c Gelderland .95 .25
1122 A429 39c Noord-Brabant .95 .25
1123 A429 39c Groningen .95 .25
1124 A429 39c Zuid-Holland .95 .25
1125 A429 39c Utrecht .95 .25
1126 A429 39c Limburg .95 .25
1127 A429 39c Overijssel .95 .25

1128 A429 39c Zeeland .95 .25
1129 A429 39c Flevoland .95 .25
Nos. 1118-1129 (12) 11.40 3.00

Nos. 1118-1129 each were issued in sheets of 10 + 5 labels.

Issued: No. 1118, 3/12; No. 1119, 3/26; No. 1120, 4/9; No. 1121, 4/23. No. 1122, 5/7; No. 1123, 5/21. No. 1124, 6/4; No. 1125, 6/18; No. 1126, 7/2. No. 1127, 7/16; No. 1128, 7/30; No. 1129, 8/13.

Efteling Theme Park, 50th Anniv. A430

Characters: a, Bald man. b, Jester. c, Fairy. d, Man with thumb extended. e, Man with mouth open.

Serpentine Die Cut 13¼x12¾

2002, May 14 Photo.

Self-Adhesive

1130 Booklet pane of 5 4.75
a.-e. A430 39c Any single .95 .25

Europa A431

Designs: No. 1131, Lions and circus tent. No. 1132, Acrobats, juggler, animal acts.

Perf. 14½x14¾

2002, June 11 Litho.

1131 A431 54c multi 1.50 .75
1132 A431 54c multi 1.50 .75
a. Tete-beche pair, #1131-1132 3.50 3.25

Landscape Paintings — A432

No. 1133: a, West Indian Landscape, by Jan Mostaert. b, Landscape with Cows, by Aelbert Cuyp. c, Grain Field, by Jacob van Ruisdael. d, Path in Middelharnis, by Meindert Hobbema. e, Italian Landscape, by Hendrik Vogel. f, Normandy Landscape, by Andreas Schelfhout. g, Landscape with Canal, by Jan Toorop. h, Landscape, by Jan Sluijters. i, Kismet, by Michael Raedecker. j, Untitled painting, by Robert Zandvliet. Names of artwork and artist are on sheet margins adjacent to stamps.

2002, June 11 Photo. *Perf. 14½*

1133 A432 Sheet of 10 9.50 2.50
a.-j. 39c Any single .95 .25

A433

Die Cut Perf. 14¼

2002, July Photo.

Coil Stamps

Self-Adhesive

1134 A433 39c blue & red .95 .20
1135 A433 78c green & red 1.90 .30

Souvenir Sheet

Amphilex 2002 Intl. Stamp Exhibition, Amsterdam — A434

No. 1136: a, One ship. b, Two ships.

2002, Aug. 30 Litho. *Perf. 14x13½*

1136 A434 Sheet of 2 1.90 1.90
a.-b. 39c Either single .95 .20

Dutch stamps, 150th anniv.; Dutch East India Company, 400th anniv.

Industrial Heritage — A435

No. 1137: a, Spakenberg shipyard, 1696. b, Dedemsvaart lime kilns, 1820. c, Cruquius steam pumping station, 1849. d, Heerlen coal mine shaft, 1898. e, Hengelo salt pumping tower, 1918. f, Weidum windmotor, 1920. g, Zevenaar brick oven, 1925. h, Breda brewery, 1926. i, Water works, Tilburg, 1927. j, Schoonebeck oil well pump, 1947.

2002, Sept. 24 *Perf. 14½x14¾*

1137 A435 Sheet of 10 9.50 9.50
a.-j. 39c Any single .95 .25

December Stamps — A436

No. 1138: a, Person, child, fence and trees. b, Man seated, trees. c, Head facing left. d, Red tree, person in black. e, Woman with white hair, tree. f, Person standing in grass. g, Man standing with legs crossed. h, Woman, windmill. i, Man on stool. j, Face with black lips. k, Man standing near tree, with bent knee. l, Man standing near trees, both hands in pockets. m, Two people seated. n, Person with black hair. o, Man with child on shoulders. p, Face, with black hair and eye looking right. q, Person with gold lips looking left. r, Head of person near shore. s, Person with sunglasses standing near shore. t, Woman with arms extended.

Serpentine Die Cut 13

2002, Nov. 26 Photo.

Self-Adhesive

1138 A436 Sheet of 20 14.00
a.-t. 29c Any single .70 .20

Paintings by Vincent Van Gogh — A437

Designs: 39c, Self-portrait, 1886. 59c, Sunflowers, 1887. 75c, The Sower, 1888.

Die Cut Perf. 14¼

2003, Jan. 2 Photo.

Booklet Stamps

Self-Adhesive

1139 A437 39c multi .95 .25
a. Booklet pane of 10 9.50

Serpentine Die Cut 13¼ Syncopated

1140 A437 59c multi + etiquette 1.40 .30
a. Booklet pane of 5+5 etiquettes 7.00
1141 A437 75c multi + etiquette 1.75 .30
a. Booklet pane of 5+5 etiquettes 8.75

A row of rouletting separates stamps from the etiquettes.

Paintings by Vincent Van Gogh — A438

No. 1142: a, Autumn Landscape with Four Trees, 1885. b, The Potato Eaters, 1885. c, Four Cut Sunflowers, 1887. d, Self-portrait with Gray Felt Hat, 1887-88. e, The Zouave, 1888. f, The Cafe Terrace on the Place du Forum, at Night, 1888. g, Pine Trees and Dandelions in the Garden of Saint-Paul Hospital, 1890. h, Blossoming Almond Tree, 1890. i, View of Auvers, 1890. j, Wheat Field with Crows, 1890.

2003, Jan. 2 Litho. *Perf. 14½*

1142 A438 Sheet of 10 8.25 8.25
a.-j. 39c Any single .80 .25

Water Control — A439

No. 1143: a, North Pier, Ijmuiden, 1869. b, Hansweert Lock, 1865. c, Damming of the Wieringermeer, 1929. d, Ijsselmeer Dam (no date). e, Water breaching dike at Willemstad, 1953. f, Repairing dike at Stavenisse, 1953. g, Damming of the Zandkreek, 1960. h, Damming of the Grevelingen, 1964. i, Oosterschelde flood barrier, 1995. j, High water in Roermond, 1993.

2003, Feb. 1 Photo.

1143 A439 Sheet of 10 8.50 8.50
a.-j. 39c Any single .85 .25

Johann Enschedé and Sons, Printers, 300th Anniv. — A440

No. 1144: a, Binary code, mathematics symbols. b, Fleischman's musical notation symbols.

Illustration reduced.

Litho. & Embossed

2003, Mar. 4 *Perf. 14x12¾*

1144 A440 Horiz. pair 1.75 1.75
a.-b. 39c Either single .85 .25

No. 1144a has photogravure back printing that can be seen through blank triangle on face of stamp.

Souvenir Sheets

Island Fauna — A441

No. 1145: a, Eurasian oyster catcher and pilings. b, Spoonbill, horiz. c, Eider. d, Harbor seal, horiz.

No. 1146: a, Sea gull. b, Stone curlew, horiz. c, Gull and seals. d, Crab, horiz.

2003, May 6 Litho. *Perf. 14½*

1145 A441 Sheet of 4 3.75 3.75
a.-d. 39c Any single .90 .25
1146 A441 Sheet of 4 5.75 5.75
a.-d. 59c Any single 1.40 .30

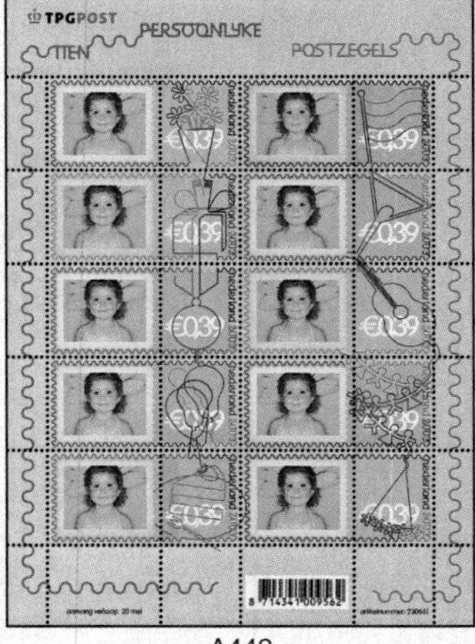

A442

Personalized Stamps — A443

No. 1147: a, Flowers. b, Flag. c, Gift. d, Martini glass. e, Medal. f, Guitar. g, Balloons. h, Paper cut-outs. i, Cake. j, Party hat.

Perf. 12½x12

1940, May 11 Engr. Unwmk.

B123 SP92 1½c +1½c brn blk 1.90 .25
B124 SP93 2½c +2½c dk grn 6.00 1.40
B125 SP94 3c +3c car 3.75 1.10
B126 SP95 5c +3c dp grn 7.75 .25
a. Booklet pane of 4 250.00
B127 SP96 12½c +3½c dp bl 6.75 .80

Surtax for social and cultural projects.

Type of 1940 Surcharged in Black

1940, Sept. 7

B128 SP95 7½c +2½c on 5c +3c dk red .50 .25
Nos. B123-B128 (6) 26.65 4.05

Child with Flowers and Doll — SP97

Perf. 14½x13½

1940, Dec. 2 Photo. Wmk. 202

B129 SP97 1½c +1½c dl bl gray .65 .20
B130 SP97 2½c +2½c dp ol 2.50 .50
B131 SP97 4c +3c royal bl 2.50 .65
B132 SP97 5c +3c dk bl grn 2.50 .20
B133 SP97 7½c +3½c hn .65 .20
Nos. B129-B133 (5) 8.80 1.75

The surtax was used for destitute children.

Dr. Antonius Mathijsen SP98

Dr. Jan Ingenhousz SP99

Aagje Deken SP100

Johannes Bosboom SP101

A. C. W. Staring — SP102

Perf. 12½x12

1941, May 29 Engr. Unwmk.

B134 SP98 1½c +1½c blk brn .80 .20
B135 SP99 2½c +2½c dk sl grn .80 .20
B136 SP100 4c +3c red .80 .20
B137 SP101 5c +3c slate grn .80 .20
B138 SP102 7½c +3½c rose vio .80 .20
Nos. B134-B138 (5) 4.00 1.00

The surtax was for cultural and social relief.

Rembrandt's Painting of Titus, His Son — SP103

Perf. 14½x13½

1941, Dec. 1 Photo. Wmk. 202

B139 SP103 1½c +1½c vio blk .30 .20
B140 SP103 2½c +2½c dk ol .30 .20
B141 SP103 4c +3c royal blue .30 .20
B142 SP103 5c +3c dp grn .30 .20
B143 SP103 7½c +3½c dp henna brn .30 .20
Nos. B139-B143 (5) 1.50 1.00

The surtax aided child welfare.

Legionary

SP104 SP105

1942, Nov. 1 *Perf. 12½x12, 12x12½*

B144 SP104 7½c +2½c dk red 1.00 1.00
a. Sheet of 10 90.00 100.00
B145 SP105 12½c +87½c ultra 7.00 10.00
a. Sheet of 4 75.00 125.00

The surtax aided the Netherlands Legion.

#B144a, B145a measure 155x111mm and 94x94mm respectively.

19th Century Mail Cart — SP108

1943, Oct. 9 Unwmk. *Perf. 12x12½*

B148 SP108 7½c +7½c henna brn .20 .20

Issued to commemorate Stamp Day.

Child and House — SP109

#B150, Mother & Child. #B151, Mother $ Children. #B152, Child Carrying Sheaf of Wheat. #B153, Mother & Children, diff.

Perf. 12½x12

1944, Mar. 6 Wmk. 202

B149 SP109 1½c +3½c dl blk .20 .20
B150 SP109 4c +3½ rose lake .20 .20
B151 SP109 5c +5c dk bl grn .20 .20
B152 SP109 7½c +7½c dp hn brn .20 .20
B153 SP109 10c +40c royal blue .20 .20
Nos. B149-B153 (5) 1.00 1.00

The surtax aided National Social Service and winter relief.

Child SP114

Fortuna SP115

1945, Dec. 1 Photo. *Perf. 14½x13½*

B154 SP114 1½c +2½c gray .20 .20
B155 SP114 2½c +3½c dk bl grn .20 .20
B156 SP114 5c +5c brn red .20 .20
B157 SP114 7½c +4½c red .20 .20
B158 SP114 12½c +5½c brt bl .20 .20
Nos. B154-B158 (5) 1.00 1.00

The surtax was for Child Welfare.

Perf. 12½x12

1946, May 1 Engr. Unwmk.

B159 SP115 1½c +3½c brn blk .45 .20
B160 SP115 2½c +5c dl grn .60 .30
B161 SP115 5c +10c dk vio .65 .40
B162 SP115 7½c +15c car lake .45 .20
B163 SP115 12½c +37½c dk bl .75 .30
Nos. B159-B163 (5) 2.90 1.40

The surtax was for victims of World War II.

Princess Irene SP116

Child on Merry-go-round SP119

Designs: Nos. B165, B167, Princess Margriet. Nos. B168-B169, Princess Beatrix.

1946, Sept. 16

B164 SP116 1½c +1½c blk brn .50 .40
B165 SP116 2½c +1½c bl grn .50 .40
B166 SP116 4c +2c magenta .50 .40
B167 SP116 5c +2c brown .50 .40
B168 SP116 7½c +2½c red .50 .20
B169 SP116 12½c +7½c dk bl .50 .40
Nos. B164-B169 (6) 3.00 2.20

The surtax was for child welfare and anti-tuberculosis work.

1946, Dec. 2 Photo. Wmk. 202

B170 SP119 2c +2c lil gray .40 .20
B171 SP119 4c +2c dk grn .40 .20
B172 SP119 7½c +2½c brt red .40 .20
B173 SP119 10c +5c dp plum .40 .20
B174 SP119 20c +5c dp bl .40 .30
Nos. B170-B174 (5) 2.00 1.10

The surtax was for child welfare.

Dr. Hendrik van Deventer SP120

Peter Cornelisz Hooft SP121

Johan de Witt SP122

Jean F. van Royen SP123

Hugo de Groot — SP124

1947, Aug. 1 Engr. Unwmk.

B175 SP120 2c +2c dark red .60 .25
B176 SP121 4c +2c dk green 1.25 .40
B177 SP122 7½c +2½c dk pur brn 1.90 .40
B178 SP123 10c +5c brown 1.40 .20
B179 SP124 20c +5c dk blue 1.10 .40
Nos. B175-B179 (5) 6.25 1.65

The surtax was for social and cultural purposes.

Children SP125

Infant SP126

1947, Dec. 1 Photo. *Perf. 13x14*

B180 SP125 2c +2c red brn .20 .20
B181 SP126 4c +2c bl grn 1.25 .40
B182 SP126 7½c +2½c sepia 1.25 .55
B183 SP126 10c +5c dk red .75 .20
B184 SP125 20c +5c blue 1.25 .65
Nos. B180-B184 (5) 4.70 2.00

The surtax was for child welfare.

Hall of Knights, The Hague — SP127

Boy in Kayak — SP128

Designs: 6c+4c, Royal Palace, Amsterdam. 10c+5c, Kneuterdyk Palace, The Hague. 20c+5c, New Church, Amsterdam.

1948, June 17 Engr. *Perf. 13½x14*

B185 SP127 2c +2c dk brn 1.50 .25
B186 SP127 6c +4c grn 1.50 .25
B187 SP127 10c +5c brt red 1.25 .20
B188 SP127 20c +5c deep blue 1.50 .65
Nos. B185-B188 (4) 5.75 1.35

The surtax was for cultural and social purposes.

1948, Nov. 15 Photo. *Perf. 13x14*

5c+3c, Swimming. 6c+4c, Sledding. 10c+5c, Swinging. 20c+8c, Figure skating.

B189 SP128 2c +2c yel grn .20 .20
B190 SP128 5c +3c dk bl grn 2.00 .65
B191 SP128 6c +4c gray .85 .20
B192 SP128 10c +5c red .20 .20
B193 SP128 20c +8c blue 2.25 .65
Nos. B189-B193 (5) 5.50 1.90

The surtax was for child welfare.

Beach Terrace SP129

Boy and Girl Hikers SP130

Campers SP131

Reaping SP132

Sailboats SP133

1949, May 2 Wmk. 202 *Perf. 14x13*

B194	SP129	2c	+2c bl & org yel	.90	.20
B195	SP130	5c	+3c bl & yel	1.50	1.00
B196	SP131	6c	+4c dk bl grn	1.50	.35
B197	SP132	10c	+5c bl & org yel	2.50	.20
B198	SP133	20c	+5c blue	1.75	1.25
			Nos. B194-B198 (5)	8.15	3.00

The surtax was for cultural and social purposes.

Hands Reaching for Sunflower SP134

"Autumn" SP135

Perf. 14½x13½

1949, Aug. 1 Photo. Unwmk.

Flower in Yellow

B199	SP134	2c	+3c gray	1.10	.20
B200	SP134	6c	+4c red brown	.70	.30
B201	SP134	10c	+5c brt blue	2.25	.20
B202	SP134	30c	+10c dk brown	6.25	2.00
			Nos. B199-B202 (4)	10.30	2.70

The surtax was for the Red Cross and for Indonesia Relief work.

1949, Nov. 14 Engr. *Perf. 13x14*

5c+3c, "Summer." 6c+4c, "Spring." 10c+5c, "Winter." 20c+7c, "New Year."

B203	SP135	2c	+3c brown	.20	.20
B204	SP135	5c	+3c red	3.25	.95
B205	SP135	6c	+4c dull green	1.10	.20
B206	SP135	10c	+5c gray	.25	.20
B207	SP135	20c	+7c blue	3.50	.85
			Nos. B203-B207 (5)	8.30	2.40

The surtax was for child welfare.

Figure from PTT Monument, The Hague SP136

Grain Binder SP137

Designs: 4c+2c, Dike repairs. 5c+3c, Apartment House, Rotterdam. 10c+5c, Bridge section being towed. 20c+5c, Canal freighter.

1950, May 2 *Perf. 12½x12, 12x12½*

B208	SP136	2c	+2c dk brown	1.50	.75
B209	SP136	4c	+2c dk green	13.00	8.00
B210	SP136	5c	+3c sepia	6.75	2.50
B211	SP137	6c	+4c purple	3.00	.70
B212	SP137	10c	+5c blue gray	3.00	.25
B213	SP137	20c	+5c deep blue	13.00	9.50
			Nos. B208-B213 (6)	40.25	21.70

The surtax was for social and cultural works.

Church Ruins and Good Samaritan SP138

Baby and Bees SP139

1950, July 17 Photo. *Perf. 12½x12*

B214	SP138	2c	+2c ol brn	3.00	1.25
B215	SP138	5c	+3c brn red	16.00	*13.00*
B216	SP138	6c	+4c dp grn	9.50	1.50
B217	SP138	10c	+5c brt lil rose	10.00	.30
B218	SP138	20c	+5c ultra	22.50	*24.00*
			Nos. B214-B218 (5)	61.00	*40.05*

The surtax was for the restoration of ruined churches.

1950, Nov. 13 *Perf. 13x12*

Designs: 5c+3c, Boy and rooster. 6c+4c, Girl feeding birds. 10c+5c, Boy and fish. 20c+7c, Girl, butterfly and toad.

B219	SP139	2c	+3c car	.20	.20
B220	SP139	5c	+3c ol grn	7.00	3.00
B221	SP139	6c	+4c dk bl grn	2.00	.65
B222	SP139	10c	+5c lilac	.20	.20
B223	SP139	20c	+7c blue	13.00	8.00
			Nos. B219-B223 (5)	22.40	12.05

The surtax was to aid needy children.

Hillenraad Castle SP140

Bergh Castle SP141

Castles: 6c+4c, Hernen. 10c+5c, Rechteren. 20c+5c, Moermond.

Perf. 12x12½, 12½x12

1951, May 15 Engr. Unwmk.

B224	SP140	2c	+2c purple	3.00	1.50
B225	SP141	5c	+3c dk red	8.00	7.75
B226	SP140	6c	+4c dk brown	1.40	1.25
B227	SP141	10c	+5c dk green	3.00	.60
B228	SP141	20c	+5c dp blue	7.00	*7.75*
			Nos. B224-B228 (5)	22.40	*18.85*

The surtax was for cultural, medical and social purposes.

Girl and Windmill SP142

Jan van Riebeeck SP143

Designs: 5c+3c, Boy and building construction. 6c+4c, Fisherboy and net. 10c+5c, Boy, chimneys and steelwork. 20c+7c, Girl and apartment house.

1951, Nov. 12 Photo. *Perf. 13x14*

B229	SP142	2c	+3c dp green	.60	.20
B230	SP142	5c	+3c sl vio	8.50	3.00
B231	SP142	6c	+4c dk brown	6.00	.50
B232	SP142	10c	+5c red brown	.40	.20
B233	SP142	20c	+7c dp bl	8.50	*6.00*
			Nos. B229-B233 (5)	24.00	*9.90*

The surtax was for child welfare.

1952, Mar. *Perf. 12½x12*

B234	SP143	2c	+3c dk gray	5.50	3.50
B235	SP143	6c	+4c dk bl grn	7.25	3.50
B236	SP143	10c	+5c brt red	9.00	3.50
B237	SP143	20c	+5c brt blue	5.25	3.50
			Nos. B234-B237 (4)	27.00	14.00

Tercentenary of Van Riebeeck's landing in South Africa. Surtax was for Van Riebeeck monument fund.

Scotch Rose — SP144

Girl and Dog — SP145

Designs: 5c+3c, Marsh marigold. 6c+4c, Tulip. 10c+5c, Ox-eye daisy. 20c+5c, Cornflower.

1952, May 1

B238	SP144	2c	+2c cer & dl grn	.85	.50
B239	SP144	5c	+3c dp grn & yel	3.25	3.25
B240	SP144	6c	+4c red & dl grn	2.75	1.00
B241	SP144	10c	+5c org yel & dl grn	2.75	.35
B242	SP144	20c	+5c bl & dl grn	17.00	8.00
			Nos. B238-B242 (5)	26.60	13.10

The surtax was for social, cultural and medical purposes.

Perf. 12x12½

1952, Nov. 17 Unwmk.

2c+3c, Boy & goat. 5c+3c, Girl on donkey. 10c+5c, Boy & kitten. 20c+7c, Boy & rabbit.

Design in Black

B243	SP145	2c	+3c olive	.20	.20
B244	SP145	5c	+3c dp rose	3.25	.90
B245	SP145	6c	+4c aqua	2.75	.30
B246	SP145	10c	+5c org yel	.20	.20
B247	SP145	20c	+7c blue	8.00	5.00
			Nos. B243-B247 (5)	14.40	6.60

The surtax was for child welfare.

No. 308 Surcharged in Black

Perf. 13½x13

1953, Feb. 10 Wmk. 202

B248	A76	10c	+10c org yel	.55	.20

The surtax was for flood relief.

Hyacinth SP146

Red Cross on Shield SP147

Designs: 5c+3c, African Marigold. 6c+4c, Daffodil. 10c+5c, Anemone. 20c+5c, Iris.

1953, May 1 Unwmk. *Perf. 12½x12*

B249	SP146	2c	+2c vio & grn	.85	.30
B250	SP146	5c	+3c dp org & grn	4.50	3.25
B251	SP146	6c	+4c grn & yel	2.10	.40
B252	SP146	10c	+5c dk red & grn	3.25	.30
B253	SP146	20c	+5c dp ultra & grn	14.50	10.50
			Nos. B249-B253 (5)	25.20	14.75

The surtax was for social, cultural and medical purposes.

1953, Aug. 24 Engr.

Designs: 6c+4c, Man holding lantern. 7c+5c, Worker and ambulance at flood. 10c+5c, Nurse giving blood transfusion. 25c+8c, Red Cross flags.

Cross in Red

B254	SP147	2c	+3c dk ol	.80	.30
B255	SP147	6c	+4c dk vio brn	5.00	2.75
B256	SP147	7c	+5c dk gray grn	1.25	.40
B257	SP147	10c	+5c red	.85	.20
B258	SP147	25c	+8c dp bl	8.25	4.00
			Nos. B254-B258 (5)	16.15	7.65

The surtax was for the Red Cross.

Spade, Flag, Bucket and Girl's Head — SP148

Head of child and: 5c+3c, Apple. 7c+5c, Pigeon. 10c+5c, Sailboat. 25c+8c, Tulip.

1953, Nov. 16 Litho. *Perf. 12x12½*

B259	SP148	2c	+3c yel & bl gray	.20	.20
B260	SP148	5c	+3c ap grn & brn car	4.00	3.00
B261	SP148	7c	+5c lt bl & sep	4.25	.70
B262	SP148	10c	+5c ol bis & lil	.20	.20
B263	SP148	25c	+8c pink & bl grn	12.00	8.50
			Nos. B259-B263 (5)	20.65	12.60

The surtax was for child welfare.

Martinus Nijhoff, Poet — SP149

Boy Flying Model Plane — SP150

5c+3c, Willem Pijper, composer. 7c+5c, H. P. Berlage, architect. 10c+5c, Johan Huizinga, historian. 25c+8c, Vincent van Gogh, painter.

1954, May 1 Photo. *Perf. 12½x12*

B264	SP149	2c	+3c dp bl	1.75	1.25
B265	SP149	5c	+3c ol brn	3.25	2.40
B266	SP149	7c	+5c dk red	3.50	.95
B267	SP149	10c	+5c dl grn	7.75	.60
B268	SP149	25c	+8c plum	13.50	9.50
			Nos. B264-B268 (5)	29.75	14.70

The surtax was for social and cultural purposes.

1954, Aug. 23 *Perf. 12½x12*

Portrait: 10c+4c, Albert E. Plesman.

B269	SP150	2c	+2c ol grn	1.25	.75
B270	SP150	10c	+4c dk gray bl	3.50	.50

The surtax was for the Netherlands Aviation Foundation.

Children Making Paper Chains — SP151

Girl Brushing Teeth — SP152

7c+5c, Boy sailing toy boat. 10c+5c, Nurse drying child. 25c+8c, Young convalescent, drawing.

Perf. 12x12½, 12½x12

1954, Nov. 15

B271	SP151	2c	+3c brn	.20	.20
B272	SP152	5c	+3c ol grn	4.25	2.75
B273	SP152	7c	+5c gray bl	1.75	.40
B274	SP152	10c	+5c brn red	.20	.20
B275	SP151	25c	+8c dp bl	10.00	4.50
			Nos. B271-B275 (5)	16.40	8.05

The surtax was for child welfare.

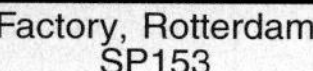
Factory, Rotterdam SP153

Amsterdam Stock Exchange SP154

5c+3c, Post office, The Hague. 10c+5c, Town hall, Hilversum. 25c+8c, Office building, The Hague.

1955, Apr. 25 **Engr.**

B276 SP153 2c +3c brnsh bis 1.25 .95
B277 SP153 5c +3c bl grn 3.00 2.00
B278 SP154 7c +5c rose brn 1.25 .80
B279 SP153 10c +5c steel bl 2.00 .20
B280 SP153 25c +8c choc 12.00 *7.50*
Nos. B276-B280 (5) 19.50 *11.45*

The surtax was for social and cultural purposes.

Microscope and Crab SP155

Willem van Loon by Dirck Santvoort SP156

1955, Aug. 15 **Photo.** ***Perf. 12½x12***
Crab in Red

B281 SP155 2c +3c dk gray .60 .35
B282 SP155 5c +3c dk grn 2.75 1.60
B283 SP155 7c +5c dk vio 1.50 .45
B284 SP155 10c +5c dk bl .95 .20
B285 SP155 25c +8c olive 7.50 4.00
Nos. B281-B285 (5) 13.30 6.60

The surtax was for cancer research.

1955, Nov. 14 **Unwmk.**

Portraits: 5+3c, Boy by Jacob Adriaanszoon Backer. 7+5c, Girl by unknown artist. 10+5c, Philips Huygens by Adriaan Hanneman. 25+8c, Constantijn Huygens by Adriaan Hanneman.

B286 SP156 2c +3c dk grn .35 .20
B287 SP156 5c +3c dp car 3.75 1.75
B288 SP156 7c +5c dl red brn 4.00 .50
B289 SP156 10c +5c dp bl .35 .20
B290 SP156 25c +8c purple 9.50 5.75
Nos. B286-B290 (5) 17.95 8.40

The surtax was for child welfare.

Farmer Wearing High Cap SP157

Sailboat SP158

Rembrandt Etchings: 5c+3c, Young Tobias with Angel. 7c+5c, Persian Wearing Fur Cap. 10c+5c, Old Blind Tobias. 25c+8c, Self-portrait of 1639.

1956, Apr. 23 **Engr.** ***Perf. 13½x14***

B291 SP157 2c +3c bluish blk 3.00 1.75
B292 SP157 5c +3c ol grn 3.00 1.75
B293 SP157 7c +5c brown 4.50 3.00
B294 SP157 10c +5c dk grn 13.00 .25
B295 SP157 25c +8c redsh brn 18.00 12.00
Nos. B291-B295 (5) 41.50 18.75

350th anniv. of the birth of Rembrandt van Rijn.
Surtax for social and cultural purposes.

1956, Aug. 27 **Litho.** ***Perf. 12½x12***

Designs: 5c+3c, Woman runner. 7c+5c, Amphora depicting runners. 10c+5c, Field hockey. 25c+8c, Waterpolo player.

B296 SP158 2c +3c brt bl & blk .90 .55
B297 SP158 5c +3c dl yel & blk 1.25 .85
B298 SP158 7c +5c red brn & blk 1.60 .85
B299 SP158 10c +5c gray & blk 3.00 .45
B300 SP158 25c +8c brt grn & blk 6.25 *4.50*
Nos. B296-B300 (5) 13.00 *7.20*

16th Olympic Games at Melbourne, Nov. 22-Dec. 8, 1956.
The surtax was for the benefit of the Netherlands Olympic Committee.

Boy by Jan van Scorel — SP159

Motor Freighter SP160

Children's Portraits: 5c+3c, Boy, 1563. 7c+5c, Girl, 1563. 10c+5c, Girl, 1590. 25c+8c, Eechie Pieters, 1592.

1956, Nov. 12 **Photo.** **Unwmk.**

B301 SP159 2c +3c blk vio .35 .20
B302 SP159 5c +3c ol grn 1.25 .90
B303 SP159 7c +5c brn vio 3.75 1.25
B304 SP159 10c +5c dp red .40 .20
B305 SP159 25c +8c dk bl 7.50 3.50
Nos. B301-B305 (5) 13.25 6.05

The surtax was for child welfare.

1957, May 13 **Photo.** ***Perf. 14x13***

Ships: 6c+4c, Coaster. 7c+5c, "Willem Barendsz." 10c+8c, Trawler. 30c+8c, S. S. "Nieuw Amsterdam."

B306 SP160 4c +3c brt bl 1.25 .75
B307 SP160 6c +4c brt vio 3.25 2.00
B308 SP160 7c +5c dk car rose 2.00 .90
B309 SP160 10c +8c grn 4.00 .25
B310 SP160 30c +8c choc 5.00 *2.75*
Nos. B306-B310 (5) 15.50 *6.65*

The surtax was for social and cultural purposes.

White Pelican Feeding Young SP161

Girl by B. J. Blommers SP162

Designs: 6c+4c, Vacation ship, "Castle of Staverden." 7c+5c, Cross and dates: 1867-1957. 10c+8c, Cross and laurel wreath. 30c+8c, Globe and Cross.

1957, Aug. 19 **Litho.** ***Perf. 12x12½***
Cross in Red

B311 SP161 4c +3c bl & red 1.25 .70
B312 SP161 6c +4c dk grn 1.60 .80
B313 SP161 7c +5c dk grn & pink 1.60 .80
B314 SP161 10c +8c yel org 1.40 .20
B315 SP161 30c +8c vio bl 3.00 *1.60*
Nos. B311-B315 (5) 8.85 *4.10*

90th anniversary of the founding of the Netherlands Red Cross.

1957, Nov. 18 **Photo.** ***Perf. 12½x12***

Girls' Portraits by: 6c+4c, William B. Tholen. 8c+4c, Jan Sluyters. 12c+9c, Matthijs Maris. 30c+9c, Cornelis Kruseman.

B316 SP162 4c +4c dp car .35 .20
B317 SP162 6c +4c ol grn 3.75 2.25
B318 SP162 8c +4c gray 3.25 1.25
B319 SP162 12c +9c dp claret .35 .20
B320 SP162 30c +9c dk bl 8.50 4.50
Nos. B316-B320 (5) 16.20 8.40

The surtax was for child welfare.

Woman from Walcheren, Zeeland SP163

Girl on Stilts and Boy on Tricycle SP164

Regional Costumes: 6c+4c, Marken. 8c+4c, Scheveningen. 12c+9c, Friesland. 30c+9c, Volendam.

1958, Apr. 28 **Photo.** **Unwmk.**

B321 SP163 4c +4c blue .70 .40
B322 SP163 6c +4c bister 2.75 1.75
B323 SP163 8c +4c dk car rose 4.50 1.10
B324 SP163 12c +9c org brn 1.60 .20
B325 SP163 30c +9c vio 7.25 *4.50*
Nos. B321-B325 (5) 16.80 *7.95*

Surtax for social and cultural purposes.

1958, Nov. 17 **Litho.**

Children's Games: 6c+4c, Boy and girl on scooters. 8c+4c, Leapfrog. 12c+9c, Roller skating. 30c+9c, Boy in toy car and girl jumping rope.

B326 SP164 4c +4c lt bl .20 .20
B327 SP164 6c +4c dp red 3.00 1.75
B328 SP164 8c +4c brt bl grn 1.75 .65
B329 SP164 12c +9c red org .20 .20
B330 SP164 30c +9c dk bl 6.25 3.00
Nos. B326-B330 (5) 11.40 5.80

The surtax was for child welfare.

Tugs and Caisson SP165

Designs: 6c+4c, Dredger. 8c+4c, Laborers making fascine mattresses. 12c+9c, Grab cranes. 30c+9c, Sand spouter.

1959, May 11 ***Perf. 14x13***

B331 SP165 4c +4c dk bl, *bl grn* 1.50 .90
B332 SP165 6c +4c red org, *gray* 1.60 1.00
B333 SP165 8c +4c bl vio, *lt bl* 2.25 1.00
B334 SP165 12c +9c bl grn, *brt yel* 4.00 .20
B335 SP165 30c +9c dk brn, *brick red* 6.75 *4.25*
Nos. B331-B335 (5) 16.10 *7.35*

Issued to publicize the endless struggle to keep the sea out and the land dry.
The surtax was for social and cultural purposes.

Child in Playpen SP166

Refugee Woman SP167

Designs: 6c+4c, Playing Indian. 8c+4c, Child feeding geese. 12c+9c, Children crossing street. 30c+9c, Doing homework.

1959, Nov. 16 ***Perf. 12½x12***

B336 SP166 4c +4c dp rose & dk bl .20 .20
B337 SP166 6c +4c red brn & emer 1.90 .85
B338 SP166 8c +4c red & bl 3.00 1.10
B339 SP166 12c +9c grnsh bl, org & gray .20 .20
B340 SP166 30c +9c yel & bl 4.50 2.75
Nos. B336-B340 (5) 9.80 5.10

The surtax was for child welfare.

1960, Apr. 7 **Photo.** ***Perf. 13x14***

B341 SP167 12c +8c dp claret .50 .30
B342 SP167 30c +10c dk ol grn 2.50 1.75

Issued to publicize World Refugee Year, July 1, 1959-June 30, 1960. The surtax was for aid to refugees.

Tulip SP168

Girl from Marken SP169

Flowers: 6c+4c, Gorse. 8c+4c, White waterlily, horiz. 12c+8c, Red poppy. 30c+10c, Blue sea holly.

Perf. 12½x12, 12x12½

1960, May 23 **Unwmk.**

B343 SP168 4c +4c gray, grn & red .80 .40
B344 SP168 6c +4c sal, grn & yel .60 .30
B345 SP168 8c +4c multi 1.75 .85
B346 SP168 12c +8c dl org, red & grn 1.75 .30
B347 SP168 30c +10c yel, grn & ultra 6.25 4.50
Nos. B343-B347 (5) 11.15 6.35

The surtax was for child welfare.

1960, Nov. 14 ***Perf. 12½x12***

Regional Costumes: 6c+4c, Volendam. 8c+4c, Bunschoten. 12c+9c, Hindeloopen. 30c+9c, Huizen.

B348 SP169 4c +4c multi .20 .20
B349 SP169 6c +4c multi 1.10 .80
B350 SP169 8c +4c multi 3.50 1.10
B351 SP169 12c +9c multi .20 .20
B352 SP169 30c +9c multi 6.00 3.50
Nos. B348-B352 (5) 11.00 5.80

The surtax was for child welfare.

Herring Gull — SP170

St. Nicholas on his Horse — SP171

Birds: 6c+4c, Oystercatcher, horiz. 8c+4c, Curlew. 12c+8c, Avocet, horiz. 30c+10c, Lapwing.

Perf. 12½x12, 12x12½

1961, Apr. 24 **Litho.** **Unwmk.**

B353 SP170 4c +4c yel & grnsh gray .85 .85
B354 SP170 6c +4c fawn & blk .40 .20
B355 SP170 8c +4c ol & red brn .85 .70
B356 SP170 12c +8c lt bl & gray 1.75 .20
B357 SP170 30c +10c grn & blk 3.50 2.75
Nos. B353-B357 (5) 7.35 4.70

The surtax was for social and cultural purposes.

1961, Nov. 13 ***Perf. 12½x12***

Holiday folklore: 6c+4c, Epiphany. 8c+4c, Palm Sunday. 12c+9c, Whitsun bride, Pentecost. 30c+9c, Martinmas.

B358 SP171 4c +4c brt red .20 .20
B359 SP171 6c +4c brt bl 1.10 .85
B360 SP171 8c +4c olive 1.10 .85

B361 SP171 12c +9c dp grn .20 .20
B362 SP171 30c +9c dp org 3.00 2.00
Nos. B358-B362 (5) 5.60 4.10

The surtax was for child welfare.

Christian Huygens' Pendulum Clock by van Ceulen SP172

Children Cooking SP173

Designs: 4c+4c, Cat, Roman sculpture, horiz. 6c+4c, Fossil Ammonite. 12c+ 8c, Figurehead from admiralty ship model. 30c+10c, Guardsmen Hendrick van Berckenrode and Jacob van Lourensz, by Frans Hals, horiz.

Perf. 14x13, 13x14

1962, Apr. 27 **Photo.**

B363 SP172 4c +4c ol grn 1.00 .85
B364 SP172 6c +4c gray .50 .40
B365 SP172 8c +4c dp claret 1.10 .85
B366 SP172 12c +8c olive bis 1.10 .20
B367 SP172 30c +10c bl blk 1.25 1.25
Nos. B363-B367 (5) 4.95 3.55

The surtax was for social and cultural purposes. Issued to publicize the International Congress of Museum Experts, July 4-11.

1962, Nov. 12 ***Perf. 12½x12***

Children's Activities: 6c+4c, Bicycling. 8c+4c, Watering flowers. 12c+9c, Feeding chickens. 30c+9c, Music making.

B368 SP173 4c +4c red .20 .20
B369 SP173 6c +4c yel bis 1.25 .30
B370 SP173 8c +4c ultra 1.50 .85
B371 SP173 12c +9c dp grn .20 .20
B372 SP173 30c +9c dk car rose 2.50 1.90
Nos. B368-B372 (5) 5.65 3.45

The surtax was for child welfare.

Gallery Windmill — SP174

Roadside First Aid Station SP175

Windmills: 6c+4c, North Holland polder mill. 8c+4c, South Holland polder mill, horiz. 12c+8c, Post mill. 30c+10c, Wip mill.

Perf. 13x14, 14x13

1963, Apr. 24 **Litho.** **Unwmk.**

B373 SP174 4c +4c dk bl 1.00 .75
B374 SP174 6c +4c dk pur 1.00 .75
B375 SP174 8c +4c dk grn 1.25 .90
B376 SP174 12c +8c blk 2.00 .25
B377 SP174 30c +10c dk car 2.00 1.75
Nos. B373-B377 (5) 7.25 4.40

The surtax was for social and cultural purposes.

1963, Aug. 20 ***Perf. 14x13***

Designs: 6c+4c, Book collection box. 8c+4c, Crosses. 12c+9c, International aid to Africans. 30c+9c, First aid team.

B378 SP175 4c +4c dk bl & red .35 .20
B379 SP175 6c +4c dl pur & red .25 .20
B380 SP175 8c +4c blk & red .85 .50
B381 SP175 12c +9c red brn & red .50 .20
B382 SP175 30c +9c yel grn & red 1.50 1.00
Nos. B378-B382 (5) 3.45 2.10

Centenary of the Intl. Red Cross. The surtax went to the Netherlands Red Cross.

"Aunt Lucy Sat on a Goosey" SP176

Seeing-Eye Dog SP177

Nursery Rhymes: 6c+4c, "In the Hague there lives a count." 8c+4c, "One day I passed a puppet's fair." 12c+9c, "Storky, storky, Billy Spoon." 30c+9c, "Ride on in a little buggy."

1963, Nov. 12 **Litho.** ***Perf. 13x14***

B383 SP176 4c +4c grnsh bl & dk bl .20 .20
B384 SP176 6c +4c org red & sl grn .70 .45
B385 SP176 8c +4c dl grn & dk brn 1.00 .45
B386 SP176 12c +9c yel & dk pur .20 .20
B387 SP176 30c +9c rose & dk bl 1.75 1.25
Nos. B383-B387 (5) 3.85 2.55

The surtax was for mentally and physically handicapped children.

1964, Apr. 21 ***Perf. 12x12½***

8c+5c, Three red deer. 12c+9c, Three kittens. 30c+9c, European bison and young.

B388 SP177 5c +5c gray ol, red & blk .35 .20
B389 SP177 8c +5c dk red, pale brn & blk .35 .20
B390 SP177 12c +9c dl yel, blk & gray .35 .20
B391 SP177 30c +9c bl, gray & blk .55 .40
Nos. B388-B391 (4) 1.60 1.00

The surtax was for social and cultural purposes.

Child Painting — SP178

View of Veere SP179

"Artistic and Creative Activities of Children": 10c+5c, Ballet dancing. 15c+10c, Girl playing the flute. 20c+10c, Little Red Riding Hood (masquerading children). 40c+15c, Boy with hammer at work bench.

Perf. 13x14

1964, Nov. 17 **Photo.** **Unwmk.**

B392 SP178 7c +3c lt ol grn & bl .45 .30
B393 SP178 10c +5c red, brt pink & grn .35 .25
B394 SP178 15c +10c yel bis, blk & yel .20 .20
B395 SP178 20c +10c brt pink, brn & red .45 .25
B396 SP178 40c +15c bl & yel grn .75 .50
Nos. B392-B396 (5) 2.20 1.50

The surtax was for child welfare.

1965, June 1 **Litho.** ***Perf. 14x13***

Views: 10c+6c, Thorn. 18c+12c, Dordrecht. 20c+10c, Staveren. 40c+10c, Medemblik.

B397 SP179 8c +6c yel & blk .35 .20
B398 SP179 10c +6c grnsh bl & blk .35 .25
B399 SP179 18c +12c sal & blk .35 .20
B400 SP179 20c +10c bl & blk .35 .25
B401 SP179 40c +10c ap grn & blk .60 .40
Nos. B397-B401 (5) 2.00 1.30

The surtax was for social and cultural purposes.

Child SP180

Designs by Children: 10c+6c, Ship. 18c+12c, Woman, vert. 20c+10c, Child, lake and swan. 40c+10c, Tractor.

Perf. 14x13, 13x14

1965, Nov. 16 **Photo.**

B402 SP180 8c +6c multi .20 .20
B403 SP180 10c +6c multi .45 .40
B404 SP180 18c +12c multi .20 .20
a. Min. sheet of 11, 5 #B402, 6 #B404 + label 20.00 18.00
B405 SP180 20c +10c multi .50 .40
B406 SP180 40c +10c multi .80 .45
Nos. B402-B406 (5) 2.15 1.65

The surtax was for child welfare.

"Help them to a safe haven" SP181

1966, Jan. 31 **Photo.** ***Perf. 14x13***

B407 SP181 18c +7c blk & org yel .40 .20
B408 SP181 40c +20c blk & red .40 .20
a. Min. sheet of 3, #B407, 2 #B408 4.00 3.00

The surtax was for the Intergovernmental Committee for European Migration (ICEM). The message on the stamps was given and signed by Queen Juliana.

Inkwell, Goose Quill and Book — SP182

Designs: 12c+8c, Fragment of Gysbert Japicx manuscript. 20c+10c, Knight on horseback, miniature from "Roman van Walewein" manuscript, 1350. 25c+10c, Initial "D" from "Ferguut" manuscript, 1350. 40c+20c, Print shop, 16th century woodcut.

1966, May 3 ***Perf. 13x14***

B409 SP182 10c +5c multi .30 .30
B410 SP182 12c +8c multi .35 .30
B411 SP182 20c +10c multi .45 .40
B412 SP182 25c +10c multi .50 .40
B413 SP182 40c +20c multi .55 .50
Nos. B409-B413 (5) 2.15 1.90

Gysbert Japicx (1603-1666), Friesian poet, and the 200th anniversary of the founding of the Netherlands Literary Society.

The surtax was for social and cultural purposes.

Infant SP183

Designs: 12c+8c, Daughter of the painter S. C. Lixenberg. 20c+10c, Boy swimming. 25c+10c, Dominga Blazer, daughter of Carel Blazer, photographer of this set. 40c+20c, Boy and horse.

1966, Nov. 15 **Photo.** ***Perf. 14x13***

B414 SP183 10c +5c dp org & bl .20 .20
B415 SP183 12c +8c ap grn & red .20 .20
B416 SP183 20c +10c brt bl & red .20 .20
a. Min. sheet of 12, 4 #B414, 5 #B415, 3 #B416 3.00 3.00
B417 SP183 25c +10c brt rose lil & dk bl .80 .75
B418 SP183 40c +20c dp car & dk grn .70 .65
Nos. B414-B418 (5) 2.10 2.00

The surtax was for child welfare.

Whelk Eggs SP184

15c+10c, Whelk. 20c+10c, Mussel with acorn shells. 25c+10c, Jellyfish. 45c+20c, Crab.

1967, Apr. 11 **Unwmk.** **Litho.**

B419 SP184 12c +8c ol grn & tan .30 .25
B420 SP184 15c +10c lt bl, ultra & blk .30 .25
B421 SP184 20c +10c gray, blk & red .30 .20
B422 SP184 25c +10c brn car, plum & ol brn .55 .50
B423 SP184 45c +20c multi .70 .65
Nos. B419-B423 (5) 2.15 1.85

Red Cross and Dates Forming Cross SP185

"Lullaby for the Little Porcupine" — SP186

15c+10c, Crosses. 20c+10c, Initials "NRK" forming cross. 25c+10c, Maltese cross and crosses. 45c+20c, "100" forming cross.

1967, Aug. 8 ***Perf. 14x13***

B424 SP185 12c +8c dl bl & red .30 .25
B425 SP185 15c +10c red .40 .35
B426 SP185 20c +10c ol & red .30 .20
B427 SP185 25c +10c ol grn & red .40 .35
B428 SP185 45c +20c gray & red .70 .50
Nos. B424-B428 (5) 2.10 1.65

Centenary of the Dutch Red Cross.

1967, Nov. 7 **Litho.** ***Perf. 13x14***

Nursery Rhymes: 15c+10c, "Little Whistling Kettle." 20c+10c, "Dikkertje Dap and the Giraffe." 25c+10c, "The Nicest Flowers." 45c+20c, "Pippeljoentje, the Little Bear."

B429 SP186 12c +8c multi .20 .20
B430 SP186 15c +10c multi .20 .20
B431 SP186 20c +10c multi .20 .20
a. Min. sheet of 10, 3 #B429, 4 #B430, 3 #B431 4.25 4.25
B432 SP186 25c +10c multi .85 .75
B433 SP186 45c +20c multi 1.00 .75
Nos. B429-B433 (5) 2.45 2.10

The surtax was for child welfare.

St. Servatius Bridge, Maastricht SP187

Bridges: 15c+10c, Narrow Bridge, Amsterdam. 20c+10c, Railroad Bridge, Culenborg. 25c+10c, Van Brienenoord Bridge, Rotterdam. 45c+20c, Zeeland Bridge, Schelde Estuary.

1968, Apr. 9 **Photo.** ***Perf. 14x13***

B434 SP187 12c +8c green .65 .85
B435 SP187 15c +10c ol brn .75 .90
B436 SP187 20c +10c rose red .65 .25
B437 SP187 25c +10c gray .65 .85
B438 SP187 45c +20c ultra 1.00 1.25
Nos. B434-B438 (5) 3.70 4.10

Goblin SP188

Fairy Tale Characters: 15c+10c, Giant. 20c+10c, Witch. 25c+10c, Dragon. 45c+20c, Magician.

1968, Nov. 12 Photo. *Perf. 14x13*

B439 SP188 12c +8c grn, pink & blk .20 .20
B440 SP188 15c +10c bl, pink & blk .20 .20
B441 SP188 20c +10c bl, emer & blk .20 .20
a. Min. sheet of 10, 3 #B439, 4 #B440, 3 #B441 8.00 8.00
B442 SP188 25c +10c org red, org & blk 2.00 1.90
B443 SP188 45c +20c yel, org & blk 1.90 1.90
Nos. B439-B443 (5) 4.50 4.40

The surtax was for child welfare.

Villa Huis ter Heide, 1915 SP189

Stylized Crab — SP190

Contemporary Architecture: 15c+10c, House, Utrecht, 1924. 20c+10c, First open-air school, Amsterdam, 1960. 25c+10c, Burgweeshuis (orphanage), Amsterdam, 1960. 45c+20c, Netherlands Congress Building, The Hague, 1969.

1969, Apr. 15 Photo. *Perf. 14x13*

B444 SP189 12c +8c lt brn & sl .85 .85
B445 SP189 15c +10c bl, gray & red .85 1.10
B446 SP189 20c +10c vio & blk .85 1.10
B447 SP189 25c +10c grn & gray 1.00 .52
B448 SP189 45c +20c gray, bl & yel 1.10 1.25
Nos. B444-B448 (5) 4.65 4.82

Surtax for social and cultural purposes.

1969, Aug. 12 Photo. *Perf. 13x14*

B449 SP190 12c +8c vio 1.00 1.10
B450 SP190 25c +10c org 1.40 .55
B451 SP190 45c +20c bl grn 1.75 2.50
Nos. B449-B451 (3) 4.15 4.15

20th anniv. of the Queen Wilhelmina Fund. The surtax was for cancer research.

Child with Violin SP191

Isometric Projection from Circle to Square SP192

12c+8c, Child with flute. 20c+10c, Child with drum. 25c+10c, Three children singing, horiz. 45c+20c, Two girls dancing, horiz.

1969, Nov. 11 *Perf. 13x14, 14x13*

B452 SP191 12c +8c ultra, blk & yel .25 .20
B453 SP191 15c +10c blk & red .25 .20
B454 SP191 20c +10c red, blk & yel 2.00 1.75
B455 SP191 25c +10c yel, blk & red .30 .20
a. Min. sheet of 10, 4 #B452, 4 #B453, 2 #B455 8.75 7.25
B456 SP191 45c +20c grn, blk & red 2.75 2.75
Nos. B452-B456 (5) 5.55 5.10

The surtax was for child welfare.

Lithographed and Engraved

1970, Apr. 7 *Perf. 13x14*

Designs made by Computer: 15c+10c, Parallel planes in a cube. 20c+10c, Two overlapping scales. 25c+10c, Transition phases of concentric circles with increasing diameters. 45c+20c, Four spirals.

B457 SP192 12c +8c yel & blk .90 .90
B458 SP192 15c +10c sil & blk .90 .90
B459 SP192 20c +10c blk .90 .90
B460 SP192 25c +10c brt bl & blk .90 .60
B461 SP192 45c +20c sil & white .90 .90
Nos. B457-B461 (5) 4.50 4.20

Surtax for social and cultural purposes.

Bleeding Heart — SP193

Toy Block — SP194

1970, July 28 Photo. *Perf. 13x14*

B462 SP193 12c +8c org yel, red & blk .65 .75
B463 SP193 25c +10c pink, red & blk .65 .40
B464 SP193 45c +20c brt grn, red & blk .70 .75
Nos. B462-B464 (3) 2.00 1.90

The surtax was for the Netherlands Heart Foundation.

1970, Nov. 10 Photo. *Perf. 13x14*

B465 SP194 12c +8c bl, vio bl & grn .25 .20
B466 SP194 15c +10c grn, bl & yel 1.25 1.25
B467 SP194 20c +10c lil rose, red & vio bl 1.25 1.25
B468 SP194 25c +10c red, yel & lil rose .40 .20
a. Min. sheet of 11, 9 #B465, 2 #B468 + label 12.00 11.00
B469 SP194 45c +20c gray & blk 1.60 1.50
Nos. B465-B469 (5) 4.75 4.40

The surtax was for child welfare.

St. Paul SP195

Detail from Borobudur SP196

Designs: 15c+10c, "50" and people. 25c+10c, Joachim and Ann. 30c+15c, John the Baptist and the Scribes. 45c+20c, St. Anne. The sculptures are wood, 15th century, and in Dutch museums.

1971, Apr. 20 Litho. *Perf. 13x14*

B470 SP195 15c +10c multi 1.25 1.25

Lithographed and Photogravure

B471 SP195 20c +10c gray, grn & blk 1.00 1.00
B472 SP195 25c +10c buff, org & blk 1.10 .50
B473 SP195 30c +15c gray, bl & blk 1.25 1.25
B474 SP195 45c +20c pink, ver & blk 1.25 1.25
Nos. B470-B474 (5) 5.85 5.25

50th anniversary of the Federation of Netherlands Universities for Adult Education.

1971, June 29 Litho. *Perf. 13x14*

B475 SP196 45c +20c pur, yel & blk 2.25 2.25

60th birthday of Prince Bernhard. Surtax for Save Borobudur Temple Fund.

"Earth" SP197

Stylized Fruits SP198

Designs: 20c+10c, "Air" (butterfly). 25c+10c, "Sun," horiz. 30c+15c, "Moon," horiz. 45c+20c, "Water" (child looking at reflection).

Perf. 13x14, 14x13

1971, Nov. 9 Photo.

B476 SP197 15c +10c blk, lil & org .30 .20
B477 SP197 20c +10c yel, blk & rose lil .35 .25
B478 SP197 25c +10c multi .40 .20
a. Min. sheet of 9, 6 #B476, #B477, 2 #B478 9.00 8.75
B479 SP197 30c +15c bl, blk & pur 1.00 .40
B480 SP197 45c +20c grn, blk & bl 1.75 1.60
Nos. B476-B480 (5) 3.80 2.65

The surtax was for child welfare.

Luminescence

Some semipostal issues from Nos. B481-B484 onward are on phosphorescent paper.

1972, Apr. 11 Litho. *Perf. 13x14*

B481 SP198 20c +10c shown .90 .80
B482 SP198 25c +10c Flower .90 .80
B483 SP198 30c +15c "Sunlit Landscape" .90 .55
B484 SP198 45c +25c "Music" .90 .80
Nos. B481-B484 (4) 3.60 2.95

Summer festivals: Nos. B481-B482 publicize the Floriade, flower festival; Nos. B483-B484 the Holland Festival of Arts.

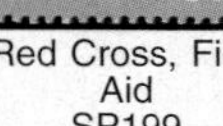

Red Cross, First Aid SP199

Prince Willem-Alexander SP200

Red Cross and: 25c+10c, Blood bank. 30c+15c, Disaster relief. 45c+25c, Child care.

1972, Aug. 15 *Perf. 13x14*

B485 SP199 20c +10c brt pink & red .55 .45
B486 SP199 25c +10c org & red .70 .80
B487 SP199 30c +15c blk & red .70 .25
B488 SP199 45c +25c ultra & red .80 .80
Nos. B485-B488 (4) 2.75 2.30

Surtax for the Netherlands Red Cross.

Perf. 13x14, 14x13

1972, Nov. 7 Photo.

Photographs of Dutch Princes: 30c+10c, Johan Friso. 35c+15c, Constantijn. 50c+20c, Johan Friso, Constantijn and Willem-Alexander. All are horizontal.

B489 SP200 25c +15c multi .45 .20
B490 SP200 30c +10c multi .75 .75
B491 SP200 35c +15c multi .75 .20
a. Min. sheet of 7, 4 #B489, #B490, 2 #B491 + label 6.00 5.25
B492 SP200 50c +20c multi 1.90 2.00
Nos. B489-B492 (4) 3.85 3.15

Surtax was for child welfare.

"W. A. Scholten," 1874 SP201

Ships: 25c+15c, Flagship "De Seven Provincien," 1673, vert. 35c+15c, "Veendam," 1923. 50c+20c, Zuider Zee fish well boat, 17th century, vert.

1973, Apr. 10 Litho.

B493 SP201 25c +15c multi 1.10 1.10
B494 SP201 30c +10c multi 1.10 1.10
B495 SP201 35c +15c multi 1.25 .65
B496 SP201 50c +20c multi 1.25 1.25
Nos. B493-B496 (4) 4.70 4.10

Tercentenary of the Battle of Kijkduin and centenary of the Holland-America Line. Surtax for social and cultural purposes.

Chessboard SP202

Games: 30c+10c, Tick-tack-toe. 40c+20c, Labyrinth. 50c+20c, Dominoes.

1973, Nov. 13 Photo. *Perf. 13x14*

B497 SP202 25c +15c multi .45 .20
B498 SP202 30c +10c multi .75 .35
B499 SP202 40c +20c multi .60 .20
a. Min. sheet of 6, 2 #B497, #B498, 3 #B499 8.25 7.50
B500 SP202 50c +20c multi 1.60 1.50
Nos. B497-B500 (4) 3.40 2.25

Surtax was for child welfare.

Music Bands SP203

Herman Heijermans SP204

Designs: 30c+10c, Ballet dancers and traffic lights. 50c+20c, Kniertje, the fisher woman, from play by Heijermans.

1974, Apr. 23 Litho. *Perf. 13x14*

B501 SP203 25c +15c multi .70 .70
B502 SP203 30c +10c multi .70 .70

Photo.

B503 SP204 40c +20c multi .70 .40
B504 SP204 50c +20c multi .75 .75
Nos. B501-B504 (4) 2.85 2.55

Surtax was for various social and cultural institutions.

Boy with Hoop — SP205

Designs: 35c+20c, Girl and infant. 45c+20c, Two girls. 60c+20c, Girl sitting on balustrade. Designs are from turn-of-the-century photographs.

1974, Nov. 12 Photo. *Perf. 13x14*

B505 SP205 30c +15c brown .50 .20
B506 SP205 35c +20c maroon .60 .40
B507 SP205 45c +20c black brn .70 .20
a. Min. sheet of 6, 4 #B505, #B506, #B507 3.50 3.25
B508 SP205 60c +20c indigo 1.00 1.10
Nos. B505-B508 (4) 2.80 1.90

Surtax was for child welfare.

Beguinage, Amsterdam SP206

Cooper's Gate, Middelburg SP207

Designs: 35c+20c, St. Hubertus Hunting Lodge, horiz. 60c+20c, Orvelte Village, horiz.

Perf. 14x13, 13x14

1975, Apr. 4 **Litho.**

B509 SP206 35c +20c multi	.60	.60
B510 SP206 40c +15c multi	.60	.60
B511 SP207 50c +20c multi	.75	.75
B512 SP207 60c +20c multi	.90	.90
Nos. B509-B512 (4)	2.85	2.85

European Architectural Heritage Year 1975. Surtax was for various social and cultural institutions.

Orphans, Sculpture, 1785 SP208

40c+15c, Milkmaid, 17th cent. 50c+25c, Aymon's 4 sons on steed Bayard, 17th cent. 60c+25c, Life at orphanage, 1557. All designs are after ornamental stones from various buildings.

1975, Nov. 11 **Photo.** ***Perf. 14x13***

B513 SP208 35c +15c multi	.55	.55
B514 SP208 40c +15c multi	.60	.60
B515 SP208 50c +25c multi	.80	.80
a. Min. sheet of 5, 3 #B513, 2 #B515 + label	3.00	3.00
B516 SP208 60c +25c multi	.95	.95
Nos. B513-B516 (4)	2.90	2.90

Surtax was for child welfare.

Hedgehog SP209

Book with "ABC" and Grain; Open Field SP210

Green Frog and Spawn SP212

People and Initials of Social Security Acts SP211

Perf. 14x13, 13x14

1976, Apr. 6 **Litho.**

B517 SP209 40c +20c multi	.65	.65
B518 SP210 45c +20c multi	.65	.65

Photo.

B519 SP211 55c +20c multi	.80	.80
B520 SP212 75c +25c multi	1.10	1.10
Nos. B517-B520 (4)	3.20	3.20

Surtax for various social and cultural institutions. #B517, B520 for wildlife protection; #B518 cent. of agricultural education and 175th anniv. of elementary education legislation; #B519 75th anniv. of social legislation and the Social Insurance Bank.

Patient Surrounded by Caring Hands — SP213

Netherlands No. 41 — SP214

1976, Sept. 2 **Litho.** ***Perf. 13x14***

B521 SP213 55c +25c multi	.90	.90

Dutch Anti-Rheumatism Assoc., 50th anniv.

1976, Oct. 8 **Litho.** ***Perf. 13x14***

Designs: No. B523, #64. No. B524, #155. No. B525, #294. No. B526, #220.

B522 SP214 55c +55c multi	1.25	1.25
B523 SP214 55c +55c multi	1.25	1.25
B524 SP214 55c +55c multi	1.25	1.25
a. Strip of 3, #B522-B524	3.75	3.75

Photo.

B525 SP214 75c +75c multi	1.60	1.60
B526 SP214 75c +75c multi	1.60	1.60
a. Pair, #B525-B526	3.25	3.25
Nos. B522-B526 (5)	6.95	6.95

Amphilex 77 Philatelic Exhibition, Amsterdam, May 26-June 5, 1977. No. B526a printed checkerwise.

See Nos. B535-B538.

Soccer SP215

Children's Drawings: 45c+20c, Sailboat. 55c+20c, Elephant. 75c+25c, Mobile home.

1976, Nov. 16 **Photo.** ***Perf. 14x13***

B527 SP215 40c +20c multi	.65	.65
B528 SP215 45c +20c multi	.65	.65
B529 SP215 55c +20c multi	.80	.80
a. Min. sheet of 6, 2 each #B527-B529	4.25	4.25
B530 SP215 75c +25c multi	1.10	1.10
Nos. B527-B530 (4)	3.20	3.20

Surtax was for child welfare.

Hot Room, Thermal Bath, Heerlen SP216

45c+20c, Altar of Goddess Nehalennia, 200 A.D., Eastern Scheldt. 55c+20c, Part of oaken ship, Zwammerdam. 75c+25c, Helmet with face, Waal River at Nijmegen.

1977, Apr. 19 **Photo.** ***Perf. 14x13***

B531 SP216 40c +20c multi	.65	.65
B532 SP216 45c +20c multi	.70	.70
B533 SP216 55c +20c multi	.80	.80
B534 SP216 75c +25c multi	1.10	1.10
Nos. B531-B534 (4)	3.25	3.25

Archaeological finds of Roman period. Surtax for various social and cultural institutions.

Type of 1976

Designs: No. B535, Netherlands #83. No. B536, Netherlands #128. No. B537, Netherlands #211. No. B538, Netherlands #302.

1977, May 26 **Litho.** ***Perf. 13x14***

B535 SP214 55c +45c multi	1.10	1.10
B536 SP214 55c +45c multi	1.10	1.10
a. Pair, #B535-B536	2.25	2.25
B537 SP214 55c +45c multi	1.10	1.10
B538 SP214 55c +45c multi	1.10	1.10
a. Souv. sheet of 2, #B535, B538	2.25	2.25
b. Pair, #B537-B538	2.25	2.25
Nos. B535-B538 (4)	4.40	4.40

Amphilex 77 International Philatelic Exhibition, Amsterdam May 26-June 5. No. B538a sold at Exhibition only.

Risk of Drowning — SP217

Childhood Dangers: 45c+20c, Poisoning. 55c+20c, Following ball into street. 75c+25c, Playing with matches.

1977, Nov. 15 **Photo.** ***Perf. 13x14***

B539 SP217 40c +20c multi	.65	.65
B540 SP217 45c +20c multi	.70	.70
B541 SP217 55c +20c multi	.80	.80
a. Min. sheet of 6, 2 each #B539-B541	4.50	4.50
B542 SP217 75c +25c multi	1.10	1.10
Nos. B539-B542 (4)	3.25	3.25

Surtax was for child welfare.

Anna Maria van Schuurman SP218

Delft Plate SP219

Designs: 45c+20c, Part of letter written by author Belle van Zuylen (1740-1805). 75c+25c, Makkum dish with dog.

1978, Apr. 11 **Litho.** ***Perf. 13x14***

B543 SP218 40c +20c multi	.65	.65
B544 SP218 45c +20c multi	.70	.70

Photo.

B545 SP219 55c +20c multi	.80	.80
B546 SP219 75c +25c multi	1.10	1.10
Nos. B543-B546 (4)	3.25	3.25

Dutch authors and pottery products.

Red Cross and World Map SP220

1978, Aug. 22 **Photo.** ***Perf. 14x13***

B547 SP220 55c +25c multi	.90	.90
a. Souvenir sheet of 3	2.75	2.75

Surtax was for Dutch Red Cross.

Boy Ringing Doorbell SP221

Designs: 45c+20c, Child reading book. 55c+20c, Boy writing "30x Children for Children," vert. 75c+25c, Girl at blackboard, arithmetic lesson.

Perf. 14x13, 13x14

1978, Nov. 14 **Photo.**

B548 SP221 40c +20c multi	.65	.65
B549 SP221 45c +20c multi	.70	.70
B550 SP221 55c +20c multi	.80	.80
a. Min. sheet of 6, 2 each #B548-B550	4.50	4.50
B551 SP221 75c +25c multi	1.10	1.10
Nos. B548-B551 (4)	3.25	3.25

Surtax was for child welfare.

Psalm Trilogy, by Jurriaan Andriessen SP222

Birth of Christ (detail) Stained-glass Window SP223

Designs: 45c+20c, Amsterdam Toonkunst Choir. 75c+25c, William of Orange, stained-glass window, 1603. Windows from St. John's Church, Gouda.

1979, Apr. 3 **Photo.** ***Perf. 13x14***

B552 SP222 40c +20c multi	.25	.20
B553 SP222 45c +20c multi	.40	.20
B554 SP223 55c +20c multi	.40	.20
B555 SP223 75c +25c multi	.55	.40
Nos. B552-B555 (4)	1.60	1.00

Surtax for social and cultural purposes.

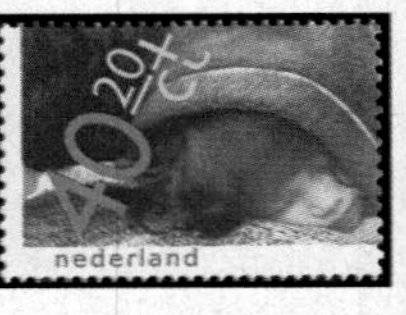
Child Sleeping Under Blanket SP224

Designs: 45c+20c, Infant. 55c+20c, African boy, vert. 75c+25c, Children, vert.

1979, Nov. 13 ***Perf. 14x13, 13x14***

B556 SP224 40c +20c blk, red & yel	.65	.65
B557 SP224 45c +20c blk & red	.70	.70
B558 SP224 55c +20c blk & yel	.80	.80
a. Min. sheet, 2 each #B556-B558	4.50	4.50
B559 SP224 75c +25c blk, ultra & red	1.10	1.10
Nos. B556-B559 (4)	3.25	3.25

Surtax was for child welfare (in conjuction with International Year of the Child).

Roads Through Sand Dunes SP225

50c+20c, Park mansion vert. 60c+25c, Sailing. 80c+35c, Bicycling, moorlands.

Perf. 14x13, 13x14

1980, Apr. 15 **Litho.**

B560 SP225 45c +20c multi	.70	.70
B561 SP225 50c +20c multi	.75	.75
B562 SP225 60c +25c multi	.95	.95
B563 SP225 80c +35c multi	1.25	1.25
Nos. B560-B563 (4)	3.65	3.65

Society for the Promotion of Nature Preserves, 75th anniv. Surtax for social and cultural purposes.

Wheelchair Basketball — SP226

1980, June 3 **Litho.** ***Perf. 13x14***

B564 SP226 60c +25c multi	.95	.95

Olympics for the Disabled, Arnhem and Veenendaal, June 21-July 5. Surtax was for National Sports for the Handicapped Fund.

Harlequin and Girl Standing in Open Book SP227

Designs: 50c+20c, Boy on flying book, vert. 60c+30c, Boy reading King of Frogs, vert. 80c+30c, Boy "engrossed" in book.

Perf. 14x13, 13x14

1980, Nov. 11 **Photo.**

B565 SP227 45c +20c multi .70 .70
B566 SP227 50c +20c multi .75 .75
B567 SP227 60c +30c multi 1.00 1.00
a. Min. sheet of 5, 2 #B565, 3 #B567 + label 4.50 4.50
B568 SP227 80c +30c multi 1.25 1.25
Nos. B565-B568 (4) 3.70 3.70

Surtax was for child welfare.

Salt Marsh with Outlet Ditch at Low Tide — SP228

Designs: 55c+25c, Dike. 60c+25c, Land drainage. 65c+30c, Cultivated land.

1981, Apr. 7 **Photo.** ***Perf. 13x14***

B569 SP228 45c +20c multi .70 .70
B570 SP228 55c +25c multi .90 .90
B571 SP228 60c +25c multi .95 .95
B572 SP228 65c +30c multi 1.00 1.00
Nos. B569-B572 (4) 3.55 3.55

Intl. Year of the Disabled SP229

Perf. 14x13, 13x14

1981, Nov. 10 **Photo.**

B573 SP229 45c +25c multi .75 .75
B574 SP229 55c +20c multi, vert .80 .80
B575 SP229 60c +25c multi, vert. .95 .95
B576 SP229 65c +30c multi 1.00 1.00
a. Min. sheet of 5, 3 #B573, 2 #B576 + label 4.50 4.50
Nos. B573-B576 (4) 3.50 3.50

Surtax was for child welfare.

Floriade '82, Amsterdam, Apr. — SP230

1982, Apr. 7 **Litho.** ***Perf. 13½x13***

B577 SP230 50c +20c shown .75 .75
B578 SP230 60c +25c Anemones .95 .95
B579 SP230 65c +25c Roses 1.00 1.00
B580 SP230 70c +30c African violets 1.10 1.10
Nos. B577-B580 (4) 3.80 3.80

Surtax was for culture and social welfare institutions.

Birds on Child's Head — SP231

Children and Animals: 60c+20c, Boy and cat. 65c+20c, Boy and rabbit. 70c+30c, Boy and bird.

1982, Nov. 16 **Photo.** ***Perf. 13x14***

B581 SP231 50c +30c multi .90 .90
B582 SP231 60c +20c multi .90 .90
a. Min. sheet of 5, 4 #B581, #B582 4.50 4.50
B583 SP231 65c +20c multi .95 .95
B584 SP231 70c +30c multi 1.10 1.10
Nos. B581-B584 (4) 3.85 3.85

Surtax was for child welfare.

Johan van Oldenbarneveldt (1547-1619), Statesman, by J. Houbraken — SP232

Paintings: 60c+25c, Willem Jansz Blaeu (1571-1638), cartographer, by Thomas de Keijser. 65c+25c, Hugo de Groot (1583-1645), statesman, by J. van Ravesteyn. 70c+30c, Portrait of Saskia van Uylenburch, by Rembrandt (1606-1669).

1983, Apr. 19 **Photo.** ***Perf. 14x13***

B585 SP232 50c +20c multi .75 .75
B586 SP232 60c +25c multi .95 .95
B587 SP232 65c +25c multi 1.00 1.00
B588 SP232 70c +30c multi 1.10 1.10
Nos. B585-B588 (4) 3.80 3.80

Surtax was for cultural and social welfare institutions.

Red Cross Workers — SP233

Designs: 60c+20c, Principles. 65c+25c, Sociomedical work. 70c+30c, Peace.

1983, Aug. 30 **Photo.** ***Perf. 13x14***

B589 SP233 50c +25c multi .80 .80
B590 SP233 60c +20c multi .90 .90
B591 SP233 65c +25c multi 1.00 1.00
B592 SP233 70c +30c multi 1.10 1.10
a. Bklt. pane, 4 #B589, 2 #B592 5.50 5.50
Nos. B589-B592 (4) 3.80 3.80

Surtax was for Red Cross.

Children's Christmas SP235

1983, Nov. 16 **Photo.** ***Perf. 14x13***

B596 SP235 50c +10c Ox & donkey .65 .65
B597 SP235 50c +25c Snowman .80 .80
B598 SP235 60c +30c Stars 1.00 1.00
B599 SP235 70c +30c Epiphany 1.10 1.10
a. Min. sheet, 4 #B597, 2 #B599 5.00 5.00
Nos. B596-B599 (4) 3.55 3.55

Surtax was for Child Welfare.

Eurasian Lapwings SP236

Birds: 60c+25c, Ruffs. 65c+25c, Redshanks, vert. 70c+30c, Black-tailed godwits, vert.

1984, Apr. 3 ***Perf. 14x13, 13x14***

B600 SP236 50c +20c multi .75 .75
B601 SP236 60c +25c multi .95 .95
B602 SP236 65c +25c multi 1.00 1.00
B603 SP236 70c +30c multi 1.10 1.10
a. Bklt. pane, 2 #B600, 2 #B603 3.75 3.75
Nos. B600-B603 (4) 3.80 3.80

Surtax for cultural and social welfare institutions.

FILACENTO '84 — SP237

Centenary of Organized Philately: 50c+20c, Eye, magnifying glass (36x25mm). 60c+25c, Cover, 1909 (34½x25mm). 70c+30c, Stamp club meeting, 1949 (34½x24mm).

1984, June 13 **Litho.** ***Perf. 14x13***

B604 SP237 50c +20c multi .75 .75
B605 SP237 60c +25c multi .95 .95
B606 SP237 70c +30c multi 1.10 1.10
a. Souv. sheet of 3, #B604-B606 3.00 3.00
Nos. B604-B606 (3) 2.80 2.80

No. B606a issued Sept. 5, 1984.

Comic Strips — SP238

1984, Nov. 14 **Litho.** ***Perf. 13x13½***

B607 SP238 50c +25c Music lesson .80 .80
B608 SP238 60c +20c Dentist .90 .90
B609 SP238 65c +25c Plumber 1.00 1.00
B610 SP238 70c +30c King 1.10 1.10
a. Min. sheet, 4 #B607, 2 #B610 5.50 5.50
Nos. B607-B610 (4) 3.80 3.80

Surtax was for child welfare.

Winterswijk Synagogue, Holy Arc — SP239

Religious architecture: 50+20c, St. Martin's Church, Zaltbommel, vert. 65+25c, Village Congregational Church, Bolsward, vert. 70+30c, St. John's Cathedral, 'S-Hertogenbosch, detail of buttress.

Perf. 13x14, 14x13

1985, Mar. 26 **Photo.**

B611 SP239 50c +20c gray & brt bl .75 .75
B612 SP239 60c +25c dk red brn, Prus bl & pck bl .95 .95
B613 SP239 65c +25c sl bl, red brn & gray ol 1.00 1.00
B614 SP239 70c +30c gray, brt bl & bis 1.10 1.10
a. Bklt. pane, 2 #B611, 2 #B614 4.00 4.00
Nos. B611-B614 (4) 3.80 3.80

Surtax for social and cultural purposes.

Traffic Safety SP240

1985, Nov. 13 **Photo.** ***Perf. 13x14***

B615 SP240 50c +25c Photograph, lock, key .80 .80
B616 SP240 60c +20c Boy, target .90 .90
B617 SP240 65c +20c Girl, hazard triangle .95 .95
B618 SP240 70c +30c Boy, traffic sign 1.10 1.10
a. Souv. sheet, 4 #B615, 2 #B618 5.50 5.50
Nos. B615-B618 (4) 3.75 3.75

Surtax was for child welfare organizations.

Antique Measuring Instruments SP241

Perf. 13½x13, 13x13½

1986, Apr. 8 **Litho.**

B619 SP241 50c +20c Balance .75 .75
B620 SP241 60c +25c Clock mechanism .95 .95
B621 SP241 65c +25c Barometer 1.00 1.00
B622 SP241 70c +30c Jacob's staff 1.10 1.10
a. Bklt. pane, 2 each #B619, B622 4.00 4.00
Nos. B619-B622 (4) 3.80 3.80

Nos. B620-B621 vert.

Youth and Culture SP242

1986, Nov. 12 **Litho.** ***Perf. 14x13***

B623 SP242 55c +25c Music .90 .90

Perf. 13½x13

B624 SP242 65c +35c Visual arts 1.10 1.10
B625 SP242 75c +35c Theater 1.25 1.25
a. Min. sheet of 5, #B623, 2 each #B624-B625, perf. 14x13 5.75 5.75
Nos. B623-B625 (3) 3.25 3.25

Surtax for child welfare organizations.

Traditional Industries SP243

Designs: 55c+30c, Steam pumping station, Nijkerk. 65c+35c, Water tower, Deventer. 75c+35c, Brass foundry, Joure.

1987, Apr. 7 **Photo.** ***Perf. 14x13***

B626 SP243 55c +30c multi .95 .95
B627 SP243 65c +35c multi 1.10 1.10
B628 SP243 75c +35c multi 1.25 1.25
a. Bklt. pane, 2 #B626, 2 #B628 4.50 4.50
Nos. B626-B628 (3) 3.30 3.30

Surtax for social and cultural welfare organizations.

Red Cross SP244

1987, Sept. 1 **Photo.** ***Perf. 14x13***

B629 SP244 55c +30c multi .95 .95
B630 SP244 65c +35c multi, diff. 1.10 1.10
B631 SP244 75c +35c multi, diff. 1.25 1.25
a. Bklt. pane, 2 #B629, 2 #B631 4.50 4.50
Nos. B629-B631 (3) 3.30 3.30

Surtax for nat'l. Red Cross.

Youth and Professions SP245

Perf. 13x14, 14x13

1987, Nov. 11 **Photo.**

B632 SP245 55c +25c Woodcutter, vert. .90 .90
B633 SP245 65c +35c Sailor 1.10 1.10
B634 SP245 75c +35c Pilot 1.25 1.25
a. Miniature sheet of 5, #B632, 2 #B633, 2 #B634 5.75 5.75
Nos. B632-B634 (3) 3.25 3.25

Surtax for child welfare organizations.

FILACEPT '88, October 18, The Hague SP246

Designs: 55c +55c, Narcissus cyclamineus and poem "I call you flowers," by Jan Hanlo. No. B636, Rosa gallica versicolor. No. B637, Eryngium maritimum and map of The Hague from 1270.

1988, Feb. 23 Litho. *Perf. 13½x13*

B635 SP246 55c +55c multi 1.25 1.25
B636 SP246 75c +70c multi 1.60 1.60
B637 SP246 75c +70c multi 1.60 1.60
a. Min. sheet of 3 + 3 labels, #B635-B637 4.50 4.50
Nos. B635-B637 (3) 4.45 4.45

Surtax helped finance exhibition.
No. B637a issued Oct. 18, 1988.

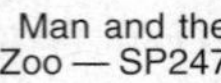
Man and the Zoo — SP247

Perf. 14x13, 13x14

1988, Mar. 22 Photo.

B638 SP247 55c +30c Equus quagga quagga .95 .95
B639 SP247 65c +35c Carribean sea cow 1.10 1.10
B640 SP247 75c +35c Sam the orangutan, vert. 1.25 1.25
a. Bklt. pane, 2 #B638, 2 #B640 4.50 4.50
Nos. B638-B640 (3) 3.30 3.30

Natural Artis Magistra zoological soc., 150th anniv. Surtax for social and cultural welfare organizations.

Royal Dutch Swimming Federation, Cent. SP248

Children's drawings on the theme "Children and Water."

1988, Nov. 16 Photo. *Perf. 14x13*

B641 SP248 55c +25c Rain .90 .90
B642 SP248 65c +35c Getting Ready for the Race 1.10 1.10
B643 SP248 75c +35c Swimming Test 1.25 1.25
a. Min. sheet of 5, #B641, 2 each #B642-B643 5.75 5.75
Nos. B641-B643 (3) 3.25 3.25

Surtax to benefit child welfare organizations.

Ships SP249

Designs: No. B644, Pleasure yacht (boyer), vert. No. B645, Zuiderzee fishing boat (smack). No. B646, Clipper.

Perf. 13x14, 14x13

1989, Apr. 11 Photo.

B644 SP249 55c +30c multi .95 .95
B645 SP249 65c +35c multi 1.10 1.10
B646 SP249 75c +35c multi 1.25 1.25
a. Bklt. pane, #B644-B645, 2 #B646 4.75 4.75
Nos. B644-B646 (3) 3.30 3.30

Surtax for social and cultural organizations.

Children's Rights SP250

1989, Nov. 8 Litho. *Perf. 13½x13*

B647 SP250 55c +25c Housing .90 .90
B648 SP250 65c +35c Food 1.10 1.10
B649 SP250 75c +35c Education 1.25 1.25
a. Min. sheet of 5, #B647, 2 each #B648-B649 5.75 5.75
Nos. B647-B649 (3) 3.25 3.25

UN Declaration of Children's Rights, 30th anniv. Surtax for child welfare.

Summer Weather SP251

Perf. 14x13, 13x14

1990, Apr. 3 Photo.

B650 SP251 55c +30c Girl, flowers .95 .95
B651 SP251 65c +35c Clouds, isobars, vert. 1.10 1.10
B652 SP251 75c +35c Weather map, vert. 1.25 1.25
a. Bklt. pane, #B650-B651, 2 #B652 4.75 4.75
Nos. B650-B652 (3) 3.30 3.30

Surtax for social & cultural welfare organizations.

Children's Hobbies SP252

1990, Nov. 7 Litho. *Perf. 13½x13*

B653 SP252 55c +25c Riding .90 .90
B654 SP252 65c +35c Computers 1.10 1.10
B655 SP252 75c +35c Philately 1.25 1.25
a. Souv. sheet of 5, #B653, 2 each #B654-B655 5.75 5.75
Nos. B653-B655 (3) 3.25 3.25

Surtax for child welfare.

Dutch Farms SP253

55c+30c, Frisian farm, Wartena. 65c+35c, Guelders T-style farm, Kesteren. 75c+35c, Closed construction farm, Nuth (Limburg).

1991, Apr. 16 Litho. *Perf. 13½x13*

B656 SP253 55c +30c multi .95 .95
a. Photo. .95 .95
B657 SP253 65c +35c multi 1.10 1.10
B658 SP253 75c +35c multi 1.25 1.25
a. Photo. 1.25 1.25
b. Bklt. pane, 2 #B656a, 3 #B658a 5.75 5.75
Nos. B656-B658 (3) 3.30 3.30

Surtax for social and cultural welfare organizations.

Children Playing SP254

1991, Nov. 6 Litho. *Perf. 13½x13*

B659 SP254 60c +30c Doll, robot 1.00 1.00
a. Photo., perf. 14x13½ 1.00 1.00
B660 SP254 70c +35c Cycle race 1.25 1.25
B661 SP254 80c +40c Hide and seek 1.40 1.40
a. Photo., perf. 14x13½ 1.40 1.40
b. Min. sheet, 4 #B659a, 2 #B661a 7.00 7.00
Nos. B659-B661 (3) 3.65 3.65

Floriade 1992, World Horticultural Exhibition SP255

Various plants and flowers.

1992, Apr. 7 Litho. *Perf. 13½x13*

B662 SP255 60c +30c multi 1.10 1.10
a. Photo., perf. 14x13½ 1.10 1.10
B663 SP255 70c +35c multi 1.25 1.25
a. Photo., perf. 14x13½ 1.25 1.25
B664 SP255 80c +40c multi 1.50 1.50
a. Photo., perf. 14x13½ 1.50 1.50
b. Booklet pane of 6, 3 #B662a, 2 #B663a, #B664a 7.50
Nos. B662-B664 (3) 3.85 3.85

Surtax for social and cultural welfare organizations.

Stamps in No. 664b are tete-beche (1 pair of B662a, 1 pair of B663a, 1 pair of B662a and B664a).

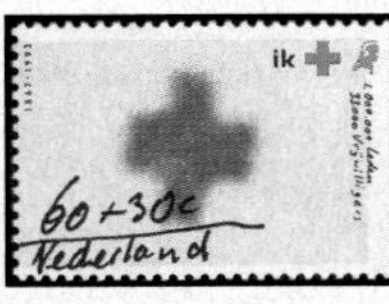

Netherlands Red Cross, 125th Anniv. SP256

1992, Sept. 8 Litho. *Perf. 13½x13*

B665 SP256 60c +30c Shadow of cross 1.10 1.10
a. Photo., perf. 14 on 3 sides 1.10 1.10
B666 SP256 70c +35c Aiding victim 1.25 1.25
a. Photo., perf. 14 on 3 sides 1.25 1.25
B667 SP256 80c +40c Red cross on bandage 1.40 1.40
a. Photo., perf. 14 on 3 sides 1.40 1.40
b. Bklt. pane, 3 #B665a, 2 #B666a, 1 #B667a 7.25
Nos. B665-B667 (3) 3.75 3.75

On normally centered stamps, the white border appears on the top, bottom and right sides only.

Children Making Music SP257

Senior Citizens SP258

1992, Nov. 11 Litho. *Perf. 13x13½*

B668 SP257 60c +30c Saxophone player 1.00 1.00
a. Photo., perf. 13½x14 1.00 1.00
B669 SP257 70c +35c Piano player 1.25 1.25
a. Photo., perf. 13½x14 1.25 1.25
B670 SP257 80c +40c Bass player 1.40 1.40
a. Photo., perf. 13½x14 1.40 1.40
b. Min. sheet, 3 #B668a, 2 #B669a, #B670a 7.00
Nos. B668-B670 (3) 3.65 3.65

1993, Apr. 20 Litho. *Perf. 13x13½*

B671 SP258 70c +35c shown 1.25 1.25
a. Photo., perf. 13½x14 1.25 1.25
B672 SP258 70c +35c couple 1.25 1.25
a. Photo., perf. 13½x14 1.25 1.25
B673 SP258 80c +40c woman 1.40 1.40
a. Photo., perf. 13½x14 1.40 1.40
b. Booklet pane, 1 #B671a, 2 #B672a, 3 #B673a 9.25
Complete booklet, #B673b 9.25
Nos. B671-B673 (3) 3.90 3.90

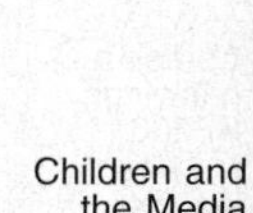

Children and the Media SP259

Designs: No. B674, Child wearing newspaper hat. No. B675, Elephant wearing earphones. 80c + 40c, Television, child's legs.

1993, Nov. 17 Litho. *Perf. 13½x13*

B674 SP259 70c +35c multi 1.25 1.25
a. Photo., perf. 14x13½ 1.25 1.25
B675 SP259 70c +35c multi 1.25 1.25
a. Photo., perf. 14x13½ 1.25 1.25
B676 SP259 80c +40c multi 1.40 1.40
a. Photo., perf. 14x13½ 1.40 1.40
b. Min. sheet, 2 each #B674a-B676a 8.00
Nos. B674-B676 (3) 3.90 3.90

FEPAPOST '94 — SP260

Birds: 70c+60c, Branta leucopsis. 80c+70c, Luscinia svecica. 90c+80c, Anas querquedula.

1994, Feb. 22 Litho. *Perf. 14x13*

B677 SP260 70c +60c multi 1.50 1.50
B678 SP260 80c +70c multi 1.75 1.75
B679 SP260 90c +80c multi 2.00 2.00
a. Min. sheet, #B677-B679 + 3 labels, perf. 13½x13 5.25
Nos. B677-B679 (3) 5.25 5.25

Issued: No. B679a, 10/17/94.

Senior Citizens — SP261

Designs: 80c+40c, Man talking on telephone seen from behind. 90c+35c, Man in suit talking on telephone.

1994, Apr. 26 Litho. *Perf. 13x13½*

B680 SP261 70c +35c shown 1.25 1.25
a. Photo., perf. 13½x14 1.25 1.25
B681 SP261 80c +40c multi 1.40 1.40
a. Photo., perf. 13½x14 1.40 1.40
B682 SP261 90c +35c multi 1.50 1.50
a. Photo., perf. 13½x14 1.50 1.50
b. Booklet pane, 2 #B680a, 3 #B681a, #B682a 8.25
Nos. B680-B682 (3) 4.15 4.15

Child Welfare Stamps SP262

Designs: 70c+35c, Holding ladder for woman painting. 80c+40c, Helping to balance woman picking cherries, vert. 90c+35c, Supporting boy on top of play house, vert.

Perf. 13½x13, 13x13½

1994, Nov. 9 Litho.

B683 SP262 70c +35c multi 1.25 1.25
B684 SP262 80c +40c multi 1.40 1.40
B685 SP262 90c +35c multi 1.50 1.50
a. SP262 Miniature sheet, 2 #B683, 3 #B684, 1 #B685, perf. 13x14 9.00
Nos. B683-B685 (3) 4.15 4.15

Senior Citizens SP263

Designs: 70c+35c, Indonesia #1422 on postcard. 80c+40c, Couple seen in bus mirror. 100c+45c, Grandparents, child at zoo.

1995, Apr. 11 Litho. *Perf. 13½x13*

B686 SP263 70c +35c multi 1.40 1.40
B687 SP263 80c +40c multi 1.50 1.50
B688 SP263 100c +45c multi 1.90 1.90
a. Miniature sheet, 2 #B686, 3 #B687, 1 #B688 9.50
Nos. B686-B688 (3) 4.80 4.80

Child Welfare Stamps SP264

Computer drawings by children: 70c+35c, Dino, by S. Stegeman. 80c+40c, The School Teacher, by L. Ensing, vert. 100c+50c, Children and Colors, by M. Jansen.

Perf. 13½x13, 13x13½

1995, Nov. 15 Litho.

B689 SP264 70c +35c multi 1.25 1.25
B690 SP264 80c +40c multi 1.50 1.50
B691 SP264 100c +50c multi 1.90 1.90
a. Min. sheet of 6, 2 #B689, 3 #B690, 1 #B691 9.75 9.75
Nos. B689-B691 (3) 4.65 4.65

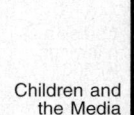

Senior Citizens SP265

1996, Apr. 23 Litho. *Perf. 13¼x12¾*

B692 SP265 70c +35c Swimming 1.25 1.25
B693 SP265 80c +40c Babysitting 1.40 1.40
B694 SP265 100c +50c Playing piano 1.75 1.75
a. Sheet of 6, 2 #B692, 3 #B693, 1 #B694, perf. 13x12½ 8.00 8.00
Nos. B692-B694 (3) 4.40 4.40

Child Welfare Stamps — SP266

Designs: 70c+35c, Baby, books. No. B696, Boy, toys. No. B697, Girl, tools.

Perf. 12¾3x13¼

1996, Nov. 6 Litho.

B695 SP266 70c +35 multi 1.10 1.10
B696 SP266 80c +40c multi 1.40 1.40
B697 SP266 80c +40c multi 1.40 1.40
a. Sheet of 2 each, #B695-B697 8.00 8.00
Nos. B695-B697 (3) 3.90 3.90

Senior Citizens SP267

Designs: No. B698, Rose in full bloom. No. B699, Stem of rose. No. B700, Rose bud.

1997, Apr. 15 Litho. *Perf. 13¼x12¾*

B698 SP267 80c +40c multi 1.40 1.40
B699 SP267 80c +40c multi 1.40 1.40
B700 SP267 80c +40c multi 1.40 1.40
a. Min. sheet, 2 each #B698-B700 8.50 8.50
Nos. B698-B700 (3) 4.20 4.20

Netherlands Red Cross — SP268

1997, May 27 Litho. *Perf. 12¾x13¼*

B701 SP268 80c +40c multi 1.40 1.40

Child Welfare Stamps SP269

Children's Fairy Tales: No. B702, Hunter with wolf, from "Little Red Riding Hood." No. B703, Dropping loaves of bread, from "Tom Thumb." No. B704, Man opening bottle, from "Genie in the Bottle."

Perf. 13¼x12¾

1997, Nov. 12 Litho.

B702 SP269 80c +40c multi 1.40 1.40
B703 SP269 80c +40c multi 1.40 1.40
B704 SP269 80c +40c multi 1.40 1.40
a. Min. sheet of 2 each, #B702-B704 8.50 8.50
Nos. B702-B704 (3) 4.20 4.20

Senior Citizens SP270

#B705, Sports shoe. #B706, Note on paper. #B707, Wrapped piece of candy.

1998, Apr. 21 Litho. *Perf. 13¼x12¾*

B705 SP270 80c +40c multi 1.40 1.40
B706 SP270 80c +40c multi 1.40 1.40
B707 SP270 80c +40c multi 1.40 1.40
a. Sheet, 2 each #B705-B707 8.50 8.50
Nos. B705-B707 (3) 4.20 4.20

Child Welfare Stamps SP271

#B708, Elephant riding horse. #B709, Pig, rabbit decorating cake. #B710, Pig, goose, rabbit carrying flower, frog carrying flag.

Perf. 13¼x12¾

1998, Nov. 11 Litho.

B708 SP271 80c +40c multi 1.40 1.40
B709 SP271 80c +40c multi 1.40 1.40
B710 SP271 80c +40c multi 1.40 1.40
a. Sheet, 2 each #B708-B710 8.50 8.50
Nos. B708-B710 (3) 4.20 4.20

Intl. Year of Older Persons SP272

1999, Apr. 13 Litho. *Perf. 13¼x12¾*

B711 SP272 80c +40c Woman 1.40 1.40
B712 SP272 80c +40c Black man 1.40 1.40
B713 SP272 80c +40c Caucasian man 1.40 1.40
a. Min. sheet, 2 ea #B711-B713 8.50 8.50
Nos. B711-B713 (3) 4.20 4.20

Child Welfare Stamps SP273

Designs: No. B714, Boy on tow truck. No. B715, Girl and chef. No. B716, Children stamping envelope.

Perf. 13¼x12¾

1999, Nov. 10 Litho.

B714 SP273 80c +40c multi 1.40 1.40
B715 SP273 80c +40c multi 1.40 1.40
B716 SP273 80c +40c multi 1.40 1.40
a. Sheet, 2 each #B714-B716 8.50 8.50
Nos. B714-B716 (3) 4.20 4.20

Senior Citizens SP274

2000, Apr. 4 Litho. *Perf. 13¼x12¾*

B717 SP274 80c +40c Swimmers 1.40 1.40
B718 SP274 80c +40c Bowlers 1.40 1.40
B719 SP274 80c +40c Fruit picker 1.40 1.40
a. Souvenir sheet, 2 each #B717-B719 8.50 8.50
Nos. B717-B719 (3) 4.20 4.20

Souvenir Sheet

Child Welfare SP275

Designs: Nos. B720a, B721, Children with masks. No. B720b, Child with ghost costume. No. B720c, Child on alligator. Nos. B720d, B722, Child in boat. Nos. B720e, B723, Children cooking. No. B720f, Children in dragon costume.

2000, Nov. 8 Litho. *Perf. 13¼x12¾*

B720 Sheet of 6 8.50 8.50
a.-f. SP275 80c +40c Any single 1.40 1.40

Self-Adhesive

Serpentine Die Cut 15

B721 SP275 80c +40c multi 1.40 1.40
B722 SP275 80c +40c multi 1.40 1.40
B723 SP275 80c +40c multi 1.40 1.40
Nos. B721-B723 (3) 4.20 4.20

Flowers SP276

Designs: No. B724a, Caryopteris. Nos. B724b, B725, Helenium. Nos. B724c, B726, Alcea rugosa. No. B724d, Euphorbia schillingii. No. B724e, B727, Centaurea dealbata. No. B724f, Inula hookeri.

2001, Apr. 24 Litho. *Perf. 13¼x12¾*

B724 Sheet of 6 6.00 6.00
a.-f. SP276 80c+40c Any single 1.00 1.00

Serpentine Die Cut 14¾x15

Self-Adhesive

B725 SP276 80c +40c multi 1.40 1.40
B726 SP276 80c +40c multi 1.40 1.40
B727 SP276 80c +40c multi 1.40 1.40
a. Booklet, 10 each #B725-727 42.50
Nos. B725-B727 (3) 4.20 4.20

Children and Computers SP277

Black figure: No. B728a, Retrieving letter from printer. No. B728b, Crossing road with letter. No. B728c, Sliding down green vine. No. B728d, Posting letter. Nos. B728e, B729, Crossing river on log. No. B728f, Swinging on rope.

2001, Nov. 6 Photo. *Perf. 14x13½*

B728 Sheet of 6 8.50 8.50
a.-f. SP277 85c +40c Any single 1.40 1.40

Self-Adhesive

Die Cut Perf. 13¼x13

B729 SP277 85c +40c multi 1.10 1.10

Surtax for Dutch Children's Stamp Foundation.

SP278

SP279

SP280

SP281

SP282

Floriade 2002 — SP283

2002, Apr. 2 Litho. *Perf. 14¾x14½*

B730 SP278 39c +19c multi 1.40 1.40
B731 SP279 39c +19c multi 1.40 1.40
B732 SP280 39c +19c multi 1.40 1.40
B733 SP281 39c +19c multi 1.40 1.40
B734 SP282 39c +19c multi 1.40 1.40
B735 SP283 39c +19c multi 1.40 1.40
a. Block of 6, #B730-B735 8.50 8.50

Nos. B730-B735 are impregnated with a floral scent.

Surtax for National Help the Aged Fund.

Blossom Walk, 10th Anniv. — SP284

2002, Apr. 27 Litho. *Perf. 14¾x14½*

B736 SP284 39c +19c multi 1.40 1.40

Surtax for Red Cross.

Children — SP285

No. B737: a, Child with red head, red cat. b, Child with green head, blue father. c, Child with red head, blue ball. d, Child with yellow head, green pet dish. e, Child with brown head, legs of child. f, Child with yellow head, blue dog.

2002, Nov. 5 Photo. *Perf. 14x13½*

B737 SP285 Sheet of 6 8.50 8.50
a.-f. 39c +19c Any single 1.40 1.40

Surtax for Dutch Children's Stamp Foundation.

Flowers — SP286

No. B738: a, Orange yellow lilies of the Incas. b, Lilac sweet peas. c, Pansies. d, Red orange and yellow trumpet creepers. e, Red campions. f, Purple, white and yellow irises.

2003, Apr. 8 Photo. *Perf. 14½x14¾*

B738 SP286 Block of 6 7.50 7.50
a.-f. 39c +19c Any single 1.25 1.25

Souvenir Sheet

Items in a Child's Life — SP287

No. B739: a, Note pad, radio, ballet shoes. b, Theater masks, book. c, Microphone, musical staff, paintbrush. d, Violin, soccer ball, television. e, Television, drum, light bulbs. f, Light bulbs, trombone, hat, headphones.

2003, Nov. 4 ***Perf. 14x13½***

B739	SP287	Sheet of 6	8.00	8.00
a.-f.		39c +19c Any single	1.25	1.25

Flowers — SP288

No. B740 — Various flowers with background color of: a, Lilac. b, Pink. c, Brownish gray. d, Ocher. e, Blue gray. f, Olive.

2004, Apr. 6 Photo. ***Perf. 14¾x14½***

B740	SP288	Block of 6	8.50	8.50
a.-f.		39c + 19c any single	1.40	1.40

Souvenir Sheet

Fruit and Sports — SP289

No. B741: a, Watermelon, soccer. b, Lemon, rope jumping. c, Orange, cycling. d, Pear, skateboarding. e, Banana, sit-ups. f, Strawberry, weight lifting.

2004, Nov. 9 Photo. ***Perf. 14½***

B741	SP289	Sheet of 6	9.00	9.00
a.-f.		39c +19c Any single	1.50	1.50

December Stamps — SP290

No. B742 — Inscriptions: a, Novib. b, Stop AIDS Now. c, Natuurmonumenten. d, KWF Kankerbestrijding. e, UNICEF. f, Plan Nederland. g, Tros Helpt. h, Greenpeace. i, Artsen Zonder Grenzen (Doctors Without Borders). j, World Food Program.

Serpentine Die Cut 8¾x9

2004, Nov. 25

Self-Adhesive

B742	Block of 10	10.50	10.50
a.-j.	SP290 29c +10c Any single	1.00	1.00

The surtax went to the various organizations named on the stamps.

Souvenir Sheets

SP291

Summer Stamps — SP292

No. B743 — Illustrations for children's stories and silhouette of: a, Children and barrel. b, Two children. c, Frying pan.

No. B744 — Illustrations for children's stories and silhouette of: a, Monkey. b, Cup, saucer and spoon. c, Cat playing with ball.

2005, Apr. 5 Litho. ***Perf. 13¼x13¾***

B743	SP291	Sheet of 3 + 2 labels	4.50	4.50
a.-c.		39c +19c Any single	1.50	1.50
B744	SP292	Sheet of 3 + 2 labels	4.50	4.50
a.-c.		39c +19c Any single	1.50	1.50

Miniature Sheet

Miffy the Bunny, by Dick Bruna — SP293

No. B745: a, Bunny and dog. b, Four bunnies. c, Bunny holding teddy bear. d, Bunny writing letter. e, White and brown bunnies. f, Six bunnies.

2005, Nov. 8 Photo. ***Perf. 14½***

B745	SP293	Sheet of 6	8.50	8.50
a.-f.		39c+19c Any single	1.40	1.40

The surtax went to the Foundation for Children's Welfare Stamps. A booklet containing four panes of two stamps sold for €9.95.

SP294 SP295

SP296 SP297

SP298 SP299

SP300 SP301

Religious Art from Museum Catharijnconvent, Utrecht

SP302 SP303

Serpentine Die Cut 8¾x9

2005, Nov. 24 **Litho.**

B746	Booklet pane of 10	9.50	
a.	SP294 29c+10c multi	.95	.95
b.	SP295 29c+10c multi	.95	.95
c.	SP296 29c+10c multi	.95	.95
d.	SP297 29c+10c multi	.95	.95
e.	SP298 29c+10c multi	.95	.95
f.	SP299 29c+10c multi	.95	.95
g.	SP300 29c+10c multi	.95	.95
h.	SP301 29c+10c multi	.95	.95
i.	SP302 29c+10c multi	.95	.95
j.	SP303 29c+10c multi	.95	.95

The surtax went to the various organizations named on the margin and backing paper of the booklet pane.

Souvenir Sheets

SP304

Illustrations From Reading Boards — SP305

No. B747: a, Monkey and birds. b, Walnut. c, Cat.

No. B748: a, Boy playing with game. b, Girl holding rattle. c, Girl playing with doll.

2006, Apr. 4 Litho. ***Perf. 13½x13¾***

B747	SP304	Sheet of 3 + 2 labels	4.25	4.25
a.-c.		39c +19c Any single	1.40	1.40
B748	SP305	Sheet of 3 + 2 labels	4.25	4.25
a.-c.		39c +19c Any single	1.40	1.40

Surtax for National Fund for Care of the Elderly.

Souvenir Sheet

Children — SP306

No. B749: a, Six children, boy in orange shirt with hands up and with foot on ball. b, Eight children, girl in red shirt with hands in air. c, Six children, girl at right standing. d, Six children, boy in orange shirt with hands down and kicking ball. e, Eight children, girl in red shirt with hands at waist. f, Six children, girl at right seated.

2006, Nov. 7 Photo. ***Perf. 14½***

B749	SP306	Sheet of 6	9.25	9.25
a.-f.		39c +19c Any single	1.50	1.50

Surtax for Dutch Children's Stamp Foundation.

SP307

SP308

SP309

SP310

SP311

SP312

SP313

SP314

SP315

Children Wearing Angel Costumes — SP316

Serpentine Die Cut 8¾x9

2006, Nov. 23 **Litho.**

Self-Adhesive

B750	Block of 10	10.50	10.50
a.	SP307 29c +10c multi	1.00	1.00
b.	SP308 29c +10c multi	1.00	1.00
c.	SP309 29c +10c multi	1.00	1.00
d.	SP310 29c +10c multi	1.00	1.00
e.	SP311 29c +10c multi	1.00	1.00
f.	SP312 29c +10c multi	1.00	1.00
g.	SP313 29c +10c multi	1.00	1.00
h.	SP314 29c +10c multi	1.00	1.00
i.	SP315 29c +10c multi	1.00	1.00
j.	SP316 29c +10c multi	1.00	1.00

The surtax went to the various organizations named in the sheet selvage.

Souvenir Sheets

Beach Activities — SP317

No. B751: a, Woman pulling dress up in surf, boy in water. b, Woman standing in surf, children on ponies on beach. c, Children on ponies on beach, children playing on beach.

No. B752: a, Children playing on beach, family posing for photograph on beach. b, Boy waving, people in large beach chair. c, Boy on sail-powered beach cart, family digging sand at shore.

2007, Apr. 4 Litho. ***Perf. 13¼x12¾***

B751 SP317 Sheet of 3 5.50 5.50
a.-c. 44c +22c Any single 1.75 1.75
B752 SP317 Sheet of 3 5.50 5.50
a.-c. 44c +22c Any single 1.75 1.75

Surtax for Natiional Fund for Senior Citizen's Help.

Netherlands Red Cross, 140th Anniv. SP318

2007, July 19 ***Perf. 13¼***

B753 SP318 44c +22c multi 1.90 1.90

Surtax for Netherlands Red Cross. Printed in sheets of 3.

Miniature Sheet

Children and Safety — SP319

No. B754 — Child: a, Watching television. b, And building at night. c, In bed. d, And computer. e, And kitten. f, Reading book.

2007, Nov. 6 Litho. ***Perf. 14½***

B754 SP319 Sheet of 6 12.00 12.00
a.-f. 44c +22c any single 2.00 2.00

Surtax for Foundation for Children's Welfare Stamps.

SP320

Forget-me-nots — SP321

No. B755: a, Forget-me-not, head-on view. b, Purple crane's bill geranium. c, Pink Japanese anemone.

No. B756: a, Purple larkspur. b, Globe thistle. c, Forget-me-not, side view.

2008, Apr. 1 Litho. ***Perf. 14½***

B755 SP320 Sheet of 3 6.25 6.25
a.-c. 44c+22c Any single 2.00 2.00
B756 SP321 Sheet of 3 6.25 6.25
a.-c. 44c+22c Any single 2.00 2.00

Surtax for National Fund for Elderly Assistance.

Miniature Sheet

Children's Education — SP322

No. B757 — Letters of word "Onderwijs" (education): a, "O." b, "ND." c, "ER." d, "W." e, "IJ." f, "S."

2008, Nov. 4 Photo. ***Perf. 14½***

B757 SP322 Sheet of 6 10.00 10.00
a.-f. 44c +22c Any single 1.60 1.60

Surtax for Foundation for Children's Welfare Stamps.

AIR POST STAMPS

Stylized Seagull — AP1

Perf. 12½

1921, May 1 Unwmk. Typo.

C1 AP1 10c red 1.25 1.50
C2 AP1 15c yellow grn 6.25 2.50
C3 AP1 60c dp blue 19.00 .25
Nos. C1-C3 (3) 26.50 4.25
Set, never hinged 190.00

Nos. C1-C3 were used to pay airmail fee charged by the carrier, KLM.

Lt. G. A. Koppen — AP2

Capt. Jan van der Hoop — AP3

Wmk. Circles (202)

1928, Aug. 20 Litho. ***Perf. 12***

C4 AP2 40c orange red .25 .25
C5 AP3 75c blue green .25 .25
Set, never hinged 1.25

Mercury AP4

Queen Wilhelmina AP5

Perf. 11½

1929, July 16 Unwmk. Engr.

C6 AP4 1½g gray 2.50 1.65
C7 AP4 4½g carmine 1.75 3.00
C8 AP4 7½g blue green 24.00 4.50
Nos. C6-C8 (3) 28.25 9.15
Set, never hinged 70.00

Perf. 12½, 14x13

1931, Sept. 24 Photo. Wmk. 202

C9 AP5 36c org red & dk bl 10.00 .60
Never hinged 70.00

Fokker Pander AP6

1933, Oct. 9 ***Perf. 12½***

C10 AP6 30c dark green .40 .60
Never hinged .80

Nos. C10-C12 were issued for use on special flights.

Crow in Flight AP7

1938-53 ***Perf. 13x14***

C11 AP7 12½c dk blue & gray .35 .25
C12 AP7 25c dk bl & gray ('53) 1.50 1.50
Set, never hinged 4.25

Catalogue values for unused stamps in this section, from this point to the end of the section, are for Never Hinged items.

Seagull — AP8

Airplane AP9

Perf. 13x14

1951, Nov. 12 Engr. Unwmk.

C13 AP8 15g gray 230.00 85.00
C14 AP8 25g blue gray 230.00 85.00
Set, hinged 260.00

1966, Sept. 2 Litho. ***Perf. 14x13***

C15 AP9 25c gray, blk & bl .35 .35

Issued for use on special flights.

AP10

1980, May 13 Photo. ***Perf. 13x14***

C16 AP10 1g multicolored .90 .90

MARINE INSURANCE STAMPS

Floating Safe Attracting Gulls — MI1

Floating Safe with Night Flare — MI2

Fantasy of Floating Safe — MI3

Perf. 11½

1921, Feb. 2 Unwmk. Engr.

GY1 MI1	15c slate grn	4.25	*37.50*
GY2 MI1	60c car rose	4.25	*42.50*
GY3 MI1	75c gray brn	6.50	*52.50*
GY4 MI2	1.50g dk blue	65.00	*425.00*
GY5 MI2	2.25g org brn	110.00	*550.00*
GY6 MI3	4½g black	165.00	*675.00*
GY7 MI3	7½g red	250.00	*925.00*
	Nos. GY1-GY7 (7)	605.00	*2,707.*
	Set, never hinged	1,500.	

POSTAGE DUE STAMPS

Postage due types of Netherlands were also used for Netherlands Antilles, Netherlands Indies and Surinam in different colors.

D1

D2

Perf. 12½x12, 13

1870, May 15 Typo. Unwmk.

J1 D1 5c brown, *org* 72.50 15.00
J2 D1 10c violet, *bl* 150.00 20.00

Type I — 34 loops. "T" of "BETALEN" over center of loop; top branch of "E" of "TE" shorter than lower branch.

Type II — 33 loops. "T" of "BETALEN" between two loops.

Type III — 32 loops. "T" of "BETALEN" slightly to the left of loop; top branch of first "E" of "BETALEN" shorter than lower branch.

Type IV — 37 loops. Letters of "PORT" larger than in the other three types.

Imperforate varieties are proofs.

Perf. 11½x12, 12½x12, 12½, 13½

1881-87

Value in Black

J3 D2	1c lt blue (III)	11.00	11.00
a.	Type I	15.00	18.00
b.	Type II	20.00	20.00
c.	Type IV	47.50	52.50
J4 D2	1½c lt blue (III)	15.00	15.00
a.	Type I	18.00	18.00
b.	Type II	24.00	24.00
c.	Type IV	75.00	75.00
J5 D2	2½c lt blue (III)	37.50	5.00
a.	Type I	45.00	5.50
b.	Type II	55.00	6.00
c.	Type IV	200.00	125.00
J6 D2	5c lt blue (III) ('87)	140.00	3.50
a.	Type I	165.00	4.50
b.	Type II	190.00	5.25
c.	Type IV	1,750.	325.00
J7 D2	10c lt blue (III) ('87)	140.00	4.00
a.	Type I	165.00	4.50
b.	Type II	190.00	5.00
c.	Type IV	2,500.	375.00
J8 D2	12½c lt blue (III)	140.00	35.00
a.	Type I	165.00	40.00
b.	Type II	190.00	45.00
c.	Type IV	475.00	140.00
J9 D2	15c lt blue (III)	125.00	4.00
a.	Type I	150.00	4.50
b.	Type II	175.00	5.00
c.	Type IV	175.00	25.00
J10 D2	20c lt blue (III)	30.00	4.00
a.	Type I	47.50	4.25
b.	Type II	50.00	5.50
c.	Type IV	137.50	27.50
J11 D2	25c lt blue (III)	300.00	3.50
a.	Type I	325.00	3.00
b.	Type II	400.00	4.50
c.	Type IV	600.00	190.00

Value in Red

J12 D2	1g lt blue (III)	110.00	30.00
a.	Type I	110.00	37.50
b.	Type II	150.00	40.00
c.	Type IV	250.00	75.00
	Nos. J3-J12 (10)	1,048.	115.00

See Nos. J13-J26, J44-J60. For surcharges see Nos. J27-J28, J42-J43, J72-J75.

1896-1910 ***Perf. 12½***

Value in Black

J13 D2	½c dk bl (I) ('01)	.20	.20
J14 D2	1c dk blue (I)	1.65	.20
a.	Type III	2.50	3.25
J15 D2	1½c dk blue (I)	.60	.30
a.	Type III	2.50	2.50
J16 D2	2½c dk blue (I)	1.50	.30
a.	Type III	3.25	.40
J17 D2	3c dk bl (I) ('10)	1.65	1.10
J18 D2	4c dk bl (I) ('09)	1.65	2.25
J19 D2	5c dk blue (I)	13.00	.30
a.	Type III	16.00	.30
J20 D2	6½c dk bl (I) ('07)	45.00	45.00
J21 D2	7½c dk bl (I) ('04)	1.65	.55
J22 D2	10c dk blue (I)	35.00	.40
a.	Type III	52.50	1.50
J23 D2	12½c dk blue (I)	30.00	1.00
a.	Type III	45.00	3.50
J24 D2	15c dk blue (I)	35.00	.90
a.	Type III	55.00	1.00
J25 D2	20c dk blue (I)	20.00	8.00
a.	Type III	20.00	8.75
J26 D2	25c dk blue (I)	45.00	.75
a.	Type III	50.00	1.00
	Nos. J13-J26 (14)	231.90	61.25

Surcharged in Black **50 CENT**

1906, Jan. 10 ***Perf. 12½***
J27 D2 50c on 1g lt bl (III) 125.00 110.00
a. 50c on 1g light blue (I) 165.00 140.00
b. 50c on 1g light blue (II) 175.00 150.00

Surcharged in Red

1906, Oct. 6
J28 D2 6½c on 20c dk bl (I) 5.50 5.00

Nos. 87-89 Surcharged

1907, Nov. 1
J29 A13 ½c on 1c claret 1.25 1.25
J30 A13 1c on 1c claret .50 .50
J31 A13 1½c on 1c claret .50 .50
J32 A13 2½c on 1c claret 1.25 1.25
J33 A13 5c on 2½c ver 1.40 .40
J34 A13 6½c on 2½c ver 3.50 3.50
J35 A13 7½c on ½c blue 2.00 1.25
J36 A13 10c on ½c blue 1.75 .75
J37 A13 12½c on ½c blue 5.00 4.75
J38 A13 15c on 2½c ver 6.00 4.00
J39 A13 25c on ½c blue 9.00 8.50
J40 A13 50c on ½c blue 42.50 40.00
J41 A13 1g on ½c blue 60.00 55.00
Nos. J29-J41 (13) 134.65 121.65

Two printings of the above surcharges were made. Some values show differences in the setting of the fractions; others are practically impossible to distinguish.

No. J20 Surcharged in Red

1909, June
J42 D2 4c on 6½c dark blue 5.50 5.00
Never hinged 20.00

No. J12 Surcharged in Black

1910, July 11
J43 D2 3c on 1g lt bl, type III 30.00 27.50
Never hinged 100.00
a. Type I 37.50 40.00
Never hinged 110.00
b. Type II 40.00 40.00
Never hinged 125.00

Type I

1912-21 ***Perf. 12½, 13½x13***
Value in Color of Stamp
J44 D2 ½c pale ultra .20 .20
J45 D2 1c pale ultra ('13) .20 .20
J46 D2 1½c pale ultra ('15) 1.10 .90
J47 D2 2½c pale ultra .20 .20
J48 D2 3c pale ultra .40 .40
J49 D2 4c pale ultra ('13) .20 .20
J50 D2 4½c pale ultra ('16) 5.25 5.00
J51 D2 5c pale ultra .20 .20
J52 D2 5½c pale ultra ('16) 5.00 5.00
J53 D2 7c pale ultra ('21) 2.25 2.25
J54 D2 7½c pale ultra ('13) 2.50 1.00
J55 D2 10c pale ultra ('13) .20 .20
J56 D2 12½c pale ultra ('13) .20 .20
J57 D2 15c pale ultra ('13) .20 .20
J58 D2 20c pale ultra ('20) .20 .20
J59 D2 25c pale ultra ('17) 80.00 .60
J60 D2 50c pale ultra ('20) .40 .20
Nos. J44-J60 (17) 98.70 17.15
Set, never hinged 225.00

D3

1921-38 Typo. ***Perf. 12½, 13½x12½***
J61 D3 3c pale ultra ('28) .20 .20
J62 D3 6c pale ultra ('27) .20 .20
J63 D3 7c pale ultra ('28) .20 .20
J64 D3 7½c pale ultra ('26) .25 .20
J65 D3 8c pale ultra ('38) .20 .20
J66 D3 9c pale ultra ('30) .20 .20
J67 D3 11c ultra ('21) 13.00 3.50
J68 D3 12c pale ultra ('28) .20 .20
J69 D3 25c pale ultra ('25) .20 .20
J70 D3 30c pale ultra ('35) .25 .20
J71 D3 1g ver ('21) .70 .20
Nos. J61-J71 (11) 15.60 5.50
Set, never hinged 40.00

Stamps of 1912-21 Surcharged

1923, Dec. ***Perf. 12½***
J72 D2 1c on 3c ultra .50 .50
J73 D2 2½c on 7c ultra .50 .45
J74 D2 25c on 1½c ultra 8.00 .40
J75 D2 25c on 7½c ultra 8.00 .35
Nos. J72-J75 (4) 17.00 1.70
Set, never hinged 45.00

Nos. 56, 58, 62, 65 Surcharged

1924, Aug.
J76 A11 4c on 3c olive grn 1.10 1.10
J77 A10 5c on 1c red .40 .20
a. Surcharge reading down 550.00 550.00
J78 A10 10c on 1½c blue .95 .20
a. Tête bêche pair 8.50 8.50
J79 A11 12½c on 5c carmine .95 .20
a. Tête bêche pair 10.00 10.00
Nos. J76-J79 (4) 3.40 1.70

The 11c on 22½c and 15c on 17½c exist. These were used by the postal service for accounting of parcel post fees.

Catalogue values for unused stamps in this section, from this point to the end of the section, are for Never Hinged items.

D5

Perf. 13½x12½
1947-58 Wmk. 202 Photo.
J80 D5 1c light blue ('48) .20 .20
J81 D5 3c light blue ('48) .40 .20
J82 D5 4c light blue 12.00 .90
J83 D5 5c light blue ('48) .45 .20
J84 D5 6c light blue ('50) .30 .35
J85 D5 7c light blue .20 .25
J86 D5 8c light blue ('48) .20 .25
J87 D5 10c light blue .20 .20
J88 D5 11c light blue .35 .45
J89 D5 12c light blue ('48) .55 1.10
J90 D5 14c light blue ('53) .90 .90
J91 D5 15c light blue .35 .20
J92 D5 16c light blue .80 1.25
J93 D5 20c light blue .35 .20
J94 D5 24c light blue ('57) 1.25 1.40
J95 D5 25c light blue ('48) .45 .20
J96 D5 26c light blue ('58) 1.90 1.75
J97 D5 30c light blue ('48) .60 .20
J98 D5 35c light blue .65 .20
J99 D5 40c light blue .75 .20
J100 D5 50c light blue ('48) .80 .20
J101 D5 60c light blue ('58) 1.00 .45
J102 D5 85c light blue ('50) 17.00 .45
J103 D5 90c light blue ('56) 2.75 .45
J104 D5 95c light blue ('57) 2.75 .60
J105 D5 1g carmine ('48) 2.50 .20
J106 D5 1.75g carmine ('57) 5.50 .40
Nos. J80-J106 (27) 55.15 13.35

OFFICIAL STAMPS

Regular Issues of 1898-1908 Overprinted

1913 Typo. Unwmk. ***Perf. 12½***
O1 A10 1c red 4.00 2.00
O2 A10 1½c ultra 1.00 1.65
O3 A10 2c yellow brn 7.00 7.00
O4 A10 2½c dp green 16.00 12.00
O5 A11 3c olive grn 4.00 1.00
O6 A11 5c carmine rose 4.00 4.50
O7 A11 10c gray lilac 35.00 37.50
Nos. O1-O7 (7) 71.00 65.65

Same Overprint in Red on No. 58

1919
O8 A10 1½c deep blue (R) 90.00 110.00

Nos. O1 to O8 were used to defray the postage on matter relating to the Poor Laws.
Counterfeit overprints exist.

For the International Court of Justice

Regular Issue of 1926-33 Overprinted in Gold

1934 Wmk. 202 ***Perf. 12½***
O9 A24 1½c red violet .60
O10 A24 2½c deep green .60
O11 A23 7½c red 1.10
O12 A31 12½c deep ultra 32.50
O13 A23 15c orange 1.25
O14 A23 30c violet 2.00
a. Perf. 13½x12½ 2.00
Nos. O9-O14 (6) 38.05

Same Overprint on No. 180 in Gold

1937 ***Perf. 13½x12½***
O15 A23 12½c ultra 16.00

"Mint" Officials
Nos. O9-O15, O20-O43 were sold to the public only canceled. Uncanceled, they were obtainable only by favor of an official or from UPU specimen copies.

Same on Regular Issue of 1940 Overprinted in Gold

1940 ***Perf. 13½x12½***
O16 A45 7½c bright red 16.00 8.75
O17 A45 12½c sapphire 16.00 8.75
O18 A45 15c lt blue 16.00 8.75
O19 A45 30c bister 16.00 8.75
Nos. O16-O19 (4) 64.00 35.00

Nos. 217 to 219, 221 and 223 Overprinted in Gold

1947
O20 A45 7½c bright red 1.10
O21 A45 10c brt red violet 1.10
O22 A45 12½c sapphire 1.10
O23 A45 20c purple 1.10
O24 A45 25c rose brown 1.10
Nos. O20-O24 (5) 5.50

O1

Perf. 14½x13½
1950 Unwmk. Photo.
O25 O1 2c ultra 8.75
O26 O1 4c olive green 8.75

Palace of Peace, The Hague — O2

Queen Juliana — O3

1951-58 ***Perf. 12½x12***
O27 O2 2c red brown .40
O28 O2 3c ultra ('53) .40
O29 O2 4c deep green .40
O30 O2 5c olive brn ('53) .40
O31 O2 6c olive grn ('53) .80
O32 O2 7c red ('53) .60

Engr.
O33 O3 6c brown vio 5.50
O34 O3 10c dull green .20
O35 O3 12c rose red .75
O36 O3 15c rose brn ('53) .20
O37 O3 20c dull blue .20
O38 O3 25c violet brn .20
O39 O3 30c rose lil ('58) .35
O40 O3 1g slate gray .80
Nos. O27-O40 (14) 11.20

1977, May Photo. ***Perf. 12½x12***
O41 O2 40c brt grnsh blue .50
O42 O2 45c brick red .50
O43 O2 50c brt rose lilac .50
Nos. O41-O43 (3) 1.50

Catalogue values for unused stamps in this section, from this point to the end of the section, are for Never Hinged items.

Peace Palace, The Hague — O4

Palm, Sun and Column — O4a

1989-94 **Litho.**
O44 O4 5c black & org yel .20 .20
O45 O4 10c black & blue .20 .20
O46 O4 25c black & red .30 .30
O47 O4 50c black & yel grn .60 .60
O48 O4 55c black & pink .55 .55
O49 O4 60c black & bister .75 .75
O50 O4 65c black & bl grn .75 .75
O51 O4 70c blk & gray bl .90 .90
O52 O4 75c black & yellow .70 .70
O53 O4 80c black & gray grn 1.00 1.00
O54 O4 1g black & orange 1.10 1.10
O55 O4 1.50g blk & blue 1.60 1.60
O56 O4 1.60g blk & rose brn 2.00 2.00

Litho. & Engr.
O57 O4a 5g multicolored 5.50 5.50
O58 O4a 7g multicolored 6.50 6.50
Nos. O44-O58 (15) 22.65 22.65

Issued: 55c, 75c, 7g, 10/24/89; 65c, 1g, 1.50g, 5g, 10/23/90; 5c, 10c, 25c, 50c, 60c, 70c, 80c, 10/22/91; 1.60g, 11/28/94.

Intl. Court of Justice — O5

Emblem of Intl. Court of Justice — O6

2004, Jan. 2 Litho. ***Perf. 14¾x14½***
O59 O5 39c multi 1.00 1.00
O60 O6 61c multi 1.60 1.60

NETHERLANDS ANTILLES

'ne-th̲ər-lən‚dz an-'ti-lēz

(Curaçao)

LOCATION — Two groups of islands about 500 miles apart in the West Indies, north of Venezuela
AREA — 383 sq. mi.
POP. — 207,333 (1995)
CAPITAL — Willemstad

Formerly a colony, Curaçao, Netherlands Antilles became an integral part of the Kingdom of the Netherlands under the Constitution of 1954. On Jan. 1, 1986, the island of Aruba achieved a separate status within the Kingdom and began issuing its own stamps.

100 Cents = 1 Gulden

Catalogue values for unused stamps in this country are for Never Hinged items, beginning with Scott 164 in the regular postage section, Scott B1 in the semi-postal section, Scott C18 in the airpost section, Scott CB9 in the airpost semi-postal section, and Scott J41 in the postage due section.

Values for unused examples of Nos. 1-44 are for stamps without gum.

Watermark

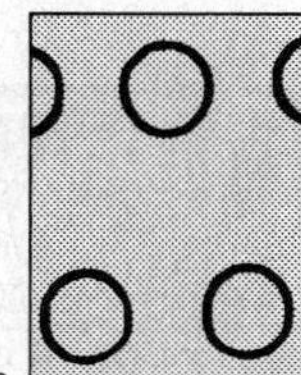

Wmk. 202 — Circles

King William III
A1

Numeral
A2

Regular Perf. 11½, 12½, 11½x12, 12½x12, 13½x13, 14

1873-79 Typo. Unwmk.

1 A1 2½c green 5.00 8.00
2 A1 3c bister 55.00 *110.00*
3 A1 5c rose 10.00 12.00
4 A1 10c ultra 60.00 17.00
5 A1 25c brown orange 45.00 10.00
6 A1 50c violet 1.75 2.50
7 A1 2.50g bis & pur ('79) 37.50 37.50
Nos. 1-7 (7) 214.25 *197.00*

See bluish paper note with Netherlands #7-22.

The gulden denominations, Nos. 7 and 12, are of larger size.

See 8-12. For surcharges see #18, 25-26.

Perf. 14, Small Holes

1b A1 2½c 12.00 15.00
2b A1 3c 60.00 *140.00*
3b A1 5c 14.50 21.00
4b A1 10c 72.50 80.00
5b A1 25c 65.00 45.00
6b A1 50c 26.00 30.00
Nos. 1b-6b (6) 250.00 *331.00*

"Small hole" varieties have the spaces between the holes wider than the diameter of the holes.

1886-89 ***Perf. 11½, 12½, 12½x12***

8 A1 12½c yellow 95.00 52.50
9 A1 15c olive ('89) 27.50 19.00
10 A1 30c pearl gray ('89) 35.00 50.00
11 A1 60c olive bis ('89) 42.50 17.00
12 A1 1.50g lt & dk bl ('89) 100.00 80.00
Nos. 7-12 (12) 587.50 587.00

Nos. 1-12 were issued without gum until 1890. Imperfs. are proofs.

1889 ***Perf. 12½***

13 A2 1c gray .85 1.00
14 A2 2c violet .65 1.25
15 A2 2½c green 4.50 3.00
16 A2 3c bister 5.00 4.50
17 A2 5c rose 21.00 1.75
Nos. 13-17 (5) 32.00 11.50

King William III
A3

Queen Wilhelmina
A4

Black Surcharge, Handstamped

1891 ***Perf. 12½x12***

Without Gum

18 A3 25c on 30c pearl gray 15.00 14.00

No. 18 exists with dbl. surch., value $225, and with invtd. surch., value $275.

1892-96 ***Perf. 12½***

19 A4 10c ultra ('95) 1.25 1.25
20 A4 12½c green 26.00 6.25
21 A4 15c rose ('93) 2.50 2.50
22 A4 25c brown orange 100.00 5.50
23 A4 30c gray ('96) 2.50 *5.50*
Nos. 19-23 (5) 132.25 21.00

A5

A6

Magenta Surcharge, Handstamped

1895 ***Perf. 12½, 13½x13***

25 A5 2½c on 10c ultra 13.00 8.00

Perf. 12½x12

Black Surcharge, Handstamped

26 A6 2½c on 30c gray 125.00 6.00

Nos. 25-26 exist with surcharge double or inverted.

No. 26 and No. 25, perf. 13½x13, were issued without gum.

Nos. 27, 29

Queen Wilhelmina — A8

1902, Jan. 1 ***Perf. 12½***

Netherlands Nos. 77, 84, 68 Surcharged in Black

27 A7 25c on 25c car & bl 2.00 2.00

1901, May 1 Engr. ***Perf. 11½x11***

28 A8 1.50g on 2.50g brn lil 20.00 21.00

1902, Mar. 1 Typo. ***Perf. 12½***

29 A7 12½c on 12½c blue 25.00 7.00

A9

A10

1904-08

30 A9 1c olive green 1.40 .90
31 A9 2c yellow brown 12.00 3.00
32 A9 2½c blue green 4.00 .35
33 A9 3c orange 7.50 4.00
34 A9 5c rose red 7.00 .35
35 A9 7½c gray ('08) 27.50 6.00
36 A10 10c slate 11.00 3.00
37 A10 12½c deep blue 1.25 .50
38 A10 15c brown 14.00 10.00
39 A10 22½c brn & ol ('08) 14.00 8.50
40 A10 25c violet 14.00 1.90
41 A10 30c brown orange 32.50 13.00
42 A10 50c red brown 27.50 8.25
Nos. 30-42 (13) 173.65 59.75

Queen Wilhelmina — A11

1906, Nov. 1 Engr. ***Perf. 11½***

Without Gum

43 A11 1½g red brown 35.00 25.00
44 A11 2½g slate blue 35.00 24.00

A12

Queen Wilhelmina
A13 A14

Perf. 12½, 11, 11½, 11x11½

1915-33 Typo.

45 A12 ½c lilac ('20) 1.60 1.10
46 A12 1c olive green .25 .20
47 A12 1½c blue ('20) .25 .20
48 A12 2c yellow brn 1.25 1.40
49 A12 2½c green .90 .20
50 A12 3c yellow 2.25 1.50
51 A12 3c green ('26) 2.60 2.50
52 A12 5c rose 2.00 .20
53 A12 5c green ('22) 3.75 2.75
54 A12 5c lilac ('26) 2.00 .20
55 A12 7½c drab 1.10 .30
56 A12 7½c bister ('20) 1.10 .20
57 A12 10c lilac ('22) 5.00 4.50
58 A12 10c rose ('26) 4.25 1.25
59 A13 10c car rose 13.00 3.00
60 A13 12½c blue 2.25 .50
61 A13 12½c red ('22) 2.00 1.60
62 A13 15c olive grn .65 .65
63 A13 15c lt blue ('26) 4.00 2.50
64 A13 20c blue ('22) 6.50 3.00
65 A13 20c ol grn ('26) 2.50 2.25
66 A13 22½c orange 2.50 2.25
67 A13 25c red violet 3.25 .90
68 A13 30c slate 3.25 .65
69 A13 35c sl & red ('22) 3.25 4.25

Perf. 11½x11, 11½, 12½, 11

Engr.

70 A14 50c green 4.00 .20
71 A14 1½g violet 13.00 11.00
72 A14 2½g carmine 21.00 20.00
a. Perf. 12½ ('33) 140.00 *300.00*
Nos. 45-72 (28) 109.45 69.25

Some stamps of 1915 were also issued without gum.

For surcharges see #74, 107-108, C1-C3.

A15

Laid Paper, without Gum

1918, July 16 Typo. ***Perf. 12***

73 A15 1c black, *buff* 6.75 3.75

"HAW" are the initials of Postmaster H. A. Willemsen.

No. 60 Surcharged in Black

1918, Sept. 1 ***Perf. 12½***

74 A13 5c on 12½c blue 3.75 2.00
a. "5" 2½mm wide 60.00 32.50
b. Double surcharge 700.00

The "5" of No. 74 is 3mm wide. Illustration shows No. 74a surcharge.

Queen Wilhelmina
A16 A17

1923 Engr. ***Perf. 11½, 11x11½***

75 A16 5c green 1.00 2.00
76 A16 7½c olive grn 1.25 1.60
77 A16 10c car rose 1.75 2.00
78 A16 20c indigo 2.50 3.50
a. Perf. 11x11½ 3.25 4.25
79 A16 1g brown vio 30.00 19.00
80 A16 2½g gray black 70.00 *170.00*
81 A16 5g brown 90.00 *200.00*
a. Perf. 11x11½ 625.00
Nos. 75-81 (7) 196.50 *398.10*

25th anniv. of the assumption of the government of the Netherlands by Queen Wilhelmina, at the age of 18.

Nos. 80-81 with clear cancel between Aug. 1, 1923 and Apr. 30, 1924, sell for considerably more.

Types of Netherlands Marine Insurance Stamps, Inscribed "CURACAO" Surcharged in Black

1927, Oct. 3

87 MI1 3c on 15c dk green .25 .30
88 MI1 10c on 60c car rose .25 .45
89 MI1 12½c on 75c gray brn .25 .45
90 MI2 15c on 1.50g dk bl 3.00 2.50
a. Double surcharge *500.00*
91 MI2 25c on 2.25g org brn 6.50 6.25
92 MI3 30c on 4½g black 13.00 11.00
93 MI3 50c on 7½g red 7.50 7.25
Nos. 87-93 (7) 30.75 28.20

Nos. 90, 91 and 92 have "FRANKEER-ZEGEL" in one line of small capitals. Nos. 90 and 91 have a heavy bar across the top of the stamp.

1928-30 Engr. ***Perf. 11½, 12½***

95 A17 6c orange red ('30) 1.50 .40
a. Booklet pane of 6
96 A17 7½c orange red .60 .45
97 A17 10c carmine 1.50 .35
98 A17 12½c red brown 1.50 1.00
a. Booklet pane of 6
99 A17 15c dark blue 1.50 .35
a. Booklet pane of 6
100 A17 20c blue black 5.75 .55
101 A17 21c yellow grn ('30) 9.25 14.00
102 A17 25c brown vio 3.50 1.40
103 A17 27½c black ('30) 12.00 14.00
104 A17 30c deep green 5.75 .55
105 A17 35c brnsh black 2.00 1.75
Nos. 95-105 (11) 44.85 34.80

No. 96 Surcharged in Black with Bars over Original Value

1929, Nov. 1

No.	Type	Description	Unused	Used
106	A17	6c on 7½c org red	1.40	1.00
a.		Inverted surcharge	275.00	260.00

No. 51 Surcharged in Red

1931, Mar. 1 Typo. *Perf. 12½*

No.	Type	Description	Unused	Used
107	A12	2½c on 3c green	1.10	1.10

No. 49 Surcharged in Red

1932, Oct. 29

No.	Type	Description	Unused	Used
108	A12	1½c on 2½c grn	3.50	3.50

Prince William I, Portrait by Van Key — A18

1933 Photo. *Perf. 12½*

No.	Type	Description	Unused	Used
109	A18	6c deep orange	1.75	1.40

400th birth anniv. of Prince William I, Count of Nassau and Prince of Orange, frequently referred to as William the Silent.

Willem Usselinx A19

Van Walbeeck's Ship A22

Designs: 2½c, 5c, 6c, Frederik Hendrik. 10c, 12½c, 15c, Jacob Binckes. 27½c, 30c, 50c, Cornelis Evertsen the Younger. 1.50g, 2.50g, Louis Brion.

1934, Jan. 1 Engr. *Perf. 12½*

No.	Type	Description	Unused	Used
110	A19	1c black	1.00	1.25
111	A19	1½c dull violet	.75	.30
112	A19	2c orange	1.00	1.25
113	A19	2½c dull green	.85	1.25
114	A19	5c black brn	.85	.85
115	A19	6c violet bl	.75	.25
116	A19	10c lake	2.00	1.00
117	A19	12½c bister brn	6.50	7.00
118	A19	15c blue	1.60	1.00
119	A22	20c black	3.00	2.00
120	A22	21c brown	11.00	13.00
121	A22	25c dull green	11.00	11.00
122	A19	27½c brown vio	14.00	16.00
123	A19	30c scarlet	11.00	5.25
124	A19	50c orange	11.00	8.25
125	A19	1.50g indigo	47.50	50.00
126	A19	2.50g yellow grn	52.50	47.50
		Nos. 110-126 (17)	176.30	167.15

3rd centenary of the founding of the colony.

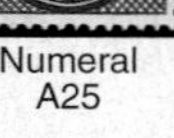

Numeral A25

Queen Wilhelmina A26

1936, Aug. 1 Litho. *Perf. 13½x13*

Size: 18x22mm

No.	Type	Description	Unused	Used
127	A25	1c brown black	.20	.20
128	A25	1½c deep ultra	.25	.20
129	A25	2c orange	.25	.25
130	A25	2½c green	.20	.20
131	A25	5c scarlet	.35	.20

Engr.

Perf. 12½

Size: 20¼x30½mm

No.	Type	Description	Unused	Used
132	A26	6c brown vio	.45	.20
133	A26	10c orange red	.85	.20
134	A26	12½c dk bl grn	1.50	.95
135	A26	15c dark blue	1.25	.60
136	A26	20c orange yel	1.25	.60
137	A26	21c dk gray	2.25	2.25
138	A26	25c brown lake	1.50	.75
139	A26	27½c violet brn	2.50	2.75
140	A26	30c olive brn	.60	.20

Perf. 13x14

Size: 22x33mm

No.	Type	Description	Unused	Used
141	A26	50c dull yel grn	3.00	.20
a.		Perf. 14	50.00	.25
142	A26	1.50g black brn	18.00	13.00
a.		Perf. 14	40.00	20.00
143	A26	2.50g rose lake	16.00	11.00
a.		Perf. 14	16.00	11.00
		Nos. 127-143 (17)	50.40	33.75

See Nos. 147-151. For surcharges see Nos. B1-B3.

Queen Wilhelmina — A27

Perf. 12½x12

1938, Aug. 27 Photo. Wmk. 202

No.	Type	Description	Unused	Used
144	A27	1½c dull purple	.20	.25
145	A27	6c red orange	.80	.75
146	A27	15c royal blue	1.50	1.25
		Nos. 144-146 (3)	2.50	2.25

Reign of Queen Wilhelmina, 40th anniv.

Numeral Type of 1936 and

Queen Wilhelmina — A28

1941-42 Unwmk. Litho. *Perf. 12½*

Thick Paper

Size: 17¾x22mm

No.	Type	Description	Unused	Used
147	A25	1c gray brn ('42)	1.50	1.25
148	A25	1½c dull blue ('42)	9.00	.20
149	A25	2c lt orange ('42)	8.00	4.00
150	A25	2½c green ('42)	1.00	.20
151	A25	5c crimson ('42)	1.00	.20

Photo.

Perf. 12½, 13

Size: 18½x23mm

No.	Type	Description	Unused	Used
152	A28	6c rose violet	2.00	2.00
153	A28	10c red orange	1.50	1.00
154	A28	12½c lt green	2.00	.90
155	A28	15c brt ultra	4.00	2.00
156	A28	20c orange	1.10	.55
157	A28	21c gray	2.25	1.75
158	A28	25c brown lake	2.25	1.60
159	A28	27½c deep brown	3.25	3.25
160	A28	30c olive bis	9.00	3.00

Size: 21x26½mm

No.	Type	Description	Unused	Used
161	A28	50c olive grn ('42)	12.00	.20
162	A28	1½g gray ol ('42)	17.00	1.75
163	A28	2½g rose lake ('42)	16.00	1.25
		Nos. 147-163 (17)	92.85	25.10

Imperfs. are proofs.

See Nos. 174-187.

Catalogue values for unused stamps in this section, from this point to the end of the section, are for Never Hinged items.

Bonaire A29

St. Eustatius — A30

Designs: 2c, View of Saba. 2½c, St. Maarten. 5c, Aruba. 6c, Curaçao.

Perf. 13x13½, 13½x13

1943, Feb. 1 Engr. Unwmk.

No.	Type	Description	Unused	Used
164	A29	1c rose vio & org brn	.20	.20
165	A30	1½c dp bl & yel grn	.20	.20
166	A29	2c sl blk & org brn	.60	.25
167	A29	2½c grn & org	.30	.20
168	A29	5c red & slate blk	1.25	.25
169	A29	6c rose lil & lt bl	.75	.60
		Nos. 164-169 (6)	3.30	1.70

Royal Family — A35

1943, Nov. 8 *Perf. 13½x13*

No.	Type	Description	Unused	Used
170	A35	1½c deep orange	.30	.30
171	A35	2½c red	.30	.30
172	A35	6c black	1.40	.70
173	A35	10c deep blue	1.40	1.25
		Nos. 170-173 (4)	3.40	2.55

Princess Margriet Francisca of the Netherlands.

Wilhelmina Type of 1941

1947 Photo. *Perf. 13½x13*

Size: 18x22mm

No.	Type	Description	Unused	Used
174	A28	6c brown vio	1.75	*2.25*
175	A28	10c orange red	1.75	*2.25*
176	A28	12½c dk blue grn	1.75	*2.25*
177	A28	15c dark blue	1.75	*3.00*
178	A28	20c orange yel	1.75	*3.75*
179	A28	21c dark gray	2.50	*3.75*
180	A28	25c brown lake	.25	.25
181	A28	27½c chocolate	2.25	3.00
182	A28	30c olive bister	2.00	1.25
183	A28	50c dull yel grn	2.10	.25

Perf. 13½x14

Engr.

Size: 25x31¼mm

No.	Type	Description	Unused	Used
184	A28	1½g dark brown	3.25	1.50
185	A28	2½g rose lake	60.00	27.50
186	A28	5g olive green	125.00	*200.00*
187	A28	10g red orange	160.00	*300.00*
		Nos. 174-187 (14)	366.10	551.00

Used values for Nos. 186-187 are for genuinely canceled copies clearly dated before the end of 1949.

A36

Queen Wilhelmina — A37

1948 Unwmk. Photo. *Perf. 13½x13*

No.	Type	Description	Unused	Used
188	A36	6c dk vio brn	1.10	1.25
189	A36	10c scarlet	1.10	*1.60*
190	A36	12½c dk blue grn	1.10	1.10

No.	Type	Description	Unused	Used
191	A36	15c deep blue	1.10	*1.25*
192	A36	20c red orange	1.10	*2.50*
193	A36	21c black	1.10	*2.50*
194	A36	25c brt red vio	.50	.25
195	A36	27½c henna brn	22.50	23.50
196	A36	30c olive brown	20.00	1.50
197	A36	50c olive green	19.00	.35

Perf. 12½x12

Engr.

No.	Type	Description	Unused	Used
198	A37	1.50g chocolate	37.50	8.50
		Nos. 188-198 (11)	106.10	44.30

Queen Wilhelmina A38

Queen Juliana A39

1948, Aug. 30 *Perf. 13x14*

No.	Type	Description	Unused	Used
199	A38	6c vermilion	.75	.60
200	A38	12½c deep blue	.75	.60

Reign of Queen Wilhelmina, 50th anniv.

Perf. 14x13½

1948, Oct. 18 Photo. Wmk. 202

No.	Type	Description	Unused	Used
201	A39	6c red brown	.75	.60
202	A39	12½c dark green	.75	.60

Investiture of Queen Juliana, Sept. 6, 1948. Nos. 201-202 were issued in Netherlands Sept. 6.

Ship of Ojeda — A40

Alonso de Ojeda — A41

Perf. 14x13, 13x14

1949, July 26 Photo. Unwmk.

No.	Type	Description	Unused	Used
203	A40	6c olive green	3.50	2.75
204	A41	12½c brown red	4.25	3.75
205	A40	15c ultra	4.75	3.75
		Nos. 203-205 (3)	12.50	10.25

450th anniversary of the discovery of Curaçao by Alonso de Ojeda, 1499.

Post Horns Entwined — A42

1949, Oct. 3 *Perf. 12x12½*

No.	Type	Description	Unused	Used
206	A42	6c brown red	4.50	3.00
207	A42	25c dull blue	4.50	1.50

UPU, 75th anniversary.

A43

A44

Queen Juliana — A45

1950-79 Photo. *Perf. 13x13½*

No.	Type	Description	Unused	Used
208	A43	1c red brown	.20	.20
209	A43	1½c blue	.20	.20
210	A43	2c orange	.20	.20

211	A43	2½c green	1.25	.20
212	A43	3c purple	.30	.20
212A	A43	4c yel grn ('59)	.80	.45
213	A43	5c dark red	.20	.20

Perf. 13½x13

214	A44	6c deep plum	1.50	.20
215	A44	7½c red brn ('54)	6.00	.20
216	A44	10c red	2.25	.20
a.		Redrawn ('79)	.20	.20
217	A44	12½c dk green	2.75	.25
218	A44	15c deep blue	2.75	.25
a.		Redrawn ('79)	.20	.20
219	A44	20c orange	3.00	.20
a.		Redrawn ('79)	.20	.20
220	A44	21c black	3.00	2.00
221	A44	22½c blue grn ('54)	6.75	.20
222	A44	25c violet	5.00	.20
a.		Redrawn ('79)	.25	.20
223	A44	27½c henna brn	7.50	2.50
224	A44	30c olive brown	13.50	.25
225	A44	50c olive green	14.00	.20

Perf. 12½x12

Engr.

226	A45	1½g slate grn	50.00	.35
227	A45	2½g black brn	60.00	2.00
228	A45	5g rose red	75.00	12.00
229	A45	10g dk vio brn	225.00	75.00
		Nos. 208-229 (23)	481.15	97.65

Nos. 216a, 218a, 219a and 222a are from booklets Nos. 427a and 428a. Background design is sharper and stamps have one or two straight edges.

See Nos. 427-429. For surcharge see No. B20.

Fort Beekenburg A46

Perf. 13½x12½

1953, June 16 **Photo.**

230 A46 22½c olive brown 7.00 .75

Founding of Fort Beekenburg, 250th anniv.

Beach at Aruba A47

1954, May 1 ***Perf. 11x11½***

231 A47 15c dk bl, sal & dp bl 5.00 3.00

3rd congress of the Caribbean Tourist Assoc., Aruba, May 3-6.

Queen Juliana — A48

1954, Dec. 15 ***Perf. 13½***

232 A48 7½c olive green 1.00 .75

Charter of the Kingdom, adopted Dec. 15, 1954. See Netherlands #366 & Surinam #264.

Beach A49

Petroleum Refinery, Aruba — A50

1955, Dec. 5 **Litho.** ***Perf. 12***

233	A49	15c chnt, bl & emer	3.00	2.00
234	A50	25c chnt, bl & emer	4.00	2.75

Caribbean Commission, 21st meeting, Aruba.

St. Annabaai Harbor and Flags — A51

1956, Dec. 6 **Unwmk.** ***Perf. 14x13***

235 A51 15c lt bl, blk & red .40 .30

Caribbean Commission, 10th anniversary.

Man Watching Rising Sun — A52

1957, Mar. 14 **Photo.** ***Perf. 11x11½***

236 A52 15c brown, blk & yel .30 .30

1st Caribbean Mental Health Conference, Aruba, Mar. 14-19.

Tourism A53

1957, July 1 **Litho.** ***Perf. 14x13***

237	A53	7½c Saba	.35	.30
238	A53	15c St. Maarten	.35	.30
239	A53	25c St. Eustatius	.35	.30
		Nos. 237-239 (3)	1.05	.90

Curaçao Intercontinental Hotel — A54

1957, Oct. 12 ***Perf. 14x13***

240 A54 15c lt ultra .25 .25

Intercontinental Hotel, Willemstad, opening.

Map of Curaçao A55

1957, Dec. 10 ***Perf. 14x13½***

241 A55 15c indigo & lt bl .55 .55

International Geophysical Year.

Flamingoes, Bonaire A56

Designs: 7½c, 8c, 25c, 1½g, Old buildings, Curaçao. 10c, 5g, Extinct volcano and palms, Saba. 15c, 30c, 1g, Fort Willem III, Aruba. 20c, 35c, De Ruyter obelisk, St. Eustatius. 12c, 40c, 2½g, Town Hall, St. Maarten.

1958-59 **Litho.** ***Perf. 14x13***

Size: 33x22mm

242	A56	6c lt ol grn & pink	2.00	.20
243	A56	7½c red brn & org	.20	.20
244	A56	8c dk bl & org ('59)	.20	.20
245	A56	10c gray & org yel	.20	.20
246	A56	12c bluish grn & gray ('59)	.20	.20
247	A56	15c grn & lt ultra	.20	.20
a.		15c green & lilac	.20	.20
248	A56	20c crim & gray	.20	.20
249	A56	25c Prus bl & yel grn	.20	.20
250	A56	30c brn & bl grn	.25	.20
251	A56	35c gray & rose ('59)	.30	.20
252	A56	40c mag & grn	.30	.20
253	A56	50c grysh brn & pink	.35	.20
254	A56	1g brt red & gray	.75	.20
255	A56	1½g rose vio & pale brn	1.10	.20
256	A56	2½g blue & citron	1.25	.30
257	A56	5g lt red brn & rose lil	3.75	.60
		Nos. 242-257 (16)	11.45	3.70

See Nos. 340-348, 400-403. For surcharge see No. B58.

Globe A57

1958, Oct. 16 ***Perf. 11x11½***

258	A57	7½c blue & lake	.20	.20
259	A57	15c red & ultra	.25	.25

50th anniv. of the Netherlands Antilles Radio and Telegraph Administration.

Hotel Aruba Caribbean A58

1959, July 18 ***Perf. 14x13***

260 A58 15c multi .30 .30

Opening of the Hotel Aruba Caribbean, Aruba.

Sea Water Distillation Plant — A59

1959, Oct. 16 **Photo.** ***Perf. 14x13***

261 A59 20c bright blue .35 .35

Opening of sea water distillation plant at Balashi, Aruba.

Netherlands Antilles Flag — A60

1959, Dec. 14 **Litho.** ***Perf. 13½***

262	A60	10c ultra & red	.30	.30
263	A60	20c ultra, yel & red	.30	.30
264	A60	25c ultra, grn & red	.30	.30
		Nos. 262-264 (3)	.90	.90

5th anniv. of the new constitution (Charter of the Kingdom).

Fokker "Snip" and Map of Caribbean A61

Designs: 20c, Globe showing route flown, and plane. 25c, Map of Atlantic ocean and view of Willemstad. 35c, Map of Atlantic ocean and plane on Aruba airfield.

1959, Dec. 22 **Unwmk.** ***Perf. 14x13***

265	A61	10c yel, lt & dk bl	.30	.25
266	A61	20c yel, lt & dk bl	.30	.25
267	A61	25c yel, lt & dk bl	.30	.20
268	A61	35c yel, lt & dk bl	.30	.35
		Nos. 265-268 (4)	1.20	1.05

25th anniv. of Netherlands-Curaçao air service.

Msgr. Martinus J. Niewindt — A62

1960, Jan. 12 **Photo.** ***Perf. 13½***

269	A62	10c deep claret	.30	.25
270	A62	20c deep violet	.40	.40
271	A62	25c olive green	.40	.40
		Nos. 269-271 (3)	1.10	1.05

Death centenary of Monsignor Niewindt, first apostolic vicar for Curaçao.

Worker, Flag and Factories — A63

1960, Apr. 29 ***Perf. 12½x13½***

272 A63 20c multi .30 .30

Issued for Labor Day, May 1, 1960.

US Brig "Andrea Doria" and Gun at Fort Orange, St. Eustatius A64

1961, Nov. 16 **Litho.** ***Perf. 14x13½***

273 A64 20c bl, red, grn & blk .50 .50

185th anniv. of 1st salute by a foreign power to the US flag flown by an American ship.

Queen Juliana and Prince Bernhard A64a

1962, Jan. 31 **Photo.** ***Perf. 14x13***

274	A64a	10c deep orange	.20	.20
275	A64a	25c deep blue	.20	.20

Silver wedding anniversary of Queen Juliana and Prince Bernhard.

Benta Player — A65

6c, Corn masher. 20c, Petji kerchief. 25c, "Jaja" (nurse) with child, sculpture.

Perf. 12½x13½

1962, Mar. 14 **Photo.**

276	A65	6c red brn & yel	.25	.20
277	A65	10c shown	.25	.20
278	A65	20c crim, ind & brt grn	.30	.30
279	A65	25c brt grn, brn & gray	.30	.30
a.		Souvenir sheet of 4, #276-279	1.25	1.25
		Nos. 276-279 (4)	1.10	1.00

Emblem of Family Relationship A66

25c, Emblem of mental health (cross).

1963, Apr. 17 Litho. *Perf. 14x13½*

280 A66 20c dk blue & ocher .30 .30
281 A66 25c blue & red .30 .30

Fourth Caribbean Conference for Mental Health, Curaçao, Apr. 17-23.

Dove with Olive Branch — A67

1963, July 1 Unwmk. *Perf. 14x13*

282 A67 25c org yel & dk brn .25 .25

Centenary of emancipation of the slaves.

Hotel Bonaire A68

1963, Aug. 31 *Perf. 14x13*

283 A68 20c dk red brown .25 .25

Opening of Hotel Bonaire on Bonaire.

Prince William of Orange Taking Oath of Allegiance — A69

1963, Nov. 21 Photo. *Perf. 13½x14*

284 A69 25c green, blk & rose .25 .25

150th anniversary of the founding of the Kingdom of the Netherlands.

Chemical Equipment A70

1963, Dec. 10 Litho. *Perf. 14x13½*

285 A70 20c bl grn, brt yel grn & red .35 .35

Opening of chemical factories on Aruba.

Airmail Letter and Wings A71

Design: 25c, Map of Caribbean, Miami-Curaçao route and planes of 1929 and 1964.

1964, June 22 Photo. *Perf. 11x11½*

286 A71 20c lt bl, red & ultra .25 .25
287 A71 25c lt grn, bl, red & blk .25 .25

35th anniversary of the first regular Curaçao airmail service.

Map of the Caribbean A72

1964, Nov. 30 Litho. Unwmk.

288 A72 20c ultra, org & dk red .25 .25

5th meeting of the Caribbean Council, Curaçao, Nov. 30-Dec. 4.

Netherlands Antilles Flags, Map of Curaçao and Crest — A73

1964, Dec. 14 Litho. *Perf. 11½x11*

289 A73 25c lt bl & multi .25 .25

10th anniversary of the Charter of the Kingdom of the Netherlands. The flags, shaped like seagulls, represent the six islands comprising the Netherlands Antilles.

Princess Beatrix — A74

1965, Feb. 22 Photo. *Perf. 13½x14*

290 A74 25c brick red .25 .25

Visit of Princess Beatrix of Netherlands.

ITU Emblem, Old and New Communication Equipment — A75

1965, May 17 Litho. *Perf. 13½*

291 A75 10c brt bl & dk bl .20 .20

ITU, centenary.

Shell Refinery, Curaçao A76

10c, Catalytic cracking installation, vert. 25c, Workers operating manifold, primary distillation plant, vert.

Perf. 13½x14, 14x13½

1965, June 22 Photo.

292 A76 10c blk, red & yel .20 .20
293 A76 20c multi .20 .20
294 A76 25c multi .25 .20
Nos. 292-294 (3) .65 .60

50th anniv. of the oil industry in Curaçao.

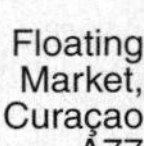

Floating Market, Curaçao A77

Designs (flag and): 2c, Divi-divi tree and Haystack Mountain, Aruba. 3c, Lace, Saba. 4c, Flamingoes, Bonaire. 5c, Church ruins, St. Eustatius. 6c, Lobster, St. Maarten.

1965, Aug. 25 Litho. *Perf. 14x13*

295 A77 1c lt grn, ultra & red .20 .20
296 A77 2c yel, ultra & red .20 .20
297 A77 3c chlky bl, ultra & red .20 .20
298 A77 4c org, ultra & red .20 .20
299 A77 5c lt bl, ultra & red .20 .20
300 A77 6c pink, ultra & red .20 .20
Nos. 295-300 (6) 1.20 1.20

Marine Guarding Beach — A78

1965, Dec. 10 Photo. *Perf. 13x10½*

301 A78 25c multi .20 .20

Netherlands Marine Corps, 300th anniv.

Budgerigars, Wedding Rings and Initials — A79

1966, Mar. 10 Photo. *Perf. 13½x14*

302 A79 25c gray & multi .25 .20

Issued to commemorate the marriage of Princess Beatrix and Claus van Amsberg.

M. A. de Ruyter and Map of St. Eustatius — A80

1966, June 19 Photo. *Perf. 13½*

303 A80 25c vio, ocher & lt bl .20 .20

Visit of Adm. Michiel Adriaanszoon de Ruyter (1607-1676) to St. Eustatius, 1666.

Liberal Arts and Grammar A81

10c, Rhetoric and dialectic. 20c, Arithmetic and geometry. 25c, Astronomy and music.

Perf. 13½x12½

1966, Sept. 19 Litho. Unwmk.

304 A81 6c yel, bl & blk .20 .20
305 A81 10c yel grn, red & blk .20 .20
306 A81 20c bl, yel & blk .20 .20
307 A81 25c red, yel grn & blk .20 .20
Nos. 304-307 (4) .80 .80

25th anniversary of secondary education.

Cruiser A82

Ships: 10c, Sailing ship. 20c, Tanker. 25c, Passenger ship.

Perf. 13½x14

1967, Mar. 29 Litho. Unwmk.

308 A82 6c lt & dk grn .20 .20
309 A82 10c org & brn .20 .20
310 A82 20c sep & brn .20 .20
311 A82 25c chlky bl & dk bl .20 .20
Nos. 308-311 (4) .80 .80

60th anniv. of *Onze Vloot* (Our Fleet), an organization which publicizes the Dutch navy and merchant marine and helps seamen.

Manuel Carlos Piar (1777-1817), Independence Hero — A83

Discobolus after Myron — A84

1967, Apr. 26 Photo. *Perf. 14x13*

312 A83 20c red & blk .20 .20

1968, Feb. 19 Litho. *Perf. 13x14*

10c, Hand holding torch, & Olympic rings. 25c, Stadium, doves & Olympic rings.

313 A84 10c multi .20 .20
314 A84 20c dk brn, ol & yel .20 .20
315 A84 25c bl, dk bl & brt yel grn .20 .20
Nos. 313-315 (3) .60 .60

19th Olympic Games, Mexico City, 10/12-27.

Friendship 500 — A84a

Designs: 20c, Beechcraft Queen Air. 25c, Friendship and DC-9.

1968, Dec. 3 Litho. *Perf. 14x13*

315A A84a 10c dl yel, blk & brt bl .20 .20
315B A84a 20c tan, blk & brt bl .20 .20
315C A84a 25c sal pink, blk & brt bl .25 .25
Nos. 315A-315C (3) .65 .65

Dutch Antillean Airlines (ALM).

Map of Bonaire, Radio Mast and Waves — A85

Code of Law — A86

1969, Mar. 6 *Perf. 14x13½*

316 A85 25c bl, emer & blk .20 .20

Opening of the relay station of the Dutch World Broadcasting System on Bonaire.

Perf. 12½x13½

1969, May 19 **Photo.**

Designs: 25c, Scales of Justice.

317 A86 20c dk grn, yel grn & gold .20 .20
318 A86 25c vio bl, bl & gold .20 .20

Court of Justice, centenary.

ILO Emblem, Cactus and House — A87

1969, Aug. 25 **Litho.** ***Perf. 14x13***

319 A87 10c bl & blk .20 .20
320 A87 25c dk red & blk .20 .20

ILO, 50th anniversary.

Queen Juliana and Rising Sun — A87a

1969, Dec. 12 **Photo.** ***Perf. 14x13***

321 A87a 25c bl & multi .20 .20

15th anniv. of the Charter of the Kingdom of the Netherlands. Phosphorescent paper.

Radio Bonaire Studio and Transmitter A88

Design: 15c, Radio waves and cross set against land, sea and air.

1970, Feb. 5 **Photo.** ***Perf. 12½x13½***

322 A88 10c multi .20 .20
323 A88 15c multi .20 .20

5th anniv. of the opening of the Trans World Missionary Radio Station, Bonaire.

Altar, St. Anna's Church, Otraband 1752 — A89

20c, Interior, Synagogue at Punda, 1732, horiz. 25c, Pulpit, Fort Church, Fort Amsterdam, 1769.

Perf. 13½x14, 14x13½

1970, May 12 **Photo.**

324 A89 10c gold & multi .25 .20
325 A89 20c gold & multi .25 .20
326 A89 25c gold & multi .25 .20
Nos. 324-326 (3) .75 .60

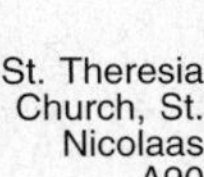

St. Theresia Church, St. Nicolaas A90

1971, Feb. 9 **Litho.** ***Perf. 14x13½***

327 A90 20c dl bl, gray & rose .20 .20

40th anniversary of the Parish of St. Theresia at St. Nicolaas, Aruba.

A91

A91a

1971, Feb. 24 ***Perf. 13½x14***

328 A91 25c Lions emblem .25 .25

Lions Club in the Netherlands Antilles, 25th anniversary.

1971, June 29 **Photo.** ***Perf. 13x14***

Prince Bernhard, Fokker F27, Boeing 747B.

329 A91a 45c multi .40 .40

60th birthday of Prince Bernhard.

Pedro Luis Brion (1782-1821), Naval Commander in Fight for South American Independence A92

1971, Sept. 27 **Photo.** ***Perf. 13x12½***

330 A92 40c multi .25 .25

Flamingoes, Bonaire A93

Ship in Dry Dock — A94

Designs: 1c, Queen Emma Bridge, Curaçao. 2c, The Bottom, Saba. 4c, Water tower, Aruba. 5c, Fort Amsterdam, St. Maarten. 6c, Fort Orange, St. Eustatius.

1972, Jan. 17 **Litho.** ***Perf. 13½x14***

331 A93 1c yel & multi .20 .20
332 A93 2c yel grn & multi .20 .20
333 A93 3c dp org & multi .20 .20
334 A93 4c brt bl & multi .20 .20
335 A93 5c red org & multi .20 .20
336 A93 6c lil rose & multi .20 .20
Nos. 331-336 (6) 1.20 1.20

1972, Apr. 7 ***Perf. 14x13½***

337 A94 30c bl gray & multi .25 .25

Inauguration of large dry dock facilities in Willemstad.

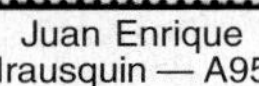

Juan Enrique Irausquin — A95

Costa Gomez — A96

1972, June 20 **Photo.** ***Perf. 13x14***

338 A95 30c deep orange .25 .25

Irausquin (1904-1962), financier and patriot.

1972, Oct. 27 **Litho.**

339 A96 30c yel grn & blk .25 .25

Moises Frumencio da Costa Gomez (1907-1966), lawyer, legislator, patriot.

Island Series Type of 1958-59

Designs: 45c, 85c, Extinct volcano and palms, Saba. 55c, 90c, De Ruyter obelisk, St. Eustatius. 65c, 75c, 10g, Flamingoes, Bonaire. 70c, Fort Willem III, Aruba. 95c, Town Hall, St. Maarten.

1973, Feb. 12 **Litho.** ***Perf. 14x13***

Size: 33x22mm

340 A56 45c vio bl & lt bl .35 .20
341 A56 55c dk car rose & emer .40 .20
342 A56 65c green & pink .45 .25
343 A56 70c gray vio & org 1.00 .25
344 A56 75c brt lilac & salmon .50 .30
345 A56 85c brn ol & apple grn .60 .30
346 A56 90c blue & ocher .65 .35
347 A56 95c orange & yellow .80 .40
348 A56 10g brt ultra & salmon 6.50 3.75
Nos. 340-348 (9) 11.25 6.00

Mailman — A97

Designs: 15c, King William III from 1873 issue. 30c, Emblem of Netherlands Antilles postal service.

1973, May 23 **Photo.** ***Perf. 13x14***

349 A97 15c lil, gold & vio .25 .20
350 A97 20c dk grn & multi .30 .25
351 A97 30c org & multi .30 .25
Nos. 349-351 (3) .85 .70

Centenary of first stamps of Netherlands Antilles.

Cable Linking Aruba, Curaçao and Bonaire A98

30c, 6 stars symbolizing the islands, cable. 45c, Saba, St. Maarten and St. Eustatius linked by cable.

1973, June 20 **Litho.** ***Perf. 14x13***

352 A98 15c multi .30 .30
353 A98 30c multi .35 .30
354 A98 45c multi .35 .30
a. Souvenir sheet of 3, #352-354 1.75 1.50
Nos. 352-354 (3) 1.00 .90

Inauguration of the inter-island submarine cable.

Queen Juliana, Netherlands Antilles and House of Orange Colors — A99a

Engr. & Photo.

1973, Sept. 4 ***Perf. 12½x12***

355 A99a 15c silver & multi .40 .40

25th anniversary of reign of Queen Juliana.

Jan Hendrik Albert Eman — A99

Lionel Bernard Scott — A100

1973, Oct. 17 **Litho.** ***Perf. 13x14***

356 A99 30c lt yel grn & blk .25 .25

Eman (1888-1957), founder of the People's Party in Aruba, member of Antillean Parliament.

1974, Jan. 28

357 A100 30c lt bl & multi .25 .25

Scott (1897-1966), architect and statesman.

Family at Supper — A101

Designs: 12c, Parents watching children at play. 15c, Mother and daughter sewing, father and son gardening.

1974, Feb. 18 **Litho.** ***Perf. 13x14***

358 A101 6c bl & multi .20 .20
359 A101 12c bis & multi .20 .20
360 A101 15c grn & multi .25 .20
Nos. 358-360 (3) .65 .60

Planned parenthood and World Population Year.

Desulphurization Plant, Lago — A102

Designs: 30c, Distillation plant. 45c, Lago refinery at night.

1974, Aug. 12 **Litho.** ***Perf. 14x13***

361 A102 15c lt bl, blk & yel .20 .20
362 A102 30c lt bl, blk & yel .30 .30
363 A102 45c dk brn & multi .40 .40
Nos. 361-363 (3) .90 .90

Oil industry in Aruba, 50th anniversary.

UPU Emblem — A103

1974, Oct. 9 Litho. *Perf. 13x14*

364 A103 15c yel grn, blk & gold .35 .30
365 A103 30c bl, blk & gold .35 .30

Centenary of Universal Postal Union.

Queen Emma Bridge A104

Willemstad Bridges: 30c, Queen Juliana Bridge. 40c, Queen Wilhelmina Bridge.

1975, Feb. 5 Litho. *Perf. 14x13*

366 A104 20c ultra & multi .30 .25
367 A104 30c ultra & multi .30 .30
368 A104 40c ultra & multi .40 .40
Nos. 366-368 (3) 1.00 .95

Dedication of new Queen Juliana Bridge spanning Curaçao Harbor.

Salt Crystals A105

Designs: 20c, Solar salt pond. 40c, Map of Bonaire and location of solar salt pond, vert.

Perf. 14x13, 13x14

1975, Apr. 24 Litho.

369 A105 15c multi .30 .25
370 A105 20c multi .30 .30
371 A105 40c multi .40 .30
Nos. 369-371 (3) 1.00 .85

Bonaire's salt industry.

Aruba Airport, 1935 and Fokker F-18 — A106

30c, Aruba Airport, 1950, & Douglas DC-9. 40c, New Princess Beatrix Airport & Boeing 727.

1975, June 19 Litho. *Perf. 14x13*

372 A106 15c vio & multi .25 .20
373 A106 30c blk & multi .35 .30
374 A106 40c yel & multi .35 .30
Nos. 372-374 (3) .95 .80

40th anniversary of Aruba Airport.

International Women's Year Emblem A107

12c, "Women's role in social development." 20c, Embryos within female & male symbols.

1975, Aug. 1 Photo. *Perf. 14x13*

375 A107 6c multi .20 .20
376 A107 12c multi .25 .20
377 A107 20c multi .30 .30
Nos. 375-377 (3) .75 .70

International Women's Year 1975.

Beach, Aruba A108

Tourist Publicity: No. 379, Beach pavilion and boat, Bonaire. No. 380, Table Mountain and Spanish Water, Curaçao.

1976, June 21 Litho. *Perf. 14x13*

378 A108 40c blue & multi .40 .40
379 A108 40c blue & multi .40 .40
380 A108 40c blue & multi .40 .40
Nos. 378-380 (3) 1.20 1.20

Julio Antonio Abraham A109

Dike and Produce A110

1976, Aug. 10 Photo. *Perf. 13x14*

381 A109 30c tan & claret .30 .30

Julio Antonio Abraham (1909-1960), founder of Democratic Party of Bonaire.

1976, Sept. 21 Litho.

382 A110 15c shown .30 .20
383 A110 35c Cattle .40 .35
384 A110 45c Fish .40 .40
Nos. 382-384 (3) 1.10 .95

Agriculture, husbandry and fishing in Netherlands Antilles.

Plaque, Fort Oranje Memorial A111

Designs: 40c, Andrea Doria in St. Eustatius harbor receiving salute. 55c, Johannes de Graaff, Governor of St. Eustatius, holding Declaration of Independence.

1976, Nov. 16 Litho. *Perf. 14x13*

385 A111 25c multi .50 .30
386 A111 40c multi .50 .30
387 A111 55c multi .50 .50
Nos. 385-387 (3) 1.50 1.10

First gun salute to US flag, St. Eustatius, Nov. 16, 1776.

Dancer with Cactus Headdress A112

Bird Petroglyph, Aruba A113

Carnival: 35c, Woman in feather costume. 40c, Woman in pompadour costume.

1977, Jan. 20 Litho. *Perf. 13x14*

388 A112 25c multi .40 .30
389 A112 35c multi .40 .30
390 A112 40c multi .40 .30
Nos. 388-390 (3) 1.20 .90

1977, Mar. 29

Indian Petroglyphs: 35c, Loops and spiral, Savonet Plantation, Curaçao. 40c, Tortoise, Onima, Bonaire.

391 A113 25c red & multi .35 .30
392 A113 35c brn & multi .35 .30
393 A113 40c yel & multi .45 .30
Nos. 391-393 (3) 1.15 .90

A114

A115

Tropical Trees: 25c, Cordia Sebestena. 40c, East Indian walnut, vert. 55c, Tamarind.

1977, July 20 *Perf. 14x13, 13x14*

394 A114 25c blk & multi .30 .30
395 A114 40c blk & multi .40 .30
396 A114 55c blk & multi .50 .50
Nos. 394-396 (3) 1.20 1.10

1977, Sept. 27 Litho. *Perf. 13x14*

Designs: 20c, Chimes, Spritzer & Fuhrmann Building. 40c, Globe with Western Hemisphere and sun over Curaçao. 55c, Diamond ring and flag of Netherlands Antilles.

397 A115 20c brt grn & multi .30 .25
398 A115 40c yel & multi .40 .35
399 A115 55c bl & multi .50 .50
Nos. 397-399 (3) 1.20 1.10

Spritzer & Fuhrmann, jewelers of Netherlands Antilles, 50th anniversary.

Type of 1958-59

Designs: 20c, 35c, 55c, De Ruyter obelisk, St. Eustatius. 40c, Town Hall, St. Maarten.

Perf. 13½ Horiz.

1977, Nov. 30 Photo.

Size: 39x22mm

400 A56 20c crim & gray .70 .50
a. Bklt. pane of 6 (2 #400, 4 #402) 5.25
401 A56 35c gray & rose 1.10 .80
a. Bklt. pane of 4 (1 #401, 3 #403) 6.00
402 A56 40c magenta & grn .70 .50
403 A56 55c dk car rose & emer 1.10 1.10
Nos. 400-403 (4) 3.60 2.90

Nos. 400-403 issued in booklets only. No. 400a has label with red inscription in size of 3 stamps; No. 401a has label with dark carmine rose inscription in size of 2 stamps.

Winding Road, Map of Saba — A116

Tourism: 35c, Ruins of Synagogue, map of St. Eustatius. 40c, Greatbay, Map of St. Maarten.

1977, Nov. 30 Litho. *Perf. 14x13*

404 A116 25c multi .20 .20
405 A116 35c multi .20 .20
406 A116 40c multi .25 .25
Nos. 404-406 (3) .65 .65

Tete-beche gutter pairs exist.

Treasure Chest — A117

Designs: 20c, Logo of Netherlands Antilles Bank. 40c, Safe deposit door.

1978, Feb. 7 Litho. *Perf. 14x13*

407 A117 15c brt & dk bl .20 .20
408 A117 20c org & gold .20 .20
409 A117 40c brt & dk grn .20 .20
Nos. 407-409 (3) .60 .60

Bank of Netherlands Antilles, 150th anniv. Tete-beche gutter pairs exist.

Flamboyant A118

Polythysana Rubrescens A119

Flowers: 25c, Erythrina velutina. 40c, Guaiacum officinale, horiz. 55c, Gliricidia sepium, horiz.

Perf. 13x14, 14x13

1978, May 31 Litho.

410 A118 15c multi .20 .20
411 A118 25c multi .25 .20
412 A118 40c multi .30 .25
413 A118 55c multi .35 .35
Nos. 410-413 (4) 1.10 1.00

1978, June 20 *Perf. 13x14*

Butterflies: 25c, Caligo eurilochus. 35c, Prepona omphale amesis. 40c, Morpho aega.

414 A119 15c multi .20 .20
415 A119 25c multi .25 .20
416 A119 35c multi .30 .25
417 A119 40c multi .35 .35
Nos. 414-417 (4) 1.10 1.00

"Conserve Energy" — A120

1978, Aug. 31 Litho. *Perf. 13x14*

418 A120 15c org & blk .20 .20
419 A120 20c dp grn & blk .20 .20
420 A120 40c dk red & blk .30 .30
Nos. 418-420 (3) .70 .70

Morse Ship-to-Shore Service A121

Designs: 40c, Ship-to-shore telex service. 55c, Future radar-satellite service, vert.

Perf. 14x13, 13x14

1978, Oct. 16 Litho.

421 A121 20c multi .25 .25
422 A121 40c multi .30 .30
423 A121 55c multi .45 .45
Nos. 421-423 (3) 1.00 1.00

Ship-to-shore communications, 70th anniv.

Villa Maria Waterworks A122

35c, Leonard B. Smith, vert. 40c, Opening of Queen Emma Bridge, Willemstadt, 1888.

1978, Dec. 13

424 A122 25c multi .20 .20
425 A122 35c multi .25 .20
426 A122 40c multi .30 .25
Nos. 424-426 (3) .75 .65

L. B. Smith, engineer, 80th death anniv.

Queen Juliana Type of 1950

1979, Jan. 11 Photo. *Perf. 13½x13*

427 A44 5c dp yel .20 .20
a. Bklt. pane of 10 (4 #427, 1 #216a, 2 #222a, 3 #429) 3.00

428 A44 30c brown .25 .20
a. Bklt. pane of 10 (1 #428, 4 #218a, 3 #219a, 2 #222a) 3.00
429 A44 40c brt bl .30 .20
Nos. 427-429 (3) .75 .60

Nos. 427-429 issued in booklets only. Nos. 427a-428a have 2 labels and selvages the size of 6 stamps. Background design of booklet stamps sharper than 1950 issue. All stamps have 1 or 2 straight edges.

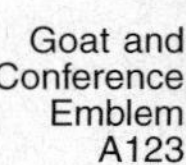

Goat and Conference Emblem A123

75c, Horse & map of Curaçao. 150c, Cattle, Netherlands Antilles flag, UN & Conf. emblems.

1979, Apr. 18 Litho. *Perf. 14x13*
437 A123 50c multi .30 .30
438 A123 75c multi .40 .40
439 A123 150c multi .75 .75
a. Souv. sheet of 3, perf. 13½x13 1.50 1.50
Nos. 437-439 (3) 1.45 1.45

12th Inter-American Meeting at Ministerial Level on Foot and Mouth Disease and Zoonosis Control, Curaçao, Apr. 17-20. No. 439a contains Nos. 437-439 in changed colors.

Dutch Colonial Soldier, Emblem — A124

1979, July 4 Litho. *Perf. 13x14*
440 A124 1g multi .55 .50
Nos. 440,B166-B167 (3) 1.15 1.05

Netherlands Antilles Volunteer Corps, 50th anniv.

A125

A126

Flowering Trees: 25c, Casearia Tremula. 40c, Cordia cylindro-stachya. 1.50g, Melochia tomentosa.

1979, Sept. 3 Litho. *Perf. 13x14*
441 A125 25c multi .20 .20
442 A125 40c multi .30 .30
443 A125 1.50g multi .75 .75
Nos. 441-443 (3) 1.25 1.25

1979, Dec. 6 Litho. *Perf. 13x14*

Designs: 65c, Dove and Netherlands flag. 1.50g, Dove and Netherlands Antilles flag.

444 A126 65c multi .50 .40
445 A126 1.50g multi .80 .80

Constitution, 25th anniversary.

Map of Aruba, Foundation Emblem A127

1g, Foundation headquarters, Aruba.

1979, Dec. 18 *Perf. 14x13*
446 A127 95c multi .60 .60
447 A127 1g multi .70 .70

Cultural Foundation Center, Aruba, 30th anniv.

Cupola, 1910, Fort Church — A128

1980, Jan. 9 *Perf. 13x14*
448 A128 100c multi .60 .60
Nos. 448,B172-B173 (3) 1.25 1.25

Fort Church, Curaçao, 210th anniv. (1979).

Rotary Emblem A129

Designs: 50c, Globe and cogwheels. 85c, Cogwheel and Rotary emblem.

1980, Feb. 22 Litho. *Perf. 14x13*
449 A129 45c multi .25 .25
450 A129 50c multi .30 .30
451 A129 85c multi .50 .50
a. Souvenir sheet of 3, #449-451, perf. 13½x13 1.10 1.10
b. Strip of 3, #449-451 1.10 1.10

Rotary Intl., 75th anniv. No. 451a has continuous design.

Coin Box, 1905 — A130

Post Office Savings Bank of Netherlands Antilles, 75th Anniv.: 150c, Coin box, 1980.

1980, Apr. 2 Litho. *Perf. 14x13*
452 A130 25c multi .20 .20
453 A130 150c multi .90 .90

Netherlands Antilles No. 200, Arms — A131

1980, Apr. 29 Photo.
454 A131 25c shown .20 .20
455 A131 60c No. 290, royal crown .30 .30
a. Bklt. pane of 5 + 3 labels (#428, 2 #454, 2 #455) 3.00

Abdication of Queen Juliana of the Netherlands.
Tete-beche gutter pairs exist.

Sir Rowland Hill (1795-1879), Originator of Penny Postage A132

1980, May 6 Litho.
456 A132 45c shown .30 .30
457 A132 60c London 1980 emblem .30 .30
458 A132 1g Airmail label .70 .70
a. Souv. sheet of 3, perf. 13½x14 1.40 1.40
Nos. 456-458 (3) 1.30 1.30

London 1980 Intl. Stamp Exhibition, May 6-14. No. 458a contains Nos. 456-458 in changed colors.

Leptotila Verreauxi A133

1980, Sept. 3 Litho. *Perf. 14x13*
459 A133 25c shown .30 .25
460 A133 60c Mockingbird .55 .55
461 A133 85c Coereba flaveola .75 .75
Nos. 459-461 (3) 1.60 1.55

Rudolf Theodorus Palm — A134

Alliance Mission Emblem, Map of Aruba A135

1981, Jan. 27 Litho. *Perf. 13x14*
462 A134 60c shown .40 .40
463 A134 1g Score, hand playing piano .75 .70

Palm, composer, birth centenary.

1981, Mar. 24 *Perf. 14x13*
464 A135 30c shown .25 .25
465 A135 50c Curaçao .40 .30
466 A135 1g Bonaire map .75 .70
Nos. 464-466 (3) 1.40 1.25

Evangelical Alliance Mission anniversaries: 35th in Aruba, 50th in Curaçao, 30th in Bonaire.

St. Elisabeth's Hospital, 125th Anniv. A136

1981, June 24 Litho. *Perf. 14x13*
467 A136 60c Gateway .40 .40
468 A136 1.50g shown 1.00 1.00

Oregano Blossom A137

Ship Pilot Service Cent. A138

1981, Nov. 24 Litho. *Perf. 13x14*
469 A137 45c shown .30 .30
470 A137 70c Flaira .50 .50
471 A137 100c Welisali .70 .70
Nos. 469-471 (3) 1.50 1.50

1982, Jan. 13 Litho. *Perf. 13x14*

Designs: Various ships.

472 A138 70c multi .55 .55
473 A138 85c multi .60 .60
474 A138 1g multi .70 .70
Nos. 472-474 (3) 1.85 1.85

A139

A140

1982, Mar. 15 Litho. *Perf. 13x14*
475 A139 75c Altar .60 .60
476 A139 85c Building .60 .60
477 A139 150c Pulpit 1.00 1.00
Nos. 475-477 (3) 2.20 2.20

Community Mikve Israel-Emanuel Synagogue, 250th anniv.

1982, Apr. 21 Litho. *Perf. 13x14*
478 A140 75c Flags, Peter Stuyvesant .70 .70
a. Souvenir sheet .75 .75

US-Netherlands diplomatic relations bicentenary.

A141

A142

1982, May 5
479 A141 35c Radar screen .30 .30
480 A141 75c Control tower .60 .60
481 A141 150c Antenna 1.00 1.00
Nos. 479-481 (3) 1.90 1.90

Intl. Air Traffic Controllers' Year.

1982, June 9 Litho. *Perf. 13x14*
482 A142 45c Emblem .30 .30
483 A142 85c Mail bag .60 .60
484 A142 150c Flags of France, Neth. Ant. 1.10 1.00
a. Souvenir sheet of 3, #482-484 2.25 2.25
Nos. 482-484 (3) 2.00 1.90

PHILEXFRANCE '82 Stamp Exhibition, Paris, June 11-21.

Brown Chromis A143

1982, Sept. 15 Litho. *Perf. 14x13*
485 A143 35c shown .50 .50
486 A143 75c Spotted trunkfish 1.00 1.00
487 A143 85c Blue tang 1.10 1.10
488 A143 100c French angelfish 1.40 1.40
Nos. 485-488 (4) 4.00 4.00

Natural Bridge, Aruba A144

1983, Apr. 12 Litho. *Perf. 14x13*
489 A144 35c shown .30 .30
490 A144 45c Lac-Bay, Bonaire .40 .40
491 A144 100c Willemstad, Curaçao .90 .90
Nos. 489-491 (3) 1.60 1.60

World Communications Year — A145

1983, May 17 Litho. *Perf. 13x14*
492 A145 1g multi .90 .90
a. Souvenir sheet .95 .95

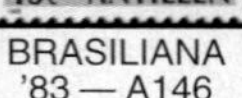

BRASILIANA '83 — A146

Fruit Tree — A147

1983, June 29 Litho. *Perf. 13x14*

493 A146 45c Ship, postal building, Waaigat .50 .50
494 A146 55c Flags, emblem .55 .55
495 A146 100c Governor's Palace, Sugar Loaf Mt. .95 .95
a. Souvenir sheet of 3, #493-495 2.25 2.25
Nos. 493-495 (3) 2.00 2.00

1983, Sept. 13 Litho. *Perf. 13x14*

496 A147 45c Mangifera indica .70 .70
497 A147 55c Malpighia punicifolia .80 .80
498 A147 100c Citrus aurantifolia 1.40 1.40
Nos. 496-498 (3) 2.90 2.90

Local Government Buildings A148

1983, Dec. 20 Litho. *Perf. 14x13*

499 A148 20c Saba .20 .20
500 A148 25c St. Eustatius .25 .25
501 A148 30c St. Maarten .30 .30
502 A148 35c Aruba *.30 .30*
503 A148 45c Bonaire .40 .40
a. Perf. 13½ horiz. ('86) .20 .20
504 A148 55c Curaçao .50 .50
a. Perf. 13½ horiz. ('86) .25 .25
b. Bklt. pane of 4 + label (2 #503a, 504a) ('86) 1.75
Nos. 499-504 (6) 1.95 1.95

See Nos. 515-520, 543A-555.

Amigoe di Curaçao Newspaper Centenary A149

1984, Jan. 5 Litho.

505 A149 45c Copy programming .40 .40
506 A149 55c Printing press .50 .50
507 A149 85c Man reading newspaper .90 .90
Nos. 505-507 (3) 1.80 1.80

40th Anniv. of Intl. Civil Aviation Org. — A150

Various emblems.

1984, Feb. 28 Litho. *Perf. 14x13*

508 A150 25c Winair .20 .20
509 A150 45c ICAO .40 .40
510 A150 55c ALM .50 .50
511 A150 100c Plane .90 .90
Nos. 508-511 (4) 2.00 2.00

Chamber of Commerce and Industry Centenary — A151

1984, May 29 Litho. *Perf. 13½*

512 A151 45c Bonnet maker .60 .60
513 A151 55c Emblem .60 .60
514 A151 100c River, bridge, boat .95 .95
Nos. 512-514 (3) 2.15 2.15

Govt. Building Type of 1983

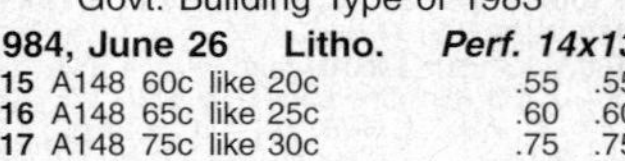

1984, June 26 Litho. *Perf. 14x13*

515 A148 60c like 20c .55 .55
516 A148 65c like 25c .60 .60
517 A148 75c like 30c .75 .75
518 A148 85c like 35c .85 .85
519 A148 90c like 45c .90 .90
520 A148 95c like 55c 1.00 1.00
Nos. 515-520 (6) 4.65 4.65

For surcharges see Nos. B306-B307.

Local Birds — A152

1984, Sept. 18 Litho. *Perf. 14x13*

521 A152 45c Tiaris bicolor .85 .85
522 A152 55c Zonotrichia capensis 1.10 1.10
523 A152 150c Chlorostilbon mellisugus 2.25 2.25
Nos. 521-523 (3) 4.20 4.20

Eleanor Roosevelt (1884-1962) — A153

1984, Oct. 11 Litho. *Perf. 13x14*

524 A153 45c At Hyde Park .50 .50
525 A153 85c Portrait .80 .80
526 A153 100c Reading to children .90 .90
Nos. 524-526 (3) 2.20 2.20

Tete-beche gutter pairs exist.

Flamingos A154

Curaçao Masonic Lodge Bicent. — A155

1985, Jan. 9 Litho. *Perf. 14x13*

527 A154 25c Adult pullets .55 .55
528 A154 45c Juveniles .90 .90
529 A154 55c Adults wading 1.10 1.10
530 A154 100c Adults flying 1.60 1.60
Nos. 527-530 (4) 4.15 4.15

1985, Feb. 21 Litho. *Perf. 13x14*

531 A155 45c Compass, sun, moon and stars .50 .50
532 A155 55c Doorway, columns and 5 steps .70 .70
533 A155 100c Star, 7 steps 1.10 1.10
Nos. 531-533 (3) 2.30 2.30

UN, 40th Anniv. A156

1985, June 5 Litho. *Perf. 14x13*

534 A156 55c multi .60 .60
535 A156 1g multi 1.00 1.00

Papiamentu, Language of the Antilles A157

45c, Pierre Lauffer (1920-1981), author and poem Patria. 55c, Waves of Papiamentu.

1985, Sept. 4 Litho. *Perf. 14x13*

536 A157 45c multi .45 .45
537 A157 55c multi .60 .60

Tete-beche gutter pairs exist.

Flora — A158

1985, Nov. 6 *Perf. 13x14*

538 A158 5c Calotropis procera .30 .20
539 A158 10c Capparis flexuosa .30 .20
540 A158 20c Mimosa distachya .45 .30
541 A158 45c Ipomoea nil .70 .50
542 A158 55c Heliotropium ternatum .85 .55
543 A158 1.50g Ipomoea incarnata 1.40 1.25
Nos. 538-543 (6) 4.00 3.00

Govt. Building Type of 1983

1985-89 *Perf. 14x13*

543A A148 70c like 20c ('88) .50 .40
543B A148 85c like 45c ('88) .60 .55
544 A148 1g like 20c 1.00 1.00
545 A148 1.50g like 25c 1.25 1.25
546 A148 2.50g like 30c ('86) 2.10 1.75
551 A148 5g like 45c ('86) 4.25 3.50
554 A148 10g like 55c ('87) 7.25 5.75
555 A148 15g like 20c ('89) 10.50 9.25
Nos. 543A-555 (8) 27.45 23.45

Issued: 70c, 85c, 3/16; 1g, 1.50g, 12/4; 2.50g, 1/8; 5g, 12/3; 10g, 5/20; 15g, 2/8.

For surcharge see No. B308.

This is an expanding set. Numbers will change if necessary.

Curaçao Town Hall, 125th Anniv. A159

1986, Jan. 8 *Perf. 14x13, 13x14*

561 A159 5c Town Hall .20 .20
562 A159 15c State room, vert. .20 .20
563 A159 25c Court room .25 .25
564 A159 55c Entrance, vert. .50 .50
Nos. 561-564 (4) 1.15 1.15

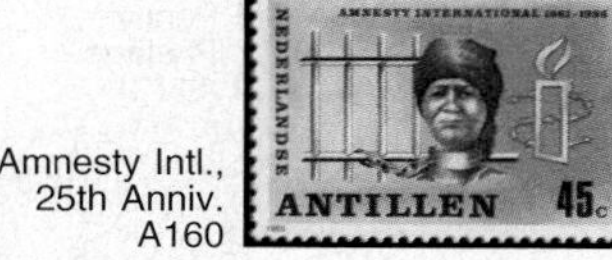

Amnesty Intl., 25th Anniv. A160

1986, May 28 Litho. *Perf. 14x13*

565 A160 45c Prisoner chained .40 .40
566 A160 55c Peace bird imprisoned .50 .50
567 A160 100c Prisoner behind bars .90 .90
Nos. 565-567 (3) 1.80 1.80

Mailboxes A161

Perf. 14x13, 13x14

1986, Sept. 3 Litho.

568 A161 10c PO mailbox .20 .20
569 A161 25c Steel mailbox .25 .25
570 A161 45c Mailbox on brick wall .35 .35
571 A161 55c Pillar box .40 .40
Nos. 568-571 (4) 1.20 1.20

Nos. 569-571 vert.

Friars of Tilburg in the Antilles, Cent. — A162

10c, Brother Mauritius Vliegendehond, residence, 1886. 45c, Monsignor Ferdinand Kieckens, St. Thomas College, Roodeweg. 55c, Father F.S. de Beer, 1st general-superior, & college courtyard.

1986, Nov. 13 Litho. *Perf. 13x14*

572 A162 10c multi .20 .20
573 A162 45c multi .35 .35
574 A162 55c multi .45 .45
Nos. 572-574 (3) 1.00 1.00

Princess Juliana & Prince Bernhard, 50th Wedding Anniv. A163

Maduro Holding, Inc., Sesquicent. A164

1987, Jan. 7 Litho. *Perf. 13x14*

575 A163 1.35g multi 1.10 1.10
a. Souvenir sheet 1.25 1.25

1987, Jan. 26

576 A164 70c Expansion map .50 .50
577 A164 85c Corporate divisions .60 .60
578 A164 1.55g S.E.L. Maduro, founder 1.10 1.10
Nos. 576-578 (3) 2.20 2.20

Curaçao Rotary Club, 50th Anniv. A165

1987, Apr. 2 Litho. *Perf. 14x13*

579 A165 15c Map of the Antilles .20 .20
580 A165 50c Rotary headquarters .40 .40
581 A165 65c Map of Curaçao .50 .50
Nos. 579-581 (3) 1.10 1.10

Bolivar-Curaçao Friendship, 175th Anniv. — A166

60c, Octagon, residence of Simon Bolivar in Curaçao. 70c, Bolivarian Soc. Headquarters, 1949, Willemstad. 80c, Octagon interior (bedroom). 90c, Manual Carlos Piar, Simon Bolivar (1783-1830) & Pedro Luis Brion.

1987, July 24 Litho. *Perf. 14x13*

582	A166	60c multi	.40	.40
583	A166	70c multi	.50	.50
584	A166	80c multi	.55	.55
585	A166	90c multi	.65	.65
		Nos. 582-585 (4)	2.10	2.10

Bolivarian Society, 50th anniv. (70c, 90c).

Antilles Natl. Parks Foundation, 25th Anniv. A167

1987, Dec. 1 Litho. *Perf. 14x13*

586	A167	70c Phaethon lepturus	.70	.70
587	A167	85c Odocoileus virginianus curassavicus	.80	.80
588	A167	1.55g Iguana iguana	1.50	1.50
		Nos. 586-588 (3)	3.00	3.00

The Curaçao Courant, 175th Anniv. A168

Designs: 55c, 19th Cent. printing press, lead type. 70c, Keyboard, modern press.

1987, Dec. 11

589	A168	55c multi	.50	.50
590	A168	70c multi	.60	.60

Mijnmaatschappij Phosphate Mining Co., Curaçao, 75th Anniv. — A169

1988, Jan. 21

591	A169	40c William Godden, founder	.30	.30
592	A169	105c Processing plant	.80	.80
593	A169	155c Tafelberg	1.25	1.25
		Nos. 591-593 (3)	2.35	2.35

States of the Netherlands Antilles, 50th Anniv. A170

Designs: 65c, John Horris Sprockel, 1st president, and natl. colors, crest. 70c, Development of state elections, women's suffrage. 155c, Natl. colors, crest, constellation representing the 5 islands and separation of Aruba.

1988, Apr. 5 Litho.

594	A170	65c multi	.50	.50
595	A170	70c multi	.50	.50
596	A170	155c multi	1.10	1.10
		Nos. 594-596 (3)	2.10	2.10

Abolition of Slavery, 125th Anniv. A171

1988, July 1 Litho. *Perf. 14x13*

597	A171	155c shown	1.25	1.25
598	A171	190c Slave Wall, Curaçao	1.40	1.40

3rd Conference for Great Cities of the Americas, Curaçao, Aug. 24-27 — A172

1988, Aug. 24 Litho.

599	A172	80c shown	.60	.60
600	A172	155c Bridge, globe	1.25	1.25

Interamerican Foundation of Cities conference on building bridges between peoples.

Charles Ernst Barend Hellmund (1896-1952) A173

Cacti A174

Men and women who initiated community development: 65c, Atthelo Maud Edwards Jackson (1901-1970). 90c, Nicolaas Debrot (1902-1981). 120c, William Charles De La Try Ellis (1881-1977).

1988, Sept. 20 *Perf. 13x14*

601	A173	55c multi	.40	.40
602	A173	65c multi	.50	.50
603	A173	90c multi	.65	.65
604	A173	120c multi	.85	.85
		Nos. 601-604 (4)	2.40	2.40

Tete-beche gutter pairs exist.

1988, Dec. 13 Litho. *Perf. 13x14*

605	A174	55c Cereus hexagonus	.55	.55
606	A174	115c Melocactus	1.10	1.10
607	A174	125c Opuntia wentiana	1.25	1.25
		Nos. 605-607 (3)	2.90	2.90

Wildlife Protection and Curaçao Foundation for the Prevention of Cruelty to Animals A175

1989, Mar. 9 Litho. *Perf. 14x13*

608	A175	65c Crested quail	.65	.65
609	A175	115c Dogs, cats	1.10	1.10

Cruise Ships at St. Maarten and Curaçao A176

1989, May 8 Litho.

610	A176	70c Great Bay Harbor	.55	.55
611	A176	155c St. Annabay	1.25	1.25

Tourism.

A177

Social and Political Figures: 40c, Paula Clementina Dorner (1901-1969), teacher. 55c, John Aniceto de Jongh (1885-1951), pharmacist, Parliament member. 90c, Jacobo Palm (1887-1982), composer. 120c, Abraham Mendes Chumaceiro (1841-1902), political reformer.

1989, Sept. 20 Litho. *Perf. 13x14*

612	A177	40c multi	.35	.35
613	A177	55c multi	.45	.45
614	A177	90c multi	.80	.80
615	A177	120c multi	1.10	1.10
		Nos. 612-615 (4)	2.70	2.70

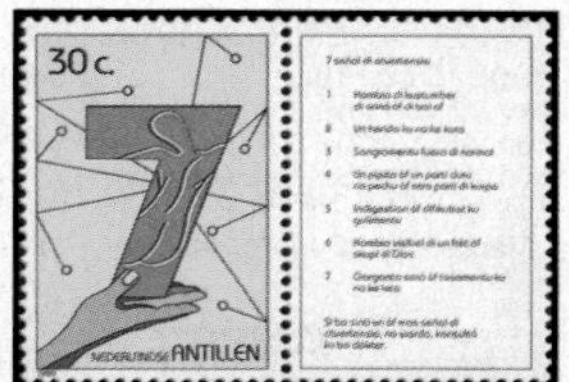

A178

1989, Nov. 7 Litho.

616	A178	30c 7 Symptoms of cancer	.30	.30
617	A178	60c Radiation treatment	.60	.60
618	A178	80c Fund emblem, healthy person	.75	.75
		Nos. 616-618 (3)	1.65	1.65

Queen Wilhelmina Fund, 40th anniv. Nos. 616-618 printed se-tenant with inscribed labels.

Souvenir Sheet

World Stamp Expo '89 and 20th UPU Congress, Washington, DC — A179

Designs: 70c, Monument, St. Eustatius, where the sovereignty of the US was 1st recognized by a foreign officer, Nov. 16, 1776. 155c, Peter Stuyvesant, flags representing bicent. of US-Antilles diplomatic relations, vert. 250c, 9-Gun salute of the *Andrea Doria.*

1989, Nov. 17 Litho. *Perf. 13*

619		Sheet of 3	3.75	3.25
a.		A179 70c multicolored	.55	.50
b.		A179 155c multicolored	1.25	1.10
c.		A179 250c multicolored	1.75	1.50

A180

1989, Dec. 1 *Perf. 13½x14*

620	A180	30c Fireworks	.25	.25
621	A180	100c Ornaments on tree	.75	.75

Christmas 1989 and New Year 1990. Nos. 620-621 printed se-tenant with labels inscribed "Merry X-mas and Happy New Year" in four languages.

A181

1990, Jan. 31 Litho. *Perf. 13x14*

Flowering plants.

622	A181	30c *Tephrosia cinerea*	.25	.25
623	A181	55c *Erithalis fruticosa*	.40	.40
624	A181	65c *Evolvulus antillanus*	.50	.50
625	A181	70c *Jacquinia arborea*	.55	.55
626	A181	125c *Tournefortia gnaphalodes*	1.00	1.00
627	A181	155c *Sesuvium portulacastrum*	1.10	1.10
		Nos. 622-627 (6)	3.80	3.80

Dominican Nuns in the Netherlands Antilles, Cent. — A182

10c, Nurse, flag, map. 55c, St. Rose Hospital and St. Martin's Home. 60c, St. Joseph School.

1990, May 7 Litho. *Perf. 14x13*

628	A182	10c multicolored	.20	.20
629	A182	55c multicolored	.60	.60
630	A182	60c multicolored	.70	.70
		Nos. 628-630 (3)	1.50	1.50

A183 A184

Poets: 40c, Carlos Alberto Nicolaas-Perez (1915-1989). 60c, Evert Stephanus Jordanus Kruythoff (1893-1967). 80c, John De Pool (1873-1947). 150c, Joseph Sickman Corsen (1853-1911).

1990, Aug. 8 Litho. *Perf. 13x14*

631	A183	40c multicolored	.45	.45
632	A183	60c multicolored	.70	.70
633	A183	80c multicolored	.95	.95
634	A183	150c multicolored	1.75	1.75
		Nos. 631-634 (4)	3.85	3.85

1990, Sept. 5 *Perf. 13x14*

Netherlands queens.

635	A184	100c Emma	1.10	1.00
636	A184	100c Wilhelmina	1.10	1.00
637	A184	100c Juliana	1.10	1.00
638	A184	100c Beatrix	1.10	1.00
		Nos. 635-638 (4)	4.40	4.00

Souvenir Sheet

Perf. 14x13

639	A184	250c Four Queens, horiz.	3.50	2.25

Oil Refining in Curaçao, 75th Anniv. A185

1990, Oct. 1 Litho. *Perf. 14x13*

640	A185	100c multicolored	1.10	1.00

Christmas A186

1990, Dec. 5 Litho. *Perf. 13½x14*

641	A186	30c Gifts	.35	.30
642	A186	100c shown	1.10	1.00

25th anniv. of Bon Bisina Project (No. 641). Nos. 641-642 each printed with se-tenant label showing holiday greetings.

Express Mail Service, 5th Anniv. A187

1991, Jan. 16 Litho. *Perf. 14x13*

643	A187	20g multicolored	20.00	20.00

Fish — A188

Designs: 10c, Scuba diver, French grunt. 40c, Spotted trunkfish. 55c, Coppersweeper. 75c, Skindiver, yellow goatfish. 100c, Blackbar soldierfish.

1991, Mar. 13 *Perf. 13x14*

644 A188 10c multicolored .20 .20
645 A188 40c multicolored .50 .50
646 A188 55c multicolored .65 .65
647 A188 75c multicolored .90 .90
648 A188 100c multicolored 1.25 1.25
Nos. 644-648 (5) 3.50 3.50

Greetings A189

1991, May 8 *Perf. 14x13*

649 A189 30c Good luck .35 .35
650 A189 30c Thank you .35 .35
651 A189 30c Love you .35 .35
652 A189 30c Happy day .35 .35
653 A189 30c Get well soon .35 .35
654 A189 30c Happy birthday .35 .35
Nos. 649-654 (6) 2.10 2.10

Lighthouses — A190

1991, June 19 **Litho.** *Perf. 13x14*

655 A190 30c Westpoint, Curaçao .35 .35
656 A190 70c Willem's Tower, Bonaire .85 .85
657 A190 115c Little Curaçao, Curaçao 1.40 1.40
Nos. 655-657 (3) 2.60 2.60

Peter Stuyvesant College, 50th Anniv. A191

Espamer '91 — A192

1991, July 5 *Perf. 14x13, 13x14*

658 A191 65c multicolored .80 .80
659 A192 125c multicolored 1.50 1.50

Christmas A193

1991, Dec. 2 **Litho.** *Perf. 13½x14*

660 A193 30c shown .35 .35
661 A193 100c Angel, shepherds 1.10 1.10

Nos. 660-661 printed with se-tenant labels.

A194

Litho. & Typo.

1991, Dec. 16 *Perf. 13x14*

662 A194 30c J. A. Correa .35 .35
663 A194 70c "75," coat of arms .90 .90
664 A194 155c I. H. Capriles 1.75 1.75
a. Strip of 3, #662-664 3.05 3.05

Maduro and Curiel's Bank NV, 75th anniv.

Odocoileus Virginianus A195

1992, Jan. 29 **Litho.** *Perf. 14x13*

666 A195 5c Fawn 2.00 1.25
667 A195 10c Two does 2.00 1.25
668 A195 30c Buck 2.00 1.25
669 A195 40c Buck & doe in water 2.00 1.25
670 A195 200c Buck drinking 2.50 2.25
671 A195 355c Buck, diff. 4.00 4.00
Nos. 666-671 (6) 14.50 11.25

World Wildlife Fund. Nos. 670-671 are airmail and do not have the WWF emblem.

Souvenir Sheet

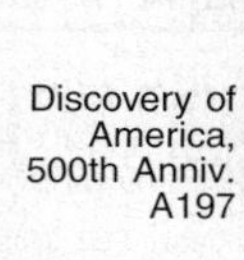

Discovery of America, 500th Anniv. — A196

Designs: a, 250c, Alhambra, Granada, Spain. b, 500c, Carthusian Monastery, Seville, Spain.

1992, Apr. 1 **Litho.** *Perf. 14x13*

672 A196 Sheet of 2, #a.-b. 9.00 8.00

#672a, Granada '92. #672b, Expo '92, Seville.

Discovery of America, 500th Anniv. A197

250c, Sailing ship. 500c, Map, Columbus.

1992, May 13 **Litho.** *Perf. 14x13*

673 A197 250c multicolored 3.00 3.00
674 A197 500c multicolored 6.00 6.00

World Columbian Stamp Expo '92, Chicago.

Container Terminal, Curaçao A198

1992, June 26

675 A198 80c multi .95 .95
676 A198 125c multi, diff. 1.50 1.50

Famous People — A199

Designs: 30c, Angela Altagracia de Lannoy-Willems (1913-1983), politician and social activist. 40c, Lodewijk Daniel Gerharts (1901-1983), politician and promoter of tourism for Bonaire. 55c, Cyrus Wilberforce Wathey (1901-1969), businessman and philanthropist. 70c, Christiaan Winkel (1899-1962), deputy governor of Netherlands Antilles. 100c, Franciscan Nuns of Roosendaal, educational and charitable group, 150th anniversary of arrival in Curaçao.

1992, Sept. 1 **Litho.** *Perf. 13x14*

677 A199 30c tan, grn & blk .40 .40
678 A199 40c tan, blue & blk .50 .50
679 A199 55c tan, yel org & blk .65 .65
680 A199 70c tan, lake & blk .85 .85
681 A199 100c tan, blue & blk 1.25 1.25
Nos. 677-681 (5) 3.65 3.65

Queen Beatrix's 1992 Visit — A200

Designs: 70c, Queen in white hat, Prince Claus. 100c, Queen signing jubilee register. 175c, Queen in black hat, Prince Claus, native girl.

1992, Nov. 9 **Litho.** *Perf. 14x13*

682 A200 70c multicolored .90 .90
683 A200 100c multicolored 1.25 1.25
684 A200 175c multicolored 2.25 2.25
Nos. 682-684 (3) 4.40 4.40

Queen Beatrix's accession to the throne, 12½ year anniv. (#683).

Christmas A201

Perf. 14x13½, 13½x14

1992, Dec. 1 **Litho.**

685 A201 30c Nativity scene .35 .35
686 A201 100c Mary, Joseph, vert. 1.25 1.25

No. 686 printed with se-tenant label.

Flowers — A202

1993, Feb. 3 **Litho.** *Perf. 13x14*

687 A202 75c Hibiscus .95 .95
688 A202 90c Helianthus annuus 1.10 1.10
689 A202 175c Ixora 2.25 2.25
690 A202 195c Rosea 2.50 2.50
Nos. 687-690 (4) 6.80 6.80

Anniversaries A203

Map of islands and: 65c, Airplane, air routes. 75c, Natl. Laboratory, scientist using microscope. 90c, Airplane at Princess Juliana Intl. Airport. 175c, Yellow and white crosses.

1993, Mar. 9 *Perf. 14x13*

691 A203 65c multicolored .80 .80
692 A203 75c multicolored .95 .95
693 A203 90c multicolored 1.25 1.25
694 A203 175c multicolored 2.25 2.25
Nos. 691-694 (4) 5.25 5.25

Princess Juliana Intl. Airport, 50th anniv. (#691, 693). Natl. Laboratory, 75th anniv. (#692). Princess Margaret White/Yellow Cross Foundation for District Nursing, 50th anniv. (#694).

Dogs — A204

1993, May 26 **Litho.** *Perf. 13x14*

695 A204 65c Pekingese .80 .80
696 A204 90c Poodle 1.10 1.10
697 A204 100c Pomeranian 1.25 1.25
698 A204 175c Papillon 2.25 2.25
Nos. 695-698 (4) 5.40 5.40

Entry of Netherlands Antilles into UPAEP A205

Designs: 150c, Indian cave painting, Bonaire. 200c, Emblem of Brasiliana '93, flag of Netherlands Antilles. 250c, Map of Central and South America, Netherlands Antilles, Spain, and Portugal, document being signed.

1993, July 15 **Litho.** *Perf. 14x13*

699 A205 150c multicolored 1.90 1.90
700 A205 200c multicolored 2.50 2.50
701 A205 250c multicolored 3.25 3.25
Nos. 699-701 (3) 7.65 7.65

Brasiliana '93 (#700).

Contemporary Art — A206

1993, July 23 **Litho.** *Perf. 13x14*

702 A206 90c silver & multi 1.10 1.10
703 A206 150c gold & multi 1.90 1.90

US Consulate General in Netherlands Antilles, Bicent. A207

1993, Nov. 16 **Litho.** *Perf. 14x13*

704 A207 65c American Consulate .80 .80
705 A207 90c Coats of Arms 1.10 1.10
706 A207 175c Eagle in flight 2.25 2.25
Nos. 704-706 (3) 4.15 4.15

Christmas — A208

Designs: 30c, Mosaic of mother and child. 115c, Painting of Mary holding Christ.

1993, Dec. 1 *Perf. 13x14*

707 A208 30c multicolored .35 .35
708 A208 115c multicolored 1.40 1.40

Dogs — A209

1994, Feb. 2 Litho. *Perf. 14x13*

709 A209 65c Basset .80 .80
710 A209 75c Pit bull terrier .95 .95
711 A209 90c Cocker spaniel 1.10 1.10
712 A209 175c Chow 2.25 2.25
Nos. 709-712 (4) 5.10 5.10

Birds — A210

A211

1994, Mar. 2 Litho. *Perf. 13x14*

713 A210 50c Polyborus plancus .60 .60
714 A210 95c Pavo muticus 1.10 1.10
715 A210 100c Ara macao 1.25 1.25
716 A210 125c Icterus icterus 1.50 1.50
Nos. 713-716 (4) 4.45 4.45

1994, Apr. 8

Famous People: 65c, Joseph Husurell Lake (1925-76), politician, journalist. 75c, Efrain Jonckheer (1917-87), diplomat. 100c, Michiel Martinus Romer (1865-1937), educator. 175c, Carel Nicolaas Winkel (1882-1973), public official, social worker.

717 A211 65c grn, olive & blk .80 .80
718 A211 75c lt brn, brn & blk .95 .95
719 A211 100c bl, grn & blk 1.25 1.25
720 A211 175c tan, brn & blk 2.25 2.25
Nos. 717-720 (4) 5.25 5.25

A212

A213

1994 World Cup Soccer Championships, US: 90c, Socks, soccer shoes, horiz. 150c, Shoe, ball. 175c, Whistle, horiz.

Perf. 14x13, 13x14

1994, May 4 Litho.

721 A212 90c multicolored 1.10 1.10
722 A212 150c multicolored 1.90 1.90
723 A212 175c multicolored 2.25 2.25
Nos. 721-723 (3) 5.25 5.25

1994, June 1 Litho. *Perf. 13x14*

ILO, 75th Anniv.: 90c, Declaration, chair, gavel. 110c, "75" over heart. 200c, Wind-blown tree.

724 A213 90c multicolored 1.10 1.10
725 A213 110c multicolored 1.40 1.40
726 A213 200c multicolored 2.50 2.50
Nos. 724-726 (3) 5.00 5.00

Wildlife A214

Designs: 10c, Ware-wara, blenchi, parakeet, dolphin. 35c, Dolphin, pelican, troupial. 50c, Iguana, fish, lobster, sea hedgehog. 125c, Sea hedgehog, sea apple, fish, turtle, flamingos, ducks.

1994, Aug. 4 Litho. *Perf. 14x13*

727 A214 10c multicolored .20 .20
728 A214 35c multicolored .45 .45
729 A214 50c multicolored .65 .65
730 A214 125c multicolored 1.60 1.60
a. Souvenir sheet, #727-730 2.75 2.75
Nos. 727-730 (4) 2.90 2.90

PHILAKOREA '94 (#730a).

FEPAPOST '94 — A215

2.50g, Netherlands #277. 5g, #109.

1994, Oct. 5 Litho. *Perf. 14x13*

731 A215 2.50g multicolored 2.75 2.75
732 A215 5g multicolored 5.50 5.50
a. Souv. sheet of 2, #731-732, perf. 13½x13 8.25 8.25

Christmas A216

1994, Dec. 1 Litho. *Perf. 14x13*

733 A216 30c shown .30 .30
734 A216 115c Hands holding earth 1.25 1.25

Curaçao Carnivals — A217

Carnival scene and: 125c, Buildings, Willemstad. 175c, Floating market. 250c, House with thatched roof.

1995, Jan. 19 Litho. *Perf. 14x13*

735 A217 125c multicolored 1.40 1.40
736 A217 175c multicolored 2.00 2.00
737 A217 250c multicolored 2.75 2.75
Nos. 735-737 (3) 6.15 6.15

Mgr. Verriet Institute for Physically Handicapped, 50th Anniv. — A218

Design: 90c, Cedric Virginie, handicapped worker at Public Library.

1995, Feb. 2 Litho. *Perf. 13x14*

738 A218 65c multicolored .75 .75
739 A218 90c multicolored 1.00 1.00

Dogs — A219

1995, Mar. 29 Litho. *Perf. 14x13*

740 A219 75c Doberman .85 .85
741 A219 85c Shepherd .95 .95
742 A219 100c Bouvier 1.10 1.10
743 A219 175c St. Bernard 2.00 2.00
Nos. 740-743 (4) 4.90 4.90

Flags, Coats of Arms of Island Territories A220

10c, Bonaire. 35c, Curaçao. 50c, St. Maarten. 65c, Saba. 75c, St. Eustatius, natl. flag, coat of arms. 90c, Flags of territories, natl. coat of arms.

1995, June 30 Litho. *Perf. 14x13*

744 A220 10c multicolored .20 .20
745 A220 35c multicolored .40 .40
746 A220 50c multicolored .55 .55
747 A220 65c multicolored .75 .75
748 A220 75c multicolored .85 .85
749 A220 90c multicolored 1.00 1.00
Nos. 744-749 (6) 3.75 3.75

Domestic Cats — A221

Designs: 25c, Siamese sealpoint. 60c, Maine coon. 65c, Egyptian silver mau. 90c, Angora. 150c, Persian blue smoke.

1995, Sept. 29 Litho. *Perf. 13x14*

750 A221 25c multicolored .30 .30
751 A221 60c multicolored .65 .65
752 A221 65c multicolored .75 .75
753 A221 90c multicolored 1.00 1.00
754 A221 150c multicolored 1.60 1.60
Nos. 750-754 (5) 4.30 4.30

Christmas and New Year — A222

Designs: 30c, Three Magi following star. 115c, Fireworks above houses, Handelskade.

1995, Dec. 1 Litho. *Perf. 13½x13*

755 A222 30c multicolored .35 .35
756 A222 115c multicolored 1.25 1.25

Nos. 755-756 each printed with se-tenant label.

A223

A224

Curaçao Lions Club, 50th Anniv.: 75c, List of services to community. 105c, Seal. 250c, Hands clasp.

1996, Feb. 26 Litho. *Perf. 13x14*

757 A223 75c multicolored .85 .85
758 A223 105c multicolored 1.25 1.25
759 A223 250c multicolored 2.75 2.75
Nos. 757-759 (3) 4.85 4.85

1996, Apr. 12 Litho. *Perf. 13x14*

760 A224 85c shown .95 .95
761 A224 175c Telegraph key 2.00 2.00

Radio, cent.

A225

A226

1996, Apr. 12

762 A225 60c shown .70 .70
763 A225 75c Tornado, sun .80 .80

Dr. David Ricardo Capriles Clinic, 60th anniv.

1996, May 8 Litho. *Perf. 13x14*

764 A226 85c shown .95 .95
765 A226 225c Bible 2.50 2.50

Translation of the Bible into Papiamentu.

CAPEX '96 — A227

Butterflies: 5c, Agraulis vanillae. 110c, Callithea philotima. 300c, Parthenos sylvia. 750c, Euphaedra francina.

1996, June 5 Litho. *Perf. 14x13*

766 A227 5c multicolored .20 .20
767 A227 110c multicolored 1.25 1.25
768 A227 300c multicolored 3.50 3.50
a. Souvenir sheet of 2, #767-768 4.75 4.75
769 A227 750c multicolored 8.50 8.50
Nos. 766-769 (4) 13.45 13.45

Famous Antillean Personalities A228

Designs: 40c, Mary Gertrude Johnson Hassel (1853-1939), introduced drawn thread (Spanish work) to Saba. 50c, Cornelis Marten (Papa Cornes) (1749-1852), spiritual care giver on Bonaire. 75c, Phelippi Benito Chakutoe (1891-1967), union leader. 85c, Christiaan Josef Hendrikus Engels (1907-80), physician, painter, pianist, poet.

1996, Aug. 21 Litho. *Perf. 14x13*

770 A228 40c orange & black .45 .45
771 A228 50c green & black .55 .55
772 A228 75c brown & black .85 .85
773 A228 85c blue & black .95 .95
Nos. 770-773 (4) 2.80 2.80

Horses A229

1996, Sept. 26 Litho. *Perf. 14x13*

774 A229 110c Shire 1.25 1.25
775 A229 225c Shetland pony 2.50 2.50
776 A229 275c Thoroughbred 3.00 3.00
777 A229 350c Przewalski 4.00 4.00
Nos. 774-777 (4) 10.75 10.75

Christmas — A230

35c, Money bag, straw hat, candy cane, gifts, poinsettias, star. 150c, Santa Claus.

Serpentine Die Cut 13x13½

1996, Dec. 2 Litho.

Self-Adhesive

778 A230 35c multicolored .40 .40
779 A230 150c multicolored 1.70 1.70

Mushrooms A231

40c, Galerina autumnalis. 50c, Amanita virosa. 75c, Boletus edulis. 175c, Amanita muscaria.

1997, Feb. 19 Litho. *Perf. 14x13*

780 A231 40c multicolored .45 .45
781 A231 50c multicolored .55 .55
782 A231 75c multicolored .85 .85
783 A231 175c multicolored 2.00 2.00
Nos. 780-783 (4) 3.85 3.85

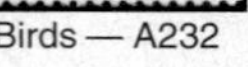

Birds — A232

Greetings Stamps — A233

5c, Melopsittacus undulatus. 25c, Cacatua leadbeateri leadbeateri. 50c, Amazona barbadensis. 75c, Ardea purperea. 85c, Chrysolampis mosquitus. 100c, Balearica pavonina. 110c, Pyrocephalus rubinus. 125c, Phoenicopteurus ruber. 200c, Pandion haliaetus. 225c, Ramphastos sulfuratus.

1997, Mar. 26 Litho. *Perf. 13x14*

784 A232 5c multicolored .20 .20
785 A232 25c multicolored .30 .30
786 A232 50c multicolored .55 .55
787 A232 75c multicolored .90 .90
788 A232 85c multicolored .95 .95
789 A232 100c multicolored 1.10 1.10
790 A232 110c multicolored 1.25 1.25
791 A232 125c multicolored 1.40 1.40
792 A232 200c multicolored 2.25 2.25
793 A232 225c multicolored 2.50 2.50
Nos. 784-793 (10) 11.40 11.40

1997, Apr. 16

794 A233 40c Love .45 .45
795 A233 75c Positivism .85 .85
796 A233 85c Mother's Day .95 .95
797 A233 100c Correspondence 1.10 1.10
798 A233 110c Success 1.25 1.25
799 A233 225c Congratulations 2.75 2.75
Nos. 794-799 (6) 7.35 7.35

Perf. 13x14 on 3 Sides

1997, Apr. 16 Litho.

#799A, like #794. #799B, Correspondence in 3 languages. #799C, Positivism, flower, sun. #799D, like #795. #799E, Success, rising sun. 85c, like #796. 100c, like #797. #799H, like #798. #799I, Love, silhouette of couple. 225c, like #799.

Booklet Stamps

Size: 21x25mm

799A A233 40c multicolored .50 .50
799B A233 40c multicolored .50 .50
799C A233 75c multicolored .95 .95
799D A233 75c multicolored .95 .95
799E A233 75c multicolored .95 .95
799F A233 85c multicolored 1.10 1.10
799G A233 100c multicolored 1.25 1.25
799H A233 110c multicolored 1.40 1.40
799I A233 110c multicolored 1.40 1.40
799J A233 225c multicolored 2.75 2.75
k. Booklet pane of 10, #799A-799J + label 11.75
Complete booklet, #799k 11.75

Stamps arranged in booklet out of Scott order.

Signs of the Chinese Calendar A234

Stylized designs.

1997, May 19 Litho. *Perf. 14x13*

800 A234 5c Rat .20 .20
801 A234 5c Ox .20 .20
802 A234 5c Tiger .20 .20
803 A234 40c Rabbit .45 .45
804 A234 40c Dragon .45 .45
805 A234 40c Snake .45 .45
806 A234 75c Horse .85 .85
807 A234 75c Goat .85 .85
808 A234 75c Monkey .85 .85
809 A234 100c Rooster 1.10 1.10
810 A234 100c Dog 1.10 1.10
811 A234 100c Pig 1.10 1.10
a. Souvenir sheet of 12, #800-811 7.75 7.75
Nos. 800-811 (12) 7.80 7.80

No. 811a for PACIFIC 97. Issued: 5/19/97.

Coins — A235

1997, Aug. 6 *Perf. 13x14*

812 A235 85c Plaka, 2½ cent 1.10 1.10
813 A235 175c Stuiver, 5 cent 2.25 2.25
814 A235 225c Fuèrtè, 2½ gulden 2.75 2.75
Nos. 812-814 (3) 6.10 6.10

A236

Shanghai '97, Intl. Stamp Exhibition — A237

15c, Nampu Grand Bridge, Shanghai. 40c, Giant panda, horiz. 75c, Tiger, New Year 1998.

90c, Buildings in downtown Shanghai.

Perf. 14x13, 13x14

1997, Nov. 19 Litho.

815 A236 15c multicolored .20 .20
816 A237 40c multicolored .45 .45
817 A237 75c multicolored .85 .85
Nos. 815-817 (3) 1.50 1.50

Souvenir Sheet

818 A236 90c multicolored 1.00 1.00

A238

A239

Christmas and New Year: 35c, Left panel of triptych from Roman Catholic Church, Willemstad. 150c, Champagne bottle being opened, calendar.

1997, Dec. 1 *Perf. 13x14*

819 A238 35c multicolored .40 .40
820 A238 150c multicolored 1.75 1.75

1998, Feb. 26 Litho. *Perf. 13x14*

Total Solar Eclipse, Curacao: 85c, Sun partially covered by moon's shadow. 110c, Outer edge of sun showing beyond moon's shadow. 225c, Total solar eclipse.

750c, Hologram of the eclipse.

821 A239 85c multicolored .95 .95
822 A239 110c multicolored 1.25 1.25
823 A239 225c multicolored 2.50 2.50
Nos. 821-823 (3) 4.70 4.70

Souvenir Sheet

824 A239 750c multicolored 9.00 9.00

No. 824 contains a hologram which may be damaged by soaking.

ISRAEL '98 World Stamp Exhibition — A240

Designs: 40c, Dead Sea. 75c, Zion Gate, Jerusalem. 110c, Masada.

225c, Mikvé Israel-Emanuel Synagogue, Curacao.

1998, Apr. 29 Litho. *Perf. 13x14*

825 A240 40c multicolored .45 .45
826 A240 75c multicolored .85 .85
827 A240 110c multicolored 1.25 1.25
Nos. 825-827 (3) 2.55 2.55

Souvenir Sheet

828 A240 225c multicolored 2.50 2.50

Elias Moreno Brandao & Sons, Car Dealership, 75th Anniv. A241

Chevrolet automobiles: 40c, 1923 Superior, Elias Moreno Brandao. 55c, 1934 Roadster. 75c, 1949 Styleline Deluxe. 110c, 1957 Bel Air Convertible. 225c, 1963 Corvette "Stingray." 500c, 1970 Chevelle SS-454.

1998, May 4 *Perf. 14x13*

829 A241 40c multicolored .45 .45
830 A241 55c multicolored .60 .60
831 A241 75c multicolored .85 .85
832 A241 110c multicolored 1.25 1.25
833 A241 225c multicolored 2.50 2.50
834 A241 500c multicolored 5.50 5.50
Nos. 829-834 (6) 11.15 11.15

A242

A243

Advisory Council, 50th Anniv.: 75c, Natl. flag, natl. arms. 85c, Gavel, stars, natl. arms.

1998, June 1 Litho. *Perf. 13x14*

835 A242 75c multicolored .85 .85
836 A242 85c multicolored .95 .95

1998, June 24 *Perf. 13*

Famous People: 40c, Christina Elizabeth Flanders (1908-96). 75c, Abraham Jesurun Dz. (1839-1918). 85c, Gerrit Simeon Newton (1884-1949). 110c, Eduardo Adriana (1925-97).

837 A243 40c multicolored .45 .45
838 A243 75c multicolored .85 .85
839 A243 85c multicolored .95 .95
840 A243 110c multicolored 1.25 1.25
Nos. 837-840 (4) 3.50 3.50

Mailboxes — A244

1998, July 29 Litho. *Perf. 13x14*

841 A244 15c Ireland .20 .20
842 A244 40c Nepal .45 .45
843 A244 75c Uruguay .85 .85
844 A244 85c Curacao .95 .95
Nos. 841-844 (4) 2.45 2.45

See Nos. 932-935.

A245

A246

Privatization of Natl. Postal Service: 75c, Globe, map of North and South America, horiz. 110c, Numbers and tree on screen. 225c, #207 and #846, horiz.

1998, Aug. 5 *Perf. 13*

845 A245 75c multicolored .85 .85
846 A245 110c multicolored 1.25 1.25
847 A245 225c multicolored 2.50 2.50
Nos. 845-847 (3) 4.60 4.60

1998, Aug. 26 *Perf. 13½*

Endangered Species: 5c, Black rhinoceros, horiz. 75c, White-tailed hawk. 125c, White-tailed deer, horiz. 250c, Tiger.

848 A246 5c multicolored .20 .20
849 A246 75c multicolored .85 .85
850 A246 125c multicolored 1.50 1.50
851 A246 250c multicolored 2.75 2.75
Nos. 848-851 (4) 5.30 5.30

Intl. Year of the Ocean A247

1998, Sept. 30 Litho. *Perf. 13*

852 A247 275c Mako shark 3.00 3.00
853 A247 350c Manta ray 4.00 4.00

1998 Philatelic Exhibition, The Hague, Netherlands A248

1998, Oct. 8 *Perf. 14x13*

854 A248 225c No. 213 2.50 2.50
855 A248 500c No. 218 5.75 5.75

Souvenir Sheet

856 A248 500c Nos. 61, 218 6.25 6.25

Price Waterhouse Coopers in Netherlands Antilles, 60th Anniv. — A249

Emblems, company buildings in Julianaplein, minerals: 75c, Lapis lazuli. 225c, Pyrite.

1998, Nov. 13 *Perf. 13½*

857 A249 75c multicolored .85 .85
858 A249 225c multicolored 2.50 2.50
a. Pair, #857-858 3.50 3.50

Christmas A250

Children's drawings: 35c, Christmas tree, vert. 150c, Mail box at Christmas.

Perf. 13x14, 14x13

1998, Dec. 1 Litho.

859 A250 35c multicolored .40 .40
860 A250 150c multicolored 1.75 1.75

Avila Beach Hotel, 50th Anniv. A251

Designs: 75c, Exterior view of hotel, Dr. Pieter Hendrik Maal. 110c, Beach, delonix regia. 225c, Mesquite tree, porposis juliflora.

1999, Feb. 3 Litho. *Perf. 14x13*

861 A251 75c multicolored .85 .85
862 A251 110c multicolored 1.25 1.25
863 A251 225c multicolored 2.50 2.50
Nos. 861-863 (3) 4.60 4.60

New Year 1999 (Year of the Rabbit) and China '99, World Stamp Exhibition, Beijing
A252

Designs: 75c, Rabbit, Great Wall of China. No. 865, Rabbit, Jade Pagoda, Beijing, vert. No. 866, Rabbit, landscape, vert.

Perf. 14x13, 13x14

1999, Mar. 30 **Litho.**

864	A252	75c multicolored	.85	.85
865	A252	225c multicolored	2.50	2.50

Souvenir Sheet

Perf. 13x13½

866	A252	225c multicolored	2.50	2.50

Government Correctional Institute (GOG) for Youth, 50th Anniv.
A253

Design, traditional musical instrument: 40c, Couple dancing, wiri. 75c, Building, bamba. 85c, Man using file and vise, triangle.

Perf. 13x14, 14x13

1999, Apr. 28 **Litho.**

867	A253	40c multi, vert.	.45	.45
868	A253	75c multi, vert.	.85	.85
869	A253	85c multi	.95	.95
		Nos. 867-869 (3)	2.25	2.25

Recorded History of Curacao, 500th Anniv.
A254

Curacao 500 emblem and: 75c, Ship launching. 110c, Houses on Rifwater, Otrobanda, Pasa Kontrami Bridge. 165c, #870-871. 225c, Fort Beeckenburg. 500c, #204, sailing ship.

1999, May 19 ***Perf. 14x13***

870	A254	75c multicolored	.85	.85
871	A254	110c multicolored	1.25	1.25
872	A254	175c multicolored	1.90	1.90
873	A254	225c multicolored	2.50	2.50
874	A254	500c multicolored	5.75	5.75
		Nos. 870-874 (5)	12.25	12.25

Wilson "Papa" Godett (1932-95), Politician — A255

1999, May 28 ***Perf. 13x14***

875	A255	75c multicolored	.85	.85

Millennium
A256

Designs: 5c, Indians, map. 10c, Indian, ship, armored horseman. 40c, Flags of islands, Autonomy monument, Curacao, autonomy document. 75c, Telephone, #5. 85c, Airplane. 100c, Oil refinery. 110c, Satellite dish, underwater cable. 125c, Tourist ship, bridge. 225c, Island residents, music box. 350c, Birds, cacti.

1999, Aug. 4 **Litho.** ***Perf. 13½***

876	A256	5c multicolored	.20	.20
877	A256	10c multicolored	.20	.20
878	A256	40c multicolored	.40	.40
879	A256	75c multicolored	.75	.75
880	A256	85c multicolored	.85	.85
881	A256	100c multicolored	1.00	1.00
882	A256	110c multicolored	1.10	1.10
883	A256	125c multicolored	1.25	1.25
884	A256	225c multicolored	2.25	2.25
885	A256	350c multicolored	3.50	3.50

Size: 31x31mm

Self-Adhesive

Serpentine Die Cut 8

886	A256	5c multicolored	.20	.20
887	A256	10c multicolored	.20	.20
888	A256	40c multicolored	.40	.40
889	A256	75c multicolored	.75	.75
890	A256	85c multicolored	.85	.85
891	A256	100c multicolored	1.00	1.00
892	A256	110c multicolored	1.10	1.10
893	A256	125c multicolored	1.25	1.25
894	A256	225c multicolored	2.25	2.25
895	A256	350c multicolored	3.50	3.50
		Nos. 876-895 (20)	23.00	23.00

A257

Designs: 150c, Church of the Conversion of St. Paul, Saba. 250c, Flamingo, Bonaire. 500c, Courthouse of Philipsburg, St. Martin.

1999, Oct. 1 **Litho.** ***Perf. 14x13***

896	A257	150c multicolored	1.60	1.60
897	A257	250c multicolored	2.75	2.75
898	A257	500c multicolored	5.50	5.50
		Nos. 896-898 (3)	9.85	9.85

Flowers — A258

Designs: No. 899, Allamanda. No. 900, Bougainvillea. No. 901, Gardenia jasminoides. No. 902, Saintpaulia ionantha. No. 903, Cymbidium. No. 904, Strelitzia. No. 905, Cassia fistula. No. 906, Phalaenopsis. No. 907, Doritaenopsis. No. 908, Guzmania. No. 909, Caralluma hexagona. No. 910, Catharanthus roseus.

1999, Nov. 15 ***Perf. 13½***

899	A258	40c multicolored	.45	.45
900	A258	40c multicolored	.45	.45
a.		Pair, #899-900	.90	.90
901	A258	40c multicolored	.45	.45
902	A258	40c multicolored	.45	.45
a.		Pair, #901-902	.90	.90
903	A258	75c multicolored	.80	.80
904	A258	75c multicolored	.80	.80
a.		Pair, #903-904	1.60	1.60
905	A258	75c multicolored	.80	.80
906	A258	75c multicolored	.80	.80
a.		Pair, #905-906	1.60	1.60
907	A258	110c multicolored	1.25	1.25
908	A258	110c multicolored	1.25	1.25
a.		Pair, #907-908	2.50	2.50
909	A258	225c multicolored	2.50	2.50
910	A258	225c multicolored	2.50	2.50
a.		Pair, #909-910	5.00	5.00
		Nos. 899-910 (12)	12.50	12.50

Christmas
A259

Year 2000
A260

1999, Dec. 1 **Litho.** ***Perf. 13x14***

911	A259	35c multi	.40	.40
912	A260	150c multi	1.60	1.60

Greetings Stamps — A261

#913, 40c, #918, 150c, Hearts, roses. #914, 40c, #919, 150c, Mothers, globe. #915, 40c, Father, baby, blocks. #916, 75c, Dog in gift box. #917, 110c, Butterfly, flowers in vase. #920, 225c, Hands, rings.

2000, Jan. 27 **Litho.** ***Perf. 13x14***

913-920	A261	Set of 8	10.00	10.00

New Year 2000 (Year of the Dragon)
A262

2000, Feb. 28 ***Perf. 14x13***

921	A262	110c shown	1.40	1.40

Souvenir Sheet

922	A262	225c Two dragons	2.75	2.75

Fauna
A263

Designs: 40c, Red eye tree toad. 75c, King penguin, vert. 85c, Killer whale, vert. 100c, African elephant, vert. 110c, Chimpanzee, vert. 225c, Indian tiger.

2000, Mar. 29 ***Perf. 14x13, 13x14***

923-928	A263	Set of 6	7.50	7.50

Space — A264

Designs: 75c, Space Shuttle. No. 930, 225c, Astronaut, flag, space station.

2000, June 21 **Litho.** ***Perf. 13x14***

929-930	A264	Set of 2	3.50	3.50

Souvenir Sheet

Perf. 13x13¼

931	A264	225c Colonized planet	2.75	2.75

World Stamp Expo 2000, Anaheim.

Mailbox Type of 1998

Mailboxes from: 110c, Mexico. 175c, Dubai. 350c, England. 500c, United States.

2000, Aug. 8 ***Perf. 13x14***

932-935	A244	Set of 4	13.50	13.50

2000 Summer Olympics, Sydney — A265

75c, Cycling. No. 937, 225c, Running.

2000, Aug. 8 **Litho.** ***Perf. 13x14***

936-937	A265	Set of 2	3.75	3.75

Souvenir Sheet

938	A265	225c Swimming	2.75	2.75

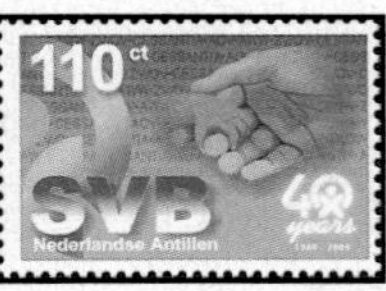

Social Insurance Bank, 40th Anniv.
A266

Designs: 75c, People, islands, vert. 110c, Hands. 225c, Emblem, vert.

2000, Sept. 1 ***Perf. 13x14, 14x13***

939-941	A266	Set of 3	5.00	5.00

Christmas
A267

Songs: 40c, Jingle Bells, vert. 150c, We Wish You a Merry Christmas.

2000, Nov. 15 ***Perf. 13x14, 14x13***

942-943	A267	Set of 2	2.25	2.25

New Year 2001 (Year of the Snake)
A268

Designs: 110c, Red milk snake. 225c, Indian cobra, vert.

2001, Jan. 17 **Litho.** ***Perf. 14x13***

944	A268	110c multi	1.25	1.25

Souvenir Sheet

Perf. 13x14

945	A268	225c multi	2.50	2.50

Hong Kong 2001 Stamp Exhibition — A269

Designs: 25c, Birds in forest. 40c, Palm trees and waterfall. 110c, Spinner dolphins.

2001, Feb. 1 ***Perf. 13x14***

946-948	A269	Set of 3	2.00	2.00

Cats and Dogs — A270

Ships — A271

Designs: 55c, Persian shaded golden. 75c, Burmese bluepoint. 110c, Beagle and American wirehair. 175c, Golden retriever. 225c, German shepherd. 750c, British shorthair black-silver marble.

2001, Mar. 7 **Litho.** ***Perf. 13x14***

949-954	A270	Set of 6	16.00	16.00

2001, Apr. 26 ***Perf. 13x14, 14x13***

Designs: 110c, Z. M. Mars. 275c, Z. M. Alphen. 350c, Z. M. Curaçao, horiz. 500c, Schooner Pioneer, horiz.

955-958	A271	Set of 4	14.00	14.00

Fedjai the Postal Worker — A272

Fedjai: 5c, On bicycle. 40c, With children. 75c, Looking at nest in mailbox. 85c, Talking with woman. 100c, Chased atop mailbox by dog. 110c, Looking at boy's stamp album.

2001, June 5 Litho. *Perf. 13x14*
959-964 A272 Set of 6 5.00 5.00

Cave Bats — A273

Designs: 85c, Map of bat species in Kueba Bosá. 110c, Leptonycteris nivalis curasaoe. 225c, Glosophaga elongata.

2001, Aug. 20 Litho. *Perf. 14x13*
965-967 A273 Set of 3 5.00 5.00

Birds — A274

No. 968: a, 10c, Trochilus polytmus. b, 85c, Pelecanus onocrotalus. c, 110c, Erythrura gouldiae. d, 175c, Passerina ciris. e, 250c, Fratercula arctica. f, 375c, Anhinga anhinga.
Illustration reduced.

2001, Sept. 28 *Perf. 12¾x13½*
968 A274 Block of 6, #a-f 12.00 12.00

Philipsburg Methodist Church, 150th Anniv. — A275

Map of St. Maarten and: 75c, Church building. 110c, Bibles.

2001, Oct. 19 *Perf. 14x13*
969-970 A275 Set of 2 2.25 2.25

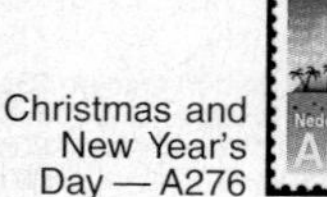

Christmas and New Year's Day — A276

Designs: 40c, Clock, people from 8 countries. 150c, Dove, poinsettias, baby Jesus, and people from 4 countries, vert.

Perf. 13½x12¾, 12¾x13½
2001, Nov. 15 Litho.
971-972 A276 Set of 2 2.25 2.25

Wedding of Prince Willem-Alexander and Máxima Zorreguieta — A277

Designs: 75c, Prince. 110c, Máxima.
No. 975: a, 2.25f, Prince. b, 2.75f, Máxima.

2002, Feb. 2 Litho. *Perf. 12¾x14*
973-974 A277 Set of 2 2.10 2.10

Souvenir Sheet
Perf. 12¾x13½
975 A277 Sheet of 2, #a-b 5.75 5.75

New Year 2002 (Year of the Horse) — A278

Designs: 25c, Horse rearing. 95c, Horse's head.

2002, Mar. 1 *Perf. 12¾x14*
976 A278 25c multi .30 .30

Souvenir Sheet
Perf. 12¾x13½
977 A278 95c multi 1.10 1.10

Flora & Fauna — A279

Designs: 50c, Chlorostilbon mellisugus and Passiflora foetida, vert. 95c, Anolis lineatus and Cordia sebestena. 120c, Odonata. 145c, Coenobita clypeatus. 285c, Polistes versicolor, vert.

Perf. 12¾x13½, 13½x12¾
2002, Mar. 27 Litho.
978-982 A279 Set of 5 8.00 8.00

Butterflies A280

Designs: 25c, Dryas iulia, vert. 145c, Danaus plexippus. 400c, Mechanitis polymnia. 500c, Pyrhapygopsis socrates.

Perf. 12¾x13½, 13½x12¾
2002, May 22 Litho.
983-986 A280 Set of 4 12.50 12.50

Fedjai the Postal Worker Type of 2001

Fedjai: 10c, Jumping rope with children, horiz. 55c, Scolding dog. 95c, Delivering letter to child. 240c, Helping elderly lady across street.

Perf. 13¾x12¾, 12¾x13¾
2002, July 31
987-990 A272 Set of 4 4.50 4.50

Amphilex 2002 Intl. Stamp Exhibition, Amsterdam — A281

Details from the 1885 version of "The Potato Eaters," by Vincent Van Gogh: 70c, 95c, 145c, 240c.
550c, Entire painting, horiz.

Perf. 12¾x13½
2002, Aug. 26 Litho.
991-994 A281 Set of 4 6.25 6.25

Souvenir Sheet
Perf. 14x12¾
995 A281 550c multi 6.25 6.25

Orchids — A282

Designs: 95c, Wingfieldara casseta. 285c, Cymbidium Magna Charta. 380c, Brassolaeliocattleya. 750c, Miltonia spectabilis.

2002, Sept. 27 *Perf. 12¾x14*
996-999 A282 Set of 4 17.00 17.00

Christmas and New Year — A283

Designs: 95c, Christmas tree decorations. 240c, Lanterns.

2002, Nov. 15 *Perf. 14x12¾*
1000-1001 A283 Set of 2 3.75 3.75

Birds — A284

No. 1002: a, 5c, Buteogallus meridionalis. b, 20c, Capito niger. c, 30c, Ara macao. d, 35c, Jacamerops aurea. e, 70c, Florisuga mellivora. f, 85c, Haematoderus militaris. g, 90c, Aratinga aurea. h, 95c, Psarocolius viridis. i, 100c, Sturnella magna, horiz. j, 145c, Aratinga solstitialis, horiz. k, 240c, Trogon viridis. l, 285c, Rhamphastos tucanus.

2002, Dec. 11 Litho. *Perf. 13x14*
1002 A284 Block of 12, #a-l 13.50 13.50

New Year 2003 (Year of the Ram) — A285

Chinese character and: 25c, Ram's head. 95c, Ram.

2003, Feb. 3
1003 A285 25c multi .30 .30

Souvenir Sheet
1004 A285 95c multi 1.10 1.10

Butterflies — A286

No. 1005: a, 5c, Rhetus arcius, vert. b, 10c, Evenus teresina. c, 25c, Bhutanitis thaidina. d, 30c, Semomesia capanea. e, 45c, Papilio machaon. f, 55c, Papilio multicaudata, vert. g, 65c, Graphium weiskei, vert. h, 95c, Ancyluris formosissima venabalis, vert. i, 100c, Euphaedra neophron. j, 145c, Ornithoptera goliath samson. k, 275c, Ancyluris colubra, vert. l, 350c, Papilio lorquinianus, vert.
Illustration reduced.

Perf. 12¾x14 (vert. stamps), 14x12¾
2003, Apr. 23 Litho.
1005 A286 Block of 12, #a-l 13.50 13.50

Printed in sheets of 2 blocks separated by a central gutter.

Miniature Sheet

Musical Instruments — A287

No. 1006: a, 20c, Trumpet. b, 75c, Percussion instruments. c, 145c, Tenor saxophone. d, 285c, Double bass.

2003, May 28 *Perf. 12¾x14*
1006 A287 Sheet of 4, #a-d 6.00 6.00

Johann Enschedé and Sons, Printers, 300th Anniv. — A288

No. 1007: a, 70c, 25-florin bank note, 1827. b, 95c, #4. c, 145c, Revenue stamp. d, 240c, Portion of 1967 bank note.
550c, Enschedé headquarters, Netherlands.

2003, June 3
1007 A288 Sheet of 4, #a-d 6.25 6.25

Souvenir Sheet
1008 A288 550c multi 6.25 6.25

Bank of the Netherlands Antilles, 175th Anniv. — A289

Designs: 95c, Portion of 10-guilder banknote with serial number magnified. 145c, Road map, Bank headquarters. 285c, Early bank document, vert.

Perf. 14x12¾, 12¾x14
2003, June 26
1009-1011 A289 Set of 3 6.00 6.00

Fedjai, the Postal Worker Type of 2001
Miniature Sheet

No. 1012: a, 30c, Fedjai giving gift to Angelina. b, 95c, Fedjai and Angelina at wedding. c, 145c, Fedjai taking pregnant wife on bicycle, horiz. d, 240c, Fedjai shows son to co-workers.

Perf. 12¾x14, 14x12¾ (#1012c)

2003, June 31

1012 A272 Sheet of 4, #a-d 5.75 5.75

Ships — A290

No. 1013: a, 5c, Egyptian boat, 15th cent. B.C. b, 5c, Ship of King Tutankhamen. c, 35c, Picture from Greek vase depicting Ulysses and the Sirens. d, 35c, Egyptian river boat. e, 40c, Greek dromond. f, 40c, Illustration from 15th cent. edition of Virgil's Aeneid. g, 60c, Javanese fusta. h, 60c, Greek trade ship. i, 75c, Venetian cog, 16th cent. j, 75c, Mora from Bayeux Tapestry. k, 85c, HMS Pembroke, ship of Capt. James Cook, vert. l, 85c, Savannah, first transatlantic steamship, 1819, vert.
Illustration reduced.

Perf. 14x12¾, 12¾x14 (vert. stamps)

2003, Aug. 7

1013 A290 Block of 12, #a-l 6.75 6.75

Miniature Sheets

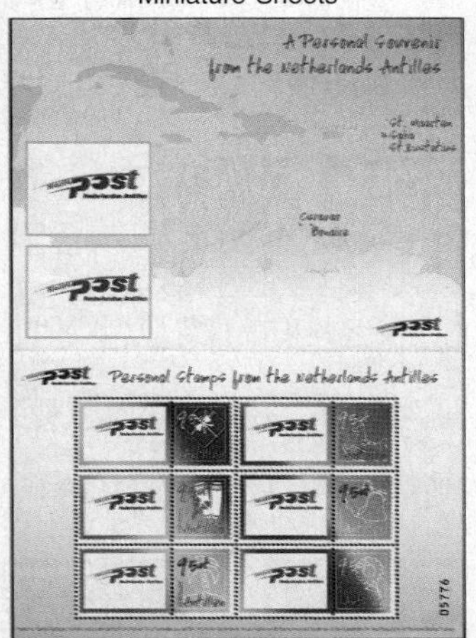

Personalized Stamps — A291

Designs: Nos. 1014a, 1015a, Gift. Nos. 1014b, 1015b, Rocking horse. Nos. 1014c, 1015c, Conga drums. Nos. 1014d, 1015d, Bells. Nos. 1014e, 1015e, Palm tree. Nos. 1014f, 1015f, Flower.

2003, Sept. 17 Litho. *Perf. 13¼x14*

1014 A291 95c Sheet of 6, #a-f, + 6 labels 12.00 12.00

1015 A291 145c Sheet of 6, #a-f, + 6 labels 17.00 17.00

Labels could be personalized. Nos. 1014-1015 each sold for $6 and $8.50 respectively in US funds.

Cats — A292

No. 1016: a, 5c, Bombay. b, 20c, Persian sealpoint. c, 25c, British shorthair blotchy. d, 50c, British blue. e, 65c, Persian chinchilla. f, 75c, Tonkinese red point. g, 85c, Balinese lilac tabbypoint. h, 95c, Persian shaded cameo. i, 100c, Burmilla. j, 145c, Chocolate tortie shaded silver eastern shorthair. k, 150c, Devon Rex silver tabby. l, 285c, Persian black tabby.

2003, Sept. 29 *Perf. 12¾x14*

1016 A292 Block of 12, #a-l 12.50 12.50

Souvenir Sheet

Christmas and New Year's Day — A293

No. 1017 — Cacti with faces and Christmas lights and: a, 75c, Star. b, 240c, Clock.

2003, Nov. 17 Litho. *Perf. 13x14*

1017 A293 Sheet of 2, #a-b 3.50 3.50

Airport Code and Local Attraction A294

Curves and Lines A295

Designs: 50c, BON (Bonaire), slave hut. 75c, CUR (Curaçao), Handelskade, Willemstad. 95c, SAB (Saba), Holy Rosary Roman Catholic Church, Hell's Gate, Anglican Church, Valley. 120c, EUX (St. Eustatius), Simon Docker House, Fort Orange. 145c, SXM (St. Maarten), bird at sunset. 240c, CUR, Queen Emma Bridge. 285c, SXM, Simpson Bay.

2003, Nov. 27 *Perf. 13½x12¾*

1018	A294 50c multi	.55	.55
1019	A294 75c multi	.85	.85
1020	A294 95c multi	1.10	1.10
1021	A294 120c multi	1.40	1.40
1022	A294 145c multi	1.60	1.60
1023	A294 240c multi	2.75	2.75
1024	A294 285c multi	3.25	3.25
1025	A295 380c multi	4.25	4.25
	Nos. 1018-1025 (8)	15.75	15.75

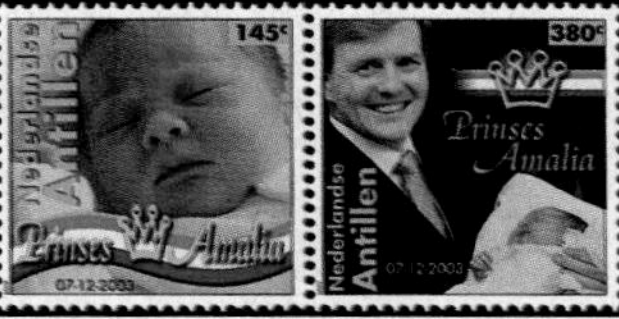

Birth of Princess Catharina-Amalia, Dec. 7, 2003 — A296

No. 1026: a, 145c, Princess Catharina-Amalia. b, 380c, Prince Willem-Alexander and Princess Catharina-Amalia.
Illustration reduced.

2004, Jan. 16 *Perf. 13½x13¾*

1026 A296 Horiz. pair, #a-b 6.00 6.00
c. Miniature sheet, #1026a, 1026b + central label 6.00 6.00

New Year 2004 (Year of the Monkey) — A297

Designs: 95c, Golden snub-nosed monkey. 145c, Monkey holding peach, on fan.

2004, Jan. 21 *Perf. 13x13½*

1027 A297 95c multi 1.10 1.10

Souvenir Sheet

1028 A297 145c multi + 2 labels 1.60 1.60

Houses and Mansions — A298

No. 1029: a, 10c, Belvedère, L. B Smithplein 3. b, 25c, Hoogstraat 27. c, 35c, Landhuis Brievengat. d, 65c, Scharlooweg 102. e, 95c, Hoogstraat 21-25. f, 145c, Villa Maria, Van den Brandhofstraat 3 t/m 6. g, 275c, Werfstraat 6. h, 350c, Landhuis Ronde Klip.
Illustration reduced.

2004, Feb. 20 *Perf. 13½x13*

1029 A298 Block of 8, #a-h 11.50 11.50

Wild Animals — A299

No. 1030: a, 5c, Loxodonta africana. b, 10c, Loxodonta africana, diff. c, 25c, Loxodonta africana, diff. d, 35c, Pan troglodytes. e, 45c, Pan troglodytes, diff. f, 55c, Pan troglodytes, diff. g, 65c, Ursus maritimus. h, 95c, Ursus maritimus, diff. i, 100c, Ursus maritimus, diff. j, 145c, Panthera leo. k, 275c, Panthera leo, diff. l, 350c, Panthera leo, diff.
Illustration reduced.

2004, Mar. 31

1030 A299 Block of 12, #a-l 13.50 13.50

Transportation — A300

No. 1031: a, 10c, Diesel locomotive, 1977. b, 55c, Water dealer and cart, 1900. c, 75c, 1903 Ford Model A. d, 85c, Oil tanker, 2004. e, 95c, 1903 Wright Flyer. f, 145c Penny Farthing bicycles, 1871.
Illustration reduced.

2004, Apr. 27

1031 A300 Block of 6, #a-f 5.25 5.25

String Instruments — A301

No. 1032: a, 70c, Harp. b, 95c, Lute. c, 145c, Violin, horiz. d, 240c, Zither, horiz.

2004, May 26 *Perf. 13x13½, 13½x13*

1032 A301 Block of 4, #a-d 6.25 6.25

Dogs — A302

No. 1033: a, 5c, Miniature pinscher. b, 5c, Pomeranian. c, 35c, Longhaired teckel. d, 35c, Shih tzu. e, 40c, Boxer. f, 40c, Jack Russell terrier. g, 60c, Basset hound. h, 60c, Braque de l'Ariege. i, 75c, Afghan hound. j, 75c, Old English sheepdog (bobtail). k, 85c, Entelbucher Sennen. l, 85c, Mastiff.
Illustration reduced.

2004, June 22 *Perf. 13x13½*

1033 A302 Block of 12, #a-l 6.75 6.75

World Stamp Championship 2004, Singapore — A303

No. 1034: a, 95c, Ship in St. Annabay Harbor, Curaçao, dragon. b, 95c, Flags of Singapore and Netherlands Antilles, lion. c, 145c, Brionplein houses, Curaçao, dragon. d, 145c, Ships at Dr. A. C. Wathey Cruise and Cargo Facility, St. Maarten, lion.
500c, Like No. 1034b.
Illustration reduced.

2004, Aug. 23 *Perf. 13½x13*
1034 A303 Block of 4, #a-d 5.50 5.50

Souvenir Sheet

1035 A303 500c multi 5.75 5.75

Fish and Ducks A304

No. 1036: a, Pomacanthus paru. b, Epinephelus guttatus. c, Mycteroperca interstitialis. d, Holacanthus isabelita. e, Epinephelus itajara. f, Holacanthus ciliaris. g, Anas americana, Sphyreana barracuda. h, Anas discors. i, Anas bahamensis. j, Aythya affinis.

2004, Sept. 28

1036	Block of 10	13.50 13.50
a.	A304 30c multi	.35 .35
b.	A304 65c multi	.75 .75
c.	A304 70c multi	.80 .80
d.	A304 75c multi	.85 .85
e.	A304 85c multi	.95 .95
f.	A304 95c multi	1.00 1.00
g.	A304 100c multi	1.10 1.10
h.	A304 145c multi	1.60 1.60
i.	A304 250c multi	2.75 2.75
j.	A304 285c multi	3.25 3.25

Birds — A305

Designs: 10c, Icterus icterus. 95c, Coereba flaveola. 100c, Zonotrichia capensis. 145c, Sterna hirundo. 250c, Phoenicopterus ruber. 500c, Buteo albicaudatus.

2004, Oct. 8
1037-1042 A305 Set of 6 12.50 12.50

Miniature Sheets

Coats of Arms and Flags — A306

Nos. 1043 and 1044 — Arms of: a, Bonaire. b, Curacao. c, Saba. d, St. Eustatius. e, St. Maarten. f, Flags of Islands of Netherlands Antilles.

2004, Oct. Litho. *Perf. 13½x13¾*
1043 A306 95c Sheet of 6, #a-f, + 6 labels *13.00 13.00*
1044 A306 145c Sheet of 6, #a-f, + 6 labels *19.00 19.00*

Labels on Nos. 1043-1044 could be personalized. The two sheets together sold for €12.42.

Turtles A307

Designs: 100c, Loggerhead turtle. 145c, Kemp's Ridley turtle. 240c, Green turtle. 285c, Olive Ridley turtle. 380c, Hawksbill turtle. 500c, Leatherback turtle.

2004, Dec. 10 Litho. *Perf. 13½x13*
1045-1050 A307 Set of 6 18.50 18.50

Buildings — A308

Beach Scene — A309

2004 Litho. *Die Cut*

Self-Adhesive

1051 A308 145c multi 4.00 4.00
1052 A309 145c multi 4.00 4.00
a. Horiz. pair, #1051-1052 8.00

Nos. 1051-1052 were printed in sheets of 10 containing five of each stamp at the right of the sheet. At the left of the sheet are three stamp-like vignettes lacking die cutting that were not valid for postage. The spaces at the right of the stamps where the birds are shown in the illustration was intended for personalization by customers on cruise ships that came to St. Maarten or Curacao. The three stamp-like vignettes at the left of the sheet also show the same personalized picture. Four different sheets, each depicting different birds in the space for personalization on each stamp and the three vignettes at the left of the sheet, were created as exemplars. The sheets, depicting birds or a personalized image, sold for $20 in US currency. The stamps were for postage for postcards mailed anywhere in the world.

Flowers A310

Designs: 65c, Hibiscus rosa sinensis. 76c, Plumbago auriculata. 97c, Tecoma stans. 100c, Ixora coccinea. 122c, Catharanthus roseus. 148c, Lantana camara. 240c, Tradescantia pallida. 270c, Nerium oleander. 285c, Plumeria obtusa. 350c, Bougainvillea spectabilis.

2005, Jan. 3 Litho. *Perf. 13½x13*

1053	A310 65c multi	.75 .75
1054	A310 76c multi	.85 .85
1055	A310 97c multi	1.10 1.10
1056	A310 100c multi	1.10 1.10
1057	A310 122c multi	1.40 1.40
1058	A310 148c multi	1.75 1.75
1059	A310 240c multi	2.75 2.75
1060	A310 270c multi	3.00 3.00
1061	A310 285c multi	3.25 3.25
1062	A310 350c multi	4.00 4.00
	Nos. 1053-1062 (10)	19.95 19.95

New Year 2005 (Year of the Rooster) — A311

Designs: 145c, Rooster and Chinese character. 500c, Two roosters.

2005, Feb. 9 *Perf. 13x13½*
1063 A311 145c multi 1.60 1.60

Souvenir Sheet

1064 A311 500c multi 5.75 5.75

Souvenir Sheet

Queen Beatrix, 25th Anniv. of Reign — A312

Photos: a, Coronation, 1980. b, Giving speech, 1991. c, With Nelson Mandela, 1999. d, Visiting colonies, 1999. e, At European Parliament, 2004.

2005, Apr. 30 *Perf. 13¼x13¾*

1065	A312 Sheet of 5	13.00 13.00
a.	50c multi	.60 .60
b.	97c multi	1.10 1.10
c.	145c multi	1.60 1.60
d.	285c multi	3.25 3.25
e.	550c multi	6.25 6.25

Houses & Mansions Type of 2004

No. 1066: a, 10c, Scharlooweg 76. b, 21c, Landhuis Zeelandia. c, 25c, Berg Altena. d, 35c, Landhuis Dokterstuin. e, 97c, Landhuis Santa Martha. f, 148c, Landhuis Seri Papaya. g, 270c, Landhuis Rooi Katooje. h, 300c, Plaza Horacio Hoyer 19.

2005, May 31 *Perf. 13½x13*
1066 A298 Block of 8, #a-h 10.50 10.50

Paintings by Vincent van Gogh — A313

No. 1067: a, 10c, Vase with Fourteen Sunflowers, detail. b, 65c, Sunflowers, detail. c, 80c, Self-portrait. d, 120c, Sunflowers, detail, diff. e, 150c, Vase with Fourteen Sunflowers. f, 175c, Joseph Roulin.
500c, Sunflowers, detail, diff.

2005, June 16 *Perf. 13x13½*
1067 A313 Block of 6, #a-f 6.75 6.75

Souvenir Sheet

1068 A313 500c multi 5.75 5.75

Otrobanda Section of Willemstad, 300th Anniv. (in 2007) — A314

No. 1069: a, 100c, Breedestraat. b, 150c, Wharf area. c, 285c, Rifwater. d, 500c, Brionplein bus stop.

Illustration reduced.

2005, July 28 *Perf. 13½x13*
1069 A314 Block of 4, #a-d 12.00 12.00

Fruit — A315

2005, Aug. 31

1070	Block of 10	15.00 15.00
a.	A315 25c Papaya	.30 .30
b.	A315 45c Pomegranates	.50 .50
c.	A315 70c Mango	.80 .80
d.	A315 75c Bananas	.85 .85
e.	A315 85c Cashews	.95 .95
f.	A315 97c Soursops	1.10 1.10
g.	A315 145c Tamarinds	1.60 1.60
h.	A315 193c Watermelons	2.25 2.25
i.	A315 270c Gennips	3.00 3.00
j.	A315 300c Sea grapes	3.50 3.50

Worldwide Fund for Nature (WWF) — A316

No. 1071: a, 51c, Blushing star coral. b, 148c, Rose coral. c, 270c, Smooth flower coral. d, 750c, Symmetrical brain coral.
Illustration reduced.

2005, Sept. 29
1071 A316 Block of 4, #a-d 14.00 14.00

Musical Instruments A317

Designs: 55c, Bandoneon. 97c, Bagpipe, vert. 145c, Vina. 195c, Samisen, vert. 240c, Shofar. 285c, Kaha di òrgel, vert.

2005, Nov. 8 *Perf. 13½x13, 13x13½*
1072-1077 A317 Set of 6 11.50 11.50

A318

A319

Santa Claus and: 10c, Children's hands. 97c, Children, horiz. 148c, Ornament, horiz. 580c, Chair.

Perf. 13x13½, 13½x13

2005, Nov. 17
1078-1081 A318 Set of 4 9.50 9.50

Christmas.

2005, Dec. 2 *Perf. 13x13½*

Designs: 97c, Aerial view of St. Elizabeth Hospital, Willemstad. 145c, Stained glass window in hospital chapel. 300c, Entrance to first community hospital.

1082-1084 A319 Set of 3 6.25 6.25

St. Elizabeth Hospital, 150th anniv.

New Year 2006 (Year of the Dog) — A320

Chinese character and: 100c, Porcelain dogs. 149c, Various dog breeds.
500c, Dog and zodiac animals.

2006, Jan. 30 ***Perf. 13½x13***

1085-1086 A320 Set of 2 2.75 2.75

Souvenir Sheet

1087 A320 500c multi 5.75 5.75

Equines A321

No. 1088: a, Turkmenian Kulan. b, Rhineland heavy draft horse. c, Donkey. d, Mule. e, Hanoverian and Arabian horses.

Perf. 13¼x12¾

2006, Feb. 24 **Litho.**

1088	Horiz. strip of 5	13.00	13.00
a.	A321 50c multi	.55	.55
b.	A321 100c multi	1.10	1.10
c.	A321 149c multi	1.75	1.75
d.	A321 285c multi	3.25	3.25
e.	A321 550c multi	6.25	6.25

Frogs A322

Designs: 55c, Hyla cinerea. 100c, Dendrobates tinctorius. 149c, Dendrobates azureus. 405c, Epipedobates tricolor.

2006, Mar. 10 ***Perf. 13¼x12¾***

1089-1092 A322 Set of 4 8.00 8.00

Butterflies A323

Designs: 24c, Danaus chrysippus. 53c, Prepona praeneste. 100c, Caligo uranus. 149c, Ituna lamirus. 285c, Euphaedra gausape. 335c, Morpho hecuba.

2006, Apr. 7

1093-1098 A323 Set of 6 11.00 11.00

Orchids A324

No. 1099: a, Brassolaeliocattleya Susan Harry M. G. R. b, Miltoniopsis Jean Sabourin. c, Promenaea xanthina Sylvan Sprite. d, Paphiopedilum Streathamense Wedgewood, vert. e, Cattleya chocoensis Linden, vert. f, Disa kewensis Rita Helen, vert.

Perf. 13¼x12¾, 12¾x13¼ (vert. stamps)

2006, Apr. 26

1099	Block of 6	21.00	21.00
a.	A324 153c multi	1.75	1.75
b.	A324 240c multi	2.75	2.75
c.	A324 285c multi	3.25	3.25
d.	A324 295c multi	3.25	3.25
e.	A324 380c multi	4.25	4.25
f.	A324 500c multi	5.75	5.75

Automobiles A325

Designs: 51c, 1976 MGB. 100c, 1963 Studebaker Avanti. 149c, 1953 Pegaso Cabriolet. 153c, 1939 Delage Aerosport. 195c, 1924 Hispano-Suiza Boulogne. 750c, 1903 Pierce Arrow Motorette.

2006, May 10 ***Perf. 13¼x12¾***

1100-1105 A325 Set of 6 16.00 16.00

Washington 2006 World Philatelic Exhibition — A326

No. 1106: a, 100c, Mailboxes of United States and Netherlands Antilles. b, 100c, Queen Emma Bridge, Curaçao, George Washington Bridge, New York and New Jersey. c, 149c, UPU emblem. d, 149c, Fokker F18-Snip, Fokker F4 airplanes.

405c, U.S. Capitol, Palace of the Governor of the Netherlands Antilles.

Illustration reduced.

2006, May 26

1106 A326 Block of 4, #a-d 5.75 5.75

Souvenir Sheet

1107 A326 405c multi 4.75 4.75

Otrobanda Type of 2005

Designs: 100c, Hoogstraat. 149c, Emmabrug. 335c, Pasa Kontrami. 500c, Seaman's Home.

2006, June 16

1108-1111 A314 Set of 4 12.50 12.50

Greetings A327

Designs: 52c, Bless you. 55c, Love. 77c, All the best. 95c, Regards. 1.00g, Go for it. 1.49g, Tolerance. 1.53g, Positivism. 2.85g, Keep on going. 3.35g, Success. 4.05g, Be good.

2006, July 31

1112-1121 A327 Set of 10 19.00 19.00

Birds — A328

No. 1122: a, Taeniopygia guttata. b, Parus caeruleus, vert. c, Pitta genus. d, Pyrrhula pyrrhula, vert. e, Calospiza fastuosa. f, Cosmopsarus regius, vert. g, Coracias caudatus, vert. h, Merops apiaster, vert. i, Icterus nigrogularis. j, Dendrocopus major, vert. k, Amazona barbadensis. l, Alcedo atthis, vert.

Perf. 13¼x12¾, 12¾x13¼ (vert. stamps)

2006, Aug. 18

1122	Block of 12	8.25	8.25
a.-b.	A328 5c Either single	.20	.20
c.-d.	A328 35c Either single	.35	.35
e.-f.	A328 60c Either single	.65	.65
g.-h.	A328 75c Either single	.85	.85
i.-j.	A328 85c Either single	.95	.95
k.-l.	A328 100c Either single	1.10	1.10

Miniature Sheets

Personalized Stamps — A329

Nos. 1123 and 1124: a, Dog, "Thank you." b, Flower, "Missing you." c, Hearts, "Love you." d, Cat, "Hello." e, Teddy bear, "Hugs & kisses." f, Dolphin, "Wish you were here."

Perf. 13¼x13¾

2006, Aug. 26 **Litho.**

Stamps Inscribed "Local Mail"

1123 A329 (1g) Sheet of 6, #a-f, + 6 labels 11.50 11.50

Stamps Inscribed "International Mail"

1124 A329 (1.49g) Sheet of 6, #a-f, + 6 labels 17.00 17.00

On day of issue, No. 1123 sold for 10g, and No. 1124 sold for 15g. Labels could be personalized. Labels shown are generic.

Rembrandt (1606-69), Painter — A330

No. 1125: a, 70c, The Nightwatch (detail of girl). b, 100c, De Staalmeesters. c, 153c, The Jewish Bride (detail). d, 285c, Self-portrait.

550c, The Nightwatch (detail of men).

Perf. 12¾x13¼

2006, Sept. 28 **Litho.**

1125 A330 Block of 4, #a-d 7.00 7.00

Souvenir Sheet

1126 A330 550c multi 6.25 6.25

Souvenir Sheet

Royal Visit of Queen Beatrix — A331

No. 1127 — Various photos of Queen Beatrix with background colors of: a, 149c, Red. b, 285c, Blue. c, 335c, Yellow. d, 750c, Orange.

2006, Nov. 13 ***Perf. 13¼x12¾***

1127 A331 Sheet of 4, #a-d 17.00 17.00

Christmas A332

Designs: 45c, Candles. 100c, Bells. 149c, Candles. 215c, Bells. 285c, Steeple. 380c, Flower.

2006, Nov. 15

1128-1133 A332 Set of 6 13.50 13.50

Fauna — A333

No. 1134: a, Cacatua leadbeateri leadbeateri. b, Aptenocytes patagonica. c, Pan troglodytes. d, Stenella longirostris. e, Anolis lineatus and Cordia sebestina, horiz. f, Passerina ciris. g, Dryas lulia. h, Bombay cat. i, Epinephelus guttatus, horiz. j, Panthera leo, horiz. k, Pomeranian dog. l, Hawksbill turtle, horiz.

Perf. 12¾x13¼, 13¼x12¾

2007, Jan. 26 **Litho.**

1134	Block of 12	14.00	14.00
a.	A333 3c multi	.20	.20
b.	A333 25c multi	.30	.30
c.	A333 53c multi	.60	.60
d.	A333 60c multi	.65	.65
e.	A333 80c multi	.90	.90
f.	A333 81c multi	.90	.90
g.	A333 95c multi	1.10	1.10
h.	A333 106c multi	1.25	1.25
i.	A333 145c multi	1.60	1.60
j.	A333 157c multi	1.75	1.75
k.	A333 161c multi	1.90	1.90
l.	A333 240c multi	2.75	2.75

New Year 2007 (Year of the Pig) — A334

Designs: 104c, Berkshire pig. 155c, Wart hog.

500c, Pig, vert.

2007, Feb. 20 ***Perf. 13¼x12¾***

1135-1136 A334 Set of 2 3.00 3.00

Souvenir Sheet

Perf. 12¾x13¼

1137 A334 500c multi 5.75 5.75

Islands — A335

Designs: 1c, Flag of Bonaire, divers and marine life. 2c, Flag of Curaçao, royal poinciana flowers. 3c, Flag of Saba, The Bottom. 4c, Flag of Statia (St. Eustatius), cannons at Fort Orange. 5c, Flag of St. Maarten, cruise ship and pier. 104c, Map of Bonaire, flamingos, horiz. 285c, Map of Curaçao, Chobolobo Landhouse, laraha tree, horiz. 335c, Map of Saba, houses, horiz. 405c, Map of Statia, oil storage tanks, horiz. 500c, Map of St. Maarten, Guavaberry Emporium, horiz.

Perf. 12¾x13¼, 13¼x12¾

2007, Mar. 1

1138	A335	1c multi	.20	.20
1139	A335	2c multi	.20	.20
1140	A335	3c multi	.20	.20
1141	A335	4c multi	.20	.20

1142	A335	5c multi	.20	.20
1143	A335	104c multi	1.25	1.25
1144	A335	285c multi	3.25	3.25
1145	A335	335c multi	3.75	3.75
1146	A335	405c multi	4.75	4.75
1147	A335	500c multi	5.75	5.75
	Nos. 1138-1147 (10)		19.75	19.75

Ananzi the Spider A336

No. 1148 — Ananzi with: a, Turtle. b, Shark. c, Parrot. d, Cow. e, Dog. f, Goat. g, Chicken. h, Donkey.

2007, Mar. 21 ***Perf. 13¼x12¾***

1148		Block of 8	10.00	10.00
a.-h.	A336	104c Any single	1.25	1.25

Saba Lace Designs — A337

Various lace designs with background colors of: 59c, Red. 80c, Green. 95c, Blue. 104c, Red. 155c, Green. 159c, Blue.

2007, Apr. 20 ***Perf. 12¾x13¼***

1149-1154 A337 Set of 6 7.50 7.50

Marine Life — A338

No. 1155: a, School of fish and sea floor. b, Portuguese man-of-war. c, Coral reef. d, Sea turtle. e, Sea anemones. f, Fish.

2007, May 22

1155		Block of 6	20.00	20.00
a.	A338	104c multi	1.25	1.25
b.	A338	155c multi	1.75	1.75
c.	A338	195c multi	2.25	2.25
d.	A338	335c multi	3.75	3.75
e.	A338	405c multi	4.75	4.75
f.	A338	525c multi	6.00	6.00

Fruits and Vegetables — A339

No. 1156: a, Grapes, Brussels sprouts, tomatoes, peppers and bananas. b, Pumpkins. c, Cucumber, tomatoes, corn, leeks. d, Strawberries, orange, peaches, pineapple. e, Avocados, horiz. f, Lemons, horiz. g, Peppers, corn, potato, mushrooms, horiz. h, Mangos, horiz.

Perf. 12¾x13¼, 13¼x12¾

2007, June 19

1156		Block of 8	11.50	11.50
a.	A339	10c multi	.20	.20
b.	A339	25c multi	.30	.30
c.	A339	35c multi	.40	.40
d.	A339	65c multi	.75	.75
e.	A339	95c multi	1.10	1.10
f.	A339	145c multi	1.60	1.60
g.	A339	275c multi	3.00	3.00
h.	A339	350c multi	4.00	4.00

Otrabanda Type of 2005

Designs: 104c, Brionplein Square. 155c, Jopi Building and Hotel Otrabanda. 285c, Kura Hulanda. 380c, Luna Blou.

2007, July 26 ***Perf. 13¼x12¾***

1157-1160 A314 Set of 4 10.50 10.50

Nature — A340

No. 1161: a, 30c, Nautilus shell. b, 65c, Turtles on beach. c, 70c, Grasshopper. d, 75c, Cactus. e, 85c, Swamp. f, 95c, Bird on cactus. g, 104c, Surf spray at rocks. h, 145c, Plants near water. i, 250c, Rainbow in rainforest. j, 285c, Sun on horizon.

Perf. 12¾x 13¼

2007, Aug. 22 **Litho.**

1161 A340 Block of 10, #a-j 13.50 13.50

Paintings by Dutch Artists — A341

No. 1162: a, 104c, Portrait of a Man (probably Nicolaes Hasselaer), by Frans Hals. b, 104c, Wedding of Isaak Abrahamsz Massa and Beatrix van der Lean, by Hals. c, 155c, The Merry Drinker, by Hals. d, 155c, Serenade, by Judith Leyster.

550c, The Meagre Company, by Hals, horiz.

2007, Sept. 20 ***Perf. 12¾x13¼***

1162 A341 Block of 4, #a-d 6.00 6.00

Souvenir Sheet

Perf. 13¼x12¾

1163 A341 550c multi 6.25 6.25

Dutch Royalty — A342

No. 1164: a, 50c, Queen Emma (1858-1934). b, 104c, Queen Wilhelmina (1880-1962). c, 155c, Queen Juliana (1909-2004). d, 285c, Queen Beatrix. e, 380c, Princess Máxima. f, 550c, Princess Catharina-Amalia.

2007, Oct. 10 ***Perf. 12¾x13¼***

1164 A342 Block of 6, #a-f 17.50 17.50

Christmas and New Year — A343

Designs: 48c, Candle. 104c, Gifts under Christmas tree. 155c, Musical notes and song lyrics, horiz. 215c, "2008" above "2007," horiz.

Perf. 12¾x13¼, 13¼x12¾

2007, Nov. 15 **Litho.**

1165-1168 A343 Set of 4 6.00 6.00

Mailboxes — A344

No. 1169 — Various mailboxes with panel color of: a, 20c, Yellow. b, 104c, Green. c, 240c, Light blue. d, 285c, Lilac. e, 380c, Orange. f, 500c, Brown.

2007, Dec. 3 ***Perf. 12¾x13¼***

1169 A344 Block of 6, #a-f 17.50 17.50

Lighthouses — A345

No. 1170: a, Fort Oranje, Bonaire. b, Malmok, Bonaire. c, Noordpunt, Curaçao. d, Klein Curaçao. e, Willemstoren, Bonaire. f, Bullenbaai, Curaçao.

2008, Jan. 21

1170 A345 158c Block of 6, #a-f 11.00 11.00

New Year 2008 (Year of the Rat) — A346

Designs: 106c, Stylized rat. 158c, Rat. 500c, Rat on branch, horiz.

2008, Feb. 7 ***Perf. 12¾x13¼***

1171-1172 A346 Set of 2 3.00 3.00

Souvenir Sheet

Perf. 13¼x12¾

1173 A346 500c multi 5.75 5.75

Dutch Royalty — A347

No. 1174: a, 75c, Princess Catharina-Amalia. b, 100c, Princess, diff. c, 125c, Crown Prince Willem-Alexander. d, 250c, Crown

Prince, diff. e, 375c, Queen Beatrix. f, 500c, Queen, diff.

2008, Feb. 28 *Perf. 12¾x13¼*
1174 A347 Block of 6, #a-f 16.00 16.00

Global Warming — A348

No. 1175: a, 50c, Smokestacks. b, 75c, Polar bear. c, 125c, Windmills. d, 250c, Beach and lighthouse.
Illustration reduced.

2008, Mar. 20 *Perf. 13¼x12¾*
1175 A348 Block of 4, #a-d 5.75 5.75

2008 Summer Olympics, Beijing — A349

No. 1176: a, 25c, Runner. b, 35c, Gymnast on rings. c, 75c, Swimmer. d, 215c, Cyclist.

2008, Apr. 1 *Perf. 12¾x13¼*
1176 A349 Block of 4, #a-d 4.00 4.00

Stamp Passion Philatelic Exhibition, the Netherlands — A350

No. 1177: a, 75c, Netherlands Antilles #C14. b, 100c, Netherlands Antilles #29. c, 125c, Netherlands Antilles #CB19. d, 250c, Netherlands #O32. e, 375c, Netherlands #134. f, 500c, Netherlands Antilles #187.

2008, Apr. 11
1177 A350 Block of 6, #a-f 16.00 16.00

Images of stamps shown on Nos. 1177a, 1177c and 1177e are distorted.

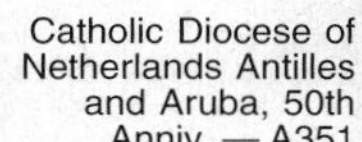

Catholic Diocese of Netherlands Antilles and Aruba, 50th Anniv. — A351

Designs: 59c, Chapel of Alto Vista, Aruba. 106c, Cross at Seru Largu, Bonaire. 158c, St. Ann Church, Curaçao. 240c, Sacred Heart Church, Saba. 285c, Roman Catholic Church of Oranjestad, St. Eustatius. 335c, Mary Star of the Sea Church, St. Maarten.

2008, Apr. 28
1178-1183 A351 Set of 6 13.50 13.50

Dolls Depicting Women Doing Work — A352

No. 1184: a, 145c, Pounding corn (Batidó di maíshi den pilon). b, 145c, Selling fish (Bendedó di piská). c, 145c, Baking fish (Hasadó di masbangu riba bleki). d, 145c, Roasting coffee beans (Totadó di kòfi). e, 155c, Scrubbing clothes on scrub board (Labadera). f, 155c, Carrying basket of clothes (Labadó di paña na laman). g, 155c, Grinding corn on coral (Muladó di maíshi chikí riba pieda). h, 155c, Weaving hat (Trahadó di sombré).

2008, May 15
1184 A352 Block of 8, #a-h 13.50 13.50

Paintings by Johannes Vermeer (1632-75) — A353

No. 1185: a, 145c, Little Street. b, 145c, Girl with Pearl Earring. c, 155c, Woman in Blue Reading Letter. d, 155c, The Love Letter.
500c, The Milkmaid.

2008, June 23
1185 A353 Sheet of 4, #a-d, + 2 labels 6.75 6.75

Souvenir Sheet

1186 A353 500c multi 5.75 5.75

Windows A354

Various windows.

2008, July 8 *Perf. 13¾*
1187 A354 5c multi .20 .20
1188 A354 106c multi, vert. 1.25 1.25
1189 A354 285c multi, vert., diff. 3.25 3.25
a. Souvenir sheet of 5, # 1187-1189, Aruba #330, Netherlands #1311, + etiquette 4.75 4.75

Nos. 1188-1189 were only available in No. 1189a. No. 1187 also was available in Aruba No. 332a and in Netherlands Nos. 1313a and 1313b.

Shells A355

Designs: 20c, Cypraea zebra. 40c, Charonia variegata. 65c, Calliostoma armillata. 106c, Strombus gigas. 158c, Pina carnea. 285c, Olivia sayana. 335c, Natica canrena. 405c, Voluta musica.

Perf. 13¼x12¾

2008, Sept. 19 **Litho.**

1190	A355	20c multi	.25	.25
1191	A355	40c multi	.45	.45
1192	A355	65c multi	.75	.75
1193	A355	106c multi	1.25	1.25
1194	A355	158c multi	1.75	1.75
1195	A355	285c multi	3.25	3.25
1196	A355	335c multi	3.75	3.75
1197	A355	405c multi	4.75	4.75
		Nos. 1190-1197 (8)	16.20	16.20

African Animals — A356

No. 1198: a, 75c, Giraffes, vert. b, 150c, Elephants. c, 175c, Cheetahs. d, 250c, Zebras.
No. 1199, Impalas, vert.
Illustration reduced.

Perf. 13¼x12¾, 12¾x13¼ (vert. stamps)

2008, Oct. 2
1198 A356 Block of 4, #a-d 7.50 7.50

Souvenir Sheet

1199 A356 250c multi 3.00 3.00

SEMI-POSTAL STAMPS

Catalogue values for unused stamps in this section are for Never Hinged items.

Nos. 132, 133 and 135 Surcharged in Black

1947, Dec. 1 **Unwmk.** *Perf. 12½*

B1	A26	1½c + 2½c on 6c	.90	.80
B2	A26	2½c + 5c on 10c	.90	.80
B3	A26	5c + 7½c on 15c	.90	.80
		Nos. B1-B3 (3)	2.70	2.40

The surtax was for the National Inspanning Welzijnszorg in Nederlandsch Indie, relief organization for Netherlands Indies.

Curaçao Children
SP1 SP2

Design: Nos. B6, B9, Girl.

1948, Nov. 3 **Photo.** *Perf. 12½x12*

B4	SP1	6c + 10c ol brn	2.25	1.75
B5	SP2	10c + 15c brt red	2.25	1.75
B6	SP2	12½c + 20c Prus grn	2.25	1.75
B7	SP1	15c + 25c brt bl	2.25	1.75
B8	SP2	20c + 30c red brn	2.25	1.75
B9	SP2	25c + 35c purple	2.25	1.75
		Nos. B4-B9 (6)	13.50	10.50

The surtax was for child welfare and the White/Yellow Cross Foundation.

Leapfrog — SP4

Ship and Gull — SP5

Designs: 5c+2½c, Flying kite. 6c+2½c, Girls swinging. 12½c+5c, "London Bridge." 25c+10c, Rolling hoops.

Perf. 14½x13½

1951, Aug. 16 **Unwmk.**

B10	SP4	1 ½c + 1c pur	1.75	2.10
B11	SP4	5c + 2 ½c brn	10.00	4.50
B12	SP4	6c + 2 ½c blue	10.00	4.50
B13	SP4	12 ½c + 5c red	10.00	4.50
B14	SP4	25c + 10c dl grn	10.00	4.00
		Nos. B10-B14 (5)	41.75	19.60

The surtax was for child welfare.

1952, July 16 ***Perf. 13x14***

Designs: 6c+4c, Sailor and lighthouse. 12 ½c+7c, Prow of sailboat. 15c+10c, Ships. 25c+15c, Ship, compass and anchor.

B15	SP5	1 ½c + 1c dk grn	1.00	1.10
B16	SP5	6c + 4c choc	8.00	3.25
B17	SP5	12 ½c + 7c red vio	8.00	3.50
B18	SP5	15c + 10c dp bl	10.00	4.25
B19	SP5	25c + 15c red	9.00	3.25
		Nos. B15-B19 (5)	36.00	15.35

The surtax was for the seamen's welfare fund.

No. 226 Surcharged in Black

1953, Feb. 21

B20	A45	22 ½c + 7 ½c on 1 ½g	.90	1.00

The surtax was for flood relief in the Netherlands.

Tribulus Cistoides SP6

Flowers: 7 ½c+5c, Yellow hibiscus. 15c+5c, Oleander. 22 ½c+7 ½c, Cactus. 25c+10c, Red hibiscus.

1955, May 17 **Photo.** ***Perf. 14x13***

Flowers in Natural Colors

B21	SP6	1 ½c + 1c bl grn & dk bl	.30	.35
B22	SP6	7 ½c + 5c dp ultra	2.50	1.75
B23	SP6	15c + 5c ol grn	2.50	1.90
B24	SP6	22 ½c + 7 ½c dk bl	2.50	1.75
B25	SP6	25c + 10c ind & gray	2.50	1.90
		Nos. B21-B25 (5)	10.30	7.65

The surtax was for child welfare.

Prince Bernhard and Queen Juliana SP7

1955, Oct. 19 ***Perf. 11x12***

B26	SP7	7 ½c + 2 ½c rose brn	.20	.20
B27	SP7	22 ½c + 7 ½c dp bl	.80	.80

Royal visit to the Netherlands Antilles, Oct. 1955.

Surtax paid for a gift.

Lord Baden-Powell SP8

1957, Feb. 22 ***Perf. 14x13½***

B28	SP8	6c + 1 ½c org yel	.40	.40
B29	SP8	7 ½c + 2 ½c dp grn	.40	.40
B30	SP8	15c + 5c red	.40	.40
		Nos. B28-B30 (3)	1.20	1.20

50th anniv. of the Boy Scout movement.

Soccer Player — SP9

Map of Central America and the Caribbean SP10

Designs: 15c+5c, Goalkeeper catching ball. 22 ½c+7 ½c, Men playing soccer.

1957, Aug. 6 ***Perf. 12x11, 11x12***

B31	SP9	6c + 2 ½c org	.40	.50
B32	SP10	7 ½c + 5c dk red	.80	.90
B33	SP9	15c + 5c brt bl grn	.90	.90
B34	SP9	22 ½c + 7 ½c brt bl	.90	.70
		Nos. B31-B34 (4)	3.00	3.00

8th Central American and Caribbean Soccer Championships, Aug. 11-25.

Surtax was for organizing costs.

American Kestrel — SP11

Flag and Map — SP12

Birds: 7 ½+1 ½c, Yellow oriole. 15+2 ½c, Common ground doves. 22 ½+2 ½c, Brown-throated parakeet.

1958, Apr. 15 **Photo.** ***Perf. 13½x14***

B35	SP11	2 ½c + 1c multi	.25	.25
B36	SP11	7 ½c + 1 ½c multi	.70	.60
B37	SP11	15c + 2 ½c multi	.80	.80
B38	SP11	22 ½c + 2 ½c multi	.90	.70
		Nos. B35-B38 (4)	2.65	2.35

The surtax was for child welfare.

1958, Dec. 1 **Litho.** ***Perf. 13½***

Cross in Red

B39	SP12	6c + 2c red brn	.30	.30
B40	SP12	7 ½c + 2 ½c bl grn	.40	.40
B41	SP12	15c + 5c org yel	.40	.40
B42	SP12	22 ½c + 7 ½c blue	.40	.40
		Nos. B39-B42 (4)	1.50	1.50

The surtax was for the Red Cross.

Community House, Zeeland SP13

Historic buildings: 7 ½c+2 ½c, Molenplein. 15c+5c, Saba, vert. 22 ½c+7 ½c, Scharlooburg. 25c+7 ½c, Community House, Brievengat.

Perf. 14x13½, 13½x14

1959, Sept. 16 **Litho.**

B43	SP13	6c + 1 ½c multi	.80	.70
B44	SP13	7 ½c + 2 ½c multi	.80	.80
B45	SP13	15c + 5c multi	.80	.80
B46	SP13	22 ½c + 7 ½c multi	.80	.80
B47	SP13	25c + 7 ½c multi	.80	.80
		Nos. B43-B47 (5)	4.00	3.90

The surtax went to the Foundation for the Preservation of Historical Monuments.

Fish — SP14

Designs. 10c+2c, SCUBA diver with spear gun, vert. 25c+5c, Two fish.

1960, Aug. 24 **Photo.** ***Perf. 13½***

B48	SP14	10c + 2c sapphire	.80	.80
B49	SP14	20c + 3c multi	1.10	1.10
B50	SP14	25c + 5c blk, brt pink & dk bl	1.10	1.10
		Nos. B48-B50 (3)	3.00	3.00

The surtax was for the fight against cancer.

Infant — SP15

Designs: 10c+3c, Girl and doll. 20c+6c, Boy on beach. 25c+8c, Children in school.

1961, July 24 **Litho.** ***Perf. 13½x14***

Designs in Black

B51	SP15	6c + 2c lt yel grn	.20	.20
B52	SP15	10c + 3c rose red	.20	.20
B53	SP15	20c + 6c yellow	.20	.20
B54	SP15	25c + 8c orange	.20	.20
		Nos. B51-B54 (4)	.80	.80

The surtax was for child welfare.

Globe and Knight — SP16

1962, May 2 ***Perf. 13½x14½***

B55	SP16	10c + 5c green	.60	.55
B56	SP16	20c + 10c carmine	.60	.55
B57	SP16	25c + 10c dk bl	.60	.55
		Nos. B55-B57 (3)	1.80	1.65

Intl. Candidates Chess Tournament, Willemstad, May-June.

No. 248 Surcharged

1963, Mar. 21

B58	A56	20c + 10c crimson & gray	.40	.40

FAO "Freedom from Hunger" campaign.

Child and Flowers — SP17

Bougainvillea SP18

Designs: 6c+3c, Three girls and flowers, horiz. 10c+5c, Girl with ball and trees, horiz. 20c+10c, Three boys with flags, horiz. 25c+12c, Singing boy.

Perf. 14½x13½, 13½x14½

1963, Oct. 23 **Photo.** **Unwmk.**

B59	SP17	5c + 2c multi	.25	.25
B60	SP17	6c + 3c multi	.25	.25
B61	SP17	10c + 5c multi	.25	.25
B62	SP17	20c + 10c multi	.25	.25
B63	SP17	25c + 12c multi	.25	.25
		Nos. B59-B63 (5)	1.25	1.25

Surtax for child welfare.

1964, Oct. 21 ***Perf. 14x13***

Designs: 10c+5c, Wild rose. 20c+10c, Chalice flower. 25c+11c, Bellisima.

Flowers in Natural Colors

B64	SP18	6c + 3c bl vio & blk	.20	.20
B65	SP18	10c + 5c yel brn, yel & blk	.20	.20
B66	SP18	20c + 10c dull red & blk	.20	.20
B67	SP18	25c + 11c citron & brn	.20	.20
		Nos. B64-B67 (4)	.80	.80

The surtax was for child welfare.

Sea Anemones and Star Coral SP19

Corals: 6c+3c, Blue cup sponges. 10c+5c, Green cup sponges. 25c+11c, Basket sponge, knobbed brain coral and reef fish.

1965, Nov. 10 **Photo.** ***Perf. 14x13½***

B68	SP19	6c + 3c multi	.20	.20
B69	SP19	10c + 5c multi	.20	.20
B70	SP19	20c + 10c multi	.20	.20
B71	SP19	25c + 11c multi	.20	.20
		Nos. B68-B71 (4)	.80	.80

The surtax was for child welfare.

ICEM Type of Netherlands

1966, Jan. 31 **Photo.** ***Perf. 14x13***

B72	SP181	35c + 15c brn & dl yel	.20	.20

The surtax was for the Intergovernmental Committee for European Migration (ICEM). The message on the stamps was given and signed by Queen Juliana.

Girl Cooking — SP20

Helping Hands Supporting Women — SP21

Youth at Work: 10c+5c, Nurse's aide with infant. 20c+10c, Young metalworker. 25c+11c, Girl ironing.

1966, Nov. 15 ***Perf. 13½***

B73	SP20	6c + 3c multi	.20	.20
B74	SP20	10c + 5c multi	.20	.20
B75	SP20	20c + 10c multi	.20	.20
B76	SP20	25c + 11c multi	.20	.20
		Nos. B73-B76 (4)	.80	.80

The surtax was for child welfare.

1967, July 4 **Litho.** ***Perf. 13x14***

B77	SP21	6c + 3c bl & blk	.20	.20
B78	SP21	10c + 5c brt pink & blk	.20	.20
B79	SP21	20c + 10c lilac	.20	.20
B80	SP21	25c + 11c dk bl	.20	.20
		Nos. B77-B80 (4)	.80	.80

The surtax was for various social and cultural institutions.

Nanzi the Spider and the Tiger — SP22

Nanzi Stories (Folklore): 6c+3c, Princess Longnose, vert. 10c+5c, The Turtle and the Monkey. 25c+11c, Adventure of Shon Arey.

Perf. 14x13, 13x14

1967, Nov. 15 **Photo.**

B81 SP22 6c + 3c dk red, pink & org .20 .20
B82 SP22 10c + 5c vio bl & org .20 .20
B83 SP22 20c + 10c grn & org .20 .20
B84 SP22 25c + 11c brt bl & org .20 .20
Nos. B81-B84 (4) .80 .80

The surtax was for child welfare.

Lintendans (Dance) and Koeoekoe House SP23

1968, May 29 **Litho.** ***Perf. 14x13***

B85 SP23 10c + 5c multi .20 .20
B86 SP23 15c + 5c multi .20 .20
B87 SP23 20c + 10c multi .20 .20
B88 SP23 25c + 10c multi .20 .20
Nos. B85-B88 (4) .80 .80

The surtax was for various social and cultural institutions.

Boy and Pet Cat — SP24

Designs: 6c+3c, Boy and goat. 10c+5c, Girl and poodle. 25c+11c, Girl and duckling.

1968, Nov. 13 **Photo.** ***Perf. 13½***

B89 SP24 6c + 3c multi .20 .20
B90 SP24 10c + 5c multi .20 .20
B91 SP24 20c + 10c multi .20 .20
B92 SP24 25c + 11c multi .20 .20
Nos. B89-B92 (4) .80 .80

The surtax was for child welfare.

Carnival Headpiece SP25

Folklore: 15c+5c, Harvest-home festival. 20c+10c, Feast of St. John (dancers & cock). 25c+10c, "Dande" New Year's celebration.

1969, July 23 **Litho.** ***Perf. 13½***

B93 SP25 10c + 5c multi .25 .25
B94 SP25 15c + 5c multi .25 .25
B95 SP25 20c + 10c multi .30 .30
B96 SP25 25c + 10c multi .30 .30
Nos. B93-B96 (4) 1.10 1.10

The surtax was for various social and cultural institutions.

Boy Playing Guitar SP26

Designs: 10c+5c, Girl with English flute. 20c+10c, Boy playing the marimula. 25c+11c, Girl playing the piano.

1969, Nov. 3 **Litho.** ***Perf. 14x13***

B97 SP26 6c + 3c org & vio .20 .20
B98 SP26 10c + 5c yel & brt grn .30 .30
B99 SP26 20c + 10c bl & car .30 .30
B100 SP26 25c + 11c pink & brn .30 .30
Nos. B97-B100 (4) 1.10 1.10

The surtax was for child welfare.

Printing Press and Quill — SP27

Mother and Child — SP28

Mass Media: 15c+5c, Filmstrip and reels. 20c+10c, Horn and radio mast. 25c+10c, Television antenna and eye focused on globe.

1970, July 14 **Litho.** ***Perf. 13½***

B101 SP27 10c + 5c multi .30 .30
B102 SP27 15c + 5c multi .30 .30
B103 SP27 20c + 10c multi .30 .30
B104 SP27 25c + 10c multi .30 .30
Nos. B101-B104 (4) 1.20 1.20

The surtax was for various social and cultural institutions.

1970, Nov. 16 ***Perf. 13½x14***

Designs: 10c+5c, Girl holding piggy bank. 20c+10c, Boys wrestling (Judokas). 25c+11c, Youth carrying small boy on his shoulders.

B105 SP28 6c + 3c multi .50 .50
B106 SP28 10c + 5c multi .50 .50
B107 SP28 20c + 10c multi .50 .50
B108 SP28 25c + 11c multi .50 .50
Nos. B105-B108 (4) 2.00 2.00

The surtax was for child welfare.

Charcoal Burner SP29

Kitchen Utensils: 15c+5c, Earthenware vessel for water. 20c+10c, Baking oven. 25c+10c, Soup plate, stirrer and kneading stick.

1971, May 12 ***Perf. 14x13½***

B109 SP29 10c + 5c multi .40 .40
B110 SP29 15c + 5c multi .40 .40
B111 SP29 20c + 10c multi .40 .40
B112 SP29 25c + 10c multi .40 .40
Nos. B109-B112 (4) 1.60 1.60

Surtax was for various social and cultural institutions.

Homemade Dolls and Comb — SP30

Homemade Toys: 20c+10c, Carts. 30c+15c, Musical top made from calabash.

1971, Nov. 16 ***Perf. 13½x14***

B113 SP30 15c + 5c multi .50 .50
B114 SP30 20c + 10c multi .50 .50
B115 SP30 30c + 15c multi .50 .50
Nos. B113-B115 (3) 1.50 1.50

Surtax was for child welfare.

Steel Band SP31

Designs: 20c+10c, Harvest festival (Seu). 30c+15c, Tambu dancers.

1972, May 16

B116 SP31 15c + 5c multi .60 .60
B117 SP31 20c + 10c multi .60 .60
B118 SP31 30c + 15c multi .60 .60
Nos. B116-B118 (3) 1.80 1.80

Surtax was for various social and cultural institutions.

Child at Play on Ground SP32

Designs: 20c+10c, Child playing in water. 30c+15c, Child throwing ball into air.

1972, Nov. 14 **Litho.** ***Perf. 14x13***

B119 SP32 15c + 5c multi .70 .70
B120 SP32 20c + 10c multi .70 .70
B121 SP32 30c + 15c multi .70 .70
Nos. B119-B121 (3) 2.10 2.10

Surtax was for child welfare.

Pedestrian Crossing, Traffic Sign — SP33

Designs: 15c+7c, School crossing. 40c+20c, Traffic light, road and car.

1973, Apr. 9 **Litho.** ***Perf. 13x14***

B122 SP33 12c + 6c multi .60 .60
B123 SP33 15c + 7c multi .60 .60
B124 SP33 40c + 20c multi .60 .60
Nos. B122-B124 (3) 1.80 1.80

Surtax was for various social and cultural institutions.

"1948-73" SP34

20c+10c, Children. 30c+15c, Mother & child.

1973, Nov. 19 **Litho.** ***Perf. 14x13***

B125 SP34 15c + 5c multi .70 .70
B126 SP34 20c + 10c multi .70 .70
a. Min. sheet, 2 ea #B125-B126 3.00 3.00
B127 SP34 30c + 15c multi 1.10 1.10
Nos. B125-B127 (3) 2.50 2.50

Child Welfare semi-postal stamps, 25th anniv.

Girl Combing her Hair — SP35

15c+7c, Young people listening to rock music. 40c+20c, Drummer, symbolizing rock music.

1974, Apr. 9 **Litho.** ***Perf. 14x13***

B128 SP35 12c + 6c multi .80 .80
B129 SP35 15c + 7c multi .80 .80
B130 SP35 40c + 20c multi .80 .80
Nos. B128-B130 (3) 2.40 2.40

Surtax was for various social and cultural institutions.

Child, Saw and Score — SP36

Designs: 20c+10c, Footprints in circle. 30c+15c, Moon and sun. Each design includes score of a children's song.

1974, Nov. 12 **Litho.** ***Perf. 13x14***

B131 SP36 15c + 5c multi .60 .60
B132 SP36 20c + 10c multi .60 .60
B133 SP36 30c + 15c multi .60 .60
Nos. B131-B133 (3) 1.80 1.80

Surtax was for child welfare.

Carved Stone Grid, Flower Pot SP37

Jewish Tombstone, Mordecai's Procession SP38

Design: 40c+20c, Ornamental stone from facade of Jewish House, 1728.

1975, Mar. 21 **Litho.** ***Perf. 13x14***

B134 SP37 12c + 6c multi .60 .60
B135 SP38 15c + 7c multi .60 .60
B136 SP37 40c + 20c multi .60 .60
Nos. B134-B136 (3) 1.80 1.80

Surtax was for various social and cultural institutions.

Children Building Curaçao Windmill SP39

Designs: 20c+10c, Girl molding clay animal. 30c+15c, Children drawing picture.

1975, Nov. 12 **Litho.** ***Perf. 14x13***

B137 SP39 15c + 5c multi .55 .55
B138 SP39 20c + 10c multi .55 .55
B139 SP39 30c + 15c multi .55 .55
Nos. B137-B139 (3) 1.65 1.65

Surtax was for child welfare.

Carrying a Child — SP40

Designs: Different ways of carrying a child. 40c+18c is vertical.

Perf. 14x13, 13x14

1976, Oct. 4 **Litho.**

B140 SP40 20c + 10c multi .45 .45
B141 SP40 25c + 12c multi .45 .45
B142 SP40 40c + 18c multi .45 .45
Nos. B140-B142 (3) 1.35 1.35

Surtax was for child welfare.

Composite: Aces of Hearts, Clubs, Diamonds and Spades — SP41

Designs: 25c+12c, "King" and inscription. 40c+18c, Hand holding cards; map of Aruba as ace of hearts, horiz.

Perf. 13x14, 14x13

1977, May 6 **Litho.**

B143	SP41	20c + 10c red & blk	.30	.30
B144	SP41	25c + 12c multi	.30	.30
a.		Min. sheet, 2 ea #B143-B144	1.40	1.10
B145	SP41	40c + 18c multi	.50	.50
		Nos. B143-B145 (3)	1.10	1.10

Central American and Caribbean Bridge Championships, Aruba.

Souvenir Sheet

1977, May 26 ***Perf. 13½x14***

B146	SP41	Sheet of 3	2.75	2.50

Amphilex 77 International Philatelic Exhibition, Amsterdam, May 26-June 5. No. B146 contains 3 stamps similar to Nos. B143-B145 with bright green background.

Children and Toys — SP42

Children playing with fantasy animals.

1977, Oct. 25 **Litho.** ***Perf. 14x13***

B147	SP42	15c + 5c multi	.30	.25
B148	SP42	20c + 10c multi	.30	.30
B149	SP42	25c + 12c multi	.40	.40
B150	SP42	40c + 18c multi	.50	.40
a.		Min. sheet, 2 ea #B148, B150	1.75	1.60
		Nos. B147-B150 (4)	1.50	1.35

Surtax was for child welfare.

Water Skiing — SP43

Roller Skating — SP45

Red Cross — SP44

Designs: 20c+10c, Sailing. 25c+12c, Soccer. 40c+18c, Baseball.

1978, Mar. 31 **Litho.** ***Perf. 13x14***

B151	SP43	15c + 5c multi	.20	.20
B152	SP43	20c + 10c multi	.20	.20
B153	SP43	25c + 12c multi	.20	.20
B154	SP43	40c + 18c multi	.25	.25
		Nos. B151-B154 (4)	.85	.85

Surtax was for sports. Tete-beche gutter pairs exist.

1978, Sept. 19 **Litho.** ***Perf. 14x13***

B155	SP44	55c + 25c red & blk	.25	.25
a.		Souv. sheet of 3, perf. 13½x13	1.60	1.60

Henri Dunant (1828-1910), founder of Red Cross. Surtax for the Red Cross.
Tete-beche gutter pairs exist.

1978, Nov. 7 **Litho.** ***Perf. 13x14***

Children's Activities: 20c+10c, Kite flying. 25c+12c, Playing marbles. 40c+ 18c, Bicycling.

B156	SP45	15c + 5c multi	.30	.30
B157	SP45	20c + 10c multi	.40	.30
a.		Min. sheet, 2 ea #B156-B157	1.75	1.50
B158	SP45	25c + 12c multi	.40	.40
B159	SP45	40c + 18c multi	.50	.45
		Nos. B156-B159 (4)	1.60	1.45

Surtax was for child welfare.

Carnival King SP46

Regatta Emblem SP47

25th Aruba Carnival: 75c+20c, Carnival Queen and coat of arms.

1979, Feb. 20 **Litho.** ***Perf. 13x14***

B160	SP46	40c + 10c multi	.40	.30
B161	SP46	75c + 20c multi	.55	.50

Perf. 13x14, 14x13

1979, May 16 **Litho.**

Designs: 35c+10c, Race. 40c+15c, Globe and yacht, horiz. 55c+25c, Yacht, birds and sun.

B162	SP47	15c + 5c multi	.20	.20
B163	SP47	35c + 10c multi	.25	.25
B164	SP47	40c + 15c multi	.30	.30
B165	SP47	55c + 25c multi	.40	.40
a.		Souv. sheet of 4, #B162-B165	1.10	1.10
		Nos. B162-B165 (4)	1.15	1.15

12th International Sailing Regatta, Bonaire.
#B164 in souvenir sheet is perf 13x14.

Volunteer Corps Type, 1979

15c+10c, Soldiers, 1929 and 1979. 40c+20c, Soldier guarding oil refinery, Guard emblem.

1979, July 4 **Litho.** ***Perf. 13x14***

B166	A124	15c + 10c multi	.20	.20
B167	A124	40c + 20c multi	.40	.35

Girls Reading Book, IYC Emblem SP48

Volleyball, Olympic Rings SP49

IYC Emblem and Children's Drawings: 25c+12c, Infant and cat. 35c+15c, Girls walking under palm trees. 50c+20c, Children wearing adult clothing.

1979, Oct. 24 **Litho.** ***Perf. 13x14***

B168	SP48	20c + 10c multi	.20	.20
B169	SP48	25c + 12c multi	.30	.30
B170	SP48	35c + 15c multi	.40	.30
a.		Souv. sheet, 2 ea #B168, B170	1.25	1.25
B171	SP48	50c + 20c multi	.50	.50
		Nos. B168-B171 (4)	1.40	1.30

International Year of the Child. Surtax for child welfare.

Fort Church Type of 1980

Designs: 20c+10c, Brass chandelier, 1909, horiz. 50c+25c, Pipe organ.

Perf. 14x13, 13x14

1980, Jan. 9 **Litho.**

B172	A128	20c + 10c multi	.20	.20
B173	A128	50c + 25c multi	.45	.45

1980, June 25 **Litho.** ***Perf. 13x14***

Designs: 25c+10c, Woman gymnast. 30c+15c, Male gymnast. 60c+25c, Basketball.

B174	SP49	25c + 10c multi	.20	.20
B175	SP49	30c + 15c multi	.30	.30
B176	SP49	45c + 20c multi	.40	.35
B177	SP49	60c + 25c multi	.50	.45
a.		Souvenir sheet of 6, 3 each #B174, B177, perf. 14x13½	2.25	1.90
		Nos. B174-B177 (4)	1.40	1.30

22nd Summer Olympic Games, Moscow, July 19-Aug. 3.

St. Maarten Landscape SP50

Children's Drawings: 30c+15c, House in Bonaire. 40c+20c, Child at blackboard. 60c+25c, Dancers, vert.

Perf. 14x13, 13x14

1980, Oct. 22 **Litho.**

B178	SP50	25c + 10c multi	.30	.25
B179	SP50	30c + 15c multi	.35	.30
B180	SP50	40c + 20c multi	.40	.40
B181	SP50	60c + 25c multi	.50	.50
a.		Souvenir sheet of 6+ 4 labels, 3 each #B178, B181	2.50	2.25
		Nos. B178-B181 (4)	1.55	1.45

Surtax was for child welfare.
#B178 in souvenir sheet is perf 13x14.

Girl Using Sign Language SP51

Tennis Player SP52

Designs: 25c+10c, Blind woman. 30c+15c, Man in wheelchair. 45c+20c, Infant in walker.

1981, Apr. 7 **Litho.** ***Perf. 13x14***

B182	SP51	25c + 10c multi	.25	.25
B183	SP51	30c + 15c multi	.30	.30
B184	SP51	45c + 20c multi	.55	.55
B185	SP51	60c + 25c multi	.60	.60
		Nos. B182-B185 (4)	1.70	1.70

International Year of the Disabled. Surtax was for handicapped children.

1981, May 27 **Litho.** ***Perf. 13x14***

B186	SP52	30c + 15c shown	.35	.35
B187	SP52	50c + 20c Diving	.55	.55
B188	SP52	70c + 25c Boxing	.75	.75
a.		Min. sheet of 3, #B186-B188	1.75	1.75
		Nos. B186-B188 (3)	1.65	1.65

Surtax was for sporting events.

Den Mother and Cub Scout — SP53

Scouting in Netherlands Antilles, 50th Anniv.: 70c+25c, van der Maarel, national founder. 1g+50c, Ronde Klip (headquarters).

1981, Sept. 16 **Litho.** ***Perf. 14x13***

B189	SP53	45c + 20c multi	.60	.60
B190	SP53	70c + 25c multi	.80	.80
B191	SP53	1g + 50c multi	1.25	1.25
a.		Min. sheet of 3, #B189-B191, perf. 13½x13	2.75	2.50
		Nos. B189-B191 (3)	2.65	2.65

Surtax was for various social and cultural institutions.

Girl and Teddy Bear — SP54

Designs: 35c+15c, Mother and child. 45c+20c, Two children. 55c+25c, Boy and cat.

1981, Oct. 21 **Litho.** ***Perf. 13x14***

B192	SP54	35c + 15c multi	.30	.30
B193	SP54	45c + 20c multi	.50	.50
B194	SP54	55c + 25c multi	.60	.60
a.		Min. sheet, 2 ea #B192, B194	2.00	2.00
B195	SP54	85c + 40c multi	.90	.90
		Nos. B192-B195 (4)	2.30	2.30

Surtax for child welfare.

Fencing SP55

1982, Feb. 17 **Litho.** ***Perf. 14x13***

B196	SP55	35c + 15c shown	.30	.30
B197	SP55	45c + 20c Judo	.50	.50
B198	SP55	70c + 35c Soccer	.80	.80
a.		Miniature sheet of 2 + label	1.75	1.75
B199	SP55	85c + 40c Bicycling	.90	.90
		Nos. B196-B199 (4)	2.50	2.50

Surtax was for sporting events.

Girl Playing Accordion SP56

1982, Oct. 20 **Litho.**

B200	SP56	35c + 15c shown	.40	.40
B201	SP56	75c + 35c Guitar	.90	.90
B202	SP56	85c + 40c Violin	1.00	1.00
a.		Min. sheet of 3, #B200-B202	2.50	2.50
		Nos. B200-B202 (3)	2.30	2.30

Surtax for child welfare.

Traditional House, Saba — SP57

1982, Nov. 17 **Litho.**

B203	SP57	35c + 15c shown	.40	.40
B204	SP57	75c + 35c Aruba	.90	.90
B205	SP57	85c + 40c Curaçao	1.00	1.00
a.		Souv. sheet of 3, #B203-B205	2.50	2.50
		Nos. B203-B205 (3)	2.30	2.30

Surtax was for various social and cultural institutions.

High Jump — SP58

1983, Feb. 22 **Litho.**

B206	SP58	35c + 15c shown	.30	.30
B207	SP58	45c + 20c Weight lifting	.60	.60

B208 SP58 85c + 40c Wind surf-ing 1.00 1.00
Nos. B206-B208 (3) 1.90 1.90

Surtax was for sporting events.

Child with Lizard
SP59

Pre-Columbian Artifacts
SP60

1983, Oct. 18 Litho. *Perf. 13x14*

B209 SP59 45c + 20c shown .60 .60
B210 SP59 55c + 25c Child with insects .75 .75
B211 SP59 100c + 50c Child with animal 1.40 1.40
a. Souv. sheet of 3, #B209-B211 2.75 2.75
Nos. B209-B211 (3) 2.75 2.75

Surtax was for Childrens' Charity.

1983, Nov. 22 Litho. *Perf. 13x14*

B212 SP60 45c + 20c multi .70 .70
B213 SP60 55c + 25c multi .80 .80
B214 SP60 85c + 40c multi 1.00 1.00
B215 SP60 100c + 50c multi 1.40 1.40
Nos. B212-B215 (4) 3.90 3.90

Curaçao Baseball Federation, 50th Anniv.
SP61

1984, Mar. 27 Litho. *Perf. 14x13*

B216 SP61 25c + 10c Catching .65 .65
B217 SP61 45c + 20c Batting 1.25 1.25
B218 SP61 55c + 25c Pitching 1.60 1.60
B219 SP61 85c + 40c Running 1.90 1.90
a. Min. sheet of 3, #B217-B219 5.00 5.00
Nos. B216-B219 (4) 5.40 5.40

Surtax was for baseball fed., 1984 Olympics.

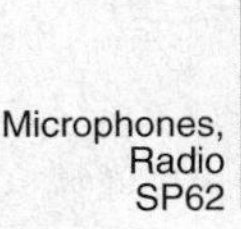

Microphones, Radio
SP62

Designs: 55c+25c, Radio, record player. 100c+50c, Record players.

1984, Apr. 24 Litho. *Perf. 14x13*

B220 SP62 45c + 20c multi .75 .75
B221 SP62 55c + 25c multi 1.00 1.00
B222 SP62 100c + 50c multi 1.25 1.25
Nos. B220-B222 (3) 3.00 3.00

Surtax was for social and cultural institutions.

Boy Reading — SP63

Designs: 55c+25c, Parents reading to children. 100c+50c, Family worship.

1984, Nov. 7 Litho. *Perf. 13x14*

B223 SP63 45c + 20c multi .75 .75
B224 SP63 55c + 25c multi 1.00 1.00
B225 SP63 100c + 50c multi 1.25 1.25
a. Souv. sheet of 3, #B223-B225 3.25 3.25
Nos. B223-B225 (3) 3.00 3.00

Surtax was for children's charity.

Soccer Players
SP64

1985, Mar. 27 Litho. *Perf. 14x13*

B226 SP64 10c + 5c multi .25 .25
B227 SP64 15c + 5c multi .25 .25
B228 SP64 45c + 20c multi .70 .70
B229 SP64 55c + 25c multi .90 .90
B230 SP64 85c + 40c multi 1.25 1.25
Nos. B226-B230 (5) 3.35 3.35

The surtax was for sporting events.

Intl. Youth Year — SP65

1985, Apr. 29 Litho.

B231 SP65 45c + 20c Youth, computer key-board .75 .75
B232 SP65 55c + 25c Girl lis-tening to mu-sic 1.00 1.00
B233 SP65 100c + 50c Youth breakdancing 1.50 1.50
Nos. B231-B233 (3) 3.25 3.25

Surtax for youth, social and cultural organizations.

Children — SP66

1985, Oct. 16 Litho. *Perf. 13x14*

B234 SP66 5c + 5c Eskimo .20 .20
B235 SP66 10c + 5c African .20 .20
B236 SP66 25c + 10c Asian .40 .40
B237 SP66 45c + 20c Dutch .70 .70
B238 SP66 55c + 25c American Indian .80 .80
a. Souv. sheet of 3, #B236-B238 2.00 2.00
Nos. B234-B238 (5) 2.30 2.30

Surtax for child welfare.

Sports
SP67

Handicrafts
SP68

1986, Feb. 19 Litho. *Perf. 13x14*

B239 SP67 15c + 5c Running .20 .20
B240 SP67 25c + 10c Horse rac-ing .40 .40
B241 SP67 45c + 20c Car racing .65 .65
B242 SP67 55c + 25c Soccer .75 .75
Nos. B239-B242 (4) 2.00 2.00

Surtax for the natl. Sports Federation.

1986, Apr. 29

B243 SP68 30c + 15c Painting .40 .40
B244 SP68 45c + 20c Sculpting .55 .55
B245 SP68 55c + 25c Ceramics .70 .70
Nos. B243-B245 (3) 1.65 1.65

Surtax for Curaçao Social & Cultural Care.

Sports
SP69

Social and Cultural Programs
SP70

1986, Oct. 15 Litho. *Perf. 13x14*

B246 SP69 20c + 10c Soccer .25 .25
B247 SP69 25c + 15c Tennis .35 .35
B248 SP69 45c + 20c Judo .50 .50
B249 SP69 55c + 25c Baseball .65 .65
a. Min. sheet of 2, #B248-B249 1.25 1.25
Nos. B246-B249 (4) 1.75 1.75

Surtax for the natl. Sports Foundation.

1987, Mar. 11 Litho.

B250 SP70 35c + 15c Musicians .40 .40
B251 SP70 45c + 25c Handi-capped .50 .50
B252 SP70 85c + 40c Pavilion .95 .95
Nos. B250-B252 (3) 1.85 1.85

Surtax for the Jong Wacht (Youth Guard) and the natl. Red Cross.

Boy in Various Stages of Growth
SP71

1987, Oct. 21 Litho. *Perf. 14x13*

B253 SP71 40c +15c Infant .45 .45
B254 SP71 55c +25c Toddler .60 .60
B255 SP71 115c +50c Boy 1.25 1.25
a. Souv. sheet of 3, #B253-B255 2.50 2.50
Nos. B253-B255 (3) 2.30 2.30

Surtax benefited Child Care programs.

Queen Emma Bridge, Cent. — SP72

55c+25c, Bridge, vert. 115c+55c, View of Willemstad Harbor and quay. 190c+60c, Flags of the Netherlands, Antilles and US, Leonard B. Smith, engineer.

1988, May 9 *Perf. 13x14, 14x13*

B256 SP72 55c +25c multi .60 .60
B257 SP72 115c +55c multi 1.25 1.25
B258 SP72 190c +60c multi 1.75 1.75
Nos. B256-B258 (3) 3.60 3.60

Surtax for social and cultural purposes.

Youth Care Campaign
SP73

1988, Oct. 26 Litho. *Perf. 14x13*

B259 SP73 55c +25c Girl, tele-vision .60 .60
B260 SP73 65c +30c Boy, port-able stereo .70 .70
B261 SP73 115c +55c Girl, com-puter 1.25 1.25
a. Souv. sheet of 3, #B259-B261 2.50 2.50
Nos. B259-B261 (3) 2.55 2.55

Surtax for child welfare.

Curaçao Stamp Assoc., 50th Anniv. — SP75

Designs: 30c+10c, Type A25 and No. 461 under magnifying glass. 55c+20c, Simulated stamp (learning to use tongs). 80c+30c, Barn owl, album, magnifying glass, tongs.

1989, Jan. 18 Litho. *Perf. 13x14*

B264 30c +10c multi .30 .30
B265 55c +20c multi .55 .55
B266 80c +30c multi .75 .75
a. SP75 Strip of 3, #B264-B266 1.60 1.60

No. B266a has a continuous design. Surtaxed for welfare organizations.

Child and Nature
SP76

1989, Oct. 25 Litho. *Perf. 14x13*

B267 SP76 40c +15c Girl, boy, tree .35 .35
B268 SP76 65c +30c Playing on beach .70 .70
B269 SP76 115c +55c Father and child 1.25 1.25
Nos. B267-B269 (3) 2.30 2.30

Souvenir Sheet

B270 SP76 155c +75c At the beach, diff. 1.60 1.60

Surtax for child welfare.

Natl. Girl Scout Movement, 60th Anniv. — SP77

Totolika, 60th Anniv. — SP78

Natl. Boy Scout Movement, 60th Anniv. — SP79

1990, Mar. 7 Litho. *Perf. 13x14*

B271 SP77 30c +10c multi .35 .35
B272 SP78 40c +15c multi .45 .45
B273 SP79 155c +65c multi 1.75 1.75
Nos. B271-B273 (3) 2.55 2.55

Parents' and Friends Association of Persons with a Mental Handicap (Totolika).
Surtax for social and cultural purposes.

SP80

SP81

1990, June 13 Litho. *Perf. 13x14*

B274 SP80 65c +30c multi .90 .90

Sport Unie Brion Trappers Soccer Club. Exists in tete-beche gutter pairs.

1990, June 13

B275 SP81 115c +55c multi 1.60 1.60

Anti-drug campaign. Exists in tete-beche gutter pairs.

Youth Care Campaign
SP82

1990, Oct. 31 Litho. *Perf. 14x13*

B276 SP82 30c +5c Bees, flowers .40 .40
B277 SP82 55c +10c Dolphins .70 .70
B278 SP82 65c +15c Donkey, bicycle .90 .90
B279 SP82 100c +20c Goat, house 1.40 1.40
B280 SP82 115c +25c Rabbit 1.60 1.60
B281 SP82 155c +55c Lizard, moon 2.25 2.25
Nos. B276-B281 (6) 7.25 7.25

Surtax for child welfare.

See Nos. B285-B288.

Social and Cultural Care — SP83

Designs: 30c+10c, Youth philately. 65c+25c, St. Vincentius Brass Band, 50th anniv. 155c+55c, Curaçao Community Center Federation.

1991, Apr. 3 Litho. *Perf. 14x13*

B282 SP83 30c +10c multi .50 .50
B283 SP83 65c +25c multi 1.10 1.10
B284 SP83 155c +55c multi 2.50 2.50
Nos. B282-B284 (3) 4.10 4.10

Youth Care Campaign Type of 1990

Fight illiteracy: 40c+15c, Octopus holding numbers and letters. 65c+30c, Birds, blackboard. 155c+65c, Turtle telling time. No. B288a, Owl, flag. b, Books, bookworms. c, Seahorse.

1991, Oct. 31 Litho. *Perf. 14x13*

B285 SP82 40c +15c multi .60 .60
B286 SP82 65c +30c multi 1.00 1.00
B287 SP82 155c +65c multi 2.40 2.40
Nos. B285-B287 (3) 4.00 4.00

Souvenir Sheet

Imperf

B288 Sheet of 3 4.25 4.25
a. SP82 55c +25c multi .90 .90
b. SP82 100c +35c multi 1.50 1.50
c. SP82 115c +50c multi 1.75 1.75

Surtax for child welfare.

SP84

1992 Summer Olympics, Barcelona: a, 30c + 10c, Triangle and oval. b, 55c + 25c, Globe showing location of Netherland Antilles, flag. c, 115c + 55c, Emblem of Netherlands Antilles Olympic Committee.

1992, Mar. 4 Litho. *Perf. 13x14*

B289 SP84 Strip of 3, #a.-c. 3.50 3.50

Netherlands Antilles Olympic Committee, 60th Anniv.

SP85

1992, Oct. 28 Litho. *Perf. 13x14*

B290 SP85 30c +10c Spaceship .50 .50
B291 SP85 70c +30c Robot 1.25 1.25
B292 SP85 100c +40c Extraterrestrial 1.75 1.75
Nos. B290-B292 (3) 3.50 3.50

Souvenir Sheet

B293 SP85 155c +70c Extraterrestrial, diff. 2.75 2.75

Surtax for child welfare.

SP86

Designs: 65c+25c, Fire safety, child playing with blocks. 90c+35c, Child fastening auto safety belt, vert. 175c+75c, Child wearing flotation equipment while swimming. 35c+15c, Alert child studying.

Perf. 14x13, 13x14

1993, Oct. 27 Litho.

B294 SP86 65c +25c multi 1.10 1.10
B295 SP86 90c +35c multi 1.50 1.50
B296 SP86 175c +75c multi 3.00 3.00
Nos. B294-B296 (3) 5.60 5.60

Souvenir Sheet

Perf. 13½x13

B297 SP86 35c +15c Sheet of 5 + label 3.00 3.00

Surtax for child welfare.

Intl. Year of the Family — SP87

1994, Oct. 26 Litho. *Perf. 13x14*

B298 SP87 35c +15c Woman, baby .60 .60
B299 SP87 65c +25c Daughter, father 1.00 1.00
B300 SP87 90c +35c Grandparents 1.40 1.40
Nos. B298-B300 (3) 3.00 3.00

Souvenir Sheet

B301 SP87 175c +75c Intl. emblem 2.75 2.75

Surtax for the benefit of the Antillean Youth Care Federation.

Slave Rebellion in Curaçao, Bicent.
SP88

Designs: 30c+10c, Monument, bird with outstretched wings. 45c+15c, Bird, bell tower.

1995, Aug. 17 Litho. *Perf. 14x13*

B302 SP88 30c +10c multi .45 .45
B303 SP88 45c +15c multi .65 .65

Youth Philately
SP89

Stamp drawings by children from: 65c+25c, Curaçao, Bonaire. 75c+35c, St. Maarten, St. Eustatius, Saba.

1995, Aug. 17

B304 SP89 65c +25c multi 1.00 1.00
B305 SP89 75c +35c multi 1.25 1.25

Nos. 516-517, 544 Surcharged in Red Brown

1995, Sept. 22 Litho. *Perf. 14x13*

B306 A148 65c +65c on #516 1.60 1.60
B307 A148 75c +75c on #517 1.90 1.90
B308 A148 1g +1g on #544 2.50 2.50
Nos. B306-B308 (3) 6.00 6.00

Surcharge for hurricane relief.

Child Welfare Stamps
SP91

Promotion of Children's Good Deeds: 35c+15c, Helping elderly across street. 65c+25c, Reading newspaper to blind person. 90c+35c, Caring for younger sibling. 175c+75c, Giving flowers to sick person.

1995, Oct. 25 Litho. *Perf. 14x13*

B309 SP91 35c +15c multi .55 .55
B310 SP91 65c +25c multi 1.00 1.00
B311 SP91 90c +35c multi 1.40 1.40
B312 SP91 175c +75c multi 2.75 2.75
Nos. B309-B312 (4) 5.70 5.70

Surtax for various youth organizations.

Child Welfare Stamps
SP92

UNICEF, 50th anniv.: 40c+15c, Child wandering streets. 75c+25c, Child labor in Asia. 110c+45c, Child in wartime (former Yugoslavia), vert. 225c+100c, Caribbean poverty, vert.

Perf. 14x13, 13x14

1996, Oct. 23 Litho.

B313 SP92 40c +15c multi .65 .65
B314 SP92 75c +25c multi 1.10 1.10
B315 SP92 110c +45c multi 1.75 1.75
B316 SP92 225c +100c multi 3.50 3.50
Nos. B313-B316 (4) 7.00 7.00

Social and Cultrual Care Stamps — SP93

Designs: 40c+15c, Curaçao Foundation for the cure and resettlement of ex-prisoners, 50th anniv. 75c+30c, ABVO (General Union of Public Servants), 60th anniv. 85+40c, 110c+50c, Red Cross Corps section, Curaçao, 65th anniv.

1997, Jan. 16 Litho. *Perf. 13x14*

B317 SP93 40c +15c multi .60 .60
B318 SP93 75c +30c multi .25 .25
B319 SP93 85c +40c multi 1.40 1.40
B320 SP93 110 +50c multi 1.60 1.60
Nos. B317-B320 (4) 3.85 3.85

Child Welfare Stamps
SP94

Musical notes, musical instruments: 40c+15c, Drums. 75c+25c, Piano. 110c+45c, Flute. 225c+100c, Guitar.

1997, Oct. 22 Litho. *Perf. 14x13*

B321 SP94 40c +15c multi .65 .65
B322 SP94 75c +25c multi 1.10 1.10
B323 SP94 110c +45c multi 1.75 1.75
B324 SP94 225c +100c multi 3.50 3.50
Nos. B321-B324 (4) 7.00 7.00

Social and Cultural Care — SP95

No. B325, Curacao Museum, 50th anniv. No. B326, Seawater Desalination, 70th anniv. 75c+25c, Water area, Lac Cai Bonaire, vert. 85c+40c, Water area, Klein-Bonaire, vert.

Perf. 14x13, 13x14

1998, Mar. 9 Litho.

B325 SP95 40c +15c multi .60 .60
B326 SP95 40c +15c multi .60 .60
B327 SP95 75c +25c multi 1.10 1.10
B328 SP95 85c +40c multi 1.40 1.40
Nos. B325-B328 (4) 3.70 3.70

Child Welfare Stamps — SP96

Universal Rights of the Child: 40c+15c, Child holding cutouts representing family. 75c+25c, Children eating watermelon. 110c+45c, Handicapped children drawing pictures. 225c+100c, Children holding cans with string to play telephone.

1998, Oct. 28 Litho. *Perf. 13x14*

B329 SP96 40c +15c multi .60 .60
B330 SP96 75c +25c multi 1.10 1.10
B331 SP96 110c +45c multi 1.75 1.75
B332 SP96 225c +100c multi 3.75 3.75
Nos. B329-B332 (4) 7.20 7.20

Buildings
SP97

Sports
SP98

Willemstad buildings on World Heritage List: 40c+15c, Houses, Ijzerstraat neighborhood, horiz. 75c+30c, Postal Museum. 110c+50c, "Bridal Cake" building, Scharloo area, horiz.

Perf. 14x13, 13x14

1999, Sept. 28 Litho.

B333 SP97 40c +15c multi .60 .60
B334 SP97 75c +30c multi 1.25 1.25
B335 SP97 110c +50c multi 1.75 1.75
Nos. B333-B335 (3) 3.60 3.60

1999, Oct. 27 *Perf. 13x14*

B336 SP98 40c +15c Basketball .60 .60
B337 SP98 75c +25c Golf 1.10 1.10
B338 SP98 110c +45c Fencing 1.75 1.75
B339 SP98 225c +100c Tennis 3.75 3.75
Nos. B336-B339 (4) 7.20 7.20

Social and Cultural Care — SP99

Designs: 75c+30c, Children playing. 110c+50c, Chemistry lesson. 225c+100c, Arithmetic lesson, vert.

Perf. 14x13, 13x14

2000, Apr. 28 Litho.

B340-B342 SP99 Set of 3 6.75 6.75

Youth Care
SP100

Designs: 40c+15c, Child reaching up, vert. 75c+25c, Children learning with computers. 110c+45c, Children playing with toy boat. 225c+100c, Children and map, vert.

Perf. 13x14, 14x13

2000, Oct. 25 **Litho.**

B343-B346 SP100	Set of 4	7.50	7.50

Caribbean Postal Union, 5th Anniv. — SP101

Designs: 75c+25c, Pen, emblem. 110c+45c, Emblem. 225c+100c, Globe, emblem.

2001, May 21 **Litho.** ***Perf. 13¼x13¾***

B347-B349 SP101	Set of 3	6.50	6.50

Youth Care — SP102

Designs: 40c+15c, Boy feeding baby. 75c+25c, Girls dancing, vert. 110c+45c, Boy pushing woman in wheelchair, vert.

Perf. 13½x12¾, 12¾x13½

2001, Oct. 24 **Litho.**

B350-B352 SP102	Set of 3	3.75	3.75

2002 World Cup Soccer Championships, Japan and Korea — SP103

Soccer player with: 95c+35c, Ball of flags. 145c+55c, Ball with map. 240c+110c, Ball.

2002, June 25 **Litho.** ***Perf. 12¾x14***

B353-B355 SP103	Set of 3	7.75	7.75

Youth Care — SP104

"Dialogue among civilizations:" 50c+15c, Lion and fish. 95c+35c, Kangaroo and iguana. 145c+55c, Goat and penguin. 240c+110c, Lizard and toucan.

2002, Oct. 24 ***Perf. 14x12¾***

B356-B359 SP104	Set of 4	8.50	8.50

Miniature Sheet

Maps of the Netherlands Antilles — SP105

No. B360: a, 25c+10c, Portion of 1688 map by Hendrick Doncker showing Curaçao and Bonaire. b, 30c+15c, Portion of Doncker map showing St. Maarten, Saba and St. Eustatius, vert. c, 55c+25c, Modern map of Curaçao and Bonaire. d, 85c+35c, Modern map of St. Maarten, Saba and St. Eustatius, vert. e, 95c+40c, Modern map of Caribbean Islands.

Perf. 14x12¾, 12¾x14 (vert. stamps)

2003, Mar. 19 **Litho.**

B360 SP105	Sheet of 5, #a-e	4.75	4.75

Miniature Sheet

Youth Care — SP106

No. B361: a, 50c+15c, Boy taking shower. b, 95c+35c, Girl with umbrella. c, 145c+55c, Boy with watering can. d, 240c+110c, Hands in water from open faucet.

2003, Oct. 22 **Litho.** ***Perf. 13x14***

B361 SP106	Sheet of 4, #a-d	8.50	8.50

Intl. Year of Fresh Water.

Youth Care SP107

No. B362: a, Boy, girl, slave huts. b, Girl, Autonomy Monument. c, Boy, girl, broken stone walls built by slaves. d, Boy, girl, wall of plantation house. e, Boy, preamble of Netherlands Constitution.

2004, Oct. 20 ***Perf. 13½x13***

B362	Horiz. strip of 5	8.25	8.25
a.	SP107 50c +15c multi	.75	.75
b.-c.	SP107 95c +35c either single	1.50	1.50
d.-e.	SP107 145c +55c either single	2.25	2.25

Autonomy of the Netherlands Antilles, 50th anniv. (Nos. B362b, B362e), Intl. Year Commemorating the Struggle Against Slavery and its Abolition (Nos. B362a, B362c, B362d).

Intl. Year of Sports and Physical Education — SP108

Designs: 55c+20c, Soccer. 97c+36c, Table tennis. 148c+56c, Tennis. 240c+110c, Baseball.

2005, Dec. 24 **Litho.** ***Perf. 13x13½***

B363-B366 SP108	Set of 4	8.75	8.75

Youth Care — SP109

Hatted globes showing: 55c+20c, North and South America. 100c+45c, Africa. 149c+61c, Europe, Africa and Asia. 285c+125c, Africa and Asia.

2006, Oct. 23 **Litho.** ***Perf. 12¾x13¼***

B367-B370 SP109	Set of 4	9.50	9.50

Youth Care SP110

Family: 59c+26c, Praying at dinner table. 104c+46c, Respecting flag. 155c+65c, As baseball team. 285c+125c, Studying together.

2007, Oct. 24 **Litho.** ***Perf. 13¼x12¾***

B371-B374 SP110	Set of 4	9.75	9.75

Youth Care — SP111

Potato: 59c+26c, As potato farmer. 1.06g+46c, Peeling potatoes. 1.58g+65c, Eating French fries. 2.85g+1.25g, Family.

2008, Oct. 23 **Litho.** ***Perf. 12¾x13¼***

B375-B378 SP111	Set of 4	9.75	9.75

Intl. Year of the Potato.

AIR POST STAMPS

Regular Issues of 1915-22 Surcharged in Black

Perf. 12½

1929, July 6 **Typo.** **Unwmk.**

C1	A13	50c on 12½c red	13.00	13.00
C2	A13	1g on 20c blue	13.00	13.00
C3	A13	2g on 15c ol grn	42.50	47.50
		Nos. C1-C3 (3)	68.50	73.50

Excellent forgeries exist.

Allegory, "Flight" — AP1

1931-39 **Engr.**

C4	AP1	10c Prus grn ('34)	.20	.20
C5	AP1	15c dull blue ('38)	.25	.20
C6	AP1	20c red	.75	.25
C7	AP1	25c gray ('38)	.75	.60
C8	AP1	30c yellow ('39)	.30	.30
C9	AP1	35c dull blue	.80	.90
C10	AP1	40c green	.60	.40
C11	AP1	45c orange	2.25	2.25
C12	AP1	50c lake ('38)	.75	.50
C13	AP1	60c brown vio	.60	.35
C14	AP1	70c black	6.50	2.50
C15	AP1	1.40g brown	4.25	5.25
C16	AP1	2.80g bister	5.00	5.50
		Nos. C4-C16 (13)	23.00	19.20

No. C6 Surcharged in Black

1934, Aug. 25

C17	AP1	10c on 20c red	19.00	17.00

Catalogue values for unused stamps in this section, from this point to the end of the section, are for Never Hinged items.

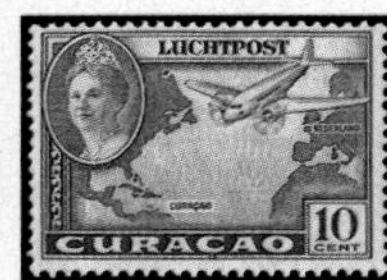

Map of the Atlantic — AP2

Plane over Islands — AP3

Map of Curaçao, Aruba and Bonaire — AP4

Planes — AP5

Plane — AP6

1942, Oct. 20 ***Perf. 13x13½***

C18	AP2	10c grn & bl	.20	.20
C19	AP3	15c rose car & yel grn	.20	.20
C20	AP4	20c red brn & grn	.25	.35
C21	AP5	25c dp ultra & org brn	.20	.20
C22	AP6	30c red & lt vio	.30	.30
C23	AP2	35c dk vio & ol grn	.45	.30
C24	AP3	40c gray ol & chnt	.50	.40
C25	AP4	45c dk red & blk	.35	.35

C26	AP5	50c	vio & blk	.85	.20
C27	AP6	60c	lt yel brn & dl bl	.85	.60
C28	AP2	70c	red brn & Prus bl	1.10	.60
C29	AP3	1.40g	bl vio & sl grn	6.75	1.40
C30	AP4	2.80g	int bl & lt bl	8.50	3.00
C31	AP5	5g	rose lake & sl grn	15.00	10.50
C32	AP6	10g	grn & red brn	20.00	18.00
			Nos. C18-C32 (15)	55.50	36.60

For surcharges see Nos. CB9-CB12.

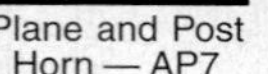

Plane and Post Horn — AP7

DC-4 above Waves — AP8

1947 Photo. ***Perf. 12½x12***

C32A	AP7	6c	gray blk	.20	.20
C33	AP7	10c	deep red	.20	.20
C33A	AP7	12½c	plum	.30	.20
C34	AP7	15c	deep blue	.30	.20
C35	AP7	20c	dl yel grn	.35	.25
C36	AP7	25c	org yel	.35	.20
C37	AP7	30c	lilac gray	.50	.35
C38	AP7	35c	org red	.60	.50
C39	AP7	40c	blue grn	.70	.60
C40	AP7	45c	brt violet	.85	.75
C41	AP7	50c	carmine	1.25	.65
C42	AP7	60c	brt blue	2.50	1.00
C43	AP7	70c	brown	2.50	1.00

Engr.

Perf. 12x12½

C44	AP8	1.50g	black	1.25	.50
C45	AP8	2.50g	dk car	10.00	2.75
C46	AP8	5g	green	20.00	6.50
C47	AP8	7.50g	dk blue	60.00	50.00
C48	AP8	10g	dk red vio	45.00	12.00
C49	AP8	15g	red org	72.50	60.00
C50	AP8	25g	chocolate	60.00	50.00
			Nos. C32A-C50 (20)	279.35	187.85

AIR POST SEMI-POSTAL STAMPS

Flags of the Netherlands and the House of Orange with Inscription "Netherlands Shall Rise Again" — SPAP1

Engr. & Photo.

1941, Dec. 11 Unwmk. ***Perf. 12***

CB1	SPAP1	10c + 10c	multi	5.25	5.25
CB2	SPAP1	15c + 25c	multi	19.00	19.00
CB3	SPAP1	20c + 25c	multi	19.00	19.00
CB4	SPAP1	25c + 25c	multi	19.00	19.00
CB5	SPAP1	30c + 50c	multi	19.00	19.00
CB6	SPAP1	35c + 50c	multi	19.00	19.00
CB7	SPAP1	40c + 50c	multi	19.00	19.00
CB8	SPAP1	50c +100c	multi	19.00	19.00
			Nos. CB1-CB8 (8)	138.25	138.25

The surtax was used by the Prince Bernhard Committee to purchase war material for the Netherlands' fighting forces in Great Britain.

Catalogue values for unused stamps in this section, from this point to the end of the section, are for Never Hinged items.

Nos. C29-C32 Surcharged in Black

1943, Dec. 1 ***Perf. 13x13½***

CB9	AP3	40c + 50c	on 1.40g	5.25	4.25
CB10	AP4	45c + 50c	on 2.80g	5.25	4.25
CB11	AP5	50c + 75c	on 5g	5.25	4.25
CB12	AP6	60c + 100c	on 10g	5.25	4.25
			Nos. CB9-CB12 (4)	21.00	17.00

The surtax was for the benefit of prisoners of war. These stamps were not sold to the public in the normal manner. All were sold in sets by advance subscription, the majority to philatelic speculators.

On No. CB9 overprint reads: "Voor / Krijgsgevangenen."

Princess Juliana — SPAP2

Engr. & Photo.

1944, Aug. 16 ***Perf. 12***

Frame in carmine & deep blue, cross in carmine

CB13	SPAP2	10c + 10c	lt brn	1.90	1.50
CB14	SPAP2	15c + 25c	turq grn	1.75	1.50
CB15	SPAP2	20c + 25c	dk ol gray	1.75	1.50
CB16	SPAP2	25c + 25c	slate	1.75	1.50
CB17	SPAP2	30c + 50c	sepia	1.75	1.50
CB18	SPAP2	35c + 50c	chnt	1.75	1.50
CB19	SPAP2	40c + 50c	grn	1.75	1.50
CB20	SPAP2	50c + 100c	dk vio	1.90	1.60
			Nos. CB13-CB20 (8)	14.30	12.10

The surtax was for the Red Cross.

Map of Netherlands Indies — SPAP3

Map of Netherlands — SPAP4

Photo. & Typo.

1946, July 1 ***Perf. 11x11½***

CB21	SPAP3	10c + 10c		.75	.75
CB22	SPAP3	15c + 25c		.85	.75
CB23	SPAP3	20c + 25c		.85	.75
CB24	SPAP3	25c + 25c		.85	.75
CB25	SPAP3	30c + 50c		.85	1.00
a.		Double impression of denomination		400.00	400.00
CB26	SPAP3	35c + 50c		.85	1.00
CB27	SPAP3	40c + 75c		.85	1.10
CB28	SPAP3	50c + 100c		.85	1.10
CB29	SPAP4	10c + 10c		.75	.75
CB30	SPAP4	15c + 25c		.85	.75
CB31	SPAP4	20c + 25c		.85	.75
CB32	SPAP4	25c + 25c		.85	.75
CB33	SPAP4	30c + 50c		.85	1.00
CB34	SPAP4	35c + 50c		.85	1.00
CB35	SPAP4	40c + 75c		.85	1.10
CB36	SPAP4	50c + 100c		.85	1.10
			Nos. CB21-CB36 (16)	13.40	14.40

The surtax on Nos. CB21 to CB36 was for the National Relief Fund.

POSTAGE DUE STAMPS

D1

D2

Type I — 34 loops. "T" of *"BETALEN"* over center of loop, top branch of "E" of *"TE"* shorter than lower branch.

Type II — 33 loops. "T" of *"BETALEN"* over center of two loops.

Type III — 32 loops. "T" of *"BETALEN"* slightly to the left of loop, top of first "E" of *"BETALEN"* shorter than lower branch.

Value in Black

1889 Unwmk. Typo. ***Perf. 12½***

Type III

J1	D1	2½c	green	3.00	3.25
J2	D1	5c	green	2.00	1.75
J3	D1	10c	green	32.50	27.50
J4	D1	12½c	green	375.00	200.00
J5	D1	15c	green	20.00	17.00
J6	D1	20c	green	9.00	9.00
J7	D1	25c	green	190.00	150.00
J8	D1	30c	green	10.00	9.00
J9	D1	40c	green	10.00	9.00
J10	D1	50c	green	40.00	37.50

Nos. J1-J10 were issued without gum.

Type I

J1a	D1	2½c	3.00	4.00
J2a	D1	5c	40.00	35.00
J3a	D1	10c	35.00	35.00
J4a	D1	12½c	375.00	200.00
J5a	D1	15c	21.00	19.00
J6a	D1	20c	65.00	65.00
J7a	D1	25c	600.00	350.00
J8a	D1	30c	75.00	75.00
J9a	D1	40c	75.00	75.00
J10a	D1	50c	45.00	40.00

Type II

J1b	D1	2½c	5.00	4.75
J2b	D1	5c	200.00	150.00
J3b	D1	10c	40.00	37.50
J4b	D1	12½c	400.00	250.00
J5b	D1	15c	25.00	20.00
J6b	D1	20c	425.00	425.00
J7b	D1	25c	*1,600.*	*1,600.*
J8b	D1	30c	400.00	400.00
J9b	D1	40c	400.00	400.00
J10b	D1	50c	47.50	45.00

Value in Black

1892-98 ***Perf. 12½***

J11	D2	2½c	green (III)	.25	.20
J12	D2	5c	green (III)	.60	.45
J13	D2	10c	green (III)	1.50	.40
J14	D2	12½c	green (III)	1.60	.60
J15	D2	15c	green (III) ('95)	2.50	1.10
J17	D2	25c	green (III)	1.25	.95
			Nos. J11-J17 (6)	7.70	3.70

Type I

J11a	D2	2½c		.50	.50
J12a	D2	5c		2.50	2.50
J13a	D2	10c		2.75	2.00
J14a	D2	12½c		2.00	1.40
J16	D2	20c	green ('95)	3.50	1.40
J17a	D2	25c		1.50	1.50
J18	D2	30c	green ('95)	25.00	13.00
J19	D2	40c	green ('95)	25.00	15.00
J20	D2	50c	green ('95)	30.00	15.00

Type II

11b	D2	2½c		20.00	20.00
12b	D2	5c		1.00	1.00
13b	D2	10c		1.75	1.10
14b	D2	12½c		9.00	8.00
17b	D2	25c		*12.50*	*12.50*
			Nos. J11b-J17b (5)	44.25	42.60

Type I

On Yellowish or White Paper

Value in Color of Stamp

1915 ***Perf. 12½, 13½x12½***

J21	D2	2½c	green	1.00	.95
J22	D2	5c	green	1.00	.95
J23	D2	10c	green	.90	.80
J24	D2	12½c	green	1.25	1.10
J25	D2	15c	green	1.90	2.00
J26	D2	20c	green	1.00	1.75
J27	D2	25c	green	.35	.20
J28	D2	30c	green	3.00	3.25
J29	D2	40c	green	3.00	3.25
J30	D2	50c	green	2.50	3.00
			Nos. J21-J30 (10)	15.90	17.25

1944 ***Perf. 11½***

J23a	D2	10c	yellow green	20.00	18.00
J24a	D2	12½c	yellow green	20.00	10.00
J27a	D2	25c	yellow green	40.00	1.00
			Nos. J23a-J27a (3)	80.00	29.00

Type of 1915

Type I

Value in Color of Stamp

Perf. 13½x13

1948-49 Unwmk. Photo.

J31	D2	2½c	bl grn ('48)	1.75	1.10
J32	D2	5c	bl grn ('48)	1.75	1.10
J33	D2	10c	blue green	15.00	10.00
J34	D2	12½c	blue green	16.00	1.75
J35	D2	15c	blue green	27.50	16.00
J36	D2	20c	blue green	25.00	16.00
J37	D2	25c	blue green	1.75	.35
J38	D2	30c	blue green	27.50	21.00
J39	D2	40c	blue green	27.50	21.00
J40	D2	50c	blue green	27.50	16.00
			Nos. J31-J40 (10)	171.25	104.30

Catalogue values for unused stamps in this section, from this point to the end of the section, are for Never Hinged items.

D3

1953-59 **Photo.**

J41	D3	1c	dk blue grn ('59)	.20	.20
J42	D3	2½c	dk blue grn	.50	.45
J43	D3	5c	dk blue grn	.20	.20
J44	D3	6c	dk blue grn ('59)	.45	.30
J45	D3	7c	dk blue grn ('59)	.45	.30
J46	D3	8c	dk blue grn ('59)	.45	.30
J47	D3	9c	dk blue grn ('59)	.45	.30
J48	D3	10c	dk blue grn	.20	.20
J49	D3	12½c	dk blue grn	.25	.20
J50	D3	15c	dk blue grn	.30	.20
J51	D3	20c	dk blue grn	.30	.30
J52	D3	25c	dk blue grn	.45	.20
J53	D3	30c	dk blue grn	1.10	.90
J54	D3	35c	dk blue grn ('59)	1.25	.90
J55	D3	40c	dk blue grn	1.10	.90
J56	D3	45c	dk blue grn ('59)	1.25	.90
J57	D3	50c	dk blue grn	1.10	.65
			Nos. J41-J57 (17)	10.00	7.40

NETHERLANDS INDIES

'ne-thər-lən,dz 'in-dēs

(Dutch Indies, Indonesia)

LOCATION — East Indies
GOVT. — Dutch colony
AREA — 735,268 sq. mi.
POP. — 76,000,000 (estimated 1949)
CAPITAL — Jakarta (formerly Batavia)

Netherlands Indies consisted of the islands of Sumatra, Java, the Lesser Sundas, Madura, two thirds of Borneo, Celebes, the Moluccas, western New Guinea and many small islands.

Netherlands Indies changed its name to Indonesia in 1948. The Netherlands transferred sovereignty on Dec. 28, 1949, to the Republic of the United States of Indonesia (see "Indonesia"), except for the western part of New Guinea (see "Netherlands New Guinea"). The Republic of Indonesia was proclaimed Aug. 15, 1950.

100 Cents = 1 Gulden
100 Sen = 1 Rupiah (1949)

Catalogue values for unused stamps in this country are for Never Hinged items, beginning with Scott 250 in the regular postage section, Scott B57 in the semi-postal section, and Scott J43 in the postage due section.

Values for unused stamps are for examples with original gum as defined in the catalogue introduction. Very fine examples of No. 2 will have perforations touching the frameline on one or more sides due to the narrow spacing of the stamps on the plates. Stamps with perfs clear of the framelines on all four sides are scarce and will command higher prices.

Watermarks

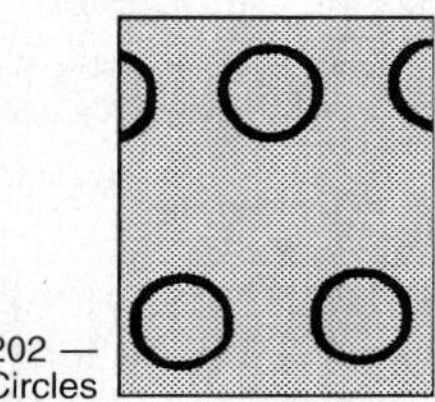

Wmk. 202 — Circles

Wmk. 228 — Small Crown and C of A Multiple

King William III
A1 A2

Unwmk.

1864, Apr. 1 **Engr.** ***Imperf.***
1 A1 10c lake 250.00 125.00

1868 ***Perf. 12½x12***
2 A1 10c lake 800.00 140.00

Privately perforated examples of No. 1 sometimes are mistaken for No. 2.

Perf. 11½x12, 12½, 12½x12, 13x14, 13½, 14, 13½x14

1870-88 **Typo.**

ONE CENT:
Type I — "CENT" 6mm long.
Type II — "CENT" 7½mm long.

3 A2 1c sl grn, type I 6.00 4.50
a. Perf. 13x14, small holes 10.00 8.00
4 A2 1c sl grn, type II 2.75 1.75
5 A2 2c red brown 6.00 4.00
a. 2c fawn 6.00 4.00
6 A2 2c violet brn 90.00 80.00
7 A2 2½c orange 35.00 20.00
8 A2 5c pale green 50.00 3.50
a. Perf. 14, small holes 60.00 4.00
b. Perf. 13x14, small holes 50.00 5.00
9 A2 10c orange brn 13.00 .20
a. Perf. 14, small holes 24.00 .80
b. Perf. 13x14, small holes 35.00 .80
10 A2 12½c gray 3.50 1.50
a. Perf. 12½x12 1,000.
11 A2 15c bister 17.00 1.50
a. Perf. 13x14, small holes 27.50 1.75
12 A2 20c ultra 80.00 2.50
a. Perf. 14, small holes 80.00 2.50
b. Perf. 13x14, small holes 80.00 2.75
13 A2 25c dk violet 14.00 .55
b. Perf. 13x14, small holes 25.00 2.50
c. Perf. 14, large holes 450.00 100.00
14 A2 30c green 27.50 3.25
15 A2 50c carmine 17.00 1.50
a. Perf. 14, small holes 22.50 1.50
b. Perf. 13x14, small holes 17.00 1.50
c. Perf. 14, large holes 25.00 2.50
16 A2 2.50g green & vio 75.00 13.00
b. Perf. 14, small holes 75.00 13.00
c. Perf. 14, large holes 85.00 13.00
Nos. 3-16 (14) 436.75 137.75

Imperforate examples of Nos. 3-16 are proofs. The 1c red brown and 2c yellow are believed to be bogus.

"Small hole" varieties have the spaces between the holes wider than the diameter of the holes.

Numeral of Value
A3

Queen Wilhelmina
A4

1883-90 ***Perf. 12½***
17 A3 1c slate grn ('88) .75 .20
a. Perf. 12½x12 1.10 .65
18 A3 2c brown ('84) .75 .20
a. Perf. 12½x12 .75 .30
b. Perf. 11½x12 65.00 22.50
19 A3 2½c yellow .75 .65
a. Perf. 12½x12 1.25 .75
b. Perf. 11½x12 12.00 4.75
20 A3 3c lilac ('90) .85 .20
21 A3 5c green ('87) 30.00 20.00
22 A3 5c ultra ('90) 9.00 .20
Nos. 17-22 (6) 42.10 21.45

For surcharges and overprint see Nos. 46-47, O4.

1892-97 ***Perf. 12½***
23 A4 10c org brn ('95) 3.75 .20
24 A4 12½c gray ('97) 7.50 12.50
25 A4 15c bister ('95) 12.00 1.25
26 A4 20c ultra ('93) 27.50 1.25
27 A4 25c violet 27.50 1.25
28 A4 30c green ('94) 37.50 1.75
29 A4 50c carmine ('93) 25.00 1.25
30 A4 2.50g org brn & ultra 110.00 27.50
Nos. 23-30 (8) 250.75 46.95

For overprints see Nos. O21-O27.

Netherlands #67-69, 74, 77, 80, 84 Surcharged in Black

1900, July 1
31 A11 10c on 10c gray lil 1.40 .20
32 A11 12½c on 12½c blue 2.25 .55
33 A11 15c on 15c yel brn 2.50 .30
34 A11 20c on 20c yel grn 13.00 .60
35 A11 25c on 25c car & bl 13.00 .70
36 A11 50c on 50c brnz grn & red brn 22.50 .90

1902 ***Perf. 11½x11***
37 A12 2.50g on 2½g brn lil 45.00 11.00
a. Perf. 11 50.00 12.50
Nos. 31-37 (7) 99.65 14.25

A6

1902-09 ***Perf. 12½***
38 A6 ½c violet .35 .20
39 A6 1c olive grn .35 .20
a. Booklet pane of 6
40 A6 2c yellow brn 2.75 .20
41 A6 2½c green 1.75 .20
a. Booklet pane of 6
42 A6 3c orange 1.75 1.10
43 A6 4c ultra ('09) 11.00 9.00
44 A6 5c rose red 4.25 .20
a. Booklet pane of 6
45 A6 7½c gray ('08) 2.25 .30
Nos. 38-45 (8) 24.45 11.40

For overprints see #63-69, 81-87, O1-O9.

Nos. 18, 20 Surcharged

1902
46 A3 ½c on 2c yel brn .20 .20
a. Double surcharge 175.00 150.00
47 A3 2½c on 3c violet .25 .25

Queen Wilhelmina
A9 A10

1903-08
48 A9 10c slate 1.00 .20
a. Booklet pane of 6
49 A9 12½c deep blue ('06) 1.50 .20
a. Booklet pane of 6
50 A9 15c chocolate ('06) 7.25 2.00
a. Ovptd. with 2 horiz. bars 1.50 .75
51 A9 17½c bister ('08) 3.00 .20
52 A9 20c grnsh slate 1.50 1.50
53 A9 20c olive grn ('05) 20.00 .20
54 A9 22½c brn & ol grn ('08) 3.75 .20
55 A9 25c violet ('04) 9.00 .20
56 A9 30c orange brn 25.00 .20
57 A9 50c red brown ('04) 19.00 .20
Nos. 48-57 (10) 91.00 5.10

For overprints and surcharges see Nos. 58, 70-78, 88-96, 139, O10-O18.

No. 52 Surcharged in Black

1905, July 6
58 A9 10c on 20c grnsh slate 1.90 1.25

1905-12 **Engr.** ***Perf. 11x11½***
59 A10 1g dull lilac ('06) 42.50 .25
a. Perf. 11½x11 42.50 .40
b. Perf. 11 52.50 3.50
60 A10 1g dl lil, *bl* ('12) 45.00 6.50
a. Perf. 11 55.00 57.50
61 A10 2½g slate bl ('05) 52.50 1.50
a. Perf. 11½ 52.50 1.60
b. Perf. 11½x11 60.00 1.60
c. Perf. 11 675.00
62 A10 2½g sl bl, *bl* ('12) 65.00 32.50
a. Perf. 11 75.00 75.00
Nos. 59-62 (4) 205.00 40.75

Sheets of Nos. 60 & 62 were soaked in an indigo solution.

For overprints and surcharge see Nos. 79-80, 97-98, 140, O19-O20.

Previous Issues Overprinted

1908, July 1
63 A6 ½c violet .25 .25
64 A6 1c olive grn .35 .25
65 A6 2c yellow brn 1.50 2.00
66 A6 2½c green .75 .20
67 A6 3c orange .65 1.10
68 A6 5c rose red 2.25 .40
69 A6 7½c gray 2.50 2.25
70 A9 10c slate .55 .20
71 A9 12½c dp blue 8.25 2.00
72 A9 15c choc (#50a) 3.75 2.00
73 A9 17½c bister 1.40 .95
74 A9 20c olive grn 7.50 1.40
75 A9 22½c brn & ol grn 5.75 3.50
76 A9 25c violet 5.75 .30
77 A9 30c orange brn 16.00 1.90
78 A9 50c red brown 7.00 .70
79 A10 1g dull lilac 52.50 3.75
80 A10 2½g slate blue 80.00 57.50
Nos. 63-80 (18) 196.70 80.65

The above stamps were overprinted for use in the territory outside of Java and Madura, stamps overprinted "Java" being used in these latter places.

The 15c is overprinted, in addition, with two horizontal lines, 2½mm apart.

The overprint also exists on #59a-59b. Same values.

Overprint Reading Down

63a A6 ½c .55 *3.25*
64a A6 1c .55 *2.50*
65a A6 2c 2.25 *4.50*
66a A6 2½c .95 *3.00*
67a A6 3c 15.00 *40.00*
68a A6 5c 2.25 *2.50*
70a A9 10c .65 *1.90*
71a A9 12½c 4.50 *8.00*
72a A9 15c 25.00 *62.50*
74a A9 20c 7.25 8.00
75a A9 22½c *1,400* *1,400.*
76a A9 25c 5.50 7.25
77a A9 30c 11.00 15.00
78a A9 50c 7.50 9.00
79a A10 1g 175.00 225.00
80a A10 2½g *2,250.* *2,500.*

Overprinted

1908, July 1
81 A6 ½c violet .20 .20
a. Inverted overprint .55 *2.25*
b. Double overprint 450.00
82 A6 1c olive grn .25 .25
a. Inverted overprint .45 *2.75*
83 A6 2c yellow brn 1.75 1.75
a. Inverted overprint 1.50 *6.00*
84 A6 2½c green .90 .20
a. Inverted overprint 2.00 *3.25*
85 A6 3c orange .75 .75
a. Inverted overprint 17.00 22.50
86 A6 5c rose red 2.25 .20
a. Inverted overprint 1.50 2.50
87 A6 7½c gray 1.90 1.75
88 A9 10c slate .55 .20
a. Inverted overprint .55 *2.00*
89 A9 12½c deep blue 2.00 .55
a. Inverted overprint 2.75 5.00
b. Dbl. ovpt., one inverted 125.00 125.00
90 A9 15c choc (on No. 50a) 3.00 2.50
a. Inverted overprint 2.75 *9.00*
91 A9 17½c bister 1.50 .65
92 A9 20c olive grn 9.25 .75
a. Inverted overprint 9.00 10.00
93 A9 22½c brn & ol grn 4.00 2.00
94 A9 25c violet 4.00 .30
a. Inverted overprint 4.50 *9.00*
95 A9 30c orange brn 24.00 2.00
a. Inverted overprint 18.00 26.00
96 A9 50c red brown 15.00 .55
a. Inverted overprint 12.00 19.00
97 A10 1g dull lilac 37.50 2.25
a. Inverted overprint 150.00 150.00
b. Perf. 11 47.50 4.00
98 A10 2½g slate blue 57.50 40.00
a. Inverted overprint *2,250.* *2,500.*
Nos. 81-98 (18) 166.30 56.85

A11

A12

Queen Wilhelmina — A13

Typo., Litho. (#114A)

1912-40 ***Perf. 12½***

No.	Type	Value	Description	Unused	Used
101	A11	½c	lt vio	.20	.20
102	A11	1c	olive grn	.20	.20
103	A11	2c	yellow brn	.40	.20
104	A11	2c	gray blk ('30)	.40	.20
105	A11	2½c	green	1.25	.20
106	A11	2½c	lt red ('22)	.25	.20
107	A11	3c	yellow	.45	.20
108	A11	3c	green ('29)	.70	.20
109	A11	4c	ultra	.65	.25
110	A11	4c	dp grn ('28)	1.25	.20
111	A11	4c	yellow ('30)	8.50	4.00
112	A11	5c	rose	1.10	.20
113	A11	5c	green ('22)	.90	.20
114	A11	5c	chlky bl ('28)	.55	.20
114A	A11	5c	ultra ('40)	.85	.20
115	A11	7½c	bister	.40	.20
116	A11	10c	lilac ('22)	.95	.20
117	A12	10c	car rose ('14)	.75	.20
118	A12	12½c	dull bl ('14)	.95	.20
119	A12	12½c	red ('22)	.95	.20
120	A12	15c	blue ('29)	7.50	.20
121	A12	17½c	red brn ('15)	.95	.20
122	A12	20c	green ('15)	1.75	.20
123	A12	20c	blue ('22)	1.75	.20
124	A12	20c	org ('32)	13.00	.20
125	A12	22½c	org ('15)	1.75	.45
126	A12	25c	red vio ('15)	1.75	.20
127	A12	30c	slate ('15)	1.90	.20
128	A12	32½c	vio & red ('22)	1.90	.20
129	A12	35c	org brn ('29)	8.50	.60
130	A12	40c	green ('22)	1.90	.20

Perf. 11½

Engr.

No.	Type	Value	Description	Unused	Used
131	A13	50c	green ('13)	4.00	.20
a.			Perf. 11x11½	4.25	.20
b.			Perf. 12½	4.25	.30
132	A13	60c	dp bl ('22)	4.75	.20
133	A13	80c	org ('22)	4.00	.20
134	A13	1g	brown ('13)	3.00	.20
a.			Perf. 11x11½	3.50	.20
135	A13	1.75g	dk vio, p. 12½ ('31)	15.00	1.90
136	A13	2½g	car ('13)	12.50	.40
a.			Perf. 11x11½	13.00	.65
b.			Perf. 12½	14.00	.60
			Nos. 101-136 (37)	107.55	13.80

For surcharges and overprints see Nos. 137-138, 144-150, 102a-123a, 158, 194-195, B1-B3, C1-C5.

Water Soluble Ink

Some values of types A11 and A12 and late printings of types A6 and A9 are in soluble ink. The design disappears when immersed in water.

Nos. 105, 109, 54, 59 Surcharged

1917-18 **Typo.** ***Perf. 12½***

No.	Type	Description	Unused	Used
137	A11	½c on 2½c	.30	.30
138	A11	1c on 4c ('18)	.55	.55
139	A9	17½c on 22½c ('18)	1.25	.55
a.		Inverted surcharge	350.00	425.00

Perf. 11x11½

No.	Type	Description	Unused	Used
140	A10	30c on 1g ('18)	7.00	1.60
a.		Perf. 11½x11	110.00	42.50
		Nos. 137-140 (4)	9.10	3.00

Nos. 121, 125, 131, 134 Surcharged in Red or Blue

On A12

On A13

Two types of 32½c on 50c:
I — Surcharge bars spaced as in illustration.
II — Bars more closely spaced.

1922, Jan. ***Perf. 12½***

No.	Type	Description	Unused	Used
144	A12	12½c on 17½c (R)	.30	.20
145	A12	12½c on 22½c (R)	.40	.20
146	A12	20c on 22½c (Bl)	.40	.20

Perf. 11½, 11x11½

No.	Type	Description	Unused	Used
147	A13	32½c on 50c (Bl) (I, perf. 11½)	1.25	.20
a.		Type II, perf. 11½	10.00	.20
b.		Type I, perf. 11x11½	1,000.	6.00
c.		Type II, perf. 11x11½	19.00	1.00
148	A13	40c on 50c (R)	3.75	.45
149	A13	60c on 1g (Bl)	6.00	.40
150	A13	80c on 1g (R)	6.75	.90
		Nos. 144-150 (7)	18.85	2.55

Stamps of 1912-22 Overprinted in Red, Blue, Green or Black

a

3de N. I. JAARBEURS
BANDOENG 1922

b

1922, Sept. 18 **Typo.** ***Perf. 12½***

No.	Type	Value	Description	Unused	Used
102a	A11(a)	1c	ol grn (R)	5.75	4.75
103a	A11(a)	2c	yel brn (Bl)	5.75	4.75
106a	A11(a)	2½c	lt red (G)	47.50	52.50
107a	A11(a)	3c	yellow (R)	5.75	5.75
109a	A11(a)	4c	ultra (R)	32.50	30.00
113a	A11(a)	5c	green (R)	11.00	8.25
115a	A11(a)	7½c	drab (Bl)	7.50	4.75
116a	A11(a)	10c	lilac (Bk)	57.50	67.50
145a	A12(b)	12½c	on 22½c org (Bl)	5.75	5.75
121a	A12(b)	17½c	red brn (Bk)	3.75	4.75
123a	A12(b)	20c	blue (Bk)	5.75	4.75
			Nos. 102a-123a (11)	188.50	193.50

Issued to publicize the 3rd Netherlands Indies Industrial Fair at Bandoeng, Java. On No. 145a the overprint is vertical.

Nos. 102a-123a were sold at a premium for 3, 4, 5, 6, 8, 9, 10, 12½, 15, 20 and 22½ cents respectively.

Queen Wilhelmina A15

Prince William I, Portrait by Van Key A16

1923, Aug. 31 **Engr.** ***Perf. 11½***

No.	Type	Description	Unused	Used
151	A15	5c myrtle green	.20	.20
a.		Perf. 11½x11	350.00	110.00
b.		Perf. 11x11½	4.50	.55
152	A15	12½c rose	.20	.20
a.		Perf. 11x11½	1.25	.20
b.		Perf. 11½x11	1.75	.25
153	A15	20c dark blue	.35	.20
a.		Perf. 11½x11	3.25	.40
154	A15	50c red orange	1.40	.60
a.		Perf. 11x11½	6.50	1.25
b.		Perf. 11½x11	2.00	.90
c.		Perf. 11	4.50	.85
155	A15	1g brown vio	2.75	.40
a.		Perf. 11½x11	7.50	.80
156	A15	2½g gray black	22.50	8.75
157	A15	5g org brn	90.00	87.50
		Nos. 151-157 (7)	117.40	97.85

25th anniversary of the assumption of the government of the Netherlands by Queen Wilhelmina, at the age of 18.

No. 123 Surcharged

1930, Dec. 13 **Typo.** ***Perf. 12½***

No.	Type	Description	Unused	Used
158	A12	12½c on 20c bl (R)	.30	.20
a.		Inverted surcharge	375.00	475.00

1933, Apr. 18 **Photo.**

No.	Type	Description	Unused	Used
163	A16	12½c deep orange	1.25	.20

400th anniv. of the birth of Prince William I, Count of Nassau and Prince of Orange, frequently referred to as William the Silent.

Rice Field Scene A17

Queen Wilhelmina A18

Queen Wilhelmina A19

1933-37 **Unwmk.** ***Perf. 11½x12½***

No.	Type	Value	Description	Unused	Used
164	A17	1c	lilac gray ('34)	.20	.20
165	A17	2c	plum ('34)	.20	.20
166	A17	2½c	bister ('34)	.20	.20
167	A17	3c	yel grn ('34)	.20	.20
168	A17	3½c	dark gray ('37)	.20	.20
169	A17	4c	dk olive ('34)	.85	.20
170	A17	5c	ultra ('34)	.20	.20
171	A17	7½c	violet ('34)	1.25	.20
172	A17	10c	ver ('34)	1.75	.20
173	A18	10c	ver ('37)	.25	.20
174	A18	12½c	dp org ('34)	.25	.20
a.			12½c light orange, perf. 12½ ('33)	6.25	.35
175	A18	15c	ultra ('34)	.25	.20
176	A18	20c	plum ('34)	.40	.20
177	A18	25c	blue grn ('34)	1.75	.20
178	A18	30c	lilac gray ('34)	2.75	.20
179	A18	32½c	bister ('34)	7.50	6.50
180	A18	35c	violet ('34)	4.25	.95
181	A18	40c	yel grn ('34)	2.50	.20
182	A18	42½c	yellow ('34)	2.50	.20

1934, Jan 16 ***Perf. 12½***

No.	Type	Value	Description	Unused	Used
183	A19	50c	lilac gray	3.25	.20
184	A19	60c	ultra	4.00	.45
185	A19	80c	vermilion	4.00	.55
186	A19	1g	violet	6.25	.40
187	A19	1.75g	yellow grn	16.00	11.00
188	A19	2.50g	plum	19.00	1.25
			Nos. 164-188 (25)	79.95	24.70

See Nos. 200-225. For overprints and surcharges see Nos. 271-275, B48, B57.

Water Soluble Ink

Nos. 164-188 and the first printing of No. 163 have soluble ink and the design disappears when immersed in water.

Nos. C6-C7, C14, C9-C10 Surcharged in Black:

a

b

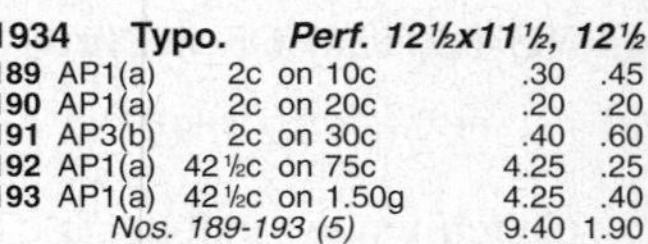

1934 **Typo.** ***Perf. 12½x11½, 12½***

No.	Type	Description	Unused	Used
189	AP1(a)	2c on 10c	.30	.45
190	AP1(a)	2c on 20c	.20	.20
191	AP3(b)	2c on 30c	.40	.60
192	AP1(a)	42½c on 75c	4.25	.25
193	AP1(a)	42½c on 1.50g	4.25	.40
		Nos. 189-193 (5)	9.40	1.90

Nos. 127-128 Surcharged with New Value in Red or Black

1937, Sept. ***Perf. 12½***

No.	Type	Description	Unused	Used
194	A12	10c on 30c (R)	2.50	.25
a.		Double surcharge	*675.00*	
195	A12	10c on 32½c (Bk)	2.75	.30

Wilhelmina — A20

Perf. 12½x12

1938, Aug. 30 **Photo.** **Wmk. 202**

No.	Type	Value	Description	Unused	Used
196	A20	2c	dull purple	.20	.20
197	A20	10c	car lake	.20	.20
198	A20	15c	royal blue	1.25	.75
199	A20	20c	red orange	.50	.30
			Nos. 196-199 (4)	2.15	1.45

40th anniv. of the reign of Queen Wilhelmina.

Types of 1933-37

1938-40 **Photo.** ***Perf. 12½x12***

No.	Type	Value	Description	Unused	Used
200	A17	1c	lilac gray ('39)	.30	*.80*
201	A17	2c	plum ('39)	.20	.20
202	A17	2½c	bister ('39)	.50	.50
203	A17	3c	yellow grn ('39)	1.50	1.25
205	A17	4c	gray ol ('39)	1.50	1.25
206	A17	5c	ultra ('39)	.20	.20
a.			Perf. 12x12½	1.25	.20
207	A17	7½c	violet ('39)	2.50	1.00
208	A18	10c	ver ('39)	.20	.20
210	A18	15c	ultra ('39)	.20	.20
211	A18	20c	plum ('39)	.20	.20
a.			Perf. 12x12½	1.25	.20
212	A18	25c	blue grn ('39)	25.00	24.00
213	A18	30c	lilac gray ('39)	6.50	.80
215	A18	35c	violet ('39)	2.75	.65
216	A18	40c	dp yel grn ('40)	5.00	.20

Perf. 12½

No.	Type	Value	Description	Unused	Used
218	A19	50c	lilac gray ('40)	275.00	
219	A19	60c	ultra ('39)	10.50	1.25
220	A19	80c	ver ('39)	62.50	26.00
221	A19	1g	violet ('39)	27.50	.85
223	A19	2g	Prus green	27.50	14.00
225	A19	5g	yellow brn	25.00	6.00
			Nos. 200-216,219-225 (19)	199.55	79.55

The note following No. 188 applies also to this issue.

The 50c was sold only at the philatelic window in Amsterdam.

War Dance of Nias Island — A23

Legong Dancer of Bali — A24

Wayang Wong Dancer of Java A25

Padjogé Dancer, Southern Celebes A26

Dyak Dancer of Borneo — A27

1941 Unwmk. *Perf. 12½*

No.	Type	Description	Unused	Used
228	A23	2½c rose violet	.20	.20
229	A24	3c green	.20	.50
230	A25	4c olive green	.20	.45
231	A26	5c blue	.20	.20
232	A27	7½c dark violet	.50	.20
		Nos. 228-232 (5)	1.30	1.55

See Nos. 279-280, 293, N38.
Imperfs. are printers waste.

A28

Queen Wilhelmina
A28a

1941 *Perf. 12½*

Size: 18x22¾mm

No.	Type	Description	Unused	Used
234	A28	10c red orange	.20	.20
a.		Perf. 13½	.40	.40
235	A28	15c ultra	1.50	1.25
236	A28	17½c orange	.40	.60
237	A28	20c plum	21.00	35.00
238	A28	25c Prus green	30.00	47.50
239	A28	30c olive bis	1.90	1.10
240	A28	35c purple	95.00	*325.00*
241	A28	40c yellow grn	8.00	2.50

Perf. 13½

Size: 20½x26mm

No.	Type	Description	Unused	Used
242	A28	50c car lake	2.00	.70
243	A28	60c ultra	1.60	.60
244	A28	80c red orange	1.90	.95
245	A28	1g purple	2.00	.30
246	A28	2g Prus green	10.00	1.10
247	A28	5g bis, perf. 12½	250.00	*675.00*
248	A28	10g green	30.00	15.00

Size: 26x32mm

No.	Type	Description	Unused	Used
249	A28a	25g orange	175.00	125.00
		Nos. 234-249 (16)	630.50	*1,231.*

Nos. 242-246 come with pin-perf 13½.

The 10c comes in two types: 1¼mm between "10" and "CENT," and 1¾mm.

For overprints and surcharge see Nos. 276-278, J43-J46.

Catalogue values for unused stamps in this section, from this point to the end of the section, are for Never Hinged items.

Rice Fields — A29

Barge on Java Lake — A30

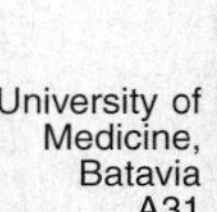
University of Medicine, Batavia A31

Palms on Shore — A32

Plane over Bromo Volcano A33

Queen Wilhelmina
A34 A35

1945-46, Oct. 1 Engr. *Perf. 12*

No.	Type	Description	Unused	Used
250	A29	1c green	.25	.20
251	A30	2c rose lilac	.25	.30
252	A31	2½c dull lilac	.25	.20
253	A32	5c blue	.20	.20
254	A33	7½c olive gray	.50	.20
255	A34	10c red brown	.20	.20
256	A34	15c dark blue	.20	.20
257	A34	17½c rose lake	.20	.20
258	A34	20c sepia	.20	.20
259	A34	30c slate gray	.30	.20
260	A35	60c gray black	.65	.20
261	A35	1g blue green	1.10	.20
262	A35	2½g red orange	3.75	.50
		Nos. 250-262 (13)	8.05	3.00

For surcharge see No. 304.
Issued: 15c, 1946, others 10/1/45.

Railway Viaduct Near Soekaboemi A36

Dam and Power Station A37

Palm Tree and Menangkabau House — A38

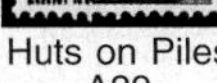
Huts on Piles A39

Buddhist Stupas A40

Perf. 14½x14

1946 Typo. Wmk. 228

No.	Type	Description	Unused	Used
263	A36	1c dark green	.20	.20
264	A37	2c black brown	.20	.20
265	A38	2½c scarlet	.20	.20
266	A39	5c indigo	.20	.20
267	A40	7½c ultra	.20	.20
		Nos. 263-267 (5)	1.00	1.00

Nos. 265, 267, 263 Surcharged

1947, Sept. 25

No.	Type	Description	Unused	Used
268	A38	3c on 2½c scar	.20	.20
269	A40	3c on 7½c ultra	.20	.20
a.		Double surcharge	150.00	150.00
270	A36	4c on 1c dk green	.20	.20
		Nos. 268-270 (3)	.60	.60

No. 219 Surcharged with New Value and Bars in Red

1947, Sept. 25 Wmk. 202 *Perf. 12½*

No.	Type	Description	Unused	Used
271	A19	45c on 60c ultra	1.25	1.25

Nos. 212, 218 and 220 Overprinted "1947" in Red or Black

1947, Sept. 25 *Perf. 12½x12, 12½*

No.	Type	Description	Unused	Used
272	A18	25c blue green (R)	.20	.20
a.		Unwmkd.		125.00
273	A19	50c lilac gray (R)	.70	.25
274	A19	80c vermilion	1.10	.75
a.		Unwmkd.	500.00	140.00
		Nos. 272-274 (3)	2.00	1.20

Bar above "1947" on No. 274.

Nos. 174, 241, 247 and Type of 1941 Overprinted "1947" in Black

Perf. 12½, 12½x12 (2g)

1947, Sept. 25 Unwmk.

No.	Type	Description	Unused	Used
275	A18	12½c deep orange	.20	.20
276	A28	40c yellow green	.40	.20
277	A28	2g Prus green	3.75	.50
278	A28	5g bister	11.00	7.50
		Nos. 275-278 (4)	15.35	8.40

The overprint is vertical on #276-278.

Dancer Types of 1941, 1945

1948, May 13 Litho. *Perf. 12½*

No.	Type	Description	Unused	Used
279	OS21	3c rose red	.20	.20
280	A24	4c dull olive grn	.20	.20

Queen Wilhelmina — A41

1948 Photo. *Perf. 12½*

Size: 18x22mm

No.	Type	Description	Unused	Used
281	A41	15c red orange	.60	.80
282	A41	20c brt blue	.20	.20
283	A41	25c dk green	.20	.20
284	A41	40c dp yellow grn	.20	.20
285	A41	45c plum	.40	.60
286	A41	50c red brown	.25	.20
287	A41	80c brt red	.30	.20

Perf. 13

Size: 20½x26mm

No.	Type	Description	Unused	Used
288	A41	1g deep violet	.25	.20
a.		Perf. 12½ x 12	.75	.40
289	A41	10g green	30.00	8.25
290	A41	25g orange	67.50	50.00
		Nos. 281-290 (10)	99.90	60.85

See #201-202. For overprints see #294-303.

Wilhelmina Type of 1948 Inscribed: "1898 1948"

1948, Aug. 31 *Perf. 12½x12*

Size: 21x26½mm

No.	Type	Description	Unused	Used
291	A41	15c orange	.30	.20
292	A41	20c ultra	.30	.20

Reign of Queen Wilhelmina, 50th anniv.

Dancer Type of 1941

1948, Sept. Photo. *Perf. 12½*

No.	Type	Description	Unused	Used
293	A27	7½c olive bister	.70	.80

Juliana Type of Netherlands 1948

Perf. 14½x13½

1948, Sept. 25 Wmk. 202

No.	Type	Description	Unused	Used
293A	A75	15c red orange	.30	.20
293B	A75	20c deep ultra	.30	.20

Investiture of Queen Juliana, Sept. 6, 1948.

Indonesia

Nos. 281 to 287 Overprinted in Black

Two types of overprint:
I — Shiny ink, bar 1.8mm wide. By G. C. T. van Dorp & Co.
II — Dull ink, bar 2.2mm. By G. Kolff & Co.

1948 *Perf. 12½*

No.	Type	Description	Unused	Used
294	A41	15c red orange (I)	.60	.20
a.		Type II	.55	.20
295	A41	20c bright blue (I)	.20	.20
a.		Type II	.25	.20
296	A41	25c dark green (I)	.25	.20
a.		Type II	.20	.20
297	A41	40c dp yel grn (I)	.25	.20
298	A41	45c plum ('49) (II)	.80	.70
299	A41	50c red brn ('49) (II)	.20	.20
300	A41	80c bright red (I)	.65	.20
a.		Type II	.65	.20

Nos. 288-290 Overprinted in Black

Two or Three Bars

Perf. 12½x12

No.	Type	Description	Unused	Used
301	A41	1g deep violet	.55	.20
a.		Perf. 13	.95	.20

Perf. 13

No.	Type	Description	Unused	Used
302	A41	10g green	50.00	6.25
303	A41	25g orange	75.00	50.00
		Nos. 294-303 (10)	128.50	58.35

Same Overprint in Black on No. 262

1949 Engr. *Perf. 12*

Bars 28½mm long

No.	Type	Description	Unused	Used
304	A35	2½g red orange	14.00	5.50

A42

Tjandi Puntadewa Temple Entrance, East Java — A43

Detail, Temple of the Dead, Bedjuning, Bali A44

Menangkabau House, Sumatra A45

Toradja House, Celebes — A46

Globe and Arms of Bern — A48

Designs: 5r, 10r, 25r, Temple entrance.

Perf. 12½, 11½

1949 Unwmk. Photo.

No.	Type	Description	Unused	Used
307	A42	1s gray	.20	.20
a.		Perf. 11½	.40	.20
308	A42	2s claret	.25	.20
a.		Perf. 11½	5.00	*14.00*
309	A42	2½s olive brown	.20	.20
a.		Perf. 11½	.25	.20
310	A42	3s rose pink	.25	.20
a.		Perf. 11½	1.10	.75
311	A42	4s green	.30	.50
312	A42	5s blue	.20	.20
a.		Perf. 11½	1.00	.20
313	A42	7½s dark green	.40	.20
a.		Perf. 11½	1.00	.75
314	A42	10s violet	.20	.20
a.		Perf. 11½		*375.00*
315	A42	12½s brt red	.30	.20
a.		Perf. 11½	4.00	4.00
316	A43	15s rose red	.25	.20
a.		Perf. 12½	.30	.20
317	A43	20s gray black	.25	.20
a.		Perf. 12½	.30	.75
318	A43	25s ultra	.30	.20
319	A44	30s brt red	.30	.20
320	A44	40s gray green	.30	.20
321	A44	45s claret	.30	.25
a.		Perf. 12½	2.75	.50
322	A45	50s orange brn	.30	.20
323	A45	60s brown	.40	.20
324	A45	80s scarlet	.30	.20
a.		Perf. 12½	4.00	.25

The 4s is perf. 12½. The 25s, 30s, 40s, 50s, 60s come both 12½ and 11½, same values.

Perf. 12½

No.	Type	Description	Unused	Used
325	A46	1r purple	.25	.20
326	A46	2r gray green	2.00	.20
327	A46	3r red violet	21.00	.20
328	A46	5r dk brown	21.00	.20
329	A46	10r gray	50.00	.35
330	A46	25r orange brn	.25	.25
		Nos. 307-330 (24)	99.50	5.35

Nos. 307-330 remained on sale in Indonesia Republic post offices until May 23, 1958, and were valid for postage until June 30, 1958.

For surcharge, see Indonesia Nos. 335-358.

1949, Oct. 1 ***Perf. 12½***

331	A48	15s bright red	.70	.35
332	A48	25s ultra	.70	.25

Nos. 307-330 remained on sale in Indonesia Republic post offices until May 23, 1958, and were valid for postage until June 30, 1958. 75th anniv. of UPU.

See Indonesia (republic) for subsequent listings.

SEMI-POSTAL STAMPS

Regular Issue of 1912-14 Surcharged in Carmine

1915, June 10 **Unwmk.** ***Perf. 12½***

B1	A11	1c + 5c ol grn	4.50	4.50
B2	A11	5c + 5c rose	4.50	4.50
B3	A12	10c + 5c rose	7.25	7.25
		Nos. B1-B3 (3)	16.25	16.25

Surtax for the Red Cross.

Bali Temple SP1

Watchtower SP2

Menangkabau Compound — SP3

Borobudur Temple, Java SP4

Perf. 11½x11, 11x11½

1930, Dec. 1 **Photo.**

B4	SP1	2c (+ 1c) vio & brn	1.00	.80
B5	SP2	5c (+ 2½c) dk grn & brn	4.75	2.50
B6	SP3	12½c (+ 2½c) dp red & brn	3.25	.50
B7	SP4	15c (+ 5c) ultra & brn	5.75	5.75
		Nos. B4-B7 (4)	14.75	9.55

Surtax for youth care.

Farmer and Carabao SP5

5c, Fishermen. 12½c, Dancers. 15c, Musicians.

1931, Dec. 1 **Engr.** ***Perf. 12½***

B8	SP5	2c (+ 1c) olive bis	3.00	2.00
B9	SP5	5c (+ 2½c) bl grn	4.25	3.75
B10	SP5	12½c (+ 2½c) dp red	3.25	.55
B11	SP5	15c (+ 5c) dl bl	8.25	7.00
		Nos. B8-B11 (4)	18.75	13.30

The surtax was for the aid of the Leper Colony at Salatiga.

Weaving SP9

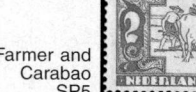

5c, Plaiting rattan. 12½c, Woman batik dyer. 15c, Coppersmith.

1932, Dec. 1 **Photo.** ***Perf. 12½***

B12	SP9	2c (+ 1c) dp vio & bis	.40	.40
B13	SP9	5c (+ 2½c) dp grn & bis	2.50	2.00
B14	SP9	12½c (+ 2½c) brt rose & bis	.85	.30
B15	SP9	15c (+ 5c) bl & bis	3.25	3.00
		Nos. B12-B15 (4)	7.00	5.70

The surtax was donated to the Salvation Army.

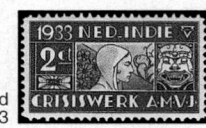

Woman and Lotus — SP13

5c, "The Light that Shows the Way." 12½c, YMCA emblem. 15c, Jobless man.

1933, Dec. 1 ***Perf. 12½***

B16	SP13	2c (+ 1c) red vio & ol bis	.65	.30
B17	SP13	5c (+ 2½c) grn & ol bis	2.25	1.90
B18	SP13	12½c (+ 2½c) ver & ol bis	2.50	.30
B19	SP13	15c (+ 5c) bl & ol bis	2.75	2.00
		Nos. B16-B19 (4)	8.15	4.50

The surtax was for the Amsterdam Young Men's Society for Relief of the Poor in Netherlands Indies.

Dowager Queen Emma — SP17

A Pioneer at Work — SP18

1934, Sept. 15 ***Perf. 13x14***

B20	SP17	12½c (+ 2½c) blk brn	1.25	.45

Issued in memory of the late Dowager Queen Emma of Netherlands. The surtax was for the Anti-Tuberculosis Society.

1935 ***Perf. 12½***

Designs: 5c, Cavalryman rescuing wounded native. 12½c, Artilleryman under fire. 15c, Bugler.

B21	SP18	2c (+ 1c) plum & ol bis	1.25	1.00
B22	SP18	5c (+ 2½c) grn & ol bis	3.25	2.25
B23	SP18	12½c (+ 2½c) red org & ol bis	3.25	.25
B24	SP18	15c (+ 5c) brt bl & ol bis	4.50	4.50
		Nos. B21-B24 (4)	12.25	8.00

The surtax was for the Indies Committee of the Christian Military Association for the East and West Indies.

Child Welfare Work — SP22

Boy Scouts — SP23

1936, Dec. 1 **Size: 23x20mm**

B25	SP22	2c (+ 1c) plum	1.00	.60

Size: 30x26½mm

B26	SP22	5c (+ 2½c) gray vio	1.25	1.10
B27	SP22	7½c (+ 2½c) dk vio	1.25	1.25
B28	SP22	12½c (+ 2½c) red org	1.25	.30
B29	SP22	15c (+5c) brt bl	2.00	1.75
		Nos. B25-B29 (5)	6.75	5.00

Surtax for Salvation Army.

1937, May 1

B30	SP23	7½c + 2½c dk ol brn	1.25	1.00
B31	SP23	12½c + 2½c rose car	1.25	.50

Fifth Boy Scout World Jamboree, Vogelenzang, Netherlands, July 31-Aug. 13, 1937. Surtax for Netherlands Indies Scout Association.

Sifting Rice — SP24

Designs: 3½c, Mother and children. 7½c, Plowing with carabao team. 10c, Carabao team and cart. 20c, Native couple.

1937, Dec. 1

B32	SP24	2c (+ 1c) dk brn & org	1.10	.80
B33	SP24	3½c (+ 1½c) gray	1.10	.80
B34	SP24	7½c (+ 2½c) Prus grn & org	1.25	.95
B35	SP24	10c (+ 2½c) car & org	1.25	.20
B36	SP24	20c (+ 5c) brt bl	1.25	1.10
		Nos. B32-B36 (5)	5.95	3.85

Surtax for the Public Relief Fund for indigenous poor.

Modern Plane — SP28

Design: 20c, Plane nose facing left.

Wmk. 202

1938, Oct. 15 **Photo.** ***Perf. 12½***

B36A	SP28	17½c (+5c) olive brn	.85	.85
B36B	SP28	20c (+ 5c) slate	.85	.55

10th anniversary of the Dutch East Indies Royal Air Lines (K. N. I. L. M.).

Surtax for the Aviation Fund in the Netherlands Indies.

Nun and Child
SP29 SP30

Designs: 7½c, Nurse examining child's arm. 10c, Nurse bathing baby. 20c, Nun bandaging child's head.

1938, Dec. 1 **Wmk. 202** ***Perf. 12½***

B37	SP29	2c (+ 1c) vio	.60	.45

Perf. 11½x12

B38	SP30	3½c (+ 1½c) brt grn	1.00	.90

Perf. 12x11½

B39	SP30	7½c (+ 2½c) cop red	.80	.85
B40	SP30	10c (+ 2½c) ver	.90	.20
B41	SP30	20c (+ 5c) brt ultra	1.00	.95
		Nos. B37-B41 (5)	4.30	3.35

The surtax was for the Central Mission Bureau in Batavia.

Social Workers SP34

Indonesian Nurse Tending Patient SP35

European Nurse Tending Patient — SP36

Perf. 13x11½, 11½x13

1939, Dec. 1 **Photo.**

B42	SP34	2c (+ 1c) purple	.25	.20
B43	SP35	3½c (+ 1½c) bl grn & pale bl grn	.30	.25
B44	SP34	7½c (+ 2½c) cop brn	.25	.20
B45	SP35	10c (+ 2½c) scar & pink	1.40	.80
B46	SP36	10c (+ 2½c) scar	1.40	.80
B47	SP36	20c (+ 5c) dk bl	.40	.35
		Nos. B42-B47 (6)	4.00	2.60

No. B44 shows native social workers.

Nos. B45 and B46 were issued se-tenant vertically and horizontally. The surtax was used for the Bureau of Social Service.

No. 174 Surcharged in Brown

1940, Dec. 2 **Unwmk.** ***Perf. 12x12½***

B48	A18	10c + 5c on 12½c dp org	1.10	.40

SP37

SP38

Netherlands coat of arms and inscription "Netherlands Shall Rise Again"

1941, May 10 **Litho.** ***Perf. 12½***

B49	SP37	5c + 5c multi	.20	.20
B50	SP37	10c + 10c multi	.25	.20
B51	SP37	1g + 1g multi	9.00	6.75
		Nos. B49-B51 (3)	9.45	7.15

The surtax was used to purchase fighter planes for Dutch pilots fighting with the Royal Air Force in Great Britain.

1941, Sept. 22 **Photo.**

Designs: 2c, Doctor and child, 3½c, Rice eater. 7½c, Nurse and patient. 10c, Nurse and children. 15c, Basket weaver.

B52	SP38	2c (+ 1c) yel grn	.60	.55
B53	SP38	3½c (+ 1½c) vio brn	4.00	3.50
B54	SP38	7½c (+ 2½c) vio	3.25	2.75
B55	SP38	10c (+ 2½c) dk red	.90	.20
B56	SP38	15c (+ 5c) saph	9.50	6.00
		Nos. B52-B56 (5)	18.25	13.00

The surtax was used for various charities.

Catalogue values for unused stamps in this section, from this point to the end of the section, are for Never Hinged items.

Indonesia

No. 208 Surcharged in Black

Perf. 12½x12

1948, Feb. 2 **Wmk. 202**

B57	A18	15c + 10c on 10c	.20	.20
	a.	Inverted surcharge	210.00	210.00

The surtax was for war victims and other charitable purposes.

AIR POST STAMPS

Regular Issues of 1913-1923 Surcharged and New Values in Black or Blue

Perf. 12½, 11½

1928, Sept. 20 **Unwmk.**

C1 A12 10c on 12½c red 1.00 1.00
C2 A12 20c on 25c red vio 2.25 2.25
C3 A13 40c on 80c org 1.90 1.50
C4 A13 75c on 1g brn (Bl) .90 .55
C5 A13 1½g on 2½g car 6.25 5.50
Nos. C1-C5 (5) 12.30 10.80

On Nos. C4 and C5 there are stars over the original values and the airplane is of different shape. On No. C3 there are no bars under "OST."

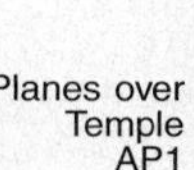

Planes over Temple
AP1

1928, Dec. 1 **Litho.** ***Perf. 12½x11½***

C6 AP1 10c red violet .30 .20
C7 AP1 20c brown .85 .55
C8 AP1 40c rose 1.00 .55
C9 AP1 75c green 2.25 .20
C10 AP1 1.50g orange 4.00 .50
Nos. C6-C10 (5) 8.40 2.00

For surcharges see Nos. 189-190, 192-193, C11-C12, C17.

No. C8 Surcharged in Black or Green

1930-32

C11 AP1 30c on 40c rose .90 .20
C12 AP1 30c on 40c rose (G) ('32) 1.25 .20

Pilot at Controls of Plane
AP2

1931, Apr. 1 **Photo.** ***Perf. 12½***

C13 AP2 1g blue & brown 11.00 11.00

Issued for the first air mail flight from Java to Australia.

Landscape and Garudas
AP3

1931, May

C14 AP3 30c red violet 2.25 .20
C15 AP3 4½g bright blue 8.00 3.00
C16 AP3 7½g yellow green 10.00 3.25
Nos. C14-C16 (3) 20.25 6.45

For surcharge see No. 191.

No. C10 Surcharged in Blue

1932, July 21 ***Perf. 12½x11½***

C17 AP1 50c on 1.50g org 2.50 .40
a. Inverted surcharge *1,800.* *2,000.*

Airplane
AP4

1933, Oct. 18 **Photo.** ***Perf. 12½***

C18 AP4 30c deep blue 2.10 1.75

MARINE INSURANCE STAMPS

Floating Safe Attracting Gulls — MI1

Floating Safe with Night Flare — MI2

Artistic Fantasy of Floating Safe — MI3

Perf. 11½

1921, Nov. 1 **Unwmk.** **Engr.**

GY1 MI1 15c slate green 2.25 *40.00*
GY2 MI1 60c rose 4.00 *50.00*
GY3 MI1 75c gray brn 4.00 *55.00*
GY4 MI2 1.50g dark blue 25.00 *250.00*
GY5 MI2 2.25g org brn 32.50 *350.00*
GY6 MI3 4½g black 65.00 *600.00*
GY7 MI3 7½g red 80.00 *700.00*
Nos. GY1-GY7 (7) 212.75 *2,045.*

POSTAGE DUE STAMPS

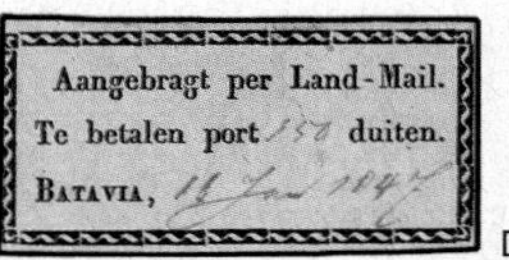
Aangebragt per Land-Mail.
Te betalen port 1/50 duiten.
BATAVIA, 18 Jan 1847

D1

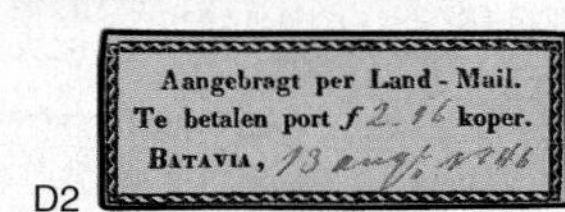
Aangebragt per Land-Mail.
Te betalen port f 2.16 koper.
BATAVIA, 13 aug 1846

D2

1845-46 **Unwmk.** **Typeset** ***Imperf.***

Bluish Paper

J1 D1 black ('46) *1,400.*
J2 D2 black *2,000.*
a. "Maill" instead of "Mail" *3,200.*

D3

Perf. 12½x12, 13x14, 10½x12

1874 **Typo.**

J3 D3 5c ocher 300.00 275.00
J4 D3 10c green, *yel* 120.00 100.00
J5 D3 15c ocher, *org* 25.00 20.00
a. Perf. 11½x12 40.00 40.00
J6 D3 20c green, *blue* 40.00 17.50
a. Perf. 11½x12 80.00 25.00
Nos. J3-J6 (4) 485.00 412.50

D4

D5

Type I — 34 loops. "T" of "Betalen" over center of loop, top branch of "E" of "Te" shorter than lower branch.

Type II — 33 loops. "T" of "Betalen" over center of two loops.

Type III — 32 loops. "T" of "Betalen" slightly to the left of loop, top branch of first "E" of "Betalen" shorter than lower branch.

Type IV — 37 loops and letters of "PORT" larger than in the other three types.

Value in Black

Perf. 11½x12, 12½, 12½x12, 13½

1882-88

Type III

J7 D4 2½c carmine .40 1.10
J8 D4 5c carmine .20 .40
J9 D4 10c carmine 2.50 3.00
J10 D4 15c carmine 3.00 3.00
J11 D4 20c carmine 95.00 .75
J12 D4 30c carmine 1.75 2.50
J13 D4 40c carmine 1.25 2.00
J14 D4 50c deep salmon .75 .60
J15 D4 75c carmine .45 .50
Nos. J7-J15 (9) 105.30 13.85

Type I

J7a D4 2½c carmine .40 1.10
J8a D4 5c carmine .25 .45
J9a D4 10c carmine 3.25 4.00
J10a D4 15c carmine 3.25 3.50
J11a D4 20c carmine 95.00 .50
J12a D4 30c carmine 3.25 4.00
J13a D4 40c carmine 1.40 2.00
J14a D4 50c deep salmon .80 .60
J15a D4 75c carmine .50 .60
Nos. J7a-J15a (9) 108.10 16.75

Type II

J7b D4 2½c carmine .50 1.40
J8b D4 5c carmine .25 .50
J9b D4 10c carmine 3.50 4.50
J10b D4 15c carmine 3.75 4.00
J11b D4 20c carmine 110.00 .65
J12b D4 30c carmine 7.00 7.50
J13b D4 40c carmine 1.50 2.50
J14b D4 50c deep salmon .85 .75
J15b D4 75c carmine .65 .85
Nos. J7b-J15b (9) 128.00 22.65

Type IV

J7c D4 2½c carmine 2.25 3.00
J8c D4 5c carmine 1.00 1.75
J9c D4 10c carmine 20.00 24.00
J10c D4 15c carmine 13.00 14.00
J11c D4 20c carmine 200.00 5.00
J13c D4 40c carmine 2.50 3.50
J14c D4 50c deep salmon 9.00 14.00
J15c D4 75c carmine 1.25 2.50
Nos. J7c-J15c (8) 249.00 67.75

1892-95 ***Perf. 12½***

Type I

J16 D5 10c carmine 2.25 .30
J17 D5 15c carmine ('95) 12.00 1.75
J18 D5 20c carmine 2.00 .20
Nos. J16-J18 (3) 16.25 2.25

Type III

J16a D5 10c dull red 2.75 2.00
J18a D5 20c dull red 3.75 1.40

Type II

J16b D5 10c dull red 13.00 13.00
J18b D5 20c dull red 18.00 6.50

1906-09

Type I

J19 D5 2½c carmine ('08) .50 .30
J20 D5 5c carmine ('09) 2.25 .20
J21 D5 30c carmine 17.50 5.75
J22 D5 40c carmine ('09) 12.50 1.50
J23 D5 50c carmine ('09) 8.50 .90
J24 D5 75c carmine ('09) 17.00 4.00
Nos. J19-J24 (6) 58.25 12.65

Value in Color of Stamp

1913-39 ***Perf. 12½***

J25 D5 1c salmon ('39) .25 *1.25*
J26 D5 2½c salmon .25 .25
J27 D5 3½c salmon ('39) .25 *1.25*
J28 D5 5c salmon .25 .25
J29 D5 7½c salmon ('22) .25 .25
J30 D5 10c salmon .25 .25
J31 D5 12½c salmon ('22) 2.75 .25
J32 D5 15c salmon 2.75 .25
J33 D5 20c salmon .25 .25
J34 D5 25c salmon ('22) .25 .25
J35 D5 30c salmon .25 .25
J36 D5 37½c salmon ('30) 22.50 22.50
J37 D5 40c salmon .25 .25
J38 D5 50c salmon 1.40 .25
J39 D5 75c salmon 2.50 .25
Nos. J25-J39 (15) 34.40 28.00

Thick White Paper
Invisible Gum
Numerals Slightly Larger

1941 **Litho.** ***Perf. 12½***

J25a D5 1c light red .60 *2.00*
J28a D5 5c light red .65 1.00
J30a D5 10c light red 10.50 10.00
J32a D5 15c light red 1.00 1.00
J33a D5 20c light red .80 .80
J35a D5 30c light red 1.25 1.00
J37a D5 40c light red 1.00 .80
Nos. J25a-J37a (7) 15.80 16.60

No. J36 Surcharged with New Value

1937, Oct. 1 **Unwmk.** ***Perf. 12½***

J40 D5 20c on 37½c salmon .25 .30

D6

D7

1939-40

J41 D6 1g salmon 5.00 7.50
J42 D6 1g blue ('40) .30 *4.50*
a. 1g lt bl, thick paper, invisible gum .90 *1.00*

Catalogue values for unused stamps in this section, from this point to the end of the section, are for Never Hinged items.

Nos. 234, 237 and 241 Surcharged or Overprinted in Black

1946, Mar. 11 **Photo.**

J43 A28 2½c on 10c red org .60 .55
J44 A28 10c red orange 1.25 1.10
J45 A28 20c plum 6.25 3.50
J46 A28 40c yellow green 60.00 45.00
Nos. J43-J46 (4) 68.10 50.15

Perf. 14½x14

1946, Aug. 14 **Wmk. 228** **Typo.**

J47 D7 1c purple 1.00 1.40
J48 D7 2½c brn org 3.50 2.00
J49 D7 3½c ultra 1.00 1.40
J50 D7 5c red orange 1.00 1.40
J51 D7 7½c Prus green 1.00 1.40
J52 D7 10c deep magenta 1.00 1.40
J53 D7 20c light ultra 1.00 1.40
J54 D7 25c olive 1.50 2.00
J55 D7 30c red brown 1.50 2.00
J56 D7 40c yellow grn 2.25 1.50
J57 D7 50c yellow 2.25 1.50
J58 D7 75c aqua 2.25 1.50
J59 D7 100c apple green 2.25 1.50
Nos. J47-J59 (13) 21.50 20.40

1948 **Litho.** **Unwmk.** ***Perf. 12½***

J59A D7 2½c brown orange .90 *2.00*

OFFICIAL STAMPS

Regular Issues of 1883-1909 Overprinted

Perf. 12½

1911, Oct. 1 Typo. Unwmk.

O1	A6	½c	violet	.20	.30
O2	A6	1c	olive grn	.20	.20
O3	A6	2c	yellow brn	.20	.20
O4	A3	2½c	yellow	.75	.75
O5	A6	2½c	blue grn	1.40	1.25
O6	A6	3c	orange	.40	.40
O7	A6	4c	ultra	.20	.20
O8	A6	5c	rose red	.80	.80
b.			Double overprint		*325.00*
O9	A6	7½c	gray	2.75	2.75
O10	A9	10c	slate	.20	.20
O11	A9	12½c	deep blue	2.00	2.25
O12	A9	15c	chocolate	.65	.65
a.			Overprinted with two bars	32.50	
b.			As "a," "Dienst" inverted	52.50	
O13	A9	17½c	bister	2.75	2.50
O14	A9	20c	olive grn	.60	.50
O15	A9	22½c	brn & ol grn	3.50	3.00
O16	A9	25c	violet	2.00	2.00
O17	A9	30c	orange brn	.90	.60
O18	A9	50c	red brown	12.00	7.00
O19	A10	1g	dull lilac	3.00	1.25
O20	A10	2½g	slate blue	27.50	30.00
			Nos. O1-O20 (20)	62.00	

The overprint reads diagonally downward on Nos. O1-O3 and O5-O9.

Overprint Inverted

O1a	A6	½c	45.00	*125.00*
O2a	A6	1c	3.00	*19.00*
O3a	A6	2c	3.00	*20.00*
O5a	A6	2½c	9.00	*30.00*
O6a	A6	3c	110.00	*40.00*
O8a	A6	5c	3.00	*20.00*
O10a	A9	10c	3.00	*7.00*
O11a	A9	12½c	32.50	*55.00*
O14a	A9	20c	175.00	70.00
O16a	A9	25c	*1,250.*	*1,000.*
O17a	A9	30c	225.00	140.00
O18a	A9	50c	32.50	32.50
O19a	A10	1g	*525.00*	*850.00*
O20a	A10	2½g	225.00	*625.00*

Regular Issue of 1892-1894 Overprinted

1911, Oct. 1

O21	A4	10c	orange brn	1.25	*.60*
O22	A4	12½c	gray	3.00	*5.50*
O23	A4	15c	bister	3.00	3.00
O24	A4	20c	blue	3.00	1.00
O25	A4	25c	lilac	12.00	10.00
O26	A4	50c	carmine	2.50	1.25
O27	A4	2.50g	org brn & bl	55.00	55.00
			Nos. O21-O27 (7)	79.75	76.35

Inverted Overprints

O21a	A4	10c	12.00	*40.00*
O22a	A4	12½c	350.00	350.00
O23a	A4	15c	350.00	350.00
O24a	A4	20c	100.00	110.00
O25a	A4	25c	550.00	*600.00*
O26a	A4	50c	15.00	*100.00*
O27a	A4	2.50g	650.00	*900.00*

OCCUPATION STAMPS

Issued under Japanese Occupation

During the Japanese occupation of the Netherlands Indies, 1942-45, the occupation forces applied a great variety of overprints to supplies of Netherlands Indies stamps of 1933-42. A few typical examples are shown above.

Most of these overprinted stamps were for use in limited areas, such as Java, Sumatra, Bangka and Billiton, etc. The anchor overprints were applied by the Japanese naval authorities for areas under their control.

For a time, stamps of Straits Settlements and some of the Malayan states, with Japanese overprints, were used in Sumatra and the Riouw archipelago. Stamps of Japan without overprint were also used in the Netherlands Indies during the occupation.

For Use in Java and Sumatra

100 Sen (Cents) = 1 Rupee (Gulden)

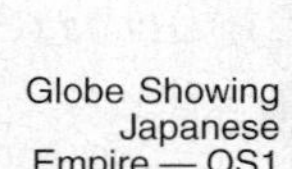

Globe Showing Japanese Empire — OS1

Farmer Plowing Rice Field — OS2

Mt. Semeru, Java's Highest Active Volcano — OS3

Bantam Bay, Northwest Java — OS4

Values in Sen

Perf. 12½

1943, Mar. 9 Unwmk. Litho.

N1	OS1	2s	red brown	1.25	4.25
N2	OS2	3½s	carmine	1.25	1.25
N3	OS3	5s	green	1.25	1.25
N4	OS4	10s	light blue	14.00	2.50
			Nos. N1-N4 (4)	17.75	9.25

Issued to mark the anniversary of Japan's "Victory" in Java.

For Use in Java (also Sumatra, Borneo and Malaya)

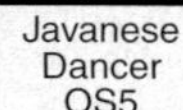

Javanese Dancer OS5

Javanese Puppet OS6

Buddha Statue, Borobudur OS7

Map of Java OS8

Sacred Dancer of Djokja Palace, and Borobudur OS9

Bird of Vishnu, Map of Java and Mt. Semeru OS10

Plowing with Carabao OS11

Terraced Rice Fields OS12

Values in Cents, Sen or Rupees

1943-44 Unwmk. *Perf. 12½*

N5	OS5	3½c	rose red	1.10	.80
N6	OS6	5s	yellow grn	1.10	.80
N7	OS7	10c	dk blue	1.10	.60
N8	OS8	20c	gray olive	1.40	1.40
N9	OS9	40c	rose lilac	3.50	3.25
N10	OS10	60c	red orange	5.00	1.60
N11	OS11	80s	fawn ('44)	11.00	5.50
N12	OS12	1r	violet ('44)	42.50	11.50
			Nos. N5-N12 (8)	66.70	25.45

Indies Soldier — OS13

1943, Apr.

N13	OS13	3½c	rose	11.00	15.00
N14	OS13	10c	blue	55.00	9.50

Issued to commemorate reaching the postal savings goal of 5,000,000 gulden.

For Use in Sumatra

Batta Tribal House OS14

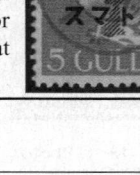

Menangkabau House OS15

Plowing with Carabao OS16

Nias Island Scene OS17

Carabao Canyon — OS18

1943 Unwmk. *Perf. 12½*

N15	OS14	1c	olive green	.55	.30
N16	OS14	2c	brt yel brn	.55	.30
N17	OS14	3c	bluish green	.55	.30
N18	OS15	3½c	rose red	2.50	.30
N19	OS15	4c	ultra	2.75	.55
N20	OS15	5c	red orange	.80	.30
N21	OS16	10c	blue gray	.80	.30
N22	OS16	20c	orange brn	1.10	.40
N23	OS17	30c	red violet	1.10	.75
N24	OS17	40c	dull brown	10.00	2.50
N25	OS18	50c	bister brn	10.00	2.50
N26	OS18	1r	lt blue vio	52.50	10.50
			Nos. N15-N26 (12)	83.20	19.00

For Use in the Lesser Sunda Islands, Molucca Archipelago and Districts of Celebes and South Borneo Controlled by the Japanese Navy

Japanese Flag, Island Scene OS19

Mt. Fuji, Kite, Flag, Map of East Indies OS20

Values in Cents and Gulden

1943 Wmk. 257 Typo. *Perf. 13*

N27	OS19	2c	brown	.40	*15.00*
N28	OS19	3c	yellow grn	.40	*15.00*
N29	OS19	3½c	brown org	3.25	*15.00*
N30	OS19	5c	blue	.40	*15.00*
N31	OS19	10c	carmine	.40	*15.00*
N32	OS19	15c	ultra	.60	*15.00*
N33	OS19	20c	dull violet	.80	*15.00*

Engr.

N34	OS20	25c	orange	5.50	*15.00*
N35	OS20	30c	blue	7.75	*10.00*
N36	OS20	50c	slate green	9.25	*25.00*
N37	OS20	1g	brown lilac	47.50	*45.00*
			Nos. N27-N37 (11)	76.25	*200.00*

Issued under Nationalist Occupation

Menari Dancer of Amboina — OS21

Perf. 12½

1945, Aug. Photo. Unwmk.

N38	OS21	2c	carmine	.20	.35

This stamp was prepared in 1941 or 1942 by Netherlands Indies authorities as an addition to the 1941 "dancers" set, but was issued in 1945 by the Nationalists (Indonesian Republic). It was not recognized by the Dutch. Exists imperforate.

NETHERLANDS NEW GUINEA

'ne-thər-lən‚d‚z 'nü 'gi-nē

(Dutch New Guinea)

LOCATION — Western half of New Guinea, southwest Pacific Ocean
GOVT. — Former Overseas Territory of the Netherlands
AREA — 151,789 sq. mi.
POP. — 730,000 (est. 1958)
CAPITAL — Hollandia

Netherlands New Guinea came under temporary United Nations administration Oct. 1, 1962, when stamps of this territory overprinted "UNTEA" were introduced to replace issues of Netherlands New Guinea. See West New Guinea (West Irian) in Vol. 6.

100 Cents = 1 Gulden

Catalogue values for all unused stamps in this country are for Never Hinged items.

A1

A2

Queen Juliana — A3

Perf. 12½x13½

1950-52 **Unwmk.** **Photo.**

1 A1 1c slate blue .20 .20
2 A1 2c deep org .20 .20
3 A1 2½c olive brn .25 .20
4 A1 3c deep plum 1.60 1.25
5 A1 4c blue grn 1.60 1.10
6 A1 5c ultra 3.25 .20
7 A1 7½c org brown .35 .20
8 A1 10c purple 1.75 .20
9 A1 12½c crimson 1.75 1.40

Perf. 13½x12½

10 A2 15c brown org 1.25 .55
11 A2 20c blue .35 .20
12 A2 25c orange red .35 .20
13 A2 30c dp blue ('52) 7.25 .30
14 A2 40c blue grn .75 .20
15 A2 45c brown ('52) 3.50 .50
16 A2 50c deep orange .75 .20
17 A2 55c brown blk ('52) 6.25 .40
18 A2 80c purple 7.25 3.00

Engr. *Perf. 12½x12*

19 A3 1g red 11.00 .20
20 A3 2g yellow brn ('52) 9.00 1.25
21 A3 5g dk olive grn 12.00 1.00
Nos. 1-21 (21) 70.65 12.95

For surcharges see Nos. B1-B3.

Bird of Paradise — A4

Queen Victoria Crowned Pigeon — A5

Queen Juliana — A6

10c, 15c, 20c, Bird of Paradise with raised wings.

Photo.; Litho. (Nos. 24, 26, 28)

1954-60 *Perf. 12½x12*

22 A4 1c ver & yel ('58) .20 .20
23 A4 5c choc & yel .20 .20
24 A5 7c org red, bl & brn vio ('59) .20 .20
25 A4 10c aqua & red brn .20 .20
26 A5 12c grn, bl & brn vio ('59) .20 .20
27 A4 15c dp yel & red brn .20 .20
28 A5 17c brn vio & bl ('59) .20 .20
29 A4 20c lt bl grn & red brn ('56) .50 .30
30 A6 25c red .20 .20
31 A6 30c deep blue .20 .20
32 A6 40c dp orange ('60) 1.75 1.75
33 A6 45c dk olive ('58) .65 .65
34 A6 55c dk blue grn .45 .20
35 A6 80c dl gray vio .80 .30
36 A6 85c dk vio brn ('56) .90 .45
37 A6 1g plum ('59) 4.50 2.00
Nos. 22-37 (16) 11.35 7.45

Stamps overprinted "UNTEA" are listed under West New Guinea in Vol. 6.
For surcharges see Nos. B4-B6.

Papuan Watching Helicopter — A7

Mourning Woman — A8

1959, Apr. 10 **Photo.** *Perf. 11½x11*

38 A7 55c red brown & blue 1.50 1.00

1959 expedition to the Star Mountains of New Guinea.

1960, Apr. 7 **Unwmk.** *Perf. 13x14*

39 A8 25c blue .70 .60
40 A8 30c yellow bister .70 .60

World Refugee Year, 7/1/59-6/30/60.

Council Building A9

1961, Apr. 5 **Litho.** *Perf. 11x11½*

41 A9 25c bluish green .30 .40
42 A9 30c rose .30 .40

Inauguration of the New Council.

School Children Crossing Street — A10

Design: 30c, Men looking at traffic sign.

1962, Mar. 16 **Photo.** *Perf. 14x13*

43 A10 25c dp blue & red .40 .40
44 A10 30c brt green & red .40 .40

Need for road safety.

Queen Juliana and Prince Bernhard A11

1962, Apr. 28 **Unwmk.** *Perf. 14x13*

45 A11 55c olive brown .45 .50

Silver wedding anniv.

Tropical Beach A12

Design: 30c, Palm trees on beach.

1962, July 18 *Perf. 14x13*

46 A12 25c multicolored .30 .40
47 A12 30c multicolored .30 .40

5th So. Pacific Conf., Pago Pago, July 1962.

SEMI-POSTAL STAMPS

Regular Issue of 1950-52 Surcharged in Black

Perf. 12½x13½

1953, Feb. 9 **Unwmk.** **Photo.**

B1 A1 5c + 5c ultra 10.00 8.00

Perf. 13½x12½

B2 A2 15c + 10c brn org 10.00 8.00
B3 A2 25c + 10c org red 10.00 8.00
Nos. B1-B3 (3) 30.00 24.00

The tax was for flood relief work in the Netherlands.

Nos. 23, 25, 27 Surcharged in Red

1955, Nov. 1 *Perf. 12½x12*

B4 A4 5c + 5c 1.50 1.50
B5 A4 10c + 10c 1.50 1.50
B6 A4 15c + 10c 1.50 1.50
Nos. B4-B6 (3) 4.50 4.50

The surtax was for the Red Cross.

Leprosarium — SP1

Papuan Girl and Beach Scene — SP2

10c+5c, 30c+10c, Young Papuan and huts.

Perf. 12x12½

1956, Dec. 15 **Unwmk.** **Photo.**

B7 SP1 5c + 5c dk slate grn 1.25 .80
B8 SP1 10c + 5c brn violet 1.25 .80
B9 SP1 25c + 10c brt blue 1.25 .80
B10 SP1 30c + 10c ocher 1.25 .80
Nos. B7-B10 (4) 5.00 3.20

The surtax was for the fight against leprosy.

1957, Oct. 1 *Perf. 12½x12*

10c+5c, 30c+10c, Papuan boy and pile dwelling.

B11 SP2 5c + 5c maroon 1.10 .90
B12 SP2 10c + 5c slate grn 1.10 .90
B13 SP2 25c + 10c brown 1.10 .90
B14 SP2 30c + 10c dark blue 1.10 .90
Nos. B11-B14 (4) 4.40 3.60

The surtax was to fight infant mortality.

Ancestral Image, North Coast New Guinea — SP3

Bignonia — SP4

Design: 10c+5c, 30c+10c, Bowl in form of human figure, Asmat-Papua.

1958, Oct. 1 **Litho.** *Perf. 12½x12*

B15 SP3 5c + 5c bl, blk & red 1.00 1.00
B16 SP3 10c + 5c rose lake, blk, red & yel 1.00 1.00
B17 SP3 25c + 10c bl grn, blk & red 1.00 1.00
B18 SP3 30c + 10c ol gray, blk, red & yel 1.00 1.00
Nos. B15-B18 (4) 4.00 4.00

The surtax was for the Red Cross.

1959, Nov. 16 **Photo.** *Perf. 12½x13*

Flowers: 10c+5c, Orchid. 25c+10c, Rhododendron. 30c+10c, Gesneriacea.

B19 SP4 5c + 5c car rose & grn .75 .75
B20 SP4 10c + 5c ol, yel & lil .75 .75
B21 SP4 25c + 10c red, org & grn .75 .75
B22 SP4 30c + 10c vio & grn .75 .75
Nos. B19-B22 (4) 3.00 3.00

Birdwing SP5

Various Butterflies.

Perf. 13x12½

1960, Sept. 1 **Unwmk.** **Litho.**

B23 SP5 5c + 5c lt bl, blk, emer & yel 1.25 1.10
B24 SP5 10c + 5c sal, blk & bl 1.25 1.10
B25 SP5 25c + 10c yel, blk & org red 1.75 1.40
B26 SP5 30c + 10c lt grn, brn & yel 1.75 1.40
Nos. B23-B26 (4) 6.00 5.00

Surtax for social care.

Rhinoceros Beetle and Coconut Palm Leaf — SP6

Beetles & leaves of host plants: 10c+5c, Ectocemus 10-maculatus Montri, a primitive weevil. 25c+10c, Stag beetle. 30c+10c, Tortoise beetle.

1961, Sept. 15 *Perf. 13x12½*

Beetles in Natural Colors

B27 SP6 5c + 5c deep org .60 .60
B28 SP6 10c + 5c lt ultra .60 .60
B29 SP6 25c + 10c citron .60 .60
B30 SP6 30c + 10c green .60 .60
Nos. B27-B30 (4) 2.40 2.40

Surtax for social care.

Crab — SP7

Designs: 10c+5c, Lobster, vert. 25c+10c, Spiny lobster, vert. 30c+10c, Shrimp.

Perf. 14x13, 13x14

1962, Sept. 17 **Unwmk.**

B31 SP7 5c + 5c red, grn, brn & yel .25 .25
B32 SP7 10c + 5c Prus bl & yel .25 .25
B33 SP7 25c + 10c multicolored .25 .25
B34 SP7 30c + 10c bl, org red & yel .25 .25
Nos. B31-B34 (4) 1.00 1.00

The surtax on Nos. B19-B34 went to various social works organizations.

POSTAGE DUE STAMPS

D1

Perf. 13½x12½

1957 **Photo.** **Unwmk.**

J1 D1 1c vermilion .40 .25
J2 D1 5c vermilion 1.00 *1.25*
J3 D1 10c vermilion 2.50 *3.00*
J4 D1 25c vermilion 3.50 2.00
J5 D1 40c vermilion 3.50 2.00
J6 D1 1g blue 4.50 *4.50*
Nos. J1-J6 (6) 15.40 13.00

NEVIS

'nē-vəs

LOCATION — West Indies, southeast of Puerto Rico
GOVT. — A former presidency of the Leeward Islands Colony (British)
AREA — 36 sq. mi.
POP. — 8,794 (1991)

Nevis stamps were discontinued in 1890 and replaced by those of the Leeward Islands. From 1903 to 1956 stamps of St. Kitts-Nevis and Leeward Islands were used concurrently. From 1956 to 1980 stamps of St. Kitts-Nevis were used. While still a part of St. Kitts-Nevis, Nevis started issuing stamps in 1980.

See Leeward Islands and St. Kitts-Nevis.

12 Pence = 1 Shilling
100 Cents = 1 Dollar

Catalogue values for unused stamps in this country are for Never Hinged items, beginning with Scott 100 in the regular postage section and Scott O1 in the officials section.

Unused examples of Nos. 1-8 almost always have no original gum, and they are valued without gum. These stamps with original gum are worth more. Other issues are valued with original gum as defined in the catalogue introduction. Very fine examples of Nos. 1-8, will have perforations touching the design on at least one side due to the narrow spacing of the stamps on the plates. Stamps with perfs clear of the design on all four sides are scarce and will command higher prices.

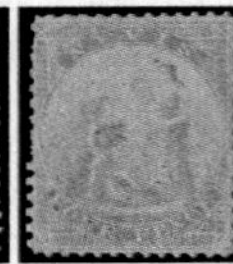

Medicinal Spring
A1 A2

A3 A4

1861 **Unwmk.** **Engr.** ***Perf. 13***

Bluish Wove Paper

1 A1 1p lake rose 275.00 140.00
2 A2 4p dull rose 850.00 200.00
3 A3 6p gray 700.00 260.00
4 A4 1sh green 1,050. 225.00

Grayish Wove Paper

5 A1 1p lake rose 82.50 52.50
6 A2 4p dull rose 110.00 62.50
7 A3 6p lilac gray 110.00 57.50
8 A4 1sh green 280.00 80.00

1867 **White Wove Paper** ***Perf. 15***

9 A1 1p red 47.50 45.00
10 A2 4p orange 110.00 22.50
11 A4 1sh yellow green 950.00 125.00
12 A4 1sh blue green 250.00 32.50

Laid Paper

13 A4 1sh yel green 17,000. *5,750.*
Manuscript cancel 1,000.

No. 13 values are for stamps with design cut into on one or two sides.

1876 **Litho.**

Wove Paper

14 A1 1p rose 22.50 17.50
14A A1 1p red 32.50 27.50
b. 1p vermilion 27.50 27.50
c. Imperf., pair 775.00
d. Half used as ½p on cover 2,250.
15 A2 4p orange 180.00 32.50
a. Imperf.
b. Vert. pair, imperf. between *5,000.*
16 A3 6p olive gray 225.00 200.00
17 A4 1sh gray green 95.00 *110.00*
a. 1sh dark green 105.00 *150.00*
b. Horiz. strip of 3, perf. all around & imperf. btwn. *6,750.*

Perf. 11½

18 A1 1p vermilion 50.00 55.00
a. Horiz. pair, imperf. btwn.
b. Half used as ½p on cover 2,250.
c. Imperf., pair 500.00
Nos. 14-18 (6) 605.00 442.50

Queen Victoria — A5

1879-80 **Typo.** **Wmk. 1** ***Perf. 14***

19 A5 1p violet ('80) 80.00 37.50
a. Diagonal half used as ½p on cover 1,100.
20 A5 2½p red brown 125.00 95.00

1882-90 **Wmk. Crown and CA (2)**

21 A5 ½p green ('83) 5.50 *14.00*
22 A5 1p violet 100.00 32.50
a. Half used as ½p on cover 800.00
23 A5 1p rose ('84) 10.00 *17.50*
24 A5 2½p red brown 125.00 55.00
25 A5 2½p ultra ('84) 20.00 17.50
26 A5 4p blue 350.00 55.00
27 A5 4p gray ('84) 11.00 4.00
28 A5 6p green ('83) 425.00 400.00
29 A5 6p brown org ('86) 25.00 *67.50*
30 A5 1sh violet ('90) 110.00 *200.00*
Nos. 21-30 (10) 1,181. *863.00*

Half of No. 22 Surcharged in Black or Violet

1883

31 A5 ½p on half of 1p *1,150.* 47.50
a. Double surcharge 350.00
b. Unsevered pair *4,000.* 600.00
32 A5 ½p on half of 1p (V) *950.00* 50.00
a. Double surcharge 350.00

Surcharge reads up or down.

Catalogue values for unused stamps in this section, from this point to the end of the section, are for Never Hinged items.

St. Kitts-Nevis Nos. 357-369 Ovptd.

Perf. 14½x14

1980, June 23 **Litho.** **Wmk. 373**

100 A61 5c multicolored .20 .20
101 A61 10c multicolored .20 .20
102 A61 12c multicolored .20 .30
103 A61 15c multicolored .20 .20
104 A61 25c multicolored .20 .20
105 A61 30c multicolored .20 .20
106 A61 40c multicolored .30 .30
107 A61 45c multicolored .75 .50
108 A61 50c multicolored .30 .30
109 A61 55c multicolored .40 .20
110 A61 $1 multicolored .30 .30
111 A61 $5 multicolored 1.50 1.00
112 A61 $10 multicolored 2.50 1.50
Nos. 100-112 (13) 7.25 5.40

The bars cover "St. Christopher" and "Anguilla."

The 25c and $1 also come on unwatermarked paper.

80th Birthday of Queen Mother Elizabeth — A6

1980, Sept. 4 ***Perf. 14***

113 A6 $2 multicolored .40 .50

Ships and Boats — A6a

1980, Oct. 8

114 A6a 5c Nevis lighter .20 .20
115 A6a 30c Local fishing boat .20 .20
116 A6a 55c *Caona* .30 .30

Size: 38x52mm

117 A6a $3 Windjammer's S.V. *Polynesia* 1.00 1.00
a. Perf. 12½x12 1.00 1.00
b. Booklet pane of 3 #117a 2.50
Nos. 114-117 (4) 1.70 1.70

No. 117b separated into three parts by roulettes running vert. through the margin surrounding the stamps. For overprint see No. 538.

Christmas A7

Landmarks A8

A9

1980, Nov. 20 ***Perf. 14***

118 A7 5c Mother and child .40 .40
119 A7 30c Heralding angel .40 .40
120 A7 $2.50 Three kings .75 .75
Nos. 118-120 (3) 1.55 1.55

1981, Feb. 5

121 A8 5c Charlestown Pier .20 .20
122 A8 10c Court House & Library .20 .20
123 A9 15c New River Mill .20 .20
124 A9 20c Nelson Museum .20 .20
125 A9 25c St. James' Parish Church .20 .20
126 A9 30c Nevis Lane .20 .20
127 A9 40c Zetland Plantation .20 .20
128 A9 45c Nisbet Plantation .25 .25
129 A9 50c Pinney's Beach .25 .25
130 A9 55c Eva Wilkin's Studio .30 .30
131 A9 $1 Nevis at dawn .55 .55
132 A9 $2.50 Ft. Charles ruins .75 .75
133 A9 $5 Old Bath House 1.50 1.50
134 A9 $10 Nisbet's Beach 3.00 3.00
Nos. 121-134 (14) 8.00 8.00

Nos. 121-134 exist inscribed "Questa 1982," issued June 9, 1982. Same values.

For surcharges see Nos. 169-181.

Prince Charles, Lady Diana, Royal Yacht Charlotte A9a

Prince Charles and Lady Diana — A9b

Illustration A9b is greatly reduced.

1981, June 23 **Wmk. 373** ***Perf. 14***

135 A9a 55c Couple, *Royal Caroline* .25 .25
a. Bklt. pane of 4, perf. 12, unwmkd. 1.10 1.10
136 A9b 55c Couple .25 .25
137 A9a $2 Couple, *Royal Sovereign* .75 .75
138 A9b $2 like No. 136 .75 .75
a. Bklt. pane of 2, perf. 12, unwmkd. 2.00 2.00
139 A9a $5 Couple, HMY *Britannia* 1.50 1.50
140 A9b $5 like No. 136 1.50 1.50
Nos. 135-140 (6) 5.00 5.00

Souvenir Sheet

1981, Dec. 14 ***Perf. 12***

141 A9b $4.50 like No. 136 2.00 2.00

Stamps of the same denomination issued in sheets of 7 (6 type A9a and 1 type A9b).

For surcharges see Nos. 453-454.

Butterflies A10

1982, Feb. 16 ***Perf. 14***

142 A10 5c Zebra .20 .20
143 A10 30c Malachite .20 .20
144 A10 55c Southern dagger tail .40 .40
145 A10 $2 Large orange sulphur 1.60 1.60
Nos. 142-145 (4) 2.40 2.40

For overprint see No. 452.

1983, June 8

146 A10 30c Tropical chequered skipper .55 .55
147 A10 55c Caribbean buckeye, vert. .55 .55

148 A10 $1.10 Common long-tailed skipper, vert. .80 .80
149 A10 $2 Mimic 1.10 1.10
Nos. 146-149 (4) 3.00 3.00

21st Birthday of Princess Diana, July 1 — A11

1982, June 22 *Perf. 13½x14*
150 A11 30c Caroline of Brunswick .25 .25
151 A11 55c Brunswick arms .35 .35
152 A11 $5 Diana 1.40 1.40
Nos. 150-152 (3) 2.00 2.00

For surcharge see No. 449.

Nos. 150-152 Overprinted "ROYAL BABY"

1982, July 12
153 A11 30c multicolored .30 .30
154 A11 55c multicolored .45 .45
155 A11 $5 multicolored 1.75 1.75
Nos. 153-155 (3) 2.50 2.50

Birth of Prince William of Wales, June 21.

Scouting, 75th Anniv. — A12

1982, Aug. 18
156 A12 5c Cycling .40 .40
157 A12 30c Running .50 .50
158 A12 $2.50 Building campfire 1.10 1.10
Nos. 156-158 (3) 2.00 2.00

For overprints see Nos. 447, 455.

Christmas — A13

Illustrations by youths. Nos. 159-160 vert.

1982, Oct. 20 *Perf. 13½x14, 14x13½*
159 A13 15c Eugene Seabrookes .30 .30
160 A13 30c Kharenzabeth Glasgow .30 .30
161 A13 $1.50 David Grant .40 .40
162 A13 $2.50 Leonard Huggins .75 .75
Nos. 159-162 (4) 1.75 1.75

Coral — A14

1983, Jan. 12 *Perf. 14*
163 A14 15c Tube sponge .25 .25
164 A14 30c Stinging coral .50 .50
165 A14 55c Flower coral .50 .50
166 A14 $3 Sea rod, red fire sponge 1.50 1.50
a. Souvenir sheet of 4, #163-166 3.00 3.00
Nos. 163-166 (4) 2.75 2.75

For overprints see Nos. 446, 448.

Commonwealth Day — A15

1983, Mar. 14
167 A15 55c HMS *Boreas* off Nevis .25 .25
168 A15 $2 Lord Nelson, *Boreas* .85 .85

Nos. 121 and 123-134 Ovptd.

No. 169

No. 170-181

1983, Sept. 23
169 A8 5c multicolored .20 .20
a. Overprint larger with serifed letters 12.00 10.00
170 A9 15c multicolored .20 .20
171 A9 20c multicolored .20 .20
172 A9 25c multicolored .20 .25
173 A9 30c multicolored .20 .25
174 A9 40c multicolored .20 .30
175 A9 45c multicolored .30 .40
176 A9 50c multicolored .30 .40
177 A9 55c multicolored .35 .45
178 A9 $1 multicolored .45 .45
179 A9 $2.50 multicolored .45 .70
180 A9 $5 multicolored .55 .85
181 A9 $10 multicolored .75 1.10
Nos. 169-181 (13) 4.35 5.75

Nos. 169 has 1982 inscription, 170-181 have 1983 inscription. Nos. 169a, 170-174, 177-181 exist without date inscription.

1st Manned Flight, Bicent. A16

10c, Montgolfier Balloon, 1783, vert. 45c, Lindbergh's Sikorsky S-38 carrying mail, 1929. 50c, Beechcraft Twin Bonanza. $2.50, Sea Harrier, 1st operational V/STOL fighter.

1983, Sept. 28 **Wmk. 380**
182 A16 10c multicolored .20 .20
183 A16 45c multicolored .30 .30
184 A16 50c multicolored .30 .30
185 A16 $2.50 multicolored .70 .70
a. Souvenir sheet of 4, #182-185 2.00 2.00
Nos. 182-185 (4) 1.50 1.50

Christmas A17

1983, Nov. 7
186 A17 5c Nativity .35 .35
187 A17 30c Shepherds, flock .35 .35
188 A17 55c Angels .35 .35
189 A17 $3 Youths 1.25 1.25
a. Souvenir sheet of 4, #186-189 2.00 2.00
Nos. 186-189 (4) 2.30 2.30

Leaders of the World

Large quantities of some Leaders of the World issues were sold at a fraction of face value when the printer was liquidated.

A18

Leaders of the World: Locomotives.

1983-86 Litho. Unwmk. *Perf. 12½*
Se-tenant Pairs, #a.-b.
a. — Side and front views.
b. — Action scene.

190 A18 1c 1882 Class Wee Bogie, UK .20 .20
191 A18 5c 1968 JNR Class EF81, Japan .20 .20
192 A18 5c 1878 Snowdon Ranger, UK .20 .20
193 A18 10c 1927 P.O. Class 5500, France .20 .20
194 A18 15c 1859 Connor Single Class .20 .20
195 A18 30c 1904 Large Belpaire Passenger, UK .20 .20
196 A18 30c 1829 Stourbridge Lion, US .20 .20
197 A18 45c 1934 Cock O' The North .30 .30
198 A18 55c 1945 County of Oxford, GB .35 .35
199 A18 60c 1940 SNCF Class 240P, France .40 .40
200 A18 60c 1851 Comet, UK .40 .40
201 A18 60c 1904 County Class, UK .40 .40
202 A18 60c 1926 JNR Class 7000, Japan .40 .40
203 A18 75c 1877 Nord L'Outrance, France .50 .50
204 A18 75c 1919 CM St.P&P Bipolar, US .50 .50
205 A18 75c 1897 Palatinate Railway Class P3, Germany .50 .50
206 A18 90c 1908 Class 8H, UK .60 .60
207 A18 $1 1927 King George V .70 .70
208 A18 $1 1951 Britannia .70 .70
209 A18 $1 1924 Pendennis Castle .70 .70
210 A18 $1 1960 Evening Star .70 .70
211 A18 $1 1934 Stanier Class 5, GB .70 .70
212 A18 $1 1946 Winston Churchill Battle of Britain .70 .70
213 A18 $1 1935 Mallard A4 .70 .70
214 A18 $1 1899 Q.R. Class PB-15, Australia .70 .70
215 A18 $1 1836 C&St.L Dorchester, Canada .70 .70
216 A18 $1.50 1953 U.P. Gas Turbine, US .90 .90
217 A18 $1.50 1969 U.P. Centennial Class, US .90 .90
218 A18 $2 1866 No. 23 Class A, UK 1.40 1.40
219 A18 $2 1955 NY, NH & HR FL9, US 1.40 1.40
220 A18 $2 1837 B&O Lafayette, US 1.40 1.40
221 A18 $2.50 1964 JNR Shin-Kansen, Japan 2.00 2.00
222 A18 $2.50 1928 DRG Class 64, Germany 2.00 2.00
223 A18 $3 1882 D&RGR Class C-16, US 2.00 2.00
Nos. 190-223 (34) 24.05 24.05

Issued: #190, 200, 218, 4/26/85; #191, 193, 199, 221, 10/29/84; #192, 195, 201, 203, 214, 222, 7/26/85; #194, 197, 202, 204, 215, 217, 220, 223, 10/1/86; #196, 205, 216, 219, 1/30/86; #198, 206-213, 11/10/83.

British Monarchs, Scenes from History — A20

#258a, Boer War. #258b, Queen Victoria. #259a, Signing of the Magna Carta. #259b, King John. #260a, Victoria, diff. #260b, Osborne House. #261a, John, diff. #261b, Newark Castle, Nottinghamshire. #262a, Battle of Dettingen. #262b, King George II. #263a, George II, diff. #263b, Bank of England, 1732. #264a, George II's coat of arms. #264b, George II, diff. #265a, John's coat of arms. #265b, John, diff. #266a, Victoria's coat of arms. #266b, Victoria, diff.

1984
258 A20 5c Pair, #a.-b. .35 .35
259 A20 5c Pair, #a.-b. .35 .35
260 A20 50c Pair, #a.-b. .35 .35
261 A20 55c Pair, #a.-b. .35 .35
262 A20 60c Pair, #a.-b. .35 .35
263 A20 75c Pair, #a.-b. .35 .35
264 A20 $1 Pair, #a.-b. .35 .35
265 A20 $2 Pair, #a.-b. .85 .85
266 A20 $3 Pair, #a.-b. .70 .70
Nos. 258-266 (9) 4.00 4.00

Issued: #258, 260, 262-264, 266, 4/11; others, 11/20.

Tourism A22

1984, May 16 **Wmk. 380** ***Perf. 14***
276 A22 55c Golden Rock Inn .50 .50
277 A22 55c Rest Haven Inn .50 .50
278 A22 55c Cliffdwellers Hotel .50 .50
279 A22 55c Pinney's Beach Hotel .50 .50
Nos. 276-279 (4) 2.00 2.00

Seal of the Colony — A22a 279A

1984, June 8 **Wmk. 380** ***Perf. 14***
279A A22a $15 dull red 2.00 4.75

Tourism Type of 1984

1985, Feb. 12
280 A22 $1.20 Croney's Old Manor Hotel .80 .80
281 A22 $1.20 Montpelier Plantation Inn .80 .80
282 A22 $1.20 Nisbet's Plantation Inn .80 .80
283 A22 $1.20 Zetland Plantation Inn .80 .80
Nos. 280-283 (4) 3.20 3.20

A23

Leaders of the World: Classic cars.

1984-86 Unwmk. *Perf. 12½*

Se-tenant Pairs, #a.-b.

a. — Side and front views.

b. — Action scene.

No.	Type	Denom.	Description	Unused	Used
285	A23	1c	1932 Cadillac V16 Fleetwood Convertible, US	.20	.20
286	A23	1c	1935 Delahaye Type 35 Cabriolet, France	.20	.20
287	A23	5c	1916 Packard Twin Six Touring Car, US	.20	.20
288	A23	5c	1929 Lagonda Speed Model Touring Car, GB	.20	.20
289	A23	5c	1958 Ferrari Testarossa, Italy	.20	.20
290	A23	10c	1934 Voisin Aerodyne, France	.20	.20
291	A23	10c	1912 Sunbeam Coupe De L'Auto, GB	.20	.20
292	A23	10c	1936 Adler Trumpf, Germany	.20	.20
293	A23	15c	1886 Daimler 2-Cylinder, Germany	.20	.20
294	A23	15c	1930 Riley Brooklands Nine, UK	.20	.20
295	A23	30c	1967 Jaguar E-Type 4.2 Liter, GB	.20	.20
296	A23	35c	1970 Porsche 911 S Targa, Germany	.20	.20
297	A23	35c	1948 Cisitalia Pinnifarina Coupe, Italy	.20	.20
298	A23	45c	1885 Benz Three-wheeler, Germany	.25	.25
299	A23	45c	1966 Alfa Romeo GTA, Italy	.30	.30
300	A23	50c	1947 Volkswagen Beetle, Germany	.30	.30
301	A23	50c	1963 Buick Riviera	.30	.30
302	A23	55c	1947 MG TC, GB	.35	.35
303	A23	60c	1960 Cooper Climax, UK	.35	.35
304	A23	60c	1957 Maserati Tipo 250F, Italy	.35	.35
305	A23	60c	1913 Pierce Arrow Type 66, US	.35	.35
306	A23	75c	1904 Ford 999, US	.40	.40
307	A23	75c	1980 Porsche 928S, Germany	.40	.40
308	A23	75c	1910 Oldsmobile Limited, US	.40	.40
309	A23	$1	1951 Jaguar C-Type, UK	.55	.55
310	A23	$1	1928 Willys-Knight 66A, US	.55	.55
311	A23	$1.15	1933 MG K3 Magnette, GB	.65	.65
312	A23	$1.50	1937 Lincoln Zephyr, US	.80	.80
313	A23	$1.50	1937 ERA 1.5 l B Type, UK	.80	.80
314	A23	$1.75	1953 Studebaker Starliner, US	.90	.90
315	A23	$2	1926 Pontiac 2-door, US	1.10	1.10
316	A23	$2.50	1966 Cobra Roadster 289, US	1.40	1.40
317	A23	$2.50	1930 MG M-Type Midget, UK	1.40	1.40
318	A23	$3	1966 Aston Martin DB6 Hardtop, GB	1.50	1.50
319	A23	$3	1932 Pierce Arrow V12, US	1.50	1.50
320	A23	$3	1971 Rolls Royce Corniche, UK	1.50	1.50
321	A23	$3	1953 Chevrolet Corvette, US	1.50	1.50
322	A23	$3	1919 Cunningham V-8, US	1.50	1.50
			Nos. 285-322 (38)	22.00	22.00

Issued: #285, 287, 293, 296, 298, 302, 316, 318, 7/25/84; #286, 289-290, 301, 303, 306, 317, 320, 2/20/85; #288, 295, 300, 319, 10/23/84; #291, 297, 307, 311-312, 315, 10/4/85; #292, 303, 308-309, 313, 321, 1/30/86; #294, 299, 305, 310, 314, 322, 8/15/86.

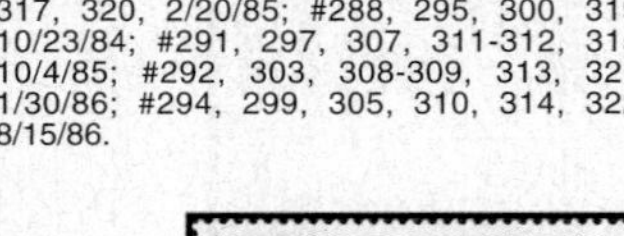

Culturama Carnival, 10th Anniv. A24a

Wmk. 380

1984, Aug. 1 Litho. *Perf. 14*

No.	Type	Denom.	Description	Unused	Used
361	A24a	30c	Carpentry	.20	.20
362	A24a	55c	Weaving mats and baskets	.25	.25
363	A24a	$1	Ceramics	.50	.50
364	A24a	$3	Carnival queen, folk dancers	1.25	1.25
			Nos. 361-364 (4)	2.20	2.20

Flowers — A24b

1984, Aug. 8

No.	Type	Denom.	Description	Unused	Used
365	A24b	5c	Yellow bell	.20	.20
366	A24b	10c	Plumbago	.20	.20
367	A24b	15c	Flamboyant	.20	.20
368	A24b	20c	Eyelash orchid	.20	.20
369	A24b	30c	Bougainvillea	.20	.20
370	A24b	40c	Hibiscus	.20	.20
371	A24b	50c	Night-blooming cereus	.25	.25
372	A24b	55c	Yellow mahoe	.25	.25
373	A24b	60c	Spider lily	.30	.30
374	A24b	75c	Scarlet cordia	.35	.35
375	A24b	$1	Shell ginger	.50	.50
376	A24b	$3	Blue petrea	1.25	1.25
377	A24b	$5	Coral hibiscus	2.25	2.25
378	A24b	$10	Passion flower	4.50	4.50
			Nos. 365-378 (14)	10.85	10.85

Nos. 368 and 370 were reissued on July 23, 1986 with date inscription. Values for those two stamps are for the 1986 printing.

Independence of St. Kitts and Nevis, 1st Anniv. — A26

1984, Sept. 18

No.	Type	Denom.	Description	Unused	Used
379	A26	15c	Picking cotton	.20	.20
380	A26	55c	Hamilton House	.30	.30
381	A26	$1.10	Self-sufficiency in food production	.65	.65
382	A26	$3	Pinney's Beach	1.75	1.75
			Nos. 379-382 (4)	2.90	2.90

Leaders of the World — A27

Cricket players and team emblems and match scenes.

1984 Unwmk. *Perf. 12½*

Pairs, #a.-b.

No.	Denom.	Description	Unused	Used
383	5c	C.P. Mead, England	.20	.20
384	5c	J.D. Love, Yorkshire	.20	.20
385	15c	S.J. Dennis, Yorkshire	.20	.20
386	25c	J.B. Statham, England	.20	.20
387	55c	Sir Learie Constantine, West Indies	.25	.25
388	55c	B.W. Luckhurst, Kent	.25	.25
389	$2.50	Sir Leonard Hutton, England	1.00	1.00
390	$2.50	B.L. D'Oliveira, England	1.00	1.00
		Nos. 383-390 (8)	3.30	3.30

Issued: #383, 386, 389, 10/23; others, 11/20.

Christmas A29

Musicians from local bands: 15c, Flutist and drummer of the Honeybees Band. 40c, Guitar and barhow players of the Canary Birds Band. 60c, Shell All Stars steel band. $3, Choir, organist, St. John's Church, Fig Tree.

1984, Nov. 2 Wmk. 380 *Perf. 14*

No.	Type	Description	Unused	Used
399-402	A29	Set of 4	2.75	2.75

Birds A30

1985, Mar. 19

No.	Type	Denom.	Description	Unused	Used
403	A30	20c	Broad-winged hawk	1.25	.25
404	A30	40c	Red-tailed hawk	1.40	.35
405	A30	60c	Little blue heron	1.40	.45
406	A30	$3	Great white heron	3.00	2.25
			Nos. 403-406 (4)	7.05	3.30

Leaders of the World — A31

Birds: #407a, Painted bunting. #407b, Golden-crowned kinglet. #408a, Eastern bluebird. #408b, Northern cardinal. #409a, Common flicker. #409b, Western tanager. #410a, Belted kingfisher. #410b, Mangrove cuckoo. #411a, Yellow warbler. #411b, Cerulean warbler. #412a, Sage thrasher. #412b, Evening grosbeak. #413a, Burrowing owl. #413b, Long-eared owl. #414a, Blackburnian warbler. #414b, Northern oriole.

1985 Unwmk. *Perf. 12½*

No.	Type	Denom.	Description	Unused	Used
407	A31	1c	Pair, #a.-b.	.20	.20
408	A31	5c	Pair, #a.-b.	.20	.20
409	A31	40c	Pair, #a.-b.	.35	.35
410	A31	55c	Pair, #a.-b.	.40	.40
411	A31	60c	Pair, #a.-b.	.45	.45
412	A31	60c	Pair, #a.-b.	.45	.45
413	A31	$2	Pair, #a.-b.	2.50	2.50
414	A31	$2.50	Pair, #a.-b.	3.00	3.00
			Nos. 407-414 (8)	7.55	7.55

John J. Audubon, ornithologist, birth bicent.
Issued: 1c, 40c, #412, $2.50, 6/3; others, 3/25.

Girl Guides, 75th Anniv. — A32

1985, June 17 Wmk. 380 *Perf. 14*

No.	Type	Denom.	Description	Unused	Used
423	A32	15c	Troop, horiz.	.20	.20
424	A32	60c	Uniforms, 1910, 1985	.40	.40
425	A32	$1	Lord and Lady Baden-Powell	.65	.65
426	A32	$3	Princess Margaret	2.00	2.00
			Nos. 423-426 (4)	3.25	3.25

Queen Mother Elizabeth — A33

#427a, 432a, Black hat, white plume. #427b, 432b, Blue hat, pink feathers. #428a, Blue hat. #428b, Tiara. #429a, Violet & blue hat. #429b, Blue hat. #430a, 433a, Light blue hat. #430b, 433b, Black hat. #431a, As a child, c. 1910. #431b, Queen consort, c. 1945.

1985, July 31 Unwmk. *Perf. 12½*

No.	Type	Denom.	Description	Unused	Used
427	A33	45c	Pair, #a.-b.	.40	.40
428	A33	75c	Pair, #a.-b.	.65	.65
429	A33	$1.20	Pair, #a.-b.	1.10	1.10
430	A33	$1.50	Pair, #a.-b.	1.40	1.40
			Nos. 427-430 (4)	3.55	3.55

Souvenir Sheets

No.	Type	Denom.	Description	Unused	Used
431	A33	$2	Sheet of 2, #a.-b.	3.00	3.00
432	A33	$3.50	Sheet of 2, #a.-b.	3.00	3.00
433	A33	$6	Sheet of 2, #a.-b.	5.00	5.00

Issued: #432-433, 12/27; others, 7/31.
For overprints see No. 450.

Great Western Railway, 150th Anniv. — A34

Railway engineers and their achievements: #438a, Isambard Brunel. #438b, Royal Albert Bridge, 1859. #439a, William Dean. #439b, *Lord of the Isles*, 1895. #440a, *Lode Star*, 1907. #440b, G.J. Churchward. #441a, Pendennis Castle Class, 1924. #441b, C.B. Collett.

1985, Aug. 31

No.	Type	Denom.	Description	Unused	Used
438	A34	25c	Pair, #a.-b.	.25	.25
439	A34	50c	Pair, #a.-b.	.55	.55
440	A34	$1	Pair, #a.-b.	1.00	1.00
441	A34	$2.50	Pair, #a.-b.	2.75	2.75
			Nos. 438-441 (4)	4.55	4.55

Nos. 163, 157, 164, 151, 427, 144, 139-140 and 158 Ovptd. or Surcharged "CARIBBEAN ROYAL VISIT 1985" in 2 or 3 Lines

Perf. 14, 12½ (45c)

1985, Oct. 23 Wmk. as Before

No.	Type	Denom.	Description	Unused	Used
446	A14	15c	No. 163	1.00	1.00
447	A12	30c	No. 157	2.00	2.00
448	A14	30c	No. 164	1.00	1.00
449	A11	40c	on 55c No. 151	2.25	2.25
450	A33	45c	Pair, #a.-b.	3.00	3.00
452	A10	55c	No. 144	2.25	2.25
453	A9a	$1.50	on $5 No. 139	3.75	3.75
454	A9b	$1.50	on $5 No. 140	15.00	*17.00*
455	A12	$2.50	No. 158	4.00	4.00
			Nos. 446-455 (9)	34.25	36.25

Christmas A36

Anglican, Roman Catholic and Methodist churches.

1985, Nov. 5 Wmk. 380 *Perf. 15*

No.	Type	Denom.	Description	Unused	Used
456	A36	10c	St. Paul's, Charlestown	.20	.20
457	A36	40c	St. Theresa, Charlestown	.30	.30
458	A36	60c	Methodist Church, Gingerland	.40	.40
459	A36	$3	St. Thomas, Lowland	2.00	2.00
			Nos. 456-459 (4)	2.90	2.90

Spitfire Fighter Plane, 50th Anniv. — A37

1986, Mar. 24 Unwmk. *Perf. 12½*

460 A37 $1 Prototype K.5054, 1936 .35 .35
461 A37 $2.50 Mk.1A, 1940 .90 .90
462 A37 $3 Mk.XII, 1944 1.00 1.00
463 A37 $4 Mk.XXIV, 1948 1.50 1.50
Nos. 460-463 (4) 3.75 3.75

Souvenir Sheet

464 A37 $6 Seafire Mk.III 4.00 4.00

Discovery of America, 500th Anniv. (in 1992) — A38

#465a, American Indian. #465b, Columbus trading with Indians. #466a, Columbus's coat of arms. #466b, Breadfruit. #467a, Galleons. #467b, Columbus.

1986, Apr. 11

465 A38 75c Pair, #a.-b. 1.00 1.00
466 A38 $1.75 Pair, #a.-b. 2.50 2.50
467 A38 $2.50 Pair, #a.-b. 3.50 3.50
Nos. 465-467 (3) 7.00 7.00

Souvenir Sheet

468 A38 $6 Columbus, diff. 7.25 7.25

Printed in continuous designs picturing various maps of Columbus's voyages.

Queen Elizabeth II, 60th Birthday — A39

Various portraits. Illustration reduced.

1986, Apr. 21

472 A39 5c multicolored .20 .20
473 A39 75c multicolored .30 .30
474 A39 $2 multicolored .75 .75
475 A39 $8 multi, vert. 3.00 3.00
Nos. 472-475 (4) 4.25 4.25

Souvenir Sheet

476 A39 $10 multicolored 7.50 7.50

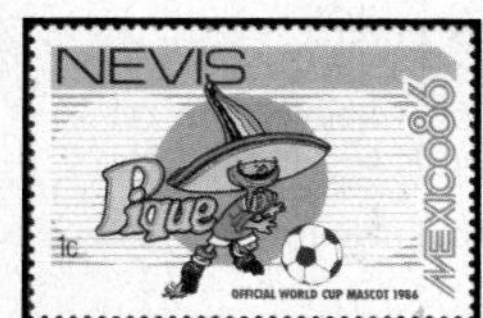

1986 World Cup Soccer Championships, Mexico — A40

Perf. 15, 12½ (75c, $1, $1.75, $6)

1986, May 16

Size of 75c, $1, $1.75, $6: 56x35½mm

477 A40 1c Character trademark .20 .20
478 A40 2c Brazilian player .20 .20
479 A40 5c Danish player .20 .20
480 A40 10c Brazilian, diff. .20 .20
481 A40 20c Denmark vs. Spain .20 .20
482 A40 30c Paraguay vs. Chile .20 .20
483 A40 60c Italy vs. W. Germany .35 .35
484 A40 75c Danish team .50 .50
485 A40 $1 Paraguayan team .70 .70
486 A40 $1.75 Brazilian team 1.25 1.25
487 A40 $3 Italy vs. England 2.00 2.00
488 A40 $6 Italian team 4.00 4.00
Nos. 477-488 (12) 10.00 10.00

Souvenir Sheets

Perf. 12½

489 A40 $1.50 like $1.75 2.25 2.25
490 A40 $2 like $6 2.50 2.50

Perf. 15

491 A40 $2 like 20c 2.50 2.50
492 A40 $2.50 like 60c 3.00 3.00
493 A40 $4 like 30c 4.00 4.00

Nos. 478-483 and 487 vert.

Local Industry A41

1986, July 18 Wmk. 380 *Perf. 14*

494 A41 15c Textile .35 .35
495 A41 40c Carpentry .50 .50
496 A41 $1.20 Agriculture 1.50 1.50
497 A41 $3 Fishing 3.50 3.50
Nos. 494-497 (4) 5.85 5.85

A42

Wedding of Prince Andrew and Sarah Ferguson — A43

#498a, Andrew. #498b, Sarah. #499a, Andrew at the races, horiz. #499b, Andrew in Africa, horiz.

1986, July 23 Unwmk. *Perf. 12½*

498 A42 60c Pair, #a.-b. .40 .40
499 A42 $2 Pair, #a.-b. 1.25 1.25

Souvenir Sheet

500 A43 $10 Couple on Balcony 4.75 4.75

Printed in vert. and horiz. pairs.
For overprints see Nos. 521-522.

Coral — A44

1986, Sept. 8 Wmk. 380 *Perf. 15*

503 A44 15c Gorgonia .20 .20
504 A44 60c Fire coral .30 .30
505 A44 $2 Elkhorn coral 1.10 1.10
506 A44 $3 Feather star 1.50 1.50
Nos. 503-506 (4) 3.10 3.10

A45

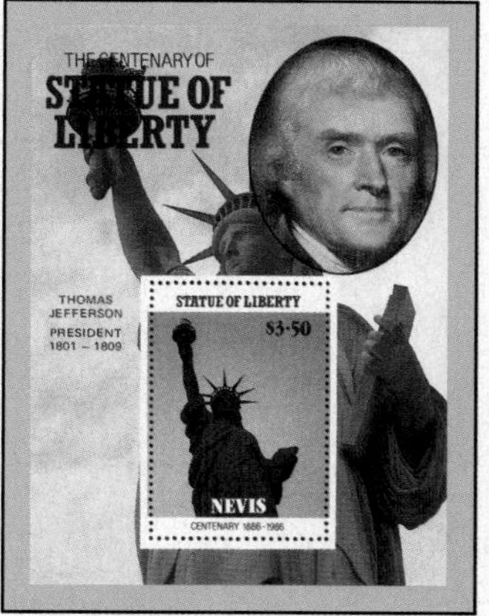

Statue of Liberty, Cent. — A46

1986, Oct. 28 Unwmk. *Perf. 14*

507 A45 15c Statue, World Trade Center .20 .20
508 A45 25c Statue, tall ship .20 .20
509 A45 40c Under renovation (front) .25 .25
510 A45 60c Renovation (side) .40 .40
511 A45 75c Statue, Operation Sail .50 .50
512 A45 $1 Tall ship, horiz. .65 .65
513 A45 $1.50 Renovation (arm, head) .95 .95
514 A45 $2 Ship flying Liberty flag 1.25 1.25
515 A45 $2.50 Statue, Manhattan 1.50 1.50
516 A45 $3 Workers on scaffold 1.90 1.90
Nos. 507-516 (10) 7.80 7.80

Souvenir Sheets

517 A46 $3.50 Statue at dusk 2.25 2.25
518 A46 $4 Head 2.50 2.50
519 A46 $4.50 Torch struck by lightning 2.75 2.75
520 A46 $5 Torch, blazing sun 3.00 3.00

Nos. 498-499 Ovptd. "Congratulations to T.R.H. The Duke & Duchess of York"

1986, Nov. 17 *Perf. 12½*

521 A42 60c Pair, #a.-b. .55 .55
522 A42 $2 Pair, #a.-b. 2.00 2.00

Sports A47

1986, Nov. 21 *Perf. 14*

525 A47 10c Sailing .30 .30
526 A47 25c Netball .30 .30
527 A47 $2 Cricket 2.10 2.10
528 A47 $3 Basketball 3.25 3.25
Nos. 525-528 (4) 5.95 5.95

Christmas — A48

Churches: 10c, St. George's Anglican Church, Gingerland. 40c, Methodist Church, Fountain. $1, Charlestown Methodist Church. $5, Wesleyan Holiness Church, Brown Hill.

1986, Dec. 8

529 A48 10c multicolored .20 .20
530 A48 40c multicolored .30 .30
531 A48 $1 multicolored .75 .75
532 A48 $5 multicolored 3.50 3.50
Nos. 529-532 (4) 4.75 4.75

US Constitution — A49

Christening of the Hamilton, 1788 — A50

US Constitution, bicent. and 230th anniv. of the birth of Alexander Hamilton: 40c, Alexander Hamilton, Hamilton House. 60c, Hamilton. $2, George Washington and members of the 1st presidential cabinet.

1987, Jan. 11

533 A49 15c shown .20 .20
534 A49 40c multicolored .30 .30
535 A49 60c multicolored .45 .45
536 A49 $2 multicolored 1.25 1.25
Nos. 533-536 (4) 2.20 2.20

Souvenir Sheet

537 A50 $5 shown 8.50 8.50

No. 117 Overprinted

1987, Feb. 20 Wmk. 373

538 A6a $3 multicolored 2.00 2.00

Wedding of Capt. Horatio Nelson and Frances Nisbet, Bicent. A51

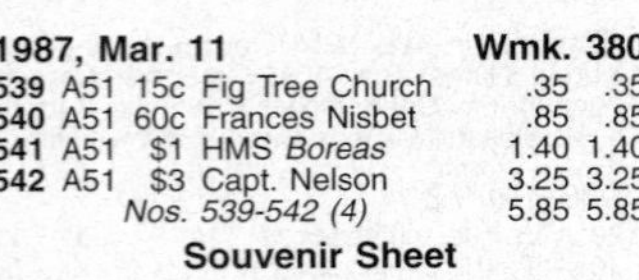

1987, Mar. 11 **Wmk. 380**

539 A51 15c Fig Tree Church .35 .35
540 A51 60c Frances Nisbet .85 .85
541 A51 $1 HMS *Boreas* 1.40 1.40
542 A51 $3 Capt. Nelson 3.25 3.25
Nos. 539-542 (4) 5.85 5.85

Souvenir Sheet

543 Sheet of 2, #542, 543a 5.25 5.25
a. A51 $3 like No. 540 3.00 3.00

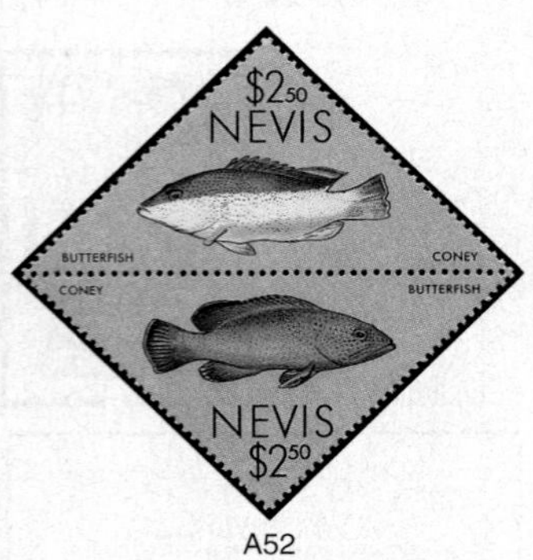

A52

#544a, Queen angelfish. #544b, Blue angelfish. #545a, Blue thum. #545b, Red thum. #546a, Red hind. #546b, Rock hind. #547a, Coney Butterfish. #547b, Coney butterfish, diff.

1987, July 22 **Unwmk.** ***Perf. 15***

544 A52 60c Pair, #a.-b. .70 .70
545 A52 $1 Pair, #a.-b. 1.25 1.25
546 A52 $1.50 Pair, #a.-b. 1.75 1.75
547 A52 $2.50 Pair, #a.-b. 3.00 3.00
Nos. 544-547 (4) 6.70 6.70

Mushrooms — A53

1987, Oct. 16 **Wmk. 384** ***Perf. 14***

552 A53 15c *Panaeolus antillarum* .50 .50
553 A53 50c *Pycnoporus sanguineus* 1.25 1.25
554 A53 $2 *Gymnopilus chrysopellus* 3.75 3.75
555 A53 $3 *Cantharellus cinnabarinus* 4.50 4.50
Nos. 552-555 (4) 10.00 10.00

Christmas — A54

1987, Dec. 4 ***Perf. 14½***

556 A54 10c Rag doll .20 .20
557 A54 40c Coconut boat .25 .25
558 A54 $1.20 Sandbox cart .70 .70
559 A54 $5 Two-wheeled cart 3.00 3.00
Nos. 556-559 (4) 4.15 4.15

Sea Shells — A55

1988, Feb. 15 ***Perf. 14x14½***

560 A55 15c Hawk-wing conch .35 .35
561 A55 40c Roostertail conch .65 .65
562 A55 60c Emperor helmet .90 .90
563 A55 $2 Queen conch 2.25 2.25
564 A55 $3 King helmet 3.00 3.00
Nos. 560-564 (5) 7.15 7.15

Intl. Red Cross and Red Crescent Organizations, 125th Annivs. — A56

Activities: 15c, Visiting the sick and the elderly. 40c, First aid training. 60c, Wheelchairs for the disabled. $5, Disaster relief.

1988, June 20 ***Perf. 14½x14***

565 A56 15c multicolored .20 .20
566 A56 40c multicolored .30 .30
567 A56 60c multicolored .45 .45
568 A56 $5 multicolored 3.75 3.75
Nos. 565-568 (4) 4.70 4.70

A57

A58

1988, Aug. 26 ***Perf. 14***

569 Strip of 4 4.75 4.75
a. A57 10c Runner at starting block .20 .20
b. A57 $1.20 Leaving block .90 .90
c. A57 $2 Full stride 1.50 1.50
d. A57 $3 Crossing finish line 2.25 2.25
e. Souvenir sheet of 4, #569a-569d 4.75 4.75

1988 Summer Olympics, Seoul. Printed se-tenant in a continuous design. Stamps in No. 569e are 23½x36½.

1988, Sept. 19 **Wmk. 373** ***Perf. 14½***

570 A58 $5 multicolored 3.75 3.75

Independence, 5th anniv.

Common Design Types pictured following the introduction.

Lloyds of London

Common Design Type

Designs: 15c, Act of Parliament incorporating Lloyds, 1871. 60c, *Cunard Countess* in Nevis Harbor, horiz. $2.50, Space shuttle, deployment of satellite in space, horiz. $3, *Viking Princess* on fire in the Caribbean, 1966.

1988, Oct. 31 **Wmk. 384** ***Perf. 14***

571 CD341 15c multicolored .45 .45
572 CD341 60c multicolored 1.00 1.00
573 CD341 $2.50 multicolored 2.75 2.75
574 CD341 $3 multicolored 5.00 5.00
Nos. 571-574 (4) 9.20 9.20

Christmas Flowers — A59

1988, Nov. 7 ***Perf. 14½***

575 A59 15c Poinsettia .20 .20
576 A59 40c Tiger claws .30 .30
577 A59 60c Sorrel flower .45 .45
578 A59 $1 Christmas candle .75 .75
579 A59 $5 Snow bush 3.25 3.25
Nos. 575-579 (5) 4.95 4.95

Battle of Frigate Bay, 1782 — A60

Exhibition emblem & maps. #580a-580c in a continuous design. Illustration reduced.

1989, Apr. 17 ***Perf. 14***

580 A60 Strip of 3 4.00 4.00
a. 50c multicolored .35 .35
b. $1.20 multicolored .90 .90
c. $2 multicolored 1.50 1.50

Size: 34x47mm

Perf. 14x13½

581 A60 $3 Map of Nevis, 1764 3.50 3.50

French revolution bicent., PHILEXFRANCE '89.

Nocturnal Insects and Frogs — A61

1989, May 15

582 A61 10c Cicada .35 .35
583 A61 40c Grasshopper .60 .60
584 A61 60c Cricket 1.00 1.00
585 A61 $5 Tree frog 5.50 5.50
a. Souvenir sheet of 4, #582-585 7.50 7.50
Nos. 582-585 (4) 7.45 7.45

Moon Landing, 20th Anniv.

Common Design Type

Apollo 12: 15c, Vehicle Assembly Building, Kennedy Space Center. 40c, Crew members Charles Conrad Jr., Richard Gordon and Alan Bean. $2, Mission emblem. $3, Moon operation in the Sun's glare. $6, Buzz Aldrin deploying passive seismic experiment package on the lunar surface, Apollo 11 mission.

1989, July 20 ***Perf. 14x13½***

Size of Nos. 587-588: 29x29mm

586 CD342 15c multicolored .20 .20
587 CD342 40c multicolored .30 .30
588 CD342 $2 multicolored 1.50 1.50
589 CD342 $3 multicolored 2.25 2.25
Nos. 586-589 (4) 4.25 4.25

Souvenir Sheet

590 CD342 $6 multicolored 4.50 4.50

Queen Conchs (*Strombus gigas*) A62

1990, Jan. 31

591 A62 10c shown .40 .40
592 A62 40c Conch, diff .75 .75
593 A62 60c Conch, diff 1.75 1.75
594 A62 $1 Conch, diff 2.75 2.75
Nos. 591-594 (4) 5.65 5.65

Souvenir Sheet

595 A62 $5 Fish and coral 6.00 6.00

World Wildlife Fund.

Wyon Portrait of Victoria — A63

Perf. 14x15

1990, May 3 **Litho.** **Unwmk.**

596 A63 15c shown .20 .20
597 A63 40c Engine-turned background .35 .35
598 A63 60c Heath's engraving .60 .60
599 A63 $4 Inscriptions added 3.50 3.50
Nos. 596-599 (4) 4.65 4.65

Souvenir Sheet

600 A63 $5 Completed design 6.00 6.00

Penny Black, 150th anniv. No. 600 for Stamp World London '90.

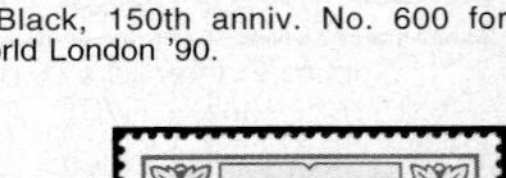

A64

1990, May 3 ***Perf. 13½***

601 A64 15c brown .25 .25
602 A64 40c deep green .40 .40
603 A64 60c violet .65 .65
604 A64 $4 bright ultra 4.00 4.00
Nos. 601-604 (4) 5.30 5.30

Souvenir Sheet

605 A64 $5 gray, lake & buff 6.00 6.00

Penny Black 150th anniversary and commemoration of the Thurn & Taxis postal service.

Crabs A65

Designs include UPAE and discovery of America anniversary emblems.

1990, June 25 **Litho.** ***Perf. 14***

606 A65 5c Sand fiddler .25 .25
607 A65 15c Great land crab .30 .30
608 A65 20c Blue crab .40 .40
609 A65 40c Stone crab .50 .50
610 A65 60c Mountain crab .75 .75
611 A65 $2 Sargassum crab 1.75 1.75
612 A65 $3 Yellow box crab 2.50 2.50
613 A65 $4 Spiny spider crab 3.50 3.50
Nos. 606-613 (8) 9.95 9.95

Souvenir Sheets

614 A65 $5 Wharf crab 5.25 5.25
615 A65 $5 Sally lightfoot 5.25 5.25

Queen Mother 90th Birthday
A66 A67

1990, July 5

616 A66 $2 shown 1.50 1.50
617 A67 $2 shown 1.50 1.50
618 A66 $2 Queen Consort, diff. 1.50 1.50
a. Strip of 3, #616-618 4.50 4.50

Souvenir Sheet

619 A67 $6 Coronation Portrait, diff. 5.25 5.25

Nos. 616-618 printed in sheet of 9.

A68

A69

Players from participating countries.

1990, Oct. 1 Litho. *Perf. 14*

620 A68 10c Cameroun .25 .25
621 A68 25c Czechoslovakia .25 .25
622 A68 $2.50 England 2.50 2.50
623 A68 $5 West Germany 5.25 5.25
Nos. 620-623 (4) 8.25 8.25

Souvenir Sheets

624 A68 $5 Spain 4.50 4.50
625 A68 $5 Argentina 4.50 4.50

World Cup Soccer Championships, Italy.

Unwmk.

1990, Nov. 19 Litho. *Perf. 14*

Christmas (Orchids): 10c, Cattleya deckeri. 15c, Epidendrum ciliare. 20c, Epidendrum fragrans. 40c, Epidendrum ibaguense. 60c, Epidendrum latifolium. $1.20, Maxillaria conferta. $2, Epidendrum strobiliferum. $3, Brassavola cucullata. $5, Rodriguezia lanceolata.

626 A69 10c multicolored .35 .35
627 A69 15c multicolored .35 .35
628 A69 20c multicolored .35 .35
629 A69 40c multicolored .55 .55
630 A69 60c multicolored .85 .85
631 A69 $1.20 multicolored 1.60 1.60
632 A69 $2 multicolored 2.75 2.75
633 A69 $3 multicolored 4.25 4.25
Nos. 626-633 (8) 11.05 11.05

Souvenir Sheet

634 A69 $5 multicolored 9.50 9.50

Peter Paul Rubens (1577-1640), Painter
A70

Details from The Feast of Achelous: 10c, Pitchers. 40c, Woman at table. 60c, Two women. $4, Achelous feasting. $5, Complete painting, horiz.

1991, Jan. 14 Litho. *Perf. 13½*

635 A70 10c multicolored .25 .25
636 A70 40c multicolored .40 .40
637 A70 60c multicolored .70 .70
638 A70 $4 multicolored 4.00 4.00
Nos. 635-638 (4) 5.35 5.35

Souvenir Sheet

639 A70 $5 multicolored 6.00 6.00

Butterflies
A71

1991-92 *Perf. 14*

640 A71 5c Gulf fritillary .25 .25
641 A71 10c Orion .25 .25
642 A71 15c Dagger wing .25 .25
643 A71 20c Red anartia .25 .25
644 A71 25c Caribbean buckeye .25 .25
645 A71 40c Zebra .35 .35
646 A71 50c Southern dagger tail .50 .50
647 A71 60c Silver spot .55 .55
648 A71 75c Doris .65 .65
648A A71 80c like #647 .70 .70
649 A71 $1 Mimic .90 .90
650 A71 $3 Monarch 2.75 2.75
651 A71 $5 Small blue grecian 4.50 4.50
652 A71 $10 Tiger 9.00 9.00
653 A71 $20 Flambeau 18.00 18.00
Nos. 640-653 (15) 39.15 39.15

#640-646, 648-653 exist dated "1992," #640-641, 644, 646, 648A, "1994."
Issued: #648A, 1992; others, 3/1/91.
For overprints see Nos. O41-O54.

Space Exploration-Discovery Voyages — A72

1991, Apr. 22 Litho. *Perf. 14*

654 A72 15c Viking Mars lander .20 .20
655 A72 40c Apollo 11 lift-off .30 .30
656 A72 60c Skylab .45 .45
657 A72 75c Salyut 6 .55 .55
658 A72 $1 Voyager 1 .75 .75
659 A72 $2 Venera 7 1.50 1.50
660 A72 $4 Gemini 4 3.00 3.00
661 A72 $5 Luna 3 4.00 4.00
Nos. 654-661 (8) 10.75 10.75

Souvenir Sheet

662 A72 $6 Sailing ship, vert. 6.00 6.00
663 A72 $6 Columbus' landfall 6.00 6.00

Discovery of America, 500th anniv. (in 1992) (No. 663).

Miniature Sheet

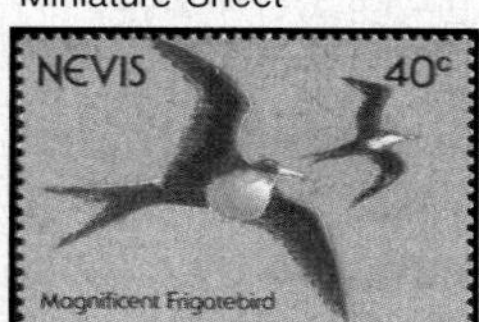

Birds
A73

Designs: a, Magnificent frigatebird. b, Roseate tern. c, Red-tailed hawk. d, Zenaida dove. e, Bananaquit. f, American kestrel. g, Grey kingbird. h, Prothonotary warbler. i, Blue-hooded euphonia. j, Antillean crested hummingbird. k, White-tailed tropicbird. l, Yellow-bellied sapsucker. m, Green-throated carib. n, Purple-throated carib. o, Black-bellied tree duck. p, Ringed kingfisher. q, Burrowing owl. r, Ruddy turnstone. s, Great white heron. t, Yellow-crowned night heron.

1991, May 28

664 A73 40c Sheet of 20, #a.-t. 16.00 16.00

Souvenir Sheet

665 A73 $6 Great egret 12.00 12.00

Royal Family Birthday, Anniversary
Common Design Type

1991, July 5 Litho. *Perf. 14*

666 CD347 10c multicolored .30 .30
667 CD347 15c multicolored .30 .30
668 CD347 40c multicolored .45 .45
669 CD347 50c multicolored .60 .60
670 CD347 $1 multicolored 1.10 1.10
671 CD347 $2 multicolored 2.25 2.25
672 CD347 $4 multicolored 4.50 4.50
673 CD347 $5 multicolored 5.50 5.50
Nos. 666-673 (8) 15.00 15.00

Souvenir Sheets

674 CD347 $5 Elizabeth, Philip 6.75 6.75
675 CD347 $5 Charles, Diana & family 6.75 6.75

10c, 50c, $1, Nos. 673, 675, Charles and Diana, 10th Wedding Anniv. Others, Queen Elizabeth II 65th birthday.

Japanese Trains
A74

Locomotives: 10c, C62 Steam, vert. 15c, C56 Steam. 40c, Streamlined C55, steam. 60c, Class 1400 Steam. $1, Class 485 bonnet type rail diesel car, vert. $2, C61 Steam, vert. $3, Class 485 express train. $4, Class 7000 electric train. No. 684, D51 Steam. No. 685, Hikari bullet train.

1991, Aug. 12

676-683 A74 Set of 8 14.00 14.00

Souvenir Sheets

684-685 A74 $5 Set of 2 11.00 11.00

Phila Nippon '91.

Christmas
A75

Paintings by Albrecht Durer: 10c, Mary Being Crowned by an Angel. 40c, Mary with the Pear. 60c, Mary in a Halo. $3, Mary with the Crown of Stars and Scepter. No. 690, The Holy Family. No. 691, Mary at the Yard Gate.

1991, Dec. 20 Litho. *Perf. 13½*

686 A75 10c yel green & blk .20 .20
687 A75 40c org brown & blk .30 .30
688 A75 60c blue & black .45 .45
689 A75 $3 brt magenta & blk 2.10 2.10
Nos. 686-689 (4) 3.05 3.05

Souvenir Sheets

690 A75 $6 black 4.25 4.25
691 A75 $6 black 4.25 4.25

A76

A77

Mushrooms: 15c, Marasmius haematocephalus. 40c, Psilocybe cubensis. 60c, Hygrocybe acutoconica. 75c, Hygrocybe occidentalis. $1, Boletellus cubensis. $2, Gymnopilus chrysopellus. $4, Cantharellus cinnabarinus. $5, Chlorophyllum molybdites. No. 700, Our Lady of the Snows (8 mushrooms). No. 701, Our Lady of the Snows (4 mushrooms), diff.

1991, Dec. 20 Litho. *Perf. 14*

692-699 A76 Set of 8 11.00 11.00

Souvenir Sheet

700-701 A76 $6 Set of 2 11.00 11.00

Queen Elizabeth II's Accession to the Throne, 40th Anniv.
Common Design Type

1992, Feb. 26 Litho. *Perf. 14*

702 CD348 10c multicolored .20 .20
703 CD348 40c multicolored .30 .30
704 CD348 $1 multicolored .75 .75
705 CD348 $5 multicolored 3.75 3.75
Nos. 702-705 (4) 5.00 5.00

Souvenir Sheets

706 CD348 $6 Queen, people on beach 5.00 5.00
707 CD348 $6 Queen, seashell 5.00 5.00

1992, May 7 Litho. *Perf. 14*

Gold medalists: 20c, Monique Knol, France, cycling. 25c, Roger Kingdom, US, 110-meter hurdles. 50c, Yugoslavia, water polo. 80c, Anja Fichtel, West Germany, foil. $1, Said Aouita, Morocco, 5000-meters. $1.50, Yuri Sedykh, USSR, hammer throw. $3, Yelena Shushunova, USSR, gymnastics. $5, Vladimir Artemov, USSR, gymnastics. No. 716, Florence Griffith-Joyner, US, 100-meter dash. No. 717, Naim Suleymanoglu, Turkey, weight lifting.

708-715 A77 Set of 8 12.50 12.50

Souvenir Sheets

716-717 A77 $6 Set of 2 9.00 9.00

1992 Summer Olympics, Barcelona. All athletes except those on $1 and $1.50 won gold medals in 1988. No. 715 incorrectly spelled "Valimir."

Spanish Art — A78

Designs: 20c, Landscape, by Mariano Fortuny, vert. 25c, Dona Juana la Loca, by Francisco Pradilla Ortiz. 50c, Idyll, by Fortuny, vert. 80c, Old Man in the Sun, by Fortuny, vert. $1, $2, The Painter's Children in the Japanese Salon (different details), vert., by Fortuny. $3, Still Life (Sea Bream and Oranges), by Luis Eugenio Melendez. $5, Still Life (Box of Sweets, Pastry, and Other Objects), by Melendez, vert. No. 726, Moroccans by Fortuny. No. 727, Bullfight, by Fortuny.

Perf. 13x13½, 13½x13

1992, June 1 Litho.

718-725 A78 Set of 8 13.50 13.50

Size: 120x95mm

Imperf

726-727 A78 $6 Set of 2 9.00 9.00

Granada '92.

A79

A80

1992, July 6 *Perf. 14*

728 A79 20c Early compass .30 .60
729 A79 50c Manatee .60 .60
730 A79 80c Green turtle .90 .90
731 A79 $1.50 Santa Maria 1.60 1.60
732 A79 $3 Queen Isabella 3.25 3.25
733 A79 $5 Pineapple 5.75 5.75
Nos. 728-733 (6) 12.40 12.70

Souvenir Sheets

734 A79 $6 Storm petrel, horiz. 5.75 5.75
735 A79 $6 Pepper, horiz. 5.75 5.75

Discovery of America, 500th anniv. World Columbian Stamp Expo '92, Chicago.

1992, Aug. 24 *Perf. 14½*

736 A80 $1 Coming ashore .85 .85
737 A80 $2 Natives, ships 1.60 1.60

Discovery of America, 500th anniv. Organization of East Caribbean States.

Wolfgang Amadeus Mozart, Bicent. of Death (in 1991) — A81

1992, Oct. Litho. *Perf. 14*

738 A81 $3 multicolored 3.25 3.25

Souvenir Sheet

739 A81 $6 Don Giovanni 5.75 5.75

Mickey's Portrait Gallery A82

1992, Nov. 9 Litho. *Perf. 13½x14*

740 A82 10c Minnie Mouse, 1930 .25 .25
741 A82 15c Mickey Mouse .35 .35
742 A82 40c Donald Duck .45 .45
743 A82 80c Mickey Mouse, 1930 .75 .75
744 A82 $1 Daisy Duck 1.00 1.00
745 A82 $2 Pluto 1.75 1.75
746 A82 $4 Goofy 3.50 3.50
747 A82 $5 Goofy, 1932 4.25 4.25
Nos. 740-747 (8) 12.30 12.30

Souvenir Sheet

Perf. 14x13½

748 A82 $6 Plane Crazy 6.75 6.75
749 A82 $6 Mickey, Home Sweet Home, horiz. 6.75 6.75

Christmas A83

Details or entire paintings: 20c, The Virgin and Child Between Two Saints, by Giovanni Bellini. 40c, The Virgin and Child Surrounded by Four Angels, by Master of the Castello Nativity. 50c, Virgin and Child Surrounded by Angels with St. Frediano and St. Augustine, by Fra Filippo Lippi. 80c, The Virgin and Child Between St. Peter and St. Sebastian, by Giovanni Bellini. $1, The Virgin and Child with St. Julian and St. Nicholas of Myra, by Lorenzo Di Credi. $2, Saint Bernardino and a Female Saint Presenting a Donor to Virgin and Child, by Francesco Bissolo. $4, Madonna and Child with Four Cherubs, Ascribed to Barthel Bruyn. $5, The Virgin and Child, by Quentin Metsys. No. 758, The Virgin and Child Surrounded by Two Angels, by Perugino. No. 759, Madonna and Child with the Infant St. John and Archangel Gabriel, by Sandro Botticelli.

1992, Nov. 16 Litho. *Perf. 13½x14*

750-757 A83 Set of 8 11.00 11.00

Souvenir Sheet

758-759 A83 $6 Set of 2 10.50 10.50

Empire State Building, New York City — A84

1992, Oct. 28 Litho. *Perf. 14*

760 A84 $6 multicolored 6.00 6.00

Postage Stamp Mega Event '92, New York City.

A85

A89

A86

A87

A88

A90

A92

A91

Anniversaries and Events — A93

Designs: 15c, Japanese launch vehicle H-2. 50c, Hindenburg on fire, 1937. 75c, Charles de Gaulle, Konrad Adenauer. No. 764, Horatio Nelson Museum, Nevis. No. 765, Red Cross emblem, Nevis. No. 766, America's Cup yacht *Resolute*, 1920, vert. No. 767, St. Thomas Anglican Church. No. 768, Care Bear, butterfly and flower. No. 770, Blue whale. No. 771, WHO, ICN, FAO emblems, graph showing population growth. vert. No. 772, Lion, Lion's Intl. emblem. No. 773, John F. Kennedy, Adenauer. No. 774, Lebaudy, first flying machine with mechanical engine. No. 775, Soviet Energia launch vehicle SL-17.

Elvis Presley: No. 776a, Portrait. b, With guitar. c, With microphone.

Details or entire paintings, by Georges de La Tour: No. 777a, The Cheater (left). b, The Cheater (center). c, The Cheater (right). d, St. Joseph, the Carpenter. e, Saint Thomas. f, Adoration of the Shepherds (left). g, Adoration of the Shepherds (right). h, La Madeleine a La Veilleuse.

No. 778, Care Bear, palm tree, vert. No. 779, Manned maneuvering unit in space. No. 780, Count Zeppelin taking off from Goppingen for Friedrichshafen. No. 781, Adenauer. No. 782, America's Cup yacht. No. 783, The Angel Departing from the Family of Tobias, by Rembrandt.

1993 Litho. *Perf. 14*

761 A85 15c multicolored .25 .25
762 A86 50c multicolored .40 .40
763 A87 75c multicolored .80 .80
764 A88 80c multicolored .90 .90
765 A88 80c multicolored .90 .90
766 A89 80c multicolored .60 .60
767 A88 80c multicolored .60 .60
768 A90 80c multicolored .60 .60
770 A88 $1 multicolored .75 .75
771 A91 $3 multicolored 3.50 3.50
772 A85 $3 multicolored 3.00 3.00
773 A87 $5 multicolored 5.00 5.00
774 A86 $5 multicolored 5.50 5.50
775 A85 $5 multicolored 5.50 5.50

Perf. 14

776 A92 $1 Strip of 3, #a.-c. 2.25 2.25
Nos. 761-776 (15) 30.55 30.55

Miniature Sheet

Perf. 12

777 A93 $1 Sheet of 8, #a.-h. + label 8.50 8.50

Souvenir Sheets

Perf. 14

778 A90 $2 multicolored 1.50 1.50
779 A85 $6 multicolored 5.75 5.75
780 A86 $6 multicolored 5.75 5.75
781 A87 $6 multicolored 6.00 6.00
782 A89 $6 multicolored 4.50 4.50

Perf. 14½

783 A92 $6 multicolored 6.75 6.75

Intl. Space Year (#761, 775, 779). Count Zeppelin, 75th anniv. of death (#762, 774, 780). Konrad Adenauer, 25th anniv. of death (#763, 773, 781). Anglican Church in Nevis, 150th anniv. Opening of Horatio Nelson Museum (#764). Nevis and St. Kitts Red Cross, 50th anniv. (#765). America's Cup yacht race (#766, 782). (#767). Lions Intl., 75th anniv. (#772). Earth Summit, Rio de Janeiro (#768, 770, 778). Intl. Conference on Nutrition, Rome (#771). Elvis Presley, 15th death anniv. (in 1992) (#776). Louvre Art Museum, bicent. (#777, 783).

Nos. 779-781 have continuous designs.
No. 783 contains one 55x89mm stamp.
Issued: No. 767, Mar.; others, Jan. 14.

Tropical Flowers — A94

1993, Mar. 26 Litho. *Perf. 14*

784 A94 10c Frangipani .25 .25
785 A94 25c Bougainvillea .25 .25
786 A94 50c Allamanda .50 .50
787 A94 80c Anthurium .80 .80
788 A94 $1 Ixora 1.00 1.00
789 A94 $2 Hibiscus 2.00 2.00
790 A94 $4 Shrimp plant 4.00 4.00
791 A94 $5 Coral vine 5.00 5.00
Nos. 784-791 (8) 13.80 13.80

Souvenir Sheets

792 A94 $6 Lantana 5.50 5.50
793 A94 $6 Petrea 5.50 5.50

Butterflies A95

1993, May 17 Litho. *Perf. 14*

794 A95 10c Antillean blue .30 .30
795 A95 25c Cuban crescentspot .30 .30
796 A95 50c Ruddy dag-gerwing .60 .60
797 A95 80c Little yellow .90 .90
798 A95 $1 Atala 1.10 1.10
799 A95 $1.50 Orange-barred giant sulphur 1.60 1.60
800 A95 $4 Tropic queen 4.50 4.50
801 A95 $5 Malachite 5.50 5.50
Nos. 794-801 (8) 14.80 14.80

Souvenir Sheets

802 A95 $6 Polydamas swallowtail 6.25 6.25
a. Ovptd. in sheet margin 5.50 5.50
803 A95 $6 West Indian Buckeye 6.25 6.25
a. Ovptd. in sheet margin 5.50 5.50

Location of Hong Kong '94 emblem on Nos. 802a-803a varies.

Nos. 802a, 803a issued Feb. 18, 1994.

Miniature Sheet

Coronation of Queen Elizabeth II, 40th Anniv. A96

Designs: a, 10c, Official coronation photograph. b, 80c, Queen, wearing Imperial Crown of State. c, $2, Queen, sitting on throne during ceremony. d, $4, Prince Charles kissing mother's hand.

$6, Portrait, "Riding on Worcran in the Great Park at Windsor," by Susan Crawford, 1977.

1993, June 2 Litho. *Perf. 13½x14*

804 A96 Sheet, 2 ea #a.-d. 10.50 10.50

Souvenir Sheet

Perf. 14

805 A96 $6 multicolored 4.50 4.50

No. 805 contains one 28x42mm stamp.

Independence of St. Kitts and Nevis, 10th Anniv. — A97

Designs: 25c, Natl. flag, anthem. 80c, Brown pelican, map of St. Kitts and Nevis.

1993, Sept. 19 Litho. *Perf. 13½*

807	A97	25c multicolored	.50	.50
808	A97	80c multicolored	1.50	1.50

1994 World Cup Soccer Championships, US — A98

Soccer players: 10c, Garaba, Hungary; Platini, France. 25c, Maradona, Argentina; Bergomi, Italy. 50c, Fernandez, France; Rats, Russia. 80c, Munoz, Spain. $1, Elkjaer, Denmark; Goicoechea, Spain. $2, Coelho, Brazil; Tigana, France. $3, Troglio, Argentina; Alejnikov, Russia. No. 816, $5, Karas, Poland; Costa, Brazil.

Each $5: No. 817, Belloumi, Algeria. No. 818, Steven, England, vert.

1993, Nov. 9 Litho. *Perf. 14*

809-816 A98 Set of 8 14.00 14.00

Souvenir Sheets

817-818 A98 Set of 2 27.00 27.00

Christmas A99

Works by Albrecht Durer: 20c, Annunciation of Mary. 40c, The Nativity. 50c, Holy Family on a Grassy Bank. 80c, The Presentation of Christ in the Temple. $1, Virgin in Glory on the Crescent. $1.60, The Nativity, diff. $3, Madonna and Child. $5, The Presentation of Christ in the Temple (detail).

Each $6: No. 827, Mary with Child and the Long-Tailed Monkey, by Durer. No. 828, The Rest on the Flight into Egypt, by Fragonard, horiz.

1993, Nov. 30 *Perf. 13*

819-826 A99 Set of 8 14.00 14.00

Souvenir Sheets

827-828 A99 Set of 2 24.00 24.00

Tuff Mickey — A100

Disney's Mickey Mouse playing: 10c, Basketball. 50c, Volleyball. $1, Soccer. $5, Boxing.

No. 837, $6, Tug-of-war. No. 838, Ringing carnival bell with hammer, vert.

Disney's Minnie Mouse: 25c, Welcome to my island, vert. 80c, Sunny and snappy, vert. $1.50, Happy hoopin', vert. $4, Jumping for joy, vert.

Perf. 14x13½, 13½x14

1994, Mar. 15 Litho.

829	A100	10c multicolored	.25	.25
830	A100	25c multicolored	.25	.25
831	A100	50c multicolored	.55	.55
832	A100	80c multicolored	.80	.80
833	A100	$1 multicolored	1.00	1.00
834	A100	$1.50 multicolored	1.50	1.50
835	A100	$4 multicolored	4.00	4.00
836	A100	$5 multicolored	5.00	5.00
		Nos. 829-836 (8)	13.35	13.35

Souvenir Sheets

837	A100	$6 multicolored	6.50	6.50
838	A100	$6 multicolored	6.50	6.50

Hummel Figurines — A101

Designs: 5c, Umbrella Girl. 25c, For Father. 50c, Apple Tree Girl. 80c, March Winds. $1, Have the Sun in Your Heart. $1.60, Blue Belle. $2, Winter Fun. $5, Apple Tree Boy.

1994, Apr. 6 Litho. *Perf. 14*

839-846	A101	Set of 8	12.50	12.50
845a		Souv. sheet, #839, 843-845	5.00	5.00
846a		Souv. sheet, #840-842, 846	7.50	7.50

Beekeeping — A102

Designs: 50c, Beekeeper cutting wild nest of bees. 80c, Group of beekeepers, 1987. $1.60, Decapping frames of honey. $3, Queen bee rearing.

$6, Queen bee, worker bees, woman extracting honey.

1994, June 13 Litho. *Perf. 14*

847-850 A102 Set of 4 7.75 7.75

Souvenir Sheet

851	A102	$6 multicolored	7.50	7.50
a.		Ovptd. in sheet margin	5.50	5.50

No. 851a Overprinted "2nd Caribbean Beekeeping Congress / August 14-18, 2000" in sheet margin. Issued 8/14/00.

Issued: No. 851a, 8/17/00.

Miniature Sheet

Cats — A103

Designs: a, Blue point Himalayan. b, Black & white Persian. c, Cream Persian. d, Red Persian. e, Persian. f, Persian black smoke. g, Chocolate smoke Persian. h, Black Persian.

Each $6: No. 853, Brown tabby Persian. No. 854, Silver tabby Persian.

1994, July 20

852 A103 80c Sheet of 8, #a.-h. 7.50 7.50

Souvenir Sheets

853-854 A103 Set of 2 24.00 24.00

Marine Life A104

Marine Life A104a

Designs: 10c, Striped burrfish. 25c, Black coral, white & yellow, vert. 40c, Black coral, white & red, vert. 50c, Black coral, yellow & green, vert. 80c, Black coral, spiral-shaped, vert. $1, Blue-striped grunt. $1.60, Blue angelfish. $3, Cocoa damselfish.

No. 864a, Flameback angelfish. b, Reef bass. c, Honey gregory. d, Saddle squirrelfish. e, Cobalt chromis. f, Cleaner goby. g, Slendertail cardinalfish. h, Royal gramma.

Each $6: No. 865, Sailfish, vert. No. 866, Blue marlin.

1994, July 25 Litho. *Perf. 14*

856-863	A104	Set of 8	8.00	8.00
860a		Strip of 4, #857-860	4.00	4.00
860b		Min. sheet, 3 each #857-860	13.00	13.00

Miniature Sheet of 8

864	A104a	50c #a.-h.	9.50	9.50
i.		Ovptd. in sheet margin	4.00	4.00

Souvenir Sheets

865-866 A104a Set of 2 25.00 25.00

Nos. 857-860, World Wildlife Fund. No. 864i overprinted in sheet margin with PHILAKOREA '94 emblem.

Issued: #864i, 8/16; #860b, 7/25.

Local Architecture — A105

Designs: 25c, Residence, Barnes Ghaut Village. 50c, House above grocery store, Newcastle. $1, Treasury Building, Charlestown. $5, House above supermarket, Charlestown. $6, Apartment houses.

1994, Aug. 22

867-870 A105 Set of 4 8.50 8.50

Souvenir Sheet

871 A105 $6 multicolored 5.50 5.50

Order of the Caribbean Community — A106

First award recipients: 25c, William Demas, economist, Trinidad and Tobago. 50c, Sir Shridath Ramphal, statesman, Guyana. $1, Derek Walcott, writer, Nobel Laureate, St. Lucia.

1994, Sept. 1

872-874 A106 Set of 3 3.00 3.00

Miniature Sheet of 8

PHILAKOREA '94 — A107

Folding screen, longevity symbols embroidered on silk, Late Choson Dynasty: a, #1. b, #2. c, #3. d, #4. e, #5. f, #6. g, #7. h, #8.

1994 Litho. *Perf. 14*

875 A107 50c #a.-h. 4.00 4.00

Christmas — A108

Different details from paintings: 20c, 40c, 50c, $5, The Virgin Mary as Queen of Heaven, by Jan Provost. 80c, $1, $1.60, $3, Adoration of the Magi, by Workshop of Hugo van der Goes.

No. 884, The Virgin Mary as Queen of Heaven (complete). $6, Adoration of the Magi (complete).

1994, Dec. 1 Litho. *Perf. 14*

876-883 A108 Set of 8 10.50 10.50

Souvenir Sheets

884	A108	$5 multicolored	5.75	5.75
885	A108	$6 multicolored	6.75	6.75

Disney Valentines — A109

Designs: 10c, Mickey, Minnie. 25c, Donald, Daisy. 50c, Pluto, Fifi. 80c, Clarabelle, Horace Horsecollar. $1, Pluto, Figaro. $1.50, Polly, Peter Penguin. $4, Prunella Pullet, Hick Rooster. $5, Jenny Wren, Cock Robin.

Each $6: No. 894, Minnie, vert. No. 895, Daisy, vert.

1995, Feb. 14 Litho. *Perf. 14x13½*

886-893 A109 Set of 8 12.50 12.50

Souvenir Sheets

Perf. 13½x14

894-895 A109 Set of 2 12.50 12.50

Birds — A110

Designs: 50c, Hooded merganser. 80c, Green-backed heron. $2, Double crested cormorant. $3, Ruddy duck.

Hummingbirds: No. 900a, Rufous-breasted hermit. b, Purple-throated carib. c, Green mango. d, Bahama woodstar. e, Hispaniolan emerald. f, Antillean crested. g, Green-throated carib. h, Antillean mango. i, Vervian. j, Jamaican mango. k, Cuban emerald. l, Blue-headed.

Each $6: No. 901, Black skimmer. No. 902, Snowy plover.

1995, Mar. 30 Litho. *Perf. 14*

896-899 A110 Set of 4 4.75 4.75

Miniature Sheet of 12

900 A110 50c #a.-l. 12.00 12.00

Souvenir Sheets

901-902 A110 Set of 2 12.00 12.00

Dogs A111

Designs: 25c, Pointer. 50c, Old Danish pointer. $1, German short-haired pointer. $2, English setter.

No. 907a, Irish setter. b, Weimaraner. c, Gordon setter. d, Britanny spaniel. e, American cocker spaniel. f, English cocker spaniel. g, Labrador retriever. h, Golden retriever. i, Flat-coated retriever.
Each $6: #908, Bloodhound. #909, German shepherd.

1995, May 23 Litho. *Perf. 14*
903-906 A111 Set of 4 2.75 2.75

Miniature Sheet of 9

907 A111 80c #a.-i. 12.00 12.00

Souvenir Sheets

908-909 A111 Set of 2 12.00 12.00

Cacti — A112

Designs: 40c, Schulumbergera truncata. 50c, Echinocereus pectinatus. 80c, Mammillaria zelmanniana alba. $1.60, Lobivia hertriehiana. $2, Hamatocatcus setispinus. $3, Astrophytum myriostigma.
Each $6: No. 916, Opuntia robusta. No. 917, Rhipsalidopsis gaertneri.

1995, June 20 Litho. *Perf. 14*
910-915 A112 Set of 6 7.00 7.00

Souvenir Sheets

916-917 A112 Set of 2 11.00 11.00

Miniature Sheets of 6 or 8

End of World War II, 50th Anniv. — A113

Famous World War II Personalities: No. 918: a, Clark Gable. b, Audie Murphy. c, Glenn Miller. d, Joe Louis. e, Jimmy Doolittle. f, John Hersey. g, John F. Kennedy. h, Jimmy Stewart.
Planes: No. 919: a, F4F Wildcat. b, F4U-1A Corsair. c, Vought SB2U Vindicator. d, F6-F Hellcat. e, SDB Dauntless. f, TBF-1 Avenger.
Each $6: No. 920, Jimmy Doolittle, vert. No. 921, Fighter plane landing on aircraft carrier.

1995, July 20
918 A113 $1.25 #a.-h. + label 11.00 11.00
919 A113 $2 #a.-f. + label 12.00 12.00

Souvenir Sheets

920-921 A113 Set of 2 16.00 16.00

UN, 50th Anniv. — A114

People of various races: No. 922a, $1.25, Two men, child. b, $1.60, Man wearing turban, man with beard, woman. c, $3, Two men in business suits, woman.
$6, Nelson Mandela.

1995, July 20 Litho. *Perf. 14*
922 A114 Strip of 3, #a.-c. 4.50 4.50

Souvenir Sheet

923 A114 $6 multicolored 5.00 5.00

No. 922 is a continuous design.

1995 Boy Scout Jamboree, Holland — A115

Scouts in various activities: No. 924a, $1, Two wearing backpacks. b, $2, One holding rope, one wearing backpack. c, $4, One crossing rope bridge, one looking at map, natl. flag.
$6, Scout in kayak.

1995, July 20
924 A115 Strip of 3, #a.-c. 5.75 5.75

Souvenir Sheet

925 A115 $6 multicolored 6.25 6.25

No. 924 is a continuous design.

Rotary Intl., 90th Anniv. A116

Designs: $5, Rotary emblem, natl. flag. $6, Rotary emblem, beach.

1995, July 20
926 A116 $5 multicolored 4.25 4.25

Souvenir Sheet

927 A116 $6 multicolored 5.00 5.00

Queen Mother, 95th Birthday — A117

No. 928: a, Drawing. b, Pink hat. c, Formal portrait. d, Green blue hat.
$6, Wearing crown jewels.

1995, July 20 *Perf. 13½x14*
928 A117 $1.50 Block or strip of 4, #a.-d. 4.50 4.50

Souvenir Sheet

928E A117 $6 multicolored 5.00 5.00

No. 928 was issued in sheets of 2.
Sheets of Nos. 928 and 928E exist with margins overprinted with black border and text "In Memoriam 1900-2002."

FAO, 50th anniv. — A118

No. 929a, 40c, Woman with tan sari over head. b, $2, FAO emblem, two infants. c, $3, Woman with blue sari over head.
$6, Man with hands around hoe handle.

1995, July 20 *Perf. 14*
929 A118 Strip of 3, #a.-c. 4.50 4.50

Souvenir Sheet

930 A118 $6 multicolored 5.00 5.00

No. 929 is a continuous design.

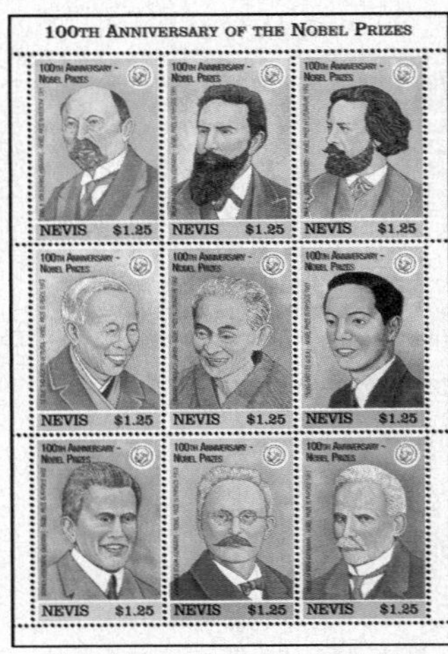

Nobel Prize Recipients — A119

1995, July 20

No. 931: a, Emil A. von Behring, medicine, 1901. b, Wilhelm Roentgen, physics, 1901. c, Paul J.L. Heyse, literature, 1910. d, Le Duc Tho, peace, 1973. e, Yasunari Kawabata, 1968. f, Tsung-Dao Lee, physics, 1957. g, Werner Hesisenberg, physics, 1932. h, Johannes Stark, physics, 1919. i, Wilhelm Wien, physics, 1911.
$6, Kenzaburo Oe, literature, 1994.

Miniature Sheet of 9

931 A119 $1.25 #a.-i. 10.00 10.00

Souvenir Sheet

932 A119 $6 multicolored 5.00 5.00

Souvenir Sheet

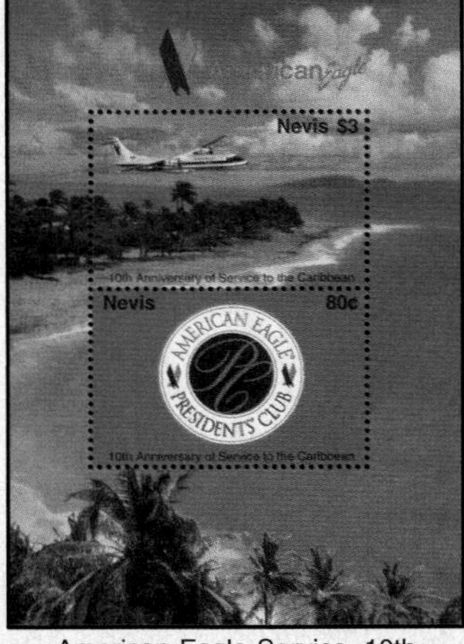

American Eagle Service, 10th Anniv. — A120

a, 80c, President's Club Emblem. b, $3, Airplane over beach. Illustration reduced.

1995, Aug. 28 Litho. *Perf. 14*
933 A120 Sheet of 2, #a.-b. 3.75 3.75

Miniature Sheet of 16

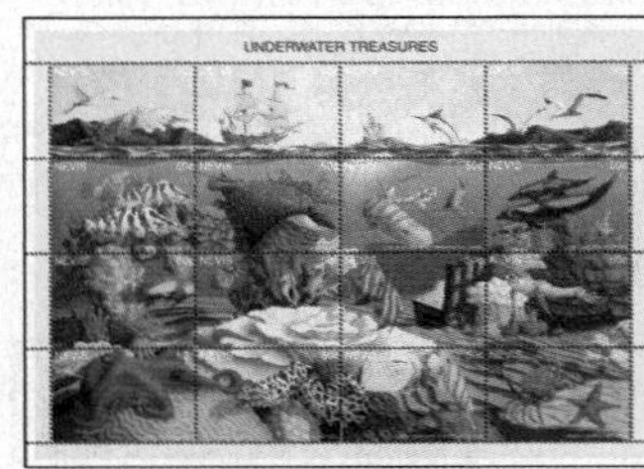

Marine Life — A121

No. 934: a, Great egrets. b, 17th cent. ship. c, Marlin. d, Herring gulls. e, Nassau groupers. f, Manta ray. g, Leopard shark, hammerhead shark. h, Hourglass dolphins. i, Spanish hogfish. j, Jellyfish, sea horses. k, Angel fish. l, Hawsbill turtle. m, Octopus vulgaris (i, j, m). n, Moray eel (o). o, Queen angelfish, butterflyfish. p, Ghost crab, sea star.

Each $6: No. 935, Nassau grouper. No. 936, Queen angelfish, vert.

1995, Sept. 1
934 A121 50c #a.-p. 8.00 8.00

Souvenir Sheets

935-936 A121 Set of 2 11.00 11.00

Singapore '95 (#935-936).

Natl. Telephone Co., SKANTEL Ltd., 10th Anniv. — A122

Designs: $1, Repairman working on telephone. $1.50, Company sign on building.
$5, Front of SKANTEL's Nevis office, horiz.

1995, Oct. 23 Litho. *Perf. 14*
937 A122 $1 multicolored .90 .90
938 A122 $1.50 multicolored 1.25 1.25

Souvenir Sheet

939 A122 $5 multicolored 4.50 4.50

Christmas Paintings, by Duccio di Buoninsegna (1250-1318) — A123

Details or entire paintings: 20c, Rucellai Madonna and Child. 50c, Border angel from Rucellai Madonna facing left. 80c, Madonna and Child. $1, The Annuniciation. $1.60, Madonna and Child. $3, Border angel from Rucellai Madonna facing right.
No. 946, Nativity with Prophets Isiah and Ezekiel. No. 947, Crevole Madonna.

1995, Dec. 1 Litho. *Perf. 13½x14*
940-945 A123 Set of 6 7.50 7.50

Souvenir Sheets

946 A123 $5 multicolored 4.75 4.75
947 A123 $6 multicolored 5.50 5.50

Four Seasons Resort, 5th Anniv. A124

Designs: 25c, Beach, resort buildings. 50c, Sailboats on beach. 80c, Golf course. $2, Premier Simeon Daniel laying cornerstone.
$6, Lounge chair on beach, sunset.

1996, Feb. 14 Litho. *Perf. 14*
948-951 A124 Set of 4 2.75 2.75

Souvenir Sheet

952 A124 $6 multicolored 5.00 5.00

New Year 1996 (Year of the Rat) — A125

Rat, various plant life, with olive margin: Nos. 953: a, Looking up at butterfly. b, Crawling left. c, Looking up at horsefly. d, Looking up at dragonfly.
Nos. 954a-954d: like Nos. 953a-953d, with yellow brown margin.
$3, Berries above rat.

1996, Feb, 28

953 A125 $1 Block of 4, #a.-d. 3.00 3.00

Miniature Sheet

954 A125 $1 Sheet of 4, #a.-d. 3.00 3.00

Souvenir Sheet

955 A125 $3 multicolored 3.00 3.00

No. 953 was issued in sheets of 16 stamps.

Pagodas of China A126

#956: a, Qian Qing Gong, 1420, Beijing. b, Qi Nian Dian, Temple of Heaven, Beijing. c, Zhongnanhai, Beijing. d, Da Zing Hall, Shenyang Palace. e, Temple of the Sleeping Buddha, Beijing. f, Huang Qiong Yu, Alter of Heaven, Beijing. g, Grand Bell Temple, Beijing. h, Imperial Palace, Beijing. i, Pu Tuo Temple.
$6, Summer Palace of emperor Wan Yanliang, 1153, Beijing, vert.

1996, May 15 Litho. *Perf. 14*

956 A126 $1 Sheet of 9, #a.-i. 6.75 6.75

Souvenir Sheet

957 A126 $6 multicolored 4.50 4.50

CHINA '96, 9th Asian Intl. Philatelic Exhibition (#956).

Queen Elizabeth II, 70th Birthday A127

Queen wearing: a, Blue dress, pearls. b, Formal white dress. c, Purple dress, hat.
$6, In uniform at trooping of the color.

1996, May 15 Litho. *Perf. 13½x14*

958 A127 $2 Strip of 3, #a.-c. 4.00 4.00

Souvenir Sheet

959 A127 $6 multicolored 4.00 4.00

No. 958 was issued in sheets of 9 stamps with each strip in a different order.

1996 Summer Olympic Games, Atlanta A128

Designs: 25c, Ancient Greek athletes boxing. 50c, Mark Spitz, gold medalist, swimming, 1972. 80c, Siegbert Horn, kayak singles gold medalist, 1972. $3, Siegestor Triumphal Arch, Munich, vert.
Pictures inside gold medals: No. 964, vert.: a, Jim Thorpe. b, Glenn Morris. c, Bob Mathias. d, Rafer Johnson. e, Bill Toomey. f, Nikolay Avilov. g, Bruce Jenner. h, Daley Thompson. i, Christian Schenk.
Each $5: No. 965, Willi Holdorf, vert. No. 966, Hans-Joachim Walde, silver medal, vert.

1996, May 28 *Perf. 14*

960-963 A128 Set of 4 4.00 4.00
964 A128 $1 Sheet of 9, #a.-i. 7.50 7.50

Souvenir Sheets

965-966 A128 Set of 2 17.00 17.00

Olymphilex '96 (#965).

UNESCO, 50th Anniv. — A129

25c, Cave paintings, Tassili N'Ajjer, Algeria. $2, Tikal Natl. Park, Guatemala, vert. $3, Temple of Hera at Samos, Greece.
$6, Pueblo, Taos, US.

1996, July 1 Litho. *Perf. 14*

967-969 A129 Set of 3 4.25 4.25

Souvenir Sheet

970 A129 $6 multicolored 4.50 4.50

UNICEF, 50th Anniv. A130

25c, Children reading book. 50c, Girl receiving innoculation. $4, Faces of young people.
$6, Girl, vert.

1996, July 1

971-973 A130 Set of 3 4.50 4.50

Souvenir Sheet

974 A130 $6 multicolored 4.50 4.50

Disney's Sweethearts — A131

Designs: a, Pocahontas, John Smith, Flit. b, Mowgli, The Girl, Kaa. c, Belle, Beast, Mrs. Potts, Chip. d, Cinderella, Prince Charming, Jaq. e, Pinocchio, Dutch Girl Marionette, Jiminy Cricket. f, Grace Martin, Henry Coy. g, Snow White, Prince. h, Aladdin, Jasmine, Abu. i, Pecos Bill, Slue Foot Sue.
Each $6: No. 977, Sleeping Beauty, Prince Phillip, vert. No. 978, Ariel, Eric.

Perf. 14x13½, 13½x14

1996, June 17 Litho.

975 A131 $2 Sheet of 9, #a.-i. 22.50 22.50

Souvenir Sheets

977-978 A131 Set of 2 14.00 14.00

A number has been reserved for an additional sheet with this set.

American Academy of Ophthalmology, Cent. — A132

1996, July 1 Litho. *Perf. 14*

979 A132 $5 multicolored 3.75 3.75

Flowers — A133

Designs: 25c, Rothmannia longiflora. 50c, Gloriosa simplex. $2, Catharanthus roseus. $3, Plumbago auriculata.
No. 984: a, Monodora myristica. b, Giraffa camelopardalis. c, Adansonia digitata. d, Ansellia gigantea. e, Geissorhiza rochensis. f, Arctotis venusta. g, Gladiohis cardinalis. h, Eucomis bicolor. i, Protea obtusifolia.
$5, Stelitzia reginae.

1996, Sept. 24 Litho. *Perf. 14*

980-983 A133 Set of 4 4.25 4.25
984 A133 $1 Sheet of 9, #a.-i. 6.75 6.75

Souvenir Sheet

985 A133 $5 multicolored 3.75 3.75

Christmas A134

Designs: 25c, Western meadowlark, vert. 50c, American goldfinch. 80c, Santa in sleigh, reindeer. $1, Western meadowlark, diff., vert. $1.60, Mockingbird, vert. $5, Yellow-rumped caleque.
Each $6: No. 992, Macaw. No. 993, Vermilion flycatcher.

1996, Dec. 2 Litho. *Perf. 14*

986-991 A134 Set of 6 6.75 6.75

Souvenir Sheets

992-993 A134 Set of 2 9.00 9.00

New Year 1997 (Year of the Ox) — A135

Painting, "Five Oxen," by Han Huang: a, 50c. b, 80c. c, $1.60. d, $2.

1997, Jan. 16 Litho. *Perf. 14x15*

994 A135 Sheet of 4, #a.-d. + label 3.75 3.75

A136

A137

Pandas: a, Eating leaves on branch. b, Face, eating. c, Paws holding object. d, Hanging upside down. e, Lying between tree branch. f, Climbing tree.
$5, Mother, cub.

1997, Feb. 12 Litho. *Perf. 14*

995 A136 $1.60 Sheet of 6, #a.-f. 9.00 9.00

Souvenir Sheet

996 A136 $5 multicolored 3.75 3.75

Hong Kong '97.

1997, May 1 Litho. *Perf. 14*

Cricket Players: 25c, Elquemedo Willet. 80c, Stuart Williams. $2, Keith Arthurton.
Each $5: No. 1000, Willet, Arthurton, Williams, 1990 Nevis team. No. 1001, Williams, Arthurton, 1994 West Indies team, vert.

997-999 A137 Set of 3 2.25 2.25

Souvenir Sheets

1000-1001 A137 Set of 2 7.50 7.50

Queen Elizabeth II, Prince Philip, 50th Wedding Anniv. A138

No. 1002: a, Queen Elizabeth II. b, Royal arms. c, Prince, Queen in red hat. d, Queen in blue coat, Prince. e, Caernarfon Castle. f, Prince Philip.
$5, Queen wearing crown.

1997, May 29 Litho. *Perf. 14*

1002 A138 $1 Sheet of 6, #a.-f. 4.50 4.50

Souvenir Sheet

1003 A138 $5 multicolored 3.75 3.75

Paintings by Hiroshige (1797-1858) A139

No. 1004: a, Scattered Pines, Tone River. b, Nakagawa River Mouth. c, Niijuku Ferry. d, Horie and Nekozane. e, View of Konodai and the Tone River. f, Maple Trees at Mama, Tekona Shrine & Bridge.
Each $6: No. 1005, Mitsumata Wakarenofuchi. No. 1006, Moto-Hachinan Shrine, Sunamura.

1997, May 29 *Perf. 13½x14*

1004 A139 $1.60 Sheet of 6, #a.-f. 7.25 7.25

Souvenir Sheets

1005-1006 A139 Set of 2 9.00 9.00

Paul Harris (1868-1947), Founder of Rotary Intl. — A140

$2, Literacy promotion, portrait of Harris.
$5, Rotary Village Corps coaching soccer for youths in Chile.

1997, May 29 *Perf. 14*

1007 A140 $2 multicolored 1.50 1.50

Souvenir Sheet

1008 A140 $5 multicolored 3.75 3.75

Heinrich von Stephan (1831-97) A141

No. 1009: a, Russian Reindeer Post, 1859. b, Von Stephan, UPU emblem. c, Steamboat, City of Cairo, 1800's.
$5, Portrait of Von Stephan, Bavarian postal messenger, 1640.

1997, May 29

1009 A141 $1.60 Sheet of 3, #a.-c. 3.50 3.50

Souvenir Sheet

1010 A141 $5 multicolored 3.75 3.75

PACIFIC 97.

Butterflies and Moths A142

10c, Crimson speckled. 25c, Purple emperor. 50c, Regent skipper. 80c, Provence burnet moth. $1, Common wall butterfly. $4, Cruiser butterfly.
No. 1017: a, Red-lined geometrid. b, Boisduval's autumnal moth. c, Blue pansy. d, Common clubtail. e, Tufted jungle queen. f, Lesser

marbled fritillary. g, Peacock royal. h, Emperor gum moth. i, Orange swallow-tailed moth.

Each $5: No. 1018, Jersey tiger. No. 1019, Japanese emperor.

1997, May 12 Litho. *Perf. 14*

1011-1016 A142 Set of 6 5.00 5.00
1017 A142 $1 Sheet of 9, #a.-i. 6.75 6.75

Souvenir Sheets

1018-1019 A142 Set of 2 7.50 7.50

Souvenir Sheet

Mother Goose — A143

1997, May 29

1020 A143 $5 Boy, two pigeons 3.75 3.75

Golf Courses of the World A144

Designs: a, Augusta National, U.S. b, Cabo Del Sol, Mexico. c, Cypress Point, U.S. d, Lost City, South Africa. e, Moscow Country Club, Russia. f, New South Wales, Australia. g, Royal Montreal, Canada. h, St. Andrews, Scotland. i, Four Seasons Resort, Nevis.

1997, July 15

1021 A144 $1 Sheet of 9, #a.-i. 6.75 6.75

Mushrooms A145

Designs: 25c, Cantharellus cibarius. 50c, Stropharia aeruginosa. $3, Lactarius turpis. $4, Entoloma Jypeatum.

No. 1026: a, Suillus luteus. b, Amanita musearia. c, Lactarius rufus. d, Amanita rubescens. e, Armillaria mellea. f, Russula sardonia.

No. 1027: a, Boletus edulis. b, Pholiota lenta. c, Cortinarius bolaris. d, Coprinus picaceus. e, Amanita phalloides. f, Cystolepiota aspera.

Each $5: No. 1028, Gymnopilus junonius. No. 1029, Galerina mutabilis, philiota auriuella.

1997, Aug. 12 Litho. *Perf. 13*

1022-1025 A145 Set of 4 6.00 6.00

Sheets of 6

1026 A145 80c #a.-f. 3.75 3.75
1027 A145 $1 #a.-f. 4.50 4.50

Souvenir Sheets

1028-1029 A145 Set of 2 7.50 7.50

Diana, Princess of Wales (1961-97) — A146

Various portraits.

1997, Sept. 19 Litho. *Perf. 14*

1030 A146 $1 Sheet of 9, #a.-i. 7.00 7.00

Trains A147

Designs: 10c, New Pacific type, Victorian Government Railways, Australia. 50c, Express locomotive, Imperial Government Railways, Japan. 80c, Turbine driven locomotive, London, Midland & Scottish Railway. $1, Electric passenger & freight locomotive, Swiss Federal Railways. $2, 3 cylinder compound express locomotive, London, Midland, Scottish Railway. $3, Express locomotive Kestrel, Great Northern Railway, Ireland.

No. 1037: a, 2-8-2 Mikado, Sudan Government Railways. b, Mohammed Ali El Kebir locomotive, Egyptian State Railways. c, "Schools" class locomotive, Southern Railway. d, Drum Battery Train, Great Southern Railways, Ireland. e, "Pacific" express locomotive, German State Railways. f, Mixed traffic locomotive, Canton-Hankow Railway, China.

Each $5: No. 1038, "King" class express, Great Western Railway. No. 1039, High pressure locomotive, London, Midland and Scottish Railway.

1997, Sept. 29 Litho. *Perf. 14*

1031-1036 A147 Set of 6 5.75 5.75
1037 A147 $1.50 Sheet of 6, #a.-f. 6.75 6.75

Souvenir Sheets

1038-1039 A147 Set of 2 7.50 7.50

Christmas — A148

Entire paintings or details: 20c, 25c, Diff. details from Selection of Angels, by Durer. 50c, Andromeda and Perseus, by Rubens. 80c, $1.60, Diff. details from Astronomy, by Raphael. $5, Holy Trinity, by Raphael.

Each $5: No. 1046, Ezekiel's Vision, by Raphael, horiz. No. 1047, Justice, by Rapahel, horiz.

1997, Nov. 26 Litho. *Perf. 14*

1040-1045 A148 Set of 6 6.25 6.25

Souvenir Sheets

1046-1047 A148 Set of 2 7.50 7.50

New Year 1998 (Year of the Tiger) — A149

Tigers: No. 1048: a, Jumping right. b, Looking back over shoulder. c, Jumping left. d, Looking forward.

No. 1049, Tiger, vert.

1998, Jan. 19 Litho. *Perf. 14*

1048 A149 80c Sheet of 4, #a.-d. 3.25 3.25

Souvenir Sheet

1049 A149 $2 multicolored 1.75 1.75

Social Security of St. Kitts and Nevis, 20th Anniv. A150

Designs: 30c, Logo, vert. $1.20, Front of Social Security building.

$6, Social Security staff, Charlestown, Nevis.

1998, Feb. 2 Litho. *Perf. 13*

1050 A150 30c multicolored .25 .25
1051 A150 $1.20 multicolored .90 .90

Souvenir Sheet

Perf. 13½x13

1052 A150 $6 multicolored 4.50 4.50

No. 1052 contains one 56x36mm stamp.

Fruit — A151

1998, Mar. 9 *Perf. 14*

1053	A151	5c	Soursop	.20	.20
1054	A151	10c	Carambola	.20	.20
1055	A151	25c	Guava	.20	.20
1056	A151	30c	Papaya	.25	.25
1057	A151	50c	Mango	.40	.40
1058	A151	60c	Golden apple	.45	.45
1059	A151	80c	Pineapple	.60	.60
1060	A151	90c	Watermelon	.70	.70
1061	A151	$1	Bananas	.75	.75
1062	A151	$1.80	Orange	1.40	1.40
1063	A151	$3	Honeydew	2.25	2.25
1064	A151	$5	Cantaloupe	3.75	3.75
1065	A151	$10	Pomegranate	7.50	7.50
1066	A151	$20	Cashew	15.00	15.00
	Nos. 1053-1066 (14)			33.65	33.65

For overprints see #O55-O66.

Nos. 1054, 1056, 1059, 1062, 1064, 1065 exist dated 2000.

Endangered Species — A152

Designs: 30c, Fish eagle. 80c, Summer tangers. 90c, Orangutan. $1.20, Tiger. $2, Cape pangolin. $3, Moatzin.

No. 1073: a, Chimpanzee. b, Keel-billed toucan. c, Chaco peccary. d, Spadefoot toad. e, Howler monkey. f, Alaskan brown bear. g, Koala. h, Brown pelican. i, Iguana.

Each $5: No. 1074, Mandrill. No. 1075, Polar bear.

1998, Mar. 31 Litho. *Perf. 14*

1067-1072 A152 Set of 6 6.25 6.25
1073 A152 $1 Sheet of 9, #a.-i. 6.75 6.75

Souvenir Sheets

1074-1075 A152 Set of 2 7.50 7.50

Aircraft A153

Designs: 10c, Boeing 747 200B. 90c, Cessna 185 Skywagon. $1.80, McDonnell Douglas DC-9 SO. $5, Airbus A300 B4.

No. 1080: a, Northrop B-2A. b, Lockheed SR-71A. c, Beechcraft T-44A. d, Sukhoi Su-27UB. e, Hawker Siddeley (BAe) Harrier GR.MK1. f, Boeing E-3A Sentry. g, Convair B-36H. h, IAI Kfir C2.

Each $5: No. 1081, Lockheed F-117A. No. 1082, Concorde G-BOAA.

1998, May 19 Litho. *Perf. 14*

1076-1079 A153 Set of 4 6.00 6.00
1080 A153 $1 Sheet of 8, #a.-h. 6.25 6.25

Souvenir Sheets

1081-1082 A153 Set of 2 8.00 8.00

#1081-1082 each contain 1 57x42mm stamp.

Chaim Topol Portraying Tevye from "Fiddler on the Roof" — A154

1998, May 17 Litho. *Perf. 13½*

1083 A154 $1.60 multicolored 1.25 1.25

Israel '98. Issued in sheets of 6.

Voice of Nevis (VON) Radio, 10th Anniv. A155

20c, Logo of Nevis Broadcasting Co., vert. 30c, Evered "Webbo" Herbert, station manager at controls. $1.20, Exterior of offices and studios.

$5, Merritt Herbert, managing director, opening ceremony, 1988.

1998, June 18 *Perf. 14*

1084-1086 A155 Set of 3 1.25 1.25

Souvenir Sheet

1087 A155 $5 multicolored 3.75 3.75

Intl. Year of the Ocean A156

30c, Butterflyfish. 80c, Bicolor cherub. $1.20, Silver badgerfish. $2, Asfur angelfish.

No. 1092, vert: a, Copperbanded butterflyfish. b, Forcepsfish. c, Double-saddled butterflyfish. d, Blue surgeonfish. e, Orbiculate batfish. f, Undulated triggerfish. g, Rock beauty. h, Flamefish. i, Queen angelfish.

No. 1093: a, Pygama cardinal fish. b, Wimplefish. c, Long-nosed filefish. d, Oriental sweetlips. e, Blue spotted boxfish. f, Blue stripe angelfish. g, Goldrim tang. h, Royal gramma. i, Common clownfish.

Each $5: No. 1094, Longhorned cowfish, vert. No. 1095, Red-faced batfish, vert.

1998, Aug. 18 Litho. *Perf. 14*

1088-1091 A156 Set of 4 5.75 5.75
1092 A156 90c Sheet of 9, #a.-i. 6.00 6.00
1093 A156 $1 Sheet of 9, #a.-i. 6.75 6.75

Souvenir Sheets

1094-1095 A156 Set of 2 8.00 8.00

Diana, Princess of Wales (1961-97) A157

1998, Oct. 15 Litho. *Perf. 14*

1096 A157 $1 multicolored .75 .75

No. 1096 was issued in sheets of 6.

Mahatma Gandhi (1869-1948) A158

Portraits: No. 1097, In South Africa, 1914. No. 1098, At Downing Street, London.

1998, Oct. 15

1097 A158 $1 multicolored .75 .75
1098 A158 $1 multicolored .75 .75

Nos. 1097-1098 were each issued in sheets of 6.

Royal Air Force, 80th Anniv. A159

Aircraft — #1100: a, Panavia Tornado F3 ADV. b, Panavia Tornado F3 IDV. c, Tristar K Mk1 Tanker refueling Panavia Tornado. d, Panavia Tornado GRI.

Each $5: No. 1101, Wessex helicopter, fighter plane. No. 1102, Early aircraft, birds.

1998, Oct. 15 **Litho.** ***Perf. 14***

1100 A159 $2 Sheet of 4, #a.-d. 6.50 6.50

Souvenir Sheets

1101-1102 A159 Set of 2 8.50 8.50

1998 World Scouting Jamboree, Chile — A160

Designs: a, Four Boy Scouts from around the world. b, Boy Scout accompanying Gettysburg veterans, 1913. c, First black troop, Virginia, 1928.

1998, Oct. 15

1103 A160 $3 Sheet of 3, #a.-c. 7.25 7.25

Independence, 15th Anniv. — A161

Design: Prime Minister Kennedy Simmonds receiving constitutional instruments from Princess Margaret, Countess of Snowden.

1998, Oct. 15 **Litho.** ***Perf. 14***

1104 A161 $1 multicolored .75 .75

Organization of American States, 50th Anniv. A162

1998, Oct. 15 ***Perf. 14***

1105 A162 $1 multicolored .75 .75

Enzo Ferrari (1898-1988), Automobile Manufacturer — A163

No. 1106: a, 365 California. b, Pininfarina's P6. c, 250 LM.

$5, 212 Export Spyder.

1998, Oct. 15

1106 A163 $2 Sheet of 3, #a.-c. 5.00 5.00

Souvenir Sheet

1107 A163 $5 multicolored 4.25 4.25

No. 1107 contains one 91x35mm stamp.

Christmas — A164

Designs: 25c Kitten, Santa. 60c, Kitten, ornament. 80c, Kitten in sock, vert. 90c, Puppy, presents. $1, Cherub sleeping, birds. $3, Child making snowball, vert.

Each $5: No. 1114, Family, vert. No. 1115, Two dogs.

1998, Nov. 24 **Litho.** ***Perf. 14***

1108-1113 A164 Set of 6 5.00 5.00

Souvenir Sheets

1114-1115 A164 Set of 2 7.50 7.50

New Year 1999 (Year of the Rabbit) — A165

Color of pairs of rabbits — #1116: a, brown & gray. b, brown & white. c, brown. d, white & black spotted.

$5, Adult white rabbit, 3 bunnies.

1999, Jan. 4 **Litho.** ***Perf. 14***

1116 A165 $1.60 Sheet of 4, #a.-d. 4.75 4.75

Souvenir Sheet

1117 A165 $5 multicolored 3.75 3.75

No. 1117 contains one 58x47mm stamp.

Disney Characters Playing Basketball A166

Basketball in background — #1118, each $1: a, Mickey in green. b, Donald. c, Minnie. d, Goofy. e, One of Donald's nephews. f, Goofy, Mickey. g, Mickey in purple. h, Huey, Dewey, Louie.

Green & white background — #1119, each $1: a, Mickey in purple. b, Goofy. c, Minnie in puple. d, Mickey in yellow & gray. e, Minnie in yellow. f, Donald. g, Donald & Mickey. h, One of Donald's nephews.

No. 1120, $5, Minnie, green bow, horiz. No. 1121, $5, Minnie, purple bow, horiz. No. 1122, $6, Mickey in purple, horiz. No. 1123, $6, Mickey in yellow, horiz.

Perf. 13½x14, 14x13½

1998, Dec. 24 **Litho.**

Sheets of 8, #a-h

1118-1119 A166 Set of 2 16.00 16.00

Souvenir Sheets

1120-1121 A166 Set of 2 8.50 8.50
1122-1123 A166 Set of 2 10.50 10.50

Mickey Mouse, 70th anniv.

1998 World Cup Soccer Players A167

No. 1124: a, Laurent Blanc, France. b, Dennis Bergkamp, Holland. c, David Sukor, Croatia. d, Ronaldo, Brazil. e, Didier Deschamps, France. f, Patrick Kluivert, Holland. g, Rivaldo, Brazil. h, Zinedine Zidane, France.

$5, Zinedine Zidane, close-up.

1999, Jan. 18 ***Perf. 13½***

1124 A167 $1 Sheet of 8, #a.-h. 6.00 6.00

Souvenir Sheet

1125 A167 $5 multicolored 3.75 3.75

Australia '99, World Stamp Expo A168

Dinosaurs: 30c, Kritosaurus. 60c, Oviraptor. 80c, Eustreptospondylus. $1.20, Tenontosaurus. $2, Ouranosaurus. $3, Muttaburrasaurus.

No. 1132, $1.20: a, Edmontosaurus. b, Avimimus. c, Minmi. d, Segnosaurus. e, Kentrosaurus. f, Deinonychus.

No. 1133, #1.20: a, Saltasaurus. b, Compsoganthus c, Hadrosaurus. d, Tuojiangosaurus. e, Euoplocephalus. f, Anchisaurus.

Each $5: #1134, Triceratops. #1135, Stegosaurus.

1999, Feb. 22 **Litho.** ***Perf. 14***

1126-1131 A168 Set of 6 6.00 6.00

Sheets of 6, #a-f

1132-1133 A168 Set of 2 11.00 11.00

Souvenir Sheets

1134-1135 A168 Set of 2 7.50 7.50

World Leaders of the 20th Century — A169

No. 1136: a, Emperor Haile Selassie (1892-1975), Ethiopia. b, Selassie, Ethiopian warriors, flag. c, David Ben-Gurion (1886-1973), Prime Minister of Israel. d, Ben-Gurion, Israeli flag. e, Pres. Franklin Roosevelt (1882-1945), Eleanor Roosevelt (1884-1962), UN emblem. f, Roosevelts campaigning, US GI in combat. g, Mao Tse-tung (1893-1976), Chinese leader, 1934 Long March. h, Poster of Mao, soldier.

Each $5: No. 1137, Gandhi. No. 1138, Nelson Mandela.

1999, Mar. 8

1136 A169 90c Sheet of 8, #a.-h. 6.00 6.00

Souvenir Sheets

1137-1138 A169 Set of 2 7.50 7.50

#1136b-1136c, 1136f-1136g are each 53x38mm.

Birds A170

No. 1139, each $1.60: a, Yellow warbler. b, Common yellowthroat. c, Painted bunting. d, Belted kingfisher. e, American kestrel. f, Northern oriole.

No. 1140, each $1.60: a, Malachite kingfisher. b, Lilac-breasted roller. c, Swallow-tailed bee-eater. d, Eurasian jay. e, Black-collared apalis. f, Gray-backed camaroptera.

Each $5: No. 1141, Banaquit. No. 1142, Ground scraper thrush, vert.

1999, May 10 **Litho.** ***Perf. 14***

Sheets of 6, #a-f

1139-1140 A170 Set of 2 15.00 15.00

Souvenir Sheets

1141-1142 A170 Set of 2 8.00 8.00

Orchids A171

Designs: 20c, Phaius hybrid, vert. 25c, Cuitlauzina pendula, vert. 50c, Bletilla striata, vert. 80c, Cymbidium "Showgirl," vert. $1.60, Zygopetalum crinitium. $3, Dendrobium nobile.

No. 1149, vert, each $1: a, Cattleya pumpernickel. b, Odontocidium Arthur Elle. c, Neostylis Lou Sneary. d, Phalaenopsis Aprodite. e, Arkundina graminieolia. f, Cymbidium Hunter's Point. g, Rynchoatylis coelestis. h, Cymbidium Elf's castle.

No. 1150, vert, each $1: a, Cattleya intermedia. b, Cattleya Sophia Martin. c, Phalaenopsis Little Hal. d, Laeliocattleya alisal "Rodeo." e, Laelia lucasiana fournieri. f, Cymbidium Red beauty. g, Sobralia sp. h, Promenaea xanthina.

Each $5: No. 1151, Philippine wind orchid. No. 1152, Dragon's mouth.

1999, June 15 **Litho.** ***Perf. 14***

1143-1148 A171 Set of 6 5.25 5.25

Sheets of 8, #a-h

1149-1150 A171 Set of 2 13.50 13.50

Souvenir Sheets

1151-1152 A171 Set of 2 8.00 8.00

Wedding of Prince Edward and Sophie Rhys-Jones A172

No. 1153, each $2: a, Sophie in checked suit. b, Couple walking across grass. c, Sophie in black hat, suit, d, Prince Edward in white shirt.

No. 1154, each $2: a, Couple standing in front of building. b, Sophie wearing large hat. c, Sophie in black dress. d, Edward in striped shirt.

Each $5: No. 1155, Couple posing for engagement photo, horiz. No. 1156, Edward kissing Sophie, horiz.

1999, June 19 Litho. *Perf. 14¼*

Sheets of 4, #a-d

1153-1154 A172 Set of 2 12.00 12.00

Souvenir Sheets

1155-1156 A172 Set of 2 7.50 7.50

IBRA '99, World Stamp Exhibition, Nuremberg — A173

Beuth 2-2-2 locomotive and: 30c, Baden #1. 80c, Brunswick #1.

Sailing ship Kruzenshstern and: 90c, Bergedorf #2 & #1a. $1, Bremen #1.

$5, Regensburg air post label on cover.

Illustration reduced.

1999, July 1 *Perf. 14x14½*

1157-1160 A173 Set of 4 4.50 4.50

Souvenir Sheet

1161 A173 $5 multicolored 3.75 3.75

Souvenir Sheets

PhilexFrance '99, World Philatelic Exhibition — A174

Trains: No. 1162, $5: First Class Carriage, 1837. No. 1163, $5: 141.R Mixed Traffic 2-8-2, 1949.

Illustration reduced.

1999, July 1 *Perf. 14x13½*

1162-1163 A174 Set of 2 3.75 3.75

Paintings by Hokusai (1760-1849) A175

Details or entire paintings — #1164: a, (Five) Women Returning Home at Sunset. b, The Blind. c, (Four) Women Returning Home at Sunset. d, A Young Man on a White Horse. e, The Blind (man with beard). f, A Peasant Crossing a Bridge.

No. 1165: a, Poppies (one in bloom). b, The Blind (man with goatee). c, Poppies. d, Abe No Nakamaro Gazing at the Moon from a Terrace. e, The Blind. f, Cranes on a Snowy Pine.

Each $5: No. 1166, Carp in a Waterfall. No. 1167, A Rider in the Snow.

1999, July 1 *Perf. 13½x14*

Sheets of 6

1164 A175 $1 #a.-f. 4.50 4.50
1165 A175 $1.60 #a.-f. 7.25 7.25

Souvenir Sheets

1166-1167 A175 Set of 2 8.00 8.00

Culturama Festival, 25th Anniv. — A176

Designs: 30c, Steel drummers. 80c, Clowns. $1.80, Masqueraders with "Big Drum." No. 1171, $5, String band.

No. 1172, Masquerade dancers.

1999, July 1 Litho. *Perf. 14*

1168-1171 A176 Set of 4 5.75 5.75

Souvenir Sheet

1172 A176 $5 multicolored 3.75 3.75

No. 1172 contains one 51x38mm stamp.

Queen Mother — A177

Christmas — A178

Queen Mother (b. 1900): No. 1173: a, In bridal gown, 1923. b, With Princess Elizabeth, 1926. c, With King George VI in World War II. d, Wearing hat, 1983.

$6, Wearing tiara, 1957.

1999, Aug. 4 *Perf. 14*

Gold Frames

Sheet of 4

1173 A177 $2 #a.-d., + label 6.00 6.00

Souvenir Sheet

Perf. 13¾

1174 A177 $6 multicolored 4.50 4.50

No. 1174 contains one 38x51mm stamp.

See Nos. 1287-1288.

1999, Nov. 12 Litho. *Perf. 14*

30c, Adoration of the Magi, by Albrecht Durer. 90c, Canigiani Holy Family, by Raphael. $1.20, The Nativity, by Durer. $1.80, Madonna Surrounded by Angels, by Peter Paul Rubens. $3, Madonna Surrounded by Saints, by Rubens.

$5, Madonna and Child by a Window, by Durer, horiz.

1175-1179 A178 Set of 5 5.50 5.50

Souvenir Sheet

1180 A178 $5 multicolored 3.75 3.75

Millennium A179

Scenes of Four Seasons Resort: a, Aerial view. b, Palm tree, beach. c, Golf course. d, Couple on beach.

1999 Litho. *Perf. 14¼x13¾*

1181 A179 30c Sheet of 4, #a.-d. .90 .90

Flowers A180

Various flowers making up a photomosaic of Princess Diana.

1999, Dec. 31 Litho. *Perf. 13¾*

1182 A180 $1 Sheet of 8, #a.-h. 6.00 6.00

New Year 2000 (Year of the Dragon) — A181

No. 1183: a, Dragon showing 9 claws. b, Dragon showing 10 claws. c, Dragon showing 5 claws. d, Dragon showing 8 claws.

$5, Dragon, vert.

2000, Feb. 5 *Perf. 14*

1183 A181 $1.60 Sheet of 4, #a.-d. 4.75 4.75

Souvenir Sheet

Perf. 13¾

1184 A181 $5 multi 3.75 3.75

No. 1184 contains one 38x50mm stamp.

Millennium A182

No. 1185 — Highlights of 1700-1750: a, Jonathan Swift writes "Gulliver's Travels." b, Manchu Dynasty flourishes in China. c, Bartolomeo Cristofori invents piano. d, Capt. William Kidd hanged for piracy. e, Astronomer William Herschel born. f, George I succeeds Queen Anne as British ruler. g, Russian treaty with China. h, Bubonic plague hits Austria and Germany. i, Kaigetsudo paints "Standing Woman." j, Queen Anne ascends to English throne. k, Anders Celsius invents centigrade scale for thermometer. l, Vitus Bering discovers Alaska and Aleutian Islands. m, Edmond Halley predicts return of comet. n, John and Charles Wesley found Methodism movement. o, Isaac Newton publishes "Opticks." p, England and Scotland form Great Britain (60x40mm). q, Johann Sebastian Bach composes "The Well-Tempered Clavier."

No. 1186 — Highlights of the 1990s: a, Boris Yeltsin becomes prime minister of Russian Federation. b, Gulf War begins. c, Civil War in Bosnia. d, Signing of the Oslo Accords. e, John Major, Albert Reynolds search for peace in Northern Ireland. f, F.W. De Klerk, Nelson Mandela end apartheid in South Africa. g, Cal Ripken, Jr. breaks record for most consecutive baseball games played. h, Kobe, Japan earthquake. i, Inca girl, believed to be 500 years old, found in ice. j, Sojourner beams back images from Mars. k, Dr. Ian Wilmot clones sheep "Dolly." l, Princess Diana dies in car crash. m, Hong Kong returned to China. n, Septuplets born and survive. o, Guggenheim Museum in Bilbao, Spain completed. p, Countdown to year 2000 (60x40mm). q, Pres. William J. Clinton impeached.

2000, Jan. 4 Litho. *Perf. 12¾x12½*

Sheets of 17

1185 A182 30c #a.-q., + label 4.50 4.50
1186 A182 50c #a.-q., + label 6.75 6.75

Misspellings and historical inaccuracies abound on Nos. 1185-1186.

Tropical Fish A183

Designs: 30c, Spotted scat. 80c, Platy variatus. 90c, Emerald betta. $4, Cowfish.

No. 1191, each $1: a, Oriental sweetlips. b, Royal gramma. c, Threadfin butterflyfish. d, Yellow tang. e, Bicolor angelfish. f, Catalina goby. g, False cleanerfish. h, Powder blue surgeon.

No. 1192, each $1: a, Sailfin tang. b, Black-capped gramma. c, Majestic snapper. d, Purple firefish. e, Clown trigger. f, Yellow long-nose. g, Clown wrasse. h, Yellow-headed jawfish.

Each $5: No. 1193, Clown coris. No. 1194, Clown killifish.

2000, Mar. 27 *Perf. 14*

1187-1190 A183 Set of 4 4.75 4.75

Sheets of 8, #a.-h.

1191-1192 A183 Set of 2 12.50 12.50

Souvenir Sheets

1193-1194 A183 Set of 2 7.75 7.75

Dogs — A184

Designs: 10c, Miniature pinscher. 20c, Pyrenean mountain dog. 30c, Welsh Springer spaniel. 80c, Alaskan malamute. $2, Bearded collie. $3, Amercian cocker spaniel.

No. 1201, horiz.: a, Beagle. b, Basset hound. c, St. Bernard. d, Rough collie. e, Shih tzu. f, American bulldog.

No. 1202, horiz.: a, Irish red and white setter. b, Dalmatian. c, Pomeranian. d, Chihuahua. e, English sheepdog. f, Samoyed.

Each $5: No. 1203, Leonberger. No. 1204, Longhaired miniature dachshund, horiz.

2000, May 1 Litho. *Perf. 14*

1195-1200 A184 Set of 6 4.75 4.75
1201 A184 90c Sheet of 6, #a-f 4.00 4.00
1202 A184 $1 Sheet of 6, #a-f 4.50 4.50

Souvenir Sheets

1203-1204 A184 Set of 2 8.00 8.00

100th Test Match at Lord's Ground — A185

Designs: $2, Elquemede Willett. $3, Keith Arthurton.

$5, Lord's Ground, horiz.

2000, June 10

1205-1206 A185 Set of 2 3.75 3.75

Souvenir Sheet

1207 A185 $5 multi 3.75 3.75

First Zeppelin Flight, Cent. — A186

No. 1208: a, LZ-129. b, LZ-1. c, LZ-11.
$5, LZ-127.
Illustration reduced.

2000, June 10 ***Perf. 14***

1208 A186 $3 Sheet of 3, #a-c 6.75 6.75

Souvenir Sheet

Perf. 14¼

1209 A186 $5 multi 4.25 4.25

No. 1208 contains three 38x25mm stamps.

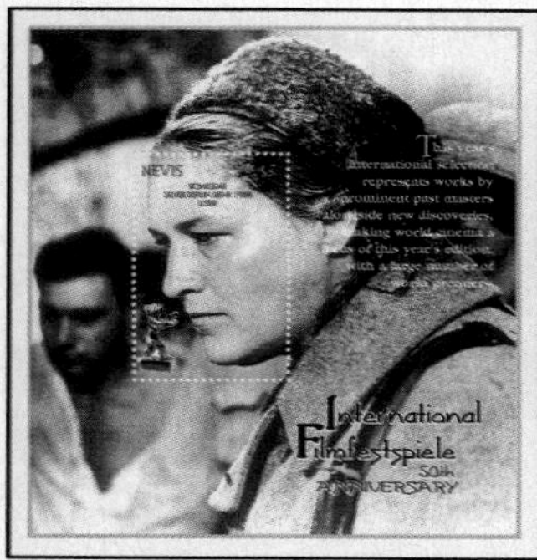

Berlin Film Festival, 50th Anniv. — A187

No. 1210: a, Rani Radovi. b, Salvatore Giuliano. c, Schoenzeit für Füchse. d, Shirley MacLaine. e, Simone Signoret. f, Sohrab Shahid Saless.
$5, Komissar.
Illustration reduced.

2000, June 10 ***Perf. 14***

1210 A187 $1.60 Sheet of 6, #a-f 7.25 7.25

Souvenir Sheet

1211 A187 $5 multi 4.25 4.25

Spacecraft — A188

No. 1212, each $1.60: a, Mars IV probe. b, Mars Water. c, Mars 1. d, Viking. e, Mariner 7. f, Mars Surveyor.

No. 1213, each $1.60: a, Mariner 9. b, Mars 3. c, Mariner 4. d, Planet B. e, Mars Express Lander. f, Mars Express.

Each $5: No. 1214, Mars Observer. No. 1215, Mars Climate Observer, vert.
Illustration reduced.

2000, June 10

Sheets of 6, #a-f

1212-1213 A188 Set of 2 14.50 14.50

Souvenir Sheets

1214-1215 A188 Set of 2 7.50 7.50

Souvenir Sheets

2000 Summer Olympics, Sydney — A189

No. 1216: a, Gisela Mauermeyer. b, Uneven bars. c, Wembley Stadium, London, and British flag. d, Ancient Greek horse racing.
Illustration reduced.

2000, June 10

1216 A189 $2 Sheet of 4, #a-d 6.00 6.00

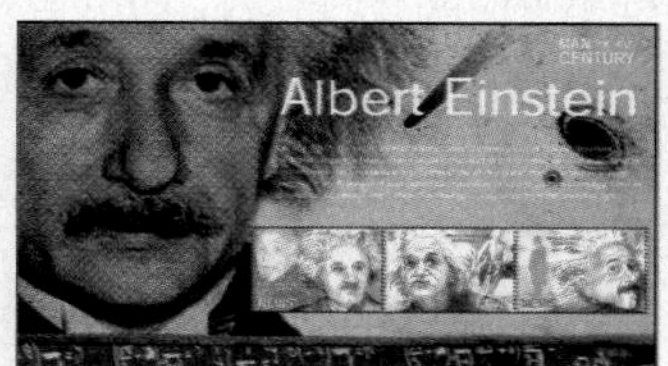

Albert Einstein (1879-1955) — A190

No. 1217: a, Sticking out tongue. b, Riding bicycle. c, Wearing hat.

2000, June 10

1217 A190 $2 Sheet of 3, #a-c 4.50 4.50

Public Railways, 175th Anniv. — A191

No. 1218: a, Locomotion No. 1, George Stephenson. b, Trevithick's 1804 drawing of locomotive.
Illustration reduced.

2000, June 10

1218 A191 $3 Sheet of 2, #a-b 4.50 4.50

Johann Sebastian Bach (1685-1750) — A192

Illustration reduced.

2000, June 10

1219 A192 $5 multi 4.00 4.00

Prince William, 18th Birthday — A193

No. 1220: a, Reaching to shake hand. b, In ski gear. c, With jacket open. d, In sweater.
$5, In suit and tie.
Illustration reduced.

2000, June 21 ***Perf. 14***

1220 A193 $1.60 Sheet of 4, #a-d 4.75 4.75

Souvenir Sheet

Perf. 13¾

1221 A193 $5 multi 4.00 4.00

No. 1220 contains four 28x42mm stamps.

Souvenir Sheets

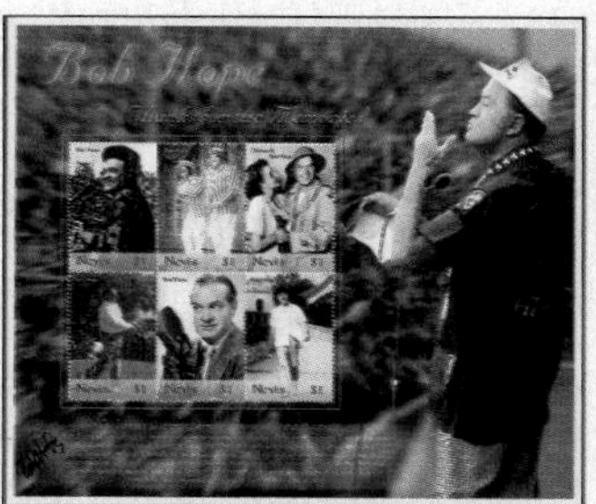

Bob Hope, Entertainer — A194

No. 1222: a, Wearing Air Force Ranger uniform. b, With Sammy Davis, Jr. c, With wife, Dolores. d, On golf course. e, In suit behind microphone. f, Walking.
Illustration reduced.

2000, July 10 ***Perf. 14***

1222 A194 $1 Sheet of 6, #a-f 5.00 5.00

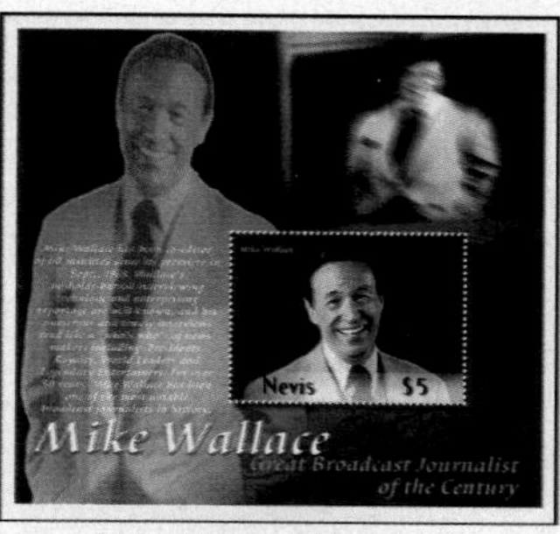

Mike Wallace, Broadcast Journalist — A195

Illustration reduced.

2000, July 10 ***Perf. 13¾***

1223 A195 $5 multi 4.00 4.00

Carifesta VII — A196

Designs: 30c, Emblem. 90c, Festival participants. $1.20, Dancer.

2000, Aug. 17 ***Perf. 14***

1224-1226 A196 Set of 3 2.00 2.00

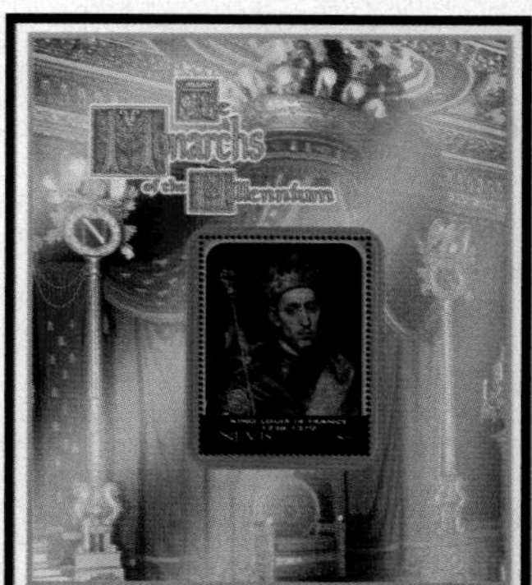

Monarchs — A197

No. 1227: a, King Edward III of England, 1327-77. b, Holy Roman Emperor Charles V (Charles I of Spain), 1520-56. c, Holy Roman Emperor Joseph II of Austria-Hungary, 1780-90. d, King Henry II of Germany, 1002-24. e, King Louis IV of France, 936-54. f, King Louis II of Bavaria, 1864-86.

$5, King Louis IX of France, 1226-70.
Illustration reduced.

2000, Aug. 1 **Litho.** ***Perf. 13¾***

1227 A197 $1.60 Sheet of 6, #a-f 7.50 7.50

Souvenir Sheet

1228 A197 $5 multi 4.25 4.25

David Copperfield, Magician — A198

2000, Aug. 10 ***Perf. 14***

1229 A198 $1.60 multi 1.75 1.75

Printed in sheets of 4.

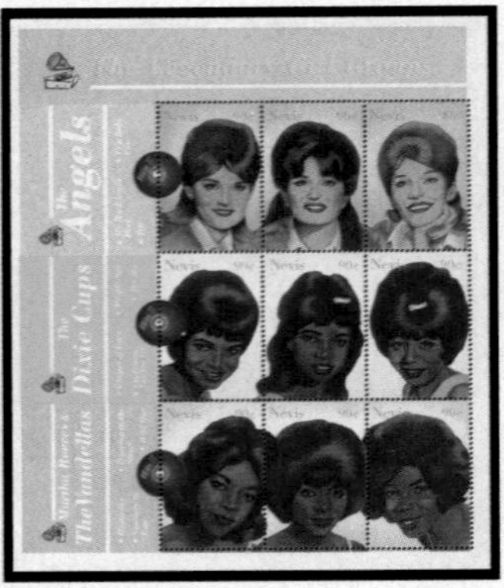
Female Singing Groups — A199

Singers from the Angels (a-c, blue background), Dixie Cups (d-f, yellow background) and Martha Reeves and the Vandellas (g-i, pink background): a, Record half. b, Woman with long hair. c, Woman with hand on chin. d, Record half. e, Woman with mole on cheek. f, Woman, no mole. g, Record half. h, Woman, not showing teeth. i, Woman showing teeth.
Illustration reduced.

2000, Aug. 10
1230 A199 90c Sheet of 9, #a-i 6.50 6.50

Butterflies A200

Designs: 30c, Zebra. 80c, Julia. $1.60, Small flambeau. $5, Purple mort bleu.
No. 1235, $1: a, Ruddy dagger. b, Common morpho. c, Banded king shoemaker. d, Figure of eight. e, Grecian shoemaker. f, Mosaic.
No. 1236, $1: a, White peacock. b, Hewitson's blue hairstreak. c, Tiger pierid. d, Gold drop helicopsis. e, Cramer's mesene. f, Red-banded pereute.
No. 1237, $5, Common mechanitis. No. 1238, $5, Hewitson's pierella.

2001, Mar. 22
1231-1234 A200 Set of 4 6.00 6.00
Sheets of 6, #a-f
1235-1236 A200 Set of 2 9.50 9.50
Souvenir Sheets
1237-1238 A200 Set of 2 7.75 7.75

Flowers A201

Designs: 30c, Golden elegance oriental lily. 80c, Frangipani. $1.60, Garden zinnia. $5, Rose elegance lily.
No. 1243, 90c: a, Star of the march. b, Tiger lily. c, Mont Blanc lily. d, Torch ginger. e, Cattleya orchid. f, Saint John's wort.
No. 1244, $1: a, Culebra. b, Rubellum lily. c, Silver elegance oriental lily. d, Chinese hibiscus. e, Tiger lily. f, Royal poinciana.
No. 1245, $1.60: a, Epiphyte. b, Enchantment lily. c, Glory lily. d, Purple granadilla. e, Jacaranda. f, Shrimp plant.
No. 1246, $5, Dahlia. No. 1247, $5, Bird of Paradise.

2000, Oct. 30
1239-1242 A201 Set of 4 6.00 6.00
Sheets of 6, #a-f
1243-1245 A201 Set of 3 17.00 17.00
Souvenir Sheets
1246-1247 A201 Set of 2 7.75 7.75

The Stamp Show 2000, London (Nos. 1243-1247).

Christmas — A203

Designs: 30c, The Coronation of the Virgin, by Diego Velazquez, vert. 80c, The Immaculate Conception, by Velazquez, vert. 90c, Madonna and Child, by Titian. $1.20, Madonna and Child With St. John the Baptist and St. Catherine, by Titian.
$6, Madonna and Child With St. Catherine, by Titian.

2000, Dec. 4 **Litho.** ***Perf. 13½***
1249-1252 A203 Set of 4 2.40 2.40
Souvenir Sheet
1253 A203 $6 multi 4.50 4.50

New Year 2001 (Year of the Snake) — A204

No. 1254: a, Snake coiled on branch, facing right. b, Snake coiled on branch, facing left. c, Snake on ground, facing right. d, Snake on ground, facing left.
$5, Snake raising head.

2001, Jan. 4 ***Perf. 14***
1254 A204 $1.60 Sheet of 4, #a-d 4.75 4.75
Souvenir Sheet
1255 A204 $5 multi 3.75 3.75

195th Annual Leeward Islands Methodist Church District Conference — A205

Churches: a, Charlestown. b, Jessups. c, Clifton. d, Trinity. e, Combermere. f, Gingerland. g, New River.

2001, Jan. 23
1256 A205 50c Sheet of 7, #a-g 2.60 2.60

Garden of Eden — A206

No. 1257, $1.60: a, Red-crested woodpecker, unicorn. b, African elephant. c, Siberian tiger. d, Greater flamingo, Adam and Eve. e, Hippopotamus. f, Harlequin frog.
No. 1258, $1.60: a, Giraffe. b, Rainbow boa constrictor. c, Mountain cottontail rabbit. d, Bluebuck antelope. e, Red fox. f, Box turtle.
No. 1259, $5, Bald eagle. No. 1260, $5, Blue and gold macaw, vert. No. 1261, $5, Toucan, vert. No. 1262, $5, Koala, vert.

2001, Jan. 31 ***Perf. 14***
Sheets of 6, #a-f
1257-1258 A206 Set of 2 14.50 14.50
Souvenir Sheets
1259-1262 A206 Set of 4 15.00 15.00

Mushrooms A207

Designs: 20c, Clavulinopsis corniculata. 25c, Cantharellus cibarius. 50c, Chlorociboria aeruginascens. 80c, Auricularia auricula judae. $2, Peziza vesiculosa. $3, Mycena acicula.
No. 1269, $1: a, Entoloma incanum. b, Entoloma nitidum. c, Stropharia cyanea. d, Otidea onotica. e, Aleuria aurantia. f, Mitrula paludosa. g, Gyromitra esculenta. h, Helvella crispa. i, Morchella semilibera.
No. 1270, $5, Omphalotus olearius. No. 1271, $5, Russula sardonia.

2001, May 15 **Litho.** ***Perf. 14***
1263-1268 A207 Set of 6 5.25 5.25
1269 A207 $1 Sheet of 9, #a-i 7.00 7.00
Souvenir Sheets
1270-1271 A207 Set of 2 7.75 7.75

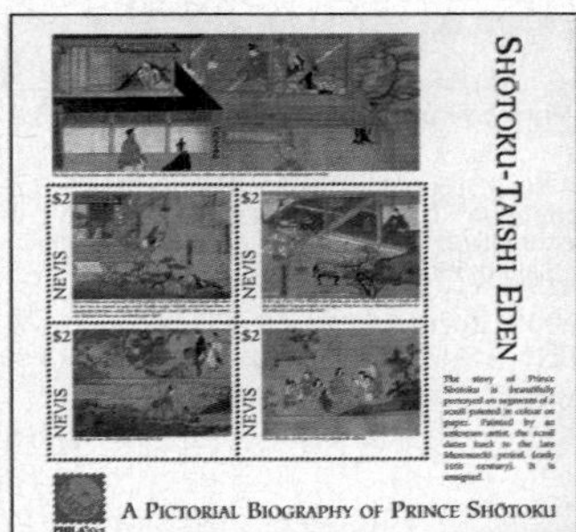
Tale of Prince Shotoku — A208

No. 1272, $2: a, Conception of Prince Shotoku. b, At six. c, At ten. d, At eleven.
No. 1273, $2: a, At sixteen (soldiers at gate). b, At sixteen (soldiers on horseback). c, At thirty-seven. d, At forty-four.

2001, May 31 ***Perf. 13¾***
Sheets of 4, #a-d
1272-1273 A208 Set of 2 12.00 12.00

Phila Nippon '01, Japan.

Queen Victoria (1819-1901) — A209

No. 1274: a, Prince Albert. b, Queen Victoria (flower in hair). c, Alexandrina Victoria. d, Duchess of Kent. e, Queen Victoria (as old woman). f, Prince of Wales.
$5, Queen Victoria (with tiara).

2001, July 9 **Litho.** ***Perf. 14***
1274 A209 $1.20 Sheet of 6, #a-f 5.50 5.50
Souvenir Sheet
1275 A209 $5 multi 3.75 3.75

Queen Elizabeth II, 75th Birthday — A210

No. 1276: a, Blue hat. b, Tiara. c, Yellow hat. d, Tan hat. e, Red hat. f, No hat.
$5, Blue hat, diff.

2001, July 9
1276 A210 90c Sheet of 6, #a-f 4.00 4.00
Souvenir Sheet
1277 A210 $5 multi 3.75 3.75

Flags of the Caribbean Community — A211

No. 1278: a, Antigua & Barbuda. b, Bahamas. c, Barbados. d, Belize. e, Dominica. f, Grenada. g, Guyana. h, Jamaica. i, Montserrat. j, St. Kitts & Nevis. k, St. Lucia. l, Surinam. m, St. Vincent & the Grenadines. n, Trinidad & Tobago.

2001, Dec. 3 **Litho.** ***Perf. 14***
1278 A211 90c Sheet of 14, #a-n 9.50 9.50

Christmas A212

Flowers: 30c, Christmas candle, vert. 90c, Poinsettia. $1.20, Snowbush. $3, Tiger claw, vert.

2001, Dec. 3
1279-1282 A212 Set of 4 4.00 4.00

2002 World Cup Soccer Championships, Japan and Korea — A213

No. 1283, $1.60: a, Moracana Stadium, Brazil, 1950. b, Ferenc Puskas, 1954. c, Luis Bellini, 1958. d, Mauro, 1962. e, Cap, 1966. f, Banner, 1970.
No. 1284, $1.60: a, Passarella, 1978. b, Dino Zoff, 1982. c, Azteca Stadium, Mexico, 1986. d, San Siro Stadium, Italy, 1990. e, Dennis Bergkamp, Netherlands, 1994. f, Stade de France, 1998.
No. 1285, $5, Head from Jules Rimet Cup, 1930. No. 1286, $5, Head and globe from World Cup trophy, 2002.

2001, Dec. 10 ***Perf. 13¾x14¼***

Sheets of 6, #a-f

1283-1284 A213 Set of 2 14.50 14.50

Souvenir Sheets

Perf. 14½x14¼

1285-1286 A213 Set of 2 7.50 7.50

Queen Mother Type of 1999 Redrawn

No. 1287: a, In bridal gown, 1923. b, With Princess Elizabeth, 1926. c, With King George VI in World War II. d, Wearing hat, 1983.
$6, Wearing tiara, 1957.

2001, Dec. 13 ***Perf. 14***

Yellow Orange Frames

1287 A177 $2 Sheet of 4, #a-d, + label 6.00 6.00

Souvenir Sheet

Perf. 13¾

1288 A177 $6 multi 4.50 4.50

Queen Mother's 101st birthday. No. 1288 contains one 38x51mm stamp with a bluer background than that found on No. 1174. Sheet margins of Nos. 1287-1288 lack embossing and gold arms and frames found on Nos. 1173-1174.

Reign of Queen Elizabeth II, 50th Anniv. — A214

No. 1289: a, Queen with Prince Philip. b, Prince Philip. c, Queen with yellow dress. d, Queen touching horse.
$5, Queen with Prince Philip, diff.

2002, Feb. 6 ***Perf. 14¼***

1289 A214 $2 Sheet of 4, #a-d 6.00 6.00

Souvenir Sheet

1290 A214 $5 multi 3.75 3.75

New Year 2002 (Year of the Horse) — A215

Horse paintings by Ren Renfa: a, Brown and white horse. b, Horse with ribs showing. c, Horse with tassel under neck. d, Gray horse.

2002, Mar. 4 ***Perf. 13¼***

1291 A215 $1.60 Sheet of 4, #a-d 4.75 4.75

Insects, Birds and Whales — A216

No. 1292, $1.20: a, Beechey's bee. b, Banded king shoemaker butterfly. c, Streaked sphinx caterpillar. d, Hercules beetle. e, South American palm beetle. f, Giant katydid.
No. 1293, $1.60: a, Roseate spoonbill. b, White-tailed tropicbird. c, Ruby-throated tropicbird. d, Black skimmer. e, Black-necked stilt. f, Mourning dove.
No. 1294, $1.60: a, Sperm whale. b, Sperm and killer whales. c, Minke whales. d, Fin whale. e, Blainville's beaked whale. f, Pygmy sperm whale.
No. 1295, $5, Click beetle. No. 1296, $5, Royal tern. No. 1297, $5, Humpback whale, vert.

2002, Aug. 15 **Litho.** ***Perf. 14***

Sheets of 6, #a-f

1292-1294 A216 Set of 3 21.00 21.00

Souvenir Sheets

1295-1297 A216 Set of 3 12.00 12.00

APS Stampshow (#1293).

United We Stand — A217

2002 Winter Olympics, Salt Lake City — A218

2002, Aug. 26

1298 A217 $2 multi 1.50 1.50

Printed in sheets of 4.

2002, Aug. 26

Designs: No. 1299, $2, Figure skating. No. 1300, $2, Freestyle skiing.

1299-1300 A218 Set of 2 3.00 3.00
a. Souvenir sheet, #1299-1300 3.00 3.00

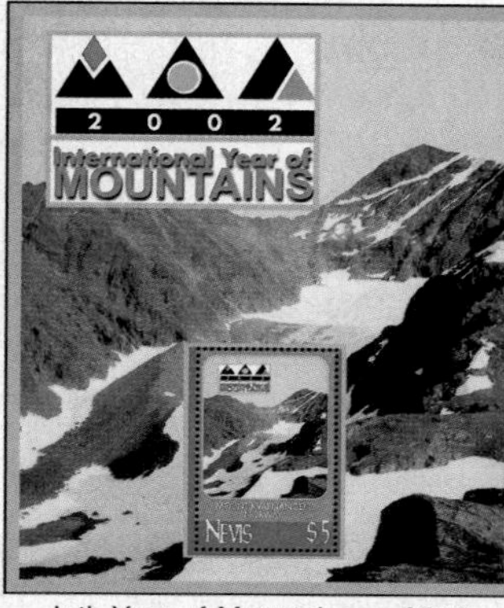

Intl. Year of Mountains — A219

No. 1301: a, Mt. Assiniboine, Canada. b, Mt. Atitlán, Guatemala. c, Mt. Adams, US. d, Matterhorn, Switzerland and Italy. e, Mt. Dhaulagiri, Nepal. f, Mt. Chamlang, Nepal.
$5, Mt. Kvaenangen, Norway.

2002, Aug. 26

1301 A219 $2 Sheet of 6, #a-f 9.00 9.00

Souvenir Sheet

1302 A219 $5 multi 3.75 3.75

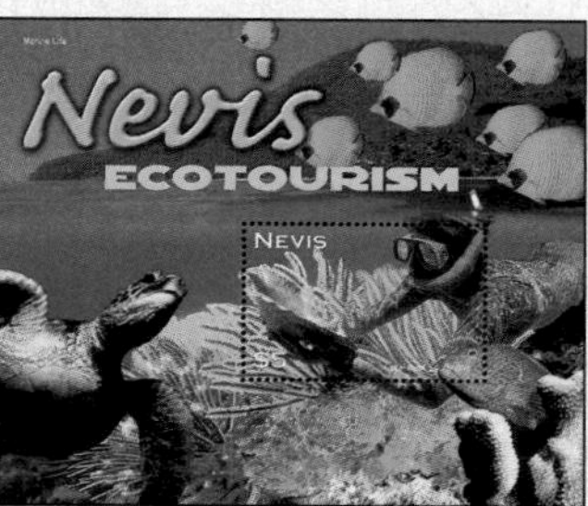

Ecotourism — A220

No. 1303: a, Horseback riding on beach. b, Windsurfing. c, Pinney's Beach. d, Cross-country hike. e, Robert T. Jones Golf Course. f, Scuba safaris.
$5, Coral reef snorkeling.

2002, Aug. 26

1303 A220 $1.60 Sheet of 6, #a-f 7.25 7.25

Souvenir Sheet

1304 A220 $5 multi 3.75 3.75

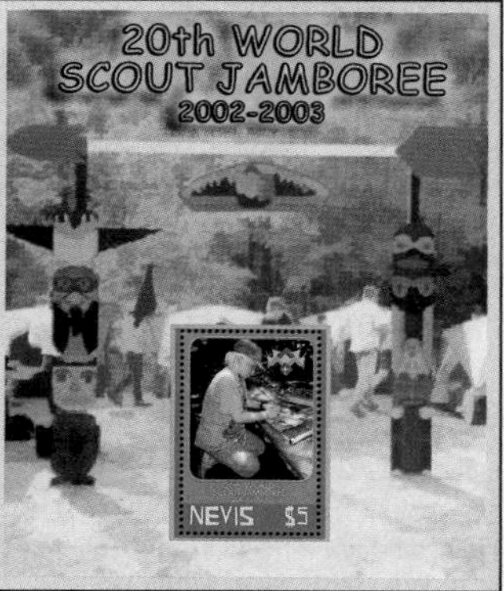

20th World Scout Jamboree, Thailand — A221

No. 1305: a, Scouts in two canoes. b, Scouts in one canoe. c, Scout on rope bridge. d, Scouts in inflatable rafts.
$5, Scout working on leatherwork project.

2002, Aug. 26

1305 A221 $2 Sheet of 4, #a-d 6.00 6.00

Souvenir Sheet

1306 A221 $5 multi 3.75 3.75

Souvenir Sheet

Artwork of Eva Wilkin (1898-1989) — A222

No. 1307: a, Unnamed painting of windmill. b, Nevis Peak (sepia toned). c, Fig Tree Church. d, Nevis Peak (full color).

2002, Sept. 23

1307 A222 $1.20 Sheet of 4, #a-d 3.75 3.75

Japanese Art — A223

No. 1308: a, Golden Pheasants and Loquat, by Shoei Kano. b, Flowers and Birds of the Four Seasons (snow-covered branches), by Koson Ikeda. c, Pheasants and Azaleas, by Kano. d, Flowers and Birds of the Four Seasons (tree and hill), by Ikeda.
No. 1309, $3: a, Flying bird from Birds and Flowers of Summer and Autumn, by Terutada Shikibu. b, Red flower, from Birds and Flowers of Summer and Autumn, by Shikibu
No. 1310, $3: a, White flower from Birds and Flowers of Summer and Autumn, by Shikibu. b, Perched bird from Birds and Flowers of Summer and Autumn, by Shikibu.
No. 1311, $3, horiz.: a, Bird facing right, from Two Birds on Willow and Peach Trees, by Buson Yosa. b, Bird facing left, from Two Birds on Willow and Peach Trees, by Yosa.
No. 1312, $5, Golden Pheasants Among Rhododendrons, by Baiitsu Yamamoto. No. 1313, $5, Muskrat and Camellias, by Neko Jako, horiz.

2002 ***Perf. 14x14¾***

1308 A223 $2 Sheet of 4, #a-d 6.00 6.00

Sheets of 2, #a-b

Perf. 13¾

1309-1311 A223 Set of 3 13.50 13.50

Souvenir Sheets

1312-1313 A223 Set of 2 7.50 7.50

No. 1308 contains four 29x80mm stamps.

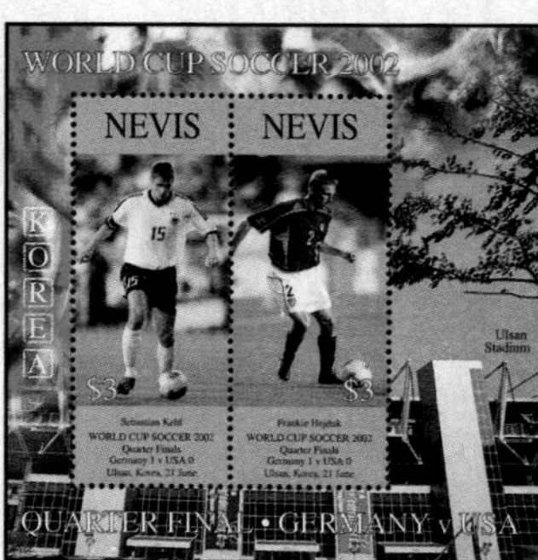

2002 World Cup Soccer Championship Quarterfinal Matches — A224

No. 1314, $1.20: a, Claudio Reyna and Torsten Frings. b, Michael Ballack and Eddie Pope. c, Sebastian Kehl and Brian McBride. d, Puyol and Eul Yong Lee. e, Jin Cheul Choi and Gaizka Mendieta. f, Juan Valeron and Jin Cheul Choi.

No. 1315, $1.60: a, Emile Heskey and Edmilson. b, Rivaldo and Sol Campbell. c, Ronaldinho and Nicky Butt. d, Ilhan Mansiz and Omar Daf. e, Hasan Sas and Papa Bouba Diop. f, Lamine Diatta and Hakan Sukur.
No. 1316, $3: a, Sebastian Kehl. b, Frankie Hejduk.
No. 1317, $3: a, Hong Myung Bo. b, Gaizka Mendieta.
No. 1318, $3: a, David Beckham and Roque Junior. b, Paul Scholes and Rivaldo.
No. 1319, $3: a, Alpay Ozalan. b, Khalilou Fadiga.

2002, Nov. 4 Litho. *Perf. 13¼*

Sheets of 6, #a-f

1314-1315 A224 Set of 2 12.50 12.50

Souvenir Sheets of 2, #a-b

1316-1319 A224 Set of 4 18.00 18.00

Christmas — A225

Religious art: 30c, Madonna and Child Enthroned with Saints, by Perugino. 80c, Adoration of the Magi, by Domenico Ghirlandaio. 90c, San Zaccaria Altarpiece, by Giovanni Bellini. $1.20, Presentation at the Temple, by Bellini. $5, Madonna and Child, by Simone Martini.
$6, Maestà, by Martini.

2002, Nov. 4 *Perf. 14¼*

1320-1324 A225 Set of 5 6.25 6.25

Souvenir Sheet

Perf. 14x14¼

1325 A225 $6 multi 4.50 4.50

New Year 2003 (Year of the Ram) — A226

2003, Feb. 10 *Perf. 14x13¾*

1326 A226 $2 multi 2.00 2.00

Printed in sheets of 4.

Pres. John F. Kennedy (1917-63) — A227

No. 1327, $2: a, Robert and Edward Kennedy. b, John F. Kennedy. c, Joseph P., Jr., and John F. Kennedy as children. d, Robert and John F. Kennedy.
No. 1328, $2: a, Taking oath of office, 1961. b, At cabinet oath ceremony, 1961. c, With Russian foreign minister Andrei Gromyko, 1963. d, Cuban Missile Crisis, 1962.

2003, Mar. 10 Litho. *Perf. 14*

Sheets of 4, #a-d

1327-1328 A227 Set of 2 12.00 12.00

Elvis Presley (1935-77) — A228

2003, Mar. 10 Litho. *Perf. 14*

1329 A228 $1.60 multi 1.25 1.25

Printed in sheets of 6.

First Non-Stop Solo Transatlantic Flight, 75th Anniv. — A229

No. 1330, $2: a, Ryan Airlines crew attaches wing to fuselage of the Spirit of St. Louis. b, Charles Lindbergh, Donald Hall and President of Ryan Flying Co. c, Lindbergh planning flight. d, Hall designing Spirit of St. Louis.
No. 1331, $2: a, Hall. b, Lindbergh. c, Automobile towing Spirit of St. Louis from Ryan factory. d, Spirit of St. Louis being towed at Curtiss Field.

2003, Mar. 10

Sheets of 4, #a-d

1330-1331 A229 Set of 2 12.00 12.00

Princess Diana (1961-97) — A230

No. 1332: a, Wearing blue dress. b, Wearing blue dress, pearl necklace. c, Wearing black gown. d, Wearing hat.
$5, Wearing black dress and necklace.

2003, Mar. 10 *Perf. 12¼*

1332 A230 $2 Sheet of 4, #a-d 6.00 6.00

Souvenir Sheet

1333 A230 $5 multi 3.75 3.75

Marlene Dietrich (1901-92) — A231

No. 1334: a, With cigarette, country name at right. b, With cigarette, country name at left. c, Close-up. d, Wearing hat and white jacket.
$5, Wearing dress.

2003, Mar. 10 *Perf. 14*

1334 A231 $1.60 Sheet, #a-b, 2 each #c-d 7.25 7.25

Souvenir Sheet

1335 A231 $5 multi 3.75 3.75

Coronation of Queen Elizabeth II, 50th Anniv. — A232

No. 1336: a, Queen as young woman. b, Queen as older woman. c, Queen wearing glasses.
$5, Queen wearing tiara.

2003, May 13

1336 A232 $3 Sheet of 3, #a-c 6.75 6.75

Souvenir Sheet

1337 A232 $5 multi 3.75 3.75

Prince William, 21st Birthday — A233

No. 1338: a, Wearing suit, showing teeth. b, Wearing suit. c, Wearing sweater.
$5, Wearing suit, diff.

2003, May 13

1338 A233 $3 Sheet of 3, #a-c 6.75 6.75

Souvenir Sheet

1339 A233 $5 multi 3.75 3.75

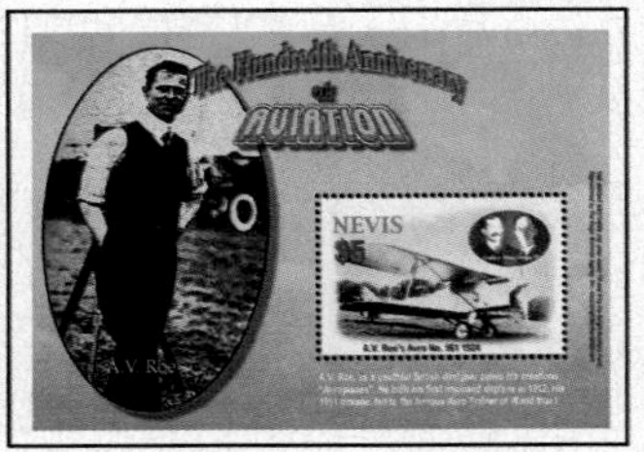

Powered Flight, Cent. — A234

No. 1340: a, A. V. Roe triplane. b, A. V. Roe Type D biplane. c, Avro Type F. d, Avro 504.
$5, Avro 561.

2003, May 13

1340 A234 $1.80 Sheet of 4, #a-d 5.75 5.75

Souvenir Sheet

1341 A234 $5 multi 4.00 4.00

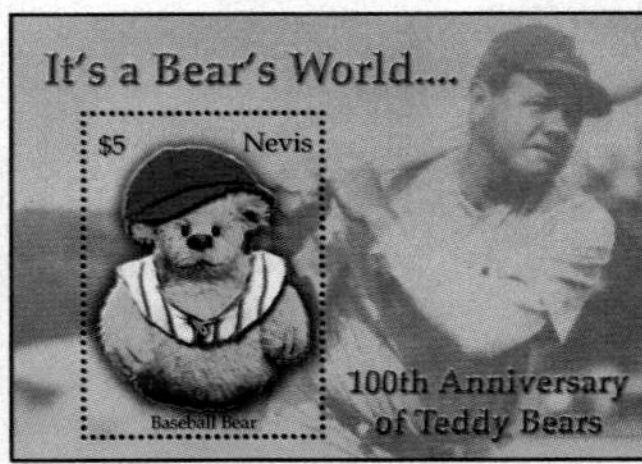

Teddy Bears, Cent. (in 2002) — A235

No. 1342: a, Abraham Lincoln bear. b, Napoleon bear. c, King Henry VIII bear. d, Charlie Chaplin bear.
$5, Baseball bear.

2003, May 13 *Perf. 13¼*

1342 A235 $2 Sheet of 4, #a-d 6.25 6.25

Souvenir Sheet

1343 A235 $5 multi 4.00 4.00

Tour de France Bicycle Race, Cent. — A236

No. 1344: a, Gustave Garrigou, 1911. b, Odile Defraye, 1912. c, Philippe Thys, 1913. d, Thys, 1914.
$5, François Faber.

2003, May 13

1344 A236 $2 Sheet of 4, #a-d 6.00 6.00

Souvenir Sheet

1345 A236 $5 multi 3.75 3.75

General Motors Automobiles — A237

No. 1346, $2 — Cadillacs: a, 1933 355-C V8 sedan. b, 1953 Eldorado. c, 1977 Coupe de Ville. d, 1980 Seville Elegante.
No. 1347, $2 — Corvettes: a, 1970. b, 1974. c, 1971. d, 1973.
No. 1348, $5, 1954 Cadillac. No. 1349, $5, 1997 C5 Corvette.

2003, May 13

Sheets of 4, #a-d

1346-1347 A237 Set of 2 12.00 12.00

Souvenir Sheets

1348-1349 A237 Set of 2 7.50 7.50

Orchids A238

Designs: 20c, Phalaenopsis joline, vert. $1.20, Vanda thonglor, vert. No. 1352, $2, Potinara. $3, Lycaste aquila.
No. 1354, $2: a, Brassolaelia cattleya. b, Cymbidium claricon. c, Calanthe vestita. d, Odontoglossum crispum.
$5, Odontioda brocade.

2003, Oct. 24 *Perf. 14*

1350-1353 A238 Set of 4 5.00 5.00
1354 A238 $2 Sheet of 4, #a-d 6.25 6.25

Souvenir Sheet

1355 A238 $5 multi 4.00 4.00

Butterflies A239

Designs: 30c, Perisama bonplandii. 90c, Danaus formosa. $1, Amauris vashti. $3, Lycorea ceres.

No. 1360: a, Kallima rumia. b, Nessaea ancaeus. c, Callicore cajetani. d, Hamadryas guatemalena.

$5, Euphaedra medon.

2003, Oct. 24

1356-1359 A239 Set of 4 4.25 4.25
1360 A239 $2 Sheet of 4, #a-d 6.25 6.25

Souvenir Sheet

1361 A239 $5 multi 4.00 4.00

Marine Life A240

Designs: 30c, Epinephelus striatus, vert. 80c, Acropora, vert. 90c, Myripristis hexagona. No. 1365, $5, Trichechus manatus.

No. 1366: a, Lioices latus. b, Chelmon rostratus. c, Epinephelus merra. d, Acanthurus coeruleus.

No. 1367, $5, Haemulon sciurus.

2003, Oct. 24

1362-1365 A240 Set of 4 5.50 5.50
1366 A240 $2 Sheet of 4, #a-d 6.25 6.25

Souvenir Sheet

1367 A240 $5 multi 4.00 4.00

Christmas A241

Designs: 30c, Madonna of the Magnificat, by Botticelli. 90c, Madonna with the Long Neck, by Il Parmigianino. $1.20, Virgin and Child With St. Anne, by Leonardo da Vinci. $5, Madonna and Child and Scenes from the Life of St. Anne, by Filippo Lippi.

$6, Conestabile Madonna, by Raphael.

2003, Nov. 5 ***Perf. 14¼***

1368-1371 A241 Set of 4 5.50 5.50

Souvenir Sheet

1372 A241 $6 multi 4.50 4.50

World AIDS Day A242

National flag, AIDS ribbon and: 90c, Stylized men. $1.20, Map.

2003, Dec. 1 ***Perf. 14***

1373-1374 A242 Set of 2 1.60 1.60

New Year 2004 (Year of the Monkey) A243

Designs: $1.60, Monkey King and Chinese text. $3, Monkey King.

2004, Feb. 16 Litho. ***Perf. 13¼***

1375 A243 $1.60 red & black 1.50 1.50

Souvenir Sheet

Perf. 13¼x13

1376 A243 $3 multi 2.50 2.50

No. 1375 printed in sheets of 4. No. 1376 contains one 30x40mm stamp.

Girl Guides in Nevis, 50th Anniv. — A244

Designs: 30c, Badges. 90c, Guide and guide leader, horiz. $1.20, Lady Olave Baden-Powell. $5, Guides wearing t-shirts.

2004, Feb. 22 ***Perf. 14***

1377-1380 A244 Set of 4 5.50 5.50

Paintings in the Hermitage, St. Petersburg, Russia — A245

Designs: 30c, Still Life with a Drapery, by Paul Cézanne. 90c, The Smoker, by Cézanne, vert. $2, Girl with a Fan, by Pierre Auguste Renoir, vert. No. 1384, $5, Grove, by André Derain, vert.

No. 1385, Lady in the Garden (Sainte Adresse), by Claude Monet.

2004, Mar. 4 ***Perf. 13¼***

1381-1384 A245 Set of 4 6.25 6.25

Imperf

Size: 94x74mm

1385 A245 $5 multi 3.75 3.75

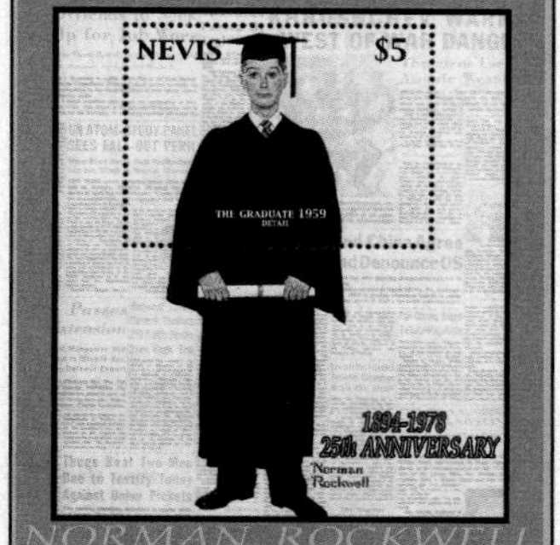

Paintings by Norman Rockwell (1894-1978) — A246

No. 1386, vert.: a, The Morning After. b, Solitaire. c, Easter Morning. d, Walking to Church.

$5, The Graduate.

2004, Mar. 4 ***Perf. 13¼***

1386 A246 $2 Sheet of 4, #a-d 6.00 6.00

Souvenir Sheet

1387 A246 $5 multi 3.75 3.75

Paintings by Pablo Picasso (1881-1973) — A247

No. 1388, $2: a, Woman with a Hat. b, Seated Woman. c, Portrait of Nusch Eluard. d, Woman in a Straw Hat.

No. 1389, $2: a, L'Arlésienne. b, The Mirror. c, Repose. d, Portrait of Paul Eluard.

No. 1390, Portrait of Nusch Eluard, diff. No. 1391, Reclining Woman with a Book, horiz.

2004, Mar. 4 ***Perf. 13¼***

Sheets of 4, #a-d

1388-1389 A247 Set of 2 12.00 12.00

Imperf

1390 A247 $5 shown 3.75 3.75

Size: 100x75mm

1391 A247 $5 multi 3.75 3.75

ASDA Mega-Event, New York (#1389).

A248

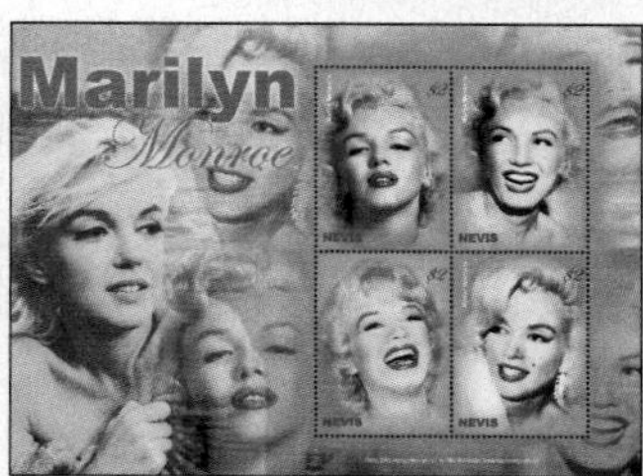

Marilyn Monroe — A249

No. 1393 — Placement of stamp on sheet: a, UL. b, UR. c, LL. d, LR.

2004, June 17 ***Perf. 13½x13¼***

1392 A248 60c multi .45 .45

Perf. 13¼

1393 A249 $2 Sheet of 4, #a-d 6.00 6.00

John Denver (1943-97), Musician — A250

Placement of stamp on sheet: a, Top left. b, Top right. c, Bottom left. d, Bottom right.

2004, June 17 ***Perf. 13¾x13½***

1394 A250 $1.20 Sheet of 4, #a-d 3.75 3.75

2004 Summer Olympics, Athens A251

Designs: 30c, Commemorative medal, 1968 Mexico City Olympics. 90c, Pentathlon. $1.80, Avery Brundage, Intl. Olympic Committee President. $3, Women's tennis, 1920 Antwerp Olympics, horiz.

2004, Sept. 7 Litho. ***Perf. 14¼***

1395-1398 A251 Set of 4 4.50 4.50

Intl. Year of Peace — A252

No. 1399: a, Country name at right, dove's feet not visible. b, Country name at left. c, Country name at right, dove's feet visible.

2004, Sept. 7

1399 A252 $3 Sheet of 3, #a-c 6.75 6.75

Souvenir Sheet

Deng Xiaoping (1904-97), Chinese Leader — A253

2004, Sept. 7 ***Perf. 14***

1400 A253 $5 multi 3.75 3.75

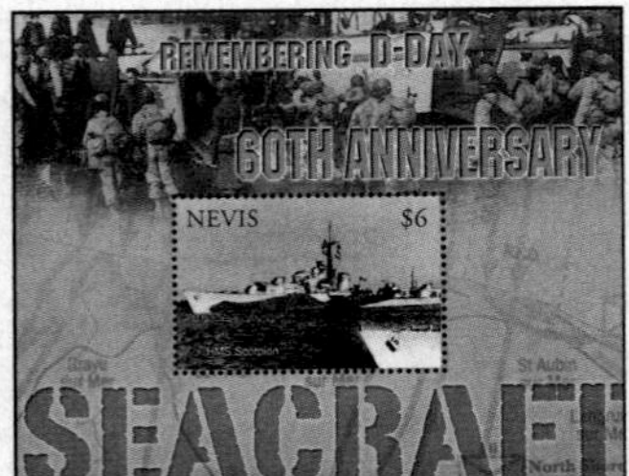

D-Day, 60th Anniv. — A254

No. 1401: a, HMCS Penetang. b, Landing Craft Infantry (Large). c, LCT (6). d, Landing Craft Tank (Rocket). e, Landing Barge Kitchen. f, Battleship Texas.
$6, HMS Scorpion.

2004, Sept. 7
1401 A254 $1.20 Sheet of 6, #a-f 5.50 5.50

Souvenir Sheet

1402 A254 $6 multi 4.50 4.50

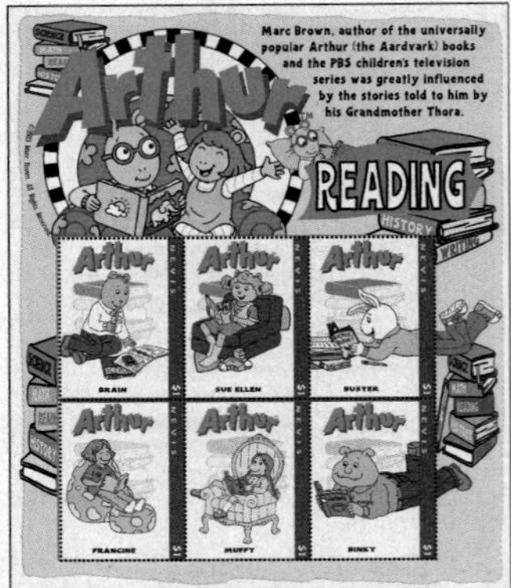

Arthur and Friends — A255

No. 1403 — Characters reading: a, Brain. b, Sue Ellen. c, Buster. d, Francine. e, Muffy. f, Binky.
No. 1404, $2 — Characters, with purple background: a, Arthur. b, D. W. c, Francine, looking right. d, Buster, diff.
No. 1405, $2 — Characters, with lilac background: a, Binky, diff. b, Sue Ellen, diff. c, Brain, diff. d, Francine, looking left.

2004, June 17 Litho. *Perf. 14¼*
1403 A255 $1 Sheet of 6, #a-f 4.50 4.50

Sheets of 4, #a-d

1404-1405 A255 Set of 2 12.00 12.00

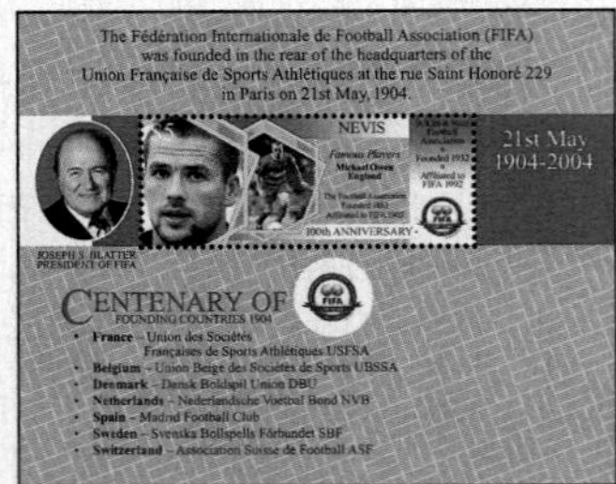

FIFA (Fédération Internationale de Football Association), Cent. — A256

Jason Berkley Joseph, Soccer Player — A257

No. 1406: a, Nery Pumpido. b, Gary Lineker. c, Thomas Hassler. d, Sol Campbell.
No. 1407, Michael Owen.

2004, Nov. 29 *Perf. 12¾x12½*
1406 A256 $2 Sheet of 4, #a-d 6.00 6.00

Souvenir Sheets

1407 A256 $5 multi 3.75 3.75
1408 A257 $5 multi 3.75 3.75

Marginal inscription on No. 1408, "100th Anniversary World Cup Soccer" is incorrect as the first World Cup was held in 1930.

Elvis Presley (1935-77) A258

No. 1409 — Wearing checked shirt: a, Blue background. b, Bright red violet background.
No. 1410 — Color of sweater: a, Red. b, Orange yellow. c, Blue. d, Blue green. e, Red violet. f, Bright green.

2004, Nov. 29 *Perf. 13½x13¼*
1409 A258 $1.20 Pair, #a-b 1.90 1.90
1410 A258 $1.20 Sheet of 6, #a-f 5.50 5.50

No. 1409 printed in sheets of 3 pairs.

Christmas A259

Paintings by Norman Rockwell: 25c, Santa's Good Boys. 30c, Ride 'em Cowboy. 90c, Christmas Sing Merrilie. No. 1414, $5, The Christmas Newsstand.
No. 1415, $5, Is He Coming.

2004, Dec. 1 *Perf. 12*
1411-1414 A259 Set of 4 5.00 5.00

Imperf

Size: 63x73mm

1415 A259 $5 multi 3.75 3.75

Locomotives, 200th Anniv. — A260

No. 1416: a, Steam Idyll, Indonesia. b, 2-8-2, Syria. c, Narrow gauge Mallet 0-4-4-0T, Portugal. d, Western Pacific Bo-Bo Road Switcher, US.
$5, LMS 5305, Great Britain.

2004, Dec. 13 *Perf. 13¼x13½*
1416 A260 $3 Sheet of 4, #a-d 9.00 9.00

Souvenir Sheet

1417 A260 $5 multi 3.75 3.75

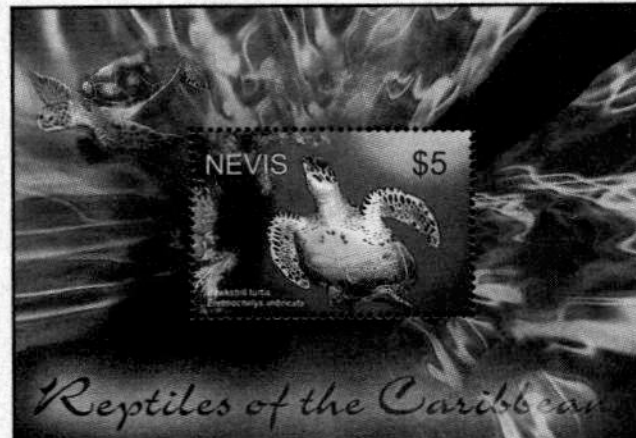

Reptiles and Amphibians — A261

No. 1418: a, Gekko gecko. b, Eyelash viper. c, Green iguana. d, Whistling frog.
$5, Hawksbill turtle.

2005, Jan. 10 *Perf. 14*
1418 A261 $1.20 Sheet of 4, #a-d 4.00 4.00

Souvenir Sheet

1419 A261 $5 multi 4.00 4.00

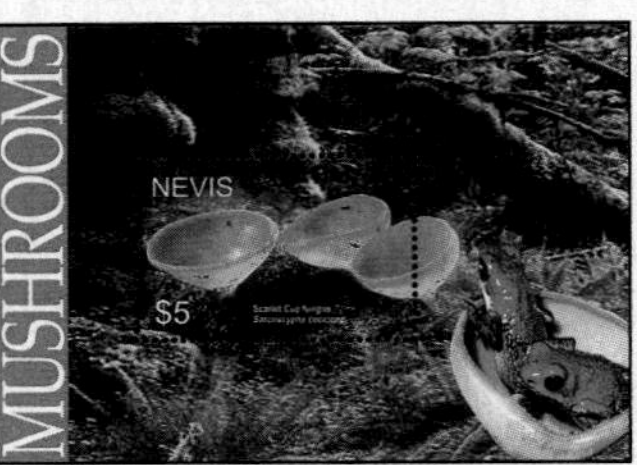

Mushrooms — A262

No. 1420: a, Xeromphalina campanella. b, Calvatia sculpta. c, Mitrula elegans. d, Aleuria aurantia.
$5, Scarlet cup.

2005, Jan. 10
1420 A262 $2 Sheet of 4, #a-d 6.25 6.25

Souvenir Sheet

1421 A262 $5 multi 4.00 4.00

Hummingbirds — A263

No. 1422: a, Rufous hummingbird. b, Green-crowned brilliant. c, Ruby-throated hummingbird. d, Purple-throated Carib.
$5, Magnificent hummingbird.

2005, Jan. 10 Litho. *Perf. 14*
1422 A263 $2 Sheet of 4, #a-d 6.25 6.25

Souvenir Sheet

1423 A263 $5 multi 4.00 4.00

Sharks — A264

No. 1424: a, Zebra shark. b, Caribbean reef shark. c, Blue shark. d, Bronze whaler.
$5, Blacktip reef shark.

2005, Jan. 10
1424 A264 $2 Sheet of 4, #a-d 6.25 6.25

Souvenir Sheet

1425 A264 $5 multi 4.00 4.00

Artist's Depictions of Hawksbill Turtles — A265

Artist: 30c, Leon Silcott. 90c, Kris Liburd. $1.20, Alice Webber. $5, Jeuaunito Huggins.

2005, Jan. 10
1426-1429 A265 Set of 4 6.00 6.00

Souvenir Sheet

New Year 2005 (Year of the Rooster) — A266

No. 1430: a, Rooster, blue green background. b, Rooster silhouette, light green background. c, Rooster silhouette, blue background. d, Rooster, red violet background.

2005, Jan. 17 *Perf. 12*
1430 A266 75c Sheet of 4, #a-d 2.50 2.50

Friedrich von Schiller (1759-1805), Writer — A267

No. 1431: a, Schiller, country name in pink. b, Schiller, country name in blue. c, Schiller's birthplace, Marbach, Germany.
$5, Statue of Schiller, Chicago.

2005, May 16 ***Perf. 12¾***

1431 A267 $3 Sheet of 3, #a-c 6.75 6.75

Souvenir Sheet

1432 A267 $5 multi 3.75 3.75

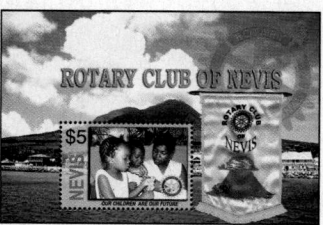

Rotary International, Cent. — A268

No. 1433, vert.: a, Barefoot child. b, Vaccination of child. c, Child with crutches and braces.

$5, Woman and children.

2005, May 16

1433 A268 $3 Sheet of 3, #a-c 6.75 6.75

Souvenir Sheet

1434 A268 $5 multi 3.75 3.75

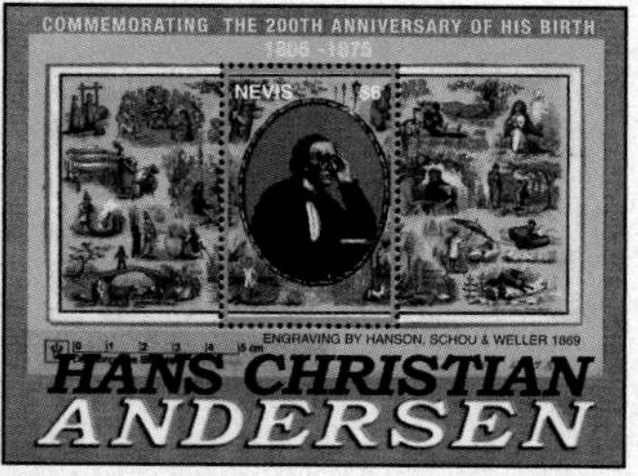

Hans Christian Andersen (1805-75), Author — A269

No. 1435: a, The Little Mermaid. b, Thumbelina. c, The Snow Queen. d, The Emperor's New Clothes.

$6, Andersen.

2005, May 16

1435 A269 $2 Sheet of 4, #a-d 6.00 6.00

Souvenir Sheet

1436 A269 $6 multi 4.50 4.50

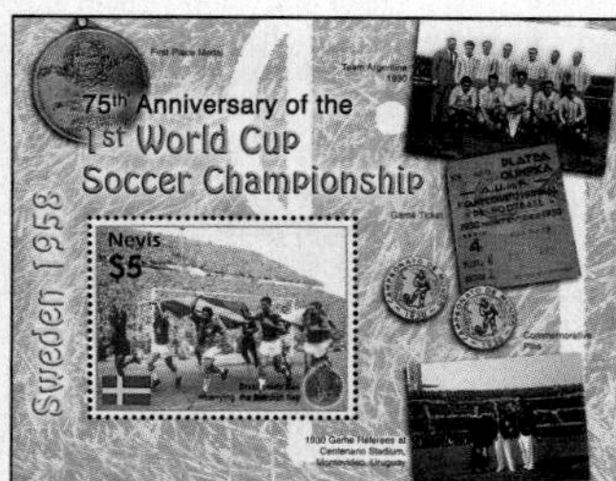

World Cup Soccer Championships, 75th Anniv. — A270

No. 1437: a, Brazil, 1958 champions. b, Scene from 1958 Brazil-Sweden final. c, Rasunda Stadium, Stockholm. d, Pele.

$5, 1958 Brazil team celebrating victory.

2005, May 16 **Litho.**

1437 A270 $2 Sheet of 4, #a-d 6.00 6.00

Souvenir Sheet

1438 A270 $5 multi 3.75 3.75

End of World War II, 60th Anniv. — A271

No. 1439, $2: a, Gen. Charles de Gaulle. b, Gen. George S. Patton. c, Field Marshal Bernard Montgomery. d, Liberation of concentration camps. e, Political cartoon about end of war.

No. 1440, $2, horiz.: a, Flight crew of the Enola Gay. b, Atomic bomb mushroom cloud. c, Souvenir of Japanese surrender ceremony. d, Japanese delegation on USS Missouri. e, Gen. Douglas MacArthur speaking at surrender ceremony.

2005, May 16 ***Perf. 12¾***

Sheets of 5, #a-e

1439-1440 A271 Set of 2 15.00 15.00

Battle of Trafalgar, Bicent. — A272

Various ships and: 30c, Admiral William Cornwallis. 90c, Capt. Maurice Suckling. $1.20, Fleet Admiral Earl Howe. $3, Sir John Jervis.

$5, Earl Howe on the quarterdeck of the Queen Charlotte.

2005, May 16 ***Perf. 12¾***

1441-1444 A272 Set of 4 4.25 4.25

Souvenir Sheet

Perf. 12

1445 A272 $5 multi 3.75 3.75

A273

Prehistoric Animals — A274

Designs: 30c, Tyrannosaurus rex. No. 1447, $5, Hadrosaur.

No. 1448, $1.20: a, Apatosaurus. b, Camarasaurus. c, Iguanodon. d, Edmontosaurus. e, Centrosaurus. f, Euoplocephalus.

No. 1449, $1.20: a, Ouranosaurus. b, Parasaurolophus. c, Psittacosaurus. d, Stegosaurus. e, Scelidosaurus. f, Hypsilophodon.

No. 1450, $1.20, vert.: a, Deinotherium. b, Platybelodon. c, Palaeoloxodon. d, Arsinotherium. e, Procoptodon. f, Macrauchenia.

No. 1451, $5, Brontotherium. No. 1452, $5, Daspletosaurus. No. 1453, $5, Pliosaur.

2005, June 7 ***Perf. 12¾***

1446-1447 A273 Set of 2 4.00 4.00

Sheets of 6, #a-f

1448-1450 A274 Set of 3 16.50 16.50

Souvenir Sheets

1451-1453 A274 Set of 3 11.50 11.50

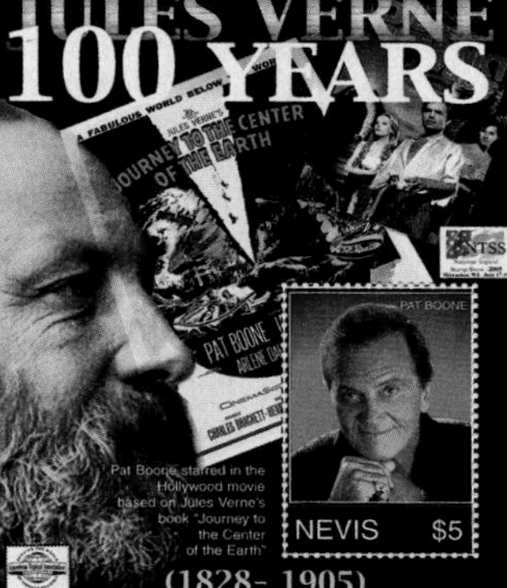

Jules Verne (1828-1905), Writer — A275

No. 1454 — Story characters: a, Captain Nemo, *20,000 Leagues Under the Sea.* b, Michael Strogoff, *Michael Strogoff.* c, Phileas Fogg, *Around the World in 80 Days.* d, Captain Cyrus Smith, *Mysterious Island.*

$5, Pat Boone, actor in movie, *Journey to the Center of the Earth.*

2005, June 17

1454 A275 $2 Sheet of 4, #a-d 6.00 6.00

Souvenir Sheet

1455 A275 $5 multi 3.75 3.75

2005 National Topical Stamp Show, Milwaukee (#1455).

Vatican City No. 66 — A276

Pope John Paul II (1920-2005) A277

2005, July 12 ***Perf. 13x13¼***

1456 A276 90c multi .70 .70

Perf. 13½x13¼

1457 A277 $4 multi 3.00 3.00

National Basketball Association Players — A278

Designs: No. 1458, $1, Shareef-Abdur Rahim (shown), Portland Trail Blazers. No. 1459, $1, Shaun Livingston, Los Angeles Clippers. No. 1460, $1, Vince Carter, New Jersey Nets. No. 1461, $1, Rasheed Wallace, Detroit Pistons.

No. 1462: a, Theo Ratliff, Portland Trail Blazers. b, Portland Trail Blazers emblem.

2005, July 26 ***Perf. 14***

1458-1461 A278 Set of 4 3.00 3.00

1462 A278 $1 Sheet, 10 #1462a, 2 #1462b 9.00 9.00

Souvenir Sheet

Sun Yat-sen (1866-1925), Chinese Leader — A279

No. 1463: a, Wearing blue suit, harbor in background. b, Wearing suit and tie. c, Wearing blue suit, statue in background. d, Wearing brown red suit.

2005, Aug. 19 **Litho.** ***Perf. 14***

1463 A279 $2 Sheet of 4, #a-d 6.00 6.00

Taipei 2005 Intl. Stamp Exhibition.

Christmas — A280

Designs: 25c, Madonna and the Angels, by Fra Angelico. 30c, Madonna and the Child, by Fra Filippo Lippi. 90c, Madonna and Child, by Giotto. $4, Madonna of the Chair, by Raphael.

$5, Adoration of the Magi, by Giovanni Batista Tiepolo, horiz.

2005, Dec. 1 ***Perf. 13½***

1464-1467 A280 Set of 4 4.25 4.25

Souvenir Sheet

1468 A280 $5 multi 3.75 3.75

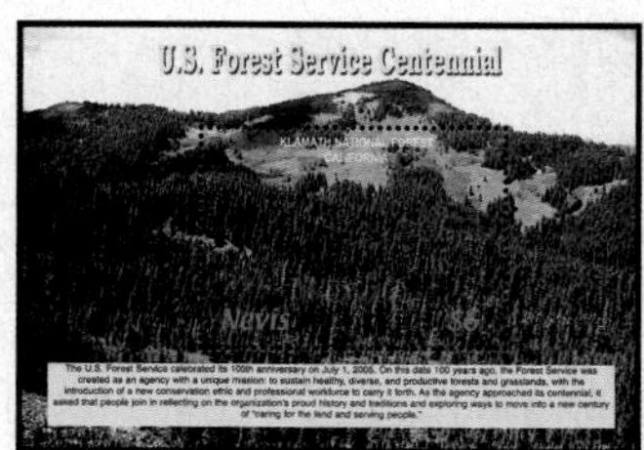

U.S. Forest Service, Cent. (in 2005) — A281

No. 1469, vert.: a, Eldorado National Forest, California. b, Pisgah National Forest, North Carolina. c, Chattahoochee-Oconee National Forests, Georgia. d, Nantahala National Forest, North Carolina. e, Bridger-Teton National Forest, Wyoming. f, Mount Hood National Forest, Oregon.

No. 1470, $6, Klamath National Forest, California. No. 1471, $6, The Source Rain Forest Walk, Nevis, vert.

2006, Jan. 3

1469 A281 $1.60 Sheet of 6, #a-f 7.25 7.25

Souvenir Sheets

1470-1471 A281 Set of 2 9.00 9.00

A Dog, by Ren Xun — A282

2006, Jan. 3
1472 A282 75c multi .70 .70

New Year 2006 (Year of the Dog). Printed in sheets of 4.

Queen Elizabeth II, 80th Anniv. — A283

No. 1473 — Queen wearing: a, Black hat with feather. b, No hat. c, Tiara. d, White hat.
$5, As young woman.

2006, Mar. 20 Litho. ***Perf. 13¼***
1473 A283 $2 Sheet of 4, #a-d 6.00 6.00

Souvenir Sheet

1474 A283 $5 multi 3.75 3.75

2006 Winter Olympics, Turin — A284

Designs: 25c, U.S. #1796. 30c, Italy #705. 90c, Italy #707. $1.20, Emblem of 1980 Lake Placid Winter Olympics, vert. $4, Italy #708. $5, Emblem of 1956 Cortina d'Ampezzo Winter Olympics.

Perf. 14¼ (25c, $1.20), 13¼

2006, Apr. 24
1475-1480 A284 Set of 6 8.75 8.75

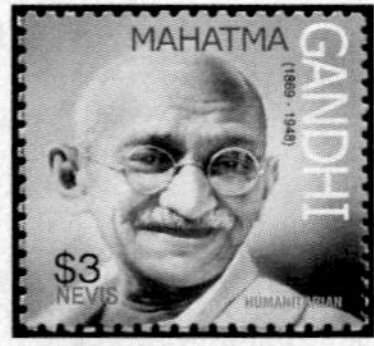

Mohandas K. Gandhi (1869-1948), Humanitarian A285

2006, May 27 ***Perf. 12x11½***
1481 A285 $3 multi 2.25 2.25

Rembrandt (1606-69), Painter — A286

No. 1482 — Various men from The Anatomy Lesson of Dr. Tulp.
$6, Bald-headed Old Man.

2006, June 23 ***Perf. 13¼***
1482 A286 $2 Sheet of 4, a-d 6.00 6.00

Imperf

Size: 70x100mm

1483 A286 $6 multi 4.50 4.50

Miniature Sheets

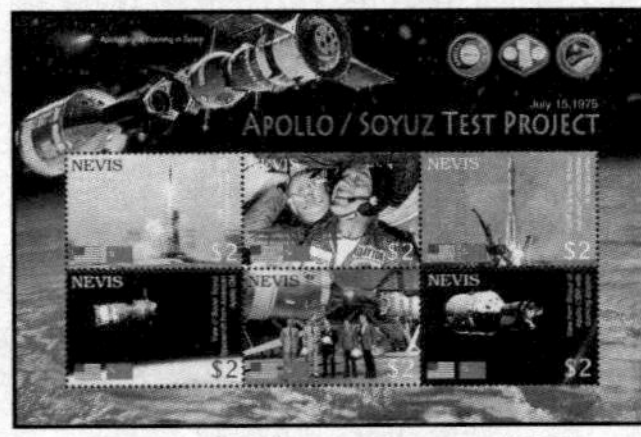

Space Achievements — A287

No. 1484 — Apollo-Soyuz: a, Liftoff of Saturn IB rocket . b, Astronaut Donald K. Slayton, Cosmonaut Aleksei A. Leonov. c, Liftoff of Soyuz 19. d, Soyuz in space. e, American and Soviet crews, model of docked spacecraft. f, Apollo in space.
No. 1485 — Viking I: a, Liftoff of Titan Centaur rocket. b, Viking I in flight. c, Model of Viking I on Mars. d, Mars.

2006, Sept. 11 ***Perf. 13¼***
1484 A287 $2 Sheet of 6, #a-f 9.00 9.00
1485 A287 $3 Sheet of 4, #a-d 9.00 9.00

Christmas A288

Designs: 25c, Charlestown Christmas tree. 30c, Snowman decoration. 90c, Reindeer decorations. $4, Christmas tree and gifts, vert.
$6, Santa Claus and children.

2006, Dec. 8
1486-1489 A288 Set of 4 4.25 4.25

Souvenir Sheet

1490 A288 $6 multi 4.50 4.50

Scouting, Cent. A289

Designs: $3, Flags, Map of Great Britain and Ireland. $5, Flags, bird, map, horiz.

2007, Jan. 29 Litho. ***Perf. 13¼***
1491 A289 $3 multi 2.25 2.25

Souvenir Sheet

1492 A289 $5 multi 3.75 3.75

No. 1491 printed in sheets of 4.

Miniature Sheet

Marilyn Monroe (1926-62), Actress — A290

No. 1493 — Monroe: a, With head tilted. b, Wearing necklace. c, With lips closed. d, Wearing sash.

2007, Jan. 29
1493 A290 $2 Sheet of 4, #a-d 6.00 6.00

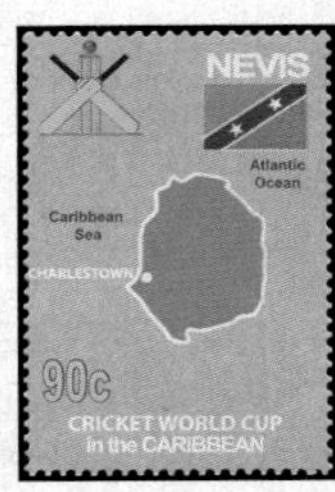

Cricket World Cup — A291

Designs: 90c, Cricket World Cup emblem, flag of St. Kitts and Nevis, map of Nevis. $2, Emblem and Runako Morton.
$6, Emblem.

2007, May 1 ***Perf. 14***
1494-1495 A291 Set of 2 2.25 2.25

Souvenir Sheet

1496 A291 $6 multi 4.50 4.50

Shells — A292

Designs: 10c, Flame helmet. 25c, Rooster tail conch. 30c, Beaded periwinkle. 60c, Emperor helmet. 80c, Scotch bonnet. 90c Milk conch. $1, Beaded periwinkle, diff. $1.20, Alphabet cone. $1.80, Measled cowrie. $3, King helmet. $5, Atlantic hairy triton. $10, White-lined mitre. $20, Reticulated cowrie.

2007, July 5 ***Perf. 12½x13¼***

1497	A292	10c	multi	.20	.20
1498	A292	25c	multi	.20	.20
1499	A292	30c	multi	.30	.30
1500	A292	60c	multi	.50	.50
1501	A292	80c	multi	.65	.65
1502	A292	90c	multi	.75	.75
1503	A292	$1	multi	.80	.80
1504	A292	$1.20	multi	1.00	1.00
1505	A292	$1.80	multi	1.50	1.50
1506	A292	$3	multi	2.40	2.40
1507	A292	$5	multi	4.00	4.00
1508	A292	$10	multi	7.75	7.75
1509	A292	$20	multi	16.00	16.00
	Nos. 1497-1509 (13)			36.05	36.05

Worldwide Fund for Nature (WWF) — A293

No. 1510 — Rainbow parrotfish: a, Facing left, white coral above fish. b, Two parrotfish. c, Facing left, ocean floor below fish. d, Facing right.

2007, July 23 ***Perf. 13½***
1510 Strip of 4 4.00 4.00
a.-d. A293 $1.20 Any single .95 .95
e. Miniature sheet, 2 each #1510a-1510d 7.75 7.75

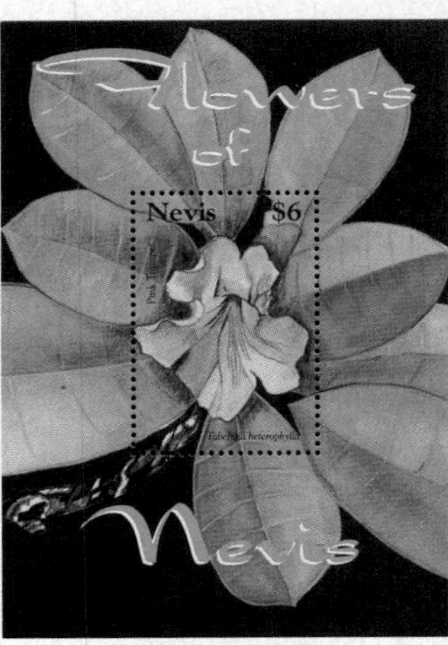

Flowers — A294

No. 1511: a, Wild cilliment. b, Jumbie beads. c, Wild sage. d, Blood flower.
$6, Pink trumpet.

2007, July 23 ***Perf. 13¼***
1511 A294 $2 Sheet of 4, #a-d 6.25 6.25

Souvenir Sheet

1512 A294 $6 multi 4.75 4.75

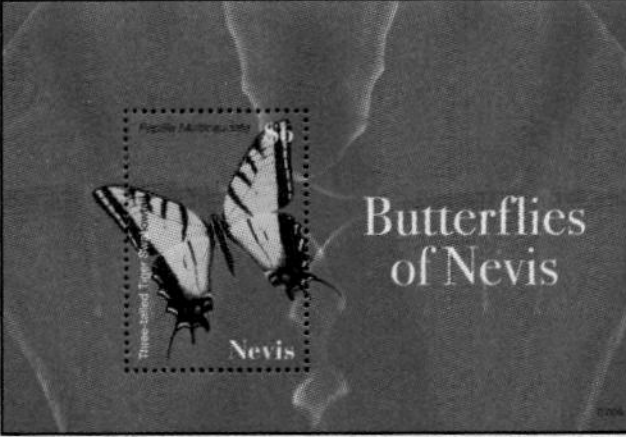

Butterflies — A295

No. 1513: a, Zetides swallowtail. b, Hahnel's Amazon swallowtail. c, Haitian mimic. d, Marbled white.
$6, Three-tailed tiger swallowtail.

2007, July 23
1513 A295 $2 Sheet of 4, #a-d 6.25 6.25

Souvenir Sheet

1514 A295 $6 multi 4.75 4.75

Miniature Sheet

Elvis Presley (1935-77) — A296

No. 1515 — Various photographs of Presley with: a, Denomination in white, country name in violet, laces showing on shirt. b, Denomination in blue. c, Denomination in bister. d, Denomination and country name in pink. e, Denomination in white, country name in pink. f, Denomination in white, country name in violet, laces not showing on shirt.

2007, Aug. 13
1515 A296 $1.20 Sheet of 6, #a-f 5.50 5.50

Princess Diana (1961-97) — A297

No. 1516: a, With head on hands. b, Wearing black dress. c, Wearing pink jacket. d, Wearing white dress.
$6, Wearing hat.

2007, Aug. 13
1516 A297 $2 Sheet of 4, #a-d 6.00 6.00

Souvenir Sheet

1517 A297 $6 multi 4.50 4.50

Miniature Sheets

Concorde — A298

No. 1518, $1.20 — Concorde with portions of globe in background: a, Western United States. b, Central United States. c, Atlantic Ocean and Eastern Canada. d, Central Pacific Ocean. e, Central America. f, Northeastern South America.
No. 1519, $1.20 — Concorde with: a, Green frame, white denomination. b, Red frame, blue denomination. c, Green frame, yellow denomination. d, Red frame, yellow denomination. e, Green frame, blue denomination. f, Red frame, white denomination.

2007, Aug. 13 Litho. *Perf. 13¼*
Sheets of 6, #a-f
1518-1519 A298 Set of 2 11.00 11.00

Pope Benedict XVI — A299

2007, Oct. 24
1520 A299 $1 multi .75 .75

Printed in sheets of 8.

Miniature Sheet

Wedding of Queen Elizabeth II and Prince Philip, 60th Anniv. — A300

No. 1521 — Couple: a, Queen wearing tiara. b, Waving. c, Wearing feathered hats. d, In gilded coach, Queen in blue, waving. e, In coach, Queen with red hat, waving. f, On balcony, Queen waving.

2007, Oct. 24
1521 A300 $1.20 Sheet of 6, #a-f 5.50 5.50

Miniature Sheet

Inauguration of Pres. John F. Kennedy, 46th Anniv. — A301

No. 1522: a, Jacqueline Kennedy. b, John F. Kennedy, hands at side. c, John F. Kennedy, clapping. d, Vice president Lyndon B. Johnson.

2007, Nov. 28
1522 A301 $3 Sheet of 4, #a-d 9.00 9.00

First Helicopter Flight, Cent. — A302

No. 1523, horiz.: a, Westland Sea King. b, Schweizer N330TT. c, Sikorsky R-4/R-5. d, PZL Swidnik.
$6, MIL V-12.

2007, Nov. 28
1523 A302 $3 Sheet of 4, #a-d 9.00 9.00

Souvenir Sheet

1524 A302 $6 multi 4.50 4.50

Paintings by Qi Baishi (1864-1957) — A303

No. 1525: a, Begonias and Rock. b, Mother and Child. c, Fish and Bait. d, Solitary Hero.
$6, Chrysanthemums and Insects.

2007, Nov. 28 *Perf. 12½*
1525 A303 $3 Sheet of 4, #a-d 9.00 9.00

Souvenir Sheet
Perf. 13¼

1526 A303 $6 multi 4.50 4.50

No. 1525 contains four 32x80mm stamps.

Christmas A304

Paintings: 25c, The Rest on the Flight Into Egypt, by Federico Barocci. 30c, The Annunciation, by Barocci. 90c, The Annunciation, by Cavalier d'Arpino. $4, The Rest on the Flight Into Egypt, by Francesco Mancini.
$5, The Virgin and Child Between Saints Peter and Paul and the Twelve Magistrates of the Rota, by Antoniazzo Romano.

2007, Dec. 3 *Perf. 11¼x11½*
1527-1530 A304 Set of 4 4.25 4.25

Souvenir Sheet
Perf. 13½

1531 A304 $5 multi 3.75 3.75

Miniature Sheet

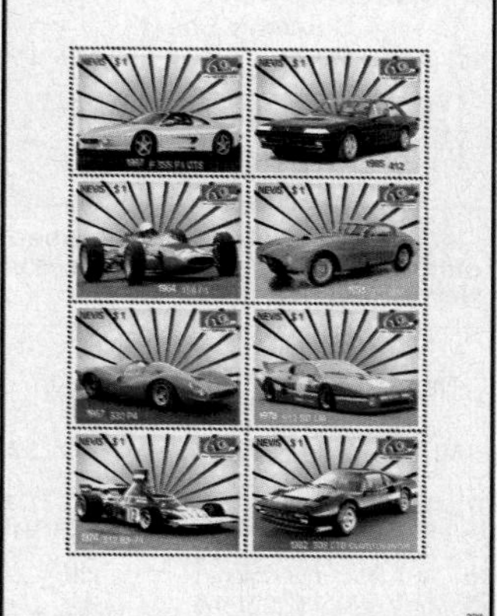
Ferrari Automobiles, 60th Anniv. — A305

No. 1532: a, 1997 F 355 F1 GTS. b, 1985 412. c, 1964 158 F1. d, 1953 375 MM. e, 1967 330 P4. f, 1978 512 BB LM. g, 1974 312 B3-74. h, 1982 308 GTB Quattrovalvole.

2007, Dec. 10 *Perf. 13¼*
1532 A305 $1 Sheet of 8, #a-h 6.00 6.00

Miniature Sheet

2008 Summer Olympics, Beijing — A306

No. 1533: a, Cycling. b, Kayaking. c, Sailing. d, Equestrian.

2008, Mar. 8 Litho. *Perf. 12¾*
1533 A306 $2 Sheet of 4, #a-d 6.00 6.00

Israel 2008 Intl. Philatelic Exhibition — A307

No. 1534 — Sites in Israel: a, Mt. Masada. b, Red Sea and mountains. c, Dead Sea. d, Sea of Galilee.
$5, Mt. Hermon.

2008, May 21 Litho. *Perf. 11½x11¼*
1534 A307 $1.50 Sheet of 4, #a-d 4.50 4.50

Souvenir Sheet

1535 A307 $5 multi 3.75 3.75

32nd America's Cup Yacht Races — A308

No. 1536 — Various yachts: a, $1.20. b, $1.80. c, $3. d, $5.

2007, Dec. 31 Litho. *Perf. 13½*
1536 A308 Block of 4, #a-d 8.25 8.25

No. 1536 was not made available until late 2008.

Miniature Sheets

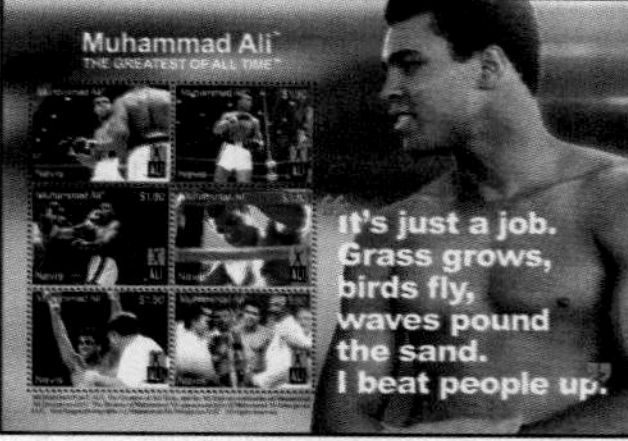

A309

Muhammad Ali, Boxer — A310

No. 1537 — Ali: a, In ring with fists at side. b, In ring, opponent at right. c, In ring, opponent punching. d, With arm on ropes. e, With arms raised. f, Receiving trophy.
No. 1538 — Ali: a, Facing left, face in background. b, With microphones, at bottom. c, Facing left, with microphone at left. d, With large microphone at LL.

2008, Sept. 3 Litho. *Perf. 11½x12*
1537 A309 $1.80 Sheet of 6, #a-f 8.25 8.25

Perf. 13¼

1538 A310 $2 Sheet of 4, #a-d 6.25 6.25

Miniature Sheet

Elvis Presley (1935-77) — A311

No. 1539 — Presley with guitar: a, Microphone at right, both hands on guitar. b, Microphone at left, hand on neck of guitar. c, With audience at LL. d, Microphone at left, no hands shown. e, Wearing blue shirt. f, Microphone at right, with hands off guitar.

2008, Sept. 3 ***Perf. 13¼***
1539 A311 $1.80 Sheet of 6, #a-f 8.25 8.25

Miniature Sheet

Visit to New York of Pope Benedict XVI — A312

No. 1540 — Pope Benedict XVI and background with: a, Gray spot to left of "N" in "Nevis." b, Left half of United Nations emblem. c, Right half of United Nations Emblem. d, Gray spot between "E" and "V" in "Nevis."

2008, Sept. 17
1540 A312 $2 Sheet of 4, #a-d 6.25 6.25

Geothermal Well — A313

2008, Sept. 19 ***Perf. 11½***
1541 A313 $5 multi 4.00 4.00

Independence, 25th anniv.

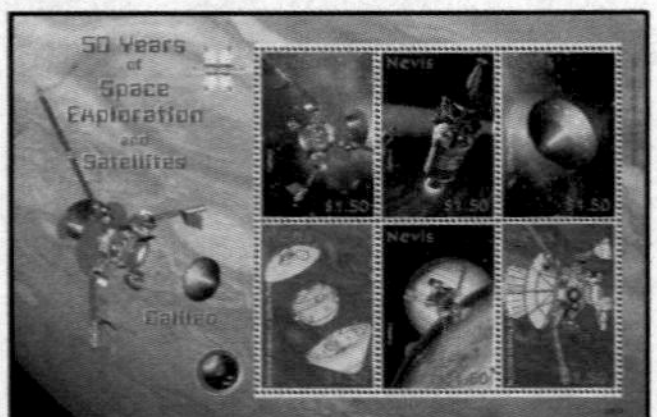

A314

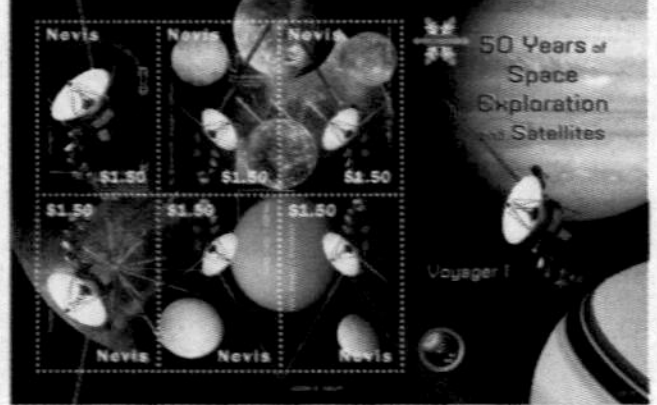

Space Exploration, 50th Anniv. — A315

No. 1542: a, Galileo spacecraft with arms extended, stars in background. b, Galileo on booster rocket. c, Galileo probe. d, Technical drawing of Galileo probe. e, Galileo, planet and moon. f, Technical drawing of Galileo.

No. 1543: a, Voyager 1 and ring diagram. b, Io, Ganymede, Voyager 1 and Callisto. c, Ganymede, Europa, Callisto and Voyager 1. d, Voyager 1 and radiating line diagram. e, Voyager 1, Titan and Dione. f, Titan, Voyager 1 and Enceladus.

No. 1544: a, Technical drawing of Apollo 11 command module. b, Saturn V rocket on launch pad. c, Edwin E. Aldrin on Moon. d, Technical drawing of Apollo 11 lunar module.

No. 1545: a, Van Allen radiation belt. b, Technical drawing of Explorer 1. c, James Van Allen. d, Explorer 1 above Earth.

2008, Dec. 3 ***Perf. 13¼***
1542 A314 $1.50 Sheet of 6, #a-f 7.00 7.00
1543 A315 $1.50 Sheet of 6, #a-f 7.00 7.00
1544 A314 $2 Sheet of 4, #a-d 6.25 6.25
1545 A315 $2 Sheet of 4, #a-d 6.25 6.25

Christmas A316

Traditional holiday foods: 25c, Roast pig. 30c, Fruit cake. 80c, Pumpkin pie. 90c, Sorrel drink. $2, Fruit cake, diff.
$6, Baked ham and turkey, vert.

2008, Dec. 5 ***Perf. 11½***
1546-1550 A316 Set of 5 3.25 3.25

Souvenir Sheet

1551 A316 $6 multi 4.75 4.75

OFFICIAL STAMPS

Catalogue values for unused stamps in this section are for Never Hinged items.

Nos. 103-112 Ovptd. "OFFICIAL"

Perf. 14½x14

1980, July 30 Litho. Wmk. 373
O1 A61 15c multicolored .20 .20
O2 A61 25c multicolored .20 .20
O3 A61 30c multicolored .20 .20
O4 A61 40c multicolored .20 .20
O5 A61 45c multicolored .25 .25
O6 A61 50c multicolored .25 .25
O7 A61 55c multicolored .25 .25
O8 A61 $1 multicolored .40 .40
O9 A61 $5 multicolored 1.90 1.90
O10 A61 $10 multicolored 3.75 3.75
Nos. O1-O10 (10) 7.60 7.60

Inverted or double overprints exist on some denominations.

Nos. 123-134 Ovptd. "OFFICIAL"

1981, Mar. ***Perf. 14***
O11 A9 15c multicolored .20 .20
O12 A9 20c multicolored .20 .20
O13 A9 25c multicolored .20 .20
O14 A9 30c multicolored .20 .20
O15 A9 40c multicolored .20 .20
O16 A9 45c multicolored .20 .20
O17 A9 50c multicolored .20 .20
O18 A9 55c multicolored .20 .20
O19 A9 $1 multicolored .35 .35
O20 A9 $2.50 multicolored .90 .90
O21 A9 $5 multicolored 1.90 1.90
O22 A9 $10 multicolored 3.75 3.75
Nos. O11-O22 (12) 8.50 8.50

Nos. 135-140 Ovptd. or Surcharged "OFFICIAL" in Blue or Black

1983, Feb. 2
O23 A9a 45c on $2 #137 .30 .30
O24 A9b 45c on $2 #138 .30 .30
O25 A9a 55c #135 .40 .40
O26 A9b 55c #136 .40 .40
O27 A9a $1.10 on $5 #139 (Bk) .80 .80
O28 A9b $1.10 on $5 #140 (Bk) .80 .80
Nos. O23-O28 (6) 3.00 3.00

Inverted or double overprints exist on some denominations.

Nos. 367-378 Ovptd. "OFFICIAL"

1985, Jan. 2 Wmk. 380
O29 A24b 15c multicolored .20 .20
O30 A24b 20c multicolored .20 .20
O31 A24b 30c multicolored .20 .20
O32 A24b 40c multicolored .25 .25
O33 A24b 50c multicolored .30 .30
O34 A24b 55c multicolored .30 .30
O35 A24b 60c multicolored .30 .30
O36 A24b 75c multicolored .40 .40
O37 A24b $1 multicolored .55 .55
O38 A24b $3 multicolored 1.60 1.60
O39 A24b $5 multicolored 2.75 2.75
O40 A24b $10 multicolored 5.50 5.50
Nos. O29-O40 (12) 12.55 12.55

Nos. 640-646, 648-653 Ovptd. "OFFICIAL"

1993 Litho. ***Perf. 14***
O41 A71 5c multicolored .20 .20
O42 A71 10c multicolored .20 .20
O43 A71 15c multicolored .20 .20
O44 A71 20c multicolored .20 .20
O45 A71 25c multicolored .20 .20
O46 A71 40c multicolored .30 .30
O47 A71 50c multicolored .40 .40
O48 A71 75c multicolored .55 .55
O49 A71 80c multicolored .60 .60
O50 A71 $1 multicolored .75 .75
O51 A71 $3 multicolored 2.25 2.25
O52 A71 $5 multicolored 3.75 3.75
O53 A71 $10 multicolored 7.50 7.50
O54 A71 $20 multicolored 15.00 15.00
Nos. O41-O54 (14) 32.10 32.10

Dated "1992."

Nos. 1055-1066 Ovptd. "OFFICIAL"

1999, Mar. 22 Litho. ***Perf. 14***
O55 A151 25c multicolored .20 .20
O56 A151 30c multicolored .25 .25
O57 A151 50c multicolored .40 .40
O58 A151 60c multicolored .45 .45
O59 A151 80c multicolored .60 .60
O60 A151 90c multicolored .70 .70
O61 A151 $1 multicolored .75 .75
O62 A151 $1.80 multicolored 1.40 1.40
O63 A151 $3 multicolored 2.25 2.25
O64 A151 $5 multicolored 3.75 3.75
O65 A151 $10 multicolored 7.50 7.50
O66 A151 $20 multicolored 15.00 15.00
Nos. O55-O66 (12) 33.25 33.25

NEW BRITAIN

'nü 'bri-tən

LOCATION — South Pacific Ocean, northeast of New Guinea
GOVT. — Australian military government
AREA — 13,000 sq. mi. (approx.)
POP. — 50,600 (approx.)
CAPITAL — Rabaul

The island Neu-Pommern, a part of former German New Guinea, was captured during World War I by Australian troops and named New Britain. Following the war it was mandated to Australia and designated a part of the Mandated Territory of New Guinea. See German New Guinea, North West Pacific Islands and New Guinea.

12 Pence = 1 Shilling

Kaiser's Yacht "The Hohenzollern"
A3 A4

Stamps of German New Guinea, 1900, Surcharged

First Setting

Surcharge lines spaced 6mm on 1p-8p, 4mm on 1sh-5sh.

Perf. 14, 14½

1914, Oct. 17 Unwmk.
1 A3 1p on 3pf brown 500.00 *600.00*
2 A3 1p on 5pf green 60.00 *90.00*
3 A3 2p on 10pf car *65.00* *100.00*
4 A3 2p on 20pf ultra 65.00 *80.00*
a. "2d." dbl., "G.R.I." omitted 3,500.
b. Inverted surcharge 7,500.
5 A3 2½p on 10pf car 85.00 *190.00*
6 A3 2½p on 20pf ultra 95.00 *200.00*
a. Inverted surcharge
7 A3 3p on 25pf org & blk, *yel* 350.00 *375.00*
8 A3 3p on 30pf org & blk, *sal* 425.00 *450.00*
a. Double surcharge *7,500.* *7,500.*
b. Triple surcharge
9 A3 4p on 40pf lake & black 425.00 *500.00*
a. Double surcharge 2,000. *2,500.*
b. Inverted surcharge *8,500.*
c. "4d." omitted
10 A3 5p on 50pf pur & blk, *sal* 600.00 *950.00*
a. Double surcharge *8,500.*
11 A3 8p on 80pf lake & blk, *rose* 900.00 *1,200.*
a. No period after "8d" *3,500.*
12 A4 1sh on 1m car 2,250. *3,500.*
13 A4 2sh on 2m blue 2,500. *3,500.*
14 A4 3sh on 3m blk vio 4,250. *5,750.*
15 A4 5sh on 5m slate & car 11,000. *13,000.*
a. No period after "I" 14,000. —

"G.R.I." stands for Georgius Rex Imperator.

Second Setting

Surcharge lines spaced 5mm on 1p-8p, 5½mm on 1sh-5sh.

1914, Dec. 16
16 A3 1p on 3pf brown 60.00 *80.00*
a. Double surcharge 750.00 *1,050.*
b. "I" for "1" 675.00
c. "1" with straight top serif 100.00 125.00
d. Inverted surcharge 2,750. —
e. "4" for "1" 9,000.
f. Small "1" 275.00
g. Double surcharge, one inverted 4,000.
17 A3 1p on 5pf green 25.00 *42.50*
a. Double surcharge 2,800.
b. "G. I. R." 7,500. *8,000.*
c. "d" inverted 1,650.
d. No periods after "G R I" *5,750.*
e. Small "1" 140.00 200.00
f. "1d" double —
g. No period after "1d"
h. Triple surcharge
18 A3 2p on 10pf car 35.00 *52.50*
a. Double surcharge *10,000.* *10,000.*
b. Dbl. surch., one inverted 8,000.
c. Surcharged "G. I. R., 3d" *8,000.*
d. Surcharged "1d" 6,750. 6,000.
e. Period before "G" *6,000.*
f. No period after "2d" 175.00 225.00
g. Inverted surcharge
h. "2d" double, one inverted
j. Pair, #18, 20 *20,000.*
19 A3 2p on 20pf ultra 37.50 *57.50*
a. Double surcharge 1,600. *2,750.*
b. Double surch., one inverted 2,800. *3,500.*
c. "R" inverted *5,000.*
d. Surcharged "1d" 7,500. 7,500.
f. Inverted surcharge 6,000. *4,600.*
h. Pair, one without surcharge 16,000.
i. Pair, #19, 21 13,750. 16,000.
20 A3 2½p on 10pf car 210.00 350.00
21 A3 2½p on 20pf ultra 2,000. 2,400.
a. Double surcharge, one invtd.
b. "2½" triple
c. Surcharged "3d"
22 A3 3p on 25pf org & blk, *yel* 150.00 *210.00*
a. Double surcharge 6,000. *7,500.*
b. Inverted surcharge 6,000. *7,500.*
c. "G. R. I." only
d. "G. I. R."
e. Pair, one without surcharge *15,000.*
f. Surcharged "G. I. R., 5d"
23 A3 3p on 30pf org & blk, *sal* 125.00 *200.00*
a. Double surcharge 1,900. *3,000.*
b. Double surcharge, one invtd. 2,400. *3,250.*
c. "d" inverted
d. Surcharged "1d" 7,000. 8,000.
e. Triple surcharge
g. Double inverted surcharge 6,750. *8,000.*
h. Pair, one without surcharge *8,750.*
24 A3 4p on 40pf lake & blk 140.00 *225.00*
a. Double surcharge 1,300. —
b. Double surcharge, one invtd. 4,000. —
e. Surcharged "1d" 4,750.
f. "1" on "4"
25 A3 5p on 50pf pur & blk, *sal* 225.00 *300.00*
a. Double surcharge 2,250.
b. Double surcharge, one invtd. 6,000. *7,500.*
c. "5" omitted
d. Inverted surcharge 5,400.
e. Double inverted surcharge 7,000. *7,500.*
f. "G. I. R." 13,000.
26 A3 8p on 80pf lake & blk, *rose* 450.00 *525.00*
a. Double surcharge 4,000. *5,000.*
b. Double surcharge, one invtd. 4,000. *5,000.*
c. Triple surcharge 4,750. *5,250.*
d. No period after "8d"
e. Inverted surcharge 7,500. *8,000.*
f. Surcharged "3d" 13,000.
27 A4 1sh on 1m car 3,750. *5,250.*
28 A4 2sh on 2m bl 3,750. *6,000.*
a. Surcharged "5s"
b. Double surcharge
29 A4 3sh on 3m blk vio 7,000. *10,500.*
a. No periods after "R I"
b. "G.R.I." double *25,000.*
29C A4 5sh on 5m sl & car 27,500. *32,500.*
d. No periods after "R I"
e. Surcharged "1s"

Nos. 18-19 Surcharged with Large "1"

1915, Jan.
29F A3 "1"(p) on 2p on 10pf carmine *40,000.* *20,000.*
29G A3 "1"(p) on 2p on 20pf ultramarine *30,000.* *12,000.*

Same Surcharge on Stamps of Marshall Islands

1914
30 A3 1p on 3pf brown 70.00 110.00
a. Inverted surcharge 5,000.

31 A3 1p on 5pf green 70.00 62.50
a. Double surcharge 1,800. *2,800.*
b. No period after "d"
c. Inverted surcharge 2,800.
32 A3 2p on 10pf car 25.00 35.00
a. Double surcharge 1,900. *3,250.*
b. Double surcharge, one invtd. 2,800. *3,250.*
c. Surcharge sideways 6,250.
d. No period after "2d"
e. No period after "G" 750.00
33 A3 2p on 20 pf ultra 25.00 40.00
a. No period after "d" 62.50 *110.00*
b. Double surcharge 2,200. 3,250.
c. Double surcharge, one invtd. 5,400. 6,000.
d. Inverted surcharge 6,250. 6,250.
e. "I" omitted
34 A3 3p on 25pf org & blk, *yel* 400.00 525.00
a. Double surcharge 2,100. *2,750.*
b. Double surcharge, one invtd. 2,100.
c. No period after "d" 675.00 925.00
d. Inverted surcharge 6,250.
35 A3 3p on 30pf org & blk, *sal* 425.00 525.00
a. No period after "d" 750.00 1,000.
b. Inverted surcharge 4,600. 5,250.
c. Double surcharge 4,000.
d. Double surcharge, one invtd.
36 A3 4p on 40pf lake & blk 140.00 190.00
a. No period after "d" 350.00 *525.00*
b. Double surcharge 4,000. *4,600.*
c. "4d" omitted
d. "1d" on "4d"
e. No period after "R"
f. Inverted surcharge 5,600.
g. Surcharged "1d" 10,500.
37 A3 5p on 50pf pur & blk, *sal* 190.00 250.00
a. "d" omitted 1,800.
b. Double surcharge 6,000.
c. "5d" double
38 A3 8p on 80pf lake & blk, *rose* 525.00 675.00
a. Inverted surcharge 6,250.
b. Double surcharge 5,250.
c. Double surcharge, one invtd.
d. Triple surcharge 8,000.
39 A4 1sh on 1m car 2,800. *5,250.*
a. Double surcharge 25,000.
b. Dbl. surch., one with "s1" for "1s"
c. No period after "I" 5,000. 6,800.
40 A4 2sh on 2m blue 1,500. 3,500.
a. Double surcharge, one invtd. 25,000. *25,000.*
b. Double surchage 25,000.
c. Large "S"
d. No period after "I" 3,100. *5,250.*
41 A4 3sh on 3m blk vio 5,000. *7,500.*
a. Double surcharge 22,500. 27,500.
b. No period after "I" 6,750.
c. No period after "R I"
d. Inverted surcharge
42 A4 5sh on 5m sl & car *11,000.* *12,500.*
a. Double surcharge, one invtd. *40,000.*

See Nos. 44-45.

A5

Surcharged in Black on Registration Label

1914 ***Perf. 12***

43 A5 3p black & red (Rabaul) 240.00 *275.00*
a. "Friedrich Wilhelmshaven" 225.00 *750.00*
b. "Herbertshohe" 250.00 *675.00*
c. "Kawieng" 300.00 *625.00*
d. "Kieta" 475.00 *800.00*
e. "Manus" 250.00 *875.00*
f. Double surcharge (Rabaul) 8,750. *8,750.*
g. As "c," double surcharge *4,500.*
h. As "e," double surcharge *5,250.*
i. As "d," pair, one without surcharge *9,000.*
j. "Deulon" *17,500.* —
k. "Stephansort" *4,000.*

Nos. 43a, 43c and 43e exist with town name in letters with serifs. The varieties Deutsch-Neuguinea, Deutsch Neu-Guinea, etc., are known.

Nos. 32-33 Surcharged with Large "1"

1915

44 A3 1p on 2p on 10pf 175. 190.
a. "1" double *9,250.*
b. "1" inverted *9,750.* *9,750.*
45 A3 1p on 2p on 20pf 3,500. 2,600.
a. "1" inverted *10,500.* *10,500.*

The stamps of Marshall Islands surcharged "G. R. I." and new values in British currency were all used in New Britain and are therefore listed here.

OFFICIAL STAMPS

O1

German New Guinea Nos. 7-8 Surcharged

1915 **Unwmk.** ***Perf. 14***

O1 O1 1p on 3pf brown 30.00 *85.00*
a. Double surcharge 2,600.
O2 O1 1p on 5pf green 200.00 *325.00*

NEW CALEDONIA

'nü ˌka-lə-'dō-nyə

LOCATION — Island in the South Pacific Ocean, east of Queensland, Australia
GOVT. — French Overseas Territory
AREA — 7,172 sq. mi.
POP. — 197,361 (1999 est.)
CAPITAL — Noumea

Dependencies of New Caledonia are the Loyalty Islands, Isle of Pines, Huon Islands and Chesterfield Islands.

100 Centimes = 1 Franc

Catalogue values for unused stamps in this country are for Never Hinged items, beginning with Scott 252 in the regular postage section, Scott B13 in the semi-postal section, Scott C14 in the airpost section, Scott J32 in the postage due section, and Scott O1 in the official section.

Watermark

Wmk. 385

Napoleon III — A1

1859 **Unwmk.** **Litho.** ***Imperf.***
Without Gum

1 A1 10c black 210.00

Fifty varieties. Counterfeits abound. See No. 315.

Type of French Colonies, 1877 Surcharged in Black:

Nos. 2-5

Nos. 6-7

1881-83

2 A8 5c on 40c red, *straw* ('82) 340.00 340.00
a. Inverted surcharge 1,250. 1,250.
3 A8 05c on 40c red, *straw* ('83) 24.00 24.00
4 A8 25c on 35c dp vio, *yel* 250.00 250.00
a. Inverted surcharge 700.00 700.00
5 A8 25c on 75c rose car, *rose* ('82) 325.00 325.00
a. Inverted surcharge 850.00 850.00

1883-84

6 A8 5c on 40c red, *straw* ('84) 17.50 17.50
a. Inverted surcharge 14.00 14.00
7 A8 5c on 75c rose car, *rose* ('83) 35.00 35.00
a. Inverted surcharge 29.00 29.00

In type "a" surcharge, the narrower-spaced letters measure 14½mm, and an early printing of No. 4 measures 13½mm. Type "b" letters measure 18mm.

French Colonies No. 59 Surcharged in Black:

No. 8

Nos. 9-10

1886 ***Perf. 14x13½***

8 A9 5c on 1fr 17.50 17.50
a. Inverted surcharge 26.00 26.00
9 A9 5c on 1fr 17.50 17.50
b. Inverted surcharge 40.00 40.00

French Colonies No. 29 Surcharged
Imperf

10 A8 5c on 1fr *8,500.* *10,000.*

Types of French Colonies, 1877-86, Surcharged in Black:

Nos. 11, 13

No. 12

1891-92 ***Imperf.***

11 A8 10c on 40c red, *straw* ('92) 27.50 27.50
a. Inverted surcharge 27.50 27.50
b. Double surcharge 72.50 72.50
c. No period after "10c" 27.50 27.50

Perf. 14x13½

12 A9 10c on 30c brn, *bis* 18.00 18.00
a. Inverted surcharge 18.00 18.00
b. Double surcharge 45.00 45.00
c. Double surcharge, inverted 55.00 55.00
13 A9 10c on 40c red, *straw* ('92) 18.00 18.00
a. Inverted surcharge 18.00 18.00
b. No period after "10c" 18.00 18.00
c. Double surcharge 45.00 45.00
Nos. 11-13 (3) 63.50 63.50

Variety "double surcharge, one inverted" exists on Nos. 11-13. Value slightly higher than for "double surcharge."

Types of French Colonies, 1877-86, Handstamped in Black

g

1892 ***Imperf.***

16 A8 20c red, *grn* 325.00 *325.00*
17 A8 35c violet, *org* 62.50 62.50
18 A8 40c red, *straw* —
19 A8 1fr bronz grn, *straw* 250.00 250.00

The 1c, 2c, 4c and 75c of type A8 are believed not to have been officially made or actually used.

1892 ***Perf. 14x13½***

23 A9 5c green, *grnsh* 14.00 12.50
24 A9 10c blk, *lavender* 100.00 57.50
25 A9 15c blue 85.00 42.50
26 A9 20c red, *grn* 82.50 45.00
27 A9 25c yellow, *straw* 21.00 12.50
28 A9 25c black, *rose* 85.00 14.00
29 A9 30c brown, *bis* 62.50 52.50
30 A9 35c violet, *org* 200.00 150.00
32 A9 75c carmine, *rose* 175.00 140.00
33 A9 1fr bronz grn, *straw* 140.00 125.00
Nos. 23-33 (10) 965.00 651.50

The note following No. 19 also applies to the 1c, 2c, 4c and 40c of type A9.

Surcharged in Blue or Black

h

1892-93 ***Imperf.***

34 A8 10c on 1fr brnz grn, *straw* (Bl) *4,400.* *3,750.*

Perf. 14x13½

35 A9 5c on 20c red, *grn* (Bk) 20.00 18.00
a. Inverted surcharge 100.00 85.00
b. Double surcharge inverted —
36 A9 5c on 75c car, *rose* (Bk) 17.50 12.50
a. Inverted surcharge 100.00 85.00
37 A9 5c on 75c car, *rose* (Bl) 14.00 10.00
a. Inverted surcharge 100.00 85.00
38 A9 10c on 1fr brnz grn, *straw* (Bk) 15.00 10.00
a. Inverted surcharge 500.00 425.00
39 A9 10c on 1fr brnz grn, *straw* (Bl) 17.50 14.00
a. Inverted surcharge 100.00 85.00
Nos. 35-39 (5) 84.00 64.50

Navigation and Commerce — A12

1892-1904 **Typo.** ***Perf. 14x13½***
Name of Colony in Blue or Carmine

40 A12 1c black, *blue* .70 .70
41 A12 2c brown, *buff* 1.40 1.10
42 A12 4c claret, *lav* 1.90 1.50
43 A12 5c green, *grnsh* 2.50 1.40
44 A12 5c yellow green ('00) 2.00 1.25
45 A12 10c blk, *lavender* 7.25 4.00
46 A12 10c rose red ('00) 7.75 1.50
47 A12 15c bl, quadrille paper 21.00 3.00
48 A12 15c gray ('00) 11.50 1.50
49 A12 20c red, *grn* 14.00 8.50
50 A12 25c black, *rose* 18.00 5.75
51 A12 25c blue ('00) 17.00 10.00
52 A12 30c brown, *bis* 18.00 10.00
53 A12 40c red, *straw* 18.50 10.50
54 A12 50c carmine, *rose* 55.00 25.00
55 A12 50c brn, *az* (name in car) ('00) 85.00 72.50
56 A12 50c brn, *az* (name in bl) ('04) 42.50 36.00
57 A12 75c violet, *org* 29.00 21.00
58 A12 1fr bronz grn, *straw* 35.00 20.00
Nos. 40-58 (19) 388.00 235.20

Perf. 13½x14 stamps are counterfeits.
For overprints and surcharges see Nos. 59-87, 117-121.

Nos. 41-42, 52, 57-58, 53 Surcharged in Black:

j

k

1900-01

59 A12 (h) 5c on 2c ('01) 18.00 14.00
a. Double surcharge 125.00 125.00
b. Inverted surcharge 110.00 110.00
60 A12 (h) 5c on 4c 3.50 3.50
a. Inverted surcharge 72.50 72.50
b. Double surcharge 80.00 80.00
61 A12 (j) 15c on 30c 4.25 3.50
a. Inverted surcharge 57.50 57.50
b. Double surcharge 62.50 62.50
62 A12 (j) 15c on 75c ('01) 17.00 14.00
a. Pair, one without surcharge —
b. Inverted surcharge 110.00 110.00
c. Double surcharge 125.00 125.00
63 A12 (j) 15c on 1fr ('01) 21.00 18.00
a. Double surcharge 150.00 150.00
b. Inverted surcharge 140.00 140.00
Nos. 59-63 (5) 63.75 53.00

1902

64 A12 (k) 5c on 30c 8.50 7.25
a. Inverted surcharge 37.50 35.00
65 A12 (k) 15c on 40c 8.50 7.25
a. Inverted surcharge 37.50 35.00

Jubilee Issue

Stamps of 1892-1900 Overprinted in Blue, Red, Black or Gold

1903

66 A12 1c blk, *lil bl* (Bl) 1.75 1.75
a. Inverted overprint 225.00 210.00
67 A12 2c brown, *buff* (Bl) 4.00 3.50
68 A12 4c claret, *lav* (Bl) 5.25 4.00
a. Double overprint 290.00 275.00
69 A12 5c dk grn, *grnsh* (R) 5.25 3.50
70 A12 5c yellow green (R) 8.50 6.75
71 A12 10c blk, *lav* (R) 14.00 12.00
72 A12 10c blk, *lav* (double G & Bk) 8.50 6.75
73 A12 15c gray (R) 11.50 6.75
74 A12 20c red, *grn* (Bl) 16.00 13.50
75 A12 25c blk, *rose* (Bl) 16.00 14.00
a. Double overprint 225.00
76 A12 30c brown, *bis* (R) 20.00 19.00
77 A12 40c red, *straw* (Bl) 27.50 24.00
78 A12 50c car, *rose* (Bl) 45.00 35.00
a. Pair, one without overprint
79 A12 75c vio, *org* (Bk) 65.00 57.50
a. Dbl. ovpt. in blk and red 400.00
80 A12 1fr brnz grn, *straw* (Bl) 100.00 85.00
a. Dbl. ovpt., one in red 400.00 375.00
Nos. 66-80 (15) 348.25 293.00

With Additional Surcharge of New Value in Blue

81 A12 1c on 2c #67 1.25 1.25
a. Numeral double 77.50 77.50
b. Numeral only 290.00
82 A12 2c on 4c #68 2.40 2.40
83 A12 4c on 5c #69 1.75 1.75
a. Small "4" 525.00 525.00
84 A12 4c on 5c #70 2.10 2.10
a. Pair, one without numeral
85 A12 10c on 15c #73 2.10 2.10
86 A12 15c on 20c #74 2.90 2.90
87 A12 20c on 25c #75 6.00 6.00
Nos. 81-87 (7) 18.50 18.50

50 years of French occupation.

Surcharge on Nos. 81-83, 85-86 is horizontal, reading down.

There are three types of numeral on No. 83. The numeral on No. 84 is identical with that of No. 83a except that its position is upright.

Nos. 66-87 are known with "I" of "TENAIRE" missing.

Kagu
A16

Landscape
A17

Ship — A18

1905-28 **Typo.** ***Perf. 14x13½***

88 A16 1c blk, *green* .25 .20
89 A16 2c red brown .25 .20
90 A16 4c bl, *org* .40 .35
91 A16 5c pale green .40 .35
92 A16 5c dl bl ('21) .35 .20
93 A16 10c carmine 1.25 .90
94 A16 10c green ('21) .65 .55
95 A16 10c red, *pink* ('25) .70 .55
96 A16 15c violet .65 .50
97 A17 20c brown .40 .35
98 A17 25c blue, *grn* .85 .45
99 A17 25c red, *yel* ('21) .50 .50
100 A17 30c brn, *org* .95 .65
101 A17 30c dp rose ('21) 1.75 1.75
102 A17 30c org ('25) .40 .35
103 A17 35c blk, *yellow* .55 .50
104 A17 40c car, *grn* .95 .85
105 A17 45c vio brn, *lav* .55 .55
106 A17 50c car, *org* 2.40 2.10
107 A17 50c dk bl ('21) 1.25 1.25
108 A17 50c gray ('25) .70 .70
109 A17 65c dp bl ('28) .55 .55
110 A17 75c ol grn, *straw* .50 .35
111 A17 75c bl, *bluish* ('25) .55 .55
112 A17 75c violet ('27) .80 .80
113 A18 1fr bl, *yel grn* 1.00 .55
114 A18 1fr dp bl ('25) 1.50 1.40
115 A18 2fr car, *bl* 3.00 1.75
116 A18 5fr blk, *straw* 5.75 5.25
Nos. 88-116 (29) 29.80 25.00

See Nos. 311, 317a. For surcharges see Nos. 122-135, B1-B3, Q1-Q3.

Nos. 96, 98, 103, 106, 113 and 115, pasted on cardboard and handstamped "TRESORIER PAYEUR DE LA NOUVELLE CALEDONIE" were used as emergency currency in 1914.

Stamps of 1892-1904 Surcharged in Carmine or Black

1912

117 A12 5c on 15c gray (C) .70 .70
a. Inverted surcharge 160.00 160.00
118 A12 5c on 20c red, *grn* 1.00 1.00
119 A12 5c on 30c brn, *bis* (C) 1.00 1.00
120 A12 10c on 40c red, *straw* 1.90 1.90
121 A12 10c on 50c brn, *az* (C) 1.90 1.90
Nos. 117-121 (5) 6.50 6.50

Two spacings between the surcharged numerals are found on Nos. 117 to 121. For detailed listings, see the *Scott Classic Specialized Catalogue of Stamps and Covers.*

No. 96 Surcharged in Brown

1918

122 A16 5c on 15c violet 1.40 1.40
a. Double surcharge 57.50 57.50
b. Inverted surcharge 35.00 35.00

The color of the surcharge on No. 122 varies from red to dark brown.

No. 96 Surcharged

1922

123 A16 5c on 15c vio (R) .60 .60
a. Double surcharge 57.50 57.50

Stamps and Types of 1905-28 Surcharged New Value and Bars in Red or Black

1924-27

124 A16 25c on 15c vio .45 .45
a. Double surcharge 57.50
125 A18 25c on 2fr car, *bl* .55 .55
126 A18 25c on 5fr blk, *straw* .55 .55
a. Double surcharge 90.00 90.00
127 A17 60c on 75c bl grn (R) .50 .50
128 A17 65c on 45c red brn 1.60 1.60
129 A17 85c on 45c red brn 1.60 1.60
130 A17 90c on 75c dp rose .70 .70
131 A18 1.25fr on 1fr dp bl (R) .65 .65
132 A18 1.50fr on 1fr dp bl, *bl* 1.10 1.10
133 A18 3fr on 5fr red vio 1.60 1.60
134 A18 10fr on 5fr ol, *lav* (R) 5.75 5.75
135 A18 20fr on 5fr vio rose, *org* 11.50 11.50
Nos. 124-135 (12) 26.55 26.55

Issue years: Nos. 125-127, 1924. Nos. 124, 128-129, 1925. Nos. 131, 134, 1926. Nos. 130, 132-133, 135, 1927.

Bay of Palétuviers Point
A19

Landscape with Chief's House
A20

Admiral de Bougainville and Count de La Pérouse — A21

1928-40 **Typo.**

136 A19 1c brn vio & ind .20 .20
137 A19 2c dk brn & yel grn .20 .20
137B A19 3c brn vio & ind .20 .20
138 A19 4c org & Prus grn .20 .20
139 A19 5c Prus bl & dp ol .35 .35
140 A19 10c gray lil & dk brn .20 .20
141 A19 15c yel brn & dp bl .35 .35
142 A19 20c brn red & dk brn .35 .35
143 A19 25c dk grn & dk brn .50 .35
144 A20 30c gray grn & bl grn .35 .35
145 A20 35c blk & brt vio .50 .50
146 A20 40c brt red & olvn .35 .35
147 A20 45c dp bl & red org 1.10 .95
147A A20 45c bl grn & dl grn .80 .80
148 A20 50c vio & brn .50 .50
149 A20 55c vio bl & car 2.75 1.75
150 A20 60c vio bl & car .50 .50
151 A20 65c org brn & bl .95 .80
152 A20 70c dp rose & brn .35 .35
153 A20 75c Prus bl & ol gray 1.10 .70
154 A20 80c red brn & grn .80 .65
155 A20 85c grn & brn 1.40 .80
156 A20 90c dp red & brt red .95 .55
157 A20 90c ol grn & rose red .70 .70
158 A21 1fr dp ol & sal red 5.50 3.50
159 A21 1fr rose red & dk car 1.75 1.25
160 A21 1fr brn red & grn .80 .80
161 A21 1.10fr dp grn & brn 9.75 8.75
162 A21 1.25fr brn red & grn .85 .85
163 A21 1.25fr rose red & dk car .80 .80
164 A21 1.40fr dk bl & red org .95 .95
165 A21 1.50fr dp bl & bl .55 .55
166 A21 1.60fr dp grn & brn 1.10 1.10
167 A21 1.75fr dk bl & red org .65 .65
168 A21 1.75fr violet bl .95 .80
169 A21 2fr red org & brn .55 .50
170 A21 2.25fr vio bl .80 .80
171 A21 2.50fr brn & lt brn 1.25 1.25
172 A21 3fr mag & brn .50 .50
173 A21 5fr dk bl & brn .80 .80
174 A21 10fr vio & brn, *pnksh* 1.00 1.00
175 A21 20fr red & brn, *yel* 2.25 2.25
Nos. 136-175 (42) 46.45 39.75

The 35c in Prussian green and dark green without overprint is listed as Wallis and Futuna No. 53a.

Issue years: 35c, 70c, 85c, #162, 167, 1933; 55c, 80c, #159, 168, 1938; #157, 163, 2.25fr, 1939; 3c, 1.40fr, 1.60fr, 2.50fr, 147A, 160, 1940; others, 1928.

For overprints see #180-207, 217-251, Q4-Q6.

Common Design Types pictured following the introduction.

Colonial Exposition Issue

Common Design Types

1931 **Engr.** ***Perf. 12½***

Country Name Typo. in Black

176 CD70 40c dp green 4.50 4.50
177 CD71 50c violet 4.50 4.50
178 CD72 90c red orange 4.50 4.50
179 CD73 1.50fr dull blue 4.50 4.50
Nos. 176-179 (4) 18.00 18.00

Paris-Nouméa Flight Issue

Regular Issue of 1928 Overprinted:

1932 ***Perf. 14x13½***

180 A20 40c brt red & olvn 400.00 400.00
181 A20 50c vio & brn 400.00 400.00

Arrival on Apr. 5, 1932 at Nouméa, of the French aviators, Verneilh, Dévé and Munch. Excellent forgeries exist of #180-181.

Types of 1928-33 Overprinted in Black or Red:

1933

182 A19 1c red vio & dl bl 5.00 5.00
183 A19 2c dk brn & yel grn 5.00 5.00
184 A19 4c dl org & Prus bl 5.00 5.00
185 A19 5c Prus grn & ol (R) 5.00 5.00
186 A19 10c gray lil & dk brn (R) 5.00 5.00
187 A19 15c yel brn & dp bl (R) 5.00 5.00
188 A19 20c brn red & dk brn 5.00 5.00
189 A19 25c dk grn & dk brn (R) 5.00 5.00
190 A20 30c gray grn & bl grn (R) 5.00 5.00
191 A20 35c blk & lt vio 5.00 5.00
192 A20 40c brt red & olvn 5.00 5.00
193 A20 45c dp bl & red org 5.00 5.00
194 A20 50c vio & brn 5.00 5.00
195 A20 70c dp rose & brn 6.25 6.25
196 A20 75c Prus bl & ol gray (R) 6.25 6.25
197 A20 85c grn & brn 6.25 6.25
198 A20 90c dp red & brt red 7.00 7.00
199 A21 1fr dp ol & sal red 7.00 7.00
200 A21 1.25fr brn red & grn 7.00 7.00
201 A21 1.50fr dp bl & bl (R) 7.00 7.00
202 A21 1.75fr dk bl & red org 7.00 7.00
203 A21 2fr red org & brn 7.00 7.00
204 A21 3fr mag & brn 7.00 7.00
205 A21 5fr dk bl & brn (R) 7.00 7.00
206 A21 10fr vio & brn, *pnksh* 8.00 8.00
207 A21 20fr red & brn, *yel* 8.00 8.00
Nos. 182-207 (26) 155.75 155.75

1st anniv., Paris-Noumea flight. Plane centered on Nos. 190-207.

Paris International Exposition Issue

Common Design Types

1937 **Engr.** ***Perf. 13***

208 CD74 20c dp vio 1.75 1.75
209 CD75 30c dk grn 1.75 1.75
210 CD76 40c car rose 1.75 1.75
211 CD77 50c dk brn & bl 1.75 1.75
212 CD78 90c red 1.75 1.75
213 CD79 1.50fr ultra 1.75 1.75
Nos. 208-213 (6) 10.50 10.50

Colonial Arts Exhibition Issue
Souvenir Sheet
Common Design Type

1937 ***Imperf.***

214	CD78	3fr sepia	21.00	*25.00*

New York World's Fair Issue
Common Design Type

1939 ***Perf. 12½x12***

215	CD82	1.25fr car lake	1.25	1.25
216	CD82	2.25fr ultra	1.25	1.25

Nouméa Roadstead and Marshal Pétain A21a

1941 **Engr.** ***Perf. 12½x12***

216A	A21a	1fr bluish green	.55	
216B	A21a	2.50fr dark blue	.55	

Nos. 216A-216B were issued by the Vichy government in France, but were not placed on sale in the colony.

For surcharges, see Nos. B12A-B12B.

Types of 1928-40 Overprinted in Black

1941 ***Perf. 14x13½***

217	A19	1c red vio & dl bl	9.00	9.00
218	A19	2c dk brn & yel grn	9.00	9.00
219	A19	3c brn vio & ind	9.00	9.00
220	A19	4c dl org & Prus bl	9.00	9.00
221	A19	5c Prus bl & dp ol	9.00	9.00
222	A19	10c gray lil & dk brn	9.00	9.00
223	A19	15c yel brn & dp bl	15.00	15.00
224	A19	20c brn red & dk brn	15.00	15.00
225	A19	25c dk grn & dk brn	15.00	15.00
226	A20	30c gray grn & bl grn	15.00	15.00
227	A20	35c blk & brt vio	15.00	15.00
228	A20	40c brt red & olvn	15.00	15.00
229	A20	45c bl grn & dl grn	15.00	15.00
230	A20	50c vio & brn	15.00	15.00
231	A20	55c vio bl & car	15.00	15.00
232	A20	60c vio bl & car	15.00	15.00
233	A20	65c org brn & bl	15.00	15.00
234	A20	70c dp rose & brn	15.00	15.00
235	A20	75c Prus bl & ol gray	15.00	15.00
236	A20	80c red brn & grn	15.00	15.00
237	A20	85c grn & brn	15.00	15.00
238	A20	90c dp red & brt red	15.00	15.00
239	A21	1fr rose red & dk car	15.00	15.00
240	A21	1.25fr brn red & grn	15.00	15.00
241	A21	1.40fr dk bl & red org	15.00	15.00
242	A21	1.50fr dp bl & bl	15.00	15.00
243	A21	1.60fr dp grn & brn	15.00	15.00
244	A21	1.75fr dk bl & red org	15.00	15.00
245	A21	2fr red org & brn	15.00	15.00
246	A21	2.25fr vio bl	15.00	15.00
247	A21	2.50fr brn & lt brn	16.00	16.00
248	A21	3fr mag & brn	16.00	16.00
249	A21	5fr dk bl & brn	16.00	16.00
250	A21	10fr vio & brn, *pnksh*	19.00	19.00
251	A21	20fr red & brn, *yel*	20.00	20.00
		Nos. 217-251 (35)	501.00	501.00

Issued to note this colony's affiliation with the "Free France" movement.

Catalogue values for unused stamps in this section, from this point to the end of the section, are for Never Hinged items.

Kagu A22

1942 **Photo.** ***Perf. 14½x14***

252	A22	5c brown	.35	.20
253	A22	10c dk gray bl	.35	.20
254	A22	25c emerald	.35	.20
255	A22	30c red org	.55	.35
256	A22	40c dk slate grn	.55	.35
257	A22	80c dl red brn	.55	.35
258	A22	1fr rose vio	.65	.50
259	A22	1.50fr red	.65	.50
260	A22	2fr gray blk	1.10	.70
261	A22	2.50fr brt ultra	1.10	.70
262	A22	4fr dl vio	1.10	.70
263	A22	5fr bister	1.10	.70
264	A22	10fr dp brn	1.40	1.10
265	A22	20fr dp grn	2.25	1.90
		Nos. 252-265 (14)	12.05	8.45

Types of 1928 Without "RF"

1944 **Typo.** ***Perf. 14x13½***

265A	A19	10c gray lil & dk brn	.50	
265B	A20	60c vio bl & car	.80	

Nos. 265A-265B were issued by the Vichy government in France, but were not placed on sale in the colony.

Stamps of 1942 Surcharged in Carmine or Black

1945-46 **Unwmk.** ***Perf. 14½x14***

266	A22	50c on 5c (C) ('46)	1.40	1.10
267	A22	60c on 5c (C)	1.40	1.10
268	A22	70c on 5c (C)	1.40	1.10
269	A22	1.20fr on 5c (C)	.70	.50
270	A22	2.40fr on 25c	.70	.50
271	A22	3fr on 25c ('46)	.70	.50
272	A22	4.50fr on 25c	1.40	1.10
273	A22	15fr on 2.50fr (C)	2.10	1.75
		Nos. 266-273 (8)	9.80	7.65

Eboue Issue
Common Design Type

1945 **Engr.** ***Perf. 13***

274	CD91	2fr black	.85	.55
275	CD91	25fr Prus grn	2.00	1.60

Kagus A23

Ducos Sanatorium A24

Porcupine Isle — A25

Nickel Foundry A26

"Towers of Notre Dame" A27

Chieftain's House — A28

1948 **Unwmk.** **Photo.** ***Perf. 13½x13***

276	A23	10c yel & brn	.30	.20
277	A23	30c grn & brn	.30	.20
278	A23	40c org & brn	.30	.20
279	A24	50c pink & brn	.45	.45
280	A24	60c yel & brn	.65	.50
281	A24	80c lt grn & bl grn	.65	.50
282	A25	1fr brn, pur & org	.65	.50
283	A25	1.20fr pale gray, brn & bl	.65	.50
284	A25	1.50fr cream, dk bl & yel	.65	.50
285	A26	2fr pck grn & brn	.65	.50
286	A26	2.40fr ver & dp rose	.95	.65
287	A26	3fr org & pur	6.00	1.60
288	A26	4fr bl & dk bl	1.90	.85
289	A27	5fr ver & pur	2.50	.85
290	A27	6fr yel & brn	2.10	1.25
291	A27	10fr org & dk bl	2.10	1.25
292	A28	15fr brn & gray	3.25	1.40
293	A28	20fr pur & yel	3.25	1.90
294	A28	25fr dk bl & org	4.50	2.60
		Nos. 276-294 (19)	31.80	16.40

Military Medal Issue
Common Design Type

1952 **Engr. & Typo.** ***Perf. 13***

295	CD101	2fr multi	6.50	5.00

Admiral Bruni d'Entrecasteaux and his Two Frigates — A29

Designs: 2fr, Msgr. Douarre and Cathedral of Nouméa. 6fr, Admiral Dumont d'Urville and map. 13fr, Admiral Auguste Febvrier-Despointes and Nouméa roadstead.

1953, Sept. 24 **Engr.**

296	A29	1.50fr org brn & dp claret	6.25	3.75
297	A29	2fr ind & aqua	5.50	2.50
298	A29	6fr dk brn, bl & car	9.25	4.50
299	A29	13fr bl grn & dk grnsh bl	11.00	5.75
		Nos. 296-299 (4)	32.00	16.50

Centenary of the presence of the French in New Caledonia.

"Towers of Notre Dame" — A30

Coffee A31

1955, Nov. 21 **Unwmk.** ***Perf. 13***

300	A30	2.50fr dk brn, ultra & grn	1.10	.70
301	A30	3fr grn, ultra & red brn	6.00	3.00
302	A31	9fr vio bl & indigo	2.25	.70
		Nos. 300-302 (3)	9.35	4.40

FIDES Issue
Common Design Type

Design: Dumbea Dam.

1956, Oct. 22 **Engr.** ***Perf. 13x12½***

303	CD103	3fr grn & bl	1.40	.80

Flower Issue
Common Design Type

Designs: 4fr, Xanthostemon. 15fr, Hibiscus.

1958, July 7 **Photo.** ***Perf. 12x12½***

304	CD104	4fr multi	2.10	.90
305	CD104	15fr grn, red & yel	5.00	1.40

Imperforates

Most stamps of New Caledonia from 1958 onward exist imperforate, in trial colors, or in small presentation sheets in which the stamps are printed in changed colors.

Human Rights Issue
Common Design Type

1958, Dec. 10 **Engr.** ***Perf. 13***

306	CD105	7fr car & dk bl	1.75	1.00

Brachyrus Zebra — A32

Lienardella Fasciata A33

Designs: 10fr, Claucus and Spirographe. 26fr, Fluorescent corals.

1959, Mar. 21 **Engr.** ***Perf. 13***

307	A32	1fr lil gray & red brn	.70	.35
308	A33	3fr bl, grn & red	1.00	.45
309	A32	10fr dk brn, Prus bl & org brn	2.75	1.10
310	A33	26fr multi	5.00	3.00
		Nos. 307-310 (4)	9.45	4.90

Types of 1859, 1905 and

Girl Operating Check Writer A34

Telephone Receiver and Exchange A35

Port-de-France (Nouméa) in 1859 — A36

Designs: 9fr, Wayside mailbox and mail bus, vert. 33fr, like 19fr without stamps.

Perf. 13½x13, 13

1960, May 20 **Unwmk.**

311	A16	4fr red	1.00	.45
312	A34	5fr claret & org brn	1.10	.60
313	A36	9fr dk grn & brn	1.10	.70
314	A35	12fr bl & blk	1.50	.80
315	A1	13fr slate blue	4.00	1.60
316	A36	19fr bl grn, dl grn & red	4.25	1.10
317	A36	33fr Prus bl & dl red	4.25	2.50
	a.	Souv. sheet of 3, #315, 311, 317 + label	13.50	12.00
		Nos. 311-317 (7)	17.20	7.75

Cent. of postal service and stamps in New Caledonia.

No. 317a has label between 4fr and 33fr stamps.

Melanesian Sailing Canoes
A37

Designs: 4fr, Spear fisherman, vert. 5fr, Sail Rock and sailboats, Noumea.

1962, July 2 Engr. *Perf. 13*

318 A37 2fr slate grn, ultra & brn 1.00 .45
319 A37 4fr brn, car & grn 1.25 .45
320 A37 5fr sepia, grn & bl 1.50 .60
Nos. 318-320 (3) 3.75 1.50

See Nos. C29-C32.

Map of Australia and South Pacific — A37a

1962, July 18 Photo. *Perf. 13x12*

321 A37a 15fr multi 3.25 1.60

Fifth South Pacific Conf., Pago Pago, 1962.

Air Currents over Map of New Caledonia and South Pacific, Barograph and Compass Rose — A38

1962, Nov. 5 *Perf. 12x12½*

322 A38 50fr multi 9.75 5.00

3rd regional assembly of the World Meteorological Association, Noumea, November 1962.

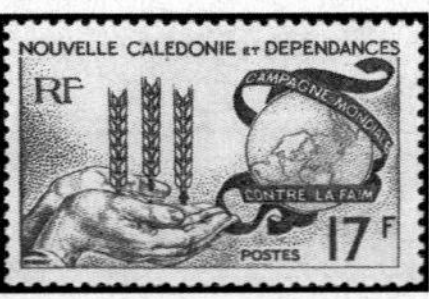

Wheat Emblem and Globe
A38a

1963, Mar. 21 Engr. *Perf. 13*

323 A38a 17fr choc & dk bl 3.75 1.10

FAO "Freedom from Hunger" campaign.

Relay Race — A39

Perf. 12½

1963, Aug. 29 Unwmk. Photo.

324 A39 1fr shown .70 .45
325 A39 7fr Tennis 1.75 .80
326 A39 10fr Soccer 2.10 1.40
327 A39 27fr Javelin 4.00 2.40
Nos. 324-327 (4) 8.55 5.05

South Pacific Games, Suva, Aug. 29-Sept. 7.

Red Cross Centenary Issue
Common Design Type

1963 Sept. 2 Engr. *Perf. 13*

328 CD113 37fr bl, gray & car 8.25 5.50

Human Rights Issue
Common Design Type

1963, Dec. 10 Unwmk. *Perf. 13*

329 CD117 50fr sl grn & dp claret 7.50 5.50

Bikkia Fritillarioides
A40

Sea Squirts
A41

Flowers: 1fr, Freycinettia Sp. 3fr, Xanthostemon Francii. 4fr, Psidiomyrtus locellatus. 5fr, Callistemon suberosum. 7fr, Montrouziera sphaeroidea, horiz. 10fr, Ixora collina, horiz. 17fr, Deplanchea speciosa.

Photogravure; Lithographed (2fr, 3fr)

1964-65 *Perf. 13x12½*

330 A40 1fr multi .70 .35
331 A40 2fr multi .85 .45
332 A40 3fr multi 1.25 .55
333 A40 4fr multi ('65) 2.50 .80
334 A40 5fr multi ('65) 3.25 .90
335 A40 7fr multi 5.25 1.25
336 A40 10fr multi 6.25 1.40
337 A40 17fr multi 8.25 2.75
Nos. 330-337 (8) 28.30 8.45

1964-65 Engr. *Perf. 13*

Design: 10fr, Alcyonium catalai. 17fr, Shrimp (hymenocera elegans).

338 A41 7fr dk bl, org & brn 1.75 1.00
339 A41 10fr dk red & dk vio bl ('65) 2.75 .70
340 A41 17fr dk bl, mag & grn 4.00 2.10
Nos. 338-340 (3) 8.50 3.80

Nouméa Aquarium. See Nos. C41-C43.

Philatec Issue
Common Design Type

1964, Apr. 9 Unwmk. *Perf. 13*

341 CD118 40fr dk vio, grn & choc 7.25 5.25

De Gaulle's 1940 Poster "A Tous les Francais"
A42

1965, Sept. 20 Engr. *Perf. 13*

342 A42 20fr red, bl & blk 12.00 7.00

25th anniv. of the rallying of the Free French.

Amedee Lighthouse
A43

Games' Emblem
A44

1965, Nov. 25

343 A43 8fr dk vio bl, bis & grn 1.50 .70

Centenary of the Amedee lighthouse.

1966, Mar. 1 Engr. *Perf. 13*

344 A44 8fr dk red, brt bl & blk 1.50 .70

2nd So. Pacific Games, Nouméa, Dec. 1966.

Red-throated Parrot Finch — A45

Design: 3fr, Giant imperial pigeon.

1966, Oct. 10 Litho. *Perf. 13x12½*
Size: 22x37mm

345 A45 1fr green & multi 3.00 1.40
346 A45 3fr citron & multi 5.00 1.75

See #361-366, 380-381, C48-C49A, C70-C71.

Dancers and UNESCO Emblem
A46

1966, Nov. 4 Engr. *Perf. 13*

347 A46 16fr pur, ocher & grn 2.10 1.00

20th anniv. of UNESCO.

High Jump and Games' Emblem
A47

1966, Dec. 8 Engr. *Perf. 13*

348 A47 17fr shown 2.10 1.10
349 A47 20fr Hurdling 4.00 1.75
350 A47 40fr Running 5.00 2.10
351 A47 100fr Swimming 8.25 5.75
a. Souv. sheet of 4, #348-351 + label 29.00 25.00
Nos. 348-351 (4) 19.35 10.70

2nd So. Pacific Games, Nouméa, Dec. 8-18.

Lekine Cliffs
A48

1967, Jan. 14 Engr. *Perf. 13*

352 A48 17fr brt grn, ultra & sl grn 2.10 1.10

Magenta Stadium, Nouméa
A49

Design: 20fr, Fish hatchery, Nouméa.

1967, June 5 Photo. *Perf. 12x13*

353 A49 10fr multi 1.25 .70
354 A49 20fr multi 3.00 1.50

ITY Emblem, Beach at Nouméa
A50

1967, June 19 Engr. *Perf. 13*

355 A50 30fr multi 4.25 2.00

Issued for International Tourist Year, 1967.

19th Century Mailman
A51

1967, July 12

356 A51 7fr dk car, bl grn & brn 3.25 1.00

Issued for Stamp Day.

Papilio Montrouzieri — A52

Butterflies: 9fr, Polyura clitarchus. 13fr, 15fr, Hypolimnas bolina, male and female respectively.

1967-68 Engr. *Perf. 13*
Size: 36x22mm

357 A52 7fr lt grn, blk & ultra 4.75 1.00
358 A52 9fr brn, lil & ind ('68) 5.75 1.00
359 A52 13fr vio bl, brn org & dk brn 7.00 2.00
360 A52 15fr dk brn, bl & yel 8.50 3.75
Nos. 357-360,C51-C53 (7) 64.00 22.00

Issued: 9fr, 3/26/68; others, 8/10/67.

Bird Type of 1966

Birds: 1fr, New Caledonian grass warbler. 2fr, New Caledonia whistler. 3fr, New Caledonia white-throated pigeon. 4fr, Kagus. 5fr, Crested parakeet. 10fr, Crow honey-eater.

1967-68 Photo. *Perf. 13x12½*
Size: 22x37mm

361 A45 1fr multi 1.50 .85
362 A45 2fr multi 2.00 1.00
363 A45 3fr multi 2.00 1.25
364 A45 4fr grn & multi 4.50 1.75
365 A45 5fr lt yel & multi 6.25 2.25
366 A45 10fr pink & multi 13.00 3.00
Nos. 361-366 (6) 29.25 10.10

Issued: #364-366, 12/16/67; others 5/14/68.

WHO Anniversary Issue
Common Design Type

1968, May 4 Engr. *Perf. 13*

367 CD126 20fr mar, vio & dk bl grn 4.00 1.50

Ferrying Mail Truck Across Tontouta River, 1900
A53

1968, Sept. 2 Engr. *Perf. 13*
368 A53 9fr dk red brn, grn & ultra 3.75 1.25

Issued for Stamp Day, 1968.

Human Rights Year Issue
Common Design Type

1968, Aug. 10 Engr. *Perf. 13*
369 CD127 12fr sl grn, dp car & org yel 3.00 .80

Conus Geographus — A54

1968, Nov. 9 Engr. *Perf. 13*
Size: 36x22mm
370 A54 10fr dk brn, brt bl & gray 4.25 1.50
Nos. 370,C58-C60 (4) 37.25 10.00

Car on Road A55

1968, Dec. 26 Engr. *Perf. 13*
371 A55 25fr dp bl, sl grn & hn brn 8.00 3.25

2nd Automobile Safari of New Caledonia.

Cattle Dip — A56

1969, May 10 Engr. *Perf. 13*
Size: 36x22mm
372 A56 9fr shown 1.25 .80
373 A56 25fr Cattle branding 3.00 1.25
Nos. 372-373,C64 (3) 9.25 4.80

Cattle breeding in New Caledonia.

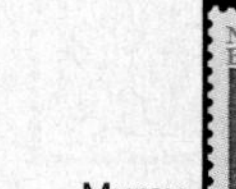

Murex Haustellum A57

Sea Shells: 5fr, Venus comb. 15fr, Murex ramosus.

1969, June 21 Engr. *Perf. 13*
Size: 35½x22mm
374 A57 2fr ver, bl & brn 1.75 .70
375 A57 5fr dl red, pur & beige 3.75 .80
376 A57 15fr ver, dl grn & gray 5.50 2.00
Nos. 374-376,C65 (4) 38.50 12.50

Judo A58

1969, Aug. 7 Engr. *Perf. 13*
Size: 36x22mm
377 A58 19fr shown 3.50 1.60
378 A58 20fr Boxers 3.50 1.60
Nos. 377-378,C66-C67 (4) 18.00 6.70

3rd South Pacific Games. Port Moresby, Papua and New Guinea, Aug. 13-23.

ILO Issue
Common Design Type

1969, Nov. 24 Engr. *Perf. 13*
379 CD131 12fr org, brn vio & brn 1.60 .85

Bird Type of 1966

15fr, Friarbird. 30fr, Sacred kingfisher.

1970, Feb. 19 Photo. *Perf. 13*
Size: 22x37mm
380 A45 15fr yel grn & multi 7.00 2.75
381 A45 30fr pale salmon & multi 12.00 5.00
Nos. 380-381,C70-C71 (4) 54.00 22.00

UPU Headquarters Issue
Common Design Type

1970, May 20 Engr. *Perf. 13*
382 CD133 12fr brn, gray & dk car 2.00 1.00

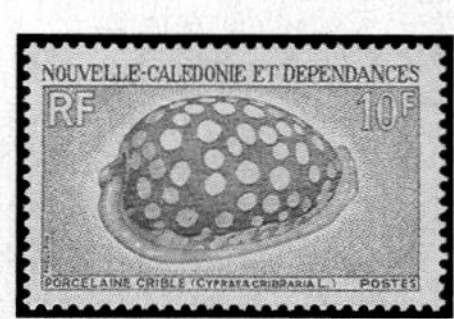

Porcelain Sieve Shell A59

Designs: 1fr, Strombus epidromis linne, vert. No. 385, Strombus variabilis swainson, vert. 21fr, Mole porcelain shell.

1970
Size: 22x36mm, 36x22mm
383 A59 1fr brt grn & multi 2.25 .50
384 A59 10fr rose & multi 5.00 1.00
385 A59 10fr blk & multi 6.50 2.00
386 A59 21fr bl grn, brn & dk brn 10.00 3.00
Nos. 383-386,C73-C76 (8) 66.75 23.00

See Nos. 395-396, C89-C90.

Packet Ship "Natal," 1883 A60

1970, July 23 Engr. *Perf. 13*
387 A60 9fr Prus bl, blk & brt grn 3.50 1.40

Issued for Stamp Day.

Dumbea Railroad Post Office A61

1971, Mar. 13 Engr. *Perf. 13*
388 A61 10fr red, slate grn & blk 4.75 1.50

Stamp Day, 1971.

Racing Yachts — A62

1971, Apr. 17 Engr. *Perf. 13*
389 A62 16fr bl, Prus bl & sl grn 5.00 3.00

Third sailing cruise from Whangarei, New Zealand, to Nouméa.

Morse Recorder, Communications Satellite — A63

1971, May 17 Engr. *Perf. 13*
390 A63 19fr red, lake & org 3.00 1.25

3rd World Telecommunications Day.

Weight Lifting — A64

1971, June 24 Engr. *Perf. 13*
391 A64 11fr shown 2.50 1.00
392 A64 23fr Basketball 3.75 1.50
Nos. 391-392,C82-C83 (4) 18.00 8.75

4th South Pacific Games, Papeete, French Polynesia, Sept. 8-19.

De Gaulle Issue
Common Design Type

Designs: 34fr, Gen. de Gaulle, 1940. 100fr, Pres. de Gaulle, 1970.

1971, Nov. 9
393 CD134 34fr dk pur & blk 8.25 3.75
394 CD134 100fr dk pur & blk 15.00 8.00

Sea Shell Type of 1970

Designs: 1fr, Scorpion conch, vert. 3fr, Common spider conch., vert.

1972, Mar. 4 Engr. *Perf. 13*
Size: 22x36mm
395 A59 1fr vio & dk brn 2.00 .70
396 A59 3fr grn & ocher 3.00 .80
Nos. 395-396,C89-C90 (4) 24.00 8.50

Carved Wooden Pillow — A66

Chamber of Commerce Emblem — A67

1972-73 Photo. *Perf. 12½x13*
397 A66 1fr Doorpost, Goa ('73) 1.25 .40
398 A66 2fr shown 1.25 .65
399 A66 5fr Monstrance 1.75 .80
400 A66 12fr Tchamba mask 4.75 1.25
Nos. 397-400,C102-C103 (6) 15.25 6.10

Objects from Nouméa Museum. Issued: 2fr-15fr, 8/5.

1972, Dec. 16
401 A67 12fr blk, yel & brt bl 1.60 .90

Junior Chamber of Commerce, 10th anniv.

Tchamba Mask — A68

Black-back Butterflyfish (Day) A69

1973, Mar. 15 Engr. *Perf. 13*
402 A68 12fr lilac 8.25 2.00
a. Booklet pane of 5 200.00

No. 402 issued in booklets only.
See No. C99.

1973, June 23 Photo. *Perf. 13x12½*
403 A69 8fr shown 2.50 1.00
404 A69 14fr same fish (night) 3.75 1.50
Nos. 403-404,C105 (3) 11.75 4.50

Nouméa Aquarium.

Emblem A70

1973, July 21 *Perf. 13*
405 A70 20fr grn, yel & vio bl 1.90 .80

School Coordinating Office, 10th anniv.

"Nature Protection" — A72

1974, June 22 Photo. *Perf. 13x12½*
406 A72 7fr multi 1.40 .55

Scorched Landscape A73

Calanthe Veratrifolia — A74

1975, Feb. 7 Photo. *Perf. 13*
407 A73 20fr multi 2.25 1.10

"Prevent brush fires."

1975, May 30 Photo. *Perf. 13*

Design: 11fr, Liperanthus gigas.

408	A74	8fr pur & multi	2.50	1.00
409	A74	11fr dk bl & multi	3.00	1.00
		Nos. 408-409,C125 (3)	13.00	4.25

Orchids. See Nos. 425-426.

Festival Emblem — A75

1975, Sept. 6 Photo. *Perf. 12½x13*

410	A75	12fr ultra, org & yel	1.10	.70

Melanesia 2000 Festival.

Birds in Flight — A76

Georges Pompidou — A77

1975, Oct. 18 Photo. *Perf. 13½x13*

411	A76	5fr ocher, yel & blk	1.10	.55

Nouméa Ornithological Society, 10th anniversary.

1975, Dec. 6 Engr. *Perf. 13*

412	A77	26fr dk grn, blk & sl	2.75	1.25

Pompidou (1911-74), president of France.

Sea Birds A78

Perf. 13x12½, 12½x13

1976, Feb. 26 Photo.

413	A78	1fr Brown booby	.90	.45
414	A78	2fr Blue-faced booby	1.40	.70
415	A78	8fr Red-footed booby, vert.	2.00	1.10
		Nos. 413-415 (3)	4.30	2.25

Festival Emblem A79

1976, Mar. 13 Litho. *Perf. 12½*

416	A79	27fr bl, org & blk	2.00	.90

Rotorua 1976, South Pacific Arts Festival, New Zealand.

Lion and Lions Emblem — A80

1976, Mar. 13 Photo. *Perf. 12½x13*

417	A80	49fr multi	4.25	2.00

Lions Club of Nouméa, 15th anniversary.

Music Pavilion — A81

Design: 30fr, Fountain, vert.

1976, July 3 Litho. *Perf. 12½*

418	A81	25fr multi	1.50	.70
419	A81	30fr blue & multi	1.75	1.00

Old Nouméa.

Polluted Shore — A82

1976, Aug. 21 Photo. *Perf. 13*

420	A82	20fr dp bl & multi	2.00	.90

Nature protection.

South Pacific People A83

1976, Oct. 23 Photo. *Perf. 13*

421	A83	20fr bl & multi	1.75	.90

16th South Pacific Commission Conference, Nouméa, Oct. 1976.

Giant Grasshopper — A84

1977, Feb. 21 Engr. *Perf. 13*

422	A84	26fr shown	1.90	1.25
423	A84	31fr Beetle and larvae	2.75	1.40

Ground Satellite Station, Nouméa — A85

1977, Apr. 16 Litho. *Perf. 13*

424	A85	29fr multi	2.10	1.10

Orchid Type of 1975

Designs: 22fr, Phajus daenikeri. 44fr, Dendrobium finetianum.

1977, May 23 Photo. *Perf. 13*

425	A74	22fr brn & multi	3.75	1.25
426	A74	44fr bl & multi	4.25	1.90

Mask, Palms, "Stamps" — A86

1977, June 25 Photo. *Perf. 13*

427	A86	35fr multi	1.75	1.00

Philately in school, Philatelic Exhibition, La Perouse Lyceum, Nouméa.

Trees A87

1977, July 23 Photo. *Perf. 13*

428	A87	20fr multi	1.50	.75

Nature protection.

Congress Emblem — A88

1977, Aug. 6 Photo. *Perf. 13*

429	A88	200fr multi	9.25	5.50

French Junior Economic Chambers Congress, Nouméa.

Young Frigate Bird — A89

22fr, Terns, horiz. 40fr, Sooty terns, horiz.

1977-78 Photo. *Perf. 13*

430	A89	16fr multi	5.75	1.00
431	A89	22fr multi	2.25	1.10
432	A89	40fr multi	3.75	1.50
		Nos. 430-432,C138 (4)	17.75	5.20

Issued: 16fr, 9/17/77; 22fr, 40fr, 2/11/78.

Mare and Foal — A90

1977, Nov. 19 Engr. *Perf. 13*

433	A90	5fr multi	1.25	.55

10th anniversary of the Society for Promotion of Caledonian Horses.

Araucaria Montana — A91

Halityle Regularis — A92

1978, Mar. 17 Photo. *Perf. 12½x13*

434	A91	16fr multi	1.25	.55

See No. C149.

1978, May 20 Photo. *Perf. 13*

436	A92	10fr vio bl & multi	1.00	.45

Nouméa Aquarium.

Stylized Turtle and Globe A93

1978, May 20

437	A93	30fr multi	3.00	1.10

Protection of the turtle.

Flying Fox — A94

1978, June 10

438	A94	20fr multi	1.75	1.00

Nature protection.

Maurice Leenhardt — A95

Soccer Player, League Emblem — A96

1978, Aug. 12 Engr. *Perf. 13*
439 A95 37fr multi 2.00 1.25

Pastor Maurice Leenhardt (1878-1954).

1978, Nov. 4 Photo. *Perf. 13*
440 A96 26fr multi 2.00 .90

New Caledonia Soccer League, 50th anniversary.

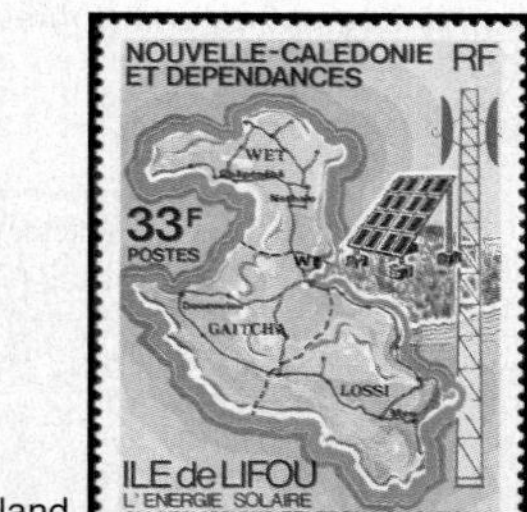

Lifu Island A97

1978, Dec. 9 Litho. *Perf. 13*
441 A97 33fr multi 1.75 .90

Petroglyph, Mère — A98

Map of Ouvea — A99

1979, Jan. 27 Engr. *Perf. 13*
442 A98 10fr brick red 1.25 .55

Perf. 12½x13, 13x12½

1979, Feb. 17 Photo.

Design: 31fr, Map of Mare Island, horiz.

443 A99 11fr multi 1.25 .55
444 A99 31fr multi 1.75 .75

House at Artillery Point — A100

1979, Apr. 28 Photo. *Perf. 13*
445 A100 20fr multi 1.40 .70

Auguste Escoffier — A101

1979, July 21 Engr. *Perf. 12½x13*
446 A101 24fr multi 1.25 .70

Auguste Escoffier Hotel School.

Regatta and Games Emblem A102

1979, Aug. 11 Photo. *Perf. 13*
447 A102 16fr multi 1.50 .70

6th South Pacific Games, Suva, Fiji, Aug. 27-Sept. 8.

Agathis Ovata A103

1979, Oct. 20 Photo. *Perf. 13x12½*
448 A103 5fr *shown* 1.00 .35
449 A103 34fr *Cyathea intermedia* 2.00 .75

Pouembout Rodeo A104

1979, Oct. 27 Engr. *Perf. 13x12½*
450 A104 12fr multi 1.25 .55

Bantamia Merleti A105

1979, Dec. 1 Photo. *Perf. 13x11½*
451 A105 23fr multi 1.50 .70

Fluorescent corals from Nouméa Aquarium.

Map of Pine Tree Island, Fishermen with Nets A106

1980, Jan. 12 Photo. *Perf. 13x12½*
452 A106 23fr multi 1.50 .45

Hibbertia Virotii A107

1980, Apr. 19 Photo. *Perf. 13x12½*
453 A107 11fr shown 1.40 .65
454 A107 12fr Grevillea meisneri 1.40 .65

Philately at School — A108

1980, May 10 Litho. *Perf. 12½*
455 A108 30fr multi 1.10 .55

Prevention of Traffic Accidents A109

1980, July 5 Photo. *Perf. 13x12½*
456 A109 15fr multi .85 .35

Parribacus Caledonicus — A110

Noumea Aquarium Crustacea: 8fr, Panulirus versicolor.

1980, Aug. 23 Litho. *Perf. 13x13½*
457 A110 5fr multi .50 .35
458 A110 8fr multi .75 .55

Solar Energy A111

1980, Oct. 11 Photo. *Perf. 13x12½*
459 A111 23fr multi 1.40 .70

Manta Birostris A112

1981, Feb. 18 Photo. *Perf. 13x12½*
460 A112 23fr shown 2.00 .90
461 A112 25fr Carcharhinus amblyrhnchos 2.00 .90

Belep Islands A113

1981, Mar. 4
462 A113 26fr multi 1.25 .55

Cypraea Stolida A114

1981, June 17 Photo. *Perf. 13*
463 A114 1fr Cymbiola rossiniana, vert. .50 .20
464 A114 2fr Connus floccatus, vert. .70 .45
465 A114 13fr shown 1.10 .70
Nos. 463-465 (3) 2.30 1.35

See Nos. 470-471.

Corvette Constantine, 1854 — A115

1981, July 22 Engr. *Perf. 13*
466 A115 10fr shown 1.25 .55
467 A115 25fr Aviso le Phoque, 1853 1.75 1.10

See Nos. 476-477.

Intl. Year of the Disabled A116

1981, Sept. 2 Litho. *Perf. 12½*
468 A116 45fr multi 1.50 .75

Nature Preservation A117

1981, Nov. 7 Photo. *Perf. 13*
469 A117 28fr multi 2.00 .90

Marine Life Type of 1981

1982, Jan. 20 Photo. *Perf. 13x13½*
470 A114 13fr Calappa calappa 1.25 .70
471 A114 25fr Etisus splendidus 1.75 1.10

Chalcantite A118

1982, Mar. 17 Photo. *Perf. 13x13½*
472 A118 15fr shown 2.25 1.10
473 A118 30fr Anorthosite 3.00 1.10

Melaleuca Quinquenervia — A119

1982, June 23 **Photo.** ***Perf. 13***

474 A119 20fr Savannah trees, vert. 1.00 .70

475 A119 29fr shown 1.25 .70

Ship Type of 1981

1982, July 7 **Engr.**

476 A115 44fr Barque Le Cher 1.75 .65

477 A115 59fr Naval dispatch vessel Kersaint 2.50 1.00

Ateou Tribe Traditional House — A120

Grey's Ptilope — A121

1982, Oct. 13 **Photo.** ***Perf. 13½x13***

478 A120 52fr multi 1.60 .90

1982, Nov. 6

479 A121 32fr shown 1.25 .70

480 A121 35fr Caledonian loriquet 2.00 .90

Central Education Coordination Office — A122

1982, Nov. 27 **Litho.** ***Perf. 13½x13***

481 A122 48fr Boat 1.75 .75

Bernheim Library, Noumea — A123

1982, Dec. 15 **Engr.** ***Perf. 13***

482 A123 36fr multi 1.10 .55

Caledonian Orchids A123a

1983, Feb. 16 **Photo.** ***Perf. 13x13½***

482A A123a 10fr Dendrobium oppositifolium .75 .35

482B A123a 15fr Dendrobium munificum 1.10 .45

482C A123a 29fr Dendrobium fractiflexum 1.75 .90

Nos. 482A-482C (3) 3.60 1.70

Xanthostemon Aurantiacum — A124

1983, Mar. 23 **Litho.** ***Perf. 13***

483 A124 1fr Crinum asiaticum .30 .20

484 A124 2fr Xanthostemon aurantiacum .30 .20

485 A124 4fr Metrosideros demonstrans, vert. .30 .20

Nos. 483-485 (3) .90 .60

25th Anniv. of Posts and Telecommunications Dept. — A125

Telephones and post offices.

1983, Apr. 30 **Litho.** ***Perf. 13***

486 A125 30fr multicolored .75 .35

487 A125 40fr multicolored .90 .45

488 A125 50fr multicolored 1.25 .55

a. Souvenir sheet of 3 11.00 10.00

b. Strip of 3, #486-488 3.75 2.00

No. 488a contains Nos. 486-488 with changed background colors.

Local Snakes A126

1983, June 22 **Photo.** ***Perf. 13***

489 A126 31fr Laticauda laticauda 1.40 .55

490 A126 33fr Laticauda colubrina 1.75 .75

A127

A128

1983, Aug. 10 **Engr.**

491 A127 16fr Volleyball .95 .55

7th South Pacific Games, Sept.

1983, Oct. 12 **Photo.** ***Perf. 12½***

492 A128 56fr multi 2.00 1.00

Nature protection.

Birds of Prey A129

1983, Nov. 16 **Litho.** ***Perf. 13***

493 A129 34fr Tyto Alba Lifuensis, vert. 1.50 .70

494 A129 37fr Pandion Haliaetus 1.90 1.00

Local Shells — A130

Arms of Noumea — A132

Steamers A131

1984, Jan. 11 **Litho. & Engr.**

495 A130 5fr Conus chenui .45 .20

496 A130 15fr Conus moluccensis .80 .55

497 A130 20fr Conus optimus 1.00 .70

Nos. 495-497 (3) 2.25 1.45

See Nos. 521-522.

1984, Feb. 8 **Engr.**

498 A131 18fr St. Joseph .90 .65

499 A131 31fr St. Antoine 1.35 .70

1984, Apr. 11 **Litho.** ***Perf. 12½x13***

500 A132 35fr multi 1.10 .50

See No. 546, 607, C214.

Environmental Preservation — A133

1984, May 23 ***Perf. 13***

501 A133 65fr Island scene 2.00 .80

Orchids — A134

1984, July 18 **Litho.** ***Perf. 12***

502 A134 16fr Diplocaulobium ou-hinnae 1.25 .55

503 A134 38fr Acianthus atepalus 1.75 1.10

Cent. of Public Schooling A135

Kagu — A137

1984, Oct. 11 **Litho.** ***Perf. 13½x13***

504 A135 59fr Schoolhouse 1.75 .70

1985-86 **Engr.** ***Perf. 13***

511 A137 1fr brt bl .20 .20

512 A137 2fr green .20 .20

513 A137 3fr brt org .20 .20

514 A137 4fr brt grn .20 .20

515 A137 5fr dp rose lil .20 .20

516 A137 35fr crimson 1.25 .35

517 A137 38fr vermilion 1.25 .55

518 A137 40fr brt rose ('86) 1.00 .55

Nos. 511-518 (8) 4.50 2.45

Issued: 1, 2, 5, 38fr, 5/22; 3, 4, 35fr, 2/13; 40fr, 7/30.

See types A179, A179a.

Sea Shell Type of 1984

Lithographed and Engraved

1985, Feb. 27 ***Perf. 13***

521 A130 55fr Conus bullatus 1.50 .90

522 A130 72fr Conus lamberti 2.00 1.40

25th World Meteorological Day — A138

1985, Mar. 20 **Litho.**

523 A138 17fr Radio communication, storm .65 .35

Red Cross, Medicine Without Frontiers — A139

1985, Apr. 10 ***Perf. 12½***

524 A139 41fr multi 1.00 .55

Telephone Switching Center Inauguration — A140

1985, Apr. 24

525 A140 70fr E 10 B installation 1.75 .90

Marguerite La Foa Suspension Bridge A141

1985, May 10 **Engr.** ***Perf. 13***

526 A141 44fr brt bl & red brn 1.25 .70

Historical Preservation Association.

Le Cagou Philatelic Society — A142

1985, June 15 **Litho.**

527 A142 220fr multi 5.00 3.25
a. Souvenir sheet, perf. 12½ 6.50 5.50

No. 527a sold for 230fr.

4th Pacific Arts Festival — A143

1985, July 3 ***Perf. 13½***

Black Overprint

528 A143 55fr multi 1.40 1.00
529 A143 75fr multi 2.00 1.25

Not issued without overprint. Festival was transferred to French Polynesia.

Intl. Youth Year — A144

1985, July 24 **Litho.** ***Perf. 13***

530 A144 59fr multi 1.75 .80

Amedee Lighthouse Electrification — A145

1985, Aug. 13

531 A145 89fr multi 2.25 1.10

Environmental Conservation A146

1985, Sept. 18

532 A146 100fr Planting trees 2.50 1.10

Birds A147

1985, Dec. 18 ***Perf. 12½***

533 A147 50fr Poule sultane 1.25 .80
534 A147 60fr Merle caledonien 1.75 1.00

Noumea Aquarium A148

1986, Feb. 19 **Litho.** ***Perf. 12½x13***

535 A148 10fr Pomacanthus imperator .45 .20
536 A148 17fr Rhinopias aphanes .65 .35

Kanumera Bay, Isle of Pines — A149

1986, Mar. 26 **Litho.** ***Perf. 12½***

537 A149 50fr shown 1.10 .55
538 A149 55fr Inland village 1.40 .80

See Nos. 547-548, 617-618.

Geckos A150

1986, Apr. 16 ***Perf. 12½x13***

539 A150 20fr Bavayia sauvagii .65 .45
540 A150 45fr Rhacodactylus leachianus 1.40 .80

1986 World Cup Soccer Championships, Mexico — A151

1986, May 28 ***Perf. 13***

541 A151 60fr multi 1.50 1.00

1st Pharmacy in New Caledonia, 120th Anniv. — A152

1986, June 25 **Litho.** ***Perf. 13***

542 A152 80fr multi 1.75 1.10

Orchids A153

1986, July 16 ***Perf. 12½x13***

543 A153 44fr Coelogynae licastioides 1.40 .80
544 A153 58fr Calanthe langei 1.75 .90

STAMPEX '86, Adelaide — A154

1986, Aug. 4 ***Perf. 12½***

545 A154 110fr Bird 2.75 1.40

Arms Type of 1984

1986, Oct. 11 **Litho.** ***Perf. 13½***

546 A132 94fr Mont Dore 3.00 1.10

Landscape Type of 1986

1986, Oct. 29 **Litho.** ***Perf. 12½***

547 A149 40fr West landscape, vert. .90 .70
548 A149 76fr South Landscape 1.60 .80

Flowers A156

Niponthes vieillardi, Syzygium ngayense, Archidendropsis Paivana, Scavola balansae.

1986, Nov. 12 ***Perf. 12½***

549 A156 73fr multi 1.75 .90

Nature Protection Assoc.

A157

A159

A158

1986, Nov. 26 ***Perf. 13x12½***

550 A157 350fr Emblem 7.50 4.25

Noumea Lions Club, 25th anniv.

1986, Dec. 23 **Litho.** ***Perf. 13***

Paintings: 74fr, Moret Point, by A. Sisley. 140fr, Butterfly Chase, by B. Morisot.

551 A158 74fr multi 2.25 1.40
552 A158 140fr multi 4.00 1.60

1987, Jan. 28 ***Perf. 13½***

553 A159 30fr Challenge France 1.00 .55
554 A159 70fr French Kiss 2.00 1.10

America's Cup.

Plants, Butterflies A160

46fr, Anona squamosa, Graphium gelon. 54fr, Albizzia granulosa, Polyura gamma.

1987, Feb. 25 **Litho.** ***Perf. 13x12½***

555 A160 46fr multi 1.75 .80
556 A160 54fr multi 2.00 .90

Pirogues A161

1987, May 13 **Engr.** ***Perf. 13x12½***

557 A161 72fr from Isle of Pines 1.75 1.00
558 A161 90fr from Ouvea 2.25 1.25

New Town Hall, Mont Dore A162

1987, May 23 **Litho.** ***Perf. 12½x13***

559 A162 92fr multi 2.10 1.00

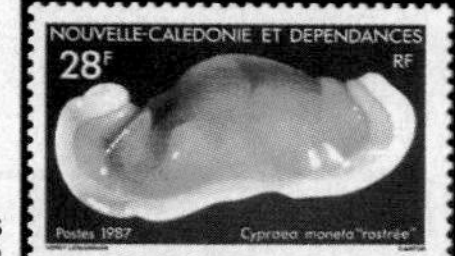

Seashells A163

1987, June 24 ***Perf. 13***

560 A163 28fr Cypraea moneta .75 .45
561 A163 36fr Cypraea martini 1.25 .70

A164

A165

1987, July 8 ***Perf. 12½x13***

562 A164 40fr multi 1.00 .55

8th South Pacific Games.

1987, July 22 ***Perf. 13½***

563 A165 270fr multi 5.75 2.75

Soroptimist Int'l. 13th Convention, Melbourne, July 26-31.

Birds A166

1987, Aug. 26 *Perf. 13*

564	A166	18fr Zosterops xanthochroa	.90	.35
565	A166	21fr Falco peregrinus nesiotes, vert.	1.10	.35

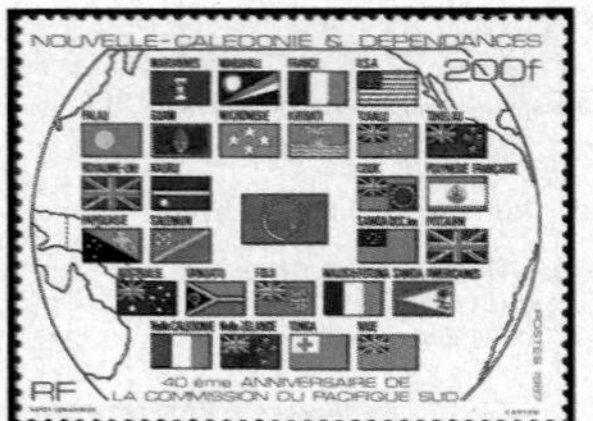

South Pacific Commission, 40th Anniv. — A167

1987, Oct. 14 **Litho.** *Perf. 13*

566	A167	200fr multi	5.00	2.50

Philately at School A168

1987, Oct. 21 *Perf. 12½*

567	A168	15fr multi	.50	.35

8th South Pacific Games, Noumea — A169

1987, Dec. 8 **Litho.** *Perf. 12½*

568	A169	20fr Golf	.55	.35
569	A169	30fr Rugby	9.00	1.00
570	A169	100fr Long jump	2.75	1.40
		Nos. 568-570 (3)	12.30	2.75

Map, Ships, La Perouse — A170

1988, Feb. 10 **Engr.** *Perf. 13*

571	A170	36fr dark rose lil	1.40	.55

Disappearance of La Perouse expedition, 200th anniv., and Jean-Francois de Galaup (1741-1788), Comte de La Perouse.

French University of the South Pacific at Noumea and Papeete A171

1988, Feb. 24 **Litho.** *Perf. 13x12½*

572	A171	400fr multi	9.25	4.25

Tropical Fish A172

1988, Mar. 23 **Litho.** *Perf. 13*

573	A172	30fr Pomacanthus semicirculatus	1.10	.55
574	A172	46fr Glyphidodontops cyaneus	1.50	.80

Intl. Red Cross and Red Crescent Organizations, 125th Annivs. — A173

1988, Apr. 27

575	A173	300fr multi	7.50	3.75

Regional Housing A174

Designs: 19fr, Mwaringou, Canala Region, vert. 21fr, Nathalo, Lifou.

1988, Apr. 13 **Engr.** *Perf. 13*

576	A174	19fr emer grn, brt blue & red brn	.45	.20
577	A174	21fr brt blue, emer grn & red brn	.70	.20

Medicinal Plants A175

1988, May 18 **Litho.** *Perf. 13x12½*

578	A175	28fr *Ochrosia elliptica*	.90	.55
579	A175	64fr *Rauvolfia levenetii*	1.90	1.10

No. 579 is airmail.

Living Fossils — A176

1988, June 11 *Perf. 13*

580	A176	51fr *Gymnocrinus richeri*	2.25	.90

Bourail Museum and Historical Soc. — A177

1988, June 25 **Litho.** *Perf. 13*

581	A177	120fr multi	3.00	1.60

SYDPEX '88 — A178

Designs: No. 582, La Perouse aboard *La Boussole*, gazing through spyglass at the First Fleet in Botany Bay, Jan. 24, 1788. No. 583, Capt. Phillip and crew ashore on Botany Bay watching the approach of La Perouse's ships *La Boussole* and *L'Astrolabe*.

1988, July 30 **Litho.** *Perf. 13x12½*

582	A178	42fr multi	1.50	.90
583	A178	42fr multi	1.50	.90
a.		Souvenir sheet of 2, #582-583, perf. 13x13½	4.25	3.75
b.		Strip of 2, #582-583 + label	3.25	2.75

No. 583a sold for 120fr.

Kagu

A179 A179a

1988-90 **Engr.** *Perf. 13*

584	A179	1fr bright blue	.50	.20
585	A179	2fr green	.50	.20
586	A179	3fr bright orange	.75	.20
587	A179	4fr bright green	.75	.20
588	A179	5fr deep rose lilac	1.00	.20
589	A179	28fr orange	1.00	.20
590	A179	40fr bright rose	1.10	.20
		Nos. 584-590 (7)	5.60	1.40

Issued: 40fr, 8/10/88; 1fr, 4fr, 1/25/89; 2fr, 3fr, 5fr, 4/19/89; 28fr, 1/15/90.

See Type A137.

1990-93 **Engr.** *Perf. 13*

591	A179a	1fr bright blue	.25	.20
592	A179a	2fr bright green	.25	.20
593	A179a	3fr brt yel org	.30	.20
594	A179a	4fr dark green	.30	.20
595	A179a	5fr bright violet	.30	.20
596	A179a	9fr blue black	.35	.20
597	A179a	12fr orange	.40	.20
598	A179a	40fr lilac rose	1.00	.20
599	A179a	50fr red	1.40	.30
		Nos. 591-599 (9)	4.55	1.90

Issued: 50fr, 9/5/90; 1fr-5fr, 1/9/91; 40fr, 1/15/92; 9fr, 12fr, 1/25/93.

See Type A137 and Nos. 675, 683. For surcharge see No. 685.

1988 Summer Olympics, Seoul — A180

1988, Sept. 14 *Perf. 12½x12*

600	A180	150fr multi	3.75	2.00

Pasteur Institute, Noumea, Cent. A181

1988, Sept. 28 **Engr.** *Perf. 13*

601	A181	100fr blk, brt ultra & dark red	2.75	1.40

Writers — A182

1988, Oct. 15 **Engr.** *Perf. 13*

602	A182	72fr Georges Baudoux (1870-1949)	1.60	.90
603	A182	73fr Jean Mariotti (1901-1975)	1.60	.90

No. 603 is airmail.

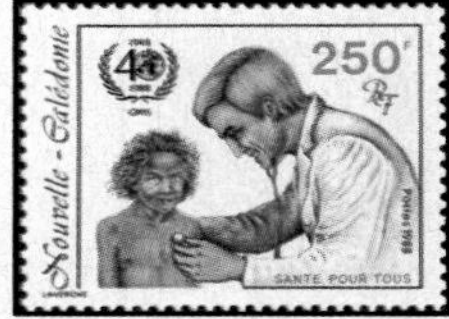

WHO, 40th Anniv. A183

1988, Nov. 16 **Litho.** *Perf. 13x12½*

604	A183	250fr multi	6.00	2.75

Art Type of 1984 Without "ET DEPENDANCES"

Paintings by artists of the Pacific: 54fr, *Land of Men*, by L. Bunckley. 92fr, *The Latin Quarter*, by Marik.

1988, Dec. 7

605	AP113	54fr multi	2.25	1.00
606	AP113	92fr multi	3.00	1.40

Arms Type of 1984 Without "ET DEPENDANCES"

1989, Feb. 22 **Litho.** *Perf. 13½*

607	A132	200fr Koumac	4.00	2.00

Indigenous Flora A184

1989, Mar. 22 **Litho.** *Perf. 13½*

608	A184	80fr *Parasitaxus ustus*, vert.	2.00	1.10
609	A184	90fr *Tristaniopsis guillainii*	2.50	1.40

Marine Life A185

1989, May 17 **Litho.** *Perf. 12½x13*

610	A185	18fr *Plesionika*	.55	.35
611	A185	66fr *Ocosia apia*	1.50	1.00
612	A185	110fr *Latiaxis*	2.75	1.60
		Nos. 610-612 (3)	4.80	2.95

See Nos. 652-653.

French Revolution, Bicent. — A186

1989, July 7 Litho. *Perf. 13½*

613 A186 40fr Liberty 2.75 .85
614 A186 58fr Equality 2.75 1.25
615 A186 76fr Fraternity 2.75 1.40
Nos. 613-615 (3) 8.25 3.50

Souvenir Sheet

616 A186 180fr Liberty, Equality, Fraternity 5.50 5.50

Nos. 614-616 are airmail.

Landscape Type of 1986 Without "ET DEPENDANCES"

1989, Aug. 23 Litho. *Perf. 13*

617 A149 64fr La Poule rookery, Hienghene 1.50 .75
618 A149 180fr Ouaieme ferry 4.00 1.60

No. 617 is airmail.

A187

A188

Litho. & Engr.

1989, Sept. 27 *Perf. 12½x13*

619 A187 70fr Carved bamboo 1.75 .70

See No. C216.

1989, Oct. 25 Litho. *Perf. 13*

620 A188 350fr multicolored 8.00 3.50

Hobie-Cat 14 10th World Championships, Nov. 3, Noumea.

Natl. Historical Soc., 20th Anniv. — A189

Cover of *Moeurs: Superstitions of New Caledonians,* cover of book on Melanesian oral literature and historians G. Pisier, R.P. Neyret and A. Surleau.

1989, Nov. 3 Engr.

621 A189 74fr brown & black 2.00 .80

Ft. Teremba — A190

1989, Nov. 18 Engr.

622 A190 100fr bl grn & dk org 2.50 1.40

Marguerite Historical Preservation Soc.

Impressionist Paintings — A191

Designs: 130fr, *The Escape of Rochefort,* by Manet. 270fr, *Self-portrait,* by Courbet.

1989, Dec. 6 Litho. *Perf. 13½*

623 A191 130fr multicolored 3.25 1.90
624 A191 270fr multicolored 7.50 4.00

Fr. Patrick O'Reilly (1900-1988), Writer — A192

1990, Jan. 24 Engr. *Perf. 13x13½*

625 A192 170fr blk & plum 4.75 1.90

Grasses and Butterflies A193

Various *Cyperacea costularia* and *Paratisiphone lyrnessa:* 18fr, Female. 50fr, Female, diff. 94fr, Male.

1990, Feb. 21 Litho. *Perf. 13½*

626 A193 18fr shown .60 .40
627 A193 50fr multicolored 1.50 .70
628 A193 94fr multicolored 2.10 1.25
Nos. 626-628 (3) 4.20 2.35

Nos. 626 and 628 are airmail.

A194

A195

1990, Mar. 16 Engr. *Perf. 12½x13*

629 A194 85fr Kanakan money 1.90 .80
630 A194 140fr money, diff. 3.00 1.40

1990, Mar. 16 Litho. *Perf. 13x13½*

631 A195 230fr multicolored 6.25 2.75

Jade and mother of pearl exhibition, New Caledonian Museum.

Noumea Aquarium A196

1990, Apr. 25 *Perf. 13x12½, 12½x13*

632 A196 10fr *Phyllidia ocellata* .35 .20
633 A196 42fr *Chromodoris kuniei,* vert. 1.25 .70

Petroglyphs A197

1990, July 11 Engr. *Perf. 13*

634 A197 40fr Neounda 1.10 .55
635 A197 58fr Kassducou 1.60 .90

No. 635 is airmail.

Meeting Center of the Pacific — A198

1990, July 25 Litho. *Perf. 13*

636 A198 320fr multicolored 6.50 3.00

World Cup Soccer Championships, Italy — A199

1990, May 30 Litho. *Perf. 13*

637 A199 240fr multicolored 6.00 3.00

Flowers A200

1990, Nov. 7 *Perf. 13x12½*

638 A200 105fr Gardenia aubryi 2.50 1.25
639 A200 130fr Hibbertia baudouinii 3.00 2.00

La Maison Celieres by M. Petron A201

365fr, Le Mont-Dore de Jade by C. Degroiselle.

1990, Dec. 5 *Perf. 12½*

640 A201 110fr multicolored 3.00 1.50
641 A201 365fr multicolored 9.50 4.25

No. 640 is airmail.

Writers — A202

Designs: #642, Louise Michel (1830-1905). #643, Charles B. Nething (1867-1947).

1991, Mar. 20 Engr. *Perf. 13*

642 A202 125fr rose lil & bl 2.50 1.50
643 A202 125fr brn & bl 2.50 1.50
a. Pair, #642-643 + label 5.75 5.50

Native Huts — A203

1991, May 15 Litho. *Perf. 12*

644 A203 12fr Houailou .25 .20
645 A203 35fr Hienghene 1.00 .50

Maps of the Provinces A204

1991, June 17 Litho. *Perf. 13½*

646 A204 45fr Northern 1.00 .45
647 A204 45fr Island 1.00 .45
648 A204 45fr Southern 1.00 .45
a. Strip of 3, #646-648 3.50 3.25

Orchids — A205

1991, July 24 Litho. *Perf. 13*

649 A205 55fr Dendrobium biflorum 1.40 .80
650 A205 70fr Dendrobium closterium 2.00 1.00

French Institute of Scientific Research — A206

1991, Aug. 26

651 A206 170fr multicolored 3.75 1.75

Marine Life Type of 1989

1991, Aug. 26 Litho. *Perf. 12*

652 A185 60fr Monocentris japonicus 1.50 .80
653 A185 100fr Tristigenys niphonia 2.50 1.10

9th South Pacific Games, Papua New Guinea
A207

1991, Sept. 6 *Perf. 12½*

654 A207 170fr multicolored 3.75 1.75

Vietnamese in New Caledonia, Cent. — A208

1991, Sept. 8 **Engr.** *Perf. 13x12½*

655 A208 300fr multicolored 7.50 2.75

Lions Club of New Caledonia, 30th Anniv. — A209

1991, Oct. 5 **Litho.** *Perf. 12½*

656 A209 192fr multicolored 5.25 2.75

First Commercial Harvesting of Sandalwood, 150th Anniv. — A210

1991, Oct. 23 **Engr.** *Perf. 13*

657 A210 200fr multicolored 5.25 2.75

Phila Nippon '91 — A211

Plants and butterflies: 8fr, Phillantus, Eurema hecabe. 15fr, Pipturus incanus, Hypolimnas octocula. 20fr, Stachytarpheta urticaefolia, Precis villida. 26fr, Malaisia scandens, Cyrestis telamon.

Butterflies: No. 662a, Cyrestis telamon, vert. b, Hypolimnas octocula, vert. c, Eurema hecabe, vert. d, Precis villida, vert.

1991, Nov. 16 **Litho.** *Perf. 12½*

658	A211	8fr multicolored	.20	.20
659	A211	15fr multicolored	.35	.35
660	A211	20fr multicolored	.45	.35
661	A211	26fr multicolored	.70	.45
a.		Strip of 4, #658-661 + label	2.75	2.50

Souvenir Sheet

662 A211 75fr Sheet of 4, #a.-d. 10.00 10.00

Central Bank for Economic Cooperation, 50th Anniv. — A212

Designs: No. 663, Nickel processing plant, dam. No. 664, Private home, tourist hotels.

1991, Dec. 2 **Litho.** *Perf. 13*

663	A212	76fr multicolored	3.00	1.25
664	A212	76fr multicolored	3.00	1.25
a.		Pair, #663-664 + label	7.00	7.00

Preservation of Nature — A213

1992, Mar. 25 **Litho.** *Perf. 13*

665 A213 15fr Madeleine waterfalls .75 .25

a. Souv. sheet, perf. 12½ 4.00 4.00

No. 665a sold for 150fr.

Immigration of First Japanese to New Caledonia, Cent.
A214

1992, June 11 **Litho.** *Perf. 13x12½*

666	A214	95fr yellow & multi	2.50	1.25
667	A214	95fr gray & multi	2.50	1.25
a.		Pair, #666-667 + label	6.25	6.25

Arrival of American Armed Forces, 50th Anniv. — A215

1992, Aug. 13

668 A215 50fr multicolored 1.50 .60

Lagoon Protection — A216

1993, Feb. 23 **Litho.** *Perf. 13*

669 A216 120fr multicolored 3.50 1.40

Kagu Type of 1990

1993-94 **Engr.** *Perf. 13*

675	A179a	55fr red	1.50	.20
676	A179a	(60fr) claret	1.50	.35

Self-Adhesive

Litho.

Die Cut Perf. 10

681	A179a	5fr bright lilac	.50	.20
a.		Bklt. pane, 8+8, gutter btwn.	8.00	
683	A179a	55fr red	2.00	.70
a.		Bklt. pane, 8+8, gutter btwn.	32.50	

Issued: Nos. 675, 683, 4/7/93; No. 676, 1/27/94; No. 681, 2/94.

No. 676 sold for 60fr on day of issue.

By their nature, Nos. 681a, 683a are complete booklets. The peelable paper backing serves as a booklet cover.

This is an expanding set. Numbers may change.

No. 599 Surcharged

1993 **Engr.** *Perf. 13*

685 A179a 55fr on 50fr red 1.40 .70

Philately in School — A217

1993, Apr. 7 **Litho.** *Perf. 13½*

686 A217 25fr multicolored .75 .30

For overprint see No. 690.

Miniature Sheet of 13

Town Coats of Arms
A218

Designs: a, Bourail. b, Noumea. c, Canala. d, Kone. e, Paita. f, Dumbea. g, Koumac. h, Ponerhouen. i, Kaamoo Hyehen. j, Mont Dore. k, Thio. l, Kaala-Gomen. m, Touho.

1993, Dec. 10 **Litho.** *Perf. 13½*

687 A218 70fr #a.-m., + 2 labels 40.00 27.50

Souvenir Sheet

Hong Kong '94 — A219

Wildlife: a, Panda. b, Kagu.

1994, Feb. 18 **Litho.** *Perf. 13*

688 A219 105fr Sheet of 2, #a.-b. 8.25 8.25

First Postal Delivery Route, 50th Anniv. — A220

1994, Apr. 28 **Engr.** *Perf. 13*

689 A220 15fr multicolored .50 .25

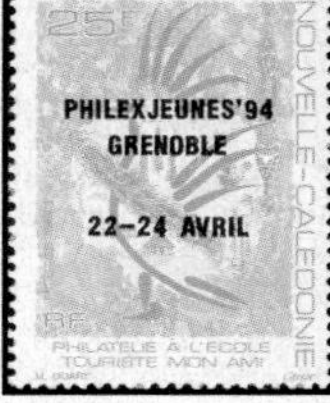

No. 686 Ovptd. in Blue

1994, Apr. 22 **Litho.** *Perf. 13½*

690 A217 25fr multicolored .70 .35

Headquarters of New Caledonian Post Office — A222

1994, June 25 **Litho.** *Perf. 13½x13*

691		Strip of 4, #a.-d.	8.00	8.00
a.	A222	30fr 1859	.75	.45
b.	A222	60fr 1936	1.50	.80
c.	A222	90fr 1967	2.10	1.40
d.	A222	120fr 1993	3.00	1.75

Pacific Sculpture — A223

Chambeyronia Macrocarpa
A224

1994, June 25 **Litho.** *Perf. 13x13½*

693 A223 60fr multicolored 1.50 .70

1994, July 7 **Litho.** *Perf. 13x13½*

694 A224 90fr multicolored 2.25 1.10

No. J46 Overprinted With Bar Over "Timbre Taxe"

1994, Aug. 8 **Litho.** *Perf. 13*

696 D5 5fr multicolored 13.50 3.25

Stag
A227

1994, Aug. 14 **Litho.** *Perf. 13½*

697 A227 150fr multicolored 3.50 1.60

Jacques Nervat, Writer — A228

1994, Sept. 15 ***Perf. 13x13½***
698 A228 175fr multicolored 4.00 1.90

Frigate Nivose A229

No. 699, 30fr, Ship at sea. No. 700, 30fr, Ship along shore. No. 701, 30fr, Ship docked. No. 702, 60fr, Painting of frigate, map of island, ship's crest. No. 703, 60fr, Ship's bell. No. 704, 60fr, Sailor looking at ship.

1994, Oct. 7 **Litho.** ***Perf. 13½***

Booklet Stamps

699	A229 30fr multicolored	1.25	.45
700	A229 30fr multicolored	1.25	.45
701	A229 30fr multicolored	1.25	.35
702	A229 60fr multicolored	2.00	.80
703	A229 60fr multicolored	2.00	.80
704	A229 60fr multicolored	2.00	.80
a.	Booklet pane, #699-704	11.00	
	Booklet, 4 #704a	55.00	

Philately at School A230

1994, Nov. 4 **Litho.** ***Perf. 13½***
705 A230 30fr multicolored .75 .35

For overprint see No. 749

Christmas A231

Top of bell starts below: a, Second "o." b, Third "e." c, "a." d, "C." e, Second "e."

1994, Dec. 17
706 Strip of 5 5.00 5.00
a.-e. A231 30fr Any single .85 .55

Nos. 706a-706e differ in location of the red ball, yellow bell and statue. No.706 is designed for stereoscopic viewing.

Le Monde Newspaper, 50th Anniv. — A232

1994, Dec. 17
707 A232 90fr multicolored 2.50 1.60

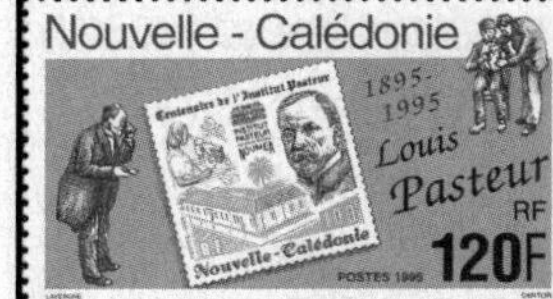

Louis Pasteur (1822-95) — A233

1995, Feb. 13 **Litho.** ***Perf. 13***
708 A233 120fr No. 601 2.75 1.40

Charles de Gaulle (1890-1970) — A234

Litho. & Embossed

1995, Mar. 28 ***Perf. 13***
709 A234 1000fr blue & gold 22.50 16.00

Teacher's Training College for the French Territories in the Pacific — A235

1995, Apr. 24 **Litho.** ***Perf. 13***
710 A235 100fr multicolored 2.25 1.25

Sylviornis Neo-Caledonia, Fossil Bird — A236

1995, May 16 **Litho.** ***Perf. 13x13½***
711 A236 60fr multicolored 1.75 .70

10th Sunshine Triathlon — A237

1995, May 26 **Engr.** ***Perf. 13x12½***
712 A237 60fr multicolored 1.50 .90

Creation of the CFP Franc, 1945 A238

Top of tree at left points to: a, Second "e." b, Second "l." c, First "l." d, First "e."

1995, June 8 **Litho.** ***Perf. 13x13½***
713 A238 10fr Strip of 4, #a.-d. 1.25 1.25

Nos. 713a-713d show coin rotating clockwise with trees, hut at different locations. No. 713 is designed for stereoscopic viewing.

1st New Caledonian Deputy in French Natl. Assembly, 50th Anniv. A239

1995, June 8 ***Perf. 13½***
714 A239 60fr multicolored 1.50 .70

End of World War II, 50th Anniv. A240

1995, June 8 ***Perf. 13x13½***
715 A240 90fr multicolored 2.00 1.10

UN, 50th Anniv. A241

1995, June 8
716 A241 90fr multicolored 2.00 1.10

Sebertia Acuminata A242

1995, July 28 **Litho.** ***Perf. 13x13½***
717 A242 60fr multicolored 1.75 .80

Singapore '95 — A243

Sea birds: 5fr, Anous stolidus. 10fr, Larus novaehollandiae. 20fr, Sterna dougallii. 35fr, Pandion haliaetus. 65fr, Sula sula. 125fr, Fregata minor.

1995, Aug. 24 **Litho.** ***Perf. 13x13½***

718	A243 5fr multicolored	.20	.20
719	A243 10fr multicolored	.25	.20
720	A243 20fr multicolored	.45	.20
721	A243 35fr multicolored	.90	.55
722	A243 65fr multicolored	1.60	1.10
723	A243 125fr multicolored	3.25	1.60
a.	Souvenir sheet, #718-723 + label	7.50	7.50
	Nos. 718-723 (6)	6.65	3.85

10th South Pacific Games A244

1995, Aug. 24
724 A244 90fr multicolored 2.50 1.25

Sculpture, The Lizard Man, by Dick Bone — A248

1995, Oct. 25 **Litho.** ***Perf. 13***
730 A248 65fr multicolored 1.60 .90

Gargariscus Prionocephalus — A249

1995, Dec. 15 **Litho.** ***Perf. 13***
731 A249 100fr multicolored 2.50 1.25

Francis Carco (1886-1958), Poet & Novelist — A250

1995, Nov. 15 **Litho.** ***Perf. 13x13½***
732 A250 95fr multicolored 2.25 1.25

Ancient Pottery — A251

1996, Apr. 12 **Litho.** ***Perf. 13***
733 A251 65fr multicolored 1.60 .90

Endemic Rubiaceous Plants — A252

Designs: 65fr, Captaincookia margaretae. 95fr, Ixora cauliflora.

1996, Apr. 17
734 A252 65fr multicolored 1.50 .80
735 A252 95fr multicolored 2.25 1.10

7th VA'A (Outrigger Canoe) World Championship, Noumea, New Caledonia — A253

Designs: a, 30fr, Islander standing on shore with early version of canoe. b, 65fr, Early single-hull canoe with islanders. c, 95fr, Early catamaran, people rowing. d, 125fr, Modern racing canoe.

1996, May 10 Litho. *Perf. 13*
736 A253 Strip of 4, #a.-d. 7.50 7.50

No. 736 is a continuous design.

CHINA '96 — A254

Marine life: 25fr, Halieutaea stellata. 40fr, Perotrochus deforgesi. 65fr, Mursia musorstomia. 125fr, Metacrinus levii.

1996, May 18

737	A254	25fr multicolored	.55	.35
738	A254	40fr multicolored	.85	.65
739	A254	65fr multicolored	1.50	.90
740	A254	125fr multicolored	2.75	1.60
		Nos. 737-740 (4)	5.65	3.50

Nos. 737-740 were each issued in sheets of 10 + 5 labels.

On Nos. 737-740 portions of the design were applied by a thermographic process producing a shiny, raised effect.

737a	Booklet pane of 6	5.00
738a	Booklet pane of 6	6.50
739a	Booklet pane of 6	12.50
740a	Booklet pane of 6	25.00
	Complete booklet, #737a-740a	49.00

CAPEX '96 — A255

Orchids: 5fr, Sarcochilus koghiensis. 10fr, Phaius robertsii. 25fr, Megastylis montana. 65fr, Dendrobium macrophyllum. 95fr, Dendrobium virotii. 125fr, Ephemerantha comata.

1996, June 25 Litho. *Perf. 13*

741	A255	5fr multicolored	.35	.20
742	A255	10fr multicolored	.35	.20
743	A255	25fr multicolored	.75	.35
744	A255	65fr multicolored	1.50	.65
745	A255	95fr multicolored	2.50	1.00
746	A255	125fr multicolored	2.50	1.25
a.		Booklet pane of 6, #741-746	7.75	
		Souvenir booklet, 4 #746a	38.00	
		Nos. 741-746 (6)	7.95	3.65

Nos. 741-746 were each issued in sheets of 10 + 5 labels.

No. 705 Ovptd. with UNICEF Emblem in Blue

1996, Sept. 12 Litho. *Perf. 13½*
749 A230 30fr multicolored .85 .45

UNICEF, 50th anniv.

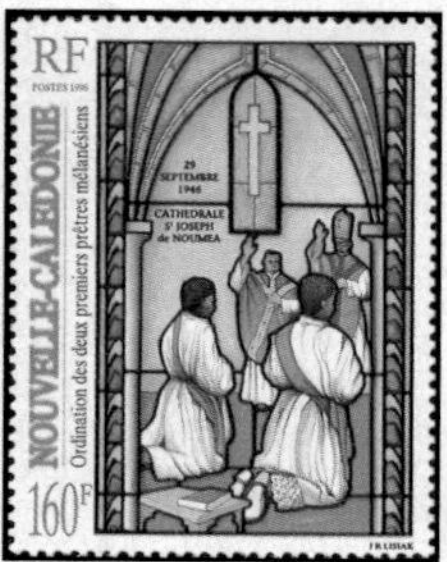

Ordination of the First Melanesian Priests A258

1996, Oct. 9 Litho. *Perf. 13*
750 A258 160fr multicolored 3.50 1.90

Portions of the design on No. 750 were applied by a thermographic process producing a shiny, raised effect.

7th Festival of South Pacific Arts A259

Designs: 100fr, Dancer, face carving. 105fr, Wood carvings of women. 200fr, Painting by Paula Boi. 500fr, Gaica Dance, Lifou.

1996, Oct. 9

751	A259	100fr multicolored	2.25	1.25
752	A259	105fr multicolored	2.25	1.25
753	A259	200fr multicolored	4.50	2.25
754	A259	500fr multicolored	11.00	5.75
		Nos. 751-754 (4)	20.00	10.50

No. 751 is airmail.

French Pres. Francois Mitterrand (1916-96) — A260

1997, Mar. 14 Litho. *Perf. 13*
755 A260 1000fr multicolored 20.00 11.25

Alphonse Daudet (1840-97), Writer — A261

Designs: No. 756, "Letters from a Windmill." No. 757, "Le Petit Chose." No. 758, "Tartarin of Tarascon." No. 759, Daudet writing.

1997, May 14 *Perf. 13*

756	A261	65fr multicolored	1.50	1.50
757	A261	65fr multicolored	1.50	1.50
758	A261	65fr multicolored	1.50	1.50
759	A261	65fr multicolored	1.50	1.50
a.		Souvenir sheet, #756-759	6.50	6.50

Henri La Fleur, First Senator of New Caledonia — A262

1997, June 12 Litho. *Perf. 13*
760 A262 105fr multicolored 2.40 1.25

Insects A263

Designs: a, Tectocoris diophthalmus. b, Kanakia gigas. c, Aenetus cohici.

1997, June 25 Litho. *Perf. 13x12½*
761 A263 65fr Strip of 3, #a.-c. 5.00 4.50

Jacques Iekawe (1946-92), First Melanesian Prefect — A264

1997, July 23 Litho. *Perf. 13*
762 A264 250fr multicolored 5.50 2.50

Kagu — A265

1997, Aug. 13 Engr. *Perf. 13*
763 A265 95fr blue 2.25 .35

See Nos. 772-773A, 878-879.

Horse Racing A266

1997, Sept. 20 Litho. *Perf. 13*

764	A266	65fr Harness racing	1.75	.80
765	A266	65fr Thoroughbred racing	1.75	.80

Early Engraving of "View of Port de France" (Noumea) — A267

Photo. & Engr.

1997, Sept. 22 *Perf. 13x12½*
766 A267 95fr multicolored 2.25 1.25

See No. 802.

A268

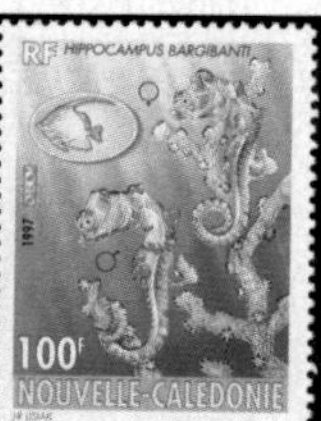

A269

1997, Sept. 22 Litho. *Perf. 13*
767 A268 150fr multicolored 3.00 1.75

First Melanesian election, 50th anniv.

1997, Nov. 3 Litho. *Perf. 13½x13*
768 A269 100fr Hippocampus Bargibanti 4.50 1.50

5th World Conf. on Fish of the Indo-Pacific. Issued in sheets of 10+5 labels.

South Pacific Arts A270

Designs: a, Doka wood carvings. b, Beizam dance mask. c, Abstract painting of primative life by Yvette Bouquet.

1997, Nov. 3 *Perf. 13*
769 A270 100fr Strip of 3, #a.-c. 7.50 6.50

Christmas A271

Designs: 95fr, Santa on surfboard pulled by dolphins. 100fr, Dolphin with banner in mouth.

1997, Nov. 17

770	A271	95fr multicolored	4.00	1.00
771	A271	100fr multicolored	4.00	1.00

Nos. 770-771 issued in sheets of 10+5 labels.

Kagu Type of 1997

1997-98 Engr. *Perf. 13*

772	A265	30fr orange	1.00	.35
773	A265	(70fr) red	2.00	.35

Self-Adhesive

773A	A265	(70fr) red	2.00	.45
b.		Booklet pane of 10	22.50	

The peelable paper backing of No. 773A serves as a booklet cover.

Issued: 30fr, 1997; (70fr), 1/2/98.

A272

A273

Mushrooms: #774, Lentinus tuber-regium. #775, Volvaria bombycina. #776, Morchella anteridiformis.

1998, Jan. 22 Litho. *Perf. 13*

774	A272	70fr multicolored	1.75	.80
775	A272	70fr multicolored	1.75	.80
776	A272	70fr multicolored	1.75	.80
		Nos. 774-776 (3)	5.25	2.40

1998, Mar. 17 Litho. *Perf. 13*

Artifacts from Territorial Museum: 105fr, Mask, Northern Region. 110fr, "Dulon" door frame pillar, Central Region.

777	A273	105fr multicolored	2.25	1.10
778	A273	110fr multicolored	2.40	1.10

Paul Gauguin (1848-1903) — A274

1998, May 15 Litho. *Perf. 13*

779 A274 405fr multicolored 9.75 5.00

1998 World Cup Soccer Championships, France — A280

1998, June 5 Photo. *Perf. 12½*

787 A280 100fr multicolored 2.25 1.25

A281

Jean-Marie Tjibaou Cultural Center — A282

Designs: 30fr, “Mitimitia,” artwork by Fatu Feu'u. No. 789, Jean-Marie Tjibaou (1936-89), Melanesian political leader. No. 790, Exterior view of building, vert. 105fr, “Man Bird,” painting by Mathias Kauage.

1998, June 21 Litho. *Perf. 13x13½*

788 A281 30fr multicolored 1.25 .35
a. Booklet pane of 6 7.50
789 A281 70fr multicolored 1.50 .85
a. Booklet pane of 6 9.00
790 A281 70fr multicolored 1.50 .85
a. Booklet pane of 6 9.00
791 A282 105fr multicolored 2.50 1.25
a. Booklet pane of 6 15.00
Complete booklet, #788a, 789a, 790a, 791a 42.50
Nos. 788-791 (4) 6.75 3.30

Abolition of Slavery, 150th Anniv. — A283

1998, July 21 Engr. *Perf. 13*

792 A283 130fr multicolored 2.75 1.50

Postman, Dogs A284

1998, Aug. 20 Litho. *Perf. 13*

793 A284 70fr multicolored 1.75 .85

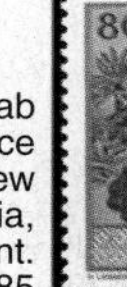

Arab Presence in New Caledonia, Cent. A285

1998, Sept. 4

794 A285 80fr multicolored 1.75 1.00

A286

Vasco da Gama's Voyage to India, 500th Anniv. A287

No. 795: a, Port in India. b, Da Gama at Cape of Good Hope, ships at sea. c, Da Gama meeting with Indians. d, Da Gama's picture in crest.

No. 796: a, Map of route. b, Vasco da Gama. c, Ship at anchor.

1998, Sept. 4

795 A286 100fr Strip of 4, #a.-d. 9.00 9.00

Souvenir Sheet

796 A287 70fr Sheet of 3, #a.-c. 5.50 5.50

Portugal '98 Intl. Philatelic Exhibition.

A288

A289

Litho. & Engr.

1998, Sept. 25 *Perf. 12½x13*

797 A288 110fr multicolored 2.25 2.25

Vincent Bouquet (1893-1971), High Chief.

1998, Oct. 20 Litho. *Perf. 13*

World Wildlife Fund — Kagu: 5fr, Male. 10fr, Female. 15fr, Two in grass. 70fr, Two in dirt, one ruffling feathers.

798 A289 5fr multicolored .25 .25
799 A289 10fr multicolored .45 .45
800 A289 15fr multicolored .75 .65
801 A289 70fr multicolored 2.00 1.75
Nos. 798-801 (4) 3.45 3.10

Early Engraving Type of 1997

1998, Nov. 4 Engr. *Perf. 13x12½*

802 A267 155fr Nou Island 3.25 2.00

Universal Declaration of Human Rights, 50th Anniv. — A290

1998, Nov. 4 Engr. *Perf. 13*

803 A290 70fr blk, bl & bl grn 1.40 1.40

Columnar Pine A291

1998, Nov. 5 Litho. *Perf. 13x13½*

804 A291 100fr shown 2.25 2.00
805 A291 100fr Coast, forest 2.25 2.00

A292

A293

Post and Telecommunications, 40th Anniv.: #806, Switchboard, bicycle, early post office. #807, Cell phone, microwave relay, motorcycle.

1998, Nov. 27 Litho. *Perf. 13½x13*

806 A292 70fr multicolored 1.60 1.60
807 A292 70fr multicolored 1.60 1.60
a. Pair, #806-807 + label 3.50 3.50

1998, Dec. 1

Underwater scenes (Greetings Stamps): No. 808, Fish, coral forming flower, Happy Anniversary. No. 809, Fish up close, Happy New Year. No. 810, Open treasure chest, Best Wishes. No. 811, Fish, starfish forming Christmas tree, Merry Christmas.

808 A293 100fr multicolored 2.25 2.00
809 A293 100fr multicolored 2.25 2.00
810 A293 100fr multicolored 2.25 2.00
811 A293 100fr multicolored 2.25 2.00
Nos. 808-811 (4) 9.00 8.00

Monument to the Disappearance of the Ship Monique, 20th Anniv. — A294

1998, Dec. 1 *Perf. 13*

812 A294 130fr multicolored 3.00 2.50

Arachnids A295

Designs: No. 813, Argiope aetherea. No. 814, Barycheloides alluvviophilus. No. 815, Latrodectus hasselti. No. 816, Crytophora moluccensis.

1999, Mar. 19 Litho. *Perf. 13x13½*

813 A295 70fr multicolored 1.60 1.40
814 A295 70fr multicolored 1.60 1.40
815 A295 70fr multicolored 1.60 1.40
816 A295 70fr multicolored 1.60 1.40
Nos. 813-816 (4) 6.40 5.60

Carcharodon Megalodon — A296

Designs: 100fr, Fossil tooth of megalodon.

No. 818: a, Shark swimming with mouth open, vert. b, Comparison of shark to man and carcharodon carcharias. c, Fossil tooth on bottom of ocean.

1999, Mar. 19 *Perf. 12½*

817 A296 100fr multicolored 3.00 2.00

Souvenir Sheet

Perf. 13

818 A296 70fr Sheet of 3, #a.-c. 6.75 6.75

Nos. 818a is 30x40mm and 818b is 40x30mm.

Australia '99, World Stamp Expo (#818).

Paul Bloc (1883-1970), Writer — A297

1999, Apr. 23 Engr. *Perf. 13x12½*

819 A297 105fr grn, bl grn & brn 2.50 2.25

Traditional Musical Instruments A298

1999, May 20 Litho. *Perf. 13½x13*

820 A298 30fr Bwanjep .75 .60
821 A298 70fr Sonnailles 1.50 1.40
822 A298 100fr Flutes 2.25 2.00
Nos. 820-822 (3) 4.50 4.00

11th South Pacific Games, Guam A299

1999, May 20 *Perf. 13x13¼*

823 A299 5fr Track & field .20 .20
824 A299 10fr Tennis .20 .20
825 A299 30fr Karate .75 .60
826 A299 70fr Baseball 1.60 1.40
Nos. 823-826 (4) 2.75 2.40

Overseas Transport Squadron 52, Humanitarian Missions — A300

1999, June 18 *Perf. 13*

827 A300 135fr multicolored 3.25 2.75

Escoffier Hotel Catering and Business School, Noumea, 20th Anniv. — A301

1999, June 17 **Litho.** *Perf. 13*

828 A301 70fr Building, computer 1.60 1.40
829 A301 70fr Building, chef's hat 1.60 1.40

New Caledonia's First Postage Stamp, 140th Anniv. — A302

Designs: No. 830, #1.

No. 831: a, Two #1. b, #1, diff. c, #1 up close. d, like #830. e, Design A265, image of Napolean III from #1, "1999."

1999, July 2 **Photo.** *Perf. 13¼*

830 A302 70fr multicolored 1.75 1.40

Souvenir Sheet

Perf. 12

831 Sheet of 5 25.00 25.00
a. A302 100fr Engraved 2.50 2.50
b. A302 100fr Litho., thermograph 2.50 2.50
c. A302 100fr Litho. 2.50 2.50
d. A302 100fr Litho. & embossed 2.50 2.50
e. A302 700fr Litho., hologram 15.00 15.00

Nos. 831a-831d are each 36x28mm. No. 831e is 44x35mm. Portions of the design on No. 831b were applied by a thermographic process producing a shiny, raised effect. No. 831e contains a holographic image. Soaking in water may affect the hologram.

PhilexFrance '99 (#831).

Tourism A303

1999, Sept. 28 **Litho.** *Perf. 13¼*

832 A303 5fr Fish, vegetables .20 .20
833 A303 30fr Lobster dish .75 .55
834 A303 70fr Tourist huts 1.50 1.25
835 A303 100fr Hotel pool 2.25 1.90
Nos. 832-835 (4) 4.70 3.90

Ratification of Noumea Accord, 1998 — A304

Illustration reduced.

1999, Nov. 10 **Litho.** *Perf. 13x13½*

836 A304 70fr multi 1.50 1.25

Aji Aboro Dance A305

1999, Nov. 10

837 A305 70fr multi 1.50 1.25

Château Hagen — A306

1999, Nov. 18 *Perf. 13*

838 A306 155fr multi 3.50 2.75

Nature Protection — A307

1999, Dec. 7

839 A307 30fr multi .75 .50

Greetings — A308

Designs: No. 840, "Joyeux Noel." No. 841, "Félicitations." No. 842, "Bon Anniversaire." No. 843, "Meilleurs Voeux 2000."

1999, Dec. 20

840 A308 100fr multi 2.50 1.75
841 A308 100fr multi 2.50 1.75
842 A308 100fr multi 2.50 1.75
843 A308 100fr multi 2.50 1.75
Nos. 840-843 (4) 10.00 7.00

Amédée Lighthouse A309

2000, Mar. 7 **Litho.** *Perf. 13½x12*

844 A309 100fr multi 2.75 1.60

Ship Emile Renouf — A310

2000, Apr. 19 **Engr.** *Perf. 13x13¼*

845 A310 135fr multi 3.50 2.25

Painting by Giles Subileau — A311

2000, June 15 **Litho.** *Perf. 13*

846 A311 155fr multi 4.00 2.25

Souvenir Sheet

New Year 2000 (Year of the Dragon) — A312

Denomination: a, at R. b, at L.

Illustration reduced.

2000, June 15

847 A312 105fr Sheet of 2, #a-b 5.00 4.50

Antoine de Saint-Exupéry (1900-44), Aviator, Writer — A313

2000, July 7

848 A313 130fr multi 3.00 2.75

World Stamp Expo 2000, Anaheim.

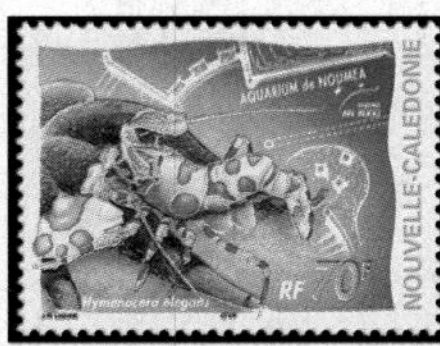

Noumea Aquarium A314

Designs: No. 849, Hymenocera elegans. No. 850, Fluorescent corals. No. 851, Chelinus undulatus.

2000, July 7 *Perf. 13x13¼*

849-851 A314 70fr Set of 3 5.00 3.00

Mangrove Heart A315

2000, Aug. 10 **Photo.** *Perf. 13*

852 A315 100fr multi 2.50 1.40

Value is for copy with surrounding selvage.

2000 Summer Olympics, Sydney A316

Designs: 10fr, Archery. 30fr, Boxing. 80fr, Cycling. 100fr, Fencing.

2000, Sept. 15 **Litho.** *Perf. 13x13¼*

853-856 A316 Set of 4 5.00 4.50

Lucien Bernheim (1856-1917), Library Founder, and Bernheim Library, Cent. — A317

2000, Oct. 24 **Engr.** *Perf. 13*

857 A317 500fr multi 11.00 7.25

A318

8th Pacific Arts Festival — A319

Kanak money and background colors of: 90fr, Orange. 105fr, Dark blue.

Festival emblem and works of art — No. 860: a, White denomination at UL, "RF" at UR. b, White denomination and "RF" at UL. c, Yellow denomination. d, White denomination at UR.

Illustration A319 reduced.

2000, Oct. 24 ***Perf. 13x13¼***

858-859 A318 Set of 2 4.50 3.00

Souvenir Sheet

860 A319 70fr Sheet of 4, #a-d 6.25 6.25

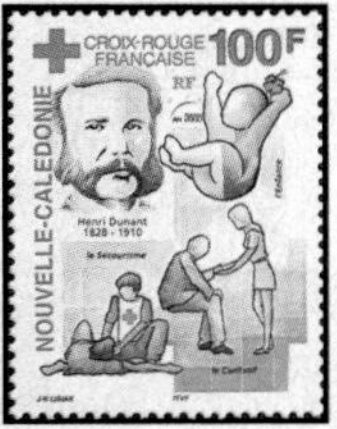

Red Cross — A320

2000, Nov. 9 Litho. ***Perf. 13¼x13***

861 A320 100fr multi 2.25 2.00

Queen Hortense (1848-1900) A321

2000, Nov. 9 Engr. ***Perf. 12½x13***

862 A321 110fr multi 2.50 2.25

Northern Province Landscapes A322

a, Fisherman in canoe. b, Motorboat near beach and cliffs. c, Fisherman on raft.

2000, Nov. 9 Litho. ***Perf. 13x13¼***

863 Horiz. strip of 3 6.50 6.50

a.-c. A322 100fr Any single 2.00 1.50

Philately in School — A323

Children's art by: a, Kévyn Pamoiloun. b, Lise-Marie Samanich. c, Alexandre Mandin.

2000, Nov. 14 ***Perf. 13¼x13***

864 Horiz. strip of 3 4.50 3.50

a.-c. A323 70fr Any single 1.40 1.10

Christmas, Holy Year 2000 A324

2000, Dec. 19 ***Perf. 13***

865 A324 100fr multi 2.00 1.60

Portions of the design were applied by a thermographic process producing a shiny, raised effect.

Greetings — A325

Kagu and: No. 866, "Meilleurs voeux de bonheur." No. 867, "Vive les vacances." No. 868, Félicitations.

2000, Dec. 19 ***Perf. 13¼x13***

866-868 A325 100fr Set of 3 6.75 6.00

No. 868 printed se-tenant with two labels.

New Year 2001 (Year of the Snake) — A326

Designs: 100fr, Snake on beach, snake wearing robe.

No. 870: a, Snake in flowers. b, Snake in city.

2001, Feb. 15 Litho. ***Perf. 13***

869 A326 100fr multi 2.50 2.00

Souvenir Sheet

Perf. 13½x13

870 A326 70fr Sheet of 2, #a-b 4.25 4.25

Size of Nos. 870a-870b: 30x40mm.

Sailing Ship France II — A327

2001, Apr. 18 Engr. ***Perf. 13x13¼***

871 A327 110fr multi 2.50 2.25

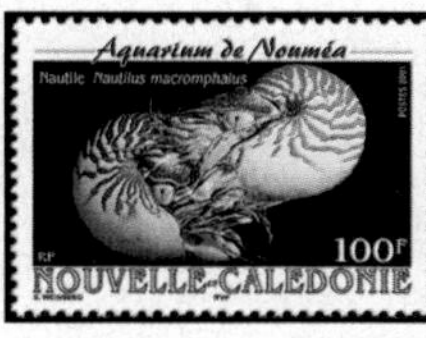

Noumea Aquarium A328

Nautilus macromphalus: a, Conjoined pair. b, Anatomical cross-section. c, Pair separated.

2001, May 22 **Litho.**

872 Horiz. strip of 3 7.00 7.00

a.-c. A328 100fr Any single 2.25 1.50

Corvus Moneduliodes and Tools — A329

2001, June 14 ***Perf. 13***

873 A329 70fr multi 1.60 1.50

Operation Cetacean A330

No. 874: a, Pair of Megaptera novaeangliae underwater. b, Whales breaching surface.

2001, July 18 ***Perf. 13x13¼***

874 Horiz. pair with central label 5.00 5.00

a.-b. A330 100fr Any single 2.25 1.50

See Vanuatu Nos. 785-787.

The Keeper of Gaia, the Eden, by Ito Waia — A331

Vision From Oceania, by Jipé Le-Bars — A332

2001, Aug. 22 ***Perf. 13***

875 A331 70fr multi 1.75 1.40

876 A332 110fr multi 2.50 2.25

Year of Dialogue Among Civilizations A333

2001, Sept. 19 Litho. ***Perf. 13x13¼***

877 A333 265fr multi 6.50 5.50

Kagu Type of 1997

2001 Engr. ***Perf. 13***

877A A265 5fr violet .35 .20

878 A265 100fr bright blue 2.75 1.50

Self-Adhesive

Litho.

Serpentine Die Cut 11

879 A265 100fr bright blue 2.75 1.50

a. Booklet pane of 10 32.50

Issued: No. 878, 9/23; No. 879, 9/20. 5fr, 4/15/02.

The Lonely Boatman, by Marik — A334

2001, Oct. 11 Litho. ***Perf. 13***

880 A334 110fr multi 2.25 2.25

Underwater Observatory — A335

2001, Oct. 11

881 A335 135fr multi 3.75 2.75

Qanono Church, Lifou — A336

2001, Oct. 11

882 A336 500fr multi 12.00 10.00

Fernande Le Riche (1884-1967), Novelist — A337

2001, Nov. 8

883 A337 155fr brown & blue 3.50 3.25

First Olympic Gold Medal Won by a New Caledonian A338

2001, Nov. 8 *Perf. 13x13¼*
884 A338 265fr multi 6.25 5.25

Kitesurfing A339

2001, Nov. 16 *Perf. 13*
885 A339 100fr multi 2.50 2.00

"The Book, My Friend" Literacy Campaign A340

2001, Nov. 27 *Perf. 13x13¼*
886 A340 70fr multi 1.75 1.40

Lifou Scenes — A341

No. 887: a, Easo. b, Jokin.

2001, Nov. 27 *Perf. 13¼x13*
887 A341 100fr Vert. pair, #a-b 4.75 4.50

Greetings A342

Flying fox and: No. 888, 100fr, Joyeux Noel (Merry Christmas). No. 889, 100fr, Meilleurs voeux (Best wishes). No. 890, 100fr, Vive la fete (Long live the holiday).

2001, Dec. 7 *Perf. 13x13¼*
888-890 A342 Set of 3 6.50 6.00

New Year 2002 (Year of the Horse) — A343

Designs: 100fr, Horse, other zodiac animals.
No. 892, vert.: a, Horse. b, Seahorse.

2002, Feb. 7 *Perf. 13*
891 A343 100fr multi 2.50 2.25

Souvenir Sheet

892 A343 70fr Sheet of 2, #a-b 3.50 3.25

Love — A344

2002, Feb. 13
893 A344 100fr multi 2.50 2.00

Value is for stamp with surrounding selvage.

Cricket — A345

2002, Mar. 20 **Litho.** *Perf. 13*
894 A345 100fr multi 2.50 2.00

Ancient Hatchet — A346

2002, Mar. 20 **Litho.**
895 A346 505fr multi 12.00 11.00

Portions of the design were applied by a thermographic process producing a shiny, raised effect.

Hobie Cat 16 World Championships — A347

2002, Apr. 1 **Litho.** *Perf. 13*
896 A347 70fr multi 1.60 1.40

Kagu Type of 1997

2002, Apr. 15 **Engr.** *Perf. 13*
897 A265 5fr purple .30 .20

2002 World Cup Soccer Championships, Japan and Korea — A348

2002, May 15 **Photo.**
898 A348 100fr multi 2.75 2.00

Values are for stamp with surrounding selvage.

Souvenir Sheet

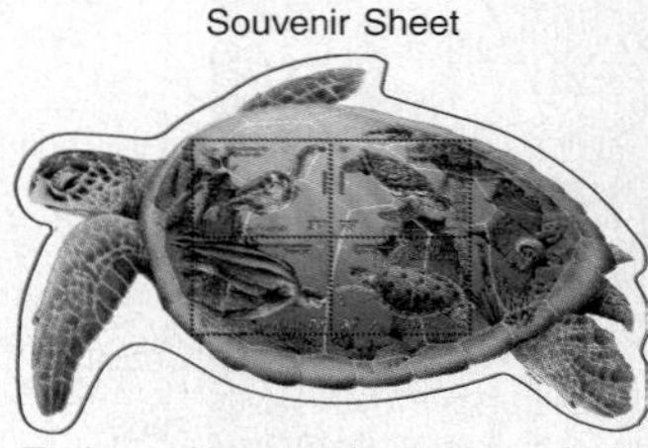
Turtles at Noumea Aquarium — A349

No. 899: a, 30fr, Caretta caretta. b, 70fr, Eretmochelys imbricat. c, 70fr, Dermochelys coriacea. d, 30fr, Chelonia mydas.

2002, May 15 **Litho.** *Perf. 13x13¼*
899 A349 Sheet of 4, #a-d 4.75 4.75
e. As #899, with inscription added in margin 4.75 4.75

Issued: No. 899e, 10/24/03. Inscription in margin of No. 899e reads "Coupe du monde 2003 / Champion du monde."

Corvette Alcmene and Map — A350

2002, June 13 **Engr.** *Perf. 13x13¼*
900 A350 210fr multi 5.00 4.25

Coffee A351

No. 901: a, Coffee plant and beans. b, Bean roasters. c, Coffee makers, woman, cup of coffee.

2002, June 13 **Litho.**
901 Horiz. strip of 3 5.00 5.00
a.-c. A351 70fr Any single 1.50 1.40

No. 901 was impregnated with coffee scent.

Edmond Caillard (1912-91), Astronomer — A352

2002, June 26 **Engr.**
902 A352 70fr multi 1.75 1.50

Statue of Emma Piffault (1861-77), by Michel Rocton — A353

2002, July 17 **Litho.** *Perf. 13¼x13*
903 A353 10fr multi .35 .20

Noumea Circus School — A354

2002, Aug. 30 *Perf. 13*
904 A354 70fr multi 1.60 1.40

Illustrations From Books by Jean Mariotti — A355

2002, Sept. 18
905 A355 70fr multi 1.60 1.40

Operation Cetacean A356

No. 906: a, Adult and young of Physeter macrocephalus. b, Physeter macrocephalus and squid.

2002, Sept. 18 *Perf. 13x13¼*
906 Horiz. pair with central label 4.75 4.75
a.-b. A356 100fr Either single 2.25 2.00

See Norfolk Island No. 783.

Intl. Year of Mountains — A357

2002, Nov. 7 **Litho.** *Perf. 13*
907 A357 100fr multi 2.50 2.00

Christmas and New Year's Day — A358

2002, Nov. 7
908 A358 100fr multi 2.00 2.00

Bourail Fort Powder Magazine — A359

Illustration reduced.

2002, Nov. 7 Engr. *Perf. 13x12½*
909 A359 1000fr multi 24.00 20.00

Mel Me Mec, by Adrien Trohmae — A360

2002, Nov. 28 Litho. *Perf. 13*
910 A360 100fr multi 2.50 2.00

New Year 2003 (Year of the Ram) A361

2003, Jan. 29
911 A361 100fr multi 2.50 2.00

Printed in sheets of 10 + 2 labels.

Valentine's Day — A362

2003, Jan. 29 Photo. *Perf. 13*
912 A362 100fr multi 2.50 2.00

Values are for copies with surrounding selvage.

Jubilee Issue, Cent. A363

Kagu A364

2003 Litho. *Perf. 13¼x13*
913 A363 70fr No. 77 1.75 1.40

Booklet Stamp
Size: 19x25mm

913A A363 70fr No. 77 1.40 1.40
b. Booklet pane of 10 14.00 —

Issued: No. 913, 2/7. No. 913A, 8/20.

2003 Engr. *Perf. 13*
914 A364 10fr green .25 .20
915 A364 15fr brown .35 .20
916 A364 30fr orange .80 .60
917 A364 (70fr) red 1.60 1.40
Nos. 914-917 (4) 3.00 2.40

Booklet Stamps

Litho. & Embossed
Perf. 13¼x13¾

918 A364 70fr gray & silver 1.60 1.40
a. Booklet pane of 10 16.00 —
Complete booklet, #913Ab, 918a 30.00

Engr.
Serpentine Die Cut 6¾ Vert.
Self-Adhesive

919 A364 (70fr) red 1.90 1.40
a. Booklet pane of 10 20.00

Issued: Nos. 914-917, 2/7; No. 918, 8/20; No. 919, 5/15.
See No. 938.

Fish at Nouméa Aquarium — A365

No. 920: a, Epinephelus maculatus. b, Plectropomus leopardus. c, Cromileptes altivelis. Illustration reduced.

2003, Apr. 9 Photo. *Perf. 12¾*
920 A365 70fr Horiz. strip of 3, #a-c 5.00 4.00

Greater Nouméa High School — A366

2003, May 14 Litho. *Perf. 13*
921 A366 70fr multi 1.75 1.40

Operation Cetacean — A367

No. 922: a, Dugong swimming (79x29mm). b, Dugong feeding (40x29mm). Illustration reduced.

2003, June 11 *Perf. 13x13¼*
922 A367 100fr Horiz. pair, #a-b 5.00 4.00

12th South Pacific Games, Suva, Fiji — A368

Designs: 5fr, Trapshooting. 30fr, Rugby. 70fr, Squash.

2003, June 11
923-925 A368 Set of 3 2.50 2.10

Man Picking Fruit From a Tree, by Paul Gauguin (1848-1903) A369

2003, June 25 Photo. *Perf. 13*
926 A369 100fr multi 2.50 1.90

Aircalin, 20th Anniv. — A370

2003, July 9 Litho.
927 A370 100fr multi 2.50 1.90

Governor Paul Feillet (1857-1903) A371

2003, July 9 Engr. *Perf. 12½x13*
928 A371 100fr bl grn & ol grn 2.50 1.90

Souvenir Sheet

Paintings by Paul Gauguin — A372

No. 929: a, Study of Heads of Tahitian Women. b, Still Life with Maori Statuette.

2003, Aug. 20 Litho. *Perf. 13*
929 A372 100fr Sheet of 2, #a-b 5.00 4.50

German Shepherd — A373

2003, Oct. 8
930 A373 105fr multi 2.50 2.10

Le Phoque, Le Prony and Le Catinat in Balade Roadstead, 1853 — A374

2003, Oct. 8 Engr. *Perf. 13x12½*
931 A374 110fr multi 2.75 2.10

Robert Tatin d'Avesnières (1925-82), Painter — A375

2003, Oct. 8 Litho. *Perf. 13*
932 A375 135fr multi 3.25 2.60

Souvenir Sheet

Geckos — A376

No. 933: a, 30fr, Bavayia cyclura. b, 30fr, Rhacodactylus chahoua. c, 70fr, Rhacodactylus ciliatus. d, 70fr, Eurydactylodes vieillardi.

2003, Oct. 8 *Perf. 13x13¼*
933 A376 Sheet of 4, #a-d 5.00 5.00

Ouen Island — A377

2003, Nov. 6 *Perf. 13*
934 A377 100fr multi 2.50 1.90

Merry Christmas and Happy New Year A378

2003, Nov. 6
935 A378 100fr multi 2.50 1.90

New Year 2004 (Year of the Monkey) — A379

Designs: 70fr, Monkeys, Hong Kong skyline. No. 937: a, Tiger and woman. b, Monkey on horse.

2004, Jan. 30 Litho. *Perf. 13*
936 A379 70fr multi 1.75 1.50

Souvenir Sheet
Perf. 13¼x13
Litho. With Foil Application

937 A379 100fr Sheet of 2, #a-b 5.00 5.00

2004 Hong Kong Stamp Expo. No. 937 contains two 30x40mm stamps.

Kagu Type of 2003

2004, Feb. 11 Engr. *Perf. 13*
938 A364 100fr blue 2.50 2.10

Love
A380

2004, Feb. 11 **Photo.**
939 A380 100fr multi 2.50 2.10

Values are for stamps with surrounding selvage.

Stamp Day — A381

2004, May 15 **Litho.**
940 A381 105fr multi 2.60 2.10

Railroads in New Caledonia — A382

2004, May 15 **Engr.** ***Perf. 13x12½***
941 A382 155fr multi 3.75 3.25

Rays
A383

No. 942: a, Dasyatis kuhlii. b, Aetobatus narinari. c, Taeniura meyeni.

2004, May 15 **Litho.** ***Perf. 13x13¼***
942 Horiz. strip of 3 7.25 7.25
a.-c. A383 100fr Any single 2.25 2.00

Souvenir Sheet

Mesoplodon Densirostris — A384

No. 943: a, Male (79x29mm). b, Female (40x29mm).

2004, May 15
943 A384 100fr Sheet of 2, #a-b 5.00 5.00

Operation Cetacean.

Flowers
A385

No. 944: a, Oxera sulfurea. b, Turbina inopinata. c, Gardenia urvillei.

2004, June 26
944 Horiz. strip of 3 7.25 7.25
a.-c. A385 100fr Any single 2.25 2.00

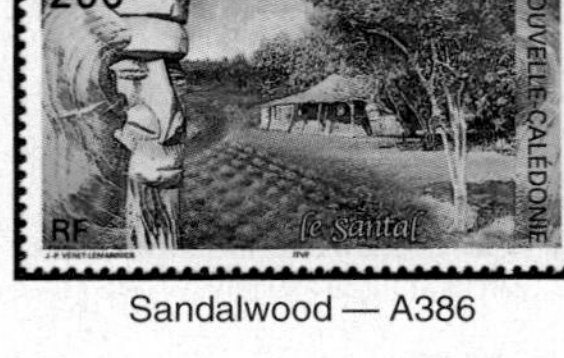

Sandalwood — A386

Designs: 200fr, Sandalwood sculpture, house.

No. 946: a, Fruit and flowers. b, Sandalwood oil extraction machinery. c, Flowerpot.

2004, June 26 ***Perf. 13***
945 A386 200fr multi 4.75 4.25

Souvenir Sheet

Perf. 13x13¼

946 A386 100fr Sheet of 3, #a-c 7.25 7.25

No. 946 contains three 40x29mm stamps.

Noumea, 150th Anniv. — A387

2004, July 8 **Litho.** ***Perf. 13***
947 A387 70fr multi 1.60 1.50

Miniature Sheet

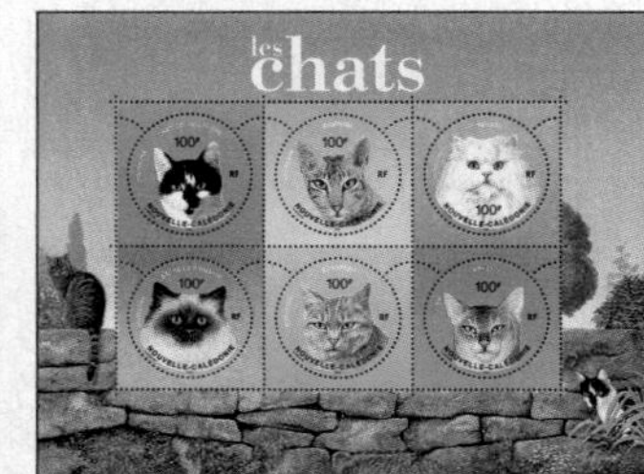

Cats — A388

No. 948: a, Mixed breed. b, Oriental. c, Persian. d, Birman. e, European. f, Abyssinian.

2004, July 25
948 A388 100fr Sheet of 6, #a-f 14.50 12.50

2004 Summer Olympics, Athens A389

Designs: No. 949, 70fr, Women's rhythmic gymnastics. No. 950, 70fr, Women's 4x400m relay. No. 951, 70fr, Beach volleyball.

2004, Aug. 5 ***Perf. 13x13¼***
949-951 A389 Set of 3 5.00 4.50

Symposium on French Research in the Pacific — A390

No. 952: a, Butterfly, hut. b, Dolphin, woman.

2004, Aug. 10 ***Perf. 13***
952 Pair 4.75 4.75
a.-b. A390 100fr Either single 2.25 2.00

Belep Island and Walla Bay — A391

2004, Nov. 10
953 A391 100fr multi 2.50 2.25

Tradimodernition, by Nathalie Deschamps — A392

2004, Nov. 10
954 A392 505fr multi 12.00 11.00

Christmas — A393

2004, Dec. 8
955 A393 100fr multi 2.50 2.25

A394

New Year 2005 (Year of the Rooster) — A395

No. 957: a, Rooster. b, Monkey.

2005, Feb. 9 **Litho.** ***Perf. 13***
956 A394 100fr multi 2.50 2.25

Souvenir Sheet

Perf. 13¼x13

957 A395 100fr Sheet of 2, #a-b 4.75 4.50

Rotary International, Cent. A396

2005, Feb. 23 **Photo.** ***Perf. 12½***
958 A396 110fr multi 2.75 2.50

Values are for stamps with surrounding selvage.

Francophone Week — A397

2005, Mar. 17 **Litho.** ***Perf. 13x13¼***
959 A397 135fr multi 3.25 3.00

Printed in sheets of 10 + 5 labels. See Wallis & Futuna Islands No. 600.

20th International Triathlon, Noumea — A398

2005, Apr. 22 **Litho.** ***Perf. 13***
960 A398 80fr multi 2.00 1.75

Coastal Tour Ship — A399

2005, May 21
961 A399 75fr multi 1.90 1.60

New Caledonian Railways — A400

2005, May 21
962 A400 745fr multi 18.00 15.00

Dolphins
A401

No. 963: a, Stenella attenuata. b, Turciop truncatus. c, Stenella longirostris.

2005, May 21 ***Perf. 13x13¼***
963 Horiz. strip of 3 7.75 7.75
a.-c. A401 100fr Any single 2.25 2.00

For surcharge, see No. 971.

Souvenir Sheet

Sharks — A402

No. 964: a, Carcharinus melanopterus. b, Nebrius ferrugineus.

2005, July 20 ***Perf. 13***
964 A402 110fr Sheet of 2, #a-b 5.25 4.50

Kagu Type of 2003

2005, Aug. 10 Engr. ***Perf. 13***
965 A364 1fr sky blue .25 .20
966 A364 3fr brt yel green .60 .20

Luengoni Beach, Lifou — A403

2005, Aug. 24 Litho.
967 A403 85fr multi 2.00 1.75

Parakeets A404

Designs: No. 968, 75fr, Eunymphicus uvaeensis. No. 969, 75fr, Eunymphicus cornutus. No. 970, 75fr, Cyanoramphus saisseti.

2005, Aug. 24 ***Perf. 13x13¼***
968-970 A404 Set of 3 5.50 4.75

No. 963 Surcharged in Silver

and Nos. 878 and 938 Surcharged

Methods and Perfs as Before

2005
971 Horiz. strip of 3 (#963) 7.00 7.00
a.-c. A401 100fr +10fr Any single 2.25 2.25
972 A265 100fr +10fr bright blue (#878) 2.25 2.25
973 A364 100fr +10fr blue (#938) 2.25 2.25
Nos. 971-973 (3) 11.50 11.50

Issued: No. 971, July. Nos. 972-973, Oct.

World Health Organization West Pacific Region Conference, Noumea — A405

Illustration reduced.

2005, Sept. 14 Litho. ***Perf. 13x13¼***
974 A405 150fr multi 3.75 3.00

World Peace Day — A406

2005, Sept. 21 ***Perf. 13¼x13***
975 A406 85fr multi 2.00 1.75

Governor Eugène du Bouzet (1805-67) A407

2005, Nov. 10 Engr.
976 A407 500fr multi 12.50 10.00

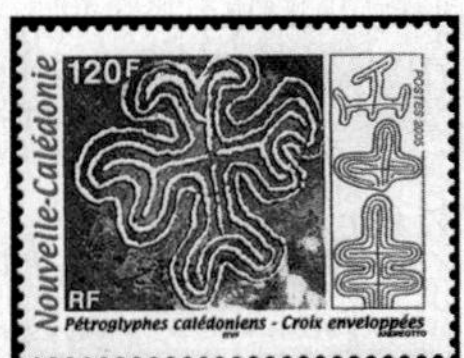

Petroglyphs — A408

Designs: No. 977, 120fr, Enclosed crosses. No. 978, 120fr, Petroglyph, Balade. No. 979, 120fr, Ouaré Petroglyph, Hienghène.

2005, Nov. 10 ***Perf. 13x12¾***
977-979 A408 Set of 3 8.75 7.25

Common Destiny, Artwork by Ito Waia and Adjé A409

2005, Dec. 7 Litho. ***Perf. 13***
980 A409 190fr multi 4.75 4.00

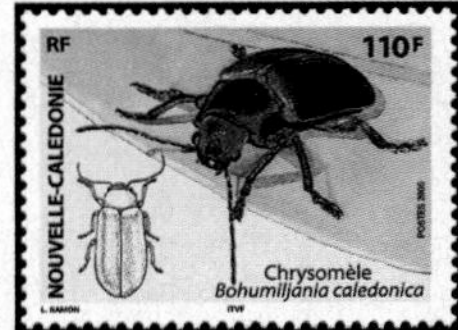

Insects A410

Designs: No. 981, 110fr, Bohumiljania caledonica. No. 982, 110fr, Bohumiljania humboldti. No. 983, 110fr, Cazeresia montana.

2005, Dec. 7 ***Perf. 13x13¼***
981-983 A410 Set of 3 8.00 6.75

Christmas A411

2005, Dec. 8 ***Perf. 13¼x13***
984 A411 110fr multi 2.75 2.25

Kagu Type of 2003

2006 Engr. ***Perf. 13***
985 A364 110fr dk blue gray 2.75 2.25

Booklet Stamp
Self-Adhesive
Serpentine Die Cut 6¾ Vert.

986 A364 110fr dk blue gray 2.75 2.25
a. Booklet pane of 10 30.00

Issued: No. 985, 1/18. No. 986, June.

Nokanhoui Islet — A412

2006, Mar. 9 Litho. ***Perf. 13***
987 A412 110fr multi 2.75 2.25

Automobiles — A413

No. 988: a, 1903 Georges Richard. b, 1925 Renault NN. c, 1925 Citroen Tréfle.

2006, Mar. 23 ***Perf. 13x13¼***
988 Horiz. strip of 3 8.00 8.00
a.-c. A413 110fr Any single 2.50 2.25

New Caledonian Red Cross, 60th Anniv. — A414

2006, Apr. 12 Litho. ***Perf. 13¼x13***
989 A414 75fr red & black 1.90 1.60

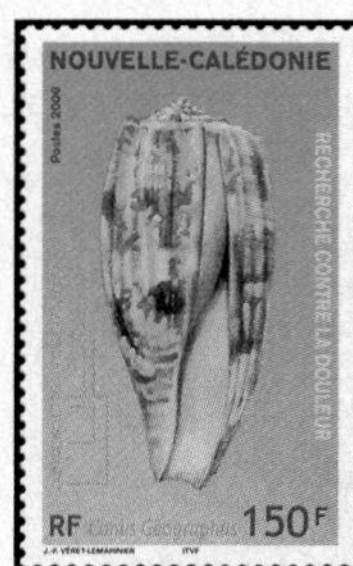

Conus Geographus A415

2006, Apr. 12 Litho. ***Perf. 13***
990 A415 150fr multi 3.75 3.25

11th World Congress on Pain, New Caledonia, 2005. Portions of the design were applied by a thermographic process producing a shiny, raised effect.

Arrival of French Colonists, 80th Anniv. — A416

2006, May 23 Engr. ***Perf. 13x12¾***
991 A416 180fr multi 4.50 3.75

2006 World Cup Soccer Championships, Germany — A417

2006, June 8 Litho. ***Perf. 13***
992 A417 110fr multi 2.75 2.25

BirdLife International A418

Designs: No. 993, 75fr, Charmosyna diadema. No. 994, 75fr, Aegotheles savesi. No. 995, 75fr, Gallirallus lafresnayanis.

2006, June 17 ***Perf. 13¼x13***
993-995 A418 Set of 3 5.50 4.75

Souvenir Sheet

Endangered Birds — A419

No. 996: a, Charmosyna diadema. b, Aegotheles savesi, vert. c, Gallirallus lafresnayanis.

2006, June 17
996 A419 110fr Sheet of 3, #a-c 8.00 7.00

Creeper Flowers A420

No. 997: a, Artia balansae. b, Oxera brevicalyx. c, Canavalia favieri.

2006, June 17 ***Perf. 13x13¼***
997 Horiz. strip of 3 8.00 8.00
a.-c. A420 110fr Any single 2.50 2.25

Mobile Post Office — A421

2006, Aug. 5 **Engr.** ***Perf. 13x12¾***
998 A421 75fr multi 1.75 1.60

Stamp Day.

New Caledonian Evacuee Voluntary Aid Association, 25th Anniv. — A422

2006, Aug. 5 **Litho.** ***Perf. 13¼x13***
999 A422 85fr multi 2.00 1.90

17th South Pacific Regional Environment Program Conference, Noumea — A423

2006, Sept. 11 **Litho.** ***Perf. 13***
1000 A423 190fr multi 4.00 4.00

Nakale 7547 Locomotive of New Caledonia Railroad — A424

2006, Sept. 19 **Engr.** ***Perf. 13x13¼***
1001 A424 320fr multi 6.75 6.75

Kaneka Music, 20th Anniv. A425

2006, Nov. 8 **Litho.** ***Perf. 13x13½***
1002 A425 75fr multi 1.90 1.75

Mobilis Mobile Phone Service, 10th Anniv. — A426

2006, Nov. 8 ***Perf. 13***
1003 A426 75fr multi 1.90 1.75

Wooden Players Puppet Theater, 30th Anniv. — A427

2006, Nov. 8
1004 A427 280fr multi 7.00 6.25

Christmas A428

Litho. & Engr.

2006, Nov. 9 ***Perf. 13***
1005 A428 110fr multi 2.75 2.50

Lizard Man, Sculpture by Joseph Poukiou A429

2006, Dec. 13 **Litho.**
1006 A429 110fr multi 2.75 2.40

Kagu Type of 2003

2007, Jan. 25 **Engr.** ***Perf. 13***
1007 A364 5fr purple .35 .20

New Year 2007 (Year of the Pig) A430

2007, Feb. 6 **Litho.** ***Perf. 13***
1008 A430 110fr multi 2.50 2.50

Printed in sheets of 10 + central label.

General Secretariat of the South Pacific Community, 60th Anniv. — A431

2007, Feb. 6
1009 A431 120fr multi 2.75 2.75

Audit Office, Bicent. A432

2007, Mar. 17 **Engr.** ***Perf. 13¼***
1010 A432 110fr multi 2.50 2.50

Treaty of Rome, 50th Anniv. A433

2007, May 10 **Litho.** ***Perf. 13x13¼***
1011 A433 110fr multi 2.50 2.50

13th South Pacific Games, Samoa — A434

2007, June 13 **Litho.** ***Perf. 13***
1012 A434 75fr multi 1.75 1.75

Submarine Cable Between Noumea and Sydney — A435

2007, June 13 **Litho. & Engr.**
1013 A435 280fr multi 6.50 6.50

Fish A436

Designs: 35fr, Siganus lineatus. 75fr, Lutianus adetii. 110fr, Naso unicornis.

2007, June 13 **Litho.** ***Perf. 13x13½***
1014-1016 A436 Set of 3 5.00 5.00

Natl. Sea Rescue Society, 40th Anniv. — A437

2007, Aug. 3 ***Perf. 13***
1017 A437 75fr multi 1.75 1.75

BirdLife International — A438

Endangered birds: 35fr, Gymnomyza aubryana. 75fr, Coracina analis. 110fr, Rhynochetos jubatus.

2007, Aug. 3 ***Perf. 13x13¼***
1018-1020 A438 Set of 3 5.00 5.00

A439

A440

A441

A442

A443

A444

A445

A446

A447

Mailboxes A448

2007, Aug. 3 ***Perf. 13¼x13, 13x13¼***

1021	Booklet pane of 10	17.50	17.50
a.	A439 75fr multi	1.75	1.75
b.	A440 75fr multi	1.75	1.75
c.	A441 75fr multi	1.75	1.75
d.	A442 75fr multi	1.75	1.75
e.	A443 75fr multi	1.75	1.75
f.	A444 75fr multi	1.75	1.75
g.	A445 75fr multi	1.75	1.75
h.	A446 75fr multi	1.75	1.75
i.	A447 75fr multi	1.75	1.75
j.	A448 75fr multi	1.75	1.75
	Complete booklet, #1021	17.50	

Stamp Day.

Souvenir Sheet

Kagu Philatelic Club, 60th Anniv. — A449

No. 1022: a, Magnifying glass over New Caledonia #262 on cover. b, Kagu.

Litho. & Silk Screened

2007, Aug. 3 ***Perf. 13x13¼***
1022 A449 110fr Sheet of 2, #a-b 5.00 5.00

Season of New Hebrides Culture in New Zealand — A450

2007, Aug. 16 **Litho.** ***Perf. 13***
1023 A450 190fr multi 4.50 4.50

New Aquarium of New Caledonia — A451

No. 1024 — Entrance of new aquarium and: a, Gymnothorax polyranodon (40x30mm). b, Entrance of old aquarium. (80x30mm). c, Monodactylus argenteus (40x30mm). d, Negaprion brevirostris (40x30mm). e, Pseudanthias bicolor (40x30mm).

2007, Aug. 31 ***Perf. 13x13¼***
1024 A451 110fr Booklet pane of 5, #a-e 13.00 13.00
Complete booklet, 2 #1024 26.00

2007 Rugby World Cup, France A452

2007, Sept. 5 **Photo.** ***Perf.***
1025 A452 110fr multi 2.60 2.60

Jules Repiquet (1874-1960), Governor of New Caledonia, 1914-23 — A453

2007, Oct. 10 **Engr.** ***Perf. 13x13¼***
1026 A453 320fr multi 7.75 7.75

Tropical Fruits A454

Designs: 35fr, Bananas and passion fruits. 75fr, Vanilla beans, vert. 110fr, Pineapples and lychees.

Perf. 13x13¼, 13¼x13

2007, Nov. 8 **Litho.**
1027-1029 A454 Set of 3 5.50 5.50

The banana, vanilla bean and pineapple portions of these stamps are covered with scratch-and-sniff coatings having those fragrances.

La Montagnarde Locomotive, New Caledonian Railways — A455

2007, Nov. 8 **Engr.** ***Perf. 13x13¼***
1030 A455 400fr multi 10.00 10.00

Tao Waterfall A456

2007, Nov. 8 **Litho.** ***Perf. 13***
1031 A456 110fr multi 2.75 2.75

The Damned, Performance by Najib Guerfi Dance Company — A457

2007, Nov. 8
1032 A457 110fr multi 2.75 2.75

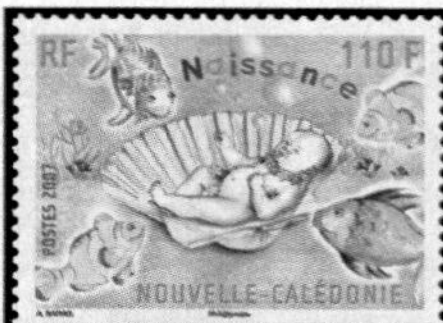
Birth Announcement — A458

2007, Nov. 8 ***Perf. 13x13¼***
1033 A458 110fr multi 2.75 2.75

New Year's Greetings A459

2007, Nov. 8
1034 A459 110fr multi 2.75 2.75

New Year 2008 (Year of the Rat) A461

2008, Feb. 6 **Litho.** ***Perf. 13***
1036 A461 110fr multi 3.00 3.00

Academic Palms, Bicent. — A462

Litho. & Embossed

2008, Mar. 17 ***Perf. 13x13¼***
1037 A462 110fr multi 3.00 3.00

Tjibaou Cultural Center, 10th Anniv. — A463

2008, June 14 **Litho.** ***Perf. 13***
1038 A463 120fr multi 3.25 3.25

Matignon Accords, 20th Anniv. — A464

2008, June 14
1039 A464 430fr multi 11.50 11.50

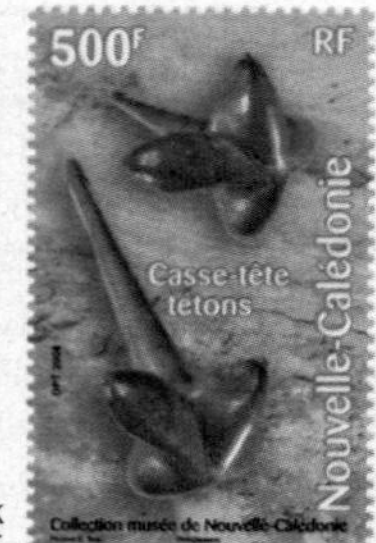

Kanak Ax — A465

2008, June 14

1040	A465 500fr multi		13.50	13.50

BirdLife International — A466

Endangered birds: No. 1041, 110fr, Pterodroma leucoptera. No. 1042, 110fr, Pseudobulweria rostrata. No. 1043, 110fr, Nesofregatta fulginosa.

2008, June 14 ***Perf. 13x13¼***

1041-1043	A466	Set of 3	8.75	8.75

Fruit A467

Designs: No. 1044, 110fr, Citrus nobilis. No. 1045, 110fr, Mangifera indica. No. 1046, 110fr, Carica papaya.

2008, June 14

1044-1046	A467	Set of 3	8.75	8.75

2008 Summer Olympics, Beijing A468

Designs: No. 1047, 75fr, Weight lifting. No. 1048, 75fr, Table tennis. No. 1049, 75fr, Taekwondo.

2008, July 31

1047-1049	A468	Set of 3	5.75	5.75

Office of Posts and Telecommunications, 50th Anniv. — A469

Designs: No. 1050, 75fr, New Caledonia #314, dish antennas, cable, map of South Pacific. No. 1051, 75fr, New Caledonia #311, savings card, person at computer. No. 1052, 75fr, New Caledonia #C106, mailbox, mail sorter.

2008, July 31

1050-1052	A469	Set of 3	5.75	5.75

Miniature Sheet

Telecommunications History — A470

No. 1053: a, Telegraph. b, Radio telephone. c, Satellite and antenna. d, Fiber-optic cables and flowers.

2008, July 31 ***Perf. 13¼x13***

1053	A470 75fr Sheet of 4, #a-d		7.50	7.50

SEMI-POSTAL STAMPS

No. 93 Surcharged

1915 Unwmk. ***Perf. 14x13½***

B1	A16	10c + 5c carmine	1.50	1.50
a.		Inverted surcharge	65.00	65.00
b.		Cross omitted	—	—

Regular Issue of 1905 Surcharged

1917

B2	A16	10c + 5c rose	.80	.80
a.		Double surcharge	75.00	—
B3	A16	15c + 5c violet	.80	.80

Curie Issue
Common Design Type

1938, Oct. 24 ***Perf. 13***

B4	CD80	1.75fr + 50c brt ultra	12.50	12.50

French Revolution Issue
Common Design Type

1939, July 5 Photo.
Name and Value Typo. in Black

B5	CD83	45c + 25c green	10.00	10.00
B6	CD83	70c + 30c brown	10.00	10.00
B7	CD83	90c + 35c red org	10.00	10.00
B8	CD83	1.25fr + 1fr rose pink	10.00	10.00
B9	CD83	2.25fr + 2fr blue	10.00	10.00
		Nos. B5-B9 (5)	50.00	50.00

Common Design Type and

Dumont d'Urville's ship, "Zélée" — SP2

New Caledonian Militiaman SP3

1941 Photo. ***Perf. 13½***

B10	SP2	1fr + 1fr red	1.50
B11	CD86	1.50fr + 3fr maroon	1.60
B12	SP3	2.50fr + 1fr dk blue	1.60
		Nos. B10-B12 (3)	4.70

Nos. B10-B12 were issued by the Vichy government in France, but were not placed on sale in New Caledonia.

Nos. 216A-216B Surcharged in Black or Red

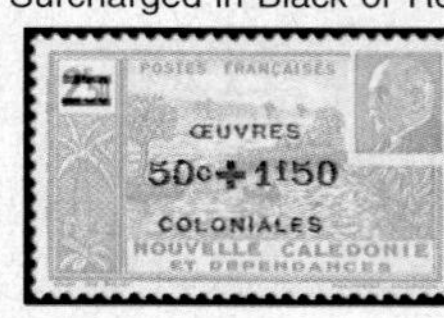

1944 Engr. ***Perf. 12½x12***

B12A	50c + 1.50fr on 2.50fr deep blue (R)	.80
B12B	+ 2.50fr on 1fr green	.80

Colonial Development Fund.

Nos. B12A-B12B were issued by the Vichy government in France, but were not placed on sale in New Caledonia.

Catalogue values for unused stamps in this section, from this point to the end of the section, are for Never Hinged items.

Red Cross Issue
Common Design Type

1944 ***Perf. 14½x14***

B13	CD90	5fr + 20fr brt scar	1.00	1.00

The surtax was for the French Red Cross and national relief.

Tropical Medicine Issue
Common Design Type

1950, May 15 Engr. ***Perf. 13***

B14	CD100	10fr + 2fr red brn & sepia	5.75	4.50

The surtax was for charitable work.

AIR POST STAMPS

Seaplane Over Pacific Ocean AP1

1938-40 Unwmk. Engr. ***Perf. 13***

C1	AP1	65c deep violet	.80	.55
a.		"65c" omitted	150.00	
C2	AP1	4.50fr red	1.25	1.10
C3	AP1	7fr dk bl grn ('40)	.80	.55
C4	AP1	9fr ultramarine	2.50	2.25
C5	AP1	20fr dk orange ('40)	1.75	1.50
C6	AP1	50fr black ('40)	2.90	2.50
		Nos. C1-C6 (6)	10.00	8.45

Type of 1938-40 Without "RF"

1942-43

C6A	AP1	65c deep violet	.20
C6B	AP1	4.50fr red	.20
C6C	AP1	5fr yellow brown	.35
C6D	AP1	9fr ultramarine	.40
C6E	AP1	10fr brown lilaca	.80
C6F	AP1	20fr dark orange	1.50
C6G	AP1	50fr black	1.50
		Nos. C6A-C6G (7)	4.95

Nos. C6A-C6G were issued by the Vichy government in France, but were not placed on sale in New Caledonia.

Common Design Type

1942 Unwmk. ***Perf. 14½x14***

C7	CD87	1fr dk orange	.50	.50
C8	CD87	1.50fr brt red	.50	.50
C9	CD87	5fr brown red	.50	.50
C10	CD87	10fr black	.80	.55
C11	CD87	25fr ultra	1.00	.90
C12	CD87	50fr dk green	1.40	.90
C13	CD87	100fr plum	1.75	1.40
		Nos. C7-C13 (7)	6.45	5.25

Eagle — AP1a

1944 ***Perf. 13***

C13A	AP1a	100fr gray green & blue green	1.25

No. C13A was issued by the Vichy government in France, but was not placed on sale in New Caledonia.

Catalogue values for unused stamps in this section, from this point to the end of the section, are for Never Hinged items.

Victory Issue
Common Design Type

1946, May 8 Engr. ***Perf. 12½***

C14	CD92	8fr brt ultra	1.50	1.10

Chad to Rhine Issue
Common Design Types

1946, June 6

C15	CD93	5fr black	1.60	1.25
C16	CD94	10fr carmine	1.60	1.25
C17	CD95	15fr dk blue	1.60	1.35
C18	CD96	20fr orange brn	1.60	1.35
C19	CD97	25fr olive grn	2.25	1.75
C20	CD98	50fr dk rose vio	3.50	2.50
		Nos. C15-C20 (6)	12.15	9.45

St. Vincent Bay — AP2

Planes over Islands — AP3

View of Nouméa — AP4

Perf. 13x12½, 12½x13
1948, Mar. 1 Photo. Unwmk.

C21	AP2	50fr org & rose vio	4.00	2.75
C22	AP3	100fr bl grn & sl bl	8.00	3.50
C23	AP4	200fr brown & yel	15.00	6.75
		Nos. C21-C23 (3)	27.00	13.00

UPU Issue
Common Design Type

1949, Nov. 21 Engr. ***Perf. 13***

C24	CD99	10fr multicolored	6.00	3.75

Liberation Issue
Common Design Type

1954, June 6

C25 CD102 3fr indigo & ultra 7.25 3.50

Conveyor for Nickel Ore — AP5

1955, Nov. 21 Unwmk. ***Perf. 13***

C26 AP5 14fr indigo & sepia 4.00 1.10

Rock Formations, Bourail — AP6

1959, Mar. 21

C27 AP6 200fr lt bl, brn & grn 27.50 12.50

Yaté Dam — AP7

1959, Sept. 21 Engr.

C28 AP7 50fr grn, brt bl & sepia 8.00 3.25

Dedication of Yaté Dam.

Fisherman with Throw-net — AP8

Skin Diver Shooting Bumphead Surgeonfish — AP9

20fr, Nautilus shell. 100fr, Yaté rock.

1962 Unwmk. ***Perf. 13***

C29 AP8 15fr red, Prus grn & sep 5.00 1.75

C30 AP9 20fr dk sl grn & org ver 10.00 3.25

C31 AP9 25fr red brn, gray & bl 9.00 2.75

C32 AP9 100fr dk brn, dk bl & sl grn 18.00 9.25

Nos. C29-C32 (4) 42.00 17.00

Telstar Issue
Common Design Type

1962, Dec. 4 Unwmk. ***Perf. 13***

C33 CD111 200fr dk bl, choc & grnsh bl 28.00 16.00

Nickel Mining, Houailou — AP10

1964, May 14 Photo.

C34 AP10 30fr multi 4.00 2.00

Isle of Pines — AP11

1964, Dec. 7 Engr. ***Perf. 13***

C35 AP11 50fr dk bl, sl grn & choc 5.50 1.90

Phyllobranchus — AP12

Design: 27fr, Paracanthurus teuthis (fish).

1964, Dec. 21 Photo.

C36 AP12 27fr red brn, yel, dp bl & blk 6.00 2.75

C37 AP12 37fr bl, brn & yel 8.25 4.25

Issued to publicize the Nouméa Aquarium.

Greco-Roman Wrestling — AP13

1964, Dec. 28 Engr.

C38 AP13 10fr brt grn, pink & blk 18.00 13.50

18th Olympic Games, Tokyo, Oct. 10-25.

Nimbus Weather Satellite over New Caledonia AP14

1965, Mar. 23 Photo. ***Perf. 13x12½***

C39 AP14 9fr multi 4.00 2.00

Fifth World Meteorological Day.

ITU Issue
Common Design Type

1965, May 17 Engr. ***Perf. 13***

C40 CD120 40fr lt bl, lil rose & lt brn 12.00 7.75

Coris Angulata (Young Fish) — AP15

15fr, Adolescent fish. 25fr, Adult fish.

1965, Dec. 6 Engr. ***Perf. 13***

C41 AP15 13fr red org, ol bis & blk 4.00 1.50

C42 AP15 15fr ind, sl grn & bis 6.00 1.50

C43 AP15 25fr ind & yel grn 8.00 4.00

Nos. C41-C43 (3) 18.00 7.00

Issued to publicize the Nouméa Aquarium.

French Satellite A-1 Issue
Common Design Type

Designs: 8fr, Diamant rocket and launching installations. 12fr, A-1 satellite.

1966, Jan. 10 Engr. ***Perf. 13***

C44 CD121 8fr rose brn, ultra & Prus bl 3.00 1.25

C45 CD121 12fr ultra, Prus bl & rose brn 3.75 1.90

a. Strip of 2, #C44-C45 + label 7.50 6.50

French Satellite D-1 Issue
Common Design Type

1966, May 16 Engr. ***Perf. 13***

C46 CD122 10fr dl bl, ocher & sep 2.75 1.25

Port-de-France, 1866 — AP16

1966, June 2

C47 AP16 30fr dk red, bl & ind 4.75 2.75

Port-de-France changing name to Nouméa, cent.

Bird Type of Regular Issue

Designs: 27fr, Uvea crested parakeet. 37fr, Scarlet honey eater. 50fr, Two cloven-feathered doves.

1966-68 Photo. ***Perf. 13***

Size: 26x46mm

C48 A45 27fr pink & multi 8.00 3.00

C49 A45 37fr grn & multi 12.00 4.25

Size: 27x48mm

C49A A45 50fr multi ('68) 15.00 6.50

Nos. C48-C49A (3) 35.00 13.75

Issued: 27fr, 37fr, Oct. 10; 50fr, May 14.

Sailboats and Map of New Caledonia-New Zealand Route — AP17

1967, Apr. 15 Engr. ***Perf. 13***

C50 AP17 25fr brt grn, dp ultra & red 6.00 2.75

2nd sailboat race from Whangarei, New Zealand, to Nouméa, New Caledonia.

Butterfly Type of Regular Issue

Butterflies: 19fr, Danaus plexippus. 29fr, Hippotion celerio. 85fr, Delias elipsis.

1967-68 Engr. ***Perf. 13***

Size: 48x27mm

C51 A52 19fr multi ('68) 8.00 3.00

C52 A52 29fr multi ('68) 10.00 4.00

C53 A52 85fr red, dk brn & yel 20.00 7.25

Nos. C51-C53 (3) 38.00 14.25

Issued: 85fr, Aug. 10; others, Mar. 26.

Jules Garnier, Garnierite and Mine — AP18

1967, Oct. 9 Engr. ***Perf. 13***

C54 AP18 70fr bl gray, brn & yel grn 8.25 4.25

Discovery of garnierite (nickel ore), cent.

Lifu Island — AP19

1967, Oct. 28 Photo. ***Perf. 13***

C55 AP19 200fr multi 14.00 6.50

Skier, Snowflake and Olympic Emblem — AP20

1967, Nov. 16 Engr. ***Perf. 13***

C56 AP20 100fr brn red, sl grn & brt bl 17.50 6.50

10th Winter Olympic Games, Grenoble, France, Feb. 6-18, 1968.

Sea Shell Type of Regular Issue

Designs: 39fr, Conus lienardi. 40fr, Conus cabriti. 70fr, Conus coccineus.

1968, Nov. 9 Engr. ***Perf. 13***

C58 A54 39fr bl grn, brn & gray 8.00 2.00

C59 A54 40fr blk, brn red & ol 8.00 2.00

C60 A54 70fr brn, pur & gray 17.00 4.50

Nos. C58-C60 (3) 33.00 8.50

Maré Dancers — AP21

1968, Nov. 30 Engr. ***Perf. 13***

C61 AP21 60fr grn, ultra & hn brn 7.25 4.25

World Map and Caudron C 600 "Aiglon" — AP22

1969, Mar. 24 Engr. ***Perf. 13***

C62 AP22 29fr lil, dk bl & dk car 5.00 2.00

Stamp Day and honoring the 1st flight from Nouméa to Paris of Henri Martinet & Paul Klein, Mar. 24, 1939.

Concorde Issue
Common Design Type

1969, Apr. 17 Engr. *Perf. 13*
C63 CD129 100fr sl grn & brt grn 28.00 17.50

Cattle Type of Regular Issue

Design: 50fr, Cowboy and herd.

1969, May 10 Engr. *Perf. 13*
Size: 48x27mm
C64 A56 50fr sl grn, dk brn & red brn 5.00 2.75

Shell Type of Regular Issue, 1969

Design: 100fr, Black murex.

1969, June 21 Engr. *Perf. 13*
Size: 48x27mm
C65 A57 100fr lake, bl & blk 27.50 9.00

Sports Type of 1969

30fr, Woman diver. 39fr, Shot put, vert.

1969, Aug. 7 Engr. *Perf. 13*
Size: 48x27mm, 27x48mm
C66 A58 30fr dk brn, bl & blk 5.00 1.50
C67 A58 39fr dk ol, brt grn & ol 6.00 2.00

Napoleon in Coronation Robes, by François P. Gerard AP23

1969, Oct. 2 Photo. *Perf. 12½x12*
C68 AP23 40fr lil & multi 16.00 9.00

200th birth anniv. of Napoleon Bonaparte (1769-1821).

Air France Plane over Outrigger Canoe — AP24

1969, Oct. 2 Engr. *Perf. 13*
C69 AP24 50fr slate grn, sky bl & choc 5.50 2.75

20th anniversary of the inauguration of the Nouméa to Paris airline.

Bird Type of Regular Issue, 1966.

39fr, Emerald doves. 100fr, Whistling kite.

1970, Feb. 19 Photo. *Perf. 13*
Size: 27x48mm
C70 A45 39fr multi 15.00 4.25
C71 A45 100fr lt bl & multi 20.00 10.00

Planes Circling Globe and Paris-Nouméa Route — AP25

1970, May 6 Engr. *Perf. 13*
C72 AP25 200fr vio, org brn & grnsh bl 16.50 8.00

10th anniversary of the Paris to Nouméa flight: "French Wings Around the World."

Shell Type of Regular Issue

22fr, Strombus sinautus humphrey, vert. 33fr, Argus porcelain shell. 34fr, Strombus vomer, vert. 60fr, Card porcelain shell.

1970 Engr. *Perf. 13*
Size: 27x48mm, 48x27mm
C73 A59 22fr bl & multi 8.00 3.75
C74 A59 33fr brn & gray bl 10.00 3.75
C75 A59 34fr pur & multi 10.00 3.50
C76 A59 60fr lt grn & brn 15.00 5.50
Nos. C73-C76 (4) 43.00 16.50

See Nos. C89-C90.

Bicyclists on Map of New Caledonia — AP26

1970, Aug. 20 Engr. *Perf. 13*
C77 AP26 40fr bl, ultra & choc 6.00 2.75

The 4th Bicycling Race of New Caledonia.

Mt. Fuji and Monorail Train — AP27

45fr, Map of Japan and Buddha statue.

1970, Sept. 3 Photo. *Perf. 13x12½*
C78 AP27 20fr blk, bl & yel grn 4.25 1.50
C79 AP27 45fr mar, lt bl & ol 6.50 2.75

EXPO '70 International Exposition, Osaka, Japan, Mar. 15-Sept. 13.

Racing Yachts AP28

1971, Feb. 23 Engr. *Perf. 13*
C80 AP28 20fr grn, blk & ver 3.75 1.25

First challenge in New Zealand waters for the One Ton Cup ocean race.

Lt. Col. Broche and Map of Mediterranean — AP29

1971, May 5 Photo. *Perf. 12½*
C81 AP29 60fr multi 8.25 3.25

30th anniversary of Battalion of the Pacific.

Pole Vault — AP30

1971, June 24 Engr. *Perf. 13*
C82 AP30 25fr shown 3.75 2.00
C83 AP30 100fr Archery 8.00 4.25

4th South Pacific Games, Papeete, French Polynesia, Sept. 8-19.

Port de Plaisance, Nouméa — AP31

1971, Sept. 27 Photo. *Perf. 13*
C84 AP31 200fr multi 17.50 7.75

Golden Eagle and Pilot's Leaflet — AP32

1971, Nov. 20 Engr. *Perf. 13*
C85 AP32 90fr dk brn, org & indigo 8.25 3.75

1st flight New Caledonia - Australia with Victor Roffey piloting the Golden Eagle, 40th anniv.

Skiing and Sapporo '72 Emblem — AP33

1972, Jan. 22 Engr. *Perf. 13*
C86 AP33 50fr brt bl, car & sl grn 6.00 2.75

11th Winter Olympic Games, Sapporo, Japan, Feb. 3-13.

South Pacific Commission Headquarters, Nouméa — AP34

1972, Feb. 5 Photo.
C87 AP34 18fr bl & multi 2.25 .85

South Pacific Commission, 25th anniv.

St. Mark's Basilica, Venice — AP35

1972, Feb. 5 Engr.
C88 AP35 20fr lt grn, bl & grn 4.25 1.25

UNESCO campaign to save Venice.

Shell Type of Regular Issue, 1970

Designs: 25fr, Orange spider conch, vert. 50fr, Chiragra spider conch, vert.

1972, Mar. 4 Engr. *Perf. 13*
Size: 27x48mm
C89 A59 25fr dp car & dk brn 8.00 3.00
C90 A59 50fr grn, brn & rose car 11.00 4.00

Breguet F-ALMV and Globe — AP36

1972, Apr. 5 Engr. *Perf. 13*
C91 AP36 110fr brt rose lil, bl & grn 12.50 7.00

40th anniversary of the first Paris-Nouméa flight, Mar. 9-Apr. 5, 1932.

Round House and Festival Emblem — AP37

1972, May 13
C92 AP37 24fr org, bl & brn 3.00 1.50

So. Pacific Festival of Arts, Fiji, May 6-20.

Hurdles and Olympic Rings — AP38

1972, Sept. 2 Engr. *Perf. 13*
C93 AP38 72fr vio, bl & red lil 7.50 3.75

20th Olympic Games, Munich, Aug. 26-Sept. 11.

New Post Office, Noumea — AP39

1972, Nov. 25 Engr. *Perf. 13*
C94 AP39 23fr brn, brt bl & grn 2.25 1.00

Molière and Scenes from Plays — AP40

1973, Feb. 24 Engr. *Perf. 13*
C95 AP40 50fr multi 7.50 2.75

300th anniversary of the death of Molière (Jean Baptiste Poquelin, 1622-1673), French actor and playwright.

Woodlands — AP41

Designs: 18fr, Palm trees on coast, vert. 21fr, Waterfall, vert.

1973, Feb. 24 Photo.
C96 AP41 11fr gold & multi 2.00 1.00
C97 AP41 18fr gold & multi 3.00 1.50
C98 AP41 21fr gold & multi 4.00 1.50
Nos. C96-C98 (3) 9.00 4.00

Concorde — AP42

1973, Mar. 15 Engr. *Perf. 13*
C99 AP42 23fr blue 18.00 3.75
a. Booklet pane of 5 300.00

No. C99 issued in booklets only.

El Kantara in Panama Canal — AP43

1973, Mar. 24 Engr. *Perf. 13*
C100 AP43 60fr brn, yel grn & blk 7.50 3.25

50th anniversary of steamship connection Marseilles to Nouméa through Panama Canal.

Sun, Earth, Wind God and Satellite — AP44

1973, Mar. 24
C101 AP44 80fr multi 7.00 2.75

Centenary of intl. meteorological cooperation and 13th World Meteorological Day.

Museum Type of Regular Issue

Designs: 16fr, Carved arrows and arrowhead. 40fr, Carved entrance to chief's house.

1973, Apr. 30 Photo. *Perf. 12½x13*
C102 A66 16fr multi 2.25 1.00
C103 A66 40fr multi 4.00 2.00

DC-10 over Map of Route Paris to Nouméa — AP45

1973, May 26 Engr. *Perf. 13*
C104 AP45 100fr brn, ultra & sl grn 7.50 3.50

First direct flight by DC-10, Nouméa to Paris.

Fish Type of Regular Issue

32fr, Old and young olive surgeonfish.

1973, June 23 Photo. *Perf. 13x12½*
C105 A69 32fr multi 5.50 2.00

Coach, 1880 — AP46

1973, Sept. 22 Engr. *Perf. 13*
C106 AP46 15fr choc, bl & sl grn 2.25 1.00

Stamp Day 1973.

Landscape — AP47

West Coast Landscapes: 8fr, Rocky path, vert. 26fr, Trees on shore.

1974, Feb. 23 Photo. *Perf. 13*
C107 AP47 8fr gold & multi 1.60 .90
C108 AP47 22fr gold & multi 2.25 1.40
C109 AP47 26fr gold & multi 3.75 1.50
Nos. C107-C109 (3) 7.60 3.80

Anse-Vata, Scientific Center, Nouméa — AP48

1974, Mar. 23 Photo. *Perf. 13x12½*
C110 AP48 50fr multi 3.00 1.60

Ovula Ovum AP49

1974, Mar. 23
C111 AP49 3fr *shown* 1.50 .55
C112 AP49 32fr *Hydatina* 4.00 1.10
C113 AP49 37fr *Dolium perdix* 4.50 2.10
Nos. C111-C113 (3) 10.00 3.75

Nouméa Aquarium.

Capt. Cook, Map of Grande Terre and "Endeavour" — AP50

Designs: 25fr, Jean F. de la Perouse, his ship and map of Grande Terre. 28fr, French sailor, 18th century, on board ship, vert. 30fr, Antoine R. J. d'Entrecasteaux, ship and map. 36fr, Dumont d'Urville, ship and map of Loyalty Islands.

1974, Sept. 4 Engr. *Perf. 13*
C114 AP50 20fr multi 3.00 .90
C115 AP50 25fr multi 4.00 1.40
C116 AP50 28fr multi 5.00 1.40
C117 AP50 30fr multi 7.00 1.60
C118 AP50 36fr multi 8.00 3.00
Nos. C114-C118 (5) 27.00 8.30

Discovery and exploration of New Caledonia and Loyalty Islands.

UPU Emblem and Symbolic Design — AP51

1974, Oct. 9 Engr. *Perf. 13*
C119 AP51 95fr multi 6.00 2.75

Centenary of Universal Postal Union.

Abstract Design — AP52

1974, Oct. 26 Photo. *Perf. 13*
C120 AP52 80fr bl, blk & org 4.25 2.00

ARPHILA 75, Philatelic Exhibition, Paris, June 6-16, 1975.

Hôtel Chateau-Royal, Nouméa — AP53

1975, Jan. 20 Photo. *Perf. 13*
C121 AP53 22fr multi 2.00 .90

Cricket — AP54

Designs: 25fr, Bougna ceremony (food offering). 31fr, Pilou dance.

1975, Apr. 5 Photo. *Perf. 13*
C122 AP54 3fr bl & multi 1.25 .45
C123 AP54 25fr olive grn & multi 2.50 .70
C124 AP54 31fr yel grn & multi 3.00 1.10
Nos. C122-C124 (3) 6.75 2.25

Tourist publicity.

Orchid Type of 1975

Design: 42fr, Eriaxis rigida.

1975, May 30
C125 A74 42fr grn & multi 7.50 2.25

Globe as "Flower" with "Stamps" and leaves — AP55

1975, June 7 Engr. *Perf. 13*
C126 AP55 105fr multi 7.50 2.75

ARPHILA 75 International Philatelic Exhibition, Paris, June 6-16.

Discus and Games' Emblem — AP56

50fr, Volleyball and Games' emblem.

1975, Aug. 23 Photo. *Perf. 13x12½*
C127 AP56 24fr emer, pur & dk bl 2.00 1.00
C128 AP56 50fr multi 3.50 2.00

5th South Pacific Games, Guam, Aug. 1-10.

Concorde — AP57

1976, Jan. 21 Engr. *Perf. 13*
C129 AP57 147fr car & ultra 12.00 7.00

First commercial flight of supersonic jet Concorde, Paris-Rio de Janeiro, Jan. 21.
For surcharge see No. C141.

Telephones 1876 and 1976, Satellite — AP58

1976, Apr. 12 Photo. *Perf. 13*
C130 AP58 36fr multi 2.25 1.25

Centenary of first telephone call by Alexander Graham Bell, Mar. 10, 1876.

Battle Scene — AP59

1976, June 14 **Engr.** ***Perf. 13***
C131 AP59 24fr red brn & ver 3.00 1.00

American Bicentennial.

Runners and Maple Leaf — AP60

1976, July 24 **Engr.** ***Perf. 13***
C132 AP60 33fr car, vio & brn 1.75 1.00

21st Olympic Games, Montreal, Canada, July 17-Aug. 1.

Whimsical Bird as Student and Collector AP61

1976, Aug. 21 **Photo.**
C133 AP61 42fr multi 3.00 1.50

Philately in School, Philatelic Exhibition in La Perouse Lyceum, Nouméa.

Old City Hall, Nouméa — AP62

Design: 125fr, New City Hall, Nouméa.

1976, Oct. 22 **Photo.** ***Perf. 13***
C134 AP62 75fr multi 5.00 2.75
C135 AP62 125fr multi 7.25 3.25

Lagoon, Women and Festival Symbols AP63

1977, Jan. 15 **Photo.** ***Perf. 13x12½***
C136 AP63 11fr multi 1.25 .55

Summer Festival 1977, Nouméa.

Training Children in Toy Cars — AP64

1977, Mar. 12 **Litho.** ***Perf. 13***
C137 AP64 50fr multi 3.00 1.60

Road safety training.

Bird Type of 1977

Design: 42fr, Male frigate bird, horiz.

1977, Sept. 17 **Photo.** ***Perf. 13***
C138 A89 42fr multi 6.00 1.60

Magenta Airport and Routes — AP65

Design: 57fr, La Tontouta airport.

1977, Oct. 22 **Litho.** ***Perf. 13***
C139 AP65 24fr multi 1.50 .90
C140 AP65 57fr multi 3.00 1.10

No. C129 Surcharged in Violet Blue: "22.11.77 PARIS NEW YORK"

1977, Nov. 22 **Engr.** ***Perf. 13***
C141 AP57 147fr car & ultra 14.00 9.00

Concorde, 1st commercial flight Paris-NY.

Old Nouméa, by H. Didonna — AP66

Valley of the Settlers, by Jean Kreber — AP67

1977, Nov. 26 **Photo.** ***Perf. 13***
C142 AP66 41fr gold & multi 3.00 1.50

Engr.

C143 AP67 42fr yel brn & dk brn 3.00 1.50

"Underwater Carnival," Aubusson Tapestry — AP68

1978, June 17 **Photo.** ***Perf. 13***
C144 AP68 105fr multi 5.50 2.25

"The Hare and the Tortoise" — AP69

1978, Aug. 19 **Photo.** ***Perf. 13x13½***
C145 AP69 35fr multi 4.50 1.50

School philately.

Bourail School Children, Map and Conus Shell — AP70

1978, Sept. 30 **Engr.** ***Perf. 13***
C146 AP70 41fr multi 3.00 1.25

Promotion of topical philately in Bourail public schools.

Old and New Candles — AP71

1978, Oct. 28 **Photo.** ***Perf. 13***
C147 AP71 36fr multi 2.00 .75

Third Caledonian Senior Citizens' Day.

Faubourg Blanchot, by Lacouture — AP72

1978, Nov. 25 **Photo.** ***Perf. 13***
C148 AP72 24fr multi 1.50 1.00

Type of 1978

Design: 42fr, Amyema scandens, horiz.

1978, Mar. 17 ***Perf. 13x12½***
C149 A91 42fr multi 3.50 1.60

Orbiting Weather Satellites, WMO Emblem AP73

1979, Mar. 24 **Photo.** ***Perf. 13***
C150 AP73 53fr multi 2.00 1.00

First world-wide satellite system in the atmosphere.

Ships and Emblem — AP74

1979, Mar. 31 **Engr.**
C151 AP74 49fr multi 2.00 .80

Chamber of Commerce and Industry, centenary.

Child's Drawing, IYC Emblem AP75

1979, Apr. 21 **Photo.** ***Perf. 13***
C152 AP75 35fr multi 2.00 .85

International Year of the Child.

Surf Casting AP76

Design: 30fr, Swordfish fishing.

1979, May 26 **Litho.** ***Perf. 12½***
C153 AP76 29fr multi 2.00 1.00
C154 AP76 30fr multi 2.00 1.00

Port-de-France, 1854, and de Montravel — AP77

1979, June 16 **Engr.** ***Perf. 13***
C155 AP77 75fr multi 4.25 2.25

125th anniversary of Noumea, formerly Port-de-France, founded by L. Tardy de Montravel.

The Eel Queen, Kanaka Legend — AP78

1979, July 7 **Photo.** ***Perf. 13***
C156 AP78 42fr multi 3.00 1.75

Nature protection.

Map of New Caledonia, Postmark, Five Races — AP79

1979, Aug. 18 Photo. *Perf. 13*
C157 AP79 27fr multi 1.50 .55

New Caledonian youth and philately.

Orstom Center, Noumea, Orstom Emblem — AP80

1979, Sept. 17 Photo. *Perf. 13*
C158 AP80 25fr multi 1.50 .55

Old Post Office, Noumea, New Caledonia No. 1, Hill — AP81

1979, Nov. 17 Engr.
C159 AP81 150fr multi 5.25 2.00

Sir Rowland Hill (1795-1879), originator of penny postage.

Pirogue AP82

1980, Jan. 26 Engr. *Perf. 13*
C160 AP82 45fr multi 2.00 1.10

Rotary Intl., 75th Anniv. — AP83

1980, Feb. 23 Photo. *Perf. 13*
C161 AP83 100fr multi 4.00 1.60

Man Holding Dolphinfish AP84

1980, Mar. 29 Photo. *Perf. 13x12½*
C162 AP84 34fr shown 1.75 1.00
C163 AP84 39fr Fishermen, sail fish, vert. 2.50 1.25

Coral Seas Air Rally — AP85

1980, June 7 Engr. *Perf. 13*
C164 AP85 31fr multi 1.50 .75

Carved Alligator, Boat — AP86

1980, June 21 Photo.
C165 AP86 27fr multi 1.50 .55

South Pacific Arts Festival, Port Moresby, Papua New Guinea.

New Caledonian Kiwanis, 10th Anniversary — AP87

1980, Sept. 10 Photo. *Perf. 13*
C166 AP87 50fr multi 1.90 .90

View of Old Noumea — AP88

1980, Oct. 25 Photo. *Perf. 13½*
C167 AP88 33fr multi 1.50 .90

Charles de Gaulle, 10th Anniversary of Death — AP89

1980, Nov. 15 Engr. *Perf. 13*
C168 AP89 120fr multi 7.00 3.50

Fluorescent Coral, Noumea Aquarium AP90

1980, Dec. 13 Photo. *Perf. 13x13½*
C169 AP90 60fr multi 2.25 1.10

Xeronema Moorei AP91

1981, Mar. 18 Photo. *Perf. 13x12½*
C170 AP91 38fr shown 1.50 1.25
C171 AP91 51fr Geissois pruinosa 2.00 1.40

Yuri Gagarin and Vostok I — AP92

20th Anniversary of First Space Flights: 155fr, Alan B. Shepard, Freedom 7.

1981, Apr. 8 Engr. *Perf. 13*
C172 AP92 64fr multi 2.75 1.10
C173 AP92 155fr multi 4.50 2.10
a. Souv. sheet of 2, #C172-C173 15.00 15.00

No. C173a sold for 225fr.

40th Anniv. of Departure of Pacific Batallion — AP93

1981, May 5 Photo. *Perf. 13*
C174 AP93 29fr multi 3.00 1.10

Ecinometra Mathaei AP94

1981, Aug. 5 Photo. *Perf. 13x13½*
C175 AP94 38fr shown 1.50 .80
C176 AP94 51fr Prionocidaris verticillata 2.25 .95

No. 4, Post Office Building AP95

1981, Sept. 16 Photo. *Perf. 13x13½*
C177 AP95 41fr multi 1.60 .75

Stamp Day.

Old Noumea Latin Quarter — AP96

1981, Oct. 14 Photo. *Perf. 13½*
C178 AP96 43fr multi 1.60 .75

New Caledonia to Australia Airmail Flight by Victor Roffey, 50th Anniv. AP97

1981, Nov. 21 Engr. *Perf. 13*
C179 AP97 37fr multi 1.25 .65

Rousette AP98

1982, Feb. 24 Engr. *Perf. 13*
C180 AP98 38fr shown 1.25 .75
C181 AP98 51fr Kagu 1.75 .85

See Nos. C188B-C188C.

50th Anniv. of Paris-Noumea Flight — AP99

1982, Apr. 5 Engr. *Perf. 13*
C182 AP99 250fr Pilots, map, plane 7.00 3.50

Scouting Year — AP100

1982, Apr. 21 Photo. *Perf. 13½x13*
C183 AP100 40fr multi 1.40 .65

PHILEXFRANCE '82 Intl. Stamp Show, Paris, June 11-21 — AP101

1982, May 12 Engr. *Perf. 13*
C184 AP101 150fr multi 3.25 2.00

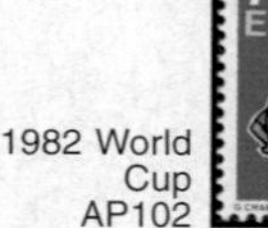

1982 World Cup AP102

1982, June 9 Photo. *Perf. 13x13½*
C185 AP102 74fr multi 2.10 1.00

French Overseas Possessions Week, Sept. 18-25 — AP103

1982, Sept. 17 *Perf. 13x12½*
C186 AP103 100fr Map, kagu, citizens 2.75 1.00

Gypsum, Poya Mines AP104

1983, Jan. 15 Photo. *Perf. 13x13½*
C187 AP104 44fr shown 2.00 1.10
C188 AP104 59fr Silica gel, Kone mine 3.00 1.40

World Communications Year — AP104a

Design: WCY emblem, map, globe.

1983, Mar. 9 Litho. *Perf. 13*
C188A AP104a 170fr multi 3.50 1.50

Aircraft Type of 1982

1983, July 6 Engr. *Perf. 13*
C188B AP98 46fr Pou-du-Ciel 1.25 .75
C188C AP98 61fr L'Aiglon Caudron 2.25 1.25

Temple and Dancers — AP105

1983, July 20 Litho. *Perf. 12½x12*
C189 AP105 47fr multi 1.25 .80

BANGKOK '83 Intl. Stamp Show, Aug. 4-13.

Oueholle Tribe, Straw Hut — AP106

1983, Sept. 7 Litho. *Perf. 13*
C190 AP106 76fr multi 2.00 1.10

Loyalty Islander by the Shore, by R. Mascart AP107

Paintings: 350fr, The Guitarist from Mare Island, by P. Neilly.

1983, Dec. 7 Photo. *Perf. 13*
C191 AP107 100fr multi 3.75 1.75
C192 AP107 350fr multi 9.00 5.25

Noumea Aquarium Fish AP108

1984, Mar. 7 Photo. *Perf. 13*
C193 AP108 46fr Amphiprion clarkii 2.25 .90
C194 AP108 61fr Centropyge bicolor 2.75 1.25

Local Plants — AP109

1984, Apr. 25 Litho. *Perf. 12½x13*
C195 AP109 51fr Araucaria columnaris 2.00 .90
C196 AP109 67fr Pritchardiopsis jeanneneyi 2.75 1.25

1984 Summer Olympics — AP110

1984, June 20 Photo. *Perf. 13½x13*
C197 AP110 50fr Swimming 1.75 1.10
C198 AP110 83fr Wind surfing 3.50 1.60
C199 AP110 200fr Running 6.00 2.75
Nos. C197-C199 (3) 11.25 5.45

Ausipex '84 — AP111

Army Day — AP112

1984, Sept. 21 Engr. *Perf. 13*
C200 AP111 150fr Exhibition Hall 4.00 1.60
a. Souvenir sheet 6.00 6.00

Se-tenant with label showing exhibition emblem. No. C200a contains No. C200 in changed colors.

1984, Oct. 27 Litho. *Perf. 13½x13*
C201 AP112 51fr multi 1.50 .70

Woman Fishing for Crabs, by Mme. Bonnet de Larbogne — AP113

Painting: 300fr, Cook Discovering New Caledonia, by Pilioko.

1984, Nov. 8 Litho. *Perf. 13x12½*
C202 AP113 120fr multi 3.50 1.75
C203 AP113 300fr multi 8.00 4.50

See Nos. 605-606.

Transpac Dragon Rapide, Map AP114

1985, Oct. 2 Litho. *Perf. 13½*
C204 AP114 80fr multi 1.75 1.25

Internal air services, 30th anniv.

UN, 40th Anniv. AP115

Perf. 12½x13
1985, Oct. 25 Wmk. 385
C205 AP115 250fr multi 5.50 2.00

Jules Garnier High School AP116

1985, Nov. 13 Unwmk. *Perf. 13*
C206 AP116 400fr multi 9.75 4.25

Paris-Noumea Scheduled Flights, 30th Anniv. — AP117

1986, Jan. 6
C207 AP117 72fr multi 2.00 1.25

Nou Island Livestock Warehouse — AP118

1986, June 14 Engr. *Perf. 13*
C208 AP118 230fr Prus bl, sep & brn 5.25 2.75

ATR-42 Inaugural Service AP119

1986, Aug. 13 Litho. *Perf. 12½x13*
C209 AP119 18fr multi .55 .45

STOCKHOLMIA '86 — AP120

1986, Aug. 29 Engr. *Perf. 13*
C210 AP120 108fr No. 1 2.75 1.25

Natl. Assoc. of Amateur Radio Operators, 25th Anniv. AP121

1987, Jan. 7 Litho. *Perf. 12½*
C211 AP121 64fr multi 1.75 .85

Nature Conservation, Fight Noise Pollution — AP122

1987, Mar. 25 Litho. *Perf. 13x12½*
C212 AP122 150fr multi 4.00 1.75

French Cricket Federation AP123

1987, Nov. 25 Litho. *Perf. 12½*
C213 AP123 94fr multi 2.25 1.75

Arms Type of 1984

1988, Jan. 13 *Perf. 12½x13*
C214 A132 76fr Dumbea 2.25 1.00

Rotary Intl. Anti-Polio Campaign — AP124

1988, Oct. 26 Litho. *Perf. 13½*
C215 AP124 220fr multi 5.25 2.75

Bamboo Type of 1989

Litho. & Engr.

1989, Sept. 27 *Perf. 12½x13*
C216 A187 44fr multi 1.25 .65

De Gaulle's Call For French Resistance, 50th Anniv. AP125

1990, June 20 Litho. *Perf. 12½*
C217 AP125 160fr multicolored 4.00 1.75

Military Cemetery, New Zealand — AP126

Auckland 1990: #C219, Brigadier William Walter Dove.

1990, Aug. 24 *Perf. 13*
C218 AP126 80fr multi 2.00 1.00
C219 AP126 80fr multi 2.00 1.00
a. Pair, #C218-C219 + label 4.75 4.75

Souvenir Sheet

New Zealand 1990 — AP126a

1990, Aug. 25 Litho. *Perf. 13x12½*
C219B AP126a 150fr multi 6.00 5.00

Crustaceans AP127

1990, Oct. 17 Litho. *Perf. 12½x13*
C220 AP127 30fr Munidopsis sp. Orstom .80 .55
C221 AP127 60fr Lyreidius tridentatus 1.75 1.10

30th South Pacific Conference — AP128

1990, Oct. 29 Litho. *Perf. 13*
C222 AP128 85fr multicolored 2.10 1.10

Gen. Charles de Gaulle (1890-1970) AP129

1990, Nov. 21 Engr. *Perf. 13*
C223 AP129 410fr dk blue 10.00 5.00

Scenic Views — AP130

1991, Feb. 13 Litho. *Perf. 13*
C224 AP130 36fr Fayawa-Ouvea Bay .90 .50
C225 AP130 90fr shown 2.40 1.25

See No. C246.

New Caledonian Cricket Players by Marcel Moutouh — AP131

Design: 435fr, Saint Louis by Janine Goetz.

1991, Dec. 18 *Perf. 13x12½*
C226 AP131 130fr multicolored 3.00 2.00
C227 AP131 435fr multicolored 10.00 5.00

See Nos. C236, C242, C260.

Blue River Nature Park — AP132

Illustration reduced.

1992, Feb. 6 Litho. *Perf. 12½*
C228 AP132 400fr multicolored 9.25 4.75
a. Souvenir sheet of 1 10.50 10.50

No. C228a sold for 450fr and was issued 2/5/92.

Native Pottery AP133

Photo. & Engr.

1992, Apr. 9 *Perf. 12½x13*
C229 AP133 25fr black & orange .75 .30

Expo '92, Seville AP134

1992, Apr. 25 Litho. *Perf. 13*
C230 AP134 10fr multicolored .35 .20

Discovery of America, 500th Anniv. AP135

#C234: a, Erik the Red, Viking longship. b, Columbus, coat of arms. c, Amerigo Vespucci.

1992, May 22 Litho. *Perf. 13½*
C231 AP135 80fr Pinta 2.00 1.00
C232 AP135 80fr Santa Maria 2.00 1.00
C233 AP135 80fr Nina 2.00 1.00
a. Strip of 3, #C231-C233 6.00 6.00
b. Bklt. pane of 3, #C231-C233 10.00 10.00

Souvenir Sheet

Perf. 12½

C234 AP135 110fr Sheet of 3, #a.-c. 10.00 10.00

World Columbian Stamp Expo '92, Chicago. No. C234 sold for 360fr.

1992 Summer Olympics, Barcelona — AP136

1992, July 25 *Perf. 13*
C235 AP136 260fr Synchronized swimming 6.75 3.25

Painters of the Pacific Type of 1991

Design: 205fr, Wahpa, by Paul Mascart

1992, Sept. 28 Litho. *Perf. 12½x13*
C236 AP131 205fr multicolored 5.00 2.50

Australian Bouvier — AP138

1992, Oct. 4 *Perf. 12*
C237 AP138 175fr multicolored 5.25 2.40

Exploration of New Caledonian Coast by Chevalier d'Entrecasteaux, Bicent. — AP139

1992, Nov. 18 Engr. *Perf. 13*
C238 AP139 110fr bl grn, ocher & olive grn 2.50 1.25

Shells — AP140

AP141

1992, Nov. 26 Litho. *Perf. 13½x13*
C239 AP140 30fr Amalda fuscolingua .75 .35
C240 AP140 50fr Cassis abbotti 1.25 .75

The vignettes on Nos. C239-C240 were applied by a thermographic process, producing a shiny, raised effect.

1992, Dec. 9 Litho. *Perf. 13½*

Comic Strip Characters from "La Brousse en Folie," by Bernard Berger: a, Dede. b. Torton Marcel in Mimine II. c, Tathan. d, Joinville.

C241 AP141 80fr Strip of 4, #a.-d. 8.00 8.00

Painters of the Pacific Type of 1991

Design: 150fr, Noumea, 1890, by Gaston Roullet (1847-1925).

1993, Mar. 25 Litho. *Perf. 13x12½*
C242 AP131 150fr multicolored 3.50 1.75

Extraction of Attar from Niaouli Flowers (Melaleuca Quinquenervia), Cent. — AP142

1993, Apr. 28 ***Perf. 13***
C243 AP142 85fr multicolored 2.00 1.00

Nicolaus Copernicus (1473-1543) — AP143

1993, May 5 **Engr.** ***Perf. 13***
C244 AP143 110fr multicolored 3.00 1.25

Polska '93.

Noumea Temple, Cent. AP144

1993, June 16 **Litho.** ***Perf. 12½x13***
C245 AP144 400fr multicolored 9.00 4.50

Scenic Views Type of 1991

1993, July 8 **Litho.** ***Perf. 13***
C246 AP130 85fr Malabou 2.00 1.00

Little Train of Thio — AP145

1993, July 24 **Engr.** ***Perf. 13***
C247 AP145 115fr multicolored 2.75 1.40

AP146

AP147

1993, Aug. 18 **Litho.**
C248 AP146 100fr multicolored 2.50 1.10

Henri Rochefort (1831-1913), writer.

1993, Oct. 1 ***Perf. 13½***

Bangkok '93: No. C249, Vanda coerulea. No. C250, Megastylis paradoxa. 140fr, Royal Palace, Bangkok, horiz.

C249 AP147 30fr multicolored .75 .35
C250 AP147 30fr multicolored .75 .35

Souvenir Sheet
Perf. 13

C251 AP147 140fr multicolored 3.00 3.00

No. C251 contains one 52x40mm stamp.

Air Caledonia, 10th Anniv. — AP148

1993, Oct. 9 ***Perf. 13***
C252 AP148 85fr multicolored 2.25 1.10

New Caledonia-Australia Telephone Cable, Cent. — AP149

1993, Oct. 15 **Engr.** ***Perf. 13x12½***
C253 AP149 200fr blue & black 4.75 2.25

Oxpleurodon Orbiculatus — AP150

1993, Oct. 15 **Litho.** ***Perf. 13½***
C254 AP150 250fr multicolored 6.00 2.75

Portions of the design on No. C254 were applied by a thermographic process producing a shiny, raised effect.

Tontouta Airport, Noumea, 25th Anniv. — AP151

1993, Nov. 29 **Litho.** ***Perf. 13***
C255 AP151 90fr multicolored 2.25 1.00

Christmas — AP152

1993, Dec. 9 **Litho.**
C256 AP152 120fr multicolored 3.00 1.25

Portions of the design on No. C256 were applied by a thermographic process producing a shiny, raised effect.

New Year 1994 (Year of the Dog) AP153

1994, Feb. 18 **Litho.** ***Perf. 13***
C257 AP153 60fr multicolored 1.75 .85

Hong Kong '94.

First Airbus A340 Flight, Paris-Noumea — AP154

1994, Mar. 31 **Litho.** ***Die Cut 8***
Self-Adhesive
C258 AP154 90fr multicolored 2.75 1.25

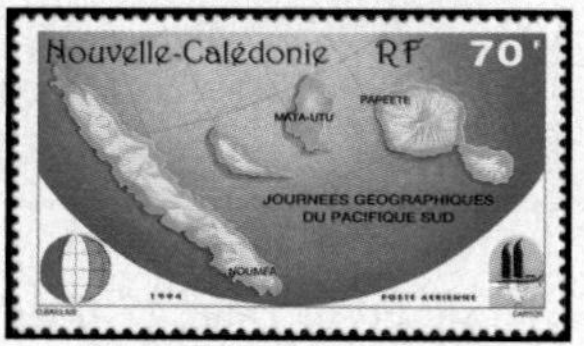
South Pacific Geography Day — AP155

1994, May 10 **Litho.** ***Perf. 13***
C259 AP155 70fr multicolored 1.75 .85

See Wallis and Futuna No. C177.

Painters of the Pacific Type of 1991

Design: 120fr, Legende du Poulpe, by Micheline Neporon.

1994, June 24 **Litho.** ***Perf. 13***
C260 AP131 120fr multicolored 3.00 1.40

Pottery, Museum of Noumea AP156

1994, July 6 **Litho.** ***Perf. 12½x13***
C261 AP156 95fr multicolored 2.50 1.10

1994 World Cup Soccer Championships, U.S. — AP156a

1994, July 12 **Litho.** ***Perf. 13***
C261A AP156a 105fr multicolored 2.50 1.50

Intl. Year of the Family AP157

PHILAKOREA '94 — AP158

Korean cuisine: No. C263a, Rice, celery, carrots, peppers. b, Lettuce, cabbage, garlic. c, Onions. d, Shrimp, oysters.

1994, Aug. 17 ***Perf. 13½x13***
C262 AP157 60fr multicolored 3.00 1.00

Souvenir Sheet
Perf. 12½

C263 Sheet of 4 4.75 4.75
a.-d. AP158 35fr any single 1.10 1.00

Research Ship Atalante — AP159

1994, Aug. 26 ***Perf. 13***
C264 AP159 120fr multicolored 2.75 1.50

Masons in New Caledonia, 125th Anniv. — AP160

1994, Sept. 16 *Perf. 13*
C265 AP160 350fr multicolored 8.00 3.75

Participation in First European Stamp Show — AP161

1994, Oct. 15 Litho. *Perf. 13*
C266 AP161 90fr Island 2.00 1.00
C267 AP161 90fr Herding cattle 2.00 1.00
a. Pair, #C266-C267 + label 4.50 4.50

ORSTOM, 50th Anniv. — AP162

1994, Nov. 14 Photo. *Perf. 13*
C268 AP162 95fr multicolored 2.50 1.25

Tiebaghi Mine — AP163

1994, Nov. 24 Litho.
C269 AP163 90fr multicolored 2.50 1.00

South Pacific Tourism Year AP164

1995, Mar. 15 Litho. *Perf. 13½*
C270 AP164 90fr multicolored 2.50 1.00

35th South Pacific Conference, Noumea — AP165

1995, Oct. 25 Litho. *Perf. 13*
C271 AP165 500fr multicolored 12.00 5.00

Kanak Dances AP166

1995, Dec. 8 Litho. *Perf. 13x13½*
C272 AP166 95fr Ouaré 2.25 1.00
C273 AP166 100fr Pothé 2.50 1.00

Mekosuchus Inexpactatus — AP167

1996, Feb. 23 Litho. *Perf. 13x13½*
C274 AP167 125fr multicolored 2.75 1.50

Indonesian Centenary AP168

1996, July 20
C275 AP168 130fr multicolored 3.00 3.00

Louis Brauquier (1900-76), Writer — AP169

1996, Aug. 7 Litho. *Perf. 12½*
C276 AP169 95fr multicolored 2.25 1.10

Ile Nou Ground Station, 20th Anniv. AP170

125fr, Guglielmo Marconi, telegraph wires.

1996, Sept. 26 Litho. *Perf. 13*
C277 AP170 95f multicolored 2.25 1.10
C278 AP170 125fr multicolored 2.75 1.50
a. Pair, #C277-C278 + label 5.00 5.00

Radio, cent. (#C278).

Regional Views — AP171

1996, Nov. 7 Litho. *Perf. 13*
C279 AP171 95fr Great reef 2.25 1.10
C280 AP171 95fr Mount Koghi 2.25 1.10
a. Pair, #C279-C280 + label 4.75 4.75

50th Autumn Philatelic Salon.

Christmas AP172

1996, Nov. 25 *Perf. 13½x13*
C281 AP172 95fr multicolored 2.25 1.10

Horned Turtle Meiolania AP173

1997, Jan. 8 Litho. *Perf. 13*
C282 AP173 95fr multicolored 3.00 1.25

Portions of the design were applied by a thermographic process producing a shiny, raised effect.

South Pacific Commission, 50th Anniv. — AP174

1997, Feb. 7 Litho. *Perf. 13X13½*
C283 AP174 100fr multicolored 2.25 1.10

Hong Kong '97 AP175

New Year 1997 (Year of the Ox) — #C285: a, Water buffalo pulling plow. b, Cattle in pasture.

1997, Feb. 12 *Perf. 13*
C284 AP175 95fr multicolored 2.50 1.10

Sheet of 2
Perf. 13x13½
C285 AP175 75fr #a.-b. 3.50 3.25

No. C285 contains two 40x30mm stamps.

Melanesian Pottery — AP176

Lapita pottery c. 1200-1000 B.C.: No. C286, With stylized faces. No. C287, With labyrinth pattern.

1997, May 14 Litho. *Perf. 13*
C286 AP176 95fr multicolored 2.25 2.25
C287 AP176 95fr multicolored 2.25 2.25

TRAPAS, French Airlines in the South Pacific, 1947-50 — AP177

Airplane, emblem, map showing: a, Australia, New Herbrides, Suva, Tahiti, New Zealand. b, Koumac, Poindimie, Noumea, Isle of Pines.

Photo. & Engr.
1997, Aug. 12 *Perf. 13*
C288 AP177 95fr multicolored 2.10 2.10
C289 AP177 95fr multicolored 2.10 2.10
a. Pair, #C288-C289 4.25 4.25

Regular Paris-Noumea Air Service, 50th Anniv. — AP178

1999, Sept. 29 Photo. *Perf. 13x12½*
C290 AP178 100fr multicolored 2.50 2.00

Inauguration of Noumea-Osaka Air Service — AP179

2001, Oct. 11 Litho. *Perf. 13*
C291 AP179 110fr multi 2.25 2.25

AIR POST SEMI-POSTAL STAMPS

French Revolution Issue
Common Design Type
Unwmk.
1939, July 5 Photo. *Perf. 13*
Name and Value Typo. in Orange
CB1 CD83 4.50fr + 4fr brn blk 25.00 25.00

Father & Child — SPAP1

1942, June 22 Engr. *Perf. 13*
CB2 SPAP1 1.50fr + 3.50fr green 1.40
CB3 SPAP1 2fr + 6fr yellow brown 1.40

Native children's welfare fund.
Nos. CB2-CB3 were issued by the Vichy government in France, but were not placed on sale in New Caledonia.

Colonial Education Fund

Common Design Type

1942, June 22

CB4	CD86a	1.20fr + 1.80fr blue & red	1.40

No. CB4 was issued by the Vichy government in France, but was not placed on sale in New Caledonia.

POSTAGE DUE STAMPS

For a short time in 1894, 5, 10, 15, 20, 25 and 30c postage stamps (Nos. 43, 45, 47, 49, 50 and 52) were overprinted with a "T" in an inverted triangle and used as Postage Due stamps.

French Colonies Postage Due Stamps Overprinted in Carmine, Blue or Silver

1903 Unwmk. *Imperf.*

J1	D1	5c blue (C)	2.25	2.25
J2	D1	10c brown (C)	8.50	6.75
J3	D1	15c yel grn (C)	17.00	6.50
J4	D1	30c carmine (Bl)	13.50	10.50
J5	D1	50c violet (Bl)	50.00	15.00
J6	D1	60c brn, *buff* (Bl)	225.00	60.00
J7	D1	1fr rose, *buff* (S)	27.50	17.50
J8	D1	2fr red brn (Bl)	1,000.	1,000.
		Nos. J1-J8 (8)	1,343.	1,118.

Nos. J1 to J8 are known with the "I" in "TENAIRE" missing.

Fifty years of French occupation.

Men Poling Boat — D2

Malayan Sambar — D3

1906 Typo. *Perf. 13½x14*

J9	D2	5c ultra, *azure*	.50	.50
J10	D2	10c vio brn, *buff*	.50	.50
J11	D2	15c grn, *greenish*	.70	.70
J12	D2	20c blk, *yellow*	.70	.70
J13	D2	30c carmine	1.25	1.10
J14	D2	50c ultra, *buff*	1.75	1.75
J15	D2	60c brn, *azure*	1.25	1.25
J16	D2	1fr dk grn, *straw*	2.00	1.90
		Nos. J9-J16 (8)	8.65	8.40

Type of 1906 Issue Surcharged

1926-27

J17	D2	2fr on 1fr vio	4.50	4.50
J18	D2	3fr on 1fr org brn	4.50	4.50

1928 Typo.

J19	D3	2c sl bl & dp brn	.20	.20
J20	D3	4c brn red & bl grn	.35	.35
J21	D3	5c red org & bl blk	.50	.50
J22	D3	10c mag & Prus bl	.50	.50
J23	D3	15c dl grn & scar	.50	.50
J24	D3	20c mar & ol grn	.75	.75
J25	D3	25c bis brn & sl bl	.55	.55
J26	D3	30c bl grn & ol grn	.75	.75
J27	D3	50c lt brn & dk red	1.00	1.00
J28	D3	60c mag & brt rose	1.00	1.00
J29	D3	1fr dl bl & Prus grn	1.40	1.40
J30	D3	2fr dk red & ol grn	1.75	1.60
J31	D3	3fr violet & brn	2.25	2.00
		Nos. J19-J31 (13)	11.50	11.10

Catalogue values for unused stamps in this section, from this point to the end of the section, are for Never Hinged items.

D4

Bat — D5

1948 Unwmk. Photo. *Perf. 13*

J32	D4	10c violet	.20	.20
J33	D4	30c brown	.20	.20
J34	D4	50c blue green	.35	.35
J35	D4	1fr orange	.35	.35
J36	D4	2fr red violet	.50	.50
J37	D4	3fr red brown	.50	.50
J38	D4	4fr dull blue	1.00	.85
J39	D4	5fr henna brown	1.00	.85
J40	D4	10fr slate green	1.75	1.40
J41	D4	20fr violet blue	2.25	1.90
		Nos. J32-J41 (10)	8.10	7.10

1983 Litho. *Perf. 13*

J42	D5	1fr multi	.20	.20
J43	D5	2fr multi	.25	.20
J44	D5	3fr multi	.25	.20
J45	D5	4fr multi	.35	.35
J46	D5	5fr multi	.45	.45
J47	D5	10fr multi	.60	.55
J48	D5	20fr multi	.75	.70
J49	D5	40fr multi	1.25	1.10
J50	D5	50fr multi	1.40	1.25
		Nos. J42-J50 (9)	5.50	5.00

For overprint see No. 696.

MILITARY STAMPS

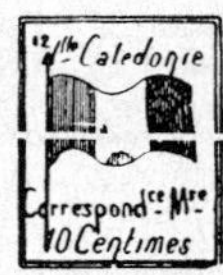

Stamps of the above types, although issued by officials, were unauthorized and practically a private speculation.

OFFICIAL STAMPS

Catalogue values for unused stamps in this section are for Never Hinged items.

Ancestor Pole — O1

Carved Wooden Pillow — O2

Various carved ancestor poles.

1959 Unwmk. Typo. *Perf. 14x13*

O1	O1	1fr org yel	.40	.20
O2	O1	3fr lt bl grn	.40	.20
O3	O1	4fr purple	.55	.35
O4	O1	5fr ultra	.75	.35
O5	O1	9fr black	.85	.45
O6	O1	10fr brt vio	1.25	.70
O7	O1	13fr yel grn	1.50	.90
O8	O1	15fr lt bl	1.75	1.10
O9	O1	24fr red lilac	2.00	1.10
O10	O1	26fr deep org	2.75	1.40
O11	O1	50fr green	4.75	2.75
O12	O1	100fr chocolate	10.00	4.75
O13	O1	200fr red	20.00	8.00
		Nos. O1-O13 (13)	46.95	22.25

1973-87 Photo. *Perf. 13*

Vignette: Green, Red Brown (2, 29, 31, 35, 38, 65, 76fr), Brown (40fr), Blue (58fr)

O14	O2	1fr yellow	.25	.20
O14A	O2	2fr green ('87)	.25	.20
O15	O2	3fr tan	.40	.20
O16	O2	4fr pale violet	.50	.20
O17	O2	5fr lilac rose	.50	.35
O18	O2	9fr light blue	.80	.35
O19	O2	10fr orange	.80	.45
O20	O2	11fr bright lilac ('76)	.50	.35
O21	O2	12fr bl grn ('73)	.95	.45
O22	O2	15fr green ('76)	.60	.35
O23	O2	20fr rose ('76)	.60	.35
O24	O2	23fr red ('80)	.85	.55
O25	O2	24fr Prus bl ('76)	.85	.35
O25A	O2	25fr gray ('81)	1.25	.55
O26	O2	26fr yellow ('76)	.95	.35
O26A	O2	29fr dl grn ('83)	1.25	.70
O26B	O2	31fr yellow ('82)	1.00	.70
O26C	O2	35fr yellow ('84)	1.25	.70
O27	O2	36fr dp lil rose ('76)	1.25	.45
O27A	O2	38fr tan	1.25	.70
O27B	O2	40fr blue ('87)	1.25	.45
O28	O2	42fr bister ('76)	1.40	.55
O29	O2	50fr blue ('76)	1.40	.75
O29A	O2	58fr blue grn ('87)	1.75	.70
O29B	O2	65fr lilac ('84)	1.75	.90
O29C	O2	76fr brt yel ('87)	2.25	.90
O30	O2	100fr red ('76)	2.75	1.25
O31	O2	200fr orange ('76)	5.00	2.10
		Nos. O14-O31 (28)	33.60	16.10

This is an expanding set. Numbers will change when complete.

PARCEL POST STAMPS

Type of Regular Issue of 1905-28 Surcharged or Overprinted

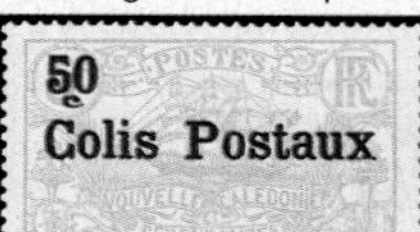

1926 Unwmk. *Perf. 14x13½*

Q1	A18	50c on 5fr olive, *lav*	1.10	.90
Q2	A18	1fr deep blue	1.50	1.40
Q3	A18	2fr car, *bluish*	1.75	1.60
		Nos. Q1-Q3 (3)	4.35	3.90

Regular Issue of 1928 Overprinted:

1930

Q4	A20	50c violet & brown	1.10	.90
Q5	A21	1fr dp ol & sal red	1.50	1.40
Q6	A21	2fr red org & brn	2.00	1.60
		Nos. Q4-Q6 (3)	4.60	3.90

NEW GUINEA

'nü 'gi-nē

LOCATION — On an island of the same name in the South Pacific Ocean, north of Australia.
GOVT. — Mandate administered by Australia
AREA — 93,000 sq. mi.
POP. — 675,369 (1940)
CAPITAL — Rabaul

The territory occupies the northeastern part of the island and includes New Britain and other nearby islands. It was formerly a German possession and should not be confused with British New Guinea (Papua) which is in the southeastern part of the same island, nor Netherlands New Guinea (Vol. 4). For previous issues see German New Guinea, New Britain, North West Pacific Islands. Issues for 1952 and later are listed under Papua.

12 Pence = 1 Shilling
20 Shillings = 1 Pound

Native Huts — A1

Bird of Paradise — A2

1925-28 **Engr.** ***Perf. 11***

1	A1	½p	orange	2.75	*8.00*
2	A1	1p	yellow green	2.75	*6.25*
3	A1	1½p	vermilion ('26)	3.75	*3.00*
4	A1	2p	claret	2.75	*5.00*
5	A1	3p	deep blue	5.00	4.50
6	A1	4p	olive green	15.00	*24.00*
7	A1	6p	yel bister ('28)	5.00	*55.00*
a.			6p light brown	22.50	55.00
b.			6p olive bister ('27)	7.00	55.00
8	A1	9p	deep violet	15.00	*50.00*
9	A1	1sh	gray green	17.50	*30.00*
10	A1	2sh	red brown	35.00	*55.00*
11	A1	5sh	olive bister	55.00	*75.00*
12	A1	10sh	dull rose	110.00	*210.00*
13	A1	£1	grnsh gray	210.00	*350.00*
			Nos. 1-13 (13)	479.50	875.75

For overprints see Nos. C1-C13, O1-O9.

1931, Aug. 2

18	A2	1p	light green	4.50	1.75
19	A2	1½p	red	5.75	*11.50*
20	A2	2p	violet brown	5.75	2.50
21	A2	3p	deep blue	5.75	5.50
22	A2	4p	olive green	7.50	*22.50*
23	A2	5p	slate green	5.75	*22.50*
24	A2	6p	bister	8.00	*30.00*
25	A2	9p	dull violet	9.00	*21.00*
26	A2	1sh	bluish gray	7.00	*17.00*
27	A2	2sh	red brown	11.50	*35.00*
28	A2	5sh	olive brown	47.50	*62.50*
29	A2	10sh	rose red	95.00	*150.00*
30	A2	£1	gray	210.00	*290.00*
			Nos. 18-30 (13)	423.00	*671.75*

10th anniversary of Australian Mandate.
For overprints see #C14-C27, O12-O22.

Type of 1931 without date scrolls

1932-34 ***Perf. 11***

31	A2	1p	light green	2.25	.25
32	A2	1½p	violet brown	2.25	*12.50*
33	A2	2p	red	2.25	.25
34	A2	2½p	dp grn ('34)	7.50	*24.00*
35	A2	3p	gray blue	2.75	.90
36	A2	3½p	magenta ('34)	15.00	*12.50*
37	A2	4p	olive green	2.75	*7.00*
38	A2	5p	slate green	2.75	.80
39	A2	6p	bister	4.50	*3.75*
40	A2	9p	dull violet	11.00	*25.00*
41	A2	1sh	bluish gray	5.00	*11.50*
42	A2	2sh	red brown	4.50	*19.00*
43	A2	5sh	olive brown	30.00	*50.00*
44	A2	10sh	rose red	55.00	*80.00*
45	A2	£1	gray	110.00	*110.00*
			Nos. 31-45 (15)	257.50	*357.45*

For overprints see #46-47, C28-C43, O23-O35. See footnote following C43.

Silver Jubilee Issue

Stamps of 1932-34 Overprinted

1935, June 27
Glazed Paper

46	A2	1p	light green	1.00	.85
47	A2	2p	red	2.25	.55
			Set, never hinged	6.00	

King George VI — A3

1937, May 18 **Engr.**

48	A3	2p	salmon rose	.20	*1.25*
49	A3	3p	blue	.20	*1.75*
50	A3	5p	green	.35	*1.75*
51	A3	1sh	brown violet	.60	*1.75*
			Nos. 48-51 (4)	1.35	6.50
			Set, never hinged	2.50	

Coronation of George VI and Queen Elizabeth.

AIR POST STAMPS

Regular Issues of 1925-28 Overprinted

1931, June ***Perf. 11***

C1	A1	½p	orange	1.75	*7.50*
C2	A1	1p	yellow green	1.75	*5.75*
C3	A1	1½p	vermilion	1.40	*5.75*
C4	A1	2p	claret	1.40	*8.00*
C5	A1	3p	deep blue	2.00	*15.00*
C6	A1	4p	olive green	1.40	*10.00*
C7	A1	6p	light brown	2.00	*16.00*
C8	A1	9p	deep violet	3.50	*19.00*
C9	A1	1sh	gray green	3.50	*19.00*
C10	A1	2sh	red brown	8.00	*47.50*
C11	A1	5sh	ol bister	22.50	*75.00*
C12	A1	10sh	light red	85.00	*110.00*
C13	A1	£1	grnsh gray	160.00	*290.00*
			Nos. C1-C13 (13)	294.20	628.50

Type of Regular Issue of 1931 and Nos. 18-30 Overprinted

1931, Aug.

C14	A2	½p	orange	3.75	3.75
C15	A2	1p	light green	4.50	*5.50*
C16	A2	1½p	red	4.25	*11.50*
C17	A2	2p	violet brown	4.25	3.50
C18	A2	3p	deep blue	7.00	*7.00*
C19	A2	4p	olive green	7.00	7.00
C20	A2	5p	slate green	7.00	*12.50*
C21	A2	6p	bister	8.00	*30.00*
C22	A2	9p	dull violet	9.00	*17.00*
C23	A2	1sh	bluish gray	8.50	*17.00*
C24	A2	2sh	red brown	18.00	*55.00*
C25	A2	5sh	olive brown	47.50	*80.00*
C26	A2	10sh	rose red	70.00	*140.00*
C27	A2	£1	gray	125.00	*290.00*
			Nos. C14-C27 (14)	323.75	679.75

10th anniversary of Australian Mandate.

Same Overprint on Type of Regular Issue of 1932-34 and Nos. 31-45

1932-34 ***Perf. 11***

C28	A2	½p	orange	.65	*1.75*
C29	A2	1p	light green	1.40	*1.75*
C30	A2	1½p	violet brown	2.00	*8.50*
C31	A2	2p	red	2.00	*.35*
C32	A2	2½p	dp grn ('34)	7.00	2.75
C33	A2	3p	gray blue	3.75	3.50
C34	A2	3½p	mag ('34)	5.00	*3.75*
C35	A2	4p	olive green	5.00	*11.50*
C36	A2	5p	slate green	8.00	*8.50*
C37	A2	6p	bister	5.00	*17.00*
C38	A2	9p	dull violet	7.00	*10.00*
C39	A2	1sh	bluish gray	7.00	*10.00*
C40	A2	2sh	red brown	11.50	*55.00*
C41	A2	5sh	olive brown	55.00	*62.50*
C42	A2	10sh	rose red	92.50	92.50
C43	A2	£1	gray	85.00	62.50
			Nos. C28-C43 (16)	297.80	351.85

No. C28 exists without overprint, but is believed not to have been issued in this condition. Value $200.

Plane over Bulolo Goldfield AP1

1935, May 1 **Engr.** **Unwmk.**

C44	AP1	£2	violet	275.00	160.00
C45	AP1	£5	green	625.00	550.00

AP2

1939, Mar. 1

C46	AP2	½p	orange	4.25	*8.00*
C47	AP2	1p	green	3.75	*5.00*
C48	AP2	1½p	vio brown	4.50	*11.00*
C49	AP2	2p	red orange	9.00	4.00
C50	AP2	3p	dark blue	15.00	*21.00*
C51	AP2	4p	ol bister	16.00	*9.75*
C52	AP2	5p	slate grn	13.50	4.25
C53	AP2	6p	bister brn	29.00	21.00
C54	AP2	9p	dl violet	29.00	*27.50*
C55	AP2	1sh	sage green	29.00	*21.00*
C56	AP2	2sh	car lake	75.00	*55.00*
C57	AP2	5sh	ol brown	150.00	*110.00*
C58	AP2	10sh	rose red	425.00	290.00
C59	AP2	£1	grnsh gray	110.00	*125.00*
			Nos. C46-C59 (14)	913.00	*712.50*

OFFICIAL STAMPS

Regular Issue of 1925 Overprinted

1925-29 **Unwmk.** ***Perf. 11***

O1	A1	1p	yellow green	1.10	*5.00*
O2	A1	1½p	vermilion ('29)	6.25	*19.00*
O3	A1	2p	claret	2.00	*4.25*
O4	A1	3p	deep blue	4.00	*8.50*
O5	A1	4p	olive green	5.00	*9.75*
O6	A1	6p	yel bister ('29)	8.00	*40.00*
a.			6p olive bister	22.50	*40.00*
O7	A1	9p	deep violet	4.50	*40.00*
O8	A1	1sh	gray green	6.25	*40.00*
O9	A1	2sh	red brown	32.50	*70.00*
			Nos. O1-O9 (9)	69.60	*236.50*

Nos. 18-28 Overprinted

1931, Aug. 2

O12	A2	1p	light green	8.00	*15.00*
O13	A2	1½p	red	9.00	*13.50*
O14	A2	2p	violet brown	11.50	*8.00*
O15	A2	3p	deep blue	7.50	*7.00*
O16	A2	4p	olive green	7.00	*9.75*
O17	A2	5p	slate green	11.50	*13.50*
O18	A2	6p	bister	16.00	*19.00*
O19	A2	9p	dull violet	18.00	*32.50*
O20	A2	1sh	bluish gray	18.00	*32.50*
O21	A2	2sh	red brown	45.00	*80.00*
O22	A2	5sh	olive brown	110.00	*200.00*
			Nos. O12-O22 (11)	261.50	*430.75*

10th anniversary of Australian Mandate.

Same Overprint on Nos. 31-43

1932-34

O23	A2	1p	light green	11.00	*12.00*
O24	A2	1½p	violet brown	12.00	*13.00*
O25	A2	2p	red	12.00	*3.75*
O26	A2	2½p	dp green ('34)	4.25	*7.00*
O27	A2	3p	gray blue	9.00	*29.00*
O28	A2	3½p	magenta ('34)	4.25	*10.00*
O29	A2	4p	olive green	11.50	*21.00*
O30	A2	5p	slate green	9.00	*21.00*
O31	A2	6p	bister	17.50	*47.50*
O32	A2	9p	dull violet	15.00	*47.50*
O33	A2	1sh	bluish gray	17.50	*32.50*
O34	A2	2sh	red brown	40.00	*85.00*
O35	A2	5sh	olive brown	140.00	*190.00*
			Nos. O23-O35 (13)	303.00	*519.25*

NEW HEBRIDES, BRITISH

'nü 'he-brə-ˌdēz

LOCATION — A group of islands in the South Pacific Ocean northeast of New Caledonia
GOVT. — Condominium under the joint administration of Great Britain and France
AREA — 5,790 sq. mi.
POP. — 100,000 (est. 1976)
CAPITAL — Vila (Port-Vila)

Stamps were issued by both Great Britain and France. In 1911 a joint issue bore the coats of arms of both countries. The British stamps bore the arms of Great Britain and the value in British currency on the right and the French arms and value at the left. On the French stamps the positions were reversed. After World War II when the franc dropped in value, both series were sold for their value in francs.

New Hebrides became the independent state of Vanuatu in 1980.

12 Pence = 1 Shilling
100 Centimes = 1 Franc
100 Centimes = 1 Hebrides Franc (FNH) (1977)

French issues (inscribed "Nouvelles Hebrides") follow after No. J20.

Catalogue values for unused stamps in this country are for Never Hinged items, beginning with Scott 62 in the regular postage section, Scott J11 in the postage due section.

British Issues

Stamps of Fiji, 1903-06, Overprinted

1908-09 Wmk. 2 Perf. 14

Colored Bar Covers "FIJI" on #2-6, 9

No.	Type	Description	Unused	Used
1	A22	½p gray grn ('09)	60.00	*92.50*
2	A22	2p vio & orange	2.25	*2.50*
3	A22	2½p vio & ultra, *bl*	2.00	*2.50*
4	A22	5p vio & green	3.50	*4.00*
5	A22	6p vio & car rose	3.50	*3.50*
6	A22	1sh grn & car rose	145.00	*290.00*
		Nos. 1-6 (6)	216.25	*395.00*

Wmk. Multiple Crown and CA (3)

No.	Type	Description	Unused	Used
7	A22	½p gray green	1.00	*8.00*
8	A22	1p carmine	.60	*1.00*
a.		Pair, one without overprint	10,000.	
9	A22	1sh grn & car rose ('09)	21.00	*4.25*
		Nos. 7-9 (3)	22.60	*13.25*

Nos. 2-6, 9 are on chalk-surfaced paper.

Stamps of Fiji, 1904-11, Overprinted in Black or Red

1910, Dec. 15

No.	Type	Description	Unused	Used
10	A22	½p green	4.00	*27.50*
11	A22	1p carmine	11.00	*9.75*
12	A22	2p gray	.80	*3.50*
13	A22	2½p ultra	1.00	*4.75*
14	A22	5p violet & ol grn	1.60	*6.25*
15	A22	6p violet	4.00	*5.75*
16	A22	1sh black, *grn* (R)	6.00	*8.50*
		Nos. 10-16 (7)	28.40	*66.00*

Nos. 14-16 are on chalk-surfaced paper.

Native Idols — A1

1911, July 25 Engr. Wmk. 3

No.	Type	Description	Unused	Used
17	A1	½p pale green	1.00	*2.00*
18	A1	1p red	4.25	*2.25*
19	A1	2p gray	9.25	4.50
20	A1	2½p ultramarine	3.50	*6.25*
21	A1	5p olive green	5.00	*8.00*
22	A1	6p claret	3.50	*5.75*
23	A1	1sh black, *green*	3.00	*15.00*
24	A1	2sh violet, *blue*	25.00	*25.00*
25	A1	5sh green, *yel*	40.00	*55.00*
		Nos. 17-25 (9)	94.50	*123.75*

See Nos. 33-37. For surcharges see Nos. 26-29, 38-39, French Issues No. 36.

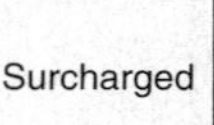

Surcharged

1920-21

No.	Type	Description	Unused	Used
26	A1	1p on 5p ol green ('21)	10.00	*70.00*
a.		Inverted surcharge	3,000.	
27	A1	1p on 1sh black, *grn*	2.25	*15.00*
28	A1	1p on 2sh violet, *blue*	1.75	*11.50*
29	A1	1p on 5sh green, *yel*	1.75	*11.50*

On French Issue No. 16

No.	Type	Description	Unused	Used
30	A2	2p on 40c red, *yel* ('21)	2.00	*21.00*
		Nos. 26-30 (5)	17.75	*129.00*

No. 31

On French Issue No. 27

Wmk. R F in Sheet

No.	Type	Description	Unused	Used
31	A2	2p on 40c red, *yel* ('21)	145.00	*625.00*

The letters "R.F." are the initials of "Republique Francaise." They are large double-lined Roman capitals, about 120mm high. About one-fourth of the stamps in each sheet show portions of the watermark, the other stamps are without watermark.

No. 26a is considered by some to be printers' waste.

Type of 1911 Issue

1921, Oct. Wmk. 4

No.	Type	Description	Unused	Used
33	A1	1p rose red	2.90	*16.00*
34	A1	2p gray	5.00	*42.50*
37	A1	6p claret	16.00	*85.00*
		Nos. 33-37 (3)	23.90	*143.50*

For surcharge see No. 40.

Stamps of 1911-21 Surcharged with New Values as in 1920-21

1924, May 1 Wmk. 3

No.	Type	Description	Unused	Used
38	A1	1p on ½p pale green	4.50	*25.00*
39	A1	5p on 2½p ultra	8.50	*24.00*
a.		Inverted surcharge	2,750.	

Wmk. 4

No.	Type	Description	Unused	Used
40	A1	3p on 1p rose red	4.50	*12.50*
		Nos. 38-40 (3)	17.50	*61.50*

No. 39a is considered by some to be printers' waste.

A3

The values at the lower right denote the currency and amount for which the stamps were to be sold. The English stamps could be bought at the French post office in French money.

1925 Engr.

No.	Type	Description	Unused	Used
41	A3	½p (5c) black	1.40	*14.00*
42	A3	1p (10c) green	1.10	*12.50*
43	A3	2p (20c) grnsh gray	2.00	*3.00*
44	A3	2½p (25c) brown	1.10	*15.00*
45	A3	5p (50c) ultra	3.50	*3.00*
46	A3	6p (60c) claret	4.00	*14.00*
47	A3	1sh (1.25fr) black, *grn*	3.75	*21.00*
48	A3	2sh (2.50fr) vio, *bl*	7.00	*25.00*
49	A3	5sh (6.25fr) grn, *yel*	7.00	*29.00*
		Nos. 41-49 (9)	30.85	*136.50*

Beach Scene A5

1938, June 1 Wmk. 4 Perf. 12

No.	Type	Description	Unused	Used
50	A5	5c green	2.90	*4.50*
51	A5	10c dark orange	1.40	*2.25*
52	A5	15c violet	4.00	*4.50*
53	A5	20c rose red	1.90	*3.00*
54	A5	25c brown	1.90	*3.00*
55	A5	30c dark blue	2.50	*2.90*
56	A5	40c olive green	5.00	*7.00*
57	A5	50c brown vio	1.90	*3.00*
58	A5	1fr car, *emerald*	4.50	*9.75*
59	A5	2fr dk blue, *emer*	35.00	19.00
60	A5	5fr red, *yellow*	80.00	55.00
61	A5	10fr violet, *blue*	225.00	85.00
		Nos. 50-61 (12)	366.00	198.90
		Set, never hinged	500.00	

Catalogue values for unused stamps in this section, from this point to the end of the section, are for Never Hinged items.

UPU Issue

Common Design Type

1949, Oct. 10 Engr. Perf. 13½

No.	Type	Description	Unused	Used
62	CD309	10c red orange	.60	*1.00*
63	CD309	15c violet	.60	*1.00*
64	CD309	30c violet blue	.75	*1.00*
65	CD309	50c rose violet	1.00	*1.25*
		Nos. 62-65 (4)	2.95	4.25

Common Design Types pictured following the introduction.

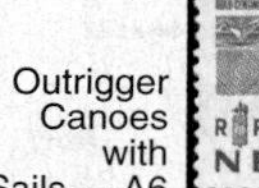

Outrigger Canoes with Sails — A6

Designs: 25c, 30c, 40c and 50c, Native Carving. 1fr, 2fr and 5fr, Island couple.

1953, Apr. 30 Perf. 12½

No.	Type	Description	Unused	Used
66	A6	5c green	.75	.20
67	A6	10c red	.75	.20
68	A6	15c yellow	.75	.20
69	A6	20c ultramarine	.75	.30
70	A6	25c olive	.75	.40
71	A6	30c light brown	.75	.50
72	A6	40c black brown	.75	.80
73	A6	50c violet	1.25	.90
74	A6	1fr deep orange	6.25	1.75
75	A6	2fr red violet	6.25	*10.00*
76	A6	5fr scarlet	11.00	*25.00*
		Nos. 66-76 (11)	30.00	*40.25*

Coronation Issue

Common Design Type

1953, June 2 Perf. 13½x13

No.	Type	Description	Unused	Used
77	CD312	10c car & black	.60	.60

Discovery of New Hebrides, 1606 — A7

20c, 50c, Britannia, Marianne, Flags & Mask.

Perf. 14½x14

1956, Oct. 20 Photo. Wmk. 4

No.	Type	Description	Unused	Used
78	A7	5c emerald	.30	.20
79	A7	10c crimson	.30	.20
80	A7	20c ultramarine	.30	.20
81	A7	50c purple	.30	.20
		Nos. 78-81 (4)	1.20	.80

50th anniv. of the establishment of the Anglo-French Condominium.

Port Vila and Iririki Islet — A8

Designs: 25c, 30c, 40c, 50c, Tropical river and spear fisherman. 1fr, 2fr, 5fr, Woman drinking from coconut (inscribed: "Franco-British Alliance 4th March 1947").

1957, Sept. 3 Engr. Perf. 13½x13

No.	Type	Description	Unused	Used
82	A8	5c green	.50	*1.25*
83	A8	10c red	.35	.20
84	A8	15c orange yellow	.60	*1.25*
85	A8	20c ultramarine	.50	.20
86	A8	25c olive	.60	.20
87	A8	30c light brown	.60	.20
88	A8	40c sepia	.60	.20
89	A8	50c violet	.90	.20
90	A8	1fr orange	1.25	1.25
91	A8	2fr rose lilac	6.00	3.50
92	A8	5fr black	12.00	5.50
		Nos. 82-92 (11)	23.90	13.95

Freedom from Hunger Issue

Common Design Type

Perf. 14x14½

1963, Sept. 2 Photo. Wmk. 314

No.	Type	Description	Unused	Used
93	CD314	60c green	.85	.35

Red Cross Centenary Issue

Common Design Type with Royal Cipher and "RF" Replacing Queen's Portrait

1963, Sept. 2 Litho. Perf. 13

No.	Type	Description	Unused	Used
94	CD315	15c black & red	.45	.20
95	CD315	45c ultra & red	.65	.25

Copra Industry A9

Designs: 5c, Manganese loading, Forari Wharf. 10c, Cacao. 20c, Map of New Hebrides, tuna, marlin, ships. 25c, Striped triggerfish. 30c, Pearly nautilus (mollusk). 40c, 60c, Turkeyfish. 50c, Lined tang (fish). 1fr, Cardinal honey-eater and hibiscus. 2fr, Buff-bellied flycatcher. 3fr, Thicket warbler. 5fr, White-collared kingfisher.

Wmk. 314 (10c, 20c, 40c, 60c, 3fr); Unwmkd. (others)

Perf. 12½ (10c, 20c, 40c, 60c); 14 (3fr); 13 (others)

Photo. (10c, 20c, 40c, 60c, 3fr); Engraved (others)

1963-67

No.	Type	Description	Unused	Used
96	A9	5c Prus bl, pur brn & cl ('66)	.20	.20
a.		5c prus blue & claret ('72)	50.00	37.50
97	A9	10c brt grn, org brn & dk brn ('65)	.20	.20
98	A9	15c dk pur, yel & brn	.25	.25
99	A9	20c brt blue, gray & cit ('65)	.40	.25
100	A9	25c vio, rose lil & org brn ('66)	.75	.50
101	A9	30c lilac, brn & cit	1.00	.75
102	A9	40c dk bl & ver ('65)	1.25	1.10
103	A9	50c Prus bl, yel & green	1.10	.80
103A	A9	60c dk bl & ver ('67)	1.90	1.25
104	A9	1fr blue grn, blk & red ('66)	3.00	2.25
105	A9	2fr ol, blk & brn	4.00	3.00
106	A9	3fr org grn, brt grn & blk ('65)	11.00	8.00
107	A9	5fr indigo, dp bl & gray ('67)	20.00	16.00
		Nos. 96-107 (13)	45.05	34.55

For surcharge see No. 141.

ITU Emblem CD317

Perf. 11x11½

1965, May 17 Litho. Wmk. 314

108 CD317 15c ver & ol bister .35 .20
109 CD317 60c ultra & ver .85 .60

Intl. Cooperation Year Issue

Common Design Type with Royal Cipher and "RF" Replacing Queen's Portrait

1965, Sept. 24 ***Perf. 14½***

110 CD318 5c blue grn & claret .25 .20
111 CD318 55c lt violet & green .40 .25

Churchill Memorial Issue

Common Design Type with Royal Cipher and "RF" Replacing Queen's Portrait

1966, Jan. 24 Photo. ***Perf. 14***

112 CD319 5c multicolored .30 .20
113 CD319 15c multicolored .50 .20
114 CD319 25c multicolored .75 .20
115 CD319 30c multicolored .75 .20
Nos. 112-115 (4) 2.30 .80

World Cup Soccer Issue

Common Design Type with Royal Cipher and "RF" Replacing Queen's Portrait

1966, July 1 Litho. ***Perf. 14***

116 CD321 20c multicolored .30 .30
117 CD321 40c multicolored .70 .70

WHO Headquarters Issue

Common Design Type with Royal Cipher and "RF" Replacing Queen's Portrait

1966, Sept. 20 Litho. ***Perf. 14***

118 CD322 25c multicolored .20 .20
119 CD322 60c multicolored .50 .25

UNESCO Anniversary Issue

Common Design Type with Royal Cipher and "RF" Replacing Queen's Portrait

1966, Dec. 1 Litho. ***Perf. 14***

120 CD323 15c "Education" .25 .25
121 CD323 30c "Science" .50 .50
122 CD323 45c "Culture" .80 .80
Nos. 120-122 (3) 1.55 1.55

Coast Watchers — A11

25c, Map of South Pacific war zone, US Marine and Australian soldier. 60c, Australian cruiser Canberra. 1fr, Flying fortress taking off from Bauer Field, & view of Vila.

Perf. 14x13

1967, Sept. 26 Photo. Wmk. 314

123 A11 15c lt blue & multi .20 .20
124 A11 25c yellow & multi .30 .30
125 A11 60c multicolored .75 .75
126 A11 1fr pale salmon & multi 1.25 1.25
Nos. 123-126 (4) 2.50 2.50

25th anniv. of the Allied Forces' campaign in the South Pacific War Zone.

Globe and World Map A12

Designs: 25c, Ships La Boudeuse and L'Etoile and map of Bougainville Strait. 60c, Louis Antoine de Bougainville, ship's figure-head and bougainvillaea.

1968, May 23 Engr. ***Perf. 13***

127 A12 15c ver, emer & dull vio .20 .20
128 A12 25c ultra, olive & brn .30 .20
129 A12 60c magenta, grn & brn .55 .30
Nos. 127-129 (3) 1.05 .70

200th anniv. of Louis Antoine de Bougainville's (1729-1811) voyage around the world.

Concorde Airliner A13

Design: 60c, Concorde, sideview.

1968, Oct. 9 Litho. ***Perf. 14x13½***

130 A13 25c vio bl, red & lt bl 1.00 .75
131 A13 60c red, ultra & black 2.00 1.50

Development of the Concorde supersonic airliner, a joint Anglo-French project to produce a high speed plane.

Kauri Pine — A14

Perf. 14x14½

1969, June 30 Wmk. 314

132 A14 20c brown & multi .25 .25

New Hebrides timber industry. Issued in sheets of 9 (3x3) on simulated wood grain background.

Relay Race, French and British Flags — A15

Design: 1fr, Runner at right.

Perf. 12½x13

1969, Aug. 13 Photo. Unwmk.

133 A15 25c ultra, car, brn & gold .20 .20
134 A15 1fr brn, car, ultra & gold .65 .65

3rd South Pacific Games, Port Moresby, Papua and New Guinea, Aug. 13-23.

Land Diver, Pentecost Island — A16

Designs: 15c, Diver in starting position on tower. 1fr, Diver nearing ground.

Wmk. 314

1969, Oct. 15 Litho. ***Perf. 12½***

135 A16 15c yellow & multi .20 .20
136 A16 25c pink & multi .25 .25
137 A16 1fr gray & multi .80 .80
Nos. 135-137 (3) 1.25 1.25

UPU Headquarters and Monument, Bern — A17

Unwmk.

1970, May 20 Engr. ***Perf. 13***

138 A17 1.05fr org, lilac & slate .85 .85

Opening of the new UPU Headquarters, Bern.

Charles de Gaulle — A18

1970, July 20 Photo. ***Perf. 13***

139 A18 65c brown & multi .50 .50
140 A18 1.10fr dp blue & multi 1.25 1.25

30th anniv. of the rallying to the Free French.
For overprints see Nos. 144-145.

No. 99 Surcharged

1970, Oct. 15 Wmk. 314 ***Perf. 12½***

141 A9 35c on 20c multi .75 .75

Virgin and Child, by Giovanni Bellini — A19

Christmas: 50c, Virgin and Child, by Giovanni Cima.

Perf. 14½x14

1970, Nov. 30 Litho. Wmk. 314

142 A19 15c tan & multi .20 .20
143 A19 50c lt green & multi .35 .35

Nos. 139-140 Overprinted with 2 Black Vertical Bars and Gold Inscription: "1890-1970 / IN MEMORIAM / 9-11-70"

Unwmk.

1971, Jan. 19 Photo. ***Perf. 13***

144 A18 65c brown & multi .50 .50
145 A18 1.10fr dp blue & multi 1.00 1.00

In memory of Gen. Charles de Gaulle (1890-1970), President of France.

Soccer — A20

Design: 65c, Basketball, vert.

1971, July 13 Photo. ***Perf. 12½***

146 A20 20c multicolored .20 .20
147 A20 65c multicolored .50 .50

4th South Pacific Games, Papeete, French Polynesia, Sept. 8-19.

Kauri Pine, Cone and Arms of Royal Society — A21

Perf. 14½x14

1971, Sept. 7 Litho. Wmk. 314

148 A21 65c multicolored .65 .65

Royal Society of London for the Advancement of Science expedition to study vegetation and fauna, July 1-October.

Adoration of the Shepherds, by Louis Le Nain — A22

Design: 50c, Adoration of the Shepherds, by Jacopo Tintoretto.

1971, Nov. 23 ***Perf. 14x13½***

149 A22 25c lt green & multi .25 .25
150 A22 50c lt blue & multi .50 .50

Christmas. See Nos. 167-168.

Drover Mk III — A23

Airplanes: 25c, Sandringham seaplane. 30c, Dragon Rapide. 65c, Caravelle.

Perf. 13½x13

1972, Feb. 29 Photo. Unwmk.

151 A23 20c lt green & multi .40 .40
152 A23 25c ultra & multi .50 .50
153 A23 30c orange & multi .70 .70
154 A23 65c dk blue & multi 1.40 1.40
Nos. 151-154 (4) 3.00 3.00

Headdress, South Malekula — A24

Baker's Pigeon — A25

Artifacts: 15c, Slit gong and carved figure, North Ambrym. 1fr, Carved figures, North Ambrym. 3fr, Ceremonial headdress, South Malekula.
Birds: 20c, Red-headed parrot-finch. 35c, Chestnut-bellied kingfisher. 2fr, Green palm lorikeet.
Sea shells: 25c, Cribraria fischeri. 30c, Oliva rubrolabiata. 65c, Strombus plicatus. 5fr, Turbo marmoratus.

1972, July 24 Photo. *Perf. 12½x13*
155 A24 5c plum & multi .20 .20
156 A25 10c blue & multi .20 .20
157 A24 15c red & multi .30 .40
158 A25 20c org brown & multi .35 .50
159 A25 25c dp blue & multi .50 .80
160 A25 30c dk green & multi .65 .85
161 A25 35c gray bl & multi .70 1.10
162 A24 65c dk green & multi 1.25 3.75
163 A24 1fr orange & multi 2.00 3.00
164 A25 2fr multicolored 4.50 4.50
165 A24 3fr yellow & multi 6.50 6.75
166 A24 5fr pink & multi 10.00 13.50
Nos. 155-166 (12) 27.15 35.55

For overprints and surcharges see #181-182, 217-228.

Christmas Type of 1971

Designs: 25c, Adoration of the Magi (detail), by Bartholomaeus Spranger. 70c, Virgin and Child, by Jan Provoost.

Perf. 14x13½
1972, Sept. 25 Litho. Wmk. 314
167 A22 25c lt green & multi .20 .20
168 A22 70c lt blue & multi .50 .50

Silver Wedding Issue, 1972
Common Design Type

Design: Elizabeth II and Prince Philip.

1972, Nov. 20 Photo. *Perf. 14x14½*
169 CD324 35c vio black & multi .25 .25
170 CD324 65c olive & multi .50 .50

Dendrobium Teretifolium A26

New Wharf, Vila A27

Orchids: 30c, Ephemerantha comata. 35c, Spathoglottis petri. 65c, Dendrobium mohlianum.

1973, Feb. 26 Litho. *Perf. 14*
171 A26 25c blue vio & multi .50 .35
172 A26 30c multicolored .70 .45
173 A26 35c violet & multi .80 .55
174 A26 65c dk green & multi 2.25 1.10
Nos. 171-174 (4) 4.25 2.45

1973, May 14 Wmk. 314

Design: 70c, New wharf, horiz.

175 A27 25c multicolored .25 .25
176 A27 70c multicolored .80 .80

New wharf at Vila, finished Nov. 1972.

Wild Horses, Tanna Island A28

Perf. 13x12½
1973, Aug. 13 Photo. Unwmk.
177 A28 35c shown .45 .45
178 A28 70c Yasur Volcano, Tanna 1.50 1.25

Mother and Child, by Marcel Moutouh — A29

Christmas: 70c, Star over Lagoon, by Tatin d'Avesnieres.

Perf. 14x13½
1973, Nov. 19 Litho. Wmk. 314
179 A29 35c tan & multi .25 .25
180 A29 70c lilac rose & multi .50 .50

Nos. 161 and 164 Overprinted in Red or Black: "ROYAL VISIT / 1974"

Perf. 12½x13
1974, Feb. 11 Photo. Unwmk.
181 A25 35c multicolored (R) .30 .30
182 A25 2fr multicolored (B) 1.45 1.45

Visit of British Royal Family, Feb. 11-12.

Pacific Dove A30

Designs: 35c, Night swallowtail. 70c, Green sea turtle. 1.15fr, Flying fox.

1974, Feb. 11 *Perf. 13x12½*
183 A30 25c gray & multi 1.25 .60
184 A30 35c gray & multi 1.75 .85
185 A30 70c gray & multi 2.75 1.65
186 A30 1.15fr gray & multi 4.75 2.25
Nos. 183-186 (4) 10.50 5.35

Nature conservation.

Old Post Office, Vila — A31

Design: 70c, New Post Office.

1974, May 6 Unwmk. *Perf. 12*
187 A31 35c blue & multi .40 .40
188 A31 70c red & multi .80 .80
a. Pair, #187-188 1.25 1.25

Opening of New Post Office, May, 1974.

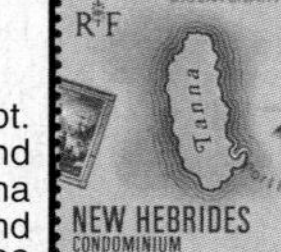

Capt. Cook and Tanna Island A32

#190, William Wales, & boat landing on island. #191, William Hodges painting islanders & landscape. 1.15fr, Capt. Cook, "Resolution" & map of New Hebrides.

Wmk. 314
1974, Aug. 1 Litho. *Perf. 13*
Size: 40x25mm
189 A32 35c multicolored 1.50 .75
190 A32 35c multicolored 1.50 .75
191 A32 35c multicolored 1.50 .75
a. Strip of 3, #189-191 4.75 3.00

Perf. 11
Size: 58x34mm
192 A32 1.15fr lilac & multi 3.00 3.00
Nos. 189-192 (4) 7.50 5.25

Bicentenary of the discovery of the New Hebrides by Capt. Cook. No. 191a has continuous design.

Exchange of Letters, UPU Emblem A33

Perf. 13x12½
1974, Oct. 9 Photo. Unwmk.
193 A33 70c multicolored .65 .65

Centenary of Universal Postal Union.

Nativity, by Gerard van Honthorst — A34

Christmas: 35c, Adoration of the Kings, by Velazquez, vert.

Wmk. 314
1974, Nov. 14 Litho. *Perf. 13½*
194 A34 35c multicolored .30 .30
195 A34 70c multicolored .50 .50

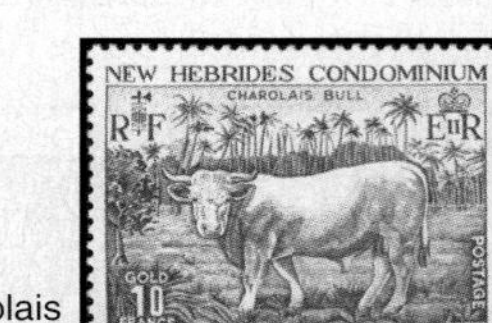

Charolais Bull — A35

1975, Apr. 29 Engr. *Perf. 13*
196 A35 10fr multicolored 10.00 17.00

For surcharge see No. 229.

A36

A37

1975, Aug. 5 Litho. *Perf. 14x13½*
197 A36 25c Kayak race .20 .20
198 A36 35c Camp cooks .25 .25
199 A36 1fr Map makers .65 .65
200 A36 5fr Fishermen 5.00 5.00
Nos. 197-200 (4) 6.10 6.10

Nordjamb 75, 14th Boy Scout Jamboree, Lillehammer, Norway, July 29-Aug. 7.

Perf. 14½x14
1975, Nov. 11 Litho. Wmk. 373

Christmas (After Michelangelo): 35c, Pitti Madonna. 70c, Bruges Madonna. 2.50fr, Taddei Madonna.

201 A37 35c ol green & multi .20 .20
202 A37 70c brown & multi .45 .45
203 A37 2.50fr blue & multi 1.50 1.50
Nos. 201-203 (3) 2.15 2.15

Concorde, British Airways Colors and Emblem — A38

Unwmk.
1976, Jan. 30 Typo. *Perf. 13*
204 A38 5fr blue & multi 7.50 7.50

First commercial flight of supersonic jet Concorde from London to Bahrain, Jan. 21.

Telephones, 1876 and 1976 — A39

Designs: 70c, Alexander Graham Bell. 1.15fr, Nouméa earth station and satellite.

1976, Mar. 31 Photo. *Perf. 13*
205 A39 25c black, car & blue .30 .30
206 A39 70c black & multi .50 .50
207 A39 1.15fr black, org & vio bl 1.20 1.20
Nos. 205-207 (3) 2.00 2.00

Centenary of first telephone call by Alexander Graham Bell, Mar. 10, 1876.

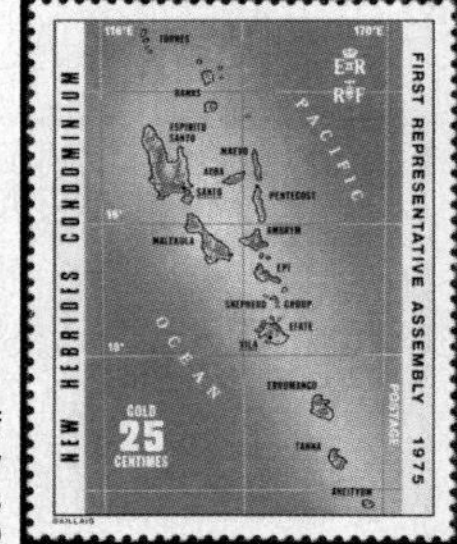

Map of New Hebrides A40

View of Santo A41

Design: 2fr, View of Vila.

1976, June 29 Photo. *Perf. 13*
208 A40 25c blue & multi .30 .30
209 A41 1fr multicolored .70 .70
210 A41 2fr multicolored 1.50 1.50
Nos. 208-210 (3) 2.50 2.50

Opening of First Representative Assembly, June 29 (25c); first Santo Municipal Council (1fr); first Vila Municipal Council (2fr).

Flight into Egypt, by Francisco Vieira Lusitano — A42

Christmas (Portuguese 16th Cent. Paintings): 70c, Adoration of the Shepherds. 2.50fr, Adoration of the Kings.

Wmk. 373

1976, Nov. 8	**Litho.**		***Perf. 14***	
211	A42	35c purple & multi	.25	.25
212	A42	70c blue & multi	.40	.40
213	A42	2.50fr lt green & multi	1.25	1.25
		Nos. 211-213 (3)	1.90	1.90

Queen's Visit, 1974 — A43

70c, Imperial state crown. 2fr, The blessing.

1977, Feb. 7			***Perf. 14x13½***	
214	A43	35c lt green & multi	.20	.20
215	A43	70c blue & multi	.25	.25
216	A43	2fr pink & multi	.60	.60
		Nos. 214-216 (3)	1.05	1.05

25th anniv. of the reign of Elizabeth II.

Nos. 155-166, 196 Surcharged with New Value, "FNH" and Bars

Paris Overprints

Perf. 12½x13

1977, July 1	**Photo.**		**Unwmk.**	
217	A24	5fr on 5c multi	.45	*.60*
218	A25	10fr on 10c multi	.90	.40
219	A24	15fr on 15c multi	.70	*1.75*
220	A25	20fr on 20c multi	1.50	.60
221	A24	25fr on 25c multi	2.00	2.00
222	A24	30fr on 30c multi	2.00	1.25
223	A25	35fr on 35c multi	2.00	1.50
224	A24	40fr on 65c multi	1.50	1.50
225	A24	50fr on 1fr multi	1.20	2.00
226	A25	70fr on 2fr multi	7.50	1.25
227	A24	100fr on 3fr multi	1.20	*4.00*
228	A24	200fr on 5fr multi	6.00	*15.00*

Wmk. 314

	Engr.		***Perf. 13***	
229	A35	500fr on 10fr multi	15.00	22.50
		Nos. 217-229 (13)	41.95	54.35

Nos. 155//166, 196 Surcharged with New Value, "FNH" and Bars

FNH FNH FNH 25 FNH
a b c d

Port Vila Overprints

Two settings of 35fr and 200fr surcharges: type 1, 1.4mm between new value and "FNH"; type 2, 2.1mm between value and "FNH."

Perf. 12½x13

1977-78	**Photo.**		**Unwmk.**	
217a	A24	5fr on 5c (a)	.60	.20
218a	A25	10fr on 10c (b)	.85	.20
219a	A24	15fr on 15c (c)	3.50	1.50
221a	A24	25fr on 25c (d)	60.00	24.00
222a	A24	30fr on 30c (d)	300.00	90.00
223a	A25	35fr on 35c (d), type 1	3.50	.90
b.		Type 2	6.00	1.20
224a	A24	40fr on 65c (d)	1.75	.65
225a	A24	50fr on 1fr (d)	30.00	20.00
227a	A24	100fr on (d)	30.00	*20.00*
228a	A24	200fr on 5fr (d), type 1	20.00	15.00
b.		Type 2	—	—
229a	A35	500fr on 10fr (d)	22.50	16.00
		Nos. 217a-229a (11)	472.70	188.45

The 50fr and 100fr values were sold only through the philatelic bureau.

Issued: 10fr, 7/10; 15fr, 7/18; 5fr, 8/10; #228a, 8/22; 25fr, 30fr, #223a, 9/10; 40fr, 9/12; 500fr, 9/14; #223b, 1/6/78; #228b, 1/13/78.

Erromango and Kaori Tree — A44

Tempi Madonna, by Raphael — A45

Designs: 10fr, Archipelago and man making copra. 15fr, Espiritu Santo Island and cattle. 20fr, Efate Island and Post Office, Vila. 25fr, Malakula Island and headdresses. 30fr, Aoba and Maewo Islands and pig tusks. 35fr, Pentecost Island and land diving. 40fr, Tanna Island and Prophet John Frum's Red Cross. 50fr, Shepherd Island and canoe with sail. 70fr, Banks Island and dancers. 100fr, Ambrym Island and carvings. 200fr, Aneityum Island and decorated baskets. 500fr, Torres Islands and fishing with bow and arrow.

1977-78	**Wmk. 373**	**Litho.**	***Perf. 14***	
238	A44	5fr multicolored	.20	.20
239	A44	10fr multicolored	.20	.20
240	A44	15fr multicolored	.25	.25
241	A44	20fr multicolored	.30	.30
242	A44	25fr multicolored	.40	.40
243	A44	30fr multicolored	.50	.50
244	A44	35fr multicolored	.55	.55
245	A44	40fr multicolored	.60	.60
246	A44	50fr multicolored	.75	.75
247	A44	70fr multicolored	1.25	1.25
248	A44	100fr multicolored	1.75	1.75
249	A44	200fr multicolored	3.50	3.50
250	A44	500fr multicolored	7.50	7.50
		Nos. 238-250 (13)	17.75	17.75

Issue dates: 5fr, 20fr, 50fr, 100fr, 200fr, Sept. 7; 15fr, 25fr, 30fr, 40fr, Nov. 23, 1977; 10fr, 35fr, 70fr, 500fr, May 9, 1978.

1977, Dec. 8	**Litho.**		***Perf. 12***	

Christmas: 15fr, Virgin and Child, by Gerard David. 30fr, Virgin and Child, by Pompeo Batoni.

251	A45	10fr multicolored	.25	.25
252	A45	15fr multicolored	.30	.30
253	A45	30fr multicolored	.55	.50
		Nos. 251-253 (3)	1.10	1.05

British Airways Concorde over New York City — A46

20fr, British Airways Concorde over London. 30fr, Air France Concorde over Washington. 40fr, Air France Concorde over Paris.

1978, May 9	**Wmk. 373**		***Perf. 14***	
254	A46	10fr multicolored	.50	.20
255	A46	20fr multicolored	.70	.40
256	A46	30fr multicolored	1.75	.60
257	A46	40fr multicolored	2.25	.80
		Nos. 254-257 (4)	5.20	2.00

Concorde, 1st commercial flight, Paris to NYC.

Elizabeth II Coronation Anniversary Issue

Common Design Types
Souvenir Sheet

1978, June 2	**Unwmk.**		***Perf. 15***	
258		Sheet of 6	3.50	3.50
a.		CD326 40fr White horse of Hanover	.70	.70
b.		CD327 40fr Elizabeth II	.70	.70
c.		CD328 40fr Gallic cock	.70	.70

No. 258 contains 2 se-tenant strips of Nos. 258a-258c, separated by horizontal gutter with commemorative and descriptive inscriptions and showing central part of coronation procession with coach.

Virgin and Child, by Dürer — A47

Dürer Paintings: 15fr, Virgin and Child with St. Anne. 30fr, Virgin and Child with Goldfinch. 40fr, Virgin and Child with Pear.

Perf. 14x13½

1978, Dec. 1	**Litho.**		**Wmk. 373**	
259	A47	10fr multicolored	.20	.20
260	A47	15fr multicolored	.25	.25
261	A47	30fr multicolored	.30	.30
262	A47	40fr multicolored	.40	.40
		Nos. 259-262 (4)	1.15	1.15

Christmas and 450th death anniv. of Albrecht Dürer (1471-1528), German painter.

Type of 1976 Surcharged with New Value, Bars over Denomination and Inscription at Right. Longitude changed to "166E."

1979, Jan. 11	**Photo.**		***Perf. 13***	
263	A40	10fr on 25c bl & multi	.30	.30
264	A40	40fr on 25c lt grn & multi	.60	.60

1st anniv. of Internal Self-Government.

New Hebrides No. 50 — A48

Rowland Hill and New Hebrides Stamps: 20fr, No. 136. 40fr, No. 43.

1979, Sept. 10	**Litho.**		***Perf. 14***	
265	A48	10fr multicolored	.20	.20
266	A48	20fr multicolored	.25	.25
a.		Souvenir sheet of 2	.90	.90
267	A48	40fr multicolored	.40	.40
		Nos. 265-267 (3)	.85	.85

Sir Rowland Hill (1795-1879), originator of penny postage. No. 266a contains New Hebrides, British, No. 266, and French, No. 286; margin shows Mulready envelope.

Arts Festival — A49

Designs: 10fr, Clubs and spears. 20fr, Ritual puppet. 40fr, Headdress.

1979, Nov. 16	**Wmk. 373**		***Perf. 14***	
268	A49	5fr multicolored	.20	.20
269	A49	10fr multicolored	.20	.20
270	A49	20fr multicolored	.25	.25
271	A49	40fr multicolored	.40	.40
		Nos. 268-271 (4)	1.05	1.05

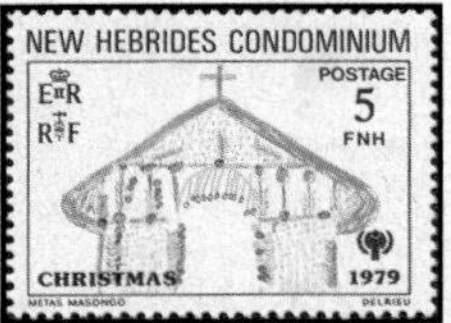

Church, IYC Emblem A50

IYC Emblem, Children's Drawings: 10fr, Father Christmas. 20fr, Cross and Bible, vert. 40fr, Stars, candle and Santa Claus, vert.

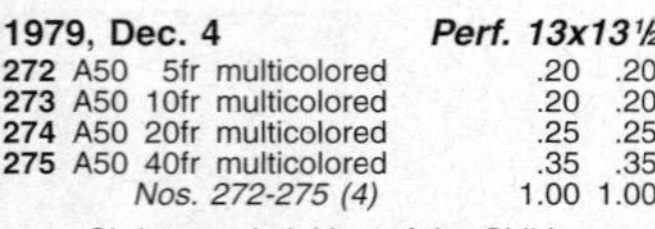

1979, Dec. 4 *Perf. 13x13½*

No.	Type	Description	Unused	Used
272	A50	5fr multicolored	.20	.20
273	A50	10fr multicolored	.20	.20
274	A50	20fr multicolored	.25	.25
275	A50	40fr multicolored	.35	.35
		Nos. 272-275 (4)	1.00	1.00

Christmas; Intl. Year of the Child.

White-bellied Honeyeater — A51

1980, Feb. 27 **Litho.** *Perf. 14*

No.	Type	Description	Unused	Used
276	A51	10fr shown	.70	.20
277	A51	20fr Scarlet robins	1.00	.45
278	A51	30fr Yellow white-eyes	1.50	.65
279	A51	40fr Fan-tailed brush cuckoo	2.00	.85
		Nos. 276-279 (4)	5.20	2.15

New Hebrides stamps were replaced in 1980 by those of Vanuatu.

POSTAGE DUE STAMPS

British Issues

Type of 1925 Overprinted

1925, June **Engr.** **Wmk. 4** *Perf. 14*

No.	Type	Description	Unused	Used
J1	A3	1p (10c) green	37.50	1.25
J2	A3	2p (20c) gray	40.00	1.25
J3	A3	3p (30c) carmine	40.00	3.25
J4	A3	5p (50c) ultra	45.00	5.50
J5	A3	10p (1fr) car, *blue*	52.50	6.50
		Nos. J1-J5 (5)	215.00	17.75

Values for Nos. J1-J5 are for toned copies.

Regular Stamps of 1938 Overprinted in Black

1938, June 1 *Perf. 12*

No.	Type	Description	Unused	Used
J6	A5	5c green	20.00	*32.50*
J7	A5	10c dark orange	20.00	*32.50*
J8	A5	20c rose red	22.50	*50.00*
J9	A5	40c olive green	27.50	*57.50*
J10	A5	1fr car, *emerald*	35.00	*67.50*
		Nos. J6-J10 (5)	125.00	*240.00*

Catalogue values for unused stamps in this section, from this point to the end of the section, are for Never Hinged items.

Regular Stamps of 1953 Overprinted in Black

1953, Apr. 30 *Perf. 12½*

No.	Type	Description	Unused	Used
J11	A6	5c green	4.75	*7.50*
J12	A6	10c red	2.25	*6.00*
J13	A6	20c ultramarine	6.00	*11.00*
J14	A6	40c black brown	8.50	*27.50*
J15	A6	1fr deep orange	5.50	*32.50*
		Nos. J11-J15 (5)	27.00	*84.50*

Same on Nos. 82-83, 85, 88 and 90

1957, Sept. 3 *Perf. 13½x13*

No.	Type	Description	Unused	Used
J16	A8	5c green	.40	*1.75*
J17	A8	10c red	.55	*2.00*
J18	A8	20c ultramarine	1.25	*2.25*
J19	A8	40c sepia	2.75	*3.50*
J20	A8	1fr orange	5.25	*8.50*
		Nos. J16-J20 (5)	10.20	*18.00*

NEW HEBRIDES, FRENCH

ˈnü ˈhe-brə-ˌdēz

LOCATION — A group of islands in the South Pacific Ocean lying north of New Caledonia

GOVT. — Condominium under the joint administration of Great Britain and France

AREA — 5,790 sq. mi.

POP. — 100,000 (est. 1976)

CAPITAL — Port-Vila (Vila)

Postage stamps are issued by both Great Britain and France. In 1911 a joint issue was made bearing the coats of arms of both countries. The British stamps bore the coat of arms of Great Britain and the value in British currency on the right and the French coat of arms and values at the left. On the French stamps the positions were reversed. This resulted in some confusion when the value of the French franc decreased following World War I but the situation was corrected by arranging that both series of stamps be sold for their value as expressed in French currency.

12 Pence = 1 Shilling
100 Centimes = 1 Franc
New Hebrides Franc (FNH) — 1977

Catalogue values for unused stamps in this country are for Never Hinged items, beginning with Scott 79 in the regular postage section, Scott J16 in the postage due section.

French Issues

Stamps of New Caledonia, 1905, Overprinted in Black or Red

Nos. 1-4

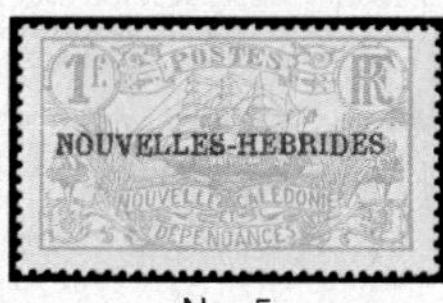

No. 5

1908 **Unwmk.** *Perf. 14x13½*

No.	Type	Description	Unused	Used
1	A16	5c green	3.75	*5.50*
2	A16	10c rose	4.50	*6.75*
3	A17	25c blue, *grnsh* (R)	7.25	*11.00*
4	A17	50c carmine, *org*	8.00	*12.00*
5	A18	1fr bl, *yel grn* (R)	16.00	*24.00*
		Nos. 1-5 (5)	39.50	*59.25*

For overprints and surcharges see #6-10, 33-35.

Stamps of 1908 with Additional Overprint

1910

No.	Type	Description	Unused	Used
6	A16	5c green	1.75	*2.40*
7	A16	10c rose	2.00	*2.75*
8	A17	25c blue, *grnsh* (R)	3.50	*5.25*
9	A17	50c car, *orange*	5.25	*7.50*
10	A18	1fr bl, *yel grn* (R)	14.00	*20.00*
		Nos. 6-10 (5)	26.50	*37.90*

A2

Perf. 14

1911, July 12 **Engr.** **Wmk. 3**

No.	Type	Description	Unused	Used
11	A2	5c pale green	.55	*1.10*
12	A2	10c red	.55	*1.10*
13	A2	20c gray	2.00	*4.00*
14	A2	25c ultramarine	2.50	*5.00*
15	A2	30c vio, *yellow*	4.00	*8.00*
16	A2	40c red, *yellow*	4.00	*8.00*
17	A2	50c olive green	4.00	*8.00*
18	A2	75c brn orange	5.25	*10.50*
19	A2	1fr brn red, *bl*	3.50	*7.00*
20	A2	2fr violet	6.75	*13.50*
21	A2	5fr brn red, *grn*	13.00	*26.00*
		Nos. 11-21 (11)	46.10	*92.20*

For surcharges see Nos. 36-37, 43 and British issue No. 30.

1912 **Wmk. R F in Sheet**

No.	Type	Description	Unused	Used
22	A2	5c pale green	1.75	1.75
23	A2	10c red	1.75	1.75
24	A2	20c gray	2.10	2.10
25	A2	25c ultramarine	2.50	2.50
26	A2	30c vio, *yellow*	2.50	2.50
27	A2	40c red, *yellow*	20.00	20.00
28	A2	50c olive green	8.50	8.50
29	A2	75c brn orange	8.50	8.50
30	A2	1fr brn red, *bl*	4.25	4.25
31	A2	2fr violet	9.25	9.25
32	A2	5fr brn red, *grn*	17.00	17.00
		Nos. 22-32 (11)	78.10	78.10

In the watermark, "R F" (République Française initials) are large double-lined Roman capitals, about 120mm high. About one-fourth of the stamps in each sheet show parts of the watermark. The other stamps are without watermark.

For surcharges see Nos. 38-42 and British issue No. 31.

Nos. 9 and 8 Surcharged

1920 **Unwmk.** *Perf. 14x13½*

No.	Type	Description	Unused	Used
33	A17	5c on 50c red, *org*	2.50	2.50
34	A17	10c on 25c bl, *grnsh*	1.40	1.40

Same Surcharge on No. 4

No.	Type	Description	Unused	Used
35	A17	5c on 50c red, *org*	900.00	*1,100.*

British Issue No. 21 and French Issue No. 15 Surcharged

1921 **Wmk. 3** *Perf. 14*

No.	Type	Description	Unused	Used
36	A1	10c on 5p ol grn	11.50	11.50
37	A2	20c on 30c vio, *yel*	13.00	11.50

Nos. 27 and 26 Surcharged

1921 **Wmk. R F in Sheet**

No.	Type	Description	Unused	Used
38	A2	5c on 40c red, *yel*	27.50	27.50
39	A2	20c on 30c vio, *yel*	11.50	11.50

Stamps of 1910-12 Surcharged with New Values as in 1920-21

1924

No.	Type	Description	Unused	Used
40	A2	10c on 5c pale grn	2.75	2.75
41	A2	30c on 10c red	2.75	2.75
42	A2	50c on 25c ultra	4.50	4.50

Wmk. 3

No.	Type	Description	Unused	Used
43	A2	50c on 25c ultra	22.50	22.50
		Nos. 40-43 (4)	32.50	32.50

A4

The values at the lower right denote the currency and amount for which the stamps were to be sold. The stamps could be purchased at the French post office and used to pay postage at the English rates.

1925 **Engr.** **Wmk. R F in Sheet**

No.	Type	Description	Unused	Used
44	A4	5c (½p) black	.90	*3.50*
45	A4	10c (1p) green	.75	*3.00*
46	A4	20c (2p) grnsh gray	.75	*3.00*
47	A4	25c (2½p) brown	.75	*3.00*
48	A4	30c (3p) carmine	.75	*3.00*
49	A4	40c (4p) car, *org*	.90	*3.50*
50	A4	50c (5p) ultra	1.25	*5.00*
51	A4	75c (7½p) bis brn	1.75	*7.00*
52	A4	1fr (10p) car, *blue*	3.00	*12.00*
53	A4	2fr (1sh 8p) gray vio	3.50	*14.00*
54	A4	5fr (4sh) car, *grnsh*	7.00	*27.50*
		Nos. 44-54 (11)	21.30	*84.50*

For overprints see Nos. J1-J5.

Beach Scene A6

1938 *Perf. 12*

No.	Type	Description	Unused	Used
55	A6	5c green	1.25	*2.50*
56	A6	10c dark orange	1.25	*2.50*
57	A6	15c violet	1.10	*2.25*
58	A6	20c rose red	1.25	*2.50*
59	A6	25c brown	2.50	*4.75*
60	A6	30c dark blue	2.50	*4.75*
61	A6	40c olive grn	2.25	*4.25*
62	A6	50c brown violet	2.25	*4.25*
63	A6	1fr dk car, *grn*	3.50	*6.75*
64	A6	2fr blue, *grn*	11.00	*21.00*
65	A6	5fr red, *yellow*	32.50	*62.50*
66	A6	10fr vio, *blue*	65.00	*110.00*
		Nos. 55-66 (12)	126.35	*228.00*

For overprints see Nos. 67-78, J6-J15.

Stamps of 1938 Overprinted in Black

1941

No.	Type	Description	Unused	Used
67	A6	5c green	8.50	*17.00*
68	A6	10c dark orange	8.50	*17.00*
69	A6	15c violet	8.50	*17.00*
70	A6	20c rose red	10.00	*20.00*
71	A6	25c brown	12.50	*25.00*
72	A6	30c dark blue	12.50	*25.00*
73	A6	40c olive green	12.50	*25.00*
74	A6	50c brn violet	12.50	*25.00*
75	A6	1fr dk car, *grn*	14.00	*27.50*
76	A6	2fr blue, *grn*	14.00	*27.50*
77	A6	5fr red, *yellow*	20.00	*40.00*
78	A6	10fr vio, *blue*	32.50	*65.00*
		Nos. 67-78 (12)	166.00	331.00

Catalogue values for unused stamps in this section, from this point to the end of the section, are for Never Hinged items.

UPU Issue

Common Design Type

Wmk. RF in Sheet

1949 **Engr.** *Perf. 13½x14*

No.	Type	Description	Unused	Used
79	CD309	10c red orange	2.25	2.25
80	CD309	15c violet	3.50	3.50
81	CD309	30c violet blue	3.75	3.75
82	CD309	50c rose violet	7.25	7.25
		Nos. 79-82 (4)	16.75	16.75

Some stamps in each sheet show part of the watermark; others show none.

Common Design Types pictured following the introduction.

Outrigger Canoes with Sails — A8

5c, 10c, 15c, 20c, Canoes with sails. 25c, 30c, 40c, 50c, Native carving. 1fr, 2fr, 5fr, Natives.

1953 ***Perf. 12½***

83 A8 5c green .40 *1.00*
84 A8 10c red .40 *1.00*
85 A8 15c yellow .40 *1.00*
86 A8 20c ultramarine .85 *2.10*
87 A8 25c olive .65 *1.60*
88 A8 30c light brown 1.25 *3.00*
89 A8 40c black brown 1.50 *3.75*
90 A8 50c violet 1.75 *4.25*
91 A8 1fr deep orange 6.00 *15.00*
92 A8 2fr red violet 15.00 *40.00*
93 A8 5fr scarlet 26.00 *65.00*
Nos. 83-93 (11) 54.20 *137.70*

For overprints see Nos. J16-J20.

Discovery of New Hebrides, 1606 — A9

20c, 50c, Britannia, Marianne, Flags and Mask.

Perf. 14½x14

1956, Oct. 20 **Unwmk.** **Photo.**

94 A9 5c emerald .75 .75
95 A9 10c crimson .75 .75
96 A9 20c ultramarine .90 .90
97 A9 50c purple 2.75 2.75
Nos. 94-97 (4) 5.15 5.15

50th anniv. of the establishment of the Anglo-French Condominium.

Port Vila and Iririki Islet — A10

Designs: 25c, 30c, 40c, 50c, Tropical river and spear fisherman. 1fr, 2fr, 5fr, Woman drinking from coconut (inscribed: "Alliance Franco-Britannique 4 Mars 1947").

Wmk. RF in Sheet

1957 **Engr.** ***Perf. 13½x13***

98 A10 5c green .60 *.75*
99 A10 10c red .60 *.75*
100 A10 15c orange yel .90 *1.10*
101 A10 20c ultramarine .90 *1.10*
102 A10 25c olive .90 *1.10*
103 A10 30c light brown 1.40 *1.60*
104 A10 40c sepia 1.60 *2.00*
105 A10 50c violet 2.50 *3.25*
106 A10 1fr orange 6.75 *8.00*
107 A10 2fr rose lilac 14.50 *17.50*
108 A10 5fr black 26.00 *32.50*
Nos. 98-108 (11) 56.65 *69.65*

For overprints see Nos. J21-J25.

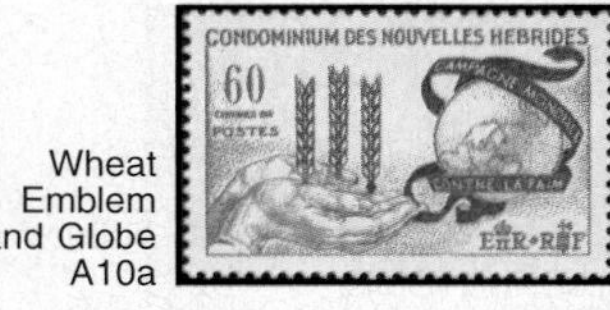

Wheat Emblem and Globe A10a

1963, Sept. 2 **Unwmk.** ***Perf. 13***

109 A10a 60c org brn & slate grn 5.00 5.00

FAO "Freedom from Hunger" campaign.

Centenary Emblem — A11

1963, Sept. 2 **Unwmk.**

110 A11 15c org, gray & car 3.00 3.00
111 A11 45c bis, gray & car 5.00 5.00

Centenary of International Red Cross.

Copra Industry A12

Designs: 5c, Manganese loading, Forari Wharf. 10c, Cacao. 20c, Map of New Hebrides, tuna, marlin and ships. 25c, Striped triggerfish. 30c, Nautilus. 40c, 60c, Turkeyfish (pterois volitans). 50c, Lined tang (fish). 1fr, Cardinal honeyeater and hibiscus. 2fr, Buff-bellied flycatcher. 3fr, Thicket warbler. 5fr, White-collared kingfisher.

Perf. 12½ (10c, 20c, 40c, 60c); 14 (3fr); 13 (others)

Photo. (10c, 20c, 40c, 60c, 3fr); Engr. (others)

1963-67 **Unwmk.**

112 A12 5c Prus bl, pur brn & cl ('66) .65 .65
a. 5c prus blue & claret ('72) 50.00 *55.00*
113 A12 10c brt grn, org brn & dk brn ("RF" at left) ('65) 2.10 1.60
114 A12 15c dk pur, yel & brn .80 .80
115 A12 20c brt bl, gray & cit ("RF" at left) ('65) 3.00 2.75
116 A12 25c vio, rose lil & org brn ('66) .80 .80
117 A12 30c lil, brn & citron 1.60 1.60
118 A12 40c dk bl & ver ('65) 5.50 4.00
119 A12 50c Prus bl, yel & grn 2.40 2.40
119A A12 60c dk bl & ver ('67) 1.90 1.50
120 A12 1fr bl grn, blk & red ('66) 3.75 3.75
121 A12 2fr ol, blk & brn 9.00 9.00
122 A12 3fr org brn, brt grn & blk ("RF" at left) ('65) 16.00 12.00
123 A12 5fr ind, dp bl & gray ('67) 30.00 30.00
Nos. 112-123 (13) 77.50 70.85

See #146-148. For surcharge see #160.

Telegraph, Syncom Satellite and ITU Emblem — A13

1965, May 17 **Unwmk.** ***Perf. 13***

124 A13 15c dk red brn, brt bl & emer 5.00 2.50
125 A13 60c Prus grn, mag & sl 12.00 7.25

ITU, centenary.

Intl. Cooperation Year Issue

Common Design Type with Royal Cipher and "RF" Replacing Queen's Portrait

1965, Oct. 24 **Litho.** ***Perf. 14½***

126 CD318 5c blue grn & claret 2.00 2.00
127 CD318 55c lt violet & grn 4.00 4.00

International Cooperation Year.

Churchill Memorial Issue

Common Design Type with Royal Cipher and "RF" Replacing Queen's Portrait

1966, Jan. 24 **Photo.** ***Perf. 14***

Design in Black, Gold and Carmine Rose

128 CD319 5c brt blue .90 .90
129 CD319 15c green 1.40 1.40
130 CD319 25c brown 3.25 3.25
131 CD319 30c violet 4.50 4.50
Nos. 128-131 (4) 10.05 10.05

World Cup Soccer Issue

Common Design Type with Royal Cipher and "RF" Replacing Queen's Portrait

1966, July 1 **Litho.** ***Perf. 14***

132 CD321 20c multicolored 1.75 1.75
133 CD321 40c multicolored 2.50 2.50

WHO Headquarters Issue

Common Design Type with Royal Cipher and "RF" Replacing Queen's Portrait

1966, Sept. 20 **Litho.** ***Perf. 14***

134 CD322 25c multicolored 1.60 1.60
135 CD322 60c multicolored 2.40 2.40

UNESCO Anniversary Issue

Common Design Type with Royal Cipher and "RF" Replacing Queen's Portrait

1966, Dec. 1 **Litho.** ***Perf. 14***

136 CD323 15c "Education" .85 .85
137 CD323 30c "Science" 1.60 1.60
138 CD323 45c "Culture" 2.10 2.10
Nos. 136-138 (3) 4.55 4.55

US Marine, Australian Soldier and Map of South Pacific War Zone — A19

Designs: 15c, The coast watchers. 60c, Australian cruiser Canberra. 1fr, Flying fortress taking off from Bauer Field, and view of Vila.

Perf. 14x13

1967, Sept. 26 **Photo.** **Unwmk.**

139 A19 15c lt blue & multi .65 .65
140 A19 25c yellow & multi .85 .85
141 A19 60c multicolored 1.50 1.50
142 A19 1fr pale salmon & multi 1.75 1.75
Nos. 139-142 (4) 4.75 4.75

25th anniv. of the Allied Forces' campaign in the South Pacific War Zone.

L. A. de Bougainville, Ship's Figurehead and Bougainvillea — A20

15c, Globe & world map. 25c, Ships La Boudeuse & L'Etoile & map of Bougainville Strait.

1968, May 23 **Engr.** ***Perf. 13***

143 A20 15c ver, emer & dl vio .25 .25
144 A20 25c ultra, ol & brn .60 .60
145 A20 60c mag, grn & brn 1.15 1.15
Nos. 143-145 (3) 2.00 2.00

200th anniv. of Louis Antoine de Bougainville's (1729-1811) voyage around the world.

Type of 1963-67 Redrawn, "E II R" at left, "RF" at Right

Designs as before.

1968, Aug. 5 **Photo.** ***Perf. 12½***

146 A12 10c brt grn, org brn & dk brn 1.00 1.00
147 A12 20c brt bl, gray & citron 1.40 1.40

Perf. 14

148 A12 3fr org brn, brt grn & blk 9.50 9.50
Nos. 146-148 (3) 11.90 11.90

On Nos. 113, 115 and 122 "RF" is at left and "E II R" is at right.

For surcharge see No. 160.

Concorde Supersonic Airliner — A21

Design: 25c, Concorde seen from above.

1968, Oct. 9 **Litho.** ***Perf. 14x13½***

149 A21 25c vio bl, red & lt bl 3.00 2.50
150 A21 60c red, ultra & blk 6.50 5.00

Development of the Concorde supersonic airliner, a joint Anglo-French project.

Kauri Pine — A22

Land Diver at Start, Pentecost Island — A24

Relay Race, British and French Flags — A23

1969, June 30 ***Perf. 14½x14***

151 A22 20c brown & multi .60 .60

New Hebrides timber industry. Issued in sheets of 9 (3x3) on simulated wood grain background.

1969, Aug. 13 **Photo.** ***Perf. 12½x13***

152 A23 25c shown .85 .85
153 A23 1fr Runner at right 1.40 1.40

3rd South Pacific Games, Port Moresby, Papua and New Guinea, Aug. 13-23.

1969, Oct. 15 **Litho.** ***Perf. 12½***

154 A24 15c shown .50 .50
155 A24 25c Diver in mid-air .60 .60
156 A24 1fr Diver near ground 2.00 2.00
Nos. 154-156 (3) 3.10 3.10

Land divers of Pentecost Island.

UPU Headquarters and Monument, Bern — A25

1970, May 20 Engr. *Perf. 13*

157	A25	1.05fr org, lilac & slate	1.75	1.75

New UPU Headquarters, Bern.

Charles de Gaulle — A26

1970, July 20 Photo. *Perf. 13*

158	A26	65c brown & multi	1.25	1.25
159	A26	1.10fr dp blue & multi	2.25	2.25

Rallying of the Free French, 30th anniv.
For overprints see Nos. 163-164.

No. 147 Surcharged

1970, Oct. 15 Photo. *Perf. 12½*

160	A12	35c on 20c multi	1.40	1.40

Virgin and Child, by Giovanni Bellini — A27

50c, Virgin and Child, by Giovanni Cima.

1970, Nov. 30 Litho. *Perf. 14½x14*

161	A27	15c tan & multi	.35	.25
162	A27	50c lt grn & multi	.75	.55

Christmas. See Nos. 186-187.

Nos. 158-159 Overprinted "1890-1970 / IN MEMORIAM / 9-11-70" in Gold, 2 Vertical Bars in Black

1971, Jan. 19 Photo. *Perf. 13*

163	A26	65c brown & multi	1.25	1.25
164	A26	1.10fr dp blue & multi	2.75	2.75

In memory of Gen. Charles de Gaulle (1890-1970), President of France.

Soccer — A28

Design: 65c, Basketball, vert.

1971, July 13 Photo. *Perf. 12½*

165	A28	20c multicolored	.75	.75
166	A28	65c multicolored	1.25	1.25

4th South Pacific Games, Papeete, French Polynesia, Sept. 8-19.

Breadfruit Tree and Fruit, Society Arms — A29

Perf. 14½x14

1971, Sept. 7 Litho. Unwmk.

167	A29	65c multicolored	1.50	1.25

Expedition of the Royal Society of London for the Advancement of Science to study vegetation and fauna, July 1-October.

Adoration of the Shepherds, by Louis Le Nain — A30

Christmas: 50c, Adoration of the Shepherds, by Jacopo Tintoretto.

1971, Nov. 23 *Perf. 14x13½*

168	A30	25c lt green & multi	.60	.40
169	A30	50c lt blue & multi	.90	.80

Drover Mk III — A31

Airplanes: 25c, Sandringham seaplane. 30c, Dragon Rapide. 65c, Caravelle.

1972, Feb. 29 Photo. *Perf. 13½x13*

170	A31	20c lt green & multi	.90	.60
171	A31	25c ultra & multi	1.00	.75
172	A31	30c orange & multi	1.10	.90
173	A31	65c dk blue & multi	3.00	2.50
		Nos. 170-173 (4)	6.00	4.75

Headdress, South Malekula — A32

Baker's Pigeon — A33

Artifacts: 15c, Slit gong and carved figure, North Ambrym. 1fr, Carved figures, North Ambrym. 3fr, Ceremonial headdress, South Malekula.

Birds: 20c, Red-headed parrot-finch. 35c, Chestnut-bellied kingfisher. 2fr, Green palm lorikeet.

Sea Shells: 25c, Cribraria fischeri. 30c, Oliva rubrolabiata. 65c, Strombus plicatus. 5fr, Turbo marmoratus.

1972, July 24 Photo. *Perf. 12½x13*

174	A32	5c plum & multi	.30	*.50*
175	A33	10c blue & multi	1.40	*1.75*
176	A32	15c red & multi	.35	.30
177	A33	20c org brn & multi	1.75	1.40
178	A32	25c dp blue & multi	1.40	1.40
179	A32	30c dk green & multi	1.40	*1.75*
180	A33	35c gray bl & multi	2.75	2.50
181	A32	65c dk green & multi	3.75	3.00
182	A32	1fr orange & multi	2.75	*4.25*
183	A33	2fr multicolored	14.00	11.50
184	A32	3fr yellow & multi	9.75	*15.00*
185	A32	5fr pink & multi	21.00	*29.00*
		Nos. 174-185 (12)	60.60	72.35

For overprints see Nos. 200-201.

Christmas Type of 1970

Christmas: 25c, Adoration of the Magi (detail), by Bartholomaeus Spranger. 70c, Virgin and Child, by Jan Provoost.

1972, Sept. 25 Litho. *Perf. 14x13½*

186	A27	25c lt green & multi	.50	.50
187	A27	70c lt blue & multi	.75	.75

Queen Elizabeth II and Prince Philip — A34

Perf. 14x14½

1972, Nov. 20 Photo. Wmk. 314

188	A34	35c violet blk & multi	.50	.50
189	A34	65c olive & multi	.75	.75

25th anniversary of the marriage of Queen Elizabeth II and Prince Philip.

Dendrobium Teretifolium A35

New Wharf, Vila A36

Orchids: 30c, Ephemerantha comata. 35c, Spathoglottis petri. 65c, Dendrobium mohlianum.

Unwmk.

1973, Feb. 26 Litho. *Perf. 14*

190	A35	25c blue vio & multi	1.40	1.40
191	A35	30c multicolored	1.60	1.60
192	A35	35c violet & multi	3.00	3.00
193	A35	65c dk green & multi	5.75	5.75
		Nos. 190-193 (4)	11.75	11.75

1973, May 14 Litho. *Perf. 14*

194	A36	25c shown	.75	.55
195	A36	70c New Wharf, horiz.	1.50	1.25

New wharf at Vila, completed Nov. 1972.

Wild Horses, Tanna A37

Design: 70c, Yasur Volcano, Tanna.

1973, Aug. 13 Photo. *Perf. 13x13½*

196	A37	35c multicolored	2.75	2.40
197	A37	70c multicolored	3.25	2.40

Christmas A38

35c, Mother and Child, by Marcel Moutouh. 70c, Star over Lagoon, by Tatin D'Avesnieres.

1973, Nov. 19 Litho. *Perf. 14x13½*

198	A38	35c tan & multi	.60	.35
199	A38	70c lil rose & multi	.90	.60

Nos. 180, 183 Overprinted in Red or Black: "VISITE ROYALE / 1974"

1974, Feb. 11 Photo. *Perf. 12½x13*

200	A33	35c multi (R)	2.40	1.00
201	A33	2fr multi (B)	7.75	4.50

Visit of British Royal Family, Feb. 15-16.

Pacific Dove A39

Designs: 35c, Night swallowtail. 70c, Green sea turtle. 1.15fr, Flying fox.

1974, Feb. 11 *Perf. 13x12½*

202	A39	25c gray & multi	2.00	1.25
203	A39	35c gray & multi	3.00	1.60
204	A39	70c gray & multi	4.50	3.25
205	A39	1.15fr gray & multi	5.00	6.50
		Nos. 202-205 (4)	14.50	12.60

Nature conservation.

Old Post Office, Vila — A40

Design: 70c, New Post Office.

Unwmk.

1974, May 6 Photo. *Perf. 12*

206	A40	35c blue & multi	.60	.50
207	A40	70c red & multi	.90	.90
a.		Pair, #206-207	1.50	1.50

Opening of New Post Office, May, 1974.

Capt. Cook and Tanna Island A41

Designs: No. 209, William Wales and boat landing on island. No. 210, William Hodges painting islanders and landscape. 1.15fr, Capt. Cook, "Resolution" and map of New Hebrides.

1974, Aug. 1 Litho. *Perf. 13*

Size: 40x25mm

208	A41	35c multicolored	3.75	2.00
209	A41	35c multicolored	3.75	2.00
210	A41	35c multicolored	3.75	2.00
a.		Strip of 3, #208-210	14.00	14.00

Size: 58x34mm

Perf. 11

211	A41	1.15fr lilac & multi	4.50	3.50

Bicentenary of the discovery of the New Hebrides by Capt. James Cook.

No. 210a has a continuous design.

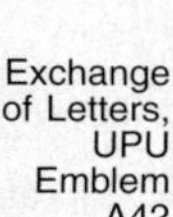

Exchange of Letters, UPU Emblem A42

1974, Oct. 9 Photo. *Perf. 13x12½*
212 A42 70c multicolored .90 .90

Centenary of Universal Postal Union.

Nativity, by Gerard Van Honthorst — A43

Christmas: 35c, Adoration of the Kings, by Velazquez, vert.

1974, Nov. 14 Litho. *Perf. 13½*
213 A43 35c multicolored .60 .50
214 A43 70c multicolored .90 .75

Charolais Bull — A44

1975, Apr. 29 Engr. *Perf. 13*
215 A44 10fr multicolored 25.00 *29.00*

Nordjamb Emblem, Kayaks — A45

Pitti Madonna, by Michelangelo A46

1975, Aug. 5 Litho. *Perf. 14x13½*
216 A45 25c shown .60 .50
217 A45 35c Camp cooks .80 .70
218 A45 1fr Map makers 1.75 1.10
219 A45 5fr Fishermen 8.50 6.00
Nos. 216-219 (4) 11.65 8.30

Nordjamb 75, 14th Boy Scout Jamboree, Lillehammer, Norway, July 29-Aug. 7.

1975, Nov. 11 Litho. *Perf. 14½x14*

Christmas (After Michelangelo): 70c, Bruges Madonna. 2.50fr, Taddei Madonna.

220 A46 35c multicolored .55 .30
221 A46 70c brown & multi .70 .45
222 A46 2.50fr blue & multi 2.75 1.90
Nos. 220-222 (3) 4.00 2.65

Concorde, Air France Colors and Emblem — A47

1976, Jan. 30 Typo. *Perf. 13*
223 A47 5fr blue & multi 15.00 11.00

1st commercial flight of supersonic jet Concorde from Paris to Rio, Jan. 21.

Telephones, 1876 and 1976 — A48

Designs: 70c, Alexander Graham Bell. 1.15fr, Nouméa Earth Station and satellite.

1976, Mar. 31 Photo. *Perf. 13*
224 A48 25c black, car & bl .40 .30
225 A48 70c black & multi 1.00 .70
226 A48 1.15fr blk, org & vio bl 1.60 .90
Nos. 224-226 (3) 3.00 1.90

Centenary of first telephone call by Alexander Graham Bell, Mar. 10, 1876.

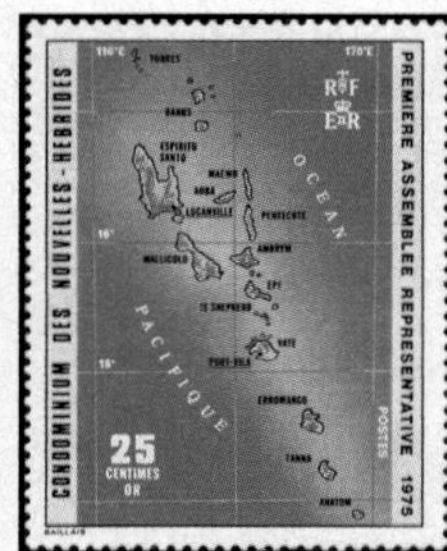

Map of New Hebrides A49

View of Luganville (Santo) A50

Design: 2fr, View of Vila.

1976, June 29 Unwmk. *Perf. 13*
227 A49 25c blue & multi .55 .35
228 A50 1fr multicolored 1.25 .70
229 A50 2fr multicolored 3.00 1.60
Nos. 227-229 (3) 4.80 2.65

Opening of first Representative Assembly, June 29, 1976 (25c); first Luganville (Santo) Municipal Council (1fr); first Vila Municipal Council (2fr).

Nos. 228-229 exist with lower inscription reading "Premiere Assemblée Representative 1975" instead of "Premiere Municipalite de Luganville" on 1fr and "Premiere Municipalite de Port-Vila" on 2fr.

For surcharges, see No. 283-284.

Flight into Egypt, by Francisco Vieira Lusitano — A51

Portuguese 16th Cent. Paintings: 70c, Adoration of the Shepherds. 2.50fr, Adoration of the Kings.

1976, Nov. 8 Litho. *Perf. 14*
230 A51 35c purple & multi .50 .40
231 A51 70c blue & multi .70 .60
232 A51 2.50fr multicolored 2.75 2.00
Nos. 230-232 (3) 3.95 3.00

Christmas 1976.

Queen's Visit, 1974 — A52

70c, Imperial State crown. 2fr, The blessing.

1977, Feb. 7 Litho. *Perf. 14x13½*
233 A52 35c lt green & multi .35 .20
234 A52 70c blue & multi .55 .50
235 A52 2fr pink & multi 1.60 1.25
Nos. 233-235 (3) 2.50 1.95

Reign of Queen Elizabeth II, 25th anniv.

Nos. 174-185, 215 Surcharged with New Value, "FNH" and Bars

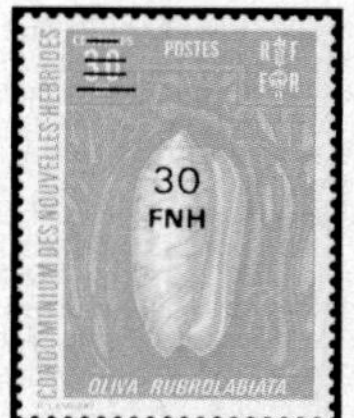

Paris Overprints

1977, July 1 Photo. *Perf. 12½x13*
236 A32 5fr on 5c multi 1.75 1.75
237 A33 10fr on 10c multi 3.00 1.50
238 A32 15fr on 15c multi 1.50 1.50
239 A33 20fr on 20c multi 3.50 1.75
240 A32 25fr on 25c multi 3.00 2.00
241 A32 30fr on 30c multi 3.00 2.50
242 A33 35fr on 35c multi 5.00 2.50
243 A32 40fr on 65c multi 3.75 3.50
244 A32 50fr on 1fr multi 3.00 *3.50*
245 A33 70fr on 2fr multi 9.00 4.50
246 A32 100fr on 3fr multi 4.00 *7.00*
247 A32 200fr on 5fr multi 15.00 *30.00*

Engr.
Perf. 13

248 A44 500fr on 10fr multi 27.50 *50.00*
Nos. 236-248 (13) 83.00 *112.00*

Nos. 155//166, 196 Surcharged with New Value, "FNH" and Bars

FNH FNH FNH 25 FNH
a b c d

Port Vila Overprints

Two settings of 35fr and 200fr surcharges: type 1, 1.4mm between new value and "FNH"; type 2, 2.1mm between value and "FNH."

Perf. 12½x13

1977-78 Photo. Unwmk.
236a A32 5fr on 5c (a) 3.00 3.00
237a A33 10fr on 10c (b) 3.50 2.50
238a A32 15fr on 15c (c) 5.00 3.25
240a A32 25fr on 25c (d) 140.00 90.00
241a A32 30fr on 30c (d) 300.00 90.00
242a A33 35fr on 35c (d), type 1 8.00 6.50
b. Type 2 37.50 22.50
243a A32 40fr on 65c (d) 7.00 7.00
244a A32 50fr on 1fr multi 80.00
245a A33 70fr on 2fr multi 80.00
246a A32 100fr on 3fr multi 80.00
247a A32 200fr on 5fr (d), type 1 55.00 *65.00*
b. Type 2 65.00 65.00
248a A44 500fr on 10fr (d) 65.00 *75.00*
Nos. 236a-248a (12) 826.50 342.25

The 50fr, 70fr and 100fr values were sold only through the philatelic bureau.

Issued: 15fr, 7/18; 10fr, 7/20; 5fr, 8/10#247a, 8/22; 25fr, 30fr, #242a, 9/10; 40fr, 9/12; 500fr, 9/14; #242b, 1/6/78; #247b, 1/13/78.

Espiritu Santo and Cattle — A53

Tempi Madonna, by Raphael — A54

Designs: 5fr, Erromango Island and Kaori tree. 10fr, Archipelago and man making copra. 20fr, Efate Island and Post Office, Vila. 25fr, Malakula Island and headdresses. 30fr, Aoba and Maewo Islands and pig tusks. 35fr, Pentecost Island and land diving. 40fr, Tanna Island and Prophet John Frum's Red Cross. 50fr, Shepherd Island and canoe with sail. 70fr, Banks Island and dancers. 100fr, Ambrym Island and carvings. 200fr, Aneityum Island and decorated baskets. 500fr, Torres Islands and fishing with bow and arrow.

1977-78 Litho. *Perf. 14*

258 A53 5fr multicolored .25 .20
259 A53 10fr multicolored .40 .35
260 A53 15fr multicolored .50 .35
261 A53 20fr multicolored .60 .45
262 A53 25fr multicolored .75 .50
263 A53 30fr multicolored 1.00 .55
264 A53 35fr multicolored 1.10 .55
265 A53 40fr multicolored 1.25 .65
266 A53 50fr multicolored 1.50 1.00
267 A53 70fr multicolored 2.50 1.60
268 A53 100fr multicolored 3.50 2.25
269 A53 200fr multicolored 6.75 5.00
270 A53 500fr multicolored 14.00 12.00
Nos. 258-270 (13) 34.10 25.45

Issued: 5fr, 20fr, 50fr, 100fr, 200fr, 9/7/77; 15fr, 25fr, 30fr, 40fr, 11/23/77; 10fr, 35fr, 70fr, 500fr, 5/9/78.

1977, Dec. 8 Litho. *Perf. 12*

Christmas: 15fr, Virgin and Child, by Gerard David. 30fr, Virgin and Child, by Pompeo Batoni.

271 A54 10fr multicolored .35 .35
272 A54 15fr multicolored .50 .35
273 A54 30fr multicolored .90 .90
Nos. 271-273 (3) 1.75 1.60

British Airways Concorde over New York — A55

Designs: 20fr, British Airways Concorde over London. 30fr, Air France Concorde over Washington. 40fr, Air France Concorde over Paris.

1978, May 9 Litho. *Perf. 14*

274 A55 10fr multicolored .90 .80
275 A55 20fr multicolored 1.90 1.40
276 A55 30fr multicolored 2.25 1.75
277 A55 40fr multicolored 3.00 2.25
Nos. 274-277 (4) 8.05 6.20

Souvenir Sheet

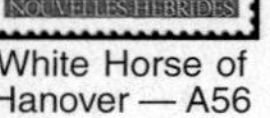

White Horse of Hanover — A56

Elizabeth II — A57

Design: No. 278c, Gallic cock.

1978, June 2 Litho. *Perf. 15*

278 Sheet of 6 7.00 7.00
a. A56 40fr greenish blue & multi 1.00 1.00
b. A57 40fr greenish blue & multi 1.00 1.00
c. A56 40fr greenish blue & multi 1.00 1.00

25th anniversary of coronation of Queen Elizabeth II.

No. 278 contains 2 se-tenant strips of Nos. 278a-278c, separated by horizontal gutter with commemorative and descriptive inscriptions and showing central part of coronation procession with coach.

Virgin and Child, by Dürer — A58

Christmas, Paintings by Albrecht Durer (1471-1528): 15fr, Virgin and Child with St. Anne. 30fr, Virgin and Child with Goldfinch. 40fr, Virgin and Child with Pear.

1978, Dec. 1 Litho. *Perf. 14x13½*

279 A58 10fr multicolored .25 .25
280 A58 15fr multicolored .40 .40
281 A58 30fr multicolored .60 .60
282 A58 40fr multicolored 1.25 .90
Nos. 279-282 (4) 2.50 2.15

Type of 1976 Surcharged with New Value, Bars over Old Denomination and Inscription at Right. Longitude changed to "166E."

1979, Jan. 11 Photo. *Perf. 13*

283 A49 10fr on 25c bl & multi .65 .40
284 A49 40fr on 25c lt grn & multi 1.40 1.00

First anniv. of Internal Self-Government.

New Hebrides No. 155 and Hill Statue A59

Rowland Hill and New Hebrides Stamps: 10fr, No. 55. 40fr, No. 46.

1979, Sept. 10 Litho. *Perf. 14*

285 A59 10fr multicolored .40 .40
286 A59 20fr multicolored .60 .60
287 A59 40fr multicolored 1.00 1.00
Nos. 285-287 (3) 2.00 2.00

Sir Rowland Hill (1795-1879), originator of penny postage. A souvenir sheet containing No. 286 and British issue No. 266 is listed as No. 266a under New Hebrides, British issues.

Arts Festival — A60

Designs: 10fr, Clubs and spears. 20fr, Ritual puppet. 40fr, Headdress.

1979, Nov. 16 Litho. *Perf. 14*

288 A60 5fr multicolored .30 .30
289 A60 10fr multicolored .50 .50
290 A60 20fr multicolored .80 .60
291 A60 40fr multicolored 1.25 .80
Nos. 288-291 (4) 2.85 2.20

Church, IYC Emblem A61

IYC Emblem, Children's Drawings: 10fr, Father Christmas. 20fr, Cross and Bible, vert. 40fr, Stars, candle and Santa Claus, vert.

1979, Dec. 4 *Perf. 13x13½*

292 A61 5fr multicolored .35 .35
293 A61 10fr multicolored .50 .40
294 A61 20fr multicolored .90 .60
295 A61 40fr multicolored 1.10 .90
Nos. 292-295 (4) 2.85 2.25

Christmas; Intl. Year of the Child.

White-bellied Honeyeater — A62

1980, Feb. 27 Litho. *Perf. 14*

296 A62 10fr shown .85 .85
297 A62 20fr Scarlet robins 1.40 1.60
298 A62 30fr Yellow white-eyes 2.75 2.75
299 A62 40fr Fan-tailed brush cuckoo 3.25 3.25
Nos. 296-299 (4) 8.25 8.45

Stamps of Vanuatu replaced those of New Hebrides in 1980.

POSTAGE DUE STAMPS

French Issues

Nos. 45-46, 48, 50, 52 Overprinted

1925 Wmk. R F in Sheet *Perf. 14*

J1 A4 10c green 50.00 4.75
J2 A4 20c greenish gray 50.00 4.75
J3 A4 30c carmine 50.00 4.75
J4 A4 50c ultramarine 50.00 4.75
J5 A4 1fr carmine, *blue* 50.00 4.75
Nos. J1-J5 (5) 250.00 23.75

Nos. 55-56, 58, 61, 63 Overprinted

1938 *Perf. 12*

J6 A6 5c green 9.00 *22.50*
J7 A6 10c dark orange 9.00 *22.50*
J8 A6 20c rose red 14.00 *35.00*
J9 A6 40c olive green 24.00 *60.00*
J10 A6 1fr dark car, *green* 42.50 *100.00*
Nos. J6-J10 (5) 98.50 *240.00*

Nos. J6-J10 Overprinted like Nos. 67-78

1941

J11 A6 5c green 11.00 *32.50*
J12 A6 10c dark orange 11.00 *32.50*
J13 A6 20c rose red 11.00 *32.50*
J14 A6 40c olive green 11.00 *32.50*
J15 A6 1fr dk car, *green* 11.00 *32.50*
Nos. J11-J15 (5) 55.00 *162.50*

Catalogue values for unused stamps in this section, from this point to the end of the section, are for Never Hinged items.

Nos. 83-84, 86, 89, 91 Overprinted "TIMBRE-TAXE"

1953 Unwmk. *Perf. 12½*

J16 A8 5c green 2.25 *5.50*
J17 A8 10c red 3.50 *8.75*
J18 A8 20c ultramarine 6.50 *16.00*
J19 A8 40c black brown 13.50 *32.50*
J20 A8 1fr deep orange 21.00 *32.50*
Nos. J16-J20 (5) 46.75 *95.25*

Nos. 98-99, 101, 104, 106 Overprinted "TIMBRE-TAXE"

Wmk. R F in Sheet

1957 Engr. *Perf. 13½x13*

J21 A10 5c green 1.25 *2.50*
J22 A10 10c red 1.50 *3.00*
J23 A10 20c ultramarine 1.75 *3.75*
J24 A10 40c sepia 6.75 *13.50*
J25 A10 1fr orange 16.00 *32.50*
Nos. J21-J25 (5) 27.25 *55.25*

NEW REPUBLIC

'nü ri-'pə-blik

LOCATION — In South Africa, located in the northern part of the present province of Natal
GOVT. — A former Republic
CAPITAL — Vryheid

New Republic was created in 1884 by Boer adventurers from Transvaal who proclaimed Dinizulu king of Zululand and claimed as their reward a large tract of country as their own, which they called New Republic. This area was excepted when Great Britain annexed Zululand in 1887, but New Republic became a part of Transvaal in 1888 and was included in the Union of South Africa.

12 Pence = 1 Shilling
20 Shillings = 1 Pound

New Republic stamps were individually handstamped on gummed and perforated sheets of paper. Naturally many of the impressions are misaligned and touch or intersect the perforations. Values are for stamps with good color and, for Nos. 37-64, sharp embossing. The alignment does not materially alter the value of the stamp.

A1

A2

Handstamped

1886 Unwmk. *Perf. 11½*

1 A1 1p violet, *yel* 12.00 14.00
1A A1 1p black, *yel* *3,500.*
2 A1 2p violet, *yel* 15.00 *20.00*
a. Without date
b. Tête bêche pair
3 A1 3p violet, *yel* 30.00 *35.00*
a. Double impression
4 A1 4p violet, *yel* 45.00
a. Without date
5 A1 6p violet, *yel* 40.00 *45.00*
a. Double impression
6 A1 9p violet, *yel* 75.00
7 A1 1sh violet, *yel* 75.00
a. "1/S" 650.00
8 A1 1/6 violet, *yel* 80.00
a. Without date
b. "1s6d" 475.00
9 A1 2sh violet, *yel* 45.00
a. Tête bêche pair 550.00
10 A1 2sh6p violet, *yel* 120.00
a. Without date
b. "2/6" 150.00
11 A1 4sh violet, *yel* 450.00
12 A1 5sh violet, *yel* 32.50 *40.00*
a. Without date
13 A1 5/6 violet, *yel* 140.00
a. "5s6d" 180.00
14 A1 7sh6p violet, *yel* 120.00
a. "7/6" 190.00
15 A1 10sh violet, *yel* 150.00 *160.00*
16 A1 10sh6p violet, *yel* 180.00
16A A1 13sh violet, *yel* 450.00
17 A1 £1 violet, *yel* 125.00
18 A1 30sh violet, *yel* 110.00
a. Tête bêche pair 550.00

Granite Paper

19 A1 1p violet, *gray* 16.00 *18.00*
20 A1 2p violet, *gray* 16.00 *18.00*
a. Without "ZUID AFRIKA"
21 A1 3p violet, *gray* 22.00 26.00
a. Tête bêche pair 350.00
22 A1 4p violet, *gray* 30.00 *35.00*
23 A1 6p violet, *gray* 50.00 *50.00*
24 A1 9p violet, *gray* 110.00

25 A1 1sh violet, *gray* 32.50 *35.00*
  a. Tête bêche pair 450.00
26 A1 1sh6p violet, *gray* 100.00
  a. Tête bêche pair 525.00
  b. "1/6" 175.00
27 A1 2sh violet, *gray* 125.00
28 A1 2sh6p violet, *gray* 150.00
  a. "2/6" 200.00
29 A1 4sh violet, *gray* 350.00
30 A1 5sh6p violet, *gray* 250.00
  a. "5/6" 250.00
31 A1 7/6 violet, *gray* 250.00
32 A1 10sh violet, *gray* 210.00 225.00
  a. Tête bêche pair 475.00
32B A1 10sh 6p vio, *gray* 220.00
  c. Without date
33 A1 12sh violet, *gray* 350.00
34 A1 13sh violet, *gray* 525.00
35 A1 £1 violet, *gray* 275.00
36 A1 30sh violet, *gray* 275.00

Same with Embossed Arms

37 A1 1p violet, *yel* 19.00 16.00
  a. Arms inverted 32.50 32.50
  b. Arms tête bêche, pair 125.00 140.00
38 A1 2p violet, *yel* 15.00 16.00
  a. Arms inverted 32.50 35.00
39 A1 4p violet, *yel* 22.50 25.00
  a. Arms inverted 110.00 80.00
  b. Arms tête bêche, pair 300.00
40 A1 6p violet, *yel* 50.00

Granite Paper

41 A1 1p violet, *gray* 16.00 17.50
  a. Imperf. vert., pair
  b. Arms inverted 40.00 45.00
  c. Arms tête bêche, pair
42 A1 2p violet, *gray* 16.00 17.50
  a. Imperf. horiz., pair
  b. Arms inverted 55.00 55.00
  c. Arms tête bêche, pair 550.00 550.00

There were several printings of the above stamps and the date upon them varies from "JAN 86" and "7 JAN 86" to "20 JAN 87."

Nos. 7, 8, 10, 13, 14, 26, 28 and 30 have the denomination expressed in two ways. Example: "1s 6d" or "1/6."

1887 Arms Embossed

43 A2 3p violet, *yel* 19.00 19.00
  a. Arms inverted 50.00 50.00
  b. Tête bêche pair 425.00 450.00
  c. Imperf. vert., pair
  d. Arms omitted
  e. Arms tête bêche, pair 260.00
44 A2 4p violet, *yel* 15.00 15.00
  a. Arms inverted 22.50 22.50
45 A2 6p violet, *yel* 11.00 11.00
  a. Arms inverted 52.50 52.50
  b. Arms omitted 200.00
  c. Arms tête bêche, pair 350.00
46 A2 9p violet, *yel* 12.00 *13.00*
47 A2 1sh violet, *yel* 13.00 13.00
  a. Arms inverted 90.00
  b. Arms omitted 55.00
48 A2 1sh6p violet, *yel* 16.00 15.00
49 A2 2sh violet, *yel* 24.00 24.00
  a. Arms inverted 75.00
  b. Arms omitted 100.00 100.00
50 A2 2sh6p violet, *yel* 21.00 21.00
  a. Arms inverted 24.00 24.00
50B A2 3sh violet, *yel* 42.50 42.50
  c. Arms inverted 47.50 47.50
51 A2 4sh violet, *yel* 15.00 14.00
  a. Arms omitted
52 A2 5sh violet, *yel* 16.00 15.00
  a. Imperf. vert., pair
  b. Arms inverted — 100.00
53 A2 5sh6p violet, *yel* 14.00 15.00
54 A2 7sh6p violet, *yel* 20.00 *22.00*
  a. Arms inverted 75.00
  b. Arms tête bêche, pair
55 A2 10sh violet, *yel* 17.00 *18.00*
  a. Arms inverted 22.50 22.50
  b. Arms omitted 90.00 75.00
  c. Imperf. vert., pair
  d. Arms tête bêche, pair 210.00
56 A2 10sh6p violet, *yel* 20.00 20.00
  a. Imperf. vert., pair
  b. Arms inverted
  c. Arms omitted
57 A2 £1 violet, *yel* 55.00 55.00
  a. Arms inverted 60.00
  b. Tête bêche pair 475.00 475.00
58 A2 30sh violet, *yel* 140.00 110.00

Granite Paper

59 A2 1p violet, *gray* 14.00 15.00
  a. Arms omitted 110.00 110.00
  b. Arms inverted 25.00 25.00
  c. Imperf. vert., pair
  d. Tête bêche pair 400.00
60 A2 2p violet, *gray* 8.00 8.00
  a. Arms omitted 100.00 100.00
  b. Arms inverted 22.50 22.50
  c. Tête bêche pair 450.00
61 A2 3p violet, *gray* 12.00 12.00
  a. Arms inverted 65.00 65.00
  b. Tête bêche pair 450.00
62 A2 4p violet, *gray* 12.00 12.00
  a. Arms inverted 90.00 90.00
  b. Tête bêche pair 450.00
63 A2 6p violet, *gray* 12.00 12.00
  a. Arms inverted 100.00 100.00
64 A2 1sh6p violet, *gray* 13.00 13.00
  a. Arms inverted 90.00
  Nos. 59-64 (6) 71.00 72.00

These stamps were valid only in New Republic.

All these stamps may have been valid for postage but bona-fide canceled specimens of any but the 1p and 2p stamps are quite rare.

NEW ZEALAND

'nü 'zē-lənd

LOCATION — Group of islands in the south Pacific Ocean, southeast of Australia

GOVT. — Self-governing dominion of the British Commonwealth

AREA — 107,241 sq. mi.

POP. — 3,662,265 (1999 est.)

CAPITAL — Wellington

12 Pence = 1 Shilling
20 Shillings = 1 Pound
100 Cents = 1 Dollar (1967)

Catalogue values for unused stamps in this country are for Never Hinged items, beginning with Scott 246 in the regular postage section, Scott AR99 in the postal-fiscal section, Scott B9 in the semi-postal section, Scott J21 in the postage due section, Scott O92 in the officials section, Scott OY29 in the Life Insurance Department section, and Scott L1 in Ross Dependency.

Watermarks

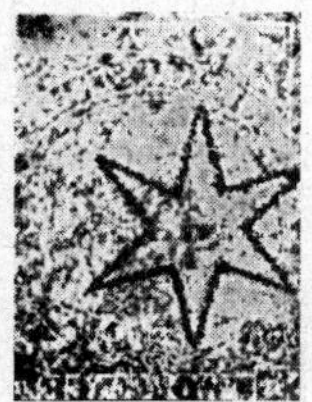
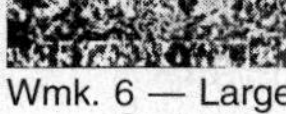
Wmk. 6 — Large Star

Wmk. 59 — N Z

Wmk. 60 — Lozenges

This watermark includes the vertical word "INVICTA" once in each quarter of the sheet.

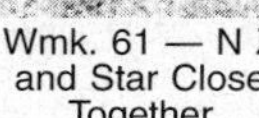
Wmk. 61 — N Z and Star Close Together

Wmk. 62 — N Z and Star Wide Apart

On watermark 61 the margins of the sheets are watermarked "NEW ZEALAND POSTAGE" and parts of the double-lined letters of these words are frequently found on the stamps. It occasionally happens that a stamp shows no watermark whatever.

Wmk. 63 — Double-lined N Z and Star

Wmk. 64 — Small Star Only

Wmk. 253 — Multiple N Z and Star

Values for unused stamps are for examples with original gum as defined in the catalogue introduction.

Very fine examples of the perforated issues between Nos. 7a-69, AR1-AR30, J1-J11, OY1-OY9 and P1-P4 will have perforations touching the framelines or design on one or more sides due to the narrow spacing of the stamps on the plates and imperfect perforating methods.

The rouletted and serrate rouletted stamps of the same period rarely have complete roulettes and are valued as sound and showing partial roulettes. Stamps with complete roulettes range from very scarce to very rare, are seldom traded, and command great premiums.

Victoria — A1

London Print
Wmk. 6

1855, July 18 Engr. *Imperf.*

White Paper

1 A1 1p dull carmine *120,000.* *15,000.*

Blued Paper

2 A1 2p deep blue *60,000.* 625.
3 A1 1sh yellow green *80,000.* *5,750.*
  a. Half used as 6p on cover *40,000.*

An imperf, engraved reproduction of No. 1 on unwatermarked paper was produced in 2005 for a sheet that was included in a book commemorating the 150th anniv. of New Zealand stamps.

The blueing of Nos. 2 and 3 was caused by chemical action in the printing process.

Auckland Print

1855-58 Blue Paper Unwmk.

4 A1 1p orange red 15,000. 2,200.
5 Al 2p blue ('56) 3,500. 350.
6 Al 1sh green ('58) *75,000.* 4,250.
  a. Half used as 6p on cover *25,000.*

Nos. 4-6 may be found with parts of the papermaker's name in double-lined letters.

1857-61 Unwmk.

Thin Hard or Thick Soft White Paper

7 A1 1p orange ('58) 3,000. 675.
  e. Wmk. 6 ('57) *100,000.*
8 A1 2p blue ('58) 1,100. 210.
9 A1 6p brown ('59) 2,300. 350.
  e. 6p bister brown ('59) 3,200. 575.
  f. 6p chestnut ('59) 3,500. 625.
10 A1 1sh blue green ('61) 16,000. 1,750.
  e. 1sh emerald 18,000. 1,750.

No. 7e is identical to a shade of No. 11. The only currently known examples are a pair on a cover front. To qualify as No. 7e, a stamp must have a cancellation prior to 1862.

1859 *Pin Rouletted 9-10*

7a A1 1p dull orange 5,750.
8a A1 2p blue 3,750.
9a A1 6p brown 4,500.
10a A1 1sh greenish blue 6,750.

1859 *Serrate Rouletted 16, 18*

7b A1 1p dull orange 5,000.
8b A1 2p blue 3,750.
9b A1 6p brown 3,500.
  g. 6p chestnut 6,750.
10b A1 1sh greenish blue 6,250.

Value for No. 10b is for a damaged stamp.

1859 ***Rouletted 7***

7c A1 1p dull orange *7,250.* 5,000.
f. Pair, imperf between —
8c A1 2p blue *7,250.* 3,400.
9c A1 6p brown *6,750.* 2,800.
10c A1 1sh greensh blue — 4,500.

1862 ***Perf. 13***

7d A1 1p orange vermilion 5,750.
8d A1 2p blue 4,250. 2,500.
9d A1 6p brown *6,250.*

1862-63 **Wmk. 6** ***Imperf.***

11 A1 1p orange ver 1,100. 250.00
d. 1p carmine vermilion ('63) 475.00 300.00
e. 1p vermilion 550.00 250.00
12 A1 2p blue 1,000. 85.00
d. 2p slate blue 2,750. 210.00
13 A1 3p brown lilac ('63) 950.00 160.00
14 A1 6p red brown ('63) 1,400. 100.00
d. 6p black brown 2,000. 125.00
e. 6p brown ('63) 1,400. 100.00
15 A1 1sh yellow green 2,750. 300.00
d. 1sh deep green 2,900. 375.00

See No. 7e.

1862 ***Pin Rouletted 9-10***

12a A1 2p deep blue — 2,800.
14a A1 6p black brown — 4,000.

1862 ***Serrate Rouletted 16, 18***

11b A1 1p orange vermilion 8,500. 1,900.
12b A1 2p blue — 1,250.
13b A1 3p brown lilac 4,000. 1,800.
14b A1 6p black brown — 1,900.
15b A1 1sh yellow green 3,750.

1862 ***Rouletted 7***

11c A1 1p vermilion 2,800. 900.
12c A1 2p blue 2,250. 625.
13c A1 3p brown lilac 2,800. 850.
14c A1 6p red brown 2,800. 525.
15c A1 1sh green 3,250. 850.

The 1p, 2p, 6p and 1sh come in two or more shades.

1863 ***Perf. 13***

16 A1 1p carmine ver 3,500. 400.00
17 A1 2p blue 650.00 85.00
18 A1 3p brown lilac 2,000. 700.00
19 A1 6p red brown 1,750. 150.00
20 A1 1sh green 2,750. 400.00

The 1p, 2p, 6p and 1sh come in two or more shades. See the *Scott Classic Specialized Catalogue.*

1862 **Unwmk.** ***Imperf.***
Pelure Paper

21 A1 1p vermilion 9,250. 2,250.
b. Rouletted 7 5,500.
22 A1 2p pale dull ultra 8,000. 950.
c. 2p gray blue 6,000. 925.
23 A1 3p brown lilac *100,000.*
24 A1 6p black brown 4,000. 400.
b. Rouletted 7 5,000. 700.
c. Serrate perf. 15 — 5,250.
25 A1 1sh deep yel green 12,000. 1,150.
b. 1sh deep green 12,000. 1,150.
c. Rouletted 7 13,000. 1,900.

No. 23 was never placed in use.

1863 ***Perf. 13***

21a A1 1p vermilion 15,000. 3,500.
22a A1 2p gray blue 6,500. 800.
b. 2p pale dull ultramarine 6,500. 800.
24a A1 6p black brown 5,500. 450.
25a A1 1sh deep green 12,000. 1,700.

1863 **Unwmk.** ***Perf. 13***
Thick White Paper

26 A1 2p dull dark blue 2,200. 550.
a. Imperf 3,250. 925.

Nos. 26 and 26a differ from 8 and 8d by a white patch of wear at right of head.

1864 **Wmk. 59** ***Imperf.***

27 A1 1p carmine ver 2,750. 325.
28 A1 2p blue 3,000. 250.
29 A1 6p red brown 8,000. 700.
30 A1 1sh green 1,750. 300.

1864 ***Rouletted 7***

27a A1 1p carmine vermilion 6,500. 3,150.
28a A1 2p blue 2,000. 875.
29a A1 6p deep red brown 7,500. 3,150.
30a A1 1sh green 5,000. 1,150.

1864 ***Perf. 12½***

27B A1 1p carmine ver 11,000. 5,000.
28B A1 2p blue 375.00 62.50
29B A1 6p red brown 1,500. 47.50
30B A1 1sh dp yel green 7,750. 2,500.

1864 ***Perf. 13***

27C A1 1p carmine ver 11,000. 5,750.
28C A1 2p blue 1,000. 190.
30C A1 1sh yellow green 1,900. 800.
d. Horiz. pair, imperf. btwn. 15,000.

1864-71 **Wmk. 6** ***Perf. 12½***

31 A1 1p vermilion 250.00 75.00
a. 1p orange ('71) 500.00 90.00
32 A1 2p blue 200.00 22.50
a. 2p blue, worn plate 225.00 24.00
b. Horiz. pair, imperf. btwn. (#32) *4,000.*
c. Perf. 10x12½ 11,000.
d. Imperf., pair (#32) 1,900. 1,700.
33 A1 3p lilac 225.00 40.00
a. 3p mauve 525.00 80.00
b. Imperf., pair (#33) 3,750. 1,900.
c. As "a", imperf., pair 3,750. 1,900.
d. 3p brown lilac *1,750.* *700.00*
34 A1 4p deep rose ('65) 5,000. 300.00
35 A1 4p yellow ('65) 450.00 110.00
a. 4p orange yellow *2,250.* 1,100.
36 A1 6p red brown 300.00 28.00
a. 6p brown 275.00 42.50
b. Horiz. pair, imperf. btwn. 1,750. 1,900.
37 A1 1sh pale yel green 325.00 100.00
a. 1sh yellow green 400.00 140.00
b. 1sh green 1,000. 350.00

The 1p, 2p and 6p come in two or more shades.

Imperforate examples of the 1p pale orange, worn plate; 2p dull blue and 6p dull chocolate brown are reprints. Value, each $100.

1871 **Wmk. 6** ***Perf. 10***

38 A1 1p deep brown 900.00 125.00

1871 ***Perf. 12½***

39 A1 1p brown 200.00 50.00
a. Imperf. 1,000.
40 A1 2p orange 175.00 32.50
a. 2p vermilion 160.00 32.50
b. Imperf., pair
41 A1 6p blue 400.00 77.50
Nos. 39-41 (3) 775.00 160.00

Shades exist.

1871 ***Perf. 10x12½***

42 A1 1p brown 450.00 52.50
43 A1 2p orange 300.00 37.50
44 A1 6p blue 2,500. 575.00
Nos. 42-44 (3) 3,250. 665.00

The 6p usually has only one side perf. 10, the 1p and 2p more rarely so.

Shades exist.

1872 **Wmk. 59** ***Perf. 12½***

45 A1 1p brown 4,600.
46 A1 2p vermilion 800.00 325.00

1872 **Unwmk.** ***Perf. 12½***

47 A1 1p brown 1,000. 200.00
48 A1 2p vermilion 175.00 57.50
49 A1 4p yellow orange 250.00 *750.00*

The watermark "T.H. SAUNDERS" in double-line capitals falls on 16 of the 240 stamps in a sheet. The 1p and 2p also are known with script "WT & CO" watermark.

1872 **Wmk. 60**

50 A1 2p vermilion *3,150.* 575.

A2

A3

A4

A5

A6

A7

Perf. 10x12½, 11½, 12, 12½

1874 **Typo.** **Wmk. 62**

51 A2 1p violet 90.00 5.75
a. Bluish paper 120.00 35.00
b. Imperf. 550.00
52 A3 2p rose 90.00 3.75
a. Bluish paper 150.00 35.00
53 A4 3p brown 225.00 62.50
a. Bluish paper 300.00 97.50
54 A5 4p claret 275.00 75.00
a. Bluish paper 500.00 125.00
55 A6 6p blue 300.00 11.50
a. Bluish paper 375.00 57.50
56 A7 1sh green 275.00 32.50
a. Bluish paper 1,150. 225.00
Nos. 51-56 (6) 1,255. 191.00

1875 **Wmk. 6** ***Perf. 12½***

57 A2 1p violet 1,400. 200.00
58 A3 2p rose 350.00 22.50

A8

1878 **Wmk. 62** ***Perf. 12x11½***

59 A8 2sh deep rose 650.00 450.00
60 A8 5sh gray 700.00 500.00

No. 60 has numeral "5" in each of the four spandrels.

Beware of cleaned fiscally used examples of Nos. 59-60.

A9 A10

A11

A12

A13

A14

A15

Perf. 10, 11, 11½, 12, 12½ and Compound

1882

61 A9 1p rose 7.50 .70
a. Vert. pair, imperf. horiz. *425.00*
b. Perf. 12x11½ 42.50 7.00
c. Perf. 12½ 275.00 150.00
62 A10 2p violet 13.50 .35
a. Vert. pair, imperf. btwn. *525.00*
b. Perf. 12½ 200.00 110.00
63 A11 3p orange 52.50 9.50
a. 3p yellow 60.00 14.00
64 A12 4p blue green 62.50 4.00
a. Perf. 10x11 80.00 13.00
65 A13 6p brown 80.00 8.00
66 A14 8p blue 80.00 52.50
67 A15 1sh red brown 125.00 8.00
Nos. 61-67 (7) 421.00 83.05

See #87. For overprints see #O1-O2, O5, O7-O8.

A15a

A16

A17

1891-95

67A A15a ½p black ('95) 4.25 .25
b. Perf. 12x11½ 35.00 *80.00*
68 A16 2½p ultramarine 57.50 5.00
a. Perf. 12½ 275.00 125.00
69 A17 5p olive gray 70.00 25.00
Nos. 67A-69 (3) 131.75 30.25

In 1893 advertisements were printed on the backs of Nos. 61-67, 68-69.

See #86C. For overprints see #O3-O4, O9.

Mt. Cook — A18

Lake Taupo — A19

Pembroke Peak — A20

Mt. Earnslaw, Lake Wakatipu — A21

Mt. Earnslaw, Lake Wakatipu — A22

Huia, Sacred Birds — A23

White Terrace, Rotomahana A24

Otira Gorge and Mt. Ruapehu A25

Kiwi A26

Maori Canoe A27

Pink Terrace, Rotomahana A28

Kea & Kaka (Hawk-billed Parrots) A29

Milford Sound A30

Mt. Cook — A31

Perf. 12 to 16

1898, Apr. 5 — Engr. — Unwmk.

70 A18 ½p lilac gray 8.00 1.10
a. Horiz. or vert. pair, imperf. btwn. 1,100. 950.00
71 A19 1p yel brn & bl 5.75 .35
a. Horiz. pair, imperf. btwn. 900.00 900.00
72 A20 2p rose brown 70.00 .30
a. Horiz. pair, imperf. vert. 475.00 475.00
73 A21 2½p bl *(Wakitipu)* 20.00 *50.00*
74 A22 2½p bl *(Wakatipu)* 50.00 10.00
75 A23 3p orange brn 45.00 10.00
76 A24 4p rose 30.00 *30.00*
77 A25 5p red brown 70.00 25.00
a. 5p violet brown 100.00 *225.00*
78 A26 6p green 150.00 60.00
79 A27 8p dull blue 70.00 32.50
80 A28 9p lilac 65.00 30.00
81 A29 1sh dull red 125.00 24.00
82 A30 2sh blue green 350.00 125.00
a. Vert. pair, imperf. btwn. 2,800. 2,800.
83 A31 5sh vermilion 400.00 *550.00*
Nos. 70-83 (14) 1,458. *948.25*

The 5sh stamps are often found with revenue cancellations that are embossed or show a crown on the top of a circle. These are worth much less.

See Nos. 84, 88-89, 91-98, 99B, 102, 104, 106-107, 111-112, 114-121, 126-128, 1508-1521. For overprint see No. O10.

A32 A33

A34

1900 — Wmk. 63 — *Perf. 11*

Thick Soft Wove Paper

84 A18 ½p green 7.00 1.10
85 A32 1p carmine rose 22.50 .65
a. 1p lake 32.50 4.50
86 A33 2p red violet 15.00 1.25
a. Vert. pair, imperf. horiz. 900.00
b. Horiz. pair, imperf. vert.
Nos. 84-86 (3) 44.50 3.00

Nos. 84 and 86 are re-engravings of Nos. 70 and 72 and are slightly smaller.

See No. 110.

1899-1900 — Wmk. 63

86C A15a ½p black ('00) 9.50 *15.00*
87 A10 2p violet ('00) 22.50 15.00

Unwmk.

88 A22 2½p blue 30.00 8.00
a. Vert. pair, imperf. horiz. 500.00 —
89 A23 3p org brown 35.00 3.00
a. Horiz. pair, imperf. vert. 500.00
b. Horiz. pair, imperf. btwn. 1,100.
90 A34 4p yel brn & bl ('00) 14.00 9.00
a. Imperf.
b. Double impression of center
91 A25 5p red brown 50.00 7.00
a. 5p violet brown 50.00 7.00
92 A26 6p green 125.00 *70.00*
a. Imperf.
93 A26 6p rose ('00) 50.00 10.00
a. 6p carmine 50.00 10.00
b. Double impression 550.00 *575.00*
c. Imperf., pair
d. Horiz. pair, imperf. vert. 425.00
94 A27 8p dark blue 45.00 20.00
95 A28 9p red lilac 52.50 22.00
96 A29 1sh red 67.50 14.00
97 A30 2sh blue green 200.00 50.00
98 A31 5sh vermilion 400.00 *450.00*
Revenue cancel 25.00
Nos. 86C-98 (13) 1,101. 693.00

See #113. For overprints see #O11-O15.

The 5sh stamps are often found with revenue cancellations that are embossed or show a crown on the top of a circle. These are worth much less.

"Commerce" — A35

1901, Jan. 1 — Unwmk. — *Perf. 12 to 16*

99 A35 1p carmine 6.00 *4.50*

Universal Penny Postage.

See Nos. 100, 103, 105, 108, 129. For overprint see No. O16. Compare design A35 with A42.

Boer War Contingent A36

Perf. 14, 11x14, 14x11

1901 — Wmk. 63

Thick Soft Paper

99B A18 ½p green 15.00 5.50

Perf. 11, 14 and Compound

100 A35 1p carmine 18.00 .20
a. Horiz. pair, imperf. vert. 325.00 325.00
101 A36 1½p brown org 25.00 8.00
a. Vert. pair, imperf. horiz. 850.00
b. Imperf., pair 800.00
Nos. 99B-101 (3) 58.00 13.70

No. 101 was issued to honor the New Zealand forces in the South African War.

See No. 109.

Thin Hard Paper

102 A18 ½p green 29.00 27.50
103 A35 1p carmine 16.00 4.75
a. Horiz. pair, imperf. vert. 300.00

1902 — Unwmk.

104 A18 ½p green 14.00 5.75
105 A35 1p carmine 14.00 3.25

1902 — *Perf. 11*

Thin White Wove Paper

106 A26 6p rose red 40.00 4.50
a. Watermarked letters 85.00 85.00

The sheets of No. 106 are watermarked with the words "LISBON SUPERFINE" in two lines, covering ten stamps.

Perf. 11, 14, 11x14, 14x13, 14x14½

1902-07 — Wmk. 61

107 A18 ½p green 6.25 .80
a. Horiz. pair, imperf. vert. 225.00
108 A35 1p carmine 5.00 .20
a. 1p rose carmine 5.00 .20
b. Imperf., pair
c. Imperf. x serrate perf. 175.00 175.00
d. Imperf. horiz. or vert. pair 200.00 200.00
f. Booklet pane of 6 225.00
109 A36 1½p brown org ('07) 21.00 *75.00*
110 A33 2p dull vio ('03) 10.00 2.00
a. Horiz. pair, imperf. vert. 425.00 *625.00*
b. Vert. pair, imperf. horiz. 450.00
111 A22 2½p blue 25.00 4.25
112 A23 3p org brown 37.50 1.75
113 A34 4p yel brn & bl 12.00 2.75
a. Horiz. pair, imperf. vert. 475.00
114 A25 5p red brown 55.00 12.00
a. 5p violet brown 52.50 8.00
115 A26 6p rose red 50.00 8.50
a. 6p rose 50.00 7.50
b. 6p pink 70.00 11.00
c. 6p brick red 80.00 18.00
d. Horiz. pair, imperf. vert. 575.00
116 A27 8p deep blue 50.00 14.00
117 A28 9p red violet 55.00 9.25
118 A29 1sh scarlet 90.00 11.00
a. 1sh orange red 95.00 8.50
b. 1sh brown red 100.00 15.00
119 A30 2sh blue green 175.00 50.00
120 A31 5sh vermilion 500.00 *400.00*
Nos. 107-120 (14) 1,091. 591.50

Wmk. 61 is normally sideways on 3p, 5p, 6p, 8p and 1sh.

The unique example of No. 113 with inverted center is used and is in the New Zealand National Philatelic Collection.

See No. 129. For overprints see Nos. O17-O22.

The 5sh stamps are often found with revenue cancellations that are embossed or show a crown on the top of a circle. These are worth much less.

In 1908 a quantity of the 1p carmine was overprinted "King Edward VII Land" and taken on a Shackleton expedition to the Antarctic. Because of the weather Shackleton landed at Victoria Land instead. The stamp was never sold to the public at face value. See No. 121a.

Similar conditions prevailed for the 1909-12 ½p green and 1p carmine overprinted "VICTORIA LAND." See Nos. 130d-131d.

1903 — Unwmk. — *Perf. 11*

Laid Paper

121 A30 2sh blue green 300.00 *225.00*

No. 108a Overprinted in Green: "King Edward VII Land" in Two Lines Reading Up

1908, Jan. 15 — *Perf. 14*

121a A35 1p rose carmine 650.00 70.00

See note after No. 120.

Christchurch Exhibition Issue

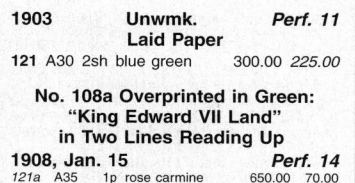

Arrival of the Maoris A37

Maori Art — A38

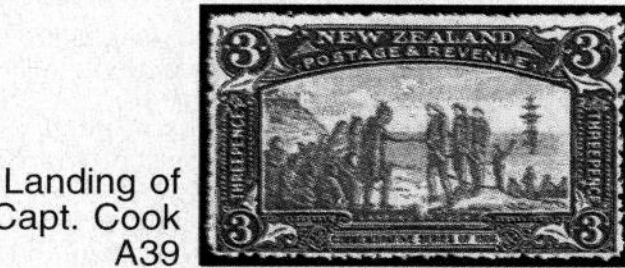

Landing of Capt. Cook A39

Annexation of New Zealand A40

Wmk. 61

1906, Nov. — Typo. — *Perf. 14*

122 A37 ½p emerald 25.00 *40.00*
123 A38 1p vermilion 20.00 30.00
a. 1p claret *12,000.* *15,000.*
124 A39 3p blue & brown 57.50 *100.00*
125 A40 6p gray grn & rose 210.00 *350.00*
Nos. 122-125 (4) 312.50 520.00

Value for No. 123a is for a fine copy.

Designs of 1902-07 Issue, but smaller

Perf. 14, 14x13, 14x14½

1907-08 — Engr.

126 A23 3p orange brown *60.00* 17.50
127 A26 6p carmine rose *70.00* 12.50
128 A29 1sh orange red *250.00* 40.00
Nos. 126-128 (3) *380.00* 70.00

The small stamps are about 21mm high, those of 1898-1902 about 23mm.

Type of 1902 Redrawn

1908 — Typo. — *Perf. 14x14½*

129 A35 1p carmine 45.00 1.75

REDRAWN, 1p: The lines of shading in the globe are diagonal and the other lines of the design are generally thicker than on No. 108.

Edward VII A41

"Commerce" A42

1909-12 — *Perf. 14x14½*

130 A41 ½p yellow green 8.00 .55
a. Booklet pane of 6 *225.00*
b. Booklet pane 5 + label *675.00*
c. Imperf., pair 225.00

131 A42 1p carmine 2.00 .20
a. Imperf., pair 350.00
b. Booklet pane of 6 160.00

Perf. 14x14½, 14x13½, 14

Engr.

Various Frames

132 A41 2p mauve 27.50 7.50
133 A41 3p orange brown 30.00 1.40
134 A41 4p red orange 35.00 *31.00*
135 A41 4p yellow ('12) 25.00 *15.00*
136 A41 5p red brown 24.00 3.50
137 A41 6p carmine rose 55.00 1.40
138 A41 8p deep blue 22.50 2.50
139 A41 1sh vermilion 85.00 7.50
Nos. 130-139 (10) 314.00 70.55

Nos. 133, 136-138 exist in vert. pairs with perf. 14x13½ on top and perf. 14x14½ on the bottom. These sell for a premium.

See #177. For overprint see Cook Islands #49.

Nos. 130-131 Overprinted in Black: "VICTORIA LAND" in Two Lines

1911-13

130d A41 ½p yellow green *1,100.* *950.00*
131d A42 1p carmine *70.00* *150.00*

See note after No. 120.

Issue dates: 1p, Feb. 9; ½p, Jan. 18, 1913.

Stamps of 1909 Overprinted in Black: "AUCKLAND EXHIBITION, 1913," in Three Lines

1913

130e A41 ½p yellow green 25.00 *55.00*
131e A42 1p carmine 35.00 *45.00*
133e A41 3p orange brown 250.00 *400.00*
137e A41 6p carmine rose 300.00 *500.00*
Nos. 130e-137e (4) 610.00 *1,000.*

This issue was valid only within New Zealand and to Australia from Dec. 1, 1913, to Feb. 28, 1914. The Auckland Stamp Collectors Club inspired this issue.

King George V — A43

1915 **Typo.** ***Perf. 14x15***

144 A43 ½p yellow green 2.00 .20
b. Booklet pane of 6 *150.00*

See Nos. 163-164, 176, 178. For overprints see No. MR1, Cook Islands No. 40.

A44

A45

Perf. 14x14½, 14x13½

1915-22 **Engr.**

145 A44 1½p gray 4.25 2.00
146 A45 2p purple 14.50 *45.00*
147 A45 2p org yel ('16) 9.50 *35.00*
148 A44 2½p dull blue 9.00 *5.75*
149 A45 3p violet brown 16.50 1.40
150 A45 4p orange yellow 9.50 *57.50*
151 A45 4p purple ('16) 22.50 .55
c. 4p blackish violet 10.00 .55
d. Vert. pair, top stamp imperf, bottom stamp perf 3 sides *1,200.*
152 A44 4½p dark green 25.00 *26.00*
153 A45 5p light blue ('21) 19.00 1.10
a. Imperf., pair 250.00 200.00
154 A45 6p carmine rose 13.00 .55
a. Horiz. pair, imperf. vert.
155 A44 7½p red brown 22.50 *26.00*
156 A45 8p blue ('21) 25.00 *50.00*
157 A45 8p red brown ('22) 35.00 4.00
158 A45 9p olive green 30.00 5.00
a. Imperf., pair *1,250.*
159 A45 1sh vermilion 30.00 .60
a. Imperf., pair 450.00
Nos. 145-159 (15) 285.25 260.45

Nos. 145-156, 158-159 exist in vert. pairs with perf 14x13½ on top and perf 14x14½ on the bottom. These sell for a premium. The 5p and No. 151c exist with the perf varieties reversed. These are rare. No. 157 only comes perf 14x13½.

The former Nos. 151a and 151b probably were listed from sheets with No. 151d. They probably do not exist.

For overprints see Cook Islands Nos. 53-60.

A46

A47

1916-19 **Typo.** ***Perf. 14x15, 14***

160 A46 1½p gray black 9.00 1.40
161 A47 1½p gray black 11.00 .60
162 A47 1½p brown orange ('18) 3.50 .60
163 A43 2p yellow 2.60 .20
164 A43 3p chocolate ('19) 12.00 1.50
Nos. 160-164 (5) 38.10 4.30

The engr. stamps have a background of geometric lathe-work; the typo. stamps have a background of crossed dotted lines.

Type A43 has three diamonds at each side of the crown, type A46 has two, and type A47 has one.

In 1916 the 1½, 2, 3 and 6p of the 1915-16 issue and the 8p of the 1909 issue were printed on paper intended for the long rectangular stamps of the 1902-07 issue. In this paper the watermarks are set wide apart, so that the smaller stamps often show only a small part of the watermark or miss it altogether.

For overprints see Cook Islands #50-52.

Victory Issue

"Peace" and British Lion — A48

Peace and Lion — A49

Maori Chief — A50

British Lion — A51

"Victory" — A52

King George V, Lion and Maori Fern at Sides — A53

1920, Jan. 27 ***Perf. 14***

165 A48 ½p yellow green 3.25 2.75
166 A49 1p carmine 2.00 .65
167 A50 1½p brown orange 3.50 .55
168 A51 3p black brown 15.00 *16.00*
169 A52 6p purple 17.00 *19.00*
170 A53 1sh vermilion 25.00 *55.00*
Nos. 165-170 (6) 65.75 *93.95*

No. 165 Surcharged in Red

1922, Mar.

174 A48 2p on ½p yellow green 6.00 1.50

Map of New Zealand — A54

1923 **Typo.** ***Perf. 14x15***

175 A54 1p carmine rose 3.50 .70

Restoration of Penny Postage. The paper varies from thin to thick.

Types of 1909-15
N Z and Star 'watermark' printed on back, usually in blue

1925 **Unwmk.** ***Perf. 14x14½***

176 A43 ½p yellow green 3.50 *3.50*
177 A42 1p carmine 3.00 .90
178 A43 2p yellow 20.00 *62.50*
Nos. 176-178 (3) 26.50 *66.90*

Exhibition Buildings A55

1925, Nov. 17 **Wmk. 61**

Surface Tinted Paper

179 A55 ½p yel green, *grnsh* 3.50 *12.50*
180 A55 1p car rose, *pink* 4.00 *6.25*
181 A55 4p red violet, *lilac* 37.50 *80.00*
Nos. 179-181 (3) 45.00 *98.75*

Dunedin Exhibition.

George V in Admiral's Uniform A56

In Field Marshal's Uniform A57

1926 ***Perf. 14, 14½x14***

182 A56 2sh blue 65.00 35.00
a. 2sh dark blue 60.00 *62.50*
183 A56 3sh violet 125.00 *160.00*
a. 3sh deep violet 100.00 *175.00*

Perf. 14, 14x14½

184 A57 1p rose red 1.25 .20
a. Booklet pane of 6 100.00
b. Imperf., pair 140.00
Nos. 182-184 (3) 191.25 195.20

For overprints see Cook Islands Nos. 74-75.

Pied Fantail and Clematis A58

Kiwi and Cabbage Palm A59

Maori Woman Cooking in Boiling Spring A60

Maori Council House (Whare) A61

Mt. Cook and Mountain Lilies — A62

Maori Girl Wearing Tiki — A63

Mitre Peak — A64

Striped Marlin A65

Harvesting — A66

Tuatara Lizard — A67

Maori Panel from Door — A68

Tui or Parson Bird — A69

Capt. Cook Landing at Poverty Bay — A70

Mt. Egmont, North Island A71

Perf. 14x14½, 14x13½, 13½x14, 13½

1935, May 1 **Engr.** **Wmk. 61**

185 A58 ½p bright green 1.75 .85
186 A59 1p copper red 2.00 .70
186A A59 1p copper red, re-engraved 6.25 3.50
b. Booklet pane of 6 + ad labels *60.00*
187 A60 1½p red brown 6.25 7.50
188 A61 2p red orange 4.00 .20
189 A62 2½p dk gray & dk brown 6.00 *15.00*
190 A63 3p chocolate 13.50 2.75
191 A64 4p blk brn & blk 4.25 2.00
192 A65 5p violet blue 26.00 20.00
193 A66 6p red 8.00 5.00
194 A67 8p dark brown 11.00 *7.50*

Litho.

Size: 18x21½mm

195 A68 9p black & scarlet 12.50 5.00

Engr.

No.	Type	Denom.	Color	Unused	Used
196	A69	1sh	dk sl green	22.50	10.00
197	A70	2sh	olive green	47.50	30.00
198	A71	3sh	yel brn & brn black	35.00	*45.00*
			Nos. 185-198 (15)	206.50	155.00
			Set, never hinged	450.00	

On No. 186A, the horizontal lines in the sky are much darker.

The 2½p, 5p, 2sh and 3sh are perf. 13½ vertically; perf. 13-14 horizontally on each stamp.

See Nos. 203-216, 244-245.

Silver Jubilee Issue

Queen Mary and King George V
A72

1935, May 7 *Perf. 11x11½*

No.	Type	Denom.	Color	Unused	Used
199	A72	½p	blue green	.75	1.00
200	A72	1p	dark car rose	1.00	.50
201	A72	6p	vermilion	17.50	*27.50*
			Nos. 199-201 (3)	19.25	*29.00*
			Set, never hinged	25.00	

25th anniv. of the reign of King George V.

Types of 1935

Perf. 12½ to 15 and Compound

1936-41 **Wmk. 253**

No.	Type	Denom.	Color	Unused	Used
203	A58	½p	bright green	1.75	.20
204	A59	1p	copper red	1.50	.20
205	A60	1½p	red brown	7.00	6.00
206	A61	2p	red orange	.20	.20
a.			Perf. 14	15.00	.90
b.			Perf. 14x15	21.00	20.00
c.			Perf. 12½	2.75	.20
207	A62	2½p	dk gray & dk brn	1.50	*6.00*
208	A63	3p	chocolate	20.00	.60
209	A64	4p	black brn & blk	2.00	.20
a.			Perf. 12½	17.50	12.50
210	A65	5p	violet blue	3.00	1.25
a.			Perf. 12½	11.00	3.50
211	A66	6p	red	1.50	.20
a.			Perf. 12½	1.75	3.50
212	A67	8p	dark brown	2.00	.75
a.			Perf. 12½	2.25	1.60

Litho.

Size: 18x21½mm

No.	Type	Denom.	Color	Unused	Used
213	A68	9p	gray & scarlet	25.00	3.50
a.			9p black & scarlet	30.00	3.50

Engr.

No.	Type	Denom.	Color	Unused	Used
214	A69	1sh	dark slate grn	4.00	.60
a.			Perf. 12½	30.00	20.00
215	A70	2sh	olive green	7.00	1.50
a.			Perf. 13½x14	200.00	3.00
b.			Perf. 12½	15.00	8.50
216	A71	3sh	yel brn & blk brn	5.75	2.25
a.			Perf. 12½ ('41)	45.00	50.00
			Nos. 203-216 (14)	82.20	23.45
			Set, never hinged	160.00	

Wool Industry
A73

Butter Industry
A74

Sheep Farming
A75

Apple Industry
A76

Shipping
A77

1936, Oct. 1 **Wmk. 61** ***Perf. 11***

No.	Type	Denom.	Color	Unused	Used
218	A73	½p	deep green	.20	.20
219	A74	1p	red	.20	.20
220	A75	2½p	deep blue	1.65	2.75
221	A76	4p	dark purple	1.25	1.90
222	A77	6p	red brown	2.00	1.65
			Nos. 218-222 (5)	5.30	6.70
			Set, never hinged	6.50	

Congress of the Chambers of Commerce of the British Empire held in New Zealand.

Queen Elizabeth and King George VI
A78

Perf. 13½x13

1937, May 13 **Wmk. 253**

No.	Type	Denom.	Color	Unused	Used
223	A78	1p	rose carmine	.20	.20
224	A78	2½p	dark blue	.20	.50
225	A78	6p	vermilion	.65	.75
			Nos. 223-225 (3)	1.05	1.45
			Set, never hinged	2.25	

Coronation of George VI and Elizabeth.

A79

A80

1938-44 **Engr.** ***Perf. 13½***

No.	Type	Denom.	Color	Unused	Used
226	A79	½p	emerald	4.50	.20
226B	A79	½p	brown org ('41)	.20	.20
227	A79	1p	rose red	3.75	.20
227A	A79	1p	lt blue grn ('41)	.20	.20
228	A80	1½p	violet brown	19.00	2.25
228B	A80	1½p	red ('44)	.20	.20
228C	A80	3p	blue ('41)	.20	.20
			Nos. 226-228C (7)	28.05	3.45
			Set, never hinged	40.00	

See Nos. 258-264. For surcharges see Nos. 242-243, 279, 285.

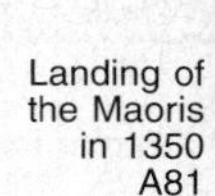

Landing of the Maoris in 1350
A81

Captain Cook, His Map of New Zealand, 1769, H.M.S. Endeavour
A82

Victoria, Edward VII, George V, Edward VIII and George VI — A83

Abel Tasman, Ship, and Chart of West Coast of New Zealand
A84

Treaty of Waitangi, 1840 — A85

Pioneer Settlers Landing on Petone Beach, 1840
A86

The Progress of Transport
A87

H.M.S. "Britomart" at Akaroa — A88

Route of Ship Carrying First Shipment of Frozen Mutton to England — A89

Maori Council
A90

Gold Mining in 1861 and Modern Gold Dredge
A91

Giant Kauri — A92

Perf. 13½x13, 13x13½, 14x13½

1940, Jan. 2 **Engr.** **Wmk. 253**

No.	Type	Denom.	Color	Unused	Used
229	A81	½p	dk blue green	.25	.20
230	A82	1p	scarlet & sepia	2.00	.20
231	A83	1½p	brt vio & ultra	.25	.50
232	A84	2p	black brown & Prussian green	1.10	.20
233	A85	2½p	dk bl & myr grn	1.50	.75
234	A86	3p	dp plum & dk vio	2.75	.75
235	A87	4p	dk red vio & vio brn	10.00	1.60
236	A88	5p	brown & lt bl	5.00	4.00
237	A89	6p	vio & brt grn	8.00	2.00
238	A90	7p	org red & black	1.25	*4.50*
239	A90	8p	org red & black	8.00	3.50
240	A91	9p	dp org & olive	5.50	2.25
241	A92	1sh	dk sl grn & ol	10.00	4.25
			Nos. 229-241 (13)	55.60	24.70
			Set, never hinged	95.00	

Centenary of British sovereignty established by the treaty of Waitangi.

Imperfs of #229-241 exist. These probably are plate proofs.

For surcharge see No. 246.

Stamps of 1938 Surcharged with New Values in Black

1941 **Wmk. 253** ***Perf. 13½***

No.	Type	Surcharge	Color	Unused	Used
242	A79	1p on ½p	emerald	.75	.20
243	A80	2p on 1½p	violet brn	.75	.20
			Set, never hinged	3.25	

Type of 1935 Redrawn

1941 **Typo.** **Wmk. 61** ***Perf. 14x15***

Size: 17½x20½mm

No.	Type	Denom.	Color	Unused	Used
244	A68	9p	int black & scarlet	65.00	30.00

Wmk. 253

No.	Type	Denom.	Color	Unused	Used
245	A68	9p	int black & scarlet	4.00	3.50
			Set, never hinged	110.00	

Catalogue values for unused stamps in this section, from this point to the end of the section, are for Never Hinged items.

No 231 Surcharged in Black

1944 ***Perf. 13½x13***

No.	Type	Surcharge	Color	Unused	Used
246	A83	10p on 1½p	brt vio & ultra	.45	.45

Peace Issue

Lake Matheson
A93

Parliament House, Wellington — A94

St. Paul's Cathedral, London — A95

The Royal Family — A96

Badge of Royal New Zealand Air Force
A97

New Zealand Army Overseas Badge
A98

Badge of Royal Navy
A99

New Zealand Coat of Arms
A100

Knight, Window of Wellington Boys' College A101

Natl. Memorial Campanile, Wellington A103

Southern Alps and Chapel Altar A102

Engr.; Photo. (1½p, 1sh)
Perf. 13x13½, 13½x13

1946, Apr. 1 **Wmk. 253**

247	A93	½p choc & dk bl grn	.20	.20
248	A94	1p emerald	.20	.20
249	A95	1½p scarlet	.20	.20
250	A96	2p rose violet	.20	.20
251	A97	3p dk grn & ultra	.20	.20
252	A98	4p brn org & ol grn	.20	.20
253	A99	5p ultra & blue grn	.20	.20
254	A100	6p org red & red brn	.20	.20
255	A101	8p brown lake & blk	.35	.20
256	A102	9p black & brt bl	.35	.25
257	A103	1sh gray black	.45	.30
		Nos. 247-257 (11)	2.75	2.35

Return to peace at the close of WWII.
Imperfs exist from the printer's archives.

George VI Type of 1938 and

King George VI — A104

1947 **Engr.** ***Perf. 13½***

258	A80	2p orange	.20	.20
260	A80	4p rose lilac	.30	.30
261	A80	5p gray	.90	.25
262	A80	6p rose carmine	.90	.20
263	A80	8p deep violet	1.00	.20
264	A80	9p chocolate	1.75	.20

Perf. 14

265	A104	1sh dk car rose & chnt	1.25	.30
266	A104	1sh3p ultra & chnt	2.00	.35
267	A104	2sh dk grn & brn org	4.75	.75
268	A104	3sh gray blk & chnt	8.00	1.25
		Nos. 258-268 (10)	21.05	4.00

Nos. 265-267 have watermark either upright or sideways. On No. 268 watermark is always sideways.

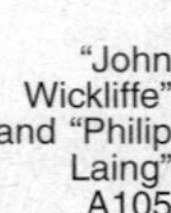

"John Wickliffe" and "Philip Laing" A105

Cromwell, Otago A106

First Church, Dunedin — A107

University of Otago A108

1948, Feb. 23 ***Perf. 13½***

269	A105	1p green & blue	.20	.20
270	A106	2p brown & green	.20	.20
271	A107	3p violet	.35	.20
272	A108	6p lilac rose & gray blk	.35	.20
		Nos. 269-272 (4)	1.10	.80

Otago Province settlement, cent.

A Royal Visit set of four was prepared but not issued. Copies of the 3p have appeared on the stamp market.

A109

Cathedral at Christchurch — A110

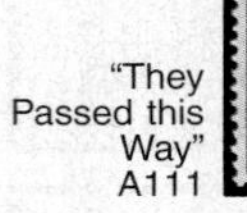

"They Passed this Way" A111

Wmk. 253

1950, July 28 **Typo.** ***Perf. 14***
Black Surcharge

273	A109	1½p rose red	.40	.40

See No. 367.

1950, Nov. 20 **Engr.** ***Perf. 13x13½***

3p, John Robert Godley. 6p, Canterbury University College. 1sh, View of Timaru.

274	A110	1p blue grn & blue	.35	.35
275	A111	2p car & red org	.35	.35
276	A110	3p indigo & blue	.35	.35
277	A111	6p brown & blue	.50	.50
278	A111	1sh claret & blue	.65	.65
		Nos. 274-278 (5)	2.20	2.20

Centenary of the founding of Canterbury Provincial District.
Imperfs of #274-278 exist.

No. 227A Surcharged in Black

1952, Dec. ***Perf. 13½***

279	A79	3p on 1p lt blue green	.30	.20

Coronation Issue

Buckingham Palace and Elizabeth II — A112

Queen Elizabeth II — A113

Westminster Abbey — A114

Designs: 4p, Queen Elizabeth and state coach. 1sh6p, Crown and royal scepter.

Perf. 13x12½, 14x14½ (3p, 8p)
Engr., Photo. (3p, 8p)

1953, May 25

280	A112	2p ultramarine	.35	.35
281	A113	3p brown	.35	.20
282	A112	4p carmine	1.40	*2.00*
283	A114	8p slate black	.90	*1.50*
284	A112	1sh6p vio blue & pur	2.25	*2.50*
		Nos. 280-284 (5)	5.25	6.55

No. 226B Surcharged in Black

1953, Sept. ***Perf. 13½***

285	A79	1p on ½p brown orange	.40	.20

Queen Elizabeth II — A115

Queen Elizabeth II and Duke of Edinburgh A116

Perf. 12½x13½, 13½x13

1953, Dec. 9 **Engr.**

286	A115	3p lilac	.20	.20
287	A116	4p deep blue	.20	.20

Visit of Queen Elizabeth II and the Duke of Edinburgh.

A117

A118

A119

1953-57 ***Perf. 13½***

288	A117	½p gray	.20	.20
289	A117	1p orange	.20	.20
290	A117	1½p rose brown	.20	.20
291	A117	2p blue green	.20	.20
292	A117	3p red	.20	.20
293	A117	4p blue	.45	.20
294	A117	6p rose violet	.75	*1.50*
295	A117	8p rose car	.65	.65
296	A118	9p emerald & org brn	.65	.50
297	A118	1sh car & blk	.70	.20
298	A118	1sh6p blue & blk	1.40	.40
298A	A118	1sh9p org & blk	9.50	1.25
298B	A119	2sh6p redsh brn	21.00	8.00
299	A119	3sh blue green	14.00	.40
300	A119	5sh rose car	25.00	4.50
301	A119	10sh vio blue	50.00	20.00
		Nos. 288-301 (16)	125.10	38.60

The 1½p was issued in 1953; 1sh9p and 2sh6p in 1957; all others in 1954.
No. 298A exists on both ordinary and chalky paper.
Two dies of the 1sh differ in shading on the sleeve.
Imperfs of Nos. 298B-301 and tete-beche pairs of No. 301 and 312 exist from the printer's archives.
See Nos. 306-312. For surcharge see No. 320.

Maori Mailman A120

Queen Elizabeth II A121

Douglas DC-3 A122

Perf. 13½ (2p), 14 (3p), 13 (4p)

1955, July 18 **Wmk. 253**

302	A120	2p deep grn & brn	.20	.20
303	A121	3p claret	.20	.20
304	A122	4p ultra & black	.50	.50
		Nos. 302-304 (3)	.90	.90

Cent. of New Zealand's 1st postage stamps.

Type of 1953-54 Redrawn

1955-59 **Wmk. 253** ***Perf. 13½***

306	A117	1p orange ('56)	.50	.20
307	A117	1½p rose brown	.60	.20
308	A117	2p bl grn ('56)	.40	.20
309	A117	3p vermilion ('56)	.50	.20
310	A117	4p blue ('58)	1.20	.75
311	A117	6p violet	11.00	.20
312	A117	8p brown red ('59)	7.50	7.50
		Nos. 306-312 (7)	21.70	9.25

The numeral has been enlarged and the ornament in the lower right corner omitted.
Nos. 306, 308-310 exist on both ordinary and chalky paper.
Imperfs exist.
For surcharges see Nos. 319, 354.

Whalers of Foveaux Strait A123

"Agriculture" with Cow and Sheep — A124

Notornis (Takahe) — A125

1956, Jan. ***Perf. 13x12½, 13 (8p)***

313	A123	2p deep green	.20	.20
314	A124	3p sepia	.20	.20
315	A125	8p car & blue vio	1.50	1.25
		Nos. 313-315 (3)	1.90	1.65

Southland centennial.

Lamb and Map of New Zealand — A126

Lamb, S. S. "Dunedin" and Refrigeration Ship — A127

Perf. 14x14½, 14½x14

1957, Feb. 15 **Photo.**

316 A126 4p bright blue .60 *1.00*
317 A127 8p brick red 1.40 1.40

New Zealand Meat Export Trade, 75th anniv.

Sir Truby King — A128

Nelson Diocese Seal — A129a

Sir Charles Kingsford-Smith and "Southern Cross" — A129

1957, May 14 **Engr.** ***Perf. 13***

318 A128 3p rose red .20 .20

Plunket Society, 50th anniversary.

Imperfs exist. These probably are plate proofs.

Nos. 307, 290 Surcharged

1958, Jan. 15 ***Perf. 13½***

319 A117 2p on 1½p (#307) .20 .20
a. Small surcharge .20 .20
320 A117 2p on 1½p (#290) 200.00 *250.00*
a. Small surcharge —

Surcharge measures 9½mm vert. on Nos. 319-320; 9mm on No. 319a-320a. Diameter of dot 4½mm on Nos. 319-320; 3¾mm on No. 319a-320a.

Counterfeits exist.

Perf. 14x14½

1958, Aug. 27 **Engr.** **Wmk. 253**

321 A129 6p brt violet blue .45 *.60*

1st air crossing of the Tasman Sea, 30th anniv.

See Australia No. 310.

1958, Sept. 29 ***Perf. 13***

322 A129a 3p carmine rose .20 .20

Centenary of Nelson City.

Imperfs exist. These probably are plate proofs.

Statue of "Pania," Napier — A130

Gannet Sanctuary, Cape Kidnappers A131

Design: 8p, Maori shearing sheep.

Perf. 13½x14½, 14½x14

1958, Nov. 3 **Photo.** **Wmk. 253**

323 A130 2p yellow green .20 .20
324 A131 3p ultramarine .20 .20
325 A130 8p red brown 1.10 *1.50*
Nos. 323-325 (3) 1.50 1.90

Centenary of Hawkes Bay province.

Jamboree Kiwi Badge — A132

1959, Jan. 5 **Engr.** ***Perf. 13***

326 A132 3p car rose & brown .25 .20

Pan-Pacific Scout Jamboree, Auckland, Jan. 3-10.

"Endeavour" at Ship Cove — A133

Designs: 3p, Shipping wool at Wairau bar, 1857. 8p, Salt Industry, Grassmere.

1959, Mar. 2 **Photo.** ***Perf. 14½x14***

327 A133 2p green .30 .20
328 A133 3p dark blue .30 .20
329 A133 8p brown 1.10 *2.50*
Nos. 327-329 (3) 1.70 2.90

Centenary of Marlborough Province.

The Explorer — A134

Westland Centennial: 3p, The Gold Digger. 8p, The Pioneer Woman.

1960, May 16 ***Perf. 14x14½***

330 A134 2p green .20 .20
331 A134 3p orange .20 .20
332 A134 8p gray 1.50 2.00
Nos. 330-332 (3) 1.90 2.40

Kaka Beak Flower A135

Timber Industry A136

Tiki A137

Maori Rock Drawing A138

Butter Making A139

Designs: ½p, Manuka flower. 1p, Karaka flower. 2½p, Titoki flower. 3p, Kowhai flower. 4p, Hibiscus. 5p, Mountain daisy. 6p, Clematis. 7p, Koromiko flower. 8p, Rata flower. 9p, Flag. 1sh3p, Rainbow trout. 1sh9p, Plane spraying farmland. 3sh, Ngauruhoe Volcano, Tongariro National Park. 5sh, Sutherland Falls. 10sh, Tasman Glacier, Mount Cook. £1, Pohutu Geyser.

Perf. 14½x14, 14x14½

1960-66 **Photo.** **Wmk. 253**

333 A135 ½p dp car, grn & pale bl .20 .20
b. Green omitted 250.00
c. Pale blue omitted 175.00
334 A135 1p brn, org & grn .20 .20
b. Orange omitted 325.00
c. Perf. 14½x13, wmkd. sideways 2.00 2.00
335 A135 2p grn, rose car, blk & yel .20 .20
b. Black omitted 350.00
c. Yellow omitted 375.00
336 A135 2½p blk, grn, red & brn .25 .20
a. Brown omitted 200.00
b. Green & red omitted 575.00
c. Green omitted 225.00
d. Red omitted 500.00
337 A135 3p Prus bl, yel, brn & grn .20 .20
b. Yellow omitted 175.00
c. Brown omitted 175.00
d. Green omitted 200.00
e. Perf. 14½x13, wmkd. sideways 2.00 2.00
338 A135 4p bl, grn, yel & lilac .20 .20
a. Yellow omitted 375.00
b. Lilac omitted 300.00
339 A135 5p pur, blk, yel & grn .30 .20
a. Yellow omitted 325.00
340 A135 6p dp grn, lt grn & lil .30 .20
a. Light green omitted 300.00
b. Lilac omitted 300.00
340C A135 7p pink, red, grn & yel .50 .60
341 A135 8p gray, grn, pink & yel .50 .20
342 A136 9p ultra & car .70 .20
a. Carmine omitted 425.00
343 A136 1sh green & brn .55 .20
344 A137 1sh3p bl, brn & carmine 1.00 .20
a. Carmine omitted 475.00
345 A137 1sh6p org brn & olive grn 1.10 .20
346 A136 1sh9p pale brown 13.00 .50
347 A138 2sh buff & blk 3.50 .20
348 A139 2sh6p red brn & yellow 3.50 .50
a. Yellow omitted 500.00
349 A139 3sh gray brown 32.50 1.25
350 A138 5sh dark green 4.50 .80
351 A139 10sh blue 8.00 4.00
352 A138 £1 magenta 16.00 10.00
Nos. 333-352 (21) 87.20 20.45

Nos. 334c and 337e were issued in coils.

Only on chalky paper: 2½p, 5p, 7p. On ordinary and chalky paper: 1p, 3p, 4p, 6p, 1sh9p, 2sh, 3sh, 5sh, 10sh. Others on ordinary paper only.

Issued: 2p, 4p, 1sh, 1sh3p, 1sh6p, 1sh9p, 2sh, 2sh6p, 3sh, 5sh, 10sh, £1, 7/11/60; ½p, 1p, 3p, 6p, 8p, 9p, 9/1/60; 2½p, 11/1/61; 5p, 5/14/62; 7p, 3/16/66; #334c, 11/63; #337e, 10/3/63.

See Nos. 360-361, 382-404.

Adoration of the Shepherds, by Rembrandt A140

Perf. 11½x12

1960, Nov. 1 **Wmk. 253**

353 A140 2p dp brown & red, *cream* .30 .20
a. Red omitted *475.00* *250.00*

Christmas. See No. 355.

No. 309 Surcharged with New Value and Bars

Two types of surcharge:
Type I — "2½d" is 5½mm wide.
Type II — "2½d" is 5mm wide.

1961, Sept. 1 **Engr.** ***Perf. 13½***

354 A117 2½p on 3p vermilion, I .40 .20
a. Type II .40 .20

Christmas Type of 1960

2½p, Adoration of the Magi, by Dürer.

1961, Oct. 16 **Photo.** ***Perf. 14½x14***
Size: 30x34mm

355 A140 2½p multicolored .20 .20

Morse Key and Port Hills, Lyttelton, 1862 A141

Design: 8p, Teleprinter and tape, 1962.

1962, June 1 **Wmk. 253**

356 A141 3p dk brn & grn .20 .20
a. Green omitted 750.00
357 A141 8p dk red & gray 1.25 .50
a. Imperf., pair 1,500.
b. Gray omitted 600.00

Centenary of the New Zealand telegraph.

Madonna in Prayer by Sassoferrato A142

1962, Oct. 15 ***Perf. 14½x14***

358 A142 2½p multicolored .20 .20

Christmas.

Holy Family by Titian A143

1963, Oct. 14 **Photo.** ***Perf. 12½***

359 A143 2½p multicolored .20 .20
a. Imperf., pair *250.00*
b. Yellow omitted *325.00*

Christmas.

Types of 1960-62

1sh9p, Plane spraying farmland. 3sh, Ngauruhoe volcano, Tongariro National Park.

1963-64 ***Perf. 14½x14***

360 A136 1sh9p brt blue, grn & yel 6.25 1.10
361 A139 3sh bl, grn & bis 3.75 1.50

Issued: 1sh9p, 11/4/63; 3sh, 4/1/64.

Old and New Engines A144

1sh9p, Express train and Mt. Ruapehu.

1963, Nov. 25 ***Perf. 14***

362 A144 3p multicolored .40 .20
a. Blue (sky) omitted *500.00*
363 A144 1sh9p bl, blk, yel & carmine 3.00 3.00
a. Carmine (value) omitted *1,750.*

Centenary of New Zealand Railways.

Cable Around World and Under Sea A144a

1963, Dec. 3 **Unwmk.** ***Perf. 13½***
364 A144a 8p yel, car, blk & bl 1.25 *1.75*

Opening of the Commonwealth Pacific (telephone) cable service (COMPAC).
See Australia No. 381.

Map of New Zealand and Steering Wheel A145

Perf. 14½x14
1964, May 1 **Wmk. 253**
365 A145 3p multicolored .20 .20

National Road Safety Campaign.

Rev. Samuel Marsden Conducting First Christian Service, Rangihoua Bay, Christmas 1814 — A146

1964, Oct. 12 ***Perf. 14x13½***
366 A146 2½p multicolored .20 .20

Christmas.

Postal-Fiscal Type of 1950
1964, Dec. 14 **Typo.** ***Perf. 14***
Black Surcharge
367 A109 7p rose red .50 *1.10*

ANZAC Issue

Anzac Cove, Gallipoli A147

Design: 5p, Anzac Cove and poppy.

Perf. 12½
1965, Apr. 14 **Unwmk.** **Photo.**
368 A147 4p light brown .20 .20
369 A147 5p green & red .20 *.40*

50th anniv. of the landing of the Australian and New Zealand Army Corps, ANZAC, at Gallipoli, Turkey, Apr. 25, 1915.

ITU Emblem, Old and New Communication Equipment — A148

Perf. 14½x14
1965, May 17 **Photo.** **Wmk. 253**
370 A148 9p lt brown & dk blue .60 *.40*

Centenary of the ITU.

Sir Winston Spencer Churchill (1874-1965) A148a

1965, May 24 **Unwmk.** ***Perf. 13½***
371 A148a 7p lt blue, gray & blk .25 *.50*

See Australia No. 389.

Provincial Council Building, Wellington A149

Perf. 14½x14
1965, July 26 **Photo.** **Wmk. 253**
372 A149 4p multicolored .20 .20

Centenary of the establishment of Wellington as seat of government. The design is from a water color by L. B. Temple, 1867.

ICY Emblem A150

1965, Sept. 28 **Litho.** ***Perf. 14***
373 A150 4p ol bister & dk red .20 .20

International Cooperation Year.

"The Two Trinities" by Murillo — A151

1965, Oct. 11 **Photo.** ***Perf. 13½x14***
374 A151 3p multicolored .20 .20
a. Gold omitted 625.00

Christmas.

Parliament House, Wellington and Commonwealth Parliamentary Association Emblem — A152

Designs: 4p, Arms of New Zealand and Queen Elizabeth II. 2sh, Wellington from Mt. Victoria.

1965, Nov. 30 **Unwmk.** ***Perf. 14***
375 A152 4p multicolored .30 .25
a. Blue omitted *600.00*
376 A152 9p multicolored .95 1.00
377 A152 2sh multicolored 5.50 5.00
a. Red omitted *600.00*
Nos. 375-377 (3) 6.75 6.25

11th Commonwealth Parliamentary Assoc. Conf.

Scout Emblem, Maori Pattern — A153

Virgin with Child, by Carlo Maratta — A154

Perf. 14x14½
1966, Jan. 5 **Photo.** **Wmk. 253**
378 A153 4p green & gold .20 .20
a. Gold omitted *600.00*

4th National Scout Jamboree, Trentham.

1966, Oct. 3 **Wmk. 253** ***Perf. 14***
379 A154 3p multicolored .20 .20

Christmas.

Queens Victoria and Elizabeth II — A155

New Zealand PO Savings Bank cent.: 9p, Reverse of half sovereign, 1867, and 1967 dollar.

Perf. 14x14½
1967, Feb. 3 **Photo.** **Wmk. 253**
380 A155 4p plum, gold & black .20 .20
381 A155 9p dk grn, bl, blk, sil & gold .20 .45

Decimal Currency
Types of 1960-62

Designs: ½c, Manuka flower. 1c, Karaka flower. 2c, Kaka beak flower. 2½c, Kowhai flower. 3c, Hibiscus. 4c, Mountain daisy. 5c, Clematis. 6c, Koromiko flower. 7c, Rata flower. 7½c, Brown trout. 8c, Flag. 10c, Timber industry. 15c, Tiki. 20c, Maori rock drawing. 25c, Butter making. 28c, Fox Glacier, Westland National Park. 30c, Ngauruhoe Volcano, Tongarino National Park. 50c, Sutherland Falls. $1, Tasman Glacier, Mount Cook. $2, Pohutu Geyser.

Wmk. 253, Unwmkd. (#400)
1967-70 **Photo.** ***Various Perfs.***
382 A135 ½c multicolored .20 .20
383 A135 1c multicolored .20 .20
a. Booklet pane of 5 + label 2.25
384 A135 2c multicolored .20 .20
385 A135 2½c multicolored .20 .20
386 A135 3c multicolored .20 .20
387 A135 4c multicolored .20 .20
388 A135 5c multicolored .30 .20
389 A135 6c multicolored .30 .20
390 A135 7c multicolored .40 .45
391 A137 7½c multicolored .30 .30
392 A136 8c ultra & car .35 .20
393 A136 10c grn & brn .45 .20
394 A137 15c org brn & slate grn .60 .40
395 A137 15c grn, sl grn & red ('68) .85 .30
396 A138 20c buff & black 1.40 .25
397 A139 25c brown & yel 1.40 1.40
398 A138 28c multi ('68) 1.10 .35
399 A139 30c multicolored 3.50 .85
400 A139 30c multi ('70) 11.00 4.25
401 A138 50c dark green 3.50 .85
402 A139 $1 blue 20.00 5.25
403 A138 $2 magenta 21.00 20.00
404 A138 $2 multi ('68) 52.50 32.50
Nos. 382-404 (23) 120.15 69.15

Perf. 13½x14: ½c to 3c, 5c, 7c. Perf. 14½x14: 4c, 6c, 8c, 10c, 25c, 30c, $1. Perf. 13½: 7½c. Perf. 14x14½: 15c, 20c, 28c, $2.

Issued: 7½c, 8/29/67; No. 395, 3/19/68; 28c, 7/30/68; No. 404, 12/10/68; No. 400, 1970; others, 7/10/67.

The 7½c was issued to commemorate the centenary of the brown trout's introduction to New Zealand, and retained as part of the regular series.

No. 395 has been redrawn. The "c" on No. 395 lacks serif; No. 394 has serif.

No. 391 exists with watermarks either sideways or upright.

Adoration of the Shepherds, by Poussin — A156

Sir James Hector — A157

Perf. 13½x14
1967, Oct. 3 **Photo.** **Wmk. 253**
405 A156 2½c multicolored .20 .20

Christmas.

1967, Oct. 10 **Litho.** ***Perf. 14***

Design: 4c, Mt. Aspiring, aurora australis and Southern Cross.

406 A157 4c multicolored .20 .20
407 A157 8c multicolored .45 .55

Centenary of the Royal Society of New Zealand to Promote Science.

Maori Bible — A158

1968, Apr. 23 **Litho.** ***Perf. 13½***
408 A158 3c multicolored .20 .20
a. Gold omitted *150.00*

Publication of the Bible in Maori, cent.

Soldiers of Two Eras and Tank A159

10c, Airmen of two eras, insigne & plane. 28c, Sailors of two eras, insigne & battleships.

1968, May 7 ***Perf. 14x13½***
409 A159 4c multicolored .20 .20
410 A159 10c multicolored .60 .60
411 A159 28c multicolored 2.75 2.75
Nos. 409-411 (3) 3.55 3.55

Issued to honor the Armed Services.

"Universal Suffrage" A160

Human Rights Flame A161

Perf. 13½
1968, Sept. 19 **Photo.** **Unwmk.**
412 A160 3c ol grn, lt bl & grn .20 .20
413 A161 10c dp grn, yel & red .60 .60

75th anniv. of universal suffrage in New Zealand; Intl. Human Rights Year.

Adoration of the Holy Child, by Gerard van Honthorst A162

Perf. 14x14½
1968, Oct. 1 **Wmk. 253**
414 A162 2½c multicolored .25 .20

Christmas.

Romney Marsh Sheep and Woolmark on Carpet A163

Designs: 7c, Trawler and catch. 8c, Apples and orchard. 10c, Radiata pines and stacked lumber. 20c, Cargo hoist and grazing cattle. 25c, Dairy farm in Taranaki, Mt. Egmont and crated dairy products.

Wmk. 253 (10c, 18c, 25c); others Unwmkd.

Perf. 13½; 14½x14 (10c, 25c)

1968-69 Litho.; Photo. (10c, 25c)

415 A163 7c multi ('69) .45 .45
416 A163 8c multi ('69) 1.00 1.00
417 A163 10c multi .60 .20
418 A163 18c multi ('69) 1.75 .35
419 A163 20c multi ('69) 1.40 .25
420 A163 25c multi 5.75 .70
Nos. 415-420 (6) 10.95 2.95

ILO Emblem A164

Perf. 14½x14

1969, Feb. 11 Photo. Wmk. 253

421 A164 7c scarlet & black .60 .60

50th anniv. of the ILO.

Law Society Coat of Arms A165

Otago University A166

Designs: 3c, Supreme Court Building, Auckland, horiz. 18c, "Justice" from memorial window of the University of Canterbury Hall, Christchurch.

1969, Apr. 8 Litho. *Perf. 13½*

422 A165 3c multicolored .25 .20
423 A165 10c multicolored .50 .55
424 A165 18c multicolored 1.10 1.10
Nos. 422-424 (3) 1.85 1.85

Centenary of New Zealand Law Society.

1969, June 3

Design: 10c, Conferring degree and arms of the University, horiz.

425 A166 3c multicolored .20 .20
426 A166 10c multicolored .60 .60

Centenary of the University of Otago.

Oldest House in New Zealand, Kerikeri A167

Design: 6c, Bay of Islands.

1969, Aug. 18 Litho. Wmk. 253

427 A167 4c multicolored .30 .30
428 A167 6c multicolored 1.10 1.25

Early European settlements in New Zealand on the 150th anniv. of the founding of Kerikeri, the oldest existing European settlement.

Nativity, by Federico Fiori — A168

Perf. 13½x14

1969, Oct. 1 Photo. Wmk. 253

429 A168 2½c multicolored .20 .20

Unwmk.

430 A168 2½c multicolored .20 .20

Christmas.

Capt. Cook, Transit of Venus and Octant A169

Designs: 6c, Joseph Banks and bark Endeavour. 18c, Dr. Daniel Solander and matata branch (rhabdothamnus solandri). 28c, Queen Elizabeth II and map showing Cook's chart of 1769.

1969, Oct. 9 *Perf. 14½x14*

431 A169 4c dk bl, blk & brt rose .25 .25
432 A169 6c sl grn & choc 2.25 *2.25*
433 A169 18c choc, sl grn & black 3.50 3.50
434 A169 28c dk ultra, blk & brt rose 5.75 *5.75*
a. Souv. sheet of 4, #431-434 27.50 22.50
Nos. 431-434 (4) 11.75 11.75

Cook's landing in New Zealand, bicent.

Child Drinking Milk, and Cattle A170

7c, Wheat and child with empty bowl.

1969, Nov. 18 Photo. *Perf. 13*

435 A170 7c multicolored 1.75 1.75
436 A170 8c multicolored 1.75 1.75

25th anniv. of CORSO (Council of Organizations for Relief Services Overseas).

Cardigan Bay A171

1970, Jan. 28 Unwmk. *Perf. 11½*

Granite Paper

437 A171 10c multicolored .35 .35

Return to New Zealand from the US of Cardigan Bay, 1st standard bred light-harness race horse to win a million dollars in stake money.

Glade Copper Butterfly A172

Scarlet Parrotfish A173

New Zealand Coat of Arms and Queen Elizabeth II — A174

Maori Fishhook A175

Egmont National Park A176

Hauraki Gulf Maritime Park — A177

Designs: 1c, Red admiral butterfly. 2c, Tussock butterfly. 2½c, Magpie moth. 3c, Lichen moth. 4c, Puriri moth. 6c, Sea horses. 7c, Leatherjackets (fish). 7½c, Garfish. 8c, John dory (fish). 18c, Maori club. 20c, Maori tattoo pattern. 30c, Mt. Cook National Park (chamois). 50c, Abel Tasman National Park. $1, Geothermal power plant. $2, Helicopter over field, molecule (agricultural technology).

1970-71 Wmk. 253 *Perf. 13½x13*

438 A172 ½c ultra & multi .20 .20
439 A172 1c dp bis & multi .20 .20
a. Bklt. pane of 3 + 3 labels ('71) 2.50
440 A172 2c ol grn & multi .20 .20
441 A172 2½c yellow & multi .20 .20
442 A172 3c brown & multi .20 .20
443 A172 4c dk brown & multi .20 .20
444 A173 5c dk green & multi .35 .20
445 A173 6c dp car & multi .45 .20
446 A173 7c brn red & multi .45 .20
447 A173 7½c dk vio & multi .60 .60
448 A173 8c blue grn & multi .50 .20

Perf. 14½x14

449 A174 10c dk bl, sil, red & ultra .45 .20

Perf. 14x13, 13x14

450 A175 15c brick red, sal & blk .35 .20
451 A177 18c yel grn, blk & red brn .45 .20
452 A175 20c yel brn & blk .50 .20

Nos. 439, 442 and 443 exist with watermark either sideways or upright.

Perf. 13½x12½

Unwmk.

453 A176 23c bl, grn & blk .60 .30

Litho.

Perf. 13½

454 A177 25c gray & multi 1.40 .45
a. Perf. 14 ('76) .60 .20
455 A177 30c tan & multi .85 .20
a. Perf. 14 ('76) 2.25 1.75

Photo.

Perf. 13½x12½

456 A176 50c sl grn & multi 1.00 .20

Perf. 11½

Granite Paper

457 A175 $1 light ultra & multi 2.25 .50
458 A175 $2 ol & multi 4.50 2.00
Nos. 438-458 (21) 15.90 7.05

The 10c for the visit of Queen Elizabeth II, Prince Philip and Princess Anne.

Issued: 10c, 3/12/70; ½c-4c, 9/2/70; 5c-8c, 11/4/70; 15c-20c, 1/20/71; 25c-50c, 9/1/71; $1-$2, 4/14/71; 23c, 12/1/71.

See Nos. 533-546. For surcharge see No. 480.

EXPO '70 Emblem, Geyser Restaurant — A178

Designs: 8c, EXPO '70 emblem and New Zealand Pavilion. 18c, EXPO '70 emblem and bush walk (part of N.Z. exhibit).

Perf. 13x13½

1970, Apr. 8 Photo. Unwmk.

459 A178 7c multicolored 1.25 1.25
460 A178 8c multicolored 1.25 1.25
461 A178 18c multicolored 2.25 2.25
Nos. 459-461 (3) 4.75 4.75

EXPO '70 Intl. Expo., Osaka, Japan.

UN Headquarters, New York — A179

UN, 25th anniv.: 10c, Plowing toward the sun and "25" with laurel.

1970, June 24 Litho. *Perf. 13½*

462 A179 3c multicolored .20 .20
463 A179 10c yellow & red .60 .60

Adoration, by Correggio — A180

Tower, Catholic Church, Sockburn A181

Christmas: 3c, Holy Family, stained glass window, First Presbyterian Church, Invercargill.

1970, Oct. 1 Unwmk. *Perf. 12½*

464 A180 2½c multicolored .20 .25
465 A180 3c multicolored .20 .25
a. Green omitted 250.00
466 A181 10c silver, org & blk .70 .70
Nos. 464-466 (3) 1.10 1.20

Chatham Islands Mollymawk — A182

1970, Dec. 2 Photo. *Perf. 13x13½*

467 A182 1c Chatham Islands lily .20 .20
468 A182 2c shown .20 .20

G Clef, Emblem and Spinning Wheel A183

Rotary Emblem and Map of New Zealand A184

1971, Feb. 10 Photo. *Perf. 13x13½*

469 A183 4c multicolored .20 .20
470 A184 10c lemon, dk blue & gold .60 .60

50th anniv. of Country Women's Inst. (4c) and Rotary Intl. in New Zealand (10c).

Ocean Racer
A185

8c, One Ton Cup and blueprint of racing yacht.

1971, Mar. 3 Litho. *Perf. 13½x13*

471	A185	5c blue, blk & red	.20	.35
472	A185	8c ultra & black	.85	.85

First challenge in New Zealand waters for the One Ton Cup ocean race.

Coats of Arms
A186

1971, May 12 Photo. *Perf. 13x13½*

473	A186	3c Palmerston North	.20	.20
474	A186	4c Auckland	.20	.20
475	A186	5c Invercargill	.45	.45
		Nos. 473-475 (3)	.85	.85

Centenary of New Zealand cities.

Map of Antarctica — A187

1971, June 9 Photo. *Perf. 13x13½*

476	A187	6c dk blue, pur & grn	1.50	*1.75*

10th anniv. of the Antarctic Treaty pledging peaceful uses of and scientific cooperation in Antarctica.

Child on Swing — A188

1971, June 9 *Perf. 13½x13*

477	188	7c yellow & multi	1.10	1.10

25th anniv. of UNICEF.

Opening of New Zealand's 1st Satellite Earth Station near Warkworth
A189

1971, July 14 *Perf. 11½*

478	A189	8c Radar Station	1.10	1.10
479	A189	10c Satellite	1.10	1.10

No. 441 Surcharged

1971 Wmk. 253 *Perf. 13½x13*

480	A172	4c on 2½c multi	.45	.20
a.		Narrow bars	.20	.20

Surcharge typographed on No. 480, photogravure or typographed on No. 480a.

Holy Night, by Carlo Maratta — A190

The Three Kings
A191

World Rose Convention
A192

Christmas: 4c, Annunciation, stained glass window, St. Luke's Anglican Church, Havelock North.

Perf. 13x13½

1971, Oct. 6 Photo. Unwmk.

481	A190	3c orange & multi	.20	.20
482	A191	4c multicolored	.20	.20
483	A191	10c dk blue & multi	.50	.50
		Nos. 481-483 (3)	.90	.90

1971, Nov. 3 *Perf. 11½*

484	A192	2c Tiffany rose	.20	.20
485	A192	5c Peace rose	.30	.30
486	A192	8c Chrysler Imperial rose	.85	.85
		Nos. 484-486 (3)	1.35	1.35

Rutherford and Alpha Particles Passing Atomic Nucleus
A193

7c, Lord Rutherford, by Sir Oswald Birley, and formula of disintegration of nitrogen atom.

1971, Dec. 1 Litho. *Perf. 13½x13*

487	A193	1c gray & multi	.25	.25
488	A193	7c multicolored	.80	.80

Centenary of the birth of Ernest Lord Rutherford (1871-1937), physicist.

Benz, 1895 — A194

Vintage Cars: 4c, Oldsmobile, 1904. 5c, Model T Ford, 1914. 6c, Cadillac service car, 1915. 8c, Chrysler, 1924. 10c, Austin 7, 1923.

1972, Feb. 2 *Perf. 14x14½*

489	A194	3c brn, car & multi	.25	.20
490	A194	4c brt lilac & multi	.25	.20
491	A194	5c lilac rose & multi	.30	.30
492	A194	6c gray grn & multi	.45	.45
493	A194	8c vio blue & multi	.70	*.70*
494	A194	10c sepia & multi	.85	*.85*
		Nos. 489-494 (6)	2.80	2.70

13th International Vintage Car Rally, New Zealand, Feb. 1972.

Asian-Oceanic Postal Union — A195

Designs: 3c, Wanganui City arms and Drurie Hill tower, vert. 5c, De Havilland DH89 and Boeing 737 planes, vert. 8c, French frigate and Maori palisade at Moturoa, vert. 10c, Stone cairn at Kaeo (site of first Methodist mission).

1972, Apr. 5 *Perf. 13x14, 14x13*

495	A195	3c violet & multi	.40	.40
496	A195	4c brn org, blk & brn	.40	.40
497	A195	5c blue & multi	.70	.70
498	A195	8c green & multi	1.75	1.75
499	A195	10c olive, yel & blk	2.00	2.00
		Nos. 495-499 (5)	5.25	5.25

Cent. of Council government at Wanganui (3c); 10th anniv. of Asian-Oceanic Postal Union (4c); 25th anniv. of Nat. Airways Corp. (5c); bicent. of the landing by Marion du Fresne at the Bay of Islands (8c); 150th anniv. of the Methodist Church in New Zealand (10c).

Black Scree Cotula — A196

Madonna and Child, by Murillo — A197

Alpine Plants: 6c, North Is. edelweiss. 8c, Haast's buttercup. 10c, Brown mountain daisy.

1972, June 7 Litho. *Perf. 13x14*

500	A196	4c orange & multi	.60	.60
501	A196	6c dp blue & multi	.75	.75
502	A196	8c rose lilac & multi	1.25	1.25
503	A196	10c yel green & multi	2.50	2.50
		Nos. 500-503 (4)	5.10	5.10

1972, Oct. 4 Photo. *Perf. 11½*

Christmas: 5c, Resurrection, stained-glass window, St. John's Methodist Church, Levin. 10c, Pohutukawa (New Zealand's Christmas flower).

504	A197	3c gray & multi	.20	.20
505	A197	5c gray & multi	.20	.20
506	A197	10c gray & multi	1.10	1.10
		Nos. 504-506 (3)	1.50	1.50

New Zealand Lakes — A198

1972, Dec. 6 Photo. Unwmk.

507	A198	6c Waikaremoana	1.40	1.25
508	A198	8c Hayes	1.75	1.75
509	A198	18c Wakatipu	3.00	*3.00*
510	A198	23c Rotomahana	4.00	*4.00*
		Nos. 507-510 (4)	10.15	10.00

Old Pollen Street
A199

Coal Mining and Landscape
A200

Cloister, University of Canterbury
A201

Forest, Birds and Lake
A202

Rowing and Olympic Emblems
A203

Progress Chart
A204

1973, Feb. 7 Litho. *Perf. 13½x13*

511	A199	3c ocher & multi	.20	.20
512	A200	4c blue & multi	.25	.25
513	A201	5c multicolored	.25	.25
514	A202	6c blue & multi	.75	.75
515	A203	8c multicolored	.85	.85
516	A204	10c blue & multi	.85	.85
		Nos. 511-516 (6)	3.15	3.15

Centenaries of Thames and Westport Boroughs (3c, 4c); centenary of the Univ. of Canterbury, Christchurch (5c); 50th anniv. of Royal Forest and Bird Protection Soc. (6c); success of New Zealand rowing team at 20th Olympic Games (8c); 25th anniv. of the Economic Commission for Asia and the Far East (ECAFE, 10c).

Class W Locomotive, 1889 — A205

New Zealand Steam Locomotives: 4c, Class X, 1908. 5c, "Passchendaele" Ab Class. 10c, Ja Class, last steam locomotive.

1973, Apr. 4 Litho. *Perf. 14½*

517	A205	3c lt green & multi	.35	.20
518	A205	4c lil rose & multi	.35	.20
519	A205	5c lt blue & multi	.60	.60
520	A205	10c cream & multi	2.50	2.50
		Nos. 517-520 (4)	3.80	3.50

Maori Woman and Child, by Hodgkins — A206

Christmas in New Zealand — A207

Paintings by Frances Hodgkins: 8c, The Hill Top. 10c, Barn in Picardy. 18c, Self-portrait, Still Life.

1973, June 6 Photo. *Perf. 12x11½*

521	A206	5c multicolored	.50	.50
522	A206	8c multicolored	1.25	1.25
523	A206	10c multicolored	1.25	1.25
524	A206	18c multicolored	2.25	2.25
		Nos. 521-524 (4)	5.25	5.25

1973, Oct. 3 Photo. *Perf. 12½x13½*

Christmas: 3c, Tempi Madonna, by Raphael. 5c, Three Kings, stained-glass window, St. Theresa's R.C. Church, Auckland.

525	A207	3c gold & multi	.20	.20
526	A207	5c gold & multi	.20	.20
527	A207	10c gold & multi	1.00	1.00
		Nos. 525-527 (3)	1.40	1.40

Mt. Ngauruhoe A208

Perf. 13x13½, 13½x13

1973, Dec. 5 **Photo.**

528 A208 6c Mitre Peak .90 .90
529 A208 8c shown 1.10 1.10
530 A208 18c Mt. Sefton, horiz. 2.00 2.00
531 A208 23c Burnett Range, horiz. 2.25 2.25
Nos. 528-531 (4) 6.25 6.25

Types of 1970-71

Designs as before.

Perf. 13½x13

1973-76 **Photo.** **Unwmk.**

533 A172 1c multicolored .30 .20
534 A172 2c multicolored .40 .20
536 A172 3c multicolored .40 .20
537 A172 4c multicolored .25 .20
538 A173 5c multicolored .55 .45
539 A173 6c multicolored 1.50 .55
540 A173 7c multicolored 4.50 2.25
542 A173 8c multicolored 3.75 2.25

Perf. 14x13½

543 A174 10c multicolored .55 .20

Perf. 13x14, 14x13

544 A175 15c multicolored .45 .25
545 A177 18c multicolored .55 .20
546 A175 20c yel brn & blk .60 .20
Nos. 533-546 (12) 13.80 7.15

Issued: 2c, 10c, 6/73; 1c, 4c, 6c, 9/7/73; 5c, 1973; 3c, 7c, 8c, 18c, 20c, 1974; 15c, 8/2/76.
For surcharges see Nos. 630-631.

Hurdles and Games' Emblem — A209

Designs: 5c, Paraplegic ballplayer. 10c, Bicycling. 18c, Rifle shooting. 23c, Lawn bowling. 4c, 10c, 18c and 23c stamps also show Commonwealth Games' emblem.

1974, Jan. 9 **Litho.** ***Perf. 13x13½***

547 A209 4c yellow & multi .30 .30
548 A209 5c violet & black .30 .30
549 A209 10c brt red & multi .60 .60
550 A209 18c brown & multi .85 .85
551 A209 23c yel green & multi 1.25 1.25
Nos. 547-551 (5) 3.30 3.30

10th British Commonwealth Games, Christchurch, 1/24-2/2. #548 for the 4th Paraplegic Games, Dunedin, 1/10-20.

Souvenir Sheet

New Zealand Day — A210

Illustration reduced.

1974, Feb. 6 **Litho.** ***Perf. 13***

552 A210 Sheet of 5 1.75 2.00
a. 4c Treaty House, Waitangi .25 .25
b. 4c Parliament extension buildings .25 .25
c. 4c Signing Treaty of Waitangi .25 .25
d. 4c Queen Elizabeth II .25 .25
e. 4c Integrated school .25 .25

New Zealand Day (Waitangi Day). No. 552 has marginal inscription and imprint.

"Spirit of Napier" Fountain — A211

Clock Tower, Bern — A212

Design: 8c, UPU emblem.

1974, Apr. 3 **Photo.** ***Perf. 11½***

553 A211 4c blue green & multi .25 .25
554 A212 5c brown & multi .25 .25
555 A212 8c lemon & multi .80 .80
Nos. 553-555 (3) 1.30 1.30

Centenaries of Napier (4c); UPU (5c, 8c).

Boeing Seaplane, 1919 A213

Designs: 4c, Lockheed Electra, 1937. 5c, Bristol freighter, 1958. 23c, Empire S30 flying boat, 1940.

1974, June 5 **Litho.** ***Perf. 14x13***

556 A213 3c multicolored .25 .25
557 A213 4c multicolored .30 .30
558 A213 5c multicolored .30 .30
559 A213 23c multicolored 2.25 2.25
Nos. 556-559 (4) 3.10 3.10

Development of New Zealand's air transport.

Adoration of the Kings, by Conrad Witz — A214

Christmas: 5c, Angels, stained glass window, St. Paul's Church, Wellington. 10c, Christmas lily (lilium candidum).

1974, Oct. 2 **Photo.** ***Perf. 11½***
Granite Paper

560 A214 3c olive & multi .20 .20
561 A214 5c lilac & multi .25 .25
562 A214 10c orange & multi 1.00 1.00
Nos. 560-562 (3) 1.45 1.45

Offshore Islands A215

1974, Dec. 4 **Photo.** ***Perf. 13½x13***

563 A215 6c Great Barrier .45 .45
564 A215 8c Stewart .70 .70
565 A215 18c White .90 .90
566 A215 23c The Brothers 1.40 1.40
Nos. 563-566 (4) 3.45 3.45

Child Using Walker A216

Farm Woman and Children A217

IWY Symbol A218

Otago Medical School A219

1975, Feb. 5 **Litho.** ***Perf. 13½x13***

567 A216 3c orange & multi .20 .20
568 A217 5c green & multi .20 .20
569 A218 10c blue & multi .50 *.50*
570 A219 18c multicolored .85 *.85*
Nos. 567-570 (4) 1.75 1.75

New Zealand Crippled Children's Soc., 40th anniv. (3c); Women's Division Federated Farmers of N. Z., 50th anniv. (5c); IWY (10c); Otago Medical School cent. (18c).

Scow "Lake Erie," 1873 A220

Historic Sailing Ships: 5c, Schooner "Herald," 1826. 8c, Brigantine "New Zealander," 1828. 10c, Topsail schooner "Jessie Kelly," 1866. 18c, Barque "Tory," 1834. 23c, Clipper "Rangitiki," 1863.

1975, Apr. 2 **Litho.** ***Perf. 13½x13***

571 A220 4c vermilion & blk .30 .30
572 A220 5c grnsh blue & blk .30 .30
573 A220 8c yellow & black .45 .45
574 A220 10c yellow grn & blk .60 .60
575 A220 18c brown & black .80 .80
576 A220 23c dull lilac & blk .90 .90
Nos. 571-576 (6) 3.35 3.35

State Forest Parks A221

1975, June 4 **Photo.** ***Perf. 13½x13***

577 A221 6c Lake Sumner .60 .60
578 A221 8c North West Nelson .85 .85
579 A221 18c Kaweka 1.40 1.40
580 A221 23c Coromandel 1.75 1.75
Nos. 577-580 (4) 4.60 4.60

Virgin and Child, by Zanobi Machiavelli (1418-1479) — A222

Stained Glass Window, Greendale Methodist/Presbyterian Church — A223

Christmas: 10c, Medieval ships and doves.

Perf. 13½x14, 14x13½

1975, Oct. 1 **Photo.**

581 A222 3c multicolored .20 .25
582 A223 5c multicolored .20 .25
583 A223 10c multicolored .70 .70
Nos. 581-583 (3) 1.10 1.20

Sterling Silver — A224

Roses: 2c, Lilli Marlene. 3c, Queen Elizabeth. 4c, Super star. 5c, Diamond jubilee. 6c, Cresset. 7c, Michele Meilland. 8c, Josephine Bruce. 9c, Iceberg.

1975, Nov. 26 **Photo.** ***Perf. 14½x14***

584 A224 1c multicolored .20 .20
585 A224 2c orange & multi .20 .20
586 A224 3c ultra & multi .20 .20
a. Perf. 14½ ('79) .25 .25
587 A224 4c purple & multi .20 .20
588 A224 5c brown & multi .20 .20
589 A224 6c multicolored ('76) .20 .20
a. Perf. 14½ .50 .50
590 A224 7c multicolored ('76) .20 .20
a. Perf. 14½ .70 .60
591 A224 8c yellow & multi ('76) .20 .20
a. Perf. 14½ .70 .60
592 A224 9c blue & multi .20 .20
Nos. 584-592 (9) 1.80 1.80

For surcharges see Nos. 693, 695, 718.

Family and Mothers' League Emblem A225

Designs: 7c, "Weight, measure, temperature and capacity." 8c, 1st emigrant ship "William Bryan" and Mt. Egmont. 10c, Maori and Caucasian women and YWCA emblem. 25c, Telecommunications network on Goode's equal area projection.

1976, Feb. 4 **Litho.** ***Perf. 14***

593 A225 6c olive & multi .20 .20
594 A225 7c lilac & multi .20 .20
595 A225 8c red & multi .30 .30
596 A225 10c yellow & multi .35 .35
597 A225 25c tan & multi .75 .75
Nos. 593-597 (5) 1.80 1.80

League of Mothers of New Zealand, 50th anniv. (6c); Metric conversion, 1976 (7c); cent. of New Plymouth (8c); YWCA in New Zealand, 50th anniv. (10c); cent. of link into intl. telecommunications network (25c).

Gig A226

Farm Vehicles: 7c, Thornycroft truck. 8c, Scandi wagon. 9c, Traction engine. 10c, Wool wagon. 25c, One-horse cart.

1976, Apr. 7 **Litho.** ***Perf. 14x13½***

598 A226 6c dk olive & multi .20 .20
599 A226 7c gray & multi .20 .20
600 A226 8c dk blue & multi .70 .20
601 A226 9c maroon & multi .55 .55
602 A226 10c brown & multi .55 .55
603 A226 25c multicolored 1.10 1.25
Nos. 598-603 (6) 3.30 2.95

Purakaunui Falls — A227

Waterfalls: 14c, Marakopa Falls. 15c, Bridal Veil Falls. 16c, Papakorito Falls.

1976, June 2 **Photo.** ***Perf. 11½***

604 A227 10c blue & multi .35 .35
605 A227 14c lilac & multi .70 .70
606 A227 15c ocher & multi .60 .60
607 A227 16c multicolored .85 .85
Nos. 604-607 (4) 2.50 2.50

Nativity, Carved Ivory, Spain, 16th Century — A228

Christmas: 11c, Risen Christ, St. Joseph's Church, Grey Lynn, Auckland, horiz. 18c, "Hark the Herald Angels Sing," horiz.

Perf. 14x14½, 14½x14

1976, Oct. 6 **Photo.**

608	A228	7c ocher & multi	.20	.20
609	A228	11c ocher & multi	.35	.35
610	A228	18c ocher & multi	.70	.70
		Nos. 608-610 (3)	1.25	1.25

Maripi (Carved Wooden Knife) — A229

Maori Artifacts: 12c, Putorino, carved flute. 13c, Wahaika, hardwood club. 14c, Kotiate, violin-shaped weapon.

1976, Nov. 24 **Photo.** ***Perf. 11½***

Granite Paper

611	A229	11c multicolored	.20	.20
612	A229	12c multicolored	.20	.20
613	A229	13c multicolored	.25	.20
614	A229	14c multicolored	.25	.20
		Nos. 611-614 (4)	.90	.80

Arms of Hamilton A230

Automobile Assoc. Emblem A231

Designs: No. 616, Arms of Gisborne. No. 617, Arms of Masterton. No. 619, Emblem of Royal Australasian College of Surgeons.

1977, Jan. 19 **Litho.** ***Perf. 13x13½***

615	A230	8c multicolored	.20	.20
616	A230	8c multicolored	.20	.20
617	A230	8c multicolored	.20	.20
a.		Strip of 3, #615-617	.60	*.75*
618	A231	10c multicolored	.30	.35
619	A230	10c multicolored	.30	.35
a.		Pair, #618-619	.60	*.75*
		Nos. 615-619 (5)	1.20	1.30

Centenaries of Hamilton, Gisborne and Masterton (cities); 75th anniv. of the New Zealand Automobile Assoc. and 50th anniv. of the Royal Australasian College of Surgeons.

Souvenir Sheet

Queen Elizabeth II, 1976 — A232

Designs: Various portraits.

1977, Feb. **Photo.** ***Perf. 14x14½***

620		Sheet of 5	1.40	*1.75*
a.-e.		A232 8c single stamp	.25	.25
f.		Sheet imperf.	*1,350.*	

25th anniv. of the reign of Elizabeth II.

Physical Education, Maori Culture A233

Education Dept., Geography, Science A234

#623, Special school for the deaf; kindergarten. #624, Language class. #625, Home economics, correspondence school, teacher training.

1977, Apr. 6 **Litho.** ***Perf. 13x13½***

621	A233	8c shown	.60	.45
622	A234	8c shown	.45	.45
623	A233	8c multicolored	.45	.45
624	A234	8c multicolored	.45	.45
625	A233	8c multicolored	.45	.45
a.		Strip of 5, #621-625	3.00	3.00
		Nos. 621-625 (5)	2.40	2.25

Cent. of Education Act, establishing Dept. of Education.

Karitane Beach — A235

Seascapes and beach scenes: 16c, Ocean Beach, Mount Maunganui. 18c, Piha Beach. 30c, Kaikoura Coast.

1977, June 1 **Photo.** ***Perf. 14½***

626	A235	10c multicolored	.20	.20
627	A235	16c multicolored	.35	.35
628	A235	18c multicolored	.35	.35
629	A235	30c multicolored	.60	.50
		Nos. 626-629 (4)	1.50	1.40

Nos. 536-537 Surcharged with New Value and Heavy Bar

1977 **Unwmk.** ***Perf. 13½x13***

630	A172	7c on 3c multicolored	.35	.35
631	A172	8c on 4c multicolored	.35	.35

Holy Family, by Correggio A236

Window, St. Michael's and All Angels Church — A237

Partridge in a Pear Tree — A238

1977, Oct. 5 **Photo.** ***Perf. 11½***

632	A236	7c multicolored	.20	.20
633	A237	16c multicolored	.45	.45
634	A238	23c multicolored	.70	.70
		Nos. 632-634 (3)	1.35	1.35

Christmas.

Merryweather Manual Pump, 1860 — A239

Fire Fighting Equipment: 11c, 2-wheel hose reel and ladder, 1880. 12c, Shand Mason Steam Fire Engine, 1873. 23c, Chemical fire engine, 1888.

1977, Dec. 7 **Litho.** ***Perf. 14x13½***

635	A239	10c multicolored	.20	.20
636	A239	11c multicolored	.20	.25
637	A239	12c multicolored	.20	.25
638	A239	23c multicolored	.40	.40
		Nos. 635-638 (4)	1.00	1.10

A240

New Zealand 24c

A240a

Parliament Building, Wellington — A241

A242

1977-82 **Photo.** ***Perf. 14½***

648	A240	10c ultra & multi	.20	.20
a.		Perf. 14½x14	.80	.50

Perf. 14½x14

649	A240a	24c blue & lt green	.30	.20
a.		Perf. 13x12½	.45	.25

Perf. 13

650	A241	$5 multicolored	6.25	4.75
		Nos. 648-650 (3)	6.75	5.15

Issued: No. 648, 2/79; No. 648a, 12/7/77; $5, 12/2/81; No. 649, 4/1/82; No. 649a, 12/13/82.

For surcharge see No. 694.

Coil Stamps

1978 **Photo.** ***Perf. 13½x13***

651	A242	1c red lilac	.20	.20
652	A242	2c orange	.20	.20
653	A242	5c brown	.20	.20

Perf. 14½x14

654	A242	10c ultramarine	.20	.20
		Nos. 651-654 (4)	.80	.80

Issue dates: 10c, May 3; others, June 9.

Ashburton A244

Stratford A245

Old Telephone — A246

Bay of Islands A247

1978, Feb. 1 **Litho.** ***Perf. 14***

656	A244	10c multicolored	.20	.20
657	A245	10c multicolored	.20	.20
a.		Pair, #656-657	.35	.45
658	A246	12c multicolored	.25	.35
659	A247	20c multicolored	.35	.35
		Nos. 656-659 (4)	1.00	1.10

Cent. of the cities of Ashburton, Stratford, the NZ Telephone Co. and Bay of Islands County.

Lincoln Univ. College of Agriculture, Cent. A248

Maui Gas Drilling Platform A249

Designs: 10c, Students and Ivey Hall. 12c, Grazing sheep. 15c, Mechanical fertilization. 16c, Furrow, plow and tractor. 20c, Combine harvester. 30c, Grazing cattle.

1978, Apr. 26 ***Perf. 14½***

660	A248	10c multicolored	.20	.20
661	A248	12c multicolored	.20	.20
662	A248	15c multicolored	.20	.20
663	A248	16c multicolored	.30	.30
664	A248	20c multicolored	.35	.35
665	A248	30c multicolored	.60	.60
		Nos. 660-665 (6)	1.85	1.85

1978, June 7 **Litho.** ***Perf. 13½x14***

The sea and its resources: 15c, Fishing boat. 20c, Map of New Zealand and 200-mile limit. 23c, Whale and bottle-nosed dolphins. 35c, Kingfish, snapper, grouper and squid.

666	A249	12c multicolored	.20	.20
667	A249	15c multicolored	.20	.20
668	A249	20c multicolored	.35	.35
669	A249	23c multicolored	.40	.40
670	A249	35c multicolored	.60	.60
		Nos. 666-670 (5)	1.75	1.75

All Saints Church, Howick A250

Christmas: 7c, Holy Family, by El Greco, vert. 23c, Beach scene.

1978, Oct. 4 **Photo.** ***Perf. 11½***

671	A250	7c gold & multi	.20	.20
672	A250	16c gold & multi	.30	.30
673	A250	23c gold & multi	.40	.40
		Nos. 671-673 (3)	.90	.90

Sea Shells — A251

20c, Paua (Haliotis Iris). 30c, Toheroa (paphies ventricosa). 40c, Coarse dosinia (dosinia anus). 50c, Spiny murex (poirieria zelandica).

1978, Nov. 29 Photo. *Perf. 13x12½*

674 A251 20c multicolored .20 .20
675 A251 30c multicolored .30 .20
676 A251 40c multicolored .45 .30
677 A251 50c multicolored .55 .40
Nos. 674-677 (4) 1.50 1.10

See Nos. 696-697.

Julius Vogel — A252

19th cent. NZ statesmen: No. 679, George Grey. No. 680, Richard John Seddon.

1979, Feb. 7 Litho. *Perf. 13x13½*

678 A252 10c light & dark brown .20 .20
679 A252 10c light & dark brown .35 .20
680 A252 10c light & dark brown .35 .20
a. Strip of 3, #678-680 1.25 1.25

Riverlands Cottage, Blenheim — A253

Early NZ Architecture: 12c, Mission House, Waimate North, 1831-32. 15c, The Elms, Anglican Church Mission, Tauranga, 1847. 20c, Provincial Council Buildings, Christchurch, 1859.

1979, Apr. 4 *Perf. 13½x13*

681 A253 10c multicolored .20 .20
682 A253 12c multicolored .20 .20
683 A253 15c black & gray .25 .25
684 A253 20c multicolored .35 .35
Nos. 681-684 (4) 1.00 1.00

Whangaroa Harbor — A254

Small Harbors: 20c, Kawau Island. 23c, Akaroa Harbor, vert. 35c, Picton Harbor, vert.

Perf. 13x13½, 13½x13

1979, June 6 Photo.

685 A254 15c multicolored .20 .20
686 A254 20c multicolored .30 .30
687 A254 23c multicolored .35 .35
688 A254 35c multicolored .50 .30
Nos. 685-688 (4) 1.35 1.15

IYC A255

1979, June 6 Litho. *Perf. 14*

689 A255 10c Children playing .20 .20

Virgin and Child, by Lorenzo Ghiberti — A256

Christmas: 25c, Christ Church, Russell, 1835. 35c, Pohutukawa ("Christmas") tree.

1979, Oct. 3 Photo. *Perf. 11½*

690 A256 10c multicolored .20 .20
691 A256 25c multicolored .40 .30
692 A256 35c multicolored .50 .40
Nos. 690-692 (3) 1.10 .90

Nos. 591a, 648 and 589a Surcharged

1979, Sept. *Perf. 14½, 14½x14 (14c)*

693 A224 4c on 8c multi .20 .20
694 A240 14c on 10c multi .20 .20
695 A224 17c on 6c multi .25 .25
Nos. 693-695 (3) .65 .65

Shell Type of 1978

$1, Scallop (pecten novaezelandiae). $2, Circular saw (astraea heliotropium).

1979, Nov. 26 Photo. *Perf. 13x12½*

696 A251 $1 multicolored 1.50 .35
697 A251 $2 multicolored 3.00 .90

Debating Chamber, House of Parliament A257

1979, Nov. 26 Litho. *Perf. 14x13½*

698 A257 14c shown .20 .20
699 A257 20c Mace, black rod .35 .35
700 A257 30c Wall hanging .50 .50
Nos. 698-700 (3) 1.05 1.05

25th Commonwealth Parliamentary Conference, Wellington, Nov. 26-Dec. 2.

NZ No. 1 A258

1980, Feb. 7 Litho. *Perf. 14x13½*

701 A258 14c shown .20 .20
702 A258 14c No. 2 .20 .20
703 A258 14c No. 3 .20 .20
a. Souvenir sheet of 3, #701-703 2.25 *3.00*
b. Strip of 3, #701-703 .60 .60

NZ postage stamps, 125th anniv. No. 703a publicizes Zeapex '80 Intl. Stamp Exhib., Auckland, Aug. 23-31; it sold for 52c, of which 10c went to exhib. fund.

Maori Wood Carving, Tudor Towers A259

Earina Autumnalis and Thelymitra Venosa — A260

Tractor Plowing, Golden Plow Trophy A261

1980, Feb. 7 *Perf. 14½*

704 A259 17c multicolored .25 .20
705 A260 25c multicolored .40 .35
706 A261 30c multicolored .50 .45
Nos. 704-706 (3) 1.15 1.00

Rotorua cent.; Intl. Orchid Conf., Auckland, Oct.; World Plowing Championship, Christchurch, May.

Ewelme Cottage, Parnell, 1864 A262

Early NZ Architecture: 17c, Broadgreen, Nelson, 1855. 25c, Courthouse, Oamaru, 1822, 30c, Government Buildings, Wellington, 1877.

1980, Apr. 2 Litho. *Perf. 13½x13*

707 A262 14c multicolored .20 .20
708 A262 17c multicolored .25 .25
709 A262 25c green & black .40 .30
710 A262 30c multicolored .45 .40
Nos. 707-710 (4) 1.30 1.15

Harbors A263

1980, June 4 Photo. *Perf. 13x13½*

711 A263 25c Auckland .40 .35
712 A263 30c Wellington .45 .35
713 A263 35c Lyttelton .55 .45
714 A263 50c Port Chalmers .75 .65
Nos. 711-714 (4) 2.15 1.80

Madonna and Child with Cherubim, by Andrea della Robbia — A264

1980, Oct. 1 Photo. *Perf. 12*

715 A264 10c shown .20 .20
716 A264 25c St. Mary's Church, New Plymouth .40 .30
717 A264 35c Picnic .55 .50
Nos. 715-717 (3) 1.15 1.00

Christmas.

No. 590 Surcharged

1980, Sept. 29 Photo. *Perf. 14½x14*

718 A224 20c on 7c multicolored .25 .20

Te Heu Heu Tukino IV, Ngati Tuwharetoa Tribal Chief — A265

Maori Leaders: 25c, Te Hau-Takiri Wharepapa. 35c, Princess Te Puea Herangi. 45, Apirana Ngata. 60c, Hakopa Te Ata-o-tu.

1980, Nov. 26 *Perf. 13*

719 A265 15c multicolored .25 .20
720 A265 25c multicolored .40 .20
721 A265 35c multicolored .55 .20
722 A265 45c multicolored .65 .20
723 A265 60c multicolored .90 .30
Nos. 719-723 (5) 2.75 1.10

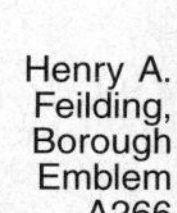

Henry A. Feilding, Borough Emblem A266

1981, Feb. 4 Litho. *Perf. 14½*

724 A266 20c multicolored .30 .20

Borough of Feilding centenary.

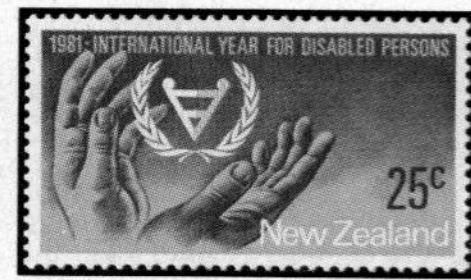

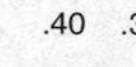
IYD A267

1981, Feb. 4

725 A267 25c orange & black .40 .35

Family and Dog — A268

1981, Apr. 1 Litho. *Perf. 13*

726 A268 20c shown .30 .20
727 A268 25c Grandparents .40 .30
728 A268 30c Parents reading to children .45 .40
729 A268 35c Family outing .55 .45
Nos. 726-729 (4) 1.70 1.35

Shotover River — A269

1981, June 3 Photo. *Perf. 13½*

730 A269 30c Kaiauai River, vert. .45 .40
731 A269 35c Mangahao River, vert. .55 .45
732 A269 40c shown .60 .50
733 A269 60c Cleddau River .90 .80
Nos. 730-733 (4) 2.50 2.15

Prince Charles and Lady Diana A270

1981, July 29 Litho. *Perf. 14½*

734 A270 20c shown .30 .30
735 A270 20c St. Paul's Cathedral .30 .30
a. Pair, #734-735 .60 .60

Royal Wedding.

Golden Tainui — A271

Christmas: 14c, Madonna and Child, by Marco d'Oggiono, 15th cent. 30c, St. John's Church, Wakefield.

1981, Oct. Photo. *Perf. 11½*
Granite Paper

736 A271 14c multicolored .20 .20
737 A271 30c multicolored .45 .40
738 A271 40c multicolored .60 .50
Nos. 736-738 (3) 1.25 1.10

SPCA Centenary A272

Intl. Science Year A273

Centenaries: No. 739, Tauranga. No. 740, Hawera. 30c, Frozen meat exports.

1982, Feb. 3 Litho. *Perf. 14½*

739 A272 20c multicolored .30 .20
740 A272 20c multicolored .30 .20
a. Pair, #739-740 .60 .60
741 A272 25c multicolored .40 .30
742 A272 30c multicolored .45 .40
743 A273 35c multicolored .55 .45
Nos. 739-743 (5) 2.00 1.55

Alberton Farmhouse, Auckland, 1867 — A274

1982, Apr. 7 Litho.

744 A274 20c shown .30 .20
745 A274 25c Caccia Birch, Palmerston North, 1893 .40 .30
746 A274 30c Dunedin Railway Station, 1904 .45 .40
747 A274 35c PO, Ophir, 1886 .55 .45
Nos. 744-747 (4) 1.70 1.35

Summer, Kaiteriteri A275

1982, June 2 Photo. *Perf. 13½*

748 A275 35c shown .55 .45
749 A275 40c Autumn, Queenstown .60 .50
750 A275 45c Winter, Mt. Ngauruhoe .70 .55
751 A275 70c Spring, Wairarapa 1.05 .85
Nos. 748-751 (4) 2.90 2.35

Madonna with Child and Two Angels, by Piero di Cosimo — A276

Christmas: 35c, Rangiatea Maori Church, Otaki. 45c, Surf life-saving patrol.

1982, Oct. 6 Photo. *Perf. 14*

752 A276 18c multicolored .25 .25
753 A276 35c multicolored .55 .50
754 A276 45c multicolored .70 .70
Nos. 752-754 (3) 1.50 1.45

Nephrite A277

Fruit Export A278

Native Birds — A279

1982-83 Litho.

755 A277 1c shown .20 .20
a. Perf 13x12½ .40 .40
756 A277 2c Agate .20 .20
a. Perf 13x12½ 1.10 1.10
757 A277 3c Iron pyrites .20 .20
758 A277 4c Amethyst .20 .20
759 A277 5c Carnelian .20 .20
760 A277 9c Native sulphur .20 .20
761 A278 10c Grapes .20 .20
762 A278 20c Citrus fruit .35 .20
763 A278 30c Nectarines .50 .20
764 A278 40c Apples .70 .20
765 A278 50c Kiwifruit .85 .20
Nos. 755-765 (11) 3.80 2.20

Issued: A277, Dec. 1; A278, Dec. 7, 1983.

1985-89 *Perf. 14½*

766 A279 30c Kakapo .50 .20
767 A279 45c Falcon .80 .50
768 A279 $1 Kokako 1.60 .45
769 A279 $2 Black Robin 3.00 .70
a. Souvenir sheet of one 13.00 13.00
770 A279 $3 Stitchbird 4.50 1.90
770A A279 $4 Saddleback 6.00 2.25
Nos. 766-770A (6) 16.40 6.00

No. 769a for PHILEXFRANCE '89 and has margin picturing progressive proofs of No. 769. No. 769a sold for $3.50.

Issued: $1, $2, 4/24; $3, $4, 4/23/86; 30c, 45c, 5/1/86; No. 769a, 7/7/89.

See Nos. 830-835, 919-933.

Salvation Army in NZ Cent. — A280

Univ. of Auckland Cent. — A281

NZ-Australia Closer Economic Relationship Agreement — A282

Introduction of Rainbow Trout Cent. — A283

WCY — A284

Perf. 14, 14x13½ (35c)

1983, Feb. 2 Litho.

771 A280 24c multicolored .35 .20
772 A281 30c multicolored .50 .50
773 A282 35c multicolored .60 .60
774 A283 40c multicolored .70 .70
775 A284 45c multicolored .75 .75
Nos. 771-775 (5) 2.90 2.75

A285

1983, Mar. 14 Litho. *Perf. 14*

776 A285 24c Queen Elizabeth II .40 .40
777 A285 35c Maori rock painting .60 .60
778 A285 40c Wool industry logos .70 .70
779 A285 45c Arms .75 .75
Nos. 776-779 (4) 2.45 2.45

Commonwealth Day.

Island Bay, by Rita Angus (1908-1970) A286

Landscapes.

1983, Apr. 6 Litho. *Perf. 14½*

780 A286 24c shown .40 .25
781 A286 30c Central Otago .60 .60
782 A286 35c Wanaka .70 .70
783 A286 45c Tree, Greymouth .75 .75
Nos. 780-783 (4) 2.45 2.30

Lake Matheson A287

Perf. 13½x13, 13x13½

1983, June 1 Photo.

784 A287 35c Mt. Egmont, vert. .60 .60
785 A287 40c Cooks Bay, vert. .70 .70
786 A287 45c shown .75 .75
787 A287 70c Lake Alexandrina 1.25 1.25
Nos. 784-787 (4) 3.30 3.30

Christmas 1983 — A288

1983, Oct. 5 Photo. *Perf. 12*

788 A288 18c Holy Family of the Oak Tree, by Raphael .25 .25
789 A288 35c St. Patrick's Church, Greymouth .60 .60
790 A288 45c Star, poinsettias .85 .85
Nos. 788-790 (3) 1.70 1.70

Antarctic Research A289

1984, Feb. 1 Litho. *Perf. 13½x13*

791 A289 24c Geology .40 .20
792 A289 40c Biology .70 .70
793 A289 58c Glaciology 1.00 1.00
794 A289 70c Meteorology 1.25 1.25
a. Souvenir sheet of 4, #791-794 3.50 3.50
Nos. 791-794 (4) 3.35 3.15

Ferry Mountaineer, Lake Wakatipu, 1879 — A290

1984, Apr. 4 Litho. *Perf. 13½*

795 A290 24c shown .40 .20
796 A290 40c Waikana, Otago Harbor, 1909 .70 .70
797 A290 58c Britannia, Waitemata Harbor, 1885 1.00 1.00
798 A290 70c Wakatere, Firth of Thames, 1896 1.25 1.25
Nos. 795-798 (4) 3.35 3.15

Skier, Mount Hutt — A291

1984, June 6 Litho. *Perf. 13½x13*

799 A291 35c shown .60 .60
800 A291 40c Coronet Peak .70 .70
801 A291 45c Turoa .75 .75
802 A291 70c Whakapapa 1.25 1.25
Nos. 799-802 (4) 3.30 3.30

Hamilton's Frog A292

1984, July 11 *Perf. 13½*

803 A292 24c shown .40 .20
804 A292 24c Great barrier skink .40 .20
a. Pair, #803-804 .80 .80
805 A292 30c Harlequin gecko .50 .50
806 A292 58c Otago skink 1.10 1.10
807 A292 70c Gold-striped gecko 1.25 1.25
Nos. 803-807 (5) 3.65 3.25

No. 804a has continuous design.

Christmas A293

Designs: 18c, Adoration of the Shepherds, by Lorenzo Di Credi. 35c, Old St. Paul's Church, Wellington, vert. 45c, Bell, vert.

Perf. 13½x14, 14x13½

1984, Sept. 26 Photo.

808 A293 18c multicolored .25 .25
809 A293 35c multicolored .60 .60
810 A293 45c multicolored .75 .75
Nos. 808-810 (3) 1.60 1.60

Military History A294

1984, Nov. 7 Litho. *Perf. 15x14*

811 A294 24c South Africa, 1901 .40 .20
812 A294 40c France, 1917 .70 .70
813 A294 58c North Africa, 1942 1.00 1.00
814 A294 70c Korea & Southeast Asia, 1950-72 1.25 1.25
a. Souvenir sheet of 4, #811-814 3.50 *3.50*
Nos. 811-814 (4) 3.35 3.15

St. John Ambulance Assoc. Cent. in NZ A295

1985, Jan. 16 Litho. *Perf. 14*
815 A295 24c multicolored .40 .20
816 A295 30c multicolored .50 .50
817 A295 40c multicolored .70 .70
Nos. 815-817 (3) 1.60 1.40

Early Transportation — A296

1985, Mar. 6 Litho. *Perf. 13½*
818 A296 24c Nelson Horse Tram, 1862 .40 .20
819 A296 30c Graham's Town-Steam, 1871 .50 .50
820 A296 35c Dunedin Cable Car, 1881 .60 .60
821 A296 40c Auckland Electric, 1902 .70 .70
822 A296 45c Wellington Electric, 1904 .75 .75
823 A296 58c Christchurch Electric, 1905 1.00 1.00
Nos. 818-823 (6) 3.95 3.75

Bridges A297

1985, June 12 Photo. *Perf. 11½*
824 A297 35c Shotover .55 .55
825 A297 40c Alexandra .60 .60
826 A297 45c So. Rangitikei .70 .70
827 A297 70c Twin Bridges 1.05 1.00
Nos. 824-827 (4) 2.90 2.85

Bird Type of 1985 and

Elizabeth II — A298

1985-89 Litho. *Perf. 14½x14*
828 A298 25c multicolored .60 .20
829 A298 35c multicolored .95 .40

Perf. 14½
830 A279 40c Blue duck .65 .20
831 A279 60c Brown teal 1.50 .65
832 A279 70c Paradise shelduck 1.05 .75
a. Souvenir sheet of 1 *10.00 10.00*
835 A279 $5 Takahe 6.00 6.00
Nos. 828-835 (6) 10.75 8.20

Size of 70c, 22x27mm.

No. 832a for World Stamp Expo '89. Sold for $1.50.

Issued: 25c, 35c, 7/1/85; 40c, 60c, 2/2/87; 70c, 6/7/88; $5, 4/20/88; #832a, 11/17/89.

Christmas A301

Carol "Silent Night, Holy Night," by Joseph Mohr (1792-1848), Austrian clergyman.

Perf. 13½x12½
1985, Sept. 18 Litho.
836 A301 18c Stable .25 .25
837 A301 40c Shepherds .65 .65
838 A301 50c Angels .80 .80
Nos. 836-838 (3) 1.70 1.70

Navy Ships A302

1985, Nov. 6 Litho. *Perf. 13½*
839 A302 25c Philomel, 1914-1947 .40 .25
840 A302 45c Achilles, 1936-1946 .75 .75
841 A302 60c Rotoiti, 1949-1965 1.00 1.00
842 A302 75c Canterbury, 1971- 1.25 1.25
a. Souvenir sheet of 4, #839-842 4.00 *5.25*
Nos. 839-842 (4) 3.40 3.25

Police Force Act, Cent. — A303

Designs: a, Radio operators, 1940-1985. b, Mounted policeman, 1890, forensic specialist in mobile lab, 1985. c, Police station, 1895, policewoman and badge, 1985. d, 1920 motorcycle, 1940s car, modern patrol cars and graphologist. e, Original Mt. Cook Training Center and modern Police College, Poriria.

1986, Jan. 15 *Perf. 14½x14*
843 Strip of 5 2.25 2.25
a.-e. A303 25c any single .40 .40

Intl. Peace Year A304

1986, Mar. 5 *Perf. 13½x13*
844 A304 25c Tree .40 .25
845 A304 25c Dove .40 .25
a. Pair, #844-845 .80 .60

Motorcycles — A305

1986, Mar. 5
846 A305 35c 1920 Indian Power Plus .60 .60
847 A305 45c 1927 Norton CS1 .70 .70
848 A305 60c 1930 BSA Sloper .95 .95
849 A305 75c 1915 Triumph Model H 1.25 1.25
Nos. 846-849 (4) 3.50 3.50

Knight's Point — A306

1986, June 11 Litho. *Perf. 14*
850 A306 55c shown .80 .75
851 A306 60c Beck's Bay .90 .85
852 A306 65c Doubtless Bay .95 .90
853 A306 80c Wainui Bay 1.20 1.10
a. Miniature sheet of one 2.25 2.25
Nos. 850-853 (4) 3.85 3.60

No. 853a sold for $1.20. Surtax benefited the "NZ 1990" executive committee.

No. 853a exists with Stockholmia '86 emblem. This sheet was sold only at the exhibition.

The Twelve Days of Christmas — A307

1986, Sept. 17 Photo. *Perf. 14½*
854 A307 25c First day .35 .20
855 A307 55c Second .85 .85
856 A307 65c Third 1.10 1.10
Nos. 854-856 (3) 2.30 2.15

Music — A308

1986, Nov. 5 Litho. *Perf. 14½x14*
857 A308 30c Conductor .45 .30
858 A308 60c Brass band .90 .85
859 A308 80c Highland pipe band 1.20 1.10
860 A308 $1 Country music 1.50 1.40
Nos. 857-860 (4) 4.05 3.65

Tourism — A309

1987, Jan. 14 *Perf. 14½x14*
861 A309 60c Boating .90 .85
862 A309 70c Aviation 1.05 1.00
863 A309 80c Camping 1.20 1.10
864 A309 85c Windsurfing 1.25 1.10
865 A309 $1.05 Mountain climbing 1.50 1.40
866 A309 $1.30 White water rafting 2.10 2.10
Nos. 861-866 (6) 8.00 7.55

Blue Water Classics A310

1987, Feb. 2 *Perf. 14x14½*
867 A310 40c Southern Cross Cup .60 .35
868 A310 80c Admiral's Cup 1.20 1.10
869 A310 $1.05 Kenwood Cup 1.50 1.40
870 A310 $1.30 America's Cup 2.10 2.10
Nos. 867-870 (4) 5.40 4.95

Vesting Day A311

a, Motor vehicles, plane. b, Train, bicycle.

1987, Apr. 1 Litho. *Perf. 13½*
871 Pair 1.20 1.10
a.-b. A311 40c any single .60 .40

Establishment of NZ Post Ltd., Apr. 1, replacing the NZ PO.

Royal NZ Air Force, 50th Anniv. A312

Designs: 40c, Avro 626, Wigram Airfield, c. 1937. 70c, P-40 Kittyhawks. 80c, Sunderland seaplane. 85c, A4 Skyhawks.

1987, Apr. 15 *Perf. 14x14½*
872 A312 40c multicolored .60 .60
873 A312 70c multicolored 1.10 1.00
874 A312 80c multicolored 1.25 1.10
875 A312 85c multicolored 1.40 1.10
a. Souvenir sheet of 4, #872-875 5.00 5.00
b. As "a," ovptd. with CAPEX '87 emblem in margin 14.00 14.00
Nos. 872-875 (4) 4.35 3.80

Natl. Parks System, Cent. — A313

1987, June 17 Litho. *Perf. 14½*
876 A313 70c Urewera 1.10 1.00
877 A313 80c Mt. Cook 1.25 1.10
878 A313 85c Fiordland 1.40 1.10
879 A313 $1.30 Tongariro 2.10 2.10
a. Souvenir sheet of one 3.50 3.50
Nos. 876-879 (4) 5.85 5.30

No. 879a sold for $1.70 to benefit the NZ 1990 World Phil. Exhib., Auckland.

No. 879a overprinted with CAPEX '87 emblem in the margin, was available only at CAPEX in Canada and was not sold in New Zealand. Value $14.

Christmas Carols — A314

1987, Sept. 16 Litho. *Perf. 14x14½*
880 A314 35c Hark! The Herald Angels Sing .55 .40
881 A314 70c Away in a Manger 1.10 1.00
882 A314 85c We Three Kings of Orient Are 1.40 1.25
Nos. 880-882 (3) 3.05 2.65

Maori Fiber Art — A315

1987, Nov. 4 Litho. *Perf. 12*
883 A315 40c Knot .65 .45
884 A315 60c Binding .95 .85
885 A315 80c Plait 1.25 1.10
886 A315 85c Flax fiber 1.40 1.10
Nos. 883-886 (4) 4.25 3.50

Royal Phil. Soc. of NZ, Cent. A316

Portrait of Queen Victoria by Chalon — A317

Queen Elizabeth II and: No. 887, No. 61 (blue background). No. 888, No. 62 (red background).

1988, Jan. 13 *Perf. 14x14½*

887 A316 40c multicolored .70 .45
888 A316 40c multicolored .70 .45
a. Pair, #887-888 1.40 1.40

Souvenir Sheet

889 A317 $1 multicolored 2.75 2.75
a. Overprinted with SYDPEX '88 emblem in margin 30.00 30.00

NZ Electrification, Cent. — A318

1988, Jan. 13 *Perf. 14x14½*

890 A318 40c Geothermal .65 .40
891 A318 60c Thermal .95 .75
892 A318 70c Gas 1.10 .90
893 A318 80c Hydroelectric 1.25 1.00
Nos. 890-893 (4) 3.95 3.05

Maori Rafter Paintings — A319

1988, Mar. 2 **Litho.** *Perf. 14½*

894 A319 40c Mangopare .65 .65
895 A319 40c Koru .65 .65
896 A319 40c Raupunga .65 .65
897 A319 60c Koiri .95 .95
Nos. 894-897 (4) 2.90 2.90

Greetings Messages A320

1988, May 18 **Litho.** *Perf. 13½x13*

Booklet Stamps

898 A320 40c Good luck .85 .85
899 A320 40c Keeping in touch .85 .85
900 A320 40c Happy birthday .85 .85

Size: 41x27mm

901 A320 40c Congratulations .85 .85
902 A320 40c Get well soon .85 .85
a. Bklt. pane of 5, #898-902 4.25

Landscapes A321

1988, June 8 *Perf. 14½*

903 A321 70c Milford Track 1.10 .90
904 A321 80c Heaphy Track 1.25 1.00
905 A321 85c Copland Track 1.40 1.10
906 A321 $1.30 Routeburn Track 2.10 2.10
a. Miniature sheet of one 3.50 3.50
Nos. 903-906 (4) 5.85 5.10

No. 906a sold for $1.70 to benefit the exhibition.

NEW ZEALAND 1990 Souvenir Sheets

Four souvenir sheets were sold by the New Zealand post to benefit NEW ZEALAND 1990 World Stamp Exhibition. They each contain three $1 and one $2 "stamps" picturing antarctic scenes. They are not valid for postage.

Australia Bicentennial A322

Caricature: Kiwi and koala around campfire.

1988, June 21

907 A322 40c multicolored .65 .65

See Australia No. 1086.

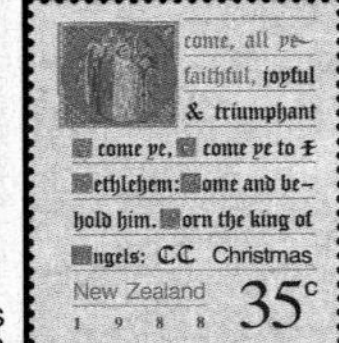

Christmas Carols — A323

Illuminated manuscripts: 35c, O, Come All Ye Faithful, by John Francis Wade, 1742. 70c, Hark! the Herald Angels Sing. 80c, Ding Dong! Merrily on High. 85c, The First Noel, first published in Davies & Gilbert's Some Ancient Christmas Carols, 1832.

1988, Sept. 14 **Litho.** *Perf. 14½*

908 A323 35c multicolored .60 .40
909 A323 70c multicolored 1.10 1.10
910 A323 80c multicolored 1.25 1.25
911 A323 85c multicolored 1.40 1.40
Nos. 908-911 (4) 4.35 4.15

New Zealand Heritage A324

The Land. Paintings by 19th cent. artists: 40c, Lake Pukaki, 1862, by John Gully. 60c, On the Grass Plain Below Lake Arthur, 1846, by William Fox. 70c, View of Auckland, 1873, by John Hoyte. 80c, Mt. Egmont from the Southward, 1840, by Charles Heaphy. $1.05, Anakiwa, Queen Charlotte Sound, 1871, by John Kinder. $1.30, White Terraces, Lake Rotomahana, 1880, by Charles Barraud.

1988, Oct. 5 **Litho.** *Perf. 14x14½*

912 A324 40c multicolored .60 .45
913 A324 60c multicolored .95 .75
914 A324 70c multicolored 1.10 .90
915 A324 80c multicolored 1.25 1.00
916 A324 $1.05 multicolored 1.60 1.40
917 A324 $1.30 multicolored 2.10 1.90
Nos. 912-917 (6) 7.60 6.40

Kiwi A325

1988, Oct. 19 **Engr.** *Perf. 14½*

918 A325 $1 green 3.00 2.50
a. Booklet pane of 6 14.00
b. Litho. 3.00 2.50

Value is for stamp with surrounding selvage. No. 918 issued in booklets only.
No. 918b is from No. 1161a.

See Nos. 1027, 1161, 1445, 1635.

Bird Type of 1985

1988-95 **Litho.** *Perf. 14½x14*

Sizes: $10, 26x31½mm, Others, 22x27mm

919 A279 5c Spotless crake .20 .20
920 A279 10c Banded dotterel .20 .20
921 A279 20c Yellowhead .30 .20
a. Perf. 13½ .75 .75
922 A279 30c Silvereye .45 .25
923 A279 40c Brown kiwi .65 .30
c. Perf. 13½x13 1.75 1.75
924 A279 45c Rock wren .70 .25
b. Booklet pane of 10 6.50
925 A279 50c Kingfisher .80 .35
926 A279 60c Spotted shag .95 .80
a. Sheet of 8, #919-926 4.50 4.50
b. Perf. 13½ 3.75 3.75
927 A279 80c Fiordland crested penguin 1.25 1.00
928 A279 80c New Zealand falcon 1.25 1.00
Complete booklet, 10 #928 12.50
c. Perf. 12 on 3 sides 3.50 3.50
d. As "c," booklet pane of 10 40.00
Complete booklet, #928d 40.00
929 A279 90c South Is. robin 1.40 1.25
930 A279 $10 Little spotted kiwi 16.00 6.75
d. Souv. sheet of 1 20.00 20.00

Self-Adhesive

Die Cut Perf 11½

931 A279 40c like #923 .65 .50
932 A279 45c like #924 .70 .55

Die Cut Perf 10½x11

933 A279 45c like #924 .70 .55
Nos. 919-933 (15) 26.20 14.15

No. 933 has a darker blue background than No. 932 and has perf "teeth" at the corners while No. 932 does not. Perf "teeth" on the top and left side are staggered to line up with perf "holes" on the bottom and right on No. 933. "Teeth" line up with "teeth" on No. 932.

PHILAKOREA '94 (#926a). POST'X '95 Postal Exhibition (#930d).

Issued: $10, 4/19/89; #931, 4/17/91; 5c, #924, 932, 7/1/91; #933, 1991; #928, 3/31/93; #926a, 8/16/94; #930d, 2/3/95; #921a, 926b, 9/22/95; #923c, 11/8/89; others, 11/2/88.

Whales of the Southern Oceans A326

1988, Nov. 2 **Litho.** *Perf. 13½*

936 A326 60c Humpback .95 .85
937 A326 70c Killer 1.10 1.00
938 A326 80c Southern right 1.25 1.10
939 A326 85c Blue 1.40 1.40
940 A326 $1.05 Southern bottlenose 1.75 1.75
941 A326 $1.30 Sperm 2.25 2.25
Nos. 936-941 (6) 8.70 8.35

Wildflowers A327

1989, Jan. 18 **Litho.** *Perf. 14½*

942 A327 40c Clover .65 .65
943 A327 60c Lotus 1.00 1.00
944 A327 70c Montbretia 1.25 1.25
945 A327 80c Wild ginger 1.40 1.40
Nos. 942-945 (4) 4.30 4.30

Authors — A328

Portraits: 40c, Katherine Mansfield (1888-1923). 60c, James K. Baxter (1926-1972). 70c, Bruce Mason (1921-1982). 80c, Ngaio Marsh (1899-1982).

1989, Mar. 1 **Litho.** *Perf. 12½*

946 A328 40c multicolored .65 .50
947 A328 60c multicolored .95 .80
948 A328 70c multicolored 1.10 .90
949 A328 80c multicolored 1.25 1.00
Nos. 946-949 (4) 3.95 3.20

New Zealand Heritage A329

The people.

1989, May 17 *Perf. 14x14½*

950 A329 40c Moriori .65 .50
951 A329 60c Prospectors .95 .80
952 A329 70c Land settlers 1.10 .90
953 A329 80c Whalers 1.25 1.00
954 A329 $1.05 Missionaries 1.60 1.40
955 A329 $1.30 Maori 2.10 1.90
Nos. 950-955 (6) 7.65 6.50

Trees — A330

1989, June 7

956 A330 80c Kahikatea 1.25 1.10
957 A330 85c Rimu 1.40 1.40
958 A330 $1.05 Totara 1.60 1.60
959 A330 $1.30 Kauri 2.10 1.90
a. Miniature sheet of one 4.25 4.25
Nos. 956-959 (4) 6.35 6.00

No. 959a sold for $1.80. Surtax benefited the "NZ 1990" executive committee.

Christmas — A331

Star of Bethlehem illuminating settings: 35c, View of One Tree Hill from a bedroom window. 65c, A shepherd overlooking snow-capped mountains. 80c, Boats in harbor. $1, Earth.

1989, Sept. 13 **Litho.** *Perf. 14½*

960 A331 35c multicolored .55 .40
a. Booklet pane of 10 5.50
961 A331 65c multicolored 1.00 .80
962 A331 80c multicolored 1.25 1.00
963 A331 $1 multicolored 1.60 1.25
Nos. 960-963 (4) 4.40 3.45

New Zealand Heritage A332

The sea.

1989, Oct. 11 **Litho.** *Perf. 14x14½*

964 A332 40c Windsurfing .65 .50
965 A332 60c Fishing .95 .80
966 A332 65c Swordfish 1.00 .85
967 A332 80c Harbor 1.25 1.00
968 A332 $1 Gulls over coast 1.60 1.25
969 A332 $1.50 Container ship 2.40 2.00
Nos. 964-969 (6) 7.85 6.40

14th Commonwealth Games, Auckland, Jan. 24-Feb. 3, 1990 — A333

1989, Nov. 8 *Perf. 14½*

970 A333 40c Emblem .65 .65
971 A333 40c Goldie character trademark .65 .65
a. Souvenir sheet of 2, #970-971, sailboats ('90) 2.75 2.75
b. As "a," stadium ('90) 2.75 2.75
972 A333 40c Gymnastics .65 .65
973 A333 50c Weight lifting .80 .70
974 A333 65c Swimming 1.00 .85
975 A333 80c Cycling 1.25 1.00
976 A333 $1 Lawn bowling 1.60 1.25
977 A333 $1.80 Hurdles 2.75 2.40
Nos. 970-977 (8) 9.35 8.15

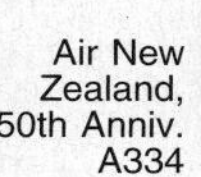

Air New Zealand, 50th Anniv. A334

1990, Jan. 17 *Perf. 13½x14½*

978 A334 80c multicolored 1.25 .95

Souvenir Sheet

Treaty of Waitangi, 150th Anniv. — A335

Painting by Leonard Mitchell: a, Maori chief signing the treaty. b, Chief Hone Heke shaking hand of Lt.-Gov. William Hobson.

1990, Jan. 17 *Perf. 13½*

979 A335 Sheet of 2 2.50 2.50
a.-b. 40c any single 1.25 1.25

New Zealand Heritage A336

The Ships.

1990, Mar. 7 Litho. *Perf. 14x14½*

980 A336 40c Polynesian double-hulled canoe, c. 1000 .65 .55
981 A336 50c *Endeavour* .80 .70
a. Souvenir sheet of 1 *20.00 20.00*
982 A336 60c *Tory* .95 .85
983 A336 80c *Crusader* 1.25 1.10
984 A336 $1 *Edwin Fox* 1.60 1.40
985 A336 $1.50 *Arawa* 2.40 1.90
Nos. 980-985 (6) 7.65 6.50

No. 981a for Stamp World London '90. Sold for $1.30. Issued May 3.

Miniature Sheet

Orchids — A337

Designs: a, Sun. b, Spider. c, Winika. d, Greenhood. e, Odd-leaved orchid.

1990, Apr. 18 Litho. *Perf. 14½*

986 Sheet of 5 7.50 7.50
a.-d. A337 40c any single 1.25 1.25
e. A337 80c multicolored 2.25 2.25

No. 986 sold for $4.90. Surcharge for the intl. stamp exhibition, Auckland, Aug. 24-Sept 2. Imperf. sheets were available only in season tickets which were sold for $25.

New Zealand Heritage A338

The Achievers: 40c, Grace Neill (1846-1926), nurse, journalist. 50c, Jean Batten (1909-1982), aviator. 60c, Katherine Sheppard (1848-1934), social worker. 80c, Richard Pearse (1877-1953), inventor. $1, Gov.-Gen. Bernard Freyberg (1889-1963). $1.50, Peter Buck (1877-1951), cabinet minister.

1990, May 16 Litho. *Perf. 14x14½*

987 A338 40c multicolored .65 .55
988 A338 50c multicolored .80 .70
989 A338 60c multicolored .95 .85
990 A338 80c multicolored 1.25 1.00
991 A338 $1 multicolored 1.60 1.25
992 A338 $1.50 multicolored 2.40 2.00
Nos. 987-992 (6) 7.65 6.35

Akaroa Harbor — A339

Early Settlements: $1, Durie Hill, Wanganui River. $1.50, Mt. Victoria, Wellington. $1.80, Rangitoto Island, Takapuna Beach, Auckland.

1990, June 13 Litho. *Perf. 14½*

993 A339 80c multicolored 1.25 1.10
994 A339 $1 multicolored 1.60 1.25
995 A339 $1.50 multicolored 2.40 2.00
996 A339 $1.80 multicolored 2.75 2.40
a. Souvenir sheet of 1 4.25 4.25
Nos. 993-996 (4) 8.00 6.75

No. 996a sold for $2.30. Surtax for world philatelic expo, New Zealand '90.

New Zealand Heritage A340

The Maori: 40c, Legend of Rangi and Papa. 50c, Maori feather cloak. 60c, Song. 80c, Maori tattoo. $1, War canoe prow. $1.50, Maori war dance.

1990, Aug. 24 Litho. *Perf. 14*

997 A340 40c multi .65 .55
998 A340 50c multi .80 .70
999 A340 60c multi .95 .85
1000 A340 80c multi 1.25 1.00
1001 A340 $1 multi 1.60 1.25
1002 A340 $1.50 multi 2.40 2.00
Nos. 997-1002 (6) 7.65 6.35

Souvenir Sheet

First Postage Stamps, 150th Anniv. — A341

Designs: a, Victoria. b, Edward VII. c, George V. d, Edward VIII. e, George VI. f, Elizabeth II.

1990, Aug. 29 Engr. *Perf. 14½x14*

1003 A341 40c Sheet of 6 5.25 5.25
a.-f. any single .85 .85

Christmas — A342

Various angels.

1990, Sept. 12 Litho. *Perf. 14*

1004 A342 40c multicolored .65 .40
1005 A342 $1 multicolored 1.60 1.10
1006 A342 $1.50 multicolored 2.40 1.75
1007 A342 $1.80 multicolored 2.75 2.25
Nos. 1004-1007 (4) 7.40 5.50

Antarctic Petrel — A343

1990, Nov. 7 *Perf. 13½x13*

1008 A343 40c shown .65 .60
1009 A343 50c Wilson's storm petrel .80 .70
1010 A343 60c Snow petrel .95 .85
1011 A343 80c Antarctic fulmar 1.25 1.10
1012 A343 $1 Chinstrap penguin 1.60 1.50
1013 A343 $1.50 Emperor penguin 2.40 2.25
Nos. 1008-1013 (6) 7.65 7.00

Sheep — A344

1991, Jan. 23 Litho. *Perf. 14½*

1014 A344 40c Coopworth .65 .50
1015 A344 60c Perendale .95 .75
1016 A344 80c Corriedale 1.25 1.00
1017 A344 $1 Drysdale 1.60 1.25
1018 A344 $1.50 South Suffolk 2.40 1.90
1019 A344 $1.80 Romney 2.75 2.40
Nos. 1014-1019 (6) 9.60 7.80

Map, Royal Albatross, Designs from Moriori House, Moriori Man, Nikau Palm, Tree Carving — A345

Design: 80c, Map, sailing ship, carving, petroglyph, Moriori house, Tommy Solomon, last full-blooded Moriori.

1991, Mar. 6 Litho. *Perf. 13½*

1020 A345 40c shown .65 .55
1021 A345 80c multicolored 1.25 1.10

Discovery of the Chatham Islands, Bicent.

New Zealand Football (Soccer) Assoc., Cent. A346

Designs: a, Goal. b, 5 players, referee.

1991, Mar. 6

1022 Pair 2.50 2.50
a.-b. A346 80c any single 1.25 1.25

Tuatara A347

Designs: No. 1023, Juvenile. No. 1024, In burrow. No. 1025, Female. No. 1026, Male.

1991, Apr. 17 Litho. *Perf. 14½*

Denomination Color

1023 A347 40c gray blue 1.50 1.50
1024 A347 40c dark brown 1.50 1.50
1025 A347 40c olive green 1.50 1.50
1026 A347 40c orange brown 1.50 1.50
Nos. 1023-1026 (4) 6.00 6.00

Kiwi Type of 1988

1991, Apr. 17 Engr. *Perf. 14½*

1027 A325 $1 red 1.60 1.25
a. Litho. 1.75 1.50

Value is for stamp with surrounding selvage.
No. 1027a is from Nos.1161a, 1635a.

Happy Birthday — A348

Thinking of You — A349

1991, May 15 Litho. *Perf. 14x13½*

Size of Nos. 1031-1032, 1036-1037: 41x27mm

1028 A348 40c Clown face 1.25 1.25
1029 A348 40c Balloons 1.25 1.25
1030 A348 40c Birthday hat 1.25 1.25
1031 A348 40c Present 1.25 1.25
1032 A348 40c Cake & candles 1.25 1.25
a. Bklt. pane of 5, #1028-1032 6.50
1033 A349 40c shown 1.25 1.25
1034 A349 40c Cat, slippers 1.25 1.25
1035 A349 40c Cat, alarm clock 1.25 1.25
1036 A349 40c Cat looking out window 1.25 1.25
1037 A349 40c Cat walking by door 1.25 1.25
a. Bklt. pane of 5, #1033-1037 6.50

See Nos. 1044-1053.

Rock Formations A350

1991, June 12 Litho. *Perf. 14½*

1038 A350 40c Punakaiki Rocks .65 .50
1039 A350 50c Moeraki Boulders .80 .65

1040 A350 80c Organ Pipes 1.25 1.00
1041 A350 $1 Castle Hill 1.60 1.25
1042 A350 $1.50 Te Kaukau Point 2.40 1.90
1043 A350 $1.80 Ahuriri River Clay Cliffs 2.75 2.40
Nos. 1038-1043 (6) 9.45 7.70

Greetings Types

1991, July 1 Litho. *Perf. 14x13½*
Size of Nos. 1047-1048, 1052-1053: 41x27mm

1044 A348 45c like #1028 1.00 1.00
1045 A348 45c like #1029 1.00 1.00
1046 A348 45c like #1030 1.00 1.00
1047 A348 45c like #1031 1.00 1.00
1048 A348 45c like #1032 1.00 1.00
a. Bklt. pane of 5, #1044-1048 5.00
1049 A349 45c like #1033 1.00 1.00
1050 A349 45c like #1034 1.00 1.00
1051 A349 45c like #1035 1.00 1.00
1052 A349 45c like #1036 1.00 1.00
1053 A349 45c like #1037 1.00 1.00
a. Bklt. pane of 5, #1049-1053 5.00

1991 Rugby World Cup — A351

1991, Aug. 21 Litho. *Perf. 14½x14*

1054 A351 80c Children's 1.25 1.00
1055 A351 $1 Women's 1.60 1.25
1056 A351 $1.50 Senior 2.40 1.90
1057 A351 $1.80 All Blacks 2.75 2.40
a. Souvenir sheet of 1 3.75 3.75
b. As "a," with Phila Nippon '91 emblem in margin 15.00 15.00
Nos. 1054-1057 (4) 8.00 6.55

No. 1057a sold for $2.40 to benefit philatelic trust for hobby support.

Christmas A352

1991, Sept. 18 Litho. *Perf. 13½x14*

1058 A352 45c Shepherds .70 .60
1059 A352 45c Wise men, camels .70 .60
1060 A352 45c Mary, Baby Jesus .70 .60
1061 A352 45c Wise man, gift .70 .60
a. Block of 4, #1058-1061 2.75 2.75
1062 A352 65c Star 1.00 .85
1063 A352 $1 Crown 1.60 1.40
1064 A352 $1.50 Angel 2.40 2.00
Nos. 1058-1064 (7) 7.80 6.65

Butterflies A354

1991-2008 Litho. *Perf. 14¼*

1075 A354 $1 Forest ringlet 1.60 1.10
a. Perf. 14x14½ on 3 sides 5.00 5.00
b. Booklet pane of 5 + 5 labels Perf. 14x14½ on 3 sides 25.00
Complete booklet, #1075b 25.00
c. Perf. 13¾x14¼ 2.00 2.00
1076 A354 $2 Southern blue 3.25 2.25
a. Perf. 13¾x14¼ 6.75 6.75
1077 A354 $3 Yellow admiral 4.75 3.75
a. Souvenir sheet of 1 10.00 10.00
b. Perf. 13¾x14¼ 10.00 5.00
1078 A354 $4 Common copper 6.25 4.50
a. Perf. 13¾x14¼ 7.00 5.25
b. Perf. 14 ('08) 6.25 4.50
1079 A354 $5 Red admiral 8.00 5.75
a. Perf. 13¾x14¼ 8.50 6.00
Nos. 1075-1079 (5) 23.85 17.35

No. 1077a issued later for Phila Nippon '91.

Issued: #1075, 1075a, 1076, 1077, 11/6/91; $4-$5, 1/25/95; #1075b, 9/1/95; #1078a, 10/97; #1079a, 10/9/96; #1075c, 1076a, 11/6/96; #1077b, Aug. 1996..

Mount Cook — A356

Die Stamped & Engr.
Perf. 14½x15

1994, Feb. 18 Wmk. 387

1084 A356 $20 gold & blue 32.50 25.00

1992 America's Cup Competition A357

1992, Jan. 22 Litho. *Perf. 14x14½*

1085 A357 45c KZ7 Kiwi Magic, 1987 .70 .60
1086 A357 80c KZ1 New Zealand, 1988 1.25 1.00
1087 A357 $1 America, 1851 1.60 1.25
1088 A357 $1.50 New Zealand, 1992 2.40 2.00
Nos. 1085-1088 (4) 5.95 4.85

Sighting of New Zealand by Abel Tasman, 350th Anniv. A358

1992, Mar. 12 *Perf. 13½x14½*

1089 A358 45c Heemskerck .65 .60
1090 A358 80c Zeehaen 1.25 1.00
1091 A358 $1 Santa Maria 1.60 1.25
1092 A358 $1.50 Pinta and Nina 2.40 2.00
a. Souvenir sheet of 2, #1091-1092, Perf. 14x14½ 7.50 7.50
Nos. 1089-1092 (4) 5.90 4.85

Discovery of America, 500th anniv. (#1091-1092).

Issue date: No. 1092a, May 22. World Columbian Stamp Expo (#1092a).

1992 Summer Olympics, Barcelona A359

1992, Apr. 3 Litho. *Perf. 13½*

1093 A359 45c Runners .70 .60

Antarctic Seals — A360

1992, Apr. 8 *Perf. 14x13½*

1094 A360 45c Weddell seal .70 .60
1095 A360 50c Crabeater seal .80 .70
1096 A360 65c Leopard seal 1.00 .85
1097 A360 80c Ross seal 1.25 1.00
1098 A360 $1 Southern elephant seal 1.60 1.40
1099 A360 $1.80 Hooker's sea lion 2.75 2.50
Nos. 1094-1099 (6) 8.10 7.05

1992 Summer Olympics, Barcelona A361

1992, May 13 Litho. *Perf. 13½*

1100 A361 45c Cycling .70 .60
1101 A361 80c Archery 1.25 1.00
1102 A361 $1 Equestrian 1.60 1.25
1103 A361 $1.50 Board sailing 2.40 2.00
a. Souvenir sheet of 4, #1100-1103, perf 14x14½ 5.75 5.75
b. No. 1103a overprinted 11.00 11.00
Nos. 1100-1103 (4) 5.95 4.85

No. 1103b overprint consists of World Columbian Stamp Expo emblem in sheet margin. Issue date: No. 1103b, May 22.

Glaciers A362

1992, June 12

1104 A362 45c Glacier ice .70 .60
1105 A362 50c Tasman glacier .80 .70
1106 A362 80c Snowball glacier 1.25 1.00
1107 A362 $1 Brewster glacier 1.60 1.25
1108 A362 $1.50 Fox glacier 2.40 2.00
1109 A362 $1.80 Franz Josef glacier 2.75 2.40
Nos. 1104-1109 (6) 9.50 7.95

Camellias — A363

1992, July 8 *Perf. 14½*

1110 A363 45c Grand finale .70 .60
1111 A363 50c Showa-no-sakae .80 .70
1112 A363 80c Sugar dream 1.25 1.00
1113 A363 $1 Night rider 1.60 1.25
1114 A363 $1.50 E.G. Waterhouse 2.40 2.00
1115 A363 $1.80 Dr. Clifford Parks 2.75 2.40
Nos. 1110-1115 (6) 9.50 7.95

Scenic Views of New Zealand — A364

1992, Sept. 1 Litho. *Perf. 14x14½*
Booklet Stamps

1116 A364 45c Tree, hills .85 .85
1117 A364 45c Hills, stream .85 .85
1118 A364 45c Hills, mountain tops .85 .85
1119 A364 45c Glacier .85 .85
1120 A364 45c Trees, green hills .85 .85
1121 A364 45c Tree branch, rapids .85 .85
1122 A364 45c Rocky shoreline .85 .85
1123 A364 45c Fjord .85 .85
1124 A364 45c Glacial runoff .85 .85
1125 A364 45c Vegetation, stream .85 .85
a. Bklt. pane of 10, #1116-1125 8.75

No. 1125a has continous design.

Christmas — A365

No. 1126, Two reindeer over village. No. 1127, Two reindeer pulling Santa's sleigh. No. 1128, Christmas tree in window. No. 1129, Two children looking out window. 65c, Fireplace, stockings. $1, Church. $1.50, People beneath pohutukawa tree at beach.

1992, Sept. 16 *Perf. 14½*

1126 A365 45c multicolored .70 .50
1127 A365 45c multicolored .70 .50
1128 A365 45c multicolored .70 .50
1129 A365 45c multicolored .70 .50
a. Block of 4, #1126-1129 2.75 2.75
1130 A365 65c multicolored 1.00 .75
1131 A365 $1 multicolored 1.60 1.10
1132 A365 $1.50 multicolored 2.40 1.75
Nos. 1126-1132 (7) 7.80 5.60

No. 1129a has continous design.

A366

The Emerging Years: The 1920s: 45c, Flaming youth. 50c, Birth of broadcasting. 80c, All Blacks rugby player. $1, The swaggie. $1.50, Motorcar brings freedom. $1.80, Arrival of the air age.

1992, Nov. 4 Litho. *Perf. 13½*

1133 A366 45c multicolored .70 .50
1134 A366 50c multicolored .80 .60
1135 A366 80c multicolored 1.25 .90
1136 A366 $1 multicolored 1.60 1.10
1137 A366 $1.50 multicolored 2.40 1.75
1138 A366 $1.80 multicolored 2.75 2.25
Nos. 1133-1138 (6) 9.50 7.10

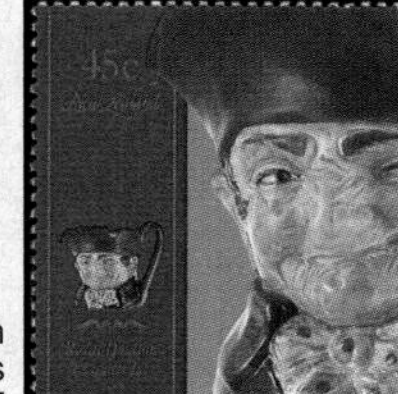

Royal Doulton Ceramics A367

45c, Character jug, "Old Charley." 50c, Plate from "Bunnykins" series. 80c, Maori art tea ware. $1, Hand painted "Ophelia" plate. $1.50, Burslem figurine of St. George. $1.80, Salt glazed vase.

1993, Jan. 20 Litho. *Perf. 13*

1139 A367 45c multicolored .70 .50
1140 A367 50c multicolored .80 .60
1141 A367 80c multicolored 1.25 .90
1142 A367 $1 multicolored 1.60 1.10
1143 A367 $1.50 multicolored 2.40 1.75
1144 A367 $1.80 multicolored 2.75 1.90
a. Souvenir sheet of 1 2.75 1.90
Nos. 1139-1144 (6) 9.50 6.75

A368

The Emerging Years: The 1930's: 45c, Buttons and bows, the new femininity. 50c, The Great Depression. 80c, Race horse, Phar Lap. $1, State housing. $1.50, Free milk for schools. $1.80, The talkies.

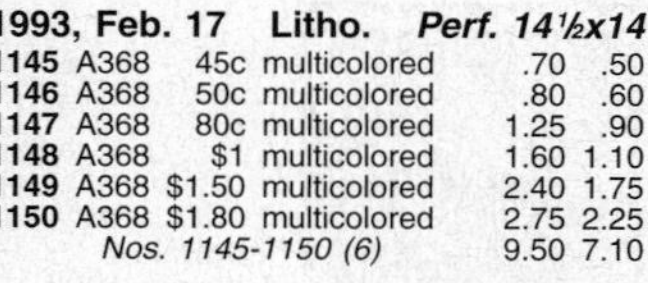

1993, Feb. 17 Litho. *Perf. 14½x14*

1145	A368	45c	multicolored	.70	.50
1146	A368	50c	multicolored	.80	.60
1147	A368	80c	multicolored	1.25	.90
1148	A368	$1	multicolored	1.60	1.10
1149	A368	$1.50	multicolored	2.40	1.75
1150	A368	$1.80	multicolored	2.75	2.25
	Nos. 1145-1150 (6)			9.50	7.10

Woman Suffrage, Cent. — A369

1993, Mar. 31 Litho. *Perf. 13½*

1151	A369	45c	First vote	.70	.50
1152	A369	80c	War work	1.25	.90
1153	A369	$1	Child care	1.60	1.10
1154	A369	$1.50	Contemporary women	2.40	1.75
	Nos. 1151-1154 (4)			5.95	4.25

Thermal Wonders A370

45c, Champagne Pool. 50c, Boiling mud, Rotorua. 80c, Emerald Pool. $1, Hakereteke Falls. $1.50, Warbrick Terrace. $1.80, Pohutu Geyser.

1993, May 5 Litho. *Perf. 12*

1155	A370	45c	multicolored	.70	.50
1156	A370	50c	multicolored	.80	.60
1157	A370	80c	multicolored	1.25	.90
1158	A370	$1	multicolored	1.60	1.10
1159	A370	$1.50	multicolored	2.40	1.75
1160	A370	$1.80	multicolored	2.75	2.25
a.	Souvenir sheet of 1			3.00	2.50
	Nos. 1155-1160 (6)			9.50	7.10

No. 1160a inscribed with Bangkok '93 emblem in sheet margin. Issue date: No. 1160a, Oct. 1.

Kiwi Type of 1988

1993, June 9 Engr. *Perf. 14½*

1161	A325	$1	blue	1.60	1.10
a.	Souv. sheet of 3, #918b, 1027a, 1161			9.00	9.00
b.	Litho.			2.25	1.75
c.	Souv. sheet of 3, #918b, 1027a, 1161b			5.50	5.50

Taipei '93, Asian Intl. Stamp Exhibition (#1161a), Hong Kong '94 (#1161c).

Value is for stamp with surrounding selvage.

Issued: #1161a, 8/14/93; #1161c, 2/18/94.

See No. 1635a.

Species Unique to New Zealand A371

Designs: No. 1162, Yellow-eyed penguin, Hector's dolphin, New Zealand fur seal. 1162A, Taiko, Mt. Cook lily, blue duck. 1162B, Giant snail, rock wren, Hamilton's frog. 1162C, Kaka, Chatham Island pigeon, giant weta.

No. 1163, Tusked weta.

1993, June 9 Litho. *Perf. 14x14½*

1162	A371	45c	multi	1.00	.75
1162A	A371	45c	multi	1.00	.75
1162B	A371	45c	multi	1.00	.75
1162C	A371	45c	multi	1.00	.75
d.	As #1162-1162C, block of 4			4.25	4.25
1163	A371	45c	multicolored	1.00	1.00
a.	Booklet pane of 10			10.00	—
	Complete booklet			10.50	

World Wildlife Fund.

Nos. 1162-1162C were issued both in sheets containing individual designs and in sheets containing the four values setenant (#1162d).

Christmas — A372

Christmas designs: No. 1164, Flowers from pohutukawa tree, denomination at UL. No. 1165, Like #1164, denomination at UR. No. 1166, Present with yellow ribbon, denomination at LL. No. 1167, Present with red ribbon, denomination at LR. $1.00, Ornaments, cracker, sailboats. $1.50, Wreath, sailboats, present.

1993, Sept. 1 Litho. *Perf. 14½x14*

1164	A372	45c	multicolored	.70	.50
1165	A372	45c	multicolored	.70	.50
1166	A372	45c	multicolored	.70	.50
1167	A372	45c	multicolored	.70	.50
a.	Block of 4, #1164-1167			2.75	2.75
1168	A372	$1	multicolored	1.60	1.10
1169	A372	$1.50	multicolored	2.40	1.75
	Nos. 1164-1169 (6)			6.80	4.85

Booklet Stamps

Perf. 12

1164a	A372	45c	multicolored	1.75	1.75
1165a	A372	45c	multicolored	1.75	1.75
1166a	A372	45c	multicolored	1.75	1.75
1167b	A372	45c	multicolored	1.75	1.75
c.	Bklt. pane, 2 ea #1166a, 1167b, 3 ea #1164a-1165a			17.50	

At least one edge of No. 1167c is guillotined.

Fish — A373

Designs: No. 1170, Paua (#1175). No. 1171, Greenshell mussels. No. 1172, Terakihi (#1171). No. 1173, Salmon (#1172). No. 1174, Southern bluefin tuna, albacore tuna, kahawai (#1173). No. 1175, Rock lobster (#1171). No. 1176, Snapper (#1177). No. 1177, Grouper ("Groper," #1178). No. 1178, Orange roughy (#1179). No. 1179, Squid, hoki, oreo dory (#1173, #1174, #1178).

1993, Sept. 1 *Perf. 13½*

Booklet Stamps

1170	A373	45c	multicolored	1.00	1.00
1171	A373	45c	multicolored	1.00	1.00
1172	A373	45c	multicolored	1.00	1.00
1173	A373	45c	multicolored	1.00	1.00
1174	A373	45c	multicolored	1.00	1.00
1175	A373	45c	multicolored	1.00	1.00
1176	A373	45c	multicolored	1.00	1.00
1177	A373	45c	multicolored	1.00	1.00
1178	A373	45c	multicolored	1.00	1.00
1179	A373	45c	multicolored	1.00	1.00
a.	Booklet pane of 10, #1170-1179 + 2 labels			10.00	

Nos. 1179a has continuous design.

Dinosaurs — A374

1993, Oct. 1

1180	A374	45c	Sauropod	.70	.50
1181	A374	80c	Pterosaur	1.25	1.10
1182	A374	$1	Ankylosaur	1.60	1.40
1183	A374	$1.20	Mauisaurus	1.90	1.50
1184	A374	$1.50	Carnosaur	2.40	2.00
a.	Souvenir sheet of 1, perf. 14½x14			2.25	2.00
b.	As "a," inscribed with Bangkok '93 emblem			3.00	2.75
	Nos. 1180-1184 (5)			7.85	6.50

Booklet Stamp

Size: 25½x23½mm

Perf. 12

1185	A374	45c	Carnosaur, sauropod	.70	.55
a.	Booklet pane of 10 + 2 labels			7.00	7.00

The 1940s — A375

Designs: 45c, New Zealand at war. 50c, Crop dusting. 80c, State produces hydroelectricity. $1, New Zealand Marching Assoc. $1.50, The American invasion. $1.80, Victory.

1993, Nov. 3 Litho. *Perf. 14*

1186	A375	45c	multicolored	.70	.50
1187	A375	50c	multicolored	.80	.60
1188	A375	80c	multicolored	1.25	.90
1189	A375	$1	multicolored	1.60	1.10
1190	A375	$1.50	multicolored	2.40	1.75
1191	A375	$1.80	multicolored	2.75	2.25
	Nos. 1186-1191 (6)			9.50	7.10

Outdoor Adventure Sports — A376

1994, Jan. 19 Litho. *Perf. 12*

1192	A376	45c	Bungy jumping	.70	.50
1193	A376	80c	Trout fishing	1.25	.90
1194	A376	$1	Jet boating, horiz.	1.60	1.10
1195	A376	$1.50	Tramping	2.40	1.75
1196	A376	$1.80	Heli-skiing	2.75	2.25
a.	Souvenir sheet of 1			3.25	3.25
	Nos. 1192-1196 (5)			8.70	6.50

No. 1196a inscribed in sheet margin with Hong Kong '94 emblem and text in English and Chinese. Issue date: No. 1196a, Feb. 18.

White Water Rafting — A377

1994, Jan. 19 Litho. *Perf. 12*

Booklet Stamp

1197	A377	45c	multicolored	.70	.55
a.	Booklet pane of 10 + 4 labels			7.00	

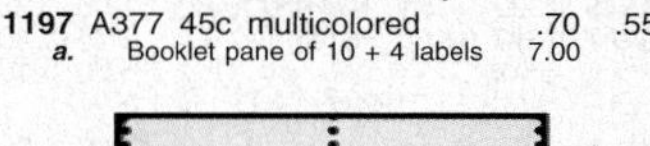

Whitbread Trans-Global Yacht Race — A378

1994, Jan. 19 *Perf. 15*

1198	A378	$1	Endeavour	1.60	1.40

Used value is for stamp with complete selvage.

The 1950's — A379

Designs: 45c, Rock and roll. 80c, Conquest of Mt. Everest. $1, Aunt Daisy, "Good Morning Everybody." $1.20, Royal visit, 1953. $1.50, Opo, the Friendly Dolphin. $1.80, The Coat Hanger (Auckland Harbor Bridge.)

1994, Mar. 24 Litho. *Perf. 14*

1199	A379	45c	multicolored	.70	.50
1200	A379	80c	multicolored	1.25	.90
1201	A379	$1	multicolored	1.60	1.10
1202	A379	$1.20	multicolored	1.90	1.40
1203	A379	$1.50	multicolored	2.40	1.75
1204	A379	$1.80	multicolored	2.75	2.25
	Nos. 1199-1204 (6)			10.60	7.90

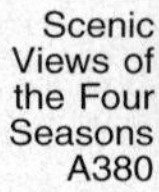

Scenic Views of the Four Seasons A380

Designs: 45c, Winter, Mt. Cook, Mt. Cook lily. 70c, Spring, Lake Hawea, kowhai flower. $1.50, Summer, Opononi, pohutukawa flower. $1.80, Autumn, Mt. Cook, Lake Pukaki, puriri flower.

1994, Apr. 27 *Perf. 12*

1205	A380	45c	multicolored	.70	.50
1206	A380	70c	multicolored	1.10	.85
1207	A380	$1.50	multicolored	2.40	1.75
1208	A380	$1.80	multicolored	2.75	2.25
a.	Strip of 4, #1205-1208			7.50	6.50

Paua Shell — A381

Pavlova Dessert A382

Jandals — A383

Bush Shirt — A384

Buzzy Bee Toy — A385

Kiwi Fruit — A386

Kiwiana: #1211, Hokey pokey ice cream. #1212, Fish and chips. #1216, Black singlet, gumboots. #1217, Rugby shoes, ball.

1994, Apr. 27 Litho. *Perf. 12*

Booklet Stamps

1209	A381	45c	shown	1.00	.70
1210	A382	45c	shown	1.00	.70
1211	A381	45c	multicolored	1.00	.70
1212	A382	45c	multicolored	1.00	.70
1213	A383	45c	shown	1.00	.70
1214	A384	45c	shown	1.00	.70

1215 A385 45c shown 1.00 .70
1216 A384 45c multicolored 1.00 .70
1217 A385 45c multicolored 1.00 .70
1218 A386 45c shown 1.00 .70
a. Booklet pane of 10, #1209-1218 10.00

Maori Myths — A387

Designs: 45c, Maui pulls up Te Ika (the fish). 80c, Rona is snatched up by Marama (moon). $1, Maui attacks Tuna (eel). $1.20, Tane separates Rangi (sky) and Papa (earth). $1.50, Matakauri slays Giant of Wakatipu. $1.80, Panenehu shows Koura (crayfish) to Tangaroa.

1994, June 8 *Perf. 13*
1219 A387 45c multicolored .70 .50
1220 A387 80c multicolored 1.25 .95
1221 A387 $1 multicolored 1.60 1.10
1222 A387 $1.20 multicolored 1.90 1.40
1223 A387 $1.50 multicolored 2.40 1.75
1224 A387 $1.80 multicolored 2.75 2.25
Nos. 1219-1224 (6) 10.60 7.95

First Manned Moon Landing, 25th Anniv. — A388

1994, July 20 **Litho.** *Perf. 12*
1225 A388 $1.50 multicolored 2.40 1.75

No. 1225 has a holographic image. Soaking in water may affect the hologram.

People Reaching People — A389

Serpentine Die Cut 11
1994, July 20 **Photo.**
Self-Adhesive
1226 A389 45c multicolored .70 .50
a. Arrow partially covering hole in "B," serpentine die cut 11¼ 1.00 .75

No. 1226a issued Aug. 1995.
See No. 1311.

Wild Animals A390

1994, Aug. 16 **Litho.** *Perf. 14*
1227 A390 45c Hippopotamus 1.00 .70
1228 A390 45c Spider monkey 1.00 .70
1229 A390 45c Giant panda 1.00 .70
1230 A390 45c Polar bear 1.00 .70
1231 A390 45c African elephant 1.00 .70
1232 A390 45c White rhinoceros 1.00 .70
1233 A390 45c African lion 1.00 .70
1234 A390 45c Plains zebra 1.00 .70
1235 A390 45c Giraffe 1.00 .70
1236 A390 45c Siberian tiger 1.00 .70
a. Block of 10, #1227-1236 10.00 7.25
b. Souvenir sheet of 6, #1229-1231, 1233, 1235-1236 4.50 4.50

PHILAKOREA '94 (#1236b). Nos. 1227-1236 printed in sheets of 100. Because of the design of these sheets, blocks or strips of Nos. 1227-1236 exist in 10 different arrangements. Value assigned to No. 1236a applies to all arrangements.

Christmas A391

Designs: No. 1237, Children, Nativity scene. 70c, Magi, father, child. 80c, Carolers, stained glass window. $1, Carolers, Christmas tree. $1.50, Children, candles. $1.80, Father, mother, infant.
No. 1243, Children, Christmas tree, Santa.

1994, Sept. 21 **Litho.** *Perf. 14*
1237 A391 45c multicolored .70 .50
1238 A391 70c multicolored 1.10 .85
1239 A391 80c multicolored 1.25 1.00
1240 A391 $1 multicolored 1.60 1.25
a. Souv. sheet, 1 ea #1237-1240 4.75 4.75
1241 A391 $1.50 multicolored 2.40 1.90
1242 A391 $1.80 multicolored 2.75 2.40
Nos. 1237-1242 (6) 9.80 7.90

Booklet Stamp
Size: 30x25mm
1243 A391 45c multicolored .70 .55
a. Booklet pane of 10 7.00

Cricket in New Zealand, Cent. — A392

Beach Cricket — A393

No. 1248: a, Woman with striped bathing suit in ocean. b, Person on bodyboard in ocean. c, Child holding float toy at water's edge. d, Boy with beach ball. e, Man holding ice cream cone. f, Beach umbrella at LL. g, Man in blue and red shorts holding cricket bat. h, Woman with cap holding cricket bat. i, Child with pail and shovel. j, Sunbather reading newspaper.

1994, Nov. 2 *Perf. 13½*
1244 A392 45c Batting .70 .50
1245 A392 80c Bowling 1.25 1.00
1246 A392 $1 Wicketkeeping 1.60 1.25
1247 A392 $1.80 Fielding 2.75 2.40
Nos. 1244-1247 (4) 6.30 5.15

Perf. 12
1248 45c Bklt. pane of 10 7.00 7.00
a.-j. A393 Any single .70 .55

New Zealand at Night A394

1995, Feb. 22 **Litho.** *Perf. 12*
1249 A394 45c Auckland .70 .50
1250 A394 80c Wellington 1.25 1.00
1251 A394 $1 Christchurch 1.60 1.25
1252 A394 $1.20 Dunedin 1.90 1.50
1253 A394 $1.50 Rotorua 2.40 1.90
1254 A394 $1.80 Queenstown 2.75 2.40
a. Souv. sheet of 6, #1249-1254 27.50 27.50
Nos. 1249-1254 (6) 10.60 8.55

Singapore '95, Jakarta '95 (#1254a).
Issued: No. 1254a, 9/1/95.

Golf Courses — A395

1995, Mar. 22 **Litho.** *Perf. 14*
1255 A395 45c Waitangi .70 .50
1256 A395 80c New Plymouth 1.25 1.00
1257 A395 $1.20 Rotorua 1.90 1.50
1258 A395 $1.80 Queenstown 2.75 2.75
Nos. 1255-1258 (4) 6.60 5.75

Environmental Protection A396

No. 1259, Native fauna, flora. No. 1260, Plant native trees, shrubs. No. 1261, Protect marine mammals. No. 1262, Conserve power, water. No. 1263, Enjoy natural environment. No. 1264, Control animal pests. No. 1265, Eliminate noxious plants. No. 1266, Return undersized catches. No. 1267, Control air, water quality. No. 1268, Dispose of trash properly.

1995, Mar. 22
1259 A396 45c multicolored .90 .70
1260 A396 45c multicolored .90 .70
1261 A396 45c multicolored .90 .70
1262 A396 45c multicolored .90 .70
1263 A396 45c multicolored .90 .70
1264 A396 45c multicolored .90 .70
1265 A396 45c multicolored .90 .70
1266 A396 45c multicolored .90 .70
1267 A396 45c multicolored .90 .70
1268 A396 45c multicolored .90 .70
a. Booklet pane, #1259-1268 9.00
Complete booklet, #1268a 9.00

Maori Language — A397

Designs: 45c, Treasured Language Nest. 70c, Sing to awaken the spirit. 80c, Acquire knowledge through stories. $1, The welcoming call. $1.50, Recite the genealogies that link people. $1.80, Tell the lore of the people.

1995, May 3 **Litho.** *Perf. 13½*
1269 A397 45c multicolored .70 .50
1270 A397 70c multicolored 1.10 .95
1271 A397 80c multicolored 1.25 1.10
1272 A397 $1 multicolored 1.60 1.40
1273 A397 $1.50 multicolored 2.40 2.00
1274 A397 $1.80 multicolored 2.75 2.75
Nos. 1269-1274 (6) 9.80 8.70

Asian Development Bank, 28th Meeting of the Board of Governors, Auckland — A398

Design: $1.50, Pacific Basin Economic Council, 28th Intl. Meeting, Auckland.

1995, May 3
1275 A398 $1 Map shown 1.60 1.40
1276 A398 $1.50 Map of Pacific 2.40 2.00

Team New Zealand, 1995 America's Cup Winner — A399

1995, May 16 *Perf. 12*
1277 A399 45c Black Magic yacht .70 .60

Rugby League, Cent. A400

Designs: No. 1278, Club Rugby League, Lion Red Cup. No. 1282, Trans Tasman. $1, Mini League. $1.50, George Smith, Albert Baskerville, Early Rugby League. $1.80, Intl. Rugby League, Courtney Intl. Goodwill Trophy.

1995, July 26 **Litho.** *Perf. 14*
1278 A400 45c multicolored .70 .50
1279 A400 $1 multicolored 1.60 1.40
1280 A400 $1.50 multicolored 2.40 2.00
1281 A400 $1.80 multicolored 2.75 2.75
a. Souvenir sheet of 1 2.75 2.75
Nos. 1278-1281 (4) 7.45 6.65

Booklet Stamp
Perf. 12 on 3 Sides
1282 A400 45c multicolored .70 .60
a. Booklet pane of 10 7.00
Complete booklet, #1282a 7.00

#1281a exists imperf from a "Limited Edition" album.

From 1995 onward, New Zealand Post has released a series of "Limited Edition" albums in editions of 2,000. Some contain souvenir sheets unique to these albums.

Farm Animals — A401

1995 **Litho.** *Perf. 14x14½*
Booklet Stamps
1283 A401 40c Sheep .65 .55
1284 A401 40c Deer .65 .55
1285 A401 40c Horses .65 .55
1286 A401 40c Cattle .65 .55
1287 A401 40c Goats .65 .55
1288 A401 40c Turkey .65 .55
1289 A401 40c Ducks .65 .55
1290 A401 40c Chickens .65 .55
1291 A401 40c Pigs .65 .55
1292 A401 40c Border collie .65 .55
a. Bklt. pane of 10, #1283-1292 6.50
Complete booklet 6.00
1293 A401 45c Sheep .80 .80
1294 A401 45c Deer .80 .80
1295 A401 45c Horses .80 .80
1296 A401 45c Cattle .80 .80
1297 A401 45c Goats .80 .80
1298 A401 45c Turkey .80 .80
1299 A401 45c Ducks .80 .80
1300 A401 45c Chickens .80 .80
1301 A401 45c Pigs .80 .80
1302 A401 45c Border collie .80 .80
a. Bklt. pane of 10, #1293-1302 8.50
Complete booklet, #1302a 8.50
b. Souvenir sheet of 5, #1298-1302, perf. 12 4.50 4.50
Nos. 1283-1302 (20) 14.50 13.50

Singapore '95 (#1302b).
#1302b exists imperf.
Issued: #1302a, 9/1/95; #1292a, 10/2/95.

Christmas A402

Stained glass windows: 40c, 45c, Archangel Gabriel. No. 1309A, Angel with trumpet. 70c, Mary. 80c, Shepherds. $1, Madonna and Child. $1.50, Two wise men. $1.80, One wise man.

1995 *Perf. 12*

1303 A402 40c multi .65 .25
1304 A402 45c multi .70 .35
1305 A402 70c multi 1.10 .90
1306 A402 80c multi 1.25 1.00
1307 A402 $1 multi 1.60 1.25
1308 A402 $1.50 multi 2.40 2.00
1309 A402 $1.80 multi 2.75 2.50
Nos. 1303-1309 (7) 10.45 8.25

Booklet Stamp
Size: 25x30mm
Perf. 14½x14

1309A A402 40c multi .65 .55
b. Booklet pane of 10 6.50
Complete booklet, #1309b 6.50

Issued: 45c-$1.80, 9/1; #1303, 10/2; #1309A, 11/9.

Nos. 1303-1309 exist in a souvenir sheet from a "Limited Edition" pack.

Nuclear Disarmament A403

1995, Sept. 1 **Litho.** ***Perf. 13½***

1310 A403 $1 multicolored 1.60 1.40

People Reaching People Type of 1994
Serpentine Die Cut 11

1995, Oct. 2 **Photo.**

Self-Adhesive

1311 A389 40c multicolored 1.50 .50
a. Arrow partially covering hole in "B," serpentine die cut 11¼ 1.00 1.00

No. 1311a, Nov. 1995.

Mitre Peak — A404

1995, Oct. 2 **Litho.** ***Perf. 13½***

1312 A404 40c multicolored .65 .55
a. Perf 12 .65 .60
b. As "a," miniature sheet of 10 6.50

Southpex '96 Stamp Show (No. 1312a).
See #1345-1360, 1405, 1412, 1636-1640.

UN, 50th Anniv. — A405

1995, Oct. 4 ***Perf. 14½***

1313 A405 $1.80 multicolored 2.75 2.50

Famous Living New Zealanders — A406

Person, career field: 40c, Dame Kiri Te Kanawa, performing arts. 80c, Charles Upham, service, business, development. $1, Barry Crump, fine arts, literature. $1.20, Sir Brian Barratt-Boyes, science, medicine, education. $1.50, Dame Whina Cooper, community leader, social campaigner. $1.80, Sir Richard Hadlee, sports.

1995, Oct. 4 ***Perf. 12***

1314 A406 40c multicolored .65 .65
1315 A406 80c multicolored 1.25 1.25
1316 A406 $1 multicolored 1.60 1.60
1317 A406 $1.20 multicolored 1.90 1.90
1318 A406 $1.50 multicolored 2.40 2.40
1319 A406 $1.80 multicolored 2.75 2.75
Nos. 1314-1319 (6) 10.55 10.55

Nos. 1314-1319 issued with se-tenant tab inscribed "STAMP / MONTH / OCTOBER / 1995."

Commonwealth Heads of Government Meeting, Auckland — A407

Designs: 40c, Fern, sky, globe, $1.80, Fern, sea, national flag.

1995, Nov. 9 **Litho.** ***Perf. 14***

1320 A407 40c multicolored .65 .50
1321 A407 $1.80 multicolored 2.75 2.50

Racehorses A408

1996, Jan. 24 **Litho.** ***Perf. 13½x14***

1322 A408 40c Kiwi .65 .50
1323 A408 80c Rough Habit 1.25 1.10
1324 A408 $1 Blossom Lady 1.60 1.25
1325 A408 $1.20 Il Vicolo 1.90 1.60
1326 A408 $1.50 Horlicks 2.40 2.00
1327 A408 $1.80 Bonecrusher 2.75 2.50
Nos. 1322-1327 (6) 10.55 8.95

Booklet

1328 A408 Souvenir bklt. 19.00

No. 1328 contains one booklet pane of Nos. 1322-1327, perf. 14, and individual panes of 1 each Nos. 1322-1327.

Maori Crafts — A409

1996, Feb. 21 **Litho.** ***Perf. 14x13½***

1329 A409 40c Basket .65 .50
1330 A409 80c Weapon 1.25 1.10
1331 A409 $1 Embroidery 1.60 1.25
1332 A409 $1.20 Greenstone 1.90 1.60
1333 A409 $1.50 Gourd 2.40 2.00
a. Souvenir sheet of 3, #1329, 1330, 1333, perf. 13 6.00 6.00
1334 A409 $1.80 Cloak 2.75 2.50
Nos. 1329-1334 (6) 10.55 8.95

No. 1333a for Hong Kong '97. Issued 2/12/97.

Seashore — A410

Designs: No. 1335, Black-backed gull. No. 1336, Sea cucumber, spiny starfish. No. 1337, Common shrimp. No. 1338, Gaudy nudibranch. No. 1339, Large rock crab, clingfish. No. 1340, Snake skin chiton, red rock crab. No. 1341, Estuarine triplefin, cat's eye shell. No. 1342, Cushion star, sea horse. No. 1343, Blue-eyed triplefin, yaldwyn's triplefin. No. 1344, Common octopus.

1996, Feb. 21 ***Perf. 14x14½***

Booklet Stamps

1335 A410 40c multicolored .65 .65
1336 A410 40c multicolored .65 .65
1337 A410 40c multicolored .65 .65
1338 A410 40c multicolored .65 .65
1339 A410 40c multicolored .65 .65
1340 A410 40c multicolored .65 .65
1341 A410 40c multicolored .65 .65
1342 A410 40c multicolored .65 .65
1343 A410 40c multicolored .65 .65
1344 A410 40c multicolored .65 .65
a. Booklet pane, Nos. 1335-1344 6.50
Complete booklet, No. 1344a 6.50

No. 1344a has a continuous design.

Serpentine Die Cut 11½

1996, Aug. 7 **Litho.**

Booklet Stamps
Self-Adhesive

1344B A410 40c like #1335 2.50 1.50
1344C A410 40c like #1336 2.50 1.50
1344D A410 40c like #1337 2.50 1.50
1344E A410 40c like #1338 2.50 1.50
1344F A410 40c like #1339 2.50 1.50
1344G A410 40c like #1340 2.50 1.50
1344H A410 40c like #1341 2.50 1.50
1344I A410 40c like #1342 2.50 1.50
1344J A410 40c like #1343 2.50 1.50
1344K A410 40c like #1344 2.50 1.50
l. Bklt pane, #1344B-1344K 25.00

No. 1344Kl is a complete booklet. The peelable paper backing serves as a booklet cover.

Scenic Views Type of 1995

5c, Mt. Cook, horiz. 10c, Champagne Pool, horiz. 20c, Cape Reinga, horiz. 30c, Mackenzie Country, horiz. 50c, Mt. Ngauruhoe, horiz. 60c, Lake Wanaka. 70c, Giant Kauri-Tane Mahuta. 80c, Doubtful Sound. 90c, Waitomo Limestone Cave.

No. 1354, Tory Channel, Marlborough Sounds. No. 1355, Lake Wakatipu. No. 1356, Lake Matheson. No. 1357, Fox Glacier. No. 1358, Mt. Egmont, Taranaki. No. 1359, Piercy Island, Bay of Islands. No. 1354-1359 horiz.

1996, Mar. 27 **Litho.** ***Perf. 13½***

1345 A404 5c multicolored .20 .20
1346 A404 10c multicolored .20 .20
1347 A404 20c multicolored .25 .25
1348 A404 30c multicolored .45 .40
1349 A404 50c multicolored .80 .70
a. Souv. sheet of 4, #1346-1349 3.00 3.00
1350 A404 60c multicolored .95 .80
1351 A404 70c multicolored 1.10 .95
1352 A404 80c multicolored 1.25 1.10
1353 A404 90c multicolored 1.40 1.25
a. Souv. sheet of 4, #1350-1353 6.50 6.50
Nos. 1345-1353 (9) 6.60 5.85

CHINA '96 (#1349a). CAPEX '96 (#1353a.)
See No. 1405.

Serpentine Die Cut 11¼

1996, May 1 **Photo.**

Size: 26x21mm
Self-Adhesive

1354 A404 40c multicolored .65 .55
1355 A404 40c multicolored .65 .55
1356 A404 40c multicolored .65 .55
1357 A404 40c multicolored .65 .55
1358 A404 40c multicolored .65 .55
1359 A404 40c multicolored .65 .55
a. Strip of 6, Nos. 1354-1359 4.00 4.00
k. Sheet of 10, #1356, 1359, 2 each #1354-1355, 1357-1358 17.50
l. Sheet of 10, #1355, 1358, 2 each #1354, 1356-1357, 1359 17.50
m. Sheet of 10, #1354, 1357, 2 each #1355-1356, 1358-1359 17.50

Serpentine Die Cut 10x9¾

1998, Jan. 14 **Litho.**

Booklet Stamps
Size: 26x21mm
Self-Adhesive

1359B A404 40c like #1358 .65 .55
1359C A404 40c like #1357 .65 .55
1359D A404 40c like #1359 .65 .55
1359E A404 40c like #1356 .65 .55
1359F A404 40c like #1354 .65 .55
h. "Marlborough Sounds" omitted 15.00
1359G A404 40c like #1355 .65 .55
i. Booklet pane, #1359D, 1359F, 1359Fh, 1359G, 2 #1359B-1359C, 1359E 16.00
j. Booklet pane #1359D, 1359G, 2 each #1359B, 1359C, 1359E, 1359F 5.50
l. Coil strip of 6, #1359B-1359G 3.60

No. 1359Gi is a complete booklet.

Serpentine Die Cut 11½

1996, Aug. 7 **Litho.**

Size: 33x22mm
Self-Adhesive

Design: $1, Pohutukawa tree, horiz.

1360 A404 $1 multicolored 1.60 1.40
a. Booklet pane of 5 8.00

By its nature No. 1360a is a complete booklet. The peelable paper backing serves as a booklet cover. The outside of the cover contains 5 peelable international airpost labels.

Rescue Services — A411

40c, Fire service, ambulance. 80c, Civil defense. $1, Air sea rescue. $1.50, Air ambulance, rescue helicopter. $1.80, Mountain rescue, Red Cross.

1996, Mar. 27 ***Perf. 14½x15***

1361 A411 40c multicolored .65 .50
1362 A411 80c multicolored 1.25 1.10
1363 A411 $1 multicolored 1.60 1.25
1364 A411 $1.50 multicolored 2.40 2.00
1365 A411 $1.80 multicolored 2.75 2.50
Nos. 1361-1365 (5) 8.65 7.35

Wildlife A412

Designs: 40c, Yellow-eyed penguin, vert. 80c, Royal albatross. $1, White heron. $1.20, Sperm whale. $1.50, Fur seal, vert. $1.80, Bottlenose dolphin, vert.

1996, May 1 **Litho.** ***Perf. 14***

1366 A412 40c multicolored .65 .50
1367 A412 80c multicolored 1.25 1.10
1368 A412 $1 multicolored 1.60 1.40
1369 A412 $1.20 multicolored 1.90 1.60
1370 A412 $1.50 multicolored 2.40 2.00
a. Sheet of 2, #1368, 1370 6.50 6.50
1371 A412 $1.80 multicolored 2.75 2.75
a. Sheet of 2, #1367, 1371 5.00 5.00
b. Block, #1366-1371, + 2 labels 10.00 10.00
Nos. 1366-1371 (6) 10.55 9.35

No. 1370a for CHINA '96. Issued May 18.
No. 1371a for Taipei '96. Issued Oct. 2.

New Zealand Symphony Orchestra, 50th Anniv. — A413

1996, July 10 Litho. *Perf. 15x14½*
1372 A413 40c Violin .65 .50
1373 A413 80c French horn 1.25 1.10

1996 Summer Olympics, Atlanta A414

1996, July 10 *Perf. 14½*
1374 A414 40c Swimming .65 .50
1375 A414 80c Cycling 1.25 1.10
1376 A414 $1 Athletics 1.60 1.40
1377 A414 $1.50 Rowing 2.40 2.00
1378 A414 $1.80 Yachting 2.75 2.75
a. Sheet of 5, #1374-1378 8.75 8.75
Nos. 1374-1378 (5) 8.65 7.75

Used value is for stamp with complete selvage.
A miniature sheet containing #1374-1378, both perf and imperf within the sheet, exists. This comes from a "Limited Edition" collectors' pack.
See No. 1383.

A415

Motion pictures, cent.: 40c, Hinemoa. 80c, Broken Barrier. $1.50, Goodbye Pork Pie. $1.80, Once Were Warriors.

1996, Aug. 7 Litho. *Perf. 14½x15*
1379 A415 40c multicolored .65 .50
1380 A415 80c multicolored 1.25 1.10
1381 A415 $1.50 multicolored 2.40 2.00
1382 A415 $1.80 multicolored 2.75 2.75
Nos. 1379-1382 (4) 7.05 6.35

Nos. 1379-1382 are printed se-tenant with scratch and win labels for a contest available to New Zealand residents.

1996 Summer Olympics Type

Design: Danyon Loader, swimmer, Blyth Tait, horseman, 1996 gold medalists from New Zealand.

1996, Aug. 28 Litho. *Perf. 14½*
1383 A414 40c multicolored .65 .65

Used value is for stamp with complete selvage.
Leaves in selvage printed in six different patterns.

A416

1996, Sept. 4 *Perf. 12*
1384 A416 40c Beehive ballot box .65 .50

Mixed member proportional election, 1966. No. 1384 was issued in sheets of 10.

Christmas A417

Scenes from the Christmas story: No. 1385, Following the star. 70c, Shepherd finding baby in manger. 80c, Angel's announcement to shepherd. $1, The Nativity. $1.50, Journey to Bethlehem. $1.80, The annunciation.
No. 1391, Adoration of the Magi. No. 1392, Heavenly host praising God.

1996, Sept. 4 *Perf. 14*
1385 A417 40c multicolored .65 .50
1386 A417 70c multicolored 1.10 1.00
1387 A417 80c multicolored 1.25 1.10
1388 A417 $1 multicolored 1.60 1.40
1389 A417 $1.50 multicolored 2.40 2.00
1390 A417 $1.80 multicolored 2.75 2.75
Nos. 1385-1390 (6) 9.75 8.75

Size: 29x24mm
Self-Adhesive
Serpentine Die Cut 11½
1391 A417 40c multicolored .65 .55
a. Booklet pane 10 6.50
1392 A417 40c multicolored .65 .55

By its nature No. 1391a is a complete booklet. The peelable paper backing serves as a booklet cover.

Extinct Birds A418

1996, Oct. 2 Litho. *Perf. 13½*
1393 A418 40c Adzebill .65 .50
1394 A418 80c Laughing owl 1.25 1.10
1395 A418 $1 Piopio 1.60 1.40
1396 A418 $1.20 Huia 1.90 1.75
1397 A418 $1.50 Giant eagle 2.40 2.10
1398 A418 $1.80 Giant moa 2.75 2.75
a. Souvenir sheet 3.00 3.00
b. As "a," with added inscription 4.50 4.50
Nos. 1393-1398 (6) 10.55 9.60

Size: 29x24mm
Self-Adhesive
Serpentine Die Cut 11½
1399 A418 40c Stout-legged wren .65 .55
a. Booklet pane of 10 6.50

Inscriptions on backs of Nos. 1393-1398 describe each species. By its nature No. 1399a is a complete booklet. The peelable backing serves as a booklet cover.
No. 1398b contains Taipei '96 exhibition emblem in sheet margin.

Scenic Gardens — A419

Designs: 40c, Seymour Square Gardens, Blenheim. 80c, Pukekura Park Gardens, New Plymouth. $1, Wintergarden, Auckland. $1.50, Botanic Gardens, Christchurch. $1.80, Marine Parade Gardens, Napier.

1996, Nov. 13 Litho. *Perf. 13½*
1400 A419 40c multicolored .65 .50
1401 A419 80c multicolored 1.25 1.10
1402 A419 $1 multicolored 1.60 1.40
1403 A419 $1.50 multicolored 2.40 2.10
1404 A419 $1.80 multicolored 2.75 2.75
Nos. 1400-1404 (5) 8.65 7.85

New Zealand Post produced and distributed three souvenir sheets as rewards for purchases made from the post office during 1996. The sheets were not available through normal philatelic channels. The sheets are inscribed "NEW ZEALAND POST / Best of 1996" and the Stamp Points emblem. Each sheet contains 3 stamps; #1327, 1365, 1334; #1378, 1382, 1371; #1390, 1404, 1398.

Scenic Views Type of 1995
Serpentine Die Cut 11½
1996, Nov. 1 Litho.
Size: 26x21mm
Self-Adhesive
1405 A404 80c like No. 1352 1.25 1.10
a. Booklet pane of 10 12.50

By its nature No. 1405a is a complete booklet. The peelable paper backing serves as a booklet cover. The outside of the cover contains 10 peelable international airpost labels.

Cattle — A420

1997, Jan. 15 *Perf. 14x14½*
1406 A420 40c Holstein-Friesian .65 .50
1407 A420 80c Jersey 1.25 1.10
1408 A420 $1 Simmental 1.60 1.40
1409 A420 $1.20 Ayrshire 1.90 1.75
1410 A420 $1.50 Angus 2.40 2.10
a. Souvenir sheet of 3, #1407, 1408, 1410 9.50 9.50
1411 A420 $1.80 Hereford 2.50 2.50
Nos. 1406-1411 (6) 10.30 9.35

No. 1410a for Hong Kong '97. Issued 2/12/97.

Souvenir Sheets
The 1997 sheets contain: Nos. 1411, 1418, 1434; Nos. 1440, 1444, 1451; Nos. 1445, 1457, 1475.
See note following No. 1404.

Scenic Views Type of 1995
1997, Feb. 12 Litho. *Perf. 13½*
Size: 37x32mm
1412 A404 $10 Mt. Ruapehu 16.00 11.50

Discoverers — A421

1997, Feb. 12 *Perf. 14*
1413 A421 40c James Cook .65 .50
1414 A421 80c Kupe 1.25 1.10
1415 A421 $1 Maui, vert. 1.60 1.40
1416 A421 $1.20 Jean de Surville, vert. 1.90 1.75
1417 A421 $1.50 Dumont d'Urville 2.40 2.10
1418 A421 $1.80 Abel Tasman 2.75 2.75
Nos. 1413-1418 (6) 10.55 9.60

#1413-1418 exist in sheet of 6 created for a hard-bound millennium book that sold for $129.

"Wackiest Letterboxes" — A422

Serpentine Die Cut 11¼
1997, Mar. 19 Litho.
Self-Adhesive
Booklet Stamps
1419 A422 40c Log house .70 .60
1420 A422 40c Owl .70 .60
1421 A422 40c Whale .70 .60
1422 A422 40c "Kilroy is Back" .70 .60
1423 A422 40c House of twigs .70 .60
1424 A422 40c Scottish piper .70 .60
1425 A422 40c Diving helmet .70 .60
1426 A422 40c Airplane .70 .60
1427 A422 40c Water faucet .70 .60
1428 A422 40c Painted buildings .70 .60
a. Bklt. pane of 10, #1419-1428 7.00
b. Sheet of 10, #1419-1428 18.00

By its nature No. 1428a is a complete booklet. The peelable paper backing serves as a booklet cover.

Vineyards — A423

1997, Mar. 19 *Perf. 14*
1429 A423 40c Central Otago .65 .40
a. Booklet pane of 1 .65
1430 A423 80c Hawke's Bay 1.25 1.10
a. Booklet pane of 1 1.25
1431 A423 $1 Marlborough 1.60 1.40
a. Booklet pane of 1 1.60
1432 A423 $1.20 Canterbury, Waipara 1.90 1.75
a. Booklet pane of 1 1.90
1433 A423 $1.50 Gisborne 2.90 2.00
a. Booklet pane of 1 2.90
b. Souvenir sheet of 3, #1429, 1431, 1433 8.00 8.00
1434 A423 $1.80 Auckland, Waiheke 2.75 2.75
a. Booklet pane of 1 2.75
b. Bklt. pane of 6, #1429-1434 10.25
Complete booklet, #1429a, 1430a, 1431a, 1432a, 1433a, 1434a, 1434b 20.00
Nos. 1429-1434 (6) 11.05 9.40

No. 1433b for PACIFIC 97. Issued: 5/29.

Pigeon Mail Service, Cent. A424

Design: 1899 local stamp.

1997, May 7 Litho. *Perf. 14*
1435 A424 40c red .65 .65
1436 A424 80c blue 1.25 1.25
a. Souv. sheet, 2 ea #1435-1436 11.00 11.00
b. As "a," diff. inscription 6.50 6.50

No. 1436a for PACIFIC 97. Issued: 5/29.
No. 1436b was inscribed in sheet margin for AUPEX '97 National Stamp Exhibition, Auckland. Issued 11/13.

Paintings by Colin McCahon (1919-87) — A425

Designs: 40c, The Promised Land, 1948. $1, Six Days in Nelson and Canterbury, 1950. $1.50, Northland Panels, 1958. $1.80, Moby Dick is sighted off Muriwai Beach, 1972.

1997, May 7
1437 A425 40c multicolored .65 .50
1438 A425 $1 multicolored 1.60 1.40
1439 A425 $1.50 multicolored 2.40 2.10
1440 A425 $1.80 multicolored 2.75 2.75
Nos. 1437-1440 (4) 7.40 6.75

See Nos. 1597-1600.

Fly Fishing
A426

Designs: 40c, Red setter fly, rainbow trout. $1, Grey ghost fly, sea-run brown trout. $1.50, Twilight beauty fly, brook trout. $1.80, Hare & copper fly, brown trout.

1997, June 18 Litho. *Perf. 13*

1441	A426	40c	multicolored	.65	.50
1442	A426	$1	multicolored	1.60	1.40
1443	A426	$1.50	multicolored	2.40	2.10
1444	A426	$1.80	multicolored	2.75	2.75
a.			Souv. sheet of 2, #1441, 1444	6.00	6.00
			Nos. 1441-1444 (4)	7.40	6.75

No.1444a issued 5/13/98 for Israel '98 World Stamp Exhibition, Tel Aviv.

Kiwi Type of 1988

1997, Aug. 6 Litho. *Perf. 14½*

1445	A325	$1	violet	1.60	1.50

Value is for copy with surrounding selvage. Selvage comes with and without gold sunbursts.

See No. 1635a.

Scenic Trains
A426a

Name of train, area scene, map of train route: 40c, Overlander, Paremata, Wellington, Wellington-Auckland. 80c, Trans-Alpine, Southern Alps, Christchurch-Greymouth. $1, Southerner, Canterbury, Invercargill-Christchurch. $1.20, Coastal Pacific, Kaikoura Coast, Christchurch-Picton. $1.50, Bay Express, Central Hawke's Bay, Wellington-Napier. $1.80, Kaimai Express, Tauranga Harbor, Tauranga-Auckland.

1997, Aug. 6 *Perf. 14x14½*

1446	A426a	40c	multicolored	.65	.45
1447	A426a	80c	multicolored	1.25	1.00
1448	A426a	$1	multicolored	1.60	1.25
1449	A426a	$1.20	multicolored	1.90	1.50
1450	A426a	$1.50	multicolored	2.40	1.90
a.			Sheet of 3, #1447-1448, 1450	7.50	7.50
1451	A426a	$1.80	multicolored	2.75	2.40
			Nos. 1446-1451 (6)	10.55	8.50

No. 1450a issued 5/13/98 for Israel '98 World Stamp Exhibition, Tel Aviv.

Nos. 1446-1451 exist in a sheet of 6 from a "Limited Edition" album.

Christmas
A427

Scenes from first Christian service, Rangihoua Bay, and words from Christmas carol, "Te Harinui:" No. 1452, Samuel Marsden's ship, Active. 70c, Marsden preaching from pulpit. 80c, Marsden extending hand to local chiefs. $1, Mother, children from Rangihoua. $1.50, Maori and Pakeha hands, Marsden's memorial cross. $1.80, Pohutukawa flowers, Rangihoua Bay. No. 1458, Cross marking spot of service, flowers, bay.

1997, Sept. 3 Litho. *Perf. 14*

1452	A427	40c	multicolored	.65	.45
1453	A427	70c	multicolored	1.10	.90
1454	A427	80c	multicolored	1.25	1.00
1455	A427	$1	multicolored	1.60	1.25
1456	A427	$1.50	multicolored	2.40	1.90
1457	A427	$1.80	multicolored	2.75	2.40
a.			Block of 6, #1452-1457	11.00	11.00
			Nos. 1452-1457 (6)	9.75	7.90

Self-Adhesive

Size: 30x24mm

Serpentine Die Cut 10

1458	A427	40c	multicolored	.65	.50
a.			Booklet pane of 10	6.50	

By its nature No. 1458a is a complete booklet. The peelable paper backing serves as a booklet cover.

"Creepy Crawlies" — A428

Serpentine Die Cut 11¼

1997, Oct. 1 Litho.

Booklet Stamps

1459	A428	40c	Huhu beetle	.65	.65
1460	A428	40c	Giant land snail	.65	.65
1461	A428	40c	Giant weta	.65	.65
1462	A428	40c	Giant dragonfly	.65	.65
1463	A428	40c	Peripatus	.65	.65
1464	A428	40c	Cicada	.65	.65
1465	A428	40c	Puriri moth	.65	.65
1466	A428	40c	Veined slug	.65	.65
1467	A428	40c	Katipo	.65	.65
1468	A428	40c	Flaxweevil	.65	.65
a.			Booklet pane, #1459-1468	6.50	
b.			Sheet of 10, #1459-1468	10.00	

By its nature No. 1468a is a complete booklet. The peelable paper backing serves as a booklet cover.

China-New Zealand Stamp Expo — A429

1997, Oct. 9 *Perf. 14*

1469	40c	Rosa rugosa	.65	.50
1470	40c	Aotearoa-New Zealand	.65	.50
a.		A429 Pair, #1469-1470	1.40	1.10
b.		Souvenir sheet, #1470a	2.00	2.00
c.		As "b," diff. inscription	2.00	2.00

No. 1470c inscribed in gold and black in sheet margin for Shanghai 1997 Intl. Stamp & Coin Expo. Issued: 11/19/97.

See People's Republic of China Nos. 2797-2798.

Queen Elizabeth II and Prince Philip, 50th Wedding Anniv. — A430

1997, Nov. 12 Litho. *Perf. 12*

1471	A430	40c	multicolored	.65	.45

Issued in sheets of 10.

Cartoonists
A431

"Kiwis Taking on the World:" 40c, Kiwi flying on bee, by Garrick Tremain. $1, Kiwi using world as egg and having it for breakfast, by Jim Hubbard. $1.50, Kiwi in yacht race against the world, by Eric Heath. $1.80, Man with chain saw, trees on mountainside cut as peace symbol, by Burton Silver.

1997, Nov. 12 *Perf. 14*

1472	A431	40c	multicolored	.65	.45
1473	A431	$1	multicolored	1.60	1.25
1474	A431	$1.50	multicolored	2.40	1.90
1475	A431	$1.80	multicolored	2.75	2.40
			Nos. 1472-1475 (4)	7.40	6.00

Performing Arts — A432

1998, Jan. 14 Litho. *Perf. 13½*

1476	A432	40c	Modern dance	.65	.45
a.			Booklet pane of 1	.65	
1477	A432	80c	Music	1.25	.95
a.			Booklet pane of 1	1.25	
b.			Perf 14	2.50	2.50
1478	A432	$1	Opera	1.60	1.25
a.			Booklet pane of 1	1.60	
1479	A432	$1.20	Theater	1.90	1.40
a.			Booklet pane of 1	1.90	
1480	A432	$1.50	Song	2.40	1.75
a.			Booklet pane of 1	2.40	
1481	A432	$1.80	Ballet	2.75	2.10
a.			Booklet pane of 1	2.75	
b.			Bklt. pane of 6, #1476-1481	11.00	
			Complete booklet, 1 each #1476a-1481a, 1481b	22.50	
c.			Perf 14	5.50	5.50
			Nos. 1476-1481 (6)	10.55	7.90

Museum of New Zealand Te Papa Tongarewa — A433

1998, Feb. 11 Litho. *Perf. 14*

1482	A433	40c	People at entrance	.65	.45
1483	A433	$1.80	Waterfront location	2.75	2.25

Souvenir Sheets

The 1998 sheets contain: Nos. 1489, 1483, 1481; Nos. 1491, 1521, 1525; Nos. 1531, 1537, 1562.

See note following No. 1404.

Domestic Cat — A434

1998, Feb. 11 *Perf. 13½*

1484	A434	40c	Moggy	.65	.45
1485	A434	80c	Burmese	1.25	.90
1486	A434	$1	Birman	1.60	1.25
1487	A434	$1.20	British blue	1.90	1.40
1488	A434	$1.50	Persian	2.40	1.75
1489	A434	$1.80	Siamese	2.75	2.25
a.			Souvenir sheet of 3, #1484, #1486, #1489	6.50	6.50
			Nos. 1484-1489 (6)	10.55	8.00

Memorial Statues — A435

40c, "With Great Respect to the Mehmetcik, Gallipoli" (Turkish soldier carrying wounded ANZAC). $1.80, "Mother with Children," Natl. War Memorial, Wellington.

1998, Mar. 18 Litho. *Perf. 13½*

1490	A435	40c	multicolored	.65	.45
1491	A435	$1.80	multicolored	2.75	2.25

See Turkey Nos. 2695-2696.

New Zealand's Multi-cultural Society — A436

Designs: 40c, The Maori. 80c, British/European settlers, 1840-1914. $1, Fortune seekers, 1800-1920. $1.20, Post-war British/European migrants, 1945-70. $1.50, Pacific Islanders, from 1960. $1.80, Asian arrivals, 1980s-90s.

1998, Mar. 18 *Perf. 14*

1492	A436	40c	multicolored	.65	.45
1493	A436	80c	multicolored	1.25	.90
1494	A436	$1	multicolored	1.60	1.10
1495	A436	$1.20	multicolored	1.90	1.40
1496	A436	$1.50	multicolored	2.40	1.75
1497	A436	$1.80	multicolored	2.75	2.25
			Nos. 1492-1497 (6)	10.55	7.85

Nos. 1492-1497 exist in sheet of 6 created for a hard-bound millennium book that sold for $129.

"Stay in Touch" Greetings Stamps
A437

Designs: No. 1498, Young and older person hugging, vert. No. 1499, Middle-aged couple wading in water at beach, vert. No. 1500, Characters giving "high five," vert. No. 1501, Stylized boy pointing way to old woman, vert. No. 1502, Cartoon of woman with tears embracing man. No. 1503, Couple kissing. No. 1504, Older couple with faces together. No. 1505, Two boys arm in arm in swimming pool. No. 1506, Stylized couple, clouds. No. 1507, Stylized couple seated on sofa.

Die Cut Perf. 10x10¼, 10¼x10

1998, Apr. 15 Litho.

Booklet Stamps

Self-Adhesive

1498	A437	40c	multicolored	.65	.65
1499	A437	40c	multicolored	.65	.65
1500	A437	40c	multicolored	.65	.65
1501	A437	40c	multicolored	.65	.65
a.			Sheet of 4, #1498-1501	5.00	
1502	A437	40c	multicolored	.65	.65
1503	A437	40c	multicolored	.65	.65
1504	A437	40c	multicolored	.65	.65
1505	A437	40c	multicolored	.65	.65
1506	A437	40c	multicolored	.65	.65
1507	A437	40c	multicolored	.65	.65
a.			Booklet pane, #1498-1507	6.50	
b.			Sheet of 6, #1502-1507	10.00	

The peelable paper backing of No. 1507a serves as a booklet cover.

Types of 1898

1998, May 20 Litho. *Perf. 14x14½*

1508	A18	40c	Mt. Cook	.65	.65
1509	A19	40c	Lake Taupo	.65	.65
1510	A20	40c	Pembroke Peak	.65	.65
1511	A23	40c	Huia	.65	.65
1512	A24	40c	White Terrace	.65	.65
1513	A26	40c	Kiwi	.65	.65

1514 A27 40c Maori canoe .65 .65
1515 A29 40c Hawk-billed parrots .65 .65

Perf. 14½

1516 A21 80c Wakitipu 1.25 1.25
1517 A22 80c Wakatipu 1.25 1.25
a. Souvenir sheet of 2, 1516-1517 4.75 4.75
1518 A25 $1 Otira Gorge 1.60 1.60
1519 A28 $1.20 Pink Terrace 1.90 1.90
1520 A30 $1.50 Milford Sound 2.40 2.40
a. Sheet of 2, #1517, 1520 4.00 4.00
1521 A31 $1.80 Mt. Cook 2.75 2.75
Nos. 1508-1521 (14) 16.35 16.35

No. 1517a issued 8/7/98 for Tarapex '98, Natl. Stamp Exhibition.

No. 1520a issued 10/23/98 for Italia '98.

Paintings by Peter McIntyre A438

Designs: 40c, Wounded at Cassino, 1944. $1, The Cliffs of Rangitikei, c. 1958. $1.50, Maori Children, King Country, 1963. $1.80, The Anglican Church, Kakahi, 1972.

1998, June 24 Litho. *Perf. 13½*

1522 A438 40c multicolored .65 .45
1523 A438 $1 multicolored 1.60 1.10
1524 A438 $1.50 multicolored 2.40 1.60
1525 A438 $1.80 multicolored 2.75 2.25
a. Souvenir sheet, #1524-1525, perf 14 6.00 6.00
Nos. 1522-1525 (4) 7.40 5.40

No. 1525a issued 10/23/98 for Italia '98.

Nos. 1524-1525 exist in an imperf souvenir sheet from a "Limited Edition" album.

Scenic Skies — A439

1998, July 29 Litho. *Perf. 14½*

1526 A439 40c Cambridge .65 .45
1527 A439 80c Lake Wanaka 1.25 .90
1528 A439 $1 Mt. Maunganui 1.60 1.10
1529 A439 $1.20 Kaikoura 1.90 1.40
1530 A439 $1.50 Whakatane 2.40 1.75
1531 A439 $1.80 Lindis Pass 2.75 2.25
a. Souv. sheet of 2, #1526, 1531 3.75 3.75
Nos. 1526-1531 (6) 10.55 7.85

No. 1531a issued 3/19/99 for Australia '99 World Stamp Expo.

Christmas A440

Designs: 40c, Madonna and Child. 70c, Shepherds approaching nativity scene. 80c, Joseph, Mary, Christ Child. $1, Magus. $1.50, Magi with gifts. $1.80, Angel telling shepherds about Messiah.

1998, Sept. 2 Litho. *Perf. 13x14*

1532 A440 40c multicolored .65 .45
1533 A440 70c multicolored 1.10 .80
1534 A440 80c multicolored 1.25 .90
1535 A440 $1 multicolored 1.60 1.10
1536 A440 $1.50 multicolored 2.40 1.75
1537 A440 $1.80 multicolored 2.75 2.25
Nos. 1532-1537 (6) 9.75 7.25

Self-adhesive

Size: 24x30mm

Serpentine Die Cut 11½

1538 A440 40c multicolored .65 .40
a. Booklet pane of 10 6.50

No. 1538a is a complete booklet. The peelable paper backing serves as a booklet cover.

Marine Life — A441

1998, Oct. 7 Litho. *Perf. 14*

1539 A441 40c Moonfish .65 .65
1540 A441 40c Mako shark .65 .65
1541 A441 40c Yellowfin tuna .65 .65
1542 A441 40c Giant squid .65 .65
a. Block of 4, #1539-1542 2.75 2.75
1543 A441 80c Striped marlin 1.25 1.25
1544 A441 80c Porcupine fish 1.25 1.25
a. Souvenir sheet of 4, #1539-1540, #1543-1544 5.25 5.25
1545 A441 80c Eagle ray 1.25 1.25
1546 A441 80c Sandager's wrasse 1.25 1.25
a. Block of 4, #1543-1546 5.00 5.00
b. Souvenir sheet of 4, #1541-1542, 1545-1546 8.00 8.00
Nos. 1539-1546 (8) 7.60 7.60

No. 1544a issued 3/19/99 for Australia '99, World Stamp Expo. No. 1546b was issued 7/2/99 for PhilexFrance '99, World Philatelic Exhibition.

#1539-1546 exist in sheets of 8 from a "Limited Edition" album.

Famous Town Icons A442 A443

Designs: No. 1547, L&P bottle, Paeroa. No. 1548, Carrot, Ohakune. No. 1549, Brown trout, Gore. No. 1550, Crayfish, Kaikoura. No. 1551, Sheep shearer, Te Kuiti. No. 1552, Pania of the Reef, Napier. No. 1553, Paua shell, Riverton. No. 1554, Kiwifruit, Te Puke. No. 1555, Border collie, Tekapo. No. 1556, Cow, Hawera.

Serpentine Die Cut 11½

1998, Oct. 7 Litho.

Self-Adhesive

1547 A442 40c multicolored .65 .45
1548 A442 40c multicolored .65 .45
1549 A443 40c multicolored .65 .45
1550 A443 40c multicolored .65 .45
1551 A443 40c multicolored .65 .45
1552 A443 40c multicolored .65 .45

Size: 25x30mm

1553 A443 40c multicolored .65 .45
1554 A443 40c multicolored .65 .45
1555 A443 40c multicolored .65 .45
1556 A443 40c multicolored .65 .45
a. Sheet of 10, #1547-1556 10.00
b. Booklet pane, #1547-1556 6.50

No. 1556b is a complete booklet. The peelable paper backing serves as a booklet cover.

Urban Transformation — A444

1998, Nov. 11 Litho. *Perf. 14x14½*

1557 A444 40c Wellington .65 .45
1558 A444 80c Auckland 1.25 .90
1559 A444 $1 Christchurch 1.60 1.10
1560 A444 $1.20 Westport 1.90 1.40
1561 A444 $1.50 Tauranga 2.40 1.75
1562 A444 $1.80 Dunedin 2.75 2.25
Nos. 1557-1562 (6) 10.55 7.85

#1557-1562 exist in sheet of 6 created for a hard-bound Millennium book that sold for $129.

Native Tree Flowers — A445

1999, Jan. 13 Litho. *Perf. 14½x14*

1563 A445 40c Kotukutuku .65 .45
1564 A445 80c Poroporo 1.25 .90
a. Souv. sheet of 2, #1563-1564 3.50 3.50
1565 A445 $1 Kowhai 1.60 1.10
1566 A445 $1.20 Weeping broom 1.90 1.40
1567 A445 $1.50 Teteaweka 2.40 1.75
1568 A445 $1.80 Southern rata 2.75 2.25
Nos. 1563-1568 (6) 10.55 7.85

No. 1564a was issued 8/21/99 for China 1999 World Philatelic Exhibition.

Nos. 1567-1568 exist in a souvenir sheet from a "Limited Edition" album.

Souvenir Sheets

The 1999 sheets contain: Nos. 1568, 1572, 1578; Nos. 1584, 1600, 1607; Nos. 1613, 1620, 1627.

See note following No. 1404.

Art Deco Buildings — A446

40c, Civic Theatre, Auckland. $1, Masonic Hotel, Napier. $1.50, Medical and Dental Offices, Hastings. $1.80, Buller County Offices, Westport.

1999, Feb. 10 Litho. *Perf. 14*

1569 A446 40c multicolored .65 .45
1570 A446 $1 multicolored 1.60 1.10
1571 A446 $1.50 multicolored 2.40 1.75
1572 A446 $1.80 multicolored 2.75 2.25
Nos. 1569-1572 (4) 7.40 5.55

Popular Pets — A447

Designs: 40c, Labrador puppy. 80c, Netherland dwarf rabbit. $1, Rabbit, tabby kitten. $1.20, Lamb. $1.50, Welsh pony. $1.80, Budgies.

1999, Feb. 10

1573 A447 40c multicolored .65 .45
1574 A447 80c multicolored 1.25 .90
1575 A447 $1 multicolored 1.60 1.10
a. Souvenir sheet, #1573-1575 4.25 4.25
b. Souvenir sheet, #1573, 1575 3.00 3.00
1576 A447 $1.20 multicolored 1.90 1.40
1577 A447 $1.50 multicolored 2.40 1.75
1578 A447 $1.80 multicolored 2.75 2.25
Nos. 1573-1578 (6) 10.55 7.85

New Year 1999, Year of the Rabbit (#1575a).

No. 1575b was issued 8/21/99 for China 1999 World Philatelic Exhibition.

Nostalgia A448

1999, Mar. 10 Litho. *Perf. 14*

1579 A448 40c Toys .65 .45
1580 A448 80c Food 1.25 .90
1581 A448 $1 Transport 1.60 1.10
1582 A448 $1.20 Household 1.90 1.40
1583 A448 $1.50 Collectibles 2.40 1.75
1584 A448 $1.80 Garden 2.75 2.25
Nos. 1579-1584 (6) 10.55 7.85

#1579-1584 exist in sheet of 6 created for a hard-bound Millennium book that sold for $129.

Victoria University of Wellington, Cent. A449

1999, Apr. 7 Litho. *Perf. 14*

1585 A449 40c multicolored .65 .45

1999 New Zealand U-Bix Rugby Super 12 — A450

Auckland Blues: a, Kicking ball. b, Running with ball.

Chiefs: c, Being tackled. d, Catching ball.

Wellington Hurricanes: e, Being tackled. f, Passing.

Canterbury Crusaders: g, Catching ball. h, Kicking ball.

Otago Highlanders: i, Falling down with ball. j, Running with ball.

1999, Apr. 7 *Perf. 14½*

1586 A450 40c Sheet of 10, #a.-j. 15.00 15.00

Booklet Stamps

Self-Adhesive

Die Cut Perf. 12

1587 A450 40c like #1586a .65 .45
1588 A450 40c like #1586b .65 .45
a. Bklt. pane, 5 ea #1587-1588 6.50
1589 A450 40c like #1586c .65 .45
1590 A450 40c like #1586d .65 .45
a. Bklt. pane, 5 ea #1589-1590 6.50
1591 A450 40c like #1586e .65 .45
1592 A450 40c like #1586f .65 .45
a. Bklt. pane, 5 ea #1591-1592 6.50
1593 A450 40c like #1586g .65 .45
1594 A450 40c like #1586h .65 .45
a. Bklt. pane, 5 ea #1593-1594 6.50
1595 A450 40c like #1586i .65 .45
1596 A450 40c like #1586j .65 .45
a. Bklt. pane, 5 ea #1595-1596 6.50

Nos. 1587-1588, 1589-1590, 1591-1592, 1593-1594, 1595-1596 were also issued as pairs without surrounding selvage.

Nos. 1588a, 1590a, 1592a, 1594a and 1596a are all complete booklets.

Paintings Type of 1997

Paintings by Doris Lusk: 40c, The Lake, Tuai, 1948. $1, The Pumping Station, 1958. $1.50, Arcade Awning, St. Mark's Square, Venice (2), 1976. $1.80, Tuan St. II, 1982.

1999, June 16 Litho. *Perf. 14*

1597 A425 40c multicolored .65 .45
1598 A425 $1 multicolored 1.60 1.10
1599 A425 $1.50 multicolored 2.40 1.75
1600 A425 $1.80 multicolored 2.75 2.25
a. Souv. sheet of 2, #1597, 1600 5.00 5.00
Nos. 1597-1600 (4) 7.40 5.55

No. 1600a was issued 7/2/99 for PhilexFrance '99, World Philatelic Exhibition.

Asia-Pacific Economic Cooperation (APEC) — A451

1999, July 21 Litho. *Perf. 14*

1601 A451 40c multicolored .65 .45

Scenic Walks A452

Designs: 40c, West Ruggedy Beach, Stewart Island. 80c, Ice Lake, Butler Valley, Westland. $1, Tonga Bay, Abel Tasman Natl. Park. $1.20, East Matakitaki Valley, Nelson Lakes Natl. Park. $1.50, Great Barrier Island. $1.80, Mt. Taranaki/Egmont.

1999, July 28

1602 A452 40c multicolored .65 .45
a. Booklet pane of 1 .65
1603 A452 80c multicolored 1.25 .90
a. Booklet pane of 1 1.25
1604 A452 $1 multicolored 1.60 1.10
a. Booklet pane of 1 1.60
1605 A452 $1.20 multicolored 1.90 1.40
a. Booklet pane of 1 1.90
1606 A452 $1.50 multicolored 2.40 1.75
a. Booklet pane of 1 2.40
1607 A452 $1.80 multicolored 2.75 2.25
a. Booklet pane of 1 2.75
b. Bklt. pane of 6, #1602-1607 11.00
Complete booklet, 1 each #1602a-1607a, 1607b 22.50
c. Souvenir sheet of 1 2.75 2.25
Nos. 1602-1607 (6) 10.55 7.85

Issued: No. 1607c, 10/1.

Christmas A453

1999, Sept. 8 Litho. *Perf. 13*

1608 A453 40c Baby in manger .65 .25
1609 A453 80c Virgin Mary 1.25 .90
1610 A453 $1.10 Joseph and Mary 1.75 1.10
1611 A453 $1.20 Angel with harp 1.90 1.40
1612 A453 $1.50 Shepherds 2.40 1.75
1613 A453 $1.80 Three Magi 2.75 2.25
Nos. 1608-1613 (6) 10.70 7.65

Self-Adhesive

Size: 23x27mm

Die Cut Perf. 9½x10

1614 A453 40c Baby in manger .65 .25
a. Booklet pane of 10 6.50

No. 1614a is a complete booklet.

Yachting — A454

1999, Oct. 20 Litho. *Perf. 14*

1615 A454 40c P Class .65 .45
1616 A454 80c Laser 1.25 .90
1617 A454 $1.10 18-foot skiff 1.75 1.25
1618 A454 $1.20 Hobie Cat 1.90 1.40
1619 A454 $1.50 Racing yacht 2.40 1.75
1620 A454 $1.80 Cruising yacht 2.75 2.25
a. Souvenir sheet of 6, #1615-1620 11.00 11.00
Nos. 1615-1620 (6) 10.70 8.00

Nos. 1615-1620 exist in an imperf souvenir sheet from a "Limited Edition" album.

Self-Adhesive

Size: 25x30mm

Die Cut Perf. 9½x10

1621 A454 40c Optimist .65 .40
a. Booklet pane of 10 6.50

No. 1621a is a complete booklet.

Millennium — A455

New Zealanders Leading the Way: 40c, Women, ballot box. 80c, Airplane of Richard Pearse, pioneer aviator. $1.10, Lord Ernest Rutherford, physicist. $1.20, Jet boat. $1.50, Sir Edmund Hillary, Mt. Everest. $1.80, Antinuclear protesters.

1999, Nov. 17 Litho. *Perf. 14x14¼*

1622 A455 40c multicolored .65 .45
1623 A455 80c multicolored 1.25 .90
1624 A455 $1.10 multicolored 1.75 1.25
1625 A455 $1.20 multicolored 1.90 1.40
1626 A455 $1.50 multicolored 2.40 1.75
1627 A455 $1.80 multicolored 2.75 2.25
Nos. 1622-1627 (6) 10.70 8.00

#1622-1627 exist in sheet of 6 created for a hard-bound millennium book that sold for $129.

Year 2000 A456

2000, Jan. 1 Litho. *Perf. 14¼*

1628 A456 40c multi .65 .45
a. Miniature sheet of 10 6.50 4.50

No. 1628 exists in a sheet of 6 created for a hard-bound Millennium book that sold for $129.

The third stamp in the left column on No. 1628a is missing the map and sun emblem between the time and country name.

New Year 2000 (Year of the Dragon) — A457

Spirits and guardians: 40c, Araiteuru. 80c, Kurangaituku. $1.10, Te Hoata and Te Pupu. $1.20, Patupaiarehe. $1.50, Te Ngarara-huarau. $1.80, Tuhirangi.

2000, Feb. 9 Litho. *Perf. 14*

1629 A457 40c multi .65 .45
1630 A457 80c multi 1.25 .90
1631 A457 $1.10 multi 1.75 1.25
1632 A457 $1.20 multi 1.90 1.40
1633 A457 $1.50 multi 2.40 1.75
1634 A457 $1.80 multi 2.75 2.25
a. Souv. sheet of 2, #1633-1634 5.25 5.25
Nos. 1629-1634 (6) 10.70 8.00

Nos. 1631-1632 exist in a souvenir sheet from a "Limited Edition" album.

Kiwi Type of 1988

2000, Mar. 6 Litho. *Perf. 14½*

1635 A325 $1.10 gold 1.75 1.75
a. Souv. sheet, #918b, 1027a, 1161b, 1445, 1635 8.25 8.25

Used value is for stamp with complete selvage.

#1635a issued 7/7 for World Stamp Expo 2000, Anaheim.

The 2000 sheets contain: #1694, 1635, 1671; #1662, 1634, 1638; #1677, 1665, 1656. See note following #1404.

Scenic Views Type of 1995

$1, Taiaroa Head. $1.10, Kaikoura Coast. $2, Great Barrier Is. $3, Cape Kidnappers.

2000 Litho. *Perf. 13¼x13½*

Size: 27x22mm

1636 A404 $1 multi 1.60 1.00
1637 A404 $1.10 multi 1.75 1.10
1638 A404 $2 multi 3.25 2.25
1639 A404 $3 multi 4.75 3.25
a. Souv. sheet, #1636, 1638-1639 9.75 9.75
Nos. 1636-1639 (4) 11.35 7.60

Self-Adhesive

Booklet Stamp

Die Cut Perf 10x9¾

1640 A404 $1.10 Like #1637 1.75 1.10
a. Booklet, 5 #1640 + 5 etiquettes 8.75

The Stamp Show 2000, London (No. 1639a).

Issued: #1639a, 5/22; #1640, 4/3; others, 3/6.

New Zealand Popular Culture — A458

Kiwi with: #1641, Insulated cooler. #1642, Pipis. #1643, Inflatable beach cushion. #1644, Chocolate fish. #1645, Beach house and surf board. #1646, Barbecue. #1647, Ug boots. #1648, Anzac biscuit. #1649, Hot dog. #1650, Meat pie.

Die Cut Perf. 9¾x10

2000, Apr. 3 Litho.

Booklet Stamps

Self-Adhesive

1641 A458 40c multi .65 .45
1642 A458 40c multi .65 .45
1643 A458 40c multi .65 .45
1644 A458 40c multi .65 .45
1645 A458 40c multi .65 .45
1646 A458 40c multi .65 .45
1647 A458 40c multi .65 .45
1648 A458 40c multi .65 .45
1649 A458 40c multi .65 .45
1650 A458 40c multi .65 .45
a. Booklet, #1641-1650 6.50
b. Sheet, #1641-1650 6.50

No. 1650b has plain backing paper.

Automobiles A459

40c, Volkswagen Beetle. 80c, Ford Zephyr MK I. $1.10, Morris Mini MK II. $1.20, Holden HQ Kingswood. $1.50, Honda Civic EB2. $1.80, Toyota Corolla.

2000, June 1 *Perf. 14*

1651 A459 40c claret .65 .45
a. Booklet pane of 1 .65
1652 A459 80c blue 1.25 .90
a. Booklet pane of 1 1.25
1653 A459 $1.10 brown 1.75 1.25
a. Booklet pane of 1 1.75
1654 A459 $1.20 green 1.90 1.40
a. Booklet pane of 1 1.90
1655 A459 $1.50 olive grn 2.40 1.75
a. Booklet pane of 1 2.40
1656 A459 $1.80 violet 2.75 2.25
a. Booklet pane of 1 2.75
b. Booklet pane, #1651-1656 11.00
Booklet, #1651a-1656a, 1656b 22.50
Nos. 1651-1656 (6) 10.70 8.00

A miniature sheet containing #1651-1656, both perf and imperf within the sheet, exists. This comes from a "Limited Edition" album.

Scenic Reflections A460

Designs: 40c, Lake Lyndon. 80c, Lake Wakatipu. $1.10, Mt. Ruapehu. $1.20, Rainbow Mountain Scenic Reserve. $1.50, Tairua Harbor. $1.80, Lake Alexandrina.

2000, July 7 Litho. *Perf. 14*

1657 A460 40c multi .65 .45
1658 A460 80c multi 1.25 .90
1659 A460 $1.10 multi 1.75 1.25
1660 A460 $1.20 multi 1.90 1.40
1661 A460 $1.50 multi 2.40 1.75
1662 A460 $1.80 multi 2.75 2.25
a. Souvenir Sheet, #1657, 1662 4.00 4.00
Nos. 1657-1662 (6) 10.70 8.00

No. 1662a issued 10/5/00 for Canpex 2000 Stamp Exhibition, Christchurch.

Queen Mother's 100th Birthday A461

Queen Mother in: 40c, 1907. $1.10, 1966. $1.80, 1997.

2000, Aug. 4

1663 A461 40c multi .65 .45
1664 A461 $1.10 multi 1.75 1.25
1665 A461 $1.80 multi 2.75 2.25
a. Souvenir sheet, #1663-1665 4.75 4.75
Nos. 1663-1665 (3) 5.15 3.95

Sports A462

2000, Aug. 4 *Perf. 14x14¼*

1666 A462 40c Rowing .65 .45
1667 A462 80c Equestrian 1.25 .90
1668 A462 $1.10 Cycling 1.75 1.25
1669 A462 $1.20 Triathlon 1.90 1.40
1670 A462 $1.50 Lawn bowling 2.40 1.75
1671 A462 $1.80 Netball 2.75 2.25
Nos. 1666-1671 (6) 10.70 8.00

2000 Summer Olympics, Sydney (Nos. 1666-1669).

Christmas A463

Designs: 40c, Madonna and child. 80c, Mary, Joseph and donkey. $1.10, Baby Jesus, cow, lamb. $1.20, Archangel. $1.50, Shepherd and lamb. $1.80, Magi.

2000, Sept. 6 *Perf. 14*

1672 A463 40c multi .65 .35
1673 A463 80c multi 1.25 .90
1674 A463 $1.10 multi 1.75 1.25
1675 A463 $1.20 multi 1.90 1.40
1676 A463 $1.50 multi 2.40 1.75
1677 A463 $1.80 multi 2.75 2.25
Nos. 1672-1677 (6) 10.70 7.90

Self-Adhesive

Size: 30x25mm

Serpentine Die Cut 11¼x11

1678 A463 40c multi .65 .25
a. Booklet of 10 6.50

Issued: No. 1678a, 11/1/00.

Scenic Views Type of 1995

Designs: 90c, Rangitoto Island. $1.30, Lake Camp, South Canterbury.

2000 Litho. *Perf. 13¼x13½*
Size: 27x22mm

1679 A404 90c multi 1.40 .75
1680 A404 $1.30 multi 2.10 1.10
a. Souvenir sheet, #1636-1637, 1679-1680 7.00 7.00

Issued: Nos. 1679-1680, 10/2/00; No. 1680a, 3/16/01. 2001: A Stamp Odyssey Philatelic Exhibition, Invercargill (#1680a).

Teddy Bears and Dolls — A464

Designs: 40c+5c, Teddy bear "Geronimo," by Rose Hill. 80c+5c, Antique French and wooden Schoenhut dolls. $1.10, Chad Valley bear. $1.20, Doll "Poppy," by Debbie Pointon. $1.50, Teddy bears "Swanni," by Robin Rive, and "Dear John," by Rose Hill. $1.80, Doll "Lia," by Gloria Young, and teddy bear.

2000, Oct. 5 *Perf. 14½x14¾*

1681 A464 40c +5c multi .65 .40
1682 A464 80c +5c multi 1.25 .70
a. Souvenir sheet, #1681-1682 1.90 1.10
1683 A464 $1.10 multi 1.75 .90
1684 A464 $1.20 multi 1.90 1.00
1685 A464 $1.50 multi 2.40 1.25
1686 A464 $1.80 multi 2.75 1.60
a. Block of 6, #1681-1686 10.00 10.00

Coil Stamp
Size: 30x25mm
Self-Adhesive
Serpentine Die Cut 11¼

1687 A464 40c +5c multi .65 .40

Endangered Birds — A465

Designs: No. 1688, Lesser kestrel. No. 1689, Orange fronted parakeet. 80c, Black stilt. $1.10, Stewart Island fernbird. $1.20, Kakapo. $1.50, North Island weka. $1.80, Okarito brown kiwi.

2000, Nov. 4 *Perf. 14*

1688 A465 40c multi .65 .45
1689 A465 40c multi .65 .45
a. Pair, #1688-1689 1.40 1.00
1690 A465 80c multi 1.25 .90
1691 A465 $1.10 multi 1.75 1.25
1692 A465 $1.20 multi 1.90 1.40
1693 A465 $1.50 multi 2.40 1.75
1694 A465 $1.80 multi 2.75 2.25
a. Souvenir sheet, #1693-1694 5.75 5.75
Nos. 1688-1694 (7) 11.35 8.45

Nos. 1689-1690 exist in a souvenir sheet from a "Limited Edition" album.

Issued: No. 1694a, 2/1/01. Hong Kong 2001 Stamp Exhibition (#1694a). See France Nos. 2790-2791.

Penny Universal Postage, Cent. — A466

Methods of mail delivery: a, Steamship. b, Horse-drawn coach. c, Early mail truck. d, Paddle steamer. e, Railway traveling post office. f, Airplane with front cargo hatch. g, Bicycle. h, Tractor trailer. i, Airplane with side cargo hatch. j, Computer mouse.

2001, Jan. 1

1695 Sheet of 10 6.50 6.50
a.-j. A466 40c Any single .65 .65
k. As No. 1695, with Belgica 2001 sheet margin 6.50 6.50

No. 1695k has no perforations running through sheet margin.

Marine Reptiles — A467

Designs: 40c, Green turtle. 80c, Leathery turtle. 90c, Loggerhead turtle. $1.30, Hawksbill turtle. $1.50, Banded sea snake. $2, Yellow-bellied sea snake.

2001, Feb. 1

1696 A467 40c multi .65 .45
1697 A467 80c multi 1.25 .90
1698 A467 90c multi 1.40 1.00
1699 A467 $1.30 multi 2.10 1.50
1700 A467 $1.50 multi 2.40 1.75
1701 A467 $2 multi 3.25 2.50
a. Souvenir sheet, #1700-1701 5.75 5.75
Nos. 1696-1701 (6) 11.05 8.10

New Year 2001 (Year of the snake) (#1701a).

Flowers A468

2001, Mar. 7

1702 A468 40c Camellia .65 .45
1703 A468 80c Siberian iris 1.25 .90
1704 A468 90c Daffodil 1.40 1.00
1705 A468 $1.30 Chrysanthemum 2.10 1.50
1706 A468 $1.50 Sweet pea 2.40 1.75
1707 A468 $2 Petunia 3.25 2.50
a. Souvenir sheet, #1702-1707 11.00 11.00
Nos. 1702-1707 (6) 11.05 8.10

No. 1707a exists imperf from a "Limited Edition" album.

Art From Nature A469

2001, Apr. 4 Litho. *Perf. 14¼*

1708 A469 40c Greenstone .65 .45
1709 A469 80c Oamaru stone 1.25 .90
1710 A469 90c Paua 1.40 1.00
1711 A469 $1.30 Kauri gum 2.10 1.50
1712 A469 $1.50 Flax 2.40 1.75
1713 A469 $2 Fern 3.25 2.50
Nos. 1708-1713 (6) 11.05 8.10

Within sheets of 25 printed for each stamp are four blocks of four showing a circular design, made by rotating each stamp design 90 degrees.

Aircraft A470

Designs: 40c, Douglas DC-3. 80c, Fletcher FU24 Topdresser. 90c, De Havilland DH82A Tiger Moth. $1.30, Fokker FVIIb/3m. $1.50, De Havilland DH100 Vampire. $2, Boeing & Westervelt Seaplane.

2001, May 2 *Perf. 14x14¼*

1714 A470 40c multi .65 .45
a. Booklet pane of 1 .65
1715 A470 80c multi 1.25 .90
a. Booklet pane of 1 1.25
1716 A470 90c multi 1.40 1.00
a. Booklet pane of 1 1.40
1717 A470 $1.30 multi 2.10 1.50
a. Booklet pane of 1 2.10
1718 A470 $1.50 multi 2.40 1.75
a. Booklet pane of 1 2.40
1719 A470 $2 multi 3.25 2.50
a. Booklet pane of 1 3.25
b. Booklet pane, #1714-1719 11.00
Booklet, #1714a-1719a, 1719b 22.50
Nos. 1714-1719 (6) 11.05 8.10

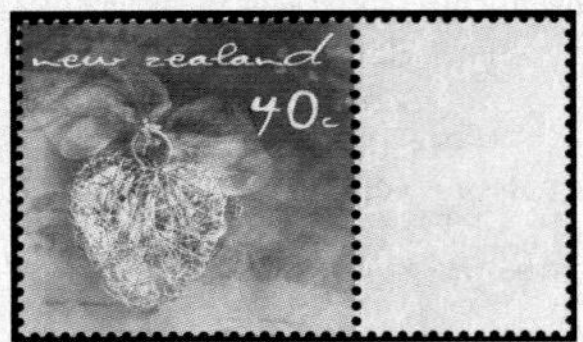

Greetings — A471

No. 1720: a, Heart. b, Balloons. c, Flower. d, Gift. e, Trumpet.

No. 1721: a, Candles. b, Stars. c, Roses and candle. d, Picture frame. e, Letter and fountain pen.

2001, June 6 *Perf. 14½x14*

1720 Vert. strip of 5 + 5 labels 3.25 2.50
a.-e. A471 40c Any single + label .65 .35
1721 Vert. strip of 5 + 5 labels 7.00 5.00
a.-e. A471 90c Any single + label 1.40 .75

Labels could be personalized on sheets that sold for $15.95 and $27.95 respectively.

Government Tourist Office, Cent. — A472

Designs: 40c, Bungee jumper, Queenstown. 80c, Canoeing on Lake Rotoiti. 90c, Sightseers on Mt. Alfred. $1.30, Fishing in Glenorchy River. $1.50, Kayakers in Abel Tasman Natl. Park. $2, Hiker in Fiordland Natl. Park.

2001 Litho. *Perf. 14¼*

1722 A472 40c multi .65 .45
1723 A472 80c multi 1.25 .80
1724 A472 90c multi 1.40 1.00
1725 A472 $1.30 multi 2.10 1.50
1726 A472 $1.50 multi 2.40 1.75
1727 A472 $2 multi 3.25 2.50
a. Souvenir sheet, #1726-1727 6.00 6.00

Size: 26x21mm
Serpentine Die Cut 11¼x11
Self-Adhesive

1728 A472 40c multi .65 .45
a. Booklet of 10 + 10 etiquettes 6.50
1729 A472 90c multi 1.40 1.00
a. Booklet of 10 + 10 etiquettes 14.00
1730 A472 $1.50 multi 2.40 1.75
a. Horiz. strip, #1728-1730 4.50
b. Booklet of 5 + 5 etiquettes 12.00

Coil Stamp
Size: 26x21mm
Self-Adhesive
Serpentine Die Cut 10x9¾

1730C A472 40c Like #1722 .65 .35
Nos. 1722-1730C (10) 16.15 11.55

Phila Nippon '01, Japan (No. 1727a). Issued: No. 1727a, 8/1; others, 7/4.

A sheet containing 3 each of Nos. 1722-1727 was included in a book that sold for $69.95.

Christmas — A473

Designs: 40c, In Excelsis Gloria. 80c, Away in the Manger. 90c, Joy to the World. $1.30, Angels We Have Heard on High. $1.50, O Holy Night. $2, While Shepherds Watched Their Flocks.

2001, Sept. 5 *Perf. 13¼x13¾*

1731 A473 40c multi .65 .35
1732 A473 80c multi 1.25 .90
1733 A473 90c multi 1.40 1.00
1734 A473 $1.30 multi 2.10 1.50
1735 A473 $1.50 multi 2.40 1.75
1736 A473 $2 multi 3.25 2.50

Size: 21x26mm
Serpentine Die Cut 9¾x10
Self-Adhesive

1737 A473 40c multi .65 .25
a. Booklet of 10 6.50
Nos. 1731-1737 (7) 11.70 8.25

Issued: No. 1737a, 11/7/01.

Visit of Queen Elizabeth II, Oct. 2001 — A474

Queen in past visits: 40c, Arriving for opening of Parliament, 1953. 80c, With crowd, 1970. 90c, With crowd, 1977. $1.30, With crowd, 1986. $1.50, At Commonwealth Games, 1990. $2, 2001 portrait.

2001, Oct. 3 Litho. *Perf. 14*

1738 A474 40c multi .65 .45
1739 A474 80c multi 1.25 .90
1740 A474 90c multi 1.40 1.00
1741 A474 $1.30 multi 2.10 1.50
1742 A474 $1.50 multi 2.40 1.75
1743 A474 $2 multi 3.25 2.50
a. Horiz. strip, #1738-1743 11.00 11.00
Nos. 1738-1743 (6) 11.05 8.10

Nos. 1738-1743 exist in a souvenir sheet from a "Limited Edition" album.

Penguins A475

Designs: 40c, Rockhopper. 80c, Little blue. 90c, Snares crested. $1.30, Erect-crested. $1.50, Fiordland crested. $2, Yellow-eyed.

2001, Nov. 7 *Perf. 14¼*

1744 A475 40c multi .65 .45
1745 A475 80c multi 1.25 .90
1746 A475 90c multi 1.40 1.00
1747 A475 $1.30 multi 2.10 1.50
1748 A475 $1.50 multi 2.40 1.75
1749 A475 $2 multi 3.25 2.40
Nos. 1744-1749 (6) 11.05 8.00

Filming in New Zealand of The Lord of the Rings Trilogy — A476

Scenes from "The Lord of the Rings: The Fellowship of the Ring:" 40c, Gandalf the Gray and Saruman the White, vert. 80c, Lady Galadriel, vert. 90c, Sam Gamgee and Frodo Baggins. $1.30, Guardian of Rivendell, vert. $1.50, Strider, vert. $2, Boromir, son of Denethor.

Perf. 14½x14, 14x14½
2001, Dec. 4 Litho.

1750 A476 40c multi .75 .50
a. Souvenir sheet of 1 2.25 1.75
b. Sheet of 10 #1750 7.50 —
1751 A476 80c multi 1.75 1.25
a. Souvenir sheet of 1 4.00 3.50
1752 A476 90c multi 2.00 2.00
a. Souvenir sheet of 1 4.75 4.00
1753 A476 $1.30 multi 2.75 2.75
a. Souvenir sheet of 1 6.50 5.75
1754 A476 $1.50 multi 3.00 3.00
a. Souvenir sheet of 1 7.50 6.50
1755 A476 $2 multi 4.00 4.00
a. Souvenir sheet of 1 11.00 8.75
b. Souvenir sheet, #1754-1755 7.50 7.50
c. Souvenir sheet, #1750, 1753, 1755 9.00 9.00

Self-Adhesive

Serpentine Die Cut 10x10¼, 10¼x10

Size: 22x33mm, 33x22mm

1756 A476 40c multi .75 .50
1757 A476 80c multi 1.75 1.75
1758 A476 90c multi 2.00 2.00
1759 A476 $1.30 multi 2.75 2.75
1760 A476 $1.50 multi 3.00 3.00
1761 A476 $2 multi 4.00 4.00
a. Pane, #1756-1761 *16.00*
b. Booklet pane, #1757, 1759-1761, 4 #1756, 2 #1758 *35.00*
Nos. 1750-1761 (12) 28.50 28.00

Issued: No. 1755b, 8/30/02; No. 1755c, 4/5/02. Other values, 12/4/01.

No. 1755b issued for Amphilex 2002 World Stamp Exhibition, Amsterdam; No. 1755c issued for Northpex 2002.

New Year 2002 (Year of the Horse) A477

Champion race horses: 40c, Christian Cullen. 80c, Lyell Creek. 90c, Yulestar. $1.30, Sunline. $1.50, Ethereal. $2, Zabeel.

2002, Feb. 7 ***Perf. 14***

1762 A477 40c multi .65 .45
1763 A477 80c multi 1.25 .90
1764 A477 90c multi 1.40 1.00
1765 A477 $1.30 multi 2.10 1.50
1766 A477 $1.50 multi 2.40 1.75
a. Souvenir sheet, #1765-1766 4.50 4.50
1767 A477 $2 multi 3.25 2.50
Nos. 1762-1767 (6) 11.05 8.10

Fungi — A478

Designs: 40c, Hygrocybe rubrocarnosa. 80c, Entoloma hochstetteri. 90c, Aseroe rubra. $1.30, Hericium coralloides. $1.50, Thaxterogaster porphyreus. $2, Ramaria aureorhiza.

2002, Mar. 6 **Litho.** ***Perf. 14***

1768 A478 40c multi .65 .45
1769 A478 80c multi 1.25 .90
1770 A478 90c multi 1.40 1.00
1771 A478 $1.30 multi 2.10 1.50
1772 A478 $1.50 multi 2.40 1.75
1773 A478 $2 multi 3.75 2.50
a. Souvenir sheet, #1768-1773 11.00 11.00
Nos. 1768-1773 (6) 11.55 8.10

No. 1773a exists as an imperforate souvenir sheet from a "Limited Edition" album.

A479

A480

Architectural Heritage — A481

Designs: 40c, War Memorial Museum, Auckland. 80c, Stone Store, Kerikeri. 90c, Arts Center, Christchurch. $1.30, Government buildings, Wellington. $1.50, Railway Station, Dunedin. $2, Sky Tower, Auckland.

2002, Apr. 3 **Litho.** ***Perf. 14½x14***

1774 A479 40c multi .65 .45
a. Booklet pane of 1 .65 —
1775 A480 80c multi 1.25 .90
a. Booklet pane of 1 1.25 —
1776 A481 90c multi 1.40 1.00
a. Booklet pane of 1 1.40 —
1777 A481 $1.30 multi 2.10 1.50
a. Booklet pane of 1 2.10 —
1778 A480 $1.50 multi 2.40 1.75
a. Booklet pane of 1 2.40 —
1779 A479 $2 multi 3.25 2.50
a. Booklet pane of 1 3.25 —
b. Block of 6, #1774-1779 11.00 11.00
c. Booklet pane, #1779b 12.00 —
Booklet, #1774a-1779a, 1779c 22.50
Nos. 1774-1779 (6) 11.05 8.10

Booklet containing Nos. 1774a-1779a, 1779c sold for $16.95.

Art from Sweden and New Zealand A482

Designs: No. 1780, Maori basket, by Willa Rogers, New Zealand. No. 1781, Starfish Vessel, by Graeme Priddle, New Zealand. 80c, Catch II, by Raewyn Atkinson, New Zealand. 90c, Silver brooch, by Gavin Hithings, New Zealand. $1.30, Glass towers, by Emma Camden, New Zealand. $1.50, Pacific Rim, by Merilyn Wiseman. $2, Rain Forest, glass vase by Ola Höglund, Sweden.

Litho. & Engr. (#1780, 1786), Litho.

Perf. 12½x12¾ (#1780, 1786), 14

2002, May 2

1780 A482 40c multi .65 .35
1781 A482 40c multi .65 .35
1782 A482 80c multi 1.25 .75
1783 A482 90c multi 1.40 .80
1784 A482 $1.30 multi 2.10 1.25
1785 A482 $1.50 multi 2.40 1.40
1786 A482 $2 multi 3.25 2.00
Nos. 1780-1786 (7) 11.70 6.90

See Sweden No. 2440.

Nos. 1780-1786 exist in a souvenir sheet from a "Limited Edition" album.

Kiwi Type of 1988

2002, June 5 **Litho.** ***Perf. 14½***

1787 A325 $1.50 brown 2.40 1.50

Used value is for stamp with complete selvage.

Queen Mother Elizabeth (1900-2002) A483

2002, June 5 ***Perf. 14¼***

1788 A483 $2 multi 2.75 2.00

Children's Book Festival Stamp Design Contest Winners A484

Art by: No. 1789, Anna Poland, Cardinal McKeefry School, Wellington. No. 1790, Hee Su Kim, Glendowie Primary School, Auckland. No. 1791, Jayne Bruce, Rangiora Borough School, Rangiora. No. 1792, Teigan Stafford-Bush (bird), Ararimu School, Auckland. No. 1793, Hazel Gilbert, Gonville School, Wanganui. No. 1794, Gerard Mackle, Temuka High School, Temuka. No. 1795, Maria Rodgers, Salford School, Invercargill. No. 1796, Paul Read (hand and ball), Ararimu School, Auckland. No. 1797, Four students, Glendene Primary School, Auckland. No. 1798, Olivia Duncan, Takapuna Normal Intermediate School, Auckland.

2002, June 5 ***Perf. 14***

1789 A484 40c multi 1.00 1.00
1790 A484 40c multi 1.00 1.00
1791 A484 40c multi 1.00 1.00
1792 A484 40c multi 1.00 1.00
1793 A484 40c multi 1.00 1.00
1794 A484 40c multi 1.00 1.00
1795 A484 40c multi 1.00 1.00
1796 A484 40c multi 1.00 1.00
1797 A484 40c multi 1.00 1.00
1798 A484 40c multi 1.00 1.00
a. Block of 10, #1789-1798 10.00 10.00
b. Sheet of 10, #1789-1798 10.00 10.00

Scenic Coastlines A485

Designs: 40c, Tongaporutu Cliffs, Taranaki. 80c, Lottin Point, East Cape. 90c, Curio Bay, Catlins. $1.30, Kaikoura Coast. $1.50, Meybille Bay, West Coast. $2, Papanui Point, Raglan.

2002, July 3 ***Perf. 14***

1799 A485 40c multi .65 .40
1800 A485 80c multi 1.25 .80
1801 A485 90c multi 1.40 .85
1802 A485 $1.30 multi 2.10 1.25
1803 A485 $1.50 multi 2.40 1.75
1804 A485 $2 multi 3.25 2.10

Size: 28x22mm

Self-Adhesive

Serpentine Die Cut 10x9¾

1805 A485 40c multi .65 .40
a. Booklet pane of 10 6.50
b. Serpentine die cut 11 .75 .55
c. Booklet pane of 10 #1805b 7.50
1806 A485 90c multi 1.40 .85
a. Booklet pane of 10 14.00
1807 A485 $1.50 multi 2.40 1.50
a. Booklet pane of 5 12.00
b. Coil strip of 3, #1805-1807 4.50

Coil Stamp

Size: 28x22mm

Self-Adhesive

Die Cut Perf. 12¾

1808 A485 40c multi .65 .40
Nos. 1799-1808 (10) 16.15 10.30

Christmas A487

Church interiors: 40c, Saint Werenfried Catholic Church, Waihi Village, Tokaannu. 80c, St. David's Anglican Church, Christchurch. 90c, Orthodox Church of the Transfiguration of Our Lord, Masterton. $1.30, Cathedral of the Holy Spirit, Palmerston North. $1.50, Cathedral of St. Paul, Wellington. $2, Cathedral of the Blessed Sacrament, Christchurch.

2002, Sept. 4 ***Perf. 14¼***

1812 A487 40c multi .65 .25
1813 A487 80c multi 1.25 .75
1814 A487 90c multi 1.40 .85
1815 A487 $1.30 multi 2.10 1.25
1816 A487 $1.50 multi 2.40 1.40
1817 A487 $2 multi 3.25 2.10

Coil Stamp

Size: 21x26mm

Self-Adhesive

Die Cut Perf. 13x12¾

1818 A487 40c multi .65 .25

Booklet Stamp

Self-Adhesive

Size: 21x26mm

1818A A487 40c Like No. 1818 .65 .25
b. Booklet pane of 10 6.50
Nos. 1812-1818A (8) 12.35 7.10

Issued: No. 1818A, 11/6/02.

Boats A488

Designs: 40c, KZ1. 80c, High 5. 90c, Gentle Spirit. $1.30, NorthStar. $1.50, OceanRunner. $2, Salperton.

2002, Oct. 2 **Litho.** ***Perf. 14***

1819 A488 40c multi .65 .35
1820 A488 80c multi 1.25 .75
1821 A488 90c multi 1.40 .85
1822 A488 $1.30 multi 2.10 1.25
1823 A488 $1.50 multi 2.40 1.40
1824 A488 $2 multi 3.25 2.10
a. Souvenir sheet, #1819-1824 11.00 11.00
Nos. 1819-1824 (6) 11.05 6.70

No. 1824a exists an an imperforate souvenir sheet from a "Limited Edition" album.

2003 America's Cup Yacht Races A489

Scenes from 2000 America's Cup finals: $1.30, Black Magic next to Luna Rossa. $1.50, Aerial view. $2, Black Magic passing Luna Rossa.

2002

1825 A489 $1.30 multi 2.10 1.25
1826 A489 $1.50 multi 2.40 1.40
1827 A489 $2 multi 3.25 2.10
a. Souvenir sheet, #1825-1827 7.75 7.75
b. As "a," with Stampshow Melbourne 02 ovpt. in margin 7.75 7.75
Nos. 1825-1827 (3) 7.75 4.75

Issued: No. 1827b, 10/4; others 10/2.

Vacation Homes A490

Various vacation homes with denominations over: No. 1828, Paua shell. No. 1829, Sunflower. No. 1830, Life preserver. No. 1831, Fish hook. No. 1832, Fish. No. 1833, Flower bouquet.

2002, Nov. 6 **Litho.** ***Perf. 14***

1828 A490 40c multi .90 .60
1829 A490 40c multi .90 .60
1830 A490 40c multi .90 .60
1831 A490 40c multi .90 .60
1832 A490 40c multi .90 .60
1833 A490 40c multi .90 .60
Nos. 1828-1833 (6) 5.40 3.60

Nativity, by Pseudo Ambrogio di Baldese — A491

2002, Nov. 21 ***Perf. 14¼x14***

1834 A491 $1.50 multi 2.40 1.50

See Vatican City No. 1232.

The Lord of the Rings Type of 2001

Scenes from *The Lord of the Rings: The Two Towers:* 40c, Aragorn and Eowyn. 80c, Orc raider. 90c, Gandalf the White, vert. $1.30, The Easterlings. $1.50, Frodo captured, vert. $2, Shield Maiden of Rohan.

2002, Dec. 4 ***Perf. 14x14½, 14½x14***

1835 A476 40c multi .65 .40
a. Souvenir sheet of 1 1.00 1.00
1836 A476 80c multi 1.25 1.25
a. Souvenir sheet of 1 2.10 2.10
1837 A476 90c multi 1.40 1.40
a. Souvenir sheet of 1 2.40 2.40

1838 A476 $1.30 multi 2.10 2.10
a. Souvenir sheet of 1 3.50 3.50
1839 A476 $1.50 multi 2.40 2.40
a. Souvenir sheet of 1 4.00 4.00
1840 A476 $2 multi 3.25 3.25
a. Souvenir sheet of 1 4.75 4.75
Set of 6 souvenir sheets of 1 each, #1835a//1840a 17.75

Self-Adhesive

Size: 34x23mm, 23x34mm

Serpentine Die Cut 10¼x10, 10x10¼

1841 A476 40c multi .65 .40
1842 A476 80c multi 1.25 1.25
1843 A476 90c multi 1.40 1.40
1844 A476 $1.30 multi 2.10 2.10
1845 A476 $1.50 multi 2.40 2.40
1846 A476 $2 multi 3.25 3.25
a. Pane, #1841-1846 11.00
b. Booklet pane, #1842, 1844-1846, 2 #1843, 4 #1841 14.50
Nos. 1835-1846 (12) 22.10 21.60

The 2002 sheets contain: #1767, 1773, 1779, 1785, 1787, 1804, 1817, 1830, B170. See note following #1404.

2003 America's Cup Yacht Races A492

Designs: 40c, Yacht and sail with sponsor's advertisements. 80c, Yachts circling. 90c, Yachts racing.

2003, Jan. 8 Litho. *Perf. 14*

1847 A492 40c multi .65 .45
1848 A492 80c multi 1.25 .85
1849 A492 90c multi 1.40 .95
a. Souvenir sheet of 3, #1847-1849 4.00 4.00
Nos. 1847-1849 (3) 3.30 2.25

New Year 2003 (Year of the Ram) A493

Designs: 40c, Sheep in high country. 90c, Sheep leaving pen. $1.30, Sheepdog and sheep. $1.50, Shearer. $2, Shearing gang.

2003, Feb. 5 Litho. *Perf. 14*

1850 A493 40c multi .65 .45
1851 A493 90c multi 1.40 1.00
1852 A493 $1.30 multi 2.10 1.40
1853 A493 $1.50 multi 2.40 1.60
1854 A493 $2 multi 3.25 2.50
a. Souvenir sheet of 2, #1852, 1854 5.25 5.25
Nos. 1850-1854 (5) 9.80 6.95

Royal New Zealand Ballet, 50th Anniv. A494

Scenes from productions of: 40c, Carmina Burana, 1971, vert. 90c, Papillon, 1989. $1.30, Cinderella, 2000, vert. $1.50, FrENZy, 2001, vert. $2, Swan lake, 2002.

2003, Mar. 5 Litho. *Perf. 14*

1855 A494 40c multi .65 .50
1856 A494 90c multi 1.40 1.10
1857 A494 $1.30 multi 2.10 1.60
1858 A494 $1.50 multi 2.40 1.90
1859 A494 $2 multi 3.25 2.75
a. Souvenir sheet, #1855, 1856, 1859 6.50 6.50
Nos. 1855-1859 (5) 9.80 7.85

No. 1859a issued for Bangkok 2003 World Philatelic Exhibition.

Nos. 1855-1859 exist in a souvenir sheet from a "Limited Edition" album.

Military Uniforms, Medals and Insignia — A495

No. 1860: a, Forest ranger, 1860s. b, Napier naval artillery volunteer officer, 1890s. c, Amuri mounted rifles officer, 1900-10. d, Mounted Rifles, South Africa, 1898-1902. e, Staff officer, France, 1918. f, Petty officer, 1914-18. g, Infantry, France, 1916-18. h, Engineer, 1939-45. i, Matron, RNZN Hospital, 1940s. j, WAAC, Egypt, 1942. k, Bomber pilot, Europe, 1943. l, Fighter pilot, Pacific, 1943. m, WAAF driver, 1943. n, Gunner, Korea, 1950-53. o, Petty officer, 1950s. p, SAS, Malaya, 1955-57. q, Canberra Pilot, 1960. r, Infantry, Viet Nam, 1960s. s, UN Peacekeeper, East Timor, 2000. t, Peace Monitor, Bougainville, 2001.

2003, Apr. 2 Litho. *Perf. 14*

1860 Sheet of 20 20.00 20.00
a.-t. A495 40c Any single 1.00 .45
u. Booklet pane, 2 each #a-d 8.00 —
v. Booklet pane, 2 each #e-h 8.00 —
w. Booklet pane, 2 each #i-l 8.00 —
x. Booklet pane, 2 each #m-p 8.00 —
y. Booklet pane, 2 each #q-t 8.00 —
Complete booklet, #u-y 40.00

Tourist Attractions A496

Designs: 50c, Ailsa Mountains. $1, Coromandel Peninsula. $1.50, Arrowtown. $2, Tongariro National Park. $5, Castlepoint.

2003, May 7 Litho. *Perf. 13¼x13½*

1861 A496 50c multi .80 .55
1862 A496 $1 multi 1.60 1.10
1863 A496 $1.50 multi 2.40 1.75
1863A A496 $1.50 multi 2.40 1.75
1864 A496 $2 multi 3.25 2.50
1865 A496 $5 multi 8.00 6.25

Self-Adhesive

Serpentine Die Cut 10x9½

1866 A496 $1.50 multi 2.25 1.75
a. Booklet pane of 5 11.00
1866B A496 $1.50 As #1866, vignette 26mm wide 2.40 2.40
c. Booklet pane of 5 #1866b + 10 etiquettes 12.00
Nos. 1861-1866 (7) 20.70 15.65

Nos. 1861-1865 exist with silver fern leaf overprints from a limited printing.

Nos. 1866b, 1866c issued 3/27/07. Vignette of No. 1866 is 27mm wide. No. 1863A issued 2007.

Nos. 1863A and 1866B show a person on the sidewalk in front of the door of the house in the foreground (above the zero in the denomination). The person is not found on Nos. 1863 and 1866.

Ascent of Mt. Everest, 50th Anniv. A497

Designs: No. 1867, Sir Edmund Hillary, Mt. Everest. No. 1868, Tenzing Norgay, climbers on mountain.

2003, May 29 *Perf. 14*

1867 A497 40c multi 1.10 1.10
1868 A497 40c multi 1.10 1.10
a. Pair, #1867-1868 2.25 2.25

Coronation Type of 1953

Perf. 14x14½, 14½x14

2003, June 4 Litho.

1869 A113 40c Like #280 .65 .50
1870 A113 90c Like #281 1.40 1.00
1871 A112 $1.30 Like #282 2.10 1.50
1872 A114 $1.50 Like #283 2.40 1.75
1873 A112 $2 Like #284 3.25 2.50
Nos. 1869-1873 (5) 9.80 7.25

Nos. 1869-1873 exist in a souvenir sheet from a "Limited Edition" album.

Test Rugby, Cent. A498

Designs: 40c, New Zealand vs. South Africa, 1937. 90c, New Zealand vs. Wales, 1963. $1.30, New Zealand vs. Australia, 1985. No.1877, New Zealand vs. France, 1986. No. 1878, All Blacks jersey. $2, New Zealand vs. England, 1997.

2003, July 2 *Perf. 14*

1874 A498 40c multi .65 .50
1875 A498 90c multi 1.40 1.00
1876 A498 $1.30 multi 2.10 1.50
1877 A498 $1.50 multi 2.40 1.75
1878 A498 $1.50 multi 2.40 1.75
1879 A498 $2 multi 3.25 2.50
a. Souvenir sheet, #1874-1879 12.50 12.50
b. Sheet, #1877-1879 8.25 8.25
c. Souvenir sheet, #1878-1879 6.00 6.00
Nos. 1874-1879 (6) 12.20 9.00

No. 1879b issued 11/7 for Welpex 2003 Stampshow, Wellington. No. 1879b sold for $6.

No. 1879c issued 1/30/04 for 2004 Hong Kong Stamp Expo (#1879c).

Waterways A499

Designs: 40c, Papaaroha, Coromandel Peninsula. 90c, Waimahana Creek, Chatham Islands. $1.30, Blue Lake, Central Otago. $1.50, Waikato River, Waikato. $2, Hooker River, Canterbury.

2003, Aug. 6 Litho. *Perf. 14¼*

1880 A499 40c multi .65 .50
1881 A499 90c multi 1.40 1.00
1882 A499 $1.30 multi 2.10 1.50
1883 A499 $1.50 multi 2.40 1.75
1884 A499 $2 multi 3.25 2.50
Nos. 1880-1884 (5) 9.80 7.25

Antique Automobiles A500

Designs: 40c, 1895 Benz Velo. 90c, 1903 Oldsmobile. $1.30, 1911 Wolseley. $1.50, 1915 Talbot. $2, 1915 Ford Model T.

2003, Sept. 3 Litho. *Perf. 13x13¼*

1885 A500 40c multi .65 .45
1886 A500 90c multi 1.40 1.10
1887 A500 $1.30 multi 2.10 1.50
1888 A500 $1.50 multi 2.40 1.75
1889 A500 $2 multi 3.25 2.50
Nos. 1885-1889 (5) 9.80 7.30

Christmas A501

Tree decorations: 40c, Christ child. 90c, Dove. $1.30, Geometric (candles). $1.50, Bells. $2, Angel.

$1, Geometric (fleur-de-lis).

2003, Oct. 1 *Perf. 13½*

1890 A501 40c multi .65 .40
1891 A501 90c multi 1.40 1.10
1892 A501 $1.30 multi 2.10 1.60
1893 A501 $1.50 multi 2.40 1.75
1894 A501 $2 multi 3.25 2.50

Self-Adhesive

Serpentine Die Cut 9½x10

Size: 21x26mm

1895 A501 40c multi .65 .40
a. Booklet pane of 10 6.50
1896 A501 $1 multi 1.60 1.25
a. Booklet pane of 8 + 8 etiquettes 13.00
Nos. 1890-1896 (7) 12.05 9.00

The Lord of the Rings Type of 2001

Scenes from *The Lord of the Rings: The Return of the King:* 40c, Legolas, vert. 80c, Frodo, vert. 90c, Merry and Pippin. $1.30, Aragorn, vert. $1.50, Gandalf the White, vert. $2, Gollum.

2003, Nov. 5 *Perf. 14½x14, 14x14½*

1897 A476 40c multi .65 .50
a. Souvenir sheet of 1 .90 .90
1898 A476 80c multi 1.25 1.25
a. Souvenir sheet of 1 1.60 1.60
1899 A476 90c multi 1.40 1.40
a. Souvenir sheet of 1 2.00 2.00
1900 A476 $1.30 multi 2.10 2.10
a. Souvenir sheet of 1 2.50 2.50
1901 A476 $1.50 multi 2.40 2.40
a. Souvenir sheet of 1 3.00 3.00
1902 A476 $2 multi 3.25 3.25
a. Souvenir sheet of 1 4.25 4.25
Set of 6 souvenir sheets of 1 each, #1897a-1902a 14.25

Self-Adhesive

Size: 23x34mm, 34x23mm

Serpentine Die Cut 10x10¼, 10¼x10

1903 A476 40c multi .65 .50
1904 A476 80c multi 1.25 1.00
1905 A476 90c multi 1.40 1.10
1906 A476 $1.30 multi 2.10 1.60
1907 A476 $1.50 multi 2.40 1.90
1908 A476 $2 multi 3.25 2.75
a. Pane, #1903-1908 11.00
b. Booklet pane, #1904, 1906-1908, 2 #1905, 4 #1903 14.00
Nos. 1897-1908 (12) 22.10 19.75

The 2003 sheets contain: #1854, 1859, 1864, 1873, 1879, 1884, 1889, 1894, 1902. See note following #1404.

Scenic Views Type of 1995

Serpentine Die Cut 10x9¾

2004, Jan. 28 Litho.

Booklet Stamp

Size: 26x21mm

Self-Adhesive

1909 A404 10c Like #1346 .20 .20
a. Booklet pane, 10 #1359F, 4 #1909 6.00

Zoo Animals — A502

Designs: 40c, Hamadryas baboon. 90c, Malayan sun bear. $1.30, Red panda. $1.50, Ring-tailed lemur. $2, Spider monkey.

2004, Jan. 28 Litho. *Perf. 13¼x13*

1910 A502 40c multi .65 .55
1911 A502 90c multi 1.40 1.25
1912 A502 $1.30 multi 2.10 1.75
1913 A502 $1.50 multi 2.40 2.00
1914 A502 $2 multi 3.25 3.25
a. Souvenir sheet, #1913-1914 5.75 5.75

Nos. 1910-1914 exist in a souvenir sheet from a "Limited Edition" album.

Self-Adhesive

Size: 21x26mm

Coil Stamp

Die Cut Perf. 12¾x12½

1915 A502 40c multi .65 .55

Booklet Stamp

Serpentine Die Cut 11¼

1916 A502 40c multi .65 .55
a. Booklet pane of 10 6.50
Nos. 1910-1916 (7) 11.10 9.90

New Year 2004 (Year of the Monkey) (#1914a).

Rugby Sevens
A503

Designs: 40c, New Zealand Sevens. 90c, Hong Kong Sevens. $1.50, Hong Kong Stadium. $2, Westpac Stadium, Wellington.

2004, Feb. 25 Litho. ***Perf. 14x14¼***

1917	A503	40c multi	.65	.55
1918	A503	90c multi	1.40	1.25
1919	A503	$1.50 multi	2.40	2.00
1920	A503	$2 multi	3.25	2.75
a.		Souvenir sheet, #1917-1920	7.75	7.75
b.		Souvenir sheet, #1877, 1878, 1920	7.25	7.25
		Nos. 1917-1920 (4)	7.70	6.55

No. 1920b issued 6/26 for Le Salon du Timbre 2004, Paris.

See Hong Kong Nos. 1084-1087.

Parliament, 150th Anniv. — A504

Designs: 40c, Parliament Building, Auckland, 1854. 90c, Parliament Buildings, Wellington (Provincial Chambers), 1865. $1.30, Parliament Buildings, Wellington, 1899. $1.50, Parliament House, Wellington, 1918. $2, Beehive, Wellington, 1977.

2004, Mar. 3 ***Perf. 14½x14¼***

1921	A504	40c blk & purple	.65	.55
1922	A504	90c blk & violet	1.40	1.25
1923	A504	$1.30 blk & gray	2.10	1.75
1924	A504	$1.50 blk & blue	2.40	2.00
1925	A504	$2 blk & green	3.25	2.75
a.		Souvenir sheet, #1921-1925	9.75	9.75
		Nos. 1921-1925 (5)	9.80	8.30

See No. 1935.

Tourist Attractions Type of 2003

Designs: 45c, Kaikoura. $1.35, Church of the Good Shepherd, Lake Tekapo.

Perf. 13¼x13½

2004, Mar. 22 Litho.

1926	A496	45c multi	.70	.70

Perf. 14x14½

1927	A496	$1.35 multi	2.10	2.10
a.		Perf. 13½ ('06)	2.10	2.10

Self-Adhesive

Serpentine Die Cut 11¼x11

1928	A496	45c multi	.70	.70
a.		Booklet pane of 10	7.00	

Coil Stamp

1928B	A496	45c multi	.70	.70
		Nos. 1926-1928B (4)	4.20	4.20

Country name on No. 1928B has an unserifed font, with horizontal bars in "e," and a symmetrical "w."

No. 1927a issued 8/2006.

Scenic Views Type of 1995

2004, Apr. 5 ***Die Cut Perf. 10x9½***

Size: 27x22mm

Self-Adhesive

1929	A404	90c Like #1679	1.25	1.25
a.		Booklet pane of 10	12.50	

Historic Farm Equipment
A505

Designs: 45c, Kinnard Haines tractor. 90c, Fordson F tractor with plow. $1.35, Burrell traction engine. $1.50, Threshing mill. $2, Duncan's seed drill.

2004, Apr. 5 ***Perf. 14***

1930	A505	45c multi	.70	.70
a.		Booklet pane of 1, perf. 14x13¼	1.00	—
1931	A505	90c multi	1.40	1.40
a.		Booklet pane of 1, perf. 14x13¼	2.00	—
1932	A505	$1.35 multi	2.10	2.10
a.		Booklet pane of 1, perf. 14x13¼	3.00	—
1933	A505	$1.50 multi	2.40	2.40
a.		Booklet pane of 1, perf. 14x13¼	3.25	—
1934	A505	$2 multi	3.25	3.25
a.		Booklet pane of 1, perf. 14x13¼	4.50	—
b.		Booklet pane of 5, #1930-1934, perf. 14x13¼	13.50	—
		Complete booklet, #1930a, 1931a, 1932a, 1933a, 1934a, 1934b	27.50	
		Nos. 1930-1934 (5)	9.85	9.85

The complete booklet sold for $19.95.

Parliament Type of 2004

2004, May 5 ***Perf. 14½x14¼***

1935	A504	45c Like #1921	.65	.65

World of Wearable Art Awards Show — A506

Designs: 45c, Dragon Fish. 90c, Persephone's Descent. $1.35, Meridian. $1.50, Taunga Ika. $2, Cailleach Na Mara (Sea Witch).

2004, May 5 ***Perf. 14***

1936	A506	45c multi	.70	.70
1937	A506	90c multi	1.40	1.40
1938	A506	$1.35 multi	2.10	2.10
1939	A506	$1.50 multi	2.40	2.40
1940	A506	$2 multi	3.25	3.25
		Nos. 1936-1940 (5)	9.85	9.85

New Zealanders — A507

Designs: No. 1941, Man outside of Pungarehu Post Office. No. 1942, Children on horse. No. 1943, Elderly man and woman in front of house.

2004, Feb. Litho. ***Die Cut Perf. 13½***

Booklet Stamps

Self-Adhesive

1941	A507	$1.50 multi	3.50	3.50
1942	A507	$1.50 multi	3.50	3.50
1943	A507	$1.50 multi	3.50	3.50
a.		Booklet pane, 2 each # 1941-1943, 6 etiquettes and 10 stickers	21.00	
		Complete booklet, #1943a	21.00	
		Nos. 1941-1943 (3)	10.50	10.50

Wild Food — A508

Designs: No. 1944, Mountain oysters. No. 1945, Huhu grubs. No. 1946, Possum paté.

2004, Feb.

Booklet Stamps

Self-Adhesive

1944	A508	$1.50 multi	3.50	3.50
1945	A508	$1.50 multi	3.50	3.50
1946	A508	$1.50 multi	3.50	3.50
a.		Booklet pane, 2 each # 1944-1946, 6 etiquettes and 6 stickers	21.00	
		Complete booklet, #1946a	21.00	
		Nos. 1944-1946 (3)	10.50	10.50

New Zealand Post Emblem — A509

2004, Feb.

Booklet Stamps

Self-Adhesive

1947	A509	$1.50 blue & red	4.00	4.00
1948	A509	$1.50 red	4.00	4.00
1949	A509	$1.50 green & red	4.00	4.00
a.		Booklet pane, 2 each # 1947-1949, 6 etiquettes	24.00	
		Complete booklet, #1949a	24.00	
		Nos. 1947-1949 (3)	12.00	12.00

Country name is at bottom on No. 1948. A pane of eight stamps containing two each of Nos. 1947-1949 and two $1.50 purple and red stamps similar to No. 1948 came unattached in a folder together with a set of four markers, a sheet of decorative magnets and two sheets of self-adhesive plastic stickers. The pane of eight was not available without purchasing the other non-stamp items, which sold as a package for $19.95.

Flowers — A510

Designs: 45c, Magnolia "Vulcan." 90c, Helleborus "Unnamed Hybrid." $1.35, Nerine "Anzac." $1.50, Rhododendron "Charisma." $2, Delphinium "Sarita."

2004, June 2 ***Perf. 13¼x13¾***

1950	A510	45c multi	.70	.70
1951	A510	90c multi	1.40	1.40
1952	A510	$1.35 multi	2.10	2.10
1953	A510	$1.50 multi	2.40	2.40
1954	A510	$2 multi	3.25	3.25
a.		Souvenir sheet, #1950-1954	10.00	10.00
		Nos. 1950-1954 (5)	9.85	9.85

The 45c stamp in the souvenir sheet was impregnated with a floral scent.

Numeral — A511

Serpentine Die Cut 5¾

2004, June 28 Litho.

Booklet Stamp

Self-Adhesive

1955	A511	5c multi	1.40	1.40
a.		Booklet pane of 10	14.00	

Postage Advertising Labels

In 2004, New Zealand Post began issuing "Postage Advertising Labels," which have the New Zealand Post emblem and curved side panel found on type A511. These stamps have various vignettes and denominations and were designed in conjunction with various private parties who contracted for and purchased the entire print run of these stamps. Though valid for domestic postage only as most of these stamps lack a country name, none of these stamps were made available to the general public by New Zealand Post.

In 2006, a limited number of Postal Advertising Labels began to be sold at face value by New Zealand Post when new contracts with the private parties were written. These agreements allowed New Zealand Post to print more items than the private party desired and to sell the overage to collectors.

Scene Locations from *The Lord of the Rings* Movie Trilogy
A512

Designs: Nos. 1956, 1965, Skippers Canyon. Nos. 1957, 1964, Skippers Canyon (Ford of Bruinden) with actors. Nos. 1958, 1967, Mount Olympus. No. 1959, 1966, Mount Olympus (South of Rivendell) with actors. No. 1960, Erewhon. No. 1961, Erewhon (Edoras) with actors. No. 1962, Tongariro National Park. No. 1963, Tongariro National Park (Emyn Muil) with actors.

2004, July 7 ***Perf. 14***

1956	A512	45c multi	.70	.70
1957	A512	45c multi	.70	.70
a.		Vert. pair, #1956-1957	1.40	1.40
1958	A512	90c multi	1.40	1.40
1959	A512	90c multi	1.40	1.40
a.		Vert. pair, #1958-1959	3.00	3.00
1960	A512	$1.50 multi	2.40	2.40
1961	A512	$1.50 multi	2.40	2.40
a.		Vert. pair, #1960-1961	4.75	4.75
b.		Souvenir sheet, #1958-1961	7.75	7.75
1962	A512	$2 multi	3.25	3.25
1963	A512	$2 multi	3.25	3.25
a.		Vert. pair, #1962-1963	6.50	6.50
b.		Horiz. block of 8, #1956-1963	16.00	16.00
c.		Souvenir sheet, #1956-1963	16.00	16.00

No. 1963c exists imperf from a "Limited Edition" album.

Self-Adhesive

Serpentine Die Cut 11¼

Size: 30x25mm

1964	A512	45c multi	.70	.70
1965	A512	45c multi	.70	.70
1966	A512	90c multi	1.40	1.40
1967	A512	90c multi	1.40	1.40
a.		Block of 4, #1964-1967	4.25	
b.		Booklet pane, 3 each #1964-1965, 2 each #1966-1967	9.75	
		Nos. 1956-1967 (12)	19.70	19.70

No. 1961b issued 8/28. World Stamp Championship (No. 1961b).

2004 Summer Olympics, Athens — A513

Gold medalists: 45c, John Walker, 1500 meters, Montreal, 1976. 90c, Yvette Williams, long jump, Helsinki, 1952. $1.50, Ian Ferguson and Paul MacDonald, 500 meters kayak doubles, Seoul, 1988. $2, Peter Snell, 800 meters, Rome, 1960.

Serpentine Die Cut 10¾

2004, Aug. 2

Litho. with 3-Dimensional Plastic Affixed

Self-Adhesive

1968	A513	45c multi	.70	.70
1969	A513	90c multi	1.40	1.40
1970	A513	$1.50 multi	2.40	2.40
1971	A513	$2 multi	3.25	3.25
a.		Horiz. strip of 4, #1968-1971	7.75	
		Nos. 1968-1971 (4)	7.75	7.75

Tourist Attractions Type of 2003

Designs: No. 1972, Lake Wakatipu, Queenstown. No. 1973, Kaikoura. No. 1974, Bath House, Rotorua. No. 1975, Pohutu Geyser, Rotorua. No. 1976, Mitre Peak, Milford Sound. No. 1977, Hawke's Bay.

2004-05 Litho. ***Perf. 13¼x13½***

1972	A496	$1.50 multi	2.40	2.40
a.		Perf. 14x14¼	2.25	2.25
1973	A496	$1.50 multi	2.40	2.40
1974	A496	$1.50 multi	2.40	2.40
1975	A496	$1.50 multi	2.40	2.40
a.		Souvenir sheet, #1973, 1975	5.00	5.00
1976	A496	$1.50 multi	2.40	2.40
a.		Perf. 14x14¼	2.25	2.25
b.		Souvenir sheet, #1972a, 1976a	4.50	4.50
1977	A496	$1.50 multi	2.40	2.40
a.		Souvenir sheet, #1639, 1977	7.25	7.25
		Nos. 1972-1977 (6)	14.40	14.40

Issued: Nos. 1972-1977, 8/28; No. 1977a, 10/29 for Baypex 2004; No. 1975a, 8/18/05 for

Taipei 2005 Stamp Exhibition; Nos. 1972a, 1976a, 1976b, 8/3/07. Bangkok 2007 Asian International Stamp Exhibition (#1976b).

A514

Christmas — A515

Designs: 45c, Candle, wine bottle, turkey, ham. 90c, Hangi. $1, Christmas cards, fruit cake. $1.35, Barbecued shrimp. $1.50, Wine bottle, pie and salad. $2, Candelabra, pavlova and plum pudding.

2004, Oct. 4 ***Perf. 14¼***

1978	A514	45c multi	.70	.70
1979	A514	90c multi	1.40	1.40
1980	A514	$1.35 multi	2.10	2.10
1981	A514	$1.50 multi	2.40	2.40
1982	A514	$2 multi	3.25	3.25
		Nos. 1978-1982 (5)	9.85	9.85

Self-Adhesive

Serpentine Die Cut 9½x10

1983	A515	45c multi	.70	.70
a.		Booklet pane of 10	7.00	
1984	A515	90c multi	1.40	1.40
1985	A515	$1 multi	1.60	1.60
a.		Booklet pane of 8 + 8 etiquettes	13.00	
b.		Horiz. strip, #1983-1985	3.75	3.75
		Nos. 1983-1985 (3)	3.70	3.70

Extreme Sports A516

Designs: 45c, Whitewater rafting. 90c, Snow sports. $1.35, Skydiving. $1.50, Jet boating. $2, Bungy jumping.

2004, Dec. 1 ***Perf. 14***

1986	A516	45c multi	.70	.70
a.		Booklet pane of 1	.85	—
1987	A516	90c multi	1.40	1.40
a.		Booklet pane of 1	1.75	—
1988	A516	$1.35 multi	2.10	2.10
a.		Booklet pane of 1	2.75	—
1989	A516	$1.50 multi	2.40	2.40
a.		Booklet pane of 1	3.00	—
1990	A516	$2 multi	3.25	3.25
a.		Booklet pane of 1	4.00	—
b.		Booklet pane, #1986-1990	12.00	—
		Complete booklet, #1986a, 1987a, 1988a, 1989a, 1990a, 1990b	24.00	
		Nos. 1986-1990 (5)	9.85	9.85

Complete booklet sold for $14.95.

The 2004 sheets contain: #1914, 1920, 1925, 1934, 1940, 1954, 1962, 1982, 1990. See note following #1404.

Farm Animals — A517

Designs: 45c, Ewe (with horns) and lambs. 90c, Scottish border collies. $1.35, Pigs. $1.50, Rooster and chicken. $2, Rooster and chicken, diff.

2005, Jan. 12 ***Perf. 14***

1991	A517	45c multi	.70	.70
1992	A517	90c multi	1.40	1.40
1993	A517	$1.35 multi	2.10	2.10
1994	A517	$1.50 multi	2.40	2.40
1995	A517	$2 multi	3.25	3.25
a.		Horiz. strip, #1991-1995	10.00	10.00
b.		Souvenir sheet, #1994-1995	5.75	5.75
		Nos. 1991-1995 (5)	9.85	9.85

Nos. 1991-1995 exist in a souvenir sheet from a "Limited Edition" album.

Self-Adhesive

Size: 22x27mm

Serpentine Die Cut 11x11¼

1996	A517	45c multi	.65	.65
a.		Booklet pane of 10	6.50	

New Year 2005 (Year of the Cock) (No. 1995b).

Community Groups A518

Designs: No. 1997, Canoeists, YMCA emblem. No. 1998, Three people holding cement, Rotary International emblem. No. 1999, People building track bed, Lions International emblem. No. 2000, Four people jumping, YMCA emblem. No. 2001, People building wall, Rotary International emblem. No. 2002, Miniature train, Lions International emblem.

2005, Feb. 2 **Litho.** ***Perf. 14***

1997	A518	45c multi	.70	.70
1998	A518	45c multi	.70	.70
1999	A518	45c multi	.70	.70
2000	A518	$1.50 multi	2.40	2.40
a.		Horiz. pair, #1997, 2000, + central label	3.00	3.00
b.		Miniature sheet, 3 #2000a	8.25	8.25
2001	A518	$1.50 multi	2.40	2.40
a.		Horiz. pair, #1998, 2001, + central label	3.00	3.00
b.		Miniature sheet, 3 #2001a	8.25	8.25
2002	A518	$1.50 multi	2.40	2.40
a.		Horiz. pair, #1999, 2002, + central label	3.00	3.00
b.		Miniature sheet, #2000a, 2001a, 2002a	9.00	9.00
c.		Miniature sheet, 3 #2002a	8.25	8.25
		Nos. 1997-2002 (6)	9.30	9.30

New Zealand Postage Stamps, 150th Anniv. — A519

2005, Mar. 2 **Litho.** ***Perf. 14***

2003	A519	45c No. 1	.70	.70
2004	A519	90c No. P1	1.40	1.40
2005	A519	$1.35 No. OY5	2.10	2.10
2006	A519	$1.50 No. 83	2.40	2.40
2007	A519	$2 No. 99	3.25	3.25
a.		Souvenir sheet, #2003-2007	10.00	10.00
		Nos. 2003-2007 (5)	9.85	9.85

New Zealand Stamps, 150th Anniv. Type of 2005

2005, Apr. 6 **Litho.** ***Perf. 14***

2008	A519	45c No. 123a	.70	.70
2009	A519	90c No. B3	1.40	1.40
2010	A519	$1.35 No. C7	2.10	2.10
2011	A519	$1.50 No. 256	2.40	2.40
2012	A519	$2 No. 301	3.25	3.25
a.		Souvenir sheet, #2008-2012	10.00	10.00
b.		Souvenir sheet, #2007, 2012	6.50	6.50
		Nos. 2008-2012 (5)	9.85	9.85

No. 2012b issued 4/21 for Pacific Explorer 2005 World Stamp Expo, Sydney.

Size: 25x30mm

Self-Adhesive

Coil Stamps

Serpentine Die Cut 12¾

2013	A519	45c No. 123a	.70	.70
2014	A519	90c No. B3	1.40	1.40
a.		Horiz. pair, #2013-2014	2.10	

Booklet Stamps

Serpentine Die Cut 11x11¼

2015	A519	45c No. 123a	.70	.70
a.		Booklet pane of 10	7.00	
2016	A519	90c No. B3	1.40	1.40
a.		Booklet pane of 10	14.00	
		Nos. 2013-2016 (4)	4.20	4.20

New Zealand Stamps, 150th Anniv. Type of 2005

2005, June 1 **Litho.** ***Perf. 14***

2017	A519	45c No. 369	.70	.70
2018	A519	90c No. 918	1.40	1.40
2019	A519	$1.35 No. 989	2.10	2.10
2020	A519	$1.50 No. 1219	2.40	2.40
a.		Souvenir sheet, #2006, 2011, 2020	7.25	7.25
2021	A519	$2 No. 1878	3.25	3.25
a.		Souvenir sheet, #2017-2021	10.00	10.00
		Nos. 2017-2021 (5)	9.85	9.85

No. 2020a issued 11/17 for New Zealand 2005 National Stamp Show, Auckland.

A miniature sheet containing Nos. 2003-2012 and 2017-2021 was sold only with a commemorative book.

Cafés — A520

2005, May 4 **Litho.** ***Die Cut***

Self-Adhesive

2022	A520	45c 1910s	.70	.70
2023	A520	90c 1940s	1.40	1.40
2024	A520	$1.35 1970s	2.10	2.10
2025	A520	$1.50 1990s	2.40	2.40
2026	A520	$2 2005	3.25	3.25
a.		Horiz. strip, #2022-2026	10.00	
		Nos. 2022-2026 (5)	9.85	9.85

Rugby Team Shirts A521

Shirts of: Nos. 2027, 2029, All Blacks. Nos. 2028, 2030, British & Irish Lions.

2005, June 1 ***Die Cut***

Self-Adhesive

2027	A521	45c multi	.70	.70
2028	A521	45c multi	.70	.70
a.		Horiz. pair, #2027-2028	1.40	
2029	A521	$1.50 multi	2.40	2.40
2030	A521	$1.50 multi	2.40	2.40
a.		Horiz. pair, #2029-2030	4.75	
		Nos. 2027-2030 (4)	6.20	6.20

Miniature Sheet

Greetings Stamps — A522

No. 2031: a, Kiwi. b, Pohutukawa flower. c, Champagne flutes. d, Balloons. e, Wedding rings. f, Gift. g, Baby's hand. h, New Zealand on globe. i, Kiwi. j, Fern.

2005, July 6 ***Perf. 14***

2031	A522	Sheet of 10	14.00	14.00
a.-g.		45c Any single	.70	.70
h.		$1.50 multi	2.40	2.40
i.-j.		$2 Either single	3.25	3.25
k.		Sheet of 20 #2031a + 20 labels	27.00	—
l.		Sheet of 20 #2031b + 20 labels	27.00	—
m.		Sheet of 20 #2031c + 20 labels	27.00	—
n.		Sheet of 20 #2031d + 20 labels	27.00	—
o.		Sheet of 20 #2031e + 20 labels	27.00	—
p.		Sheet of 20 #2031f + 20 labels	27.00	—
q.		Sheet of 20 #2031g + 20 labels	27.00	—
r.		Sheet of 20 #2031h + 20 labels	60.00	—
s.		Sheet of 20 #2031i + 20 labels	75.00	—
t.		Sheet of 20 #2031j + 20 labels	75.00	—

Nos. 2031k-2031q each sold for $19.95; No. 2031r sold for $44.95; Nos. 2031s-2031t each sold for $54.95.

Examples of Nos. 2031a and 2031h without the "2005" year date were produced in sheets of 20 stamps + 20 labels for the Washington 2006 World Philatelic Exhibition and sold only at that show.

See No. 2070.

Worldwide Fund for Nature (WWF) A523

Kakapo and text: No. 2032, "Nocturnal bird living on the forest floor." No. 2033, "Endangered — only 86 known surviving." No. 2034, "Relies heavily on camouflage for defence." No. 2035, "Night Parrot unique to New Zealand."

2005, Aug. 3

2032	A523	45c multi	.70	.70
2033	A523	45c multi	.70	.70
2034	A523	45c multi	.70	.70
2035	A523	45c multi	.70	.70
a.		Strip of 4, #2032-2035	2.75	2.75
		Nos. 2032-2035 (4)	2.80	2.80

A524

Christmas — A525

Designs: 45c, Baby Jesus. 90c, Mary and Joseph. $1.35, Shepherd and sheep. $1.50, Magi. $2, Star of Bethlehem.

2005 **Litho.** ***Perf. 14¼***

2036	A524	45c multi	.70	.70
2037	A524	90c multi	1.40	1.40
2038	A524	$1.35 multi	2.10	2.10
2039	A524	$1.50 multi	2.40	2.40
2040	A524	$2 multi	3.25	3.25
a.		Horiz. strip, #2036-2040	10.00	10.00
		Nos. 2036-2040 (5)	9.85	9.85

Booklet Stamps

Size: 22x27mm

Self-Adhesive

Serpentine Die Cut 11x11¼

2041	A524	45c multi	.70	.70
a.		Booklet pane of 10	7.00	
2042	A525	$1 multi	1.60	1.60
a.		Booklet pane of 10	16.00	

Issued: $1, 10/5; Nos. 2036-2041, 11/2.

Premiere of Movie, *King Kong* — A526

Characters: 45c, King Kong. 90c, Carl Denham. $1.35, Ann Darrow. $1.50, Jack Driscoll. $2, Darrow and Driscoll.

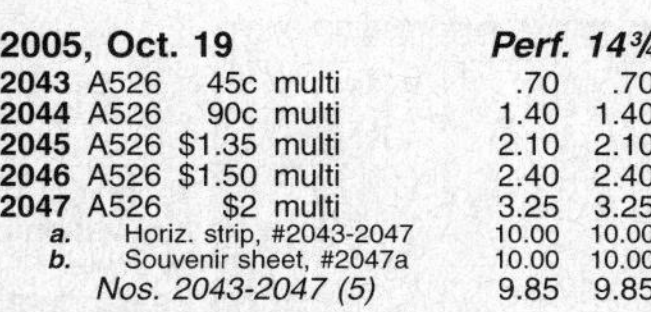

2005, Oct. 19 *Perf. 14¾*

2043	A526	45c multi	.70	.70
2044	A526	90c multi	1.40	1.40
2045	A526	$1.35 multi	2.10	2.10
2046	A526	$1.50 multi	2.40	2.40
2047	A526	$2 multi	3.25	3.25
a.		Horiz. strip, #2043-2047	10.00	10.00
b.		Souvenir sheet, #2047a	10.00	10.00
		Nos. 2043-2047 (5)	9.85	9.85

Premiere of Film *Narnia: The Lion, The Witch and the Wardrobe* A527

Designs: 45c, Lucy and the Wardrobe. 90c, Lucy, Edmund, Peter and Susan, horiz. $1.35, White Witch and Edmund, horiz. $1.50, Frozen Army. $2, Aslan and Lucy, horiz.

Perf. 14x14¼, 14¼x14

2005, Dec. 1 **Litho.**

2048	A527	45c multi	.70	.70
a.		Souvenir sheet of 1	1.00	1.00
2049	A527	90c multi	1.40	1.40
a.		Souvenir sheet of 1	1.90	1.90
2050	A527	$1.35 multi	2.10	2.10
a.		Souvenir sheet of 1	3.00	3.00
2051	A527	$1.50 multi	2.40	2.40
a.		Souvenir sheet of 1	3.25	3.25
2052	A527	$2 multi	3.25	3.25
a.		Souvenir sheet of 1	4.25	4.25
		Nos. 2048-2052 (5)	9.85	9.85

Self-Adhesive

Serpentine Die Cut 12½x12, 12x12½

2053	Sheet of 5	10.00	
a.	A527 45c multi, 26x37mm	.70	.70
b.	A527 90c multi, 37x26mm	1.40	1.40
c.	A527 $1.35 multi, 37x26mm	2.10	2.10
d.	A527 $1.50 multi, 26x37mm	2.40	2.40
e.	A527 $2 multi, 37x26mm	3.25	3.25

Nos. 2048a-2052a sold as a set for $8.70.

The 2005 sheets contain: #2003, 2006, 2007, 2008, 2011, 2012, 2017, 2020, 2021. See note following #1404.

New Year 2006 (Year of the Dog) — A528

Designs: 45c, Labrador retriever. 90c, German shepherd. $1.35, Jack Russell terrier. $1.50, Golden retriever. $2, Huntaway.

Litho. & Embossed

2006, Jan. 4 *Perf. 14*

2054	A528	45c multi	.70	.70

Litho.

2055	A528	90c multi	1.40	1.40
2056	A528	$1.35 multi	2.10	2.10
2057	A528	$1.50 multi	2.40	2.40
2058	A528	$2 multi	3.25	3.25
a.		Souvenir sheet, #2057-2058	5.75	5.75
		Nos. 2054-2058 (5)	9.85	9.85

No. 2058a exists imperf in a limited edition album.

Self-Adhesive

Size: 25x30mm

Coil Stamp

Die Cut Perf. 12¾

2059	A528	45c multi	.70	.70

Booklet Stamp

Serpentine Die Cut 11x11¼

2060	A528	45c multi	.70	.70
a.		Booklet pane of 10	7.00	

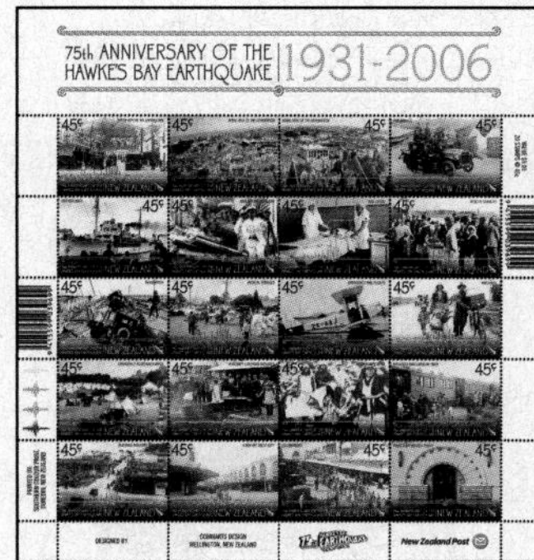

Hawke's Bay Earthquake, 75th Anniv. — A529

No. 2061: a, Napier before the earthquake. b, Aerial view of the devastation (denomination at left). c, Aerial view of the devastation (denomination at right). d, Fire service. e, HMS Veronica. f, HMS Veronica sailors. g, Red Cross. h, Rescue services. i, Devastation. j, Medical services. k, Emergency mail flights. l, Refugees. m, Emergency accommodation. n, Makeshift cooking facilities. o, Community spirit. p, Refugees evacuated by train. q, Building industry. r, A new Art Deco city. s, Celebrations. t, Hawke's Bay region today.

2006, Feb. 3 **Litho.** *Perf. 14*

2061	A529	Sheet of 20	14.00	14.00
a.-t.		45c Any single	.70	.70
u.		Booklet pane, 2 each #2061a-2061c	4.75	—
v.		Booklet pane, 2 each #2061r-2061t	4.75	—
w.		Booklet pane, 2 each #2061d-2061f	4.75	—
x.		Booklet pane, 2 each #2061g-2061h + 2 labels	3.25	—
y.		Booklet pane, 2 each #2061i, 2061k, 2061p	4.75	—
z.		Booklet pane, 2 each #2061j, 2061l, 2061m	4.75	—
aa.		Booklet pane, 2 each #2061n, 2061o, 2061q	4.75	—
		Complete booklet, #2061u-2061aa	32.50	

Complete booklet sold for $19.95.

Tourist Attractions Type of 2003

Designs: No. 2062, Franz Josef Glacier, West Coast. No. 2063, Halfmoon Bay, Stewart Island. No. 2064, Cathedral Cove, Coromandel. No. 2065, Mount Taranaki. No. 2066, Huka Falls, Taupo. No. 2067, Lake Wanaka.

2006, Mar. 1 *Perf. 13¼x13½*

2062	A496	$1.50 multi	2.40	2.40
2063	A496	$1.50 multi	2.40	2.40
2064	A496	$1.50 multi	2.40	2.40
2065	A496	$1.50 multi	2.40	2.40
2066	A496	$1.50 multi	2.40	2.40
2067	A496	$1.50 multi	2.40	2.40
		Nos. 2062-2067 (6)	14.40	14.40

Queen Elizabeth II, 80th Birthday A530

Litho. & Embossed with Foil Application

2006, Apr. 21 *Perf. 13½*

2068	A530	$5 dk bl & multi	8.00	8.00
a.		$5 Prussian blue & multi	8.00	8.00
b.		Souvenir sheet, #2068a, Jersey #1215a	27.50	27.50

Printed in sheets of 4.

No. 2068b sold for $17.50. See Jersey No. 1215.

Miniature Sheet

Greetings Stamps — A531

No. 2069: a, Champagne flutes. b, Child's toy. c, Fern. d, Pohutukawa flower. e, Stars. f, Wedding and engagement rings. g, Rose. h, Fern. i, Pohutukawa flower. j, Stars.

2006, May 3 **Litho.** *Perf. 14*

2069	A531	Sheet of 10 + 5 labels	14.00	14.00
a.-g.		45c Any single	.70	.70
h.		$1.50 multi	2.40	2.40
i.-j.		$2 Either single	3.25	3.25
k.		Souvenir sheet, #2069i, 2 #2069h	8.00	8.00
l.		Sheet of 20 #2069h + 20 labels	67.50	—
m.		Sheet of 20 #2069i + 20 labels	82.50	—
n.		Sheet of 20 #2069j + 20 labels	82.50	—

No. 2069k issued 11/16. Belgica'06 World Philatelic Exhibition, Brussels (#2069k).

Nos. 2069l-2069n issued 2007. No. 2069l sold for $44.90; Nos. 2069m and 2069n, each sold for $54.90. Labels could be personalized

A sheet of 20 #2069c + 20 labels depicting New Zealand's America's Cup Emirates Team yacht sold for $19.90. Labels on this sheet could not be personalized.

Greetings Type of 2005 Redrawn

Souvenir Sheet

No. 2070: a, Like #2031i, without "2005" year date. b, Like #2031j, without "2005" year date.

2006, May 27 **Litho.** *Perf. 14*

2070		Sheet of 2 + central label	6.50	6.50
a.-b.		A522 $2 Either single	3.25	3.25
c.		Souvenir sheet, #2070a-2070b	6.75	6.75

Washington 2006 World Philatelic Exhibition.

No. 2070c issued 11/2. Kiwipex 2006 National Stamp Exhibition, Christchurch (#2070c). No. 2070c lacks label, and sold for $5, with the extra $1 going to the NZ Philatelic Foundation.

A set of five gummed stamps, a self-adhesive coil stamp and a self-adhesive booklet stamp depicting Traditional Maori Performing Arts was prepared for release on June 7, 2006 but was withdrawn on June 2. Some mail orders for these stamps were fulfilled and shipped out inadvertantly prior to June 7, but apparently no examples were sold over post office counters. The editors request any evidence of sale of any of these stamps over post office counters.

Renewable Energy A532

Designs: 45c, Wind farm, Tararua. 90c, Roxburgh Hydroelectric Dam. $1.35, Biogas facility, Waikato. $1.50, Geothermal Power Station, Wairakei. $2, Solar panels on Cape Reinga Lighthouse, vert.

2006, July 5

2071	A532	45c multi	.70	.70
2072	A532	90c multi	1.40	1.40
2073	A532	$1.35 multi	2.10	2.10
2074	A532	$1.50 multi	2.40	2.40
2075	A532	$2 multi	3.25	3.25
		Nos. 2071-2075 (5)	9.85	9.85

Fruits and Vegetables A533

Slogan "5 + a day," and: 45c+5c, Tomatoes and "5." 90c+10c, Oranges and "+." $1.35, Onions and "a" (30x30mm). $1.50, Kiwi fruit and "Day," horiz. $2, Radicchio and hand.

2006, Aug. 2 **Litho.** *Perf. 14*

2076	A533	45c +5c multi	.70	.70
2077	A533	90c +10c multi	1.40	1.40
2078	A533	$1.35 multi	2.10	2.10
2079	A533	$1.50 multi	2.40	2.40
2080	A533	$2 multi	3.25	3.25
a.		Souvenir sheet, #2076-2080	10.00	10.00
		Nos. 2076-2080 (5)	9.85	9.85

Self-Adhesive

Size: 24x29mm

Serpentine Die Cut 9¾x10

2081	A533	45c +5c multi	.70	.70

New Zealand Gold Rush — A534

Designs: 45c, Gold panner, c. 1880. 90c, Miners, Kuranui Creek, c. 1868, horiz. $1.35, Chinese miners, Tuapeka, c. 1900, horiz. $1.50, Gold escort coach, Roxburgh, 1901, horiz. $2, Dunedin harbor, c. 1900, horiz.

2006, Sept. 9 *Perf. 14*

2082	A534	45c multi	.70	.70
2083	A534	90c multi	1.40	1.40
2084	A534	$1.35 multi	2.10	2.10
2085	A534	$1.50 multi	2.40	2.40
2086	A534	$2 multi	3.25	3.25
		Nos. 2082-2086 (5)	9.85	9.85

Souvenir Sheet

Litho. With Foil Application

2087	Sheet of 5	10.00	10.00
a.	A534 45c gold & multi	.70	.70
b.	A534 90c gold & multi	1.40	1.40
c.	A534 $1.35 gold & multi	2.10	2.10
d.	A534 $1.50 gold & multi	2.40	2.40
e.	A534 $2 gold & multi	3.25	3.25

Portions of the design of Nos. 2082 and 2087a are printed with a thermochromic ink that changes color when warmed that is applied by a thermographic process producing a shiny, raised effect.

No. 2087 exists imperf in a limited edition album.

Christmas A535

Children's art by: Nos. 2088, 2098, Hanna McLachlan. No. 2089, Isla Hewitt. No. 2090, Caitlin Davidson. No. 2091, Maria Petersen. No. 2092, Deborah Yoon. No. 2093, Hannah Webster. 90c, Pierce Higginson. $1.35, Rosa Tucker. $1.50, Sylvie Webby. $2, Gemma Baldock.

2006, Oct. 4 **Litho.** *Perf. 14¼*

2088	A535	45c multi	.70	.70
2089	A535	45c multi	.70	.70
2090	A535	45c multi	.70	.70
2091	A535	45c multi	.70	.70
2092	A535	45c multi	.70	.70
2093	A535	45c multi	.70	.70
a.		Miniature sheet, #2088-2093	4.25	4.25
b.		Horiz. strip of 5, #2089-2093	3.50	3.50
2094	A535	90c multi	1.40	1.40
2095	A535	$1.35 multi	2.10	2.10

2096 A535 $1.50 multi 2.40 2.40
2097 A535 $2 multi 3.25 3.25
Nos. 2088-2097 (10) 13.35 13.35

Self-Adhesive

Size: 21x26mm

Serpentine Die Cut 9¾x10

2098 A535 45c multi .70 .70
a. Booklet pane of 10 7.00
2099 A535 $1.50 multi 2.40 2.40
a. Horiz. pair, #2098-2099 3.00
b. Booklet pane of 10 24.00

No. 2099b sold for $13.50.

Summer Festivals A536

Designs: 45c, Dragon boat racing. 90c, Race day. $1.35, Teddy Bears' Picnic. $1.50, Outdoor concerts. $2, Jazz festivals.

2006, Nov. 1 ***Perf. 14¼***
2100 A536 45c multi .70 .70
2101 A536 90c multi 1.40 1.40
2102 A536 $1.35 multi 2.10 2.10
2103 A536 $1.50 multi 2.40 2.40
2104 A536 $2 multi 3.25 3.25
a. Horiz. strip of 5, #2100-2104 10.00 10.00
b. Miniature sheet, #2104a 10.00 10.00
Nos. 2100-2104 (5) 9.85 9.85

The 2006 sheets contain: #2058, 2061e, 2066, 2069i, 2075, 2080, 2086, 2097, 2104. See note following #1404.

Scott Base, Antarctica, 50th Anniv. — A537

Designs: 45c, Opening ceremony, 1957. 90c, Scott Base, 1990. $1.35, Aerial view, 2000. $1.50, Sign, 2003-04. $2, Aerial view, 2005.

2007, Jan. 20 ***Perf. 14¼x14***
2105 A537 45c multi .70 .70
a. Souvenir sheet of 1 1.00 1.00
2106 A537 90c multi 1.40 1.40
a. Souvenir sheet of 1 1.90 1.90
2107 A537 $1.35 multi 2.10 2.10
a. Souvenir sheet of 1 2.75 2.75
2108 A537 $1.50 multi 2.40 2.40
a. Souvenir sheet of 1 3.50 3.50
2109 A537 $2 multi 3.25 3.25
a. Souvenir sheet of 1 4.50 4.50
Nos. 2105-2109 (5) 9.85 9.85

Nos. 2105a-2109a sold as a set for $8.70. The souvenir sheets exist overprinted in a limited edition album.

New Year 2007 (Year of the Pig) A538

Pig breeds: 45c, Kunekune. 90c, Kunekune, diff. $1.35, Arapawa. $1.50, Auckland Island. $2, Kunekune, diff.

2007, Feb. 7 ***Perf. 14½x14***
2110 A538 45c multi .70 .70
2111 A538 90c multi 1.40 1.40
2112 A538 $1.35 multi 2.10 2.10
2113 A538 $1.50 multi 2.40 2.40
2114 A538 $2 multi 3.25 3.25
a. Souvenir sheet, #2113-2114 5.75 5.75

Nos. 2111-2112 exist in a souvenir sheet in a limited edition album.

Indigenous Animals — A539

Designs: 45c, Tuatara. 90c, Kiwi. $1.35, Hamilton's frog. $1.50, Yellow-eyed penguin. $2, Hector's dolphin.

Serpentine Die Cut

2007, Mar. 7 **Litho.**

Self-Adhesive

2115 A539 45c multi .65 .65
2116 A539 90c multi 1.25 1.25
2117 A539 $1.35 multi 1.90 1.90
2118 A539 $1.50 multi 2.10 2.10
2119 A539 $2 multi 2.75 2.75
a. Horiz. strip of 5, #2115-2119 8.65

Greetings Type of 2005 Redrawn

Souvenir Sheet

2007, Mar. 30 **Litho.** ***Perf. 14***
2120 Sheet, #2075, 2120a 6.00 6.00
a. A531 $2 Like #2069i, without "2006" year date 3.00 3.00

Northland 2007 National Stamp Exhibition, Whangarei.

Centenaries — A540

Designs: No. 2121, Scouts and Lieutenant Colonel David Cossgrove, founder of scouting movement in New Zealand. No. 2122, Infant, nurse, Dr. Frederic Truby King, founder of Plunket Society. No. 2123, Rugby players, Hercules "Bumper" Wright, first team captain. No. 2124, Sister of Compassion teaching children, Suzanne Aubert, founder of Sisters of Compassion. $1, Plunket Society emblem, family. $1.50, Sisters of Compassion emblem, women reading book. No. 2127, New Zealand Rugby League emblem, rugby players. No. 2128, Scouting emblem, scouts.

2007, Apr. 24 ***Perf. 14***
2121 A540 50c multi .75 .75
2122 A540 50c multi .75 .75
2123 A540 50c multi .75 .75
2124 A540 50c multi .75 .75
a. Horiz. strip of 4, #2121-2124 3.00 3.00
2125 A540 $1 multi 1.50 1.50
2126 A540 $1.50 multi 2.25 2.25
2127 A540 $2 multi 3.00 3.00
2128 A540 $2 multi 3.00 3.00
a. Block of 8, #2121-2128 12.75 12.75
b. Horiz. pair, #2127-2128 6.00 6.00

Tourist Attractions Type of 2003

Designs: 5c, Whakarewarewa geothermal area. 10c, Central Otago. 20c, Rainbow Falls, Northland. 50c, Lake Coleridge. $1, Rangitoto Island. $2.50, Abel Tasman National Park. $3, Tongaporutu, Taranaki.

2007, May 9 ***Perf. 13¼x13½***
2129 A496 5c multi .20 .20
2130 A496 10c multi .20 .20
2131 A496 20c multi .30 .30
2132 A496 50c multi .75 .75
2133 A496 $1 multi 1.50 1.50
2134 A496 $2.50 multi 3.75 3.75
2135 A496 $3 multi 4.50 4.50
Nos. 2129-2135 (7) 11.20 11.20

Self-Adhesive

Serpentine Die Cut 10x9½

2136 A496 50c multi .75 .75
a. Booklet pane of 10 7.50
2137 A496 $1 multi 1.50 1.50
a. Horiz. pair, #2136-2137 2.25 2.25
b. Booklet pane of 10 15.00

Greetings Type of 2006 Redrawn

No. 2138: a, Child's toy. b, Pohutukawa flower. c, Wedding and engagement rings. d, Fern. e, Champagne flutes. f, Rose. g, Stars.

2007, May 9 ***Perf. 14***
2138 A531 Sheet of 7 + 8 labels 5.25 5.25
a.-g. 50c Any single .75 .75
h. Sheet of 20 #2138a + 20 labels 32.50 —
i. Sheet of 20 #2138b + 20 labels 32.50 —
j. Sheet of 20 #2138c + 20 labels 32.50 —
k. Sheet of 20 #2138d + 20 labels 32.50 —
l. Sheet of 20 #2138e + 20 labels 32.50 —
m. Sheet of 20 #2138f + 20 labels 32.50 —
n. Sheet of 20 #2138g + 20 labels 32.50 —

Nos. 2138h-2138n each sold for $20.90.

Southern Skies and Observatories — A541

Designs: 50c, Southern Cross, Stardome Observatory. $1, Pleiades, McLellan Mt. John Observatory. $1.50, Trifid Nebula, Ward Observatory. $2, Southern Pinwheel, MOA telescope, Mt. John Observatory. $2.50, Large Magellanic Cloud, Southern African Large Telescope.

2007, June 6 ***Perf. 13x13¼***
2139 A541 50c multi .80 .80
a. Perf. 14 1.00 1.00
b. Booklet pane of 1 #2139a 1.00 —
2140 A541 $1 multi 1.60 1.60
a. Perf. 14 2.00 2.00
b. Booklet pane of 1 #2140a 2.00 —
2141 A541 $1.50 multi 2.40 2.40
a. Perf. 14 3.00 3.00
b. Booklet pane of 1 #2141a 3.00 —
2142 A541 $2 multi 3.00 3.00
a. Perf. 14 4.25 4.25
b. Booklet pane of 1 #2142a 4.25 —
2143 A541 $2.50 multi 3.75 3.75
a. Perf. 14 5.25 5.25
b. Booklet pane of 1 #2143a 5.25 —
c. Booklet pane of 5, #2139a-2143a 15.50 —
Complete booklet, #2139b, 2140b, 2141b, 2142b, 2143b, 2143c 31.00
d. Souvenir sheet, #2142a, 2143a 6.75 6.75
Nos. 2139-2143 (5) 11.55 11.55

No. 2143d issued 8/31. Huttpex 2007 Stampshow (#2143d).

Miniature Sheet

New Zealand Slang — A542

No. 2144 — Designs: a, "Good as gold," gold nugget. b, "Sweet as," kiwi fruit. c, "She'll be right," hand with thumb up. d, "Hissy fit," insect. e, "Sparrow fart," sun in sky. f, "Cuz," kiwi bird. g, "Away laughing," sandals. h, "Tiki tour," road sign. i, "Away with the fairies," cookies. j, "Wop-wops," house. k, "Hard yakka," shirt. l, "Cods wollop," fish. m, "Boots and all," rugby ball and athletic shoes. n, "Shark and taties," fish and chips. o, "Knackered," boots. p, "Laughing gear," mug. q, "Everyman and his dog," dog. r, "Bit of a dag," sheep. s, "Dreaded lurgy," box of tissues. t, "Rark up," hand pointing.

2007, July 4 ***Perf. 14***
2144 A542 Sheet of 20 16.00 16.00
a.-t. 50c Any single .80 .80

Portions of the design were covered with a thermographic ink that allowed printing below (definitinons of the slang phrases) to appear when the ink was warmed.

Technical Innovations by New Zealanders A543

Designs: 50c, Gallagher electric fence. $1, Spreadable butter. $1.50, Mountain buggy. $2, Hamilton jet boat. $2.50, Tranquilizer gun.

2007, Aug. 1
2145 A543 50c multi .75 .75
2146 A543 $1 multi 1.50 1.50
2147 A543 $1.50 multi 2.25 2.25
2148 A543 $2 multi 3.00 3.00
2149 A543 $2.50 multi 3.75 3.75
Nos. 2145-2149 (5) 11.25 11.25

Wedding of Queen Elizabeth II and Prince Philip, 60th Anniv. — A544

Queen and Prince: 50c, In 2007. $2, On wedding day, 1947.

2007, Sept. 5 **Litho.** ***Perf. 14***
2150 A544 50c multi .70 .70
2151 A544 $2 multi 2.75 2.75
a. Souvenir sheet, #2150-2151 3.50 3.50

Christmas A545

Children's art by: 50c, Sione Vao. $1, Reece Cateley. $1.50, Emily Wang. $2, Alexandra Eathorne. $2.50, Jake Hooper.

2007, Oct. 3 ***Perf. 14¼***
2152 A545 50c multi .80 .80
2153 A545 $1 multi 1.50 1.50
2154 A545 $1.50 multi 2.40 2.40
2155 A545 $2 multi 3.00 3.00
2156 A545 $2.50 multi 4.00 4.00
Nos. 2152-2156 (5) 11.70 11.70

Size: 25x30mm

Self-Adhesive

Coil Stamps

Die Cut Perf. 13x12¾

2157 A545 50c multi .80 .80
2158 A545 $1.50 multi 2.40 2.40
a. Horiz. pair, #2157-2158 3.25

Booklet Stamps

Serpentine Die Cut 11x11¼

2159 A545 50c multi .80 .80
a. Booklet pane of 10 8.00
2160 A545 $1.50 multi 2.10 2.10
a. Booklet pane of 10 21.00

No. 2160a sold for $13.50.

Miniature Sheet

Greetings Stamps — A546

No. 2161: a, "Go You Good Thing." b, "Look Who It Is." c, "Love Always." d, "Thanks a Million." e, "We've Got News." f, "Wish You Were Here." g, "Time to Celebrate." h, "Kia Ora." i, "You Gotta Love Christmas." j, Chinese characters.

2007, Nov. 7 *Perf. 14*

2161 A546 Sheet of 10 + 5 labels 13.00 13.00
a.-f. 50c Any single .75 .75
g.-h. $1 Either single 1.50 1.50
i. $1.50 multi 2.40 2.40
j. $2 multi 3.00 3.00
k. Sheet of 20 #2161c + 20 labels 32.50 —
l. Sheet of 20 #2161d + 20 labels 32.50 —
m. Sheet of 20 #2161e + 20 labels 32.50 —
n. Sheet of 20 #2161f + 20 labels 32.50 —
o. Sheet of 20 #2161g + 20 labels 47.50 —
p. Sheet of 20 #2161h + 20 labels 47.50 —
q. Sheet of 20 #2161i + 20 labels 70.00 —
r. Sheet of 20 #2161j + 20 labels 85.00 —

Nos. 2161k-2161n each sold for $20.90; Nos. 2161o-2161p, for $30.90; No. 2161q, for $44.90; No. 2161r, for $54.90. Labels were personalizable on Nos. 2161k-2161r.

Reefs A547

Marine life from: 50c, Dusky Sound, Fiordland. $1, Mayor Island, Bay of Plenty. $1.50, Fiordland. $2, Volkner Rocks, White Island, Bay of Plenty.

2008, Jan. 9 **Litho.** *Perf. 13x13¼*

2162 A547 50c multi .80 .80
2163 A547 $1 multi 1.60 1.60
2164 A547 $1.50 multi 2.40 2.40
2165 A547 $2 multi 3.25 3.25
a. Souvenir sheet, #2162-2165 8.25 8.25
Nos. 2162-2165 (4) 8.05 8.05

Self-Adhesive

Size: 26x21mm

Serpentine Die Cut 11¼

2166 A547 50c multi .80 .80
a. Booklet pane of 10 8.00
2167 A547 $1 multi 1.60 1.60
a. Horiz. pair, #2166-2167 2.40
b. Booklet pane of 10 #2167 16.00

Pocket Pets A548

2008, Feb. 7 *Perf. 14*

2168 A548 50c Rabbits .80 .80
2169 A548 $1 Guinea pigs 1.60 1.60
2170 A548 $1.50 Rats 2.40 2.40
2171 A548 $2 Mice 3.25 3.25
a. Souvenir sheet, #2170-2171 5.75 5.75
b. As #2171, perf. 13½x13¼ 3.25 3.25
c. Souvenir sheet, #2161j, 2171b 6.50 6.50

New Year 2008 (Year of the Rat), No. 2171a.
Nos. 2171b, 2171c issued 3/7. Taipei 2008 International Stamp Exhibition (#2171c).

Weather Extremes A549

Designs: No. 2172, Drought, Gisborne, 1998. No. 2173, Wind, Auckland, 2007. $1, Storm, Wellington, 2001. $1.50, Flooding, Hikurangi, 2007. $2, Snow storm, Southland, 2001. $2.50, Heat, Matarangi, 2005.

2008, Mar. 5 **Litho.** *Perf. 14*

2172 A549 50c multi .80 .80
2173 A549 50c multi .80 .80
2174 A549 $1 multi 1.60 1.60
2175 A549 $1.50 multi 2.40 2.40
2176 A549 $2 multi 3.25 3.25
2177 A549 $2.50 multi 4.00 4.00
Nos. 2172-2177 (6) 12.85 12.85

Australian and New Zealand Army Corps (ANZAC) A550

Designs: No. 2178, Dawn Parade. No. 2179, Soldiers at Gallipoli, 1915. $1, Soldiers at Western Front, 1916-18. $1.50, Chalk kiwi made by soldiers, England, 1919. $2, Soldier's Haka dance, Egypt, 1941. $2.50, Soldiers in Viet Nam, 1965-71.

2008, Apr. 2

2178 A550 50c multi .80 .80
a. Booklet pane of 1 1.00 —
2179 A550 50c multi .80 .80
a. Booklet pane of 1 1.00 —
2180 A550 $1 multi 1.60 1.60
a. Booklet pane of 1 2.00 —
2181 A550 $1.50 multi 2.40 2.40
a. Booklet pane of 1 3.00 —
b. Souvenir sheet, #2179-2181 3.50 3.50
2182 A550 $2 multi 3.25 3.25
a. Booklet pane of 1 4.00 —
2183 A550 $2.50 multi 4.00 4.00
a. Booklet pane of 1 5.00 —
b. Booklet pane of 6, #2178-2183 16.00 —
Complete booklet, #2178a, 2179a, 2180a, 2181a, 2182a, 2183a, 2183b 32.00
Nos. 2178-2183 (6) 12.85 12.85

No. 2181b issued 10/20. End of World War I, 90th anniv. (#2181b).

Maori King Movement, 150th Anniv. — A551

Various unnamed artworks by Fred Graham and English text: 50c, "There is but one eye of the needle. . ." $1.50, "Taupiri is the mountain. . ." $2.50, "After I am gone. . .," horiz.

2008, May 2 **Litho.** *Perf. 14*

2184 A551 50c multi .80 .80
2185 A551 $1.50 multi 2.40 2.40
2186 A551 $2.50 multi 4.00 4.00
Nos. 2184-2186 (3) 7.20 7.20

Premiere of Film, *The Chronicles of Narnia: Prince Caspian* — A552

Designs: 50c, The Pevensie children. $1, Queen Susan. $1.50, High King Peter. $2, Prince Caspian.

2008, May 7 *Perf. 14½x14*

2187 A552 50c multi .80 .80
a. Souvenir sheet of 1 1.10 1.10
2188 A552 $1 multi 1.60 1.60
a. Souvenir sheet of 1 2.25 2.25
2189 A552 $1.50 multi 2.40 2.40
a. Souvenir sheet of 1 3.25 3.25
2190 A552 $2 multi 3.25 3.25
a. Souvenir sheet of 1 4.50 4.50
Nos. 2187-2190 (4) 8.05 8.05

Nos. 2187a-2190a were sold as a set for $7.

Matariki (Maori New Year) A553

Inscriptions: No. 2191, Ranginui. No. 2192, Te Moana nui a Kiwa. $1, Papatuanuku. $1.50, Whakapapa. $2, Takoha. $2.50, Te Tau Hou.

2008, June 5 **Litho.** *Perf. 14*

2191 A553 50c multi .80 .80
2192 A553 50c multi .80 .80
2193 A553 $1 multi 1.60 1.60
2194 A553 $1.50 multi 2.40 2.40
2195 A553 $2 multi 3.25 3.25
a. Souvenir sheet, #2192, 2194, 2195 6.50 6.50
2196 A553 $2.50 multi 4.00 4.00
a. Miniature sheet, #2191-2196, perf. 13½x13¼ 13.00 13.00
Nos. 2191-2196 (6) 12.85 12.85

No. 2195a issued 9/18. Vienna Intl. Postage Stamp Exhibition (#2195a).

2008 Summer Olympics, Beijing — A554

2008, July 2 *Perf. 14¼*

2197 A554 50c Rowing .80 .80
2198 A554 50c Cycling .80 .80
2199 A554 $1 Kayaking 1.60 1.60
2200 A554 $2 Running 3.00 3.00
Nos. 2197-2200 (4) 6.20 6.20

Compare with Type SP82.

Miniature Sheet

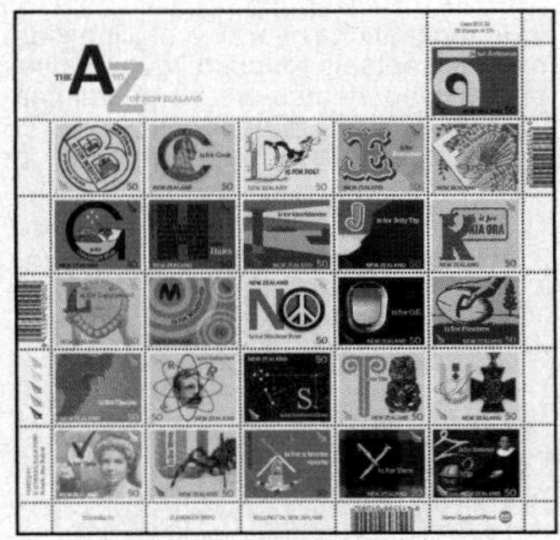

Alphabet — A555

No. 2201 — Inscriptions: a, A is for Aotearoa (Maori name for New Zealand). b, B is for Beehive (Parliament Building). c, C is for Cook (Capt. James Cook). d, D is for Dog (comic strip character). e, E is for Edmonds (Thomas J. Edmonds, cookbook producer). f, F is for Fantail (bird). g, G is for Goodnight Kiwi (cartoon). h, H is for Haka (Maori dance). i, I is for Interislander (ferry). j, J is for Jelly tip (ice cream bar). k, K is for Kia ora. l, L is for Log O'Wood (rugby trophy). m, M is for Mudpots. n, N is for Nuclear free. o, O is for O.E. (overseas experience). p, P is for Pinetree (Colin "Pinetree" Meads, rugby player). q, Q is for Quake. r, R is for Rutherford (Sir Ernest Rutherford, chemist and physicist). s, S is for Southern Cross (constellation). t, T is for Tiki (rock carving). u, U is for Upham (Capt. Charles Upham, war hero). v, V is for Vote. w, W is for Weta (insect). x, X is for X-treme sports. y, Y is for Yarn. z, Z is for Zeeland (Dutch province for which New Zealand was named).

2008, Aug. 6 *Perf. 14¼*

2201 A555 Sheet of 26 18.50 18.50
a.-z. 50c Any single .70 .70

North Island Main Trunk Line, Cent. A556

Designs: 50c, Last spike ceremony, Manganui-o-te-Ao, 1908. $1, Locomotive at Taumarunui Station, 1958. $1.50, Train on Makatote Viaduct, 1963. $2, Train on Raurimi Spiral, 1964. $2.50, Train on Hapuawhenua Viaduct, 2003.

2008, Sept. 3 **Litho.** *Perf. 14*

2202 A556 50c multi .70 .70
2203 A556 $1 multi 1.40 1.40
2204 A556 $1.50 multi 2.00 2.00
2205 A556 $2 multi 2.75 2.75
2206 A556 $2.50 multi 3.50 3.50
Nos. 2202-2206 (5) 10.35 10.35

Christmas A557

Winning art in children's stamp design competition: 50c, Sheep With Stocking Cap, by Kirsten Fisher-Marsters. $2, Pohutukawa and Koru, by Tamara Jenkin. $2.50, Kiwi and Pohutukawa, by Molly Bruhns.

2008, Oct. 1 *Perf. 14¼*

2207 A557 50c multi .70 .70
2208 A557 $2 multi 2.75 2.75
2209 A557 $2.50 multi 3.25 3.25
Nos. 2207-2209 (3) 6.70 6.70

Christmas A558

Designs: 50c, Nativity. $1, Holy Family. $1.50, Madonna and Child.

2008, Oct. 1 *Perf. 14¼*

2210 A558 50c multi .70 .70
2211 A558 $1 multi 1.40 1.40
2212 A558 $1.50 multi 2.00 2.00
Nos. 2210-2212 (3) 4.10 4.10

Size: 21x26mm

Self-Adhesive

Coil Stamps

Die Cut Perf. 12¾

2213 A558 50c multi .70 .70
2214 A558 $1.50 multi 2.00 2.00
a. Horiz. pair, #2213-2214 2.75

Booklet Stamps

Serpentine Die Cut 11¼

2215 A558 50c multi .70 .70
a. Booklet pane of 10 7.00
2216 A558 $1.50 multi 2.00 2.00
a. Booklet pane of 10 20.00
Nos. 2213-2216 (4) 5.40 5.40

Sir Edmund Hillary (1919-2008), Mountaineer A559

New Zealand flag and: 50c, Hillary. $1, Hillary and Tenzing Norgay on Mt. Everest, 1953. $1.50, Hillary on Trans-Antarctic Expedition, 1958. $2, Hillary with Nepalese people, 1964. $2.50, Hillary at Order of the Garter ceremony, 1995.

2008, Nov. 5 **Litho.** *Perf. 14¾*

2217 A559 50c multi .60 .60
2218 A559 $1 multi 1.25 1.25
2219 A559 $1.50 multi 1.75 1.75
2220 A559 $2 multi 2.40 2.40
2221 A559 $2.50 multi 3.00 3.00
Nos. 2217-2221 (5) 9.00 9.00

Tourist Attractions Type of 2003

Souvenir Sheet

No. 2222: a, Like #2065, without year date. b, Like #2135, without year date.

2008, Nov. 7 *Perf. 13¼x13½*

2222	Sheet of 2	5.50	5.50
a.	A496 $1.50 multi	1.75	1.75
b.	A496 $3 multi	3.75	3.75

Tarapex 2008 Philatelic Exhibition, New Plymouth.

New Year 2009 (Year of the Ox) — A560

Designs: 50c, Chinese character for "ox." $1, Ox. $2, Chinese lanterns and Auckland Harbor Bridge.

2009, Jan. 7 *Perf. 13¼x13*

2223	A560	50c multi	.60	.60
2224	A560	$1 multi	1.25	1.25
2225	A560	$2 multi	2.40	2.40
a.		Souvenir sheet, #2223-2225	4.25	4.25
		Nos. 2223-2225 (3)	4.25	4.25

Lighthouses — A561

Designs: 50c, Pencarrow Lighthouse. $1, Dog Island Lighthouse. $1.50, Cape Brett Lighthouse. $2, Cape Egmont Lighthouse. $2.50, Cape Reinga Lighthouse.

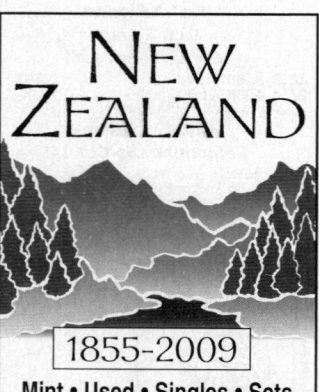

2009, Jan. 7 *Perf. 13x13¼*

2226	A561	50c multi	.60	.60
2227	A561	$1 multi	1.25	1.25
2228	A561	$1.50 multi	1.75	1.75
2229	A561	$2 multi	2.40	2.40
2230	A561	$2.50 multi	3.00	3.00
		Nos. 2226-2230 (5)	9.00	9.00

Motor Sports Champions A562

Designs: 50c, Scott Dixon. $1, Bruce McLaren. $1.50, Ivan Mauger. $2, Denny Hulme. $2.50, Hugh Anderson.

2009, Feb. 4 **Litho.** *Perf. 14*

2231	A562	50c multi	.50	.50
2232	A562	$1 multi	1.00	1.00
2233	A562	$1.50 multi	1.50	1.50
2234	A562	$2 multi	2.10	2.10
2235	A562	$2.50 multi	2.60	2.60
a.		Sheet, #2231-2235	7.75	7.75
		Nos. 2231-2235 (5)	7.70	7.70

Self-Adhesive

Size: 26x21mm

Serpentine Die Cut 10x9¾

2236	A562	50c multi	.50	.50
a.		Booklet pane of 10	5.00	
2237	A562	$1 multi	1.00	1.00
a.		Booklet pane of 10	10.00	
b.		Horiz. pair, #2236-2237	1.50	

POSTAL-FISCAL STAMPS

In 1881 fiscal stamps of New Zealand of denominations over one shilling were made acceptable for postal duty. Values for canceled stamps are for postal cancellations. Denominations above £5 appear to have been used primarily for fiscal purposes.

Queen Victoria
PF1 PF2

Perf. 11, 12, 12½

1882 **Typo.** **Wmk. 62**

AR1	PF1	2sh blue	100.00	15.00
AR2	PF1	2sh6p dk brown	125.00	15.00
AR3	PF1	3sh violet	200.00	16.00
AR4	PF1	4sh brown vio	250.00	35.00
AR5	PF1	4sh red brown	250.00	35.00
AR6	PF1	5sh green	300.00	35.00
AR7	PF1	6sh rose	400.00	60.00
AR8	PF1	7sh ultra	400.00	90.00
AR9	PF1	7sh6p ol gray	1,500.	400.00
AR10	PF1	8sh dull blue	400.00	85.00
AR11	PF1	9sh org red	600.00	175.00
AR12	PF1	10sh red brown	300.00	60.00

1882-90

AR13	PF2	15sh dk grn	1,500.	400.00
AR15	PF2	£1 rose	600.00	125.00
AR16	PF2	25sh blue		—
AR17	PF2	30sh brown		—
AR18	PF2	£1 15sh yellow		—
AR19	PF2	£2 purple		—

PF3

PF4

AR20	PF3	£2 10sh red brn		—
AR21	PF3	£3 yel green		—
AR22	PF3	£3 10sh rose		—
AR23	PF3	£4 ultramarine		—
AR24	PF3	£4 10sh olive brn		—
AR25	PF3	£5 dark blue		—
AR26	PF4	£6 org red		—
AR27	PF4	£7 brn red		—
AR28	PF4	£8 green		—
AR29	PF4	£9 rose		—
AR30	PF4	£10 blue		—
AR30A	PF4	£20 yellow	—	—

No. AR31

With "COUNTERPART" at Bottom

1901

AR31	PF1	2sh6p brown	250.00	225.00

Perf. 11, 14, 14½x14

1903-15 **Wmk. 61**

AR32	PF1	2sh blue ('07)	80.00	12.00
AR33	PF1	2sh6p brown	80.00	12.00
AR34	PF1	3sh violet	150.00	14.00
AR35	PF1	4sh brown red	175.00	30.00
AR36	PF1	5sh green ('06)	225.00	30.00
AR37	PF1	6sh rose	350.00	50.00
AR38	PF1	7sh dull blue	350.00	80.00
AR39	PF1	7sh6p ol gray ('06)	1,250.	350.00
AR40	PF1	8sh dark blue	350.00	75.00
AR41	PF1	9sh dl org ('06)	500.00	150.00
AR42	PF1	10sh dp claret	250.00	50.00
AR43	PF2	15sh blue grn	1,250.	350.00
AR44	PF2	£1 rose	500.00	150.00

Perf. 14½

AR45	PF2	£2 deep vio ('25)	600.00	150.00
a.		Perf. 14	700.00	150.00
		Nos. AR32-AR45 (14)	6,110.	1,503.

For overprints see Cook Islands Nos. 67-71.

Coat of Arms — PF5

1931-39 **Wmk. 61** *Perf. 14*

Type PF5

AR46	1sh3p lemon	30.00	40.00
AR47	1sh3p orange ('32)	8.00	9.00
AR48	2sh6p brown	16.00	5.25
AR49	4sh dull red ('32)	17.00	7.50
AR50	5sh green	21.00	12.50
AR51	6sh brt rose ('32)	37.50	15.00
AR52	7sh gray blue	32.50	25.00
AR53	7sh6p olive gray ('32)	75.00	92.50
AR54	8sh dark blue	50.00	37.50
AR55	9sh brn org	52.50	32.50
AR56	10sh dark car	27.50	10.50
AR57	12sh6p brn vio ('35)	250.00	250.00
AR58	15sh ol grn ('32)	70.00	42.50
AR59	£1 pink ('32)	75.00	22.50
AR60	25sh turq bl ('38)	550.00	600.00
AR61	30sh dk brn ('36)	300.00	200.00
AR62	35sh yellow ('37)	5,000.	*6,500.*
AR63	£2 violet ('33)	400.00	70.00
AR64	£2 10sh dark red ('36)	400.00	*550.00*
AR65	£3 light grn ('32)	400.00	210.00
AR66	£3 10sh rose ('39)	2,250.	2,250.
AR67	£4 light blue	400.00	175.00
AR68	£4 10sh dk ol gray ('39)	2,250.	2,500.
AR69	£5 dk blue ('32)	400.00	100.00

For overprints see Cook Islands Nos. 80-83.

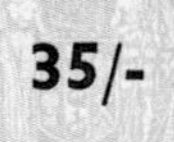

No. AR62 Surcharged in Black

1939 *Perf. 14*

AR70	PF5 35sh on 35sh yel	500.00	350.00

Type PF5 Surcharged in Black

1940

AR71	3sh6p on 3sh6p dl green	28.50	21.00
AR72	5sh6p on 5sh6p rose lilac	60.00	57.50
AR73	11sh on 11sh pale yellow	125.00	150.00
AR74	22sh on 22sh scar	275.00	350.00
	Nos. AR71-AR74 (4)	488.50	578.50

Type of 1931

1940-58 **Wmk. 253** *Perf. 14*

Type PF5

AR75	1sh3p orange	5.75	.60
AR76	2sh6p brown	5.75	.60
AR77	4sh dull red	6.75	.60
AR78	5sh green	11.50	.90
AR79	6sh brt rose	20.00	4.00
AR80	7sh gray bl	20.00	6.75
AR81	7sh6p ol gray ('50)	70.00	*70.00*
AR82	8sh dk blue	45.00	25.00
AR83	9sh orange ('46)	50.00	30.00
AR84	10sh dk carmine	25.00	3.25
AR85	15sh olive ('45)	55.00	20.00
AR86	£1 pink('45)	29.00	8.50
a.	Perf. 14x13½ ('58)	32.50	15.00
AR87	25sh blue ('46)	500.00	*550.00*
AR88	30sh choc ('46)	250.00	200.00
AR89	£2 violet ('46)	100.00	60.00
AR90	£2 10sh dk red ('51)	400.00	*525.00*
AR91	£3 lt grn ('46)	150.00	125.00
AR92	£3 10sh rose ('48)	2,250.	2,250.
AR93	£4 lt blue ('52)	150.00	160.00
AR94	£5 dk blue ('40)	175.00	150.00

Type PF5 Surcharged in Black

1942-45 **Wmk. 253**

AR95	3sh6p on 3sh6p grn	12.50	8.00
AR96	5sh6p on 5sh6p rose lil ('44)	26.00	8.50
AR97	11sh on 11sh yel	67.50	52.50
AR98	22sh on 22sh car ('45)	250.00	*250.00*
	Nos. AR95-AR98 (4)	356.00	319.00

Catalogue values for unused stamps in this section, from this point to the end of the section, are for Never Hinged items.

Type of 1931 Redrawn Surcharged in Black

1953 **Typo.**

AR99	PF5 3sh6p on 3sh6p green	32.50	35.00

Denomination of basic stamp is in small, sans-serif capitals without period after "sixpence."

Type of 1931

1955 **Wmk. 253** *Perf. 14*

Denomination in Black

AR100	PF5 1sh3p orange	2.75	.90

1956 **Denomination in Blue**

AR101	PF5 1sh3p orange yel	17.50	14.50

1967, July 10 ***Perf. 14***

AR102 PF5	$4 purple		10.00	2.50
AR103 PF5	$6 green		9.00	4.00
AR104 PF5	$8 light blue		12.00	5.50
AR105 PF5	$10 dark blue		17.00	6.50
	Nos. AR102-AR105 (4)		48.00	18.50

1987 **Unwmk.**

AR103a	PF5	$6 green	9.00	9.00
AR104a	PF5	$8 light blue	12.00	12.00
AR105a	PF5	$10 dark blue	15.00	15.00
	Nos. AR103a-AR105a (3)		36.00	36.00

SEMI-POSTAL STAMPS

Nurse
SP1 SP2

Inscribed: "Help Stamp out Tuberculosis, 1929"

Wmk. 61

1929, Dec. 11 **Typo.** ***Perf. 14***
B1 SP1 1p + 1p scarlet 12.50 *20.00*

Inscribed: "Help Promote Health, 1930"

1930, Oct. 29
B2 SP2 1p + 1p scarlet 30.00 *45.00*

Boy — SP3

Hygeia, Goddess of Health — SP4

1931, Oct. 31 ***Perf. 14½x14***
B3 SP3 1p + 1p scarlet 100.00 90.00
B4 SP3 2p + 1p dark blue 100.00 75.00

1932, Nov. 18 **Engr.** ***Perf. 14***
B5 SP4 1p + 1p carmine 22.50 *30.00*
Never hinged 55.00

Road to Health — SP5

1933, Nov. 8
B6 SP5 1p + 1p carmine 15.00 *20.00*
Never hinged 35.00

Crusader — SP6

1934, Oct. 25 ***Perf. 14x13½***
B7 SP6 1p + 1p dark carmine 12.50 *20.00*
Never hinged 25.00

Child at Bathing Beach — SP7

Anzac — SP8

1935, Sept. 30 ***Perf. 11***
B8 SP7 1p + 1p scarlet 3.00 3.25
Never hinged 5.00

Catalogue values for unused stamps in this section, from this point to the end of the section, are for Never Hinged items.

1936, Apr. 27
B9 SP8 ½p + ½p green .70 *2.00*
B10 SP8 1p + 1p red .70 *1.60*

21st anniv. of Anzac landing at Gallipoli.

"Health" SP9

1936, Nov. 2
B11 SP9 1p + 1p red 2.00 *4.25*

Boy Hiker — SP10

Children at Play — SP11

1937, Oct. 1
B12 SP10 1p + 1p red 3.00 *4.00*

Perf. 14x13½

1938, Oct. 1 **Wmk. 253**
B13 SP11 1p + 1p red 6.25 3.25

Children at Play — SP12

Children in Swing — SP13

1939, Oct. 16 **Wmk. 61** ***Perf. 11½***

Black Surcharge

B14 SP12 1p on ½p + ½p grn 5.00 5.00
B15 SP12 2p on 1p + 1p scar 5.00 5.00

1940, Oct. 1
B16 SP12 1p + ½p green 16.00 17.50
B17 SP12 2p + 1p org brown 16.00 17.50

The surtax was used to help maintain children's health camps.

Semi-Postal Stamps of 1940, Overprinted in Black "1941"

1941, Oct. 4 ***Perf. 11½***
B18 SP12 1p + ½p green 3.00 *3.50*
B19 SP12 2p + 1p org brown 3.00 *3.50*

1942, Oct. 1 **Engr.**
B20 SP13 1p + ½p green .35 *1.10*
B21 SP13 2p + 1p dp org brown .35 *1.10*

Imperf plate proofs on card exist for #B22-B27, B32-B33, B38-B39, B46-B48, B59-B60. Imperfs exist for B44-B45, B49-B51. These are from the printer's archives.

Princess Margaret Rose — SP14

Design: 2p+1p, Princess Elizabeth.

1943, Oct. 1 **Wmk. 253** ***Perf. 12***
B22 SP14 1p + ½p dark green .20 .40
a. Vert. pair, imperf. between
B23 SP14 2p + 1p red brown .20 .40
a. Vert. pair, imperf. between

Princesses Margaret Rose and Elizabeth SP16

1944, Oct. 9 ***Perf. 13½***
B24 SP16 1p + ½p blue green .35 .45
B25 SP16 2p + 1p chalky blue .35 .45

Peter Pan Statue, London — SP17

Statue of Eros, London — SP19

Soldier Helping Child over Stile SP18

1945, Oct. 1
B26 SP17 1p + ½p gray green & bister brown .20 .35
B27 SP17 2p + 1p car & olive bis .20 .35

1946, Oct. 24 ***Perf. 13½x13***
B28 SP18 1p + ½p dk grn & org brn .20 .35
B29 SP18 2p + 1p dk brn & org brn .20 .35

1947, Oct. 1 **Engr.** ***Perf. 13x13½***
B30 SP19 1p + ½p deep green .20 .35
B31 SP19 2p + 1p deep carmine .20 .35

Children's Health Camp SP20

1948, Oct. 1 ***Perf. 13½x13***
B32 SP20 1p + ½p blue grn & ultra .20 .35
B33 SP20 2p + 1p red & dk brn .20 .35

Nurse and Child SP21

Princess Elizabeth and Prince Charles SP22

1949, Oct. 3 **Photo.** ***Perf. 14x14½***
B34 SP21 1p + ½p deep green .30 .35
B35 SP21 2p + 1p ultramarine .30 .35

1950, Oct. 2
B36 SP22 1p + ½p green .20 *.35*
B37 SP22 2p + 1p violet brown .20 .35

Racing Yachts SP23

Perf. 13½x13

1951, Nov. 1 **Engr.** **Wmk. 253**
B38 SP23 1½p + ½p red & yel .20 .35
B39 SP23 2p + 1p dp grn & yel .20 .35

Princess Anne SP24

Prince Charles SP25

Perf. 14x14½

1952, Oct. 1 **Wmk. 253** **Photo.**
B40 SP24 1½p + ½p crimson .20 .35
B41 SP25 2p + 1p brown .20 .35

Girl Guides Marching SP26

Boy Scouts at Camp SP27

1953, Oct. 7
B42 SP26 1½p + ½p bright blue .20 .35
B43 SP27 2p + 1p deep green .20 .35

The border of No. B43 consists of Morse code reading "Health" at top and bottom and "New Zealand" on each side. On No. B42 the top border line is replaced by "Health" in Morse code.

Young Mountain Climber Studying Map — SP28

1954, Oct. 4 Engr. *Perf. 13½*

B44 SP28 1½p + ½p pur & brown .20 *.35*
B45 SP28 2p + 1p vio gray & brn .20 *.35*

Child's Head — SP29

Children Picking Apples — SP30

1955, Oct. 3 Wmk. 253 *Perf. 13*

B46 SP29 1½p + ½p brn org & sep .20 *.35*
B47 SP29 2p + 1p grn & org brn .20 *.35*
B48 SP29 3p + 1p car & sepia .20 .35
Nos. B46-B48 (3) .60 1.05

1956, Sept. 24

B49 SP30 1½p + ½p chocolate .20 *.35*
B50 SP30 2p + 1p blue green .20 *.35*
B51 SP30 3p + 1p dark carmine .20 .35
Nos. B49-B51 (3) .60 1.05

Life-Saving Team SP31

3p+1p, Children playing and boy in canoe.

1957, Sept. 25 *Perf. 13½*

B52 SP31 2p + 1p emer & blk .20 .35
a. Miniature sheet of 6 5.25 *25.00*
B53 SP31 3p + 1p car & ultra .20 .35
a. Miniature sheet of 6 5.25 *25.00*

The watermark is sideways on Nos. B52a and B53a. In a second printing, the watermark is upright; values double.

Girls' Life Brigade Cadet — SP32

Design: 3p+1p, Bugler, Boys' Brigade.

1958, Aug. 20 Photo. *Perf. 14x14½*

B54 SP32 2p + 1p green .20 .45
a. Miniature sheet of 6 4.00 *25.00*
B55 SP32 3p + 1p ultramarine .20 .45
a. Miniature sheet of 6 4.00 *25.00*

75th anniv. of the founding of the Boys' Brigade.

The surtax on this and other preceding semi-postals was for the maintenance of children's health camps.

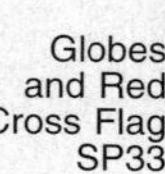

Globes and Red Cross Flag SP33

1959, June 3 *Perf. 14½x14*

B56 SP33 3p + 1p ultra & car .25 .20
a. Red Cross omitted *1,750.*

The surtax was for the Red Cross.

Gray Teal (Tete) SP34

Sacred Kingfisher (Kotare) SP35

Design: 3p+1p, Pied stilt (Poaka).

1959, Sept. 16 *Perf. 14x14½*

B57 SP34 2p + 1p pink, blk, yel & gray .60 .75
a. Miniature sheet of 6 4.50 *20.00*
B58 SP34 3p + 1p blue, black & pink .60 .75
a. Miniature sheet of 6 4.50 *20.00*
b. Pink omitted *125.00*

1960, Aug. 10 Engr. *Perf. 13x13½*

Design: 3p+1p, NZ pigeon (Kereru).

B59 SP35 2p + 1p grnsh blue & sepia .60 .85
a. Min. sheet of 6, perf. 11½x11 15.00 *32.50*
B60 SP35 3p + 1p org & sepia .60 .85
a. Min. sheet of 6, perf. 11½x11 15.00 *32.50*

Type of 1959

Birds: 2p+1p, Great white egret (kotuku). 3p+1p, NZ falcon (karearea).

1961, Aug. 2 Wmk. 253

B61 SP34 2p + 1p pale lil & blk .60 .80
a. Miniature sheet of 6 15.00 *22.50*
B62 SP34 3p + 1p yel grn & blk brn .60 .80
a. Miniature sheet of 6 15.00 *22.50*

Type of 1959

Birds: 2½p+1p, Red-fronted parakeet (kakariki). 3p+1p, Saddleback (tieke).

1962, Oct. 3 Photo. *Perf. 15x14*

B63 SP34 2½p + 1p lt bl, blk, grn & org .60 .80
a. Miniature sheet of 6 20.00 *29.00*
B64 SP34 3p + 1p salmon, blk, grn & org .60 .80
a. Miniature sheet of 6 20.00 *35.00*
b. Orange omitted

Prince Andrew — SP36

Design: 3p+1p, Prince without book.

1963, Aug. 7 Engr. *Perf. 14*

B65 SP36 2½p + 1p ultra .35 .80
a. Miniature sheet of 6 13.00 *25.00*
B66 SP36 3p + 1p rose car .35 .20
a. Miniature sheet of 6 13.00 *25.00*

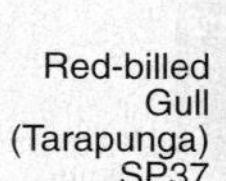

Red-billed Gull (Tarapunga) SP37

Design: 3p+1p, Blue penguin (korora).

1964, Aug. 5 Photo. *Perf. 14*

B67 SP37 2½p + 1p lt bl, pale yel, red & blk .45 .75
a. Miniature sheet of 8 22.50 *55.00*
b. Red omitted
c. Yellow omitted
B68 SP37 3p + 1p blue, yellow & black .45 .75
a. Miniature sheet of 8 22.50 *55.00*

Kaka — SP38

Bellbird & Bough of Kowhai Tree — SP39

Design: 4p+1p, Fantail (piwakawaka).

1965, Aug. 4 *Perf. 14x14½*

B69 SP38 3p + 1p gray, red, brn & yellow .60 .85
a. Miniature sheet of 6 12.50 *32.50*
B70 SP38 4p + 1p yel, blk, emer & brn .60 .85
a. Miniature sheet of 6 12.50 *32.50*

1966, Aug. 3 Photo. Wmk. 253

4p+1p, Flightless rail (weka) and fern.

B71 SP39 3p + 1p lt bl & multi .60 .85
a. Miniature sheet of 6 12.50 *27.50*
B72 SP39 4p + 1p lt grn & multi .60 .85
a. Miniature sheet of 6 12.50 *27.50*
b. Brown omitted *1,500.*

National Team Rugby Player and Boy — SP40

Design: 3c+1c, Man and boy placing ball for place kick, horiz.

1967, Aug. 2 *Perf. 14½x14, 14x14½*

B73 SP40 2½c + 1c multi .20 .20
a. Miniature sheet of 6 13.00 *22.50*
B74 SP40 3c + 1c multi .20 .20
a. Miniature sheet of 6 13.00 *22.50*

Boy Running and Olympic Rings — SP41

3c+1c, Girl swimming and Olympic rings.

1968, Aug. 7 *Perf. 14½x14*

B75 SP41 2½c + 1c multi .20 .20
a. Miniature sheet of 6 10.00 *24.00*
B76 SP41 3c + 1c multi .20 .20
a. Miniature sheet of 6 10.00 *24.00*

Boys Playing Cricket SP42

Dr. Elizabeth Gunn — SP43

Design: 3c+1c, playing cricket.

Perf. 13½x13, 13x13½

1969, Aug. 6 Litho. Unwmk.

B77 SP42 2½c + 1c multi .45 .75
a. Miniature sheet of 6 12.00 *27.50*
B78 SP42 3c + 1c multi .45 .75
a. Miniature sheet of 6 12.00 *27.50*
B79 SP43 4c + 1c multi .45 2.25
Nos. B77-B79 (3) 1.35 3.75

50th anniv. of Children's Health Camps, founded by Dr. Elizabeth Gunn.

Boys Playing Soccer SP44

2½c+1c, Girls playing basketball, vert.

1970, Aug. 5 Unwmk. *Perf. 13½*

B80 SP44 2½c + 1c multi .30 .80
a. Miniature sheet of 6 10.00 *26.00*
B81 SP44 3c + 1c multi .30 .80
a. Miniature sheet of 6 10.00 *26.00*

Hygienist and Child SP45

Designs: 3c+1c, Girls playing hockey. 4c+1c, Boys playing hockey.

1971, Aug. 4 Litho. *Perf. 13½*

B82 SP45 3c + 1c multicolored .50 .75
a. Miniature sheet of 6 11.00 *26.00*
B83 SP45 4c + 1c multicolored .50 .75
a. Miniature sheet of 6 11.00 *26.00*
B84 SP45 5c + 1c multicolored 1.25 2.25
Nos. B82-B84 (3) 2.25 3.75

50th anniv. of School Dental Service (No. B84).

Boy Playing Tennis SP46

Prince Edward SP47

Design: 4c+1c, Girl playing tennis.

1972, Aug. 2 Litho. *Perf. 13x13½*

B85 SP46 3c + 1c gray & lt brn .35 .60
a. Miniature sheet of 6 10.50 *22.50*
B86 SP46 4c + 1c brown, yellow & gray .35 .60
a. Miniature sheet of 6 10.50 *22.50*

1973, Aug. 1 Photo.

B87 SP47 3c + 1c grn & brn .35 .60
a. Miniature sheet of 6 9.00 *20.00*
B88 SP47 4c + 1c dk red & blk .35 .60
a. Miniature sheet of 6 9.00 *20.00*

Children with Cat and Dog — SP48

Designs: 4c+1c, Girl with dogs and cat. 5c+1c, Children and dogs.

1974, Aug. 7 Litho. *Perf. 13½x14*

B89 SP48 3c + 1c multicolored .20 .60
B90 SP48 4c + 1c multicolored .30 .60
a. Miniature sheet of 10 22.50 *50.00*
B91 SP48 5c + 1c multicolored 1.10 1.75
Nos. B89-B91 (3) 1.60 2.95

Girl Feeding Lamb SP49

Designs: 4c+1c, Boy with hen and chicks. 5c+1c, Boy with duck and duckling.

1975, Aug. 6 Litho. *Perf. 14x13½*

B92 SP49 3c + 1c multicolored .20 .35
B93 SP49 4c + 1c multicolored .20 .35
a. Miniature sheet of 10 17.50 *50.00*
B94 SP49 5c + 1c multicolored .75 1.75
Nos. B92-B94 (3) 1.15 2.45

Boy and Piebald Pony SP50

Girl and Bluebird SP51

Designs: 8c+1c, Farm girl and calf. 10c+1c, 2 girls watching nest-bound thrush.

1976, Aug. 4 Litho. *Perf. 13½x14*

B95 SP50 7c + 1c multicolored .20 .35
B96 SP50 8c + 1c multicolored .20 .35
B97 SP50 10c + 1c multicolored .45 1.00
a. Min. sheet, 2 each #B95-B97 3.50 7.00
Nos. B95-B97 (3) .85 1.70

1977, Aug. 3 Litho. *Perf. 13½x14*

8c+2c, Boy & frog. 10c+2c, Girl & butterfly.

B98 SP51 7c + 2c multi .20 .60
B99 SP51 8c + 2c multi .25 .65
B100 SP51 10c + 2c multi .50 1.10
a. Miniature sheet of 6 2.00 7.50
Nos. B98-B100 (3) .95 2.35

No. B100a contains 2 each of Nos. B98-B100 in 2 strips of continuous design.

NZ No. B1 SP52

Heart Surgery SP53

1978, Aug. 2 Litho. *Perf. 13½x14*

B101 SP52 10c + 2c multi .35 .40
B102 SP53 12c + 2c multi .35 .45
a. Min. sheet, 3 ea #B101-B102 1.40 4.50

50th Health Stamp issue (No. B101) and National Heart Foundation (No. B102).

Demoiselle Fish SP54

Designs: No. B104, Sea urchin. 12c+2c, Underwater photographer and red mullet, vert.

1979, July 25 *Perf. 13½x13, 13x13½*

B103 SP54 10c + 2c multi .35 .70
B104 SP54 10c + 2c multi .35 .70
a. Pair, #B103-B104 .70 1.25
B105 SP54 12c + 2c multi .35 .70
a. Min. sheet, 2 ea #B103-B105 1.50 3.25
Nos. B103-B105 (3) 1.05 2.10

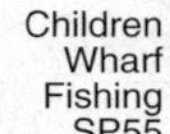

Children Wharf Fishing SP55

1980, Aug. 6 Litho. *Perf. 13½x13*

B106 SP55 14c + 2c shown .35 .95
B107 SP55 14c + 2c Surfcasting .35 .95
a. Pair, #B106-B107 .70 1.75
B108 SP55 17c + 2c Underwater fishing .35 .65
a. Min. sheet, 2 ea #B106-B108 1.90 3.75
Nos. B106-B108 (3) 1.05 2.55

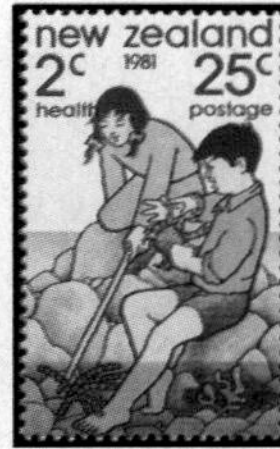
Boy and Girl at Rock Pool — SP56

1981, Aug. 5 Litho. *Perf. 14½*

B109 SP56 20c + 2c Girl, starfish .30 .75
B110 SP56 20c + 2c Boy fishing .30 .75
a. Pair, #B109-B110 .60 1.50
B111 SP56 25c + 2c shown .30 .40
a. Min. sheet, 2 ea #B109-B111 1.50 3.50
Nos. B109-B111 (3) .90 1.90

Cocker Spaniel — SP57

Persian Cat — SP58

1982, Aug. 4 Litho. *Perf. 13x13½*

B112 SP57 24c + 2c Labrador .90 1.10
B113 SP57 24c + 2c Border collie .90 1.10
a. Pair, #B112-B113 1.90 2.25
B114 SP57 30c + 2c shown .90 1.10
a. Min. sheet, 2 each #B112-B114, perf. 14x13½ 5.00 7.50
Nos. B112-B114 (3) 2.70 3.30

1983, Aug. 3 Litho. *Perf. 14½*

B115 SP58 24 + 2c Tabby .70 .85
B116 SP58 24 + 2c Siamese .70 .85
a. Pair, #B115-B116 1.40 1.75
B117 SP58 30 + 2c shown .95 1.10
a. Min. sheet, 2 ea #B115-B117 3.00 3.50
Nos. B115-B117 (3) 2.35 2.80

Thoroughbreds — SP59

1984, Aug. 1 Litho. *Perf. 13½x13*

B118 SP59 24c + 2c Clydesdales .60 .85
B119 SP59 24c + 2c Shetlands .60 .85
a. Pair, #B118-B119 1.25 1.75
B120 SP59 30c + 2c shown .60 .85
a. Min. sheet, 2 ea #B118-B120 2.50 3.75
Nos. B118-B120 (3) 1.80 2.55

Health — SP60

Princess Diana and: No. B121, Prince William. No. B122, Prince Henry. No. B123, Princes Charles, William and Henry.

1985, July 31 Litho. *Perf. 13½*

B121 SP60 25c + 2c multi 1.00 1.50
B122 SP60 25c + 2c multi 1.00 1.50
a. Pair, #B121-B122 2.10 3.00
B123 SP60 35c + 2c multi 1.00 1.50
a. Min. sheet, 2 ea #B121-B123 4.75 7.00
Nos. B121-B123 (3) 3.00 4.50

Surtax for children's health camps.

Children's Drawings — SP61

1986, July 30 Litho. *Perf. 14½x14*

B124 SP61 30c + 3c shown .50 .75
B125 SP61 30c + 3c Children playing .50 .75
a. Pair, #B124-B125 1.00 1.50
B126 SP61 45c + 3c Skipping rope, horiz. .75 .90
a. Min. sheet, 2 ea #B124-B126 3.50 4.00
Nos. B124-B126 (3) 1.75 2.40

Surtax for children's health camps.

No. B126a exists with Stockholmia '86 emblem. This sheet was sold only at the exhibition.

Children's Drawings SP62

1987, July 29 Litho. *Perf. 14½*

B127 SP62 40c + 3c shown .90 1.75
B128 SP62 40c + 3c Swimming .90 1.75
a. Pair, #B127-B128 1.90 3.50
B129 SP62 60c + 3c Riding horse, vert. 1.50 7.75
a. Min. sheet, 2 ea #B127-B129 5.75 8.00
Nos. B127-B129 (3) 3.30 11.25

Surtax benefited children's health camps.

1988 Summer Olympics, Seoul — SP63

1988, July 27 Litho. *Perf. 14½*

B130 SP63 40c + 3c Swimming .70 .80
B131 SP63 60c + 3c Running .95 1.25
B132 SP63 70c + 3c Rowing 1.10 1.25
B133 SP63 80c + 3c Equestrian 1.25 1.60
a. Souv. sheet of 4, #B130-B133 4.00 5.00
Nos. B130-B133 (4) 4.00 4.90

Children's Health — SP64

Designs: No. B134, Duke and Duchess of York, Princess Beatrice. No. B135, Duchess, princess. No. B136, Princess.

1989, July 23

B134 SP64 40c + 3c multi .90 1.75
B135 SP64 40c + 3c multi .90 1.75
a. Pair, #B134-B135 1.90 3.50
B136 SP64 80c + 3c multi 1.60 2.00
a. Min. sheet, 2 ea #B134-B136 6.75 8.75
b. As "a," overprinted with World Stamp Expo '89 emblem in margin 17.50 17.50
Nos. B134-B136 (3) 3.40 5.50

Athletes SP65

40c+5c, Jack Lovelock (1910-1949), runner. 80c+5c, George Nepia (1905-1986), rugby player.

1990, July 25 Litho. *Perf. 14½x14*

B137 SP65 40c +5c multi .60 .95
B138 SP65 80c +5c multi 1.25 1.60
a. Min. sheet, 2 ea #B137-B138 3.75 4.25

Hector's Dolphin SP66

1991, July 24 Litho. *Perf. 14½*

B139 SP66 45c +5c 3 swimming 1.00 1.40
B140 SP66 80c +5c 2 jumping 1.40 2.25
a. Souv. sheet, 2 ea #B139-B140 5.75 7.50

Surtax benefited children's health camps.

Anthony F. Wilding (1883-1915), Tennis Player — SP67

Design: No. B142, C.S. "Stewie" Dempster (1903-1974), cricket player.

1992, Aug. 12 Litho. *Perf. 14x13½*

B141 SP67 45c +5c multi 1.10 1.40
B142 SP67 80c +5c multi 1.40 1.75
a. Souv. sheet, 2 each #B141-B142, perf. 14½ 4.50 6.25

Surtax for children's health camps.

SP68

1993, July 21 Litho. *Perf. 13½x14*

B143 SP68 45c +5c Boy, puppy .80 1.00
B144 SP68 80c +5c Girl, kitten 1.40 1.75
a. Souvenir sheet, 2 each #B143-B144, perf. 14½ 4.50 5.00
b. As "a," inscribed in sheet margin 7.00 7.00

Surtax for children's health camps.

No. B144b inscribed with "TAIPEI '93" emblem.

Issue date: No. B144b, Aug. 14.

SP69

Children's Health Camps, 75th Anniv.: No. B145, #B15, Children playing with ball. No. B146, #B34, Nurse holding child. No. B147, #B79, Children reading. 80c+5c, #B4, Boy.

1994, July 20 Litho. *Perf. 14*

B145 SP69 45c +5c multi .80 .90
B146 SP69 45c +5c multi .80 .90
B147 SP69 45c +5c multi .80 .90
B148 SP69 80c +5c multi 1.40 1.40
a. Souv. sheet of 4, #B145-B148 4.50 5.00
Nos. B145-B148 (4) 3.80 4.10

Surtax for children's health camps.

Children's Health Camps — SP70

Designs: 45c+5c, Boy on skateboard. 80c+5c, Child on bicycle.

1995, June 21 Litho. *Perf. 14½*

B149 SP70 45c +5c multi .85 1.25
B150 SP70 80c +5c multi 2.10 2.10
a. Souv. sheet, 2 ea #B149-B150 4.75 5.75
b. As "a," with added inscription 8.00 8.00

No. B150b inscribed with Stampex '95 emblem in sheet margin.
Surtax for children's health camps.

SP71 SP72

Children's Health: Nos. B151, B153, Infant buckled into child safety seat. 80c, Child holding adult's hand on pedestrian crossing.

1996, June 5 Litho. *Perf. 14x13½*

B151 SP71 40c +5c multi .80 .95
B152 SP71 80c +5c multi 1.40 1.50
a. Souvenir sheet, 2 each Nos. B151-B152, perf. 14x14½ 4.00 4.00
b. As "a" with added inscription 5.50 5.50

Self-Adhesive

Serpentine Die Cut 11½

B153 SP71 40c +5c multi .60 .85

No. B152b inscribed with CAPEX '96 emblem in sheet margin.

Original Design

1996, June 5 Litho. *Perf. 14x13½*

B154 SP72 40c +5c multi *1,000.* 1,200.

Self-Adhesive

Serpentine Die Cut 11½

B155 SP72 40c +5c multi 1,750. 1,750.

Nos. B154 and B155 were withdrawn before issue by New Zealand Post. Slightly over 1,000 copies of No. B154 and 500 copies of No. B155 were sold in error by two post offices within three days of June 5. A total of 402 copies of the souvenir sheet containing No. B154 were made available by the printer, but none were sold at post offices.

The stamps were withdrawn because the inclusion of the stuffed animal indicated that the infant was improperly belted into the vehicle.

Children's Health SP73

Children's designs of "Healthy Living:" No. B156, Child on beach. 80c+5c, Child riding horse on waterfront. No. B158, Mosaic of person collecting fruit from tree, vert.

1997, June 18 Litho. *Perf. 14*

B156 SP73 40c +5c multi .80 .85
B157 SP73 80c +5c multi 1.40 1.40

Souvenir Sheet

B157A Sheet of 3, #B156-B157, B157Ab 3.50 3.50
b. SP73 40c +5c like #B158 1.30 1.30

Self-Adhesive

Serpentine Die Cut 10½

B158 SP73 40c +5c multi .75 .70

Children's Water Safety — SP74

Designs: 40c+5c, Child in life jacket. 80c+5c Child learning to swim.

1998, June 24 Litho. *Perf. 13½*

B159 SP74 40c +5c multicolored .75 .60
B160 SP74 80c +5c multicolored 1.40 1.40
a. Sheet, 2 each #B159-B160 4.25 4.25

Self-Adhesive

Serpentine Die Cut 11½

B161 SP74 40c +5c multicolored .75 .45

Children's Health SP75

Scenes from children's books: #B162, Hairy Maclary's Bone, by Lynley Dodd. #B163, Lion in the Meadow, by Margaret Mahy. 80c+5c, Greedy Cat, by Joy Cowley.

Serpentine Die Cut 11½

1999, June 16 Litho.

Self-Adhesive (#B162)

B162 SP75 40c +5c multi .75 .60

Perf. 14¼

B163 SP75 40c +5c multi .75 .60
B164 SP75 80c +5c multi 1.40 1.40

Souvenir Sheet

B165 Sheet of 3, #B163-B164, B165a 3.50 3.50
a. SP75 40c +5c like #B162 1.35 1.35

Nos. B162, B165a are 37x26mm.

For 2000 semi-postals, see Nos. 1681, 1682, 1682a and 1687.

Children's Health SP76

Designs: No. B166, Four cyclists. 90c+5c, Cyclist in air. No. B168, Cyclist riding through puddle.

2001, Aug. 1 Litho. *Perf. 14*

B166 SP76 40c +5c multi .75 .60
a. Sheet of 10 7.50 7.50
B167 SP76 90c +5c multi 1.50 1.40
a. Souvenir sheet, #B166-B167 2.10 2.10

Size: 30x25mm

Serpentine Die Cut 10x9¾

Self-Adhesive

B168 SP76 40c +5c multi .60 .60
Nos. B166-B168 (3) 2.85 2.60

Healthy Living SP77

Designs: B169, 40c+5c, Fruits. 90c+5c, Vegetables.

No. B171a, Fruits, diff. B172, Fruits diff. (like B171a).

2002, Aug. 7 *Perf. 14¼x14*

B169 SP77 40c +5c multi .75 .60
B170 SP77 90c +5c multi 1.50 1.50

Souvenir Sheet

B171 Sheet, #B169-B170, B171a 3.50 3.50
a. SP77 40c +5c multi (21x26mm) 1.25 1.25

Coil Stamp

Size: 21x26mm

Self-Adhesive

Serpentine Die Cut 9¾x10

B172 SP77 40c +5c multi .75 .50

Children's Health SP78

Designs: No. B173, 40c+5c, Children on swings. 90c+5c, Child with ball, girl playing hopscotch.

Nos. B175a, B176, 40c+ 5c, Girl on monkey bars.

2003, Aug. 6 Litho. *Perf. 14*

B173 SP78 40c +5c multi .75 .55
B174 SP78 90c +5c multi 1.50 1.50

Souvenir Sheet

B175 Sheet, #B173-B174, B175a 3.50 3.50
a. SP78 40c +5c multi (21x26mm), perf. 14½x14 1.25 1.25

Coil Stamp

Size: 21x26mm

Self-Adhesive

Serpentine Die Cut 9¾x10

B176 SP78 40c +5c multi .75 .55

Children's Health — SP79

Designs: No. B177, Children playing with beach ball in water. No. B178, People in boat. Nos. B179a, B180, People fishing.

2004, Sept. 1 Litho. *Perf. 14*

B177 SP79 45c +5c multi .75 .65
B178 SP79 90c +5c multi 1.50 1.50

Souvenir Sheet

B179 Sheet, #B177-B178, B179a 3.50 3.50
a. SP79 45c +5c multi (22x27mm), perf. 14¼x14 1.25 1.25

Self-Adhesive

Size: 22x27mm

Serpentine Die Cut 9½x10

B180 SP79 45c +5c multi .75 .65

Children's Health — SP80

Designs: No. B181, Girl and horse. 90c+5c, Boy and rabbit. Nos. B183a, B184, Children and dog.

2005, Aug. 3 Litho. *Perf. 14*

B181 SP80 45c +5c multi .75 .65
B182 SP80 90c +5c multi 1.50 1.50
B183 Souvenir sheet, #B181-B182, B183a 3.50 3.50
a. SP80 45c +5c multi, 20x25mm, perf. 14½x14 1.25 1.25

Self-Adhesive

Size: 20x25mm

Serpentine Die Cut 9½x10

B184 SP80 45c +5c multi .75 .65

Children's Health — SP81

Designs: No. B185, Girl releasing dove. $1+10c, Boy with origami bird. Nos. B187a, B188, Two children, peace lily (25x30mm).

2007, Sept. 5 Litho. *Perf. 14*

B185 SP81 50c +10c multi .85 .85
a. Perf. 13½ .85 .85
B186 SP81 $1 +10c multi 1.50 1.50
a. Perf. 13½ 1.50 1.50

Souvenir Sheet

B187 Sheet, #B185-B186, B187a 3.75 3.75
a. SP81 50c +10c multi, perf. 14½x14 1.40 1.40
b. As "a," perf. 14½x13½x14½x14 .85 .85
c. Souvenir sheet, #B185a, B186a, B187b 3.25 3.25

Self-Adhesive

Serpentine Die Cut 9½x10

B188 SP81 50c +10c multi .85 .85

Surtax for Children's Health Camps.

Children's Health — SP82

Child: No. B189, Cycling. $1+10c, Kayaking. Nos. B191a, B192, Running.

2008, July 2 Litho. *Perf. 14¼*

B189 SP82 50c +10c multi .95 .95
B190 SP82 $1 +10c multi 1.75 1.75

Souvenir Sheet

B191 Sheet, #B189-B190, B191a 3.75 3.75
a. SP82 50c +10c multi (36x36mm), perf. 14x14½ .95 .95

Self-Adhesive

Serpentine Die Cut 9¾

Size: 34x34mm

B192 SP82 50c +10c multi .95 .95

Surtax for Children's Health Camps.

AIR POST STAMPS

Plane over Lake Manapouri AP1

Perf. 14x14½

1931, Nov. 10 Typo. Wmk. 61

C1 AP1 3p chocolate 27.50 22.50
a. Perf. 14x15 150.00 *500.00*
C2 AP1 4p dark violet 27.50 27.50
C3 AP1 7p orange 30.00 27.50
Nos. C1-C3 (3) 85.00 77.50

Most copies of No. C1a are poorly centered.

Type of 1931 Surcharged in Red

1931, Dec. 18 *Perf. 14x14½*

C4 AP1 5p on 3p yel green 20.00 25.00

Type of 1931 Overprinted in Dark Blue

1934, Jan. 17

C5 AP1 7p bright blue 50.00 55.00

1st official air mail flight between NZ and Australia.

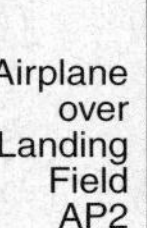

Airplane over Landing Field AP2

1935, May 4 Engr. *Perf. 14*

C6 AP2 1p rose carmine 1.10 .80
C7 AP2 3p dark violet 5.75 3.75
C8 AP2 6p gray blue 11.50 5.75
Nos. C6-C8 (3) 18.35 10.30
Set, never hinged 40.00

SPECIAL DELIVERY STAMPS

SD1

Perf. 14x½,14x15

1903-26 Typo. Wmk. 61

E1 SD1 6p purple & red ('26) 60.00 40.00
a. 6p violet & red, perf. 11 70.00 50.00

Mail Car — SD2

1939, Aug. 16 Engr. *Perf. 14*

E2 SD2 6p violet 1.75 6.00
Never hinged 5.00

POSTAGE DUE STAMPS

D1

D2

Wmk. 62

1899, Dec. 1 Typo. *Perf. 11*

J1 D1 ½p green & red .90 *19.00*
a. No period after "D" 75.00 60.00
J2 D1 1p green & red 12.50 2.10
J3 D1 2p green & red 40.00 6.25
J4 D1 3p green & red 20.00 6.00
J5 D1 4p green & red 42.50 25.00
J6 D1 5p green & red 45.00 *60.00*
J7 D1 6p green & red 45.00 *60.00*
J8 D1 8p green & red 110.00 *150.00*
J9 D1 10p green & red 175.00 *200.00*
J10 D1 1sh green & red 140.00 97.50
J11 D1 2sh green & red 225.00 *250.00*
Nos. J1-J11 (11) 855.90 875.85

Nos. J1-J11 may be found with N. Z. and D. varying in size.

1902, Feb. 28 Unwmk.

J12 D2 ½p gray grn & red 3.00 7.50

Wmk. 61

J13 D2 ½p gray grn & red 3.00 2.10
J14 D2 1p gray grn & red 12.00 4.00
J15 D2 2p gray grn & red 150.00 150.00

1904-28 *Perf. 14, 14x14½*

J16 D2 ½p green & car 3.75 4.25
J17 D2 1p green & car 7.00 1.00
J18 D2 2p green & car 9.00 3.50
J19 D2 3p grn & rose ('28) 50.00 25.00
Nos. J16-J19 (4) 69.75 33.75

N Z and Star printed on the back in Blue

1925 Unwmk. *Perf. 14x14½, 14x15*

J20 D2 ½p green & rose 4.00 *26.00*
J21 D2 2p green & rose 9.00 *35.00*

Catalogue values for unused stamps in this section, from this point to the end of the section, are for Never Hinged items.

D3

1939 Wmk. 61 Typo. *Perf. 15x14*

J22 D3 ½p turquoise green 13.00 *9.00*
J23 D3 1p rose pink 5.00 .60
J24 D3 2p ultramarine 9.00 1.75
J25 D3 3p brown orange 26.00 29.00
Nos. J22-J25 (4) 53.00 40.35

1945-49 Wmk. 253

J27 D3 1p rose pink ('49) 5.00 25.00
J28 D3 2p ultramarine ('47) 7.00 9.00
J29 D3 3p brown orange 15.00 5.75
Nos. J27-J29 (3) 27.00 39.75

The use of postage due stamps was discontinued in Sept., 1951.

WAR TAX STAMP

No. 144 Overprinted in Black

Perf. 14x14½

1915, Sept. 24 Wmk. 61

MR1 A43 ½p green 2.10 .60

OFFICIAL STAMPS

Regular Issues Ovptd. "O. P. S. O." Handstamped on Stamps of 1882-92

Overprinted in Black

1892 Wmk. 62 *Perf as Before*

Rose or Magenta Handstamp

O1 A9 1p rose *250.*
O2 A10 2p violet *425.*
O3 A16 2½p ultramarine *325.*
O4 A17 5p olive gray *500.*
O5 A13 6p brown *700.*

Violet Handstamp

O6 N1 ½p rose *625.*
O7 A9 1p rose *210.*
O8 A10 2p violet

Handstamped on No. 67A in Rose

1899 *Perf. 10, 10x11*

O9 A15a ½p black *250.*

Handstamped on No. 79 in Violet

Unwmk. *Perf. 14, 15*

O10 A27 8p dull blue *575.*

Handstamped on Stamps of 1899-1900 in Violet

1902 *Perf. 11*

O11 A22 2½p blue *425.*
O12 A23 3p org brown *525.*
O13 A25 5p red brown *525.*
O14 A27 8p dark blue *625.*

Green Handstamp

O15 A25 5p red brown *500.*

Handstamped on Stamp of 1901 in Violet

Wmk. 63 *Perf. 11*

O16 A35 1p carmine *275.*

Handstamped on Stamps of 1902-07 in Violet or Magenta

1905-07 Wmk. 61 *Perf. 11, 14*

O17 A18 ½p green *250.*
O18 A35 1p carmine *275.*
O19 A22 2½p blue *350.*
O20 A25 5p red brown
O21 A27 8p deep blue
O22 A30 2sh blue green *1,600.*

The "O. P. S. O." handstamp is usually struck diagonally, reading up, but on No. O19 it also occurs horizontally. The letters stand for "On Public Service Only."

Overprinted in Black

On Stamps of 1902-07

1907 *Perf. 14, 14x13, 14x14½*

O23 A18 ½p green 12.00 2.00
O24 A35 1p carmine 12.00 1.00
a. Booklet pane of 6 110.00
O25 A33 2p violet 20.00 2.00
O26 A23 3p orange brn 60.00 6.00
O27 A26 6p carmine rose 250.00 40.00
a. Horiz. pair, imperf. vert. *925.00*
O28 A29 1sh brown red 125.00 25.00
O29 A30 2sh blue green 175.00 150.00
a. Horiz. pair, imperf. vert. *1,400.*
O30 A31 5sh vermilion 350.00 350.00
Nos. O23-O30 (8) 1,004. 576.00

On No. 127

Perf. 14x13, 14x14½

O31 A26 6p carmine rose 275.00 65.00

On No. 129

1909 *Perf. 14x14½*

O32 A35 1p car (redrawn) 90.00 3.00

On Nos. 130-131, 133, 137, 139

1910 *Perf. 14, 14x13½, 14x14½*

O33 A41 ½p yellow green 10.00 1.00
a. Inverted overprint 1,600.
O34 A42 1p carmine 3.75 .20
O35 A41 3p orange brown 20.00 2.00
O36 A41 6p carmine rose 30.00 10.00
O37 A41 1sh vermilion 70.00 40.00
Nos. O33-O37 (5) 133.75 53.20

For 3p see note on perf varieties following No. 139.

On Postal-Fiscal Stamps No. AR32, AR36, AR44

1911-14

O38 PF1 2sh blue ('14) 75.00 52.50
O39 PF1 5sh green ('13) 125.00 *200.00*
O40 PF2 £1 rose 1,000. 625.00
Nos. O38-O40 (3) 1,200. 877.50

On Stamps of 1909-19

Perf. 14x13½, 14x14½

1915-19 Typo.

O41 A43 ½p green 1.60 .20
O42 A46 1½p gray black ('16) 8.00 3.00
O43 A47 1½p gray black ('16) 5.75 1.00
O44 A47 1½p brown org ('19) 5.75 .60
O45 A43 2p yellow ('17) 5.75 .50
O46 A43 3p chocolate ('19) 16.00 1.50

Engr.

O47 A45 3p vio brn ('16) 8.00 1.50
O48 A45 6p car rose ('16) 12.00 1.00
O49 A41 8p dp bl (R) ('16) 20.00 *30.00*
O50 A45 1sh vermilion ('16) 20.00 4.00
a. 1sh orange 20.00 4.00
Nos. O41-O50 (10) 102.85 *43.30*

For 8p see note on perf varieties following No. 139.

On No. 157

1922

O51 A45 8p red brown 100.00 *125.00*

On Nos. 151, 158

1925

O52 A45 4p purple 20.00 4.25
O53 A45 9p olive green 45.00 42.50

On No. 177

1925 *Perf. 14x14½*

O54 A42 1p carmine 5.00 5.00

On Nos. 184, 182

1927-28 Wmk. 61 *Perf. 14, 14½x14*

O55 A57 1p rose red 2.50 .20
O56 A56 2sh blue 125.00 140.00

On No. AR50

1933 *Perf. 14*

O57 PF5 5sh green 350.00 350.00

Nos. 186, 187, 196 Overprinted in Black

1936 *Perf. 14x13½, 13½x14, 14*

O58 A59 1p copper red 2.00 1.40
O59 A60 1½p red brown 14.00 *30.00*
O60 A69 1sh dark slate grn 20.00 *52.50*
Nos. O58-O60 (3) 36.00 83.90
Set, never hinged 80.00

Same Overprint Horizontally in Black or Green on Stamps of 1936

Perf. 12½, 13½, 13x13½, 14x13½, 13½x14, 14

1936-42 Wmk. 253

O61 A58 ½p brt grn ('37) 1.50 5.25
O62 A59 1p copper red 3.00 .60
O63 A60 1½p red brown 4.00 5.25
O64 A61 2p red org ('38) 1.00 .20
a. Perf. 12½ ('42) 110.00 62.50
O65 A62 2½p dk gray & dk brown 8.00 24.00
O66 A63 3p choc ('38) 27.50 4.00
O67 A64 4p blk brn & blk 5.00 1.10
O68 A66 6p red ('37) 5.75 .35
O68B A67 8p dp brn ('42) 8.50 20.00
O69 A68 9p black & scar (G) ('38) 80.00 45.00
O70 A69 1sh dk slate grn 14.00 1.60
a. Perf. 12½ ('42) 27.50 1.75

Overprint Vertical

O71 A70 2sh ol grn ('37) 24.00 8.50
a. Perf. 12½ ('42) 90.00 25.00
Nos. O61-O71 (12) 182.25 115.85
Set, never hinged 375.00

Same Overprint Horizontally in Black on Nos. 226, 227, 228

1938

O72 A79 ½p emerald 5.75 1.75
O73 A79 1p rose red 7.25 .30
O74 A80 1½p violet brn 37.50 10.50
Nos. O72-O74 (3) 50.50 12.55
Set, never hinged 95.00

Same Overprint on No. AR50

1938 Wmk. 61 *Perf. 14*

O75 PF5 5sh green 75.00 47.50
Never hinged 150.00

Nos. 229-235, 237, 239-241 Overprinted in Red or Black

Perf. 13½x13, 13x13½, 14x13½

1940 Wmk. 253

O76 A81 ½p dk bl grn (R) .60 .75
a. "ff" joined 29.00 70.00
O77 A82 1p scar & sepia 2.25 .30
a. "ff" joined 29.00 70.00
O78 A83 1½p brt vio & ultra 1.10 *4.25*
O79 A84 2p black brn & Prus green 2.25 .30
a. "ff" joined 35.00 70.00
O80 A85 2½p dk bl & myr grn 1.40 4.50
a. "ff" joined 29.00 77.50
O81 A86 3p deep plum & dark vio (R) 5.75 .95
a. "ff" joined 24.00 55.00
O82 A87 4p dark red vio & violet brn 14.50 1.60
a. "ff" joined 70.00 92.50
O83 A89 6p vio & brt grn 14.50 1.60
a. "ff" joined 40.00 80.00
O84 A90 8p org red & blk 14.50 13.00
a. "ff" joined 40.00 110.00
O85 A91 9p dp org & olive 5.75 5.75
O86 A92 1sh dk sl grn & ol 35.00 5.25
Nos. O76-O86 (11) 97.60 38.25
Set, never hinged 190.00

Nos. 227A, 228C Overprinted in Black

1941 Wmk. 253 *Perf. 13½*
O88 A79 1p light blue green .30 .30
O89 A80 3p blue .75 .30
Set, never hinged 2.25

Same Overprint on No. 245

1944 *Perf. 14x15*

Size: 17¼x20¼mm

O90 A68 9p int black & scar 20.00 17.00
Never Hinged 45.00

Same Overprint on No. AR78

Perf. 14

O91 PF5 5sh green 12.00 7.00
Never Hinged 20.00

Catalogue values for unused stamps in this section, from this point to the end of the section, are for Never Hinged items.

Same Ovpt. on Stamps of 1941-47

1946-51 *Perf. 13½, 14*
O92 A79 ½p brn org ('46) 1.75 1.25
O92B A80 1½p red 5.75 1.25
O93 A80 2p orange .90 .30
O94 A80 4p rose lilac 4.00 1.25
O95 A80 6p rose carmine 5.75 1.25
O96 A80 8p deep violet 10.00 4.50
O97 A80 9p chocolate 11.50 5.75
O98 A104 1sh dk car rose & chestnut 11.50 1.75
O99 A104 2sh dk green & brown org 26.00 8.50
Nos. O92-O99 (9) 77.15 25.80

Queen Elizabeth II — O1

Perf. 13½x13

1954, Mar. 1 Engr. Wmk. 253
O100 O1 1p orange 1.10 .50
O101 O1 1½p rose brown 4.25 5.75
O102 O1 2p green .45 .20
O103 O1 3p red .45 .20
O104 O1 4p blue 1.10 .60
O105 O1 9p rose carmine 10.50 2.50
O106 O1 1sh rose violet 1.10 .20
Nos. O100-O106 (7) 18.95 9.95

Exist imperf.

Nos. O102, O101 Surcharged with New Value and Dots

1959-61
O107 O1 2½p on 2p green ('61) 1.10 1.75
O108 O1 6p on 1½p rose brn .60 1.25

Exist imperf.

1963, Mar. 1
O109 O1 2½p dark olive 4.00 1.75
O111 O1 3sh slate 47.50 57.50

Exist imperf.

LIFE INSURANCE

Lighthouses
LI1 LI2

Perf. 10, 11, 10x11, 12x11½

1891, Jan. 2 Typo. Wmk. 62
OY1 LI1 ½p purple 100.00 7.00
OY2 LI1 1p blue 80.00 2.00
OY3 LI1 2p red brown 125.00 4.25
OY4 LI1 3p chocolate 425.00 22.50
OY5 LI1 6p green 550.00 70.00
OY6 LI1 1sh rose pink 800.00 140.00
Nos. OY1-OY6 (6) 2,080. 245.75

Stamps from outside rows of the sheets sometimes lack watermark.

1903-04 Wmk. 61 *Perf. 11, 14x11*
OY7 LI1 ½p purple 90.00 7.00
OY8 LI1 1p blue 75.00 1.10
OY9 LI1 2p red brown 140.00 10.00
Nos. OY7-OY9 (3) 305.00 18.10

1905-32 *Perf. 11, 14, 14x14½*
OY10 LI2 ½p yel grn ('13) 1.40 .90
OY11 LI2 ½p green ('32) 5.75 2.75
OY12 LI2 1p blue ('06) 375.00 29.00
OY13 LI2 1p dp rose ('13) 9.75 1.10
OY14 LI2 1p scarlet ('31) 4.25 2.00
OY15 LI2 1½p gray ('17) 14.00 4.25
OY16 LI2 1½p brn org ('19) 1.75 1.40
OY17 LI2 2p red brown 2,750. 20.00
OY18 LI2 2p violet ('13) 20.00 17.00
OY19 LI2 2p yellow ('21) 6.00 6.00
OY20 LI2 3p ocher ('13) 29.00 20.00
OY21 LI2 3p choc ('31) 11.00 26.00
OY22 LI2 6p carmine rose ('13) 20.00 26.00
OY23 LI2 6p pink ('31) 20.00 45.00
Nos. OY10-OY23 (14) 3,267. 201.40

#OY15, OY16 have "POSTAGE" at each side.
Stamps from outside rows of the sheets sometimes lack watermark.

1946-47 Wmk. 253 *Perf. 14x15*
OY24 LI2 ½p yel grn ('47) 1.90 1.90
OY25 LI2 1p scarlet 1.40 1.25
OY26 LI2 2p yellow 2.25 *15.00*
OY27 LI2 3p chocolate 10.50 *30.00*
OY28 LI2 6p pink ('47) 8.50 *25.00*
Nos. OY24-OY28 (5) 24.55 73.15
Set, never hinged 42.50

Catalogue values for unused stamps in this section, from this point to the end of the section, are for Never Hinged items.

New Zealand Lighthouses

Castlepoint LI3

Taiaroa — LI4

Cape Palliser LI5

Cape Campbell LI6

Eddystone (England) LI7

Stephens Island LI8

The Brothers LI9

Cape Brett — LI10

Perf. 13½x13, 13x13½

1947-65 Engr. Wmk. 253
OY29 LI3 ½p dk grn & red orange 1.75 .70
OY30 LI4 1p dk ol grn & blue 1.75 1.10
OY31 LI5 2p int bl & gray .90 .90
OY32 LI6 2½p ultra & blk ('63) 11.00 15.00
OY33 LI7 3p red vio & bl 3.50 .75
OY34 LI8 4p dk brn & org 4.50 1.75
a. Wmkd. sideways ('65) 4.50 16.00
OY35 LI9 6p dk brn & bl 4.25 2.50
OY36 LI10 1sh red brn & bl 4.25 3.50
Nos. OY29-OY36 (8) 31.90 26.20

Set first issued Aug. 1, 1947.
Exist imperf.

Nos. OY30, OY32-OY33, OY34a, OY35-OY36 and Types Surcharged

Perf. 13½x13, 13x13½

1967-68 Engr. Wmk. 253
OY37 LI4 1c on 1p 2.50 4.75
a. Wmkd. upright ('68) 1.10 4.75
OY38 LI6 2c on 2½p 11.00 16.00
OY39 LI7 2½c on 3p, wmkd. upright 1.75 5.50
a. Watermarked sideways ('68) 2.75 5.50
OY40 LI8 3c on 4p 5.25 6.25
OY41 LI9 5c on 6p .85 7.00
OY42 LI10 10c on 1sh, wmkd. sideways .85 4.75
a. Watermarked upright 2.40 11.50
Nos. OY37-OY42 (6) 22.20 44.25

The surcharge is different on each stamp and is adjusted to obliterate old denomination. One dot only on 2½c.
Set first issued July 10, 1967.

Moeraki Point Lighthouse — LI11

Lighthouses: 2½c, Puysegur Point, horiz. 3c, Baring Head. 4c, Cape Egmont, horiz. 8c, East Cape. 10c, Farewell Spit. 15c, Dog Island.

Perf. 13x13½, 13½x13, 14 (8c, 10c)

1969-76 Litho. Unwmk.
OY43 LI11 ½c pur, bl & yel .75 2.00
OY44 LI11 2½c yel, ultra & grn .60 1.40
OY45 LI11 3c yellow & brown .60 .85
OY46 LI11 4c lt ultra & ocher .60 1.10
OY47 LI11 8c multicolored .60 3.25
OY48 LI11 10c multicolored .40 3.25
OY49 LI11 15c multicolored .40 2.40
a. Perf. 14 ('78) 1.00 2.50
Nos. OY43-OY49 (7) 3.95 14.25

Cent. of Government Life Insurance Office.
Issued: #OY47-OY48, 11/17/76; others 3/27/69.

No. OY44 Surcharged with New Value and 4 Diagonal Bars

Perf. 13½x13

1978, Mar. 8 Litho. Wmk. 253
OY50 LI11 25c on 2½c multi .85 2.00

Lighthouse — LI12

1981, June 3 Litho. *Perf. 14½*
OY51 LI12 5c multicolored .20 .20
OY52 LI12 10c multicolored .20 .20
OY53 LI12 20c multicolored .20 .20
OY54 LI12 30c multicolored .30 .30
OY55 LI12 40c multicolored .35 .35
OY56 LI12 50c multicolored .35 .50
Nos. OY51-OY56 (6) 1.60 1.75

Government Life Insurance Stamps have been discontinued.

NEWSPAPER STAMPS

Queen Victoria — N1

Wmk. 59

1873, Jan. 1 Typo. *Perf. 10*
P1 N1 ½p rose 140.00 47.50
a. Perf. 12½x10 160.00 75.00
b. Perf. 12½ 210.00 75.00

The "N Z" watermark (illustrated over No. 27) is widely spaced and intended for larger stamps. About a third of the stamps in each sheet are unwatermarked. They are worth a slight premium.
For overprint, see No. O6.

1875, Jan. Wmk. 64 *Perf. 12½*
P3 N1 ½p rose 25.00 5.00
a. Pair, imperf. between 800.00 500.00
b. Perf. 12 70.00 12.50

1892 Wmk. 62 *Perf. 12½*
P4 N1 ½p bright rose 11.00 1.50
a. Unwatermarked 20.00 10.00

ROSS DEPENDENCY

Catalogue values for unused stamps in this section are for Never Hinged items.

H.M.S. Erebus and Mount Erebus A1

Ernest H. Shackleton and Robert F. Scott — A2

Map Showing Location of Ross Dependency
A3

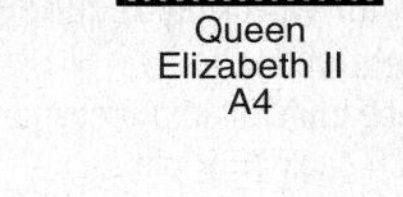

Queen Elizabeth II
A4

Perf. 14, 13 (A4)

1957, Jan. 11 Engr. Wmk. 253

L1	A1	3p dark blue	3.00	1.25
L2	A2	4p dark carmine	3.00	1.25
L3	A3	8p ultra & car rose	3.00	1.25
L4	A4	1sh6p dull violet	3.00	1.25
		Nos. L1-L4 (4)	12.00	5.00

1967, July 10

L5	A1	2c dark blue	21.00	15.00
L6	A2	3c dark carmine	12.00	10.00
L7	A3	7c ultra & car rose	12.00	10.00
L8	A4	15c dull violet	12.00	10.00
		Nos. L5-L8 (4)	57.00	45.00

Skua — A5

Scott Base — A6

Designs: 4c, Hercules plane unloading at Williams Field. 5c, Shackleton's hut, Cape Royds. 8c, Naval supply ship Endeavour unloading. 18c, Tabular ice floe.

Perf. 13x13½

1972, Jan. 18 Litho. Unwmk.

L9	A5	3c lt bl, blk & gray	1.00	1.75
L10	A5	4c black & violet	.25	1.75
L11	A5	5c rose lil, blk & gray	.25	1.75
L12	A5	8c blk, dk gray & brn	.25	1.75

Perf. 14x13½

L13	A6	10c slate grn, brt grn & blk ('79)	.70	1.75
a.		Perf. 14½x14	.25	1.90
L14	A6	18c pur & black ('79)	1.60	3.00
a.		Perf. 14½x14	.25	1.90
		Nos. L9-L14 (6)	4.05	11.75

25th Anniv. of Scott Base — A7

1982, Jan. 20 Litho. *Perf. 15½*

L15	A7	5c Adelie penguins	1.40	1.60
L16	A7	10c Tracked vehicles	.20	.75
L17	A7	20c shown	.20	.75
L18	A7	30c Field party, Upper Taylor Valley	.20	.45
L19	A7	40c Vanda Station	.20	.45
L20	A7	50c Scott's hut, Cape Evans, 1911	.20	.45
		Nos. L15-L20 (6)	2.40	4.45

Wildlife — A8

1994-95 Litho. *Perf. 13½*

L21	A8	5c South polar skua	.20	.20
L22	A8	10c Snow petrel chick	.20	.20
L23	A8	20c Black-browed albatross	.30	.30
L23A	A8	40c like No. 24	.65	.65
L24	A8	45c Emperor penguins	.70	.70
L25	A8	50c Chinstrap penguins	.80	.80
L26	A8	70c Adelie penguins	1.10	1.10
L27	A8	80c Elephant seals	1.25	1.25
L28	A8	$1 Leopard seal	1.60	1.60
L29	A8	$2 Weddell seal	3.25	3.25
L30	A8	$3 Crabeater seal pup	4.75	4.75
		Nos. L21-L30 (11)	14.80	14.80

Issued: 40c, 10/2/95; others, 11/2/94.

Antarctic Explorers
A9

Explorer, ships: 40c, James Cook, Resolution & Adventure. 80c, James Clark Ross, Erebus & Terror. $1, Roald Amundsen, Fram. $1.20, Robert Falcon Scott, Terra Nova. $1.50, Ernest Henry Shackleton, Endurance. $1.80, Richard Evelyn Byrd, Floyd Bennett (airplane).

1995, Nov. 9 Litho. *Perf. 14½*

L31	A9	40c multicolored	.65	.65
L32	A9	80c multicolored	1.25	1.25
L33	A9	$1 multicolored	1.60	1.60
L34	A9	$1.20 multicolored	1.90	1.90
L35	A9	$1.50 multicolored	2.40	2.40
L36	A9	$1.80 multicolored	2.75	2.75
		Nos. L31-L36 (6)	10.55	10.55

Antarctic Landscapes — A10

Designs: 40c, Inside ice cave, vert. 80c, Base of glacier, vert. $1, Glacier ice fall, vert. $1.20, Climbers on crater rim. $1.50, Pressure ridges. $1.80, Fumarole ice tower.

1996, Nov. 13 Litho. *Perf. 14*

L37	A10	40c multicolored	.65	.65
L38	A10	80c multicolored	1.25	1.25
L39	A10	$1 multicolored	1.60	1.60
L40	A10	$1.20 multicolored	1.90	1.90
L41	A10	$1.50 multicolored	2.40	2.40
L42	A10	$1.80 multicolored	2.75	2.75
		Nos. L37-L42 (6)	10.55	10.55

Antarctic Sea Birds — A11

1997, Nov. 12 Litho. *Perf. 14*

L43	A11	40c Snow petrel	.65	.65
L44	A11	80c Cape petrel	1.25	1.25
L45	A11	$1 Antarctic prion	1.75	1.50
L46	A11	$1.20 Antarctic fulmar	2.25	2.00
L47	A11	$1.50 Antarctic petrel	2.50	2.25
L48	A11	$1.80 Antarctic tern	3.00	2.75
a.		Block of 6, #L43-L48	15.00	15.00

World Wildlife Fund.

Ice Formations
A12

Designs: 40c, Sculptured sea ice. 80c, Glacial tongue. $1, Stranded tabular iceberg. $1.20, Autumn at Cape Evans. $1.50, Sea ice in summer thaw. $1.80, Sunset on tabular icebergs.

1998, Nov. 11 Litho. *Perf. 14*

L49	A12	40c multicolored	.65	.65
L50	A12	80c multicolored	1.25	1.25
L51	A12	$1 multicolored	1.60	1.60
L52	A12	$1.20 multicolored	1.90	1.90
L53	A12	$1.50 multicolored	2.40	2.40
L54	A12	$1.80 multicolored	2.75	2.75
a.		Block of 6, #L49-L54	11.00	11.00

Night Skies
A13

Designs: 40c, Sea smoke, McMurdo Sound. 80c, Alpenglow, Mt. Erebus. $1.10, Sunset, Black Island. $1.20, Pressure ridges, Ross Sea. $1.50, Evening light, Ross Island. $1.80, Mother of pearl clouds, Ross Island.

1999, Nov. 17 Litho. *Perf. 14*

L55	A13	40c multicolored	.65	.65
L56	A13	80c multicolored	1.25	1.25
L57	A13	$1.10 multicolored	1.75	1.75
L58	A13	$1.20 multicolored	1.90	1.90
L59	A13	$1.50 multicolored	2.40	2.40
L60	A13	$1.80 multicolored	2.75	2.75
		Nos. L55-L60 (6)	10.70	10.70

Antarctic Transportation — A14

Designs: 40c, RNZAF C130 Hercules. 80c, Hagglunds BV206 All-terrain carrier. $1.10, Tracked 4x4 motorbike. $1.20, ASV Track truck. $1.50, Squirrel helicopter. $1.80, Elan Skidoo.

2000, Nov. 4 Litho. *Perf. 14*

L61	A14	40c multi	.65	.65
L62	A14	80c multi	1.25	1.25
L63	A14	$1.10 multi	1.75	1.75
L64	A14	$1.20 multi	1.90	1.90
L65	A14	$1.50 multi	2.40	2.40
L66	A14	$1.80 multi	2.75	2.75
		Nos. L61-L66 (6)	10.70	10.70

Penguins Type of 2001 of New Zealand

Designs: 40c, Emperor. 80c, Adelie. 90c, Emperor, diff. $1.30, Adelie, diff. $1.50, Emperor, diff. $2, Adelie, diff.

2001, Nov. 7 *Perf. 14¼*

L67	A475	40c multi	.65	.65
L68	A475	80c multi	1.25	1.25
L69	A475	90c multi	1.40	1.40
L70	A475	$1.30 multi	2.10	2.10
L71	A475	$1.50 multi	2.40	2.40
L72	A475	$2 multi	3.25	3.25
		Nos. L67-L72 (6)	11.05	11.05

Discovery Expedition of Capt. Robert Falcon Scott, 1901-04
A15

Designs: 40c, Three men with sleds. 80c, HMS Discovery. 90c, HMS Discovery trapped in ice. $1.30, Edward Wilson, Ernest Shackleton and sleds. $1.50, Explorers with flags and dog. $2, Base hut.

2002, Nov. 6 Litho. *Perf. 14*

L73	A15	40c multi	.65	.65
L74	A15	80c multi	1.25	1.25
L75	A15	90c multi	1.40	1.40
L76	A15	$1.30 multi	2.10	2.10
L77	A15	$1.50 multi	2.40	2.40
L78	A15	$2 multi	3.25	3.25
		Nos. L73-L78 (6)	11.05	11.05

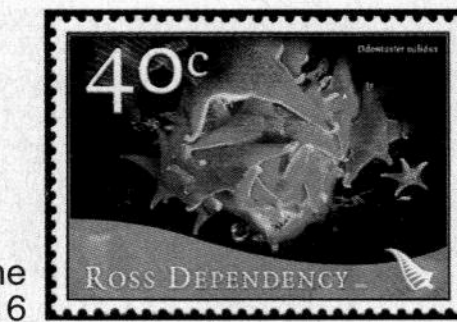

Marine Life — A16

Designs: 40c, Odontaster validus. 90c, Beroe cucumis. $1.30, Macroptychaster accrescens. $1.50, Sterechinus neumayeri. $2, Perkinsiana littoralis.

2003, Oct. 1 Litho. *Perf. 13x13¼*

L79	A16	40c multi	.65	.65
L80	A16	90c multi	1.40	1.40
L81	A16	$1.30 multi	2.10	2.10
L82	A16	$1.50 multi	2.40	2.40
L83	A16	$2 multi	3.25	3.25
		Nos. L79-L83 (5)	9.80	9.80

Emperor Penguins and Map of Antarctica — A17

Various pictures of penguins.

2004, Nov. 3 Litho. *Perf. 13¼x14*

Color of Denomination

L84	A17	45c yellow orange	.70	.70
L85	A17	90c dark brown	1.40	1.40
L86	A17	$1.35 lilac	2.10	2.10
L87	A17	$1.50 red brown	2.40	2.40
L88	A17	$2 gray blue	3.25	3.25
		Nos. L84-L88 (5)	9.85	9.85

Photographs — A18

Designs: 45c, Dry Valleys, by Craig Potton. 90c, Emperor Penguins, by Andris Apse. $1.35, Fur Seal, by Mark Mitchell. $1.50, Captain Scott's Hut, by Colin Monteath. $2. Minke Whale, by Kim Westerskov.

2005, Nov. 2 Litho. *Perf. 13¼*

L89	A18	45c multi	.70	.70
L90	A18	90c multi	1.40	1.40
L91	A18	$1.35 multi	2.10	2.10
L92	A18	$1.50 multi	2.40	2.40
L93	A18	$2 multi	3.25	3.25
		Nos. L89-L93 (5)	9.85	9.85

A sheet containing Nos. L89-L93 was in a limited edition album.

New Zealand Antarctic Program, 50th Anniv.
A19

Designs: 45c, Biologist. 90c, Hydrologist. $1.35, Geologist. $1.50, Meteorologist. $2, Marine biologist.

2006, Nov. 1 Litho. *Perf. 14*

L94	A19	45c multi	.70	.70
L95	A19	90c multi	1.40	1.40
L96	A19	$1.35 multi	2.10	2.10
L97	A19	$1.50 multi	2.40	2.40
L98	A19	$2 multi	3.25	3.25
		Nos. L94-L98 (5)	9.85	9.85

Commonwealth Trans-Antarctic Expedition, 50th Anniv. — A20

Designs: 50c, Man and Beaver airplane. $1, Man and sled. $1.50, Sled dogs. $2, TE20 Ferguson tractor. $2.50, HMNZS Endeavour.

2007, Nov. 7 Litho. *Perf. 14*

L99	A20	50c	multi	.80	.80
L100	A20	$1	multi	1.50	1.50
L101	A20	$1.50	multi	2.40	2.40
L102	A20	$2	multi	3.25	3.25
L103	A20	$2.50	multi	4.00	4.00
a.	Souvenir sheet, #L102-L103			7.25	7.25
	Nos. L99-L103 (5)			11.95	11.95

1907-09 British Antarctic Expedition A21

Designs: 50c, Departure of Nimrod from Lyttleton. $1, Expedition Hut, Cape Royds. $1.50, First vehicle on Antarctica. $2, First men to reach South Magnetic Pole. $2.50, First ascent of Mt. Erebus.

2008, Nov. 5 Litho. *Perf. 13½x13¼*

L104	A21	50c	multi	.60	.60
L105	A21	$1	multi	1.25	1.25
L106	A21	$1.50	multi	1.75	1.75
L107	A21	$2	multi	2.40	2.40
L108	A21	$2.50	multi	3.00	3.00
	Nos. L104-L108 (5)			9.00	9.00

NICARAGUA

ˌni-kə-ˈrä-gwə

LOCATION — Central America, between Honduras and Costa Rica
GOVT. — Republic
AREA — 50,439 sq. mi.
POP. — 4,384,400 (1997 est.)
CAPITAL — Managua

100 Centavos = 1 Peso
100 Centavos = 1 Córdoba (1913)

Catalogue values for unused stamps in this country are for Never Hinged items, beginning with Scott 689 in the regular postage section, Scott C261 in the airpost section, Scott CO37 in the airpost official section, and Scott RA60 in the postal tax section.

Watermarks

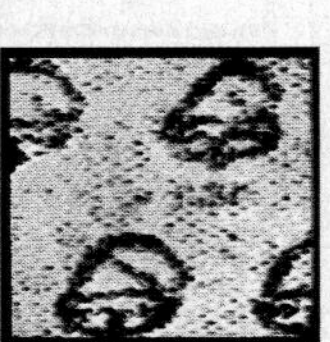

Wmk. 117 — Liberty Cap

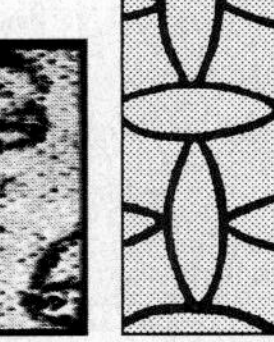

Wmk. 209 — Multiple Ovals

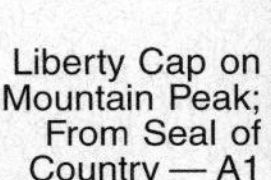

Liberty Cap on Mountain Peak; From Seal of Country — A1

A2

A3

Unwmk.

1862, Dec. 2 Engr. *Perf. 12*

Yellowish Paper

1	A1	2c	dark blue	75.00	20.00
2	A1	5c	black	150.00	60.00

Designs of Nos. 1-2 measure 22½x18½mm. Perforations are invariably rough.

Values are for copies without gum. Copies with gum sell for more. Nos. 1-2 were canceled only by pen.

See No. C509.

1869-71

White Paper

3	A1	1c	bister ('71)	3.00	1.25
4	A1	2c	blue	3.00	1.25
5	A1	5c	black	100.00	1.00
6	A2	10c	vermilion	4.00	1.75
7	A3	25c	green	7.50	4.00
			Nos. 3-7 (5)	117.50	9.25

Designs of Nos. 3-7 measure 22½x19mm. Perforations are clean cut.

1878-80 *Rouletted 8½*

8	A1	1c	brown	2.00	1.25
9	A1	2c	blue	2.00	1.25
10	A1	5c	black	50.00	1.00
11	A2	10c	ver ('80)	2.50	1.50
12	A3	25c	green ('79)	2.50	4.00
			Nos. 8-12 (5)	59.00	9.00

Most values exist on thicker soft paper.

Stamps with letter/numeral cancellations other than "3 G," "6 M," "9 C" sell for more.

Nos. 3-12 were reprinted in 1892. The corresponding values of the two series are printed in the same shades which is not usually true of the originals. They are, however, similar to some of the original shades and the only certain test is comparison. Originals have thin white gum; reprints have rather thick yellowish gum. Value 50c each. Unused examples of Nos. 3-12 without gum should be presumed to be reprints. Nos. 5 and 10 unused are extremely scarce and should be purchased with original gum and should be expertized.

Seal of Nicaragua — A4

Locomotive and Telegraph Key — A5

1882 Engr. *Perf. 12*

13	A4	1c	green	.20	.25
14	A4	2c	carmine	.20	.25
15	A4	5c	blue	.20	.25
16	A4	10c	dull violet	.25	.75
17	A4	15c	yellow	.60	*25.00*
18	A4	20c	slate gray	.90	*5.00*
19	A4	50c	dull violet	1.25	*25.00*
			Nos. 13-19 (7)	3.60	*56.50*

Used Values

of Nos. 13-120 are for stamps with genuine cancellations applied while the stamps were valid. Various counterfeit cancellations exist.

1890 Engr.

20	A5	1c	yellow brown	.20	.25
21	A5	2c	vermilion	.20	.25
22	A5	5c	deep blue	.20	.25
23	A5	10c	lilac gray	.20	.25
24	A5	20c	red	.20	*1.75*
25	A5	50c	purple	.20	*5.00*
26	A5	1p	brown	.25	*8.50*
27	A5	2p	dark green	.25	*9.00*
28	A5	5p	lake	.25	
29	A5	10p	orange	.25	
			Nos. 20-29 (10)	2.20	

The issues of 1890-1899 were printed by the Hamilton Bank Note Co., New York, to the order of N. F. Seebeck who held a contract for stamps with the government of Nicaragua. Reprints were made, for sale to collectors, of the 1896, 1897 and 1898, postage, postage due and official stamps. See notes following those issues.

For overprints see Nos. O1-O10.

Perforation Varieties

Imperfs and part perfs of all the Seebeck issues, Nos. 20-120, exist for all except originals of the 1898 issue, Nos. 99-109M.

Goddess of Plenty — A6

Columbus Sighting Land — A7

1891 Engr.

30	A6	1c	yellow brn	.25	.35
31	A6	2c	red	.25	.35
32	A6	5c	dk blue	.25	.25
33	A6	10c	slate	.25	.50
34	A6	20c	plum	.25	*2.00*
35	A6	50c	purple	.25	*5.00*
36	A6	1p	black brn	.25	*5.00*
37	A6	2p	green	.25	*8.50*
38	A6	5p	brown red	.25	
39	A6	10p	orange	.25	
			Nos. 30-39 (10)	2.50	

For overprints see Nos. O11-O20.

1892 Engr.

40	A7	1c	yellow brn	.20	.25
41	A7	2c	vermilion	.20	.20
42	A7	5c	dk blue	.20	.20
43	A7	10c	slate	.20	.25
44	A7	20c	plum	.20	*2.00*
45	A7	50c	purple	.20	*7.00*
46	A7	1p	brown	.20	*7.00*
47	A7	2p	blue grn	.20	*8.50*
48	A7	5p	rose lake	.20	
49	A7	10p	orange	.20	
			Nos. 40-49 (10)	2.00	

Commemorative of the 400th anniversary of the discovery of America by Columbus.

Stamps of the 1892 design were printed in other colors than those listed and overprinted "Telegrafos". The 1c blue, 10c orange, 20c slate, 50c plum and 2p vermilion are telegraph stamps which did not receive the overprint.

For overprints see Nos. O21-O30.

Arms — A8

"Victory" — A9

1893 Engr.

51	A8	1c	yellow brn	.20	.20
52	A8	2c	vermilion	.20	.20
53	A8	5c	dk blue	.20	.20
54	A8	10c	slate	.20	.25
55	A8	20c	dull red	.20	*1.50*
56	A8	50c	violet	.20	*4.00*
57	A8	1p	dk brown	.20	*7.00*
58	A8	2p	blue green	.20	*8.50*
59	A8	5p	rose lake	.20	
60	A8	10p	orange	.20	
			Nos. 51-60 (10)	2.00	

The 1c blue and 2c dark brown are telegraph stamps which did not receive the "Telegrafos" overprint.

For overprints see Nos. O31-O41.

1894 Engr.

61	A9	1c	yellow brn	.20	*.30*
62	A9	2c	vermilion	.20	*.40*
63	A9	5c	dp blue	.20	*.30*
64	A9	10c	slate	.20	*.40*
65	A9	20c	lake	.20	*2.00*
66	A9	50c	purple	.20	*5.00*
67	A9	1p	brown	.20	*9.50*
68	A9	2p	green	.20	*17.50*
69	A9	5p	brown red	.20	*45.00*
70	A9	10p	orange	.20	*45.00*
			Nos. 61-70 (10)	2.00	

There were three printings of this issue. Only the first is known postally used. Unused values are for the third printing.

Used values are for stamps with "DIRECCION" cancels in black that were removed from post office new year cards.

Specialists believe the 25c yellow green, type A9, is a telegraph denomination never issued for postal purposes. Stamps in other colors are telegraph stamps without the usual "Telegrafos" overprint.

For overprints see Nos. O42-O51.

Coat of Arms A10

Map of Nicaragua A11

1895 Engr.

71	A10	1c	yellow brn	.20	.30
72	A10	2c	vermilion	.20	.30
73	A10	5c	deep blue	.20	.25
74	A10	10c	slate	.20	.25
75	A10	20c	claret	.20	*.75*
76	A10	50c	lt violet	50.00	*5.00*
77	A10	1p	dk brown	.20	*5.00*
78	A10	2p	dp green	.20	*8.00*
79	A10	5p	brown red	.20	*11.00*
80	A10	10p	orange	.20	—
			Nos. 71-80 (10)	51.80	

Frames of Nos. 71-80 differ for each denomination.

A 50c violet blue exists. Its status is questioned. Value 20c.

There was little use of No. 80. Canceled stamps are almost always c-t-o or faked cancels, though it is known properly used.

For overprints see Nos. O52-O71.

1896 Engr.

81	A11	1c	violet	.30	*1.00*
82	A11	2c	blue grn	.30	*.50*
83	A11	5c	brt rose	.30	*.30*
84	A11	10c	blue	.50	*.50*
85	A11	20c	bister brn	3.00	*4.00*
86	A11	50c	blue gray	.60	*8.00*
87	A11	1p	black	.75	*11.00*
88	A11	2p	claret	.75	*15.00*
89	A11	5p	deep blue	.75	*15.00*
			Nos. 81-89 (9)	7.25	*55.30*

There were two printings of this issue. Only the first is known postally used. Unused values are for the second printing.

See italic note after No. 109M.

For overprints see Nos. O82-O117.

Wmk. 117

89A	A11	1c	violet	3.75	.90
89B	A11	2c	bl grn	3.75	1.25
89C	A11	5c	brt rose	15.00	.30
89D	A11	10c	blue	25.00	.90
89E	A11	20c	bis brn	22.50	4.25
89F	A11	50c	bl gray	42.50	*9.00*
89G	A11	1p	black	37.50	*12.50*
89H	A11	2p	claret		*18.00*
89I	A11	5p	dp bl		*40.00*

Same, dated 1897

1897 Engr. Unwmk.

90	A11	1c	violet	.50	.50
91	A11	2c	bl grn	.50	.60
92	A11	5c	brt rose	.50	.30
93	A11	10c	blue	6.25	.75
94	A11	20c	bis brn	2.50	*3.75*
95	A11	50c	bl gray	9.00	*9.50*
96	A11	1p	black	9.00	*15.00*
97	A11	2p	claret	20.00	*19.00*
98	A11	5p	dp bl	20.00	*42.50*
			Nos. 90-98 (9)	68.25	*91.90*

See italic note after No. 109M.

Wmk. 117

98A	A11	1c	violet	14.00	.50
98B	A11	2c	bl grn	14.00	.50
98C	A11	5c	brt rose	20.00	.40
98D	A11	10c	blue	22.50	.90
98E	A11	20c	bis brn	22.50	4.25
98F	A11	50c	bl gray	22.50	*8.00*
98G	A11	1p	black	25.00	*16.00*
98H	A11	2p	claret	25.00	*25.00*
98I	A11	5p	dp bl	125.00	*50.00*
			Nos. 98A-98I (9)	290.50	*105.55*

Coat of Arms of "Republic of Central America" — A12

1898 Engr. Wmk. 117

99	A12	1c	brown	.25	.40
100	A12	2c	slate	.25	.40
101	A12	4c	red brown	.25	.50
102	A12	5c	olive green	40.00	22.50
103	A12	10c	violet	15.00	.60
104	A12	15c	ultra	.40	1.50
105	A12	20c	blue	10.00	2.00
106	A12	50c	yellow	10.00	*9.50*
107	A12	1p	violet blue	.40	*16.00*
108	A12	2p	brown	19.00	*22.50*
109	A12	5p	orange	25.00	*32.50*
			Nos. 99-109 (11)	120.55	*108.40*

Unwmk.

109A	A12	1c	brown	1.25	.30
109B	A12	2c	slate	1.25	
109D	A12	4c	red brown	2.25	.60
109E	A12	5c	olive green	25.00	.20
109G	A12	10c	violet	25.00	.60
109H	A12	15c	ultra	25.00	
109I	A12	20c	blue	25.00	
109J	A12	50c	yellow	25.00	
109K	A12	1p	deep ultra	25.00	
109L	A12	2p	olive brown	25.00	
109M	A12	5p	orange	25.00	
			Nos. 109A-109M (11)	204.75	

The paper of Nos. 109A to 109M is slightly thicker and more opaque than that of Nos. 81 to 89 and 90 to 98. The 5c and 10c also exist on very thin, semi-transparent paper.

Many reprints of Nos. 81-98, 98F-98H, 99-109M are on thick, porous paper, with and without watermark. The watermark is sideways. Paper of the originals is thinner for Nos. 81-109 but thicker for Nos. 109A-109M. Value 15 cents each.

In addition, reprints of Nos. 81-89 and 90-98 exist on thin paper, but with shades differing slightly from those of originals.

For overprints see Nos. O118-O128.

"Justice" A13

Mt. Momotombo A14

1899 Litho.

110	A13	1c	gray grn	.20	*.35*
111	A13	2c	brown	.20	*.25*
112	A13	4c	dp rose	.35	*.40*
113	A13	5c	dp bl	.20	*.25*
114	A13	10c	buff	.20	*.30*
115	A13	15c	chocolate	.20	*.65*
116	A13	20c	dk grn	.35	*.75*

117 A13 50c brt rose .20 *3.00*
118 A13 1p red .20 *8.50*
119 A13 2p violet .20 *20.00*
120 A13 5p lt bl .20 *25.00*
Nos. 110-120 (11) 2.50 *59.45*

Nos. 110-120 exist imperf. and in horizontal pairs imperf. between.

Nos. 110-111, 113 exist perf 6x12 due to defective perforating equipment.

For overprints see Nos. O129-O139.

Imprint: "American Bank Note Co. NY"

1900, Jan. 1 **Engr.**

121 A14 1c plum .50 .20
122 A14 2c vermilion .50 .20
123 A14 3c green .75 .25
124 A14 4c ol grn 1.00 .25
125 A14 5c dk bl 4.00 .20
126 A14 6c car rose 14.00 5.00
127 A14 10c violet 7.00 .25
128 A14 15c ultra 8.00 .65
129 A14 20c brown 8.00 .65
130 A14 50c lake 7.00 1.10
131 A14 1p yellow 12.00 4.00
132 A14 2p salmon 10.00 2.25
133 A14 5p black 10.00 3.00
Nos. 121-133 (13) 82.75 18.00

Used values for #123, 126, 130-133 are for canceled to order copies.

See Nos. 159-161. For overprints and surcharges see Nos. 134-136, 144-151, 162-163, 175-178, O150-O154, 1L1-1L13, 1L16-1L19, 1L20, 2L1-2L10, 2L16-2L24, 2L36-2L39.

Nos. 131-133 Surcharged in Black or Red

1901, Mar. 5

134 A14 2c on 1p yel 5.00 *3.00*
a. Bar below date 14.00 *9.00*
b. Inverted surcharge *35.00*
c. Double surcharge *50.00*
135 A14 10c on 5p blk (R) 6.50 4.50
a. Bar below date 14.00 8.00
136 A14 20c on 2p salmon 7.50 7.50
a. Bar below date 14.00 10.00
Nos. 134-136 (3) 19.00 15.00

A 2c surcharge on No. 121, the 1c plum, was not put on sale, though some are known used from a few sheets distributed by the post office to "government friends."

The 2c on 1p yellow without ornaments is a reprint.

Postage Due Stamps of 1900 Overprinted in Black or Gold

1901, Mar.

137 D3 1c plum 4.50 3.50
138 D3 2c vermilion 4.50 3.50
139 D3 5c dk bl 6.00 3.50
140 D3 10c pur (G) 8.50 5.00
a. Double overprint 14.00 14.00
141 D3 20c org brn 10.00 6.50
142 D3 30c dk grn 10.00 6.50
143 D3 50c lake 8.50 4.00
a. "1091" for "1901" 35.00 35.00
b. "Correo" 37.50
Nos. 137-143 (7) 52.00 32.50

In 1904 an imitation of this overprint was made to fill a dealer's order. The date is at top and "Correos" at bottom. The overprint is printed in black, sideways on the 1c and 2c and upright on the 5c and 10c. Some copies of the 2c were further surcharged "1 Centavo." None of these stamps was ever regularly used.

Nos. 126, 131-133 Surcharged

Black Surcharge

1901, Oct. 20

144 A14 3c on 6c rose 6.00 5.00
a. Bar below value 7.00 5.50
b. Inverted surcharge 8.00 8.00
c. Double surcharge 8.00 8.00
d. Double surch., one inverted 25.00 25.00
145 A14 4c on 6c rose 5.00 4.00
a. Bar below value 5.50 4.50
b. "1 cent" instead of "4 cent" 8.00 8.00
c. Double surcharge 20.00 20.00
146 A14 5c on 1p yellow 5.00 4.00
a. Three bars below value 6.00 4.50
b. Ornaments at each side of "1901" 6.00 4.50
c. Double surcharge, one in red 15.00 15.00
147 A14 10c on 2p salmon 5.50 4.00
a. Inverted surcharge 12.50 12.50
b. Double surcharge

Blue Surcharge

148 A14 3c on 6c rose 6.00 4.50
a. Bar below value 7.00 5.50
b. Double surcharge 8.00 8.00
149 A14 4c on 6c rose 6.50 5.00
a. Bar below value 7.50 7.50
b. "1 cent" instead of "4 cent" 10.00 10.00
c. Inverted surcharge 20.00 20.00

Red Surcharge

150 A14 5c on 1p yellow 7.50 6.50
a. Three bars below value 9.00 7.00
b. Ornaments at each side of "1901" 9.00 7.00
c. Inverted surcharge 12.00 12.00
d. Double surcharge, inverted 17.50 17.50
151 A14 20c on 5p black 5.00 3.50
a. Inverted surcharge 16.00 16.00
b. Double surcharge 22.50 22.50
c. Triple surcharge
Nos. 144-151 (8) 46.50 36.50

In 1904 a series was surcharged as above, but with "Centavos" spelled out. About the same time No. 122 was surcharged "1 cent." and "1901," "1902" or "1904." All of these surcharges were made to fill a dealer's order and none of the stamps was regularly issued or used.

Postage Due Stamps of 1900 Overprinted in Black

1901, Oct.

152 D3 1c red violet 1.00 .40
a. Ornaments at each side of the stamp 1.10 .65
b. Ornaments at each side of "1901" 1.10 .65
c. "Correos" in italics 1.50 1.50
d. Double overprint 14.00 14.00
153 D3 2c vermilion .75 .40
a. Double overprint 8.50 5.50
154 D3 5c dark blue 1.00 .60
a. Double overprint, one inverted
b. Double overprint 7.00 7.00
155 D3 10c purple 1.00 .60
b. Double overprint 10.00 10.00
c. Double overprint, one inverted 12.00 12.00
156 D3 20c org brn 1.25 1.25
b. Double overprint 7.00 7.00
157 D3 30c dk grn 1.00 1.10
a. Double overprint 9.00 9.00
b. Inverted overprint 19.00 19.00
158 D3 50c lake 1.00 1.10
a. Triple overprint 25.00 25.00
b. Double overprint 16.00 16.00
Nos. 152-158 (7) 7.00 5.45

One stamp in each group of 25 has the 2nd "o" of "Correos" italic. Value twice normal.

Momotombo Type of 1900 Without Imprint

1902 **Litho.** ***Perf. 14***

159 A14 5c blue .50 .25
a. Imperf., pair 3.75
160 A14 5c carmine .50 .20
a. Imperf., pair 3.75
161 A14 10c violet 1.50 .20
a. Imperf., pair 3.75
Nos. 159-161 (3) 2.50 .65

No. 161 was privately surcharged 6c, 1p and 5p in black in 1903. Not fully authorized but known postally used. Value of c-t-o peso denominations, $5 each.

Nos. 121 and 122 Surcharged in Black

1902, Oct. ***Perf. 12***

162 A14 15c on 2c ver 2.00 .75
a. Double surcharge 32.50
b. Blue surcharge 90.00
163 A14 30c on 1c plum 1.00 2.25
a. Double surcharge 9.00
b. Inverted surcharge 27.50

Counterfeits of No. 163 exist in slightly smaller type.

President José Santos Zelaya — A15

1903, Jan. **Engr.**

167 A15 1c emer & blk .35 .50
168 A15 2c rose & blk .70 .50
169 A15 5c ultra & blk .35 .50
170 A15 10c yel & blk .35 .85
171 A15 15c lake & blk .60 2.00
172 A15 20c vio & blk .60 2.00
173 A15 50c ol & blk .60 5.00
174 A15 1p red brn & blk .60 6.00
Nos. 167-174 (8) 4.15 17.35

10th anniv. of 1st election of Pres. Zelaya.

The so-called color errors-1c orange yellow and black, 2c ultramarine and black, 5c lake and black and 10c emerald and black-were also delivered to postal authorities. They were intended for official use though not issued as such. Value, $4 each.

Nos. 175-176

No. 177b

No. 161 Surcharged with New Values in Blue

1904-05

175 A14 5c on 10c vio ('05) 1.75 .25
a. Inverted surcharge 2.00 1.40
b. Without ornaments 2.00 .70
c. Character for "cents" inverted 1.75 .40
d. As "b," inverted
e. As "c," inverted 2.75 2.75
f. Double surcharge 8.00 8.00
g. "5" omitted 2.75 2.75
176 A14 15c on 10c vio ('05) .30 .30
a. Inverted surcharge 1.40 1.40
b. Without ornaments 1.40 1.40
c. Character for "cents" inverted 1.10 1.10
d. As "b," inverted
e. As "c," inverted 1.75 1.75
f. Imperf. 6.50
h. As "a," imperf. 9.00 9.00
i. Double surcharge 14.00 14.00
177 A14 15c on 10c vio 4.50 2.75
a. Inverted surcharge 6.00 6.00
b. "Centcvos" 6.00 4.50
c. "5" of "15" omitted 7.50
d. As "b," inverted 8.50 8.50
e. Double surcharge 11.00 11.00
f. Double surcharge, inverted 13.00 13.00
g. Imperf., pair 9.00 9.00
Nos. 175-177 (3) 6.55 3.30

There are two settings of the surcharge on No. 175. In the 1st the character for "cents" and the figure "5" are 2mm apart and in the 2nd 4mm.

The 2c vermilion, No. 122, with surcharge "1 cent. / 1904" was not issued.

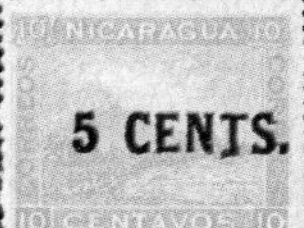

No. 161 Surcharged in Black

1905, June

178 A14 5c on 10c violet .60 .35
a. Inverted surcharge 2.75 2.75
b. Double surcharge 4.50 4.50
c. Surcharge in blue *75.00*

Coat of Arms — A18

Imprint: "American Bank Note Co. NY"

1905, July 25 **Engr.** ***Perf. 12***

179 A18 1c green .30 .20
180 A18 2c car rose .30 .20
181 A18 3c violet .45 .25
182 A18 4c org red .45 .25
183 A18 5c blue .45 .20
184 A18 6c slate .60 .40
185 A18 10c yel brn .85 .25
186 A18 15c brn olive .75 .35
187 A18 20c lake .60 .40
188 A18 50c orange 3.00 1.50
189 A18 1p black 1.50 1.50
190 A18 2p dk grn 1.50 2.00
191 A18 5p violet 1.75 2.50
Nos. 179-191 (13) 12.50 10.00

See Nos. 202-208, 237-248. For overprints and surcharges see Nos. 193-201, 212-216, 235-236, 249-265, O187-O198, O210-O222, 1L21-1L62, 1L73-1L95, 1LO1-1LO3, 2L26-2L35, 2L42-2L46, 2L48-2L72, 2LO1-2LO4.

Nos. 179-184 and 191 Surcharged in Black or Red Reading Up or Down

1906-08

193 A18 10c on 2c car rose (up) 7.00 4.00
a. Surcharge reading down 13.00 13.00
194 A18 10c on 3c vio (up) .60 .20
a. "¢" normal 2.75 1.35
b. Double surcharge 4.50 4.50
c. Double surch., up and down 7.00 5.00
d. Pair, one without surcharge 9.50
e. Surcharge reading down .30 .20
195 A18 10c on 4c org red (up) ('08) *35.00 20.00*
a. Surcharge reading down *32.50 22.50*
196 A18 15c on 1c grn (up) .60 .30
a. Double surcharge 7.50 7.50
b. Dbl. surch., one reading down 11.00 11.00
c. Surcharge reading down .40 .25
197 A18 20c on 2c car rose (down) ('07) .50 .30
a. Double surcharge 13.00 13.00
b. Surcharge reading up 37.50 32.50
c. "V" omitted 10.00 10.00
198 A18 20c on 5c bl (down) .75 .50
a. Surcharge reading up 35.00
199 A18 50c on 6c sl (R) (down) .60 .50
a. Double surcharge
b. Surcharge reading up 30.00 30.00
c. Yellow brown surcharge .60 .40
200 A18 1p on 5p vio (down) ('07) 42.50 25.00
Nos. 193-200 (8) *87.55 50.80*

There are several settings of these surcharges and many varieties in the shapes of the figures, the spacing, etc.

Surcharged in Red Vertically Reading Up

1908, May

201 A18 35c on 6c slate 3.00 2.25
a. Double surcharge (R) 25.00
b. Double surcharge (R + Bk) 65.00
c. Carmine surcharge 3.00 2.25

Arms Type of 1905

Imprint: "Waterlow & Sons, Ltd."

1907, Feb. ***Perf. 14 to 15***

202 A18 1c green .70 .40
203 A18 2c rose .80 .25
204 A18 4c brn org 2.00 .30
205 A18 10c yel brn 3.00 .25
206 A18 15c brn olive 4.50 .90
207 A18 20c lake 8.00 1.25
208 A18 50c orange 20.00 4.25
Nos. 202-208 (7) 39.00 7.60

Nos. 202-204, 207-208 Surcharged in Black or Blue (Bl) Reading Down

1907-08

212 A18 10c on 2c rose 1.50 .50
a. Double surcharge 10.00
b. "Vale" only 22.50
c. Surcharge reading up 14.00 6.50
213 A18 10c on 4c brn org (up) ('08) 2.25 .85
a. Double surcharge 10.00
b. Surcharge reading down 5.50
214 A18 10c on 20c lake ('08) 3.25 1.40
b. Surcharge reading up 80.00
215 A18 10c on 50c org (Bl) ('08) 2.00 .60
216 A18 15c on 1c grn ('08) 32.50 4.00
Nos. 212-216 (5) 41.50 7.35

Several settings of this surcharge provide varieties of numeral font, spacing, etc.

Revenue Stamps Overprinted "CORREO-1908" — A19

1908, June

217 A19 5c yel & blk .60 .40
a. "CORROE" 2.75 2.75
b. Overprint reading down 7.00
c. Double overprint 13.00
218 A19 10c lt bl & blk .50 .25
a. Double overprint 4.50 4.50
b. Overprint reading down .50 .25
c. Double overprint, up and down 13.00 13.00
219 A19 1p yel brn & blk .50 *2.00*
a. "CORROE" 7.50 7.50
220 A19 2p pearl gray & blk .50 *2.50*
a. "CORROE" 10.00 10.00
Nos. 217-220 (4) 2.10 *5.15*

The overprint exists on a 5p in green (value $200) and on a 50p in black (value $300).

Revenue Stamps Surcharged Vertically Reading Up in Red (1c, 15c), Blue(2c), Green (4c) or Orange (35c)

221 A19 1c on 5c yel & blk .40 .25
a. "1008" 1.50 1.50
b. "8908" 1.50 1.50
c. Surcharge reading down 4.00 4.00
d. Double surcharge 4.00 4.00
222 A19 2c on 5c yel & blk .50 .30
a. "ORREO" 1.75 1.75
c. "1008" 1.75 1.75
d. "8908" 1.75 1.75
f. Double surcharge 7.00 7.00
g. Double surcharge, one inverted 7.00 7.00
h. Surcharge reading down 9.00 9.00
223 A19 4c on 5c yel & blk .65 .35
a. "ORREO" 2.50 2.50
b. "1008" 2.00 2.00
c. "8908" 2.00 2.00
224 A19 15c on 50c ol & blk .60 .40
a. "1008" 4.00 4.00
b. "8908" 4.00 4.00
c. Surcharge reading down 10.00 10.00
225 A19 35c on 50c ol & blk 4.00 1.00
a. Double surcharge, one inverted 12.00 12.00
b. Surcharge reading down 12.00 12.00
c. Double surcharge, one in black
Nos. 221-225 (5) 6.15 2.30

For surcharges and overprints see Nos. 225D-225H, 230-234, 266-278, 1L63-1L72A, 1L96-1L106, 2L47.

Revenue Stamps Surcharged Vertically Reading Up in Blue, Black or Orange

1908, Nov.

225D A19 2c on 5c yel & blk (Bl) 20.00 12.50
e. "9c" instead of "2c" 75.00 75.00
225F A19 10c on 50c ol & blk (Bk) *850.00 325.00*
g. Double surcharge *425.00*
225H A19 35c on 50c ol & blk (O) 17.50 10.00

In this setting there are three types of the character for "cents."

Revenue Stamps Overprinted or Surcharged in Various Colors

No. 226

1908, Dec.

226 2c org (Bk) 3.50 2.00
a. Double overprint 6.00 6.00
b. Overprint reading up 5.00 5.00
227 4c on 2c org (Bk) 1.75 .90
a. Surcharge reading up 5.00 5.00
b. Blue surcharge 80.00 80.00
228 5c on 2c org (Bl) 1.50 .60
a. Surcharge reading up 6.00 6.00
229 10c on 2c org (G) 1.50 .30
a. "1988" for "1908" 4.00 3.00
b. Surcharge reading up 5.00 5.00
c. "¢" inverted 4.00 4.00
d. Double surcharge 7.50
Nos. 226-229 (4) 8.25 3.80

Two printings of No. 229 exist. In the first, the initial of "VALE" is a small capital, and in the second a large capital.

The overprint "Correos-1908." 35mm long, handstamped on 1c blue revenue stamp of type A20, is private and fraudulent.

Revenue Stamps Surcharged in Various Colors

1909, Feb.

Color: Olive & Black

230 A19 1c on 50c (V) 4.00 1.60
231 A19 2c on 50c (Br) 7.00 3.00
232 A19 4c on 50c (G) 7.00 3.00
233 A19 5c on 50c (C) 4.00 1.75
a. Double surcharge 12.50 12.50
234 A19 10c on 50c (Bk) 1.10 .75
Nos. 230-234 (5) 23.10 10.10

Nos. 230 to 234 are found with three types of the character for "cents."

Nos. 190 and 191 Surcharged in Black

1909, Mar. ***Perf. 12***

235 A18 10c on 2p dk grn 20.00 12.00
236 A18 10c on 5p vio *100.00 70.00*

There are three types of the character for "cents."

Arms Type of 1905

Imprint: "American Bank Note Co. NY"

1909, Mar.

237 A18 1c yel grn .35 .20
238 A18 2c vermilion .35 .20
239 A18 3c red org .35 .20
240 A18 4c violet .35 .20
241 A18 5c dp bl .35 .20
242 A18 6c gray brn 3.00 1.50
243 A18 10c lake .85 .20
244 A18 15c black .85 .20
245 A18 20c brn olive .85 .20
246 A18 50c dp grn 1.25 .40
247 A18 1p yellow 1.25 .40
248 A18 2p car rose 1.25 .40
Nos. 237-248 (12) 10.80 4.30

Nos. 239 and 244, Surcharged in Black or Red

1910, July

249 A18 2c on 3c red org 2.75 1.10
250 A18 10c on 15c blk (R) 1.25 .30
a. "VLEA" 3.50 2.00
b. Double surcharge 17.50 17.50

There are two types of the character for "cents."

Nos. 239, 244, 245 Surcharged in Black or Red

1910

252 A18 2c on 3c (Bk) 1.50 1.25
a. Double surcharge 6.00 6.00
b. Pair, one without surcharge
c. "Vale" omitted 10.00 10.00
254 A18 5c on 20c (R) .40 .30
a. Double surcharge (R) 6.00 5.00
b. Inverted surcharge (R) 3.50 2.50
c. Black surcharge 100.00
d. Double surcharge (Bk) 140.00
e. Inverted surcharge (Bk) 110.00
255 A18 10c on 15c (Bk) .90 .30
a. "c" omitted 2.00 1.10
b. "10c" omitted 2.50 1.50
c. Inverted surcharge 4.00 4.00
d. Double surcharge 6.00 6.00
e. Double surch., one inverted 12.00
Nos. 252-255 (3) 2.80 1.85

There are several minor varieties in this setting, such as italic "L" and "E" and fancy "V" in "VALE," small italic "C," and italic "I" for "1" in "10."

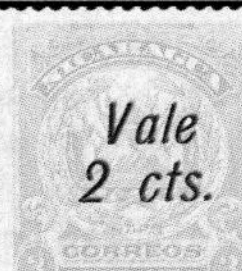

Nos. 239, 244, 246 and 247, Surcharged in Black

1910, Dec. 10

256 A18 2c on 3c red org .85 .45
a. Without period 1.00 .75
b. Inverted surcharge 6.00 6.00
c. Double surcharge 6.00 6.00
257 A18 10c on 15c blk 2.00 .75
a. Without period 3.50 1.25
b. Double surcharge 3.50 3.00
c. Inverted surcharge 5.00 5.00
258 A18 10c on 50c dp grn 1.25 .40
a. Without period 1.50 .75
b. Double surcharge 3.00 3.00
c. Inverted surcharge 3.00 3.00
259 A18 10c on 1p yel .90 .40
a. Without period 1.25 .75
b. Double surcharge 3.00 3.00
Nos. 256-259 (4) 5.00 2.00

The 15c on 50c deep green is a telegraph stamp from which the "Telegrafos" overprint was omitted. It appears to have been pressed into postal service, as all examples are used with postal cancels. Value $450.

Nos. 240, 244-248 Surcharged in Black

Surcharge as on Nos. 256-259 but lines wider apart.

1911, Mar.

260 A18 2c on 4c vio .30 .20
a. Without period .35 .30
b. Double surcharge 3.50 3.00
c. Double surcharge, inverted 4.00 4.00
d. Double surcharge, one invtd. 3.50 3.50
e. Inverted surcharge 7.50 7.50
261 A18 5c on 20c brn ol .30 .20
a. Without period .60 .50
b. Double surcharge 2.50 2.50
c. Inverted surcharge 2.50 2.00
d. Double surcharge, one invtd. 6.00 6.00
262 A18 10c on 15c blk .40 .20
a. Without period 1.00 .50
b. "Yale" 12.00 12.00
c. Double surcharge 3.00 3.00
d. Inverted surcharge 3.00 3.00
e. Double surch., one inverted 5.00 4.00
f. Double surch., both inverted 12.00 12.00
263 A18 10c on 50c dp grn .25 .20
a. Without period 1.00 .50
b. Double surcharge 3.00 2.50
c. Double surcharge, one invtd. 5.00 4.00
d. Inverted surcharge 5.00 5.00
264 A18 10c on 1p yel 1.50 .40
a. Without period 2.00 1.50
b. Double surcharge 4.00 4.00
c. Double surcharge, one invtd. 7.50
265 A18 10c on 2p car rose .60 .50
a. Without period 2.00 1.50
b. Double surcharge 2.50 2.50
c. Double surcharge, one invtd. 6.00 6.00
d. Inverted surcharge 6.00 6.00
Nos. 260-265 (6) 3.35 1.70

Revenue Stamps Surcharged in Black

1911, Apr. 10 ***Perf. 14 to 15***

266 A19 2c on 5p dl bl 1.00 *1.25*
a. Without period 1.25 *1.50*
b. Double surcharge 2.50 2.00
267 A19 2c on 5p ultra .35 *.40*
a. Without period .75 *1.25*
b. Double surcharge *3.50*
268 A19 5c on 10p pink .75 .40
a. Without period 1.50 1.00
b. "cte" for "cts" 1.50 1.00
c. Double surcharge 4.00 4.00
d. Inverted surcharge 2.50 2.50
269 A19 10c on 25c lilac .40 .25
a. Without period 1.00 .75
b. "cte" for "cts" 1.25 1.00
c. Inverted surcharge 4.00 4.00
d. Double surcharge 2.50 2.50
e. Double surcharge, one inverted 4.00 4.00
270 A19 10c on 2p gray .40 .25
a. Without period 1.00 .75
b. "cte" for "cts" 1.25 1.00
c. Double surcharge 5.00 5.00
d. Double surcharge, one inverted 4.00 3.00
271 A19 35c on 1p brown .40 .30
a. Without period 1.00 .75
b. "cte" for "cts" 1.25 1.00
c. "Corre" 1.50 1.50
d. Double surcharge 2.50 2.50
e. Double surcharge, one inverted 2.50 2.50
f. Double surcharge inverted 3.00 3.00
g. Inverted surcharge *5.00*
Nos. 266-271 (6) 3.30 2.85

These surcharges are in settings of twenty-five. One stamp in each setting has a large square period after "cts" and two have no period. One of the 2c has no space between "02" and "cts" and one 5c has a small thin "s" in "Correos."

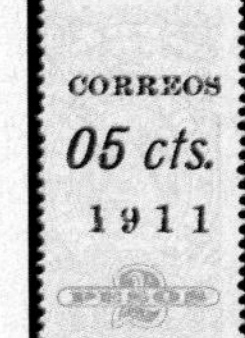

Surcharged in Black

1911, June

272 A19 5c on 2p gray 1.50 1.00
a. Inverted surcharge 6.00 5.00

In this setting one stamp has a large square period and another has a thick up-right "c" in "cts."

Surcharged in Black

1911, June 12

273 A19 5c on 25c lilac 1.50 1.25
274 A19 5c on 50c ol grn 5.00 5.00
275 A19 5c on 5p blue 7.00 7.00
276 A19 5c on 5p ultra 6.00 6.00
a. Inverted surcharge 45.00
277 A19 5c on 50p ver 5.00 5.00
278 A19 10c on 50c ol grn 1.50 .50
Nos. 273-278 (6) 26.00 24.75

This setting has the large square period and the thick "c" in "cts." Many of the stamps have no period after "cts." Owing to broken type and defective impressions letters sometimes appear to be omitted.

A21

Revenue Stamps Surcharged on the Back in Black:

a

b

Railroad coupon tax stamps (1st class red and 2nd class blue) are the basic stamps of Nos. 279-294. They were first surcharged for revenue use in 1903 in two types: I — "Timbre Fiscal" and "ctvs." II — "TIMBRE FISCAL" and "cents" (originally intended for use in Bluefields).

1911, July

279 A21 (a) 2c on 5c on 2 bl .25 .30
a. New value in yellow on face 6.00 6.00
b. New value in black on face 10.00 5.00
c. New value in red on face *100.00*
d. Inverted surcharge .75
e. Double surch., one inverted 7.50 7.50
f. "TIMBRE FISCAL" in black .75 .75
280 A21 (b) 2c on 5c on 2 bl .25 .30
a. New value in yellow on face 3.00 3.00
b. New value in black on face 9.00 4.00
c. New value in red on face *100.00*
d. Inverted surcharge .90 1.00
e. Double surch., one inverted 7.50 7.50
f. "TIMBRE FISCAL" in black 1.00 1.00
281 A21 (a) 5c on 5c on 2 bl .20 .20
a. Inverted surcharge .50 .35
b. "TIMBRE FISCAL" in black 1.00 1.00
c. New value in yellow on face
282 A21 (b) 5c on 5c on 2 bl .25 .20
a. Inverted surcharge .40 .35
b. "TIMBRE FISCAL" in black 1.00 1.00
c. New value in yellow on face
283 A21 (a) 10c on 5c on 2 bl .20 .20
a. Inverted surcharge .75 .50
b. "TIMBRE FISCAL" in black 1.00 1.00
c. New value in yellow on face *100.00*
d. Double surcharge 6.00 6.00
284 A21 (b) 10c on 5c on 2 bl .20 .20
a. Inverted surcharge .75 .50
b. "TIMBRE FISCAL" in black 1.00 1.00
c. Double surcharge 6.00 6.00
d. New value in yellow on face *110.00*
285 A21 (a) 15c on 10c on 1 red .25 .25
a. Inverted surcharge 1.00 1.25
b. "Timbre Fiscal" double 5.00
286 A21 (b) 15c on 10c on 1 red .40 .35
a. Inverted surcharge 1.00 1.00
b. "Timbre Fiscal" double 5.00
Nos. 279-286 (8) 2.00 2.00

These surcharges are in settings of 20. For listing, they are separated into small and large figures, but there are many other varieties due to type and arrangement.

The colored surcharges on the face of the stamps were trial printings. These were then surcharged in black on the reverse. The olive yellow surcharge on the face of the 2c was later applied to prevent use as a 5c revenue stamps. Other colors known on the face are orange and green. Forgeries exist.

For overprints and surcharges see Nos. 287-294, O223-O244, 1L107-1L108.

Surcharged on the Face in Black

1911, Oct.

287 A21 2c on 10c on 1 red 6.50 6.50
a. Inverted surcharge 1.40 1.40
b. Double surcharge 10.00 10.00
288 A21 20c on 10c on 1 red 4.50 4.50
a. Inverted surcharge 5.25 5.00
289 A21 50c on 10c on 1 red 5.25 4.50
a. Inverted surcharge 10.00 10.00
Nos. 287-289 (3) 16.25 15.50

There are two varieties of the figures "2" and "5" in this setting.

Surcharged on the Back in Black

Vale
10 cts.
CORREO DE
1911

1911, Nov.

289B A21 5c on 10c on 1 red 37.50
c. Inverted surcharge 20.00
289D A21 10c on 10c on 1 red 12.50
e. Inverted surcharge 24.00

Surcharged on the Face

1911, Dec.

Dark Blue Postal Surcharge

290 A21 2c on 10c on 1 red .25 .20
a. Inverted surcharge 2.50 2.50
b. Double surcharge 5.00 5.00
291 A21 5c on 10c on 1 red .30 .20
a. Double surcharge 2.50 2.50
b. Inverted surcharge 2.50 2.50
292 A21 10c on 10c on 1 red .35 .20
a. Inverted surcharge 2.50 2.50
b. Double surcharge 2.50 2.50
c. "TIMBRE FISCAL" on back 3.50 3.50

Black Postal Surcharge

293 A21 10c on 10c on 1 red 1.50 1.00
a. Inverted surcharge 7.00 7.00
b. New value surch. on back 12.00 12.00

Red Postal Surcharge

293C A21 5c on 5c on 2 blue 1.40 1.25
d. "TIMBRE FISCAL" in black 2.50 1.75
e. "5" omitted 3.75 3.75
f. Inverted surcharge 4.75 4.75
Nos. 290-293C (5) 3.80 2.85

Bar Overprinted on No. O234 in Dark Blue

294 A21 10c on 10c on 1 red 1.25 1.00
a. Inverted surcharge 2.50 2.50
b. Bar at foot of stamp 5.00 5.00

Nos. 290-294 each have three varieties of the numerals in the surcharge.

"Liberty" A22

Coat of Arms A23

1912, Jan. Engr. *Perf. 14, 15*

295 A22 1c yel grn .30 .20
296 A22 2c carmine .40 .20
297 A22 3c yel brn .30 .20
298 A22 4c brn vio .30 .20
299 A22 5c blue & blk .25 .20
300 A22 6c olive bister .30 .80
301 A22 10c red brn .25 .20
302 A22 15c vio .25 .20
303 A22 20c red .25 .20
304 A22 25c blue grn & blk .30 .20
305 A23 35c grn & chnt 2.00 1.50
306 A22 50c lt blue 1.00 .40
307 A22 1p org 1.40 2.00
308 A22 2p dark blue grn 1.50 2.25
309 A22 5p blk 3.50 3.50
Nos. 295-309 (15) 12.30 12.25

For overprints and surcharges see Nos. 310-324, 337A-348, 395-396, O245-O259.

No. 305 Surcharged in Violet

1913, Mar.

310 A23 15c on 35c .40 .25
a. "ats" for "cts" 6.00 6.00

Stamps of 1912 Surcharged in Red or Black

1913-14

311 A22 ½c on 3c yel brn (R) .40 .35
a. "Corooba" 2.50 2.50
b. "do" for "de" 2.50 2.50
c. Inverted surcharge 22.50
312 A22 ½c on 15c vio (R) .25 .20
a. "Corooba" 1.00 1.00
b. "do" for "de" 1.25 1.25
313 A22 ½c on 1p org .25 .20
a. "VALB" 1.50 1.00
b. "ALE" 4.00 3.50
c. "LE" 6.00 5.00
d. "VALE" omitted 3.50 3.50
314 A22 1c on 3c yel brn .75 .60
315 A22 1c on 4c brn vio .25 .20
316 A22 1c on 50c lt blue .25 .20
317 A22 1c on 5p blk .25 .20
318 A22 2c on 4c brn vio .35 .25
a. "do" for "de" 1.25 1.25
319 A22 2c on 20c red 3.50 *4.50*
a. "do" for "de" 17.50 12.50
320 A22 2c on 25c blue grn & blk .35 .20
a. "do" for "de" 3.50 2.50
321 A23 2c on 35c grn & chnt .25 .40
a. "9131" 3.00 2.00
b. "do" for "de" 2.50 2.00
322 A22 2c on 50c lt blue .25 .20
a. "do" for "de" 1.25 1.25
323 A22 2c on 2p dark blue grn .20 .20
a. "VALB" 1.25 .75
b. "ALE" 2.50 1.25
c. "VALE" omitted 6.00
d. "VALE" and "dos" omitted 6.00
324 A22 3c on 6c olive bis .20 .20
a. "VALB" *35.00*
Nos. 311-324 (14) 7.50 7.90

Nos. 311, 312 surcharged in black were not regularly issued.

Surcharged on Zelaya Issue of 1912

325 Z2 ½c on 2c ver .60 .45
a. "Corooba" 1.25 1.25
b. "do" for "de" 1.25 1.25
326 Z2 1c on 3c org brn .50 .20
327 Z2 1c on 4c car .50 .20
328 Z2 1c on 6c red brn .40 .20
329 Z2 1c on 20c dark vio .50 .20
330 Z2 1c on 25c grn & blk .50 .20
331 Z2 2c on 1c yel grn ('14) 6.75 1.25
a. "Centavos" 7.50 1.50
332 Z2 2c on 25c grn & blk 2.25 *3.00*
333 Z2 5c on 35c brn & blk .40 .20
334 Z2 5c on 50c ol grn .40 .20
a. Double surcharge 22.50
335 Z2 6c on 1p org .40 .20
336 Z2 10c on 2p org brn .40 .20
337 Z2 1p on 5p dk bl grn .50 .40
Nos. 325-337 (13) 14.00 6.90

On No. 331 the surcharge has a space of 2½mm between "Vale" and "dos."

Space between "Vale" and "dos" 2½mm instead of 1mm, "de Cordoba" in different type.

1914, Feb.

337A A22 2c on 4c brn vio 27.50 4.00
b. "Ccntavos" 12.00
337C A22 2c on 20c red 13.00 1.25
d. "Ccntavos" 4.00
337E A22 2c on 25c bl grn & blk 6.00
f. "Ccntavos" 12.00
337G A23 2c on 35c grn & chnt 8.50
h. "Ccntavos" 15.00
337I A22 2c on 50c lt bl 22.50 4.00
j. "Ccntavos" 10.00

No. 310 with Additional Surcharge

medio
cvo. Córdoba

1913, Dec.

337K A23 ½c on 15c on 35c *300.00*

The word "Medio" is usually in heavy-faced, shaded letters. It is also in thinner, unshaded letters and in letters from both fonts mixed.

No. 310 Surcharged in Black and Violet

338 A23 ½c on 15c on 35c .20 .20
a. Double surcharge 3.50
b. Inverted surcharge 3.50
c. Surcharged on No. 305 12.00
339 A23 1c on 15c on 35c .25 .20
a. Double surcharge 4.00

Official Stamps of 1912 Surcharged

1914, Feb.

340 A22 1c on 25c lt bl .40 .25
a. Double surcharge 9.00
341 A23 1c on 35c lt bl .40 .25
a. "0.10" for "0.01" 10.00 10.00
341B A22 1c on 50c lt bl *200.00*
342 A22 1c on 1p lt bl .25 .20
342A A22 2c on 20c lt bl *200.00 150.00*
b. "0.12" for "0.02"
343 A22 2c on 50c lt bl .40 .20
a. "0.12" for "0.02" 150.00
344 A22 2c on 2p lt bl .40 .20
345 A22 2c on 5p lt bl *250.00*
346 A22 5c on 5p lt bl .25 .20

Red Surcharge

347 A22 5c on 1p lt bl *75.00*
348 A22 5c on 5p lt bl *500.00*

National Palace, Managua — A24

León Cathedral — A25

Various Frames

1914, May 13 Engr. *Perf. 12*

349 A24 ½c lt blue .85 .20
350 A24 1c dk green .85 .20
351 A25 2c red orange .85 .20
352 A24 3c red brown 1.25 .30
353 A25 4c scarlet 1.25 .40
354 A24 5c gray black .45 .20
355 A25 6c black brn 9.00 5.50
356 A25 10c orange yel .85 .20
357 A24 15c dp violet 5.75 2.00
358 A25 20c slate 11.00 5.50
359 A24 25c orange 1.50 .45
360 A25 50c pale blue 1.40 .40
Nos. 349-360 (12) 35.00 15.55

In 1924 the 5c, 10c, 25c, 50c were issued in slightly larger size, 27x22¾mm. The original set was 26x22½mm.

No. 356 with overprint "Union Panamericana 1890-1940" in green is of private origin.

See Nos. 408-415, 483-495, 513-523, 652-664. For overprints and surcharges see Nos. 361-394, 397-400, 416-419, 427-479, 500, 540-548, 580-586, 600-648, 671-673, 684-685, C1-C3, C9-C13, C49-C66, C92-C105, C121-C134, C147-C149, C155-C163, C174-C185, CO1-CO24, O260-O294, O296-O319, O332-O376, RA1-RA5, RA10-RA11, RA26-RA35, RA39-RA40, RA44, RA47, RA52.

No. 355 Surcharged in Black

1915, Sept.

361 A25 5c on 6c blk brn 1.50 .40
a. Double surcharge 7.00 7.00

Stamps of 1914 Surcharged in Black or Red

New Value in Figures

1918-19

362 A24 1c on 3c red brn 6.50 2.25
a. Double surch., one invtd. 12.50
363 A25 2c on 4c scarlet 32.50 22.50
364 A24 5c on 15c dp vio (R) 7.50 1.50
a. Double surcharge 12.00
364C A24 5c on 15c dp vio 350.00

Surcharged in Black

365 A25 2c on 20c slate 200.00 100.00
a. "ppr" for "por" *500.00* *300.00*
b. Double surcharge *300.00*
c. "Cordobo" *500.00* *300.00*
365D A25 5c on 20c slate — *200.00*
e. Double surcharge (Bk + R) *300.00*
f. "Cordobo" *300.00*

The surcharge on No. 365 is in blue black, and that on No. 365D usually has an admixture of red.

Used only at Bluefields and Rama.

Surcharged in Black, Red or Violet

New Value in Words

366 A25 ½c on 6c blk brn 4.00 1.50
a. "Meio" 15.00
b. Double surcharge 12.00
367 A25 ½c on 10c yellow 2.50 .30
a. "Val" for "Vale" 3.00
b. "Codoba" 3.00
c. Inverted surcharge 5.00
d. Double surch., one inverted 10.00
368 A24 ½c on 15c dp vio 2.50 .60
a. Double surcharge 7.50
b. "Codoba" 4.00
c. "Meio" 6.00
369 A24 ½c on 25c orange 5.00 2.00
a. Double surcharge 8.00
b. Double surch., one inverted 6.00
370 A25 ½c on 50c pale bl 2.50 .30
a. "Meio" 6.00
b. Double surcharge 5.00
c. Double surch., one inverted 7.00
371 A25 ½c on 50c pale bl (R) 4.50 1.50
a. Double surcharge 10.00
372 A24 1c on 3c red brown 3.00 .30
a. Double surcharge 3.50
373 A25 1c on 6c blk brn 12.50 3.50
a. Double surcharge 9.00
374 A25 1c on 10c yellow 24.00 8.00
a. "nu" for "un" 22.50
375 A24 1c on 15c dp vio 4.50 .75
a. Double surcharge 10.00
b. "Codoba" 6.00
376 A25 1c on 20c slate *200.00* *100.00*
a. Black surch. normal and red surch. invtd. *150.00*
b. Double surch., red & black *150.00*
c. Blue surcharge *200.00*
377 A25 1c on 20c sl (V) 110.00 70.00
a. Double surcharge (V + Bk) *150.00*
378 A25 1c on 20c sl (R) 2.50 .30
a. Double surch., one inverted
b. "Val" for "Vale" 3.50 3.00
379 A24 1c on 25c orange 4.50 1.00
a. Double surcharge 11.00
380 A25 1c on 50c pale bl 14.00 4.50
a. Double surcharge 17.50
381 A25 2c on 4c scarlet 3.50 .30
a. Double surcharge 10.00
b. "centavo" 5.00
c. "Val" for "Vale"
382 A25 2c on 6c blk brn 24.00 8.00
a. "Centavoss"
b. "Cordobas"
383 A25 2c on 10c yellow 24.00 4.50
a. "centavo"
384 A25 2c on 20c sl (R) 13.00 3.25
a. "pe" for "de" 15.00
b. Double surch., red & blk 27.50
c. "centavo" 12.00
d. Double surcharge (R) 17.50
385 A24 2c on 25c orange 5.50 .40
a. "Vle" for "Vale" 7.50
b. "Codoba" 7.50
c. Inverted surcharge 10.00
386 A25 5c on 6c blk brn 10.00 4.25
a. Double surcharge 13.50
387 A24 5c on 15c dp vio 3.50 .60
a. "cincoun" for "cinco" 15.00
b. "Vle" for "Vale" 12.50
c. "Codoba" 12.50
Nos. 366-387 (22) 479.50 215.85

No. 378 is surcharged in light red and brown red: the latter color is frequently offered as the violet surcharge (No. 377).

Official Stamps of 1915 Surcharged in Black or Blue

1919-21

388 A24 1c on 25c lt blue 1.50 .25
a. Double surcharge 10.00
b. Inverted surcharge 12.00
389 A25 2c on 50c lt blue 1.50 .25
a. "centavo" 4.00 4.00
b. Double surcharge 12.00
390 A25 10c on 20c lt blue 1.40 .40
a. "centovos" 5.00 5.00
b. Double surcharge 8.00
390F A25 10c on 20c lt bl (Bl) 65.00
Nos. 388-390 (3) 4.40 .90

There are numerous varieties of omitted, inverted and italic letters in the foregoing surcharges.

No. 358 Surcharged in Black

VALE
5 Centavos

Types of the numerals:

2 I, 2 II, 2 III
2 IV, 2 V, 2 VI, 2 VII, 2 VIII
5 I, 5 II, 5 III, 5 IV
5 V, 5 VI, 5 VII, 5 VIII

1919, May

391 A25 2c on 20c (I) *200.00* *150.00*
a. Type II
b. Type III
c. Type IV
d. Type VI
e. Type VIII
392 A25 5c on 20c (I) 110.00 40.00
a. Type II 110.00 45.00
b. Type III 125.00 50.00
c. Type IV 125.00 50.00
d. Type V 140.00 60.00
e. Type VI 140.00 60.00
f. Type VII 400.00 250.00
h. Double surch., one inverted

No. 358 Surcharged in Black

VALE
2 Cents

393 A25 2 Cents on 20c (I) *200.00* *150.00*
a. Type II
b. Type III
c. Type IV
d. Type V
e. Type VI
f. Type VII
393G A25 5 Cents on 20c sl, (VIII) 140.00 55.00

Nos. 391-393G used only at Bluefields and Rama.

No. 351 Surcharged in Black

1920, Jan.

394 A25 1c on 2c red org 1.50 .25
a. Inverted surcharge
b. Double surcharge

Official Stamps of 1912 Overprinted in Carmine

1921, Mar.

395 A22 1c lt blue 1.50 .60
a. "Parricular" 5.00 5.00
b. Inverted overprint 10.00
396 A22 5c lt blue 1.50 .40
a. "Parricular" 5.00 5.00

Official Stamps of 1915 Surcharged in Carmine

1921, May

397 A25 ½c on 2c light blue .50 .20
a. "Mddio" 2.50 2.50
398 A25 ½c on 4c light blue 1.25 .20
a. "Mddio" 2.50 2.50
399 A24 1c on 3c light blue 1.25 .30
Nos. 397-399 (3) 3.00 .70

No. 354 Surcharged in Red

1921, Aug.

400 A24 ½c on 5c gray blk .75 .75

Trial printings of this stamp were surcharged in yellow, black and red, and yellow and red. Some of these were used for postage.

Gen. Manuel José Arce — A26

José Cecilio del Valle — A27

Miguel Larreinaga A28

Gen. Fernando Chamorro A29

Gen. Máximo Jérez — A30

Gen. Pedro Joaquín Chamorro — A31

Rubén Darío — A32

1921, Sept. **Engr.**

401 A26 ½c lt bl & blk 1.00 1.00
402 A27 1c grn & blk 1.00 1.00
403 A28 2c rose red & blk 1.00 1.00
404 A29 5c ultra & blk 1.00 1.00
405 A30 10c org & blk 1.00 1.00
406 A31 25c yel & blk 1.00 1.00
407 A32 50c vio & blk 1.00 1.00
Nos. 401-407 (7) 7.00 7.00

Centenary of independence.

For overprints and surcharges see Nos. 420-421, RA12-RA16, RA19-RA23.

Types of 1914 Issue Various Frames

1922

408 A24 ½c green .20 .20
409 A24 1c violet .20 .20
410 A25 2c car rose .20 .20
411 A24 3c ol gray .30 .20
411A A25 4c vermilion .35 .25
412 A25 6c red brn .20 .20
413 A24 15c brown .35 .20
414 A25 20c bis brn .50 .20
415 A25 1cor blk brn .90 .50
Nos. 408-415 (9) 3.20 2.15

In 1924 Nos. 408-415 were issued in slightly larger size, 27x22¾mm. The original set was 26x22½mm.

Nos. 408, 410 exist with signature controls. See note before No. 600. Same values.

No. 356 Surcharged in Black

1922, Nov.

416 A25 1c on 10c org yel 1.00 .35
417 A25 2c on 10c org yel 1.00 .25

Nos. 354 and 356 Surcharged in Red

1923, Jan.

418 A24 1c on 5c gray blk 1.25 .20
419 A25 2c on 10c org yel 1.25 .20
a. Inverted surcharge

Nos. 401 and 402 Overprinted in Red

1923

420 A26 ½c lt blue & blk 7.50 7.50
421 A27 1c green & blk 2.50 .85
a. Double overprint 7.50

Francisco Hernández de Córdoba — A33

1924 **Engr.**

422 A33 1c deep green 1.50 .30
423 A33 2c carmine rose 1.50 .30
424 A33 5c deep blue 1.00 .30
425 A33 10c bister brn 1.00 .60
Nos. 422-425 (4) 5.00 1.50

Founding of León & Granada, 400th anniv.

For overprint & surcharges see #499, 536, O295.

Stamps of 1914-22 Overprinted

Black, Red or Blue Overprint

1927, May 3

427 A24 ½c green (Bk) .25 .20
428 A24 1c violet (R) .20 .20
a. Double overprint 3.00

428B A24 1c violet (Bk) 85.00 55.00
429 A25 2c car rose (Bk) .20 .20
a. Inverted overprint 5.00
b. Double overprint 5.00
430 A24 3c ol gray (Bk) 1.25 1.25
a. Inverted overprint 5.00
b. Double overprint 6.00
c. Double ovpt., one inverted 9.00 7.00
430D A24 3c ol gray (Bl) 8.00 3.25
431 A25 4c ver (Bk) 16.00 13.00
a. Inverted overprint 30.00
432 A24 5c gray blk (R) 1.25 .25
a. Inverted overprint 7.50
432B A24 5c gray blk (Bk) .75 .25
c. Double ovpt., one inverted 8.00
d. Double overprint 8.00
433 A25 6c red brn (Bk) 13.00 11.00
a. Inverted overprint 17.50
b. Double overprint
c. "1297" for "1927" 250.00
434 A25 10c yellow (Bl) .65 .40
a. Double overprint 12.50
b. Double ovpt., one inverted 10.00
435 A24 15c brown (Bk) 6.00 2.50
436 A25 20c bis brn (Bk) 6.00 2.50
a. Double overprint 17.50
437 A24 25c orange (Bk) 27.50 5.00
438 A25 50c pale bl (Bk) 7.50 3.00
439 A25 1cor blk brn (Bk) 15.00 9.00
Nos. 427-439 (16) 188.55 107.00

Most stamps of this group exist with tall "1" in "1927." Counterfeits exist of normal stamps and errors of Nos. 427-478.

Violet Overprint

1927, May 19

440 A24 ½c green .20 .20
a. Inverted overprint 2.00 2.00
b. Double overprint 2.00 2.00
441 A24 1c violet .20 .20
a. Double overprint 2.00 2.00
442 A25 2c car rose .20 .20
a. Double overprint 2.00 2.00
b. "1927" double 5.00
d. Double ovpt., one inverted 2.00 2.00
443 A24 3c ol gray .25 .20
a. Inverted overprint 6.00
b. Overprinted "1927" only 12.00
c. Double ovpt., one inverted 9.00
444 A25 4c vermilion 37.50 27.50
a. Inverted overprint 75.00
445 A24 5c gray blk 1.00 .25
a. Double overprint, one inverted 6.00
446 A25 6c red brn 37.50 27.50
a. Inverted overprint 75.00
447 A25 10c yellow .35 .20
a. Double overprint 2.00 2.00
448 A24 15c brown .75 .30
a. Double overprint 5.00
b. Double overprint, one inverted 8.00
449 A25 20c bis brn .35 .20
a. Double overprint
450 A24 25c orange .40 .20
451 A25 50c pale bl .40 .20
a. Double ovpt., one inverted 4.00 4.00
452 A25 1cor blk brn .75 .20
a. Double overprint 3.00
b. "1927" double 5.00
c. Double ovpt., one inverted 6.00
Nos. 440-452 (13) 79.85 57.35

Stamps of 1914-22 Overprinted in Violet

1928, Jan. 3

453 A24 ½c green .25 .20
a. Double overprint 3.00
b. Double overprint, one inverted 4.00
454 A24 1c violet .20 .20
a. Inverted overprint 2.00
b. Double overprint 2.00
c. Double overprint, one inverted 2.00
d. "928" for "1928" 2.50
455 A25 2c car rose .20 .20
a. Inverted overprint 2.00
b. Double overprint 2.00
c. "1928" omitted 5.00
d. "928" for "1928" 2.50
e. As "d," inverted
f. "19" for "1928"
456 A24 3c ol gray .40 .20
457 A25 4c vermilion .20 .20
458 A24 5c gray blk .20 .20
a. Double overprint 5.00
b. Double overprint, one inverted 5.00
459 A25 6c red brn .20 .20
460 A25 10c yellow .25 .20
a. Double overprint 2.50
c. Inverted overprint
461 A24 15c brown .35 .25
462 A25 20c bis brn .50 .25
a. Double overprint
463 A24 25c orange .75 .25
a. Double overprint, one inverted 4.00
464 A25 50c pale bl 1.25 .20
465 A25 1cor blk brn 1.25 .35
Nos. 453-465 (13) 6.00 2.90

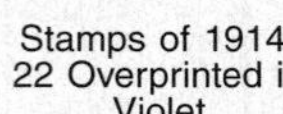
Stamps of 1914-22 Overprinted in Violet

1928, June 11

466 A24 ½c green .20 .20
467 A24 1c violet .20 .20
a. "928" omitted
469 A24 3c ol gray .75 .25
a. Double overprint 6.00
470 A25 4c vermilion .35 .20
471 A24 5c gray blk .25 .20
a. Double overprint 4.00
472 A25 6c red brn .40 .20
a. Double overprint 5.00
473 A25 10c yellow .50 .20
474 A24 15c brown 1.75 .20
a. Double overprint
475 A25 20c bis brn 2.00 .20
476 A24 25c orange 2.00 .25
a. Double overprint, one inverted 6.00
477 A25 50c pale bl 2.00 .25
478 A25 1cor blk brn 5.00 2.50
a. Double overprint 10.00
Nos. 466-478 (12) 15.40 4.85

No. 410 with above overprint in black was not regularly issued.

No. 470 with Additional Surcharge in Violet

1928

479 A25 2c on 4c ver 1.25 .35
a. Double surcharge 9.00

A34

Inscribed: "Timbre Telegrafico"
Red Surcharge

1928

480 A34 1c on 5c bl & blk .30 .20
a. Double surcharge 5.00
b. Double surcharge, one inverted
481 A34 2c on 5c bl & blk .30 .20
a. Double surcharge 5.00
482 A34 3c on 5c bl & blk .30 .20
Nos. 480-482 (3) .90 .60

Stamps similar to Nos. 481-482, but with surcharge in black and with basic stamp inscribed "Timbre Fiscal," are of private origin.

See designs A36, A37, A44, PT1, PT4, PT6, PT7.

Types of 1914 Issue
Various Frames

1928

483 A24 ½c org red .40 .20
484 A24 1c orange .40 .20
485 A25 2c green .40 .20
486 A24 3c dp vio .40 .25
487 A25 4c brown .40 .25
488 A24 5c yellow .40 .20
489 A25 6c lt bl .40 .25
490 A25 10c dk bl .90 .20
491 A24 15c car rose 1.40 .50
492 A25 20c dk grn 1.40 .50
493 A24 25c blk brn 27.50 6.00
494 A25 50c bis brn 3.25 1.00
495 A25 1cor dl vio 6.25 3.00
Nos. 483-495 (13) 43.50 12.75

No. 425 Overprinted in Violet

1929

499 A33 10c bis brn .75 .60

No. 408 Overprinted in Red

1929

500 A24 ½c green (R) .25 .20
a. Inverted overprint 2.50
b. Double overprint 2.50
c. Double overprint, one inverted 3.50

A36

A37

Ovptd. Horiz. in Black "R. de T."
Surcharged Vert. in Red

1929

504 A36 1c on 5c bl & blk (R) .25 .20
a. Inverted surcharge 3.00
b. Surcharged "0.10" for "0.01" 3.00
c. "0.0" instead of "0.01" 5.00
509 A36 2c on 5c bl & blk (R) .20 .20
a. Double surcharge 2.50
b. Double surcharge, one inverted 3.50
c. Inverted surcharge 5.00

Overprinted Horizontally in Black "R. de C." Surcharged Vertically in Red

510 A36 2c on 5c bl & blk (R) 22.50 1.25
a. Dbl. surcharge, one inverted 25.00

Surcharged in Red

511 A37 1c on 10c dk grn & blk (R) .25 .20
a. Double surcharge
512 A37 2c on 5c bl & blk (R) .25 .20
Nos. 504-512 (5) 23.45 2.05

The varieties tall "1" in "0.01" and "O$" for "C$" are found in this surcharge.

Nos. 500, 504, 509-512 and RA38 were surcharged in red and sold in large quantities to the public. Surcharges in various other colors were distributed only to a favored few and not regularly sold at the post offices.

Types of 1914 Issue
Various Frames

1929-31

513 A24 1c ol grn .20 .20
514 A24 3c lt bl .30 .20
515 A25 4c dk bl ('31) .30 .20
516 A24 5c ol brn .40 .20
517 A25 6c bis brn ('31) .50 .30
518 A25 10c lt brn ('31) .60 .20
519 A24 15c org red ('31) .90 .25
520 A25 20c org ('31) 1.25 .35
521 A24 25c dk vio .25 .20
522 A25 50c grn ('31) .50 .20
523 A25 1cor yel ('31) 4.50 1.25
Nos. 513-523 (11) 9.70 3.55

Nos. 513-523 exist with signature controls. See note before No. 600. Same values.

New Post Office at Managua — A38

1930, Sept. 15 **Engr.**

525 A38 ½c olive gray 1.25 1.25
526 A38 1c carmine 1.25 1.25
527 A38 2c red org .90 .90
528 A38 3c orange 1.75 1.75
529 A38 4c yellow 1.75 1.75
530 A38 5c ol grn 2.25 2.25
531 A38 6c bl grn 2.25 2.25
532 A38 10c black 2.75 2.75
533 A38 25c dp bl 5.50 5.50
534 A38 50c ultra 9.00 9.00
535 A38 1cor dp vio 25.00 25.00
Nos. 525-535 (11) 53.65 53.65

Opening of the new general post office at Managua. The stamps were on sale on day of issuance and for an emergency in April, 1931.

No. 499 Surcharged in Black and Red

1931, May 29

536 A33 2c on 10c bis brn .50 1.60
a. Red surcharge omitted 2.50
b. Red surcharge double 5.00
c. Red surcharge inverted 3.50
d. Red surcharge double, one invtd.

Surcharge exists in brown.

Types of 1914-31 Issue Overprinted

1931, June 11

540 A24 ½c green .35 .20
a. Double overprint .80
b. Double ovpt., one inverted 1.40
c. Inverted overprint .80
541 A24 1c ol grn .35 .20
a. Double overprint .80
b. Double ovpt., one inverted 1.40
c. Inverted overprint
542 A25 2c car rose .35 .20
a. Double overprint .80
b. Double ovpt., both inverted 2.50
c. Inverted overprint 1.40
543 A24 3c lt bl .35 .20
a. Double overprint .80
b. Double ovpt., one inverted 1.40
c. Inverted overprint 1.40
544 A24 5c yellow 3.50 2.25
545 A24 5c ol brn 1.00 .20
a. Double overprint 4.50
b. Inverted overprint 4.50
546 A24 15c org red 1.25 .40
a. Double overprint 3.50
547 A24 25c blk brn 10.00 6.50
a. Double overprint 11.00 7.00
b. Inverted overprint 11.00 7.00
548 A24 25c dk vio 4.00 2.50
a. Double overprint 6.50
Nos. 540-548 (9) 21.15 12.65

Counterfeits exist of the scarcer values. The 4c brown and 6c light blue with this overprint are bogus.

Managua P.O. Before and After Earthquake A40

1932, Jan. 1 **Litho.** ***Perf. 11½***
Soft porous paper, Without gum

556 A40 ½c emerald 1.50
557 A40 1c yel brn 1.90
558 A40 2c dp car 1.50
559 A40 3c ultra 1.50
560 A40 4c dp ultra 1.50
561 A40 5c yel brn 1.60
562 A40 6c gray brn 1.60
563 A40 10c yel brn 2.50
564 A40 15c dl rose 3.75
565 A40 20c orange 3.50
566 A40 25c dk vio 2.50
567 A40 50c emerald 2.50
568 A40 1cor yellow 6.25
Nos. 556-568 (13) 32.10

Issued in commemoration of the earthquake at Managua, Mar. 31, 1931. The stamps were on sale on Jan. 1, 1932, only. The money received from this sale was for the reconstruction of the Post Office building and for the improvement of the postal service. Many shades exist.

Sheets of 10.

Reprints are on thin hard paper and do not have the faint horiz. ribbing that is on the front or back of the originals. Fake cancels abound. Value 75 cents each.

See Nos. C20-C24. For overprints and surcharges see Nos. C32-C43, C47-C48.

Rivas Railroad Issue

"Fill" at El Nacascolo — A41

1c, Wharf at San Jorge. 5c, Rivas Station. 10c, San Juan del Sur. 15c, Train at Rivas Station.

1932, Dec. 17 Litho. *Perf. 12*
Soft porous paper

570 A41 1c yellow 16.00
a. 1c ocher 18.00
571 A41 2c carmine 16.00
572 A41 5c blk brn 16.00
573 A41 10c chocolate 16.00
574 A41 15c yellow 16.00
a. 15c deep orange 18.00
Nos. 570-574 (5) 80.00

Inauguration of the railroad from San Jorge to San Juan del Sur. On sale only on Dec. 17, 1932.

Sheets of 4, without gum. See #C67-C71.

Reprints exist on five different papers ranging from thick soft light cream to thin very hard paper and do not have the faint horiz. ribbing that is normally on the front or back of the originals. Originals are on very white paper. Value of reprints, $5 each.

Leon-Sauce Railroad Issue

Bridge No. 2 at Santa Lucia — A42

Designs: 1c, Environs of El Sauce. 5c, Santa Lucia. 10c, Works at Km. 64. 15c, Rock cut at Santa Lucia.

1932, Dec. 30 *Perf. 12*
Soft porous paper

575 A42 1c orange 16.00
576 A42 2c carmine 16.00
577 A42 5c blk brn 16.00
578 A42 10c brown 16.00
579 A42 15c orange 16.00
Nos. 575-579 (5) 80.00

Inauguration of the railroad from Leon to El Sauce. On sale only on Dec. 30, 1932.

Sheets of 4, without gum. See #C72-C76.

Reprints exist on thin hard paper and do not have the faint horiz. ribbing that is on the front or back of the originals. Value $5 each.

Nos. 514-515, 543 Surcharged in Red

1932, Dec. 10

580 A24 1c on 3c lt bl (514) .35 .20
a. Double surcharge 3.50
581 A24 1c on 3c lt bl (543) 4.00 3.50
582 A25 2c on 4c dk bl (515) .25 .20
a. Double surcharge 2.50
Nos. 580-582 (3) 4.60 3.90

Nos. 514, 516, 545 and 518 Surcharged in Black or Red

1933

583 A24 1c on 3c lt bl (Bk) (514) .20 .20
a. "Censavo" 4.00 2.25
b. Double surcharge, one inverted 4.00

584 A24 1c on 5c ol brn (R) (516) .20 .20
a. Inverted surcharge
b. Double surcharge
585 A24 1c on 5c ol brn (R) (545) 6.50 5.00
a. Red surcharge double 12.00
586 A25 2c on 10c lt brn (Bk) (518) .20 .20
a. Double surcharge 4.00 2.50
b. Inverted surcharge 3.50 3.50
c. Double surcharge, one inverted 4.00 2.50
Nos. 583-586 (4) 7.10 5.60

On No. 586 "Vale Dos" measures 13mm and 14mm.

No. 583 with green surcharge and No. 586 with red surcharge are bogus.

Flag of the Race Issue

Flag with Three Crosses for Three Ships of Columbus A43

1933, Aug. 3 Litho. *Rouletted 9*
Without gum

587 A43 ½c emerald 1.75 1.75
588 A43 1c green 1.50 1.50
589 A43 2c red 1.50 1.50
590 A43 3c dp rose 1.50 1.50
591 A43 4c orange 1.50 1.50
592 A43 5c yellow 1.75 1.75
593 A43 10c dp brn 1.75 1.75
594 A43 15c dk brn 1.75 1.75
595 A43 20c vio bl 1.75 1.75
596 A43 25c dl bl 1.75 1.75
597 A43 30c violet 4.50 4.50
598 A43 50c red vio 4.50 4.50
599 A43 1cor ol brn 4.50 4.50
Nos. 587-599 (13) 30.00 30.00

Commemorating the raising of the symbolical "Flag of the Race"; also the 441st anniversary of the sailing of Columbus for the New World, Aug. 3, 1492. Printed in sheets of 10.

See Nos. C77-C87, O320-O331.

In October, 1933, various postage, airmail and official stamps of current issues were overprinted with facsimile signatures of the Minister of Public Works and the Postmaster-General. These overprints are control marks.

Nos. 410 and 513 Overprinted in Black

1935 *Perf. 12*

600 A24 1c ol grn .20 .20
a. Inverted overprint 1.40 1.60
b. Double overprint 1.40 1.60
c. Double overprint, one inverted 1.60 1.60
601 A25 2c car rose .20 .20
a. Inverted overprint 1.60
b. Double overprint 1.60
c. Double overprint, one inverted 1.60
d. Double overprint, both inverted 2.50 2.25

No. 517 Surcharged in Red as in 1932

1936, June

602 A25 ½c on 6c bis brn .35 .20
a. "Ccentavo" .80 .80
b. Double surcharge 3.50 3.50

Regular Issues of 1929-35 Overprinted in Blue

1935, Dec.

603 A25 ½c on 6c bis brn .65 .20
604 A24 1c ol grn (#600) .80 .20
605 A25 2c car rose (#601) .80 .20
a. Black overprint inverted 6.00
606 A24 3c lt bl .80 .25
607 A24 5c ol brn 1.00 .25
608 A25 10c lt brn 1.60 .80
Nos. 603-608 (6) 5.65 1.90

Nos. 606-608 have signature control overprint. See note before No. 600.

Same Overprint in Red

1936, Jan.

609 A24 ½c dk grn .20 .20
610 A25 ½c on 6c bis brn (602) .20 .20
a. Double surch., one inverted 6.00 6.00
611 A24 1c ol grn (513) .25 .20
612 A24 1c ol grn (600) .25 .20
613 A25 2c car rose (410) .50 .20
614 A25 2c car rose (601) .25 .20
a. Black overprint inverted 2.50 2.50
b. Black ovpt. double, one invtd. 3.50 3.50
615 A24 3c lt bl .25 .20
616 A25 4c dk bl .25 .20
617 A24 5c ol brn .22 .20
618 A25 6c bis brn .25 .20
619 A25 10c lt brn .50 .20
620 A24 15c org red .20 .20
621 A25 20c orange .80 .25
622 A24 25c dk vio .25 .20
623 A25 50c green .35 .20
624 A25 1cor yellow .40 .25
Nos. 609-624 (16) 5.12 3.30

Red or blue "Resello 1935" overprint may be found inverted or double. Red and blue overprints on same stamp are bogus.

Nos. 615-624 have signature control overprint. See note before No. 600.

Regular Issues of 1922-29 Overprinted in Carmine

1936, May

625 A24 ½c green .20 .20
626 A24 1c olive green .20 .20
627 A25 2c carmine rose .50 .20
628 A24 3c light blue .20 .20
Nos. 625-628 (4) 1.10 .80

No. 628 has signature control overprint. See note before No. 600.

Nos. 514, 516 Surcharged in Black

1936, June

629 A24 1c on 3c lt bl .20 .20
a. "1396" for "1936" 1.00 1.00
b. "Un" omitted 1.40 1.40
c. Inverted surcharge 1.60 1.60
d. Double surcharge 1.60 1.60
630 A24 2c on 5c ol brn .20 .20
a. "1396" for "1936" 1.40 1.40
b. Double surcharge 3.50 3.50

Regular Issues of 1929-31 Surcharged in Black or Red

1936

631 A24 ½c on 15c org red (R) .20 .20
a. Double surcharge 4.00
632 A25 1c on 4c dk bl (Bk) .25 .20
633 A24 1c on 5c ol brn (Bk) .25 .20
634 A25 1c on 6c bis brn (Bk) .40 .20
a. "1939" instead of "1936" 2.50 1.60
635 A24 1c on 15c org red (Bk) .25 .20
a. "1939" instead of "1936" 2.50 1.60
636 A25 1c on 20c org (Bk) .20 .20
a. "1939" intead of "1936" 2.50 1.60
b. Double surcharge 4.00
637 A25 1c on 20c org (R) .20 .20
638 A25 2c on 10c lt brn (Bk) .25 .20
639 A24 2c on 15c org red (Bk) 1.00 .80
640 A25 2c on 20c org (Bk) .50 .25
641 A24 2c on 25c dk vio (R) .35 .20
642 A24 2c on 25c dk vio (Bk) .35 .20
a. "1939" instead of "1936" 2.50 1.60
643 A25 2c on 50c grn (Bk) .35 .25
a. "1939" instead of "1936" 2.50 1.60
644 A25 2c on 1 cor yel (Bk) .35 .20
a. "1939" instead of "1936" 2.50 1.60
645 A25 3c on 4c dk bl (Bk) .65 .50
a. "1939" instead of "1936" 2.50 1.60
b. "s" of "Centavos" omitted and "r" of "Tres" inverted 2.50
Nos. 631-645 (15) 5.55 4.00

Nos. 634, 639, 643-644 exist with and without signature controls. Same values, except for No. 639, which is rare without the signature control. Nos. 635-636, 642, 645 do not have signature controls. Others have signature controls only. See note before No. 600.

Regular Issues of 1929-31 Overprinted in Black

1936, Aug.

646 A24 3c lt bl .35 .20
647 A24 5c ol brn .25 .20
648 A25 10c lt brn .50 .35
Nos. 646-648 (3) 1.10 .75

No. 648 bears script control mark.

A44

Surcharged in Red

1936, Oct. 19

649 A44 1c on 5c grn & blk .20 .20
650 A44 2c on 5c grn & blk .20 .20

Types of 1914

1937, Jan. 1 Engr.

652 A24 ½c black .20 .20
653 A24 1c car rose .20 .20
654 A25 2c dp bl .20 .20
655 A24 3c chocolate .20 .20
656 A25 4c yellow .20 .20
657 A24 5c org red .20 .20
658 A25 6c dl vio .20 .20
659 A25 10c ol grn .20 .20
660 A24 15c green .20 .20
661 A25 20c red brn .25 .20
663 A25 50c brown .35 .20
664 A25 1cor ultra .60 .25
Nos. 652-664 (12) 3.00 2.45

See note after No. 360.

Mail Carrier — A45

1c, Mule carrying mail. 2c, Mail coach. 3c, Sailboat. 5c, Steamship. 7½c, Train.

1937, Dec. Litho. *Perf. 11*

665 A45 ½c green .20 .20
666 A45 1c magenta .20 .20
667 A45 2c brown .20 .20
668 A45 3c purple .20 .20
669 A45 5c blue .20 .20
670 A45 7½c red org .55 .35
Nos. 665-670 (6) 1.55 1.35

Postal service in Nicaragua, 75th anniv.

Nos. 665-670 were also issued in sheets of 4, value, set of sheets, $7.

The miniature sheets are ungummed, and also exist imperf. and part-perf.

Nos. 662, 663 and 664 Surcharged in Red

1938 *Perf. 12*

671 A24 3c on 25c org .20 .20
672 A25 5c on 50c brn .25 .20
a. "e" of "Vale" omitted 1.60 1.00
673 A25 6c on 1cor ultra .20 .20
Nos. 671-673 (3) .65 .60

No. 672 has a script signature control and the surcharge is in three lines.

Dario Park A46

1939, Jan. **Engr.** ***Perf. 12½***

674 A46 1½c yel grn .20 .20
675 A46 2c dp rose .20 .20
676 A46 3c brt bl .20 .20
677 A46 6c brn org .20 .20
678 A46 7½c dp grn .20 .20
679 A46 10c blk brn .20 .20
680 A46 15c orange .20 .20
681 A46 25c lt vio .20 .20
682 A46 50c brt yel grn .20 .20
683 A46 1cor yellow .65 .40
Nos. 674-683 (10) 2.45 2.20

Nos. 660 and 661 Surcharged in Red

1939 ***Perf. 12***

684 A24 1c on 15c grn .20 .20
a. Inverted surcharge 2.00 2.00
685 A25 1c on 20c red brn .20 .20

No. C236 Surcharged in Carmine

1941 **Unwmk.** ***Perf. 12***

686 AP14 10c on 1c brt grn .20 .20
a. Double surcharge 10.00 2.50
b. Inverted surcharge 10.00 2.50

Rubén Darío A47

1941, Dec. **Engr.** ***Perf. 12½***

687 A47 10c red .40 .20
Nos. 687,C257-C260 (5) 2.00 1.10

25th anniversary of the death of Rubén Darío, poet and writer.

No. C236 Surcharged in Carmine

1943 ***Perf. 12***

688 AP14 10c on 1c brt grn 4.00 .20
a. Inverted surcharge 10.00
b. Double surcharge 10.00

Catalogue values for unused stamps in this section, from this point to the end of the section, are for Never Hinged items.

"Victory" A48

Columbus and Lighthouse A49

1943, Dec. 8 **Engr.**

689 A48 10c vio & cerise .20 .20
690 A48 30c org brn & cerise .20 .20

2nd anniv. of Nicaragua's declaration of war against the Axis. See Nos. C261-C262.

1945, Sept. 1 **Unwmk.** ***Perf. 12½***

691 A49 4c dk grn & blk .20 .20
692 A49 6c org & blk .25 .25
693 A49 8c dp rose & blk .35 .35
694 A49 10c bl & blk .40 .40
Nos. 691-694,C266-C271 (10) 6.20 5.40

Issued in honor of the discovery of America by Columbus and the Columbus Lighthouse near Ciudad Trujillo, Dominican Republic.

Franklin D. Roosevelt, Philatelist A50

Roosevelt Signing Declaration of War Against Japan — A51

8c, F. D. Roosevelt, Winston Churchill. 16c, Gen. Henri Giraud, Roosevelt, de Gaulle & Churchill. 32c, Stalin, Roosevelt, Churchill. 50c, Sculptured head of Roosevelt.

Engraved, Center Photogravure
1946, June 15 **Unwmk.** ***Perf. 12½***
Frame in Black

695 A50 4c sl grn .20 .20
696 A50 8c violet .30 .30
697 A51 10c ultra .30 .30
698 A50 16c rose red .40 .40
699 A50 32c org brn .30 .30
700 A51 50c gray .30 .30
Nos. 695-700 (6) 1.80 1.80

Issued to honor US Pres. Franklin D. Roosevelt (1882-1945). See Nos. C272-C276.

Projected Provincial Seminary — A56

Designs: 4c, Metropolitan Cathedral, Managua. 5c, Sanitation Building. 6c, Municipal Building. 75c, Communications Building.

1947, Jan. 10
Frame in Black

701 A56 4c carmine .20 .20
702 A56 5c blue .20 .20
703 A56 6c green .20 .20
704 A56 10c olive .20 .20
705 A56 75c golden brn .30 .30
Nos. 701-705 (5) 1.10 1.10

Centenary of the founding of the city of Managua. See Nos. C277-C282.

San Cristóbal Volcano A61

Designs: 3c, Tomb of Rubén Darío. 4c, Grandstand. 5c, Soldiers' monument. 6c, Sugar cane. 8c, Tropical fruit. 10c, Cotton industry. 20c, Horse race. 30c, Nicaraguan coffee. 50c, Steer. 1cor, Agriculture.

Engraved, Center Photogravure
1947, Aug. 29
Frame in Black

706 A61 2c orange .20 .20
707 A61 3c violet .20 .20
708 A61 4c gray .25 .20
709 A61 5c rose car .55 .25
710 A61 6c green .30 .20
711 A61 8c org brn .40 .20
712 A61 10c red .55 .25
713 A61 20c brt ultra 1.90 .50
714 A61 30c rose lilac 1.50 .50
715 A61 50c dp claret 3.25 .95
716 A61 1cor brn org 1.10 .50
Nos. 706-716 (11) 10.20 3.95

The frames differ for each denomination.
For surcharge see No. 769.

Softball A62

Boy Scout, Badge and Flag — A63

Designs: 3c, Pole vault. 4c, Diving. 5c, Bicycling. 10c, Proposed stadium. 15c, Baseball. 25c, Boxing. 35c, Basketball. 40c, Regatta. 60c, Table tennis. 1 cor, Soccer. 2 cor, Tennis.

1949, July 15 **Photo.** ***Perf. 12***

717 A62 1c henna brn .20 .20
718 A63 2c ultra .75 .20
719 A63 3c bl grn .30 .20
720 A62 4c dp claret .20 .20
721 A63 5c orange .50 .20
722 A62 10c emerald .50 .20
723 A62 15c cerise .75 .20
724 A63 25c brt bl .75 .20
725 A63 35c olive grn 1.25 .25
726 A62 40c violet 1.75 .30
727 A62 60c olive gray 2.00 .40
728 A62 1cor scarlet 2.50 1.25
729 A62 2cor red vio 4.50 2.50
Nos. 717-729 (13) 15.95 6.30
Nos. 717-729,C296-C308 (26) 35.95 16.55

10th World Series of Amateur Baseball, 1948.

Each denomination was also issued in a souvenir sheet containing four stamps and marginal inscriptions. Value, set of 13 sheets, $100.

Rowland Hill — A64

Designs: 25c, Heinrich von Stephan. 75c, UPU Monument. 80c, Congress medal, obverse. 4cor, as 80c, reverse.

1950, Nov. 23 **Engr.** ***Perf. 13***
Frame in Black

730 A64 20c car lake .20 .20
731 A64 25c yel grn .20 .20
732 A64 75c ultra .50 .20
733 A64 80c green .25 .25
734 A64 4cor blue .90 .80
Nos. 730-734 (5) 2.05 1.65
Nos. 730-734,C309-C315,CO45-CO50 (18) 9.70 8.90

75th anniv. (in 1949) of the UPU.

Each denomination was also issued in a souvenir sheet containing 4 stamps. Size: 115x123mm. Value, set of 5 sheets, $30.

For surcharge see #771.

Queen Isabella I — A65

Ships of Columbus A66

Designs: 98c, Santa Maria. 1.20cor, Map. 1.76cor, Portrait facing left.

1952, June 25 ***Perf. 11½***

735 A65 10c lilac rose .20 .20
736 A66 96c deep ultra .75 .75
737 A65 98c carmine .75 .75
738 A65 1.20cor brown .90 .90
739 A65 1.76cor red violet 1.25 1.25
a. Souvenir sheet of 5, #735-739 3.75 3.75
Nos. 735-739 (5) 3.85 3.85
Nos. 735-739,C316-C320 (10) 16.35 13.85

Queen Isabella I of Spain, 500th birth anniv.

ODECA Flag — A67

Designs: 5c, Map of Central America. 6c, Arms of ODECA. 15c, Presidents of Five Central American Republics. 50c, ODECA Charter and Flags.

1953, Apr. 15 ***Perf. 13½x14***

740 A67 4c dk bl .20 .20
741 A67 5c emerald .20 .20
742 A67 6c lt brn .20 .20
743 A67 15c lt ol grn .20 .20
744 A67 50c blk brn .20 .20
Nos. 740-744,C321-C325 (10) 2.60 2.50

Founding of the Organization of the Central American States (ODECA).

For surcharge see #767.

Pres. Carlos Solorzano — A68

Presidents: 6c, Diego Manuel Chamorro. 8c, Adolfo Diaz. 15c, Gen. Anastasio Somoza. 50c, Gen. Emiliano Chamorro.

Engr. (frames); Photo. (heads)
1953, June 25 ***Perf. 12½***
Heads in Gray Black

745 A68 4c dk car rose .20 .20
746 A68 6c dp ultra .20 .20
747 A68 8c brown .20 .20
748 A68 15c car rose .20 .20
749 A68 50c bl grn .20 .20
Nos. 745-749,C326-C338 (18) 4.60 4.35

For surcharges see Nos. 768, 853.

Sculptor and UN Emblem — A69

Capt. Dean L. Ray, USAF — A70

4c, Arms of Nicaragua. 5c, Globe. 15c, Candle & Charter. 1cor, Flags of Nicaragua & UN.

Perf. 13½

1954, Apr. 30 Engr. Unwmk.

750 A69 3c olive .20 .20
751 A69 4c olive green .20 .20
752 A69 5c emerald .20 .20
753 A69 15c deep green .90 .20
754 A69 1cor blue green .75 .30
Nos. 750-754,C339-C345 (12) 10.75 6.90

UN Organization.

Engraved; Center Photogravure

1954, Nov. 5 ***Perf. 13***

Designs: 2c, Sabre jet plane. 3c, Plane, type A-20. 4c, B-24 bomber. 5c, Plane, type AT-6. 15c, Gen. Anastasio Somoza. 1cor, Air Force emblem.

Frame in Black

755 A70 1c gray .20 .20
756 A70 2c gray .20 .20
757 A70 3c dk gray grn .20 .20
758 A70 4c orange .20 .20
759 A70 5c emerald .20 .20
760 A70 15c aqua .20 .20
761 A70 1cor purple .20 .20
Nos. 755-761,C346-C352 (14) 3.20 3.10

National Air Force.

Rotary Slogans and Wreath — A71

Map of the World and Rotary Emblem A72

20c, Handclasp, Rotary emblem & globe. 35c, Flags of Nicaragua & Rotary. 90c, Paul P. Harris.

1955, Aug. 30 Photo. ***Perf. 11½***

Granite Paper.

762 A71 15c dp orange .20 .20
763 A71 20c dk olive grn .20 .20
764 A71 35c red violet .20 .20
765 A72 40c carmine .20 .20
766 A71 90c black & gray .35 .35
a. Souvenir sheet of 5, #762-766 4.25 4.25
Nos. 762-766,C353-C362 (15) 3.50 3.40

50th anniversary of Rotary International.
For surcharges see Nos. 770, 772, 876.

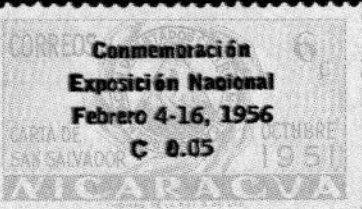

Issues of 1947-55 Surcharged in Various Colors

Perf. 13½x14, 12½, 11½, 13

Engraved, Photogravure

1956, Feb. 4 Unwmk.

767 A67 5c on 6c lt brn .20 .20
768 A68 5c on 6c ultra & gray blk (Ult) .20 .20
769 A61 5c on 8c blk & org brn .20 .20
770 A71 15c on 35c red vio (G) .20 .20
771 A64 15c on 80c blk & grn .20 .20
772 A71 15c on 90c blk & gray (Bl) .20 .20
Nos. 767-772,C363-C366 (10) 2.60 2.55

Spacing of surcharge varies to fit shape of stamps.
National Exhibition, Feb. 4-16, 1956.

Gen. Máximo Jerez — A73

Battle of San Jacinto A74

10c, Gen. Fernando Chamorro. 25c, Burning of Granada. 50c, Gen. José Dolores Estrada.

Perf. 12½x12, 12, 12½

1956, Sept. 14 Engr.

773 A73 5c brown .20 .20
774 A73 10c dk car rose .20 .20
775 A74 15c blue gray .20 .20
776 A74 25c brt red .20 .20
777 A73 50c brt red vio .40 .20
Nos. 773-777,C367-C371 (10) 4.50 4.05

National War, cent.

Boy Scout — A75

Pres. Luis A. Somoza — A76

Designs: 15c, Cub Scout. 20c, Boy Scout. 25c, Lord Baden-Powell. 50c, Joseph A. Harrison.

Perf. 13½x14

1957, Apr. 9 Photo. Unwmk.

778 A75 10c violet & ol .20 .20
779 A75 15c dp plum & gray blk .20 .20
780 A75 20c ultra & brn .20 .20
781 A75 25c dl red brn & dp bluish grn .20 .20
782 A75 50c red & olive .20 .20
a. Souvenir sheet of 5, #778-782 2.50 2.50
Nos. 778-782,C377-C386 (15) 3.15 3.15

Centenary of the birth of Lord Baden-Powell, founder of the Boy Scouts.
For surcharge see #C754.

1957, July 2 ***Perf. 14x13½***

Portrait in Dark Brown

783 A76 10c brt red .20 .20
784 A76 15c deep blue .20 .20
785 A76 35c rose violet .25 .20
786 A76 50c brown .30 .20
787 A76 75c gray green .65 .55
Nos. 783-787,C387-C391 (10) 3.65 3.40

President Luis A. Somoza.

Leon Cathedral A77

Bishop Pereira y Castellon — A78

Designs: 5c, Managua Cathedral. 15c, Archbishop Lezcano y Ortega. 50c, De la Merced Church, Granada. 1cor, Father Mariano Dubon.

1957, July 12 ***Perf. 13½x14, 14x13½***

Centers in Olive Gray

788 A77 5c dull green .20 .20
789 A78 10c dk purple .20 .20
790 A78 15c dk blue .20 .20
791 A77 20c dk brown .20 .20
792 A77 50c dk slate grn .20 .20
793 A78 1cor dk violet .30 .30
Nos. 788-793,C392-C397 (12) 3.20 3.20

Honoring the Catholic Church in Nicaragua.

M. S. Honduras A79

5c, Gen. Anastasio Somoza & freighter. 6c, M. S. Guatemala. 10c, M. S. Salvador. 15c, Ship between globes. 50c, Globes & ship.

1957, Oct. 15 Litho. ***Perf. 14***

794 A79 4c green, bl & blk .20 .20
795 A79 5c multi .20 .20
796 A79 6c red, bl & blk .20 .20
797 A79 10c brn, bl grn & blk .20 .20
798 A79 15c dk car, ultra & ol brn .25 .20
799 A79 50c violet, bl & mar .40 .25
Nos. 794-799,C398-C403 (12) 4.45 4.25

Issued to honor Nicaragua's Merchant Marine. For surcharge see No. C691.

Melvin Jones and Lions Emblem A80

Designs: 5c, Arms of Central American Republics. 20c, Dr. Teodoro A. Arias. 50c, Edward G. Barry. 75c, Motto and emblem. 1.50 cor, Map of Central America.

1958, May 8 Unwmk. ***Perf. 14***

Emblem in Yellow, Red and Blue

800 A80 5c blue & multi .20 .20
801 A80 10c blue & org .20 .20
802 A80 20c blue & olive .20 .20
803 A80 50c blue & lilac .25 .20
804 A80 75c blue & pink .35 .25
805 A80 1.50cor blue, gray ol & sal .60 .45
a. Souvenir sheet of 6, #800-805 2.50 2.50
Nos. 800-805,C410-C415 (12) 5.10 4.40

17th convention of Lions Intl. of Central America, May, 1958.
For surcharge see #C686.

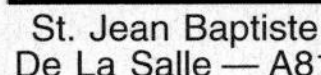

St. Jean Baptiste De La Salle — A81

UN Emblem and Globe — A82

Christian Brothers: 5c, Arms of La Salle. 10c, School, Managua, horiz. 20c, Bro. Carlos. 50c, Bro. Antonio. 75c, Bro. Julio. 1cor, Bro. Argeo.

1958, July 13 Photo. ***Perf. 14***

806 A81 5c car, bl & yel .20 .20
807 A81 10c emer, blk & ultra .20 .20
808 A81 15c red brn, bis & blk .20 .20
809 A81 20c car, bis & blk .20 .20
810 A81 50c org, bis & brn blk .20 .20
811 A81 75c bl, lt grn & dk brn .25 .20
812 A81 1cor vio, bis & grnsh blk .30 .30
Nos. 806-812,C416-C423 (15) 6.55 5.30

For surcharges see Nos. C539A, C755-C756.

1958, Dec. 15 Litho. ***Perf. 11½***

15c, UNESCO building. 25c, 45c, "UNESCO." 40c, UNESCO building and Eiffel tower.

813 A82 10c brt pink & bl .20 .20
814 A82 15c blue & brt pink .20 .20
815 A82 25c green & brn .20 .20
816 A82 40c red org & blk .20 .20
817 A82 45c dk bl & rose lil .20 .20
818 A82 50c brown & grn .20 .20
a. Miniature sheet of 6, #813-818 .75 .75
Nos. 813-818,C424-C429 (12) 5.00 3.60

UNESCO Headquarters in Paris opening, Nov. 3.

Pope John XXIII and Cardinal Spellman — A83

Abraham Lincoln — A84

Designs: 10c, Spellman coat of arms. 15c, Cardinal Spellman. 20c, Human rosary and Cardinal, horiz. 25c, Cardinal with Ruben Dario order.

1959, Nov. 26 Unwmk. ***Perf. 12½***

819 A83 5c grnsh bl & brn .20 .20
820 A83 10c yel, bl & car .20 .20
821 A83 15c dk grn, blk & dk car .20 .20
822 A83 20c yel, dk bl & grn .20 .20
823 A83 25c ultra, vio & mag .20 .20
a. Min. sheet of 5, #819-823, perf. or imperf. 1.00 1.00
Nos. 819-823,C430-C436 (12) 4.55 3.55

Cardinal Spellman's visit to Managua, Feb. 1958.
For surcharges see #C638, C747, C752.

1960, Jan. Engr. ***Perf. 13x13½***

Center in Black

824 A84 5c dp carmine .20 .20
825 A84 10c green .20 .20
826 A84 15c dp orange .20 .20
827 A84 1cor plum .20 .20
828 A84 2cor ultra .35 .30
a. Souv. sheet of 5, #824-828, imperf. .90 .90
Nos. 824-828,C437-C442 (11) 3.70 3.10

150th anniv. of the birth of Abraham Lincoln.
For surcharges see #C500, C539, C637, C680, C753.

Nos. 824-828 Overprinted in Red

1960, Sept. 19

Center in Black

829 A84 5c deep carmine .20 .20
830 A84 10c green .20 .20
831 A84 15c deep orange .20 .20
832 A84 1cor plum .25 .20
833 A84 2cor ultra .50 .40
Nos. 829-833,C446-C451 (11) 4.20 3.50

Issued for the Red Cross to aid earthquake victims in Chile.

Gen. Tomas Martinez and Pres. Luis A. Somoza — A85

Arms of Nueva Segovia — A86

5c, Official decrees. 10c, Two envelopes.

Perf. 13½

1961, Aug. 29 Unwmk. Litho.

834 A85 5c grnsh bl & lt brn .25 .20
835 A85 10c green & lt brn .25 .20
836 A85 15c pink & brn .25 .20
Nos. 834-836 (3) .75 .60

Cent. (in 1960) of the postal rates regulation.

1962, Nov. 22 ***Perf. 12½x13***

Coats of Arms: 3c, León. 4c, Managua. 5c, Granada. 6c, Rivas.

Arms in Original Colors; Black Inscriptions

837 A86 2c pink .20 .20
838 A86 3c lt blue .20 .20
839 A86 4c pale lilac .20 .20
840 A86 5c yellow .20 .20
841 A86 6c buff .20 .20
Nos. 837-841,C510-C514 (10) 2.75 2.65

For surcharge see #854.

No. RA73 Overprinted in Red: "CORREOS"

1964 Photo. ***Perf. 11½***

842 PT13 5c gray, red & org .20 .20
a. Inverted overprint

Nos. RA66-RA75 Overprinted

1965 Photo. ***Perf. 11½***

Orchids in Natural Colors

843 PT13 5c pale lilac & grn .50
844 PT13 5c yellow & grn .50
845 PT13 5c pink & grn .50
846 PT13 5c pale vio & grn .50
847 PT13 5c lt grnsh bl & red .50
848 PT13 5c buff & lil .50
849 PT13 5c yel grn & brn .50
850 PT13 5c gray & red .50
851 PT13 5c lt blue & dk bl .50
852 PT13 5c lt green & brn .50
Nos. 843-852 (10) 5.00

7th Central American Scout Camporee at El Coyotete. This overprint was also applied to each stamp on souvenir sheet No. C386a.

Use of Nos. 843-852 for postage was authorized by official decree.

Nos. 746 and 841 Surcharged with New Value and "RESELLO"

1968, May Engr. ***Perf. 12½***

853 A68 5c on 6c dp ultra & gray blk .50 .50

Litho. ***Perf. 12½x13***

854 A86 5c on 6c multi .50 .50

Nos. RA66-RA67, RA69 and RA71 Overprinted

1969 Photo. ***Perf. 11½***

Orchids in Natural Colors

855 PT13 5c pale lil & grn .60 .60
856 PT13 5c yellow & grn .60 .60
857 PT13 5c pale vio & grn .60 .60
858 PT13 5c buff & lilac .60 .60
Nos. 855-858 (4) 2.40 2.40

Nos. RA66-RA75 Overprinted

1969 Photo. ***Perf. 11½***

Orchids in Natural Colors

859 PT13 5c pale lil & grn .30 .30
860 PT13 5c yellow & grn .30 .30
861 PT13 5c pink & grn .30 .30
862 PT13 5c pale vio & grn .30 .30
863 PT13 5c lt grnsh bl & red .30 .30
864 PT13 5c buff & lil .30 .30
865 PT13 5c yel grn & brn .30 .30
866 PT13 5c gray & red .30 .30
867 PT13 5c lt & dk blue .30 .30
868 PT13 5c lt grn & brn .30 .30
Nos. 859-868 (10) 3.00 3.00

International Labor Organization, 50th anniv.

Pelé, Brazil — A87

Soccer Players: 10c, Ferenc Puskás, Hungary. 15c, Sir Stanley Matthews, England. 40c, Alfredo di Stefano, Argentina. 2cor, Giacinto Facchetti, Italy. 3cor, Lev Yashin, USSR. 5cor, Franz Beckenbauer, West Germany.

1970, May 11 Litho. ***Perf. 13½***

869 A87 5c multicolored .20 .20
870 A87 10c multicolored .20 .20
871 A87 15c multicolored .20 .20
872 A87 40c multicolored .25 .20
873 A87 2cor multicolored .90 .75
874 A87 3cor multicolored 1.25 .90
875 A87 5cor multicolored 1.25 1.25
Nos. 869-875,C712-C716 (12) 7.65 6.50

Issued to honor the winners of the 1970 poll for the International Soccer Hall of Fame. Names of players and their achievements printed in black on back of stamps.

For surcharges and overprint see Nos. 899-900, C786-C788.

No. 766 Surcharged with New Value and Overprinted "RESELLO" and Bar Through Old Denomination

1971, Mar. Photo. ***Perf. 11***

876 A71 30c on 90c blk & gray *200.00 100.00*

Egyptian Using Fingers to Count — A88

Symbolic Designs of Scientific Formulas: 15c, Newton's law (gravity). 20c, Einstein's theory (relativity). 1cor, Tsiolkovski's law (speed of rockets). 2cor, Maxwell's law (electromagnetism).

1971, May 15 Litho. ***Perf. 13½***

877 A88 10c lt bl & multi .20 .20
878 A88 15c lt bl & multi .20 .20
879 A88 20c lt bl & multi .30 .20
880 A88 1cor lt bl & multi 1.00 .60
881 A88 2cor lt bl & multi 2.10 1.25
Nos. 877-881,C761-C765 (10) 7.80 4.15

Mathematical equations which changed the world. On the back of each stamp is a descriptive paragraph.

Symbols of Civilization, Peace Emblem with Globe — A89

1971, Sept. 6 Litho. ***Perf. 14***

882 A89 10c blk & bl .20 .20
883 A89 15c vio bl, bl & blk .20 .20
884 A89 20c brn bl & blk .20 .20
885 A89 40c emer, bl & blk .30 .30
886 A89 50c mag, bl & blk .40 .40
887 A89 80c org, bl & blk .60 .60
888 A89 1cor ol, bl & blk .75 .75
889 A89 2cor vio, bl & blk 1.50 1.50
Nos. 882-889 (8) 4.15 4.15

"Is there a formula for peace?" issue.

Moses with Tablets of the Law, by Rembrandt A90

The Ten Commandments (Paintings): 15c, Moses and the Burning Bush, by Botticelli (I). 20c, Jephthah's Daughter, by Degas, (II), horiz. 30c, St. Vincent Ferrer Preaching in Verona, by Domenico Morone (III). 35c, The Nakedness of Noah, by Michelangelo (IV), horiz. 40c, Cain and Abel, by Francesco Trevisani (V), horiz. 50c, Potiphar's wife, by Rembrandt (VI). 60c, Isaac Blessing Jacob, by Gerbrand van den Eeckhout (VII), horiz. 75c, Susanna and the Elders, by Rubens (VIII), horiz.

1971, Nov. 1 ***Perf. 11***

890 A90 10c ocher & multi .20 .20
891 A90 15c ocher & multi .20 .20
892 A90 20c ocher & multi .20 .20
893 A90 30c ocher & multi .20 .20
894 A90 35c ocher & multi .25 .25
895 A90 40c ocher & multi .25 .25
896 A90 50c ocher & multi .35 .35
897 A90 60c ocher & multi .50 .50
898 A90 75c ocher & multi .75 .75
Nos. 890-898,C776-C777 (11) 5.30 4.15

Descriptive inscriptions printed in gray on back of stamps.

Nos. 873-874 Surcharged

1972, Mar. 20 Litho. ***Perf. 13½***

899 A87 40c on 2cor multi .20 .20
900 A87 50c on 3cor multi .20 .20
Nos. 899-900,C786-C788 (5) 1.90 1.80

20th Olympic Games, Munich, 8/26-9/10.

Nos. RA66-RA69, RA71-RA74 Overprinted in Blue

1972, July 29 Photo. ***Perf. 11½***

Granite Paper

901 PT13 5c (#RA66) .25 .25
902 PT13 5c (#RA67) .25 .25
903 PT13 5c (#RA68) .25 .25
904 PT13 5c (#RA69) .25 .25
905 PT13 5c (#RA71) .25 .25
906 PT13 5c (#RA72) .25 .25
907 PT13 5c (#RA73) .25 .25
908 PT13 5c (#RA74) .25 .25
Nos. 901-908 (8) 2.00 2.00

Gown by Givenchy, Paris — A91

1973, July 26 Litho. ***Perf. 13½***

909 A91 1cor shown .30 .25
910 A91 2cor Hartnell, London .55 .50
911 A91 5cor Balmain, Paris 1.40 1.20
Nos. 909-911,C839-C844 (9) 3.45 3.15

Gowns by famous designers, modeled by Nicaraguan women. Inscriptions on back printed on top of gum give description of gown in Spanish and English.

Nos. 909-911 in perf. 11, see No. C844a.

Christmas A92

2c, 5c, Virginia O'Hanlon writing letter, father. 3c, 15c, letter. 4c, 20c, Virginia, father reading letter.

1973, Nov. 15 Litho. ***Perf. 15***

912 A92 2c multicolored .20
913 A92 3c multicolored .20
914 A92 4c multicolored .20
915 A92 5c multicolored .20
916 A92 15c multicolored .20
917 A92 20c multicolored .20
Nos. 912-917,C846-C848 (9) 3.20

Sir Winston Churchill (1874-1965) A93

Designs: 2c, Churchill speaking. 3c, Military planning. 4c, Cigar, lamp. 5c, Churchill with Roosevert and Stalin. 10c, Churchill walking ashore from landing craft.

1974, Apr. 30 ***Perf. 14½***

918 A93 2c multicolored .20
919 A93 3c multicolored .20
920 A93 4c multicolored .20
921 A93 5c multicolored .20
922 A93 10c multicolored .20
Nos. 918-922,C849-C850 (7) 4.15

World Cup Soccer Championships, Munich — A94

Scenes from previous World Cup Championships with flags and scores of finalists.

1974, May 8 ***Perf. 14½***

923 A94 1c 1930 .20
924 A94 2c 1934 .20
925 A94 3c 1938 .20
926 A94 4c 1950 .20
927 A94 5c 1954 .20
928 A94 10c 1958 .20
929 A94 15c 1962 .20
930 A94 20c 1966 .20
931 A94 25c 1970 .20
Nos. 923-931,C853 (10) 4.55

For overprint see No. C856.

A95

A96

Wild Flowers and Cacti: 2c, Hollyhocks. 3c, Paguira insignis. 4c, Morning glory. 5c, Pereschia autumnalis. 10c, Cultivated morning glory. 15c, Hibiscus. 20c, Pagoda tree blossoms.

1974, June 11 Litho. *Perf. 14*

932	A95	2c grn & multi	.20	.20
933	A95	3c grn & multi	.20	.20
934	A95	4c grn & multi	.20	.20
935	A95	5c grn & multi	.20	.20
936	A95	10c grn & multi	.20	.20
937	A95	15c grn & multi	.20	.20
938	A95	20c grn & multi	.20	.20
		Nos. 932-938,C854-C855 (9)	2.25	2.15

1974, July 10 *Perf. 14½*

Nicaraguan stamps,

939	A96	2c No. 670	.20
940	A96	3c No. 669	.20
941	A96	4c No. C110, horiz.	.20
942	A96	5c No. 667	.20
943	A96	10c No. 666	.20
944	A96	20c No. 665	.20
		Nos. 939-944,C855A-C855C (9)	3.70

UPU, Cent.

Four-toed Anteater A97

Designs: 2c, Puma. 3c, Raccoon. 4c, Ocelot. 5c, Kinkajou. 10c, Coypu. 15c, Peccary. 20c, Tapir.

1974, Sept. 10 Litho. *Perf. 14½*

946	A97	1c multi	.20	.20
947	A97	2c multi	.20	.20
948	A97	3c multi	.20	.20
949	A97	4c multi	.20	.20
950	A97	5c multi	.20	.20
951	A97	10c multi	.20	.20
952	A97	15c multi	.20	.20
953	A97	20c multi	.20	.20
		Nos. 946-953,C857-C858 (10)	3.25	3.05

Wild animals from San Diego and London Zoos.

Prophet Zacharias, by Michelangelo A98

Works of Michelangelo: 2c, The Last Judgment. 3c, The Creation of Adam, horiz. 4c, Sistine Chapel. 5c, Moses. 10c, Mouscron Madonna. 15c, David. 20c, Doni Madonna.

1974, Dec. 15

954	A98	1c dp rose & multi	.20	.20
955	A98	2c yellow & multi	.20	.20
956	A98	3c sal & multi	.20	.20
957	A98	4c blue & multi	.20	.20
958	A98	5c tan & multi	.20	.20
959	A98	10c multicolored	.20	.20
960	A98	15c multicolored	.20	.20
961	A98	20c blue & multi	.20	.20
		Nos. 954-961,C859-C862 (12)	3.00	2.90

Christmas 1974 and 500th birth anniversary of Michelangelo Buonarroti (1475-1564), Italian painter, sculptor and architect.

Giovanni Martinelli, Othello A99

Opera Singers and Scores: 2c, Tito Gobbi, Simone Boccanegra. 3c, Lotte Lehmann, Der Rosenkavalier. 4c, Lauritz Melchior, Parsifal. 5c, Nellie Melba, La Traviata. 15c, Jussi Bjoerling, La Bohème. 20c, Birgit Nilsson, Turandot.

1975, Jan. 22 *Perf. 14x13½*

962	A99	1c rose lil & multi	.20	.20
963	A99	2c brt bl & multi	.20	.20
964	A99	3c yel & multi	.20	.20
965	A99	4c dl bl & multi	.20	.20
966	A99	5c org & multi	.20	.20
967	A99	15c lake & multi	.20	.20
968	A99	20c gray & multi	.20	.20
		Nos. 962-968,C863-C870 (15)	6.10	3.50

Famous opera singers.

Jesus Condemned A100

The Spirit of 76, by Archibald M. Willard — A101

Stations of the Cross: 2c, Jesus Carries the Cross. 3c, Jesus falls the first time. 4c, Jesus meets his mother. 5c, Simon of Cyrene carries the Cross. 15c, St. Veronica wipes Jesus' face. 20c, Jesus falls the second time. 25c, Jesus meets the women of Jerusalem. 35c, Jesus falls the third time. Designs from Leon Cathedral.

1975, Mar. 20 *Perf. 14½*

969	A100	1c ultra & multi	.20	.20
970	A100	2c ultra & multi	.20	.20
971	A100	3c ultra & multi	.20	.20
972	A100	4c ultra & multi	.20	.20
973	A100	5c ultra & multi	.20	.20
974	A100	15c ultra & multi	.20	.20
975	A100	20c ultra & multi	.20	.20
976	A100	25c ultra & multi	.20	.20
977	A100	35c ultra & multi	.20	.20
		Nos. 969-977,C871-C875 (14)	3.50	3.40

Easter 1975.

1975, Apr. 16 *Perf. 14*

Designs: 2c, Pitt Addressing Parliament, by K. A. Hickel. 3c, The Midnight Ride of Paul Revere, horiz. 4c, Statue of George III Demolished, by W. Walcutt, horiz. 5c, Boston Massacre. 10c, Colonial coin and seal, horiz. 15c, Boston Tea Party, horiz. 20c, Thomas Jefferson, by Rembrandt Peale. 25c, Benjamin Franklin, by Charles Willson Peale. 30c, Signing Declaration of Independence, by John Trumbull, horiz. 35c, Surrender of Cornwallis, by Trumbull, horiz.

978	A101	1c tan & multi	.20	.20
979	A101	2c tan & multi	.20	.20
980	A101	3c tan & multi	.20	.20
981	A101	4c tan & multi	.20	.20
982	A101	5c tan & multi	.20	.20
983	A101	10c tan & multi	.20	.20
984	A101	15c tan & multi	.20	.20
985	A101	20c tan & multi	.20	.20
986	A101	25c tan & multi	.20	.20
987	A101	30c tan & multi	.20	.20
988	A101	35c tan & multi	.20	.20
		Nos. 978-988,C876-C879 (15)	5.45	5.20

American Bicentennial.

Scouts Saluting Flag, Scout Emblems A102

2c, Two-men canoe. 3c, Scouts of various races shaking hands. 4c, Scout cooking. 5c, Entrance to Camp Nicaragua. 20c, Group discussion.

1975, Aug. 15 *Perf. 14½*

989	A102	1c multi	.20	.20
990	A102	2c multi	.20	.20
991	A102	3c multi	.20	.20
992	A102	4c multi	.20	.20
993	A102	5c multi	.20	.20
994	A102	20c multi	.20	.20
		Nos. 989-994,C880-C883 (10)	3.20	3.05

Nordjamb 75, 14th World Boy Scout Jamboree, Lillehammer, Norway, July 29-Aug. 7.

Pres. Somoza, Map and Arms of Nicaragua — A103

1975, Sept. 10 *Perf. 14*

995	A103	20c multi	.20	.20
996	A103	40c org & multi	.20	.20
		Nos. 995-996,C884-C886 (5)	6.60	5.40

Reelection of Pres. Anastasio Somoza D.

King's College Choir, Cambridge — A104

Famous Choirs: 2c, Einsiedeln Abbey. 3c, Regensburg. 4c, Vienna Choir Boys. 5c, Sistine Chapel. 15c, Westminster Cathedral. 20c, Mormon Tabernacle.

1975, Nov. 15 *Perf. 14½*

997	A104	1c silver & multi	.20	.20
998	A104	2c silver & multi	.20	.20
999	A104	3c silver & multi	.20	.20
1000	A104	4c silver & multi	.20	.20
1001	A104	5c silver & multi	.20	.20
1002	A104	15c silver & multi	.20	.20
1003	A104	20c silver & multi	.20	.20
		Nos. 997-1003,C887-C890 (11)	3.15	2.95

Christmas 1975.

The Chess Players, by Ludovico Carracci A105

History of Chess: 2c, Arabs Playing Chess, by Delacroix. 3c, Cardinals Playing Chess, by Victor Marais-Milton. 4c, Albrecht V of Bavaria and Anne of Austria Playing Chess, by Hans Muelich, vert. 5c, Chess Players, Persian manuscript, 14th century. 10c, Origin of Chess, Indian miniature, 17th century. 15c, Napoleon Playing Chess at Schönbrunn, by Antoni Uniechowski, vert. 20c, The Chess Game, by J. E. Hummel.

1976, Jan. 8 *Perf. 14½*

1004	A105	1c brn & multi	.20	.20
1005	A105	2c lt vio & multi	.20	.20
1006	A105	3c ocher & multi	.20	.20
1007	A105	4c multi	.20	.20
1008	A105	5c multi	.20	.20
1009	A105	10c multi	.20	.20
1010	A105	15c blue & multi	.20	.20
1011	A105	20c ocher & multi	.20	.20
		Nos. 1004-1011,C891-C893 (11)	4.05	3.60

Olympic Rings, Danish Crew — A107

Winners, Rowing and Sculling Events: 2c, East Germany, 1972. 3c, Italy, 1968. 4c, Great Britain, 1936. 5c, France, 1952. 35c, US, 1920, vert.

1976, Sept. 7 Litho. *Perf. 14*

1022	A107	1c blue & multi	.20	.20
1023	A107	2c blue & multi	.20	.20
1024	A107	3c blue & multi	.20	.20
1025	A107	4c blue & multi	.20	.20
1026	A107	5c blue & multi	.20	.20
1027	A107	35c blue & multi	.20	.20
		Nos. 1022-1027,C902-C905 (10)	6.35	5.55

Candlelight — A108

#1028, The Smoke Signal, by Frederic Remington. #1029, Space Signal Monitoring Center. #1031, Edison's laboratory & light bulb. #1032, Agriculture, 1776. #1033, Agriculture, 1976. #1034, Harvard College, 1726. #1035, Harvard University, 1976. #1036, Horse-drawn carriage. #1037, Boeing 747.

1976, May 25 Litho. *Perf. 13½*

1028	A108	1c gray & multi	.20	.20
1029	A108	1c gray & multi	.20	.20
a.		Pair, #1028-1029	.20	.20
1030	A108	2c gray & multi	.20	.20
1031	A108	2c gray & multi	.20	.20
a.		Pair, #1030-1031	.20	.20
1032	A108	3c gray & multi	.20	.20
1033	A108	3c gray & multi	.20	.20
a.		Pair, #1032-1033	.20	.20
1034	A108	4c gray & multi	.20	.20
1035	A108	4c gray & multi	.20	.20
a.		Pair, #1034-1035	.20	.20
1036	A108	5c gray & multi	.20	.20
1037	A108	5c gray & multi	.20	.20
a.		Pair, #1036-1037	.20	.20
		Nos. 1028-1037,C907-C912 (16)	4.70	4.20

American Bicentennial, 200 years of progress.

Mauritius No. 2 — A109

Rare Stamps: 2c, Western Australia #3a. 3c, Mauritius #1. 4c, Jamaica #83a. 5c, US #C3a. 10c, Basel #3L1. 25c, Canada #387a.

1976, Dec. *Perf. 14*

1038	A109	1c multi	.20	.20
1039	A109	2c multi	.20	.20
1040	A109	3c multi	.20	.20
1041	A109	4c multi	.20	.20
1042	A109	5c multi	.20	.20
1043	A109	10c multi	.20	.20
1044	A109	25c multi	.20	.20
		Nos. 1038-1044,C913-C917 (12)	4.20	3.95

Back inscriptions printed on top of gum describe illustrated stamp.

Zeppelin in Flight — A110

1c, Zeppelin in hangar. 3c, Giffard's dirigible airship, 1852. 4c, Zeppelin on raising stilts coming out of hangar. 5c, Zeppelin ready for take-off.

1977, Oct. 31 Litho. *Perf. 14½*

1045 A110 1c multi .20 .20
1046 A110 2c multi .20 .20
1047 A110 3c multi .20 .20
1048 A110 4c multi .20 .20
1049 A110 5c multi .20 .20
Nos. 1045-1049,C921-C924 (9) 4.55 3.65

75th anniversary of Zeppelin.

Lindbergh, Map of Nicaragua — A111

2c, Spirit of St. Louis, map of Nicaragua. 3c, Lindbergh, vert. 4c, Spirit of St. Louis & NYC-Paris route. 5c, Lindbergh & Spirit of St. Louis. 20c, Lindbergh, NYC-Paris route & plane.

1977, Nov. 30

1050 A111 1c multi .20 .20
1051 A111 2c multi .20 .20
1052 A111 3c multi .20 .20
1053 A111 4c multi .20 .20
1054 A111 5c multi .20 .20
1055 A111 20c multi .20 .20
Nos. 1050-1055,C926-C929 (10) 4.00 3.50

Charles A. Lindbergh's solo transatlantic flight from NYC to Paris, 50th anniv.

Nutcracker Suite — A112

1c, Christmas party. 2c, Dancing dolls. 3c, Clara and Snowflakes. 4c, Snowflake and prince. 5c, Snowflake dance. 15c, Sugarplum fairy and prince. 40c, Waltz of the flowers. 90c, Chinese tea dance. 1cor, Bonbonnière. 10cor, Arabian coffee dance.

1977, Dec. 12

1056 A112 1c multi .20 .20
1057 A112 2c multi .20 .20
1058 A112 3c multi .20 .20
1059 A112 4c multi .20 .20
1060 A112 5c multi .20 .20
1061 A112 15c multi .20 .20
1062 A112 40c multi .20 .20
1063 A112 90c multi .20 .20
1064 A112 1cor multi .30 .20
1065 A112 10cor multi 2.25 2.00
Nos. 1056-1065 (10) 4.15 3.80

Christmas 1977. See No. C931.

Mr. and Mrs. Andrews, by Gainsborough — A113

Paintings: 2c, Giovanna Bacelli, by Gainsborough. 3c, Blue Boy by Gainsborough. 4c, Francis I, by Titian. 5c, Charles V in Battle of Muhlberg, by Titian. 25c, Sacred Love, by Titian.

1978, Jan. 11 Litho. *Perf. 14½*

1066 A113 1c multi .20 .20
1067 A113 2c multi .20 .20
1068 A113 3c multi .20 .20
1069 A113 4c multi .20 .20
1070 A113 5c multi .20 .20
1071 A113 25c multi .20 .20
Nos. 1066-1071,C932-C933 (8) 4.20 3.65

Thomas Gainsborough (1727-1788), 250th birth anniv.; Titian (1477-1576), 500th birth anniv.

Gothic Portal, Lower Church, Assisi — A114

Designs: 2c, St. Francis preaching to the birds. 3c, St. Francis, painting. 4c, St. Francis and Franciscan saints, 15th century tapestry. 5c, Portiuncola, cell of St. Francis, now in church of St. Mary of the Angels, Assisi. 15c, Blessing of St. Francis for Brother Leo (parchment). 25c, Stained-glass window, Upper Church of St. Francis, Assisi.

1978, Feb. 23 Litho. *Perf. 14½*

1072 A114 1c red & multi .20 .20
1073 A114 2c brt grn & multi .20 .20
1074 A114 3c bl grn & multi .20 .20
1075 A114 4c ultra & multi .20 .20
1076 A114 5c rose & multi .20 .20
1077 A114 15c yel & multi .20 .20
1078 A114 25c ocher & multi .20 .20
Nos. 1072-1078,C935-C936 (9) 3.50 3.35

St. Francis of Assisi (1182-1266), 750th anniversary of his canonization, and in honor of Our Lady of the Immaculate Conception, patron saint of Nicaragua.

Passenger and Freight Locomotives — A115

Locomotives: 2c, Lightweight freight. 3c, American. 4c, Heavy freight Baldwin. 5c, Light freight and passenger Baldwin. 15c, Presidential coach.

1978, Apr. 7 Litho. *Perf. 14½*

1079 A115 1c lil & multi .20 .20
1080 A115 2c rose lil & multi .20 .20
1081 A115 3c bl & multi .20 .20
1082 A115 4c ol & multi .20 .20
1083 A115 5c yel & multi .20 .20
1084 A115 15c dp org & multi .20 .20
Nos. 1079-1084,C938-C940 (9) 4.30 4.05

Centenary of Nicaraguan railroads.

Michael Strogoff, by Jules Verne — A116

Jules Verne Books: 2c, The Mysterious Island. 3c, Journey to the Center of the Earth (battle of the sea monsters). 4c, Five Weeks in a Balloon.

1978, Aug. Litho. *Perf. 14½*

1085 A116 1c multi .20 .20
1086 A116 2c multi .20 .20
1087 A116 3c multi .20 .20
1088 A116 4c multi .20 .20
Nos. 1085-1088,C942-C943 (6) 2.75 2.50

Jules Verne (1828-1905), science fiction writer.

Montgolfier Balloon — A117

1c, Icarus. 3c, Wright Brothers' Flyer A. 4c, Orville Wright at control of Flyer, 1908.

Perf. 14½, horiz.

1978, Sept. 29 Litho.

1089 A117 1c multi, horiz. .20 .20
1090 A117 2c multi .20 .20
1091 A117 3c multi, horiz. .20 .20
1092 A117 4c multi .20 .20
Nos. 1089-1092,C945-C946 (6) 2.40 2.00

History of aviation & 75th anniv. of 1st powered flight.

Ernst Ocwirk and Alfredo Di Stefano — A118

St. Peter, by Goya — A119

Soccer Players: 25c, Ralf Edstroem and Oswaldo Piazza.

1978, Oct. 25 Litho. *Perf. 13½x14*

1093 A118 20c multicolored .20 .20
1094 A118 25c multicolored .20 .20
Nos. 1093-1094,C948-C949 (4) 1.60 1.45

11th World Soccer Cup Championship, Argentina, June 1-25. See No. C950.

1978, Dec. 12 Litho. *Perf. 13½x14*

Paintings: 15c, St. Gregory, by Goya.

1095 A119 10c multi .20 .20
1096 A119 15c multi .20 .20
Nos. 1095-1096,C951-C952 (4) 2.20 1.75

Christmas 1978. See No. C953.

San Cristobal Volcano and Map — A120

Designs: No. 1098, Lake Cosiguina. No. 1099, Telica Volcano. No. 1100, Lake Jiloa.

1978, Dec. 29 *Perf. 14x13½*

1097 A120 5c multi .20 .20
1098 A120 5c multi .20 .20
a. Pair, #1097-1098 .25 .25
1099 A120 20c multi .20 .20
1100 A120 20c multi .20 .20
a. Pair, #1099-1100 .25 .25
Nos. 1097-1100,C954-C961 (12) 5.80 4.80

Volcanos, lakes and their locations.

Souvenir Sheet

Quetzal — A121

1981, May 18 Litho. *Perf. 13*

1101 A121 10cor multi 1.75 1.25

WIPA 1981 Phil. Exhib., Vienna, May 22-31.

1982 World Cup A122

Various soccer players and stadiums.

1981, June 25 *Perf. 12x12½*

1102 A122 5c multi .20 .20
1103 A122 20c multi .20 .20
1104 A122 25c multi .20 .20
1105 A122 30c multi .20 .20
1106 A122 50c multi .20 .20
1107 A122 4cor multi .45 .25
1108 A122 5cor multi .55 .30
1109 A122 10cor multi 1.10 .65
Nos. 1102-1109 (8) 3.10 2.20

Souvenir Sheet

Perf. 13

1110 A122 10cor multi 1.40 1.00

2nd Anniv. of Revolution — A123

1981, July 19 *Perf. 12½x12*

1111 A123 50c Adult education .20 .20
Nos. 1111,C973-C975 (4) 1.70 1.10

20th Anniv. of the FSLN A124

1981, July 23

1112 A124 50c Armed citizen .20 .20

See No. C976.

Postal Union of Spain and the Americas, 12th Congress, Managua — A125

1981, Aug. 10

1113 A125 50c Mailman .20 .20
Nos. 1113,C977-C979 (4) 1.35 .95

Aquatic Flowers (Nymphaea...) A126

1981, Sept. 15 ***Perf. 12½***

1114 A126 50c Capensis .20 .20
1115 A126 1cor Daubenyana .20 .20
1116 A126 1.20cor Marliacea .25 .20
1117 A126 1.80cor GT Moore .35 .20
1118 A126 2cor Lotus .35 .20
1119 A126 2.50cor BG Berry .50 .30
Nos. 1114-1119,C981 (7) 3.25 2.20

Tropical Fish A127

1981, Oct. 19

1120 A127 50c Cheirodon axelrodi .20 .20
1121 A127 1cor Poecilia reticulata .20 .20
1122 A127 1.85cor Anostomus anostomus .35 .20
1123 A127 2.10cor Corydoras arcuatus .40 .20
1124 A127 2.50cor Cynolebias nigripinnis .50 .30
Nos. 1120-1124,C983-C984 (7) 2.70 1.70

Dryocopus Lineatus — A128

1981, Nov. 30 ***Perf. 12½***

1125 A128 50c shown .20 .20
1126 A128 1.20cor Ramphastos sulfuratus, horiz. .25 .20
1127 A128 1.80cor Aratinga finschi, horiz. .40 .25
1128 A128 2cor Ara macao .40 .25
Nos. 1125-1128,C986-C988 (7) 3.75 2.10

Space Communications — A129

Various communications satellites.

1981, Dec. 15 ***Perf. 13x12½***

1129 A129 50c multi .20 .20
1130 A129 1cor multi .20 .20
1131 A129 1.50cor multi .25 .20
1132 A129 2cor multi .30 .20
Nos. 1129-1132,C989-C991 (7) 3.95 1.70

Vaporcito 93 A130

1981, Dec. 30 ***Perf. 12½***

1133 A130 50c shown .20 .20
1134 A130 1cor Vulcan Iron Works, 1946 .20 .20
1135 A130 1.20cor 1911 .25 .20
1136 A130 1.80cor Hoist & Derriel, 1909 .40 .20
1137 A130 2cor U-10B, 1956 .40 .25
1138 A130 2.50cor Ferrobus, 1945 .40 .30
Nos. 1133-1138,C992 (7) 3.35 1.90

1982 World Cup — A131

Designs: Various soccer players. 3.50cor horiz.

1982, Jan. 25

1139 A131 5c multi .20 .20
1140 A131 20c multi .20 .20
1141 A131 25c multi .20 .20
1142 A131 2.50cor multi .40 .35
1143 A131 3.50cor multi .55 .35
Nos. 1139-1143,C993-C994 (7) 3.55 2.40

Cocker Spaniels A132

1982, Feb. 18

1144 A132 5c shown .20 .20
1145 A132 20c German shepherds .20 .20
1146 A132 25c English setters .20 .20
1147 A132 2.50cor Brittany spaniels .45 .30
Nos. 1144-1147,C996-C998 (7) 3.05 2.00

Dynamine Myrrhina A133

1982, Mar. 26

1148 A133 50c shown .20 .20
1149 A133 1.20cor Eunica alcmena .25 .20
1150 A133 1.50cor Callizona acesta .30 .20
1151 A133 2cor Adelpha leuceria .35 .25
Nos. 1148-1151,C1000-C1002 (7) 3.60 1.85

Satellite A134

Designs: Various satellites. 5c, 50c, 1.50cor, 2.50cor horiz.

1982, Apr. 12

1152 A134 5c multi .20 .20
1153 A134 15c multi .20 .20
1154 A134 50c multi .20 .20
1155 A134 1.50cor multi .25 .20
1156 A134 2.50cor multi .45 .25
Nos. 1152-1156,C1003-C1004 (7) 3.05 1.95

UPU Membership Centenary — A135

1982, May 1 **Litho.** ***Perf. 13***

1157 A135 50c Mail coach .20 .20
1158 A135 1.20cor Ship .20 .20
Nos. 1157-1158,C1005-C1006 (4) 1.90 1.35

14th Central American and Caribbean Games (Cuba '82) — A136

1982, May 13

1159 A136 10c Bicycling, vert. .20 .20
1160 A136 15c Swimming .20 .20
1161 A136 25c Basketball, vert. .20 .20
1162 A136 50c Weight lifting, vert. .20 .20
Nos. 1159-1162,C1007-C1009 (7) 3.80 2.15

3rd Anniv. of Revolution — A137

1982, July 19

1163 A137 50c multi .20 .20
Nos. 1163,C1012-C1014 (4) 2.45 1.45

George Washington (1732-1799) A138

19th Century Paintings. 1cor horiz. Size of 50c: 45x35mm.

Perf. 13x12½, 12½x13

1982, June 20 **Litho.**

1164 A138 50c Mount Vernon .20 .20
1165 A138 1cor Signing the Constitution .20 .20
1166 A138 2cor Riding through Trenton .40 .25
Nos. 1164-1166,C1015-C1018 (7) 3.80 2.25

Flower Arrangement, by R. Penalba A139

Paintings: 50c, Masked Dancers, by M. Garcia, horiz. 1cor, The Couple, by R. Perez. 1.20cor, Canales Valley, by A. Mejias, horiz. 1.85cor, Portrait of Mrs. Castellon, by T. Jerez. 2cor, Street Vendors, by L. Cerrato. 10cor, Cock Fight, by Gallos P. Ortiz.

1982, Aug. 17 ***Perf. 13***

1167 A139 25c multi .20 .20
1168 A139 50c multi .20 .20
1169 A139 1cor multi .20 .20
1170 A139 1.20cor multi .20 .20
1171 A139 1.85cor multi .30 .20
1172 A139 2cor multi .30 .20
Nos. 1167-1172,C1019 (7) 3.15 2.00

Souvenir Sheet

1173 A139 10cor multi 1.60 1.00

No. 1173 contains one 36x28mm stamp.

George Dimitrov, First Pres. of Bulgaria — A140

1982, Sept. 9

1174 A140 50c Lenin, Dimitrov, 1921 .20 .20
Nos. 1174,C1020-C1021 (3) 1.20 .85

26th Anniv. of End of Dictatorship — A141

1982, Sept. 21 ***Perf. 13x12½***

1175 A141 50c Ausberto Narvaez .20 .20
1176 A141 2.50cor Cornelio Silva .50 .30
Nos. 1175-1176,C1022-C1023 (4) 2.30 1.50

Ruins, Leon Viejo A142

1982, Sept. 25 ***Perf. 13***

1177 A142 50c shown .20 .20
1178 A142 1cor Ruben Dario Theater and Park .20 .20
1179 A142 1.20cor Independence Plaza, Granada .20 .20
1180 A142 1.80cor Corn Island .30 .20
1181 A142 2cor Santiago Volcano crater, Masaya .30 .20
Nos. 1177-1181,C1024-C1025 (7) 1.90 1.45

Karl Marx (1818-1883) — A143

1982, Oct. 4 *Perf. 12½*
1182 A143 1cor Marx, birthplace .20 .20

Se-tenant with label showing Communist Manifesto titlepage. See No. C1026.

World Food Day (Oct. 16) A144

1982, Oct. 10 *Perf. 13*
1183 A144 50c Picking fruit .20 .20
1184 A144 1cor Farm workers, vert. .20 .20
1185 A144 2cor Cutting sugar cane .30 .25
1186 A144 10cor Emblems 1.50 1.25
Nos. 1183-1186 (4) 2.20 1.90

Discovery of America, 490th Anniv. — A145

1982, Oct. 12 *Perf. 12½x13*
1187 A145 50c Santa Maria .20 .20
1188 A145 1cor Nina .25 .20
1189 A145 1.50cor Pinta .30 .20
1190 A145 2cor Columbus, fleet .40 .30
Nos. 1187-1190,C1027-C1029 (7) 3.65 2.25

A146

A147

1982, Nov. 13 *Perf. 12½*
1191 A146 50c Lobelia laxiflora .20 .20
1192 A146 1.20cor Bombacopsis quinata .25 .20
1193 A146 1.80cor Mimosa albida .40 .25
1194 A146 2cor Epidendrum alatum .40 .25
Nos. 1191-1194,C1031-C1033 (7) 3.00 1.90

1982, Dec. 10 *Perf. 13*
1195 A147 10c Coral snake .20 .20
1196 A147 50c Iguana, horiz. .20 .20
1197 A147 2cor Lachesis muta, horiz. .40 .25
Nos. 1195-1197,C1034-C1037 (7) 7.20 1.95

Telecommunications Day — A148

1982, Dec. 12 **Litho.** *Perf. 12½*
1198 A148 50c Radio transmission station .20 .20
1199 A148 1cor Telcor building, Managua .20 .20

50c airmail.

Jose Marti, Cuban Independence Hero, 130th Birth Anniv. — A149

1983, Jan. 28 *Perf. 13*
1200 A149 1cor multi .25 .20

Boxing A150

Local Flowers A151

1983, Jan. 31 *Perf. 12½*
1201 A150 50c shown .20 .20
1202 A150 1cor Gymnast .20 .20
1203 A150 1.50cor Running .20 .20
1204 A150 2cor Weightlifting .25 .20
1205 A150 4cor Women's discus .65 .30
1206 A150 5cor Basketball .80 .40
1207 A150 6cor Bicycling 1.00 .50
Nos. 1201-1207 (7) 3.30 2.00

Souvenir Sheet

Perf. 13

1208 A150 15cor Sailing 2.25 1.25

23rd Olympic Games, Los Angeles, July 28-Aug. 12, 1984. Nos. 1205-1208 airmail. No. 1208 contains one 31x39mm stamp.

1983, Feb. 5 *Perf. 12½*
1209 A151 1cor Bixa orellana .20 .20
1210 A151 1cor Brassavola nodosa .20 .20
1211 A151 1cor Cattleya lueddemanniana .20 .20
1212 A151 1cor Cochlospermum spec. .20 .20
1213 A151 1cor Hibiscus rosa-sinensis .20 .20
1214 A151 1cor Laelia spec. .20 .20
1215 A151 1cor Malvaviscus arboreus .20 .20
1216 A151 1cor Neomarica coerulea .20 .20
1217 A151 1cor Plumeria rubra .20 .20
1218 A151 1cor Senecio spec. .20 .20
1219 A151 1cor Sobralla macrantha .20 .20
1220 A151 1cor Stachytarpheta indica .20 .20
1221 A151 1cor Tabebula ochraceae .20 .20
1222 A151 1cor Tagetes erecta .20 .20
1223 A151 1cor Tecoma stans .20 .20
1224 A151 1cor Thumbergia alata .20 .20
Nos. 1209-1224 (16) 3.20 3.20

See #1515-1530, 1592-1607, 1828-1843.

Visit of Pope John Paul II A152

1983, Mar. 4 *Perf. 13*
1225 A152 50c Peace banner .20 .20
1226 A152 1cor Map, girl picking coffee beans .25 .20
1227 A152 4cor Pres. Rafael Rivas, Pope .95 .60
1228 A152 7cor Pope, Managua Cathedral 1.60 1.00
Nos. 1225-1228 (4) 3.00 2.00

Souvenir Sheet

1229 A152 15cor Pope, vert. 3.25 1.75

Nos. 1227-1229 airmail. No. 1229 contains one 31x39mm stamp.

Nocturnal Moths — A153

1983, Mar. 10
1230 A153 15c Xilophanes chiron .20 .20
1231 A153 50c Protoparce ochus .20 .20
1232 A153 65c Pholus lasbruscae .20 .20
1233 A153 1cor Amphypterus gannascus .20 .20
1234 A153 1.50cor Pholus licaon .20 .20
1235 A153 2cor Agrius cingulata .35 .20
1236 A153 10cor Rothschildia jurulla, vert. 1.50 .80
Nos. 1230-1236 (7) 2.85 2.00

No. 1236 airmail.

26th Anniv. of the Anti-Somoza Movement — A154

Various monuments and churches. 2cor, 4cor vert. 4cor airmail.

1983, Mar. 25 *Perf. 12½*
1237 A154 50c Church of Subtiava, Leon .20 .20
1238 A154 1cor La Immaculata Castle, Rio San Juan .20 .20
1239 A154 2cor La Recoleccion Church, Leon .35 .20
1240 A154 4cor Ruben Dario monument, Managua .65 .40
Nos. 1237-1240 (4) 1.40 1.00

Railroad Cars A155

1983, Apr. 15
1241 A155 15c Passenger .20 .20
1242 A155 65c Freight .20 .20
1243 A155 1cor Tank .20 .20
1244 A155 1.50cor Ore .20 .20
1245 A155 4cor Passenger, diff. .55 .30
1246 A155 5cor Flat .70 .40
1247 A155 7cor Rail bus .95 .50
Nos. 1241-1247 (7) 3.00 2.00

Nos. 1245-1247 airmail.

Red Cross Flood Rescue A156

1983, May 8 *Perf. 13*
1248 A156 50c shown .20 .20
1249 A156 1cor Putting patient in ambulance .20 .20
1250 A156 4cor 1972 earthquake & fire rescue .65 .40
1251 A156 5cor Nurse examining soldier, 1979 Liberation War .70 .40
Nos. 1248-1251 (4) 1.75 1.20

4cor, 5cor airmail. 4cor vert.

World Communications Year — A157

1983, May 17
1252 A157 1cor multi .40 .20

9th Pan-American Games, Aug. — A158

1983, May 30 **Litho.** *Perf. 13*
1253 A158 15c Baseball .20 .20
1254 A158 50c Water polo .20 .20
1255 A158 65c Running .20 .20
1256 A158 1cor Women's basketball, vert. .20 .20
1257 A158 2cor Weightlifting, vert. .35 .20
1258 A158 7cor Fencing 1.10 .55
1259 A158 8cor Gymnastics 1.25 .65
Nos. 1253-1259 (7) 3.50 2.20

Souvenir Sheet

1260 A158 15cor Boxing 2.50 1.25

Nos. 1258-1260 airmail. No. 1260 contains one 39x31mm stamp.

4th Anniv. of Revolution — A159

1983, July 19 **Litho.** *Perf. 12½*
1261 A159 1cor Port of Corinto .20 .20
1262 A159 2cor Telecommunications Bldg., Leon .40 .20

Founders of FSLN (Sandinista Party) — A160

1983, July 23 Litho. *Perf. 13*

1263 A160 50c multi .20 .20
1264 A160 1cor multi .20 .20
1265 A160 4cor multi, vert. .60 .35
Nos. 1263-1265 (3) 1.00 .75

No. 1265, airmail, 33x44mm.

Simon Bolivar, 200th Birth Anniv. A161

1983, July 24 Litho. *Perf. 12½*

1266 A161 50c Bolivar and Sandino .20 .20
1267 A161 1cor Bolivar on horseback, vert. .20 .20

14th Winter Olympic Games, Sarajevo, Yugoslavia, Feb. 8-19, 1984 — A162

1983, Aug. 5 Litho. *Perf. 13*

1268 A162 50c Speed skating .20 .20
1269 A162 1cor Slalom .20 .20
1270 A162 1.50cor Luge .20 .20
1271 A162 2cor Ski jumping .40 .20
1272 A162 4cor Ice dancing .65 .35
1273 A162 5cor Skiing .75 .40
1274 A162 6cor Biathlon 1.00 .50
Nos. 1268-1274 (7) 3.40 2.05

Souvenir Sheet

1983, Aug. 25 Litho. *Perf. 13*

1275 A162 15cor Hockey 2.50 1.40

No. 1275 contains one 39x32mm stamp. Nos. 1272-1275 airmail.

Chess Moves — A163

Archaeological Finds — A164

1983, Aug. 20 Litho. *Perf. 13*

1276 A163 15c Pawn .20 .20
1277 A163 65c Knight .20 .20
1278 A163 1cor Bishop .20 .20
1279 A163 2cor Castle .35 .20
1280 A163 4cor Queen .60 .35
1281 A163 5cor King .70 .40
1282 A163 7cor Player 1.00 .55
Nos. 1276-1282 (7) 3.25 2.10

Nos. 1280-1282 airmail.

1983, Aug. 20 *Perf. 13x12½*

1283 A164 50c Stone figurine .20 .20
1284 A164 1cor Covered dish .20 .20
1285 A164 2cor Vase .35 .20
1286 A164 4cor Platter .60 .35
Nos. 1283-1286 (4) 1.35 .95

No. 1286 airmail.

Madonna of the Chair, by Raphael (1483-1517) A165

Paintings: 1cor, The Eszterhazy Madonna. 1.50cor, Sistine Madonna. 2cor, Madonna of the Linnet. 4cor, Madonna of the Meadow. 5cor, La Belle Jardiniere. 6cor, Adoration of the Kings. 15cor, Madonna of Foligno. 4, 5, 6, 15cor airmail.

1983, Sept. 15

1287 A165 50c multi .20 .20
1288 A165 1cor multi .20 .20
1289 A165 1.50cor multi .20 .20
1290 A165 2cor multi .35 .20
1291 A165 4cor multi .60 .35
1292 A165 5cor multi .70 .40
1293 A165 6cor multi .90 .45
Nos. 1287-1293 (7) 3.15 2.00

Souvenir Sheet

1984, Sept. 15 Litho. *Perf. 13*

1293A A165 15cor multi 2.50 1.25

Mining Industry Nationalization — A166

1983, Oct. 2 *Perf. 13*

1294 A166 1cor Pouring molten metal .20 .20
1295 A166 4cor Mine headstock, workers .60 .40

4cor airmail.

Ship-to-Shore Communications — A167

1983, Oct. 7 *Perf. 12½*

1296 A167 1cor shown .20 .20
1297 A167 4cor Radio tower, view .60 .40

FRACAP '83, Federation of Central American and Panamanian Radio Amateurs Cong., Oct. 7-9.

Agrarian Reform — A168

1983, Oct. 16

1298 A168 1cor Tobacco .20 .20
1299 A168 2cor Cotton .35 .20
1300 A168 4cor Corn .60 .25
1301 A168 5cor Sugar cane .70 .35
1302 A168 6cor Cattle .90 .40
1303 A168 7cor Rice paddy 1.00 .45
1304 A168 8cor Coffee beans 1.20 .55
1305 A168 10cor Bananas 1.50 .65
Nos. 1298-1305 (8) 6.45 3.05

See Nos. 1531-1538, 1608-1615.

Fire Engine A169

Various Fire Engines.

1983, Oct. 17 *Perf. 13*

1306 A169 50c multi .20 .20
1307 A169 1cor multi .20 .20
1308 A169 1.50cor multi .20 .20
1309 A169 2cor multi .35 .20
1310 A169 4cor multi .60 .35
1311 A169 5cor multi .70 .40
1312 A169 6cor multi .90 .45
Nos. 1306-1312 (7) 3.15 2.00

Nos. 1308-1311 airmail.

Nicaraguan-Cuban Solidarity — A170

1983, Oct. 24

1313 A170 1cor José Marti, Gen. Sandino .20 .20
1314 A170 4cor Education, health, industry .60 .40

4cor airmail.

A171

A172

Christmas (Adoration of the Kings Paintings by): 50c, Hugo van der Goes. 1 cor, Ghirlandaio. 2cor, El Greco. 7cor, Konrad von Soest. 7cor airmail.

1983, Dec. 1

1315 A171 50c multi .20 .20
1316 A171 1cor multi .20 .20
1317 A171 2cor multi .30 .20
1318 A171 7cor multi .90 .40
Nos. 1315-1318 (4) 1.60 1.00

1984, Jan. 10

1319 A172 50c Biathlon .20 .20
1320 A172 50c Bobsledding .20 .20
1321 A172 1cor Speed skating .20 .20
1322 A172 1cor Slalom .20 .20
1323 A172 4cor Downhill skiing .65 .35
1324 A172 5cor Ice dancing .80 .40
1325 A172 10cor Ski jumping 1.40 .75
Nos. 1319-1325 (7) 3.65 2.30

Souvenir Sheet

1326 A172 15cor Hockey 3.00 1.50

1984 Winter Olympics. No. 1326 contains one 31x39mm stamp. Nos. 1323-1326 airmail.

Domestic Cats — A173

1984, Feb. 15 *Perf. 12½*

1327 A173 50c Chinchilla .20 .20
1328 A173 50c Long-haired Angel .20 .20
1329 A173 1cor Red tabby .25 .20
1330 A173 2cor Tortoiseshell .50 .20
1331 A173 3cor Siamese .40 .30
1332 A173 4cor Blue Burmese .85 .40
1333 A173 7cor Silver long-haired 1.50 .60
Nos. 1327-1333 (7) 3.90 2.10

Nos. 1331, 1333 airmail.

Augusto Cesar Sandino (d. 1934) — A174

1984, Feb. 21

1334 A174 1cor Arms .20 .20
1335 A174 4cor Portrait .60 .40

4cor airmail.

Intl. Women's Day — A175

1984, Mar. 8

1336 A175 1cor Blanca Arauz .20 .20

Bee-pollinated Flowers A176

1984, Mar. 20

1337 A176 50c Poinsettia .20 .20
1338 A176 50c Sunflower .20 .20
1339 A176 1cor Antigonan leptopus .20 .20
1340 A176 1cor Cassia alata .20 .20
1341 A176 3cor Bidens pilosa .40 .25
1342 A176 4cor Althea rosea .60 .35
1343 A176 5cor Rivea corymbosa .70 .40
Nos. 1337-1343 (7) 2.50 1.80

Nos. 1341-1343 airmail.

Space Annivs. — A177

1984, Apr. 20

1344	A177	50c	Soyuz 6,7,8, 1969	.20	.20
1345	A177	50c	Soyuz 6,7,8, diff.	.20	.20
1346	A177	1cor	Apollo 11, 1969	.20	.20
1347	A177	2cor	Luna 1, 1959	.35	.20
1348	A177	3cor	Luna 2, 1959	.50	.25
1349	A177	4cor	Luna 3, 1959	.65	.35
1350	A177	9cor	Painting by Koroliov, 1934	1.40	.50
			Nos. 1344-1350 (7)	3.50	1.90

Nos. 1348-1350 airmail.

Noli Me Tangere, by Correggio
A178

1984, May 17 Litho. *Perf. 12½*

1351	A178	50c	shown	.20	.20
1352	A178	50c	Madonna of San Girolamo	.20	.20
1353	A178	1cor	Allegory of the Virtues	.20	.20
1354	A178	2cor	Allegory of Placer	.35	.20
1355	A178	3cor	Ganimedes	.50	.25
1356	A178	5cor	Danae	.80	.40
1357	A178	8cor	Leda	1.25	.65
			Nos. 1351-1357 (7)	3.50	2.10

Souvenir Sheet

1358	A178	15cor	St. John the Evangelist	3.00	1.25

No. 1358 contains one 31x39mm stamp. Nos. 1355-1358 airmail.

Vintage Cars
A179

1984, May 18

1359	A179	1cor	Abadal, 1914	.20	.20
1360	A179	1cor	Daimler, 1886, vert.	.20	.20
1361	A179	2cor	Ford, 1903, vert.	.35	.20
1362	A179	2cor	Renault, 1899, vert.	.35	.20
1363	A179	3cor	Rolls Royce, 1910	.50	.25
1364	A179	4cor	Metallurgique, 1907	.65	.35
1365	A179	7cor	Bugatti Mode 40	1.10	.60
			Nos. 1359-1365 (7)	3.35	2.00

Birth sesquicentennial of Gottlieb Daimler. Nos. 1363-1365 airmail.

1984 Summer Olympics
A180

1984, July 6

1366	A180	50c	Volleyball	.20	.20
1367	A180	50c	Basketball	.20	.20
1368	A180	1cor	Field hockey	.20	.20
1369	A180	2cor	Tennis	.35	.20
1370	A180	3cor	Soccer	.50	.25
1371	A180	4cor	Water polo	.65	.35
1372	A180	9cor	Net ball	1.40	.70
			Nos. 1366-1372 (7)	3.50	2.10

Souvenir Sheet
Perf. 13

1373	A180	15cor	Baseball	2.25	1.25

No. 1373 contains one 40x31mm stamp. Nos. 1370-1373 airmail and horiz.

5th Anniv. of Revolution — A181

1984, July 19

1374	A181	50c	Construction	.20	.20
1375	A181	1cor	Transportation	.20	.20
1376	A181	4cor	Agriculture	.65	.35
1377	A181	7cor	Govt. building	1.25	.55
			Nos. 1374-1377 (4)	2.30	1.30

Nos. 1376-1377 airmail.

UNESCO Nature Conservation Campaign — A182

1984, Aug. 3 *Perf. 12½x13, 13x12½*

1378	A182	50c	Children dependent on nature	.20	.20
1379	A182	1cor	Forest	.20	.20
1380	A182	2cor	River	.35	.20
1381	A182	10cor	Seedlings, field, vert.	1.50	.80
			Nos. 1378-1381 (4)	2.25	1.40

No. 1381 airmail.

Nicaraguan Red Cross, 50th Anniv. — A183

1984, Sept. 16 *Perf. 12½x12*

1382	A183	1cor	Air ambulance	.20	.20
1383	A183	7cor	Battle field	1.00	.55

No. 1383 airmail.

History of Baseball — A184

Portraits and national colors: #1384, Ventura Escalante, Dominican Republic. #1385, Daniel Herrera, Mexico. #1386, Adalberto Herrera, Venezuela. #1387, Roberto Clemente, Puerto Rico. #1388, Carlos Colas, Cuba. #1389, Stanley Cayasso, Nicaragua. #1390, Babe Ruth, US.

1984, Oct. 25 Litho. *Perf. 12½*

1384	A184	50c	multi	.20	.20
1385	A184	50c	multi	.20	.20
1386	A184	1cor	multi	.35	.20
1387	A184	1cor	multi	.35	.20
1388	A184	3cor	multi	.90	.20
1389	A184	4cor	multi	1.25	.25
1390	A184	5cor	multi	1.50	.35
			Nos. 1384-1390 (7)	4.75	1.60

Nos. 1388-1390 are airmail.

Tapirus Bairdii
A185

1984, Dec. 28 *Perf. 13*

1391	A185	25c	In water	.30	.20
1392	A185	25c	In field	.30	.20
1393	A185	3cor	Baring teeth	.60	.20
1394	A185	4cor	Female and young	.80	.25
			Nos. 1391-1394 (4)	2.00	.85

Wildlife conservation. Nos. 1393-1394 are airmail. Compare with type A202.

1986 World Cup Soccer Championships, Mexico — A186

Evolution of soccer.

1985, Jan. 20

1395	A186	50c	1314	.20	.20
1396	A186	50c	1500	.20	.20
1397	A186	1cor	1846	.20	.20
1398	A186	1cor	1872	.20	.20
1399	A186	2cor	1883	.20	.20
1400	A186	4cor	1890	.40	.20
1401	A186	6cor	1953	.60	.30
			Nos. 1395-1401 (7)	2.00	1.50

Souvenir Sheet
Perf. 12½

1402	A186	10cor	1985	1.25	.80

Nos. 1399-1402 are airmail. No. 1402 contains one 40x32mm stamp.

Mushrooms
A187

1985, Feb. 20

1403	A187	50c	Boletus calopus	.20	.20
1404	A187	50c	Strobilomyces retisporus	.20	.20
1405	A187	1cor	Boletus luridus	.20	.20
1406	A187	1cor	Xerocomus illudens	.20	.20
1407	A187	4cor	Gyrodon merulioides	.50	.20
1408	A187	5cor	Tylopilus plumbeoviolaceus	.60	.25
1409	A187	8cor	Gyroporus castaneus	1.00	.40
			Nos. 1403-1409 (7)	2.90	1.65

Nos. 1406-1409 are airmail.

City Railway Engine
A189

Various locomotives.

1985, Apr. 5 *Perf. 12½*

1412	A189	1cor	Electric	.20	.20
1413	A189	1cor	Steam	.20	.20
1414	A189	9cor	shown	.80	.25
1415	A189	9cor	Tram	.80	.25
1416	A189	15cor	steam, diff.	1.40	.40
1417	A189	21cor	steam, diff.	2.00	.35
			Nos. 1412-1417 (6)	5.40	1.65

Souvenir Sheet
Perf. 13

1418	A189	42cor	steam, diff.	5.75	5.75

German Railroads, 150th Anniv. #1418 also for 100th anniv. of Nicaraguan railroads. #1418 contains one 40x32mm stamp. #1414-1418 are airmail.

Motorcycle Cent. — A190

1985, Apr. 30 Litho. *Perf. 12½*

1419	A190	50c	F.N., 1928	.25	.20
1420	A190	50c	Douglas, 1928	.25	.20
1421	A190	1cor	Puch, 1938	.40	.20
1422	A190	2cor	Wanderer, 1939	.50	.20
1423	A190	4cor	Honda, 1949	1.00	.20
1424	A190	5cor	BMW, 1984	1.40	.25
1425	A190	7cor	Honda, 1984	1.75	.40
			Nos. 1419-1425 (7)	5.55	1.65

Nos. 1419-1425 se-tenant with labels picturing manufacturers' trademarks. Nos. 1422-1425 are airmail.

Flowers — A194

1985, May 20 Litho. *Perf. 13*

1454	A194	50c	Metelea quirosii	.20	.20
1455	A194	50c	Ipomea nil	.20	.20
1456	A194	1cor	Lysichitum americanum	.40	.20
1457	A194	2cor	Clusia sp.	.70	.20
1458	A194	4cor	Vanilla planifolia	1.40	.35
1459	A194	7cor	Stemmadenia obovata	2.50	.60
a.			Miniature sheet of 6, #1454-1459	5.75	
			Nos. 1454-1459 (6)	5.40	1.75

Nos. 1457-1459 are airmail.
Stamps in No. 1459a do not have white border.

End of World War II, 40th Anniv. — A195

1985, May *Perf. 12x12½, 12½x12*

1460	A195	9.50cor	German army surrenders	.40	.20
1461	A195	28cor	Nuremberg trials, horiz.	1.10	.50

No. 1461 is airmail.

Lenin, 115th Birth Anniv. A196

Design: 21cor, Lenin speaking to workers.

1985, June Litho. *Perf. 12x12½*

1462 A196 4cor multicolored .50 .20
1463 A196 21cor multicolored 2.50 1.10

Souvenir Sheet

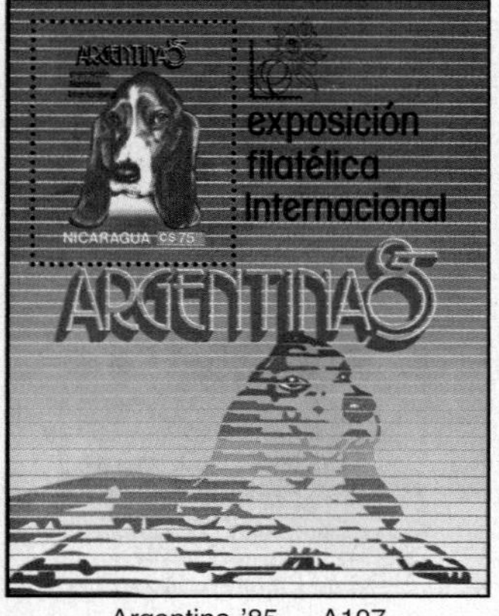

Argentina '85 — A197

1985, June 5 Litho. *Perf. 13*

1464 A197 75cor multicolored 4.25 2.00

World Stamp Exposition.

Birds — A198

1985, Aug. 25

1465 A198 50c Ring-neck pheasant .20 .20
1466 A198 50c Chicken .20 .20
1467 A198 1cor Guinea hen .30 .20
1468 A198 2cor Goose .60 .20
1469 A198 6cor Turkey 1.90 .60
1470 A198 8cor Duck 2.40 .80
Nos. 1465-1470 (6) 5.60 2.20

Intl. Music Year A199

1985, Sept. 1

1471 A199 1cor Luis A. Delgadillo, vert. .20 .20
1472 A199 1cor shown .20 .20
1473 A199 9cor Parade .90 .30
1474 A199 9cor Managua Cathedral .90 .30
1475 A199 15cor Masked dancer 1.40 .50
1476 A199 21cor Parade, diff. 1.90 .65
Nos. 1471-1476 (6) 5.50 2.15

Nos. 1473-1476 are airmail.

Natl. Fire Brigade, 6th Anniv. A200

1985, Oct. 18

1477 A200 1cor Fire station .20 .20
1478 A200 1cor Fire truck .20 .20
1479 A200 1cor shown .20 .20
1480 A200 3cor Ambulance .30 .20
1481 A200 9cor Airport fire truck .90 .30
1482 A200 15cor Waterfront fire 1.50 .50
1483 A200 21cor Hose team, fire 2.10 .75
a. Min. sheet of 7, #1474-1483 + 2 labels 5.50
Nos. 1477-1483 (7) 5.40 2.35

Stamps from No. 1483a have orange borders. Nos. 1480-1483 are airmail.

Halley's Comet — A201

1985, Nov. 26

1484 A201 1cor Edmond Halley .20 .20
1485 A201 3cor Map of comet's track, 1910 .35 .20
1486 A201 3cor Tycho Brahe's observatory .35 .20
1487 A201 9cor Astrolabe, map .90 .25
1488 A201 15cor Telescopes 1.50 .40
1489 A201 21cor Telescope designs 2.25 .60
Nos. 1484-1489 (6) 5.55 1.85

Nos. 1487-1489 are airmail.

Tapirus Bairdii A202

1985, Dec. 30

1490 A202 1cor Eating .30 .20
1491 A202 3cor Drinking .50 .20
1492 A202 5cor Grazing in field .85 .25
1493 A202 9cor With young 1.60 .45
Nos. 1490-1493 (4) 3.25 1.10

Nos. 1491-1493 are airmail.

Roses — A203

1986, Jan. 15 *Perf. 12½*

1494 A203 1cor Spinosissima .20 .20
1495 A203 1cor Canina .20 .20
1496 A203 3cor Eglanteria .40 .20
1497 A203 5cor Rubrifolia .40 .20
1498 A203 9cor Foetida .40 .20
1499 A203 100cor Rugosa 4.00 1.10
Nos. 1494-1499 (6) 5.60 2.10

Nos. 1497-1499 are airmail.

Birds — A204 A205

1986, Feb. 10 *Perf. 13x12½*

1500 A204 1cor Colibri topacio .20 .20
1501 A204 3cor Paraulata picodorado .30 .20
1502 A204 3cor Troupial .30 .20
1503 A204 5cor Vereron pintado .30 .20
1504 A204 10cor Tordo ruisenor .40 .20
1505 A204 21cor Buho real .80 .25
1506 A204 75cor Gran kiskadee 2.75 .90
Nos. 1500-1506 (7) 5.05 2.15

Nos. 1504-1506 are airmail.

1986, Mar. 20 *Perf. 12½*

World Cup Soccer Championships, Mexico: Soccer players and pre-Columbian artifacts. No. 1514, Player's foot, ball.

Shirt Colors

1507 A205 1cor blue & yel .20 .20
1508 A205 1cor yel & green .20 .20
1509 A205 3cor blue & white .20 .20
1510 A205 3cor red & white .20 .20
1511 A205 5cor red .20 .20
1512 A205 9cor blk & yel .25 .20
1513 A205 100cor red & grn 2.25 1.10
Nos. 1507-1513 (7) 3.50 2.30

Souvenir Sheet

Perf. 13

1514 A205 100cor multicolored 2.50 1.25

Nos. 1509-1514 are airmail.

Flower Type of 1983

1986, Mar. Litho. *Perf. 12½*

1515 A151 5cor like #1209 .35 .20
1516 A151 5cor like #1210 .35 .20
1517 A151 5cor like #1211 .35 .20
1518 A151 5cor like #1212 .35 .20
1519 A151 5cor like #1213 .35 .20
1520 A151 5cor like #1214 .35 .20
1521 A151 5cor like #1215 .35 .20
1522 A151 5cor like #1216 .35 .20
1523 A151 5cor like #1217 .35 .20
1524 A151 5cor like #1218 .35 .20
1525 A151 5cor like #1219 .35 .20
1526 A151 5cor like #1220 .35 .20
1527 A151 5cor like #1221 .35 .20
1528 A151 5cor like #1222 .35 .20
1529 A151 5cor like #1223 .35 .20
1530 A151 5cor like #1224 .35 .20
Nos. 1515-1530 (16) 5.60 3.20

Agrarian Reform Type of 1983

1986, Apr. 15 *Perf. 12½*

1531 A168 1cor dk brown .20 .20
1532 A168 9cor purple .20 .20
1533 A168 15cor rose violet .30 .20
1534 A168 21cor dk car rose .45 .25
1535 A168 33cor orange .75 .35
1536 A168 42cor green .95 .45
1537 A168 50cor brown 1.10 .55
1538 A168 100cor blue 2.25 1.10
Nos. 1531-1538 (8) 6.20 3.30

Writers A207

1986, Apr. 23 *Perf. 12½x13*

1539 A207 1cor Alfonso Cortes .20 .20
1540 A207 3cor Salomon de la Selva .20 .20
1541 A207 3cor Azarias H. Pallais .20 .20
1542 A207 5cor Ruben Dario .20 .20
1543 A207 9cor Pablo Neruda .25 .20
1544 A207 15cor Alfonso Reyes .35 .20
1545 A207 100cor Pedro Henriquez Urena 2.50 1.10
Nos. 1539-1545 (7) 3.90 2.30

Nos. 1544-1545 are airmail.

Nuts & Fruits — A208

1986, June 20 *Perf. 12x12½*

1546 A208 1cor Maranon (cashew) .20 .20
1547 A208 1cor Zapote .20 .20
1548 A208 3cor Pitahaya .30 .20
1549 A208 3cor Granadilla .30 .20
1550 A208 5cor Anona .30 .20
1551 A208 21cor Melocoton (starfruit) .75 .25
1552 A208 100cor Mamey 3.25 1.10
Nos. 1546-1552 (7) 5.30 2.35

FAO, 40th Anniv. Nos. 1550-1552 are airmail.

Lockheed L-1011 Tristar — A209

Airplanes: No. 1554, YAK 40. No. 1555, BAC 1-11. No. 1556, Boeing 747. 9cor, A-300. 15cor, TU-154. No. 1559, Concorde, vert. No. 1560, Fairchild 340.

1986, Aug. 22 *Perf. 12½*

1553 A209 1cor multicolored .20 .20
1554 A209 1cor multicolored .20 .20
1555 A209 3cor multicolored .20 .20
1556 A209 3cor multicolored .30 .20
1557 A209 9cor multicolored .40 .20
1558 A209 15cor multicolored .50 .20
1559 A209 100cor multicolored 3.50 1.10
Nos. 1553-1559 (7) 5.30 2.30

Souvenir Sheet

Perf. 13

1560 A209 100cor multicolored 3.75 3.75

Stockholmia '86. No. 1560 contains one 40x32mm stamp.
Nos. 1557-1560 airmail.

A210

A210a

Discovery of America, 500th Anniv. (in 1992) — A210b

1986, Oct. 12 *Perf. 12½x12*
1561 A210 1cor shown .20 .20
1562 A210 1cor 2 of Columbus' ships .20 .20
a. Pair, #1561-1562 .20 .20
b. Souv. sheet of 2, #1561-1562 .30 .20

Perf. 12x12½
1563 A210a 9cor Juan de la Cosa .30 .20
1564 A210a 9cor Columbus .30 .20
a. Pair, #1563-1564 .65 .20
1565 A210b 21cor Ferdinand, Isabella .80 .25
1566 A210b 100cor Columbus before throne 3.50 1.10
a. Pair, #1565-1566 4.50 1.40
b. Souv. sheet of 4, #1563-1566 5.00 1.50
Nos. 1561-1566 (6) 5.30 2.15

Nos. 1563-1566 are airmail. Nos. 1564a, 1566a have continuous design.

Butterflies A211

1986, Dec. 12 *Perf. 12½*
1567 A211 10cor Theritas coronata .40 .20
1568 A211 15cor Charayes nitebis .60 .20
1569 A211 15cor Salamis cacta .60 .20
1570 A211 15cor Papilio maacki .60 .20
1571 A211 25cor Euphaedro cyparissa 1.00 .30
1572 A211 25cor Palaeochrysophonus hippothoe 1.00 .30
1573 A211 30cor Ritra aurea 1.25 .35
Nos. 1567-1573 (7) 5.45 1.75

Nos. 1568-1573 are airmail.

Ruben Dario Order of Cultural Independence A212

Dario Order Winning Writers: No. 1574, Ernesto Mejia Sanchez. No. 1575, Fernando Gordillo C. No. 1576, Francisco Perez Estrada. 30cor, Julio Cortazar. 60cor, Enrique Fernandez Morales.

1987, Jan. 18 **Litho.** *Perf. 13*
1574 A212 10cor multicolored .25 .20
1575 A212 10cor multicolored .25 .20
1576 A212 10cor multicolored .25 .20
1577 A212 15cor multicolored .30 .20
1578 A212 30cor multicolored .65 .30
1579 A212 60cor multicolored 1.25 .65
a. Strip of 6, #1574-1579 2.90 1.50
b. Min. sheet of 6, #1574-1579 2.90 2.90

1988 Winter Olympics, Calgary — A213

#1580, Speed skating. #1581, Ice hockey. #1582, Women's figure skating. #1583, Ski jumping. 20cor, Biathalon. 30cor, Slalom skiing. 40cor, Downhill skiing. 110cor, Ice hockey, diff., horiz.

1987, Feb. 3 *Perf. 13*
1580 A213 10cor multi .45 .20
1581 A213 10cor multi .45 .20
1582 A213 15cor multi .60 .20
1583 A213 15cor multi .60 .20
1584 A213 20cor multi .75 .20
1585 A213 30cor multi 1.10 .30
1586 A213 40cor multi 1.75 .40
Nos. 1580-1586 (7) 5.70 1.70

Souvenir Sheet
Perf. 12½
1587 A213 110cor multi 3.75 3.75

Nos. 1582-1587 are airmail. No. 1587 contains one 40x32mm stamp.

Children's Welfare Campaign A214

1987, Mar. 18 *Perf. 13*
1588 A214 10cor Growth & development .25 .20
1589 A214 25cor Vaccination .60 .30
1590 A214 30cor Rehydration .75 .35
1591 A214 50cor Breastfeeding 1.25 .60
Nos. 1588-1591 (4) 2.85 1.45

Nos. 1589-1591 are airmail.

Flower Type of 1983

1987, Mar. 25 *Perf. 12½*
1592 A151 10cor Bixa orellana .35 .20
1593 A151 10cor Brassavola nodosa .35 .20
1594 A151 10cor Cattleya lueddemanniana .35 .20
1595 A151 10cor Cochlospermum spec. .35 .20
1596 A151 10cor Hibiscus rosasinensis .35 .20
1597 A151 10cor Laella spec. .35 .20
1598 A151 10cor Malvaviscus arboreus .35 .20
1599 A151 10cor Neomarica coerulea .35 .20
1600 A151 10cor Plumeria rubra .35 .20
1601 A151 10cor Senecio spec. .35 .20
1602 A151 10cor Sobralia macrantha .35 .20
1603 A151 10cor Stachytarpheta indica .35 .20
1604 A151 10cor Tabebula ochraceae .35 .20
1605 A151 10cor Tagetes erecta .35 .20
1606 A151 10cor Tecoma stans .35 .20
1607 A151 10cor Thumbergia alata .35 .20
Nos. 1592-1607 (16) 5.60 3.20

Agrarian Reform Type of 1983 Inscribed "1987"

Designs: No. 1608, Tobacco. No. 1609, Cotton. 15cor, Corn. 25cor, Sugar. 30cor, Cattle. 50cor, Coffee Beans. 60cor, Rice. 100cor, Bananas.

1987, Mar. 25 *Perf. 12½*
1608 A168 10cor dk brown .30 .20
1609 A168 10cor purple .30 .20
1610 A168 15cor rose violet .45 .25
1611 A168 25cor dk car rose .70 .35
1612 A168 30cor orange .85 .45
1613 A168 50cor brown 1.40 .65
1614 A168 60cor green 1.75 .90
1615 A168 100cor blue 2.75 1.40
Nos. 1608-1615 (8) 8.50 4.40

77th Interparliamentary Conf., Managua — A215

1987, Apr. 27
1616 A215 10cor multicolored .20 .20

Prehistoric Creatures — A216

1987, May 25 *Perf. 13*
1617 A216 10cor Mammoth .35 .20
1618 A216 10cor Dimetrodon .35 .20
1619 A216 10cor Triceratops .35 .20
1620 A216 15cor Dinichthys .60 .20
1621 A216 15cor Uintaterium .60 .20
1622 A216 30cor Pteranodon 1.25 .25
1623 A216 40cor Tilosaurus 1.75 .30
Nos. 1617-1623 (7) 5.25 1.55

Nos. 1620-1623 are airmail.

CAPEX '87 — A217

Various tennis players in action.

1987, June 2 *Perf. 13*
1624 A217 10cor Male player .30 .20
1625 A217 10cor Female player .30 .20
1626 A217 15cor Player at net .60 .20
1627 A217 15cor Female player, diff. .60 .20
1628 A217 20cor multi .70 .20
1629 A217 30cor multi 1.25 .30
1630 A217 40cor multi 1.90 .40
Nos. 1624-1630 (7) 5.65 1.70

Souvenir Sheet
Perf. 12½
1631 A217 110cor Doubles partners, vert. 3.75 3.75

Nos. 1626-1631 are airmail. No. 1631 contains one 32x40mm stamp.

Dogs — A218

1987, June 25 *Perf. 13*
1632 A218 10cor Doberman pinscher .20 .20
1633 A218 10cor Bull Mastiff .20 .20
1634 A218 15cor Japanese Spaniel .60 .20
1635 A218 15cor Keeshond .60 .20
1636 A218 20cor Chihuahua .80 .20
1637 A218 30cor St. Bernard 1.25 .30
1638 A218 40cor West Gotha spitz 1.75 .40
Nos. 1632-1638 (7) 5.40 1.70

Nos. 1634-1638 are airmail.

Cacti A219

1987, July 25 *Perf. 12½*
1639 A219 10cor Lophocereus schottii .30 .20
1640 A219 10cor Opuntia acanthocarpa .30 .20
1641 A219 10cor Echinocereus engelmanii .30 .20
1642 A219 20cor Lemaireocereus thurberi .80 .20
1643 A219 20cor Saguaros .80 .20
1644 A219 30cor Opuntia fulgida 1.25 .30
1645 A219 50cor Opuntia ficus 2.00 .50
Nos. 1639-1645 (7) 5.75 1.80

Nos. 1642-1645 are airmail.

10th Pan American Games, Indianapolis — A220

1987, Aug. 7 *Perf. 13*
1646 A220 10cor High jump .30 .20
1647 A220 10cor Volleyball .30 .20
1648 A220 15cor Sprinter .55 .25
1649 A220 15cor Gymnastics .55 .25
1650 A220 20cor Baseball .70 .30
1651 A220 30cor Synchronized swimming 1.10 .45
1652 A220 40cor Weightlifting 1.50 .60
Nos. 1646-1652 (7) 5.00 2.25

Souvenir Sheet
1653 A220 110cor Rhythmic gymnastics 3.50 3.50

Nos. 1648-1653 are airmail. No. 1653 contains one 32x40mm stamp. Nos. 1651-1653 are vert.

Satellites A221

1987, Oct. 4
1654 A221 10cor Sputnik .30 .20
1655 A221 10cor Cosmos .30 .20
1656 A221 15cor Proton .50 .20
1657 A221 25cor Meteor .90 .25
1658 A221 25cor Luna .90 .25
1659 A221 30cor Electron 1.00 .30
1660 A221 50cor Mars 1 1.60 .50
Nos. 1654-1660 (7) 5.50 1.90

Cosmonauts' Day. Nos. 1656-1660 are airmail.

Fish A222

Designs: No. 1661, Tarpon atlanticus. No. 1662, Cichlasoma managuense. No. 1663, Atractoteus tropicus. No. 1664, Astyana fasciatus. No. 1665, Cichlasoma citrimellum. 20cor, Cichlosoma dowi. 50cor, Caracharhinus nicaraguensis.

1987, Oct. 18 *Perf. 12½*

No.	Type	Denom.	Description	Unused	Used
1661	A222	10cor	multicolored	.35	.20
1662	A222	10cor	multicolored	.35	.20
1663	A222	10cor	multicolored	.35	.20
1664	A222	15cor	multicolored	.60	.20
1665	A222	15cor	multicolored	.60	.20
1666	A222	20cor	multicolored	.80	.20
1667	A222	50cor	multicolored	2.00	.50
			Nos. 1661-1667 (7)	5.05	1.70

Nos. 1663-1667 are airmail.

October Revolution, 70th Anniv. — A223

Designs: 30cor, Cruiser Aurora, horiz. 50cor, USSR natl. arms.

1987, Nov. 7 *Perf. 13*

No.	Type	Denom.	Description	Unused	Used
1668	A223	10cor	multicolored	.25	.20
1669	A223	30cor	multicolored	.60	.35
1670	A223	50cor	multicolored	1.00	.60
			Nos. 1668-1670 (3)	1.85	1.15

Nos. 1669-1670 are airmail.

Christmas Paintings by L. Saenz — A224

1987, Nov. 15 *Perf. 13*

No.	Type	Denom.	Description	Unused	Used
1671	A224	10cor	Nativity	.25	.20
1672	A224	20cor	Adoration of the Magi	.35	.20
1673	A224	25cor	Adoration of the Magi, diff.	.40	.20
1674	A224	50cor	Nativity, diff.	.80	.40
			Nos. 1671-1674 (4)	1.80	1.00

1988 Winter Olymmpics, Calgary — A225

1988, Jan. 30 **Litho.** *Perf. 12½*

No.	Type	Denom.	Description	Unused	Used
1675	A225	10cor	Biathlon	.25	.20
1676	A225	10cor	Cross-country skiing, vert.	.25	.20
1677	A225	15cor	Hockey, vert.	.50	.20
1678	A225	20cor	Women's figure skating, vert.	.75	.20
1679	A225	25cor	Slalom skiing, vert.	1.00	.30
1680	A225	30cor	Ski jumping	1.10	.40
1681	A225	40cor	Men's downhill skiing, vert.	1.50	.50
			Nos. 1675-1681 (7)	5.35	2.00

Souvenir Sheet

Perf. 13

No.	Type	Denom.	Description	Unused	Used
1682	A225	100cor	Pairs figure skating	3.75	3.75

Nos. 1675-1681 printed with se-tenant label showing Canadian flag and wildlife.

No. 1682 contains one 40x32mm stamp.

Nicaraguan Journalists Assoc., 10th Anniv. — A226

Design: 5cor, Churches of St. Francis Xavier and Fatima, and speaker addressing journalists, horiz.

1988, Feb. 10

No.	Type	Denom.	Description	Unused	Used
1683	A226	1cor	shown	.20	.20
1684	A226	5cor	multicolored	.75	.40

No. 1684 is airmail.

1988 Summer Olympics, Seoul — A227

1988, Feb. 28

No.	Type	Denom.	Description	Unused	Used
1685	A227	10cor	Gymnastics	.25	.20
1686	A227	10cor	Basketball	.25	.20
1687	A227	15cor	Volleyball	.50	.20
1688	A227	20cor	Long jump	.75	.20
1689	A227	25cor	Soccer	1.00	.25
1690	A227	30cor	Water polo	1.10	.40
1691	A227	40cor	Boxing	1.75	.55
			Nos. 1685-1691 (7)	5.60	2.00

Souvenir Sheet

No.	Type	Denom.	Description	Unused	Used
1692	A227	100cor	Baseball	3.75	3.75

No. 1692 contains one 40x32mm stamp.

European Soccer Championships, Essen — A228

Designs: Various soccer players in action.

1988, Apr. 14 *Perf. 13x12½, 12½x13*

No.	Type	Denom.	Description	Unused	Used
1693	A228	50c	multicolored	.35	.20
1694	A228	1cor	multicolored	.35	.20
1695	A228	2cor	multi, vert.	.40	.20
1696	A228	3cor	multi, vert.	.70	.25
1697	A228	4cor	multi, vert.	.95	.25
1698	A228	5cor	multi, vert.	1.25	.35
1699	A228	6cor	multicolored	1.50	.40
			Nos. 1693-1699 (7)	5.50	1.85

Souvenir Sheet

Perf. 13

No.	Type	Denom.	Description	Unused	Used
1700	A228	15cor	multi, vert.	3.75	3.75

Nos. 1695-1700 are airmail. No. 1700 contains one 32x40mm stamp.

Sandinista Revolution, 9th Anniv. — A229

1988, July 19 *Perf. 13*

No.	Type	Denom.	Description	Unused	Used
1701	A229	1cor	shown	.20	.20
1702	A229	5cor	Volcanoes, dove	.60	.30

No. 1702 is airmail.

Animals — A230

1988, Mar. 3 *Perf. 13x12½*

No.	Type	Denom.	Description	Unused	Used
1703	A230	10c	Bear, cub	.20	.20
1704	A230	15c	Lion, cubs	.20	.20
1705	A230	25c	Spaniel, pups	.25	.20
1706	A230	50c	Wild boars	.25	.20
1707	A230	4cor	Cheetah, cubs	1.10	.35
1708	A230	7cor	Hyenas	1.60	.70
1709	A230	8cor	Fox, kit	2.00	.80
			Nos. 1703-1709 (7)	5.60	2.65

Souvenir Sheet

Perf. 12½

No.	Type	Denom.	Description	Unused	Used
1710	A230	15cor	House cat, kittens, vert.	3.75	3.75

Nos. 1707-1710 are airmail. No. 1710 contains one 32x40mm stamp.

Helicopters — A231

Illustration reduced.

1988, June 1 *Perf. 12½x12*

No.	Type	Denom.	Description	Unused	Used
1711	A231	4cor	B-206B-JRIII	.25	.20
1712	A231	12cor	BK-117A-3	.25	.20
1713	A231	16cor	B-360	.50	.20
1714	A231	20cor	109-MRII	.60	.20
1715	A231	24cor	S-61	.80	.20
1716	A231	28cor	SA-365N-D2	.90	.25
1717	A231	56cor	S-76	1.75	.50
			Nos. 1711-1717 (7)	5.05	1.75

Souvenir Sheet

Perf. 13

No.	Type	Denom.	Description	Unused	Used
1718	A231	120cor	NH-90	3.75	3.75

Nos. 1712-1718 are airmail. No. 1718 contains one 40x32mm stamp.

Shells — A232

1988, Sept. 20 *Perf. 13*

No.	Type	Denom.	Description	Unused	Used
1719	A232	4cor	Strombus pugilis	.25	.20
1720	A232	12cor	Polymita picta	.30	.20
1721	A232	16cor	Architectonica maximum	.50	.20
1722	A232	20cor	Pectens laqueatus	.70	.20
1723	A232	24cor	Guildfordia triumphans	.90	.25
1724	A232	28cor	Ranella pustulosa	.95	.30
1725	A232	50cor	Trochus maculatus	1.75	.50
			Nos. 1719-1725 (7)	5.35	1.85

Nos. 1720-1725 are airmail.

Insects — A233

1988, Nov. 10

No.	Type	Denom.	Description	Unused	Used
1726	A233	4cor	Chrysina macropus	.25	.20
1727	A233	12cor	Plusiotis victoriana	.30	.20
1728	A233	16cor	Ceratotrupes bolivari	.55	.20
1729	A233	20cor	Gymnetosoma stellata	.70	.20
1730	A233	24cor	Euphoria lineoligera	.90	.25
1731	A233	28cor	Euphoria candezei	.95	.30
1732	A233	50cor	Sulcophanaeus chryseicollis	1.75	.50
			Nos. 1726-1732 (7)	5.40	1.85

Nos. 1727-1732 are airmail.

Heroes of the Revolution — A234

Designs: 4cor, Casimiro Sotelo Montenegro. 12cor, Ricardo Morales Aviles. 16cor, Silvio Mayorga Delgado. 20cor, Pedro Arauz Palacios. 24cor, Oscar A. Turcios Chavarrias. 28cor, Julio C. Buitrago Urroz. 50cor, Jose B. Escobar Perez. 100cor, Eduardo E. Contreras Escobar.

1988, Aug. 27 *Perf. 12½x12*

No.	Type	Denom.	Description	Unused	Used
1733	A234	4cor	sky blue	.20	.20
1734	A234	12cor	red lilac	.25	.20
1735	A234	16cor	yel grn	.30	.20
1736	A234	20cor	org brown	.40	.20
1737	A234	24cor	brown	.45	.25
1738	A234	28cor	purple	.55	.30
1739	A234	50cor	henna brn	.95	.50
1740	A234	100cor	plum	1.90	.95
			Nos. 1733-1740 (8)	5.00	2.80

Nos. 1734-1740 are airmail.

Flowers — A235

Designs: 4cor, Acacia baileyana. 12cor, Anigozanthos manglesii. 16cor, Telopia speciosissima. 20cor, Eucalyptus ficifolia. 24cor, Boronia heterophylla. 28cor, Callistemon speciosus. 30cor, Nymphaea caerulea, horiz. 50cor, Clianthus formosus.

1988, Aug. 30 *Perf. 13*

No.	Type	Denom.	Description	Unused	Used
1741	A235	4cor	multicolored	.20	.20
1742	A235	12cor	multicolored	.35	.20
1743	A235	16cor	multicolored	.45	.20
1744	A235	20cor	multicolored	.60	.20
1745	A235	24cor	multicolored	.70	.25
1746	A235	28cor	multicolored	.80	.50
1747	A235	30cor	multicolored	.90	.30
1748	A235	50cor	multicolored	1.50	.45
			Nos. 1741-1748 (8)	5.50	2.30

Nos. 1742-1748 are airmail.

Pre-Columbian Art — A236

Designs: 4cor, Zapotec funeral urn. 12cor, Mochica ceramic kneeling man. 16cor,

Mochica ceramic head. 20cor, Taina ceramic vase. 28cor, Nazca cup, horiz. 100cor, Inca pipe, horiz. 120cor, Aztec ceramic vessel, horiz.

1988, Oct. 12 ***Perf. 12x12½, 12½x12***

1749 A236 4cor multi + label .20 .20
1750 A236 12cor multi + label .35 .20
1751 A236 16cor multi + label .45 .20
1752 A236 20cor multi + label .60 .20
1753 A236 28cor multi + label .80 .30
1754 A236 100cor multi + label 2.75 1.00
Nos. 1749-1754 (6) 5.15 2.10

Souvenir Sheet

Perf. 13x13½

1755 A236 120cor multicolored 3.75 3.75

Discovery of America, 500th anniv. (in 1992). Nos. 1750-1755 are airmail. No. 1755 contains one 40x32mm stamp.

Publication of Blue, by Ruben Dario, Cent. — A237

1988, Oct. 12 ***Perf. 12x12½***

1756 A237 25cor multi + label .45 .20

Tourism — A238

1989, Feb. 5 ***Perf. 12½x12***

1757 A238 4cor Pochomil .20 .20
1758 A238 12cor Granada .35 .20
1759 A238 20cor Olof Palme Convention Center .65 .20
1760 A238 24cor Masaya Volcano Natl. Park .70 .25
1761 A238 28cor La Boquita .90 .25
1762 A238 30cor Xiloa .95 .25
1763 A238 50cor Hotels of Managua 1.75 .45
Nos. 1757-1763 (7) 5.50 1.80

Souvenir Sheet

Perf. 13

1764 A238 160cor Montelimar 3.75 3.75

Nos. 1758-1764 are airmail. No. 1764 contains one 40x32mm stamp.

French Revolution, Bicentennial — A240

Designs: 50cor, Procession of the Estates General, Versailles. 300cor, Oath of the Tennis Court. 600cor, 14th of July, vert. 1000cor, Dancing Around the Liberty Tree. 2000cor, Liberty Guiding the People, vert. 3000cor, Storming the Bastille. 5000cor, Lafayette Swearing Allegiance to the Constitution, vert. 9000cor, La Marsiellaise, vert.

Perf. 12½x13 (50cor), 13x12½ (600, 2000cor), 12½

1989, July 14

Sizes: 50cor, 40x25mm

600cor, 2000cor, 33x44mm

1773 A240 50cor multicolored .20 .20
1774 A240 300cor shown .25 .20
1775 A240 600cor multicolored .30 .20
1776 A240 1000cor multicolored .45 .20
1777 A240 2000cor multicolored .80 .30
1778 A240 3000cor multicolored 1.40 .40
1779 A240 5000cor multicolored 2.10 .65
Nos. 1773-1779 (7) 5.50 2.15

Souvenir Sheet

Perf. 12½

1780 A240 9000cor multicolored 4.50 4.50

Philexfrance '89. #1774-1780 are airmail. #1780 contains one 32x40mm stamp.

Currency Reform

Currency reform took place Mar. 4, 1990. Until stamps in the new currency were issued, mail was to be handstamped "Franqueo Pagado," (Postage Paid). Stamps were not used again until Apr. 25, 1991. The following four sets and one airmail set were sold by the post office but were not valid for postage.

Ships

Stamp World London '90: 500cor, Director. 1000cor, Independence. 3000cor, Orizaba. 5000cor, SS Lewis. 10,000cor, Golden Rule. 30,000cor, Santiago de Cuba. 75,000cor, Bahia de Corinto. 100,000cor, North Star.

1990, Apr. 3 ***Perf. 12½x12***

500cor-100,000cor

Souvenir Sheet

Perf. 12½

75,000cor

World Cup Soccer Championships, Italy

Designs: Various soccer players in action.

1990, Apr. 30 ***Perf. 13***

500cor-100,000cor

Souvenir Sheet

Perf. 12½

75,000cor

1992 Winter Olympics, Albertville

Designs: 500cor, Ski jumping. 1000cor, Downhill skiing. 3000cor, Figure skating, vert. 5000cor, Speed skating, vert. 10,000cor, Biathlon, vert. 30,000cor, Cross country skiing, vert. 75,000cor, Two-man bobsled, vert. 100,000cor, Ice hockey, vert.

1990, July 25 ***Perf. 13***

500cor-100,000cor

Souvenir Sheet

Perf. 12½

75,000cor

1992 Summer Olympics, Barcelona

Designs: 500cor, Javelin. 1000cor, Steeplechase. 3000cor, Handball. 5000cor, Basketball. 10,000cor, Gymnastics. 30,000cor, Cycling. 75,000cor, Soccer. 100,000cor, Boxing, horiz.

1990, Aug. 10 ***Perf. 13***

500cor-100,000cor

Souvenir Sheet

75,000cor

Birds A245

Designs: No. 1813, Apteryx owenii. No. 1814, Notornis mantelli. 10c, Cyanoramphus novaezelandiae. 20c, Gallirallus australis. 30c, Rhynochetos jubatus, vert. 60c, Nestor notabilis. 70c, Strigops habroptilus. 1.50cor, Cygnus atratus.

1990, Aug. 14 **Litho.** ***Perf. 12½***

1813 A245 5c multicolored .20 .20
1814 A245 5c multicolored .20 .20
1815 A245 10c multicolored .25 .20
1816 A245 20c multicolored .45 .20
1817 A245 30c multicolored .70 .30
1818 A245 60c multicolored 1.40 .65
1819 A245 70c multicolored 1.60 .75
Nos. 1813-1819 (7) 4.80 2.50

Souvenir Sheet

1820 A245 1.50cor multicolored 3.75 3.75

New Zealand '90, Intl. Philatelic Exhibition.

Fauna A246

1990, Oct. 10

1821 A246 5c Panthera onca .20 .20
1822 A246 5c Felis pardalis, vert. .20 .20
1823 A246 10c Atelles geoffrogi, vert. .25 .20
1824 A246 20c Tapirus bairdi .50 .20
1825 A246 30c Dasypus novencintus .85 .30
1826 A246 60c Canis latrans 1.60 .65
1827 A246 70c Choloepus hoffmanni 2.00 .75
Nos. 1821-1827 (7) 5.60 2.50

FAO, 45th anniv.

Flower Type of 1983 Redrawn Without Date

1991, Apr. 24 **Litho.** ***Perf. 14x13½***

Size: 19x22mm

1828 A151 1cor like #1220 .40 .20
1829 A151 2cor like #1212 .80 .20
1830 A151 3cor like #1218 1.25 .20
1831 A151 4cor like #1219 1.60 .20
1832 A151 5cor like #1217 2.00 .20
1833 A151 6cor like #1210 2.40 .20
1834 A151 7cor like #1216 2.75 .20
1835 A151 8cor like #1215 3.25 .20
1836 A151 9cor like #1211 3.50 .20
1837 A151 10cor like #1221 4.00 .20
1838 A151 11cor like #1214 4.50 .20
1839 A151 12cor like #1222 4.75 .20
1840 A151 13cor like #1213 5.25 .20
1841 A151 14cor like #1224 5.50 .20
1842 A151 15cor like #1223 6.00 .20
1843 A151 16cor like #1209 6.50 .20
Nos. 1828-1843 (16) 54.45 3.20

Dr. Pedro Joaquin Chamorro — A247

1991, Apr. 25 ***Perf. 14½x14***

1844 A247 2.25cor multicolored .95 .45

1990 World Cup Soccer Championships, Italy — A248

Designs: No. 1845, Two players. No. 1846, Four players, vert. 50c, Two players, referee. 1cor, Germany, five players, vert. 1.50cor, One player, vert. 3cor, Argentina, five players, vert. 3.50cor, Italian players. 7.50cor, German team with trophy.

1991, July 16 ***Perf. 14x14½, 14½x14***

1845 A248 25c multicolored .20 .20
1846 A248 25c multicolored .20 .20
1847 A248 50c multicolored .20 .20
1848 A248 1cor multicolored .40 .20
1849 A248 1.50cor multicolored .60 .30
1850 A248 3cor multicolored 1.25 .60
1851 A248 3.50cor multicolored 1.40 .70
Nos. 1845-1851 (7) 4.25 2.40

Souvenir Sheet

1852 A248 7.50cor multicolored 3.00 1.50
a. Overprinted in sheet margin ('93) 3.25 1.60

No. 1852a overprint reads "COPA DE FOOTBALL / U.S.A. '94."

Butterflies — A249

Designs: No. 1853, Prepona praeneste. No. 1854, Anartia fatima. 50c, Eryphanis aesacus. 1cor, Heliconius melpomene. 1.50cor, Chlosyne janais. 3cor, Marpesia iole. 3.50cor, Metamorpha epaphus. 7.50cor, Morpho peleides.

1991, July 16 ***Perf. 14½x14***

1853 A249 25c multicolored .20 .20
1854 A249 25c multicolored .20 .20
1855 A249 50c multicolored .20 .20
1856 A249 1cor multicolored .40 .20
1857 A249 1.50cor multicolored .60 .30
1858 A249 3cor multicolored 1.25 .60
1859 A249 3.50cor multicolored 1.40 .70
Nos. 1853-1859 (7) 4.25 2.40

Souvenir Sheet

1860 A249 7.50cor multicolored 3.00 1.50

Fauna of Rainforest A250

No. 1861 a, Yellow-headed amazon. b, Toucan. c, Scarlet macaw (lapa roja). d, Quetzal. e, Spider monkey (mono arana). f, Capuchin monkey. g, Sloth (cucala). h, Oropendola. i, Violet sabrewing (colibri violeta). j, Tamandua. k, Jaguarundi. l, Boa constrictor. m, Iguana. n, Jaguar. o, White-necked jacobin. p, Doxocopa clothilda. q, Dismorphia deione. r, Golden arrow-poison frog (rana venenosa). s, Callithomia hezia. t, Chameleon.

1991, Aug. 7 Litho. *Perf. 14x14½*

1861	A250	2.25cor Sheet of 20, #a.-t.	19.00	9.50

America Issue — A251

1990, Oct. 12 *Perf. 14½x14*

1862	A251	2.25cor Concepcion volcano	.95	.50

Orchids A252

Designs: No. 1863, Isochilus major. No. 1864, Cycnoches ventricosum. 50c, Vanilla odorata. 1cor, Helleriella nicaraguensis. 1.50cor, Barkeria spectabilis. 3cor, Maxillaria hedwigae. 3.50cor, Cattleya aurantiaca. 7.50cor, Psygmorchis pusilla, vert.

1991 Litho. *Perf. 14x14½*

1863	A252	25c multicolored	.20	.20
1864	A252	25c multicolored	.20	.20
1865	A252	50c multicolored	.25	.20
1866	A252	1cor multicolored	.35	.20
1867	A252	1.50cor multicolored	.60	.25
1868	A252	3cor multicolored	1.10	.50
1869	A252	3.50cor multicolored	1.40	.55
		Nos. 1863-1869 (7)	4.10	2.10

Souvenir Sheet

Perf. 14½x14

1870	A252	7.50cor multicolored	3.00	1.50

Locomotives of South America — A253

Birds — A254

Various steam locomotives.

1991, Apr. 21 *Perf. 14½x14*

1871	A253	25c Bolivia	.20	.20
1872	A253	25c Peru	.20	.20
1873	A253	50c Argentina	.20	.20
1874	A253	1.50cor Chile	.50	.25
1875	A253	2cor Colombia	.65	.30
1876	A253	3cor Brazil	.95	.50
1877	A253	3.50cor Paraguay	1.10	.55
		Nos. 1871-1877 (7)	3.80	2.20

Souvenir Sheets

1878	A253	7.50cor Nicaragua	3.00	3.00
1879	A253	7.50cor Guatemala	3.00	3.00

1991 *Perf. 14½x14, 14x14½*

Designs: 50c, Eumomota supercilliosa. 75c, Trogon collaris. 1cor, Electron platyrhynchum. 1.50cor, Teleonema filicauda. 1.75cor, Tangara chilensis, horiz. No. 1885, Pharomachrus mocino. No. 1886, Phlegopsis nigromaculata. No. 1887, Hylophylax naevioides, horiz. No. 1888, Aulacorhynchus haematopygius, horiz.

1880	A254	50c multicolored	.20	.20
1881	A254	75c multicolored	.30	.20
1882	A254	1cor multicolored	.40	.20
1883	A254	1.50cor multicolored	.65	.25
1884	A254	1.75cor multicolored	.70	.30
1885	A254	2.25cor multicolored	1.00	.35
1886	A254	2.25cor multicolored	1.00	.35
		Nos. 1880-1886 (7)	4.25	1.85

Souvenir Sheets

1887	A254	7.50cor multicolored	3.00	3.00
1888	A254	7.50cor multicolored	3.00	3.00

Paintings by Vincent Van Gogh A255

Designs: No. 1889, Head of a Peasant Woman Wearing a Bonnet. No. 1890, One-Eyed Man. 50c, Self-Portrait. 1cor, Vase with Carnations and Other Flowers. 1.50cor, Vase with Zinnias and Geraniums. 3cor, Portrait of Pere Tanguy. 3.50cor, Portrait of a Man, horiz. 7.50cor, Path Lined with Poplars, horiz.

1991 *Perf. 14x13½, 13½x14*

1889	A255	25c multicolored	.20	.20
1890	A255	25c multicolored	.20	.20
1891	A255	50c multicolored	.25	.20
1892	A255	1cor multicolored	.35	.20
1893	A255	1.50cor multicolored	.60	.25
1894	A255	3cor multicolored	1.10	.50
1895	A255	3.50cor multicolored	1.40	.55
		Nos. 1889-1895 (7)	4.10	2.10

Size: 128x102mm

Imperf

1896	A255	7.50cor multicolored	2.50	1.25

Phila Nippon '91 A256

Designs: 25c, Golden Hall. 50c, Phoenix Hall. 1cor, Bunraku puppet head. 1.50cor, Japanese cranes. 2.50cor, Himeji Castle. 3cor, Statue of the Guardian. 3.50cor, Kabuki warrior. 7.50cor, Vase.

1991 *Perf. 14x14½*

1897	A256	25c multicolored	.20	.20
1898	A256	50c multicolored	.25	.20
1899	A256	1cor multicolored	.45	.20
1900	A256	1.50cor multicolored	.65	.25
1901	A256	2.50cor multicolored	1.00	.40
1902	A256	3cor multicolored	1.25	.50
1903	A256	3.50cor multicolored	1.40	.55
		Nos. 1897-1903 (7)	5.20	2.30

Souvenir Sheet

1904	A256	7.50cor multicolored	3.00	3.00

Inscriptions are switched on 50c and 2.50cor.

Child's Drawing A257

1991

1905	A257	2.25cor multicolored	.95	.35

Central American Bank of Economic Integration, 30th Anniv. — A258

1991, Aug. 1 Litho. *Perf. 14*

1906	A258	1.50cor multicolored	.65	.50

No. 1906 printed with se-tenant label.

Discovery of America, 500th Anniv. (in 1992) — A259

1991, Oct. 12 *Perf. 14½x14*

1907	A259	2.25cor Columbus' fleet	.95	.75

Swiss Confederation, 700th Anniv. (in 1991) — A260

1992, Aug. 1 Litho. *Perf. 14x14½*

1908	A260	2.25cor black & red	.95	.75

Contemporary Art — A261

Designs: No. 1909, Pitcher, by Jose Ortiz. No. 1910, Black jar, by Lorenza Pineda Cooperative, vert. 50c, Vase, by Elio Gutierrez, vert. 1cor, Christ on Cross, by Jose de Los Santos, vert. 1.50cor, Sculpture of family, by Erasmo Moya, vert. 3cor, Bird and fish, by Silvio Chavarria Cooperative. 3.50cor, Filigree jar, by Maria de Los Angeles Bermudez, vert. 7.50cor, Masks by Jose Flores.

Perf. 14x14½, 14½x14

1992, Sept. 17 Litho.

1909	A261	25c multicolored	.20	.20
1910	A261	25c multicolored	.20	.20
1911	A261	50c multicolored	.25	.20
1912	A261	1cor multicolored	.45	.25
1913	A261	1.50cor multicolored	.65	.30
1914	A261	3cor multicolored	1.25	.65
1915	A261	3.50cor multicolored	1.50	.75
		Nos. 1909-1915 (7)	4.50	2.55

Imperf

Size: 100x70mm

1916	A261	7.50cor multicolored	3.25	1.60

Miniature Sheet

Fauna and Flora of Rainforest — A262

No. 1917: a, Colibri magnifico (b). b, Aguila arpia (f). c, Orchids. d, Toucan, Mariposa morpho. e, Quetzal (i). f, Guardabarranco (g, k). g, Mono aullador (howler monkey). h, Perezoso (sloth). i, Mono ardilla (squirrel monkey). j, Guacamaya (macaw) (n). k, Boa esmeralda, Tanagra escarlata (emerald boa, scarlet tanager). l, Rana flecha venenosa (arrow frog). m, Jaguar. n, Oso hormiguero (anteater) (o). o, Ocelot. p, Coati.

1992, Nov. 12 *Perf. 14½x14*

1917	A262	1.50cor Sheet of 16, #a.-p.	10.00	5.00

1992 Winter Olympics, Albertville A263

Perf. 14x14½, 14½x14

1992, Sept. 17

1918	A263	25c Ice hockey	.20	.20
1919	A263	25c 4-man bobsled	.20	.20
1920	A263	50c Combined slalom, vert.	.25	.20
1921	A263	1cor Speed skating	.45	.25
1922	A263	1.50cor Cross-country skiing	.65	.30
1923	A263	3cor Double luge	1.40	.65
1924	A263	3.50cor Ski jumping, vert.	1.50	.75
		Nos. 1918-1924 (7)	4.65	2.55

Imperf

Size: 100x70mm

1925	A263	7.50cor Slalom	3.25	1.60
a.		Overprinted ('93)	3.25	1.60

No. 1925a overprint reads "JUEGOS PRE OLIMPICOS DE INVIERNO / LILLEHAMMER, NORUEGA."

1992 Summer Olympics, Barcelona A264

Perf. 14x14½, 14½x14

1992, Sept. 17 Litho.

1926	A264	25c Javelin	.20	.20
1927	A264	25c Fencing	.20	.20
1928	A264	50c Basketball	.25	.20
1929	A264	1.50cor 1500-meter race	.65	.30
1930	A264	2cor Long jump	.85	.40
1931	A264	3cor Women's 10,000-meter race	1.25	.65
1932	A264	3.50cor Equestrian	1.50	.75
		Nos. 1926-1932 (7)	4.90	2.70

Imperf

Size: 100x70mm

1933	A264	7.50cor Canoeing	3.25	1.60
a.		Overprinted ('93)	3.25	1.60

Nos. 1927-1932 are vert. Dated 1991.

No. 1933a overprint reads "JUEGOS PRE OLIMPICOS DE VERANO / ATLANTA, GA. / ESTADOS UNIDOS DE AMERICA."

Father R. M. Fabretto and Children A265

1992, Nov. 12 Litho. *Perf. 14x14½*

1934	A265	2.25cor multicolored	.95	.50

Nicaraguan Natives, by Claudia Gordillo — A266

1992, Nov. 12

1935	A266	2.25cor black & brn	.95	.50

Nicaraguan Caciques, by Milton Jose Cruz — A267

1992, Nov. 12

1936 A267 2.25cor multicolored .95 .50

Contemporary Paintings — A268

Paintings by: No. 1937, Alberto Ycaza, vert. No. 1938, Alejandro Arostegui, vert. 50c, Bernard Dreyfus. 1.50cor, Orlando Sobalvarro. 2cor, Hugo Palma. 3cor, Omar D'Leon. 3.50cor, Carlos Montenegro, vert. 7.50cor, Federico Nordalm.

Perf. 14½x14, 14x14½

1992, Nov. 12

1937 A268 25c multicolored .20 .20
1938 A268 25c multicolored .20 .20
1939 A268 50c multicolored .25 .20
1940 A268 1.50cor multicolored .65 .30
1941 A268 2cor multicolored .85 .40
1942 A268 3cor multicolored 1.25 .65
1943 A268 3.50cor multicolored 1.50 .75
Nos. 1937-1943 (7) 4.90 2.70

Imperf

Size: 100x70mm

1944 A268 7.50cor multicolored 3.25 1.60

Monument to Columbus, Rivas — A269

Catholic Religion in Nicaragua, 460th Anniv. — A270

1993, Mar. 22 ***Perf. 14½x14***

1945 A269 2.25cor multicolored .95 .50

UPAEP issue. Dated 1992.

1993, Mar. 22

Designs: 25c, Eucharistic gonfalon. 50c, Statue of Virgin Mary. 1cor, Document, 1792-93. 1.50cor, Baptismal font. 2cor, Statue of Madonna and Child. 2.25cor, Monsignor Diego Alvarez Osario. 3cor, Christ on cross.

1946 A270 25c multicolored .20 .20
1947 A270 50c multicolored .25 .20
1948 A270 1cor multicolored .40 .20
1949 A270 1.50cor multicolored .65 .30
1950 A270 2cor multicolored .85 .40
1951 A270 2.25cor multicolored .95 .50
1952 A270 3cor multicolored 1.25 .65
Nos. 1946-1952 (7) 4.55 2.45

Dated 1992.

A271

A272

Archdiocese of Managua: a, 3cor, Cathedral of the Immaculate Conception. b, 4cor, Cross, map.

1993, Apr. 30

1953 A271 Pair, #a.-b. 3.00 1.50

Dated 1992.

1994, Jan. 28 **Litho.** ***Perf. 14***

Player, country: 50c, Brolin, Sweden. No. 1955, Karas, Poland; Costa, Brazil. No. 1956, Bossis, Platini, France. 1.50cor, Schumacher, Germany. 2cor, Zubizarreta, Spain. 2.50cor, Matthaeus, Germany; Maradona, Argentina. 3.50cor, Robson, England; Santos, Portugal. 10cor, Biyik, Cameroun; Valderrama, Colombia.

1954 A272 50c multicolored .25 .20
1955 A272 1cor multicolored .40 .25
1956 A272 1cor multicolored .40 .25
1957 A272 1.50cor multicolored .65 .30
1958 A272 2cor multicolored .85 .40
1959 A272 2.50cor multicolored 1.10 .55
1960 A272 3.50cor multicolored 1.50 .75
Nos. 1954-1960 (7) 5.15 2.70

Souvenir Sheet

1961 A272 10cor multicolored 4.25 2.00

1994 World Cup Soccer Championships, US.

Sonatina, by Alma Iris Prez — A272a

1993, Oct. 29 **Litho.** ***Perf. 13½x14***

1961A A272a 3cor multicolored 1.00 1.00

Butterflyfish A273

No. 1962: a, Chaetodon lunula. b, Chaetodon rainfordi. c, Chaetodon reticulatus. d, Chaetodon auriga. e, Heniochus acuminatus. f, Coradion fulvocinctus. g, Chaetodon speculum. h, Chaetodon lineolatus. i, Chaetodon bennetti. j, Chaetodon melanotus. k, Chaetodon aureus. l. Chaetodon ephippium. m, Hemitaurichthys polylepis. n, Chaetodon semeion. o, Chaetodon kleinii. p, Chelmon rostratus.

1993, Nov. 18 **Litho.** ***Perf. 14***

1962 Sheet of 16 10.00 5.00
a.-p. A273 1.50cor Any single .60 .30
q. Inscribed with Bangkok '93 emblem in sheet margin 10.00 5.00
r. Inscribed with Indopex '93 emblem in sheet margin 10.00 5.00

Issue date: No. 1962, Nov. 1, 1993.

No. 1962 inscribed with Taipei '93 emblem in sheet margin.

1994 Winter Olympics, Lillehammer, 1996 Summer Olympics, Atlanta — A274

1993, Nov. 18

1963 A274 25c Downhill skiing .20 .20
1964 A274 25c Four-man bobsled .20 .20
1965 A274 25c Swimming .20 .20
1966 A274 25c Diving .20 .20
1967 A274 50c Speed skating .25 .20
1968 A274 50c Race walking .25 .20
1969 A274 1cor Hurdles .40 .20
1970 A274 1.50cor Ski jumping .65 .30
1971 A274 1.50cor Women's gymnastics .65 .30
1972 A274 2cor Women's figure skating .85 .40
1973 A274 3cor Pairs figure skating 1.25 .65
1974 A274 3cor Javelin 1.25 .65
1975 A274 3.50cor Biathlon 1.50 .75
1976 A274 3.50cor Running 1.50 .75
Nos. 1963-1976 (14) 9.35 5.20

Souvenir Sheets

1977 A274 7.50cor Torch, hands 3.25 1.50
1978 A274 7.50cor Flags 3.25 1.50

1994 Winter Olympics (#1963-1964, 1967, 1970, 1972-1973, 1975, 1978). Others, 1996 Summer Olympics.

Pan-American Health Organization, 90th Anniv. — A275

1993, June 16 ***Perf. 14½***

1979 A275 3cor multicolored 1.25 .65

Organization of American States, 23rd General Assembly — A276

1993, June 7 ***Perf. 13½x14***

1980 A276 3cor multicolored 1.25 .65

Christmas — A276a

Paintings: 1cor, Holy Family, by unknown painter. 4cor, Birth of Christ, by Lezamon.

1994, Feb. 23 **Litho.** ***Perf. 13½x14***

1980A A276a 1cor multicolored .35 .20
1980B A276a 4cor multicolored 1.40 .70

Fauna and Flora of Rainforest — A277

No. 1981: a, Bromeliacae. b, Tilmatura dupontii. c, Anolis biporcatus (b). d, Fulgara laternaria. e, Bradypus. f, Spizaetus ornatus. g, Cotinga amabilis. h, Bothrops schlegelii. i, Odontoglossum. j, Agalychnis callidryas. k, Heliconius spaho. l, Passiflora vitifolia.

No. 1982, Dasyprocta punctata. No. 1983, Melinaea lilis.

1994, Jan. 20 ***Perf. 14***

1981 A277 2cor Sheet of 12, #a.-l. 10.00 5.00

Souvenir Sheets

1982 A277 10cor multicolored 3.50 1.75
1983 A277 10cor multicolored 3.50 1.75

Hong Kong '94 A278

No. 1984 — Butterflies: a, Callicore patelina. b, Chlosyne narva. c, Anteos maerula. d, Marpesia petreus. e, Pierella helvetia. f, Eurytides epidaus. g, Heliconius doris. h, Smyrna blomfildia. i, Eueides lybia. j, Adelpha heraclea. k, Heliconius hecale. l, Parides montezuma. m, Morpho polyphemus. n, Eresia alsina. o, Prepona omphale. p, Morpho granadensis.

1994, Feb. 18 **Litho.** ***Perf. 14***

1984 A278 1.50cor Sheet of 16 8.25 4.00

Astronomers — A279

No. 1985 — Copernicus and: a, Satellite. b, Tycho Brahe (1546-1601), making observations. c, Galileo probe, Galileo. d, Isaac Newton, Newton telescope. e, Giotto probe to Halley's comet, Edmund Halley. f, James Bradley (1693-1762), Grenwich Observatory. g, 1793 telescope, William Herschel (1738-1822). h, John Goodricke (1764-86), stellar eclipse. i, Gottingen observatory, Karl Fredrich Gauss (1777-1855). j, Friedrich Bessell (1784-1846), astronomical instrument. k, Harvard College Observatory, William Granch (1783-1859). l, George B. Airy (1801-92), stellar disc. m, Lowell Observatory, Flagstaff, Arizona, Percival Lowell (1855-1916). n, George A. Halle (1868-1938), solar spectrograph. o, Space telescope, Edwin Hubble (1889-1953). p, Gerard Kuiper (1905-73), Uranus' moon Miranda.

10cor, Nicolas Copernicus, interstellar probe.

1994, Apr. 4

1985 A279 1.50cor Sheet of 16 8.25 4.00

Souvenir Sheet

1986 A279 10cor multicolored 3.50 1.75

Automotive Anniversaries — A280

No. 1987: a, 1886 Benz three-wheel car. b, 1909 Benz Blitzen. c, 1923 Mercedes Benz 24/100/140. d, 1928 Mercedes Benz SSK. e, 1934 Mercedes Benz Cabriolet 500k. f, 1949 Mercedes Benz 170S. g, 1954 Mercedes Benz W196. h, 1954 Mercedes Benz 300SL. i, 1896 Ford four-wheel car. j, 1920 Ford taxi. k, 1928 Ford Roadster. l, 1932 Ford V-8. m, 1937 Ford 78 (V-8). n, 1939 Ford 91 Deluxe Tudor Sedan. o, 1946 Ford V-8 Sedan Coupe. p, 1958 Ford Custom 300.

10cor, Henry Ford (1863-1947), 1903 Ford Model A; Karl Benz (1844-1929), 1897 Benz 5CH.

1994, Apr. 5

1987 A280 1.50cor Sheet of 16 8.25 4.00

Souvenir Sheet

1988 A280 10cor multicolored 3.50 1.75

First Benz four-wheeled vehicle, cent. (Nos. 1987a-1987h). First Ford gasoline engine, cent. (Nos. 1987i-1987p).

Graf Zeppelin A281

No. 1989 — Graf Zeppelin and: a, Dr. Hugo Eckener, Count Zeppelin (inside cabin). b, New York City, 1928. c, Tokyo, 1929. d, San Simeon, California, 1929. e, Col. Charles Lindbergh, Dr. Hugo Eckener, 1929. f, Moscow, 1930. g, Paris, 1930. h, Cairo, 1931. i, Arctic waters. j, Rio de Janeiro, 1932. k, London, 1935. l, St. Peter's Basilica, Vatican City. m, Swiss Alps. n, Brandenburg Gate. o, Eckener in control room. p, Ernest A. Lehman, DO-X.

No. 1990, Graf Zeppelin, Count Zeppelin. No. 1991, Zeppelin, Eckener.

1994, Apr. 6

1989 A281 1.50cor Sheet of 16 8.25 4.00

Souvenir Sheets

1990 A281 10cor multicolored 3.50 1.75
1991 A281 10cor multicolored 3.50 1.75

Dr. Hugo Eckener (1868-1954) (#1991).

Contemporary Crafts — A282

Designs: No. 1992, 50c, Basket weaving, by Rosalia Sevilla, horiz. No. 1993, 50c, Wood carving, by Julio Lopez. No. 1994, 1cor, Woman carrying sack, by Indiana Robleto. No. 1995, 1cor, Church, by Auxiliadora Bush. 2.50cor, Carving, by Jose de Los Santos. 3cor, Costumed doll with horse's head, by Ines Gutierrez de Chong. 4cor, Ceramic container, by Elio Gutierrez.

10cor, Metate, by Saul Carballo.

Perf. 13½x14, 14x13½

1994, Feb. 15 **Litho.**

1992-1998 A282 Set of 7 4.25 2.00

Imperf

Size: 96x66mm

1999 A282 10cor multicolored 3.25 1.60

Dated 1993.

Stone Carvings, Chontal Culture — A283

Color of inscription tablet: No. 2000, 50c, Yellow. No. 2001, 50c, Yellow brown. No. 2002, 1cor, Green. No. 2003, 1cor, Yellow green. 2.50cor, Greenish blue. 3cor, Blue. 4cor, Grey green.

10cor, Two stone totems seen against landscape painting.

1994, Feb. 23 ***Perf. 14***

2000-2006 A283 Set of 7 4.25 2.00

Imperf

Size: 96x66mm

2007 A283 10cor multicolored 3.25 1.60

Dated 1993.

Contemporary Art — A284

Designs: No. 2008, 50c, Lady Embroidering, by Guillermo Rivas Navas. No. 2009, 50c, Virgin of Nicaragua, by Cella Lacayo. No. 2010, 1cor, The Dance, by June Beer. No. 2011, 1cor, Song of Peace, by Alejandro Canales. 2.50cor, Fruits, by Genaro Lugo, horiz. 3cor, Figures and Fragments, by Leonel Vanegas. 4cor, Eruption of Volcano of Water, by Asilia Guillen, horiz.

10cor, Still life, by Alejandro Alonso Rochi.

1994, Mar. 15 ***Perf. 14x13½, 13½x14***

2008-2014 A284 Set of 7 4.25 2.00

Imperf

Size: 96x66mm

2015 A284 10cor multicolored 3.25 1.60

Dated 1993.

Prominent Nicaraguan Philatelists — A285

Designs: 1cor, Gabriel Horvilleur (1907-91). 3cor, Jose S. Cuadra A. (1932-92). 4cor, Alfredo Pertz (1864-1948).

1994, Apr. 18 **Litho.** ***Perf. 14***

2016-2018 A285 Set of 3 2.75 1.40

Dated 1993.

First Tree Conference of Nicaragua A286

1994, June 5 ***Perf. 14x13½***

2019 A286 4cor multicolored 1.40 .70

Souvenir Sheets

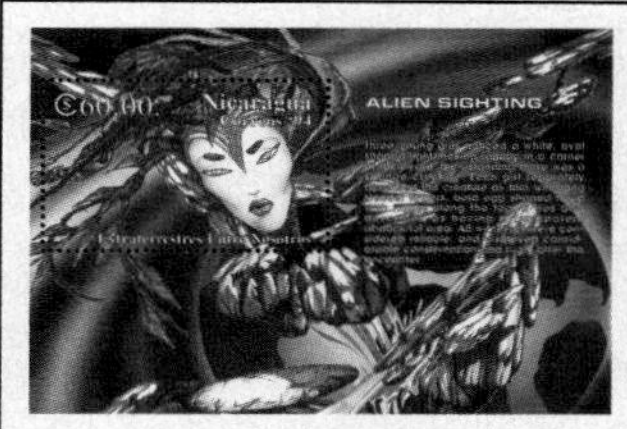

Reported Alien Sightings — A287

Date and location of sighting: No. 2020, 60cor, July 21, 1991, Missouri. No. 2021, 60cor, July 28, 1965, Argentina. No. 2022, 60cor, Aug. 21, 1955, Kentucky. No. 2023, 60cor, Oct. 25, 1973, Pennsylvania. No. 2024, 60cor, Sept. 19, 1961, New Hampshire. No. 2025, 60cor, Nov. 7, 1989, Kansas. No. 2026, 60cor, Sept. 26, 1976, Grand Canary Island. No. 2027, 60cor, May 8, 1973, Texas.

1994, May 25 **Litho.** ***Perf. 14***

2020-2027 A287 Set of 8 170.00 170.00

Sacred Art — A288

Designs: No. 2028, 50c, Pulpit, Cathedral of Leon. No. 2029, 50c, Statue of Saint Ann, Chinandega Parish. No. 2030, 1cor, Statue of St. Joseph, San Pedro Parish, Rivas. No. 2031, 1cor, Statue of St. James, Jinotepe Parish. 2.50cor, Chalice, Subtiava Temple, Leon. 3cor, Processional cross, Nequinohoma Parish, Masaya. 4cor, Crucifix, Temple of Miracles, Managua.

10cor, Silver frontal, San Pedro Parish, Rivas.

1994, July 11 **Litho.** ***Perf. 14***

2028-2034 A288 Set of 7 4.25 2.25

Size: 96x66mm

Imperf

2036 A288 10cor multicolored 3.50 1.75

No. 2035 is unassigned.

A289

A290

1994, July 4 **Litho.** ***Perf. 14***

2037 A289 3cor multicolored 1.00 1.00

Intl. Conference of New or Restored Democracies.

1994, Aug. 2

2038 A290 4cor multicolored 1.50 1.50

32nd World Amateur Baseball Championships.

PHILAKOREA '94 — A291

No. 2039: a, Soraksan. b, Statue of Kim Yu-Shin. c, Solitary Rock. d, Waterfall, Hallasan Valley. e, Mirukpong and Pisondae. f, Chonbuldong Valley. g, Bridge of the Seven Nymphs. h, Piryong Falls.

No. 2040, Boy on first birthday, gifts of fruit.

1994, Aug. 16

2039 A291 1.50cor Sheet of 8, #a.-h. 4.00 4.00

Souvenir Sheet

2040 A291 10cor multicolored 3.00 3.00

Dinosaurs A292

No. 2041: a, Tyrannosaurus rex. b, Plateosaurus (f-g). c, Pteranodon (b). d, Camarasaurus (c). e, Euplocephalus. f, Sacuanjoche. g, Deinonychus (h). h, Chasmosaurus (d). i, Dimorphodon. j, Ametriorhynchids (i). k, Ichthyosaurus (j). l, Pterapsis, Compsognathus. m, Cephalopod. n, Archelon (o). o, Griphognatus, Gyroptychius. p, Plesiosaur (o), Navtiloid.

1994, Sept. 1

2041 A292 1.50cor Sheet of 16, #a.-p. 8.50 8.50

1994 World Cup Soccer Championships, US — A293

Players: a, Rai. b, Freddy Rincon. c, Luis Garcia. d, Thomas Dooley. e, Franco Baresi. f, Tony Meola. g, Enzo Francescoli. h, Roy Wegerle.

No. 2043, 10cor, Faustino Asprilla. No. 2044, 10cor, Adolfo Valencia, horiz.

1994, Sept. 19

2042 A293 3cor Sheet of 8, #a.-h. 7.50 7.50

Souvenir Sheets

2043-2044 A293 Set of 2 6.00 6.00

D-Day, 50th Anniv. A294

No. 2045: a, British fighter plane. b, C-47 transports dropping paratroopers. c, HMS Mauritius bombards Houlgate. d, Mulberry artificial harbor. e, Churchill tank. f, Landing craft approaching beach.

1994, Sept. 26

2045 A294 3cor Sheet of 6, #a.-f. 6.00 6.00

Ruben Dario National Theater, 25th Anniv. A295

1994, Sept. 30

2046 A295 3cor multicolored 1.00 1.00

A296

Intl. Olympic Committee, Cent. — A297

Gold Medalists: No. 2047, Cassius Clay (Muhammad Ali), boxing, 1960. No. 2048, Renate Stecher, track, 1972, 1976. 10cor, Claudia Pechstein, speed skating, 1994.

1994, Oct. 3

2047 A296 3.50cor multicolored 1.25 1.25

2048 A296 3.50cor multicolored 1.25 1.25

Souvenir Sheet

2049 A297 10cor multicolored 3.25 3.25

La Carreta Nagua, by Erick Joanello Montoya A298

1994, Oct. 19

2050 A298 4cor multicolored 1.25 1.25

Motion Pictures, Cent. — A299

No. 2051 — Film and director: a, The Kid, Charlie Chaplin. b, Citizen Kane, Orson Welles. c, Lawrence of Arabia, David Lean. d, Ivan the Terrible, Sergei Eisenstein. e, Metropolis, Fritz Lang. f, The Ten Commandments, Cecil B. DeMille. g, Gandhi, Richard Attenborough. h, Casablanca, Michael Curtis. i, Platoon, Oliver Stone. j, The Godfather, Francis Ford Coppola. k, 2001: A Space Odyssey, Stanley Kubrick. l, The Ocean Depths, Jean Renoir.

No. 2052, Gone With the Wind, Victor Fleming.

1994, Nov. 14

2051 A299 2cor Sheet of 12, #a.-l. 8.00 8.00

Souvenir Sheet

2052 A299 15cor multicolored 5.00 5.00

Wildlife A300

No. 2053: a, Nyticorax nyticorax. b, Ara macao. c, Bulbulcus ibis. d, Coragyps atratus. e, Epicrates cenchria. f, Cyanerpes cyaneus. g, Ortalis vetula. h, Bradypus griseus. i, Felis onca. j, Anhinga anhinga. k, Tapirus bairdi. l, Myrmecophaga jubata. m, Iguana iguana. n, Chelydra serpentina. o, Dendrocygna autumnalis. p, Felis paradalis.

1994, Oct. 31

2053 A300 2cor Sheet of 16, #a.-p. 10.50 10.50

First Manned Moon Landing, 25th Anniv. — A301

No. 2054: a, Docking command, lunar modules. b, Lift-off. c, Entering lunar orbit. d, Footprint on moon. e, Separation of first stage. f, Trans-lunar insertion. g, Lander descending toward moon. h, Astronaut on moon.

No. 2055, 10cor, Astronaut saluting, flag. No. 2056, 10cor, Astronauts in quarantine, horiz.

1994, Oct. 17

2054 A301 3cor Sheet of 8, #a.-h. 8.00 8.00

Souvenir Sheets

2055-2056 A301 Set of 2 6.50 6.50

Nos. 2055-2056 each contain one 29x47mm stamp.

Contemporary Paintings by Rodrigo Penalba — A302

Designs: 50c, Discovery of America. 1cor, Portrait of Maurice. 1.50cor, Portrait of Franco. 2cor, Portrait of Mimi Hammer. 2.50cor, Seated Woman. 3cor, Still Life, horiz. 4cor, Portrait of Maria Augusta. 15cor, Entrance to Anticoli.

1994, Nov. 15

2057-2063 A302 Set of 7 4.75 4.75

Size: 66x96mm

Imperf

2064 A302 15cor multicolored 4.75 4.75

Domestic Cats — A303

No. 2065: a, Chocolate point Himalayan. b, Red Somalian. c, American long hair. d, Russian blue. e, Scottish folded ear. f, Persian chinchilla. g, Egyptian mau. h, Manx blue cream. i, Burmese blue Malaysian. j, Balinesian seal point. k, Oriental long-haired blue. l, Persian chinchilla cameo. m, Angora. n, Siamese. o, Burmese seal point. p, Mixed red.

15cor, Golden shoulder Persian.

1994, Dec. 20 Litho. *Perf. 14*

2065 A303 1.50cor Sheet of 16, #a.-p. 8.00 8.00

Souvenir Sheet

2066 A303 15cor multicolored 5.00 5.00

No. 2066 contains one 38x51mm stamp.

Wild Fowl A304

No. 2067 — Penelopina nigra: a, 50c, Male, female on tree branch. b, 1cor, Head of male, male on tree branch. c, 2.50cor, Head of female, female on tree branch. d, 3cor, Male spreading wings, female.

No. 2068, 15cor, Heads of male and female Penelopina nigra. No. 2069, 15cor, Anhinga anhinga.

1994, Dec. 20 Litho. *Perf. 14*

2067 A304 Vert. strip of 4, #a.-d. 2.25 2.25

Souvenir Sheets

2068-2069 A304 Set of 2 11.00 11.00

World Wildlife Fund (#2067).

No. 2067 was issued in minature sheets of 3 strips.

Sculpture — A305

Designs: 50c, Truth, by Aparicio Arthola. 1cor, Owl, by Orlando Sobalvarro. 1.50cor, Small Music Player, by Noel Flores Castro. 2cor, Exodus II, by Miguel Angel Abarca. 2.50cor, Raza, by Fernando Saravia. 3cor, Dolor Incognito, by Edith Gron. 4cor, Heron, by Ernesto Cardenal.

No. 2077, 15cor, Atlante, by Jorge Navas Cordonero. No. 2078, 15cor, Motherhood, by Rodrigo Penalba.

1995, Feb. 23 Litho. *Perf. 14½*

2070-2076 A305 Set of 7 4.50 4.50

Size: 66x96mm

Imperf

2077-2078 A305 Set of 2 9.00 9.00

Historic Landmarks — A306

Designs: 50c, Animas Chapel, Granada, vert. 1cor, San Francisco Convent, Granada. 1.50cor, Santiago Tower, Leon, vert. 2cor, Santa Ana Church, Nindiri. 2.50cor, Santa Ana Church, Nandaime, vert. 3cor, Lion Gate, Granada. 4cor, Castle of the Immaculate Conception, Rio San Juan.

15cor, Hacienda San Jacinto, Managua.

1995 Litho. *Perf. 14*

2079-2085 A306 Set of 7 4.50 4.50

Size: 96x66mm

2086 A306 15cor multicolored 4.50 4.50

Korean Baseball Championships — A307

No. 2087, 3.50cor — LG Twins: No. 2087a, D.H. Han. b, Y.S. Kim. c, J.H. Yoo. d, Y.B. Seo. e, Team logo. f, J.H. Park. g, S.H. Lee. h, D.S. Kim. i, J.H. Kim.

No. 2088, 3.50cor — Samsung Lions: a, J.L. Ryu. b, S.Y. Kim. c, S.R. Kim. d, B.C. Dong. e, Team logo. f, K.W. Kang. g, C.S. Park. h, J.H. Yang. i, T.H. Kim.

No. 2089, 3.50cor — SBW Raiders: a, H.J. Park. b, K.J. Cho. c, K.T. Kim. d, W.H. Kim. e, Team logo. f, I.H. Baik. g, S.K. Park. h, K.L. Kim. i, J.S. Park.

No. 2090, 3.50cor — Doosan OB Bears: a, M.S. Lee. b, C.S. Park. c, H.S. Lim. d, K.W. Kim. e, Team logo. f, J.S. Kim. g, T.H. Kim. h, H.S. Kim. i, S.J. Kim.

No. 2091, 3.50cor — Pacific Dolphins: a, M.W. Jung. b, K.K. Kim. c, H.J. Kim. d, M.T. Chung. e, Team logo. f, B.W. An. g, D.G. Yoon. h, S.D. Choi. i, D.K. Kim.

No. 2092, 3.50cor — Hanwha Eagles: a, J.H. Jang. b, Y.D. Han. c, K.D. Lee. d, J.S. Park. e, Team logo. f, M.C. Jeong. g, J.W. Song. h, J.G. Kang. i, D.S. Koo.

No. 2093, 3.50cor — Lotte Giants: a, H.K. Yoon. b, D.H. Park. c, H.K. Joo. d, E.G. Kim. e, Team logo. f, J.T. Park. g, P.S. Kong. h, J.S. Yeom. i, M.H. Kim.

No. 2094, 3.50cor — Haitai Tigers: a, D.Y. Sun. b, J.B. Lee. c, J.S. Kim. d, S.H. Kim. e, Team logo. f, G.C. Lee. g, G.H. Cho. h, S.H. Kim. i, S.C. Lee.

1995, Mar. 25 Litho. *Perf. 14*

Sheets of 9, #a-i

2087-2094 A307 Set of 8 77.50 77.50

Nature Paintings — A308

Designs: 1cor, Advancing Forward, by Maria Jose Zamora. 2cor, Natural Death, by Rafael Castellon. 4cor, Captives of Water, by Alvaro Gutierrez.

1995, Apr. 4 Litho. *Perf. 14*

2095-2097 A308 Set of 3 2.25 2.25

British-Nicaragua Expedition, San Juan River — A309

1995, May 5

2098 A309 4cor multicolored 1.25 1.25

Boaco Festival — A310

1995, May 10

2099 A310 4cor multicolored 1.25 1.25

Printed with se-tenant label.

Contemporary Paintings, by Armando Morales — A311

Designs: 50c, Ferry Boat. 1cor, Oliverio Castañeda, vert. 1.50cor, Sitting Nude, vert. 2cor, Señoritas at the Port of Cabeza. 2.50cor, The Automobile and Company, vert. 3cor, Bullfight, vert. 4cor, Still life.

15cor, Woman Sleeping.

1995, Oct. 31 Litho. *Perf. 14*

2100-2106 A311 Set of 7 4.50 4.50

Size: 96x66mm

2107 A311 15cor multicolored 4.50 4.50

Louis Pasteur (1822-95) — A312

1995, Sept. 28 Litho. *Perf. 14*

2108 A312 4cor multicolored 1.25 1.25

First Place in Childrens' Painting Contest A313

Nature scene, by Brenda Jarquin Gutierrez.

1995, Oct. 9

2109 A313 3cor multicolored .90 .90

Animals A314

No. 2110: a, Crocodile. b, Opossum. c, Zahina. d, Guardatinale. e, Frog. f, Iguana. g, Macaw. h, Capybara. i, Vampire bat.

No. 2111, 15cor, Jaguar, vert. No. 2112, 15cor, Eagle, vert.

1995, Oct. 9

2110 A314 2.50cor Sheet of 9, #a.-i. 6.75 6.75

Souvenir Sheets

2111-2112 A314 Set of 2 9.00 9.00

Issued: #2112, 4/15; #2110-2111, 10/9.

FAO, 50th Anniv. — A315

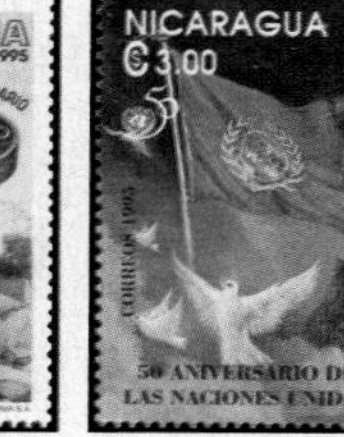

UN, 50th Anniv. — A316

1995, Oct. 16

2113 A315 4cor multicolored 1.25 1.25

1995, Oct. 31

No. 2114: a, 3cor, UN flag, doves, rainbow. b, 4cor, Rainbow, lion, lamb. c, 5cor, Rainbow, dove on soldier's helmet.

No. 2115, Children holding hands under sun, dove.

2114 A316 Strip of 3, #a.-c. 3.75 3.75

Souvenir Sheet

2115 A316 10cor multicolored 3.00 3.00

No. 2114 is a continuous design.

Rotary Intl., 90th Anniv. — A317

1995, Nov. 17

2116 A317 15cor Paul Harris, logo 4.50 4.50

Souvenir Sheet

2117 A317 25cor Old, new logos 7.50 7.50

Butterflies, Moths — A318

No. 2118: a, Cyrestis camillus. b, Salamis cacta. c, Charaxes castor. d, Danaus formosa. e, Graphium ridleyanus. f, Hewitsonia boisduvali. g, Charaxes zoolina. h, Kallima cymodoce i, Precis westermanni. j, Papilo antimachus. k, Cymothoe sangaris. l, Papillo zalmoxis.

No. 2119, Danaus formosa, vert.

1995, Nov. 17

2118 A318 2.50cor Sheet of 12, #a.-l. 9.00 9.00

Souvenir Sheet

2119 A318 15cor multicolored 4.50 4.50

1996 Summer Olympics, Atlanta — A319

No. 2120: a, Michael Jordan. b, Heike Henkel. c, Linford Christie. d, Vitaly Chtcherbo. e, Heike Drechsler. f, Mark Tewksbury.

Pierre de Coubertin and: No. 2121, 20cor, Javelin thrower, horiz. No. 2122, 20cor, Runner.

1995, Dec. 1 Litho. *Perf. 14*

2120 A319 5cor Sheet of 6, #a.-f. 9.00 9.00

Souvenir Sheets

2121-2122 A319 Set of 2 12.00 12.00

John Lennon (1940-80) — A320

1995, Dec. 8

2123 A320 2cor multicolored .60 .60

Issued in sheets of 16.

Trains A321

Designs: No. 2124, 2cor, Mombasa mail train, Uganda. No. 2125, 2cor, Steam locomotive, East Africa. No. 2126, 2cor, Electric locomotive, South Africa. No. 2127, 2cor, Beyer-Garrat steam locomotive, South Africa. No. 2128, 2cor, Beyer-Garrat steam locomotive, Rhodesia. No. 2129, 2cor, Class 30 steam locomotive, East Africa.

No. 2130: a, New York Central & Hudson River RR 4-4-0, #999, US. b, Australian Class 638, 4-6-2, Pacific. c, Baldwin 2-10-2, Bolivia. d, Vulcan 4-8-4, China. e, Paris-Orleans 4-6-2 Pacific, France. f, Class 062, 4-6-4, Japan.

No. 2131, 15cor, Siberian cargo train. No. 2132, 15cor, Midland 4-4-0 train, Great Britain. No. 2133, 15cor, Soviet steam locomotive.

1995, Dec. 11

2124-2129 A321 Set of 6 3.75 3.75

Miniature Sheet

2130 A321 4cor Sheet of 6, #a.-f. 7.25 7.25

Souvenir Sheets

2131-2133 A321 Set of 3 13.50 13.50

#2131-2133 each contain one 85x28mm stamp.

Establishment of Nobel Prize Fund, Cent. — A322

No. 2134: a, Otto Meyerhof, medicine, 1922. b, Léon Bourgeois, peace, 1920. c, James Franck, physics, 1925. d, Leo Esaki, physics, 1973. e, Miguel Angel Asturias, literature, 1967. f, Henri Bergson, literature, 1927. g, Friedrich Bergius, chemistry, 1931. h, Klaus von Klitzing, physics, 1985. i, Eisaku Sato, Japan, peace, 1974.

No. 2135: a, Wilhelm C. Roentgen, physics, 1901. b, Theodor Mommsen, literature, 1902. c, Philipp E.A. von Lenard, physics, 1905. d, Walther H. Nernst, chemistry, 1920. e, Hans Spemann, medicine, 1935. f, Jean Paul Sartre, literature, 1964. g, T.S. Eliot, literature, 1948. h, Albert Camus, literature, 1957. i, Ludwig Quidde, peace, 1927. j, Werner Heisenberg, physics, 1932. k, Joseph Brodsky, literature, 1987. l, Carl von Ossietzky, peace, 1935.

No. 2136, 15cor, Sin-itiro Tomonaga, physics, 1965. No. 2137, 15cor, Johannes Stark, physics, 1919. No. 2138, 15cor, Oscar Arias Sánchez, peace, 1987.

1995, Dec. 11

2134 A322 2.50cor Sheet of 9, #a.-i. 6.75 6.75

2135 A322 2.50cor Sheet of 12, #a.-l. 9.00 9.00

Souvenir Sheets

2136-2138 A322 Set of 3 13.50 13.50

Orchids A323

No. 2139: a, Cattleya dowinana. b, Odontoglossum maculatum. c, Barkeria lindleyana. d, Rossioglossum grnde. e, Brassavpia digbyana. f, Miltonia schroederiana. g, Ondidium ornithorhynchum. h, Odontoglossum cervantesii. i, Chysis tricostata.

No. 2140: a, Lycaste auburn. b, Lemboglossum cordatum. c, Cyrtochilum macranthum. d, Miltassia Aztec "Nalo." e, Masdevaltia ignea. f, Oncidium sniffen "Jennifer Dauro." g, Brassolaeliocattleya Alma Kee. h, Ascocenda blue boy. i, Phalaenopsis.

15cor, Odontogiossum uro-skinneri.

1995, Dec. 15

2139 A323 2.50cor Sheet of 9, #a.-i. 6.75 6.75

2140 A323 3cor Sheet of 9, #a.-i. 8.25 8.25

Souvenir Sheet

2141 A323 15cor multicolored 4.50 4.50

World War II, 50th Anniv. A324

No. 2142: a, Patton's troops crossing the Rhine. b, Churchill, Roosevelt, and Stalin at Yalta. c, US flag being raised at Iwo Jima. d, Marine infantry taking possession of Okinawa. e, US troops greeting Russian troops at Torgau. f, Liberation of concentration camps. g, Signing UN Charter, June 1945. h, Ships arriving at Tokyo after war's end.

10cor, German Bf-109 fighter plane.

1996, Jan. 24 Litho. *Perf. 14*

2142 A324 3cor Sheet of 8, #a.-h. + label 7.25 7.25

Souvenir Sheet

2143 A324 10cor multicolored 3.00 3.00

Miniature Sheet

Exotic Birds — A325

No. 2144: a, Paradisiaea apoda. b, Dryocopus galeatus. c, Psarisomus dalhousiae (g). d, Psarocolius montezuma. e, Halcyon pileata. f, Calocitta formosa. g, Ara chloroptera. h, Platycercus eximius. i, Polyplectron emphanum. j, Cariama cristata. k, Opisthocomus hoatzin. l, Coracias cyanogaster.

10cor, Dryocopus galeatus.

1996, Feb. 1

2144 A325 2cor Sheet of 12, #a.-l. 7.25 7.25

Souvenir Sheet

2145 A325 10cor multicolored 3.00 3.00

Town of Rivas, 275th Anniv. — A326

1995, Sept. 23 Litho. *Perf. 14*

2146 A326 3cor multi +label .90 .90

Christmas A327

1995, Dec. 8

2147 A327 4cor multicolored 1.25 1.25

20th Century Writers — A328

No. 2148 — Writer, country flag: a, C. Drummond de Andrade (1902-87), Brazil. b, Cesar Vallejo (1892-1938), Peru. c, J. Luis Borges (1899-1986), Argentina. d, James Joyce (1882-1941), Italy. e, Marcel Proust (1871-1922), France. f, William Faulkner (1897-1962), US. g, Vladmir Maiakovski (1893-1930), Russia. h, Ezra Pound (1885-1972), US. i, Franz Kafka (1883-1924), Czechoslovakia. j, T.S. Eliot (188-1965), United Kingdom. k, Rainer Rilke (1875-1926), Austria. l, Federico G. Lorca (1898-1936), Spain.

1995, Oct. 15 *Perf. 14½x14*

2148 A328 3cor Sheet of 12, #a.-l. 11.00 11.00

Classic Sailing Ships A329

No. 2149, 2.50cor: a, Mayflower, England. b, Young America, US. c, Preussen, Germany. d, Lateen-rigged pirate ship, Caribbean Sea. e, Cutty Sark, England. f, Square-rigged pirate ship, Caribbean Sea. g, Galeón, Spain. h, The Sun King, France. i, Santa Maria, Spain.

No. 2150, 2.50cor: a, HMS Bounty, England. b, The President, US. c, Prince William, Holland. d, Flying Cloud, US. e, Markab, Nile River, Egypt. f, Europa, Holland. g, Vasa, Sweden. h, Foochow junk, China. i, San Gabriel, Portugal.

No. 2151, 15cor, Passat, Germany. No. 2152, 15cor, Japanese junk, vert.

1996, Jan. 10 Litho. *Perf. 14*

Sheets of 9, #a-i

2149-2150 A329 Set of 2 13.50 13.50

Souvenir Sheets

2151-2152 A329 Set of 2 9.00 9.00

Visit of Pope John Paul II — A330

1996, Feb. 7

2153 A330 5cor multicolored 1.50 1.50

Puppies — A331

Various breeds: No. 2154, 1cor, Holding red leash in mouth. No. 2155, 1cor, With red bandanna around neck. No. 2156, 2cor, Spaniel playing with ball. No. 2157, 2cor, With dog biscuit in mouth. No. 2158, 3cor, Akita. No. 2159, 3cor, Bull dog. No. 2160, 4cor, With newspaper in mouth. No. 2161, 4cor, Dalmatian with cat.

No. 2162, 16cor, Bending down on front paws. No. 2163, 16cor, Poodle.

1996, Mar. 6

2154-2161 A331 Set of 8 7.25 7.25

Souvenir Sheets

2162-2163 A331 Set of 2 9.50 9.50

Famous Women — A332

No. 2164: a, Indira Gandhi. b, Mme. Chiang Kai-shek. c, Mother Teresa. d, Marie Curie. e, Margaret Thatcher. f, Eleanor Roosevelt. g, Eva Perón. h, Golda Meir. i, Violeta Barrios de Chamorro.

No. 2165, 15cor, Jacqueline Kennedy Onassis, vert. No. 2166, 15cor, Aung San Suu Kyi, vert. No. 2167, 15cor, Valentina Tereshkova, vert.

1996, Mar. 8 *Perf. 14x13½*

2164 A332 2.50cor Sheet of 9, #a.-i. 6.75 6.75

Souvenir Sheets

Perf. 13½x14

2165-2167 A332 Set of 3 13.50 13.50

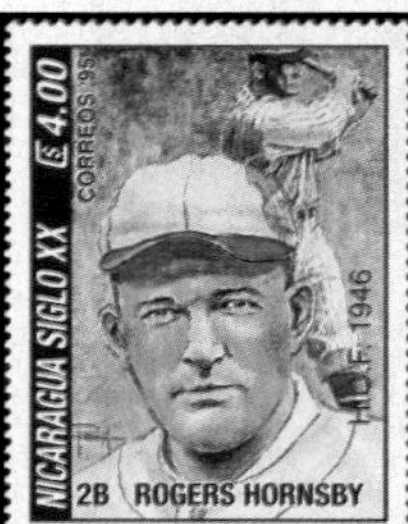

Members of Baseball's Hall of Fame A333

No. 2168 — Player, year inducted: a, Lou Gehrig, 1944. b, Rogers Hornsby, 1946. c, Mike Schmidt, 1995. d, Honus Wagner, 1936. e, Ty Cobb, 1936. f, Roberto Clemente, 1973. g, Babe Ruth, 1936. h, Johnny Bench, 1987. i, Tom Seaver, 1993.

10cor, Reggie Jackson, 1993.

1996, Mar. 15 Litho. *Perf. 13½x14*

2168 A333 4cor Sheet of 9, #a.-i. 11.00 11.00

Souvenir Sheet

2169 A333 10cor multicolored 9.25 9.25

1996 Summer Olympics, Atlanta A334

Designs: 1cor, Takehide Nakatani, Japan. 2cor, Olympic Stadium, Tokyo, 1964. 3cor, Al Oerter, US, vert. 10cor, Discus thrower from ancient games.

No. 2174, 2.50cor, vert. — Gold medal winners in boxing: a, Andrew Maynard, U.S. b, Rudi Fink, Germany. c, Peter Lessov, Bulgaria. d, Angel Herrera, Cuba. e, Patrizio Oliva, Italy. f, Armando Martinez, Cuba. g, Slobodan Kacar, Yugoslavia. h, Teofilo Stevenson, Cuba. i, George Foreman, U.S.

No. 2175, 2.50cor — Events: a, Basketball. b, Baseball. c, Boxing. d, Long jump. e, Judo. f, Team handball. g, Volleyball. h, Water polo. i, Tennis.

25cor, Cassius Clay (Muhammad Ali), US.

1996, Mar. 28 *Perf. 14*

2170-2173 A334 Set of 4 4.75 4.75

Sheets of 9, #a-i

2174-2175 A334 Set of 2 13.50 13.50

Souvenir Sheet

2176 A334 25cor multicolored 7.50 7.50

Race Horses A335

Carousel Horses — A336

Race horses: 1cor, "Wave." 2cor, "Charming Traveler." 2.50cor, "Noble Vagabond." No. 2180, 3cor, "Golden Dancer," vert. No. 2181, 3cor, "Wave Runner." No. 2182, 4cor, "Ebony Champion." No. 2183, 4cor, "Wave Tamer."

Antique carousel horses: No. 2184a, Persian light infantry horse, 18th cent. b, Italian parade horse, 15th cent. c, German armored horse, 15th cent. d, Turkish light infantry horse, 17th cent.

16cor, "Proud Heart." 25cor, German armored horse, 16th cent.

1996, Apr. 15

2177-2183 A335 Set of 7 6.00 6.00

2184 A336 2cor Sheet of 4, #a.-d. 2.50 2.50

Souvenir Sheets

2185 A335 16cor multi 4.75 4.75

2186 A336 25cor multi 7.50 7.50

Marine Life A337

No. 2187, 2.50cor: a, Butterflyfish (d). b, Barracuda (a). c, Manatee. d, Jellyfish. e, Octopus (b, d, f, g, h). f, Small yellow-striped fish. g, Lemon shark. h, Striped fish. i, Red fish.

No. 2188, 2.50cor: a, Reef shark. b, Diver, hammerhead shark (c, e). c, Moray eel (f). d, Macrela ojos de caballo (a, b, e). e, Hammerhead shark. f, Butterflyfish. g, Mediterranean grouper. h, Octopus, diff. i, Manta ray.

No. 2189, 20cor, Angelfish. No. 2190, 20cor, Saddleback butterflyfish.

1996, Apr. 29 Litho. *Perf. 14*

Sheets of 9, #a-i

2187-2188 A337 Set of 2 14.50 14.50

Souvenir Sheets

2189-2190 A337 Set of 2 13.00 13.00

Chinese Lunar Calendar A338

Year signs: a, Rat. b, Ox. c, Tiger. d, Hare. e, Dragon. f, Snake. g, Horse. h, Sheep. i, Monkey. j, Rooster. k, Dog. l, Boar.

1996, May 6

2191 A338 2cor Sheet of 12, #a.-l. 6.50 6.50

China'96.

Central American Integration System (SICA) A339

1996, May 8 *Perf. 14½*

2192 A339 5cor multicolored 1.60 1.60

20th Century Events A340

No. 2193: a, Russian revolution, 1917. b, Chinese revolution, 1945. c, Creation of the UN, 1945. d, Tearing down the Berlin Wall, 1989. e, World War I, vert. f, Creation of the State of Israel, 1948, vert. g, World War II, vert. h, 2nd Vatican Council, 1962-65, vert. i, Atom bombing of Hiroshima, 1945. j, Viet Nam War, 1962-73. k, Persian Gulf War, 1991. l, End of Apartheid, 1991.

1996 *Perf. 14*

2193 A340 3cor Sheet of 12, #a.-l. + label 11.50 11.50

Souvenir Sheet

New Year 1997 (Year of the Ox) — A341

Illustration reduced.

1996 Litho. *Perf. 15x14*

2194 A341 10cor multicolored 3.00 3.00

Wuhan Huanghelou — A342

1996, May 20 Litho. *Perf. 14*

2195 A342 4cor multicolored 1.25 1.25

China '96. No. 2195 was not available until March 1997.

Red Parrot, by Ernesto Cardenal — A343

1996, June 5 Litho. *Perf. 14½x14*

2196 A343 4cor multicolored 1.25 1.25

Friendship Between Nicaragua and Republic of China A344

Designs: 10cor, Painting, "Landscape with Bags," by Fredrico Nordalm, vert. 20cor, Dr. Lee Teng-Hui, Pres. of Republic of China and Violeta Barrios de Chamorro, President of Nicaragua.

Perf. 14½x14, 14x14½

1996, June 26 Litho.

2197 A344 10cor multicolored 1.75 1.75

2198 A344 20cor multicolored 3.50 3.50

Violeta Barrios de Chamorro, President, 1990-96 A345

Serpentine Die Cut

1997, Jan. 27 Litho.

Self-Adhesive

2199 A345 3cor multicolored .90 .90

a. Booklet pane of 9 + 2 labels 8.25

The peelable paper backing serves as a booklet cover.

"Plan International," Intl. Children's Organization, 60th Anniv. — A346

1997, Feb. 24 *Serpentine Die Cut*

Self-Adhesive

2200 A346 7.50cor multicolored 2.25 2.25

a. Booklet pane of 12 27.00

The peelable paper backing serves as a booklet cover.

"Iberoamerica," Spanish-America Art Exhibition — A347

Painting, "Night with Two Figures," by Alejandro Aróstegui.

1998, May 8 *Perf. 13½*

2201 A347 7.50cor multicolored 2.00 2.00

Butterflies — A348

No. 2202: a, Metamorpha stelenes. b, Erateina staudingeri. c, Premolis semirufa. d, Heliconius eisini. e, Phoebis phlea. f, Dione juno. g, Helicopis cupido. h, Catonephele numili. i, Anteos clorinde.

No. 2203, 25cor, Thecla coronata. No. 2204, 25cor, Ufefheisa bela.

1999, Mar. 15 Litho. *Perf. 14*

2202 A348 2.50cor Sheet of 9, #a.-i. 4.25 4.25

Souvenir Sheets

2203-2204 A348 Set of 2 15.50 15.50

Dated 1996.

Fauna of Central America — A349

No. 2205, 2cor: a, Red banded parrot. b, Sloth. c, Porcupine. d, Toucan. e, Howler monkey. f, Anteater. g, Kinkajou. h, Owl monkey. i, Red-footed land turtle. j, Red deer. k, Armadillo. l, Paca.

No. 2206, 2cor: a, Vulture. b, Tarantula. c, Palm viper. d, Ocelot. e, Fighting spider. f, Large fruit bat. g, Jaguar. h, Venomous tree frog. i, Viper. j, Grison. k, Rattlesnake. l, Puma.

No. 2207, 25cor, Tapir. No. 2208, 25cor, Caiman.

1999, Mar. 15

Sheets of 12, #a-l

2205-2206 A349 Set of 2 9.00 9.00

Souvenir Sheets

2207-2208 A349 Set of 2 9.00 9.00

Dated 1996.

Endangered Species — A350

No. 2209, 2.50cor: a, Owls, gorilla. b, Cheetahs. c, Giraffes. d, Gazelle, elephants. e, Elephants. f, Lion, okapi. g, Rhinoceros. h, Hippopotamus. i, Lion.

No. 2210, 2.50cor, vert: a, Lemurs. b, Blue gliding parrot. c, Toucan. d, Boa. e, Jaguar. f, Margay. g, Loris. h, White egret. i, Armadillo.

No. 2211, 2.50cor, vert: a, Prezwalski horse. b, Red deer. c, Zebra. d, Golden lion monkey. e, African elephant. f, Black bear. g, Tiger. h, Orangutan. i, Snow leopard.

25cor, Chimpanzee. 25.50cor, Panda, vert.

1999, Mar. 15

Sheets of 9, #a-i

2209-2211 A350 Set of 3 13.00 13.00

Souvenir Sheets

2212 A350 25cor multicolored 4.50 4.50

2213 A350 25.50cor multicolored 4.75 4.75

Dated 1996.

India's Independence, 50th Anniv. — A351

1998, Aug. 13 Litho. *Perf. 14½*

2214 A351 3cor blue & multi .50 .50

2215 A351 9cor brn yel & multi 1.50 1.50

Dated 1997.

Nature Reserves and Natl. Parks A352

Designs: 1.50cor, Mombacho Volcano Nature Reserve. 2.50cor, La Flor Wildlife Refuge. 3cor, Zapatera Archipelago Natl. Park. 3.50cor, Miraflor Nature Reserve. 5cor, Cosigüina Volcano Natl. Park. 6.50cor, Masaya Volcano Natl. Park. 7.50cor, Juan Venado Island Nature Reserve. 8cor, Escalante Chacocente River Wildlife Refuge. 10cor, Protected Areas, Natl. Park System.

12cor, Trees, first Biosphere Reserve.

1998, Aug. 20 *Perf. 10½*

2216 A352 1.50cor multicolored .25 .25

2217 A352 2.50cor multicolored .45 .45

2218 A352 3cor multicolored .50 .50

2219 A352 3.50cor multicolored .60 .60

2220 A352 5cor multicolored .85 .85

2221 A352 6.50cor multicolored 1.10 1.10

2222 A352 7.50cor multicolored 1.25 1.25

2223 A352 8cor multicolored 1.40 1.40

2224 A352 10cor multicolored 1.75 1.75

Nos. 2216-2224 (9) 8.15 8.15

Size: 65x95mm

Imperf

2225 A352 12cor multicolored 2.00 2.00

National Museum, Cent A353

1998, Aug. 25

2226 A353 3.50cor Footprints .60 .60

Paintings by Rodrigo Peñalba (1908-1979) A354

Designs: 2.50cor, "Descendimiento." 3.50cor, "Victoria y Piere With Child." 5cor, "Motherhood."

10cor, "El Güegüense."

1998, Aug. 26 *Perf. 10½*

2227 A354 2.50cor multicolored .45 .45

2228 A354 3.50cor multicolored .60 .60

2229 A354 5cor multicolored .85 .85

Nos. 2227-2229 (3) 1.90 1.90

Size: 95x65mm

Imperf

2230 A354 10cor multicolored 1.75 1.75

Child's Painting, "Children Love Peace" — A355

1998, Aug. 28 *Perf. 14½*

2231 A355 50c multicolored .20 .20

Dated 1997.

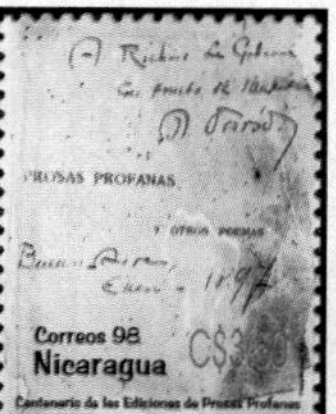

Publishing of "Profane Prose and Other Poems," by Rubén Darío (1867-1916), Cent. — A356

1998, Sept. 11 *Perf. 10½*

2232 A356 3.50cor shown .60 .60

2233 A356 5cor Portrait .85 .85

Naturaleza '98 — A357

Painting by Bayron Gómez Chavarría.

1998, Sept. 25

2234 A357 3.50cor multicolored .60 .60

World Stamp Day — A358

1998, Oct. 9

2235 A358 6.50cor multicolored 1.10 1.10

Dialogue of Nicaragua A359

1998, Oct. 12

2236 A359 5cor multicolored .85 .85

Famous Nicaraguan Women — A360

America issue: 3.50cor, Lolita Soriano de Guerrero (b. 1922), writer. 7.50cor, Violeta Barrios de Chamorro (b. 1929), former president.

1998, Oct. 16

2237 A360 3.50cor multicolored .60 .60
2238 A360 7.50cor multicolored 1.25 1.25

Universal Declaration of Human Rights, 50th Anniv. A361

1998, Dec. 10 ***Perf. 13½***

2239 A361 12cor multicolored 2.10 2.10

Christmas — A362

Nativity scenes: 50c, Molded miniature, vert. 1cor, Drawing on pottery, vert. 2cor, Adoration of the Magi. 3cor, Painting.

7.50cor, Painting of angel over modern village.

1998, Dec. 14 ***Perf. 14***

2240 A362 50c multicolored .20 .20
2241 A362 1cor multicolored .20 .20
2242 A362 2cor multicolored .35 .35
2243 A362 3cor multicolored .50 .50
Nos. 2240-2243 (4) 1.25 1.25

Size: 95x64mm

Imperf

2244 A362 7.50cor multicolored 1.25 1.25

Dated 1997.

Managua Earthquake, 25th Anniv. (in 1997) — A363

Designs: 3cor, Managua in 1997, vert. 7.50cor, Devastation after earthquake in 1972. 10.50cor, Buildings toppling, clock, vert.

1998, Dec. 23

2245 A363 3cor multicolored .50 .50
2246 A363 7.50cor multicolored 1.25 1.25

Souvenir Sheet

2247 A363 10.50cor multicolored 1.75 1.75

Dated 1997.

Diana, Princess of Wales (1961-97) — A364

Designs: 5cor, Wearing hat. 7.50cor, Wearing tiara. 10cor, Wearing white dress.

1999, Apr. 29 **Litho.** ***Perf. 13½***

2248-2250 A364 Set of 3 3.75 3.75

Nos. 2248-2250 were each issued in sheets of 6.

Butterflies A365

Designs: 3.50cor, Papilionidae ornithoptera. 8cor, Nymphalidae cepheuptychia. 12.50cor, Pieridae phoebis.

No. 2254: a, Nymphalidae eryphanis. b, Nymphalidae callicore. c, Nymphalidae hypolimmas. d, Nymphalidae precis. e, Papilionidae troides. f, Nymphalidae cithaerias. g, Papilionidae parides. h, Nymphalidae heliconius. i, Nymphalidae morpho.

15cor, Papilionidae papilio.

1999, Apr. 30 ***Perf. 14***

2251-2253 A365 Set of 3 4.25 4.25
2254 A365 9cor Sheet of 9, #a.-i. 14.00 14.00

Souvenir Sheet

2255 A365 15cor multicolored 2.50 2.50

Sailing Ships — A366

Paintings: 2cor, Eagle, 1851, US. 4cor, Contest, 1800, US. 5cor, Architect, 1847, US. 10cor, Edward O'Brien, 1863, UK.

No. 2260, vert: a, HMS Rodney, 1830, UK. b, Boyne, 1700's, Great Britain. c, Castor, 1800's, UK. d, Mutin, 1800's, UK. e, Britainnia, 1820, UK. f, Gouden Leeuw, 1600, Holland. g, Hercules, 1600, Holland. h, Resolution, 1667, Great Britain. i, Royal George, 1756, Great Britain. j, Vanguard, 1700's, Great Britain. k, Prince Royal, 1600, Great Britain. l, Zeven Provincien, 1600, Holland.

No. 2261, 15cor, Pamir, 1905, US. No. 2262, 15cor, Great Expedition, 1700's, Great Britain.

1999, May 31 **Litho.** ***Perf. 14x13½***

2256-2259 A366 Set of 4 3.75 3.75

Perf. 14½x14¼

2260 A366 3cor Sheet of 12, #a.-l. 6.50 6.50

Souvenir Sheets

Perf. 13½x14

2261-2262 A366 Set of 2 5.50 5.50

No. 2260 contains twelve 28x36mm stamps.

Flora and Fauna A367

Designs: 5cor, Anteos clorinde. 6cor, Coereba flaveola. No. 2265, 7.50cor, Rynchops niger. No. 2266, 7.50cor, Chaetodon striatus.

No. 2267, vert: a, Palm tree. b, Phaethon lepturus. c, Cinclocerthia ruficauda. d, Myadestes genibarbis. e, Rosa sinesis. f, Cyanophala bicolor. g, Delphinus delphis. h, Anolis carolinensis (l). i, Dynastes tityus. j, Heliconia psittacorum. k, Iguana iguana (j). l, Propona meander.

No. 2268, 10cor, Ceryle torquata, vert. No. 2269, 10cor, Anisotremus virginicus.

1999, June 14 ***Perf. 14x14¼***

2263-2266 A367 Set of 4 4.75 4.75

Perf. 14¼x14

2267 A367 5cor Sheet of 12, #a.-l. 11.00 11.00

Souvenir Sheet

2268-2269 A367 Set of 2 3.50 3.50

No. 2267 l is inscribed 3cor, but the editors believe the sheet was sold as sheet of 5cor stamps.

Birds — A368

Designs: 5cor, Eudyptes chrysocome. 5.50cor, Spheniscus magellanious. 6cor, Pygoscelis antarctica. 7.50cor, Magadyptes antipodes.

No. 2274, horiz.: a, Phalacrocorax punctatus featherstoni. b, Phalacrocorax bougainvillii. c, Anhinga anhinga. d, Phalacrocorax punctatus punctatus. e, Phalacrocorax sulcirostris. f, Pelecanus occidentalis.

No. 2275, 12cor, Aptenodytes forsteri, horiz. No. 2276, 12cor, Pygoscelis papua.

1999, May 25 **Litho.** ***Perf. 14***

2270-2273 A368 Set of 4 4.00 4.00
2274 A368 6cor Sheet of 6, #a.-f. 6.00 6.00

Souvenir Sheets

2275-2276 A368 Set of 2 4.00 4.00

Dated 1998.

Dinosaurs A369

No. 2277: a, Sordes. b, Dimorphodon. c, Anurognathus. d, Rhamphorhynchus. e, Pterodaustro. f, Pteranodon.

No. 2278: a, Macroplata. b, Coelurus. c, "Stegosaurus." d, "Corythosaurus." e, Thadeosaurus. f, "Brachisaurus."

No. 2279, 12cor, Platecarpus. No. 2280, 12cor, Pterodactylus.

1999, June 1 **Litho.** ***Perf. 14***

2277 A369 5cor Sheet of 6, #a.-f. 5.00 5.00
2278 A369 6cor Sheet of 6, #a.-f. 6.00 6.00

Souvenir Sheets

2279-2280 A369 Set of 2 4.00 4.00

Dated 1998. Stamp inscriptions on Nos. 2278c, 2278d and 2278f, and perhaps others, are incorrect or misspelled.

Trains A370

Designs: 1cor, U25B, Rock Island Line. 5cor, C-630 Santa Fe Railroad. 6.50cor, Class D. D. 40 AX, Union Pacific Railroad. 7.50cor, F Series B. B. EMD, Maryland Department of Transportation.

No. 2285: a, CR Alco RS11. b, Metra EMD F40. c, British Columbia Railways GF6C. d, Amtrak AEM7. e, C-40-9, Norfolk Southern. f, C-630, Reading Railroad.

No. 2286: a, British Columbia Railways GF6C, diff. b, Indian Railways WDM C-C. c, Class 421, Australia. d, Class M821, Australia. e, LRC B.B., Via Canada. f, GM Class X, Victorian Railways, Australia.

No. 2287, 15cor, Queen Victoria. No. 2288, 15cor, Donald Smith driving last spike of Trans-Canada Railway, vert.

1999, June 28 **Litho.** ***Perf. 14***

2281-2284 A370 Set of 4 3.25 3.25
2285 A370 5cor Sheet of 6, #a.-f. 5.00 5.00
2286 A370 6cor Sheet of 6, #a.-f. 6.00 6.00

Souvenir Sheets

2287-2288 A370 Set of 2 5.00 5.00

Dated 1998. Stamp inscription on No. 2284, and perhaps others, is misspelled.

Mushrooms and Insects — A371

No. 2289: a, Tricholoma ustaloides, leaf beetle. b, Tricholoma pardinum, grasshopper. c, Amanita echinocephala, crickets. d, Tricholoma saponaceum, red-tipped clearwing moth. e, Amanita inaurata, hanging scorpionfly. f, Amanita rubescens, assassin bug.

No. 2290: a, Amanita citrina, banded agrion. b, Cryoptotrama asprata, clouded yellow butterfly. c, Amanita gemmata, mayfly. d, Catathelasma imperiale, variable reed beetle. e, Collybia fusipes, black swallowtail caterpillar. f, Collybia butyracea, South African savannah grasshopper.

No. 2291, 12.50cor, Tricholomopsis rutilans, lesser cloverleaf weevil. No. 2292, 12.50cor, Tricholoma virgatum, rose weevil.

1999, Oct. 27 **Litho.** ***Perf. 13¼x13½***

2289 A371 5.50cor Sheet of 6, #a.-f. 5.50 5.50
2290 A371 7.50cor Sheet of 6, #a.-f. 7.25 7.25

Souvenir Sheets

2291-2292 A371 Set of 2 4.00 4.00

Dated 1998.

Ballooning — A372

No. 2293, 12cor: a, Solo Spirit 3. b, Emblem of Breitling Orbiter 3, first balloon to make non-stop circumnavigation, 1999. c, ICO Global.

No. 2294, 12cor: a, Breitling Orbiter 3 over mountains. b, Leonardo da Vinci. c, Brian Jones and Bertrand Piccard, pilots of Breitling Orbiter 3.

No. 2295, 12cor: a, Tiberius Cavallo. b, Breitling Orbiter 3 on ground. c, Piccard and Jones, diff.

No. 2296, 12cor: a, Jones. b, Breitling Orbiter 3 in flight. c, Piccard.

No. 2297, 25cor, Jean-Francois Pilatre de Rozier. No. 2298, 25cor, Jean-Pierre Blanchard. No. 2299, 25cor, Madame Thible. No. 2300, 25cor, J. A. C. Charles.

1999, Nov. 12 ***Perf. 13½x13¼***

Sheets of 3, #a-c

2293-2296 A372 Set of 4 24.00 24.00

Souvenir Sheets

2297-2300 A372 Set of 4 16.00 16.00

Dated 1998.

Orchids — A373

Designs: 2cor, Cattleya, skinneri. 4cor, Lycaste aromatica. 5cor, Odontoglossum cervantesii. 10cor, Brassia verrucosa.

No. 2305, 3cor: a, Odontoglossum rossii. b, Cattleya aurantiaca. c, Encyclia cordigera. d, Phragmipedium bessae. e, Brassavola nodosa. f, Cattleya forbesii.

No. 2306, 3cor: a, Barkeria spectabilis. b, Dracula erythrochaete. c, Cochleanthes discolor. d, Encyclia cochleata. e, Lycaste aromatica. f, Brassia maculata.
No. 2307, 25cor, Odontoglossum rossii, diff. No. 2308, 25cor, Phragmipedium longifolium.

1999, Nov. 10

2301-2304 A373 Set of 4 3.50 3.50

Sheets of 6, #a.-f.

2305-2306 A373 Set of 2 6.00 6.00

Souvenir Sheets

2307-2308 A373 Set of 2 8.00 8.00

Rubén Darío Natl. Theater, 30th Anniv. A374

1999, Dec. 6 ***Perf. 13¼x13½***

2309 A374 7.50cor multi 1.25 1.25

Inter-American Development Bank, 40th Anniv. — A375

1999, Nov. 18 ***Perf. 13¼***

2310 A375 7.50cor multi 1.25 1.25

America Issue, A New Millennium Without Arms — A376

1999, Nov. 25 ***Perf. 13½***

2311 A376 7.50cor multi 1.25 1.25

Japanese-Nicaraguan Friendship — A377

Designs: a, 3.50cor, Fishing boats, Puertos Cabezas. b, 9cor, Hospital. c, 5cor, Combine in field. d, 6cor, Japanese school. e, 7.50cor, Bridge on Pan-American Highway. f, 8cor, Aqueduct.

1999, Nov. 12 ***Perf. 13x13¼***

2312 A377 Sheet of 6, #a.-f. 6.50 6.50

UPU, 125th Anniv. — A378

1999, Dec. 20 Litho. ***Perf. 13½***

2313 A378 7.50cor multi 1.25 1.25

Cities of Granada and León, 475th Anniv. A379

No. 2314 — Granada: a, City Hall. b, Guadalupe Church. c, Buildings on central square. d, Houses with porches. e, House of the Leones. f, El Consulado Street.
No. 2315 — León: a, Cathedral. b, Municipal theater. c, La Recolección Church. d, Rubén Dario Museum. e, Post and Telegraph office. f, Cural de Subtiava house.

1999, Dec. 13 ***Perf. 13x13½***

2314 A379 3.50cor Sheet of 6, #a.-f. 3.50 3.50
2315 A379 7.50cor Sheet of 6, #a.-f. 7.25 7.25

Dogs and Cats — A380

Designs: 1cor, Azawakh. 2cor, Chihuahua. 2.50cor, Chocolate colorpoint Birman, horiz. 3cor, Norwegian Forest cat, horiz.
No. 2320: a, Clumber spaniel. b, Australian shepherd. c, German wire-haired pointer. d, Unnnamed. e, Ibizan hound. f, Norwegian elkhound.
No. 2321, horiz.: a, Blue European Shorthair. b, Turkish Angora. c, Red Tiffany. d, Persian. e, Calico Shorthair. f, Russian Blue.
No. 2322, 12cor, Braque du Bourbonnais. No. 2323, 12cor, Burmese, horiz.

Perf. 13¾x13½, 13½x13¾

2000, July 20 **Litho.**

2316-2319 A380 Set of 4 1.50 1.50
2320 A380 6cor Sheet of 6, #a-f 6.25 6.25
2321 A380 6.50cor Sheet of 6, #a-f 6.75 6.75

Souvenir Sheets

2322-2323 A380 Set of 2 4.25 4.25

No. 2322 contains one 42x56mm stamp; No. 2323 contains one 56x42mm stamp.

Trains A381

Designs: 3cor, Class 470 APT-P, Great Britain. 4cor, X-2000, Sweden. 5cor, XPT, Australia. 10cor, High speed train, Great Britain.
No. 2328: a, Metro North B-25-7. b, Long Island Railroad EMD DE30. c, EMD F40 PHM-2C. d, Pennsylvania Railroad GG1. e, New Jersey Transit MK GP40 FH-2. f, Amtrak EMD F59 PHI.
No. 2329: a, DM-3, Sweden. b, EW 165, New Zealand. c, Class 87, Great Britain. d, Class 40, Great Britain. e, GE 6/6, Switzerland. f, Class 277, Spain.
No. 2330, Metra EMD P69PN-AC. No. 2331, Class 44, Great Britain.

2000, Aug. 21 Litho. ***Perf. 14***

2324-2327 A381 Set of 4 3.75 3.75

Sheets of 6, #a-f

2328-2329 A381 3cor Set of 2 6.25 6.25

Souvenir Sheets

2330-2331 A381 25cor Set of 2 8.50 8.50

Marine Life A382

Designs: 3.50cor, Great white shark. 5cor, Humpback whale. 6cor, Sea turtle. 9cor, Sperm whale.
No. 2336, 7.50cor: a, Puffer fish. b, Manta ray. c, Black grouper. d, Tiger grouper. e, Golden-tailed eel. f, Atlantic squid.
No. 2337, 7.50cor: a, Hawksbill turtle. b, Moon jellyfish. c, Caribbean reef shark. d, Turtle. e, Spotted dolphin. f, Southern sting ray.
No. 2338, Tiger shark. No. 2339, Spotted dolphins.

2000, Aug. 22 ***Perf. 14***

2332-2335 A382 Set of 4 4.00 4.00

Sheets of 6, #a-f

2336-2337 A382 Set of 2 15.00 15.00

Souvenir Sheets

2338-2339 A382 25cor Set of 2 8.50 8.50

Queen Mother, 100th Birthday — A383

No. 2340: a, As young woman. b, In 1970. c, With King George VI. d, As old woman.

Litho. (Margin Embossed)

2000, July 25 ***Perf. 14***

2340 A383 10cor Sheet of 4, #a-d + label 7.00 7.00

Souvenir Sheet

Perf. 13¾

2341 A383 25cor In 1948 4.25 4.25

No. 2341 contains one 38x51mm stamp.

History of Aviation — A384

No. 2342, 7.50cor: a, Montgolfier balloon (blue background), vert. b, Hawker Hart. c, Lysander. d, Bleriot and Fox Moth, vert. e, Harrier. f, VC10.
No. 2343, 7.50cor: a, Montgolfier balloon (tan background), vert. b, Bristol F2B. c, Jet Provost. d, Avro 504K and Redwing II trainer, vert. e, Hunter. f, Wessex.
No. 2344, 25cor, Spartan Arrow (top) and Tiger Moth. No. 2345, 25cor, Tiger Moth (top) and Spartan Arrow.

2000, July 27 Litho. ***Perf. 14½x14***

Sheets of 6, #a-d

2342-2343 A384 Set of 2 15.00 15.00

Souvenir Sheets

2344-2345 A384 Set of 2 8.50 8.50

Size of Nos. 2342a, 2342d, 2343a, 2343d: 41x60mm.

Birds — A385

Designs: 5cor, Cotinga amabilis. 7.50cor, Galbula ruficauda. 10cor, Guiraca caerulea. 12.50cor, Momotus momota.
No. 2350: a, Ara macao. b, Amazona ochrocephala. c, Chloroceryle americana. d, Archilocus colubris. e, Pharamachrus mocinno. f, Ramphastos sulfuratus. g, Coereba flaveola. h, Piculus rubiginosus. i, Passerina ciris. j, Busarellus nigricollis.
No. 2351, 25cor, Aulacorhynchus prasinus. No. 2352, 25cor, Ceryle alcyon.

2000, Aug. 23 ***Perf. 14***

2346-2349 A385 Set of 4 6.00 6.00
2350 A385 3cor Sheet of 10, #a-j 5.25 5.25

Souvenir Sheets

2351-2352 A385 Set of 2 8.50 8.50

Space Exploration — A386

No. 2353, 5cor: a, Donald K. Slayton. b, M. Scott Carpenter. c, Walter M. Schirra. d, John H. Glenn, Jr. e, L. Gordon Cooper. f, Virgil I. Grissom. g, Mercury Redsone 3 rocket. h, Alan B. Shepard.
No. 2354, 5cor, horiz.: a, Recovery of Mercury 8. b, View of Earth from space. c, Carpenter in life raft. d, Shepard in water. e, USS Intrepid. f, Friendship 7. g, Mercury 9 splashdown. h, Recovery of Mercury 6.
No. 2355, 25cor, Glenn, diff. No. 2356, 25cor, Shepard, horiz.

2000, Aug. 25 **Litho.**

Sheets of 8, #a-h

2353-2354 A386 Set of 2 14.00 14.00

Souvenir Sheets

2355-2356 A386 Set of 2 8.50 8.50

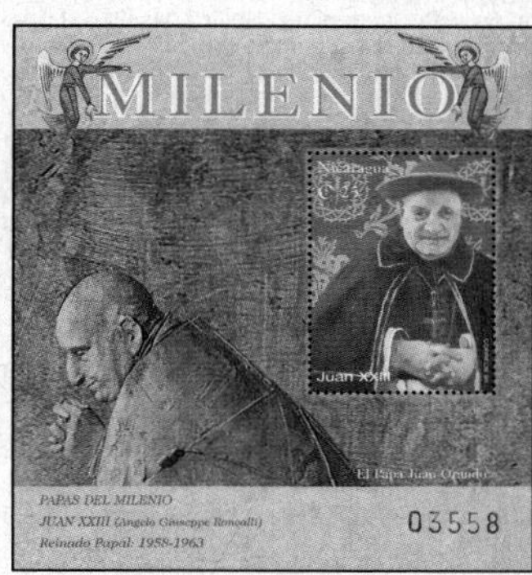

Millennium — A387

No. 2357: a, Pope Leo XIII. b, Rerum Novarum. c, Pope Pius X. d, Revision of ecclesiatic music. e, Pope Benedict XV. f, Canonization of Joan of Arc. g, Pope Pius XI. h, Establishment of Radio Vatican. i, Pope John XXIII. j, Peace symbol. k, Pope Paul VI. l, Arms of Paul VI. m, Pope John Paul I. n, Lamb and cross. o, Pope John Paul II. p, Globe, hands holding dove.

No. 2358, 25cor, John XXIII. No. 2359, 25cor, John Paul II.

2000, Sept. 7 *Perf. 13¼*

2357 A387 3cor Sheet of 16, #a-p + label 8.25 8.25

Souvenir Sheets

2358-2359 A387 Set of 2 8.50 8.50

No. 2357 contains sixteen 30x40mm stamps.

Butterflies — A388

No. 2360, 8cor: a, Catonephele numilla esite. b, Marpesia marcella. c, Heliconius hecalesia. d, Actinote thalia anteas. e, Doxocopa larentia cherubina. f, Napeogenes tolosa mombachoensis.

No. 2361, 9cor: a, Heliconius cydno galanthus. b, Nessaea agiaura. c, Godyris zavaleta sosunga. d, Caligo atreus dionysos. e, Morpho amatonte. f, Eryphanis polyxena lycomedon.

No. 2362, 25cor, Papilio garamas. No. 2363, 25cor, Cithaerias menander.

2000, Sept. 27 *Perf. 14*

Sheets of 6, #a-f

2360-2361 A388 Set of 2 17.50 17.50

Souvenir Sheets

2362-2363 A388 Set of 2 8.50 8.50

20th Century National Leaders — A389

No. 2364, 5cor: a, Kemal Ataturk, dam. b, Ataturk, Turkish flag, horiz. c, John F. Kennedy, wife Jacqueline, Soviet missiles, horiz. d, John F. Kennedy, rocket. e, Winston Churchill, bomb explosion. f, Churchill, airplane, horiz. g, Jomo Kenyatta, tribesman, animals, horiz. h, Kenyatta, Mt. Kenya.

No. 2365, 5cor: a, Indira Gandhi. b, Indira Gandhi, soldier, elephant, horiz. c, Ronald Reagan, airplanes, horiz. d, Reagan, American flags. e, Lenin. f, Lenin, hammer and sickle, horiz. g, Charles de Gaulle, Eiffel Tower, horiz. h, De Gaulle, monument.

No. 2366, 25cor, Chiang Kai-shek. No. 2367, 25cor, Theodore Roosevelt.

2000, Oct. 5 *Perf. 14*

Sheets of 8, #a-h

2364-2365 A389 Set of 2 14.00 14.00

Souvenir Sheets

2366-2367 A389 Set of 2 8.50 8.50

Horizontal stamps are 56x42mm.

Lions Intl. — A390

No. 2368, horiz.: a, Melvin Jones and other founding members, Chicago, 1917. b, Old headquarters building, Chicago. c, Helen Keller and dog. d, UN Secretary General Kofi Annan greeting Lions Intl. Pres. Kajit Hadananda. e, Jones and globe. f, André de Villiers, winner of 1998-99 Peace Poster contest.

2000, Oct. 26 **Litho.**

2368 A390 5cor Sheet of 6, #a-f 5.25 5.25

Souvenir Sheet

2369 A390 25cor Melvin Jones 4.25 4.25

Rotary Intl. — A391

No. 2370: a, Clowns and child in Great Britain. b, Polio vaccination in Egypt. c, Burkina Faso natives at well. d, School for girls in Nepal. e, Assisting the disabled in Australia. f, Discussing problem of urban violence.

2000, Oct. 26 *Perf. 14*

2370 A391 7cor Sheet of 6, #a-f 7.25 7.25

Souvenir Sheet

2371 A391 25cor Rotary emblem 4.25 4.25

Campaign Against AIDS A392

2000, Dec. 1 **Litho.** *Perf. 13¼*

2372 A392 7.50cor multi 1.25 1.25

Third Conference of States Signing Ottawa Convention — A393

Designs: 7.50cor, People, world map. 10cor, People opposing land mines on globe.

2001, Sept. 18 *Perf. 13x13½*

2373-2374 A393 Set of 2 2.60 2.60

Miniature Sheet

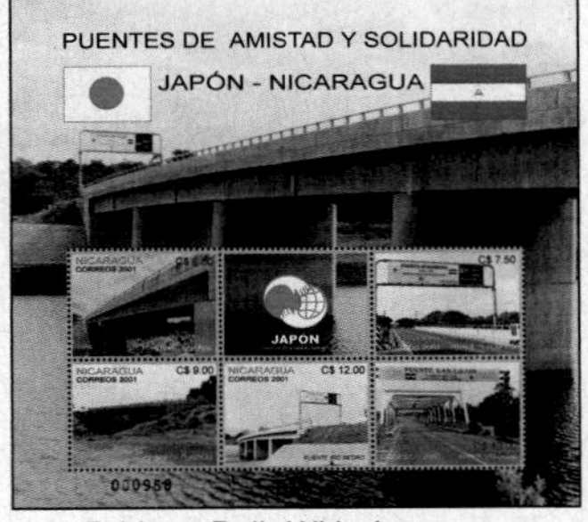

Bridges Built With Japanese Assistance — A394

No. 2375: a, 6.50cor, Tamarindo Bridge. b, 7.50cor, Ochomogo Bridge. c, 9cor, Gil González Bridge. d, 10cor, Las Lajas Bridge. e, 12cor, Río Negro Bridge.

2001, Oct. 23 *Perf. 13x13¼*

2375 A394 Sheet of 5, #a-e, + label 6.75 6.75

World Post Day — A395

2001, Nov. 21 *Perf. 13½*

2376 A395 6.50cor multi .95 .95

Dated 2000.

America Issue — Old Léon Ruins, UNESCO World Heritage Site A396

2001, Nov. 23 *Perf. 13½*

2377 A396 10cor multi 1.50 1.50

Order of Piarists in Nicaragua, 50th Anniv. — A397

Perf. 13¼x13½

2001, Nov. 27 **Litho.**

2378 A397 7cor multi 1.00 1.00

Dated 2000.

Miniature Sheet

Endangered Wildlife — A398

No. 2379: a, 5cor, Rhamphastos swaisonii. b, 6.50cor, Amazona auropalliata. c, 8cor, Buteo magnirostris. d, 9cor, Atteles geoffroyi. 10cor, Leopardus wiedii. 12cor, Puma concolor.

2001, Nov. 27 *Perf. 13¼x13*

2379 A398 Sheet of 6, #a-f 7.50 7.50

Dated 2000.

SOS Children's Villages, 50th Anniv. — A399

2001, Dec. 6 *Perf. 13¼x13½*

2380 A399 5.50cor multi .80 .80

Dated 2000.

Miguel Cardinal Obando Bravo A400

2002, Jan. 3 **Litho.** *Perf. 13½*

2381 A400 6.50cor multi —

Visit of UN Secretary General Kofi Annan to Nicaragua A402

2002, Mar. 15 **Litho.** *Perf. 13¼*

2383 A402 14cor multi 2.25 2.25

Sister Maria Romero A403

2002, Apr. 9 *Perf. 13x13¼*

2384 A403 7.50cor multi 1.25 1.25

Discovery of Nicaragua, 500th Anniv. A404

Design: 12cor, Natives watching ships on horizon, vert.

2002, Sept. 12 **Litho.** *Perf. 13x13¼*

2385 A404 7.50cor shown 1.25 1.25

Souvenir Sheet

Perf. 13¼x13

2386 A404 12cor multi 1.75 1.75

America Issue - Youth, Education and Literacy — A405

2002, Nov. 29 Litho. ***Perf. 13¼x13***
2387 A405 7.50cor multi 1.25 1.25

Canonization of St. Josemaría Escrivá de Balaguer — A406

2002, Nov. 29 ***Perf. 13x13¼***
2388 A406 2.50cor multi .40 .40

Port of Corinto A407

2002, Dec. 10
2389 A407 5cor multi .80 .80

Managua Earthquake, 30th Anniv. — A408

Pictures of earthquake damage: 3.50cor, Avenida del Mercado Central. 7.50cor, Managua Cathedral, vert.
Illustration reduced.

Perf. 13¼x13½, 13½x13¼
2002, Dec. 13
2390-2391 A408 Set of 2 1.75 1.75

Visit of Grand Duke Henri and Princess Maria Teresa of Luxembourg A409

2003, Feb. 5 ***Perf. 13¼x13***
2392 A409 12cor multi 1.90 1.90

Paintings — A410

Designs: 3cor, En Diriamba de Nicaragua, Capturaronme Amigo, by Roger Pérez de la Rocha. 5cor, San Gabriel Arcangel, by Orlando Sobalvarro. 6.50cor, Ava Fénix, by Alejandro Aróstegui. 7.50cor, Abstracción de Frutas, by Leonel Vanegas. 8cor, Suite en Turquesa y Azules, by Bernard Dreyfus, horiz. 9cor, Ana III, by Armando Morales, horiz. 10cor, Coloso IV, by Arnoldo Guillén, horiz.

Perf. 14x13½, 13½x14
2003, Oct. 23 Litho.
2393-2399 A410 Set of 7 6.50 6.50

Souvenir Sheet

Pontificate of Pope John Paul II, 25th Anniv. — A411

No. 2400: a, 3cor, Pope wearing zucchetto. b, 10cor, Pope wearing miter.

2003, Oct. 28 Litho. ***Perf. 13¼x13***
2400 A411 Sheet of 2, #a-b 1.90 1.90

Christian Brothers (La Salle Order) in Nicaragua, Cent. — A412

Designs: 3cor, San Juan de Dios Hospice, horiz. 5cor, Brother Octavio de Jesús. 6.50cor, Brother Bodrán Marie. 7.50cor, Brother Agustin Hervé. 9cor, Brother Vauthier de Jesús. 10cor, Father Mariano Dubón.
12cor, St. Jean-Baptiste de la Salle.

Perf. 13½x14, 14x13½
2003, Nov. 14 Litho.
2401-2406 A412 Set of 6 5.50 5.50

Souvenir Sheet

2407 A412 12cor multi 1.60 1.60

Insects — A413

No. 2408, 6.50cor: a, Fulgora laternaria. b, Acraephia perspicillata. c, Copidocephala guttata. d, Pterodictya reticularis. e, Phrictus quinquepartitus. f, Odontoptera carrenoi.
No. 2409, 8cor: a, Golofa pizarro. b, Phaneus pyrois. c, Plusiotis aurigans. d, Polyphylla concurrens. e, Dynastes hercules septentrionalis. f, Phaneus demon excelsus.

2003, Nov. 19 ***Perf. 13x13½***
Sheets of 6, #a-f
2408-2409 A413 Set of 2 11.50 11.50

Contemporary Crafts — A414

Designs: 3cor, Marble sculpture, vert. 5cor, Dolls. 6.50cor, Balsa wood fish and birds. 7.50cor, Cord and jipijapa hats. 8cor, Ceramics. 9cor, Saddle. 10cor, Clay rendition of Léon Cathedral.

Perf. 14x13½, 13½x14
2003, Nov. 20
2410-2416 A414 Set of 7 6.50 6.50

Lake and River Mail Steamships A415

Designs: 3cor, Victoria. 5cor, Irma. 6.50cor, Hollenbeck. 7.50cor, Managua.

2003, Nov. 28 ***Perf. 13½x14***
2417-2420 A415 Set of 4 3.00 3.00

America Issue - Flora and Fauna A416

Designs: 10cor, Corytophanes cristatus. 12.50cor, Guaiacum sanctum.

2003, Dec. 4 ***Perf. 13x13¼***
2421-2422 A416 Set of 2 3.00 3.00

San Juan del Sur, 150th Anniv. A417

2003, Dec. 9 Litho.
2423 A417 10cor multi 1.40 1.40

Miniature Sheet

Toyota Motor Vehicles — A418

No. 2424: a, 1936 Model AA. b, 1936 Model AB Phaeton. c, 1947 Model SA. d, 1951 Model BJ. e, 1955 Model Crown RSD. f, 1958 Model FJ28VA.

2003, Dec. 11
2424 A418 7.50cor Sheet of 6, #a-f 6.00 6.00

Publication of Tierras Solares, by Rubén Darío, Cent. A419

2004, June 22 ***Perf. 13x13¼***
2425 A419 10cor multi 1.25 1.25

Flora A420

Designs: 3cor, Tabebuia rosea. 5cor, Cassia fistula. 6.50cor, Delonix regia.

2004, June 24
2426-2428 A420 Set of 3 1.90 1.90

America Issue - Environmental Protection — A421

Designs: No. 2429, 7.50cor, Bosawas Río Bocay Biosphere Reserve. No. 2430, 7.50cor, Cerro Kilambé Nature Reserve.

2004, June 30
2429-2430 A421 Set of 2 1.90 1.90

2004 Summer Olympics, Athens — A422

Designs: 7.50cor, Track athletes. 10cor, Swimmers. 12cor, Rifleman.

2004, Aug. 13 ***Perf. 13¼x13***
2431-2433 A422 Set of 3 3.75 3.75

Central American Student's Games, Managua A423

Designs: 3cor, Judo. 5cor, Soccer, baseball. 6.50cor, High jump, swimming.

2004, Sept. 17
2434-2436 A423 Set of 3 1.90 1.90

Birds — A424

Designs: 5cor, Selenidera spectabilis. 6.50cor, Nycticorax nycticorax. 7.50cor, Caracara plancus. 10cor, Myiozetetes similis.

2004, Sept. 28 Litho.
2437-2440 A424 Set of 4 3.75 3.75

Granada Railroad Station A425

2004, Oct. 8 ***Perf. 13x13¼***
2441 A425 3cor multi .40 .40

Tourist Attractions A426

Designs: No. 2442, 7.50cor, Río Tapou, Río San Juan Forest Refuge. No. 2443, 7.50cor, Mombacho Volcano Natural Reserve.

2004, Oct. 12
2442-2443 A426 Set of 2 1.90 1.90

Contemporary Paintings — A427

Designs: 3cor, Frutas Ocultas, by Federico Nordalm. 7.50cor, Nicaraguapa, by Efrén Medina, vert. 10cor, Bambues, by Genaro Lugo.

2004, Nov. 4 ***Perf. 13x13¼, 13¼x13***
2444-2446 A427 Set of 3 2.60 2.60

Dogma of the Immaculate Conception, 150th Anniv. — A428

2004, Dec. 6 ***Perf. 13¼x13***
2447 A428 3cor multi .40 .40

Pablo Neruda (1904-73), Poet — A429

2004, Dec. 16
2448 A429 7.50cor multi .95 .95

Publication of *Songs of Life and Hope,* by Rubén Darío, Cent. — A430

Illustration reduced.

2005, Feb. 7 Litho. ***Perf. 13¼x13½***
2449 A430 7.50col multi + label .95 .95

Souvenir Sheet

Nicaragua — Japan Diplomatic Relations, 70th Anniv. — A431

No. 2450: a, 3col, Adult volunteer teaching student. b, 7.50col, Momotombo Volcano. c, 10col, Vado Bridge, Bocana de Paiwas. d, 12col, Flowers.

2005, Feb. 21 ***Perf. 13x13¼***
2450 A431 Sheet of 4, #a-d 4.00 4.00

Orchids — A432

Designs: 3.50cor, Eleanthus hymeniformis. 5cor, Laelia superbens. 6.50cor, Cattleya aurentiaca. 7.50cor, Bletia roezlii. 10cor, Dimerandra emarginata. 12cor, Epidendrum werckleii.
25cor, Cyhysis tricostata.

2005 Litho. ***Perf. 13¼x13***
2451-2456 A432 Set of 6 5.50 5.50

Souvenir Sheet

2457 A432 25cor multi 3.00 3.00

Endangered Reptiles and Amphibians — A433

Designs: 3cor, Dendrobates pumilio. 6.50cor, Drymodius melanotropis. 7.50cor, Cochranella granulosa. 10cor, Bolitoglossa mombachoensis. 12cor, Caiman crocodilus. 15cor, Polychrus gutturosus.
25cor, Lepidochelys olivacea.

2005 Litho. ***Perf. 13x13¼***
2458-2463 A433 Set of 6 6.75 6.75

Souvenir Sheet

2464 A433 25cor multi 3.00 3.00

Intl. Year of Microcredit A434

2005 Litho. ***Perf. 13¼x13***
2465 A434 3.50col multi .45 .45

Europa Stamps, 50th Anniv. A435

Designs: Nos. 2466, 2470a, 14col, Morpho peleides. Nos. 2467, 2470b, 14col, Amazona autumnalis. Nos. 2468, 2470c, 15col, Rubén Dario Monument. Nos. 2469, 2470d, 25col, Antigua Cathedral, Managua.

2006 ***Perf. 13¾x13½***
2466-2469 A435 Set of 4 8.00 8.00

Souvenir Sheet

Imperf

2470 A435 Sheet of 4, #a-d 8.00 8.00

No. 2470 contains four 40x30mm stamps.

Souvenir Sheet

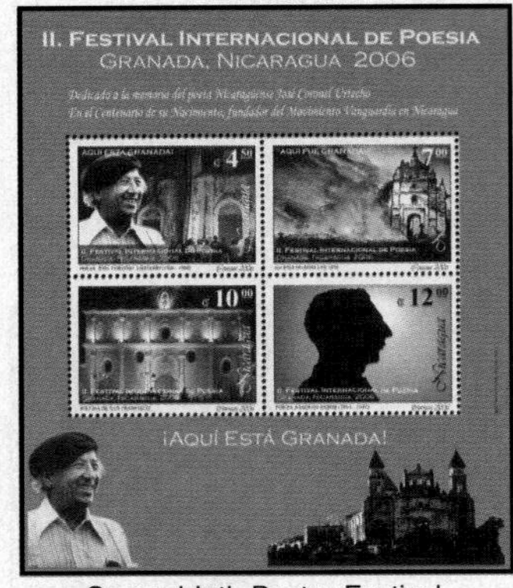

Second Intl. Poetry Festival, Granada — A436

No. 2471: a, 4.50col, Jose Coronel Urtecho (1906-94), poet. b, 7col, Guadalupe Church, 1856. c, 10col, Church of St. Francis. d, 12col, Joaquin Pasos (1914-47), poet.

2006 Litho. ***Perf. 14***
2471 A436 Sheet of 4, #a-d 3.75 3.75

Environmental Protection — A437

Designs: 4.50col, Casmerodius albus. 11.50col, Amazilia tzacatl. 13.50col, Jacana spinosa. 14.50col, Mico River.

2007 Litho. ***Perf. 13x13¼***
2472-2475 A437 Set of 4 4.75 4.75

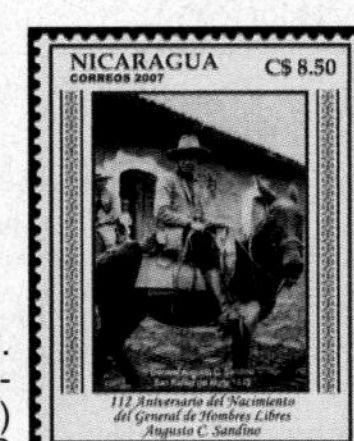

Gen. Augusto C. Sandino (1893-1934) A438

Various photographs of Sandino: 8.50col, 10.50col, 12.50col.

2007 ***Perf. 13¼x13***
2476-2478 A438 Set of 3 3.50 3.50

Land Mine Clearance Program, 15th Anniv. A439

2007 Litho. ***Perf. 13x13¼***
2479 A439 19col multi 2.10 2.10

Literacy Campaign, 27th Anniv. — A440

Various literacy campaign workers and students: 1col, 2col, 2.50col, 4.50col.

2007 ***Perf. 13¼x13***
2480-2483 A440 Set of 4 1.10 1.10

AIR POST STAMPS

Counterfeits exist of almost all scarce surcharges among Nos. C1-C66.

Regular Issues of 1914-28 Overprinted in Red

1929, May 15 Unwmk. ***Perf. 12***

C1	A24 25c orange	1.75	1.75
a.	Double overprint, one inverted	50.00	
b.	Inverted overprint	50.00	
c.	Double overprint	50.00	
C2	A24 25c blk brn	2.25	2.25
a.	Double overprint, one inverted	50.00	
b.	Double overprint	50.00	
c.	Inverted overprint	30.00	

There are numerous varieties in the setting of the overprint. The most important are: Large "1" in "1929" and large "A" in "Aereo" and "P. A. A."

Similar Overprint on Regular Issue of 1929 in Red

1929, June

C3	A24 25c dk vio	1.25	.75
a.	Double overprint	50.00	
b.	Inverted overprint	50.00	
c.	Double overprint, one inverted	50.00	
	Nos. C1-C3 (3)	5.25	4.75

The stamps in the bottom row of the sheet have the letters "P. A. A." larger than usual.

Similar overprints, some including an airplane, have been applied to postage issues of 1914-20, officials of 1926 and Nos. 401-407. These are, at best, essays.

Airplanes over Mt. Momotombo — AP1

1929, Dec. 15 **Engr.**

C4	AP1 25c olive blk	.50	.40
C5	AP1 50c blk brn	.75	.75
C6	AP1 1cor org red	1.00	1.00
	Nos. C4-C6 (3)	2.25	2.15

See Nos. C18-C19, C164-C168. For surcharges and overprints see Nos. C7-C8, C14-C17, C25-C31, C106-C120, C135-C146, C150-C154, C169-C173, CO25-CO29.

No. C4 Surcharged in Red or Black

1930, May 15

C7 AP1 15c on 25c ol blk (R) .50 .40
 a. "$" inverted 3.50
 b. Double surcharge (R + Bk) 7.00
 c. As "b," red normal, blk invtd. 7.00
 d. Double red surch., one inverted 7.00
C8 AP1 20c on 25c ol blk (Bk) .75 .60
 a. "$" inverted 7.00
 b. Inverted surcharge 15.00

Nos. C1, C2 and C3 Surcharged in Green

1931, June 7

C9 A24 15c on 25c org 50.00 50.00
C10 A24 15c on 25c blk brn 100.00 100.00
C11 A24 15c on 25c dk vio 15.00 15.00
 c. Inverted surcharge 30.00
C12 A24 20c on 25c dk vio 10.00 10.00
 c. Inverted surcharge 50.00
 d. Double surcharge 50.00
C13 A24 20c on 25c blk brn *375.00*

No. C13 was not regularly issued.

"1391"

C9a A24 15c on 25c
C10a A24 15c on 25c
C11a A24 15c on 25c 60.00
 d. As "a," inverted 400.00
C12a A24 20c on 25c 25.00
 e. As "a," inverted 400.00
 g. As "a," double 400.00
C13a A24 20c on 25c

"1921"

C9b A24 15c on 25c
C10b A24 15c on 25c 400.00
C11b A24 15c on 25c 60.00
 e. As "b," inverted 400.00
C12b A24 20c on 25c 25.00
 f. As "b," inverted 400.00
 h. As "b," double 400.00
C13b A24 20c on 25c

Nos. C8, C4-C6 Surcharged in Blue

1931, June

C14 AP1 15c on 20c on 25c 9.00 9.00
 b. Blue surcharge inverted 25.00
 c. "$" in blk, surch. invtd. 50.00
 d. Blue surch. dbl., one invtd. 25.00
C15 AP1 15c on 25c 5.50 5.50
 b. Blue surcharge inverted 25.00
 c. Double surch., one invtd. 25.00
C16 AP1 15c on 50c 40.00 40.00
C17 AP1 15c on 1cor 100.00 100.00
 Nos. C14-C17 (4) 154.50 154.50

"1391"

C14a AP1 15c on 20c on 25c 50.00
C15a AP1 15c on 25c 30.00
C16a AP1 15c on 50c 80.00
C17a AP1 15c on 1cor 225.00
 Nos. C14a-C17a (4) 385.00

Momotombo Type of 1929

1931, July 8

C18 AP1 15c deep violet .20 .20
C19 AP1 20c deep green .40 .40

Managua Post Office Before and After Earthquake AP2

Without gum, Soft porous paper

1932, Jan. 1 **Litho.** ***Perf. 11***

C20 AP2 15c lilac 1.50 *1.25*
 a. 15c violet 22.50
 b. Vert. pair, imperf. btwn. 35.00
C21 AP2 20c emerald 2.00
 b. Horizontal pair, imperf. between 35.00
C22 AP2 25c yel brn 6.50
 b. Vertical pair, imperf. between 60.00
C23 AP2 50c yel brn 8.00
C24 AP2 1cor dp car 12.00
 a. Vert. or horiz. pair, imperf. btwn. 80.00
 Nos. C20-C24 (5) 30.00

Sheets of 10. See note after No. 568.

For overprint and surcharges see #C44-C46.

Reprints: see note following No. 568. Value $1 each.

Nos. C5 and C6 Surcharged in Red or Black

1932, July 12 ***Perf. 12***

C25 AP1 30c on 50c (Bk) 1.50 1.50
 a. "Valc" 25.00
 b. Double surcharge 15.00
 c. Double surch., one inverted 15.00
 d. Period omitted after "O" 25.00
 e. As "a," double 300.00
C26 AP1 35c on 50c (R) 1.50 1.50
 a. "Valc" 30.00
 b. Double surcharge 12.00
 c. Double surch., one inverted 12.00
 d. As "a," double 300.00
C27 AP1 35c on 50c (Bk) 35.00 35.00
 a. "Valc" 250.00
C28 AP1 40c on 1cor (Bk) 1.75 1.75
 a. "Valc" 25.00
 b. Double surcharge 15.00
 c. Double surch., one inverted 15.00
 d. Inverted surcharge 15.00
 e. As "a," inverted 300.00
 f. As "a," double 300.00
C29 AP1 55c on 1cor (R) 1.75 1.75
 a. "Valc" 25.00
 b. Double surcharge 12.00
 c. Double surch., one inverted 12.00
 d. Inverted surcharge 12.00
 e. As "a," inverted 300.00
 f. As "a," double 300.00
 Nos. C25-C29 (5) 41.50 41.50

No. C18 Overprinted in Red

1932, Sept. 11

C30 AP1 15c dp vio 70.00 70.00
 a. "Aerreo" 150.00 150.00
 b. Invtd. "m" in "Septiembre" 150.00

International Air Mail Week.

No. C6 Surcharged

1932, Oct. 12

C31 AP1 8c on 1 cor org red 20.00 20.00
 a. "1232" 30.00 30.00
 b. 2nd "u" of "Inauguration" invtd. 30.00 30.00

Inauguration of airmail service to the interior.

Regular Issue of 1932 Overprinted in Red

1932, Oct. 24 ***Perf. 11½***

Without Gum

C32 A40 1c yel brn 20.00 20.00
 a. Inverted overprint 125.00 125.00
C33 A40 2c carmine 20.00 20.00
 a. Inverted overprint 125.00 125.00
 b. Double overprint 100.00 100.00
C34 A40 3c ultra 9.50 9.50
 a. Inverted overprint 150.00 150.00
 b. As "a," vert. pair, imperf. btwn. 500.00
C35 A40 4c dp ultra 9.50 9.50
 a. Inverted overprint 125.00 125.00
 b. Double overprint 100.00 100.00
 c. Vert. or horiz. pair, imperf. btwn. 300.00
C36 A40 5c yel brn 9.50 9.50
 a. Inverted overprint 125.00 125.00
 b. Vert. pair, imperf. btwn. 75.00
C37 A40 6c gray brn 9.50 9.50
 a. Inverted overprint 100.00 100.00
C38 A40 50c green 9.00 9.00
 a. Inverted overprint 125.00 125.00
C39 A40 1cor yellow 9.50 9.50
 a. Inverted overprint 125.00 125.00
 b. Horiz. pair, imperf. btwn. 200.00
 Nos. C32-C39 (8) 96.50 96.50

Nos. 564, C20-C21 exist overprinted as C32-C39. The editors believe they were not regularly issued.

Surcharged in Red

1932, Oct. 24

C40 A40 8c on 10c yel brn 9.00 9.00
 a. Inverted surcharge 125.00 125.00
C41 A40 16c on 20c org 9.00 9.00
 a. Inverted surcharge 125.00 125.00
C42 A40 24c on 25c dp vio 9.00 9.00
 a. Inverted surcharge 125.00 125.00
 b. Horiz. pair, imperf. vert. 300.00

Surcharged in Red as No. C40 but without the word "Vale"

C43 A40 8c on 10c yel brn 45.00 45.00
 a. Inverted surcharge 125.00 125.00
 b. Horiz. pair, imperf. vert. 300.00

No. C22 Overprinted in Red

1932, Oct. 24

C44 AP2 25c yel brn 8.00 8.00
 a. Inverted overprint 125.00 125.00

Nos. C23 and C24 Surcharged in Red

Interior—1932

Vale C 0.32

1932, Oct. 24

C45 AP2 32c on 50c yel brn 9.50 9.50
 a. Inverted surcharge 125.00 125.00
 b. "Interior-1932" inverted 150.00 150.00
 c. "Vale $0.32" inverted 150.00 150.00
 d. Horiz. pair, imperf. btwn. 200.00
C46 AP2 40c on 1cor car 7.00 7.00
 a. Inverted surcharge 125.00 125.00
 b. "Vale $0.40" inverted 200.00 200.00

Nos. 557-558 Overprinted in Black like Nos. C32 to C39

1932, Nov. 16

C47 A40 1c yel brn 25.00 22.50
 a. "1232" 45.00 45.00
 b. Inverted overprint 125.00 125.00
 c. Double ovpt., one invtd. 125.00 125.00
 d. As "a," inverted 500.00
C48 A40 2c dp car 20.00 17.50
 a. "1232" 45.00 45.00
 b. Inverted overprint 125.00 125.00
 c. As "a," inverted 500.00

Excellent counterfeits exist of Nos. C27, C30-C48. Forged overprints and surcharges as on Nos. C32-C48 exist on reprints of Nos. C20-C24.

Regular Issue of 1914-32 Surcharged in Black

1932 ***Perf. 12***

C49 A25 1c on 2c brt rose .35 .30
C50 A24 2c on 3c lt bl .35 .30
C51 A25 3c on 4c dk bl .35 .30
C52 A24 4c on 5c gray brn .35 .30
C53 A25 5c on 6c ol brn .35 .30
C54 A25 6c on 10c lt brn .35 .30
 a. Double surcharge 25.00
C55 A24 8c on 15c org red .35 .30
C56 A25 16c on 20c org .35 .35
C57 A24 24c on 25c dk vio 1.40 1.00
C58 A24 25c on 25c dk vio 1.40 1.00
 a. Double surcharge 25.00
C59 A25 32c on 50c grn 1.40 1.25
C60 A25 40vc on 50c grn 1.60 1.40
C61 A25 50c on 1cor yel 2.25 2.25
C62 A25 1cor on 1cor yel 3.00 3.00
 Nos. C49-C62 (14) 13.85 12.35

Nos. C49-C62 exist with inverted surcharge.

In addition to C49 to C62, four other stamps, Type A25, exist with this surcharge:
40c on 50c bister brown, black surcharge.
1cor on 2c bright rose, black surcharge.
1cor on 1cor yellow, red surcharge.
1cor on 1cor dull violet, black surcharge.
The editors believe they were not regularly issued.

Surcharged on Nos. 548, 547

1932

C65 A24 24c on 25c dk vio 45.00 45.00
C66 A24 25c on 25c blk brn 50.00 50.00

Counterfeits of Nos. C65 and C66 are plentiful.

Rivas Railroad Issue

La Chocolata Cut — AP3

El Nacascola — AP4

Designs: 25c, Cuesta cut. 50c, Mole of San Juan del Sur. 1cor, View of El Estero.

1932, Dec. **Litho.**

Soft porous paper

C67 AP3 15c dk vio 20.00
C68 AP4 20c bl grn 20.00
C69 AP4 25c dk brn 20.00
C70 AP4 50c blk brn 20.00
C71 AP4 1cor rose red 20.00
 Nos. C67-C71 (5) 100.00

Inauguration of the railroad from San Jorge to San Juan del Sur, Dec. 18, 1932. Printed in sheets of 4, without gum.

Reprints: see note following No. 574. Value, $6 each.

Leon-Sauce Railroad Issue

"Fill" at Santa Lucia River AP5

Designs: 15c, Bridge at Santa Lucia. 25c, Malpaicillo Station. 50c, Panoramic view. 1cor, San Andres.

1932, Dec. 30

Soft porous paper

No.	Type	Description	Unused	Used
C72	AP5	15c purple	20.00	
C73	AP5	20c bl grn	20.00	
C74	AP5	25c dk brn	20.00	
C75	AP5	50c blk brn	20.00	
C76	AP5	1cor rose red	20.00	
		Nos. C72-C76 (5)	100.00	

Inauguration of the railroad from Leon to El Sauce, 12/30/32. Sheets of 4, without gum.

Reprints: see note following No. 579. Value, $6 each.

Flag of the Race Issue

1933, Aug. 3 Litho. *Rouletted 9*

Without gum

No.	Type	Description	Unused	Used
C77	A43	1c dk brn	1.50	1.50
C78	A43	2c red vio	1.50	1.50
C79	A43	4c violet	2.50	2.25
C80	A43	5c dl bl	2.25	2.25
C81	A43	6c vio bl	2.25	2.25
C82	A43	8c dp brn	.70	.70
C83	A43	15c ol brn	.70	.70
C84	A43	20c yellow	2.25	2.25
a.		Horiz. pair, imperf. btwn.	15.00	
b.		Horiz. pair, imperf. vert.	15.00	
C85	A43	25c orange	2.25	2.25
C86	A43	50c rose	2.25	2.25
C87	A43	1cor green	11.00	11.00
		Nos. C77-C87 (11)	29.15	28.90

See note after No. 599. Printed in sheets of 10.

Reprints exist, shades differ from postage and official stamps.

Imperf., Pairs

No.	Type	Description	Value
C78a	A43	2c	14.00
C79a	A43	4c	10.00
C81a	A43	6c	10.00
C82a	A43	8c	10.00
C83a	A43	15c	10.00
C87a	A43	1cor	30.00

AP7

1933, Nov. *Perf. 12*

No.	Type	Description	Unused	Used
C88	AP7	10c bis brn	1.50	1.50
a.		Vert. pair, imperf. between	35.00	
C89	AP7	15c violet	1.25	1.25
a.		Vert. pair, imperf. between	37.50	
C90	AP7	25c red	1.40	1.40
a.		Horiz. pair, imperf. between	22.50	
C91	AP7	50c dp bl	1.50	1.50
		Nos. C88-C91 (4)	5.65	5.65

Intl. Air Post Week, Nov. 6-11, 1933. Printed in sheets of 4. Counterfeits exist.

Stamps and Types of 1928-31 Surcharged in Black

1933, Nov. 3

No.	Type	Description	Unused	Used
C92	A25	1c on 2c grn	.20	.20
C93	A24	2c on 3c ol gray	.20	.20
C94	A25	3c on 4c car rose	.20	.20
C95	A24	4c on 5c lt bl	.20	.20
C96	A25	5c on 6c dk bl	.20	.20
C97	A25	6c on 10c ol brn	.20	.20
C98	A24	8c on 15c bis brn	.20	.20
C99	A25	16c on 20c brn	.20	.20
C100	A24	24c on 25c ver	.20	.20
C101	A25	25c on 25c org	.25	.20
C102	A25	32c on 50c vio	.20	.20
C103	A25	40c on 50c grn	.20	.20
C104	A25	50c on 1cor yel	.20	.20
C105	A25	1cor on 1cor org red	.35	.25
		Nos. C92-C105 (14)	3.00	2.85

Nos. C100, C102-C105 exist without script control overprint. Value, each $1.50.

Type of Air Post Stamps of 1929 Surcharged in Black

1933, Oct. 28

No.	Type	Description	Unused	Used
C106	AP1	30c on 50c org red	.25	.20
C107	AP1	35c on 50c lt bl	.25	.20
C108	AP1	40c on 1cor yel	.40	.20
C109	AP1	55c on 1cor grn	.30	.25
		Nos. C106-C109 (4)	1.20	.85

No. C19 Surcharged in Red

1934, Mar. 31

No.	Type	Description	Unused	Used
C110	AP1	10c on 20c grn	.30	.25
a.		Inverted surcharge	15.00	
b.		Double surcharge, one inverted	15.00	
c.		"Ceutroamericano"	10.00	

No. C110 with black surcharge is believed to be of private origin.

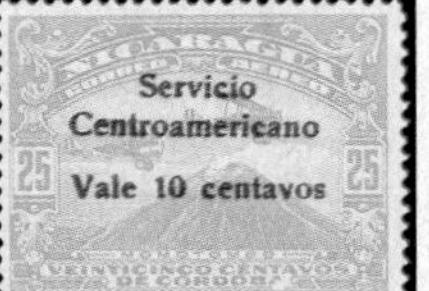

No. C4 Surcharged in Red

1935, Aug.

No.	Type	Description	Unused	Used
C111	AP1	10c on 25c ol blk	.25	.25
a.		Small "v" in "vale" (R)	5.00	
b.		"centrvos" (R)	5.00	
c.		Double surcharge (R)	25.00	
d.		Inverted surcharge (R)	25.00	
g.		As "a," inverted	400.00	
h.		As "a," double	400.00	

No. C111 with blue surcharge is believed to be private origin.

The editors do not recognize the Nicaraguan air post stamps overprinted in red "VALIDO 1935" in two lines and with or without script control marks as having been issued primarily for postal purposes.

Nos C4-C6, C18-C19 Overprinted Vertically in Blue, Reading Up:

1935-36

No.	Type	Description	Unused	Used
C112	AP1	15c dp vio	1.00	1.00
C113	AP1	20c dp grn	1.75	1.75
C114	AP1	25c ol blk	2.25	2.25
C115	AP1	50c blk brn	5.00	5.00
C116	AP1	1cor org red	40.00	40.00
		Nos. C112-C116 (5)	50.00	50.00

Same Overprint on Nos. C106-C109 Reading Up or Down

No.	Type	Description	Unused	Used
C117	AP1	30c on 50c org red	1.50	1.40
C118	AP1	35c on 50c lt bl	6.50	6.50
C119	AP1	40c on 1cor yel	6.50	6.50
C120	AP1	55c on 1cor grn	6.50	6.50
		Nos. C117-C120 (4)	21.00	20.90
		Nos. C112-C120 (9)	71.00	70.90

Same Overprint in Red on Nos. C92-C105

1936

No.	Type	Description	Unused	Used
C121	A25	1c on 2c grn	.20	.20
C122	A24	2c on 3c ol gray	.20	.20
C123	A25	3c on 4c car rose	.20	.20
C124	A24	4c on 5c lt bl	.20	.20
C125	A25	5c on 6c dk bl	.20	.20
C126	A25	6c on 10c ol brn	.20	.20
C127	A24	8c on 15c bis brn	.20	.20
C128	A25	16c on 20c brn	.25	.25
C129	A24	24c on 25c ver	.35	.30
C130	A24	25c on 25c org	.25	.25
C131	A25	32c on 50c vio	.20	.20
C132	A25	40c on 50c grn	.55	.50
C133	A25	50c on 1cor yel	.40	.25
C134	A25	1cor on 1cor org red	1.40	.65
		Nos. C121-C134 (14)	4.80	3.80

Nos. C121 to C134 are handstamped with script control mark.

Overprint Reading Down on No. C110

No.	Type	Description	Unused	Used
C135	AP1	10c on 20c grn	*350.00*	

This stamp has been extensively counterfeited.

Overprinted in Red on Nos. C4 to C6, C18 and C19

No.	Type	Description	Unused	Used
C136	AP1	15c dp vio	.55	.20
C137	AP1	20c dp grn	.65	.60
C138	AP1	25c ol blk	.65	.55
C139	AP1	50c blk brn	.55	.55
C140	AP1	1cor org red	1.10	.55

On Nos. C106 to C109

No.	Type	Description	Unused	Used
C141	AP1	30c on 50c org red	.65	.60
C142	AP1	35c on 50c lt bl	.65	.40
C143	AP1	40c on 1cor yel	.65	.55
C144	AP1	55c on 1cor grn	.65	.50

Same Overprint in Red or Blue on No. C111 Reading Up or Down

No.	Type	Description	Unused	Used
C145	AP1	10c on 25c, down	.55	.45
a.		"Centrvos"	25.00	
C146	AP1	10c on 25c (Bl), up	1.25	1.00
a.		"Centrvos"	25.00	
		Nos. C136-C146 (11)	7.90	5.95

Overprint on No. C145 is at right, on No. C146 in center.

Nos. C92, C93 and C98 Overprinted in Black

Resello 1936

1936

No.	Type	Description	Unused	Used
C147	A25	1c on 2c grn	.20	.20
C148	A24	2c on 3c ol gray	.20	.20
a.		"Resello 1936" dbl., one invtd.	2.50	
C149	A24	8c on 15c bis brn	.25	.25
		Nos. C147-C149 (3)	.65	.65

With script control handstamp.

Nos. C5 and C6 Surcharged in Red

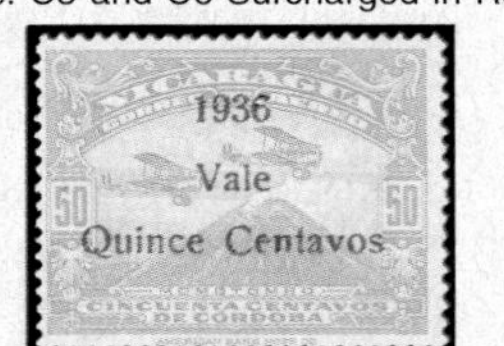

1936, Nov. 26

No.	Type	Description	Unused	Used
C150	AP1	15c on 50c blk brn	.20	.20
C151	AP1	15c on 1cor org red	.20	.20

Nos. C18 and C19 Overprinted in Carmine

1936, July 2

No.	Type	Description	Unused	Used
C152	AP1	15c dp vio	.35	.20
C153	AP1	20c dp grn	.35	.25

Overprint reading up or down.

No. C4 Surcharged and Overprinted in Red

No.	Type	Description	Unused	Used
C154	AP1	10c on 25c olive blk	.30	.30
a.		Surch. and ovpt. inverted	3.50	

Same Overprint in Carmine on Nos. C92 to C99

No.	Type	Description	Unused	Used
C155	A25	1c on 2c green	.20	.20
C156	A24	2c on 3c olive gray	.65	.65
C157	A25	3c on 4c car rose	.20	.20
C158	A24	4c on 5c light blue	.20	.20
C159	A25	5c on 6c dark blue	.20	.20
C160	A25	6c on 10c olive brn	.20	.20
C161	A24	8c on 15c bister brn	.20	.20
C162	A25	16c on 20c brown	.20	.20
		Nos. C154-C162 (9)	2.35	2.35

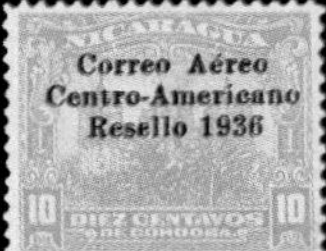

No. 518 Overprinted in Black

No.	Type	Description	Unused	Used
C163	A25	10c lt brn	.20	.20
a.		Overprint inverted	2.25	
b.		Double overprint	2.25	

Two fonts are found in the sheet of #C163.

Momotombo Type of 1929

1937

No.	Type	Description	Unused	Used
C164	AP1	15c yel org	.20	.20
C165	AP1	20c org red	.20	.20
C166	AP1	25c black	.20	.20
C167	AP1	50c violet	.25	.20
C168	AP1	1cor orange	.55	.20
		Nos. C164-C168 (5)	1.40	1.00

Surcharged in Black

1937

No.	Type	Description	Unused	Used
C169	AP1	30c on 50c car rose	.20	.20
C170	AP1	35c on 50c olive grn	.20	.20
C171	AP1	40c on 1cor green	.25	.20
C172	AP1	55c on 1cor blue	.20	.20
		Nos. C169-C172 (4)	.85	.80

No. C168 Surcharged in Violet

1937 Unwmk. *Perf. 12*

No.	Type	Description	Unused	Used
C173	AP1	10c on 1cor org	.20	.20
a.		"Centauos"	10.00	

No. C98 with Additional Overprint "1937"

No.	Type	Description	Unused	Used
C174	A24	8c on 15c bis brn	.45	.20
a.		"1937" double	6.50	

Nos. C92-C102 with Additional Overprint in Blue reading "HABILITADO 1937"

No.	Type	Description	Unused	Used
C175	A25	1c on 2c grn	.20	.20
a.		Blue overprint double	*2.50*	
C176	A24	2c on 3c ol gray	.20	.20
a.		Double surch., one inverted	*2.50*	
C177	A25	3c on 4c car rose	.20	.20
C178	A24	4c on 5c lt bl	.20	.20
C179	A25	5c on 6c dk bl	.20	.20
C180	A25	6c on 10c ol brn	.20	.20
C181	A24	8c on 15c bis brn	.20	.20
a.		"Habilitado 1937" double	3.50	
C182	A25	16c on 20c brn	.20	.20
a.		Double surcharge	2.50	
C183	A24	24c on 25c ver	.20	.20
C184	A24	25c on 25c org	.25	.20
C185	A25	32c on 50c vio	.25	.25
		Nos. C175-C185 (11)	2.30	2.25

Map of Nicaragua AP8

For Foreign Postage

1937, July 30 Engr.

No.	Type	Description	Unused	Used
C186	AP8	10c green	.20	.20
C187	AP8	15c dp bl	.20	.20
C188	AP8	20c yellow	.20	.20
C189	AP8	25c bl vio	.20	.20
C190	AP8	30c rose car	.25	.20
C191	AP8	50c org yel	.35	.20
C192	AP8	1cor ol grn	.70	.55
		Nos. C186-C192 (7)	2.10	1.75

Presidential Palace AP9

For Domestic Postage

C193 AP9 1c rose car .20 .20
C194 AP9 2c dp bl .20 .20
C195 AP9 3c ol grn .20 .20
C196 AP9 4c black .20 .20
C197 AP9 5c dk vio .20 .20
C198 AP9 6c chocolate .20 .20
C199 AP9 8c bl vio .20 .20
C200 AP9 16c org yel .25 .20
C201 AP9 24c yellow .20 .20
C202 AP9 25c yel grn .25 .20
Nos. C193-C202 (10) 2.10 2.00

No. C201 with green overprint "Union Panamericana 1890-1940" is of private origin.

Managua AP10

Designs: 15c, Presidential Palace. 20c, Map of South America. 25c, Map of Central America. 30c, Map of North America. 35c, Lagoon of Tiscapa, Managua. 40c, Road Scene. 45c, Park. 50c, Another park. 55c, Scene in San Juan del Sur. 75c, Tipitapa River. 1cor, Landscape.

Wmk. 209

1937, Sept. 17 Typo. *Perf. 11*

Center in Dark Blue

C203 AP10 10c yel grn 1.60 1.20
C204 AP10 15c orange 1.60 1.40
C205 AP10 20c red 1.00 1.00
C206 AP10 25c vio brn 1.00 1.00
C207 AP10 30c bl grn 1.00 1.00
a. Great Lakes omitted 40.00 40.00
C208 AP10 35c lemon .50 .45
C209 AP10 40c green .40 .40
C210 AP10 45c brt vio .40 .35
C211 AP10 50c rose lil .40 .35
a. Vert. pair, imperf. btwn. 140.00
C212 AP10 55c lt bl .40 .35
C213 AP10 75c gray grn .40 .35

Center in Brown Red

C214 AP10 1cor dk bl 1.00 .50
Nos. C203-C214 (12) 9.70 8.35

150th anniv. of the Constitution of the US.

Diriangen — AP11

Designs: 4c, 10c, Nicarao. 5c, 15c, Bartolomé de Las Casas. 8c, 20c, Columbus.

For Domestic Postage
Without gum

1937, Oct. 12 Unwmk. *Perf. 11*

C215 AP11 1c green .20 .20
C216 AP11 4c brn car .20 .20
C217 AP11 5c dk vio .20 .20
a. Without imprint .40
C218 AP11 8c dp bl .20 .20
a. Without imprint .50

For Foreign Postage
Wmk. 209
With Gum

C219 AP11 10c lt brn .20 .20
C220 AP11 15c pale bl .20 .20
a. Without imprint 1.00
C221 AP11 20c pale rose .20 .20
Nos. C215-C221 (7) 1.40 1.40

Nos. C215-C221 printed in sheets of 4.

Imperf., Pairs

C215a AP11 1c .20 .20
C216a AP11 4c .20 .20
C217b AP11 5c .20 .20
C217c AP11 5c Without imprint
C218b AP11 8c .20
C218c AP11 8c Without imprint
C219a AP11 10c .20 .20
C220b AP11 15c .25 .25
C220c AP11 15c Without imprint
C221a AP11 20c .35 .35

Gen. Tomas Martinez — AP11a

Design: 10c-50c, Gen. Anastasio Somoza.

For Domestic Postage
Without Gum

Perf. 11½, Imperf.

1938, Jan. 18 Typo. Unwmk.

Center in Black

C221B AP11a 1c orange .20 .20
C221C AP11a 5c red vio .20 .20
C221D AP11a 8c dk bl .25 .25
C221E AP11a 16c brown .25 .25
f. Sheet of 4, 1c, 5c, 8c, 16c 1.25 1.25

For Foreign Postage

C221G AP11a 10c green .25 .20
C221H AP11a 15c dk bl .25 .25
C221J AP11a 25c violet .40 .40
C221K AP11a 50c carmine .50 .45
m. Sheet of 4, 10c, 15c, 25c, 50c 2.00 2.00
Nos. C221B-C221K (8) 2.30 2.20

75th anniv. of postal service in Nicaragua. Printed in sheets of four.

Stamps of type AP11a exist in changed colors and with inverted centers, double centers and frames printed on the back. These varieties were private fabrications.

Lake Managua AP12

President Anastasio Somoza — AP13

For Domestic Postage

1939 Unwmk. Engr. *Perf. 12½*

C222 AP12 2c dp bl .20 .20
C223 AP12 3c green .20 .20
C224 AP12 8c pale lil .20 .20
C225 AP12 16c orange .20 .20
C226 AP12 24c yellow .20 .20
C227 AP12 32c dk grn .20 .20
C228 AP12 50c dp rose .20 .20

For Foreign Postage

C229 AP13 10c dk brn .20 .20
C230 AP13 15c dk bl .20 .20
C231 AP13 20c org yel .20 .20
C232 AP13 25c dk pur .20 .20
C233 AP13 30c lake .20 .20
C234 AP13 50c dp org .25 .20
C235 AP13 1cor dk ol grn .35 .40
Nos. C222-C235 (14) 3.00 3.00

For Domestic Postage

Will Rogers and View of Managua AP14

Designs: 2c, Rogers standing beside plane. 3c, Leaving airport office. 4c, Rogers and U.S. Marines. 5c, Managua after earthquake.

1939, Mar. 31 Engr. *Perf. 12*

C236 AP14 1c brt grn .20 .20
C237 AP14 2c org red .20 .20
C238 AP14 3c lt ultra .20 .20
C239 AP14 4c dk bl .20 .20
C240 AP14 5c rose car .20 .20
Nos. C236-C240 (5) 1.00 1.00

Will Rogers' flight to Managua after the earthquake, Mar. 31, 1931.

For surcharges see Nos. 686, 688.

Pres. Anastasio Somoza in US House of Representatives — AP19

President Somoza and US Capitol AP20

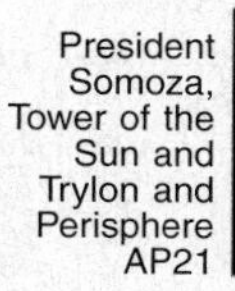

President Somoza, Tower of the Sun and Trylon and Perisphere AP21

For Domestic Postage

1940, Feb. 1

C241 AP19 4c red brn .20 .20
C242 AP20 8c blk brn .20 .20
C243 AP19 16c grnsh bl .20 .20
C244 AP20 20c brt plum .50 .30
C245 AP21 32c scarlet .20 .20

For Foreign Postage

C246 AP19 25c dp bl .20 .20
C247 AP19 30c black .20 .20
C248 AP20 50c rose pink .45 .40
C249 AP21 60c green .50 .30
C250 AP19 65c dk vio brn .50 .20
C251 AP19 90c ol grn .65 .30
C252 AP21 1cor violet 1.00 .55
Nos. C241-C252 (12) 4.80 3.25

Visit of Pres. Somoza to US in 1939.

For surcharge see No. C636.

L. S. Rowe, Statue of Liberty, Nicaraguan Coastline, Flags of 21 American Republics, US Shield and Arms of Nicaragua — AP22

1940, Aug. 2 Engr. *Perf. 12½*

C253 AP22 1.25cor multi .65 .60

50th anniversary of Pan American Union.

For overprint see No. C493.

First Nicaraguan Postage Stamp and Sir Rowland Hill — AP23

1941, Apr. 4

C254 AP23 2cor brown 2.50 .80
C255 AP23 3cor dk bl 8.25 1.40
C256 AP23 5cor carmine 22.50 3.50
Nos. C254-C256 (3) 33.25 5.70

Centenary of the first postage stamp.

Nos. C254-C256 imperf. are proofs.

Rubén Darío AP24

1941, Dec. 23

C257 AP24 20c pale lil .25 .20
C258 AP24 35c yel grn .30 .20
C259 AP24 40c org yel .40 .20
C260 AP24 60c lt bl .65 .30
Nos. C257-C260 (4) 1.60 .90

25th anniversary of the death of Rubén Dario, poet and writer.

Catalogue values for unused stamps in this section, from this point to the end of the section, are for Never Hinged items.

Victory Type

1943, Dec. 8 *Perf. 12*

C261 A48 40c dk bl grn & cer .20 .20
C262 A48 60c lt bl & cer .30 .20

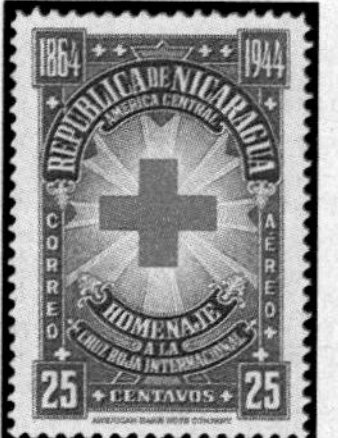
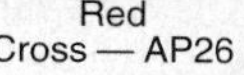
Red Cross — AP26

Cross and Globes — AP27

Red Cross Workers AP28

1944, Oct. 12 Engr.

C263 AP26 25c red lil & car .65 .30
C264 AP27 50c ol brn & car 1.00 .55
C265 AP28 1cor dk bl grn & car 2.00 2.00
Nos. C263-C265 (3) 3.65 2.85

International Red Cross Society, 80th anniv.

Caravels of Columbus and Columbus Lighthouse AP29

Landing of Columbus AP30

1945, Sept. 1 *Perf. 12½*

C266 AP29 20c dp grn & gray .20 .20
C267 AP29 35c dk car & blk .35 .30
C268 AP29 75c ol grn & rose pink .50 .40
C269 AP29 90c brick red & aqua .80 .75
C270 AP29 1cor blk & pale bl .90 .30
C271 AP30 2.50cor dk bl & car rose 2.25 2.25
Nos. C266-C271 (6) 5.00 4.20

Issued in honor of the discovery of America by Columbus and the Columbus Lighthouse near Ciudad Trujillo, Dominican Republic.

Roosevelt Types

Designs: 25c, Franklin D. Roosevelt and Winston Churchill. 75c, Roosevelt signing declaration of war against Japan. 1cor, Gen. Henri Giraud, Roosevelt, Gen. Charles de Gaulle and Churchill. 3cor, Stalin, Roosevelt and Churchill. 5cor, Sculptured head of Roosevelt.

Engraved, Center Photogravure

1946, June 15 *Perf. 12½*

Frame in Black

C272 A50 25c orange .20 .20
a. Horiz. pair, imperf. btwn. 225.00
b. Imperf., pair 175.00
C273 A51 75c carmine .25 .25
a. Imperf., pair 175.00

C274 A50 1cor dark green .40 .40
C275 A50 3cor violet 3.75 3.75
C276 A51 5cor greenish blue 5.00 5.00
Nos. C272-C276 (5) 9.60 9.60

Issued to honor Franklin D. Roosevelt.

Projected Provincial Seminary — AP36

Designs: 20c, Communications Building. 35c, Sanitation Building. 90c, National Bank. 1cor, Municipal Building. 2.50cor, National Palace.

1947, Jan. 10

Frame in Black

C277 AP36 5c violet .20 .20
a. Imperf., pair 125.00
C278 AP36 20c gray grn .20 .20
C279 AP36 35c orange .20 .20
C280 AP36 90c red lil .40 .30
C281 AP36 1cor brown .60 .45
C282 AP36 2.50cor rose lil 1.75 1.50
Nos. C277-C282 (6) 3.35 2.85

City of Managua centenary.

Rubén Darío Monument — AP42

Designs: 6c, Tapir. 8c, Stone Highway. 10c, Genizaro Dam. 20c, Detail of Dario Monument. 25c, Sulphurous Lake of Nejapa. 35c, Mercedes Airport. 50c, Prinzapolka River delta. 1cor, Tipitapa Spa. 1.50cor, Tipitapa River. 5cor, United States Embassy. 10cor, Indian fruit vendor. 25cor, Franklin D. Roosevelt Monument.

Engraved, Center Photogravure

1947, Aug. 29 Unwmk. *Perf. 12½*

C283 AP42 5c dk bl grn & rose car .20 .20
C284 AP42 6c blk & yel .20 .20
C285 AP42 8c car & ol .20 .20
C286 AP42 10c brn & bl .20 .20
C287 AP42 20c bl vio & org .30 .30
C288 AP42 25c brn red & emer .35 .35
C289 AP42 35c gray & bis .30 .30
C290 AP42 50c pur & sep .25 .25
C291 AP42 1cor blk & lil rose .75 .75
C292 AP42 1.50cor red brn & aqua .80 .80
C293 AP42 5cor choc & car rose 6.25 6.25
C294 AP42 10cor vio & dk brn 5.00 5.00
C295 AP42 25cor dk bl grn & yel 10.00 10.00
Nos. C283-C295 (13) 24.80 24.80

The frames differ for each denomination.
For surcharge see No. C750.

Tennis — AP43

Designs: 2c, Soccer. 3c, Table tennis. 4c, Proposed stadium. 5c, Regatta. 15c, Basketball. 25c, Boxing. 30c, Baseball. 40c, Bicycling. 75c, Diving. 1cor, Pole vault. 2cor, Boy Scouts. 5cor, Softball.

1949, July Photo. *Perf. 12*

C296 AP43 1c cerise .20 .20
C297 AP43 2c ol gray .20 .20
C298 AP43 3c scarlet .20 .20
C299 AP43 4c dk bl gray .20 .20
C300 AP43 5c aqua .30 .20
C301 AP43 15c bl grn .90 .20
C302 AP43 25c red vio 2.00 .30
C303 AP43 30c red brn 1.75 .30
C304 AP43 40c violet .50 .30
C305 AP43 75c magenta 4.50 2.75
C306 AP43 1cor lt bl 5.00 1.40
C307 AP43 2cor brn ol 2.00 1.75
C308 AP43 5cor lt grn 2.25 2.25
a. Set of 13 souv. sheets of 4 125.00 125.00
Nos. C296-C308 (13) 20.00 10.25

10th World Series of Amateur Baseball, 1948.

Rowland Hill — AP44

Designs: 20c, Heinrich von Stephan. 25c, First UPU Bldg. 30c, UPU Bldg., Bern. 85c, UPU Monument. 1.10cor, Congress medal, obverse. 2.14cor, as 1.10cor, reverse.

1950, Nov. 23 Engr. *Perf. 13*

Frames in Black

C309 AP44 16c cerise .20 .20
C310 AP44 20c orange .20 .20
C311 AP44 25c gray .20 .20
C312 AP44 30c cerise .30 .20
C313 AP44 85c dk bl grn .65 .65
C314 AP44 1.10cor chnt brn .50 .45
C315 AP44 2.14cor ol grn 2.25 2.25
Nos. C309-C315 (7) 4.30 4.15

75th anniv. (in 1949) of the UPU.
Each denomination was also issued in a souvenir sheet containing four stamps and marginal inscriptions. Size: 126x114mm. Value, set of 7 sheets, $35.
For surcharges see Nos. C501, C758.

Queen Isabela I Type

Designs: 2.30cor, Portrait facing left. 2.80cor, Map. 3cor, Santa Maria. 3.30cor, Columbus' ships. 3.60cor, Portrait facing right.

1952, June 25 Unwmk. *Perf. 11½*

C316 A65 2.30cor rose car 2.50 2.00
C317 A65 2.80cor red org 2.25 1.75
C318 A65 3cor green 2.50 2.00
C319 A66 3.30cor lt bl 2.50 2.00
C320 A65 3.60cor yel grn 2.75 2.25
a. Souv. sheet of 5, #C316-C320 12.50 12.50
Nos. C316-C320 (5) 12.50 10.00

For overprint see No. C445.

Arms of ODECA AP47

Designs: 25c, ODECA Flag. 30c, Presidents of five Central American countries. 60c, ODECA Charter and Flags. 1cor, Map of Central America.

1953, Apr. 15 *Perf. 13½x14*

C321 AP47 20c red lil .20 .20
C322 AP47 25c lt bl .20 .20
C323 AP47 30c sepia .20 .20
C324 AP47 60c dk bl grn .30 .25
C325 AP47 1cor dk vio .70 .65
Nos. C321-C325 (5) 1.60 1.50

Founding of the Organization of Central American States (ODECA).

Leonardo Arguello — AP48

Presidents: 5c, Gen. Jose Maria Moncada. 20c, Juan Bautista Sacasa. 25c, Gen. Jose Santos Zelaya. 30c, Gen. Anastasio Somoza. 35c, Gen. Tomas Martinez. 40c, Fernando Guzman. 45c, Vicente Cuadra. 50c, Pedro Joaquin Chamorro. 60c, Gen. Joaquin Zavala. 85c, Adan Cardenas. 1.10cor, Evaristo Carazo. 1.20cor, Roberto Sacasa.

Engraved (frames); Photogravure (heads)

1953, June 25 *Perf. 12½*

Heads in Gray Black

C326 AP48 4c dp car .20 .20
C327 AP48 5c dp org .20 .20
C328 AP48 20c dk Prus bl .20 .20
C329 AP48 25c blue .20 .20
C330 AP48 30c red brn .20 .20
C331 AP48 35c dp grn .20 .20
C332 AP48 40c dk vio brn .25 .20
C333 AP48 45c olive .25 .25
C334 AP48 50c carmine .30 .20
C335 AP48 60c ultra .30 .25
C336 AP48 85c brown .40 .35
C337 AP48 1.10cor purple .45 .45
C338 AP48 1.20cor ol bis .45 .45
Nos. C326-C338 (13) 3.60 3.35

For surcharges see Nos. C363-C364, C757.

Torch and UN Emblem — AP49

Capt. Dean L. Ray, USAF — AP50

Designs: 4c, Raised hands. 5c, Candle and charter. 30c, Flags of Nicaragua and UN. 2cor, Globe. 3cor, Arms of Nicaragua. 5cor, Type A69 inscribed "Aereo."

1954, Apr. 30 Engr. *Perf. 13½*

C339 AP49 3c rose pink .20 .20
C340 AP49 4c dp org .20 .20
C341 AP49 5c red .20 .20
C342 AP49 30c cerise 1.00 .20
C343 AP49 2cor magenta 1.40 1.00
C344 AP49 3cor org brn 2.50 1.75
C345 AP49 5cor brn vio 3.00 2.25
Nos. C339-C345 (7) 8.50 5.80

Honoring the United Nations.
For overprint & surcharge see #C366, C443.

Engraved; Center Photogravure

1954, Nov. 5 *Perf. 13*

Designs: 15c, Sabre jet plane. 20c, Air Force emblem. 25c, National Air Force hangars. 30c, Gen. A. Somoza. 50c, AT-6's in formation. 1cor, Plane, type P-38.

Frame in Black

C346 AP50 10c gray .20 .20
C347 AP50 15c gray .20 .20
C348 AP50 20c claret .20 .20
C349 AP50 25c red .20 .20
C350 AP50 30c ultra .20 .20
C351 AP50 50c blue .45 .45
C352 AP50 1cor green .35 .25
Nos. C346-C352 (7) 1.80 1.70

Issued to honor the National Air Force.

Rotary Intl. Type

Designs: 1c, 1cor, Paul P. Harris. 2c, 50c, Handclasp, Rotary emblem and globe. 3c, 45c, Map of world and Rotary emblem. 4c, 30c, Rotary slogans and wreath. 5c, 25c, Flags of Nicaragua and Rotary.

Perf. 11½

1955, Aug. 30 Unwmk. Photo.

Granite Paper

C353 A71 1c vermilion .20 .20
C354 A71 2c ultra .20 .20
C355 A72 3c pck grn .20 .20
C356 A71 4c violet .20 .20
C357 A71 5c org brn .20 .20
C358 A71 25c brt grnsh bl .20 .20
C359 A71 30c dl pur .20 .20
C360 A72 45c lil rose .35 .30
C361 A71 50c lt bl grn .25 .20
C362 A71 1cor ultra .35 .35
a. Souv. sheet of 5, #C358-C362 9.50 9.50
Nos. C353-C362 (10) 2.35 2.25

For surcharge see No. C365.

Nos. C331, C333, C360, C345 Surcharged in Green or Black

Engraved, Photogravure

1956, Feb. 4 *Perf. 13½x13, 11½*

C363 AP48 30c on 35c (G) .20 .20
C364 AP48 30c on 45c (G) .20 .20
C365 A72 30c on 45c .20 .20
C366 AP49 2cor on 5cor .80 .75
Nos. C363-C366 (4) 1.40 1.35

National Exhibition, Feb. 4-16, 1956.
See note after No. 772.

Gen. Jose D. Estrada — AP53

The Stoning of Andres Castro AP54

1.50 cor, Emanuel Mongalo. 2.50 cor, Battle of Rivas. 10 cor, Com. Hiram Paulding.

1956, Sept. 14 Engr. *Perf. 12½*

C367 AP53 30c dk car rose .20 .20
C368 AP54 60c chocolate .20 .20
C369 AP53 1.50cor green .25 .25
C370 AP54 2.50cor dk ultra .40 .40
C371 AP53 10cor red org 2.25 2.00
Nos. C367-C371 (5) 3.30 3.05

Centenary of the National War.
For overprint and surcharge see #C444, C751.

President Somoza — AP55

1957, Feb. 1 Photo. *Perf. 14x13½*

Various Frames: Centers in Black

C372 AP55 15c gray blk .20 .20
C373 AP55 30c indigo .20 .20
C374 AP55 2cor purple 1.00 1.00
C375 AP55 3cor dk grn 2.00 2.00
C376 AP55 5cor dk brn 3.25 3.25
Nos. C372-C376 (5) 6.65 6.65

President Anastasio Somoza, 1896-1956.

Type of Regular Issue and

Handshake and Globe — AP56

Designs: 4c, Scout emblem, globe and Lord Baden-Powell. 5c, Cub Scout. 6c, Crossed flags and Scout emblem. 8c, Scout symbols. 30c, Joseph A. Harrison. 40c, Pres. Somoza receiving decoration at first Central American Camporee. 75c, Explorer Scout. 85c, Boy Scout. 1cor, Lord Baden-Powell.

1957, Apr. 9 Unwmk. *Perf. 13½x14*

C377 AP56 3c red org & ol .20 .20
C378 A75 4c dk brn & dk Prus grn .20 .20
C379 A75 5c grn & brn .20 .20
C380 A75 6c pur & ol .20 .20
C381 A75 8c grnsh blk & red .20 .20
C382 A75 30c Prus grn & gray .20 .20
C383 AP56 40c dk bl & grysh blk .20 .20
C384 A75 75c mar & brn .20 .20
C385 A75 85c red & gray .25 .25

C386 A75 1cor dl red brn & sl grn .30 .30
a. Souv. sheet of 5, #C382-C386, imperf. 2.50 2.50
Nos. C377-C386 (10) 2.15 2.15

Centenary of the birth of Lord Baden-Powell, founder of the Boy Scouts.

No. C386a with each stamp overprinted "CAMPOREE SCOUT 1965" was issued in 1965 along with Nos. 843-852.

For surcharge see No. C754.

Pres. Luis A. Somoza — AP57

1957, July 2 *Perf. 14x13½*
Portrait in Dark Brown

C387 AP57 20c dp bl .20 .20
C388 AP57 25c lil rose .20 .20
C389 AP57 30c blk brn .20 .20
C390 AP57 40c grnsh bl .20 .20
C391 AP57 2cor brt vio 1.25 1.25
Nos. C387-C391 (5) 2.05 2.05

Issued to honor President Luis A. Somoza.

Church Types of Regular Issue

Designs: 30c, Archbishop Lezcano y Ortega. 60c, Managua Cathedral. 75c, Bishop Pereira y Castellon. 90c, Leon Cathedral. 1.50cor, De la Merced Church, Granada. 2cor, Father Mariano Dubon.

1957, July 16 **Unwmk.**
Centers in Olive Gray

C392 A78 30c dk grn .20 .20
C393 A77 60c chocolate .20 .20
C394 A78 75c dk bl .20 .20
C395 A77 90c brt red .30 .30
C396 A77 1.50cor Prus grn .40 .40
C397 A78 2cor brt pur .60 .60
Nos. C392-C397 (6) 1.90 1.90

Merchant Marine Type of 1957

Designs: 25c, M. S. Managua. 30c, Ship's wheel and map. 50c, Pennants. 60c, M. S. Costa Rica. 1 cor, M. S. Nicarao. 2.50 cor, Flag, globe & ship.

1957, Oct. 24 **Litho.** *Perf. 14*

C398 A79 25c ultra grysh bl & gray .20 .20
C399 A79 30c red brn, gray & yel .20 .20
C400 A79 50c vio, ol gray & bl .30 .30
C401 A79 60c lake, grnsh bl & blk .35 .35
C402 A79 1cor crim, brt bl & blk .45 .45
C403 A79 2.50cor blk, bl & red brn 1.50 1.50
Nos. C398-C403 (6) 3.00 3.00

For surcharge see No. C691.

Fair Emblem — AP58

Designs: 30c, 2cor, Arms of Nicaragua. 45c, 10cor, Pavilion of Nicaragua, Brussels.

1958, Apr. 17 **Unwmk.** *Perf. 14*

C404 AP58 25c bluish grn, blk & yel .20 .20
C405 AP58 30c multi .20 .20
C406 AP58 45c bis, bl & blk .25 .20
C407 AP58 1cor pale brn, lt bl & blk .25 .20
C408 AP58 2cor multi .40 .30
C409 AP58 10cor pale bl, lil & brn 2.10 1.60
a. Souv. sheet of 6, #C404-C409 12.00 12.00
Nos. C404-C409 (6) 3.40 2.70

World's Fair, Brussels, Apr. 17-Oct. 19.

Lions Type of Regular Issue

Designs: 30c, Dr. Teodoro A. Arias. 60c, Arms of Central American Republics. 90c, Edward G. Barry. 1.25cor, Melvin Jones. 2cor, Motto and emblem. 3cor, Map of Central America.

1958, May 8 **Litho.**
Emblem in Yellow, Red and Blue

C410 A80 30c bl & org .20 .20
C411 A80 60c multi .25 .20
C412 A80 90c blue .35 .30
C413 A80 1.25cor bl & ol .45 .40
C414 A80 2cor bl & grn .80 .70
C415 A80 3cor bl, lil & pink 1.25 1.10
a. Souv. sheet of 6, #C410-C415 4.25 4.25
Nos. C410-C415 (6) 3.30 2.90

For surcharge see No. C686.

Christian Brothers Type of 1958

Designs: 30c, Arms of La Salle. 60c, School, Managua, horiz 85c, St. Jean Baptiste De La Salle. 90c, Bro. Carlos. 1.25cor, Bro. Julio. 1.50cor, Bro. Antonio. 1.75cor, Bro. Argeo. 2cor, Bro. Eugenio.

1958, July 13 **Photo.** *Perf. 14*

C416 A81 30c bl, car & yel .20 .20
C417 A81 60c gray, brn & lil .35 .25
C418 A81 85c red, bl & grnsh blk .35 .30
C419 A81 90c ol grn, ocher & blk .50 .35
C420 A81 1.25cor car, ocher & blk .70 .50
C421 A81 1.50cor lt grn, gray & vio blk .80 .55
C422 A81 1.75cor brn, bl & grnsh blk .85 .65
C423 A81 2cor ol grn, gray & vio blk 1.25 1.00
Nos. C416-C423 (8) 5.00 3.80

For surcharges see Nos. C539A, C755-C756.

UNESCO Building, Paris — AP59

75c, 5cor, "UNESCO." 90c, 3cor, UNESCO building, Eiffel tower. 1cor, Emblem, globe.

Perf. 11½
1958, Dec. 15 **Unwmk.** **Litho.**

C424 AP59 60c brt pink & bl .30 .20
C425 AP59 75c grn & red brn .30 .20
C426 AP59 90c lt brn & grn .30 .20
C427 AP59 1cor ultra & brt pink .30 .20
C428 AP59 3cor gray & org 1.00 .65
C429 AP59 5cor rose lil & dk bl 1.60 .95
a. Min. sheet of 6, #C424-C429 4.00 4.00
Nos. C424-C429 (6) 3.80 2.40

UNESCO Headquarters Opening in Paris, Nov. 3.

For overprints see Nos. C494-C499.

Type of Regular Issue, 1959 and

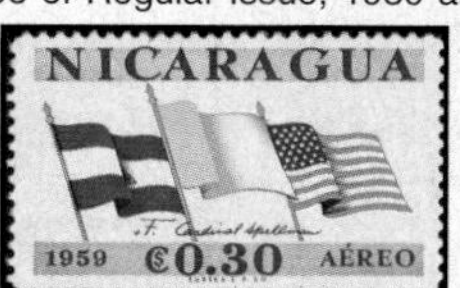

Nicaraguan, Papal and US Flags — AP60

Designs: 35c, Pope John XXIII and Cardinal Spellman. 1cor, Spellman coat of arms. 1.05cor, Cardinal Spellman. 1.50cor, Human rosary and Cardinal, horiz. 2cor, Cardinal with Ruben Dario order.

1959, Nov. 26 *Perf. 12½*

C430 AP60 30c vio bl, yel & red .20 .20
C431 A83 35c dp org & grnsh blk .20 .20
C432 A83 1cor yel, bl & car .25 .25
C433 A83 1.05cor red, blk & dk car .40 .30
C434 A83 1.50cor dk bl & yel .40 .30
C435 A83 2cor multi .50 .40
C436 AP60 5cor multi 1.60 .90
a. Min. sheet of 7, #C430-C436, perf. or imperf. 4.00 4.00
Nos. C430-C436 (7) 3.55 2.55

Visit of Cardinal Spellman to Managua, Feb. 1958.

For surcharges see #C538, C638, C747, C752.

Type of Lincoln Regular Issue and

AP61

Perf. 13x13½, 13½x13
1960, Jan. 21 **Engr.** **Unwmk.**
Portrait in Black

C437 A84 30c indigo .20 .20
C438 A84 35c brt car .20 .20
C439 A84 70c plum .25 .20
C440 A84 1.05cor emerald .25 .20
C441 A84 1.50cor violet .40 .30
C442 AP61 5cor int blk & bis 1.25 .90
a. Souv. sheet of 6, #C437-C442, imperf. 4.00 4.00
Nos. C437-C442 (6) 2.55 2.00

150th anniv. of the birth of Abraham Lincoln.

For overprints and surcharges see Nos. C446-C451, C500, C539, C637, C680, C753.

Nos. C343, C370 and C318 Overprinted: "X Aniversario Club Filatelico S.J.-C.R."

1960, July 4 **Engr.**

C443 AP49 2cor magenta .90 .70
C444 AP54 2.50cor dk ultra .90 .75
C445 A65 3cor green 1.25 1.10
Nos. C443-C445 (3) 3.05 2.55

10th anniversary of the Philatelic Club of San Jose, Costa Rica.

Nos. C437-C442 Overprinted in Red

Perf. 13x13½, 13½x13
1960, Sept. 19 **Unwmk.**
Center in Black

C446 A84 30c indigo .20 .20
C447 A84 35c brt car .20 .20
C448 A84 70c plum .25 .20
C449 A84 1.05cor emerald .30 .25
C450 A84 1.50cor violet .50 .35
C451 AP61 5cor int blk & bis 1.40 1.10
Nos. C446-C451 (6) 2.85 2.30

Issued for the Red Cross to aid earthquake victims in Chile. The overprint on No. C451 is horizontal and always inverted.

People and World Refugee Year Emblem AP62

5cor, Crosses, globe and WRY emblem.

1961, Dec. 30 **Litho.** *Perf. 11x11½*

C452 AP62 2cor multi .50 .30
C453 AP62 5cor multi 1.00 .65
a. Souv. sheet of 2, #C452-C453 2.50 2.50

World Refugee Year, July 1, 1959-June 30, 1960.

AP63

Consular Service Stamps Surcharged "Correo Aéreo" and New Denomination in Red, Black or Blue

Unwmk.
1961, Feb. 21 **Engr.** *Perf. 12*
Red Marginal Number

C454 AP63 20c on 50c dp bl (R) .20 .20
C455 AP63 20c on 1cor grnsh blk (R) .20 .20
C456 AP63 20c on 2cor grn (R) .20 .20
C457 AP63 20c on 3cor dk car .20 .20
C458 AP63 20c on 5cor org (Bl) .20 .20
C459 AP63 20c on 10cor vio (R) .20 .20
C460 AP63 20c on 20cor red brn (R) .20 .20
C461 AP63 20c on 50cor brn (R) .20 .20
C462 AP63 20c on 100cor mag .20 .20
Nos. C454-C462 (9) 1.80 1.80

See Nos. CO51-CO59, RA63-RA64.

Charles L. Mullins, Anastasio Somoza and Franklin D. Roosevelt AP64

Standard Bearers with Flags of Nicaragua and Academy — AP65

Designs: 25c, 70c, Flags of Nicaragua and Academy. 30c, 1.05cor, Directors of Academy: Fred T. Cruse, LeRoy Bartlett, Jr., John F. Greco, Anastasio Somoza Debayle, Francisco Boza, Elias Monge. 40c, 2cor, Academy Emblem. 45c, 5cor, Anastasio Somoza Debayle and Luis Somoza Debayle.

Perf. 11x11½, 11½x11
1961, Feb. 24 **Litho.** **Unwmk.**

C463 AP64 20c rose lil, gray & buff .20 .20
C464 AP65 25c bl, red & blk .20 .20
C465 AP64 30c bl, gray & yel .20 .20
C466 AP65 35c multi .20 .20
C467 AP65 40c multi .20 .20
C468 AP64 45c pink, gray & buff .20 .20
a. Min. sheet of 6, #C463-C468, imperf. .55 .55
C469 AP64 60c brn, gray & buff .20 .20
C470 AP65 70c multi .20 .20
C471 AP64 1.05cor lil, gray & yel .20 .20
C472 AP65 1.50cor multi .20 .20
C473 AP65 2cor multi .30 .25
C474 AP64 5cor gray & buff .70 .55
a. Min. sheet of 6, #C469-C474, imperf. 2.50 2.50
Nos. C463-C474 (12) 3.00 2.80

20th anniversary (in 1959) of the founding of the Military Academy of Nicaragua.

In 1977, Nos. C468a and C474a were overprinted in black: "1927-1977 50 ANIVERSARIO / Guardia Nacional de Nicaragua." Value, $7 for both.

For surcharges see #C692, C748, C759.

Emblem of Junior Chamber of Commerce — AP66

Designs: 2c, 15c, Globe showing map of Americas, horiz. 4c, 35c, Globe and initials, horiz. 5c, 70c, Chamber credo. 6c, 1.05cor, Handclasp. 10c, 5cor, Regional map.

Perf. 11x11½, 11½x11
1961, May 16 **Unwmk.**

C475 AP66 2c multi .20 .20
C476 AP66 3c yel & blk .20 .20
C477 AP66 4c multi .20 .20
C478 AP66 5c crim & blk .20 .20
C479 AP66 6c brn, yel & blk .20 .20
C480 AP66 10c red org, blk & bl .20 .20
C481 AP66 15c bl, blk & grn .20 .20
C482 AP66 30c bl & blk .20 .20

C483	AP66	35c multi	.20	.20
C484	AP66	70c yel, blk & crim	.20	.20
C485	AP66	1.05cor multi	.20	.20
C486	AP66	5cor multi	.55	.55
		Nos. C475-C486 (12)	2.75	2.75

13th Regional Congress of the Junior Chamber of Commerce of Nicaragua and the Intl. Junior Chamber of Commerce.

The imperforates of Nos. C475-C486 were not authorized.

For overprints and surcharges see Nos. C504-C508, C537, C634, C687, C749.

Rigoberto Cabezas — AP67

Map of Mosquito Territory and View of Cartago — AP68

Designs: 45c, Newspaper. 70c, Building. 2cor, Cabezas quotation. 10cor, Map of lower Nicaragua with Masaya area.

1961, Aug. 29 Litho. *Perf. 13½*

C487	AP67	20c org & dk bl	.20	.20
C488	AP68	40c lt bl & claret	.20	.20
C489	AP68	45c citron & brn	.20	.20
C490	AP68	70c beige & grn	.20	.20
C491	AP68	2cor pink & dk bl	.30	.25
C492	AP68	10cor grnsh bl & cl	1.40	1.10
		Nos. C487-C492 (6)	2.50	2.15

Centenary of the birth of Rigoberto Cabezas, who acquired the Mosquito Territory (Atlantic Littoral) for Nicaragua.

No. C253 Overprinted in Red: "Convención Filatélica-Centro-América-Panama-San Salvador-27 Julio 1961"

1961, Aug. 23 Engr. *Perf. 12½*

C493	AP22	1.25cor multi	.40	.40
a.		Inverted overprint	75.00	

Central American Philatelic Convention, San Salvador, July 27.

Nos. C424-C429 Overprinted in Red: "Homenaje a Hammarskjold Sept. 18-1961"

1961 Litho. *Perf. 11½*

C494	AP59	60c brt pink & bl	.25	.25
C495	AP59	75c grn & red brn	.30	.30
C496	AP59	90c lt brn & grn	.30	.30
C497	AP59	1cor ultra & brt pink	.30	.30
C498	AP59	3cor gray & org	.65	.65
C499	AP59	5cor rose lil & dk bl	1.75	1.75
		Nos. C494-C499 (6)	3.55	3.55

Issued in memory of Dag Hammarskjold, Secretary General of the United Nations, 1953-61.

Nos. C314 and C440 Surcharged in Red

Perf. 13x13½, 13

1962, Jan. 20 Engr.

C500	A84	1cor on 1.05cor	.20	.20
C501	AP44	1cor on 1.10cor	.20	.20

UNESCO Emblem and Crowd — AP69

Design: 5cor, UNESCO and UN Emblems.

Unwmk.

1962, Feb. 26 Photo. *Perf. 12*

C502	AP69	2cor multi	.40	.25
C503	AP69	5cor multi	.85	.70
a.		Souv. sheet of 2, #C502-C503, imperf.	1.25	1.25

15th anniv. (in 1961) of UNESCO.

Nos. C480 and C483-C486 Overprinted

Perf. 11x11½, 11½x11

1962, July Litho.

C504	AP66	10c multi	.30	.20
C505	AP66	35c multi	.40	.20
C506	AP66	70c multi	.50	.30
C507	AP66	1.05cor multi	.65	.45
C508	AP66	5cor multi	1.10	1.40
		Nos. C504-C508 (5)	2.95	2.55

WHO drive to eradicate malaria.

Souvenir Sheet

Stamps and Postmarks of 1862 — AP69a

1962, Sept. 9 Litho. *Imperf.*

C509	AP69a	7cor multi	2.75	2.75

Cent. of Nicaraguan postage stamps.

Arms Type of Regular Issue, 1962

30c, Nueva Segovia. 50c, León. 1cor, Managua. 2cor, Granada. 5cor, Rivas.

1962, Nov. 22 *Perf. 12½x13*

Arms in Original Colors; Black Inscriptions

C510	A86	30c rose	.20	.20
C511	A86	50c salmon	.20	.20
C512	A86	1cor lt grn	.20	.20
C513	A86	2cor gray	.30	.30
C514	A86	5cor lt bl	.85	.75
		Nos. C510-C514 (5)	1.75	1.65

Liberty Bell AP70

1963, May 15 Litho. *Perf. 13x12*

C515	AP70	30c lt bl, blk & ol bis	.25	.20

Sesquicentennial of the 1st Nicaraguan declaration of Independence (in 1961).

Paulist Brother Comforting Boy — AP71

Map of Central America — AP72

60c, Nun comforting girl. 2cor, St. Vincent de Paul and St. Louisa de Marillac, horiz.

1963, May 15 Photo. *Perf. 13½*

C516	AP71	60c gray & ocher	.20	.20
C517	AP71	1cor salmon & blk	.30	.20
C518	AP71	2cor crimson & blk	.50	.50
		Nos. C516-C518 (3)	1.00	.90

300th anniv. of the deaths of St. Vincent de Paul and St. Louisa de Marillac (in 1960).

Lithographed and Engraved

1963, Aug. 2 Unwmk. *Perf. 12*

C519	AP72	1cor bl & yel	.25	.20

Issued to honor the Federation of Central American Philatelic Societies.

Cross over World — AP73

Wheat and Map of Nicaragua AP74

1963, Aug. 6

C520	AP73	20c yel & red	.25	.20

Vatican II, the 21st Ecumenical Council of the Roman Catholic Church.

1963, Aug. 6

Design: 25c, Dead tree on parched earth.

C521	AP74	10c lt grn & grn	.20	.20
C522	AP74	25c yel & dk brn	.20	.20

FAO "Freedom from Hunger" campaign.

Boxing — AP75

Flags of Central American States — AP75a

Lithographed and Engraved

1963, Dec. 12 Unwmk. *Perf. 12*

C523	AP75	2c shown	.20	.20
C524	AP75	3c Running	.20	.20
C525	AP75	4c Underwater	.20	.20
C526	AP75	5c Soccer	.20	.20
C527	AP75	6c Baseball	.20	.20
C528	AP75	10c Tennis	.20	.20
C529	AP75	15c Bicycling	.20	.20
C530	AP75	20c Motorcycling	.20	.20
C531	AP75	35c Chess	.25	.25
C532	AP75	60c Deep-sea fishing	.30	.30
C533	AP75	1cor Table tennis	.40	.40
C534	AP75	2cor Basketball	.80	.80
C535	AP75	5cor Golf	2.00	2.00
		Nos. C523-C535 (13)	5.35	5.35

Publicizing the 1964 Olympic Games.

For overprints and surcharge see Nos. C553-C558, C635.

Central American Independence Issue

1964, Sept. 15 Litho. *Perf. 13x13½*

Size: 27x43mm

C536	AP75a	40c multi	.25	.25

Nos. C479, C430, C437 and C416 Surcharged in Black or Red

a

b

1964 Litho. *Perf. 11½x11*

C537	AP66 (a)	5c on 6c	.25	.20
		Perf. 12½		
C538	AP60 (a)	10c on 30c	.50	.20
		Engr.		
		Perf. 13x13½		
C539	A84 (a)	15c on 30c (R)	.65	.20
		Photo.		
		Perf. 14		
C539A	A81 (b)	20c on 30c	.20	.20
		Nos. C537-C539A (4)	1.60	.80

Floating Red Cross Station AP76

Designs: 5c, Alliance for Progress emblem, vert. 15c, Highway. 20c, Plowing with tractors, and sun. 25c, Housing development. 30c, Presidents Somoza and Kennedy and World Bank Chairman Eugene Black. 35c, Adult education. 40c, Smokestacks.

1964, Oct. 15 Litho. *Perf. 12*

C540 AP76 5c yel, brt bl, grn & gray .20 .20
C541 AP76 10c multi .20 .20
C542 AP76 15c multi .20 .20
C543 AP76 20c org brn, yel & blk .20 .20
C544 AP76 25c multi .20 .20
C545 AP76 30c dk bl, blk & brn .20 .20
C546 AP76 35c lil rose, dk red & blk .20 .20
C547 AP76 40c dp car, blk & yel .25 .20
Nos. C540-C547 (8) 1.65 1.60

Alliance for Progress.
For surcharges see Nos. C677, C693.

Map of Central America and Central American States AP77

Designs (Map of Central America and): 25c, Grain. 40c, Cogwheels. 50c, Heads of cattle.

1964, Nov. 30 Litho. *Perf. 12*

C548 AP77 15c ultra & multi .20 .20
C549 AP77 25c multi .20 .20
C550 AP77 40c multi .20 .20
C551 AP77 50c multi .20 .20
Nos. C548-C551 (4) .80 .80

Central American Common Market.
For surcharge see No. C678.

Nos. C523-C525, C527 and C533-C534 Overprinted: "OLIMPIADAS / TOKYO-1964"

Lithographed and Engraved

1964, Dec. 19 Unwmk. *Perf. 12*

C553 AP75 2c multi .25 .20
C554 AP75 3c multi .25 .20
C555 AP75 4c multi .25 .20
C556 AP75 6c multi .25 .20
C557 AP75 1cor multi 2.25 2.00
C558 AP75 2cor multi 2.75 2.50
Nos. C553-C558 (6) 6.00 5.30

18th Olympic Games, Tokyo, Oct. 10-25.

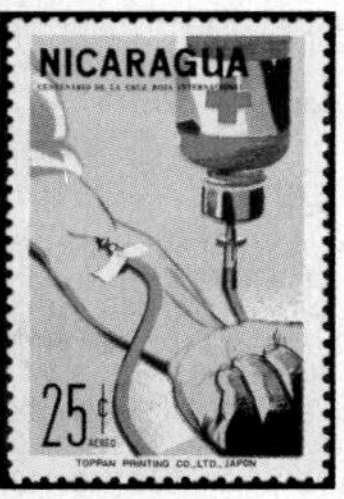

Blood Transfusion AP78

Stele — AP79

Designs: 20c, Volunteers and priest rescuing wounded man. 40c, Landscape during storm. 10cor, Red Cross over map of Nicaragua.

1965, Jan. 28 Litho. *Perf. 12*

C559 AP78 20c yel, blk & red .20 .20
C560 AP78 25c red, blk & ol bis .20 .20
C561 AP78 40c grn, blk & red .20 .20
C562 AP78 10cor multi 1.75 1.10
Nos. C559-C562 (4) 2.35 1.70

Centenary (in 1963) of the Intl. Red Cross.

Perf. 13½x13, 13x13½

1965, Mar. 24 Litho. Unwmk.

Antique Indian artifacts: 5c, Three jadeite statuettes, horiz. 15c, Dog, horiz. 20c, Talamanca pendant. 25c, Decorated pottery bowl and vase, horiz. 30c, Stone pestle and mortar on animal base. 35c, Three statuettes, horiz. 40c, Idol on animal pedestal. 50c, Decorated pottery bowl and vase. 60c, Vase and metate (tripod bowl), horiz. 1cor, Metate.

Black Margin and Inscription

C563 AP79 5c yel & multi .20 .20
C564 AP79 10c multi .20 .20
C565 AP79 15c multi .20 .20
C566 AP79 20c sal & dk brn .20 .20
C567 AP79 25c lil & multi .20 .20
C568 AP79 30c lt grn & multi .20 .20
C569 AP79 35c multi .20 .20
C570 AP79 40c cit & multi .20 .20
C571 AP79 50c ocher & multi .20 .20
C572 AP79 60c multi .20 .20
C573 AP79 1cor car & multi .30 .20
Nos. C563-C573 (11) 2.30 2.20

For surcharges see Nos. C596-597, C679, C688-C690.

Pres. John F. Kennedy (1917-63) — AP80

Photogravure & Lithographed

1965, Apr. 28 *Perf. 12½x13½*

C574 AP80 35c blk & brt grn .20 .20
C575 AP80 75c blk & brt pink .35 .20
C576 AP80 1.10cor blk & dk bl .50 .40
C577 AP80 2cor blk & yel brn 1.25 1.00
Nos. C574-C577 (4) 2.30 1.80
Set of 4 souvenir sheets 5.50 5.50

Nos. C574-C577 each exist in souvenir sheets containing one imperf. block of 4.
For surcharge see No. C760.

Andrés Bello AP81

1965, Oct. 15 Litho. *Perf. 14*

C578 AP81 10c dk brn & red brn .20 .20
C579 AP81 15c ind & lt bl .20 .20
C580 AP81 45c blk & dl lil .20 .20
C581 AP81 80c blk & yel grn .20 .20
C582 AP81 1cor dk brn & yel .20 .20
C583 AP81 2cor blk & gray .30 .30
Nos. C578-C583 (6) 1.30 1.30

Centenary of the death of Andrés Bello (1780?-1864), Venezuelan writer and educator.

Winston Churchill — AP82

Pope John XXIII — AP83

Winston Churchill: 35c, 1cor, Broadcasting, horiz. 60c, 3cor, On military inspection. 75c, As young officer.

1966, Feb. 7 Unwmk. *Perf. 14*

C584 AP82 20c cer & blk .20 .20
C585 AP82 35c dk ol grn & blk .20 .20
C586 AP82 60c brn & blk .20 .20
C587 AP82 75c rose red .20 .20
C588 AP82 1cor vio blk .30 .25
C589 AP82 2cor lil & blk .55 .50
a. Souv. sheet of 4 1.40 1.40
C590 AP82 3cor ind & blk .85 .70
Nos. C584-C590 (7) 2.50 2.25

Sir Winston Spencer Churchill (1874-1965), statesman and World War II leader.
No. C589a contains four imperf. stamps similar to Nos. C586-C589 with simulated perforations.

1966, Dec. 15 Litho. *Perf. 13*

35c, Pope Paul VI. 1cor, Archbishop Gonzalez y Robleto. 2cor, St. Peter's, Rome. 3cor, Arms of Pope John XXIII & St. Peter's.

C591 AP83 20c multi .20 .20
C592 AP83 35c multi .20 .20
C593 AP83 1cor multi .25 .20
C594 AP83 2cor multi .40 .35
C595 AP83 3cor multi .65 .50
Nos. C591-C595 (5) 1.70 1.45

Closing of the Ecumenical Council, Vatican II.

Nos. C571-C572 Surcharged in Red

1967 *Perf. 13x13½, 13½x13*

C596 AP79 10c on 50c multi .20 .20
C597 AP79 15c on 60c multi .20 .20

Rubén Dario and Birthplace — AP84

Portrait and: 10c, Monument, Managua. 20c, Leon Cathedral, site of Dario's tomb. 40c, Centaurs. 75c, Swans. 1cor, Roman triumphal march. 2cor, St. Francis and the Wolf. 5cor, "Faith" defeating "Death."

1967, Jan. 18 Litho. *Perf. 13*

C598 AP84 5c lt brn, tan & blk .20 .20
C599 AP84 10c org, pale org & blk .20 .20
C600 AP84 20c vio, lt bl & blk .20 .20
C601 AP84 40c grn, dk grn & blk .20 .20
a. Souv. sheet of 4, #C598-C601 .50 .50
C602 AP84 75c ultra, pale bl & blk .20 .20
C603 AP84 1cor red, pale red & blk .20 .20
C604 AP84 2cor rose pink, car & blk .30 .30
C605 AP84 5cor dp ultra, vio bl, & blk .75 .65
a. Souv. sheet of 4, #C602-C605 3.50 3.50
Nos. C598-C605 (8) 2.25 2.15

Rubén Dario (pen name of Felix Rubén Garcia Sarmiento, 1867-1916), poet, newspaper correspondent and diplomat.
Sheets were issued perf. and imperf.

Megalura Peleus AP85

Designs: Various butterflies. 5c, 10c, 30c, 35c, 50c and 1cor are vertical.

1967, Apr. 20 Litho. *Perf. 14*

C606 AP85 5c multi .20 .20
C607 AP85 10c multi .20 .20
C608 AP85 15c multi .20 .20
C609 AP85 20c multi .20 .20
C610 AP85 25c multi .20 .20
C611 AP85 30c multi .20 .20
C612 AP85 35c multi .20 .20
C613 AP85 40c multi .20 .20
C614 AP85 50c multi .25 .25
C615 AP85 60c multi .25 .25
C616 AP85 1cor multi .40 .40
C617 AP85 2cor multi .75 .75
Nos. C606-C617 (12) 3.25 3.25

Com. James McDivitt and Maj. Edward H. White AP86

Gemini 4 Space Flight: 10c, 40c, Rocket launching and astronauts. 15c, 75c, Edward H. White walking in space. 20c, 1cor, Recovery of capsule.

1967, Sept. 20 Litho. *Perf. 13*

C618 AP86 5c red & multi .20 .20
C619 AP86 10c org & multi .20 .20
C620 AP86 15c multi .20 .20
C621 AP86 20c multi .20 .20
C622 AP86 35c ol & multi .20 .20
C623 AP86 40c ultra & multi .20 .20
C624 AP86 75c brn & multi .20 .20
C625 AP86 1cor multi .25 .25
Nos. C618-C625 (8) 1.65 1.65

Saquanjoche, National Flower of Nicaragua AP87

Presidents of Nicaragua and Mexico AP88

National Flowers: No. C626, White nun orchid, Guatemala. No. C627, Rose, Honduras. No. C629, Maquilishuat, Salvador. No. C630, Purple guaria orchid, Costa Rica.

1967, Nov. 22 Litho. *Perf. 13½*

C626 AP87 40c multi .20 .20
C627 AP87 40c multi .20 .20
C628 AP87 40c multi .20 .20
C629 AP87 40c multi .20 .20
C630 AP87 40c multi .20 .20
a. Strip of 5, #C626-C630 .75 .50

5th anniversary of the General Treaty for Central American Economic Integration.

1968, Feb. 28 Litho. *Perf. 12½*

Designs: 40c Pres. Gustavo Diáz Ordaz of Mexico and Pres. René Schick of Nicaragua signing statement, horiz. 1cor, President Diáz.

C631 AP88 20c black .20 .20
C632 AP88 40c slate grn .20 .20
C633 AP88 1cor dp brn .25 .20
Nos. C631-C633 (3) .65 .60

Issued to commemorate the visit of the President of Mexico, Gustavo Diáz Ordaz.

Nos. C479, C527, C242, C440 and C434 Surcharged "Resello" and New Value in Black, Red (#C637) or Yellow (#C638)

1968, May Litho.; Engr.

C634 AP66 5c on 6c multi .20 .20
C635 AP75 5c on 6c multi .20 .20
C636 AP20 5c on 8c blk brn .20 .20
C637 A84 1cor on 1.05cor emer & blk .20 .20
C638 A83 1cor on 1.50cor dk bl & yel .20 .20
Nos. C634-C638 (5) 1.00 1.00

Mangos — AP89

1968, May 15 Litho. *Perf. 14*

C639 AP89 5c shown .20 .20
C640 AP89 10c Pineapples .20 .20
C641 AP89 15c Orange .20 .20
C642 AP89 20c Papaya .20 .20
C643 AP89 30c Bananas .20 .20
C644 AP89 35c Avocado .20 .20
C645 AP89 50c Watermelon .20 .20
C646 AP89 75c Cashews .25 .20

C647 AP89 1cor Sapodilla .40 .25
C648 AP89 2cor Cacao .75 .45
Nos. C639-C648 (10) 2.80 2.30

The Last Judgment, by Michelangelo — AP90

Paintings: 10c, The Crucifixion, by Fra Angelo, horiz. 35c, Madonna with Child and St. John, by Raphael. 2cor, The Disrobing of Christ, by El Greco. 3cor, The Immaculate Conception, by Murillo. 5cor, Christ of St. John of the Cross, by Salvador Dali.

1968, July 22 Litho. *Perf. 12½*

C649 AP90 10c gold & multi .20 .20
C650 AP90 15c gold & multi .20 .20
C651 AP90 35c gold & multi .20 .20
C652 AP90 2cor gold & multi .45 .40
C653 AP90 3cor gold & multi .65 .55
Nos. C649-C653 (5) 1.70 1.55

Miniature Sheet

C654 AP90 5cor gold & multi 2.75 2.75

Nos. C649-C652 Overprinted: "Visita de S.S. Paulo VI C.E. de Bogota 1968"

1968, Oct. 25 Litho. *Perf. 12½*

C655 AP90 10c gold & multi .20 .20
C656 AP90 15c gold & multi .20 .20
C657 AP90 35c gold & multi .20 .20
C658 AP90 2cor gold & multi .50 .40
Nos. C655-C658 (4) 1.10 1.00

Visit of Pope Paul VI to Bogota, Colombia, Aug. 22-24. The overprint has 3 lines on the 10c stamp and 5 lines on others.

Basketball AP91

Sports: 15c, Fencing, horiz. 20c, Diving. 35c, Running. 50c, Hurdling, horiz. 75c, Weight lifting. 1cor, Boxing, horiz. 2cor, Soccer.

1968, Nov. 28 Litho. *Perf. 14*

C659 AP91 10c multi .20 .20
C660 AP91 15c org red, blk & gray .20 .20
C661 AP91 20c multi .20 .20
C662 AP91 35c multi .20 .20
C663 AP91 50c multi .20 .20
C664 AP91 75c multi .20 .20
C665 AP91 1cor yel & multi .30 .30
C666 AP91 2cor gray & multi .80 .80
a. Souv. sheet of 4, #C663-C666 1.75 1.75
Nos. C659-C666 (8) 2.30 2.30

19th Olympic Games, Mexico City, 10/12-27.

Cichlasoma Citrinellum — AP92

Fish: 15c, Cichlasoma nicaraguensis. 20c, Carp. 30c, Gar (lepisosteus tropicus). 35c, Swordfish. 50c, Phylipnus dormitor, vert. 75c, Tarpon atlanticus, vert. 1cor, Eulamia nicaraguensis, vert. 2cor, Sailfish, vert. 3cor, Sawfish, vert.

Perf. 13½x13, 13x13½

1969, Mar. 12 Litho.

C667 AP92 10c vio bl & multi .20 .20
C668 AP92 15c org & multi .20 .20
C669 AP92 20c grn & multi .20 .20
C670 AP92 30c pur & multi .20 .20
C671 AP92 35c yel & multi .20 .20
C672 AP92 50c brn & multi .20 .20
C673 AP92 75c ultra & multi .20 .20
C674 AP92 1cor org & multi .20 .20
C675 AP92 2cor dk bl & multi .40 .25
C676 AP92 3cor multi .65 .40
a. Min. sheet of 4, #C673-C676 3.00 3.00
Nos. C667-C676 (10) 2.65 2.25

Nos. C544, C549, C567 and C439 Surcharged in Black or Red

1969, Mar. Litho. *Perf. 12, 13½x13*

C677 AP76 10c on 25c multi .20 .20
C678 AP77 10c on 25c multi .20 .20
C679 AP79 15c on 25c multi .20 .20

Engr.

C680 A84 50c on 70c (R) .20 .20
Nos. C677-C680 (4) .80 .80

Size of 50c surcharge: 11½x9mm.

View, Exhibition Tower and Emblem — AP93

1969, May 30 Litho. *Perf. 13½x13*

C681 AP93 30c dk vio bl & red .20 .20
C682 AP93 35c blk & red .20 .20
C683 AP93 75c car rose & vio bl .20 .20
C684 AP93 1cor dp plum & blk .25 .20
C685 AP93 2cor dk brn & blk .45 .35
a. Souv. sheet of 4, #C681-C682, C684-C685 1.25 1.25
Nos. C681-C685 (5) 1.30 1.15

HEMISFAIR 1968 Exhibition.

Nos. C410, C482, C567-C569, C399, C465, C546 Surcharged in Black or Red

1969 Litho. *Perfs. as before*

C686 A80 10c on 30c multi .20 .20
C687 AP66 10c on 30c bl & blk (R) .20 .20
C688 AP79 10c on 25c multi .20 .20
C689 AP79 10c on 30c multi .20 .20
C690 AP79 15c on 35c multi (R) .20 .20
C691 A79 20c on 30c multi .20 .20
C692 AP64 20c on 30c multi .20 .20
C693 AP76 20c on 35c multi .20 .20
Nos. C686-C693 (8) 1.60 1.60

Fishing AP94

Products of Nicaragua: 5c, Minerals (miner). 15c, Bananas. 20c, Timber (truck). 35c, Coffee. 40c, Sugar cane. 60c, Cotton. 75c, Rice and corn. 1cor, Tobacco. 2cor, Meat.

1969, Sept. 22 Litho. *Perf. 13x13½*

C694 AP94 5c gold & multi .20 .20
C695 AP94 10c gold & multi .20 .20
C696 AP94 15c gold & multi .20 .20
C697 AP94 20c gold & multi .20 .20
C698 AP94 35c gold & multi .20 .20
C699 AP94 40c gold & multi .20 .20
C700 AP94 60c gold & multi .20 .20
C701 AP94 75c gold & multi .20 .20
C702 AP94 1cor gold & multi .20 .20
C703 AP94 2cor gold & multi .40 .20
Nos. C694-C703 (10) 2.20 2.00

Woman Carrying Jar, Conference Emblem — AP95

1970, Feb. 26 Litho. *Perf. 13½x14*

C704 AP95 10c multi .20 .20
C705 AP95 15c grn & multi .20 .20
C706 AP95 20c ultra & multi .20 .20
C707 AP95 35c multi .20 .20
C708 AP95 50c multi .20 .20
C709 AP95 75c multi .25 .20
C710 AP95 1cor lil & multi .45 .30
C711 AP95 2cor multi .85 .50
Nos. C704-C711 (8) 2.55 2.00

8th Inter-American Conf. on Savings & Loans.

Soccer Type of Regular Issue and

Flags of Participating Nations, World Cup, 1970 — AP96

Soccer Players: 20c, Djalma Santos, Brazil. 80c, Billy Wright, England. 4cor, Jozef Bozsik, Hungary. 5cor, Bobby Charlton, England.

1970, May 11 Litho. *Perf. 13½*

C712 A87 20c multi .20 .20
C713 A87 80c multi .25 .20
C714 AP96 1cor multi .30 .25
C715 A87 4cor multi 1.25 .90
C716 A87 5cor multi 1.40 1.25
Nos. C712-C716 (5) 3.40 2.80

Issued to honor the winners of the 1970 poll for the International Soccer Hall of Fame. No. C714 also publicizes the 9th World Soccer Championships for the Jules Rimet Cup, Mexico City, May 30-June 21, 1970.

Names of players and their achievements printed in black on back of stamps.

For overprint and surcharges see Nos. C786-788.

EXPO Emblem, Mt. Fuji and Torii — AP97

1970, July 5 Litho. *Perf. 13½x14*

C717 AP97 25c multi .20 .20
C718 AP97 30c multi .20 .20
C719 AP97 35c multi .20 .20
C720 AP97 75c multi .25 .20
C721 AP97 1.50cor multi .40 .30
C722 AP97 3cor multi .75 .75
a. Souv. sheet of 3, #C720-C722, imperf. 1.00 1.00
Nos. C717-C722 (6) 2.00 1.85

EXPO '70 International Exhibition, Osaka, Japan, Mar. 15-Sept. 13, 1970.

Moon Landing, Apollo 11 Emblem and Nicaragua Flag AP98

Apollo 11 Emblem, Nicaragua Flag and: 40c, 75c, Moon surface and landing capsule. 60c, 1cor, Astronaut planting US flag.

1970, Aug. 12 Litho. *Perf. 14*

C723 AP98 35c multi .20 .20
C724 AP98 40c multi .20 .20
C725 AP98 60c pink & multi .20 .20
C726 AP98 75c yel & multi .25 .20
C727 AP98 1cor vio & multi .40 .20
C728 AP98 2cor org & multi .65 .40
Nos. C723-C728 (6) 1.90 1.40

Man's 1st landing on the moon, July 20, 1969. See note after US No. C76.

Franklin D. Roosevelt AP99

Christmas 1970 AP100

Roosevelt Portraits: 15c, 1cor, as stamp collector. 20c, 50c, 2cor, Full face.

1970, Oct. 12

C729 AP99 10c blk & bluish blk .20 .20
C730 AP99 15c blk & brn vio .20 .20
C731 AP99 20c blk & ol grn .20 .20
C732 AP99 35c blk & brn vio .20 .20
C733 AP99 50c brown .20 .20
C734 AP99 75c blue .20 .20
C735 AP99 1cor rose red .20 .20
C736 AP99 2cor black .40 .25
Nos. C729-C736 (8) 1.80 1.65

Franklin Delano Roosevelt (1882-1945).

1970, Dec. 1 Litho. *Perf. 14*

Paintings: No. C737, 15c, Annunciation, by Matthias Grunewald. No. C738, 20c, Nativity, by El Greco. No. C739, 35c, Adoration of the Magi, by Albrecht Dürer. No. C740, 75c, Virgin and Child, by J. van Hemessen. No. C741, 1cor, Holy Shepherd, Portuguese School, 16th century.

C737 AP100 10c multi .20 .20
C738 AP100 10c multi .20 .20
C739 AP100 10c multi .20 .20
C740 AP100 10c multi .20 .20
C741 AP100 10c multi .20 .20
C742 AP100 15c multi .20 .20
C743 AP100 20c multi .20 .20
C744 AP100 35c multi .20 .20
C745 AP100 75c multi .20 .20
C746 AP100 1cor multi .20 .20
Nos. C737-C746 (10) 2.00 2.00

Nos. C737-C741 printed se-tenant.

Issues of 1947-67 Surcharged

1971, Mar.

C747 A83 10c on 1.05cor, #C433 .30 .30
C748 AP64 10c on 1.05cor, #C471 .30 .30
C749 AP66 10c on 1.05cor, #C485 .30 .30
C750 AP42 15c on 1.50cor, #C292 .40 .40
C751 AP53 15c on 1.50cor, #C369 .40 .40
C752 A83 15c on 1.50cor, #C434 .40 .40
C753 A84 15c on 1.50cor, #C441 .40 .40
C754 A75 20c on 85c, #C385 .50 .50
C755 A81 20c on 85c, #C418 .50 .50

C756	A81	25c on 90c, #C419	.70	.70
C757	AP48	30c on 1.10cor, #C337	.85	.85
C758	AP44	40c on 1.10cor, #C314	1.10	1.10
C759	AP65	40c on 1.50cor, #C472	1.10	1.10
C760	AP80	1cor on 1.10cor, #C576	2.75	2.75
		Nos. C747-C760 (14)	10.00	10.00

The arrangement of the surcharge differs on each stamp.

Mathematics Type of Regular Issue

Symbolic Designs of Scientific Formulae: 25c, Napier's law (logarithms). 30c, Pythagorean theorem (length of sides of right-angled triangle). 40c, Boltzman's equation (movement of gases). 1cor, Broglie's law (motion of particles of matter). 2cor, Archimedes' principle (displacement of mass).

1971, May 15 Litho. *Perf. 13½*

C761	A88	25c lt bl & multi	.25	.20
C762	A88	30c lt bl & multi	.30	.20
C763	A88	40c lt bl & multi	.45	.20
C764	A88	1cor lt bl & multi	1.10	.35
C765	A88	2cor lt bl & multi	1.90	.75
		Nos. C761-C765 (5)	4.00	1.70

On the back of each stamp is a descriptive paragraph.

Montezuma Oropendola AP101

Birds: 15c, Turquoise-browed motmot. 20c, Magpie-jay. 25c, Scissor-tailed flycatchers. 30c, Spot-breasted oriole, horiz. 35c, Rufous-naped wren. 40c, Great kiskadee. 75c, Red-legged honeycreeper, horiz. 1cor, Great-tailed grackle, horiz. 2cor, Belted kingfisher.

1971, Oct. 15 Litho. *Perf. 14*

C766	AP101	10c multi	.20	.20
C767	AP101	15c multi	.20	.20
C768	AP101	20c gray & multi	.20	.20
C769	AP101	25c multi	.20	.20
C770	AP101	30c multi	.20	.20
C771	AP101	35c multi	.20	.20
C772	AP101	40c multi	.20	.20
C773	AP101	75c yel & multi	.25	.20
C774	AP101	1cor org & multi	.30	.20
C775	AP101	2cor org & multi	.65	.30
		Nos. C766-C775 (10)	2.60	2.10

Ten Commandments Type of Regular Issue

Designs: 1cor, Bathsheba at her Bath, by Rembrandt (IX). 2cor, Naboth's Vineyard, by James Smetham (X).

1971, Nov. 1 *Perf. 11*

C776	A90	1cor ocher & multi	.90	.45
C777	A90	2cor ocher & multi	1.50	.80

Descriptive inscriptions printed in gray on back of stamps.

U Thant, Anastasio Somoza, UN Emblem AP102

1972, Feb. 15 *Perf. 14x13½*

C778	AP102	10c pink & mar	.20	.20
C779	AP102	15c green	.20	.20
C780	AP102	20c blue	.20	.20
C781	AP102	25c rose claret	.20	.20
C782	AP102	30c org & brn	.20	.20
C783	AP102	40c gray & sl grn	.20	.20
C784	AP102	1cor ol grn	.25	.20
C785	AP102	2cor brown	.45	.25
		Nos. C778-C785 (8)	1.90	1.65

25th anniv. of the United Nations (in 1970).

Nos. C713, C715, C716 Surcharged or Overprinted Like Nos. 899-900

1972, Mar. 20 Litho. *Perf. 13½*

C786	A87	20c on 80c multi	.20	.20
C787	A87	60c on 4cor multi	.20	.20
C788	A87	5cor multi	1.10	1.00
		Nos. C786-C788 (3)	1.50	1.40

20th Olympic Games, Munich, 8/26-9/11.

Ceramic Figure, Map of Nicaragua — AP103

Pre-Columbian ceramics (700-1200 A.D.) found at sites indicated on map of Nicaragua.

1972, Sept. 16 Litho. *Perf. 14x13½*

C789	AP103	10c blue & multi	.20	.20
C790	AP103	15c blue & multi	.20	.20
C791	AP103	20c blue & multi	.20	.20
C792	AP103	25c blue & multi	.20	.20
C793	AP103	30c blue & multi	.20	.20
C794	AP103	35c blue & multi	.20	.20
C795	AP103	40c blue & multi	.20	.20
C796	AP103	50c blue & multi	.20	.20
C797	AP103	60c blue & multi	.20	.20
C798	AP103	80c blue & multi	.20	.20
C799	AP103	1cor blue & multi	.20	.20
C800	AP103	2cor blue & multi	.40	.25
		Nos. C789-C800 (12)	2.60	2.45

Lord Peter Wimsey, by Dorothy L. Sayers AP104

Designs (Book and): 10c, Philip Marlowe, by Raymond Chandler. 15c, Sam Spade, by Dashiell Hammett. 20c, Perry Mason, by Erle S. Gardner. 25c, Nero Wolfe, by Rex Stout. 35c, Auguste Dupin, by Edgar Allan Poe. 40c, Ellery Queen, by Frederick Dannay and Manfred B. Lee. 50c, Father Brown, by G. K. Chesterton. 60c, Charlie Chan, by Earl Derr Biggers. 80c, Inspector Maigret, by Georges Simenon. 1cor, Hercule Poirot, by Agatha Christie. 2cor, Sherlock Holmes, by A. Conan Doyle.

1972, Nov. 13 Litho. *Perf. 14x13½*

C801	AP104	5c blue & multi	.30	.20
C802	AP104	10c blue & multi	.30	.20
C803	AP104	15c blue & multi	.30	.20
C804	AP104	20c blue & multi	.30	.20
C805	AP104	25c blue & multi	.30	.20
C806	AP104	35c blue & multi	.40	.25
C807	AP104	40c blue & multi	.40	.25
C808	AP104	50c blue & multi	.50	.30
C809	AP104	60c blue & multi	.70	.40
C810	AP104	80c blue & multi	.85	.50
C811	AP104	1cor blue & multi	1.10	.65
C812	AP104	2cor blue & multi	2.25	1.25
		Nos. C801-C812 (12)	7.70	4.60

50th anniv. of INTERPOL, intl. police organization. Designs show famous fictional detectives. Inscriptions on back, printed on top of gum, give thumbnail sketch of character and author.

Shepherds Following Star AP105

Legend of the Christmas Rose: 15c, Adoration of the kings and shepherds. 20c, Shepherd girl alone crying. 35c, Angel appears to girl. 40c, Christmas rose (Helleborus niger). 60c, Girl thanks angel. 80c, Girl and Holy Family. 1cor, Girl presents rose to Christ Child. 2cor, Adoration.

1972, Dec. 20

C813	AP105	10c multi	.20	.20
C814	AP105	15c multi	.20	.20
C815	AP105	20c multi	.20	.20
C816	AP105	35c multi	.20	.20
C817	AP105	40c multi	.20	.20
C818	AP105	60c multi	.20	.20
C819	AP105	80c multi	.20	.20
C820	AP105	1cor multi	.20	.20
C821	AP105	2cor multi	.40	.30
a.		Souv. sheet of 9, #C813-C821	1.25	1.25
		Nos. C813-C821 (9)	2.00	1.90

Christmas 1972.

No. C821a exists with red marginal overprint, "TERREMOTO DESASTRE," for the Managua earthquake of Dec. 22-23, 1972. It was sold abroad, starting in Jan. 1973.

Sir Walter Raleigh, Patent to Settle New World — AP106

Events and Quotations from Contemporary Illustrations: 15c, Mayflower Compact, 1620. 20c, Acquittal of Peter Zenger, 1735, vert. 25c, William Pitt, 1766, vert. 30c, British revenue stamp for use in America No. RM31, vert. 35c, "Join or Die" serpent, 1768. 40c, Boston Massacre and State House, 1770, vert. 50c, Boston Tea Party and 3p coin, 1774. 60c, Patrick Henry, 1775, vert. 75c, Battle scene ("Our cause is just, our union is perfect," 1775). 80c, Declaration of Independence, 1776. 1cor, Liberty Bell, Philadelphia. 2cor, Seal of US, 1782, vert.

1973, Feb. 22 Photo. *Perf. 13½*

C822	AP106	10c olive & multi	.20	.20
C823	AP106	15c olive & multi	.20	.20
C824	AP106	20c olive & multi	.20	.20
C825	AP106	25c olive & multi	.20	.20
C826	AP106	30c olive & multi	.20	.20
C827	AP106	35c ol, gold & blk	.35	.20
C828	AP106	40c olive & multi	.35	.20
C829	AP106	50c olive & multi	.35	.35
C830	AP106	60c olive & multi	.40	.35
C831	AP106	75c olive & multi	.50	.40
C832	AP106	80c olive & multi	.50	.40
C833	AP106	1cor olive & multi	.80	.50
C834	AP106	2cor olive & multi	1.50	1.00
		Nos. C822-C834 (13)	5.75	4.40

Inscriptions on back, printed on top of gum, give brief description of subject and event.

Baseball, Player and Map of Nicaragua AP107

1973, May 25 Litho. *Perf. 13½x14*

C835	AP107	15c lil & multi	.20	.20
C836	AP107	20c multi	.20	.20
C837	AP107	40c multi	.20	.20
C838	AP107	10cor multi	1.75	1.50
a.		Souvenir sheet of 4	2.50	2.50
		Nos. C835-C838 (4)	2.35	2.10

20th International Baseball Championships, Managua, Nov. 15-Dec. 5, 1972. No. C838a contains 4 stamps similar to Nos. C835-C838 with changed background colors (15c, olive; 20c, gray; 40c, lt. green; 10cor, lilac), and 5 labels.

Fashion Type of 1973

1973, July 26 Litho. *Perf. 13½*

C839	A91	10c Lourdes Nicaragua	.20	.20
C840	A91	15c Halston, New York	.20	.20
C841	A91	20c Pino Lancetti, Rome	.20	.20
C842	A91	35c Madame Ges, Paris	.20	.20
C843	A91	40c Irene Galitzine, Rome	.20	.20
C844	A91	80c Pedro Rodriguez, Barcelona	.20	.20
a.		Souv. sheet of 9, #909-911, C839-C844, perf. 11 + 3 labels	3.00	3.00
		Nos. C839-C844 (6)	1.20	1.20

Inscriptions on back printed on top of gum give description of gown in Spanish and English.

Type of Air Post Semi-Postal Issue

Design: 2cor, Pediatric surgery.

1973, Sept. 25

C845	SPAP1	2cor multi	.40	.35
		Nos. C845,CB1-CB11 (12)	2.70	2.60

Planned Children's Hospital. Inscription on back, printed on top of gum gives brief description of subject shown.

Christmas Type

1cor, Virginia O'Hanlon writing letter, father. 2cor, Letter. 4cor, Virginia, father reading letter.

1973, Nov. 15 Litho. *Perf. 15*

C846	A92	1cor multicolored	.30	
C847	A92	2cor multicolored	.60	
C848	A92	4cor multicolored	1.10	
a.		Souvenir sheet of 3, #C846-C848, perf. 14½	4.00	
		Nos. C846-C848 (3)	2.00	

Churchill Type

#C851, Silhouette, Parliament. #C852, Silhouette, #10 Downing St. 5cor, Showing "V" sign. 6cor, "Bulldog" Churchill protecting England.

1974, Apr. 30 *Perf. 14½*

C849	A93	5cor multicolored	1.40	
C850	A93	6cor multicolored	1.75	

Souvenir Sheets

Perf. 15

C851	A93	4cor blk, org & bl	1.10	
C852	A93	4cor blk, org, & grn	1.10	

Nos. C851-C852 contain one 28x42mm stamp.

World Cup Type

Scenes from previous World Cup Championships with flags and scores of finalists.

1974, May 8 *Perf. 14½*

C853	A94	10cor Flags of participants	2.75	

Souvenir Sheets

C853A	A94	4cor like No. 928	1.10	
C853B	A94	5cor like No. 930	1.40	

For overprint see No. C856.

Flower Type of 1974

Wild Flowers and Cacti: 1 cor, Centrosema. 3 cor, Night-blooming cereus.

1974, June 11 Litho. *Perf. 14*

C854	A95	1cor green & multi	.20	.20
C855	A95	3cor green & multi	.65	.55

Nicaraguan Stamps Type

1974, July 10 *Perf. 14½*

C855A	A96	40c #835	.20	
C855B	A96	3cor #C313, horiz.	.90	
C855C	A96	5cor #734	1.40	
		Nos. C855A-C855C (3)	2.50	

Souvenir Sheet

Imperf

C855D		Sheet of 3	2.25	
e.	A96	1cor #665	.30	
f.	A96	2cor #C110, horiz.	.55	
g.	A96	4cor Globe, stars	1.40	

UPU, Cent.

No. C853 Ovptd.

1974, July 12

C856	A94	10cor Flags	2.75	

Animal Type of 1974

3cor, Colorado deer. 5cor, Jaguar.

1974, Sept. 10 Litho. *Perf. 14½*

C857	A97	3cor multi	.65	.55
C858	A97	5cor multi	1.00	.90

Christmas Type of 1974

Works of Michelangelo: 40c, Madonna of the Stairs. 80c, Pitti Madonna. 2cor, Pietà. 5cor, Self-portrait.

1974, Dec. 15

C859	A98	40c multi	.20	.20
C860	A98	80c multi	.20	.20
C861	A98	2cor multi	.30	.25
C862	A98	5cor multi	.70	.65
		Nos. C859-C862 (4)	1.40	1.30

An imperf. souvenir sheet exists containing 2cor and 5cor stamps.

Opera Type of 1975

Opera Singers and Scores: 25c, Rosa Ponselle, Norma. 35c, Giuseppe de Luca, Rigoletto. 40c, Joan Sutherland, La Figlia del Reggimento. 50c, Ezio Pinza, Don Giovanni. 60c, Kirsten Flagstad, Tristan and Isolde. 80c, Maria Callas, Tosca. 2cor, Fyodor Chaliapin, Boris Godunov. 5cor, Enrico Caruso, La Juive.

1975, Jan. 22 *Perf. 14x13½*

C863	A99	25c grn & multi	.30	.20
C864	A99	35c multi	.30	.20
C865	A99	40c multi	.30	.20
C866	A99	50c org & multi	.30	.20
C867	A99	60c rose & multi	.30	.20
C868	A99	80c lake & multi	.40	.20
C869	A99	2cor sep & multi	.80	.25
C870	A99	5cor multi	2.00	.65
a.		Souvenir sheet of 3	2.50	
		Nos. C863-C870 (8)	4.70	2.10

No. C870a contains one each of Nos. C869-C870 and a 1cor with design and colors of No. C868. Exists imperf.

Easter Type of 1975

Stations of the Cross: 40c, Jesus stripped of his clothes. 50c, Jesus nailed to the Cross. 80c, Jesus dies on the Cross. 1cor, Descent from the Cross. 5cor, Jesus laid in the tomb.

1975, Mar. 20 *Perf. 14½*

C871	A100	40c ultra & multi	.20	.20
C872	A100	50c ultra & multi	.20	.20
C873	A100	80c ultra & multi	.20	.20
C874	A100	1cor ultra & multi	.20	.20
C875	A100	5cor ultra & multi	.90	.80
		Nos. C871-C875 (5)	1.70	1.60

American Bicentennial Type of 1975

Designs: 40c, Washington's Farewell, 1783. 50c, Washington Addressing Continental Congress by J. B. Stearns. 2cor, Washington Arriving for Inauguration. 5cor, Statue of Liberty and flags of 1776 and 1976. 40c, 50c, 2cor, horiz.

1975, Apr. 16 *Perf. 14*

C876	A101	40c tan & multi	.20	.20
C877	A101	50c tan & multi	.25	.20
C878	A101	2cor tan & multi	.80	.70
C879	A101	5cor tan & multi	2.00	1.90
		Nos. C876-C879 (4)	3.25	3.00

Perf. and imperf. 7cor souv. sheets exist.

Nordjamb 75 Type of 1975

Designs (Scout and Nordjamb Emblems and): 35c, Camp. 40c, Scout musicians. 1cor, Campfire. 10cor, Lord Baden-Powell.

1975, Aug. 15 *Perf. 14½*

C880	A102	35c multi	.20	.20
C881	A102	40c multi	.20	.20
C882	A102	1cor multi	.20	.20
C883	A102	10cor multi	1.40	1.25
		Nos. C880-C883 (4)	2.00	1.85

Two airmail souvenir sheets of 2 exist. One, perf., contains 2cor and 3cor with designs of Nos. 992 and 990. The other, imperf., contains 2cor and 3cor with designs of Nos. 993 and C882. Size: 125x101mm.

Pres. Somoza Type of 1975

1975, Sept. 10 *Perf. 14*

C884	A103	1cor vio & multi	.20	.25
C885	A103	10cor bl & multi	2.00	1.75
C886	A103	20cor multi	4.00	3.00
		Nos. C884-C886 (3)	6.20	5.00

Choir Type of 1975

Famous Choirs: 50c, Montserrat Abbey. 1cor, St. Florian Choir Boys. 2cor, Choir Boys of the Wooden Cross, vert. 5cor, Boys and Pope Paul VI (Pueri Cantores International Federation).

1975, Nov. 15 *Perf. 14½*

C887	A104	50c sil & multi	.20	.20
C888	A104	1cor sil & multi	.20	.20
C889	A104	2cor sil & multi	.35	.30
C890	A104	5cor sil & multi	1.00	.85
		Nos. C887-C890 (4)	1.75	1.55

A 10cor imperf. souvenir sheet exists (Oberndorf Memorial Chapel Choir and score of "Holy Night-Silent Night").

Chess Type of 1976

Designs: 40c, The Chess Players, by Thomas Eakins. 2cor, Bobby Fischer and Boris Spasski in Reykjavik, 1972. 5cor, Shakespeare and Ben Johnson Playing Chess, by Karel van Mander.

1976, Jan. 8 *Perf. 14½*

C891	A105	40c multi	.20	.20
C892	A105	2cor vio & multi	.75	.55
C893	A105	5cor multi	1.50	1.25
		Nos. C891-C893 (3)	2.45	2.00

A souvenir sheet contains one each of Nos. C892-C893, perf. and imperf. Size: 143x67mm.

Olympic Winner Type 1976

Winners, Rowing and Sculling Events: 55c, USSR, 1956, 1960, 1964, vert. 70c, New Zealand, 1972, vert. 90c, New Zealand, 1968. 10cor, Women's rowing crew, US, 1976, vert. 20cor, US, 1956.

1976, Sept. 7 **Litho.** *Perf. 14*

C902	A107	55c bl & multi	.20	.20
C903	A107	70c bl & multi	.20	.20
C904	A107	90c bl & multi	.25	.20
C905	A107	20cor bl & multi	4.50	3.75
		Nos. C902-C905 (4)	5.15	4.35

Souvenir Sheet

C906	A107	10cor multi	3.00	

No. C906 for the 1st participation of women in Olympic rowing events, size of stamp: 37x50mm.

The overprint "Republica Democratica Alemana Vencedor en 1976" was applied in 1976 to No. C905 in black in 3 lines and to the margin of No. C906 in gold in 2 lines.

Bicentennial Type of 1976

American Bicentennial Emblem and: #C907, Philadelphia, 1776. #C908, Washington, 1976. #C909, John Paul Jones' ships. #C910, Atomic submarine. #C911, Wagon train. #C912, Diesel train.

1976, May 25 **Litho.** *Perf. 13½*

C907	A108	80c multi	.20	.20
C908	A108	80c multi	.20	.20
a.		Pair, #C907-C908	.35	.30
C909	A108	2.75cor multi	.50	.40
C910	A108	2.75cor multi	.50	.40
a.		Pair, #C909-C910	1.00	.80
C911	A108	4cor multi	.65	.50
C912	A108	4cor multi	.65	.50
a.		Pair, #C911-C912	1.30	1.00
		Nos. C907-C912 (6)	2.70	2.20

A souvenir sheet contains two 10cor stamps showing George Washington and Gerald R. Ford with their families. Size: 140x111mm.

Rare Stamps Type of 1976

Rare Stamps: 40c, Hawaii #1. 1cor, Great Britain #1. 2cor, British Guiana #13. 5cor, Honduras #C12. 10cor, Newfoundland #C1.

1976, Dec. *Perf. 14*

C913	A109	40c multi	.20	.20
C914	A109	1cor multi	.20	.20
C915	A109	2cor multi	.30	.25
C916	A109	5cor multi	.70	.65
C917	A109	10cor multi	1.40	1.25
		Nos. C913-C917 (5)	2.80	2.55

Inscriptions on back printed on top of gum give description of illustrated stamp. A 4cor imperf. souvenir sheet shows 1881 Great Britain-Nicaragua combination cover. Size: 140x101mm.

Olga Nuñez de Saballos — AP108

Designs: 1cor, Josefa Toledo de Aguerri. 10cor, Hope Portocarrero de Somoza.

1977, Feb. **Litho.** *Perf. 13½*

C918	AP108	35c multi	.20	.20
C919	AP108	1cor red & multi	.20	.20
C920	AP108	10cor multi	2.00	1.75
		Nos. C918-C920 (3)	2.40	2.15

Famous Nicaraguan women and for International Women's Year (in 1975).

Zeppelin Type of 1977

Designs: 35c, Ville de Paris airship. 70c, Zeppelin "Schwaben." 3cor, Zeppelin in flight. 10cor, Vickers "Mayfly" before take-off. 20cor, Zeppelin with leadlines extended.

1977, Oct. 31 **Litho.** *Perf. 14½*

C921	A110	35c multi	.20	.20
C922	A110	70c multi	.20	.20
C923	A110	3cor multi	.65	.50
C924	A110	10cor multi	2.50	1.75
		Nos. C921-C924 (4)	3.55	2.65

Souvenir Sheet

C925	A110	20cor multi	4.50	2.75

Lindbergh Type of 1977

Designs: 55c, Lindbergh's plane approaching Nicaraguan airfield, 1928. 80c, Spirit of St. Louis and map of New York-Paris route. 2cor, Plane flying off Nicaragua's Pacific Coast. 10cor, Lindbergh flying past Momotombo Volcano on way to Managua. 20cor, Spirit of St. Louis.

1977, Nov. 30

C926	A111	55c multi	.20	.20
C927	A111	80c multi	.20	.20
C928	A111	2cor multi	.40	.30
C929	A111	10cor multi	2.00	1.60
		Nos. C926-C929 (4)	2.80	2.30

Souvenir Sheet

C930	A111	20cor multi	4.50	3.50

Christmas Type of 1977

Souvenir Sheet

Design: 20cor, Finale of Nutcracker Suite.

1977, Dec. 12

C931	A112	20cor multi	4.50	4.50

Painting Type of 1978

Rubens Paintings: 5cor, Hippopotamus and Crocodile Hunt. 100cor, Duke de Lerma on Horseback. 20cor, Self-portrait.

1978, Jan. 11 **Litho.** *Perf. 14½*

C932	A113	5cor multi	1.00	.85
C933	A113	10cor multi	2.00	1.60

Souvenir Sheet

C934	A113	20cor multi	4.75	4.00

Peter Paul Rubens (1577-1640), 400th birth anniversary.

St. Francis Type of 1978

Designs: 80c, St. Francis and the wolf. 10cor, St. Francis, painting. 20cor, Our Lady of Conception, statue in Church of El Viejo.

1978, Feb. 23 **Litho.** *Perf. 14½*

C935	A114	80c lt brn & multi	.20	.20
C936	A114	10cor bl & multi	1.90	1.75

Souvenir Sheet

C937	A114	20cor multi	3.50	

Railroad Type of 1978

Locomotives: 35c, Light-weight American. 4cor, Heavy Baldwin. 10cor, Juniata, 13-ton. 20cor, Map of route system.

1978, Apr. 7 **Litho.** *Perf. 14½*

C938	A115	35c lt grn & multi	.20	.20
C939	A115	4cor dp org & multi	.90	.75
C940	A115	10cor cit & multi	2.00	1.90
		Nos. C938-C940 (3)	3.10	2.85

Souvenir Sheet

C941	A115	20cor multi	6.00	

Jules Verne Type of 1978

Designs: 90c, 20,000 Leagues under the Sea. 10cor, Around the World in 80 Days. 20cor, From the Earth to the Moon.

1978, Aug. **Litho.** *Perf. 14½*

C942	A116	90c multi	.20	.20
C943	A116	10cor multi	1.75	1.50

Souvenir Sheet

C944	A116	20cor multi	5.00	

Aviation History Type of 1978

Designs: 55c, Igor Sikorsky in his helicopter, 1913, horiz. 10cor, Space shuttle, horiz. 20cor, Flyer III, horiz.

1978, Sept. 29 **Litho.** *Perf. 14½*

C945	A117	55c multi	.20	.20
C946	A117	10cor multi	1.40	1.00

Souvenir Sheet

C947	A117	20cor multi	5.00	

Soccer Type of 1978

Soccer Players: 50c, Denis Law and Franz Beckenbauer. 5cor, Dino Zoff and Pelé. 20cor, Dominique Rocheteau and Johan Neeskens.

1978, Oct. 25 **Litho.** *Perf. 13½x14*

C948	A118	50c multi	.20	.20
C949	A118	5cor multi	1.00	.85

Souvenir Sheet

C950	A118	20cor multi	4.50	

Christmas Type of 1978

Paintings: 3cor, Apostles John and Peter, by Dürer. 10cor, Apostles Paul and Mark, by Dürer. 20cor, Virgin and Child with Garlands, by Dürer.

1978, Dec. 12 **Litho.** *Perf. 13½x14*

C951	A119	3cor multi	.40	.35
C952	A119	10cor multi	1.40	1.00

Souvenir Sheet

C953	A119	20cor multi	3.50	

Volcano Type of 1978

Designs: No. C954, Cerro Negro Volcano. No. C955, Lake Masaya. No. C956, Momotombo Volcano. No. C957, Lake Asososca. No. C958, Mombacho Volcano. No. C959, Lake Apoyo. No. C960, Concepcion Volcano. No. C961, Lake Tiscapa.

1978, Dec. 29 *Perf. 14x13½*

C954	A120	35c multi	.20	.20
C955	A120	35c multi	.20	.20
a.		Pair, #C549-C955	.30	.30
C956	A120	90c multi	.20	.20
C957	A120	90c multi	.20	.20
a.		Pair, #C956-C957	.35	.30
C958	A120	1cor multi	.20	.20
C959	A120	1cor multi	.20	.20
a.		Pair, #C958-C959	.40	.30
C960	A120	10cor multi	1.90	1.40
C961	A120	10cor multi	1.90	1.40
a.		Pair, #C960-C961	4.00	3.00
		Nos. C954-C961 (8)	5.00	4.00

Bernardo O'Higgins AP109

1979, Mar. 7 **Litho.** *Perf. 14*

C962	AP109	20cor multi	4.25	3.25

Bernardo O'Higgins (1778-1842), Chilean soldier and statesman.

Red Ginger and Rubythroated Hummingbird — AP110

Designs: 55c, Orchid. 70c, Poinsettia. 80c, Flower and bees. 2cor, Lignum vitae and blue morpho butterfly. 4cor, Cattleya.

1979, Apr. 6 **Litho.** *Perf. 14x13½*

C963	AP110	50c multi	.20	.20
C964	AP110	55c multi	.20	.20
C965	AP110	70c multi	.20	.20
C966	AP110	80c multi	.20	.20
C967	AP110	2cor multi	.35	.30
C968	AP110	4cor multi	.70	.50
		Nos. C963-C968 (6)	1.85	1.60

Revolution Type of 1981

1981, July 19 **Litho.** *Perf. 12½x12*

C973	A123	2.10cor March	.30	.20
C974	A123	3cor Construction	.40	.25
C975	A123	6cor Health programs	.80	.45
		Nos. C973-C975 (3)	1.50	.90

FSLN Type of 1981

1981, July 23

C976	A124	4cor Founder	.55	.35

Postal Union Type of 1981

1981, Aug. 10

C977	A125	2.10cor Pony express	.25	.20
C978	A125	3cor Headquarters	.30	.20
C979	A125	6cor Members' flags	.60	.35
		Nos. C977-C979 (3)	1.15	.75

1300th Anniv. of Bulgaria — AP112

1981, Sept. 2 *Imperf.*

C980	AP112	10cor multi	2.50	1.00

Size: 96x70mm.

Aquatic Flower Type of 1981

1981, Sept. 15 *Perf. 12½*

C981 A126 10cor Nymphaea gladstoniana 1.40 .90

Souvenir Sheet

Panda Bear — AP113

1981, Oct. 9 *Perf. 13*

C982 AP113 10cor multi 1.25 1.00

Philatokyo Stamp Exhibition, Tokyo.

Tropical Fish Type of 1981

1981, Oct. 19 *Perf. 12½*

C983 A127 3.50cor Pterolebias longipinnis .50 .30

C984 A127 4cor Xiphophorus helleri .55 .30

Souvenir Sheet

Frigate — AP114

1981, Nov. 2 *Perf. 13*

C985 AP114 10cor multi 1.50 .85

Espamer '81 Stamp Exhibition, Buenos Aires, Nov. 13-22.

Bird Type of 1981

1981, Nov. 30 *Perf. 12½*

C986 A128 3cor Trogon massena .65 .25

C987 A128 4cor Campylo-pterus hemileucurus, horiz. .75 .40

C988 A128 6cor Momotus momota 1.10 .55

Nos. C986-C988 (3) 2.50 1.20

Satellite Type of 1981

1981, Dec. 15 *Perf. 13x12½*

C989 A129 3cor multi .75 .25

C990 A129 4cor multi 1.00 .30

C991 A129 5cor multi 1.25 .35

Nos. C989-C991 (3) 3.00 .90

Railroad Type of 1981

1981, Dec. 30 *Perf. 12½*

C992 A130 6cor Ferrobus, 1967 1.50 .55

World Cup Type of 1982

1982, Jan. 25

C993 A131 4cor multi .60 .30

C994 A131 10cor multi, horiz. 1.40 .80

Souvenir Sheet

Perf. 13

C995 A131 10cor multi 2.75 1.10

No. C995 contains one 39x31mm stamp.

Dog Type of 1982

1982, Feb. 18

C996 A132 3cor Boxers .50 .30

C997 A132 3.50cor Pointers .55 .30

C998 A132 6cor Collies .95 .50

Nos. C996-C998 (3) 2.00 1.10

Intl. ITU Congress — AP115

1982, Mar. 12

C999 AP115 25cor multi 3.50 2.25

Butterfly Type of 1982

1982, Mar. 26

C1000 A133 3cor Parides iphidamas .75 .30

C1001 A133 3.50cor Consul hippona .85 .30

C1002 A133 4cor Morpho peleides .90 .40

Nos. C1000-C1002 (3) 2.50 1.00

Satellite Type of 1982

1982, Apr. 12

C1003 A134 5cor multi, horiz. .75 .40

C1004 A134 6cor multi 1.00 .50

UPU Type of 1982

1982, May 1 **Litho.** *Perf. 13*

C1005 A135 3.50cor Train .40 .25

C1006 A135 10cor Jet 1.10 .70

Sports Type of 1982

1982, May 13

C1007 A136 2.50cor Women's volleyball, vert. .50 .25

C1008 A136 3cor Boxing .60 .30

C1009 A136 9cor Soccer 1.90 .80

Nos. C1007-C1009 (3) 3.00 1.35

Souvenir Sheet

C1010 A136 10cor Baseball, vert. 2.00 .80

No. C1010 contains one 29x36mm stamp.

Souvenir Sheet

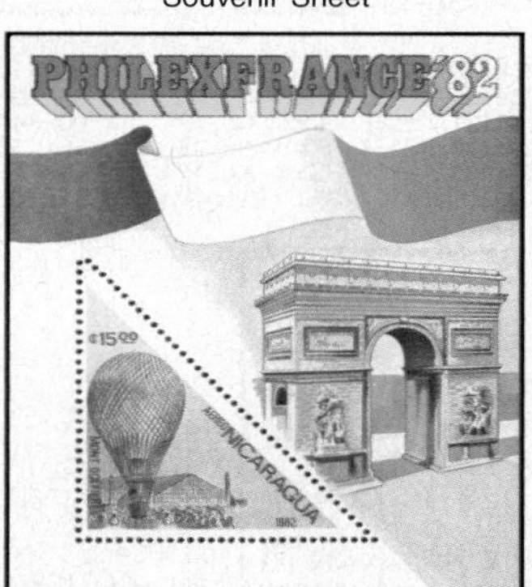

PHILEXFRANCE '82 Intl. Stamp Exhibition, Paris, June 11-21 — AP116

1982, June 9 *Perf. 13x12½*

C1011 AP116 15cor multi 2.50 1.00

Revolution Type of 1982

Symbolic doves. 2.50cor, 4cor vert.

1982, July 19 *Perf. 13*

C1012 A137 2.50cor multi .45 .25

C1013 A137 4cor multi .70 .40

C1014 A137 6cor multi 1.10 .60

Nos. C1012-C1014 (3) 2.25 1.25

Washington Type of 1982

2.50cor, Crossing the Delaware. 3.50cor, At Valley Forge. 4cor, Battle of Trenton. 6cor, Washington in Princeton.

Perf. 12½x13, 13x12½

1982, June 20 **Litho.**

C1015 A138 2.50cor multi, horiz. .50 .25

C1016 A138 3.50cor multi, horiz. .65 .35

C1017 A138 4cor multi .75 .40

C1018 A138 6cor multi 1.10 .60

Nos. C1015-C1018 (4) 3.00 1.60

Painting Type of 1982

1982, Aug. 17 *Perf. 13*

C1019 A139 9cor Seated Woman, by A. Morales 1.75 .80

Dimitrov Type of 1982

1982, Sept. 9

C1020 A140 2.50cor Dimitrov, Yikov, Sofia, 1946 .40 .25

C1021 A140 4cor Portrait, flag .60 .40

Dictatorship Type of 1982

1982, Sept. 21 *Perf. 13x12½*

C1022 A141 4cor Rigoberto Lopez Perez .60 .40

C1023 A141 6cor Edwin Castro 1.00 .60

Tourism Type of 1982

1982, Sept. 25 *Perf. 13*

C1024 A142 2.50cor Coyotepe Fortress, Masaya .30 .20

C1025 A142 3.50cor Velazquez Park, Managua .40 .25

Marx Type of 1982

1982, Oct. 4 *Perf. 12½*

C1026 A143 4cor Marx, Highgate Monument .55 .35

Discovery of America Type of 1982

1982, Oct. 12 *Perf. 12½x13*

C1027 A145 2.50cor Trans-atlantic voyage .50 .25

C1028 A145 4cor Landing of Columbus .75 .40

C1029 A145 7cor Death of Columbus 1.25 .70

a. Sheet, 2 each #1187-1190, C1027-C1029, + 2 labels — —

Nos. C1027-C1029 (3) 2.50 1.35

Souvenir Sheet

Perf. 13

C1030 A145 10cor Columbus' fleet 2.00 1.00

No. C1030 contains one 31x39mm stamp.

Flower Type of 1982

1982, Nov. 13 *Perf. 12½*

C1031 A146 2.50cor Pasiflora foetida .40 .25

C1032 A146 3.50cor Clitoria sp. .55 .30

C1033 A146 5cor Russelia sarmentosa .80 .45

Nos. C1031-C1033 (3) 1.75 1.00

Reptile Type of 1982

1982, Dec. 10 *Perf. 13*

C1034 A147 2.50cor Turtle, horiz. 1.25 .25

C1035 A147 3cor Boa constrictor 1.40 .30

C1036 A147 3.50cor Crocodile, horiz. 1.50 .30

C1037 A147 5cor Sistrurus catenatus, horiz. 2.25 .45

Nos. C1034-C1037 (4) 6.40 1.30

Non-aligned States Conference, Jan. 12-14 — AP117

1983, Jan. 10 **Litho.** *Perf. 12½x13*

C1038 AP117 4cor multi .90 .40

Geothermal Electricity Generating Plant, Momotombo Volcano — AP118

1983, Feb. 25 *Perf. 13*

C1039 AP118 2.50cor multi .40 .25

Souvenir Sheet

TEMBAL '83 Philatelic Exhibition, Basel, Switzerland — AP119

1983, May 21 **Litho.** *Perf. 13*

C1040 AP119 15cor Chamoix 2.25 1.25

Souvenir Sheet

1st Nicaraguan Philatelic Exhibition — AP120

1983, July 17 **Litho.** *Perf. 13*

C1041 AP120 10cor Nicaragua Airlines jet 2.25 1.25

Armed Forces AP121

1983, Sept. 2 **Litho.** *Perf. 13*

C1042 AP121 4cor Frontier guards, watch dog .40 .25

Souvenir Sheet

BRASILIANA '83 Intl. Stamp Show, Rio de Janeiro, July 29-Aug. 7 — AP122

1983

C1043 AP122 15cor Jaguar 5.00 1.25

Cuban Revolution, 25th Anniv. AP122a

1984, Jan. 1 **Litho.** *Perf. 13*

C1043A AP122a 4cor shown .60 .30

C1043B AP122a 6cor Castro, Guevara, flag .95 .45

Souvenir Sheet

Cardinal Infante Don Fernando, by Diego Velazquez — AP123

1984, May 2 **Litho.** ***Perf. 13***
C1044 AP123 15cor multi 3.75 1.00

ESPANA '84.

Souvenir Sheet

Hamburg '84 — AP124

1984, June 19 **Litho.** ***Perf. 13***
C1045 AP124 15cor Dirigible 3.75 .90

1984 UPU Congress — AP125

1984, June 24 ***Perf. 12½***
C1046 AP125 15cor Mail transport 1.75 .90

Souvenir Sheet

Expofilnic '84 (2nd Natl. Stamp Exhibition) — AP126

1984, July 15
C1047 AP126 15cor Communications Museum 1.75 .90

Souvenir Sheet

Ausipex '84 — AP127

1984, Sept. 21
C1048 AP127 15cor Explorer ship 1.75 .90

Souvenir Sheet

OLYMPHILEX '85 — AP128

1985, Mar. 18 **Litho.** ***Perf. 12½***
C1049 AP128 15cor Bicycle race 1.10 .60

Souvenir Sheet

ESPAMER '85, Havana, Mar. 19-24 — AP129

1985, Mar. 19
C1050 AP129 10cor Crocodylus rhombifer 1.00 .40

Victory of Sandanista Revolution, 6th Anniv. AP134

1985, July 19 **Litho.** ***Perf. 12½***
C1125 AP134 9cor Soldier, flag .90 .60
C1126 AP134 9cor Sugar mill .90 .60

Benjamin Zeledon, Birth Cent. — AP135

1985, Oct. 4 **Litho.** ***Perf. 12½***
C1127 AP135 15cor multicolored .75 .40

Henri Dunant (1828-1910), Founder of Red Cross — AP136

1985, Oct. 10 ***Perf. 12½x12***
C1128 AP136 3cor shown .30 .20
C1129 AP136 15cor Dunant, air ambulance 1.10 .45
a. Pair, #C1128-C1129 + label 1.45 .55

Nicaraguan Stamps, 125th Anniv. AP137

1986, May 22 ***Perf. 12½x13***
C1130 AP137 30cor No. C1 .80 .30
C1131 AP137 40cor No. 174 1.00 .40
C1132 AP137 50cor No. 48 1.25 .50
C1133 AP137 100cor No. 1 2.40 1.10
Nos. C1130-C1133 (4) 5.45 2.30

Intl. Peace Year — AP138

1986, July 19 ***Perf. 12½***
C1134 AP138 5cor shown .20 .20
C1135 AP138 10cor Globe, dove .25 .20

Carlos Fonseca, 10th Death Anniv. — AP139

1986, Aug. 11 **Litho.** ***Perf. 12½***
C1136 AP139 15cor multicolored .30 .20

Formation of the Sandinista Front, 25th anniv.

AP140

AP141

1986, Nov. 20 ***Perf. 13***
C1137 AP140 15cor Rhinoceros .30 .20
C1138 AP140 15cor Zebra .30 .20
C1139 AP140 25cor Elephant .55 .30
C1140 AP140 25cor Giraffe .55 .30
C1141 AP140 50cor Mandrill 1.10 .55
C1142 AP140 50cor Tiger 1.10 .55
Nos. C1137-C1142 (6) 3.90 2.10

1986, Dec. 20 ***Perf. 13***

World Cup Soccer Championships, Mexico: Various soccer players and natl. flags.

Shirt Colors

C1143 AP141 10cor blue .30 .20
C1144 AP141 10cor blk & white .30 .20
C1145 AP141 10cor blue & white .30 .20
C1146 AP141 15cor pink & white .45 .20
C1147 AP141 15cor grn & blk .45 .20
C1148 AP141 25cor blk & white, red .70 .30
C1149 AP141 50cor grn & yel, red, horiz. 1.40 .55
Nos. C1143-C1149 (7) 3.90 1.85

Souvenir Sheet

Perf. 12½

C1150 AP141 100cor blk & white, bl & white 2.75 1.10

Vassil Levski, 150th Birth Anniv. — AP142

1987, Apr. 18 ***Perf. 13***
C1151 AP142 30cor multicolored .70 .30

Intl. Year of Shelter for the Homeless — AP143

1987, Aug. 2
C1152 AP143 20cor multicolored .45 .25
C1153 AP143 30cor Housing, diff. .70 .35

Souvenir Sheet

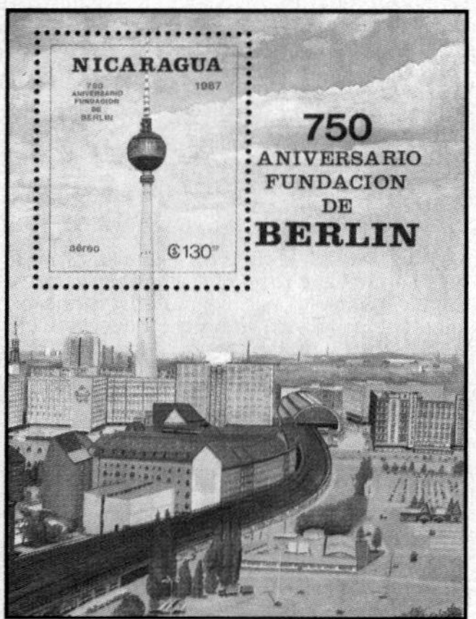

Berlin, 750th Anniv. — AP144

1987, Sept. 25 Litho. *Perf. 13*

C1154	AP144	130cor multi	2.95	.70

Discovery of America, 500th Anniv. (in 1992) — AP145

1987, Oct. 12 *Perf. 13*

C1155	AP145	15cor Indian village	.50	.20
C1156	AP145	15cor Sailing ships	.50	.20
C1157	AP145	20cor Battle in village	.65	.25
C1158	AP145	30cor Battle, prisoners	1.00	.30
C1159	AP145	40cor Spanish town	1.40	.40
C1160	AP145	50cor Cathedral	1.60	.50
a.		Min. sheet of 6, #C1155-C1160	5.75	5.75
		Nos. C1155-C1160 (6)	5.65	1.85

Cuban Revolution, 30th Anniv. — AP146

1989, Jan. 1 *Perf. 13*

C1161	AP146	20cor multicolored	.45	.25

AP147

AP148

Designs: Various soccer players in action.

1989, Feb. 20 *Perf. 13x12½*

C1162	AP147	100cor multi	.30	.20
C1163	AP147	200cor multi	.30	.20
C1164	AP147	600cor multi	.30	.20
C1165	AP147	1000cor multi	.40	.20
C1166	AP147	2000cor multi	.80	.45
C1167	AP147	3000cor multi	1.25	.40
C1168	AP147	5000cor multi	2.00	.65
		Nos. C1162-C1168 (7)	5.35	2.30

Souvenir Sheet

Perf. 13

C1169	AP147	9000cor multi	3.75	2.25

World Cup Soccer Championships, Italy. No. C1169 contains one 32x40mm stamp.

1989, July 19 *Perf. 13*

Design: 9000cor, Concepcion Volcano.

C1170	AP148	300cor multi	.20	.20

Souvenir Sheet

C1171	AP148	9000cor multi	2.25	2.25

Sandinista Revolution, 10th Anniv. No. C1171 contains one 40x32mm stamp.

AP149

AP150

Birds: 100cor, Anhinga anhinga. 200cor, Elanoides forficatus. 600cor, Eumomota superciliosa. 1000cor, Setophaga picta. 2000cor, Taraba major, horiz. 3000cor, Onychorhynchus mexicanus. 5000cor, Myrmotherula axillaris, horiz. 9000cor, Amazona ochrocephala.

1989, July 18 *Perf. 13x12½, 12½x13*

C1172	AP149	100cor multi	.25	.20
C1173	AP149	200cor multi	.25	.20
C1174	AP149	600cor multi	.25	.20
C1175	AP149	1000cor multi	.40	.20
C1176	AP149	2000cor multi	.80	.30
C1177	AP149	3000cor multi	1.25	.45
C1178	AP149	5000cor multi	2.00	.75
		Nos. C1172-C1178 (7)	5.20	2.30

Souvenir Sheet

Perf. 13

C1179	AP149	9000cor multi	3.75	1.60

Brasiliana '89. No. C1179 contains one 32x40mm stamp.

1989, Mar. 25 *Perf. 13*

Designs: 50cor, Downhill skiing. 300cor, Ice hockey. 600cor, Ski jumping. 1000cor, Pairs figure skating. 2000cor, Biathalon. 3000cor, Slalom skiing. 5000cor, Cross country skiing. 9000cor, Two-man luge.

C1180	AP150	50cor multi	.60	.20
C1181	AP150	300cor multi	.60	.20
C1182	AP150	600cor multi	.60	.20
C1183	AP150	1000cor multi	.60	.20
C1184	AP150	2000cor multi	1.00	.20
C1185	AP150	3000cor multi	1.10	.20
C1186	AP150	5000cor multi	1.25	.25
		Nos. C1180-C1186 (7)	5.75	1.45

Souvenir Sheet

C1187	AP150	9000cor multi	3.75	.45

1992 Winter Olympics, Albertville. No. C1187 contains one 32x40mm stamp.

AP151

AP152

Designs: 100cor, Water polo. 200cor, Running. 600cor, Diving. 1000cor, Gymnastics. 2000cor, Weight lifting. 3000cor, Volleyball. 5000cor, Wrestling. 9000cor, Field hockey.

1989, Apr. 23

C1188	AP151	100cor multi	.60	.20
C1189	AP151	200cor multi	.60	.20
C1190	AP151	600cor multi	.60	.20
C1191	AP151	1000cor multi	.60	.20
C1192	AP151	2000cor multi	1.00	.20
C1193	AP151	3000cor multi	1.10	.20
C1194	AP151	5000cor multi	1.25	.25
		Nos. C1188-C1194 (7)	5.75	1.45

Souvenir Sheet

C1195	AP151	9000cor multi	3.75	.45

1992 Summer Olympics, Barcelona. No. C1195 contains one 32x40mm stamp.

1989, Oct. 12

C1196	AP152	2000cor Vase	.70	.30

Discovery of America, 500th Anniv. (in 1992).

Currency Reform

Currency reform took place Mar. 4, 1990. Until stamps in the new currency were issued, mail was to be hand-stamped "Franqueo Pagado," (Postage Paid). Stamps were not used again until Apr. 25, 1991. The following set was sold by the post office but was not valid for postage. Value $5.65

Mushrooms

Designs: 500cor, Morchella esculenta. 1000cor, Boletus edulis. 5000cor, Lactarius deliciosus. 10,000cor, Panellus stipticus. 20,000cor, Craterellus cornucopioides. 40,000cor, Cantharellus cibarius. 50,000cor, Armillariella mellea.

1990, July 15 *Perf. 13*

500cor-50,000cor

AIR POST SEMI-POSTAL STAMPS

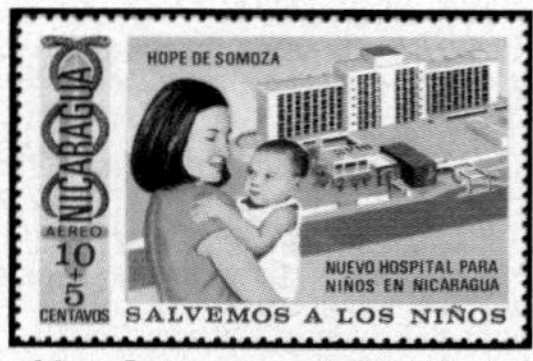

Mrs. Somoza and Children's Hospital — SPAP1

Designs: 5c+5c, Children and weight chart. 15c+5c, Incubator and Da Vinci's "Child in Womb." 20c+5c, Smallpox vaccination. 30c+5c, Water purification. 35c+5c, 1cor+50c, like 10c+5c. 50c+10c, Antibiotics. 60c+15c, Malaria control. 70c+10c, Laboratory. 80c+20c, Gastroenteritis (sick and well babies).

1973, Sept. 25 Litho. *Perf. 13½x14*

CB1	SPAP1	5c + 5c multi	.20	.20
CB2	SPAP1	10c + 5c multi	.20	.20
CB3	SPAP1	15c + 5c multi	.20	.20
CB4	SPAP1	20c + 5c multi	.20	.20
CB5	SPAP1	30c + 5c multi	.20	.20
CB6	SPAP1	35c + 5c multi	.20	.20
CB7	SPAP1	50c + 10c multi	.20	.20
CB8	SPAP1	60c + 15c multi	.20	.20
CB9	SPAP1	70c + 10c multi	.20	.20
CB10	SPAP1	80c + 20c multi	.20	.20
CB11	SPAP1	1cor + 50c multi	.30	.25
		Nos. CB1-CB11 (11)	2.30	2.25

The surtax was for hospital building fund. See No. C845. Inscriptions on back, printed on top of gum give brief description of subjects shown.

AIR POST OFFICIAL STAMPS

OA1

"Typewritten" Overprint on #O293

1929, Aug. Unwmk. *Perf. 12*

CO1	OA1	25c orange	50.00	45.00

Excellent counterfeits of No. CO1 are plentiful.

Official Stamps of 1926 Overprinted in Dark Blue

1929, Sept. 15

CO2	A24	25c orange	.50	.50
a.		Inverted overprint	25.00	
b.		Double overprint	25.00	
CO3	A25	50c pale bl	.75	.75
a.		Inverted overprint	25.00	
b.		Double overprint	25.00	
c.		Double overprint, one inverted	25.00	

Nos. 519-523 Overprinted in Black

1932, Feb.

CO4	A24	15c org red	.40	.40
a.		Inverted overprint	25.00	
b.		Double overprint	25.00	
c.		Double overprint, one invtd.	25.00	
CO5	A25	20c orange	.45	.45
a.		Double overprint	25.00	

CO6 A24 25c dk vio .45 .45
CO7 A25 50c green .55 .55
CO8 A25 1cor yellow 1.00 1.00
Nos. CO4-CO8 (5) 2.85 2.85

Nos. CO4-CO5, CO7-CO8 exist with signature control overprint. Value, each, $2.50.

Overprinted on Stamp No. 547

CO9 A24 25c blk brn 42.50 42.50

The varieties "OFICAL", "OFIAIAL" and "CORROE" occur in the setting and are found on each stamp of the series.

Counterfeits of No. CO9 are plentiful.

Stamp No. CO4 with overprint "1931" in addition is believed to be of private origin.

Type of Regular Issue of 1914 Overprinted Like Nos. CO4-CO8

1933

CO10 A24 25c olive .20 .20
CO11 A25 50c ol grn .25 .25
CO12 A25 1cor org red .40 .40

On Stamps of 1914-28

CO13 A24 15c dp vio .20 .20
CO14 A25 20c dp grn .20 .20
Nos. CO10-CO14 (5) 1.25 1.25

Nos. CO10-CO14 exist without signature control mark. Value, each $2.50.

Air Post Official Stamps of 1932-33 Overprinted in Blue

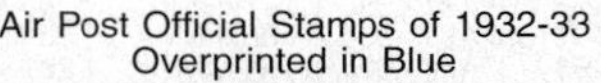

1935

CO15 A24 15c dp vio 1.00 .80
CO16 A25 20c dp grn 2.00 1.60
CO17 A24 25c olive 3.00 2.50
CO18 A25 50c ol grn 35.00 30.00
CO19 A25 1cor org red 40.00 37.50
Nos. CO15-CO19 (5) 81.00 72.40

Overprinted in Red

CO20 A24 15c dp vio .25 .25
CO21 A25 20c dp grn .25 .25
CO22 A24 25c olive .25 .25
CO23 A25 50c ol grn .80 .80
CO24 A25 1cor org red .80 .80
Nos. CO20-CO24 (5) 2.35 2.35

Nos. CO15 to CO24 are handstamped with script control mark. Counterfeits of blue overprint are plentiful.

The editors do not recognize the Nicaraguan air post Official stamps overprinted in red "VALIDO 1935" in two lines and with or without script control marks as having been issued primarily for postal purposes.

Nos. C164-C168 Overprinted in Black

1937

CO25 AP1 15c yel org .80 .55
CO26 AP1 20c org red .80 .60
CO27 AP1 25c black .80 .70
CO28 AP1 50c violet .80 .70
CO29 AP1 1cor orange .80 .70
Nos. CO25-CO29 (5) 4.00 3.25

Pres. Anastasio Somoza — OA2

1939, Feb. 7 Engr. *Perf. 12½*

CO30 OA2 10c brown .25 .25
CO31 OA2 15c dk bl .25 .25
CO32 OA2 20c yellow .25 .25
CO33 OA2 25c dk pur .25 .25
CO34 OA2 30c lake .25 .25
CO35 OA2 50c dp org .65 .65
CO36 OA2 1cor dk ol grn 1.25 1.25
Nos. CO30-CO36 (7) 3.15 3.15

Catalogue values for unused stamps in this section, from this point to the end of the section, are for Never Hinged items.

Mercedes Airport — OA3

Designs: 10c, Sulphurous Lake of Nejapa. 15c, Ruben Dario Monument. 20c, Tapir. 25c, Genizaro Dam. 50c, Tipitapa Spa. 1cor, Stone Highway. 2.50cor, Franklin D. Roosevelt Monument.

Engraved, Center Photogravure

1947, Aug. 29

Various Frames in Black

CO37 OA3 5c org brn .20 .20
CO38 OA3 10c blue .20 .20
CO39 OA3 15c violet .20 .20
CO40 OA3 20c red org .20 .20
CO41 OA3 25c blue .20 .20
CO42 OA3 50c car rose .20 .20
CO43 OA3 1cor slate .45 .45
CO44 OA3 2.50cor red brn 1.25 1.25
Nos. CO37-CO44 (8) 2.90 2.90

Rowland Hill — OA4

Designs: 10c, Heinrich von Stephan. 25c, 1st UPU Bldg. 50c, UPU Bldg., Bern. 1cor, UPU Monument. 2.60cor, Congress medal, reverse.

1950, Nov. 23 Engr. *Perf. 13*

Frames in Black

CO45 OA4 5c rose vio .20 .20
CO46 OA4 10c dp grn .20 .20
CO47 OA4 25c rose vio .20 .20
CO48 OA4 50c dp org .20 .20
CO49 OA4 1cor ultra .30 .30
CO50 OA4 2.60cor gray blk 2.25 2.00
Nos. CO45-CO50 (6) 3.35 3.10

75th anniv. (in 1949) of the UPU.

Each denomination was also issued in a souvenir sheet containing four stamps and marginal inscriptions. Size: 121x96mm. Value, set of 6 sheets, $35.

Consular Service Stamps Surcharged "Oficial Aéreo" and New Denomination in Red, Black or Blue

1961, Nov. Unwmk. Engr. *Perf. 12*

Red Marginal Number

CO51 AP63 10c on 1cor grnsh blk (R) .20 .20
CO52 AP63 15c on 20cor red brn (R) .20 .20
CO53 AP63 20c on 100cor mag .20 .20
CO54 AP63 25c on 50c dp bl (R) .20 .20
CO55 AP63 35c on 50cor brn (R) .20 .20
CO56 AP63 50c on 3cor dk car .20 .20
CO57 AP63 1cor on 2cor grn (R) .20 .20
CO58 AP63 2cor on 5cor org (Bl) .40 .40
CO59 AP63 5cor on 10cor vio (R) 1.00 1.00
Nos. CO51-CO59 (9) 2.80 2.80

POSTAGE DUE STAMPS

D1

D2

1896 Unwmk. Engr. *Perf. 12*

J1 D1 1c orange .50 *1.25*
J2 D1 2c orange .50 *1.25*
J3 D1 5c orange .50 *1.25*
J4 D1 10c orange .50 *1.25*
J5 D1 20c orange .50 *1.25*
J6 D1 30c orange .50 *1.25*
J7 D1 50c orange .50 *1.50*
Nos. J1-J7 (7) 3.50 *9.00*

Wmk. 117

J8 D1 1c orange 1.00 *1.50*
J9 D1 2c orange 1.00 *1.50*
J10 D1 5c orange 1.00 *1.50*
J11 D1 10c orange 1.00 *1.50*
J12 D1 20c orange 1.25 *1.50*
J13 D1 30c orange 1.00 *1.50*
J14 D1 50c orange 1.00 *1.50*
Nos. J8-J14 (7) 7.25 *10.50*

1897 Unwmk.

J15 D1 1c violet .50 *1.50*
J16 D1 2c violet .50 *1.50*
J17 D1 5c violet .50 *1.50*
J18 D1 10c violet .50 *1.50*
J19 D1 20c violet 1.25 *2.00*
J20 D1 30c violet .50 *1.50*
J21 D1 50c violet .50 *1.50*
Nos. J15-J21 (7) 4.25 *11.00*

Wmk. 117

J22 D1 1c violet .50 *1.50*
J23 D1 2c violet .50 *1.50*
J24 D1 5c violet .50 *1.50*
J25 D1 10c violet .50 *1.50*
J26 D1 20c violet 1.00 *2.00*
J27 D1 30c violet .50 *1.50*
J28 D1 50c violet .50 *1.50*
Nos. J22-J28 (7) 4.00 *11.00*

Reprints of Nos. J8-J28 are on thick, porous paper. Color of 1896 reprints, reddish orange; or 1897 reprints, reddish violet. On watermarked reprints, liberty cap is sideways. Value 25c each.

1898 Litho. Unwmk.

J29 D2 1c blue green .20 *2.00*
J30 D2 2c blue green .20 *2.00*
J31 D2 5c blue green .20 *2.00*
J32 D2 10c blue green .20 *2.00*
J33 D2 20c blue green .20 *2.00*
J34 D2 30c blue green .20 *2.00*
J35 D2 50c blue green .20 *2.00*
Nos. J29-J35 (7) 1.40 *14.00*

1899

J36 D2 1c carmine .20 *2.00*
J37 D2 2c carmine .20 *2.00*
J38 D2 5c carmine .20 *2.00*
J39 D2 10c carmine .20 *2.00*
J40 D2 20c carmine .20 *2.00*
J41 D2 50c carmine .20 *2.00*
Nos. J36-J41 (6) 1.20 *12.00*

Some denominations are found in se-tenant pairs.

Various counterfeit cancellations exist on #J1-J41.

D3

1900 Engr.

J42 D3 1c plum .75
J43 D3 2c vermilion .75
J44 D3 5c dk bl .75
J45 D3 10c purple .75
J46 D3 20c org brn .75
J47 D3 30c dk grn 1.50
J48 D3 50c lake 1.50
Nos. J42-J48 (7) 6.75

Nos. J42-J48 were not placed in use as postage due stamps. They were only issued with "Postage" overprints. See Nos. 137-143, 152-158, O72-O81, 2L11-2L15, 2L25, 2L40-2L41.

OFFICIAL STAMPS

Types of Postage Stamps Overprinted in Red Diagonally Reading up

1890 Unwmk. Engr. *Perf. 12*

O1 A5 1c ultra .20 *.30*
O2 A5 2c ultra .20 *.30*
O3 A5 5c ultra .20 *.30*
O4 A5 10c ultra .20 *.40*
O5 A5 20c ultra .20 *.45*
O6 A5 50c ultra .20 *.75*
O7 A5 1p ultra .20 *1.25*
O8 A5 2p ultra .20 *1.50*
O9 A5 5p ultra .20 *2.00*
O10 A5 10p ultra .20 *3.25*
Nos. O1-O10 (10) 2.00 *10.50*

All values of the 1890 issue are known without overprint and most of them with inverted or double overprint, or without overprint and imperforate. There is no evidence that they were issued in these forms.

Official stamps of 1890-1899 are scarce with genuine cancellations. Forged cancellations are plentiful.

Overprinted Vertically Reading Up

1891 Litho.

O11 A6 1c green .20 *.30*
O12 A6 2c green .20 *.30*
O13 A6 5c green .20 *.30*
O14 A6 10c green .20 *.30*
O15 A6 20c green .20 *.50*
O16 A6 50c green .20 *1.10*
O17 A6 1p green .20 *1.25*
O18 A6 2p green .20 *1.25*
O19 A6 5p green .20 *2.00*
O20 A6 10p green .20 *3.50*
Nos. O11-O20 (10) 2.00 *10.80*

All values of this issue except the 2c and 5p exist without overprint and several with double overprint. They are not known to have been issued in this form.

Many of the denominations may be found in se-tenant pairs.

Overprinted in Dark Blue

1892 Engr.

O21 A7 1c yellow brown .20 *.30*
O22 A7 2c yellow brown .20 *.30*
O23 A7 5c yellow brown .20 *.30*
O24 A7 10c yellow brown .20 *.30*
O25 A7 20c yellow brown .20 *.50*
O26 A7 50c yellow brown .20 *1.00*
O27 A7 1p yellow brown .20 *1.25*
O28 A7 2p yellow brown .20 *1.50*
O29 A7 5p yellow brown .20 *2.25*
O30 A7 10p yellow brown .20 *3.50*
Nos. O21-O30 (10) 2.00 *11.20*

The 2c and 1p are known without overprint and several values exist with double or inverted overprint. These probably were not regularly issued.

Commemorative of the 400th anniversary of the discovery of America by Christopher Columbus.

Overprinted in Red

1893 Engr.

O31 A8 1c slate .20 *.30*
O32 A8 2c slate .20 *.30*
O33 A8 5c slate .20 *.30*
O34 A8 10c slate .20 *.30*
O35 A8 20c slate .20 *.50*
O36 A8 25c slate .20 *.75*
O37 A8 50c slate .20 *.85*
O38 A8 1p slate .20 *1.00*
O39 A8 2p slate .20 *2.00*
O40 A8 5p slate .20 *2.50*
O41 A8 10p slate .20 *5.50*
Nos. O31-O41 (11) 2.20 *14.30*

The 2, 5, 10, 20, 25, 50c and 5p are known without overprint but probably were not regularly issued. Some values exist with double or inverted overprints.

Overprinted in Black

1894

O42	A9	1c orange	.30	.35
O43	A9	2c orange	.30	.35
O44	A9	5c orange	.30	.35
O45	A9	10c orange	.30	.35
O46	A9	20c orange	.30	*.50*
O47	A9	50c orange	.30	*.75*
O48	A9	1p orange	.30	*1.50*
O49	A9	2p orange	.30	*2.00*
O50	A9	5p orange	2.00	*3.00*
O51	A9	10p orange	2.00	*4.00*
		Nos. O42-O51 (10)	6.40	*13.15*

Reprints are yellow.

1895

Overprinted in Blue

O52	A10	1c green	.20	*.35*
O53	A10	2c green	.20	*.35*
O54	A10	5c green	.20	*.35*
O55	A10	10c green	.20	*.35*
O56	A10	20c green	.20	*.50*
O57	A10	50c green	.20	*1.00*
O58	A10	1p green	.20	*1.50*
O59	A10	2p green	.20	*2.00*
O60	A10	5p green	.20	*3.00*
O61	A10	10p green	.20	*4.00*
		Nos. O52-O61 (10)	2.00	*13.40*

Wmk. 117

O62	A10	1c green
O63	A10	2c green
O64	A10	5c green
O65	A10	10c green
O66	A10	20c green
O67	A10	50c green
O68	A10	1p green
O69	A10	2p green
O70	A10	5p green
O71	A10	10p green

Nos. O62-O71 probably exist only as reprints. Value, each 15 cents.

Postage Due Stamps of Same Date Handstamped in Violet

1896 **Unwmk.**

O72	D1	1c orange	7.00
O73	D1	2c orange	7.00
O74	D1	5c orange	5.00
O75	D1	10c orange	5.00
O76	D1	20c orange	5.00
		Nos. O72-O76 (5)	29.00

Wmk. 117

O77	D1	1c orange	7.00
O78	D1	2c orange	7.00
O79	D1	5c orange	4.00
O80	D1	10c orange	4.00
O81	D1	20c orange	4.00
		Nos. O77-O81 (5)	26.00

Nos. O72-O81 were handstamped in rows of five. Several handstamps were used, one of which had the variety "Oftcial." Most varieties are known inverted and double.

Forgeries exist.

Types of Postage Stamps Overprinted in Red

1896 **Unwmk.**

O82	A11	1c red	2.50	3.00
O83	A11	2c red	2.50	3.00
O84	A11	5c red	2.50	3.00
O85	A11	10c red	2.50	3.00
O86	A11	20c red	3.00	3.00
O87	A11	50c red	5.00	*5.00*
O88	A11	1p red	12.00	*12.00*
O89	A11	2p red	12.00	*12.00*
O90	A11	5p red	16.00	*16.00*
		Nos. O82-O90 (9)	58.00	*60.00*

Wmk. 117

O91	A11	1c red	3.00	3.50
O92	A11	2c red	3.00	3.50
O93	A11	5c red	3.00	3.50
O94	A11	10c red	3.00	3.50
O95	A11	20c red	5.00	5.00
O96	A11	50c red	3.00	*5.00*
O97	A11	1p red	14.00	*14.00*
O98	A11	2p red	16.00	*16.00*
O99	A11	5p red	25.00	*25.00*
		Nos. O91-O99 (9)	75.00	*79.00*

Used values for Nos. O88-O90, O97-O99 are for CTO copies. Postally used copies are not known.

Same, Dated 1897

1897 **Unwmk.**

O100	A11	1c red	3.00	3.00
O101	A11	2c red	3.00	3.00
O102	A11	5c red	3.00	2.50
O103	A11	10c red	3.00	3.00
O104	A11	20c red	3.00	4.00
O105	A11	50c red	5.00	*5.00*
O106	A11	1p red	12.00	*12.00*
O107	A11	2p red	12.00	*12.00*
O108	A11	5p red	16.00	*16.00*
		Nos. O100-O108 (9)	60.00	*60.50*

Wmk. 117

O109	A11	1c red	5.00	5.00
O110	A11	2c red	5.00	5.00
O111	A11	5c red	5.00	5.00
O112	A11	10c red	10.00	10.00
O113	A11	20c red	10.00	10.00
O114	A11	50c red	12.00	*12.00*
O115	A11	1p red	20.00	*20.00*
O116	A11	2p red	20.00	*20.00*
O117	A11	5p red	20.00	*20.00*
		Nos. O109-O117 (9)	107.00	*107.00*

Reprints of Nos. O82-O117 are described in notes after No. 109M. Value 15c each.

Used values for Nos. O106-O108, O115-O117 are for CTO copies. Postally used copies are not known.

Overprinted in Blue

1898 **Unwmk.**

O118	A12	1c carmine	3.25	3.25
O119	A12	2c carmine	3.25	3.25
O120	A12	4c carmine	3.25	3.25
O121	A12	5c carmine	2.50	2.50
O122	A12	10c carmine	4.00	4.00
O123	A12	15c carmine	6.00	6.00
O124	A12	20c carmine	6.00	6.00
O125	A12	50c carmine	8.50	*8.50*
O126	A12	1p carmine	11.00	*11.00*
O127	A12	2p carmine	11.00	*11.00*
O128	A12	5p carmine	11.00	*11.00*
		Nos. O118-O128 (11)	69.75	*69.75*

Stamps of this set with sideways watermark 117 or with black overprint are reprints. Value 25c each.

Used values for Nos. O126-O128 are for CTO copies. Postally used copies are not known.

Overprinted in Dark Blue

1899

O129	A13	1c gray grn	.20	*1.00*
O130	A13	2c bis brn	.20	*1.00*
O131	A13	4c lake	.20	*1.00*
O132	A13	5c dk bl	.20	*.50*
O133	A13	10c buff	.20	*1.00*
O134	A13	15c chocolate	.20	*2.00*
O135	A13	20c dk grn	.20	*3.00*
O136	A13	50c car rose	.20	*3.00*
O137	A13	1p red	.20	*10.00*
O138	A13	2p violet	.20	*10.00*
O139	A13	5p lt bl	.20	*15.00*
		Nos. O129-O139 (11)	2.20	*47.50*

Counterfeit cancellations on Nos. O129-O139 are plentiful.

"Justice" — O5

1900 **Engr.**

O140	O5	1c plum	.60	.60
O141	O5	2c vermilion	.50	.50
O142	O5	4c ol grn	.60	.60
O143	O5	5c dk bl	1.25	.45
O144	O5	10c purple	1.25	.35
O145	O5	20c brown	.90	.35
O146	O5	50c lake	1.25	.50
O147	O5	1p ultra	3.50	2.50
O148	O5	2p brn org	4.00	4.00
O149	O5	5p grnsh blk	5.00	5.00
		Nos. O140-O149 (10)	18.85	14.85

For surcharges see Nos. O155-O157.

Nos. 123, 161 Surcharged in Black

1903 ***Perf. 12, 14***

O150	A14	1c on 10c violet	.25	.30
	a.	"Centovo"	1.00	
	b.	"Contavo"	1.00	
	c.	With ornaments	.30	
	d.	Inverted surcharge	1.00	
	e.	"1" omitted at upper left	2.00	
O151	A14	2c on 3c green	.30	.40
	a.	"Centovos"	1.00	
	b.	"Contavos"	1.00	
	c.	With ornaments	.35	
	d.	Inverted surcharge	1.00	
O152	A14	4c on 3c green	1.25	1.25
	a.	"Centovos"	2.50	
	b.	"Contavos"	2.50	
	c.	With ornaments	2.50	
	d.	Inverted surcharge		
O153	A14	4c on 10c violet	1.25	1.25
	a.	"Centovos"	2.50	
	b.	"Contavos"	2.50	
	c.	With ornaments	2.00	
	d.	Inverted surcharge		
O154	A14	5c on 3c green	.20	.20
	a.	"Centovos"	1.00	
	b.	"Contavos"	1.00	
	c.	With ornaments	.30	
	d.	Double surcharge	2.00	
	e.	Inverted surcharge		
		Nos. O150-O154 (5)	3.25	3.40

These surcharges are set up to cover 25 stamps. Some of the settings have bars or pieces of fancy border type below "OFICIAL." There are 5 varieties on #O150, 3 on #O151, 1 each on #O152, O153, O154.

In 1904 #O151 was reprinted to fill a dealer's order. This printing lacks the small figure at the upper right. It includes the variety "OFICILA." At the same time the same setting was printed in carmine on official stamps of 1900, 1c on 10c violet and 2c on 1p ultramarine. Also the 1, 2 and 5p official stamps of 1900 were surcharged with new values and the dates 1901 or 1902 in various colors, inverted, etc. It is doubtful if any of these varieties were ever in Nicaragua and certain that none of them ever did legitimate postal duty.

No. O145 Surcharged in Black

1904 ***Perf. 12***

O155	O5	10c on 20c brn	.20	.20
	a.	No period after "Ctvs"	1.00	.75
O156	O5	30c on 20c brn	.20	.20
O157	O5	50c on 20c brn	.50	.35
	a.	Lower "50" omitted	2.50	2.50
	b.	Upper figures omitted	2.50	2.50
	c.	Top left and lower figures omitted	3.50	3.50
		Nos. O155-O157 (3)	.90	.75

Coat of Arms — O6

1905, July 25 **Engr.**

O158	O6	1c green	.25	.25
O159	O6	2c rose	.25	.25
O160	O6	5c blue	.25	.25
O161	O6	10c yel brn	.25	.25
O162	O6	20c orange	.25	.25
O163	O6	50c brn ol	.25	.25
O164	O6	1p lake	.25	.25
O165	O6	2p violet	.25	.25
O166	O6	5p gray blk	.25	.25
		Nos. O158-O166 (9)	2.25	2.25

Surcharged Vertically Up or Down

1907

O167	O6	10c on 1c grn	.75	.75
O168	O6	10c on 2c rose	25.00	22.50
O169	O6	20c on 2c rose	22.50	17.50
O170	O6	50c on 1c grn	1.50	1.50
O171	O6	50c on 2c rose	22.50	12.50

Surcharged

O172	O6	1p on 2c rose	1.50	1.50
O173	O6	2p on 2c rose	1.50	1.50
O174	O6	3p on 2c rose	1.50	1.50
O175	O6	4p on 2c rose		
O176	O6	4p on 5c blue	2.25	2.25

The setting for this surcharge includes various letters from wrong fonts, the figure "1" for "l" in "Vale" and an "l" for "1" in "$1.00."

Surcharged

O177	O6	20c on 1c green	1.00	1.00
	a.	Double surcharge	5.00	5.00
		Nos. O167-O174,O176-O177 (10)	80.00	62.50

The preceding surcharges are vertical, reading both up and down.

O7

Revenue Stamps Surcharged

1907 ***Perf. 14 to 15***

O178	O7	10c on 2c org (Bk)	.20	.20
O179	O7	35c on 1c bl (R)	.20	.20
	a.	Inverted surcharge	3.00	3.00
O180	O7	70c on 1c bl (V)	.20	.20
	a.	Inverted surcharge	3.00	3.00
O181	O7	70c on 1c bl (O)	.20	.20
	a.	Inverted surcharge	3.00	3.00
O182	O7	1p on 2c org (G)	.20	.20
	a.	Inverted surcharge	2.50	2.50
O183	O7	2p on 2c org (Br)	.20	.20
O184	O7	3p on 5c brn (Bl)	.20	.20
O185	O7	4p on 5c brn (G)	.20	.20
	a.	Double surcharge	3.00	3.00
O186	O7	5p on 5c brn (G)	.20	.20
	a.	Inverted surcharge	3.50	3.50
		Nos. O178-O186 (9)	1.80	1.80

Letters and figures from several fonts were mixed in these surcharges.

See Nos. O199-O209.

No. 202 Surcharged

1907, Nov.

Black or Blue Black Surcharge

O187 A18 10c on 1c grn 15.00 13.00
O188 A18 15c on 1c grn 15.00 13.00
O189 A18 20c on 1c grn 15.00 13.00
O190 A18 50c on 1c grn 15.00 13.00

Red Surcharge

O191 A18 1(un)p on 1c grn 14.00 13.00
O192 A18 2(dos)p on 1c grn 14.00 13.00
Nos. O187-O192 (6) 88.00 78.00

No. 181 Surcharged 

1908 Yellow Surcharge ***Perf. 12***

O193 A18 10c on 3c vio 15.00 15.00
O194 A18 15c on 3c vio 15.00 15.00
O195 A18 20c on 3c vio 15.00 15.00
O196 A18 35c on 3c vio 15.00 15.00
O197 A18 50c on 3c vio 15.00 15.00
Nos. O193-O197 (5) 75.00 75.00

Black Surcharge

O198 A18 35c on 3c vio *100.00 100.00*

Revenue Stamps Surcharged like 1907 Issue Dated "1908"

1908 ***Perf. 14 to 15***

O199 O7 10c on 1c bl (V) .75 .50
a. Inverted surcharge 3.50 3.50
O200 O7 35c on 1c bl (Bk) .75 .50
a. Inverted surcharge 3.50 3.50
b. Double surcharge 4.00 4.00
O201 O7 50c on 1c bl (R) .75 .50
O202 O7 1p on 1c bl (Br) 37.50 37.50
a. Inverted surcharge 65.00 65.00
O203 O7 2p on 1c bl (G) .90 .75
O204 O7 10c on 2c org (Bk) 1.10 .65
O205 O7 35c on 2c org (R) 1.10 .65
a. Double surcharge 3.50
O206 O7 50c on 2c org (Bk) 1.10 .65
O207 O7 70c on 2c org (Bl) 1.10 .65
O208 O7 1p on 2c org (G) 1.10 .65
O209 O7 2p on 2c org (Br) 1.10 .65
Nos. O199-O209 (11) 47.25 43.65

There are several minor varieties in the figures, etc., in these surcharges.

Nos. 243-248 Overprinted in Black 

1909 ***Perf. 12***

O210 A18 10c lake .20 .20
a. Double overprint 2.50 2.50
O211 A18 15c black .60 .50
O212 A18 20c brn ol 1.00 .75
O213 A18 50c dp grn 1.50 1.00
O214 A18 1p yellow 1.75 1.25
O215 A18 2p car rose 2.75 2.00
Nos. O210-O215 (6) 7.80 5.70

Overprinted in Black **OFICIAL**

1910

O216 A18 15c black 1.50 1.25
a. Double overprint 4.00 4.00
O217 A18 20c brn ol 2.50 2.00
O218 A18 50c dp grn 2.50 2.00
O219 A18 1p yellow 2.75 2.50
a. Inverted overprint 7.50 7.50
O220 A18 2p car rose 4.00 3.00
Nos. O216-O220 (5) 13.25 10.75

Nos. 239-240 Surcharged in Black

OFICIAL
Vale 10 *cts.*

1911

O221 A18 5c on 3c red org 6.00 6.00
O222 A18 10c on 4c vio 5.00 5.00
a. Double surcharge 10.00 10.00
b. Pair, one without new value 20.00

Railroad Stamps Surcharged in Black 

1911, Nov. ***Perf. 14 to 15***

O223 A21 10c on 1 red 3.00 3.00
a. Inverted surcharge 4.50
b. Double surcharge 4.50
O224 A21 15c on 1 red 3.00 3.00
a. Inverted surcharge 5.00
b. Double surcharge 4.50
O225 A21 20c on 1 red 3.00 3.00
a. Inverted surcharge 5.00
O226 A21 50c on 1 red 3.75 3.75
a. Inverted surcharge 4.50
O227 A21 1p on 1 red 5.00 *7.00*
a. Inverted surcharge 6.00
O228 A21 2p on 1 red 5.50 *10.00*
a. Inverted surcharge 7.50
b. Double surcharge 7.50
Nos. O223-O228 (6) 23.25 29.75

Surcharged in Black

CORREO
OFICIAL
15 centavos

1911, Nov.

O229 A21 10c on 1 red 22.50
O230 A21 15c on 1 red 22.50
O231 A21 20c on 1 red 22.50
O232 A21 50c on 1 red 16.00
Nos. O229-O232 (4) 83.50

Surcharged in Black

Correo oficial
Vale
5 cts.
1911

1911, Dec.

O233 A21 5c on 1 red 4.50 *6.00*
a. Double surcharge 7.50
b. Inverted surcharge 7.50
c. "5" omitted 6.00
O234 A21 10c on 1 red 5.50 *7.00*
O235 A21 15c on 1 red 6.00 *7.50*
O236 A21 20c on 1 red 6.50 *8.50*
O237 A21 50c on 1 red 7.50 *10.00*
Nos. O233-O237 (5) 30.00 39.00

Nos. O233 to O237 have a surcharge on the back like Nos. 285 and 286 with "15 cts" obliterated by a heavy bar.

Surcharged Vertically in Black 

1912

O238 A21 5c on 1 red 8.00 8.00
O239 A21 10c on 1 red 8.00 8.00
O240 A21 15c on 1 red 8.00 8.00
O241 A21 20c on 1 red 8.00 8.00
O242 A21 35c on 1 red 8.00 8.00
O243 A21 50c on 1 red 8.00 8.00
O244 A21 1p on 1 red 8.00 8.00
Nos. O238-O244 (7) 56.00 56.00

Nos. O238 to O244 are printed on Nos. 285 and 286 but the surcharge on the back is obliterated by a vertical bar.

Types of Regular Issue of 1912 Overprinted in Black 

1912 ***Perf. 12***

O245 A22 1c light blue .20 .20
O246 A22 2c light blue .20 .20
O247 A22 3c light blue .20 .20
O248 A22 4c light blue .20 .20
O249 A22 5c light blue .20 .20
O250 A22 6c light blue .20 .20
O251 A22 10c light blue .20 .20
O252 A22 15c light blue .20 .20
O253 A22 20c light blue .20 .20
O254 A22 25c light blue .20 .20
O255 A22 35c light blue .25 .25
O256 A22 50c light blue 1.50 1.50
O257 A22 1p light blue .30 .30
O258 A22 2p light blue .35 .35
O259 A22 5p light blue .50 .50
Nos. O245-O259 (15) 4.90 4.90

On the 35c the overprint is 15½mm wide, on the other values it is 13mm.

Types of Regular Issue of 1914 Overprinted in Black 

1915, May

O260 A24 1c light blue .20 .20
O261 A25 2c light blue .20 .20
O262 A24 3c light blue .20 .20
O263 A25 4c light blue .20 .20
O264 A24 5c light blue .20 .20
O265 A25 6c light blue .20 .20
O266 A25 10c light blue .20 .20
O267 A24 15c light blue .20 .20
O268 A25 20c light blue .20 .20
O269 A24 25c light blue .30 .30
O270 A25 50c light blue .60 .60
Nos. O260-O270 (11) 2.70 2.70

Regular Issues of 1914-22 Overprinted in Red 

1925

O271 A24 ½c dp grn .20 .20
a. Double overprint 2.50 2.50
O272 A24 1c violet .20 .20
O273 A25 2c car rose .20 .20
O274 A24 3c ol grn .20 .20
O275 A25 4c vermilion .20 .20
a. Double overprint 2.50 2.50
O276 A24 5c black .20 .20
a. Double overprint 2.50 2.50
O277 A25 6c red brn .25 .25
O278 A25 10c yellow .30 .30
a. Double overprint 3.50 3.50
O279 A24 15c red brn .40 .40
O280 A25 20c bis brn .50 .50
O281 A24 25c orange .60 .60
a. Inverted overprint 4.00 4.00
O282 A25 50c pale bl .75 .75
a. Double overprint 5.00 5.00
Nos. O271-O282 (12) 4.00 4.00

Type II overprint has "f" and "i" separated. Comes on Nos. O272-O274 and O276.

Regular Issues of 1914-22 Overprinted in Black 

1926

O283 A24 ½c dk grn .20 .20
O284 A24 1c dp vio .20 .20
O285 A25 2c car rose .20 .20
O286 A24 3c ol gray .20 .20
O287 A25 4c vermilion .20 .20
O288 A24 5c gray blk .20 .20
O289 A25 6c red brn .20 .20
O290 A25 10c yellow .20 .20
O291 A24 15c dp brn .20 .20
O292 A25 20c bis brn .20 .20
O293 A24 25c orange .20 .20
O294 A25 50c pale bl .25 .25
Nos. O283-O294 (12) 2.45 2.45

No. 499 Surcharged in Black 

1931

O295 A33 5c on 10c bis brn .20 .20

Nos. 517-518 Overprinted in Red 

1931

O296 A25 6c bis brn .20 .20
O297 A25 10c lt brn .20 .20

Nos. 541, 543, 545 With Additional Overprint in Black 

O298 A24 1c ol grn .20 .20
O299 A24 3c lt bl .20 .20
a. "OFICIAL" inverted .80 .80
O300 A24 5c gray brn .20 .20
a. "1931" double .80 .80
Nos. O298-O300 (3) .60 .60

Regular Issues of 1914-31 Overprinted in Black 

1932, Feb. 6

O301 A24 1c ol grn .20 .20
a. Double overprint 1.40 1.40
O302 A25 2c brt rose .20 .20
a. Double overprint 1.40 1.40
O303 A24 3c lt bl .20 .20
a. Double overprint .50 .50
O304 A25 4c dk bl .20 .20
O305 A24 5c ol brn .20 .20
O306 A25 6c bis brn .20 .20
a. Double overprint 2.00 2.00
O307 A25 10c lt brn .30 .20
O308 A24 15c org red .40 .25
a. Double overprint 2.25 2.25
O309 A25 20c orange .70 .35
O310 A24 25c dk vio 2.00 .50
O311 A25 50c green .20 .20
O312 A25 1cor yellow .20 .20
Nos. O301-O312 (12) 5.00 2.90

With Additional Overprint in Black 

1932, Feb. 6

O313 A24 1c ol grn 5.50 5.50
O314 A25 2c brt rose 6.50 6.50
a. Double overprint 8.25 8.25
O315 A24 3c lt bl 5.00 5.00
O316 A24 5c ol brn 5.00 5.00
O317 A24 15c org red .65 .65
O318 A24 25c blk brn .65 .65
O319 A24 25c dk vio 1.50 1.50
Nos. O313-O319 (7) 24.80 24.80

The variety "OFIAIAL" occurs once in each sheet of Nos. O301 to O319 inclusive.

Flag of the Race Issue

1933, Aug. 9 Litho. ***Rouletted 9***

Without gum

O320 A43 1c orange 1.00 1.00
O321 A43 2c yellow 1.00 1.00
O322 A43 3c dk brn 1.00 1.00
O323 A43 4c dp brn 1.00 1.00
O324 A43 5c gray brn 1.00 1.00
O325 A43 6c dp ultra 1.25 1.25
O326 A43 10c dp vio 1.25 1.25
O327 A43 15c red vio 1.25 1.25
O328 A43 20c dp grn 1.25 1.25
O329 A43 25c green 2.00 2.00
O330 A43 50c carmine 2.50 2.50
O331 A43 1cor red 4.00 4.00
Nos. O320-O331 (12) 18.50 18.50

See note after No. 599.

Reprints of Nos. O320-O331 exist.

A 25c dull blue exists. Its status is questioned.

Regular Issue of 1914-31 Overprinted in Red

1933, Nov. *Perf. 12*

O332 A24 1c ol grn .20 .20
O333 A25 2c brt rose .20 .20
O334 A24 3c lt bl .20 .20
O335 A25 4c dk bl .20 .20
O336 A24 5c ol brn .20 .20
O337 A25 6c bis brn .20 .20
O338 A25 10c lt brn .20 .20
O339 A24 15c red org .20 .20
O340 A25 20c orange .20 .20
O341 A24 25c dk vio .20 .20
O342 A25 50c green .20 .20
O343 A25 1cor yellow .35 .20
Nos. O332-O343 (12) 2.55 2.40

Nos. O332-O343 exist with or without signature control overprint. Values are the same.

Official Stamps of 1933 Overprinted as Nos. CO15-CO19 in Blue

1935, Dec.

O344 A24 1c ol grn .65 .40
O345 A25 2c brt rose .65 .50
O346 A24 3c lt bl 1.60 .50
O347 A25 4c dk bl 1.60 1.60
O348 A24 5c ol brn 1.60 1.60
O349 A25 6c bis brn 2.00 2.00
O350 A25 10c lt brn 2.00 2.00
O351 A24 15c org red 27.50 27.50
O352 A25 20c orange 27.50 27.50
O353 A24 25c dk vio 27.50 27.50
O354 A25 50c green 27.50 27.50
O355 A25 1cor yellow 27.50 27.50
Nos. O344-O355 (12) 147.60 146.10

Nos. O344-O355 have signature control overprints. Counterfeits of overprint abound.

Same Overprinted in Red

1936, Jan.

O356 A24 1c ol grn .20 .20
O357 A25 2c brt rose .20 .20
O358 A24 3c lt bl .20 .20
a. Double overprint
O359 A25 4c dk bl .20 .20
O360 A24 5c ol brn .20 .20
O361 A25 6c bis brn .20 .20
O362 A25 10c lt brn .20 .20
O363 A24 15c org red .20 .20
O364 A25 20c orange .20 .20
O365 A24 25c dk vio .20 .20
O366 A25 50c green .20 .20
O367 A25 1cor yellow .35 .35
Nos. O356-O367 (12) 2.55 2.55

Have signature control overprints.

Nos. 653 to 655, 657, 659 660, 662 to 664 Overprinted in Black

1937

O368 A24 1c car rose .20 .20
O369 A25 2c dp bl .20 .20
O370 A24 3c chocolate .25 .25
O371 A24 5c org red .35 .25
O372 A25 10c ol grn .65 .40
O373 A24 15c green .80 .50
O374 A24 25c orange 1.00 .65
O375 A25 50c brown 1.40 .80
O376 A25 1cor ultra 2.50 1.25
Nos. O368-O376 (9) 7.35 4.50

Islands of the Great Lake
O9

1939, Jan. **Engr.** *Perf. 12½*

O377 O9 2c rose red .20 .20
O378 O9 3c lt bl .20 .20
O379 O9 6c brn org .20 .20
O380 O9 7½c dp grn .20 .20
O381 O9 10c blk brn .20 .20
O382 O9 15c orange .20 .20
O383 O9 25c dk vio .25 .25
O384 O9 50c brt yel grn .45 .45
Nos. O377-O384 (8) 1.90 1.90

POSTAL TAX STAMPS

Official Stamps of 1915 Surcharged in Black

1921, July **Unwmk.** *Perf. 12*

RA1 A24 1c on 5c lt bl 1.50 .60
RA2 A25 1c on 6c lt bl .65 .20
a. Double surcharge, one inverted
RA3 A25 1c on 10c lt bl 1.00 .25
a. Double surcharge 3.50 3.50
RA4 A24 1c on 15c lt bl 1.50 .25
a. Double surcharge, one inverted 5.00 5.00
Nos. RA1-RA4 (4) 4.65 1.30

"R de C" signifies "Reconstruccion de Comunicaciones." The stamps were intended to provide a fund for rebuilding the General Post Office which was burned in April, 1921. One stamp was required on each letter or parcel, in addition to the regular postage. In the setting of one hundred there are five stamps with antique "C" and twenty-one with "R" and "C" smaller than in the illustration. One or more stamps in the setting have a dotted bar, as illustrated over No. 388, instead of the double bar.

The use of the "R de C" stamps for the payment of regular postage was not permitted.

Official Stamp of 1915 Overprinted in Black

1921, July

RA5 A24 1c light blue 6.00 1.75

This stamp is known with the dotted bar as illustrated over No. 388, instead of the double bar.

Coat of Arms — PT1

PT2

1921, Sept.

Red Surcharge

RA6 PT1 1c on 1c ver & blk .20 .20
RA7 PT1 1c on 2c grn & blk .20 .20
a. Double surcharge 3.00 3.00
b. Double surcharge, one inverted 4.00 4.00
RA8 PT1 1c on 4c org & blk .20 .20
a. Double surcharge 4.00 4.00
RA9 PT1 1c on 15c dk bl & blk .20 .20
a. Double surcharge 3.00 3.00
Nos. RA6-RA9 (4) .80 .80

1922, Feb.

Black Surcharge

RA10 PT2 1c on 10c yellow .20 .20
a. Period after "de" .50 .40
b. Double surcharge 2.00 2.00
c. Double inverted surcharge 3.75 3.75
d. Inverted surcharge 3.00 3.00
e. Without period after "C" 1.00 1.00

No. 409 Overprinted in Black

1922

RA11 A24 1c violet .20 .20
a. Double overprint 2.00 2.00

This stamp with the overprint in red is a trial printing.

Nos. 402, 404-407 Surcharged in Black

1922, June

RA12 A27 1c on 1c grn & blk .75 .75
RA13 A29 1c on 5c ultra & blk .75 .75
RA14 A30 1c on 10c org & blk .75 .40
RA15 A31 1c on 25c yel & blk .75 .30
a. Inverted surcharge 5.00 5.00
RA16 A32 1c on 50c vio & blk .30 .25
a. Double surcharge 4.00 4.00
Nos. RA12-RA16 (5) 3.30 2.45

PT3

Surcharge in Red or Dark Blue

1922, Oct. *Perf. 11½*

RA17 PT3 1c yellow (R) .20 .20
a. No period after "C" 1.00 1.00
RA18 PT3 1c violet (DBl) .20 .20
a. No period after "C" 1.00 1.00

Surcharge is inverted on 22 out of 50 of No. RA17, 23 out of 50 of No. RA18.

Nos. 403-407 Surcharged in Black

1923 *Perf. 12*

RA19 A28 1c on 2c rose red & black .50 .45
RA20 A29 1c on 5c ultra & blk .55 .20
RA21 A30 1c on 10c org & blk .25 .20
RA22 A31 1c on 25c yel & blk .35 .30
RA23 A32 1c on 50c vio & blk .25 .20
Nos. RA19-RA23 (5) 1.90 1.35

The variety no period after "R" occurs twice on each sheet.

Red Surcharge

Wmk. Coat of Arms in Sheet

Perf. 11½

RA24 PT3 1c pale blue .20 .20

Unwmk.

Type of 1921 Issue

Without Surcharge of New Value

RA25 PT1 1c ver & blk .20 .20
a. Double overprint, one inverted 3.00 3.00

No. 409 Overprinted in Blue

1924

RA26 A24 1c violet .20 .20
a. Double overprint 8.00 8.00

There are two settings of the overprint on No. RA26, with "1924" 5½mm or 6½mm wide.

No. 409 Overprinted in Blue

1925

RA27 A24 1c violet .20 .20

No. 409 Overprinted in Blue

1926

RA28 A24 1c violet .25 .20

No. RA28 Overprinted in Various Colors

1927

RA29 A24 1c vio (R) .20 .20
a. Double overprint (R) 2.00 2.00
b. Inverted overprint (R) 3.00 3.00
RA30 A24 1c vio (V) .20 .20
a. Double overprint 2.50 2.50
b. Inverted overprint 2.50 2.50
RA31 A24 1c vio (Bl) .20 .20
a. Double overprint 5.00 5.00
RA32 A24 1c vio (Bk) .20 .20
a. Double ovpt., one invtd. 4.25 4.25
b. Double overprint 4.25 4.25

Same Overprint on No. RA27

RA33 A24 1c vio (Bk) 15.00 10.00
Nos. RA29-RA33 (5) 15.80 10.80

No. RA28 Overprinted in Violet

1928

RA34 A24 1c violet .20 .20
a. Double overprint 2.00 2.00
b. "928" 1.00 1.00

Similar to No. RA34 but 8mm space between "Resello" and "1928"

Black Overprint

RA35 A24 1c violet .40 .20
a. "1828" 2.00 2.00

PT4

Inscribed "Timbre Telegrafico" Horiz. Surch. in Black, Vert. Surch. in Red

RA36 PT4 1c on 5c bl & blk .60 .20
a. Comma after "R" 1.25 1.25
b. No period after "R" 1.25 1.25
c. No periods after "R" and "C" 1.25 1.25

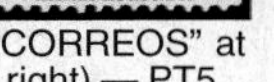

("CORREOS" at right) — PT5

PT6

1928 **Engr.** *Perf. 12*

RA37 PT5 1c plum .25 .20

See Nos. RA41-RA43. For overprints see Nos. RA45-RA46, RA48-RA51.

1929

Surcharged in Red

RA38 PT6 1c on 5c bl & blk .20 .20
a. Inverted surcharge 3.00 3.00
b. Double surcharge 2.00 2.00
c. Double surcharge, one inverted 2.00 2.00
d. Period after "de" 1.25 1.25
e. Comma after "R" 1.25 1.25

See note after No. 512.

Regular Issue of 1928 Overprinted in Blue

RA39 A24 1c red orange .20 .20

No. RA39 exists both with and without signature control overprint.

An additional overprint, "1929" in black or blue on No. RA39, is fraudulent.

No. 513 Overprinted in Red

1929

RA40 A24 1c ol grn .20 .20
a. Double overprint .75 .75

No. RA40 is known with overprint in black, and with overprint inverted. These varieties were not regularly issued, but copies have been canceled by favor.

Type of 1928 Issue Inscribed at right "COMUNICACIONES"

1930-37

RA41 PT5 1c carmine .20 .20
RA42 PT5 1c orange ('33) .20 .20
RA43 PT5 1c green ('37) .20 .20
Nos. RA41-RA43 (3) .60 .60

No. RA42 has signature control. See note before No. 600.

No. RA39 Overprinted in Black

1931

RA44 A24 1c red orange .20 .20
a. "1931" double overprint .35 .35
b. "1931" double ovpt., one invtd. .40 .40

No. RA44 exists with signature control overprint. See note before No. 600. Value is the same.

No. RA42 Overprinted Up or Down, in Black

1935

RA45 PT5 1c orange .20 .20
a. Double overprint 1.00 1.00
b. Double ovpt., one inverted

No. RA45 and RA45a Overprinted Reading Down, in Blue

RA46 PT5 1c orange .50 .20
a. Black overprint double 2.00 2.00

Same Overprint in Red on Nos. RA39, RA42 and RA45

RA47 A24 1c red org (#RA39) *50.00 50.00*
RA48 PT5 1c org (#RA42) .20 .20
RA49 PT5 1c org (#RA45) .20 .20
a. Black overprint double .80 .80

Overprint is horizontal on No. RA47 and vertical, reading down, on Nos. RA48-RA49.

No. RA48 exists with signature control overprint. See note before No. 600. Same values.

No. RA42 Overprinted Reading Down, in Carmine

1935 **Unwmk.** ***Perf. 12***

RA50 PT5 1c orange .20 .20

No. RA45 with Additional Overprint "1936", Vertically, Reading Down, in Red

1936

RA51 PT5 1c orange .50 .20

No. RA39 with Additional Overprint "1936" in Red

RA52 A24 1c red orange .50 .20

No. RA52 exists only with script control mark.

PT7

Vertical Surcharge in Red

1936

RA53 PT7 1c on 5c grn & blk .20 .20
a. "Cenavo" 1.40 1.40
b. "Centavos" 1.40 1.40

Horizontal Surcharge in Red

RA54 PT7 1c on 5c grn & blk .20 .20
a. Double surcharge 1.40 1.40

Baseball Player PT8

1937 **Typo.** ***Perf. 11***

RA55 PT8 1c carmine .35 .20
RA56 PT8 1c yellow .35 .20
RA57 PT8 1c blue .35 .20
RA58 PT8 1c green .35 .20
b. Sheet of 4, #RA55-RA58 3.00 3.00
Nos. RA55-RA58 (4) 1.40 .80

Issued for the benefit of the Central American Caribbean Games of 1937.

Control mark in red is variously placed. See dark oval below "OLIMPICO" in illustration.

Tête bêche Pairs

RA55a PT8 1c .75 .75
RA56a PT8 1c .75 .75
RA57a PT8 1c .75 .75
RA58a PT8 1c .75 .75
Nos. RA55a-RA58a (4) 3.00 3.00

Catalogue values for unused stamps in this section, from this point to the end of the section, are for Never Hinged items.

PT9 PT10

1949 **Photo.** ***Perf. 12***

RA60 PT9 5c greenish blue .25 .20
a. Souvenir sheet of 4 3.75 3.75

10th World Series of Amateur Baseball, 1948. The tax was used toward the erection of a national stadium at Managua.

Type Similar to 1949, with "Correos" omitted

1952

RA61 PT9 5c magenta .25 .20

The tax was used toward the erection of a national stadium at Managua.

1956 **Engr.** ***Perf. 12½x12***

RA62 PT10 5c deep ultra .20 .20

The tax was used for social welfare.

Jesus and Children

PT11 PT12

Surcharged in Red or Black

1959 **Unwmk.** ***Perf. 12***

Red Marginal Number

RA63 PT11 5c on 50c vio bl (R) .20 .20
RA64 PT11 5c on 50c vio bl (B) .20 .20

Nos. RA63-RA64 are surcharged on consular revenue stamps. Surcharge reads "Sobre Tasa Postal CO.O5." Vertical surcharge on No. RA63, horizontal on No. RA64.

1959 **Photo.** ***Perf. 16***

RA65 PT12 5c ultra .20 .20

Hexisia Bidentata — PT13

Orchids: No. RA67, Schomburgkia tibicinus. No. RA68, Stanhopea ecornuta. No. RA69, Lycaste macrophylla. No. RA70, Maxillaria tenuifolia. No. RA71, Cattleya skinneri. No. RA72, Cycnoches egertonianum. No. RA73, Bletia roezlii. No. RA74, Sobralia pleiantha. No. RA75, Oncidium cebolleta and ascendens.

1962, Feb. **Photo.** ***Perf. 11½***

Granite Paper

Orchids in Natural Colors

RA66 PT13 5c pale lil & grn .20 .20
RA67 PT13 5c yel & grn .20 .20
RA68 PT13 5c pink & grn .20 .20
RA69 PT13 5c pale vio & grn .20 .20
RA70 PT13 5c lt grnsh bl & red .20 .20
RA71 PT13 5c buff & lil .20 .20
RA72 PT13 5c yel grn & brn .20 .20
RA73 PT13 5c gray & red .20 .20
RA74 PT13 5c lt bl & dk bl .20 .20
RA75 PT13 5c lt grn & brn .20 .20
Nos. RA66-RA75 (10) 2.00 2.00

For overprints see #842-852, 855-868, 901-908.

Exist imperf. Value, each pair $100.

PROVINCE OF ZELAYA

(Bluefields)

A province of Nicaragua lying along the eastern coast. Special postage stamps for this section were made necessary because for a period two currencies, which differed materially in value, were in use in Nicaragua. Silver money was used in Zelaya and Cabo Gracias a Dios while the rest of Nicaragua used paper money. Later the money of the entire country was placed on a gold basis.

Dangerous counterfeits exist of most of the Bluefields overprints.

Regular Issues of 1900-05 Handstamped in Black (4 or more types)

1904-05 **Unwmk.** ***Perf. 12, 14***

On Engraved Stamps of 1900

1L1 A14 1c plum 1.50 .75
1L2 A14 2c vermilion 1.50 .75
1L3 A14 3c green 1.90 1.50
1L4 A14 4c ol grn 11.00 9.00
1L5 A14 15c ultra 3.00 1.90
1L6 A14 20c brown 3.00 1.90
1L7 A14 50c lake 10.50 9.00
1L8 A14 1p yellow 21.00
1L9 A14 2p salmon 30.00
1L10 A14 5p black 37.50
Nos. 1L1-1L10 (10) 120.90
Nos. 1L1-1L7 (7) 24.80

On Lithographed Stamps of 1902

1L11 A14 5c blue 3.00 .75
1L12 A14 5c carmine 1.90 .90
1L13 A14 10c violet 1.50 .75
Nos. 1L11-1L13 (3) 6.40 2.40

On Postage Due Stamps Overprinted "1901 Correos"

1L14 D3 20c brn (No. 156) 4.50 1.90
1L15 D3 50c lake (No. 158) — —

On Surcharged Stamps of 1904-05

1L16 A16 5c on 10c (#175) 1.50 1.10
1L17 A14 5c on 10c (#178) 3.00 1.50
1L18 A16 15c on 10c vio 1.50 1.50
1L19 A17 15c on 10c vio 14.00 4.50
Nos. 1L16-1L19 (4) 20.00 8.60

On Surcharged Stamp of 1901

1L20 A14 20c on 5p blk 18.00 3.00

On Regular Issue of 1905

1906-07 ***Perf. 12***

1L21 A18 1c green .30 .30
1L22 A18 2c car rose .30 .30
1L23 A18 3c violet .30 .30
1L24 A18 4c org red .45 .45
1L25 A18 5c blue .25 .25
1L26 A18 10c yel brn 3.00 1.50
1L27 A18 15c brn ol 4.50 1.75
1L28 A18 20c lake 9.00 7.50
1L29 A18 50c orange 35.00 30.00
1L30 A18 1p black 30.00 27.50
1L31 A18 2p dk grn 37.50
1L32 A18 5p violet 45.00
Nos. 1L21-1L32 (12) 165.60
Nos. 1L21-1L32 (10) 69.85

On Surcharged Stamps of 1906-08

1L33 A18 10c on 3c vio .40 .40
1L34 A18 15c on 1c grn .50 .50
1L35 A18 20c on 2c rose 3.50 3.50
1L36 A18 20c on 5c bl 1.50 1.50
1L37 A18 50c on 6c sl (R) 1.50 3.00
Nos. 1L33-1L37 (5) 7.40 8.90

B **B**

Dpto. Zelaya **Dto. Zelaya**

Stamps with the above overprints were made to fill dealers' orders but were never regularly issued or used. Stamps with similar overprints handstamped are bogus.

Surcharged Stamps of 1906 Overprinted in Red, Black or Blue

1L38 A18 15c on 1c grn (R) 2.75 2.75
a. Red overprint inverted
1L39 A18 20c on 2c rose (Bk) 1.90 1.90
1L40 A18 20c on 5c bl (R) 3.00 3.00
1L41 A18 50c on 6c sl (Bl) 14.00 14.00
Nos. 1L38-1L41 (4) 21.65 21.65

Stamps of the 1905 issue overprinted as above No. 1L38 or similarly overprinted but with only 2¼mm space between "B" and "Dpto. Zelaya" were made to fill dealers' orders but not placed in use.

No. 205 Handstamped in Black

Perf. 14 to 15

1L42 A18 10c yel brn 24.00 24.00

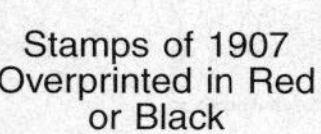

Stamps of 1907 Overprinted in Red or Black

1L43 A18 15c brn ol (R) 3.00 3.00
1L44 A18 20c lake .90 .90
a. Inverted overprint 11.00 11.00

With Additional Surcharge

1L45 A18 5c brn org .50 .45
a. Inverted surcharge 7.50 7.50

With Additional Surcharge **5 cent.**

1L46 A18 5c on 4c brn org 12.00 12.00

On Provisional Postage Stamps of 1907-08 in Black or Blue

1L47 A18 10c on 2c rose (Bl) 4.50 4.50
1L48 A18 10c on 2c rose *300.00*
1L48A A18 10c on 4c brn org *300.00*
1L49 A18 10c on 20c lake 3.00 3.00
1L50 A18 10c on 50c org (Bl) 3.00 2.25

Arms Type of 1907 Overprinted in Black or Violet

1907
1L51 A18 1c green .30 .22
1L52 A18 2c rose .30 .22
1L53 A18 3c violet .38 .38
1L54 A18 4c brn org .45 .45
1L55 A18 5c blue 4.50 2.25
1L56 A18 10c yel brn .38 .30
1L57 A18 15c brn ol .75 .38
1L58 A18 20c lake .75 .45
1L59 A18 50c orange 2.25 1.50
1L60 A18 1p blk (V) 2.25 1.50
1L61 A18 2p dk grn 2.25 1.90
1L62 A18 5p violet 3.75 2.25
Nos. 1L51-1L62 (12) 18.31 11.80

Nos. 217-225 Overprinted in Green

1908
1L63 A19 1c on 5c yel & blk (R) .45 .40
1L64 A19 2c on 5c yel & blk (Bl) .45 .40
1L65 A19 4c on 5c yel & blk (G) .45 .40
a. Overprint reading down 11.00 11.00
b. Double overprint, reading up and down 18.00 18.00
1L66 A19 5c yel & blk .45 .45
a. "CORROE" 4.50
b. Double overprint 11.00 11.00
c. Double overprint, reading up and down 19.00 19.00
d. "CORREO 1908" double 15.00 15.00
1L67 A19 10c lt bl & blk .45 .45
a. Ovpt. reading down .50 .50
b. "CORREO 1908" triple 37.50
1L68 A19 15c on 50c ol & blk (R) .90 .90
a. "1008" 4.50
b. "8908" 4.50
1L69 A19 35c on 50c ol & blk 1.40 1.40
1L70 A19 1p yel brn & blk 1.90 1.90
a. "CORROE" 12.00 12.00
1L71 A19 2p pearl gray & blk 2.25 2.25
a. "CORROE" 15.00 15.00
Nos. 1L63-1L71 (9) 8.70 8.55

Overprinted Horizontally in Black or Green

1L72 A19 5c yel & blk 9.00 7.50
1L72A A19 2p pearl gray & blk (G) *300.00*

On Nos. 1L72-1L72A, space between "B" and "Dpto. Zelaya" is 13mm.

Nos. 237-248 Overprinted in Black

Imprint: "American Bank Note Co. NY"

1909 ***Perf. 12***
1L73 A18 1c yel grn .25 .25
1L74 A18 2c vermilion .25 .25
a. Inverted overprint
1L75 A18 3c red org .25 .25
1L76 A18 4c violet .25 .25
1L77 A18 5c dp bl .30 .25
a. Inverted overprint 9.00 9.00
b. "B" inverted 7.50 7.50
c. Double overprint 12.00 12.00
1L78 A18 6c gray brn 4.50 3.00
1L79 A18 10c lake .30 .30
a. "B" inverted 9.00 9.00
1L80 A18 15c black .45 .40
a. "B" inverted 11.00 11.00
b. Inverted overprint 12.00 12.00
c. Double overprint 14.00 14.00
1L81 A18 20c brn ol .50 .50
a. "B" inverted 19.00 19.00
1L82 A18 50c dp grn 1.50 1.50
1L83 A18 1p yellow 2.25 2.25
1L84 A18 2p car rose 3.00 3.00
a. Double overprint 27.50 27.50
Nos. 1L73-1L84 (12) 13.80 12.20

One stamp in each sheet has the "o" of "Dpto." sideways.

Overprinted in Black

1910
1L85 A18 3c red org .40 .40
1L86 A18 4c violet .40 .40
a. Inverted overprint 14.00 14.00
1L87 A18 15c black 4.50 2.25
1L88 A18 20c brn ol .25 .30
1L89 A18 50c dp grn .30 .40
1L90 A18 1p yellow .30 .45
a. Inverted overprint 7.50
1L91 A18 2p car rose .40 .75
Nos. 1L85-1L91 (7) 6.55 4.95

Z1

Black Ovpt., Green Surch., Carmine Block-outs

1910
1L92 Z1 5c on 10c lake 3.75 3.00

There are three types of the letter "B." It is stated that this stamp was used exclusively for postal purposes and not for telegrams.

No. 247 Surcharged in Black

1911
1L93 A18 5c on 1p yellow .75 .75
a. Double surcharge 14.00
1L94 A18 10c on 1p yellow 1.50 1.50
1L95 A18 15c on 1p yellow .75 .75
a. Inverted surcharge 9.00
b. Double surcharge 9.00
c. Double surcharge, one invtd. 9.00
Nos. 1L93-1L95 (3) 3.00 3.00

Revenue Stamps Surcharged in Black

Perf. 14 to 15
1L96 A19 5c on 25c lilac .75 1.10
a. Without period 1.50 1.50
b. Inverted surcharge 9.00 9.00
1L97 A19 10c on 1p yel brn 1.10 .75
a. Without period 1.90 1.90
b. "01" for "10" 9.00 7.50
c. Inverted surcharge 13.00 13.00

Surcharged in Black

1L98 A19 5c on 1p yel brn 1.50 1.50
a. Without period 2.25
b. "50" for "05" 14.00 14.00
c. Inverted surcharge 15.00 15.00
1L99 A19 5c on 10p pink 1.50 1.50
a. Without period 2.25 2.25
b. "50" for "05" 11.00 11.00
1L100 A19 10c on 1p yel brn 82.50 82.50
a. Without period 95.00 95.00
1L101 A19 10c on 25p grn .75 .75
a. Without period 2.25 2.25
b. "1" for "10" 7.50
1L102 A19 10c on 50p ver 11.00 11.00
a. Without period 16.00
b. "1" for "10" 22.50
Nos. 1L98-1L102 (5) 97.25 97.25

With Additional Overprint "1904"

1L103 A19 5c on 10p pink 14.00 14.00
a. Without period 24.00 24.00
b. "50" for "05" 110.00 110.00
1L104 A19 10c on 2p gray .75 .75
a. Without period 1.90
b. "1" for "10" 7.50
1L105 A19 10c on 25p grn 92.50
a. Without period 100.00
1L106 A19 10c on 50p ver 7.50 7.50
a. Without period 14.00
b. "1" for "10" 18.00
c. Inverted surcharge

The surcharges on Nos. 1L96 to 1L106 are in settings of twenty-five. One stamp in each setting has a large square period after "cts" and another has a thick upright "c" in that word. There are two types of "1904".

B

No. 293C Overprinted

Dpto. Zelaya

1911
1L107 A21 5c on 5c on 2c bl (R) 32.50
a. "5" omitted 37.50
b. Red overprint inverted 40.00
c. As "a" and "b" 47.50

Same Overprint On Nos. 290, 291, 292 and 289D with Lines of Surcharge spaced 2½mm apart Reading Down

1L107D A21 2c on 10c on 1c red *250.00*
e. Overprint reading up *250.00*
1L107F A21 5c on 10c on 1c red *150.00*
1L107G A21 10c on 10c on 1c red (#292) *200.00*
1L108 A21 10c on 10c on 1c red (#289D) *200.00*

Locomotive — Z2

1912 **Engr.** ***Perf. 14***
1L109 Z2 1c yel grn .75 .50
1L110 Z2 2c vermilion .50 .25
1L111 Z2 3c org brn .75 .45
1L112 Z2 4c carmine .75 .30
1L113 Z2 5c dp bl .75 .45
1L114 Z2 6c red brn 4.00 2.50
1L115 Z2 10c slate .75 .30
1L116 Z2 15c dl lil .75 .60
1L117 Z2 20c bl vio .75 .60
1L118 Z2 25c grn & blk 1.00 .80
1L119 Z2 35c brn & blk 1.25 1.00
1L120 Z2 50c ol grn 1.25 1.00
1L121 Z2 1p orange 1.75 1.50
1L122 Z2 2p org brn 4.00 3.00
1L123 Z2 5p dk bl grn 7.00 6.50
Nos. 1L109-1L123 (15) 26.00 19.75

The stamps of this issue were for use in all places on the Atlantic Coast of Nicaragua where the currency was on a silver basis.

For surcharges see Nos. 325-337.

PROVINCE OF ZELAYA OFFICIAL STAMPS

Oficial

B

Regular Issue of 1909 Overprinted in Black

1909 **Unwmk.** ***Perf. 12***
1LO1 A18 20c brn ol 15.00 12.00
a. Double overprint 30.00

Official Stamp of 1909 Overprinted in Black

B

1LO2 A18 15c black 15.00 10.00

Same Overprint on Official Stamp of 1911

1911
1LO3 A18 5c on 3c red org 22.50 17.50

CABO GRACIAS A DIOS

A cape and seaport town in the extreme northeast of Nicaragua. The name was coined by Spanish explorers who had great difficulty finding a landing place along the Nicaraguan coast and when eventually locating this harbor expressed their relief by designating the point "Cape Thanks to God." Special postage stamps came into use for the same reasons as the Zelaya issues. See Zelaya.

Dangerous counterfeits exist of most of the Cabo Gracias a Dios overprints. Special caution should be taken with double and inverted handstamps of Nos. 2L1-2L25, as most are counterfeits. Expert opinion is required.

Regular Issues of 1900-04 Handstamped in Violet

On Engraved Stamps of 1900

1904-05 Unwmk. *Perf. 12, 14*

2L1 A14 1c plum 2.25 1.10
2L2 A14 2c vermilion 4.50 1.25
2L3 A14 3c green 6.00 4.50
2L4 A14 4c ol grn 9.75 9.75
2L5 A14 15c ultra 35.00 22.50
2L6 A14 20c brown 3.00 2.25
Nos. 2L1-2L6 (6) 60.50 41.35

On Lithographed Stamps of 1902

2L7 A14 5c blue 24.00 24.00
2L8 A14 10c violet 24.00 24.00

On Surcharged Stamps of 1904

2L9 A16 5c on 10c vio 22.50 22.50
2L10 A16 15c on 10c vio

On Postage Due Stamps

Violet Handstamp

2L11 D3 20c org brn (#141) 5.00 1.25
2L12 D3 20c org brn (#156) 3.50 1.25
2L13 D3 30c dk grn (#157) 14.00 14.00
2L14 D3 50c lake (#158) 3.75 .75
Nos. 2L11-2L14 (4) 26.25 17.25

Black Handstamp

2L15 D3 30c dk grn (#157) 24.00 24.00

Stamps of 1900-05 Handstamped in Violet

On Engraved Stamps of 1900

2L16 A14 1c plum 2.75 2.25
2L17 A14 2c vermilion 27.50 24.00
2L18 A14 3c green 37.50 27.50
2L19 A14 4c ol grn 40.00 37.50
2L20 A14 15c ultra 45.00 45.00
Nos. 2L16-2L20 (5) 152.75 136.25

On Lithographed Stamps of 1902

2L22 A14 5c dk bl 95.00 50.00
2L23 A14 10c violet 27.50 24.00

On Surcharged Stamp of 1904

2L24 A14 5c on 10c vio

On Postage Due Stamp

2L25 D3 20c org brn (#141)

Cabo

The editors have no evidence that stamps with this handstamp were issued. Copies were sent to the UPU and covers are known.

Stamps of 1900-08 Handstamped in Violet

1905

On Stamps of 1905

2L26 A18 1c green 1.10 1.10
2L27 A18 2c car rose 1.50 1.50
2L28 A18 3c violet 1.50 1.50
2L29 A18 4c org red 3.75 3.75
2L30 A18 5c blue 1.50 1.10
2L31 A18 6c slate 3.75 3.75
2L32 A18 10c yel brn 3.00 1.90
2L33 A18 15c brn ol 4.50 4.50
2L34 A18 1p black 20.00 20.00
2L35 A18 2p dk grn 35.00 35.00
Nos. 2L26-2L35 (10) 75.60 74.10

Magenta Handstamp

2L26a A18 1c 3.75 3.00
2L27a A18 2c 3.00 2.75
2L28a A18 3c 3.75 3.00
2L30a A18 5c 7.50 6.00
2L33a A18 15c 13.50 11.00
Nos. 2L26a-2L33a (5) 31.50 25.75

On Stamps of 1900-04

2L36 A14 5c on 10c vio 14.00 14.00
2L37 A14 10c violet
2L38 A14 20c brown 12.00 12.00
2L39 A14 20c on 5p blk 95.00

On Postage Due Stamps Overprinted "Correos"

2L40 D3 20c org brn (#141) 9.00 9.00
2L41 D3 20c org brn (#156) 5.00 4.50

On Surcharged Stamps of 1906-08

2L42 A18 10c on 3c vio 250.00
2L43 A18 20c on 5c blue 9.00 9.00
2L44 A18 50c on 6c slate 24.00 24.00

On Stamps of 1907

Perf. 14 to 15

2L44A A18 2c rose 250.00
2L45 A18 10c yel brn *100.00* 75.00
2L46 A18 15c brn ol *90.00* 75.00

On Provisional Stamp of 1908 in Magenta

2L47 A19 5c yel & blk 7.50 7.50

Stamps with the above large handstamp in black instead of violet, are bogus. There are also excellent counterfeits in violet.

The foregoing overprints being handstamped are found in various positions, especially the last type.

Stamps of 1907 Type A18, Overprinted in Black or Violet

1907

2L48 A18 1c green .30 .30
2L49 A18 2c rose .30 .30
2L50 A18 3c violet .30 .30
a. Vert. pair, imperf. btwn. 350.00
2L51 A18 4c brn org .40 .40
2L52 A18 5c blue .50 .50
2L53 A18 10c yel brn .40 .40
2L54 A18 15c brn ol .75 .75
2L55 A18 20c lake .75 .75
2L56 A18 50c orange 1.90 1.50
2L57 A18 1p blk (V) 2.25 1.90
2L58 A18 2p dk grn 3.00 2.25
2L59 A18 5p violet 4.50 3.75
Nos. 2L48-2L59 (12) 15.35 13.10

Nos. 237-248 Overprinted in Black

Imprint: American Bank Note Co.

1909 *Perf. 12*

2L60 A18 1c yel grn .35 .40
2L61 A18 2c vermilion .35 .40
2L62 A18 3c red org .35 .40
2L63 A18 4c violet .35 .40
2L64 A18 5c dp bl .35 .60
2L65 A18 6c gray brn 6.00 6.00
2L66 A18 10c lake .60 .75
2L67 A18 15c black .90 .90
2L68 A18 20c brn ol 1.00 1.10
2L69 A18 50c dp grn 2.50 2.50
2L70 A18 1p yellow 4.00 4.00
2L71 A18 2p car rose 5.75 5.75
Nos. 2L60-2L71 (12) 22.50 23.20

No. 199 Overprinted Vertically

2L72 A18 50c on 6c slate (R) 7.50 7.50

CABO GRACIAS A DIOS OFFICIAL STAMPS

Official Stamps of 1907 Overprinted in Red or Violet

CÂBO

1907

2LO1 A18 10c on 1c green *60.00*
2LO2 A18 15c on 1c green *75.00*
2LO3 A18 20c on 1c green *100.00*
2LO4 A18 50c on 1c green *125.00*

NIGER

ˈnī-jər

LOCATION — Northern Africa, directly north of Nigeria
GOVT. — Republic
AREA — 458,075 sq. mi.
POP. — 9,962,242 (1999 est.)
CAPITAL — Niamey

The colony, formed in 1922, was originally a military territory. The Republic of the Niger was proclaimed December 19, 1955. In the period between issues of the colony and the republic, stamps of French West Africa were used.

100 Centimes = 1 Franc

Catalogue values for unused stamps in this country are for Never Hinged items, beginning with Scott 91 in the regular postage section, Scott B14 in the semi-postal section, Scott C14 in the airpost section, Scott J22 in the postage due section, and Scott O1 in the official section.

Watermark

TOR CARTO (mirrored)

Wmk. 385

Camel and Rider — A1

Stamps of Upper Senegal and Niger Type of 1914, Overprinted

1921-26 Unwmk. *Perf. 13½x14*

1 A1 1c brn vio & vio .20 .20
2 A1 2c dk gray & dl vio .20 .20
3 A1 4c black & blue .25 .25
4 A1 5c ol brn & dk brn .25 .25
5 A1 10c yel grn & bl grn 1.10 1.10
6 A1 10c mag, *bluish* ('26) .45 .45
7 A1 15c red brn & org .30 .30
8 A1 20c brn vio & blk .25 .25
9 A1 25c blk & bl grn .45 .45
10 A1 30c red org & rose 2.00 2.00
11 A1 30c bl grn & red org ('26) .60 .60
12 A1 35c rose & violet .75 .75
13 A1 40c gray & rose .60 .60
14 A1 45c blue & ol brn .95 .95
15 A1 50c ultra & bl .60 .60
16 A1 50c dk gray & bl vio ('25) 1.00 1.00
17 A1 60c org red ('26) .90 .90
18 A1 75c yel & ol brn 1.00 1.00
19 A1 1fr dk brn & dl vio 1.10 1.10
20 A1 2fr green & blue 1.25 1.25
21 A1 5fr violet & blk 2.00 2.00
Nos. 1-21 (21) 16.20 16.20

Stamps and Type of 1921 Surcharged New Value and Bars in Black or Red

1922-26

22 A1 25c on 15c red brn & org ('25) .60 .60
a. Multiple surcharge 125.00
b. "25c" inverted 90.00
23 A1 25c on 2fr grn & bl (R) ('24) .50 .50
24 A1 25c on 5fr vio & blk (R) ('24) .60 .60
a. Double surcharge 125.00
25 A1 60c on 75c vio, *pnksh* .50 .50
26 A1 65c on 45c bl & ol brn ('25) 2.00 2.00
27 A1 85c on 75c yel & ol brn ('25) 2.00 2.00
28 A1 1.25fr on 1fr dp bl & lt bl (R) ('26) .65 .65
a. Surcharge omitted 200.00
Nos. 22-28 (7) 6.85 6.85

Nos. 22-24 are surcharged "25c," No. 28, "1f25." Nos. 25-27 are surcharged like illustration.

Drawing Water from Well — A2

Zinder Fortress — A4

Boat on Niger River — A3

Perf. 13x14, 13½x14, 14x13, 14x13½

1926-40 Typo.

29 A2 1c lilac rose & olive .20 .20
30 A2 2c dk gray & dl red .20 .20
31 A2 3c red vio & ol gray ('40) .20 .20
32 A2 4c amber & gray .20 .20
33 A2 5c ver & yel grn .20 .20
34 A2 10c dp bl & Prus bl .20 .20
35 A2 15c gray grn & yel grn .40 .35
36 A2 15c gray lil & lt red ('28) .20 .20
37 A3 20c Prus grn & ol brn .25 .20
38 A3 25c black & dl red .25 .20
39 A3 30c bl grn & yel grn .60 .55
40 A3 30c yel & red vio ('40) .25 .20
41 A3 35c brn org & turq bl, *bluish* .50 .50
42 A3 35c bl grn & dl grn ('38) .75 .70
43 A3 40c red brn & slate .25 .20
44 A3 45c yel & red vio .95 .95
45 A3 45c bl grn & dl grn ('40) .25 .20
46 A3 50c scar & grn, *grnsh* .25 .20
47 A3 55c dk car & brn ('38) 1.40 1.40
48 A3 60c dk car & brn ('40) .40 .35
49 A3 65c ol grn & rose .25 .20
50 A3 70c ol grn & rose ('40) 1.25 1.25
51 A3 75c grn & vio, *pink* 1.25 1.25
52 A3 80c cl & ol grn ('38) 1.10 1.10
53 A3 90c brn red & ver 1.00 1.00
54 A3 90c brt rose & yel grn ('39) 1.25 1.25
55 A4 1fr rose & yel grn 6.25 5.00
56 A4 1fr dk red & red org ('38) 1.40 1.40
57 A4 1fr grn & red ('40) .60 .60
58 A4 1.10fr ol brn & grn 2.75 2.75
59 A4 1.25fr grn & red ('33) 1.25 1.25
60 A4 1.25fr dk red & red org ('39) .60 .55
61 A4 1.40fr red vio & dk brn ('40) .60 .55

62 A4 1.50fr dp bl & pale bl .30 .30
63 A4 1.60fr ol brn & grn ('40) 1.10 1.10
64 A4 1.75fr red vio & dk brn ('33) 2.40 2.25
65 A4 1.75fr dk bl & vio bl ('38) .95 .95
66 A4 2fr red org & ol brn .25 .20
67 A4 2.25fr dk bl & vio bl ('39) .80 .80
68 A4 2.50fr blk brn ('40) .75 .70
69 A4 3fr dl vio & blk ('27) .40 .35
70 A4 5fr vio brn & blk, *pink* .50 .50
71 A4 10fr chlky bl & mag 1.10 1.10
72 A4 20fr yel grn & red org 1.25 1.25
Nos. 29-72 (44) 37.25 35.05

For surcharges see Nos. B7-B10.

Common Design Types pictured following the introduction.

Colonial Exposition Issue
Common Design Types

1931 Typo. *Perf. 12½*
Name of Country in Black

73 CD70 40c deep green 4.00 4.00
74 CD71 50c violet 4.00 4.00
75 CD72 90c red orange 4.25 4.25
76 CD73 1.50fr dull blue 4.25 4.25
Nos. 73-76 (4) 16.50 16.50

Paris International Exposition Issue
Common Design Types

1937 *Perf. 13*

77 CD74 20c deep violet 1.10 1.10
78 CD75 30c dark green 1.10 1.10
79 CD76 40c carmine rose 1.25 1.25
80 CD77 50c dark brown 1.40 1.40
81 CD78 90c red 1.50 1.50
82 CD79 1.50fr ultra 1.50 1.50
Nos. 77-82 (6) 7.85 7.85

Colonial Arts Exhibition Issue
Souvenir Sheet
Common Design Type

1937 *Imperf.*

83 CD74 3fr magenta 6.50 *8.00*

Caillie Issue
Common Design Type

1939 *Perf. 12½x12*

84 CD81 90c org brn & org .80 .80
85 CD81 2fr brt violet .80 .80
86 CD81 2.25fr ultra & dk bl .80 .80
Nos. 84-86 (3) 2.40 2.40

New York World's Fair Issue
Common Design Type

1939, May 10

87 CD82 1.25fr carmine lake .85 .70
88 CD82 2.25fr ultra .95 .80

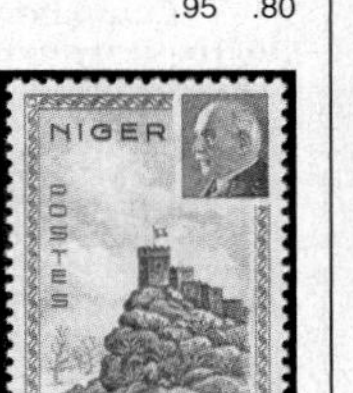

Zinder Fortress and Marshal Pétain — A5

1941 Unwmk. Engr. *Perf. 12x12½*

89 A5 1fr green .75
90 A5 2.50fr dark blue .75

Nos. 89-90 were issued by the Vichy government in France, but were not placed on sale in Niger.

For surcharges, see Nos. B13A-B13B.

See French West Africa No. 68 for additional stamp inscribed "Niger" and "Afrique Occidentale Francaise."

Catalogue values for unused stamps in this section, from this point to the end of the section, are for Never Hinged items.

Republic of the Niger

Giraffes — A6

1fr, 2fr, Crested cranes. 5fr, 7fr, Saddle-billed storks. 15fr, 20fr, Barbary sheep. 25fr, 30fr, Giraffes. 50fr, 60fr, Ostriches. 85fr, 100fr, Lion.

1959-60 Unwmk. Engr. *Perf. 13*

91 A6 1fr multi .35 .20
92 A6 2fr multi .35 .20
93 A6 5fr blk, car & ol .50 .20
94 A6 7fr grn, blk & red .60 .25
95 A6 15fr grnsh bl & dk brn .20 .20
96 A6 20fr vio, blk & ind .25 .20
97 A6 25fr multi .35 .20
98 A6 30fr multi .45 .30
99 A6 50fr ind & org brn 4.75 .70
100 A6 60fr dk brn & emer 6.50 1.00
101 A6 85fr org brn & bis 2.25 .80
102 A6 100fr bis & yel grn 3.00 1.25
Nos. 91-102 (12) 19.55 5.50

Issue years: #97, 1959; others, 1960.

For surcharge see No. 103.

Imperforates

Most stamps of the republic exist imperforate in issued and trial colors, and also in small presentation sheets in issued color.

No. 102 Surcharged with New Value and: "Indépendance 3-8-60"

1960

103 A6 200fr on 100fr 14.00 14.00

Niger's independence.

C.C.T.A. Issue
Common Design Type

1960 Engr. *Perf. 13*

104 CD106 25fr buff & red brn .85 .45

Emblem of the Entente — A6a

Pres. Diori Hamani — A7

1960, May 29 Photo. *Perf. 13x13½*

105 A6a 25fr multi .85 .45

1st anniversary of the Entente (Dahomey, Ivory Coast, Niger and Upper Volta).

1960, Dec. 18 Engr. *Perf. 13*

106 A7 25fr ol bis & blk .60 .30

2nd anniversary of the proclamation of the Republic of the Niger.

Dugong A8

1962, Jan. 29 Unwmk. *Perf. 13*

107 A8 50c grn & dk sl grn .40 .25
108 A8 10fr red brn & dk grn .65 .25

Abidjan Games Issue
Common Design Type

25fr, Basketball & Soccer. 85fr, Track, horiz.

1962, May 26 Photo. *Perf. 12x12½*

109 CD109 15fr multi .40 .20
110 CD109 25fr multi .60 .25
111 CD109 85fr multi 1.60 .60
Nos. 109-111 (3) 2.60 1.05

African-Malgache Union Issue
Common Design Type

1962, Sept. 8 *Perf. 12½x12*

112 CD110 30fr multi .80 .40

Pres. Diori Hamani and Map of Niger in Africa A10

1962, Dec. 18 Photo. *Perf. 12½x12*

113 A10 25fr multi .60 .25

Woman Runner A11

Woodworker A12

15fr, Swimming, horiz. 45fr, Volleyball.

Unwmk.

1963, Apr. 11 Engr. *Perf. 13*

114 A11 15fr brt bl & dk brn .25 .25
115 A11 25fr dk brn & red .60 .25
116 A11 45fr grn & blk 1.10 .40
Nos. 114-116 (3) 1.95 .90

Friendship Games, Dakar, Apr. 11-21.

Perf. 12x12½, 12½x12

1963, Aug. 30 Photo.

10fr, Tanners, horiz. 25fr, Goldsmith. 30fr, Mat makers, horiz. 85fr, Decoy maker.

117 A12 5fr brn & multi .25 .20
118 A12 10fr dk grn & multi .35 .25
119 A12 25fr blk & multi .60 .25
120 A12 30fr vio & multi .90 .30
121 A12 85fr dk bl & multi 2.00 .80
Nos. 117-121,C26 (6) 7.10 3.30

Berberi (Nuba) Woman's Costume — A13

Costume Museum, Niamey — A14

Costumes: 20fr, Hausa woman. 25fr, Tuareg woman. 30fr, Tuareg man. 60fr, Djerma woman.

Perf. 12x12½, 12½x12

1963, Oct. 15 Photo.

122 A13 15fr multi .35 .25
123 A13 20fr blk & bl .50 .25
124 A13 25fr multi .70 .25
125 A13 30fr multi .75 .25
126 A13 60fr multi 1.75 .60
127 A14 85fr multi 2.00 .70
Nos. 122-127 (6) 6.05 2.30

Man, Globe and Scales — A15

Parkinsonia Aculeata — A16

Unwmk.

1963, Dec. 10 Engr. *Perf. 13*

128 A15 25fr lt ol grn, ultra & brn org .65 .30

15th anniversary of the Universal Declaration of Human Rights.

1964-65 Photo. *Perf. 13½x13*

Flowers: 10fr, Russelia equisetiformis. 15fr, Red sage (lantana). 20fr, Argyreia nervosa. 25fr, Luffa cylindrica. 30fr, Hibiscus rosa sinensis. 45fr, Red jasmine (frangipani). 50fr, Catharanthus roseus. 60fr, Caesalpinia pulcherrima.

129 A16 5fr dk red, grn & yel .75 .30
130 A16 10fr multi .60 .30
131 A16 15fr multi 1.00 .40
132 A16 20fr multi 1.00 .40
133 A16 25fr multi 1.00 .40
134 A16 30fr multi 1.25 .55
135 A16 45fr multi ('65) 2.25 .85
136 A16 50fr dk red, brt pink & grn ('65) 2.25 .85
137 A16 60fr multi ('65) 4.00 1.10
Nos. 129-137 (9) 14.10 5.15

Solar Flares and IQSY Emblem — A17

1964, May 12 Engr. *Perf. 13*

138 A17 30fr dp org, vio & blk .75 .40

International Quiet Sun Year, 1964-65.

Mobile Medical Unit — A18

30fr, Mobile children's clinic. 50fr, Mobile women's clinic. 60fr, Outdoor medical laboratory.

1964, May 26

139 A18 25fr bl, org & ol .40 .20
140 A18 30fr multi .50 .25
141 A18 50fr vio, org & bl .80 .30
142 A18 60fr grnsh bl, org & dk brn .90 .40
Nos. 139-142 (4) 2.60 1.15

Nigerian mobile health education organization, OMNES (Organisation Médicale Mobile Nigérienne d'Education Sanitaire).

Cooperation Issue
Common Design Type

1964, Nov. 7 Unwmk. *Perf. 13*

143 CD119 50fr vio, dk brn & org .80 .40

Tuareg Tent of Azawak A19

Designs: 20fr, Songhai house. 25fr, Wogo and Kourtey tents. 30fr, Djerma house. 60fr, Huts of Sorkawa fishermen. 85fr, Hausa town house.

1964-65 Engr.

144 A19 15fr ultra, dl grn & red brn .25 .25
145 A19 20fr multi .30 .25
146 A19 25fr Prus bl, dk brn & org brn .35 .25
147 A19 30fr multi ('65) .50 .30
148 A19 60fr red, grn & bis ('65) .85 .30
149 A19 85fr multi ('65) 1.25 .50
Nos. 144-149 (6) 3.50 1.85

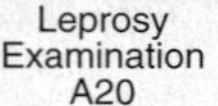

Leprosy Examination A20

Abraham Lincoln A21

1964, Dec. 15 Photo. *Perf. 13x12½*
150 A20 50fr multi .70 .40

Issued to publicize the fight against leprosy.

1965, Apr. 3 *Perf. 13x12½*
151 A21 50fr vio bl, blk, & ocher .90 .45

Centenary of death of Abraham Lincoln.

Teaching with Radio and Pictures — A22

Designs: 25fr, Woman studying arithmetic: "A better life through knowledge." 30fr, Adult education class. 50fr, Map of Niger and 5 tribesmen, "Literacy for adults."

1965, Apr. 16 Engr. *Perf. 13*
152 A22 20fr dk bl, dk brn & ocher .40 .25
153 A22 25fr sl grn, brn & ol brn .50 .25
154 A22 30fr red, sl grn & vio brn .60 .25
155 A22 50fr dp bl, brn & vio brn .85 .35
Nos. 152-155 (4) 2.35 1.10

Issued to promote adult education and "a better life through knowledge."

Ader Portable Telephone A23

Runner A24

Designs: 30fr, Wheatstone telegraph interrupter. 50fr, Early telewriter.

1965, May 17 Unwmk. *Perf. 13*
156 A23 25fr red brn, dk grn & ind .60 .25
157 A23 30fr lil, slate grn & red .70 .30
158 A23 50fr red, slate grn & pur 1.00 .40
Nos. 156-158 (3) 2.30 .95

International Telecommunication Union, cent.

1965, July 1 Engr. *Perf. 13*

Designs: 10fr, Hurdler, horiz. 20fr, Pole vaulter, horiz. 30fr, Long jumper.

159 A24 10fr brn, ocher & blk .25 .20
160 A24 15fr gray, brn & red .45 .25
161 A24 20fr dk grn, brn & vio bl .60 .25
162 A24 30fr maroon, brn & grn .70 .25
Nos. 159-162 (4) 2.00 .95

African Games, Brazzaville, July 18-25.

Radio Interview and Club Emblem A25

45fr, Recording folk music, vert. 50fr, Group listening to broadcast, vert. 60fr, Public debate.

1965, Oct. 1 Engr. *Perf. 13*
163 A25 30fr brt vio, emer & red brn .40 .20
164 A25 45fr blk, car & buff .55 .20
165 A25 50fr dk car, bl & lt brn .60 .30
166 A25 60fr bis, ultra & brn .75 .35
Nos. 163-166 (4) 2.30 1.05

Issued to promote radio clubs.

Water Cycle — A26

1966, Feb. 28 Engr. *Perf. 13*
167 A26 50fr vio, ocher & bl .80 .30

Hydrological Decade, 1965-74.

Carvings, Mask and Headdresses — A27

50fr, Carvings and wall decorations. 60fr, Carvings and arch. 100fr, Architecture and handicraft.

1966, Apr. 12
168 A27 30fr red brn, blk & brt grn .50 .30
169 A27 50fr brt bl, ocher & pur .75 .30
170 A27 60fr car lake, dl pur & yel brn .85 .45
171 A27 100fr brt red, bl & blk 1.75 .80
Nos. 168-171 (4) 3.85 1.85

Intl. Negro Arts Festival, Dakar, Senegal, Apr. 1-24.

Soccer Player — A28

Color Guard — A29

50fr, Goalkeeper, horiz. 60fr, Player kicking ball.

1966, June 17 Engr. *Perf. 13*
172 A28 30fr dk brn, brt bl & rose red .60 .25
173 A28 50fr bl, choc & emer .75 .30
174 A28 60fr bl, lil & brn .90 .45
Nos. 172-174 (3) 2.25 1.00

8th World Soccer Cup Championship, Wembley, England, July 11-30.

Perf. 12½x13, 13x12½

1966, Aug. 23 Photo.

20fr, Parachutist, horiz. 45fr, Tanks, horiz.

175 A29 20fr multi .40 .25
176 A29 30fr multi .50 .25
177 A29 45fr multi .65 .30
Nos. 175-177 (3) 1.55 .80

5th anniv. of the National Armed Forces.

Cow Receiving Injection A30

1966, Sept. 26 Litho. *Perf. 12½x13*
178 A30 45fr org brn, bl & blk 1.25 .45

Campaign against cattle plague.

UNESCO Emblem — A31

1966, Nov. 4 Litho. *Perf. 13x12½*
179 A31 50fr multi .70 .35

20th anniversary of UNESCO.

Cement Works Malbaza A32

Designs: 10fr, Furnace, vert. 20fr, Electric center. 50fr, Handling of raw material.

1966, Dec. 17 Engr. *Perf. 13*
180 A32 10fr ind, brn & org .30 .20
181 A32 20fr dk ol grn & dl bl .45 .25
182 A32 30fr bl, gray & red brn .45 .25
183 A32 50fr ind, bl & brn .70 .30
Nos. 180-183 (4) 1.90 1.00

Redbilled Hornbill A33

Birds: 2fr, Pied kingfisher. 30fr, Barbary shrike. 45fr, 65fr, Little weaver and nest.

1967 Engr. *Perf. 13*
184 A33 1fr red, sl grn & dk brn .70 .35
185 A33 2fr brn, brt grn & blk .70 .35
186 A33 30fr multi 3.50 .60
187 A33 45fr multi 1.75 .35
188 A33 65fr multi ('81) 3.00 .70
189 A33 70fr multi 3.00 .60
Nos. 184-189 (6) 12.65 2.95

Issued: 45fr, 70fr, 11/18; others, 2/8. See #237.

Villard-de-Lans and Olympic Emblem — A34

Lions Emblem and Family — A35

Olympic Emblem and Mountains: 45fr, Autrans and ski jump. 60fr, Saint Nizier du Moucherotte and ski jump. 90fr, Chamrousse and course for downhill and slalom races.

1967, Feb. 24
190 A34 30fr grn, ultra & brn .50 .25
191 A34 45fr grn, ultra & brn .65 .40
192 A34 60fr grn, ultra & brn .85 .45
193 A34 90fr grn, ultra & brn 1.40 .65
Nos. 190-193 (4) 3.40 1.75

10th Winter Olympic Games, Grenoble, 1968.

1967, Mar. 4
194 A35 50fr dk grn, brn red & ultra 1.00 .40

Lions International, 50th anniversary.

ITY Emblem, Views, Globe and Plane A36

1967, Apr. 28 Engr. *Perf. 13*
195 A36 45fr vio, brt grn & red lil .60 .30

International Tourist Year, 1967.

1967 Jamboree Emblem and Scouts — A37

Red Cross Aides Carrying Sick Man — A38

Designs (Jamboree Emblem and): 45fr, Scouts gathering from all directions, horiz. 80fr, Campfire.

1967, May 25 Engr. *Perf. 13*
196 A37 30fr mar, Prus bl & ol .50 .25
197 A37 45fr org, vio bl & brn ol .70 .30
198 A37 80fr multi 1.25 .75
Nos. 196-198 (3) 2.45 1.30

12th Boy Scout World Jamboree, Farragut State Park, Idaho, Aug. 1-9.

1967, July 13 Engr. *Perf. 13*

Designs: 50fr, Nurse, mother and infant. 60fr, Physician examining woman.

199 A38 45fr blk, grn & car .65 .30
200 A38 50fr grn, blk & car .90 .50
201 A38 60fr blk, grn & car 1.00 .50
Nos. 199-201 (3) 2.55 1.30

Issued for the Red Cross.

Europafrica Issue, 1967

Map of Europe and Africa — A39

1967, July 20 Photo. *Perf. 12½x12*
202 A39 50fr multi .75 .30

Women and UN Emblem — A40

1967, Oct. 21 Engr. *Perf. 13*
203 A40 50fr brn, brt bl & yel .70 .35

UN Commission on Status of Women.

Monetary Union Issue

Common Design Type

1967, Nov. 4 Engr. *Perf. 13*
204 CD125 30fr grn & dk gray .45 .25

Human Rights Flame, Globe, People and Statue of Liberty
A41

1968, Feb. 19 Engr. *Perf. 13*
205 A41 50fr brn, indigo & brt bl .70 .35

International Human Rights Year.

Woman Dancing and WHO Emblem — A42

1968, Apr. 8 Engr. *Perf. 13*
206 A42 50fr brt bl, blk & red brn .75 .30

20th anniv. of WHO.

Gray Hornbill
A43

Birds: 10fr, Woodland kingfisher. 15fr, Senegalese coucal. 20fr, Rose-ringed parakeets. 25fr, Abyssinian roller. 50fr, Cattle egret.

Dated "1968"

1968, Nov. 15 Photo. *Perf. 12½x13*
207 A43 5fr dk grn & multi .60 .40
208 A43 10fr grn & multi .70 .40
209 A43 15fr bl vio & multi 1.25 .40
210 A43 20fr pink & multi 1.25 .50
211 A43 25fr ol & multi 2.00 .60
212 A43 50fr pur & multi 2.75 1.50
Nos. 207-212 (6) 8.55 3.80

See Nos. 233-236, 316.

ILO Emblem and "Labor Supporting the World"
A44

1969, Apr. 22 Engr. *Perf. 13*
213 A44 30fr yel grn & dk car .45 .25
214 A44 50fr dk car & yel grn .60 .35

50th anniv. of the World Labor Organization.

Red Crosses, Mother and Child — A45

Designs: 50fr, People, globe, red crosses, horiz. 70fr, Man with gift parcel and red crosses.

1969, May 5 Engr. *Perf. 13*
215 A45 45fr bl, red & brn ol .80 .25
216 A45 50fr dk grn, red & gray .80 .30
217 A45 70fr ocher, red & dk brn 1.25 .55
Nos. 215-217 (3) 2.85 1.10

50th anniv. of the League of Red Cross Societies.

Mouth and Ear — A46

1969, May 20 Photo. *Perf. 12½x12*
218 A46 100fr multi 1.10 .50

First (cultural) Conference of French-speaking Community at Niamey.

National Administration College — A47

1969, July 8 Photo. *Perf. 12½x12*
219 A47 30fr emer & dp org .75 .30

Development Bank Issue
Common Design Type

1969, Sept. 10 Engr. *Perf. 13*
220 CD130 30fr pur, grn & ocher .60 .25

ASECNA Issue
Common Design Type

1969, Dec. 12 Engr. *Perf. 12*
221 CD132 100fr car rose 1.25 .60

Classical Pavilion, National Museum
A48

Pavilions, National Museum: 45fr, Temporary exhibitions. 50fr, Audio-visual. 70fr, Nigerian musical instruments. 100fr, Craftsmanship.

1970, Feb. 23 Engr. *Perf. 13*
222 A48 30fr brt bl, sl grn & brn .30 .20
223 A48 45fr emer, Prus bl & brn .50 .25
224 A48 50fr sl grn, vio bl & brn .50 .25
225 A48 70fr brn, sl grn & lt bl .75 .40
226 A48 100fr sl grn, vio bl & brn 1.10 .50
Nos. 222-226 (5) 3.15 1.60

Map of Africa and Vaccination Gun — A49

1970, Mar. 31 Engr. *Perf. 13*
227 A49 50fr ultra, dp yel grn & mag .75 .40

Issued to commemorate the 100 millionth smallpox vaccination in West Africa.

Mexican Figurine and Soccer Player
A50

Designs: 70fr, Figurine, globe and soccer ball. 90fr, Figurine and 2 soccer players.

1970, Apr. 25
228 A50 40fr dk brn, red lil & emer .75 .30
229 A50 70fr red brn, bl & plum .95 .45
230 A50 90fr blk & red 1.25 .65
Nos. 228-230 (3) 2.95 1.40

9th World Soccer Championship for the Jules Rimet Cup, Mexico City, 5/29-6/21.

UPU Headquarters Issue
Common Design Type

1970, May 20 Engr. *Perf. 13*
231 CD133 30fr brn, dk gray & dk red .40 .25
232 CD133 60fr vio bl, dk car & vio .60 .30

Bird Types of 1967-68

Birds: 5fr, Gray hornbill. 10fr, Woodland kingfisher. 15fr, Senegalese coucal. 20fr, Rose-ringed parakeets. 40fr, Red bishop.

Dated "1970"

1970-71 Photo. *Perf. 13*
233 A43 5fr multi ('71) .60 .25
234 A43 10fr multi ('71) .60 .25
235 A43 15fr multi ('71) .60 .25
236 A43 20fr multi ('71) .90 .30

Engr.

237 A33 40fr multi 2.75 1.00
Nos. 233-237 (5) 5.45 2.05

Issue dates: 40fr, Dec. 9; others Jan. 4.

World Map with Niamey in Center
A51

1971, Mar. 3 Photo. *Perf. 12½x12*
238 A51 40fr brn & multi .60 .35

First anniversary of founding of the cooperative agency of French-speaking countries.
For overprint see No. 289.

Scout Emblem, Merit Badges, Mt. Fuji, Japanese Flag — A52

Designs: 40fr, Boy Scouts and flags, vert. 45fr, Map of Japan, Boy Scouts and compass rose, vert. 50fr, Tent and "Jamboree."

1971, July 5 Engr. *Perf. 13*
239 A52 35fr rose lil, dp car & org .45 .25
240 A52 40fr dk pur, grn & mar .45 .25
241 A52 45fr ultra, cop red & grn .65 .30
242 A52 50fr multi .65 .30
Nos. 239-242 (4) 2.20 1.10

13th Boy Scout World Jamboree, Asagiri Plain, Japan, Aug. 2-10.

Maps of Europe and Africa — A53

1971, July 29 Photo. *Perf. 13x12*
243 A53 50fr lt bl & multi .70 .35

Renewal of the agreement on economic association between Europe and Africa, 2nd anniv.

Broad-tailed Whydah
A54

1971, Aug. 17 *Perf. 12½x12*
244 A54 35fr yel grn & multi 3.00 1.10

See No. 443.

Garaya, Haoussa — A55

UNICEF Emblem, Children of 4 Races — A56

Stringed Instruments of Niger: 25fr, Gouroumi, Haoussa. 30fr, Molo, Djerma. 40fr, Godjie, Djerma-Sonrai. 45fr, Inzad, Tuareg. 50fr, Kountigui, Sonrai.

1971-72 Engr. *Perf. 13*
245 A55 25fr red, emer & brn .40 .25
246 A55 30fr emer, pur & brn .40 .25
247 A55 35fr brn red, emer & ind .40 .30
248 A55 40fr emer, org & dk brn .40 .30
249 A55 45fr Prus bl, grn & bis .60 .35
250 A55 50fr blk, red & brn .80 .35
Nos. 245-250 (6) 3.00 1.80

Issued: 35, 40, 45fr, 10/13/71; others, 6/16/72.

1971, Dec. 11 Photo. *Perf. 11*
251 A56 50fr multi .60 .35

25th anniversary of UNICEF.

Star with Globe, Book, UNESCO Emblem
A57

Design: 40fr, Boy reading, UNESCO emblem, sailing ship, plane, mosque.

1972, Mar. 27 Engr. *Perf. 13*
252 A57 35fr mag & emer .40 .25
253 A57 40fr dk car & Prus bl .40 .25

International Book Year 1972.

Cattle Egret
A58

1972, July 31 Photo. *Perf. 12½x12*
254 A58 50fr tan & multi 5.00 2.75

See No. 425.

Cattle at Salt Pond of In-Gall
A59

1972, Aug. 25 *Perf. 13*
255 A59 35fr shown .75 .30
256 A59 40fr Cattle wading in pond .75 .30

Salt cure for cattle.
For surcharge see No. 282.

Lottery Drum — A60

1972, Sept. 18
257 A60 35fr multi .65 .40

6th anniversary of the national lottery.

West African Monetary Union Issue
Common Design Type

Design: 40fr, African couple, city, village and commemorative coin.

1972, Nov. 2 Engr. *Perf. 13*
258 CD136 40fr brn, lil & gray .45 .30

Dromedary Race — A61

Design: 40fr, Horse race.

1972, Dec. 15 Engr. *Perf. 13*
259 A61 35fr brt bl, dk red & brn .90 .45
260 A61 40fr sl grn, mar & brn 1.10 .55

Pole Vault, Map of Africa A62

Knight, Pawn, Chessboard A63

Map of Africa and: 40fr, Basketball. 45fr, Boxing. 75fr, Soccer.

1973, Jan. 15 Engr. *Perf. 13*
261 A62 35fr claret & multi .35 .25
262 A62 40fr grn & multi .45 .25
263 A62 45fr red & multi .55 .30
264 A62 75fr dk bl & multi .75 .40
Nos. 261-264 (4) 2.10 1.20

2nd African Games, Legos, Nigeria, 1/7-18.

1973, Feb. 16 Engr. *Perf. 13*
265 A63 100fr dl red, sl grn & bl 2.50 1.25

World Chess Championship, Reykjavik, Iceland, July-Sept. 1972.

Abutilon Pannosum A64

Interpol Emblem A65

Rare African Flowers: 45fr, Crotalaria barkae. 60fr, Dichrostachys cinerea. 80fr, Caralluma decaisneana.

1973, Feb. 26 Photo. *Perf. 12x12½*
266 A64 30fr dk vio & multi .65 .35
267 A64 45fr red & multi .90 .35
268 A64 60fr ultra & multi 1.25 .60
269 A64 80fr ocher & multi 1.60 .60
Nos. 266-269 (4) 4.40 1.90

1973, Mar. 13 Typo. *Perf. 13x12½*
270 A65 50fr brt grn & multi .60 .40

50th anniversary of International Criminal Police Organization (INTERPOL).

Dr. Hansen, Microscope and Petri Dish — A66

Nurse Treating Infant, UN and Red Cross Emblems — A67

1973, Mar. 29 Engr. *Perf. 13*
271 A66 50fr vio bl, sl grn & dk brn 1.25 .50

Centenary of the discovery by Dr. Armauer G. Hansen of the Hansen bacillus, the cause of leprosy.

1973, Apr. 3 Engr. *Perf. 13*
272 A67 50fr red, bl & brn .60 .25

25th anniversary of WHO.

Crocodile A68

Animals from W National Park: 35fr, Elephant. 40fr, Hippopotamus. 80fr, Wart hog.

1973, June 5 Typo. *Perf. 12½x13*
273 A68 25fr gray & blk .90 .25
274 A68 35fr blk, gold & gray 1.25 .30
275 A68 40fr red, lt bl & blk 1.25 .35
276 A68 80fr multi 2.50 .50
Nos. 273-276 (4) 5.90 1.40

Eclipse over Mountains A69

1973, June 21 Engr. *Perf. 13*
277 A69 40fr dk vio bl .60 .40

Solar eclipse, June 30, 1973.

Palominos — A70

Horses: 75fr, French trotters. 80fr, English thoroughbreds. 100fr, Arabian thoroughbreds.

1973, Aug. 1 Photo. *Perf. 13x12½*
278 A70 50fr ultra & multi 1.00 .40
279 A70 75fr gray & multi 1.25 .40
280 A70 80fr emer & multi 1.60 .60
281 A70 100fr ocher & multi 2.00 .85
Nos. 278-281 (4) 5.85 2.25

No. 255 Surcharged with New Value, 2 Bars, and Overprinted in Ultramarine: "SECHERESSE/SOLIDARITE AFRICAINE"

1973, Aug. 16 *Perf. 13*
282 A59 100fr on 35fr multi 1.50 1.00

African solidarity in drought emergency.

Diesel Engine and Rudolf Diesel A71

Designs: Various Diesel locomotives.

1973, Sept. 7 *Perf. 13x12½*
283 A71 25fr gray, choc & Prus bl .60 .25
284 A71 50fr sl bl, gray & dk grn 1.10 .35
285 A71 75fr red lil, sl bl & gray 1.50 .55
286 A71 125fr brt grn, vio bl & car 2.75 1.00
Nos. 283-286 (4) 5.95 2.15

Rudolf Diesel (1858-1913), inventor of an internal combustion engine, later called Diesel engine.

African Postal Union Issue
Common Design Type

1973, Sept. 12 Engr. *Perf. 13*
287 CD137 100fr ol, dk car & sl grn .90 .50

TV Set, Map of Niger, Children A72

1973, Oct. 1 Engr. *Perf. 13*
288 A72 50fr car, ultra & brn .75 .30

Educational television.

Type of 1971 Overprinted

1973, Oct. 12 Photo. *Perf. 13*
289 A51 40fr red & multi .75 .30

3rd Conference of French-speaking countries, Liège, Sept. 15-Oct. 14.

Apollo of Belvedère — A73

Classic Sculpture: No. 291, Venus of Milo. No. 292, Hercules. No. 293, Atlas.

1973, Oct. 15 Engr.
290 A73 50fr brn & sl grn 1.00 .40
291 A73 50fr rose car & pur 1.00 .40
292 A73 50fr red brn & dk brn 1.00 .40
293 A73 50fr red brn & blk 1.00 .40
Nos. 290-293 (4) 4.00 1.60

Beehive, Bees and Globes A74

1973, Oct. 31 Engr. *Perf. 13*
294 A74 40fr dl red, ocher & dl bl .65 .30

World Savings Day.

Tcherka Songhai Blanket — A75

Design: 35fr, Kounta Songhai blanket, vert.

Perf. 12½x13, 13x12½
1973, Dec. 17 Photo.
295 A75 35fr brn & multi .75 .40
296 A75 40fr brn & multi .75 .40

Textiles of Niger.

WPY Emblem, Infant and Globe A76

1974, Mar. 4 Engr. *Perf. 13*
297 A76 50fr multi .65 .35

World Population Year 1974.

Locomotives, 1938 and 1948 — A77

1974, May 24 Engr. *Perf. 13*
298 A77 50fr shown .95 .35
299 A77 75fr Locomotive, 1893 1.50 .50
300 A77 100fr Locomotives, 1866 and 1939 2.10 .75
301 A77 150fr *Locomotives, 1829* 3.25 1.25
Nos. 298-301 (4) 7.80 2.85

Map and Flags of Members A78

1974, May 29 Photo. *Perf. 13x12½*
302 A78 40fr bl & multi .70 .30

15th anniversary of the Council of Accord.

Marconi Sending Radio Signals to Australia — A79

1974, July 1 Engr. *Perf. 13*
303 A79 50fr pur, bl & dk brn .75 .35

Centenary of the birth of Guglielmo Marconi (1874-1937), Italian inventor and physicist.

Hand Holding Sapling — A80

Camel Saddle — A81

1974, Aug. 2 Engr. *Perf. 13*

304 A80 35fr multi .75 .30

National Tree Week.

1974, Aug. 20 Engr. *Perf. 13*

Design: 50fr, 3 sculptured horses, horiz.

305 A81 40fr ol brn, bl & red .60 .30
306 A81 50fr ol brn, bl & red .75 .35

Chopin and Polish Eagle A82

Design: No. 308, Ludwig van Beethoven and allegory of Ninth Symphony.

1974

307 A82 100fr multi 1.50 .70
308 A82 100fr multi 1.50 .70

125th anniversary of the death of Frederic Chopin (1810-1849), composer and 150th anniversary of Beethoven's Ninth Symphony, composed 1823.

Issue dates: #307, Sept. 4; #308, Sept. 19.

Don-Don Drum — A83

1974, Nov. 12 Engr. *Perf. 13*

309 A83 60fr multi 1.10 .50

Tenere Tree, Compass Rose and Caravan — A84

1974, Nov. 24 Engr. *Perf. 13*

310 A84 50fr multi 2.50 1.10

Tenere tree, a landmark in Sahara Desert, first death anniversary.

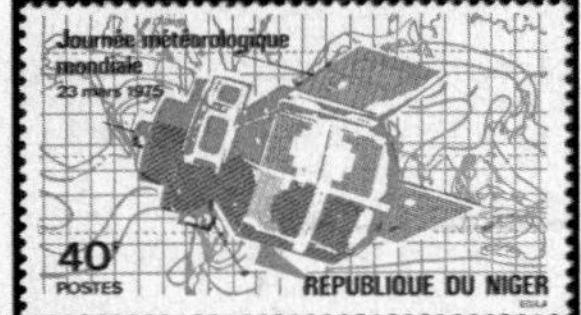

Satellite over World Weather Map — A85

1975, Mar. 23 Litho. *Perf. 13*

311 A85 40fr bl, blk & red .60 .30

World Meteorological Day, Mar. 23, 1975.

"City of Truro," English, 1903 — A86

Locomotives and Flags: 75fr, "5.003," Germany, 1937. 100fr, "The General," United States, 1863. 125fr, "Electric BB 15.000," France, 1971.

1975, Apr. 24 Typo. *Perf. 13*

312 A86 50fr org & multi 1.50 .35
313 A86 75fr yel grn & multi 2.00 .65
314 A86 100fr lt bl & multi 2.40 .80
315 A86 125fr multi 3.00 1.00
Nos. 312-315 (4) 8.90 2.80

Bird Type of 1968 Dated "1975"

1975, Apr. Photo. *Perf. 13*

316 A43 25fr ol & multi 1.75 .55

Zabira Leather Bag — A87

Handicrafts: 40fr, Damier tapestry. 45fr, Vase. 60fr, Gourd flask.

1975, May 28 Litho. *Perf. 12½*

317 A87 35fr dp bl & multi .40 .25
318 A87 40fr dp grn & multi .60 .30
319 A87 45fr brn & multi .80 .40
320 A87 60fr dp org & multi 1.25 .40
Nos. 317-320 (4) 3.05 1.35

Mother and Child, IWY Emblem — A88

1975, June 9 Engr. *Perf. 13*

321 A88 50fr claret, brn & bl .90 .30

International Women's Year 1975.

Dr. Schweitzer and Lambarene Hospital — A89

1975, June 23 Engr. *Perf. 13*

322 A89 100fr brn, grn & blk 1.40 .75

Dr. Albert Schweitzer (1875-1965), medical missionary.

Peugeot, 1892 — A90

Early Autos: 75fr, Daimler, 1895. 100fr, Fiat, 1899. 125fr, Cadillac, 1903.

1975, July 16 Engr. *Perf. 13*

323 A90 50fr rose & vio bl 1.25 .40
324 A90 75fr bl & vio brn 1.60 .45
325 A90 100fr brt grn & mag 2.75 .70
326 A90 125fr brick red & brt grn 3.00 .80
Nos. 323-326 (4) 8.60 2.35

Sun, Tree and Earth — A91

Boxing — A92

1975, Aug. 2 Engr. *Perf. 13*

327 A91 40fr multi .80 .35

National Tree Week.

1975, Aug. 25 Engr. *Perf. 13*

Designs: 35fr, Boxing, horiz. 45fr, Wrestling, horiz. 50fr, Wrestling.

328 A92 35fr blk, org & brn .45 .25
329 A92 40fr bl grn, brn & blk .50 .30
330 A92 45fr blk, brt bl & brn .80 .35
331 A92 50fr red, brn & blk .85 .40
Nos. 328-331 (4) 2.60 1.30

Lion's Head Tetradrachma, Leontini, 460 B.C. — A93

Greek Coins: 75fr, Owl tetradrachma, Athens, 500 B.C. 100fr, Crab diadrachma, Himera, 480 B.C. 125fr, Minotaur tetradrachma, Gela, 460 B.C.

1975, Sept. 12 Engr. *Perf. 13*

332 A93 50fr red, dl bl & blk .90 .30
333 A93 75fr lil, brt bl & blk 1.25 .35
334 A93 100fr bl, org & blk 1.60 .60
335 A93 125fr grn, pur & blk 2.25 .70
Nos. 332-335 (4) 6.00 1.95

Starving Family A94

45fr, Animal skeletons. 60fr, Truck bringing food.

1975, Oct. 21 Engr. *Perf. 13x12½*

336 A94 40fr multi .90 .40
337 A94 45fr ultra & brn 1.60 .60
338 A94 60fr grn, org & dk bl 1.50 .50
Nos. 336-338 (3) 4.00 1.50

Fight against drought.

Niger River Crossing — A95

Designs: 45fr, Entrance to Boubon camp. 50fr, Camp building.

1975, Nov. 10 Litho. *Perf. 12½*

339 A95 40fr multi .70 .30
340 A95 45fr multi .75 .30
341 A95 50fr multi .80 .40
Nos. 339-341 (3) 2.25 1.00

Tourist publicity.

Teacher and Pupils A96

Each stamp has different inscription in center.

1976, Jan. 12 Photo. *Perf. 13*

342 A96 25fr ol & multi .25 .20
343 A96 30fr vio bl & multi .25 .20
344 A96 40fr multi .25 .20
345 A96 50fr multi .40 .20
346 A96 60fr multi .50 .20
Nos. 342-346 (5) 1.65 1.00

Literacy campaign 1976.
For overprints see Nos. 371-375.

12th Winter Olympic Games, Innsbruck — A97

1976, Feb. 20 Litho. *Perf. 14x13½*

347 A97 40fr Ice hockey .35 .25
348 A97 50fr Luge .55 .30
349 A97 150fr Ski jump 1.10 .55
Nos. 347-349,C266-C267 (5) 5.75 2.80

Satellite, Telephone, ITU Emblem — A98

1976, Mar. 10 Litho. *Perf. 13*

350 A98 100fr org, bl & vio bl 1.25 .55

Centenary of first telephone call by Alexander Graham Bell, Mar. 10, 1876.

WHO Emblem, Red Cross Truck, Infant — A99

1976, Apr. 7 Engr. *Perf. 13*
351 A99 50fr multi .75 .25

World Health Day 1976.

Statue of Liberty and Washington Crossing the Delaware — A100

50fr, Statue of Liberty and call to arms.

1976, Apr. 8 Litho. *Perf. 14x13½*
352 A100 40fr multi .30 .20
353 A100 50fr multi .40 .25
Nos. 352-353,C269-C271 (5) 5.65 2.30

American Bicentennial.

The Army Helping in Development — A101

Design: 50fr, Food distribution, vert.

Perf. 12½x13, 13x12½
1976, Apr. 15 Litho.
354 A101 50fr multi .45 .25
355 A101 100fr multi .90 .40

National Armed Forces, 2nd anniv. of takeover.

Europafrica Issue 1976

Maps, Concorde, Ship and Grain — A102

1976, June 9 Litho. *Perf. 13*
356 A102 100fr multi 1.25 .50

Road Building A103

Design: 30fr, Rice cultivation.

1976, June 26 *Perf. 12½*
357 A103 25fr multi .25 .20
358 A103 30fr multi .35 .20

Community labor.

Motobecane 125, France — A104

Motorcycles: 75fr, Norton Challenge, England. 100fr, BMW 90 S, Germany. 125fr, Kawasaki 1000, Japan.

1976, July 16 Engr. *Perf. 13*
359 A104 50fr vio bl & multi .70 .30
360 A104 75fr dp grn & multi 1.00 .35
361 A104 100fr dk brn & multi 1.50 .70
362 A104 125fr slate & multi 1.75 .80
Nos. 359-362 (4) 4.95 2.15

Boxing A105

Designs: 50fr, Basketball. 60fr, Soccer. 80fr, Cycling, horiz. 100fr, Judo, horiz.

1976, July 17 Litho. *Perf. 14*
363 A105 40fr multi .50 .30
364 A105 50fr multi .60 .30
365 A105 60fr multi .70 .30
366 A105 80fr multi .80 .30
367 A105 100fr multi 1.10 .35
Nos. 363-367 (5) 3.70 1.55

21st Summer Olympic games, Montreal. See No. C279.

Map of Niger, Planting Seedlings A106

Designs: 50fr, Woman watering seedling, vert. 60fr, Women planting seedlings, vert.

1976, Aug. 1 Litho. *Perf. 12½x13*
368 A106 40fr org & multi .45 .25
369 A106 50fr yel & multi .50 .25
370 A106 60fr grn & multi .65 .30
Nos. 368-370 (3) 1.60 .80

Reclamation of Sahel Region.

Nos. 342-346 Overprinted: "JOURNEE / INTERNATIONALE / DE L'ALPHABETISATION"

1976, Sept. 8 Photo. *Perf. 13*
371 A96 25fr ol & multi .25 .20
372 A96 30fr vio bl & multi .25 .20
373 A96 40fr multi .30 .25
374 A96 50fr multi .40 .25
375 A96 60fr multi .45 .25
Nos. 371-375 (5) 1.65 1.15

Literacy campaign.

Hairdresser — A107

Designs: 40fr, Woman weaving straw, vert. 50fr, Women potters, vert.

1976, Oct. 6 *Perf. 13*
376 A107 40fr buff & multi .40 .25
377 A107 45fr bl & multi .45 .25
378 A107 50fr red & multi .65 .30
Nos. 376-378 (3) 1.50 .80

Niger Women's Association.

Rock Carvings A108

Archaeology: 50fr, Neolithic sculptures. 60fr, Dinosaur skeleton.

1976, Nov. 15 Photo. *Perf. 13x12½*
379 A108 40fr blk, sl & yel 1.25 .40
380 A108 50fr blk, red & bis 1.60 .40
381 A108 60fr bis, blk & brn 2.25 .50
Nos. 379-381 (3) 5.10 1.30

Benin Head — A109

Weaver, Dancers and Musicians — A110

1977, Jan. 15 Engr. *Perf. 13*
382 A109 40fr dk brn .45 .25
383 A110 50fr gray bl 1.00 .30

2nd World Black and African Festival, Lagos, Nigeria, Jan. 15-Feb. 12.

First Aid, Student, Blackboard and Plow — A111

Midwife — A112

Designs: Inscriptions on blackboard differ on each denomination.

1977, Jan. 23 Photo. *Perf. 12½x13*
384 A111 40fr multi .35 .25
385 A111 50fr multi .45 .25
386 A111 60fr multi .65 .35
Nos. 384-386 (3) 1.45 .85

Literacy campaign.

1977, Feb. 23 Litho. *Perf. 13*

Design: 50fr, Midwife examining newborn.

387 A112 40fr multi .45 .25
388 A112 50fr multi .75 .30

Village health service.

Titan Rocket Launch A113

80fr, Viking orbiter near Mars, horiz.

1977, Mar. 15 Litho. *Perf. 14*
389 A113 50fr multi .45 .25
390 A113 80fr multi .75 .25
Nos. 389-390,C283-C285 (5) 4.70 1.60

Viking Mars project.
For overprints see #497-498, C295-C297.

Marabous A114

Design: 90fr, Harnessed antelopes.

1977, Mar. 18 Engr. *Perf. 13*
391 A114 80fr multi 2.00 1.00
392 A114 90fr multi 2.25 1.00

Nature protection.

Weather Map, Satellite, WMO Emblem A115

1977, Mar. 23
393 A115 100fr multi 1.00 .50

World Meteorological Day.

Group Gymnastics — A116

50fr, High jump. 80fr, Folk singers.

1977, Apr. 7 Litho. *Perf. 13x12½*
394 A116 40fr dl yel & multi .45 .25
395 A116 50fr bl & multi .60 .30
396 A116 80fr org & multi .75 .35
Nos. 394-396 (3) 1.80 .90

2nd Tahoua Youth Festival, Apr. 7-14.

Red Cross, WHO Emblems and Children — A117

1977, Apr. 25 **Engr.** ***Perf. 13***
397 A117 80fr lil, org & red .75 .35

World Health Day: "Immunization means protection of your children."

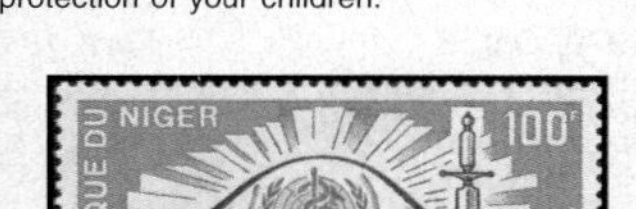

Eye with WHO Emblem, and Sword Killing Fly — A118

1977, May 7
398 A118 100fr multi 1.00 .50

Fight against onchocerciasis, a roundworm infection, transmitted by flies, causing blindness.

Guirka Tahoua Dance A119

50fr, Mailfilafili Gaya. 80fr, Naguihinayan Loga.

1977, June 7 **Photo.** ***Perf. 13x12½***
399 A119 40fr multi .50 .30
400 A119 50fr multi .75 .35
401 A119 80fr multi 1.00 .50
Nos. 399-401 (3) 2.25 1.15

Popular arts and traditions.

Cavalry — A120

Traditional chief's cavalry, different groups.

1977, July 7 **Litho.** ***Perf. 13x12½***
402 A120 40fr multi .60 .30
403 A120 50fr multi .75 .35
404 A120 60fr multi 1.00 .50
Nos. 402-404 (3) 2.35 1.15

Planting and Cultivating — A121

1977, Aug. 10
405 A121 40fr multi .60 .30

Reclamation of Sahel Region.

Albert John Luthuli Peace — A122

Designs: 80fr, Maurice Maeterlinck, literature. 100fr, Allan L. Hodgkin, medicine. 150fr, Albert Camus, literature. 200fr, Paul Ehrlich, medicine.

1977, Aug. 20 **Litho.** ***Perf. 14***
406 A122 50fr multi .35 .25
407 A122 80fr multi .45 .25
408 A122 100fr multi .70 .25
409 A122 150fr multi 1.10 .40
410 A122 200fr multi 1.50 .50
Nos. 406-410 (5) 4.10 1.65

Nobel prize winners. See No. C287.

Mao Tse-tung — A123

1977, Sept. 9 **Engr.** ***Perf. 13***
411 A123 100fr blk & red 3.25 1.25

Argentina '78 Emblem, Soccer Players and Coach, Vittorio Pozzo, Italy — A124

Designs (Argentina '78 emblem, soccer players and coach): 50fr, Vincente Feola, Spain. 80fr, Aymore Moreira, Portugal. 100fr, Sir Alf Ramsey, England. 200fr, Helmut Schoen, Germany. 500fr, Sepp Herberger, Germany.

1977, Oct. 12 **Litho.** ***Perf. 13½***
412 A124 40fr multi .35 .25
413 A124 50fr multi .45 .25
414 A124 80fr multi .60 .25
415 A124 100fr multi .95 .35
416 A124 200fr multi 1.60 .65
Nos. 412-416 (5) 3.95 1.75

Souvenir Sheet

417 A124 500fr multi 4.25 1.75

World Cup Soccer championship, Argentina '78.
For overprints see Nos. 453-458.

Horse's Head, Parthenon and UNESCO Emblem — A125

1977, Nov. 12 **Engr.** ***Perf. 13***
418 A125 100fr multi 1.50 .75

Woman Carrying Water Pots — A126

Design: 50fr, Women pounding corn.

1977, Nov. 23 **Photo.** ***Perf. 12½x13***
419 A126 40fr multi .45 .25
420 A126 50fr red & multi .55 .30

Niger Women's Association.

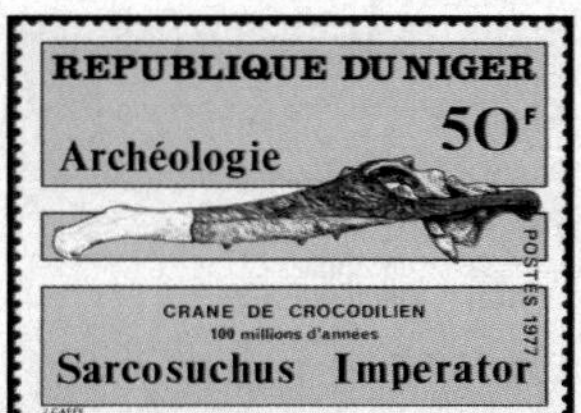

Crocodile's Skull, 100 Million Years Old — A127

Design: 80fr, Neolithic flint tools.

1977, Dec. 14 ***Perf. 13***
421 A127 50fr multi 1.10 .50
422 A127 80fr multi 1.50 .70

Raoul Follereau and Lepers A128

40fr, Raoul Follereau and woman leper, vert.

1978, Jan. 28 **Engr.** ***Perf. 13***
423 A128 40fr multi .45 .25
424 A128 50fr multi .50 .30

25th anniversary of Leprosy Day. Follereau (1903-1977) was "Apostle to the Lepers" and educator of the blind.

Bird Type of 1972 Redrawn

1978, Feb. **Photo.** ***Perf. 13***
425 A58 50fr tan & multi 3.00 1.00

No. 425 is dated "1978" and has only designer's name in imprint. No. 254 has printer's name also.

Assumption, by Rubens A129

Rubens Paintings: 70fr, Rubens and Friends, horiz. 100fr, History of Marie de Medici. 150fr, Alathea Talbot and Family. 200fr, Marquise de Spinola. 500fr, Virgin and St. Ildefonso.

1978, Feb. 25 **Litho.** ***Perf. 14***
426 A129 50fr multi .35 .20
427 A129 70fr multi .40 .25
428 A129 100fr multi .75 .30
429 A129 150fr multi 1.10 .40
430 A129 200fr multi 1.60 .50
Nos. 426-430 (5) 4.20 1.65

Souvenir Sheet
Perf. 13½

431 A129 500fr gold & multi 4.50 1.50

Peter Paul Rubens (1577-1640), 400th birth anniversary.

Shot Put A130

1978, Mar. 22 **Photo.** ***Perf. 13***
432 A130 40fr shown .25 .20
433 A130 50fr Volleyball .35 .25
434 A130 60fr Long jump .40 .25
435 A130 100fr Javelin .70 .35
Nos. 432-435 (4) 1.70 1.05

Natl. University Games' Championships.

First Aid and Red Crosses A131

1978, May 13 **Litho.**
436 A131 40fr red & multi .35 .25

Niger Red Cross.

Goudel Earth Station A132

1978, May 23
437 A132 100fr multi .75 .40

Soccer Ball, Flags of Participants A133

Argentina '78 Emblem and: 50fr, Ball in net. 100fr, Globe with South America, Soccer field. 200fr, Two players, horiz. 300fr, Player and globe.

1978, June 18 **Litho.** ***Perf. 13½***
438 A133 40fr multi .30 .20
439 A133 50fr multi .50 .20
440 A133 100fr multi .75 .35
441 A133 200fr multi 1.50 .60
Nos. 438-441 (4) 3.05 1.35

Souvenir Sheet

442 A133 300fr multi 2.50 1.25

11th World Cup Soccer Championship, Argentina, June 1-25.

Bird Type of 1971 Redrawn

1978, June **Photo.** ***Perf. 13***
443 A54 35fr bl & multi 3.00 .80

No. 443 has no year date, nor Delrieu imprint.

Post Office, Niamey — A134

Design: 60fr, Post Office, different view.

1978, Aug. 12 **Litho.**
444 A134 40fr multi .30 .25
445 A134 60fr multi .45 .25

Goudel Water Works A135

1978, Sept. 25 **Photo.** ***Perf. 13***
446 A135 100fr multi .75 .40

Giraffe — A136

Animals and Wildlife Fund Emblem: 50fr, Ostrich. 70fr, Cheetah. 150fr, Oryx, horiz. 200fr, Addax, horiz. 300fr, Hartebeest, horiz.

1978, Nov. 20 **Litho.** ***Perf. 15***
447 A136 40fr multi *2.00* .50
448 A136 50fr multi *3.00* .60
449 A136 70fr multi *3.25* .75
450 A136 150fr multi *7.50* 1.00
451 A136 200fr multi *10.00* 1.75
452 A136 300fr multi *14.00* 2.25
Nos. 447-452 (6) 39.75 6.85

Endangered species.

Nos. 412-417 Overprinted in Silver
a. "EQUIPE QUATRIEME: ITALIE"
b. "EQUIPE TROISIEME: BRESIL"
c. "EQUIPE / SECONDE: / PAYS BAS"
d. "EQUIPE VAINQUEUR: ARGENTINE"
e. "ARGENTINE-PAYS BAS 3-1"

1978, Dec. 1 ***Perf. 13½***
453 A124(a) 40fr multi .35 .25
454 A124(b) 50fr multi .45 .25
455 A124(c) 80fr multi .70 .30
456 A124(d) 100fr multi 1.00 .40
457 A124(e) 200fr multi 1.75 .75
Nos. 453-457 (5) 4.25 1.95

Souvenir Sheet

458 A124(e) 500fr multi 4.25 1.75

Winners, World Soccer Cup Championship, Argentina, June 1-25.

Tinguizi — A137

Musicians: No. 460, Dan Gourmou. No. 461, Chetima Ganga, horiz.

1978, Dec. 11 **Litho.** ***Perf. 13***
459 A137 100fr multi .95 .40
460 A137 100fr multi .95 .40
461 A137 100fr multi .95 .40
Nos. 459-461 (3) 2.85 1.20

Virgin Mary, by Dürer A138

50fr, The Homecoming, by Honoré Daumier (1808-79). 150fr, 200fr, 500fr, Virgin and Child, by Albrecht Dürer (1471-1528), diff.

1979, Jan. 31 **Litho.** ***Perf. 13½***
462 A138 50fr multi .70 .25
463 A138 100fr multi .75 .30
464 A138 150fr multi 1.10 .40
465 A138 200fr multi 1.50 .60
Nos. 462-465 (4) 4.05 1.55

Souvenir Sheet

466 A138 500fr multi 4.50 1.50

Solar Panels and Tank — A139

Design: 40fr, Tank and panels on roof, vert.

1979, Feb. 28 ***Perf. 12½x12, 12x12½***
467 A139 40fr multi .35 .25
468 A139 50fr multi .45 .25

Hot water from solar heat.

Children with Building Blocks — A140

Children and IYC Emblem: 100fr, Reading books. 150fr, With model plane.

1979, Apr. 10 **Litho.** ***Perf. 13½***
469 A140 40fr multi .35 .25
470 A140 100fr multi .70 .30
471 A140 150fr multi 1.40 .40
Nos. 469-471 (3) 2.45 .95

International Year of the Child.

The Langa, Traditional Sport A141

Design: 50fr, The langa, diff.

1979, Apr. 10 **Litho.** ***Perf. 12½x12***
472 A141 40fr multi .35 .25
473 A141 50fr multi .45 .25

Rowland Hill, Mail Truck and France No. 8 — A142

Designs (Hill and): 100fr, Canoes and Austria #P4. 150fr, Air Niger plane and US #122. 200fr, Streamlined mail train and Canada type A6. 400fr, Electric train and Niger #51.

1979, June 6 **Litho.** ***Perf. 14***
474 A142 40fr multi .40 .25
475 A142 100fr multi .90 .30
476 A142 150fr multi 1.25 .40
477 A142 200fr multi 1.50 .55
Nos. 474-477 (4) 4.05 1.50

Souvenir Sheet

478 A142 400fr multi 3.75 1.50

Sir Rowland Hill (1795-1879), originator of penny postage.

Zabira Handbag and Niger No. 135 — A143

Design: 150fr, Heads with communications waves, world map, UPU emblem and satellite.

1979, June 8 **Litho.** ***Perf. 12x12½***
479 A143 50fr multi 1.10 .50

Engr. ***Perf. 13***
480 A143 150fr brt red & ultra 3.00 1.50

Philexafrique II, Libreville, Gabon, June 8-17. Nos. 479, 480 each printed in sheets of 10 and 5 labels showing exhibition emblem.

Djermakoye Palace — A144

1979, Sept. 26 **Litho.** ***Perf. 13x12½***
481 A144 100fr multi .75 .40

Bororo Festive Headdress — A145

60fr, Bororo women's traditional costumes.

Perf. 13x12½, 12½x13
1979, Sept. 26
482 A145 45fr multi .35 .25
483 A145 60fr multi, vert. .50 .30

Annual Bororo Festival.

Olympic Emblem, Flame and Boxers — A146

Designs: 100fr, 150fr, 250fr, 500fr, Olympic emblem, flame and boxers, diff.

1979, Oct. 6 ***Perf. 13½***
484 A146 45fr multi .35 .20
485 A146 100fr multi .75 .30
486 A146 150fr multi 1.10 .40
487 A146 250fr multi 2.00 .65
Nos. 484-487 (4) 4.20 1.55

Souvenir Sheet

488 A146 500fr multi 3.75 1.75

Pre-Olympic Year.

John Alcock, Arthur Whitten Brown, Vickers-Vimy Biplane — A147

1979, Sept. 3 ***Perf. 13½***
489 A147 100fr multi 1.25 .50

First Transatlantic flight, 60th anniversary.

Road and Traffic Safety — A148

1979, Nov. 20 **Litho.** ***Perf. 12½***
490 A148 45fr multi .45 .30

Four-Man Bobsledding, Lake Placid '80 Emblem — A149

Lake Placid '80 Emblem and: 60fr, Downhill skiing. 100fr, Speed skating. 150fr, Two-man bobsledding. 200fr, Figure skating. 300fr, Cross-country skiing.

1979, Dec. 10 ***Perf. 14½***
491 A149 40fr multi .30 .20
492 A149 60fr multi .45 .20
493 A149 100fr multi .75 .30
494 A149 150fr multi 1.10 .40
495 A149 200fr multi 1.50 .75
Nos. 491-495 (5) 4.10 1.85

Souvenir Sheet

496 A149 300fr multi 2.50 1.00

13th Winter Olympic Games, Lake Placid, NY, Feb. 12-24, 1980.
For overprints see Nos. 501-506.

Nos. 389, 390 Overprinted in Silver or Black "alunissage/apollo XI/juillet 1969" and Emblem

1979, Dec. 20 **Litho.** ***Perf. 14***
497 A113 50fr multi (S) .35 .25
498 A113 80fr multi .60 .30
Nos. 497-498,C295-C296 (4) 3.80 2.10

Apollo 11 moon landing, 10th anniv. See #C297.

Court of Sultan of Zinder — A150

1980, Mar. 25 **Litho.** ***Perf. 13x12½***

499 A150 45fr shown .35 .25
500 A150 60fr Sultan's court, diff. .45 .25

Nos. 491-496 Overprinted
a. VAINQUEUR/R.D.A.
b. VAINQUEUR/STENMARK/SUEDE
c. VAINQUEUR/HEIDEN/Etats-Unis
d. VAINQUEURS/SCHAERER-BENZ/Suisse
e. VAINQUEUR/COUSINS/ Grande Bretagne
f. VAINQUEUR/ZIMIATOV/U.R.S.S.

1980, Mar. 31 **Litho.** ***Perf. 14½***

501 A149 (a) 40fr multi .30 .20
502 A149 (b) 60fr multi .45 .25
503 A149 (c) 100fr multi .75 .40
504 A149 (d) 150fr multi 1.10 .50
505 A149 (e) 200fr multi 1.50 .70
Nos. 501-505 (5) 4.10 2.05

Souvenir Sheet

506 A149 (f) 300fr multi 2.40 1.50

Javelin, Olympic Rings — A151

Man Smoking Cigarette, Runner — A152

1980, Apr. 17

507 A151 60fr shown .45 .20
508 A151 90fr Walking .75 .25
509 A151 100fr High jump, horiz. .90 .30
510 A151 300fr Marathon runners, horiz. 2.00 .80
Nos. 507-510 (4) 4.10 1.55

Souvenir Sheet

511 A151 500fr High jump, diff. 3.50 1.50

22nd Summer Olympic Games, Moscow, July 19-Aug. 3.

For overprints see Nos. 527-531.

1980, Apr. 7 ***Perf. 13***

512 A152 100fr multi .70 .40

World Health Day; fight against cigarette smoking.

Health Year A153

1980, May 15 **Photo.** ***Perf. 13x12½***

513 A153 150fr multi 1.00 .55

Shimbashi-Yokohama Locomotive — A154

1980, June **Litho.** ***Perf. 12½***

514 A154 45fr shown .50 .30
515 A154 60fr American type .75 .35
516 A154 90fr German Reichsbahn series 61 .95 .50
517 A154 100fr Prussian Staatsbahn P2 1.10 .65
518 A154 130fr L'Aigle 1.40 .85
Nos. 514-518 (5) 4.70 2.65

Souvenir Sheet

519 A154 425fr Stephenson's Rocket 7.50 2.25

For overprint see No. 674.

Steve Biko, 4th Anniversary of Death — A155

1980, Sept. 12 **Litho.** ***Perf. 13***

520 A155 150fr org & blk 1.00 .60

Soccer Players — A156

Designs: Various soccer scenes.

1980, Oct. 15 ***Perf. 12½***

521 A156 45fr multi .25 .20
522 A156 60fr multi .35 .20
523 A156 90fr multi .60 .25
524 A156 100fr multi .75 .30
525 A156 130fr multi .80 .35
Nos. 521-525 (5) 2.75 1.30

Souvenir Sheet

526 A156 425fr multi 3.50 1.10

World Soccer Cup 1982.

Nos. 507-511 Overprinted in Gold with Winner's Name and Country

1980, Sept. 27 **Litho.** ***Perf. 14½***

527 A151 60fr multi .40 .20
528 A151 90fr multi .60 .30
529 A151 100fr multi .70 .35
530 A151 300fr multi 2.00 1.00
Nos. 527-530 (4) 3.70 1.85

Souvenir Sheet

531 A151 500fr multi 3.50 1.75

African Postal Union, 5th Anniversary A157

Terra Cotta Kareygorou Head A158

1980, Dec. 24 **Photo.** ***Perf. 13½***

532 A157 100fr multi .75 .40

1981, Jan. 23 **Litho.** ***Perf. 13***

Designs: Terra Cotta Kareygorou Statues, 5th-12th cent. 45fr, 150fr, horiz.

533 A158 45fr multi .30 .25
534 A158 60fr multi .45 .25
535 A158 90fr multi .60 .30
536 A158 150fr multi 1.10 .50
Nos. 533-536 (4) 2.45 1.30

Ostrich — A159

1981, Mar. 17 **Litho.** ***Perf. 12½***

537 A159 10fr shown 1.00 .30
538 A159 20fr Oryx .40 .30
539 A159 25fr Gazelle .40 .30
540 A159 30fr Great bustard 1.60 .50
541 A159 60fr Giraffe .75 .30
542 A159 150fr Addax 1.60 .80
Nos. 537-542 (6) 5.75 2.50

7th Anniv. of the F.A.N. A160

1981, Apr. 14 **Litho.** ***Perf. 13***

543 A160 100fr multi .75 .40

One-armed Archer — A161

1981, Apr. 24 **Engr.**

544 A161 50fr shown .65 .30
545 A161 100fr Draftsman 1.00 .60

Intl. Year of the Disabled.

Scene from Mahalba Ballet, 1980 Youth Festival, Dosso A162

1981, May 17 **Litho.**

546 A162 100fr shown .75 .40
547 A162 100fr Ballet, diff. .75 .40

Prince Charles and Lady Diana, Coach — A163

Designs: Couple and coaches.

1981, July 15 **Litho.** ***Perf. 14½***

548 A163 150fr multi .90 .45
549 A163 200fr multi 1.25 .65
550 A163 300fr multi 1.75 .90
Nos. 548-550 (3) 3.90 2.00

Souvenir Sheet

551 A163 400fr multi 3.00 1.50

Royal wedding.

For overprints see Nos. 595-598.

Hegira 1500th Anniv. — A164

Alexander Fleming (1881-1955) A165

1981, July 15 ***Perf. 13½x13***

552 A164 100fr multi .80 .40

1981, Aug. 6 **Engr.** ***Perf. 13***

553 A165 150fr multi 1.75 .85

25th Intl. Letter Writing Week, Oct. 6-12 — A167

1981, Oct. 9 **Surcharged in Black**

554 A167 65fr on 40fr multi .45 .30
555 A167 85fr on 60fr multi .65 .50

Nos. 554-555 not issued without surcharge.

World Food Day — A168

1981, Oct. 16 **Litho.**

556 A168 100fr multi .75 .40

65F
REPUBLIQUE DU NIGER
COUPE DU MONDE DE FOOTBALL ESPANA 1982

Espana '82 World Cup Soccer — A169

Designs: Various soccer players.

1981, Nov. 18 **Litho.** ***Perf. 14x13½***

557 A169 40fr multi .30 .20
558 A169 65fr multi .50 .20
559 A169 85fr multi .60 .25
560 A169 150fr multi 1.10 .45
561 A169 300fr multi 2.00 .90
Nos. 557-561 (5) 4.50 2.00

Souvenir Sheet

562 A169 500fr multi 3.50 1.75

For overprints see Nos. 603-608.

75th Anniv. of Grand Prix — A170

Designs: Winners and their cars.

1981, Nov. 30 *Perf. 14*
563 A170 20fr Peugeot, 1912 .40 .25
564 A170 40fr Bugatti, 1924 .55 .25
565 A170 65fr Lotus-Climax, 1962 .80 .25
566 A170 85fr Georges Boillot, 1912 1.00 .50
567 A170 150fr Phil Hill, 1960 1.50 1.00
Nos. 563-567 (5) 4.25 2.25

Souvenir Sheet

568 A170 450fr Race 5.00 2.00

For overprint see No. 675.

Christmas 1981 — A171

Designs: Virgin and Child paintings.

1981, Dec. 24
569 A171 100fr Botticelli .70 .35
570 A171 200fr Botticini 1.40 .75
571 A171 300fr Botticelli, diff. 2.00 1.00
Nos. 569-571 (3) 4.10 2.10

School Gardens A172

1982, Feb. 19 **Litho.** *Perf. 13x13½*
572 A172 65fr shown .45 .30
573 A172 85fr Garden, diff. .60 .45

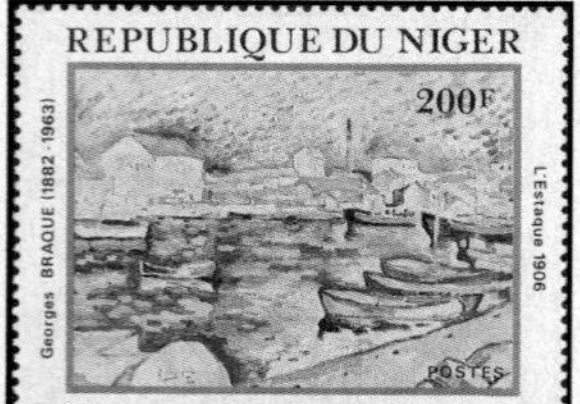

L'Estaque, by Georges Braque (1882-1963) — A173

Anniversaries: 120fr, Arturo Toscanini (1867-1957), vert. 140fr, Fruit on a Table, by EdouardManet (1832-1883). 300fr, George Washington (1732-99), vert. 400fr, Goethe (1749-1832), vert. Nos. 579-580, 21st birthday of Diana, Princess of Wales (portraits), vert.

1982, Mar. 8 **Litho.** *Perf. 13*
574 A173 120fr multi 1.00 .40
575 A173 140fr multi 1.40 .45
576 A173 200fr multi 2.50 .65
577 A173 300fr multi 3.00 1.00
578 A173 400fr multi 3.75 1.25
579 A173 500fr multi 4.50 1.75
Nos. 574-579 (6) 16.15 5.50

Souvenir Sheet

580 A173 500fr multi 3.75 1.75

Palace of Congress — A174

1982, Mar. 17
581 A174 150fr multi 1.00 .60

7th Youth Festival, Agadez — A175

Reafforestation Campaign — A176

1982, Apr. 7 *Perf. 12½*
582 A175 65fr Martial arts, horiz. .45 .30
583 A175 100fr Wrestling .70 .50

1982, Apr. 16 *Perf. 13*
584 A176 150fr Tree planting 1.00 .50
585 A176 200fr Trees, Desert 1.25 .65

For overprints see Nos. 668-669.

Scouting Year A177

1982, May 13
586 A177 65fr Canoeing .45 .25
587 A177 85fr Scouts in rubber boat .70 .30
588 A177 130fr Canoeing, diff. 1.00 .45
589 A177 200fr Rafting 1.50 .75
Nos. 586-589 (4) 3.65 1.75

Souvenir Sheet

590 A177 400fr Beach scene 3.00 1.75

For overprint see No. 673.

13th Meeting of Islamic Countries Foreign Affairs Ministers, Niamey, Aug. 20-27 A178

1982, June 6
591 A178 100fr multi .90 .40

West African Economic Community — A179

1982, June 28
592 A179 200fr Map 1.25 .85

Fishermen in Canoe A180

1982, July 18 *Perf. 13x12½*
593 A180 65fr shown .60 .35
594 A180 85fr Bringing in nets .75 .40

Nos. 548-551 Overprinted in Blue: "NAISSANCE ROYALE 1982"

1982, Aug. 4 *Perf. 14½*
595 A163 150fr multi 1.00 .50
596 A163 200fr multi 1.40 .70
597 A163 300fr multi 2.25 1.00
Nos. 595-597 (3) 4.65 2.20

Souvenir Sheet

598 A163 400fr multi 2.50 1.25

Flautist, by Norman Rockwell A181

1982, Sept. 10 **Litho.** *Perf. 14*
599 A181 65fr shown .45 .25
600 A181 85fr Clerk .70 .30
601 A181 110fr Teacher and Pupil .90 .35
602 A181 150fr Girl Shopper 1.10 .50
Nos. 599-602 (4) 3.15 1.40

Nos. 557-562 Overprinted with Past and Present Winners in Black on Silver

1982, Sept. 28 *Perf. 14x13½*
603 A169 40fr multi .30 .20
604 A169 65fr multi .45 .25
605 A169 85fr multi .50 .30
606 A169 150fr multi 1.10 .45
607 A169 300fr multi 2.00 1.00
Nos. 603-607 (5) 4.35 2.20

Souvenir Sheet

608 A169 500fr multi 3.50 2.25

Italy's victory in 1982 World Cup.

ITU Plenipotentiaries Conference, Nairobi, Sept. — A182

1982, Sept. 28 *Perf. 13*
609 A182 130fr black & blue .90 .50

Laboratory Workers A183

Various laboratory workers.

1982, Nov. 9 **Litho.** *Perf. 13*
610 A168 65fr multi .60 .35
611 A183 115fr multi .90 .55

Self-sufficiency in Food Production — A184

1983, Feb. 16 **Litho.** *Perf. 13½x13*
612 A184 65fr Rice harvest .60 .30
613 A184 85fr Planting rice, vert. .90 .40

Grand Ducal Madonna, by Raphael A185

Raphael Paintings: 65fr, Miraculous Catch of Fishes. 100fr, Deliverance of St. Peter. 150fr, Sistine Madonna. 200fr, Christ on the Way to Calvary. 300fr, Deposition. 400fr, Transfiguration. 500fr, St. Michael Slaying the Dragon.

1983, Mar. 30 **Litho.** *Perf. 14*
614 A185 65fr multi, vert. .50 .20
615 A185 85fr multi .60 .25
616 A185 100fr multi, vert. .80 .25
617 A185 150fr multi 1.25 .40
618 A185 200fr multi 1.50 .55
619 A185 300fr multi, vert. 2.25 .80
620 A185 400fr multi 3.25 1.10
621 A185 500fr multi 4.25 1.25
Nos. 614-621 (8) 14.40 4.80

African Economic Commission, 25th Anniv. — A186

1983, Mar. 18 *Perf. 12½x13*
622 A186 120fr multi .90 .45
623 A186 200fr multi 1.40 .85

Army Surveyors A187

1983, Apr. 14 *Perf. 13x12½*
624 A187 85fr shown .60 .40
625 A187 150fr Road building 1.10 .75

Agadez Court A188

1983, Apr. 26 **Litho.** *Perf. 13x12½*
626 A188 65fr multi .45 .25

Mail Van — A189

1983, June 25 **Litho.**
627 A189 65fr Van .45 .40
628 A189 100fr Van, map .75 .45

Palestine Solidarity — A190

1983, Aug. 21 **Litho.** ***Perf. 12½***
629 A190 65fr multi .60 .25

Intl. Literacy Year — A191

Various adult education classes. 65fr, 150fr vert.

Perf. 13½x14½, 14½x13½
1983, Sept. 8 **Litho.**
630 A191 40fr multi .35 .20
631 A191 65fr multi .45 .25
632 A191 85fr multi .60 .30
633 A191 100fr multi .75 .40
634 A191 150fr multi 1.25 .90
Nos. 630-634 (5) 3.40 2.05

7th Ballet Festival of Dosso Dept. A192

Various dancers.

1983, Oct. 7 ***Perf. 14½x13½***
635 A192 65fr multi .45 .35
636 A192 85fr multi .65 .40
637 A192 120fr multi 1.00 .55
Nos. 635-637 (3) 2.10 1.30

World Communications Year — A193

1983, Oct. 18 ***Perf. 13x12½, 12½x13***
638 A193 80fr Post Office, mail van .60 .45
639 A193 120fr Sorting mail .75 .50
640 A193 150fr Emblem, vert. 1.10 .60
Nos. 638-640 (3) 2.45 1.55

Solar Energy For Television — A194

1983, Nov. 26 ***Perf. 13***
641 A194 85fr Antenna .60 .40
642 A194 130fr Car 1.00 .40

Local Butterflies — A195

1983, Dec. 9 ***Perf. 12½***
643 A195 75fr Hypolimnas misippus .90 .40
644 A195 120fr Papilio demodocus 1.25 .50
645 A195 250fr Vanessa antiopa 2.25 1.00
646 A195 350fr Charesex jasius 3.50 1.25
647 A195 500fr Danaus chrisippus 5.50 2.00
Nos. 643-647 (5) 13.40 5.15

SAMARIYA Natl. Development Movement — A196

1984, Jan. 18 **Litho.** ***Perf. 13x13½***
648 A196 80fr multi .60 .40

Alestes Bouboni A197

1984, Mar. 28 **Litho.** ***Perf. 13***
649 A197 120fr multi 2.50 .70

Military Pentathlon A198

1984, Apr. 10
650 A198 120fr Hurdles .85 .40
651 A198 140fr Shooting 1.00 .55

Radio Broadcasting Building Opening A199

1984, May 14 **Litho.** ***Perf. 13***
652 A199 120fr multi .90 .40

25th Anniv. of Council of Unity — A200

1984, May 29 ***Perf. 12½***
653 A200 65fr multi .45 .35
654 A200 85fr multi .75 .45

Renault, 1902 — A201

Vintage cars (#656, 658, 660, 662) & ships.

1984, June 12 ***Perf. 12½***
655 A201 80fr Paris .60 .30
656 A201 100fr Gottlieb Daimler .75 .40
657 A201 120fr Three-master Jacques Coeur .75 .40
658 A201 140fr shown 1.00 .50
659 A201 150fr Barque Bosphorus 1.10 .60
660 A201 250fr Delage D8 1.90 .75
661 A201 300fr Three-master Comet 2.00 .75
662 A201 400fr Maybach Zeppelin 3.00 1.00
Nos. 655-662 (8) 11.10 4.70

1984 UPU Congress A202

1984, June 20 **Engr.** ***Perf. 13x12½***
663 A202 300fr Ship, emblems 3.00 1.75

Ayerou Market Place A203

1984, July 18 **Litho.** ***Perf. 12½***
664 A203 80fr shown .75 .50
665 A203 120fr River scene 1.10 .60

Vipere Echis Leucogaster — A204

1984, Aug. 16 ***Perf. 13x12½***
666 A204 80fr multi .95 .50

West African Union, CEAO, 10th Anniv. A205

1984, Oct. 26 **Litho.** ***Perf. 13½***
667 A205 80fr multi .60 .40

UN Disarmament Campaign, 20th Anniv. — A205a

1984, Oct. 31 ***Perf. 13***
667A A205a 400fr brt grn & blk 2.75 1.50
667B A205a 500fr brt bl & blk 3.25 2.00

Nos. 584-585 Overprinted "Aide au Sahel 84"

1984 **Litho.** ***Perf. 13***
668 A176 150fr multi 1.40 .75
669 A176 200fr multi 1.60 1.10

World Tourism Organization, 10th Anniv. — A206

1984, Jan. 2 **Litho.** ***Perf. 12½***
670 A206 110fr WTO emblem .75 .40

Infant Survival Campaign A207

1985, Jan. 28 **Litho.** ***Perf. 12½***
671 A207 85fr Breastfeeding .65 .35
672 A207 110fr Weighing child, giving liquids .90 .50

Nos. 590, 519 and 568 Overprinted with Exhibitions in Red Souvenir Sheets

Perf. 13, 12½, 14
1985, Mar. 11 **Litho.**
673 A177 400fr MOPHILA '85 / HAMBOURG 4.00 4.00
674 A154 425fr TSUKUBA EXPO '85 4.00 4.00
675 A170 450fr ROME, ITALIA '85 emblem 4.00 4.00

See Nos. C356-C357.

Technical & Cultural Cooperation Agency, 15th Anniv. — A208

1985, Mar. 20 *Perf. 13*
676 A208 110fr vio, brn & car rose .75 .40

8th Niamey Festival A209

Gaya Ballet Troupe. No. 678 vert.

1985, Apr. 8 *Perf. 12½x13, 13x12½*
677 A209 85fr multi .60 .40
678 A209 110fr multi .75 .55
679 A209 150fr multi 1.10 .70
Nos. 677-679 (3) 2.45 1.65

Intl. Youth Year — A210

Authors and scenes from novels: 85fr, Jack London (1876-1916). 105fr, Joseph Kessel (1898-1979). 250fr, Herman Melville. 450fr, Rudyard Kipling.

1985, Apr. 29 *Perf. 13*
680 A210 85fr multi .75 .35
681 A210 105fr multi .75 .40
682 A210 250fr multi 2.00 .70
683 A210 450fr multi 3.00 1.40
Nos. 680-683 (4) 6.50 2.85

PHILEXAFRICA '85, Lome, Togo — A211

1985, May 6 *Perf. 13x12½*
684 A211 200fr Tree planting 1.50 1.00
685 A211 200fr Industry 1.50 1.00
a. Pair, Nos. 684-685 + label 4.50 4.50

Victor Hugo and His Son Francois, by A. de Chatillon — A212

1985, May 22 *Perf. 12½*
686 A212 500fr multi 4.00 1.60

Europafrica A213

1985, June 3 *Perf. 13*
687 A213 110fr multi .95 .50

World Wildlife Fund — A214

50fr, 60fr, Addax. 85fr, 110fr, Oryx.

1985, June 15
688 A214 50fr Head, vert. *4.75 .75*
689 A214 60fr Grazing *5.75 1.00*
690 A214 85fr Two adults *7.50 1.25*
691 A214 110fr Head, vert. *9.00 1.50*
Nos. 688-691 (4) *27.00 4.50*

Environ-destroying Species — A215

1985, July 1 *Perf. 13x12½, 12½x13*
692 A215 85fr Oedaleus sp. .85 .35
693 A215 110fr Dysdercus volkeri 1.00 .40
694 A215 150fr Tolyposporium ehrenbergii, Sclerospora graminicola, horiz. 1.60 .60
695 A215 210fr Passer luteus 2.25 .90
696 A215 390fr Quelea quelea 4.00 1.75
Nos. 692-696 (5) 9.70 4.00

Official Type of 1988 and

Cross of Agadez — A216

1985-94 **Engr.** *Perf. 13*
697 A216 85fr green .75 .40
698 O2 110fr brown 1.00 .50
699 A216 125fr blue green — —
700 A216 175fr emerald — —
701 A216 210fr orange — —
Nos. 697-701 (2) 1.75 .90

Issued: 85fr, 110fr, 7/85; 125fr, 175fr, 210fr, 5/15/94.

Natl. Independence, 25th Anniv. — A217

1985, Aug. 3 **Litho.** *Perf. 13x12½*
707 A217 110fr multi .90 .40

Protected Trees A218

Designs: 30fr, No. 711, Adansonia digitata and pod, vert. 85fr, 210fr, Acacia albida. No. 710, 390fr, Adansonia digitata, diff. Nos. 708-710 inscribed "DES ARBRES POUR LE NIGER."

1985 *Perf. 13x12½, 12½x13*
708 A218 30fr grn & multi .50 .40
709 A218 85fr brn & multi .75 .50
710 A218 110fr mag & multi 1.10 .60
711 A218 110fr blk & multi .95 .55
712 A218 210fr blk & multi 1.50 1.00
713 A218 390fr blk & multi 3.00 1.40
Nos. 708-713 (6) 7.80 4.45

Issued: #708-710, 10/1; #711-713, 8/19.

Niamey-Bamako Motorboat Race — A219

1985, Sept. 16 *Perf. 13½*
714 A219 110fr Boats on Niger River .75 .40
715 A219 150fr Helicopter, competitor 1.00 .60
716 A219 250fr Motorboat, map 1.75 1.00
Nos. 714-716 (3) 3.50 2.00

Mushrooms — A220

1985, Oct. 3
717 A220 85fr Boletus .80 .35
718 A220 110fr Hypholoma fasciculare 1.10 .40
719 A220 200fr Coprinus comatus 1.90 .75
720 A220 300fr Agaricus arvensis 3.25 1.10
721 A220 400fr Geastrum fimbriatum 4.25 1.60
Nos. 717-721 (5) 11.30 4.20

Nos. 717-719 vert.

PHILEXAFRICA '85, Lome, Togo — A221

1985, Oct. 21 *Perf. 13x12½*
722 A221 250fr Village water pump 2.00 1.10
723 A221 250fr Children playing dili 2.00 1.10
a. Pair, Nos. 722-723 4.50 4.50

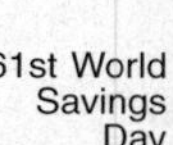

61st World Savings Day A222

1985, Oct. 31 *Perf. 12½x13*
724 A222 210fr multi 1.60 .80

European Music Year A223

Traditional instruments.

1985, Nov. 4 *Perf. 13½*
725 A223 150fr Gouroumi, vert. 1.10 .70
726 A223 210fr Gassou 1.60 1.10
727 A223 390fr Algaita, vert. 2.75 1.50
Nos. 725-727 (3) 5.45 3.30

Souvenir Sheet

Perf. 12½

728 A223 500fr Biti 4.00 4.00

Civil Statutes Reform — A224

1986, Jan. 2 **Litho.** *Perf. 13x12½*
729 A224 85fr Natl. identity card .60 .40
730 A224 110fr Family services .85 .50

Traffic Safety — A225

1986, Mar. 26 **Litho.** *Perf. 12½x13*
731 A225 85fr Obey signs .60 .35
732 A225 110fr Speed restriction .85 .50

Artists — A226

60fr, Oumarou Ganda, filmmaker. 85fr, Ida Na Dadaou, entertainer. 100fr, Dan Gourmou, entertainer. 130fr, Koungoui, comedian.

1986, Apr. 11 *Perf. 12½*
733 A226 60fr multi .45 .30
734 A226 85fr multi .60 .40
735 A226 100fr multi .75 .50
736 A226 130fr multi 1.00 .55
Nos. 733-736 (4) 2.80 1.75

Hunger Relief Campaign, Trucks of Hope — A227

1986, Aug. 27 Litho. *Perf. 12½*

737 A227 85fr Relief supply truck .75 .40
738 A227 110fr Mother, child, vert. 1.00 .50

Intl. Solidarity Day — A228

200fr, Nelson Mandela and Walter Sisulu, Robben Island prison camp. 300fr, Mandela.

1986, Oct. 8 *Perf. 13½*

739 A228 200fr multi 1.60 .80
740 A228 300fr multi 2.75 1.40

FAO, 40th Anniv. A229

1986, Oct. 16 *Perf. 13*

741 A229 50fr Cooperative peanut farm .40 .30
742 A229 60fr Fight desert encroachment .45 .30
743 A229 85fr Irrigation management .60 .40
744 A229 100fr Breeding livestock .75 .40
745 A229 110fr Afforestation 1.00 .40
Nos. 741-745 (5) 3.20 1.80

Improved Housing for a Healthier Niger — A230

1987, Feb. 26 Litho. *Perf. 13½*

746 A230 85fr Albarka .75 .30
747 A230 110fr Mai Sauki .95 .50

Insects Protecting Growing Crops — A231

1987, Mar. 26 *Perf. 13x12½*

748 A231 85fr Sphodromantis 1.25 .50
749 A231 110fr Delta 1.75 .60
750 A231 120fr Cicindela 2.00 .85
Nos. 748-750 (3) 5.00 1.95

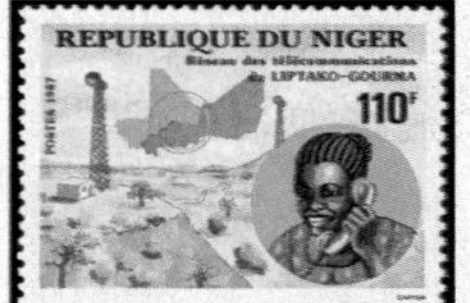

Liptako-Gourma Telecommunications Link Inauguration — A232

1987, Apr. 10 *Perf. 13½*

751 A232 110fr multi .75 .50

Samuel Morse — A233

1987, May 21 Litho. *Perf. 12x12½*

752 A233 120fr Telegraph key, operator, horiz. .75 .40
753 A233 200fr shown 1.50 .75
754 A233 350fr Receiver, horiz. 3.00 1.50
Nos. 752-754 (3) 5.25 2.65

Invention of the telegraph, 150th anniv.

1988 Seoul Summer Olympics — A234

1987, July 15

755 A234 85fr Tennis .50 .40
756 A234 110fr Pole vault .75 .40
757 A234 250fr Soccer 1.90 .85
Nos. 755-757 (3) 3.15 1.65

Souvenir Sheet

758 A234 500fr Running 3.75 2.50

1988 Winter Olympics, Calgary — A235

1987, July 28 Litho. *Perf. 12½*

759 A235 85fr Ice hockey .60 .35
760 A235 110fr Speed skating .75 .35
761 A235 250fr Pairs figure skating 1.60 .80
Nos. 759-761 (3) 2.95 1.50

Souvenir Sheet

762 A235 500fr Downhill skiing 3.75 2.00

For overprints see Nos. 783-785.

African Games, Nairobi — A236

1987, Aug. 5 *Perf. 13*

763 A236 85fr Runners .60 .35
764 A236 110fr High jump .75 .40
765 A236 200fr Hurdles 1.50 .75
766 A236 400fr Javelin 3.00 1.50
Nos. 763-766 (4) 5.85 3.00

Natl. Tourism Office, 10th Anniv. A237

1987, Sept. 10 *Perf. 13½*

767 A237 85fr Chief's stool, scepter, vert. .50 .35
768 A237 110fr Nomad, caravan, scepter 1.00 .40
769 A237 120fr Moslem village 1.00 .40
770 A237 200fr Bridge over Niger River 1.75 .75
Nos. 767-770 (4) 4.25 1.90

Aga Khan Architecture Prize, 1986 — A238

1987, Oct. 7 *Perf. 13*

771 A238 85fr Yaama Mosque, dawn .60 .30
772 A238 110fr At night .80 .40
773 A238 250fr In daylight 1.75 .90
Nos. 771-773 (3) 3.15 1.60

Niamey Court of Appeal A239

1987, Nov. 17 *Perf. 13x12½*

774 A239 85fr multi .60 .30
775 A239 110fr multi .75 .40
776 A239 140fr multi 1.00 .50
Nos. 774-776 (3) 2.35 1.20

Christmas 1987 — A240

Paintings: 110fr, The Holy Family with Lamb, by Raphael. 500fr, The Adoration of the Magi, by Hans Memling (c. 1430-1494).

Wmk. 385

1987, Dec. 24 Litho. *Perf. 12½*

777 A240 110fr multi 1.00 .50

Souvenir Sheet

778 A240 500fr multi 3.75 2.00

No. 778 is airmail.

Modern Services for a Healthy Community — A241

1988, Jan. 21 *Perf. 13*

779 A241 85fr Water drainage .95 .50
780 A241 110fr Sewage 1.10 .70
781 A241 165fr Garbage removal 1.90 .80
Nos. 779-781 (3) 3.95 2.00

Dan-Gourmou Prize — A242

1988, Feb. 16 Litho. *Perf. 13½*

782 A242 85fr multi 1.10 .70

Natl. modern music competition.

Nos. 759-761 Ovptd. "Medaille d'or" and Name of Winner in Gold

1988, Mar. 29 *Perf. 12½*

783 A235 85fr USSR .60 .35
784 A235 110fr Gusafson, Sweden .80 .40
785 A235 250fr Gordeeva and Grinkov, USSR 2.00 1.00
Nos. 783-785 (3) 3.40 1.75

New Market Building, Niamey A243

1988, Apr. 9 Litho. *Perf. 13x12½*

786 A243 85fr multi .75 .40

WHO 40th Anniv., Universal Immunization Campaign — A244

1988, May 26 Litho. *Perf. 12½x13*

787 A244 85fr Mother and child .65 .40
788 A244 110fr Visiting doctor .80 .45

Organization for African Unity (OAU), 25th Anniv. — A245

1988, June 28 *Perf. 12½*

789 A245 85fr multi .65 .35

Construction of a Sand Break to Arrest Desert Encroachment — A246

1988, Sept. 27 Litho. *Perf. 12½x13*

790 A246 85fr multi .95 .50

Intl. Red Cross and Red Crescent Organizations, 125th Annivs. — A247

1988, Oct. 26 ***Perf. 13x12½***
791 A247 85fr multi .60 .35
792 A247 110fr multi .80 .40

Niger Press Agency A248

1989, Jan. 31 **Litho.** ***Perf. 12½***
793 A248 85fr blk, org & grn .65 .35

Fight Against AIDS — A249

1989, Feb. 28 ***Perf. 13½***
794 A249 85fr multi .65 .35
795 A249 110fr multi .80 .40

Intl. Maritime Organization, 30th Anniv. — A250

1989, Mar. 29 **Litho.** ***Perf. 12½x13***
796 A250 100fr multi .80 .40
797 A250 120fr multi .95 .50

FAN Seizure of Government, 15th Anniv. — A251

1989, Apr. 14
798 A251 85fr Gen. Ali Saibou .60 .30
799 A251 110fr Raising of the flag .80 .35

PHILEXFRANCE '89 — A252

1989, July 1 **Litho.** ***Perf. 13***
800 A252 100fr Eiffel Tower .75 .40
801 A252 200fr Simulated stamps 1.50 .70

French Revolution, Bicent. — A253

1989, July 1
802 A253 250fr Planting a tree for liberty 2.25 1.10

Zinder Regional Museum — A253a

Perf. 14¾x14¼
1989, Aug. 23 **Litho.**
802A A253a 85fr multi *15.00*

African Development Bank, 25th Anniv. — A254

1989, Aug. 30 **Litho.** ***Perf. 13½***
803 A254 100fr multi .75 .35

Communication and Postal Organization of West Africa (CAPTEAO), 30th Anniv. — A255

1989, July 3 **Litho.** ***Perf. 13½***
804 A255 85fr multi .65 .35

Verdant Field, Field After Locust Plague — A256

1989, Oct. 1 **Litho.** ***Perf. 13***
805 A256 85fr multicolored .65 .35

Lumiere Brothers, Film Pioneers A256a

Designs: 150fr, Auguste Lumiere (1862-1954). 250fr, Louis Lumiere (1864-1948).

1989, Nov. 21 **Litho.** ***Perf. 13½***
805A A256a 150fr multicolored 1.50 .75
805B A256a 250fr multicolored 2.25 1.00
805C A256a 400fr multicolored 3.50 1.75
Nos. 805A-805C (3) 7.25 3.50

Rural Development Council, 30th Anniv. — A256b

1989 **Litho.** ***Perf. 15x14***
805D A256b 75fr multicolored *15.00*

Flora — A257

1989, Dec. 12 **Litho.** ***Perf. 13***
806 A257 10fr *Russelia equisetiformis* .20 .20
807 A257 20fr *Argyreia nervosa* .25 .20
808 A257 30fr *Hibiscus rosa-sinensis* .25 .20
809 A257 50fr *Catharanthus roseus* .45 .25
810 A257 100fr *Cymothoe sangaris,* horiz. 1.00 .40
Nos. 806-810 (5) 2.15 1.25

Dunes of Temet A257a

1989 **Litho.** ***Perf. 15x14***
810A A257a 145fr Caravan *40.00* —
810B A257a 165fr shown *40.00* —

Pan-African Postal Union, 10th Anniv. — A258

1990, Jan. 18 ***Perf. 12½***
811 A258 120fr multicolored 1.00 .50

Intl. Literacy Year — A259

1990, Feb. 27 ***Perf. 13½x13***
812 A259 85fr shown .65 .30
813 A259 110fr Class, diff. .95 .40

Islamic Conference Organization, 20th anniv. — A260

1990, Mar. 15 ***Perf. 13x12½***
814 A260 85fr OCI emblem .70 .35

U.S. Congressman Mickey Leland — A261

1990, Mar. 29 **Litho.** ***Perf. 13½***
815 A261 300fr multicolored 2.40 1.25
816 A261 500fr multicolored 4.00 2.00

Leland died Aug. 7, 1989 in a plane crash on a humanitarian mission.

Natl. Development Society, 1st Anniv. — A262

1990, May 15 **Litho.** ***Perf. 13½***
817 A262 85fr multicolored .70 .35

Multinational Postal School, 20th Anniv. — A263

1990, May 31 ***Perf. 13x12½***
818 A263 85fr multicolored .70 .35

1992 Summer Olympics, Barcelona — A263a

1990, June 4 **Litho.** ***Perf. 13½***
818A A263a 85fr Gymnastics .65 .30
818B A263a 110fr Hurdles .85 .40
818C A263a 250fr Running 2.00 1.00
818D A263a 400fr Equestrian 3.00 1.50
818E A263a 500fr Long jump 4.00 2.00
Nos. 818A-818E (5) 10.50 5.20

Souvenir Sheet

818F A263a 600fr Cycling 4.75 2.25

Nos. 818D-818F are airmail.

Independence, 30th Anniv. — A264

1990, Aug. 3 ***Perf. 12½***
819 A264 85fr gray grn & multi .60 .35
820 A264 110fr buff & multi .90 .45

UN Development Program, 40th Anniv. — A265

1990, Oct. 24	Litho.	Perf. 13½	
821 A265 100fr multicolored		.80	.40

A266

Butterflies and Mushrooms — A266a

Designs: 85fr, Amanita rubescens. 110fr, Graphum pylades. 200fr, Pseudacraea hostilia. 250fr, Russula virescens. 400fr, Boletus impolitus. 500fr, Precis octavia. 600fr, Cantharellus cibarius & pseudacraea boisduvali.

1991, Jan. 15	Litho.	Perf. 13½	
822 A266	85fr multicolored	.65	.30
823 A266	110fr multicolored	.85	.40
824 A266	200fr multicolored	1.50	.80
825 A266	250fr multicolored	2.00	1.00
826 A266	400fr multicolored	3.00	1.50
827 A266	500fr multicolored	4.00	2.00
	Nos. 822-827 (6)	12.00	6.00

Souvenir Sheet

828 A266a	600fr multicolored	6.00	5.00

Nos. 826-828 are airmail. No. 828 contains one 30x38mm stamp.

Palestinian Uprising — A267

1991, Mar. 30	Litho.	Perf. 12½	
829 A267 110fr multicolored		1.00	.45

Christopher Columbus (1451-1506) A268

Hypothetical portraits and: 85fr, Santa Maria. 110fr, Frigata, Portuguese caravel, 15th cent. 200fr, Four-masted caravel, 16th cent. 250fr, Estremadura, Spanish caravel, 1511. 400fr, Vija, Portuguese caravel, 1600. 500fr, Pinta. 600fr, Nina.

1991, Mar. 19	Litho.	Perf. 13½	
830 A268	85fr multicolored	.75	.40
831 A268	110fr multicolored	1.00	.45
832 A268	200fr multicolored	1.75	1.00
833 A268	250fr multicolored	2.25	1.25
834 A268	400fr multicolored	3.50	1.75
835 A268	500fr multicolored	4.50	2.25
	Nos. 830-835 (6)	13.75	7.10

Souvenir Sheet

835A A268	600fr multicolored	5.00	3.50

Nos. 834-835A are airmail.

Timia Falls — A269

African Tourism Year — A270

Designs: 85fr, Boubon Market, horiz. 130fr, Ruins of Assode, horiz.

1991, July 10			
836 A269	85fr multicolored	.70	.30
837 A269	110fr multicolored	.95	.45
838 A269	130fr multicolored	1.10	.50
839 A270	200fr multicolored	1.75	.85
	Nos. 836-839 (4)	4.50	2.10

Anniversaries and Events — A270a

85fr, Chess players Anatoly Karpov and Garry Kasparov. 110fr, Race car drivers Ayrton Senna and Alain Prost. 200fr, An official swears allegiance to the constitution, Honoré-Gabriel Riqueti (Comte de Mirabeau). 250fr, Gen. Dwight D. Eisenhower, Winston Churchill, Field Marshal Bernard Montgomery and Republic P-4D Thunderbolt. 400fr, Charles de Gaulle and Konrad Adenauer. 500fr, German Chancellor Helmut Kohl, Brandenburg Gate. 600fr, Pope John Paul II's visit to Africa.

1991, July 15	Litho.	Perf. 13½	
839A A270a	85fr multicolored	.45	.20
839B A270a	110fr multicolored	.60	.25
839C A270a	200fr multicolored	1.10	.35
839D A270a	250fr multi	6.00	1.25
839E A270a	400fr multicolored	2.25	.75
839F A270a	500fr multicolored	2.75	.85
839G A270a	600fr multi	5.00	5.00

French Revolution, bicent. (#839C). Franco-German Cooperation Agreement, 28th anniv. (#839E). #839E is airmail & exists in a souvenir sheet of 1. German reunification (#839F). No. 839F is airmail and exists in a souvenir sheet of 1.

For surcharge see No. 865.

Women's Hairstyles A271

1991			
840 A271	85fr multicolored	.95	.30
841 A271	110fr multicolored	1.25	.40
842 A271	165fr multicolored	1.90	.65
843 A271	200fr multicolored	2.10	.75
	Nos. 840-843 (4)	6.20	2.10

Transportation — A271a

Design: 250fr, Congo-Ocean BB.BB.301.

1991, Oct. 15	Litho.	Perf. 13½x13¼	
843B A271a	110fr multi	.60	.20
843C A271a	200fr multi	2.10	.35
843D A271a	250fr multi	2.50	.40
843E A271a	400fr multi	3.75	.55
843F A271a	500fr multi	2.75	.50

Nos. 843E and 843F are airmail. Nos. 843C-843F exist in souvenir sheets of one.

Two additional items were issued in this set. The editors would like to examine any examples.

Natl. Conference of Niger — A272

1991, Dec. 17	Litho.	Perf. 12½	
844 A272 85fr multicolored		.70	.35

House Built Without Wood A273

1992, May 25	Litho.	Perf. 12½	
845 A273 85fr multicolored		.75	.40

World Population Day — A274

Designs: 85fr, Assembling world puzzle. 110fr, Globe on a kite string.

1992, July 11	Litho.	Perf. 12½	
846 A274	85fr multicolored	.75	.40
847 A274	110fr multicolored	.95	.50

Discovery of America, 500th Anniv. — A275

1992, Sept. 16		Perf. 13	
848 A275 250fr multicolored		2.25	1.10

Hadjia Haoua Issa (1927-1990), Singer — A276

1992, Sept. 23		Perf. 12½x13	
849 A276 150fr multicolored		1.25	.65

Intl. Conference on Nutrition, Rome — A277

1992	Litho.	Perf. 12½	
850 A277	145fr tan & multi	1.25	.60
851 A277	350fr blue & multi	3.00	1.50

African School of Meteorology and Civil Aviation, 30th Anniv. — A278

1993, Feb. 7		Perf. 13½	
852 A278 110fr bl, grn & blk		.90	.45

Environmental Protection A279

1993, June 26	Litho.	Perf. 12½	
853 A279	85fr salmon & multi	.75	.40
854 A279	165fr green & multi	1.50	.75

World Population Day A280

110fr, Buildings, person with globe as head, tree.

1993, July 11	Litho.	Perf. 13½	
855 A280	85fr multicolored	.65	.30
856 A280	110fr multicolored	.85	.40

Holy City of Jerusalem — A281

1993, Nov. 8 Litho. *Perf. 13x12½*

857 A281 110fr multicolored .95 .45

Artisans at Work — A282b

1994 Litho. *Perf. 13x13¼*

857D A282b 125fr Tailor —

857E A282b 175fr Weaver, vert. — —

Nelson Mandela, F.W. De Klerk, Winners of 1993 Nobel Peace Prize — A282

1994, Feb. 11 Litho. *Perf. 13*

858 A282 270fr multicolored 1.10 .55

A282a

1994 Litho. *Perf. 12½x13*

858B A282a 110fr Hills —

858C A282a 165fr Mountain —

An 85fr stamp was released with this set. The editors would like to examine that stamp.

Cultural Cooperation & Technique Agency, 25th Anniv. — A283

1995 Litho. *Perf. 13½x13*

859 A283 100fr multicolored .50 .25

Animals Used for Transportation — A284

1995 *Perf. 13x13½*

860 A284 500fr Donkey cart 2.25 1.10

861 A284 1000fr Man, saddled horse 4.50 2.25

Economic Community of West African States (ECOWAS), 20th Anniv. — A285

1995 Litho. *Perf. 13½*

862 A285 125fr multicolored .70 .35

Cattle Ranching A286

Design: 300fr, Irrigating fields.

1995 *Perf. 13½x13*

863 A286 125fr shown .70 .35

864 A286 300fr multicolored 1.50 .75

Souvenir Sheet of No. 839E Ovptd.

1995, Nov. 8 Litho. *Perf. 13½*

865 A270a 400fr multicolored *6.50 3.25*

African Development Bank, 30th Anniv. — A287

1995 Litho. *Perf. 14*

866 A287 300fr green & red 1.60 .80

Boy Scouts A288

1996 *Perf. 13½*

867 A288 350fr Robert Baden-Powell 1.50 .75

868 A288 500fr Scout saluting 2.25 1.10

Nos. 867-868 exist imperf. and in souvenir sheets of 1 both perf. and imperf.

UN, UNICEF, 50th Anniv. — A289

Designs: 150fr, Child with head bandaged, UNICEF emblem. 225fr, Boy carrying bowl of food on head, dove, globes. 475fr, Woman, boy playing on artillery piece, space station Mir. 550fr, Boy, race car driver Michael Schumacher, UNICEF emblem.

1996

869 A289 150fr multicolored .70 .35

870 A289 225fr multicolored 1.00 .50

871 A289 475fr multicolored 2.25 1.10

a. Sheet of 2, #870-871 + label *11.00 5.50*

872 A289 550fr multicolored 2.50 1.25

a. Sheet of 2, #869, 872 + label *11.00 5.50*

Nos. 869-872 (4) 6.45 3.20

Entertainers — A290

1996

873 A290 175fr Bob Marley .80 .45

874 A290 300fr Janis Joplin 1.25 .80

874A A290 400fr Madonna 1.75 1.00

875 A290 600fr Jerry Garcia 2.75 1.50

876 A290 700fr Elvis Presley 3.00 1.75

877 A290 700fr Marilyn Monroe 3.00 1.75

878 A290 750fr John Lennon 3.50 2.10

879 A290 800fr Monroe, diff. 3.50 2.10

880 A290 800fr Presley, diff. 3.50 2.10

Nos. 873-880 (9) 23.05 13.55

Souvenir Sheets

881 A290 2000fr Presley, diff. 9.00 5.00

882 A290 2000fr Monroe, diff. 9.00 5.00

Nos. 873-882 exist imperf. and in souvenir sheets of 1 both perf. and imperf.

No. 874A exists in a souvenir sheet of 1.

Butterflies A291

Boy Scout Jamboree emblem and: 150fr, Chrysiridia riphearia. 200fr, Palla ussheri. 750fr, Mylothris chloris. 800fr, Papilo dardanus.

1996 Litho. *Perf. 13½*

883 A291 150fr multicolored .70 .35

884 A291 200fr multicolored .90 .50

885 A291 750fr multicolored 3.25 2.00

886 A291 800fr multicolored 3.50 2.00

Nos. 883-886 (4) 8.35 4.85

Nos. 883-886 exist imperf. and in souvenir sheets of 1 both perf. and imperf.

Wild Animals — A292

Boy Scout Jamboree emblem, Rotary emblem and: 150fr, Erythrocebus patas. 200fr, Panthera pardus. 900fr, Balearica regulorum. 1000fr, Alcelaphus buselaphus.

2000fr, Panthera leo.

1996

887 A292 150fr multicolored .60 .35

888 A292 200fr multicolored .90 .55

889 A292 900fr multicolored 4.00 2.25

890 A292 1000fr multicolored 4.50 2.50

Nos. 887-890 (4) 10.00 5.65

Souvenir Sheet

891 A292 2000fr multicolored 9.00 5.00

Nos. 887-890 exist in souvenir sheets of 1.

Rotary International A292a

Designs: 200fr, Boy holding fruits and vegetables. 700fr, Girl holding sheaves of grain.

1996 Litho. *Perf. 13½*

891A A292a 200fr multicolored 1.10 .55

891B A292a 700fr multicolored 3.75 1.90

Intl. Red Cross and Lions Intl. — A293

Designs: 250fr, Jean-Henri Dunant as young man. 300fr, Lions Intl. emblems, boy with books. 400fr, Dunant as old man. 600fr, Older boy carrying younger boy, Lions Intl. emblems.

1996 Litho. *Perf. 13½*

892 A293 250fr multicolored 1.10 .60

893 A293 300fr multicolored 1.40 .70

894 A293 400fr multicolored 1.75 .90

895 A293 600fr multicolored 2.75 1.40

Nos. 892-895 (4) 7.00 3.60

Traditional Musical Instruments A294

1996 Litho. *Perf. 13½*

896 A294 125fr violet & multi .55 .30

897 A294 175fr pink & multi .80 .40

Sports A295

1996

898 A295 300fr Golf 1.40 .70

899 A295 500fr Tennis 2.25 1.10

900 A295 700fr Table tennis 3.25 1.50

Nos. 898-900 (3) 6.90 3.30

Nos. 898-900 exist in souvenir sheets of one.

1996 Summer Olympic Games, Atlanta A296

Designs: 250fr, Track & field. 350fr, Women's gymnastics, table tennis. 400fr, Tennis, swimming. 600fr, Hurdles, pole vault.

1500fr, Men's track and field.

1996 Litho. *Perf. 13½*

901 A296 250fr multicolored 1.10 .55
902 A296 350fr multicolored 1.50 .75
903 A296 400fr multicolored 1.75 .90
904 A296 600fr multicolored 2.75 1.40
Nos. 901-904 (4) 7.10 3.60

Souvenir Sheet

904A A296 1500fr multicolored 7.00 7.00

Souvenir Sheet

CHINA '96 — A297

Statues from Yunguang Grottoes, Datong, China: a, Head of Buddha. b, Side view.

1996

905 A297 140fr Sheet of 2, #a.-b. 1.50 .75

1998 Winter Olympic Games, Nagano A298

1996

906 A298 85fr Hockey .40 .25
907 A298 200fr Downhill skiing .90 .45
908 A298 400fr Slalom skiing 1.75 .90
909 A298 500fr Pairs figure skating 2.25 1.10
Nos. 906-909 (4) 5.30 2.70

Nos. 906-909 were not issued without metallic blue overprint on stamps dated 1991. Nos. 908-909 are airmail.

Nos. 906-909 exist with red metallic overprint. A 600fr souvenir sheet with red metallic overprint exists in limited quantities.

Formula I Race Car Drivers A299

Designs: 450fr, Jacques Villeneuve. 2000fr, Ayrton Senna (1960-94).

1996

910 A299 450fr multicolored 2.00 1.00

Souvenir Sheet

911 A299 2000fr multicolored 9.00 4.50

No. 910 exists in souvenir sheet of 1. No. 911 contains one 39x57mm stamp.

Tockus Nasutus A300

Coracias Abyssinica A301

Designs: 15fr, Psittacula krameri. 25fr, Coracias abyssinica. 35fr, Bulbucus ibis.

1996 Litho. *Perf. 13½x13*

912 A300 5fr multi
912A A300 15fr multi
912B A300 25fr multi
912C A300 35fr multi

Perf. 13

913 A301 25fr multi
914 A301 35fr multi

Compare type A300 to types A301 and A309. The editors would like to examine two stamps of type A301 with 5fr and 15fr denominations.

1998 Winter Olympic Games, Nagano, Japan A302

1996 Litho. *Perf. 13x13½*

915 A302 125fr Ice hockey .55 .30
916 A302 175fr Slalom skiing .75 .35
917 A302 700fr Pairs figure skating 3.00 1.50
918 A302 800fr Speed skating 3.50 1.75
Nos. 915-918 (4) 7.80 3.90

Souvenir Sheet

919 A302 1500fr Downhill skiing 6.50 3.25

No. 919 contains one 57x51mm stamp. Nos. 915-918 exist in souvenir sheets of 1.

Minerals A303

No. 920: a, Brookite. b, Elbaite indicolite. c. Elbaite rubellite verdelite. d, Olivine.

No. 921: a, Topaz. b, Autunite. c, Leucite. d, Struvite.

1996 Litho. *Perf. 13½*

920 A303 375fr Sheet of 4, #a.-d. 6.50 3.25
921 A303 500fr Sheet of 4, #a.-d. 8.75 4.50

Souvenir Sheet

922 A303 2000fr Pyrargyrite 6.50 3.25

No. 922 contains one 42x39mm stamp.

World Driving Champion Michael Schumacher A304

Schumacher: a, Grand Prix of Spain. b, In race car in pit. c, Ahead of another car. d, Behind another car.

1996 Litho. *Perf. 13½*

923 A304 375fr Sheet of 4, #a.-d. 6.50 3.25

German Soccer Team, Euro '96 Champions A305

No. 924: a, Oliver Bierhoff, player jumping up. b, Bierhoff, player holding up arms. c, ChancellorHelmut Kohl, Queen Elizabeth II, Klinsmann. d, Stadium, Mathias Sammer. logos.

1996 Litho. *Perf. 13½*

924 A305 400fr Sheet of 4, #a.-d. 7.00 3.50

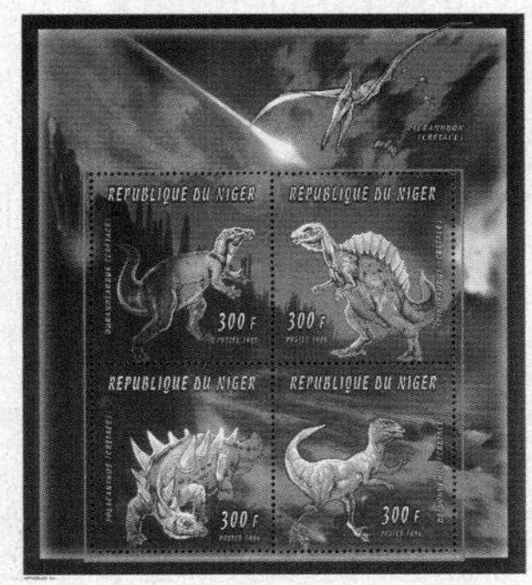

Dinosaurs — A306

No. 925: a, Ouranosaurus. b, Spinosaurus. c, Polacanthus. d, Deinonychus.

No. 926: a, Camptosaurus. b, Allosaurus. c, Nodosaurus. d, Kritosaurus.

2000fr, Protoceratops, oviraptor, horiz.

1996

925 A306 300fr Sheet of 4, #a.-d. 9.00 9.00
926 A306 450fr Sheet of 4, #a.-d. 14.00 14.00

Souvenir Sheet

927 A306 2000fr multicolored 7.25 6.00

France '98, World Soccer Cup Championships — A307

World Cup Trophy and: 125fr, American player. 175fr, Brazilian player. 750fr, Italian player. 1000fr, German player.

1500fr, Player in action scene.

1996

928 A307 125fr multicolored .55 .25
929 A307 175fr multicolored .75 .40
930 A307 750fr multicolored 3.25 1.60
931 A307 1000fr multicolored 4.25 2.10
Nos. 928-931 (4) 8.80 4.35

Souvenir Sheet

932 A307 1500fr multicolored 6.50 3.25

No. 932 contains one 57x51mm stamp.

New Year 1997 (Year of the Ox) — A308

1997 Litho. *Perf. 13½*

933 A308 500fr shown 2.00 1.00
934 A308 500fr Riding three oxen 2.00 1.00

Nos. 933-934 exist in souvenir sheets of 1, design extending to perfs on No. 933.

Birds A309

5fr, Tockus nasutus. 15fr, Psittacula kramer. 25fr, Coracias abyssinica. 35fr, Bulbucus ibis.

1997 Litho. *Perf. 13½*

935 A309 5fr multicolored .30 .25
936 A309 15fr multicolored .30 .25
937 A309 25fr multicolored .30 .25
938 A309 35fr multicolored .30 .25
Nos. 935-938 (4) 1.20 1.00

See No. 1050.

19th Dakar-Agades-Dakar Rally — A310

Designs: 125fr, Truck, child in traditional dress. 175fr, Ostrich, three-wheel vehicle. 300fr, Camel, heavy-duty support truck. 500fr, Motorcycles.

1997

939 A310 125fr multicolored .60 .30
940 A310 175fr multicolored .85 .40
941 A310 300fr multicolored 1.50 .75
942 A310 500fr multicolored 2.40 1.25
a. Souvenir sheet, #939-942 5.50 5.50
b. Strip of 4, #939-942 5.50 5.50

Deng Xiaoping (1904-97), Chinese Leader — A311

Designs: a, Deng, flag, eating at table, Deng as young man. b, Farming with oxen, Deng holding girl, flag. c, Flag, Deng with soldiers, camp. d, Deng bathing, ships in port, combining grain, launching space vehicle. e, Huts, heavy equipment vehicle, men working. f, Airplane, man holding up flask, operating room, Deng.

Illustration reduced.

1997

943 A311 150fr Sheet of 6, #a.-f. 3.50 1.75

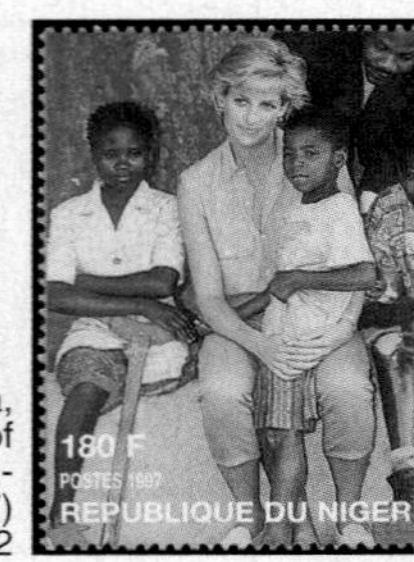

Diana, Princess of Wales (1961-97) A312

No. 944: Various portraits performing humanitarin deeds, on world tours, with various figures.
No. 945: Various portraits in designer dresses.
No. 946: With Mother Teresa (in margin).

1997, Sept. 30 Litho. *Perf. 13½*

944 A312	180fr	Sheet of 9, #a.-i.	7.00	3.50
945 A312	180fr	Sheet of 9, #a.-i.	7.00	3.50

Souvenir Sheets

946 A312	2000fr	multicolored	8.75	4.50
947 A312	4000fr	multicolored	14.00	14.00

No. 947 contains one 40x46mm stamp.

Famous Americans A313

No. 948 — Various portraits: a-b, John F. Kennedy. c-d, Pres. Bill Clinton.
No. 949 — Various pprtraits: a, Kennedy. b, Dr. Martin Luther King (1929-68). c-d, Clinton.
2000fr, John F. Kennedy.

1997 Litho. *Perf. 13½*

948 A313	350fr	Sheet of 4, #a.-d.	5.50	2.75
949 A313	400fr	Sheet of 4, #a.-d.	6.25	6.25

Souvenir Sheet

950 A313	2000fr	multicolored	7.75	4.00

No. 950 contains one 42x60mm stamp.

Stars of American Cinema A314

No. 951: a, Eddie Murphy. b, Elizabeth Taylor. c, Bruce Willis. d, James Dean. e, Clint Eastwood. f, Elvis Presley. g, Michelle Pfeiffer. h, Marilyn Monroe. i, Robert Redford.

1997 Litho. *Perf. 13½*

951 A314	300fr	Sheet of 9, #a.-i.	10.50	5.25

Communications — A315

No. 952: a, 80fr, Satellite transmission, radios. b, 100fr, Computers. c, 60fr, Cellular phone transmission around world. d, 120fr, Hand holding car phone. e, 180fr, Satellite, earth. f, 50fr, Transmission tower, cellular phone.

1997

952 A315		Sheet of 6, #a.-f.	2.25	1.10

Prof. Abdou Moumouni Dioffo — A316

1997 Litho. *Perf. 13½x13*

953 A316	125fr	multicolored	.60	.30

Methods of Transportation — A317

Bicycles, motorcycles: No. 954: a, Jan Ullrich, 1997 Tour de France winner, Eiffel Tower. b, Diana 250, Harley Davidson. c, MK VIII motorcycle, bicycles of 1819, 1875. d, Brands Match Motorcycle Race, Great Britain.
Modern locomotives, country flags: No. 955: a, Pendolino ETR 470, Italy. b, Rame TGV 112, France. c, Eurostar, France, Belgium, UK. d, Intercity Express ICE train, Germany.
Early locomotives, country flags: No. 956: a, Trevithick, UK. b, Pacific North Chapelon, France. c, Buddicom, UK, France. d, PLM "C", France.
Trains of Switzerland: No. 957: a, Crocodile, St. Gothard. b, RE 460. c, Red Streak, RAE 2/4 1001. d, Limmat.
Classic cars, modern sports cars: No. 958: a, Mercedes 300 SL Gullwing, Mercedes E320 Cabriolet. b, Aston Martin V8, Aston Martin DBR2. c. Ferrari F50, Ferrari 250 GT Berlinette. d, Ford Thunderbird, Ford GT40.
Air flight: No. 959: a, Clement Ader's Avion 111, dirigible R101. b, Concorde jet, X36 NASA/MCDD prototype. c, Aile volante FW900, Airbus A340. d, Gaudron GIII, Montgolfier's balloon.
Space travel: No. 960: a, HII rocket, Japan, Copernicus. b, Galileo, Ariane rocket. c, Space shuttle, Neil Armstrong. d, Yuri Gagarin, orbital space station, Soyuz.
1500fr, Swiss train, RE 4/4 II 11349, vert. No. 962, Hubble Space Telescope, Concorde jet. No. 963, TGV mail train, 1958 Chevrolet Corvette.

1997 Litho. *Perf. 13½*

954 A317	300fr	Sheet of 4, #a.-d.	4.75	4.75
955 A317	350fr	Sheet of 4, #a.-d.	5.50	5.50
956 A317	375fr	Sheet of 4, #a.-d.	6.00	6.00
957 A317	400fr	Sheet of 4, #a.-d.	6.25	6.25
958 A317	450fr	Sheet of 4, #a.-d.	7.00	7.00
959 A317	500fr	Sheet of 4, #a.-d.	7.75	7.75
960 A317	600fr	Sheet of 4, #a.-d.	9.50	9.50

Souvenir Sheets

961 A317	1500fr	multicolored	5.75	5.75
962 A317	2000fr	multicolored	7.75	7.75
963 A317	2000fr	multicolored	7.75	7.75

Swiss Railroad, 150th anniv. (#957, #961).
Nos. 961-963 each contain one 50x60mm stamp.

Diana, Princess of Wales (1961-97) — A318

Various portraits.
1500fr, Wearing red dress. No. 966, Wearing blue dress.

1997 Litho. *Perf. 13½*

964 A318	250fr	Sheet of 9, #a.-i.	8.75	4.50
964J A318	300fr	Sheet of 9, #k.-s.	10.50	5.25

Souvenir Sheets

965 A318	1500fr	multicolored	5.75	3.00
966 A318	2000fr	multicolored	7.75	4.00

Nos. 965-966 contain one 42x60mm stamp.

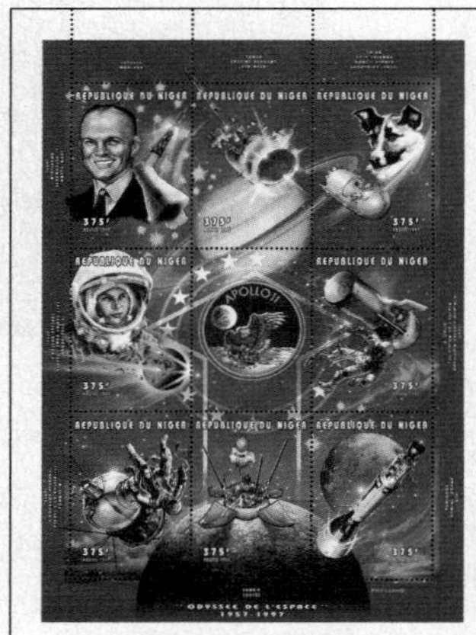

Man in Space — A319

No. 967: a, John Glenn, Mercury capsule. b, Cassini/Huygens satellite. c, Laika, first dog in space, Sputnik 2. d, Valentina Tereshkova, first woman in space, Vostok 6. e. Edward White, first American to walk in space, Gemini 4. f, Alexi Leonov, first Soviet to walk in space. g, Luna 9. h, Gemini capsule docked to Agena.
No. 968: a, Skylab space station. b, Pioneer 13, Venus 2. c, Giotto probe, Halley's Comet. d, Apollo-Soyuz mission. e, Mariner 10. f, Viking 1. g, Venera 11. h, Surveyor 1.
No. 969, 2000fr, Yuri Gagarin, first man in space, Sergei Korolev, RD107 rocket. No. 970, 2000fr, John F. Kennedy, Apollo 11, Neil Armstrong, first man to set foot on the moon.

1997 Litho. *Perf. 13½*

967 A319	375fr	Sheet of 8 + label	12.00	6.00
968 A319	450fr	Sheet of 8 + label	14.00	7.00

Souvenir Sheets

969-970 A319		Set of 2	15.50	8.00

Nos. 969-970 each contain one 42x60mm stamp.

Pres. Ibrahim Mainassara-Bare — A320

1997 Litho. & Embossed *Perf. 13½*

971 A320	500fr	gold & multi	1.75	.90

Scouting, Intl., 90th Anniv. (in 1997) — A321

No. 972 — Scout and: a, Lion. b, Rhinoceros. c, Giraffe. d, Elephant.
No. 972E — Girl Scout: f, Building bird house. g, Examining flower with magnifying glass. h, Identifying flower from book. i, Playing with bird.
No. 973: a, Butterfly. b, Bird with berries in mouth. c, Bird. d, Brown & white butterfly.
No. 974: a, Holding up rock to light. b, Using magnifying glass. c, Looking at rock. d, On hands and knees.
No. 975 — Scout, mushroom, with background color of: a, Yellow. b, White. c, Pink. d, Green.
2000fr, Robert Baden-Powell, Scouts chasing butterflies, mushroom.

1998 Litho.

972 A321	350fr	Sheet of 4, #a.-d.	5.00	2.50
972E A321	400fr	Sheet of 4, #f.-i.	5.75	3.00
973 A321	450fr	Sheet of 4, #a.-d.	6.50	3.25
974 A321	500fr	Sheet of 4, #a.-d.	7.00	3.50
975 A321	600fr	Sheet of 4, #a.-d.	8.50	4.25

Souvenir Sheet

975E A321	2000fr	multicolored	7.00	3.50

Greenpeace — A322

No. 976 — Turtles: a, Being caught in net. b, One swimming right. c, Mating. d, One swimming left.

1998

976 A322	400fr	Block of 4, #a-d	7.50	3.75
e.		Souvenir sheet, #976	16.00	16.00

Sheets overprinted "CHINA 99 World Philatelic Exhibition" are not authorized.

A323

No. 977 — Turtles: a, Pelomedusa subruta. b, Megacephalum shiui. c, Eretmochelus imbricata. d, Platycephala platycephala. e, Spinifera spinifera. f, Malayemys subtrijuga.
No. 978 — Raptors: a, Aquila uerreauxii. b, Asia otus. c, Bubo bubo. d, Surnia ulula. e, Asio flammeus. f, Falco biarnicus.
No. 979 — Orchids: a, Oeceoclades saundersiana. b, Paphiopedilum venustum. c, Maxillaria picta. d, Masdevallia triangularis. e, Zugopetalum. f, Encyllia nemoralis.

No. 980 — Butterflies: a, Danaus plexippus. b, Leto venus. c, Callioratis millari. d, Hippotion celerio. e, Euchloron megaera. f, Teracotona euprepia.

No. 981 — Mushrooms: a, Phaeolepotia aurea. b, Disciotis venosa. c, Gomphidius glutinosus. d, Amanita vaginata. e, Tremellodon gelatinosum. f, Voluariella voluacea.

1998, Sep. 29 Litho. *Perf. 13½*

977 A323 250fr Sheet of 6, #a.-f. 5.50 2.25
978 A323 300fr Sheet of 6, #a.-f. 6.50 3.25
979 A323 350fr Sheet of 6, #a.-f. 7.50 3.75
980 A323 400fr Sheet of 6, #a.-f. 8.50 4.25
981 A323 450fr Sheet of 6, #a.-f. 9.75 4.75

Marine Life — A324

No. 982: a, Tursiops truncatus. b, Phocoenoides dalli. c, Sousa teuszii. d, Stegostoma fasciatum. e, Delphinus delphis, balaenoptera musculus. f, Carcharodon carcharias. g, Argonauta argo, heterodontus portusjacksoni. h, Mitsukurina owstoni. i, Sphyrna mokarran. j, Homarus gammarus, prostheceraeus vittatus. k, Glossodoris valenciennesi, cephalopodes decapodes. l, Nemertien anople, elysia viridis.

1998, Sep. 29 Litho. *Perf. 13½*

982 A324 175fr Sheet of 12, #a-l 7.50 3.75

World Wildlife Fund A325

Gazella dorcas: No. 983, Doe, fawn. No. 984, Adult lying down. No. 985, Two adults standing still. No. 986 Adult walking.

1998

983 A325 250fr multicolored 1.25 .85
984 A325 250fr multicolored 1.25 .85
985 A325 250fr multicolored 1.25 .85
986 A325 250fr multicolored 1.25 .85
a. Souvenir sheet, #983-986 *50.00 40.00*
Nos. 983-986 (4) 5.00 3.40

Similar items without WWF emblem are not authorized.

Pope John Paul II — A326

Various portraits of pontiff thoughout his life.

1998, Sep. 29 Litho. *Perf. 13½*

987 A326 250fr Sheet of 9, #a.-i. 8.75 4.50

Souvenir Sheet

988 A326 2000fr multicolored 7.75 3.75

No. 988 contains one 57x51mm stamp.

Frank Sinatra (1915-98) A327

Various portraits.

1998

989 A327 300fr Sheet of 9, #a.-i. 10.50 5.25

Explorers — A328

No. 990: a, Juan Sebastian del Cano (1476-1526), commander of vessel that completed circumnavigation of globe. b, Globe, sailing ships. c, Ferdinand Magellan (1480-1521).

No. 991 — Vasco da Gama (1469-1524): a. Portrait. b, Angels, explorers, soldiers, flag. c, Sailing ship, da Gama's tomb, Lisbon.

No. 992 — Aviator Roland Garros (1888-1918): a, Arriving at Utrecht. b, Flying across Mediterranean, 1913. c, Portrait.

1998, Sep. 29

990 A328 350fr Sheet of 3, #a.-c. 4.00 2.00
991 A328 400fr Sheet of 3, #a.-c. 4.75 2.25
992 A328 450fr Sheet of 3, #a.-c. 5.25 2.50

Nos. 990b, 991b, 992b are 60x51mm.

Jacques-Yves Cousteau (1910-97), Environmentalist A329

No. 993: a, Whales. b, Fish, diver, whales, sled dog team. c, Portrait of Cousteau surrounded by ship, explorers in polar region, whale, fish.

No. 994: a, Cousteau, children, bird. b, Ship, marine life. c, Cousteau in diving gear, fish.

1998, Sep. 29

993 A329 500fr Sheet of 3, #a.-c. 5.75 3.00
994 A329 600fr Sheet of 3, #a.-c. 7.00 3.50

Nos. 993b and 994b are 60x51mm.

1998 World Cup Soccer Championships, France — A330

No. 995: a, Emmanuel Petit. b, Zinedine Zidane. c, Fabien Barthez. d, Lilian Thuram. e, Didier Deschamps. f, Youri Djorkaeff. g, Marcel Desailly, Christian Karembeu. h, Bixente Lizarazu. i, Frank Leboeuf, Stephane Guivarc'h.

1998

995 A330 250fr Sheet of 9, #a.-i. 8.75 4.50

A331

A332

FIMA Niger '98 African Fashion Festival

1998 Litho. *Perf. 13½x13*

996 A331 175fr multi 1.50 .75
997 A332 225fr multi 1.50 .75

Flowers — A333

Designs: 10fr, Roses and anemone. 20fr, Asystasia vogeliana, horiz. 30fr, Agrumes, horiz. 40fr, Angraecum sesquipedale. 45fr, Dissotis rotundifolia. 50fr, Hibiscus rosa-sinensis. 100fr, Datura.

1998 Litho. *Perf. 13¼x13½*

997A A333 10fr multi — —
997B A333 20fr multi — —
997C A333 30fr multi — —
997D A333 40fr multi — —
997E A333 45fr multi — —
998 A333 50fr multi — —
999 A333 100fr multi — —

A number of items inscribed "Republique du Niger" were not authorized by Niger postal authorities. These include:

Dated 1996: Overprinted 500fr souvenir sheet for 20th anniv. first commercial flight of the Concorde.

Dated 1998: Martin Luther King, Jr., 2000fr souvenir sheet;

Ferrari automobile, 2000fr stamp and souvenir sheet;

Trains, 650fr sheet of 4, 2500fr souvenir sheet, two 3000fr souvenir sheets;

Titanic, 650fr sheet of 4, four 650fr souvenir sheets, 2500fr souvenir sheet;

Paintings by Toulouse-Lautrec, Gauguin, Renoir, Matisse, Delacroix, Van Gogh, sheets of nine 250fr, 300fr, 375fr 400fr, 425fr, 500fr stamps, sheet of three 725fr Matisse stamps, 200fr, Delacroix souvenir sheet;

French and Italian performers, sheet of nine 675fr stamps;

Sailing vessels, sheets of four 525fr, 875fr stamps;

Events of the 20th Century, 3 sheets of nine 225fr stamps, 2 sheets of nine 375fr stamps, 3 sheets of nine 500fr stamps, fourteen 225fr souvenir sheets, three 2000fr souvenir sheets;

Space events of the 20th Century, two 2000fr souvenir sheets;

Papal visits, sheet of nine 500fr stamps, sheet of two 1500fr stamps;

Cats, sheetlet of 5 stamps, various denominations, 500fr souvenir sheet;

African Music, sheet of nine 225fr stamps;

Pinocchio, sheet of nine 200fr stamps;

Dated 1999: History of the Cinema (Marilyn Monroe), sheet of nine 275fr stamps, 2000fr souvenir sheet;

History of American Cinema (various actors), sheet of nine 400fr stamps;

John F. Kennedy, Jr., sheet of nine 500fr stamps;

Sheets of nine stamps of various denominations depicting Cats, Panda, Dinosaurs, Kennedy Space Center, Mushrooms, Butterflies, Eagles, Tiger Woods, Chess Pieces (2 different sheets);

Sheets of six stamps of various denominations depicting Butterflies, Cartoon Network Cartoon Characters.

Additional issues may be added to this list.

Wildlife — A334

Designs: No. 1000, 180fr, Tiger, Rotary emblem, vert. No. 1001, 250fr, Tigers, Lions emblem. No. 1002, 375fr, Tiger, Scouting, scouting jamboree emblems.

No. 1003, vert. — Rotary emblem and: a, Lions. b, Leopard. c, Red-headed cranes. d, Owl. e, Buzzards. f, Gazelles (long horns). g, Elands (twisted horns). h, Antelope (short horns).

No. 1004 — Lions emblem and: a, Lion, looking left. b, Lion, lioness. c, Lion reclining. d, Leopards. e, Leopard on rock. f, Lion, looking right. g, Lion in grass. h, Lion cub.

No. 1005 — Scouting and scouting jamboree emblems and: a, Leopard, mouth open. b, Leopard overlooking plains. c, Leopard looking right. d, Cat. e, Pair of leopards. f, Leopard and trees. g, Leopard reclining. h, Leopard standing on rock.

1000fr, Tiger in water, horiz. 2500fr, Leopards.

1998 Litho. *Perf. 13½*

1000-1002 A334 Set of 3
1003 A334 180fr Sheet of 9, #a-h, 1000
1004 A334 250fr Sheet of 9, #a-h, 1001
1005 A334 375fr Sheet of 9, #a-h, 1002

Souvenir Sheets

1006 A334 1000fr mutli
1007 A334 2500fr multi

New Year 1998, Year of the Tiger, Nos. 1000-1002, 1006. Nos. 1006-1007 each contain one 46x40mm stamp.

Jerry Garcia — A335

No. 1008: a, In brown shirt. b, In blue shirt, with flower. c, In yellow shirt. d, in green shirt. e, With fists clenched. f, In blue shirt. g, In black jacket. h, Holding glasses. i, In black shirt, with black guitar strap.
Illustration reduced.

1998
1008 A335 350fr Sheet of 9, #a-i

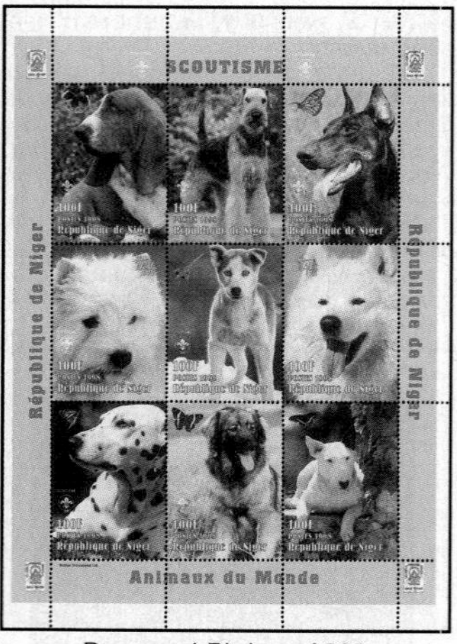

Dogs and Birds — A336

No. 1009, 100fr — Scouting emblem and: a, Beagle, butterfly. b, Airedale terrier, Italia 98 emblem. c, Doberman pinscher, butterfly. d, Small white dog, Italia emblem. e, Husky pup, Concorde. f, White Eskimo dog, Italia emblem. g, Dalmatian, butterfly. h, Retriever, butterfly. i, Pit bull, butterfly.
No. 1010, 300fr — a-i, Scouting jamboree emblem and various penguins.
No. 1011, 500fr — a-i, Various parrots.
Illustration reduced.

1999

Sheets of 9, #a-i

1009-1011 A336 Set of 3

Intl. Year of the Ocean (No. 1010). Dated 1998.

Sailing — A337

No. 1012: a, Sailboat, lighthouse. b, Man, woman in sailboat. c, Sailor, large waves. d, Yachts racing.
Illustration reduced.

1999
1012 A337 750fr Sheet of 4, #a-d

Dated 1998. Sheets of four 525fr and 875fr stamps were not authorized by Niger Post.

Trains — A338

Various trains. Sheets of 4, each stamp denominated: 225fr, 325fr, 375fr, 500fr, or 750fr.
Illustration reduced.

1999

Sheets of 4, #a-d

1013-1017 A338 Set of 5

Dated 1998. PhilexFrance 99 (#1017). A sheet of four similar stamps with 650fr denominations, a 2500fr souvenir sheet, and two 3000fr souvenir sheets were not authorized by Niger Post.

Astronauts — A339

No. 1018, 450fr: a, James Lovell. b, Alan Shepard. c, David Scott. d, John Young.
No. 1019, 500fr: a, Neil Armstrong. b, Michael Collins. c, Edwin Aldrin. d, Alan Bean.
No. 1020, 600fr: a, Walter Schirra. b, Robert Crippen. c, Thomas Stafford. d, Owen Garriott.
No. 1021, 750fr: a, John Glenn. b, Gordon Cooper. c, Scott Carpenter. d, Virgil Grissom.
2000fr, Collins, Armstrong and Aldrin.
Illustration reduced.

1999

Sheets of 4, #a-d

1018-1021 A339 Set of 4

Souvenir Sheet

1022 A339 2000fr multi

No. 1022 contains one 56x51mm stamp.

Chess — A340

No. 1023, 350fr: a, Tigran Petrosian. b, Robert Fischer. c, Boris Spassky. d, Viktor Korchnoi. e, Garry Kasparov. f, Anatoly Karpov.
No. 1024, 400fr: a, Richard Reti. b, Alexander Alekhine. c, Max Euwe. d, Paul Keres. e, Mikhail Botvinnik. f, Mikhail Tal.
No. 1025, 500fr: a, Philidor. b, Adolf Anderssen. c, Joseph Henry Blackburne. d, Emanuel Lasker. e, Frank Marshall. f, José Raul Capablanca.
2000fr, head of Kasparov, Leo Tolstoy playing chess.
Illustration reduced.

1999

Sheets of 6, #a-f

1023-1025 A340 Set of 3

Souvenir Sheet

1026 A340 2000fr multi

Nos. 1023-1025 each contain six 51x36mm stamps. Dated 1998.

Baseball Players — A341

No. 1027, 200fr, Various views of Lou Gehrig.
No. 1028, 250fr, Various views of Ty Cobb.
Nos. 1029, 1031, Gehrig, diff. Nos. 1030, 1032, Cobb, diff.
Illustration reduced.

1999

Sheets of 9, #a-i

1027-1028 A341 Set of 2

Souvenir Sheets

1029-1030 A341 1500fr Set of 2
1031-1032 A341 2000fr Set of 2

Animals and Mushrooms — A342

No. 1033, 300fr: a, Snake. b, Tortoise. c, Scorpion. d, Lizard.
No. 1034, 400fr: a, Vulture. b, Gray cuckoo. c, Jackdaw. d, Turtle dove.
No. 1035, 600fr: a, Ham the chimpanzee. b, Laika the dog. c, Cat. d, Spider.
No. 1036, 750fr: a, Nymphalidae palla. b, Nymphalidae perle. c, Nymphalidae diademe-bleu. d, Nymphalidae pirate.
No. 1037, 1000fr: a, Cliotcybe rouge brique. b, Lactaire a odeur de camphre. c, Strophaire vert-de-gris. d, Lepiote a ecailles aigues.
Illustration reduced.

1999, Nov. 23

Sheets of 4, #a-d

1033-1037 A342 Set of 5

Council of the Entente, 40th Anniv. A343

1999, May 29 Litho. *Perf. 13x13¼*
1039 A343 175fr multi — —

An additional stamp was issued in this set. The editors would like to examine any examples.

First French Stamps, 150th Anniv. A344

Litho. With Hologram Applied

1999, Oct. 7 *Perf. 13*
1040 A344 200fr France Type A1 .95 .95

Fire Fighting Equipment — A345

No. 1041 — Automobiles: a, Bugatti Type 37. b, Chevrolet Corvette. c, Lotus Elise. d, Ferrari 550 Maranello.
No. 1042: a, Canadair airplane. b, Hook and ladder truck. c, Water pumper of middle ages. d, 1914 pumper.
No. 1043 — Trains: a, Union Pacific, 1869. b, Prussian State Railway P8, 1905. c, Pennsylvania Railroad T1, 1942. d, German Railways Series 015, 1962.
No. 1044 — Airplanes: a, De Havilland Comet. b, Airbus A340. c, Boeing 747. d, Concorde.
No. 1045 — Trains: a, Diesel-electric locomotive. b, Bullet train, Japan. c, Thalys. d, X2000, China.
No. 1046 — Spacecraft: a, Atlas rocket, Mercury capsule. b, RD-107 Soyuz. c, Saturn V rocket, Apollo capsule. d, Space shuttle.

1999, Nov. 23 Litho. *Perf. 13½*
1041 A345 450fr Sheet of 4, #a-d — —
1042 A345 500fr Sheet of 4, #a-d — —
1043 A345 600fr Sheet of 4, #a-d — —
1044 A345 650fr Sheet of 4, #a-d — —
1045 A345 750fr Sheet of 4, #a-d — —
1046 A345 800fr Sheet of 4, #a-d — —

Intl. Anti-Desertification Day — A346

Designs: 150fr, Trenches. 200fr, Men in field. 225fr, Trees in desert.

2000, June 17 Litho. *Perf. 13½*
1047-1049 A346 Set of 3 1.75 1.75

Bird Type of 1997

2000, June 20 *Perf. 13¼*
1050 A309 150fr Psittacula krameri .45 .45

2000 Summer Olympics, Sydney — A347

No. 1051: a, 50fr, Men's singles, badminton. b, 50fr, Men's doubles, badminton. c, 50fr, Softball. d, 50fr, Men's floor exercises. e, 50fr, Women's singles, badminton. f, 50fr, Women's doubles, badminton. g, 50fr, Baseball. h, 50fr, Men's long horse vault. i, 50fr, Women's cycling. j, 50fr, Women's pursuit cycling. k, 50fr, Women's road race cycling. l, 50fr, Women's shot put. m, 900fr, Men's singles, table tennis. n, 900fr, Men's doubles, table tennis. o, 900fr, Women's singles, table tennis. p, 900fr, Women's doubles, table tennis.
No. 1052: a, 100fr, Women's freestyle swimming. b, 100fr, Women's butterfly. c, 100fr, Men's prone rifle. d, 100fr, Women's sport pistol. e, 100fr, Women's 3-meter diving. f, 100fr, Women's 10-meter diving. g, 100fr, Women's three-position rifle. h, 100fr, Women's double trap. i, 100fr, Women's beach volleyball. j, 100fr, Women's volleyball. k, 100fr, Women's handball. l, 100fr, Men's sailboarding. m,

700fr, Women's kayak singles. n, 700fr, Women's kayak pairs. o, 700fr, Women's kayak fours. p, 700fr, Women's eight-oared shell with coxswain.

2000, July 27 **Litho.**
Sheets of 16, #a-p
1051-1052 A347 Set of 2 27.50 27.50

Modern and Prehistoric Fauna — A348

No. 1053, 200fr — Butterflies: a, Epiphora bauhiniae. b, Cymothoe sangaris. c, Cyrestris camillus. d, Precis clelia. e, Precis octavia amestris. f, Nudaurelia zambesina.
No. 1054, 200fr — Insects: a, Stenocara eburnea. b, Chalcocoris anchorago. c, Scarabaeus aeratus. d, Pseudocreobotra wahlbergi. e, Schistocera gregaria. f, Anopheles gambiae.
No. 1055, 225fr — Prehistoric winged animals: a, Sordes pilosus. b, Quetzalcoatlus. c, Dimorphodon. d, Podopteryx. e, Archaeopteryx. f, Pteranodon.
No. 1056, 225fr — Birds: a, Bec-en-sabot. b, Euplecte ingnicolore. c, Spreo royal. d, Calao trompette. e, Pseudocanari parasite. f, Gonolek rouge et noir.
No. 1057, 400fr — Cats: a, Egyptian mau. b, Domestic. c, African wildcat. d, Chat dore. e, Chat a pieds noirs. f, Chat des sables.
No. 1058, 400fr — Dogs: a, Chien du pharaon. b, Saluki. c, Rhodesian ridgeback. d, Beagle. e, Spitz. f, Basenji.
No. 1059, 450fr — Modern and prehistoric African animals: a, Proconsul africanus. b, Chimpanzee. c, Metamynodon planifrons. d, Black rhinoceros. e, Hyrachius eximus. f, White rhinoceros.
No. 1060, 450fr — Modern and prehistoric African animals: a, Canis familiaris. b, Black and white basenji. c, Hipparion mediterraneum. d, Burchell zebra. e, Moeritherium. f, African elephant.
No. 1061, 475fr — Modern and prehistoric reptiles: a, Palaeobatrachus. b, African frog. c, Metoposaurus. d, Salamander. e, Tylosaurus. f, Varan du Nil.
No. 1062, 475fr — Modern and prehistoric African animals: a, Basilosaurus. b, Solalie du Cameroun. c, Mesosaurus. d, Cordylus giganteus. e, Sarcosuchus. f, Nile crocodile

2000, Oct. 27 ***Perf. 13¼***
Sheets of 6, #a-f
1053-1062 A348 Set of 10 57.50 57.50

2002 World Cup Soccer Championships, Japan and Korea — A349

No. 1063, 400fr: a, Castro. b, Orsi. c, Piola. d, Ghiggia.
No. 1064, 400fr: a, Morlock. b, Pele. c, Amarildo. d, Hurst.
No. 1065, 400fr: a, Jairzinho. b, Müller. c, Kempes. d, Rossi.
No. 1066, 400fr: a, Burruchaga. b, Brehme. c, Dunga. d, Petit.

2001, Jan. 16
Sheets of 4, #a-d
1063-1066 A349 Set of 4 19.00 19.00
Dated 2000.

Universal Postal Union, 125th Anniv. (in 1999) — A350

No. 1067, 150fr — Ships: a, Transat, Citta di Catania. b, Great Eastern, Julius Caesar. c, Caledonia, Mercury. d, Braganza, Westland.
No. 1068, 225fr — Vehicles: a, Horse-drawn omnibus, postal bus. b, 1899 automobile, rural omnibus. c, 1904 van, postal automobile and bicycle. d, 1906 automobile, Swiss postal bus.
No. 1069, 450fr — Trains: a, 25NC Modder Kimberley locomotive, CDJR diesel. b, Pacific Karoo, Budd diesel. c, 141 Maghreb locomotive, EAR Diesel-electric locomotive. d, 230 Series 6 C.G.A., Postal TGV train.
No. 1070, 500fr — Airplanes: a, Late-28, Super Constellation. b, Douglas DC-4, Nord Atlas. c, Boeing 707, Concorde. d, Boeing 747, Airbus A3XX.
No. 1071, 550fr — Spacecraft: a, 1934 postal rocket, Asian telecommunications satellite. b, Space capsules. c, Apollo 15, Astra 1 H telecommunications satellite. d, Voyager, Space Station and shuttle.
No. 1072, 700fr — Trains: a, 230 locomotive, Senegal, 141 locomotive, Tanganyika. b, 141 locomotive, Niger. 242 locomotive, South Africa. c, 130+031 locomotive, Ivory Coast, Garrat 242+242. d, 040 locomotive, Cameroun, 14R locomotive.

2001, Jan. 16 ***Perf. 13¼***
Sheets of 4, #a-d
1067-1072 A350 Set of 6 30.00 30.00
Dated 2000.

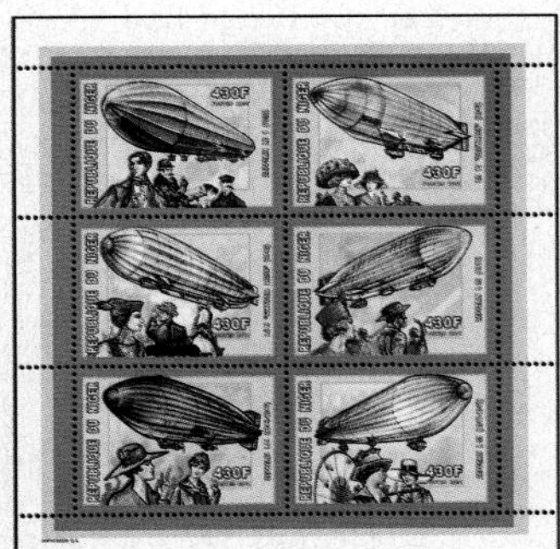

Zeppelins and Satellites — A351

No. 1073, 430fr — Zeppelins: a, LZ-1. b, LZ-10 Schwaben. c, LZ II Viktoria Luise. d, L-30. e, L-11. f, L-59.
No. 1074, 460fr — Zeppelins: a, LZ-120 Bodensee. b, L-72 Dixmude. c, LZ-127 Graf Zeppelin. d, LZ-129 Hindenburg. e, LZ-130. f, D-LZFN.
No. 1075, 750fr, vert. — Satellites: a, Meteosat. b, GOMS. c, GMS. d, Insat 1A. e, GOES. f, FY-2.

2001, June 20 **Litho.**
Sheets of 6, #a-f
1073-1075 A351 Set of 3 27.50 27.50

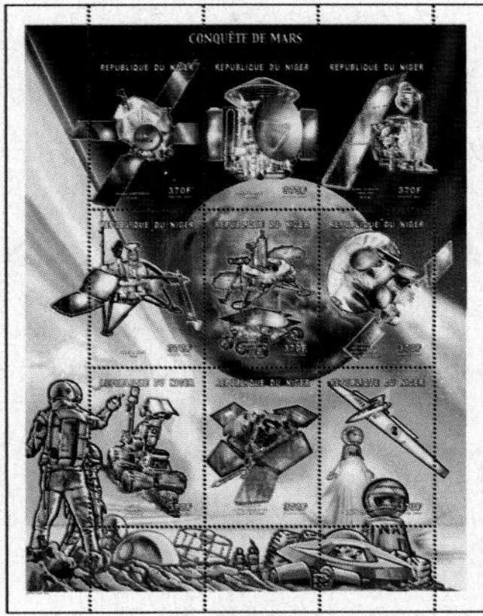

Space Exploration — A352

No. 1076, 370fr — Conquest of Mars: a, Mariner 9. b, Mars 3. c, Mars Climate Orbiter. d, Mars Lander. e, Mars Rover. f, Netlander. g, Robot on Mars. h, Beagle 2. i, Ames Research plane for Mars.
No. 1077, 390fr — Orbital and Lunar Exploration: a, Yuri Gagarin, Vostok capsule. b, John Glenn, Mercury capsule. c, Space shuttle. d, Alan Shepard, Apollo 14. e, Neil Armstrong, Apollo 11. f, Charles Conrad, Apollo 12. g, Edward White, Gemini 4. h, James Irwin, Apollo 15. i, Lunar base and shuttle.
No. 1078, 490fr — Planetary and Interstellar Exploration: a, Pioneer 10. b, Mariner 10. c, Venera 13. d, Pioneer 13, Venus 2. e, Probe for detecting "Big Bang." f, Interstellar spacecraft. g, Inhabited space station. h, Giotto probe, Astronaut on comet. i, Galileo probe.

2001, June 20 **Litho.**
Sheets of 9, #a-i
1076-1078 A352 Set of 3 32.50 32.50

African History — A353

No. 1079, 390fr: a, Gahna Empire, 10th cent. b, Kankou Moussa, Emperor of Mali, 1324. c, Sankore, University of Tombouctou, 15th cent. d, Sonni Ali Ber, Songhai Emperor. e, Bantu migrations, 15th and 16th cents. f, Slave trade, 1513.
No. 1080, 490fr: a, Ramses II, 1301-1235 B.C., Battle of Qadesh. b, Mummification. c, Religion. d, Instruction. e, Justice. f, Artisans.
No. 1081, 530fr: a, Djoser, Third Dynasty, 2650 B.C. b, Rahotep and wife, Fourth Dynasty, 2570 B.C. c, Cheops and Pyramid, Fourth Dynasty, 2600 B.C. d, Chephren, Fourth Dynasty, 2500 B.C. e, Akhenaton and Nefertiti, 18th Dynasty, 1372-1354 B.C. f, Tutankhamen, 18th Dynasty, 1354-1346 B.C.

2001, July 24 **Litho.**
Sheets of 6, #a-f
1079-1081 A353 Set of 3 25.00 25.00

Air Chiriet — A354

2001 ***Perf. 13x13¼***
1082 A354 150fr multi — —

Intl. Volunteers Year — A355

2001
1083 A355 150fr multi — —

Birds, Butterflies, Meteorites, and Mushrooms — A356

No. 1084, 530fr — Birds: a, Falco peregrinus. b, Falco biarmicus. c, Vultur gryphus.
No. 1085, 575fr — Butterflies: a, Junonia orithya. b, Salamis parhassus. c, Amauris echeria.
No. 1086, 750fr — Meteorites: a, P. Pallas, 1772. b, Iron meteorite. c, Bouvante rock.
No. 1087, 825fr — Mushrooms: a, Otidea onotica. b, Lentinus sajor-caju. c, Pleurotus luteoalbus.

2002, Apr. 24 ***Perf. 13¼***
Sheets of 3, #a-c
1084-1087 A356 Set of 4 22.50 22.50

Souvenir sheets of 1 of each of the individual stamps exist.

Cow's Head A357

2002, Sept. 17 **Litho.** ***Perf. 13¼***
1088 A357 50fr multi .50 .50

Toubou Spears — A358

2002, Sept. 17 **Litho.** ***Perf. 13x12½***
1089 A358 100fr multi .90 .90

Birds — A359

2002, Sept. 17 **Litho.** ***Perf. 13***
1090 A359 225fr multi .75 .75

Hippopotamus in Captivity — A360

Boudouma Cow A361

Boudouma Calf — A362

Illustration A360 reduced.

2003, Dec. 3 Litho. *Perf. 13x13¼*

1091 A360 100fr multi .60 .60

Perf. 13

1092 A361 150fr multi .80 .80

Perf. 13¼

1093 A362 225fr multi 1.10 1.10
Nos. 1091-1093 (3) 2.50 2.50

Values for No. 1092 are for stamps with surrounding selvage.

Pottery — A363

Camel and Rider A364

Illustration A363 reduced.

2004 *Perf. 13x13¼*

1094 A363 150fr multi 1.00 1.00

Perf. 13

1095 A364 1000fr multi 5.00 5.00

Values for No. 1095 are for stamps with surrounding selvage.

In Universal Postal Union Circular 388, issued Nov. 28, 2005, Niger postal officials declared illegal additional items bearing the inscription "Republique du Niger." As this circular contains a somewhat unintelligible list of items which lacks specifics as to denominations found on the illegal items or the sizes of sheets, some of the items may be duplicative of items mentioned in the note on illegal stamps following No. 999. Also, because of the lack of clarity of the list, some catalogued items may now be items cited as "illegal" in Circular 388. The text of this circular can be seen on the UPU's WNS website, www.wnsstamps.ch.

Emblem of 2005 Francophone Games — A365

2005, May 12 Litho. *Perf. 13x13¼*

1096 A365 150fr multi .65 .65

World Summit on the Information Society, Tunis — A366

2005, May 26 *Perf. 13¼*

1097 A366 225fr multi 1.10 1.10

Mascot of 2005 Francophone Games — A367

2005, Aug. 22 *Perf. 13*

1098 A367 225fr multi 1.00 1.00

Léopold Sédar Senghor (1906-2001), First President of Senegal — A368

2006, Apr. 6 Litho. *Perf. 12¾*

1099 A368 175fr multi .85 .85

Pres. Tandja Mamadou — A369

2006, July 14

1100 A369 750fr multi 3.50 3.50

Boubou Hama (1906-82), Writer — A370

Background colors: 150fr, Green. 175fr, Orange brown. 325fr, Light blue.

2006, Sept. 23 Litho. *Perf. 13x12¾*

1101-1103 A370 Set of 3 3.50 3.50

24th UPU Congress, Geneva, Switzerland — A373

2007, Nov. 9 Litho. *Perf. 13*

1106 A373 500fr multi 2.25 2.25

Values are for stamps with surrounding selvage. UPU Congress was moved to Geneva after political violence in Nairobi, Kenya.

Wildlife A374

Designs: 200fr, Giraffes. 400fr, Addax. 600fr, Ostriches.

2007, Nov. 9 *Perf. 12¾*

1107-1109 A374 Set of 3 5.50 5.50

SEMI-POSTAL STAMPS

Curie Issue
Common Design Type

1938 Unwmk. Engr. *Perf. 13*

B1 CD80 1.75fr + 50c brt ultra 14.00 14.00

French Revolution Issue
Common Design Type

1939 Photo. *Perf. 13*

Name and Value Typo. in Black

B2 CD83 45c + 25c grn 9.25 9.25
B3 CD83 70c + 30c brn 9.25 9.25
B4 CD83 90c + 35c red org 9.25 9.25
B5 CD83 1.25fr + 1fr rose pink 9.25 9.25
B6 CD83 2.25fr + 2fr blue 9.25 9.25
Nos. B2-B6 (5) 46.25 46.25

Stamps of 1926-38, Surcharged in Black

1941 *Perf. 14x13½, 13½x14*

B7 A3 50c + 1fr scar & grn, *grnsh* 1.75 1.75
B8 A3 80c + 2fr cl & ol grn 5.75 5.75
B9 A4 1.50fr + 2fr dp bl & pale bl 5.75 5.75
B10 A4 2fr + 3fr red org & ol brn 5.75 5.75
Nos. B7-B10 (4) 19.00 19.00

Common Design Type and

Colonial Cavalry — SP1

Soldiers and Tank SP2

1941 Unwmk. Photo. *Perf. 13½*

B11 SP2 1fr + 1fr red .85
B12 CD86 1.50fr + 3fr claret .85
B13 SP1 2.50fr + 1fr blue .85
Nos. B11-B13 (3) 2.55

Nos. B11-B13 were issued by the Vichy government in France, but were not placed on sale in Niger.

Nos. 89-90 Surcharged in Black or Red

1944 Engr. *Perf. 12x12½*

B13A 50c + 1.50fr on 2.50fr deep blue (R) .60
B13B + 2.50fr on 1fr green .60

Colonial Development Fund.

Nos. B13A-B13B were issued by the Vichy government in France, but were not placed on sale in Niger.

Catalogue values for unused stamps in this section, from this point to the end of the section, are for Never Hinged items.

Republic of the Niger
Anti-Malaria Issue
Common Design Type

Perf. 12½x12

1962, Apr. 7 Engr. Unwmk.

B14 CD108 25fr + 5fr brn .60 .60

Freedom from Hunger Issue
Common Design Type

1963, Mar. 21 *Perf. 13*

B15 CD112 25fr + 5fr gray ol, red lil & brn .60 .60

Dome of the Rock — SP3

1978, Dec. 11 Litho. *Perf. 12½*

B16 SP3 40fr + 5fr multi .45 .30

Surtax was for Palestinian fighters and their families.

AIR POST STAMPS

Common Design Type

1940 Unwmk. Engr. *Perf. 12½x12*

C1 CD85 1.90fr ultra .35 .20
C2 CD85 2.90fr dk red .50 .30
C3 CD85 4.50fr dk gray grn .80 .60
C4 CD85 4.90fr yel bis .80 .80
C5 CD85 6.90fr dp org .80 .80
Nos. C1-C5 (5) 3.25 2.70

Common Design Types

1942

C6 CD88 50c car & bl .20
C7 CD88 1fr brn & blk .20
C8 CD88 2fr multi .35
C9 CD88 3fr multi .35
C10 CD88 5fr vio & brn red .45

Frame Engraved, Center Typographed

C11 CD89 10fr multi	.80	
C12 CD89 20fr multi	.90	
C13 CD89 50fr multi	1.10	
Nos. C6-C13 (8)	4.35	

There is doubt whether Nos. C6-C13 were officially placed in use. They were issued by the Vichy government.

Catalogue values for unused stamps in this section, from this point to the end of the section, are for Never Hinged items.

Republic of the Niger

Wild Animals, W National Park — AP1

1960, Apr. 11 Engr. *Perf. 13*

C14 AP1 500fr multi 20.00 8.00

For overprint see No. C112.

Nubian Carmine Bee-eater — AP2

1961, Dec. 18 Unwmk. *Perf. 13*

C15 AP2 200fr multi 9.00 3.75

UN Headquarters and Emblem, Niger Flag and Map — AP3

1961, Dec. 16

C20 AP3 25fr multi	.60	.35
C21 AP3 100fr multi	2.00	1.25

Niger's admission to the United Nations.
For overprints see Nos. C28-C29.

Air Afrique Issue
Common Design Type

1962, Feb. 17 Unwmk. *Perf. 13*

C22 CD107 100fr multi 1.75 .90

Mosque at Agadez and UPU Emblem — AP4

Designs: 85fr, Gaya Bridge. 100fr, Presidential Palace, Niamey.

1963, June 12 Photo. *Perf. 12½*

C23 AP4 50fr multi	1.00	.50
C24 AP4 85fr multi	1.75	.70
C25 AP4 100fr multi	1.75	.80
Nos. C23-C25 (3)	4.50	2.00

2nd anniv. of Niger's admission to the UPU.

Type of Regular Issue, 1963
Design: 100fr, Building boats (kadei), horiz.

1963, Aug. 30 *Perf. 12½x12*
Size: 47x27mm

C26 A12 100fr multi 3.00 1.50

African Postal Union Issue
Common Design Type

1963, Sept. 8 *Perf. 12½*

C27 CD114 85fr multi 1.25 .60

Nos. C20-C21 Overprinted "Centenaire de la Croix-Rouge" and Cross in Red

1963, Sept. 30 Engr. *Perf. 13*

C28 AP3 25fr multi	.85	.50
C29 AP3 100fr multi	2.00	.90

Centenary of International Red Cross.

White and Black before Rising Sun — AP5

1963, Oct. 25 Photo. *Perf. 12x13*

C30 AP5 50fr multi 3.75 2.25

See note after Mauritania No. C28.

Peanut Cultivation — AP6

Designs: 45fr, Camels transporting peanuts to market. 85fr, Men closing bags. 100fr, Loading bags on truck.

1963, Nov. 5 Engr. *Perf. 13*

C31 AP6 20fr grn, bl & red brn	.60	.25
C32 AP6 45fr red brn, bl & grn	1.00	.40
C33 AP6 85fr multi	2.00	.70
C34 AP6 100fr red brn, ol bis & bl	2.25	1.00
a. Souv. sheet of 4, #C31-C34	6.00	6.00
Nos. C31-C34 (4)	5.85	2.35

To publicize Niger's peanut industry.

1963 Air Afrique Issue
Common Design Type

1963, Nov. 19 Photo. *Perf. 13x12*

C35 CD115 50fr multi .90 .50

Telstar and Capricornus and Sagittarius Constellations — AP7

100fr, Relay satellite, Leo & Virgo constellations.

1964, Feb. 11 Engr. *Perf. 13*

C36 AP7 25fr olive gray & vio	.50	.30
C37 AP7 100fr grn & rose claret	1.40	.85

Ramses II Holding Crook and Flail, Abu Simbel — AP8

1964, Mar. 9

C38 AP8 25fr bis brn & dl bl grn	.80	.50
C39 AP8 30fr dk bl & org brn	1.25	.65
C40 AP8 50fr dp claret & dk bl	2.25	1.25
Nos. C38-C40 (3)	4.30	2.40

Issued to publicize the UNESCO world campaign to save historic monuments in Nubia.

Tiros I Weather Satellite over Globe and WMO Emblem — AP9

1964, Mar. 23 Unwmk. *Perf. 13*

C41 AP9 50fr emer, dk bl & choc 1.25 .65

4th World Meteorological Day, Mar. 23.

Rocket, Stars and "Stamp" — AP10

1964, June 5 Engr.

C42 AP10 50fr dk bl & magenta 1.00 .65

"PHILATEC," International Philatelic and Postal Techniques Exhibition, Paris, June 5-21, 1964.

Europafrica Issue, 1963
Common Design Type

50fr, European & African shaking hands, emblems of industry & agriculture.

1964, July 20 Photo. *Perf. 12x13*

C43 CD116 50fr multi .85 .50

John F. Kennedy — AP11

Discobolus and Discus Thrower — AP12

Perf. 12½

1964, Sept. 25 Unwmk. Photo.

C44 AP11 100fr multi	1.90	1.25
a. Souvenir sheet of 4	8.50	8.50

President John F. Kennedy (1917-1963).

1964, Oct. 10 Engr. *Perf. 13*

60fr, Water polo, horiz. 85fr, Relay race, horiz. 250fr, Torch bearer & Pierre de Coubertin.

C45 AP12 60fr red brn & sl grn	1.00	.50
C46 AP12 85fr ultra & red brn	1.50	.60
C47 AP12 100fr brt grn, dk red & sl	1.50	.70
C48 AP12 250fr yel brn, brt grn & sl	3.50	1.75
a. Min. sheet of 4, #C45-C48	10.50	10.50
Nos. C45-C48 (4)	7.50	3.55

18th Olympic Games, Tokyo, Oct. 10-25.

Pope John XXIII (1881-1963) AP13

1965, June 3 Photo. *Perf. 12½x13*

C49 AP13 100fr multi 1.50 .75

Hand Crushing Crab — AP14

Sir Winston Churchill — AP15

1965, July 15 Engr. *Perf. 13*

C50 AP14 100fr yel grn, blk & brn 1.40 .85

Issued to publicize the fight against cancer.

Perf. 12½x13

1965, Sept. 3 Photo. Unwmk.

C51 AP15 100fr multi 1.40 .85

Symbols of Agriculture, Industry, Education AP16

Flags and Niamey Fair — AP17

1965, Oct. 24 Engr. *Perf. 13*
C52 AP16 50fr henna brn, blk & ol .85 .40

International Cooperation Year, 1965.

1965, Dec. 10 Photo. *Perf. 13x12½*
C53 AP17 100fr multi 1.25 .70

International Fair at Niamey.

Dr. Schweitzer, Crippled Hands and Symbols of Medicine, Religion and Music — AP18

1966, Jan. 4 Photo. *Perf. 12½x13*
C54 AP18 50fr multi 1.00 .50

Weather Survey Frigate and WMO Emblem — AP19

1966, Mar. 23 Engr. *Perf. 13*
C55 AP19 50fr brt rose lil, dl grn & dk vio bl 1.50 .50

6th World Meteorological Day, Mar. 23.

Edward H. White Floating in Space and Gemini IV — AP20

#C57, Alexei A. Leonov & Voskhod II.

1966, Mar. 30
C56 AP20 50fr dk red brn, blk & brt grn 1.00 .40
C57 AP20 50fr pur, slate & org 1.00 .40

Issued to honor astronauts Edward H. White and Alexei A. Leonov.

A-1 Satellite and Earth — AP21

45fr, Diamant rocket and launching pad. 90fr, FR-1 satellite. 100fr, D-1 satellite.

1966, May 12 Photo. *Perf. 13*
C58 AP21 45fr multi, vert. .65 .40
C59 AP21 60fr multi .80 .40
C60 AP21 90fr multi 1.00 .60
C61 AP21 100fr multi 1.50 .80
Nos. C58-C61 (4) 3.95 2.20

French achievements in space.

Maps of Europe and Africa and Symbols of Industry — AP22

1966, July 20 Photo. *Perf. 12x13*
C62 AP22 50fr multi .55 .40

Third anniversary of economic agreement between the European Economic Community and the African and Malgache Union.

Air Afrique Issue, 1966
Common Design Type

1966, Aug. 31 Photo. *Perf. 13*
C63 CD123 30fr gray, yel grn & blk .60 .35

Gemini 6 and 7 — AP23

1966, Oct. 14 Engr. *Perf. 13*
C64 AP23 50fr Voskhod 1, vert. .75 .40
C65 AP23 100fr shown 1.50 .75

Russian & American achievements in space.

Torii and Atom Destroying Crab — AP24

1966, Dec. 2 Photo. *Perf. 13*
C66 AP24 100fr dp claret, brn, vio & bl grn 1.50 .70

9th Intl. Anticancer Cong., Tokyo, Oct. 23-29.

New Mosque, Niamey — AP25

1967, Jan. 11 Engr. *Perf. 13*
C67 AP25 100fr grn & brt bl 1.60 .80

Albrecht Dürer, Self-portrait AP26

Self-portraits: 100fr, Jacques Louis David. 250fr, Ferdinand Delacroix.

1967, Jan. 27 Photo. *Perf. 12½*
C68 AP26 50fr multi 1.25 .70
C69 AP26 100fr multi 2.00 1.00
C70 AP26 250fr multi 4.25 2.10
Nos. C68-C70 (3) 7.50 3.80

See No. C98.

Maritime Weather Station — AP27

1967, Apr. 28 Engr. *Perf. 13*
C71 AP27 50fr brt bl, dk car rose & blk 1.50 .70

7th World Meteorological Day.

View of EXPO '67, Montreal — AP28

1967, Apr. 28 Engr. *Perf. 13*
C72 AP28 100fr lil, brt bl & blk 1.40 .70

Issued for EXPO '67, International Exhibition, Montreal, Apr. 28-Oct. 27, 1967.

Audio-visual Center, Stylized Eye and People — AP29

1967, June 22 Engr. *Perf. 13*
C73 AP29 100fr brt bl, pur & grn 1.25 .60

National Audio-Visual Center.

Konrad Adenauer (1876-1967), Chancellor of West Germany (1949-63) — AP30

1967, Aug. 11 Photo. *Perf. 12½*
C74 AP30 100fr dk bl, gray & sep 1.75 .70
a. Souv. sheet of 4 7.50 7.50

African Postal Union Issue, 1967
Common Design Type

1967, Sept. 9 Engr. *Perf. 13*
C75 CD124 100fr emer, red & brt lil 1.40 .60

Jesus Teaching in the Temple, by Ingres — AP31

Design: 150fr, Jesus Giving the Keys to St. Peter, by Ingres, vert.

1967, Oct. 2 Photo. *Perf. 12½*
C76 AP31 100fr multi 2.25 1.10
C77 AP31 150fr multi 3.25 1.60

Jean Dominique Ingres (1780-1867), French painter.

Children and UNICEF Emblem — AP32

1967, Dec. 11 Engr. *Perf. 13*
C78 AP32 100fr bl, brn & grn 1.50 .85

21st anniv. of UNICEF.

O.C.A.M. Emblem — AP33

1968, Jan. 12 Engr. *Perf. 13*
C79 AP33 100fr brt bl, grn & org 1.25 .55

Conf. of the Organization Communitée Afrique et Malgache (OCAM), Niamey, Jan. 1968.

Vincent van Gogh, Self-portrait AP34

Self-portraits: 50fr, Jean Baptiste Camille Corot. 150fr, Francisco de Goya.

1968, Jan. 29 Photo. *Perf. 12½*
C80 AP34 50fr multi 1.00 .45
C81 AP34 150fr multi 2.75 1.10
C82 AP34 200fr multi 4.25 1.75
Nos. C80-C82 (3) 8.00 3.30

See No. C98.

Breguet 27 — AP35

Planes: 80fr, Potez 25 on the ground. 100fr, Potez 25 in the air.

1968, Mar. 14 Engr. *Perf. 13*
C83 AP35 45fr ind, car & dk grn 1.00 .40
C84 AP35 80fr indigo, bl & brn 1.50 .75
C85 AP35 100fr sky bl, brn blk & dk grn 2.50 .90
Nos. C83-C85 (3) 5.00 2.05

25th anniversary of air mail service between France and Niger.

Splendid Glossy Starling — AP36

Design: 100fr, Amethyst starling, vert.

1968-69 Photo. *Perf. 13*
C86 AP36 100fr gold & multi ('69) 2.75 1.10

Engr.

C87 AP36 250fr mag, sl grn & brt bl 2.75 1.40

See No. C255.

Dandy Horse, 1818, and Racer, 1968 — AP37

1968, May 17 Engr. *Perf. 13*
C88 AP37 100fr bl grn & red 2.00 .75

150th anniversary of the invention of the bicycle.

Sheet Bend Knot — AP37a

1968, July 20 Photo. *Perf. 13*
C89 AP37a 50fr gray, blk, red & grn .80 .45

Fifth anniversary of economic agreement between the European Economic Community and the African and Malgache Union.

Fencing — AP38

Designs: 100fr, Jackknife dive, vert. 150fr, Weight lifting, vert. 200fr, Equestrian.

1968, Sept. 10 Engr. *Perf. 13*
C90 AP38 50fr pur & blk .60 .40
C91 AP38 100fr choc, ultra & blk 1.10 .60
C92 AP38 150fr choc & org 1.60 .75
C93 AP38 200fr brn, emer & ind 2.25 1.50
a. Min. sheet of 4, #C90-C93 7.50 7.50
Nos. C90-C93 (4) 5.55 3.25

19th Olympic Games, Mexico City, 10/12-27.
No. C93a is folded down the vertical gutter separating Nos. C90-C91 se-tenant at left and Nos. C92-C93 se-tenant at right.

Robert F. Kennedy — AP39

#C94, John F. Kennedy. #C95, Rev. Dr. Martin Luther King, Jr. #C96, Mahatma Gandhi.

1968, Oct. 4 Photo. *Perf. 12½*
C94 AP39 100fr blk & dl org 1.25 .70
C95 AP39 100fr blk & aqua 1.40 .70
C96 AP39 100fr blk & gray 1.25 .70
C97 AP39 100fr blk & yel 1.25 .70
a. Souv. sheet of 4, #C94-C97 6.50 6.50
Nos. C94-C97 (4) 5.15 2.80

Issued to honor proponents of non-violence.

PHILEXAFRIQUE Issue
Painting Type of 1968

Design: 100fr, Interior Minister Paré, by J. L. La Neuville (1748-1826).

1968, Oct. 25 Photo. *Perf. 12½*
C98 AP34 100fr multi 2.75 2.00

Issued to publicize PHILEXAFRIQUE, Philatelic Exhibition in Abidjan, Feb. 14-23, 1969. Printed with alternating light blue label.

Arms and Flags of Niger — AP40

1968, Dec. 17 Litho. *Perf. 13*
C99 AP40 100fr multi 1.50 .65

10th anniv. of the proclamation of the Republic.

Bonaparte as First Consul, by Ingres AP41

Paintings: 100fr, Napoleon Visiting the Plague House in Jaffa, by Antoine Jean Gros. 150fr, Napoleon on the Imperial Throne, by Jean Auguste Dominique Ingres. 200fr, Napoleon's March Through France, by Jean Louis Ernest Meissonier, horiz.

Perf. 12½x12, 12x12½
1969, Jan. 20 Photo.
C100 AP41 50fr multi 1.90 .95
C101 AP41 100fr grn & multi 3.00 1.50
C102 AP41 150fr pur & multi 4.00 1.75
C103 AP41 200fr brn & multi 6.00 3.00
Nos. C100-C103 (4) 14.90 7.20

Napoleon Bonaparte (1769-1821).

2nd PHILEXAFRIQUE Issue
Common Design Type

Designs: 50fr, Niger No. 41 and giraffes.

1969, Feb. 14 Engr. *Perf. 13*
C104 CD128 50fr slate, brn & org 2.75 1.60

Weather Observation Plane in Storm and Anemometer — AP42

1969, Mar. 23 Engr. *Perf. 13*
C105 AP42 50fr blk, brt bl & grn .70 .45

9th World Meteorological Day.

Panhard Levassor, 1900 — AP43

Early Automobiles: 45fr, De Dion Bouton 8, 1904. 50fr, Opel, 1909. 70fr, Daimler, 1910. 100fr, Vermorel 12/16, 1912.

1969, Apr. 15 Engr. *Perf. 13*
C106 AP43 25fr gray, lt grn & bl grn .50 .30
C107 AP43 45fr gray, bl & vio .65 .30
C108 AP43 50fr gray, yel bis & brn 1.25 .40
C109 AP43 70fr gray, brt pink & brt lil 1.90 .65
C110 AP43 100fr gray, lem & sl grn 2.10 .90
Nos. C106-C110 (5) 6.40 2.55

Apollo 8 Trip around Moon AP44

Embossed on Gold Foil
1969, Mar. 31 *Die-cut Perf. 10½*
C111 AP44 1000fr gold 19.00 19.00

US Apollo 8 mission, which put the 1st men into orbit around the moon, Dec. 21-27, 1968.

No. C14 Overprinted in Red with Lunar Landing Module and: "L'HOMME / SUR LA LUNE / JUILLET 1969 / APOLLO 11"

1969, July 25 Engr. *Perf. 13*
C112 AP1 500fr multi 7.50 7.50

See note after Mali No. C80.

Toys — AP45

1969, Oct. 13 Engr. *Perf. 13*
C113 AP45 100fr bl, red brn & grn 1.40 .55

International Nuremberg Toy Fair.

Europafrica Issue

Links — AP46

1969, Oct. 30 Photo.
C114 AP46 50fr vio, yel & blk .75 .50

Camels and Motor Caravan Crossing Desert — AP47

100fr, Motor caravan crossing mountainous region. 150fr, Motor caravan in African village. 200fr, Map of Africa showing tour, Citroen B-2 tractor, African & European men shaking hands.

1969, Nov. 22 Engr. *Perf. 13*
C115 AP47 50fr lil, pink & brn .95 .40
C116 AP47 100fr dk car rose, lt bl & vio bl 2.00 .75
C117 AP47 150fr multi 2.50 1.25
C118 AP47 200fr sl grn, bl & blk 4.00 1.75
Nos. C115-C118 (4) 9.45 4.15

Black Tour across Africa from Colomb-Bechar, Algeria, to Mombassa, Dar es Salaam, Mozambique, Tananarive and the Cape of Good Hope.

EXPO '70 at Osaka — AP48

1970, Mar. 25 Photo. *Perf. 12½*
C119 AP48 100fr multi 1.25 .50

Issued to publicize EXPO '70 International Exhibition, Osaka, Japan, Mar. 15-Sept. 13.

Education Year Emblem and Education Symbols — AP49

1970, Apr. 6 Engr. *Perf. 13*
C120 AP49 100fr plum, red & gray 1.25 .60

Issued for International Education Year.

Rotary Emblem, Globe and Niamey Club Emblem — AP50

1970, Apr. 30 Photo. *Perf. 12½*
C121 AP50 100fr gold & multi 1.60 .70

65th anniversary of Rotary International.

Modern Plane, Clement Ader and his Flying Machine — AP51

Designs: 100fr, Joseph and Jacques Montgolfier, rocket and balloon. 150fr, Isaac Newton, planetary system and trajectories. 200fr, Galileo Galilei, spaceship and trajectories. 250fr, Leonardo da Vinci, his flying machine, and plane.

1970, May 11 Engr. *Perf. 13*

C122 AP51 50fr bl, cop red & sl .90 .35
C123 AP51 100fr cop red, bl & sl 1.60 .70
C124 AP51 150fr brn, grn & ocher 1.75 .90
C125 AP51 200fr dk car rose, dp vio & bis 2.40 1.40
C126 AP51 250fr cop red, gray & pur 3.75 1.60
Nos. C122-C126 (5) 10.40 4.95

Pioneers of space research.

For overprints and surcharges see Nos. C129-C130, C141-C142.

Bay of Naples, Buildings, Mt. Vesuvius and Niger No. 97 — AP52

1970, May 5 Photo. *Perf. 12½*

C127 AP52 100fr multi 1.25 .55

Issued to publicize the 10th Europa Philatelic Exhibition, Naples, Italy, May 2-10.

TV Tube, Books, Microscope, Globe and ITU Emblem — AP53

1970, May 16 Engr. *Perf. 13*

C128 AP53 100fr grn, brn & red 1.40 .60

Issued for World Telecommunications Day.

Nos. C123 and C125 Overprinted: "Solidarité Spatiale / Apollo XIII / 11-17 Avril 1970"

1970, June 6 Engr. *Perf. 13*

C129 AP51 100fr multi 1.25 .55
C130 AP51 200fr multi 2.25 .70

Abortive flight of Apollo 13, 4/11-17/70.

UN Emblem, Man, Woman and Doves — AP54

1970, June 26 Photo. *Perf. 12½*

C131 AP54 100fr brt bl, dk bl & org 1.25 .55
C132 AP54 150fr multi 1.75 .70

25th anniversary of the United Nations.

European and African Men, Globe and Fleur-de-lis — AP55

Lithographed; Embossed on Gold Foil

1970, July 22 *Perf. 12½*

C133 AP55 250fr gold & ultra 4.00 4.00

French Language Cong., Niamey, Mar. 1970.

Europafrica Issue

European and African Women — AP56

1970, July 29 Engr. *Perf. 13*

C134 AP56 50fr slate grn & dl red .65 .30

EXPO Emblem, Geisha and Torii — AP57

Design: 150fr, EXPO emblem, exhibition at night and character from Noh play.

1970, Sept. 16 Engr. *Perf. 13*

C135 AP57 100fr multi 1.10 .50
C136 AP57 150fr bl, dk brn & grn 1.60 .65

EXPO '70 International Exhibition, Osaka, Japan, Mar. 15-Sept. 13.

Gymnast on Parallel Bars — AP58

Beethoven and Piano — AP59

Sports: 100fr, Vaulting, horiz. 150fr, Flying jump, horiz. 200fr, Rings.

1970, Oct. 26 Engr. *Perf. 13*

C137 AP58 50fr brt bl .65 .35
C138 AP58 100fr brt grn 1.40 .60
C139 AP58 150fr brt rose lil 2.25 .80
C140 AP58 200fr red org 2.75 1.10
Nos. C137-C140 (4) 7.05 2.85

17th World Gymnastics Championships, Ljubljana, Oct. 22-27.

Nos. C124 and C126 Surcharged and Overprinted: "LUNA 16 - Sept. 1970 / PREMIERS PRELEVEMENTS / AUTOMATIQUES SUR LA LUNE"

1970, Nov. 5

C141 AP51 100fr on 150fr multi 1.60 .55
C142 AP51 200fr on 250fr multi 3.25 1.10

Unmanned moon probe of the Russian space ship Luna 16, Sept. 12-24.

1970, Nov. 18 Photo. *Perf. 12½*

Design: 150fr, Beethoven and dancers with dove, symbolic of Ode to Joy.

C143 AP59 100fr multi 1.60 .55
C144 AP59 150fr multi 2.40 .85

Ludwig van Beethoven (1770-1827), composer.

John F. Kennedy Bridge, Niamey — AP60

1970, Dec. 18 Photo. *Perf. 12½*

C145 AP60 100fr multicolored 1.40 .50

Proclamation of the Republic, 12th anniv.

Gamal Abdel Nasser (1918-70), President of Egypt — AP61

Design: 200fr, Nasser with raised arm.

1971, Jan. 5 Photo. *Perf. 12½*

C146 AP61 100fr blk, org brn & grn 1.00 .40
C147 AP61 200fr grn, org & blk brn 1.75 .75

Charles de Gaulle AP62

Embossed on Gold Foil

1971, Jan. 22 *Die-cut Perf. 10*

C148 AP62 1000fr gold *65.00 65.00*

In memory of Gen. Charles de Gaulle (1890-1970), President of France.

Olympic Rings and "Munich" — AP63

1971, Jan. 29 Engr. *Perf. 13*

C149 AP63 150fr dk bl, rose lil & grn 1.90 .70

1972 Summer Olympic Games, Munich.

Landing Module over Moon — AP64

Masks of Hate — AP65

1971, Feb. 5 Engr. *Perf. 13*

C150 AP64 250fr ultra, sl grn & org 3.00 1.50

Apollo 14 mission, Jan. 31-Feb. 9.

1971, Mar. 20 Engr. *Perf. 13*

200fr, People & 4-leaf clover (symbol of unity).

C151 AP65 100fr red, sl & brt bl 1.10 .45
C152 AP65 200fr slate, red & grn 2.25 .85

Intl. Year against Racial Discrimination.

Map of Africa and Telecommunications System — AP66

1971, Apr. 6 Photo. *Perf. 12½*

C153 AP66 100fr grn & multi .80 .45

Pan-African telecommunications system.

African Mask and Japan No. 580 — AP67

Design: 100fr, Japanese actors, stamps of Niger, No. 95 on cover and No. 170.

1971, Apr. 23 Engr. *Perf. 13*

C154 AP67 50fr dk brn, emer & blk .80 .40
C155 AP67 100fr brn & multi 1.40 .55

Philatokyo 71, Tokyo Philatelic Exposition, Apr. 19-29.

Longwood, St. Helena, by Carle Vernet — AP68

Napoleon Bonaparte: 200fr, Napoleon's body on camp bed, by Marryat.

1971, May 5 Photo. Perf. 13
C156 AP68 150fr gold & multi 2.25 .75
C157 AP68 200fr gold & multi 3.25 1.25

Satellite, Waves and Earth — AP69

Olympic Rings, Athletes and Torch — AP70

1971, May 17 Engr. Perf. 13
C158 AP69 100fr org, ultra & dk brn 1.40 .55

3rd World Telecommunications Day.

1971, June 10

Designs: 50fr, Pierre de Coubertin, discus throwers, horiz. 150fr, Runners, horiz.

C159 AP70 50fr red & slate .80 .30
C160 AP70 100fr sl, brn & grn 1.25 .50
C161 AP70 150fr plum, bl & rose lil 2.10 1.10
Nos. C159-C161 (3) 4.15 1.90

75th anniv. of modern Olympic Games.

Astronauts and Landing Module on Moon — AP71

Charles de Gaulle — AP72

1971, July 26 Engr. Perf. 13
C162 AP71 150fr red brn, pur & sl 1.90 .75

US Apollo 15 moon mission, 7/26-8/7/71.

1971, Nov. 9 Photo. Perf. 12½x12
C163 AP72 250r multi 9.50 5.25

First anniversary of the death of Charles de Gaulle (1890-1970), president of France.

African Postal Union Issue, 1971
Common Design Type

Design: 100fr, Water carrier, cattle and UAMPT headquarters, Brazzaville, Congo.

1971, Nov. 13 Photo. Perf. 13x13½
C164 CD135 100fr blue & multi 1.25 .50

Al Hariri Holding Audience, Baghdad, 1237 — AP73

Designs from Mohammedan Miniatures: 150fr, Archangel Israfil, late 14th century, vert. 200fr, Horsemen, 1210.

1971, Nov. 25 Perf. 13
C165 AP73 100fr multi 1.25 .55
C166 AP73 150fr multi 2.00 .85
C167 AP73 200fr multi 3.00 1.50
Nos. C165-C167 (3) 6.25 2.90

Louis Armstrong AP74

Design: 150fr, Armstrong with trumpet.

1971, Dec. 6
C168 AP74 100fr multi 1.75 .75
C169 AP74 150fr multi 2.75 1.00

Armstrong (1900-71), American jazz musician.

Adoration of the Kings, by Di Bartolo — AP75

Christmas (Paintings): 150fr, Nativity, by Domenico Ghirlandaio, vert. 200fr, Adoration of the Shepherds, by Il Perugino.

1971, Dec. 24 Photo. Perf. 13
C170 AP75 100fr blk & multi 1.25 .45
C171 AP75 150fr blk & multi 1.90 .75
C172 AP75 200fr blk & multi 2.25 1.00
Nos. C170-C172 (3) 5.40 2.20

See Nos. C210-C212, C232-C234.

Presidents Pompidou and Diori Hamani, Flags of Niger and France — AP76

1972, Jan. 22
C173 AP76 250fr multi 6.75 3.75

Visit of President Georges Pompidou of France, Jan. 1972.

Snowflakes, Olympic Torch and Emblem — AP77

Design: 100fr, Torii made of ski poles and skis, and dwarf tree, vert.

1972, Jan. 27 Engr.
C174 AP77 100fr dk vio, grn & car 1.25 .55
C175 AP77 150fr dk vio, lil & red 1.90 .75
a. Souv. sheet of 2, #C174-C175 3.25 3.25

11th Winter Olympic Games, Sapporo, Japan, Feb. 3-13.

The Masked Ball, by Guardi — AP78

50fr, 100fr, 150fr, Details from "The Masked Ball," by Francesco Guardi (1712-93); all vert.

1972, Feb. 7 Photo.
C176 AP78 50fr gold & multi 1.10 .50
C177 AP78 100fr gold & multi 1.90 .85
C178 AP78 150fr gold & multi 3.00 1.10
C179 AP78 200fr gold & multi 3.75 1.40
Nos. C176-C179 (4) 9.75 3.85

UNESCO campaign to save Venice.
See Nos. C215-C216.

Johannes Brahms and "Lullaby" — AP79

Scout Sign and Tents — AP80

1972, Mar. 17 Engr. Perf. 13
C180 AP79 100fr multicolored 1.60 .75

75th anniversary of death of Johannes Brahms (1833-1897), German composer.

1972, Mar. 22
C181 AP80 150fr pur, org & slate bl 1.60 .75

World Boy Scout Seminar, Cotonou, Dahomey, March 1972.

Surgical Team, Heart-shaped Globe and Emblem — AP81

1972 Engr. Perf. 13
C182 AP81 100fr deep brown & car 1.40 .55

"Your heart is your health," World Health Day.

Famous Aircraft — AP82

50fr, Bleriot XI Crossing English Channel. 75fr, Spirit of St. Louis crossing Atlantic. 100fr, 1st flight of Concorde supersonic jet.

1972, Apr. 24
C183 AP82 50fr shown .90 .35
C184 AP82 75fr multicolored 1.40 .50
C185 AP82 100fr multicolored 2.50 1.25
Nos. C183-C185 (3) 4.80 2.10

ITU Emblem, Satellite, Stars and Earth — AP83

1972, May 17 Engr. Perf. 13
C186 AP83 100fr pur, car & blk 1.40 .50

4th World Telecommunications Day.

20th Olympic Games, Munich — AP84

50fr, Boxing and Opera House. 100fr, Broad jump & City Hall. 150fr, Soccer & Church of the Theatines, vert. 200fr, Running and Propylaeum.

1972, May 26
C187 AP84 50fr blue & grn .70 .30
C188 AP84 100fr yel grn & dk brn 1.00 .50
C189 AP84 150fr org red & dk brn 1.60 .70
C190 AP84 200fr violet & dk brn 2.10 .90
a. Min. sheet of 4, #C187-C190 6.00 6.00
Nos. C187-C190 (4) 5.40 2.40

For overprints see Nos. C196-C199.

"Alexander Graham Bell," Telephone — AP85

1972, July 7

C191 AP85 100fr car, dk pur & slate 1.25 .60

Alexander Graham Bell (1847-1922), inventor of the telephone. Stamp pictures Samuel F. B. Morse.

Europafrica Issue

Stylized Maps of Africa and Europe — AP86

1972, July 29 Engr. *Perf. 13*

C192 AP86 50fr red brn, bl & grn .60 .25

Mail Runner, UPU Emblem — AP87

Designs: 100fr, Mail truck, UPU emblem. 150fr, Mail plane, UPU emblem.

1972, Oct. 9 Engr. *Perf. 13*

C193	AP87	50fr multicolored	.80	.35
C194	AP87	100fr multicolored	1.25	.55
C195	AP87	150fr multicolored	2.00	.85
		Nos. C193-C195 (3)	4.05	1.75

Universal Postal Union Day.

Nos. C187-C190 Overprinted in Red or Violet Blue

a. WELTER / CORREA / MEDAILLE D'OR
b. TRIPLE SAUT / SANEEV / MEDAILLE D'OR
c. FOOTBALL / POLOGNE / MEDAILLE D'OR
d. MARATHON / SHORTER / MEDAILLE D'OR

1972, Nov. 10

C196	AP84(a)	50fr multi (R)	.65	.30
C197	AP84(b)	100fr multi (R)	1.00	.50
C198	AP84(c)	150fr multi (VBl)	1.75	.70
C199	AP84(d)	200fr multi (R)	2.25	.85
		Nos. C196-C199 (4)	5.65	2.35

Gold medal winners in 20th Olympic Games: Emilio Correa, Cuba, welterweight boxing; Victor Saneev, USSR, triple jump; Poland, soccer; Frank Shorter, US, marathon.

Fables — AP88

25fr, The Crow and The Fox. 50fr, The Lion and the Mouse. 75fr, The Monkey and the Leopard.

1972, Nov. 23

C200	AP88	25fr emer, blk & brn	1.10	.40
C201	AP88	50fr brt pink, bl grn & brn	1.50	.50
C202	AP88	75fr lt brn, grn & dk brn	2.40	.80
		Nos. C200-C202 (3)	5.00	1.70

Jean de La Fontaine (1621-1695), French fabulist.

Astronauts on Moon — AP89

1972, Dec. 12 Photo. *Perf. 13*

C203 AP89 250fr multi 3.50 1.50

Apollo 17 US moon mission, Dec. 7-19.

Young Athlete AP90

Design: 100fr, Head of Hermes.

1973, Feb. 7 Engr. *Perf. 13*

C204	AP90	50fr dk car	.60	.35
C205	AP90	100fr purple	1.25	.50

Treasures of antiquity.

Boy Scouts and Radio Transmission — AP91

Niger Boy Scouts: 50fr, Red Cross, first aid. 100fr, Scout and gazelle. 150fr, Scouts with gazelle and bird.

1973, Mar. 21 Engr. *Perf. 13*

C206	AP91	25fr multicolored	.40	.30
C207	AP91	50fr multicolored	.75	.35
C208	AP91	100fr multicolored	1.25	.60
C209	AP91	150fr multicolored	1.60	.75
		Nos. C206-C209 (4)	4.00	2.00

For overprints see Nos. C217-C218.

Christmas Type of 1971

Paintings: 50fr, Crucifixion, by Hugo van der Goes, vert. 100fr, Burial of Christ, by Cima da Conegliano. 150fr, Pietà, by Giovanni Bellini.

1973, Apr. 20 Photo. *Perf. 13*

C210	AP75	50fr gold & multi	.70	.30
C211	AP75	100fr gold & multi	1.40	.55
C212	AP75	150fr gold & multi	2.00	.70
		Nos. C210-C212 (3)	4.10	1.55

Easter 1973.

Air Afrique Plane and Mail Truck — AP92

1973, Apr. 30 Engr. *Perf. 13*

C213 AP92 100fr brt grn, choc & car 1.60 .65

Stamp Day 1973.

WMO Emblem, Pyramids with Weather Symbols, Satellite — AP93

1973, May 7

C214 AP93 100fr multicolored 1.25 .50

Cent. of intl. meteorological cooperation.

Painting Type of 1972

Paintings by Delacroix: 150fr, Prowling lioness. 200fr, Tigress and cub.

1973, May 22 Photo. *Perf. 13x12½*

C215	AP78	150fr blk & multi	2.50	1.25
C216	AP78	200fr blk & multi	4.00	1.90

175th anniversary of the birth of Ferdinand Delacroix (1798-1863), French painter.

Nos. C208-C209 Overprinted: "24 * Conference Mondiale / du Scoutisme / NAIROBI 1973"

1973, July 19 Engr. *Perf. 13*

C217	AP91	100fr multi	1.25	.50
C218	AP91	150fr multi	1.75	.70

Boy Scout 24th World Jamboree, Nairobi, Kenya, July 16-21.

Head and City Hall, Brussels AP93a

1973, Sept. 17 Engr. *Perf. 13*

C219 AP93a 100fr multicolored 1.25 .80

Africa Weeks, Brussels, Sept. 15-30, 1973.

Men Emptying Cornucopia, FAO Emblem, People — AP94

1973, Nov. 2 Engr. *Perf. 13*

C220 AP94 50fr ultra, pur & ver .80 .35

10th anniversary of the World Food Program.

AP95

AP96

Copernicus, Sputnik 1, Heliocentric System.

1973, Nov. 12

C221 AP95 150fr mag, vio bl & brn 1.75 .90

1973, Nov. 22 Photo. *Perf. 12½*

C222 AP96 100fr redsh brn & multi 1.25 .60

Souvenir Sheet

Perf. 13

C223 AP96 200fr dp ultra & multi 2.40 2.40

10th anniv. of the death of Pres. John F. Kennedy.

Barge on Niger River — AP97

Design: 75fr, Tug Baban Maza.

1974, Jan. 18 Engr. *Perf. 13*

C224	AP97	50fr mar, vio bl & grn	1.00	.50
C225	AP97	75fr yel grn, bl & lil rose	1.40	.50

1st anniv. of the upstream voyage of the Flotilla of Hope.

Lenin — AP98

1974, Jan. 21

C226 AP98 50fr dk red brn 2.10 .60

Skiers AP99

1974, Feb. 8 Engr. *Perf. 11½x11*

C227 AP99 200fr bl, sepia & car 3.00 1.00

50th anniversary of the first Winter Olympic Games, Chamonix, France.

Soccer and Emblem — AP100

Designs: Various views of soccer game.

1974, Apr. 8 Engr. *Perf. 13*

C228	AP100	75fr vio & blk	.85	.40
C229	AP100	150fr brn, lt & sl grn	1.75	.75
C230	AP100	200fr Prus bl, grn & brn	2.40	1.25
		Nos. C228-C230 (3)	5.00	2.40

Souvenir Sheet

C231 AP100 250fr yel grn, brn & ol brn 3.25 3.25

World Soccer Championship, Munich, June 13-July 7.

For overprint see No. C239.

Christmas Type of 1971

Paintings: 50fr, Crucifixion, by Matthias Grunewald. 75fr, Avignon Pietà, attributed to Enguerrand Quarton. 125fr, Burial of Christ, by G. Isenmann.

1974, Apr. 12 Litho. *Perf. 13x12½*

C232 AP75 50fr blk & multi .70 .30

C233 AP75 75fr blk & multi .95 .40

C234 AP75 125r blk & multi 1.60 .70

Nos. C232-C234 (3) 3.25 1.40

Easter 1974.

21st Chess Olympiad, Nice, June 6-30 — AP101

1974, June 3 Engr. *Perf. 13*

C235 AP101 50fr Knights 2.50 .75

C236 AP101 75fr Kings 3.00 1.25

Astronaut and Apollo 11 Badge AP102

1974, July 20 Engr. *Perf. 13*

C237 AP102 150fr multi 1.60 .75

5th anniversary of the first manned moon landing.

Europafrica Issue

The Rhinoceros, by Pietro Longhi — AP103

1974, Aug. 10 Photo. *Perf. 12½x13*

C238 AP103 250fr multi 7.00 3.50

No. C231 Overprinted in Red: "R.F.A. 2 / HOLLANDE 1"

1974, Sept. 27 Engr. *Perf. 13*

Souvenir Sheet

C239 AP100 250fr multi 3.25 3.25

World Cup Soccer Championship, Munich, 1974, victory of German Federal Republic. No. C239 has additional red inscription in margin: "7 JUILLET 1974 / VAINQUEUR REPUBLIQUE FEDERALE ALLEMANDE."

Caucasian Woman, Envelope, UPU Emblem and Jets — AP104

Skylab over Africa — AP105

Designs (UPU emblem, Envelope and): 100fr, Oriental woman and trains. 150fr, Indian woman and ships. 200fr, Black woman and buses.

1974, Oct. 9 Engr. *Perf. 13*

C240 AP104 50fr multi .75 .35

C241 AP104 100fr multi 1.40 .45

C242 AP104 150fr bl & multi 2.00 .75

C243 AP104 200fr multi 2.75 1.00

Nos. C240-C243 (4) 6.90 2.55

Centenary of Universal Postal Union.

1974, Nov. 4 Engr. *Perf. 13*

C244 AP105 100fr multi 1.25 .50

Virgin and Child, by Correggio AP106

150fr, Virgin and Child with St. Hilary, by Filippo Lippi. 200fr, Virgin and Child, by Murillo.

1974, Dec. 24 Litho. *Perf. 12½x13*

C245 AP106 100fr multi 1.25 .45

C246 AP106 150fr multi 2.00 .65

C247 AP106 200fr multi 2.50 1.00

Nos. C245-C247 (3) 5.75 2.10

Christmas 1974. See Nos. C252-C254, C260-C262, C280-C282.

Apollo and Emblem AP107

Designs (Emblem of Soyuz-Apollo Space Docking): 100fr, Docking in space over earth. 150fr, Soyuz in space.

1975, Jan. 31 Engr. *Perf. 13*

C248 AP107 50fr bl & multi .55 .35

C249 AP107 100fr multi 1.00 .50

C250 AP107 150fr multi 1.60 .70

Nos. C248-C250 (3) 3.15 1.55

Russo-American space cooperation. For overprints see Nos. C263-C265.

Europafrica Issue

European and African Women, Globe — AP108

1975, Feb. 28 Engr. *Perf. 13*

C251 AP108 250fr brn, lil & red 3.00 1.50

Painting Type of 1974

Easter: 75fr, Jesus in Garden of Olives, by Delacroix, horiz. 125fr, Crucifixion, by El Greco. 150fr, Resurrection, by Leonard Limosin.

Perf. 13x12½, 12½x13

1975, Mar. 27 Litho.

C252 AP106 75fr multi .75 .35

C253 AP106 125fr multi 1.40 .50

C254 AP106 150fr multi 1.75 .75

Nos. C252-C254 (3) 3.90 1.60

Bird Type of 1968-69 Dated "1975"

100fr, Cinnyricinclus leucogaster, vert.

1975, Apr. Photo. *Perf. 13*

C255 AP36 100fr gold & multi 3.00 1.10

Lt. Col. Seyni Kountche AP109

1975, Apr. 15 Litho. *Perf. 12½x13*

C256 AP109 100fr multi 1.25 .50

Military Government, first anniversary.

Shot Put, Maple Leaf, Montreal Olympic Emblem AP110

Design: 200fr, Gymnast on rings, Canadian flag, Montreal Olympic emblem.

1975, Oct. 6 Engr. *Perf. 13*

C257 AP110 150fr blk & red 1.40 .70

C258 AP110 200fr red & blk 2.00 1.00

Pre-Olympic Year 1975.

UN Emblem and Dove — AP111

1975, Nov. 26 Engr. *Perf. 13*

C259 AP111 100fr grn & bl 1.00 .50

United Nations, 30th anniversary.

Painting Type of 1974

50fr, Virgin of Seville, by Murillo. 75fr, Adoration of the Shepherds, by Tintoretto, horiz. 125fr, Virgin with Angels, Florentine, 15th cent.

1975, Dec. 24 Litho. *Perf. 12½x13*

C260 AP106 50fr multi .55 .30

C261 AP106 75fr multi .85 .40

C262 AP106 125fr multi 1.40 .75

Nos. C260-C262 (3) 2.80 1.45

Christmas 1975.

Nos. C248-C250 Overprinted: "JONCTION / 17 Juillet 1975"

1975, Dec. 30 Engr. *Perf. 13*

C263 AP107 50fr bl & multi .65 .25

C264 AP107 100fr multi .90 .50

C265 AP107 150fr multi 1.60 .80

Nos. C263-C265 (3) 3.15 1.55

Apollo-Soyuz link-up in space, July 17, 1975.

12th Winter Olympic Games Type, 1976

Designs: 200fr, Women's figure skating. 300fr, Biathlon. 500fr, Speed skating.

1976, Feb. 20 Litho. *Perf. 14x13½*

C266 A97 200fr multi 1.50 .70

C267 A97 300fr multi 2.25 1.00

Souvenir Sheet

C268 A97 500fr multi 4.25 1.75

American Bicentennial Type, 1976

Design (Statue of Liberty and): 150fr, Joseph Warren, martyr at Bunker Hill. 200fr, John Paul Jones on the bridge of the "Bonhomme Richard." 300fr, Molly Pitcher, Monmouth battle heroine. 500fr, Start of the fighting.

1976, Apr. 8

C269 A100 150fr multi 1.10 .35

C270 A100 200fr multi 1.60 .65

C271 A100 300fr multi 2.25 .85

Nos. C269-C271 (3) 4.95 1.85

Souvenir Sheet

C272 A100 500fr multi 4.25 1.50

LZ-129 over Lake Constance — AP112

Designs: 50fr, LZ-3 over Würzburg. 150fr, LZ-9 over Friedrichshafen. 200fr, LZ-2 over Rothenburg, vert. 300fr, LZ-130 over Essen. 500fr, LZ-127 over the Swiss Alps.

1976, May 18 Litho. *Perf. 11*

C273 AP112 40fr multi .50 .25

C274 AP112 50fr multi .60 .25

C275 AP112 150fr multi 1.75 .50

C276 AP112 200fr multi 2.00 .55

C277 AP112 300fr multi 3.00 .70

Nos. C273-C277 (5) 7.85 2.25

Souvenir Sheet

C278 AP112 500fr multi 5.00 1.75

75th anniversary of the Zeppelin.

Olympic Games Type, 1976

Souvenir Sheet

1976, July 17 Litho. *Perf. 14*

C279 A105 150fr Sprint 1.60 .70

Christmas Type of 1974

Paintings: 50fr, Nativity, by Rubens. 100fr, Virgin and Child, by Correggio. 150fr, Adoration of the Kings, by Gerard David, horiz.

1976, Dec. 24 Litho. *Perf. 12½*

C280 AP106 50fr multi .60 .25

C281 AP106 100fr multi 1.25 .50

C282 AP106 150fr multi 2.00 .85

Nos. C280-C282 (3) 3.85 1.60

Christmas 1976.

Viking Mars Project Type, 1977

100fr, Viking lander & nprobe, horiz. 150fr, Descent phases of Viking lander. 200fr, Titan rocket start for Mars. 400fr, Viking orbiter in flight.

1977, Mar. 15 Litho. *Perf. 14*

C283 A113 100fr multi .80 .25
C284 A113 150fr multi 1.10 .35
C285 A113 200fr multi 1.60 .50
Nos. C283-C285 (3) 3.50 1.10

Souvenir Sheet

C286 A113 400fr multi 3.00 1.10

For overprints see Nos. C295-C297.

Nobel Prize Type, 1977
Souvenir Sheet

Design: 500fr, Theodore Roosevelt, peace.

1977, Aug. 20 Litho. *Perf. 14*

C287 A122 500fr multi 4.25 1.25

Games' Emblem, Wheels and Colors AP113

150fr, Rings, colors and Games' emblem.

1978, July 13 Litho. *Perf. 12½x13*

C288 AP113 40fr multi .40 .30
C289 AP113 150fr multi 1.40 .60

Third African Games, Algiers, July 13-28.

Emblem AP114

1978, Oct. 6 Litho. *Perf. 13*

C290 AP114 150fr multi 1.25 .60

Niger Broadcasting Company, 20th anniversary.

Philexafrique II — Essen Issue
Common Design Types

Designs: No. C291, Giraffes and Niger No. 92. No. C292, Eagle and Oldenburg No. 7.

1978, Nov. 1 Litho. *Perf. 13x12½*

C291 CD138 100fr multi 2.25 1.40
C292 CD139 100fr multi 2.25 1.40
a. Pair, #C291-C292 + label 6.00 4.50

View of Campus and Laying Cornerstone — AP115

1978, Dec. 11 Litho. *Perf. 12½*

C293 AP115 100fr multi .80 .40

Islamic University of Niger.

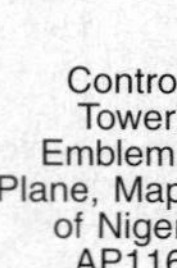

Control Tower, Emblem, Plane, Map of Niger AP116

1979, Dec. 12 Litho. *Perf. 12½*

C294 AP116 150fr multi 1.25 .65

ASECNA (Air Safety Board), 20th anniversary.

Nos. C284-C286 Overprinted in Silver or Black: "alunissage / apollo XI / juillet 1969" and Emblem

1979, Dec. 20 Litho. *Perf. 14*

C295 A113 150fr multi 1.25 .70
C296 A113 200fr multi (S) 1.60 .85

Souvenir Sheet

C297 A113 400fr multi 3.25 2.00

Apollo 11 moon landing, 10th anniversary.

Gaweye Hotel AP117

1980, Jan. 10 Litho. *Perf. 13*

C298 AP117 100fr multi .80 .40

Self-portrait, by Rembrandt AP118

Rembrandt Portraits: 90fr, Hendrickje at the Window. 100fr, Old Man. 130fr, Maria Trip. 200fr, Self-portrait, diff. 400fr, Saskia.

1981, Feb. 12 Litho. *Perf. 12½*

C299 AP118 60fr multi .50 .30
C300 AP118 90fr multi .70 .40
C301 AP118 100fr multi .80 .50
C302 AP118 130fr multi 1.25 .60
C303 AP118 200fr multi 1.75 1.00
C304 AP118 400fr multi 3.25 2.00
Nos. C299-C304 (6) 8.25 4.80

Apollo 11, 1969 — AP119

Space Conquest: Views of Columbia space shuttle, 1981.

1981, Mar. 30 Litho. *Perf. 12½*

C305 AP119 100fr multi .80 .30
C306 AP119 150fr multi 1.25 .45
C307 AP119 200fr multi 1.40 .70
C308 AP119 300fr multi 2.25 1.00
Nos. C305-C308 (4) 5.70 2.45

Souvenir Sheet

C309 AP119 500fr multi 4.00 1.75

For overprint see No. C356.

Girl in a Room, by Picasso — AP120

Picasso Birth Centenary: 60fr, Olga in an Armchair. 90fr, Family of Acrobats. 120fr, Three Musicians. 200fr, Paul on a Donkey. All vert.

1981, June 25 Litho. *Perf. 12½*

C310 AP120 60fr multi .55 .25
C311 AP120 90fr multi .80 .30
C312 AP120 120fr multi 1.00 .40
C313 AP120 200fr multi 2.00 .60
C314 AP120 400fr multi 3.50 1.10
Nos. C310-C314 (5) 7.85 2.65

Christmas 1982 AP121

Rubens Paintings.

1982, Dec. 24 Litho. *Perf. 14*

C315 AP121 200fr Adoration of the Kings 1.60 .50
C316 AP121 300fr Mystical Marriage of St. Catherine 2.50 .90
C317 AP121 400fr Virgin and Child 3.25 1.00
Nos. C315-C317 (3) 7.35 2.40

Manned Flight Bicentenary AP122

1983, Jan. 24

C318 AP122 65fr Montgolfiere balloon, 1783, vert. .50 .20
C319 AP122 85fr Hydrogen balloon, 1783, vert. .75 .25
C320 AP122 200fr Zeppelin 1.50 .55
C321 AP122 250fr Farman plane 2.00 .65
C322 AP122 300fr Concorde 2.25 .80
C323 AP122 500fr Apollo 11, vert. 4.00 1.40
Nos. C318-C323 (6) 11.00 3.85

Pre-Olympic Year — AP123

1983, May 25 Litho. *Perf. 13*

C324 AP123 85fr Javelin .60 .25
C325 AP123 200fr Shot put 1.50 .55
C326 AP123 250fr Hammer, vert. 1.75 .70
C327 AP123 300fr Discus 2.25 .80
Nos. C324-C327 (4) 6.10 2.30

Souvenir Sheet

C328 AP123 500fr Shot put, diff. 3.75 1.75

For overprint see No. C357.

Christmas 1983 — AP124

Botticelli Paintings. 120fr, 500fr vert.

Wmk. 385 Cartor

1983 Litho. *Perf. 13*

C329 AP124 120fr Virgin and Child with Angels .90 .40
C330 AP124 350fr Adoration of the Kings 2.75 1.00
C331 AP124 500fr Virgin of the Pomegranate 3.75 1.25
Nos. C329-C331 (3) 7.40 2.65

1984 Summer Olympics — AP125

Unwmk.

1984, Feb. 22 Litho. *Perf. 13*

C332 AP125 80fr Sprint .55 .25
C333 AP125 120fr Pole vault .80 .25
C334 AP125 140fr High jump 1.25 .35
C335 AP125 200fr Triple jump, vert. 1.75 .40
C336 AP125 350fr Long jump, vert. 2.75 .75
Nos. C332-C336 (5) 7.10 2.00

Souvenir Sheet

C337 AP125 500fr 110-meter hurdles 3.75 1.50

1984, Oct. 8 Litho.

Designs: Winners of various track events. Nos. C338-C341 vert.

C338 AP125 80fr Carl Lewis .60 .35
C339 AP125 120fr J. Cruz 1.00 .45
C340 AP125 140fr A. Cova 1.25 .50
C341 AP125 300fr Al Joyner 2.25 1.10
Nos. C338-C341 (4) 5.10 2.40

Souvenir Sheet

C342 AP125 500fr D. Mogenburg, high jump 3.75 2.00

World Soccer Cup — AP126

1984, Nov. 19 Litho. *Perf. 13*

C345 AP126 150fr multi 1.00 .50
C346 AP126 250fr multi 1.75 .85
C347 AP126 450fr multi 3.25 1.40
C348 AP126 500fr multi 3.50 1.60
Nos. C345-C348 (4) 9.50 4.35

Christmas 1984 AP127

Paintings: 100fr, The Visitation, by Ghirlandajo. 200fr, Virgin and Child, by the Master of Santa Verdiana. 400fr, Virgin and Child, by J. Koning.

1984, Dec. 24 Litho. *Perf. 13*

C349 AP127 100fr multi .80 .45
C350 AP127 200fr multi 1.60 .85
C351 AP127 400fr multi 3.25 1.10
Nos. C349-C351 (3) 5.65 2.40

Audubon Birth Bicentennial — AP128

1985, Feb. 6 Litho. *Perf. 13*

C352 AP128 110fr Himantopus mexicanus .90 .50
C353 AP128 140fr Phoenicopterus ruber, vert. 1.40 .55
C354 AP128 200fr Fratercula arctica 1.75 .85
C355 AP128 350fr Sterna paradisaea, vert. 3.25 1.40
Nos. C352-C355 (4) 7.30 3.30

Nos. C309, C328 Ovptd. in Silver with Exhibition Emblems

1985, Mar. 11 Litho. *Perf. 12½, 13*

C356 AP119 500fr ARGENTINA '85 BUENOS AIRES 4.75 3.00
C357 AP123 500fr OLYMPHILEX '85 LAUSANNE 4.75 3.00

Religious Paintings by Bartolome Murillo (1617-1682) AP129

1985, Dec. 19 Litho. *Perf. 13*

C358 AP129 110fr Virgin of the Rosary .80 .45
C359 AP129 250fr The Immaculate Conception 1.90 .85
C360 AP129 390fr Virgin of Seville 3.25 1.40
Nos. C358-C360 (3) 5.95 2.70

Christmas 1985.

Halley's Comet — AP130

1985, Dec. 26

C361 AP130 110fr Over Paris, 1910 .80 .35
C362 AP130 130fr Over New York 1.00 .50
C363 AP130 200fr Giotto space probe 1.75 .70
C364 AP130 300fr Vega probe 2.50 1.00
C365 AP130 390fr Planet A probe 3.25 1.40
Nos. C361-C365 (5) 9.30 3.95

Martin Luther King, Jr. (1929-1968), Civil Rights Activist — AP131

1986, Apr. 28 Litho. *Perf. 13½*

C366 AP131 500fr multi 3.75 1.60

1986 World Cup Soccer Championships, Mexico — AP132

Various soccer plays, stamps and labels.

1986, May 21 *Perf. 13*

C367 AP132 130fr No. 228 1.00 .50
C368 AP132 210fr No. 229 1.75 .70
C369 AP132 390fr No. 230 3.25 1.50
C370 AP132 400fr Aztec drawing 3.25 1.50
Nos. C367-C370 (4) 9.25 4.20

Souvenir Sheet

C371 AP132 500fr World Cup 4.00 2.25

Statue of Liberty, Cent. AP133

1986, June 19

C372 AP133 300fr Bartholdi, statue 2.40 1.25

1988 Summer Olympics, Seoul AP134

Olympic Rings, Pierre de Coubertin and: 85fr, One-man kayak, vert. 165fr, Crew racing. 200fr, Two-man kayak. 600fr, One-man kayak, diff., vert. 750fr, One-man kayak, diff., vert.

1988, June 22 Litho. *Perf. 13*

C373 AP134 85fr multi .65 .30
C374 AP134 165fr multi 1.25 .55
C375 AP134 200fr multi 1.60 .70
C376 AP134 600fr multi 4.50 2.00
Nos. C373-C376 (4) 8.00 3.55

Souvenir Sheet

C377 AP134 750fr multi 6.00 6.00

First Moon Landing, 20th Anniv. AP135

1989, July 27 Litho. *Perf. 13*

C378 AP135 200fr Launch 1.60 .75
C379 AP135 300fr Crew 2.40 1.25
C380 AP135 350fr Lunar experiments 2.75 1.40
C381 AP135 400fr Raising flag 3.25 1.50
Nos. C378-C381 (4) 10.00 4.90

1990 World Cup Soccer Championships, Italy — AP136

Athletes & views or symbols of Italian cities.

1990, Mar. 6 Litho. *Perf. 13*

C382 AP136 130fr Florence .90 .40
C383 AP136 210fr Verona 1.50 .75
C384 AP136 500fr Bari 3.50 1.75
C385 AP136 600fr Rome 4.25 2.10
Nos. C382-C385 (4) 10.15 5.00

1992 Winter Olympics, Albertville — AP138

1991, Mar. 28 Litho. *Perf. 13*

C392 AP138 110fr Speed skating .80 .35
C393 AP138 300fr Ice hockey 2.40 1.25
C394 AP138 500fr Downhill skiing 4.00 2.00
C395 AP138 600fr Luge 4.75 2.40
Nos. C392-C395 (4) 11.95 6.00

AIR POST SEMI-POSTAL STAMPS

Dahomey types SPAP1-SPAP3 inscribed Niger

Perf. 13½x12½, 13 (#CB3)

Photo, Engr. (#CB3)

1942, June 22

CB1 SPAP1 1.50fr + 3.50fr green .70 —
CB2 SPAP2 2fr + 6fr brown .70 —
CB3 SPAP3 3fr + 9fr car red .70 —
Nos. CB1-CB3 (3) 2.10

Native children's welfare fund.

Colonial Education Fund

Common Design Type

Perf. 12½x13½

1942, June 22 Engr.

CB4 CD86a 1.20fr + 1.80fr blue & red .70 —

POSTAGE DUE STAMPS

D1

D2

Postage Due Stamps of Upper Senegal and Niger, 1914, Overprinted

1921 Unwmk. *Perf. 14x13½*

J1 D1 5c green .60 .60
J2 D1 10c rose .60 .60
J3 D1 15c gray .70 .70
J4 D1 20c brown .70 .70
J5 D1 30c blue .85 .85
J6 D1 50c black .85 .85
J7 D1 60c orange 1.40 1.40
J8 D1 1fr violet 1.50 1.50
Nos. J1-J8 (8) 7.20 7.20

1927 Typo.

J9 D2 2c dk bl & red .20 .20
J10 D2 4c ver & blk .20 .20
J11 D2 5c org & vio .25 .25
J12 D2 10c red brn & blk vio .25 .25
J13 D2 15c grn & org .35 .35
J14 D2 20c cer & ol brn .50 .50
J15 D2 25c blk & ol brn .50 .50
J16 D2 30c dl vio & blk 1.10 1.10
J17 D2 50c dp red, *grnsh* .85 .85
J18 D2 60c gray vio & org, *bluish* .60 .60
J19 D2 1fr ind & ultra, *bluish* .85 .85
J20 D2 2fr rose red & vio .95 .95
J21 D2 3fr org brn & ultra 1.50 1.50
Nos. J9-J21 (13) 8.10 8.10

Catalogue values for unused stamps in this section, from this point to the end of the section, are for Never Hinged items.

Republic of the Niger

Cross of Agadez D3

Native Metalcraft: 3fr, 5fr, 10fr, Cross of Iferouane. 15fr, 20fr, 50fr, Cross of Tahoua.

Perf. 12½

1962, July 1 Unwmk. Photo.

J22 D3 50c emerald .20 .20
J23 D3 1fr violet .20 .20
J24 D3 2fr slate green .20 .20
J25 D3 3fr lilac rose .20 .20
J26 D3 5fr green .20 .20
J27 D3 10fr orange .20 .20
J28 D3 15fr deep blue .20 .20
J29 D3 20fr carmine .25 .25
J30 D3 50fr chocolate .35 .35
Nos. J22-J30 (9) 2.00 2.00

1993 Litho. *Perf. 12½*

Designs as Before

Size: 50x50mm

J31 D3 5fr green .20 .20
J32 D3 10fr orange .20 .20
J33 D3 15fr blue .20 .20
J34 D3 20fr red .20 .20
J35 D3 50fr chocolate .40 .40
Nos. J31-J35 (5) 1.20 1.20

Imprint on Nos. J31-J35 is in black.

OFFICIAL STAMPS

Catalogue values for unused stamps in this section are for Never Hinged items.

Djerma Girl Carrying Jug
O1 O2

Perf. 14x13½

1962-71 Typo. Unwmk.

Denomination in Black

O1 O1 1fr dark purple .20 .20
O2 O1 2fr yel grn .20 .20
O3 O1 5fr brt blue .20 .20
O4 O1 10fr deep red .20 .20
O5 O1 20fr vio blue .20 .20
O6 O1 25fr orange .20 .20
O7 O1 30fr light blue ('65) .30 .20
O8 O1 35fr pale grn ('71) .40 .30
O9 O1 40fr brown ('71) .40 .30
O10 O1 50fr black .40 .30
O11 O1 60fr rose red .60 .35
O12 O1 85fr blue green .90 .35
O13 O1 100fr red lilac .95 .35
O14 O1 200fr dark blue 2.00 .75
Nos. O1-O14 (14) 7.15 4.10

1988, Nov. Typo. *Perf. 13*

O15 O2 5fr brt blue .20 .20
O16 O2 10fr henna brn .25 .20
O17 O2 20fr vio blue .25 .20
O18 O2 50fr greenish blk .50 .25

1989-96(?)

O19 O2 15fr bright yellow .20 .20
O20 O2 45fr orange .30 .20
O21 O2 85fr blue green
O22 O2 100fr red lilac
Nos. O15-O20 (6) 1.70 1.25

Issued: 15, 45fr, 3/89; 85, 100fr, 1996(?).
See No. 698.
This is an expanding set. Numbers will change when complete.

NIGER COAST PROTECTORATE

ˈnī-jər ˈkōst prə-ˈtek-t(ə-)rət

(Oil Rivers Protectorate)

LOCATION — West coast of Africa on Gulf of Guinea
GOVT. — British Protectorate

This territory was originally known as the Oil Rivers Protectorate, and its affairs were conducted by the British Royal Niger Company. The Company surrendered its charter to the Crown in 1899. In 1900 all of the territories formerly controlled by the Royal Niger Company were incorporated into the two protectorates of Northern and Southern Nigeria, the latter absorbing the area formerly known as Niger Coast Protectorate. In 1914 Northern and Southern Nigeria joined to form the Crown Colony of Nigeria. (See Nigeria, Northern Nigeria, Southern Nigeria and Lagos.)

12 Pence = 1 Shilling

Stamps of Great Britain, 1881-87, Overprinted in Black

1892 Wmk. 30 *Perf. 14*

1 A54 ½p vermilion 14.00 9.00
2 A40 1p lilac 8.50 9.00
a. "OIL RIVERS" at top 8,500.
b. Half used as ½p on cover 3,000.
3 A56 2p green & car 27.50 9.00
a. Half used as 1p on cover —
4 A57 2½p violet, *bl* 7.50 2.50
5 A61 5p lilac & blue 12.00 7.25
6 A65 1sh green 62.50 *85.00*
Nos. 1-6 (6) 132.00 121.75

For surcharges see Nos. 7-36, 50.

Dangerous forgeries exist of all surcharges.

No. 2 Surcharged in Red or Violet

1893

7 A40 ½p on half of 1p (R) 175.00 160.00
c. Unsevered pair 550.00 500.00
d. "½" omitted
7A A40 ½p on half of 1p (V) *5,000.* *4,750.*
b. Surcharge double *21,000.*
c. Unsevered pair *15,000.* *14,000.*

Nos. 3-6 Handstamp Surcharged in Violet, Red, Carmine, Bluish Black, Deep Blue, Green or Black

1893 Wmk. 30 *Perf. 14*

8 A56 ½p on 2p (V) *425.* 250.
9 A57 ½p on 2½p (V) 3,500.
10 A57 ½p on 2½p (R) 325. 325.
11 A57 ½p on 2½p (C) *9,000.* *6,500.*
12 A57 ½p on 2½p (B) *10,000.* *6,500.*
13 A57 ½p on 2½p (G) 475. 525.

14 A56 ½p on 2p (V) 425. 375.
15 A56 ½p on 2p (Bl) 1,900. 800.
16 A57 ½p on 2½p (V) *6,000.*
17 A57 ½p on 2½p (R) 575. *700.*
18 A57 ½p on 2½p (Bl) 425. 400.
19 A57 ½p on 2½p (G) 450. *475.*

20 A56 ½p on 2p (V) 400. 300.
21 A57 ½p on 2½p (R) 350. 350.
22 A57 ½p on 2½p (C) 200. 200.
23 A57 ½p on 2½p (Bl Bk) *3,000.*
24 A57 ½p on 2½p (Bl) 325. 400.
25 A57 ½p on 2½p (G) 250. 250.
26 A57 ½p on 2½p (Bk) *3,500.*

HALF
PENNY

27 A57 ½p on 2½p (R) *8,500.*
28 A57 ½p on 2½p (G) 500. 475.

29 A56 1sh on 2p (V) 475. 400.
30 A56 1sh on 2p (R) 675. *4,250.*
31 A56 1sh on 2p (Bk) *6,250.*

32 A56 5sh on 2d (V) *10,250.* *11,500.*
33 A61 10sh on 5p (R) *6,750.* *9,000.*
34 A65 20sh on 1sh (V) *110,000.*
35 A65 20sh on 1sh (R) *110,000.*
36 A65 20sh on 1sh (Bk) *110,000.*

The handstamped 1893 surcharges are known inverted, vertical, etc.

Queen Victoria
A8 A9

A10 A11

A12 A13

1893 Unwmk. *Perf. 12 to 15*

37 A8 ½p vermilion 5.50 5.50
38 A9 1p light blue 6.75 3.75
a. Half used as ½p on cover 650.00
39 A10 2p green 32.50 27.50
a. Half used as 1p on cover *800.00*
b. Horiz. pair, imperf. between *15,000.*
40 A11 2½p car lake 9.50 4.00
41 A12 5p gray lilac 19.00 13.50
a. 5p lilac 15.00 20.00
42 A13 1sh black 15.00 13.00
Nos. 37-42 (6) 88.25 67.25

For surcharge see No. 49.

A15 A16

A17 A18

A19 A20

1894 Engr.

43 A15 ½p yel green 5.00 5.00
44 A16 1p vermilion 15.00 9.00
a. 1p orange vermilion 17.50 11.00
b. Diagonal half, used as ½p on cover 600.00
45 A17 2p car lake 35.00 7.25
a. Half used as 1p on cover —
46 A18 2½p blue 15.00 4.25
47 A19 5p dp violet 7.25 6.00
48 A20 1sh black 55.00 16.00
Nos. 43-48 (6) 132.25 47.50

See #55-59, 61. For surcharges see #51-54.

Halves of Nos. 38, 3 and 44 Surcharged in Red, Blue, Violet or Black:

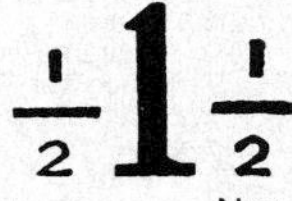

No. 49 No. 50 Nos. 51-53

1894

49 A9 ½p on half of 1p (R) 900. 375.
a. Inverted surcharge *5,000.*

Perf. 14

Wmk. 30

50 A56 1p on half of 2p (R) 1,950. 400.
a. Double surcharge 5,750. 1,350.
b. Inverted surcharge 1,800.

Perf. 12 to 15

Unwmk.

51 A16 ½p on half of 1p (Bl) 2,500. 475.
a. Double surcharge
52 A16 ½p on half of 1p (V) 3,500. 750.
53 A16 ½p on half of 1p (Bk) *4,500.* *1,150.*

This surcharge is found on both vertical and diagonal halves of the 1p.

No. 46 Surcharged in Black

1894

54 A18 ½p on 2½p blue 425. 250.
a. Double surcharge 4,500. 1,750.

The surcharge is found in eight types. The "OIE" variety is broken type.

A27 A28

A29

1897-98 Wmk. 2

55 A15 ½p yel green 3.75 1.75
56 A16 1p vermilion 5.00 1.60
57 A17 2p car lake 4.50 2.50
58 A18 2½p blue 9.50 2.25
a. 2½p slate blue 8.50 2.25
59 A19 5p dp violet 10.00 *75.00*
60 A27 6p yel brn ('98) 8.00 7.25
61 A20 1sh black 17.50 *32.50*
62 A28 2sh6p olive bister 25.00 *90.00*
63 A29 10sh dp pur ('98) 110.00 *190.00*
a. 10sh bright purple 110.00 *190.00*
Nos. 55-63 (9) 193.25 *402.85*

The stamps of Niger Coast Protectorate were superseded in Jan. 1900, by those of Northern and Southern Nigeria.

NIGERIA

nī-ˈjir-ē-ə

LOCATION — West coast of Africa, bordering on the Gulf of Guinea
GOVT. — Republic
AREA — 356,669 sq. mi.
POP. — 113,828,587 (1999 est.)
CAPITAL — Abuja

The colony and protectorate were formed in 1914 by the union of Northern and Southern Nigeria. The mandated territory of Cameroons (British) was also attached for administrative purposes. The Federation of Nigeria was formed in 1960. It became a republic in 1963. See Niger Coast Protectorate, Lagos, Northern Nigeria and Southern Nigeria.

12 Pence = 1 Shilling
20 Shillings = 1 Pound
100 Kobo = 1 Naira (1973)

Catalogue values for unused stamps in this country are for Never Hinged items, beginning with Scott 71 in the regular postage section, Scott B1 in the semi-postal section and Scott J1 in the postage due section.

Watermarks

Wmk. 335 — FN Multiple

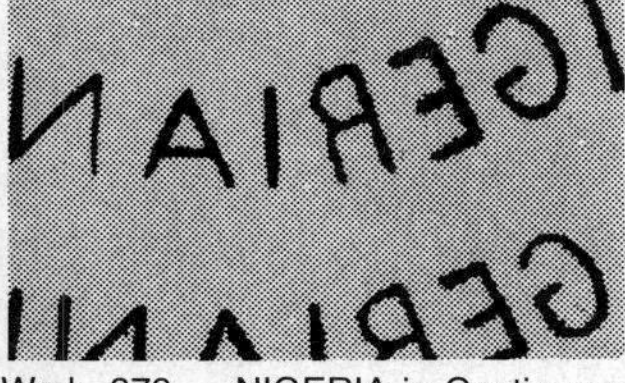
Wmk. 379 — NIGERIA in Continuous Wavy Lines

King George V — A1

Numerals of 3p, 4p, 6p, 5sh and £1 of type A1 are in color on plain tablet.
Dies I and II are described in the back of this volume.

Wmk. Multiple Crown and CA (3)
1914-27 Typo. *Perf. 14*
Die I
Ordinary Paper

1 A1 ½p green 3.00 .50
a. Booklet pane of 6
2 A1 1p carmine 5.25 .20
a. Booklet pane of 6
b. 1p scarlet 7.50 .25
3 A1 2p gray 9.00 3.00
4 A1 2½p ultramarine 7.25 3.25

Chalky Paper

5 A1 3p violet, *yel* 1.60 3.00
6 A1 4p black & red, *yel* 1.10 *4.75*
7 A1 6p dull vio & red vio 10.00 11.00
8 A1 1sh black, *green* 1.10 *10.00*
a. 1sh black, *emerald,* 1.40 *15.00*
b. 1sh black, *bl grn,* ol back 30.00 30.00
c. As "a," olive back ('20) 9.00 *42.50*
9 A1 2sh6p blk & red, *bl* 17.50 7.25
10 A1 5sh grn & red, *yel,* white back 15.00 *62.50*

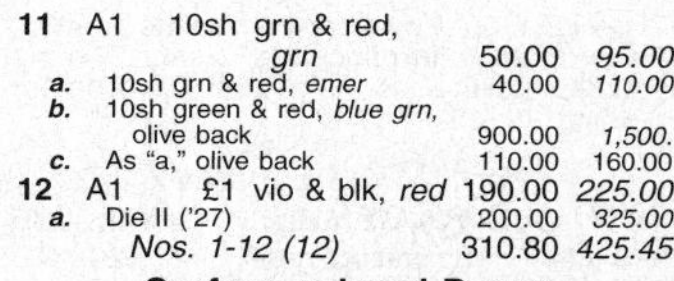

11 A1 10sh grn & red, *grn* 50.00 *95.00*
a. 10sh grn & red, *emer* 40.00 *110.00*
b. 10sh green & red, *blue grn,* olive back 900.00 *1,500.*
c. As "a," olive back 110.00 160.00
12 A1 £1 vio & blk, *red* 190.00 *225.00*
a. Die II ('27) 200.00 *325.00*
Nos. 1-12 (12) 310.80 *425.45*

Surface-colored Paper

13 A1 3p violet, *yel* 3.50 *11.00*
14 A1 4p black & red, *yel* 1.60 *11.50*
15 A1 1sh black, *green* 1.60 *25.00*
a. 1sh black, *emerald*
16 A1 5sh grn & red, *yel* 15.00 *55.00*
17 A1 10sh grn & red, *grn* 50.00 *150.00*
Nos. 13-17 (5) 71.70 *252.50*

1921-33 Wmk. 4
Die II
Ordinary Paper

18 A1 ½p green 4.00 .90
a. Die I 1.25 .40
19 A1 1p carmine 1.75 .55
a. Booklet pane of 6 27.50
b. Die I 3.00 .35
c. Booklet pane of 6, Die I 35.00
20 A1 1½p orange ('31) 4.50 .20
21 A1 2p gray 8.50 .50
a. Die I 1.60 *5.50*
b. Booklet pane of 6, Die I 55.00
22 A1 2p red brown ('27) 5.00 1.00
a. Booklet pane of 6 60.00
23 A1 2p dk brown ('28) 1.40 .20
a. Booklet pane of 6 27.50
b. Die I ('32) 6.00 .50
24 A1 2½p ultra (die I) 1.10 6.75
25 A1 3p dp violet 11.00 1.10
a. Die I ('24) 5.50 3.50
26 A1 3p ultra ('31) 6.75 1.10

Chalky Paper

27 A1 4p blk & red, *yel* .70 .60
a. Die I ('32) 6.25 7.75
28 A1 6p dull vio & red vio 8.00 9.00
a. Die I 14.00 22.50
29 A1 1sh black, *emerald* 1.40 *2.25*
30 A1 2sh6p blk & red, *bl* 7.25 *29.00*
a. Die I ('32) 45.00 *72.50*
31 A1 5sh green & red, *yel* ('26) 16.00 *72.50*
a. Die I ('32) 72.50 *200.00*
32 A1 10sh green & red, *emer* 67.50 *200.00*
a. Die I ('32) 110.00 *450.00*
Nos. 18-32 (15) 144.85 325.65

Silver Jubilee Issue
Common Design Type

1935, May 6 Engr. *Perf. 11x12*

34 CD301 1½p black & ultra .75 *.75*
35 CD301 2p indigo & green 1.50 *1.10*
36 CD301 3p ultra & brown 3.25 *11.50*
37 CD301 1sh brown vio & ind 3.25 *26.50*
Nos. 34-37 (4) 8.75 *39.85*
Set, never hinged 16.50

Wharf at Apapa — A2

Picking Cacao Pods — A3

Dredging for Tin — A4

Timber — A5

Fishing Village — A6

Ginning Cotton — A7

Minaret at Habe — A8

Fulani Cattle — A9

Victoria-Buea Road — A10

Oil Palms A11

View of Niger at Jebba A12

Nigerian Canoe A13

1936, Feb. 1 *Perf. 11½x13*

38 A2 ½p green .50 .50
39 A3 1p rose car .30 .30
40 A4 1½p brown 1.50 .30
a. Perf. 12½x13½ 60.00 4.50
41 A5 2p black .50 .50
42 A6 3p dark blue 1.75 1.00
a. Perf. 12½x13½ 110.00 25.00
43 A7 4p red brown 2.00 2.00
44 A8 6p dull violet .70 .60
45 A9 1sh olive green 2.25 *10.00*

Perf. 14

46 A10 2sh6p ultra & blk 5.00 *22.50*
47 A11 5sh ol grn & blk 14.00 *27.50*
48 A12 10sh slate & blk 50.00 *90.00*
49 A13 £1 orange & blk 80.00 *160.00*
Nos. 38-49 (12) 158.50 *315.20*
Set, never hinged 325.00

Common Design Types pictured following the introduction.

Coronation Issue
Common Design Type

1937, May 12 *Perf. 11x11½*

50 CD302 1p dark carmine .20 .20
51 CD302 1½p dark brown .55 .25
52 CD302 3p deep ultra .65 .30
Nos. 50-52 (3) 1.40 .75
Set, never hinged 3.50

George VI — A14

Victoria-Buea Road — A15

Niger at Jebba A16

1938-51 Wmk. 4 *Perf. 12*

53 A14 ½p deep green .20 .30
a. Perf. 11½ ('50) .20 .20
54 A14 1p dk carmine .20 .30
55 A14 1½p red brown .20 .30
a. Perf. 11½ ('50) .20 .20
56 A14 2p black .30 .30
57 A14 2½p orange ('41) .20 .30
58 A14 3p deep blue .20 .30
59 A14 4p orange 32.50 7.25
60 A14 6p brown violet .20 .30
a. Perf. 11½ ('51) .30 .20
61 A14 1sh olive green .35 .30
a. Perf. 11½ ('50) .35 .20
62 A14 1sh3p turq blue ('40) .50 .30
a. Perf. 11½ ('50) .50 .20
63 A15 2sh6p ultra & blk ('51) 4.50 4.75
a. Perf. 13½ ('42) 1.90 .70
b. Perf. 14 ('42) 1.90 .70
c. Perf. 13x11½ 42.50 9.50
64 A16 5sh org & blk, perf. 13½ ('42) 3.00 1.90
a. Perf. 12 ('49) 5.00 1.10
b. Perf. 14 ('48) 3.00 1.10
c. Perf. 13x11½ 75.00 9.00

1944, Dec. 1 *Perf. 12*

65 A14 1p red violet .20 .30
a. Perf. 11½ ('50) .20 .20
66 A14 2p deep red .20 .30
a. Perf. 11½ ('50) .20 .20
67 A14 3p black .20 .30
68 A14 4p dark blue .20 .30
Nos. 53-68 (16) 43.15 17.80
Set, never hinged 80.00

Issue date: Nos. 65a, 66a, Feb. 15.

Catalogue values for unused stamps in this section, from this point to the end of the section, are for Never Hinged items.

Peace Issue
Common Design Type

1946, Oct. 21 Engr. *Perf. 13½x14*

71 CD303 1½p brown .35 .20
72 CD303 4p deep blue .35 .35

Silver Wedding Issue
Common Design Types

1948, Dec. 20 Photo. *Perf. 14x14½*

73 CD304 1p brt red violet .35 .30

Perf. 11½x11
Engraved; Name Typographed

74 CD305 5sh brown orange 6.75 *9.00*

UPU Issue
Common Design Types
Engr.; Name Typo. on 3p, 6p
Perf. 13½, 11x11½

1949, Oct. 10 Wmk. 4

75 CD306 1p red violet .20 .20
76 CD307 3p indigo .40 .30
77 CD308 6p rose violet .90 .75
78 CD309 1sh olive 1.50 1.25
Nos. 75-78 (4) 3.00 2.50

Coronation Issue
Common Design Type

1953, June 2 Engr. *Perf. 13½x13*

79 CD312 1½p brt green & black .45 .20

Manilla (Bracelet) Currency A17

Olokun Head, Ife — A18

Designs: 1p, Bornu horsemen. 1½p, Peanuts, Kano City. 2p, Mining tin. 3p, Jebba Bridge over Niger River. 4p, Cocoa industry. 1sh, Logging. 2sh6p, Victoria harbor. 5sh, Loading palm oil. 10sh, Goats and Fulani cattle. £1, Lagos waterfront, 19th and 20th centuries.

1953, Sept. 1 *Perf. 14*

Size: 35½x22½mm

80	A17	½p red orange & blk	.20	.20
81	A17	1p ol gray & blk	.20	.20
82	A17	1½p blue green	.45	.20
83	A17	2p bister & blk	4.00	.20
84	A17	3p purple & blk	.50	.20
85	A17	4p ultra & black	2.50	.20
86	A18	6p blk & org brn	.25	.20
87	A17	1sh brn vio & blk	.35	.20

Size: 40½x24½mm

88	A17	2sh6p green & black	6.00	.50
89	A17	5sh ver & black	3.50	1.00
90	A17	10sh red brown & blk	12.50	2.50

Size: 42x31½mm

91	A17	£1 violet & black	22.50	6.00
		Nos. 80-91 (12)	52.95	11.60

Booklet panes of 4 of Nos. 80, 81, 84, 87 were issued in 1957. They are identical to margin blocks of 4 from sheets.

See No. 93.

No. 83 Overprinted in Black

1956, Jan. 28 **Wmk. 4** *Perf. 13½*

92	A17	2p bister & black	.35	.20

Visit of Queen Elizabeth II to Nigeria, Jan.-Feb., 1956.

Mining Tin Type of 1953

Two types:
I — Broken row of dots between "G" and miner's head.
II — Complete row of dots.

1956-57

93	A17	2p bluish gray (shades) (I)	2.75	1.25
b.		2p gray (shades) (II)	3.00	.30

Booklet pane of 4 of No. 83 was issued in 1957. See note after No. 91.

Ambas Bay, Victoria Harbor A19

Wmk. 314

1958, Dec. 1 **Engr.** *Perf. 13½*

94	A19	3p purple & black	.35	.20

Cent. of the founding of Victoria, Southern Cameroons.

1959, Mar. 14

3p, Lugard Hall, Kaduna. 1sh, Kano Mosque.

95	A19	3p purple & black	.30	.20
96	A19	1sh green & black	.40	.30

Attainment of self-government by the Northern Region, Mar. 15, 1959.

Federation of Nigeria

Federal Legislature A20

3p, Man Paddling Canoe. 6p, Federal Supreme Court. 1sh3p, Map of Africa, dove and torch.

Wmk. 335

1960, Oct. 1 **Photo.** *Perf. 13½*

Size: 35x22mm

97	A20	1p carmine & black	.20	.20
98	A20	3p blue & black	.20	.20
99	A20	6p dk red brn & emer	.20	.20

Size: 39½x23½mm

100	A20	1sh3p ultra & yellow	.30	.25
		Nos. 97-100 (4)	.90	.85

Nigeria's independence, Oct. 1, 1960.

Peanuts — A21

Central Bank, Lagos A22

Designs: 1p, Coal miner. 1½p, Adult education. 2p, Potter. 3p, Oyo carver. 4p, Weaver. 6p, Benin mask. 1sh, Yellow-casqued hornbill. 1sh3p, Camel train and map. 5sh, Nigeria museum and sculpture. 10sh, Kano airport. £1, Lagos terminal.

Perf. 14½x14

1961, Jan. 1 **Wmk. 335**

101	A21	½p emerald	.20	.30
102	A21	1p purple	.20	.30
a.		Booklet pane of 6	.45	
103	A21	1½p rose red	.20	.30
104	A21	2p ultra	.20	.30
105	A21	3p dark green	.20	.30
a.		Booklet pane of 6	.50	
106	A21	4p blue	.20	.30
107	A21	6p black & yel	.20	.30
a.		Booklet pane of 6	1.00	
b.		Yellow omitted		375.00
108	A21	1sh yellow green	.35	.30
109	A21	1sh3p orange	.60	.30
a.		Booklet pane of 6	3.75	
110	A22	2sh6p yellow & blk	1.50	.55
111	A22	5sh emerald & blk	3.00	2.00
112	A22	10sh dp ultra & blk	4.75	3.75
113	A22	£1 dp car & blk	7.50	7.50
		Nos. 101-113 (13)	19.10	16.50

For overprint see No. 198.

Globe and Train A23

1961, July 25 **Wmk. 335**

114	A23	1p shown	.20	.20
115	A23	3p Truck	.25	.25
116	A23	1sh3p Plane	.35	.35
117	A23	2sh6p Ship	.75	.75
		Nos. 114-117 (4)	1.55	1.55

Nigeria's admission to the UPU.

Coat of Arms — A24

Map and Natural Resources — A25

Designs: 6p, Eagle carrying banner. 1sh3p, Flying eagles forming flag. 2sh6p, Young couple looking at flag and government building.

Perf. 14½x14, 14x14½

1961, Oct. 1 **Photo.** **Wmk. 335**

118	A24	3p multicolored	.20	.20
119	A25	4p org, yel grn & dk red	.20	.20
120	A25	6p emerald	.20	.20
121	A25	1sh3p ultra, emer & gray	.30	.30
122	A25	2sh6p blue, emer & sep	.60	.60
		Nos. 118-122 (5)	1.50	1.50

First anniversary of independence.

Map of Africa and Staff of Aesculapius — A26

Map of Africa and: 3p, Lyre, book and scroll. 6p, Cogwheel. 1sh, Radio beacon. 1sh3p, Hands holding globe.

1962, Jan. 25 *Perf. 14x14½*

123	A26	1p bister	.20	.20
124	A26	3p deep magenta	.20	.20
125	A26	6p blue green	.20	.20
126	A26	1sh chestnut	.30	.20
127	A26	1sh3p bright blue	.40	.35
		Nos. 123-127 (5)	1.30	1.15

Issued to honor the conference of heads of state of African and Malagasy Governments.

Malaria Eradication Emblem and Larvae — A27

Emblem and: 6p, Man with spray gun. 1sh3p, Plane spraying insecticide. 2sh6p, Microscope, retort and patient.

1962, Apr. 7 *Perf. 14½*

128	A27	3p emerald, brn & ver	.20	.20
129	A27	6p lilac rose & dk blue	.20	.20
130	A27	1sh3p dk blue & lil rose	.25	.20
131	A27	2sh6p yel brown & blue	.55	.55
		Nos. 128-131 (4)	1.20	1.15

WHO drive to eradicate malaria.

National Monument, Lagos A28

Ife Bronze Head and Flag — A29

Perf. 14½x14, 14x14½

1962, Oct. 1 **Wmk. 335** **Photo.**

132	A28	3p lt ultra & emerald	.20	.20
a.		Emerald omitted		
133	A29	5sh vio, emer & org red	1.75	1.75

Second anniversary of independence.

Fair Emblem — A30

Globe and Arrows — A31

Designs (horizontal): 6p, "Wheels of Industry." 1sh, Cornucopia, goods and trucks. 2sh6p, Oil derricks and tanker.

1962, Oct. 27 **Wmk. 335**

134	A30	1p brown olive & org	.20	.20
135	A30	6p crimson & blk	.20	.20
136	A30	1sh dp orange & blk	.25	.20
137	A30	2sh6p dk ultra, yel & blk	.55	.50
		Nos. 134-137 (4)	1.20	1.10

Lagos Intl. Trade Fair, Oct. 27-Nov. 8.

1962, Nov. 5

4p, Natl. Hall & Commonwealth emblem, horiz. 1sh3p, Palm tree, emblem & doves.

138	A31	2½p sky blue	.20	.20
139	A31	4p dp rose & slate bl	.20	.20
140	A31	1sh3p gray & yellow	.45	.45
		Nos. 138-140 (3)	.85	.85

8th Commonwealth Parliamentary Conf., Lagos.

Herdsman with Cattle — A32

US Mercury Capsule over Kano Tracking Station — A33

Design: 6p, Tractor and corn, horiz.

1963, Mar. 21 **Photo.** *Perf. 14½*

141	A32	3p olive green	1.25	.20
142	A32	6p brt lilac rose	1.50	.35

FAO "Freedom from Hunger" campaign.

1963, June 21 *Perf. 14½*

Design: 1sh3p, Syncom II satellite and US tracking ship "Kingsport," Lagos harbor.

143	A33	6p dk blue & yel grn	.20	.20
144	A33	1sh3p black & dp green	.40	.40

Peaceful uses of outer space.

Printed in sheets of 12 (4x3) with ornamental borders and inscriptions.

Nigerian and Greek Scouts Shaking Hands and Jamboree Emblem — A34

1sh, Scouts dancing around campfire.

1963, Aug. 1 **Photo.** *Perf. 14*

145	A34	3p gray olive & red	.35	.25
146	A34	1sh red & black	.65	.65
a.		Souvenir sheet of 2, #145-146	1.75	1.75

11th Boy Scout Jamboree, Marathon, Greece, Aug. 1963.

Republic

First Aid — A35

Designs: 6p, Blood donors and ambulances. 1sh3p, Helping the needy.

1963, Sept. 1 Wmk. 335 *Perf. 14½*

147 A35 3p dk blue & red .35 .30
148 A35 6p dk green & red .60 .50
149 A35 1sh3p black & red 1.75 1.75
a. Souvenir sheet of 4, #149 11.00 11.00
Nos. 147-149 (3) 2.70 2.55

Cent. of the Intl. Red Cross.

Pres. Nnamdi Azikiwe and State House — A36

"Freedom of Worship" — A37

Designs: 1sh3p, President and Federal Supreme Court. 2sh6p, President and Parliament Building.

1963, Oct. 1 Unwmk. *Perf. 14x13*

150 A36 3p dull green & yel grn .20 .20
151 A36 1sh3p brown & bister .25 .20
a. Bister (head) omitted
152 A36 2sh6p vio bl & brt grnsh bl .50 .50
Nos. 150-152 (3) .95 .90

Independence Day, Oct. 1, 1963.

1963, Dec. 10 Wmk. 335 *Perf. 13*

3p, Charter & broken whip, horiz. 1sh3p, "Freedom from Want." 2sh6p, "Freedom of Speech."

153 A37 3p vermilion .20 .20
154 A37 6p green .20 .20
155 A37 1sh3p deep ultra .20 .20
156 A37 2sh6p red lilac .50 .50
Nos. 153-156 (4) 1.10 1.10

15th anniv. of the Universal Declaration of Human Rights.

Queen Nefertari — A38

1964, Mar. 8 Photo. *Perf. 14*

157 A38 6p shown 1.00 .35
158 A38 2sh6p Ramses II 2.00 2.00

UNESCO world campaign to save historic monuments in Nubia.

John F. Kennedy, US and Nigerian Flags A39

1sh3p, Kennedy bust & laurel. 5sh, Kennedy coin (US), flags of US & Nigeria at half-mast.

1964, Aug. 20 Unwmk. *Perf. 13x14*

159 A39 1sh3p black & lt vio .25 .25
160 A39 2sh6p multicolored .75 .75
161 A39 5sh multicolored 1.75 1.75
a. Souvenir sheet of 4 9.00 9.00
Nos. 159-161 (3) 2.75 2.75

Pres. John F. Kennedy (1917-63). No. 161a contains 4 imperf. stamps similar to No. 161 with simulated perforations.

Pres. Nnamdi Azikiwe — A40

Herbert Macaulay — A41

Design: 2sh6p, King Jaja of Opobo.

Perf. 14x13, 14

1964, Oct. 1 Photo. Unwmk.

162 A40 3p red brown .20 .20
163 A41 1sh3p green .30 .30
164 A41 2sh6p slate green .65 .65
Nos. 162-164 (3) 1.15 1.15

First anniversary of the Republic.

Boxing Gloves and Torch A42

Hurdling — A43

6p, High jump. 1sh3p, Woman runner, vert.

1964, Oct. *Perf. 14½*

165 A42 3p olive grn & sepia .25 .25
166 A42 6p dk blue & emer .35 .35
167 A42 1sh3p olive & brown .55 .55

Perf. 14

168 A43 2sh6p orange red & brn 1.50 1.50
a. Souvenir sheet of 4 4.50 4.50
Nos. 165-168 (4) 2.65 2.65

18th Olympic Games, Tokyo, Oct. 10-25. No. 168a contains 4 imperf. stamps similar to No. 168 with simulated perforations.

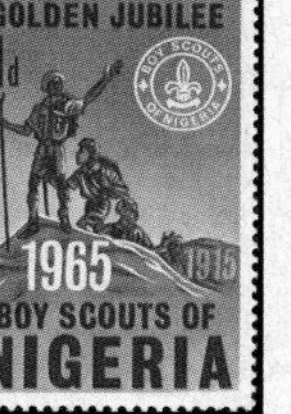

Mountain Climbing Scouts — A44

IQSY Emblem and Telstar, Map of Africa — A45

3p, Golden Jubilee emblem. 6p, Nigeria's Scout emblem & merit badges. 1sh3p, Lord Baden-Powell & Nigerian Boy Scout.

1965, Jan. Photo. *Perf. 14½*

169 A44 1p brown .20 .20
170 A44 3p emer, blk & red .20 .20
171 A44 6p yel grn, red & blk .25 .25
172 A44 1sh3p sep, yel & dk grn .75 .75
a. Souvenir sheet of 4 7.50 7.50
Nos. 169-172 (4) 1.40 1.40

Founding of the Nigerian Boy Scouts, 50th anniv.

No. 172a contains four imperf. stamps similar to No. 172 with simulated perforation.

1965, Apr. 1 Unwmk. *Perf. 14x13*

1sh3p, Explorer XII over map of Africa.

173 A45 6p grnsh bl & vio .20 .20
174 A45 1sh3p lilac & green .40 .40

Intl. Quiet Sun Year, 1964-65. Printed in sheets of 12 (4x3) with ornamental borders and inscriptions.

ITU Emblem, Drummer, Man at Desk and Telephone A46

Cent. of the ITU: 1sh3p, ITU emblem and telecommunication tower, vert. 5sh, ITU emblem, Relay satellite and map of Africa showing Nigeria.

Perf. 11x11½, 11½x11

1965, Aug. 2 Photo. Unwmk.

175 A46 3p ocher, red & blk .35 .25
176 A46 1sh3p ultra, grn & blk 1.50 1.50
177 A46 5sh multicolored 6.00 6.00
Nos. 175-177 (3) 7.85 7.75

ICY Emblem, Diesel Locomotive and Camel Caravan A47

ICY Emblem and: 1sh, Students and hospital, Lagos. 2sh6p, Kainji Dam, Niger River.

Perf. 14x15

1965, Sept. 1 Wmk. 335

178 A47 3p orange, grn & car 3.00 .35
179 A47 1sh ultra, blk & yel 3.00 .50
180 A47 2sh6p ultra, yel & grn 10.00 7.50
Nos. 178-180 (3) 16.00 8.35

Intl. Cooperation Year and 20th anniv. of the UN.

Stone Images, Ikom — A48

Designs: 3p, Carved frieze, horiz. 5sh, Seated man, Taba bronze.

Perf. 14x15, 15x14

1965, Oct. 1 Photo. Unwmk.

181 A48 3p ocher, black & red .20 .20
182 A48 1sh3p lt ultra, grn & reddish brn .40 .40
183 A48 5sh emer, dk brn & reddish brn 1.75 1.75
Nos. 181-183 (3) 2.35 2.35

Second anniversary of the Republic.

Elephants A49

Designs: ½p, Lioness and cubs, vert. 1½p, Splendid sunbird. 2p, Weaverbirds. 3p, Cheetah. 4p, Leopard and cubs. 6p, Saddle-billed storks, vert. 9p, Gray parrots. 1sh, Kingfishers. 1sh3p, Crowned cranes. 2sh6p, Buffon's kobs (antelopes). 5sh, Giraffes. 10sh, Hippopotami, vert. £1, Buffalos.

"MAURICE FIEVET" below Design.*

Perf. 12x12½, 12½x12, 14x13½ (1p, 2p, 3p, 4p, 9p)

1965-66 Photo.

Size: 23x38mm, 38x23mm

184 A49 ½p multicolored 1.00 *1.60*
185 A49 1p red & multi .50 .20
186 A49 1½p lt blue & multi 7.50 *9.00*
187 A49 2p brt red & multi 3.25 .20
a. White "2d" ('70) 7.50 2.50
188 A49 3p brt grn, yel & dl brn 1.25 .25
189 A49 4p lilac & multi .50 *3.00*
a. Perf 12½x12 .60 .20
b. "4" 5mm wide ('71) 4.00 1.25
190 A49 6p violet & multi 2.10 .30
191 A49 9p blue & orange 3.00 .50

Perf. 12½

Size: 45x26mm, 26x45mm

192 A49 1sh gray & multi 2.75 .60
a. Red omitted
193 A49 1sh3p brt bl & multi 10.00 1.00
194 A49 2sh6p dk brn, yel & ocher 1.00 *1.75*
195 A49 5sh brn, yel & red brown 2.25 3.00
196 A49 10sh grnsh bl & multi 7.50 3.00
197 A49 £1 brt green & multi 17.50 8.00
Nos. 184-197 (14) 60.10 32.40

* The designer's name, Maurice Fievet, appears at right or left, in small or large capitals. Nos. 187a and 189b have "MAURICE FIEVET" at right, 5mm wide. No. 187a has "2d" in white instead of yellow. No. 189b has "REPUBLIC" and "4d" larger, bolder.

Issued: ½p, 1p, 11/1/65; 2p, 4/1/66; 1½p, #189a, 6p, 1sh, 1sh3p, 2sh6p, 5sh, 10sh, 1£, 5/2/66; 3p, 9p, 10/17/66; 4p, 1966.

Nine values were overprinted "F. G. N./ F. G. N." (Federal Government of Nigeria) in 1969. They were not issued, but some were irregularly sold. Later the Nigerian Philatelic Service sold copies, stating they were not postally valid.

See Nos. 258-267.

No. 110 Overprinted in Red: "COMMONWEALTH / P.M. MEETING / 11. Jan. 1966"

Perf. 14½x14

1966, Jan. 11 Photo. Wmk. 335

198 A22 2sh6p yellow & black .50 .50

Conf. of British Commonwealth Prime Ministers, Lagos.

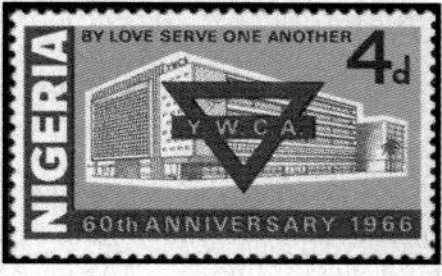

YWCA Building, Lagos A50

Unwmk.

1966, Sept. 1 Litho. *Perf. 14*

199 A50 4p yel, green & multi .20 .20
200 A50 9p brt green & multi .30 .30

60th anniv. of the Nigerian YWCA.

Lineman and Telephone A51

Designs: 4p, Flag and letter carrying pigeon, vert. 2sh6p, Niger Bridge.

Perf. 14½x14, 14x14½

1966, Oct. 1 Photo. Wmk. 335

201 A51 4p green .20 .20
202 A51 1sh6p lilac, blk & sep .60 .60
203 A51 2sh6p multicolored 1.00 1.00
Nos. 201-203 (3) 1.80 1.80

Third anniversary of the Republic.

Book, Chemical Apparatus, Carved Head and UNESCO Emblem A52

1966, Nov. 4 *Perf. 14½x14*

204 A52 4p dl org, mar & blk .50 .20
205 A52 1sh6p bl grn, plum & blk 2.00 2.00
206 A52 2sh6p pink, plum & blk 3.75 3.75
Nos. 204-206 (3) 6.25 5.95

20th anniv. of UNESCO.

Surveyors and Hydrological Decade Emblem — A53

Design: 2sh6p, Water depth gauge on dam and Hydrological Decade emblem, vert.

Perf. 14½x14, 14x14½

1967, Feb. 1 Photo. Wmk. 335

207 A53 4p multicolored .20 .20
208 A53 2sh6p multicolored 1.25 1.25

Hydrological Decade (UNESCO), 1965-74.

Weather Satellite Orbiting Earth A54

1sh6p, Storm over land & sea & World Meteorological Organization emblem.

1967, Mar. 23 Photo. *Perf. 14½x14*

209 A54 4p dp ultra & brt rose .25 .20
210 A54 1sh6p ultra & yellow 1.00 1.00

World Meteorological Day, March 23.

Eyo Masqueraders — A55

1sh6p, Acrobat. 2sh6p, Stilt dancer, vert.

Perf. 11x11½, 11½x11

1967, Oct. 1 Photo. Unwmk.

211 A55 4p multicolored .25 .20
212 A55 1sh6p turq bl & multi 1.00 1.00
213 A55 2sh6p pale grn & multi 1.50 1.25
Nos. 211-213 (3) 2.75 2.45

4th anniversary of the Federal Republic.

Vaccination of Cattle A56

1967, Dec. 1 *Perf. 14½x14*

214 A56 4p maroon & multi .20 .20
215 A56 1sh6p ultra & multi .80 *1.00*

Campaign to eradicate cattle plague.

Anopheles Mosquito and Sick Man — A57

20th anniv. of the WHO: 4p, WHO emblem and vaccination.

1968, Apr. 7 Litho. *Perf. 14*

216 A57 4p dp lil rose & blk .20 .20
217 A57 1sh6p org yel & blk .60 .35

Shackled Hands, Map of Nigeria and Human Rights Flame A58

Design: 1sh6p, Flag of Nigeria and human rights flame, vert.

1968, July 1 Photo. *Perf. 14*

218 A58 4p dp blue, yel & blk .20 .20
219 A58 1sh6p green, blk & red .55 .55

International Human Rights Year.

Hand and Doves — A59

1968, Oct. 1 Unwmk. *Perf. 14*

220 A59 4p brt blue & multi .20 .20
221 A59 1sh6p black & multi .25 .25

5th anniversary of the Federal Republic.

Olympic Rings, Nigerian Flag and Athletes A60

4p, Map of Nigeria and Olympic rings.

1968, Oct. 14 Photo. *Perf. 14*

222 A60 4p red, blk & emer .20 .20
223 A60 1sh6p multicolored .50 .50

19th Olympic Games, Mexico City, 10/12-27.

G.P.O., Lagos A61

1969, Apr. 11 Unwmk. *Perf. 14*

224 A61 4p emerald & black .20 .20
225 A61 1sh6p dk blue & black .25 .25

Opening of the Nigerian Philatelic Service of the GPO, Lagos.

Gen. Yakubu Gowon and Victoria Zakari A62

Perf. 13x13½

1969, Sept. 20 Litho. Unwmk.

226 A62 4p emerald & choc .35 .20
227 A62 1sh6p emerald & black .80 .60

Wedding of Yakubu Gowon, head of state of Nigeria, and Miss Victoria Zakari, Apr. 19, 1969.

Development Bank Emblem and "5" — A63

Design: 1sh6p, Emblem and rays.

1969, Oct. 18 Litho. *Perf. 14*

228 A63 4p dk bl, blk & org .20 .20
229 A63 1sh6p dk pur, yel & blk .25 *.50*

African Development Bank, 5th anniv.

ILO Emblem A64

50th anniv. of the ILO: 1sh6p, ILO emblem and world map.

1969, Nov. 15 Photo.

230 A64 4p purple & black .20 .20
231 A64 1sh6p green & black .55 *.80*

Tourist Year Emblem and Musicians A65

12-Spoke Wheel and Arms of Nigeria A66

Designs: 4p, Olumo Rock and Tourist Year emblem, horiz. 1sh6p, Assob Falls.

1969, Dec. 30 Photo. *Perf. 14*

232 A65 4p blue & multi .20 .20
233 A65 1sh emerald & black .35 .30
234 A65 1sh6p multicolored 1.40 .75
Nos. 232-234 (3) 1.95 1.25

International Year of African Tourism.

Perf. 11½x11, 11x11½

1970, May 28 Photo. Unwmk.

Designs: 4p, Map of Nigeria and tree with 12 fruits representing 12 tribes. 1sh6p, People bound by common destiny and map of Nigeria. 2sh, Torch with 12 flames and map of Africa, horiz.

235 A66 4p gold, blue & blk .20 .20
236 A66 1sh gold & multi .20 .20
237 A66 1sh6p green & black .25 .20
238 A66 2sh bl, org, gold & black .40 .30
Nos. 235-238 (4) 1.05 .90

Establishment of a 12-state administrative structure in Nigeria.

Opening of New UPU Headquarters, Bern — A67

1970, June 29 Unwmk. *Perf. 14*

239 A67 4p purple & yellow .30 .20
240 A67 1sh6p blue & vio blue .50 .35

UN Emblem and Charter — A68

Student — A69

25th anniv. of the UN: 1sh6p, UN emblem and headquarters, New York.

1970, Sept. 1 Photo. *Perf. 14*

241 A68 4p brn org, buff & blk .20 .20
242 A68 1sh6p dk bl, gold & bis brn .30 .20

1970, Sept. 30 Litho. *Perf. 14x13½*

Designs: 2p, Oil drilling platform. 6p, Durbar horsemen. 9p, Soldier and sailors raising flag. 1sh, Soccer player. 1sh6p, Parliament Building. 2sh, Kainji Dam. 2sh6p, Export products: Timber, rubber, peanuts, cocoa and palm produce.

243 A69 2p blue & multi .20 .20
244 A69 4p blue & multi .20 .20
245 A69 6p blue & multi .30 .20
246 A69 9p blue & multi .45 .20
247 A69 1sh blue & multi .45 .20
248 A69 1sh6p blue & multi .45 .25
249 A69 2sh blue & multi .90 .90
250 A69 2sh6p blue & multi .90 .90
Nos. 243-250 (8) 3.85 3.05

Ten years of independence.

Black and White Men Uprooting Racism — A70

Ibibio Mask, c. 1900 — A71

Designs: 4p, Black and white school children and globe, horiz. 1sh6p, World map with black and white stripes. 2sh, Black and white men, shoulder to shoulder, horiz.

Perf. 13½x14, 14x13½

1971, Mar. 22 Photo. Unwmk.

251 A70 4p multicolored .20 .20
252 A70 1sh yellow & multi .20 .20
253 A70 1sh6p blue, yel & blk .20 .35
254 A70 2sh multicolored .20 .60
Nos. 251-254 (4) .80 1.35

Intl. year against racial discrimination.

1971, Sept. 30 *Perf. 13½x14*

Nigerian Antiquities: 1sh3p, Bronze mask of a King of Benin, c. 1700. 1sh9p, Bronze figure of a King of Ife.

255 A71 4p lt blue & black .20 .20
256 A71 1sh3p yellow bis & blk .20 .35
257 A71 1sh9p apple grn, dp grn & blk .45 .60
Nos. 255-257 (3) .85 1.15

Type of 1965-66 Redrawn
Imprint: "N.S.P. & M. Co. Ltd."
Added to "MAURICE FIEVET"

Perf. 13x13½; 14x13½ (6p)

1969-72 Photo.

Size: 38x23mm

258 A49 1p red & multi 4.25 1.50
259 A49 2p brt red & multi 3.00 .60
260 A49 3p multi ('71) .75 *1.40*
261 A49 4p lilac & multi 11.00 .20
262 A49 6p brt vio & multi ('71) 2.25 .20
263 A49 9p dl bl & dp org ('70) 8.50 .40

Size: 45x26mm

264 A49 1sh multi ('71) 3.00 .20
265 A49 1sh3p multi ('71) 14.00 2.50
266 A49 2sh6p multi ('72) 12.50 4.50
267 A49 5sh multi ('72) 4.25 *8.50*
Nos. 258-267 (10) 63.50 20.00

"Maurice Fievet" imprint on No. 259 exists in two lengths, 5mm and 5½mm.

"Maurice Fievet" imprint on No. 260 exists in two lengths, 5½mm and 8½mm..

UNICEF Emblem and Children — A72

Satellite Earth Station — A73

UNICEF 25th anniv.: 1sh3p, Mother and child. 1sh9p, African mother carrying child on back.

1971, Dec. 11 *Perf. 14*

270 A72 4p purple & yellow .20 .20
271 A72 1sh3p org, pur & plum .20 *.45*
272 A72 1sh9p blue & dk blue .20 *.65*
Nos. 270-272 (3) .60 1.30

1971, Dec. 30 Photo. *Perf. 14*

Various views of satellite communications earth station, Lanlate, Nigeria. All horiz.

273 A73 4p multicolored .20 .20
274 A73 1sh3p blue, blk & grn .35 .65
275 A73 1sh9p orange & blk .60 .95
276 A73 3sh brt pink & blk 1.10 1.50
Nos. 273-276 (4) 2.25 3.30

Satellite communications earth station, Lanlate, Nigeria.

Fair Emblem — A74

Fair Emblem and: 1sh3p, Map of Africa, horiz. 1sh9p, Globe with map of Africa.

Perf. 13½x13, 13x13½

1972, Feb. 23 Litho.

277 A74 4p multicolored .20 .20
278 A74 1sh3p dull pur, yel & gold .20 *.40*
279 A74 1sh9p orange, yel & blk .20 *.70*
Nos. 277-279 (3) .60 1.30

First All-Africa Trade Fair, Nairobi, Kenya, Feb. 23-Mar. 5.

Traffic A75

Designs: 1sh3p, Traffic flow at circle. 1sh9p, Car and truck on road. 3sh, Intersection with lights and pedestrians.

1972, June 23 Photo. *Perf. 13x13½*

280 A75 4p orange & blk .50 .20
281 A75 1sh3p lt blue & multi 1.50 1.00
282 A75 1sh9p emerald & multi 2.00 1.25
283 A75 3sh yellow & multi 3.00 *3.50*
Nos. 280-283 (4) 7.00 5.95

Introduction of right-hand driving in Nigeria, Apr. 2, 1972.

Nok Style Terra-cotta Head, Katsina Ala — A76

1sh3p, Roped bronze vessel, Igbo Ukwu. 1sh9p, Bone harpoon, Daima, horiz.

Perf. 13½x13, 13x13½

1972, Sept. 1 Litho.

284 A76 4p dk blue & multi .20 .20
285 A76 1sh3p gold & multi .45 *.55*
286 A76 1sh9p dp blue & multi .60 *.75*
Nos. 284-286 (3) 1.25 1.50

All-Nigeria Festival of the Arts, Kaduna, Dec. 9.

Games Emblem and Soccer A77

Designs: 5k, Running. 18k, Table tennis. 25k, Stadium, vert.

1973, Jan. 8 Litho. *Perf. 13x13½*

287 A77 5k lilac, blue & blk .20 .20
288 A77 12k multicolored .45 .55
289 A77 18k yellow & multi .75 *1.10*
290 A77 25k brown & multi 1.25 *1.40*
Nos. 287-290 (4) 2.65 3.25

2nd All-Africa Games, Lagos, Jan. 7-18.

Hides and Skins A78

Designs: 2k, Natural gas tanks. 3k, Cement works. 5k, Cattle ranching. 7k, Lumbermill. 8k, Oil refinery. 10k, Leopards, Yankari Game Reserve. 12k, New civic building. 15k, Sugar cane harvesting. 18k, Palm oil production, vert. 20k, Vaccine production. 25k, Modern docks. 30k, Argungu Fishing Festival, vert. 35k, Textile industry. 50k, Pottery, vert. 1n, Eko Bridge. 2n, Teaching Hospital, Lagos.

Imprint at left: "N S P & M Co Ltd" 6mm on Litho. Stamps, 5¼ mm on Photo. Stamps

Litho.; Photo. (50k)

1973-74 Unwmk. *Perf. 14*

291 A78 1k multi, buff imprint *.20 .20*
292 A78 2k multi ('74) *2.00 .75*
293 A78 3k multi ('74) *.20 .20*
294 A78 5k grn & multi ('74) *2.85 .80*
295 A78 7k multicolored *.60 .60*
296 A78 8k multicolored *.40 .20*
297 A78 10k multicolored *3.75 .20*
298 A78 12k multicolored *.75 .75*
299 A78 15k multicolored *.40 .40*
300 A78 18k multicolored *.50 .25*
301 A78 20k multicolored *.65 .25*
302 A78 25k multicolored *.85 .45*
303 A78 30k multicolored *.60 .60*
304 A78 35k multicolored *5.00 3.00*
305 A78 50k black background *3.25 2.25*
306 A78 1n multicolored *1.25 1.10*
307 A78 2n multicolored *2.50 2.50*
Nos. 291-307 (17) 25.75 14.50

Imprint on 35k has periods.

Imprint at left: "N S P & M Co Ltd"

1973 Photo., Imprint 5¼mm

291a A78 1k multi, dk grn foliage *1.20 .60*
291b A78 1k multi, brt grn foliage *.20 .20*
292a A78 2k multicolored *.35 .20*
294a A78 5k multi, emer fields *.60 .50*
294b A78 5k multi, yel grn fields *.50 .20*
297a A78 10k multicolored *.75 .65*
298a A78 12k multicolored *9.00 6.50*
300a A78 18k multicolored *9.00 1.65*
301a A78 20k multicolored *9.00 3.00*
303a A78 30k multicolored *10.00 6.00*
305a A78 50k dk brn background *1.25 .75*
306a A78 1n multicolored *6.75 6.75*
Nos. 291a-306a (12) 48.60 27.00

Nos. 300a, 305a and 306a have periods in the imprint.

1975-80 Wmk. 379

291c A78 1k multi, dk grn foliage *.60 .60*
292b A78 2k multi ('75) *.85 .20*
293a A78 3k multi ('75) *.20 .20*
294c A78 5k emerald fields ('76) *1.00 .20*
295a A78 7k multi ('80) *1.25 1.00*
296a A78 8k multi ('76) *1.50 .75*
297b A78 10k multi ('76) *.90 .20*
299a A78 15k multicolored *1.50*
300b A78 18k multi ('78) *2.00 2.00*
301b A78 20k multi, pale pink table, door, windows ('79) *2.00 2.00*
302a A78 25k multi, pur barges *2.75 .25*
302b A78 25k multi, brn barges *2.75 .25*
305b A78 50k dk brn background, grn imprint *3.50 3.00*
307a A78 2n multicolored *6.00 6.00*

OAU Headquarters — A79

Designs: 18k, OAU flag, vert. 30k, Stairs leading to OAU emblem, vert.

1973, May 25 Litho. *Perf. 14*

308 A79 5k blue & multi .20 .20
309 A79 18k olive grn & multi .40 *.50*
310 A79 30k lilac & multi .65 *.80*
Nos. 308-310 (3) 1.25 1.50

Org. for African Unity, 10th anniv.

WMO Emblem, Weather Vane A80

1973, Sept. 4 Litho. *Perf. 13*

311 A80 5k multicolored .30 .25
312 A80 30k multicolored 1.60 *2.25*

Cent. of intl. meteorological cooperation.

View of Ibadan University A81

Designs: 12k, Campus, crest and graph showing growth, vert. 18k, Campus, students and crest. 30k, Teaching hospital.

1973, Nov. 17 *Perf. 14*

313 A81 5k lt blue & multi .20 .20
314 A81 12k lilac & multi .30 .30
315 A81 18k orange & multi .50 .50
316 A81 30k blue, org & blk .75 *1.00*
Nos. 313-316 (4) 1.75 2.00

University of Ibadan, 25th anniversary.

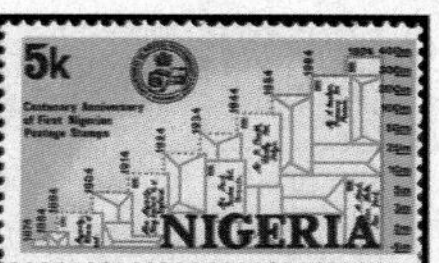

Growth of Mail, 1874-1974 A82

12k, Nigerian Post emblem & Northern Nigeria #18A. 18k, Postal emblem & Lagos #1. 30k, Map of Nigeria &means of transportation.

1974, June 10 Litho. *Perf. 14*

317 A82 5k green, black & org .20 .20
318 A82 12k green & multi .60 .60
319 A82 18k green, lilac & blk 1.40 1.40
320 A82 30k black & multi 1.75 1.75
Nos. 317-320 (4) 3.95 3.95

Centenary of first Nigerian postage stamps.

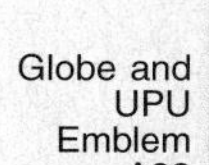

Globe and UPU Emblem A83

UPU cent.: 18k, World map and means of transportation. 30k, Letters.

1974, Oct. 9

321 A83 5k blue & multi .30 .20
322 A83 18k orange & multi 3.00 .75
323 A83 30k brown & multi 2.50 1.75
Nos. 321-323 (3) 5.80 2.70

Hungry and Well-fed Children — A84

Designs: 12k, Chicken farm, horiz. 30k, Irrigation project.

1974, Nov. 25 Litho. *Perf. 14*

324 A84 5k orange, blk & grn .20 .20
325 A84 12k multicolored .45 .55
326 A84 30k multicolored 1.10 *1.25*
Nos. 324-326 (3) 1.75 2.00

Freedom from Hunger.

A85

Map of Nigeria with Telex Network, Teleprinter — A86

1975, July 3 Litho. *Perf. 14*

327 A85 5k multicolored .20 .20
328 A85 12k multicolored .25 .25
329 A86 18k multicolored .35 .35
330 A86 30k multicolored .70 .70
Nos. 327-330 (4) 1.50 1.50

Inauguration of Nigeria Telex Network.

Queen Amina of Zaria (1536-1566) A87

Alexander Graham Bell A88

1975, Aug. 18 Litho. *Perf. 14*

331 A87 5k multicolored .20 .20
332 A87 18k multicolored 1.25 1.25
333 A87 30k multicolored 1.60 *1.90*
Nos. 331-333 (3) 3.05 3.35

International Women's Year.

1976, Mar. 10 Wmk. 379

Designs: 18k, Hands beating gong, modern telephone operator, horiz. 25k, Telephones, 1876, 1976.

334 A88 5k pink, black & ocher .20 .20
335 A88 18k deep lilac & multi .50 .55
336 A88 25k lt bl, vio bl & blk 1.00 1.10
Nos. 334-336 (3) 1.70 1.85

Centenary of first telephone call by Alexander Graham Bell, Mar. 10, 1876.

Children Going to School — A89

Designs: 5k, Child learning to write, horiz. 25k, Classroom.

1976, Sept. 20 Litho. *Perf. 14*

337 A89 5k multicolored .20 .20
338 A89 18k multicolored .60 .65
339 A89 25k multicolored .80 .90
Nos. 337-339 (3) 1.60 1.75

Launching of universal primary education in 1976.

Traditional Musical Instruments A90

5k, Carved mask (festival emblem). 10k, Natl. Arts Theater, Lagos. 12k, Nigerian & African women's hair styles. 30k, Nigerian carvings.

1976-77 **Wmk. 379**

340 A90 5k black, gold & grn .25 .25
341 A90 10k multicolored .40 .40
342 A90 12k multicolored .75 .75
343 A90 18k brown, ocher & blk 1.00 1.00
344 A90 30k multicolored 1.25 1.25
Nos. 340-344 (5) 3.65 3.65

2nd World Black and African Festival of Arts and Culture, Lagos, Jan. 15-Feb. 12, 1977.

Issued: 5k, 18k, 11/1; others 1/15/77.

Gen. Muhammed Broadcasting and Map of Nigeria — A91

Designs: 18k, Gen. Muhammed as Commander in Chief, vert. 30k, in battle dress, vert.

1977, Feb. 13 **Litho.** ***Perf. 14***

345 A91 5k multicolored .20 .20
346 A91 18k multicolored .60 .60
347 A91 30k multicolored 1.00 1.00
Nos. 345-347 (3) 1.80 1.80

Gen. Murtala Ramat Muhammed, Head of State and Commander in Chief, 1st death anniversary.

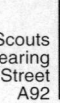

Scouts Clearing Street A92

5k, Senior and Junior Boy Scouts saluting, vert. 25k, Scouts working on farm. 30k, African Scout Jamboree emblem, map of Africa.

1977, Apr. 1 **Wmk. 379**

348 A92 5k multicolored .35 .35
349 A92 18k multicolored .75 .75
350 A92 25k multicolored 1.10 1.10
351 A92 30k multicolored 1.50 1.50
Nos. 348-351 (4) 3.70 3.70

First All-Africa Boy Scout Jamboree, Sherehills, Jos, Nigeria, Apr. 2-8, 1977.

Trade Fair Emblem A93

Emblem and: 5k, View of Fair grounds. 30k, Weaver and potter.

1977, Nov. 27 **Litho.** ***Perf. 13***

352 A93 5k multicolored .20 .20
353 A93 18k multicolored .55 .55
354 A93 30k multicolored .95 .95
Nos. 352-354 (3) 1.70 1.70

1st Lagos Intl. Trade Fair, Nov. 27-Dec. 11.

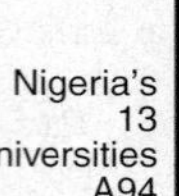

Nigeria's 13 Universities A94

12k, Map of West African highways and telecommunications network. 18k, Training of technicians, and cogwheel. 30k, World map and map of Argentina with Buenos Aires.

1978, Apr. 28 **Wmk. 379**

355 A94 5k multicolored .20 .20
356 A94 12k multicolored .30 .30
357 A94 18k multicolored .40 .40
358 A94 30k multicolored .80 .80
Nos. 355-358 (4) 1.70 1.70

Global Conf. on Technical Cooperation among Developing Countries, Buenos Aires.

Antenna and ITU Emblem A95

1978, May 17 **Litho.** ***Perf. 14***

359 A95 30k multicolored 1.00 1.00

10th World Telecommunications Day.

Students on Cassava Plantation A96

"Operation Feed the Nation": 18k, Woman working in backyard vegetable garden. 30k, Plantain harvest, vert.

1978, July 7 **Litho.** ***Perf. 14***

360 A96 5k multicolored .20 .20
361 A96 18k multicolored .40 .40
362 A96 30k multicolored .65 .65
Nos. 360-362 (3) 1.25 1.25

Mother Holding Sick Child A97

Designs: 12k, Sick boy at health station. 18k, Vaccination of children. 30k, Syringe and WHO emblem, vert.

1978, Aug. 31 **Wmk. 379**

363 A97 5k multicolored .20 .20
364 A97 12k multicolored .35 .35
365 A97 18k multicolored .50 .50
366 A97 30k multicolored .85 .85
Nos. 363-366 (4) 1.90 1.90

Global eradication of smallpox.

Bronze Horseman from Benin — A98

Anti-Apartheid Emblem — A99

Nigerian antiquities: 5k, Nok terracotta figure from Bwari. 12k, Bronze snail and animal from Igbo-Ukwu. 18k, Bronze statue of a king of Ife.

1978, Oct. 27 **Litho.** ***Perf. 14***

367 A98 5k multicolored .20 .20
368 A98 12k multicolored, horiz. .30 .30
369 A98 18k multicolored .40 .40
370 A98 30k multicolored .70 .70
Nos. 367-370 (4) 1.60 1.60

1978, Dec. 10 ***Perf. 14***

371 A99 18k red, yellow & black .45 .45

Anti-Apartheid Year.

Wright Brothers, Flyer A A100

18k, Nigerian Air Force fighters in formation.

1978, Dec. 28

372 A100 5k multicolored .30 .30
373 A100 18k multicolored .60 .60

75th anniversary of powered flight.

Murtala Muhammed Airport A101

1979, Mar. 15 **Litho.** ***Perf. 14***

374 A101 5k bright blue & black .50 .30

Inauguration of Murtala Muhammed Airport.

Young Stamp Collector A102

1979, Apr. 11

375 A102 5k multicolored .35 .20

Philatelic Week; Natl. Philatelic Service, 10th anniv.

Mother Nursing Child, IYC Emblem A103

18k, Children at study. 25k, Children at play, vert.

1979, June 28 **Wmk. 379** ***Perf. 14***

376 A103 5k multicolored .20 .20
377 A103 18k multicolored .35 .35
378 A103 25k multicolored .40 .40
Nos. 376-378 (3) .95 .95

International Year of the Child.

A104

A105

Design: 10k, Preparation of audio-visual material. 30k, Adult education class.

1979, July 25 **Photo. & Engr.**

379 A104 10k multicolored .20 .20
380 A104 30k multicolored .55 .55

Intl. Bureau of Education, Geneva, 50th anniv.

1979, Sept. 20 **Litho.** ***Perf. 13½x14***

381 A105 10k Necom house, Lagos .30 .30

Intl. Radio Consultative Committee (CCIR) of the ITU, 50th anniv.

Trainees and Survey Equipment A106

1979, Dec. 12 **Photo.** ***Perf. 14***

382 A106 10k multicolored .30 .30

Economic Commission for Africa, 21st anniv.

Soccer Cup and Ball on Map of Nigeria A107

1980, Mar. 8

383 A107 10k shown .20 .20
384 A107 30k Player, vert. .75 .75

12th African Cup of Nations Soccer Championship, Lagos and Ibadan, Mar.

Swimming, Moscow '80 Emblem A108

Litho. & Engr.

1980, July 19 ***Perf. 14***

385 A108 10k Wrestling, vert. .20 .20
386 A108 20k Long jump, vert. .30 .30
387 A108 30k shown .50 .50
388 A108 45k Women's basketball, vert. .75 .75
Nos. 385-388 (4) 1.75 1.75

22nd Summer Olympic Games, Moscow, July 19-Aug. 3.

Men Holding OPEC Emblem A109

1980, Sept. 15 **Litho. & Engr.**

389 A109 10k shown .20 .20
390 A109 45k Anniversary emblem, vert. .80 .80

OPEC, 20th anniversary.

First Steam Locomotive in Nigeria A110

1980, Oct. 2 **Wmk. 379** ***Perf. 14***

391 A110 10k shown .50 .50
392 A110 20k Unloading freight car 1.50 1.50
393 A110 30k Freight train 2.25 2.25
Nos. 391-393 (3) 4.25 4.25

Nigerian Railway Corp., 75th anniv.

Technician Performing Quality Control Test A111

1980, Oct. 14

394 A111 10k Scale, ruler, vert. .20 .20
395 A111 30k shown .55 .55

World Standards Day.

Map of West Africa showing ECOWAS Members, Modes of Communication — A112

1980, Nov. 5 **Litho. & Engr.**

396 A112 10k shown .20 .20
396A A112 25k Transportation .40 .40
397 A112 30k Map, cow, cocoa .60 .60
398 A112 45k Map, industrial symbols .85 .85
Nos. 396-398 (4) 2.05 2.05

Woman with Cane Sweeping — A113

Wmk. 379

1981, June 25 Litho. *Perf. 14*

399 A113 10k shown .20 .20
400 A113 30k Amputee photographer .50 .50

Intl. Year of the Disabled.

World Food Day A114

1981, Oct. 16 Litho. & Engr.

401 A114 10k Pres. Shenu Shagari .20 .20
402 A114 25k Produce, vert. .50 .50
403 A114 30k Tomato crop, vert. .60 .60
404 A114 45k Pig farm .90 .90
Nos. 401-404 (4) 2.20 2.20

Anti-apartheid Year — A115

1981, Dec. 10 Litho.

405 A115 30k Soweto riot .55 .55
406 A115 45k Police hitting man, vert. .80 .80

Scouting Year A116

1982, Feb. 22 Litho. *Perf. 14*

407 A116 30k Animal first aid .75 .75
408 A116 45k Baden-Powell, scouts 1.25 1.25

TB Bacillus Centenary A117

1982, Mar. 24 Litho. *Perf. 14*

409 A117 10k Inoculation .30 .30
410 A117 30k Research .55 .55
411 A117 45k Patient being x-rayed, vert. .90 .90
Nos. 409-411 (3) 1.75 1.75

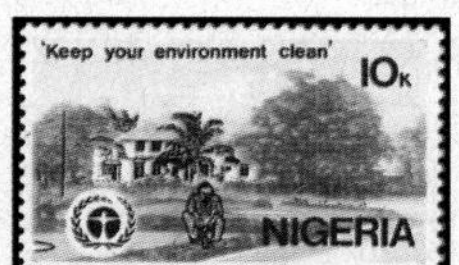

10th Anniv. of UN Conference on Human Environment — A118

1982, June 10 Litho.

412 A118 10k Keep your environment clean .20 .20
413 A118 20k Check air pollution .30 .30
414 A118 30k Preserve natural environment .40 .40
415 A118 45k Reafforestation concerns all .70 .70
Nos. 412-415 (4) 1.60 1.60

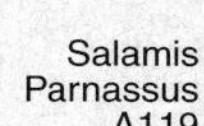

Salamis Parnassus A119

1982, Sept. 15 Litho.

416 A119 10k shown .30 .25
417 A119 20k Papilio zalmoxis .65 .55
418 A119 30k Pachylophus beckeri 1.25 1.00
419 A119 45k Papilio hesperus 1.75 1.40
Nos. 416-419 (4) 3.95 3.20

25th Anniv. of Natl. Museum A120

1982, Nov. 18 Wmk. 379

420 A120 10k Statuettes, vert. .20 .20
421 A120 20k Bronze leopard .40 .40
422 A120 30k Soapstone seated figure, vert. .55 .55
423 A120 45k Wooden helmet mask .90 .90
Nos. 420-423 (4) 2.05 2.05

Family Day — A121

Commonwealth Day — A122

1983, Mar. 8 Litho. *Perf. 14*

424 A121 10k Extended family, house, horiz. .25 .25
425 A121 30k Family .75 .75

1983, Mar. 14

426 A122 10k Satellite view, horiz. .20 .20
427 A122 25k Natl. Assembly buildings, horiz. .50 .50
428 A122 30k Oil exploration .65 .65
429 A122 45k Runners .90 .90
Nos. 426-429 (4) 2.25 2.25

10th Anniv. of Natl. Youth Service Corps A123

1983, May 25 Litho. *Perf. 14*

430 A123 10k Construction .25 .25
431 A123 25k Climbing wall, vert. .55 .55
432 A123 30k Marching, vert. .75 .75
Nos. 430-432 (3) 1.55 1.55

World Communications Year — A124

Wmk. 379

1983, July 22 Litho. *Perf. 14*

433 A124 10k Mailman, vert. .20 .20
434 A124 25k Newspaper stand .50 .50
435 A124 30k Traditional horn messenger .65 .65
436 A124 45k TV news broadcast .95 .95
Nos. 433-436 (4) 2.30 2.30

World Fishery A125

1983, Sept. 22 Litho. Wmk. 379

437 A125 10k Pink shrimp .20 .20
438 A125 25k Long neck groaker .50 .50
439 A125 30k Barracuda .60 .60
440 A125 45k Fishing technique .90 .90
Nos. 437-440 (4) 2.20 2.20

Boys' Brigade, 75th Anniv. A126

1983, Oct. 14 *Perf. 14*

441 A126 10k Boys, emblem, vert. .30 .30
442 A126 30k Food production 1.50 1.50
443 A126 45k Skill training 2.50 2.50
Nos. 441-443 (3) 4.30 4.30

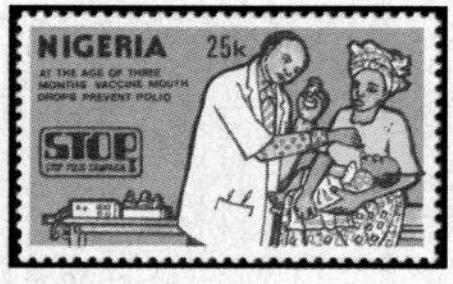

Fight Against Polio Campaign A127

1984, Feb. 29 Litho. *Perf. 14*

444 A127 10k Crippled boy, vert. .20 .20
445 A127 25k Vaccination .60 .60
446 A127 30k Healthy child, vert. .80 .80
Nos. 444-446 (3) 1.60 1.60

Hartebeests — A128

1984, May 25 Wmk. 379 *Perf. 14*

447 A128 10k Waterbuck, vert. .30 .30
448 A128 25k shown .60 .60
449 A128 30k Buffalo .75 .75
450 A128 45k African golden monkey, vert. 1.10 1.10
Nos. 447-450 (4) 2.75 2.75

Central Bank of Nigeria, 25th Anniv. A129

1984, July 2 Wmk. 379

451 A129 10k £1 note, 1968 .20 .20
452 A129 25k Bank .55 .55
453 A129 30k £5 note, 1959 .70 .70
Nos. 451-453 (3) 1.45 1.45

1984 Summer Olympics, Los Angeles A130

African Development Bank, 20th Anniv. A131

Wmk. 379

1984, Aug. 9 Litho. *Perf. 14*

454 A130 10k Boxing .20 .20
455 A130 25k Discus .40 .40
456 A130 30k Weight lifting .50 .50
457 A130 45k Bicycling .75 .75
Nos. 454-457 (4) 1.85 1.85

1984, Sept. 10

10k, Irrigation project, Lesotho. 25k, Bomi Hills roadway, Liberia. 30k, Education development, Seychelles. 45k, Coal mining & transportation, Niger. #459-461 horiz.

458 A131 10k multicolored .30 .30
459 A131 25k multicolored .55 .55
460 A131 30k multicolored .75 .75
461 A131 45k multicolored 1.20 1.20
Nos. 458-461 (4) 2.80 2.80

A132

A132a

A132b

A132c

Rare bird species.

1984, Oct. 24

462 A132 10k Pin-tailed whydah .50 .50
463 A132a 25k Spur-winged plover 2.00 2.00
464 A132b 30k Red bishop 2.25 2.25
465 A132c 45k Francolin 3.50 3.50
Nos. 462-465 (4) 8.25 8.25

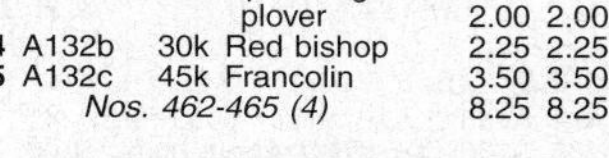

Intl. Civil Aviation Organization, 40th Anniv. — A132d

1984, Dec. 7 Litho. *Perf. 14*

465A A132d 10k shown .50 .50
465B A132d 45k Jet circling Earth 2.00 2.00

Fight Against Indiscipline A133

1985, Feb. 27

466 A133 20k Encourage punctuality .35 .35
467 A133 50k Discourage bribery .95 .95

Intl. Youth Year — A134

OPEC, 25th Anniv. — A135

1985, June 5

468 A134 20k Sports, horiz. .25 .25
469 A134 50k Nationalism .65 .65
470 A134 55k Service organizations .75 .75
Nos. 468-470 (3) 1.65 1.65

1985, Sept. 15

471	A135	20k	shown	1.00	1.00
472	A135	50k	World map, horiz.	2.00	2.00

Natl. Independence, 25th Anniv. — A136

1985, Sept. 25

473	A136	20k	Oil refinery	.30	.30
474	A136	50k	Map of states	.75	.75
475	A136	55k	Monument	.80	.80
476	A136	60k	Eleme Oil Refinery	.90	.90
a.			Souvenir sheet of 4, #473-476	6.50	
			Nos. 473-476 (4)	2.75	2.75

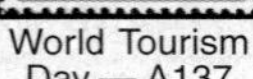

World Tourism Day — A137

UN, 40th Anniv. — A138

1985, Sept. 27

477	A137	20k	Waterfalls	.25	.25
478	A137	50k	Crafts, horiz.	.60	.60
479	A137	55k	Carved calabashes, flag	.65	.65
480	A137	60k	Leather goods, rug	.75	.75
			Nos. 477-480 (4)	2.25	2.25

1985, Oct. 7

481	A138	20k	Emblem, map, flag	.40	.40
482	A138	50k	UN building, horiz.	1.00	1.00
483	A138	55k	Emblem, horiz.	1.10	1.10
			Nos. 481-483 (3)	2.50	2.50

Admission of Nigeria to UN, 25th anniv.

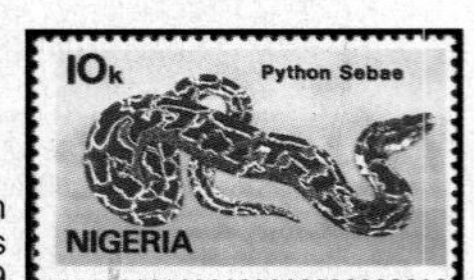

African Reptiles A139

1986, Apr. 15 Wmk. 379 *Perf. 14*

484	A139	10k	Python	.20	.20
485	A139	20k	Crocodile	.70	.70
486	A139	25k	Gopher tortoise	.85	.85
487	A139	30k	Chameleon	1.00	1.00
			Nos. 484-487 (4)	2.75	2.75

Volkswagen Automobile Assembly Factory A140

Designs: 1k, Social worker with children, vert. 5k, Modern housing development. 10k, Modern method of harvesting coconuts, vert. 15k, Port activities. 20k, Tecoma stans, flower, vert. 25k, Medical care. 30k, Birom folk dancers. 35k, Telephone operators. 40k, Nkpokiti dancers, vert. 45k, Hibiscus. 50k, Modern p.o. 1n, Stone quarry. 2n, Technical education.

1986, June 16 Wmk. 379 *Perf. 14*

488	A140	1k	multicolored	.20	.20
489	A140	2k	multicolored	.20	.20
490	A140	5k	multicolored	.20	.20
491	A140	10k	multicolored	.20	.20
492	A140	15k	multicolored	.20	.20
493	A140	20k	multicolored	.20	.20
494	A140	25k	multicolored	.20	.20
494A	A140	30k	multicolored	.20	.20
495	A140	35k	multicolored	.20	.20
496	A140	40k	multicolored	.20	.20
497	A140	45k	multicolored	.25	.25
498	A140	50k	multicolored	.25	.25
499	A140	1n	multicolored	.50	.50
500	A140	2n	multicolored	1.00	1.00
			Nos. 488-500 (14)	4.00	4.00

Use of some denominations began as early as 1984. Date of issue of the 30k is not definite.

Intl. Peace Year A141

1986, June 20 Litho. *Perf. 14*

501	A141	10k	Emblem	.30	.30
502	A141	20k	Hands touching globe	.60	.60

Insects A142

1986, July 14

503	A142	10k	Goliath beetle	.25	.25
504	A142	20k	Wasp	.75	.75
505	A142	25k	Cricket	.90	.90
506	A142	30k	Carpet beetle	1.25	1.25
a.			Souvenir sheet of 4, #503-506	6.00	6.00
			Nos. 503-506 (4)	3.15	3.15

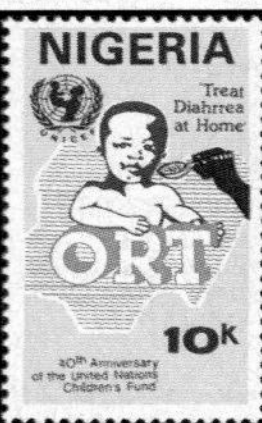

UNICEF, 40th Anniv. — A143

Institute of Intl. Affairs, 25th Anniv. — A144

1986, Nov. 11

507	A143	10k	Oral rehydration	.20	.20
508	A143	20k	Immunization	.40	.40
509	A143	25k	Breast-feeding	.80	.80
510	A143	30k	Mother playing with child	.90	.90
			Nos. 507-510 (4)	2.30	2.30

UN Child Survival Campaign.

1986, Dec. 13

511	A144	20k	Intl. understanding, horiz.	.70	.70
512	A144	30k	shown	.90	.90

Seashells A145

1987, Mar. 31

513	A145	10k	Freshwater clam	1.75	1.75
514	A145	20k	Periwinkle	1.75	1.75
515	A145	25k	Bloddy cockle	1.75	1.75
516	A145	30k	Mangrove oyster	1.75	1.75
			Nos. 513-516 (4)	7.00	7.00

A146

A147

1987, May 28

517	A146	10k	Blue pea but	.20	.20
518	A146	20k	Hibiscus	.20	.20
519	A147	25k	Acanthus montanus	.20	.20
520	A147	30k	Combretum racemosum	.20	.20
			Nos. 517-520 (4)	.80	.80

Hair Styles A148

Intl. Year of Shelter for the Homeless A149

1987, Sept. 15 Wmk. 379 *Perf. 14*

521	A148	10k	Doka	.20	.20
522	A148	20k	Eting	.20	.20
523	A148	25k	Agogo	.20	.20
524	A148	30k	Goto	.20	.20
			Nos. 521-524 (4)	.80	.80

1987, Dec. 10 Litho.

525	A149	20k	Homeless family	.20	.20
526	A149	30k	Moving to new home	.20	.20

A150

A152

A151

1988, Feb. 17 Litho. *Perf. 14*

527	A150	20k	Help the Needy	.75	.50
528	A150	30k	Care for the sick	1.25	.90

Intl. Red Cross and Red Crescent Organizations, 125th annivs.

1988, Apr. 7 Wmk. 379 *Perf. 14*

529	A151	10k	Immunization	.30	.25
530	A151	20k	Map, globe, emblem	.70	.50
531	A151	30k	Mobile hospital	.80	.75
			Nos. 529-531 (3)	1.80	1.50

WHO, 40th anniv.

1988, May 25

532	A152	10k	shown	.20	.20
533	A152	20k	Emblem, map, 4 men	.20	.20

Organization of African Unity, 25th anniv.

Shrimp A153

1988, June 2

534	A153	10k	Pink shrimp	.20	.20
535	A153	20k	Tiger shrimp	.60	.60
536	A153	25k	Deepwater roseshrimp	.70	.70
537	A153	30k	Estuarine prawn	.75	.75
a.			Miniature sheet of 4, #534-537	2.75	2.75
			Nos. 534-537 (4)	2.25	2.25

1988 Summer Olympics, Seoul A154

1988, Sept. 6 Wmk. 379 *Perf. 14*

538	A154	10k	Weight lifting	.30	.30
539	A154	20k	Boxing	.30	.30
540	A154	30k	Running, vert.	.30	.30
			Nos. 538-540 (3)	.90	.90

A155

A156

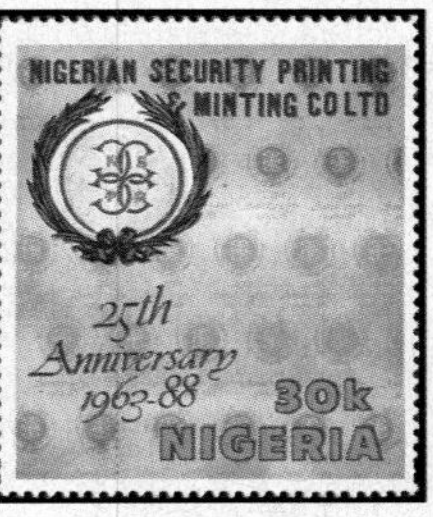

Nigerian Security Printing and Minting Co., Ltd., 25th Anniv. A157

1988, Oct. 28

541	A155	10k	Bank note production	.35	.35
542	A155	20k	Coin production	.35	.35
543	A156	25k	Products	.35	.35
544	A157	30k	Anniv. emblem	.35	.35
			Nos. 541-544 (4)	1.40	1.40

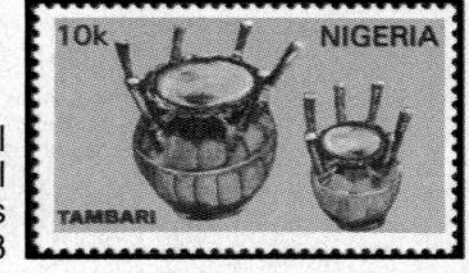

Traditional Musical Instruments A158

Wmk. 379

1989, June 29 Litho. *Perf. 14*

545	A158	10k	Tambari	.40	.40
546	A158	20k	Kundung	.40	.40
547	A158	25k	Ibid	.40	.40
548	A158	30k	Dundun	.40	.40
			Nos. 545-548 (4)	1.60	1.60

African Development Bank, 25th Anniv. — A159

Nigerian Girl Guides Assoc., 70th Anniv. — A160

1989, Sept. 10

549	A159	10k	Reservoir, Mali	.25	.25
550	A159	20k	Irrigation project, Gambia	.25	.25
551	A159	25k	Bank headquarters	.25	.25
552	A159	30k	shown	.25	.25
			Nos. 549-552 (4)	1.00	1.00

Nos. 549-551 horiz.

1989, Sept. 16

553	A160	10k	Campfire, horiz.	.55	.55
554	A160	20k	shown	.55	.55

A161

A162

Traditional costumes.

1989, Oct. 26

555	A161	10k Etubom	.40	.40
556	A161	20k Fulfulde	.40	.40
557	A161	25k Aso-ofi	.40	.40
558	A161	30k Fuska Kura	.40	.40
		Nos. 555-558 (4)	1.60	1.60

1990, Jan. 18

559	A162	10k shown	.35	.35
560	A162	20k Map, delivery	.40	.40

Pan-African Postal Union, 10th anniv.

Ancient Wall, Kano A162a

50n, Rock Bridge. 100n, Ekpe masquerade, vert. 500n, National Theater.

1990, May 23 Litho. *Perf. 14*

560A	A162a	20n multicolored	—	
560B	A162a	50n multicolored	—	
560C	A162a	100n multicolored	—	
560D	A162a	500n multi	—	—
		Set of 4	*50.00*	

Postal counterfeits are known of No. 560B.

Pottery A163

1990, May 24

561	A163	10k Oil lamp	.20	.20
562	A163	20k Water pot	.20	.20
563	A163	25k Musical pots	.20	.20
564	A163	30k Water jug	.20	.20
a.		Sheet of 4, #561-564 with yellow frames, + 4 labels	2.50	2.50
		Nos. 561-564 (4)	.80	.80

Inscriptions, including country name, denomination and descriptions vary widely in size and style.

Intl. Literacy Year A164

1990, Aug. 8

565	A164	20k multicolored	.20	.20
566	A164	30k multicolored	.20	.20

A165

A166 A167

1990, Sept. 14

567	A165	10k shown	.20	.20
568	A166	20k Flags	.20	.20
569	A165	25k Globe	.20	.20
570	A166	30k shown	.20	.20
		Nos. 567-570 (4)	.80	.80

Organization of Petroleum Exporting Countries (OPEC), 30th anniv.

1990, Nov. 8

571	A167	20k Grey parrot	.20	.20
572	A167	30k Roan antelope	.30	.30
573	A167	1.50n Grey-necked rock fowl	1.50	1.50
574	A167	2.50n Mountain gorilla	2.00	2.00
a.		Souvenir sheet of 4, #571-574	4.50	4.50
		Nos. 571-574 (4)	4.00	4.00

Inscriptions vary widely in size and style.

A168

A170

A169

1991, Mar. 20

575	A168	10k Eradication	.25	.25
576	A169	20k shown	.25	.25
577	A168	30k Prevention	.30	.30
		Nos. 575-577 (3)	.80	.80

Natl. Guineaworm Eradication Day.

1991, May 26

578	A170	20k Progress	.20	.20
579	A170	30k Unity	.20	.20
580	A170	50k Freedom	.20	.20
		Nos. 578-580 (3)	.60	.60

OAU Heads of State Meeting, Abiya.

ECOWAS Summit, Abuja A171

1991, July 4

581	A171	20k Flags	.40	.40
582	A171	50k Map of West Africa	.40	.40

Economic Community of West African States.

Fish A172

1991, July 10

583	A172	10k Electric catfish	.40	.40
584	A172	20k Niger perch	.40	.40
585	A172	30k Talapia	.40	.40
586	A172	50k African catfish	.40	.40
a.		Souvenir sheet of 4, #583-586	3.00	3.00
		Nos. 583-586 (4)	1.60	1.60

Telecom '91 — A173

1991, Oct. 7

587	A173	20k shown	.30	.30
588	A173	50k multi, vert.	.45	.45

Sixth World Forum and Exposition on Telecommunications, Geneva, Switzerland.

1992 Summer Olympics, Barcelona A174

1992, Jan. 24 Unwmk.

589	A174	50k Boxing	.30	.30
590	A174	1n Running	.30	.30
591	A174	1.50n Table tennis	.40	.40
592	A174	2n Taekwondo	.50	.50
a.		Souvenir sheet of 4, #589-592, wmk. 379	5.00	5.00
		Nos. 589-592 (4)	1.50	1.50

1992 Summer Olympics, Barcelona A175

World Health Day A176

Wmk. 379

1992, Apr. 3 Litho. *Perf. 14*

593	A175	1.50n multicolored	.65	.65

1992, Apr. 7 Unwmk.

Designs: 50k, Heart and blood pressure gauge. 1n, Globe and blood pressure guage. 1.50n, Heart in rib cage. 2n, Cross-section of heart.

594	A176	50k multicolored	.20	.20
595	A176	1n multicolored	.25	.25
596	A176	1.50n multicolored	.35	.35
597	A176	2n multicolored	.50	.50
a.		Souvenir sheet of 4, #594-597	1.60	1.60
		Nos. 594-597 (4)	1.30	1.30

Intl. Institute of Tropical Agriculture, 25th Anniv. A177

Designs: 50k, Plantain, vert. 1n, Food products. 1.50n, Harvesting cassava tubers, vert. 2n, Yam barn, vert.

1992, July 17

598	A177	50k multicolored	.20	.20
599	A177	1n multicolored	.25	.25
600	A177	1.50n grn, blk & brown	.35	.35
601	A177	2n multicolored	.50	.50
a.		Souvenir sheet of 4, #598-601	2.40	2.40
		Nos. 598-601 (4)	1.30	1.30

Olymphilex '92 — A178

1.50n, Stamp under magnifying glass.

Wmk. 379

1992, July 3 Litho. *Perf. 14*

602	A178	50k multicolored	.30	.30
603	A178	1.50n multicolored	.45	.45
a.		Souvenir sheet of 2, #602-603 + 4 labels, unwmkd.	2.25	2.25

Maryam Babangida, Natl. Center for Women's Development
A179 A180

A180a

Designs: 50k, Emblem of Better Life Program. 1n, Women harvesting corn. 1.50n, Natl. Center, horiz. 2n, Woman using loom.

1992, Oct. 16

604	A179	50k multicolored	.20	.20
605	A180	1n multicolored	.25	.25
606	A180	1.50n multicolored	.35	.35
607	A180a	2n multicolored	.50	.50
		Nos. 604-607 (4)	1.30	1.30

Traditional Dances — A181

Unwmk.

1992, Dec. 15 Litho. *Perf. 14*

608	A181	50k Sabada	.20	.20
609	A181	1n Sato	.25	.25
610	A181	1.50n Asian Ubo Ikpa	.35	.35
611	A181	2n Dundun	.50	.50
a.		Souvenir sheet of 4, #608-611	2.40	2.40
		Nos. 608-611 (4)	1.30	1.30

Intl. Conference on Nutrition, Rome A182

1992, Dec. 1 Litho. *Perf. 14*

612	A182	50k Vegetables	.20	.20
613	A182	1n Child eating	.25	.25
614	A182	1.50n Fruits, vert.	.35	.35
615	A182	2n Vegetables, diff.	.50	.50
a.		Souvenir sheet of 4, #611-615	2.40	2.40
		Nos. 612-615 (4)	1.30	1.30

Lekki Beach — A182a

Stanlyey crane — A182b

Roan Antelopes — A182c

Designs: 1.50n, African elephant. 30n, Lion.

1992-93 Litho. *Perf. 14*

615A	A182a	1.50n multi	4.00	1.50
615B	A182b	5n multi	1.00	.35
615C	A182a	10n multi	1.60	.75

615D A182c 20n multi 7.00 3.00
615E A182a 30n multi 9.50 4.00
Nos. 615A-615E (5) 23.10 9.60

World Environment Day — A183

Designs: 1n, Clean environment ensures good health. 1.50n, Check water polution. 5n, Preserve your environment. 10n, Environment and nature.

1993, June 4 Litho. *Perf. 14*
616 A183 1n multicolored .20 .20
617 A183 1.50n multicolored .30 .30
618 A183 5n multicolored .90 .90
619 A183 10n multicolored 1.10 1.10
Nos. 616-619 (4) 2.50 2.50

Natl. Commission for Museums and Monuments, 50th Anniv. — A184

1993, July 28 Litho. *Perf. 14*
620 A184 1n Oni figure, vert. .20 .20
621 A184 1.50n Queen Mother head, vert. .30 .30
622 A184 5n Pendant .50 .50
623 A184 10n Nok head, vert. .80 .80
Nos. 620-623 (4) 1.80 1.80

Orchids — A185

1993, Oct. 28 Litho. *Perf. 14*
624 A185 1n Bulbophyllum distans .20 .20
625 A185 1.50n Eulophia cristata .30 .30
626 A185 5n Eulophia horsfalli .60 .60
627 A185 10n Eulophia quartiniana 1.25 1.25
a. Souv. sheet of 4, #624-627 *3.50 3.50*
Nos. 624-627 (4) 2.35 2.35

No. 627a exists with perforations through either the bottom or top margins.

Intl. Year of the Family A186

1.50n, Child abuse, classroom scene. 10n, Fending for the family, market scene.

1994, Mar. 30 Litho. *Perf. 14*
628 A186 1.50n multicolored .50 .50
629 A186 10n multicolored 1.10 1.10

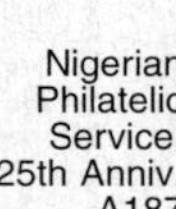

Nigerian Philatelic Service, 25th Anniv. A187

1n, #224. 1.50n, Bureau building. 5n, Map made of stamps. 10n, Counter staff, customers.

1994, Apr. 11
630 A187 1n multicolored .20 .20
631 A187 1.50n multicolored .30 .30
632 A187 5n multicolored .60 .60
633 A187 10n multicolored 1.30 1.30
Nos. 630-633 (4) 2.40 2.40

First Nigerian Postage Stamps, 120th Anniv. A188

Designs: 1n, "I love stamps." 1.50n, "I collect stamps." 5n, Methods of transporting mail. 10n, Lagos type A1 on airmail envelope.

1994, June 10 Litho. *Perf. 14*
634 A188 1n multicolored .20 .20
635 A188 1.50n multicolored .30 .30
636 A188 5n multicolored .60 .60
637 A188 10n multicolored 1.30 1.30
Nos. 634-637 (4) 2.40 2.40

PHILAKOREA '94 — A189

1994, Aug. 16 Litho. *Perf. 14*
638 A189 30n multicolored 3.00 3.00
a. Souvenir sheet of 1, #638 5.25 5.25

Crabs A190

1994, Aug. 12 Litho. *Perf. 14*
639 A190 1n Geryon quinquedens .25 .25
640 A190 1.50n Spider crab .40 .40
641 A190 5n Red spider .75 .75
642 A190 10n Geryon maritae 1.60 1.60
Nos. 639-642 (4) 3.00 3.00

African Development Bank, 30th Anniv. — A191

1994, Sept. 16
643 A191 1.50n Water treatment plant .20 .20
644 A191 30n Emblem, field 2.75 2.75

NIPOST/NITEL, 10th Anniv. — A192

Designs: 1n, Putting letter into mailbox, vert. 1.50n, Airmail letter. 5n, NIPOST, NITEL logos. 10n, Telephones, vert.

1995, Jan. 1 Litho. *Perf. 14*
645 A192 1n multicolored .20 .20
646 A192 1.50n multicolored .20 .20
647 A192 5n multicolored .45 .45
648 A192 10n multicolored .90 .90
Nos. 645-648 (4) 1.75 1.75

Family Support Program A194

Designs: 1n, Feed the family. 1.50n, Monitoring child education. 5n, Caring for the family. 10n, Support agriculture.

1995, July 20 Litho. *Perf. 14*
653 A194 1n multicolored .20 .20
654 A194 1.50n multicolored .20 .20
655 A194 5n multicolored .45 .45
656 A194 10n multicolored .90 .90
Nos. 653-656 (4) 1.75 1.75

First Telephone in Nigeria, Cent. — A195

Designs: 1.50n, Dial telephone, c. 1919. 10n, Crank telephone, c. 1885.

1995, Oct. 9 Litho. *Perf. 14*
657 A195 1.50n multicolored .35 .35
658 A195 10n multicolored 1.25 1.25

FAO, 50th Anniv. A196

1995, Oct. 16
659 A196 1.50n shown .25 .25
660 A196 30n Fishing boats 3.00 3.00

UN, 50th Anniv. A197

Designs: 1n, Emblem of justice, vert. 1.50n, Against illegal dumping of toxic chemicals. 5n, Tourism. 10n, Peace-keeping soldiers.

1995, Oct. 24
661 A197 1n multicolored .20 .20
662 A197 1.50n multicolored .20 .20
663 A197 5n multicolored .45 .45
664 A197 10n multicolored .90 .90
Nos. 661-664 (4) 1.75 1.75

Niger Dock, 10th Anniv. A198

5n, Overall view of dock. 10n, Boat being lifted. 20n, Boats in dock area. 30n, Boat on water.

1996, Apr. 29 Litho. *Perf. 14*
665 A198 5n multicolored .50 .50
666 A198 10n multicolored 1.10 1.10
667 A198 20n multicolored 2.00 2.00
668 A198 30n multicolored 3.00 3.00
Nos. 665-668 (4) 6.60 6.60

Economic Community of West African States (ECOWAS), 21st Anniv. A199

5n, Developing agriculture and scientific research. 30n, Free movement of people.

1996, May 5 Litho. *Perf. 14*
669 A199 5n multicolored .60 .60
670 A199 30n multicolored 3.00 3.00

A200

A201

1996, June 28
671 A200 5n Judo .50 .50
672 A200 10n Tennis 1.10 1.10
673 A200 20n Relay race 2.00 2.00
674 A200 30n Soccer 3.00 3.00
Nos. 671-674 (4) 6.60 6.60

1996 Summer Olympic Games, Atlanta.

1996, Oct. 10 Litho. *Perf. 14*
675 A201 30n Natl. flag, logo 3.00 3.00

Istanbul '96.

Mushrooms A202

Designs: 5n, Volvariella esculenta. 10n, Lentinus subnudus. 20n, Tricholoma lobayensis. 30n, Pleurotus tuber-regium.

1996, Nov. 19
676 A202 5n multicolored .50 .50
677 A202 10n multicolored 1.00 1.00
678 A202 20n multicolored 2.25 2.25
679 A202 30n multicolored 3.25 3.25
Nos. 676-679 (4) 7.00 7.00

UNICEF, 50th Anniv. A203

Designs: 5n, "Child's right to play," vert. 30n, "Educate the girl child."

1996, Dec. 10
680 A203 5n multicolored .50 .50
681 A203 30n multicolored 3.00 3.00

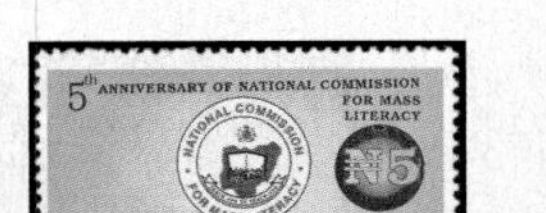

Mass Literacy Commission, 5th Anniv. — A204

Designs: 5n, "Teach one to teach one." 30n, "Education through co-operation."

1996, Dec. 30
682 A204 5n grn, blk & dk grn .45 .45
683 A204 30n grn, blk & dk grn 2.75 2.75

1998 World Cup Soccer Championships, France — A205

1998, June 10 Litho. *Perf. 13*
684 A205 5n shown .45 .45
685 A205 10n Player, vert. .90 .90
686 A205 20n Player, diff., vert. 1.75 1.75
687 A205 30n Two players 2.75 2.75
Nos. 684-687 (4) 5.85 5.85

ECOMOG (Military Co-operation Organization), 8th Anniv. — A206

Designs: 5n, Silhouette of ship. 30n, Flag colors of Gambia, Ghana, Guinea, Mali, Nigeria, Senegal, Sierra Leone. 50n, Flag colors of Gambia, Ghana, Nigeria, Guinea, Mali, Senegal, Sierra Leone, Niger, Ivory Coast, Benin, Burkina Faso.

1998, Nov. 30 Litho. *Perf. 14*

688	A206	5n multicolored	.50	.50
689	A206	30n multicolored	2.50	2.50
690	A206	50n multicolored	4.25	4.25
		Nos. 688-690 (3)	7.25	7.25

Nigerian Railroad, Cent. A207

5n, Caged locomotive. 10n, Iddo Terminal. 20n, Locomotive. 30n, Passenger tram.

1999, Jan. 20 *Perf. 13*

691	A207	5n multicolored	.45	.45
692	A207	10n multicolored	.90	.90
693	A207	20n multicolored	1.75	1.75
694	A207	30n multicolored	2.75	2.75
		Nos. 691-694 (4)	5.85	5.85

Rain Forest — A207a

1999, May 10 Litho. *Perf. 13*

694A	A207a	10n multi	—	—

University of Ibadan, 50th Anniv. A208

1998, Nov. 17 Litho. *Perf. 14*

695	A208	5n University building	.50	.50
696	A208	30n "50," Crest	2.50	2.50

Federal Environmental Protection Agency, 10th Anniv. — A209

1999, June 8 Litho. *Perf. 13*

697	A209	5n Water resources	.50	.50
698	A209	10n Natural resources	.75	.75
699	A209	20n Endangered species	1.75	1.75
700	A209	30n One earth, one family	2.50	2.50
		Nos. 697-700 (4)	5.50	5.50

NICON Insurance Corp., 30th Anniv. A210

Emblem and: 5n, Airplane, ship, oil refinery, vert. 30n, Building.

Perf. 12¾x13, 13x12¾
1999, Aug. 31 Litho.

701	A210	5n multi	.50	.50
702	A210	30n multi	2.00	2.00

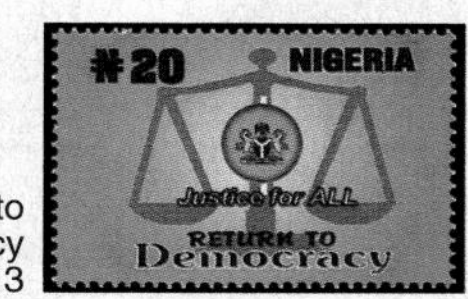

Millennium A211

Designs: 10n, Map of Northern and Southern Protectorates, 1900-14. 20n, Map of Nigeria, 1914. 30n, Coat of arms. 40n, Map of 36 states, 1996.

2000 Litho. *Perf. 13*

703-706	A211	Set of 4	2.25	2.25

World Meteorological Organization, 50th Anniv. — A212

Designs: 10n, Sunshine hour recorder, vert. 30n, Meteorological station.

2000 *Perf. 12¾x13, 13x12¾*

707-708	A212	Set of 2	1.25	1.25

Return to Democracy A213

Designs: 10n, Flag, "Freedom of the press," vert. 20n, Scales of justice. 30n, Legislative mace, vert. 40n, Pres. Olusegun Obasanjo, flag, vert.

2000 *Perf. 14¾*

709-712	A213	Set of 4	3.50	3.50
712a		Souvenir sheet, #709-712	6.00	6.00

2000 Summer Olympics, Sydney A214

Designs: 10n, Boxing. 20n, Weight lifting. 30n, Soccer. 40n, Soccer, diff.

2000, Sept. 7 Litho. *Perf. 13x12¾*

713-716	A214	Set of 4	3.50	3.50
a.		Souvenir sheet, #713-716 + 4 labels	6.00	6.00

A215

A216

Independence, 40th anniv.: 10n, Obafemi Awolowo (1909-87), promoter of federal constitution. 20n, Prime Minister Abubakar Tafawa Balewa (1912-66). 30n, Pres. Nnamdi Azikiwe (1904-96). 40n, Liquified gas refinery, horiz. 50n, Ship carrying exports, horiz.

Perf. 12¾x13, 13x12¾
2000, Sept. 27 Litho.

717-721	A215	Set of 5	4.00	4.00

2001, Jan. 16 *Perf. 14*

Fruit: 20n, Hug plum. 30n, White star apple. 40n, African breadfruit. 50n, Akee apple.

722-725	A216	Set of 4	3.25	3.25

Nigeria Daily Times Newspaper, 75th Anniv. A217

Designs: 20n, Corporate headquarters, Lagos. 30n, First issue. 40n, Daily Times complex, Lagos. 50n, Masthead.

2001, June 1 Litho. *Perf. 13x12¾*

726-729	A217	Set of 4	3.50	3.50

Fauna A218

Designs: 10n, Broad-tailed paradise whydahs, vert. 15n, Fire-bellied woodpeckers, vert. 20n, Grant's zebras. 25n, Aardvark. 30n, Preuss's guenon, vert. 40n, Giant ground pangolin. 50n, Bonobo. 100n, Red-eared guenon, vert.

2001, June 15 *Perf. 14*

730	A218	10n multi	.20	.20
731	A218	15n multi	.30	.30
732	A218	20n multi	.45	.40
a.		Thinner inscriptions, perf. 13x13¼ ('05)	.30	.30
733	A218	25n multi	.60	.55
734	A218	30n multi	.85	.70
735	A218	40n multi	1.00	.90
736	A218	50n multi	1.50	1.25
a.		Thinner inscriptions, perf. 13x13¼ ('05)	.80	.80
737	A218	100n multi	3.50	3.25
		Nos. 730-737 (8)	8.40	7.55

Inscriptions vary widely in size and style. Nos. 732a, 736a issued 2005

Year of Dialogue Among Civilizations — A219

2001, Oct. 9 Litho. *Perf. 13*

738	A219	20n multi	.90	.90

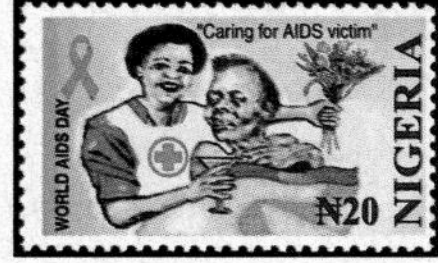

New Millennium A220

Designs: 20n, Peace. 30n, Age of globalization. 40n, Reconciliation. 50n, Love.

2002, Feb. 13 Litho. *Perf. 13x12¾*

739-742	A220	Set of 4	3.25	3.25

Crops A221

Designs: 20n, Kola nuts. 30n, Oil palm. 40n, Cassava. 50n, Corn, vert.

2002, May 10 *Perf. 13x12¾, 12¾x13*

743-746	A221	Set of 4	2.75	2.75

2002 World Cup Soccer Championships, Japan and Korea — A222

Emblem and: 20n, Nigerian player and opponent, vert. 30n, Globe and soccer balls, vert. 40n, Player's legs and ball. 50n, World Cup trophy, vert.

Perf. 12¾x13, 13x12¾
2002, June 14

747-750	A222	Set of 4	2.90	2.90

World AIDS Day — A223

Designs: 20n, Nurse, patient, flowers. 50n, AIDS counseling.

2003, May 3 Litho. *Perf. 13x12¾*

751-752	A223	Set of 2	1.80	1.80
752a		Souvenir sheet, #751-752	1.80	1.80

A224

A225

Universal basic education: 20n, Students. 50n, Student writing, horiz.

Perf. 12¾x13, 13x12¾
2003, Sept. 22 Litho.

753-754	A224	Set of 2	2.00	2.00

2003, Oct. 4

Eighth All Africa Games: 20n, Runner. 30n, High jump, horiz. 40n, Taekwondo, horiz. 50n, Long jump

755-758	A225	Set of 4	2.50	2.50
758a		Souvenir sheet, #755-758 + 4 labels	3.00	3.00

Worldwide Fund for Nature (WWF) A226

Side-striped jackal: 20n, Adult and pups. 40n, Adult in grass. 80n, Two adults. 100n, Adult in grass, diff.

2003, Dec. 12 *Perf. 13x12¾*

759-762	A226	Set of 4	3.75	3.75
a.		Block of 4, #759-762	4.50	4.50

Commonwealth Heads of Government Meeting, Abuja — A227

Emblem and: 20n, Map of Nigeria. 50n, Flag of Nigeria, vert.

Perf. 13x12¾, 12¾x13
2003, Dec. 7 Litho.

763-764	A227	Set of 2	2.00	2.00

2004 Summer Olympics, Athens — A228

Designs: 50n, Runners. 120n, Basketball.

2004, Aug. 18 Litho. *Perf. 12¾x13*

765-766	A228	Set of 2	3.00	3.00

A229 A232

A230

Winning Children's Stamp Art Contest Designs — A231

Perf. 12¾x13, 13x12¾

2004, Oct. 29 **Litho.**
767 A229 50n multi .75 .75
768 A230 90n multi 1.40 1.40
769 A231 120n multi 1.90 1.90
770 A232 150n multi 2.25 2.25
a. Souvenir sheet, #767-770, + 12 labels 6.50 6.50
Nos. 767-770 (4) 6.30 6.30

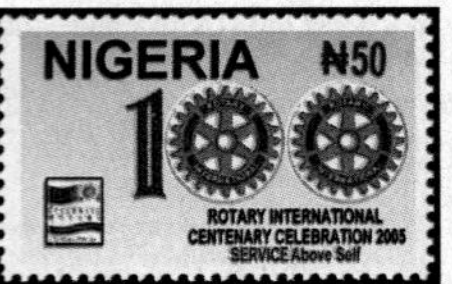

Rotary International, Cent. — A233

Designs: 50n, "100" with Rotary emblems for zeroes. 120n, Rotary emblem and world map.

2005, Aug. 9 **Litho.** ***Perf. 13x12¾***
771-772 A233 Set of 2 3.00 3.00
772a Horiz. pair, #771-772 2.50 2.50

Nigerian Postage Stamps, 131st Anniv. A234

Designs: 50n, Text in simulated stamp. 90n, Map of Nigeria, simulated stamp. 120n, Map of Nigeria, years "1874" and "2005." 150n, Nigeria #118, 746, vert.

2005, Oct. 9 ***Perf. 13x12¾, 12¾x13***
773-776 A234 Set of 4 6.50 6.50

World Summit on the Information Society, Tunis A235

Summit emblems, globe and: 20n, Nigeria Post emblem. 50n, Postman on motorcycle, vert. 120n, Like 20n.

Perf. 13x12¾, 12¾x13

2005, Nov. 4 **Litho.**
777-779 A235 Set of 3 3.00 3.00

Writers A236

Designs: 20n, Prof. Chinua Achebe. 40n, Dr. Abubakar Imam (1911-81). 50n, Prof. Wole Soyinka.

2006, Jan. 18 ***Perf. 13x12¾***
780-782 A236 Set of 3 1.75 1.75

Scholars — A237

Designs: No. 783, 50n, No. 786, 100n, Prof. Ayodele Awojobi (1937-84), engineer. No. 784, 50n, No. 787, 120n, Prof. Gabriel Oyibo, mathematician. No. 785, 50n, No. 788, 150n, Philip Emeagwali, computer scientist.

2006, Jan. 18 ***Perf. 12¾x13***
783-788 A237 Set of 6 8.25 8.25

Queen Elizabeth II, 80th Birthday A239

Designs: 20n, Queen at public ceremony, in pink hat. 50n, Queen in pink hat, vert.

2006, Oct. 9 **Litho.** ***Perf. 13***
792-793 A239 Set of 2 1.10 1.10

Agbani Darego, 2001 Miss World — A240

Darego and: 20n, Map of Nigeria. 50n, Map of world, horiz.

2006, Nov. 9
794-795 A240 Set of 2 1.10 1.10

Abuja, 30th Anniv. A241

Designs: 20n, Gate, fireworks, palm trees, map of Nigeria. 50n, Emblem, hands beating drum, vert.

2006, Dec. 13
796-797 A241 Set of 2 1.10 1.10

143rd Extraordinary Conference of OPEC, Abuja — A242

2006, Dec. 14
798 A242 50n multi .80 .80

Mungo Park (1771-1806), Explorer — A243

Park and: 20n, Monument. 50n, River, horiz.

2007, Mar. 29 **Litho.** ***Perf. 13***
799-800 A243 Set of 2 1.10 1.10

Second World Black and African Festival of Arts and Culture, 30th Anniv. A244

2007, Mar. 29 **Litho.** ***Perf. 13***
801 A244 50n multi .80 .80

A245 A246

Cross river gorilla: 20n, Adult. 50n, Two adults, horiz. 100n, Adult and juvenile, horiz. 150n, Head.

2008, Mar. 26 **Litho.** ***Perf. 13***
802-805 A245 Set of 4 3.75 3.75

Worldwide Fund for Nature (WWF).

2008, Apr. 10

Designs: 20n, Hands, money. 50n, Campaign to end violation of 419 law. 100n, Clasped hands.

806-808 A246 Set of 3 3.00 3.00

Economic & Financial Crimes Commission anti-corruption campaign.

2008 Summer Olympics, Beijing A247

Designs: 20n, Runners at finish line. 50n, Soccer. 100n, Wrestling, vert.

2008, Aug. 8
809-811 A247 Set of 3 3.00 3.00

SEMI-POSTAL STAMPS

Catalogue values for unused stamps in this section are for Never Hinged items.

Children Drinking Milk at Orphanage SP1

Designs: 1sh6p+3p, Civilian first aid, vert. 2sh6p+3p, Military first aid.

1966, Dec. 1 **Photo.** ***Perf. 14½x14***
B1 SP1 4p + 1p pur, blk & red .25 .25
B2 SP1 1sh6p + 3p multi 1.00 1.00
B3 SP1 2sh6p + 3p multi 1.75 1.75
Nos. B1-B3 (3) 3.00 3.00

The surtax was for the Nigerian Red Cross.

Dr. Armauer G. Hansen — SP2

1973, July 30 **Litho.** ***Perf. 14***
B4 SP2 5k + 2k blk, brn & buff .55 .55

Centenary of the discovery of the Hansen bacillus, the cause of leprosy. The surtax was for the Nigerian Anti-Leprosy Association.

Nigeria '99, FIFA World Youth Championships — SP3

5n+5n, Soccer ball, FIFA emblem. 10n+5n, Throwing ball. 20n+5n, Kicking ball into goal. 30n+5n, Map of Nigeria. 40n+5n, FIFA emblem, eagle, soccer ball. 50n+5n, Tackling.

1999, Mar. 31 **Litho.** ***Perf. 13x14***
B5 SP3 5n +5n multi .25 .25
B6 SP3 10n +5n multi .35 .35
B7 SP3 20n +5n multi .60 .60
B8 SP3 30n +5n multi .75 .75
B9 SP3 40n +5n multi 1.00 1.00
B10 SP3 50n +5n multi 1.40 1.40
a. Souvenir sheet of 6, #B5-B10 4.50 4.50
Nos. B5-B10 (6) 4.35 4.35

POSTAGE DUE STAMPS

Catalogue values for unused stamps in this section are for Never Hinged items.

D1

Caravansary Near Timbuktu — D2

Perf. 14½x14

1959, Jan. 4 **Wmk. 4** **Litho.**
J1 D1 1p orange .20 .20
J2 D1 2p orange .20 .20
J3 D1 3p orange .20 .20
J4 D1 6p orange 1.00 *5.25*
J5 D1 1sh black 2.25 *10.50*
Nos. J1-J5 (5) 3.85 *16.35*

1961, Aug. 1 **Wmk. 335**
J6 D1 1p red .20 .20
J7 D1 2p blue .20 .20
J8 D1 3p emerald .20 .20
J9 D1 6p yellow .25 1.50
J10 D1 1sh dark blue .75 *3.75*
Nos. J6-J10 (5) 1.60 *5.85*

Perf. 12½x13½

1973, May 3 **Litho.** **Unwmk.**
J11 D2 2k red .20 .20
J12 D2 3k blue .20 .20
J13 D2 5k orange .20 .20
J14 D2 10k yellow green .35 .35
Nos. J11-J14 (4) .95 .95

1987-94 ***Rouletted 9***
J15 D2 2k red 1.50
J16 D2 5k yellow 5.00
J17 D2 10k green 10.00
Nos. J15-J17 (3) 16.50

NIUE

nē-'ü-ˌāˌā

LOCATION — Island in the south Pacific Ocean, northeast of New Zealand
GOVT. — Self-government, in free association with New Zealand
AREA — 100 sq. mi.
POP. — 1,708 (1997 est.)
CAPITAL — Alofi

Niue, also known as Savage Island, was annexed to New Zealand in 1901 with the Cook Islands. Niue achieved internal self-government in 1974.

12 Pence = 1 Shilling
20 Shillings = 1 Pound
100 Cents = 1 Dollar (1967)

Catalogue values for unused stamps in this country are for Never Hinged items, beginning with Scott 90 in the regular postage section, Scott B1 in the semi-postal section, Scott C1 in the air post section, and Scott O1 in the officials section.

Watermarks

Wmk. 61 — Single-lined NZ and Star Close Together

Wmk. 253 — NZ and Star

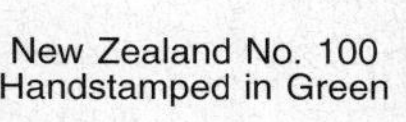

New Zealand No. 100 Handstamped in Green

1902 **Wmk. 63** ***Perf. 11***

Thick Soft Paper

1	A35 1p carmine		375.00	375.00

Stamps of New Zealand Surcharged in Carmine, Vermilion or Blue:

1/2p

1p

2 1/2p

Perf. 14

Thin Hard Paper

3	A18	½p green (C)	3.00	*4.50*
a.		Inverted surcharge	300.00	*500.00*
4	A35	1p carmine (Bl), perf. 11x14	2.00	*2.75*
a.		No period after "PENI"	35.00	*50.00*
b.		Perf. 14	22.50	*25.00*
c.		As "a," perf. 14	300.00	*350.00*

Perf. 14

Wmk. 61

6	A18	½p green (V)	1.10	1.10
7	A35	1p carmine (Bl)	.85	1.10
a.		No period after "PENI"	9.00	*16.00*
b.		Double surcharge	*1,400.*	1,500.

Perf. 11

Unwmk.

8	A22	2½p blue (C)	4.00	4.50
a.		No period after "PENI"	45.00	47.50
9	A22	2½p blue (V)	1.75	2.00
a.		No period after "PENI"	20.00	25.00

The surcharge on the ½ & 1p stamps is printed in blocks of 60. Two stamps in each block have a space between the "U" and "E" of "NIUE" and one of the 1p stamps has a broken "E" like an "F."

Blue Surcharge on Stamps of New Zealand, Types of 1898:

e

f

g

h

1903 **Wmk. 61** ***Perf. 11***

10	A23(e)	3p yellow brown	11.00	5.50
11	A26(f)	6p rose	14.00	12.50
13	A29(g)	1sh brown red	40.00	40.00
a.		1sh scarlet	40.00	40.00
b.		1sh orange red	50.00	*52.50*
c.		As "b," surcharge "h" (error)	750.00	
		Nos. 10-13 (3)	65.00	58.00

Surcharged in Carmine or Blue on Stamps of New Zealand

j

1911-12 ***Perf. 14, 14x14½***

14	A41(j)	½p yellow grn (C)	.60	.70
15	A41(f)	6p car rose (Bl)	2.50	*7.50*
16	A41(g)	1sh vermilion (Bl)	8.00	*50.00*
		Nos. 14-16 (3)	11.10	*58.20*

1915 ***Perf. 14***

18	A22(d)	2½p dark blue (C)	17.50	*35.00*

Surcharged in Brown or Dark Blue on Stamps of New Zealand

1917 ***Perf. 14x13½, 14x14½***

19	A42	1p carmine (Br)	12.50	6.25
a.		No period after "PENI"	350.00	
20	A45(e)	3p violet brn (Bl)	50.00	*90.00*
a.		No period after "Pene"	850.00	

New Zealand Stamps of 1909-19 Overprinted in Dark Blue or Red

k

1917-20 **Typo.**

21	A43	½p yellow grn (R)	.80	*2.75*
22	A42	1p carmine (Bl)	11.00	10.00
23	A47	1½p gray black (R)	1.10	*2.50*
24	A47	1½p brown org (R)	1.00	*4.75*
25	A43	3p chocolate (Bl)	1.60	*30.00*

Engr.

26	A44	2½p dull blue (R)	3.00	*8.50*
27	A45	3p violet brown (Bl)	1.75	*2.25*
28	A45	6p car rose (Bl)	7.00	*26.00*
29	A45	1sh vermilion (Bl)	10.00	*27.50*
		Nos. 21-29 (9)	37.25	114.25

Same Overprint On Postal-Fiscal Stamps of New Zealand, 1906-15

Perf. 14, 14½ and Compound

1918-23

30	PF1	2sh blue (R)	18.00	*35.00*
31	PF1	2sh6p brown (Bl) ('23)	24.00	*55.00*
32	PF1	5sh green (R)	29.00	*57.50*
33	PF1	10sh red brn (Bl) ('23)	110.00	*150.00*
34	PF2	£1 rose (Bl) ('23)	160.00	*210.00*
		Nos. 30-34 (5)	341.00	507.50

Landing of Captain Cook A16

Avarua Waterfront A17

Capt. James Cook — A18

Coconut Palm — A19

Arorangi Village — A20

Avarua Harbor — A21

Unwmk.

1920, Aug. 23 **Engr.** ***Perf. 14***

35	A16	½p yel grn & blk	4.25	*4.25*
36	A17	1p car & black	2.25	1.40
37	A18	1½p red & black	2.75	*9.00*
38	A19	3p pale blue & blk	1.00	*16.00*
39	A20	6p dp grn & red brn	2.00	*21.00*
a.		Center inverted	*500.00*	
40	A21	1sh blk brn & blk	2.00	*21.00*
		Nos. 35-40 (6)	14.25	*72.65*

See Nos. 41-42. For surcharge see No. 48.

Types of 1920 Issue and

Rarotongan Chief (Te Po) — A22

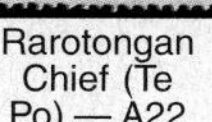

Avarua Harbor — A23

1925-27 **Wmk. 61**

41	A16	½p yel grn & blk ('26)	1.60	*9.00*
42	A17	1p car & black	2.00	1.00
43	A22	2½p dk blue & blk ('27)	4.50	*12.00*
44	A23	4p dull vio & blk ('27)	8.00	*22.50*
		Nos. 41-44 (4)	16.10	44.50

New Zealand No. 182 Overprinted Type "k" in Red

1927

47	A56	2sh blue	18.00	*35.00*
a.		2sh dark blue	17.00	*37.50*

No. 37 Surcharged

1931 **Unwmk.** ***Perf. 14***

48	A18	2p on 1½p red & blk	2.00	1.10

New Zealand Postal-Fiscal Stamps of 1931-32 Overprinted Type "k" in Blue or Red

1931, Nov. 12 **Wmk. 61**

49	PF5	2sh6p deep brown	5.00	13.00
50	PF5	5sh green (R)	40.00	*75.00*
51	PF5	10sh dark car	40.00	*100.00*
52	PF5	£1 pink ('32)	65.00	*150.00*
		Nos. 49-52 (4)	150.00	338.00

See Nos. 86-89D, 116-119.

Landing of Captain Cook — A24

Capt. James Cook — A25

Polynesian Migratory Canoe — A26

Islanders Unloading Ship — A27

View of Avarua Harbor — A28

R.M.S. Monowai — A29

King George V — A30

Perf. 13, 14 (4p, 1sh)

1932, Mar. 16 **Engr.** **Unwmk.**

53	A24	½p yel grn & blk	10.00	*25.00*
a.		Perf. 14x13	275.00	
54	A25	1p dp red & blk	1.10	.55
55	A26	2p org brn & blk	2.75	*4.50*
56	A27	2½p indigo & blk	8.50	*80.00*
57	A28	4p Prus blue & blk	16.00	*57.50*
a.		Perf. 13	15.00	*62.50*
58	A29	6p dp org & blk	2.75	2.25
59	A30	1sh dull vio & blk	2.50	*5.50*
		Nos. 53-59 (7)	43.60	*175.30*

For types overprinted see Nos. 67-69.

1933-36 **Wmk. 61** ***Perf. 14***

60	A24	½p yel grn & blk	.50	*3.50*
61	A25	1p deep red & blk	.50	*1.50*
62	A26	2p brown & blk ('36)	.50	*1.50*
63	A27	2½p indigo & blk	.50	*4.75*
64	A28	4p Prus blue & blk	2.00	*4.00*
65	A29	6p org & blk ('36)	.80	*.90*
66	A30	1sh dk vio & blk ('36)	9.00	*25.00*
		Nos. 60-66 (7)	13.80	41.15

See Nos. 77-82.

Silver Jubilee Issue

Types of 1932 Overprinted in Black or Red

1935, May 7 ***Perf. 14***

67	A25	1p car & brown red	.80	*2.00*
68	A27	2½p indigo & bl (R)	3.50	*6.00*
a.		Vert. pair, imperf. horiz.	275.00	
69	A29	6p dull org & grn	3.50	*5.00*
		Nos. 67-69 (3)	7.80	13.00
		Set, never hinged	14.50	

The vertical spacing of the overprint is wider on No. 69.

No. 68a is from proof sheets.

Coronation Issue

New Zealand Stamps of 1937 Overprinted in Black

Perf. 13½x13

1937, May 13 **Wmk. 253**

70 A78 1p rose carmine .20 .20
71 A78 2½p dark blue .20 *1.00*
72 A78 6p vermilion .30 .30
Nos. 70-72 (3) .70 1.50
Set, never hinged 1.25

George VI — A31

Village Scene — A32

Coastal Scene with Canoe — A33

Mt. Ikurangi behind Avarua — A34

1938, May 2 **Wmk. 61** ***Perf. 14***

73 A31 1sh dp violet & blk 7.50 6.00
74 A32 2sh dk red brown & blk 10.00 *12.00*
75 A33 3sh yel green & blue 27.50 12.00
Nos. 73-75 (3) 45.00 30.00
Set, never hinged 65.00

See Nos. 83-85.

Perf. 13½x14

1940, Sept. 2 **Engr.** **Wmk. 253**

76 A34 3p on 1½p rose vio & blk .75 .75
Never hinged 1.00

Examples without surcharge are from printer's archives.

Types of 1932-38

1944-46 **Wmk. 253** ***Perf. 14***

77 A24 ½p yel grn & blk .40 *2.25*
78 A25 1p dp red & blk ('45) .40 *1.25*
79 A26 2p org brn & blk ('46) 4.00 *6.00*
80 A27 2½p dk bl & blk ('45) .50 *1.00*
81 A28 4p Prus blue & blk 3.00 .90
82 A29 6p dp orange & blk 1.40 1.40
83 A31 1sh dp vio & blk .85 1.00
84 A32 2sh brn car & blk ('45) 9.00 3.75
85 A33 3sh yel grn & bl ('45) 12.00 8.50
Nos. 77-85 (9) 31.55 26.05
Set, never hinged 40.00

New Zealand Postal-Fiscal Stamps Overprinted Type "k" (narrow "E") in Blue or Red

1941-45 **Wmk. 61** ***Perf. 14***

86 PF5 2sh6p brown 55.00 *60.00*
87 PF5 5sh green (R) 225.00 150.00
88 PF5 10sh rose 95.00 *150.00*
89 PF5 £1 pink 150.00 *225.00*
Nos. 86-89 (4) 525.00 *585.00*
Set, never hinged 725.00

Wmk. 253

89A PF5 2sh6p brown 2.50 *10.00*
89B PF5 5sh green (R) 5.25 *11.00*
e. 5sh light yellow green, wmkd. sideways ('67) 35.00 *95.00*
89C PF5 10sh rose 37.50 *100.00*
89D PF5 £1 pink 30.00 *60.00*
Nos. 89A-89D (4) 75.25 181.00
Set, never hinged 110.00

No. 89Be exists in both line and comb perf.

Catalogue values for unused stamps in this section, from this point to the end of the section, are for Never Hinged items.

Peace Issue

New Zealand Nos. 248, 250, 254 and 255 Overprinted in Black or Blue:

p

q

1946, June 4 ***Perf. 13x13½, 13½x13***

90 A94 (p) 1p emerald .35 .35
91 A96 (q) 2p rose violet (Bl) .35 .35
92 A100 (p) 6p org red & red brn .35 .35
93 A101 (p) 8p brn lake & blk (Bl) .45 .45
Nos. 90-93 (4) 1.50 1.50

Map of Niue — A35

Thatched Dwelling — A36

Designs: 1p, H.M.S. Resolution. 2p, Alofi landing. 4p, Arch at Hikutavake. 6p, Alofi bay. 9p, Fisherman. 1sh, Cave at Makefu. 2sh, Gathering bananas. 3sh, Matapa Chasm.

Perf. 14x13½, 13½x14

1950, July 3 **Engr.** **Wmk. 253**

94 A35 ½p red orange & bl .20 .20
95 A36 1p green & brown 2.50 2.50
96 A36 2p rose car & blk 1.10 1.40
97 A36 3p blue vio & blue .25 .20
98 A36 4p brn vio & ol grn .40 .40
99 A36 6p brn org & bl grn .70 *1.40*
100 A35 9p dk brn & brn org .85 *1.40*
101 A36 1sh black & purple 1.00 1.10
102 A35 2sh dp grn & brn org 1.35 *4.00*
103 A35 3sh black & dp blue 4.00 4.00
Nos. 94-103 (10) 12.35 16.60

For surcharges see Nos. 106-115.

Coronation Issue

Queen Elizabeth II — A36a

Westminster Abbey — A36b

1953, May 24 **Photo.** ***Perf. 14x14½***

104 A36a 3p brown .50 .50
105 A36b 6p slate black 1.25 1.25

Nos. 94-103 Surcharged

Perf. 14x13½, 13½x14

1967, July 10 **Engr.** **Wmk. 253**

106 A35 ½c on ½p red org & blue .20 .20
107 A36 1c on 1p green & brn .50 .25
108 A36 2c on 2p rose car & black .20 .20
109 A36 2½c on 3p bl vio & bl .20 .20
110 A36 3c on 4p brn vio & ol grn .20 .20
111 A36 5c on 6p brn org & green .20 .20
112 A35 8c on 9p dk brn & brn org .25 .25
113 A36 10c on 1sh blk & pur .50 .50
114 A35 20c on 2sh dp grn & brown org .65 .65
115 A35 30c on 3sh blk & dp bl 1.00 1.00
Nos. 106-115 (10) 3.90 3.65

The position of the numeral varies on each denomination. The surcharge on the ½c, 2½c, 8c, 10c and 20c contains one dot only.

New Zealand Arms — A37

Wmk. 253

1967, July 10 **Typo.** ***Perf. 14***

Black Surcharge

116 A37 25c yellow brown .70 .65
117 A37 50c green 1.25 1.25
118 A37 $1 cerise .80 2.50
119 A37 $2 pale pink 1.25 4.25
Nos. 116-119 (4) 4.00 8.65

1967 ***Perf. 11***

116a A37 25c 7.25 13.00
117a A37 50c 8.50 15.00
118a A37 $1 10.75 15.00
119a A37 $2 13.50 20.00
Nos. 116a-119a (4) 40.00 63.00

The perf. 11 stamps were produced when a normal perforating machine broke down and 2,500 of each denomination were perforated on a treadle machine first used by the N.Z. Post Office in 1899.

Christmas Issues

Adoration of the Shepherds, by Poussin — A37a

Nativity, by Federico Fiori — A37b

Perf. 13½x14

1967, Oct. 3 **Photo.** **Wmk. 253**

120 A37a 2½c multicolored .25 .25

1969, Oct. 1 **Photo.** **Wmk. 253**

121 A37b 2½c multicolored .25 .25

Pua — A38

Flowers (except 20c): 1c, Golden shower. 2c, Flamboyant. 2½c, Frangipani. 3c, Niue crocus. 5c, Hibiscus. 8c, Passion fruit. 10c, Kamapui. 20c, Queen Elizabeth II. 30c, Tapeu orchid.

Perf. 12½x13

1969, Nov. 27 **Litho.** **Unwmk.**

122 A38 ½c green & multi .20 .20
123 A38 1c orange & multi .20 .20
124 A38 2c gray & multi .20 .20
125 A38 2½c bister & multi .20 .20
126 A38 3c blue & multi .20 .20
127 A38 5c ver & multi .25 .20
128 A38 8c violet & multi .35 .20
129 A38 10c yellow & multi .40 .20
130 A38 20c dk blue & multi 1.00 *1.50*
131 A38 30c olive grn & multi 1.25 *2.00*
Nos. 122-131 (10) 4.25 5.10

See Nos. 678.

Edible Crab A39

Perf. 13½x12½

1969, Aug. 19 **Litho.**

132 A39 3c Kalahimu .20 .20
133 A39 5c Kalavi .20 .20
134 A39 30c Unga .75 .75
Nos. 132-134 (3) 1.15 1.15

Christmas Issue

Adoration, by Correggio — A39a

1970, Oct. 1 **Litho.** ***Perf. 12½***

135 A39a 2½c multicolored .35 .20

Plane over Outrigger Canoe A40

Designs: 5c, Plane over ships in harbor. 8c, Civair plane over island.

1970, Dec. 9 **Litho.** ***Perf. 13½***

136 A40 3c multicolored .20 .20
137 A40 5c multicolored .20 .20
138 A40 8c multicolored .20 .20
Nos. 136-138 (3) .60 .60

Opening of Niue Airport.

Polynesian Triller (Heahea) A41

Birds: 10c, Crimson-crowned fruit pigeon (kulukulu). 20c, Blue-crowned lory (henga).

1971, June 23 **Litho.** ***Perf. 13½x13***

139 A41 5c multicolored .25 .25
140 A41 10c multicolored .50 .25
141 A41 20c multicolored 1.00 .25
Nos. 139-141 (3) 1.75 .75

Christmas Issue

Holy Night, by Carlo Maratta — A41a

1971, Oct. 6 **Photo.** ***Perf. 13x13½***

142 A41a 3c orange & multi .35 .20

People of Niue — A42

Octopus Lure and Octopus — A43

1971, Nov. 17

143	A42	4c	Boy	.20	.20
144	A42	6c	Girl	.20	.20
145	A42	9c	Man	.20	.30
146	A42	14c	Woman	.20	.40
			Nos. 143-146 (4)	.80	1.10

1972, May 3 Litho. ***Perf. 13x13½***

5c, Warrior and weapons. 10c, Sika (spear) throwing, horiz. 25c, Vivi dance, horiz.

147	A43	3c	blue & multi	.20	.20
148	A43	5c	rose & multi	.20	.20
149	A43	10c	blue & multi	.25	.25
150	A43	25c	yellow & multi	.35	.35
			Nos. 147-150 (4)	1.00	1.00

So. Pacific Festival of Arts, Fiji, May 6-20.

Alofi Wharf A44

South Pacific Commission Emblem and: 5c, Health service. 6c, School children. 18c, Cattle and dwarf palms.

1972, Sept. 6 Litho. ***Perf. 13½x14***

151	A44	4c	blue & multi	.20	.20
152	A44	5c	blue & multi	.20	.20
153	A44	6c	blue & multi	.20	.20
154	A44	18c	blue & multi	.40	.25
			Nos. 151-154 (4)	1.00	.85

So. Pacific Commission, 25th anniv.

Christmas Issue, 1972

Madonna and Child, by Murillo — A44a

1972, Oct. 4 Photo. ***Perf. 11½***

155	A44a	3c	gray & multi	.35	.20

Pempheris Oualensis A45

Designs: Various fish.

Perf. 13½x13

1973, June 27 Litho. Unwmk.

156	A45	8c	shown	.45	.45
157	A45	10c	Cephalopholis	.45	.45
158	A45	15c	Variola louti	.50	.50
159	A45	20c	Etelis carbunculus	.55	.55
			Nos. 156-159 (4)	1.95	1.95

Flowers, by Jan Breughel — A46

Paintings of Flowers: 5c, by Hans Bollongier. 10c, by Rachel Ruysch.

1973, Nov. 21 Litho. ***Perf. 13½x13***

160	A46	4c	bister & multi	.20	.20
161	A46	5c	orange brn & multi	.20	.20
162	A46	10c	emerald & multi	.25	.25
			Nos. 160-162 (3)	.65	.65

Christmas.

Capt. Cook and "Resolution" — A47

Capt. Cook and: 3c, Cook's landing place and ship. 8c, Map of Niue. 20c, Administration Building and flag of 1774.

1974, June 20 Litho. ***Perf. 13½x14***

163	A47	2c	multicolored	.30	.30
164	A47	3c	multicolored	.30	.30
165	A47	8c	multicolored	.30	.30
166	A47	20c	multicolored	.35	.35
			Nos. 163-166 (4)	1.25	1.25

Bicentenary of Cook's landing on Niue.

King Fataaiki — A48

Annexation Day, Oct. 19, 1900 — A49

Village Meeting A50

Design: 10c, Legislative Assembly Building.

Perf. 14x13½, 13½x14

1974, Oct. 19 Litho.

167	A48	4c	multicolored	.20	.20
168	A49	8c	multicolored	.20	.20
169	A50	10c	multicolored	.25	.25
170	A50	20c	multicolored	.35	.35
			Nos. 167-170 (4)	1.00	1.00

Referendum for Self-government, 9/3/74.

Decorated Bicycle — A51

Christmas: 10c, Decorated motorcycle. 20c, Going to church by truck.

1974, Nov. 13 Litho. ***Perf. 12½***

171	A51	3c	green & multi	.20	.20
172	A51	10c	dull blue & multi	.20	.20
173	A51	20c	brown & multi	.25	.25
			Nos. 171-173 (3)	.65	.65

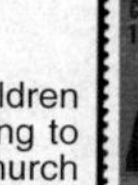

Children Going to Church A52

Children's Drawings: 5c, Child on bicycle trailing balloons. 10c, Balloons and gifts hanging from tree.

1975, Oct. 29 Litho. ***Perf. 14½***

174	A52	4c	multicolored	.20	.20
175	A52	5c	multicolored	.20	.20
176	A52	10c	multicolored	.25	.25
			Nos. 174-176 (3)	.65	.65

Christmas.

Opening of Tourist Hotel A53

Design: 20c, Hotel, building and floor plan.

1975, Nov. 19 Litho. ***Perf. 14x13½***

177	A53	8c	multicolored	.20	.20
178	A53	20c	multicolored	.20	.20

Preparing Ground for Taro A54

2c, Planting taro (root vegetable). 3c, Banana harvest. 4c, Bush plantation. 5c, Shellfish gathering. 10c, Reef fishing. 20c, Luku (fern) harvest. 50c, Canoe fishing. $1, Husking coconuts. $2, Hunting uga (land crab).

1976, Mar. 3 Litho. ***Perf. 13½x14***

179-188	A54	Set of 10	4.50	4.50

See #222-231. For surcharges see #203-210.

Water Tower, Girl Drawing Water — A55

15c, Teleprinter & Niue radio station. 20c, Instrument panel, generator & power station.

1976, July 7 Litho. ***Perf. 14x14½***

189	A55	10c	multicolored	.20	.20
190	A55	15c	multicolored	.20	.20
191	A55	20c	multicolored	.25	.25
			Nos. 189-191 (3)	.65	.65

Technical achievements.

Christmas Tree (Flamboyant) and Administration Building — A56

Christmas: 15c, Avatele Church, interior.

1976, Sept. 15 Litho. ***Perf. 14½***

192	A56	9c	orange & multi	.20	.20
193	A56	15c	orange & multi	.20	.20

Elizabeth II, Coronation Portrait, and Westminster Abbey — A57

Design: $2, Coronation regalia.

1977, June 7 Photo. ***Perf. 13½***

194	A57	$1	multicolored	1.25	.75
195	A57	$2	multicolored	2.50	1.25
a.			Souvenir sheet of 2, #194-195	3.75	3.75

25th anniv. of reign of Elizabeth II. Nos. 194-195 each printed in sheets of 5 stamps and label showing Niue flag and Union Jack.

For surcharge see No. 213.

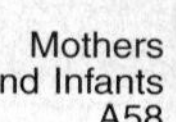

Mothers and Infants A58

Designs: 15c, Mobile school dental clinic. 20c, Elderly couple and home.

1977, June 29 Litho. ***Perf. 14½***

196	A58	10c	multicolored	.20	.20
197	A58	15c	multicolored	.20	.20
198	A58	20c	multicolored	.25	.25
			Nos. 196-198 (3)	.65	.65

Personal (social) services.

For surcharges see Nos. 211-212.

Annunciation, by Rubens — A59

Rubens Paintings (details, Virgin and Child): 12c, Adoration of the Kings. 20c, Virgin with Garland. 35c, Holy Family.

1977, Nov. 15 Photo. ***Perf. 13x13½***

199	A59	10c	multicolored	.20	.20
200	A59	12c	multicolored	.20	.20
201	A59	20c	multicolored	.50	.50
202	A59	35c	multicolored	.75	.75
a.			Souvenir sheet of 4, #199-202	2.00	2.00
			Nos. 199-202 (4)	1.65	1.65

Christmas and 400th birth anniversary of Peter Paul Rubens (1577-1640). Nos. 199-202 each printed in sheets of 6 stamps.

Stamps of 1976-77 Surcharged with New Value and 4 Bars in Black or Gold

Printing and Perforations as Before

1977, Nov. 15

203	A54	12c on 1c (#179)	.70	.25
204	A54	16c on 2c (#180)	.85	.30
205	A54	30c on 3c (#181)	.85	.40
206	A54	35c on 4c (#182)	.85	.45
207	A54	40c on 5c (#183)	.85	.50
208	A54	60c on 20c (#185)	.85	.50
209	A54	70c on $1 (#187)	.85	.50
210	A54	85c on $2 (#188)	.85	.60
211	A58	$1.10 on 10c (#196)	.85	.60
212	A58	$2.60 on 20c (#198)	1.40	.65
213	A57	$3.20 on $2 (#195, G)	1.75	.75
		Nos. 203-213 (11)	10.65	5.50

"An Inland View in Atooi," by John Webber — A60

Scenes in Hawaii, by John Webber: 16c, A View of Karakooa in Owyhee. 20c, An Offering Before Capt. Cook in the Sandwich Islands. 30c, Tereoboo, King of Owyhee, bringing presents (boats). 35c, Masked rowers in boat.

1978, Jan. 18 Photo. *Perf. 13½*

214 A60 12c gold & multi .85 .35
215 A60 16c gold & multi .90 .40
216 A60 20c gold & multi .90 .50
217 A60 30c gold & multi 1.00 .60
218 A60 35c gold & multi 1.10 .65
a. Souv. sheet, #214-218 + label 4.75 2.75
Nos. 214-218 (5) 4.75 2.50

Bicentenary of Capt. Cook's arrival in Hawaii. Nos. 214-218 printed in sheets of 5 stamps and one label showing flags of Hawaii and Niue.

Descent from the Cross, by Caravaggio A61

Easter: 20c, Burial of Christ, by Bellini.

1978, Mar. 15 Photo. *Perf. 13x13½*

219 A61 10c multicolored .20 .20
220 A61 20c multicolored .40 .20
a. Souv. sheet, #219-220, perf. 13½ 1.00 1.00

Nos. 219-220 issued in sheets of 8.
See Nos. B1-B2.

Souvenir Sheet

Elizabeth II — A62

1978, June 26 Photo. *Perf. 13*

221 Sheet of 6 3.75 3.75
a. A62 $1.10 Niue and UK flags .50 .75
b. A62 $1.10 shown .50 .75
c. A62 $1.10 Queen's New Zealand flag .50 .75
d. Souvenir sheet of 3 3.25 3.25

25th anniv. of coronation of Elizabeth II. No. 221 contains 2 horizontal se-tenant strips of Nos. 221a-221c, separated by horizontal gutter showing coronation coach. No. 221d contains a vertical se-tenant strip of Nos. 221a-221c.

Type of 1977

12c, Preparing ground for taro. 16c, Planting taro. 30c, Banana harvest. 35c, Bush plantation. 40c, Shellfish gathering. 60c, Reef fishing. 75c, Luku (fern) harvest. $1.10, Canoe fishing. $3.20, Husking coconuts. $4.20, Hunting uga (land crab).

1978, Oct. 27 Litho. *Perf. 14*

222-231 A54 Set of 10 8.00 8.00

Celebration of the Rosary, by Dürer — A63

Designs: 30c, Nativity, by Dürer. 35c, Adoration of the Kings, by Dürer.

1978, Nov. 30 Photo. *Perf. 13*

232 A63 20c multicolored .35 .35
233 A63 30c multicolored .50 .50
234 A63 35c multicolored .55 .55
a. Souv. sheet, #232-234 + label 1.75 1.75
Nos. 232-234 (3) 1.40 1.40

Christmas and 450th death anniversary of Albrecht Dürer (1471-1528). Nos. 232-234 each printed in sheets of 5 stamps and descriptive label.
See Nos. B3-B5.

Pietà, by Gregorio Fernandez — A64

Easter: 35c, Burial of Christ, by Pedro Roldan.

1979, Apr. 2

235 A64 30c multicolored .45 .45
236 A64 35c multicolored .55 .55
a. Souvenir sheet of 2, #235-236 1.75 1.75

See Nos. B6-B7.

Child, by Franz Hals — A65

IYC (Emblem and Details from Paintings): 16c, Nurse and Child. 20c, Child of the Duke of Osuna, by Goya. 30c, Daughter of Robert Strozzi, by Titian. 35c, Children Eating Fruit, by Murillo.

1979, May 31 Photo. *Perf. 14*

237 A65 16c multicolored .35 .35
238 A65 20c multicolored .45 .45
239 A65 30c multicolored .60 .60
240 A65 35c multicolored .75 .75
a. Souvenir sheet of 4, #237-240 3.00 3.00
Nos. 237-240 (4) 2.15 2.15

See Nos. B8-B11.

Penny Black, Bath Mail Coach, Rowland Hill — A66

30c, Basel #3L1 & Alpine village coach. 35c, US #1 & 1st US transatlantic mail ship. 50c, France #3 & French railroad mail car, 1849. 60c, Bavaria #1 & Bavarian mail coach.

1979, July 3 Photo. *Perf. 14*

241 A66 20c Pair, #a.-b. .50 .50
242 A66 30c Pair, #a.-b. .75 .75
243 A66 35c Pair, #a.-b. .85 .85
244 A66 50c Pair, #a.-b. 1.30 1.30
245 A66 60c Pair, #a.-b. 1.50 1.50
a. Souv. sheet of 10, #241-245 + 2 labels 5.00 5.00
Nos. 241-245 (5) 4.90 4.90

Sir Rowland Hill (1795-1879), originator of penny postage.
For overprints and surcharges see Nos. 281-285, B16, B21, B26, B30, B33, B41.

Cook's Landing at Botany Bay A68

18th Century Paintings: 30c, Cook's Men during a Landing on Erromanga. 35c, Resolution and Discovery in Queen Charlotte's Sound. 75c, Death of Capt. Cook on Hawaii, by Johann Zoffany.

1979, July 30 Photo. *Perf. 14*

251 A68 20c multicolored .70 .30
252 A68 30c multicolored .90 .40
253 A68 35c multicolored 1.25 .50
254 A68 75c multicolored 1.25 1.10
a. Souv. sheet, #251-254, perf. 13½ 4.00 4.00
Nos. 251-254 (4) 4.10 2.30

200th death anniv. of Capt. James Cook.
For surcharges see Nos. B18, B23, B28, B36.

Apollo 11 Lift-off — A69

Virgin and Child, by P. Serra — A70

1979, Sept. 27 Photo. *Perf. 13½*

255 A69 30c shown .40 .40
256 A69 35c Lunar module .45 .45
257 A69 60c Splashdown .90 .90
a. Souvenir sheet of 3 2.00 2.00
Nos. 255-257 (3) 1.75 1.75

Apollo 11 moon landing, 10th anniversary. #257a contains #255-257 in changed colors.
For surcharges see Nos. B24, B29, B35.

1979, Nov. 29 Photo. *Perf. 13*

Virgin and Child by: 25c, R. di Mur. 30c, S. diG. Sasseta. 50c, J. Huguet.

258 A70 20c multicolored .30 .30
259 A70 25c multicolored .35 .35
260 A70 30c multicolored .40 .40
261 A70 50c multicolored .70 .70
a. Souvenir sheet of 4, #258-261 2.25 2.25
Nos. 258-261 (4) 1.75 1.75

Christmas. See Nos. B12-B15. For surcharges see Nos. B19-B20, B25, B32.

Pietà, by Giovanni Bellini — A71

Easter (Pietà, Paintings by): 30c, Botticelli. 35c, Anthony Van Dyck.

1980, Apr. 2 Photo. *Perf. 13*

262 A71 25c multicolored .35 .35
263 A71 30c multicolored .40 .40
264 A71 35c multicolored .45 .45
Nos. 262-264 (3) 1.20 1.20

See Nos. B37-B40.

A72

#265a, Ceremonial Stool, New Guinea (shown). #265b, Ku-Tagwa plaque. #265c, Suspension hook. #266a, Platform post. #266b, Canoe ornament. #266c, Carved figure. #266d, Woman and child. #267a, God A'a, statue. #267b, Tangaroa, statue. #267c, Ivory pendant. #267d, Tapa cloth. #268a, Maori feather box. #268b, Hei-tiki. #268c, House post. #268d, God Ku, feather image.

1980, July 30 Photo. *Perf. 13*

265 A72 20c Strip of 4, #a.-d. .80 .80
266 A72 25c Strip of 4, #a.-d. 1.00 1.00
267 A72 30c Strip of 4, #a.-d. 1.25 1.25
268 A72 35c Strip of 4, #a.-d. 1.40 1.40

Souvenir Sheets of 4

e. #265a, 266a, 267a, 268a 1.50 1.50
f. #265b, 266b, 267b, 268b 1.50 1.50
g. #265c, 266c, 267c, 268c 1.50 1.50
h. #265d, 266d, 267d, 268d 1.50 1.50
Nos. 265-268 (4) 4.45 4.45

3rd South Pacific Festival of Arts, Port Moresby, Papua New Guinea, June 30-July 12. Stamps in souvenir sheets have 2c surtax.
For surcharges see Nos. 626-629.

Nos. 241-250, Overprinted in Black on Silver

1980, Aug. 22 *Perf. 14*

281 A66 20c Pair, #a.-b. .60 .60
282 A66 30c Pair, #a.-b. .85 .85
283 A66 35c Pair, #a.-b. .95 .95
284 A66 50c Pair, #a.-b. 1.30 1.30
285 A66 60c Pair, #a.-b. 1.60 1.60
Nos. 281-285 (5) 5.30 5.30

ZEAPEX '80, New Zealand International Stamp Exhibition, Auckland, Aug. 23-31.

Queen Mother Elizabeth, 80th Birthday — A73

1980, Sept. 15 Photo. *Perf. 13x13½*

291 A73 $1.10 multicolored 1.40 1.40

Souvenir Sheet

292 A73 $3 multicolored 3.50 3.50

No. 291 issued in sheets of 5 and label showing coad of arms.

A74

#293a, 100-meter dash. #293b, Allen Wells, England. #294a, 400-Meter freestyle. #294b, Ines Diers, DDR. #295a, Soling class yachting. #295b, Denmark. #296a, Soccer. #296b, Czechoslovakia.

1980, Oct. 30 Photo. *Perf. 14*

293 A74 20c Pair, #a.-b. .60 .60
294 A74 25c Pair, #a.-b. .70 .70
295 A74 30c Pair, #a.-b. .80 .80
296 A74 35c Pair, #a.-b. .90 .90
Nos. 293-296 (4) 3.00 3.00

22nd Summer Olympic Games, Moscow, July 19-Aug. 3.
See No. B42.

Virgin and Child, by del Sarto — A76

Paintings of Virgin & Child, by Andrea del Sarto.

1980, Nov. 28 Photo. *Perf. 13x13½*

301 A76 20c multicolored .25 .25
302 A76 25c multicolored .30 .30
303 A76 30c multicolored .35 .35
304 A76 35c multicolored .45 .45
a. Souvenir sheet of 4, #301-304 1.60 1.60
Nos. 301-304 (4) 1.35 1.35

Christmas and 450th death anniversary of Andrea del Sarto.
See Nos. B43-B46.

A77

Golden Shower Tree — A77a

#317a, Phalaenopsis sp. #317b, Moth Orchid. #318a, Euphorbia pulcherrima. #318b, Poinsettia. #319a, Thunbergia alata. #319b, Black-eyed Susan. #320a, Cochlospermum hibiscoides. #320b, Buttercup tree. #321a, Begonia sp. #321b, Begonia. #322a, Plumeria sp. #322b, Frangipani. #323a, Sterlitzia reginae. #323b, Bird of paradise. #324a, Hibiscus syriacus. #324b, Rose of Sharon. #325a, Nymphaea sp. #325b, Water lily. #326a, Tibouchina sp. #326b, Princess flower. #327a, Nelumbo sp. #327b, Lotus. #328a, Hybrid hibiscus. #328b, Yellow hibiscus.

1981-82 Photo. *Perf. 13x13½*

317 A77 2c Pair, #a.-b. .20 .20
318 A77 5c Pair, #a.-b. .20 .20
319 A77 10c Pair, #a.-b. .25 .25
320 A77 15c Pair, #a.-b. .35 .35
321 A77 20c Pair, #a.-b. .50 .50
322 A77 25c Pair, #a.-b. .65 .65
323 A77 30c Pair, #a.-b. .70 .70
324 A77 35c Pair, #a.-b. .80 .80
325 A77 40c Pair, #a.-b. .90 .90
326 A77 50c Pair, #a.-b. 1.25 1.25
327 A77 60c Pair, #a.-b. 1.40 1.40
328 A77 80c Pair, #a.-b. 2.00 2.00

Perf. 13½

329 A77a $1 shown 1.25 1.25
330 A77a $2 Orchid var. 2.50 2.50
331 A77a $3 Orchid sp. 3.50 3.50
332 A77a $4 Poinsettia 5.00 5.00
333 A77a $6 Hybrid hibiscus 7.25 7.25
334 A77a $10 Hibiscus rosa-sinensis 12.50 12.50
Nos. 317-334 (18) 41.20 41.20

Issued: 2c, 5c, 10c, 15c, 20c, 25c, Apr. 2; 30c, 35c, 40c, 50c, 60c, 80c, May 26; $1, $2, $3, Dec. 9, 1981; $4, $6, $10, Jan. 15, 1982.
For surcharges and overprints see Nos. 406-409, 413E, 594-595, O14, O16, O19.

Jesus Defiled, by El Greco A78

Easter (Paintings): 50c, Pieta, by Fernando Gallego. 60c, The Supper of Emaus, by Jacopo da Pontormo.

1981, Apr. 10 *Perf. 14*

337 A78 35c multicolored .50 .50
338 A78 50c multicolored .80 .80
339 A78 60c multicolored .95 .95
Nos. 337-339 (3) 2.25 2.25

See Nos. B47-B50.

Prince Charles and Lady Diana — A79

1981, June 26 Photo. *Perf. 14*

340 A79 75c Charles .80 .80
341 A79 95c Lady Diana 1.00 1.00
342 A79 $1.20 shown 1.40 1.40
a. Souvenir sheet of 3, #340-342 4.00 4.00
Nos. 340-342 (3) 3.20 3.20

Royal Wedding. Nos. 340-342 each printed in sheets of 5 plus label showing St. Paul's Cathedral.
For overprints and surcharges see Nos. 357-359, 410, 412, 455, 596-598, B52-B55.

1982 World Cup Soccer A80

1981, Oct. 16 Photo. *Perf. 13*

343 Strip of 3 1.10 1.10
a. A80 30c any single .35 .35
344 Strip of 3 1.40 1.40
a. A80 35c any single .45 .45
345 Strip of 3 1.50 1.50
a. A80 40c any single .50 .50
Nos. 343-345 (3) 4.00 4.00

See No. B51.

Christmas 1981 — A81

Rembrandt Paintings: 20c, Holy Family with Angels, 1645. 35c, Presentation in the Temple, 1631. 50c, Virgin and Child in Temple, 1629. 60c, Holy Family, 1640.

1981-82 Photo. *Perf. 14x13*

346 A81 20c multicolored .40 .40
347 A81 35c multicolored .90 .90
348 A81 50c multicolored 1.20 1.20
349 A81 60c multicolored 1.50 1.50
a. Souvenir sheet of 4, #346-349 4.00 4.00
Nos. 346-349 (4) 4.00 4.00

Souvenir Sheets

350 A81 80c + 5c like #346 1.10 1.10
351 A81 80c + 5c like #347 1.10 1.10
352 A81 80c + 5c like #348 1.10 1.10
353 A81 80c + 5c like #349 1.10 1.10

Surtax was for school children.
Issued: #346-349, 12/11; others, 1/22/82.

21st Birthday of Princess Diana — A82

1982, July 1 *Perf. 14*

354 A82 50c Charles .50 .50
355 A82 $1.25 Wedding 1.25 1.25
356 A82 $2.50 Diana 2.50 2.50
a. Souvenir sheet of 3, #354-356 7.00 7.00
Nos. 354-356 (3) 4.25 4.25

Nos. 354-356 each printed in sheets of 5 plus label showing wedding day picture.
For overprints and surcharges see Nos. 359B-359D, 411, 413, 456.

Nos. 340-342a Overprinted

Type I: "COMMEMORATING THE ROYAL BIRTH 21 JUNE 1982."Type II: "BIRTH OF PRINCE WILLIAM OF WALES 21 JUNE 1982." Type III): "PRINCE WILLIAM OF WALES 21 JUNE 1982."

1982, July 23 *Perf. 14*

357 A79 75c multi (I) 1.40 1.40
357A A79 75c multi (II) 1.40 1.40
358 A79 95c multi (I) 1.75 1.75
358A A79 95c multi (II) 1.75 1.75
359 A79 $1.20 multi (I) 2.25 2.25
359A A79 $1.20 multi (II) 2.25 2.25
Nos. 357-359A (6) 10.80 10.80

Souvenir Sheet

359B A79 Sheet of 3, #a.-c. 7.50 7.50
a. 75c multi (III) 2.00 2.00
b. 95c multi (III) 2.00 2.00
c. $1.20 multi (III) 2.00 2.00

Nos. 357/357A, 358/358A and 359/359A were printed in small sheets containing three stamps overprinted Type I, two overprinted type II and one label.

Birthday Type of 1982 Inscribed in Silver "COMMEMORATING THE BIRTH OF PRINCE WILLIAM OF WALES—21 JUNE 1982."

1982 Photo. *Perf. 14*

359C A82 50c like #354 .75 .75
359D A82 $1.25 like #355 1.80 1.80
359E A82 $2.50 like #356 3.50 3.50
a. Souvenir sheet of 3 8.00 8.00
Nos. 359C-359E (3) 6.05 6.05

Christmas — A83

Princess Diana Holding Prince William and Paintings of Infants by: 40c, Bronzino (1502-1572). 52c, Murillo (1617-1682). 83c, Murillo, diff. $1.05, Boucher (1703-1770). Singles in No. 363a: 34x30mm, showing paintings only.

1982, Dec. 3 Photo. *Perf. 13½x14½*

360 A83 40c multicolored 1.40 1.40
361 A83 52c multicolored 1.60 1.60
362 A83 83c multicolored 2.75 2.75
363 A83 $1.05 multicolored 3.75 3.75
a. Souvenir sheet of 4, #364-367 8.00 8.00
Nos. 360-363 (4) 9.50 9.50

Souvenir Sheets

364 A83 80c + 5c like #360 2.75 2.75
365 A83 80c + 5c like #361 2.75 2.75
366 A83 80c + 5c like #362 2.75 2.75
367 A83 80c + 5c like #363 2.75 2.75

Nos. 364-367 each contain one 30x42mm stamp showing Royal family. Surtax was for children's funds.

Commonwealth Day — A84

1983, Mar. 14 Photo. *Perf. 13*

368 A84 70c Flag, Premier Robert R. Rex .85 .85
369 A84 70c Resolution, Adventurer .85 .85
370 A84 70c Passion flower .85 .85
371 A84 70c Lime branch .85 .85
a. Block of 4, #368-371 3.40 3.40

For overprints see Nos. 484-487.

Scouting Year — A85

1983, Apr. 28 Photo. *Perf. 13*

372 A85 40c Flag signals .85 .85
373 A85 50c Tree planting 1.00 1.00
374 A85 83c Map reading 1.80 1.80
Nos. 372-374 (3) 3.65 3.65

Souvenir Sheet

375 Sheet of 3 3.75 3.75
a. A85 40c + 3c like 40c .90 .90
b. A85 50c + 3c like 50c 1.00 1.00
c. A85 83c + 3c like 83c 1.60 1.60

Nos. 372-375 Overprinted in Black on Silver: "XV WORLD JAMBOREE CANADA"

1983, July 14 Photo.

376 A85 40c multicolored .85 .85
377 A85 50c multicolored 1.00 1.00
378 A85 83c multicolored 1.60 1.60
Nos. 376-378 (3) 3.45 3.45

Souvenir Sheet

379 Sheet of 3 4.00 4.00
a. A85 40c + 3c multicolored .90 .90
b. A85 50c + 3c multicolored 1.00 1.00
c. A85 83c + 3c multicolored 2.00 2.00

Save the Whales Campaign — A86

1983, Aug. 15 *Perf. 13x14*

380 A86 12c Right whale 1.00 .50
381 A86 25c Fin whale 1.40 .60
382 A86 35c Sei whale 1.90 .95
383 A86 40c Blue whale 2.25 1.10
384 A86 58c Bowhead whale 2.40 1.25
385 A86 70c Sperm whale 3.00 1.25
386 A86 83c Humpback whale 3.25 1.75
387 A86 $1.05 Lesser rorqual 4.00 1.90
388 A86 $2.50 Gray whale 5.50 3.25
Nos. 380-388 (9) 24.70 12.55

Manned Flight Bicentenary — A87

1983, Oct. 14 Photo. *Perf. 14*

389 A87 25c Montgolfier, 1783 .40 .40
390 A87 40c Wright Bros. Flyer, 1903 .60 .60
391 A87 58c Graf Zeppelin, 1928 1.10 1.10
392 A87 70c Boeing 247, 1933 1.50 1.50
393 A87 83c Apollo VIII, 1968 1.75 1.75
394 A87 $1.05 Columbia space shuttle 2.00 2.00
a. Souvenir sheet of 6 6.25 6.25
Nos. 389-394 (6) 7.35 7.35

No. 394a contains Nos. 389-394 inscribed "AIRMAIL."

Christmas A87a

Paintings by Raphael (1483-1520): 30c, Garvagh Madonna, National Gallery, London. 40c, Granduca Madonna, Pitti Gallery, Florence. 58c, Goldfinch Madonna, Uffizi Gallery, Florence. 70c, Holy Family of Francis I, Louvre, Paris. 83c, Holy Family with Saints, Alte Pinakothek, Munich.

1983 Photo. *Perf. 14*

395 A87a 30c multicolored .75 .75
396 A87a 40c multicolored 1.00 1.00
397 A87a 58c multicolored 1.50 1.50
398 A87a 70c multicolored 1.60 1.60
399 A87a 83c multicolored 2.10 2.10
Nos. 395-399 (5) 6.95 6.95

Souvenir Sheets

Perf. 13½

400 Sheet of 5 4.50 4.50
a. A87a 30c + 3c like #395 .45 .45
b. A87a 40c + 3c like #396 .60 .60
c. A87a 58c + 3c like #397 .90 .90
d. A87a 70c + 3c like #398 1.00 1.00
e. A87a 83c + 3c like #399 1.25 1.25
401 A87a 85c + 5c like #395 1.50 1.50
402 A87a 85c + 5c like #396 1.50 1.50
403 A87a 85c + 5c like #397 1.50 1.50
404 A87a 85c + 5c like #398 1.50 1.50
405 A87a 85c + 5c like #399 1.50 1.50

500th birth anniv. of Raphael.
Issued: #395-400, 11/25; #401-405, 12/29.

Nos. 323, 326-328, 341, 355, 342, 356 and 331 Surcharged in Black or Gold with One or Two Bars

1983, Nov. 30 Photo.
Pairs, #a.-b. (#406-409)

406 A77 52c on 30c 1.75 1.75
407 A77 58c on 50c 1.90 1.90
408 A77 70c on 60c 2.50 2.50
409 A77 83c on 80c 3.00 3.00
410 A79 $1.10 on 95c #341 1.80 1.80
411 A82 $1.10 on $1.25 #355 (G) 1.80 1.80
412 A79 $2.60 on $1.20 #342 4.50 4.50
413 A82 $2.60 on $2.50 #356 (G) 4.50 4.50
413A A77a $3.70 on $3 #331 6.00 6.00
Nos. 406-413A (9) 27.75 27.75

World Communications Year — A88

1984, Jan. 23 Photo. *Perf. 13x13½*
414 A88 40c Telegraph sender .50 .50
415 A88 52c Early telephone .70 .70
416 A88 83c Satellite 1.25 1.25
a. Souvenir sheet of 3, #414-416 2.25 2.25
Nos. 414-416 (3) 2.45 2.45

Moth Orchid — A89

Golden Shower Tree A90

1984 *Perf. 13x13½*
417 A89 12c shown .20 .20
418 A89 25c Poinsettia .45 .45
419 A89 30c Buttercup tree .65 .65
420 A89 35c Begonia .65 .65
421 A89 40c Frangipani .70 .70
422 A89 52c Bird of paradise .90 .90
423 A89 58c Rose of Sharon 1.00 1.00
424 A89 70c Princess flower 1.25 1.25
425 A89 83c Lotus 1.40 1.40
426 A89 $1.05 Yellow hibiscus 2.00 2.00
427 A90 $1.75 shown 2.10 2.10
428 A90 $2.30 Orchid var. 2.75 2.75
429 A90 $3.90 Orchid sp. 4.50 4.50
430 A90 $5 Poinsettia, diff. 5.75 5.75
431 A90 $6.60 Hybrid hibiscus 7.50 7.50
431A A90 $8.30 Hibiscus rosasinensis 10.00 10.00
Nos. 417-431A (16) 41.80 41.80

Issued: #417-426, 2/20; #427-429, 5/10; others 6/18.
For overprints see #O1-O13, O15, O17-O18.

1984 Summer Olympics A91

Designs: Greek pottery designs, 3rd cent. BC. 30c, 70c vert.

1984, Mar. 15 Photo. *Perf. 14*
432 A91 30c Discus .50 .50
433 A91 35c Running .55 .55
434 A91 40c Equestrian .60 .60
435 A91 58c Boxing .90 .90
436 A91 70c Javelin 1.10 1.10
Nos. 432-436 (5) 3.65 3.65

For overprints and surcharges see #446-450, 480-483.

AUSIPEX '84, Australian Animals — A92

1984 Photo. *Perf. 14*
437 A92 25c Koala .35 .35
438 A92 35c Koala, diff. .45 .45
439 A92 40c Koala, diff. .75 .75
440 A92 58c Koala, diff. 1.20 1.20
441 A92 70c Koala, diff. 1.50 1.50
442 A92 83c Kangaroo with joey 1.75 1.75
443 A92 $1.05 Kangaroo with joey, diff. 2.00 2.00
444 A92 $2.50 Kangaroo, diff. 4.75 4.75
Nos. 437-444 (8) 12.75 12.75

Souvenir Sheets

445 Sheet of 2 + label 6.00 6.00
a. A92 $1.75 Wallaby 3.00 3.00
b. A92 $1.75 Koala, diff. 3.00 3.00
c. Sheet, #437-441, 445b, perf 13½ 5.00 5.00
d. Sheet, #442-444, 445a, perf 13½ 7.25 7.25

Nos. 442-444 airmail.
Issued: #437-444, Aug. 24; $445, Sept. 20.

Nos. 432-436 Ovptd. with Event, Names of Gold Medalists, Country in Gold or Red

1984, Sept. 7 *Perf. 14*
446 A91 30c Danneberg .50 .50
447 A91 35c Coe (R) .60 .60
448 A91 40c Todd .70 .70
449 A91 58c Biggs 1.00 1.00
450 A91 70c Haerkoenen 1.25 1.25
Nos. 446-450 (5) 4.05 4.05

10th Anniv. of Self Government — A93

1984, Oct. 19 Photo. *Perf. 13*
451 A93 40c Niue flag .60 .60
452 A93 58c Niue map 1.10 1.10
453 A93 70c Ceremony 1.25 1.25
a. Souvenir sheet of 3, #451-453 3.00 3.00
Nos. 451-453 (3) 2.95 2.95

Souvenir Sheet

454 A93 $2.50 like 70c 3.00 3.00

For overprints and surcharges see Nos. 655-660.

Nos. 340, 354 Surcharged: "Prince Henry / 15.9.84" and Bars and New Values in Red or Silver

1984, Oct. 22 Photo. *Perf. 14*
455 A79 $2 on 75c multi (R) 2.50 2.50
456 A82 $2 on 50c multi (S) 2.50 2.50

Nos. 455-456 issued in sheets of 5 + label.

Christmas A94

Paintings: 40c, The Nativity, by A. Vaccaro. 58c, Virgin with Fly, anonymous. 70c, Adoration of the Shepherds, by B. Murillo. 83c, Flight into Egypt, by B. Murillo.

1984, Oct. 19 Photo. *Perf. 13x13½*
457 A94 40c multicolored .60 .60
458 A94 58c multicolored .85 .85
459 A94 70c multicolored 1.10 1.10
460 A94 83c multicolored 1.25 1.25
Nos. 457-460 (4) 3.80 3.80

Souvenir Sheets

461 Sheet of 4 4.00 4.00
a. A94 40c + 5c Like 40c .65 .65
b. A94 58c + 5c Like 58c .85 .85
c. A94 70c + 5c Like 70c 1.10 1.10
d. A94 83c + 5c Like 83c 1.20 1.20

Perf. 13½
462 A94 95c + 10c Like 40c 1.50 1.50
463 A94 95c + 10c Like 58c 1.50 1.50
464 A94 95c + 10c Like 70c 1.50 1.50
465 A94 95c + 10c Like 83c 1.50 1.50

Audubon Birth Bicentenary A95

Illustrations of North American bird species by artist/naturalist John J. Audubon.

1985, Apr. 15 Photo. *Perf. 14½*
466 A95 40c House wren 1.50 1.50
467 A95 70c Veery 2.00 2.00
468 A95 83c Grasshopper sparrow 2.75 2.75
469 A95 $1.05 Henslow's sparrow 3.25 3.25
470 A95 $2.50 Vesper sparrow 7.50 7.50
Nos. 466-470 (5) 17.00 17.00

Souvenir Sheets

Perf. 14
471 A95 $1.75 like #466 3.00 3.00
472 A95 $1.75 like #467 3.00 3.00
473 A95 $1.75 like #468 3.00 3.00
474 A95 $1.75 like #469 3.00 3.00
475 A95 $1.75 like #470 3.00 3.00
Nos. 471-475 (5) 15.00 15.00

Queen Mother, 85th Birthday A96

Designs: 70c, Wearing mantle of the Order of the Garter. $1.15, With Queen Elizabeth II. $1.50, With Prince Charles. $3, Writing letter.

1985, June 14 *Perf. 13½x13*
476 A96 70c multicolored 1.25 1.25
477 A96 $1.15 multicolored 1.50 1.50
478 A96 $1.50 multicolored 2.25 2.25
a. Souvenir sheet of 3 + label, #476-478 5.50 5.50
Nos. 476-478 (3) 5.00 5.00

Souvenir Sheet

Perf. 13½
479 A96 $3 multicolored 5.00 5.00

Nos. 476-478 issued in sheets of 5 plus label. No. 479 contains one 39x36mm stamp. No. 478a issued 8/4/86, for 86th birthday.

Nos. 432-433, 435-436 Overprinted: "Mini South Pacific Games, Rarotonga" and Surcharged with Gold Bar and New Value in Black

1985, July 26 *Perf. 14*
480 A91 52c on 95c multi .60 .60
481 A91 83c on 58c multi 1.25 1.25
482 A91 95c on 35c multi 1.40 1.40
483 A91 $2 on 30c multi 2.75 2.75
Nos. 480-483 (4) 6.00 6.00

Nos. 368-371 Overprinted with Conference Emblem and: "Pacific Islands Conference, Rarotonga"

1985, July 26 *Perf. 13½x13*
484 A84 70c on #368 .85 .85
485 A84 70c on #369 .85 .85
486 A84 70c on #370 .85 .85
487 A84 70c on #371 .85 .85
a. Block of 4, #484-487 3.50 3.50

A97

A98

Paintings of children: 58c, Portrait of R. Strozzi's Daughter, by Titian. 70c, The Fifer, by Manet. $1.15, Portrait of a Young Girl, by Renoir. $1.50, Portrait of M. Berard, by Renoir.

1985, Oct. 11 *Perf. 13*
488 A97 58c multicolored 2.00 2.00
489 A97 70c multicolored 2.25 2.25
490 A97 $1.15 multicolored 3.75 3.75
491 A97 $1.50 multicolored 5.00 5.00
Nos. 488-491 (4) 13.00 13.00

Souvenir Sheets

Perf. 13x13½
492 A97 $1.75 + 10c like #488 5.50 5.50
493 A97 $1.75 + 10c like #489 5.50 5.50
494 A97 $1.75 + 10c like #490 5.50 5.50
495 A97 $1.75 + 10c like #491 5.50 5.50

Intl. Youth Year.

1985, Nov. 29 Photo. *Perf. 13x13½*

Christmas, Paintings (details) by Correggio: 58c, No. 500a, Virgin and Child. 85c, No. 500b, Adoration of the Magi. $1.05, No. 500c, Virgin and Child, diff. $1.45, No. 500d, Virgin and Child with St. Catherine.

496 A98 58c multicolored 1.50 1.50
497 A98 85c multicolored 2.50 2.50
498 A98 $1.05 multicolored 3.00 3.00
499 A98 $1.45 multicolored 4.25 4.25
Nos. 496-499 (4) 11.25 11.25

Souvenir Sheets

500 Sheet of 4 6.00 6.00
a.-d. A98 60c + 10c, any single 1.50 1.50

Imperf
501 A98 65c like #496 1.50 1.50
502 A98 95c like #497 2.00 2.00
503 A98 $1.20 like #498 2.75 2.75
504 A98 $1.75 like #499 4.00 4.00
Nos. 500-504 (5) 16.25 16.25

Nos. 501-504 each contain one 61x71mm stamp.

Halley's Comet — A99

The Constellations, fresco by Giovanni De Vecchi, Farnesio Palace, Caprarola, Italy.

1986, Jan. 24 *Perf. 13½*

505 A99 60c multicolored 1.00 1.00
506 A99 75c multicolored 1.25 1.25
507 A99 $1.10 multicolored 1.75 1.75
508 A99 $1.50 multicolored 2.75 2.75
Nos. 505-508 (4) 6.75 6.75

Souvenir Sheet

509 Sheet of 4 9.00 9.00
a. A99 95c like #505 2.25 2.25
b. A99 95c 95c like #506 2.25 2.25
c. A99 95c like #507 2.25 2.25
d. A99 95c like #508 2.25 2.25

A100

A102

A101

Elizabeth II, 60th Birthday: $1.10, No. 513a, Elizabeth and Prince Philip at Windsor Castle. $1.50, No. 513b, At Balmoral. $2, No. 513c, Elizabeth at Buckingham Palace. $3, Elizabeth seated and Prince Philip.

1986, Apr. 28 *Perf. 14½x13½*

510 A100 $1.10 multicolored 1.10 1.10
511 A100 $1.50 multicolored 1.60 1.60
512 A100 $2 multicolored 2.25 2.25
Nos. 510-512 (3) 4.95 4.95

Souvenir Sheets

513 Sheet of 3 2.75 2.75
a.-c. A100 75c any single .90 .90
514 A100 $3 multicolored 3.50 3.50

For surcharges see Nos. 546-547.

1986, May 22 **Photo.** *Perf. 14*

AMERIPEX '86: #515a, Washington, US #1. #515b, Jefferson, Roosevelt, Lincoln.

515 A101 $1 Pair, #a.-b. 9.00 9.00

1986, July 4 *Perf. 13x13½*

Paintings: $1, Statue under construction, 1883, by Victor Dargaud. $2.50, Unveiling the Statue of Liberty, 1886, by Edmund Morand (1829-1901).

517 A102 $1 multicolored 2.50 2.50
518 A102 $2.50 multicolored 6.00 6.00

Souvenir Sheet

519 Sheet of 2 4.50 4.50
a. A102 $1.25 like #517 2.25 2.25
b. A102 $1.25 like #518 2.25 2.25

Statue of Liberty, cent.

Wedding of Prince Andrew and Sarah Ferguson — A103

Designs: $2.50, Portraits, Westminster Abbey. $5, Portraits.

1986, July 23 *Perf. 13½x13*

520 A103 $2.50 multicolored 4.50 4.50

Souvenir Sheet

521 A103 $5 Portraits 10.00 10.00

No. 520 printed in sheets of 4. No. 521 contains one 45x32mm stamp.

STAMPEX '86, Adelaide, Aug. 4-10 — A104

Birds.

Perf. 13x13½, 13½x13

1986, Aug. 4 **Photo.**

522 A104 40c Egretta alba, vert. 1.25 1.25
523 A104 60c Emblema picta 1.75 1.75
524 A104 75c Aprosmictus scapularis, vert. 2.50 2.50
525 A104 80c Malurus lamberti 2.75 2.75
526 A104 $1 Falco peregrinus, vert. 3.25 3.25
527 A104 $1.65 Halcyon azurea 5.25 5.25
528 A104 $2.20 Melopsittacus undulatus, vert. 7.50 7.50
529 A104 $4.25 Dromaius novaehollandiae 14.00 14.00
Nos. 522-529 (8) 38.25 38.25

Christmas A105

Paintings in the Vatican Museum: 80c, No. 534a, Virgin and Child, by Perugino (1446-1523). $1.15, No. 534b, Virgin of St. N. dei Frari, by Titian. $1.80, No. 534c, Virgin with Milk, by Lorenzo di Credi (1459-1537). $2.60, $7.50, No. 534d, Foligno Madonna, by Raphael.

1986, Nov. 14 **Litho.** *Perf. 14*

530 A105 80c multi 1.75 1.75
531 A105 $1.15 multi 2.50 2.50
532 A105 $1.80 multi 4.25 4.25
533 A105 $2.60 multi 6.50 6.50
Nos. 530-533 (4) 15.00 15.00

Souvenir Sheets

Perf. 13½

534 Sheet of 4 14.00 14.00
a.-d. A105 $1.50 any single 3.50 3.50

Perf. 14½x13½

535 A105 $7.50 multi 15.00 15.00

For surcharges see Nos. B56-B61.

Souvenir Sheets

Statue of Liberty, Cent. — A106

Photographs: No. 536a, Tall ship, bridge. No. 536b, Workmen, flame from torch. No. 536c, Workman, flame, diff. No. 536d, Ships, New York City. No. 536e, Tall ship, sailboat, bridge. No. 537a, Statue, front. No. 537b, Statue, left side. No. 537c, Torch dismantled. No. 537d, Statue, right side. No. 537e, Welder.

1987, May 20

536 Sheet of 5 + label 4.50 4.50
a.-e. A106 75c any single .90 .90
537 Sheet of 5 + label 4.50 4.50
a.-e. A106 75c any single .90 .90

Tennis Champions — A107

Olympic emblem, coin and: 80c, $1.15, $1.40, $1.80, Boris Becker. 85c, $1.05, $1.30, $1.75, Steffi Graf. Various action scenes.

1987

538 A107 80c multi 3.00 3.00
539 A107 85c multi 2.50 2.50
540 A107 $1.05 multi 3.00 3.00
541 A107 $1.15 multi 3.25 3.25
542 A107 $1.30 multi 3.00 3.00
543 A107 $1.40 multi 3.75 3.75
544 A107 $1.75 multi 3.75 3.75
545 A107 $1.80 multi 4.50 4.50
Nos. 538-545 (8) 26.75 26.75

Issued: 80c, $1.15, $1.40, $1.80, 9/25; others, 10/20.

For overprints see Nos. 560-563.

Nos. 511-512 Surcharged "40th /WEDDING / ANNIV." with Denomination in Black on Gold

Perf. 14½x13½

1987, Nov. 20 **Photo.**

546 A100 $4.85 on $1.50 #511 6.00 6.00
547 A100 $4.85 on $2 #512 6.00 6.00

40th Wedding anniv. of Queen Elizabeth II and Prince Philip, Duke of Edinburgh.

Christmas — A108

Paintings (details) by Albrecht Durer (Angel with Lute on 80c, $1.05, $2.80): 80c, No. 551a, The Nativity. $1.05, No. 551b, Adoration of the Magi. $2.80, No. 551c, $7.50, Celebration of the Rosary.

1987, Dec. 4 **Photo.** *Perf. 13½*

548 A108 80c multi 2.00 2.00
549 A108 $1.05 multi 2.50 2.50
550 A108 $2.80 multi 6.00 6.00
Nos. 548-550 (3) 10.50 10.50

Souvenir Sheets

551 Sheet of 3 10.00 10.00
a.-c. A108 $1.30 any single 3.25 3.25
552 A108 $7.50 multi 12.00 12.00

Size of Nos. 551a-551c: 49½x38½mm. No. 552 contains one 51x33mm stamp.

European Soccer Championships — A109

Highlights from Franz Beckenbauer's career: 20c, Match scene. 40c, German all-star team. 60c, Brussels, 1974. 80c, England, 1966. $1.05, Mexico, 1970. $1.30, Munich, 1974. $1.80, FC Bayern Munchen vs. Athletico Madrid.

1988, June 20 **Litho.** *Perf. 14*

553 A109 20c multi .50 .50
554 A109 40c multi 1.00 1.00
555 A109 60c multi 1.50 1.50
556 A109 80c multi 2.00 2.00
557 A109 $1.05 multi 2.75 2.75
558 A109 $1.30 multi 3.50 3.50
559 A109 $1.80 multi 4.50 4.50
Nos. 553-559 (7) 15.75 15.75

Nos. 539-540, 542 and 543 Ovptd.

a. "Australia 24 Jan 88 / French Open 4 June 88"

b. "Wimbledon 2 July 88 / U S Open 10 Sept. 88"

c. "Women's Tennis Grand / Slam: 10 September 88"

d. "Seoul Olympic Games / Gold Medal Winner"

1988, Oct. 14 **Litho.** *Perf. 13½x14*

560 A107(a) 85c on No. 539 2.00 2.00
561 A107(b) $1.05 on No. 540 2.50 2.50
562 A107(c) $1.30 on No. 542 3.00 3.00
563 A107(d) $1.75 on No. 543 4.00 4.00
Nos. 560-563 (4) 11.50 11.50

Steffi Graf, 1988 Olympic gold medalist; opportunities for youth in sports.

Christmas A110

Adoration of the Shepherds, by Rubens: 60c, Angels. 80c, Joseph and witness. $1.05, Madonna. $1.30, Christ child. $7.20, Entire painting.

1988, Oct. 28 **Photo.** *Perf. 13½*

564 A110 60c multi 1.75 1.75
565 A110 80c multi 3.00 3.00
566 A110 $1.05 multi 4.25 4.25
567 A110 $1.30 multi 5.00 5.00
Nos. 564-567 (4) 14.00 14.00

Souvenir Sheet

568 A110 $7.20 multi 12.00 12.00

No. 568 contains one 40x50mm stamp.

First Moon Landing, 20th Anniv. A111

Apollo 11: #a, Mission emblem and astronaut. #b, Earth, Moon and simplified flight plan. #c, Olive branch, Apollo 1 mission emblem and astronaut on Moon. Printed in continuous design.

1989, July 20 **Photo.** *Perf. 14*

571 A111 $1.50 Strip of 3, #a.-c. 17.50 17.50

Souvenir Sheet of 3

Perf. 13½x13

572 A111 $1.15 #a.-c. 10.00 10.00

Christmas — A112

Details of Presentation in the Temple, 1631, by Rembrandt, Royal Cabinet of Paintings, The Hague: 70c, Priests. 80c, Madonna. $1.05, Joseph. $1.30, Christ child. $7.20, Entire painting.

1989, Nov. 22 Photo. *Perf. 13x13½*

573	A112	70c	multicolored	3.00	3.00
574	A112	80c	multicolored	3.25	3.25
575	A112	$1.05	multicolored	4.25	4.25
576	A112	$1.30	multicolored	5.25	5.25
			Nos. 573-576 (4)	15.75	15.75

Souvenir Sheet

Perf. 13½

577	A112	$7.20	multicolored	16.00	16.00

No. 577 contains one 39x50mm stamp.

Emblem of the German Natl. Soccer Team and Signatures — A113

Former team captains: 80c, Fritz Walter. $1.15, Franz Beckenbauer. $1.40, Uwe Seeler.

1990, Feb. 5 Photo. *Perf. 13½*

578	A113	80c	multicolored	2.50	2.50
579	A113	$1.15	multicolored	3.00	3.00
580	A113	$1.40	multicolored	5.00	5.00
581	A113	$1.80	shown	6.00	6.00
			Nos. 578-581 (4)	16.50	16.50

1990 World Cup Soccer Championships, Italy.

First Postage Stamp, 150th Anniv. — A114

Paintings by Rembrandt showing letters: 80c, No. 586d, Merchant Maarten Looten (1632). $1.05, No. 586c, Rembrandt's son Titus holding pen (1655). $1.30, No. 586b, The Shipbuilder and his Wife (1633). $1.80, No. 586a, Bathsheba with King David's letter (1654).

1990, May 2 Photo. *Perf. 13½*

582	A114	80c	multicolored	2.25	2.25
583	A114	$1.05	multicolored	3.00	3.00
584	A114	$1.30	multicolored	4.50	4.50
585	A114	$1.80	multicolored	6.00	6.00
			Nos. 582-585 (4)	15.75	15.75

Souvenir Sheet

586		Sheet of 4	12.00	12.00
a.-d.	A114 $1.50	any single	3.00	3.00

A115

A116

1990, July 23 *Perf. 13x13½*

587	A115	$1.25	multicolored	6.00	6.00

Souvenir Sheet

588	A115	$7	multicolored	17.50	17.50

Queen Mother, 90th birthday.

1990, Nov. 27 Litho. *Perf. 14*

Christmas (Paintings): 70c, Adoration of the Magi by Bouts. 80c, Holy Family by Fra Bartolomeo. $1.05, The Nativity by Memling. $1.30, Adoration of the King by Pieter Bruegel, the Elder. $7.20, Virgin and Child Enthroned by Cosimo Tura.

589	A116	70c	multicolored	2.50	2.50
590	A116	80c	multicolored	3.25	3.25
591	A116	$1.05	multicolored	4.00	4.00
592	A116	$1.30	multicolored	5.00	5.00
			Nos. 589-592 (4)	14.75	14.75

Souvenir Sheet

593	A116	$7.20	multicolored	16.00	16.00

No. 334 Overprinted in Silver

1990, Dec. 5 *Perf. 13x13½*

594	A77a	$10	multicolored	17.50	17.50

Birdpex '90, 20th Intl. Ornithological Congress, New Zealand.

No. 333 Overprinted "SIXTY FIFTH BIRTHDAY QUEEN ELIZABETH II"

1991, Apr. 22 Litho. *Perf. 13x13½*

595	A77a	$6	multicolored	9.50	9.50

Nos. 340-342 Overprinted in Black or Silver

Typo. Litho.

1991, June 26 Photo. *Perf. 14*

596	A79	75c on #340 (S)		1.75	1.75
a.		Litho. overprint		1.75	1.75
597	A79	95c on #341		2.50	2.50
a.		Litho. overprint		2.50	2.50
598	A79	$1.20 on #342		3.50	3.50
a.		Litho. overprint		3.50	3.50
			Nos. 596-598 (3)	7.75	7.75
			Nos. 596a-598a (3)	7.75	7.75

Nos. 596-598 issued in miniature sheets of 5 with typo. overprint. Nos. 596a-598a issued in uncut panes of 4 miniature sheets of 5. Letters of typo. overprint are taller and thinner than litho. overprint.

Christmas — A117

Birds — A118

Paintings: 20c, The Virgin and Child with Saints Jerome and Dominic, by Filippino Lippi. 50c, The Isenheim Altarpiece, The Virgin and Child, by Grunewald. $1, The Nativity, by Pittoni. $2, Adoration of the Kings, by Jan Brueghel, the Elder. $7, The Adoration of the Shepherds, by Reni.

1991, Nov. 11 Litho. *Perf. 14*

599	A117	20c	multicolored	.40	.40
600	A117	50c	multicolored	1.25	1.25
601	A117	$1	multicolored	2.75	2.75
602	A117	$2	multicolored	5.00	5.00
			Nos. 599-602 (4)	9.40	9.40

Souvenir Sheet

603	A117	$7	multicolored	11.00	11.00

1992-93 Litho. *Perf. 14x13½*

604	A118	20c	Banded rail	.30	.30
605	A118	50c	Red-tailed tropicbird	.70	.70
606	A118	70c	Purple swamphen	1.00	1.00
607	A118	$1	Pacific pigeon	1.50	1.50
608	A118	$1.50	White-collared kingfisher	2.00	2.00
609	A118	$2	Blue-crowned lory	2.75	2.75
610	A118	$3	Crimson-crowned fruit dove	4.25	4.25
611	A118	$5	Barn owl	6.50	6.50

Perf. 13

Size: 51x38mm

612	A118	$7	Longtailed cockoo	9.00	9.00

Size: 49x35mm

613	A118	$10	Reef heron	12.50	12.50
614	A118	$15	Polynesian triller	20.00	20.00
			Nos. 604-614 (11)	60.50	60.50

Issued $1.50, $2, 3/20; $3, 4/16; $5, 5/15; $7, 3/26/93; $10, 4/16/93; $15, 8/10/93; others, 2/92.

For overprints & surcharges see Nos. O20-O25, 676-677.

This is an expanding set. Numbers may change.

Discovery of America, 500th Anniv. — A119

$2, Queen Isabella supports Columbus. $3, Columbus' fleet. $5, Columbus landing in America.

1992 Litho. *Perf. 13*

621	A119	$2	multicolored	3.00	3.00
622	A119	$3	multicolored	5.25	5.25
623	A119	$5	multicolored	8.75	8.75
			Nos. 621-623 (3)	17.00	17.00

1992 Summer Olympics, Barcelona — A120

#624: a, $10 coin, tennis player. b, Flags, torch. c, Gymnast, $10 coin. $5, Water polo player.

1992, July 22 Litho. *Perf. 13½x13*

624	A120	$2.50	Strip of 3, #a.-c.	19.00	19.00

Souvenir Sheet

625	A120	$5	multicolored	13.00	13.00

Nos. 265-268 Surcharged

1992, Sept. 30 Photo. *Perf. 13*

Strips of 4, #a.-d.

626	A72	$1 on 20c	5.50	5.50
627	A72	$1 on 25c	5.50	5.50
628	A72	$1 on 30c	5.50	5.50
629	A72	$1 on 35c	5.50	5.50
		Nos. 626-629 (4)	22.00	22.00

6th South Pacific Festival of the Arts.

Christmas A121

Design: Different details from St. Catherine's Mystic Marriage, by Hans Memling.

1992, Nov. 18 Litho. *Perf. 13½*

642	A121	20c	multicolored	.35	.35
643	A121	50c	multicolored	1.00	1.00
644	A121	$1	multicolored	2.50	2.50
645	A121	$2	multicolored	4.50	4.50
			Nos. 642-645 (4)	8.35	8.35

Souvenir Sheet

646	A121	$7	like #643	14.00	14.00

No. 646 contains one 39x48mm stamp.

Queen Elizabeth II's Accession to the Throne, 40th Anniv. — A122

Various portraits of Queen Elizabeth II.

1992, Dec. 7 *Perf. 14*

647	A122	70c	multicolored	.75	.75
648	A122	$1	multicolored	2.25	2.25
649	A122	$1.50	multicolored	4.50	4.50
650	A122	$2	multicolored	5.50	5.50
			Nos. 647-650 (4)	13.00	13.00

Dolphins A123

Designs: 20c, Rough-toothed dolphin. 50c, Fraser's dolphin. 75c, Pantropical spotted dolphin. $1, Risso's dolphin.

1993, Jan. 13 **Litho.** ***Perf. 14***

651	A123	20c multicolored	1.25	.75
652	A123	50c multicolored	3.50	1.50
653	A123	75c multicolored	4.75	2.50
654	A123	$1 multicolored	6.00	4.50
		Nos. 651-654 (4)	15.50	9.25

World Wildlife Fund.

Nos. 451-453 Ovptd.

1993, Mar. 15 **Photo.** ***Perf. 13***

655	A93	40c on #451 multi	.75	.75
656	A93	58c on #452 multi	1.50	1.50
657	A93	70c on #453 multi	2.00	2.00

Nos. 655-657 Surcharged

1993, Mar. 15

658	A93	$1 on 40c #655	3.50	3.50
659	A93	$1 on 58c #656	3.50	3.50
660	A93	$1 on 70c #657	3.50	3.50
		Nos. 655-660 (6)	14.75	14.75

Queen Elizabeth II, 40th Anniv. of Coronation — A124

1993, June 2 **Litho.** ***Perf. 14***

661	A124	$5 multicolored	13.50	13.50

Christmas A125

Details from Virgin of the Rosary, by Guido Reni: 20c, Infant Jesus. 70c, Cherubs. $1, Two men, one pointing upward. $1.50, Two men looking upward. $3, Madonna and child.

1993, Oct. 29 **Litho.** ***Perf. 14***

662	A125	20c multicolored	.40	.40
663	A125	70c multicolored	1.50	1.50
664	A125	$1 multicolored	2.25	2.25
665	A125	$1.50 multicolored	4.00	4.00

Size: 32x47mm

Perf. 13½

666	A125	$3 multicolored	7.50	7.50
		Nos. 662-666 (5)	15.65	15.65

1994 World Cup Soccer Championships, U.S. — A126

Illustration reduced.

1994, June 17 **Litho.** ***Perf. 14***

667	A126	$4 multicolored	10.00	10.00

First Manned Moon Landing, 25th Anniv. — A127

Designs: a, Flight to Moon, astronaut opening solar wind experiment lunar surface. b, Astronaut holding flag. c, Astronaut standing by lunar experiment package.

1994, July 20 **Litho.** ***Perf. 14***

668	A127	$2.50 Tryptic, #a.-c.	24.00	24.00

Christmas A128

Entire paintings or details: No. 669a, The Adoration of the Kings, by Jan Gossaert. b, Madonna & Child with Saints John & Catherine, by Titian. c, The Holy Family and Shepherd, by Titian. d, Virgin & Child with Saints, by Gerard David.

No. 670: a-b, Adoration of the Shepherds, by N. Poussin. c, Madonna & Child with Saints Joseph & John, by Sebastiano. d, Adoration of the Kings, by Veronese.

1994, Nov. 28 **Litho.** ***Perf. 14***

669	A128	70c Block of 4, #a.-d.	6.00	6.00
670	A128	$1 Block of 4, #a.-d.	9.00	9.00

Robert Louis Stevenson (1850-94), Writer — A129

a, Treasure Island. b, Dr. Jekyll and Mr. Hyde. c, Kidnapped. d, Stevenson, tomb, inscription.

1994, Dec. 14 ***Perf. 15x14***

671	A129	$1.75 Block of 4, #a.-d.	17.50	17.50

Flowers — A130

1996, May 10 **Litho.** ***Perf. 14½x14***

672	A130	70c Tapeu orchid	1.10	1.10
673	A130	$1 Frangipani	1.60	1.60
674	A130	$1.20 Golden shower	2.00	2.00
675	A130	$1.50 Pua	2.50	2.50
		Nos. 672-675 (4)	7.20	7.20

Nos. 606, 608 Surcharged

1996, Feb. 19 **Litho.** ***Perf. 14x13½***

676	A118	50c on 70c #606	11.50	8.50
677	A118	$1 on $1.50 #608	13.50	10.50

Flower Type of 1969 Redrawn

Design: 20c, Hibiscus.

1996, Aug. 22 **Litho.** ***Rouletted 7***

678	A38	20c red & green	.55	.55

Yachting A131

1996 **Litho.** ***Perf. 14½***

679	A131	70c Jackfish	1.10	1.10
680	A131	$1 S/V Jennifer	1.60	1.60
681	A131	$1.20 Mikeva	2.25	2.25
682	A131	$2 Eye of the Wind	3.75	3.75
		Nos. 679-682 (4)	8.70	8.70

Souvenir Sheet

Perf. 14

683	A131	$1.50 Desert Star	2.75	2.75

Issued: Nos. 679-682, 9/30/96. No. 683, 10/96 (Taipei '96). No. 683 contains one 30x30mm stamp.

Coral A132

20c, Acropora gemmifera. 50c, Acropora nobilis. 70c, Goniopora lobata. $1, Stylaster. $1.20, Alveopora catalai. $1.50, Fungia scutaria. $2, Porites solida. $3, Millepora. $4, Pocillopora eydouxi. $5, Platygyra pini.

1996, Dec. 20 **Litho.** ***Perf. 14***

684-693	A132	Set of 10	29.00	29.00

Souvenir Sheet

New Year 1997 (Year of the Ox) — A133

1997, Feb. 10 **Litho.** ***Perf. 13***

694	A133	$1.50 multicolored	2.50	2.50

Hong Kong '97.

Humpback Whale — A134

20c, Whale in water. 50c, Killer whale. 70c, Minke whale. $1, Adult, young whale swimming upward. $1.20, Sperm whale. $1.50, Whale breaching.

1997 **Litho.** ***Perf. 14***

695	A134	20c multi	.35	.35
696	A134	50c multi, vert.	.80	.80
697	A134	70c multi, vert.	1.10	1.10
698	A134	$1 multi, vert.	1.75	1.75
699	A134	$1.20 multi, vert.	2.00	2.00
700	A134	$1.50 multi, vert.	2.75	2.75
a.		Souvenir sheet, #695, 698, 700	5.00	5.00
		Nos. 695-700 (6)	8.75	8.75

Pacific '97 (#700a).

Issued: 20c, $1, $1.50, 5/29; others, 9/3.

Island Scenes — A135

Designs: a, Steps leading over island along inlet. b, Island, vegetagion, sky. c, Coral reef, undersea vegetation. d, Reef, vegetation, diff.

1997, Apr. 18 **Litho.** ***Perf. 13½x14***

701	A135	$1 Block of 4, #a.-d.	5.75	5.75

Christmas A136

Bouquets of various flowers.

1997, Nov. 26 **Litho.** ***Perf. 14***

702	A136	20c deep plum & multi	.35	.35
703	A136	50c green & multi	.85	.85
704	A136	70c blue & multi	1.25	1.25
705	A136	$1 red & multi	1.75	1.75
		Nos. 702-705 (4)	4.20	4.20

Diana, Princess of Wales (1961-97)

Common Design Type

Various portraits: a, 20c. b, 50c. c, $1. d, $2.

1998, Apr. 29 **Litho.** ***Perf. 14½x14***

706	CD355	Sheet of 4, #a.-d.	5.50	5.50

No. 706 sold for $3.70 + 50c, with surtax from international sales being donated to the Princess of Wales Memorial fund and surtax from national sales being donated to designated local charity.

Diving A137

Designs: 20c, Two snorkeling beneath water's surface. 70c, One diver, coral. $1, Diving into underwater canyon, vert. $1.20, Two divers, coral. $1.50, Divers exploring underwater cavern.

Wmk. Triangles

1998, May 20 **Litho.** ***Perf. 14½***

707	A137	20c multicolored	.35	.35
708	A137	70c multicolored	.85	.85
709	A137	$1 multicolored	1.25	1.25
710	A137	$1.20 multicolored	1.50	1.50
711	A137	$1.50 multicolored	2.00	2.00
		Nos. 707-711 (5)	5.95	5.95

Sea Birds A138

Designs: 20c, Pacific black duck. 70c, Fairy tern. $1, Great frigatebird, vert. $1.20, Lesser golden plover. $2, Brown noddy.

Perf. 14½x14, 14x14½
Wmk. Triangles

1998, July 23 Litho.
712 A138 20c multicolored .45 .45
713 A138 70c multicolored 1.00 1.00
714 A138 $1 multicolored 1.75 1.75
715 A138 $1.20 multicolored 2.00 2.00
716 A138 $2 multicolored 3.00 3.00
Nos. 712-716 (5) 8.20 8.20

Shells A139

Two views of various shells from the Pacific Ocean.

Perf. 14½
1998, Sept. 23 Litho. Unwmk.
717 A139 20c multicolored .45 .45
718 A139 70c multicolored 1.00 1.00
719 A139 $1 multicolored 2.00 2.00
720 A139 $5 multicolored 6.50 6.50
Nos. 717-720 (4) 9.95 9.95

Ancient Weapons — A140

Perf. 14x14½
1998, Nov. 18 Litho. Unwmk.
721 A140 20c Clubs .45 .45
722 A140 $1.20 Spears 1.40 1.40
723 A140 $1.50 Spears, diff. 1.75 1.75
724 A140 $2 Throwing stones 2.50 2.50
Nos. 721-724 (4) 6.10 6.10

Nos. 722-723 are each 60x23mm.

Maritime Heritage — A141

Designs: 70c, First migration of Niue Fekai. $1, Crew of Resolution discover Niue. $1.20, LMS John Williams. $1.50, Captain James Cook (1728-79).

1999, Feb. 24 Litho. *Perf. 14½x14*
725 A141 70c bright violet blue .85 .85
726 A141 $1 bright violet blue 1.25 1.25
727 A141 $1.20 bright violet blue 1.60 1.60
728 A141 $1.50 bright violet blue 2.00 2.00
Nos. 725-728 (4) 5.70 5.70

Nudibranchs A142

World Wide Fund for Nature: 20c, Risbecia tryoni. $1, Chromodoris lochi. $1.20, Chromodoris elizabethina. $1.50, Chromodoris bullocki.

1999, Mar. 17 Litho. *Perf. 14½*
729 A142 20c multicolored .40 .40
730 A142 $1 multicolored 1.40 1.40
731 A142 $1.20 multicolored 1.50 1.50
732 A142 $1.50 multicolored 2.25 2.25
a. Souv. sheet, 2 ea #729-732 11.50 11.50
Nos. 729-732 (4) 5.55 5.55

Scenic Views A143

1999, June 16 Litho. *Perf. 14*
734 A143 $1 Togo Chasm, vert. 1.25 1.25
735 A143 $1.20 Matapa Chasm, vert. 1.40 1.40
736 A143 $1.50 Tufukia 1.75 1.75
737 A143 $2 Talava Arches 2.50 2.50
Nos. 734-737 (4) 6.90 6.90

Woven Baskets A144

Various styles and patterns: #738a, 20c. #738b, $1. #739a, 70c. #739b, $3.

1999, Sept. 18 Litho. *Perf. 12*
738 A144 Pair, a.-b. 2.00 2.00
739 A144 Pair, a.-b. 4.00 4.00

Nos. 738b, 739b are each 45x35mm.

Souvenir Sheet

Self-Government, 25th Anniv. — A145

Designs: a, 20c, Natives, boats. b, $5, Fish, tree, diver, child.

Litho. with Foil application
1999, Dec. 1 *Perf. 15x14¾*
740 A145 Sheet of 2, #a.-b 6.00 6.00

Millennium — A146

a, 20c, Man in outrigger canoe. b, 70c, Women pointing up. c, $4, Swimmers, bird, fish.

1999, Dec. 31 Litho. *Perf. 14¼x15*
741 A146 Strip of 3, #a.-c. 6.50 6.50

Birds and Flora — A147

20c, Purple-capped fruit dove, mamane. $1, Purple swamphen, fig. $1.20, Barn owl, koa. $2, Blue-crowned lory, ohia lehua.

2000, Apr. 5 Litho. *Perf. 13x13¼*
742-745 A147 Set of 4 7.00 7.00

Royal Birthdays A148

Designs: $1.50, Queen Mother, 100th birthday, vert. $3, Prince William, 18th birthday, and Queen Mother.

2000, May 22 *Perf. 13¼x13, 13x13¼*
746-747 A148 Set of 2 6.00 6.00

2000 Summer Olympics, Sydney A149

Designs: 50c, Pole vault. 70c, Diving. $1, Hurdles. $3, Gymnastics.

Perf. 13½x13¼
2000, Sept. 16 Litho.
748-751 A149 Set of 4 5.50 5.50

Dancers — A150

No. 752: a, Couple. b, Woman with red garments. c, Woman with white garments. d, Child with garments made of leaves.

2000, Nov. 22 Litho. *Perf. 13¼x13*
752 Horiz. strip of 4 6.00 6.00
a. A150 20c multi .35 .35
b. A150 70c multi .80 .80
c. A150 $1.50 multi 1.60 1.60
d. A150 $3 multi 3.25 3.25

Niue Postage Stamps, Cent. (in 2002) — A151

Designs: 70c, #1. $3, #34.

2001, Jan. 31
753-754 A151 Set of 2 4.25 4.25

Butterflies A152

No. 755: a, Large green-banded blue. b, Leafwing. c, Cairns birdwing. d, Meadow argus.

2001, Mar. 22 *Perf. 13½x13¼*
755 Horiz. strip of 4 5.00 5.00
a. A152 20c multi .25 .25
b. A152 70c multi .75 .75
c. A152 $1.50 multi 1.75 1.75
d. A152 $2 multi 2.25 2.25

Turtles A153

Designs: 50c, Green turtle hatching. $1, Hawksbill turtle. $3, Green turtle on beach.

2001, May 10
756-758 A153 Set of 3 5.25 5.25

Coconut Crabs — A154

Crab: 20c, In water. 70c, On beach. $1.50, Climbing tree. $3, With coconut.

2001, July 7 *Perf. 14*
759-762 A154 Set of 4 6.00 6.00

Annexation by New Zealand, Cent. A155

Designs: $1.50, Building. $2, Man and woman.

2001, Oct. 19 Litho. *Perf. 13½x13¼*
763-764 A155 Set of 2 4.00 4.00

Christmas — A156

Designs: 20c, Magi. 70c, Dove. $1, Angel. $2, Star.

2001, Dec. 13 *Perf. 13x13¼*
765-768 A156 Set of 4 4.50 4.50
a. Horiz. strip, #765-768 4.50 4.50

No. 729 Surcharged

2002, July 7 Litho. *Perf. 14½*
769 A142 $10 on 20c multi *55.00 45.00*

Worldwide Fund for Nature (WWF) — A156a

Various depictions of small giant clam.

2002, Nov. 7 Litho. *Perf. 13¼x13*
769A Horiz. strip of 4 4.50 4.50
b. A156a 50c multi .60 .60
c. A156a 70c multi .75 .70
d. A156a $1 multi 1.10 1.10
e. A156a $1.50 multi 1.60 1.60

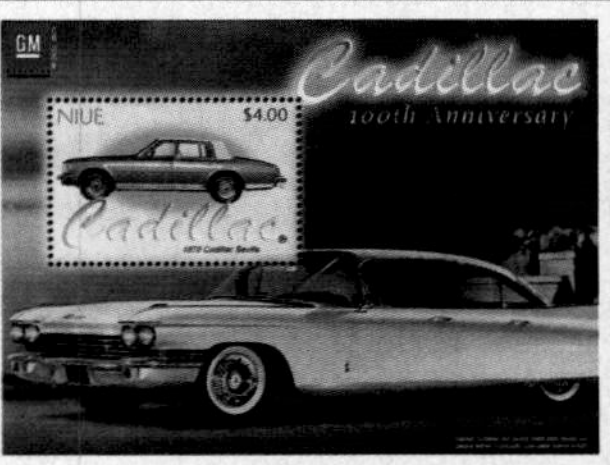

General Motors Automobiles — A157

No. 770, $1.50 — Cadillacs: a, 1953 Eldorado. b, 2002 Eldorado. c, 1967 Eldorado. d, 1961 Sedan de Ville.
No. 771, $1.50 — Corvettes: a, 1954 convertible. b, 1979. c, 1956 convertible. d, 1964 Stingray.
No. 772, $4, 1978 Cadillac Seville. No. 773, $4, 1979 Corvette.

2003 Litho. *Perf. 14*
Sheets of 4, #a-d

770-771 A157 Set of 2 24.00 24.00

Souvenir Sheets

772-773 A157 Set of 2 22.00 22.00

Issued: Nos. 770, 772, 8/25; Nos. 771, 773, 9/2.

Coronation of Queen Elizabeth II, 50th Anniv. — A158

No. 774: a, Wearing crown as younger woman. b, Wearing tiara. c, Wearing crown as older woman.
$4, Wearing hat.

2003, Sept. 2

774 A158 $1.50 Sheet of 3, #a-c 9.25 9.25

Souvenir Sheet

775 A158 $4 multi 9.25 9.25

Prince William, 21st Birthday — A159

No. 776: a, Wearing blue checked tie. b, Wearing shirt and jacket. c, Wearing striped shirt and tie.
$4, Wearing shirt.

2003, Sept. 2

776 A159 $1.50 Sheet of 3, #a-c 9.25 9.25

Souvenir Sheet

777 A159 $4 multi 8.75 8.75

Tour de France Bicycle Race, Cent. — A160

No. 778: a, Nicholas Frantz, 1927. b, Frantz, 1928. c, Maurice de Waele, 1929. d, André Leducq, 1930.
$4, Leducq, 1930, diff.

2003, Sept. 2 ***Perf. 13½x13¼***

778 A160 $1.50 Sheet of 4, #a-d 11.00 11.00

Souvenir Sheet

779 A160 $4 multi 9.25 9.25

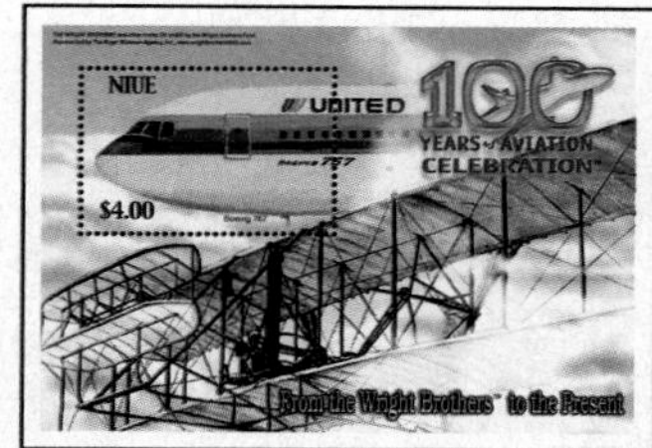

Powered Flight, Cent. — A161

No. 780: a, Boeing 737-200. b, Boeing Stratocruiser. c, Boeing Model SA-307B. d, Douglas DC-2. e, Wright Flyer I. f, De Havilland D.H.4A.
$4, Boeing 767.

2003, Sept. 2 ***Perf. 14***

780 A161 80c Sheet of 6, #a-f 9.00 9.00

Souvenir Sheet

781 A161 $4 multi 9.00 9.00

Birds, Butterflies and Fish — A162

No. 782, $1.50, vert. — Birds: a, Wrinkled hornbill. b, Toco toucan. c, Roseate spoonbill. d, Blue and gold macaw.
No. 783, $1.50 — Butterflies: a, Agrias beata. b, Papilio blumei. c, Cethosia bibbis. d, Cressida cressida.
No. 784, $1.50 — Fish: a, Garibaldi fish. b, Golden damselfish. c, Squarespot anthias. d, Orange-fin anemonefish.
No. 785, $3, Green-wing macaw. No. 786, $3, Blue morpho butterfly. No. 787, $3, Maculosus angelfish.

Perf. 13½x13¼, 13¼x13½
2004, Aug. 16 Litho.
Sheets of 4, #a-d

782-784 A162 Set of 3 24.00 24.00

Souvenir Sheets

785-787 A162 Set of 3 12.00 12.00

Miniature Sheet

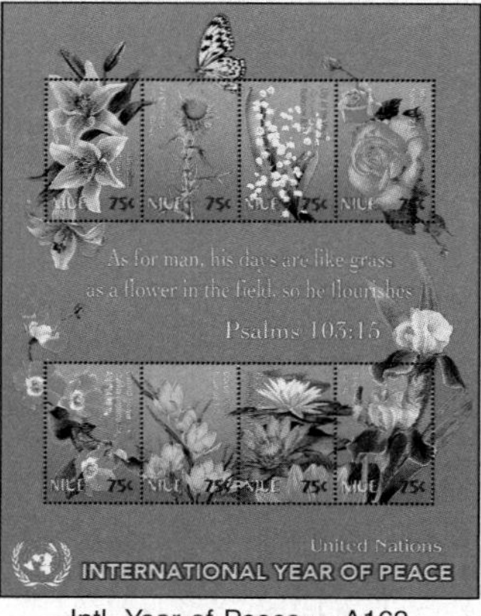

Intl. Year of Peace — A163

No. 788: a, Lily. b, Thistle. c, Lily of the valley. d, Rose. e, Garland flower. f, Crocus. g, Lotus. h, Iris.

2004, Oct. 13 ***Perf. 13½x13¼***

788 A163 75c Sheet of 8, #a-h 8.25 8.25

Miniature Sheet

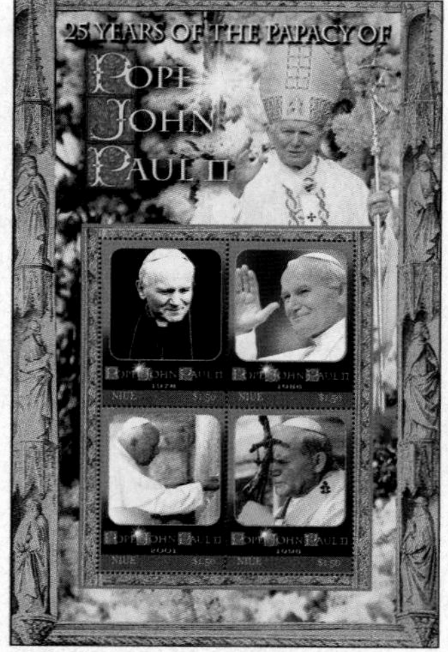

Election of Pope John Paul II, 25th Anniv. (in 2003) — A164

No. 789 — Pope in: a, 1978. b, 1986. c, 2001. d, 1996.

2004, Oct. 13 ***Perf. 13¼***

789 A164 $1.50 Sheet of 4, #a-d 8.25 8.25

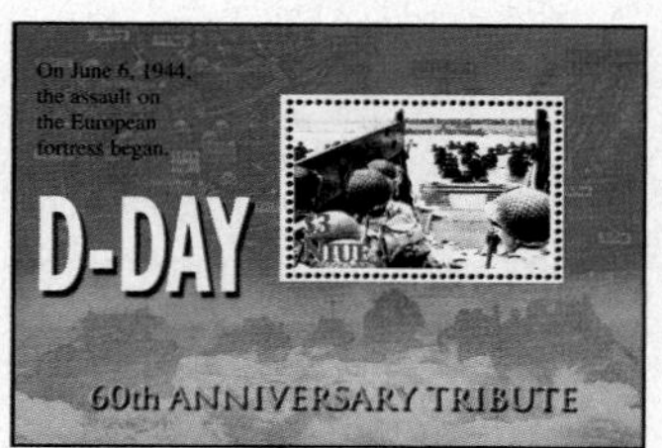

D-Day, 60th Anniv. — A165

No. 790: a, Allied Air Forces begin bombing German coastal batteries. b, Allied naval guns pound Atlantic Wall. c, Paratroopers drop over Normandy. d, Allies advance and the Germans begin to surrender.
$3, Assault troops disembark on the shores of Normandy.

2004, Oct. 13 ***Perf. 13¼x13½***

790 A165 $1.50 Sheet of 4, #a-d 8.25 8.25

Souvenir Sheet

791 A165 $3 multi 4.25 4.25

Locomotives, 200th Anniv. — A166

No. 792: a, 520 Class 4-8-4, Australia. b, FEF-2 Class 4-8-4, US. c, Royal Scot Class 4-6-0, Great Britain. d, A4 Class 4-6-2, Great Britain.
$3, Class GS-4 4-8-4, US.

2004, Oct. 13

792 A166 $1.50 Sheet of 4, #a-d 8.25 8.25

Souvenir Sheet

793 A166 $3 multi 4.25 4.25

Pope John Paul II (1920-2005) — A167

2005, Dec. 13 Litho. *Perf. 13¼*

794 A167 $2 multi 2.75 2.75

Printed in sheets of 4.

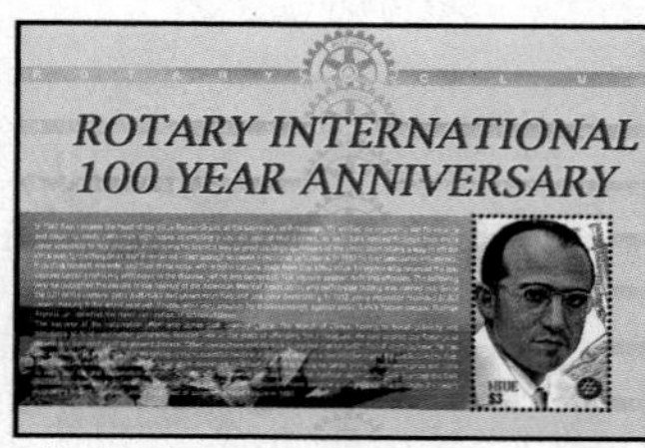

Rotary International, Cent. — A168

No. 795: a, Children. b, Paul P. Harris, Rotary founder. c, Carlo Ravizza, 1999-2000 Rotary International President.
$3, Dr. Jonas Salk, polio vaccine pioneer.

2005, Dec. 22

795 A168 $1.50 Sheet of 3, #a-c 6.25 6.25

Souvenir Sheet

796 A168 $3 multi 4.25 4.25

Pope Benedict XVI — A169

2005, Dec. 27

797 A169 $1.50 multi 2.10 2.10

Printed in sheets of 4.

Hans Christian Andersen (1805-75), Author — A170

No. 798 — Andersen and country name and denomination in: a, Lilac. b, Ocher. c, Red.
$3, Andersen facing left.

2005, Dec. 27

798 A170 $1.50 Sheet of 3, #a-c 6.25 6.25

Souvenir Sheet

799 A170 $3 multi 4.25 4.25

World Cup Soccer Championships, 75th Anniv. — A171

No. 800: a, Frank Bauman. b, Marcus Babbel. c, Dietmar Hamann.
$3, Christian Worns.

2005, Dec. 27
800 A171 $1.50 Sheet of 3, #a-c 6.25 6.25

Souvenir Sheet

801 A171 $3 multi 4.25 4.25

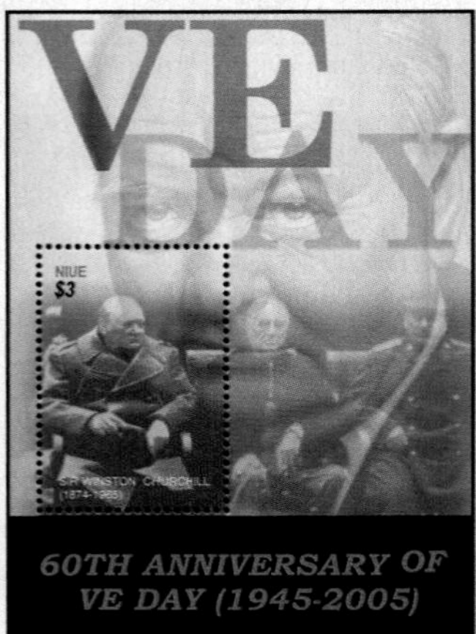

End of World War II, 60th Anniv. — A172

No. 802, horiz.: a, Entertaining the troops in the Pacific. b, USS Argonaut sailors reading letters from home. c, Japan surrenders on USS Missouri. d, A toast to peace. e, Entertainment at sea. f, Welcoming peace.
No. 803: a, D-Day invasion, Normandy, France. b, Lt. Meyrick Clifton-James, double for Field Marshal Bernard Montgomery. c, RAF Hawker Typhoon over French coast. d, Allied war cemetery, St. Laurent-sur-Mer, France.
No. 804, $3, Sir Winston Churchill. No. 805, $3, Pres. Franklin D. Roosevelt.

2005, Dec. 27
802 A172 75c Sheet of 6, #a-f 6.25 6.25
803 A172 $1.25 Sheet of 4, #a-d 7.00 7.00

Souvenir Sheets

804-805 A172 Set of 2 8.50 8.50

Souvenir Sheets

National Basketball Association Players and Team Emblems — A173

No. 806, $4.50: a, LeBron James. b, Cleveland Cavaliers emblem.
No. 807, $4.50: a, Tim Duncan. b, San Antonio Spurs emblem.
No. 808, $4.50: a, Allen Iverson. b, Denver Nuggets emblem.
No. 809, $4.50: a, Kobe Bryant. b, Los Angeles Lakers emblem.
No. 810, $4.50: a, Tracy McGrady. b, Houston Rockets emblem.
No. 811, $4.50: a, Jermaine O'Neal. b, Indiana Pacers emblem.

Litho. & Embossed
2007, Feb. 4 *Imperf.*
Without Gum
Sheets of 2, #a-b
806-811 A173 Set of 6 75.00 75.00

Miniature Sheet

Elvis Presley (1935-77) — A174

No. 812 — Presley: a, With hands resting on guitar. b, In green shirt, playing guitar. c, In brown red shirt, playing guitar. d, Holding guitar by neck.

2007, Feb. 15 Litho. *Perf. 12¾*
812 A174 $1.50 Sheet of 4, #a-d 8.25 8.25

Miniature Sheets

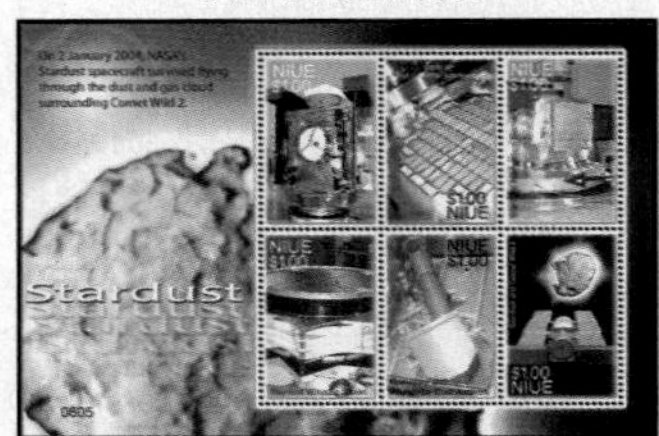

Space Achievements — A175

No. 813: a, Stardust probe at Kennedy Space Center. b, Stardust dust collector with aerogel. c, Stardust navigational camera. d, Stardust Whipple shield. e, Cometary and interstellar dust analyzer. f, Stardust and Comet Wild 2.
No. 814, horiz. — Artist's rendition of future projects: a, Astrobiology field laboratory. b, Deep-drill lander. c, Mars science laboratory. d, Phoenix lander.

2007, Feb. 15
813 A175 $1 Sheet of 6, #a-f 8.25 8.25
814 A175 $1.50 Sheet of 4, #a-d 8.25 8.25

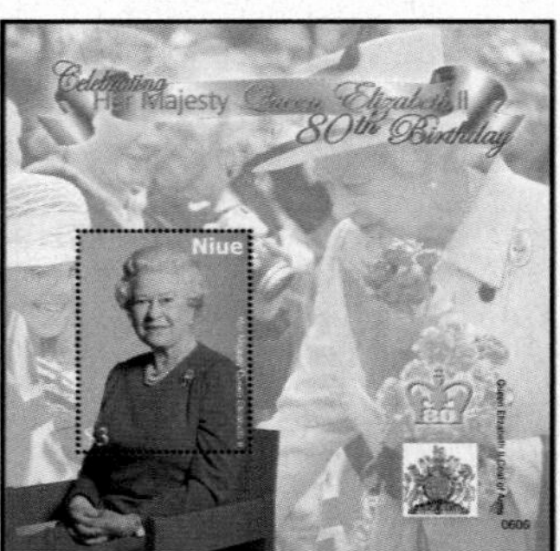

Queen Elizabeth II, 80th Birthday (in 2006) — A176

No. 815 — Dress color: a, Brown. b, Pink. c, Red. d, White.
$3, Purple.

2007, Feb. 15 *Perf. 12¼x12*
815 A176 $1.50 Sheet of 4, #a-d 8.25 8.25

Souvenir Sheet
Perf. 13¼

816 A176 $3 multi 4.25 4.25

Rembrandt (1606-69), Painter A177

Designs: 75c, Life Study of a Young Man Pulling a Rope. $1.25, Self-portrait. $1.50, Joseph Telling His Dreams. $2, The Blindness of Tobit.
$3, Christ in the Storm on the Lake of Galilee.

2007, Feb. 15 *Perf. 12¼x12*
817-820 A177 Set of 4 7.75 7.75

Imperf
Size: 70x100mm

821 A177 $3 multi 4.25 4.25

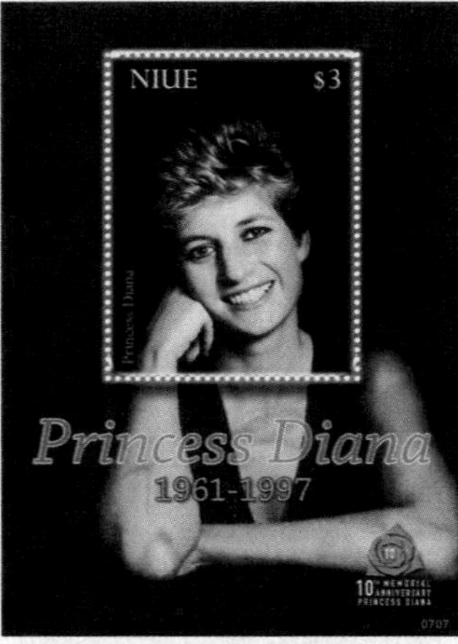

Princess Diana (1961-97) — A178

No. 822 — Diana wearing: a, Purple dress. b, Tiara and black dress. c, Green dress, close-up. d, Purple dress, close-up. e, Tiara, close-up. f, Green dress.
$3, Diana with head on hand.

2007, May 3 *Perf. 13½x13¼*
822 A178 $1 Sheet of 6, #a-f 9.00 9.00

Souvenir Sheet

823 A178 $3 multi 4.50 4.50

Local Attractions, Flora and Fauna — A179

Designs: 20c, Palaha Cave. 70c, White pua flower. $1, Talava Natural Arch. $1.20, Avaiki Pool. $1.50, Coral rock spears. $2, Humpback whale. $3, Spinner dolphins.

2007, July 9 Litho. *Perf. 14x14¾*

824	A179	20c multi	.30	.30
825	A179	70c multi	1.10	1.10
826	A179	$1 multi	1.50	1.50
827	A179	$1.20 multi	1.90	1.90
828	A179	$1.50 multi	2.25	2.25
829	A179	$2 multi	3.00	3.00
830	A179	$3 multi	4.50	4.50
		Nos. 824-830 (7)	14.55	14.55

Miniature Sheets

Concorde — A180

No. 831, $1: a, Concorde and hangar, blue tint. b, Concorde in air, normal tint. c, Concorde and hangar, red tint. d, Concorde in air, pink tint. e, Concorde and hangar, normal tint. f, Concorde in air, blue tint.
No. 832, $1: a, Concorde landing, yellow green frame. b, Concorde being towed, gray frame. c, Concorde landing, green gray frame. d, Concorde being towed, brown frame. e, Concorde landing, gray frame. f, Concorde being towed, blue frame.

2007, July 21 *Perf. 13¼*
Sheets of 6, #a-f
831-832 A180 Set of 2 18.00 18.00

Wedding of Queen Elizabeth II and Prince Philip, 60th Anniv. — A181

No. 833, vert.: a, Queen and Prince, "N" of "Niue" and denomination over white area, parts of flag in faded area between country name and denomination. b, Queen, "N" of "Niue" and denomination over white and blue areas. c, Queen, flower buds in faded area between country name and denomination. d, Queen and Prince, "N" of "Niue" and denomination over gray area, parts of flag in faded area between country name and denomination. e, Queen and Prince, country name and denomination over solid gray area. f, Queen, country name and denomination over solid gray area.
$3, Queen and Prince.

2007, July 21 *Perf. 13¼*
833 A181 $1 Sheet of 6, #a-f 9.00 9.00

Souvenir Sheet

834 A181 $3 multi 4.50 4.50

Miniature Sheets

A182

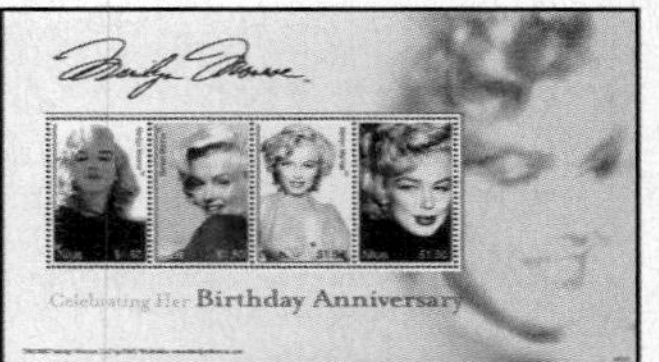

Marilyn Monroe (1926-62), Actress — A183

Various portraits.

2007, Aug. 21
835 A182 $1.50 Sheet of 4, #a-d 8.50 8.50
836 A183 $1.50 Sheet of 4, #a-d 8.50 8.50

Jamestown, Virginia, 400th Anniv. — A184

No. 837: a, Marriage of John Rolfe to Pocahontas. b, First settlers reach Jamestown. c, Tobacco plant. d, Capt. John Smith. e, Jamestown Tercentenary Monument. f, Map of Jamestown.

$3, Queen Elizabeth II and Prince Philip at Jamestown.

2007, Aug. 21

837 A184 $1 Sheet of 6, #a-f 8.50 8.50

Souvenir Sheet

838 A184 $3 multi 4.25 4.25

Pope Benedict XVI — A185

2007, Dec. 3 Litho. *Perf. 13¼*

839 A185 70c multi 1.10 1.10

Printed in sheets of 8.

Miniature Sheet

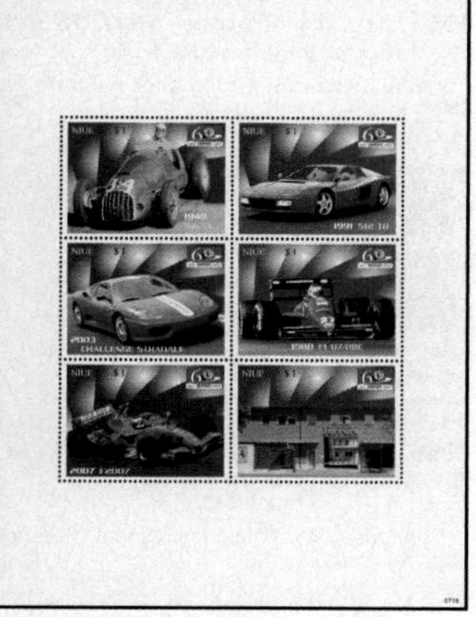

Ferrari Automobiles, 60th Anniv. — A186

No. 840: a, 1949 166 FL. b, 1991 512 TR. c, 2003 Challenge Stradale. d, 1988 F1 87/88C. e, 2007 F2007. f, Building with Ferrari sign.

2007, Dec. 10

840 A186 $1 Sheet of 6, #a-f 9.50 9.50

SEMI-POSTAL STAMPS

Catalogue values for unused stamps in this section are for Never Hinged items.

Easter Type of 1978
Souvenir Sheets

Designs: No. B1, Descent from the Cross, by Caravaggio. No. B2, Burial of Christ, by Bellini. Sheets show paintings from which stamp designs were taken.

1978, Mar. 15 Photo. *Perf. 13½*

B1 A61 70c + 5c multi 1.25 1.25
B2 A61 70c + 5c multi 1.25 1.25

Surtax was for school children in Niue.

Christmas Type of 1978
Souvenir Sheets

1978, Nov. 30 Photo. *Perf. 13*

B3 A63 60c + 5c like #232 1.25 1.25
B4 A63 60c + 5c like #233 1.25 1.25
B5 A63 60c + 5c like #234 1.25 1.25
Nos. B3-B5 (3) 3.75 3.75

Surtax was for school children of Niue. The sheets show paintings from which designs of stamps were taken.

Easter Type of 1979
Souvenir Sheets

1979, Apr. 2

B6 A64 70c + 5c like #235 1.50 1.50
B7 A64 70c + 5c like #236 1.50 1.50

Surtax was for school children of Niue. The sheets show altarpiece from which designs of stamps were taken.

IYC Type of 1979
Souvenir Sheets

1979, May 31 Photo. *Perf. 13*

B8 A65 70c + 5c like #237 1.25 1.25
B9 A65 70c + 5c like #238 1.25 1.25
B10 A65 70c + 5c like #239 1.25 1.25
B11 A65 70c + 5c like #240 1.25 1.25
Nos. B8-B11 (4) 5.00 5.00

Sheets show paintings from which designs of stamps were taken.

Christmas Type of 1979
Souvenir Sheets

1979, Nov. 29 Photo. *Perf. 13*

B12 A70 85c + 5c like #258 1.25 1.25
B13 A70 85c + 5c like #259 1.25 1.25
B14 A70 85c + 5c like #260 1.25 1.25
B15 A70 85c + 5c like #261 1.25 1.25
Nos. B12-B15 (4) 5.00 5.00

Multicolored margins show entire paintings.

Nos. 241-245, 251-254, 255-257, 258-261 Surcharged in Black (2 lines) or Silver (3 lines):

HURRICANE RELIEF Plus 2c

1980, Jan. 25 Photo. *Perf. 14, 13½*

B16 A66 20c + 2c pair .60 .60
B18 A68 20c + 2c multi (S) .30 .30
B19 A70 20c + 2c multi (S) .30 .30
B20 A70 25c + 2c multi (S) .40 .40
B21 A66 30c + 2c pair .90 .90
B23 A68 30c + 2c multi (S) .45 .45
B24 A69 30c + 2c multi (S) .45 .45
B25 A70 30c + 2c multi (S) .45 .45
B26 A66 35c + 2c pair 1.10 1.10
B28 A68 35c + 2c multi (S) .55 .55
B29 A69 35c + 2c multi (S) .55 .55
B30 A66 50c + 2c pair 1.40 1.40
B32 A70 50c + 2c multi (S) .70 .70
B33 A66 60c + 2c pair 1.75 1.75
B35 A69 60c + 2c multi (S) .90 .90
B36 A68 75c + 2c multi (S) 1.10 1.10
Nos. B16-B36 (16) 11.90 11.90

Easter Type of 1980
Souvenir Sheets

1980, Apr. 2 Photo. *Perf. 13*

B37 Sheet of 3 1.05 1.05
a. A71 25c + 2c like #262 .30 .30
b. A71 30c + 2c like #263 .35 .35
c. A71 35c + 2c like #264 .40 .40

1980, Apr. 2

B38 A71 85c + 5c like #262 1.10 1.10
B39 A71 85c + 5c like #263 1.10 1.10
B40 A71 85c + 5c like #264 1.10 1.10
Nos. B38-B40 (3) 3.30 3.30

Surtax was for hurricane relief.

No. 245a Overprinted Like Nos. 281-285 and Surcharged

Souvenir Sheet

1980, Aug. 22 Photo. *Perf. 14*

B41 Sheet of 10 6.00 6.00
a. A66 20c + 2c pair .60 .60
b. A66 30c + 2c pair .80 .80
c. A66 35c + 2c pair 1.00 1.00
d. A66 50c + 2c pair 1.50 1.50
e. A66 60c + 2c pair 2.00 2.00

ZEAPEX '80, New Zealand Intl. Stamp Exhib., Auckland, Aug. 23-31.

Souvenir Sheet

1980, Oct. 30 Photo. *Perf. 14*

B42 Sheet of 8, #a.-h. 3.75 3.75

22nd Summer Olympic Games, Moscow, July 19-Aug. 3.

#B42a-B42h are #293a-296a with 2c surtax.

Christmas Type of 1980
Souvenir Sheets

1980, Nov. 28 Photo. *Perf. 13½x13*

B43 A76 80c + 5c like #301 .90 .90
B44 A76 80c + 5c like #302 .90 .90
B45 A76 80c + 5c like #303 .90 .90
B46 A76 80c + 5c like #304 .90 .90
Nos. B43-B46 (4) 3.60 3.60

Nos. B43-B46 each contain one 31x39mm stamp.

Easter Type of 1981
Souvenir Sheets

1981, Apr. 10 Photo. *Perf. 13½*

B47 Sheet of 3 2.25 2.25
a. A78 35c + 2c like #337 .52 .52
b. A78 50c + 2c like #338 .65 .65
c. A78 60c + 2c like #339 .80 .80
B48 A78 80c + 5c like #337 1.00 1.00
B49 A78 80c + 5c like #338 1.00 1.00
B50 A78 80c + 5c like #339 1.00 1.00
Nos. B47-B50 (4) 5.25 5.25

Soccer Type of 1981

1981, Oct. 16 Photo. *Perf. 13*

B51 A80 Sheet of 9 4.50 4.50

#B51 contains #343-345 each with 3c surtax.

Royal Wedding Type of 1981
Nos. 340-342a Surcharged

1981, Nov. 3 Photo. *Perf. 14*

B52 A79 75c + 5c like #340 1.60 1.60
B53 A79 95c + 5c like #341 2.00 2.00
B54 A79 $1.20 + 5c like #342 2.50 2.50
Nos. B52-B54 (3) 6.10 6.10

Souvenir Sheet

B55 Sheet of 3 6.50 6.50
a. A79 75c + 10c like #340 1.75 1.75
b. A79 95c + 10c like #341 2.10 2.10
c. A79 $1.20 + 10c like #342 2.60 2.60

Intl. Year of the Disabled. Surtax was for disabled.

Nos. 530-535 Surcharged "CHRISTMAS VISIT TO SOUTH PACIFIC OF / POPE JOHN PAUL II, NOVEMBER 21-24 1986" in Black on Silver

1986, Nov. 21 Litho. *Perf. 14*

B56 A105 80c + 10c multi 3.00 3.00
B57 A105 $1.15 + 10c multi 4.25 4.25
B58 A105 $1.80 + 10c multi 6.00 6.00
B59 A105 $2.60 + 10c multi 9.00 9.00
Nos. B56-B59 (4) 22.25 22.25

Souvenir Sheets

Perf. 13½

B60 Sheet of 4 22.00 22.00
a.-d. A105 $1.50 + 10c on #534a-534d 5.50 5.50

Perf. 14½x13½

B61 A105 $7.50 + 50c multi 22.00 22.00

No. B60 ovptd. "FIRST VISIT OF A POPE TO SOUTH PACIFIC" and "HIS HOLINESS POPE JOHN PAUL II" on margin. No. B61 ovptd. on margin only "Visit of Pope John Paul II, Nov 21-24 1986 / First Papal Visit to the South Pacific."

Souvenir Sheets

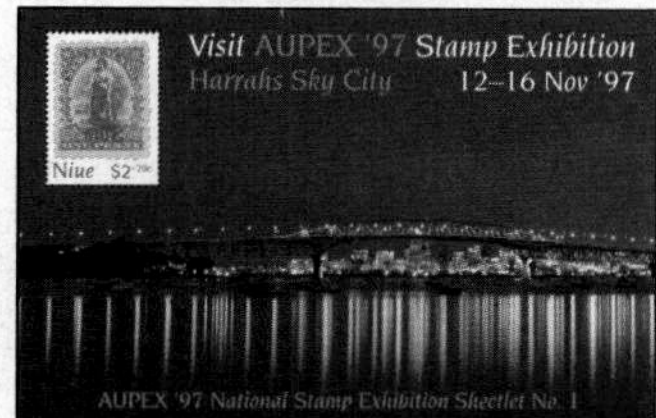

Aupex '97 Stamp Exhibition — SP1

1997, June 9 Litho. *Perf. 14x15*

B62 SP1 $2 +20c like #1 3.25 3.25

Perf. 14½x15

B63 SP1 $2 +20c like #34 2.75 2.75

No. B63 contains one 31x60mm stamp.

AIR POST STAMPS

Catalogue values for unused stamps in this section are for Never Hinged items.

Type of 1977

Designs: 15c, Preparing ground for taro. 20c, Banana harvest. 23c, Bush plantation. 50c, Canoe fishing. 90c, Reef fishing. $1.35, Preparing ground for taro. $2.10, Shellfish gathering. $2.60, Luku harvest.

1979 Litho. *Perf. 14*

C1 A54 15c gold & multi .20 .20
C2 A54 20c gold & multi .25 .25
C3 A54 23c gold & multi .30 .30
C4 A54 50c gold & multi .55 .55
C5 A54 90c gold & multi .85 .85
C6 A54 $1.35 gold & multi 1.30 1.30
C7 A54 $2.10 gold & multi 2.10 2.10
C8 A54 $2.60 gold & multi 2.60 2.60
C9 A54 $5.10 like #187 5.00 5.00
C10 A54 $6.35 like #188 6.50 6.50
Nos. C1-C10 (10) 19.65 19.65

Issue dates: Nos. C1-C5, Feb. 26. Nos. C6-C8, Mar. 30. C9-C10, May 28.

OFFICIAL STAMPS

Catalogue values for unused stamps in this section are for Never Hinged items.

Nos. 417-430, 332-334, 431-431A Overprinted "O.H.M.S." in Metallic Blue or Gold

Perf. 13½, 13½x13, 13x13½, 13

1985-87 Photo.

O1 A89 12c multi .20 .20
O2 A89 25c multi .20 .20
O3 A89 30c multi .25 .25
O4 A89 35c multi .25 .25
O5 A89 40c multi .30 .30
O6 A89 52c multi .40 .40
O7 A89 58c multi .50 .50
O8 A89 70c multi .55 .55
O9 A89 83c multi .65 .65
O10 A89 $1.05 multi .75 .75
O11 A90 $1.75 multi 1.50 1.50
O12 A90 $2.30 multi 2.50 2.50
O13 A90 $3.90 multi 4.75 4.75
O14 A77a $4 multi (G) 4.50 4.50
O15 A90 $5 multi 5.50 5.50
O16 A77a $6 multi ('87) (G) 11.00 11.00
O17 A90 $6.60 multi ('86) 7.00 7.00
O18 A90 $8.30 multi ('86) 9.00 9.00
O19 A77a $10 multi ('87) (G) 17.50 17.50
Nos. O1-O19 (19) 67.30 67.30

Nos. 604-613 Ovptd. "O.H.M.S." in Gold

1993-94 Litho. *Perf. 14x13½*

O20 A118 20c multicolored .30 .30
O21 A118 50c multicolored .55 .55
O22 A118 70c multicolored .80 .80
O23 A118 $1 multicolored 1.25 1.25
O24 A118 $1.50 multicolored 2.00 2.00
O25 A118 $2 multicolored 3.50 3.50
O26 A118 $3 multicolored 4.50 4.50
O27 A118 $5 multicolored 7.00 7.00
O28 A118 $7 multicolored 10.00 10.00
O29 A118 $10 multicolored 14.00 14.00
O30 A118 $15 multicolored 21.00 21.00
Nos. O20-O30 (11) 64.90 64.90

Nos. O20-O30 were not sold unused to local customers.

Issued: 20c-$2, 12/10/93; $3, $5, 4/27/94; $7, $10, 9/1/94; $15, 9/30/94.

NORFOLK ISLAND

'nor-fək 'ī-lənd

LOCATION — Island in the south Pacific Ocean, 900 miles east of Australia
GOVT. — Territory of Australia
AREA — 13½ sq. mi.
POP. — 1,905 (1999 est.)

12 Pence = 1 Shilling
100 Cents = 1 Dollar (1966)

Catalogue values for all unused stamps in this country are for Never Hinged items.

Watermark

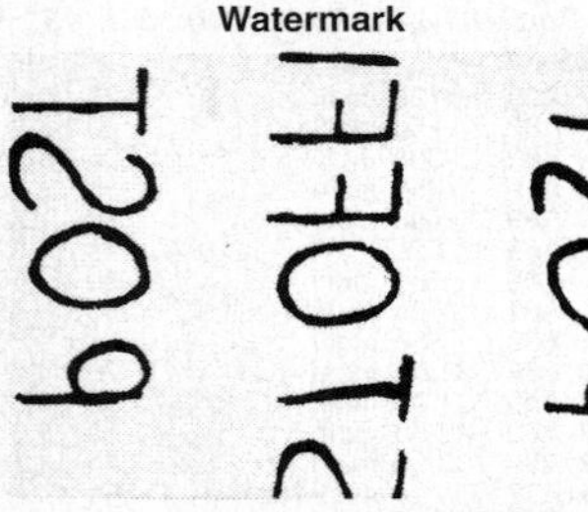

Wmk. 380 — "POST OFFICE"

View of Ball Bay — A1

Unwmk.

1947, June 10 Engr. *Perf. 14*

No.	Type	Value	Color	Unused	Used
1	A1	½p	deep orange	.40	.30
2	A1	1p	violet	.40	.35
3	A1	1½p	bright green	.60	.30
4	A1	2p	red violet	.65	.30
5	A1	2½p	red	.85	.50
6	A1	3p	brown orange	.80	.40
7	A1	4p	rose lake	1.25	.40
8	A1	5½p	slate	1.25	.50
9	A1	6p	sepia	1.50	.50
10	A1	9p	lilac rose	2.25	.75
11	A1	1sh	gray green	2.25	.75
12	A1	2sh	olive bister	6.75	1.25
			Nos. 1-12 (12)	18.95	6.30

See Nos. 23-24.

Warder's Tower — A2

Airfield — A3

Designs: 7½p, First Governor's Residence. 8½p, Barracks entrance. 10p, Salt House. 5sh, Bloody Bridge.

1953, June 10 *Perf. 14½*

No.	Type	Value	Color	Unused	Used
13	A2	3½p	rose brown	2.10	1.00
14	A3	6½p	dark green	3.00	1.25
15	A3	7½p	deep ultra	6.25	2.50
16	A2	8½p	chocolate	7.50	3.25
17	A2	10p	rose lilac	6.25	.65
18	A3	5sh	dark brown	22.50	9.75
			Nos. 13-18 (6)	47.60	18.40

See Nos. 35, 40. For surcharges see Nos. 21-22, 27. For types surcharged see Nos. 26, 28.

Original Norfolk Seal and First Settlers — A4

1956, June 8

No.	Type	Value	Color	Unused	Used
19	A4	3p	bluish green	.75	.50
20	A4	2sh	violet	3.75	*4.00*

Cent. of the landing of the Pitcairn Islanders on Norfolk Island.

Nos. 15 and 16 Surcharged with New Value and Bars

1958, July 1

No.	Type	Value	Color	Unused	Used
21	A3	7p on 7½p	dp ultra	1.50	*1.50*
22	A2	8p on 8½p	choc	1.50	*2.00*

Ball Bay Type of 1947

1959, July 6 Engr. *Perf. 14*

No.	Type	Value	Color	Unused	Used
23	A1	3p	green	12.50	6.00
24	A1	2sh	dark blue	20.00	9.50

A5

Australia #332 Surcharged in Red

1959, Dec. 7

No.	Type	Value	Color	Unused	Used
25	A5	5p on 4p	dk gray blue	1.60	1.60

No. 14 and Types of 1953 Surcharged with New Values and Bars

1960, Sept. 26 *Perf. 14½*

No.	Type	Value	Color	Unused	Used
26	A2	1sh1p on 3½p	dk bl	4.00	3.00
27	A3	2sh5p on 6½p	dk grn	5.50	4.50
28	A3	2sh8p on 7½p	dk brn	7.25	6.25
			Nos. 26-28 (3)	16.75	13.75

Types of 1953 and

Island Hibiscus — A6

Fairy Tern — A7

Red-Tailed Tropic Bird — A8

Designs: 2p, Lagunaria patersonii (flowers). 5p, Lantana. 8p, Red hibiscus. 9p, Cereus and Queen Elizabeth II. 10p, Salt House. 1sh1p, Fringed hibiscus. 2sh, Providence petrel, vert. 2sh5p, Passion flower. 2sh8p, Rose apple. 5sh, Bloody Bridge.

1960-62 Unwmk. Engr. *Perf. 14½*

No.	Type	Value	Color	Unused	Used
29	A6	1p	blue green	.20	.20
30	A6	2p	gray grn & brt pink	.20	.20
31	A7	3p	brt green ('61)	.45	.20
32	A6	5p	lilac	.95	.60
33	A6	8p	vermilion	1.75	1.25
34	A6	9p	ultramarine	1.75	1.25
35	A2	10p	pale pur & brn ('61)	3.00	1.50
36	A6	1sh1p	dark red ('61)	2.25	1.25
37	A6	2sh	sepia ('61)	2.25	1.50
38	A6	2sh5p	dk purple ('62)	2.25	1.50
39	A6	2sh8p	green & sal ('62)	3.75	1.75
40	A3	5sh	green & gray ('61)	5.50	2.50

Perf. 14½x14

No.	Type	Value	Color	Unused	Used
41	A8	10sh	green ('61)	37.50	25.00
			Nos. 29-41 (13)	61.80	38.70

See #585-586. For surcharges see #71-82.

Map of Norfolk Island — A9

1960, Oct. 24 Engr. *Perf. 14*

No.	Type	Value	Color	Unused	Used
42	A9	2sh8p	rose violet	16.00	16.00

Introduction of local government for Norfolk Island.

Open Bible and Candle — A9a

Page from Book of Hours, 15th Century A9b

Madonna and Child — A9c

1960, Nov. 21 *Perf. 14½*

No.	Type	Value	Color	Unused	Used
43	A9a	5p	bright lilac rose	2.75	2.75

Christmas.

1961, Nov. 20 *Perf. 14½x14*

No.	Type	Value	Color	Unused	Used
44	A9b	5p	slate blue	1.00	1.00

Nos. 43-44 were issued to mark the beginning and the end of the 350th anniversary year of the publication of the King James translation of the Bible.

1962, Nov. 19 *Perf. 14½*

No.	Type	Value	Color	Unused	Used
45	A9c	5p	blue	1.25	1.00

Christmas.

Overlooking Kingston — A10

Dreamfish — A11

Designs: 6p, Tweed trousers (fish). 8p, Kingston scene. 9p, "The Arches." 10p, Slaughter Bay. 11p, Trumpeter fish. 1sh, Po'ov (wrasse). 1sh6p, Queensland grouper. 2sh3p, Ophie (carangidae).

Perf. 14½x14

1962-64 Unwmk. Photo.

No.	Type	Value	Color	Unused	Used
49	A10	5p	multi ('64)	.50	.45
50	A11	6p	multi	.60	.60
51	A10	8p	multi ('64)	.75	.65
52	A10	9p	multi ('64)	1.10	1.00
53	A10	10p	multi ('64)	1.25	1.25
54	A11	11p	multi ('63)	1.90	1.25
55	A11	1sh	olive, bl & pink	2.25	1.75
57	A11	1sh3p	bl, mar & grn ('63)	2.50	2.25
58	A11	1sh6p	bl, brn & lil ('63)	2.75	2.75
60	A11	2sh3p	dl bl, yel & red ('63)	3.25	3.00
			Nos. 49-60 (10)	16.85	14.95

Star of Bethlehem A11a

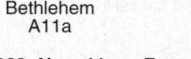

Symbolic Pine Tree A12

1963, Nov. 11 Engr. *Perf. 14½*

No.	Type	Value	Color	Unused	Used
65	A11a	5p	vermilion	1.00	1.00

Christmas.

1964, July 1 Photo. *Perf. 13½x13*

No.	Type	Value	Color	Unused	Used
66	A12	5p	orange, blk & red	.75	.75
67	A12	8p	gray green, blk & red	1.00	1.00

50th anniv. of Norfolk Island as an Australian Territory.

Child Looking at Nativity Scene A12a

"Simpson and His Donkey" by Wallace Anderson A12b

1964, Nov. 9 *Perf. 13½*

No.	Type	Value	Color	Unused	Used
68	A12a	5p	multicolored	.90	.90

Christmas.

1965, Apr. 14 Photo. *Perf. 13½x13*

No.	Type	Value	Color	Unused	Used
69	A12b	5p	brt grn, sepia & blk	.55	.45

ANZAC issue. See note after Australia No. 387.

Nativity — A12c

1965, Oct. 25 Unwmk. *Perf. 13½*

No.	Type	Value	Color	Unused	Used
70	A12c	5p	gold, blk, ultra & redsh brn	.50	.50

Christmas. No. 70 is luminescent. See note after Australia No. 331.

Nos. 29-33 and 35-41 Surcharged in Black on Overprinted Metallic Rectangles

Two types of 1c on 1p:
I. Silver rectangle 4x5½mm.
II. Silver rectangle 5½x5¼mm.
Two types of $1 on 10sh:
I. Silver rectangle 7x6½mm.
II. Silver rectangle 6x4mm.

Perf. 14½, 14½x14

1966, Feb. 14 Engr.

No.	Type	Value	Color	Unused	Used
71	A6	1c on 1p	bl grn (I)	.20	.20
a.			Type II	.30	.30
72	A6	2c on 2p	gray grn & brt pink	.20	.20
73	A7	3c on 3p	brt green	.35	*.60*
74	A6	4c on 5p	lilac	.20	.20
75	A6	5c on 8p	vermilion	.20	.20
76	A2	10c on 10p	pale pur & brn	.70	.20
77	A6	15c on 1sh1p	dark red	.30	.40
78	A6	20c on 2sh	sepia	2.75	2.25
79	A6	25c on 2sh5p	dk pur	1.10	.30
80	A6	30c on 2sh8p	grn & sal	.75	.40
81	A3	50c on 5sh	grn & gray	2.75	.55
82	A8	$1 on 10sh	green (I)	2.50	2.00
a.			Type II	5.00	5.00
			Nos. 71-82 (12)	12.00	7.50

Headstone Bridge — A13

1966, June 27 Photo. *Perf. 14½*

No.	Type	Value	Color	Unused	Used
88	A13	7c	shown	.30	.30
89	A13	9c	Cemetary road	.50	.50

St. Barnabas Chapel — A14

Design: 4c, Interior of St. Barnabas Chapel.

Perf. 14x14½

1966, Aug. 23 Photo. Unwmk.

97 A14 4c multicolored .20 .20
98 A14 25c multicolored .65 .65

Centenary of the Melanesian Mission.

Star over Philip Island — A15

1966, Oct. 24 Photo. *Perf. 14½*

99 A15 4c violet, grn, blue & sil .35 .35

Christmas.

H.M.S. Resolution, 1774 — A16

Ships: 2c, La Boussole and Astrolabe, 1788. 3c, Brig Supply, 1788. 4c, Sirius, 1790. 5c, The Norfolk, 1798. 7c, Survey cutter Mermaid, 1825. 9c, The Lady Franklin, 1853. 10c The Morayshire, 1856. 15c, Southern Cross, 1866. 20c, The Pitcairn, 1891. 25c, Norfolk Island whaleboat, 1895. 30c, Cable ship Iris, 1907. 50c, The Resolution, 1926. $1, S.S. Morinda, 1931.

1967-68 Photo. *Perf. 14x14½*

100 A16 1c multicolored .20 .20
101 A16 2c multicolored .20 .20
102 A16 3c multicolored .20 .20
103 A16 4c multicolored .40 .20
104 A16 5c multicolored .20 .20
105 A16 7c multicolored .20 .20
106 A16 9c multicolored .30 .25
107 A16 10c multicolored .40 .35
108 A16 15c multicolored .60 .55
109 A16 20c multicolored .90 .80
110 A16 25c multicolored 1.40 1.25
111 A16 30c multicolored 1.75 1.50
112 A16 50c multicolored 2.25 2.00
113 A16 $1 multicolored 3.50 3.25
Nos. 100-113 (14) 12.50 11.15

Issued: #100-103, 4/17; #104-107, 8/19; #108-110, 3/18/68; #111-113, 6/18/68.

Lions Intl., 50th Anniv. — A16a

1967, June 7 Photo. *Perf. 13½*

114 A16a 4c citron, blk & bl grn .35 .35

Printed on luminescent paper; see note after Australia No. 331.

John Adams' Prayer A17

1967, Oct. 16 Photo. *Perf. 14x14½*

115 A17 5c brick red, blk & buff .35 .35

Christmas.

Queen Elizabeth II Type of Australia, 1966-67

Coil Stamps

Perf. 15 Horizontally

1968-71 Photo. Unwmk.

116 A157 3c brn org, blk & buff .20 .20
117 A157 4c blue grn, blk & buff .20 .20
118 A157 5c brt purple, blk & buff .20 .20
118A A157 6c dk red, brn, blk & buff .35 .35
Nos. 116-118A (4) .95 .95

Issued: 6c, 8/2/71; others, 8/5/68.

DC-4 Skymaster and Lancastrian Plane — A18

1968, Sept. 25 *Perf. 14½x14*

119 A18 5c dk car, sky bl & ind .20 .20
120 A18 7c dk car, bl grn & sep .25 .25

21st anniv. of the Sydney to Norfolk Island air service by Qantas Airways.

Star and Hibiscus Wreath — A19

Photo.; Silver Impressed (Star)

1968, Oct. 24 *Perf. 14½x14*

121 A19 5c sky blue & multi .30 .30

Christmas.

Map of Pacific, Transit of Venus before Sun, Capt. Cook and Quadrant A20

1969, June 3 Photo. *Perf. 14x14½*

122 A20 10c brn, ol, pale brn & yel .35 .35

Bicent. of the observation at Tahiti by Capt. James Cook of the transit of the planet Venus across the sun.

Map of Van Diemen's Land and Norfolk Island A21

1969, Sept. 29 *Perf. 14x14½*

123 A21 5c multicolored .20 .20
124 A21 30c multicolored .70 .70

125th anniv. of the annexation of Norfolk Island by Van Diemen's Land (Tasmania).

Nativity (Mother-of-Pearl carving) — A22

1969, Oct. 27 Photo. *Perf. 14½x14*

125 A22 5c brown & multi .30 .30

Christmas.

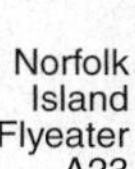

Norfolk Island Flyeater A23

Birds of Norfolk Island from Book by Gregory Mathews: 1c, Robins, vert. 2c, Norfolk Island whistlers (thickheads), vert. 4c, Long-tailed cuckoos. 5c, Red-fronted parakeet, vert. 7c, Long-tailed trillers, vert. 9c, Island thrush. 10c, Owl, vert. 15c, Norfolk Island pigeon (extinct; vert.). 20c, White-breasted white-eye. 25c, Norfolk Island parrots, vert. 30c, Gray fantail. 45c, Norfolk Island starlings. 50c, Crimson rosella, vert. $1, Sacred kingfisher.

Perf. 14x14½, 14½x14

1970-71 Photo. Unwmk.

126 A23 1c multicolored .25 .20
127 A23 2c multicolored .25 .30
128 A23 3c multicolored .25 .20
129 A23 4c multicolored .45 .30
130 A23 5c multicolored 1.25 .80
131 A23 7c multicolored .35 .20
132 A23 9c multicolored .55 .30
133 A23 10c multicolored 1.40 1.75
134 A23 15c multicolored 1.25 .75
135 A23 20c multicolored 5.75 3.75
136 A23 25c multicolored 2.00 1.25
137 A23 30c multicolored 5.75 3.25
138 A23 45c multicolored 2.50 1.50
139 A23 50c multicolored 3.00 2.50
140 A23 $1 multicolored 8.25 8.00
Nos. 126-140 (15) 33.25 25.05

Issued: 3c, 4c, 9c, 45c, 2/25; 1c, 7c, 10c, 25c, 7/22; 2c, 2c, 5c, 15c, 50c, 2/24/71; 20c, 30c, $1, 6/16/71.

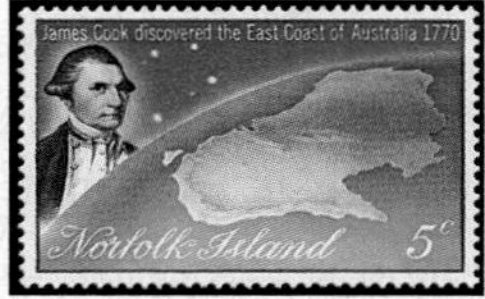

Map of Australia, James Cook and Southern Cross A24

Design: 10c, "Endeavour" entering Botany Bay, Apr. 29, 1770, and aborigine with spear. The 1776 portrait of James Cook on the 5c is by John Webber.

1970, Apr. 29 Photo. *Perf. 14x14½*

141 A24 5c multicolored .20 .20
142 A24 10c multicolored .30 .20

200th anniv. of Cook's discovery and exploration of the eastern coast of Australia.

First Christmas, Sydney Bay, 1788 — A25

1970, Oct. 15 Photo. *Perf. 14x14½*

143 A25 5c multicolored .20 .20

Christmas.

Bishop Patteson, Open Bible — A26

#145, Bible opened to Acts Chap. 7, martyrdom of St. Stephen, & knotted palm fronds. #146, Bishop Patteson, rose window of Melanesian Mission Chapel on Norfolk Island. #147, Cross erected at Nukapu where Patteson died & his arms.

1971, Sept. 20

144 A26 6c brown & multi .20 .20
145 A26 6c brown & multi .20 .20
a. Pair, #144-145 .45 .45
146 A26 10c purple & multi .20 .20
147 A26 10c purple & multi .20 .20
a. Pair, #146-147 .55 .55
Nos. 144-147 (4) .80 .80

Centenary of the death of Bishop John Coleridge Patteson (1827-1871), head of the Melanesian mission.

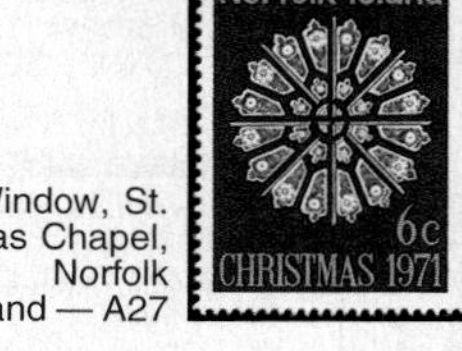

Rose Window, St. Barnabas Chapel, Norfolk Island — A27

1971, Oct. 25 *Perf. 14x13½*

148 A27 6c dk vio blue & multi .25 .25

Christmas.

Map of South Pacific and Commission Flag — A28

1972, Feb. 7 *Perf. 14x14½*

149 A28 7c multicolored .30 .30

So. Pacific Commission, 25th anniv.

Stained-glass Window — A29

Cross, Church, Pines — A30

1972, Oct. 16 Photo. *Perf. 14x14½*

150 A29 7c dark olive & multi .25 .25

Christmas. The stained-glass window by Edward Coley Burne-Jones is in All Saints Church, Norfolk Island.

1972, Nov. 20

151 A30 12c multicolored .25 .25

Centenary of All Saints Church, first built by Pitcairners on Norfolk Island.

"Resolution" in Antarctica — A31

1973, Jan. 17 Photo. *Perf. 14½x14*

152 A31 35c multicolored 2.50 2.50

200th anniv. of the 1st crossing of the Antarctic Circle by Cook, Jan. 17, 1773.

Sleeping Child, and Christmas Tree — A32

Christmas: 35c, Star over lagoon.

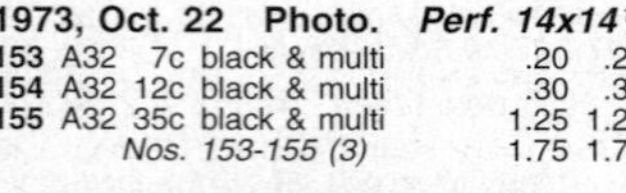

1973, Oct. 22 Photo. *Perf. 14x14½*

153	A32	7c black & multi	.20	.20
154	A32	12c black & multi	.30	.30
155	A32	35c black & multi	1.25	1.25
		Nos. 153-155 (3)	1.75	1.75

Protestant Clergyman's House — A33

Designs: 2c, Royal Engineer Office. 3c, Double quarters for free overseers. 4c, Guard House. 5c, Pentagonal Gaol entrance. 7c, Pentagonal Gaol, aerial view. 8c, Convict barracks. 10c, Officers' quarters, New Military Barracks. 12c, New Military Barracks. 14c, Beach stores. 15c, Magazine. 20c, Old Military Barracks, entrance. 25c, Old Military Barracks. 30c, Old stores, Crankmill. 50c, Commissariat stores. $1, Government House.

1973-75 Photo. *Perf. 14x14½*

156	A33	1c multicolored	.20	.20
157	A33	2c multicolored	.20	.20
158	A33	3c multicolored	.35	*.75*
159	A33	4c multicolored	.25	.25
160	A33	5c multicolored	.30	.20
161	A33	7c multicolored	.40	.40
162	A33	8c multicolored	1.50	1.50
163	A33	10c multicolored	.55	.55
164	A33	12c multicolored	.55	.45
165	A33	14c multicolored	.55	*.70*
166	A33	15c multicolored	1.40	1.00
167	A33	20c multicolored	.55	.55
168	A33	25c multicolored	1.50	1.50
169	A33	30c multicolored	.55	.55
170	A33	50c multicolored	.60	*1.25*
171	A33	$1 multicolored	1.25	*2.00*
		Nos. 156-171 (16)	10.70	12.05

Issued: 1c, 5c, 10c, 50c, 11/19/73; 2c, 7c, 12c, 30c, 5/1/74; 4c, 14c, 20c, $1, 7/12/74; 3c, 8c, 15c, 25c, 2/19/75.

Map of Norfolk Island A34

1974, Feb. 8 Photo. *Perf. 14x14½*

172	A34	7c red lilac & multi	.40	.40
173	A34	25c dull blue & multi	1.10	1.10

Visit of Queen Elizabeth II and the Duke of Edinburgh, Feb. 11-12.

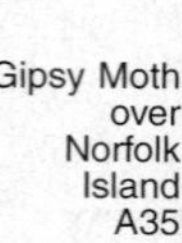

Gipsy Moth over Norfolk Island A35

1974, Mar. 28 Litho. *Perf. 14x14½*

174	A35	14c multicolored	1.25	1.25

1st aircraft to visit Norfolk, Sir Francis Chichester's "Mme. Elijah," Mar. 28, 1931.

Capt. Cook — A36

Nativity — A37

Designs: 10c, "Resolution," by Henry Roberts. 14c, Norfolk Island pine, cone and seedling. 25c, Norfolk Island flax, by George Raper, 1790. Portrait of Cook on 7c by William Hodges, 1770.

1974, Oct. 8 Litho. *Perf. 14*

175	A36	7c multicolored	.80	.80
176	A36	10c multicolored	2.00	2.00
177	A36	14c multicolored	1.60	1.60
178	A36	25c multicolored	1.60	1.60
		Nos. 175-178 (4)	6.00	6.00

Bicentenary of the discovery of Norfolk Island by Capt. James Cook.

1974, Oct. 18 Photo. *Perf. 14*

179	A37	7c rose & multi	.30	.30
180	A37	30c violet & multi	1.50	1.50

Christmas.

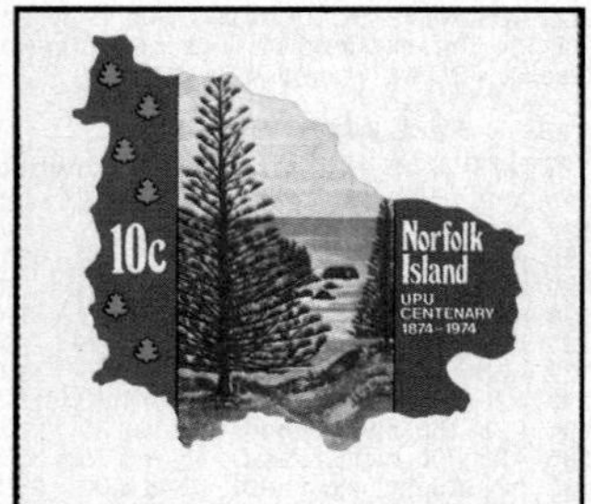

Norfolk Island Pine — A38

15c, Off-shore islands. 35c, Crimson rosella and sacred kingfisher. 40c, Map showing Norfolk's location. Stamps in shape of Norfolk Island.

1974, Dec. 16 Litho. *Imperf.*
Self-adhesive

181	A38	10c brown & multi	.35	.35
182	A38	15c dk blue & multi	.50	.50
183	A38	35c dk purple & multi	1.25	1.25
184	A38	40c dk blue grn & multi	1.50	2.50
a.		Souvenir sheet of 4	22.50	22.50
		Nos. 181-184 (4)	3.60	4.60

Cent. of UPU. Stamps printed on peelable paper backing. No. 184a contains 4 imperf. stamps similar to Nos. 181-184 in reduced size on a background of map of Norfolk Island. Peelable paper backing shows beach scene on Norfolk Island.

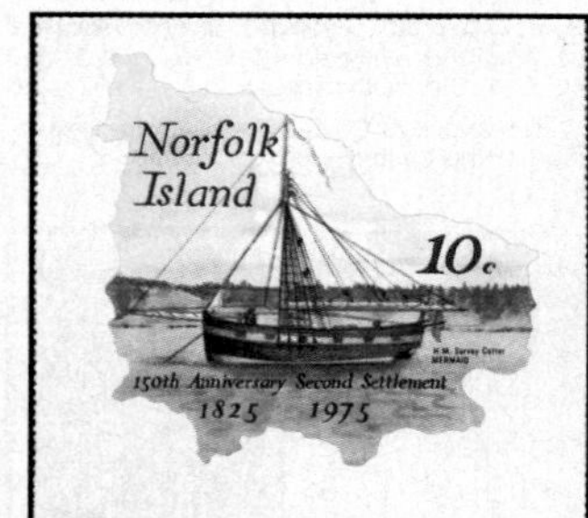

Survey Cutter "Mermaid," 1825 — A39

Design: 35c, Kingston, 1835, after painting by Thomas Seller. Stamps outlined in shape of Norfolk Island map.

1975, Aug. 18 Litho. *Imperf.*
Self-adhesive

185	A39	10c multicolored	.35	.35
186	A39	35c multicolored	.65	.65

Sesquicentennial of 2nd settlement of Norfolk Island. Printed on peelable paper backing with green and black design and inscription.

Star over Norfolk Island Pine and Map — A40

Brass Memorial Cross — A41

1975, Oct. 6 Photo. *Perf. 14½x14*

187	A40	10c lt blue & multi	.30	.30
188	A40	15c lt brown & multi	.45	.45
189	A40	35c lilac & multi	.65	.65
		Nos. 187-189 (3)	1.40	1.40

Christmas.

Perf. 14½x14, 14x14½
1975, Nov. 24 Photo.

Design: 60c, Laying foundation stone, 1875, and chapel, 1975, horiz.

190	A41	30c multicolored	.40	.40
191	A41	60c multicolored	1.00	1.00

St. Barnabas Chapel, centenary.

Launching "Resolution" A42

Design: 45c, "Resolution" under sail.

1975, Dec. 1 *Perf. 14x14½*

192	A42	25c multicolored	.40	.40
193	A42	45c multicolored	.85	.85

50th anniversary of launching of schooner "Resolution."

Bedford Flag, Charles W. Morgan Whaler A43

Designs: 25c, Grand Union Flag, church interior. 40c, 15-stari flag, 1795, and plane over island, WWII. 45c, 13-star flag and California quail.

1976, July 5 Photo. *Perf. 14*

194	A43	18c multicolored	.30	.35
195	A43	25c multicolored	.30	.30
196	A43	40c multicolored	.65	.75
197	A43	45c multicolored	.75	.85
		Nos. 194-197 (4)	2.00	2.25

American Bicentennial.

Bird in Flight, Brilliant Sun — A44

1976, Oct. 4 Photo. *Perf. 14*

198	A44	18c blue grn & multi	.30	.30
199	A44	25c dp blue & multi	.55	.55
200	A44	45c violet & multi	.90	.90
		Nos. 198-200 (3)	1.75	1.75

Christmas.

Bassaris Itea — A45

Butterflies and Moths: 2c, Utetheisa pulchelloides vaga. 3c, Agathia asterias jowettorum. 4c, Cynthia kershawi. 5c, Leucania loreyimima. 10c, Hypolimnas bolina nerina. 15c, Pyrrhorachis pyrrhogona. 16c, Austrocarea iocephala millsi. 17c, Pseudocoremia christiani. 18c, Cleora idiocrossa. 19c, Simplicia caeneusalis buffetti. 20c, Austrocidaria ralstonae. 30c, Hippotion scrofa. 40c, Papilio ilioneus. 50c, Tiracola plagiata. $1, Precis villida. $2, Cepora perimale.

1976-77 Photo. *Perf. 14*

201	A45	1c multicolored	.20	*.35*
202	A45	2c multicolored	.20	*.35*
203	A45	3c multicolored	.20	.20
204	A45	4c multicolored	.20	.20
205	A45	5c multicolored	.20	*.60*
206	A45	10c multicolored	.25	*.60*
207	A45	15c multicolored	.25	.25
208	A45	16c multicolored	.25	.25
209	A45	17c multicolored	.30	.25
210	A45	18c multicolored	.30	.25
211	A45	19c multicolored	.30	.25
212	A45	20c multicolored	.35	.25
213	A45	30c multicolored	.45	.50
214	A45	40c multicolored	.50	.30
215	A45	50c multicolored	.65	.65
216	A45	$1 multicolored	.70	.65
217	A45	$2 multicolored	1.10	1.10
		Nos. 201-217 (17)	6.40	7.00

Issued: 1c, 5c, 10c, 16c, 18c, $1, 11/17; others, 1977.

View of Kingston A46

1977, June 10

218	A46	25c multicolored	.50	.50

25th anniv. of reign of Elizabeth II.

Hibiscus and 19th Century Whaler's Lamp — A47

Capt. Cook, by Nathaniel Dance — A48

1977, Oct. 4 Photo. *Perf. 14½*

219	A47	18c multicolored	.25	.25
220	A47	25c multicolored	.25	.25
221	A47	45c multicolored	.50	.50
		Nos. 219-221 (3)	1.00	1.00

Christmas.

1978, Jan. 18 Photo. *Perf. 14½*

Designs: 25c, Discovery of Northern Hawaiian Islands (Cook aboard ship), horiz. 80c, British flag and Island, horiz.

222	A48	18c multicolored	.30	.30
223	A48	25c multicolored	.30	.30
224	A48	80c multicolored	.65	.65
		Nos. 222-224 (3)	1.25	1.25

Bicentenary of Capt. Cook's arrival in Hawaiian Islands.

World Guides Flag and Globe — A49

Designs: 25c, Norfolk Guides' scarf badge and trefoil. 35c, Elizabeth II and trefoil. 45c, FAO Ceres medal with portrait of Lady Olive Baden-Powell, and trefoil. Stamps outlined in shape of Norfolk Island map.

1978, Feb. 22 Litho. *Imperf.*
Self-adhesive

225	A49	18c lt ultra & multi	.25	.25
226	A49	25c yellow & multi	.25	.25
227	A49	35c lt green & multi	.40	.40
228	A49	45c yellow grn & multi	.50	.50
		Nos. 225-228 (4)	1.40	1.40

50th anniversary of Norfolk Island Girl Guides. Printed on peelable paper backing with green multiple pines and tourist publicity inscription.

St. Edward's Crown A50

Design: 70c, Coronation regalia.

1978, June 29 Photo. *Perf. 14½*

229 A50 25c multicolored .30 .30
230 A50 70c multicolored .70 .70

25th anniv. of coronation of Elizabeth II.

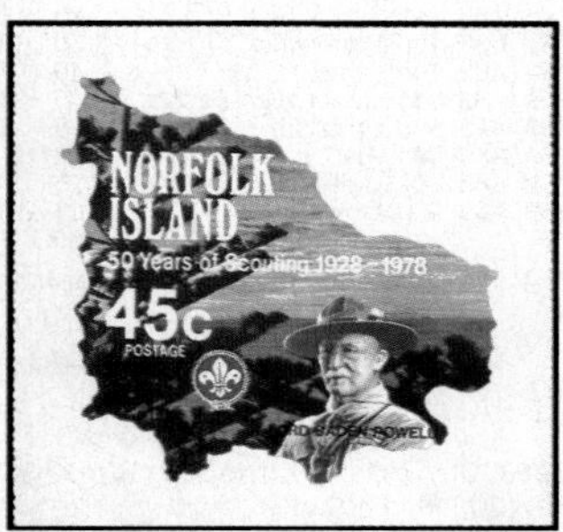

Norfolk Island Boy Scouts, 50th Anniv. — A51

Designs: 20c, Cliffs, Duncombe Bay, Scout Making Fire. 25c, Emily Bay, Philip and Nepean Islands from Kingston. 35c, Anson Bay, Cub and Boy Scouts. 45c, Sunset and Lord Baden-Powell. Stamps outlined in shape of Norfolk Island map.

1978, Aug. 22 Litho. *Imperf.*
Self-adhesive

231 A51 20c multicolored .35 .35
232 A51 25c multicolored .40 .40
233 A51 35c multicolored .55 .55
234 A51 45c multicolored .60 .60
Nos. 231-234 (4) 1.90 1.90

Printed on peelable paper backing with green multiple pines and tourist publicity inscription and picture.

Map of Bering Sea and Pacific Ocean, Routes of Discovery and Resolution — A52

Design: 90c, Discovery and Resolution trapped in ice, by John Webber.

1978, Aug. 29 Photo. *Perf. 14½*

235 A52 25c multicolored .40 .40
236 A52 90c multicolored 1.00 1.00

Northernmost point of Cook's voyages.

Poinsettia and Bible — A53

Christmas: 30c, Native oak (flowers) and Bible. 55c, Hibiscus and Bible.

1978, Oct. 3 Photo. *Perf. 14½*

237 A53 20c multicolored .20 .20
238 A53 30c multicolored .30 .30
239 A53 55c multicolored .60 .60
Nos. 237-239 (3) 1.10 1.10

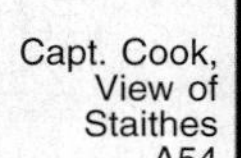

Capt. Cook, View of Staithes A54

80c, Capt. Cook and view of Whitby harbor.

1978, Oct. 27

240 A54 20c multicolored .40 *.50*
241 A54 80c multicolored 1.10 *1.25*

Resolution, Map of Asia and Australia — A55

Designs: No. 243, Map of Hawaii and Americas, Cook's route and statue. No. 244, Capt. Cook's death. No. 245, Ships off Hawaii.

1979, Feb. 14 Photo. *Perf. 14½*

242 A55 20c multicolored .25 .25
243 A55 20c multicolored .25 .25
a. Pair, #242-243 .50 .50
244 A55 40c multicolored .50 .50
245 A55 40c multicolored .50 .50
a. Pair, #244-245 1.00 1.00
Nos. 242-245 (4) 1.50 1.50

Bicentenary of Capt. Cook's death.

Rowland Hill and Tasmania No. 1 A56

Rowland Hill and: 30c, Great Britain No. 8. 55c, Norfolk Island No. 2.

1979, Aug. 27 *Perf. 14x14½*

246 A56 20c multicolored .20 .20
247 A56 30c multicolored .25 .25
248 A56 55c multicolored .35 .35
a. Souvenir sheet of 1 1.00 1.00
Nos. 246-248 (3) .80 .80

Sir Rowland Hill (1795-1879), originator of penny postage.

Legislative Assembly — A57

1979, Aug. Photo. *Perf. 14½x14*

249 A57 $1 multicolored .90 .90

First session of Legislative Assembly.

Map of Pacific Ocean, IYC Emblem A58

1979, Sept. 25 Litho. *Perf. 15*

250 A58 80c multicolored .70 .70

International Year of the Child.

Emily Bay Beach — A59

1979, Oct. 2 Photo. *Perf. 12½x13*

251 A59 15c shown .25 .25
252 A59 20c Emily Bay .25 .25
253 A59 30c Salt House .30 .30
a. Souv. sheet of 3, #251-253, perf. 14x14½ 1.25 1.25
b. Strip of 3, #251-253 .80 .80

Christmas. #253b has continuous design.

Lions District Convention 1980 — A60

1980, Jan. 25 Litho. *Perf. 15*

254 A60 50c multicolored .50 .50

Rotary International, 75th Anniversary — A61

1980, Feb. 21

255 A61 50c multicolored .50 .50

DH-60 "Gypsy Moth" A62

1980-81 Litho. *Perf. 14½*

256 A62 1c Hawker Siddeley HS-748 .20 .20
257 A62 2c shown .20 .20
258 A62 3c Curtiss P-40 Kittyhawk .20 .20
259 A62 4c Chance Vought Corsair .20 .20
260 A62 5c Grumman Avenger .20 .20
261 A62 15c Douglas Dauntless .30 .30
262 A62 20c Cessna 172 .35 .35
262A A62 25c Lockheed Hudson .45 .45
263 A62 30c Lockheed PV-1 Ventura .55 .55
264 A62 40c Avro York .70 .70
265 A62 50c DC-3 .90 .90
266 A62 60c Avro 691 Lancastrian 1.00 1.00
267 A62 80c DC-4 1.50 1.50
268 A62 $1 Beechcraft Super King Air 1.75 1.75
269 A62 $2 Fokker Friendship 2.25 2.25
270 A62 $5 Lockheed C-130 Hercules 5.75 5.75
Nos. 256-270 (16) 16.50 16.50

Issued: 2, 3, 20c, $5, 3/25; 4, 5, 15c, $2, 8/19; 30, 50, 60, 80c, 1/13/81; 1, 25, 40c, $1, 3/3/81.

Queen Mother Elizabeth, 80th Birthday A63

1980, Aug. 4 Litho. *Perf. 14½*

271 A63 22c multicolored .30 .30
272 A63 60c multicolored .75 .75

Red-tailed Tropic Birds — A64

1980, Oct. 28 Litho. *Perf. 14x14½*

273 A64 15c shown .20 .20
274 A64 22c Fairy terns .30 .30
275 A64 35c White-capped noddys .50 .50
a. Strip of 3, #273-275 1.10 1.10
276 A64 60c Fairy terns, diff. .90 .90
Nos. 273-276 (4) 1.90 1.90

Christmas. No. 275a has continuous design.

Citizens Arriving at Norfolk Island A65

1981, June 5 Litho. *Perf. 14½*

277 A65 5c Departure .20 .20
278 A65 35c shown .50 .50
279 A65 60c Settlement .85 .85
a. Souvenir sheet of 3, #277-279 1.65 1.65
Nos. 277-279 (3) 1.55 1.55

Pitcairn migration to Norfolk Island, 125th anniv.

Common Design Types pictured following the introduction.

Royal Wedding Issue
Common Design Type

1981, July 22 Litho. *Perf. 14*

280 CD331 35c Bouquet .40 .40
281 CD331 55c Charles .65 .65
282 CD331 60c Couple .70 .70
Nos. 280-282 (3) 1.75 1.75

#280-282 each se-tenant with decorative label.

Uniting Church of Australia A66

1981, Sept. 15 Litho. *Perf. 14½*

283 A66 18c shown .20 .20
284 A66 24c Seventh Day Adventist Church .30 .30
285 A66 30c Church of the Sacred Heart .35 .35
286 A66 $1 St. Barnabas Church 1.25 1.25
Nos. 283-286 (4) 2.10 2.10

Christmas.

White-breasted Silvereye — A67

1981, Nov. 10 Litho. *Perf. 14½*

287 Strip of 5 4.00 4.00
a.-e. A67 35c any single .70 .70

Philip Island A68

Views, Flora and Fauna: No. 288, Philip Isld. No. 289, Nepean Island.

1982, Jan. 12 Litho. *Perf. 14*

288 Strip of 5 1.50 1.50
a.-e. A68 24c any single .30 .30
289 Strip of 5 2.50 2.50
a.-e. A68 35c any single .50 .50

Sperm Whale A69

1982, Feb. 23 Litho. *Perf. 14½*

290 A69 24c shown .50 .50
291 A69 55c Southern right whale 1.00 1.00
292 A69 80c Humpback whale 1.75 1.75
Nos. 290-292 (3) 3.25 3.25

Shipwrecks — A70

1982 Litho. *Perf. 14½*

293 A70 24c Sirius, 1790 .40 .40
294 A70 27c Diocet, 1873 .45 .45
295 A70 35c Friendship, 1835 .55 .55
296 A70 40c Mary Hamilton, 1873 .65 .65
297 A70 55c Fairlie, 1840 .80 .80
298 A70 65c Warrigal, 1918 1.00 1.00
Nos. 293-298 (6) 3.85 3.85

Christmas and 40th Anniv. of Aircraft Landing A71

1982, Sept. 7 *Perf. 14*

299 A71 27c Supplies drop .35 .35
300 A71 40c Landing .60 .60
301 A71 75c Sharing supplies 1.10 1.10
Nos. 299-301 (3) 2.05 2.05

A72

A73

British Army Uniforms, Second Settlement, 1839-1848: 27c, Battalion Company Officer, 50th Regiment, 1835-1842. 40c, Light Company Officer, 58th Reg., 1845. 55c, Private, 80th Bat., 1838. 65c, Bat. Company Officer, 11th Reg., 1847.

1982, Nov. 9 *Perf. 14½*

302 A72 27c multicolored .35 .35
303 A72 40c multicolored .60 .60
304 A72 55c multicolored .70 .70
305 A72 65c multicolored .90 .90
Nos. 302-305 (4) 2.55 2.55

1983, Mar. 29 Litho. *Perf. 14x13½*

Local mushrooms.

306 A73 27c Panaeolus papilonaceus .40 .40
307 A73 40c Coprinus domesticus .65 .65
308 A73 55c Marasmius niveus .80 .80
309 A73 65c Cymatoderma elegans 1.00 1.00
Nos. 306-309 (4) 2.85 2.85

Manned Flight Bicentenary A74

1983, July 12 Litho. *Perf. 14½x14*

310 A74 10c Beech 18, aerial mapping .20 .20
311 A74 27c Fokker F-28 .35 .35
312 A74 45c DC4 .75 .75
313 A74 75c Sikorsky helicopter 1.10 1.10
a. Souvenir sheet of 4, #310-313 2.75 2.75
Nos. 310-313 (4) 2.40 2.40

Christmas — A75

Stained-glass Windows by Edward Burne-Jones (1833-1898), St. Barnabas Chapel.

1983, Oct. 4 Litho. *Perf. 14*

314 A75 5c multicolored .20 .20
315 A75 24c multicolored .40 .40
316 A75 30c multicolored .45 .45
317 A75 45c multicolored .65 .65
318 A75 85c multicolored 1.25 1.25
Nos. 314-318 (5) 2.95 2.95

World Communications Year — A76

ANZCAN Cable Station: 30c, Chantik, Cable laying Ship. 45c, Shore end. 75c, Cable Ship Mercury. 85c, Map of cable route.

1983, Nov. 15 Litho. *Perf. 14½x14*

319 A76 30c multicolored .40 .40
320 A76 45c multicolored .65 .65
321 A76 75c multicolored 1.10 1.10
322 A76 85c multicolored 1.25 1.25
Nos. 319-322 (4) 3.40 3.40

Local Flowers — A77

1984 Litho. *Perf. 14*

323 A77 1c Myoporum obsurum .20 .20
324 A77 2c Ipomoea pes-caprae .20 .20
325 A77 3c Phreatia crassiuscula .20 .20
326 A77 4c Streblorrhiza speciosa .20 .20
327 A77 5c Rhopalostylis baueri .20 .20
328 A77 10c Alyxia gynopogon .20 .20
329 A77 15c Ungeria floribunda .20 .20
330 A77 20c Capparis nobilis .25 .25
331 A77 25c Lagunaria patersonia .35 .35
332 A77 30c Cordyline obtecta .45 .45
333 A77 35c Hibiscus insularis .50 .50
334 A77 40c Millettia australis .55 .55
335 A77 50c Jasminum volubile .75 .75
336 A77 $1 Passiflora aurantia 1.50 1.50
337 A77 $3 Oberonia titania 4.50 4.50
338 A77 $5 Araucaria heterophylla 7.50 7.50
Nos. 323-338 (16) 17.75 17.75

Issued: 2-3, 10, 20-25, 40-50c, $5, 1/10; others 3/27.

Reef Fish — A78

Perf. 13½x14

1984, Apr. 17 Litho. Wmk. 373

339 A78 30c Painted morwong .50 .50
340 A78 45c Black-spot goatfish .70 .70
341 A78 75c Ring-tailed surgeon fish 1.25 1.25
342 A78 85c Three-striped butterfly fish 1.40 1.40
Nos. 339-342 (4) 3.85 3.85

Boobook Owl — A79

Designs: a, Laying eggs. b, Standing at treehole. c, Sitting on branch looking sideways. d, Looking head on. e, Flying.

Wmk. 373

1984, July 17 Litho. *Perf. 14*

343 Strip of 5 4.25 4.25
a.-e. A79 30c any single .85 .85

AUSIPEX '84 — A80

1984, Sept. 18 Litho. *Perf. 14½*

344 A80 30c Nos. 15 and 176 .55 .55
345 A80 45c First day cover .85 .85
346 A80 75c Presentation pack 1.65 1.65
a. Souvenir sheet of 3, #344-346 3.50 3.50
Nos. 344-346 (3) 3.05 3.05

Christmas — A81

A82

1984, Oct. 9 Litho. *Perf. 13½*

347 A81 5c The Font .20 .20
348 A81 24c Church at Kingston, interior .35 .35
349 A81 30c Pastor and Mrs. Phelps .45 .45
350 A81 45c Phelps, Church of Chester .70 .70
351 A81 85c Phelps, Methodist Church, modern interior 1.40 1.40
Nos. 347-351 (5) 3.10 3.10

1984, Nov. 6 Litho. *Perf. 14x15*

352 A82 30c As teacher .45 .45
353 A82 45c As minister .65 .65
354 A82 75c As chaplain 1.10 1.10
355 A82 85c As community leader 1.40 1.40
Nos. 352-355 (4) 3.60 3.60

Rev. George Hunn Nobbs, death centenary.

Whaling Ships — A83

1985 Litho. *Perf. 13½x14*

356 A83 5c Fanny Fisher .20 .20
357 A83 15c Waterwitch .30 .30
358 A83 20c Canton .40 .40
359 A83 33c Costa Rica Packet .60 .60
360 A83 50c Splendid .90 .90
361 A83 60c Aladin 1.50 1.50
362 A83 80c California 1.75 1.75
363 A83 90c Onward 2.25 2.25
Nos. 356-363 (8) 7.90 7.90

Issued: 5c, 33c, 50c, 90c, 2/19; others 4/30.

Queen Mother 85th Birthday
Common Design Type

Perf. 14½x14

1985, June 6 Litho. Wmk. 384

364 CD336 5c Portrait, 1926 .20 .20
365 CD336 33c With Princess Anne .55 .55
366 CD336 50c Photograph by N. Parkinson .80 .80
367 CD336 90c Holding Prince Henry 1.65 1.65
Nos. 364-367 (4) 3.20 3.20

Souvenir Sheet

368 CD336 $1 With Princess Anne, Ascot Races 2.25 2.25

Intl. Youth Year — A84

Children's drawings.

1985, July 9 Litho. *Perf. 13½x14*

369 A84 33c Swimming .75 .75
370 A84 50c Nature walk 1.25 1.25

Girl, Prize-winning Cow — A85

Designs: 90c, Embroidery, jam-making, baking, animal husbandry.

1985, Sept. 10 Litho. *Perf. 13½x14*

371 A85 80c multicolored 1.10 1.10
372 A85 90c multicolored 1.25 1.25
a. Souvenir sheet of 2, #371-372 3.25 3.25

Royal Norfolk Island Agricultural & Horticultural Show, 125th anniv.

Christmas — A86

1985, Oct. 3 *Perf. 13½*

373 A86 27c Three Shepherds .45 .45
374 A86 33c Journey to Bethlehem .60 .60
375 A86 50c Three Wise Men .80 .80
376 A86 90c Nativity 1.65 1.65
Nos. 373-376 (4) 3.50 3.50

Marine Life — A87

1986, Jan. 14 *Perf. 13½x14*

377 A87 5c Long-spined sea urchin .20 .20
378 A87 33c Blue starfish .60 .60
379 A87 55c Eagle ray 1.00 1.00
380 A87 75c Moray eel 1.40 1.40
a. Souvenir sheet of 4, #377-380 3.75 3.75
Nos. 377-380 (4) 3.20 3.20

Halley's Comet — A88

Designs: a, Giotto space probe. b, Comet.

1986, Mar. 11 *Perf. 15*

381 A88 Pair 4.00 4.00
a.-b. $1 any single 2.00 2.00

Se-tenant in continuous design.

AMERIPEX '86 — A89

Designs: 33c, Isaac Robinson, US consul in Norfolk, 1887-1908, vert. 50c, Ford Model-T. 80c, Statue of Liberty.

1986, May 22 **Litho.** *Perf. 13½*

382 A89 33c multicolored .60 .60
383 A89 50c multicolored .90 .90
384 A89 80c multicolored 1.50 1.50
a. Souvenir sheet of #382-384 3.25 3.25
Nos. 382-384 (3) 3.00 3.00

Queen Elizabeth II, 60th Birthday — A90

Various portraits.

1986, June 12

385 A90 5c As Princess .20 .20
386 A90 33c Contemporary photograph .65 .65
387 A90 80c Opening N.I. Golf Club 1.40 1.40
388 A90 90c With Prince Philip 1.75 1.75
Nos. 385-388 (4) 4.00 4.00

Christmas A91

1986, Sept. 23 **Litho.** *Perf. 13½x14*

389 A91 30c multicolored .50 .50
390 A91 40c multicolored .65 .65
391 A91 $1 multicolored 1.60 1.60
Nos. 389-391 (3) 2.75 2.75

Commission of Gov. Phillip, Bicent. — A92

1986 **Litho.** *Perf. 14x13½*

392 A92 36c British prison, 1787 .55 .55
393 A92 55c Transportation, Court of Assize .85 .85
394 A92 90c Gov. meeting Home Society 1.40 1.40
395 A92 90c Gov. meeting Home Secretary 1.40 1.40
396 A92 $1 Gov. Phillip, 1738-1814 1.50 1.50
Nos. 392-396 (5) 5.70 5.70

No. 395 was issued because No. 394 is incorrectly inscribed.

Issued: #395, Dec. 16; others, Oct. 14.

See #417-420, 426-436.

Commission of Gov. Phillip, Bicent. — A93

1986, Dec. 16 *Perf. 13½*

397 A93 36c Maori chief .75 .75
398 A93 36c Bananas, taro .75 .75
399 A93 36c Stone tools .75 .75
400 A93 36c Polynesian outrigger .75 .75
Nos. 397-400 (4) 3.00 3.00

Pre-European occupation of the Island.

Island Scenery — A94 A96

1987-88 **Litho.** *Perf. 13½*

401 A94 1c Cockpit Creek Bridge .20 .20
402 A94 2c Cemetery Bay Beach .20 .20
403 A94 3c Guesthouse .20 .20
404 A94 5c Philip Island from Point Ross .20 .20
405 A94 15c Cattle grazing .20 .20
406 A94 30c Rock fishing .45 .45
407 A94 37c Old home .55 .55
408 A94 40c Shopping center .60 .60
409 A94 50c Emily Bay .75 .75
410 A94 60c Bloody Bridge .85 .85
411 A94 80c Pitcairner-style shop 1.10 1.10
412 A94 90c Government House 1.25 1.25
413 A94 $1 Melanesian Memorial Chapel 1.50 1.50
414 A94 $2 Kingston convict settlement 3.00 3.00
415 A94 $3 Ball Bay 4.50 4.50
416 A94 $5 Northerly cliffs 10.00 10.00
Nos. 401-416 (16) 25.55 25.55

Issued: 5c, 50c, 90c, $1, 2/17; 30c, 40c, 80c, $2, 4/17; 15c, 37c, 60c, $3, 7/27; 1c, 2c, 3c, $5, 5/17/88.

Bicentennial Type of 1986

Designs: 5c, Loading supplies at Deptford, England, 1787. No. 418, First Fleet sailing from Spithead (buoy in water). No. 419, Sailing from Spithead (ship flying British merchant flag). $1, Convicts below deck.

1987, May 13 **Litho.** *Perf. 14x13½*

417 A92 5c multicolored .20 .20
418 A92 55c multicolored .80 .80
419 A92 55c multicolored .80 .80
a. Pair, #418-419 1.60 1.60
420 A92 $1 multicolored 1.50 1.50
Nos. 417-420 (4) 3.30 3.30

No. 419a has a continuous design.

1987, Sept. 16 **Unwmk.**

World Wildlife Fund: Green parrot.

421 Strip of 4 *19.50 19.50*
a. A96 5c Parrot facing right *3.25 2.50*
b. A96 15c Parrot, chick, egg *3.75 2.00*
c. A96 36c Parrots *5.25 4.00*
d. A96 55c Parrot facing left *7.00 5.00*

Christmas A97

Children's party: 30c, Norfolk Island pine tree, restored convicts' settlement. 42c, Santa Claus, children opening packages. 58c, Santa, children, gifts in fire engine. 63c, Meal.

Perf. 13½x14

1987, Oct. 13 **Litho.** **Wmk. 384**

422 A97 30c multicolored .45 .45
423 A97 42c multicolored .65 .65
424 A97 58c multicolored .85 .85
425 A97 63c multicolored .95 .95
Nos. 422-425 (4) 2.90 2.90

Bicentennial Type of 1986

Designs: 5c, Lt. Philip Gidley King. No. 427, La Perouse and Louis XVI of France. No. 428, Gov. Phillip sailing in ship's cutter from Botany Bay to Port Jackson. No. 429, Flag raising on Norfolk Is. 55c, Lt. King and search party exploring the island. 70c, Landfall, Sydney Bay. No. 432, L'Astrolabe and La Boussole off coast of Norfolk. No. 433, HMS Supply. No. 434, Wrecking of L'Astrolabe off the Solomon Isls. No. 435, First Fleet landing at Sydney Cove. No. 436, First settlement, Sydney Bay, 1788.

1987-88 **Litho.** *Perf. 14x13½*

426 A92 5c multicolored .20 .20
427 A92 37c multicolored .85 .85
428 A92 37c multicolored .85 .85
429 A92 37c multicolored .85 .85
430 A92 55c multicolored 1.25 1.25
431 A92 70c multicolored 1.50 1.50
432 A92 90c multicolored 2.00 2.00
433 A92 90c multicolored 2.00 2.00
434 A92 $1 multicolored 2.50 2.50
435 A92 $1 multicolored 2.50 2.50
436 A92 $1 multicolored 2.50 2.50
Nos. 426-436 (11) 17.00 17.00

Visit of Jean La Perouse (1741-88), French navigator, to Norfolk Is. (Nos. 427, 432, 434); arrival of the First Fleet at Sydney Cove (Nos. 428, 435); founding of Norfolk Is. (Nos. 426, 429-431, 433, 436).

Issued: #427, 432, 434, Dec. 8, 1987; #428, 435, Jan. 25, 1988; others, Mar. 4, 1988.

SYDPEX '88, July 30-Aug. 7 A98

Sydney-Norfolk transportation and communication links.

Perf. 14x13½ 13½x14

1988, July 30 **Litho.**

437 A98 37c Air and sea transports, vert. .75 .75
438 A98 37c shown .75 .75
439 A98 37c Telecommunications, vert. .75 .75
a. Souvenir sheet of 3, #437-439 3.50 3.50
Nos. 437-439 (3) 2.25 2.25

No. 438 exists perf. 13½ within No. 439a.

Christmas — A99

1988, Sept. 27 **Litho.** *Perf. 14x13½*

440 A99 30c shown .55 .55
441 A99 42c Flowers, diff. .75 .75
442 A99 58c Trees, fish 1.10 1.10
443 A99 63c Trees, sailboats 1.10 1.10
Nos. 440-443 (4) 3.50 3.50

Convict Era Georgian Architecture, c. 1825-1850 A100

Designs: 39c, Waterfront shop and boat shed. 55c, Royal Engineers' Building. 90c, Old military barracks. $1, Commissary and new barracks.

1988, Dec. 6 **Litho.** *Perf. 13½x14*

444 A100 39c multicolored .60 .60
445 A100 55c multicolored .85 .85
446 A100 90c multicolored 1.40 1.40
447 A100 $1 multicolored 1.65 1.65
Nos. 444-447 (4) 4.50 4.50

Indigenous Insects A101

Perf. 13½x14

1989, Feb. 14 **Litho.** **Unwmk.**

448 A101 39c *Lamprima aenea* .75 .75
449 A101 55c *Insulascirtus nythos* 1.00 1.00
450 A101 90c *Caedicia araucariae* 1.50 1.50
451 A101 $1 *Thrincophora aridela* 2.00 2.00
Nos. 448-451 (4) 5.25 5.25

Mutiny on the Bounty A102

Designs: 5c, *Bounty's* landfall, Adventure Bay, Tasmania. 39c, Mutineers and Polynesian maidens, c. 1790. 55c, Cumbria, Christian's home county. $1.10, Capt. Bligh and crewmen cast adrift.

Perf. 13½

1989, Apr. 28 **Litho.** **Unwmk.**

452 A102 5c multicolored .20 .20
453 A102 39c multicolored .75 .75
454 A102 55c multicolored 1.10 1.10
455 A102 $1.10 multicolored 1.90 1.90
Nos. 452-455 (4) 3.95 3.95

Souvenir Sheet

456 Sheet of 3 + label (#453, 456a-456b) 5.75 5.75
a. A102 90c Isle of Man No. 393 2.25 2.25
b. A102 $1 Pitcairn Isls. No. 321d 2.50 2.50

See Isle of Man Nos. 389-394 and Pitcairn Isls. Nos. 320-322.

A103

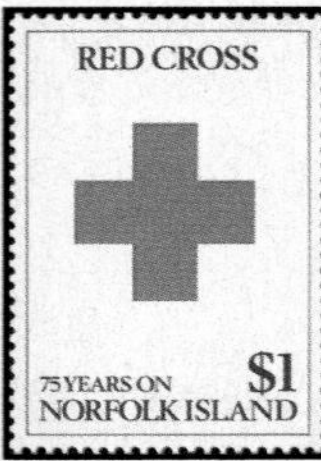

A104

Perf. 14x13½

1989, Aug. 10 Litho. Unwmk.

457 A103 41c Flag .65 .65
458 A103 55c Ballot box .85 .85
459 A103 $1 Norfolk Is. Act of 1979 1.50 1.50
460 A103 $1.10 Norfolk Is. crest 1.65 1.65
Nos. 457-460 (4) 4.65 4.65

Self-Government, 10th anniv.

Perf. 13½x13

1989, Sept. 25 Litho. Unwmk.

461 A104 $1 dark ultra & dark red 2.00 2.00

Natl. Red Cross, 75th anniv.

Bounty Hymns A105

Designs: 36c, "While nature was sinking in stillness to rest, The last beams of daylight show dim in the west." 60c, "There's a land that is fairer than day, And by faith we can see it afar." 75c, "Let the lower lights be burning, Send a gleam across the wave." 80c, "Oh, have you not heard of that beautiful stream That flows through our father's lands."

1989, Oct. 9 *Perf. 13½x14*

462 A105 36c multicolored .55 .55
463 A105 60c multicolored .95 .95
464 A105 75c multicolored 1.25 1.25
465 A105 80c multicolored 1.25 1.25
Nos. 462-465 (4) 4.00 4.00

A106

A107

1989, Nov. 21 *Perf. 14x13½*

466 A106 41c Announcer John Royle .75 .75
467 A106 65c Sound waves on map 1.25 1.25
468 A106 $1.10 Jacko, the laughing kookaburra 2.00 2.00
Nos. 466-468 (3) 4.00 4.00

Radio Australia, 50th anniv.

Perf. 15x14½

1990, Jan. 23 Litho. Unwmk.

Settlement of Pitcairn (The Norfolk Islanders): 70c, The *Bounty* on fire. $1.10, Armorial ensign of Norfolk.

469 A107 70c multicolored 1.25 1.25
470 A107 $1.10 multicolored 2.00 2.00

Salvage Team at Work A108

Designs: No. 471, HMS *Sirius* striking reef. No. 472, HMS *Supply* clearing reef. $1, Map of salvage sites, artifacts.

1990, Mar. 19 *Perf. 14x13½*

Size of Nos. 471-472: 40x27

471 A108 41c multicolored .70 .70
472 A108 41c multicolored .70 .70
a. Pair, #471-472 1.40 1.40
473 A108 65c shown 1.10 1.10
474 A108 $1 multicolored 1.65 1.65
Nos. 471-474 (4) 4.15 4.15

Wreck of HMS *Sirius,* 200th anniv. No. 472a has continuous design.

Lightering Cargo Ashore, Kingston A109

MV Ile de Lumiere A110

1990-91 Litho. *Perf. 14x14½*

479 A109 5c like #480 .20 .20
480 A109 10c shown .20 .20

Perf. 14½

481 A110 45c La Dunkerquoise .65 .65
482 A110 50c Dmitri Mendeleev .75 .75
483 A110 65c Pacific Rover .95 .95
484 A110 70c shown 1.00 1.00
485 A110 75c Norfolk Trader 1.10 1.10
486 A110 80c Roseville 1.10 1.10
487 A110 90c Kalia 1.25 1.25
488 A110 $1 HMS Bounty 1.50 1.50
489 A110 $2 HMAS Success 3.00 3.00
490 A110 $5 HMAS Whyalia 7.50 7.50
Nos. 479-490 (12) 19.20 19.20

Issued: 5c, 10c, 70c, $2, 7/17/90; 45c, 50c, 65c, $5, 2/19/91; 75c, 80c, 90c, $1, 8/13/91.

Christmas — A111

A112

1990, Sept. 25 Litho. *Perf. 14½*

491 A111 38c Island home .65 .65
492 A111 43c New post office .75 .75
493 A111 65c Sydney Bay, Kingston, horiz. 1.10 1.10
494 A111 85c Officers' Quarters, 1836, horiz. 1.50 1.50
Nos. 491-494 (4) 4.00 4.00

1990, Oct. 11 Litho. *Perf. 15x14½*

Designs: 70c, William Charles Wentworth (1790-1872), Australian politician. $1.20, Thursday October Christian (1790-1831).

495 A112 70c brown 1.25 1.25
496 A112 $1.20 brown 2.00 2.00

Norfolk Island Robin
A113 A114

1990, Dec. 3 Litho. *Perf. 14½*

497 A113 65c multicolored 1.50 1.50
498 A113 $1 shown 2.50 2.50
499 A113 $1.20 multi, diff. 3.00 3.00
Nos. 497-499 (3) 7.00 7.00

Souvenir Sheet

500 Sheet of 2 8.00 8.00
a. A114 $1 shown 3.50 3.50
b. A114 $1 Two robins 3.50 3.50

Birdpex '90, 20th Intl. Ornithological Congress, New Zealand.

Ham Radio — A115

1991, Apr. 9 Litho. *Perf. 14½*

501 A115 43c Island map .75 .75
502 A115 $1 World map 1.75 1.75
503 A115 $1.20 Regional location 2.25 2.25
Nos. 501-503 (3) 4.75 4.75

Museum Displays A116

1991, May 16 Litho. *Perf. 14½*

504 A116 43c Ship's bow, Sirius Museum, vert. .70 .70
505 A116 70c House Museum 1.25 1.25
506 A116 $1 Carronade, Sirius Museum 1.65 1.65
507 A116 $1.20 Pottery, Archaeology Museum, vert. 2.00 2.00
Nos. 504-507 (4) 5.60 5.60

Wreck of HMS Pandora, Aug. 28, 1791 A117

Design: $1.20, HMS Pandora searching for Bounty mutineers.

1991, July 2 Litho. *Perf. 13½x14*

508 A117 $1 shown 1.65 1.65
509 A117 $1.20 multicolored 2.00 2.00

Christmas A118

1991, Sept. 23 Litho. *Perf. 14½*

510 A118 38c multicolored .60 .60
511 A118 43c multicolored .65 .65
512 A118 65c multicolored 1.00 1.00
513 A118 85c multicolored 1.40 1.40
Nos. 510-513 (4) 3.65 3.65

Start of World War II in the Pacific, 50th Anniv. A119

1991, Dec. 9 Litho. *Perf. 14½*

514 A119 43c Tank and soldier .75 .75
515 A119 70c B-17 1.10 1.10
516 A119 $1 War ships 1.65 1.65
Nos. 514-516 (3) 3.50 3.50

A120

A121

1992, Feb. 11 Litho. *Perf. 14½*

517 A120 45c Columbus' Coat of Arms .70 .70
518 A120 $1.05 Santa Maria 1.65 1.65
519 A120 $1.20 Columbus at globe 1.90 1.90
Nos. 517-519 (3) 4.25 4.25

Discovery of America, 500th anniv.

1992, May 4 Litho. *Perf. 14½*

Designs: No. 520, Map of Coral Sea Battle area. No. 521, Battle area, Midway. No. 522, HMAS Australia. No. 523, Catalina PBY5. No. 524, USS Yorktown. No. 525, Dauntless dive bomber.

520 A121 45c multicolored .75 .75
521 A121 45c multicolored .75 .75
522 A121 70c multicolored 1.25 1.25
523 A121 70c multicolored 1.25 1.25
524 A121 $1.05 multicolored 1.90 1.90
525 A121 $1.05 multicolored 1.90 1.90
Nos. 520-525 (6) 7.80 7.80

Battles of the Coral Sea and Midway, 50th anniv.

US Invasion of Guadalcanal, 50th Anniv. A122

Designs: 45c, Troops landing on beach. 70c, Troops in battle. $1.05, Map, flags.

1992, Aug. 6 Litho. *Perf. 14½*

526 A122 45c multicolored .65 .65
527 A122 70c multicolored 1.10 1.10
528 A122 $1.05 multicolored 1.65 1.65
Nos. 526-528 (3) 3.40 3.40

Christmas — A123

Scenes of Norfolk Island: 40c, Ball Bay, looking over Point Blackbourne. 45c, Headstone Creek. 75c, Ball Bay. $1.20, Rocky Point Reserve.

1992, Oct. 29 Litho. *Perf. 15x14½*

529 A123 40c multicolored .65 .65
530 A123 45c multicolored .70 .70
531 A123 75c multicolored 1.25 1.25
532 A123 $1.20 multicolored 1.90 1.90
Nos. 529-532 (4) 4.50 4.50

Tourism A124

Tourist sites at Kingston: a, Boat shed, flaghouses. b, Old military barracks. c, All Saints Church. d, Officers quarters. e, Quality row.

1993, Feb. 23 Litho. *Perf. 14½*

533 A124 45c Strip of 5, #a.-e. 3.50 3.50

Emergency Services A125

1993, May 18 Litho. *Perf. 14½*

534 A125 45c Volunteer fire service .75 .75
535 A125 70c Rescue squad 1.10 1.10
536 A125 75c St. John ambulance 1.25 1.25
537 A125 $1.20 Police service 2.00 2.00
Nos. 534-537 (4) 5.10 5.10

Nudibranchs A126

1993, July 7 Litho. *Perf. 14½*

538 A126 45c Phyllidia ocellata .65 .65
539 A126 45c Glaucus atlanticus .65 .65
540 A126 75c Bornella sp. 1.10 1.10
541 A126 85c Glossodoris rubroannolata 1.40 1.40
542 A126 95c Halgerda willeyi 1.60 1.60
543 A126 $1.05 Chromodoris amoena 1.75 1.75
Nos. 538-543 (6) 7.15 7.15

No. 539 identified as "glauc."

A127 A128

Designs: 70c, Maori patus. $1.20, First Maori map of New Zealand on paper, 1793.

1993, Oct. 28 Litho. *Perf. 14½*

544 A127 70c tan, buff & black 1.00 1.00
545 A127 $1.20 tan, buff & black 2.00 2.00

Cultural contact with New Zealand, bicent.

1993, Oct. 28

546 A128 40c blue & multi .60 .60
547 A128 45c red & multi .65 .65
548 A128 75c green & multi 1.10 1.10
549 A128 $1.20 black & multi 1.75 1.75
Nos. 546-549 (4) 4.10 4.10

Early Pacific Explorers A129

Explorer, ship: 5c, Vasco Nunez de Balboa, Barbara. 10c, Ferdinand Magellan, Victoria. 20c, Juan Sebastian de Elcano, Victoria. 50c, Alvaro de Saavedra, Florida. 70c, Ruy Lopez de Villalobos, San Juan. 75c, Miguel Lopez de Legaspi, San Lesmes. 80c, Sir Frances Drake, Golden Hinde. 85c, Alvaro de Mendana, Santiago. 90c, Pedro Fernandes de Quiros, San Pedro Paulo. $1, Luis Baez de Torres, San Perico. $2, Abel Tasman, Heemskerk. $5, William Dampier, Cygnet. No. 562, Golden Hinde (Francis Drake).

1994 Litho. *Perf. 14½*

550 A129 5c multicolored .30 .30
551 A129 10c multicolored .35 .35
552 A129 20c multicolored .70 .70
554 A129 50c multicolored 1.00 1.00
556 A129 70c multicolored 1.25 1.25
557 A129 75c multicolored 1.40 1.40
558 A129 80c multicolored 1.40 1.40
559 A129 85c multicolored 1.50 1.50
560 A129 90c multicolored 1.75 1.75
560A A129 $1 multicolored 2.00 2.00
561 A129 $2 multicolored 4.00 4.00
561A A129 $5 multicolored 9.00 9.00
Nos. 550-561A (12) 24.65 24.65

Souvenir Sheet

Perf. 13

562 A129 $1.20 multicolored 3.00 3.00

No. 562 contains one 32x52mm stamp.

Issued: 50c, 70c, 75c, $2, No. 562, 2/8/94; 5c, 10c, 20c, $5, 5/3/94. 80c, 85c, 90c, $1, 7/26/94.

This is an expanding set. Numbers may change.

A130

A131

Seabirds: a, Sooty tern. b, Red-tailed tropic bird. c, Australasian gannet. d, Wedge-tail shearwater. e, Masked booby.

1994, Aug. 17 Litho. *Perf. 14½x14*

565 A130 45c Strip of 5, #a.-e. 4.00 4.00
Booklet, 2 #565 8.00

1994, Oct. 27 Litho. *Die Cut*

Christmas: 45c, Church, flowers, words from Pitcairn anthem. 75c, Stained glass windows, "To God be the glory." $1.20, Rainbow, ship, "Ship of Fame."

Self-Adhesive

566 A131 45c multicolored .75 .75
567 A131 75c multicolored 1.25 1.25
568 A131 $1.20 multicolored 2.25 2.25
Nos. 566-568 (3) 4.25 4.25

Vintage Cars — A132

1995, Feb. 7 Litho. *Perf. 14x14½*

569 A132 45c 1926 Chevrolet .75 .75
570 A132 75c 1928 Model A Ford 1.25 1.25
571 A132 $1.05 1929 Model A A/C Ford truck 1.75 1.75
572 A132 $1.20 1930 Model A Ford 2.00 2.00
Nos. 569-572 (4) 5.75 5.75

Humpback Whales A133

Perf. 14x14½, 14½x14

1995, May 9 Litho.

573 A133 45c Tail fluke .75 .75
574 A133 75c Mother & calf 1.40 1.40
575 A133 $1.05 Breaching, vert. 2.00 2.00
Nos. 573-575 (3) 4.15 4.15

Souvenir Sheet

Perf. 14x14½

576 A133 $1.20 Bubble netting, vert. 1.75 1.75
a. Overprinted in gold & black 1.75 1.75

No. 576 contains one 30x50mm stamp and is a continuous design.

Overprint in margin of No. 576a has "Selamat Hari Merdeka" and JAKARTA '95 exhibition emblem.

Butterfly Fish — A134

Chaetodon...: 5c, pelewensis. 45c, plebeius. $1.20, tricinctus. $1.50, auriga.

1995, June 15 Litho. *Perf. 14*

577 A134 5c multicolored .25 .25
578 A134 45c multicolored .75 .75
579 A134 $1.20 multicolored 2.00 2.00
580 A134 $1.50 multicolored 2.50 2.50
Nos. 577-580 (4) 5.50 5.50

World War II Vehicles A135

Designs: 5c, 1942 Intl. 4x4 refueler. 45c, 1942 Ford 5 passenger sedan. $1.20, 1942 Ford 3-ton tipper. $2, D8 Caterpillar with scraper.

1995, Aug. 8 Litho. *Perf. 14x15*

Black Vignettes

581 A135 5c brown & tan .20 .20
582 A135 45c blue & red lilac .65 .65
583 A135 $1.20 green & orange 1.90 1.90
584 A135 $2 red & gray 3.25 3.25
Nos. 581-584 (4) 6.00 6.00

Island Flower Type of 1960

1995, Sept. 1 Litho. *Rouletted 7*

Booklet Stamps

585 A6 5c like No. 30 .20 .20
a. Booklet pane of 18 + 3 labels 2.00
586 A6 5c like No. 33 .20 .20
a. Booklet pane of 18 + 3 labels 2.00
Complete booklet, 1 each #585a-586a 4.00

A136

Victory in the Pacific Day, 50th Anniv. — A136a

Designs: 5c, Fighter plane en route. 45c, Sgt. T.C. Derrick, VC, vert. 75c, Gen. MacArthur, vert. $1.05, Girls at victory party.

1995, Sept. 1 Litho. *Perf. 12*

587 A136 5c multicolored .25 .25
588 A136 45c multicolored .75 .75
589 A136 75c multicolored 1.25 1.25
590 A136 $1.05 multicolored 1.75 1.75
Nos. 587-590 (4) 4.00 4.00

Litho. & Embossed

591 A136a $10 Medals 22.50 22.50

Singapore '95.

UN, 50th Anniv. — A137

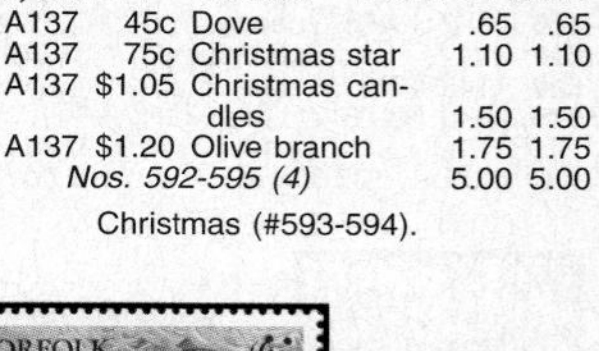

1995, Nov. 7 Litho. *Perf. 14½x14*

592 A137 45c Dove .65 .65
593 A137 75c Christmas star 1.10 1.10
594 A137 $1.05 Christmas candles 1.50 1.50
595 A137 $1.20 Olive branch 1.75 1.75
Nos. 592-595 (4) 5.00 5.00

Christmas (#593-594).

Skinks and Geckos A138

World Wildlife Fund: a, 45c, Skink crawling left. b, 5c, Skink crawling right. c, 45c, Gecko crawling right. d, 5c, Gecko crawling left, flower.

1996, Feb. 7 Litho. *Perf. 14½x15*

596 A138 Strip of 4, #a.-d. 4.00 4.00

No. 596 was issued in sheets of 4 strips with stamps in each strip in different order.

Royal Australian Air Force, 75th Anniv. — A139

1996, Apr. 22 Litho. *Perf. 14*

597 A139 45c Sopwith pup .75 .75
598 A139 45c Wirraway .75 .75
599 A139 75c F-111C 1.25 1.25
600 A139 85c F/A-18 Hornet 1.40 1.40
Nos. 597-600 (4) 4.15 4.15

Souvenir Sheet

New Year 1996 (Year of the Rat) — A140

Illustration reduced.

1996, May 17 Litho. *Perf. 12*

601 A140 $1 multicolored 2.00 2.00
a. With addl. inscription in sheet margin 2.00 2.00

No. 601a is inscribed in sheet margin with China '96 exhibition emblem.

Shells — A141

Designs: No. 602, Argonauta nodosa. No. 603, Janthina janthina. No. 604, Naticarius oncus. No. 605, Cypraea caputserpentis.

1996, July 2 Litho. *Perf. 14*

602 A141 45c multicolored .75 .75
603 A141 45c multicolored .75 .75
604 A141 45c multicolored .75 .75
605 A141 45c multicolored .75 .75
Nos. 602-605 (4) 3.00 3.00

Tourism A142

1996, Sept. 17 Litho. *Perf. 13½x14*

606 A142 45c Shopping .75 .75
607 A142 75c Bounty day 1.25 1.25
608 A142 $2.50 Horse riding 4.25 4.25
609 A142 $3.70 Working the ship 6.25 6.25
Nos. 606-609 (4) 12.50 12.50

A143

A144

Christmas: Cow, star, Bible verse, and: No. 610, Nativity scene. No. 611, Boats, boathouses. 75c, House, trees. 85c, Flowers, fruits.

1996, Nov. 5 Litho. *Perf. 15*

610 A143 45c multicolored .75 .75
611 A143 45c multicolored .75 .75
612 A143 75c multicolored 1.25 1.25
613 A143 85c multicolored 1.40 1.40
Nos. 610-613 (4) 4.15 4.15

1997, Jan. 22 Litho. *Roulette 7*

No. 614, Natl. Arms. No. 615, Natl. Seal.

614 A144 5c yellow & green .20 .20
a. Booklet pane of 10 .80
615 A144 5c tan & brown .20 .20
a. Booklet pane of 10 .80
Complete booklet, 2 each #614a-615a 3.25

Souvenir Sheet

Beef Cattle — A145

1997, Feb. 11 *Perf. 13½x13*

616 A145 $1.20 multicolored 3.00 3.00
a. Inscribed in sheet margin 30.00 25.00

No. 616a is inscribed with Hong Kong '97 exhibition emblem.

Butterflies A146

Designs: 75c, Cepora perimale perimale. 90c, Danaus chrysippus petilia. $1, Danaus bamata bamata. $1.20, Danaus plexippus.

1997, Mar. 28 *Perf. 14½*

617 A146 75c multicolored 1.50 1.50
618 A146 90c multicolored 1.75 1.75
619 A146 $1 multicolored 2.00 2.00
620 A146 $1.20 multicolored 2.50 2.50
Nos. 617-620 (4) 7.75 7.75

Dolphins — A147

1997, May 29 Litho. *Perf. 14*

621 A147 45c Dusky dolphin 1.50 1.50
622 A147 75c Common dolphin 3.00 3.00

Souvenir Sheet

623 A147 $1.05 Dolphin, diff. 3.00 3.00
a. Inscribed in sheet margin 4.00 4.00

No. 623a is inscribed in sheet margin with PACIFIC 97 exhibition emblem.

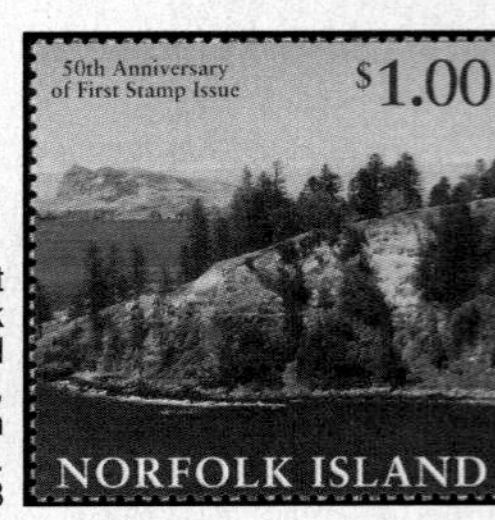

First Norfolk Island Stamp, 50th Anniv. A148

Designs: $1, View of Ball Bay. $1.50, #4. $8, #12, view of Ball Bay.

1997, June 10 *Perf. 12*

624 A148 $1.00 multicolored 2.00 2.00
625 A148 $1.50 multicolored 3.00 3.00
a. Pair, #624-625 5.00 5.00

Size: 90x45mm

626 A148 $8 multicolored 15.00 15.00

Queen Elizabeth II & Prince Philip, 50th Wedding Anniv. — A149

Designs: 20c, Queen. No. 628, Prince guiding 4-in-hand team. No. 629, Prince in formal suit, hat. 50c, Queen riding in royal coach.
$1.50, Younger picture of Queen, Prince riding in carriage.

1997, Aug. 12 Litho. *Perf. 14½*

627 A149 20c multicolored .35 .35
628 A149 25c multicolored .40 .40
a. Pair, #627-628 .75 .75
629 A149 25c multicolored .40 .40
630 A149 50c multicolored .80 .80
a. Pair, #629-630 1.20 1.20

Souvenir Sheet

631 A149 $1.50 multicolored 2.40 2.40

Souvenir Sheet

Return of Hong Kong to China — A150

1997, Sept. 16 Litho. *Perf. 14*

632 A150 45c Royal Yacht Britannia .85 .85

Greetings Stamps — A151

1997, Nov. 4 Litho. *Perf. 13x13½*

633 A151 45c Christmas .75 .75
634 A151 75c New Year's Eve 1.25 1.25
635 A151 $1.20 Valentine's Day 2.00 2.00
Nos. 633-635 (3) 4.00 4.00

Souvenir Sheet

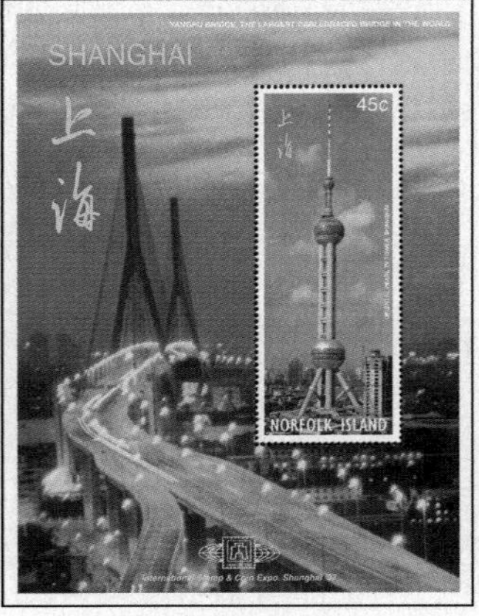

Oriental Pearl TV Tower, Shanghai — A152

Illustration reduced.

1997, Nov. 18 *Perf. 14½*

636 A152 45c multicolored 1.50 1.50

Shanghai '97, Intl. Stamp & Coin Expo.

Souvenir Sheet

New Year 1998 (Year of the Tiger) — A153

Illustration reduced.

1998, Feb. 12 Litho. *Perf. 12*

637 A153 45c multicolored 1.50 1.50

Paintings of Cats — A154

1998, Feb. 26 *Perf. 14½*

638 A154 45c "Pepper" .75 .75
639 A154 45c "Tabitha" .75 .75
640 A154 75c "Midnight" 1.25 1.25
641 A154 $1.20 "Rainbow" 2.00 2.00
Nos. 638-641 (4) 4.75 4.75

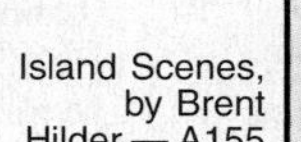

Island Scenes, by Brent Hilder — A155

Designs: No. 642, Penal Settlement, 1825-56. No. 643, First settlement, 1788-1814.

1998, Feb. 27 *Rouletted 7*

642 A155 5c blue & black .20 .20
a. Booklet pane of 10 1.25
643 A155 5c blue green & black .20 .20
a. Booklet pane of 10 .75
Complete booklet, 2 each 1642a-1643a 4.00

Diana, Princess of Wales (1961-97)
Common Design Type

#645: a, Wearing blue & white dress. b, Wearing pearl pendant earrings. c, In striped dress.

1998, Apr. 28 Litho. *Perf. 14½x14*

644 CD355 45c multicolored .85 .85

Sheet of 4

645 CD355 45c #a.-c., #644 3.75 3.75

No. 644 sold for $1.80 + 45c, with surtax from international sales being donated to the Princess Diana Memorial fund and surtax from national sales being dontated to designated local charity.

Reef Fish — A156

Designs: 10c, Tweed trousers. 20c, Conspicuous angelfish. 30c, Moon wrasse. 45c, Wide-stiped clownfish. 50c, Raccoon butterfly fish. 70c, Artooti. 75c, Splendid hawkfish. 85c, Scorpion fish. 90c, Orange fairy basslet. $1, Sweetlip. $3, Moorish idol. $4, Gold ribbon soapfish.
$1.20, Shark.

1998 Litho. *Perf. 14½*

646 A156 10c multicolored .20 .20
647 A156 20c multicolored .30 .30
648 A156 30c multicolored .45 .45
649 A156 45c multicolored .65 .65
650 A156 50c multicolored .75 .75
651 A156 70c multicolored 1.00 1.00
652 A156 75c multicolored 1.10 1.10
653 A156 85c multicolored 1.25 1.25
654 A156 90c multicolored 1.25 1.25
655 A156 $1 multicolored 1.50 1.50
656 A156 $3 multicolored 4.50 4.50
657 A156 $4 multicolored 6.00 6.00
Nos. 646-657 (12) 18.95 18.95

Souvenir Sheet
Perf. 14x14½

658 A156 $1.20 multicolored 2.00 2.00

No. 658 contains 30x40mm stamp.
Issued: 10c, 30c, 50c, 75c, 90c, $1.20, $4, 5/5; others, 6/29.

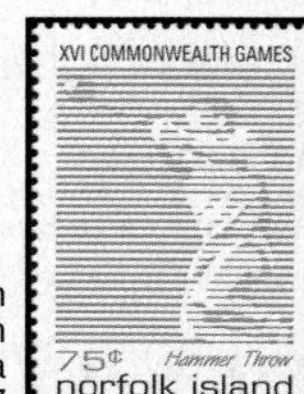

16th Commonwealth Games, Kuala Lumpur — A157

Designs: 75c, Hammer throw, vert. 95c, Trap shooting. $1.05, Lawn bowling, vert.
85c, Flag bearer, vert.

1998, July 23 Litho. *Perf. 14½*

659 A157 75c black & red 1.10 1.10
660 A157 95c black & violet blue 1.40 1.40
661 A157 $1.05 black & red lilac 1.50 1.50
Nos. 659-661 (3) 4.00 4.00

Souvenir Sheet

662 A157 85c black & greenish blue 1.75 1.75

The Norfolk, Bicent. A158

1998, Sept. 24 Litho. *Perf. 13*

663 A158 45c multicolored .80 .80

Souvenir Sheet

664 A158 $1.20 multicolored 2.00 2.00

Souvenir Sheet

Whales — A159

Illustration reduced.

1998, Oct. 23 Litho. *Perf. 13½x14*
665 A159 $1.50 multicolored 4.00 4.00

See Namibia No. 919, South Africa No. 1095.

Christmas A160

Designs: 45c, "Peace on earth." 75c, "Joy to the World." $1.05, Doves, "A season of love." $1.20, Candle, "Light of the World."

1998, Nov. 10 *Perf. 13x13½*
666 A160 45c multicolored .65 .65
667 A160 75c multicolored 1.10 1.10
668 A160 $1.05 multicolored 1.50 1.50
669 A160 $1.20 multicolored 1.75 1.75
Nos. 666-669 (4) 5.00 5.00

Airplanes A161

1999, Jan. 28 Litho. *Roulette 7*
Booklet Stamps
670 A161 5c S23 Sandringham .20 .20
a. Booklet pane of 10 1.25
671 A161 5c DC4 "Norfolk Trader" .20 .20
a. Booklet pane of 10 1.25
Complete booklet, 2 ea #670a-671a 5.00

Souvenir Sheet

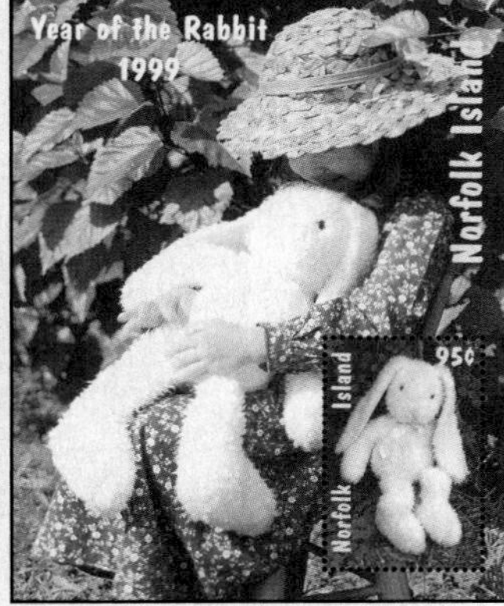

New Year 1999 (Year of the Rabbit) — A162

Illustration reduced.

1999, Feb. 9 Litho. *Perf. 14*
672 A162 95c multicolored 1.75 1.75
a. With additional sheet margin inscription 1.75 1.75

No. 672a is inscribed in sheet margin with China '99 exhibition emblem. Issued: 8/23/99.

Trading Ship Resolution A163

Designs: No. 673, Under construction. No. 674, Launch day. No. 675, Emily Bay. No. 676, Cascade. No. 677, Docked at Auckland.

1999, Mar. 19 *Perf. 13x13½*
Booklet Stamps
673 A163 45c multicolored .90 .90
674 A163 45c multicolored .90 .90
675 A163 45c multicolored .90 .90
676 A163 45c multicolored .90 .90
677 A163 45c multicolored .90 .90
a. Booklet pane, #673-677 + label 4.50
Complete booklet, #677a 4.50

Australia '99, World Stamp Expo.

Souvenir Sheet

Pacific Black Duck — A164

Illustration reduced.

1999, Apr. 27 Litho. *Perf. 14*
678 A164 $2.50 multicolored 4.50 4.50

IBRA '99, Intl. Philatelic Exhibition, Nuremberg, Germany.

Providence Petrel A165

1999, May 27 Litho. *Perf. 14½*
679 A165 75c In flight, vert. 1.50 1.50
680 A165 $1.05 Up close 2.00 2.00
681 A165 $1.20 Adult, young 2.50 2.50
Nos. 679-681 (3) 6.00 6.00

Souvenir Sheet
Perf. 13
682 A165 $4.50 In flight 7.50 7.50

No. 682 contains one 35x51mm stamp.

Roses — A166

1999, July 30 Litho. *Perf. 14½x14*
683 A166 45c Cecile Brunner 1.00 1.00
684 A166 75c Green 1.50 1.50
685 A166 $1.05 David Buffett 2.25 2.25
Nos. 683-685 (3) 4.75 4.75

Souvenir Sheet
686 A166 $1.20 A Country Woman 3.00 3.00

Handicrafts A167

Designs: a, 45c, Pottery. b, 45c, Woodcarving. c, 75c, Quilting. d, $1.05, Weaving.

1999, Sept. 16 *Perf. 14¼x14¾*
687 A167 Strip of 4, #a.-d. 4.00 4.00

Queen Mother's Century
Common Design Type

Queen Mother: No. 688, Inspecting bomb damage at Buckingham Palace, 1940. No. 689, With royal family at Abergeldy Castle, 1955. 75c, With Queen Elizabeth, Prince William, 94th birthday. $1.20, As colonel-in-chief of King's Regiment.

$3, With Amy Johnson, pilot of 1930 flight to Australia.

Wmk. 384
1999, Oct. 12 Litho. *Perf. 13½*
688 CD358 45c multicolored .65 .65
689 CD358 45c multicolored .65 .65
690 CD358 75c multicolored 1.10 1.10
691 CD358 $1.20 multicolored 1.75 1.75
Nos. 688-691 (4) 4.15 4.15

Souvenir Sheet
692 CD358 $3 multicolored 5.00 5.00

Melanesian Mission, 150th Anniv. — A168

Christmas: a, 45c, Bishop George Augustus Selwyndd. b, 45c, Bishop John Coleridge Patteson. c, 75c, Text. d, $1.05, Stained glass. e, $1.20, Southern Cross.

1999, Nov. 10 Litho. *Perf. 14*
693 A168 Strip of 5, #a.-e. 6.00 6.00

See Solomon Islands No. 890.

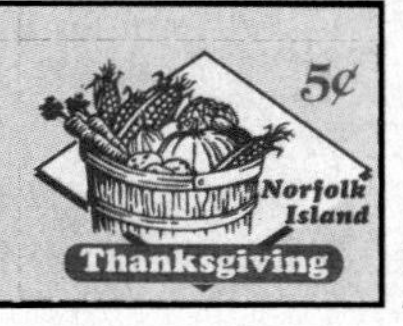

Festivals A169

2000, Jan. 31 Litho. *Roulette 5¾*
Booklet Stamps
694 A169 5c Thanksgiving .20 .20
695 A169 5c Country music festival .20 .20
a. Booklet pane, 5 each #694-695 1.00
Complete booklet, 4 #695a 4.00

Souvenir Sheet

New Year 2000 (Year of the Dragon) — A170

Illustration reduced.

2000, Feb. 7 Litho. *Perf. 13¼*
696 A170 $2 multi 3.00 3.00

Fowl — A171

Designs: 45c, Domestic goose. 75c, Pacific black duck. $1.05, Mallard drake. $1.20, Aylesbury duck.

2000, Feb. 18 Litho. *Perf. 14¼*
697 A171 45c multi 1.00 1.00
698 A171 75c multi 1.50 1.50
699 A171 $1.05 multi 2.00 2.00
700 A171 $1.20 multi 2.50 2.50
Nos. 697-700 (4) 7.00 7.00

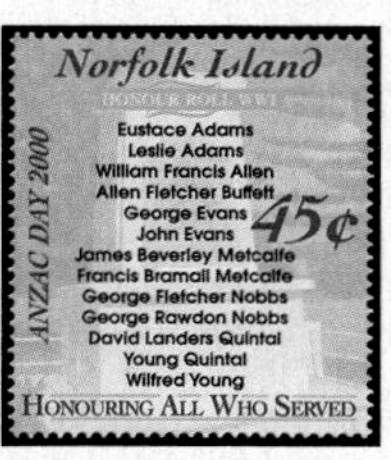

Anzac Day — A172

Monument and lists of war dead from: 45c, WWI. 75c, WWII and Korean War.

2000, Apr. 25 Litho. *Perf. 14x14¾*
701-702 A172 Set of 2 2.00 2.00

Souvenir Sheets

Whaler Project — A173

Designs: No. 703, shown. No. 704, As #703, with gold overprints for The Stamp Show 2000, London, and Crown Agents.

Perf. 14¼, Imperf. (#704)
2000, May 1
703-704 A173 $4 Set of 2 14.00 14.00

Bounty Day — A174

Designs: 45c, Capt. William Bligh. 75c, Fletcher Christian.

2000, June 8 *Perf. 14¼*
705-706 A174 Set of 2 1.75 1.75

Eighth Festival of Pacific Arts, New Caledonia — A175

Designs: 45c, Pot and broom.
No. 708: a, 75c, Turtle and shells. $1.05, Paintings. $1.20, Spear, mask. $2, Decorated gourds.

2000, June 19 *Die cut 9x9½*
Self-Adhesive
707 A175 45c multi .80 .80

Souvenir Sheet
Perf. 13¾
Water-Activated Gum

708 A175 Sheet of 4, #a-d 8.50 8.50

No. 708 contains four 30x38mm stamps.

Souvenir Sheet

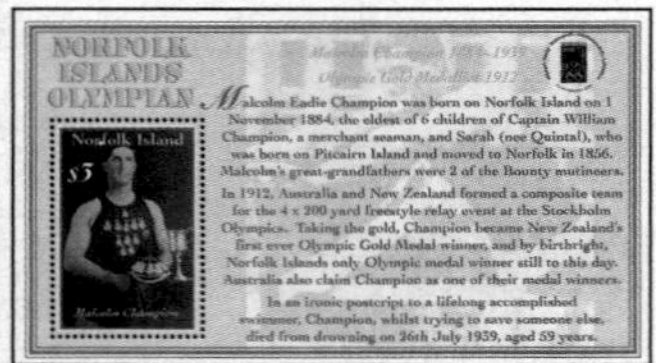

Malcolm Eadie Champion, 1912 Olympic Gold Medalist — A176

2000, Sept. 15 Litho. *Perf. 14x14¼*
709 A176 $3 multi 5.00 5.00

Olymphilex 2000 Stamp Exhibition, Sydney.

Providence Petrel Type of 1999
Souvenir Sheet

2000, Oct. 5 *Perf. 14½x14¾*
710 Sheet of 2 #710a 4.00 4.00
a. A165 $1.20 Like #681, 32x22mm, with white frame 2.00 2.00

Canpex 2000 Stamp Exhibition, Christchurch, New Zealand.

Christmas A177

Words from "Silent Night" and: 45c, Sun. 75c, Candle. $1.05, Moon. $1.20, Stars.

2000, Oct. 20 *Perf. 13¼x13*
711-714 A177 Set of 4 5.00 5.00

Millennium A178

Children's art by: No. 715, 45c, Jessica Wong and Mardi Pye. No. 716, 45c, Roxanne Spreag. No. 717, 75c, Tara Grube. No. 718, 75c, Tom Greenwood.

2000, Nov. 26 *Perf. 14¾x14½*
715-718 A178 Set of 4 3.50 3.50

Green Parrot — A179

Tarler Bird — A180

2001, Jan. 26 *Rouletted 5½*
Booklet Stamp
719 A179 5c green & red .20 .20
a. Booklet pane of 10 2.00
Booklet, 4 #719a 8.00

2001, Feb. 1 *Perf. 13¼*

Designs: $2.30, Norfolk island eel and tarler bird.

720 A180 45c multi 1.00 1.00

Imperf
Size: 110x70mm
721 A180 $2.30 multi 5.00 5.00

No. 720 issued in sheet of 5 + label. New Year 2001 (Year of the snake), Hong Kong 2001 Stamp Exhibition (#721).

Australian Federation, Cent. — A181

Pre-federation political cartoons from The Bulletin Magazine: No. 722, 45c, Promises, Promises! No. 723, 45c, The Gout of Federation. No. 724, 45c, The Political Garotters. No. 725, 45c, Tower of Babel. No. 726, 45c, Old Clothes. No. 727, 45c, The Federal Spirit. 75c, Australia Faces the Dawn. $1.05, The Federal Capital Question. $1.20, The Imperial Fowl Yard.

2001, Mar. 12 Litho. *Perf. 14x14¾*
722-730 A181 Set of 9 8.00 8.00

Souvenir Sheet

2001 A Stamp Odyssey Stamp Show, Invercargill, New Zealand — A182

Blue portion of background at: a, Right. b, Left. c, Top.

2001, Mar. 16 *Perf. 13*
731 A182 75c Sheet of 3, #a-c, + 3 labels 3.75 3.75

Bounty Day — A183

2001, June 8 *Rouletted 6*
732 A183 5c green & black .20 .20
a. Booklet pane of 10 1.00
Booklet, 4 #732a 4.00

Tourism A184

Perfume bottle and: 45c, Jasminium simplicifolium. 75c, Woman's face in perfume bottle. $1.05, Woman with roses. $1.20, Taylors Road. $1.50, Couple shopping for perfume. $3, Woman and Norfolk pine trees.

2001, June 9 *Perf. 13¼*
733 A184 45c multi .75 .75
734 A184 75c multi 1.75 1.75
a. Booklet pane, #733-734 2.50 —
735 A184 $1.05 multi 1.75 1.75
736 A184 $1.20 multi 2.00 2.00
a. Booklet pane, #735-736 3.75 —
737 A184 $1.50 multi 2.75 2.75
a. Booklet pane of 1 2.75 —

Souvenir Sheet
738 A184 $3 multi 5.00 5.00

Booklet Stamp
Size: 154x97mm
Microrouletted at Left
739 A184 $3 Like #738 5.00 5.00
a. Booklet pane of 1 5.00 —
Booklet, #734a, 736a, 737a, 739a 14.00

Nos. 733-739 are impregnated with jasmine perfume. No. 738 contains one 60x72mm stamp.

No. 739 has perfume bottle at LR, country name moved on one line at UL, and is impregnated with jasmine perfume. No. 739a has binding stub at left. Booklet sold for $10 and includes postal card.

Boats A185

Designs: 45c, Whaler, vert. No. 741, $1, Rowers in boat. No. 742, $1, Motorboat, vert. $1.50, Men in cutter.

Perf. 14½x14¼, 14¼x14½
2001, Aug. 1 Litho.
740-743 A185 Set of 4 6.00 6.00

Coil Stamp
Self-Adhesive
Die Cut Perf. 14¼x14¾
744 A185 45c multi .80 .80

Peace Keepers in Japan — A186

No. 745: a, Australian soldiers playing cards. b, Soldiers with birthday cake.

No. 746: a, Soldiers on Christmas float. b, Soldiers controlling traffic.

2001, Sept. 9 *Perf. 14½x14¾*
745 Pair with central label 2.75 2.75
a. A186 45c multi .85 .85
b. A186 $1 multi 1.90 1.90
746 Pair with central label 2.75 2.75
a. A186 45c multi .85 .85
b. A186 $1 multi 1.90 1.90

6th South Pacific Mini Games — A187

2001, Oct. 1 *Rouletted 6*
747 A187 10c green & brown .30 .30
a. Booklet pane of 10 3.00 —
Booklet, 2 #747a 6.00

Two souvenir sheets publicizing the 6th South Pacific Mini-Games, featuring four 45c and four $1 values, respectively, were scheduled for release but were withdrawn from sale upon arrival in Norfolk, when serious design errors were discovered. A small quantity had previously been sold by Crown Agents. Value for pair of sheets, $150.

Christmas A188

Christmas carols and flora: No. 748, 45c, Hark, the Herald Angels Sing, strawberry guava. No. 749, 45c, Deck the Halls, poinsettia. No., 750, $1, The First Noel, hibiscus. No. 751, $1, Joy to the World, Christmas croton. $1.50, We Wish You a Merry Christmas, Indian shot.

2001, Oct. 26 *Perf. 12½*
748-752 A188 Set of 5 6.50 6.50

Sacred Kingfisher — A189

2002, Jan. 15 Litho. *Rouletted 5¾*
Booklet Stamp
753 A189 10c aqua & dk bl .20 .20
a. Booklet pane of 10 1.75 —
Booklet, 2 #753a 3.50

Cliff Ecology A190

Designs: 45c, Red-tailed tropicbird. No. 755, $1, White oak tree. No. 756, $1, White oak flower. $1.50, Eagle ray.

2002, Jan. 21 Unwmk. *Perf. 13*
754-757 A190 Set of 4 6.00 6.00

Reign Of Queen Elizabeth II, 50th Anniv. Issue
Common Design Type

Designs: Nos. 758, 762a, 45c, Queen Mother with Princesses Elizabeth and Margaret, 1930. Nos. 759, 762b, 75c, Wearing scarf, 1977. Nos. 760, 762c, $1, Wearing crown, 1953. Nos. 761, 762d, $1.50, Wearing yellow hat, 2000. No. 762e, $3, 1955 portrait by Annigoni (38x50mm).

Perf. 14¼x14½, 13¾ (#762e)
2002, Feb. 6 Litho. Wmk. 373
With Gold Frames
758-761 CD360 Set of 4 6.00 6.00

Souvenir Sheet
Without Gold Frames
762 CD360 Sheet of 5, #a-e 10.00 10.00

The Age of Steam — A191

Perf. 14½x14¾
2002, Mar. 21 Litho. Unwmk.
763 A191 $4.50 multi 6.50 6.50

South Pacifc Mini Games — A192

Designs: 50c, Track and field. $1.50, Tennis.

2002, Mar. 21 *Perf. 13¾x14¼*
764-765 A192 Set of 2 3.00 3.00

2002 Bounty Bowls Tournament A193

2002, May 6 *Rouletted 6*
Booklet Stamp
766 A193 10c multi .20 .20
a. Booklet pane of 10 1.75 —
Booklet, 2 #766a 3.50

Phillip Island Flowers — A194

Designs: 10c, Streblorrhiza specioca. 20c, Plumbago zeylanica. 30c, Canavalia rosea. 40c, Ipomoea pes-caprae. 45c, Hibiscus insularis. 50c, Solanum laciniatum. 95c, Phormium tenax. $1, Lobelia anceps. $1.50, Carpobrotus glaucescens. $2, Abutilon julianae. $3, Wollastonia biflora. $5, Oxalis corniculata.

2002 ***Perf. 14½***

767 A194	10c multi	.25	.25
768 A194	20c multi	.35	.35
769 A194	30c multi	.50	.50
770 A194	40c multi	.65	.65
771 A194	45c multi	.70	.70
772 A194	50c multi	.80	.80
773 A194	95c multi	1.75	1.75
774 A194	$1 multi	2.00	2.00
775 A194	$1.50 multi	2.75	2.75
776 A194	$2 multi	3.75	3.75
777 A194	$3 multi	5.50	5.50
778 A194	$5 multi	9.00	9.00
	Nos. 767-778 (12)	28.00	28.00

Issued: 20c, 40c, 45c, 95c, $2, $5, 5/21; others 9/18.

2002 Commonwealth Games, Manchester, England — A195

Designs: 10c, Track and field, vert. 45c, Cycling. $1, Lawn bowling, vert. $1.50, Shooting.

2002, July 25

779-782 A195 Set of 4 5.00 5.00

Operation Cetacean A196

No. 783: a, Sperm whale and calf. b, Sperm whale and squid.

2002, Sept. 18 ***Perf. 14***

783 Horiz. pair with central label 5.00 5.00
a.-b. A196 $1 Either single 2.25 2.25

See New Caledonia No. 906.

Christmas A197

White tern: No. 784, 45c, Hatchling. No. 785, 45c, Bird on egg in nest. $1, Pair in flight. $1.50, One in flight.

2002, Nov. 12 Litho. ***Perf. 14***

784-787 A197 Set of 4 6.00 6.00

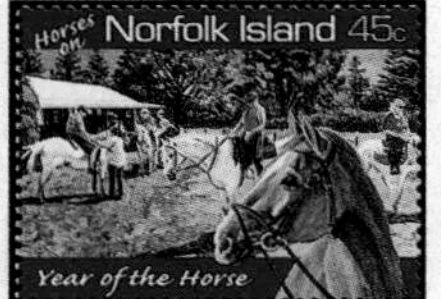

Horses on Norfolk Island A198

No. 788: a, Horses with riders near stable. b, Horses grazing. c, Show jumping. d, Horse racing. e, Horses pulling carriage.

2003, Jan. 14

788 Horiz. strip of 5 5.00 5.00
a.-c. A198 45c Any single 1.00 1.00
d.-e. A198 75c Either single 2.00 2.00

Year of the horse (in 2002).

Island Scenes — A199

Photographs by Mary Butterfield: 50c, Buildings. 95c, Boat on beach. $1.10 Cattle grazing. $1.65 Tree near water.

2003, Mar. 18 ***Perf. 14x14¼***

789-792 A199 Set of 4 6.75 6.75

Day Lilies — A200

No. 793: a, Southern Prize. b, Becky Stone. c, Cameroons. d, Chinese Autumn. e, Scarlet Orbit. f, Ocean Rain. g, Gingerbread man. h, Pink Corduroy. i, Elizabeth Hinrichsen. j, Simply Pretty.

2003, June 10 Litho. ***Perf. 14¼***

793 Block of 10 7.50 7.50
a.-j. A200 50c Any single .75 .75
Complete booklet, #793 7.50

Island Views — A201

No. 794: a, Large trees at left, ocean. b, Beach. c, Rocks at shoreline. d, Cattle grazing.

2003, July 21 ***Perf. 14***

794 Horiz. strip of 4 + 4 labels 3.00 3.00
a.-d. A201 50c Any single + label .75 .75

No. 794 was issued in sheets of five strips that had labels that could be personalized for an additional fee.

First Norfolk Island Writer's Festival — A202

No. 795: a, Maeve and Gil Hitch. b, Alice Buffett. c, Nan Smith. d, Archie Bigg. e, Colleen McCullough. f, Peter Clarke. g, Bob Tofts. h, Merval Hoare.

2003, July 21 ***Perf. 14½***

795 Block of 8 + 2 labels 3.25 3.25
a.-d. A202 10c Any single .20 .20
e.-h. A202 50c Any single .65 .65

Souvenir Sheet

Coronation of Queen Elizabeth II, 50th Anniv. — A203

No. 796: a, 10c, Queen wearing crown. b, $3, Queen wearing hat.

2003, July 29 ***Perf. 14½***

796 A203 Sheet of 2, #a-b 4.50 4.50

Christmas — A204

Designs: No. 797, 50c, Dove, rainbow, "Joy to the World." No. 798, 50c, Earth, "Peace on Earth." $1.10, Heart, "Give the gift of Love." $1.65, Candle, "Trust in Faith."

2003, Oct. 21 ***Perf. 14¼x14***

797-800 A204 Set of 4 6.00 6.00

Powered Flight, Cent. A205

Designs: 50c, Seaplane. $1.10, QANTAS airliner in flight. No. 803, $1.65, QANTAS airliner on ground.
No. 804, $1.65, Wright Flyer.

2003, Dec. 2 ***Perf. 14x14¼***

801-803 A205 Set of 3 5.00 5.00

Souvenir Sheet

Perf. 14½x14

804 A205 $1.65 multi 2.75 2.75

No. 804 contains one 48x30mm stamp.
Limited quantities of No. 804 exist with an 85c surcharge and a 2004 Hong Kong Stamp Expo emblem in the margin. These were sold only at the exhibition. Value, mint never hinged or cto, $60.

Island Scenes Type of 2003

Designs: 50c, Houses, boat prow with foliage, vert. 95c, Waterfall, vert. $1.10, Cattle, vert. $1.65, Sea shore, vert.

2004, Feb. 10 Litho. ***Perf. 14¼x14***

805-808 A199 Set of 4 7.00 7.00

Sharks — A206

Designs: 10c, Whale shark. 50c, Hammerhead shark. $1.10, Tiger shark. $1.65, Bronze whaler shark.

2004, Apr. 6 ***Perf. 14¾***

809-812 A206 Set of 4 7.25 7.25

Spiders A207

Designs: No. 813, 50c, Golden orb spider. No. 814, 50c, Community spider. $1, St. Andrew's cross spider. $1.65, Red-horned spider.
$1.50, Red-horned spider, diff.

2004, June 1 ***Perf. 14½***

813-816 A207 Set of 4 5.75 5.75

Souvenir Sheet

Perf. 14½x14

817 A207 $1.50 multi 2.50 2.50

No. 817 contains one 47x40mm stamp.

Unloading of Ship Cargo — A208

Designs: 50c, Men climbing on cargo nets. $1.10, Small boat with men and cargo. No. 820, $1.65, Two small boats.
No. 821, $1.65, Two small boats at dock.

2004, July 13 Litho. ***Perf. 14¾***

818-820 A208 Set of 3 4.75 4.75

Souvenir Sheet

821 A208 $1.65 multi 2.75 2.75

Souvenir Sheet

Quota International, 25th Anniv. on Norfolk Island — A209

No. 822: a, 50c, Three children. b, $1.10, "We Care" on feet. c, $1.65, Child drawing "Quota" in sand.

2004, Aug. 16 ***Perf. 14¼***

822 A209 Sheet of 3, #a-c 5.50 5.50

Day Lilies A210

No. 823 — Hippeastrum varieties: a, Apple Blossom. b, Carnival. c, Cherry Blossom. d, Lilac Wonder. e, Millenium Star. f, Cocktail. g, Milady. h, Pacific Sunset. i, Geisha Girl. j, Lady Jane.

2004, Aug. 16 ***Perf. 14½***

823 Block of 10 8.00 8.00
a.-j. A210 50c Any single .80 .80
Complete booklet, #823 8.00

No. 824 Overprinted in Silver

Souvenir Sheet

2004, Aug. Litho. ***Perf. 13¼***

824 A184 $3 multi 5.00 5.00

No. 824 is impregnated with jasmine perfume.

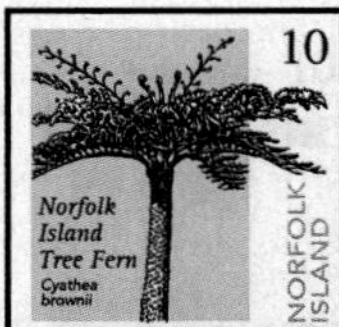

Flora — A211

Designs: No. 825, Norfolk Island tree fern. No. 826, Norfolk Island palm.

2004, Sept. 28 ***Rouletted 6***

Booklet Stamps

825 A211 10c bl grn & blk .20 .20
a. Booklet pane of 10 1.75 —
826 A211 10c yel & blk .20 .20
a. Booklet pane of 10 1.75 —
Complete booklet, #825a, 826a 3.50

Christmas — A212

Norfolk pine and words from: No. 827, 50c, Silent Night. No. 828, 50c, 'Twas the Night Before Christmas. $1.10, On the First Day of Christmas. $1.65, Oh, Holy Night.

2004, Oct. 26 ***Perf. 14¼***
827-830 A212 Set of 4 5.75 5.75

Legislative Assembly, 25th Anniv. — A213

2004, Dec. 14 ***Perf. 14***
831 A213 $5 multi 8.00 8.00

Worldwide Fund for Nature (WWF) — A214

Sacred kingfisher: No. 832, 50c, Two birds on tree branch. No. 833, 50c, Bird in flight with insect in beak. $1, Bird on branch. $2, Bird on branch, diff.

2004, Dec. 14
832-835 A214 Set of 4 8.00 8.00
835a Miniature sheet, 2 each #832-835 15.00 15.00

Rotary International, Cent. A215

Emblem and: No. 836, 50c, Beach Carnival. No. 837, 50c, Tree planting, vert. $1.20, Paul Harris. $1.80, Rotary Youth Leadership Awards, vert.
$2, District 9910 ceremony.

2005, Feb. 23 **Litho.** ***Perf. 14½***
836-839 A215 Set of 4 6.50 6.50

Souvenir Sheet

840 A215 $2 multi 3.25 3.25

No. 840 contains one 40x30mm stamp.

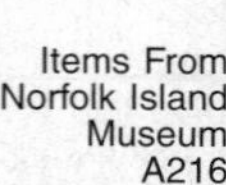

Items From Norfolk Island Museum A216

Designs: No. 841, 50c, Teacup, 1856. No. 842, 50c, Salt cellar from HMAV Bounty, 1856. $1.10, Medicine cups, 1825-55. $1.65, Stoneware jar, 1825-55.

2005, Apr. 5
841-844 A216 Set of 4 6.00 6.00

Pacific Explorers A217

Designs: 50c, Polynesian explorer, boat and fish. $1.20, Magellan's ship and bird. $1.80, Captain James Cook, ship and flower.
$2, Old map of world, horiz.

2005, Apr. 21 ***Perf. 14***
845-847 A217 Set of 3 5.50 5.50

Souvenir Sheet

Perf. 14¾

848 A217 $2 multi 3.25 3.25

Pacific Explorer 2005 World Stamp Expo, Sydney. No. 848 contains one 46x32mm stamp.

Old Houses A218

Designs: No. 849, 50c, Greenacres. No. 850, 50c, Branka House. $1.20, Ma Annas. $1.80, Naumai.

2005, June 16 **Litho.** ***Perf. 14½***
849-852 A218 Set of 4 6.00 6.00

Sea Birds — A219

Designs: 10c, Red-tailed tropicbird. 50c, Australasian gannet. $1.50 Gray ternlet. $2, Masked booby. $5, White-necked petrel.
$4, Red-tailed tropicbird, horiz.

2005, Aug. 9
853-857 A219 Set of 5 20.00 20.00

Souvenir Sheet

858 A219 $4 multi 8.00 8.00

Hibiscus Varieties A220

No. 859: a, Marjory Brown. b, Aloha. c, Pulau Tree. d, Ann Miller. e, Surfrider. f, Philip Island. g, Rose of Sharon. h, D. J. O'Brien. i, Elaine's Pride. j, Castle White. k, Skeleton Hibiscus. l, Pink Sunset.

2005, Aug. 30 ***Perf. 14¼x14***
859 Block of 12 9.25 9.25
a.-l. A220 50c Any single .90 .90
Complete booklet, #859 9.25

Christmas — A221

Designs: 50c, Anson Bay. $1.20, Cascade Bay. $1.80, Ball Bay.

2005, Oct. 25 **Litho.** ***Perf. 14¼x14***
860-862 A221 Set of 3 5.25 5.25

Jazz Festival — A222

Designs: 50c, Drummer. $1.20, Saxophonist. $1.80, Guitarist.

2005, Dec. 6 ***Perf. 14x14¼***
863-865 A222 Set of 3 5.25 5.25

Queen's Baton Relay for 2006 Commonwealth Games — A223

No. 866: a, 50c, Baton relay runner, boat's prow. b, $1.50, Baton.
Illustration reduced.

2006, Jan. 16 **Litho.** ***Perf. 14½x14¾***
866 A223 Horiz. pair, #a-b 3.00 3.00

2006 Commonwealth Games, Melbourne — A224

Norfolk Island flag and: 50c, Shooting. $1.50, Lawn bowling. $2, Squash.

2006, Mar. 14 **Litho.** ***Perf. 14½***
867-869 A224 Set of 3 5.75 5.75

Pitcairn Migration, 150th Anniv. — A225

Pitcairn Island history: No. 870, 50c, The Bounty at Portsmouth. No. 871, 50c, Collecting breadfruit at Tahiti. $1.20, The mutiny. $1.50, Burning of the Bounty at Pitcairn Island. $1.80, Pitcairners arrive at Norfolk Island, 1856.

2006, May 4 ***Perf. 14x14½***
870-874 A225 Set of 5 7.25 7.25

Bounty Anniversary Day — A226

Designs: 10c, Re-enactment procession. 30c, Remembering old soldiers. No. 877, 50c, Honoring ancestors. No. 878, 50c, Community picnic. $4, Bounty Ball.

2006, June 7
875-879 A226 Set of 5 8.25 8.25

See Pitcairn Islands No. 643.

Traditional Hat Making — A227

No. 880, 50c — Purple panel: a, Hat with flowers on brim. b, Hat with no flowers.
No. 881, 50c — Blue green panel: a, Hat with flowers on brim. b, Hat with feather at right.
No. 882, 50c — Green panel: a, Hat with flowers on brim. b, Hat with no flowers.

2006, June 7 ***Perf. 15¼x14¾***

Horiz. Pairs, #a-b

880-882 A227 Set of 3 4.50 4.50

Sea Birds Type of 2005

Designs: 25c, White tern. 40c, Sooty tern. 70c, Black-winged petrel. $1, Black noddy. $3, Wedge-tailed shearwater.
$2.50, Sooty tern, diff.

2006, Aug. 9 ***Perf. 14½***
883-887 A219 Set of 5 8.25 8.25

Souvenir Sheet

888 A219 $2.50 multi 4.00 4.00

Dogs — A228

Dogs named: 10c, Wal. 50c, Axel. $1, Wag. $2.65, Gemma.

2006, Sept. 12 ***Perf. 14½***
889-892 A228 Set of 4 6.50 6.50

Norfolk Island Central School, Middlegate, Cent. — A229

Designs: No. 893, $2, Sepia-toned photograph. No. 894, $2, Color photograph.

2006, Oct. 3
893-894 A229 Set of 2 6.00 6.00

Christmas — A230

Ornaments showing: No. 895, 50c, Birds. No. 896, 50c, House. $1.20, Building. $1.80, Flower.

2006, Nov. 21 **Litho.**

Stamp + Label

895-898 A230 Set of 4 6.50 6.50

Weeds A231

Designs: No. 899, 50c, Ageratina riparia. No. 900, 50c, Lantana camara. $1.20, Ipomoea cairica. $1.80, Solanum mauritianum.

2007, Feb. 6 ***Perf. 14¼***
899-902 A231 Set of 4 6.25 6.25

Adventure Sports A232

Designs: No. 903, 50c, Wind surfing. No. 904, 50c, Sea kayaking. $1.20, Mountain biking. $1.80, Surfing.

2007, Apr. 3 **Litho.** ***Perf. 14½***
903-906 A232 Set of 4 6.50 6.50

Souvenir Sheet

Kentia Palm Seed Harvest — A233

No. 907: a, Ladder and trees, vert. b, Dog and buckets of seeds. c, Man pouring seeds into box. d, Seeds on tree, vert.

Perf. 14 (14½ on Short Side Not Adjacent to Another Stamp)

2007, May 29
907 A233 50c Sheet of 4, #a-d, + central label 3.50 3.50

Ghosts A234

Queen Victoria A235

Designs: 10c, Violinist, musical notes, building. 50c, Graveyard. $1, Female ghost on dock steps. $1.80, Ghosts on building steps.

2007, June 26 ***Perf. 14½***
908-911 A234 Set of 4 5.75 5.75

2007, July 31 ***Die Cut***

Self-Adhesive

Booklet Stamp (10c)

912 A235 10c multi .20 .20
a. Booklet pane of 10 2.00

Size: 21x28mm

913 A235 $5 multi 8.50 8.50

Queen Victoria Scholarship, 120th anniv.

13th South Pacific Games, Samoa — A236

Designs: 50c, Squash. $1, Golf. $1.20, Netball. $1.80, Running.

$2, Games emblem.

2007, Aug. 28 ***Perf. 14¼***
914-917 A236 Set of 4 7.50 7.50

Souvenir Sheet

918 A236 $2 multi 3.25 3.25

Closure of First Convict Settlement, Bicent. A237

Designs: 10c, HMS Sirius and Supply off Kingston. 50c, Shipping signal, Kingston. $1.20, First settlement, Kingston. $1.80, Ship Lady Nelson leaving for Tasmania.

2007, Nov. 13
919-922 A237 Set of 4 6.75 6.75

Banyan Park Play Center A238

Children and slogans: 50c, "Friendship." $1, "Community." $1.20, "Play, learn, grow together." $1.80, "Read books."

2007, Nov. 27 **Litho.** ***Perf. 14x14¼***
923-926 A238 Set of 4 8.00 8.00

Christmas A239

Items with Christmas lights: 50c, Christmas tree. $1.20, Building. $1.80, Rowboat.

2007, Nov. 27
927-929 A239 Set of 3 6.25 6.25

Automobiles A240

Designs: 50c, 1965 Ford Falcon XP. $1, 1952 Chevrolet Styleline. $1.20, 1953 Pontiac Silver Arrow. $1.80, 1971 Rolls Royce Silver Shadow.

2008, Feb. 5
930-933 A240 Set of 4 8.25 8.25

Norfolk Islanders With Pitcairn Islands Heritage — A241

Designs: 50c, Andre Nobbs. $1, Darlene Buffett. $1.20, Colin "Boonie" Lindsay Buffett. $1.80, Tania Grube.

2008, Apr. 4 **Litho.** ***Perf. 14½***
934-937 A241 Set of 4 8.50 8.50

Jewish Gravestones A242

Gravestone of: 50c, Carl Hans Nathan Strauss. $1.20, Meta Kienhuize. $1.80, Johan Jacobus Kienhuize.
$2, Sally Kadesh.

2008, May 14 ***Perf. 14½***
938-940 A242 Set of 3 6.75 6.75

Souvenir Sheet

Perf. 13½

941 A242 $2 multi 4.00 4.00

2008 World Stamp Championship, Israel (#941). No. 941 contains one 30x40mm stamp.

Calves A243

Designs: 50c, Limousin Cross. $1, Murray Grey. $1.20, Poll Hereford. $1.80, Brahman Cross.

2008, May 30 ***Perf. 14¼***
942-945 A243 Set of 4 8.75 8.75

St. John Ambulance, 25th Anniv. on Norfolk Island — A244

Designs: 30c, Past and present members. 40c, Re-enactment of treatment of accident victim at scene. 95c, Accident victim being placed in ambulance. $4, Accident victim entering hospital.

2008, June 27 ***Perf. 14½***
946-949 A244 Set of 4 11.00 11.00

Ferns — A245

No. 950, 20c: a, Netted brakefern. b, Pteris zahlbruckneriana.
No. 951, 50c: a, Robinsonia. b, Asplenium australasicum.
No. 952, 80c: a, Hanging fork fern. b, Tmesipteris norfolkensis.
No. 953, $2: a, King fern. b, Marattia salicina.
Illustration reduced.

2008, Aug. 1 **Litho.** ***Perf. 14¼***

Horiz. Pairs, #a-b

950-953 A245 Set of 4 13.00 13.00

Ships Built On Norfolk Island — A246

Designs: 50c, Sloop Norfolk, 1798. $1.20, Schooner Resolution, 1925. $1.80, Schooner Endeavour, 1808.

2008, Sept. 2
954-956 A246 Set of 3 5.75 5.75

A247 A248

Designs: 25c, Prison buildings. 55c, Gate and prison buildings. $1.75, Graveyard. $2.50, Building and walls.

2008, Oct. 27 **Litho.** ***Perf. 14½***
957-960 A247 Set of 4 6.75 6.75

Isles of Exile Conference, Norfolk Island.

2008, Nov. 7 ***Perf. 14¼***

Christmas: 55c, Adoration of the Shepherds. $1.40, Madonna and Child. $2.05, Adoration of the Magi.

961-963 A248 Set of 3 5.50 5.50

Mosaics A249

Designs: 5c, Fish. No. 965, 15c, Flower. 55c, Bird. $1.40, Tree.
No. 968, 15c, Turtle. No. 969, 15c, Starfish.

2009, Feb. 16 ***Perf. 14x14¼***
964-967 A249 Set of 4 2.75 2.75

Booklet Stamps

Self-Adhesive

Serpentine Die Cut 9½x10

968-969 A249 Set of 2 .40 .40
969a Booklet pane of 12, 6 each #968-969 2.40

NORTH BORNEO

'north 'bor-nē-ˌō

LOCATION — Northeast part of island of Borneo, Malay archipelago
GOVT. — British colony
AREA — 29,388 sq. mi.
POP. — 470,000 (est. 1962)
CAPITAL — Jesselton

The British North Borneo Company administered North Borneo, under a royal charter granted in 1881, until 1946 when it became a British colony. Labuan (q.v.) became part of the new colony. As "Sabah," North Borneo joined with Singapore, Sarawak and Malaya to form the Federation of Malaysia on Sept. 16, 1963.

100 Cents = 1 Dollar

Quantities of most North Borneo stamps through 1912 have been canceled to order with an oval of bars. Values given for used stamps beginning with No. 6 are for those with this form of cancellation. Stamps from No. 6 through Nos. 159 and J31 that do not exist CTO have used values in italics. Stamps with dated town cancellations sell for much higher prices.

Catalogue values for unused stamps in this country are for Never Hinged items, beginning with Scott 238.

North Borneo

Coat of Arms — A1

1883-84 Unwmk. Litho. *Perf. 12*

1 A1 2c brown 30.00 *60.00*
  a. Horiz. pair, imperf. btwn.
2 A1 4c rose ('84) 52.50 *60.00*
3 A1 8c green ('84) 90.00 *60.00*
  Nos. 1-3 (3) 172.50 *180.00*

For surcharges see Nos. 4, 19-21.

No. 1 Surcharged in Black

4 A1 8c on 2c brown 500.00 *210.00*
  a. Double surcharge *4,500.*

Coat of Arms with Supporters
A4 A5

Perf. 14

6 A4 50c violet 160.00 27.50
7 A5 $1 red 140.00 15.00

1886 *Perf. 14*

8 A1 ½c magenta 110.00 *200.00*
9 A1 1c orange *210.00* *350.00*
  a. Imperf., pair 300.00
  b. Vert. pair, imperf horiz. 1,100.
10 A1 2c brown 27.50 25.00
  a. Horiz. pair, imperf. between 675.00
11 A1 4c rose 20.00 *50.00*
12 A1 8c green 21.00 *50.00*
  a. Horiz. pair, imperf. between 900.00
13 A1 10c blue 32.50 *50.00*
  a. Imperf., pair 375.00
  Nos. 8-13 (6) 421.00 *725.00*

Nos. 8, 11, 12 and 13 Surcharged or Overprinted in Black:

b

c

d

1886

14 A1 (b) ½c magenta 150.00 *250.00*
15 A1 (c) 3c on 4c rose 120.00 *130.00*
16 A1 (d) 3c on 4c rose 1,800.
17 A1 (c) 5c on 8c green 120.00 *130.00*
  a. Inverted surcharge 2,500.
18 A1 (b) 10c blue 200.00 *250.00*

On Nos. 2 and 3

Perf. 12

19 A1 (c) 3c on 4c rose 225.00 *300.00*
20 A1 (d) 3c on 4c rose *7,000.*
  a. Double surcharge, both types of "3"
21 A1 (c) 5c on 8c green 250.00 *300.00*

British North Borneo

A9

1886 Unwmk. Litho. *Perf. 12*

22 A9 ½c lilac rose 225.00 *400.00*
23 A9 1c orange 175.00 *250.00*

Perf. 14

25 A9 ½c lilac rose 3.50 *14.00*
  a. ½c lilac rose *16.00* 50.00
  b. Imperf., pair 45.00
26 A9 1c orange 2.25 *10.00*
  a. Imperf., pair 42.50
27 A9 2c brown 2.25 *9.50*
  a. Imperf., pair 42.50
  b. Horiz. pair, imperf. between *57.50*
28 A9 4c rose 3.50 *14.00*
  a. Cliché of 1c in plate of 4c 300.00 *800.00*
  b. Imperf., pair 45.00
  c. As "a," imperf. in pair with #28 4,750.
  d. Horiz. pair, imperf vert. 325.00
29 A9 8c green 17.50 *22.50*
  a. Imperf., pair 45.00
30 A9 10c blue 8.00 *30.00*
  a. Imperf., pair 45.00
  b. Vert. pair, imperf btwn. 425.00
  Nos. 25-30 (6) 37.00 *100.00*

For surcharges see Nos. 54-55.

A10 A11

A12 A13

31 A10 25c slate blue 210.00 14.00
  a. Imperf., pair 325.00 30.00
32 A11 50c violet 375.00 20.00
  a. Imperf., pair 425.00 40.00
33 A12 $1 red 350.00 18.50
  a. Imperf., pair 475.00 40.00
34 A13 $2 sage green 450.00 25.00
  a. Imperf., pair 400.00 42.50
  Nos. 31-34 (4) 1,385. 77.50
  Nos. 22-34 (12) 1,822. *827.50*

See Nos. 44-47.

A14

1887-92 *Perf. 14*

35 A14 ½c rose 1.25 .50
  a. ½c magenta 4.00 *3.00*
36 A14 1c orange 2.25 .50
37 A14 2c red brown 9.50 1.00
  a. Horiz. pair imperf. between *425.00*
38 A14 3c violet 2.75 .40
39 A14 4c rose 6.75 .40
  a. Horiz. pair, imperf. vert.
40 A14 5c slate 3.00 .40
41 A14 6c lake ('92) 9.00 .40
42 A14 8c green 21.00 .90
  a. Horiz. pair, imperf. between
43 A14 10c blue 7.25 .40
  Nos. 35-43 (9) 62.75 4.90

Exist imperf. Value $8 each, unused, $4.50 used. Forgeries exist, perf. 11½.

For surcharges see Nos. 52-53, 56-57.

Redrawn

25c. The letters of "BRITISH NORTH BORNEO" are 2mm high instead of 1½mm.

50c. The club of the native at left does not touch the frame. The 0's of "50" are flat at top and bottom instead of being oval.

$1.00. The spear of the native at right does not touch the frame. There are 14 pearls at each side of the frame instead of 13.

$2.00. "BRITISH" is 11mm long instead of 12mm. There are only six oars at the side of the dhow.

1888

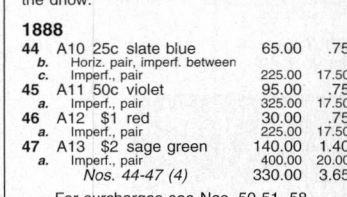

44 A10 25c slate blue 65.00 .75
  b. Horiz. pair, imperf. between
  c. Imperf., pair 225.00 17.50
45 A11 50c violet 95.00 .75
  a. Imperf., pair 325.00 17.50
46 A12 $1 red 30.00 .75
  a. Imperf., pair 225.00 17.50
47 A13 $2 sage green 140.00 1.40
  a. Imperf., pair 400.00 20.00
  Nos. 44-47 (4) 330.00 3.65

For surcharges see Nos. 50-51, 58.

A15

A16

1889

48 A15 $5 red violet 250.00 9.00
  a. Imperf., pair 650.00 45.00
49 A16 $10 brown 300.00 12.50
  b. Imperf., pair 800.00 55.00

e f

No. 44 Surcharged Type "e" in Red

1890

50 A10 2c on 25c slate blue 75.00 *100.00*
  a. Inverted surcharge 450.00 *450.00*
  b. With additional surcharge "2 cents" in black
51 A10 8c on 25c slate blue 105.00 *125.00*

Surcharged Type "f" in Black On #42-43

1891-92

52 A14 6c on 8c green 25.00 *11.00*
  a. "c" of "cents" inverted 500.00 *550.00*
  b. "cetns" 500.00 *550.00*
  c. Inverted surcharge 450.00 *500.00*
53 A14 6c on 10c blue 160.00 *27.50*

On Nos. 29 and 30

54 A9 6c on 8c green 9,000. *4,750.*
55 A9 6c on 10c blue 67.50 *22.50*
  a. Inverted surcharge 275.00 *290.00*
  b. Double surcharge 1,000.
  c. Triple surcharge 500.00

Nos. 39, 40 and 44 Surcharged in Red:

8 Cents.

1892

56 A14 1c on 4c rose 25.00 15.00
a. Double surcharge 1,350.
b. Surcharged on face & back *675.00*
57 A14 1c on 5c slate 8.00 6.50
58 A10 8c on 25c blue 150.00 *175.00*
Nos. 56-58 (3) 183.00 *196.50*

North Borneo

Dyak Chief — A21

Malayan Sambar — A22

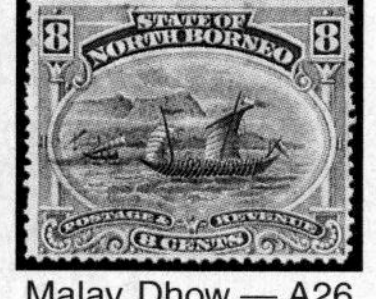

Malay Dhow — A26

Sago Palm — A23

Saltwater Crocodile — A27

Argus Pheasant A24

Mt. Kinabalu A28

Coat of Arms — A25

Coat of Arms with Supporters — A29

A30 A31

A32 A33

A34

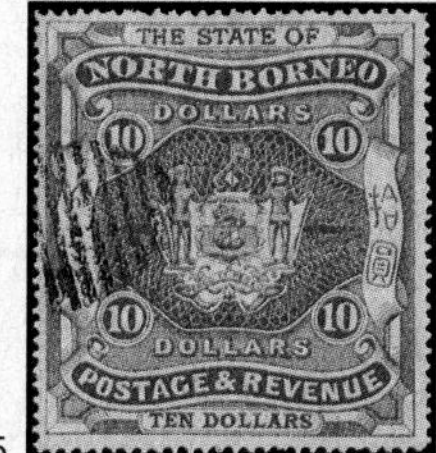

A35

Perf. 12 to 15 and Compound

1894 **Engr.** **Unwmk.**

59 A21 1c bis brn & blk 1.40 .40
a. Vert. pair, imperf. btwn.
60 A22 2c rose & black 4.00 .75
61 A23 3c vio & ol green 4.00 .55
a. Horiz. pair, imperf. btwn. — *725.00*
62 A24 5c org red & blk 3.25 .75
a. Horiz. pair, imperf. btwn. 625.00
63 A25 6c brn ol & blk 3.00 .55
64 A26 8c lilac & black 2.50 .75
a. Vert. pair, imperf. btwn. 475.00 *350.00*
b. Horiz. pair, imperf. btwn. *475.00*
65 A27 12c ultra & black 45.00 3.00
a. 12c blue & black 30.00 2.75
66 A28 18c green & black 30.00 2.00
67 A29 24c claret & blue 25.00 2.00

Litho. ***Perf. 14***

68 A30 25c slate blue 10.00 .80
a. Imperf., pair 40.00 9.00
69 A31 50c violet 25.00 2.00
a. Imperf., pair 9.00
70 A32 $1 red 12.50 1.25
a. Perf. 14x11 275.00
b. Imperf., pair 37.50 9.50
71 A33 $2 gray green 22.50 2.75
a. Imperf., pair 14.00
72 A34 $5 red violet 225.00 9.00
a. Imperf., pair 425.00 45.00
73 A35 $10 brown 250.00 16.00
a. Imperf., pair 425.00 45.00
Nos. 59-73 (15) 663.15 42.55

For #68-70 in other colors see Labuan #63a-65a.

For surcharges & overprints see #74-78, 91-94, 97-102, 115-119, 130-135, 115-119, 150-151, 158-159, J1-J8.

No. 70 Surcharged in Black

1895, June

74 A32 4c on $1 red 7.00 1.25
a. Double surcharge 1,000.
75 A32 10c on $1 red 21.00 .60
76 A32 20c on $1 red 45.00 .60
77 A32 30c on $1 red 32.50 .75
78 A32 40c on $1 red 32.50 .80
Nos. 74-78 (5) 138.00 4.00

See No. 99.

A37

A38

A39

A40

A41

A42

A43

"Postal Revenue" — A44

No "Postal Revenue" — A45

Perf. 13 to 16 and Compound

1897-1900 **Engr.**

79 A37 1c bis brn & blk 12.00 .55
a. Horiz. pair, imperf. btwn. 525.00
80 A38 2c dp rose & blk 25.00 .55
81 A38 2c grn & blk ('00) 50.00 .55
82 A39 3c lilac & ol green 20.00 .55
83 A40 5c orange & black 100.00 .50
84 A41 6c ol brown & blk 30.00 .45
85 A42 8c brn lilac & blk 12.50 .50
86 A43 12c blue & black 100.00 1.50
87 A44 18c green & black 25.00 1.50
a. Vert. pair, imperf. btwn. *350.00*
b. Horiz. pair, imperf. vert. *95.00*
c. Imperf, pair *200.00*
88 A45 24c claret & blue 11.00 .85
Nos. 79-88 (10) 385.50 7.50

For overprints and surcharges see Nos. 105-107, 109-112, 124-127, J9-J17, J20-J22, J24-J26, J28.

A46

"Postage & Revenue" — A47

1897

89 A46 18c green & black 100.00 1.75
90 A47 24c claret & blue 80.00 2.10

For surcharges & overprints see #95-96, 128-129, 113-114, J18-J19, J30-J31.

Stamps of 1894-97 Surcharged in Black

1899

91 A40 4c on 5c org & blk 27.50 *12.50*
92 A41 4c on 6c ol brn & blk 20.00 *25.00*
93 A42 4c on 8c brn lil & blk 16.00 *13.00*
94 A43 4c on 12c bl & blk 25.00 *15.00*
a. Horiz. pair, imperf. btwn. 675.00
b. Vert. pair, imperf. btwn. 725.00
95 A46 4c on 18c grn & blk 11.00 *18.00*
96 A47 4c on 24c cl & blue 20.00 *20.00*
a. Perf. 16 55.00 *55.00*
97 A30 4c on 25c sl blue 6.00 *10.00*
98 A31 4c on 50c violet 10.00 *18.00*
99 A32 4c on $1 red 6.25 *14.00*
100 A33 4c on $2 gray grn 6.25 *19.00*

"CENTS" 8½mm below "4"

101 A34 4c on $5 red vio 7.25 *18.00*
a. Normal spacing 160.00 *250.00*
102 A35 4c on $10 brown 7.25 *18.00*
a. Normal spacing 125.00 *250.00*
Nos. 91-102 (12) 162.50 *200.50*

No. 99 differs from No. 74 in the distance between "4" and "cents" which is 4¾mm on No. 99 and 3¾mm on No. 74.

Orangutan — A48

1899-1900 **Engr.**

103 A48 4c green & black 10.00 1.75
104 A48 4c dp rose & blk ('00) 40.00 .75

For overprints see Nos. 108, J23.

Stamps of 1894-1900 Overprinted in Red, Black, Green or Blue

m

1901-05

105 A37 1c bis brn & blk (R) 4.00 .35
106 A38 2c grn & blk (R) 2.75 .35
107 A39 3c lil & ol grn (Bk) 2.00 .35
108 A48 4c dp rose & blk (G) 10.00 .35
109 A40 5c org & blk (G) 16.00 .35
110 A41 6c ol brn & blk (R) 4.50 .75
111 A42 8c brn & blk (Bl) 4.25 .55
a. Vert. pair, imperf. btwn. 425.00
112 A43 12c blue & blk (R) 57.50 1.50
113 A46 18c grn & blk (R) 12.50 1.40
114 A47 24c red & blue (Bk) 18.00 1.75
115 A30 25c slate blue (R) 3.00 .60
a. Inverted overprint 550.00
116 A31 50c violet (R) 7.50 .70
117 A32 $1 red (R) 20.00 3.75
118 A32 $1 red (Bk) 10.00 2.75
a. Double overprint 425.00
119 A33 $2 gray green (R) 35.00 4.00
a. Double overprint 1,250.
Nos. 105-119 (15) 207.00 19.50

Nos. 110, 111 and 122 are known without period after "PROTECTORATE."

See Nos. 122-123, 150-151.

Bruang (Sun Bear) — A49

Railroad Train — A50

1902 **Engr.**

120 A49 10c slate & dk brn 110.00 3.25
a. Vertical pair, imperf. between 575.00
121 A50 16c yel brn & grn 150.00 3.75

Overprinted type "m" in Red or Black

No.	Type	Description	Unused	Used
122	A49	10c sl & dk brn (R)	62.50	1.10
a.		Double overprint	800.00	350.00
123	A50	16c yel brn & grn (Bk)	150.00	2.50
		Nos. 120-123 (4)	472.50	10.60

For overprints see Nos. J27, J29.

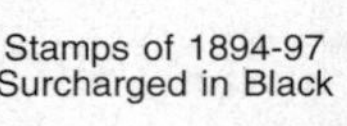
Stamps of 1894-97 Surcharged in Black

1904

No.	Type	Description	Unused	Used
124	A40	4c on 5c org & blk	40.00	14.00
125	A41	4c on 6c ol brn & blk	8.00	14.00
a.		Inverted surcharge	275.00	
126	A42	4c on 8c brn lil & blk	15.00	14.00
a.		Inverted surcharge	350.00	
127	A43	4c on 12c blue & blk	30.00	14.00
128	A46	4c on 18c grn & blk	16.00	14.00
129	A47	4c on 24c cl & bl	20.00	14.00
130	A30	4c on 25c sl blue	5.00	14.00
131	A31	4c on 50c violet	5.50	14.00
132	A32	4c on $1 red	7.00	14.00
133	A33	4c on $2 gray grn	10.50	14.00
134	A34	4c on $5 red vio	14.00	14.00
135	A35	4c on $10 brown	14.00	14.00
a.		Inverted surcharge	2,100.	
		Nos. 124-135 (12)	185.00	168.00

Malayan Tapir — A51

Traveler's Palm — A52

Railroad Station — A53

Meeting of the Assembly — A54

Elephant and Mahout A55

Sumatran Rhinoceros A56

Natives Plowing — A57

Wild Boar — A58

Palm Cockatoo A59

Rhinoceros Hornbill A60

Banteng (Wild Ox)
A61 A62

Cassowary A63

1909-22 Unwmk. Engr. *Perf. 14*
Center in Black

No.	Type	Description	Unused	Used
136	A51	1c chocolate	4.25	.20
b.		Perf. 13½		
c.		Perf. 15	17.00	.40
137	A52	2c green	.90	.20
b.		Perf. 15	1.90	.20
138	A53	3c deep rose	2.25	.30
b.		Perf. 15		.40
139	A53	3c green ('22)	6.50	*.40*
140	A54	4c dull red	1.75	.20
b.		Perf. 13½	*11.00*	*10.50*
c.		Perf. 15	7.75	.40
141	A55	5c yellow brn	7.25	.30
b.		Perf. 15		
142	A56	6c olive green	5.50	.30
b.		Perf. 15	42.50	1.00
143	A57	8c rose	2.25	.30
b.		Perf 15		—
144	A58	10c blue	14.00	.30
b.		Perf. 13½		*2.50*
c.		Perf. 15	32.50	*6.50*
145	A59	12c deep blue	20.00	.60
c.		Perf. 15		—
146	A60	16c red brown	16.00	1.25
b.		Perf. 13½	20.00	6.50
147	A61	18c blue green	72.50	1.25
148	A62	20c on 18c bl grn (R)	5.50	.55
b.		Perf. 15	150.00	*75.00*
149	A63	24c violet	22.50	1.50
		Nos. 136-149 (14)	181.15	7.65

Issued: #139, 1922; others, July 1, 1909.
See #167-178. #136a-149a follow #162.
For surcharges and overprints see #160-162, 166, B1-B12, B14-B24, B31-B41, J32-J49.

Nos. 72-73 Overprinted type "m" in Red

1910

No.	Type	Description	Unused	Used
150	A34	$5 red violet	100.00	4.50
151	A35	$10 brown	92.50	6.75
a.		Double overprint		
b.		Inverted overprint		

A64 A65

1911 Engr. *Perf. 14*
Center in Black

No.	Type	Description	Unused	Used
152	A64	25c yellow green	4.00	1.00
a.		Perf. 15	10.00	
b.		Imperf., pair	50.00	
153	A64	50c slate blue	7.00	1.25
a.		Perf. 15	24.00	*8.50*
b.		Imperf., pair	67.50	
154	A64	$1 brown	14.00	1.50
a.		Perf. 15	32.50	*6.75*
c.		Imperf., pair	67.50	
155	A64	$2 dk violet	32.50	3.25
156	A65	$5 claret	57.50	20.00
a.		Perf. 13½	*82.50*	
b.		Imperf., pair	100.00	
157	A65	$10 vermilion	140.00	40.00
a.		Imperf., pair	100.00	
		Nos. 152-157 (6)	255.00	*67.00*

See #179-184. #152c-153c follow #162.
For overprint and surcharges see Nos. B13, B25-B30, B42-B47.

Nos. 72-73 Overprinted in Red

1912

No.	Type	Description	Unused	Used
158	A34	$5 red violet	900.00	9.25
159	A35	$10 brown	1,400.	9.25

Nos. 158 and 159 were prepared for use but not regularly issued.

Nos. 138, 142 and 145 Surcharged in Black or Red

1916 Center in Black *Perf. 14*

No.	Type	Description	Unused	Used
160	A53	2c on 3c dp rose	15.00	6.50
a.		Inverted "S"	87.50	87.50
161	A56	4c on 6c ol grn (R)	13.00	6.50
a.		Inverted "S"	100.00	100.00
162	A59	10c on 12c bl (R)	35.00	37.50
a.		Inverted "S"	110.00	110.00
		Nos. 160-162 (3)	63.00	50.50

Stamps and Types of 1909-11 Overprinted in Red or Blue in Three Lines: "MALAYA-BORNEO EXHIBITION 1922."

1922

Center in Black

No.	Type	Description	Unused	Used
136a	A51	1c brown	5.50	*22.50*
137a	A52	2c green	1.90	*13.00*
138a	A53	3c deep rose (B)	4.75	*18.00*
140a	A54	4c dull red (B)	2.50	*13.00*
141a	A55	5c yel brown (B)	5.50	*22.50*
142a	A56	6c olive green	4.75	*27.50*
143a	A57	8c rose (B)	4.75	*27.50*
144a	A58	10c gray blue	5.25	*35.00*
145a	A59	12c deep blue	7.50	*45.00*
146a	A60	16c red brown (B)	7.50	*50.00*
148a	A62	20c on 18c bl grn	13.00	*57.50*
149a	A63	24c violet	11.00	*55.00*
152c	A64	25c yel green	11.00	*40.00*
153c	A64	50c slate blue	9.50	*45.00*
		Nos. 136a-153c (14)	94.40	*471.50*

Industrial fair, Singapore, 3/31-4/15/22.

No. 140 Surcharged in Black

1923

No.	Type	Description	Unused	Used
166	A54	3c on 4c dull red & blk	1.50	1.60
a.		Double surcharge		

Types of 1909-22 Issues

1926-28 Engr. *Perf. 12½*
Center in Black

No.	Type	Description	Unused	Used
167	A51	1c chocolate	.55	.50
168	A52	2c lake	.40	.40
169	A53	3c green	1.25	.75
170	A54	4c dull red	.40	.25
171	A55	5c yellow brown	3.50	3.50
172	A56	6c yellow green	3.75	.45
173	A57	8c rose	2.25	.30
174	A58	10c bright blue	1.90	.65
175	A59	12c deep blue	5.00	.65
176	A60	16c orange brn	12.50	*22.50*
177	A62	20c on 18c bl grn (R)	3.50	4.00
178	A63	24c dull violet	35.00	*50.00*
179	A64	25c yellow grn	5.50	5.50
180	A64	50c slate blue	8.50	*12.50*
181	A64	$1 brown	30.00	*75.00*
182	A64	$2 dark violet	50.00	*125.00*
183	A65	$5 deep rose	85.00	250.00
184	A65	$10 dull vermilion	200.00	350.00
		Nos. 167-184 (18)	449.00	901.95

Murut — A66

Orangutan — A67

Dyak — A68

Mt. Kinabalu A69

Clouded Leopard A70

Arms with Supporters and Motto A72

Coat of Arms — A71

Arms with Supporters — A73

1931, Jan. 1 Engr. *Perf. 12½*
Center in Black

No.	Type	Description	Unused	Used
185	A66	3c blue green	.65	*1.50*
186	A67	6c orange red	13.00	4.75
187	A68	10c carmine	2.75	6.25
188	A69	12c ultra	3.25	4.00
189	A70	25c deep violet	30.00	22.50
190	A71	$1 yellow green	18.00	30.00
191	A72	$2 red brown	40.00	37.50
192	A73	$5 red violet	110.00	*225.00*
		Nos. 185-192 (8)	217.65	*331.50*

50th anniv. of the North Borneo Co.

Buffalo Transport A74

Palm Cockatoo — A75

Murut — A76

Proboscis Monkey — A77

Bajaus — A78

Map of North Borneo and Surrounding Lands — A79

Orangutan — A80

Murut with Blowgun — A81

Dyak — A82

River Scene — A83

Proa — A84

Mt. Kinabalu — A85

Coat of Arms — A86

Arms with Supporters A87

1939, Jan. 1 ***Perf. 12½***

No.	Type	Description	Unused	Used
193	A74	1c red brn & dk grn	1.90	1.50
194	A75	2c Prus bl & red vio	3.25	1.50
195	A76	3c dk grn & sl blue	2.25	2.00
196	A77	4c rose vio & ol grn	4.00	.50
197	A78	6c dp cl & dk blue	3.75	7.00
198	A79	8c red	6.00	1.50
199	A80	10c olive grn & vio	26.00	6.00
200	A81	12c ultra & grn	17.50	5.50
201	A82	15c bis brn & brt bl grn	15.00	7.50
202	A83	20c ind & rose vio	9.50	3.75
203	A84	25c dk brn & bl grn	12.00	10.00
204	A85	50c purple & brn	13.50	8.00
205	A86	$1 car & brown	50.00	20.00
206	A86	$2 ol grn & pur	75.00	95.00
207	A87	$5 blue & indigo	200.00	200.00
		Nos. 193-207 (15)	439.65	369.75
		Set, never hinged	700.00	

For overprints see #208-237, MR1-MR2, N1-N15, N16-N31.

Nos. 193 to 207 Overprinted in Black

1945, Dec. 17 **Unwmk.** ***Perf. 12½***

No.	Type	Description	Unused	Used
208	A74	1c red brn & dk grn	4.25	1.75
209	A75	2c Prus bl & red vio	10.00	1.75
210	A76	3c dk grn & sl bl	.90	1.10
211	A77	4c rose vio & ol grn	11.50	14.00
212	A78	6c dp cl & dk bl	.90	.90
213	A79	8c red	2.10	.65
214	A80	10c ol green & vio	2.10	.35
215	A81	12c ultra & green	4.25	2.50
216	A82	15c bis brn & brt bl grn	1.10	1.10
217	A83	20c ind & rose vio	3.00	.90
218	A84	25c dk brn & bl grn	4.75	1.10
219	A85	50c purple & brn	2.10	1.25
220	A86	$1 carmine & brn	35.00	32.50
221	A86	$2 ol green & pur	32.50	27.50
a.		Double overprint	3,600.	
222	A87	$5 blue & indigo	13.50	12.50
		Nos. 208-222 (15)	127.95	99.85
		Set, never hinged	210.00	

"BMA" stands for British Military Administration.

Nos. 193 to 207 Overprinted in Black or Carmine With Bars

1947

No.	Type	Description	Unused	Used
223	A74	1c red brn & dk grn	.20	.90
224	A75	2c Prus bl & red vio	1.25	.80
225	A76	3c dk grn & sl bl (C)	.20	.80
226	A77	4c rose vio & ol grn	.25	.80
227	A78	6c dp cl & dk bl (C)	.20	.20
228	A79	8c red	.25	.20
229	A80	10c olive grn & vio	1.10	.35
230	A81	12c ultra & grn	1.50	2.50
231	A82	15c bis brn & brt bl grn	1.75	.25
232	A83	20c ind & rose vio	1.75	.75
233	A84	25c dk brn & bl grn	1.90	.45
234	A85	50c purple & brn	1.75	.75
235	A86	$1 carmine & brn	3.50	1.50
236	A86	$2 ol green & pur	9.00	15.00
237	A87	$5 blue & ind (C)	16.00	15.00
		Nos. 223-237 (15)	40.60	40.25
		Set, never hinged	60.00	

The bars obliterate "The State of" and "British Protectorate."

Catalogue values for unused stamps in this section, from this point to the end of the section, are for Never Hinged items.

Silver Wedding Issue

Common Design Types

Perf. 14x14½

1948, Nov. 1 **Wmk. 4** **Photo.**

No.	Type	Description	Unused	Used
238	CD304	8c scarlet	.30	.50

Engraved; Name Typographed

Perf. 11½x11

No.	Type	Description	Unused	Used
239	CD305	$10 purple	20.00	*30.00*

Common Design Types pictured following the introduction.

UPU Issue

Common Design Types

Engr.; Name Typo. on 10c and 30c

1949, Oct. 10 ***Perf. 13½, 11x11½***

No.	Type	Description	Unused	Used
240	CD306	8c rose carmine	.25	.20
241	CD307	10c chocolate	.35	.30
242	CD308	30c deep orange	1.10	.85
243	CD309	55c blue	1.75	1.40
		Nos. 240-243 (4)	3.45	2.75

Mount Kinabalu — A88

Coconut Grove — A89

Designs: 2c, Musician. 4c, Hemp drying. 5c, Cattle at Kota Belud. 8c, Map. 10c, Logging. 15c, Proa at Sandakan. 20c, Bajau Chief. 30c, Suluk Craft. 50c, Clock tower. $1, Bajau horsemen. $2, Murut with blowgun. $5, Net fishing. $10, Arms.

Perf. 13½x14½, 14½x13½

1950, July 1 **Photo.**

No.	Type	Description	Unused	Used
244	A88	1c red brown	.20	.90
245	A88	2c blue	.20	.40
246	A89	3c green	.20	.20
247	A89	4c red violet	.20	.20
248	A89	5c purple	.20	.20
249	A88	8c red	.75	.75
250	A88	10c violet brn	1.25	.20
251	A88	15c brt ultra	2.00	.55
252	A88	20c dk brown	1.25	.20
253	A89	30c brown	3.50	.20
254	A89	50c cer *(Jessleton)*	.85	2.50
255	A89	$1 red orange	3.75	1.75
256	A88	$2 dark green	4.75	11.00
257	A88	$5 emerald	15.00	17.50
258	A88	$10 gray blue	40.00	40.00
		Nos. 244-258 (15)	74.10	76.55

Redrawn

1952, May 1 ***Perf. 14½x13½***

No.	Type	Description	Unused	Used
259	A89	50c cerise *(Jesselton)*	6.50	1.75

Coronation Issue

Common Design Type

1953, June 3 **Engr.** ***Perf. 13½x13***

No.	Type	Description	Unused	Used
260	CD312	10c carmine & black	.35	.35

Types of 1950 with Portrait of Queen Elizabeth II

Perf. 13½x14½, 14½x13½

1954-57 **Photo.**

No.	Type	Description	Unused	Used
261	A88	1c red brown	.25	.25
262	A88	2c brt blue ('56)	.60	.20
263	A89	3c green ('57)	.50	1.25
264	A89	4c red violet ('55)	.75	.20
265	A89	5c purple	.90	.20
266	A88	8c red	.60	.25
267	A88	10c violet brown	.40	.20
268	A88	15c brt ultra ('55)	.90	.20
269	A88	20c dk brown	.40	.20
270	A89	30c brown	2.50	.20
271	A89	50c cerise ('56)	6.25	.20
272	A89	$1 red orange ('55)	7.50	.20
273	A88	$2 dk green ('55)	15.00	.80
274	A88	$5 emerald ('57)	12.50	14.50
275	A88	$10 gray blue ('57)	27.50	22.50
		Nos. 261-275 (15)	76.55	41.35

Issued: 10c, 3/1; 5c, 7/1; 20c, 30c, 8/3; 1c, 8c, 10/1; $1, 4/1/55; 4c, 15c, 5/16/55; $2, 10/1/55; 50c, 2/10/56; 2c, 6/1/56; 3c, $5, $10, 2/1/57.

In 1960, the 30c plate was remade, using a finer, smaller-dot (250) screen instead of the 200 screen. The background appears smoother. Value, $2.75 unused.

Borneo Railway, 1902 — A90

Comp. Arms — A91

15c, Proa (sailboat). 35c, Mount Kinabalu.

Perf. 13x13½, 13½x13

1956, Nov. 1 **Engr.** **Wmk. 4**

No.	Type	Description	Unused	Used
276	A90	10c rose car & blk	.20	.20
277	A90	15c red brown & blk	.30	.30
278	A90	35c green & blk	.50	.50
279	A91	$1 slate & blk	1.25	1.25
		Nos. 276-279 (4)	2.25	2.25

75th anniv. of the founding of the Chartered Company of North Borneo.

Malayan Sambar — A92

Orangutan — A93

Designs: 4c, Honey bear. 5c, Clouded leopard. 6c, Dusun woman with gong. 10c, Map of Borneo. 12c, Banteng (wild ox). 20c, Butterfly orchid. 25c, Rhinoceros. 30c, Murut with blowgun. 35c, Mount Kinabalu. 50c, Dusun with buffalo transport. 75c, Bajau horsemen. $2, Rhinoceros hornbill. $5, Crested wood partridge. $10, Coat of arms.

Perf. 13x12½, 12½x13

1961, Feb. 1 **Wmk. 314** **Engr.**

No.	Type	Description	Unused	Used
280	A92	1c lt red brn & grn	.25	.20
281	A92	4c orange & olive	.25	.75
282	A92	5c violet & sepia	.30	.20
283	A92	6c bluish grn & sl	.50	.35
284	A92	10c rose red & lt grn	.30	.20
285	A92	12c dull grn & brn	.30	.20
286	A92	20c ultra & bl grn	3.25	.20
287	A92	25c rose red & gray	.65	.75
288	A92	30c gray ol & sep	.70	.20
289	A92	35c redsh brn & stl bl	1.60	.80
290	A92	50c brn org & bl grn	1.60	.20
291	A92	75c red vio & sl bl	7.00	.80
292	A93	$1 yel grn & brn	10.00	.65
293	A93	$2 slate & brown	21.00	2.50
294	A93	$5 brn vio & grn	35.00	10.50
295	A93	$10 blue & car	22.50	19.00
		Nos. 280-295 (16)	105.20	37.50

Freedom from Hunger Issue
Common Design Type

1963, June 4 Photo. *Perf. 14x14½*
296 CD314 12c ultramarine .90 .40

SEMI-POSTAL STAMPS

Nos. 136-138, 140-146, 148-149, 152 Overprinted in Carmine or Vermilion

1916 Unwmk. *Perf. 14*
Center in Black

B1 A51 1c chocolate 7.50 *30.00*
B2 A52 2c green 32.50 *80.00*
a. Perf. 15 50.00 *80.00*
B3 A53 3c deep rose 27.50 *47.50*
B4 A54 4c dull red 7.25 *32.50*
a. Perf. 15 225.00 *160.00*
B5 A55 5c yellow brown 45.00 *55.00*
B6 A56 6c olive green 65.00 *75.00*
a. Perf. 15 225.00 225.00
B7 A57 8c rose 24.00 *60.00*
B8 A58 10c brt blue 45.00 *70.00*
B9 A59 12c deep blue 95.00 *95.00*
B10 A60 16c red brown 95.00 *95.00*
B11 A62 20c on 18c bl grn 48.00 *95.00*
B12 A63 24c violet 120.00 *120.00*

Perf. 15

B13 A64 25c yellow green 450.00 *475.00*
Nos. B1-B13 (13) 1,061. *1,330.*

All values exist with the vermilion overprint and all but the 4c with the carmine.

Of the total overprinting, a third was given to the National Philatelic War Fund Committee in London to be auctioned for the benefit of the wounded and veterans' survivors. The balance was lost en route from London to Sandakan when a submarine sank the ship. Very few were postally used.

Nos. 136-138, 140-146, 149, 152-157 Surcharged

1918 *Perf. 14*
Center in Black

B14 A51 1c + 2c choc 3.25 *7.00*
B15 A52 2c + 2c green .70 *7.00*
B16 A53 3c + 2c dp rose 5.00 *13.00*
a. Perf. 15 25.00 *60.00*
B17 A54 4c + 2c dull red .50 *4.00*
a. Inverted surcharge 275.00
B18 A55 5c + 2c yel brn 5.50 *21.00*
B19 A56 6c + 2c olive grn 4.50 *15.00*
a. Perf. 15 125.00
B20 A57 8c + 2c rose 4.50 *6.00*
B21 A58 10c + 2c brt blue 5.00 *20.00*
B22 A59 12c + 2c deep bl 12.50 *35.00*
a. Inverted surcharge 550.00
B23 A60 16c + 2c red brn 14.00 *30.00*
B24 A63 24c + 2c violet 15.00 *30.00*
B25 A64 25c + 2c yel grn 12.00 *35.00*
B26 A64 50c + 2c sl blue 14.00 *35.00*
B27 A64 $1 + 2c brown 35.00 *45.00*
B28 A64 $2 + 2c dk vio 50.00 *85.00*
B29 A65 $5 + 2c claret 240.00 *325.00*
B30 A65 $10 + 2c ver 240.00 *325.00*
Nos. B14-B30 (17) 661.45 *1,038.*

On Nos. B14-B24 the surcharge is 15mm high, on Nos. B25-B30 it is 19mm high.

Nos. 136-138, 140-146, 149, 152-157 Surcharged in Red

1918
Center in Black

B31 A51 1c + 4c choc .40 *4.00*
B32 A52 2c + 4c green .60 *6.00*
B33 A53 3c + 4c dp rose .60 *3.00*
B34 A54 4c + 4c dull red .40 *4.00*
B35 A55 5c + 4c yel brn 1.40 *15.00*
B36 A56 6c + 4c olive grn 1.40 *10.00*
a. Vert. pair, imperf. btwn. 900.00
B37 A57 8c + 4c rose 1.00 *8.50*
B38 A58 10c + 4c brt blue 3.25 *10.00*
B39 A59 12c + 4c dp blue 6.00 *10.00*
B40 A60 16c + 4c red brn 4.25 *15.00*
B41 A63 24c + 4c violet 4.25 *17.50*
B42 A64 25c + 4c yel grn 5.00 *40.00*
B43 A64 50c + 4c sl blue 13.00 *40.00*
a. Perf. 15 50.00
B44 A64 $1 + 4c brown 15.00 *50.00*
a. Perf. 15 *60.00*
B45 A64 $2 + 4c dk vio 35.00 *65.00*
B46 A65 $5 + 4c claret 250.00 *400.00*
B47 A65 $10 + 4c ver 250.00 *375.00*
Nos. B31-B47 (17) 591.55 *1,073.*

POSTAGE DUE STAMPS

Regular Issues Overprinted

Reading Up Vert. (V), or Horiz. (H)

1895, Aug. 1 Unwmk. *Perf. 14, 15*
On Nos. 60 to 67

J1 A22 2c rose & blk (V) 15.00 .95
J2 A23 3c vio & ol grn (V) 5.00 .80
J3 A24 5c org red & blk (V) 25.00 1.25
a. Period after "DUE" (V) 45.00
J4 A25 6c ol brn & blk (V) 12.00 1.50
J5 A26 8c lilac & blk (H) 32.50 2.00
a. Double ovpt. (H)
J6 A27 12c blue & blk (H) 60.00 1.50
a. Double ovpt (H) *325.00*
J7 A28 18c green & blk (V) 65.00 3.00
a. Ovpt. reading down 400.00 *275.00*
b. Overprinted horizontally 20.00 2.75
c. Same as "b" inverted 300.00 *275.00*
J8 A29 24c claret & bl (H) 60.00 1.60
Nos. J1-J8 (8) 274.50 12.60

On Nos. 80 and 85

1897

J9 A38 2c dp rose & blk (V) 6.00 .45
a. Overprinted horizontally 12.00 *15.00*
J10 A42 8c brn lil & blk (H) 40.00 *40.00*
a. Period after "DUE" 30.00 *60.00*

On Nos. 81-88 and 104
Vertically reading up

1901

J11 A38 2c green & blk 21.00 .55
a. Overprinted horizontally 27.50
J12 A39 3c lilac & ol grn 8.00 .35
a. Period after "DUE" 18.00 *30.00*
J13 A48 4c dp rose & blk 18.00 .45
J14 A40 5c orange & blk 21.00 .55
a. Period after "DUE" 30.00
J15 A41 6c olive brn & blk 3.50 .45
J16 A42 8c brown & blk 7.00 .45
a. Overprinted horizontally 30.00
b. Period after "DUE" (H) 60.00
J17 A43 12c blue & blk 65.00 .90
J18 A46 18c green & blk 35.00 .90
J19 A47 24c red & blue 17.50 .90
Nos. J11-J19 (9) 196.00 5.50

On Nos. 105-114, 122-123
Horizontally

1903-11 *Perf. 14*

J20 A37 1c bis brn & blk, period after "DUE" 13.00 13.00
a. Period omitted
J21 A38 2c green & blk 6.00 .25
a. Ovpt. vert., perf. 16 *150.00*
b. Perf 15 (ovpt. horiz.) 55.00 *55.00*
J22 A39 3c lilac & ol grn 6.00 .35
a. Ovpt. vert. 110.00 *110.00*
b. Perf. 15 (ovpt. horiz.) 95.00 *17.00*
J23 A48 4c dp rose & blk, perf. 15 4.50 .45
a. "Postage Due" double 110.00
b. Perf. 14 4.75 1.00
J24 A40 5c orange & blk 7.00 .45
a. Ovpt. vert., perf. 15 160.00 *110.00*
b. Perf. 13½ (ovpt. horiz.)
c. Perf. 15 (ovpt. horiz.) 13.00 *10.00*
J25 A41 6c olive brn & blk 7.25 .35
a. "Postage Due" double
b. "Postage Due" inverted *110.00*
c. Perf. 16 25.00 *25.00*
J26 A42 8c brown & blk 14.00 .50
a. Overprint vertical 150.00 *125.00*
J27 A49 10c slate & brn 35.00 .90
J28 A43 12c blue & blk 10.50 .75
J29 A50 16c yel brn & grn 18.00 .90
J30 A46 18c green & blk 7.00 .60
a. "Postage Due" double *70.00*
J31 A47 24c claret & blue 15.00 1.25
a. "Postage Due" double *125.00*
b. Overprint vertical *85.00*
Nos. J20-J31 (12) 143.25 19.75

On Nos. 137 and 139-146

1921-31 *Perf. 14, 15*

J32 A52 2c green & blk 11.00 60.00
a. Perf. 13½ 15.00 12.00
J33 A53 3c green & blk 5.25 20.00
J34 A54 4c dull red & blk 1.25 1.25
J35 A55 5c yel brn & blk 5.25 10.00
J36 A56 6c olive grn & blk 13.00 11.00
J37 A57 8c rose & blk 5.25 4.25
J38 A58 10c blue & blk 6.50 12.00
a. Perf. 15 47.50 60.00
J39 A59 12c dp vio & blk 8.50 25.00
J40 A60 16c red brn & blk 24.00 65.00
Nos. J32-J40 (9) 80.00 208.50

On Nos. 168 to 176

1926-28 *Perf. 12½*

J41 A52 2c lake & blk .45 *2.00*
J42 A53 3c green & blk 2.00 *12.50*
J43 A54 4c dull red & blk 3.25 *1.00*
J44 A55 5c yel brown & blk 5.75 *50.00*
J45 A56 6c yel green & blk 8.00 *3.00*
J46 A57 8c rose & black 7.00 8.50
J47 A58 10c brt blue & blk 9.00 *50.00*
J48 A59 12c dp blue & blk 16.00 *85.00*
J49 A60 16c org brn & blk 35.00 *125.00*
Nos. J41-J49 (9) 86.45 *337.00*

Crest of British North Borneo Company — D1

1939, Jan. 1 Engr. *Perf. 12½*

J50 D1 2c brown 4.00 *25.00*
J51 D1 4c carmine 4.00 *32.50*
J52 D1 6c dp rose violet 13.50 *42.50*
J53 D1 8c dk blue green 14.00 *52.50*
J54 D1 10c deep ultra 29.00 *70.00*
Nos. J50-J54 (5) 64.50 *222.50*
Set, never hinged 100.00

WAR TAX STAMPS

Nos. 193-194 Overprinted

No. MR1

No. MR2

1941, Feb. 24 Unwmk. *Perf. 12½*

MR1 A74 1c red brn & dk grn .30 .30
MR2 A75 2c Prus blue & red vio .50 .55

For overprints see Nos. N15A-N15B.

OCCUPATION STAMPS

Issued under Japanese Occupation

Nos. 193-207 Handstamped in Violet or Black

On Nos. N1-N15B, the violet overprint is attributed to Jesselton, the black to Sandakan. Nos. N1-N15 are generally found with violet overprint, Nos. N15A-N15B with black.

1942 Unwmk. *Perf. 12½*

N1 A74 1c 125.00 120.00
N2 A75 2c 110.00 125.00
N3 A76 3c 110.00 125.00
N4 A77 4c 65.00 95.00
N5 A78 6c 125.00 125.00
N6 A79 8c 110.00 125.00
N7 A80 10c 110.00 125.00
N8 A81 12c 175.00 190.00
N9 A82 15c 175.00 190.00
N10 A83 20c 275.00 *250.00*
N11 A84 25c 250.00 *250.00*
N12 A85 50c 400.00 *300.00*
N13 A86 $1 300.00 *400.00*
N14 A86 $2 425.00 *550.00*
N15 A87 $5 600.00 *700.00*
Nos. N1-N15 (15) 3,355. *3,670.*

For overprints see Nos. N22a, N31a.

Same Overprint on Nos. MR1-MR2 in Black or Violet

1942

N15A A74 1c *625.00* 190.00
N15B A75 2c *1,300.* 250.00

Nos. 193 to 207 Overprinted in Black

1944, Sept. 30 Unwmk. *Perf. 12½*

N16 A74 1c 3.50 6.25
N17 A75 2c 6.75 6.25
N18 A76 3c 2.50 3.50
N19 A77 4c 3.50 5.00
N20 A78 6c 3.25 3.50
N21 A79 8c 5.00 *11.00*
N22 A80 10c 6.00 *9.00*
a. On No. N7 150.00
N23 A81 12c 4.50 *9.00*
N24 A82 15c 3.50 *9.00*
N25 A83 20c 12.50 *21.00*
N26 A84 25c 12.50 *21.00*
N27 A85 50c 45.00 *57.50*
N28 A86 $1 72.50 *95.00*
Nos. N16-N28 (13) 181.00 *257.00*

Nos. N1 and 205 Surcharged in Black

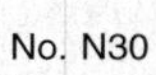

No. N30

本 日 大

No. N31

1944, May

N30 A74 $2 on 1c *4,250.* *3,250.*
N31 A86 $5 on $1 *4,500.* 3,800.
a. On No. N13 2,750. 2,750.

Mt. Kinabalu OS1

Boat and Traveler's Palm OS2

1943, Apr. 29 Litho.

N32 OS1 4c dull rose red 15.00 18.00
N33 OS2 8c dark blue 15.00 18.00

Aviator Saluting and Japanese Flag — A150

Miyajima Torii, Itsukushima Shrine — A96

Stamps of Japan, 1938-43, Overprinted in Black

1s, War factory girl. 2s, Gen. Maresuke Nogi. 3s, Power plant. 4s, Hyuga Monument and Mt. Fuji. 5s, Adm. Heihachiro Togo. 6s, Garambi Lighthouse, Formosa. 8s, Meiji Shrine, Tokyo. 10s, Palms and map of "Greater East Asia." 20s, Mt. Fuji and cherry blossoms. 25s, Horyu Temple, Nara. 50s, Golden Pavilion, Kyoto. 1y, Great Buddha, Kamakura. See Burma, Vol. 1, for illustrations of 2s, 3s, 5s, 8s, 20s and watermark. For others, see Japan.

Wmk. Curved Wavy Lines (257)

1944, Sept. 30 ***Perf. 13***

No.	Type	Description	Unused	Used
N34	A144	1s orange brown	5.25	12.00
N35	A84	2s vermilion	5.25	12.00
N36	A85	3s green	3.50	12.00
N37	A146	4s emerald	5.25	12.00
N38	A86	5s brown lake	6.25	13.00
N39	A88	6s orange	5.75	13.00
N40	A90	8s dk purple & pale vio	3.25	13.00
N41	A148	10s crim & dull rose	4.75	13.00
N42	A150	15s dull blue	4.75	13.00
N43	A94	20s ultra	100.00	200.00
N44	A95	25s brown	65.00	55.00
N45	A96	30s peacock blue	225.00	125.00
N46	A97	50s olive	70.00	55.00
N47	A98	1y lt brown	65.00	100.00
		Nos. N34-N47 (14)	569.00	648.00

The overprint translates "North Borneo."

NORTHERN NIGERIA

'nor-thə̦r̦n nī-'jir-ē-ə

LOCATION — Western Africa
GOVT. — British Protectorate
AREA — 281,703 sq. mi.
POP. — 11,866,250
CAPITAL — Zungeru

In 1914 Northern Nigeria united with Southern Nigeria to form the Colony and Protectorate of Nigeria.

12 Pence = 1 Shilling
20 Shillings = 1 Pound

Victoria — A1

Edward VII — A2

Numerals of 5p and 6p, types A1 and A2, are in color on plain tablet.

Wmk. Crown and C A (2)

1900, Mar. **Typo.** ***Perf. 14***

No.	Type	Description	Unused	Used
1	A1	½p lilac & grn	3.50	*14.00*
2	A1	1p lilac & rose	3.75	3.75
3	A1	2p lilac & yel	12.50	*50.00*
4	A1	2½p lilac & blue	10.00	*37.50*
5	A1	5p lilac & brn	25.00	*55.00*
6	A1	6p lilac & vio	24.00	*37.50*
7	A1	1sh green & blk	25.00	*75.00*
8	A1	2sh6p green & blue	125.00	*475.00*
9	A1	10sh green & brn	275.00	*700.00*
		Nos. 1-9 (9)	503.75	*1,447.*

1902, July 1

No.	Type	Description	Unused	Used
10	A2	½p violet & green	2.00	1.00
11	A2	1p vio & car rose	2.50	.75
12	A2	2p violet & org	2.25	*3.00*
13	A2	2½p violet & ultra	2.00	*9.00*
14	A2	5p vio & org brn	3.50	*5.00*
15	A2	6p violet & pur	11.00	*4.75*
16	A2	1sh green & black	4.50	*6.00*
17	A2	2sh6p green & ultra	11.00	*60.00*
18	A2	10sh green & brown	55.00	*60.00*
		Nos. 10-18 (9)	93.75	*149.50*

1904, Apr. **Wmk. 3**

No.	Type	Description	Unused	Used
18A	A2	£25 green & car	*45,000.*	

No. 18A was available for postage but probably was used only for fiscal purposes.

1905

No.	Type	Description	Unused	Used
19	A2	½p violet & grn	6.75	5.50
20	A2	1p violet & car rose	6.75	1.00
21	A2	2p violet & org	15.00	*32.50*
22	A2	2½p violet & ultra	7.25	8.00
23	A2	5p violet & org brn	25.00	70.00
24	A2	6p violet & pur	27.50	42.50
25	A2	1sh green & black	24.00	*55.00*
26	A2	2sh6p green & ultra	37.50	55.00
		Nos. 19-26 (8)	149.75	*269.50*

All values exist on ordinary paper and all but the 2½p on chalky paper.

1910-11 **Ordinary Paper**

No.	Type	Description	Unused	Used
28	A2	½p green	2.25	1.25
29	A2	1p carmine	2.00	1.25
30	A2	2p gray	5.00	*2.75*
31	A2	2½p ultra	2.50	*7.00*

Chalky Paper

No.	Type	Description	Unused	Used
32	A2	3p violet, *yel*	4.50	.75
33	A2	5p vio & ol grn	5.00	*12.50*
34	A2	6p vio & red vio ('11)	5.50	*6.00*
a.		6p violet & deep violet	7.50	*17.50*
35	A2	1sh black, *green*	3.00	.75
36	A2	2sh6p blk & red, *bl*	12.00	*32.50*
37	A2	5sh grn & red, *yel*	25.00	*75.00*
38	A2	10sh grn & red, *grn*	52.50	*50.00*
		Nos. 28-38 (11)	119.25	189.75

George V — A3

For description of dies I and II see back of this section of the Catalogue.

Die I

1912 **Ordinary Paper**

No.	Type	Description	Unused	Used
40	A3	½p green	2.25	.60
41	A3	1p carmine	2.00	.60
42	A3	2p gray	3.50	*9.00*

Chalky Paper

No.	Type	Description	Unused	Used
43	A3	3p violet, *yel*	2.25	1.25
44	A3	4p blk & red, *yel*	1.25	*2.25*
45	A3	5p vio & ol grn	4.00	11.00
46	A3	6p vio & red vio	4.25	*4.50*
47	A3	9p violet & scar	2.25	*12.00*
48	A3	1sh blk, *green*	5.00	2.25
49	A3	2sh6p blk & red, *bl*	8.75	*45.00*
50	A3	5sh grn & red, *yel*	25.00	*90.00*
51	A3	10sh grn & red, *grn*	45.00	*50.00*
52	A3	£1 vio & blk, *red*	200.00	120.00
		Nos. 40-52 (13)	305.50	*348.45*

Numerals of 3p, 4p, 5p and 6p, type A3, are in color on plain tablet.

Stamps of Northern Nigeria were replaced in 1914 by those of Nigeria.

NORTHERN RHODESIA

'nor-thə̦r̦n rō-'dē-zhə̦-ə

LOCATION — In southern Africa, east of Angola and separated from Southern Rhodesia by the Zambezi River.
GOVT. — British Protectorate
AREA — 287,640 sq. mi.
POP. — 2,550,000 (est. 1962)
CAPITAL — Lusaka

Prior to April 1, 1924, Northern Rhodesia was administered by the British South Africa Company. It joined the Federation of Rhodesia and Nyasaland in 1953 and used its stamps in 1954-63. It resumed issuing its own stamps in December, 1963, after the Federation was dissolved. On Oct. 24, 1964, Northern Rhodesia became the independent republic of Zambia. See Rhodesia, Southern Rhodesia, Rhodesia and Nyasaland, Zambia.

12 Pence = 1 Shilling
20 Shillings = 1 Pound

Catalogue values for unused stamps in this country are for Never Hinged items, beginning with Scott 46 in the regular postage section and Scott J5 in the postage due section.

King George V
A1 A2

1925-29 **Engr.** **Wmk. 4** ***Perf. 12½***

No.	Type	Description	Unused	Used
1	A1	½p dk green	1.75	.70
2	A1	1p dk brown	1.75	.20
3	A1	1½p carmine	2.50	.25
4	A1	2p brown org	2.75	.20
5	A1	3p ultra	2.75	1.30
6	A1	4p dk violet	5.00	.45
7	A1	6p gray	5.00	.40
8	A1	8p rose lilac	4.75	*60.00*
9	A1	10p olive grn	5.00	*50.00*
10	A2	1sh black & org	4.00	2.25
11	A2	2sh ultra & brn	20.00	*30.00*
12	A2	2sh6p green & blk	21.00	*12.00*
13	A2	3sh indigo & vio	30.00	25.00
14	A2	5sh dk vio & gray	40.00	22.50
15	A2	7sh6p blk & lil rose	125.00	*175.00*
16	A2	10sh black & green	100.00	*100.00*
17	A2	20sh rose lil & red	190.00	*225.00*
		Nos. 1-17 (17)	561.25	*705.25*

High values with revenue cancellations are inexpensive.

Issue dates: 3sh, 1929; others, Apr. 1.

Common Design Types pictured following the introduction.

Silver Jubilee Issue

Common Design Type

1935, May 6 ***Perf. 13½x14***

No.	Type	Description	Unused	Used
18	CD301	1p olive grn & ultra	.90	.90
19	CD301	2p indigo & grn	1.50	1.75
20	CD301	3p blue & brown	3.50	3.50
21	CD301	6p brt vio & indigo	4.50	3.75
		Nos. 18-21 (4)	10.40	9.90

Coronation Issue

Common Design Type

1937, May 12 ***Perf. 11x11½***

No.	Type	Description	Unused	Used
22	CD302	1½p dark carmine	.25	.25
23	CD302	2p yellow brown	.50	.50
24	CD302	3p deep ultra	.75	1.00
		Nos. 22-24 (3)	1.50	1.75

King George VI — A3

1938-52 **Wmk. 4** ***Perf. 12½***

Size: 19x24mm

No.	Type	Description	Unused	Used
25	A3	½p green	.20	.20
26	A3	½p dk brown ('51)	1.40	*1.50*
a.		Perf. 12½x14	1.50	*6.00*
27	A3	1p dk brown	.25	.25
28	A3	1p green ('51)	.75	*2.00*
29	A3	1½p carmine	35.00	.75
a.		Horiz. pair, imperf. between	*14,000.*	
30	A3	1½p brown org ('41)	.30	.25
31	A3	2p brown org	45.00	1.75
32	A3	2p carmine ('41)	.30	.50
33	A3	2p rose lilac ('51)	.45	*1.50*
34	A3	3p ultra	.50	.30
35	A3	3p red ('51)	.45	*2.50*
36	A3	4p dk violet	.30	.40
37	A3	4½p dp blue ('52)	1.00	*7.50*
38	A3	6p dark gray	.30	.25
39	A3	9p violet ('52)	1.00	*7.00*

Size: 21½x26¾mm

No.	Type	Description	Unused	Used
40	A3	1sh blk & brn org	1.75	.60
41	A3	2sh6p green & blk	5.00	4.75
42	A3	3sh ind & dk vio	9.00	12.50
43	A3	5sh violet & gray	9.00	13.00
44	A3	10sh black & green	10.00	*20.00*
45	A3	20sh rose lil & red	22.50	*55.00*
		Nos. 25-45 (21)	144.45	*132.50*

Catalogue values for unused stamps in this section, from this point to the end of the section, are for Never Hinged items.

Peace Issue

Common Design Type

1946, Nov. 26 **Engr.** ***Perf. 13½x14***

No.	Type	Description	Unused	Used
46	CD303	1½p deep orange	.50	.50
a.		Perf. 13½	14.00	*13.00*
47	CD303	2p carmine	.25	*.50*

Silver Wedding Issue

Common Design Types

1948, Dec. 1 **Photo.** ***Perf. 14x14½***

No.	Type	Description	Unused	Used
48	CD304	1½p orange	.30	.20

Engr. ***Perf. 11½x11***

No.	Type	Description	Unused	Used
49	CD305	20sh rose brown	62.50	*77.50*

UPU Issue

Common Design Types

Engr.; Name Typo. on 3p, 6p

Perf. 13½, 11x11½

1949, Oct. 10 **Wmk. 4**

No.	Type	Description	Unused	Used
50	CD306	2p rose carmine	.50	.50
51	CD307	3p indigo	1.00	*2.00*
52	CD308	6p gray	1.50	1.50
53	CD309	1sh red orange	1.50	1.50
		Nos. 50-53 (4)	4.50	5.50

Victoria Falls and Railway Bridge, Cecil Rhodes and Elizabeth II — A4

1953, May 30 **Engr.** ***Perf. 12x11***

No.	Type	Description	Unused	Used
54	A4	½p brown	.30	*.40*
55	A4	1p green	.30	*.40*
56	A4	2p deep claret	.35	*.30*
57	A4	4½p deep blue	.85	*2.00*
58	A4	1sh gray & orange	1.10	*3.00*
		Nos. 54-58 (5)	2.90	6.10

Cecil Rhodes (1853-1902).

Exhibition Seal — A5

1953, May 30 ***Perf. 14x13½***

No.	Type	Description	Unused	Used
59	A5	6p purple	.60	*1.25*

Central African Rhodes Centenary Exhib.

Coronation Issue

Common Design Type

1953, June 2 ***Perf. 13½x13***

No.	Type	Description	Unused	Used
60	CD312	1½p orange & black	.40	.25

Elizabeth II
A6

Coat of Arms
A7

Perf. 12½x13½

1953, Sept. 15 **Engr.**

Size: 19x23mm

No.	Type	Description	Unused	Used
61	A6	½p dark brown	.65	.20
62	A6	1p green	.75	.20
63	A6	1½p brown orange	1.25	.20
64	A6	2p rose lilac	1.40	.20
65	A6	3p red	.80	.20
66	A6	4p dark violet	1.25	1.75
67	A6	4½p deep blue	2.00	*4.00*
68	A6	6p dark gray	1.50	.55
69	A6	9p violet	1.50	*4.00*

Size: 21x27mm

No.	Type	Description	Unused	Used
70	A6	1sh black & brn org	1.00	.20
71	A6	2sh6p green & blk	8.50	4.00
72	A6	5sh violet & gray	10.00	*12.00*
73	A6	10sh black & green	7.50	22.50
74	A6	20sh rose lilac & red	21.00	*28.00*
		Nos. 61-74 (14)	59.10	78.00

Perf. 14½

1963, Dec. 1 **Unwmk.** **Photo.**

Size: 23x19mm

Arms in Black, Blue and Orange

No.	Type	Description	Unused	Used
75	A7	½p violet & blk	.60	.40
a.		Value omitted	900.00	
76	A7	1p blue & blk	1.00	.20
a.		Value omitted	12.50	

77 A7 2p brown & blk .70 .20
78 A7 3p orange & blk .20 .20
a. Bklt. pane of 4 .85
b. Value omitted 90.00
c. Orange (eagle) omitted *1,200.* —
d. Value and orange (eagle) omitted 200.00
79 A7 4p green & blk .60 .20
a. Value omitted 110.00
80 A7 6p yel grn & blk .75 .20
a. Value omitted 650.00
81 A7 9p ocher & blk .50 .20
a. Value omitted 475.00
b. Value and orange (eagle) omitted 350.00
82 A7 1sh dk gray & blk .40 .20
83 A7 1sh3p brt red lil & blk 2.25 .20

Perf. 13

Size: 27x23mm

84 A7 2sh dp orange & blk 2.00 2.00
85 A7 2sh6p maroon & blk 2.00 1.75
86 A7 5sh dk car rose & blk 7.50 7.50
a. Value omitted *1,900.*
87 A7 10sh brt pink & blk 9.00 *16.00*
88 A7 20sh dk blue & blk 12.50 *20.00*
a. Value omitted 1,000.
Nos. 75-88 (14) 40.00 *49.25*

Stamps of Northern Rhodesia were replaced by those of Zambia, starting Oct. 24, 1964.

POSTAGE DUE STAMPS

D1

1929 Typo. Wmk. 4 *Perf. 14*
J1 D1 1p black 2.75 *2.75*
a. Wmk. 4a (error) 2,500.
J2 D1 2p black 3.50 *3.50*
a. Bisected, used as 1d, on cover *850.00*
J3 D1 3p black 6.75 *27.50*
a. Crown in watermark missing 375.00
b. Wmk. 4a (error) 200.00
J4 D1 4p black 9.00 *35.00*
Nos. J1-J4 (4) 22.00 *68.75*

Catalogue values for unused stamps in this section, from this point to the end of the section, are for Never Hinged items.

D2

1964 Unwmk. Litho. *Perf. 12½*
J5 D2 1p orange 1.25 *3.50*
J6 D2 2p dark blue 1.50 *3.75*
J7 D2 3p rose claret 1.75 *6.00*
J8 D2 4p violet blue 1.75 *8.00*
J9 D2 6p purple 6.00 *9.00*
J10 D2 1sh emerald 7.50 *25.00*
Nos. J5-J10 (6) 19.75 *55.25*

NORTH INGERMANLAND

'north 'iŋ-gər-mən-ˌland

LOCATION — In Northern Russia lying between the River Neva and Finland
CAPITAL — Kirjasalo

In 1920 the residents of this territory revolted from Russian rule and set up a provisional government. The new State existed only a short period as the revolution was quickly quelled by Soviet troops.

100 Pennia = 1 Markka

Arms — A1

Perf. 11½

1920, Mar. 21 Unwmk. Litho.
1 A1 5p green 2.00 *3.50*
2 A1 10p rose red 2.00 *3.50*
3 A1 25p bister 2.00 *3.50*
4 A1 50p dark blue 2.00 *3.50*
5 A1 1m car & black 26.00 *42.50*
6 A1 5m lilac & black 175.00 *175.00*
7 A1 10m brown & blk 225.00 *250.00*
Nos. 1-7 (7) 434.00 *481.50*

Well centered examples sell for twice the values shown.

Imperf., Pairs

1a A1 5p 5.25
2a A1 10p 5.25
3a A1 25p 5.25
4a A1 50p 5.25
5a A1 1m 20.00
6a A1 5m 125.00
7a A1 10m 200.00

Arms — A2

Peasant — A3

Plowing — A4

Milking — A5

Planting A6

Ruins of Church A7

Peasants Playing Zithers A8

1920, Aug. 2
8 A2 10p gray grn & ultra 3.00 *7.00*
9 A3 30p buff & gray grn 3.00 *7.00*
10 A4 50p ultra & red brn 3.00 *7.00*
11 A5 80p claret & slate 3.00 *7.00*
12 A6 1m red & slate 22.50 *45.00*
13 A7 5m dk vio & dl rose 9.00 *18.00*
14 A8 10m brn & violet 9.00 *18.00*
a. Center inverted 1,000.
Nos. 8-14 (7) 52.50 *109.00*

Counterfeits abound.

Nos. 8-14 exist imperf. Value for set in pairs, $200.

NORTH WEST PACIFIC ISLANDS

'north 'west pə-'si-fik 'ī-ləndz

LOCATION — Group of islands in the West Pacific Ocean including a part of New Guinea and adjacent islands of the Bismarck Archipelago
GOVT. — Australian military government
AREA — 96,160 sq. mi.
POP. — 636,563

Stamps of Australia were overprinted for use in the former German possessions of Nauru and German New Guinea which Australian troops had captured. Following the League of Nations' decision which placed these territories under mandate to Australia, these provisional issues were discontinued. See German New Guinea, New Britain, Nauru and New Guinea.

12 Pence = 1 Shilling
20 Shillings = 1 Pound

Stamps of Australia Overprinted — a

Type a: "P" of "PACIFIC" above "S" of "ISLANDS."

There are two varieties of the letter "S" in the Type "a" overprint. These occur in three combinations: a, both normal "S"; b, 1st "S" with small head and long bottom stroke, 2nd "S" normal; c, both "S" with small head and long bottom stroke.

DESIGN A1

Die I — The inside frameline has a break at left, even with the top of the letters of the denomination.

Die II — The frameline does not show a break.

Die IV — As Die III, with a break in the top outside frameline above the "ST" of "AUSTRALIA." The upper right inside frameline has an incomplete corner.

Dies are only indicated when there are more than one for any denomination.

1915-16 Wmk. 8 *Perf. 12*
1 A1 2p gray 32.50 *75.00*
2 A1 2½p dark blue 10.00 *30.00*
3 A1 3p ol bis, die I 40.00 *90.00*
a. Die II 350.00 *450.00*
b. Pair, #3, 3a 575.00 *800.00*
4 A1 6p ultra 80.00 *85.00*
5 A1 9p violet 55.00 *62.50*
6 A1 1sh blue green 57.50 *62.50*
8 A1 5sh yel & gray ('16) 1,400. *1,750.*
9 A1 10sh pink & gray 125.00 *190.00*
Revenue cancel 27.50
10 A1 £1 ultra & brown *700.00* *900.00*
Nos. 1-6,8-10 (9) *2,500.* *3,245.*

For surcharge see No. 27.

Wmk. Wide Crown and Narrow A (9)
Perf. 12, 14

ONE PENNY

Die I — Normal die, having outside the oval band with "AUSTRALIA" a white line and a heavy colored line.

Die Ia — As die I with a small white spur below the right serif at foot of the "1" in left tablet.

Dies are only indicated when there are more than one for any denomination.

11 A4 ½p emerald 5.00 *12.00*
a. Double overprint
12 A4 1p car (Die I) 10.00 *12.00*
a. 1p carmine rose (Die I) 10.00 *10.00*
b. 1p carmine (Die Ia) 160.00 *175.00*
13 A1 2p gray 25.00 *40.00*
14 A1 2½p dk bl ('16) *17,500.* *17,500.*
16 A4 4p orange 12.00 *25.00*
17 A4 5p org brown 13.00 *26.00*
18 A1 6p ultra 18.00 *32.50*
19 A1 9p violet 27.50 *37.50*
20 A1 1sh blue green 16.00 *40.00*
21 A1 2sh brown 150.00 *200.00*
22 A1 5sh yellow & gray 110.00 *150.00*
Nos. 11-13,16-22 (10) 386.50 *575.00*

For surcharge see No. 28.

1915-16 Wmk. 10 *Perf. 12*
23 A1 2p gray, die I 9.50 *25.00*
24 A1 3p ol bis, die I 9.00 *20.00*
a. Die II 125.00 *200.00*
b. Pair, #24, 24a 600.00
25 A1 2sh brown ('16) 50.00 *75.00*
26 A1 £1 ultra & brn ('16) 425.00 *575.00*
Nos. 23-26 (4) 493.50 *695.00*

Nos. 6 and 17 Surcharged

1918, May 23 Wmk. 8 *Perf. 12*
27 A1 1p on 1sh bl grn 150.00 140.00

Wmk. 9 *Perf. 14*
28 A4 1p on 5p org brn 150.00 125.00

Stamps of Australia Overprinted

b

Type "b": "P" of "PACIFIC" above space between "I" and "S" of "ISLANDS."

1918-23 Wmk. 10 *Perf. 12*
29 A1 2p gray 11.00 *30.00*
a. Die II 14.00 *70.00*
30 A1 2½p dk bl ('19) 10.00 *27.50*
a. "1" of fraction omitted *10,000.* *12,000.*
31 A1 3p ol bis, die I 32.50 *40.00*
a. Die II 100.00 *175.00*
b. Pair, #31, 31a 600.00 *800.00*
c. 3p lt olive, die IV 32.50 *50.00*
32 A1 6p ultra ('19) 15.00 *25.00*
a. chalky blue 70.00 *95.00*
33 A1 9p violet ('19) 17.00 *60.00*
34 A1 1sh bl grn ('18) 21.00 *50.00*
35 A1 2sh brown 37.50 *57.50*
36 A1 5sh yel & gray ('19) 90.00 100.00
37 A1 10sh pink & gray ('19) 225.00 *300.00*
38 A1 £1 ultra & brn 4,000. *6,000.*
Nos. 29-37 (9) 459.00 *690.00*

1919 Wmk. 11
39 A4 ½p emerald 5.00 *6.00*

1918-23 Wmk. 9
40 A4 ½p emerald 3.00 *6.00*
41 A4 1p car red, die 1 5.00 2.00
a. 1p carmine red, die Ia 150.00 100.00

42	A4	1p scar, die I, rough paper	650.00	200.00
a.		1p rose red, die Ia, rough paper	1,200.	600.00
43	A4	1p violet ('22)	4.50	*10.00*
44	A4	2p orange	15.00	*10.00*
45	A4	2p red ('22)	17.00	14.00
46	A4	4p yel org	6.00	*22.50*
47	A4	4p violet ('22)	30.00	*42.50*
48	A4	4p light ultra ('22)	20.00	*70.00*
49	A4	5p brown	10.00	*20.00*
		Nos. 40-41,43-49 (9)	110.50	*197.00*

North West Pacific Islands stamps were largely used in New Britain. Some were used in Nauru. They were intended to serve the Bismarck Archipelago and other places.

NUMBER CHANGES

Old No.	New No.
new	3a, 3b
11	11, 40
12	12, 41, 42
12b	12b, 41a, 42a
16	16, 46
17	17, 49
27	23, 29
new	29a
28, 28a	30, 30a
29	24, 31
new	24a, 24b
new	31a, 31b, 31c
35	25, 35
38	26, 38
39-40	27-28
41	39
42-44	43-45
45-46	47-48

NORWAY

'nor-,wā

LOCATION — Western half of the Scandinavian Peninsula in northern Europe
GOVT. — Kingdom
AREA — 125,051 sq. mi.
POP. — 4,644,457 (2008 est.)
CAPITAL — Oslo

120 Skilling = 1 Specie Daler
100 Ore = 1 Krone (1877)

Catalogue values for unused stamps in this country are for Never Hinged items, beginning with Scott 275 in the regular postage section, Scott B27 in the semi-postal section, and Scott O65 in the official section.

Watermarks

Wmk. 159 — Lion

Wmk. 160 — Post Horn

Coat of Arms — A1

King Oscar I — A2

Wmk. 159

1855, Jan. 1 Typo. *Imperf.*

1	A1	4s blue	*6,400.*	130.
a.		Double foot on right hind leg of lion		2,600.

Only a few genuine unused exmaples of No. 1 exist. Stamps often offered have had penmarkings removed. The unused catalogue value is for a copy without gum. Stamps with original gum sell for much more.

No. 1 was reprinted in 1914 and 1924 unwatermarked. Lowest value reprint, $95.

REPRINTS

The various reprints of the early issues were never valid for postage and are not known canceled.

Rouletted Reprints

1963: No. 1, value $25; Nos. 2-5, 15, value each $15.

1965: Nos. 57, 70a, 100, 152, J1, O1. Value each $10.

1969: Nos. 69, 92, 107, 114, 128, J12. Value each $10.

1856-57 Unwmk. *Perf. 13*

2	A2	2s yellow ('57)	650.00	150.00
3	A2	3s lilac ('57)	475.00	95.00
4	A2	4s blue	375.00	17.00
a.		Imperf.		*10,000.*
b.		Half used as 2s on cover		
5	A2	8s dull lake	1,300.	55.00

Nos. 2-5 were reprinted in 1914 and 1924, perf. 13½. Lowest valued reprint, $50 each.

A3

A4

1863 Litho. *Perf. 14½x13½*

6	A3	2s yellow	1,150.	210.00
7	A3	3s gray lilac	850.00	475.00
8	A3	4s blue	200.00	12.00
9	A3	8s rose	1,000.	65.00
10	A3	24s brown	45.00	50.00
		Nos. 6-10 (5)	3,245.	812.00

There are four types of the 2, 3, 8 and 24 skilling and eight types of the 4 skilling. See note on used value of No. 10 following No. 21.

No. 8 exists imperf. Value, unused $900.

1867-68 Typo.

11	A4	1s black ('68)	85.00	55.00
12	A4	2s orange	30.00	25.00
b.		Vert. pair, imperf between	*1,750.*	
13	A4	3s dl lil ('68)	525.00	100.00
14	A4	4s blue	125.00	12.00
15	A4	8s car rose	550.00	55.00
a.		8s rose, clear impression	1,600.	450.00
		Nos. 11-15 (5)	1,315.	247.00

See note on used value of #12 following #21.

For surcharges see Nos. 59-61, 149.

No. 15 was reprinted in 1914 and 1924, perf. 13½. Lowest valued reprint, $50.

Post Horn and Crown — A5

1872-75 Wmk. 160

16	A5	1s yel grn ('75)	11.50	*20.00*
a.		1s deep green ('73)	300.00	65.00
b.		"E.EN"	25.00	*55.00*
d.		Vert. pair, imperf between	—	
17	A5	2s ultra ('74)	20.00	*35.00*
a.		2s Prussian blue ('74)	*17,000.*	*5,000.*
b.		2s gray blue	15.00	*30.00*
18	A5	3s rose	85.00	14.00
a.		3s carmine	85.00	14.00
b.		3s carmine, *bluish* thin paper	350.00	32.50
19	A5	4s lilac ('73)	19.00	*45.00*
a.		4s dark violet, *bluish* thin paper	625.00	175.00
b.		4s brown violet, *bluish* thin paper ('73)	575.00	210.00
20	A5	6s org brn ('75)	575.00	65.00
21	A5	7s red brn ('73)	60.00	50.00
		Nos. 16-21 (6)	770.50	229.00

In this issue there are 12 types each of Nos. 16, 17, 18 and 19; 12 types of No. 20 and 20 types of No. 21. The differences are in the words of value.

Nos. 10, 12, 16, 17, 19 and 21 were rereleased in 1888 and used until March 31, 1908. Used values of these stamps are for specimens canceled in this later period, usually with a two-ring cancellation. Examples bearing clear dated cancellations before 1888 are worth considerably more, as follows: No. 10 $125, No. 12 $55, No. 16 $45, No. 17 $70, No. 17b $250, No. 19 $65, No. 21 $70.

No. 21 exists imperf. Value, unused without gum $800.

No. 19 comes on thin and thick paper.

For surcharges see Nos. 62-63.

Post Horn — A6

King Oscar II — A7

"NORGE" in Sans-serif Capitals, Ring of Post Horn Shaded

1877-78

22	A6	1o drab	8.50	*10.00*
23	A6	3o orange	100.00	35.00
24	A6	5o ultra	37.50	12.50
a.		5o dull blue	700.00	125.00
b.		5o bright blue	250.00	70.00
c.		No period after "Postfrim"	57.50	13.00
d.		Retouched plate	175.00	20.00
e.		As "c," retouched plate	200.00	27.50
25	A6	10o rose	95.00	3.25
b.		Retouched plate	85.00	4.00
26	A6	12o lt green	125.00	20.00
27	A6	20o orange brn	375.00	14.00
28	A6	25o lilac	475.00	125.00
29	A6	35o bl grn ('78)	25.00	15.00
a.		Retouched plate	250.00	110.00
30	A6	50o maroon	47.50	10.00
31	A6	60o dk bl ('78)	47.50	10.00
32	A7	1k gray grn & grn ('78)	30.00	8.50
33	A7	1.50k ultra & bl ('78)	70.00	32.50
34	A7	2k rose & mar ('78)	50.00	22.50
		Nos. 22-34 (13)	1,486.	318.25

There are 6 types each of Nos. 22, 26 and 28 to 34; 12 types each of Nos. 23, 24, 25 and 27. The differences are in the numerals.

A 2nd plate of the 5o ultramarine has 100 types, the 10o, 200 types.

The retouch on 5o, 10o and 35o shows as a thin white line between crown and post horn.

Post Horn — A8

"NORGE" in Sans-serif Capitals, Ring of Horn Unshaded

1882-93 Wmk. 160 *Perf. 14½x13½*

35	A8	1o black brn ('86)	19.00	*25.00*
a.		No period after "Postfrim"	60.00	60.00
b.		Small "N" in "NORGE"	60.00	60.00
36	A8	1o gray ('93)	11.00	*12.50*
37	A8	2o brown ('90)	6.00	*6.50*
38	A8	3o yellow ('89)	85.00	12.50
a.		3o orange ('93)	200.00	17.50
b.		Perf. 13½x12½ ('93)	10,000.	3,250.
39	A8	5o bl grn ('89)	75.00	2.00
a.		5o gray green ('86)	100.00	4.50
b.		5o emerald ('88)	225.00	10.00
c.		5o yellow green ('91)	100.00	3.50
d.		Perf. 13½x12½ ('93)	*4,250.*	*950.00*
40	A8	10o rose	70.00	1.25
a.		10o rose red ('86)	70.00	1.50
b.		10o carmine ('91)	70.00	1.50
c.		As "b," imperf. ('91)	*2,250.*	*2,000.*
41	A8	12o green ('84)	1,450.	425.00
42	A8	12o orange brn ('84)	35.00	25.00
a.		12o bister brown ('83)	70.00	60.00
43	A8	20o brown	175.00	19.00
44	A8	20o blue ('86)	100.00	2.50
a.		20o ultramarine ('83)	350.00	22.50
b.		No period after "Postfrim" ('85)	550.00	20.00
c.		As "a," imperf. ('90)	*1,750.*	*2,000.*
d.		0o Prussian blue	300.00	20.00
45	A8	25o dull vio ('84)	20.00	15.00

Dies vary from 20 to 21mm high. Numerous types exist due to different production methods, including separate handmade dies for value figures. Many shades exist.

No. 42 and 42a Surcharged in Black

1888 *Perf. 14½x13½*

No.				
46	A8	2o on 12o org brn	2.50	3.00
a.		2o on 12o bister brown	3.50	3.75

Post Horn — A10

"NORGE" in Roman instead of Sans-serif capitals

Perf. 14½x13½

1893-1908 **Wmk. 160**

Size: 16x20mm

47	A10	1o gray ('99)	3.25	*3.50*
48	A10	2o pale brn ('99)	2.60	2.25
49	A10	3o orange yel	2.00	.40
50	A10	5o dp green ('98)	7.00	.20
b.		Booklet pane of 6		
51	A10	10o carmine ('98)	15.00	.20
b.		Booklet pane of 6		
d.		10o rose ('94)	350.00	4.00
e.		Imperf		*2,500.*
52	A10	15o brown ('08)	50.00	11.50
53	A10	20o dp ultra	27.50	.40
b.		Booklet pane of 6		
54	A10	25o red vio ('01)	62.50	4.00
55	A10	30o sl gray ('07)	50.00	5.00
56	A10	35o dk bl grn ('98)	16.00	8.00
57	A10	50o maroon ('94)	75.00	2.25
58	A10	60o dk blue ('00)	62.50	8.00
		Nos. 47-58 (12)	373.35	45.70

Two dies exist of 3, 10 and 20o.

See Nos. 74-95, 162-166, 187-191, 193, 307-309, 325-326, 416-419, 606, 709-714, 960-968, 1141-1145.

For overprints and surcharge see Nos. 99, 207-211, 220-224, 226, 329, 1282A-1291©.

1893-98 **Wmk. 160** *Perf. 13½x12½*

No.				
47a	A10	1o gray ('95)	17.50	*35.00*
49a	A10	3o orange ('95)	40.00	7.00
50a	A10	5o green	27.50	1.25
51a	A10	10o carmine ('96)	35.00	1.50
c.		10o rose ('95)	100.00	3.25
53a	A10	20o dull ultra ('95)	95.00	5.50
54a	A10	25o red violet ('98)	85.00	25.00
56a	A10	35o dark blue green ('95)	85.00	25.00
57a	A10	50o maroon ('97)	275.00	22.50
		Nos. 47a-57a (8)	660.00	122.75

Two dies exist of each except 25 and 35o.

No. 12 Surcharged in Green, Blue or Carmine

1905 **Unwmk.** *Perf. 14½x13½*

No.				
59	A4	1k on 2s org (G)	45.00	37.50
60	A4	1.50k on 2s org (Bl)	85.00	75.00
61	A4	2k on 2s org (C)	80.00	65.00
		Nos. 59-61 (3)	210.00	177.50

Used values are for stamps canceled after 1910. Stamps used before that sell for twice as much.

Nos. 19 and 21 Surcharged in Black

1906-08 **Wmk. 160** *Perf. 14½x13½*

No.				
62	A5	15o on 4s lilac ('08)	6.00	6.00
a.		15o on 4s violet ('08)	17.50	12.00
63	A5	30o on 7s red brown	12.50	8.50
a.		Inverted overprint		*9,000.*

Used values are for stamps canceled after 1914. Stamps used before that sell for twice as much.

King Haakon VII — A11

Die A

Die B

Die C

Die A — Background of ruled lines. The coils at the sides are ornamented with fine cross-lines and small dots. Stamps 20¼mm high.

Die B — Background of ruled lines. The coils are ornamented with large white dots and dashes. Stamps 21¼mm high.

Die C — Solid background. The coils are without ornamental marks. Stamps 20¾mm high.

1907 **Typo.** *Perf. 14½x13½*

Die A

64	A11	1k yellow grn	50.00	30.00
65	A11	1.50k ultra	90.00	75.00
66	A11	2k rose	150.00	110.00
		Nos. 64-66 (3)	290.00	215.00

Used values are for stamps canceled after 1910. Stamps used before that sell for twice as much.

1909-10

Die B

67	A11	1k green	190.00	110.00
68	A11	1.50k ultra	225.00	*300.00*
69	A11	2k rose	175.00	6.00
		Nos. 67-69 (3)	590.00	*416.00*

Used values are for stamps canceled after 1914. Stamps used before that sell for twice as much.

1911-18

Die C

70	A11	1k light green	.70	.20
a.		1k dark green	75.00	3.00
71	A11	1.50k ultra	2.50	.20
72	A11	2k rose ('15)	3.00	.20
73	A11	5k dk violet ('18)	5.50	2.50
		Nos. 70-73 (4)	11.70	3.10
		Set, never hinged	35.00	

See note following No. 180.

Post Horn Type Redrawn

Original Redrawn

In the redrawn stamps the white ring of the post horn is continuous instead of being broken by a spot of color below the crown. On the 3 and 30 ore the top of the figure "3" in the oval band is rounded instead of flattened.

1910-29 *Perf. 14½x13½*

No.				
74	A10	1o pale olive	.40	*.50*
75	A10	2o pale brown	.40	.40
76	A10	3o orange	.40	.40
77	A10	5o green	3.50	.20
a.		Booklet pane of 6	250.00	
		Complete booklet, 4 #77a	2,500.	
78	A10	5o magenta ('22)	.80	.20
79	A10	7o green ('29)	.80	.20
80	A10	10o car rose	4.50	.20
a.		Booklet pane of 6	150.00	
		Complete booklet, 2 #80a	450.00	
81	A10	10o green ('22)	10.00	.20
82	A10	12o purple ('17)	.80	.80
83	A10	15o brown	8.00	.30
a.		Booklet pane of 6	30.00	
		Complete booklet, 2 #83a	70.00	
84	A10	15o indigo ('20)	7.00	.20
85	A10	20o deep ultra	6.50	.20
a.		Booklet pane of 6	500.00	
		Complete booklet, 2 #85a	*3,500.*	
86	A10	20o ol grn ('21)	7.00	.20
87	A10	25o red lilac	40.00	.30
88	A10	25o car rose ('22)	7.00	.80
89	A10	30o slate gray	10.00	.25
90	A10	30o lt blue ('27)	10.00	6.00

91	A10	35o dk olive ('20)	10.00	.30
92	A10	40o ol grn ('17)	4.00	.30
93	A10	40o dp ultra ('22)	27.50	.30
94	A10	50o claret	21.00	.30
95	A10	60o deep blue	27.50	.30
		Nos. 74-95 (22)	207.10	12.85
		Set, never hinged	1,050.	

Constitutional Assembly of 1814 — A12

1914, May 10 **Engr.** *Perf. 13½*

96	A12	5o green	1.00	.50
97	A12	10o car rose	2.50	.50
98	A12	20o deep blue	8.50	7.00
		Nos. 96-98 (3)	12.00	8.00
		Set, never hinged	60.00	

Norway's Constitution of May 17, 1814.

No. 87 Surcharged

1922, Mar. 1 *Perf. 14½x13½*

No.				
99	A10	5o on 25o red lilac	1.00	.60
		Never hinged	2.00	

Lion Rampant A13

Polar Bear and Airplane A14

"NORGE" in Roman capitals, Line below "Ore"

1922-24 **Typo.** *Perf. 14½x13½*

No.				
100	A13	10o dp grn ('24)	10.00	.30
101	A13	20o dp vio	14.00	.20
102	A13	25o scarlet ('24)	27.50	.60
103	A13	45o blue ('24)	1.50	1.25
		Nos. 100-103 (4)	53.00	2.35
		Set, never hinged	200.00	

For surcharge see No. 129.

1925, Apr. 1

No.				
104	A14	2o yellow brn	2.25	*3.00*
105	A14	3o orange	3.25	*5.50*
106	A14	5o magenta	8.25	*16.00*
107	A14	10o yellow grn	11.00	*27.50*
108	A14	15o dark blue	10.00	*25.00*
109	A14	20o plum	16.00	*32.50*
110	A14	25o scarlet	3.25	*7.00*
		Nos. 104-110 (7)	54.00	116.50
		Set, never hinged	125.00	

Issued to help finance Roald Amundsen's attempted flight to the North Pole.

A15

A16

1925, Aug. 19

111	A15	10o yellow green	5.00	*14.00*
112	A15	15o indigo	4.25	*8.00*
113	A15	20o plum	4.75	*2.25*
114	A15	45o dark blue	4.75	*7.50*
		Nos. 111-114 (4)	18.75	31.75
		Set, never hinged	62.50	

Annexation of Spitsbergen (Svalbard). For surcharge see No. 130.

"NORGE" in Sans-serif Capitals, No Line below "Ore"

1926-34 **Wmk. 160**

Size: 16x19½mm

115	A16	10o yel grn	.70	.20
116	A16	14o dp org ('29)	2.25	2.25
117	A16	15o olive gray	.85	.20
118	A16	20o plum	27.50	.20
119	A16	20o scar ('27)	2.00	.20
a.		Booklet pane of 6	110.00	
		Complete booklet, 2 #119a	300.00	
120	A16	25o red	12.00	1.75
121	A16	25o org brn ('27)	1.25	.20
122	A16	30o dull bl ('28)	1.25	.20
123	A16	35o ol brn ('27)	52.50	.20
124	A16	35o red vio ('34)	2.00	.20
125	A16	40o dull blue	3.25	.90
126	A16	40o slate ('27)	2.00	.20
127	A16	50o claret ('27)	2.00	.20
128	A16	60o Prus bl ('27)	2.00	.20
		Nos. 115-128 (14)	111.55	7.10
		Set, never hinged	550.00	

See Nos. 167-176, 192, 194-202A. For overprints and surcharges see Nos. 131, 212-219, 225, 227-234, 237-238, 302-303.

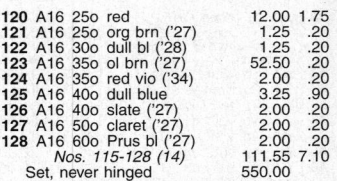

Nos. 103 and 114 Surcharged

1927, June 13

No.				
129	A13	30o on 45o blue	11.00	2.50
130	A15	30o on 45o dk blue	5.00	8.00
		Set, never hinged	47.50	

No. 120 Surcharged

1928

No.				
131	A16	20o on 25o red	2.50	2.50
		Never hinged	10.00	

See Nos. 302-303.

Henrik Ibsen — A17

Niels Henrik Abel — A18

1928, Mar. 20 **Litho.**

132	A17	10o yellow grn	9.00	4.00
133	A17	15o chnt brown	3.00	*3.25*
134	A17	20o carmine	3.00	.75
135	A17	30o dp ultra	6.00	5.00
		Nos. 132-135 (4)	21.00	13.00
		Set, never hinged	55.00	

Ibsen (1828-1906), dramatist.

Postage Due Stamps of 1889-1923 Overprinted

a

b

1929, Jan.

136	D1	(a)	1o gray	.75	*1.25*
137	D1	(a)	4o lilac rose	.60	.60
138	D1	(a)	10o green	2.25	*4.00*
139	D1	(b)	15o brown	3.00	*6.00*
140	D1	(b)	20o dull vio	1.25	1.00
141	D1	(b)	40o deep ultra	1.90	1.00
142	D1	(b)	50o maroon	8.50	*9.00*
143	D1	(a)	100o orange yel	3.00	*3.50*
144	D1	(b)	200o dk violet	5.00	4.00
			Nos. 136-144 (9)	26.25	30.35
			Set, never hinged	55.00	

1929, Apr. 6 **Litho.** *Perf. 14½x13½*

145	A18	10o green	3.00	1.00
146	A18	15o red brown	2.50	1.60
147	A18	20o rose red	1.25	.35
148	A18	30o deep ultra	3.00	2.50
		Nos. 145-148 (4)	9.75	5.45
		Set, never hinged	40.00	

Abel (1802-1829), mathematician.

No. 12 Surcharged

Perf. 14½x13½

1929, July 1 **Unwmk.**

149 A4 14o on 2s orange 2.25 6.00
Never hinged 5.00

Saint Olaf A19

Trondheim Cathedral A20

Death of Olaf in Battle of Stiklestad A21

Typo.; Litho. (15o)
Perf. 14½x13½

1930, Apr. 1 **Wmk. 160**

150 A19 10o yellow grn 10.00 .35
151 A20 15o brn & blk 1.75 .45
152 A19 20o scarlet 1.25 .30

Engr.
Perf. 13½

153 A21 30o deep blue 3.50 4.00
Nos. 150-153 (4) 16.50 5.10
Set, never hinged 60.00

King Olaf Haraldsson (995-1030), patron saint of Norway.

Björnson A22

Holberg A23

1932, Dec. 8 ***Perf. 14½x13½***

154 A22 10o yellow grn 8.00 .40
155 A22 15o black brn 1.50 1.50
156 A22 20o rose red 1.00 .30
157 A22 30o ultra 2.50 *3.00*
Nos. 154-157 (4) 13.00 5.20
Set, never hinged 40.00

Björnstjerne Björnson (1832-1910), novelist, poet and dramatist.

1934, Nov. 23

158 A23 10o yellow grn 3.00 .75
159 A23 15o brown .75 .75
160 A23 20o rose red 15.00 .25
161 A23 30o ultra 3.25 3.50
Nos. 158-161 (4) 22.00 5.25
Set, never hinged 65.00

Ludvig Holberg (1684-1754), Danish man of letters.

Types of 1893-1900, 1926-34
Second Redrawing
Perf. 13x13½

1937 **Wmk. 160** **Photo.**
Size: 17x21mm

162 A10 1o olive .70 1.00
163 A10 2o yellow brn .70 1.00
164 A10 3o deep orange 1.75 *2.50*
165 A10 5o rose lilac .55 .20
a. Booklet pane of 6 55.00
166 A10 7o brt green .70 .20
167 A16 10o brt green .45 .20
a. Booklet pane of 6 50.00
Complete booklet, 2 #167a 550.00
168 A16 14o dp orange 2.50 4.50
169 A16 15o olive bis 1.50 .20
170 A16 20o scarlet 1.10 .20
a. Booklet pane of 6 50.00
Complete booklet, 2 #170a 1,000.
Complete booklet, 1 ea #165a, 167a, 170a 400.00
171 A16 25o dk org brn 5.50 .25
172 A16 30o ultra 3.00 .25
173 A16 35o brt vio 2.50 .25
174 A16 40o dk slate grn 3.00 .25
175 A16 50o deep claret 3.50 .40
176 A16 60o Prussian bl 2.25 .20
Nos. 162-176 (15) 29.70 11.60
Set, never hinged 100.00

Nos. 162 to 166 have a solid background inside oval. Nos. 74, 75, 76, 78, 79 have background of vertical lines.

King Haakon VII — A24

1937-38

177 A24 1k dark green .20 .20
178 A24 1.50k sapphire ('38) 1.00 1.00
179 A24 2k rose red ('38) 1.00 1.00
180 A24 5k dl vio ('38) 5.00 5.75
Nos. 177-180 (4) 7.20 7.95
Set, never hinged 18.00

Nos. 64-66, 67-69, 70-73 and B11-B14 were demonitized on Sept. 30, 1940. Nos. 267, B19, B32-B34 and B38-B41 were demonetized on May 15, 1945. All of these stamps became valid again Sept. 1, 1981. Nos. 64-66, 67-69 and 70-73 rarely were used after 1981, and values represent stamps used in the earlier period. Values for Nos. B11-B14 used are for stamps used in the earlier period, and used examples in the later period are worth the same as mint stamps. Values for the other stamps used are for examples used in the later period, and stamps with dated cancellations prior to May 15, 1945 sell for more. False cancellations exist.

Reindeer — A25

Borgund Church — A26

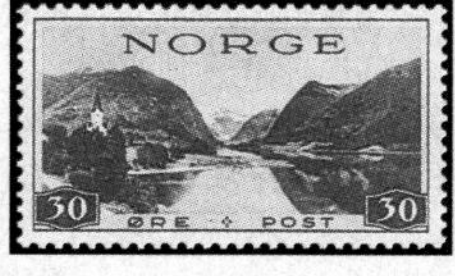
Jolster in Sunnfiord A27

Perf. 13x13½, 13½x13

1938, Apr. 20 **Wmk. 160**

181 A25 15o olive brn .75 .75
182 A26 20o copper red 4.00 .55
183 A27 30o brt ultra 3.75 2.50
Nos. 181-183 (3) 8.50 3.80
Set, never hinged 30.00

1939, Jan. 16 **Unwmk.**

184 A25 15o olive brn .50 .50
185 A26 20o copper red .50 .20
186 A27 30o brt ultra .50 .35
Nos. 184-186 (3) 1.50 1.05
Set, never hinged 2.75

Types of 1937
Perf. 13x13½

1940-49 **Unwmk.** **Photo.**
Size: 17x21mm

187 A10 1o olive grn ('41) .20 .20
188 A10 2o yellow brn ('41) .20 .20
189 A10 3o dp orange ('41) .20 .20
190 A10 5o rose lilac ('41) .35 .20
191 A10 7o brt green ('41) .40 .20
192 A16 10o brt green .35 .20
Complete booklet, 2 panes of 6 #192 50.00
193 A10 12o brt vio .80 1.10
194 A16 14o dp org ('41) 1.00 2.00
195 A16 15o olive bister .50 .20
196 A16 20o red .45 .20
Complete booklet, 2 panes of 6 #196 60.00
Complete booklet, pane of 6 ea of #190, 192, 196 150.00
Complete booklet, pane of 10 ea of #190, 192, 196 100.00
197 A16 25o dk org brn 1.25 .20
197A A16 25o scarlet ('46) .40 .20
Complete booklet, pane of 10 ea of #190, 192, 197A 100.00
Complete booklet, pane of 10 ea of #192, 195, 197A 80.00
198 A16 30o brt ultra ('41) 1.25 .20
198A A16 30o gray ('49) 5.75 .20
199 A16 35o brt vio ('41) 1.50 .20
200 A16 40o dk sl grn ('41) 1.00 .20
200A A16 40o dp ultra ('46) 1.50 .20
201 A16 50o dp claret ('41) 1.00 .20
201A A16 55o dp org ('46) 15.00 .20
202 A16 60o Prus bl ('41) 1.00 .20
202A A16 80o dk org brn ('46) 12.50 .20
Nos. 187-202A (21) 46.60 6.90
Set, never hinged 125.00

Lion Rampant — A28

1940 **Unwmk.** **Photo.** ***Perf. 13x13½***

203 A28 1k brt green 1.00 .20
204 A28 1½k deep blue 1.50 .30
205 A28 2k bright red 2.50 1.25
206 A28 5k dull purple 5.00 *5.50*
Nos. 203-206 (4) 10.00 7.25
Set, never hinged 27.50

For overprints see Nos. 235-238.

Stamps of 1937-41, Types A10, A16, A28, Overprinted "V" in Black

1941 **Wmk. 160** ***Perf. 13x13½***

207 A10 1o olive .40 *7.00*
208 A10 2o yellow brn .40 *8.50*
209 A10 3o orange 2.00 *16.00*
210 A10 5o rose lilac .50 *1.40*
211 A10 7o brt green .50 *3.50*
212 A16 10o brt green 7.50 *40.00*
213 A16 14o dp orange 1.00 *16.00*
214 A16 15o olive bis .30 *1.00*
215 A16 30o ultra 2.25 *3.50*
216 A16 35o brt violet 1.00 *.80*
217 A16 40o dk slate grn 7.50 *11.00*
218 A16 50o dp claret 250.00 *600.00*
Never hinged 425.00
219 A16 60o Prus blue 1.00 *1.75*
Nos. 207-217,219 (12) 24.35 *110.45*
Set, never hinged 50.00

The "V" overprint exists on Nos. 170-171, but these were not regularly issued.

Unwmk.

220 A10 1o olive .35 *4.25*
221 A10 2o yellow brn .35 *6.00*
222 A10 3o deep orange .35 *4.75*
223 A10 5o rose lilac .35 .40
224 A10 7o brt green .95 *7.00*
225 A16 10o brt green .35 .25
226 A10 12o brt violet 1.10 *15.00*
227 A16 15o olive bis 1.90 *15.00*
228 A16 20o red .35 .20
a. Inverted overprint 925.00 1,500.
Never hinged 1,300.
229 A16 25o dk orange brn .40 .40
230 A16 30o brt ultra 1.50 *3.00*
231 A16 35o brt violet 1.00 .70
232 A16 40o dk slate grn .70 .55
233 A16 50o dp claret .80 *2.25*
234 A16 60o Prus blue 1.90 1.25
235 A28 1k brt green 1.25 .50
236 A28 1½k dp blue 3.75 *12.00*
237 A28 2k bright red 10.50 *50.00*
238 A28 5k dull purple 19.00 *100.00*

Coil Stamp

Lion Rampant with "V" — A29

239 A29 10o brt green 1.25 *10.00*
Nos. 220-239 (20) 48.10 *233.50*
Set, never hinged 85.00

No. 239 has a white "V" incorporated into design, rather than an overprint.

Dream of Queen Ragnhild A30

Snorri Sturluson A32

Einar Tambarskjelve in Fight at Svolder — A31

Designs: 30o, King Olaf sailing in wedding procession to Landmerket. 50o, Syipdag's sons and followers going to Hall of Seven Kings. 60o, Before Battle of Stiklestad.

1941 ***Perf. 13½x13, 13x13½***

240 A30 10o bright green .35 .40
241 A31 15o olive brown .40 .55
242 A32 20o dark red .35 .20
243 A31 30o blue 1.50 *2.25*
244 A31 50o dull violet 1.10 *2.00*
245 A31 60o Prus blue 2.00 2.00
Nos. 240-245 (6) 5.70 7.40
Set, never hinged 12.00

700th anniversary of the death of Snorri Sturluson, writer and historian.

University of Oslo — A36

1941, Sept. 2 ***Perf. 13x13½***

246 A36 1k dk olive grn 40.00 65.00
Never hinged 65.00

Centenary of cornerstone laying of University of Oslo building.

Richard (Rikard) Nordraak (1842-66), Composer — A37

"Broad Sails Go over the North Sea" A38

View of Coast and Lines of National Anthem A39

1942, June 12 *Perf. 13*

247 A37 10o dp green 1.50 *4.00*
248 A38 15o dp brown 1.50 *2.50*
249 A37 20o rose red 1.50 *3.00*
250 A39 30o sapphire 1.50 *2.50*
Nos. 247-250 (4) 6.00 12.00
Set, never hinged 14.00

Johan Herman Wessel (1742-1785), Author — A40

1942, Oct. 6

251 A40 15o dull brown .30 .50
252 A40 20o henna .30 .50
Set, never hinged .90

Designs of 1942 and 1855 Stamps of Norway A41

1942, Oct. 12

253 A41 20o henna .25 1.00
254 A41 30o sapphire .35 2.25
Set, never hinged .90

European Postal Congress at Vienna, October, 1942.

Edvard Grieg (1843-1907), Composer A42

Destroyer Sleipner A43

1943, June 15

255 A42 10o deep green .25 *.50*
256 A42 20o henna .25 *.50*
257 A42 40o grnsh black .25 *.50*
258 A42 60o dk grnsh blue .25 *.50*
Nos. 255-258 (4) 1.00 2.00
Set, never hinged 2.00

1943-45 Unwmk. Engr. *Perf. 12½*

5o, 10o, "Sleipner." 7o, 30o, Convoy under midnight sun. 15o, Plane and pilot. 20o, "We will win." 40o, Ski troops. 60o, King Haakon VII.

259 A43 5o rose vio ('45) .20 .20
260 A43 7o grnsh blk ('45) .20 .45
261 A43 10o dk blue grn .20 .20
262 A43 15o dk olive grn .60 *1.50*
263 A43 20o rose red .20 .20
264 A43 30o dp ultra .65 1.00

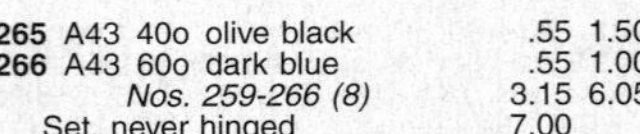
265 A43 40o olive black .55 1.50
266 A43 60o dark blue .55 1.00
Nos. 259-266 (8) 3.15 6.05
Set, never hinged 7.00

Nos. 261-266 were used for correspondence carried on Norwegian ships until after the liberation of Norway, when they became regular postage stamps.

Nos. 261-266 exist with overprint "London 17-5-43" and serial number. Value for set, unused, $1,000; canceled $1,200.

Gran's Plane and Map of His North Sea Flight Route A49

1944, July 30 *Perf. 13*

267 A49 40o dk grnsh blue .40 .20
Never hinged .60

20th anniv. of the 1st flight over the North Sea, made by Tryggve Gran on July 30, 1914.
For used value see note following No. 180.

New National Arms of 1943 — A50

1945, Feb. 15 Typo. *Perf. 13*

268 A50 1½k dark blue .85 .60
Never hinged 2.50

Henrik Wergeland A51

Lion Rampant A52

1945, July 12 **Photo.**

269 A51 10o dk olive green .30 .30
270 A51 15o dark brown .85 1.00
271 A51 20o dark red .25 .30
Nos. 269-271 (3) 1.40 1.60
Set, never hinged 2.00

Wergeland, poet & playwright, death cent.

1945, Dec. 19

272 A52 10o dk olive green .35 .30
273 A52 20o red .35 .30
Set, never hinged 2.00

Norwegian Folklore Museum, 50th anniv.

Pilot and Mechanic — A53

King Haakon VII — A54

1946, Mar. 22 Engr. *Perf. 12*

274 A53 15o brown rose .40 1.00
Never hinged .90

Issued in honor of Little Norway, training center in Canada for Norwegian pilots.

Catalogue values for unused stamps in this section, from this point to the end of the section, are for Never Hinged items.

1946, June 7 Photo. *Perf. 13*

275 A54 1k bright green 2.00 .20
276 A54 1½k Prus blue 6.00 .20
277 A54 2k henna brown 50.00 .20
278 A54 5k violet 35.00 .40
Nos. 275-278 (4) 93.00 1.00

Hannibal Sehested — A55

Designs: 10o, Letter carrier, 1700. 15o, Adm. Peter W. Tordenskjold. 25o, Christian Magnus Falsen. 30o, Cleng Peerson and "Restaurationen." 40o, Post ship "Constitution." 45o, First Norwegian locomotive. 50o, Sven Foyn and whaler. 55o, Fridtjof Nansen and Roald Amundsen. 60o, Coronation of King Haakon VII and Queen Maud, 1906. 80o, Return of King Haakon, June 7, 1945.

1947, Apr. 15 Photo. *Perf. 13*

279 A55 5o red lilac .40 .20
280 A55 10o green .65 .20
281 A55 15o brown 1.00 .20
282 A55 25o orange red .65 .20
283 A55 30o gray 1.00 .20
284 A55 40o blue 3.00 .20
285 A55 45o violet 2.25 .50
286 A55 50o orange brn 3.75 .20
287 A55 55o orange 6.00 .25
288 A55 60o slate gray 5.00 1.50
289 A55 80o dk brown 5.00 .25
Nos. 279-289 (11) 28.70 3.90

Establishment of the Norwegian Post Office, 300th anniv.

Petter Dass — A66

King Haakon VII — A67

1947, July 1 **Unwmk.**

290 A66 25o bright red 2.00 1.00

300th birth anniv. of Petter Dass, poet.

1947, Aug. 2

291 A67 25o orange red .90 .75

75th birthday of King Haakon.

Axel Heiberg — A68

Alexander L. Kielland — A69

1948, June 15

292 A68 25o deep carmine 1.25 .45
293 A68 80o dp red brown 2.25 .30

50th anniv. of the Norwegian Society of Forestry; birth cent. of Axel Heiberg, its founder.

1949, May 9

295 A69 25o rose brown 1.75 .50
296 A69 40o greenish blue 1.75 .50
297 A69 80o orange brown 2.25 .65
Nos. 295-297 (3) 5.75 1.65

Birth cent. of Alexander L. Kielland, author.

Symbols of UPU Members A70

Stylized Pigeons and Globe A71

Symbolical of the UPU A72

1949, Oct. 9 *Perf. 13*

299 A70 10o dk green & blk .75 .60
300 A71 25o scarlet .60 .25
301 A72 40o dull blue .60 .50
Nos. 299-301 (3) 1.95 1.35

75th anniv. of the formation of the UPU.

Nos. 196 and 200A Surcharged with New Value and Bar in Black

1949 *Perf. 13x13½*

302 A16 25o on 20o red .75 .20
303 A16 45o on 40o dp ultra 3.00 .65

King Harald Haardraade and Oslo City Hall — A73

1950, May 15 Photo. *Perf. 13*

304 A73 15o green .90 1.00
305 A73 25o red .80 .35
306 A73 45o ultramarine .80 .75
Nos. 304-306 (3) 2.50 2.10

900th anniversary of Oslo.

Redrawn Post Horn Type of 1937

1950-51 Photo. *Perf. 13x13½*

Size: 17x21mm

307 A10 10o grnsh gray .50 .20
Complete booklet, pane of 10 #307 150.00
308 A10 15o dark green 2.00 .40
309 A10 20o chnt brn ('51) 5.00 2.25
Nos. 307-309 (3) 7.50 2.85

King Haakon VII — A74

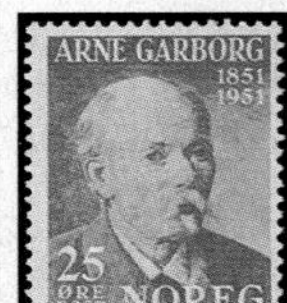

Arne Garborg — A75

1950-51 Photo. *Perf. 13x13½*

310 A74 25o dk red ('50) .90 .20
Complete booklet, pane of 10 ea of #307, 308, 310 80.00
311 A74 30o gray 9.00 .60
312 A74 35o red brn 19.00 .20
313 A74 45o brt blue 2.00 2.00
314 A74 50o olive brn 3.50 .20
315 A74 55o orange 2.00 1.10
316 A74 60o gray blue 13.50 .20
317 A74 80o chnt brn 3.00 .40
Nos. 310-317 (8) 52.90 4.90

See Nos. 322-324, 345-352. For surcharge see No. 321.

1951, Jan. 25 *Perf. 13*

318 A75 25o red .65 .25
319 A75 45o dull blue 2.25 2.25
320 A75 80o brown 3.50 1.25
Nos. 318-320 (3) 6.40 3.75

Birth cent. of Arne Garborg, poet.

No. 310 Surcharged with New Value in Black

1951 *Perf. 13x13½*

321 A74 30o on 25o dk red .75 .30

Haakon Type of 1950-51

1951-52 **Photo.**

322 A74 25o gray 20.00 .20
323 A74 30o dk red ('52) .90 .20
Complete booklet, pane of 10 ea of #307, 308, 323 175.00
Complete booklet, pane of 10 ea of #307, 325, 323 100.00
324 A74 55o blue ('52) 1.75 .50
Nos. 322-324 (3) 22.65 .90

Redrawn Post Horn Type of 1937

1952, June 3 ***Perf. 13x13½***
325 A10 15o org brn .70 .20
326 A10 20o green .70 .20

King Haakon VII A76

Medieval Sculpture, Nidaros Cathedral A77

1952, Aug. 3 **Unwmk.** ***Perf. 13***
327 A76 30o red .50 .20
328 A76 55o deep blue 1.10 1.00

80th birthday of King Haakon VII.

No. 308 Surcharged with New Value

1952, Nov. 18 ***Perf. 13x13½***
329 A10 20o on 15o dk grn .60 .20

1953, July 15 ***Perf. 13***
330 A77 30o henna brn 1.00 .60

800th anniv. of the creation of the Norwegian Archbishopric of Nidaros.

Train of 1854 and Horse-drawn Sled — A78

Carsten T. Nielsen — A79

Designs: 30o, Diesel train. 55o, Engineer.

1954, Apr. 30 **Photo.**
331 A78 20o green .85 .60
332 A78 30o red .85 .20
333 A78 55o ultra 2.00 1.25
Nos. 331-333 (3) 3.70 2.05

Inauguration of the first Norwegian railway, cent.

1954, Dec. 10

Designs: 30o, Government radio towers. 55o, Lineman and telegraph poles in snow.

334 A79 20o ol grn & blk .40 .60
335 A79 30o brt red .40 .20
336 A79 55o blue 1.50 1.25
Nos. 334-336 (3) 2.30 2.05

Centenary (in 1955) of the inauguration of the first Norwegian public telegraph line.

Norway No. 1 — A80

Stamp Reproductions: 30o, Post horn type A5. 55o, Lion type A13.

1955, Jan. 3 ***Perf. 13***
337 A80 20o dp grn & gray bl .45 .30
338 A80 30o red & carmine .20 .20
339 A80 55o gray bl & dp bl .95 .50
Nos. 337-339 (3) 1.60 1.00

Centenary of Norway's first postage stamp.

Nos. 337-339 Overprinted in Black

1955, June 4
340 A80 20o dp grn & gray bl 15.00 *18.00*
341 A80 30o red & carmine 15.00 *18.00*
342 A80 55o gray bl & dp bl 15.00 *18.00*
Nos. 340-342 (3) 45.00 54.00

Norway Philatelic Exhibition, Oslo, 1955. Sold at exhibition post office for face value plus 1kr admission fee.

King Haakon VII and Queen Maud in Coronation Robes — A81

1955, Nov. 25 **Photo.** ***Perf. 13***
343 A81 30o rose red .40 .20
344 A81 55o ultra .60 .50

Haakon's 50th anniv. as King of Norway.

Haakon Type of 1950-51

1955-57 **Unwmk.** ***Perf. 13x13½***
345 A74 25o dk grn ('56) 1.50 .20
346 A74 35o brn red ('56) 6.00 .20
Complete booklet, pane of 10 ea of #307, 325, 346 100.00
347 A74 40o pale pur 2.25 .20
Complete booklet, pane of 10 ea of #307, 325, 347 70.00
348 A74 50o bister ('57) 5.00 .20
349 A74 65o ultra ('56) 1.50 .40
350 A74 70o brn ol ('56) 20.00 .20
351 A74 75o mar ('57) 3.00 .20
352 A74 90o dp org 1.75 .20
Nos. 345-352 (8) 41.00 1.80

Northern Countries Issue

Whooper Swans — A81a

1956, Oct. 30 **Engr.** ***Perf. 12½***
353 A81a 35o rose red .95 .60
354 A81a 65o ultra .95 .85

Close bonds connecting the northern countries: Denmark, Finland, Iceland, Norway and Sweden.

Jan Mayen Island A82

Map of Spitsbergen A83

King Haakon VII A84

Design: 65o, Map of South Pole with Queen Maud Land.

Perf. 12½x13, 13x12½

1957, July 1 **Photo.** **Unwmk.**
355 A82 25o slate green .65 .40
356 A83 35o dk red & gray .65 .20
357 A83 65o dk grn & bl .65 .50
Nos. 355-357 (3) 1.95 1.10

Intl. Geophysical Year, 1957-58.

1957, Aug. 2 ***Perf. 13***
358 A84 35o dark red .60 .30
359 A84 65o ultra .85 .85

85th birthday of King Haakon VII.

A85

King Olav V — A86

1958-60 **Photo.** ***Perf. 13x13½***
360 A85 25o emerald 1.50 .20
Complete booklet, pane of 4 of #360 100.00
361 A85 30o purple ('59) 2.00 .20
361A A85 35o brown car ('60) 1.25 .20
362 A85 40o dark red 1.25 .20
Complete booklet, pane of 10 of ea of #307, 325, 362 100.00
363 A85 45o scarlet 1.90 .20
Complete booklet, pane of 10 of #363 70.00
Complete booklet, pane of 10 ea of #307, 325, 363 100.00
364 A85 50o bister ('59) 8.50 .20
365 A85 55o dk gray ('59) 2.25 1.00
366 A85 65o blue 3.25 .50
367 A85 80o org brn ('60) 12.50 .50
368 A85 85o olive brn ('59) 2.25 .20
369 A85 90o orange ('59) 1.90 .20
Nos. 360-369 (11) 38.55 3.60

See Nos. 408-412.

1959, Jan. 12
370 A86 1k green 1.50 .20
371 A86 1.50k dark blue 3.00 .20
372 A86 2k crimson 4.00 .20
373 A86 5k lilac 55.00 .20
374 A86 10k dp orange 8.50 .20
Nos. 370-374 (5) 72.00 1.00

See Phosphorescence note following No. 430.

Asbjörn Kloster — A87

Agricultural Society Medal — A88

1959, Feb. 2
375 A87 45o violet brown .70 .25

Centenary of the founding of the Norwegian Temperance Movement; Asbjörn Kloster, its founder.

1959, May 26
376 A88 45o red & ocher .80 .25
377 A88 90o blue & gray 2.25 2.25

150th anniversary of the Royal Agricultural Society of Norway.

Sower — A89

Society Seal — A90

Design: 90o, Grain, vert.

1959, Oct. 1 **Photo.** ***Perf. 13***
378 A89 45o ocher & blk .80 .25
379 A89 90o blue & blk 1.50 1.50

Agricultural College of Norway, cent.

1960, Feb. 26 **Unwmk.**
380 A90 45o carmine .75 .25
381 A90 90o dark blue 2.00 1.40

Bicentenary of the Royal Norwegian Society of Sciences, Trondheim.

Viking Ship A91

25o, Caravel & fish. 45o, Sailing ship & nautical knot. 55o, Freighter & oil derricks. 90o, Passenger ship & Statue of Liberty.

1960, Aug. 27 ***Perf. 12½x13***
382 A91 20o gray & blk 2.50 1.50
383 A91 25o yel grn & blk 1.25 1.25
384 A91 45o ver & blk 1.25 .40
385 A91 55o ocher & blk 3.25 3.00
386 A91 90o Prus bl & blk 4.00 2.00
Nos. 382-386 (5) 12.25 8.15

Norwegian shipping industry.

Common Design Types pictured following the introduction.

Europa Issue, 1960
Common Design Type

1960, Sept. 19 ***Perf. 13***
Size: 27x21mm
387 CD3 90o blue 1.25 1.25

DC-8 Airliner — A91a

Javelin Thrower — A92

1961, Feb. 24 **Photo.** ***Perf. 13***
388 A91a 90o dark blue 1.00 .60

Scandinavian Airlines System, SAS, 10th anniv.

1961, Mar. 15
389 A92 20o shown .80 .50
390 A92 25o Skater .80 .50
391 A92 45o Ski jumper .80 .20
392 A92 90o Sailboat 1.40 1.40
Nos. 389-392 (4) 3.80 2.60

Norwegian Sports Federation centenary.

Haakonshallen — A93

1961, May 25 ***Perf. 12½x13***
393 A93 45o maroon & gray .70 .20
394 A93 1k gray green & gray 1.10 .30

700th anniv. of Haakonshallen, castle in Bergen.

Domus Media, Oslo University A94

1961, Sept. 2 **Photo.** ***Perf. 12½x13***
395 A94 45o dark red .60 .20
396 A94 1.50k Prus blue 1.25 .30

150th anniversary of Oslo University.

Fridtjof Nansen — A95

1961, Oct. 10 ***Perf. 13***

397 A95 45o orange red & gray 1.00 .40
398 A95 90o chlky blue & gray 1.50 1.50

Birth centenary of Fridtjof Nansen, explorer.

Roald Amundsen A96

Design: 90o, Explorers and tent at Pole.

1961, Nov. 10 **Unwmk.** ***Perf. 13***

399 A96 45o dl red brn & gray 1.50 .50
400 A96 90o dk & lt blue 2.25 1.50

50th anniversary of Roald Amundsen's arrival at the South Pole.

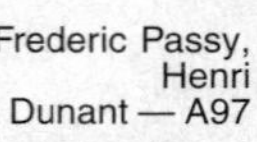

Frederic Passy, Henri Dunant — A97

Vilhelm Bjerknes — A98

1961, Dec. 9 **Photo.**

401 A97 45o henna brown .50 .25
402 A97 1k yellow green 1.50 .50

Winners of the first Nobel Peace prize. Frederic Passy, a founder of the Interparliamentary Union, and Henri Dunant, founder of the International Red Cross.

1962, Mar. 14 ***Perf. 13***

403 A98 45o dk red & gray .50 .25
404 A98 1.50k dk blue & gray 1.25 .35

Vilhelm Bjerknes (1862-1951), physicist, mathematician, meteorologist, etc.

German Rumpler Taube over Oslo Fjord A99

1962, June 1 **Photo.**

405 A99 1.50k dl bl & blk 4.00 .70

50th anniversary of Norwegian aviation.

Fir Branch and Cone — A100

1962, June 15

406 A100 45o salmon & blk .75 .45
407 A100 1k pale grn & blk 6.75 .30

Olav Type of 1958-60

1962 **Unwmk.** ***Perf. 13x13½***

408 A85 25o slate grn 1.25 .20
Complete booklet, pane of 4 of #408 100.00
Complete booklet, pane of 10 ea of #190, 307, 408 30.00
409 A85 35o emerald 5.00 .20
410 A85 40o gray 4.25 2.00
411 A85 50o scarlet 9.50 .20
Complete booklet, pane of 10 of #411 200.00
412 A85 60o violet 7.50 .75
Nos. 408-412 (5) 27.50 3.35

Europa Issue, 1962

Common Design Type

1962, Sept. 17 **Photo.** ***Perf. 13***

Size: 37x21mm

414 CD5 50o dp rose & maroon .50 .40
415 CD5 90o blue & dk blue 1.50 1.10

Post Horn Type of 1893-1908 Redrawn and

Rock Carvings A101

Boatswain's Knot A102

Designs: 30o, 55o, 85o, Rye and fish. 65o, 80o, Stave church and northern lights.

1962-63 **Engr.** ***Perf. 13x13½***

416 A10 5o rose cl .20 .20
417 A10 10o slate .20 .20
Complete booklet, pane of 10 of #417 20.00
418 A10 15o orange brn .30 .20
419 A10 20o green .20 .20
Complete booklet, pane of 4 ea of #416, 419 15.00
420 A101 25o gray grn ('63) 1.10 .20
Complete booklet, pane of 4 of #420 16.00
Complete booklet, pane of 10 ea of #416, 417, 420 15.00
421 A101 30o olive brn ('63) 4.50 4.50
422 A102 35o brt green ('63) .30 .20
423 A101 40o lake ('63) 3.00 .20
424 A102 50o vermilion 4.75 .20
Complete booklet, pane of 10 of #424 100.00
425 A101 55o orange brn ('63) .50 .55
426 A102 60o dk grnsh gray ('63) 11.50 .20
427 A102 65o dk blue ('63) 3.50 .20
Complete booklet, pane of 10 of #427 100.00
428 A102 80o rose lake ('63) 2.25 2.25
429 A101 85o sepia ('63) .50 .25
430 A101 90o blue ('63) .30 .20
Nos. 416-430 (15) 33.10 9.75

Nos. 416-419 have been redrawn and are similar to 1910-29 issue, with vertical lines inside oval and horizontal lines in oval frame. See Nos. 462-470, 608-615.

> Phosphorescence
> Nos. 370-372, 416-419, 423, 425, 428, 430, 462, 466, O65-O68, O75, O78-O82, O83-O84 and O88 have been issued on both ordinary and phosphorescent paper.

Camilla Collett (1813-1895), Author — A103

1963, Jan. 23 **Photo.** ***Perf. 13***

431 A103 50o red brn & tan .50 .20
432 A103 90o slate & gray 1.50 1.10

Girl in Boat Loaded with Grain — A104

Still Life A105

1963, Mar. 21 **Unwmk.** ***Perf. 13***

433 A104 25o yellow brown .45 .25
434 A104 35o dark green .65 .65
435 A105 50o dark red .65 .35
436 A105 90o dark blue 1.50 1.10
Nos. 433-436 (4) 3.25 2.35

FAO "Freedom from Hunger" campaign.

River Boat A106

Design: 90o, Northern sailboat.

1963, May 20 **Unwmk.** ***Perf. 13***

437 A106 50o brown red 1.50 .70
438 A106 90o blue 2.50 2.50

Tercentenary of regular postal service between Northern and Southern Norway.

Ivar Aasen — A107

1963, Aug. 5 **Photo.**

439 A107 50o dk red & gray .75 .30
440 A107 90o dk blue & gray 1.50 1.25

150th birth anniv. of Ivar Aasen, poet and philologist.

Europa Issue, 1963

Common Design Type

1963, Sept. 14 **Unwmk.** ***Perf. 13***

Size: 27x21½mm

441 CD6 50o dull rose & org .75 .40
442 CD6 90o blue & yel grn 3.75 2.00

Patterned Fabric A108

1963, Sept. 24

443 A108 25o olive & ol grn .65 .55
444 A108 35o Prus bl & dk bl 1.00 .85
445 A108 50o dk car rose & plum .85 .40
Nos. 443-445 (3) 2.50 1.80

Norwegian textile industry, 150th anniv.

"Loneliness" A109

Eilert Sundt — A110

Paintings by Edvard Munch (1863-1944): 25o, Self-portrait, vert. 35o, "Fertility." 90o, "Girls on Bridge," vert.

1963, Dec. 12 **Litho.** ***Perf. 13***

446 A109 25o black .35 .25
447 A109 35o dark green .45 .35
448 A109 50o deep claret .40 .30
449 A109 90o gray bl & dk bl 1.25 1.00
Nos. 446-449 (4) 2.45 1.90

1964, Feb. 17 **Photo.**

50o, Beehive, Workers' Society emblem.

450 A110 25o dark green .50 .45
451 A110 50o dk red brown .75 .25

Centenary of the Oslo Workers' Society.

Cato M. Guldberg and Peter Waage by Stinius Fredriksen A111

1964, Mar. 11 **Unwmk.** ***Perf. 13***

452 A111 35o olive green .90 .45
453 A111 55o bister 2.00 1.75

Centenary of the presentation of the Law of Mass Action (chemistry) by Professors Cato M. Guldberg and Peter Waage in the Oslo Scientific Society.

Eidsvoll Building A112

Design: 90o, Storting (Parliament House).

1964, May 11 **Photo.**

454 A112 50o hn brn & blk .75 .30
455 A112 90o Prus bl & dk bl 1.75 1.10

150th anniv. of Norway's constitution.

Church and Ships in Harbor A113

1964, Aug. 17 ***Perf. 13***

456 A113 25o dk sl grn & buff .50 .40
457 A113 90o dk bl & gray 2.00 2.00

Centenary of the Norwegian Seamen's Mission, which operates 32 stations around the world.

Europa Issue, 1964

Common Design Type

1964, Sept. 14 **Photo.** ***Perf. 13***

458 CD7 90o dark blue 4.00 4.00

Herman Anker and Olaus Arvesen A114

1964, Oct. 31 **Litho.** **Unwmk.**

459 A114 50o rose .65 .30
460 A114 90o blue 2.75 1.90

Centenary of the founding of Norwegian schools of higher education (Folk High Schools).

Types of Regular Issue, 1962-63

Designs: 30o, 45o, Rye and fish. 40o, 100o, Rock carvings. 50o, 60o, 65o, 70o, Boatswain's knot.

Two types of 60o:
I — Four twists across bottom of knot.
II — Five twists.

1964-70 **Engr.** ***Perf. 13x13½***

462 A101 30o dull green .80 .20
463 A101 40o lt bl grn ('68) .50 .20
464 A101 45o lt yel grn ('68) 1.10 .55
465 A102 50o indigo ('68) .50 .20
466 A102 60o brick red, II ('75) 2.50 .30
a. Type I 2.75 .30
Complete booklet, pane of 10 of #466a 80.00
467 A102 65o lake ('68) .65 .20
Complete booklet, pane of 10 of #467 40.00
468 A102 70o brown ('70) .50 .20
Complete booklet, pane of 10 of #468 25.00
469 A101 100o violet bl ('70) 1.10 .20
Complete booklet, pane of 4 ea of #416, 419, 469 8.00
Nos. 462-469 (8) 7.65 2.05

See Phosphorescence note following #430.

Coil Stamp

1965 ***Perf. 13½ Horiz.***

470 A101 30o dull green 5.00 2.00

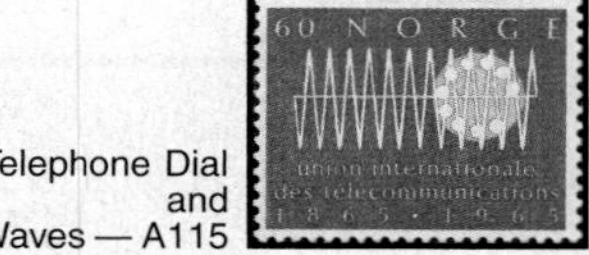

Telephone Dial and Waves — A115

Design: 90o, Television mast and antenna.

1965, Apr. 1 Engr. *Perf. 13*

471 A115 60o redsh brown .40 .40
472 A115 90o slate 1.60 1.50

ITU, centenary.

Mountain Scene A116

Design: 90o, Coastal view.

1965, June 4 Unwmk. *Perf. 13*

473 A116 60o brn blk & car .75 .35
474 A116 90o slate bl & car 4.00 3.25

Centenary of the Norwegian Red Cross.

Europa Issue, 1965

Common Design Type

1965, Sept. 25 Photo. *Perf. 13*

Size: 27x21mm

475 CD8 60o brick red 1.25 .60
476 CD8 90o blue 2.75 2.00

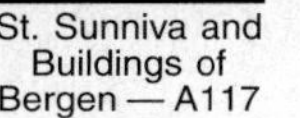

St. Sunniva and Buildings of Bergen — A117

Rondane Mountains by Harold Sohlberg — A118

90o, St. Sunniva and stylized view of Bergen.

1965, Oct. 25 *Perf. 13*

477 A117 30o dk green & blk .55 .30
478 A117 90o blue & blk, horiz. 1.60 1.25

Bicentenary of Bergen's philharmonic society "Harmonien."

1965, Nov. 29 Photo. *Perf. 13*

484 A118 1.50k dark blue 2.50 .20

Rock Carving of Skier, Rodoy Island, c. 2000 B.C. — A120

Designs: 55o, Ski jumper. 60o, Cross country skier. 90o, Holmenkollen ski jump, vert.

1966, Feb. 8 Engr. *Perf. 13*

486 A120 40o sepia 1.50 1.50
487 A120 55o dull green 1.50 1.40
488 A120 60o dull red 1.00 .50
489 A120 90o blue 2.00 2.00
Nos. 486-489 (4) 6.00 5.40

World Ski Championships, Oslo, Feb. 17-27.

Open Bible and Chrismon A121

1966, May 20 Photo. *Perf. 13*

490 A121 60o dull red .40 .20
491 A121 90o slate blue 1.40 1.00

150th anniv. of the Norwegian Bible Society.

Engine-turned Bank Note Design — A122

Bank of Norway — A123

1966, June 14 Engr.

492 A122 30o green .55 .55
493 A123 60o dk carmine rose .55 .20

150th anniversary of Bank of Norway.

Johan Sverdrup A124

Nitrogen Molecule in Test Tube A125

1966, July 30 Photo. *Perf. 13*

494 A124 30o green .50 .50
495 A124 60o rose lake .50 .50

Johan Sverdrup (1816-92), Prime Minister of Norway (1884-89).

Canceled to Order

The Norwegian philatelic agency began in 1966 to sell commemorative and definitive issues canceled to order at face value.

Europa Issue, 1966

Common Design Type

1966, Sept. 26 Engr. *Perf. 13*

Size: 21x27mm

496 CD9 60o dark carmine 1.75 .50
497 CD9 90o blue gray 3.25 1.75

1966, Oct. 29 Photo. *Perf. 13x12½*

Design: 55o, Wheat and laboratory bottle.

498 A125 40o bl & dp bl 1.25 .95
499 A125 55o red, org & lil rose 2.25 1.60

Centenary of the birth of Kristian Birkeland (1867-1917), and of Sam Eyde (1866-1940), who together developed the production of nitrates.

EFTA Emblem — A126

1967, Jan. 16 Engr. *Perf. 13*

500 A126 60o rose red .50 .20
501 A126 90o dark blue 2.25 2.25

European Free Trade Association. Tariffs were abolished Dec. 31, 1966, among EFTA members: Austria, Denmark, Finland, Great Britain, Norway, Portugal, Sweden, Switzerland.

Sabers, Owl and Oak Leaves A127

1967, Feb. 16 Engr. *Perf. 13*

502 A127 60o chocolate 1.00 .75
503 A127 90o black 3.00 2.00

Higher military training in Norway, 150th anniv.

Europa Issue, 1967

Common Design Type

1967, May 2 Photo. *Perf. 13*

Size: 21x27mm

504 CD10 60o magenta & plum 1.00 .50
505 CD10 90o bl & dk vio bl 3.75 2.25

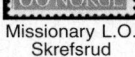

Johanne Dybwad, by Per Ung — A128

1967, Aug. 2 Photo. *Perf. 13*

506 A128 40o slate blue .55 .45
507 A128 60o dk carmine rose .55 .30

Johanne Dybwad (1867-1950), actress.

Missionary L.O. Skrefsrud A129

Ebenezer Church, Benagaria, Santal A130

1967, Sept. 26 Engr. *Perf. 13*

508 A129 60o red brown .55 .30
509 A130 90o blue gray 1.25 1.10

Norwegian Santal (India) mission, cent.

Mountaineers A131

Designs: 60o, Mountain view. 90o, Glitretind mountain peak.

1968, Jan. 22 Engr. *Perf. 13*

510 A131 40o sepia 1.25 1.00
511 A131 60o brown red .75 .30
512 A131 90o slate blue 1.25 1.10
Nos. 510-512 (3) 3.25 2.40

Centenary of the Norwegian Mountain Touring Association.

Two Smiths A132

1968, Mar. 30 Photo. *Perf. 12½x13*

513 A132 65o dk car rose & brn .45 .20
514 A132 90o blue & brown 1.50 1.10

Issued to honor Norwegian craftsmen.

A. O. Vinje — A133

Cross and Heart — A134

1968, May 21 Engr. *Perf. 13*

515 A133 50o sepia .55 .35
516 A133 65o maroon .50 .25

Aasmund Olafsson Vinje (1818-1870), poet, journalist and language reformer.

1968, Sept. 16 Photo.

517 A134 40o brt grn & brn red 3.25 2.75
518 A134 65o brn red & vio bl .45 .25

Centenary of the Norwegian Lutheran Home Mission Society.

Cathinka Guldberg — A135

1968, Oct. 31 Engr. *Perf. 13*

519 A135 50o bright blue .50 .35
520 A135 65o dull red .50 .20

Nursing profession; centenary of Deaconess House in Oslo. Cathinka Guldberg was a pioneer of Norwegian nursing and the first deaconess.

Klas P. Arnoldson and Fredrik Bajer — A136

1968, Dec. 10 Engr. *Perf. 13*

521 A136 65o red brown .50 .30
522 A136 90o dark blue 1.50 .80

60th anniv. of the awarding of the Nobel Peace prize to Klas P. Arnoldson (1844-1916), Swedish writer and statesman, and to Fredrik Bajer (1837-1922), Danish writer and statesman.

Nordic Cooperation Issue

Five Ancient Ships — A136a

1969, Feb. 28 Engr. *Perf. 13*

523 A136a 65o red .35 .30
524 A136a 90o blue 1.40 1.00

50th anniv. of the Nordic Society and centenary of postal cooperation among the northern countries. The design is taken from a coin found on the site of Birka, an ancient Swedish town.

See Demark Nos. 454-455, Finland No. 481, Iceland Nos. 404-405 and Sweden Nos. 808-810.

Ornament from Urnes Stave Church — A137

Traena Island A138

1969 Engr. *Perf. 13*

526 A137 1.15k sepia 1.25 .50
529 A138 3.50k bluish blk 1.75 .20

Issue dates: 1.15k, Jan. 23, 3.50k, June 18.

Plane, Train, Ship and Bus A139

Child Crossing Street
A140

1969, Mar. 24 Photo. *Perf. 13*
531 A139 50o green 1.00 1.00
532 A140 65o slate grn & dk red .40 .25

No. 531 for the centenary of the publication of "Rutebok of Norway" (Communications of Norway); No. 532 publicizes traffic safety.

Europa Issue, 1969
Common Design Type

1969, Apr. 28
Size: 37x21mm
533 CD12 65o dk red & gray 1.75 .35
534 CD12 90o chalky bl & gray 2.75 2.00

Johan Hjort — A141

King Olav V — A142

Design: 90o, different emblem.

1969, May 30 Engr. *Perf. 13*
535 A141 40o brn & bl .90 .60
536 A141 90o bl & grn 2.10 1.50

Zoologist and oceanographer (1869-1948).

1969-83 Engr. *Perf. 13*
537 A142 1k lt ol grn ('70) 1.25 .20
538 A142 1.50k dk blue ('70) .85 .20
539 A142 2k dk red ('70) .85 .20
540 A142 5k vio bl ('70) 2.50 .20
541 A142 10k org brn ('70) 5.00 .20
542 A142 20k brown 11.00 .20
543 A142 50k dk olive grn ('83) 18.50 .40
Nos. 537-543 (7) 39.95 1.60

Man, Woman and Child, by Vigeland
A143

65o, Mother and Child, by Gustav Vigeland.

1969, Sept. 8 Photo. *Perf. 13*
545 A143 65o car rose & blk .50 .35
546 A143 90o blue & black 1.25 .90

Gustav Vigeland (1869-1943), sculptor.

People
A144

1969, Oct. 10
547 A144 65o Punched card .50 .35
548 A144 90o shown 1.25 1.00

1st Norwegian census, 200th anniv.

Queen Maud
A145

Pulsatilla Vernalis
A146

1969, Nov. 26 Engr. *Perf. 13*
549 A145 65o dk carmine .80 .40
550 A145 90o violet blue 1.10 1.00

Queen Maud (1869-1938), wife of King Haakon VII.

1970, Apr. 10 Photo. *Perf. 13*

European Nature Conservation Year: 40o, Wolf. 70o, Voringsfossen (waterfall). 100o, White-tailed sea eagle, horiz.

551 A146 40o sep & pale bl 1.50 1.50
552 A146 60o lt brn & gray 2.50 2.50
553 A146 70o pale bl & brn 1.40 .60
554 A146 100o pale bl & brn 2.00 2.00
Nos. 551-554 (4) 7.40 6.60

"V" for Victory
A147

"Citizens"
A148

Design: 100o, Convoy, horiz.

Perf. 13x12½, 12½x13

1970, May 8 Photo.
555 A147 70o red & lilac 1.75 .45
556 A147 100o vio bl & brt grn 1.75 1.75

Norway's liberation from the Germans, 25th anniv.

1970, June 23 Engr. *Perf. 13*

Designs: 70o, "The City and the Mountains." 100o, "Ships."

557 A148 40o green 2.25 2.00
558 A148 70o rose claret 2.50 .35
559 A148 100o violet blue 2.00 2.00
Nos. 557-559 (3) 6.75 4.35

City of Bergen, 900th anniversary.

Olive Wreath and Hands Upholding Globe
A149

Georg Ossian Sars (1837-1927)
A150

1970, Sept. 15 Engr. *Perf. 13*
560 A149 70o dk car rose 2.75 .50
561 A149 100o steel blue 1.75 1.25

25th anniversary of the United Nations.

1970, Oct. 15 Engr. *Perf. 13*

Portraits: 50o, Hans Strom (1726-1797). 70o, Johan Ernst Gunnerus (1718-1773). 100o, Michael Sars (1805-1869).

562 A150 40o brown 1.50 1.50
563 A150 50o dull purple 1.25 1.00
564 A150 70o brown red 1.25 .35
565 A150 100o bright blue 1.50 1.50
Nos. 562-565 (4) 5.50 4.35

Issued to honor Norwegian zoologists.

Leapfrog — A151

1970, Nov. 17 Photo. *Perf. 13*
566 A151 50o Ball game .55 .40
567 A151 70o shown 1.50 .20

Central School of Gymnastics, Oslo, cent.

Seal of Tonsberg
A152

1971, Jan. 20 Photo. *Perf. 13*
568 A152 70o dark red .75 .30
569 A152 100o blue black 1.50 1.50

City of Tonsberg, 1,100th anniversary.

Parliament
A153

1971, Feb. 23
570 A153 70o red brn & lil .50 .30
571 A153 100o dk bl & sl grn 1.50 1.50

Centenary of annual sessions of Norwegian Parliament.

Hand, Heart and Eye
A154

1971, Mar. 26 Photo. *Perf. 13*
572 A154 50o emerald & blk .75 .75
573 A154 70o scarlet & blk .55 .30

Joint northern campaign for the benefit of refugees.

"Haugianerne" by Adolph Tiedemand — A155

1971, Apr. 27 Photo. *Perf. 13*
574 A155 60o dark gray .45 .45
575 A155 70o brown .45 .25

Hans Nielsen Hauge (1771-1824), church reformer.

Worshippers Coming to Church — A156

Design: 70o, Building first church, vert.

1971, May 21
576 A156 70o black & dk red .50 .35
577 A156 1k black & blue 2.00 2.00

900th anniversary of the Bishopric of Oslo.

Roald Amundsen, Antarctic Treaty Emblem
A157

The Farmer and the Woman — A158

1971, June 23 Engr. *Perf. 13*
578 A157 100o blue & org red 3.50 2.75

Antarctic Treaty pledging peaceful uses of and scientific cooperation in Antarctica, 10th anniv.

1971, Nov. 17 Photo. *Perf. 13*

Designs: 50o, The Preacher and the King, horiz. 70o, The Troll and the Girl. Illustrations for legends and folk tales by Erik Werenskiold.

579 A158 40o olive & blk 1.00 .35
580 A158 50o blue & blk 1.00 .25
581 A158 70o magenta & blk .85 .25
Nos. 579-581 (3) 2.85 .85

Engine Turning
A159

1972, Apr. 10 Photo. *Perf. 13*
582 A159 80o red & gold .80 .30
583 A159 1.20k ultra & gold 1.25 1.25

Norwegian Savings Bank sesquicentennial.

Norway #18 — A160

Dragon's Head, Oseberg Viking Ship — A161

Engr. & Photo.

1972, May 6 *Perf. 12*
584 A160 80o shown .50 .35
585 A160 1k Norway #17 .50 .40
a. Souvenir sheet of 2, #584-585 6.00 10.00

Centenary of the post horn stamps. No. 585a sold for 2.50k.

1972, June 7 Engr. *Perf. 13*

Ancient Artifacts: 50o, Horseman from Stone of Alstad. 60o, Horseman, wood carving, stave church, Hemsedal. 1.20k, Sword hilt, found at Lodingen.

586 A161 50o yellow grn .75 .55
587 A161 60o brown 1.25 1.25
588 A161 80o dull red 1.75 .45
589 A161 1.20k ultra 1.75 1.50
Nos. 586-589 (4) 5.50 3.75

1,100th anniversary of unification.

King Haakon VII (1872-1957)
A162

"Joy"
A163

1972, Aug. 3 Engr. *Perf. 13*
590 A162 80o brown orange 2.50 .35
591 A162 1.20k Prussian bl 1.50 1.50

1972, Aug. 15 Photo. *Perf. 13x13½*

Design: 1.20k, "Solidarity."

592 A163 80o brt magenta .75 .30
593 A163 1.20k Prussian blue 1.50 1.50

2nd Intl. Youth Stamp Exhib., INTERJUNEX 72, Kristiansand, Aug. 25-Sept. 3.

Same Overprinted "INTERJUNEX 72"

1972, Aug. 25

594 A163 80o brt magenta 3.00 3.50
595 A163 1.20k Prussian blue 3.00 3.50

Opening of INTERJUNEX 72. Sold at exhibition only together with 3k entrance ticket.

"Fram." — A164

"Little Man" — A165

Polar Exploration Ships: 60o, "Maud." 1.20k, "Gjoa."

1972, Sept. 20 ***Perf. 13½x13***

596 A164 60o olive & green 1.50 1.25
597 A164 80o red & black 3.00 .35
598 A164 1.20k blue & red brn 2.00 1.75
Nos. 596-598 (3) 6.50 3.35

1972, Nov. 15 Litho. ***Perf. 13½x13***

Illustrations for folk tales by Theodor Kittelsen (1857-1914): 60o, The Troll who wondered how old he was. 80o, The princess riding the polar bear.

599 A165 50o green & blk .75 .25
600 A165 60o blue & blk 1.00 1.00
601 A165 80o pink & blk .75 .25
Nos. 599-601 (3) 2.50 1.50

Dr. Armauer G. Hansen and Leprosy Bacillus Drawing — A166

Design: 1.40k, Dr. Hansen and leprosy bacillus, microscopic view.

1973, Feb. 28 Engr. ***Perf. 13x13½***

602 A166 1k henna brn & bl .75 .25
603 A166 1.40k dk bl & dp org 1.50 1.50

Centenary of the discovery of the Hansen bacillus, the cause of leprosy.

Europa Issue 1973

Common Design Type

1973, Apr. 30 Photo. ***Perf. 12½x13***

Size: 37x20mm

604 CD16 1k red, org & lil *2.50 .40*
605 CD16 1.40k dk grn, grn & bl *1.50 1.25*

Types of 1893 and 1962-63

Designs: 75o, 85o, Rye and fish. 80o, 140o, Stave church. 100o, 110o, 120o, 125o, Rock carvings.

1972-75 Engr. ***Perf. 13x13½***

606 A10 25o ultra ('74) .20 .20
Complete booklet, pane of 4 of #606 1.50
608 A101 75o green ('73) .25 .20
609 A102 80o red brown .25 .20
Complete booklet, pane of 10 of #609 50.00
610 A101 85o bister ('74) .25 .20
611 A101 100o red ('73) .65 .20
Complete booklet, pane of 10 of #611 30.00
612 A101 110o rose car ('74) .50 .20
613 A101 120o gray blue .40 .30
614 A101 125o red ('75) .50 .20
Complete booklet, pane of 10 of #614 18.00
615 A102 140o dk blue ('73) .60 .20
Nos. 606-615 (9) 3.60 1.90

Nordic Cooperation Issue

Nordic House, Reykjavik A167

1973, June 26 Engr. ***Perf. 12½***

617 A167 1k multi .85 .40
618 A167 1.40k multi 1.50 1.50

A century of postal cooperation among Denmark, Finland, Iceland, Norway and Sweden; Nordic Postal Conference, Reykjavik, Iceland.

King Olav V — A168

Jacob Aall — A169

1973, July 2 Engr. ***Perf. 13***

619 A168 1k car & org brn 1.50 .25
620 A168 1.40k blue & org brn 1.50 1.50

70th birthday of King Olav V.

1973, Aug. 22 Engr. ***Perf. 13***

621 A169 1k deep claret .75 .20
622 A169 1.40k dk blue gray 1.50 1.50

Jacob Aall (1773-1844), mill owner and industrial pioneer.

Blade Decoration A170

Viola Biflora A171

Handicraft from Lapland: 1k, Textile pattern. 1.40k, Decoration made of tin.

1973, Oct. 9 Photo. ***Perf. 13x12½***

623 A170 75o blk brn & buff .60 .60
624 A170 1k dp car & buff 1.00 .30
625 A170 1.40k blk & dl bl 1.25 1.25
Nos. 623-625 (3) 2.85 2.15

1973, Nov. 15 Litho. ***Perf. 13***

626 A171 65o shown .60 .50
627 A171 70o Veronica Fruticans .75 .75
628 A171 1k Phyllodoce corrulea .75 .25
Nos. 626-628 (3) 2.10 1.50

See Nos. 754-756, 770-771.

Surveyor in Northern Norway, 1907 — A172

1.40k, South Norway Mountains map, 1851.

1973, Dec. 14 Engr. ***Perf. 13***

629 A172 1k red orange .50 .25
630 A172 1.40k slate blue 1.50 1.50

Geographical Survey of Norway, bicent.

Lindesnes A173

Design: 1.40k, North Cape.

1974, Apr. 25 Photo. ***Perf. 13***

631 A173 1k olive 1.25 .50
632 A173 1.40k dark blue 3.00 3.00

Ferry in Hardanger Fjord, by A. Tidemand and H. Gude A174

Classical Norwegian paintings: 1.40k, Stugunoset from Filefjell, by Johan Christian Dahl.

1974, May 21 Litho. ***Perf. 13***

633 A174 1k multi .75 .25
634 A174 1.40k multi 1.50 1.25

Gulating Law Manuscript, 1325 A175

King Magnus VI Lagaböter A176

1974, June 21 Engr.

635 A175 1k red & brn .75 .25
636 A176 1.40k ultra & brn 1.50 1.50

700th anniv. of the National Code given by King Magnus VI Lagaböter (1238-80).

Saw Blade and Pines — A177

J.H.L. Vogt — A178

Design: 1k, Cog wheel and guard.

1974, Aug. 12 Photo. ***Perf. 13***

637 A177 85o grn, ol & dk grn 2.25 2.25
638 A177 1k org, plum & dk red 1.50 .40

Safe working conditions.

1974, Sept. 4 Engr. ***Perf. 13***

Geologists: 85o, V. M. Goldschmidt. 1k, Theodor Kjerulf. 1.40k, Waldemar C. Brogger.

639 A178 65o olive & red brn .30 .20
640 A178 85o mag & red brn 1.50 1.50
641 A178 1k org & red brn .75 .25
642 A178 1.40k blue & red brn 1.25 1.25
Nos. 639-642 (4) 3.80 3.20

"Man's Work," Famous Buildings A179

Design: 1.40k, "Men, our brethren," people of various races.

1974, Oct. 9 Photo. ***Perf. 13***

643 A179 1k green & brn .75 .25
644 A179 1.40k brn & grnsh bl 1.25 1.25

Centenary of Universal Postal Union.

Horseback Rider A180

Flowers A181

1974, Nov. 15 Litho. ***Perf. 13***

645 A180 85o multicolored .50 .35
646 A181 1k multicolored .50 .25

Norwegian folk art, rose paintings from furniture decorations.

Woman Skier, c. 1900 A182

1975, Jan. 15 Litho. ***Perf. 13***

647 A182 1k shown 1.00 .25
648 A182 1.40k Telemark turn 1.25 1.25

"Norway, homeland of skiing."

Women — A183

Nusfjord Fishing Harbor — A184

Design: Detail from wrought iron gates of Vigeland Park, Oslo.

1975, Mar. 7 Litho. ***Perf. 13***

649 A183 1.25k brt rose lil & dk bl .65 .20
650 A183 1.40k bl & dk bl 1.25 1.25

International Women's Year.

1975, Apr. 17 Litho. ***Perf. 13***

1.25k, Street in Stavanger. 1.40k, View of Roros.

651 A184 1k yellow green 1.00 .65
652 A184 1.25k dull red .75 .20
653 A184 1.40k blue 1.25 1.25
Nos. 651-653 (3) 3.00 2.10

European Architectural Heritage Year.

Norwegian Krone, 1875 — A185

Ole Jacob Broch — A186

1975, May 20 Engr. ***Perf. 13***

654 A185 1.25k dark carmine 1.00 .20
655 A186 1.40k blue 1.25 1.25

Centenary of Monetary Convention of Norway, Sweden and Denmark (1.25k); and of Intl. Meter Convention, Paris, 1875. Ole Jacob Broch (1818-1889) was first director of Intl. Bureau of Weights and Measures.

Scouting in Summer A187

Design: 1.40k, Scouting in winter (skiers).

1975, June 19 Litho. ***Perf. 13***

656 A187 1.25k multicolored 1.00 .35
657 A187 1.40k multicolored 1.25 1.25

Nordjamb 75, 14th Boy Scout Jamboree, Lillehammer, July 29-Aug. 7.

Sod Hut and Settlers
A188

Cleng Peerson and Letter from America, 1874
A189

1975, July 4

658	A188	1.25k red brown	.85	.20
659	A189	1.40k bluish blk	1.25	1.25

Sesquicentennial of Norwegian emigration to America.

Templet, Tempelfjord, Spitsbergen
A190

Miners Leaving Coal Pit — A191

Design: 1.40k, Polar bear.

1975, Aug. 14 **Engr.** ***Perf. 13***

660	A190	1k olive black	1.25	1.00
661	A191	1.25k maroon	1.00	.20
662	A191	1.40k Prus blue	2.50	2.00
		Nos. 660-662 (3)	4.75	3.20

50th anniversary of union of Spitsbergen (Svalbard) with Norway.

Microphone with Ear Phones — A192

Radio Tower and Houses — A193

Designs after children's drawings.

1975, Oct. 9 **Litho.** ***Perf. 13***

663	A192	1.25k multi	.60	.20
664	A193	1.40k multi	1.10	1.10

50 years of broadcasting in Norway.

Annunciation
A194

Nativity — A195

Painted vault of stave church of Al, 13th cent: 1k, Visitation. 1.40k, Adoration of the Kings.

1975, Nov. 14

665	A194	80o red & multi	.60	.25
666	A194	1k red & multi	.75	.40
667	A195	1.25k red & multi	.60	.20
668	A195	1.40k red & multi	1.00	1.00
		Nos. 665-668 (4)	2.95	1.85

Sigurd and Regin
A196

Halling, Hallingdal Dance
A197

1976, Jan. 20 **Engr.** ***Perf. 13***

669	A196	7.50k brown	6.50	.20

Norwegian folk tale, Sigurd the Dragon-killer. Design from portal of Hylestad stave church, 13th century.

1976, Feb. 25 **Litho.** ***Perf. 13***

Folk Dances: 1k, Springar, Hordaland region. 1.25k, Gangar, Setesdal.

670	A197	80o black & multi	1.00	.75
671	A197	1k black & multi	1.00	.75
672	A197	1.25k black & multi	.75	.20
		Nos. 670-672 (3)	2.75	1.70

Silver Sugar Shaker, Stavanger, c. 1770 — A198

1.40k, Goblet, Nostetangen glass, c. 1770.

1976, Mar. 25 **Engr.** ***Perf. 13***

673	A198	1.25k multicolored	.85	.40
674	A198	1.40k multicolored	1.00	1.00

Oslo Museum of Applied Art, centenary.

Ceramic Bowl Shaped Like Bishop's Mitre
A199

Europa: 1.40k, Plate and CEPT emblem. Both designs after faience works from Herrebo Potteries, c. 1760.

1976, May 3 **Litho.** ***Perf. 13***

675	A199	1.25k rose mag & brn	*1.00*	*.40*
676	A199	1.40k brt bl & vio bl	*1.75*	*.70*

The Pulpit, Lyse Fjord — A200

Gulleplet (Peak), Sogne Fjord — A201

Perf. 13 on 3 Sides

1976, May 20 **Litho.**

677	A200	1k multi	.60	.20
a.		Booklet pane of 10	6.50	
		Complete booklet, #677a	7.50	
678	A201	1.25k multi	.80	.20
a.		Booklet pane of 10	8.00	
		Complete booklet, #678a	10.00	

Nos. 677-678 issued only in booklets.

Graph Paper, Old and New Subjects — A202

Design: 2k, Graph of national product.

1976, July 1 **Engr.** ***Perf. 13***

679	A202	1.25k red brown	.50	.20
680	A202	2k dark blue	.80	.25

Central Bureau of Statistics, centenary.

Olav Duun on Dun Mountain
A203

1976, Sept. 10 **Engr.** ***Perf. 13***

681	A203	1.25k multi	.50	.20
682	A203	1.40k multi	1.00	1.00

Olav Duun (1876-1939), novelist.

"Birches" by Th. Fearnley (1802-1842)
A204

Design: 1.40k, "Gamle Furutraer" (trees), by L. Hertervig (1830-1902).

1976, Oct. 8 **Litho.** ***Perf. 13***

683	A204	1.25k multi	.65	.25
684	A204	1.40k multi	1.10	1.10

"April" — A205

"May" — A206

Baldishol Tapestry — A207

80o, 1k, Details from 13th cent. Baldishol tapestry, found in Baldishol stave church.

1976, Nov. 5 **Litho.** ***Perf. 13***

685	A205	80o multi	.25	.25
686	A206	1k multi	.45	.25
687	A207	1.25k multi	.60	.20
		Nos. 685-687 (3)	1.30	.70

Five Water Lilies — A208

Photo. & Engr.

1977, Feb. 2 ***Perf. 12½***

688	A208	1.25k multi	.75	.30
689	A208	1.40k multi	.75	.60

Nordic countries cooperation for protection of the environment and 25th Session of Nordic Council, Helsinki, Feb. 19.

Akershus Castle, Oslo — A209

Steinviksholm Fort, Asen Fjord — A210

Torungen Lighthouses, Arendal — A211

1977, Feb. 24 **Engr.** ***Perf. 13***

690	A209	1.25k red	.45	.20
		Complete booklet, horiz. pane of 8 of #690	8.00	
		Complete booklet, vert. pane of 8 of #690	6.00	
691	A210	1.30k olive brown	.50	.20
692	A211	1.80k blue	.65	.25
		Nos. 690-692 (3)	1.60	.65

See Nos. 715-724, 772-774.

Europa Issue

Hamnoy, Lofoten, Fishing Village — A212

Huldre Falls, Loen — A213

Perf. 13 on 3 Sides

1977, May 2 **Litho.**

693	A212	1.25k multi	1.75	.25
a.		Booklet pane of 10	17.50	
		Complete booklet, #693a	18.50	
694	A213	1.80k multi	1.50	1.00
a.		Booklet pane of 10	15.00	
		Complete booklet, #694a	16.00	

Nos. 693-694 issued only in booklets.

Norwegian Trees — A214

1977, June 1 **Engr.** ***Perf. 13***

695	A214	1k Spruce	.75	.30
696	A214	1.25k Fir	.75	.25
697	A214	1.80k Birch	1.10	1.00
		Nos. 695-697 (3)	2.60	1.55

"Constitutionen," Norway's 1st Steamship, at Arendal — A215

Designs: 1.25k, "Vesteraalen" off Bodo, 1893. 1.30k, "Kong Haakon," 1904 and "Dronningen," 1893, off Stavanger. 1.80k, "Nordstjernen" and "Harald Jari" at pier, 1970.

1977, June 22

698	A215	1k brown	.60	.20
699	A215	1.25k red	1.00	.20
700	A215	1.30k green	1.50	1.40
701	A215	1.80k blue	1.50	1.25
		Nos. 698-701 (4)	4.60	3.05

Norwegian ships serving coastal routes.

Fishermen and Boats — A216

Fish and Fishhooks
A217

1977, Sept. 22 **Engr.** ***Perf. 13***

702	A216	1.25k buff, lt brn & dk brn	1.00	.20
703	A217	1.80k lt bl, bl & dk bl	1.25	1.10

Men, by Halfdan Egedius A218

Landscape, by August Cappelen A219

1977, Oct. 7 **Litho.** ***Perf. 13***
704 A218 1.25k multi .60 .25
705 A219 1.80k multi 1.10 1.10

Norwegian classical painting.

David with the Bells — A220

Christmas: 1k, Singing Friars. 1.25k, Virgin and Child, horiz. Designs from Bible of Bishop Aslak Bolt, 13th century.

1977, Nov. 10 **Litho.** ***Perf. 13***

Size: 21x27mm

706 A220 80o multi .25 .25
707 A220 1k multi .50 .20

Size: 34x27mm

708 A220 1.25k multi .50 .25
Nos. 706-708 (3) 1.25 .70

Post Horn Type of 1893 and Scenic Types of 1977

Designs: 1k, Austrat Manor, 1650. 1.10k, Trondenes Chruch, early 13th Cent. 1.40k, Ruins of Hamar Cathedral, 12th Cent. 1.75k, Seamen's Hall, Stavern, 1926, vert. 2k, Tofte Estate, Dovre, 16-17th cent., vert. 2.25k, Oscarhall, Oslofijord, 1847, vert. 2.50k, Log house, Breiland, 1785. 2.75k, Damsgard Building, Lakesvag, 1770. 3k, Selje Monastery, 11th cent. 3.50k, Lighthouse, Lindesnes, 1655.

Perf. 13x13½, 13½x13

1978-83 **Engr.**
709 A10 40o olive .30 .20
710 A10 50o dull purple .30 .20
711 A10 60o vermilion .30 .20
712 A10 70o orange .30 .30
713 A10 80o red brown .30 .20
714 A10 90o brown .30 .30
715 A209 1k green .30 .20
Complete booklet, pane of 4 ea #416, 419, 715 10.00
716 A209 1.10k rose mag .50 .20
717 A209 1.40k dark purple .90 .30
718 A211 1.75k green ('82) .50 .20
719 A211 2k brown red ('82) .50 .20
720 A211 2.25k dp vio ('82) .75 .30
721 A209 2.50k brn red ('83) .75 .20
722 A209 2.75k dp mag ('82) 1.25 .75
723 A209 3k dk bl ('82) .75 .20
724 A209 3.50k dp vio ('83) 1.25 .30
Nos. 709-724 (16) 9.25 4.25

See Nos. 772-774.

Peer Gynt, and Reindeer by Per Krogh — A222

Henrik Ibsen, by Erik Werenskiold, 1895 — A223

1978, Mar. 10 **Litho.** ***Perf. 13***
725 A222 1.25k buff & blk .60 .20
726 A223 1.80k multicolored 1.00 1.00

Ibsen (1828-1906), poet and dramatist.

Heddal Stave Church, c. 1250 A224

Lenangstindene and Jaegervasstindene A225

Europa: 1.80k, Borgund stave church.

1978, May 2 **Engr.** ***Perf. 13***
727 A224 1.25k dk brn & red 1.75 .45
728 A224 1.80k sl grn & bl 2.50 1.50

Perf. 13 on 3 Sides

1978, June 1 **Litho.**

1.25k, Gaustatoppen, mountain, Telemark.

729 A225 1k multi .55 .40
a. Booklet pane of 10 6.50
Complete booklet, #729a 6.50
730 A225 1.25k multi .70 .20
a. Booklet pane of 10 9.00
Complete booklet, #730a 8.00

Nos. 729-730 issued only in booklets.

Olav V Sailing A226

Design: 1.80k, King Olav delivering royal address in Parliament, vert.

1978, June 30 **Engr.** ***Perf. 13***
731 A226 1.25k red brown 1.00 .20
732 A226 1.80k violet blue 1.10 1.10

75th birthday of King Olav V.

Norway No. 107 — A227

Stamps: b, #108. c, #109. d, #110. e, #111. f, #112. g, #113. h, #114.

Perf. 13 on 3 Sides

1978, Sept. 19 **Litho.**
733 Booklet pane of 8 6.00 6.75
a.-h. A227 1.25k, any single .75 .75
Complete booklet, #733 6.75

NORWEX '80 Philatelic Exhibition, Oslo, June 13-22, 1980. Booklet sold for 15k; the additional 5k went for financing the exhibition.

Willow Pipe Player A228

Musical Instruments: 1.25k, Norwegian violin. 1.80k, Norwegian zither. 7.50k, Ram's horn.

1978, Oct. 6 **Engr.** ***Perf. 13***
734 A228 1k deep green .35 .20
735 A228 1.25k dk rose car .55 .20
736 A228 1.80k dk violet blue 1.00 .50
737 A228 7.50k gray 3.25 .20
Nos. 734-737 (4) 5.15 1.10

Wooden Doll, 1830 — A229

Ski Jump, Huseby Hill, c. 1900 — A230

Christmas: 1k, Toy town 1896-97. 1.25k, Wooden horse from Torpo in Hallingdal.

1978, Nov. 10 **Litho.**
738 A229 80o multi .35 .25
739 A229 1k multi .45 .25
740 A229 1.25k multi .45 .20
Nos. 738-740 (3) 1.25 .70

1979, Mar. 2 **Engr.** ***Perf. 13***

1.25k, Crown Prince Olav, Holmenkollen ski jump competition, 1922. 1.80k, Cross-country race, Holmenkollen, 1976.

741 A230 1k green .75 .25
742 A230 1.25k red .75 .25
743 A230 1.80k blue 1.10 1.10
Nos. 741-743 (3) 2.60 1.60

Huseby Hills and Holmenkollen ski competitions, centenary.

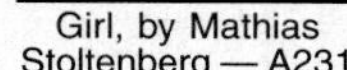

Girl, by Mathias Stoltenberg — A231

Road to Briksdal Glacier — A232

1.80k, Boy, by H. C. F. Hosenfelder.

1979, Apr. 26 **Litho.** ***Perf. 13***
744 A231 1.25k multi .75 .20
745 A231 1.80k multi 1.00 1.00

International Year of the Child.

1979, June 13 ***Perf. 13 on 3 Sides***

1.25k, Boat on Skjernoysund, near Mandal.

746 A232 1k multi .55 .20
a. Booklet pane of 10 5.50
Complete booklet, #746a 6.00
747 A232 1.25k multi .75 .20
a. Booklet pane of 10 7.50
Complete booklet, #747a 7.50

Nos. 746-747 issued only in booklets.

Johan Falkberget, by Harald Dal — A233

Kylling Bridge, Verma, 1923 — A234

1.80k, "Ann-Magritt and the Hovi Bullock" (by Falkberget), monument by Kristofer Leirdal.

1979, Sept. 4 **Engr.** ***Perf. 13***
748 A233 1.25k deep claret .75 .20
749 A233 1.80k Prus blue 1.10 1.00

Johan Falkberget (1879-1967), novelist.

1979, Oct. 5

Norwegian Engineering: 2k, Vessingsjo Dam, Nea, 1960. 10k, Stratfjord A, oil drilling platform in North Sea.

750 A234 1.25k gray brown .60 .20
751 A234 2k gray blue 1.00 .20
752 A234 10k brown olive 4.25 .45
Nos. 750-752 (3) 5.85 .85

Souvenir Sheet

Dornier Wal over Polar Map — A235

Arctic Aviation and Polar Maps: 2k, Dirigible Norge. 2.80k, Loening air yacht amphibian. 4k, Reidar Viking DC-7C.

1979, Oct. 5 **Litho.** ***Perf. 13***
753 Sheet of 4 6.50 6.50
a. A235 1.25k multi 1.25 1.25
b. A235 2k multi 1.25 1.25
c. A235 2.80k multi 1.25 1.25
d. A235 4k multi 1.25 1.25

Norwex '80 Intl. Phil. Exhib., Oslo, June 13-22, 1980. No. 753 sold for 15k.

Mountain Flower Type of 1973

1979, Nov. 22 **Litho.** ***Perf. 13½***
754 A171 80o Ranunculus glacialis .30 .20
755 A171 1k Potentilla crantzii .35 .20
756 A171 1.25k Saxiflora oppositifolia .35 .20
Nos. 754-756 (3) 1.00 .60

Norwegian Christian Youth Assn. Centenary A237

1980, Feb. 26 **Litho.** ***Perf. 13***
757 A237 100o shown .60 .20
758 A237 180o Emblems and doves 1.00 1.00

Oyster Catcher — A238

Perf. 13 on 3 Sides

1980, Apr. 18 **Litho.**
759 A238 100o shown .35 .20
760 A238 100o Mallard .35 .20
a. Bklt. pane, 5 #759, 5 #760 4.00
Complete booklet, #760a 4.50
761 A238 125o Dipper .55 .20
762 A238 125o Great tit .55 .20
a. Bklt. pane, 5 #761, 5 #762 4.50
Complete booklet, #762a 6.00
Nos. 759-762 (4) 1.80 .80

Nos. 759-762 issued in booklets only.
See Nos. 775-778, 800-801, 821-822.

Dish Antenna, Old Phone A239

National Telephone Service Centenary: 1.80k, Erecting telephone pole.

1980, May 9 **Litho.** ***Perf. 13½***
763 A239 1.25k multi .60 .20
764 A239 1.80k multi 1.00 1.00

Souvenir Sheet

Paddle Steamer "Bergen" A240

1980, June 13

765 Sheet of 4 6.00 6.00
a. A240 1.25k shown 1.25 1.25
b. A240 2k Train, 1900 1.25 1.25
c. A240 2.80k Bus, 1940 1.25 1.25
d. A240 4k Boeing 737 1.25 1.25

NORWEX '80 Stamp Exhibition, Oslo, June 13-22. Sold for 15k.

Nordic Cooperation Issue

Vulcan as an Armourer, by Henrich Bech, 1761 — A241

Henrich Bech Cast Iron Stove Ornament: 1.80k, Hercules at a Burning Altar, 1769.

1980, Sept. 9 Engr. *Perf. 13*

766 A241 1.25k dk vio brn .60 .20
767 A241 1.80k dark blue 1.00 1.00

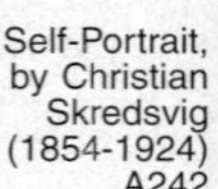

Self-Portrait, by Christian Skredsvig (1854-1924) A242

Paintings: 1.25k, Fire, by Nikolai Astrup.

1980, Nov. 14 Litho. *Perf. 13½x13*

768 A242 1.25k multi .60 .20
769 A242 1.80k multi 1.00 1.00

Mountain Flower Type of 1973

1980, Nov. 14 *Perf. 13*

770 A171 80o Sorbus aucuparia .30 .20
771 A171 1k Rosa canina .30 .20

Scenic Type of 1977

1.50k, Stavanger Cathedral, 13th cent. 1.70k, Rosenkrantz Tower, Bergen, 13th-16th cent. 2.20k, Church of Tromsdalen (Arctic Cathedral), 1965.

Perf. 13x13½, 13½x13

1981, Feb. 26 Engr.

772 A211 1.50k brown red .50 .20
773 A211 1.70k olive green .55 .45
774 A209 2.20k dark blue .70 .45
Nos. 772-774 (3) 1.75 1.10

Bird Type of 1980

Perf. 13 on 3 Sides

1981, Feb. 26 Litho.

775 A238 1.30k Anser erythropus .50 .30
776 A238 1.30k Peregrine falcon .50 .30
a. Booklet pane of 10 (5 each) 5.50
Complete booklet, #776a 5.50
777 A238 1.50k Black guillemot .65 .20
778 A238 1.50k Puffin .65 .20
a. Booklet pane of 10 (5 each) 6.50
Complete booklet, #778a 7.50
Nos. 775-778 (4) 2.30 1.00

Nos. 775-778 issued in booklets. See Nos. 800-801, 821-822.

Nat'l Milk Producers Assn. Centenary A244

1981, Mar. 24 Litho. *Perf. 13x13½*

779 A244 1.10k Cow .45 .25
780 A244 1.50k Goat .55 .20

A245

A246

Europa: 1.50k, The Mermaid, painted dish, Hol. 2.20k, The Proposal, painted box, Nes.

1981, May 4 Litho. *Perf. 13*

781 A245 1.50k multi 1.50 .50
782 A245 2.20k multi 2.00 1.00

1981, May 4 Engr.

Designs: 1.30k, Weighing anchor. 1.50k, Climbing rigging, vert. 2.20k, Training Ship Christian Radich.

783 A246 1.30k dk olive grn .75 .25
784 A246 1.50k orange red .75 .20
785 A246 2.20k dark blue 1.25 .75
Nos. 783-785 (3) 2.75 1.20

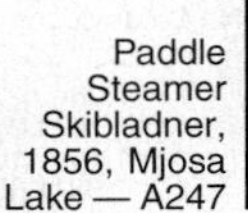

Paddle Steamer Skibladner, 1856, Mjosa Lake — A247

Lake Transportation: 1.30k, Victoria, 1882, Bandak Channel. 1.50k, Faemund II, 1905, Fermund Lake. 2.30k, Storegut, 1956, Tinnsjo Lake.

1981, June 11 Engr. *Perf. 13*

786 A247 1.10k dark brown .75 .20
787 A247 1.30k green .75 .40
788 A247 1.50k red .60 .20
789 A247 2.30k dark blue 1.10 .40
Nos. 786-789 (4) 3.20 1.20

Group Walking Arm in Arm — A248

1981, Aug. 25 Engr.

790 A248 1.50k shown .50 .20
791 A248 2.20k Group, diff. 1.00 1.00

Intl. Year of the Disabled.

A249

A250

Paintings: 1.50k, Interior in Blue, by Harriet Backer (1845-1932). 1.70k, Peat Moor on Jaeren, by Kitty Lange Kielland (1843-1914).

1981, Oct. 9 Litho. *Perf. 13*

792 A249 1.50k multi .75 .20
793 A249 1.70k multi 1.00 .75

1981, Nov. 25 Litho. *Perf. 13½*

Tapestries: 1.10k, One of the Three Kings, Skjak, 1625. 1.30k, Adoration of the Infant Christ, tapestry, Skjak, 1625. 1.50k, The Marriage of Cana, Storen, 18th cent.

794 A250 1.10k multi .40 .25
795 A250 1.30k multi .40 .25

Size: 29x37mm

796 A250 1.50k multi .55 .20
Nos. 794-796 (3) 1.35 .70

1921 Nobel Prize Winners Christian L. Lange (1869-1938) and Hjalmar Branting (1860-1925) A251

1981, Nov. 25 Engr. *Perf. 13*

797 A251 5k black 2.50 .40

World Skiing Championship, Oslo — A252

1982, Feb. 16 *Perf. 13½*

798 A252 2k Poles .75 .20
799 A252 3k Skis 1.10 .40

Bird Type of 1980

Perf. 13 on 3 Sides

1982, Apr. 1 Litho.

Booklet Stamps

800 A238 2k Blue-throat .65 .20
801 A238 2k Robin .65 .20
a. Bklt. pane, 5 each #800-801 7.00
Complete booklet, #801a 8.00

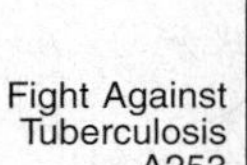

Fight Against Tuberculosis A253

1982, Apr. 1 *Perf. 13*

802 A253 2k Nurse .50 .20
803 A253 3k Microscope 1.00 .50

Jew's Harp — A254

1982, May 3 Engr. *Perf. 13*

804 A254 15k sepia 5.50 .35

Europa 1982 — A255

1982, May 3

805 A255 2k Haakon VII, 1905 4.00 .40
806 A255 3k Prince Olav, King Haakon VII, 1945 3.50 .75

Girls from Telemark, by Erik Werenskiold (1855-1938) A256

Design: 2k, Tone Veli at the Fence, by Henrik Sorensen (1882-1962), vert.

1982, June 23 Litho. *Perf. 13*

807 A256 1.75k multi .75 .40
808 A256 2k multi .75 .20

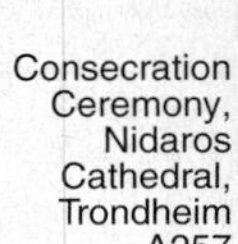

Consecration Ceremony, Nidaros Cathedral, Trondheim A257

Sigrid Undset (1882-1949), Writer, by A.C. Svarstad — A258

1982, Sept. 2 Engr. *Perf. 13x13½*

809 A257 3k blue 1.75 1.00

Reign of King Olav, 25th anniv.

1982, Oct. 1 Litho. *Perf. 13*

Painting: 1.75k, Bjornstjerne Bjornson (1832-1910), writer, by Erik Werenskiold, horiz.

810 A258 1.75k multi 1.00 .25
811 A258 2k multi 1.00 .20

A souvenir sheet containing Nos. 810-811 was prepared by the Norwegian Philatelic Association.

Graphical Union of Norway Centenary A259

1982, Oct. 1

812 A259 2k "A" .75 .25
813 A259 3k Type 1.10 .75

Fridtjof Nansen A260

Christmas A261

1982, Nov. 15 Engr. *Perf. 13½x13*

814 A260 3k dark blue 2.00 1.00

Fridtjof Nansen (1861-1930) polar explorer, 1922 Nobel Peace Prize winner.

Perf. 13 on 3 Sides

1982, Nov. 15 Litho.

Painting: Christmas Tradition, by Adolf Tidemand (1814-1876).

815 A261 1.75k multi .50 .20
a. Booklet pane of 10 6.00
Complete booklet, #815a 6.00

Farm Dog — A262

1983, Feb. 16 Litho. *Perf. 13x13½*

816 A262 2k shown 1.10 .40
817 A262 2.50k Elk hound 1.50 .20
818 A262 3.50k Hunting dog 1.60 .75
Nos. 816-818 (3) 4.20 1.35

Nordic Cooperation Issue — A263

1983, Mar. 24 Litho. *Perf. 13*
819 A263 2.50k Mountains 1.00 .20
820 A263 3.50k Fjord 1.50 1.00

Bird Type of 1980

1983, Apr. 14 *Perf. 13 on 3 Sides*
821 A238 2.50k Goose 1.10 .20
822 A238 2.50k Little auk 1.10 .20
a. Bklt. pane, 5 each #821-822 11.00
Complete booklet, #822a 11.00

Nos. 821-822 issued only in booklets.

Europa A264

Designs: 2.50k, Edvard Grieg (1843-1907), composer and his Piano Concerto in A-minor. 3.50k, Niels Henrik Abel (1802-1829), mathematician, by Gustav Vigeland, vert.

1983, May 3 Engr. *Perf. 13*
823 A264 2.50k red orange 3.75 .40
824 A264 3.50k dk bl & grn 4.00 1.00

World Communications Year — A265

Symbolic arrow designs.

1983, May 3 Litho.
825 A265 2.50k multi 1.25 .20
826 A265 3.50k multi 1.25 .75

80th Birthday of King Olav V, July 2 — A266

1983, June 22 Engr. *Perf. 13x13½*
827 A266 5k green 3.00 .40

Jonas Lie (1833-1908), Writer — A267

Northern Ships — A268

1983, Oct. 7 Engr. *Perf. 13½x13*
828 A267 2.50k red 1.00 .20

1983, Oct. 7 Litho.
829 A268 2k Nordlandsfemboring 1.25 .30
830 A268 3k Nordlandsjekt 1.50 .50

Christmas 1983 — A269

Paintings: 2k, The Sleigh Ride by Axel Ender (1853-1920). 2.50k, The Guests are Arriving by Gustav Wenzel (1859-1927).

Perf. 13 on 3 sides

1983, Nov. 17 Litho.
831 A269 2k multi .90 .25
a. Booklet pane of 10 9.00
Complete booklet, #831a 10.00
832 A269 2.50k multi 1.10 .25
a. Booklet pane of 10 9.00
Complete booklet, #832a 10.00

Postal Services A270

1984, Feb. 24 Litho. *Perf. 13½x13*
833 A270 2k Counter service 1.00 .25
834 A270 2.50k Sorting 1.10 .20
835 A270 3.50k Delivery 1.50 1.00
Nos. 833-835 (3) 3.60 1.45

Freshwater Fishing A271

Christopher Hansteen (1784-1873), Astronomer A272

1984, Apr. 10 Engr. *Perf. 13*
836 A271 2.50k shown 1.00 .20
837 A271 3k Salmon fishing 1.25 .75
838 A271 3.50k Ocean fishing 1.50 1.00
Nos. 836-838 (3) 3.75 1.95

1984, Apr. 10
839 A272 3.50k Magnetic meridians, parallels, horiz. 1.50 1.00
840 A272 5k shown 2.00 .40

Europa (1959-84) — A273

Produce, Spices — A274

1984, June 4 Litho. *Perf. 13*
841 A273 2.50k multi 3.75 .40
842 A273 3.50k multi 4.00 1.20

1984, June 4 *Perf. 13*
843 A274 2k shown 1.00 .25
844 A274 2.50k Flowers 1.10 .20

Horticultural Society centenary.

A275

A276

1984, June 4
845 A275 2.50k Worker bees 1.00 .20
846 A275 2.50k Rooster 1.00 .20

Centenaries: Beekeeping Society (No. 845); Poultry-breeding Society (No. 846).

1984, Oct. 5 Engr. *Perf. 13*
847 A276 2.50k lake 1.10 .20

Ludvig Holberg (1684-1754), writer, by J.M. Bernigeroth.

A277

A278

1984, Oct. 5 Litho. & Engr.
848 A277 2.50k Children reading .65 .20
849 A277 3.50k First edition 1.10 1.00

Norwegian Weekly Press sesquicentennial.

Perf. 13½x13 on 3 sides

1984, Nov. 15 Litho.

Illustrations from Children's Stories by Thorbjorn Egner.

Booklet Stamps

850 A278 2k Karius & Baktus 1.50 .30
851 A278 2k Tree Shrew 1.50 .30
a. Bklt. pane, 5 each #850-851 15.00
Complete booklet, #851a 22.50
852 A278 2.50k Cardamom Rovers 2.25 .20
853 A278 2.50k Chief Constable Bastian 2.25 .20
a. Bklt. pane, 5 each #852-853 22.50
Complete booklet, #853a 25.00
Nos. 850-853 (4) 7.50 1.00

Parliament Centenary — A279

1984, Nov. 15 Engr. *Perf. 13½x13*
854 A279 7.50k Sverdrup Govt. parliament, 1884 4.25 1.00

Antarctic Mountains A280

1985, Apr. 18 Litho. *Perf. 13*
855 A280 2.50k The Saw Blade 1.50 .20
856 A280 3.50k The Chopping Block 2.00 1.00

Liberation from the German Occupation Forces, 40th Anniv. A281

1985, May 8 Engr. *Perf. 13x13½*
857 A281 3.50k dk bl & red 2.00 1.00

Norwegian Artillery A282

Anniv.: 3k, Norwegian Artillery, 300th. 4k, Artillery Officers Training School, 200th.

1985, May 22 Litho. *Perf. 13½x13*
858 A282 3k multi 1.50 .75
859 A282 4k multi 1.75 .50

Kongsten Fort, 300th Anniv. A283

1985, May 22
860 A283 2.50k multi 1.25 .20

Europa — A284

Intl. Youth Year — A285

Designs: 2.50k, Torgeir Augundsson (1801-1872), fiddler. 3.50k, Ole Bull (1810-1880), composer, violinist.

1985, June 19 Engr.
861 A284 2.50k brown lake 3.75 .45
862 A284 3.50k dark blue 4.00 .85

1985, June 19 Litho.

Stone and bronze sculptures: 2k, Boy and Girl, detail, Vigeland Museum, Oslo. 3.50k, Fountain, detail, Vigeland Park, Oslo.

863 A285 2k multi .75 .40
864 A285 3.50k multi 1.25 1.25

Electrification of Norway, Cent. — A286

1985, Sept. 6 Engr. *Perf. 13½x13*
865 A286 2.50k Glomfjord Dam penstock 1.00 .20
866 A286 4k Linemen 1.50 .40

Public Libraries, 200th Anniv. A287

Designs; 2.50k, Carl Deichman (1705-1780), Public Libraries System founder. 10k, Modern library interior, horiz.

1985, Oct. 4
867 A287 2.50k hn brn & yel brn 1.00 .20
868 A287 10k dark green 5.00 .50

Ship Navigation A288

Lithographed & Engraved

1985, Nov. 14 *Perf. 13x13½*
869 A288 2.50k Dredger Berghavn, 1980 1.00 .20
870 A288 5k Sextant and chart, 1791 2.00 .45

Port Authorities, 250th anniv., Hydrographic Services, bicent.

Christmas Wreath A289

Bullfinches A290

Booklet Stamps
Perf. 13½ on 3 Sides

1985, Nov. 14 **Litho.**

871 A289 2k multi 2.00 .25
a. Booklet pane of 10 20.00
Complete booklet, #871a 22.50
872 A290 2.50k multi 2.00 .20
a. Booklet pane of 10 20.00
Complete booklet, #872a 22.50

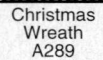

World Biathlon Championships, Feb. 18-23 — A290a

1986, Feb. 18 *Perf. 13x13½*

873 A290a 2.50k shown 1.25 .20
874 A291 3.50k Shooting upright 1.50 1.00

Ornaments A291

Fauna A292

Mushrooms — A293

Litho. & Engr.
1986-90 *Perf. 13½x13*

875 A291 2.10k Sun 1.00 .20
876 A291 2.30k Fish .90 .20
877 A292 2.60k Fox 1.00 .20
878 A291 2.70k Flowers, wheat 1.25 .20
879 A292 2.90k Capercaillie 1.50 .20
880 A292 3k Ermine 1.50 .20
881 A292 3.20k Mute swan 1.50 .20
882 A292 3.80k Reindeer 2.00 .20
883 A291 4k Star 1.50 .30
883A A292 4k Squirrel 1.50 .20
883B A292 4.50k Beaver 1.50 .20
Nos. 875-883B (11) 15.15 2.30

Issued: 2.10k, #883, 2/18/86; 2.30k, 2.70k, 2/12/87; 2.90k, 3.80k, 2/18/88; 2.60k, 3k, #883A, 2/20/89; 3.20k, 4.50k, 2/23/90.
See Nos. 958-959.

Booklet Stamps
Perf. 13½x13 on 3 Sides

1987-89 **Litho.**

884 A293 2.70k Cantharellus tubaeformis 1.25 .20
885 A293 2.70k Rozites caperata 1.25 .20
a. Bklt. pane, 5 #884, 5 #885 12.50
Complete booklet, #885a 16.00
886 A293 2.90k Lepista nuda 1.25 .20
887 A293 2.90k Lactarius deterrimus 1.25 .20
a. Bklt. pane, 5 #886, 5 #887 12.50
Complete booklet, #887a 13.50
888 A293 3k Cantharellus cibarius 1.10 .20
889 A293 3k Suillus luteus 1.10 .20
a. Bklt. pane, 5 #888, 5 #889 11.00
Complete booklet, #889a 15.00
Nos. 884-889 (6) 7.20 1.20

Issued: 2.70k, 5/8; 2.90k, 4/26/88; 3k, 2/20/89.

Natl. Federation of Craftsmen, Cent. — A294

1986, Apr. 11 **Engr.**

890 A294 2.50k Stone cutter 1.00 .20
891 A294 7k Carpenter 3.25 1.00

Europa A295

1986, Apr. 11 **Litho.** *Perf. 13*

892 A295 2.50k Bird, industry 3.50 .40
893 A295 3.50k Acid rain 3.75 1.00

Nordic Cooperation Issue A296

Sister towns.

1986, May 27 *Perf. 13½x13*

894 A296 2.50k Moss 1.25 .20
895 A296 4k Alesund 2.00 .75

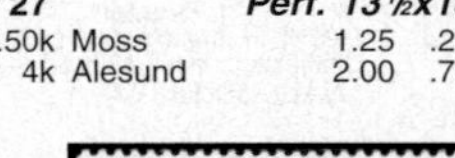

Famous Men — A297

Designs: 2.10k, Hans Poulson Egede (1686-1758), missionary, and map of Norway and Greenland. 2.50k, Herman Wildenvey (1886-1959), poet, and poem carved in Seaman's Commemoration Hall, Stavern. 3k, Tore Orjasaeter (1886-1968), poet, and antique cupboard, Skjak. 4k, Engebret Soot, engineer, and canal lock, Orje.

Engr., Litho. & Engr. (#897)
1986, Oct. 17 *Perf. 13x13½*

896 A297 2.10k multi 1.10 1.00
897 A297 2.50k multi 1.10 .25
898 A297 3k multi 1.50 .65
899 A297 4k multi 2.00 .40
Nos. 896-899 (4) 5.70 2.30

A298

A299

Christmas (Stained glass windows by Gabriel Kielland, Nidaros Cathedral, Trondheim): 2.10k, Olav Kyrre Founding The Diocese in Nidaros. 2.50k, The King and the Peasant at Sul.

Perf. 13½ on 3 Sides
1986, Nov. 26 **Litho.**
Booklet Stamps

900 A298 2.10k multi 1.50 .40
a. Booklet pane of 10 15.00
Complete booklet, #900a 16.00
901 A298 2.50k multi 1.50 .20
a. Booklet pane of 10 15.00
Complete booklet, #901a 16.00

Lithographed & Engraved
1986, Nov. 26 *Perf. 13½x13*

902 A299 15k brt grn, org & lt bl 7.50 .75

Intl. Peace Year.

A300

1987, Feb. 12 **Litho.** *Perf. 13½*

903 A300 3.50k red, yel & dk bl 1.50 .75
904 A300 4.50k bl, yel & grn 1.75 .50

Europa A301

Modern architecture: 2.70k, Wood. 4.50k, Glass and stone.

1987, Apr. 3 **Litho.** *Perf. 13½x13*

905 A301 2.70k multi 3.00 .40
906 A301 4.50k multi 4.25 .75

Odelsting (Norwegian Assembly) Voting on Law Administering Local Councils, 150th Anniv. A302

1987, Apr. 3 **Engr.** *Perf. 13x13½*

907 A302 12k dark green 6.00 .55

Miniature Sheet

Red Crescent-Red Cross Rehabilitation Center, Mogadishu, Somalia — A303

Illustration reduced.

1987, May 8 **Litho.** *Perf. 13½x13*

908 A303 4.50k multi 2.50 2.00

See Somalia Nos. 576-577.

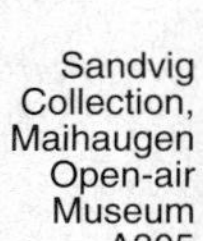

Sandvig Collection, Maihaugen Open-air Museum A305

1987, June 10 **Engr.** *Perf. 13x13½*

911 A305 2.70k Bjornstad Farm, Vaga 1.25 .30
912 A305 3.50k Horse and Rider, by Christen E. Listad 1.75 .80

Churchyard, Inspiration for Valen's Churchyard by the Sea — A306

Fartein Valen (1887-1952), Composer — A306a

Perf. 13x13½, 13½x13
1987, Aug. 25 **Engr.**

913 A306 2.30k emer grn & dark blue 1.00 .75
914 A306a 4.50k dark brown 1.75 .50

Tempest at Sea, by Christian Krogh (1852-1925) A307

Painting: 5k, The Farm, by Gerhard Munthe (1849-1929).

1987, Oct. 9 **Litho.** *Perf. 13½x13*

915 A307 2.70k multi 1.25 .30
916 A307 5k multi 2.00 .40

Norwegian Horse Breeds A308

Litho. & Engr.
1987, Nov. 12 *Perf. 13x13½*

917 A308 2.30k Dales 1.25 .60
918 A308 2.70k Fjord 1.25 .30
919 A308 4.50k Nordland 2.00 .40
Nos. 917-919 (3) 4.50 1.30

Christmas A309

Perf. 13½x13 on 3 sides
1987, Nov. 12 **Litho.**
Booklet Stamps

920 A309 2.30k Children making tree ornaments 1.40 .40
a. Booklet pane of 10 14.00
Complete booklet, #920a 15.00
921 A309 2.70k Baking gingersnaps 1.25 .20
a. Booklet pane of 10 12.50
Complete booklet, #921a 13.00

Salvation Army in Norway, Cent. A310

4.80k, Othilie Tonning, early Salvation Army worker in Norway.

1988, Feb. 18 *Perf. 13½*

922 A310 2.90k multi 1.25 .30
923 A310 4.80k multi 2.00 .65

European North-South Solidarity Campaign — A311

1988, Apr. 26 *Perf. 13x13½*

924 A311 25k multi 10.00 1.00

Defense Forces Activities A312

Defense Forces, 300th anniv.: 2.50k, Fortress construction. 2.90k, Army Signal Corps on duty. 4.60k, Pontoon bridge under construction, Corps of Engineers.

1988, Apr. 26 **Engr.**
925 A312 2.50k dark green 1.25 .60
926 A312 2.90k carmine lake 1.10 .30
927 A312 4.60k dark blue 1.75 .50
Nos. 925-927 (3) 4.10 1.40

Europa A313

Transport: 2.90k, *Prinds Gustav* passing Lofoten Isls., 1st passenger steamer in northern Norway, sesquicent. 3.80k, Heroybrua Bridge, between Leinoy and Blankholm, 1976.

Litho. & Engr.
1988, July 1 ***Perf. 13x13½***
928 A313 2.90k multi 3.50 .50
929 A313 3.80k multi 4.00 1.75

A souvenir sheet containing 2 No. 928 exists, though it is invalid for postage. Sold for 30k.

85th Birthday of King Olav V — A314

Reign of King Christian IV (1577-1648), 400th Anniv. — A315

Designs: No. 930, Portrait, c. 1988. No. 931a, Arrival in 1905 after Norway declared independence from Sweden. No. 931b, Olav in snowstorm at Holmenkollen.

1988, July 1 **Litho.** ***Perf. 13½x13***
930 A314 2.90k multi 1.25 .30

Souvenir Sheet

931 Sheet of 3 6.00 4.50
a. A314 2.90k org red, black & ultra 1.50 1.25
b. A314 2.90k multi 1.50 1.25
c. A314 2.90k like No. 930, no date 1.50 1.25

Litho. & Engr.
1988, Oct. 7 ***Perf. 13½x13***

Designs: 10k, Reverse of a rixdaler struck in Christiania (Oslo), 1628, and excerpt of a mining decree issued by Christian IV.

932 A315 2.50k black & buff 1.50 .60
933 A315 10k multi 5.75 .60

Miniature Sheet

Handball A316

Ball sports: b, Soccer. c, Basketball. d, Volleyball.

1988, Oct. 7 **Litho.** ***Perf. 13½x13***
934 Sheet of 4 10.00 10.00
a.-d. A316 2.90k any single 2.50 2.50

Stamp Day. No. 934 sold for 15k.

Christmas — A317

Ludvig, a cartoon character created by Kjell Aukrust: No. 935, With ski pole. No. 936, Reading letter.

Perf. 13½x13 on 3 sides
1988, Nov. 15 **Litho.**
Booklet Stamps
935 A317 2.90k multi 1.75 .20
936 A317 2.90k multi 1.75 .20
a. Bklt. pane, 5 #935, 5 #936 17.50
Complete booklet, #936a 18.00

World Cross-Country Running Championships, Stavanger, Mar. 19 — A318

1989, Feb. 20 **Litho.** ***Perf. 13x13½***
937 A318 5k multi 2.00 .30

Port City Bicentennials A319

Nordic Cooperation Issue A320

Litho. & Engr.
1989, Apr. 20 ***Perf. 13½x13***
938 A319 3k Vardo 1.50 .30
939 A319 4k Hammerfest 2.00 1.10

1989, Apr. 20 **Litho.** ***Perf. 13x13½***

Folk costumes.

940 A320 3k Setesdal (woman) 1.50 .30
941 A320 4k Kautokeino (man) 2.00 1.10

Europa 1989 — A321

Public Primary Schools, 250th Anniv. — A322

Children's games.

1989, June 7 **Litho.** ***Perf. 13x13½***
942 A321 3.70k Building snowman 3.50 1.00
943 A321 5k Cat's cradle 5.50 1.25

Litho. & Engr.
1989, June 7 ***Perf. 13½x13***
944 A322 2.60k shown 1.10 .60

Engr.
945 A322 3k Child learning to write 1.25 .30

Souvenir Sheet

Winter Olympic Gold Medalists from Norway — A323

Portraits: a, Bjoerg Eva Jensen, women's 3000-meter speed skating, 1980. b, Eirik Kvalfoss, 10k biathlon, 1984. c, Tom Sandberg, combined cross-country and ski jumping, 1984. d, Women's Nordic ski team, 20k relay, 1984.

1989, Oct. 6 **Litho.** ***Perf. 13½x13***
946 Sheet of 4 9.00 9.00
a.-d. A323 4k any single 2.00 2.00

Sold for 20k to benefit Olympic sports promotion.

See Nos. 984, 997, 1021, 1035.

Souvenir Sheet

Impression of the Countryside, 1982, by Jakob Weidemann — A324

Illustration reduced.

1989, Oct. 6
947 A324 Sheet of 4 10.00 10.00
a.-d. 3k any single 2.00 2.00

Stamp Day. Sold for 15k to benefit philatelic promotion.

Writers A325

3k, Arnulf Overland (1889-1968), poet. 25k, Hanna Winsnes (1789-1872), author.

Litho. & Engr.
1989, Nov. 24 ***Perf. 13x13½***
948 A325 3k dk red & brt bl 1.25 .30
949 A325 25k multicolored 10.00 1.10

Manors A326

1989, Nov. 24 **Engr.** ***Perf. 13***
950 A326 3k Manor at Larvik 1.50 .30
951 A326 3k Rosendal Barony 1.50 .30

A327

A328

Christmas decorations.

Perf. 13 on 3 sides
1989, Nov. 24 **Litho.**
Booklet Stamps
952 A327 3k Star 1.10 .20
953 A327 3k Round ornament 1.10 .20
a. Bklt. pane of 10, 5 #952, 5 #953 11.00
Complete booklet, #953a 12.50

1990, Feb. 23 **Litho.** ***Perf. 13½***
954 A328 5k multicolored 2.00 .35

Winter City events, Tromso.

Fauna Type of 1988 and

Scenes of Norway — A329

Designs: 4k, Cable cars. 4.50k, Goat Mountain. 5.50k, Top of the World outpost.

1991-94 **Litho.** ***Perf. 13***
955 A329 4k multicolored 1.50 .60
956 A329 4.50k multicolored 2.25 .60
957 A329 5.50k multicolored 2.00 .45

Litho. & Engr.
958 A292 5.50k Lynx 2.00 .20
959 A292 6.40k Owl 2.25 .40
Nos. 955-959 (5) 10.00 2.25

Issued: #958-959, 2/21/91; #955-957, 4/19/94.

Posthorn Type of 1893

1991-92 **Engr.** ***Perf. 12½x13***
960 A10 1k orange & black .40 .20
961 A10 2k emerald & lake 1.00 .20
962 A10 3k blue & green 1.10 .20
963 A10 4k org & henna brn 1.50 .20
964 A10 5k green & dark blue 2.00 .20
965 A10 6k grn & red vio 2.00 .20
966 A10 7k red brn & bl 2.25 .20
967 A10 8k red vio & grn 2.50 .25
968 A10 9k ultra & red brn 3.00 .35
Nos. 960-968 (9) 15.75 2.00

Issued: 1k-5k, 11/23/92; others, 11/22/91.

A332

A334

Orchids.

Perf. 13½x13 on 3 Sides
1990-92 **Litho.** **Booklet Stamps**
970 A332 3.20k *Dactylorhiza fuchsii* 1.25 .20
971 A332 3.20k *Epipactis atrorubens* 1.25 .20
a. Bklt. pane, 5 #970, 5 #971 12.50
Complete booklet, #971a 13.00
972 A332 3.30k *Cypripedium calceolus* 1.25 .20
973 A332 3.30k *Ophrys insectifera* 1.25 .20
a. Bklt. pane, 5 each #972-973 12.50
Complete booklet, #973a 14.00
Nos. 970-973 (4) 5.00 .80

Issued: #970-971, 2/23; #972-973, 2/21/92.

1990, Apr. 9 **Litho.** ***Perf. 13x13½***

German Invasion of Norway, 50th Anniv.: 3.20k, King Haakon VII's monogram, merchant navy, air force, Norwegian Home Guard and cannon Moses. 4k, Recapture of Narvik, May 28, 1940, by the Polish, British, Norwegian and French forces.

975 A334 3.20k shown 2.25 .25
976 A334 4k multicolored 2.50 1.10

A335

A336

Souvenir Sheet

Stamps on stamps: b, Norway #1.

1990, Apr. 9 ***Perf. 13½x13***

977 Sheet of 2 7.50 7.50
a.-b. A335 5k any single 3.00 3.00

Penny Black, 150th anniv. Sold for 15k.

1990, June 14 **Litho. & Engr.**

978 A336 3.20k Portrait 1.50 .25
979 A336 5k Coat of arms 2.00 .40

Tordenskiold (Peter Wessel, 1690-1720), naval hero.

A337

A338

Europa: Post offices.

1990, June 14 **Litho.** ***Perf. 13x13½***

980 A337 3.20k Trondheim 6.75 .40
981 A337 4k Longyearbyen 6.75 1.25

1990, Oct. 5 **Litho. & Engr.** ***Perf. 13***

982 A338 2.70k Svendsen 1.25 .55
983 A338 15k Monument by Fredriksen 6.00 1.00

Johan Severin Svendsen (1840-1911), composer.

Winter Olympic Type of 1989
Souvenir Sheet

Gold medal winners: a, Thorleif Haug, skier, 1924. b, Sonja Henie, figure skater, 1928, 1932, 1936. c, Ivar Ballangrud, speed skater, 1928, 1936. d, Hjalmar Andersen, speed skater, 1952.

1990, Oct. 5 **Litho.** ***Perf. 13½x13***

984 Sheet of 4 10.00 10.00
a.-d. A323 4k any single 2.00 2.00

Sold for 20k to benefit Olympic sports promotion.

A339

A340

Litho & Engr.

1990, Nov. 23 ***Perf. 13***

985 A339 30k bl, brn & car rose 11.00 1.00

Lars Olof Jonathan Soderblom (1866-1931), 1930 Nobel Peace Prize winner.

Perf. 13 on 3 sides

1990, Nov. 23 **Litho.**

Christmas (Children's drawings): No. 987, Church, stars, and Christmas tree.

986 A340 3.20k multicolored 1.25 .20
987 A340 3.20k multicolored 1.25 .20
a. Bklt. pane, 5 each #986-987 12.50
Complete booklet, #987a 13.00

Ship Building Industry A341

1991, Feb. 21 **Litho.** ***Perf. 13½x13***

988 A341 5k multicolored 2.00 .60

Europa — A342

1991, Apr. 16 **Litho.** ***Perf. 13***

989 A342 3.20k ERS-1 7.00 .50
990 A342 4k Andoya rocket range 7.00 1.50

City of Christiansand, 350th Anniv. — A343

Litho. & Engr.

1991, Apr. 16 ***Perf. 13***

991 A343 3.20k Early view 1.25 .25
992 A343 5.50k Modern view 2.00 .35

Lifeboat Service, Cent. A344

Tourism A345

Designs: 3.20k, Rescue boat, Skomvaer III, horiz. 27k, Sailboat Colin Archer.

Litho & Engr.

1991, June 7 ***Perf. 13***

993 A344 3.20k multicolored 1.25 .25
994 A344 27k multicolored 11.00 1.50

1991, June 7 **Litho.** ***Perf. 13½x13***

Designs: 3.20k, Fountain, Vigeland Park. 4k, Globe, North Cape.

995 A345 3.20k multicolored 1.25 .25
996 A345 4k multicolored 3.00 2.00

Winter Olympics Type of 1989
Souvenir Sheet

Gold medal winners: a, Birger Ruud, ski jumping. b, Johan Grottumsbraten, cross country skiing. c, Knut Johannesen, speed skating. d, Magnar Solberg, biathlon.

1991, Oct. 11 **Litho.** ***Perf. 13½x13***

997 Sheet of 4 7.75 7.75
a.-d. A323 4k any single 1.75 1.75

Sold for 20k to benefit Olympic sports promotion.

A346

A347

Natl. Stamp Day: a, Hands engraving. b, Magnifying glass above hands. c, View of hands through magnifying glass. d, Printed label being removed from plate.

1991, Oct. 11 ***Perf. 13x13½***

Souvenir Sheet

998 Sheet of 4 9.00 9.00
a. A346 2.70k multicolored 2.00 2.00
b. A346 3.20k multicolored 2.00 2.00
c. A346 4k multicolored 2.00 2.00
d. A346 5k multicolored 2.00 2.00

Sold for 20k.

Perf. 13½x13 on 3 Sides

1991, Nov. 22 **Litho.**

Christmas: No. 1000, People with lantern.

Booklet Stamps

999 A347 3.20k multicolored 1.25 .20
1000 A347 3.20k multicolored 1.25 .20
a. Bklt. pane, 5 each #999-1000 12.50
Complete booklet, #1000a 13.00

Queen Sonja A348

King Harald A349

A349a

Perf. 13x13½, 12½x13½ (6.50k), 13½x13 (30k)

Litho. & Engr., Engr. (6.50k)

1992-2002

1004 A348 2.80k multi 1.50 .20
1005 A348 3k multi 1.50 .20
1007 A349 3.30k multi 1.50 .20
1008 A349 3.50k multi 1.50 .20
1009 A349 4.50k carmine 2.00 .50
1011 A349 5.50k multi 2.25 .25
1012 A349 5.60k multi 2.25 .30
1014 A349 6.50k green 2.50 .40
1015 A349 6.60k multi 2.50 .50
1016 A349 7.50k violet 3.25 1.50
1016A A349 8.50k brown 3.50 2.00

Engr.

Perf. 13½x13

1017 A349a 10k dark grn 5.00 .20
a. Perf. 13½x13¾ 4.00 .50
1019 A349a 20k deep vio 10.00 .50
b. Perf. 13½x13¾ 8.50 .50
1019A A349a 30k dark blue 11.00 .40
1020 A349a 50k olive black 15.00 1.00
a. Perf. 13½x13¾ 14.00 1.00
Nos. 1004-1020 (15) 65.25 8.35

Issued: 2.80k, 3.30k, 5.60k, 6.60k, 2/21/92; 50k, 6/12/92; 3k, 3.50k, 5.50k, 2/23/93; 10k, 20k, 6/17/93; 6.50k, 2/12/94; 30k, 11/18/94; 4.50k, 7.50k, 8.50k, 11/24/95; Nos. 1019b, 1020a, Dec. 2001. No. 1017a, 2002. This is an expanding set. Numbers may change.

Winter Olympics Type of 1989
Souvenir Sheet

Gold Medal winners: a, Hallgeir Brenden, cross-country skiing. b, Arnfinn Bergmann, ski jumping. c, Stein Eriksen, giant slalom. d, Simon Slattvik, Nordic combined.

1992, Feb. 21 **Litho.** ***Perf. 13½x13***

1021 Sheet of 4 8.00 8.00
a.-d. A323 4k any single 1.75 1.75

Sold for 20k to benefit Olympic sports promotion.

Expo '92, Seville A350

Designs: 3.30k, Norwegian pavilion, ship. 5.20k, Mountains, boat and fish.

1992, Apr. 20 **Litho.** ***Perf. 13x13½***

1022 A350 3.30k multicolored 1.25 .25
1023 A350 5.20k multicolored 2.00 .60

Discovery of America, 500th Anniv. A351

Europa: 3.30k, Sailing ship Restauration at sea, 1825. 4,20k, Stavangerfjord in New York Harbor, 1918.

Litho. & Engr.

1992, Apr. 21 ***Perf. 13x13½***

1024 A351 3.30k multicolored 3.75 .30
1025 A351 4.20k multicolored 5.00 1.00

Kristiansund, 250th Anniv. — A352

Litho. & Engr.

1992, June 12 ***Perf. 13***

1026 A352 3.30k brn, bl & blk 1.25 .25
1027 A352 3.30k View of Molde 1.50 .25

Molde, 250th anniv. (#1027).

Souvenir Sheet

Glass — A353

Stamp Day: a, Decorated vase. b, Carafe with gold design. c, Cut glass salad bowl. d, Decorated cup.

1992, Oct. 9 **Litho.** ***Perf. 13x13½***

1028 Sheet of 4 10.00 10.00
a. A353 2.80k multicolored 2.00 2.00
b. A353 3.30k multicolored 2.00 2.00
c. A353 4.20k multicolored 2.00 2.00
d. A353 5.20k multicolored 2.00 2.00

No. 1028 sold for 20k.

A354

A355

Designs: 3.30k, Flags, buildings in Lillehammer. 4.20k, Flag.

1992, Oct. 9 **Litho.** ***Perf. 13x13½***

1029 A354 3.30k multicolored 1.25 .25
1030 A354 4.20k multicolored 1.75 .60

1994 Winter Olympics, Lillehammer. See Nos. 1047-1048, 1053-1058.

Perf. 13 on 3 Sides

1992, Nov. 23 **Litho.**

Christmas: No. 1031, Elves in front of mailbox. No. 1032, One elf holding other on shoulders to mail letters.

Booklet Stamps

1031 A355 3.30k multicolored 1.50 .20
1032 A355 3.30k multicolored 1.50 .20
b. Booklet pane, 5 each #1031-1032 15.00
Complete booklet, #1032b 15.00

Butterflies — A356

Designs: No. 1033, Anthocharis cardamines. No. 1034, Aglais urticae.

Perf. 13½x13 on 3 Sides
1993, Feb. 23 **Litho.**
Booklet Stamps

1033 A356 3.50k multicolored 1.50 .20
1034 A356 3.50k multicolored 1.50 .20
b. Booklet pane, 5 each #1033-1034 15.00
Complete booklet, #1034b 15.00

See Nos. 1051-1052.

Winter Olympics Type of 1989
Souvenir Sheet

1992 Gold Medal winners: a, Finn Christian Jagge, slalom. b, Bjorn Daehlie, cross-country skiing. c, Geir Karlstad, speed skating. d, Vegard Ulvang, cross-country skiing.

1993, Feb. 23 ***Perf. 13½x13***
1035 Sheet of 4 8.00 8.00
a.-d. A323 4.50k any single 1.75 1.75

No. 1035 sold for 22k to benefit Olympic sports promotion.

Norden — A357

1993, Apr. 23 **Litho.** ***Perf. 13½x13***
1036 A357 4k Canoe on lake 1.50 .50
1037 A357 4.50k River rafting 2.00 .50

Edvard Grieg A358

Litho. & Engr.
1993, Apr. 23 ***Perf. 13x13½***
1038 A358 3.50k Portrait 1.50 .25
1039 A358 5.50k Landscape 2.00 .50

1993 World Championships in Norway — A359

1993, June 17 **Litho.** ***Perf. 13½x13***
1040 A359 3.50k Team handball 1.50 .25
1041 A359 5.50k Cycling 2.00 .50

Hurtigruten Shipping Line, Cent. A360

Litho. & Engr.
1993, June 17 ***Perf. 12½x13***
1042 A360 3.50k Richard With, ship 2.00 .25
1043 A360 4.50k Ship, officers 1.75 .75

Worker's Organization, Cent. A361

1993, Sept. 24 **Engr.** ***Perf. 13x13½***
1044 A361 3.50k Johan Castberg 2.00 .40
1045 A361 12k Betzy Kjelsberg 4.00 .75

Souvenir Sheet

Carvings — A362

Stamp Day: a, Spiral leaf scroll. b, Interlocking scroll. c, "1754" surrounded by scroll. d, Face with scroll above.

1993, Sept. 24 **Litho.** ***Perf. 13½x13***
1046 Sheet of 4, #a.-d. 10.00 10.00
a. A362 3k multicolored 2.00 2.00
b. A362 3.50k multicolored 2.00 2.00
c. A362 4.50k multicolored 2.00 2.00
d. A362 5.50k multicolored 2.00 2.00

No. 1046 sold for 21k.
See No. 1069.

1994 Winter Olympics Type of 1992

#1047, Flags, cross country skiier. #1048, Flags, buildings in Lillehammer.

1993, Nov. 27 **Litho.** ***Perf. 13x13½***
1047 A354 3.50k multicolored 1.50 .25
1048 A354 3.50k multicolored 1.50 .25
a. Pair, #1047-1048 3.00 1.60

No. 1048a has a continuous design.

Christmas — A363

Designs: No. 1049, Store Mangen Chapel. No. 1050, Church of Stamnes, Sandnes.

Perf. 13½x13 on 3 Sides
1993, Nov. 27
Booklet Stamps

1049 A363 3.50k shown 1.50 .20
1050 A363 3.50k multicolored 1.50 .20
b. Booklet pane, 5 each #1049-1050 15.00
Complete booklet, #1050b 15.00

Butterfly Type of 1993
Perf. 13½x13 on 3 Sides
1994, Feb. 12 **Litho.**
Booklet Stamps

1051 A356 3.50k Colias hecla 1.25 .20
1052 A356 3.50k Clossiana freija 1.25 .20
b. Booklet pane, 5 each #1051-1052 12.50
Complete booklet, #1052b 12.50

1994 Winter Olympics Type of 1992

Designs: No. 1053, Stylized Norwegian flag, Olympic rings UR. No. 1054, Stylized Norwegian flag, Olympic rings, UL. No. 1055, Olympic rings, buildings in Lillehammer. No. 1056, Olympic rings, ski jump. 4.50k, Flags of Norway, Belgium, Greece, Switzerland, Sweden, Germany, United Kingdom. 5.50k, Flags of Australia, New Zealand, Brazil, Canada, US, Japan, Mexico, South Korea.

1994, Feb. 12 ***Perf. 13x13½***
1053 A354 3.50k multicolored 1.50 .30
1054 A354 3.50k multicolored 1.50 .30
1055 A354 3.50k multicolored 1.50 .30
1056 A354 3.50k multicolored 1.50 .30
a. Block of 4, #1053-1056 6.00 6.00
1057 A354 4.50k multicolored 1.50 .60
1058 A354 5.50k multicolored 2.00 .50
Nos. 1053-1058 (6) 9.50 2.30

1994 Paralympics A365

1994, Mar. 10 **Litho.** ***Perf. 13***
1059 A365 4.50k Skier 1.50 .60
1060 A365 5.50k Skier, diff. 2.00 .50

Tromso Charter, Bicent. A366

Litho. & Engr.
1994, Apr. 19 ***Perf. 13***
1061 A366 3.50k Royal seal 1.50 .25
1062 A366 4.50k Cathedral 2.00 .50

Norwegian Folk Museum, Cent. A367

Designs: 3k, Log buildings, Osterdal Valley. 3.50k, Sled, 1750.

Litho. & Engr.
1994, June 14 ***Perf. 12½x13***
1063 A367 3k multicolored 1.25 .50
1064 A367 3.50k multicolored 1.50 .25

Research in Norway A368

Abstract designs with various formulas, microchips, glass flasks.

1994, June 14 **Litho.**
1065 A368 4k multicolored 1.50 .60
1066 A368 4.50k multicolored 2.00 .60

Electric Tram Lines, Cent. A369

Litho. & Engr.
1994, Sept. 23 ***Perf. 13x13½***
1067 A369 3.50k Early tram, map 1.50 .25
1068 A369 12k Modern tram, map 5.00 .60

Stamp Day Type of 1993

Ornamental broaches: a, Gold, embossed designs. b, Silver, embossed designs. c, Silver, circular designs. d, Gold, jeweled center.

1994, Sept. 23 **Litho.** ***Perf. 13½x13***
1069 Sheet of 4, #a.-d. 10.00 10.00
a. A362 3k multicolored 2.00 2.00
b. A362 3.50k multicolored 2.00 2.00
c. A362 4.50k multicolored 2.00 2.00
d. A362 5.50k multicolored 2.00 2.00

No. 1069 sold for 21k.

Christmas — A370

Perf. 13½x13 on 3 Sides
1994, Nov. 18 **Litho.**
Booklet Stamps

1070 A370 3.50k Sled 1.50 .20
1071 A370 3.50k Kick sled 1.50 .20
a. Booklet pane, 5 each 15.00
Complete booklet, #1071a 15.00

Berries — A371

1995-96 **Litho.** ***Perf. 13½x13***
Booklet Stamps

1086 A371 3.50k Vaccinium vitis 1.25 .20
1087 A371 3.50k Vaccinium myrtillus 1.25 .20
a. Bklt. pane, 4 ea #1086-1087 10.00
Complete booklet, #1087a 10.00
1088 A371 3.50k Fragaria vesca 1.25 .20
1089 A371 3.50k Rubus chamaemorus 1.25 .20
a. Bklt. pane, 4 ea #1088-1089 10.00
Complete booklet, #1089a 10.00
Nos. 1086-1089 (4) 5.00 .80

Issued: #1086-1087, 2/23/95; #1088-1089, 2/22/96.

A372

A373

Apothecary Shops, 400th Anniv.: 3.50k, Swan Pharmacy, Bergen. 25k, Apothecary's tools.

Litho. & Engr.
1995, Feb. 23 ***Perf. 13½x13***
1090 A372 3.50k multicolored 1.50 .25
1091 A372 25k multicolored 9.00 1.00

1995, May 8 **Litho.** ***Perf. 13½x13***

Tourism: 4k, Skudeneshavn Harbor. 4.50k, Torghatten mountain, Helgeland coastline.

Booklet Stamps

1092 A373 4k multicolored 1.50 .60
a. Booklet pane of 8 12.00
Complete booklet, #1092a 12.00
1093 A373 4.50k multicolored 1.50 .60
a. Booklet pane of 8 12.00
Complete booklet, #1093a 12.00

Christianity in Norway A374

3.50k, Old Moster Church, c. 1100. 15k, Slettebakken Church, Bergen, 1970.

Litho. & Engr.
1995, May 8 ***Perf. 13x13½***
1094 A374 3.50k multicolored 1.50 .25
1095 A374 15k multicolored 5.00 1.00

End of World War II, 50th Anniv. A375

Designs: 3.50k, German commander saluting Terje Rollem in 1945, German forces marching down Karl Johans Gate from Royal Palace, 1940. 4.50k, King Haakon VII, Crown Prince leaving Norway in 1940, King saluting upon return in 1945. 5.50k, Children waving Norwegian flags, 1945.

1995, May 8 Litho. *Perf. 13½x13*
1096 A375 3.50k multicolored 1.50 .25
1097 A375 4.50k multicolored 1.75 .60
1098 A375 5.50k multicolored 2.00 .50
Nos. 1096-1098 (3) 5.25 1.35

Kirsten Flagstad (1895-1962), Opera Singer — A376

Design: 5.50k, In Lohengrin.

1995, June 26 Litho. *Perf. 13*
1099 A376 3.50k multicolored 1.50 .25
1100 A376 5.50k multicolored 2.00 .50

Conciliation Boards, Bicent. A377

Designs: 7k, Three-man board between two people facing away from each other. 12k, Seated board member, two people talking to each other.

1995, June 26 *Perf. 13½*
1101 A377 7k multicolored 2.25 .60
1102 A377 12k multicolored 4.50 .60

UN, 50th Anniv. A378

UN emblem and: 3.50k, Trygve Lie, Secretary General 1946-53. 5.50k, Woman drinking from clean water supply.

Litho. & Engr.

1995, Sept. 22 *Perf. 13*
1103 A378 3.50k multicolored 1.50 .25
1104 A378 5.50k multicolored 2.25 .50

Norway Post, 350th Anniv. A379

#1105, Signature, portrait of Hannibal Sehested, letter post, 1647. #1106, Wax seal, registered letters, 1745. #1107, Christiania, etc. postmarks. #1108, Funds transfer, coins, canceled envelopes, 1883. #1109, "Norske Intelligenz-Seddeler," first newspaper, newspapers, magazines, 1660. #1110, Postmarks, label, parcel post, 1827. #1111, No. 1, Type A5, stamps, 1855. #1112, Savings book stamps, bank services, 1950.

1995, Sept. 22 Litho.

Booklet Stamps

1105 A379 3.50k multicolored 1.10 .85
1106 A379 3.50k multicolored 1.10 .85
1107 A379 3.50k multicolored 1.10 .85
1108 A379 3.50k multicolored 1.10 .85
1109 A379 3.50k multicolored 1.10 .85
1110 A379 3.50k multicolored 1.10 .85
1111 A379 3.50k multicolored 1.10 .85
a. Missing gray stamp at LR *20.00* 3.00
1112 A379 3.50k multicolored 1.10 .85
a. Booklet pane, #1105-1112 12.50 12.50
Complete booklet, #1112a 12.50
b. Booklet pane, #1105-1110, #1111a, 1112 25.00 25.00
Complete booklet, #1112b 25.00

Christmas — A380

Perf. 13 on 3 Sides

1995, Nov. 24 Litho.

Booklet Stamps

1113 A380 3.50k Knitted cap 1.25 .20
1114 A380 3.50k Knitted mitten 1.25 .20
a. Bklt. pane, 4 ea #1113-1114 10.00
Complete booklet, #1114a 10.00

Svalbard Islands A381

1996, Feb. 22 Litho. *Perf. 13*
1115 A381 10k Advent Bay 5.00 .50
1116 A381 20k Polar bear 7.50 1.00

Olympic Games, Cent. A382

Tourism A383

Children's drawings: 3.50k, Cross country skier. 5.50k, Runner.

1996, Apr. 18 Litho. *Perf. 13½*
1117 A382 3.50k multicolored 1.50 .25
1118 A382 5.50k multicolored 2.00 .50

1996, Apr. 18 *Perf. 13*
1119 A383 4k Besseggen 1.25 .50
a. Booklet pane of 8 10.00
Complete booklet, #1119a 10.00
1120 A383 4.50k Urnes Stave Church 1.40 .50
a. Booklet pane of 8 11.00
Complete booklet, #1120a 11.00
1121 A383 5.50k Alta Rock Carvings 1.75 .50
a. Booklet pane of 8 14.00
Complete booklet, #1121a 14.00
Nos. 1119-1121 (3) 4.40 1.50

See Nos. 1155-1157.

Railway Centennials — A384

Litho. & Engr.

1996, June 19 *Perf. 13*
1122 A384 3k Urskog-Holand 1.25 .50
1123 A384 4.50k Setesdal 1.75 .60

The Troll Offshore Gasfield A385

3.50k, Size of Troll platform compared to Eiffel Tower. 25k, Troll platform, map of gas pipelines.

1996, June 19 Litho.
1124 A385 3.50k multicolored 1.25 .25
1125 A385 25k multicolored 9.00 1.25

Norway Post, 350th Anniv. A386

#1126, Postal courier on skis. #1127, Fjord boat, SS "Framnaes," 1920's. #1128, Mail truck, Oslo, 1920's. #1129, Early airmail service. #1130, Unloading mail, East Railroad Station, Oslo, 1950's. #1131, Using bicycle for rural mail delivery, 1970's. #1132, Customer, mail clerk, Elverum post office. #1133, Computer, globe, E-mail service.

1996, Sept. 20 Litho. *Perf. 13*

Booklet Stamps

1126 A386 3.50k multicolored 1.10 .85
1127 A386 3.50k multicolored 1.10 .85
1128 A386 3.50k multicolored 1.10 .85
1129 A386 3.50k multicolored 1.10 .85
1130 A386 3.50k multicolored 1.10 .85
1131 A386 3.50k multicolored 1.10 .85
1132 A386 3.50k multicolored 1.10 .85
1133 A386 3.50k multicolored 1.10 .85
a. Booklet pane, #1126-1133 10.00 9.00
Complete booklet, #1133a 10.00

Motion Pictures, Cent. A387

Film strips showing: 3.50k, Leif Juster, Sean Connery, Liv Ullmann, The Olsen Gang Films, Il Temp Gigante. 5.50k, Wenche Foss, Jack Fjeldstad, Marilyn Monroe, murder, blood, shooting. 7k, Charlie Chaplin, Ottar Gladvedt, Laurel & Hardy, Marlene Dietrich.

1996, Sept. 20
1134 A387 3.50k multicolored 1.10 .25
1135 A387 5.50k multicolored 1.75 .50
1136 A387 7k multicolored 2.25 .60
Nos. 1134-1136 (3) 5.10 1.35

A388

A389

Christmas (Embroidered motif from Norwegian folk costume): Denomination at UL (#1137), UR (#1138).

Perf. 13 on 3 Sides

1996, Nov. 21 Litho.
1137 A388 3.50k multicolored 1.25 .20
1138 A388 3.50k multicolored 1.25 .20
a. Bklt. pane, 4 ea #1137-1138 10.00
Complete booklet, #1138a 10.00

1996, Nov. 21 Engr.

Amalie Skram (1846-1905), Novelist: 3.50k, Portrait. 15k, Scene from performance of Skram's "People of Hellemyr."

1139 A389 3.50k claret 1.25 .25
1140 A389 15k claret & dk blue 5.00 1.25

Posthorn Type of 1893 Redrawn

1997, Jan. 2 Litho. *Perf. 13x13½*

Color of Oval

1141 A10 10o red .20 .20
1142 A10 20o blue .20 .20
a. Perf. 13¾x13¼ .50 .50
1143 A10 30o orange .20 .20
1144 A10 40o gray .20 .20
1145 A10 50o green, green numeral .20 .20
Nos. 1141-1145 (5) 1.00 1.00

Numerous design differences exist in the vertical shading lines, the size and shading of the posthorn, and in the corner wings.

See No. 1282A for stamp similar to No. 1145 but with blue numeral.

Issued: No. 1142a, Dec. 2000.

Insects A390

Flowers A391

1997, Jan. 2 *Perf. 13 on 3 Sides*
1146 A390 3.70k Bumblebee 1.25 .20
1147 A390 3.70k Ladybug 1.25 .20
a. Bklt. pane, 4 ea #1146-1147 10.00
Complete booklet 10.00

See Nos. 1180-1181.

1997, Jan. 2 *Perf. 13*
1148 A391 3.20k Red clover 1.25 .30
1149 A391 3.70k Coltsfoot 1.50 .35
1150 A391 4.30k Lily of the Valley 1.75 .40
1151 A391 5k Harebell 2.00 .45
1152 A391 6k Oxeye daisy 2.00 .55
Nos. 1148-1152 (5) 8.50 2.05

See #1182-1187, 1210-1212, 1244-1247.

World Nordic Skiing Championships, Trondheim A392

1997, Feb. 20
1153 A392 3.70k Ski jumping 1.50 .40
1154 A392 5k Cross-country skiing 2.00 .60

Tourism Type of 1996

Perf. 13 on 3 Sides

1997, Apr. 16 Litho.

Booklet Stamps

1155 A383 4.30k Roros 1.40 .50
a. Booklet pane of 8 11.50
Complete booklet, #1155a 11.50
1156 A383 5k Faerder Lighthouse 1.60 .50
a. Booklet pane of 8 13.00
Complete booklet, #1156a 13.00
1157 A383 6k Nusfjord 1.90 .60
a. Booklet pane of 8 15.00
Complete booklet #1157a 15.00

King Harald, Queen Sonja, 60th Birthdays A393

1997, Apr. 16 Litho. *Perf. 13*
1158 A393 3.70k shown 1.50 .40
1159 A393 3.70k King Harald, vert. 1.50 .40

Norway Post, 350th Anniv. A394

Post-World War II development: No. 1160, Tools for construction, 1945. No. 1161, Kon-Tiki Expedition, 1947. No. 1162, Environmental protection, establishing national parks, 1962. No. 1163, Welfare, help for the elderly, 1967. No. 1164, Off-shore oil drilling, 1969. No. 1165, Grete Waitz, marathon winner, 1983. No. 1166, Askoy Bridge, 1992. No. 1167, Winter Olympic Games, Lillehammer, 1994.

1997, Apr. 16

Booklet Stamps

1160 A394 3.70k multicolored 1.25 .85
1161 A394 3.70k multicolored 1.25 .85
1162 A394 3.70k multicolored 1.25 .85
1163 A394 3.70k multicolored 1.25 .85
1164 A394 3.70k multicolored 1.25 .85
1165 A394 3.70k multicolored 1.25 .85
1166 A394 3.70k multicolored 1.25 .85
1167 A394 3.70k multicolored 1.25 .85
a. Booklet pane, #1160-1167 12.00 12.00
Complete booklet, #1167a 12.00 12.00

City of Trondheim, Millenium A395

Stylized designs: 3.70k, New Trondheim. 12k, Ships entering harbor, King, early settlements in Old Nidaros.

1997, June 6 Litho. *Perf. 13½x13*

1168 A395 3.70k multicolored 1.50 .40
1169 A395 12k multicolored 4.50 .75

Einar Gerhardsen (1897-1987), Prime Minister — A396

Caricatures: 3.70k, In front on government buildings. 25k, Scenes of Norway.

1997, June 6 *Perf. 13½*

1170 A396 3.70k multicolored 1.50 .40
1171 A396 25k multicolored 9.00 1.50

Junior Stamp Club A397

Harald Saeverud (1897-1992), Composer A398

Topics found on stamps: No. 1172, Insect, butterfly (silhouette of person's face), cartoon character, fish, flag, hand holding pen, heart, tiger, horn, boy with dog, globe. No. 1173, Flag, hand holding pen, tree, butterfly (silhouette of person's face), ladybug, cartoon character, antique postal vehicle, soccer ball, stylized bird, man on bicycle, lighthouse.

1997, Sept. 29 Litho. *Perf. 13*

1172 A397 3.70k multicolored 1.50 .40
1173 A397 3.70k multicolored 1.50 .40

Litho. & Engr.

1997, Sept. 19 *Perf. 13½x13*

15k, Tarjei Vesaas (1897-1970), writer.

1174 A398 10k blue 5.00 .75
1175 A398 15k green 5.75 1.00

Petter Dass (1647-1706), Poet, Priest — A399

Designs: 3.20k, Dass standing in rowboat, verse. 3.70k, Dass, church on island of Alsten.

Litho. & Engr.

1997, Nov. 26 *Perf. 13*

1176 A399 3.20k multicolored 1.25 .50
1177 A399 3.70k multicolored 1.50 .40

Christmas A400

Various designs from Norwgian calendar stick, medieval forerunner of modern day calendar.

Serpentine Die Cut 13½ on 3 Sides

1997, Nov. 26 Litho.

Self-Adhesive

Booklet Stamps

1178 A400 3.70k yellow & multi 1.25 .30
1179 A400 3.70k blue & multi 1.25 .30
a. Bklt. pane, 2 ea #1178-1179 5.00
Complete booklet, 2 #1179a 20.00

Insect Type of 1997

1998, Jan. 2 *Perf. 13½ on 3 Sides*

Booklet Stamps

1180 A390 3.80k Dragonfly 1.25 .20
1181 A390 3.80k Grasshopper 1.25 .20
a. Bklt. pane, 4 ea #1180-1181 10.00
Complete booklet, #1181a 12.00

Flower Type of 1997

1998, Jan. 2 Litho. *Perf. 13*

1182 A391 3.40k Marsh marigold 1.10 .25
1183 A391 3.80k Wild pansy 1.25 .25
1184 A391 4.50k White clover 1.50 .40
1185 A391 5.50k Hepatica 2.00 .40
1186 A391 7.50k Pale pasqueflower 2.50 .50
1187 A391 13k Purple saxifrage 4.50 .50
Nos. 1182-1187 (6) 12.85 2.30

Valentine's Day — A401

1998, Feb. 9 *Die Cut Perf. 14x13*

Self-Adhesive

1188 A401 3.80k multicolored 1.00 .50

No. 1188 was issued in sheets of 3 + 4 labels.

A402

A403

Coastal Shipping: 3.80k, Mail boat, SS Hornelen. 4.50k, Catamaran, Kommandoren.

Litho. & Engr.

1998, Apr. 20 *Perf. 13x13½*

1189 A402 3.80k dark bl & grn 1.50 .30
1190 A402 4.50k bl & dark grn 1.75 .75

Perf. 13 on 3 Sides

1998, Apr. 20 Litho.

Tourism: 3.80k, Holmenkollen ski jump, Oslo. 4.50k, Fisherman, city of Alesund. 5.50k, Summit of Hamaroyskaftet Mountain.

1191 A403 3.80k multicolored 1.25 .20
a. Booklet pane of 8 10.00
Complete booklet, #1191a 11.00
1192 A403 4.50k multicolored 1.50 .50
a. Booklet pane of 8 12.00
Complete booklet, #1192a 13.00
1193 A403 5.50k multicolored 1.75 .50
a. Booklet pane of 8 14.00
Complete booklet, #1193a 15.00
Nos. 1191-1193 (3) 4.50 1.20

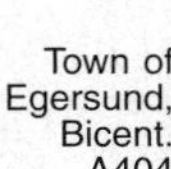

Town of Egersund, Bicent. A404

Designs: 3.80k, Port, herring boats. 6k, Pottery, white stoneware.

Litho. & Engr.

1998, Apr. 20 *Perf. 13*

1194 A404 3.80k dk blue & pink 1.50 .30
1195 A404 6k mag & dp bl 2.25 .40

Minerals — A405

1998, June 18 Litho. *Perf. 13*

1196 A405 3.40k Silver 1.10 .50
1197 A405 5.20k Cobaltite 2.00 .50

Contemporary Art — A406

Designs: 6k, "Water Rider," painting by Frans Widerberg. 7.50k, "Red Moon," tapestry by Synnove Anker Aurdal. 13k, "King Haakon VII," sculpture by Nils Aas.

1998, June 18

1198 A406 6k multicolored 2.00 .50
1199 A406 7.50k multicolored 2.50 1.00
1200 A406 13k multicolored 4.50 1.00
Nos. 1198-1200 (3) 9.00 2.50

Children's Games A407

1998, Sept. 18 Litho. *Perf. 13*

1201 A407 3.80k Hopscotch 1.25 .40
1202 A407 5.50k Pitching coins 2.00 1.00

New Airport, Gardermoen — A408

1998, Sept. 18 *Perf. 13½*

1203 A408 3.80k DC-3 1.50 .40
1204 A408 6k Boeing 737 2.50 1.00
1205 A408 24k New airport 9.00 1.00
Nos. 1203-1205 (3) 13.00 2.40

The Royal Palace A409

1998, Nov. 20 Engr. *Perf. 13x13½*

1206 A409 3.40k Royal Guard 1.25 1.00
1207 A409 3.80k Facade 1.50 .40

Christmas A410

Serpentine Die Cut 14x13 on 3 Sides

1998, Nov. 20 Photo.

Self-Adhesive

Booklet Stamps

1208 A410 3.80k red & multi 1.10 .30
1209 A410 3.80k blue & multi 1.10 .30
a. Bklt. pane, 2 ea #1208-1209 4.50
Complete booklet, 2 #1209a 9.00

Flower Type of 1997

1999, Jan. 2 Litho. *Perf. 13*

1210 A391 3.60k Red campion 1.10 .30
1211 A391 4k Wood anemone 1.25 .25
1212 A391 7k Yellow wood violet 2.25 .50
Nos. 1210-1212 (3) 4.60 1.05

Norwegian Inventions — A411

Designs: 3.60k, Cheese slicer, by Thor Bjorklund. 4k, Paper clip, by Johan Vaaler.

Die Cut Perf. 13

1999, Jan. 2 Photo.

Self-Adhesive

1213 A411 3.60k blue & black 1.10 .25
1214 A411 4k red & gray 1.25 .25

See No. 1260.

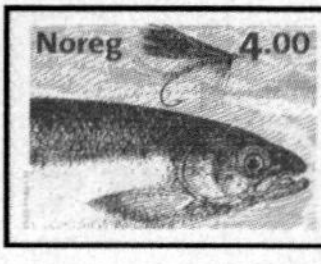

Salmon — A412

Cod — A413

Die Cut Perf. 14x13

1999, Jan. 2 Litho. & Photo.

Self-Adhesive

Booklet Stamps

1215 A412 4k multicolored 1.25 .20
1216 A413 4k multicolored 1.25 .20
a. Bklt. pane, 2 ea #1215-1216 5.00
Complete booklet, 2 #1216a 10.00

No. 1216a is a complete booklet.

St. Valentine's Day — A414

1999, Feb. 14 Litho. *Perf. 13x13½*

1217 A414 4k multicolored 1.50 .30

A415

A416

Litho. & Engr.

1999, Apr. 12 *Perf. 13*

1218 A415 4k multicolored 1.50 .30

Norwegian Confederation of Trade Unions, Cent.

1999, Apr. 12 Litho. *Perf. 13*

Tourism: 4k, Swans on lake. 5k, Hamar Cathedral. 6k, Man in traditional attire.

Booklet Stamps

1219 A416 4k multicolored 1.25 .40
a. Booklet pane of 8 10.00
Complete booklet, #1219a 10.00
1220 A416 5k multicolored 1.60 .50
a. Booklet pane of 8 13.00
Complete booklet, #1220a 13.00
1221 A416 6k multicolored 1.90 .50
a. Booklet pane of 8 15.00
Complete booklet, #1221a 15.00

Ice Hockey World Championships — A417

Designs: 4k, Poland vs Norway, 1998 Class B Championships. 7k, Sweden vs Switzerland, 1998 Class A Championships.

1999, Apr. 12 *Perf. 13½*

1222 A417 4k multicolored 1.25 .30
1223 A417 7k multicolored 2.25 .50

Millennium Stamps A418

Events from 1000-1899: 4k, Family leaving Sejestad Station, emigration period, 1800's. 6k, Statue of St. Olav (995-1030), Christian III Bible, 1550, Christianization period. 14k, King Christian IV speciedaler, miners, union period, 1380-1814. 26k, Textile factory, paper mill on Aker River, Oslo, 1850's, industrialization period.

Litho. & Engr.

1999, June 11 *Perf. 12¾x13*

1224 A418 4k multicolored 1.25 .30
1225 A418 6k multicolored 1.90 .50
1226 A418 14k multicolored 4.50 1.00
1227 A418 26k multicolored 8.25 1.25
Nos. 1224-1227 (4) 15.90 3.05

Pictures of Everyday Life — A419

1999, Sept. 9 **Litho.** *Perf. 13*

1228 A419 4k Carriage on ferry 1.25 .30
1229 A419 4k Men with hammers 1.25 .30
1230 A419 4k Pumping gasoline 1.25 .30
1231 A419 4k Milking cow 1.25 .30
1232 A419 4k Rakers 1.25 .30
1233 A419 4k Skier 1.25 .30
1234 A419 4k Boat captain 1.25 .30
1235 A419 4k Soccer player 1.25 .30
a. Souv. sheet of 8, #1228-1235 10.00 8.00

Children's Games — A420

1999, Sept. 9 **Litho.** *Perf. 13¼*

1236 A420 4k Skateboarder 1.25 .30
1237 A420 6k Roller skater 1.90 .50

National Theater, Cent. A421

Designs: 3.60k, Scene from "An Ideal Husband." 4k, Scene from "Peer Gynt."

1999, Nov. 19 **Engr.** *Perf. 12¾x13¼*

1238 A421 3.60k claret & org yel 1.10 .75
1239 A421 4k dk bl & royal bl 1.25 .30

Christmas — A422

Designs: No. 1240, Mother, children at door. No. 1241, Mother, children at window.

Die Cut Perf. 14x13 on 3 sides

1999, Nov. 19 **Litho.**

Self-Adhesive

1240 A422 4k multi 1.25 .30
1241 A422 4k multi 1.25 .30
a. Bklt. pane, 2 ea #1240-1241 4.50
Complete booklet, 2 #1241a 9.00

No. 1241a is a complete booklet.

Millennium A423

Winners of photo competition: No. 1242, "Winter Night." No. 1243, "Sunset."

Die Cut Perf. 13¼x13

1999, Dec. 31 **Litho. & Photo.**

Self-Adhesive

1242 A423 4k multi 1.50 .30
1243 A423 4k multi 1.50 .30
a. Bklt. pane of 2, #1242-1243 3.00
Complete booklet, #1243a 21.00
b. Bklt. pane, 2 ea #1242-1243 7.00
Complete booklet, 2 #1243b 14.00

One complete booklet containing No. 1243a was given free to each Norwegian household in January 2000.

Flower Type of 1997

Designs: 5.40k, Oeder's lousewort. 8k, White water lily. 14k, Globe flower. 25k, Melancholy thistle.

2000, Feb. 9 **Litho.** *Perf. 12¾x13¼*

1244 A391 5.40k multi 1.75 .30
1245 A391 8k multi 2.50 .50
1246 A391 14k multi 4.50 .75
1247 A391 25k multi 8.00 1.00
Nos. 1244-1247 (4) 16.75 2.55

Love — A424

2000, Feb. 9 *Perf. 13x13¼*

1248 A424 4k multi 1.25 .30

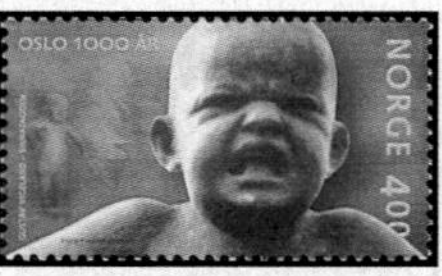

Oslo, 1000th Anniv. A425

4k, Angry Child sculpture, Frogner Park. 6k, Statue of King Christian IV, by C. L. Jacobsen. 8k, Oslo City Hall. 27k, Oslo Stock Exchange.

2000, Apr. 7 **Litho.** *Perf. 13¼*

1249 A425 4k multi 1.25 .30
1250 A425 6k multi 1.90 .50
1251 A425 8k multi 2.50 .75
1252 A426 27k multi 8.50 1.25
Nos. 1249-1252 (4) 14.15 2.80

Fauna — A426

2000, Apr. 7 *Perf. 13¼ on 3 sides*

Booklet Stamps

1253 A426 5k Golden eagle 1.60 .50
a. Booklet pane of 8 13.00
Booklet, #1253a 13.00
1254 A426 6k Elk 1.90 .50
a. Booklet pane of 8 15.00
Booklet, #1254a 15.00
1255 A426 7k Whale 2.25 .50
a. Booklet pane of 8 18.00
Complete booklet, #1255a 18.00
Nos. 1253-1255 (3) 5.75 1.50

Expo 2000, Hanover A427

Artwork of Marianne Heske: 4.20k, The Quiet Room. 6.30k, Power and Energy.

2000, June 1 *Perf. 13¼*

1256 A427 4.20k multi 1.40 .50
1257 A427 6.30k multi 2.00 .50

Royal Norwegian Military Academy, 250th Anniv. — A428

Litho. & Engr.

2000, June 2 *Perf. 13x13¼*

1258 A428 3.60k 1750 Cadets 1.25 *2.00*
1259 A428 8k 2000 Cadets 2.50 .85

Inventions Type of 1999

4.20k, Aerosol container, by Erik Rotheim.

Die Cut Perf. 12¾

2000, June 2 **Photo.**

Self-Adhesive

1260 A411 4.20k green & black 1.40 .25

Mackerel — A429

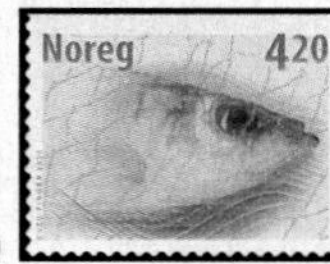

Herring — A430

Die Cut Perf. 14x13 on 3 sides

2000, June 2 **Photo. & Litho.**

Self-Adhesive

Booklet Stamps

1261 A429 4.20k multi 1.40 .20
1262 A430 4.20k multi 1.40 .20
a. Booklet pane, 2 each #1261-1262 5.50
Complete booklet, 2#1262a 11.00

A431

A432

Litho. & Engr.

2000, Sept. 15 *Perf. 13¼x13*

1263 A431 5k multi 1.60 .60

Lars Levi Laestadius (1800-61), botanist.

Perf. 13¼x13¾

2000, Sept. 15 **Litho.**

Intl. Museum of Children's Art, Oslo: 4.20k, Astronaut, by May-Therese Vorland. 6.30k, Rocket, by Jann Fredrik Ronning.

1264 A432 4.20k multi 1.40 .30
1265 A432 6.30k multi 2.00 .60

Skien, 1000th Anniv. — A433

Designs: 4.20k, Monument to loggers. 15k, Skien Church.

2000, Sept. 15 *Perf. 13¼x13*

1266 A433 4.20k multi 1.40 .50
1267 A433 15k multi 4.75 1.25

Church Altar Pieces A434

2000, Nov. 17 **Litho.** *Perf. 13x13¼*

1268 A434 3.60k Hamaroy Church 1.10 .60
1269 A434 4.20k Ski Church 1.40 .50

Comic Strips — A435

Designs: No. 1270, Nils og Blamman, by Sigurd Winsnes and Ivar Mauritz-Hansen. No. 1271, Nr. 91 Stomperud, by Ernst Garvin and Torbjorn Wen.

Die Cut Perf. 14x13 on 3 sides

2000, Nov. 17 **Photo. & Litho.**

Booklet Stamps

Self-Adhesive

1270 A435 4.20k multi 1.40 .20
1271 A435 4.20k multi 1.40 .20
a. Booklet pane, 2 each #1270-1271 5.50
Complete booklet, 2 #1271a 11.00

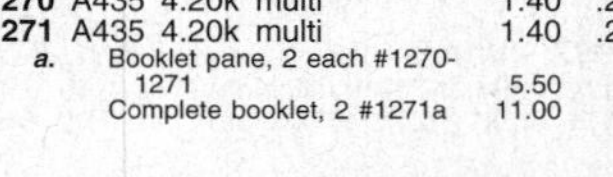

Rose Varieties A436

Designs: No. 1272, Sekel (green denomination). No. 1273, Namdal (brown denomination).

Die Cut Perf.13¼ on 3 sides

2001, Jan. 2 **Photo.**

Booklet Stamps

Self-Adhesive

1272 A436 4.50k multi 1.40 .20
1273 A436 4.50k multi 1.40 .20
a. Booklet pane, 2 each #1272-1273 5.50
Complete booklet, 2 #1273a 11.00

Crafts — A437

Designs: 4k, Mat of bound birch roots. 4.50k, Birch bark basket. 7k, Embroidered bunad.

2001, Jan. 2 ***Die Cut Perf. 12¾***

Coil Stamps

Self-Adhesive

1274 A437 4k multi 1.25 .30
1275 A437 4.50k multi 1.40 .25
1276 A437 7k multi 2.25 .50
Nos. 1274-1276 (3) 4.90 1.05

See also No. 1354.

Actors and Actresses A438

Designs: 4k, Aase Bye (1904-91). 4.50k, Per Aabel (1902-99). 5.50k, Alfred Maurstad (1896-1967). 7k, Lillebil Ibsen (1899-1989). 8k, Tore Segelcke (1901-79).

2001, Jan. 2 **Litho.** *Perf. 14x12¾*

1277 A438 4k brn & blk 1.25 .50
1278 A438 4.50k bl & blk 1.40 .30
1279 A438 5.50k gold & blk 1.75 .50
1280 A438 7k pur & blk 2.25 .60
1281 A438 8k bl gray & blk 2.50 .75
Nos. 1277-1281 (5) 9.15 2.65

Ties That Bind, by Magne Furuholmen
A439

2001, Feb. 7 Litho. *Perf. 14¾x14*
1282 A439 4.50k multi 1.40 1.00

A439a

Posthorn Type of 1893 Redrawn

2001-6 Litho. *Perf. 13¾x13¼*
Color of Oval

1282A A439a 50o green, blue denomination *1.00* .20
1283 A439a 1k green .30 .20
a. Horiz. rows of dots between vert. lines .30 .20
1284 A439a 2k Prus blue .65 .45
a. Horiz. rows of dots between vert. lines .60 .45
1285 A439a 3k blue .95 .70
1287 A439a 5k purple 1.60 .25
a. Horiz. rows of dots between vert. lines *4.00 4.00*
1288 A439a 6k purple 1.90 .45
1289 A439a 7k brown 2.25 1.75
1291 A439a 9k orange brn 2.90 .30
a. Horiz. rows of dots between vert. lines *4.00 4.00*
Nos. 1282A-1291 (8) 11.55 4.30

Numerous design differences exist between types A10 and A439a in the vertical shading lines, the size and shading of the posthorn and in the corner wings.

No. 1282A has no dots between vertical lines. Dots between vertical lines on Nos. 1283-1284, 1287, 1288 and 1291 are arranged diagonally. Nos. 1285 and 1289 have horizontal rows of dots between vertical lines.©©©©©

Issued: 1k (#1283), 2k (#1284), 6k, 2/7/01; 50o, 3/01; 5k, 9k, 2/11/02; 1k (#1283a), 2k (#1284a), 2003; 3k, 7k, 4/15/05; No. 1287a, 2006; No. 1291a, 2003.

See No. 1145 for green 50o stamp with green denomination.

School Bands, Cent.
A440

Designs: 4.50k, Tuba player. 9k, Drum majorette.

2001, Apr. 20 Litho. *Perf. 14¾x14*
1292 A440 4.50k multi 1.50 .30
1293 A440 9k multi 2.75 1.00

Adventure Sports — A441

Designs: 4.50k, Kayaking. 7k, Rock climbing.

Serpentine Die Cut 14x13 on 3 Sides

2001, Apr. 20 Photo. & Litho.
Booklet Stamps
Self-Adhesive

1294 A441 4.50k multi 1.50 .30
a. Booklet of 8 10.00
1295 A441 7k multi 2.25 .60
a. Booklet of 8 18.00

Norwegian Architecture
A442

Designs: 5.50k, Bank of Norway, Oslo, by Christian Heinrich Grosch. 8.50k, Ivar Aasen Center, Orsta, by Sverre Fehn.

2001, June 22 Litho. *Perf. 14¾x14*
1296 A442 5.50k multi 1.75 .30
1297 A442 8.50k multi 2.75 .60

Actors and Actresses — A443

Designs: 5k, Lalla Carlsen (1889-1967). 5.50k, Leif Juster (1910-95). 7k, Kari Diesen (1914-87). 9k, Arvid Nilssen (1913-76). 10k, Einar Rose (1898-1979).

2001, June 22 *Perf. 13x14*
1298 A443 5k multi 1.60 .50
1299 A443 5.50k multi 1.75 .30
1300 A443 7k multi 2.25 .60
1301 A443 9k multi 2.75 .60
1302 A443 10k multi 3.25 .60
Nos. 1298-1302 (5) 11.60 2.60

Rose Type of 2001

Die Cut Perf. 13¼x13 on 3 Sides

2001, June 22 Photo. & Litho.
Booklet Stamps
Self-Adhesive

1303 A436 5.50k Red roses 1.75 .30
1304 A436 5.50k Pink roses 1.75 .30
a. Booklet pane, 2 each #1303-1304 7.00
Booklet, 2 #1304a 14.00

Nos. 1303-1304 are impregnated with a rose scent.

Roses on No. 1303 have white centers. Compare with Illustration A460.

Crafts Type of 2001

Designs: 5k, Carved bird-shaped drinking vessel. 5.50k, Doll with crocheted clothing. 8.50k, Knitted cap.

Die Cut Perf. 14½

2001, June 22 Photo.
Coil Stamps
Self-Adhesive

1305 A437 5k multi 2.00 2.00
1306 A437 5.50k multi 2.00 2.00
1307 A437 8.50k multi 3.50 3.50
Nos. 1305-1307 (3) 7.50 7.50

2001, June 22 Photo.
Coil Stamps
Self-Adhesive

1305a Die cut perf. 12¾ 1.60 .30
1306a Die cut perf. 12¾ 1.75 .20
1307a Die cut perf. 12¾ 2.75 .50

Nobel Peace Prize, Cent.
A444

Designs: No. 1308, 1991 winner Aung San Suu Kyi. No. 1309, 1993 winner Nelson Mandela. No. 1310, Alfred Nobel. No. 1311, 1901 winner Henri Dunant. No. 1312, 1922 winner Fridjof Nansen. No. 1313, 1990 winner, Mikhail S. Gorbachev. No. 1314, 1964 winner, Dr. Martin Luther King, Jr. No. 1315, 1992 winner Dr. Rigoberta Menchú Tum.

Perf. 13¼x13¾

2001, Sept. 14 Litho. & Engr.
1308 A444 5.50k multi 1.75 .60
1309 A444 5.50k multi 1.75 .60
a. Vert. pair, #1308-1309 3.50 1.50
1310 A444 7k multi 2.25 .60
a. Souvenir sheet of 1 3.00 2.00
1311 A444 7k multi 2.25 .60
a. Vert. pair, #1310-1311 4.50 1.50
1312 A444 9k multi 2.75 .75
1313 A444 9k multi 2.75 .75
a. Vert. pair, #1312-1313 5.50 1.75
1314 A444 10k multi 3.25 1.00
1315 A444 10k multi 3.25 1.00
a. Vert. pair, #1314-1315 6.50 2.50
Nos. 1308-1315 (8) 20.00 5.90

Pets — A445

2001, Sept. 14 Litho. *Perf. 14x13¼*
1316 A445 5.50k Kittens 1.75 .30
1317 A445 7.50k Goat 2.40 .60

Aurora Borealis
A446

2001, Nov. 15
1318 A446 5k Trees 1.60 .50
1319 A446 5.50k Reindeer 1.75 .30

Christmas — A447

Gingerbread: No. 1320, Man. No. 1321, House.

Serp. Die Cut 14x13 on 3 Sides

2001, Nov. 15 Photo. & Litho.
Booklet Stamps
Self-Adhesive

1320 A447 5.50k multi 1.75 .30
1321 A447 5.50k multi 1.75 .30
a. Booklet pane, 2 each #1320-1321 7.00
Complete booklet, 2 #1321a 14.00

Actors and Actresses — A448

Designs: 5k, Tordis Maurstad (1901-97). 5.50k, Rolf Just Nilsen (1931-81). 7k, Lars Tvinde (1886-1973). 9k, Henry Gleditsch (1902-42). 10k, Norma Balean (1907-89).

2002, Feb. 11 Litho. *Perf. 13x14*
Background Color

1322 A448 5k rose lilac 1.60 .50
1323 A448 5.50k lilac 1.75 .30
1324 A448 7k beige 2.25 .60
1325 A448 9k light green 2.75 .60
1326 A448 10k dull rose 3.25 .60
Nos. 1322-1326 (5) 11.60 2.60

Contemporary Sculpture — A449

Designs: 7.50k, Monument to Whaling, by Sivert Donali. 8.50k, Throw, by Kare Groven.

2002, Apr. 12 Litho. *Perf. 13¼x13¾*
1327 A449 7.50k multi 2.40 .75
1328 A449 8.50k multi 2.75 .60

Fairy Tales
A450 A451

Designs: No. 1329, Askeladden and the Good Helpers, by Ivo Caprino. No. 1330, Giant Troll on Karl Johan, by Theodor Kittelsen.

Serpentine Die Cut 13x14 on 3 Sides

2002, Apr. 12 Photo. & Litho.
Booklet Stamps
Self-Adhesive

1329 A450 5.50k multi 1.75 .25
a. Booklet pane of 4 7.00
Booklet, 2 #1329a 14.00
1330 A451 9k multi 2.75 .50
a. Booklet pane of 4 11.00
Booklet, 2 #1330a 22.00

Norwegian Soccer Association, Cent. — A452

No. 1331: a, Boys playing soccer. b, Referee pointing, player. c, Girls playing soccer. d, Boy kicking ball.

2002, Apr. 12 *Die Cut Perf.*
Self-Adhesive

1331 Booklet pane of 4 7.00
a.-d. A452 5.50k Any single 1.75 .30
Booklet, 2 #1331 14.00

The margins of the two panes in the booklet differ.

Niels Henrik Abel (1802-29), Mathematician — A453

Designs: 5.50k, Abel, formula and curves. 22k, Formula, front page of book by Abel, curve.

Perf. 13¼x13¾

2002, June 5 Litho. & Engr.
1332 A453 5.50k multi 1.75 .30
1333 A453 22k multi 7.00 1.75

For overprints, see No. 1346-1347.

City Charter Anniversaries — A454

Designs: No. 1334, Holmestrand, 250th anniv. No. 1335, Kongsberg, 200th anniv.

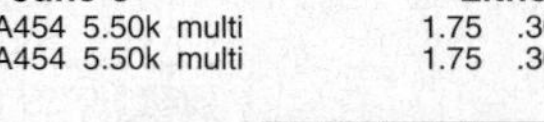
2002, June 5 Litho.
1334 A454 5.50k multi 1.75 .30
1335 A454 5.50k multi 1.75 .30

Authors — A455

Designs: 11k, Johan Collett Muller Borgen (1902-79). 20k, Nordahl Grieg (1902-43).

2002, June 5 *Perf. 14¼x14*
1336 A455 11k multi 3.50 .75
1337 A455 20k multi 6.50 1.50

Europa — A456

Designs: 5.50k, Clown juggling balls. 8.50k, Elephant, monkey on rocking horse.

2002, Sept. 20 *Perf. 14x14¾*

1338	A456	5.50k multi	1.75	.35
1339	A456	8.50k multi	3.00	.80

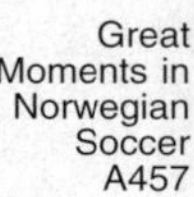

Great Moments in Norwegian Soccer
A457

Players involved in: 5k, Victory against Germany in 1936 Olympics. No. 1341, Victory against Brazil in 1998 World Cup tournament. No. 1342, Victory of women's team against US in 2000 Olympics. 7k, Victory against Sweden, 1960. 9k, Victory against England, 1981. 10k, Rosenborg's victory against Milan, in Champions League tournament, 1996.

2002, Sept. 20 *Perf. 13¼x13¾*

1340	A457	5k multi	1.60	.50
1341	A457	5.50k multi	1.75	.30
1342	A457	5.50k multi	1.75	.30
1343	A457	7k multi	2.25	.60
1344	A457	9k multi	2.75	.60
1345	A457	10k multi	3.25	.60
a.		Souvenir sheet, #1340-1345 + 6 labels	13.50	13.50
		Nos. 1340-1345 (6)	13.35	2.90

Norwegian Soccer Association, cent.

Nos. 1332-1333 Overprinted

Perf. 13¼x13¾

2002, Oct. 10 **Litho. & Engr.**

1346	A453	5.50k multi	4.00	4.00
1347	A453	22k multi	11.00	11.00

Pastor Magnus B. Landstad (1802-80), Hymn Writer and Folk Song Collector
A458

Designs: 5k, Landstad on horse, front page of 1853 book of folk songs. 5.50k, Church's hymn board, front page of 1870 hymn book, portrait of Landstad.

2002, Nov. 20

1348	A458	5k multi	1.60	.50
1349	A458	5.50k multi	1.75	.30

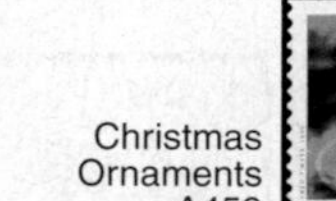

Christmas Ornaments
A459

Die Cut Perf. 13½x13 on 3 Sides

2002, Nov. 20 **Photo.**

Booklet Stamps

Self-Adhesive

1350	A459	5.50k Hearts	1.75	.30
1351	A459	5.50k Star	1.75	.30
a.		Booklet pane, 2 each #1350-1351	7.00	
		Booklet, 2 #1351a	14.00	

Rose Type of 2001 and

Grand Prix Rose — A460

Design: No. 1353, Champagne roses (light yellow).

Die Cut Perf. 13¼x13 on 3 Sides

2003, Feb. 10 **Photo. & Litho.**

Booklet Stamps

Self-Adhseive

1352	A460	5.50k multi	1.75	.20
1353	A436	5.50k multi	1.75	.20
a.		Booklet pane, 2 each #1352-1353	7.00	
		Booklet, 2 #1353a	14.00	

Roses on No. 1303 have white centers, while those on No. 1352 do not.

Crafts Type of 2001

2003, Feb. 10 *Die Cut Perf. 12¾*

Self-Adhesive

1354	A437	5.50k Duodji knife handle	1.75	.20

Graphic Arts — A461

Designs: 5k, Nordmandens Krone, by Kaare Espolin Johnson. 8.50k, Bla Hester, by Else Hagen. 9k, Dirigent og Solist, by Niclas Gulbrandsen. 11k, Olympia, by Svein Strand. 22k, Still Life XVII, by Rigmor Hansen.

Perf. 13¼x12¾

2003, Feb. 10 **Litho.**

1355	A461	5k multi	1.75	.75
1356	A461	8.50k multi	2.75	1.00
1357	A461	9k multi	3.00	1.00
1358	A461	11k multi	3.50	1.25
1359	A461	22k multi	7.25	1.50
a.		Perf. 14x12¾	6.75	5.00
		Nos. 1355-1359 (5)	18.25	5.50

St. Valentine's Day — A462

Inscriptions beneath scratch-off heart: b, Elsker deg! c, Jusen kyss! d, Glad i dag! e, Klem fra meg! f, Du er sot! g, Min beste venn! h, Yndlings-bror. i, Yndlings-soster. j, Verdens beste far. k, Verdens beste mor.

2003, Feb. 10 *Perf. 14¾x14*

1360		Sheet of 10	17.50	8.00
a.		A462 5.50k Any single, unscratched	1.75	.65
b.-k.		A462 5.50k Any single, scratched		.65

Unused value for No. 1360a is for stamp with attached selvage. Inscriptions are shown in selvage next to each stamp.

Fairy Tale Illustrations by Theodor Kittelsen (1857-1914)
A463 A464

Serpentine Die Cut 13x14 on 3 Sides

2003, May 22 **Photo. & Litho.**

Booklet Stamps

Self-Adhesive

1361	A463	5.50k Forest troll	1.75	.30
a.		Booklet pane of 4	7.00	
		Complete booklet, 2 #1361a	14.00	

Serpentine Die Cut 14x13 on 3 Sides

1362	A464	9k Water sprite	2.75	.80
a.		Booklet pane of 4	11.00	
		Complete booklet, 2 #1362a	22.00	

Bergen Intl. Music Festival, 50th Anniv.
A465

Musical score and: 5.50k, Violinist. 10k, Children.

2003, May 22 **Litho.** *Perf. 13¼x14*

1363	A465	5.50k multi	1.75	.80
1364	A465	10k multi	3.25	1.10

Public Health Service, 400th Anniv.
A466

Designs: 5.50k, Heart transplant operation. 7k, Infant welfare clinic.

2003, May 22

1365	A466	5.50k multi	1.75	.80
1366	A466	7k multi	2.25	1.10

Norwegian Refugee Council, 50th Anniv.
A467

Designs: 5.50k, Child with bread. 10k, Line of refugees.

2003, June 20

1367	A467	5.50k multi	1.75	.80
1368	A467	10k multi	3.25	1.10

King Olav V (1903-91) — A468

Designs: 5.50k, As child, with parents. 8.50k, With Crown Princess Märtha. 11k, In uniform.

Litho. & Engr.

2003, June 20 *Perf. 14x13¼*

1369	A468	5.50k multi	1.75	.30
1370	A468	8.50k multi	2.75	1.00
1371	A468	11k multi	3.50	1.50
a.		Souvenir sheet, #1369-1371	8.00	8.00
		Nos. 1369-1371 (3)	8.00	2.80

Norwegian Nobel Laureates
A469

Designs: 11k, Bjornsterne Bjornson, Literature, 1903. 22k, Lars Onsager, Chemistry, 1968.

Perf. 13¼x13¾

2003, Sept. 19 **Litho. & Engr.**

1372	A469	11k multi	3.50	1.25
1373	A469	22k multi	7.00	2.00

Europa — A470

Poster art: 8.50k, Dagbladet newspaper poster, by Per Krohg. 9k, Travel poster, by Knut Yran. 10k, 1985 North of Norway Music Festival poster, by Willibald Storn.

2003, Sept. 19 **Litho.** *Perf. 13¾*

1374	A470	8.50k multi	3.00	1.25
1375	A470	9k multi	3.00	1.50
1376	A470	10k multi	3.25	1.75
		Nos. 1374-1376 (3)	9.25	4.50

Special Occasions
A471

Designs: No. 1377, Baby, children's names. No. 1378, Children, birthday cake, toys. No. 1379, Man and woman at party, musical notes. No. 1380, Hands, Cupid. No. 1381, Lily.

Die Cut Perf. 13x13½

2003, Sept. 19 **Photo.**

Self-Adhesive

1377	A471	5.50k multi	1.75	.65
1378	A471	5.50k multi	1.75	.65
1379	A471	5.50k multi	1.75	.65
1380	A471	5.50k multi	1.75	.65
1381	A471	5.50k multi	1.75	.65
		Nos. 1377-1381 (5)	8.75	3.25

Graphic Arts — A472

Designs: 5k, Winter Landscape, woodcut by Terje Grostad. 5.50k, Goatherd and Goats, by Rolf Nesch.

Perf. 13¾x12¾

2003, Nov. 21 **Litho.**

1382	A472	5k multi	1.60	.80
1383	A472	5.50k multi	1.75	.80

Christmas
A473

Serpentine Die Cut 13¼x13 on 3 Sides

2003, Nov. 21 **Photo.**

Booklet Stamps

Self-Adhesive

1384	A473	5.50k Santa Claus	1.75	.30
1385	A473	5.50k Gift	1.75	.30
a.		Booklet pane, 2 each #1384-1385	9.50	
		Complete booklet, 2 #1385a	19.00	

Paintings — A474

Designs: 6k, Idyll, by Christian Skredsvig. 9.50k, Stetind in Fog, by Peder Balke. 10.50k, Worker's Protest, by Reidar Aulie.

2004, Jan. 2 **Litho.** *Perf. 13x14*

1386	A474	6k multi	1.90	.60
1387	A474	9.50k multi	3.00	1.25
1388	A474	10.50k multi	3.25	1.25
		Nos. 1386-1388 (3)	8.15	3.10

Marine Life — A475

Designs: 5.50k, Periphylla periphylla. 6k, Anarhichas lupus. 9k, Sepiola atlantica.

Die Cut Perf. 15½x14¼

2004, Jan. 2 **Photo.**

Self-Adhesive

1389	A475	5.50k multi	1.75	.30
1390	A475	6k multi	2.00	.20
1391	A475	9k multi	2.75	.75
		Nos. 1389-1391 (3)	6.50	1.25

"Person to Person" A476

Stylized: No. 1392, Man and woman. No. 1393, Globe.

Serpentine Die Cut 13¼x13 on 3 Sides

2004, Jan. 2 Photo. & Litho.

Self-Adhesive

Booklet Stamps

1392 A476 6k multi 1.90 .20
1393 A476 6k multi 1.90 .20
a. Booklet pane, 2 each #1392-1393 8.00
Complete booklet, 2 #1393a 16.00

Sunflower Heart — A477

2004, Feb. 6 Litho. *Perf. 14x13¼*
1394 A477 6k multi 1.90 .60

Printed in sheets of 6 stamps and 3 labels.

Europa A478

Designs: 6k, Bicyclist in Moskenes. 7.50k, Kayaker on Oslo Fjord. 9.50k, Hikers crossing Stygge Glacier.

Die Cut Perf. 13½x13 on 3 Sides

2004, Mar. 26 Photo. & Litho.

Self-Adhesive

Booklet Stamps

1395 A478 6k multi 1.75 1.25
a. Booklet pane of 4 7.00
Complete booklet, 2 #1395a 14.00
1396 A478 7.50k multi 2.25 1.75
a. Booklet pane of 4 9.00
Complete booklet, 2 #1396a 18.00
1397 A478 9.50k multi 2.75 2.10
a. Booklet pane of 4 11.00
Complete booklet, 2 #1397a 22.00
Nos. 1395-1397 (3) 6.75 5.10

Otto Sverdrup (1854-1930), Arctic Explorer — A479

Litho. & Engr.

2004, Mar. 26 *Perf. 13¼*
1398 A476 6k shown 1.75 1.25
1399 A476 9.50k Ship "Fram" 2.75 2.10
a. Souvenir sheet, #1398-1399 + label 4.50 4.50

See Canada Nos. 2026-2027, Greenland No. 426.

Norse Mythology A480

Designs: 7.50k, Njord, god of wind, sea and fire and ship. 10.50k, Nanna, wife of Balder, Balder's horse, ship.

Perf. 14¼x13¾

2004, Mar. 26 Litho.
1400 A480 7.50k multi 2.25 1.75
1401 A480 10.50k multi 3.00 2.25
a. Souvenir sheet, #1400-1401 5.25 5.25

Souvenir Sheet

Birth of Princess Ingrid Alexandra — A481

2004, Apr. 17 *Perf. 13¾*
1402 A481 6k multi 1.75 1.75

King Haakon IV Haakonson (1204-63) A482

Designs: 12k, Silhouette of King Haakon IV Haakonson, bows of Viking ships. 22k, Sword and Haakon's Hall, Bergen.

2004, June 18 *Perf. 14¼x14¾*
1403 A482 12k multi 3.50 2.60
1404 A482 22k multi 6.50 5.00

Railways in Norway, 150th Anniv. A483

Designs: 6k, Koppang Station. 7.50k, Dovre Station. 9.50k, Locomotive, Kylling Bridge. 10.50k, Airport Express train.

2004, June 18 *Perf. 13¼*
1405 A483 6k multi 1.75 1.25
1406 A483 7.50k multi 2.25 1.75
1407 A483 9.50k multi 2.75 2.10
1408 A483 10.50k multi 3.00 2.25
Nos. 1405-1408 (4) 9.75 7.35

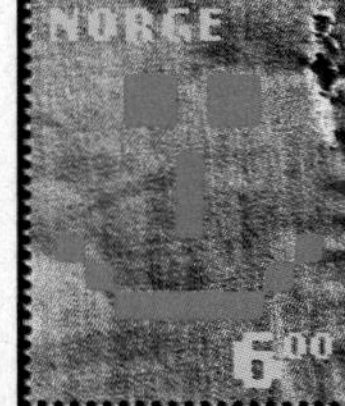

A484

Children's Stamps — A485

2004, Sept. 17 *Perf. 13¼x14*
1409 A484 6k multi 1.75 1.25
1410 A485 9k multi 2.60 2.00

Oseberg Excavations, Cent. — A486

Designs: 7.50k, Archaeologists uncovering ship's stern, excavated containers. 9.50k, Textile fragment, ceremonial sleigh. 12k, Bed and rattle.

Litho. & Engr.

2004, Sept. 17 *Perf. 13x13¼*
1411 A486 7.50k multi 2.25 1.75
1412 A486 9.50k multi 2.75 2.10
1413 A486 12k multi 3.50 2.60
Nos. 1411-1413 (3) 8.50 6.45

Norwegian Nobel Laureates Type of 2003

Designs: 5.50k, Odd Hassel, Chemistry, 1969. 6k, Christian Lous Lange, Peace, 1921.

Perf. 13¼x13¾

2004, Nov. 19 Litho. & Engr.
1414 A469 5.50k multi 1.90 1.40
1415 A469 6k multi 2.00 1.50

Christmas — A487

Winning art in UNICEF children's stamp design contest: No. 1416, Children and sun, by Hanne Soteland. No. 1417, Child on woman's lap, by Synne Amalie Lund Kallak.

Serpentine Die Cut 13x13¼ on 3 Sides

2004, Nov. 19 Photo. & Litho.

Self-Adhesive

Booklet Stamps

1416 A487 6k multi 2.00 1.50
1417 A487 6k multi 2.00 1.50
a. Booklet pane, 2 each #1416-1417 8.00
Complete booklet, 2 #1417a 16.00

Illustrations From "The Three Princesses in the Blue Hill," by Erik Werenskiold (1855-1936) A488

Designs: 7.50k, Princesses and guard. 9.50k, Baby in cradle.

2005, Jan. 7 Litho. *Perf. 14¼x14*
1418 A488 7.50k multi 2.40 1.75
1419 A488 9.50k multi 3.00 2.25

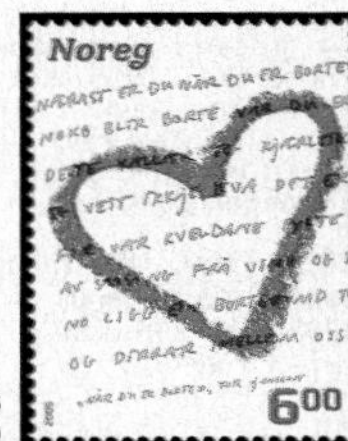

St. Valentine's Day — A489

2005, Feb. 4 *Perf. 13¼x13¾*
1420 A489 6k red & silver 1.90 1.40

Church City Missions, 150th Anniv. A490

Designs: 5.50k, Soup kitchen. 6k, Ministers administering communion.

2005, Feb. 4 *Perf. 13¾x14¼*
1421 A490 5.50k multi 1.75 1.25
1422 A490 6k multi 1.90 1.40

Children's Mental Health Pioneers — A491

Designs: 12k, Nic Waal (1905-60), first Norwegian child psychiatrist. 22k, Aase Gruda Skard (1905-85), first Norwegian child psychologist.

2005, Feb. 4 *Perf. 14¼x14¾*
1423 A491 12k multi 3.75 2.75
1424 A491 22k multi 7.00 5.25

A492

Children's Drawings of Norway in 2105 — A493

2005, Apr. 15 Litho. *Perf. 14x12¾*
1425 A492 6k multi 1.90 1.40
1426 A493 7.50k multi 2.40 1.75

Tourism — A494

Designs: 6k, Geiranger Fjord. 9.50k, Kjofossen Waterfall, Flam. 10.50k, Polar bear, Svalbard.

Die Cut Perf. 13x13¼ on 3 Sides

2005, Apr. 15 Photo. & Litho.

Booklet Stamps

Self-Adhesive

1427 A494 6k multi 1.90 1.40
a. Booklet pane of 4 7.75
Complete booklet, 2 #1427a 15.50
1428 A494 9.50k multi 3.00 2.25
a. Booklet pane of 4 12.00
Complete booklet, 2 #1428a 24.00
1429 A494 10.50k multi 3.25 2.40
a. Booklet pane of 4 13.00
Complete booklet, 2 #1429a 26.00
Nos. 1427-1429 (3) 8.15 6.05

Dissolution of Union with Sweden, Cent. — A495

Designs: 6k, Norwegian Prime Minister Christian Michelsen, Norwegian negotiators and signatures. 7.50k, King Haakon VII, ships.

Perf. 12½x12¾

2005, May 27 Litho. & Engr.

1430 A495 6k multi 1.90 1.40
1431 A495 7.50k multi 2.40 1.75
a. Souvenir sheet, #1430-1431 4.50 4.50

See Sweden No. 2514.

Historic Events Since Dissolution of Union with Sweden A496

Designs: No. 1432, King Haakon VII taking oath of allegiance, 1905. No. 1433, Crown Prince Olav celebrating end of World War II, 1945. No. 1434, King Olav V at inauguration of Norwegian television broadcasting, 1960. No. 1435, Prime Minister Trygve Bratteli opening Ekofisk oil field, 1971. No. 1436, Victory of Norwegian World Cup soccer team over Brazil, 1998.

2005, June 7 Litho. *Perf. 13¾*

1432 A496 6k multi 1.90 1.40
1433 A496 6k multi 1.90 1.40
1434 A496 6k multi 1.90 1.40
1435 A496 6k multi 1.90 1.40
1436 A496 9k multi 2.75 2.10
Nos. 1432-1436 (5) 10.35 7.70

Tall Ships — A497

Designs: 6k, Christian Radich. 9.50k, Sorlandet. 10.50k, Statsraad Lehmkuhl.

2005, June 7 *Perf. 13¾x13½*

1437 A497 6k multi 1.90 1.40
1438 A497 9.50k multi 3.00 2.25
1439 A497 10.50k multi 3.25 2.40
Nos. 1437-1439 (3) 8.15 6.05

Marine Life Type of 2004

Designs: B, Orcinus orca. A, Urticina eques.

Die Cut Perf. 15½x14¼

2005, Sept. 1 Photo.

Self-Adhesive

1440 A475 B multi 1.75 1.40
1441 A475 A multi 2.00 1.50

No. 1440 sold for 5.50k and No. 1441 sold for 6k on day of issue.

Lighthouses A498

Designs: No. 1442, Jomfruland (white lighthouse). No. 1443, Tranoy (red and white lighthouse).

Die Cut Perf. 13¼x13 on 3 Sides

2005, Sept. 1 Photo. & Litho.

Self-Adhesive

Booklet Stamps

1442 A498 A multi 2.00 1.50
1443 A498 A multi 2.00 1.50
a. Booklet pane, 2 each #1442-1443 8.00
Complete booklet, 2 #1443a 16.00

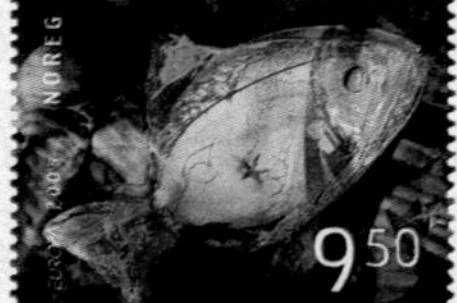

Europa A499

2005, Sept. 16 Litho. *Perf. 14¾x14*

1444 A499 9.50k Fish 3.00 2.25
1445 A499 10.50k Table 3.50 2.60

Norwegian Telegraph Service, 150th Anniv. A500

Designs: 6k, Telegraph key and poles. 10.50k, Woman and symbols of modern communication.

Perf. 13½x13¾

2005, Sept. 16 Litho. & Engr.

1446 A500 6k multi 1.90 1.40
1447 A500 10.50k multi 3.50 2.60

Geological Society of Norway, Cent. — A501

Designs: 5.50k, Thortveitite and feldspar. 6k, Oil rig, ship, map of Norway, microfossil and stylized rock layers.

2005, Sept. 16 Litho. *Perf. 13¾*

1448 A501 5.50k multi 1.75 1.40
1449 A501 6k multi 1.90 1.40

Norwegian Postage Stamps, 150th Anniv. — A502

Designs: A, Eye, vignette and spandrels of Norway #1. 12k, Norway #1, woman writing letter.
Illustration reduced.

Litho., Engr. & Silk Screened

2005, Nov. 17 *Perf. 14x14¼*

1450 A502 A multi 2.00 1.50

Souvenir Sheet

1451 Sheet, #1450, 1451a 6.00 6.00
a. A502 12k multi 4.00 3.00

No. 1450 sold for 6k on day of issue.

Royal House, Cent. — A503

Designs: No. 1452, Norwegian Prime Minister greeting King Haakon VII and Crown Prince Olav, 1905. No. 1453, Royal coat of arms, King Haakon VII, Queen Maud and Crown Prince Olav, 1945, King Harald V, Crown Prince Haakon, and Princess Ingrid Alexandra, 2004.

2005, Nov. 18 Litho. *Perf. 14x13½*

1452 A503 6k multi 2.00 1.50
1453 A503 6k multi 2.00 1.50

Christmas — A504

Designs: No. 1454, Gingerbread Christmas tree. No. 1455, Oranges studded with cloves on bed of nuts.

Serpentine Die Cut 13x13¼ on 3 Sides

2005, Nov. 19 Photo. & Litho.

Booklet Stamps

Self-Adhesive

1454 A504 A multi 2.00 1.50
1455 A504 A multi 2.00 1.50
a. Booklet pane, 2 each #1454-1455 8.00
Complete booklet, 2, #1455a 16.00

Nos. 1454-1455 each sold for 6k on day of issue and are impregnated with a cinnamon scent.

Norwegian Language Society, Cent. — A505

2006, Feb. 3 Litho. *Perf. 13¼x13¾*

1456 A505 6k multi 1.90 1.40

St. Valentine's Day — A506

2006, Feb. 3 *Perf. 13¾x14¼*

1457 A506 A multi 1.90 1.40

Sold for 6k on day of issue.

2006 Winter Olympics, Turin — A507

Designs: 6k, Kari Traa, freestyle skier. 22k, Ole Einar Bjorndalen, biathlon.

2006, Feb. 3 *Perf. 14¼x14¾*

1458 A507 6k multi 1.90 1.40
1459 A507 22k multi 6.75 5.00

Norwegian Lifesaving Society, Cent. — A508

Designs: 10k, Lifeguard carrying man. 10.50k, Child swimming.

2006, Feb. 24 *Perf. 13¾*

1460 A508 10k multi 3.00 2.25
1461 A508 10.50k multi 3.25 2.40

Greetings A509

Designs: No. 1462, Baby and spoon. No. 1463, Birthday cake. No. 1464, Heart and wedding rings. No. 1465, Flower.

2006, Feb. 24 *Die Cut Perf. 13¼*

Self-Adhesive

1462 A509 A multi 1.75 1.40
1463 A509 A multi 1.75 1.40
1464 A509 A multi 1.75 1.40
1465 A509 A multi 1.75 1.40
Nos. 1462-1465 (4) 7.00 5.60

Each stamp sold for 6k on day of issue. Each stamp was issued on a white paper backing with surrounding selvage and in coils on a translucent paper backing without surrounding selvage.

Polycera Quadrilineata A510

Die Cut Perf. 15½x14½

2006, Mar. 29 Photo.

Coil Stamp

1466 A510 10k multi 3.00 2.25

Wildlife A511

2006, Mar. 29 Litho. *Perf. 13¼x14*

1467 A511 6.50k Lynx 2.00 1.50
1468 A511 8.50k Capercaillie 2.60 2.00
1469 A511 10k Golden eagle 3.00 2.25
1470 A511 10.50k Arctic fox 3.25 2.40
1471 A511 13k Arctic hare 4.00 3.00
Nos. 1467-1471 (5) 14.85 11.15

Souvenir Sheet

Norse Mythology — A512

No. 1472: a, Design on Sami shaman's drum. b, Carved door post from Hylestad Stave Church depicting dragon and dragon slayer.

2006, Mar. 29 *Perf. 14x14¼*

1472 A512 Sheet of 2 5.00 5.00
a. A multi 1.75 1.40
b. 10.50k multi 3.25 2.25

No. 1472a sold for 6k on day of issue.

Norwegian Arctic Expeditions, Cent. — A513

Designs: 6.50k, Gunnar Isachsen and assistant surveying terrain. 8.50k, Coal cable car terminal, Store Norske Spitzbergen mines. 22k, Longyearbyen.

Litho. & Engr.

2006, June 9 *Perf. 13½x14*

1473 A513 6.50k multi 2.10 2.10
1474 A513 8.50k multi 2.75 2.75

Litho.

1475 A513 22k multi 7.00 7.00
a. Souvenir sheet, #1473-1475 12.00 12.00
Nos. 1473-1475 (3) 11.85 11.85

Tourism A514

Designs: No. 1476, Paddle steamer Skibladner. No. 1477, Maihaugen Museum, Lillehammer. No. 1478, Kirkeporten natural arch. No. 1479, North Cape. No. 1480, Bryggen UNESCO World Heritage Site. No. 1481, Storeseisundet Bridge on Atlantic Road.

Die Cut Perf. 13¼x13½

2006, June 9 Photo.

Self-Adhesive

Booklet Stamps

1476	A514	6.50k multi	2.10	2.10
1477	A514	6.50k multi	2.10	2.10
a.		Booklet pane, 5 each #1476-1477	21.00	
1478	A514	8.50k multi	2.75	2.75
1479	A514	8.50k multi	2.75	2.75
a.		Booklet pane, 5 each #1478-1479	27.50	
1480	A514	10.50k multi	3.50	3.50
1481	A514	10.50k multi	3.50	3.50
a.		Booklet pane, 5 each #1480-1481	35.00	
		Nos. 1476-1481 (6)	16.70	16.70

Consumer Cooperatives, Cent. — A515

2006, June 9 Litho. ***Perf. 13½x14***

1482	A515	6.50k multi	2.10	2.10

Personalized Stamp — A516

Serpentine Die Cut 11¾ Syncopated

2006, Aug. 22

Self-Adhesive

1483	A516	A multi	2.00	2.00

No. 1483 sold for 6.50k on the day of issue. The image shown is the generic image sold at face value. Stamps could be personalized, presumably for an extra fee.

Marine Life — A517

Designs: B, Strongylocentrotus droebachiensis. A, Labrus bimaculatus.

Die Cut Perf. 15½x14½

2006, Sept. 15 Photo.

Self-Adhesive

Coil Stamps

1484	A517	B multi	1.90	1.90
1485	A517	A multi	2.00	2.00

On day of issue, No. 1484 sold for 6k; No. 1485 for 6.50k.

King's Guard, 150th Anniv. A518

Designs: 6.50k, King's Guard in dress uniforms. 13k, In field uniforms, with helicopter.

2006, Sept. 15 Litho. ***Perf. 14x13¼***

1486	A518	6.50k multi	2.00	2.00
1487	A518	13k multi	4.00	4.00
a.		Souvenir sheet, #1486-1487	6.00	6.00

Europa A519

Designs: 8.50k, Five children. 13k, Three children playing soccer.

2006, Nov. 17 ***Perf. 13¾***

1488	A519	8.50k multi	2.75	2.75
1489	A519	13k multi	4.25	4.25

Christmas A520

Designs: No. 1490, Children and Christmas tree. No. 1491, Child and snowman.

Die Cut Perf. 13¼x13½

2006, Nov. 17 Photo. & Litho.

Self-Adhesive

Booklet Stamps

1490	A520	A multi	2.10	2.10
1491	A520	A multi	2.10	2.10
a.		Booklet pane, 5 each #1490-1491	21.00	

On day of issue each stamp sold for 6.50k.

Personalized Stamp — A521

Serpentine Die Cut 11¾ Syncopated

2006, Nov. 17 Litho.

Self-Adhesive

1492	A521	A multi	2.10	2.10

No. 1492 sold for 6.50k on the day of issue. The image shown is the generic image sold at face value. Stamps could be personalized, presumably for an extra fee.

St. Valentine's Day — A522

2007, Feb. 6 Litho. ***Perf. 13¼***

1493	A522	A multi	2.10	2.10

Sold for 6.50k on day of issue. Values are for stamps with surrounding selvage.

Winter Rally Race Cars A523

Designs: No. 1494, Petter Solberg's Subaru Impreza. No. 1495, Henning Solberg's Peugeot 307. No. 1496, Thomas Schie's Ford Focus.

Litho. With Foil Application

2007, Feb. 6 ***Perf. 13¼x13¾***

1494	A523	A Innland multi	2.10	2.10
1495	A523	A Europa multi	2.75	2.75
1496	A523	A Verden multi	3.50	3.50
a.		Souvenir sheet, #1494-1496	8.50	8.50
		Nos. 1494-1496 (3)	8.35	8.35

On day of issue, No. 1494 sold for 6.50k; No. 1495, for 8.50k; No. 1496, for 10.50k.

King Harald V, 70th Birthday — A524

Perf. 13¾x13¼

2007, Feb. 21 Litho.

1497	A524	6.50k multi	2.10	2.10

Mammals A525

Designs: 12k, Hedgehog. 22k, Red squirrel.

2007, Feb. 21 ***Perf. 13¼x13¾***

1498	A525	12k multi	4.00	4.00
1499	A525	22k multi	7.25	7.25

Souvenir Sheet

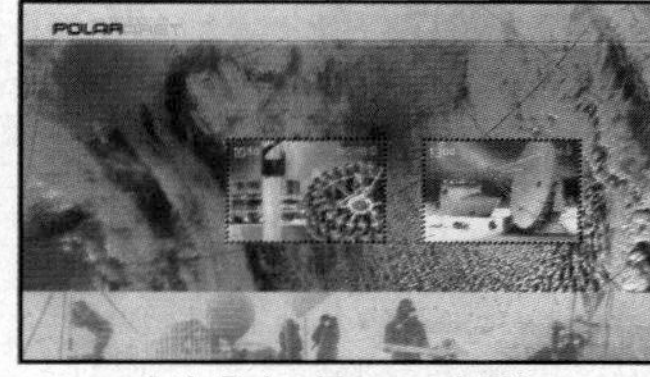
Intl. Polar Year — A526

No. 1500: a, Ice core, oceanographic equipment. b, K/V Svalbard, dish antenna.

2007, Feb. 21

1500	A526	Sheet of 2	7.75	7.75
a.		10.50k multi	3.50	3.50
b.		13k multi	4.25	4.25

Porsgrunn, Bicent. — A527

2007, Apr. 27

1501	A527	A Innland multi	2.40	2.40

Sold for 7k on day of issue.

Illustrations by Theodor Kittelsen (1857-1914) A528

Designs: No. 1502, An Attack (grasshoppers, mosquito, flower). No. 1503, Premature Delivery (frogs, hatched bird).

2007, Apr. 27 ***Perf. 14x13½***

1502	A528	A Europa multi	3.00	3.00
1503	A528	A Verden multi	3.75	3.75

On day of issue, No. 1502 sold for 9k; No. 1503, for 11k.

Skydivers A529

Cyclists A530

Buildings, Roros A531

Bridge, Fredrikstad A532

Pilot House, Portor A533

Reine Harbor A534

Die Cut Perf. 13¼x13¾

2007, Apr. 27

Self-Adhesive

Booklet Stamps

1504	A529	A Innland multi	2.40	2.40
1505	A530	A Innland multi	2.40	2.40
a.		Booklet pane, 5 each #1504-1505	24.00	
1506	A531	A Europa multi	3.00	3.00
1507	A532	A Europa multi	3.00	3.00
a.		Booklet pane, 5 each #1506-1507	30.00	
1508	A533	A Verden multi	3.75	3.75
1509	A534	A Verden multi	3.75	3.75
a.		Booklet pane, 5 each #1508-1509	37.50	
		Nos. 1504-1509 (6)	18.30	18.30

On day of issue, Nos. 1504-1505 each sold for 7k; Nos. 1506-1507 each sold for 9k; Nos. 1508-1509 each sold for 11k.

Marine Life — A535

Designs: No. 1510, Pandalus montagui. No. 1511, Homarus gammarus. No. 1512, Cancer pagurus. No. 1513, Galathea strigosa. 11k, Scomber scombrus.

2007 ***Die Cut Perf. 15½x14½***

Self-Adhesive

Coil Stamps

1510	A535	A Innland multi	2.60	2.60
1511	A535	A Innland multi	2.60	2.60
1512	A535	A Innland multi	2.60	2.60
1513	A535	A Innland multi	2.60	2.60
a.		Horiz. strip of 4, #1510-1513	10.50	
1514	A535	11k multi	3.75	3.75
		Nos. 1510-1514 (5)	14.15	14.15

Issued; Nos. 1510-1513, 9/21; No. 1514, 5/2. On day of issue, Nos. 1510-1513 each sold for 7k.

Europa
A536

Designs: 9k, Scouts, knots. 11k, Hitch diagrams, camp gateway.

Perf. 13¼x13¾

2007, May 11 **Litho. & Engr.**

1515 A536 9k multi	3.00	3.00
1516 A536 11k multi	3.75	3.75

Scouting, cent.

Building Anniversaries — A537

Designs: 14k, Church of Our Lady, Trondheim, 800th anniv. 23k, Vardohus Fortress, 700th anniv.

2007, May 11

1517 A537 14k multi	4.75	4.75
1518 A537 23k multi	7.75	7.75

Riksmaal Society, Cent.
A538

2007, June 15 **Litho.**

1519 A538 7k multi	2.40	2.40

Personalized Stamp — A539

Serpentine Die Cut 11½ Syncopated

2007, June 15

1520 A539 A Innland multi	2.40	2.40

No. 1520 sold for 7k on day of issue. The image shown is the generic image sold at face value. Stamps could be personalized, presumably for an extra fee.

Ona Lighthouse, Romsdal
A540

Tungeneset Lighthouse, Ersfjorden
A541

Die Cut Perf. 13¼x13¾

2007, June 15

1521 A540 A Innland multi	2.40	2.40
1522 A541 A Innland multi	2.40	2.40
a. Booklet pane, 5 each #1521-1522	24.00	

Nos. 1521-1522 each sold for 7k on day of issue.

Haldis Moren Vesaas (1907-95), Poet — A542

Litho. With Foil Application

2007, Sept. 21 ***Perf. 14x13½***

1523 A542 23k multi	8.50	8.50

Mining Academy, Kongsberg, 250th Anniv. — A543

Norwegian Academy of Science and Letters, 150th Anniv. — A544

Perf. 13¼x13¾

2007, Nov. 23 **Litho. & Engr.**

1524 A543 14k multi	5.25	5.25
1525 A544 14k multi	5.25	5.25

Personalized Stamp — A545

Serpentine Die Cut 10¼ Syncopated

2007, Nov. 23

Self-Adhesive

Booklet Stamp

1526 A545 A Innland multi	2.60	2.60
a. Booklet pane of 8	21.00	

No. 1526 sold for 7k on day of issue. The image shown is the generic image sold at face value. Stamps could be personalized, presumably for an extra fee.

Christmas Star — A546

Adoration of the Magi — A547

Die Cut Perf. 13¼x13¾

2007, Nov. 23 **Photo.**

Self-Adhesive

Booklet Stamps

1527 A546 A Innland multi	2.60	2.60
1528 A547 A Innland multi	2.60	2.60
a. Booklet pane, 5 each #1527-1528	26.00	

On day of issue, Nos. 1527-1528 each sold for 7k.

A548

St. Valentine's Day — A549

2008, Feb. 8 **Litho.** ***Perf. 13¼x13¾***

1529 A548 A Innland multi	2.75	2.75
1530 A549 A Europa multi	3.50	3.50

On day of issue, Nos. 1529-1530 sold for 7k and 9k, respectively.

Mammals
A550

2008, Feb. 21

1531 A550 11k Elk	4.25	4.25
1532 A550 14k Bear	5.50	5.50
1533 A550 23k Wolf	9.00	9.00
Nos. 1531-1533 (3)	18.75	18.75

Thorleif Haug, 1924 Olympic Cross-country Skiing Gold Medalist — A551

Espen Bredesen, 1994 Olympic Ski Jumping Gold Medalist
A552

Children Skiing
A553

Kjetil André Aamodt, 1992, 2002, and 2006 Olympic Alpine Skiing Gold Medalist
A554

Die Cut Perf. 15½x14½

2008, Mar. 14 **Photo.**

Coil Stamps

Self-Adhesive

1534 A551 A Innland multi	2.75	2.75
1535 A552 A Innland multi	2.75	2.75
1536 A553 A Innland multi	2.75	2.75
1537 A554 A Innland multi	2.75	2.75
a. Horiz. strip of 4, #1534-1537	11.00	

On day of issue, Nos. 1534-1537 each sold for 7k. Norwegian Ski Federation, cent.

Souvenir Sheet

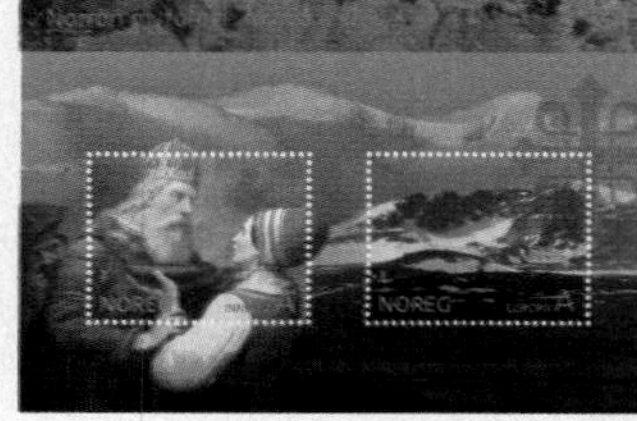

Norse Mythology — A555

No. 1538: a, Harald Fairhair meeting Snofrid. b, Snohetta Mountain.

2008, Mar. 27 **Litho.** ***Perf. 14x14¼***

1538 A555 Sheet of 2	6.50	6.50
a. A Innland multi	2.75	2.75
b. A Europa multi	3.75	3.75

On day of issue, No. 1538a sold for 7k, and No. 1538b sold for 9k.

Opera House, Oslo — A556

Litho. With Foil Application

2008, Apr. 12 ***Perf. 14x13½***

1539 A556 A Innland multi	2.75	2.75

Sold for 7k on day of issue.

Famous Men — A557

Designs: No. 1540, Frederik Stang (1808-84), Interior Minister. No. 1541, Henrik Wergeland (1808-45), lyricist.

Perf. 13¼x13¾

2008, Apr. 12 **Litho. & Engr.**

1540 A557 A Innland multi	2.75	2.75
1541 A557 A Innland multi	2.75	2.75

On day of issue, Nos. 1540-1541 each sold for 7k.

Oslo Harbor
A558

Divers, Sculpture, by Ola Enstad, Oslo — A559

The Blade, Sunnmore Alps — A560

Kjerag Boulder
A561

Sailboat and Lyngor Lighthouse
A562

Lyngor A563

Die Cut Perf. 13¼x13¾

2008, Apr. 12 **Photo.**

Booklet Stamps

Self-Adhesive

1542 A558 A Innland multi 2.75 2.75
1543 A559 A Innland multi 2.75 2.75
a. Booklet pane of 10, 5 each #1542-1543 27.50
1544 A560 A Europa multi 3.50 3.50
1545 A561 A Europa multi 3.50 3.50
a. Booklet pane of 10, 5 each #1544-1545 35.00
1546 A562 A Varden multi 4.25 4.25
1547 A563 A Varden multi 4.25 4.25
a. Booklet pane of 10, 5 each #1546-1547 42.50
Nos. 1542-1547 (6) 21.00 21.00

On day of issue, Nos. 1542-1543 each sold for 7k; Nos. 1544-1545, for 9k; Nos. 1546-1547, for 11k.

Stavanger, 2008 European Cultural Capital — A564

Designs: 7k, Dancer in a Cultural Landscape, photograph by Marcel Lelienhof. 14k, Swords in Rock, sculpture by Fritz Roed. 23k, Scene from musical, The Thousandth Heart, vert.

Perf. 14x13½, 13½x14

2008, June 6 **Litho.**

1548 A564 7k multi 2.75 2.75
1549 A564 14k multi 5.75 5.75
1550 A564 23k multi 9.25 9.25
a. Souvenir sheet, #1548-1550 13.50 13.50
Nos. 1548-1550 (3) 17.75 17.75

No. 1550a issue 10/23. Nordia 2008 Philatelic Exhibition, Stavenger (#1550a).

Transportation Centenaries — A565

Designs: 7k, SS Boroysund. 9k, SS Oster. 25k, Automobile used on first bus route. 30k, Train on Thamshavn electric railroad line.

Perf. 13¼x13¾

2008, June 6 **Litho. & Engr.**

1551 A565 7k ocher & green 2.75 2.75
1552 A565 9k rose pink & blue 3.75 3.75
1553 A565 25k lt bl & brown 10.00 10.00
1554 A565 30k pur & green 12.00 12.00
Nos. 1551-1554 (4) 28.50 28.50

2008 Summer Olympics, Beijing A566

Designs: 9k, Andreas Thorkildsen, javelin thrower. 23k, Women's handball player, Gro Hammerseng.

2008, Aug. 8 **Litho.** *Perf. 14¾x14¼*

1555 A566 9k multi 3.50 3.50
1556 A566 23k multi 8.75 8.75

Personalized Stamp — A567

Serpentine Die Cut 11¾ Syncopated

2008, Sept. 5 **Litho.**

Self-Adhesive

1557 A567 A Innland multi 2.50 2.50

No. 1557 sold for 7k on day of issue. The image shown is the generic image sold at face value. Stamps could be personalized for an extra fee.

Art — A568

Designs: No. 1559, In the Forecourt of the Revolution, by Arne Ekeland. No. 1560, Svalbard Motif, by Kare Tveter. No. 1561, Composition in Red, by Inger Sitter. No. 1562, From Sagorsk, c. 1985, by Terje Bergstad.

Die Cut Perf. 15½x14½

2008, Oct. 24 **Photo.**

Coil Stamps

Self-Adhesive

1559 A568 A Innland multi 2.10 2.10
1560 A568 A Innland multi 2.10 2.10
1561 A568 A Innland multi 2.10 2.10
1562 A568 A Innland multi 2.10 2.10
a. Horiz. strip of 4, #1559-1562 8.40
Nos. 1559-1562 (4) 8.40 8.40

On day of issue, Nos. 1559-1562 each sold for 7k.

Gnomes, Amperhaugen Farm, Stor-Elvdal A569

Gnome, Nordre Lien Farm, Stor-Elvdal A570

Die Cut Perf. 13¼x13¾

2008, Nov. 17

Booklet Stamps

Self-Adhesive

1563 A569 A Innland multi 2.00 2.00
1564 A570 A Innland multi 2.00 2.00
a. Booklet pane of 10, 5 each #1563-1564 20.00

Christmas. On day of issue, Nos. 1563-1564 each sold for 7k.

Wildlife A571

2009, Jan. 2 **Litho.** *Perf. 13¼x13¾*

1565 A571 11.50k Roe deer 3.50 3.50
1566 A571 15.50k Reindeer 4.50 4.50
1567 A571 25k Willow grouse 7.25 7.25
Nos. 1565-1567 (3) 15.25 15.25

Art — A572

Designs: B, Summer Night, a Tribute to E. M., by Kjell Nupen. 12k, Light at Whitsuntide, by Irma Salo Jaeger.

Die Cut Perf. 15½x14½

2009, Jan. 2 **Photo.**

Coil Stamps

Self-Adhesive

1568 A572 B Innland multi 2.25 2.25
1569 A572 12k multi 3.50 3.50

No. 1568 sold for 7.50k on day of issue.

Souvenir Sheet

Global Warming — A573

No. 1570: a, Warm globe. b, Globe with melting ice at meridians.

Litho. (#1570a), Litho and Embossed (#1570b)

2009, Feb. 20 *Perf. 13½*

1570 A573 Sheet of 2 4.50 4.50
a.-b. 8k Either single 2.25 2.25

SEMI-POSTAL STAMPS

North Cape Issue

North Cape — SP1

Perf. 13½x14

1930, June 28 **Wmk. 160** **Photo.**

Size: 33¼x21½mm

B1 SP1 15o + 25o blk brn 2.00 *5.00*
B2 SP1 20o + 25o car 32.50 *50.00*
B3 SP1 30o + 25o ultra 85.00 *110.00*
Nos. B1-B3 (3) 119.50 165.00
Set, never hinged 225.00

The surtax was given to the Tourist Association. See Nos. B9-B10, B28-B30, B54-B56, B59-B61.

Radium Hospital SP2

1931, Apr. 1 *Perf. 14½x13½*

B4 SP2 20o + 10o carmine 12.00 6.00
Never hinged 40.00

The surtax aided the Norwegian Radium Hospital.

Fridtjof Nansen — SP3

Queen Maud — SP4

1935, Dec. 13 *Perf. 13½*

B5 SP3 10o + 10o green 3.25 *6.00*
B6 SP3 15o + 10o red brn 10.00 *12.00*
B7 SP3 20o + 10o crimson 5.00 3.50
B8 SP3 30o + 10o brt ultra 12.00 *15.00*
Nos. B5-B8 (4) 30.25 36.50
Set, never hinged 50.00

The surtax aided the International Nansen Office for Refugees.

North Cape Type of 1930

1938, June 20 *Perf. 13x13½*

Size: 27x21mm

B9 SP1 20o + 25o brn car 3.25 *8.00*
B10 SP1 30o + 25o dp ultra 11.00 21.00
Set, never hinged 25.00

Surtax given to the Tourist Assoc.

Perf. 13x13½

1939, July 24 **Photo.** **Unwmk.**

B11 SP4 10o + 5o brt grn .40 10.00
B12 SP4 15o + 5o red brn .40 10.00
B13 SP4 20o + 5o scarlet .40 7.50
B14 SP4 30o + 5o brt ultra .40 12.00
Nos. B11-B14 (4) 1.60 39.50
Set, never hinged 4.00

The surtax was used for charities.

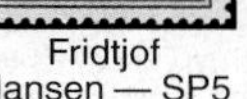

Fridtjof Nansen — SP5

SP6

1940, Oct. 21

B15 SP5 10o + 10o dk grn 2.50 3.50
B16 SP5 15o + 10o henna brn 3.00 4.75
B17 SP5 20o + 10o dark red .50 1.10
B18 SP5 30o + 10o ultra 1.25 2.25
Nos. B15-B18 (4) 7.25 11.60
Set, never hinged 13.00

The surtax was used for war relief work.

1941, May 16

Ancient Sailing Craft off Lofoten Islands.

B19 SP6 15o + 10o deep blue .90 .60
Never hinged 3.50

Haalogaland Exposition. Surtax for relief fund for families of lost fishermen.

Nos. 70-73, 177-180, 267, B19, B32-B34 and B38-B41 were demonetized from May 15, 1945 until Sept. 1, 1981. Used values are for stamps canceled after this period. Stamps with dated cancellations prior to May 15, 1945 sell for more. False cancellations exist.

Colin Archer and Lifeboat — SP7

Lifeboat — SP8

1941, July 9 *Perf. 13x13½, 13½x13*

B20 SP7 10o + 10o yel grn .95 2.25
B21 SP7 15o + 10o dk ol brn 1.25 2.25
B22 SP8 20o + 10o brt red .45 .50
B23 SP8 30o + 10o ultra 4.50 6.00
Nos. B20-B23 (4) 7.15 11.00
Set, never hinged 12.00

Norwegian Lifeboat Society, 50th anniv.

Legionary, Norwegian and Finnish Flags SP9

Vidkun Quisling SP10

1941, Aug. 1 *Perf. 13½x13*

B24 SP9 20o + 80o scar ver 50.00 85.00
Never hinged 72.50

The surtax was for the Norwegian Legion.

1942, Feb. 1

B25 SP10 20o + 30o henna 5.00 *20.00*
Never hinged 7.00

Overprinted in Red

B26 SP10 20o + 30o henna 5.00 *20.00*
Never hinged 7.00

Inauguration of Quisling as prime minister.

Catalogue values for unused stamps in this section, from this point to the end of the section, are for Never Hinged items.

Vidkun Quisling SP11

Frontier Guardsmen Emblem SP12

1942, Sept. 26 *Perf. 13*

B27 SP11 20o + 30o henna .75 *6.00*

8th annual meeting of Nasjonal Samling, Quisling's party. The surtax aided relatives of soldiers killed in action.

North Cape Type of 1930

1943, Apr. 1

Size: 27x21mm

B28 SP1 15o + 25o olive brn 1.50 1.50
B29 SP1 20o + 25o dark car 3.00 3.00
B30 SP1 30o + 25o chalky blue 2.50 2.50
Nos. B28-B30 (3) 7.00 7.00

The surtax aided the Tourist Association.

1943, Aug. 2 **Unwmk.**

B31 SP12 20o + 30o henna .75 *6.00*

The surtax aided the Frontier Guardsmen (Norwegian Nazi Volunteers).

Fishing Village — SP13

Drying Grain — SP14

Barn in Winter — SP15

1943, Nov. 10

B32 SP13 10o + 10o gray green 1.50 .60
B33 SP14 20o + 10o henna 1.50 .60
B34 SP15 40o + 10o grnsh blk 1.50 .60
Nos. B32-B34 (3) 4.50 1.80

The surtax was for winter relief.

The Baroy Sinking — SP16

Sanct Svithun Aflame — SP17

Design: 20o+10o, "Irma" sinking.

1944, May 20

B35 SP16 10o + 10o gray grn 1.40 *7.00*
B36 SP17 15o + 10o dk olive 1.40 *7.00*
B37 SP16 20o + 10o henna 1.40 *7.00*
Nos. B35-B37 (3) 4.20 *21.00*

The surtax aided victims of wartime ship sinkings, and their families.

Spinning SP19

Plowing SP20

Tree Felling — SP21

Child Care — SP22

1944, Dec. 1

B38 SP19 5o + 10o deep mag 1.25 .40
B39 SP20 10o + 10o dark yel grn 1.25 .40
B40 SP21 15o + 10o chocolate 1.25 .40
B41 SP22 20o + 10o henna 1.25 .40
Nos. B38-B41 (4) 5.00 1.60

The surtax was for National Welfare.

Red Cross Nurse — SP23

Crown Prince Olav — SP24

1945, Sept. 22

B42 SP23 20o + 10o red 1.00 1.10

80th anniv. of the founding of the Norwegian Red Cross. The surtax was for that institution.
For surcharge see No. B47.

1946, Mar. 4 **Unwmk.**

B43 SP24 10o + 10o ol grn .75 .40
B44 SP24 15o + 10o ol brn .75 .40
B45 SP24 20o + 10o dk red .75 .40
B46 SP24 30o + 10o brt bl 2.25 1.50
Nos. B43-B46 (4) 4.50 2.70

The surtax was for war victims.

No. B42 Surcharged with New Value and Bar in Black

1948, Dec. 1

B47 SP23 25o + 5o on 20o+10o .85 .85

The surtax was for Red Cross relief work.

Child Picking Flowers — SP25

1950, Aug. 15 **Photo.** *Perf. 13*

B48 SP25 25o + 5o brt red 2.50 1.10
B49 SP25 45o + 5o dp bl 7.00 6.50

The surtax was for poliomyelitis victims.

Skater — SP26

Winter Scene SP27

Design: 30o+10o, Ski jumper.

1951, Oct. 1

B50 SP26 15o + 5o olive grn 2.50 2.50
B51 SP26 30o + 10o red 2.75 2.75
B52 SP27 55o + 20o blue 12.50 12.50
Nos. B50-B52 (3) 17.75 17.75

Olympic Winter Games, Oslo, 2/14-29/52.

Kneeling Woman SP28

Crown Princess Martha SP29

1953, June 1 **Photo. & Litho.**

B53 SP28 30o + 10o red & cr 2.50 2.00

The surtax was for cancer research.

North Cape Type of 1930

1953, June 15 **Photo.**

Size: 27x21mm

B54 SP1 20o + 10o green 11.00 10.00
B55 SP1 30o + 15o red 11.00 10.00
B56 SP1 55o + 25o gray blue 18.00 14.00
Nos. B54-B56 (3) 40.00 34.00

The surtax aided the Tourist Association.

1956, Mar. 28 *Perf. 13*

B57 SP29 35o + 10o dark red 1.75 1.50
B58 SP29 65o + 10o dark blue 4.25 3.50

The surtax was for the Crown Princess Martha Memorial Fund.

North Cape Type of 1930

1957, May 6

Size: 27x21mm

B59 SP1 25o + 10o green 6.00 6.00
B60 SP1 35o + 15o red 7.00 7.00
B61 SP1 65o + 25o gray blue 4.50 3.50
Nos. B59-B61 (3) 17.50 16.50

The surtax aided the Tourist Association.

White Anemone SP30

Mother, Child, WRY Emblem SP31

Design: 90o+10o, Hepatica.

1960, Jan. 12 **Litho.** *Perf. 13*

B62 SP30 45o + 10o brt red & grn 2.50 2.75
B63 SP30 90o + 10o bl, org & grn 7.50 8.00

The surtax was for anti-tuberculosis work.

1960, Apr. 7 **Photo.** **Unwmk.**

B64 SP31 45o + 25o rose & blk 5.00 6.00
B65 SP31 90o + 25o bl & blk 10.00 10.50

World Refugee Year, July 1, 1959-June 30, 1960. The surtax was for aid to refugees.

Severed Chain and Dove SP32

Design: 60o+10o, Norwegian flags.

1965, May 8 **Photo.** *Perf. 13*

B66 SP32 30o + 10o grn, blk & tan .75 .70
B67 SP32 60o + 10o red & dk bl .75 .75

20th anniversary of liberation from the Germans. The surtax was for war cripples.

Souvenir Sheet

Offshore Oil Drilling SP33

Designs: a, Ekofisk Center. b, Treasure Scout drilling rig and Odin Viking supply vessel at Tromsoflaket, 1982. c, Statfjord C oil platform, 1984. d, Men working on deck of Neptune Nordraug.

1985, Oct. 4 **Litho.** *Perf. 13½x13*

B68 Sheet of 4 10.00 10.00
a.-d. SP33 2k + 1k, any single 2.00 2.00

Stamp Day 1985. Surtax for philatelic promotion.

Souvenir Sheet

Paper Industry SP34

Paper mill: a, Wood aging containers. b, Boiling plant. c, Paper-making machine. d, Paper dryer.

1986, Oct. 17 **Litho.** *Perf. 13½*

B69 Sheet of 4 13.00 13.00
a.-d. SP34 2.50k + 1k, any single 2.75 2.75

Surtax for philatelic promotion. Nos. B69a-B69b and B69c-B69d printed in continuous designs.

Souvenir Sheet

Salmon Industry SP35

Designs: a, Eggs and milt pressed out of fish by hand. b, Cultivation of eggs in tanks. c, Outdoor hatchery. d, Market.

1987, Oct. 9 Litho. *Perf. 13½x13*
B70 Sheet of 4 13.00 13.00
a. SP35 2.30k +50o multi 2.75 2.75
b. SP35 2.70k +50o multi 2.75 2.75
c. SP35 3.50k +50o multi 2.75 2.75
d. SP35 4.50k +50o multi 2.75 2.75

AIR POST STAMPS

Airplane over Akershus Castle
AP1 AP2

Perf. 13½x14½

1927-34 Typo. Wmk. 160
C1 AP1 45o lt bl, strong frame line ('34) 5.25 3.00
Never hinged 20.00
a. Faint or broken frame line 20.00 6.00
Never hinged 125.00

1937, Aug. 18 Photo. *Perf. 13*
C2 AP2 45o Prussian blue 1.25 .55
Never hinged 3.00

1941, Nov. 10 Unwmk.
C3 AP2 45o indigo .40 .25
Never hinged 1.25

POSTAGE DUE STAMPS

Numeral of Value — D1

Perf. 14½x13½

1889-1914 Typo. Wmk. 160
Inscribed "at betale"
J1 D1 1o olive green 1.10 1.25
J2 D1 4o magenta 1.75 .80
J3 D1 10o carmine rose 4.25 .65
a. 10o rose red 72.50 16.00
J4 D1 15o brown ('14) 1.75 .75
J5 D1 20o ultra 3.00 .65
a. Perf. 13½x12½ 210.00 90.00
J6 D1 50o maroon 6.00 2.50
Nos. J1-J6 (6) 17.85 6.60

See #J7-J12. For overprint see #136-144.

1922-23
Inscribed "a betale"
J7 D1 4o lilac rose 7.75 10.00
Never hinged 19.00
J8 D1 10o green 2.40 2.00
Never hinged 6.00
J9 D1 20o dull violet 5.50 4.50
Never hinged 12.00
J10 D1 40o deep ultra 8.50 .50
Never hinged 19.00
J11 D1 100o orange yel 30.00 9.00
Never hinged 77.50
J12 D1 200o dark violet 72.50 20.00
Never hinged 110.00
Nos. J7-J12 (6) 126.65 46.00

OFFICIAL STAMPS

Coat of Arms
O1 O2

Perf. 14½x13½

1926 Typo. Wmk. 160
O1 O1 5o rose lilac .75 *1.50*
O2 O1 10o yellow green .35 *.40*
O3 O1 15o indigo 2.00 *3.50*
O4 O1 20o plum .35 .20
O5 O1 30o slate 4.00 *6.00*
O6 O1 40o deep blue 1.25 *2.00*
O7 O1 60o Prussian blue 5.00 *8.00*
Nos. O1-O7 (7) 13.70 21.60
Set, never hinged 27.50

Official Stamp of 1926 Surcharged

1929, July 1
O8 O1 2o on 5o magenta .60 *1.25*

Perf. 14½x13½

1933-34 Litho. Wmk. 160
Size: 35x19¼mm
O9 O2 2o ocher .60 *1.50*
O10 O2 5o rose lilac 3.00 *6.50*
O11 O2 7o orange 4.50 *9.00*
O12 O2 10o green 25.00 1.25
O13 O2 15o olive .60 *1.25*
O14 O2 20o vermilion 25.00 .60
O15 O2 25o yellow brn .60 *1.00*
O16 O2 30o ultra .75 *1.00*
O18 O2 40o slate 27.50 1.00
O19 O2 60o blue 14.00 1.50
O20 O2 70o olive brn 1.50 *3.50*
O21 O2 100o violet 2.00 3.00
Nos. O9-O16,O18-O21 (12) 105.05 31.10
Same, never hinged 400.00

On the lithographed stamps, the lion's left leg is shaded.

Typo.
Size: 34x18¾mm
O10a O2 5o rose lilac 1.25 2.50
O11a O2 7o orange 7.50 *20.00*
O12a O2 10o green .70 .60
O13a O2 15o olive 5.00 *14.00*
O14a O2 20o vermilion .70 .25
O17 O2 35o red violet ('34) .85 .75
O18a O2 40o slate .85 .75
O19a O2 60o blue 1.25 .90
Nos. O10a-O14a,O17,O18a-O19a (8) 18.10 39.75
Same, never hinged 40.00

Coat of Arms — O3

Norwegian Nazi Party Emblem — O4

1937-38 Photo. *Perf. 13½x13*
O22 O3 5o rose lilac ('38) .65 1.00
O23 O3 7o dp orange .65 2.00
O24 O3 10o brt green .40 .25
O25 O3 15o olive bister .55 .90
O26 O3 20o carmine ('38) .55 2.00
O27 O3 25o red brown ('38) 1.00 .70
O28 O3 30o ultra 1.00 .60
O29 O3 35o red vio ('38) 1.00 .60
O30 O3 40o Prus grn ('38) .85 .40
O31 O3 60o Prus bl ('38) 1.00 .60
O32 O3 100o dk vio ('38) 2.00 1.50
Nos. O22-O32 (11) 9.65 10.55
Set, never hinged 23.00

See Nos. O33-O43, O55-O56. For surcharge see No. O57.

1939-47 Unwmk.
O33 O3 5o dp red lil ('41) .40 .20
O34 O3 7o dp orange ('41) .40 1.00
O35 O3 10o brt green ('41) .25 .20
O36 O3 15o olive ('45) .40 .25
O37 O3 20o carmine .25 .20
O38 O3 25o red brown 2.00 6.00
O38A O3 25o scarlet ('46) .25 .20
O39 O3 30o ultra 2.75 1.50
O39A O3 30o dk gray ('47) .65 .55
O40 O3 35o brt lilac ('41) .55 .25
O41 O3 40o grnsh blk ('41) .55 .25
O41A O3 40o dp ultra ('46) 1.25 .25
O42 O3 60o Prus blue ('41) .65 .25
O43 O3 100o dk violet ('41) .65 .25
Nos. O33-O43 (14) 11.00 11.35
Set, never hinged 27.50

1942-44
O44 O4 5o magenta .35 *1.50*
O45 O4 7o yellow org .35 *1.50*
O46 O4 10o emerald .20 .20
O47 O4 15o olive ('44) 2.00 *15.00*
O48 O4 20o bright red .20 .20
O49 O4 25o red brn ('43) 4.00 *25.00*
O50 O4 30o brt ultra ('44) 3.00 *25.00*
O51 O4 35o brt pur ('43) 3.00 *15.00*
O52 O4 40o grnsh blk ('43) .25 .40
O53 O4 60o indigo ('43) 2.25 *15.00*
O54 O4 1k blue vio ('43) 2.25 *17.50*
Nos. O44-O54 (11) 17.85 *116.30*
Set, never hinged 32.50

Type of 1937

1947, Nov. 1
O55 O3 50o deep magenta 1.10 .25
O56 O3 200o orange 3.25 .65
Set, never hinged 6.50

No. O37 Surcharged with New Values and Bars in Black

1949, Mar. 15
O57 O3 25o on 20o carmine .60 .35
Never hinged 1.00

Norway Coat of Arms
O5 O6

1951-52 Unwmk. Photo. *Perf. 13*
O58 O5 5o rose lilac 1.50 .50
O59 O5 10o dk gray 1.25 .20
O60 O5 15o dp org brn ('52) 2.00 .70
O61 O5 30o scarlet .60 .20
O62 O5 35o red brn ('52) 2.00 .70
O63 O5 60o blue gray 1.60 .20
O64 O5 100o vio bl ('52) 2.50 .30
Nos. O58-O64 (7) 11.45 2.80
Set, never hinged 20.00

Catalogue values for unused stamps in this section, from this point to the end of the section, are for Never Hinged items.

1955-61
O65 O6 5o rose lilac .25 .20
O66 O6 10o slate .25 .20
O67 O6 15o orange brn 1.60 1.50
O68 O6 20o bl grn ('57) .35 .20
O69 O6 25o emer ('59) .70 .20
O70 O6 30o scarlet 2.50 .65
O71 O6 35o brown red .70 .20
O72 O6 40o blue lilac 1.10 .20
O73 O6 45o scar ('58) .90 .20
O74 O6 50o gldn brn ('57) 2.50 .25
O75 O6 60o blue 7.00 .50
O76 O6 70o brn olive 4.25 1.10
O77 O6 75o maroon ('57) 14.00 12.00
O78 O6 80o org brn ('58) 5.00 .70
O79 O6 90o org ('58) 1.10 .20
O80 O6 1k vio ('57) 1.60 .20
O81 O6 2k gray grn ('60) 2.75 .20
O82 O6 5k red lil ('61) 6.25 .85
Nos. O65-O82 (18) 52.80 19.55

See Phosphorescence note after No. 430.

1962-74 Photo.
O83 O6 30o green ('64) 1.00 .20
O84 O6 40o ol grn ('68) .50 .50
O85 O6 50o scarlet 1.50 .25
O86 O6 50o slate ('69) .50 .20
O87 O6 60o dk red ('64) 1.10 .20
O87A O6 60o grnsh bl ('72) 3.75 4.00
O88 O6 65o dk red ('68) 1.10 .20
O89 O6 70o dk red ('70) .30 .20
O90 O6 75o lt grn ('73) .75 .75
O90A O6 80o red brn ('72) .75 .25
O91 O6 85o ocher ('74) .95 1.50
O92 O6 1k dp org ('73) .45 .20
O93 O6 1.10k car lake ('74) .75 .60
Nos. O83-O93 (13) 13.40 9.05

Shades exist of several values of type O6.
Nos O87A, O90A are on phosphored paper.

1975-82 Litho.
O94 O6 5o rose lil ('80) .60 1.50
O95 O6 10o bluish gray ('82) .80 2.50
O96 O6 15o henna brn 1.25 2.50
O97 O6 20o green ('82) 1.00 3.50
O98 O6 25o yellow grn .40 .20
O99 O6 40o ol grn ('79) 1.00 5.00
O100 O6 50o grnsh gray ('76) .40 .20
O101 O6 60o dk grnsh bl 1.00 5.00
O102 O6 70o dk red ('82) 4.00 10.00
O103 O6 80o red brn ('76) .60 .20
O104 O6 1k vio ('80) 1.40 .35
O105 O6 1.10k red ('80) 1.25 2.00
O106 O6 1.25k dull red .60 .20
O107 O6 1.30k lilac ('81) 1.75 1.75
O108 O6 1.50k red ('81) .70 .20
O109 O6 1.75k dl bl grn ('82) 1.40 1.25
O110 O6 2k dk gray grn 1.00 .20
O111 O6 2k cerise ('82) 1.40 .30
O112 O6 3k purple ('82) 2.00 .80
O113 O6 5k lt vio 25.00 2.50
O114 O6 5k blue ('77) 2.75 .25
Nos. O94-O114 (21) 50.30 40.40

In lithographed set, shield's background is dotted; on photogravure stamps it is solid color.
Official stamps invalid as of Apr. 1, 1985.

NOSSI-BE

ˌno-sē-ˈbā

LOCATION — Island in the Indian Ocean, off the northwest coast of Madagascar
GOVT. — French Protectorate
AREA — 130 sq. mi.
POP. — 9,000 (approx. 1900)
CAPITAL — Hellville

In 1896 the island was placed under the authority of the Governor-General of Madagascar and postage stamps of Madagascar were placed in use.

100 Centimes = 1 Franc

Stamps of French Colonies Surcharged in Blue:

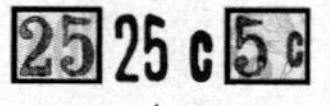
a b c

On the following issues the colors of the French Colonies stamps, type A9, are: 5c, green, *greenish*; 10c, black, *lavender*; 15c, blue; 20c, red, *green*; 30c, brown, *bister*; 40c, vermilion, *straw*; 75c, carmine, *rose*; 1fr, bronze green, *straw*.

1889 Unwmk. *Imperf.*
1 A8(a) 25 on 40c red, *straw* 2,200. 850.
a. Double surcharge *1,600.*
2 A8(b) 25c on 40c red, *straw* 2,600. 1,700.

Perf. 14x13½
3 A9(b) 5c on 10c 2,750. 775.
4 A9(b) 5c on 20c 2,900. 1,950.
5 A9(c) 5c on 10c 3,100. 1,150.
6 A9(c) 5c on 20c 3,500. 1,300.
7 A9(a) 15 on 20c 2,300. 775.
a. 15 on 30c (error) *27,500. 24,000.*
8 A9(a) 25 on 30c 2,300. 700.
9 A9(a) 25 on 40c 2,000. 625.

d

f

g

Black Surcharge

1890
10 A9(d) 0.25 on 20c 350.00 225.00
11 A9(d) 0.25 on 75c 350.00 225.00
12 A9(d) 0.25 on 1fr 350.00 225.00
a. Without ornament 350.00 225.00
16 A9(f) 25c on 20c 350.00 225.00
17 A9(f) 25c on 75c 350.00 225.00
18 A9(f) 25c on 1fr 350.00 225.00
19 A9(g) 25 on 20c 775.00 550.00
20 A9(g) 25 on 75c 775.00 550.00
21 A9(g) 25 on 1fr 775.00 550.00

The 25c on 20c with surcharge composed of "25 c." as in "f," "N S B" as in "d," and frame as in "g" is an essay.

Surcharged or Overprinted in Black, Carmine, Vermilion or Blue:

j

k

m

1893
23 A9(j) 25 on 20c (Bk) 37.50 35.00
24 A9(j) 50 on 10c (Bk) 50.00 37.50
a. Inverted surcharge 300.00 200.00
25 A9(j) 75 on 15c (Bk) 250.00 200.00
26 A9(j) 1fr on 5c (Bk) 92.50 85.00
a. Inverted surcharge 275.00 225.00
27 A9(k) 10c (C) 19.00 15.00
a. Inverted overprint 100.00 85.00
28 A9(k) 10c (V) 19.00 15.00
29 A9(k) 15c (Bk) 19.00 15.00
a. Inverted overprint 110.00 85.00
30 A9(k) 20c (Bk) 425.00 57.50
a. Double overprint
31 A9(m) 20c (Bl) 100.00 55.00
a. Inverted overprint 140.00 130.00

Counterfeits exist of surcharges and overprints of Nos. 1-31.

Navigation and Commerce — A14

1894 Typo. *Perf. 14x13½*
Name of Colony in Blue or Carmine
32 A14 1c blk, *lil bl* 1.10 1.10
33 A14 2c brn, *buff* 1.50 1.50
34 A14 4c claret, *lav* 2.00 1.75
35 A14 5c grn, *greenish* 3.00 2.10
36 A14 10c blk, *lav* 7.25 5.00
37 A14 15c blue, quadrille paper 10.50 5.00
38 A14 20c red, *grn* 7.75 5.25
39 A14 25c blk, *rose* 11.50 7.75
40 A14 30c brn, *bister* 13.00 11.00
41 A14 40c red, *straw* 17.00 12.50
42 A14 50c carmine, *rose* 17.00 12.50
43 A14 75c dp vio, *orange* 29.00 29.00
44 A14 1fr brnz grn, *straw* 21.00 21.00
Nos. 32-44 (13) 141.60 115.45

Perf. 13½x14 stamps are counterfeits.

POSTAGE DUE STAMPS

Stamps of French Colonies Surcharged in Black:

n

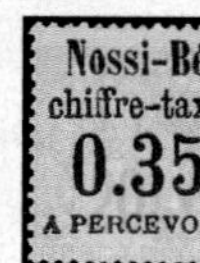
o

1891 Unwmk. *Perf. 14x13½*
J1 A9(n) 20 on 1c blk, *lil bl* 350.00 250.00
a. Inverted surcharge 700.00 500.00
b. Surcharged vertically 850.00 925.00
c. Surcharge on back 775.00 700.00
J2 A9(n) 30 on 2c brn, *buff* 350.00 250.00
a. Inverted surcharge 700.00 500.00
b. Surcharge on back 775.00 700.00
J3 A9(n) 50 on 30c brn, *bister* 92.50 75.00
a. Inverted surcharge 700.00 500.00
b. Surcharge on back 775.00 700.00
J4 A9(o) 35 on 4c cl, *lav* 375.00 275.00
a. Inverted surcharge 700.00 500.00
b. Surcharge on back 775.00 700.00
c. Pair, one without surcharge
J5 A9(o) 35 on 20c red, *green* 390.00 275.00
a. Inverted surcharge 700.00 500.00
J6 A9(o) 1fr on 35c vio, *orange* 390.00 190.00
a. Inverted surcharge 700.00 500.00
b. Surcharge on back 775.00 700.00

p

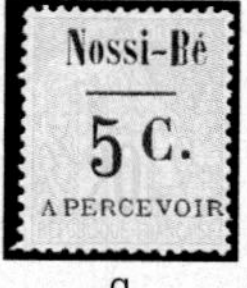
q

r

1891
J7 A9(p) 5c on 20c 190.00 190.00
J8 A9(q) 5c on 20c 225.00 225.00
J9 A9(r) 0.10c on 5c 23.00 19.00
J10 A9(p) 10c on 15c 190.00 190.00
J11 A9(q) 10c on 15c 225.00 225.00
J12 A9(p) 15c on 10c 160.00 160.00
J13 A9(q) 15c on 10c 170.00 170.00
J14 A9(r) 0.15c on 20c 25.00 23.00
a. 25c on 20c (error) *36,000. 29,000.*
J15 A9(p) 25c on 5c 140.00 140.00
J16 A9(q) 25c on 5c 160.00 160.00
J17 A9(r) 0.25c on 75c 575.00 500.00

Inverted Surcharge
J7a A9(p) 5c on 20c 350.00 350.00
J8a A9(q) 5c on 20c 350.00 350.00
J10a A9(p) 10c on 15c 350.00 350.00
J11a A9(q) 10c on 15c 350.00 350.00
J12a A9(p) 15c on 10c 350.00 350.00
J13a A9(q) 15c on 10c 350.00 350.00
J15a A9(p) 25c on 5c 300.00 300.00
J16a A9(q) 25c on 5c 300.00 300.00
J17a A9(r) 0.25c on 75c 1,400. 1,150.

Stamps of Nossi-Be were superseded by those of Madagascar.
Counterfeits exist of surcharges on #J1-J17.

NYASALAND PROTECTORATE

nī-ˈa-sə-ˌland prə-ˈtek-t(ə-)rət

LOCATION — In southern Africa, bordering on Lake Nyasa
GOVT. — British Protectorate
AREA — 49,000 sq. mi.
POP. — 2,950,000 (est. 1962)
CAPITAL — Zomba

For previous issues, see British Central Africa.

Nyasaland joined the Federation of Rhodesia and Nyasaland in 1953, using its stamps until 1963. As the Federation began to dissolve in 1963, Nyasaland withdrew its postal services and issued provisional stamps. On July 6, 1964, Nyasaland became the independent state of Malawi.

12 Pence = 1 Shilling
20 Shillings = 1 Pound

Catalogue values for unused stamps in this country are for Never Hinged items, beginning with Scott 68 in the regular postage section and Scott J1 in the postage due section.

A1

King Edward VII — A2

Wmk. Crown and C A (2)
1908, July 22 Typo. *Perf. 14*
Chalky Paper
1 A1 1sh black, *green* 3.50 *14.00*

Wmk. Multiple Crown and C A (3)
Ordinary Paper
2 A1 ½p green 2.00 2.25
3 A1 1p carmine 4.50 1.10

Chalky Paper
4 A1 3p violet, *yel* 1.75 *4.75*
5 A1 4p scar & blk, *yel* 1.75 *1.75*
6 A1 6p red vio & vio 4.25 *12.50*
7 A2 2sh 6p car & blk, *bl* 55.00 *100.00*
8 A2 4sh black & car 92.50 *140.00*
9 A2 10sh red & grn, *grn* 125.00 *250.00*
10 A2 £1 blk & vio, *red* 500.00 *625.00*
11 A2 £10 ultra & lilac 9,000. *5,500.*
Nos. 1-10 (10) 790.25 *1,151.*

King George V
A3 A4

1913-19
Ordinary Paper
12 A3 ½p green .80 1.00
13 A3 1p scarlet 2.25 .75
a. 1p carmine 1.25 1.00
14 A3 2p gray 3.00 1.00
15 A3 2½p ultra 2.00 *3.00*

Chalky Paper
16 A3 3p violet, *yel* 4.50 4.50
17 A3 4p scar & blk, *yel* 2.00 *2.50*
18 A3 6p red vio & dull vio 3.75 *10.00*
19 A3 1sh black, *green* 1.90 *9.00*
a. 1sh black, *emerald* 4.00 *6.00*
b. 1sh blk, *bl grn,* olive back 6.00 1.60
20 A4 2sh6p red & blk, *bl* ('18) 12.50 12.50
21 A4 4sh blk & red ('18) 20.00 *50.00*
22 A4 10sh red & grn, *grn* 85.00 *100.00*
23 A4 £1 blk & vio, *red* ('18) 200.00 150.00
24 A4 £10 brt ultra & slate vio ('19) *3,750. 2,000.*
Revenue cancel 250.00
a. £10 pale ultra & dull vio ('14) 6,000.
Revenue cancel 275.00
Nos. 12-23 (12) 337.70 *344.25*

Stamps of Nyasaland Protectorate overprinted "N. F." are listed under German East Africa.

1921-30 Wmk. 4
Ordinary Paper
25 A3 ½p green 1.50 .50
26 A3 1p rose red 2.00 .50
27 A3 1½p orange 7.00 17.50
28 A3 2p gray 1.25 .50

Chalky Paper
29 A3 3p violet, *yel* 10.00 3.00
30 A3 4p scar & blk, *yel* 3.25 *9.00*
31 A3 6p red vio & dl vio 3.50 3.00
32 A3 1sh blk, *grn* ('30) 9.00 4.50
33 A4 2sh ultra & dl vio, *bl* 14.50 *15.00*
34 A4 2sh6p red & blk, *bl* ('24) 22.50 17.50
35 A4 4sh black & car 19.00 *27.50*
36 A4 5sh red & grn, *yel* ('29) 45.00 *75.00*
37 A4 10sh red & grn, *emer* 97.50 *110.00*
Nos. 25-37 (13) 236.00 *283.50*

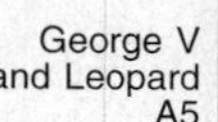
George V and Leopard
A5

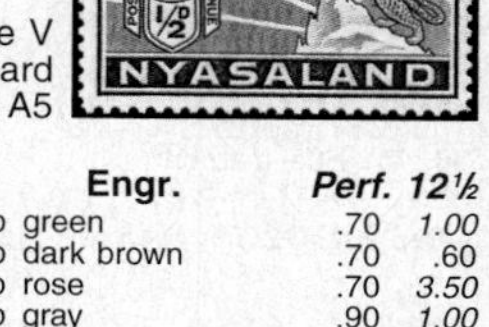

1934-35 Engr. *Perf. 12½*
38 A5 ½p green .70 *1.00*
39 A5 1p dark brown .70 .60
40 A5 1½p rose .70 *3.50*
41 A5 2p gray .90 *1.00*
42 A5 3p dark blue 2.25 1.50
43 A5 4p rose lilac ('35) 3.00 4.00
44 A5 6p dk violet 3.50 3.00
45 A5 9p olive bis ('35) 7.00 *10.00*
46 A5 1sh orange & blk 9.00 *15.00*
Nos. 38-46 (9) 27.75 *39.60*

Common Design Types pictured following the introduction.

Silver Jubilee Issue
Common Design Type
1935, May 6 *Perf. 11x12*
47 CD301 1p gray blk & ultra .65 *2.50*
48 CD301 2p indigo & grn 3.75 2.75
49 CD301 3p ultra & brn 5.50 *15.00*
50 CD301 1sh brown vio & ind 15.00 *50.00*
Nos. 47-50 (4) 24.90 *70.25*
Set, never hinged 44.00

Coronation Issue
Common Design Type

1937, May 12 *Perf. 11x11½*

No.	Type	Description	Unused	Used
51	CD302	½p deep green	.20	.20
52	CD302	1p dark brown	.35	.20
53	CD302	2p gray black	.35	.35
		Nos. 51-53 (3)	.90	.75
		Set, never hinged	1.75	

A6

King George VI — A7

1938-44 **Engr.** *Perf. 12½*

No.	Type	Description	Unused	Used
54	A6	½p green	.20	*1.50*
54A	A6	½p dk brown ('42)	.20	*2.00*
55	A6	1p dark brown	1.75	*.35*
55A	A6	1p green ('42)	.20	*.90*
56	A6	1½p dark carmine	3.00	*4.50*
56A	A6	1½p gray ('42)	.20	*5.75*
57	A6	2p gray	4.00	1.25
57A	A6	2p dark car ('42)	.20	*2.00*
58	A6	3p blue	.50	.50
59	A6	4p rose lilac	1.50	1.25
60	A6	6p dark violet	2.00	1.25
61	A6	9p olive bister	2.00	*3.25*
62	A6	1sh orange & blk	1.75	*2.00*

Typo.
Perf. 14
Chalky Paper

No.	Type	Description	Unused	Used
63	A7	2sh ultra & dl vio, *bl*	7.00	*11.00*
64	A7	2sh6p red & blk, *bl*	8.00	*13.00*
65	A7	5sh red & grn, *yel*	25.00	22.50
a.		5sh dk red & dp grn, *yel* ('44)	55.00	*80.00*
66	A7	10sh red & grn, *grn*	35.00	*45.00*

Wmk. 3

No.	Type	Description	Unused	Used
67	A7	£1 blk & vio, *red*	22.50	*32.50*
		Nos. 54-67 (18)	115.00	*150.50*
		Set, never hinged	200.00	

Catalogue values for unused stamps in this section, from this point to the end of the section, are for Never Hinged items.

Canoe on Lake Nyasa — A8

Soldier of King's African Rifles — A9

Tea Estate, Mlanje Mountain A10

Map and Coat of Arms — A11

Fishing Village, Lake Nyasa — A12

Tobacco Estate — A13

Arms of Nyasaland and George VI A14

1945, Sept. 1 **Engr.** *Perf. 12*

No.	Type	Description	Unused	Used
68	A8	½p brn vio & blk	.45	.20
69	A9	1p dp green & blk	.20	.20
70	A10	1½p gray grn & blk	.35	.20
71	A11	2p scarlet & blk	.85	.20
72	A12	3p blue & blk	.45	.20
73	A13	4p rose vio & blk	1.40	.55
74	A10	6p violet & blk	1.40	.55
75	A8	9p ol grn & blk	1.40	*2.75*
76	A11	1sh myr grn & ind	1.10	.55
77	A12	2sh dl red brn & grn	3.75	3.75
78	A13	2sh6p ultra & green	8.75	4.50
79	A14	5sh ultra & lt vio	5.25	*5.50*
80	A11	10sh green & lake	16.50	13.00
81	A14	20sh black & scar	22.50	*27.50*
		Nos. 68-81 (14)	64.35	59.65

Peace Issue
Common Design Type
Perf. 13½x14

1946, Dec. 16 **Wmk. 4**

No.	Type	Description	Unused	Used
82	CD303	1p bright green	.20	.20
83	CD303	2p red orange	.25	.25

A15

1947, Oct. 20 *Perf. 12*

No.	Type	Description	Unused	Used
84	A15	1p emerald & org brn	.60	.30

Silver Wedding Issue
Common Design Types

1948, Dec. 15 **Photo.** *Perf. 14x14½*

No.	Type	Description	Unused	Used
85	CD304	1p dark green	.20	.20

Engr.; Name Typo.
Perf. 11½x11

No.	Type	Description	Unused	Used
86	CD305	10sh purple	15.00	*26.00*

UPU Issue
Common Design Types
Engr.; Name Typo. on 3p, 6p
Perf. 13½, 11x11½

1949, Nov. 21 **Wmk. 4**

No.	Type	Description	Unused	Used
87	CD306	1p blue green	.35	.35
88	CD307	3p Prus blue	2.25	2.25
89	CD308	6p rose violet	.85	.85
90	CD309	1sh violet blue	.35	.35
		Nos. 87-90 (4)	3.80	3.80

Arms of British Central Africa and Nyasaland Protectorate — A16

1951, May 15 **Engr.** *Perf. 11x12*
Arms in Black

No.	Type	Description	Unused	Used
91	A16	2p rose	1.25	1.10
92	A16	3p blue	1.25	1.10
93	A16	6p purple	1.25	*1.90*
94	A16	5sh deep blue	3.50	*7.75*
		Nos. 91-94 (4)	7.25	*11.85*

60th anniv. of the Protectorate, originally British Central Africa.

Exhibition Seal — A17

1953, May 30 *Perf. 14x13½*

No.	Type	Description	Unused	Used
95	A17	6p purple	.45	.50

Central African Rhodes Cent. Exhib.

Coronation Issue
Common Design Type

1953, June 2 *Perf. 13½x13*

No.	Type	Description	Unused	Used
96	CD312	2p orange & black	.60	.50

Types of 1945-47 with Portrait of Queen Elizabeth II and

Grading Cotton A18

1953, Sept. 1 *Perf. 12*

No.	Type	Description	Unused	Used
97	A8	½p red brn & blk	.25	*1.00*
a.		Booklet pane of 4	3.75	
b.		Perf. 12x12½ ('54)	.25	*1.00*
98	A15	1p emer & org brn	.65	.25
a.		Booklet pane of 4	3.75	
99	A10	1½p gray grn & blk	.25	*1.90*
100	A11	2p orange & blk	.30	.30
a.		Booklet pane of 4	3.75	
b.		Perf. 12x12½ ('54)	.30	.30
101	A18	2½p blk & brt grn	.25	*.50*
102	A13	3p scarlet & blk	.30	.30
103	A12	4½p blue & blk	.45	.45
104	A10	6p violet & blk	1.90	.85
a.		Booklet pane of 4	11.50	
b.		Perf. 12x12½ ('54)	1.90	.85
105	A8	9p olive & blk	.80	*2.75*
106	A11	1sh myr grn & ind	2.00	.45
107	A12	2sh rose brn & grn	2.00	*3.00*
108	A13	2sh6p ultra & grn	3.50	*4.25*
109	A14	5sh Prus bl & rose lil	7.25	4.50
110	A11	10sh green & lake	4.75	*17.00*
111	A14	20sh black & scar	16.00	*21.50*
		Nos. 97-111 (15)	40.65	*59.00*

Issue date: Nos. 97b, 100b, 104b, Mar. 8.

Revenue Stamps Overprinted "POSTAGE" and Bars in Black

Arms of Nyasaland A19

Perf. 11½x12

1963, Nov. 1 **Engr.** **Unwmk.**

No.	Type	Description	Unused	Used
112	A19	½p on 1p blue	.25	.25
113	A19	1p green	.25	.25
114	A19	2p rose red	.25	.25
115	A19	3p dark blue	.25	.25
116	A19	6p rose lake	.25	.25
117	A19	9p on 1sh car rose	.40	.40
118	A19	1sh purple	.45	.25
119	A19	2sh6p black	.65	*1.25*
120	A19	5sh brown	2.25	1.75
121	A19	10sh gray olive	3.25	*4.50*
122	A19	£1 violet	3.75	*8.00*
		Nos. 112-122 (11)	12.00	*17.40*

Nos. 112, 117 have 3 bars over old value.

Mother and Child — A20

Designs: 1p, Chambo fish. 2p, Zebu bull. 3p, Peanuts. 4p, Fishermen in boat. 6p, Harvesting tea. 1sh, Lumber and tropical pine branch. 1sh3p, Tobacco industry. 2sh6p, Cotton industry. 5sh, Monkey Bay, Lake Nyasa. 10sh, Afzelia tree (pod mahogany). £1, Nyala antelope, vert.

Perf. 14½

1964, Jan. 1 **Unwmk.** **Photo.**

Size: 23x19mm

No.	Type	Description	Unused	Used
123	A20	½p lilac	.25	*.35*
124	A20	1p green & blk	.25	*.30*
125	A20	2p red brown	.25	*.30*
126	A20	3p pale brn, brn red & grn	.25	*.30*
127	A20	4p org yel & indigo	.30	*.35*

Size: 41½x25mm, 25x41½mm

No.	Type	Description	Unused	Used
128	A20	6p bl pur & brt yel grn	.50	*.65*
129	A20	1sh yel brn & dk grn	.75	.30
130	A20	1sh3p red brn & olive	.80	.30
131	A20	2sh6p blue & brn	1.40	.65
132	A20	5sh grn, bl, sep & yel	2.00	1.60
133	A20	10sh org brn grn & gray	3.25	*4.00*
134	A20	£1 yel & dk brn	7.00	*7.75*
		Nos. 123-134 (12)	17.00	16.85

POSTAGE DUE STAMPS

Catalogue values for unused stamps in this section are for Never Hinged items.

D1

Perf. 14

1950, July 1 **Wmk. 4** **Typo.**

No.	Type	Description	Unused	Used
J1	D1	1p rose red	2.75	*8.75*
J2	D1	2p ultramarine	6.50	*17.50*
J3	D1	3p green	10.00	*11.00*
J4	D1	4p claret	17.50	*40.00*
J5	D1	6p ocher	27.50	*72.50*
		Nos. J1-J5 (5)	64.25	*149.75*

NYASSA

nī-ˈa-sə

LOCATION — In the northern part of Mozambique in southeast Africa
AREA — 73,292 sq. mi.
POP. — 3,000,000 (estimated)
CAPITAL — Porto Amelia

The district formerly administered by the Nyassa Company is now a part of Mozambique.

1000 Reis = 1 Milreis
100 Centavos = 1 Escudo (1919)

Mozambique Nos. 24-35 Overprinted in Black

1898 Unwmk. *Perf. 11½, 12½*

No.	Type	Description	Unused	Used
1	A3	5r yellow	2.00	1.50
2	A3	10r redsh violet	2.00	1.50
3	A3	15r chocolate	2.00	1.50
4	A3	20r gray violet	2.00	1.50
5	A3	25r blue green	2.00	1.50
6	A3	50r light blue	2.00	1.50
a.		Inverted overprint		
b.		Perf. 12½	6.00	3.50
7	A3	75r rose	2.50	2.00
8	A3	80r yellow grn	2.50	2.00
9	A3	100r brown, *buff*	2.50	2.00
10	A3	150r car, *rose*	6.50	4.00
11	A3	200r dk blue, *blue*	4.50	3.00
12	A3	300r dk blue, *salmon*	4.50	3.00
		Nos. 1-12 (12)	35.00	25.00

Reprints of Nos. 1, 5, 8, 9, 10 and 12 have white gum and clean-cut perforation 13½. Value of No. 9, $15; others $3 each.

Same Overprint on Mozambique Issue of 1898

1898 *Perf. 11½*

No.	Type	Description	Unused	Used
13	A4	2½r gray	1.40	.80
14	A4	5r orange	1.40	.80
15	A4	10r light green	1.40	.80
16	A4	15r brown	1.75	1.00
17	A4	20r gray violet	1.75	1.00
18	A4	25r sea green	1.75	1.00
19	A4	50r blue	1.75	1.00
20	A4	75r rose	2.10	1.00
21	A4	80r violet	2.25	.80
22	A4	100r dk bl, *bl*	2.25	.80
23	A4	150r brown, *straw*	2.25	.80
24	A4	200r red lilac, *pnksh*	2.25	1.00
25	A4	300r dk blue, *rose*	3.00	1.00
		Nos. 13-25 (13)	25.30	11.80

Giraffe — A5

Camels — A6

1901 Engr. *Perf. 14*

No.	Type	Description	Unused	Used
26	A5	2½r blk & red brn	1.60	.55
27	A5	5r blk & violet	1.60	.55
28	A5	10r blk & dp grn	1.60	.55
29	A5	15r blk & org brn	1.60	.55
30	A5	20r blk & org red	1.60	.70
31	A5	25r blk & orange	1.60	.70
32	A5	50r blk & dl bl	1.60	.70
33	A6	75r blk & car lake	1.75	.70
34	A6	80r blk & lilac	1.75	.90
35	A6	100r blk & brn bis	1.75	.90
36	A6	150r blk & dp org	1.90	1.00

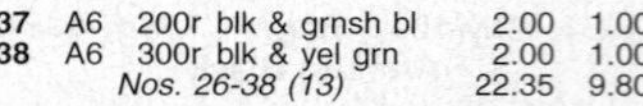

No.	Type	Description	Unused	Used
37	A6	200r blk & grnsh bl	2.00	1.00
38	A6	300r blk & yel grn	2.00	1.00
		Nos. 26-38 (13)	22.35	9.80

Nos. 26 to 38 are known with inverted centers but are believed to be purely speculative and never regularly issued. Value $50 each.

Perf 13½, 14½, 15½ & compound also exist.

For overprints and surcharges see Nos. 39-50, 63-80.

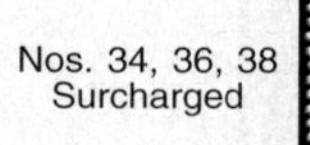

Nos. 34, 36, 38 Surcharged

1903

No.	Type	Description	Unused	Used
39	A6	65r on 80r	1.00	.75
40	A6	115r on 150r	1.00	.75
41	A6	130r on 300r	1.00	.75
		Nos. 39-41 (3)	3.00	2.25

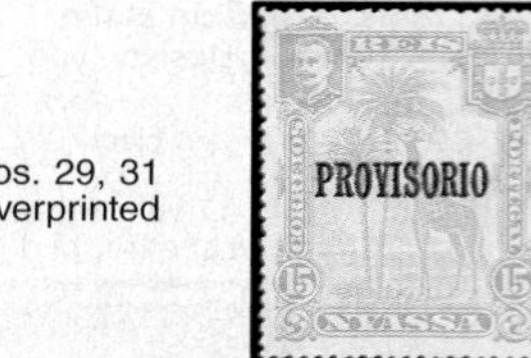

Nos. 29, 31 Overprinted

1903

No.	Type	Description	Unused	Used
42	A5	15r black & org brn	1.00	.75
43	A5	25r black & orange	1.00	.75

Nos. 34, 36, 38 Surcharged

1903

No.	Type	Description	Unused	Used
44	A6	65r on 80r	32.50	25.00
45	A6	115r on 150r	32.50	25.00
46	A6	130r on 300r	32.50	25.00
		Nos. 44-46 (3)	97.50	75.00

Nos. 29, 31 Overprinted

1903

No.	Type	Description	Unused	Used
47	A5	15r black & org brn	400.00	100.00
48	A5	25r black & orange	150.00	100.00

Forgeries exist of Nos. 44-48.

Nos. 26, 35 Surcharged

1910

No.	Type	Description	Unused	Used
49	A5	5r on 2½r	1.00	.75
50	A6	50r on 100r	1.00	.75
a.		"50 REIS" omitted	300.00	

Reprints of Nos. 49-50, made in 1921, have 2mm space between surcharge lines, instead of 1½mm. Value, each 25 cents.

Zebra — A7

Vasco da Gama's Flagship "San Gabriel" — A8

Red Overprint

Designs: Nos. 51-53, Camels. Nos. 57-59, Giraffe and palms.

1911

No.	Type	Description	Unused	Used
51	A7	2½r blk & dl vio	1.00	.55
52	A7	5r black	1.00	.55
53	A7	10r blk & gray grn	1.00	.55
54	A7	20r blk & car lake	1.00	.55
55	A7	25r blk & vio brn	1.00	.55
56	A7	50r blk & dp bl	1.00	.55
57	A8	75r blk & brn	1.00	.55
58	A8	100r blk & brn, *grn*	1.00	.55
59	A8	200r blk & dp grn, *sal*	1.10	1.00
60	A8	300r blk, *blue*	2.40	1.60
61	A8	400r blk & dk brn	3.00	2.00
a.		Pair, one without overprint		
62	A8	500r ol & vio brn	4.00	3.00
		Nos. 51-62 (12)	18.50	12.00

Nos. 51-62 exist without overprint but were not issued in that condition. Value $5 each.

For surcharges see Nos. 81-105.

Stamps of 1901-03 Surcharged

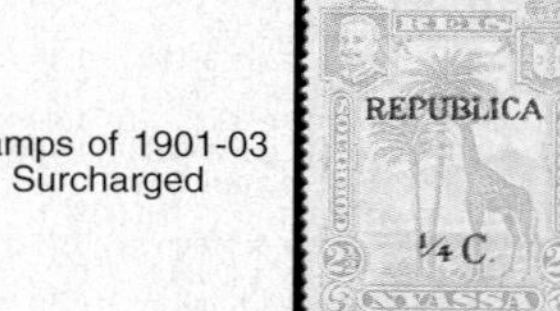

1918

On Nos. 26-38

No.	Type	Description	Unused	Used
63	A5	¼c on 2½r	140.00	95.00
64	A5	½c on 5r	140.00	95.00
65	A5	1c on 10r	140.00	95.00
66	A5	1½c on 15r	2.10	1.10
67	A5	2c on 20r	1.25	1.00
68	A5	3½c on 25r	1.50	1.00
69	A5	5c on 50r	1.25	1.00
70	A6	7½c on 75r	1.25	1.00
71	A6	8c on 80r	1.25	1.00
72	A6	10c on 100r	1.25	1.00
73	A6	15c on 150r	2.10	2.00
74	A6	20c on 200r	2.00	2.00
75	A6	30c on 300r	3.25	2.40

On Nos. 39-41

No.	Type	Description	Unused	Used
76	A6	40c on 65r on 80r	18.00	16.50
77	A6	50c on 115r on 150r	2.75	2.00
78	A6	1e on 130r on 300r	2.75	2.00

On Nos. 42-43

No.	Type	Description	Unused	Used
79	A5	1½c on 15r	5.00	3.00
80	A5	3½c on 25r	2.00	1.00
		Nos. 63-80 (18)	467.70	323.00

On Nos. 70-78 there is less space between "REPUBLICA" and the new value than on the other stamps of this issue.

On Nos. 76-78 the 1903 surcharge is canceled by a bar.

The surcharge exists inverted on #64, 66-70, 72, 76, 78-80, and double on #64, 67, 69.

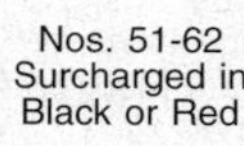

Nos. 51-62 Surcharged in Black or Red

1921

Lisbon Surcharges

Numerals: The "1" (large or small) is thin, sharp-pointed, and has thin serifs. The "2" is italic, with the tail thin and only slightly wavy. The "3" has a flat top. The "4" is open at the top. The "7" has thin strokes.

Centavos: The letters are shaded, i.e., they are thicker in some parts than in others. The "t" has a thin cross bar ending in a downward stroke at the right. The "s" is flat at the bottom and wider than in the next group.

No.	Type	Description	Unused	Used
81	A7	¼c on 2½r	3.25	2.75
83	A7	½c on 5r (R)	3.25	2.75
a.		½c on 2½r (R) (error)	275.00	250.00
84	A7	1c on 10r	3.25	2.75
a.		Pair, one without surcharge		
85	A8	1½c on 300r (R)	3.25	2.75
86	A7	2c on 20r	3.25	2.75
87	A7	2½c on 25r	3.25	2.75
88	A8	3c on 400r	3.25	2.75
a.		"Republica" omitted		
89	A7	5c on 50r	3.25	2.75
90	A8	7½c on 75r	3.25	2.75
91	A8	10c on 100r	3.25	2.75
92	A8	12c on 500r	3.25	2.75
93	A8	20c on 200r	3.25	2.75
		Nos. 81-93 (12)	39.00	33.00

The surcharge exists inverted on Nos. 83-85, 87-88 and 92, and double on Nos. 81, 83 and 86.

Forgeries exist of Nos. 81-93.

London Surcharges

Numerals: The "1" has the vertical stroke and serifs thicker than in the Lisbon printing. The "2" is upright and has a strong wave in the tail. The small "2" is heavily shaded. The "3" has a rounded top. The "4" is closed at the top. The "7" has thick strokes.

Centavos: The letters are heavier than in the Lisbon printing and are of even thickness throughout. The "t" has a thick cross bar with scarcely any down stroke at the end. The "s" is rounded at the bottom and narrower than in the Lisbon printing.

No.	Type	Description	Unused	Used
94	A7	¼c on 2½r	1.50	1.25
95	A7	½c on 5r (R)	1.50	1.25
96	A7	1c on 10r	1.50	1.25
97	A8	1½c on 300r (R)	1.50	1.25
98	A7	2c on 20r	1.50	1.25
99	A7	2½c on 25r	1.50	1.25
100	A8	3c on 400r	1.50	1.25
101	A7	5c on 50r	1.50	1.25
102	A8	7½c on 75r	1.50	1.25
a.		Inverted surcharge		
103	A8	10c on 100r	1.50	1.25
104	A8	12c on 500r	1.50	1.25
105	A8	20c on 200r	1.50	1.25
		Nos. 94-105 (12)	18.00	15.00

A9

Zebra and Warrior — A10

Designs: 2c-6c, Vasco da Gama. 7½c-20c, "San Gabriel." 2e-5e, Dhow and warrior.

Perf. 12½, 13½-15 & Compound

1921-23 Engr.

No.	Type	Description	Unused	Used
106	A9	¼c claret	1.00	.70
107	A9	½c steel blue	1.00	.70
108	A9	1c grn & blk	1.00	.70
109	A9	1½c blk & ocher	1.00	.70
110	A9	2c red & blk	1.00	.70
111	A9	2½c blk & ol grn	1.00	.70
112	A9	4c blk & org	1.00	.70
113	A9	5c ultra & blk	1.00	.70
114	A9	6c blk & vio	1.00	.70
115	A9	7½c blk & blk brn	1.00	.70
116	A9	8c blk & ol grn	1.00	.70
117	A9	10c blk & red brn	1.00	.70
118	A9	15c blk & carmine	1.00	.70
119	A9	20c blk & pale bl	1.00	.70
120	A10	30c blk & bister	1.00	.70
121	A10	40c blk & gray bl	1.00	.70
122	A10	50c blk & green	1.00	.70
123	A10	1e blk & red brn	1.00	.70
124	A10	2e red brn & blk ('23)	3.25	2.50
125	A10	5e ultra & red brn ('23)	3.00	2.25
		Nos. 106-125 (20)	24.25	17.35

POSTAGE DUE STAMPS

Giraffe — D1

½c, 1c, Giraffe. 2c, 3c, Zebra. 5c, 6c, 10c, "San Gabriel." 20c, 50c, Vasco da Gama.

1924 Unwmk. Engr. *Perf. 14*

No.	Type	Description	Unused	Used
J1	D1	½c deep green	1.00	*1.75*
J2	D1	1c gray	1.00	*1.75*
J3	D1	2c red	1.00	*1.75*
J4	D1	3c red orange	1.00	*1.75*
J5	D1	5c dark brown	1.00	*1.75*
J6	D1	6c orange brown	1.00	*1.75*
J7	D1	10c brown violet	1.00	*1.75*
J8	D1	20c carmine	1.00	*1.75*
J9	D1	50c lilac gray	1.00	*1.75*
		Nos. J1-J9 (9)	9.00	*15.75*

Used values are for c-t-o copies.

NEWSPAPER STAMP

Mozambique No. P6 Overprinted Like Nos. 1-25 in Black

1898 Unwmk. *Perf. 13½*

No.	Type	Description	Unused	Used
P1	N3	2½r brown	1.75	1.00

Reprints have white gum and clean-cut perf. 13½. Value $1.

POSTAL TAX STAMPS

Pombal Issue

Mozambique Nos. RA1-RA3 Overprinted "NYASSA" in Red

1925 Unwmk. *Perf. 12½*

No.	Type	Description	Unused	Used
RA1	CD28	15c brown & blk	5.00	5.00
RA2	CD29	15c brown & blk	5.00	5.00
RA3	CD30	15c brown & blk	5.00	5.00
		Nos. RA1-RA3 (3)	15.00	15.00

POSTAL TAX DUE STAMPS

Pombal Issue

Mozambique Nos. RAJ1-RAJ3 Overprinted "NYASSA" in Red

1925 Unwmk. *Perf. 12½*

No.	Type	Description	Unused	Used
RAJ1	CD28	30c brown & blk	12.50	7.75
RAJ2	CD29	30c brown & blk	12.50	7.75
RAJ3	CD30	30c brown & blk	12.50	7.75
		Nos. RAJ1-RAJ3 (3)	37.50	23.25

OBOCK

'ō-ˌbäk

LOCATION — A seaport in eastern Africa on the Gulf of Aden, directly opposite Aden.

Obock was the point of entrance from which French Somaliland was formed. The port was acquired by the French in 1862 but was not actively occupied until 1884 when Sagallo and Tadjoura were ceded to France. In 1888 Djibouti was made into a port and the seat of government moved from Obock to the latter city. In 1902 the name Somali Coast was adopted on the postage stamps of Djibouti, these stamps superseding the individual issues of Obock.

100 Centimes = 1 Franc

Counterfeits exist of Nos. 1-31.

Stamps of French Colonies Handstamped in Black:

#1-11, J1-J4

#12-20, J5-J18

1892 Unwmk. *Perf. 14x13½*

No.	Type	Description	Unused	Used
1	A9	1c blk, *lil bl*	28.00	28.00
2	A9	2c brn, *buff*	28.00	28.00
3	A9	4c claret, *lav*	325.00	*350.00*
4	A9	5c grn, *grnsh*	25.00	20.00
5	A9	10c blk, *lavender*	55.00	28.00
6	A9	15c blue	52.50	35.00
7	A9	25c blk, *rose*	70.00	55.00
8	A9	35c vio, *org*	325.00	325.00
9	A9	40c red, *straw*	275.00	*300.00*
10	A9	75c car, *rose*	325.00	*350.00*
11	A9	1fr brnz grn, *straw*	375.00	375.00
		Nos. 1-11 (11)	1,883.	1,894.

No. 3 has been reprinted. On the reprints the second "O" of "OBOCK" is 4mm high instead of 3½mm. Value $20.

1892

No.	Type	Description	Unused	Used
12	A9	4c claret, *lav*	17.50	14.00
13	A9	5c grn, *grnsh*	17.50	14.00
14	A9	10c blk, *lavender*	22.50	17.50
15	A9	15c blue	21.00	17.50
16	A9	20c red, *grn*	35.00	27.50
17	A9	25c blk, *rose*	24.00	17.50
18	A9	40c red, *straw*	42.50	45.00
19	A9	75c car, *rose*	250.00	190.00
20	A9	1fr brnz grn, *straw*	62.50	55.00
		Nos. 12-20 (9)	492.50	398.00

Exists inverted or double on all denominations.

Nos. 14, 15, 17, 20 with Additional Surcharge Handstamped in Red, Blue or Black:

Nos, 21-30

No. 31

1892

No.	Type	Description	Unused	Used
21	A9	1c on 25c blk, *rose*	10.00	10.00
22	A9	2c on 10c blk, *lav*	47.50	35.00
23	A9	2c on 15c blue	12.50	12.50
24	A9	4c on 15c bl (Bk)	14.00	14.00
25	A9	4c on 25c blk, *rose* (Bk)	14.00	14.00
26	A9	5c on 25c blk, *rose*	22.00	17.50
27	A9	20c on 10c blk, *lav*	70.00	70.00
28	A9	30c on 10c blk, *lav*	82.50	75.00
29	A9	35c on 25c blk, *rose*	70.00	62.50
a.		"3" instead of "35"	525.00	500.00
30	A9	75c on 1fr brnz grn, *straw*	75.00	70.00
b.		"57" instead of "75"	*6,500.*	*6,500.*
c.		"55" instead of "75"	*6,500.*	*6,500.*
31	A9	5fr on 1fr brnz grn, *straw*(Bl)	600.00	550.00
		Nos. 21-31 (11)	1,017.	930.50

Exists inverted on most denominations.

Navigation and Commerce A4

Camel and Rider A5

1892 Typo. *Perf. 14x13½*

Obock in Red (1c, 5c, 15c, 25c, 75c, 1fr) or Blue

No.	Type	Description	Unused	Used
32	A4	1c blk, *lil bl*	2.10	1.75
33	A4	2c brn, *buff*	1.40	1.25
34	A4	4c claret, *lav*	2.10	2.00
35	A4	5c grn, *grnsh*	3.50	2.75
36	A4	10c blk, *lavender*	5.50	3.50
37	A4	15c bl, quadrille paper	14.00	7.00
38	A4	20c red, *grn*	20.00	19.00
39	A4	25c blk, *rose*	19.00	16.00
40	A4	30c brn, *bis*	18.00	14.00
41	A4	40c red, *straw*	17.50	14.00
42	A4	50c car, *rose*	20.00	15.00
43	A4	75c vio, *org*	24.50	17.50
a.		Name double	250.00	250.00
b.		Name inverted	*3,100.*	*3,100.*
44	A4	1fr brnz grn, *straw*	35.00	27.50
		Nos. 32-44 (13)	182.60	141.25

Perf. 13½x14 stamps are counterfeits.

1893 *Imperf.*

Quadrille Lines Printed on Paper

Size: 32mm at base

No.	Type	Description	Unused	Used
44A	A5	2fr brnz grn	45.00	42.50

Size: 45mm at base

No.	Type	Description	Unused	Used
45	A5	5fr red	100.00	90.00

Somali Warriors A7

A8

1894 *Imperf.*

Quadrille Lines Printed on Paper

No.	Type	Description	Unused	Used
46	A7	1c blk & rose	1.75	1.75
47	A7	2c vio brn & grn	1.75	1.75
48	A7	4c brn vio & org	1.75	1.75
49	A7	5c bl grn & brn	2.40	2.40
50	A7	10c blk & grn	6.50	5.50
a.		Half used as 5c on cover		210.00
51	A7	15c bl & rose	6.50	4.75
52	A7	20c brn org & mar	6.50	5.50
a.		Half used as 10c on cover		210.00
53	A7	25c blk & bl	7.00	5.00
a.		Right half used as 5c on cover ('01)		210.00
b.		Left half used as 2c on cover ('03)		210.00
54	A7	30c bis & yel grn	14.00	10.50
a.		Half used as 15c on cover		1,600.
55	A7	40c red & bl grn	11.50	9.00
56	A7	50c rose & bl	11.00	8.25
a.		Half used as 25c on cover		2,500.
57	A7	75c gray lil & org	12.50	9.00
58	A7	1fr ol grn & mar	11.00	7.00

Size: 37mm at base

No.	Type	Description	Unused	Used
60	A8	2fr vio & org	82.50	82.50

Size: 42mm at base

No.	Type	Description	Unused	Used
61	A8	5fr rose & bl	70.00	65.00

Size: 46mm at base

No.	Type	Description	Unused	Used
62	A8	10fr org & red vio	110.00	110.00
63	A8	25fr brn & bl	625.00	600.00
64	A8	50fr red vio & grn	700.00	700.00

Counterfeits exist of Nos. 63-64.

Stamps of Obock were replaced in 1901 by those of Somali Coast. The 5c on 75c, 5c on 25fr and 10c on 50fr of 1902 are listed under Somali Coast.

POSTAGE DUE STAMPS

Postage Due Stamps of French Colonies Handstamped Like #1-20

1892 Unwmk. *Imperf.*

No.	Type	Description	Unused	Used
J1	D1	5c black	*7,500.*	
J2	D1	10c black	175.00	*200.00*
J3	D1	30c black	275.00	*350.00*
J4	D1	60c black	350.00	*400.00*
J5	D1	1c black	37.50	37.50
J6	D1	2c black	30.00	30.00
J7	D1	3c black	35.00	35.00
J8	D1	4c black	27.50	27.50
J9	D1	5c black	10.00	10.00
J10	D1	10c black	24.00	24.00
J11	D1	15c black	17.50	17.50
J12	D1	20c black	21.00	21.00
J13	D1	30c black	24.00	24.00
J14	D1	40c black	42.50	42.50
J15	D1	60c black	55.00	55.00
J16	D1	1fr brown	165.00	165.00
J17	D1	2fr brown	180.00	180.00
J18	D1	5fr brown	400.00	400.00
		Nos. J2-J18 (17)	1,869.	2,019.

These handstamped overprints may be found double or inverted on some values. Counterfeits exist of Nos. J1-J18.

No. J1 has been reprinted. The overprint on the original measures 12½x3¾mm and on the reprint 12x3¼mm. Value, $200.

OLTRE GIUBA

ˌōl-trā-ˈjü-bə

(Italian Jubaland)

LOCATION — A strip of land, 50 to 100 miles in width, west of and parallel to the Juba River in East Africa
GOVT. — Former Italian Protectorate
AREA — 33,000 sq. mi.
POP. — 12,000
CAPITAL — Kismayu

Oltre Giuba was ceded to Italy by Great Britain in 1924 and in 1926 was incorporated with Italian Somaliland. In 1936 it became part of Italian East Africa.

100 Centesimi = 1 Lira

Watermark

Wmk. 140 — Crown

Italian Stamps of 1901-26 Overprinted

On #1-15

On #16-20

1925, July 29 Wmk. 140 *Perf. 14*

No.	Type	Description	Unused	Used
1	A42	1c brown	3.50	*22.50*
a.		Inverted overprint	425.00	
2	A43	2c yel brown	2.50	*22.50*
3	A48	5c green	2.25	*10.50*
4	A48	10c claret	2.25	*10.50*
5	A48	15c slate	2.25	*14.00*
6	A50	20c brn orange	2.25	*14.00*
7	A49	25c blue	2.50	*14.00*
8	A49	30c org brown	3.50	*17.50*
9	A49	40c brown	5.25	13.00
10	A49	50c violet	5.25	13.00
11	A49	60c carmine	5.25	*17.50*
12	A46	1 l brn & green	10.50	22.00
13	A46	2 l dk grn & org	70.00	47.50
14	A46	5 l blue & rose	105.00	65.00
15	A51	10 l gray grn & red	12.00	*70.00*
		Nos. 1-15 (15)	234.25	*373.50*

1925-26

No.	Type	Description	Unused	Used
16	A49	20c green	6.00	*15.00*
17	A49	30c gray	8.00	*19.00*
18	A46	75c dk red & rose	40.00	*65.00*
19	A46	1.25 l bl & ultra	57.50	*87.50*
20	A46	2.50 l dk grn & org	80.00	*175.00*
		Nos. 16-20 (5)	191.50	*361.50*

Issue years: #18-20, 1926; others 1925.

Victor Emmanuel Issue

Italian Stamps of 1925 Overprinted

1925-26 Unwmk. *Perf. 11*

No.	Type	Description	Unused	Used
21	A78	60c brown car	1.75	*12.00*
a.		Perf. 13½	*10,500.*	
22	A78	1 l dark blue	1.75	*20.00*
a.		Perf. 13½	440.00	*1,400.*
23	A78	1.25 l dk bl ('26)	3.50	*25.00*
a.		Perf. 13½	4.25	*30.00*
		Nos. 21-23 (3)	7.00	*57.00*

Saint Francis of Assisi Issue

Italian Stamps and Type of 1926 Overprinted

Overprinted in Red

1926, Apr. 12 Wmk. 140 *Perf. 14*

No.	Type	Description	Unused	Used
24	A79	20c gray green	2.50	*36.00*
25	A80	40c dark violet	2.50	*36.00*
26	A81	60c red brown	2.50	*47.50*

Unwmk.

No.	Type	Description	Unused	Used
27	A82	1.25 l dk bl, perf. 11	2.50	*67.50*
28	A83	5 l + 2.50 l ol grn, perf. 13½	7.00	*105.00*
		Nos. 24-28 (5)	17.00	*292.00*

Map of Oltre Giuba — A1

1926, Apr. 21 Typo. Wmk. 140

No.	Type	Description	Unused	Used
29	A1	5c yellow brown	1.00	*24.00*
30	A1	20c blue green	1.00	*24.00*
31	A1	25c olive brown	1.00	*24.00*
32	A1	40c dull red	1.00	*24.00*
33	A1	60c brown violet	1.00	*24.00*
34	A1	1 l blue	1.00	*24.00*
35	A1	2 l dark green	1.00	*24.00*
		Nos. 29-35 (7)	7.00	*168.00*

Oltre Giuba was incorporated with Italian Somaliland on July 1, 1926, and stamps inscribed "Oltre Giuba" were discontinued.

SEMI-POSTAL STAMPS

Note preceding Italy semi-postals applies to No. 28.

Colonial Institute Issue

"Peace" Substituting Spade for Sword — SP1

Wmk. 140

1926, June 1 Typo. *Perf. 14*

No.	Type	Description	Unused	Used
B1	SP1	5c + 5c brown	1.00	*8.50*
B2	SP1	10c + 5c olive green	1.00	*8.50*
B3	SP1	20c + 5c blue green	1.00	*8.50*
B4	SP1	40c + 5c brown red	1.00	*8.50*
B5	SP1	60c + 5c orange	1.00	*8.50*
B6	SP1	1 l + 5c blue	1.00	*19.00*
		Nos. B1-B6 (6)	6.00	*61.50*

Surtax for Italian Colonial Institute.

SPECIAL DELIVERY STAMPS

Special Delivery Stamps of Italy Overprinted

1926 Wmk. 140 *Perf. 14*

No.	Type	Description	Unused	Used
E1	SD1	70c dull red	25.00	*52.50*
E2	SD2	2.50 l blue & red	50.00	*130.00*

POSTAGE DUE STAMPS

Italian Postage Due Stamps of 1870-1903 Overprinted Like Nos. E1-E2

1925, July 29 Wmk. 140 *Perf. 14*

No.	Type	Description	Unused	Used
J1	D3	5c buff & magenta	21.00	20.00
J2	D3	10c buff & magenta	21.00	20.00
J3	D3	20c buff & magenta	21.00	*32.50*
J4	D3	30c buff & magenta	21.00	*32.50*
J5	D3	40c buff & magenta	21.00	*36.00*
J6	D3	50c buff & magenta	30.00	*45.00*
J7	D3	60c buff & brown	30.00	*52.50*
J8	D3	1 l blue & magenta	35.00	*65.00*
J9	D3	2 l blue & magenta	150.00	*190.00*
J10	D3	5 l blue & magenta	190.00	190.00
		Nos. J1-J10 (10)	540.00	*683.50*

PARCEL POST STAMPS

These stamps were used by affixing them to the waybill so that one half remained on it following the parcel, the other half staying on the receipt given the sender. Most used halves are right halves. Complete stamps were obtainable canceled, probably to order. Both unused and used values are for complete stamps.

Italian Parcel Post Stamps of 1914-22 Overprinted

1925, July 29 Wmk. 140 *Perf. 13½*

No.	Type	Description	Unused	Used
Q1	PP2	5c brown	17.50	*36.00*
Q2	PP2	10c blue	13.00	*36.00*
Q3	PP2	20c black	13.00	*36.00*
Q4	PP2	25c red	13.00	*36.00*
Q5	PP2	50c orange	17.50	*36.00*
Q6	PP2	1 l violet	13.00	*80.00*
a.		Double overprint	550.00	
Q7	PP2	2 l green	17.50	*80.00*
Q8	PP2	3 l bister	55.00	*110.00*
Q9	PP2	4 l slate	24.00	*110.00*
Q10	PP2	10 l rose lilac	87.50	*175.00*
Q11	PP2	12 l red brown	175.00	*275.00*
Q12	PP2	15 l olive green	160.00	*275.00*
Q13	PP2	20 l brown violet	160.00	*275.00*
		Nos. Q1-Q13 (13)	766.00	1,560.

Halves Used

Q1-Q4	1.60
Q5-Q7	2.50
Q8-Q9	4.25
Q10	8.50
Q11	13.00
Q12-Q13	8.50

OMAN

ˈō-ˌmän

Muscat and Oman

LOCATION — Southeastern corner of the Arabian Peninsula
GOVT. — Sultanate
AREA — 105,000 sq. mi.
POP. — 2,446,645 (1999 est.)
CAPITAL — Muscat

Nos. 16-93, the stamps with 'value only' surcharges, were used not only in Muscat, but also in Dubai (Apr. 1, 1948 - Jan. 6, 1961), Qatar (Aug. 1950 - Mar. 31, 1957), and Abu Dhabi (Mar. 30, 1963 - Mar. 29, 1964). Occasionally they were also used in Bahrain and Kuwait.

The Sultanate of Muscat and Oman changed its name to Oman in 1970.

12 Pies = 1 Anna
16 Annas = 1 Rupee
100 Naye Paise = 1 Rupee (1957)
64 Baizas = 1 Rupee (1966)
1000 Baizas = 1 Rial Saidi (1970)

Catalogue values for all unused stamps in this country are for Never Hinged items.

Muscat

Stamps of India 1937-43 Overprinted in Black

On #1-13 the overprint is 13x6mm.

Wmk. Multiple Stars (196)

1944, Nov. 20 *Perf. 13½x14*

No.	Type	Description	Unused	Used
1	A83	3p slate	.65	*5.25*
2	A83	½a rose violet	.65	*5.25*
3	A83	9p lt green	.65	*5.25*
4	A83	1a carmine rose	.65	*5.25*
5	A84	1½a dark purple	.65	*5.25*
a.		Double overprint	400.00	
6	A84	2a scarlet	.75	*5.25*
7	A84	3a violet	1.50	*5.25*
8	A84	3½a ultra	1.50	*5.25*
9	A85	4a chocolate	1.75	*5.25*
10	A85	6a pck blue	2.00	*5.25*
11	A85	8a blue violet	2.50	*6.00*
12	A85	12a car lake	2.75	*6.00*
13	A81	14a rose violet	5.00	*7.50*
14	A82	1r brown & slate	2.75	*10.00*
15	A82	2r dk brn & dk vio	5.00	*16.50*
		Nos. 1-15 (15)	28.75	*98.50*

200th anniv. of A1 Busaid Dynasty.

Great Britain, Nos. 258 to 263, 243, 248, 249A Surcharged

Perf. 14½x14

1948, Apr. 1 Wmk. 251

No.	Type	Description	Unused	Used
16	A101	½a on ½p green	2.50	*6.75*
17	A101	1a on 1p vermilion	2.75	.30
18	A101	1½a on 1½p lt red brn	5.00	1.50
19	A101	2a on 2p lt org	2.00	1.00
20	A101	2½a on 2½p ultra	3.25	*6.00*
21	A101	3a on 3p violet	3.25	.20
22	A102	6a on 6p rose lilac	3.50	.20
23	A103	1r on 1sh brown	4.50	.75

Wmk. 259 *Perf. 14*

No.	Type	Description	Unused	Used
24	A104	2r on 2sh6p yel grn	14.00	*40.00*
		Nos. 16-24 (9)	40.75	*56.70*

Silver Wedding Issue

Great Britain, Nos. 267 and 268, Surcharged

Perf. 14½x14, 14x14½

1948, Apr. 26 Wmk. 251

No.	Type	Description	Unused	Used
25	A109	2½a on 2½p brt ultra	2.75	1.50
26	A110	15r on £1 dp chlky bl	32.50	32.50

Three bars obliterate the original denomination on No. 26.

Olympic Games Issue

Great Britain, Nos. 271-274, Surcharged

1948, July 29 *Perf. 14½x14*

No.	Type	Description	Unused	Used
27	A113	2½a on 2½p brt ultra	.75	*1.00*
28	A114	3a on 3p dp violet	.85	*1.75*
29	A115	6a on 6p red violet	1.00	*2.00*
30	A116	1r on 1sh dk brown	2.50	*3.00*
a.		Double surcharge	1,200.	
		Nos. 27-30 (4)	5.10	*7.75*

A square of dots obliterates the original denomination on Nos. 28-30.

UPU Issue

Great Britain Nos. 276 to 279 Surcharged with New Value and Square of Dots

1949, Oct. 10 **Photo.**

31 A117 2½a on 2½p brt ultra .75 *2.75*
32 A118 3a on 3p brt violet 1.00 *3.00*
33 A119 6a on 6p red violet 1.50 *2.25*
34 A120 1r on 1sh brown 3.50 3.25
Nos. 31-34 (4) 6.75 *11.25*

Great Britain Nos. 280-286 Surcharged

1951

35 A101 ½a on ½p lt org .90 *9.00*
36 A101 1a on 1p ultra .50 *6.75*
37 A101 1½a on 1½p green 11.00 *25.00*
38 A101 2a on 2p lt red brn 1.00 *8.00*
39 A101 2½a on 2½p vermilion 2.25 *16.00*
40 A102 4a on 4p ultra 2.00 *3.00*

Perf. 11x12

Wmk. 259

41 A121 2r on 2sh6p green 30.00 7.00
Nos. 35-41 (7) 47.65 *74.75*

Two types of surcharge on No. 41.

Stamps of Great Britain, 1952-54, Surcharged with New Value in Black and Dark Blue

1952-54 **Wmk. 298** ***Perf. 14½x14***

42 A126 ½a on ½p red org ('53) .20 *1.00*
43 A126 1a on 1p ultra ('53) .20 *1.00*
44 A126 1½a on 1½p green ('52) .45 *1.00*
45 A126 2a on 2p red brn ('53) .25 .20
46 A127 2½a on 2½p scar ('52) .55 .25
47 A127 3a on 3p dk pur (Dk Bl) .30 *.50*
48 A128 4a on 4p ultra ('53) 1.40 *1.50*
49 A129 6a on 6p lilac rose .70 .45
50 A132 12a on 1sh3p dk grn ('53) 5.50 1.40
51 A131 1r on 1sh6p dk bl ('53) 5.25 1.60
Nos. 42-51 (10) 14.80 *8.90*

Coronation Issue

Great Britain Nos. 313-316 Surcharged

1953, June 10

52 A134 2½a on 2½p scarlet 2.25 1.50
53 A135 4a on 4p brt ultra 2.75 1.10
54 A136 12a on 1sh3p dk green 5.00 3.50
55 A137 1r on 1sh6p dk blue 6.25 1.00
Nos. 52-55 (4) 16.25 7.10

Squares of dots obliterate the original denominations on Nos. 54-55.

Great Britain Stamps of 1955-56 Surcharged

Perf. 14½x14

1955-57 **Wmk. 308** **Photo.**

56 A126 1a on 1p ultra .50 *.60*
56A A126 1½a on 1½p grn 5,000. *800.00*
57 A126 2a on 2p red brn 1.00 *1.25*
58 A127 2½a on 2½p scar 1.25 *2.00*
59 A127 3a on 3p dk pur 1.40 *3.75*
60 A128 4a on 4p ultra 6.50 *16.00*
61 A129 6a on 6p lilac rose 1.40 *5.75*
62 A131 1r on 1sh6p dk bl 5.50 *1.40*

Engr. ***Perf. 11x12***

63 A133 2r on 2sh6p dk brown 9.00 *8.50*
64 A133 5r on 5sh crimson 18.00 *15.00*
Nos. 56,57-64 (9) 44.55 *54.25*

Surcharge on No. 63 exists in three types, on No. 64 in two types.

Issued: 2r, 9/23/55; 2a, 2½a, 6/8/56; 1r, 8/2/56; 4a, 12/9/56; 1½a, 1956; 3a, 2/3/57; 6a, 2/10/57; 5r, 3/1/57; 1a, 3/4/57.

Great Britain Nos. 317-325, 328, 332 Surcharged

1957, Apr. 1 ***Perf. 14½x14***

65 A129 1np on 5p lt brown .25 *.70*
66 A126 3np on ½p red org .35 *1.60*
67 A126 6np on 1p ultra .45 *1.60*
68 A126 9np on 1½p green .65 *1.00*
69 A126 12np on 2p red brown .80 *1.25*
70 A127 15np on 2½p scar, I .90 .80
a. Type II .60 *2.00*
71 A127 20np on 3p dk pur .55 .30
72 A128 25np on 4p ultra 1.40 *3.50*
73 A129 40np on 6p lilac rose .90 .80
74 A130 50np on 9p dp ol grn 2.75 2.00
75 A132 75np on 1sh3p dk grn 5.25 .75
Nos. 65-75 (11) 14.25 *14.30*

The arrangement of the surcharge varies on different values; there are three bars through value on No. 74.

Jubilee Jamboree Issue

Great Britain Nos. 334-336 Surcharged with New Value and Square of Dots

Perf. 14½x14

1957, Aug. 1 **Wmk. 308**

76 A138 15np on 2½p scar 2.75 1.50
77 A138 25np on 4p ultra 2.75 1.50
78 A138 75np on 1sh3p dk grn 3.00 1.50
Nos. 76-78 (3) 8.50 4.50

50th anniv. of the Boy Scout movement and the World Scout Jubilee Jamboree, Aug. 1-12.

Great Britain Stamps of 1958-60 Surcharged

Perf. 14½x14

1960-61 **Wmk. 322** **Photo.**

79 A129 1np on 5p lt brown .20 .30
80 A126 3np on ½p red org 1.60 1.50
81 A126 5np on 1p ultra 1.20 *2.00*
82 A126 6np on 1p ultra 3.75 3.00
83 A126 10np on 1½p green 1.10 1.10
84 A126 12np on 2p red brn 11.00 6.00
85 A127 15np on 2½p scar .65 .25
86 A127 20np on 3p dk pur .65 .20
87 A128 30np on 4½p hn brn 1.00 *1.25*
88 A129 40np on 6p lil rose 1.00 .30
89 A130 50np on 9p dp ol grn 1.75 *2.25*
90 A132 75np on 1sh3p dk grn 3.50 1.75
91 A131 1r on 1sh6p dk blue 12.00 4.00
92 A133 2r on 2sh6p dk brn 18.00 *27.50*
93 A133 5r on 5sh crimson 45.00 *55.00*
Nos. 79-93 (15) 102.40 *106.40*

Issued: 15np, 4/26; 3np, 6np, 12np, 6/21; 1np, 8/8; 20np, 40np, 9/28; 5np, 10np, 30np, 50np-5r, 4/8/61.

Muscat and Oman

Crest — A1

View of Harbor — A2

Nakhal Fort — A3

Baizas

Crest and: 50b, Samail Fort. 1r, Sohar Fort. 2r, Nizwa Fort. 5r, Matrah Fort. 10r, Mirani Fort.

Perf. 14½x14 (A1), 14x14½ (A2), 14x13½ (A3)

1966, Apr. 29 **Photo.** **Unwmk.**

94 A1 3b plum .20 .20
95 A1 5b brown .20 .20
96 A1 10b red brown .20 .20
97 A2 15b black & violet .65 .25
98 A2 20b black & ultra .90 .25
99 A2 25b black & orange 1.25 .35
100 A3 30b dk blue & lil rose 1.75 .45
101 A3 50b red brn & brt grn 2.25 .90
a. Value in "baizas" in Arabic 150.00 25.00
102 A3 1r org & dk bl 4.50 1.10
103 A3 2r grn & brn org 8.25 2.75
104 A3 5r dp car & vio 19.00 9.00
105 A3 10r dk vio & car rose 37.50 17.50
Nos. 94-105 (12) 76.65 33.15

No. 101 has value in rupees in Arabic.

See Nos. 110-121. For overprints & surcharges see Nos. 122-133C.

Mina al Fahal Harbor A4

Designs: 25b, Oil tanks. 40b, Oil installation in the desert. 1r, View of Arabian Peninsula from Gemini IV.

Perf. 13½x13

1969, Jan. 1 **Litho.** **Unwmk.**

106 A4 20b multicolored 3.00 .60
107 A4 25b multicolored 3.75 .80
108 A4 40b multicolored 5.50 1.50
109 A4 1r multicolored 14.50 3.75
Nos. 106-109 (4) 26.75 6.65

1st oil shipment from Muscat & Oman, July, 1967.

Types of 1966

Designs: 50b, Nakhal Fort. 75b, Samail Fort. 100b, Sohar Fort. ¼r, Nizwa Fort. ½r, Matrah Fort. 1r, Mirani Fort.

Perf. 14½x14 (A1), 14x14½ (A2), 14x13½ (A3)

1970, June 27 **Photo.** **Unwmk.**

110 A1 5b plum .60 .20
111 A1 10b brown 1.00 .20
112 A1 20b red brown 1.25 .25
113 A2 25b black & vio 2.25 .30
114 A2 30b black & ultra 2.50 .45
115 A2 40b black & org 3.00 .50
116 A3 50b dk blue & lil rose 4.50 .60
117 A3 75b red brn & brt grn 6.00 1.25
118 A3 100b orange & dk bl 7.50 1.25
119 A3 ¼r grn & brn org 20.00 3.75
120 A3 ½r brn car & vio 35.00 7.50
121 A3 1r dk vio & car rose 62.50 12.50
Nos. 110-121 (12) 146.10 28.75

Sultanate of Oman

Nos. 110-121 Overprinted

a

b

c

5b, 10b 20b:

Type 1 — Lower bars 15¼mm long; letter "A" has low, thick crossbar.

Type 2 — Lower bars 14¾mm; "A" crossbar high, thin.

Perf. 14½x14, 14x14½, 14x13½

1971, Jan. 16 **Photo.** **Unwmk.**

122 A1 (a) 5b plum .50 .20
a. Type 2 9.50 4.00
123 A1 (a) 10b brown .75 .20
a. Type 2 9.50 4.00
124 A1 (a) 20b red brown 1.50 .40
a. Type 2 9.50 4.00
125 A2 (b) 25b black & vio 1.40 .40
126 A2 (b) 30b black & ultra 2.10 .70
127 A2 (b) 40b black & org 2.75 .75
128 A3 (c) 50b dk bl & lil rose 3.50 1.00
129 A3 (c) 75b red brn & brt grn 5.25 1.50
130 A3 (c) 100b org & dk bl 7.25 2.00
131 A3 (c) ¼r grn & brn org 18.00 6.00
132 A3 (c) ½r brn car & vio 35.00 8.50
133 A3 (c) 1r dk vio & car rose 72.50 17.50
Nos. 122-133 (12) 150.50 39.15

For surcharge see No. 133B.

No. 94 Surcharged Type "a," Nos. 127, 102 Surcharged

Perf. 14½x14, 14x14½, 14½x13½

1971-72

133A A1 5b on 3b *140.00* *14.00*
133B A2 25b on 40b *110.00* *100.00*
133C A3 25b on 1r *110.00* *100.00*
Nos. 133A-133C (3) *360.00* *214.00*

No. 133C surcharge resembles type "c" with "Sultanate of Oman" omitted and bars of criss-cross lines.

No. 133A exists with inverted surchagre and in pair, one with surcharge omitted. No. 133C exists with Arabic "2" or "5" omitted.

Issued: 5b, Nov; #133C, 6/6/7; #133B, 7/1/72.

Sultan Qaboos bin Said and New Buildings — A5

National Day: 40b, Sultan Qaboos and freedom symbols. 50b, Crest of Oman and health clinic. 100b, Crest of Oman, classrooms and school.

1971, July 23 **Litho.** ***Perf. 13½x14***

134 A5 10b multicolored 2.00 .30
135 A5 40b multicolored 7.50 .75
136 A5 50b multicolored 10.00 1.25
137 A5 100b multicolored 19.00 3.50
Nos. 134-137 (4) 38.50 5.80

Open Book A6

1972, Jan. 3 ***Perf. 14x14½***

138 A6 25b ap grn, dk bl & dk red 17.50 2.50

International Book Year, 1972.

View of Muscat, 1809 A7

Designs: 5, 10, 20, 25b, View of Matrah, 1809. 30, 40, 50, 75b, View of Shinas, 1809.

Wmk. 314 Sideways

1972, July 23 **Litho.** ***Perf. 14x14½***

Size: 21x17mm

139 A7 5b tan & multi .60 .20
140 A7 10b blue & multi .75 .20
141 A7 20b gray grn & multi 1.25 .20
142 A7 25b violet & multi 1.50 .25

Perf. 14½x14

Size: 25x21mm

143 A7 30b tan & multi 2.00 .30
144 A7 40b gray blue & multi 2.00 .35
145 A7 50b rose brn & multi 2.50 .50
146 A7 75b olive & multi 6.00 .75

Perf. 14

Size: 41x25mm

147 A7 100b lilac & multi 8.00 1.00
148 A7 ¼r green & multi 18.00 2.00
149 A7 ½r bister & multi 35.00 5.50
150 A7 1r dull bl grn & multi 60.00 10.00
Nos. 139-150 (12) 137.60 21.25

Perf. 14x14½, 14½x14

1972-75 **Wmk. 314 Upright**

139a A7 5b tan & multi ('75) .35 .20
140a A7 10b blue & multi ('75) .70 .35
141a A7 20b gray grn & multi ('75) 1.50 .65
142a A7 25b violet & multi ('75) 2.25 .90
143a A7 30b tan & multi 3.25 1.20
144a A7 40b blue & multi 4.25 1.50

145a	A7	50b rose brn & multi	5.00	1.75
146a	A7	75b olive & multi	7.00	3.00
		Nos. 139a-146a (8)	24.30	9.55

Issue dates: Nov. 17, 1972, Sept. 11, 1975.

Perf. 14x14½, 14½x14, 14

1976-82 **Wmk. 373**

139b	A7	5b tan & multi ('78)	.40	.25
140b	A7	10b blue & multi ('78)	.50	.30
141b	A7	20b gray grn & multi ('82)	.90	.30
142b	A7	25b vio & multi ('78)	1.00	.30
143b	A7	30b tan & multi	1.50	.35
144b	A7	40b blue & multi	1.75	.55
145b	A7	50b rose brn & multi	2.00	.65
146b	A7	75b olive & multi	5.00	.90
147b	A7	100b lilac & multi	5.00	1.50
148a	A7	¼r grn & multi ('78)	14.00	3.50
149a	A7	½r bister & multi	19.50	7.00
150a	A7	1r dull bl grn & multi	55.00	12.00
		Nos. 139b-150a (12)	106.55	27.60

Issued: 4/12/76; 1/27/78; 3/15/82.

Ministerial Complex — A8

Litho.; Date Typo.

1973, Sept. 20 **Unwmk.** ***Perf. 13***

151	A8	25b emerald & multi	2.75	.75
152	A8	100b brown org & multi	9.50	2.00

Opening of ministerial complex.

Nos. 151-152 exist with date omitted and hyphen omitted.

Dhows — A9

Perf. 12½x12

1973, Nov. 18 **Litho.** **Wmk. 314**

153	A9	15b shown	1.50	.35
154	A9	50b Seeb Airport	7.00	1.40
155	A9	65b Dhow and tanker	8.00	1.75
156	A9	100b Camel rider	10.00	2.50
		Nos. 153-156 (4)	26.50	6.00

National Day.

Port Qaboos — A10

1974, July 30 **Litho.** ***Perf. 13***

157	A10	100b multicolored	11.00	2.00

Opening of Port Qaboos.

Open Book, Map of Arab World A11

100b, Hands reaching for book, vert.

1974, Sept. 8 **Wmk. 314** ***Perf. 14½***

158	A11	25b multicolored	2.75	.50
159	A11	100b multicolored	8.50	2.50

International Literacy Day, Sept. 8.

Sultan Qaboos, UPU and Arab Postal Union Emblems — A12

1974, Oct. 29 **Litho.** ***Perf. 13½***

160	A12	100b multicolored	3.00	1.50

Centenary of Universal Postal Union.

Arab Scribe A13

1975, May 8 **Photo.** ***Perf. 13x14***

161	A13	25b multicolored	8.00	2.00

Eradication of illiteracy.

New Harbor at Mina Raysoot — A14

Designs: 50b, Stadium and map of Oman. 75b, Water desalination plant. 100b, Oman color television station. 150b, Satellite earth station and map. 250b, Telephone, radar, cable and map.

Perf. 14x13½

1975, Nov. 18 **Litho.** **Wmk. 373**

162	A14	30b multicolored	1.00	.35
163	A14	50b multicolored	2.00	.40
164	A14	75b multicolored	2.50	.75
165	A14	100b multicolored	3.50	1.25
166	A14	150b multicolored	5.00	1.75
167	A14	250b multicolored	10.00	3.50
		Nos. 162-167 (6)	24.00	8.00

National Day 1975.

For surcharges see Nos. 190A-190C.

Mother with Child, Nurse, Globe, Red Crescent, IWY Emblem — A15

Design: 150b, Hand shielding mother and children, Omani flag, IWY emblem, vert.

Perf. 13½x14, 14x13½

1975, Dec. 27 **Litho.**

168	A15	75b citron & multi	2.50	1.10
169	A15	150b ultra & multi	4.00	2.00

International Women's Year 1975.

Sultan Presenting Colors and Opening Seeb-Nizwa Road — A16

National Day: 40b, Paratroopers bailing out from plane and mechanized harvester. 75b, Helicopter squadron and Victory Day procession. 150b, Army building road and Salalah television station.

1976, Nov. 15 **Litho.** ***Perf. 14½***

173	A16	25b multicolored	1.00	.25
174	A16	40b multicolored	3.00	.50
175	A16	75b multicolored	5.75	1.25
176	A16	150b multicolored	7.50	2.25
		Nos. 173-176 (4)	17.25	4.25

Great Bath at Mohenjo-Daro — A17

1977, Jan. 6 **Wmk. 373** ***Perf. 13½***

177	A17	125b multicolored	7.50	2.50

UNESCO campaign to save Mohenjo-Daro excavations in Pakistan.

APU Emblem, Members' Flags — A18

Coffeepots — A19

1977, Apr. 4 **Litho.** ***Perf. 12***

178	A18	30b emerald & multi	2.75	.65
179	A18	75b blue & multi	5.50	1.75

Arab Postal Union, 25th anniversary.

1977, Nov. 18 **Litho.** ***Perf. 13½***

Designs: 75b, Earthenware. 100b, Stone tablet, Khor Rori, 100 B.C. 150b, Jewelry.

180	A19	40b multicolored	1.50	.35
181	A19	75b multicolored	3.00	.65
182	A19	100b multicolored	4.75	1.00
183	A19	150b multicolored	7.75	1.40
		Nos. 180-183 (4)	17.00	3.40

National Day 1977.

Forts A20

Wmk. 373

1978, Nov. 18 **Litho.** ***Perf. 14***

184	A20	20b Jalali	1.00	.25
185	A20	25b Nizwa	1.00	.40
186	A20	40b Rostaq	2.25	.60
187	A20	50b Sohar	2.50	.65
188	A20	75b Bahla	3.50	1.00
189	A20	100b Jibrin	5.00	1.25
		Nos. 184-189 (6)	15.25	4.15

National Day 1978.

Pilgrims, Mt. Arafat, Holy Kaaba A21

1978, Nov. 1 **Litho.** ***Perf. 13½***

190	A21	40b multicolored	5.25	2.00

Pilgrimage to Mecca.

Nos. 166, 169 and 167 Surcharged

Perf. 14x13½

1978, July 30 **Litho.** **Wmk. 373**

190A	A14	40b on 150b	*450.00*	*450.00*
190B	A15	50b on 150b	*450.00*	*450.00*
190C	A14	75b on 250b	*2,250.*	*2,250.*
		Nos. 190A-190C (3)	*3,150.*	*3,150.*

World Map, Book, Symbols of Learning A22

1979, Mar. 22 **Litho.** ***Perf. 14x13½***

191	A22	40b multicolored	2.00	.45
192	A22	100b multicolored	4.25	1.10

Cultural achievements of the Arabs.

Girl on Swing, IYC Emblem A23

1979, Oct. 28 **Litho.** ***Perf. 14***

193	A23	40b multicolored	3.25	2.00

International Year of the Child.

Sultan on Horseback, Military Symbols — A25

Gas Plant — A24

National Day: 75b, Fisheries.

1979, Nov. 18 **Photo.** ***Perf. 11½***

194	A24	25b multicolored	2.50	.75
195	A24	75b multicolored	7.25	2.25

Design: 100b, Soldier, parachutes, tank.

1979, Dec. 11

196	A25	40b multicolored	5.00	1.25
197	A25	100b multicolored	11.00	3.00

Armed Forces Day.

Hegira (Pilgrimage Year) — A26

1980, Nov. 9 Photo. *Perf. 11½*

198 A26 50b shown 3.00 .75
199 A26 150b Hegira emblem 7.75 2.50

Omani Women — A27

1980, Nov. 18

Granite Paper

200 A27 75b Bab Alkabir 2.00 .75
201 A27 100b Corniche High-way 2.50 1.00
202 A27 250b Polo match 5.50 3.50
203 A27 500b shown 10.00 6.50
Nos. 200-203 (4) 20.00 11.75

10th National Day.
For surcharges see Nos. 212-213.

Sultan and Patrol Boat — A28

1980, Dec. 11

Granite Paper

204 A28 150b shown 5.00 2.25
205 A28 750b Sultan, mounted troops 29.00 10.00

Armed Forces Day.
For surcharges see Nos. 210-211.

Policewoman and Children Crossing Street — A29

1981, Feb. 7 Litho. *Perf. 13½x14*

206 A29 50b shown 3.75 .70
207 A29 100b Marching band 4.75 1.25
208 A29 150b Mounted police on beach 5.50 2.00
209 A29 ½r Headquarters 11.00 3.50
Nos. 206-209 (4) 25.00 7.45

First National Police Day.

Nos. 204-205, 200, 203 Surcharged in Black on Silver

1981, Apr. 8 Photo. *Perf. 11½*

210 A28 20b on 150b multi 3.75 .55
211 A28 30b on 750b multi 5.00 .85
212 A27 50b on 75b multi 5.75 1.40
213 A27 100b on 500b multi 9.50 2.50
Nos. 210-213 (4) 24.00 5.30

Welfare of the Blind — A30

1981, Oct. 14 Photo. *Perf. 11½*

214 A30 10b multicolored 22.50 1.75

World Food Day — A31

1981, Oct. 16 Photo. *Perf. 12*

215 A31 50b multicolored 6.25 1.75

Hegira (Pilgrimage Year) — A32

1981, Oct. 25 Litho. *Perf. 14½*

216 A32 50b multicolored 8.00 2.00

11th Natl. Day — A32a

1981, Nov. 18 Photo. *Perf. 12*

216A A32a 160b Al-Razha match (sword vs. stick) 5.00 2.00
216B A32a 300b Sultan, map, vert. 9.00 3.25

Voyage of Sinbad A33

1981, Nov. 23 Litho. *Perf. 14½x14*

217 A33 50b Muscat Port, 1981 2.50 .75
218 A33 100b Dhow Shohar 4.75 1.75
219 A33 130b Map 5.75 2.25
220 A33 200b Muscat Harbor, 1650 8.00 3.25
a. Souvenir sheet of 4, #217-220 55.00 55.00
Nos. 217-220 (4) 21.00 8.00

Armed Forces Day — A34

1981, Dec. 11 Photo. *Perf. 11½*

221 A34 100b Sultan, planes 5.00 1.75
222 A34 400b Patrol boats 12.50 4.25

Natl. Police Day A35

1982, Jan. 5 Litho. *Perf. 14½*

223 A35 50b Patrol launch 3.50 .75
224 A35 100b Band, vert. 6.00 1.50

Nerium Mascatense A36

Red-legged Partridge A37

1982, July 7 Photo. *Perf. 12½*

Granite Paper

225 A36 5b shown .30 .25
226 A36 10b Dionysia mira .30 .25
227 A36 20b Teucrium mas-catense .60 .25
228 A36 25b Geranium mas-catense .60 .25
229 A36 30b Cymatium bos-chi, horiz. .90 .40
230 A36 40b Acteon eloiseae, horiz. .90 .50
231 A36 50b Cypraea teuler-ei, horiz. 1.00 .60
232 A36 75b Cypraea pul-chra, horiz. 1.25 .90
233 A37 100b shown 4.25 1.10
234 A37 ¼r Hoopoe 10.00 4.00

Size: 25x38mm

235 A37 ½r Tahr 12.50 5.50
236 A37 1r Arabian oryx 20.00 11.00
Nos. 225-236 (12) 52.60 25.00

2nd Municipalities Week (1981) — A38

1982, Oct. 28 Litho. *Perf. 13½x14½*

237 A38 40b multicolored 8.00 2.00

ITU Plenipotentiaries Conference, Nairobi, Sept. — A39

1982, Nov. 6 *Perf. 14½x13½*

238 A39 100b multicolored 9.25 2.50

12th Natl. Day A40

1982, Nov. 18 *Perf. 12*

239 A40 40b State Consultative Council inaugural session 3.75 1.25
240 A40 100b Oil refinery 7.75 2.50

Armed Forces Day — A41

1982, Dec. 11 *Perf. 13½x14*

241 A41 50b Soldiers 3.00 1.00
242 A41 100b Mounted band 7.50 2.00

Arab Palm Tree Day — A42

Perf. 13½x14½

1982, Sept. 19 Litho.

243 A42 40b Picking coconuts 3.50 1.75
244 A42 100b Dates 7.25 2.75

Natl. Police Day — A43

1983, Jan. 5 Litho. *Perf. 14x13½*

245 A43 50b multicolored 6.75 1.75

World Communications Year — A44

1983, May 17 *Perf. 13½x14*

246 A44 50b multicolored 6.75 2.25

Bees — A45

Designs: a, Beehive. b, Bee, flower.

1983, Aug. 15 Litho. *Perf. 13½*

247 A45 Pair 16.50 16.50
a.-b. A45 50b any single 3.50 2.00

Hegira (Pilgrimage Year) — A46

1983, Sept. 14 Photo. ***Perf. 13½***
248 A46 40b multicolored 9.25 2.25

Youth Year — A47

Perf. 12½x13½
1983, Nov. 15 Litho.
249 A47 50b multicolored 6.25 1.75

National Day 1983 — A48

1983, Nov. 18 Litho. ***Perf. 13½x14***
250 A48 50b Sohar Copper Factory 3.25 1.00
251 A48 100b Sultan Qaboos University 6.50 2.25

Armed Forces Day A49

1983, Dec. 11 Litho. ***Perf. 13½x14***
252 A49 100b multicolored 8.00 2.25

Police Day A50

1984, Jan. 5 Litho. ***Perf. 13½x14***
253 A50 100b multicolored 9.00 2.25

7th Arabian Gulf Soccer Tournament, Muscat, Mar. 9-26 — A51

1984, Mar. 9 Litho. ***Perf. 13½***
254 A51 40b Players, cup, vert. 3.00 1.00
255 A51 50b Emblem 4.75 1.50

Pilgrims at Stone-Throwing Ceremony — A52

1984, Sept. 5 Litho. ***Perf. 13½x14***
256 A52 50b multicolored 5.50 1.25

Pilgrimage to Mecca.

National Day 1984 — A53

Perf. 13½x14, 14x13½
1984, Nov. 18 Litho.
257 A53 130b Mail sorting, new p.o. 4.75 1.25
258 A53 160b Map, vert. 7.50 1.50

Inauguration of the new Central P.O., development of telecommunications.

16th Arab Scout Conference, Muscat — A54

1984, Dec. 5 Litho. ***Perf. 14½***
259 A54 50b Setting-up camp 1.50 .75
260 A54 50b Map reading 1.50 .75
a. Pair, #259-260 6.50 6.50
261 A54 130b Saluting natl. flag 4.25 1.75
262 A54 130b Scouts and girl guides 4.25 1.75
a. Pair, #261-262 14.50 14.50
Nos. 259-262 (4) 11.50 5.00

Armed Forces Day A55

1984, Dec. 11 ***Perf. 13½x14***
263 A55 100b multicolored 8.00 2.50

Police Day — A56

1985, Jan. 5 ***Perf. 14x13½***
264 A56 100b multicolored 9.00 2.50

Hegira (Pilgrimage Year) — A57

1985, Aug. 20 Litho. ***Perf. 13½x14***
265 A57 50b Al-Khaif Mosque, Mina 4.75 1.00

Intl. Youth Year A58

1985, Sept. 22 Litho. ***Perf. 13½x14***
266 A58 50b Emblems 2.50 .75
267 A58 100b Emblem, youth activities 4.50 1.50

Jabrin Palace Restoration — A59

1985, Sept. 22 Litho. ***Perf. 13½x14***
268 A59 100b Interior 3.00 1.00
269 A59 250b Restored ceiling 7.00 3.25

Intl. Symposium on Traditional Music — A60

1985, Oct. 6 Litho. ***Perf. 13½x14***
270 A60 50b multicolored 4.00 1.00

UN Child Survival Campaign — A61

1985, Oct. 25 Litho. ***Perf. 13½x14***
271 A61 50b multicolored 4.00 1.00

Flags, Map and Sultan Qaboos — A62

1985, Nov. 3 Litho. ***Perf. 12½***
272 A62 40b shown 2.50 1.25
273 A62 50b Supreme Council, vert. 4.00 1.50

6th Session of Arab Gulf States Supreme Council, Muscat.

Natl. Day 1985 — A63

Progress and development. 20b, Sultan Qaboos University. 50b, Date picking, plowing field. 100b, Port Qaboos Cement Factory. 200b, Post, transportation and communications. 250b, Sultan Qaboos, vert.

1985, Nov. 18
274 A63 20b multicolored .90 .25
275 A63 50b multicolored 1.75 .60
276 A63 100b multicolored 3.00 1.00
277 A63 200b multicolored 5.00 2.00
278 A63 250b multicolored 6.75 2.75
Nos. 274-278 (5) 17.40 6.60

Armed Forces Day A64

1985, Dec. 11 ***Perf. 13½x14***
279 A64 100b multicolored 8.25 1.50

Fish and Crustaceans A65

Perf. 11½x12, 12x11½
1985, Dec. 15 Photo.
280 A65 20b Chaetodon collaris .60 .20
281 A65 50b Chaetodon melapterus 1.10 .40
282 A65 100b Chaetodon gardineri 1.75 .85
283 A65 150b Scomberomorus commerson 2.50 1.25
284 A65 200b Panulirus homarus 3.75 1.75
Nos. 280-284 (5) 9.70 4.45

Nos. 280-282, vert.

Frankincense Trees in Oman — A66

1985, Dec. 15 Litho. ***Perf. 13½x14***
285 A66 100b multicolored 1.25 .90
286 A66 3r multicolored 37.50 22.50

Police Day A67

1986, Jan. 5 Litho. ***Perf. 13½x14***
287 A67 50b Camel Corps, Muscat 5.50 1.00

Statue of Liberty, Cent. A68

Maps and: 50b, Sultanah, voyage from Muscat to US 1840. 100b, Statue, Shabab Oman voyage from Oman to US, 1986, and fortress.

1986, July 4 *Perf. 14½*

288 A68 50b multicolored 4.00 1.00
289 A68 100b multicolored 7.00 1.75
a. Souvenir sheet of 2, #288-289 25.00 10.00

No. 289a sold for 250b.

Pilgrimage to Mecca — A69

1986, Aug. 9

290 A69 50b Holy Kaaba 3.00 .75

17th Arab Scout Camp — A70

1986, Aug. 20

291 A70 50b Erecting tent 2.75 .75
292 A70 100b Surveying 4.75 1.50

Sultan Qaboos Sports Complex Inauguration — A71

1986, Oct. 18 Litho. *Perf. 14½*

293 A71 100b multicolored 3.25 1.25

Intl. Peace Year A72

1986, Oct. 24 *Perf. 13½x13*

294 A72 130b multicolored 3.25 1.10

A73

A74

Natl. Day 1986 — A75

1986, Nov. 18 *Perf. 14½*

295 A73 50b mutlicolored 1.50 .60
296 A74 100b multicolored 4.00 1.25

Perf. 13½x13

297 A75 130b multicolored 4.50 1.50
Nos. 295-297 (3) 10.00 3.35

Police Day A76

1987, Jan. 5 *Perf. 13½x14*

298 A76 50b multicolored 3.25 1.00

Second Arab Gulf Week for Social Work, Bahrain A77

1987, Mar. 21 *Perf. 13½x13*

299 A77 50b multicolored 2.75 .75

Intl. Environment Day — A78

Perf. 13½x13, 13x13½

1987, June 5 **Litho.**

300 A78 50b Flamingos in flight 3.00 .65
301 A78 130b Irrigation canal, vert. 5.00 1.00

Pilgrimage to Mecca A79

Stages of Pilgrimage (not in consecutive order): a, Pilgrims walking the tawaf, circling the Holy Kaaba 7 times. b, Tent City, Mina. c, Symbolic stoning of Satan. d, Pilgrims in Muzdalifah at dusk, picking up stones. e, Veneration of the prophet (pilgrims praying), Medina. f, Pilgrims wearing ihram, Pilgrim's Village, Jeddah.

1987, July 29 Litho. *Perf. 13½*

302 Strip of 6 17.50 17.50
a.-f. A79 50b any single 1.25 .70

Third Municipalities Month — A80

1987, Oct. 1 *Perf. 13x13½*

303 A80 50b multicolored 2.25 .70

Natl. Day A81

Designs: 50b, Marine Biology and Fisheries Center. 130b, Royal Hospital.

1987, Nov. 18 Litho. *Perf. 13½x13*

304 A81 50b multicolored .85 .40
305 A81 130b multicolored 2.75 1.25

Royal Omani Amateur Radio Soc., 15th Anniv. — A82

1987, Dec. 23 Litho. *Perf. 13½x13*

306 A82 130b multicolored 3.25 1.25

Traditional Handicrafts — A83

1988, June 1 Photo. *Perf. 12x11½*

Granite Paper

307 A83 50b Weaver 1.25 .50
308 A83 100b Potter 1.75 .75
309 A83 150b Halwa maker 2.50 1.40
310 A83 200b Silversmith 3.00 1.75
a. Souvenir sheet of 4, #307-310 16.50 14.50
Nos. 307-310 (4) 8.50 4.40

No. 310a sold for 600b.

A84

A85

1988, Sept. 17 Litho. *Perf. 14½*

311 A84 100b Equestrian 1.25 .70
312 A84 100b Field hockey 1.25 .70
313 A84 100b Soccer 1.25 .70
314 A84 100b Running 1.25 .70
315 A84 100b Swimming 1.25 .70
316 A84 100b Shooting 1.25 .70
a. Block of 6, #311-316 17.50 17.50
b. Souvenir sheet of 6, #311-316 30.00 30.00

1988 Summer Olympics, Seoul.

1988, Nov. 1 Litho. *Perf. 13½*

317 A85 100b multicolored 2.25 1.10

WHO, 40th anniv.

Natl. Day, Agriculture Year A86

1988, Nov. 18 *Perf. 14½x13½*

318 A86 100b Tending crops 1.75 1.00
319 A86 100b Animal husbandry 1.75 1.00
a. Pair, #318-319 5.25 5.25

No. 319a has a continuous design.

Women Wearing Regional Folk Costume — A87

Designs: 200b-1r, Men wearing regional folk costumes.

1989 Photo. *Perf. 11½x12*

Granite Paper

320 A87 30b Dhahira .75 .25
321 A87 40b Eastern 1.00 .40
322 A87 50b Batinah 1.25 .55
323 A87 100b Interior 2.25 1.00
324 A87 130b Southern 3.00 2.00
325 A87 150b Muscat 4.00 2.25
a. Souvenir sheet of 6, #320-325 20.00 20.00
326 A87 200b Dhahira 2.00 1.40
327 A87 ¼r Eastern 2.50 1.60
328 A87 ½r Southern 5.00 5.00
329 A87 1r Muscat 8.75 6.75
a. Souvenir sheet of 4, #326-329 24.00 24.00
Nos. 320-329 (10) 30.50 21.20

No. 325a sold for 700b, No. 329a for 2r.
Issued: 30b-150b, 8/26; 200b-1r, 11/11.

National Day, Agriculture Year — A88

1989, Nov. 18 *Perf. 12½x13*

330 A88 100b Fishing 1.25 .60
331 A88 100b Farming 1.25 .60
a. Pair, #330-331 4.00 4.00

Printed se-tenant in a continuous design.

10th Session of Supreme Council of the Cooperation Council for Arab Gulf States — A89

1989, Dec. 18 Litho. *Perf. 13x12*

332 A89 50b Flags, Omani crest .80 .40
333 A89 50b Sultan Qaboos, council emblem .80 .40
a. Pair, #332-333 3.50 3.50

No. 333a has a continuous design.

Gulf Investment Corp., 5th Anniv. (in 1989) — A90

1990, Jan. 1 Litho. *Perf. 13x12*

334 A90 50b multicolored 2.00 .70
335 A90 130b multicolored 3.25 1.00

Gulf Air, 40th Anniv. A91

1990, Mar. 24 *Perf. 13x13½*

336 A91 80b multicolored 4.75 1.00

Symposium on the Oman Ophiolite — A92

1990, Apr. 22 Photo. *Perf. 11½*
Granite Paper

337 A92 80b shown 1.10 .50
338 A92 150b multicolored 2.25 1.00

First Omani Envoy to the U.S., 150th Anniv. A93

1990, Apr. 30 Litho. *Perf. 13*

339 A93 200b multicolored 3.00 1.10

Sultan Qaboos Rose — A94

1990, May 5 Photo. *Perf. 11½*
Granite Paper

340 A94 200b multicolored 2.50 1.00

20th National Day A95

100b, Natl. Day emblem. 200b, Sultan Qaboos.

Litho. & Embossed
1990, Nov. 18 *Perf. 12x11½*
Granite Paper

341 A95 100b gold, red & green 1.50 .60
342 A95 200b gold, green & red 3.25 1.25
a. Souvenir sheet of 2, #341-342 5.50 5.50

No. 342a sold for 500b.

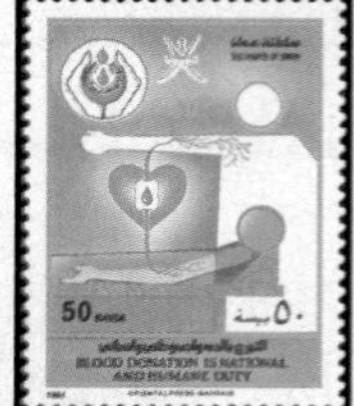

Blood Donors — A96

1991, Apr. 22 Litho. *Perf. 13½x13*

343 A96 50b multicolored .60 .35
344 A96 200b multicolored 2.75 1.50
a. Pair, #343-344 25.00 25.00

National Day — A97

1991, Nov. 18 Photo. *Perf. 13½*

345 A97 100b shown 2.75 .65
346 A97 200b Sultan Qaboos 5.50 1.25
a. Souvenir sheet of 2, #345-346 9.00 7.00

No. 346a sold for 400b.

Armed Forces Day A98

1991, Dec. 11 Litho. *Perf. 14½*

347 A98 100b multicolored 2.00 .90

A99

A100

1992, Jan. 29 Litho. *Perf. 13½x14*

348 A99 100b multicolored 1.50 .65
a. Sheet of 1, perf. 13x13½ 11.00 9.00

Inauguration of Omani-French Museum, Muscat. No. 348a sold for 300b.

1992, Mar. 23 Litho. *Perf. 14½*

349 A100 200b multicolored 3.50 1.25

World Meteorological Day.

A101

A102

1992, June 5 Litho. *Perf. 13x13½*

350 A101 100b multicolored 2.00 .75

World Environment Day.

1992, Sept. 26 Litho. *Perf. 13½x14*

351 A102 70b multicolored 1.40 .55

Welfare of Handicapped Children.

Sultan Qaboos Encyclopedia of Arab Names — A103

1992, Oct. 10 *Perf. 14½*

352 A103 100b gold & multi 2.00 .70

National Day — A104

Sultan Qaboos and emblems of: 100b, Year of Industry. 200b, Majlis As'shura.

1992, Nov. 18 Litho. *Perf. 14x13½*

353 A104 100b multicolored 1.50 .70
354 A104 200b multicolored 3.50 1.10

Royal Oman Police Day A105

1993, Jan. 5 Litho. *Perf. 13½x14*

355 A105 80b multicolored 1.75 .70

1993 Census A106

1993, Sept. 4 Litho. *Perf. 14x13½*

356 A106 100b multicolored 1.50 .70

Royal Navy Day — A107

1993, Nov. 3 Litho. *Perf. 13*

357 A107 100b multicolored 2.25 .70

23rd National Day A108

1993, Nov. 18 Photo. *Perf. 12*
Granite Paper

358 A108 100b Year of Youth emblem 1.50 .70
359 A108 200b Sultan Qaboos 2.50 1.10

Scouting — A109

#360, Emblem of Scouts & Guides, Scout Headquarters. #361, Scout camp, Sultan Qaboos.

1993, Nov. 20 Litho. *Perf. 13x13½*

360 A109 100b multicolored 1.10 .70
361 A109 100b multicolored 1.10 .70
a. Pair, #360-361 5.00 5.00

Scouting movement in Oman, 61st anniv. (#360). Installation of Sultan Qaboos as chief scout, 10th anniv. (#361).

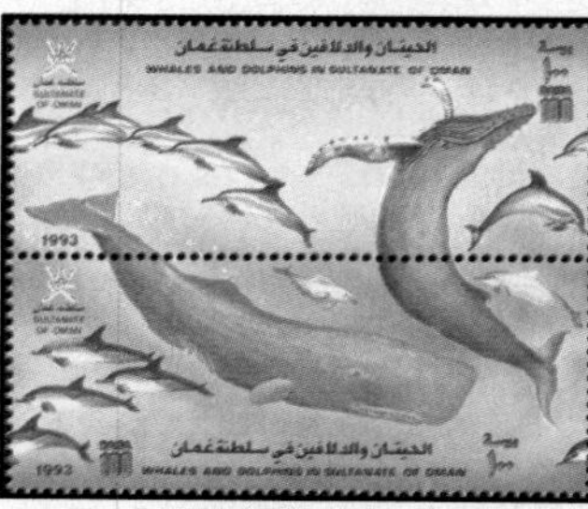

Whales and Dolphins — A110

#362, Dolphins, humpback whale. #363, Dolphins, sperm whale. Illustration reduced.

1993, Dec. 8 *Perf. 14½*

362 100b multicolored 3.00 1.00
363 100b multicolored 3.00 1.00
a. A110 Pair, #362-363 10.00 10.00
b. Souvenir sheet of 2, #362-363 45.00 45.00

No. 363a has a continuous design. No. 363b sold for 400b and has a white border surrounding the stamps.

World Day for Water — A111

Muscat Municipality, 70th Anniv. — A112

1994, Mar. 22 Litho. *Perf. 13½*

364 A111 50b multicolored 1.75 .40

1994, Apr. 16

365 A112 50b multicolored 1.60 .40

Intl. Olympic Committee, Cent. — A113

1994, Aug. 29 Litho. *Perf. 13½*

366 A113 100b multicolored 11.00 3.50

Al Busaid Dynasty, 250th Anniv. — A114

Natl. arms or sultan, dates: a, 1744-75. b, 1775-79. c, 1779-92. d, 1792-1804. e, 1804-7. f, Sa'id ibn Sultan, 1807-56. g, 1856-65. h, 1866-68. i, 1868-71. j, Sultan, 1871-88. k, Sultan, 1888-1913. l, Sultan Taymur ibn Faysal, 1913-32. m, Sultan Qaboos, laurel tree. n, Sultan Sa'id ibn Taymur, 1932-70. o, Sultan Qaboos, 1970-.

200b, Sultan Qaboos atop family "tree," Arabic listing of former Sultans, years in power.

Litho. & Embossed

1994, Dec. 28 *Perf. 11½*

367 A114 50b Block of 15, #a.-o. 47.50 47.50

Litho. & Typo.

Imperf

Size: 140x110mm

367P A114 200b gold & multi 4.50 4.00

Nos. 367f, 367j-367o contain portraits of sultans.

Open Parliament — A115

1995, Jan. 7 Litho. *Perf. 14*

Granite Paper

368 A115 50b silver & multi 1.25 .55

24th National Day, Year of the Heritage — A116

1994, Nov. 18 Litho. *Perf. 13½*

369 A116 50b Emblem .85 .35

370 A116 50b Sultan Qaboos .85 .35

a. Pair, #369-370 6.25 6.25

ICAO, 50th Anniv. A117

1994, Dec. 7 *Perf. 13½x14*

371 A117 100b multicolored 3.75 1.00

Arab League, 50th Anniv. — A118

1995, Mar. 22 Litho. *Perf. 13*

372 A118 100b multicolored 2.00 .65

UN, 50th Anniv. A119

1995, Sept. 2 *Perf. 13½*

373 A119 100b multicolored 3.50 .65

16th Session of Supreme Council of the Co-operative Council for Arab Gulf States A120

Designs: 100b, Emblem. 200b, Flags of Arab Gulf States, map, Sultan Qaboos.

1995, Dec. 4 *Perf. 12*

Granite Paper

374 A120 100b multicolored 2.00 .70

375 A120 200b multicolored 4.00 1.25

a. Pair, #374-375 *30.00 20.00*

25th National Day A121

Portraits of Sultan Qaboos: 50b, In traditional attire. 100b, In military uniform.

Litho. & Embossed

1995, Nov. 18 *Perf. 11½*

Granite Paper

376 A121 50b multicolored 1.25 .40

377 A121 100b multicolored 2.75 .65

a. Souvenir sheet of 2, #376-377 6.00 3.50

No. 377a sold for 300b.

1996 Summer Olympic Games, Atlanta — A122

a, Shooting. b, Swimming. c, Cycling. d, Running.

1996, July 19 Litho. *Perf. 14½*

378 A122 100b Strip of 4, #a.-d. 27.50 22.50

13th Arabian Gulf Cup Soccer Tournament — A123

1996, Oct. 15 *Perf. 13½*

379 A123 100b multicolored 2.00 .75

UN Decade Against Drug Abuse — A124

1996, June 26 *Perf. 13½x14*

380 A124 100b multicolored 15.00 6.75

UNICEF, 50th Anniv. A125

1996, Dec. 11 Litho. *Perf. 14½*

381 A125 100b multicolored 1.75 .60

26th National Day — A126

Designs: No. 382, Sultan Qaboos waving, boats in harbor. No. 383, Boats in harbor, Sultan Qaboos.

1996, Nov. 26 *Perf. 13½*

382 A126 50b multicolored .75 .40

383 A126 50b multicolored .75 .40

a. Pair, #382-383 4.25 4.25

No. 383a is a continuous design.

Traditional Boats — A127

1996, Apr. 15 Photo. *Perf. 13½x14*

384 A127 50b Ash'Shashah .25 .25

385 A127 100b Al-Battil .50 .50

386 A127 200b Al-Boum 1.00 1.00

387 A127 250b Al-Badan 1.25 1.25

388 A127 350b As'Sanbuq 1.75 1.75

389 A127 450b Al-Galbout 2.25 2.25

390 A127 650b Al-Baghlah 3.50 3.50

391 A127 1r Al-Ghanjah 5.25 5.25

Nos. 384-391 (8) 15.75 15.75

Souvenir Sheet

Imperf

392 A127 600b Designs of #384-391 8.00 6.75

No. 392 has simulated perfs. and individual stamps are defaced and not valid for postage.

Tourism A128

a, Oasis fort among palm trees. b, Small waterfalls, trees. c, Highway, coastline, castle on hilltop. d, Lake, mountains. e, Ruins of ancient fort on cliff. f, Waterfall, mountain stream.

1997 Litho. *Perf. 13½x14*

393 A128 100b Block of 6, #a.-f. 11.00 11.00

27th National Day — A129

Waterfall, Sultan Qaboos wearing: No. 394, Multicolored outfit. No. 395, Wearing white outfit.

1997, Nov. 18 Litho. *Perf. 13½*

394 A129 100b multicolored 1.25 .70

395 A129 100b multicolored 1.25 .70

a. Pair, #394-395 4.00 4.00

Girl Guides in Oman, 25th Anniv. A130

1997, Nov. 30 *Perf. 14½*

396 A130 100b multicolored 2.75 .85

Amateur Radio Society, 25th Anniv. — A131

1997, Dec. 23 *Perf. 13½*

397 A131 100b multicolored 2.75 .85

Al-Khanjar Assaidi — A132

1997 *Perf. 11½*

Granite Paper

398	A132	50b red & multi	.55	.30
399	A132	50b green & multi	.55	.30
400	A132	100b purple & multi	1.00	.60
401	A132	200b brown & multi	2.75	1.25
		Nos. 398-401 (4)	4.85	2.45

See No. 418.

Traffic Week A133

1998 *Perf. 13½*

402 A133 100b multicolored 5.00 1.50

Tourism — A134

Designs: a, Fort. b, Rocky mountainside, lake. c, City. d, Men raising swords, drummers. e, Stream running through countryside. f, Girls standing beside stream, trees.

1998 *Perf. 13½x13*

403 A134 100b Block of 6, #a.-f. 11.00 11.00

4th Arab Gulf Countries Philatelic Exhibition, Muscat — A135

1998 **Litho.** *Perf. 13½*

404 A135 50b multicolored 1.50 .50

Sultan Qaboos, Recipient of Intl. Peace Award A136

1998

405 A136 500b multicolored 11.00 5.00

28th National Day — A137

1998 *Perf. 12½*

406	A137	100b Sultan Qaboos	2.75	1.00
407	A137	100b Emblem, map	2.75	1.00
a.		Pair, #406-407	6.00	6.00
b.		Souvenir sheet, #406-407	*25.00*	*25.00*

Opening of Raysut Port-Salalah Container Terminal — A138

1998 *Perf. 13x13½*

408 A138 50b multicolored 3.00 1.00

World Stamp Day — A139

1998 *Perf. 13½*

409 A140 100b multicolored 1.50 .70

Royal Air Force of Oman, 40th Anniv. — A140

1999 **Litho.** *Perf. 13½x13¾*

410 A140 100b multicolored 1.75 .85

Butterflies A141

Designs: a, Danaus chrysippus. b, Papilio demoleus. c, Precis orithya. d, Precis hierta.

1999 **Litho.** *Perf. 13¼*

411	A141	100b Block of 4, #a.-d.	*12.50*	*12.50*
e.		Souvenir sheet of 4, #a.-d.	*50.00*	*50.00*

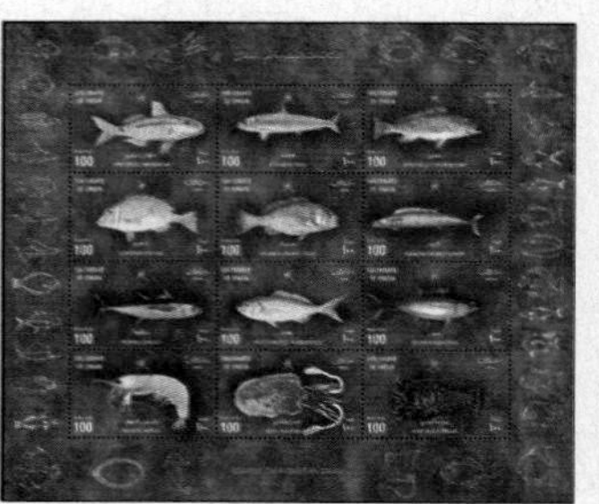

Marine Life — A142

Designs: a, Parupeneus macronema. b, Etrumeus teres. c, Epinephelus chlorostigma. d, Lethrinus lentjan. e, Lutjanus erythropterus. f, Acanthocybium solandri. g, Thunnus tongol. h, Pristipomoides filamentosus. i, Thunnus albacares. j, Penaeus indicus. k, Sepia pharaonis. l, Panulirus homarus.

1999 **Litho.** *Perf. 13½x13*

412 A142 100b Sheet of 12, #a.-l. 11.00 11.00

Wildlife — A143

Designs: a, Sand cat. b, Genet. c, Leopard. d, Sand fox. e, Caracal lynx. f, Hyena.

1999 **Litho.** *Perf. 13½x13*

413	A143	100b Block of 6, #a.-f.	10.00	10.00
g.		Souvenir sheet, #a.-f.	24.00	24.00

UPU, 125th Anniv. A144

1999 *Perf. 11*

414 A144 200b multi 1.75 1.10

29th National Day — A145

1999 **Litho.** *Perf. 13½*

415	A145	100b shown	1.40	.70
416	A145	100b Sultan in white	1.40	.70
a.		Pair, #415-416	4.00	4.00

Souvenir Sheet

Millennium — A146

Illustration reduced.

Litho. & Embossed with Foil Application

2000, Jan. 1 *Perf. 13¼*

417 A146 500b multi 10.00 10.00

Al-Khanjar Assaidi Type of 1997

2000, Feb. 12 **Litho.** *Perf. 11½*

Granite Paper

418 A132 80b orange & multi 1.25 .45

GCC Water Week — A147

2000 **Litho.** *Perf. 13¼*

419 A147 100b multi 1.50 .70

Gulf Air, 50th Anniv. — A148

2000 *Perf. 13½*

420 A148 100b multi 1.10 .60

Butterfly Type of 1999

No. 421: a, Colotis danae. b, Anaphaeis aurota. c, Tarucus rosaceus. d, Lampides boeticus.

2000 **Litho.** *Perf. 13½*

421		Block of 4	8.50	8.50
a.-d.	A141	100b Any single	1.75	.85
e.		Souvenir sheet, #421	21.00	21.00

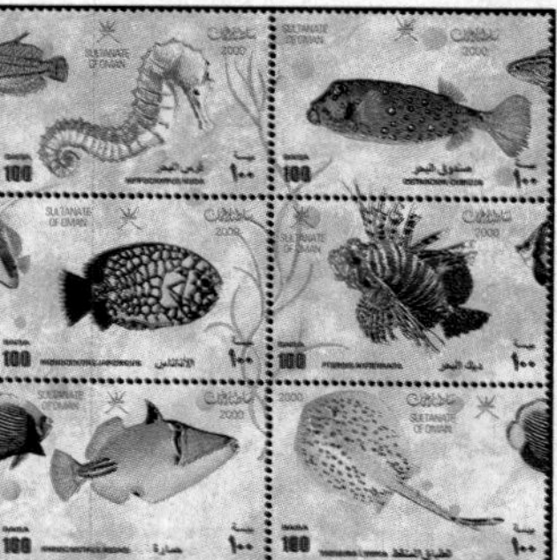

Fish — A148a

No. 421F: g, Hippocampus kuda. h, Ostracion cubicus. i, Monocentris japonicus. j, Pterois antennata. k, Phinecanthus assasi. l, Taenura lymma.
Illustration reduced.

Perf. 13½x13¾

2000, June 12 **Litho.**

421F A148a 100b Block of 6, #g-l		11.00	6.00
m.	Souvenir sheet, #421F	20.00	10.00

2000 Summer Olympics, Sydney — A149

Designs: a, Shooting. b, Emblem of Sydney Games. c, Running. d, Swimming.
Illustration reduced.

2000, Sept. 15 ***Perf. 13½x13¾***

422 A149 100b Block of 4, #a-d		8.50	8.50
e.	Souvenir sheet, #422	22.50	22.50

Coup by Sultan Qaboos, 30th Anniv. — A150

No. 423: a, Emblem, Sultan in blue hat. b, Emblem, Sultan seated. c, Emblem, Sultan in red beret. d, Emblem, Sultan in white hat. e, Emblem. f, Emblem, Sultan in black hat.

Litho. & Embossed

2000, Nov. 18 ***Perf. 13½***

423	Block of 6	10.00	7.50
a.-f.	A150 100b Any single	1.50	.75
g.	Souvenir sheet, #423	9.00	8.00

Wildlife — A151

No. 424: a, Arabian tahr. b, Nubian ibex. c, Arabian oryx. d, Arabian gazelle.

2000, July 23 **Litho.** ***Perf. 13½x13***

424 A151 100b Block of 4, #a-d		8.50	8.50
e.	Souvenir sheet, #424	16.50	16.50

Souvenir Sheet

Environment Day — A152

2001, Jan. 8 **Litho.** ***Perf. 13¾x14¼***

425 A152 200b multi	9.50	7.00

Souvenir Sheet

Palestinian Uprising in Jerusalem — A153

Litho. & Embossed

2001, July 31 ***Perf. 13½x13***

426 A153 100b multi	5.25	2.00

Al-Khanjar A'Suri — A154

Perf. 14½x13¾

2001, Mar. 19 **Litho.**

427 A154	50b red & multi	.65	.45
428 A154	80b yel org & multi	1.00	.75

Size: 26x34mm

Perf. 13¼x13

429 A154	100b blue & multi	1.25	.90
430 A154	200b multi	2.50	1.50
a.	Miniature sheet, #427-430	8.00	4.75

See Nos. 474-476.

Souvenir Sheets

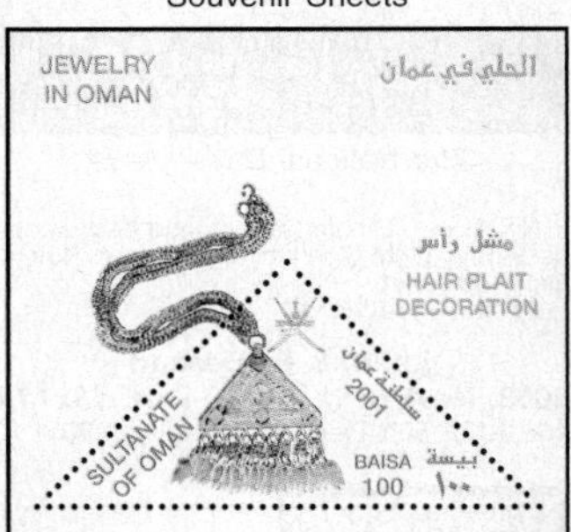

Jewelry — A155

Litho., Typo. & Embossed

2001 ***Perf. 12¾x12½***

431 A155 100b Hair plait decoration	3.50	1.75

Stamp Size: 62x27mm

Perf. 13¼x13¾

432 A155 100b Pendant	3.50	1.75

Stamp Size: 44x44mm

Perf. 12¾

433 A155 100b Necklace	3.50	1.75

Stamp Size: 38mm Diameter

Perf.

434 A155 100b Mazrad	3.50	1.75
Nos. 431-434 (4)	14.00	7.00

Supreme Council of Arab Gulf Cooperation Council States, 22nd Session A156

Designs: 50b, Map. 100b, Sultan Qaboos.

2001 **Litho. & Typo.** ***Perf. 14x14¼***

435-436 A156	Set of 2	1.50	1.00

Year of Dialogue Among Civilizations A157

2001 **Litho.** ***Perf. 13¾x13¼***

437 A157 200b multi	3.75	2.25

Shells — A157a

No. 437A: b, Nassarius coronatus. c, Epitoneum pallasii d, Cerithium caeruleum. e, Cerithidea cingulata.

2001 **Litho.** ***Perf. 13¼***

437A A157a 100b Block of 4, #a-d	5.00	4.00

31st National Day — A158

No. 438: a, Map of Oman, tree. b, Sultan Qaboos.
Illustration reduced.

2001 ***Perf. 13¼***

438 A158 100b Horiz. pair, #a-b	2.25	1.75

Turtles — A159

No. 439: a, Olive Ridley. b, Green. c, Hawksbill. d, Loggerhead.
Illustration reduced.

2002, Aug. 12 **Litho.** ***Perf. 13¼x13***

439 A159 100b Block of 4, #a-d		4.50	4.00
e.	Souvenir sheet, #439a-439d	7.75	6.00

Sultan Qaboos Grand Mosque — A160

No. 440: a, Interior view of dome and chandelier. b, Exterior view of mosque and minaret. c, Exterior view of archway. d, Interior view of corner arches.
100b, Aerial view of mosque.

Litho. With Foil Application

2002, May 25 ***Perf. 13¼***

440 A160 50b Block of 4, #a-d	4.25	2.75

Size: 120x90mm

Imperf

441 A160 100b multi	5.50	3.00

Souvenir Sheet

32nd National Day — A160a

Design: 100b, Sultan Qaboos, flowers in corners.

Litho. With Foil Application

2002, Nov. 18 ***Perf. 13x13¼***

441A A160a 100b multi	1.50	1.25
441B A160a 200b shown	3.25	2.75

Birds — A161

No. 442: a, Streptopelia decaocto. b, Tchagra senegala. c, Ploceus galbula. d, Hieraaetus fasciatus. e, Pycnonotus xanthopygos. f, Bubo bubo. g, Eremalauda dunni. h, Burhinus capensis. i, Prinia gracilis. j, Francolinus pondicerianus. k, Onychognathus tristramii. l, Hoplopterus indicus. m, Corvus splendens. n, Chlamydotis undulata. o, Halcyon chloris. p, Pterocles coronatus.

2002, Dec. 15 ***Perf. 13x13¼***

442 A161 50b Sheet of 16, #a-p	16.50	12.50

Early Intervention for Children With Special Needs — A161a

2002, Oct. 30 Litho. ***Perf. 13x13¼***
442Q A161a 100b multi 1.50 .50

Booklet Stamp
Self-Adhesive

442R A161a 100b multi 2.00 .70
s. Booklet pane of 10 20.00 —

Muscat Festival 2003 A162

2003, Jan. 8 ***Perf. 14½***
443 A162 100b multi 1.25 .75

Oman - People's Republic of China Diplomatic Relations, 25th Anniv. — A163

Illustration reduced.

2003, May 25 Litho. ***Perf. 12***
444 A163 70b multi 1.50 1.00

Souvenir Sheets

A164

Arabian Horses — A165

2003, Apr. 8 ***Perf. 13¼x12¾***
445 A164 100b shown 1.50 1.00
446 A165 100b shown 1.50 1.00
447 A165 100b White horse facing left 1.50 1.00
448 A165 100b Brown horse 1.50 1.00
Nos. 445-448 (4) 6.00 4.00

Census — A166

No. 449: a, Emblem, buildings. b, Emblem, blue circle.
Illustration reduced.

2003, Sept. 16 Litho. ***Perf. 13***
449 A166 50b Horiz. pair, #a-b 1.50 .75

Intl. Day of Peace — A167

2003, Sept. 21 ***Perf. 13¼x12¾***
450 A167 200b multi 2.00 2.00

Organization of the Islamic Conference — A168

Litho. & Embossed

2003, Sept. 25 ***Perf. 13***
451 A168 100b multi .85 .85

Self-Employment and National Autonomous Development Program — A169

2003, Oct. 6 Litho. ***Perf. 13¼***

Souvenir Sheet

452 A169 100b multi 1.25 1.25

Booklet Stamp
Self-Adhesive
Serpentine Die Cut 12½

453 A169 100b multi .75 .75
a. Booklet pane of 4 3.00
Complete booklet, 3 #453a 9.00

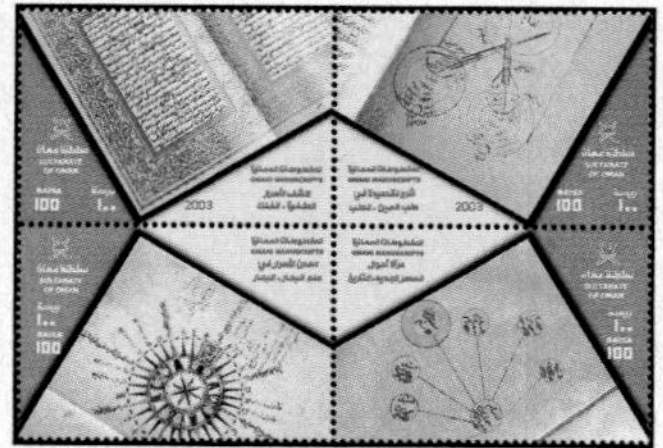

A170

Manuscripts — A171

No. 454: a, Denomination at lower left. b, Denomination at lower right. c, Denomination at left center. d, Denomination at right center.
No. 455: a, Illustrations of ships. b, Illustration of connected circles. c, Illustration of concentric circles. d, Text in large red circle.

2003, Oct. 14 Litho. ***Perf. 13½x13¼***
454 A170 100b Block of 4, #a-d 4.00 4.00

Miniature Sheet
Litho. With Foil Application
Perf. 13¼

455 A171 50b Sheet of 4, #a-d 4.75 4.00

33rd National Day — A172

No. 456 — Sultan Qaboos and background color of: a, Light green. b, Light blue. c, Buff. d, Light red violet.
Illustration reduced.

Litho. & Embossed

2003, Nov. 18 ***Perf. 13x13¼***
456 A172 50b Block fo 4, #a-d 1.75 1.75

Flowers — A173

No. 457: a, Anogeissus dhofarica. b, Tecomella undulata. c, Euryops pinifolius. d, Aloe dhufarensis. e, Cleome glaucescens. f, Cassia italica. g, Cibirhiza dhofarensis. h, Ipomoea nil. i, Viola cinerea. j, Dyschoriste dalyi. k, Calotropis procera. l, Lavandula dhofarensis. m, Teucrium mascatense. n, Capparis mucronifolia. o, Geranium mascatense. p, Convolvulus arvensis.

2004, Jan. 24 Litho. ***Perf. 14½***
457 Sheet of 16 6.25 6.25
a.-p. A173 50b Any single .35 .35

FIFA (Fédération Internationale de Football Association), Cent. — A174

Litho. & Embossed

2004, May 21 ***Perf. 13¾***
458 A174 250b multi 1.75 1.75

Worldwide Fund for Nature (WWF) — A175

No. 459 — Arabian leopard: a, Front feet on mound. b, Pair of leopards. c, Rear feet on mound. d. Feet in depression.

2004, June 5 Litho. ***Perf. 13¾x13½***
459 Horiz. strip of 4 5.00 5.00
a.-d. A175 50b Any single .85 .75

Corals A176

No. 460: a, Montipora. b, Porites. c, Acropora. d, Cycloseris.

2004, Aug. 1 ***Perf. 13¾***
460 Horiz. strip of 4 3.25 3.25
a.-d. A176 100b Any single .70 .70

Intl. Day of Peace — A177

Designs: 50b, Dove and green circle. 100b, Doves and Earth.

2004, Sept. 21 ***Perf. 13½x13¾***
461-462 A177 Set of 2 1.10 1.10

Souvenir Sheet

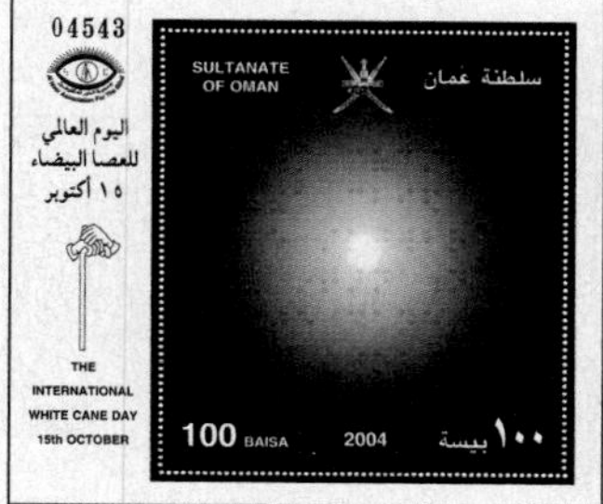

Intl. White Cane Day — A178

2004 Litho. ***Perf. 14x13¼***
463 A178 100b black 2.25 2.25

Braille text was applied by a thermographic process producing a shiny, raised effect.

34th National Day — A179

No. 464 — Sultan Qaboos with kaffiyah in: a, Red. b, Blue green. c, Gray and white. d, Black and white.
Illustration reduced.

Litho. & Embossed With Foil Application

2004, Nov. 18 ***Perf. 13¾x13½***
464 A179 100b Block of 4, #a-d 3.00 3.00

Water Supply Projects — A180

No. 465: a, Al Massarat. b, Ash'Sharqiyah.
Illustration reduced.

2004, Dec. 1 **Litho.** ***Perf. 14***
465 A180 50b Horiz. pair, #a-b 1.50 1.50

10th Gulf Cooperation Council Stamp Exhibition — A181

2004, Dec. 4 ***Perf. 13½***
466 A181 50b multi .50 .50

Self-Adhesive
Booklet Stamp
Serpentine Die Cut 12½

467 A181 50b multi .50 .50
a. Booklet pane of 4 2.00
Complete booklet, 3 #467a 6.00

Civil Defense — A182

Designs: 50b, Civil defense workers, Omani people. 100b, Rescue workers in action.

2005, May 14 **Litho.** ***Perf. 14***
468-469 A182 Set of 2 1.40 1.40

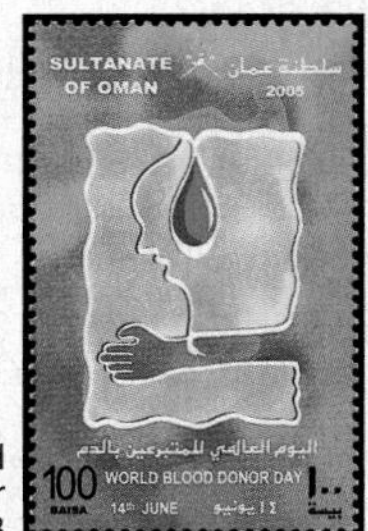
World Blood Donor Day — A183

2005, June 14 **Litho.** ***Perf. 13¾x14***
470 A183 100b multi .85 .85

Agricultural Census — A184

No. 471 — Census taker and: a, Herder and livestock. b, Farmer and crops.
Illustration reduced.

2005, July 18 ***Perf. 14x13¼***
471 A184 100b Horiz. pair, #a-b 1.50 1.50

World Summit on the Information Society, Tunis — A185

2005, Nov. 16 ***Perf. 14***
472 A185 100b multi 1.10 1.10

Miniature Sheet

35th National Day — A186

No. 473: a, Airplane, dish antennas. b, Helicopter, mounted soldiers. c, Sultan Qaboos. d, People in costumes. e, Military aircraft, ship, vehicle. f, Tower, highway. g, Tower, people at computers. h, Emblem of 35th National Day. i, Man at oasis. j, Petroleum facility.

Litho., Litho. & Embossed With Foil Application (#473c)

2005, Nov. 18 ***Perf. 13¼x13½***
473 A186 100b Sheet of 10, #a-j 7.00 7.00

Al-Khanjar A'Suri Type of 2001

2005, Dec. 7 **Litho.** ***Perf. 13¼x13***
Size: 26x34mm

474 A154 250b bl grn & multi 1.40 1.40
475 A154 300b red vio & multi 1.60 1.60
476 A154 400b yel brn & multi 2.10 2.10
Nos. 474-476 (3) 5.10 5.10

A187

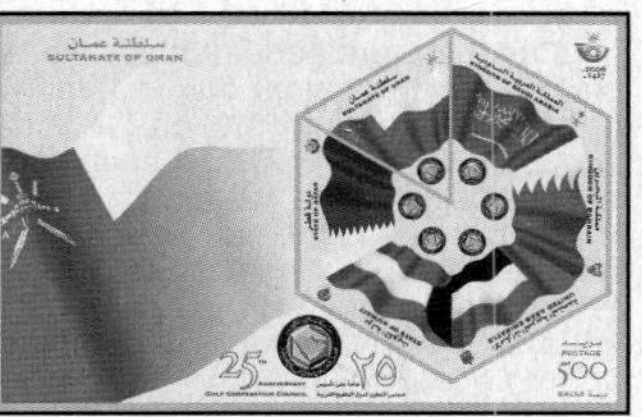
Gulf Cooperation Council, 25th Anniv. — A188

Litho. With Foil Application

2006, May 25 ***Perf. 14***
477 A187 100b multi .80 .80

Imperf
Size: 165x100mm

478 A188 500b multi 3.50 3.50

See Bahrain Nos. 628-629, Kuwait Nos. 1646-1647, Qatar Nos. 1007-1008, Saudi Arabia No. 1378, and United Arab Emirates Nos. 831-832.

Souvenir Sheet

Muscat, 2006 Capital of Arab Culture — A189

2006, Aug. 26 **Litho.** ***Perf. 14***
479 A189 100b multi 1.00 1.00

Tourism — A190

No. 480: a, Man picking flowers, houses on mountain. b, Six men, building. c, Scuba diver, turtle on beach. d, Women with clothing on line, camels.
Illustration reduced.

2006, Sept. 27 **Litho.** ***Perf. 14***
480 A190 100b Block of 4, #a-d 2.75 2.75

Oman Post Emblem A191

Text in: 100b, Blue. 250b, White.

Litho. With Foil Application

2006, Nov. 6 ***Perf. 13¾x13½***
481-482 A191 Set of 2 2.50 2.50

36th National Day — A192

2006, Nov. 18 ***Perf. 13x13½***
483 A192 100b multi .85 .85

Sultan Qaboos Prize for Cultural Innovation — A193

2006, Dec. 24 **Litho.** ***Perf. 13¼x13***
484 A193 250b multi 1.75 1.75

Exportation of Crude Oil, 40th Anniv. — A194

No. 485: a, Oil tanker and oil storage facility. b, Oil storage facility and oil well.
Illustration reduced.

2007, July 27 **Litho.** ***Perf. 13¾***
485 A194 100b Horiz. pair, #a-b 1.40 1.40

Symposium on Agricultrual Development A195

2007, Oct. 1 **Litho.** ***Perf. 13¾x14***
486 A195 100b multi .55 .55

37th National Day — A196

2008, Nov. 18 ***Perf. 13***
487 A196 100b multi .55 .55

Khasab Castle — A197

No. 488: a, Exterior of castle. b, Man behind table. c, People reading. d, Men and cannons near door.
Illustration reduced.

2007, Dec. 1 ***Perf. 13¼x13***
488 A197 100b Block of 4, #a-d 2.10 2.10

Scouting, Cent., and Scouting in Oman, 75th Anniv. — A198

2007, Dec. 20 *Perf. 13¾x13¼*
489 A198 250b multi 1.40 1.40

SEMI-POSTAL STAMP

UNICEF Emblem, Girl with Book — SP1

Wmk. 314
1971, Dec. 25 Litho. *Perf. 14*
B1 SP1 50b + 25b multicolored 17.50 5.00

25th anniv. of UNICEF.

OFFICIAL STAMPS

Official Stamps of India 1938-43 Overprinted in Black

Perf. 13½x14
1944, Nov. 20 **Wmk. 196**

O1	O8	3p slate	1.10	*9.00*
O2	O8	½a dk rose violet	1.10	*9.00*
O3	O8	9p green	1.10	*9.00*
O4	O8	1a carmine rose	1.10	*9.00*
O5	O8	1½a dull purple	1.10	*9.00*
O6	O8	2a scarlet	1.60	*9.00*
O7	O8	2½a purple	5.25	*9.00*
O8	O8	4a dark brown	2.25	*9.00*
O9	O8	8a blue violet	4.50	*10.00*
O10	A82	1r brown & slate	5.25	*17.50*
		Nos. O1-O10 (10)	24.35	*99.50*

Al Busaid Dynasty, 200th anniv. On Nos. O1-O9 the overprint is smaller — 13x6mm.

ORANGE RIVER COLONY

'är-inj 'ri-vər 'kä-lə-nē

(Orange Free State)

LOCATION — South Africa, north of the Cape of Good Hope between the Orange and Vaal Rivers
GOVT. — A former British Crown Colony
AREA — 49,647 sq. mi.
POP. — 528,174 (1911)
CAPITAL — Bloemfontein

Orange Free State was an independent republic, 1854-1900. Orange River Colony existed from May, 1900, to June, 1910, when it united with Cape of Good Hope, Natal and the Transvaal to form the Union of South Africa.

12 Pence = 1 Shilling

Values for unused stamps are for examples with original gum as defined in the catalogue introduction. Very fine examples of Nos. 1-60c will have perforations touching the design on one or more sides due to the narrow spacing of the stamps on the plates. Stamps with perfs clear of the design on all four sides are scarce and will command higher prices.

Een = 1
Twee = 2
Drie = 3
Vier = 4

Issues of the Republic

Orange Tree — A1

1868-1900 Unwmk. Typo. *Perf. 14*

1	A1	½p red brown ('83)	3.00	.75
2	A1	½p orange ('97)	2.00	.35
a.		½p yellow ('97)	2.00	.35
3	A1	1p red brown	12.50	.45
a.		3p pale brown	20.00	1.50
b.		3p deep brown	20.00	.45
4	A1	1p violet ('94)	3.25	.35
5	A1	2p violet ('83)	15.00	.75
a.		2p pale mauve ('83-'84)	15.00	.30
6	A1	3p ultra ('83)	3.25	1.75
7	A1	4p ultra ('78)	4.50	2.50
a.		4p pale blue ('78)	20.00	3.25
8	A1	6p car rose ('90)	22.50	12.50
a.		6p rose ('71)	25.00	8.00
b.		6p pale rose ('68)	50.00	7.50
c.		6p bright carmine ('94)	14.00	2.00
9	A1	6p ultramarine ('00)	100.00	
10	A1	1sh orange	42.50	2.00
a.		1sh orange buff	*80.00*	*6.75*
11	A1	1sh brown ('97)	22.50	1.60
12	A1	5sh green ('78)	10.50	*12.50*
		Nos. 1-8,10-12 (11)	141.50	35.50

No. 8b was not placed in use without surcharge.

For surcharges see #13-53, 44j-53c, 57-60.

No. 8a Surcharged:

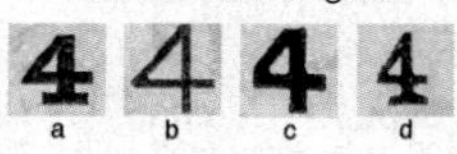

a b c d

1877

13	(a) 4p on 6p rose		350.00	50.00
a.	Inverted surcharge		*1,500.*	500.00
b.	Double surcharge, one inverted ("a" + "c" inverted)			*3,500.*
c.	Double surcharge, one inverted ("a" inverted + "c"			*6,000.*
14	(b) 4p on 6p rose		2,000.	225.00
a.	Inverted surcharge		—	1,250.
b.	Double surcharge, one inverted ("b" and "d")		—	
15	(c) 4p on 6p rose		200.00	27.50
a.	Inverted surcharge		—	750.00
16	(d) 4p on 6p rose		350.00	60.00
a.	Inverted surcharge		*1,500.*	600.00
b.	Double surcharge, one inverted ("d" and "c" inverted)		—	*3,500.*
c.	Double surcharge, one inverted ("d" inverted and "c")		—	*6,000.*

No. 20

No. 12 Surcharged with Bar and:

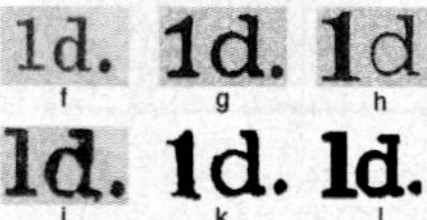

f g h
i k l

1881

First Printing

17	(f) 1p on 5sh green	120.00	22.50

Second Printing

18	(g) 1p on 5sh green	240.00	80.00
a.	Inverted surcharge	—	*1,250.*
b.	Double surcharge		*1,450.*
19	(h) 1p on 5sh green	210.00	67.50
a.	Inverted surcharge	—	*1,200.*
b.	Double surcharge	—	*1,400.*
20	(i) 1p on 5sh green	100.00	22.50
a.	Double surcharge	—	*1,200.*
b.	Inverted surcharge	*2,000.*	*1,000.*
21	(k) 1p on 5sh green	600.00	250.00
a.	Inverted surcharge	—	*2,250.*
b.	Double surcharge		*2,250*

Third Printing

21C	(l) 1p on 5sh green	800.00	22.50
a.	Inverted surcharge	—	*800.00*
b.	Double surcharge		*900.00*
	Nos. 17-21C (6)	2,070.	465.00

No. 12 Surcharged:

1882

22	A1 ½p on 5sh green	15.00	4.00
a.	Double surcharge	450.00	375.00
b.	Inverted surcharge	*1,350.*	*900.00*

No. 7 Surcharged with Thin Line and:

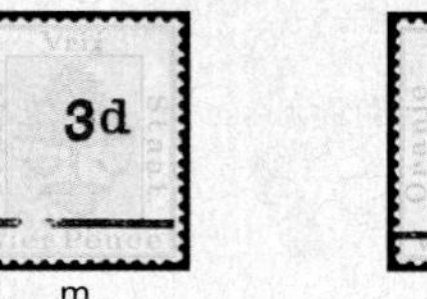

m n

o p

q

1882

23	(m) 3p on 4p ultra	95.00	20.00
a.	Double surcharge		1,400.
24	(n) 3p on 4p ultra	95.00	19.00
a.	Double surcharge		1,400.
25	(o) 3p on 4p ultra	37.50	17.50
a.	Double surcharge		1,400.
26	(p) 3p on 4p ultra	240.00	67.50
a.	Double surcharge		3,500.
27	(q) 3p on 4p ultra	95.00	25.00
a.	Double surcharge		1,500.
	Nos. 23-27 (5)	562.50	149.00

No. 6 Surcharged

1888

28	A1 2p on 3p ultra	32.50	2.25
a.	Wide "2" at top	57.50	10.00
b.	As No. 28, invtd. surch.		350.00
c.	As No. 28a, invtd. surch.		800.00
d.	Curved base on "2"	*1,350.*	*575.00*

Nos. 6 and 7 Surcharged:

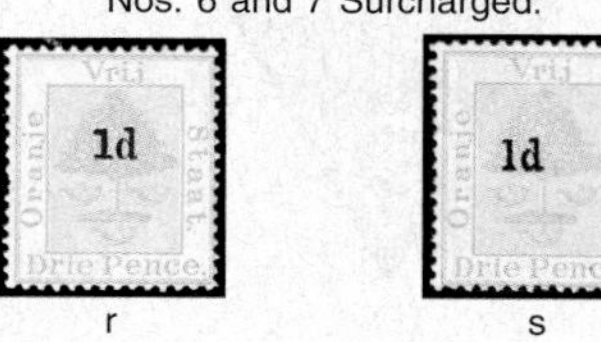

r s

t

1890-91

29	(r) 1p on 3p ultra ('91)	2.00	.75
a.	Double surcharge	77.50	75.00
b.	"1" and "d" wide apart	140.00	100.00
30	(r) 1p on 4p ultra	17.50	4.00
a.	Double surcharge	140.00	125.00
31	(s) 1p on 3p ultra ('91)	11.00	2.75
a.	Double surcharge	200.00	225.00
32	(s) 1p on 4p ultra	75.00	50.00
a.	Double surcharge	350.00	300.00
b.	Triple surcharge		*2,250.*
33	(t) 1p on 4p ultra	*2,500.*	*550.00*

No. 6 Surcharged

1892

34	A1 2½p on 3p ultra	5.00	.80
a.	Without period	60.00	45.00

No. 6 Surcharged:

v

w

x

y

z

1896

35	(v) ½p on 3p ultra	2.50	6.50
a.	Double surcharge "v" and "y"	14.00	12.00
36	(w) ½p on 3p ultra	5.25	2.75
a.	Double surcharge "w" and "y"	15.00	15.00
37	(x) ½p on 3p ultra	5.25	2.75
38	(y) ½p on 3p ultra	3.00	2.50
a.	Double surcharge	12.50	11.00
39	(z) ½p on 3p ultra	4.50	2.75

Surcharged as "v" but "1" with Straight Serif

40	A1 ½p on 3p ultra	5.50	5.50
a.	Double surcharge, one type "y"	13.00	13.00

Surcharged as "z" but "1" with Straight Serif

41	A1 ½p on 3p ultra	6.00	7.00
a.	Double surcharge, one type "y"	12.50	11.00
	Nos. 35-41 (7)	32.00	29.75

No. 6 Surcharged

1896

42	A1 ½p on 3p ultra	.65	.65
a.	No period after "Penny"	10.00	15.00
b.	"Peuny"	8.50	8.50
c.	Inverted surcharge	60.00	60.00
d.	Double surch., one inverted	160.00	160.00
e.	Without bar	5.00	5.00
f.	With additional surcharge as on Nos. 35-41	75.00	75.00

No. 6 Surcharged

1897

43	A1	2½p on 3p ultra	2.00	.75
a.		Roman "I" instead of "1" in "½"	150.00	90.00

Issued under British Occupation

Nos. 2-8, 8a, 10-12 Surcharged or Overprinted

1900, Mar.-Apr. Unwmk. *Perf. 14*

Periods in "V.R.I." Level with Bottoms of Letters

44	A1	½p on ½p org	1.50	1.50
a.		No period after "V"	15.00	15.00
b.		No period after "I"	175.00	175.00
c.		"I" and period after "R" omitted		
f.		"½" omitted	*175.00*	*175.00*
g.		Small "½"	45.00	45.00
h.		Double surcharge	125.00	*125.00*
i.		As "g," double surcharge	300.00	
45	A1	1p on 1p violet	1.60	.75
a.		No period after "V"	10.50	10.50
b.		"I" and period after "R" omitted	160.00	175.00
d.		"1" of "1d" omitted	160.00	175.00
e.		"d" omitted	300.00	300.00
f.		"1d" omitted, "V.R.I." at top	375.00	
45O	A1	1p on 1p brown	*675.00*	*400.00*
y.		No period after "V"	*2,250.*	
46	A1	2p on 2p violet	.35	.60
a.		No period after "V"	10.00	12.00
b.		No period after "R"	250.00	
c.		No period after "I"	250.00	
47	A1	'2½' on 3p ultra	4.50	4.00
a.		No period after "V"	70.00	65.00
b.		Roman "I" in "½"	160.00	275.00
48	A1	3p on 3p ultra	1.50	1.00
a.		No period after "V"	13.00	13.00
b.		Dbl. surch. one diagonal	600.00	
49	A1	4p on 4p ultra	4.50	6.00
a.		No period after "V"	50.00	52.50
50	A1	6p on 6p car rose	35.00	35.00
a.		No period after "V"	250.00	300.00
b.		"6" omitted	300.00	300.00
51	A1	6p on 6p ultra	2.75	3.25
a.		No period after "V"	30.00	30.00
c.		"6" omitted	65.00	65.00
52	A1	1sh on 1sh brown	3.50	3.50
a.		No period after "V"	30.00	30.00
c.		"1" of "1s" omitted	110.00	110.00
52G	A1	1sh on 1sh org	*3,000.*	*2,000.*
53	A1	5sh on 5sh green	18.00	30.00
a.		No period after "V"	175.00	175.00
b.		"5" omitted	950.00	950.00

#47, 47c overprinted "V.R.I." on #43.

No. 45f ("1d" omitted) with "V.R.I." at bottom is a shift which sells for a fifth of the value of the listed item. Varieties such as "V.R.I." omitted, denomination omitted and pair, one without surcharge are also the result of shifts.

For surcharges see Nos. 57, 60.

1900-01

Periods in "V.R.I." Raised Above Bottoms of Letters

44j	A1	½p on ½p orange	.25	.20
k.		Mixed periods	1.75	1.75
l.		Pair, one with level periods	8.00	13.00
m.		No period after "V"	3.00	3.00
n.		No period after "I"	25.00	25.00
o.		"V" omitted	400.00	400.00
p.		Small "½"	12.00	13.00
q.		"1" for "I" in "V.R.I."	9.00	9.00
r.		Thick "V"	.30	.45
45i	A1	1p on 1p violet	.30	.20
j.		Mixed periods	1.50	1.60
k.		Pair, one with level periods	17.00	17.00
l.		No period after "V"	6.00	6.00
m.		No period after "R"	12.00	12.00
n.		No period after "I"	12.00	12.00
p.		Double surcharge	90.00	90.00
q.		Inverted surcharge	200.00	
s.		Small "1" in "1d"	160.00	160.00
t.		"1" for "I" in "V.R.I."	13.00	13.00
u.		Thick "V"	.30	.25
v.		As "u," invtd. "1" for "I" in "V.R.I."	7.25	7.25
w.		As "u," double surcharge	300.00	300.00
z.		As "u," no period after "R"	30.00	30.00
46e	A1	2p on 2p violet	.50	.25
f.		Mixed periods	4.50	4.50
g.		Pair, one with level periods	7.25	7.25
h.		Inverted surcharge	500.00	400.00
i.		Thick "V"	.35	.30
j.		As "i," invtd. "1" for "I" in "V.R.I."	15.00	15.00
47c	A1	'2½' on 3p ultra	190.00	160.00
d.		Thick "V"	350.00	350.00
f.		As "d," Roman "I" on "½"		
48d	A1	3p on 3p ultra	.35	.20
e.		Mixed periods	5.00	5.00
f.		Pair, one with level periods	15.00	15.00
g.		Double surcharge	425.00	
h.		Thick "V"	.90	.90
i.		As "h," invtd. "1" for "I" in "V.R.I."	80.00	80.00
49b	A1	4p on 4p ultra	1.10	2.00
c.		Mixed periods	7.00	7.00
d.		Pair, one with level periods	15.00	18.00
50c	A1	6p on 6p car rose	35.00	47.50
d.		Mixed periods	175.00	175.00
e.		Pair, one with level periods	175.00	
f.		Thick "V"	*450.00*	*450.00*
51d	A1	6p on 6p ultra	.60	.30
e.		Mixed periods	6.00	6.00
f.		Pair, one with level periods	15.00	15.00
g.		Thick "V"	3.00	3.00
52e	A1	1sh on 1sh brown	1.00	.45
f.		Mixed periods	10.00	10.00
h.		Pair, one with level periods	25.00	26.00
i.		Thick "V"	1.75	1.50
52j	A1	1sh on 1sh orange	*1,500.*	*1,500.*
53c	A1	5sh on 5sh green	6.50	9.00
d.		Mixed periods	325.00	325.00
e.		Pair, one with level periods	*1,600.*	*2,500.*
f.		"5" with short flag	60.00	60.00
g.		Thick "V"	18.00	18.00

Stamps with mixed periods have one or two periods level with the bottoms of letters. One stamp in each pane had all periods level. Later settings had several stamps with thick "V." Forgeries of the scarcer varieties exist.

"V.R.I." stands for Victoria Regina Imperatrix. On No. 59, "E.R.I." stands for Edward Rex Imperator.

Cape of Good Hope Stamps of 1893-98 Overprinted

1900 Wmk. 16

54	A15	½p green	.40	.20
a.		No period after "COLONY"	8.50	12.00
b.		Double overprint	900.00	600.00
55	A13	2½p ultramarine	.60	.30
a.		No period after "COLONY"	45.00	57.50

Overprinted as in 1900

1902, May

56	A15	1p carmine rose	.60	.30
a.		No period after "COLONY"	10.00	15.00

Nos. 51d, 53c, Surcharged and No. 8b Surcharged like No. 51 but Reading "E.R.I."

Carmine or Vermilion and Black Surcharges

1902 Unwmk.

57	A1	4p on 6p on 6p ultra	1.50	.70
a.		Thick "V"	2.00	1.25
b.		As "a," invtd. "1" instead of "I"	4.50	4.50
c.		No period after "R"	30.00	30.00

Black Surcharge

59	A1	6p on 6p ultra	3.00	6.00
a.		Double surcharge, one invtd.	*600.00*	*600.00*

Orange Surcharge

60	A1	1sh on 5sh on 5sh grn	5.00	6.00
a.		Thick "V"	13.00	18.00
b.		"5" with short flag	60.00	60.00
c.		Double surcharge		
		Nos. 57-60 (3)	9.50	12.70

"E.R.I." stands for Edward Rex Imperator.

King Edward VII — A8

1903-04 Wmk. 2 Typo.

61	A8	½p yellow green	8.75	1.25
62	A8	1p carmine	4.50	.20
63	A8	2p chocolate	6.00	.85
64	A8	2½p ultra	1.75	.45
65	A8	3p violet	7.50	.90
66	A8	4p olive grn & car	32.50	2.50
67	A8	6p violet & car	9.00	1.00
68	A8	1sh bister & car	30.00	2.00
69	A8	5sh red brn & bl ('04)	80.00	22.00
		Nos. 61-69 (9)	180.00	31.15

Some of the above stamps are found with the overprint "C. S. A. R." for use by the Central South African Railway.

The "IOSTAGE" variety on the 4p is the result of filled in type.

Issue dates: 1p, Feb. 3. ½p, 2p, 2½p, 3p, 4p, 6p, 1sh, July 6. 5sh, Oct. 31.

1907-08 Wmk. 3

70	A8	½p yellow green	7.00	.45
71	A8	1p carmine	7.00	.20
72	A8	4p olive grn & car	4.50	1.75
73	A8	1sh bister & car	42.00	13.50
		Nos. 70-73 (4)	60.50	15.90

The "IOSTAGE" variety on the 4p is the result of filled-in type.

Stamps of Orange River Colony were replaced by those of Union of South Africa.

Vol. 4 Number Additions, Deletions & Changes

Number in 2009 Catalogue	Number in 2010 Catalogue
Japan	
new	9d
Korea DPRK	
new	1722a
new	1723a
new	1724a
new	1725a
new	1758a
new	1759a
new	1760a
new	1803a
new	1804a
new	1805a
new	1806a
new	2033a
new	2034a
new	2035a
new	2039a
new	2040a
new	2041a
new	2042a
new	2287a
new	2288a
new	2289a
new	2290a
new	2291a
new	2353a
new	2354a
new	2356a
new	2357a
new	2405a
new	2495a
new	2496a
new	2497a
new	2498a
new	2499a
new	2500a
new	2501a
new	2502a
new	2503a
new	2516a
new	2517a
new	2518a
new	2519a
new	2521a
new	2584a
new	2607e
new	2610a
new	2611a
new	2612a
new	2613a
new	2625a
new	2626a
new	2627a
new	2722a
new	2734a
new	2735a
new	2736a
new	2739a
new	2771a
new	2814a
new	2822a
new	2823a
new	2824a
new	2825a
new	2825b
new	2829a
new	2836a
new	2883a
new	2884a
new	2885a

Number in 2009 Catalogue	Number in 2010 Catalogue
Korea DPRK	
new	2887a
new	2890a
new	2897a
new	3434A-3434E
new	3512B-3512f
new	4121b
new	4323a
Latvia	
new	1N14-1N24
Leeward Islands	
new	9b
new	29a
new	33a
new	63b
new	71a
new	77a
new	103a
new	105b
new	107a
new	108a
new	110a
new	110b
new	111a
new	112a
new	113a
new	114a
new	114b
new	114c
Mexico	
new	344d
new	607a
new	676a
new	2312a
Guadalajara	
new	2a
new	4a
new	5a
new	6a
new	7b
new	12A
new	19A
new	34A
47a	deleted
new	47a
Montserrat	
new	501-502
Mozambique	
new	149a
new	149b
new	151a
new	156a
new	157a
new	157b
New Zealand	
new	17
17c	deleted
Nicaragua	
new	433c
Niue	
357-359	357-359A
359a	359B
359B-359D	359C-359E

Number in 2009 Catalogue	Number in 2010 Catalogue
Niue	
359De	359Ea
Norway	
25a	deleted
new	44d
new	51e
new	63a
Oman	
new	375a
new	421Fm
Orange River Colony	
new	2a
new	3a
new	3b
new	5a
new	7a
new	8a
new	8b
new	8c
8b	9
new	13b
new	13c
new	21C
new	21Cd
new	21Ce

Illustrated Identifier

This section pictures stamps or parts of stamp designs that will help identify postage stamps that do not have English words on them.

Many of the symbols that identify stamps of countries are shown here as well as typical examples of their stamps.

See the Index and Identifier on the previous pages for stamps with inscriptions such as "sen," "posta," "Baja Porto," "Helvetia," "K.S.A.", etc.

Linn's Stamp Identifier is now available. The 144 pages include more 2,000 inscriptions and over 500 large stamp illustrations. Available from Linn's Stamp News, P.O. Box 29, Sidney, OH 45365-0029.

1. HEADS, PICTURES AND NUMERALS

GREAT BRITAIN

Great Britain stamps never show the country name, but, except for postage dues, show a picture of the reigning monarch.

Victoria

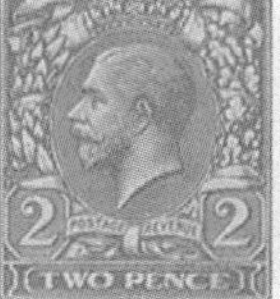

Edward VII George V Edward VIII

George VI

Elizabeth II

Some George VI and Elizabeth II stamps are surcharged in annas, new paisa or rupees. These are listed under Oman.

Silhouette (sometimes facing right, generally at the top of stamp)

The silhouette indicates this is a British stamp. It is not a U.S. stamp.

VICTORIA

Queen Victoria

INDIA

Other stamps of India show this portrait of Queen Victoria and the words "Service" and "Annas."

AUSTRIA

YUGOSLAVIA

(Also BOSNIA & HERZEGOVINA if imperf.)

BOSNIA & HERZEGOVINA

Denominations also appear in top corners instead of bottom corners.

HUNGARY

Another stamp has posthorn facing left

BRAZIL

AUSTRALIA

Kangaroo and Emu

GERMANY

Mecklenburg-Vorpommern

SWITZERLAND

PALAU

2. ORIENTAL INSCRIPTIONS

CHINA

Any stamp with this one character is from China (Imperial, Republic or People's Republic). This character appears in a four-character overprint on stamps of Manchukuo. These stamps are local provisionals, which are unlisted. Other overprinted Manchukuo stamps show this character, but have more than four characters in the overprints. These are listed in People's Republic of China.

Some Chinese stamps show the Sun.

Most stamps of Republic of China show this series of characters.

Stamps with the China character and this character are from People's Republic of China.

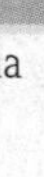

Calligraphic form of People's Republic of China

(一)	(二)	(三)	(四)	(五)	(六)
1	2	3	4	5	6
(七)	(八)	(九)	(十)	(一十)	(二十)
7	8	9	10	11	12

Chinese stamps without China character

REPUBLIC OF CHINA

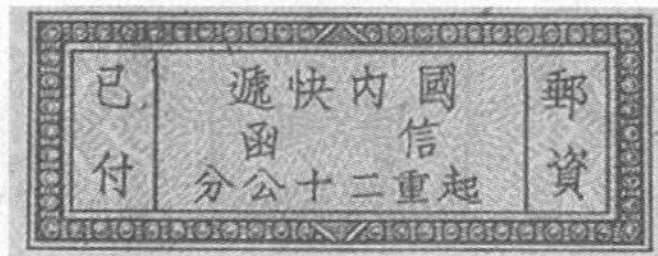

PEOPLE'S REPUBLIC OF CHINA

Mao Tse-tung

MANCHUKUO

Temple

Emperor Pu-Yi

The first 3 characters are common to many Manchukuo stamps.

The last 3 characters are common to other Manchukuo stamps.

Orchid Crest

Manchukuo stamp without these elements

JAPAN

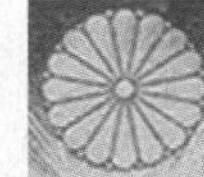

Chrysanthemum Crest

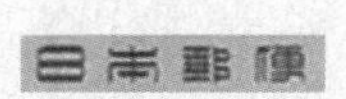

Country Name

Japanese stamps without these elements

The number of characters in the center and the design of dragons on the sides will vary.

RYUKYU ISLANDS

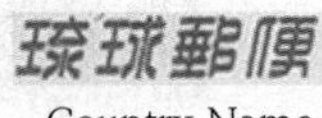

Country Name

PHILIPPINES

(Japanese Occupation)

Country Name

NORTH BORNEO (Japanese Occupation)

Indicates Japanese Occupation

Country Name

MALAYA (Japanese Occupation)

Indicates Japanese Occupation

Country Name

BURMA

Union of Myanmar

ပြည်ထောင်စုမြန်မာနိုင်ငံတော်

Union of Myanmar

(Japanese Occupation)

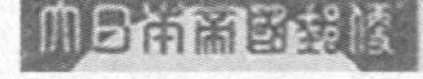

Indicates Japanese Occupation

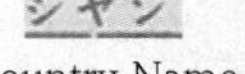

Country Name

Other Burma Japanese Occupation stamps without these elements

Burmese Script

KOREA

These two characters, in any order, are common to stamps from the Republic of Korea (South Korea) or of the People's Democratic Republic of Korea (North Korea).

This series of four characters can be found on the stamps of both Koreas. Most stamps of the Democratic People's Republic of Korea (North Korea) have just this inscription.

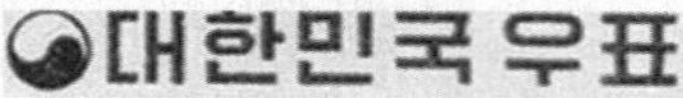

Indicates Republic of Korea (South Korea)

South Korean postage stamps issed after 1952 do not show currency expressed in Latin letters. Stamps wiith "HW," "HWAN," "WON," "WN," "W" or "W" with two lines through it, if not illustrated in listings of stamps before this date, are revenues. North Korean postage stamps do not have currency expressed in Latin letters.

Yin Yang appears on some stamps.

THAILAND

Country Name

King Chulalongkorn

King Prajadhipok and Chao P'ya Chakri

3. CENTRAL AND EASTERN ASIAN INSCRIPTIONS

INDIA - FEUDATORY STATES

Alwar **Bhor**

Bundi

Similar stamps come with different designs in corners and differently drawn daggers (at center of circle).

Dhar **Faridkot**

Hyderabad

Similar stamps exist with straight line frame around stamp, and also with different central design which is inscribed "Postage" or "Post & Receipt."

Indore **Jhalawar**

A similar stamp has the central figure in an oval.

Nandgaon

Nowanuggur

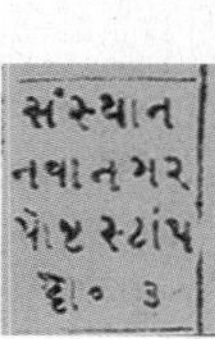

Poonch

Similar stamps exist in various sizes

Rajpeepla

Soruth

BANGLADESH

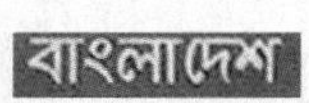

Country Name

NEPAL

Similar stamps are smaller, have squares in upper corners and have five or nine characters in central bottom panel.

TANNU TUVA

ISRAEL

GEORGIA

This inscription is found on other pictorial stamps.

Country Name

ARMENIA

The four characters are found somewhere on pictorial stamps. On some stamps only the middle two are found.

4. AFRICAN INSCRIPTIONS

ETHIOPIA

5. ARABIC INSCRIPTIONS

١	٢	٣	٤	٥
1	2	3	4	5
٦	٧	٨	٩	٠
6	7	8	9	0

AFGHANISTAN

Many early Afghanistan stamps show Tiger's head, many of these have ornaments protruding from outer ring, others show inscriptions in black.

Arabic Script

Mosque Gate & Crossed Cannons
The four characters are found somewhere on pictorial stamps. On some stamps only the middle two are found.

BAHRAIN

EGYPT

Postage

INDIA - FEUDATORY STATES

Jammu & Kashmir

Text and thickness of ovals vary. Some stamps have flower devices in corners.

India-Hyderabad

IRAN

Country Name

Royal Crown

Lion with Sword

Symbol

IRAQ

JORDAN

LEBANON

Similar types have denominations at top and slightly different design.

LIBYA

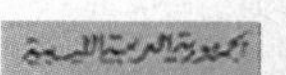

Country Name in various styles

Other Libya stamps show Eagle and Shield (head facing either direction) or Red, White and Black Shield (with or without eagle in center).

Without Country Name

SAUDI ARABIA

Tughra (Central design)

Palm Tree and Swords

SYRIA

THRACE

YEMEN

PAKISTAN

PAKISTAN - BAHAWALPUR

Country Name in top panel, star and crescent

TURKEY

Star & Crescent is a device found on many Turkish stamps, but is also found on stamps from other Arabic areas (see Pakistan-Bahawalpur)

Tughra (similar tughras can be found on stamps of Turkey in Asia, Afghanistan and Saudi Arabia)

Mohammed V

Mustafa Kemal

Plane, Star and Crescent

TURKEY IN ASIA

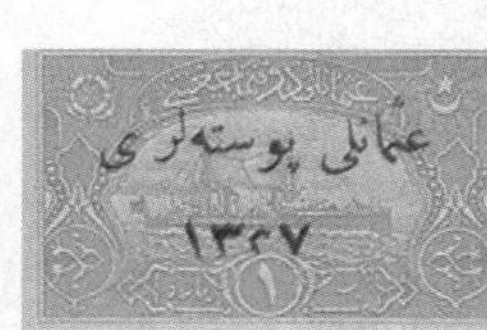

Other Turkey in Asia pictorials show star & crescent.
Other stamps show tughra shown under Turkey.

6. GREEK INSCRIPTIONS

GREECE

Country Name in various styles
(Some Crete stamps overprinted with the Greece country name are listed in Crete.)

Lepta

Drachma Drachmas Lepton

Abbreviated Country Name 

Other forms of Country Name

No country name

CRETE

Country Name

These words are on other stamps

Grosion

Crete stamps with a surcharge that have the year "1922" are listed under Greece.

EPIRUS **IONIAN IS.**

Country Name

7. CYRILLIC INSCRIPTIONS

RUSSIA

Postage Stamp

Imperial Eagle

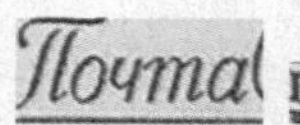

Postage in various styles

Abbreviation for Kopeck

Abbreviation for Ruble

Russian

Abbreviation for Russian Soviet Federated Socialist Republic
RSFSR stamps were overprinted (see below)

Abbreviation for Union of Soviet Socialist Republics

This item is footnoted in Latvia

RUSSIA - Army of the North

"OKCA"

RUSSIA - Wenden

RUSSIAN OFFICES IN THE TURKISH EMPIRE

These letters appear on other stamps of the Russian offices.

The unoverprinted version of this stamp and a similar stamp were overprinted by various countries (see below).

ARMENIA

BELARUS

FAR EASTERN REPUBLIC

Country Name

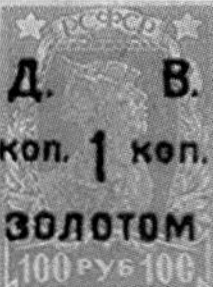

SOUTH RUSSIA

Country Name

FINLAND

Circles and Dots on stamps similar to Imperial Russia issues

BATUM

Forms of Country Name

TRANSCAUCASIAN FEDERATED REPUBLICS

Abbreviation for Country Name

KAZAKHSTAN

ҚАЗАҚСТАН

Country Name

KYRGYZSTAN

КЫРГЫЗСТАН Country Name

ROMANIA

TADJIKISTAN

Country Name & Abbreviation

UKRAINE

України

Україhu

Country Name in various forms

УС РР

The trident appears on many stamps, usually as an overprint.

Abbreviation for Ukrainian Soviet Socialist Republic

WESTERN UKRAINE

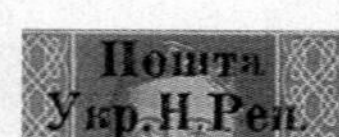

Abbreviation for Country Name

AZERBAIJAN

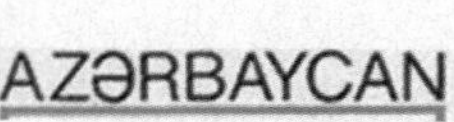

Country Name

А.С.С.Р. Abbreviation for Azerbaijan Soviet Socialist Republic

MONTENEGRO

ЦРНЕГОРЕ

ЦРНА ГОРА

Country Name in various forms

Ц.Р.ГОРЕ

Abbreviation for country name

No country name (A similar Montenegro stamp without country name has same vignette.)

SERBIA

СРПСКА СРБИЈА

Country Name in various forms

СРП. К. С.

Abbreviation for country name

No country name

SERBIA & MONTENEGRO

YUGOSLAVIA

Showing country name

No Country Name

MACEDONIA

МАКЕДОНИЈА

МАКЕДОНИЈА

Country Name

МАКЕДОНСКИ
11 Октомври 1997

Different form of Country Name

BOSNIA & HERZEGOVINA (Serb Administration)

РЕПУБЛИКА СРПСКА

Country Name

РЕПУБЛИКЕ СРПСКЕ

Different form of Country Name

No Country Name

BULGARIA

Country Name   Postage

Stotinka

Stotinki (plural)   Abbreviation for Stotinki

Country Name in various forms and styles

No country name

Abbreviation for Lev, leva

MONGOLIA

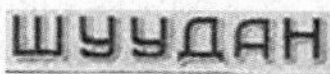

Country name in one word   Tugrik in Cyrillic

Country name in two words   Mung in Cyrillic

Mung in Mongolian

Tugrik in Mongolian

Arms

No Country Name

INDEX AND IDENTIFIER

All page numbers shown are those in this Volume 4.

Postage stamps that do not have English words on them are shown in the Identifier which begins on page 1627.

D....Vol. 3

E.A.F. overprinted on stamps of Great Britain....Vol. 3

15 August 1947 (Pakistan #23)... Vol. 5

Pronunciation Symbols

ə .... banana, collide, abut

ˈə, ˌə .... humdrum, abut

ᵊ .... immediately preceding \l\, \n\, \m\, \ŋ\, as in battle, mitten, eaten, and sometimes open \ˈō-pᵊm\, lock and key \-ᵊŋ-\; immediately following \l\, \m\, \r\, as often in French table, prisme, titre

ər .... further, merger, bird

ˈər- / ˈə-r .... as in two different pronunciations of hurry \ˈhər-ē, ˈhə-rē\

a .... mat, map, mad, gag, snap, patch

ā .... day, fade, date, aorta, drape, cape

ä .... bother, cot, and, with most American speakers, father, cart

ȧ .... father as pronounced by speakers who do not rhyme it with *bother*; French patte

au̇ .... now, loud, out

b .... baby, rib

ch .... chin, nature \ˈnā-chər\

d .... did, adder

e .... bet, bed, peck

ˈē, ˌē .... beat, nosebleed, evenly, easy

ē .... easy, mealy

f .... fifty, cuff

g .... go, big, gift

h .... hat, ahead

hw .... whale as pronounced by those who do not have the same pronunciation for both *whale* and *wail*

i .... tip, banish, active

ī .... site, side, buy, tripe

j .... job, gem, edge, join, judge

k .... kin, cook, ache

k̲ .... German ich, Buch; one pronunciation of loch

l .... lily, pool

m .... murmur, dim, nymph

n .... no, own

ⁿ .... indicates that a preceding vowel or diphthong is pronounced with the nasal passages open, as in French *un bon vin blanc* \œⁿ-bōⁿ-vaⁿ-bläⁿ\

ŋ .... sing \ˈsiŋ\, singer \ˈsiŋ-ər\, finger \ˈfiŋ-gər\, ink \ˈiŋk\

ō .... bone, know, beau

ȯ .... saw, all, gnaw, caught

œ .... French boeuf, German Hölle

œ̄ .... French feu, German Höhle

ȯi .... coin, destroy

p .... pepper, lip

r .... red, car, rarity

s .... source, less

sh .... as in shy, mission, machine, special (actually, this is a single sound, not two); with a hyphen between, two sounds as in *grasshopper* \ˈgras-ˌhä-pər\

t .... tie, attack, late, later, latter

th .... as in thin, ether (actually, this is a single sound, not two); with a hyphen between, two sounds as in *knighthood* \ˈnīt-ˌhu̇d\

t̲h̲ .... then, either, this (actually, this is a single sound, not two)

ü .... rule, youth, union \ˈyün-yən\, few \ˈfyü\

u̇ .... pull, wood, book, curable \ˈkyu̇r-ə-bəl\, fury \ˈfyu̇r-ē\

ue .... German füllen, hübsch

ue̅ .... French rue, German fühlen

v .... vivid, give

w .... we, away

y .... yard, young, cue \ˈkyü\, mute \ˈmyüt\, union \ˈyün-yən\

ʸ .... indicates that during the articulation of the sound represented by the preceding character the front of the tongue has substantially the position it has for the articulation of the first sound of *yard*, as in French *digne* \dēnʸ\

z .... zone, raise

zh .... as in vision, azure \ˈa-zhər\ (actually, this is a single sound, not two); with a hyphen between, two sounds as in *hogshead* \ˈhȯgz-ˌhed, ˈhägz-\

\ .... slant line used in pairs to mark the beginning and end of a transcription: \ˈpen\

ˈ .... mark preceding a syllable with primary (strongest) stress: \ˈpen-mən-ˌship\

ˌ .... mark preceding a syllable with secondary (medium) stress: \ˈpen-mən-ˌship\

\- .... mark of syllable division

( ) .... indicate that what is symbolized between is present in some utterances but not in others: *factory* \ˈfak-t(ə-)rē\

÷ .... indicates that many regard as unacceptable the pronunciation variant immediately following: *cupola* \ˈkyü-pə-lə, ÷-ˌlō\

INDEX TO ADVERTISERS
2010 VOLUME 4

2010
VOLUME 4
DEALER DIRECTORY YELLOW PAGE LISTINGS

This section of your Scott Catalogue contains advertisements to help you conveniently find what you need, when you need it...!

Accessories

BROOKLYN GALLERY COIN & STAMP, INC.
8725 4th Ave.
Brooklyn, NY 11209
PH: 718-745-5701
FAX: 718-745-2775
info@brooklyngallery.com
www.brooklyngallery.com

Appraisals

HERITAGE AUCTION GALLERIES
3500 Maple Ave, 17th Floor
Dallas, TX 75219
PH: 800-872-6467
FAX: 214-409-1425
Stamps@HA.com
HA.com

PHILIP WEISS AUCTIONS
1 Neil Ct.
Oceanside, NY 11572
PH: 516-594-0731
FAX: 516-594-9414

Asia

MICHAEL ROGERS, INC.
415 S. Orlando Ave.
Winter Park, FL 32789-3683
PH: 407-644-2290
PH: 800-843-3751
FAX: 407-645-4434
Stamps@michaelrogersinc.com
www.michaelrogersinc.com

Asia

THE STAMP ACT
PO Box 1136
Belmont, CA 94002
PH: 650-703-2342
PH: 650-592-3315
FAX: 650-508-8104
thestampact@sbcglobal.net
www.thestampact.com

Auctions

DANIEL F. KELLEHER CO., INC.
20 Walnut St.
Suite 213
Wellesley, MA 02481
PH: 781-235-0990
FAX: 781-235-0945

JACQUES C. SCHIFF, JR., INC.
195 Main St.
Ridgefield Park, NJ 07660
PH: 201-641-5566
FAX: 201-641-5705

MICHAEL ROGERS, INC.
415 S. Orlando Ave.
Winter Park, FL 32789-3683
PH: 407-644-2290
PH: 800-843-3751
FAX: 407-645-4434
Stamps@michaelrogersinc.com
www.michaelrogersinc.com

Auctions

PHILIP WEISS AUCTIONS
1 Neil Ct.
Oceanside, NY 11572
PH: 516-594-0731
FAX: 516-594-9414

R. MARESCH & SON LTD.
5th Floor - 6075 Yonge St.
Toronto, ON M2M 3W2
CANADA
PH: 416-363-7777
FAX: 416-363-6511
www.maresch.com

THE STAMP CENTER DUTCH COUNTRY AUCTIONS
4115 Concord Pike
Wilmington, DE 19803
PH: 302-478-8740
FAX: 302-478-8779
auctions@thestampcenter.com
www.thestampcenter.com

Auctions - Public

ALAN BLAIR STAMPS/ AUCTIONS
5405 Lakeside Ave.
Suite 1
Richmond, VA 23228
PH: 800-689-5602
FAX: 804-262-9307
alanblair@verizon.net
www.alanblairstamps.com

Auctions - Public

HERITAGE AUCTION GALLERIES
3500 Maple Ave, 17th Floor
Dallas, TX 75219
PH: 800-872-6467
FAX: 214-409-1425
Stamps@HA.com
HA.com

British Asia

THE STAMP ACT
PO Box 1136
Belmont, CA 94002
PH: 650-703-2342
PH: 650-592-3315
FAX: 650-508-8104
thestampact@sbcglobal.net
www.thestampact.com

British Commonwealth

ARON R. HALBERSTAM PHILATELISTS, LTD.
PO Box 150168
Van Brunt Station
Brooklyn, NY 11215-0168
PH: 718-788-3978
FAX: 718-965-3099
arh@arhstamps.com
www.arhstamps.com

Auctions

Schiff Auctions

Buyers, Auctioneers & Appraisers of U.S. & Worldwide Stamps & Covers

We have been catering to the individual buyer and seller since 1947. Let us put our over **60 years** of experience to work for you when selling your stamps, covers or your collection. Whether you prefer consigning to public auction or selling outright, call us first. Describe your material before sending. Please include your address and telephone numbers.

CATALOG SUBSCRIPTIONS	N. AMERICA	OVERSEAS
1 Year Catalogs & Prices Realized	$10.00	$18.00
1 Year Catalog Only	$7.50	$15.00
1 Catalog with Prices Realized	$1.50	$2.50
1 Catalog Only	$1.00	$1.50

Send a self-addressed, stamped envelope for our complimentary brochure "How to auction your stamps and covers".

JACQUES C. SCHIFF, JR., INC.

195 Main St., Ridgefield Park, NJ 07660 USA
Telephone 201-641-5566 FAX 201-641-5705

OFFICIAL AUCTIONEERS:
AMERIPEX 1986.
WORLD STAMP EXPO 1989.
WORLD COLUMBIAN STAMP EXPO 1992.
AMERICAN PHILATELIC SOCIETY 2000-2003

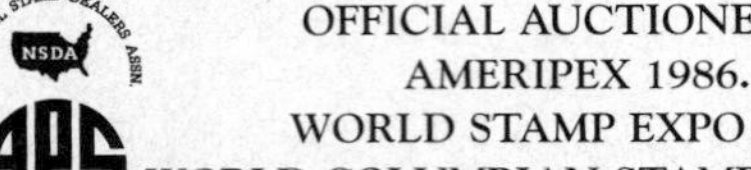

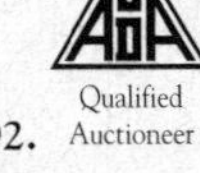

Qualified Auctioneer

British Commonwealth

Aden to Zululand Mint & Used
Most complete stock in North America

For over 35 years we have helped our customers build some of the worlds finest known collections. Our expert ***Want Lists Services*** can do the same for you. With over 50 volumes filled with singles, sets and rare stamps, I am sure we have what you need. We welcome your Want Lists in Scott or Gibbons numbers. Monthly payment plans available for larger purchases.

Put our expertise to work for you today!
You'll be glad you did!!

Colonial Stamp Company
5757 Wilshire Blvd., Penthouse 8
Los Angeles, CA 90036 USA
Tel: +1 (323) 933-9435 Fax: +1 (323) 939-9930
Toll Free in North America
Tel: 1 (877) 272-6693 Fax: 1 (877) 272-6694
E-Mail: *info@colonialstampcompany.com*
URL: *www.colonialstampcompany.com*

Ask for your free Public Auction Catalogue today!

CCNY, IFSDA, INTERNATIONAL SOCIETY OF APPRAISERS

British Commonwealth

WWW.WORLDSTAMPS.COM
242 West Saddle River Road
Suite C
Upper Saddle River, NJ 07458
PH: 201-236-8122
FAX: 201-236-8133
by mail:
Frank Geiger Philatelists
info@WorldStamps.com
www.WorldStamps.com

Central America

GUY SHAW
PO Box 27138
San Diego, CA 92198
PH/FAX: 858-485-8269
guyshaw@guyshaw.com
www.guyshaw.com

China

MICHAEL ROGERS, INC.
415 S. Orlando Ave.
Winter Park, FL 32789-3683
PH: 407-644-2290
PH: 800-843-3751
FAX: 407-645-4434
Stamps@michaelrogersinc.com
www.michaelrogersinc.com

Ducks

MICHAEL JAFFE
PO Box 61484
Vancouver, WA 98666
PH: 360-695-6161
PH: 800-782-6770
FAX: 360-695-1616
mjaffe@brookmanstamps.com
www.brookmanstamps.com

Egypt

KAMAL SHALABY
3, Aly Basha Fahmy St.
8th Floor, Gleem
Alexandria
EGYPT
PH/FAX: +203-5840254
Cell: +2-0105838213
alexstamplover@yahoo.com
www.stampsofegypt.com

German Colonies

COLONIAL STAMP COMPANY
5757 Wilshire Blvd. PH #8
Los Angeles, CA 90036
PH: 323-933-9435
FAX: 323-939-9930
Toll Free in North America
PH: 877-272-6693
FAX: 877-272-6694
info@colonialstampcompany.com
www.colonialstampcompany.com

Great Britain

COLONIAL STAMP COMPANY
5757 Wilshire Blvd. PH #8
Los Angeles, CA 90036
PH: 323-933-9435
FAX: 323-939-9930
Toll Free in North America
PH: 877-272-6693
FAX: 877-272-6694
info@colonialstampcompany.com
www.colonialstampcompany.com

Japan

MICHAEL ROGERS, INC.
415 S. Orlando Ave.
Winter Park, FL 32789-3683
PH: 407-644-2290
PH: 800-843-3751
FAX: 407-645-4434
Stamps@michaelrogersinc.com
www.michaelrogersinc.com

THE STAMP ACT
PO Box 1136
Belmont, CA 94002
PH: 650-703-2342
PH: 650-592-3315
FAX: 650-508-8104
thestampact@sbcglobal.net
www.thestampact.com

WWW.WORLDSTAMPS.COM
242 West Saddle River Road
Suite C
Upper Saddle River, NJ 07458
PH: 201-236-8122
FAX: 201-236-8133
by mail:
Frank Geiger Philatelists
info@WorldStamps.com
www.WorldStamps.com

British Commonwealth

Kenya, Uganda, Tanzania

COLONIAL STAMP COMPANY
5757 Wilshire Blvd. PH #8
Los Angeles, CA 90036
PH: 323-933-9435
FAX: 323-939-9930
Toll Free in North America
PH: 877-272-6693
FAX: 877-272-6694
info@colonialstampcompany.com
www.colonialstampcompany.com

Kiauchau (German)

COLONIAL STAMP COMPANY
5757 Wilshire Blvd. PH #8
Los Angeles, CA 90036
PH: 323-933-9435
FAX: 323-939-9930
Toll Free in North America
PH: 877-272-6693
FAX: 877-272-6694
info@colonialstampcompany.com
www.colonialstampcompany.com

Korea

MICHAEL ROGERS, INC.
415 S. Orlando Ave.
Winter Park, FL 32789-3683
PH: 407-644-2290
PH: 800-843-3751
FAX: 407-645-4434
Stamps@michaelrogersinc.com
www.michaelrogersinc.com

THE STAMP ACT
PO Box 1136
Belmont, CA 94002
PH: 650-703-2342
PH: 650-592-3315
FAX: 650-508-8104
thestampact@sbcglobal.net
www.thestampact.com

Latin America

GUY SHAW
PO Box 27138
San Diego, CA 92198
PH/FAX: 858-485-8269
guyshaw@guyshaw.com
www.guyshaw.com

Leeward Islands

COLONIAL STAMP COMPANY
5757 Wilshire Blvd. PH #8
Los Angeles, CA 90036
PH: 323-933-9435
FAX: 323-939-9930
Toll Free in North America
PH: 877-272-6693
FAX: 877-272-6694
info@colonialstampcompany.com
www.colonialstampcompany.com

Liechtenstein

HENRY GITNER PHILATELISTS, INC.
PO Box 3077-S
Middletown, NY 10940
PH: 845-343-5151
PH: 800-947-8267
FAX: 845-343-0068
hgitner@hgitner.com
www.hgitner.com

Luxembourg

HENRY GITNER PHILATELISTS, INC.
PO Box 3077-S
Middletown, NY 10940
PH: 845-343-5151
PH: 800-947-8267
FAX: 845-343-0068
hgitner@hgitner.com
www.hgitner.com

Macau

THE STAMP ACT
PO Box 1136
Belmont, CA 94002
PH: 650-703-2342
PH: 650-592-3315
FAX: 650-508-8104
thestampact@sbcglobal.net
www.thestampact.com

Madagascar (British Issues)

COLONIAL STAMP COMPANY
5757 Wilshire Blvd. PH #8
Los Angeles, CA 90036
PH: 323-933-9435
FAX: 323-939-9930
Toll Free in North America
PH: 877-272-6693
FAX: 877-272-6694
info@colonialstampcompany.com
www.colonialstampcompany.com

Malaya

COLONIAL STAMP COMPANY
5757 Wilshire Blvd. PH #8
Los Angeles, CA 90036
PH: 323-933-9435
FAX: 323-939-9930
Toll Free in North America
PH: 877-272-6693
FAX: 877-272-6694
info@colonialstampcompany.com
www.colonialstampcompany.com

THE STAMP ACT
PO Box 1136
Belmont, CA 94002
PH: 650-703-2342
PH: 650-592-3315
FAX: 650-508-8104
thestampact@sbcglobal.net
www.thestampact.com

Manchukuo

MICHAEL ROGERS, INC.
415 S. Orlando Ave.
Winter Park, FL 32789-3683
PH: 407-644-2290
PH: 800-843-3751
FAX: 407-645-4434
Stamps@michaelrogersinc.com
www.michaelrogersinc.com

Mariana Islands (Ger & Sp)

COLONIAL STAMP COMPANY
5757 Wilshire Blvd. PH #8
Los Angeles, CA 90036
PH: 323-933-9435
FAX: 323-939-9930
Toll Free in North America
PH: 877-272-6693
FAX: 877-272-6694
info@colonialstampcompany.com
www.colonialstampcompany.com

Marshall Islands

COLONIAL STAMP COMPANY
5757 Wilshire Blvd. PH #8
Los Angeles, CA 90036
PH: 323-933-9435
FAX: 323-939-9930
Toll Free in North America
PH: 877-272-6693
FAX: 877-272-6694
info@colonialstampcompany.com
www.colonialstampcompany.com

Mauritius

COLONIAL STAMP COMPANY
5757 Wilshire Blvd. PH #8
Los Angeles, CA 90036
PH: 323-933-9435
FAX: 323-939-9930
Toll Free in North America
PH: 877-272-6693
FAX: 877-272-6694
info@colonialstampcompany.com
www.colonialstampcompany.com

Mesopotamia

COLONIAL STAMP COMPANY
5757 Wilshire Blvd. PH #8
Los Angeles, CA 90036
PH: 323-933-9435
FAX: 323-939-9930
Toll Free in North America
PH: 877-272-6693
FAX: 877-272-6694
info@colonialstampcompany.com
www.colonialstampcompany.com

Middle East-Arab

MICHAEL ROGERS, INC.
415 S. Orlando Ave.
Winter Park, FL 32789-3683
PH: 407-644-2290
PH: 800-843-3751
FAX: 407-645-4434
Stamps@michaelrogersinc.com
www.michaelrogersinc.com

Monaco

WULFF'S STAMPS
PO Box 661746
Sacramento, CA 95866
PH/FAX: 800-884-0656
PH/FAX: 916-489-0656
service@wulffstamps.com
www.wulffstamps.com

Natal

COLONIAL STAMP COMPANY
5757 Wilshire Blvd. PH #8
Los Angeles, CA 90036
PH: 323-933-9435
FAX: 323-939-9930
Toll Free in North America
PH: 877-272-6693
FAX: 877-272-6694
info@colonialstampcompany.com
www.colonialstampcompany.com

Netherlands

HENRY GITNER PHILATELISTS, INC.
PO Box 3077-S
Middletown, NY 10940
PH: 845-343-5151
PH: 800-947-8267
FAX: 845-343-0068
hgitner@hgitner.com
www.hgitner.com

New Britain

COLONIAL STAMP COMPANY
5757 Wilshire Blvd. PH #8
Los Angeles, CA 90036
PH: 323-933-9435
FAX: 323-939-9930
Toll Free in North America
PH: 877-272-6693
FAX: 877-272-6694
info@colonialstampcompany.com
www.colonialstampcompany.com

New Issues

DAVIDSON'S STAMP SERVICE
PO Box 36355
Indianapolis, IN 46236-0355
PH: 317-826-2620
ed-davidson@earthlink.net
www.newstampissues.com

New Issues - Retail

BOMBAY PHILATELIC INC.
PO Box 90937
Raleigh, NC 27675
PH: 561-499-7990
FAX: 561-499-7553
sales@bombaystamps.com
www.bombaystamps.com

New Zealand

ARON R. HALBERSTAM PHILATELISTS, LTD.
PO Box 150168
Van Brunt Station
Brooklyn, NY 11215-0168
PH: 718-788-3978
FAX: 718-965-3099
arh@arhstamps.com
www.arhstamps.com

COLONIAL STAMP COMPANY
5757 Wilshire Blvd. PH #8
Los Angeles, CA 90036
PH: 323-933-9435
FAX: 323-939-9930
Toll Free in North America
PH: 877-272-6693
FAX: 877-272-6694
info@colonialstampcompany.com
www.colonialstampcompany.com

Niger Coast Protectorate

COLONIAL STAMP COMPANY
5757 Wilshire Blvd. PH #8
Los Angeles, CA 90036
PH: 323-933-9435
FAX: 323-939-9930
Toll Free in North America
PH: 877-272-6693
FAX: 877-272-6694
info@colonialstampcompany.com
www.colonialstampcompany.com

Orange River Colony

COLONIAL STAMP COMPANY
5757 Wilshire Blvd. PH #8
Los Angeles, CA 90036
PH: 323-933-9435
FAX: 323-939-9930
Toll Free in North America
PH: 877-272-6693
FAX: 877-272-6694
info@colonialstampcompany.com
www.colonialstampcompany.com

Postal History

TILL NEUMANN CLASSIC PHILATELY
PO Box 10 29 40
28029 Bremen
GERMANY
PH: +49.421.79 40 260
FAX: +49.421.79 40 261
tn@klassische-philatelie.de
www.klassische-philatelie.de

Proofs & Essays

HENRY GITNER PHILATELISTS, INC.
PO Box 3077-S
Middletown, NY 10940
PH: 845-343-5151
PH: 800-947-8267
FAX: 845-343-0068
hgitner@hgitner.com
www.hgitner.com

Rhodesia

COLONIAL STAMP COMPANY
5757 Wilshire Blvd. PH #8
Los Angeles, CA 90036
PH: 323-933-9435
FAX: 323-939-9930
Toll Free in North America
PH: 877-272-6693
FAX: 877-272-6694
info@colonialstampcompany.com
www.colonialstampcompany.com

South America

GUY SHAW
PO Box 27138
San Diego, CA 92198
PH/FAX: 858-485-8269
guyshaw@guyshaw.com
www.guyshaw.com

New Issues

Stamp Shows

STAMP STORES

California

BROSIUS STAMP, COIN & SUPPLIES
2105 Main St.
Santa Monica, CA 90405
PH: 310-396-7480
FAX: 310-396-7455

COLONIAL STAMP CO./ BRITISH EMPIRE SPECIALIST
5757 Wilshire Blvd. PH #8
(by appt.)
Los Angeles, CA 90036
PH: 323-933-9435
FAX: 323-939-9930
Toll Free in North America
PH: 877-272-6693
FAX: 877-272-6694
info@colonialstampcompany.com
www.colonialstampcompany.com

FISCHER-WOLK PHILATELICS
22762 Aspan St.
Suite 211
Lake Forest, CA 92630
PH: 949-837-2932
fw@occoxmail.com

NATICK STAMPS & HOBBIES
411 E. Huntington Dr.
Suite 209
Arcadia, CA 91006
PH: 626-445-2185
natickco@att.net

Colorado

SHOWCASE STAMPS
3865 Wadsworth
Wheat Ridge, CO 80033
PH: 303-425-9252
kbeiner@colbi.net
www.showcasestamps.com

Connecticut

SILVER CITY COIN & STAMP
41 Colony St.
Meriden, CT 06451
PH: 203-235-7634
FAX: 203-237-4915

Georgia

STAMPS UNLIMITED OF GEORGIA, INC.
100 Peachtree St.
Suite 1460
Atlanta, GA 30303
PH: 404-688-9161
tonyroozen@yahoo.com

Illinois

DR. ROBERT FRIEDMAN & SONS
2029 W. 75th St.
Woodridge, IL 60517
PH: 800-588-8100
FAX: 630-985-1588
drbobstamps@yahoo.com
www.drbobfriedmanstamps.com

SIDMORE STAMPS
145 E. Lincoln Hwy.
DeKalb, IL 60115
PH: 815-787-7000
sidmorestamps@verizon.net
www.sidmorestamps.net
Authorized APS Dealer

Indiana

KNIGHT STAMP & COIN CO.
237 Main St.
Hobart, IN 46342
PH: 219-942-4341
PH: 800-634-2646
knight@knightcoin.com
www.knightcoin.com

Massachusetts

KAPPY'S COINS & STAMPS
534 Washington St.
Norwood, MA 02062
PH: 781-762-5552
kappyscoins@aol.com

New Jersey

BERGEN STAMPS & COLLECTIBLES
306 Queen Anne Rd.
Teaneck, NJ 07666
PH: 201-836-8987

PHILLY STAMP & COIN CO., INC.
683 Haddon Ave.
Collingswood, NJ 08108
PH: 856-854-5333
FAX: 856-854-5377
phillysc@verizon.net
www.phillystampandcoin.com

TRENTON STAMP & COIN CO.
Thomas DeLuca
Store: Forest Glen Plaza
1804 Route 33
Hamilton Square, NJ 08690
Mail: PO Box 8574
Trenton, NJ 08650
PH: 800-446-8664
PH: 609-584-8100
FAX: 609-587-8664
TOMD4TSC@aol.com

New York

CHAMPION STAMP CO., INC.
432 W. 54th St.
New York, NY 10019
PH: 212-489-8130
FAX: 212-581-8130
championstamp@aol.com
www.championstamp.com

Ohio

HILLTOP STAMP SERVICE
Richard A. Peterson
PO Box 626
Wooster, OH 44691
PH: 330-262-8907
PH: 330-262-5378
hilltop@bright.net

THE LINK STAMP CO.
3461 E. Livingston Ave.
Columbus, OH 43227
PH/FAX: 614-237-4125
PH/FAX: 800-546-5726

Texas

HERITAGE AUCTION GALLERIES
3500 Maple Ave, 17th Floor
Dallas, TX 75219
PH: 800-872-6467
FAX: 214-409-1425
Stamps@HA.com
HA.com

Virginia

KENNEDY'S STAMPS & COINS, INC.
7059 Brookfield Plaza
Springfield, VA 22150
PH: 703-569-7300
FAX: 703-569-7644
j.w.kennedy@verizon.net

LATHEROW & CO., INC.
5054 Lee Hwy.
Arlington, VA 22207
PH: 703-538-2727
PH: 800-647-4624
FAX: 703-538-5210
latherow@filatco.com

Topicals

E. JOSEPH MCCONNELL
PO Box 683
Monroe, NY 10949
PH: 845-783-9791
FAX: 845-782-0347
ejstamps@gmail.com
www.EJMcConnell.com

Topicals-Columbus

MR. COLUMBUS
PO Box 1492
Fennville, MI 49408
PH: 269-543-4755
columbus@acen.org

United States

ACS STAMP COMPANY
10831 Chambers Way
Commerce City, CO 80022
PH: 303-841-8666
ACS@ACSStamp.com
www.acsstamp.com

BROOKMAN STAMP CO.
PO Box 90
Vancouver, WA 98666
PH: 360-695-1391
PH: 800-545-4871
FAX: 360-695-1616
larry@brookmanstamps.com
www.brookmanstamps.com

U.S.-Collections Wanted

DR. ROBERT FRIEDMAN & SONS
2029 W. 75th St.
Woodridge, IL 60517
PH: 800-588-8100
FAX: 630-985-1588
drbobstamps@yahoo.com
www.drbobfriedmanstamps.com

U.S.-Rare Stamps

HERITAGE AUCTION GALLERIES
3500 Maple Ave, 17th Floor
Dallas, TX 75219
PH: 800-872-6467
FAX: 214-409-1425
Stamps@HA.com
HA.com

U.S.-Trust Territories

HENRY GITNER PHILATELISTS, INC.
PO Box 3077-S
Middletown, NY 10940
PH: 845-343-5151
PH: 800-947-8267
FAX: 845-343-0068
hgitner@hgitner.com
www.hgitner.com

Want Lists

CHARLES P. SCHWARTZ
PO Box 165
Mora, MN 55051
PH: 320-679-4705
charlesp@ecenet.com

Want Lists-British Empire 1840-1935 German Cols./Offices

COLONIAL STAMP COMPANY
5757 Wilshire Blvd. PH #8
Los Angeles, CA 90036
PH: 323-933-9435
FAX: 323-939-9930
Toll Free in North America
PH: 877-272-6693
FAX: 877-272-6694
info@colonialstampcompany.com
www.colonialstampcompany.com

Wanted-Estates

HERITAGE AUCTION GALLERIES
3500 Maple Ave, 17th Floor
Dallas, TX 75219
PH: 800-872-6467
FAX: 214-409-1425
Stamps@HA.com
HA.com

Wanted to Buy

HERITAGE AUCTION GALLERIES
3500 Maple Ave, 17th Floor
Dallas, TX 75219
PH: 800-872-6467
FAX: 214-409-1425
Stamps@HA.com
HA.com

Wanted-U.S.

HERITAGE AUCTION GALLERIES
3500 Maple Ave, 17th Floor
Dallas, TX 75219
PH: 800-872-6467
FAX: 214-409-1425
Stamps@HA.com
HA.com

Wanted-U.S. Collections

BROOKMAN STAMP CO.
PO Box 90
Vancouver, WA 98666
PH: 360-695-1391
PH: 800-545-4871
FAX: 360-695-1616
larry@brookmanstamps.com
www.brookmanstamps.com

Wanted-Worldwide Collections

DR. ROBERT FRIEDMAN & SONS
2029 W. 75th St.
Woodridge, IL 60517
PH: 800-588-8100
FAX: 630-985-1588
drbobstamps@yahoo.com
www.drbobfriedmanstamps.com

THE STAMP CENTER DUTCH COUNTRY AUCTIONS
4115 Concord Pike
Wilmington, DE 19803
PH: 302-478-8740
FAX: 302-478-8779
auctions@thestampcenter.com
www.thestampcenter.com

Websites

ACS STAMP COMPANY
10831 Chambers Way
Commerce City, CO 80022
PH: 303-841-8666
ACS@ACSStamp.com
www.acsstamp.com

HERITAGE AUCTION GALLERIES
3500 Maple Ave, 17th Floor
Dallas, TX 75219
PH: 800-872-6467
FAX: 214-409-1425
Stamps@HA.com
HA.com

Worldwide-Year Sets

WWW.WORLDSTAMPS.COM
242 West Saddle River Road
Suite C
Upper Saddle River, NJ 07458
PH: 201-236-8122
FAX: 201-236-8133
by mail:
Frank Geiger Philatelists
info@WorldStamps.com
www.WorldStamps.com

Worldwide